WATERLOO
PUBLIC LIBRARY

THE OFFICIAL ENCYCLOPEDIA
OF MAJOR LEAGUE BASEBALL

TOTAL BASEBALL

SEVENTH EDITION

EDITED BY

JOHN THORN, PETE PALMER,

AND MICHAEL GERSHMAN

WITH MATTHEW SILVERMAN, SEAN LAHMAN, AND GREG SPIRA

Official Publication—Major League Baseball

For information about permission to reproduce selections from this book, please write to:
Permissions
Total Sports Publishing
100 Enterprise Drive
Kingston, NY 12401
www.totalsportspublishing.com

ISBN: 1-930844-01-8
CIP data available

Printed in Canada
Designed by Marc Cheshire

Contents

PART TWO

The Registers, Leaders, and Rosters

Appendixes

Acknowledgments

This seventh edition of *Total Baseball* could not have been published without legions of writers, researchers, editors, designers, and production people. The principal contributors in these areas are credited in the table of contents; others may be acknowledged within the text or in the separate introductions to the various sections of Part 2.

We owe our stylish jacket to Todd Radom with assists from Donna Harris, Ann Sullivan, and Chad Lawrence. Dianne Robinson, production chief at Total Sports Publishing, and Robert Wilson, editorial director, led the process. The skills of Jed Thorn and Mikhail Horowitz were integral in the copy editing process. Ed Dinger came in to help at a key time. At Major League Baseball, Don Hintze supported us every step of the way and Jerome Holtzman, baseball's official historian, worked with us to effect some significant changes in scoring practices for 19th century baseball. If you picked up this copy of *Total Baseball* at your local bookstore, the credit goes to our Publishers Group West, and their able sales force, and VistaInfo, which printed the book.

We were fortunate to extend our relationship with Starkey & Henricks, which has been the typographer for every edition of *Total Baseball.* To Peter and Doug Bird, and Peter Compton, George Galgoczi, and Ellen Curcio go our admiration and gratitude.

Marc Cheshire's splendid design for the first edition has stood the test of time, and Gypsy da Silva earned the *croix de guerre* for her production work on the second. Jacquie Roland was important to the third edition, as Ray Shaw was to the fourth, and adding James Charlton's day-by-day history of baseball has informed the Annual Record in both editions five and six. Gary Gillette's groundbreaking work in situational statistics and his editorial assistance were crucial contributions to this seventh edition.

We will also not forget our friends at Sony, who published *Total Baseball* in digital form way back in 1991. The pioneers at CMC (Creative Multimedia Corporation) issued the encyclopedia in CD-ROM in 1994, one year before Microsoft incorporated it in its *Complete Baseball.* Franklin Electronic Publishing and Headland Digital Media also published electronic versions that enlarged our audience.

We are forever indebted to David Reuther, whose contributions to the editorial, production, and business aspects of the first two editions of *Total Baseball* were truly awesome. Likewise, *Total Baseball* will always reflect the contributions of Mike Gershman, who was a principal editor of editions three through six before passing away in January 2000.

For research help, particularly into the years before 1920, we extend heartfelt thanks (alphabetically) to the Society for American Baseball Research colleagues Bill Carle, Bob McConnell, David Neft, Bob Tiemann, and Frank Williams. Bill Carle helped us with biographical data, especially debut dates. Bob McConnell lent his personal expertise and his knowledge of the John Tattersall research collection to clear up a variety of perplexing areas. David Neft supplied us with heretofore unknown RBI data for the National League of 1880–1885 and inspired us by his example, as the man who headed the Information Concepts, Inc., team that produced *The Baseball Encyclopedia* of 1969. Bob Tiemann provided game scores and sites for a host of pre-1900 games that were most helpful in deriving, for the first time, home-road stats for the 19th century; he also headed the SABR research project that yielded new National Association data. And Frank Williams continued his remarkable efforts in correcting pitcher won-lost records before 1920. Since our debut in 1989, an army of readers has taken us up on our invitation to write with their corrections and suggestions, from the mathematical to the typographical; we thank them in the aggregate here and list them by name in the Notes on Contributors near the end of the book.

And last, we thank some giants of baseball research whose work informs these pages but who are no longer with us to receive the tribute: in no particular order, Ernie Lanigan, John Tattersall, S.C. Thompson, Alex Haas, Preston D. Orem, Len Gettelson, Lee Allen, and Harold Seymour.

For Mike Gershman (1939–2000), who lives on in these pages and in the hearts of his colleagues.

Introduction

When it first appeared, in 1989, *Total Baseball* was the most complete, most authoritative, and most informative—not to mention the biggest—baseball book ever published. It came into being because its creators saw that there was nothing else like it and because its publishers had faith that fans would want such a book—a virtual baseball library in one volume. In fact, it could be said that *Total Baseball* is the first true baseball encyclopedia because it offers not only the game's numbers but also the stories and statistical principles that underlie them.

In this seventh edition, *Total Baseball* builds upon that foundation to provide new stories, new stats, and a thorough review of all the data that went into the first six editions. We welcomed the endorsement of *Total Baseball* by Major League Baseball as the official encyclopedia of the game in 1995, and we are pleased to continue our partnership in this edition.

This book is divided into two parts. The first consists of prose features on subjects of interest to all baseball fans, from the general reader who wishes to know more about the game's trivia and lore to the advanced fan who wants to know about its humble beginnings and evolving institutions.

Simply be assured that *Total Baseball* will be totally absorbing. The writers gathered together here are experts in their fields, as befits an encyclopedic reference work, and even the most erudite reader will learn countless new things about our great game.

The same holds true for Part 2, which contains the playing and pitching registers, a variety of rosters, a year-by-year statistical summary of major league play since 1871, and more. The stats will please the devotee of sabermetrics, who can use the Total Player Ranking to compare Mark McGwire's record-shattering 1998 season against Roger Maris's legendary 1961 season—or the reader can take both those performances and find that they barely equal Babe Ruth's best season. The traditional computations will appeal to baseball scholars, who know what a tangle of briars the historical record has become over the last two decades, as individual player records have been altered without corresponding changes to other players on the same team. (For more on this, see the essay, "The History of Major League Baseball Statistics.") And the cornucopia of stats old and new of baseball's 15,416 players—for everyone from all-time leaders to cup-of-coffee nonentities—will provide days, months, and years of archaeological delight for baseball fans of all stripes. In an exciting yet odd pairing of new features, this seventh edition of *Total Baseball* offers, for the first time, lifetime situational statistics for all regular players from 1978 through 2000, as well as completely revised batting averages for all men who played in 1876 and 1887. Whether from the distant past or the current era, the records are equally important to us.

Total Baseball joins the game's most knowledgeable writers, most of them members of the Society for American Baseball Research (SABR), with the game's great historical database, the one built up over two decades by Pete Palmer. Benefiting from the painstaking research of hundreds of friends and colleagues in SABR, we have corrected many errors and omissions in other reference works, relying not upon the numbers enshrined by tradition or official edict but upon the evidence. How many hours have been spent scanning the handwritten official records of the early years of the century, or reviewing box scores and scoresheets and game summaries! It would have been easier not to bother, to accept, for example, a game mistakenly entered twice in the record for 1910 so that Ty Cobb could keep his career total of 4,191 hits. But there can be no statute of limitations on historical error; the researcher and historian must go where the evidence leads them.

This book is as good as we know how to make it, but we do want to hear from you about our blunders (we know there will be some) or about your research (which may be as important to subsequent editions of *Total Baseball* as that of, say, Gary Gillette has been for this one). We believe that history is process, not product, and our aim has been for *Total Baseball* to reflect the state of the art in baseball research and to convey its editors' love for the game.

CHAPTER 1

Our Game

John Thorn

Baseball has been, most often for better but occasionally for worse, the American game. It has given our people rest and recreation, myths and memories, heroes and history, and hope. It has mirrored our society, sometimes propelling it with models for democracy, community, commerce, and common humanity, sometimes lagging behind with equally instructive models of futility and resistance to change. And as our national game, baseball in no small measure defines us as Americans, connecting us with our countrymen across all barriers of generation, class, race, and creed.

Baseball in the Americas is more than a game, an observation to which the scope of this book is testimony and tribute. But it is first and foremost about play, a fact obscured amid today's ferment of free agency, salary caps, and sky boxes. Some 150 years ago, an overly solemn America was first indebted to baseball for the freedom it gave to play. As overture to this volume's chronicle of baseball's history, let's look at how child's play came to be our national pastime.

America Learns to Play

Even when baseball was in its infancy in the 1850s—having just evolved from the boyhood game of rounders and its more formalized derivative, town ball—the sport was already shaping the life of the country. Americans of the previous generation had been blind to the virtue of play, much perplexing our European cousins. We permitted ourselves few amusements that could not be justified in terms of social or business utility, or "seriousness." Nonconformists like the Olympic Town Ball Club of Philadelphia in the 1830s had to put up with a lot of guff, as this contemporary account details:

The first day that the Philadelphia men took the field . . . only four men were found to play, so they started in by playing a game called cat ball. All the players were over twenty-five years of age, and to see them playing a game like this caused much merriment among the friends of the players. It required "sand" in those days to go out on the field and play, as the prejudice against the game was very great. It took nearly a whole season to get men enough together to make a team, owing to the ridicule heaped upon the players for taking part in such childish sports.

What brought scorn upon the heads of these staunch devotees of town ball (also known as "Boston Ball" or the "Massachusetts Game") was that although the game had regularly positioned fielders and demanded a modicum of strategic play, it still bore the childish essence of rounders: the retirement of a baserunner by throwing the ball at him, which necessitated a softer, less resilient ball than that used in the manly sport of cricket.

Who was the genius who came up with the idea of retiring a runner by touching him with the ball or securing it "in the hands of an adversary on the base" ? Perhaps it was Alexander Cartwright, who is known to many as "the man who invented baseball," though baseball was not invented; it evolved. But it may have been Daniel Lucius Adams or William Wheaton or Lewis F. Wadsworth.

No matter—this was the first step toward making an American game that could challenge boys and men alike, and that could take its place in the life of our nation as cricket had done in England. Henry Chadwick, the English-born cricket reporter who coined the term "national pastime" and became known as the "Father of Baseball," wrote that early on he

. . . was struck with the idea that base ball was just the game for a national sport for Americans and . . . that from this game of ball a powerful lever might be made by which our people could be lifted into a position of more devotion to physical exercise and healthful out-door recreation than they had, hitherto, been noted for. . . . In fact, as is well-known, we were the regular target for the shafts of raillery and even abuse from our outdoor-sport-loving cousins of England, in consequence of our national neglect of sports and pastimes, and our too great devotion to business and the "Almighty Dollar." But thanks to Base Ball . . . we have been transformed into quite another people. . . .

The transformation was from a hard-working but grim citizenry to a nation devoted to fresh air and exercise, not unlike the current rage for jogging, aerobics, and body building. Amateur baseball clubs sprang up like dandelions in the years immediately before the Civil War, but these were formed more for camaraderie and calisthenics than the pursuit of victory or the honing of skills. The demands of the new game on athleticism were few, as the one-bound rule remained in effect (an out was recorded if a ball was caught on a bounce), and a couple of weeks' practice were enough to make a novice of forty a creditable player.

Men viewed baseball as a mild pastime, or relief from the mental strains of work; as a tonic, restorative of the physical energies needed for work; or as a release of the surplus nervous energy that impedes young men in their pursuit of purposeful work. America in the mid-1850s was learning how to play, but still viewed sport in terms of its salutary effects on commerce; not until the close of the War Between the States would the focus shift to learning how to play well—for its own sake.

The Charm of the Game

Today we think of baseball as an anachronism, a last vestige of America's agrarian paradise—an idyllic game that takes us back to a more innocent time. But baseball originated in New York City, not rural Cooperstown, and in truth it was an exercise in nostalgia from the beginning. Alexander Cartwright and his Knickerbockers began play in Madison Square in 1842, and the city's northward progress soon compelled them to move uptown to Murray Hill.

When the grounds there were also threatened by the march of industry, the Knicks ferried across the Hudson River to the Elysian Fields of Hoboken, a landscaped retreat of picnic grounds and scenic vistas that was designed by its proprietors to relieve New Yorkers of city air and city care. In other words, the purpose of baseball's primal park was the same as that of New York's Central Park or, much later, Boston's Fenway Park—to give an increasingly urban populace a park within the city, a place reminiscent of the idealized farms that had sent all these lads to the metropolis.

Thus the attraction of the game in its earliest days was first the novelty and exhilaration of play; second the opportunity for deskbound city clerks to expend surplus energy in a sylvan setting, freed from the tyranny of the clock; and third, to harmonize with an American golden age that was almost entirely legendary.

Simple charms, simple pleasures. In the late 1860s, advancing skills led to heightened appetites for victory, which led to hot pursuit of the game's gifted players, which inevitably led to sub rosa payments and, by 1870, rampant professionalism. (Doesn't that chain reaction put one in mind of college football or basketball?) The gentlemanly players of baseball's first generation retreated from the field, shaking their heads in dismay at how greed had perverted the "grand old game" —now barely 20 years old—and probably ruined it forever.

Sound familiar? It should—the same dire and premature announcements of the demise of the game have been issued ever since, spurred by free-agent signings, long-term contracts, no-trade provisions, strikes and lockouts, integration, night ball, rival leagues, ad infinitum. The only conclusions a calm head might draw from this recurring cycle of disdain for the present and glorification of the past are that (a) things aren't what they used to be and never were; (b) accurate assessment of a present predicament is impossible, for it requires perspective; and (c) no matter what the owners or players or rulesmakers or fans do, they can't kill baseball. All three conclusions are correct. In baseball, the distinction between amateur and professional is not clear-cut: an amateur may play for devotion to the game (*amat* being the Latin for he loves), but a professional does not play for pursuit of gain alone; he plays for love, too.

Oh, don't you remember the game of base-ball we saw twenty years ago played,
When contests were true, and the sight free to all, and home-runs in plenty were made?
When we lay on the grass, and with thrills of delight, watched the ball squarely pitched at the bat,
And easily hit, and then mount out of sight along with our cheers and our hat?
And then, while the fielders raced after the ball, the men on the bases flew round,
And came in together—four batters in all. Ah! That was the old game renowned.
Now salaried pitchers, who throw the ball curved at padded and masked catchers lame
And gate-money music and seats all reserved is all that is left of the game.
Oh, give us the glorious matches of old, when love of true sport made them great,
And not this new-fashioned affair always sold for the boodle they take at the gate.

H. C. Dodge

That doomsday ditty was published in 1886.

The National Pastime

America before the Civil War was still populated by a handful of veterans of the Revolutionary War and many who remembered vividly the War of 1812. The era of Anglo-American amity had not yet dawned; our country's spiritual separation from the Mother Country, though effected by treaty in 1783, was still in process. And having baseball to rival and replace cricket was an important step in that process. Moreover when England, seeking to maintain its supply of cotton from the American South, appeared over-cordial to the Confederate cause, anti-British feeling swept the North. An America long suffering from an inferiority complex toward England now turned against cricket and embraced baseball with increased fervor.

From 1856 on, Henry Chadwick had been eager for baseball to rise to the status in America that cricket held in his native England. He championed the game tirelessly, helping to refine its rules and practices to make it the equal of cricket as a "manly" and "scientific" game. And baseball soon became, in his words, like cricket "a game requiring the mental powers of judgment, calculation and quick perception to excel in it—while in its demands upon the vigor, endurance and courage of manhood, its requirements excel those requisite to become equally expert as a cricketer."

Chadwick invented a method of scorekeeping and statistical compilation patterned on those which were inaugurated in cricket. Baseball was an elemental game—pitch, hit, catch, throw—like other games of ball; but keeping records of the contests and later printing box scores and individual averages elevated it from rounders and placed it on an equal footing with its transatlantic counterpart. (As important, the records served to legitimize men's concern with what had been merely a boys' exercise by making it more systematic, like the numerically annotated world of business.) Today a baseball without records is inconceivable: They are what keep Babe Ruth and Ty Cobb and Walter Johnson alive in our minds in a way that President James K. Polk, Walter Reed, or Admiral Dewey—arguably greater men—are not.

By the end of the Civil War cricket in this country remained a pastime for a shrinking band of Anglophiles, while the New York Game of Baseball (as it was then called to differentiate it from the nearly vanished Massachusetts Game) was spreading across the country, courtesy of returning veterans whose first exposure to baseball might have come in a prisoner-of-war camp. In the press, baseball was typically proclaimed The National Game—the same term Britons used for cricket.

Play for Pay

From its creation in 1871 to its crash five years later, the National Association had a rocky time as America's first professional league. Franchises came and went with dizzying speed, often folding in midseason. Schedules were not played out if a club slated to go on the road saw little prospect of gain. Drinking and gambling and game-fixing were rife. And the Boston Red Stockings of Al Spalding and the Wright brothers dominated play, going 71–8 in the last of their four straight championship seasons; their predictable and one-sided victories crushed the competition and, at last, interest in the entire circuit.

But from the ashes of the National Association emerged the Red Stockings' model of success and the entrepreneurial genius of Chicago's William Hulbert. After raiding Boston to obtain four of the biggest stars in the game—Spalding, Ross Barnes, Deacon White, and Cal McVey—and lining up the services of the Philadelphia Athletics' Adrian "Cap" Anson, the White Stockings were ready to roll in the National League of Professional Base Ball Clubs, founded on February 2, 1876 in New York's Grand Central Hotel.

The first five years of the NL were nearly as unsettled as the final years of the NA, with franchises appearing and then disappearing in such cities as Syracuse, Indianapolis, and Hartford while major cities like New York and Philadelphia were, after the league's inaugural year, unrepresented. In 1878 the fledgling circuit was forced to cut back to six teams: Milwaukee, Indianapolis, Chicago, Providence, Cincinnati, and Boston. National League? National Game? It seemed Americans had plenty of appetite for playing the game, but not much for watching it.

Yet as the National League suffered with growing pains, it was introducing some elements that were critical to the explosion of interest that came with the 1880s. It created a professional (paid) umpiring crew; insisted that the league schedule be honored; banned pool selling and hard-liquor consumption in the stands; and created a system of management-owned teams as opposed to the player-run cooperatives that had largely characterized the NA. As the public's renewed faith in the integrity of the game coincided with an upswing in the national economy, not only did the National League flourish, along came an interloper, the rival American Association, to offer patrons 25-cent baseball (NL admissions were 50 cents), Sunday games, and beer. With the public's new appetite for the game seeming insatiable, a group of investors led by St. Louis' Henry Lucas launched a third major league, the Union Association, for 1884.

As brash stars like Cap Anson, Tim Keefe, Dan Brouthers, and the larger-than-life King Kelly captured the newspaper headlines and the nation's imagination, the age of the baseball idol arrived. Before this decade, men like Jim Creighton, Joe Start, and George Wright had been admired in New York and New England, but now a baseball hero's image could be mass-produced for nationwide sale, or licensed for advertising, or inspire odes and songs. Kelly inspired "Slide, Kelly, Slide," its arcane references now largely forgotten but once the most popular song in the land:

Slide, Kelly, slide!
Your running's a disgrace!
Slide, Kelly, slide!
Stay there, hold your base!
If someone doesn't steal ya,
And your batting doesn't fail ya,
They'll take you to Australia!
Slide, Kelly, slide!

And although Ernest Lawrence Thayer always denied it, Kelly could well have been the model for "Casey at the Bat," the immortal lyric ballad Thayer penned in 1888. ("Casey" was sometimes reprinted in the newspapers of the 1880s as "Kelly at the Bat," changing the locale from Mudville to Beantown.)

Baseball was ascendant in the 1880s, and like the budding nation whose pastime it was, pretty cocksure of itself. In the same year that "Casey" made his debut, Albert Spalding led a contingent of baseball players on a round the world tour, spreading the gospel of bat and ball to such places as Egypt, Italy, England, Hawaii, and the above-mentioned Australia. Baseball, America thought, was too grand a game to be merely a national pastime; it ought to be the international pastime.

At a New York banquet for Spalding's returning "world tourists" in 1889, speaker Mark Twain declared, "Baseball is the very symbol, the outward and visible expression of the drive and push and rush and struggle of the raging, tearing, booming nineteenth century." Spalding himself later wrote:

I claim that Base Ball owes its prestige as our National Game to the fact that as no other form of sport it is the exponent of American Courage, Confidence, Combativeness; American Dash, Discipline, Determination; American Energy, Eagerness, Enthusiasm; American Pluck, Persistency, Performance; American Spirit, Sagacity, Success; American Vim, Vigor, Virility.

In fact baseball had become more than the mere reflection of our rising industrial and political power and its propensity for bluster and hokum: the national game was beginning to supply emblems for democracy, industry, and community that would change America and the world—not in the ways that Spalding's Tourists may have envisioned, but indisputably for the better.

A Model Institution

Father Henry Chadwick had been typically prescient when he wrote in 1876, the inaugural year of the National League and the centenary of America's birth:

What Cricket is to an Englishman, Base-Ball has become to an American. . . . On the Cricket-field—and there only—the Peer and the Peasant meet on equal terms; the possession of courage, nerve, judgment, skill, endurance and activity alone giving the palm of superiority. In fact, a more democratic institution does not exist in Europe than this self-same Cricket; and as regards its popularity, the records of the thousands of Commoners, Divines and Lawyers, Legislators and Artisans, and Literateurs as well as Mechanics and Laborers, show how great a hold it has on the people. If this is the characteristic of Cricket in aristocratic and monarchical England, how much more will the same characteristics mark Base-Ball in democratic and republican America.

Chadwick's vision of baseball as a model democratic institution would have to wait for the turn of the century to be fully articulated, and for Jackie Robinson and Branch Rickey to be fully realized. But Chadwick's belief that baseball could be more than a game, could become a model of and for American life, presaged baseball's golden age of 1903–1930.

The tumultuous 1890s witnessed a player revolt against high-handed and monopolistic management, epitomized by a cap on salaries, followed by a nearly ruinous contraction from three major leagues to one 12-team circuit. The national economy suffered a panic in 1893 and a sluggish recovery thereafter; baseball attendance dwindled; and the lack of postseason interleague competition after 1890 (as there had been since 1884) was sorely felt. The game was in a period of consolidation, or hibernation, or stagnation; one's perspective depended upon whether he were an owner, fan, or player.

But then Ban Johnson came along, fired by the same vision of a rival league that had inflamed the Players League and the American and Union Associations before him, and that would beckon to the Federal and Continental Leagues later on. With the declaration by the American League that it would conduct business as a major league in 1901, and the signing of a peace treaty with the Nationals two years later, the World Series was resumed, prosperity returned, and the popularity and influence of the game exploded.

Baseball mania seized America as new heroes like Christy Mathewson, Honus Wagner, Ty Cobb, Walter Johnson, and Nap Lajoie found a public hungry for knowledge of their every action, their every thought. A fan's affiliation with his team could exceed in vigor his attachment to his church, his trade, his political party—all but family and country, and even these were wrapped up in baseball. The national pastime became the great repository of national ideals, the symbol of all that was good in American life: fair play (sportsmanship); the rule of law (objective arbitration of disputes); equal opportunity (each side has its innings); the brotherhood of man (bleacher harmony); and more.

The baseball boom of the early 20th century built on the game's simple charms of exercise and communal celebration, adding the psychological and social complexities of vicarious play: civic pride, role models, and hero worship. It became routine for the President to throw out the first ball of the season. Supreme Court Justices had inning-by-inning scores from the World Series relayed to their chambers. Business leaders, perhaps disingenuously, praised baseball as a model of competition and fair play. "Baseball," opined a writer for American Magazine in 1913, "has given our public a fine lesson in commercial morals. . . . Some day all business will be reorganized and conducted by baseball standards."

Leaders of recent immigrant groups advised their peoples to learn the national game if they wanted to become Americans, and foreign-language newspapers devoted space to educating their readers about America's strange and wonderful game. (New York's *Staats-Zeitung*, for example, applauded Kraftiges Schlagen—hard hitting—and cautioned German fans not to kill the Unparteiischer.) As historian Harold Seymour wrote, "The argot of baseball supplied a common means of communication and strengthened the bond which the game helped to establish among those sorely in need of it—the mass of urban dwellers and immigrants living in the anonymity and impersonal vortex of large industrial cities. . . . With the loss of the traditional ties known in a rural society, baseball gave to many the feeling of belonging." And rooting for a baseball team permitted city folk, newcomers and native-born, the sense of pride in community that in former times—when they may have lived in small towns—was commonplace.

Thus baseball offered a model of how to be an American, to be part of the team: Baseball was "second only to death as a leveler," wrote essayist Allen Sangree. Even in those horrifically leveling years of 1941–1945, when so many of our bravest and best gave their lives to defend American ideals, baseball's role as a vital enterprise was confirmed by President Franklin Delano Roosevelt's "green light" for continued play. Many of baseball's finest players—Ted Williams, Joe DiMaggio, Hank Greenberg, Bob Feller, to name a few—swapped their baseball gear for Uncle Sam's, and served with military distinction or helped to boost the nation's morale. Even oldtimers like Babe Ruth, Walter Johnson, and Ty Cobb donned uniforms in service of their country—baseball uniforms, as they staged exhibitions on behalf of war bonds. Servicemen overseas looked to letters from home and the box scores in *The Sporting News* to keep them in touch with what they had left behind, and what they were fighting for—an American way of life that was a beacon for a world in which the light of freedom had been nearly extinguished.

I was one of the countless immigrants who from the 1860s on saw baseball as the "open sesame" to the door of their adopted land. A Polish Jew born in occupied Germany to Holocaust survivors, I arrived on these shores at age 2. After checking in at Ellis Island, I happened by chance to spend the first night in my new land in the no-longer-elegant hotel where in 1876 the National League had been founded. I learned to read by studying the backs of Topps baseball cards, and to be an American by attaching myself passionately to the Brooklyn Dodgers (who also taught me about the fickleness of love).

The Brooklyn Dodgers, in the persons particularly of Rickey and Robinson, also taught America a lesson: that baseball's integrative and democratic models, by the 1940s long held to be verities, were hollow at the core. David Halberstam has written:

. . . it was part of our folklore, basic to our national democratic myth, that sports was the great American equalizer, that money and social status did not matter upon the playing fields. Elsewhere life was assumed to be unfair: those who had privilege passed it on to their children, who in turn had easier, softer lives. Those without privilege were doomed to accept the essential injustices of daily life. But according to the American myth, in sports the poor but honest kid from across the tracks could gain (often in competition with richer, snottier kids) recognition and acclaim for his talents.

Until October 23, 1945, when Robinson signed a contract to play for the Montreal Royals, Brooklyn's top farm club, the myth as far as African Americans were concerned was not a sustaining legend but a mere falsehood.

Rickey's rectitude and Robinson's courage have become central parables of baseball and America, exemplars of decency and strength that inspire all of us. Their "great experiment" came too late for such heroes of black ball as Josh Gibson and Oscar Charleston and Ray Dandridge, but its success has been complete. Once the integrative or leveling model of baseball—all America playing and working in harmony—was extended to African Americans, the effect on the nation was profound. Eighty years after the Civil War, America had proved itself unable to practice the values for which it was fought; baseball showed the way. This is what Commissioner Ford Frick said to the St. Louis Cardinals, rumored to be planning a strike in May 1947:

If you do this you will be suspended from the league. You will find that the friends you think you have in the press box will not support you, that you will be outcasts. I do not care if half the league strikes. Those who do it will encounter quick retribution. They will be suspended and I don't care if it wrecks the National League for five years. This is the United States of America, and one citizen has as much right to play as any other. The National League will go down the line with Robinson whatever the consequence.

As Monte Irvin said, "Baseball has done more to move America in the right direction than all the professional patriots with their billions of cheap words." The Supreme Court decision of Brown v. Topeka Board of Education; civil rights heroes like Martin Luther King Jr., James Meredith, Thurgood Marshall, and others; the freedom marches and the voting rights act—all were vital to America's progress toward unity, but the title of one of Jackie Robinson's books may not overstate the case: *Baseball Has Done It*.

A final way in which baseball supplies models for America is one that has been present from the game's beginning: a model for children wishing to be grownups, wrestling with their insecurities and wondering, What does it mean to be a man? What does a man do? (Most of us old boys occasionally wonder this as well.) The answers in baseball, at least, are unequivocal; as Satchel Paige said in his later years, "I loved baseball. There wasn't no 'maybe so' about it."

Baseball gives children a sense of how wide the world is, in its possibilities but also in its geography. Reading the summations of minor league ball in *The Sporting News* each week piqued the curiosity of baseball-mad boys like me: where were Kokomo and Mattoon and Thibodeaux and Nogales? How did people behave in Salinas or Rocky Mount? What did they eat in Artesia? How many exciting, exotic places this enormous country contained! But a note of comfort—they couldn't be all that strange if baseball was played there.

And to that other vast terra incognita—the world of adults—baseball also offered a road map. How many boys and girls learned to talk with adults, principally their fathers, by nodding wisely at an assessment of a shortstop's range or a pitcher's heart, and mock-confidently venturing an opinion about the hometown team's chances? Our dads are our first heroes (and, decades later, our last); but in between, baseball players are what we want to be. For heroes are larger than life, and when as adults we have taken the measure of ourselves and found we are no more than life-size, and on our bad days seemingly less than that, baseball can puff us up a bit.

Douglass Wallop put it nicely:

. . . only yesterday the fan was a kid of nine or ten bolting his breakfast on Saturday morning and hurtling from the house with a glove buttoned over his belt and a bat over his shoulder, rushing to the nearest vacant lot, perhaps the nearest alley, where the other guys were gathering, a place where it would always be spring. For him, baseball would always have the sound and look and smell of that morning and of other mornings just like it. Only by an accident of chance would he find himself, in the years to come, up in the grandstand, looking on. But for a quirk of fate, he himself would be down on that field; it would be his likeness on the television screen and his name in the newspaper high on the list of .300 hitters. He was a fan, but a fan only incidentally. He was, first and always, himself a baseball player.

The Fifties

If the America that was survives anywhere as more than a memory, it is in baseball, that strangely pastoral game in no matter what setting—domed stadium or Little League field. As hindsight improves upon foresight, memory improves upon reality, so that the endless monotony and grinding physical labor of small-town life before the Civil War are now thought quite romantic. For all our complaints today, it may likewise be argued that America is better than it ever was.

Today's players are better than those in the game's golden age; the strategy of the game and even its execution are more adept (forget all that moaning about how nobody knows the "fundamentals" any more . . . the average player of fifty years ago didn't know them either); and the opportunities to watch baseball, if not to play it, far exceed those of say, the 1950s, today broadly regarded as the game's halcyon era. (A golden age may be defined flexibly, it seems, so as to coincide with the period of one's youth.) For all its pull toward the good old days, for all its statistical illusions of an Olympian era when titans strode the basepaths, for all its seeming permanence in a world aswirl with change, baseball has in fact moved with America, and improved with it.

The period after World War II was a heady time for the nation and its pastime, both of them buoyed by returning veterans and removed restrictions. But in 1946 the major leagues still represented only the sixteen cities that had participated in the National Agreement of 1903, none west of St. Louis; a handful of African Americans were just entering the minor leagues after a half-century's exclusion; and because television was not yet a staple of the American home, most baseball fans had never seen even a single big-league game.

Women had been courted as patrons (even nonpaying patrons) ever since the game's dawn. Baseball management hoped that their presence would lend "tone" to the proceedings and keep a lid on the rowdies, in the stands and on the field. But women's participation in the game's labor force and management was even more limited than their role in the nation's business and industry—Rosie the Riveter and Eleanor Roosevelt as yet had no counterparts in Organized Baseball. The All-American Girls Baseball League made its debut in 1943, the brainchild of Chicago Cubs' owner Philip K. Wrigley. The women's "league of their own" won many admirers over the next decade, but the majors always regarded it as separate and unequal.

On the amateur level, while American Legion Junior Baseball had begun as early as 1928, and Little League in 1939, neither attained their heights until after the War ended. Naysayers will point out that baseball has lost ground as more kids today play football, basketball, soccer, and tennis than fifty years ago—but far more play baseball, too, and not only in America. The annual pursuit of the Little League championship in Williamsport, Pa. (like the Pan-American Games), has become an international affair, an instrument of diplomacy that State Department officials envy. Indeed, baseball may yet hold the key to neighborly relations with all nations in the hemisphere.

Baseball in the colleges, now so vibrant and so fertile with major league talent, was on the path to extinction by the end of the War, only to be brought back from the brink by the G.I. Bill: the explosive growth in enrollment that the returning veterans produced also created a sudden need for expanded athletic programs, and baseball was the prime beneficiary. The NCAA's introduction of the College World Series in 1947 affirmed the game's recovery on campus, and since locating in Omaha three years later it has grown steadily.

In 1951 Major League Baseball, as dated from the inception of the National League in 1876, reached the august age of 75 and proclaimed its "diamond jubilee." Celebratory banquets were held, a plaque was erected at the old hotel where the league was founded, and all NL players wore a commemorative patch on their sleeves. (Coincidentally but less flashily the American League marked its fiftieth birthday as a major circuit.) Let's take a moment to look at where baseball stood at that point.

There was no question it was booming. On the professional level, a whopping 59 leagues contained 448 teams employing about 8,000 players—or 19 minor leaguers competing for each of the then 400 spots in the big show. Little League would soon send its first alumnus to the majors, which had already accepted hundreds of graduates from Legion and other programs. Happy Chandler secured from television a then mind-boggling but now quaint $6 million for broadcast rights to the next six World Series. And with the game's most powerful teams bunched in New York City—the Yankees, the Dodgers, and the Giants—the publicity mills and the turnstiles were spinning as they had never spun before.

But the excitement of the first five postwar years was not confined to New York: even such perennial tailenders as the Boston Braves, the Philadelphia Phillies, and the Cleveland Indians fought their way into the World Series; and staid old Cleveland, under Bill Veeck's carnival-barker aegis, set staggering new attendance records. Many of the newly admitted African-American players had become stars and—satisfyingly, though few but Branch Rickey had predicted it—box-office attractions: Jackie Robinson, Roy Campanella, and Don Newcombe of the Dodgers; Monte Irvin and rookie Willie Mays of the Giants; Sam Jethroe of the Braves; Larry Doby and Satchel Paige of the Indians. Many prewar stars continued to shine, like Bob Feller, Stan Musial, and Ted Williams (though with the Korean War he answered Uncle Sam's call yet again), and new ones like Gotham's center field trio of Duke Snider, Mickey Mantle, and Mays replenished the stock as heroes like Joe DiMaggio hung up their spikes.

But most of these blessings had their downside. Opening the game to African Americans was indubitably right, but it killed the Negro Leagues, ruining owners and abruptly ending many playing careers. The increasing organization of youth baseball, particularly the rise of Little League, heightened the stress of the game at its formative levels and drained much of the fun, as driven parents began to see their Junior as tomorrow's big leaguer, not as just a boy having fun while learning a thing or two. The game on the field was dominated by the home run, making for a brand of ball that some might term dull. League champs registered such stolen-base totals as Dom DiMaggio's 15 or Jackie Jensen's 22; Early Wynn led the AL in ERA one year with a mark of 3.20; and the three-base hit, despite the big old parks still prevalent, went the way of the dodo. And the pennant domination by the three New York teams—principally the Yankees, of course—made the national pastime a rather parochial pleasure; it was hard for fans in Pittsburgh or Detroit to wax rhapsodic over a Subway Series. No, the blessings of the 1950s were not unmitigated, any more than on the national scene the tranquility of the Eisenhower years was without cost.

Take television, for instance: the revenues were great, and so was the publicity value of electronically extending major league play to people in southern and western areas. But the novelty of big-time heroes on the small screen kept those folks at home when formerly they had gone to the local ballpark. The minors began their long decline, one that didn't bottom out until 1964; by then the 59 leagues of 1951 had become 19, and the 8,000-odd professional players had dwindled to fewer than 2,500.

Moreover, television whetted the baseball appetites of Californians and Texans (and Georgians and Washingtonians and more). That demand plus the development of faster passenger planes gave ideas to owners of two of baseball's decaying franchises. Walter O'Malley, owner of the Brooklyn Dodgers, and Giants' owner Horace Stoneham had seen the solidarity of the original 16-city composition broken in 1953, when the venerable Boston Braves (a franchise established in the first year of the National Association, 1871) became the darlings of Milwaukee, and further weakened by the defections in 1954–55 of the St. Louis Browns to Baltimore and the Philadelphia Athletics to Kansas City. Amid weeping and gnashing of teeth that continue to this day, the Dodgers and Giants left for the Golden West in 1958.

In a strange twist, the architect of the move, Walter O'Malley, was (and in the East, still is) widely reviled as the man responsible for ending the grand old game's paradisical age. Yet the placement of franchises in California, as distressing as it was for Brooklyn and Manhattan and as roundly condemned as it was by traditionalists, may now be seen as the best thing to happen to baseball in the decade. And Walter O'Malley, if you will permit your mind a considerable stretch, may be viewed not as the snake offering baseball the mortal apple but as a latter-day Johnny Appleseed (in the footsteps of Alexander Cartwright, who in 1849 also headed for California in pursuit of gold, yet who is remembered not for his venality but for bringing the New York Game to the West).

It was imperative that baseball take the game to where the people were, precisely as it had in 1903. America's population had already begun the westward and southward shift that was to become so pronounced in the 1960s and 1970s. The move to Los Angeles and San Francisco, rather than confirming those cities' stature as "big-league," as is so often written, brought baseball into step with America, which had long recognized them as such. Baseball could now call itself the national pastime without apology.

The Sixties

A chaotic decade for our country, the 1960s were worrisome, stormy years for baseball as well, with dramatic changes in league composition, playing styles, competitive balance and, most distressingly, the game's appeal to the American people. Baseball endured its ordeal by fire, and came through not unscathed but strengthened.

The departure of the Dodgers and Giants in 1958 created a vacuum in New York and an increased hunger for baseball in new boomtowns like Houston, Atlanta, and Minneapolis. Enter Branch Rickey, nearly eighty but still possessed of a keen nose for new opportunity. The great innovator who had already brought baseball the farm system and integration now created the Continental League, a paper league with paper franchises. Nonetheless, Rickey's mirage worried Organized Baseball into expansion.

Two of the Continental "franchises"—the future New York Mets and Houston Colt .45s—were admitted for 1962. The American League was authorized to commence its western foray one year earlier with the expansion-draft Los Angeles Angels and the relocated Minnesota Twins (the latter being the transplanted Washington Senators, who were replaced in the nation's capital by an ill-fated expansion team).

Other franchise shifts and startups in the decade saw baseball's original vagabonds, the Milwaukee Braves by way of Boston, move to Atlanta in 1966. Two years later the erstwhile Athletics of Philadelphia, having failed in Kansas City, directed their caravan toward Oakland.

The A's were quickly replaced in KC by the Royals, one of two new teams introduced in each league with the expansion of 1969. This in turn precipitated divisional play and the League Championship Series, both inventions much decried at the time but now generally applauded. And in one of baseball's more forgettable debacles, the expansion Pilots of 1969 lost their course in Seattle after only one year and ran aground in Milwaukee, where they were rechristened as the Brewers. The National League's expansion into San Diego and Montreal proceeded more smoothly, although Padres' attendance lagged expectations and the Expos' Olympic Stadium (replacing the stopgap Jarry Park) took longer to open its dome than Michelangelo took to paint St. Peter's.

On the field, the big-bang game of the 1950s was giving way to a pitching-and-defense formula, at least in the National League, which began to outstrip its long-time tormentor at the box office and in World Series and All Star confrontations. Speed returned to the equation, too, as personified by first Maury Wills and then Lou Brock (though both were preceded, in the AL, by Luis Aparicio). And a revolution in baseball strategy was brewing, as the 1959 success of such relievers as Larry Sherry, Lindy McDaniel, and Roy Face paved the way for the universal adoption of the bullpen stopper in the 1960s.

In the American League expansion year of 1961, the first played to a 162-game schedule, the Bronx Bombers hit a whopping 240 homers. Sluggers Harmon Killebrew, Norm Cash, and Rocky Colavito all hit more than 40 homers; Mickey Mantle hit more than 50. These totals were troubling to Commissioner Ford Frick, but nowhere near as consternating as the 61 homers struck by Roger Maris to top the game's most famous record, the 60 that Babe Ruth had walloped in 1927. After seeing the National League's scoring increase in 1962, its first year of expansion, Frick became concerned that pitchers were becoming an endangered species. He said:

I would even like the spitball to come back. Take a look at the batting, home run, and slugging record for recent seasons, and you become convinced that the pitchers need help urgently.

Disastrously, Frick convinced the owners to widen the strike zone for 1963 to its pre-1950 dimensions: top of the armpit to bottom of the knee. The result was to increase strikeouts, reduce walks, and shrink batting averages within five years to levels unseen since 1908, the nadir of the Dead Ball Era. The once-proud Yankees, who had continued their long domination of the American League to mid-decade, saw their team batting average sink to an incredible .214 in 1968. That year produced an overall AL mark of .230 and a batting champion, Carl Yastrzemski, with an average of .301.

As pitchers vanquished batters, seemingly for all eternity, the bottom line was that the fans stayed away in droves. Attendance in the National League, which in 1966 reached 15 million, fell by 1968 to only 11.7 million. In fact, despite the addition of four new clubs in 1961–62, attendance in 1968 was only 3 million more than it had been in 1960. Critics charged that baseball was a geriatric vestige of an America that had vanished, a game too slow for a nation that was rushing toward the moon; its decline would only steepen, they claimed, as that more with-it national pastime, pro football, extended its mastery of the airwaves.

But the sky was not falling, despite the alarms. The owners acted quickly to redress the game's balance between offense and defense, reducing the strike zone and lowering the pitcher's mound. But the most important change may have been one that was introduced in 1965 and was only beginning to take effect: the amateur free-agent draft. Typically successful teams like the Yankees, Dodgers, Braves, and Cardinals had stayed successful because of their attention to scouting. Consistently they were able to garner more top prospects for their farm systems than clubs with less deep pockets or more volatile management. Now, teams that had fallen on hard times need not look toward a generation of famine before returning to the feast. Now, dynasties—awe-inspiring but not healthy for the game—were suddenly rendered implausible. Now, baseball had a competitive balance that could produce a rotation of electrifying successes among the leagues' cities, like the ascension of the Boston Red Sox from ninth place in 1966 to the pennant the next, and the amazing rise of the New York Mets from the netherworld they had known to World Champions in 1969. The game would still have some hard rows to hoe in the 1970s, but there was no mistaking the reversal of its downturn: in the new age of "relevance," baseball was back.

The Seventies

The 1970s saw a continuation of the trend toward new stadium construction that had marked the 1960s and may well have triggered that decade's batting drought, as hitter's havens like Ebbets Field, the Polo Grounds, and Sportsman's Park fell to the wrecker's ball. The 1960s had brought new ballparks to 11 cities—San Francisco, Los Angeles, Washington, Bloomington (Minn.), New York (NL), Houston, Atlanta, Anaheim, St. Louis, Oakland, and San Diego. In 1970–1971, baseball bade farewell to old friends Crosley Field, Forbes Field, and Shibe Park as new stadiums—artificial-turf clones of each other—sprang up in Cincinnati, Pittsburgh, and Philadelphia. Other new parks were built in Arlington, Kansas City, Montreal, Seattle, and Toronto (the latter two, expansion franchises added to the American League in 1977), and Yankee Stadium underwent a massive facelift.

All this construction activity seemed to bespeak the game's profitability. Indeed, attendance was climbing in almost all major league cities, as heroes like Henry Aaron, Johnny Bench, Reggie Jackson, and Pete Rose, to name but a few, gave the fans plenty to cheer about. And the controversial adoption of the designated hitter innovation by the American League in 1973 gave a further boost to hitting while giving fans much to argue about, which after all is one of the game's great pleasures.

But the game's financial health was imperiled by rising unrest over labor issues, centered on the reserve clause which bound a player to his team in perpetuity while denying him the opportunity to gauge his worth in the free market. The reformulation of the relationship between players and management became the hallmark of the decade and sorely tested fans' devotion to the game.

It began with the momentous case brought against Organized Baseball by veteran outfielder Curt Flood in 1970, challenging the legality of the reserve clause. The Supreme Court ruled against Flood the following year, but the tenor for the 1970s had been set. A 13-day player strike delayed the opening of the 1972 season, and arbitrator Peter Seitz ruled in 1975 (in what has come to be known as the Messersmith-McNally case) that a player could establish his right of free agency by playing out his option year without a signed contract. The writing on the wall was clear: free agency was the wave of the future.

Big-name players like Jim Hunter, Reggie Jackson, and Rich Gossage migrated to New York, and lesser lights like Wayne Garland and Oscar Gamble signed elsewhere for figures that seemed incredible. In the race to sign available talent some owners spun out of control while others like Minnesota's Cal Griffith, without corporate coffers behind them, had no choice but to sit on the sidelines. Player movement among stars jeopardized fan allegiances, pundits alleged, as Gossage and Jackson played for three teams in three years and championship teams like the Oakland A's and Boston Red Sox were broken up through trades that were forced by the specter of impending—and uncompensated—free-agent departures.

(Comfortingly to the historian, all this hubbub had occurred in very much the same way in 1869–1870, before the advent of the reserve clause, when Henry Chadwick was fulminating about the perniciousness of players "revolving" from one team to another simply to advance their fortunes. Also, baseball's first avowedly professional team, Harry Wright's Cincinnati Red Stockings of 1869 and 1870, were roundly abused for constructing their powerhouse team with "mercenaries" from other states—thus scorning baseball's core appeal to civic pride.)

What actually compromised fan loyalties in the 1970s was not player movement—it took Yankee fans, oh, maybe, ten minutes to regard Reggie as a born pinstriper—but player salaries. When the major league minimum was under $5,000 or so and only a Mantle, Williams, Musial, and DiMaggio made $100,000 a year, fans saw with their heroes as, by and large, working colleagues who had the supreme good fortune to play ball for a living. If a star made a splendiferous salary, that was socially useful as a proof that any worker could make it big if only he had sufficient ability to emerge from the pack. But when stars began routinely to command seven-figure salaries, and, more importantly, the annual wage of the average major leaguer rose to six-figure levels, and eventually seven figures, many adult breadwinners struggled to remain fans.

That they succeeded is testament to their love of the game, for fans have had a difficult assignment in reshaping their views of baseball players along the lines of media stars. The princely compensations of actors and pop musicians have long been accepted by the public as the verdict of the marketplace. If the movie *The Terminator* makes hundreds of millions of dollars for its studio and distributor, then Arnold Schwarzenegger's multimillion-dollar fee for the film seems not out of line. Analogously, if the Dodgers were fabulously lucrative for ownership, then a lofty salary for Steve Garvey ought not to have given rise in the 1970s to resentment among the fans. This sort of reeducation is by no means complete, but barroom banter about baseball in the in the ensuing decades was not as bitterly one-note about "greedy players" as it had been.

And one didn't hear a peep about pro football replacing baseball as the national game.

The Eighties and Nineties

The game on the field in the 1970s had been marked by an unprecedented commingling of power and speed; the great teams of Cincinnati, Baltimore, and Oakland; the return to prominence of the Yankees; and the historic exploits of Henry Aaron and Pete Rose. The game in the 1980s would begin with the Philadelphia Phillies, led by free-agent Rose and future Hall of Famers Mike Schmidt and Steve Carlton, ridding themselves of a historic stain. Until their victory over the Kansas City Royals, the Phils were the only one of the original sixteen major-league franchises never to have won a World Series (the St. Louis Browns had to accept the help of their modern incarnation, the Baltimore Orioles).

The next year brought baseball's darkest moment since the Brotherhood revolt and ensuing Players League of 1890, as major league players walked off their jobs at the height of the season and didn't return for fifty days. By that time even diehard fans were thoroughly fed up with baseball's seeming inability to resolve its problems fairly and with dispatch. Talk of a fan boycott never amounted to much, but as players and management looked toward their Basic Agreement negotiation in 1989—the centenary of the Brotherhood's break with Organized Baseball—both reflected back on the damage wrought in 1981.

The 1980s brought unprecedented parity on the playing field and misery off it. The drug problem endemic in our society struck baseball, inevitably as well, and Pete Rose's itch for gambling disgraced him and the game. Baseball's victims are highly publicized and their fall from grace is judged more reprehensible for all the advantages that today's players enjoy—but the game is an American institution reflecting what is wrong with our people as well as what is right with them. Let's hope that in this most difficult area of addictive behavior baseball can again—as it did with integration—lead America rather than follow it.

The year of 1989 became a nightmare, with Commissioner Bart Giamatti's expulsion of Rose followed by his own sudden and shocking death days later, a second finding of collusion by owners to undermine the free-agent market, and a Bay Area World Series rudely interrupted by an earthquake. But baseball recovered even from these calamities, as well as a spring training lockout in 1990, to embark upon an era that gave promise of unprecedented prosperity. The attendance of the Toronto Blue Jays exceeded the 4 million mark while the team captured back-to-back World Series, the first such feat since the Cincinnati Reds of 1975–1976. And in 1993 the National League expanded to 14 teams, welcoming franchises in Miami and Colorado that were instantly and wildly prosperous, with the Rockies setting an all-time attendance peak of nearly 4.5 million fans.

And then came 1994, a year of wonderment on the playing fields, as Ken Griffey Jr., Matt Williams, Frank Thomas, Jeff Bagwell, Tony Gwynn, Greg Maddux, and a host of others appeared to be initiating a new golden age of baseball . . . until play stopped on August 12 and did not resume. The leagues, which had divided into three divisions for the first time, now had no opportunity to try out their new idea of an additional round of postseason play, with the introduction of a Wild Card team that had not been a division winner.

As fans, we were presented with a dilemma: to side with the players, who went on strike hoping to extend their gains of the previous two decades? Or to side with the owners, who stood fast in insisting upon a balance between costs and revenues? As fans, we tried to side with the game of baseball, and to wish that its most intense contests would soon reconvene to the field of play.

And they did, with splendid seasons in 1995 and 1996, though some fans continued to withhold their affections, hoping that baseball owners and players would give peace a chance—as at last they did.

Baseball is not a conventional industry. It belongs neither to the players nor management, but to all of us. It is our national pastime, our national symbol, and our national treasure.

The monumental 1998 season enriched that treasure in so many ways, from the excitement of the home run race between Mark McGwire and Sammy Sosa to the awesome victory total of the New York Yankees. Gloriously, baseball's ghosts came back to life, in the daily press and in dinner-table conversations everywhere. Roger Maris, Babe Ruth, Hack Wilson, even Tinker and Evers and Chance, played invisibly alongside our heroes of today. Yankee heroics in succeeding Octobers even included an eerily nostalgic Subway Series victory.

The Weather of Our Lives

Ever changing in ways that are so small as to preserve the illusion that "nothing changes in baseball," the game has introduced, in the lifetime of many of us: night ball, plane travel, television, integration, bullpen stoppers, expansion, the amateur draft, competitive parity, indoor stadiums, artificial turf, free agency, the designated hitter, Wild Card contestants, interleague contests, international play, and expansion to 30 teams in 1998. Not far off, perhaps, are further expansion to 32 teams and intercontinental championships.

For fans accustomed to the game's languorous rhythms and conservative resistance to innovation, the changes of the past twenty years in particular seem positively frenetic. Yet for all its changes, baseball has not strayed far from its origins, and in fact has changed far less than other American institutions of equivalent antiquity. What sustains baseball in the hearts of Americans, finally, is not its responsiveness to changes in society nor its propensity for novelty, but its myths, its lore, its records, and its essential stability. As historian Bruce Catton noted in 1959:

A gaffer from the era of William McKinley, abruptly brought back to the second half of the twentieth century, would find very little in modern life that would not seem new, strange, and rather bewildering, but put in a good grandstand seat back of first base he would see nothing that was not completely familiar.

It's still a game of bat and ball, played without regard for the clock; a game of 90-foot basepaths, nine innings, nine men in the field; three outs, all out; and three strikes still send you to the bench, no matter whom you know in city hall. It's the national anthem before every game; it's playing catch with your son or daughter; it's learning how to win and how to deal with loss, and how to connect with something larger than our selves.

"Baseball," wrote Thomas Wolfe, "has been not merely 'the great national game' but really a part of the whole weather of our lives, of the thing that is our own, of the whole fabric, the million memories of America." Spring comes in America not on the vernal equinox but on Opening Day; summer sets in with a Memorial Day doubleheader and does not truly end until the last out of the regular season. Winter begins the day after the World Series.

Where were you when Bobby Thomson hit the shot heard 'round the world? Or the night Carlton Fisk hit his homer in the 12th? Or when the Mets, with batter after batter one strike away from their loss in the World Series, staged their famous rally? These are milestones in the lives of America and Americans.

We grow up with baseball; we mark—and, for a moment, stop—the passage of time with it; and we grow old with it. It is our game, for all our days.

CHAPTER 2

Team Histories

Frederick Ivor-Campbell and Matthew Silverman

When the Tampa Bay Devil Rays and Arizona Diamondbacks began play in 1998 they brought to 112 the number of clubs (plus those of the Negro major leagues) that have played major league ball at one time or another since baseball's first professional league—the National Association—was organized in 1871. Some of the early teams dropped out after only a few games, but several have played for more than a century, and one—the present Atlanta Braves—has played every season from 1871 to the present. The only existing franchise older than Atlanta's (which originated as the Boston Red Stockings, then became the Boston and Milwaukee Braves before moving to Atlanta) is the Chicago Cubs, which organized in 1870, a year before league play began. The White Stockings (as they were first known) missed two seasons (1872-1873) in the aftermath of the great Chicago fire, but have since then continuously represented the same city longer than any other club in baseball history.

Here are brief histories of 30 current big-league clubs, arranged alphabetically by city or state. These are followed by summary histories of the 82 other clubs—now defunct—that at one time also represented their cities in the major leagues.

Anaheim Angels

Of the 10 teams added to the major leagues in the 1960s and '70s, the Angels were quickest to put together a winning season, finishing third in the American League in only their second year of play.

Former cowboy actor and singer Gene Autry brought the club into being as the Los Angeles Angels in December 1960. They played their first season, 1961, in Los Angeles' Wrigley Field, a former minor league park with power alleys only five feet deeper than the foul poles; five Angels hit 20 or more home runs that year. Though the team finished seventh in the standings, they were second in homers only to the mighty Yankees.

What the Angels lost in home runs in 1962 (when they moved out of Wrigley Field into the Dodgers' new stadium), they more than made up in pitching. Paced by rookie Dean Chance, the Angels nearly doubled their wins on the road, and, as late as mid-August, stood in second place, within striking distance of New York. Though they tailed off in September, they finished a respectable third, 10 games back.

The team collapsed to ninth the next year, but in 1964 Chance's pitching and splendid relief by rookie Bob Lee helped lift the team back into the first division. Among Chance's league-leading 11 shutouts were six 1-0 victories.

Los Angeles became the California Angels in 1965 in anticipation of their move south to a new stadium in Anaheim the following year, but neither the name change nor the new location stirred them out of the second division. In 1967 with below-average run production but the league's third-best pitching, the Angels shot up from ninth to third in midseason before leveling off to fifth. After dismal seasons in 1968-1969, career years in 1970 by pitcher Clyde Wright (22 wins, including a no-hitter) and newly acquired left fielder Alex Johnson (202 hits and a league-high .329 batting average) helped the Angels snap back with an 86-76 record that matched their previous best (1962).

The seven losing seasons which followed 1970 were somewhat redeemed by the arrival in 1972 of pitcher Nolan Ryan, who burst into superstardom as an Angel, setting a modern record of 383 strikeouts in 1973 and hurling four no-hitters in three years (1973-1975). Ryan's effectiveness dipped in 1978, but the club as a whole came to life, contending closely for the Western Division title all season until Kansas City shot ahead in September.

In 1979 Don Baylor became the first (and, so far, only) DH to be named league Most Valuable Player, as a renewed offense powered California to its first division title. Baltimore stopped the Angels in the ALCS, though. The team's run production dropped off dramatically the next year, and the club followed up its best season with its worst.

After another losing season in 1981 (during which Jim Fregosi was replaced as manager by 20-year veteran Gene Mauch), California lured free agent Reggie Jackson from the Yankees. With Jackson leading a resurgent offense and Geoff Zahn headlining the league's second-best pitching staff, the Angels rebounded to 93 wins in 1982 and their second division title. They defeated Milwaukee in the first two games of the ALCS, but lost the next three. A disappointed Mauch retired.

Again, in 1983, the Angels followed a championship with a poor season—not quite as bad as 1980, but still their third worst to that point. In 1984 they rebounded to .500, good enough for second in a weak division. Pitcher Mike Witt concluded his rise to staff ace with a perfect game on the season's last day.

Gene Mauch came out of retirement to manage the Angels again in 1985. With pitching that featured splendid relief from newly acquired Donnie Moore (31 saves; 1.92 ERA), the team led the division much of the season, but lost three of four to Kansas City in the final week to fall a game behind the Royals into second.

With Witt's 18 wins and 2.84 ERA pacing the staff and rookie first baseman Wally Joyner leading the offense, California won the 1986 division crown with ease. In the ALCS against Boston, the Angels took three of the first four games, and were within one pitch of capturing their first pennant in Game 5, but the Red Sox rallied to win.

For the third time the Angels followed up their division championship with a losing season, this time dropping the 1987 season finale to tie for last place in the AL West. Manager Mauch retired again, this time for good. After another losing season brought them home a distant fourth in 1988, the Angels signed Doug Rader to manage the club. They also acquired a veteran pitcher—Bert Blyleven—who led a resurgence that lifted the club to its third best won-lost record ever. Since the West was now the stronger AL division, the team's 91 wins carried them only into third place. In 1990 they dropped just one place in the standings, but finished again below .500, 23 games out of first.

The Angels began strong in 1991, and moved into the division lead on July 3, but seven straight losses plunged them to fifth; although they finished at .500 for the season, just 14 games out of first, they wound up in the division cellar.

After four sub-500 seasons the Angels (paced by Jim Edmonds' 107 RBIs and Mark Langston's 15-7 mark) led the AL West for most of the 1995 season, only to fade and finish in a tie in the division race with the upstart Seattle Mariners. The AL West title was decided by a one-game playoff in which the Mariners' Randy Johnson made the difference. California's improvement made it one of only three major league clubs to register an increase in per-game attendance over 1994.

The Angels fell to last in 1996, resulting in manager Marcel Lachemann's firing. He was replaced by John McNamara on an interim basis, and former Astros pilot Terry Collins took over the post later. At the end of 1996 the Angels changed their name (to Anaheim Angels), owners (the Walt Disney Company purchased the team), and manager (Collins arrived from Houston). In 1998 they changed their stadium (a reconstructed ballpark was renamed Edison Field), but they could not change their luck. In 1997 the Angels chased both the Mariners for the AL West title and the Yankees for the AL Wild Card before coming up short of both. Injuries, which hurt the team's chances in 1997, caught up to them again in '98. The Texas Rangers supplanted the Angels atop the standings in the final week of the season to win the AL West title.

The Angels fell apart in 1999. Dissension between Collins and the players, especially new first baseman Mo Vaughn, resulted in the manager getting axed at season's end. Rookie skipper Mike Scioscia led the Angels to 82 wins in 2000 despite the fact that no one on the inexperienced starting staff won in double figures. Troy Glaus emerged as one of the league's best third baseman, and his AL-best 47 home runs helped Anaheim set a club mark with 236 homers. Left fielder Darin Erstad set team records with a .355 average and 240 hits, the highest hit total in the major leagues in 15 years.

Arizona Diamondbacks

Along with the Tampa Bay Devil Rays, the Arizona Diamondbacks were granted a $130 million NL expansion franchise on March 9, 1995.

Jerry Colangelo, owner of the National Basketball Association's Phoenix Suns, headed the Diamondbacks ownership group. Joe Garagiola Jr., a former player agent, was named the team's first general manager. In November 1994, more than three years before the first scheduled game, the Diamondbacks named former Yankees manager Buck Showalter as the franchise's first field manager.

In Bank One Ballpark, a $335 million retractable-roofed, natural-grass facility in downtown Phoenix, the Diamondbacks drew 3,602,856 fans their first season. After getting off to a rocky start—they lost their first five games—the Diamondbacks finished strong and posted key victories in the closing weeks of the season against the Chicago Cubs, San Francisco Giants, and New York Mets, who were locked in a fight-to-the-finish struggle for the final playoff berth. Mound ace Andy Benes came within two outs of a September no-hitter, and Travis Lee, who had the first hit and home run in club history, was one of the year's top rookies. Devon White was the team's first All-Star.

Arizona became the first team to reach the postseason in just its second year of existence. The Diamondbacks won 100 games, including 17 wins by National League Cy Young Award winner Randy Johnson. He also led the NL in complete games, innings, and his 364 strikeouts were the fourth most in the 20th century. Jay Bell, Matt Williams, and Steve Finley each hit 30 home runs and drove in 100 runs, and Luis Gonzalez batted .336 with 111 RBIs. Arizona, however, fell to the Mets in the 1999 Division Series.

The Diamondbacks seemed poised to repeat as NL West champion for the first two months of the 2000 season, but the Giants took over first place. Despite the mid-season acquisition of Curt Schilling, who, along with Johnson, gave Arizona one of baseball's best righty-lefty combinations, the Diamondbacks finished third. Showalter was fired the day after the season ended and was replaced by Bob Brenly, who had been a broadcaster for the team.

Atlanta Braves

The Atlanta Braves, who first played in 1871 as Boston's Red Stockings, are the only club to field a team every season of professional league baseball.

When the game's first openly professional club, the Cincinnati Red Stockings, decided to revert to amateur status, manager/outfielder Harry Wright and three of his teammates took their talents and club nickname to Boston, where, with infielders Ross Barnes and Harry Schafer and pitcher Al Spalding, they formed the nucleus of a team that would dominate the five-year history of the first professional league, the National Association. After a close second-place finish in their first year, the Red Stockings won four pennants in convincing fashion, including a 71-8 record in 1875 with an .899 winning percentage that has never since been approached in major league ball.

When the National League replaced the NA in 1876, four of Boston's best players, including Spalding and Barnes, deserted the club for Chicago. After a fourth-place finish in 1876, the Red Stockings lured pitcher Tommy Bond from Hartford and finished at the top in 1877 and '78. Bond dominated NL pitching, winning 80 games (40 each year), 22 more than his nearest rival. Although he won 43 more in 1879, Boston slipped to second.

In 1880 the Red Stockings suffered their first losing season. After a second consecutive sixth-place finish the next year, Wright left to manage Providence, but Boston rebounded to third in 1882 and surprised everyone in 1883 by outplaying favored Chicago and Providence to capture their seventh pennant.

Providence knocked them out of the race late in 1884, and Boston remained out of contention the next four seasons. In 1889, though, with several players signed from the defunct Detroit Wolverines (including batting champ Dan Brouthers), and 49 wins from pitcher John Clarkson, the Beaneaters (as they were now more commonly known) waged a two-team race for the championship with the New York Giants. Boston won as many games as the Giants, but lost two more and finished a game behind their New York rivals.

Frank Selee, who had managed two straight minor league pennant winners, was hired from Omaha along with his star pitcher, Charles "Kid" Nichols. Their arrival in 1890 ushered in Boston's second golden era. When they left the club 12 years later, the Beaneaters had won five more NL pennants. Nichols won 27 games in his rookie season, but Boston—decimated by defections to the outlaw Players League— finished only fifth. With the return of some of the defectors in 1891, Clarkson won 33 games, Nichols recorded the first of seven 30-win seasons, and the Beaneaters returned to the top.

When the NL expanded in 1892 from eight teams to 12, the schedule was also expanded, and the season divided into two halves. Boston won the first half, and the Cleveland Spiders the second. In a World Series to determine the league champion, the Beaneaters (102-48) defeated the Spiders.

The split season was abandoned and the schedule reduced in 1893—and Boston captured its third straight pennant. Center fielder Hugh Duffy hit .363. The next year Duffy led the way with .440, which is still the major league record. His Beaneaters didn't win the pennant, but they became the first club in a decade (and the last until 1920) to hit over 100 home runs. Five Beaneaters drove in 100 runs or more, and the team set a big league record for runs scored (1,220).

Boston dropped out of contention for a couple of years, but bounced back in 1897 to edge Baltimore for the pennant. In the Temple Cup series, though, played between the first-and second-place teams for the world title, the Orioles overwhelmed Boston, four games to one. The next year Boston won 102 games to lead the league, but the league had abandoned the four-year-old Temple Cup.

After coming in second in 1899, Boston dropped out of pennant contention for 14 years, finishing as far back as 66½ games (in 1906) and losing as many as 108 (in 1909). The Braves (as they were now known) rose to fifth in 1913 under new manager George Stallings. Through the first half of 1914, however, the Braves seemed to be destined for another cellar finish.

In mid-July they stood a last-place eighth in a tight field. Six days and six wins later they were third. By mid-August they had climbed to second; on Aug. 26 they replaced the New York Giants in first. For two weeks they alternated between first and second, then broke out of the pack to win the pennant by 10½ games.

Boston's heroes were pitchers Dick Rudolph and Bill James, both in only their second full big league seasons. Rudolph won 26 games in 1914 and James won 26; then they added two more each in the "Miracle" Braves' World Series sweep of the heavily favored Philadelphia Athletics.

A seven-game losing streak in early September dropped them out of a tie for first in 1916. They rallied, but finished third. It was the Braves' last close race for 32 years.

From 1917 through 1945 the Braves finished only as high as fourth three seasons and only once as close as nine games from the top. With four years in the cellar and 11 in seventh place, the team finished near the bottom of the league more than half the time.

In 1946, with dynamic new ownership headed by contractor Lou Perini, a new manager—Billy Southworth, who had led the Cardinals to three pennants and two world championships—and the return of war veterans like pitchers Warren Spahn and Johnny Sain, the Braves had their first winning season in eight years. At the end of the season Boston acquired third baseman Bob Elliott from Pittsburgh. He enjoyed a career year in 1947, powering the Braves to third place. Spahn and Sain won 21 games each.

Spahn dropped to 15 wins in 1948, but Sain won 24. Four veterans—plus rookie shortstop Alvin Dark—hit over .300. With the league's best pitching and hitting, the Braves moved out in front in June, and shook off their last challengers with a September spurt. From there on, the Braves' path in Boston was downhill. Cleveland beat them in the World Series, and the club dropped to fourth for the next three years. Southworth resigned part way through the 1951 season. In 1952 the team fell to seventh; home attendance was less than one-fifth what it had been four years earlier. The next spring Perini moved the franchise to Milwaukee in the league's first realignment since 1900.

The move was a spectacular success. Not only did the Braves rebound to second place, but attendance jumped 649 percent over their previous year in Boston to set an NL record of more than 1.8 million. The league's best pitching staff was led by the trio that would anchor Milwaukee's years of greatness: veteran Warren Spahn, sophomore Lew Burdette, and rookie Bob Buhl. In 1953 Eddie Mathews led the league in home runs, a category the Braves would own in the coming years as Hank Aaron joined the team the following year.

The Braves were slightly ahead through much of the 1956 season until five straight losses in early September brought them even with the surging Dodgers. It was not settled until the final day, when a Dodger victory over Pittsburgh left Milwaukee a game back in second.

The acquisition of veteran second baseman Red

Schoendienst from St. Louis in June 1957 steadied the infield and gave the team a baserunner for Mathews and Aaron to drive home. In August the Braves drew away from the pack, and recovered from a September slump to win the pennant by eight games over St. Louis. The Yankees took them to seven games in the World Series, but Burdette's shutout in the finale brought the Braves their first world championship since 1914.

Milwaukee repeated as league champions in 1958, but in the Fall Classic, after taking the first two games from the Yankees, they lost the Series in seven. The race was much tighter in 1959 until the Giants moved away from the Dodgers and Braves in August. In September the Giants faltered as the others surged past them, and the season ended with the Braves and Dodgers tied. In a best-of-three playoff, the Dodgers took the pennant in two games—but both by only one run and the second only after 12 innings.

A portent for the Braves' future could be seen in the crowd of under 20,000 that attended the first playoff game in Milwaukee. After setting a third NL record in 1957, Milwaukee attendance had gradually declined, dropping below 2 million in 1958, the club's second pennant year, and even farther in this year of the tight pennant race. When attendance dropped in 1965 to a new Milwaukee low of just over half a million, the club pulled up stakes again and moved to Atlanta.

The Braves' won-lost records in 1965 and '66 were nearly identical. But in Atlanta attendance improved by almost a million. Aaron was still at the height of his powers, and younger players were beginning to make their mark. Reliever Phil Niekro was converted to a starter in 1967 and responded with the league's best ERA.

After finishing no higher than fifth in their first three seasons in Atlanta, the Braves celebrated 1969, the first year of divisional play, with a late-season drive that carried them to the championship of the West. Veteran Orlando Cepeda, newly acquired from St. Louis, joined Aaron in supplying power, and Niekro won 23 games as the Braves won 10 in a row to clinch the title in their next-to-last game. In the league's first Championship Series, though, the "Miracle" Mets of New York swept Atlanta in three games.

From there it was mostly downhill for the next decade. After breaking Babe Ruth's career home run record in the 1974 home opener, Aaron returned to Milwaukee (to the AL Brewers) in 1975. Attendance in Atlanta dwindled without Aaron. Yachtsman Ted Turner bought the club in 1976 and attendance rose, but the team sank to the bottom of the division for four years.

In 1982, though, with power from outfielder Dale Murphy and third baseman Bob Horner, and exceptional pitching from Niekro (17-4) and reliever Gene Garber (30 saves), Atlanta grabbed the division lead with a season-opening 13-game winning streak and recovered from a midsummer collapse to edge Los Angeles by one game for their second divisional crown. But they were swept by St. Louis in the NLCS.

For the next two seasons Murphy's league-leading slugging carried the Braves to second place. By 1986, though, they had sunk into the division cellar. Murphy boosted them up a notch in 1987 with the most productive season of his career, but as his power at the plate dropped the next year, the Braves sunk to their worst finish in 53 years.

With the first bottom-to-top comeback in NL history, the Braves captured the West in 1991. As Atlanta's home attendance zoomed back above 2 million for the first time since 1983, the Braves won a battle with Los Angeles that saw 11 ties or lead changes in the season's final weeks. The Braves captured the city's first pennant with a victory over Pittsburgh in seven games. Free agent Terry Pendleton (the NL MVP) joined David Justice and Ron Gant to power Atlanta's offense, while a trio of young pitchers—Tom Glavine, Steve Avery, and John Smoltz—anchored one of the league's best staffs.

In the World Series the Braves overcame a two-game deficit to take a Series lead before falling short by one extra-inning run in each of the final two games. The following season was very similar. Once again the Braves won the NL West and edged Pittsburgh for the pennant, although this time it took a come-from-behind win in the final at bat of Game 7 to beat the Pirates. Once again they faltered in the World Series, this time succumbing to Toronto in six games.

For the third season in a row the Braves topped the NL West in 1993, this time charging from 10 games back in July to a four-game lead in mid-September, then holding off resurgent San Francisco to clinch the crown on the season's final day. After building a 2-1 lead in the NLCS, though, they fell to the Phillies in six games.

When the players' strike ended the 1994 season in August, pitcher Greg Maddux, en route to a record third consecutive Cy Young Award, was fashioning one of the greatest seasons in years. Atlanta's 68-46 record ranked second in the NL only to Montreal's 74-40. But a new divisional alignment had moved the Braves from the NL West to the East—Montreal's division—so they finished second, six games behind the Expos.

Behind Maddux (19-2, 1.63 ERA), who won his fourth straight Cy Young, and rookie star Chipper Jones, the Braves bounced back in 1995, romping to the NL East title. Atlanta also charged past Wild Card Colorado in the first round of the new postseason format and swept the Reds in the NLCS. In the World Series the Braves met the Indians in a rematch of the 1948 Fall Classic. This time the results were far different as Atlanta triumphed in six games.

The Braves won the NL East again in 1996. Atlanta's staff was paced this time by Cy Young Award winner John Smoltz (24-8, 276 strikeouts), Tom Glavine (15-10), and Mark Wohlers (39 saves); its offense was led by Chipper Jones (.309, 30 HR, 110 RBIs), Ryan Klesko (34 HR, 93 RBIs), and Fred McGriff (28 HR, 107 RBIs). In the first round of the postseason Atlanta rolled over Los Angeles. In the NLCS, the club had its back to the wall. Down three games to one, it rallied with 12-1, 3-1, and 15-0 wins over Tony LaRussa's Cards. The Braves kept it up in the first two games of the World Series, stomping Joe Torre's Yankees 12-1 and 4-0. The pundits were about to anoint the Braves as one of history's greatest teams. Then, suddenly, they ran out of gas, losing the next four straight to New York.

The Braves won the NL East again in 1997 and swept Houston in the Division Series. But Florida, the NL Wild Card, knocked the Braves out of the NLCS. The Braves were never challenged in 1998 as they won the East by 18 games and won a club-record 106 times. Atlanta had five pitchers win at least 15 games and Kerry Ligtenberg (30 saves) emerged as the team's new closer. Andres Galarraga, who replaced Fred McGriff at first base, brought more power to an already potent lineup. After the Braves swept the Cubs in the Division Series, however, they scored just three runs in losing the first three games of the NLCS to San Diego. Although Atlanta became the first team in major league history to go down 3-0 and still force a sixth game, the Padres won Game 6 and the NL pennant.

Atlanta continued to dominate the NL East, winning division titles the next two years. In 1999 league MVP Chipper Jones led the Braves to 100 wins and controversial reliever John Rocker emerged as one of baseball's top closers. Atlanta reached the World Series but fell to the Yankees in four straight games. Turner Field hosted the 2000 All-Star Game and first baseman Andres Galarraga received a prolonged ovation for his return to All-Star form after missing an entire season while undergoing cancer treatments. National League Rookie of the Year Rafael Furcal gave the Braves speed at the top of the lineup. Atlanta lost John Smoltz for the year but Glavine and Maddux won 20 and 19 games, respectively. The postseason ended abruptly as the Cardinals swept the Braves, who had never lost in five previous Division Series.

Baltimore Orioles

The history of major league baseball in Baltimore dates back to 1872, to the Lord Baltimores of the National Association, and includes the great National League Orioles of the 1890s. The city was also represented in the American League's first big league seasons, 1901-1902. But when those Orioles moved to New York in 1903 and became the Highlanders (later Yankees), Baltimore was without a big league club for more than half a century, until the transfer of the Browns from St. Louis in 1954.

The current Orioles didn't get their start in St. Louis, though. Their first home was Milwaukee, where they finished in the AL cellar in 1901. When they moved to St. Louis the next year, they lured several valuable players from the city's NL Cardinals—including 1901 batting champ Jesse Burkett, star shortstop Bobby Wallace, and the Cards' three best pitchers. They also took on the Cardinals' discarded nickname: becoming the new St. Louis Browns.

The Browns finished a strong second to the Philadelphia Athletics in their first St. Louis season, but fell to sixth the next year and, except for a fourth-place finish in 1908 (thanks to the pitching of newly acquired veteran Rube Waddell), remained mired in the second division until 1920. Late in the 1913 season a young Branch Rickey was hired to manage the Browns. In his two full seasons he was unable to lift the club out of the second division, but he did sign college star George Sisler (whom he had coached at the University of Michigan)

In 1916, his first full season, Sisler led the Browns in hitting as they caught fire in August to record their first winning season in eight years. Pitcher Urban Shocker was obtained from the Yankees two years later and by 1920 had developed into a 20-game winner. Also in 1920, Sisler connected for what is still a major league record 257 hits and batted .407 to help move the Browns up to fourth, their first finish that high since 1908. The next year Shocker's 27 victories brought them a winning season and third place. And in 1922 the team recorded its finest record ever in St. Louis: 93 wins and a .604 winning percentage.

The 1922 Browns, led by Sisler's sizzling .420 average, hit .313 as a team to lead the league. Left fielder Ken Williams ran away with the RBI title and beat out Babe Ruth and Tilly Walker for the home run crown. (Ruth, to be honest, did miss nearly a third of the season that year.) Sisler and Williams even finished one-two in stolen bases. And though Shocker slipped a bit to 24 wins, he led a pitching staff that recorded the league's lowest ERA. The team led the league in the standings throughout July and into August before the Yankees nudged ahead of them. The Browns never regained the lead, remaining second, a heartbreaking single game back, at season's end.

Falling back to fifth the next year, as Sisler missed the whole season with a sinus infection, the Browns remained out of contention for the next 21 years, dropping to their lowest point in 1939 with 111 losses. They had three winning seasons in the war years 1942-1945. The Browns captured their only pennant in 1944, edging the Detroit Tigers on the final day after trailing them through most of September. The World Series—an all-St. Louis affair—proved anticlimactic for the Browns as they lost to the Cardinals in six games.

The Browns finished third in 1945 before sinking back into the second division. Even the club's purchase by the dynamic Bill Veeck in July 1951 couldn't rouse them. (A month after buying the Browns, Veeck made his best-remembered move; bringing in midget Eddie Gaedel for one plate appearance—he walked.)

Unable to earn either victories or money in St. Louis, Veeck sold the club in September 1953 to a Baltimore group, who relocated and renamed them the Orioles. The new owners hired the brilliant Paul Richards to rebuild the team as manager. It took him (and Lee MacPhail, who became general manager and president in 1958) several years to move the Orioles above .500. In 1960 young third baseman Brooks Robinson and rookie Jim Gentile led the team as it made its first run for the pennant since 1944. In first place in early September, they finished second when the Yanks won 15 straight.

The next year the O's did even better, winning six more games than they had in 1960. Gentile hit 46 home runs and drove in 141. But the Yankees and Tigers had even better years and the Orioles finished a distant third.

When Hank Bauer was brought in to manage the Orioles in 1964, the team entered its golden decades—20 years which saw them win seven division titles, six pennants, and three world championships, with only two finishes below third. With Robinson driving in runs and left fielder Boog Powell slugging at a league-leading pace, the O's finished with wins in seven of their final eight games. But the White Sox won their last nine and the Yankees put together an 11-game streak near the end to take the pennant and leave Baltimore third, two games back.

After another third-place finish in 1965, the Orioles acquired slugging Frank Robinson from Cincinnati and moved second-year pitcher Jim Palmer into the starting rotation. Palmer won 15 to lead a balanced staff, and Frank Robinson captured the Triple Crown. With both Robinsons and Powell driving in 100 runs or more, the O's romped to their first pennant. They continued the romp in the World Series, holding Los Angeles to a total of just two runs as they swept to their first world title.

A drop in offensive production and the loss of Palmer to injuries for most of the season plunged Baltimore into a tie for sixth in 1967. Palmer was out the next year, too, but pitchers Dave McNally and Jim Hardin burst to the forefront with fine seasons to lift the club back to second.

Baltimore coach Earl Weaver, a pennant-winning manager in the O's farm system, replaced Hank Bauer at the Orioles' helm in mid-1968 to begin what became one of the longest and most successful managerial tenures of recent times. In 14 full seasons Weaver led his club to six Eastern Division titles and six second-place finishes, with one season each in third and fourth. In seven of the 14 years the Orioles compiled the league's lowest ERA, including five consecutive seasons (1969-1973). Baltimore pitchers put together 21 different 20-game seasons in those 14 seasons (eight of them by Jim Palmer), and garnered six Cy Young Awards.

In the first three years of divisional play Baltimore ran away with the East championship and swept the American League Championship Series to capture the pennant each time. The 1969 team (despite an embarrassingly easy loss to the New York Mets in the World Series) is often ranked among the greatest clubs of all time. With overwhelming pitching and fielding, the Orioles took the division crown by 19 games, winning a club-record 109. The Orioles also were tops in fielding and their pitchers gave up nearly a run less per game than the league average.

Baltimore's performance in 1970 was nearly as impressive. Mike Cuellar and Dave McNally won 24 games each, and Jim Palmer contributed 20 more wins to the O's total of 108. This time they won the World Series as well, rolling over Cincinnati in five games behind an unforgettable performance by Series MVP Brooks Robinson.

In the 1971 World Series, though, Pittsburgh came back from losses in the first two games to defeat the Orioles by a run in Game 7. The O's captured divisional titles in 1973 and '74, but it was 1979 before they again triumphed in the ALCS. Once again, however, they faced the Pirates in the World Series, and once again took the Series lead, only to fall again in the seventh game.

The 1979 pennant was Weaver's last, as late-season Oriole surges in 1980 and '82 fell just short. But in 1983 the O's—paced by the pitching of veteran Scott McGregor and rookie Mike Boddicker, and the hitting and fielding of Cal Ripken, Jr. at short, and Eddie Murray at first—made new manager Joe Altobelli look good. After a comfortable divisional win, they trounced the Chicago White Sox in the ALCS and the Philadelphia Phillies in the World Series.

Despite the return of Earl Weaver in 1985-1986, the Orioles finished last in the East in 1986. Though they rose to sixth in 1987, their .414 winning percentage was their lowest in 32 years. Then in 1988 they hit rock bottom, not only finishing last but also beginning the season with an AL record-setting 21 consecutive defeats.

Baltimore's rebound was even more startling than its plummet. Under manager Frank Robinson (who had been handed the hapless O's early in the 1988 season) the 1989 Orioles took over first place in late April, held the lead through August, and stayed within the reach of the division title until Toronto defeated them in the season's penultimate game to clinch the crown. The newly potent bat of catcher Mickey Tettleton and splendid relief from rookie Gregg Olson highlighted the Baltimore resurgence. Olson remained effective in 1990, but the offense faltered, and an August-September slide dropped the Orioles out of the race.

The O's began slowly in 1991, and manager Robinson was replaced by coach Johnny Oates in May, with the club in last place. But although Cal Ripken put together an MVP season, the O's never caught fire, and finished sixth, 24 games out. In 1992, at festive new Orioles Park at Camden Yards, Baltimore snapped back to challenge Toronto through much of the season before slipping to third.

At a bankruptcy auction in August 1993, a group led by Peter Angelos agreed to purchase the club for a record $173 million. On the field, 1993 was much like 1992. Only half a game out of first as late as Sept. 9, the Orioles finished 10 games back, tied for third with Detroit. They challenged again in 1994, but Baltimore's second-place finish was not good enough to save manager Oates' job.

Cal Ripken, Jr. had twice won AL MVP honors and was a fixture on the All-Star team, but none of these accomplishments could compare to the spectacle at Camden Yards in 1995. He finally broke Lou Gehrig's consecutive game playing streak on Sept. 6 in an uplifting ceremony that highlighted an otherwise disappointing season.

Under new manager Davey Johnson, the Orioles (88-74) underperformed until midseason. Owner Angelos resisted temptations to break up the team and instead acquired veteran Eddie Murray, who hit his 500th home run and helped spark a successful stretch run for a Wild Card berth. Offense was the name of the game for this team as it slammed a major league record 257 homers. Standouts included Brady Anderson (50 HR, 110 RBIs), Rafael Palmeiro (39 HR, 142 RBIs), Roberto Alomar (22 HR, 94 RBIs), Cal Ripken (26 HR, 102 RBIs), and pitcher Mike Mussina (19-11).

Baltimore's 1996 postseason appearance (its first since 1983) was overshadowed, however, by Alomar's spitting on umpire John Hirschbeck. Baltimore upset the favored Indians in the Division Series, but in the ALCS (aided by a controversial Game 1 home run that should have been ruled fan interference) the O's fell to Joe Torre's Yankees in five games.

The Orioles won the AL East in 1997 and knocked off the Seattle Mariners in the Division Series with surprising ease. Nothing was easy in the ALCS. Mussina's dominating performance—25 strikeouts in 15 innings and a 0.60 ERA—was wasted as the Orioles lost both his starts to Cleveland in extra innings. On the day that Davey Johnson was named AL Manager of the Year he resigned as the result of a dispute with Angelos.

Ray Miller moved from pitching coach to manager in 1998, but the Orioles suffered through an up-and-down season that culminated with Ripken unexpectedly ending his consecutive game streak at 2,632 in Baltimore's final home game. Mike Hargrove replaced Miller as manager following a disappointing 1999.

The 2000 season began with Ripken reaching his 3,000th career hit, but it ended with a long-speculated fire sale of Baltimore's veteran talent. The Orioles traded former All-Stars Will Clark, Mike Bordick, Charles Johnson, and B.J. Surhoff, among others, for a number of unproven younger players. For the first time in a decade, the Orioles were in a position of starting over.

Boston Red Sox

Since the end of World War II, the Red Sox have won the American League pennant four times, only to lose the World Series each time in the seventh game. It was not always thus. In their first two decades they were the league's most successful club, winners of six pennants and five world championships. (No World Series was played the year of their second pennant.)

Organized in 1901 as one of four new eastern clubs in Ban Johnson's newly-formed American League, Boston's Americans (or Pilgrims, Puritans, Plymouth Rocks, or Somersets, as they were variously called) quickly established themselves as one of the game's strongest teams. Star third baseman Jimmy Collins was lured from Boston's NL club to manage the new Americans, and he assembled a team that included such former NL standouts as slugger Buck Freeman and pitcher Cy Young. Finishing a strong second in the AL's inaugural major league season, the Pilgrims quickly supplanted their mediocre NL counterparts in the hearts and wallets of Boston fans.

After a third-place finish in 1902, the Pilgrims ran away from the rest of the league in 1903 to take their first pennant by 14½ games over Philadelphia. Young led the league in victories for the third straight season, Freeman took titles in home runs, total bases, and RBIs and second-year outfielder Patsy Dougherty finished first in hits and runs scored. In the first modern World Series, Boston overcame Pittsburgh's favored Pirates, thereby confirming the AL's claim to major league status in the public mind.

Boston repeated as pennant winners in 1904, but by a much narrower margin, after a struggle with the New York Highlanders that wasn't settled until the next-to-last game of the season. The NL Giants refused to play Boston in a World Series that year.

Over the next few years, as the Pilgrims dropped into the league cellar, new owner John I. Taylor (whose father, *Boston Globe* publisher Charles Taylor, was said to have bought the club for his son to give him something useful to do) rid the team of many of the players who had brought it glory. Eventually Taylor was himself maneuvered out of the club presidency, but it turned out he had not been a wanton destroyer. In driving out the old guard he had been making room for new young players: pitcher Joe Wood, for example, and a sprightly outfield of Tris Speaker, Harry Hooper, and Duffy Lewis. The club—now known as the Red Sox—rose out of its depths in the final years of Taylor's presidency, even challenging the league leaders through much of 1909 before dropping away in late August. In 1911, in one of the last acts of his presidency, Taylor had, with his father, purchased land in Boston's Fenway section and built a new ballpark.

Sparked by the spectacular pitching of Wood and Speaker's play at the bat and in center field, the Red Sox of 1912 took the league lead in early June and were never headed, finishing with a club-record 105 victories. In the World Series they edged John McGraw's Giants and Christy Mathewson in one of the most exciting Series ever, four games to three, with one tie. Three years later, with a staff that boasted the AL's four top pitchers in winning percentage (including rookie Babe Ruth), the Sox captured their fourth pennant. After a first-game loss to the Phillies in the World Series, Boston recovered to sweep the next four by one run apiece.

Joe Wood's ailing arm finally gave out, and Tris Speaker was traded to Cleveland at the start of the 1916 season following a salary dispute. But with Ruth winning 23 games to lead the team, the Sox slid past the White Sox and Tigers in mid-September to take their fifth pennant and waltzed over Brooklyn in the Series.

Incipient disaster struck the Red Sox that December when New York theatrical entrepreneurs Hugh Ward and Harry Frazee bought the club. They put little cash into the deal, counting on future profits to pay the bulk of the purchase price. Ward sailed for Australia, leaving Frazee to run the club. For a while the future looked bright. After a second-place finish in 1917, Frazee hired minor league executive Ed Barrow as manager, and when many of the team's regulars left for military service in World War I, Frazee bought and traded for worthy replacements. In a season shortened a month because of the war, the Sox edged Cleveland for their sixth pennant and defeated the Chicago Cubs for their fifth world championship.

Frazee's theater losses put him in a financial bind and gradually forced him to sell off the best of his players—mostly to the Yankees, who had plenty of money, and an office just a short hop from Frazee's New York theater. Though the Sox fell to sixth place in 1919, Babe Ruth kept attention fixed on the team as he went to the outfield and startled the baseball world with a record 29 home runs. But that winter Frazee sold Ruth to the Yankees for $100,000 and a $300,000 mortgage on Fenway Park.

The Red Sox were on a 15-year sojourn in the second division that even a 1923 change in ownership was powerless to end. From 1922 through 1932 the Sox emerged from last place only twice. In 1932 they reached their nadir, losing 111 games and finishing 64 games out of first.

Young and wealthy Tom Yawkey bought the club in 1933 and promptly began what would be a lifetime effort to restore Boston to its former glory. His first efforts to buy success ready-made with such established stars as Lefty Grove, Jimmie Foxx, and Joe Cronin pulled the club out of the cellar but failed to lift it into pennant contention. But as general manager Eddie Collins began turning up young players to join the veterans, the club's fortune rose. The emergence between 1938 and 1942 of players like Bobby Doerr, Ted Williams, and pitcher Tex Hughson brought Boston a level of success not seen since 1918. In four of the five years they finished second to the Yankees, achieving, in 1942, their highest winning percentage since 1915.

The loss of most of these newcomers to military service in World War II delayed further progress. But with the arrival of rookie pitching sensation Dave Ferriss in 1945, and the acquisition of slugging first baseman Rudy York that winter, the club was prepared for its returning war veterans to join in bringing Boston its greatest season since 1912. With 104 victories, the 1946 Sox won their long-delayed seventh pennant by 12 games over second-place Detroit. In the World Series the favored Sox bowed to the Cardinals in Game 7 by one run.

The Yankees ran away from the pack in 1947, but the three years that followed saw the Red Sox three times in the throes of pennant fever. In 1948, after falling back a bit in late September, the Sox won four at the very end to tie Cleveland for first—but lost the one-game playoff. The next year they were 12 games behind the Yankees on July 4 but pulled up gradually to take a one-game lead into the final two-game series in New York. One Sox victory would win the pennant, but the Yankees took both games. In 1950 Boston played the league's best ball through July and August, to pull within a game of the Yankees on Sept. 18 but then lost four in a row and all hope of the pennant.

In 1951 the Sox collapsed at season's end to finish third, 11 games back. They came no closer the next 15 years, finishing with eight consecutive losing seasons from 1959 through 1966.

In 1967 the Sox awakened from their long slumber. A 10-game win streak in mid-July shot them out of mediocrity into the midst of a four-team race for the pennant that was not settled until Boston beat Minnesota and Detroit split a doubleheader on the final day, leaving the Sox on top. Carl Yastrzemski, who had replaced Ted Williams in left field seven years earlier, clinched the Triple Crown with a game-winning home run and six other hits in the final two must-win games. But Boston lost the World Series to St. Louis in seven games.

It was eight years before the Red Sox won another pennant, but they came close in 1972, losing the AL East crown by half a game to Detroit in the season's final series. They led the division two years later from mid-July through early September, then fell apart and finished third. But the next year, 1975, they maintained to the end the lead they first took in May, and swept Oakland in the ALCS for their ninth pennant. Television viewers will long remember Carlton Fisk's home run that won Game 6 of the World Series from Cincinnati, but Red Sox fans also remember that the Sox lost Game 7 the next day, 4-3. Owner Tom Yawkey died the following July without winning the world championship he had sought for more than 40 years.

Boston contended seriously in 1977 in a tight three-way race, pulling ahead for a time in June and again in August, but ultimately falling 2½ games short. The next year, though, the Sox pulled off another amazing finish. After blowing a 7½-game late-August lead, they won their final eight scheduled games to tie the Yankees. But in the one-game playoff, Yankees shortstop Bucky Dent's three-run pop-fly homer over Fenway's cozy left field wall proved Boston's ruin. The Sox rallied in the eighth to draw within a run, but with two out and a man on third in the ninth, Yastrzemski popped up and the season was history.

Yaz retired in 1983, but outfielders Jim Rice and Dwight Evans remained from the 1975 champions. In Wade Boggs, the Red Sox had their most consistent hitter since Ted Williams, and, in Roger Clemens, Boston had its most exciting pitcher since Joe Wood. In 1986 the Red Sox won their 10th pennant, with an amazing comeback over California from a 3-1 deficit in the ALCS. Against the New York Mets in the World Series, the Red Sox were within one pitch of capturing their first world title in 68 years, but they lost the game, and again lost Game 7.

When a pitching decline dropped the Sox to fifth place in 1987, and the All-Star break the next year found them barely above .500, manager John McNamara was replaced by coach Joe Morgan. The Sox responded with 19 wins in their next 20 games and, despite a slump at season's end, took the title in the AL East by one game. In the ALCS, though, Oakland swept to the pennant in four games.

In 1990, with Clemens back in peak form after a season and a half below par, the Sox arrived at midseason in first place. After trading the lead back and forth with Toronto, they captured the crown of the East on the season's final day. But in the ALCS Oakland again swept past them to the pennant.

Roger Clemens won his third Cy Young award in 1991, and the Sox came from 11½ games back in August to within half a game of first-place Toronto in September. But they dropped back and finished in a second-place tie with Detroit. Manager Joe Morgan was replaced by Butch Hobson for 1992, but the downhill slide continued.

Hobson's disappointing tenure was filled with fast starts and sudden collapses. The Sox, who started 1994 with the majors' best record, were one game out of last place the day the players' strike ended the season. Hobson's days in Boston ended shortly thereafter.

His replacement, Kevin Kennedy, constantly juggled lineups to give the Sox the 1995 AL East by the surprisingly comfortable margin of seven games over the Yankees. Key to the club's victory was AL RBI king Mo Vaughn, who captured MVP honors in a tight race over Cleveland's Albert Belle. Boston, however, was no match for the powerful Indians, falling to them, 3-0, in the first round of the postseason, with Vaughn and Jose Canseco particularly ineffective at bat.

In 1996 the Sox got off to a sluggish start, but finished strong—not strong enough, however, to save manager Kennedy's job (he was replaced by longtime Braves coach Jimy Williams). Standouts for the third-place (85-77) Red Sox included Vaughn (44 HR, 143 RBIs, 207 hits) and Clemens (an AL-best 257 strikeouts, including a record-tying 20 in one game against Detroit.)

After a disappointing 78-84 season in 1997—the lone bright spot was AL Rookie of the Year Nomar Garciaparra—the Red Sox put a dramatically retooled team on the field in 1998. The Sox traded for 1997 NL Cy Young Award winner Pedro Martinez and made him the highest-paid player in the game. Mo Vaughn narrowly missed his first batting title in 1998, but more importantly for Red Sox fans, the team held off a late charge by Toronto to win the AL Wild Card. In the Division Series, the Red Sox ended a 13-game losing streak in the post-season (dating back to Game 5 of the 1986 World Series), but the Sox got little other than what their stars could provide: Vaughn and Garciaparra drove in 19 of the team's 20 runs, and Martinez won his only start as Cleveland took the series in four games.

In 1999 the Red Sox played their archrivals in the postseason for the first time ever. Boston met the Yankees in the ALCS following a stunning comeback from two games to none against Cleveland in the Division Series. Boston lost to the Yanks, however, in five games. In 2000 Garciaparra won his second consecutive batting crown and Martinez won the AL Cy Young for the second year running, but the Red Sox were left out of the postseason for the first time since 1997.

Chicago Cubs

The Cubs have represented the same city in the major leagues longer than any other club. Organized in 1870 to provide a professional challenge to Cincinnati's Red Stockings, the next year the White Stockings (as they were originally known) were one of the founding members of the game's first professional league—the National Association.

Despite the great Chicago fire, which destroyed their ballpark, uniforms, and club business records late in the 1871 season, the White Stockings completed their schedule, finishing third to the Athletics of Philadelphia. But they dropped out of the NA for the next two years because of the fire's devastation. In 1875, in the midst of a second losing season following their return, the club arranged for four of champion Boston's best players to jump to Chicago for the 1876 season. That winter, White Stockings president William A. Hulbert and pitcher/manager Al Spalding (one of the jumpers) led in forming a new league to replace the NA.

Sparked by its Boston players and infielder Adrian "Cap" Anson (lured from the Athletics), the 1876 White Stockings outscored their opponents by more than five runs per game and handily won the first championship of the new National League. The next year, when Spalding (whose pitching had brought Chicago 47 of its 52 victories in 1876) switched over to first base, the club fell to fifth. Spalding retired from the field in 1878 to attend to his young sporting goods firm (though he returned as club president from 1882 through 1891).

In 1879 Anson was named to manage the team. For the next 12 years the White Stockings ranked among baseball's best, garnering five pennants (1880-1882, 1885-1886) and four second-place finishes. Anson's strict discipline did not make him popular with his often rowdy teammates, but his consistency as a player set an example, and his innovative management made the most of his players' abilities. Anson's forcefulness, however, contributed to baseball's most grievous setback: His adamant refusal in the mid-1880s to take the field against black players prevented the racial integration of the major leagues.

After a close finish behind Boston in 1891, the White Stockings' first era as an NL power ended. In each of the next 11 seasons they fell at least 15 games short of the top. The team's youthful ineptitude was reflected in the nicknames that succeeded "White Stockings": the "Colts," the "Orphans" (in 1898, after Anson—known as "Pop"—was fired after 19 years at the helm), and finally, the "Cubs."

When Frank Selee (who had led Boston to greatness in the 1890s) was hired to manage the Cubs in 1902, he inherited a team that had ended the 1901 season 37 games out. By 1903 he had turned catcher/outfielder Frank Chance into a first baseman, moved Joe Tinker from third to short, and brought Johnny Evers up from Troy to play second. The new double-play combination flourished not only in the field but at the bat. The Cubs finished third in 1903 with their best record since 1898.

That winter Selee traded for pitcher Mordecai "Three Finger" Brown. After leading the Cubs to second place in 1904, Selee signed rookie hurler Ed Reulbach, but, ill with tuberculosis, he took a leave of absence in the middle of the 1905 season. Chance took his place and brought the team to third; Selee never returned, but he had gone a long way toward building a championship team.

Trades for outfielder Jimmy Sheckard and third baseman Harry Steinfeldt, the signing of rookie pitcher Jack Pfiester, and the acquisition during the 1906 season of pitchers Orval Overall and Jack Taylor completed one of the greatest teams of all time. The Cubs passed the Giants to take the lead early in May and kept on rising. New York and Pittsburgh made a race of it through July, but the Cubs won 55 of their final 65 games to finish with a record 116 victories, 20 games ahead of second-place New York.

Brown's 1.04 ERA was the league's best, with Pfiester and Reulbach second and third. The team ERA was a remarkably low 1.76. Overall, Chicago scored 80 more runs than its nearest rival, and yielded 89 fewer. But in the World Series, the crosstown "Hitless Wonder" White Sox matched the Cubs' hitting and pitched twice as effectively to take the crown in six games.

The Cubs' hitting and run production fell off in 1907, but their pitching did not (ERA: 1.73). With 107 wins, they captured their second straight pennant, by 17 games. This time their dominance carried over into the World Series as they swept Detroit after an opening-game tie.

The pennant race of 1908 was one of the tightest in baseball history. On Sept. 22 the Cubs won two from the Giants to pull into a virtual tie for first (with Pittsburgh third, 1½ games back). The next day the Giants appeared to have beaten the Cubs with an RBI single in the last of the ninth. But young Fred Merkle, on first when the hit was made, failed to continue on to second and was forced out by alert Cubs second baseman Johnny Evers for the third out, which negated the Giant run. Because of increasing darkness and the mood of excited fans on the field, the game was called and ruled a tie.

After another week and a half in which all three teams took turns in front, Chicago defeated Pittsburgh to pull ahead by half a game, leaving the Pirates and Giants tied for second. But New York had one more game—and defeated the Boston Braves to pull into a tie with the Cubs. The "Merkle boner" game thus had to be replayed, and, this time, the Cubs won to take their third straight pennant. In the World Series they again beat Detroit in five games. Their second straight world title was also, to date, their last.

The Cubs won 104 games in 1909 as their pitching staff recorded an ERA under 2.00 for the third time in four years. Chicago still finished second to the powerful Pirates, who won 110 and captured the World Series.

In 1910 their 104 wins carried them to another pennant, by a comfortable 13 games. After a World Series loss to the Philadelphia Athletics, and seasons in second and third place, Chance resigned, protesting the unwillingness of owner Charles Murphy to spend money for top players.

The Cubs got a new owner in 1916, and with him a new ballpark. Charles Weeghman, who had owned the Chicago Whales in the short-lived Federal League, purchased the Cubs when the FL went under, and moved them into the park he had built for the Whales.

The team that next carried Chicago to the pennant, in the war-shortened season of 1918, featured only one name familiar to Cubs fans from earlier championship seasons—Fred Merkle. The man whose rookie boner as a Giant had made possible their pennant in 1908 was now their leading run producer. As in earlier pennant-winning seasons, fine pitching predominated, with veteran James "Hippo" Vaughn the league's best pitcher on the league's top staff.

Several years of decline followed the Cubs' World Series loss to the Boston Red Sox. The club hit bottom in 1925 with its first cellar finish in 53 years of league play, but a new era of greatness was at hand. In 1921 wealthy chewing-gum manufacturer William Wrigley had purchased control of the Cubs, with a determination to spend what was needed to produce a winner.

The seeds Wrigley planted eventually bore fruit. In 1926 he hired Joe McCarthy—a successful minor league manager—to lead the club and drafted outfielder Lewis "Hack" Wilson from Toledo. Wilson immediately became one of the league's leading offensive threats, and the Cubs rebounded to the first division. In 1927 they even led the league through August before dropping back to fourth. A postseason trade brought them outfielder Hazen "Kiki" Cuyler and a close third-place finish in 1928. Then the Cubs traded with the Braves for second baseman Rogers Hornsby, and in 1929 returned to the top. Led by Wilson's 159 RBIs and Hornsby's 149, five Cubs drove in more than 90 runs each. After battling Pittsburgh for the lead through mid-July, the Cubs hurtled ahead to take the pennant by 10½ games, despite a late-season slump. The slump continued through the World Series, though, as the Athletics humbled the Cubs in five games.

Just four games from the end of the hot pennant race in 1930 (the year Wilson set the major league RBI record with 191), McCarthy—still smarting from criticism arising from the World Series loss—quit as manager. With Hornsby at the helm, the Cubs preserved a second-place finish. They dropped to third the next year, but returned to the top in 1932. Hornsby, near the end of his playing days, was dropped as manager in August, with the Cubs in second, and replaced by first baseman Charlie Grimm. Pitcher Lon Warneke, in his first full season as a starter, led the league in wins and ERA. The club enjoyed a hot streak in August to move out in front of slumping Pittsburgh and hung on to take the flag by four games. The Yankees provided the World Series humiliation this time, a four-game sweep that provided McCarthy (now the Yankees manager) with sweet revenge for the Chicago fans' criticism three years earlier.

It had become a pattern: three years, another pennant. In 1935 a balanced offense (led by catcher Gabby Hartnett and second baseman Billy Herman) and the league's best pitching brought the Cubs up from fourth in late June to first in September. They clinched the pennant with three games to go, with their 20th win of a 21-game streak. In the World Series, Detroit stopped the Cubs in six games.

After two seasons in second, it was time for another pennant. Bill Lee, the club's top pitcher in 1935, was now the league's finest, as was the Cubs' staff. With the club languishing six and a half games back in midseason, Grimm quit as manager and was replaced by catcher Hartnett. In September the Cubs came to life, rising to second early in the month. They overtook Pittsburgh with their ninth consecutive win on Hartnett's homer against the Pirates in the growing darkness with two away in the bottom of the ninth, which became known as the "Home Run in the Gloaming." The Cubs clinched the pennant four games later, on the next-to-last day of the season. The Yankees swept Chicago to hand the Cubs their sixth straight World Series loss.

In 1940, after 14 straight winning seasons, the Cubs began a five-year stretch below .500. Jimmie Wilson replaced Hartnett as manager in 1941; then Grimm returned near the start of the 1944 season. The club finished a distant fourth that year, but in 1945, after a middling start, they won 26 of 30 midseason games to take a lead they never relinquished. Balanced pitching (sparked by Hank Borowy, who went 11-2 after coming over from the Yankees in July) and the hitting of veteran first baseman Phil Cavarretta (.355) and center fielder Andy Pafko (110 RBIs) held off the pressing St. Louis Cardinals to preserve a 16th Cubs pennant. Although they battled Detroit through a full seven games in the World Series, they ended up losing again.

For the next 23 years the Cubs remained out of pennant contention. But in 1969, the first year of divisional play, under the lively management of Leo Durocher, they took an early lead in the NL East. With a potent offense led by veteran sluggers Ron Santo, Ernie Banks, and Billy Williams, the team continued rising through early August. But the New York Mets rose even faster and farther; they didn't pause when Chicago leveled off in late August, and while the Cubs were losing eight straight in September the Mets were winning 10 in a row. The Cubs wound up eight games back.

The 1970s were a disappointing decade, with several division leads melting away in the summertime sun at Wrigley. In 1981 the Wrigley family sold the club to the Chicago Tribune Company. Three years later, with a new manager, Jim Frey, and an almost wholly different roster, the new management capped its rebuilding program with the acquisition of pitcher Rick Sutcliffe from Cleveland in mid-June 1984. As Sutcliffe fashioned a 16-1 record for his new club, the Cubs went on to capture their first division title. After winning the first two games of the NLCS against San Diego, the pennant was swept out from under them as the Padres took the final three.

In 1989 the team, now managed by Don Zimmer, bounced back to duplicate its 1984 success. With a balanced offense and pitching vastly improved over the previous season, the Cubs took the NL East lead for good on Aug. 7. Once again, though, they were unable to persevere to the pennant, losing the best-of-seven NLCS to San Francisco in five games.

As they had done in 1989, Andre Dawson, Mark Grace and Ryne Sandberg continued to provide offensive clout over the next three years, and in 1992 Cy Young Award winner Greg Maddux and newly acquired Mike Morgan fashioned sterling seasons on the mound. But the team could not carve out a winning season, finishing tied for fourth in 1990, and fourth by themselves in 1991 and '92. Ownership snarled when baseball commissioner Fay Vincent proposed transferring the club from the NL East to the West in 1993, but the threat passed when Vincent, under pressure from owners dissatisfied with his leadership, resigned before the end of the 1992 season.

Free agents Dawson and Maddux left for greener pastures in 1993, but catcher Rick Wilkins and outfielder Sammy Sosa blossomed into power hitters, and newly acquired closer Randy Myers garnered a league-record 53 saves. While the Cubs once again finished only fourth, they put together their first winning season in four years. The improvement wasn't enough to satisfy management, though, and second-year manager Jim Lefebvre was replaced by coach Tom Treblehorn at the end of the 1993 season.

Ryne Sandberg, claiming to have lost his competitive drive, retired during the 1994 season, and the Cubs followed suit, settling themselves firmly in the cellar of the newly formed Central division.

Chicago, under manager Jim Riggleman, bounced back to third (73-71) in 1995 as Mark Grace led the NL with 51 doubles. And at season's end Sandberg, now 36, announced he was ending his retirement and returning to the Cubs. The 1996 Cubs fell to fourth place and the 1997 team lost a National League-record 14 games to start the season and finished last in the NL Central.

But if 1997 was a nightmare for Chicago, 1998 was a sweet dream. The Cubs bolstered the team through free agent signings (Rod Beck, Henry Rodriguez, and Jeff Blauser), brought up a rookie (Kerry Wood) who tied the major league record with 20 strikeouts in his third start on his way to NL Rookie of the Year, and found a savior on the waiver wire (Gary Gaetti).

Even those contributions paled in comparison to the season put forth by Sammy Sosa. Sosa set a major league record with 20 home runs in June and his longball exploits challenged even those of Mark McGwire. Sosa was at Busch Stadium when McGwire hit his record-breaking 62nd home run off Cubs teammate Steve Trachsel and a few days later Sosa also hit number 62. He finished the season with 66 home runs and became just the fourth player with 50 home runs, 150 RBIs, and 400 total bases. More importantly, the Cubs survived many bullets in the closing days of the season to force a one-game playoff for the NL Wild Card. The Cubs beat the Giants to advance to the NL Division Series against the Braves. But Atlanta, winners of 106 games during the season, swept the Cubs in three games.

Don Baylor replaced Jim Riggleman after a poor 1999 season. The following year began with a win in Tokyo—the first regular-season major league game ever played in Japan—but the club's fortunes turned sour once the Cubs returned home. Sosa was again the team's bright spot. The All-Star right fielder, fresh off consecutive 60-homer seasons, was the only major leaguer to reach 50 home runs in 2000. All-Star righthander Jon Lieber, who led the major leagues in innings, had the best season of his career.

Chicago White Sox

When minor league owner Charlie Comiskey transferred his club from St. Paul to Chicago as part of the move to upgrade the American League to major league status, he called it the White Stockings, after the Chicago team that dominated the National League in its early years. The new Chicago team revived memories of the old White Stockings, winning the AL championship in 1900, and repeating the triumph in 1901, the league's first major league season. Manager Clark Griffith (who had jumped to the White Stockings from Chicago's NL Cubs) was the team's star pitcher in 1901, winning 24 of 31 decisions as his team took the lead in May and held off the threatening Boston Somersets the rest of the way.

Griffith's effectiveness fell off in 1902, as did the team, (now called the White Sox) which took a sizable lead in July, only to slide back to fourth in August. Griffith left the next year and the White Sox sank to seventh. It would take 18 years and baseball's biggest scandal for the Sox to finish that low again.

In 1904, after center fielder Fielder Jones replaced left fielder Nixey Callahan as manager, the Sox rose into first place for a moment in August before settling back to third. The next year they made up a seven-game deficit in September to catch the Philadelphia Athletics, but the loss of two games to the A's stalled their drive and left them in second.

Nothing stalled the White Sox drive in 1906. Although they ranked at the very bottom of the league in hitting and entered June five games below .500, their pitching and hustle pulled them through. "Big Ed" Walsh, who had finally mastered the spitball after two years of trying, won 17 games, including a league-high 10 shutouts. Doc White contributed 18 wins with a league-best 1.52 ERA, and Frank Owen and Nick Altrock won 22 and 20, respectively. The Sox shot to the top in August with a 19-game win streak (including eight shutouts). Early in September, New York's Highlanders passed them, but after the two teams had traded the lead back and forth for a couple of weeks the Sox spurted to take the pennant by three games. If the race was close, so were the individual games: the Sox achieved nearly one-third of their victories by the margin of a single run. The "Hitless Wonders" carried their momentum through the World Series, shocking the mighty crosstown Cubs (who had won a record 116 games that year) in six games.

In 1907, after leading the league much of the first half, the Sox slipped to third. The next year Walsh pitched in the final seven games on his way to a career-high 40 wins. In a tight finish he pulled the Sox to within a half game of first-place Detroit before they dropped back to third with a loss to the Tigers on the final day.

It was 1915 before the Sox (piloted by rookie manager Clarence H. "Pants" Rowland) next finished that high, and 1916 before they again challenged seriously for the pennant. Comiskey, though accused of pinching pennies in his payment of players, was willing to spend what was needed to acquire them. After the 1914 season he purchased star second baseman Eddie Collins from the A's, and promising young Oscar "Happy" Felsch from minor league Milwaukee. The following August he acquired the great "Shoeless" Joe Jackson from Cleveland. Together with the league's best pitching staff, they carried the Sox into the thick of a three-way race and a close second-place finish in 1916. A year later the Sox took the pennant with the best winning percentage the club has ever compiled. Ten-year veteran pitcher Eddie Cicotte enjoyed his first 20-win season with a league-high 28 victories, and a league-and career-best 1.53 ERA. After dueling the Boston Red Sox most of the season, Chicago streaked out of reach in late August to finish with 100 wins. In the World Series against the New York Giants they captured their second (and, to date, their last) world title, in six games.

With several key players out much of 1918 for military or civilian war service, the White Sox finished out of the running, a dismal sixth. But in 1919, with the team back at full strength, the race once again went to Chicago. If their pitching didn't have quite the depth of the 1917 squad, its best hurlers were in peak form. Cicotte, after an off-year in 1918, attained a career high with 29 wins, as did Lefty Williams with 23 victories. Collins and Jackson enjoyed their best seasons in several years, and Buck Weaver had never been better. Old-time pitcher/second baseman Kid Gleason was a rookie as a big league manager, but his Sox began strong and, after slipping briefly into second in midseason, pulled ahead in July to stay.

When the Sox lost the World Series to underdog Cincinnati, there were rumors of a fix, but nothing came to light for nearly a year. The White Sox looked better than ever in 1920. Though they fell back in May after a hot April, by mid-August they had risen to the thick of a tight three-team race. Felsch, Collins, and Weaver had never played better, Jackson was enjoying one of his very best seasons, and four pitchers were on their way to more than 20 wins. Chicago might not have caught Cleveland's rampaging Indians, but it didn't help that talk of a White Sox scandal revived late in the season, or that the grand jury convened only eight games from the end, or that eight Sox players were indicted and suspended with just three games to play. The team finished two games back, in second place.

The indicted players—infielders Chick Gandil, Swede Risberg, and Fred McMullin, plus Cicotte, Felsch, Jackson, Weaver, and Williams—were acquitted in court when three crucial confessions disappeared, but they were banned for life from organized baseball by Commissioner Kenesaw Mountain Landis. The White Sox did not soon recover from the loss. In 1921 they began 15 years of wandering in the second division. The Sox finished last three times in that span, plus a seventh-place finish in 1932 that left the Sox a club-worst 56½ games out of first.

Two of the club's greatest and most durable players arrived during these years: pitcher Ted Lyons (who won 260 games for the Sox in 21 years) in 1923, and in 1930 shortstop Luke Appling (who averaged .310 in his 20 years with the club). Owner Comiskey died in 1931, in the midst of his Sox's most dismal era, but Lyons and Appling were around long enough to enjoy a few fourth- and third-place seasons. But neither saw the Sox contend seriously for the pennant. After his playing career was over, Lyons managed the team for a few years—until 1948, when the Sox lost 101 games and finished last.

That year Frank Lane was lured from the presidency of the American Association to take charge as Chicago's general manager. When Lane hired Paul Richards to manage the club in 1951, the Sox began what became a 17-year string of winning seasons.

In 1951, Richards' first season, the Sox spent a month in first place before drifting down to fourth, and the next year began a five-year run in third place. In 1954 they won 94 games but were out of the race by August—that was the year Cleveland won 111 and the second-place Yankees 103. Richards moved on to Baltimore, but Marty Marion, who replaced him, kept the Sox in third place.

After the Sox fell from first place in early September, Frank Lane left at the end of the 1955 season. Young Chuck Comiskey (one of the grandchildren of Charlie Comiskey who now owned the club) took over the front office. A year later Comiskey replaced Marion with Al Lopez, who had piloted the great Cleveland club of 1954 and whose teams, in his six seasons of managing, had never finished below second. Lopez continued his success in Chicago: the Sox moved up to second (though well behind the Yankees) in 1957 and '58. In March 1959, Bill Veeck (who had in previous years owned the Cleveland Indians and the St. Louis Browns) bought a controlling interest in the White Sox from the Comiskey family and stepped into instant success.

With the Yankees suffering an off-year in 1959, Chicago and Cleveland battled for the lead throughout the summer, until the White Sox pulled away in late August. The same 94-60 record that had given them only a distant third in 1954 now carried them to their first pennant in 40 years. The close and successful pennant race, and the club's dynamic new ownership, pushed Sox home attendance up more than 78 percent to a new club record.

As they had in 1906, pitching and hustle won the Sox their 1959 pennant. The league's best staff was led by veteran Early Wynn (enjoying his last big season with a league high of 22 wins) and young Bob Shaw (with a career high of 18), and featured the league's top relievers in Gerry Staley and Turk Lown. Shortstop Luis Aparicio, in the midst of a nine-year reign as stolen-base leader, set a personal high in runs scored as the club went 35-15 in one-run games. But in the World Series, Los Angeles stopped Chicago in six games.

The next year the Sox remained competitive until September, but finished third. After dropping to fourth and fifth the next two years (in a league now expanded to 10 teams), they returned to second in 1963. The next year the Sox finished a season-long three-way race with nine straight wins, enough to pull them past Baltimore, but a game short of catching the Yankees, whose 11-game streak a week earlier had put them out in front. After a third straight second-place finish in 1965, manager Lopez resigned for health reasons.

Under Eddie Stanky—and with the AL's stingiest pitching staff in 49 years—the Sox competed into the final week of a hot 1967 race, when five straight losses at the end dropped them to fourth. They would rise above .500 only twice in the next 13 years. In 1970 they lost a club-record 106 games to finish at the bottom of the AL West. Two years later they took the division lead briefly in late August before dropping back to second, and in 1977 they held the lead through much of the summer before tailing off to third.

Bill Veeck had sold the club and repurchased it in 1976. But in January 1981, after three losing seasons and troubled by poor health and skyrocketing player salaries, he sold the Sox once again, to a group headed by Jerry Reinsdorf and Eddie Einhorn. With Reinsdorf heading the club's baseball operations and lawyer Tony LaRussa piloting the team on the field, the Sox briefly became one of the best teams in baseball. With their best record since 1920, the 1983 Sox carried the AL West by 20 games. Rookie slugger Ron Kittle led the attack, backed up by fourth-year outfielder Harold Baines and resurgent old-timers Greg Luzinski and Carlton Fisk. Pitchers LaMarr Hoyt and Rich Dotson attained personal bests to lead the majors in wins (with 24 and 22), and White Sox home attendance for the first time topped 2 million. In the ALCS, though, after a close win over Baltimore in the opener, Chicago lost the next three games and the pennant. Chicago's pitching and offense (except for Baines) collapsed the next season, and the team remained out of serious contention for six years.

Most forecasters predicted another dismal season for the Sox in 1990, but as fans watched a new Comiskey Park arise next door, they also saw their club celebrate its final year in the old yard with an astonishing resurgence. With their best start in decades, the Sox stayed close to mighty Oakland through the first half of the season, and even took over first place for brief periods in June and July before Oakland pulled away. Anchoring a strong bullpen, closer Bobby Thigpen shattered the major league record for saves, passing the old record of 46 with a month to go and finishing with 57.

First baseman Frank Thomas helped keep the Sox competitive through much of 1991, the inaugural season of their new park. Rookie Wilson Alvarez's no-hitter capped a seven-game win streak in August that pulled the team to just a game from the top, but 15 losses in their next 17 games stifled their pennant hopes and they finished second. Thomas continued his awesome offense in 1992, and Jack McDowell showed himself one of the AL's best pitchers, but the team won one game fewer than the year before, and finished third.

McDowell, Alvarez, and Alex Fernandez led the league's stingiest pitching staff in 1993, and Thomas turned in an MVP season as the Sox carried a narrow lead into the All-Star break, held it into late September, then pulled away to an eight-game margin of victory at the finish. In the postseason, though, the Sox came up short, losing the AL pennant to Toronto in six games.

In 1994 Frank Thomas was rising to even greater heights and became the first American Leaguer since Roger Maris in 1960 and 1961 to be named MVP in back-to-back seasons. The Sox were hanging on to a slim first-place lead over Cleveland in the new Central division when the players struck to end the season.

Despite another strong season by Thomas (.308, 40 HR, 111 RBIs) the club slumped to third in 1995, 32 games back of Cleveland. In 1996 the Sox again finished second to the Tribe. After the season they shocked the baseball world by signing Albert Belle to a $10 million per year contract, but the highlight of the 1997 season was the first-ever Cubs-Sox interleague series. Terry Bevington was fired after the season and his replacement, Jerry Manuel, struggled through the first half of 1998 before the White Sox surged to a 45-31 record in the second half to end the season in second place.

Although Chicago finished second for the fourth straight year in 1999, the club's 75 wins was its lowest total over a 162-game season in a decade. The team's young talent prospered the following year, however, as the White Sox were the surprise team of baseball. Chris Singleton, Carlos Lee, and Magglio Ordonez became one of the most promising—and successful—outfields in the American League. Frank Thomas rebounded from a dismal season to bat .328 with 43 home runs and 143 RBIs while shortstop Jose Hernandez had the best season of his career. The pitching staff, led by veteran James Baldwin, helped fend off the five-time defending division champion Indians and lead the White Sox to the league's best record. Manuel was the overwhelming choice for AL Manager of the year. The team's first postseason appearance since 1993 was brief, though, as the Mariners knocked off the White Sox in three tight games in the Division Series.

Cincinnati Reds

Red Stockings was the nickname of two pioneering Cincinnati ballclubs—the first avowedly professional team, which was undefeated in 1869, and the charter member club in the National League of 1876-1880. After a year on the sidelines, the reformed Reds joined the new American Association and captured the 1882 pennant by 11½ games, with a .688 winning percentage that is still the club record. Seven Reds enjoyed career highs in batting, pitcher Will White led the association with 40 wins, and rookie second baseman John "Bid" McPhee proved himself already one of the game's classiest fielders.

McPhee remained 18 years with the Reds and established himself as the finest second baseman of the 19th century. But the club would go 37 years before it won another pennant. Twice in their seven remaining years in the AA the Reds finished second, and they enjoyed six winning seasons. Transferring from the AA to the NL in 1890, they finished fourth; at 10½ games out of first it was their closest finish in 34 years between 1884 and their next pennant-winning season, 1919.

In 1902 club owner John T. Brush sold out to a group of Cincinnati's political bosses, who in mid-August named August "Garry" Herrmann (formerly head of the water works commission) to run it. Herrmann not only remained president of the Reds for 25 years, but he also chaired the three-man National Commission that oversaw organized baseball, from its establishment in 1903 until 1920 (when his resignation brought about the commission's demise).

A midseason trade in 1916 brought the Reds Christy Mathewson (at the end of his pitching career) to manage the team, plus outfielder Edd Roush. The next year, with Roush leading the league in batting, the Reds edged above .500 and into fourth place. In 1918 an August spurt boosted the Reds into third place, in a season shortened by a month at the end because of World War I. Roush enjoyed another banner year, but Mathewson left for the Army just before the season ended.

First baseman Hal Chase—suspected of throwing games—was traded away after the season and replaced by veteran Jake Daubert. Southpaw Slim Sallee was purchased from the Giants and right-hander Ray Fisher from the Yankees. Pat Moran (who had led the Phillies to a pennant in 1915) was hired to replace Mathewson at the Cincinnati helm. Thus fortified, the Reds in 1919 won their second pennant. Three pitchers—Sallee (21-7), Hod Eller (20-9), and Dutch Ruether (19-7, 1.82 ERA)—reached career peaks, Fisher (14-5) enjoyed one of his best years, Roush won another batting title and finished second in NL RBIs, and three Reds finished in the league's top four in runs scored. The Reds drove quickly from the gate, but faltered in May and didn't pass the Giants for first place until July. They finished nine games in front. Rumors of a White Sox fix to throw the World Series clouded the Reds' Series triumph—and spoiled it entirely when, a year later, the scandal became public and the truth of the rumors was confirmed.

In 1920 Cincinnati led the league entering September, but Brooklyn spurted and the Reds slumped to a third-place finish, 10½ games out. They dropped to sixth in 1921, but recovered for five years in the first division, including three second-place finishes.

The Reds finished in the second division for 11 years, hitting bottom with four straight cellar finishes from 1931 through 1934. President Herrmann retired after the 1927 season, and within two years a controlling interest in the Reds was sold to a wealthy Cincinnatian, Sidney Weil. But Weil lost his fortune in the stock market crash of 1929. While he continued to run the Reds for four years, his stock in the club was held by the Central Trust Company. In his efforts to turn the club around, Weil acquired catcher Ernie Lombardi from Brooklyn in March 1932 and pitcher Paul Derringer from the St. Louis Cardinals the following May. Derringer lost 25 games in his first season in Cincinnati and 21 the next, but both remained with the club long enough to star in its return to glory. Owner Weil, however, relinquished his control to the bank in 1933, at the depth of the Depression and of the team's fortunes.

The bank hired Larry MacPhail (who had rescued minor league Columbus by introducing night baseball there) to run the Reds. MacPhail in turn hired Frank Lane to develop a minor league farm system, and persuaded Cincinnati industrialist Powel Crosley, Jr., to invest in the club. On May 24, 1935, Crosley and MacPhail brought night ball to the major leagues (the Reds, with Derringer pitching, beat the Phillies, 2-1), and with it a sharp upswing in attendance at Crosley Field. By June 1936, Crosley's increased investment in the Reds had made him the majority owner. The temperamental MacPhail quit suddenly in mid-September 1936, but the Reds replaced him with another successful minor league executive, Warren Giles, who ran the club until his selection in 1952 as president of the NL.

After rising to sixth place in 1935 and fifth the next year, the Reds dropped back into the cellar in 1937. But the following year, under new manager Bill McKechnie, they rose into the first division once again—even holding second place briefly in September before slipping to fourth. Derringer enjoyed the first of three peak seasons, young Johnny Vander Meer contributed 15 wins (including two consecutive no-hitters) and Bucky Walters, after his acquisition from the Phillies in June, compiled his first winning season since converting from third baseman to pitcher in 1935. Lombardi led the NL in batting, and first baseman Frank McCormick, in his first full season, led the league in hits. The stage was set for the club's first back-to-back pennants.

Several Reds reached the apex of their careers in 1939, among them Walters (27-11) and Derringer (25-7), who between them topped most of the league's pitching stats, and McCormick, who led the league in RBIs and hits and finished second in batting. The club pulled out of the pack to the front before the end of May and held the lead to the end, although St. Louis closed the gap with a late-season surge before slipping four and a half games back.

Cincinnati's sweep by the Yankees in the World Series was something of a shock, but the club had recovered its poise by the next spring. Starting strong and—except for a small dip in August—pushing steadily upward throughout the season, the Reds shook off the persistent Dodgers in midseason and finished 12 games in front with their first 100-win season. McCormick and Lombardi powered the offense, and Walters for the second year in a row took NL crowns in wins and ERA. This time the team's triumph carried through the World Series as Walters and Derringer won two games apiece to edge the Tigers in seven games to win their second world championship.

The Reds' pitching remained strong in 1941, but their hitting and run production fell off and the team struggled to finish third. They remained in the upper division through 1944, but then dropped into an 11-year trough of losing seasons.

Ted Kluszewski was in his ninth season as the Reds' slugging first baseman when Cincinnati next offered a serious run for the pennant in 1956 under manager Birdie Tebbetts. Kluszewski led the club in hitting and RBIs, but his 35 home runs were good enough only for third behind rookie Frank Robinson's 38 and Wally Post's 36 on a team that hammered 221 during the season to tie the then-major league record set nine years earlier by the Giants. The Reds' offense led the league in runs scored and kept them in the thick of a three-team race throughout the season. That same year, for the first time ever they drew more than a million fans at home.

The Reds dropped out of a tight race in August 1957, and suffered losing seasons the next three years. Gabe Paul, who had succeeded Warren Giles as club president and general manager, left to help organize the new Houston club after the 1960 season. Owner Crosley died the following spring. Bill DeWitt, who replaced Paul as president (and ultimately purchased control of the club), acquired pitcher Joey Jay from the Milwaukee Braves and third baseman Gene Freese from the White Sox. Jay in 1961 tied for the league lead with 21 wins, and Freese homered 26 times and drove in 87 runs—both career highs. Most of the team improved on their 1960 stats, and despite a poor start that saw them enter May in last place, the Reds had risen to the top by mid-June. The streaking Dodgers caught them briefly in August, but then fell away. In the World Series, though, it was the Yankees winning in five games.

The Reds next threatened in 1964 when, in a wild three-way finish, they won nine straight in late September to take first place for a day before slipping into a tie for second, one game behind St. Louis. In 1965 a young Pete Rose recorded the first of his 10 seasons with 200 hits as the Reds battled among the leaders much of the summer before dropping off to fourth.

That December, after a decade of standout offense in Cincinnati, Frank Robinson was traded to Baltimore. The next year, while Robinson won the Triple Crown in assisting his new team to the world championship, the Reds suffered their first losing season in six years and sank to seventh place. That winter, owner DeWitt completed the sale of the team to a group led by Cincinnati newspaper publisher Francis Dale and brothers James and William Williams who later acquired a controlling interest in the club.

In 1969, the first year of divisional play, the Reds rose into the thick of a five-way race in the NL West before stumbling as Atlanta and San Francisco surged in the final three weeks. But the season provided a foretaste of the decade to come as the team captured league crowns in slugging and home runs.

At midseason in 1970 the Reds moved out of Crosley Field—their home for 58 years—into the new Riverfront Stadium. Catcher Johnny Bench and third baseman Tony Perez, with the finest seasons of their long careers, paced an overwhelming offense as the team hammered out a new club-high 102 wins to reward rookie manager Sparky Anderson with victory in the NL West by 14½ games, and gain the name "Big Red Machine." In the National League Championship Series the Reds continued their triumph with a three-game sweep of East winner Pittsburgh. But mighty Baltimore humbled the Reds in the World Series, 4-1.

Cincinnati's hitting and run production fell off sharply the next year, and the club dropped to fourth with their only losing season of the decade. But in 1972—spurred on after a slow start by Johnny Bench's recovery of power, Gary Nolan's finest season on the mound, and the all-around mastery of newly acquired second baseman Joe Morgan—the Reds cruised to a division title. Victory in the NLCS came harder, as powerful Pittsburgh carried the series to the full five games before handing the Reds the pennant with a wild pitch in the last of the ninth inning of the final game. Cincinnati's defeat in the World Series was also close: the Reds won three, and Oakland's four wins were each achieved by a margin of just one run.

The Reds repeated in the NL West in 1973 with a second-half surge from fourth place that carried them past front-runner Los Angeles in September. But the much weaker New York Mets ended Cincinnati's pennant hopes in a five-game loss in the NLCS best remembered for Rose's brawl with Bud Harrelson.

In 1974 the Reds finished four games behind the Dodgers in second place. But over the next two years the Big Red Machine flattened all opposition. In 1975, after hovering around .500 through mid-May, the Reds began an ascent that carried them to what are still club records: 108 victories and a winning margin of 20 games. The team featured balanced pitching (six starters won in double figures), an offense in which every regular drove in more than 45 runs (averaging nearly 77 apiece), the best fielding in the majors, and a big NL lead in stolen bases. After a three-game sweep of Pittsburgh in the NLCS, the Reds subdued the stubborn Boston Red Sox in seven games for their first world title in 35 years, and their third overall.

They won their fourth the next year. Joe Morgan, at the peak of his career, led the NL in slugging, finished second to teammate George Foster in RBIs, and stole 60 bases as he won his second consecutive MVP award. Balanced pitching and offense again put the Reds in front to stay in June, carrying the team to 102 wins and a 10-game lead over Los Angeles at the finish. The NLCS produced another sweep—of Philadelphia this time. The World Series was also a sweep as the Reds dispatched the Yankees as the Reds became the first team to go through the Championship Series and World Series without losing a game.

Two years of second-place finishes followed, and the Reds replaced Sparky Anderson at the helm with John McNamara, who led the club back to the top of the NL West in 1979. Pete Rose, after 16 years in Cincinnati, had signed with the Phillies as a free agent, but Ray Knight (who replaced Rose at third base) minimized the loss with a team-high .318 batting average. Houston led the division much of the summer, but a sustained Reds' surge in August brought them even, then pulled them ahead in early September, where they hung on to take the title by just 1½ games. But that was the end of the Reds' decade of splendor; Pittsburgh swept past them to the pennant in the NLCS.

Joe Morgan left the club after the season, returning as a free agent to Houston, whence he had come eight years earlier. In 1980 the Reds dipped in midseason, recovering to make a race of it in August, only to fade a bit and finish third. The next year, in a season shortened and split in two by a players' strike, the Reds compiled the best overall record in the majors. But they came away empty-handed by finishing half a game behind Los Angeles in the first half-season and 1½ games back of Houston in the second half, losing a chance at postseason play when the owners decided to pit the half-season winners against each other.

As a penurious front office continued to trade away its stars or lose them to free agency, the dispirited Reds dropped to the bottom of the NL West in 1982 with a club-worst 101 losses. Manager McNamara yielded in midseason to coach Russ Nixon, who was himself replaced by Vern Rapp after another last-place finish in 1983. Robert Howsam, Sr., whose shrewd trading as general manager had been instrumental in building the mighty Reds of the 1970s, was called out of semiretirement to restore the club to respectability. Howsam signed free-agent slugger Dave Parker from Pittsburgh, and late in the 1984 season brought Pete Rose back as player-manager. Early in 1985 the NL approved the sale of the Reds to Marge Schott, a Cincinnati automobile dealer. With Parker enjoying his most productive seasons in several years, and the emergence of outfielder Eric Davis and reliever John Franco, owner Schott's public enthusiasm for her team was rewarded with four straight second-place finishes. The highlight of that period came in 1985 when Rose broke Ty Cobb's record for most career hits.

Turmoil ruled the Reds in 1989. Disabling injuries to a dozen players, including such 1988 standouts as pitcher Danny Jackson (whose 23 wins tied for the league high) and infielders Barry Larkin and Chris Sabo, contributed most to the team's drop to fifth place. Baseball's investigation of manager Pete Rose on charges of gambling on baseball games and other offenses—an investigation which resulted in Rose's lifetime banishment from the game in August—did nothing to bolster Cincinnati's play on the field. The team had its lowest win total in five years.

The distress of 1989 was all but forgotten in 1990 as the Reds, under new manager Lou Piniella, leaped to a 9-0 start and, surviving threats from San Francisco in August and Los Angeles in September, held on to first place through the entire season. Larkin and Sabo—whole again—anchored a balanced offense, while pitchers Randy Myers (acquired from the Mets in a trade for John Franco), Rob Dibble, and Norm Charlton (nicknamed "The Nasty Boys") provided All-Star relief to a solid core of starters. In the NLCS, the Reds overcame an opening-game loss to capture the pennant from Pittsburgh in six games, then startled Oakland's heavily favored Athletics with a four-game sweep.

The Reds remained in the thick of the 1991 race through mid-season, despite a 10-game losing streak in July. But as Atlanta rose to battle early leader Los Angeles, Cincinnati settled into a long decline that at the end left them 20 games back, in fifth place. Barry Larkin and Bip Roberts sparked the league's strongest offense in 1992, as the Reds rebounded to win 90 games. But they let a six-game midseason lead get away and finished eight games behind repeat champion Atlanta.

Piniella was replaced by Cincinnati hero—but managing novice—Tony Perez for 1993. Perez lasted only until May 24, when veteran manager Davey Johnson took his place. Meanwhile, Marge Schott's fellow NL owners banned her for the season from active participation in club affairs for making racial slurs. With their season further marred by injuries and backbiting, the Reds finished fifth, 31 games out.

With Kevin Mitchell pacing a strong, balanced offense, the Reds turned their fortunes around in 1994 and reached the All-Star break atop the new Central division by 2½ games. They were still clinging to a half-game lead over Houston when the strike ended the season. When play resumed in 1995 the Reds showed they had indeed been for real, winning the division by nine games. Standouts included MVP Barry Larkin (.319, 15 HR, 66 RBIs), Mets discard Pete Schourek (18-7), Ron Gant (29 HR, 88 RBIs), Reggie Sanders (28 HR, 99 RBIs), and Jeff Brantley (28 saves). The Reds swept LA in the first round of playoffs but in turn were swept by the Braves in the NLCS. At season's end manager Davey Johnson left the team for Baltimore and was replaced by Ray Knight.

By mid-1997 the Reds were floundering under Knight and Jack McKeon took over as a field manager. Jeff Shaw, whose career high was four saves a year earlier, led the NL with 42 saves. Shaw, along with pitcher Dave Burba, were traded in separate deals in 1998 to bring in young players.

Several shrewd moves by general manager Jim Bowden, plus the maturation of first baseman Sean Casey and a solid bullpen, made Cincinnati the surprise team of the National League in 1999. Ron Villone, who had never started a major league game in 157 appearances before the season, started and won three one-hitters; 16-game winner Pete Harnisch, who battled through injuries all year, also tossed a one-hit game. The Reds seemed to have a firm grasp on the National League Wild Card when the Mets lost eight of nine games going into the final weekend of the season. The Reds, however, lost consecutive games in Milwaukee while the Mets swept the Pirates. Cincinnati won its last scheduled game of the season, following a rain delay of more than eight hours, to force a one-game playoff. The Reds fell to the Mets at Cinergy Field to bring a sour end to a successful year.

Cincinnati's failure in the final days of the season turned into triumph in the offseason when Bowden landed Ken Griffey Jr. in a historic trade. Expectations faded, however, when the Cardinals started off hot and never let the Reds get within striking distance. McKeon, the NL Manager of the Year a season before, was fired after an 85-win season and replaced with Bob Boone, the father of Reds third baseman Aaron Boone.

Cleveland Indians

The Indians finished in the top half of the league nearly 70 percent of the time through their first 68 years, and wound up in the cellar only once (in 1914). Cleveland then experienced only five winning seasons from 1969 through 1993. The team's greatest period of success has come since 1995.

The Indians (who were at first called the Blues because of the color of their uniforms) succeeded Cleveland's National League Spiders, who in 1899, their final season, lost a major league record 134 games. When the NL dropped the Spiders at the end of the season, Ban Johnson, president of the emerging American League, grasped the opportunity to move into this major market. In 1901, when Johnson proclaimed the AL a major league, Cleveland lured several players from NL clubs and played much better than the Spiders had, but still finished next-to-last in their first big league season. The next year the Bronchos (as they decided to call themselves) languished in last place through June. But during the season they acquired several players through trade and purchase—most notably star second baseman Napoleon "Nap" Lajoie and pitcher Bill Bernhard—who turned the Bronchos around in midseason and lifted them above .500 (and into fifth place) by season's end.

With Lajoie sparkling in the field and dominating the league at the plate, the fans soon settled on another nickname for the club—the Naps—that lasted as long as Lajoie remained in Cleveland. Late in the 1904 season, Lajoie was named manager. After enjoying moderate success in two of the next three seasons, the Naps in 1908 experienced their best year and one of the team's most exciting finishes ever.

With a 10-game winning streak near the end of the season, they moved from fourth to first, only to be surpassed by Detroit's 10-game streak. Both teams won their season finale, but the Tigers, because they had not made up an earlier rainout, took the pennant by half a game. Cleveland protested that if Detroit had played the missed game and lost, Cleveland would have gained a tie, forcing a playoff that might have brought them the championship. The dispute eventually led to a rules change requiring ties or washouts to be replayed if their outcome could determine the pennant winner.

Poor seasons alternated with good the next few years. Lajoie quit as manager but remained as player. Pitching ace Addie Joss pitched a second no-hitter (he had hurled a perfect game at the height of the 1908 race), but before the start of the 1911 season, he was dead of tubercular meningitis. Outfielder Joe Jackson—acquired from the Athletics—hit .408 in his first full big league season. The club reached bottom in 1914 with a last-place finish that found them 18½ games out of seventh place, 48½ out of first. After the season Lajoie went to Philadelphia (the fans then voted to rename the club the Indians), and the next August Jackson was sold to the Chicago White Sox as attendance dropped to its lowest level since 1901.

By the time the 1916 season began, though, new ownership had acquired the great Tris Speaker from Boston and brought up from the minors a pair of promising pitchers, Jim Bagby (Sr.) and Stan Coveleski. Sparked by the three newcomers, the Indians rose to third in 1917, and to close second-place finishes the next two years. In 1920 everything came together. Speaker, who had taken over as manager the previous July, hit .388. Coveleski also had one of his best years with 24 wins. Bagby, in the finest season of his career, led the league with 31 victories, and veteran pitcher Ray Caldwell (picked up from the Boston Red Sox the previous summer) added another 20. Six regulars hit over .300; the club as a whole hit .303.

The team rebounded from the devastating loss of Ray Chapman, who was killed by a pitch from Carl Mays. The Yankees dropped back a bit in mid-September, but the White Sox hung close until the final week, when eight of their players were indicted and suspended as suspects in the Black Sox scandal of 1919. The Sox lost two of their final three games and all hope of tying Cleveland to force a playoff. The Indians defeated Brooklyn in a World Series that is best remembered for second baseman Bill Wambsganss' unassisted triple play in Game 5.

Cleveland led much of the way in 1921 before a late slump and a New York surge gave the Yankees their first pennant. Through the next quarter century the Indians came close to a pennant only twice. In 1926, with two veteran Georges—pitcher Uhle and first baseman Burns—enjoying their finest seasons, the Indians came to life in midseason and drew within three games of the Yankees by season's end. Fourteen years later, in 1940, behind the 27 wins of 21-year-old Bob Feller and the inspired play (in the field and at the bat) of second-year shortstop Lou Boudreau, Cleveland made an even closer run for the flag. Throughout the summer the Indians were in or near first place, but six losses in nine games with a resurgent Detroit in late August and September left them a game back at the finish.

Two years later Boudreau, at age 24, was named to manage the Tribe. His team stirred little interest through the war years. But in 1946, with Feller back from military service, Cleveland fans boosted home attendance above a million for the first time. The next year, their first full season under new president Bill Veeck, the Indians climbed to fourth. More significantly, Veeck hired the league's first black player, Larry Doby, who became a mainstay of the Indians for the next eight years.

In 1948 the Indians began a nine-year era of excellence with a victory in one of the closest pennant races ever. Through June they ran a three-way race with the Yankees and the surprisingly lively Philadelphia Athletics; in July the Red Sox rose out of nowhere to make it a four-way struggle. In September the A's fell behind, but the three remaining clubs stayed close, and on Sept. 24 found themselves in a three-way tie. Cleveland moved ahead with a four-game win streak, but Boston, after a pair of losses, won their final four (including two to eliminate New York). Cleveland's final-day loss to Detroit left them tied with Boston. In a one-game playoff in Boston the next day (the first playoff in AL history), manager-shortstop Boudreau capped his MVP season with two home runs to help give rookie Gene Bearden his 20th win and the Tribe their second pennant. The exciting race drew more than 2.6 million Cleveland fans to Municipal Stadium, a new major league record. The World Series against the Boston Braves was anticlimactic—a Cleveland triumph in six games.

By 1951 both owner Veeck and manager Boudreau had moved on, but under new manager Al Lopez the Indians fashioned a six-year stretch in which they finished second to the Yankees five times, and in 1954 they won their third pennant with 111 victories. The Lopez years, 1951-1956, were punctuated by the power of players like Doby, Luke Easter, Al Rosen, and Vic Wertz. But it was pitching that gave the team its consistency. Bob Lemon and Early Wynn won between 17 and 23 games in every one of the six years, as did Mike Garcia through 1954. As Garcia and Feller (who won 22 in 1951) faded, Art Houtteman was acquired from Detroit for a couple of good years, and Herb Score came along for his two explosive seasons.

The 1954 season was the Yankees' best season in 18 years from 1943 through 1960, a period in which they won 12 pennants, but it turned out to be the best year in Cleveland history. The Yankees kept the race close until the end of July and finished with 103 wins. But the Indians became the first American League team to reach 111 wins. Wynn and Lemon tied for the league lead with 23 wins apiece, and Garcia copped the ERA crown. Doby led the league in homers and RBIs, and second baseman Bobby Avila took the batting title. Heavily favored to defeat the Giants in the World Series, the Tribe and their fans were shocked when the NL champs swept them in four games.

After Lopez left to manage the White Sox in 1957, the Indians slipped below .500 for the first time in a decade. Rocky Colavito's power and Cal McLish's pitching brought them back in 1959, when they finished second to Lopez's White Sox. Their next highest post-Lopez finish came nine years later, in 1968, when Luis Tiant and Sam McDowell pitched them into third.

From 1969 through 1989 the Indians completed every season in the bottom half of the AL East, rising above .500 in only four seasons while finishing seven years in the division cellar. In 1990, though, with three straight wins at season's end, they passed Baltimore by half a game to wind up fourth.

The effort proved too much. In July 1991, the Indians dropped into the cellar to stay, and spiraled down to a club-record 105 losses. With nowhere to go but up, the 1992 team, spurred by the offense of Carlos Baerga and Albert Belle and the impressive pitching of Charles Nagy, played the best ball in the AL after the All-Star break, lifting themselves out of the cellar into a fourth place-tie with the Yankees.

The tragic preseason deaths of relievers Tim Crews and Steve Olin and severe injury to starter Bob Ojeda in a boating accident cast a pall over the team's final season in Cleveland Stadium. With Nagy also out much of the season, the Indians' pitching was among the league's worst. Offensively, though, they ranked among the better clubs, paced by Baerga, Belle, and sophomore Kenny Lofton, whose league-leading 70 stolen bases set a new club record. The team finished sixth.

The Indians—playing in brand-new Jacobs Field—were up for 1994. Belle, who ranked among AL leaders in almost every offensive category, and Lofton, who added the league lead in hits to another stolen base title, paced a powerful offense that kept the team in the thick of a tight race with Chicago in the league's new Central division. With their best chance in decades to bring Cleveland a winner, the Indians trailed the White Sox by just one game when the season ended prematurely.

The Indians dominated the AL in 1995, rolling to a 100-44 record and capturing the AL Central division by a phenomenal 30 games. Paced by Albert Belle (who despite the shortened season led the AL with 50 homers, 121 runs, 377 total bases, 52 doubles, and a .690 slugging percentage), the Indians batted .291 and slugged 207 homers. Meanwhile Tribe pitchers posted a league-best 3.83 ERA (the only AL ERA under 4.00). Jose Mesa led league relievers with 46 saves.

The Indians swept the Red Sox in the first round of the postseason, then edged the upstart Mariners in the ALCS, before falling to Atlanta, 4-2, in the World Series. The fans appreciated their team's superb effort, however, and in the offseason the club became the first to sell out every seat for the entire upcoming campaign.

Despite discarding Eddie Murray and Carlos Baerga in midseason, the 1996 Indians (99-62, with a league-leading .293 team batting average) repeated as AL Central champions. Team standouts included Albert Belle (48 home runs and an AL-best 148 RBIs), Kenny Lofton (.317 and a league-leading 75 stolen bases), Jim Thome (38 HR), Jose Mesa (39 saves), and Charles Nagy (17-5, 3.41). The Tribe fell, however, to Wild Card Baltimore in the first round of the postseason.

The Indians returned to the World Series in 1997, surprising both the Yankees and the Orioles along the way. Sandy Alomar Jr., who had been the MVP at the All-Star Game at Jacobs Field in July, continued his heroics in October. His home run off New York's Mariano Rivera in the eighth inning of Game 4 of the Division Series tied the game as the Indians rallied to win the series. The Indians beat the favored Orioles in the ALCS on a series-deciding home run by Tony Fernandez in the top of the 11th inning of Game 6. The World Series went seven games and was also decided in the 11th inning, but the Florida Marlins were the winners.

The 1998 Indians won the AL Central Division for the fourth consecutive season. Second-year pitchers Bartolo Colon and Jaret Wright combined to win 26 games and Charles Nagy and newcomer Dave Burba won 15 games apiece. Manny Ramirez led the offense with 45 home runs and 145 RBIs and shortstop Omar Vizquel won his sixth consecutive Gold Glove. The Indians lost the first game of the Division Series to the Red Sox, but won the next three games to take the series. Next came the Yankees, who had bettered Cleveland's AL record with 114 wins in 1998, and the Indians briefly held a 2-1 series lead before New York won in six games. Still, the Indians were the only team to win any postseason games against the eventual world champions.

The 1999 Indians won the Central Division title for the fifth consecutive year, but it was not enough. Cleveland won the first two games of the Division Series before losing three straight to the Red Sox. Mike Hargrove, winner of 721 games for Cleveland since 1991, was replaced with Charlie Manuel. Manny Ramirez, who had broken Hal Trosky's 63-year-old record with 165 RBIs in 1999, batted .351 with 122 RBIs and a .457 on-base percentage in 2000. Several late-season acquisitions, including David Segui (.334), helped the Indians rebound from a poor first half, but the Tribe was eliminated on the final day of the season.

Colorado Rockies

Denver was one of two cities awarded a National League franchise in June 1991 (Miami was the other), in the league's first expansion since Montreal and San Diego were added in 1969. The new teams took the field for the first time in 1993, their rosters stocked primarily with players selected from the other major league clubs in a special expansion draft. Denver, which chose to call itself the Colorado Rockies, drew nearly 4.5 million fans to cavernous Mile High Stadium, the highest season attendance in the history of sport.

Though their 5.41 ERA was by far the worst in the majors, the Rockies, under rookie manager Don Baylor, not only avoided the NL West cellar, but they also set a new league record for most wins by an expansion team, with 67. Andres Galarraga, Charlie Hayes, and Dante Bichette headed a solid offense, with Galarraga hitting more than 100 points above his previous major league career average to lead the NL in batting at .370.

Galarraga was in the midst of another fine season in 1994 when a pitch broke his hand on July 28. Despite a 50-54 record, the Rockies stood in second place in the weak NL West, just half a game out of first. By the time the season ended two weeks later, though, they had slipped to third, 6 1/2 games out.

In 1995 the Rockies moved into Coors Field (drawing 3.3 million fans), and Baylor won NL Manager of the Year honors as Colorado finished just one game behind LA in the NL West and earned a wild card playoff slot in the process. Key Rockies were Galarraga (31 HR, 106 RBIs), Vinny Castilla (32 HR, 90 RBIs, .309), Dante Bichette (.340 and a league-leading 40 HR, 128 RBIs, 359 total bases, and a .620 slugging mark), Eric Young (.317 and an NL-leading nine triples), and Larry Walker (36 HR, 101 RBIs). The dream ended in the first round of the playoffs, however, as Colorado fell to Atlanta, three games to one.

The 1996 Rockies finished third, eight games behind surprising San Diego. Standouts included Galarraga (a league-leading 47 HR and 150 RBIs), Bichette (141 RBIs, 198 hits), Young (a league-leading 53 stolen bases) and Ellis Burks (40 HR,.344, 211 hits, 128 RBIs, and an NL-best 142 runs scored).

The 1997 and 1998 seasons were similar in that the team continued to lead the league in hitting (1998 marked the fourth straight time), but, in the thin air of Colorado, their pitching staff was among the worst in baseball. (Even the 1998 All-Star Game was a typical Mile High slugfest, a 13-8 AL win at Coors Field). After a strong finish in 1997, Galarraga left for Atlanta and Darryl Kile came to Denver as a free agent. Larry Walker, the 1997 NL MVP, won the batting title in 1998, while Dante Bichette finished third in the '98 batting race. First baseman Todd Helton emerged as one of the league's top rookies, and Vinny Castilla had his finest professional season. But all the offense couldn't save the job of the team's first manager, Don Baylor. Jim Leyland, who won the 1997 World Series with the other team born in 1993, the Florida Marlins, was hired to manage the Rockies.

Leyland lasted just one year in Denver before he retired. The Rockies made several wholesale changes, trading in their old slow-footed power models like Bichette and Castilla for faster, younger, line drive hitters like Jeffrey Hammonds and Jeff Cirillo. Todd Helton flirted with .400 for a large portion of the 2000 season before finishing at a league-best .372; he also led the NL with 147 RBIs, 216 hits, 59 doubles, 405 total bases, a .463 on-base percentage, and a .698 slugging average.

Detroit Tigers

One of the more successful clubs in the American League, the Tigers have enjoyed winning seasons nearly 70 percent of the time. In 18 of their 61 winning seasons, they have remained in contention into the final days, 11 times emerging triumphant as league or division champions.

Detroit was one of the clubs from Ban Johnson's Western League that (renamed the American League) raised itself to major league status in 1901 with a talent raid on the long-established National League. In their first six big league seasons, the Tigers displayed little bite, finishing four times in the second division and never threatening for the league lead.

In 1907 all that changed. Sparked by a young right fielder, Ty Cobb (who in his first full big league season led the league in batting, slugging, hits, RBIs, and stolen bases) and led by a dynamic new manager, Hugh "Eeyah" Jennings (who knew enough not to try to tell Cobb how to play the game), the Tigers clawed their way to the pennant in a four-way race. The outcome might have been different if two late-season games with second-place Philadelphia had not been rained out. (Today's rules would require that the games be made up.)

The 1908 race was even closer, with four teams contending into late September. The race wasn't settled until the final day, when Detroit beat Chicago to edge Cleveland by half a game. Once again the pennant hinged on a rainout that had not been made up. And once again Cobb dominated the league's hitters (though he slipped to fourth in stolen bases).

The Tigers had a slightly easier time of it the next year. It was a three-way race into September, but Detroit then pulled away to finish three and a half games ahead of Philadelphia. Cobb, in his best season yet, took the Triple Crown and returned to the top in stolen bases. But the Tigers were again unable to win a World Series. In 1907, after an opening-game tie, the Chicago Cubs swept the next four. The Cubs lost Game 3 the next year, but won the other four. And in 1909 Pittsburgh and Detroit alternated victories, with the Pirates emerging world champions in seven games.

Jennings managed Detroit for 11 more seasons; then Cobb took the reins for six years before leaving for Philadelphia. But the Tigers won no more pennants in the Cobb era. Cobb himself continued to dominate the league offensively through 1919. In 1911 he achieved career highs in most offensive categories, including a batting average of .420, but the Tigers managed no better than a distant second to the Athletics. In 1915 they started strong and remained in the race throughout the season. Cobb stole what was for 47 years a modern-record 96 bases, and the team's 100 wins proved to be the highest total in their first 33 years. But after running neck and neck with the Red Sox through most of August, the Tigers slumped a bit in early September—just enough for the Sox to take the flag by two and a half games. A close third-place finish the next year marked the Tigers' last serious challenge for 18 years.

In 1934, after six straight years in the second division, and only three years after their most distant finish ever (47 games out), the Tigers turned themselves around to win the pennant with a 101-53 record and a .656 winning percentage, the highest in club history. Two newly acquired veterans—manager/catcher Mickey Cochrane and outfielder Goose Goslin—enjoyed fine seasons at the bat, as did first baseman Hank Greenberg (.339, 139 RBIs) in his first full season, and second baseman Charlie Gehringer (.356, 127 RBIs). The two other infielders, third baseman Marv Owen and shortstop Billy Rogell enjoyed their finest seasons at the plate for a club whose batting average led the league at .300. It took the Tigers a month to get going, but by mid-July they had shot ahead of the Yankees to win by seven games. But once again, victory in the World Series eluded them as the St. Louis Cardinals blew them away, 11-0, in Game 7.

Paced by Greenberg's 170 RBIs in 1935, Detroit—after another slow start—moved up so sharply in July and August that even a September slump gave the Yankees no opportunity to catch them. And finally, in their fifth try, the Tigers won a world championship, overcoming Chicago in six games despite the loss of Greenberg, who broke his wrist in Game 2. Part-owner Frank Navin, who had run the club for three decades, had finally seen his Tigers reach the very top. A month later, after falling from a horse, he suffered a heart attack and died.

Del Baker had replaced Cochrane as manager when Detroit next made a run for the pennant in 1940. In a tight race the Tigers caught up with Cleveland in early September and traded the lead with them for two weeks before pulling ahead to stay with two wins in a three-game series. In the pennant clincher, Detroit's Floyd Giebell outdueled Cleveland great Bob Feller 2-0 for his third—and last—big league victory. In the World Series the Tigers lost once again, as Cincinnati came from behind in Game 7 for a 2-1 win.

Two losing seasons followed, and Steve O'Neill replaced Baker at the helm. In 1944, the wartime Tigers, behind the splendid pitching of workhorses Dizzy Trout and Hal Newhouser (one-two in ERA and innings pitched, and winners of 27 and 29 games), joined the race in late August and found themselves tied with the St. Louis Browns for first going into the last game of the season. But the Browns beat the Yankees, and Detroit lost to Washington.

Hank Greenberg's release from military service in mid-1945 sparked another run for the pennant. They held the lead from mid-June through August, but in September a surging Washington caught up with them. The race once again went down to the final day, and the final inning, when Greenberg's grand slam overcame a St. Louis lead to give Detroit the flag over the idle Senators. Newhouser, with 25 wins and a 1.81 ERA, was named AL MVP for the second straight year. In the World Series his ERA shot up to 6.10, but he still managed to win two games (including the finale) as the Tigers took the Cubs in seven for their second world title.

In the 23 years that passed before their next pennant, the Tigers came close only twice. In 1950 they led the race through the middle of the season, but were caught by the Yankees late in August. After retaking the lead in early September, the two clubs ran neck-and-neck for a while before Detroit fell away to second.

Two years later the Tigers reached their nadir: their first cellar finish. After a decade in which they finished no higher than fourth, they rebounded in 1961 as first baseman Norm Cash and left fielder Rocky Colavito both enjoyed the most explosive seasons of their careers. Compiling their best season record since 1934, Detroit led the league through parts of June and July. But this was the year of Maris and Mantle and 109 Yankee victories; when the season ended, the Tigers' 101 wins had earned them only second place.

They came much closer six years later in the great four-way race of 1967 that saw three clubs still contending on the final day, when the Tigers split a doubleheader to tie with Minnesota for second. If 1967 was a scramble, 1968 belonged to Detroit. Denny McLain won 31 games (the last major leaguer to win 30) to lead the team to a 103-win finish, 12 games ahead of Baltimore. Down three games to one in the World Series, the pitching of McLain in Game 6 and Mickey Lolich in Games 5 and 7 brought the Tigers back against the Cardinals and gave them their third world championship.

A strike at the start of 1972 contributed to the Tigers' first divisional title, which culminated a four-way race in the AL East. Detroit defeated Boston two games out of three at season's end, to edge the Sox by half a game. But if the strike had not wiped out an unequal number of games, the end of the season could have seen the two clubs tied.

The Tigers lost the pennant to Oakland with a 2-1 loss in the finale of a close American League Championship Series, and dropped out of contention for a decade. In 1974 they finished at the bottom of the division and the next year lost 102 games to post the worst record in the majors.

Finally, after seven seasons in the second division, Detroit put together a strong second half in strike-divided 1981, fading only at the end to tie for second. Three years later the Tigers were back on top with one of their best years. Opening the season 9-0, they ended April at 18-2, stretched their mark to 35-5 by late May, and were never headed, finishing a team-record 15 games in front with 104 wins, their most ever. Their balanced pitching staff led the league in ERA, even though none of their starters finished among the top ten. Willie Hernandez (who with Aurelio Lopez compiled a 19-4 record from the bullpen, with 46 saves) earned both Cy Young and MVP awards. After sweeping Kansas City in the ALCS, the Tigers took the world championship—their fourth—from San Diego in five games.

In 1987 the Tigers caught the Blue Jays in the season's final series, tying them for the lead in the first game, moving to the front with a 12-inning win in the second game, and clinching the division crown in the finale, 1-0. In the ALCS, though, Minnesota stopped the favored Tigers, four games to one.

Injuries sidelined veteran keystoners Alan Trammell and Lou Whitaker more than a month each and derailed the season of starter Jeff Robinson in August just as he was emerging as ace of Detroit's pitchers. All the same, the Tigers led the AL East much of the 1988 season before falling back and rallied at season's end to finish second, one game behind Boston.

The next year, though, as new waves of injury broke over an aging lineup, the Tigers dropped into the division cellar in June and kept sinking, finishing with 103 losses and the worst record in the majors. But in 1990 Trammell rebounded from one of his worst seasons with one of his best and, with newly acquired first baseman Cecil Fielder, sparked a recovery to third place. Fielder, back in the AL after a season in Japan, topped the majors in home runs (with 51, the most in the AL since 1961), slugging percentage, and runs batted in.

The 1991 Tigers clawed their way back from an eight-game deficit in mid-July into a tie with first-place Toronto seven weeks later; they finished tied for second with Boston. In 1992, for the third year in a row, Detroit led the AL in home runs, but this time their big bats couldn't lift the club above sixth place. Texas edged the Tigers for the home run crown in 1993, but Detroit challenged for their division lead through August and, after a dip in September, surged to tie Baltimore for third place. In strike-shortened 1994 they finished last in the AL East, 18 games out.

On the field in 1995 little of substance changed for the Tigers, as Fielder slammed 31homers and the team finished a distant fourth (60-84), but momentous changes occurred off it. Sparky Anderson retired as manager at season's end, and plans to replace Tiger Stadium with another downtown ballpark accelerated.

The Buddy Bell-led 1996 Tigers compiled baseball's worst record (53-109). The season saw Cecil Fielder leave for the Yankees in midseason and Alan Trammell retire at season's end. The 1997 Tigers, however, were 26 games better than the previous season's club and paced by 100 RBIs from both first baseman Tony Clark and outfielder Bobby Higginson, the team finished third. The Tigers shifted to the AL Central in 1998 and the team foundered. Bell was dismissed late in the season and was replaced by Larry Parrish.

The 1999 season was the team's last at Tiger Stadium, and it also turned out to be the last in Detroit for Larry Parrish. He was hurriedly dismissed as manager after the season as the Tigers rushed to sign Phil Garner. Garner proved to be worth the effort. At spacious new Comerica Park, the pitching improved dramatically—the club's 4.71 ERA was fifth in the league and was lower than that of the eventual world champion Yankees. Juan Gonzalez, who came over from Texas in a blockbuster trade, was a disappointment, but Bobby Higginson enjoyed one of his finest seasons. Todd Jones finished tied for the league lead with 42 saves.

Florida Marlins

One of two new clubs to join the National League in 1993, the Florida Marlins were formed after the selection, in June 1991, of Miami and Denver as cities for the league's first expansion teams since 1969. Headed by entertainment magnate H. Wayne Huizenga, the Marlins played in Joe Robbie Stadium (which Huizenga partially owned). In their first season the Marlins featured one of the game's premier relievers in Bryan Harvey, whose 45 saves ranked third in the NL and contributed to 70 percent of the club's 64 victories. Though the Marlins lost their final six games, they finished ahead of the New York Mets for sixth place in the NL East.

In the strike-shortened seasons of 1994 and 1995 they finished in the division cellar. In 1995, however, Pat Rapp showed signs of promise with a 14-7 mark and rookie second baseman Quilvio Veras led the NL with 56 stolen bases. Even though the Marlins fired manager Rene Lachemann in midseason 1996 (replacing him with interim manager John Boles) they moved up to third place (80-82) with help from Gary Sheffield (42 HR, 120 RBIs, 118 runs scored), Al Leiter (200 strikeouts), Kevin Brown (league-leading 1.89 ERA), and Robb Nen (35 saves).

In the offseason, the Marlins signed manager Jim Leyland and within a few months they had practically a whole new team. In less than three weeks the Marlins signed six free agents—Bobby Bonilla, Moises Alou, Alex Fernandez, Jim Eisenreich, John Cangelosi, and Dennis Cook—and suddenly they were one of the best teams in baseball. The Marlins battled Atlanta for the NL East title (they went 8-4 against the Braves during the season), but failing that, they still managed to hold off the Mets for the Wild Card. The Marlins swept the Giants in the Division Series and then shocked the Braves in six games to win the pennant.

Rookie Livan Hernandez, who was Most Valuable Player of the NLCS, earned MVP honors for the World Series as well. It was second-year shortstop Edgar Rentaria, however, who won the World Series with a single in the bottom of the 11th inning of Game 7 to score Craig Counsell, whose sacrifice fly had tied the game in the ninth. Their victory over Cleveland not only made the Marlins the first Wild Card team to win the World Series, but in only their fifth season of existence, they were also the first expansion team to win a world championship.

As quickly as success had come, it disappeared. Quoting huge financial losses on the championship team, owner Huizenga looked to sell the Marlins, and in the meantime, traded away the nucleus of the world champions before they ever got a chance to defend the title. By the end of the year, only everyday players Renteria and Counsel remained (and Renteria was traded to St. Louis during the winter meetings). The Marlins were finally sold to commodities trader John Henry and John Boles was named manager of the team for the second time after the 1998 season, replacing Jim Leyland, who resigned. General manager Dave Dombrowski, who, in Huizenga's "house cleaning" had secured several top prospects from other organizations, signed a five-year contract to remain with the club.

Despite the sale of the team to financier John Henry, the Marlins finished last for the second straight year in 1999. The team received solid seasons from shortstop Alex Gonzalez and rookie center fielder Preston Wilson—between them they led the Marlins in a dozen offensive categories. Florida's 15-game improvement in 2000, however, was mainly due to pitching. All-Star Ryan Dempster led the staff with 14 wins, including a one-hit shutout of the Mets. Antonio Alfonseca led the major leagues in saves as the Marlins developed one of baseball's best young bullpens. Luis Castillo led the majors in stolen bases and batted .334 atop a lineup that included Cliff Floyd and Mike Lowell, who both enjoyed solid comeback seasons.

Houston Astros

The Colt .45s (as the Astros were originally known) had hoped to begin their history in the Harris County Domed Stadium. When the start of the vast project was delayed, a temporary outdoor park was built for them next door in time for their 1962 inaugural. Heat, humidity, and giant mosquitoes held Colt home attendance below a million in each of their three outdoor seasons. In 1965, they brought big league baseball indoors for the first time, and the fans arrived—more than 2 million the first year. The original grass under the dome was real, but when the skylight panels were coated over so fielders wouldn't lose sight of high flies, the grass died. In 1966 the club (now known as the Astros) and the stadium (now called the Astrodome) brought to baseball yet another innovation—AstroTurf.

The Houston franchise, conceived as an entry in the abortive Continental League, first took the field instead in the National League. Houston and the New York Mets were part of the league's first expansion since shrinking from 12 teams to eight in 1900. Shrewd player selection by general manager Paul Richards kept the new team from being as bad as the Mets. Although they suffered just as long playing below .500 (seven years), they finished below New York in the standings only once.

When the NL added two more teams in 1969 and split into two divisions, the Astros for the first time made a serious title run. Though they wound up fifth in the West (ahead of only the expansion San Diego Padres), they rose to within two games of the top in August, and again in September before a six-game losing streak dropped them out of contention. With an 81-81 record, they finished out of the ranks of losers for the first time.

After dropping below .500 again in 1970 and '71, the Astros made their second run for the division title in 1972. At the end of June they were battling with Cincinnati for the lead, but the Reds pulled away over the rest of the season while Houston leveled off for an eventual second-place finish 10½ games back. With a record of 84-

69, the Astros had fashioned their first winning season.

In 1975 they endured their worst year ever, losing 97 games to finish at the bottom of the West, 43½ games behind the Reds. But the next year pitcher J.R. Richard, with the first of several fine seasons, brought the club up to third with his 20 wins. By 1979 Richard was the NL's most overwhelming pitcher, leading the league with 313 strikeouts and a 2.71 ERA. His 18 wins and teammate Joe Niekro's 21 sparked a team that spent much of the summer in first place before falling to a game and a half behind Cincinnati at the end.

Houston and Los Angeles battled back and forth for the division lead throughout 1980. Richard began strong and seemed headed for his finest year. With a 10-4 record, he was the starting pitcher in the All-Star Game. But shortly after midseason he suffered a stroke that ended his big league career. Led by Joe Niekro, Nolan Ryan, and Vern Ruhle (who replaced Richard in the rotation and finished 12-4), the best pitching staff in baseball kept the Astros in the race to season's end, although three straight losses to the Dodgers had left the clubs tied for first. In a one-game playoff, Houston rebounded with a 7-1 win (Niekro's 20th) to capture the division title. In the National League Championship Series, the Astros took the Phillies to the 10th inning of the final game before bowing three games to two.

When a player strike cut the middle out of the 1981 season, intradivisional playoffs were scheduled between the winners of the two halves. Houston, the second-half champion, defeated first-half victor Los Angeles in the first two games, but lost the next three, and the division title.

After four years in the middle of the division, the Astros stormed back in 1986 with their best season ever, winning 15 of their last 19 games to conquer the West. Pitcher Mike Scott, who had developed a deceptive split-finger fastball, won 18 and led the NL in strikeouts, innings, and ERA. On Sept. 25 he clinched the division crown with a no-hitter. In the NLCS the Astros lost to the Mets in six games, but three of New York's wins came in its final at bat, including a 16-inning victory in Game 6.

In each of the next three seasons the Astros drew within a game and a half of first place in August, only to tumble out of the race in the season's final weeks. Rookie first baseman Jeff Bagwell's strong performance at the plate gave Astros fans one of their few reasons to cheer in 1991 as their team plummeted to last place.

The offense set club records in batting average and home runs in 1993, and the pitching staff compiled the second lowest ERA in the majors, as ace Mark Portugal concluded his brilliant 18-4 season with 12 straight wins. But the Astros couldn't approach powerful Atlanta and San Francisco, and finished third in their division, 19 games out.

Free agent Portugal departed for San Francisco in 1994, but pitcher Doug Drabek rebounded after an off year, and MVP Bagwell's slugging dominated the NL. Playing in the Central division under new manager Terry Collins, the Astros struggled to catch division leader Cincinnati, and had drawn within half a game of the Reds when the season ended. The following year was almost a replay of 1994, as the Astros again finished second to Cincinnati. In 1996 the Astros were bridesmaids again, this time finishing second, six games behind St. Louis.

At season's end Astros broadcaster Larry Dierker replaced Collins as manager. Dierker, the ace of the Astros pitching staff more than two decades earlier, let developing pitchers like Shane Reynolds, Mike Hampton, and Jose Lima stay in games longer and they quickly learned from their mistakes and gained confidence. After three years of finishing second, the Astros finally won the NL Central in Dierker's rookie season as manager. They were quickly swept by Atlanta in the playoffs.

Even though 1997 ace Darryl Kile (19-7, 2.57 ERA) left for Colorado as a free agent, the Astros repeated as division champs in 1998. A last-minute trade for Randy Johnson of Seattle fortified an already solid pitching staff and helped Houston to a club record 102 wins. The hot Astros ran into an even hotter Padres team and lost in the Division Series, three games to one.

The Astros won their third consecutive division title in 1999 behind 20-game winners Hampton and Lima and a solid batting order that featured Craig Biggio, Carl Everett, and Bagwell, yet the team lost in the Division Series for the third year running. After several offseason changes—including Everett to Boston plus Hampton and Derek Bell to the Mets—the Astros fell flat in their new home. Enron Field proved to be popular with both fans and hitters, but Houston's vaunted pitching staff took a beating. While the Astros placed third in batting and led the league in home runs, including 47 by Bagwell and 44 by Richard Hidalgo, the club allowed the most homers and had the worst ERA. The lone bright spot on the pitching staff was the emergence of Scott Elarton, who finished the season at 17-7.

Kansas City Royals

Two years after the Athletics abandoned Kansas City for the West Coast, patent medicine millionaire Ewing Kauffman bankrolled an expansion club for the city. Where the A's had been unable in 13 years to fashion even one winning season, the Royals did it in 1971, their third year. One of the most successful of all expansion clubs, the Royals finished either first or second in their division in 14 of their first 20 years.

In their fifth season, 1973, the year they moved into new Royals Stadium, the Royals also made their first serious run for the division title. A midsummer spurt carried them into first place in August before they leveled off to another second-place finish behind Oakland.

After a third second-place race with Oakland in 1975 (during which manager Jack McKeon was replaced by Whitey Herzog), the Royals won the division crown in 1976, taking the lead two months into the season and holding it to the end. Third baseman George Brett won his first AL batting championship by one point over teammate Hal McRae. The Royals and New York were tied after four games in the American League Championship Series, but the Yankees snatched the pennant on Chris Chambliss' home run in the bottom of the ninth inning of the final game.

For two more years the Royals dominated the AL West but failed to stop the Yankees in the ALCS. In 1977, with a pitching staff that led the league in ERA and a balanced offense that included four players with more than 20 home runs and 80 RBIs, the Royals compiled a record of 102-60—their finest to date. Though they didn't move into the division lead until mid-August, they were nearly unstoppable the rest of the way. In the ALCS they once again battled New York all the way, only to lose the Series and pennant for the second time in the final inning of Game 5.

The American League West divisional race was a bit tighter in 1978, as California hung close to Kansas City through much of August and into September, before the Royals finally pulled away. In the ALCS, the Royals tied the series with a big win in Game 2, but the Yankees came back to take the next two by one run each for their third straight flag.

The Royals slipped to second place in 1979, but the next year (led now by rookie manager Jim Frey) they overwhelmed the rest of a weak division. Despite a month-long decline in September, Kansas City finished the season 14 games ahead of Oakland for their fourth divisional title. This was the year Brett chased .400 (ending at .390, the highest major league average since Ted Williams hit .406 in 1941), reliever Dan Quisenberry enjoyed his first big season (12 wins, 33 saves), and starter Dennis Leonard came back from an off-year to record his third 20-win season in four years. It was also the year the Royals finally beat the Yankees to capture their first pennant—with a three-game sweep in the ALCS. In the World Series, though, it was Philadelphia in six games.

The player strike of 1981 divided the season into two halves. In the first half the Royals finished fifth, but part way through the second half Dick Howser (who had managed the Yankees to the East title the previous year) replaced Frey as Royals manager.

The Royals rallied to finish first, a game ahead of Oakland. But in the special playoffs, the A's (who had won the first-half race) beat Kansas City for the division title with a three-game sweep.

Two more second-place finishes in 1982 (a close race with California) and 1983 (20 games behind the Chicago White Sox) were followed in 1984 by a fifth division championship in a three-way race with California and Minnesota. But Detroit swept away the Royals' pennant hopes in the ALCS, in the minimum three games.

For Kansas City, 1985 was a season of catching up. Few picked the Royals to win the West, but with starters Charlie Leibrandt (17-9) and Bret Saberhagen (20-6) finishing two-three in the league ERA race, reliever Quisenberry leading the league in saves for the fourth straight year, and veteran George Brett healthy and enjoying one of his best seasons ever, the Royals chased California throughout the summer and caught them in the final week to take their sixth division crown by a single game.

In the ALCS against Toronto, the Royals fell behind three games to one, which would have eliminated them in earlier years. Saved by the expansion of the series from five games to seven, they came back with three straight wins for their second pennant. Repeating the suspense in the World Series, the Royals again fell behind 3-1 to St. Louis, before rallying once again to win three straight for their first world championship.

During the 1986 season, manager Howser left the club because of a brain tumor. The Royals dropped below .500 and finished third, their lowest rank in a dozen years. Howser was unable to return to the helm in 1987 as he had hoped and died during the summer.

In 1989 Bret Saberhagen, with his most sparkling season yet (23-6, 2.16 ERA), hurled the Royals to their best record since 1980, but their 92 wins earned them only a ninth second-place finish—although Saberhagen earned his second Cy Young Award. Confounding predictions of another strong season, following free agent acquisitions Mark Davis and Storm Davis, the Royals in 1990 floundered in the division cellar much of the summer. They wound up in sixth place, 27½ games out. George Brett, now 37, rallied from the worst start of his career (a .200 batting average in early May) to hit .329 and capture his third AL batting title.

Slugging outfielder Danny Tartabull enjoyed a peak season in 1991, and helped lift Kansas City back above .500. But in the strong AL West no club suffered a losing season, so the Royals again had to settle for sixth. When Tartabull left for the Yankees in 1992, the Royals faltered again. But as the West was now the weaker division, the club's 72-90 record was good enough for a fifth-place tie.

In the final season of his playing career at Kansas City, George Brett led his team in RBIs in 1993, and Kevin Appier led AL pitchers in ERA, as the Royals returned above .500 to finish third. Ewing Kauffman, the club's founder and owner, died in August, and Royals Stadium was renamed in his honor.

In 1994, after a sluggish first half, the Royals picked up the pace to challenge Chicago and Cleveland in the new American League Central division. At season's end, the Royals were still third but—thanks largely to Cy Young Award winner David Cone's 16-5 season—only four games behind first-place Chicago. Manager Bob Boone's Royals finished second again in 1995—but this time 30 games back of Cleveland. In 1996, playing on natural turf for the first time in Kauffman Stadium's history, the Royals finished last again (75-86, 24 games out).

The 1997 Royals had an eight-game losing streak heading into the All-Star Game; after the break they had a new manager, Tony Muser, and lost four more before they finally won in 14 innings. The Royals finished last, but Kansas City rebounded to finish third in 1998, despite losing Chili Davis and Jay Bell to free agency and seeing Kevin Appier miss most of the season with injuries.

The 1990s ended with the club's fifth consecutive losing season, but 2000 saw the Royals reach peak numbers offensively. Kansas City tied Cleveland for the American League's best batting average and had the most hits and the fewest strikeouts of any team in the league. Mike Sweeney was one of the game's most productive hitters, batting .333 and driving in a club-record 144 runs. Jermaine Dye, meanwhile, had 57 multi-hit games and Johnny Damon batted .327 with league highs in stolen bases (46) and runs scored (136). The team's fielding was among the best in the AL, but Kansas City's pitching was second from the bottom in ERA while also allowing the most home runs, walks, and wild pitches.

Los Angeles Dodgers

When the Dodgers left Brooklyn for Los Angeles, an era ended. From baseball's earliest days Brooklyn had been prominent; the city's Atlantics were the nation's best in the mid-1860s, and since 1884 Brooklyn had been home to major league ball. But before the start of the 1958 season, its link to the big time was severed by an owner who saw greener fields to the west.

The club's origins were modest. After winning the championship of the minor Inter-State Association in 1883, Brooklyn moved up to the major league American Association in 1884 and endured three losing seasons in its first four years. But in 1888, after signing three regulars from New York's newly defunct Mets and buying pitching/hitting stars Bob Caruthers and Dave Foutz from the AA champion St. Louis Browns, Brooklyn finished second to St. Louis, and the next year dethroned the Browns for their first big league pennant. In a World Series against the National League champion New York Giants, the Bridegrooms (as the Brooklyns had been nicknamed) won three of the first four games, but lost the next five.

Before the start of the 1890 season, Brooklyn transferred from the AA to the more prestigious NL. Many NL clubs performed below par that year, weakened by the loss of players to the outlaw Players League. But Brooklyn held on to most of its players and swept to its second straight pennant. In postseason play, poor weather and lack of fan support caused the World Series against AA winner Louisville to be called off after each team had won three games and tied one. The next year, with other NL teams renewed by players from the failed PL, Brooklyn finished sixth.

When the AA folded after the 1891 season, Brooklyn picked up slugger Dan Brouthers and pitcher George Haddock from pennant-winning Boston, and rebounded in 1892 to finish second and third in the two halves of a divided season. But for the next five years they finished no higher than fifth, and in 1898 sank to 10th in what was then a 12-team league.

Help was on the way, however. The owners of the Baltimore Orioles—Harry Von der Horst and Ned Hanlon—seeing an opportunity to move into the more lucrative Brooklyn market, purchased a half interest in the Bridegrooms. Hanlon retained his Baltimore presidency, but took over as manager in Brooklyn, bringing along with him the core of the Orioles—shortstop Hughie Jennings and outfielders Joe Kelley and Willie Keeler—plus his two best pitchers, Jim Hughes and Doc McJames.

The infusion of new talent worked wonders, as Brooklyn in 1899 (with a new nickname, the Superbas) took the NL lead in late May, during a 22-game winning streak, and held it the rest of the way. That winter, when Baltimore was dropped as the NL cut back from 12 teams to eight, Hanlon moved more Orioles to Brooklyn (including pitcher Joe "Iron Man" McGinnity), and once again led the Superbas to the pennant. That year they also won their first world championship in a series played with second-place Pittsburgh for the elegant Chronicle-Telegraph Cup.

Charley Ebbets, who had risen from ticket seller to president, took over majority ownership with the purchase of Von der Horst's stock, thereby quashing Hanlon's proposed move back to Baltimore. Ebbets' clashes with Hanlon hastened the club's decline. In 1903 the team began a 12-year sojourn in the second division, including a last-place finish in 1905 with their worst record ever (48-104, 56½ games out). Perhaps the most memorable events of these years were the change in nickname to Dodgers, and their move to brand-new Ebbets Field in 1913.

Hanlon was fired as manager after the disastrous 1905 season, but it was not until Wilbert Robinson took over in 1914 that the team began to pull out of its doldrums. Pitcher Jack Pfeffer, in his first full big-league season, won 23 games for the fifth-place Dodgers that year, and two years later led them to the pennant with 25 wins on a sparkling 1.92 ERA.

But the Dodgers lost the 1916 World Series to the Boston Red Sox, and in 1917 fell all the way to seventh. After three years in the second division, they bounced back in 1920, turning a three-way race into a rout with 16 wins in their final 18 games. After another World Series loss, to Cleveland, the Dodgers returned to the second division for another three years. In 1924 they began slowly, but leaped from 12 games back to an early-September lead, only to slip 1½ games behind the Giants at the finish.

Charley Ebbets died the following April, and Robinson was named to replace him. In his five years as president the club suffered on the field, finishing sixth each year. Fired as president but retained as manager, "Uncle Robby" saw his Robins (as the Dodgers were now known) lead the league in 1930 most of the time from mid-May to a mid-August decline, then retake the lead for a day in mid-September before tailing off once more to finish fourth. That was Uncle Robby's last hurrah. When the Robins provided no serious challenge in their fourth-place run the next year, he resigned after 18 years at the wheel.

A succession of managers followed, but it was not until the Dodgers brought in the free-spending Larry MacPhail as general manager in 1938 that the club began to pull itself back into contention. The highlight of MacPhail's first year with the Dodgers was not the team's finish (seventh) but the introduction of night baseball to Ebbets Field (on June 15, when Cincinnati's Johnny Vander Meer defeated Brooklyn with his second consecutive no-hitter).

MacPhail's most brilliant move may have been his conversion of shortstop Leo Durocher into manager Leo Durocher. The loud, driven Durocher alienated many (including MacPhail himself), but provided inspired leadership and a will to win that overcame complaints against him. After a third-place finish in 1939 and second place in 1940, the Dodgers battled the St. Louis Cardinals through all of 1941 before pulling ahead to clinch the pennant with just two games remaining. Veteran first baseman Dolf Camilli led the league in home runs and RBIs, sophomore outfielder Pete Reiser led the league in batting, slugging, and runs scored, and pitchers Kirby Higbe and Whitlow Wyatt tied for the league lead with 22 wins apiece, as the Dodgers won 100 games. Only their loss to the Yankees in the World Series marred their finest season in 42 years.

In 1942 they played even better, winning 104 games. But a late-season five-game slump dropped them behind the surging Cardinals. MacPhail and many of his players left for the war, and though the club finished third in 1943 and 1945, it was not until 1946 that the Dodgers again presented a serious challenge. Once again the Cards and Dodgers made a two-team race of it, but this time the race ended in a tie, forcing the first league playoff ever. St. Louis won the pennant with wins in the first two games.

When MacPhail left for the Army, Branch Rickey was hired to run the club. MacPhail had left the club financially sound; Rickey set about to make it a consistent winner. Famed as the developer of the Cardinals farm system, he was determined at Brooklyn to tap the one source of talent that the major leagues had willfully neglected: black players. He signed Jackie Robinson to Montreal (Brooklyn's leading farm team), and after a year there promoted him to the Dodgers for the 1947 season. Thus began the club's golden Brooklyn decade: 10 years in which they won six pennants and—in 1955—a World Series. Two other races went right to the wire; only once did they finish as low as third.

With manager Durocher suspended from baseball for a year for consorting with gamblers, the Dodgers in 1947 were led by grandfatherly Burt Shotton, brought out of his Florida retirement. Robinson's hustle put him at the top of the league in stolen bases and second in runs scored. The team pulled up from fourth in June to first in July, and held the lead to the end. In the World Series they lost to the Yankees in an exciting seven games.

Durocher returned to the helm in 1948, but was replaced by Shotton in midsummer, with the Dodgers in fifth place. Shotton saw the team rise to third that season, then battle back and forth with the Cardinals throughout 1949 before edging them by a game on the final day. Robinson, in his finest season, led the NL in hitting and stolen bases, and finished among the leaders in most other offensive categories. Rookie pitcher Don Newcombe led the team in victories with 17, and Preacher Roe led the league in winning percentage. Again the World Series was a loss to the Yankees, this time in only five games.

In 1950 the Dodgers nearly caught the staggering Phillies, losing out only in the 10th inning of the final game. President Rickey left the club for Pittsburgh and was replaced by Walter O'Malley, who replaced manager Shotton with Charlie Dressen. The slugging of catcher Roy Campanella and first baseman Gil Hodges, and 20-win seasons by Roe (22-3) and Newcombe (20-9) kept the Dodgers in front through most of 1951, but New York's surging Giants closed from 13 games back in August to tie for the lead at the finish. The teams split the first two playoff games. In Game 3 the Dodgers were leading by two runs in the last of the ninth when Bobby Thomson's three-run homer gave New York the flag.

The next year, though, the Giants fell short and Brooklyn took the pennant with relative ease. But not the World Series. Although Brooklyn held a 3-2 lead after five games, the Yankees came back to take the final two.

The Dodgers repeated as NL champions in 1953 with their best season ever. The Dodgers overwhelmed the league, hitting 19 points and slugging 63 points above the league average, as the team outscored its nearest rival by more than a run per game. With a club-record 105 wins, the Dodgers cruised to the pennant by 13 games. But again the Yankees took the World Series, in six games.

Dressen wanted a three-year contract and was let go when he turned down another for only one year. Minor league manager Walter Alston wasn't so demanding, and signed for 1954 the first of a historic string of 23 one-year Dodger contracts that would see him into the Hall of Fame. After a second-place finish in Alston's rookie season, the Dodgers in 1955 took the lead from the start and—never challenged—walked away with their 11th pennant. Outfielder Duke Snider, with one of his most productive seasons, led the league's most powerful squad; Newcombe (20-5) paced the league's best pitching staff.

Once more in the World Series, Brooklyn faced the Yankees, and once more the Series went seven games. But this time there was joy in Brooklyn—Johnny Podres shut out New York in the finale! In an exciting three-way fight in 1956, the Dodgers repeated as pennant-winners, taking their final three games to edge the Milwaukee Braves. Newcombe, in his greatest year, clinched the flag on the final day with his 27th win. In the World Series, though, it was deja vu time—a sixth Yankee triumph, in seven games. The golden decade was over.

The Dodgers (despite the league's best pitching) vacated the 1957 race in August, finishing third. Before the start of the next season, they had vacated Brooklyn as well, for Los Angeles. Playing in Memorial Coliseum (a converted football stadium) the L.A. Dodgers sank to seventh place in 1958. But the next year the reawakened bats of aging Duke Snider and Gil Hodges, the fiery pitching of young Don Drysdale, and the late-season pitching heroics of Roger Craig (recalled from Spokane) kept the team in the thick of a tight race that found them tied with the Braves at season's end. The Dodgers won the first playoff game in Milwaukee, and captured big league baseball's first West Coast pennant at home the next day, in the 12th inning. Then they defeated the Chicago White Sox to give the West its first World Series winner.

After finishes of fourth and second, the Dodgers produced record-breaking excitement in 1962 as they moved into brand-new Dodger Stadium in the hills above Los Angeles. Between the new ballpark and the excitement generated on the field, more than 2.75 million fans passed through the turnstiles—a new attendance record that would last until the Dodgers themselves broke it 15 years later. As pitcher Don Drysdale and left fielder Tommy Davis ignited the league with career-high seasons, and shortstop Maury Wills became the first major leaguer of the century to steal 100 bases, the team locked into a season-long struggle for first place with archrival San Francisco. But after holding a narrow lead much of the season, the Dodgers dropped their last four games to finish in yet another tie. The playoff must have reminded fans of 1951. As they had then, the Giants and Dodgers split the first two games, and the Dodgers once again brought a 4-2 lead into the ninth inning of the third game. This time, though, it was not a home run that undid them, but a bases-loaded walk.

Sandy Koufax—who had won 14 games in 1962 (and the first of five straight ERA crowns) despite losing half the year with circulation problems in his fingers—rose to dominate the world of pitching the next four years. For three of those years his Dodgers dominated the NL. In

1963 Koufax's 25-5 season carried Los Angeles into the World Series against the Yankees, where two more wins helped put the New Yorkers away in the minimum four games. The next year Koufax slipped to 19 wins, but the Dodgers fell all the way to a tie for sixth.

They rebounded to the top in 1965. Koufax won 26 and Drysdale 23 in a tight four-team race that saw them fall behind the Giants in early September, only to retake the lead for good later in the month with 13 straight wins. The World Series against Minnesota went to the seventh game before Koufax nailed down another world title with his second shutout in three days.

The race in 1966 was just as close as in '65, with three teams switching leads throughout the season. But the Dodgers, third at the end of August, put together streaks of five and seven wins in September to move to the top, where Koufax clinched the pennant on the final day with his 27th victory. And then it was all over. After a losing effort in Game 2 of the World Series (a Baltimore sweep), Koufax, at age 30, retired because of arthritis in his pitching elbow. The Dodgers sank to eighth the next year and rose only to seventh in 1968.

In 1969, the first season of divisional play, Los Angeles found itself in the thick of a five-team race in the West until eight straight losses in late September dropped them to fourth. No one challenged Cincinnati in 1970, but the next year the Dodgers closed to within a game of the front-running Giants in September before their drive stalled.

A late-season slump let Cincinnati get to the top in 1973, but the Dodgers held their lead to the end in 1974. Newly acquired veteran outfielder Jimmy Wynn and first baseman Steve Garvey, in his first full season, led the club offensively; pitcher Mike Marshall set a modern major league record with 106 appearances in relief of a staff that was the league's best (which earned him the Cy Young Award). The Dodgers beat Pittsburgh handily in the National League Championship Series for their fifth Los Angeles pennant, but lost the World Series to Oakland in five games.

Cincinnati proved untouchable in 1975 and '76, but in 1977 the Dodgers—under new manager Tom Lasorda, who moved up from the coaching staff when Alston retired—jumped to an early lead and held it all the way. Garvey's 33 home runs led a balanced offense in which four players hit 30 or more homers. Again the Dodgers won the NLCS (in four games, against Philadelphia), and again they lost the World Series (to the Yankees, in six games).

Although the divisional race was closer—and the Dodgers broke baseball's 3 million attendance barrier for the first time—1978 was in most respects a replay of 1977. Garvey again led the club offensively, the Dodgers again beat out Cincinnati in the West and Philadelphia in a four-game NLCS, and the Yankees again defeated the Dodgers in a six-game World Series.

A season-long back-and-forth battle with Houston in 1980 ended in a tie for first—the fifth tie for the Dodgers, three more than any other club. In the playoff (reduced from three games to one to bring the NL into line with AL practice), Houston won easily.

When the players went out on strike part way through 1981, the Dodgers, paced by the spectacular pitching of rookie Fernando Valenzuela, found themselves half a game in front of Cincinnati. In a special playoff with Houston, the winner of the NL West second half of the split season, the Dodgers defeated the Astros in five games for the division title, and also went the distance in beating Montreal for the pennant. Facing the Yankees for the 11th time in World Series play, they lost the first two games, but swept the next four to capture their sixth world title.

In 1982, after a poor start, the Dodgers fought back to take the lead in August and again in September before dropping back to second, a game out. More successful drives in 1983 and '85 led to their fifth and sixth division titles, but culminated in defeat in the NLCS—to Philadelphia in 1983 and St. Louis two years later.

In 1988, with an infusion of talent from the American League—most notably slugger Kirk Gibson and relief ace Jay Howell—and a spectacular season from starter Orel Hershiser (who concluded his 23-8 year with a major-league record 59 consecutive scoreless innings), the Dodgers bounced back to the top of the NL West. It took them the full seven games to down the favored Mets in the NLCS, but in the World Series they humbled Oakland's powerful Athletics in just five games for their seventh world crown. Kirk Gibson's pinch-hit two-run homer in the bottom of the ninth off Dennis Eckersley in Game 1 was the turning point of the series. A panel of local experts later selected the home run by the gimpy Gibson as the greatest moment in Los Angeles sports history.

Led by Hershiser (whose 15-15 record belied another strong season) the Dodgers yielded the fewest runs in the NL in 1989. A lack of offense, however, left the team no better than fourth. Hershiser underwent shoulder surgery in April 1991, but young Ramon Martinez picked up the slack and won 20 games for the second-place Dodgers.

From early May to late August 1991, the Dodgers occupied first place in their division, paced by the majors' stingiest pitching staff and the hot bats of free agent signees Brett Butler and Darryl Strawberry. Seven straight losses after the All-Star break began the team's descent into a great struggle with ascendant Atlanta. From Aug. 21 through season's end the two clubs stayed within two games of each other. With four games to go, Los Angeles held a one-game lead. But they lost their next three games, and all hope of the division crown.

In 1992 everything fell apart. Unable to parry the twin blows of injury and inexperience, the Dodgers stumbled to the worst record in the majors, and finished last for only the second time in their 109 years of major league play. Rookie catcher Mike Piazza burst upon the scene in 1993 to rank among NL leaders in batting, slugging, home runs, and RBIs, as the Dodgers recovered to finish in fourth place. A final-game victory over San Francisco brought their season record to .500, and deprived the Giants of a tie for the division title.

Japanese rookie sensation Hideo Nomo paced the NL with 236 strikeouts in 1995 and led the Dodgers to the NL West title—by just one game over the power-hitting Colorado Rockies. But in the first round of the postseason, Los Angeles fell to Cincinnati in three straight.

In mid-1996 a heart attack felled Lasorda, and he handed over the club's reins to Bill Russell. Mike Piazza (.344, 36 HR, 105 RBIs,), Eric Karros (34 HR, 121 RBIs), and Raul Mondesi (.297, 24 HR) led the offense. Outfielder Todd Hollandsworth (.291) became the fifth consecutive Dodger to win NL Rookie of the Year honors. Ramon Martinez (15-6), Ismael Valdes (15-7), Hideo Nomo (16-11, 234 strikeouts), and Todd Worrell (44 saves) paced a staff that led the majors with a 3.46 ERA. Los Angeles (90-72) lost the West Division title to San Diego on the final day of the season but achieved a postseason berth via the Wild Card route. The 1996 Dodgers faced Atlanta in the playoffs and met the same fate as the 1995 team had at the hands of the Reds: a humiliating three-game sweep.

The Dodgers, the model of stability in baseball for decades, underwent huge changes over the next two years. First, major league owners grudgingly approved Rupert Murdoch and the Fox Corporation as the new owners of the team. Then, the team traded its biggest star, Mike Piazza, after he turned down a sizeable contract offer from the Dodgers. The trade, which brought Bobby Bonilla, Gary Sheffield, and Charles Johnson from the Marlins, was made by Fox executives and didn't go through general manager Fred Claire. Russell and Claire were both dismissed soon after and were replaced by minor-league manager Glenn Hoffman and Tommy Lasorda, who returned as interim GM. The Dodgers ended the season in third place, their lowest finish since 1993. Kevin Malone was hired as full-time general manager late in 1998 and Davey Johnson became the team's third manager in six months after the franchise had just two managers from 1954 to 1996. To cap off the changes, they signed Kevin Brown to a seven-year, $105 million contract.

The new-look Dodgers were a disappointment in 1999. Los Angeles won just 77 games, the fewest wins ever by one of Johnson's clubs over a full season, and, after Brown, the club's vaunted pitching looked ordinary. The Dodgers finished the 20th century behind only the Yankees and Giants for overall wins, but they began the 21st century a distant second in both the NL West and Wild Card standings. The pitching staff returned to form—including an ERA title by Brown and an outstanding year by Chan Ho Park—but the Dodgers batted just .257 and left more runners on base than any other club in the league. Despite a strong finish, aided by Gary Sheffield's .325 average and 43 home runs, Johnson was replaced with coach Jim Tracy at season's end.

Milwaukee Brewers

When in 1969 the new Seattle Pilots played their home opener in the refurbished minor league Sick's Stadium, 7,000 seats and the left field fence were still unfinished. The Pilots may not have needed the seats. Fewer than 700,000 fans came to see them play—the third-worst attendance in the league—as they drifted into the cellar of the American League West with 98 losses. (In fact the most memorable thing about that season was a controversial book, *Ball Four,* by Pilots pitcher Jim Bouton.). That winter the Pilots—renamed the Brewers—moved to Milwaukee, where a genuine big league stadium (vacated by the Braves five years earlier) awaited them.

Attendance improved nearly 38 percent in Milwaukee, although the Brewers of 1970 won only one game more than the Pilots had in Seattle. It would be eight more years before they experienced their first winning season. Meanwhile, in 1972, they switched divisions from West to East, trading places with the Washington Senators, who moved West to become the Texas Rangers. Hank Aaron came to the Brewers in 1975 to finish his career where it had started in 1954 (with the Milwaukee Braves), but Aaron's presence helped the club at the gate more than in the standings.

The Brewers broke their losing pattern in 1978. One key front-office move leading to the turnaround was the signing of free agent Larry Hisle (who the previous year with Minnesota had led the league in RBIs). Hisle proved his worth in 1978, leading an offense that sprang to life under rookie manager George Bamberger to top the league in hitting, slugging, homers, and runs scored. On the mound Mike Caldwell won 22 games in the best season of his career. Although the Brewers never threatened the Boston Red Sox or the New York Yankees for the lead, they did rise from below .500 in early June to finish a solid third, 24 games above .500.

A shoulder injury the next April marked the beginning of the end of Hisle's career and perhaps cost Milwaukee the division title. Even without him the team compiled what is still their best winning percentage (.590), as outfielder Gorman Thomas (45 home runs, 123 RBIs) and several other hitters attained new career peaks of productivity. While they never seriously threatened front-running Baltimore, they rose past Boston in late August to finish second.

Most of the Milwaukee bats remained hot in 1980, but injuries, ragged pitching, and Bamberger's heart attack (which caused him to miss the first part of the season and retire in early September) contributed to a distant third-place finish. In strike-divided 1981, league-leading performances by two newly acquired pitchers—starter Pete Vuckovich (14-4) and reliever Rollie Fingers (28 saves)—helped give the Brewers the best overall record in the AL East, and the second-half championship. But in the special intradivisional playoffs with first-half winner New York, the Yankees captured the division crown three games to two.

The Brewers started slowly in 1982; at the end of May they were two games below .500, near the bottom of the division. A day later Buck Rodgers, the Milwaukee coach who had replaced Bamberger as manager two years earlier, was himself replaced by coach Harvey Kuenn. By mid-July the team had risen to first place, and they led the West by more than six games as September neared. Baltimore had cut the lead to three games by the time Milwaukee arrived for the season's final four games. One win would give the Brewers their first division championship, but they lost the first three games by five, six, and eight runs. Don Sutton, who had been acquired from Houston a month earlier, faced Oriole Jim Palmer in the season finale: the Brewers took the division title with a 10-2 win.

Milwaukee's offense—"Harvey's Wallbangers"—had been awesome, scoring more than a run per game above the league average. Just about every offensive category featured one or two Brewers among the league's top three: in hits they took all three top spots. Shortstop Robin Yount, who finished first in slugging, hits, total bases, and doubles, was named major league player of the year.

In postseason play California took a 2-0 lead in the ALCS, but Milwaukee came back to take the final three games and the pennant. In the World Series against St. Louis, the Brewers twice took the lead in games, but the Cardinals scored the last five runs of Game 7 to win the Series.

Milwaukee dropped to fifth in 1983, then to a last-place seventh the next year, 36½ games back. It was not until 1987 that they returned to the winning track, finishing third with 91 victories. As veterans Robin Yount and Paul Molitor continued to spark the team's offense, and starter Ted Higuera and reliever Dan Plesac headlined the AL East's best pitching staff, the Brewers in 1988 rose above .500 to stay at the end of August, and finished in a tie for third, just two games behind champion Boston. With Yount and Molitor enjoying even more productive seasons in 1989, and reliever Plesac on a club-record pace for saves, the Brewers drew within half a game of first place in August. But injuries and league-worst fielding took their toll, and the club finished fourth, right at .500. In 1990, as poor fielding led to more than 100 unearned runs, the Brewers dropped to sixth.

Paul Molitor enjoyed a banner season in 1991, and, from the first week in August to the finish, the Brewers played at a torrid .750 clip. But they had begun their comeback 15 games behind, and too late to raise themselves more than one place in the standings. With another sterling season from Molitor in 1992, plus Robin Yount's milestone 3,000th hit, and another strong finish (after a better first half), Milwaukee drew within two games of ultimately victorious Toronto in the season's final week. Still, the Brewers' 92-70 record and second-place finish were their best since their pennant-winning season a decade earlier. In 1993, though, free agent Molitor departed for Toronto, sparking the Blue Jays' run for a second straight world championship as the Brewers fell into the AL East cellar, 26 games behind the Jays.

In 1994 the Brewers were one of five clubs inserted into the AL's new Central Division, thus becoming the only club to play in three different divisions. They finished last once again, dropping behind Minnesota just three days before the season concluded in August. Only marginal improvement occurred in 1995 as manager Phil Garner's Brewers finished fourth (65-79). In 1996, despite slugger Greg Vaughn's midseason departure to San Diego, Milwaukee moved up to third (80-82) thanks to Dave Nilsson (.331) and Mike Fetters (32 saves).

The 1997 Brewers pulled within 2½ games of first-place Cleveland on Sept. 2, but faded to eight games back by season's end. Garner, the Brewers' all-time winningest manager, guided the team to fifth place in the first league switch of the century. Because of the addition of a new team to each league in 1998, it was decided that one existing team had to switch leagues to make both leagues have an even number of teams for scheduling purposes. Milwaukee, which had been home to the Braves from 1953-1965, returned to the National League with a game between the Brewers and, fittingly, the Braves in Atlanta on March 31. Bud Selig, who had been acting commissioners since 1992, put his shares of the Brewers in a trust and handed ownership of the club to his daughter when he was officially named commissioner in 1998.

Davey Lopes replaced Garner as manager, and Dean Taylor followed Sal Bando as general manager while the Brewers set about rebuilding in 2000. A trade with Cleveland brought slugger Richie Sexson, who combined with Geoff Jenkins to give Milwaukee some pop in a batting order with the league's lowest batting average and on-base percentage. County Stadium, which remained open a year longer than planned because of a fatal crane accident at the new ballpark site, hosted its final game 47 years after major league baseball was played there for the first time.

Minnesota Twins

The Twins' beginnings as the Washington Senators were inauspicious. When American League president Ban Johnson established the Senators as part of his move in 1901 to raise the league to major league status, he staffed it with the manager and many of the players from his disbanded Kansas City franchise. Within a decade, four of the eight teams in the new major league had won two or more pennants, and three others had enjoyed at least one season in second place. But the Senators, after sixth-place finishes in their first two seasons, spent the next nine years in seventh or eighth.

Even the arrival of promising young fireballer Walter Johnson didn't seem to help. By 1909 he was the league's second-best strikeout artist, but he lost 25 games and the Senators finished farther back than ever—56 games from the top. Johnson turned his record around the next two years, winning 25 games in 1910 and in 1911, but the team rose only to seventh.

When Clark Griffith—a 42-year-old former pitching great and one of the founders of the American League—was hired to manage the Senators after the 1911 season, the club's fortunes took an immediate turn for the better. Griffith revamped the lineup—most strikingly in the acquisition of first baseman Chick Gandil from minor league Montreal. The Senators in 1912 won 17 straight games after Gandil was put into the lineup, and found themselves in the midst of a pennant race. The Boston Red Sox eventually ran away from the field, but the Senators held off Philadelphia for second place. Johnson won 33 games, and his 1.39 ERA led the league.

The next season was Johnson's finest. His league-leading 36 wins, 11 shutouts, and 1.14 ERA were also career bests and enabled Washington to overtake Cleveland late in the season for another second-place finish. But while Johnson continued to top 20 wins per season for several years before beginning to fade, his team was unable to stay competitive.

Griffith wanted the Senators to spend more to attract good players; when his demands were rejected, he bought a controlling interest in the club and named himself president. A year later, in 1921, he retired as field manager. Under a succession of veteran player-managers the team showed some improvement over the next three years, but Griffith's surprise appointment of 27-year-old second baseman Bucky Harris to manage the team in 1924 worked wonders. Left fielder Goose Goslin drove in more runs than Babe Ruth, and Walter Johnson put together his best season in years to head the league's best pitching staff. A hot streak in June shot the team from fifth to first, and a strong stretch drive in August and September brought home their first pennant. In the World Series a ground ball's lucky bounce over the head of the Giants' third baseman brought the Senators victory in the last of the 12th inning of the seventh game.

Though the Senators, aided by the acquisition of veteran pitcher Stan Coveleski from Cleveland, fought off the A's to repeat as pennant winners in 1925, they were less successful in postseason play. Once again the Series went the full seven games, but this time Pittsburgh won the world title.

The Senators enjoyed winning seasons in five of the next seven years, as Johnson retired from the mound and replaced Harris as manager. But it was not until 1933, when Johnson was replaced by 26-year-old shortstop Joe Cronin, that the team again pursued the pennant beyond midseason. Two veteran pitchers at the top of their form—Alvin "General" Crowder and Earl Whitehill—and a balanced offense led by Cronin and first baseman Joe Kuhel kept the Senators close to New York through July, and then, as the Yankees leveled off in August, shot the team up out of reach. Although they tailed off a bit at the end, the Senators won the pennant handily, compiling a .651 winning percentage that is still the club record. The New York Giants, though, took Washington's measure in the World Series and overcame them in five games.

The following October a drop from third place in June to a distant seventh at season's end had plunged home attendance nearly 25 percent below the previous year. With finances always a problem in Washington, Griffith traded Joe Cronin, his manager, star shortstop, and (since September) son-in-law, to the Boston Red Sox for a lesser shortstop and $225,000.

Only twice in their remaining quarter century in Washington did the Senators rise higher than fourth or finish closer than 17 games from the top. In 1943 they placed second, 13½ games behind the runaway Yankees. And two years later, after a poor start, they caught up with frontrunner Detroit in September, only to stall and finish one and a half games out. The Senators finished in the cellar in four of their last six seasons in Washington.

Calvin Griffith, Clark's adopted son, assumed the club presidency when his father died in 1955. Within three years he was making plans to move the club to Minneapolis. There were threats from Congress and a plea from President Eisenhower not to move the Senators—and at first the league itself opposed the move. But Washington was not a good baseball town even when the Senators were playing well, and in October 1960 a solution was reached. The league would let Griffith move his club to Minnesota, and Washington would be granted a new expansion team.

Players like outfielders Bob Allison and Harmon Killebrew, and pitcher Camilo Pascual, who had enjoyed productive seasons before the move, were even more productive at Metropolitan Stadium in Minnesota. Other standouts became regulars or joined the club after the move—Zoilo Versalles at shortstop, Rich Rollins at third, Jim Kaat on the mound, and (arriving in 1964) outfielder Tony Oliva and pitcher Jim "Mudcat" Grant. Infielder Rod Carew began a remarkable 12-year stint with the Twins in 1967.

Former outfielder Sam Mele made his major league managerial debut during 1961, and in 1962 saw his Twins come close to catching the Yankees in mid-September, finishing second. The next year they didn't catch fire until August and wound up third. In 1964 they dropped below .500 into a tie for sixth. But after the end of June 1965 no one challenged them as they breezed to their first Minnesota pennant. Oliva led the league in batting for the second straight year, and Versalles (in what was far and away his finest season) led the league in total bases and runs scored. Mudcat Grant led the league with 21 victories (his only 20-win season) and six shutouts, and Kaat's 18 wins were the league's third best. In the World Series it took a three-hitter by Los Angeles' Sandy Koufax to stop the Twins in the seventh game.

After a poor start in 1966 that saw them enter July deep in fifth place, the Twins played better than anyone else the rest of the season to sneak ahead of Detroit into second. Killebrew, who had been injured much of the previous year, returned with his old power in '66, and Kaat enjoyed a career-high season with 25 wins.

The Twins began 1967 with another poor start. With the team in disarray and in sixth place, the easygoing Mele was replaced in June by hard-driving Cal Ermer, a longtime minor league manager. By mid-July the team had risen to second, and a month later (after dropping back to fourth) moved to the top in one of the greatest pennant races ever. Four clubs battled for the title, with three still in the running on the final day. But Boston defeated Minnesota to win the pennant, and Detroit split a doubleheader to tie the Twins for second. The next year Minnesota finished seventh.

Fiery rookie manager Billy Martin replaced Ermer in 1969 and, in this first season of divisional play, piloted the Twins to the championship of the West. Killebrew exploded for the best season of his career (49 home runs, 140 runs driven in), and Carew won the first of his seven batting titles. The first American League Championship Series, though, was a disaster for the Twins as Baltimore swept to the pennant in three games. Veteran manager Bill Rigney replaced the difficult Martin at the helm, and piloted Minnesota to an almost identical division crown in 1970, again by a nine-game margin. Pitcher Jim Perry, with 24 victories, enjoyed his second straight 20-win season, and the best of his career. The ALCS, though, was another repeat performance—a Baltimore sweep.

For the next 13 years the Twins remained out of contention; it was not until the flowering of a new generation of young players in 1984 that a Minnesota title threat could be taken seriously.

The Twins' decline on the field was matched by a decline in attendance, which even their move indoors to the Hubert H. Humphrey Metrodome in 1982 did not significantly redress. The Griffith family, unwilling to risk the high cost of luring proven talent, decided to give up the club after more than 60 years of family ownership. Early in 1984 a buyer was found in Carl Pohlad, a wealthy Minneapolis banker. By the time Pohlad's purchase was completed at the end of July, the Twins' young team had blossomed into the West's front-runner, paced by pitcher Frank Viola's sudden development into a winner, and by the arrival in May of rookie centerfield sparkplug Kirby Puckett. Although the Twins leveled off in August and lost their final six games, to fall to .500 and a tie for second, they had brought the crowds back to the ballpark. The 1984 team drew more than 1.5 million fans for the first time ever and remained well above a million the next two years despite a pair of losing seasons.

In 1987, under manager Tom Kelly, the Minnesota fans were rewarded for their faithfulness. Although the Twins lost their last five games to finish only eight above .500, their winning record at home was the best in the league, and their title in the West was never in doubt. More surprising was their decisive triumph over favored Detroit in the ALCS, four games to one. In the first World Series to feature indoor play, the Twins won the four games played in their Metrodome to capture Minnesota's first baseball world championship in seven games.

Although the Twins in 1988 improved on their 1987 won-lost record—and Frank Viola, Kirby Puckett, and relief ace Jeff Reardon enjoyed career peaks—they finished well back of Oakland in the race for the division crown. But their home attendance, which had jumped 66 percent in 1987 to top 2 million for the first time, bounded another 45 percent in 1988 to make the Twins the first AL club ever to attract more than 3 million fans in a season.

As the team suffered a general decline in pitching and hitting in 1989, Viola—in the middle of a disappointing season—was traded to the Mets; and the Twins finished fifth. Reardon, a free agent, left for Boston after the season. The Twins continued their downhill slide in 1990, slipping from fifth place at midseason to their first cellar finish in eight years.

On May 27, 1991, the Twins stood sixth in the AL West. Three weeks later, after winning 18 of 19 games, they were first. There they finished, becoming (like Atlanta in the NL) the first AL team to rise from last place to first in successive seasons. Minnesota's attack featured a balanced offense in which seven players drove in 50 runs or more, and a pitching revival that starred veteran free agent Jack Morris and a pair of young hurlers with their first big seasons, Scott Erickson (who won 12 in a row before the end of June) and Kevin Tapani (16-9, 2.99 ERA). In the ALCS, the Twins overcame Toronto in five games, then came back from a 3-2 World Series deficit to defeat Atlanta with a pair of extra-inning victories, including a 10-inning win in Game 7 as Morris pitched the shutout and Gene Larkin drove in the only run.

After his single starring season in Minnesota, Morris moved on to Toronto to hurl the Blue Jays into the championship. The Twins, meanwhile, arrived at midseason-1992 first in the AL West, where they remained into early August before drifting back into a second-place finish behind Oakland. Veteran superstar Dave Winfield left Toronto for Minnesota in 1993, where in September he passed the 3,000 hit mark. But the Twins slid out of contention early, and finished tied for fifth.

In early August 1994, now playing in the new Central Division, they finished fourth. In 1995 the Twins tied Toronto for the majors' worst record (56-88) and saw attendance drop 38 percent from the previous season. Among the few bright spots were Chuck Knoblauch (.333) and AL Rookie of the Year Marty Cordova (24 HR, 84 RBIs, .277).

Minnesota rebounded back to fourth (78-84) in 1996, helped largely by the efforts of Knoblauch and Paul Molitor (.341 and an AL-best 225 hits). Molitor, a Minnesota native, recorded his 3,000th hit during the season, and became the first player in history to reach the milestone with a triple. The season was also tinged with sadness as Puckett officially retired due to glaucoma.

Brad Radke was the brightest spot for Minnesota in 1997. He tied a club record with wins in 12 consecutive starts and became the team's first 20-game winner since 1991. Solid pitching bolstered the Twins in the first half of 1998, but the club slipped to fourth in the AL Central in the second half.

Twins southpaw Eric Milton pitched the last no-hitter of the 20th century on September 1, 1999. The following year Cristian Guzman led the major leagues with 20 triples and also stole 28 bases as the Twins tried to make up for a lack of power with speed. Despite some emerging young players, the Twins finished with the American League's worst record in both 1999 and 2000.

Montreal Expos

In the spring of 1969, in an unfinished "temporary" ballpark that would be the Expos' home for eight years, major league baseball came to Canada. One of two clubs added to the National League in this first year of divisional play—Montreal in the East and San Diego in the West—the Expos finished 48 games out of first. Although they matched San Diego's 52-110 record and last-place divisional finish, they outdrew the Padres by better than two to one, with a home attendance of more than 1.2 million fans.

After a second last-place (but much improved at 73-89) season in 1970, the Expos moved a notch out of the cellar to fifth in 1971 and '72, and into pennant contention in 1973. Outfielder Ken Singleton became the first Expo to drive in 100 or more runs, rookie pitcher Steve Rogers compiled a sparkling 1.54 ERA, and reliever Mike Marshall set a new major-league record with 92 pitching appearances (winning 14 games and saving a league-high 31). In the tightest race of the century, all six clubs remained in contention into September, when Philadelphia dropped away. In mid-September Montreal won six straight to catch front-running Pittsburgh, but the Expos finished the season in fourth place, three and a half games behind the champion New York Mets.

Center fielder Willie Davis (acquired from Los Angeles in a trade for Mike Marshall) led the Expos' offense in another fourth-place season in 1974. The club sank back to a tie for last in 1975 and sole possession of the cellar a year later, with a 55-107 record nearly as bad as their first season (and a home attendance little more than half that of 1969).

But with the acquisition of heavy-hitting Tony Perez from Cincinnati, a new manager—the controversial Dick Williams—and strong seasons from catcher Gary Carter, sophomore outfielder Ellis Valentine, and rookie Andre Dawson, the club snapped back in 1977 to win 20 more games than the previous year and rise to fifth. And with their move into the new Olympic Stadium (built for the 1976 Olympics), attendance rebounded from a club low to a new high.

After climbing another notch to fourth in 1978 (as the

newly acquired Ross Grimsley became their first—and, to date, only—20-game winner), the Expos put on a run for the title that drove attendance in 1979 to over 2 million. Third baseman Larry Parrish, with a career-high season, led the club in batting and home runs in a balanced attack that saw five players drive in more than 70 runs. The pitching too was balanced, with six pitchers winning 10 games or more on a staff that compiled the league's lowest ERA. With a fast start in April, the Expos led the East through much of June and into July, when a surging Pittsburgh caught up with them. Both clubs climbed away from the pack to the end of the season. Montreal fell back a bit in August but caught up with the Pirates in September and carried the race to the final day before dropping off to second.

The 1980 race was just as exciting. A three-way struggle with Philadelphia and Pittsburgh through most of the summer narrowed to two teams in September as the Pirates fell away. In a crucial late-September series, the Expos beat the Phillies two games of three to take a half-game lead, but in the final series a week later Philadelphia won two games to clinch the crown.

In a 1981 season divided by a players' strike, Montreal finished the first part of the season in third place, but held off St. Louis to win the second part by half a game. The Expos then won the division championship in a special playoff with first-half winner Philadelphia—their first title—but lost the National League Championship Series to Los Angeles.

As the Expos declined gradually over the next five years, most of the regulars left through trade, free agency, or retirement. But in 1987, two 1981 rookies who had remained in Montreal—outfielder Tim Raines and third baseman Tim Wallach—helped lead the Expos to third place, just four games back, with 91 wins.

Strong midsummer surges in 1988 and 1989 propelled the Expos into the thick of the race in the NL East, in 1989 lifting them into the lead for six straight weeks following the acquisition from Seattle of mound ace Mark Langston. But in both years, late-season slumps dropped the club to identical 81-81 finishes. In 1990 strong pitching (despite the loss of free agents Langston, Bryn Smith, and Pascual Perez) kept the Expos competitive well into September before they fell out of the race.

The collapse of a huge cement beam at Olympic Stadium in September 1991—which forced the Expos to play all their remaining games on the road—was emblematic of the team's collapse into the cellar with their worst record in 15 years. But the club revived in 1992 under new manager Felipe Alou, who was promoted from coach in late May. The Expos rose from fifth place to second behind the pitching of Ken Hill and veteran ace Dennis Martinez, and the offensive leadership of right fielder Larry Walker. The Expos finished an even closer second in 1993, just three games behind Philadelphia, with a record of 94-68. On Aug. 7, 1994, pitcher Hill moved into the NL lead with his 16th win of the season. Walker and Moises Alou—manager Felipe's son—dueled for the club's offensive leadership. Montreal stood atop the mountain with the best record in the majors. Five days later, the season was over when the players went on strike.

Even though the club fell to last (66-78) in 1995, the club turned a $40,000 profit—a dramatic turnaround from 1994 when due to the strike the club lost an estimated $15.9 million. Helping the Expos balance sheet was the modesty of their payroll—just $10 million. The Expos (88-74) challenged for a postseason berth in 1996 but fell short in the final week despite the efforts of Henry Rodriguez (36 HR, 103 RBIs), Mark Grudzielanek (.306, 201 hits), Jeff Fassero (15-11, 222 strikeouts), and Mel Rojas (36 saves).

Pedro Martinez became the first Expos pitcher to win the NL Cy Young Award in 1997. He was the first pitcher to combine 300 strikeouts and an ERA below 2.00. since Steve Carlton in 1972, but it was a bittersweet year for Montreal. Escalating salaries forced the Expos to trade Martinez as well as second baseman Mike Lansing and to allow first baseman David Segui, catcher Darrin Fletcher, and outfielder Henry Rodriguez to leave as free agents.

The 1998 Expos spent most of the season in fourth place, but Vladimir Guerrero established club records in several categories while Ugueth Urbina emerged as one of the league's top closers. General manager Jim Beattie signed both players to long-term contracts. After the season, just when it seemed like Felipe Alou would reluctantly leave the team, Beattie was able to sign his manager as well.

Jeffrey Loria took over as chairman of the franchise in 1999, but the team's future in Montreal remained clouded during a horrific 2000 season. Free agent Graeme Lloyd and high-priced acquisition Hideki Irabu both spent most of the season on the disabled list, as did several other members of the pitching staff. The Expos stood at 31-23 on June 5, yet the club won just 25 games between them—topped off with a nine-game losing streak to end the year. The bright spots for the Expos were found in the middle of the lineup. Vladimir Guerrero had another outstanding season and broke his own team records with a .345 average and 44 home runs, while second baseman Jose Vidro hit .330 with 24 homers and 97 RBIs.

New York Mets

Branch Rickey's projected Continental League never materialized, but its New York and Houston franchises were admitted to the National League, expanding the league to 10 clubs in 1962. Few major league teams have been as inept as the New York Mets were in their first season. Despite the presence of such New York favorites as manager Casey Stengel, pitcher Roger Craig, and first baseman Gil Hodges, and of players like outfielders Richie Ashburn and Frank Thomas who were still near peak form, the Mets finished at the bottom of the league in batting, fielding, and pitching. They won only one game in four and suffered a 20th-century record 120 losses.

New York fans—deprived of National League baseball since the defection of the Dodgers and Giants to the West Coast four years earlier—found their ineptitude lovable. By their third season, having moved out of the old Polo Grounds into brand-new Shea Stadium, the last-place Mets were regularly outdrawing the pennant-bound Yankees.

Former New York Giants catcher Wes Westrum replaced the aging Stengel as manager part way through the 1965 season, and the next year saw the club rise out of the cellar for the first time. They fell back to 10th in 1967 (despite rookie Tom Seaver's 16 wins), and Westrum was replaced at the helm by Gil Hodges. With Jerry Koosman joining Seaver in the starting rotation and setting a new club record with 19 victories, Hodges led the Mets in 1968 back up to ninth place with their first season of more than 70 victories.

In 1969 the majors inaugurated divisional play, but the Mets got off to their usual indifferent start. At the end of May, however, they began to win consistently. By early June they were second in the NL East, though well back of the explosive Chicago Cubs. By September, though, the Cubs were faltering. The "Miracle Mets" caught and passed them with a 10-game winning streak and continued on to take the division title. In Tom Seaver's Hall of Fame career, it was probably his finest season. He won his last 10 starts, sparking the team's final push to triumph, and finished with a league-high 25 wins that still stands as the club record. After a three-game sweep of West champion Atlanta in the league's first Championship Series, the Mets faced the mighty Baltimore Orioles—regarded by many as one of baseball's all-time greatest teams—for the world championship. The Met miracle continued; after an opening game loss, the New Yorkers humbled the Orioles with four straight wins.

The Mets of 1970 remained competitive into mid-September as they sought to repeat their '69 triumph. But they fell back at the end while Pittsburgh spurted, and finished third. Just before the start of the 1972 season, coach Yogi Berra moved up to manage the club after Hodges suffered a fatal heart attack two days before his 48th birthday.

In 1973 the NL East experienced the tightest major league race of the century. Chicago moved out in front of the pack early in the season, but folded in July and August. So did the Mets, who fell from third to a last-place sixth. Although the Mets were last in late August, they were less than seven games out of first. A series of bursts in September, culminating in a seven-game winning streak, shot the Mets through the division into first place by Sept. 21. Although they finished the season only three games above .500, they topped the division by a game and a half. In the NLCS they held off the favored Cincinnati Reds to take the pennant in the maximum five games, but they lost the World Series in seven when Oakland won the final two games.

The Mets then entered a decade-long decline. Though they won as often in 1975 and '76 as they had in 1973, they didn't come close to winning the East, and dropped into a seven-year trough in 1977 which included five seasons in last place. Seaver was traded to Cincinnati in 1977, and Koosman (after two disastrous seasons) was sent to Minnesota in the fall of 1978 (where he won 20 the next year). The heirs of original owner Joan Whitney Payson sold the club to Nelson Doubleday (of the publishing company) and Fred Wilpon in January 1980. In February the new owners hired Frank Cashen as general manager, hoping he could rebuild the Mets as he had the Baltimore Orioles in the late 1960s.

It took a few years to achieve the right blend, but when outfielder Darryl Strawberry was brought up from the minors early in 1983 and first baseman Keith Hernandez was acquired from St. Louis in June, the mix had nearly all the needed ingredients. In 1984, under new manager Davey Johnson, and with rookie pitchers Dwight Gooden and Ron Darling combining for 29 wins, the Mets rebounded to second place with their second-best season record up till then.

The rise continued in 1985. With catcher Gary Carter (newly acquired from Montreal) leading the club in homers and RBIs, and Gooden cementing his superstardom at age 20 with a phenomenal 24-4, 1.53 ERA season, the Mets won 98 games—eight more than the year before—and came within a game of tying St. Louis late in September before slipping three games back at the finish.

When the Mets acquired pitcher Bob Ojeda from the Boston Red Sox after the season, many predicted an easy division title for them in 1986. For once, the pundits were right. With Carter, Strawberry, and Hernandez powering the offense, and Ojeda, Darling, and Gooden all placing among the league's top five pitchers in ERA, the Mets won two of every three games (108 in all) to capture the division title by 21½ games.

The postseason battles were tougher. The Mets won the pennant from Houston with a 16-inning victory in Game 6 of the NLCS, but came within a strike of elimination by the Red Sox in Game 6 of the World Series before rallying to take that game and the next for their second world crown.

Strawberry enjoyed his finest season yet in 1987, and pitchers Terry Leach and Rick Aguilera put together a combined won-lost record of 22-4. But Ojeda was lost to injury early in the season, and the Mets, though they hung close and posted 92 wins, lost out—as in 1985—to St. Louis by three games.

David Cone (20-3, 2.22 ERA) emerged in 1988 as the ace of the league's best pitching staff, which, with the power of Darryl Strawberry and Kevin McReynolds behind it, carried the Mets back to the top of the NL East, 15 games ahead of runner-up Pittsburgh. But the favored Mets lost the pennant to underdog Los Angeles in seven games.

With co-captains Carter and Hernandez injured and in decline, the Mets floundered through 1989, salvaging a narrow second-place finish with four wins in the season's final three days. The two captains were released after the season. Early the following season, with the Mets mired almost 10 games out, manager Davey Johnson was replaced by coach Bud Harrelson. In June the team took off, ignited by Strawberry's suddenly hot bat and propelled themselves into first place before the end of the month. Through July and August the Mets and Pittsburgh lobbed the division lead back and forth, until the Pirates consigned the New Yorkers to second place for good with a three-game sweep in early September.

Free agent Strawberry signed with Los Angeles for 1991, but the Mets competed strongly into July before tumbling to fifth place with their first losing season in eight years. Manager Harrelson was fired in the final week of the season. Jeff Torborg was hired to manage and ex-Pirates star Bobby Bonilla signed with the Mets as a free agent in 1992, but injuries plagued the team throughout the season, and the finish found them once again a distant fifth.

Things only got worse in 1993. Dallas Green replaced Torborg in May, and even a six-game win streak at the end of the season couldn't keep them from the worst record in the majors and, with 103 losses, the club's worst season in 28 years.

The Mets crawled to within three games of .500 in 1994, but the club also stumbled out of the gate in 1995. When they rid themselves of such high-priced talent as Bret Saberhagen, Bonilla, and center fielder Brett Butler, it appeared the club might hit a very deep bottom. Instead, new talent such as Bill Pulsipher and Jason Isringhausen lifted manager Dallas Green's young team to a surprising second place finish (69-75).

Adding another highly-rated pitching prospect, Paul Wilson, to the starting rotation gave Mets fans high hopes for 1996 but these were not realized. Despite standout seasons from Bernard Gilkey (.317, 117 RBIs), Lance Johnson (.333, 227 hits, 21 triples), and Todd Hundley (a record 41 home runs for a catcher), the club faltered, and Bobby Valentine replaced Green as manager. New York's 71-91 record was good only for fourth place.

The Mets had their best season in seven years in 1997. They had the most come-from-behind victories in baseball (47) and the Mets won the first-ever regular season game against the Yankees. The Mets were full of surprises, but the biggest was Rick Reed, a former replacement player who finished sixth in the league with a 2.89 ERA. In 1998 the Mets had the same record as the year before (88-74), but the club remained in the hunt for the Wild Card until the final day of the season. Two players acquired from the Marlins, pitcher Al Leiter (17-6, 2.47 ERA) and catcher Mike Piazza, who batted .328 with 32 home runs and 111 RBIs while playing for three teams during the season, teamed with John Olerud (.353) to help put the Mets in a position to reach the postseason for the first time in a decade. The year ended in agonizing fashion as New York lost its last five games of the season and finished one game shy of the Giants and Cubs in what would have been the first three-way playoff in major league history.

The Mets finished second in each of the next two years, but the team reached the playoffs on both occasions—the first repeat postseason performance in franchise history. In 1999 the Mets crumbled in late September by losing eight of nine games. New York rallied in the closing days of the season, however, to force a tie for the Wild Card, and then won a one-game playoff in Cincinnati on Leiter's two-hit shutout. Backup catcher Todd Pratt beat the Diamondbacks with a series-ending home run in the bottom of the 10th inning of Game 4 of the Division Series. The Mets eventually lost to rival Atlanta in six games in the NLCS, with each of the last three games decided in the home team's final at bat.

Edgardo Alfonzo and Piazza each batted .324 while Leiter and fellow southpaw Mike Hampton combined for 31 wins—each member of the starting staff won at least 10 games—to lead the Mets to the Wild Card again in 2000. Against the favored Giants, the Mets won twice in extra innings and Bobby J. Jones pitched a one-hitter to clinch the Division Series. The Mets flew past the Cardinals to claim their first league championship since 1986. Under the glare of the Subway Series, though, the Mets fell to the crosstown Yankees in a taut five-game World Series.

New York Yankees

In its first 20 seasons, the club that became the New York Yankees won no league championships and finished second only twice. But for the next 44 years the Yankees dominated the American League, winning nearly two of every three pennants and 20 World Series. After another pennant drought of 12 years, the club in six years won five division titles, four pennants, and two world championships. Their next pennant drought, which ended in 1996, lasted 14 years, and was the second longest in their history. That year the Yankees started yet another streak, with four World Series titles in five years—including three in a row.

The Yankees began as the Baltimore Orioles in 1901. But AL president Ban Johnson really wanted a club in New York and, after outmaneuvering the politically influential Giants (who didn't want a competing big league team in their city), Johnson moved the Orioles to the northern end of Manhattan in 1903.

In 1904 the Highlanders (as they were known during their first years in New York because of the high land on which their park was built) chased the Boston Pilgrims through midsummer, catching them in August and trading first place back and forth into October. After Jack Chesbro defeated Boston on Oct. 7 to give New York a half-game lead (his 41st win, a 20th-century major league record), the Pilgrims came back to win the next two. In the fourth game of the series, with Chesbro again pitching and the score tied, 2-2, in the top of the ninth, a wild pitch over the New York catcher's head let in Boston's pennant-clinching run.

The Highlanders again led the league in late September two years later, before tailing off to finish three games behind Chicago. But that was the last time they contended seriously for the title for 14 years. In that span they finished last twice: in 1908 they lost 103 games, and in 1912 the team suffered through its most distant finish ever—55 games behind the Red Sox.

In 1914 Colonel Jake Ruppert and Tillinghast Huston bought the Yankees, and the next year they purchased pitcher Bob Shawkey from the Philadelphia A's. Shawkey's 24 victories in 1916 led the Yankees to their first winning season in six years, and in 1919, on returning from military service, his 20 wins (plus nine by Carl Mays, who came to the club in a controversial mid-season deal with the Red Sox) brought the Yankees to third—their closest finish in 13 years.

That winter, on the recommendation of manager Miller Huggins, the Yankees paid a then-record $125,000 (plus a $300,000 loan) to the Red Sox for Babe Ruth. Ruth, with 54 home runs in 1920, obliterated the record of 29 he had set the year before, and Mays and Shawkey won 46 games in a three-way pennant race that ended with New York a close third.

At season's end Ruppert hired Ed Barrow as general manager. While managing the Red Sox, Barrow had converted Ruth from a pitcher to outfielder. His December trade with Boston that gave the Yankees pitcher Waite Hoyt and catcher Wally Schang was just the improvement needed to bring the Yankees their first pennant in 1921. Ruth's 59 homers and his career-high 171 RBIs didn't hurt, either.

The prickly Carl Mays, staff ace in 1921 with a 27-9 record, slipped to 13-14 the next year. But the Yankees continued to decimate the Red Sox roster with trades that brought them pitchers "Bullet Joe" Bush and "Sad Sam" Jones, and infielders Everett Scott and Joe Dugan. Bush's 26 wins in 1922 made up for Mays' decline, and the Yankees captured their second straight league championship.

Both races had been tight two-way struggles—with Cleveland in 1921 and the St. Louis Browns in 1922—and both pennants had been followed by a World Series loss to the Giants. But in 1923 the Yankees at last put everything together. After sharing the Giants' Polo Grounds since 1913, they were at home in brand-new Yankee Stadium just across the Harlem River in the Bronx. With the addition of yet another pitcher from the Red Sox—Herb Pennock—and a .393 year from Ruth, they took the lead from the start and built it over the summer to a 16-game margin by the end. For the third time the Yankees faced the Giants in the World Series; this time they beat them, in six games, for their first world championship.

The Yankees lost a close race to Washington in 1924 and collapsed into seventh place in 1925—a year in which Ruth was lost much of the season to surgery and suspension. It wasn't all bad. Center fielder Earle Combs, in his first full season, hit .342 to lead Yankee regulars. Left fielder Bob Meusel filled Ruth's shoes as AL home run and RBI leader, and first baseman Lou Gehrig arrived to stay. With Ruth's return to full strength in 1926 and the establishment of a new middle infield of Tony Lazzeri and Mark Koenig, the Yankees took their fourth pennant. They lost a close World Series to the Cardinals.

Many observers rank the 1927 Yankees as baseball's greatest team ever. Ruth hit his 60 home runs, and Gehrig drove in 175 as the Yankees fashioned a remarkable 110-44 mark. Waite Hoyt led the league in ERA, and rookie Wilcy Moore proved the league's premier reliever. As a team the Yankees led the league in hitting (.307) and slugging (.489); their pitchers compiled a 3.20 ERA (the next best team, the White Sox, had an ERA of 3.91). In the World Series they swept the Pittsburgh Pirates.

The resurgent Athletics made the 1928 race much closer, but New York won three in a row from the A's in mid-September to pull ahead, and held on for their sixth pennant. Another Series sweep (this time against the Cardinals) gave them their third world title.

An ill Huggins yielded the club's reins in September 1929 and died before the season ended. By the time the Yankees returned to the top in 1932, their manager was Joe McCarthy. He had led the Chicago Cubs to the NL pennant in 1929; in 15 seasons at New York he would lead his club to eight more pennants and seven world championships.

A New York pennant and World Series triumph over the Cubs in 1932 was followed by three second-place finishes to Washington (in 1933) and Detroit (in 1934 and 1935). Ruth had retired by the time the Bronx Bombers returned to the top in 1936, but Gehrig was still in top form, catcher Bill Dickey and outfielder George Selkirk developed into formidable sluggers, and Joe DiMaggio arrived to take over center field. New York finished 19½ games in front and buried the Giants in the World Series.

Three more pennants and three more world titles followed in 1937-1939. Lefty Gomez emerged as the league's premier pitcher in 1937, and DiMaggio picked up the home run and slugging crowns. Again the Giants were vanquished in the World Series. Rookie second baseman Joe Gordon and sophomore outfielder Tommy Henrich joined Dickey, DiMaggio, and a declining Gehrig in leading the slugging Yankees to the 1938 crown and a Series sweep of the Cubs. A balanced attack in 1939 saw seven of the eight starters (including Babe Dahlgren, who replaced the dying Gehrig at first) drive in 80 runs or more as the Yankees won 106 to run away with their 11th pennant—and eighth World Series, another sweep, with Cincinnati the victim. For the fourth straight year the offense topped the league in slugging, and overshadowed the steady—if unspectacular—pitching staff, which compiled the league's stingiest ERA for the sixth consecutive year.

After catching the Tigers with a 19-4 spurt in late summer, the 1940 Yankees fell away to finish a close third. But then came another three convincing pennant wins and a pair of Series triumphs as the nation moved into World War II. Outfielders DiMaggio and Charlie Keller dominated the offense in 1941, and rookie shortstop Phil Rizzuto hit .307. Brooklyn was the loser in a five-game World Series.

Keller, DiMaggio, and Gordon provided the power, and Tiny Bonham (with 21 wins), Spud Chandler, and rookie Hank Borowy headed the league-leading pitching staff that propelled the Yankees to 103 wins and another easy pennant in 1942. But after winning their previous eight World Series, the Yankees were finally stopped, in five games, by the St. Louis Cardinals.

By 1943 many Yankees were in military service. But pitchers Chandler, Bonham, Borowy, and Murphy were not, and they led the charge to the team's seventh pennant in eight years. In the Series the Yankees reversed the results of the previous year, turning back St. Louis in five.

In January 1945, Dan Topping and Del Webb bought the club and installed Larry MacPhail as president, giving him a third of the club and a 10-year contract to run it. The volatile, innovative MacPhail had previously brought life to Cincinnati and Brooklyn. But manager McCarthy, who couldn't get along with MacPhail, quit early in the 1946 season, and the team finished a distant third.

DiMaggio and the others were back from the war by 1946, but it was not until 1947—under new manager Bucky Harris, and with sparkling pitching from Allie Reynolds (acquired from Cleveland), rookie Frank "Spec" Shea, and reliever Joe Page—that the Yankees returned to the top of the heap with an easy pennant win and a narrow World Series triumph over Brooklyn. On the day the Yankees won the Series, though, president MacPhail embarrassed the club and undid himself by brawling in public. Topping and Webb bought out his contract and share of the ownership. Topping took over the presidency, promoting farm director George Weiss to run the club as general manager.

After the Yankees dropped a pair of season-ending games to the Red Sox to finish third in a tight 1948 race, Weiss replaced manager Harris with Casey Stengel, who in nine years of managing the Braves and Dodgers had only twice seen his club finish as high as fifth. But with

Weiss providing a steady stream of talented players via the farm system and canny trades, the Yankees under Stengel proved all but invincible into the '60s.

Stengel's Yankees began by putting together a record string of five world championships. No major league club had ever won five pennants in a row, let alone five World Series, and the Yankees didn't accomplish the feat easily. In 1949, for example, they saw the Red Sox come from 12 games back in midseason to pass them with a three-game series sweep in late September, only to rescue the title with two close must-win victories over the Sox in the season's final games. In the World Series, Brooklyn was again the victim, in five games.

After losing much of 1949 to injury, DiMaggio returned with power in 1950, shortstop Rizzuto and catcher Yogi Berra enjoyed the finest seasons of their careers, and pitcher Whitey Ford broke into the majors, winning all nine of his decisions as a starter (he lost once in relief). Though three of the games in the World Series were decided by just one run, New York took Philadelphia's "Whiz Kids" in four straight.

No Yankee drove in as many as 90 runs in 1951, and Whitey Ford was drafted for two years of military service. But the remaining pitchers doubled their shutout production and lowered the team ERA by more than half a run per game, enough to propel the club ahead of Cleveland in mid-September. In the World Series the Yankees shook the Giants, four games to two. Cleveland challenged once again in 1952, and again fell just short, as did Brooklyn in carrying the World Series to seven games.

Finally, in 1953, Stengel's Yankees won with relative ease. Ford, back from the Army, won 18 to lead the club to a finish eight and a half games in front. Once again it was Brooklyn in the World Series, and once again the Yankees beat them. In 1954 New York won 103 games—the most in Stengel's 12-year tenure. But Cleveland won an AL-record 111 to take the flag by eight games.

In 1955, though, it was back to second place for Cleveland as New York, with Mickey Mantle now established as one of the game's most productive hitters, settled in for another four pennants. As August passed into September, three teams were within a game of each other at the top. But the Chicago White Sox faltered, leaving the Yankees and Indians to fight it out. With two weeks left, New York won eight straight to pass Cleveland for good. Facing the Dodgers in the World Series for the sixth time, the Yankees finally lost, as Johnny Podres shut them out in Game 7 to give Brooklyn its first world title since 1900.

From 1956 through 1958 the Yankees seldom found themselves out of first place. In postseason play, they went the full seven games all three years, winning twice—from the Dodgers for the sixth time in 1956, and from the Milwaukee Braves in 1958, after losing to the Braves the year before.

In 1959 the Yankees started poorly and never did rise much above .500, finishing a distant third with their worst won-lost record in 34 years. After the season, George Weiss sent an aging Hank Bauer to Kansas City in a trade that brought Roger Maris to New York. In 1960 Maris, with AL titles in slugging and RBIs, won the MVP award. He and Mantle dominated the power stats and led the charge back to the top as the Yankees won their final 15 games to bury the faltering Orioles.

New York's 1960 pennant was the first in another five-flag streak, but it was the last for Stengel. After Pittsburgh toppled the Yankees in the World Series on Bill Mazeroski's famous home run, president Topping retired both the 70-year-old Stengel and general manager Weiss, 65, who had been with the club for 28 years.

With the season lengthened by eight games in 1961, Maris broke Ruth's home-run record and rookie manager Ralph Houk led the club to 109 wins. Ford enjoyed a splendid 25-4 season and celebrated with two more wins in the World Series as the Yankees humbled Cincinnati in five games.

Pitcher Ralph Terry moved out of Ford's shadow in 1962 with 23 wins. Though the Yankees finished just five games ahead of Minnesota, there was little doubt about the outcome from midseason on. In a close World Series with San Francisco, Terry won two, including the clincher with a 1-0 shutout.

Though New York won pennants the next two years, the 1962 world title was to be their last until the Steinbrenner era 15 years later. Despite the loss to injuries of Mantle and Maris for much of 1963, New York dominated the AL, winning by 10½ games with 104 wins. But in postseason play the Yankees were themselves dominated by the Dodgers (now in Los Angeles), who held them to just four runs in a Series sweep.

Yogi Berra replaced Houk as manager for 1964. In a season-long three-way race with the White Sox and Orioles that found the clubs virtually tied in mid-September, only an 11-game win streak gave the Yankees the space they needed for their final one-game margin of victory. Pitcher Jim Bouton won a pair in the World Series, but the Cardinals took the crown in seven. Berra was fired.

During the 1964 season Topping had sold the Yankees to CBS. The next year the club, which had gone 40 years without a losing season, dropped to sixth place, and in 1966 fell to a last-place 10th, their first cellar finish in more than half a century. Even Houk's return as manager in 1967—though it led to some winning seasons—failed to restore the once-proud club to pennant contention, except once, in 1972, when it was mid-September before they fell out of a tight race to finish fourth.

In January 1973 a syndicate headed by Cleveland shipping magnate George Steinbrenner purchased the Yankees from CBS. Although he had vowed not to take a prominent role in running the club, Steinbrenner soon emerged as one of baseball's most active owners. Through a series of shrewd trades, offers of big contracts to free agents, and what became a round robin of managerial changes, Steinbrenner's Yankees became competitive again in 1974 (finishing a close second to Baltimore) and returned to the top with three successive pennants and a pair of world championships.

Manager Billy Martin (a former Yankees second baseman) led the renewed club to a runaway division title in 1976. First baseman Chris Chambliss homered in the last of the ninth of the final game of the American League Championship Series to give the Yankees the pennant over the Kansas City Royals. Cincinnati swept New York in the World Series, but the Yankees came back the next year to edge Baltimore and Boston in a three-way race that saw the teams shift back and forth in the standings throughout the season. Slugger Reggie Jackson, signed as a free agent the previous autumn, turned the club's power trio of Chambliss, Graig Nettles, and Thurman Munson into a quartet as the Yankees recorded their first 100-win season in 14 years. After another ninth-inning win over Kansas City in the ALCS finale, New York won the World Series in six games over Los Angeles. Jackson became "Mr. October" with five home runs—three of them in successive at-bats in the final game.

The 1978 season provided as exciting a race as baseball is likely to see. In mid-July it looked like a Red Sox romp, but the fourth-place Yankees put on a great surge, catching the faltering Sox with a four-game series sweep in early September. Boston dropped three and a half games back, but won their final eight games to catch New York on the final day. In the one-game tiebreaker, shortstop Bucky Dent lofted a wind-blown three-run homer over Boston's close left field wall in the seventh, and Jackson homered an inning later for New York's final run in the 5-4 win. Again the Royals were the victims in the ALCS, as were the Dodgers in the World Series.

After dropping to fourth in 1979, the Yankees held off Baltimore in 1980 to win their fourth division title—but this time Kansas City swept to the pennant in three games. In 1981 the Yankees found themselves in first place when the players struck in June and were thus admitted to an intradivisional playoff with the season's second-half winner, Milwaukee. Narrowly defeating the Brewers for the division title, New York swept Oakland for the pennant in the ALCS. But after taking the first two games from Los Angeles in the World Series, they were stopped cold as the Dodgers won the next four.

The Yankees fell below .500 the next year, and although they revived to win 91 games in 1983, they failed to frighten the division leaders until 1985. First baseman Don Mattingly drove in more runs than any other American Leaguer since 1953 and newcomer (from Oakland) Rickey Henderson scored more often than any major leaguer since 1949 to keep the Yankees in the running until Toronto eliminated them with just one game to go.

But constant roster manipulation and managerial rotation (Billy Martin alone was hired and fired five times) at last set in motion a steady drop in effectiveness. While the team remained in the thick of a tight 1988 divisional race until three season-ending losses set them back into fifth place, their won-lost record showed a third straight season of decline. In 1989 the Yankees sank to their worst finish in 22 years and in 1990 they dropped to the floor of the AL East with the club's worst record since 1913.

Before the 1990 season ended, Steinbrenner was gone. As penalty for his dealings with a gambler named Howard Spira in an attempt to gain information damaging to Yankees outfielder Dave Winfield, Steinbrenner relinquished his controlling interest in the club in August. When fans at Yankee Stadium heard the news, they stood and applauded for 90 seconds.

Their string of consecutive losing seasons stretched to four, something that hadn't happened to the Yankees in 76 years. In 1993 the Yankees bounced back and—bolstered by the league's best hitting and a strong season from newly acquired pitcher Jimmy Key—contended seriously into September, finishing second to Toronto.

They were even better in 1994. With Key in the midst of one of his best seasons ever, and a solid offense paced by right fielder Paul O'Neill (whose .603 slugging average stood 99 points above his previous career high), the Yankees were enjoying the league's best won-lost record and a 6½-game lead in the AL East when the players' strike cut the season short in August.

The 1995 Yankees earned the first-ever AL Wild Card slot. Standouts included Wade Boggs (.324), Paul O'Neill (24 HR), Bernie Williams (.307), David Cone (9-2 with New York after coming over from Toronto), and Jack McDowell (15-10). After taking a tough loss to Seattle in the Division Series, the Yankees saw the departure of McDowell, veteran Don Mattingly, and manager Buck Showalter (who became manager of the new Arizona Diamondbacks). Joe Torre replaced Showalter, continuing a tradition of managers—Casey Stengel, Yogi Berra, and Dallas Green—who have managed both the Mets and the Yankees.

In 1996, despite a late season swoon, Torre's Yankees (92-70) captured the AL East championship. Standout Yankees included Bernie Williams (.305, 29 HR, 102 RBIs), Paul O'Neill (.302, 19 HR, 91 RBIs), Tino Martinez (.292, 25 HR, 117 RBIs), AL Rookie of the Year Derek Jeter (.314), Andy Pettitte (21-8), and John Wetteland (43 saves). In the first round of the postseason, New York overcame Texas in four games.

In the ALCS, the Yanks rolled over Baltimore in five games. Assisting the Bombers was the "Angel in the Outfield," a 12-year-old boy who caught Jeter's flyball over the right field wall in Game 1. Instead of a fan interference call, Jeter was credited with a pivotal homer.

In the first two games of the World Series against Atlanta the Yankees looked outclassed, losing, 12-1, and 4-0. But New York rebounded to win the next four, including a 10-inning Game 4 comeback from a 6-0 deficit. The victory was particularly sweet for manager Torre, whose brother, Frank, received a long-awaited heart transplant the day before Game 6.

In 1997 the Yankees reached the postseason as a Wild Card team and seemed to have the easier assignment in facing Cleveland, but the Indians had the Yankees' number. Cleveland rallied to take the last two games to end New York's season.

The Yankees dominated baseball in 1998. They eclipsed the AL record with 114 wins as they rolled through the regular season. They allowed Texas just one run in three Division Series games, but ran into trouble again with the Indians. A controversial Game 2 loss in the ALCS was followed by another loss in Cleveland as the Yankees trailed 2-1 in the series. From there, New York ran the table, winning the last three games in the ALCS and winning four straight against the Padres. It marked the Yankees' seventh sweep and 24th world championship.

Two more world championships followed: one seemingly easy and the other as the team with the worst record of any postseason participant. The 1999 Yankees won 16 fewer games than the previous season, and still won 98 times. The Yankees lost just once during the postseason and swept the World Series for the second straight year—this time against Atlanta. The following year the Yankees lost 15 of their final 18 games, but won 11 of 16 postseason games to become the third Yankees club—and fourth team in history—to capture three or more world championships in succession. Making it sweeter was the first Subway Series since 1956. The Yankees won a memorable five-game Series from the Mets.

Oakland Athletics

The history of the Athletics is a tale of three cities—a story of the best of teams and of the worst of teams. With a 13-year sojourn in Kansas City between residence in Philadelphia and Oakland, the A's are the only club to include a stop in Middle America in their trek from the East Coast to West. While the A's are second only to the Yankees in AL championships (with 15), they have also finished last in the league or division 27 times, and in 16 seasons have lost 100 games or more—both AL worsts, by far. A club of extremes, they have been either at the top or at the bottom in nearly one season out of two.

When Ban Johnson established four eastern clubs for his American League in 1901, he chose Connie Mack to manage the new Philadelphia Athletics and gave him a quarter ownership of the club. Mack, who had been managing the league's Milwaukee franchise, settled in at Philadelphia and set a record for managerial longevity—50 years—that is unlikely ever to be surpassed.

In his first 14 years the A's dominated the league with six pennants and two close second-place finishes. After finishing fourth in 1901, the club won its first pennant the next year, pulling away from the field with spurts in August and September. Rube Waddell led the team with 24 wins, and six regulars hit over .300. The next two years saw the A's fade in August, but in 1905, after forging ahead in early August and hanging on to the lead with two crucial wins over Chicago's surging White Sox in late September, the A's opened October with a five-game winning streak to clinch their second flag. Waddell, with 26 wins, once again led the club (followed closely by Eddie Plank's 25) and compiled a league-leading 1.48 ERA. In the Athletics' first World Series appearance, though, New York's Christy Mathewson provided most of the pitching heroics, shutting out the A's three times in the Giants' 4-1 Series triumph.

Another August decline in 1906 was followed in 1907 by a comeback struggle from fifth place in late May to a 2½-game lead in mid-September. But the loss of a crucial game to Detroit several days later, and the failure to make up a rainout and a tie, left the A's 1½ games behind the Tigers at the finish.

In 1908 the A's suffered their first losing season, but they rebounded in 1909 to chase the Tigers throughout the summer before tailing off to second. In 1910, with a pitching staff that compiled a stunning 1.79 ERA (paced by Jack Coombs, whose 31 wins included 13 shutouts) and with league-leading fielding and hitting, the A's pulled ahead for good in June, increasing their lead through the rest of the season to finish 14½ games in front. In the World Series they continued to dominate, outscoring the Chicago Cubs 35-15 as they took their first world title, in five games. The A's repeated just as convincingly in 1911. With their "$100,000 infield" of Stuffy McInnis, Eddie Collins, Jack Barry, and Frank "Home Run" Baker averaging .323 at the bat, and Jack Coombs winning 28 games to again lead the club (and the league), the A's overtook Detroit in August to win by 13½ games. In the World Series, Baker homered against the Giants, and the A's defeated Mathewson twice, avenging their 1905 humiliation with a victory in six games.

A third-place finish in 1912 broke the pennant streak, but the Athletics came back for two more in 1913 and '14, in both seasons pulling away in early June for easy wins. In the 1913 World Series the A's again felled the Giants, this time in just five games, but the next year they were in turn humiliated by the upstart Boston Braves, who stunned Philadelphia with the first sweep since the renewal of World Series play in 1903.

That winter, Mack began to dismantle his championship club, selling second baseman Collins to the White Sox and watching Chief Bender go to the Federal League. Third baseman Baker, unable to work out a contract, sat out the 1915 season before moving on to the Yankees.

The A's sank immediately to last place, where they remained for seven years. In 1915 they lost 109 games and finished 58½ games out. The next year they lost 117 games to set a league record for ineptitude that has never been matched.

It was a decade before Mack was able to restore the club to respectability. In 1924 he brought up Al Simmons, and the next year Jimmie Foxx and pitcher Lefty Grove. Thus renewed, the A's in 1925 battled Washington to the end of August before backing off to second. In 1927 they won 91 games, though their second-place finish was 19 games back of the overwhelming Yankees. In 1928 the A's battled from well back of New York in midseason to overtake them briefly in September, only to lose three of four games in a critical Yankee series and slip back to second.

From 1929 through 1931, though, the A's interrupted New York's domination of the AL with three spectacular seasons. In 1929 sophomore pitcher George Earnshaw blossomed into the league's big winner with 24 victories and Grove led the league's stingiest staff with a league-low 2.81 ERA. Six players drove in 79 runs or more (led by Simmons' league-high 157) in powering the A's to 104 wins and an impressive finish 18 games ahead of the second-place Yankees.

After swamping the Cubs in the World Series (including a record-setting 10-run eighth inning at Shibe Park that wiped out an 8-0 deficit in Game 4), the A's repeated as pennant winners in 1930. Simmons led the league in batting (.381), and Grove led its pitchers in just about everything: wins (28), ERA, strikeouts—even saves (nine). Again the World Series was no contest as the A's downed the Cardinals in six.

Earnshaw won more than 20 games for his third successive season in 1931, Simmons repeated as batting leader (.390), and Grove enjoyed what would be the finest season of his career (31-4, 2.06 ERA) in carrying the A's to 107 wins—their best record ever. But in Game 7 the Cardinals ended Philadelphia's championship run.

Following a second-place finish in 1932, Mack began selling off his stars again. This time the reason was primarily economic. Home attendance—never robust—fell off sharply after 1931, as the Great Depression and the A's decline made their impact felt. By 1935 the Athletics were back in the cellar, where they finished in 10 of Mack's final 16 seasons as manager in Philadelphia.

In 1946 Mack, who had been the A's majority stockholder since 1940, divided his shares among his three sons, provoking a family squabble over control of the club. In 1950 the two eldest, Roy and Earle, bought out Connie Jr. and pressured their 87-year-old father to retire. But with Connie Sr. gone, attendance (which had risen to new highs in the baseball boom that followed World War II) dropped off again. When the A's finished 60 games behind champion Cleveland and attendance dropped to an 18-year low in 1954, the Macks sold the club to Chicagoan Arnold Johnson, who moved it to Kansas City.

Attendance increased by more than a million the first season in Kansas City and the team rose a couple of places to sixth. But 1955 was the high point of their 13-year stay in the Midwest; the Kansas City A's never again rose above seventh, and they finished last six times.

Owner Johnson died in March 1960, and that December his heirs sold the club to the enterprising but abrasive Charles O. Finley. Finley brought in a succession of new managers over the next few years, and in 1965 outfitted his players in new bright green-and-yellow uniforms. But with the league's expansion to 10 teams in 1961, the A's had two places lower to sink—and did. After finishing 10th in 1967 for the third time in four years, Finley moved the club to California.

In 1968, their first year on the West Coast, they put together their first winning season in 16 years. The next year, with the start of divisional play, the A's took second in the AL West. Reggie Jackson, in only his second full big league season, enjoyed his finest year, with 47 home runs, 118 RBIs, and AL highs in slugging (.608) and runs scored (123).

After another second-place finish in 1970, the A's were ready for a return to glory. In the next five years they won five division titles, winning both the AL pennant and the World Series from 1972 to 1974. In 1971, with a new manager, Dick Williams, and three pitchers (Vida Blue, Catfish Hunter, and reliever Rollie Fingers) who reached their prime all at once, the A's enjoyed their best season in 40 years and won the West by a whopping 16 games. Baltimore swept them in the American League Championship Series, but they came back to take the West again the next year. Detroit took them to the limit in the ALCS, as did Cincinnati in the World Series, but in both series the A's prevailed in the deciding game by the margin of a single run.

The next year, 1973, Jackson led the league in slugging, homers, and RBIs, Ken Holtzman joined Blue and Hunter in the 20-win column, and home attendance crept over a million for the first time in Oakland as the A's ran their string of Western Division titles to three. Once again they were pushed to the limit in the postseason—by Baltimore in the ALCS and the New York Mets in the World Series—and once again they emerged as world champions.

Manager Williams quit in a dispute with Finley and was replaced by Alvin Dark, but the outcome in 1974 (except for a drop in attendance to under a million) was the same. Hunter bore more of the pitching load and wound up tied for the AL lead with 25 wins. His 2.49 ERA also led the league, as the staff ended Baltimore's five-year hold on the ERA title. The A's toppled the Orioles in the ALCS and (in the first World Series held entirely on the West Coast) won their third consecutive world title in five closely fought games with Los Angeles.

Catfish Hunter moved to the Yankees as a free agent, and Baltimore regained the ERA crown in 1975, but pitchers Paul Lindblad and newcomer Dick Bosman combined for a 20-5 record to supplement the efforts of Blue, Holtzman, and Fingers and carry Oakland to an unprecedented fifth straight division title. But there the magic stopped, as Boston swept to the pennant in the ALCS.

Finley, with moves reminiscent of Connie Mack, tried to sell off his star players: Blue, Jackson, Fingers, Holtzman, and outfielder/first baseman Joe Rudi, one of the team's steadiest hitters. The proposed sales made some sense: the players planned to leave the club at the end of their 1976 option year, and by disposing of them before they played out their option Finley could at least be compensated for his loss. The Jackson and Holtzman deals were approved, but baseball commissioner Bowie Kuhn blocked the sale of the others, citing the "best interests of baseball."

The weakened A's came back from a poor start to close within two and a half games of the Kansas City Royals in 1976, but they dropped to last place the next year. After another last-place finish in 1979, Finley hired fiery Billy Martin to manage the club. Martin brought the A's in second in 1980 (and his propensity for leaving starters in resulted in an astounding 94 complete games, almost twice as many as Milwaukee's second-best total) . The A's finished first in the first half of strike-divided 1981. They won the Western Division championship by sweeping Kansas City in the special intradivisional playoffs but were swept by the Yankees in the ALCS.

Finley's sale of the club in 1981 to the folks who bring us Levi's jeans signaled a turn toward normalcy and popularity. Despite a losing season in 1982, the club set a home attendance record as over 1.7 million fans came to watch Rickey Henderson's successful assault on the stolen-base record. In 1987 the A's finished right at .500—for the first time in their history a perfectly average team.

The next season they inaugurated a new multiyear reign as the league's best. Starter Dave Stewart and closer Dennis Eckersley anchored the league's strongest pitching staff and "Bash Brothers" Jose Canseco and Mark McGwire headlined an awesome offense. From 1988 through 1990 the team had its second run of three straight pennants since moving to Oakland (and the third three-pennant run in franchise history). In 1988 they built a 13-game margin of victory over runner-up Minnesota, winning 104 games and drawing more than 2 million fans to their home games for the first time. They swept Boston in the ALCS, but faltered in the World Series, losing to underdog Los Angeles in five games.

Injuries to several key players—especially Canseco, who missed the first half of the season with a broken wrist—kept the A's from dominating AL play through most of 1989. But the preseason signing of free agent starter Mike Moore had strengthened the pitching, and a June trade that brought Rickey Henderson back after more than four years with the Yankees gave the A's the push they needed to prevail.

At full strength by season's end, the A's overwhelmed Toronto in five games for their 14th pennant, then swept San Francisco for their ninth world title as a franchise.

Only the surprising White Sox challenged Oakland in 1990, and they too fell away in the latter half of the season as the A's walked to the division title with 103 wins. The potent offense was made even more formidable by the late-season acquisition of Harold Baines from Texas and Willie McGee from St. Louis. But the key to Oakland's dominance was its pitchers, who for the third year in a row compiled the league's lowest earned run average. Bob Welch led the majors with 27 wins, Dave Stewart put together his fourth straight 20-win season, and Dennis Eckersley rebounded from an injury-hampered 1989 with his finest relief year yet. The A's swept Boston to take their third straight pennant, but—shades of 1988!—floundered in the World Series, succumbing in just four games to Cincinnati's aroused Reds.

In 1991 the A's stayed at or near the top into late June before slipping to fourth. Eckersley remained in top form, however, and in 1992 proved almost invincible, with 51 saves to earn the Cy Young Award. Jose Canseco's trade to Texas during the season severed the Bash Brothers' tandem offense, but Mark McGwire enjoyed a banner season at the bat. Despite a wave of injuries that would have sunk most teams, the A's stayed afloat near the front through the first half season and held steady in the second half to win their fourth division title in five years. In the ALCS the A's fell to Toronto in six games.

With an injury to McGwire that sidelined him more than four months, plus a general decline on the mound and at the bat that saw the team finish with the league's worst batting and earned run averages, the 1993 A's did what only two major league clubs before them (the 1915 Athletics and 1885 St. Louis Maroons) had ever done before: tumble into the cellar after a first-place finish the year before.

The A's weren't winning much more often in 1994 when the players' strike halted play in August, but in the weak AL West their 51-63 record was good enough to land them in second place, just a game out of first. In 1995 their 67-77 mark earned them last place in the AL West. More significant, though, was the sale of the club by the Haas family to Bay Area businessmen Steve Schott and Ken Hofmann and the departure at season's end of manager Tony La Russa.

The power-hitting 1996 A's (78-84) edged up to third place, largely on the basis of McGwire's 52 homers. The 1997 season was a disappointment all around: the A's failed to have a pitcher win 10 games for the second straight year, third baseman Scott Brosius batted 101 points lower than in 1996, and the team was forced to trade McGwire rather than lose him to free agency. Pitcher Kenny Rogers, who came from the Yankees in a trade for Brosius, was the team's top winner in 1998, and Ben Grieve (the AL Rookie of the Year) gave the A's a young power bat to go along with sluggers Matt Stairs and Jason Giambi.

Oakland became a contender in 1999 as general manager Billy Beane acquired several solid players—Randy Velarde, Jason Isringhausen, Kevin Appier, and Omar Olivares—at the July 30 trading deadline. Oakland immediately won nine of its next 10 and remained in the hunt for the Wild Card until the closing weeks of the season. The A's exceeded all expectations the following year. Jason Giambi hit 43 home runs with 137 RBIs and batted .333 to lead one of the league's most explosive offenses. Second-year starter Tim Hudson flourished as the staff ace, winning his 20th game on the last day of the season to clinch Oakland's first postseason berth since 1992. The A's forced the Yankees to five games in the Division Series, but New York held on to win Game 5 to end the season for the AL West champs.

Philadelphia Phillies

It took the Phillies 32 years to win their first pennant, and 97 years to win their first world championship. They have finished last in their league or division 30 times—one season in four. In the nine years from 1975 through 1983, though, they were one of the most formidable teams in baseball.

Alfred J. Reach, a sporting goods entrepreneur and former player, and Colonel John Rogers, a Philadelphia lawyer and politician, organized the Phillies in 1883 to bring Philadelphia back into the National League after a six-year absence. In their first season, the Phillies won only 17 of 98 decisions to finish last, as far out of seventh as the seventh-place team was from first.

Reach hired the respected Harry Wright to manage the Phillies in 1884, and while Wright failed to lead them to a pennant in a decade at the helm, he did make them respectable. His fourth-place 1886 team, in fact, compiled a winning percentage of .623 that remained the club's best for 90 years. In 1887 the Phillies, with three pitchers winning more than 20 games, finished second, just three and a half games behind Detroit— their closest finish until their first pennant 28 years later.

The Phillies remained in the upper division 12 of the next 14 years. For five years—1891-1895— they fielded an outfield of Ed Delahanty, Billy Hamilton, and Sam Thompson—Hall of Famers who rank among the top hitters of all time. In the three heavy-hitting seasons that followed the lengthening of the pitching distance to its present 60 feet, 6 inches in 1893, Delahanty, Hamilton, and Thompson—with help from players like catcher Jack Clements (.394 in 1895) and utility outfielder Tuck Turner (.416 in 1894)— sparked the Phillies to three team batting titles with batting averages of over .300. In 1894 the big three joined Turner in batting over .400 and the team hit .349—still the major league club record.

In 1899, with Delahanty's .410 leading the way, the Phillies once again topped .300 to lead the league. Though the team finished third, they won 94 games, a club high they would not surpass for 77 years. President Reach sold his interest in the club after a dispute with co-owner Rogers, and Rogers lost star second baseman Nap Lajoie in a salary dispute to the Athletics (Philadelphia's new entry in the rival American League). But the Phillies chased front-runner Pittsburgh through much of 1901. Though they slumped in August, they recovered to finish second.

It was the end of an era. Delahanty deserted to the AL the next season, and the Phillies dropped to seventh. Rogers sold the club to a syndicate. By 1904 the team was in last place, losing 100 games for the first time. They rose into the first division the next season, but didn't mount a serious pennant run until 1911, when the pitching of rookie Grover Cleveland Alexander kept them in the thick of the race into midseason. Two years later the Phillies enjoyed first place through most of June until they faded to a distant second.

In 1915 Alexander brought his ERA down more than a run per game to a league-low and career-best 1.22, with 12 shutouts among his 31 wins. Right fielder Gavvy Cravath and first baseman Fred Luderus finished one-two among NL sluggers, and Cravath won home run and RBI crowns. For half a season all eight clubs were in the thick of a tight race, with the Cubs and Phillies at the top of the heap. But in July the Cubs folded, and in August and September the Phillies took off to outdistance the late-surging Boston Braves for their first pennant.

The World Series was a Phillies' heartbreak. Four of the five games were decided by a single run— but the runs belonged to the Boston Red Sox, who swept four after the Phillies had taken the opener.

Alexander shut out a record-tying 16 opponents the following year, winning a career-high 33, and teammate Eppa Rixey had his first big year with 22 wins. Through most of the season, the club trailed the leading Dodgers but caught them in September, only to fall away again in the final week.

After Alexander's 30 wins had brought the Phillies another second-place finish in 1917, the club dealt him to Chicago and embarked on 31 years of wandering in the desert. After 14 losing seasons (eight of them in last place), Philadelphia climbed to fourth, two games above .500, in 1932, but dropped back the next year into the second division (including nine last-place finishes) for 16 more years.

Several outstanding players spent time in Philadelphia during these years: Dave Bancroft (a rookie in their pennant season), Cy Williams, Freddy Leach, Chuck Klein, Lefty O'Doul, and Dick Bartell. Of these, only Williams and Klein retired as Phillies. The financially strapped management traded away the others at the height of their careers in deals that included cash as well as players. Even Klein—perhaps the greatest of them all—was sold twice before returning a third time to Philly to end his career.

The Phillies in 1930 produced a season that ranks among the most extraordinary of all time. With Klein and O'Doul leading the way at .386 and .383, every regular hit at least .280, to give the Phillies a team batting average of .315. But Phillies pitchers yielded a record 1199 runs while compiling the worst big league ERA ever—6.71. The club lost 102 games and finished last.

The Phillies' move in 1938 out of tiny, antiquated Baker Bowl into the Athletics' Shibe Park did nothing for attendance—or for performance. The team strung together a club-record five consecutive last-place finishes from 1938 to 1942, in which they averaged 107 losses per season and finished between 43 and 62½ games out of first.

In February 1943 the league took control of the debt-ridden club and sold it to a group headed by New York sportsman William D. Cox. Cox didn't last long; before the year was out he was barred from baseball for betting on the Phillies. His controlling interest was sold to Robert M. Carpenter, who installed his son, Robert Jr., as president. The younger Carpenter hired former pitcher Herb Pennock as general manager with instructions to build a farm system, and a new era began in the club's history.

Outfielder Del Ennis had come up to hit .313 in 1946, but Pennock died (in January 1948) before he could see the full fruits of his labor. First baseman Dick Sisler would be purchased in March; rookie outfielder Richie Ashburn would lead Philadelphia hitters in 1948 with a .333 average. Willie Jones wouldn't nail down third base for another year, and rookie pitchers Robin Roberts and Curt Simmons wouldn't overawe the opposition for a couple of seasons yet. But the team that would be dubbed the "Whiz Kids" was gathering. Triple A manager Eddie Sawyer was brought up in late July.

The loss of first baseman Eddie Waitkus (shot in the chest by a crazed young woman) and midseason complacency threatened to strand the Phillies in the second division in 1949. Sawyer fired up his players in a special team meeting, and the Phillies rallied to finish third with the club's best record in 32 years.

With new red-pinstripe uniforms and a recovered Eddie Waitkus, the 1950 Phillies pulled away from a tightly bunched first division in July and August, but late in September they fell to within two games of onrushing Brooklyn. The Dodgers took the first game of a season-ending two-game series to narrow the gap to one. In the finale Ashburn threw out a Dodger at the plate in the ninth to preserve a tie and Sisler gave the Phillies the lead with a three-run homer the next inning. When Brooklyn failed to score in the bottom of the tenth, the Whiz Kids had their pennant.

Curt Simmons, who was called up for military service in September after winning 17 games, missed the World Series. As in 1915, the result for Philadelphia was frustration and heartbreak, as the Phillies were swept by the Yankees—in the first three games by a single run.

Roberts' pitching kept the Phillies in the first division for four of the next five years, but the team made no serious run at another pennant. And when Roberts began to lose his effectiveness the team kept sinking, to fifth for two years, then to four years in the cellar, culminating in 1961 with the longest big league losing streak of the century—23 games.

The club stuck with new manager Gene Mauch, and the 1962 Phillies edged above .500 for the first time in nine years (finishing seventh in a league newly expanded to 10 teams). In 1963 they moved up to fourth with a strong second half. In 1964, with the acquisition of pitcher Jim Bunning from Detroit and infielder Richie (later Dick) Allen's productive rookie season, Mauch's Phillies moved way out in front in August. But they blew their lead with 10 straight losses in late September while Cincinnati was winning nine and St. Louis eight in a row. Only victories in their final two games salvaged a second-place tie.

Pitcher Steve Carlton, acquired from St. Louis in an off-season trade, accounted for nearly half the Phillies' 59 wins in 1972. His 27 victories for the league's worst team gave the club a ray of hope for the future and earned Carlton the Cy Young Award. Carlton lost a league-high 20 games the next year. He regained his form over the next three seasons, and the Phillies gradually rose to the top of the division.

In 1974 sophomore third baseman Mike Schmidt burst to the forefront of the league's power hitters. The Phillies dropped out of contention in August, but wound up third, their best finish since the league split into divisions in 1969. The next year outfielder Greg Luzinski joined Schmidt among the league's top sluggers, and the club rose to second, with their first winning season since 1967.

In 1976 they enjoyed their finest regular season ever. With Schmidt and Luzinski providing the power, Carlton returning to the ranks of 20-game winners and Jim Lonborg climaxing a long comeback with 18 wins, the Phillies took the division lead in May and pulled away, recovering from a late-season dive to finish well ahead of Pittsburgh. Their 101 wins, .624 winning percentage, and nine-game margin of victory remain club records.

The Phillies were swept by Cincinnati in the National League Championship Series, but they came back the next season to duplicate their record 101 wins for another comfortable first-place finish. Carlton won 23 (and his second Cy Young Award), and Luzinski enjoyed the best season of his career, driving in 130 runs. After defeating Los Angeles in the NLCS opener, though, the Phillies lost the pennant with three straight defeats.

In 1978, even though Schmidt and Carlton had off-years, the Phillies led much of the season and captured the division title a third straight time. But it was a tight race, and they barely survived a late-season Pittsburgh surge to finish a game and a half in front. For the third time, their triumph in the East was followed by defeat in the NLCS—for the second time at the hands of Los Angeles in four games.

Danny Ozark, in his seventh year as Phillies manager, was replaced by Dallas Green late in a disappointing 1979 season that saw the club stumble after a strong start. The club rallied in September to finish fourth. But Schmidt was back in top form, and Pete Rose had arrived via free agency to add his bat and hustle.

In a three-way race in 1980 that remained close through August, the Phillies hung tight without being able to move into the lead. But as Pittsburgh folded in late August and early September, the Phillies edged in front briefly, then battled back and forth with Montreal. Tied with the Expos as the clubs met in Montreal for the season's final three games, Philadelphia took the first, 2-1, then—in 11 innings—the second, to clinch their fourth division title in five years. Schmidt, with perhaps his finest season, drove in 121 runs and was named NL MVP; Carlton, with 24 wins, won his third Cy Young Award; and veteran reliever Tug McGraw enjoyed his best season in years. In an NLCS in which four of the five games went into extra innings, the Phillies prevailed over Houston, capturing their first pennant since the Whiz Kids 30 years earlier. And in the World Series, fortune finally smiled on the team as they overcame Kansas City in six games.

The Phillies won the first half of the strike-divided 1981 season. In the special intradivisional playoff against Montreal, Philadelphia fought back to tie the series after losing the first two games—only to lose the finale. The Carpenter family—citing the prohibitive cost of running a major league club—sold the team. Manager Dallas Green also left and was replaced by Pat Corrales, who kept the club in the thick of the 1982 race until the final month, when the Phillies slipped 3½ games back, to second. And Steve Carlton did it again: his 23 wins earned him the Cy Young trophy, making him the first pitcher to win the award four times.

Mike Schmidt again dominated the Phillies' offense in 1983, but Carlton yielded to John Denny as the team's pitching ace. Newly acquired reliever Al Holland emerged as one of the league's best. After general manager Paul Owens took over for Corrales as manager in midseason, the Phillies came alive and took the division title by six games. Carlton dominated the NLCS with an 0.66 ERA and two wins as the Phillies won their fourth pennant.

But their golden age ended in the World Series, when Baltimore triumphed in five games. The Phillies dropped to .500 and fourth place in 1984, and suffered a losing fifth-place season in 1985. They rebounded to second in 1986 (but 21½ games behind New York), then dropped back below .500 in 1987. Mike Schmidt, the only remaining member of the 1980 world champions, continued to power the offense. Despite an impressive lineup of everyday players in 1988, the Phils collapsed, finishing in the division cellar for the first time in 15 years. Unable to recover from a shoulder injury, Schmidt retired in May 1989, and despite several midseason trades the Phillies again finished last in the NL East. The Phillies followed that with a tie for fourth in 1990, a distant third in 1991, and, in 1992, their third last-place finish in five years.

Strengthened by the signing of several free agents and sustained by solid performances throughout the roster, the Phillies reversed course in 1993. Led by Len Dykstra's peak season at the plate, the team grabbed the division lead at the start of the year and never let go, fending off Montreal's late-season surge to take the NL East title by three games. In the NLCS they won their fifth NL pennant, defeating Atlanta in six games, but in the World Series they blew a pair of late-inning leads and fell in six games to repeat champion Toronto. Plagued by illness and injury, the Phillies never caught fire in 1994, finishing a distant fourth in the NL East. In 1995 they finished tied for second (but 21 games back).

The following year saw the Phillies riddled by injuries and falling to last (67-95), with the worst record in the NL. The club's failure led to manager Jim Fregosi's firing at season's end. Standouts in the futile effort were outfielder Jim Eisenreich (.361), starter Curt Schilling (3.19 ERA), reliever Ricky Bottalico (34 saves), and catcher Benito Santiago (30 home runs).

Under new manager Terry Francona, the Phillies started from scratch in 1997. At first, the results were disastrous. The Phils were 24-61 in the first half, but had a 44-33 mark after the All-Star break as Scott Rolen earned NL Rookie of the Year honors and Curt Schilling reached 300 strikeouts. Schilling notched 300 strikeouts again in 1998 as the Phillies actually competed for the NL Wild Card until an August slump pushed them out of the running. Still, the team's 75 wins were the most in Philadelphia since the team won the 1993 pennant.

Although the Phillies finished third in 1999, they slipped to last the following season. Rookie first baseman Pat Burrell, catcher Mike Lieberthal, and right fielder Bobby Abreu had solid seasons in 2000, but the Phils scored the fewest runs in the National League and had the most losses. At the end of the season Francona was replaced with former fiery Phillies shortstop Larry Bowa.

Pittsburgh Pirates

Pittsburgh became a big league city in 1882, when its Allegheny baseball club joined with five other teams to form the American Association. Allegheny president H.D. McKnight was named president of the new league, but Allegheny made little stir until the club hired Horace Phillips to manage it and replaced its team in 1885 with players from the defunct Columbus club, which had finished second in the AA the year before. The new Alleghenys finished a distant third in 1885, but after purchasing Pud Galvin from Buffalo they improved in 1886 to finish a respectable second behind the invincible St. Louis Browns.

Flushed with success, Allegheny in 1887 became the first club to desert the AA for the older and more highly regarded National League. There they found the competition stiffer and sank back into the second division. In 1890, when most of the team jumped to the rival Pittsburgh Players' League club, Allegheny (known that year as the Innocents) suffered the worst season in Pittsburgh major league history, finishing last, 66½ games out of first place (and 23 out of seventh), with a won-lost record of 23-113.

When the Players League folded after just one season, Allegheny merged with its PL counterpart to form the Pittsburgh Athletic Company, thereby retrieving many of its old regulars. The club also hired a second baseman—Lou Bierbauer—whose signing (or theft, as his old club saw it) gave the Innocents a new and more enduring nickname: the Pirates. The renewed club still finished last in 1891, but 36 games closer to the top than the year before, and only fractionally out of seventh place.

In 1893 a rules change moved the pitcher 10½ feet farther back from home plate. Of all the NL clubs, the Pirates benefited most from the change: their batting average jumped 63 points—28 more than that of the league as a whole—while their pitchers suffered less than most. The club finished second, with a .628 winning percentage that was their best of the century. Lefty Frank Killen, acquired from Washington, led the club's resurgence with a league-leading 34 wins.

Although catcher Connie Mack was called upon to manage the club toward the end of the 1894 season and led them to winning seasons the next two years, the Pirates did not make another serious run for the pennant until 1900. With a team transformed yet again by players from a defunct club—this time the Louisville Colonels—the Pirates battled Brooklyn's Superbas almost to the end of the season before dropping four and a half games back, a solid second. Although they lost the postseason Chronicle-Telegraph Cup games (that year's World Series) to the Superbas, the Pirates were embarked on an era of greatness.

In the merger that brought the Louisville players to Pittsburgh, the Colonels' owner Barney Dreyfuss acquired half ownership of the Pirates. A year later he bought the other half. His perennial hope for the club was a first-division finish; the Pirates reached that goal in 26 of his 32 years as owner.

Four of the former Louisville players—outfielder-turned-shortstop Honus Wagner, outfielder/manager Fred Clarke, third baseman/outfielder Tommy Leach, and pitcher Deacon Phillippe—and one carryover from the old Pirates, pitcher Sam Leever, remained with Pittsburgh long enough to help lead them to four pennants and, in 1909, their first world championship. In the 16 years Clarke managed the Pirates, they also finished second five times and slipped out of the first division only in Clarke's final two seasons at the helm.

In contrast to the club's devastation by the Players League raid of 1890, the Pirates were unaffected in 1901 by raiders from the American League (which that year turned itself into a major league largely by drawing off talent from National League clubs). Only third baseman Jimmy Williams defected to the Americans, and he was ably replaced by Tommy Leach. The Pirates, with the league's best pitching (Jesse Tannehill and Deacon Phillippe finished one-two in ERA, and Jack Chesbro at 21-10 led in winning percentage), captured their first pennant by a comfortable seven and a half games over the Philadelphia Phillies.

The Pirates repeated as pennant winners in 1902 and 1903. The 1902 team was overwhelming. One Pirate or another led the league in nearly every offensive category: Ginger Beaumont in hits and batting; Tommy Leach in home runs; and Honus Wagner in slugging, RBIs, runs scored, doubles, and stolen bases. Pitcher Jack Chesbro's 28 wins led the league, and the top five NL pitchers in winning percentage were all Pirates. The club held the lead the whole season, finishing 27½ games ahead of second-place Brooklyn, still a major league record.

Pitchers Chesbro and Tannehill deserted to the AL's New York Highlanders the next season, but their loss merely made Pittsburgh's pennant-winning margin (6½ games) smaller than it might have been. Wagner beat out teammate Fred Clarke for the NL batting crown and finished second to Clarke in slugging. Beaumont took the titles in hits, runs, and total bases. Pitcher Sam Leever, with his finest season, led the club with 25 wins and the league in ERA and winning percentage. Owner Dreyfuss arranged with the AL champion Boston Pilgrims for a best-of-nine World Series—the first between NL and AL champions—but the Pirates lost it in eight games as their tired pitchers at last succumbed to overwork.

Although the Pirates twice finished second over the next four years, they didn't come close to capturing another pennant until 1908, when, in one of the tightest NL races ever, they were edged out by the Chicago Cubs and finished one game back, tied with the New York Giants for second.

The following year, though, they moved in June into the new concrete-and-steel Forbes Field and celebrated by returning to the top of the league with a club record 110 wins—holding off the dogged Cubs throughout the season to win the pennant by six and a half games. And this time they won the World Series, too, although they needed the full seven games to subdue the Detroit Tigers.

Honus Wagner remained the league's dominant offensive force. Aging pitchers Leever and Phillippe were overshadowed by a new crop of standouts: Vic Willis, Howie Camnitz, Nick Maddox, and Lefty Leifield—and the astonishing rookie Babe Adams, who after going 12-3 (with a 1.11 ERA) during the season, won three more games in the World Series.

The Series triumph ended an era. Wagner was past his

prime and wound down his long career over the next several seasons as the Pirates dropped out of contention for a dozen years. Only Babe Adams remained of the world championship team when Pittsburgh next made a contest of the pennant race in 1921. That season saw the Pirates take an early lead and hold it most of the summer until a late-season decline dropped them to second place.

Former Pittsburgh infielder Bill McKechnie replaced George Gibson as manager during the following season with the club in fifth place, and saw the Pirates spurt to second before fading to third at the finish. Two more third-place seasons—with the Pirates finishing just three games out of first in 1924—paved the way for another pennant in 1925.

The 1925 Pirates fielded several stars: shortstop Glenn Wright, who led the club with 121 RBIs; sophomore right fielder Kiki Cuyler, who led the team in hitting (.357) and the league in runs scored; third baseman Pie Traynor, who shone on the field and at the bat; and Max Carey, who beat out Cuyler for the league stolen base title and enjoyed his finest season (.343) at the plate. The team as a whole hit .307 to lead the league and ran away with the pennant, spurting to catch the front-running Giants in midseason and pushing ahead to an eight and a half-game lead by season's end.

The World Series was tougher, but the Pirates prevailed over the Washington Senators, defeating veteran Walter Johnson in a seventh-game slugfest, 9-7. Babe Adams, hero of the 1909 Series and now, at 43, nearing the end of his long career, pitched one shutout inning in Game 4.

Rookie outfielder Paul Waner arrived the next season and hit .336, but the team, which had led the race going into August, fell into decline late in the month and finished third, four and a half games out. Max Carey sparked an unsuccessful player uprising against the management and was sold to Brooklyn just before the Pirates collapsed in August, and manager McKechnie was replaced after the season by former Washington manager Donie Bush.

In 1927, his first season at the helm, Bush won the pennant, even though Kiki Cuyler was benched for half the season for refusing to bat second in the order. But Paul Waner's younger brother Lloyd arrived to join Paul in the outfield, and the pair tore up the league, finishing one-two in hits (237 and 223) as Paul also took crowns in batting (.380; Lloyd was third at .355), RBIs, and total bases, while Lloyd led in runs scored. In and out of first place throughout the season, the Pirates moved into the lead a final time at the start of September and held on to edge the St. Louis Cardinals by a game and a half. In the World Series, though (played with Cuyler on the bench), the Pirates were swept by the imposing '27 Yankees, a team widely acclaimed as the greatest of all time.

Barney Dreyfuss died in February 1932. Ownership of the Pirates passed to his widow, who named their son-in-law Bill Benswanger president. The team finished a competitive second in 1932 and 1933, but then fell back until 1938. With Pie Traynor now manager, they moved out in front in midseason and held their lead comfortably until late September, when 10 straight Chicago victories (including three against Pittsburgh) dropped the Pirates to second place, where they finished two games back.

The Pirates showcased some great players in their lean years, like shortstop Arky Vaughan in the 1930s and early '40s, and slugger Ralph Kiner, who won or shared the league home run title all seven of his seasons with Pittsburgh in the 1940s and '50s. But after 1938 the club finished no closer than eight games from the top for 21 years.

The Pirates were purchased in 1946 by a four-man syndicate that included singer Bing Crosby and real estate tycoon John W. Galbreath. Galbreath later bought a majority interest in the club and, as president, hired Branch Rickey to rebuild the Pirates into contenders.

Barney Dreyfuss had resisted the development of minor league systems and preferred to scour unaffiliated minor league teams himself in search of young talent. Rickey, who pioneered the farm system in St. Louis and Brooklyn, laid the foundation for Pittsburgh's resurgence. Six of the eight regulars who would lead the Pirates to their next championship in 1960 were already in the 1958 lineup, including Dick Groat, Bill Mazeroski, and Roberto Clemente; and the leading pitchers of 1958—Bob Friend, Vern Law, and reliever Roy Face—topped the 1960 staff, too.

They began strong in 1960 and, shaking off their last challenger in late July, built up a seven-game margin of victory by season's end. League batting champion Groat paced a balanced offense that led the league in hitting, and pitcher Law, with 20 wins, enjoyed the finest season of his career. Facing the Yankees in the World Series, the Pirates were overwhelmed in the three games they lost, but they won the world title with four close wins, capped by Mazeroski's famous home run in the bottom of the ninth inning of the final game.

Pittsburgh again led the league in batting in 1961, with Clemente (whose .351 batting average led the league) and first baseman Dick Stuart (35 home runs, 117 RBIs) enjoying especially fine seasons. But the pitching fell apart, and the club dropped to sixth place.

When the Pirates next made a serious run for the pennant, in 1966, Harry Walker managed the team and center fielder Matty Alou (newly acquired from San Francisco) won the batting crown. (His brother Felipe of Atlanta was runner-up—the only one-two brother finish ever.) In a season-long three-way race, the Pirates took a lead in August but lost it early in September and finished third, three games out. They dropped to sixth again the next season and remained out of the pennant race for three years.

In 1970 John Galbreath's son Daniel was named Pirates' president, and Danny Murtaugh returned a third time to pilot the Pirates. (His second stint was for half a season in 1967.) The team began slowly and entered June with a record under .500. But they were already on their way up, and they moved out of aging Forbes Field into the brand-new Three Rivers Stadium in mid-July. They slipped into a three-way tangle for first in the NL East in mid-September, but shot ahead later in the month to take the division title. The power was now supplied by first baseman Bob Robertson and outfielder Willie Stargell, but Roberto Clemente was still in top form and Bill Mazeroski was still at second base, though nearing the end of his career.

In the 1970 National League Championship Series, the Pirates were swept by Cincinnati. But they came back the next season to overwhelm the East in a race that was no race after June, then defeated San Francisco for their eighth pennant, three games to one. Their slugging—paced by Stargell's league-leading 48 home runs—was tops in the NL, and reliever Dave Giusti saved a league-leading 30 games in support of a balanced pitching staff. Clemente hit .414 in the World Series (with half his hits going for extra bases) as the Pirates overcame a 2-0 deficit to edge Baltimore in seven games for their fourth world title.

In 1972, after a slow start, Pittsburgh (now managed by their former center fielder Bill Virdon) rocketed to their third straight division championship—by 11 games over Chicago. The club lost, narrowly, to Cincinnati in the NLCS, then suffered an even greater loss when Clemente was killed that winter in a plane crash. Clemente, who had collected exactly 3,000 hits with the Pirates, had the usual five-year waiting period waved by the Hall of Fame and was enshrined in Cooperstown in 1973.

The Pirates played poorly the next season, yet even with a losing record finished third in a five-way divisional race. Danny Murtaugh returned as manager a fourth (and final) time late in the season and piloted the club to two more NL East titles the next two years.

The 1974 championship drive featured a comeback from last place in early July to first by late August, followed by a nip-and-tuck race in September with St. Louis that was settled by a 10th-inning Pittsburgh victory over Chicago in the season's final game. Stargell's bat was joined by those of Al Oliver and Richie Zisk as the Pirates outhit the rest of the league. In the NLCS, though, the Los Angeles Dodgers overcame Pittsburgh handily, three games to one.

The Pirates won the 1975 race more easily, holding the lead from early June as right fielder Dave Parker, in his first full big league season, led the club in home runs and RBIs, and the league in slugging. Rennie Stennett, now the second baseman, tied Wilbert Robinson's 1892 record by going 7-for-7 in a nine-inning game at Wrigley Field. Their regular season success failed to carry over to the postseason as Pittsburgh fell in the NLCS for the fourth time in five tries.

A distant second-place finish in 1976 was followed that December by manager Murtaugh's untimely death. His successor, Chuck Tanner (acquired in a trade with Oakland), kept the Pirates competitive in his first two seasons, steering them to within five games of the champion Phillies in 1977, then—with an amazing August-September spurt from way below .500—to within a game and a half of the Phillies in 1978.

In 1979 the Pirates again started slowly but began to move up in May and pushed to the front, ahead of Montreal, in late July. By mid-September, though, the Expos had caught up, and it was not until the final day that Pittsburgh had its sixth NL East title. Parker and the aging Stargell (now called "Pops") were still the club's big bats. Submariner Kent Tekulve had emerged as the bullpen ace and was one of six Pittsburgh pitchers to win 10 games or more.

In the NLCS the Pirates repaid Cincinnati for their 1975 humiliation, sweeping to the pennant in three games. In the World Series they seemed to have met their match in Baltimore, falling behind, three games to one. But Pops rallied his "family" to victory in the final three must-win contests, and Pittsburgh for a fifth time reigned at the top of the baseball world. Stargell was a three-time MVP that season, winning the honor in the NLCS and World Series, and sharing the regular season MVP trophy with Keith Hernandez of St. Louis.

For seven years the Pirates drifted downhill. The club's family spirit disintegrated, fans deserted the team, and it seemed for a time that the Pirates would leave Pittsburgh. But in 1985 a group of local corporations and individuals purchased the club from the Galbreaths, determined (with the assistance of a loan from the city of Pittsburgh) to keep the Pirates in town. Syd Thrift, a trader of consummate skill, was named general manager, and Chicago White Sox coach Jim Leyland was hired to his first job as a big league pilot. Under the new regime the club improved gradually, until in 1988 it once again proved itself a serious contender in the NL East. Thrift had built a team second only to New York's mighty Mets, one that drew more than 1.8 million fans in Pittsburgh—a club record. Thrift, however, clashed with the team's directors and he was fired at season's end.

Plagued all season by injuries, Pittsburgh plunged to fifth in 1989. But in 1990, as Doug Drabek put together a career season on the mound and the bats of Barry Bonds and Bobby Bonilla boomed, the Pirates arrived at the All-Star break in first place by half a game over New York. With Drabek and Zane Smith (newly acquired from Montreal) all but unbeatable down the stretch, the Pirates, after exchanging the lead with New York several times, swept a series against the Mets in early September to extend a narrow lead. The Bucs clinched the NL East title at the end of the month with eight straight wins.

The Pirates repeated as division champions in 1991 and 1992. Bonds and Bonilla again led the offense in 1991, and pitcher John Smiley won 20 games as the team built an early lead and enlarged it to 14 games by season's end. In 1992, even the departure of Bonilla (who signed with the Mets as a free agent) and Smiley (dealt to Minnesota) didn't hamper the Pirates. Center fielder Andy Van Slyke took up the offensive slack with one of his best seasons, and pitcher Tim Wakefield rose from the minors at the end of July to compile an 8-1 record as the Pirates breezed to the title by nine games. But the three-time division champions could not win a pennant. In the 1990 NLCS they fell to Cincinnati in six games. The next year they built a 3-2 lead over Atlanta, but lost the final two games. And in 1992, down three games to two, the Bucs fought back to within one out of victory in Game 7 before an Atlanta pinch hit cut them down once again.

The departure of free agent Barry Bonds to San Francisco was the most crucial of many roster changes for 1993, which saw more than half the 1992 NL East championship squad replaced. The revamped Pirates fielded near the top of the league and batted near the middle, but their pitching fell apart and the team finished fifth.

When the strike ended the 1994 season, the Pirates' .465 winning percentage was only two points better than the year before, but in the NL's new Central Division, that was good enough for a third-place tie with St. Louis. However, financial problems continued to haunt the team, and the payroll was slashed to the bone in 1995, resulting in the Pirates posting the NL's worst record (58-86). In February 1996 Sacramento newspaper heir Kevin

McClatchy, 32, moved to purchase the club for $90 million.

Despite an 11-game winning streak in September, the Pirates (73-89) remained in the basement in 1996, prompting Jim Leyland to resign at season's end. Several of Pittsburgh's best players followed Leyland out of town in cost-cutting trades, but the Pirates turned out to be one of baseball's biggest surprises in 1997. Manager Gene Lamont kept the Pirates alive in the NL Central chase until the final week of the season. The highlight of the year came when Francisco Cordova and Ricardo Rincon combined for a no-hitter against first-place Houston at sold-out Three Rivers Stadium. The 1998 Pirates, however, slid to sixth place in the NL Central as the team lost its last eight games.

Brian Giles emerged as one of the leagues most consistent outfielders, averaging 37 home runs, 119 RBIs, and 110 runs scored over the next two seasons. Despite a devastating injury to Jason Kendall, the Pirates managed to finish third in 1999. The following year, however, the Pirates stumbled just when management thought the team could become a contender. Kendall had a successful comeback and Kris Benson proved to be one of the National League's better young pitchers, but the Bucs slid to a distant fifth in the club's final year at Three Rivers Stadium. Gene Lamont was replaced with coach Lloyd McClendon at year's end.

St. Louis Cardinals

The club that is now the Cardinals first fielded a team in 1881, and the next season became a charter member of the American Association, a new major league formed in part to offer fans the beer and Sunday baseball forbidden by the older National League. Chris Von der Ahe, one of the club's founders and its first president, at first saw in baseball simply a source of customers for his St. Louis saloon and beer garden, but he developed a love for the game itself as his Brown Stockings—or Browns—developed into one of the era's greatest teams.

After a losing season in 1882, Von der Ahe hired Ted Sullivan, a noted judge of baseball talent, to manage the Browns. Sullivan brought in third baseman Arlie Latham and pitcher Tony Mullane to strengthen a team that already boasted a fine pitcher in Jumbo McGinnis (25-18 in 1882) and one of the game's premier first baseman in Charlie Comiskey. Although Sullivan quit before the end of his first season because of the continued interference of the volatile Von der Ahe, the Browns finished second in the AA, just a game behind champion Philadelphia.

When Mullane bolted the Browns in 1884, the club slipped to fourth. But help was on the way. In July Von der Ahe purchased the Bay City, Michigan, club to acquire its heavy-hitting pitcher Dave Foutz, and in September added another hitting pitcher, "Parisian Bob" Caruthers, to the roster. In 1885— with Comiskey now the manager, left fielder Tip O'Neill blossoming into one of baseball's best hitters, and Caruthers and Foutz winning 40 and 33 games—the Browns rose to the top, 16 games ahead of second-place Cincinnati. They finished on top four years in a row, tying Chicago's White Stockings (3-3-1) in the 1885 World Series and defeating them, four games to two, the next year for the AA's only Series triumph over their NL rivals.

Pitcher Silver King joined the club in 1887, and outfielder Tommy McCarthy arrived the following year. They helped keep the Browns at the top of the AA through 1888 (although the team lost the World Series both years). But Von der Ahe's sale of Foutz and Caruthers to Brooklyn following the 1887 season boosted Brooklyn to second place in 1888. The next year Brooklyn edged the Browns for the pennant, and the club's first era of greatness was over.

When the AA folded after the 1891 season, the Browns were taken into the NL, but fared poorly there, finishing ninth and then 11th in the divided season of 1892. They rose no higher than ninth in the remaining years of Von der Ahe's ownership, dropping into the cellar (63½ games out) in 1897 and returning to the bottom with a club-worst 111 losses the next season.

New owners Frank and Stanley Robison (who also controlled the Cleveland club) transferred the best Cleveland players and their manager to St. Louis in 1899. Dubbed the Perfectos, the revitalized St. Louis club fell short of perfection, but did rise to a first-division fifth place that year and (now known as the Cardinals) rose to fourth in 1901 before sinking back into the second division for a dozen years.

After Stanley Robison died in 1911 (his brother Frank had died in 1905), the club passed into the possession of Frank's daughter Helene Britton, who ran it behind the scenes until, in 1916, she sold it to a syndicate headed by her attorney James C. Jones. Jones hired Branch Rickey away from the AL Browns to run the club.

Rickey took over a team with two chief assets: manager Miller Huggins and a promising young infielder, Rogers Hornsby. Huggins had managed the Cards to third place in 1914, before Hornsby arrived, and, after a pair of losing seasons brought them up to third again in 1917. Huggins was lost to the New York Yankees the next year, and Rickey left the club temporarily for military service in the Great War. When Rickey returned in 1919, he took over as manager himself. In 1921 and 1922 the team finished third, closer to the leaders than the club had finished since joining the NL in 1891. Led by Hornsby's .397 and .401 batting, the team hit over .300 both seasons.

Sam Breadon increased his investment in the Cardinals until he was majority stockholder and club president in 1920, with Rickey as vice president and general manager. Breadon moved the Cards out of the inadequate wooden Cardinal Park during the 1920 season into the more modern Sportsman's Park, owned by the Browns and built on the site of Von der Ahe's original ground.

Early in the 1925 season, with the Cards in last place, Breadon replaced Rickey as field manager with second baseman Hornsby. The switch worked. In 1925 the Cards rebounded to fourth, and in 1926 they captured their first pennant since the glory days of the old Browns four decades earlier—edging Cincinnati in the final week of the season. The season was made perfect by victory in the World Series over Miller Huggins' Yankees as midseason pickup Grover Cleveland Alexander won Game 6 and saved Game 7 for the Cardinals.

But Breadon and his irascible player-manager had a falling out, and Hornsby was traded that winter to the

New York Giants for second baseman Frank Frisch and pitcher Jimmy Ring. The trade enraged fans, but the team finished a close second in 1927, and returned to the top (under new manager Bill McKechnie) in a tight race the following season.

McKechnie, fired after the Yankees swept the Cards in the 1928 World Series and rehired in the midst of a St. Louis slump the next season, left to manage the Boston Braves in 1930. Former catcher Gabby Street, who replaced him, led the Cards back to the top again for successive pennants in 1930 and 1931, and in 1931 to a World Series victory over the Philadelphia Athletics. The 1930 race saw the club shoot from below .500 in mid-June to 30 games over .500 by season's end, overtaking three other teams to clinch the flag just three games from the finish. The 1931 team ran away with the pennant, leading all the way and finishing 13 games in front. Outfielder Chick Hafey and first baseman Jim Bottomley finished first and third in NL batting, and pitcher Bill Hallahan led the league in strikeouts (for the second year in a row) and tied for the lead in wins, with 19. Four of the league's top five base stealers—led by Frank Frisch and including outfielder Pepper Martin in his first full season—were Cardinals.

When the Cards dropped to sixth place in 1932 and showed little improvement the following year, Breadon replaced manager Street with Frisch. Breadon's move paid immediate dividends. Though the club finished fifth that season, their record improved after Frisch took over, and the next year, in a season-long uphill struggle, the Cards won 13 of their final 15 games to pass the front-running New York Giants in the final week.

Writers labeled the 1934 Cardinals the "Gashouse Gang" for their rowdy and daring play. In addition to team veterans Frisch and Martin (who had been shifted from the outfield to third base), the gang included shortstop Leo Durocher, left fielder Joe "Ducky"Medwick, and the team's leading hitter and slugger, first baseman Rip Collins, who in a career-best season led the league in slugging average and tied for first in home runs.

The pitching staff was headed by the league-leading Jerome "Dizzy" Dean (30-7) and his rookie brother Paul (19-11). Of the team's final nine wins, Diz and Paul accounted for seven. Each won another pair in the Cards' World Series triumph over Detroit.

The next two seasons the Cardinals moved into the lead late in the season only to wind up second. After the team slipped into the second division in 1938, Breadon replaced Frisch as manager with Ray Blades, who led a late-season run for the flag in 1939 but finished second. When the Cards failed to contend in 1940, Breadon brought up Rochester manager Billy Southworth for a second time. Southworth had failed as McKechnie's replacement in 1929, but this time he stuck, becoming one of the club's greatest skippers.

Through all these years Branch Rickey was revolutionizing baseball as he built the game's first and most extensive "farm system" of minor league clubs. The Cardinals' farm teams would—until the other major league clubs caught on and caught up—provide St. Louis with a competitive advantage in recruitment and development.

In the closing days of the 1941 season, perhaps that system's greatest product arrived at the big club: Stan Musial. Southworth brought the club in a close second that year after a season-long back-and-forth struggle with Brooklyn. The next year—Musial's first full season—the Cardinals enjoyed their winningest season ever: 106 victories.

They needed them all, too, for Brooklyn won 104 games, leading the race until mid-September, when the Cardinals passed them and held on to a narrow lead by winning 12 of their final 13 games. St. Louis pitchers Mort Cooper and Johnny Beazley finished one-two in National League wins and ERA, while Enos Slaughter and Musial paced the offense. The club maintained its momentum in the World Series, taking the Yankees in five games.

St. Louis retained its preeminence for two more years as baseball gradually lost players to military service in World War II. Slaughter and Beazley were gone by 1943. But Cooper remained to compile two more 20-plus winning seasons, and Musial was not called until after the 1944 season. With 105 wins in both 1943 and 1944, the Cards ran away with two more pennants, losing to the Yankees in the 1943 World Series, but taking their sixth world title the next year from their St. Louis landlords, the AL champion Browns.

Owner Breadon had fired Branch Rickey in 1942 (objecting to the personal profit Rickey made from selling the club's unneeded farm players) and Southworth left to manage the Boston Braves after the 1945 season. Rickey went to head the Brooklyn Dodgers, building for them a farm system and tapping the large reservoir of black players. In 1946, the last year of all-white major league ball, the Cards (managed now by Eddie Dyer) and the Dodgers waged a two-team pennant race, ending the season in the first major league tie for first place. St. Louis won the first two games in a best-of-three playoff against Brooklyn and went on to surprise the favored Boston Red Sox in the World Series in seven games.

St. Louis was slow to integrate and the Cards lost ground to teams like Brooklyn, whose black players brought an immediate upswing in the club's success. After the 1947 season Breadon sold the club to Fred Saigh and Robert Hannegan (the U.S. Postmaster General). Musial enjoyed his finest season in 1948, but the club finished second again in a lackluster race. The next year, though, the Cards and Dodgers tangled in a season-long struggle for first place that was not resolved until the season's last day—with Brooklyn on top.

The Cardinals threatened to move to Milwaukee, but beer magnate August Busch, Jr., purchased the club early in 1953 and the same year bought Sportsman's Park from the Browns (who were moving to Baltimore). With Busch's infusion of money and enthusiasm, the club slowly revived. They made runs for the pennant in 1957, 1960, and 1963, but each time tailed off sharply in the final week of the season.

The Cards were playing below .500, in seventh place, in mid-June 1964 when the arrival (via a trade with the Cubs) of speedy young Lou Brock sparked a revival of both the team and player. Brock, who had been hitting .251 in Chicago, with 10 stolen bases, hit .348 the rest of the season and stole 33 more bases as the Cards hurtled into the midst of a four-way race for the pennant that was settled only when they took the flag with an 11-5 win on the final day. After surprising the Yankees in seven games in the World Series, the Cardinals were themselves surprised when manager Johnny Keane left to take the helm of the Yankees. The club slipped into the second division for a couple of years under the management of their great former second baseman Red Schoendienst.

Busch built them a striking new stadium in 1966, and the next season the team rebounded to the top again, running away from the field in the last half of the season behind the heavy hitting of Orlando Cepeda, the bat and speed of Brock, and a pitching staff of remarkable breadth and balance. Bob Gibson's three World Series wins over Boston edged the Cards to a ninth world title and set the stage for Gibson's astonishing season the following year.

With his 22 wins leading the Cards to another pennant in 1968, Gibson hurled 13 shutouts and compiled an ERA of just 1.12—both feats the best in more than half a century, both ranking among the top five big league performances ever. After winning two World Series games, Gibson lost Game 7 as Detroit took the crown.

Red Schoendienst continued as manager through 1976—a club record 12 years—but led the team to no more championships. When divisional play was inaugurated in 1969, geography was ignored as the Cards were installed in the East to add strength to what seemed the weaker division. But it was 14 years before they won their first divisional championship. Four times they finished second, losing twice by only a game and a half in the back-to-back tight races of 1973 and 1974.

In the strike-shortened divided season of 1981, manager Dorrel "Whitey" Herzog's Cards compiled the best overall record in the NL East, but because they had finished the two halves of the season second to Philadelphia and Montreal they were ineligible for postseason play.

With the defensive wizard shortstop Ozzie Smith (acquired from San Diego) and rookie speedster Willie McGee bolstering an already strong team, the Cardinals of 1982 prevailed against the Phillies in the race for the East. St. Louis then swept West champion Atlanta for the pennant and captured their 10th World Series crown in a seven-game struggle with Milwaukee.

After two seasons out of the running, the Cards in 1985 gained the power of veteran Jack Clark (acquired from San Francisco) and the speed of rookie Vince Coleman. With career-best seasons from Willie McGee and newly acquired pitcher John Tudor, the team edged the New York Mets for the division title and defeated Los Angeles for the pennant but lost the World Series in seven games to Kansas City.

Jack Clark missed two-thirds of the 1986 season to injury, and the Cards finished below .500, but they rebounded to edge the Mets again for the championship of the East in 1987 as Clark and Vince Coleman enjoyed their finest seasons at the bat. The reinjured Clark made only a token appearance as the Cards edged San Francisco for the league championship, and he missed the World Series entirely as St. Louis bowed to Minnesota in seven games. That winter Clark signed as a free agent with the Yankees, and, in 1988, the Cardinals dropped to fifth place, 25 games out.

With solid pitching and hitting, and the league's best fielding, the 1989 Cardinals drew within half a game of the division lead on Sept. 8, then fell out of the race with six straight losses, finishing third. As the season drew to a close, long-time owner August Busch, Jr., died at age 90. The next July, with the club uncharacteristically mired at the bottom of the NL East, manager Whitey Herzog resigned. Under new manager Joe Torre (a former NL MVP in St. Louis) the Cards revived briefly, but then dropped their final seven games to insure their first basement finish in 72 years.

Reliever Lee Smith provided the key to St. Louis' 1991 rebound to second place: his 47 saves—a new NL record—preserved more than half the wins of a team that won 37 games by a single run. Smith saved another 43 games in 1992 and the Cards won nearly as often as they had the previous year, but this time finished third. The defense developed a leak in 1993, and the pitching faltered, but four regulars— Bernard Gilkey, Todd Zeile, and newcomers Gregg Jefferies and Mark Whiten (who became the 12th player to hit four home runs in a game)—scaled new heights offensively to keep the Cardinals competitive through much of the season and give them another third place finish. In 1994 the team—now playing in the NL's new Central Division—performed below .500 for the first time since 1990.

The weak-hitting Cards slipped to fourth in 1995. Manager Joe Torre was fired as the season wound down and was replaced by interim manager Mike Jorgensen and ultimately by former A's pilot Tony LaRussa. The big news of the year, however, came in December when Anheuser-Busch sold the club for $150 million to an investment group headed by St. Louis banker Andrew Baur and William DeWitt Jr., whose father had once owned the Browns and the Reds.

In 1996, Ozzie Smith's last season, the LaRussa-led Cards (88-74) outpaced Houston and Cincinnati for the NL Central championship. Aiding St. Louis's effort were Ron Gant (30 HR, 82 RBIs), Brian Jordan (17 HR, 104 RBIs), Andy Benes (18-10), and Dennis Eckersley (30 saves). In the first round of the postseason the Cards rolled over San Diego in three straight but in the NLCS ran into the Atlanta buzzsaw. Ahead three games to one, the Cards couldn't put away the pennant as the Braves rolled to 12-1, 3-1, and 15-0 victories in the last three games.

The 1997 and 1998 seasons were disappointing in the standings, but the Cardinals nonetheless became a top drawing card at home and on the road. A 1997 trading deadline deal with Oakland for Mark McGwire was worth its weight in gold. McGwire's combined total of 58 homers in 1997 was the most since Roger Maris broke Babe Ruth's mark with 61 home runs in 1961. In 1998 McGwire obliterated that record. As fans packed the left field stands across the country just to see McGwire take batting practice, "Big Mac" became the first player to hit 50 home runs in three straight seasons. Before a national television audience, McGwire hit his record-breaking 62nd home run on Sept. 8. He finished with an astounding 70 home runs, beating out Sammy Sosa, who blasted 66 homers for the Cubs.

McGwire followed his epic 1998 season with 65 home runs the next year, and also collected his 500th career blast, but little else went right for the Cardinals. General manager Walt Jocketty made several key moves in the offseason, acquiring Darryl Kile from Colorado and Jim

Edmonds from Anaheim. Kile won 20 games and Edmonds hit 40 home runs, marking the first time in history that two acquisitions both reached those plateaus in their first season with a new club. McGwire, however, was lost to regular duty for the second half as a knee injury limited him to a pinch-hitting role. So Jocketty made another key deal by bringing 36-year-old first baseman Will Clark to St. Louis. Clark, who would announce his retirement at the end of the season, batted .345 in 51 games for the division champs. Clark and Edmonds keyed a shocking sweep of the Braves in the Division Series, but St. Louis succumbed to the Mets in five games in the NLCS.

San Diego Padres

In their first 15 years the Padres put together only one winning season. In their 16th, they won the National League pennant. Founded in the 1969 expansion that saw the two major leagues divide into East and West divisions, the Padres finished last in the six-team NL West their first six seasons, ending each year from 28½ to 42 games behind the division champion.

Their first season was their worst. With 110 losses, the Padres finished not only 41 games out of first but 29 games out of fifth. First baseman Nate Colbert, with 24 home runs, provided San Diego's brightest ray of hope. He proved to be one of the Padres' standout performers through their last-place years, and in 1972 became the first Padre to drive in more than 100 runs. Colbert also had the greatest day in club history with five home runs and 13 RBIs in a doubleheader against Atlanta on Aug. 1, 1972.

Big league baseball was not an instant hit in San Diego. Home attendance barely topped half a million in the Padres' first year, and, though it rose a little over the next few seasons, the increase was not enough to make the club viable. Owner C. Arnholt Smith decided early in 1974 to sell the franchise to a buyer who planned to move the team to Washington, D.C. New uniforms had been manufactured and the club's files were packed for the move, when the builder of the McDonald's fast-food empire, longtime baseball fan Ray Kroc, stepped in with an offer to buy the Padres for cash and keep them in San Diego.

Though Kroc's 1974 Padres finished last with the same 60-102 record they had posted the year before, his sense of showmanship drew spectators. Home attendance shot up 76 percent, rising above a million for the first time. The Padres then began to draw fans on their own merits as they finally pulled themselves out of the cellar. Pitcher Randy Jones, who in 1974 had led the league with 22 losses, turned his record around and for two years shone as one of the game's finest pitchers. He halved his 1974 ERA to a league-leading 2.24, winning 20 games as the Padres rose to fourth place in 1975 and posted a winning percentage over .400 for the first time. The next year Jones won a league-high 22 games and earned the Cy Young Award—the first major award to come to a San Diego player.

Outfielder Dave Winfield came up as a rookie in 1973, and the following year became the team RBI leader, a position he held in six of his seven full seasons with the Padres. Reliever Rollie Fingers signed as a free agent. In each of his four seasons in San Diego (1977-1980) he led the team in saves, twice also leading the league. In 1978 the Padres acquired veteran pitcher Gaylord Perry from Texas and installed rookie Ozzie Smith at shortstop. Perry's sparkling 21-6 season gave San Diego its second Cy Young winner, and together with Smith's play in the field, Winfield's bat (.308, 97 RBIs) and Fingers' 37 saves, brought the Padres their first winning season.

All these stars had gone—and owner Kroc had recently died—by the time the Padres recorded a second winning season six years later, and won the division title and NL pennant with a new blend of experience and youth. Sparked by recently acquired veterans Steve Garvey at first, Graig Nettles at third, and Goose Gossage in the bullpen, and by a bevy of younger stars like batting champ Tony Gwynn and hard-hitting outfielder Kevin McReynolds, the Padres moved into first place to stay in early June. From Aug. 3 to the end of the season, they played only .500 ball but still won the championship of the weak Western Division by 12 games. Underdogs in the National League Championship Series, the Padres lost the first two games in Chicago, but pulled themselves together to take the pennant with three come-from-behind wins at home.

Their decline began with their World Series loss to Detroit. The end of 1985 saw them tied for third, and in 1986 they slipped below .500 and into fourth place. In 1987 Gwynn won his second batting title, and rookie catcher Benito Santiago capped the season with a 34-game hitting streak to cop Rookie of the Year honors. But with most of the 1984 standouts faded or traded, the Padres' decline was complete: the club for the ninth time in its 19 years finished last.

In late May 1988, with the team at 16-30, general manager Jack McKeon took over as field manager from Larry Bowa. Under McKeon the Padres went 67-48, with nine wins in their final 10 games, and shot from sixth place to third in the NL West.

In 1989 a trio of veteran pitchers—starters Bruce Hurst (lured from Boston as a free agent) and Ed Whitson and closer Mark Davis—attained new peaks of performance. Slugger Jack Clark (newly acquired from the Yankees) turned on the power after a slow start to complement Tony Gwynn's fourth season as NL batting leader. The Padres stumbled through the first half, arriving at the All-Star break four games below .500, but climbed steadily through the final two months to a second-place finish with their second-best winning percentage ever.

With the loss of free agent Davis in 1990, plus injuries to Clark and catcher Santiago, even the new power of Joe Carter (traded from Cleveland) could not lift the club above a tie for fourth. New owners, headed by TV producer Tom Werner, took control of the Padres from Ray Kroc's widow Joan in mid-June. Jack McKeon resigned his managerial position, which went to coach Greg Riddoch a month later, and was fired as general manager in September.

Slugger Fred McGriff arrived for 1991 (in a trade that sent Carter and young Roberto Alomar to Toronto) and helped power the Padres into third place. In 1992 he was joined by Gary Sheffield, who revived after an injury-ridden season at Milwaukee to lead the NL in batting and rank with McGriff among the league leaders in home runs and RBIs. The Padres again finished third, but Sheffield and McGriff were traded away during the 1993 season in cost-cutting moves that, combined with poor team pitching and fielding, dumped the Padres into the NL West cellar, a club record 43 games out of first.

Although the Padres had improved their winning percentage somewhat over 1993 by the time the 1994 season was cut short in August by the strike, their 47-70 record was the worst in the majors. One of San Diego's few reasons to cheer in 1994 was the hitting of Tony Gwynn, whose .394 batting average was the best in the NL since Bill Terry's .401 in 1930.

In December 1994 a group led by Larry Lucchino and John Moores acquired the club. GM Randy Smith resigned in midseason 1995, but the club rebounded slightly to a third place finish (70-74) as Gwynn (.368) won his sixth batting title.

The 1996 Padres (91-71) surprised virtually everyone by catching the Dodgers and capturing the NL West title on the last day of the season. Standout Padres included Tony Gwynn (with a league-leading .353 average), NL MVP Ken Caminiti (40 HR, 130 RBIs), Steve Finley (30 HR, 95 RBIs), Rickey Henderson (37 stolen bases), and Trevor Hoffman (42 saves). Their Cinderella season, however, came to an end in the first round of the postseason as they lost in three straight to St. Louis.

Other than Gwynn winning his eighth batting crown (tying Honus Wagner for the most in NL history), the 1997 season was a disappointment in San Diego. The Padres rebounded for a franchise-best 98 wins in 1998. New acquisition Kevin Brown anchored the rotation (18-7, 2.38 ERA, 257 strikeouts), Trevor Hoffman shattered the Padres record with 53 saves, and Greg Vaughn exploded for a club-record 50 home runs. The Padres surprised the favored Astros in the Division Series and then won the pennant in six games against Atlanta. They were tied or held a lead late in three of the four World Series games, but they could not stop the Yankees' march to a sweep. The Padres' biggest victory of the year, however, came on Nov. 3, when voters approved a new stadium for the ballclub.

Much like the Padres quickly sank in the standings after their 1984 pennant, San Diego plummeted again after the 1998 National League championship. Several players defected via free agency while trades sent away other key personnel. Still, the Padres popped into contention briefly with a franchise-record 14-game winning streak in June. San Diego's abysmal 28-53 mark on the road, however, consigned the club to fourth place. The high point of 1999 came in Montreal when Tony Gwynn singled for his 3,000th career hit.

The addition of Ryan Klesko and continued success from Phil Nevin and Eric Owens were the most satisfying developments in 2000. Injuries early in the season to Gwynn and Sterling Hitchcock helped keep the Padres from ever contending in the NL West.

San Francisco Giants

The expulsion of Troy and Worcester from the National League after the 1882 season cleared the way for the league to reestablish clubs in the major markets of Philadelphia and New York. Manufacturer John B. Day was awarded the New York franchise. Purchasing the defunct Troy club, he divided their players between the new NL Gothams and his other club, the Metropolitans of the American Association, and set them up on adjoining grounds north of Central Park, on a field once used for polo.

The Mets fared better than the Gothams, finishing fourth in 1883 to the Gothams' sixth, and winning the AA pennant the next year while the Gothams rose only to fifth in the NL. Since the NL, with greater prestige and higher ticket prices, offered potentially greater profit, Day switched some of his Mets to the Gothams in 1885, including ace hurler Tim Keefe and manager Jim Mutrie. The results were immediate: the Mets sank to seventh place while the Gothams (dubbed "my Giants" by an enthusiastic Mutrie) rose to the thick of a pennant race with Chicago. At the finish Chicago was on top by two games, but the Giants had won more than three games out of four for a .759 winning percentage that is not only the club's best ever, but one of the highest in major-league history. Pitchers Keefe and Mickey Welch together won 76 of the team's 85 victories, and first-baseman Roger Connor led the league in batting.

The Giants won their first pennant in 1888 and their second the next year in a one-game squeaker over Boston. Keefe and Welch, still going strong, combined for 61 wins in '88 and 55 in '89. Continuing their winning ways in the World Series, the Giants triumphed easily over St. Louis in 1888, and overcame a three-games-to-one deficit to vanquish Brooklyn the next year.

In 1890, ravaged by the loss of players to the rival Players League, the Giants finished sixth, but they recovered several players when the PL folded at the end of the season. (They also moved into the PL ballpark, named it after their original Polo Grounds, and played there for 67 years). They rose to third in 1891, but Day could no longer afford to maintain the team and sold out to financier Edward Talcott. Talcott brought back former Giants star J.M. Ward to manage the club and in 1894 saw the team rise to a close second-place finish behind Baltimore. Pitchers Amos Rusie and Jouett Meekin tied for the league lead with 36 wins apiece. In postseason Temple Cup play, the Giants swept Baltimore in four games for their third world championship.

That winter Talcott sold control of the club to Tammany Hall politician Andrew Freedman. The club's fortunes sank under Freedman's abrasive and heavy-handed rule. In 1902, his final year of ownership, the Giants suffered their lowest winning percentage—.353—and most distant finish ever—53½ games behind champion Pittsburgh.

In the midst of the 1902 season, though, a skirmish in the war between the NL and the upstart American League led to a Giants turnaround. John T. Brush, owner of the NL Cincinnati Reds, bought the AL Baltimore Orioles, then released Orioles manager John McGraw and several key players to sign with NL clubs. Five joined the Giants, including McGraw, catcher Roger Bresnahan, and pitcher Joe "Iron Man" McGinnity. That winter, Brush sold the Reds and Orioles and bought the Giants.

In 1903, with Bresnahan hitting .350 and McGinnity winning a league-high 31 games (closely followed by third-year phenom Christy Mathewson's 30 wins), manager McGraw saw his Giants win 36 more games than they had in 1902 and finish a solid second in the standings. In McGraw's 29 full seasons at the helm, the team won 10 pennants and finished second 11 times.

Just two years after their worst season ever, McGraw in 1904 led the Giants to one of their best. Their 106 wins and 13-game winning margin remain franchise records. The club led the NL in pitching, hitting, fielding, and base stealing. McGinnity led league pitchers in several categories with a career-best 35-8, 1.61 ERA season. Mathewson, right behind with 33 wins, led the league in strikeouts.

The only disappointment of 1904 was McGraw's refusal to face Boston in a World Series. His rejection of the AL champions as worthy opponents was the last shot fired in a war between the two leagues. By the time the Giants had repeated as NL pennant winners a year later, the World Series was an official and permanent feature of the baseball landscape.

Mathewson led NL pitchers in 1905 with 31 wins and an ERA of 1.27, and outfielder "Turkey Mike" Donlin, acquired from Cincinnati the previous July, erupted with the best season of his career, batting a team-high .356 and scoring a league-high 124 runs. The Giants won only one game less than the year before and held a comfortable lead throughout the season. Matty's three shutouts against the Philadelphia Athletics in the World Series secured the club's fourth world crown.

It was 1911 before the Giants won their next pennant. Despite 96 wins in 1906 they finished a distant second to the Chicago Cubs, who won a record 116 games. In 1908 the Giants came within a disputed play of the pennant. On Sept. 23, playing Chicago (with whom they were tied at the top of a three-way race), Giants baserunner Fred Merkle failed to run to second on a single by Al Bridwell that would have driven in the winning run from third. Merkle was forced at second after the ball (or a second ball—the argument still rages) was recovered amid the horde of fans who overran the field. The force out at second negated the run, and the game was ruled a tie. At season's end, when the two clubs found themselves again tied at the top, the "Merkle boner" game was replayed. The Cubs won the game and flag, leaving the Giants in a second-place tie with Pittsburgh.

In 1911 the Giants pulled away from the Cubs in September for the first of three straight pennants. (Early in the season most of the Polo Grounds was rebuilt in concrete after fire destroyed the wooden stands.) The following year the Giants took the lead in May and held it comfortably the rest of the way. In 1913 they didn't move into first until late June, but then they quickly put the flag out of reach and finished 12½ games ahead of the faltering Phillies. Mathewson led the team in victories over the three years, with 74, followed closely by Rube Marquard, who enjoyed the three best seasons of his career with 73 wins. Matty led the NL in ERA in 1911 and 1913, and rookie Jeff Tesreau took the honors in 1912 (winning 17 games that season and 22 the next). Giants pitching led the league all three seasons, as did their hitting, which featured a balanced offense paced by infielders Larry Doyle and Art Fletcher and catcher John "Chief" Myers.

In the World Series, though, the Giants fell short of the title three times. The Philadelphia Athletics defeated them handily in 1911 and 1913, but the Giants carried the 1912 Series against the Boston Red Sox to the 10th inning of the final game before a pair of fielding lapses by the Giants enabled Boston to rally for the win.

Boston's "Miracle" Braves, in their 1914 surge from last place to the pennant, passed the front-running Giants for good in early September. The next year, five of the eight NL clubs found themselves bunched within three and a half games of one another at the lower end of the standings as the season ended—with the Giants at the very bottom. The 1916 season was characterized by dips and surges, but even a 26-game winning streak in September couldn't raise the team higher than fourth. In 1917 a balanced pitching staff— paced by Ferdie Schupp's one big season (21-7, 1.95 ERA)—hurled the Giants to the front early in June and kept them there to the finish. Once more, though, the World Series proved to be a disappointment, with a loss to the Chicago White Sox in six games.

Three years of second-place finishes followed, in the midst of which the Giants changed owners. Brush had died in 1912 and was succeeded as president by his son-in-law Harry Hempstead. But in January 1919 Brush's heirs sold the club to financier and racehorse fancier Charles A. Stoneham, with manager McGraw becoming a minority stockholder.

In 1921 McGraw brought home the first of four straight winners for Stoneham. Seven regulars hit over .300 (led by third baseman Frank Frisch's .341); first baseman George Kelly's 23 home runs topped the NL. The club hung close to Pittsburgh through August, then broke into a lead which the fading Pirates could not challenge. In postseason play the Giants lost the first two games to the Yankees, but charged back to win their fifth world title. The next year outfielder Emil "Irish" Meusel celebrated his first full season in New York with a team-high 132 RBIs, as the Giants fended off a midseason challenge from St. Louis to pull away to a comfortable margin at the end. The World Series was especially sweet: a four-game sweep of the Yankees.

Cincinnati and Pittsburgh hung just behind the Giants through much of 1923, but never quite caught up. The Giants' league-leading offense was led by individual NL highs in RBIs (Meusel), runs scored (outfielder Ross Youngs), and hits and total bases (Frisch). But the Yankees finally caught the Giants in the World Series, 4-2.

George Kelly took the NL RBI title in 1924. The club's hitting remained the league's best, and by early August the Giants had taken a 10-game lead. But they then leveled off while Brooklyn and Pittsburgh surged. Brooklyn, in fact, took over the lead for a day in early September, but the Giants emerged triumphant at the end by 1½ games. The World Series, though, was as heartbreaking as the pennant race had been heartstopping: the Giants lost to Washington in the last of the 12th inning of the seventh game when a grounder bounced over the head of Giants rookie third baseman Fred Lindstrom to drive in the Series-ending run.

Close finishes in 1927 and 1928 were the nearest McGraw's Giants came to another pennant. Ill and tired, he quit early in the 1932 season with the team in last place, naming first baseman Bill Terry to replace him. Under Terry the Giants rose only to sixth that season, but McGraw had built a squad fit for a new era of greatness. He had persuaded Terry to leave a career with Standard Oil for one with the Giants; he had saved Mel Ott's unique but effective batting stance from revision by well-meaning minor league managers by keeping Ott out of the minors; and he had rescued pitcher Carl Hubbell from mediocrity by encouraging the screwball pitch other managers had tried to suppress in the minors.

Hubbell and Ott formed the heart of the club that would win a trio of pennants under Terry's management. In 1933 the Giants moved to the front in June and, despite a late-September slump, finished well ahead of runner-up Pittsburgh. Ott, with what was for him an off-year, powered the offense with 23 homers and 103 RBIs, while Hubbell led the league in wins, shutouts, and ERA. Hubbell also hurled two wins against Washington in the World Series, and Ott won it all for New York with a 10th-inning home run in Game 5. McGraw, still the club's vice president, threw a party for "his" Giants after the Series. The following February he died, at age 60.

As they had the previous season, the Giants of 1934 emerged from the crowd to take and hold first place into late September. They rose higher than they had in 1933 and didn't slump as far at the end. But their five end-of-season losses were enough to drop them two games behind the surging Cardinals at the finish. Again in 1935 they led the league much of the season. But they had begun to level off in mid-July and finished the season well back in third. Charles Stoneham died in January 1936, and his son Horace— who at age 33 had already run the club for a year—assumed the club presidency.

In 1936, and again in 1937, the Giants came from behind to take the flag. Hubbell sparked their second-half resurgence in 1936, winning his final 16 decisions of the season as the Giants rose from fourth to first. In the World Series, though, Hubbell, after one win, was stopped by the Yankees in his try for a second. The Yankees took the Series in six games.

Again the next year the Giants hid behind the leaders most of the season until a surge in late August coincided with a Chicago decline and shot the Giants to the front. The Cubs recovered, but New York continued its winning ways and finished ahead by three games. But again the Yankees dominated the World Series, winning in five games.

Hubbell's years of greatness were now over, and while the Giants led the NL through the first half of 1938, they finished five games out in third place. It would be 12 years before they again finished that close to the top. Mel Ott replaced Terry as manager in 1942, but the Giants sank to the cellar in 1943 with their second-worst season ever, and finished last again three years later.

Halfway through the 1948 season the baseball world was startled to learn that Leo Durocher, the fiery manager of the Brooklyn Dodgers, had switched his allegiance to their arch foes, the Giants. Durocher discarded the club's top three home run hitters of 1947 and added agile infielders Alvin Dark and Eddie Stanky to the roster. By 1950, with the blossoming of Sal Maglie into a first-rank pitcher and the timely midseason purchase of hurler Jim Hearn, the Giants were once more a challenger, spurting in the second half from below .500 to within five games of the top.

After losing their first 11 games the next year, the Giants began a long climb. A 16-game August winning streak and a seven-game streak at season's end tied them with Brooklyn and forced a three-game playoff. After a win and a loss, the Giants entered the last of the ninth inning of Game 3 trailing by a 4-1 score. Two singles and a double cut the deficit by a run and brought on Ralph Branca to face Bobby Thomson. Thomson homered to left and the Giants won the pennant. Their defeat by the Yankees in the World Series dimmed the miracle a bit, but it couldn't detract from the career bests of pitchers Maglie and Larry Jansen, who tied for the NL lead with 23 wins apiece, and of former Negro League great Monte Irvin, who hit .312 and led the league in RBIs.

The next year Irvin was lost until August with a broken ankle, Jansen (with a back problem) fell off to 11-11, and Willie Mays—a promising rookie in 1951—left early in the season for a hitch in the Army. Still, the Giants hung close to Brooklyn for much of the summer and finished second. In 1953, though, they fell apart in midseason and wound up in fifth, 35 games out.

Mays returned in 1954 to enjoy one of his strongest seasons, and pitchers Johnny Antonelli (newly acquired from Milwaukee), sophomore Ruben Gomez, and reliever Marv Grissom all burst forth with the best seasons of their careers. The Giants pulled away from Brooklyn in July and held on with a late-season rush to win by five games. Underdogs to powerful Cleveland in the World Series, they stunned the Indians (and the rest of the baseball world) with a four-game sweep. It was their eighth world title—and, so far, their last.

Manager Durocher retired after a distant third-place finish in 1955, and Bill Rigney, who replaced him (the first of seven straight rookie managers to be hired by the Giants over the next 20 years), presided over a pair of sixth-place seasons in the club's final years in New York. Persuaded by the Dodgers' Walter O'Malley that California was the land of baseball opportunity, Giants owner Stoneham announced in August 1957 his decision to move the club to San Francisco before the next season.

The move succeeded. Home attendance doubled, even though the team had to play in a former minor league park that seated fewer than 23,000 fans. When new Candlestick Park opened in 1960 attendance climbed to nearly 1.8 million, a new club high. Better still, rookie sensations like Orlando Cepeda in 1958 and Willie McCovey in 1959, plus the continuing mastery of Willie Mays, made the Giants competitive once again. In their first 14 San Francisco seasons, they compiled winning records—a longer string than they had ever known in New York.

Candlestick Park, though, proved a cold and windy place to watch baseball, and after its inaugural season fans began to drift away. Attendance picked up some in 1962, however, as the Giants battled for first all summer with the Los Angeles Dodgers. Mays, Cepeda, and Felipe Alou headlined the league's best offense, and a pair of veteran pitchers—Jack Sanford and Billy O'Dell—garnered the most wins of their careers (24 and 19) as part of a balanced staff that also got 16 wins from veteran Billy Pierce and 18 from the emerging great Juan Marichal. Still, the Giants trailed the Dodgers most of the season until the Giants won and the Dodgers lost on the final day to force another playoff. As in 1951, the Giants won the first game and lost the second, and overcame a ninth-inning deficit in the finale to win the pennant. Also as in

1951, they lost the World Series to the Yankees, although this time they held on until the final out of Game 7 before losing their grip on the crown.

The 1963 Giants offered little challenge to the leaders after June, but the next three years found them locked to the end in tight struggles for the flag. Although they finished fourth in 1964, they were still in contention with just two games to play, in one of the closest four-way races ever. The next year they took the lead from the Dodgers early in September, only to lose it in the final week. And in 1966, in a season-long three-way race with the Dodgers and Pirates, the Giants weren't eliminated until the final day.

The turbulence of these races was reflected in the team itself. Cepeda (until traded to St. Louis in 1966) continually railed against his managers and his low pay. Alvin Dark, after four winning seasons as manager, was fired in 1964 when some of his racist comments ended up in print. And Marichal was fined and suspended for nine days in 1965 for hitting Dodgers catcher John Roseboro over the head with his bat.

After a pair of distant second-place finishes, the Giants in 1969 (with the fine work of Marichal and McCovey augmented by the speed and power of young outfielder Bobby Bonds) found themselves in the thick of a five-way race for the championship of the newly created NL West. The race wasn't settled until the final week, when Atlanta's 10-game winning streak knocked the Giants out of first. Two years later, with Bonds the chief source of offensive power and fine pitching from starters Marichal and Gaylord Perry and reliever Jerry Johnson, the Giants moved out in front at the start of the season and held their lead all the way. In the National League Championship Series, though, they succumbed to Pittsburgh with three losses after an opening-game win.

The NLCS loss signaled the end of an era. McCovey was past his prime and Marichal had enjoyed his last big year. Mays, after 20 seasons as a Giant was sent to the Mets in 1972 so he could close out his career in New York, where it began. That year the Giants suffered their first losing season in San Francisco, and attendance for the first time dropped below what it had been in their final New York season.

Attendance had reached such a low point by the mid-1970s that Stoneham negotiated the club's sale to a Canadian brewery which planned to move it to Toronto. But San Francisco's mayor George Moscone delayed the sale until a buyer could be found who would keep the Giants in the city. San Francisco realtor Robert Lurie stepped forth with half the purchase price, and Arizona cattleman Arthur "Bud" Herseth provided the rest. (Toronto settled for an expansion club, the Blue Jays.)

After six years out of the running, the Giants in 1978 played at the top of the NL West through much of the summer before dropping to third (and home attendance jumped more than a million above the previous year). But they fell below .500 the next two years—making seven losing seasons in the nine that followed their division title of 1971.

In 1982 the Giants—paced by the slugging of Jack Clark and Greg Minton's sparkling relief pitching—made one of the most impressive comebacks since divisional play was instituted in 1969, driving from 10 games below .500 to within two games of champion Atlanta at season's end. But they dropped to fifth the following year, and to a last-place sixth in 1984 and 1985.

When Roger Craig was called on to manage the final weeks of the 1985 season, there was no stopping the Giants' slide to a club-record 100 losses. But the next year, inspiring a "can do" spirit among the players, Craig turned the club around. Veteran hurler Mike Krukow won a career-high 20 games, eight players contributed more than 40 RBIs each, and the team captured 26 of their 83 wins in their final at bat. In first place at midseason, the Giants slipped (in part because of injuries) to third by season's end, but the fans were back—over 700,000 more than a year earlier.

The club set a new home attendance record of more than 1.9 million in 1987 as it returned to the top of the NL West for the first time in 16 years. Sophomore first baseman Will Clark led a balanced offense, and several shrewd in-season acquisitions by the front office spurred a second-half drive from five games back to a six-game lead at the finish. But after taking a three-games-to-two advantage over St. Louis in the NLCS, the Giants failed to score in the final two games and the Cardinals captured the flag.

Injuries contributed to the Giants' decline to fourth place the next year, but in 1989 Clark enjoyed his strongest season yet, and left fielder Kevin Mitchell erupted with league-high power, pacing the NL in homers (47), RBIs (125), and slugging percentage (.635) to lead a San Francisco assault on the division title. For the first time, the Giants passed the 2 million mark in home attendance. After holding first place from mid-June to the finish, they pushed past the stubborn Cubs in the NLCS to win the first Giants pennant in 27 years and the 19th in franchise history. But the earthquake that delayed Game 3 of the World Series only postponed a sweep by mighty Oakland.

The Giants' downward slide over the next three years—to third place in 1990, fourth in 1991, and fifth in 1992—coincided with futile efforts to persuade Bay area voters to approve public funding for a new stadium to replace unpopular Candlestick Park. In August 1992, owner Bob Lurie arranged to sell the club to a group of investors who planned to move it to St. Petersburg, Florida. In November, though, the sale and move were blocked by the other major league owners.

The signing of free agent Barry Bonds ignited a turnaround in 1993. As Bonds put together another Ruthian season, and Matt Williams rebounded from his worst season to his best, starting pitchers John Burkett and Bill Swift developed into 20-game winners and closer Rod Beck saved the second most games (48) in NL history. The Giants lost their once-big lead to surging Atlanta in September, but revived to tie the Braves with three games to go. Although a final-game loss to Los Angeles cost them the division title, their 103 wins tied for third best in club history.

On Aug. 11, 1994, the Giants stood five games below .500, but only three and a half games out of first place in the weak NL West. Barry Bonds was enjoying another fine season at the bat, but Matt Williams' 43 home runs (within legitimate striking distance of Roger Maris' record of 61) stole the headlines. When the players went out on strike the next day, one of the most exciting offensive seasons ever went down the drain.

In 1995 manager Dusty Baker's Giants fell to last (67-77) despite Barry Bonds' 33 homers and 104 RBIs. The Giants (68-94) remained in the NL basement in 1996 as Bonds (.308, 42 HR, 129 RBIs) again compiled superstar numbers.

The Giants were transformed from "worst to first" in 1997. The additions of second baseman Jeff Kent (28 HR, 118 RBIs) and three pitchers from the White Sox (Wilson Alvarez, Roberto Hernandez, and Danny Darwin) plus the emergence of starter Shawn Estes (19-5, 3.48 ERA) helped push the Giants to the division title. The eventual world champion Florida Marlins beat the Giants twice in their last at bat on the way to a sweep in the Division Series. In 1998 the Giants put together a 10-game winning streak in the final week of the season to come from four games behind to tie the Cubs and force a one-game playoff for the NL Wild Card. Despite a late rally by the Giants in the playoff game, the Cubs held on to win at Wrigley Field.

The 1999 season, the club's last at Candlestick, yielded 86 wins yet left the team a distant second to division champ Arizona. The franchise finished the 20th century with the most wins of any National League team. The new century brought a new ballpark and success.

The club christened beautiful Pacific Bell Park and sold out every game. After winning just once in the park's first month, the Giants were unstoppable at home and finished the season with the best record of any team in baseball. Bonds hit 49 home runs and scored 129 times, while Kent drove in 125; Ellis Burks, meanwhile, battled through injuries to bat .344. San Francisco's starting staff was good, but its bullpen was even better with Felix Rodriguez and Robb Nen providing one of baseball's best setup-closer tandems. The Giants won the division by 11 games over Los Angeles. Game 1 of the Division Series was San Francisco's first postseason win in 11 years, but the Mets won the next three to bring an abrupt end to the season.

Seattle Mariners

The Mariners began play in 1977, returning major league baseball to the Pacific Northwest eight years after the Seattle Pilots had moved to Milwaukee after only one season. With a 64-98 inaugural season, the Mariners avoided last place in the American League West only because the Oakland A's had plummeted faster and farther. The hitting of first baseman Dan Meyer, outfielder Leroy Stanton, and rookie center fielder Ruppert Jones—who combined for 73 home runs—and the relief pitching of rookie Enrique Romo, who contributed 16 saves and eight wins, provided most of the high points of that first season.

There was less to cheer about the next year as the production of the first-season heroes fell off and the Mariners took early possession of the cellar and lost a club-record 104 games. They finished 12 games out of sixth place, 35 out of first. Much of the offense that was generated came from outfielder Leon Roberts. Acquired from Houston over the winter, Roberts became the Mariners' first .300 hitter.

The club moved up a notch in 1979, to sixth place (and Seattle also hosted that year's All-Star Game). Meyer and Jones regained much of their earlier power, first baseman Bruce Bochte hit .316 and drove in 100 runs, and DH Willie Horton, near the end of a long career, enjoyed one of his finest seasons, driving in 106 runs and leading the club with 29 homers.

As the Mariners, with the league's weakest hitting, dropped back into the cellar the next season, attendance fell to a new low, and some of the original owners decided to sell out. In January 1981 California real-estate magnate George Argyros purchased control of the club, and later bought out the remaining partners to take sole ownership.

Pitching finally arrived in 1982 in the form of Bill Caudill and rookie Ed Vande Berg. The pair, working in relief, combined for 21 wins and 31 saves. Starter Floyd Bannister led the league in strikeouts while winning 12 games (tying Caudill for the team lead), and veteran Gaylord Perry added 10 victories, including his 300th career win in May. The team finished above .450 for the first time, fourth in the AL West, a new high.

Caudill's 26 saves in 1983 couldn't prevent a slide back into last place. But the club's farm system was beginning to produce quality talent, and 1984 saw the arrival of two standouts: first baseman Alvin Davis, whose 27 homers and 116 RBIs earned him AL Rookie of the Year honors, and pitcher Mark Langston, a 17-game winner in 1984 and AL strikeout leader in three of his first four seasons. Rookie third baseman Jim Presley hit 10 home runs in 70 games and proceeded to blossom into one of the Seattle club's leading power hitters the next year.

After sixth-place finishes in 1984 and '85, the Mariners fell off to last again in 1986. Langston's 19 wins led the team's 1987 rebound to fourth. Infielder Harold Reynolds stole his 60th base in the final game to give the Mariners their first league leader in an offensive category.

After dropping back into the cellar in 1988 and rising a notch to sixth in 1989, the Mariners revived under new ownership in 1990 to challenge the .500 barrier. Center fielder Ken Griffey, Jr., began to fulfill the promise he had shown as a 19-year-old rookie the previous summer. Sophomore hurler Erik Hanson—with 18 wins and an ERA among the league's best—replaced the traded Mark Langston as ace of a young pitching staff that compiled the league's third lowest ERA. The Mariners entered August third in the strong AL West, with a winning record which they maintained through mid-month before stumbling to fifth place with their 14th straight losing season.

At last, in 1991, Seattle produced its first winning season, rising from an even .500 with six wins in the final eight games. Griffey Jr. overcame a lackluster first half to reach new Mariner heights in batting (.327) and slugging (.527), but the club still finished fifth, and manager Jim Lefebvre was fired. It also continued to lose money, so in June 1992, as the Mariners sailed for the sixth time to the bottom of the AL West, the club was sold. The new ownership group included (for the first time) substantial local representation, but as major financing came from Hiroshi Yamauchi, the Japanese president of computer game giant Nintendo, and his son-in-law, a Washington State resident but Japanese national, the sale was delayed until jingoistic opposition to it subsided—and the deal was restructured to insure American control of the club. On the field Griffey enjoyed another strong season, and third baseman Edgar Martinez hit .343 to give Seattle its first league batting champion.

A torn hamstring sidelined Martinez much of 1993, but Griffey shone brighter than ever at the bat, and pitcher Randy Johnson finished with nine straight wins (for a 19-8 season record) and 308 strikeouts (a 15-year AL high). Their exploits lifted the Mariners into third place for a day in late September before they settled into fourth, with their second winning season ever.

In 1994 the Mariners again enjoyed stellar performances from Griffey and Johnson, but despite six straight wins before the season ended in August, they wound up 14 games below .500. In the weak AL West, though, their ministreak brought them within two games of division leader Texas—and a third place finish, their highest ever.

After a long climb during the 1995 season, the Mariners (paced by Edgar Martinez's league-leading .356 average and Randy Johnson's league-leading 294 strikeouts and 2.48 ERA) caught the Angels in the AL West division race and forced a one-game playoff. Behind Johnson, Seattle took the game and went on to nip the New York Yankees in the first round of the postseason in one of the most exciting series in baseball history. But in the ALCS the powerhouse Indians proved too much for Seattle, defeating them in six games.

Injuries to Johnson and Edgar Martinez hampered the 1996 Mariners and they slipped to second (85-76) despite shortstop Alex Rodriguez's major league-best .358 average and 54 doubles. The Mariners survived a rocky bullpen to stave off the Angels for the AL West title in 1997. Griffey earned AL MVP honors and led the league with 56 home runs, 147 RBIs, 125 runs, .646 slugging, and 393 total bases. Attendance, which topped 1 million just twice in the team's first eight seasons reached 3 million in 1997. The Mariners faltered in the Division Series, however, falling to the Orioles in four games.

Poor pitching buried the Mariners early in 1998 and not even 56 home runs from Griffey could save the Mariners from a distant third-place finish. The 1999 season was a learning experience for Seattle. The club moved into its new ballpark in midseason, and the pitchers learned it was to their liking. Rookie Freddy Garcia won 17 games and Jamie Moyer added 14. Griffey learned, however, that he did not like spacious Safeco Field and asked to be traded at season's end. Griffey, with the power to veto any trade, left new general manager Pat Gillick little choice but to send him to Cincinnati.

Free-agent first baseman John Olerud and new center fielder Mike Cameron anchored the defense, and the pitching continued to blossom in 2000. American League Rookie of the Year Kazuhiro Sasaki brought stability to a traditionally porous bullpen, and free agent Aaron Sele won 17 games. The Mariners had the league's best home record, yet the AL's worst home batting average. Alex Rodriguez and Edgar Martinez combined for 79 home runs and drove in 277 runs, including a league-best 145 RBIs by Martinez. Seattle clinched a Wild Card berth on the final day of the season. The Mariners shocked the White Sox with a three-game sweep in the Division Series. Seattle blanked the Yankees for the first 16 innings of the ALCS, but New York rallied to take the series in six games.

Tampa Bay Devil Rays

Along with the Arizona Diamondbacks, the Tampa Bay Devil Rays were granted a $130 million major league expansion franchise on March 9, 1995. The Devil Rays played their first game at the newly-renovated (and renamed) Tropicana Field in St. Petersburg on March 31, 1998. The first pitch in franchise history, by Wilson Alvarez, was a long time in coming to finally bring baseball to the Tampa area.

The White Sox had planned to move to St. Petersburg in the late 1980s and only remained in the Windy City when funding was approved for a new Comiskey Park. The Mariners had considered moving to St. Petersburg in 1991. And in late 1992 a Tampa Bay group led by businessman Vince Naimoli thought it had purchased the San Francisco Giants from Bob Lurie for $115 million, but NL owners voted against moving the club from one Bay Area to another. Naimoli was eventually awarded the Devil Rays franchise and he named Chuck LaMar as the club's first general manager. Shortly after the Florida Marlins won the 1997 World Series, Tampa Bay scooped up Marlins pitching coach Larry Rothschild and made him the team's first manager.

Rookie Rolando Arrojo, the team's first All-Star, won 14 games to break the single-season expansion record. By contrast, the rest of the starters won just 25 games between them. There were plenty of whiffs at Tropicana Field: Tampa Bay pitchers fanned 1,003 batters and their hitters struck out 1,101 times. Highlights of their first season included Tampa native Wade Boggs hitting the first home run in club history; Quinton McCracken setting the expansion record for hits and outfield assists; and the Devil Rays becoming the first expansion team to be four games over .500 in their first season at 10-6. Their fast start was all that kept the Devil Rays from hitting the century mark in losses as the team finished its inaugural season with the AL's worst record at 63-99.

After three years the Devil Rays had still not reached 100 losses in a season, but they had not escaped the cellar either. Tampa Bay had difficulty drawing crowds and even more trouble earning wins. The 1999 team won just 33 of 81 games at Tropicana Field. Their highlights were memorable but brief: Wade Boggs achieved his 3,000th hit, becoming the first to do so with a home run; Jim Morris, 35, made the impressive jump from high school teacher to major league pitcher in one year; Jose Canseco hit 32 home runs in half a season before having back surgery; and Roberto Hernandez won or saved 45 games—unfortunately the team won just 24 other times.

In 2000 they avoided the league's worst record by going 8-2 to close out the season, including their first-ever sweep of the Yankees. It was hardly the season that the team had envisioned, however. The Devil Rays had fashioned a powerful new look: acquisitions Greg Vaughn and Vinny Castilla, plus holdovers Fred McGriff and Jose Canseco. Vaughn battled through injuries to hit 28 home runs, one more than Fred McGriff, who hit his 400th career homer during the season. Castilla, however, hit just six homers and Canseco homered nine times before the club placed him on waivers.

Texas Rangers

As part of the first American League expansion, a new Washington club was added to the league in November 1960, to replace the old Senators, who were moving to Minnesota to become the Twins. The old Senators had languished in the second division their final 14 years in Washington, and the new Senators scarcely improved on that record. In each of their first four seasons they lost 100 games or more, tying for last place in 1961 and holding down the bottom all by themselves for two years before rising to ninth in 1964.

Although as an expansion team the new Senators had to make do at first with expendable players from the established clubs, they were not devoid of talent. In their first season, pitcher Dick Donovan led the league with a 2.40 earned run average, though injuries and the lack of offensive support held his won-lost record to 10-10. Perhaps their most promising player, he was traded with two teammates to Cleveland for outfielder Jimmy Piersall. Piersall proved a major disappointment in Washington, batting only .244 while Donovan was winning 20 games for his new club.

Not all the Senators' trades proved disastrous. In late 1964 they sent another promising pitcher— Claude Osteen—to the Dodgers in a deal that brought them five players, including third baseman Ken McMullen and outfielder Frank Howard. Osteen blossomed into a consistent winner in Los Angeles, but at the same time, McMullen brought strength to the Washington infield and Howard became one of the league's offensive stars.

The Senators' blend of youth and experience jelled in 1969 under rookie manager Ted Williams, as several key players—including McMullen and Howard—enjoyed career-best seasons. The club finished above .500 for the first time, driving with a late-season spurt to within a game of third-place Boston in the league's Eastern Division.

But 1969 was a one-year phenomenon. After losing seasons in 1970 and '71 (and the loss of much of their fan support), owner Bob Short pulled up stakes and moved the club to Arlington, Texas (midway between Fort Worth and Dallas), where, as the Texas Rangers, they have been ever since. Their first summer in Texas resembled their first in Washington: they lost 100 games (despite a strike-shortened season) and finished last. Williams was replaced by a new rookie manager—Whitey Herzog—but the club did no better in 1973.

Before the season's end Herzog gave way to Billy Martin. Martin came too late to save the Rangers from another lost season, but the next year he spurred the team to the kind of turnaround Williams had managed five years earlier. Behind the 25-12 pitching of Ferguson Jenkins (acquired in the offseason from the Cubs) and the hitting of league MVP Jeff Burroughs and AL Rookie of the Year Mike Hargrove, the Rangers spurted in the second half of 1974 from a sub-.500 record to second place in the American League West, only five games behind Oakland.

The Rangers rebounded from two losing seasons to their finest season yet in 1977 (94-68, .580) and second place, behind strong pitching and the blooming of Jim Sundberg as a hitter to go along with his league-leading catching. The return of Fergie Jenkins (after two years in Boston), the sparkling 11-5 season of rookie Steve Comer, and a September surge kept the club competitive in 1978. Jim Kern's brilliant relief work the next season helped the club recover from a nosedive in July and August to edge Minnesota for a strong third-place finish.

After a losing season in 1980, the Rangers bounced back in 1981 to record their second-best winning percentage ever (.543)—and finishes of second and third in the two halves of the strike-divided season. Then they slipped below .500 again for four more years. Pitcher Charlie Hough's knuckleball, and strong seasons at the bat from Pete O'Brien, Larry Parrish, Scott Fletcher, and rookie Pete Incaviglia helped new manager Bobby Valentine guide the Rangers to a second-place finish after last-place seasons in 1984 and '85.

Once more, though, the turnaround was brief: in 1987 losses in their final games of the season dropped the Rangers into a tie at the bottom of the division, and in 1988 they finished only two games out of the cellar, in sixth place.

A group of investors headed by George W. Bush—the President's son—purchased control of the Rangers in March 1989, and strikeout king Nolan Ryan returned to the American League as a Ranger after nine years in Houston. The strong arms of starter Ryan (who recorded his 5,000th career strikeout during the season) and reliever Jeff Russell, the potent bats of outfielder Ruben Sierra and second baseman Julio Franco (newly acquired from Cleveland), and a 10-1 start that put the club in first place for a month (before they settled back to fourth) highlighted a return to the winning side of the ledger. In 1990 Ryan hurled his 300th win and sixth no-hitter, first baseman Rafael Palmeiro peaked at the plate, and pitcher Bobby Witt enjoyed his finest season, with 17 wins. After a slow first half, the Rangers rose from sixth place to third, compiling an 83-79 record identical to that of the year before.

A 14-game win streak in May 1991 boosted the Rangers into first place for several days, although they again finished third. Jose Guzman joined Ryan (who fashioned a seventh no-hitter) among the league's top pitchers, and young slugger Juan Gonzalez formed with Franco, Palmeiro, and Sierra a powerful quartet that made the Rangers the top scoring team in the majors. In 1992 pitcher Kevin Brown won 21 games, and Gonzalez topped the majors in home runs. But an overall decline in offense, and disastrous fielding and relief pitching dropped the team below .500 after a competitive first half as manager Valentine was fired in July. In the year's biggest in-season trade, the club acquired Jose Canseco from Oakland for Sierra, Witt, and Russell.

The Rangers surged to within a game of first place in mid-July 1993 and remained competitive into September, finishing second. Canseco injured his elbow in a relief pitching stint in June and was lost for the season, but Gonzalez again led the league in home runs (with 46), while also leading his team in batting and RBIs. Nolan Ryan retired after an injury-shortened season, and as the Rangers ended their tenure at Texas Stadium, their new home arose on the other side of the parking lot.

In the weak AL West of 1994, it didn't matter that the Rangers played losing ball in the new Ballpark in Arlington. Despite their worst record in six years—a .456 winning percentage that would have consigned them to the cellar of the East or Central divisions—the Rangers were a game ahead of Oakland, in first place, when the strike ended the season. Texas's won-lost percentage improved to .538 in 1995 but that was only good enough for third.

In 1996 the Rangers (90-72) won their first division title on the heavy hitting of MVP Juan Gonzalez (47 HR, 144 RBIs), Dean Palmer (38 HR, 107 RBIs), Rusty Greer (.321, 100 RBIs), and Kevin Elster (24 HR, 99 RBIs). The Rangers boasted an unusually well-balanced rotation—Ken Hill (16-10), Roger Pavlik (15-8), Bobby Witt (16-12), and Darren Oliver (14-6)—along with reliever Mike Henneman (31 saves) and late season addition John Burkett (5-2). The Yankees, however, rolled over Texas in the first round of the postseason despite five home runs by Gonzalez.

Johnny Oates, who shared AL Manager of the Year honors in 1996, could do little with the Rangers in 1997. The most significant thing that happened in Texas was the first-ever interleague game on June 12; later in the month, Texas starter Bobby Witt became the first AL pitcher to homer in the regular season in 25 years. The Rangers jousted with the Angels for first place in the AL West for much of 1998 before they swept Anaheim in the final week of the season to capture the title. Trades for Royce Clayton and Todd Zeille revitalized the left side of the infield while new acquisition Todd Stottlemyre won several big games down the stretch. Juan Gonzalez, who had 100 RBIs at the All-Star break, drove in 157 runs and won his second AL MVP. Rick Helling became the third 20-game winner in Rangers history and John Wetteland set the club record with 42 saves. Just as in 1996, they ran into the Yankees in the Division Series and the Rangers were quickly dispatched.

The 1999 ended with a club-record 95 wins, another MVP Award (this time for Ivan Rodriguez), and a smashing return to Texas by Rafael Palmeiro, but for the third time in four years the Yankees knocked off the Rangers in the Division Series. The club tried a new direction, trading Gonzalez to the Tigers for several young players. Gabe Kapler had the biggest impact of any new player. He had a 28-game hitting streak, while his .302 average and 32 doubles were better numbers than Gonzalez put together in Detroit. Palmeiro followed up a 47-homer, 140-RBI season with 39 homers and 120 RBIs in 2000. But it was pitching and defense that was the team's undoing. Texas was last in the league in ERA and had the lowest fielding percentage as well. Part of that certainly had to do with the absence of nine-time Gold Glove catcher Rodriguez, who missed the second half of the year with a broken thumb.

Toronto Blue Jays

For a while, in February 1976, it looked as if the National League's San Francisco Giants would move to Toronto, where there were buyers eager for the club. But when the Giants were sold in March to new owners determined to keep them in San Francisco, the American League jumped in to establish Toronto as an American League city, setting up an expansion club, the Blue Jays, who began play the next year in Exhibition Stadium.

It took seven years for the Jays to lift themselves out of last place in the seven-team American League East. For five years they had the cellar all to themselves, never finishing closer than 11 games behind the sixth-place club.

In their first season, the Jays' 107 losses left them 45½ games out of first, as the team performed at the bottom of the division in hitting, fielding, and pitching. In 1978 their fielding improved dramatically, but the Jays still lost over 100 games, and there was little doubt after April who would finish last.

The next year was the team's worst ever. While every other Eastern Division club was compiling a winning record, Toronto plunged relentlessly downward and, despite a brief rally in September, finished 28½ games out of sixth place (50½ out of first), with 109 losses.

The club's turnaround began in 1980. It was late June before the Jays began their drop away from the rest of the division, and for the first time they finished with fewer than 100 losses. Pitchers Jim Clancy and Dave Stieb each had an ERA below 4.00 for the first time, and newly acquired second baseman Damaso Garcia combined with shortstop Alfredo Griffin to form the league's best double-play combination. There were still two more seasons in the cellar, but in strike-divided 1981 the Jays played a creditable second half for the first time, and in 1982 they spurted in September to tie the Indians for sixth at season's end. Garcia in 1982 became a .300 hitter and a leading base stealer, Clancy put together his first winning season and Stieb his second, and Stieb's five shutouts led the league.

In 1983, with seven of the Blue Jays' eight principal pitchers enjoying winning seasons, and the Jays' hitters leading the league in team batting and slugging, Toronto recorded its first winning season—in fourth place, only nine games out of first. Their balanced pitching and offense carried them to a repeat 89-73 record in 1984—this time for second place (though they finished a distant 15 games behind Detroit).

In 1985 the Blue Jays topped their division with 99 victories, edging the Yankees by two games. Their pitching was better than ever. Doyle Alexander won 17 games, Jimmy Key and Dave Stieb contributed 14 each, and reliever Dennis Lamp compiled an impressive 11-0 record. Stieb led the league in ERA, with Key fourth. Tony Fernandez, in his first full big league season, sparkled as expected at short, but also proved unexpectedly solid at the bat. Eight Jays drove in more than 50 runs, with outfielders George Bell (95), Jesse Barfield (84), and Lloyd Moseby (71) pacing the club's balanced attack.

In the ALCS the Jays won three of their first four games against Kansas City, but lost the next three—and the pennant. Equally discouraging was their drop to fourth place in 1986. Barfield, Bell, and Fernandez all improved at the plate, but the league-leading pitchers of 1985 dropped back to the middle of the pack in '86 (though rookie Mark Eichorn sparkled in long relief).

Toronto sprang back stronger than ever in 1987. Jim Clancy (15-11, 3.54 ERA) enjoyed his best season yet, as did Jimmy Key (17-8), whose 2.76 ERA led the league. Once again, as in 1985, the team ERA was the league's lowest. And the offense remained strong. (George Bell, league RBI leader with 134, was named the American League MVP at season's end.) The Jays led their division going into the season's final series against second-place Detroit, though four straight losses had reduced the lead to just one game. Needing to win two of the three games to take the AL East title, or one to tie the Tigers and force a playoff, Toronto lost the first two games. In the season finale, Jimmy Key hurled a three-hitter, striking out eight. But one of the hits was a home run—the only run of the game, as it turned out. Toronto's seven-game losing streak had cost them what would have been their second title in three years.

In 1988, a rocky season made worse by George Bell's feud with manager Jimy Williams (who wanted the unwilling outfielder to serve as designated hitter), the Jays surged at the end—with six straight wins—into a tie for third place. Dave Steib pitched two one-hitters in September, both of which were no-hitters through 8⅔ innings.

When Toronto's front office replaced manager Williams with batting coach Cito Gaston in mid-May 1989, the Jays were drowning near the bottom of the AL East with a record of 12-24. By mid-August they had bobbed above .500 to stay, and on Sept. 1 replaced Baltimore in first place. With a pair of one-run victories over the Orioles at the end of September, the Jays preserved their narrow lead and clinched the division title. But Oakland outplayed them in the ALCS, taking the pennant in five games.

From mid-June 1990 to the final day of the season, the Blue Jays battled Boston for the division lead before settling for second. Dave Stieb (after two more one-hitters in 1989) at last hurled a no-hitter, and third baseman Kelly Gruber earned a place with Bell and McGriff among Toronto's power elite. But the brightest Toronto star of 1989-90 was the new SkyDome, with its 11,000-ton retractable roof and its restaurants and hotel rooms above the outfield wall. After the Jays moved into the Dome on June 5, 1989, attendance zoomed, and by season's end the club set a new American League home attendance record of nearly 3.4 million. In 1990, with a full season in the Dome, the Jays attracted a new major league record of 3,885,284. Attendance surpassed 4 million in 1991 and 1992.

McGriff and Bell had departed by 1991, but an improved Devon White, plus newly acquired slugger Joe Carter and second-baseman Roberto Alomar, led an offense that—together with the league's stingiest pitching staff—brought the Jays through a tight race to their third divisional title. For the third time, though, they crashed in the ALCS, this time trampled by Minnesota in five games. With the addition of a pair of free-agent veterans—pitcher Jack Morris (who went 21-6) and Dave Winfield (108 RBIs)—Toronto in 1992 finally completed the puzzle. The Jays sported a balanced offense (six players drove in 60 runs or more) and outstanding pitching from starter Juan Guzman (16-5; 2.64 ERA) and relievers Tom Henke and Duane Ward. In the ALCS the Jays defeated Oakland in six games to bring Canada its first major league baseball pennant, and then they stopped stubborn Atlanta in six games to carry home the championship of the world.

Nearly half the team was new in 1993, but after a tight battle with several clubs through most of the season, the Blue Jays pulled away to capture their fourth divisional title in five years, by a comfortable seven-game margin. John Olerud hit over .400 through the first half of the season and finished with a league-high .363. Paul Molitor, signed from Milwaukee as a free agent, hit better than anyone else in the league from midseason on, and finished second in the AL. Together with Roberto Alomar, Olerud and Molitor became the first teammates since 1893 to take the top three spots in a major league batting race. In the ALCS the Blue Jays bowled over the Chicago White Sox for the AL pennant in six games. The World Series wasn't necessarily pretty (Toronto beat the Philadelphia Phillies in Game 4 by a dizzying 15-14 score), but it was memorable. Joe Carter's two-out, three-run home run off Mitch Williams in climactic Game 6 made it just the second World Series to end on a home run.

The glory faded fast in 1994. At the July All-Star break the Blue Jays lay at the bottom of the AL East. While they pulled themselves up to third before the players' strike ended the season in August, they remained 16 games out of first, their first losing season in a dozen years. The losing continued in 1995 as the Jays stripped their roster of most of the veterans of its world championship squad. Toronto tied Minnesota for the dubious honor of worst won-lost record (56-88).

Toronto edged up slightly in 1996, to fourth (74-88) in the AL East. Pat Hentgen (20-10, 181 strikeouts) won the 1996 AL Cy Young Award and Roger Clemens—with a league-leading 21 wins, 2.05 ERA, and 292 strikeouts—kept the award in Toronto in 1997. Clemens won it again in 1998 (his record fifth Cy Young), in a season in which he earned his 3,000th strikeout, ended the year with 15 consecutive wins, and copped his second consecutive Triple Crown. Offensively, Jose Canseco socked 46 home runs and Tony Fernandez batted .321 in his third tour of duty with the Blue Jays. Led by new manager Tim Johnson, who replaced Cito Gaston, Toronto made a late run at the Red Sox for the AL Wild Card. The Blue Jays won 11 straight games and 14 of 16 in the closing weeks of the season, but Toronto finished four games behind Boston.

The 1999 season looked gloomy while the team was still in spring training. An unhappy Clemens was traded to the division rival Yankees for David Wells, Homer Bush, and Graeme Lloyd. Johnson, meanwhile, was fired as manager because his untrue comments regarding his military career had caused dissention on the team. With a new ace and a new manager, Jim Fregosi, the Blue Jays took the lead in the Wild Card race in August. A nine-game SkyDome losing streak, however, doomed Toronto to a third-place finish.

For the second year in a row, a star player asked to be traded and was sent to a large U.S. market. Many, including Wells, wondered if the Blue Jays got equal value from Los Angeles in the Shawn Green-Raul Mondesi deal. Mondesi had 24 homers and 67 RBIs in 96 games, and provided ample protection in the lineup for red-hot Carlos Delgado (.344, 41 homers, 137 RBIs, 99 extra-base hits), but Mondesi missed the final two months with an injury. The Jays became the second team in history to have seven 20-homer players (Tony Batista, Brad Fullmer, Jose Cruz Jr., Shannon Stewart, Darrin Fletcher, Mondesi, and Delgado), and led the AL in home runs. Toronto finished third again despite a 20-win season by Wells and 10 wins each from Frank Castillo, Esteban Loaizia, Chris Carpenter, and Kelvim Escobar. After the season Fregosi was replaced by Buck Martinez, a broadcaster with the club.

Defunct Clubs

In addition to the many Negro League teams, some 112 ballclubs have played in the major leagues since the first professional association was formed in 1871. The 30 that still do are described above; here are the other 82, listed according to the league and year in which they first played major league ball. Official club names precede the name of the city; nicknames follow.

National Association, 1871-1875

Two of the 23 clubs that played at one time or another in baseball's first professional league still play in the majors: the Atlanta Braves (then the Boston Red Stockings) and the Chicago Cubs (then the White Stockings). The other 21 are:

Athletic of Philadelphia: NA 1871-1875, NL 1876. Organized in 1860 as an amateur club, the Athletics became one of the dominant teams of the decade. As professionals they won the first NA pennant in 1871. After one year in the NL, they were expelled for failing to make the final western trip of the season.

Forest City of Cleveland, NA 1871-1872. In the midst of a second losing season, the club disbanded in August 1872.

Forest City of Rockford, Illinois, NA 1871. As an amateur club, Forest City (with its 16-year-old pitcher Al Spalding) was the only team to defeat the famous Washington Nationals on their pioneering midwestern tour of 1867. As professionals, Forest City finished seventh of the nine NA teams in 1871.

Kekionga of Fort Wayne, NA 1871. The Kekiongas won the first NA game ever played but dropped out of the association before the end of the season.

Mutual of New York, NA 1871-1875, NL 1876. Organized as an amateur club in 1857, the Mutuals were said to be backed financially by New York's notorious William M. "Boss" Tweed. Frequently accused of corrupt practices, the club was one of the leading eastern teams of the late 1860s. They were declared national champions of 1868 and proclaimed themselves national champions of 1870. On the demise of the NA the Mutuals entered the NL, but they were expelled after one season (along with the Athletics) for failing to play their final games in the West.

Olympic of Washington, D.C., NA 1871-1872. Unsuccessful in 1872 after playing well the year before, the Olympics disbanded about midseason.

Union of Troy, New York, NA 1871-1872. The Haymakers, as they were popularly known, dropped out of the NA halfway through the 1872 season.

Atlantic of Brooklyn, NA 1872-1875. One of the greatest of the amateur clubs, the Atlantics (organized in 1855) went undefeated in 1864 and 1865 and won three successive national championships, 1864-1866. But in four NA seasons their combined won-lost record was only 49-139, including a dismal 2-42 in 1875.

Eckford of Brooklyn, NA 1872. Another great early amateur club—like the Atlantics, organized in 1855—they won the national championship in 1862 and again (with an undefeated season of 10 games) the next year. The Eckfords actually joined the NA in August 1871, replacing Kekionga, but their 1871 games were later erased from the record because they had failed to enter the association at the start of the season.

Lord Baltimore of Baltimore, NA 1872-1874. After twice finishing third, the Lord Baltimores (or "Canaries," for their yellow silk jerseys) disbanded two games before the end of the 1874 season, while in last place.

Mansfield of Middletown, Connecticut, NA 1872. Disbanded in late August.

National of Washington, D.C., NA 1872-1873, 1875. Organized as amateurs in 1859, the Nationals were the first eastern club to tour as far west as Chicago and St. Louis. After skipping the 1874 race, the Nationals reentered the NA in 1875, but dropped out in July.

Maryland of Baltimore, NA 1873. Dropped out after only six games.

Philadelphia, NA 1873-1875. Known successively as the "White Stockings," "Pearls," and "Phillies," the team finished a strong second to Boston in their first season, but slipped to fourth and fifth the next two years.

Resolute of Elizabeth, New Jersey, NA 1873. Disbanded in August with a 2-21 record.

Hartford Dark Blues, NA 1874-1875, NL 1876-1877. After a weak first season, the Dark Blues finished third in its next three seasons, as standings are presently reckoned. But by the 1876 guidelines (which used the number of games won rather than winning percentage), Hartford that year placed second. In 1877 the club played its home games in Brooklyn.

Centennial of Philadelphia, NA 1875. Dropped out in late May.

New Haven Elm Citys, NA 1875. Failed to play out their schedule.

St. Louis Brown Stockings, NA 1875, NL 1876-1877. George Bradley pitched all but five of the Browns' 39 wins in 1875, when they finished fourth, and all 45 victories in 1876, when they finished a strong third in number of victories; they were second in winning percentage. With Bradley lost to Chicago the next year, St. Louis dropped below .500—and out of the league.

St. Louis Red Stockings, NA 1875. A successful amateur club that decided to take a fling at pro ball, the Red Stockings played only a few games in the NA.

Western of Keokuk, Iowa, NA 1875. Disbanded in mid-June.

National League, 1876-

When the National League was founded to replace the ill-organized National Association, it included six of the stronger NA clubs plus independent clubs in Cincinnati and Louisville. The league's composition was in continual flux to the end of the century as clubs were dropped and added, shrinking the league to as few as six teams and expanding it to as many as 12. Two clubs that first played major league ball in the NL still do: the Philadelphia Phillies and the San Francisco (originally New York) Giants, both organized in 1883. (The Boston and Chicago franchises—that continue to this day as the Atlanta Braves and Chicago Cubs—had their starts in the National Association.) Those that have not survived:

Cincinnati Red Stockings, NL 1876-1880. From last place in 1876 (and 1877, when their games were not counted because of the club's reorganization and failure to pay its dues), the Reds—with seven new regulars—rose to second in 1878, only to fall back to fifth in 1879 and last again in 1880. That fall, when they refused to accept a new rule abolishing liquor sales and Sunday baseball on club grounds, they were dropped from league membership.

Louisville Grays, NL 1876-1877. The strong Louisville team led the league in mid-August 1877, but seven suspicious losses to chief rivals Boston and Hartford dropped the Grays out of first place. After Boston clinched the pennant, Louisville revived to secure second place, but four players—including pitching ace Jim Devlin—were expelled from baseball for throwing games. Their expulsion showed the NL's determination to wipe out corruption, but it also caused the St. Louis Browns, who had planned to sign three of the four Louisville players for 1878, to resign from the league. Louisville, too, dropped out of the league before the next season, unable to find adequate replacements for the four.

Indianapolis Browns, NL 1878. Finished fifth of six teams.

Milwaukee Grays (or Cream Citys), NL 1878. Finished a last-place sixth, 26 games back of Boston.

Providence Grays, NL 1878-1885. One of the great teams in the NL's early years, Providence won pennants in 1879 and 1884, finishing no lower than third in seven of their eight seasons. In 1884, pitcher Charley "Old Hoss" Radbourn won a record 59 games, then pitched the Grays to victory in baseball's first World Series with a three-game sweep of the American Association champion New York Mets. But as they dropped to fourth place the next year, finishing for the first time below .500, their fans deserted them. Late that autumn the club was dissolved.

Buffalo Bisons, NL 1879-1885. Buffalo moved up to the majors after winning the International Association pennant in 1878. Jim "Pud" Galvin pitched nearly 70 percent of Buffalo's victories as he led them to four first-division finishes in seven big league seasons. First baseman Dan Brouthers, in his five years with Buffalo, twice won the batting title and led NL sluggers five times.

Cleveland Blues, NL 1879-1884. Cleveland's fortunes rested in large measure with pitcher Jim McCormick (who also managed the club their first two seasons). In 1880, their best season, McCormick won a career-high 45 games to bring the Blues in third. In 1883 Cleveland was in first place when McCormick's injured arm put him out for the season after he had won 23 games. The Blues dropped to fourth. The club folded after a seventh-place finish in 1884, a season that saw McCormick and two other Blues jump to the Union Association.

Stars of Syracuse, NL 1879. After finishing a close second to Buffalo in the International League in 1878, the Stars moved up with the Bisons to the NL, but disbanded after a single unsuccessful season.

Troy, New York, Trojans, NL 1879-1882. After four losing seasons the franchise was expelled to make room for a club in New York City.

Worcester, Massachusetts, Brown Stockings, NL 1880-1882. After a pair of losing minor league seasons, Worcester was admitted to the NL to replace the defunct Stars of Syracuse. After finishing a respectable fifth in 1880, Worcester dropped into the cellar for two seasons before being ousted in 1883 for a new Philadelphia club.

Detroit Wolverines, NL 1881-1888. Buffalo's sale of its "big four" (Dan Brouthers, Hardy Richardson, Jack Rowe, and Deacon White) to Detroit late in 1885 transformed a perennial also-ran into a contender. The club finished second in 1886 and won the pennant in 1887. In a World Series played in 10 different cities, the Wolverines trounced St. Louis 10 games to five. In 1888, after finishing fifth, they expired.

Kansas City Cowboys, NL 1886. They finished seventh, 58½ games out.

Washington Senators, NL 1886-1889. In their four seasons, the Senators finished out of the cellar only once: next to last in 1887.

Indianapolis Hoosiers, NL 1887-1889. After dropping below Washington into the cellar in 1887, the Hoosiers and Senators traded places for their final two years.

American Association, 1882-1891

Three of the six clubs that formed the AA in 1882 still represent their cities in the majors today: Allegheny (Pittsburgh), Cincinnati, and St. Louis. Brooklyn, which entered the AA two years later, today represents Los Angeles. The others:

Athletic of Philadelphia, AA 1882-1890. After finishing a distant second in the AA's first season, the Athletics in 1883 took the pennant from St. Louis by a single game. First baseman Harry Stovey, who led AA batters in most offensive categories that year, was even more productive in 1884. The A's dropped to seventh and never challenged for the crown again. Expelled from the AA after the 1890 season for financial reasons, they were replaced by the Philadelphia club from the defunct Players League.

Baltimore Orioles, AA 1882-1889, 1890-1891, NL 1892-1899. After eight seasons out of pennant contention (including four in last place), the Orioles dropped out of the AA to play minor league ball in 1890. Toward the end of the season, when Brooklyn's new franchise went under, the Orioles returned to complete Brooklyn's season (finishing a combined last). After rising to third in 1891, the AA's final year, the Orioles were invited into the expanding NL, where they dropped to a 12th-place last (54½ games out) in 1892.

Ned Hanlon, hired to manage Baltimore early in the 1892 season, set about building a championship club. By 1894, with a lineup that included six future Hall of Famers, Hanlon led his club to a narrow pennant victory over New York, though the Giants swept the Orioles in the first Temple Cup World Series, 4-0.

For five years Hanlon's brand of scrappy, hustling play made the Orioles the terror of the NL. Led by shortstop Hughie Jennings and outfielders Willie Keeler and Joe Kelley, the club repeated as NL champions in 1895 and 1896, and finished second to Boston the next two years. They lost the Temple Cup to Cleveland (four games to one) in 1895, but swept the Spiders the next year, 4-0, and took the cup again in 1897, defeating Boston, 4-1, in what turned out to be the Series swan song.

Baltimore owners Hanlon and Harry Von der Horst purchased a half-interest in the Brooklyn club in 1899 (retaining a half-interest in Baltimore), and switched Jennings, Kelley, and Keeler to Brooklyn. Hanlon also went over as manager, leaving third baseman John McGraw in charge of the Orioles. McGraw hit .391 and rookie pitcher Joe McGinnity won 28 games to bring the team in fourth. But Hanlon's Superbas won the pennant, and, when the NL cut back to eight teams after the season, Baltimore got the ax.

Eclipse of Louisville/Louisville Colonels (or Cyclones), AA 1882-1891, NL 1892-1899. The club, which changed its official name from Eclipse to Louisville after the 1883 season, was one of only two teams to play all 10 seasons of the major league AA. (St. Louis—the present Cardinals—was the other.) Louisville finished above .500 in five of its first six years, but only once in that time closed within 10 games of the top—in 1884, when Guy Hecker's 52 wins brought the team in third. Slugger Pete Browning paced the offense in their early years, winning batting titles in 1882 (his rookie season), 1885, and 1886, and hammering a second-best .402 in 1887. (A bat made for him by woodworker John Hillerich inspired the creation of the Louisville Slugger.)

By 1889, though, the club had sunk to last place, finishing 66½ games out of first, with 111 losses. The next year, although Hecker and Browning defected to the outlaw PL, the club was less affected by deserters than other AA teams. The Colonels (paced by the league's best hitter, William "Chicken" Wolf, and its best pitcher, Scott Stratton) made one of the greatest turnarounds in big league history, winning the pennant by 10 games over second-place Columbus. In the World Series against Brooklyn, poor weather and small crowds ended play after the teams had tied once and won three apiece.

Even though the Colonels finished next to last in 1891, they were one of four clubs taken into the NL after the AA folded. They never finished higher than ninth in the NL, and for three straight years (1894-1896) they occupied the cellar. When the league cut back from 12 teams to eight after the 1899 season, Louisville merged with the Pittsburgh Pirates.

Columbus Colts (or Senators), AA 1883-1884. From sixth place in 1883, Columbus climbed to second in 1884 behind the 34-13 pitching of rookie Ed Morris. But when the AA dropped back from 12 clubs to eight in 1885, Columbus was out.

Metropolitan of New York, AA 1883-1887. After success in minor league and independent play since 1880, the Mets entered the AA in 1883 as the association expanded from six clubs to eight. With 41 victories from pitcher Tim Keefe (who was picked up from disbanded Troy), the Mets finished fourth. The next season, with first baseman Dave Orr hitting .354 in his first full major league season and pitcher Jack Lynch matching Keefe with 37 wins apiece, the Mets won the AA pennant handily. But they lost baseball's first World Series to the Providence Grays. When manager Jim Mutrie, third baseman Dude Esterbrook, and pitcher Keefe were transferred in 1885 to the New York Giants (the two clubs had the same owner), the Mets sank to seventh place, where they finished in their final three seasons.

Indianapolis Blues, AA 1884. Finished 11th of 12 clubs, 46 games behind.

Toledo Blue Stockings, AA 1884. Catcher Fleet Walker (who played in 42 games) and his brother Welday (five games) were the major leagues' first black players and the only blacks until Jackie Robinson broke the color bar for good in 1947.

Washington, D.C., AA 1884. The popularity of the city's Union Association Nationals proved too much for this inept AA club, which went under in early August.

Virginia of Richmond, AA 1884. When Washington disbanded in August, the Wilmington club of the Eastern League was invited to join the AA as its replacement. Wilmington declined (and later jumped to the UA), but Virginia—also a member of the EL—accepted the invitation and took over Washington's remaining games. Washington-Virginia finished a combined 24-81, in last place.

Cleveland Spiders, AA 1887-1888, NL 1889-1899. After two losing seasons in the AA, the Spiders moved to the NL, where they continued below .500 for three more years. But in 1892 Cy Young's league-leading pitching brought them the second-half championship of the league's experimental split season. Cleveland lost the World Series to first-half winner Boston, losing five after tying the first game.

Second-place finishes in 1895 and 1896 qualified the Spiders for the Temple Cup series against champion Baltimore. In 1895 they beat the Orioles for the world title four games to one, but were swept the next year.

In 1899, when owner Frank Robison transferred all the team's best players to St. Louis (which he also owned), Cleveland suffered the worst season in major league history, winning only 20 games while losing a record 134. They finished 35 games behind 11th-place Washington and 84 games out of first. After the season the Spiders died, as the NL cut back from 12 teams to eight.

Kansas City Blues, AA 1888-1889. Finished last in 1888, next to last in 1889.

Columbus Colts (or Solons), AA 1889-1891. In 1890, with the AA weakened by the replacement of half its franchises with new clubs and by defections to the outlaw PL, Columbus (which retained several of its regulars) rose from its 1889 sixth-place finish to second behind Louisville. When the PL folded and the defectors returned in 1891, Columbus dropped back to sixth.

Brooklyn Gladiators, AA 1890. Formed as a replacement for the Brooklyn club that forsook the AA for the NL in 1890, the Gladiators floundered and were replaced by Baltimore late in the season.

Rochesters, AA 1890. Played .500 ball, finishing fifth.

Syracuse Stars, AA 1890. Finished sixth.

Toledo Maumees, AA 1890. Finished fourth.

Cincinnati Porkers, AA 1891. Also known as "Kelly's Killers" for their manager Mike "King" Kelly, the club went bankrupt in August and was replaced by Milwaukee.

Milwaukee Brewers, AA 1891. This Western League club moved up to the AA in August. Taking five players and the 43-57 record from the defunct Cincinnati club, Milwaukee went 21-15 the rest of the way to lift the Cincinnati-Milwaukee combination from seventh to fifth by season's end.

Washington Senators, AA 1891, NL 1892-1899. Despite a cellar finish in the AA's final year, the Senators were taken into the expanding NL. Of its nine losing seasons, the best was a tie for sixth in the 12-team NL of 1897.

Union Association, 1884

Formed in opposition to the reserve rule that governed players in the National League and American Association, the Union Association struggled through one season. The first eight clubs listed here began the season. The other five are listed according to the month they entered the UA as replacement teams. All 13—like the Union Association itself—are long extinct:

Altoona, Pennsylvania, Unions, UA 1884. The first of several Union Association clubs to drop out of competition during the season, Altoona disbanded on May 31, but reorganized as an independent club two days later with many of the same players taking the field.

Baltimore Unions, UA 1884. Bill Sweeney's league-leading 40 wins accounted for 70 percent of third-place Baltimore's victories.

Boston Unions, UA 1884. Outfielder Tom McCarthy, the UA's only Hall of Famer, hit .215 in this, his rookie big league season. Boston finished fourth.

Chicago Browns/Pittsburgh Stogies, UA 1884. Financial woes caused the Chicago Browns to relocate in Pittsburgh in late August, but the club quit altogether less than a month later.

Cincinnati Outlaw Reds, UA 1884. With three 20-game winners—including Jim McCormick, who won 21 after defecting from the NL in midseason—Cincinnati compiled a strong 69-36 record, but still finished 21 games behind champion St. Louis.

Keystone of Philadelphia, UA 1884. In early August Keystone dropped out of the league and reorganized as an independent semipro club.

National of Washington, D.C., UA 1884. Finished sixth, 46½games back.

St. Louis Maroons, UA 1884, NL 1885-1886. Batting 47 points above the league average, the Maroons scored 184 runs more than the next-best club to run away with the pennant. They were the only UA club to survive 1884 as a major league team. In the NL, where they were dubbed "the black diamonds," because of their previously expelled players, they were unable to fashion a winning season or finish higher than sixth.

Kansas City Unions, UA 1884. Formed to replace Altoona, Kansas City went 16-63 in its partial season.

Wilmington, Delaware, UA 1884. After Wilmington had gone 51-12 to sew up the Eastern League championship, they jumped to the UA in August to replace Philadelphia's Keystones. But as several players failed to make the jump with them, the move was a disaster on the field (2-16) and financially. They failed in mid-September.

Milwaukee Grays, UA 1884. One of only two teams left in the deteriorating Northwestern League, Milwaukee moved up to the UA in September to complete the schedule of dropout Pittsburgh.

St. Paul White Caps, UA 1884. With the disbanding of the Northwestern League in September, St. Paul joined the UA to take over Wilmington's remaining games.

Players League, 1890

Formed in rebellion against the NL owner John T. Brush's classification plan, a scheme to limit players' pay, the PL drew many of the finest players from the NL and AA, and proved the most popular league with the fans. But when only one club turned a profit, the clubs' financial backers deserted and the league died. Two clubs were admitted to the AA, and many of the rest merged with their National League counterparts:

Boston Red Stockings, PL 1890, AA 1891. Boston won the PL pennant with such stars as Dan Brouthers, Charley Radbourn, Hardy Richardson, and manager Michael "King" Kelly. The only PL club to make money, Boston joined the AA the next year and won another pennant. But when the popular Kelly defected to Boston's NL Beaneaters (who also won a pennant for the city in 1891), the fans defected too, and the Red Stockings died along with the AA at the end of the season.

Brooklyn Wonders, PL 1890. At the end of a season in which they edged New York for second place, the Wonders merged with Brooklyn's NL pennant-winners.

Buffalo Bisons, PL 1890. After a last-place finish 20

games back of their nearest competitor, the Bisons simply went out of business.

Chicago Pirates, PL 1890. Mark Baldwin, with a league-high 34 wins, and Charles "Silver" King, with 30, pitched Chicago into fourth place. Both went to Pittsburgh the next year, although the franchise was absorbed by Chicago's NL Colts.

Cleveland Infants, PL 1890. Like Cleveland's NL Spiders of 1890, the Infants finished next to last. But one of their three managers, infielder Oliver Wendell "Patsy" Tebeau, would go on to lead the Spiders to their finest seasons.

Philadelphia Quakers, PL 1890, *Philadelphia Athletic,* AA 1891. Although they finished sixth in their PL season, the Quakers compiled a winning record. When the Athletics of the AA were expelled following the 1890 season, the Quakers were admitted in their place and awarded the name "Athletic." The team finished fourth in 1891, but was not among the four clubs taken into the NL when the AA folded, because Philadelphia already had an NL team (the Phillies).

New York Giants, PL 1890. Paced by the hitting of first baseman Roger Connor and outfielder Jim O'Rourke, New York's PL Giants finished third. In November the club merged with the city's NL Giants.

Pittsburgh Burghers, PL 1890. After a sixth-place finish, the Pittsburgh PL club and the NL Allegheny Club combined to form the new Pittsburgh Athletic Club, which still represents Pittsburgh in the NL.

American League, 1901-

When Western League president Ban Johnson renamed the circuit in 1900 and proclaimed it a major league the next year, he little knew how stable it would be. For over half a century (1903-1953) the same eight clubs represented the same eight cities. Even today, although the league has expanded and several clubs have moved to new cities, not one franchise has perished.

Federal League, 1914-1915

After an inaugural season as a six-team minor league in 1913, the FL expanded to eight teams and declared war on the NL and AL for their players. After two big league seasons, and despite two of the game's most exciting pennant races ever, the league died for lack of patronage, and with it went its eight franchises:

Baltimore Terrapins, FL 1914-1915. Jack Quinn and George Suggs, with 26 and 25 wins, pitched Baltimore to third place in 1914. But when Quinn and Suggs lost their stuff the next year, the club sank out of sight, 24 games behind seventh-place Brooklyn.

Brooklyn Tip-Tops (or Brookfeds), FL 1914-1915. The Brookfeds finished fifth in 1915 and not even the acquisition of batting and base-stealing champ Benny Kauff could stop Brooklyn from slipping to seventh the next year.

Buffalo Buffeds, FL 1914-1915. Finished fourth in 1914, sixth the next year.

Chicago Chifeds (or Whales), FL 1914-1915. After leading the league through July and much of August in 1914, only to lose out after a late-season struggle with Indianapolis, the Whales came back in 1915 to triumph in an even tighter race that saw the three top teams separated at the finish by only half a game. Owner Charles Weeghman was permitted to buy the NL Cubs in 1916, and many Whales joined the Cubs to play at what was then Weeghman Park and is now known as Wrigley Field.

Indianapolis Federals (or Hoosiers), FL 1914; Newark Peps, FL 1915. Five regulars hit over .300 (paced by Benny Kauff's league-leading .370) in 1914, and the team as a whole hit 22 points above the league average. From fourth place in August the Hoosiers fought back to capture the flag from Chicago by 1½ games, with seven consecutive wins at the end. The only major league pennant winner to move to a new city the next year, the Hoosiers became the Peps in 1915. Though they remained competitive into September, an eight-game losing streak dropped them out of the race and they finished fifth.

Kansas City Packers, FL 1914-1915. After a sixth-place finish in 1914, the Packers competed in a five-way race through much of 1915. But from first place on Aug. 21 they dropped to fifth a week later and finished fourth.

Pittsburgh Rebels, FL 1914-1915. After avoiding last place in 1914 only by St. Louis' late-season nosedive, Pittsburgh turned itself around the next year, luring first baseman Ed Konetchy from their NL rival Pirates, and pitcher Frank Allen from the NL Brooklyn Robins. Both enjoyed the best season of their careers to lead the Rebels into first place in late August, where they remained until they were dropped to third by losing three out of four at the end to the champion Whales.

St. Louis Terriers, FL 1914-1915. After finishing last in 1914, St. Louis added veteran pitcher Eddie Plank to its roster. From a club with two 20-game losers, the Terriers became in 1915 a team with three 20-game winners (including Plank), pulling up from fifth late in August to catch the leaders with a nine-game winning streak. At the finish, though, they ranked second—by less than one percentage point, the narrowest big league pennant margin ever. In 1916 Terriers owner Phil Ball took over the AL St. Louis Browns.

CHAPTER 3

Major League Attendance

Robert L. Tiemann

If you have the patience to sift through them, the figures on the following pages, dating from 1871 through 2000, tell a remarkable story. Season attendance has approached 4.5 million in Colorado in 1993, and it has been as little as 6,088 in Cleveland in 1899, when the awful Spiders went 20–134. The first club to pass the million mark was the New York Yankees of 1920, featuring a newcomer named Ruth and a ballpark borrowed from the Giants (who did not reach the mark themselves until 1945). In the depths of the Depression, the St. Louis Browns posted annual attendance figures (80,922 in 1935; 88,113 in 1933) below what a weekend set produces in many major league venues today.

Why did attendance stagnate in the 1890s? How much did the entry of the American League into National League strongholds New York, Chicago, Philadelphia, and St. Louis hurt the senior franchises? Were the Dodgers justified in leaving Brooklyn? How did baseball survive in Washington as long as it did, surpassing the million mark only once from 1892 to 1971? Did anyone notice that Atlanta's attendance of 1990 doubled, and then tripled, over the next two years? Or that while major league attendance increased by 25.8 percent from 1992 to 1993, almost all of that gain came from the senior circuit? (The American League rose a modest 5 percent while the National League posted a whopping gain of 53 percent. That season the league not only added two teams, Colorado and Florida, but the NL also started to count tickets sold, which followed the long-standing practice in the AL.

You get the picture. There's stuff here that permits you to chart trends in baseball that you already know about, and if you are eagle-eyed you may pick up a figure that prompts you to rethink what you thought you knew.

A researcher's goldmine, the tables that follow tell an interesting story for the average fan as well. Does winning a pennant correlate with higher attendance? Are first-division teams more profitable than those in the second division? What is the impact on attendance of a new stadium?

By the time the next edition rolls around we may be able to gather figures going back to the dawn of professional baseball. Here are some scattered tidbits:

- In their first year of existence, 1871, the Boston Red Stockings counted 32,600 fans in 18 home games.
- In 1882, the last year of its existence as an NL franchise, the Troy Haymakers drew a whopping 26,000 attendees for its 42 home games, with one late season date posting a recorded crowd of 12 (that's not a typo).
- The 1891 American Association, in its final year of operation, counted 1,296,000 fans, or an average of 162,000 per team, a figure very comparable to the 169,060 of the National League. In 1892, with the AA gone and the NL a 12-team circuit, the average team attendance was less than 152,000. Is there a lesson to be drawn from this?

Yes, and the lesson is plain for magnates no less than for fans and students of the game.

	1871	1872	1873	1874	1875	1876	1877	1878	1879	1880
NATIONAL LEAGUE										
ATH	51,000	61,000	36,000	33,000	45,500					
ATL		10,000	20,000	21,000	11,000					
BAL		40,500	25,000	12,000						
BOS	36,500	38,500	52,000	46,500	50,000	51,000	55,240	48,915	36,501	34,000
BUF									26,000	20,000
CEN					4,500					
CHI	69,000			66,000	60,323	65,441	46,454	58,691	67,687	66,708
CIN						24,000	28,000	41,000	28,000	21,000
CLE	16,000	7,500							25,000	35,000
ECK		4,000								
HAR				30,500	41,000	18,000	22,000			
IND								12,000		
KEK	3,500									
LOU						25,000	24,000			
MAN		5,500								
MAR			1,500							
MIL								17,000		
MUT	40,500	48,500	29,000	37,000	32,000					
NAT		1,500								
NH					17,500					
NY						23,000				
OLY	26,000	3,000								
PHI			50,000	23,000	29,500	24,000				
PRO								46,000	47,595	37,220
RES		3,000								
RS					6,500					
ROK	6,500									
STL					78,500	36,000	29,000			
SYR									9,000	
TRO	17,500	17,000							12,000	18,500
WAS			8,000		7,500					
WES					4,000					
WOR										24,000
TOT	266,500	237,000	224,500	269,000	387,823	266,441	204,694	223,606	251,783	256,428

	1881	1882	1883	1884	1885	1886	1887	1888	1889	1890
NATIONAL LEAGUE										
BOS	34,343	50,971	128,968	146,777	110,290	133,683	261,000	265,015	283,257	147,539
BRO										121,412
BUF	32,173	28,000	32,000	42,000	35,000					
CHI	82,000	125,452	124,880	87,667	117,519	142,438	217,070	228,906	149,175	102,536
CIN										131,980
CLE	34,000	30,000	63,000	38,000					144,425	47,478
DET	53,720	75,000	70,000	32,000	43,000	105,000	95,000	75,000		
IND							84,000	78,000	105,850	
KC						55,000				
NY			75,000	105,000	185,000	189,000	270,945	305,455	201,989	60,667
PHI			55,992	100,475	150,698	175,623	253,671	151,804	281,869	148,366
PIT							140,000	112,000	117,338	16,064
PRO	30,000	57,477	61,314	64,409	49,000					
STL					62,000	99,000				
TRO	18,000	26,488								
WAS						60,000	80,000	57,000	68,652	
WOR	17,000	11,000								
TOT	301,236	404,388	611,154	616,328	752,507	959,744	1,401,686	1,273,180	1,352,555	776,042

	1882	1883	1884	1885	1886	1887	1888	1889	1890	1891
AMERICAN ASSOCIATION										
BAL	36,000	110,000	120,000	60,000	70,000	142,000	38,000	115,000	34,000	150,000
BOS										170,000
BRO			65,000	85,000	185,000	273,000	245,000	353,690	37,000	
CIN	65,000	86,000	110,000	120,000	138,563	185,397	132,606	131,000		63,000
CLE						72,000	60,000			
COL		48,000	66,000					90,000	85,000	105,000
IND			56,000							
KC							50,000	85,000		
LOU	50,000	78,000	111,000	108,000	123,000	128,000	76,000	60,000	206,200	140,000
MIL										45,000
NY		50,000	68,000	64,000	67,000	105,000				
PHI	72,000	305,000	116,000	169,000	179,000	163,000	201,000	220,000	134,000	168,000
PIT	42,000	85,000	60,000	82,000	195,000					
RIC			16,000							
ROC									82,000	
STL	135,000	243,000	212,000	129,000	205,000	244,000	166,000	175,000	105,000	220,000
SYR									50,000	
TOL			55,000						70,000	
WAS			25,000							112,000
TOT	400,000	1,005,000	1,080,000	817,000	1,162,563	1,312,397	968,606	1,229,690	803,200	1,173,000
ML	804,388	1,616,154	1,696,328	1,569,507	2,122,307	2,714,083	2,241,786	2,582,245	1,579,242	2,525,487

	1891	1892	1893	1894	1895	1896	1897	1898	1899	1900
NATIONAL LEAGUE										
BAL		93,589	143,000	328,000	293,000	249,448	273,046	123,416	121,935	
BOS	184,472	146,421	193,300	152,800	242,000	240,000	334,800	229,275	200,384	190,000
BRO	181,477	183,727	235,000	214,000	230,000	201,000	220,831	122,514	269,641	170,000
CHI	201,188	109,067	223,500	239,000	382,300	317,500	327,160	424,352	352,130	248,577
CIN	97,500	196,473	194,250	158,000	281,000	373,000	336,800	336,378	259,536	155,000
CLE	132,000	139,928	130,000	82,000	143,000	152,000	115,250	70,496	6,088	
LOU		131,159	53,683	75,000	92,000	133,000	145,210	128,980	109,319	
NY	210,568	130,566	290,000	387,000	240,000	274,000	390,340	206,700	121,384	175,000
PHI	217,282	193,731	293,019	352,773	474,971	357,025	288,816	265,414	388,933	301,913
PIT	128,000	177,205	184,000	159,000	188,000	197,000	165,950	150,900	251,834	250,000
STL		192,442	195,000	155,000	170,000	184,000	136,400	151,700	373,909	255,000
WAS		128,279	90,000	125,000	153,000	223,000	151,028	103,250	86,392	
TOT	1,352,487	1,822,587	2,224,752	2,427,573	2,889,271	2,900,973	2,885,631	2,313,375	2,541,485	1,745,490
ML	2,525,487	1,822,587	2,224,752	2,427,573	2,889,271	2,900,973	2,885,631	2,313,375	2,541,485	1,745,490

	1901	1902	1903	1904	1905	1906	1907	1908	1909	1910
NATIONAL LEAGUE										
BOS	146,502	116,960	143,155	140,694	150,003	143,280	203,221	253,750	195,188	149,027
BRO	198,200	199,868	224,670	214,600	227,924	277,400	312,500	275,600	321,300	279,321
CHI	205,071	263,700	386,205	439,100	509,900	654,300	422,550	665,325	633,480	526,152
CIN	205,728	217,300	351,680	391,915	313,927	330,056	317,500	399,200	424,643	380,622
NY	297,650	302,875	579,530	609,826	552,700	402,850	538,350	910,000	783,700	511,785
PHI	234,937	112,066	151,729	140,771	317,932	294,680	341,216	420,660	303,177	296,597
PIT	251,955	243,826	326,855	340,615	369,124	394,877	319,506	382,444	534,950	436,586
STL	379,988	226,417	226,538	386,750	292,800	283,770	185,377	205,129	299,982	355,668
TOT	1,920,031	1,683,012	2,390,362	2,664,271	2,734,310	2,781,213	2,640,220	3,512,108	3,496,420	2,935,758
AMERICAN LEAGUE										
BAL	141,952	174,606								
BOS	289,448	348,567	379,338	623,295	468,828	410,209	436,777	473,048	668,965	584,619
CHI	354,350	337,898	286,183	557,123	687,419	585,202	666,307	636,096	478,400	552,084
CLE	131,380	275,395	311,280	264,749	316,306	325,733	382,046	422,262	354,627	293,456
DET	259,430	189,469	224,523	177,796	193,384	174,043	297,079	436,199	490,490	391,288
MIL	139,034									
NY			211,808	438,919	309,100	434,700	350,020	305,500	501,700	355,857
PHI	206,329	420,078	422,473	512,294	554,576	489,129	625,581	455,062	674,915	588,905
STL		272,283	380,405	318,108	339,112	389,157	419,025	618,947	366,274	249,889
WAS	161,661	188,158	128,878	131,744	252,027	129,903	221,929	264,252	205,199	254,591
TOT	1,683,584	2,206,454	2,344,888	3,024,028	3,120,752	2,938,076	3,398,764	3,611,366	3,740,570	3,270,689
ML	3,603,615	3,889,466	4,735,250	5,688,299	5,855,062	5,719,289	6,038,984	7,123,474	7,236,990	6,206,447

	1911	1912	1913	1914	1915	1916	1917	1918	1919	1920
NATIONAL LEAGUE										
BOS	116,000	121,000	208,000	382,913	376,283	313,495	174,253	84,938	167,401	162,483
BRO	269,000	243,000	347,000	122,671	297,766	447,747	221,619	83,831	360,721	808,722
CHI	576,000	514,000	419,000	202,516	217,058	453,685	360,218	337,256	424,430	480,783
CIN	300,000	344,000	258,000	100,791	218,878	255,846	269,056	163,009	532,501	568,107
NY	675,000	638,000	630,000	364,313	391,850	552,056	500,264	256,618	708,857	929,609
PHI	416,000	250,000	470,000	138,474	449,898	515,365	354,428	122,266	240,424	330,998
PIT	432,000	384,000	296,000	139,620	225,743	289,132	192,807	213,610	276,810	429,037
STL	447,768	241,759	203,531	256,099	252,666	224,308	288,491	110,599	167,059	326,836
TOT	3,231,768	2,735,759	2,831,531	1,707,397	2,430,142	3,051,634	2,361,136	1,372,127	2,878,203	4,036,575
AMERICAN LEAGUE										
BOS	503,961	597,096	437,194	481,359	539,885	496,397	387,856	249,513	417,291	402,445
CHI	583,208	602,241	644,501	469,290	539,461	679,923	684,521	195,081	627,186	833,492
CLE	406,296	336,844	541,000	185,997	159,285	492,106	477,298	295,515	538,135	912,832
DET	484,988	402,870	398,502	416,225	476,105	616,772	457,289	203,719	643,805	579,650
NY	302,444	242,194	357,551	359,477	256,035	469,211	330,294	282,047	619,164	1,289,422
PHI	605,749	517,653	571,896	346,641	146,223	184,471	221,432	177,926	225,209	287,888
STL	207,984	214,070	250,330	244,714	150,358	335,740	210,486	122,076	349,350	419,311
WAS	244,884	350,663	325,831	243,888	167,332	177,265	89,682	182,122	234,096	359,260
TOT	3,339,514	3,263,631	3,526,805	2,747,591	2,434,684	3,451,885	2,858,858	1,707,999	3,654,236	5,084,300
ML	6,571,282	5,999,390	6,358,336	4,454,988	4,864,826	6,503,519	5,219,994	3,080,126	6,532,439	9,120,875

	1921	1922	1923	1924	1925	1926	1927	1928	1929	1930
NATIONAL LEAGUE										
BOS	318,627	167,965	227,802	177,478	313,528	303,598	288,685	227,001	372,351	464,835
BRO	613,245	498,865	564,666	818,883	659,435	650,819	637,230	664,863	731,886	1,097,329
CHI	410,107	542,283	703,705	716,922	622,610	885,063	1,159,168	1,143,740	1,485,166	1,463,624
CIN	311,227	493,754	575,063	473,707	464,920	672,987	442,164	490,490	295,040	386,727
NY	973,477	945,809	820,780	844,068	778,993	700,362	858,190	916,191	868,806	868,714
PHI	273,961	232,471	228,168	299,818	304,905	240,600	305,420	182,168	281,200	299,007
PIT	701,567	523,675	611,082	736,883	804,354	798,542	869,720	495,070	491,377	357,795
STL	384,773	536,998	338,551	272,885	404,959	668,428	749,340	761,574	399,887	508,501
TOT	3,986,984	3,941,820	4,069,817	4,340,644	4,353,704	4,920,399	5,309,917	4,881,097	4,925,713	5,446,532

	1921	1922	1923	1924	1925	1926	1927	1928	1929	1930
AMERICAN LEAGUE										
BOS	279,273	259,184	229,688	448,556	267,782	285,155	305,275	396,920	394,620	444,045
CHI	543,650	602,860	573,778	606,658	832,231	710,339	614,423	494,152	426,795	406,123
CLE	748,705	528,145	558,856	481,905	419,005	627,426	373,138	375,907	536,210	528,657
DET	661,527	861,206	911,377	1,015,136	820,766	711,914	773,716	474,323	869,318	649,450
NY	1,230,696	1,026,134	1,007,066	1,053,533	697,267	1,027,675	1,164,015	1,072,132	960,148	1,169,230
PHI	344,430	425,356	534,122	531,992	869,703	714,508	605,529	689,756	839,176	721,663
STL	355,978	712,918	430,296	533,349	462,898	283,986	247,879	339,497	280,697	152,088
WAS	456,069	458,552	357,406	584,310	817,199	551,580	528,976	378,501	355,506	614,474
TOT	4,620,328	4,874,355	4,602,589	5,255,439	5,186,851	4,912,583	4,612,951	4,221,188	4,662,470	4,685,730
ML	8,607,312	8,816,175	8,672,406	9,596,083	9,540,555	9,832,982	9,922,868	9,102,285	9,588,183	10,132,262

	1931	1932	1933	1934	1935	1936	1937	1938	1939	1940
NATIONAL LEAGUE										
BOS	515,005	507,606	517,803	303,205	232,754	340,585	385,339	341,149	285,994	241,616
BRO	753,133	681,827	526,815	434,188	470,517	489,618	482,481	663,087	955,668	975,978
CHI	1,086,422	974,688	594,112	707,525	692,604	699,370	895,020	951,640	726,663	534,878
CIN	263,316	356,950	218,281	206,773	448,247	466,345	411,221	706,756	981,443	850,180
NY	812,163	484,868	604,471	730,851	748,748	837,952	926,887	799,633	702,457	747,852
PHI	284,849	268,914	156,421	169,885	205,470	249,219	212,790	166,111	277,973	207,177
PIT	260,392	287,262	288,747	322,622	352,885	372,524	459,679	641,033	376,734	507,934
STL	608,535	279,219	256,171	325,056	506,084	448,078	430,811	291,418	400,245	324,078
TOT	4,583,815	3,841,334	3,162,821	3,200,105	3,657,309	3,903,691	4,204,228	4,560,827	4,707,177	4,389,693
AMERICAN LEAGUE										
BOS	350,975	182,150	268,715	610,640	558,568	626,895	559,659	646,459	573,070	716,234
CHI	403,550	233,198	397,789	236,559	470,281	440,810	589,245	338,278	594,104	660,336
CLE	483,027	468,953	387,936	391,338	397,615	500,391	564,849	652,006	563,926	902,576
DET	434,056	397,157	320,972	919,161	1,034,929	875,948	1,072,276	799,557	836,279	1,112,693
NY	912,437	962,320	728,014	854,682	657,508	976,913	998,148	970,916	859,785	988,975
PHI	627,464	405,500	297,138	305,847	233,173	285,173	430,738	385,357	395,022	432,145
STL	179,126	112,558	88,113	115,305	80,922	93,267	123,121	130,417	109,159	239,591
WAS	492,657	371,396	437,533	330,074	255,011	379,525	397,799	522,694	339,257	381,241
TOT	3,883,292	3,133,232	2,926,210	3,763,606	3,688,007	4,178,922	4,735,835	4,445,684	4,270,602	5,433,791
ML	8,467,107	6,974,566	6,089,031	6,963,711	7,345,316	8,082,613	8,940,063	9,006,511	8,977,779	9,823,484

	1941	1942	1943	1944	1945	1946	1947	1948	1949	1950
NATIONAL LEAGUE										
BOS	263,680	285,332	271,289	208,691	374,178	969,673	1,277,361	1,455,439	1,081,795	944,391
BRO	1,214,910	1,037,765	661,739	605,905	1,059,220	1,796,824	1,807,526	1,398,967	1,633,747	1,185,896
CHI	545,159	590,972	508,247	640,110	1,036,386	1,342,970	1,364,039	1,237,792	1,143,139	1,165,944
CIN	643,513	427,031	379,122	409,567	290,070	715,751	899,975	823,386	707,782	538,794
NY	763,098	779,621	466,095	674,483	1,016,468	1,219,873	1,600,793	1,459,269	1,218,446	1,008,878
PHI	231,401	230,183	466,975	369,586	285,057	1,045,247	907,332	767,429	819,698	1,217,035
PIT	482,241	448,897	498,740	604,278	604,694	749,962	1,283,531	1,517,021	1,449,435	1,166,267
STL	633,645	553,552	517,135	461,968	594,630	1,061,807	1,247,913	1,111,440	1,430,676	1,093,411
TOT	4,777,647	4,353,353	3,769,342	3,974,588	5,260,703	8,902,107	10,388,470	9,770,743	9,484,718	8,320,616
AMERICAN LEAGUE										
BOS	718,497	730,340	358,275	506,975	603,794	1,416,944	1,427,315	1,558,798	1,596,650	1,344,080
CHI	677,077	425,734	508,962	563,539	657,981	983,403	876,948	777,844	937,151	781,330
CLE	745,948	459,447	438,894	475,272	558,182	1,057,289	1,521,978	2,620,627	2,233,771	1,727,464
DET	684,915	580,087	606,287	923,176	1,280,341	1,722,590	1,398,093	1,743,035	1,821,204	1,951,474
NY	964,722	922,011	618,330	789,995	881,845	2,265,512	2,178,937	2,373,901	2,283,676	2,081,380
PHI	528,894	423,487	376,735	505,322	462,631	621,793	911,566	945,076	816,514	309,805
STL	176,240	255,617	214,392	508,644	482,986	526,435	320,474	335,564	270,936	247,131
WAS	415,663	403,493	574,694	525,235	652,660	1,027,216	850,758	795,254	770,745	699,697
TOT	4,911,956	4,200,216	3,696,569	4,798,158	5,580,420	9,621,182	9,486,069	11,150,099	10,730,647	9,142,361
ML	9,689,603	8,553,569	7,465,911	8,772,746	10,841,123	18,523,288	19,874,540	20,920,842	20,215,364	17,462,976

	1951	1952	1953	1954	1955	1956	1957	1958	1959	1960
NATIONAL LEAGUE										
BOS	487,475	281,278								
BRO	1,282,628	1,088,704	1,163,419	1,020,531	1,033,589	1,213,562	1,028,258			
CHI	894,415	1,024,826	763,658	748,183	875,800	720,118	670,629	979,904	858,255	809,770
CIN	588,268	604,197	548,086	704,167	693,662	1,125,928	1,070,850	788,582	801,298	663,486
LA								1,845,556	2,071,045	2,253,887
MIL			1,826,397	2,131,388	2,005,836	2,046,331	2,215,404	1,971,101	1,749,112	1,497,799
NY	1,059,539	984,940	811,518	1,155,067	824,112	629,179	653,923			
PHI	937,658	755,417	853,644	738,991	922,886	934,798	1,146,230	931,110	802,815	862,205
PIT	980,590	686,673	572,757	475,494	469,397	949,878	850,732	1,311,988	1,359,917	1,705,828
STL	1,013,429	913,113	880,242	1,039,698	849,130	1,029,773	1,183,575	1,063,730	929,953	1,096,632
SF								1,272,625	1,422,130	1,795,356
TOT	7,244,002	6,339,148	7,419,721	8,013,519	7,674,412	8,649,567	8,819,601	10,164,596	9,994,525	10,684,963
AMERICAN LEAGUE										
BAL				1,060,910	852,039	901,201	1,029,581	829,991	891,926	1,187,849
BOS	1,312,282	1,115,750	1,026,133	931,127	1,203,200	1,137,158	1,181,087	1,077,047	984,102	1,129,866
CHI	1,328,234	1,231,675	1,191,353	1,231,629	1,175,684	1,000,090	1,135,668	797,451	1,423,144	1,644,460
CLE	1,704,984	1,444,607	1,069,176	1,335,472	1,221,780	865,467	722,256	663,805	1,497,976	950,985

	1951	1952	1953	1954	1955	1956	1957	1958	1959	1960
DET	1,132,641	1,026,846	884,658	1,079,847	1,181,838	1,051,182	1,272,346	1,098,924	1,221,221	1,167,669
KC					1,393,054	1,015,154	901,067	925,090	963,683	774,944
NY	1,950,107	1,629,665	1,537,811	1,475,171	1,490,138	1,491,784	1,497,134	1,428,438	1,552,030	1,627,349
PHI	465,469	627,100	362,113	304,666						
STL	293,790	518,796	297,238							
WAS	695,167	699,457	595,594	503,542	425,238	431,647	457,079	475,288	615,372	743,404
TOT	8,882,674	8,293,896	6,964,076	7,922,364	8,942,971	7,893,683	8,196,218	7,296,034	9,149,454	9,226,526
ML	16,126,676	14,633,044	14,383,797	15,935,883	16,617,383	16,543,250	17,015,820	17,460,630	19,143,980	19,911,488

	1961	1962	1963	1964	1965	1966	1967	1968	1969	1970
NATIONAL LEAGUE										
ATL						1,539,801	1,389,222	1,126,540	1,458,320	1,078,848
CHI	673,057	609,802	979,551	751,647	641,361	635,891	977,226	1,043,409	1,674,993	1,642,705
CIN	1,117,603	982,095	858,805	862,466	1,047,824	742,958	958,300	733,354	987,991	1,803,568
HOU		924,456	719,502	725,773	2,151,470	1,872,108	1,348,303	1,312,887	1,442,995	1,253,444
LA	1,804,250	2,755,184	2,538,602	2,228,751	2,553,577	2,617,029	1,664,362	1,581,093	1,784,527	1,697,142
MIL	1,101,441	766,921	773,018	910,911	555,584					
MON									1,212,608	1,424,683
NY		922,530	1,080,108	1,732,597	1,768,389	1,932,693	1,565,492	1,781,657	2,175,373	2,697,479
PHI	590,039	762,034	907,141	1,425,891	1,166,376	1,108,201	828,888	664,546	519,414	708,247
PIT	1,199,128	1,090,648	783,648	759,496	909,279	1,196,618	907,012	693,485	769,369	1,341,947
STL	855,305	953,895	1,170,546	1,143,294	1,241,201	1,712,980	2,090,145	2,011,167	1,682,783	1,629,736
SD									512,970	643,679
SF	1,390,679	1,592,594	1,571,306	1,504,364	1,546,075	1,657,192	1,242,480	837,220	873,603	740,720
TOT	8,731,502	11,360,159	11,382,227	12,045,190	13,581,136	15,015,471	12,971,430	11,785,358	15,094,946	16,662,198
AMERICAN LEAGUE										
BAL	951,089	790,254	774,343	1,116,215	781,649	1,203,366	955,053	943,977	1,062,094	1,057,069
BOS	850,589	733,080	942,642	883,276	652,201	811,172	1,727,832	1,940,788	1,833,246	1,595,278
CAL					566,727	1,400,321	1,317,713	1,025,956	758,388	1,077,741
CHI	1,146,019	1,131,562	1,158,848	1,250,053	1,130,519	990,016	985,634	803,775	589,546	495,355
CLE	725,547	716,076	562,507	653,293	934,786	903,359	662,980	857,994	619,970	729,752
DET	1,600,710	1,207,881	821,952	816,139	1,029,645	1,124,293	1,447,143	2,031,847	1,577,481	1,501,293
KC	683,817	635,675	762,364	642,478	528,344	773,929	726,639		902,414	693,047
LA	603,510	1,144,063	821,015	760,439						
MIL										933,690
MIN	1,256,723	1,433,116	1,406,652	1,207,514	1,463,258	1,259,374	1,483,547	1,143,257	1,349,328	1,261,887
NY	1,747,725	1,493,574	1,308,920	1,305,638	1,213,552	1,124,648	1,259,514	1,185,666	1,067,996	1,136,879
OAK								837,466	778,232	778,355
SEA									677,944	
WAS	597,287	729,775	535,604	600,106	560,083	576,260	770,868	546,661	918,106	824,789
TOT	10,163,016	10,015,056	9,094,847	9,235,151	8,860,764	10,166,738	11,336,923	11,317,387	12,134,745	12,085,135
ML	18,894,518	21,375,216	20,477,074	21,280,340	22,441,900	25,182,208	24,308,352	23,102,744	27,229,692	28,747,332

	1971	1972	1973	1974	1975	1976	1977	1978	1979	1980
NATIONAL LEAGUE										
ATL	1,006,320	752,973	800,655	981,085	534,672	818,179	872,464	904,494	769,465	1,048,411
CHI	1,653,007	1,299,163	1,351,705	1,015,378	1,034,819	1,026,217	1,439,834	1,525,311	1,648,587	1,206,776
CIN	1,501,122	1,611,459	2,017,601	2,164,307	2,315,603	2,629,708	2,519,670	2,532,497	2,356,933	2,022,450
HOU	1,261,589	1,469,247	1,394,004	1,090,728	858,002	886,146	1,109,560	1,126,145	1,900,312	2,278,217
LA	2,064,594	1,860,858	2,136,192	2,632,474	2,539,349	2,386,301	2,955,087	3,347,845	2,860,954	3,249,287
MON	1,290,963	1,142,145	1,246,863	1,019,134	908,292	646,704	1,433,757	1,427,007	2,102,173	2,208,175
NY	2,266,680	2,134,185	1,912,390	1,722,209	1,730,566	1,468,754	1,066,825	1,007,328	788,905	1,192,073
PHI	1,511,223	1,343,329	1,475,934	1,808,648	1,909,233	2,480,150	2,700,070	2,583,389	2,775,011	2,651,650
PIT	1,501,132	1,427,460	1,319,913	1,110,552	1,270,018	1,025,945	1,237,349	964,106	1,435,454	1,646,757
STL	1,604,671	1,196,894	1,574,046	1,838,413	1,695,270	1,207,079	1,659,287	1,278,215	1,627,256	1,385,147
SD	557,513	644,273	611,826	1,075,399	1,281,747	1,458,478	1,376,269	1,670,107	1,456,967	1,139,026
SF	1,106,043	647,744	834,193	519,987	522,919	626,868	700,056	1,740,477	1,456,402	1,096,115
TOT	17,324,856	15,529,730	16,675,322	16,978,314	16,600,490	16,660,529	19,070,228	20,106,922	21,178,416	21,124,086
AMERICAN LEAGUE										
BAL	1,023,037	899,950	958,667	962,572	1,002,157	1,058,609	1,195,769	1,051,724	1,681,009	1,797,438
BOS	1,678,732	1,441,718	1,481,002	1,556,411	1,748,587	1,895,846	2,074,549	2,320,643	2,353,114	1,956,092
CAL	926,373	744,190	1,058,206	917,269	1,058,163	1,006,774	1,432,633	1,755,386	2,523,575	2,297,327
CHI	833,891	1,177,318	1,302,527	1,149,596	750,802	914,945	1,657,135	1,491,100	1,280,702	1,200,365
CLE	591,361	626,354	615,107	1,114,262	977,039	948,776	900,365	800,584	1,011,644	1,033,827
DET	1,591,073	1,892,386	1,724,146	1,243,080	1,058,836	1,467,020	1,359,856	1,714,893	1,630,929	1,785,293
KC	910,784	707,656	1,345,341	1,173,292	1,151,836	1,680,265	1,852,603	2,255,493	2,261,845	2,288,714
MIL	731,531	600,440	1,092,158	955,741	1,213,357	1,012,164	1,114,938	1,601,406	1,918,343	1,857,408
MIN	940,858	797,901	907,499	662,401	737,156	715,394	1,162,727	787,878	1,070,521	769,206
NY	1,070,771	966,328	1,262,103	1,273,075	1,288,048	2,012,434	2,103,092	2,335,871	2,537,765	2,627,417
OAK	914,993	921,323	1,000,763	845,693	1,075,518	780,593	495,599	526,999	306,763	842,259
SEA							1,338,511	877,440	844,447	836,204
TEX		662,974	686,085	1,193,902	1,127,924	1,164,982	1,250,722	1,447,963	1,519,671	1,198,175
TOR							1,701,052	1,562,585	1,431,651	1,400,327
WAS	655,156									
TOT	11,868,560	11,438,538	13,433,604	13,047,294	13,189,423	14,657,802	19,639,552	20,529,964	22,371,980	21,890,052
ML	29,193,416	26,968,268	30,108,926	30,025,608	29,789,912	31,318,332	38,709,780	40,636,888	43,550,396	43,014,136

	1981	1982	1983	1984	1985	1986	1987	1988	1989	1990
NATIONAL LEAGUE										
ATL	535,418	1,801,985	2,119,935	1,724,892	1,350,137	1,387,181	1,217,402	848,089	984,930	980,129
CHI	565,637	1,249,278	1,479,717	2,107,655	2,161,534	1,859,102	2,035,130	2,089,034	2,491,942	2,243,791
CIN	1,093,730	1,326,528	1,190,419	1,275,887	1,834,619	1,692,432	2,185,205	2,072,528	1,979,320	2,400,892
HOU	1,321,282	1,558,555	1,351,962	1,229,862	1,184,314	1,734,276	1,909,902	1,933,505	1,834,908	1,310,927
LA	2,381,292	3,608,881	3,510,313	3,134,824	3,264,593	3,023,208	2,797,409	2,980,262	2,944,653	3,002,396
MON	1,534,564	2,318,292	2,320,651	1,606,531	1,502,494	1,128,981	1,850,324	1,478,659	1,783,533	1,373,087
NY	704,244	1,323,036	1,112,774	1,842,695	2,761,601	2,767,601	3,034,129	3,055,445	2,918,710	2,732,745
PHI	1,638,752	2,376,394	2,128,339	2,062,693	1,830,350	1,933,335	2,100,110	1,990,041	1,861,985	1,992,484
PIT	541,789	1,024,106	1,225,916	773,500	735,900	1,000,917	1,161,193	1,866,713	1,374,141	2,049,908
STL	1,010,247	2,111,906	2,317,914	2,037,448	2,637,563	2,471,974	3,072,122	2,892,799	3,080,980	2,573,225
SD	519,161	1,607,516	1,539,815	1,983,904	2,210,352	1,805,716	1,454,061	1,506,896	2,009,031	1,856,396
SF	632,274	1,200,948	1,251,530	1,001,545	818,697	1,528,748	1,917,168	1,785,297	2,059,701	1,975,528
TOT	12,478,390	21,507,424	21,549,284	20,781,436	22,292,156	22,333,472	24,734,156	24,499,268	25,323,834	24,491,508
AMERICAN LEAGUE										
BAL	1,024,247	1,613,031	2,042,071	2,045,784	2,132,387	1,973,176	1,835,692	1,660,738	2,535,208	2,415,189
BOS	1,060,379	1,950,124	1,782,285	1,661,618	1,786,633	2,147,641	2,231,551	2,464,851	2,510,012	2,528,986
CAL	1,441,545	2,807,360	2,555,016	2,402,997	2,567,427	2,655,872	2,696,299	2,340,925	2,647,291	2,555,688
CHI	946,651	1,567,787	2,132,821	2,136,988	1,669,888	1,424,313	1,208,060	1,115,749	1,045,651	2,002,357
CLE	661,395	1,044,021	768,941	734,079	655,181	1,471,805	1,077,898	1,411,610	1,285,542	1,225,240
DET	1,149,144	1,636,058	1,829,636	2,704,794	2,286,609	1,899,437	2,061,830	2,081,162	1,543,656	1,495,785
KC	1,279,403	2,284,464	1,963,875	1,810,018	2,162,717	2,320,794	2,392,471	2,350,181	2,477,700	2,244,956
MIL	874,292	1,978,896	2,397,131	1,608,509	1,360,265	1,265,041	1,909,244	1,923,238	1,970,735	1,752,900
MIN	469,090	921,186	858,939	1,598,692	1,651,814	1,255,453	2,081,976	3,030,672	2,277,438	1,751,584
NY	1,614,353	2,041,219	2,257,976	1,821,815	2,214,587	2,268,030	2,427,672	2,633,701	2,170,485	2,006,436
OAK	1,304,052	1,735,489	1,294,941	1,353,281	1,334,599	1,314,646	1,678,921	2,287,335	2,667,225	2,900,217
SEA	636,276	1,070,404	813,537	870,372	1,128,696	1,029,045	1,134,255	1,022,398	1,298,443	1,509,727
TEX	850,076	1,154,432	1,363,469	1,102,471	1,112,497	1,692,002	1,763,053	1,581,901	2,043,993	2,057,911
TOR	755,083	1,275,978	1,930,415	2,110,009	2,468,925	2,455,477	2,778,429	2,595,175	3,375,883	3,885,284
TOT	14,065,986	23,080,448	23,991,052	23,961,428	24,532,220	25,172,732	27,277,350	28,499,636	29,849,264	30,332,260
ML	26,544,376	44,587,872	45,540,336	44,742,864	46,824,376	47,506,204	52,011,504	52,998,904	55,173,096	54,823,768

	1991	1992	1993	1994	1995	1996	1997	1998	1999	2000
NATIONAL LEAGUE										
ARI								3,600,412	3,019,654	2,942,516
ATL	2,140,217	3,077,400	3,884,725	2,539,240	2,561,831	2,901,242	3,464,488	3,361,350	3,284,897	3,234,301
CHI	2,314,250	2,126,720	2,653,763	1,845,208	1,918,265	2,219,110	2,190,308	2,623,000	2,813,854	2,789,511
CIN	2,372,377	2,315,946	2,453,232	1,897,681	1,837,649	1,861,428	1,785,788	1,793,679	2,061,222	2,577,351
COL			4,483,350	3,281,511	3,390,037	3,891,014	3,888,453	3,789,347	3,481,065	3,285,710
FLA			3,064,847	1,937,467	1,700,466	1,746,767	2,364,387	1,750,395	1,369,421	1,218,326
HOU	1,196,152	1,211,412	2,084,546	1,561,136	1,363,801	1,975,888	2,046,781	2,450,451	2,706,017	3,056,139
LA	3,348,170	2,473,266	3,170,392	2,279,355	2,766,251	3,188,454	3,319,504	3,089,201	3,095,346	3,010,819
MIL								1,811,548	1,701,796	1,573,621
MON	934,742	1,669,077	1,641,437	1,276,250	1,309,618	1,616,709	1,497,609	914,717	773,277	926,263
NY	2,284,484	1,779,534	1,873,183	1,151,471	1,273,183	1,588,323	1,766,174	2,287,942	2,725,668	2,800,221
PHI	2,050,012	1,927,448	3,137,674	2,290,971	2,043,598	1,801,677	1,490,638	1,715,702	1,825,337	1,612,769
PIT	2,065,302	1,829,395	1,650,593	1,222,520	905,517	1,332,150	1,657,022	1,560,950	1,638,023	1,748,908
STL	2,448,699	2,418,483	2,844,328	1,866,544	1,756,727	2,654,718	2,634,014	3,194,092	3,225,334	3,336,493
SD	1,804,289	1,722,102	1,375,432	953,857	1,041,805	2,187,886	2,089,333	2,555,901	2,523,538	2,423,149
SF	1,737,478	1,561,987	2,606,354	1,704,608	1,241,500	1,413,922	1,690,869	1,925,634	2,078,399	3,315,330
TOT	24,696,174	24,112,770	36,923,856	25,807,820	25,110,248	30,379,288	31,885,364	38,424,324	38,322,848	39,851,424
AMERICAN LEAGUE										
ANA							1,767,330	2,519,107	2,253,123	2,066,977
BAL	2,552,753	3,567,819	3,644,965	2,535,359	3,098,475	3,646,950	3,711,132	3,685,194	3,433,150	3,295,128
BOS	2,562,435	2,468,574	2,422,021	1,775,818	2,164,410	2,315,231	2,226,136	2,343,947	2,446,162	2,586,032
CAL	2,416,236	2,065,444	2,057,460	1,512,622	1,748,680	1,820,521				
CHI	2,934,154	2,681,156	2,581,091	1,697,398	1,609,773	1,676,403	1,864,782	1,391,146	1,338,851	1,947,799
CLE	1,051,863	1,224,274	2,177,908	1,995,174	2,842,745	3,318,174	3,404,750	3,467,299	3,468,456	3,456,278
DET	1,641,661	1,423,963	1,971,421	1,184,783	1,180,979	1,168,610	1,365,157	1,409,391	2,026,441	2,533,752
KC	2,161,537	1,867,689	1,934,578	1,400,494	1,233,530	1,435,997	1,517,638	1,494,875	1,506,068	1,677,915
MIL	1,478,729	1,857,314	1,688,080	1,268,399	1,087,560	1,327,155	1,444,027			
MIN	2,293,842	2,482,428	2,048,673	1,398,565	1,057,667	1,437,352	1,411,064	1,165,980	1,202,829	1,059,715
NY	1,863,733	1,748,733	2,416,965	1,675,556	1,705,263	2,250,877	2,580,325	2,919,046	3,292,736	3,227,657
OAK	2,713,493	2,494,160	2,035,025	1,242,692	1,174,310	1,148,380	1,264,218	1,232,339	1,434,610	1,728,888
SEA	2,147,905	1,651,398	2,051,853	1,104,206	1,643,203	2,723,850	3,192,237	2,644,305	2,916,346	3,148,317
TB								2,261,158	1,562,827	1,549,052
TEX	2,297,720	2,198,231	2,244,616	2,503,198	1,985,910	2,889,020	2,945,228	2,927,409	2,771,469	2,800,147
TOR	4,001,527	4,028,318	4,057,947	2,907,933	2,826,483	2,559,573	2,589,297	2,454,283	2,163,464	1,819,886
TOT	32,117,584	31,759,506	33,332,598	24,202,196	25,358,990	29,718,094	31,283,320	31,915,480	31,816,532	32,897,544
ML	56,813,760	55,872,276	70,256,456	50,010,016	50,469,240	60,097,384	63,168,684	70,339,808	70,139,376	72,748,968

1884 UNION ASSOCIATION

ALT	11,000	KC	54,000	WAS	56,000
BAL	45,000	MIL	10,000	WIL	3,000
BOS	28,000	PHI	19,000	TOT	411,000
CIN	41,000	STL	116,000		
CP	28,000	STP	0		

1890 PLAYERS LEAGUE

BOS	197,346	NY	148,197
BRO	79,272	PHI	170,399
BUF	61,244	PIT	117,123
CHI	148,876	TOT	980,887
CLE	58,430		

CHAPTER 4

The Changing Game

Bill Felber and Gary Gillette

In 1906, at the arguable heights of their careers, the Hall of Fame-bound trio of Joe Tinker, Johnny Evers, and Frank Chance completed approximately 50 double plays. In 2000, the primary players in the last-place Tampa Bay Devil Rays infield—Fred McGriff at first base, Miguel Cairo and Bobby Smith at second, and Kevin Stocker and Felix Martinez at shortstop—turned roughly twice that number. May we infer that the finest middle infield of a bygone era would be rejected as unfit for duty on a perfectly nondescript modern team?

For the five-year period between 1921 and 1925, Rogers Hornsby batted better than .400. In the past 60 seasons, not a single major league hitter has reached that level of excellence as much as once, let alone for half a decade. May we conclude that, were he in his prime today, Hornsby would shame Tony Gwynn into anonymity?

The answers to those questions are, of course, two resounding calls of "no."

Baseball is not played in a time capsule, and neither its record book nor its archives should be read as if it were. The game played on the artificial turf of Veterans Stadium that you watch today on television holds the same lure as the contest your grandfather took a surrey to see at Chicago's old West Side Park. Teams contest for the same end, using fundamentally the same objects in a format scribed basically by the same rules. However, technological, sociological, strategic, and cultural forces have over decades refined those elements, so that today's performances cannot easily be accurately measured relative to yesterday's. Nor can judgment be precisely made as to the superiority of either, save subjectively in the mind's eye.

Baseball today is different from the game of the early 20th century in many ways, just as contemporary American culture is different from the horse-and-buggy era. Imagine paying a quarter for admission to the ballpark, another quarter for access to the grandstand, and a third quarter for a seat. Imagine games played before audiences of a few hundred, maybe a thousand, fans. Imagine visiting teams arriving in town on trains, bunking two to a bed, then caravaning to the ballyard in a grand parade through the streets—though never at night and never, ever on Sunday. Now imagine baseball as the only sport of widespread popularity. No football to speak of, no basketball, no hockey; no golf, no tennis, no track of consequence. Moreover, horse racing was only for the elite, and boxing only for the disreputable. There *was* such a time in America, and it was only a century ago.

In many ways, the game of baseball has changed precisely because America itself has changed. Whether all that change has been for the good may be argued. One might contend, for instance, that a laudable part of Americana died out when the practice of uniformed players publicly trolleying to the game (as a means of stirring fan attention) was halted in the first decade of the 20th century. However, most, if not all, aspects of baseball's growth alongside society were inevitable. The 50-cent admission charge established by the National League in 1876 held for many years, but so did the rather unsavory practice of treating players as peons, to the point of doubling up sleeping arrangements. Philadelphia Athletics catcher Ossie Schreckengost once actually had it written into his contract that teammate (and bunkmate) Rube Waddell would be barred from eating animal crackers in bed because the crumbs irritated the catcher. Players today sleep in luxury hotels, and most do not even share rooms, much less beds. As the cost of living and the cost of operating a franchise have both increased strikingly, so have the size of the grandstand and the cost of a general admission ticket, the latter by a factor of 15 or 20.

In any era and at any price, a great championship battle has always held the American populace in thrall. Tens of millions of fans watched on their living room televisions in October 2000 as the Yankees and Mets waged their crosstown World Series struggle long into the night. Those fans studied every decisive play from a half dozen angles on instant replay as they second-guessed managerial moves and controversial umpiring decisions. Was that excitement any greater, measure for measure, than the grip in which the cities of Boston and Baltimore were held during the final days of the race for the 1897 National League pennant?

There was neither television nor radio then, but that did not stay the enthusiasm of hundreds of thousands of rooters nationwide as the pulsating battle for supremacy wound to a close. The principals were the two most dominant sporting teams of their generation: The Boston Beaneaters and Baltimore Orioles had divided the previous six pennants. Now, with less than a week remaining in the 1897 season, they were locked in a virtual tie for first, each having won better than seven of every 10 games played and fated by the schedule to meet for three conclusive games in Baltimore.

So all encompassing was interest in the games that Associated Press telegraphers dispatched play-by-play accounts to every major subscribing newspaper east of the Rockies. More than three dozen correspondents—an unheard-of number for the era—covered the games. Twenty more telegraphers tapped out accounts to cities where fans had gathered in theaters or outside newspaper offices to follow the events on chalkboards. In Boston, fan interest was so great that the game reports received triple the front-page space accorded the activities of President William McKinley, who was in Boston at the same time. Throngs numbering in the thousands massed daily along Washington Street, Boston's Newspaper Row, to watch mechanical re-creations, which can be considered a distant precursor to graphical coverage of the World Series on the World Wide Web. There was a published report of 4,000 fans jamming Boston's Music Hall to watch a similar simulation. The games at Baltimore's Union Grounds drew as many as 25,000 spectators, more than twice the previous record attendance for that facility!

The excitement of a great pennant race is a constant; only the modes of sensing that excitement change. Consider only a few of the more obvious changes: The player pool has changed, albeit at times tardily, to reflect the nation's ethnic populations. When that pool expanded to encompass Southerners, Irish, Jews, Latins, or African Americans, it did so in reaction to fundamental changes such as the gradual dying out of post-Civil War prejudice, the assimilation of immigrant populations, and the eventual willingness of white society to acknowledge blacks as equals.

Technology has worked on the grand old game in many ways. Basic improvements in the construction of the ball and glove have dramatically changed the play on the field. The field itself has changed in ways as grandiose and obvious as the abandonment of the unfenced pasture in favor of the comparative luxury of the wooden park. Intimate brick and steel stadiums of the early 20th century were followed half a century later by huge, impersonal concrete multipurpose facilities that are now being retired by atavistic retro ballparks evoking the golden years of the game.

Sociological alterations, as exemplified by population shifts from city to suburb and by the replacement of the trolley in favor of the automobile, resulted in the abandonment of many inner-city ballparks after World War II. At the turn of the millennium, ironically, high-tech new downtown ballparks are viewed by many cities as key components in reviving aging sections of their urban cores.

Changes in national attitudes have been mirrored in the game on the field. America was a prim and proper country in 1908, and its national game was a prim and proper one, heavy on the sacrifice bunt and very short on the long ball. Americans were a comparatively profligate bunch in the late 1920s, winning and losing with abandon on Wall Street, and these restless capitalists adopted baseball heroes like Babe Ruth and Hack Wilson, who hit 'em far during the day and swigged 'em long into the night. The difference of only two decades is strikingly underscored in a baseball statistic that also speaks volumes about off-field attitudes: for the five years between 1906 and 1910, the Chicago White Sox hit a total of only 27 home runs. Ruth hit more than that by himself in every season save one between 1919 and 1933.

Baseball's labor-management relations have also generally mirrored national patterns. The present major leagues can trace their ancestry back to the 1870s, an age when even the legality of organized labor was questioned. The motivation behind the organizers of the National League was to take control of the game that had been essentially run by players' cooperatives. The 1890s, the era of some of the most violent union-management conflicts (e.g., the Haymarket riot, the Pullman strike), also witnessed the last direct player challenge to the authority of ownership, the Brotherhood War, which produced the Players League. Unionization very gradually gained favor, although both nationally and in baseball that process took decades. True player free agency in the National Pastime, as with worker rights in other businesses, often arrived only under the aegis of the courts.

Finally, as the educational level of America itself has changed, the strategies of baseball have evolved. The dominant function of today's late-inning reliever could hardly have been envisioned by the game's greatest minds as little as three decades ago. The stolen base, the home run, and the sacrifice have all come and gone as strategic coups (and, in some cases, have come back again). It is as judgmental to speculate on whether the game of today is better than the game of 1907 as it is to posit whether Joe Tinker was a better shortstop than Nomar Garciaparra.

No one would contend that baseball has been, or is today, any more than a general mirror of its times. Neither can it seriously be suggested that the National Pastime has failed to reflect many of the historical trends that have occurred during its existence. For purposes of this discussion, it is vital to recognize both of those realities. Paradoxically, only by appreciating the game's evolution can one truly begin to sense the marvelous continuum represented therein.

So, by what context does one measure Hornsby's feats of the 1920s relative to Gwynn's of the 1980s and 1990s? By the context of the technological, strategic, societal, and cultural changes that wrought both of them. Could Joe Tinker play shortstop for the Cubs of today? For that matter, could Ozzie Smith have adapted to the scrub fields, primitive travel methods, incompetent training aides, and all-but-useless equipment of Tinker's day?

These questions cannot be answered with finality. But without considering the many changing aspects of the game, attempts to even provide an answer become frivolous. What follows is an effort to examine some of the major causes of change and to provide context to a discussion of the evolving nature of baseball. It is a sport has possessed for more than a century only one enduring and vital characteristic: it has, from the outset, been America's National Pastime.

Equipment

The bat, the ball, and the glove are baseball's utensils. Virtually every child old enough to root, root, root for the home team owns at least one of each. Their omnipresence serves as immutable evidence of the game's penetration into American culture. Yet today's equipment is as changed from its predecessors of generations ago as is baseball itself. Even the seemingly simple functions of each have been redefined, in part a cause and in part an effect of the changing game.

Only a few of those changes are reflected in the rulebook; to most the book has proven adaptable. Examination of the adjustments made to the game's basic tools illuminates the changes that the baseball itself has made.

For obvious reasons, rulemakers have always felt the need to define how the ball shall be made. Curiously, that definition has changed very little over more than a century. Notice how similar are the two definitions that follow, the first from an 1861 convention of the National Association of Base Ball Players, and the second taken from the Official Baseball Rules of 2000:

1861—*The ball must weigh not less than five and one-half, nor more than five and three-fourths ounces avoirdupois. It must measure not less than nine and one-half, nor more than nine and three fourths inches in circumference. It must be composed of India rubber and yarn, covered with leather."*

2000—*The ball shall be a sphere formed by yarn wound around a small core of cork, rubber or similar material, covered with two stripes of white horsehide or cowhide, tightly stitched together. It shall weigh not less than five nor more than five and one quarter ounces avoirdupois and measure not less than nine nor more than nine and one quarter inches in circumference."*

How greatly has the ball changed in 139 years? It is about 5 percent smaller, about 9 percent lighter. Rather than an India rubber center, it may have—and in professional ball does have—a cork center. The stitching must be tight, though precisely how tight is not defined. And that's it. In every other respect, the ball put in play in the amateur games of 1861 would pass muster by modern rules.

That is not to say that the baseball of Civil War Days and the Rawlings Official model of today are virtually identical. Today's ball is far more resilient and travels greater distances. This is due to several factors.

Most obviously the modern baseball undergoes far less wear and tear. For the first half century of professional play, it was customary for a game ball—whether mushy, discolored, or lopsided—to be kept in play until it was irretrievably lost. The key word here is *irretrievably.* In the 19th century, if a ball was hit into the stands, the ushers collected the ball so that play could continue. If hit out of sight, it was searched for—for as long as five minutes! Then and only then might the host team be required to furnish a second ball. The idea of going through dozens of balls per game, as is the modern custom, would have seemed frivolously wasteful to Great-Grandpa.

The original policy moderated somewhat with the passing years, but it was not until 1920 that league officials stipulated the use of only clean and new baseballs. This was mandated to enhance offense as well as out of concern for player safety: worn and discolored balls frequently were hard to control or even see, as the tragic beaning death of Ray Chapman demonstrated. Those directives lent a new measure of consistency to the game, so that the ball a batter swung at in the bottom of the ninth was not different from the one used in the first-pitch ceremonies.

The only rule change of significance affecting the ball came in 1910, and it authorized the use of a cushioned cork center as an alternative to the rubber-centered ball that had been in vogue until that time. The cork-centered ball was found to be more lively, an especially desirable trait considering the depressed (and, to the baseball-going public, depressing) league batting averages. The cork-centered ball was introduced in time for the 1910 World Series between the Philadelphia Athletics and Chicago Cubs; as a result, the two clubs batted .272, which was about 20 points higher than the regular season league average. For the 1911 regular season, both leagues used the cork-centered ball: National League averages rose by only four points; however, in the American League, the climb was a heady 30 points and the league leader, Detroit's Ty Cobb, hit a stunning .420. A total of 21 American League regulars bettered .300 that season; only eight had done so the year before. In the National League, Chicago's Frank Schulte hit 21 home runs. Schulte had tied for the home run title in 1910 with 10.

All other changes in the makeup of the ball itself—tighter winding of the yarn, introduction of different and supposedly better kinds of yarn, raised or depressed stitches—have been products of technology, not of the rulemakers. About 1920, as batting averages soared and Babe Ruth began to crash home runs in unheard-of profusion, there was controversy over the substitution of Australian wool for the generic type in making baseball yarn. Surely, fans speculated, this new wool must be the reason behind the livelier ball. In fact, the explanation probably had more to do with improved methods of winding the wool than with the wool itself.

The same rulebook that has licensed virtually no change in the parameters of the baseball itself has brooked only minor adjustment with the bat, and then, generally, only by way of greater specificity. Again, compare the rules governing play in 1861 with the slightly more elaborate section from the modern rulebook:

1861—*The bat must be round and must not exceed two and one half inches in diameter in the thickest part. It must be made of wood, and may be of any length to suit the striker.*

2000—*The bat shall be a smooth, rounded stick not more than two and three quarter inches in diameter at the thickest part and not more than 42 inches in length. The bat shall be one piece of solid wood, or formed from a block of wood consisting of two or more pieces of wood bonded together with an adhesive in such way that the grain direction in all pieces is essentially parallel to the length of the bat. Any such laminated bat shall contain only wood or adhesive.*

The modern rule also contains an allowance for a small cupping of up to one inch at the bat's end, and for use of a grip-improving substance on the bat handle. But again, the stipulated differences of almost a century and a half of development are comparatively minimal.

There is a length limit where once there was none; however, at least in practice, the limit is functionally irrelevant. In today's major leagues, it is virtually unheard-of for a bat to exceed 36 inches in length, much less 42. The modern bat has gained one-quarter of an inch in girth over its ancestor, and it need no longer necessarily be of a single piece of wood, though no such laminated bats have been used in big-league play to date.

Changes in the bat have tended to develop stylistically, more so than with the ball, generally under the influence of the batters themselves. Bats, of course, always have been highly personalized objects. With such a broad allowance by the rules (no weight limit, no functional length limit) hitters have tended to individualize their sticks within widely recognized norms.

Many hitters before 1920 coveted heavy "wagon-tongue" models with thick barrels capable of driving the ball over the infield, even at the expense of bat speed. Cap Anson, legendary star of the Chicago White Stockings, used just such a bat, reputedly weighing in at a manly three pounds and then some. In the 1920s Babe Ruth menaced opposing pitchers with a 48-ounce bat, though Ruth saw to it that the bat handle was tapered to accommodate his smaller-than-normal hands.

Heinie Groh, third baseman of the Cincinnati Reds and New York Giants, was no slugger of Ruthian proportion. Yet Groh's innovative "bottle" bat, with its narrow handle expanding precipitously at the hitting area to a broad surface, not only served as a personal trademark but also helped him to a .292 lifetime average and a starting role on four pennant winners.

The modern bat bears no resemblance to any of those models. It is sleeker, usually no more than 35 inches in length and no heavier than 33 ounces. The reason is simple: batting instructors, who once looked upon mass as the key factor behind a mighty poke, now focus on bat speed instead. The faster a batter can swing a bat through the strike zone, the greater the force applied to the ball. And the greater the force applied, the farther the ball travels. Presto, light bats generating greater bat speed generating more home runs.

As for gloves . . . well, in the game's early days, they did not exist: Players were expected to catch the ball barehanded. For a time, they received something of an aid in that effort by a rule recording an out if a ball was caught on the first bounce. That made things a little easier.

The use of gloves was never formally barred, as were, for instance, black players in the old National Association rulebook; it simply was looked upon as sort of sissified. There is no clear record of who first conceived the notion of fielding with a glove. Al Spalding wrote that the first to don a glove was an 1875 player for the National Association's St. Louis team named Charlie Waitt. In a game that year, Waitt donned a street-dress leather glove on his fielding hand. Waitt, reportedly, was ridiculed league-wide. Despite that attitude, as more prominent players adopted Waitt's concept, the notion gradually came to be accepted.

Two points should be made about the use of early-day gloves. First, their function was utterly different than it is today. The first gloves, lacking webbing and lacing, merely provided protection for the hands when fielding the ball. Today's larger, better-padded, webbed, laced and pocketed gloves might more appropriately be described as fielding devices, because it is the glove, not the fielder's hands, that does much of the actual fielding work.

Second, as verification of the first point, players of the 19th century often wore gloves on both hands. For the throwing hand, they would simply snip the glove at the fingers for dexterity. Those photographs that remain of players from that era, especially the ones portraying fielding sequences, confirm that tendency.

It was not until 1895 that stipulations concerning gloves were included in the rules. Those limited the size of gloves to 10 ounces and 14 inches in circumference for all players except catchers and first basemen, who were permitted to use any size glove. Today's rulebook, by contrast, takes a page and a half to specify dimensions, materials, lacings, and webbings for gloves. There are 13 different size limitations on the standard fielder's glove, ranging from palm width to the length of each separate finger. The transition from the glove as protection to the glove as a tightly defined fielding aid came gradually but inexorably.

The first advance was development of a pocket, an indentation in the palm of the hand where the ball was most easily and most naturally caught. As with the origination of the glove itself, there is no firm and fast date for the pocket's appearance: it simply happened, though it did not happen immediately.

To the contrary, for several years after the introduction of the glove, fielders adopted a sort of "reverse pocket" when they would excise the leather from the palm area and leave it bare, presumably for better a touch or feel. In all probability, the pocket was not invented by glove makers, but by players themselves, taking advantage of the natural stretching the glove's leather underwent with use. Today this is called "breaking a glove in." Today, however, pockets are made in the manufacturing process.

Credit commonly is given to a pitcher, spitballer Bill Doak of the St. Louis Cardinals, for advancing glove technology from the primordial state. In 1920 Doak approached a glove manufacturer with a plan for a new personalized glove. Many players liked personalized glove models, but Doak's was different. It envisioned a pre-formed pocket, not one that would be fashioned through constant wear. And it included a square of reinforced webbing between the thumb and finger sections as an additional aid to fielding. Previously, the fingers simply had been tied together, if they were not allowed to act independently. Doak's model remained popular for almost 30 years. Every subsequent advance in glove design, whether it be the hinged heel, short- or long-fingered design, or advanced webbing, can be traced to a concept originated by Doak.

In the 1930s rulemakers mandated the use of only leather in the making of gloves—the first change in glove rules since the initial size and weight limitations were set in 1895. In 1939, acting in response to Hank Greenberg's introduction of an oversized mitt with a netted webbing, they outlawed the use of netting, limited webbing to four inches from thumb to palm (the present rule is four and one-half inches), and restricted the size of first basemen's gloves as well. Weight restrictions were dropped in 1950, and size limitations further defined.

For many years, no limitation was placed on the size of the catcher's mitt; after all, the larger the catcher's mitt, the harder it was for a catcher to dig the ball out of the glove and make a throw. In 1960, however, Baltimore manager Paul Richards knew that there was something worse than having catchers who could not evict the ball from an oversized mitt—that was having catchers who could not catch the ball at all.

The manager's problem was that his most effective pitcher was Hoyt Wilhelm, and Wilhelm's most effective pitch was a knuckleball that proved as difficult to catch as it was to hit. As Baltimore catchers soared to the top of league in passed balls, Richards devised a catcher's mitt of nearly 50 inches in circumference—perhaps twice the standard size. If Baltimore catchers could not throw out base stealers with the new mitt, they could at least have a fighting chance at preventing Wilhelm's pitches from rolling to the backstop. Shortly after the appearance of Baltimore's oversized mitt, the rule was amended to set a 38-inch circumference and 15½-inch diameter limit on catchers' gloves as well.

Even after catchers' gloves were restricted in size, however, questions remained about enforcement of the 1950 size limits. So, in 1972 the rules committee drafted the present 13-point measuring system. Fortunately, there is no record of a game ever being halted while a manager challenged the legality of a fielder's glove on all 13 points.

The Playing Field

Charley "Old Hoss" Radbourn was a pitcher of considerable note in the National League of the 1880s, and a hitter of no special renown. In 1882 he won 31 games for Providence while hitting only one home run. But this story isn't about any of his 31 victories, nor even about his home run—it's about playing conditions.

On August 17, 1882, Radbourn was playing right field (as he occasionally did when not pitching) against Detroit. The Providence field was not unlike most baseball fields of the day: it was, in the literal sense, a *field.* There was little groundskeeping and often no outfield barriers; even if there were, well-heeled fans who wished to simply pulled their carriages onto the playing surface and watched from there.

On this particular date, John Ward of Providence and Stump Weidman of Detroit allowed no runs to cross home over 17 innings. When Radbourn advanced to the plate with one out in the 18th, the sky was growing dark. In his then-brief big league career, Hoss had never hit a home run. He was not alone in that distinction, for four-base hits were a rare sight. (That season's league leader, George Wood of Detroit, hit only seven; the league record was nine.) But Radbourn lashed at Weidman's pitch and sent it scurrying past Wood in left field. As some witnesses reported, the ball rolled close to the leg of an especially spirited black horse hitched to a wagon.

Wood raced to the spot and reached for the ball. He was prevented by, of all things, the horse's hind hoof, which swished through the air and barely missed conking him. Wood reached again; again the horse kicked. Radbourn, meanwhile, raced past second. Desperately, Wood grabbed for a handful of grass, hopeful of appeasing the critter. That did not work. Finally, Ed Hanlon obtained a stick, reached in and swatted the ball clear of danger. It was too late; as Hanlon prepared to throw, Radbourn was being carried from the field in triumph.

The mere concept of what constitutes a major league ballpark has evolved through at least five distinct transformations, each markedly different from its predecessor and each spurred by changes both in the game's strategy and in the nation's sociology. The conditions surrounding Charley Radbourn's home run in Providence in 1882 may seem bizarre to us. No more bizarre, perhaps, than artificial turf will seem three generations hence.

The parks in the first few decades of professional ball were simple open spaces with ruts worn by the players marking the baselines. At games that attracted large crowds, the fans circling the field often defined the playing area. In 1871 the National Association club in Rockford, Illinois, played on a field called by ballpark expert Phil Lowry "the strangest in major league history." The aptly-named Forest City club had a field in which trees virtually lined the baselines, so players chasing popups took their chances. Third base was on a hill, home plate in a depression, and the outfield framed by a gutter draining an adjacent horseracing track.

For several reasons, there were few of the niceties we presently associate with a ballpark. Not the least of these was that, since the game itself was new, club owners often lacked the capital necessary to develop the grounds beyond a rudimentary level. A grandstand might hold about 1,500 customers if it was expansive, but usually it held fewer. It was desirable, but by no means certain, that the playing ground be level and free of gravel, though horse droppings might literally pockmark areas of play.

Except in Rockford, trees were not much of a hazard but, even at the best of diamonds, infields were poorly sculpted and ill-cared for. There were rarely such things as a scoreboard or dugout and, where outfield fences existed—first used at Brooklyn's Union Grounds—they might be as close as 180 feet from home plate or as distant as 500 feet at all points. Some fields like Brooklyn's doubled over the winter as skating rinks, when they were deliberately flooded.

Gradually, ballfields assumed a more standardized and slightly more familiar appearance. By the mid-1880s, most playing fields were at least semi-enclosed. Still, however, distances to the fences commonly were dictated as much by topography as any other consideration. When built in 1883, Chicago's Lake Front Park was considered the archetypal modern facility, seating almost 10,000. Yet its cramped site near the lake permitted only a 180-foot carry to left field, and only 300 feet to dead center! Such a field would be considered inadequate for 15-year-olds today. In contrast, at Boston's spacious Huntington Avenue Grounds a few years later, the barrier in left field was a comfortable 440 feet from home plate; it was a very long 635 feet to the fence in center. For part of the 1896 season, Robison Field in St. Louis did not even have a fence entirely circling the grounds. At one point that year, it was possible to hit a ball in-play through a gap in the barrier in right field; if so, the ball could roll unimpeded for more than 600 feet . . . to a lake.

If there was a single, overriding concern about ballparks in the game's first few decades, it was the danger of fire. Because wood was the common building material, facilities were susceptible to that danger, and it intruded on the game more than once, sometimes with dire results. Baltimore's Union Park was damaged by fire in 1894, while a blaze destroyed Boston's South End

Grounds in the third inning of a game between the Orioles and Beaneaters that same season. A game was halted by fire at Chicago's West Side Park; several years earlier a contest actually had continued at the nearby 23rd Street Grounds while fire consumed the grandstand. Brooklyn's Washington Park fell to flames in 1889; New York's Polo Grounds was virtually destroyed in 1911.

With all of its inherent and obvious disadvantages, the wooden ballpark may seem to have been an anachronism as early as 1910; furthermore, its role in the development of the game may seem to have been quite fleeting. Was it really anachronistic? Yes. Was its role fleeting? No. The era of wood, from the opening of Brooklyn's Union Grounds in 1862 until the closing of the last wooden grandstand at Philadelphia's Baker Bowl in 1938, encompasses three quarters of a century and better than half the lifespan of the professional game to date.

The demise of the wooden park was occasioned by a number of factors, fire hazard being not the least of them. Some wooden parks were deemed to be particularly dangerous. In 1903 hundreds of fans fell (and 12 died) when a wooden rail gave way at Baker Bowl in Philadelphia. In 1907 and again in 1908, the building inspector for the city of Cincinnati submitted a detailed bill of particulars on the hazards at the Palace of the Fans. Cracked girders, decayed supports, unsafe flooring, and a defective bleacher platform were only some of the problems. Construction problems were documented in St. Louis and other cities as well. Nonetheless, the gradually widening acceptance of baseball as an important cultural event also played a part in the transition to more permanent structures.

The average attendance climbed from 100,000 per franchise in 1890 to 365,000 in 1905. Larger, stronger, and more durable venues were needed and, because of the game's growing popularity, club owners were able to provide such facilities. Motivation for the owners also came from the fact that, as new parks were constructed, they could increase the numbers of more costly box seats, thus increasing potential revenues. Sound familiar?

Concrete and steel thus became the materials of choice. In 1909 Philadelphia Athletics owner Benjamin Shibe conceived and executed plans for a baseball plant upon a former brickyard at the corner of 21st and Lehigh north of Center City. The facility would be easily accessible from the city's center by trolley line and would supplant old, wooden Columbia Park, which had the added disadvantage of being located near several breweries, thus subjecting patrons to the constant odor of barley and yeast.

Shibe Park would not only smell better: it would be the grandest facility of its type ever conceived. A French Renaissance-style dome at the home plate entrance gave the stadium a distinctive, almost church-like, appearance. The concrete grandstand and bleachers followed the first and third base foul lines, seating 20,000. A huge scoreboard was installed in left field. The facility's price tag was a breathtaking half million dollars, yet the opening of Shibe Park set a standard that was soon widely matched.

In Pittsburgh Barney Dreyfuss already had begun construction of a replacement for old Exposition Park, the riverfront facility that had been in use since 1890. Named Forbes Field, the new ballpark opened June 30 near Schenley Park, and it included elevators, lighting in the grandstand, telephones, and even maids in the ladies rooms. Dreyfuss also conceived of providing access to the upper levels of the triple-decked grandstand by means of ramps rather than stairs, a practice in effect today. The larger capacity of Forbes paid almost immediate dividends when the Pirates celebrated the new home's inaugural season by winning a world championship.

If there is one hallmark of the concrete and steel stadiums raised in a dozen different cities between the years 1909 and 1923, it is their individuality. When Charles Comiskey developed plans for his new concrete and steel structure at 35th and Shields in Chicago in 1910, he asked his own star, pitcher Ed Walsh, to take a hand in the work. It may not be surprising, then, that Comiskey Park, both at its opening and for decades afterward, was considered one of the most tasking layouts for hitters. The original Comiskey featured 363-foot foul lines, 382-foot power alleys, and a center field of 420 feet (that, year by year, was enlarged to 455 feet). Particularly in the Dead Ball Era, the center field fence may as well not have existed at all.

In Brooklyn's 22,000 seat Ebbets Field, which opened in 1913, the original carry to the barrier in left was 419 feet, though a street limited the distance to the fence in right field to a mere 301. (Construction of bleachers in the 1930s brought the left field wall within a more manageable distance.)

The most unusual design of all the old parks was New York's bathtub-shaped Polo Grounds, which replaced the wooden facility of the same name after it was damaged by fire in 1911. The "new" Polo Grounds featured foul poles only about 260 feet distant from the plate, coupled with a cavernous center field that arced to distances of nearly 500 feet.

With a few exceptions, these classic-era parks served their host teams well for generations. Nevertheless, gradually at first in the 1940s and 1950s, then increasingly so in the 1960s, interior wear and exterior conditions rendered most unsatisfactory in the eyes of their tenants. Those conditions varied, but they can be summarized as follows:

Access: The classic-era parks had been dependent on trolley, subway, or bus lines to deliver fans to their gates. By the 1950s, though, America was a motorized nation, and club owners felt the need for expansive parking lots as well as proximity to modern freeways. Brooklyn club owner Walter O'Malley moved his team to Los Angeles when the city failed to deliver on his demands for such a new facility. The Giants, beset at the Polo Grounds by many of the same problems, fled the same year to San Francisco.

Size: When most of the so-called classic era parks were constructed, crowds of 30,000 were considered exceptional. By the mid-1960s, increased costs as well as increasing attendance made such limited capacity a serious operating problem for many clubs. Neither Forbes Field in Pittsburgh, Shibe Park in Philadelphia nor Crosley Field in Cincinnati was capable of seating much more than 35,000; when new and larger multipurpose stadiums were built in those cities, the clubs gladly moved into them.

Cost: Without exception, classic-era parks had been

constructed using private capital. By the 1960s, the cost of developing the kind of 50,000-seat stadium required by a major league team was more than the club owner was able to afford or willing to spend. Fortunately, local governments, which had come to view teams as community assets, proved willing in many cases to finance or subsidize the construction. This happened as early as the 1930s in Cleveland, and again in 1954 when the city of Baltimore captured the Browns from St. Louis. Since Dodger Stadium opened in Los Angeles in 1962, more than three dozen new ballparks have opened for major league use, have been extensively renovated, or are currently under construction. Of the billions of dollars spent on these parks, only the renovation of Pro Player Stadium in Miami and the construction of Pacific Bell Park in San Francisco were not government-financed. (Even the Giants new palace, however, was subsidized by government aid in land acquisition and infrastructure development.) Oftentimes, that public involvement has taken place as one part of a larger urban-development effort, with the new park situated on once-blighted or undeveloped land near the city core and forming the centerpiece of a massive redevelopment project. This was the case earlier in cities like St. Louis as well as more recently in Baltimore, Cleveland, and Denver.

Concurrent with that last trend, a new and significant factor has emerged. In the past, ballparks were forced by the exigency of private construction to conform to their surrounding, thus imbuing each park inevitably with an individual flavor. Public involvement, however, eliminated that limitation. Since the opening of Dodger Stadium, Shea Stadium, and the Astrodome in the 1960s, surroundings were altered to conform to the design of the park, rather than the opposite. Freed from the constrictions of neighborhood geography, architects gave their parks a symmetry bordering on sameness in an effort to maximize utility. The result was the virtually indistinguishable trio of much-scorned 1970s "superstadiums": Riverfront in Cincinnati, Three Rivers in Pittsburgh, and Veterans in Philadelphia—and each seemed best suited for the football teams in those towns, despite the success of the local baseball clubs in the years after these stadiums opened.

In truth, neither stadium designers nor club owners fell headlong into the new age of the anonymous modern multipurpose facility. In fact, the modern era of generic ballparks started with a two-decade transitional period during which these factors were gradually assimilated into the classic motif.

Cleveland's Municipal Stadium provided the introduction to this transitional period. Constructed in 1932 by the city, it was vast (potentially holding more than 80,000, it was built in a failed bid to secure the summer Olympics), virtually symmetrical, yet situated close in the central city on the lakefront. Evidence that the symbiotic relationship between a private ballclub and a public stadium had not yet taken hold is that, for 15 years after Municipal Stadium was built, the Indians occupied it only in fits and starts. Unless a large crowd was expected, Cleveland generally played its weekend games at Municipal, maintaining staid old League Park (smaller and cheaper to operate) as their weekday habitat. Not until 1947 did the Indians become full-time tenants of what became derisively known as the "Mistake by the Lake."

For the first time in 1953, then again in 1954 and 1955, public facilities were developed with the specific aim of attracting major league teams. It worked in all three cases: luring the Braves from Boston to Milwaukee, the Browns from St. Louis to Baltimore, and the Athletics from Philadelphia to Kansas City. The moves were unprecedented in the previous half-century, yet sensible in that all three teams left cities which had proved incapable or unwilling of supporting two clubs (the perennial losing records of these three teams certainly didn't help). The stadiums in Milwaukee and Baltimore were constructed from scratch; in Kansas City, Municipal Stadium, which had served for many years as a minor league facility, was extensively renovated. None of these three parks abandoned the city for the open country, but none was reliant on mass transit, either.

The era of the modern public superstadium ironically probably dated from the opening of the last private stadium, Dodger Stadium in Los Angeles in 1962. Yet the species' zenith was achieved in 1965, when the Harris County Domed Stadium, dubbed the Astrodome, opened in Houston. The $35.5 million project broke so many traditional rules of stadium design that it literally changed the way the game was played—and not just in Houston.

The first and most obvious change, of course, was the roof that covered the facility. Baseball had come indoors; no more would rain, wind, or other weather be a factor in a game's outcome. Beyond that, it changed the surface on which the game could be played. When the dome's translucent roof panels were painted to give the fielders a chance to follow flyballs, the lack of sunlight killed the grass, and artificial turf had to be installed. "AstroTurf," as it came to be called, was faster and more durable than grass but also was harder on the players' legs, so it required substantial changes in strategy.

Swifter, agile fielders replaced their slow-footed but hard-hitting predecessors. Speed, whether for basestealing or cutting off base hits in the outfield gaps, supplanted brawn in the new game played on artificial turf, whether inside or outside. Within a span of little more than a decade, artificial turf became the most copied aspect of any single new ballpark built in America since the owners of the Union Grounds in Brooklyn fenced their lot. Not only did it not wear out, not only was it easier to maintain, not only did it minimize rainouts, but it also withstood far better the strain of multipurpose use for events such as football games and musical concerts. Municipalities installed the plastic stuff in most stadiums built for use by more than one team, and its widespread adoption in the NL greatly changed the character of play in the Senior Circuit.

The city of St. Louis originally built new Busch Stadium in 1966 with a grass surface, then replaced it with turf after a few years. So faddish had artificial turf become that, in 1970 when Kansas City officials developed plans for separate and individually designed football and baseball stadiums, they still installed artificial turf on the baseball field.

Thanks to the willingness of local government to subsidize new, baseball-only ballparks in the 1990s, however, baseball has seen a reversal of this trend toward artificial surfaces. Every new ballpark opened since 1989—save

Tropicana Field in Tampa Bay, which quickly abandoned its traditional rug and installed a new artificial turf with simulated grass—has featured grass. Moreover, three existing parks joined the flight from AstroTurf and its derivatives since 1995, as Kauffman Stadium in Kansas City, Busch Stadium in St. Louis, and Cinergy Field in Cincinnati have reinstalled grass fields.

The design of indoor stadiums, which started the era of artificial turf, has been dramatically altered by the debut of the high-tech ballpark with a movable roof. Of the six enclosed venues, SkyDome in Toronto, BankOne Ballpark in Phoenix, and Safeco Field in Seattle all feature retractable covers, with only SkyDome, the oldest of the retractable stadiums, retaining artificial turf. Miller Park in Milwaukee, which will open in 2001, also will boast a movable roof and a grass field.

The superstadium boom of the 1960s and 1970s produced a series of parks that shared most, if not all, of the following characteristics: they altered the landscape to conform to the "ideal" of a park, rather than vice versa; they were built on large open areas that included acres of parking; they were symmetrical and predictable in design; they were proximate to interstate highways; they were built from the ground up to be multipurpose venues; they eliminated structural pillars, but in doing so sacrificed proximity of upper deck seats to the playing field; and they used artificial surfaces.

The multipurpose stadium, which a few decades ago appeared to be a fixture of the modern game, is now universally viewed as a dinosaur awaiting its doom. While only two facilities that opened after Dodger Stadium in the 1960s, 1970s, or 1980s were exclusively reserved for baseball (Arlington Stadium and Royals/Kauffman Stadium), every new ballpark opened since 1990 has been baseball-only. Three others (Shea, Busch, and Anaheim/Edison International) have reverted to baseball-only status after their football tenants fled for greener pastures.

The stunning success of Baltimore's Oriole Park at Camden Yards revolutionized baseball park design as well as greatly influencing stadium and arena design in other sports. Making its debut on Opening Day 1992, the retro brick-and-steel ballpark in the shadow of an old railroad warehouse in downtown Baltimore wowed fans, players, writers, broadcasters, and politicians alike. Though Camden Yards opened only one year after the new Comiskey Park in Chicago, the difference in design between these two parks was half a century apart—even though the same architectural firm designed both. Comiskey Park was a traditional modern stadium, a drab concrete structure with blue seats, clean sight lines, and no character. Camden Yards was nothing like that.

The exterior of Baltimore's new jewel featured an arched brick façade that evoked memories of long-gone Ebbets Field. Like the famous Brooklyn park, it was built within the context of its urban environment, not built on top of an expansive concrete plain surrounded by an asphalt sea of parking lots. The color scheme of the new park, where structural steel girders were left exposed and painted green like the seats, was chosen in deliberate contrast to dominant blues, reds, and concrete grays of existing modern stadiums. Though not really constrained by dense urban geography like the ballparks of the classic era, Camden Yards also boasted asymmetrical dimensions in the outfield and quirky features in the outfield wall, another homage to the past. The striking differences between Camden Yards and all the other ballparks it made instantly obsolete didn't stop with the park's appearance, however.

Equally important in earning the park universal acclaim was its attention to the needs of the fans. Like historic Wrigley Field, Fenway Park, and Tiger Stadium, the seats in Camden Yards were closer to the field than those in multipurpose stadiums. The ballpark featured a spectacular view of the downtown Baltimore skyline through an open center field, giving the interior an airy character totally unlike the claustrophobic feeling engendered by the enclosed superstadiums, whose 360-degree, multi-tiered construction completely surrounded the field. Broad concourses, expanded concessions, plentiful restrooms, and a dozen other thoughtful touches pampered the patrons as well as thrilled management, which saw a huge increase in discretionary spending by its satisfied customers.

Perhaps the most significant moneymaking component of Baltimore's new park was the space devoted to the large number of luxury suites. Leased by corporations and wealthy individuals by the season at unheard-of prices for baseball, these suites provided a lucrative new stream of revenue for the Orioles' ownership—a revenue source that all other team owners soon wanted to tap. The popularity of the new park also guaranteed sellouts for most games, allowing the Orioles to raise ticket prices early and often and reap unforeseen windfall profits.

Proving that cloning is the sincerest form of flattery, other owners rushed to persuade their local politicians that they, too, needed such a moneymaking machine if they were going to survive and compete in baseball's brave new world. Derivative new ballparks quickly arose in downtown Cleveland and in suburban Arlington, Texas. When these also proved instantly successful, the escalation of the arms race was unstoppable, and the economic balance of the game was forever altered.

What can be said today, and what could always be said, is that in baseball, more so than in any other sport, the term "home field advantage" should be taken literally. Baseball clubs spend far more time trying to tailor their teams to the home field than in any other team sport. This is true, paradoxically, despite the fact that the home-field advantage in major league baseball, where only 53 to 54 percent of games are won by the home team, is far smaller than in football, basketball, or hockey, where the home team wins approximately 60 percent of the time.

Origins of Spring Training

The precise origin of spring training, that marvelously contrived ritual that today amounts to a six-week paid vacation in the sun for athletes, media, and club officials, is unknown. With few exceptions, early-day ballplayers trained privately at home. It is known that in 1870 the Chicago White Stockings organized a trip to New Orleans, but that may have been mere barnstorming rather than preparation for the coming season. The generally accepted beginning of spring training is 1886, when the

White Stockings and Philadelphia Phillies traveled to Little Rock and Charleston, respectively.

The standard regimen of spring training has varied greatly from decade to decade. Today, for instance, little actual training is done in the spring, since players are expected to report in shape. Instead, the emphasis is on narrowing a roster of 40 players (plus many other spring training invitees) to the requisite 25 by Opening Day. Modern spring training amounts to an extended advertisement for the season to come, with a bit of tryout camp thrown in for effect.

That was not always the case. Players in the 19th and early 20th century commonly received salaries of a few hundred or a few thousand dollars, supplementing their salaries with off-season jobs, many of questionable value to their athletic careers. These players literally required a period of a month or so to work back into shape before the start of the season. In the early 1900s the New York Giants trained in the little Texas town of Marlin, and their training was, by the strictest definition, training.

Each day began and ended with what amounted to a two-mile forced march along the railroad tracks from the hotel to the park. The routine consisted of batting and fielding practice, along with drills on the fundamentals of play. If there was a scrimmage, it usually was an intrasquad effort, or perhaps a game against a local team or minor league club. In 1906 the 16 major league teams trained in 10 different states as far north as Illinois. The notion of grouping in Florida and Arizona to make exhibition games between them more convenient would not gain full currency for the better part of another decade. In 1911 the Yankees set up their spring camp in Bermuda.

At most early camps, players oversaw their own conditioning since, as a rule, teams employed only a manager and a single coach—if that. Teams now have coaches they employ just for spring training and will occasionally even attach a coach to a player who is making a position change. Complexes are usually used to house minor league teams when spring training is over; the municipalities, which see spring training as a major source of tourism dollars, often pay for construction of these complexes. A list of past and present spring training sites can be found in the Appendixes.

Pitching

How prized is the pitcher? Consider that of the nine positions, candidates for eight are winnowed principally by their skill with the bat. Middle infielders can progress through the professional ranks on the strength of superior range, outfielders may prosper by dint of speed, or catchers thanks to a God-given arm. Fundamentally, however, not even an Ozzie Smith or an Ivan Rodriguez can become a regular professional player until they establish at least a minimal offensive ability. The only exception is the pitcher.

Pitchers always have been the exception, even before the designated hitter rule legislated many of them out of that *terra incognita* known as the batter's box. In any analysis of Ty Cobb's value as a player, the first thing that comes up is his lifetime .366 batting average, yet no one would think of discussing Sandy Koufax's value to the Dodgers in terms of his .097 batting average.

In fact, the pitcher is the one and only player whose defensive contribution is so vital that the ability to hit is considered irrelevant—as is his fielding skill. Red Ruffing, the fine righthander for the New York Yankees of the 1930s and 1940s, compiled one of the best batting records of any pitcher in the past three quarters of a century, including a .268 career average. But when he was voted into the Hall of Fame in 1967, it was on the strength of a 273–225 record, 3.80 earned run average, and on his status as the leading moundsman for seven pennant winners.

Pitching has been the staple of most successful big league franchises since batters lost the right to call for the type of pitch they liked. Connie Mack is variously quoted as having called it anywhere from 70 to 90 percent of the game. The precise figure is not important: What is important is that Mr. Mack's axiom remains generally accepted today, though logical analysis of baseball shows that pitching and fielding together comprise 50 percent of the game.

Yet, despite the constancy of the importance placed on quality pitching, both pitching styles and the rules governing pitching have undergone more major changes than any other aspect of on-field play. This change has been so great that the best pitchers of today have virtually nothing in common with the best pitchers of a century ago. Furthermore, pitchers today bear strikingly little resemblance to their predecessors of as little as three decades earlier.

Much of this evolution took place during the game's formative years, and came via efforts by the rule makers to settle on the proper balance of batting to pitching. In the early years of professional ball in the 1860s and 1870s, pitching bore more similarity to the style employed today in fast-pitch softball than in baseball. The ball was delivered underhand and without a wrist snap from a box set at a distance of 45 feet from the plate, although pitchers fudged so much that, by 1872, wrist movement was legalized. Legalization of the wrist snap quickly spawned the development of various "trick" pitches, notably the curveball, commonly credited to William "Candy" Cummings, a much-traveled moundsman of that era who compiled a 124–72 record in the only six seasons he played as a top-level professional. Whether Cummings or any of several other pitchers of his era first perfected the art of making a ball curve, Candy generally got the credit (being elected to the Hall of Fame in 1939 for that accomplishment).

Nineteenth-century pitchers worked under virtually ever-changing conditions. For instance, the pitcher's "box" was moved back to 50 feet from home plate after 1880, then eliminated in 1893 in favor of a "rubber" placed at 60 feet, 6 inches. The underhand delivery requirement gradually was modified to allow what in effect was a sidearm pitch in 1883, and a full overhand delivery the following year. Rules governing the ball-and-strike count—at one time nine balls were required to give the batter a walk— changed frequently until they were stabilized at four and three, respectively, in 1889. At various times, pitchers were required to deliver a high or low pitch, as requested by the batter; windups were banned, then permitted again; the size of the "box" was altered almost routinely before being consigned to extinction.

It would be difficult to generalize as to whether all of those changes helped or hurt pitchers. Certainly, batting averages tended to improve as the distance between the mound and plate increased. Yet the underhand pitching style, physically much easier on the arm, enabled most teams to play an entire schedule with only one or two pitchers. And the best of them attained results that would be unthinkable today.

By way of illustration, compare the statistics of Providence's Old Hoss Radbourn compiled in 1884 with the record of the last pitcher to win 30 or more games, Detroit's Denny McLain, in 1968, and of the pitcher with the best statistics in 2000, Boston's Pedro Martinez.

Radbourn's numbers seem even more impressive when it is noted that his Providence team played only a 112-game schedule. Of course, the comparisons are fair only as illustration of how greatly the pitching environment—the rules, conditions, and strategies—changed between 1884, 1968, and the present.

At least as dynamic a force as the rulebook in the evolution of the modern pitcher has been the development of pitching strategy, notably new pitches. For while the broad regulations under which pitchers work today are not vastly different from 1893, the arsenal of pitches that have come into vogue— and occasionally passed from it—has ranged widely and sometimes wildly.

Cummings's introduction of the curveball marked the first major deviation toward finesse from what had fundamentally been a power pitcher's game to up that time. Other innovators included Phonney Martin, who threw a drop or slowball, and Al Spalding and Tim Keefe, masters of the change-of-pace. However, such bolder experimentation was limited to a handful of hurlers.

While pitchers of the latter part of the 19th century occasionally dabbled in "outshoots" or "rises," the best built their reputations with speed. "Cyclone" Young in Cleveland and Amos Rusie, New York's "Hoosier Thunderbolt," were the best—and in all likelihood—the fastest of them. Young won 27 games for Cleveland in 1891, his first full season, and then accumulated 511 victories over a remarkable 22-year career. The magnificence of Cy Young's record is best illustrated by the fact that the all-time runner-up, Washington's Walter Johnson, trails by almost a hundred wins. Young's 2,799 strikeouts—a record when he retired—further testify to his velocity. As for Rusie, he won 36 games in 1894 and led the league in strikeouts five times between 1890 and 1895. He also led five times in walks, initiating the popular linkage between hard throwers and control trouble.

By the mid-1890s, earned run averages rose as a reaction to the shift of the mound back to 60 feet, 6 inches. The legendary Baltimore Orioles of Wee Willie Keeler had batted .343 as a team in 1894, yet did not even lead the league—Philadelphia did, at .349! In response, pitchers began to experiment more readily with changes of speed as well as with the ball itself. Chicago's Clark Griffith scraped the ball against his spikes and discovered that the scuffs added to the break of his curve, making him a 20-game winner for six consecutive seasons. Philadelphia's Al Orth, a "one-pitch wonder," mastered the art of changing speeds and won 203 games in 15 years.

Equally as significant as changes in the approach to pitching was the increase in the numbers of pitchers needed. In 1876 Chicago's Albert Spalding had been able to pitch in all but five of his team's 66 games. By the early 1880s, the top teams were using two pitchers. Within another decade—as the increased pitching distance, longer playing schedules, and more tiresome overhand motion became accepted—staffs of fewer than four to five were uncommon. The Detroit team of the 1884 National League utilized perhaps the first pitching "staff" *per se,* with four hurlers (Frank Meinke, Stump Weidman, Charley Getzien, and Dupee Shaw) each working between 147 and 289 innings. Detroit's strategy did not count for much as the club finished last but, within a decade, Baltimore rode what amounted to a four-to-six-pitcher rotation to the league championship. That staff's ace, Sadie McMahon, pitched only about one-quarter of the total number of innings worked by the sextet. In 1876, the eight National League teams basically employed a total of 13 pitchers; by 1886, that number was 24; by 1896, for 12 teams, it was 51.

By the turn of the century, the popularization of two theretofore lightly used pitches helped reestablish the pitcher as the game's dominant player. Christy Mathewson, a fresh-faced college graduate from Bucknell, brought to the New York Giants a pitch he called the "fadeaway," actually a reworked version of something known in the 1880s as an "outshoot." Today, Matty's legendary fadeaway would be called a screwball, though the popularity of that pitch has declined in recent years.

The pitch acts like a reverse curve: when thrown by a righthanded pitcher, it breaks toward a righthanded batter. Mathewson might very well have become a great pitcher even without the fadeaway, but with it he won 373 games, four times winning 30 or more, and five times helping the Giants to pennants. So difficult was the pitch to throw and control that no other major league pitcher of the era could master it.

The other dominant pitch of the first part of the 20th century was the spitball, advocated principally by two men, Jack Chesbro and Ed Walsh.

Chesbro came to the major leagues with Pittsburgh in 1899 and, by 1901, had incorporated the spitball into his routine. He became a 20-game winner throwing the wet one; it would not be illegal to doctor a baseball with a foreign substance for two more decades. Chesbro won 28 games with the pennant-winning Pirates in 1902, so greatly increasing his value that he became one of a cadre of "free agents" who were recruited to the fledgling American League during the three-year interleague war. With the New York Highlanders of the young league in 1904, Chesbro's spitball took him to a 20th-century record 41 victories, although it also set up one of the most ironic finishes to any pennant race. Because of its wild break, the spitball was one of the least predictable of pitches, yet Chesbro had walked only 88 batters that season, fewer than two every nine innings. His control of the devious delivery was impeccable.

On the final weekend of that season, Boston and New York—virtually tied for first—engaged in a five-game series, with the winner of that series becoming the champion. Chesbro's 41st victory came in the series opener, but Boston claimed the ensuing two. In the climactic fourth game, the opening contest of a last-day doubleheader, Chesbro held a 2–2 tie entering the ninth.

An infield hit, a sacrifice and a groundout moved Boston's pennant winning run to third base. The great pitcher had been masterful to that point, walking just one and striking out five. However, in that most pivotal of situations, a Chesbro spitball bounced in the dirt and skipped toward the backstop, a wild pitch that cost New York a pennant.

Walsh, like Chesbro, perfected control of the elusive spitter and parlayed that to remarkable feats. A moundsman of modest ability prior to employing the pitch in 1906, he won 17 games that season, 24 the next, and an astonishing 40 the year after that. Irony played a central role in Walsh's career as well, for perhaps his best performance in that 40-win season of 1908 came in defeat. At the climax of a three-team race involving Cleveland, Detroit, and Chicago, Walsh's White Sox came to Cleveland needing a victory to remain in contention. Walsh pitched a four-hitter and struck out 15 batters, but Cleveland's Addie Joss achieved a rare perfect game and won 1–0. The only run scored on a passed ball.

Other so-called "freak" pitches came into vogue during that era as well. Pitchers altered balls not only with spit or spikes, but also with emery paper, paraffin, mud, slippery elm, and who knows what else. But the ranks of pitchers who relied on tampering for their success still constituted a minority. Most, like Washington's Walter Johnson continued to rely on the basic fastball. Of course, most pitchers did not have a fastball the caliber of Walter Johnson's to rely on.

And on that basis, pitchers and batters lived in happy coexistence for about a decade, pausing only to occasionally admire the ascendancy of a new star like Philadelphia's Grover Cleveland Alexander. Master both of the fastball and curve, Alexander emerged in 1911 as a rookie 28-game winner and, by 1915, he was leading the Phillies to the National League pennant on the strength of a 31-victory season. With Philadelphia and later with the Chicago Cubs, he led the league in victories six times between 1911 and 1920, becoming generally acknowledged as the pre-eminent pitcher of the latter half of what is commonly called baseball's Dead Ball Era.

Alexander, along with Walter Johnson, continued to pitch in form beyond 1920, but that was not true of major league pitchers as a whole. A series of factors, some mechanical, some societal, reshaped the game again following World War I and, in most instances, it was pitchers who suffered in the reshaping.

The catalyst for much of that reshaping, ironically, was a former pitcher—and a very good one. As a 20-year-old rookie in 1915, Babe Ruth won 18 games to help the Boston Red Sox to the world championship. By the following season, Ruth, a 23-game winner who added another victory in the World Series, was coming to be recognized as Boston's ace. He led the American League in earned run average (1.75), starts (41), and shutouts (9), and paced it in complete games (35) the following season as well.

By 1918, however, Ruth the pitcher was recognized as less of a hero than Ruth the slugger. He pitched in 20 games that season, winning 13 of them, but started nearly three times as often in the outfield, a response both to his hitting and to the box-office value of the fans' clamoring to see him hit. Although by no means an everyday player, the Babe tied for the league lead in home runs that season with a modest 11. More significantly, he drew crowds, both at Fenway Park and on the road. So in 1919, Boston manager Ed Barrow converted him almost exclusively to the outfield. Ruth's response was to break the all-time record for home runs—with 29—and to lead the league in runs, runs batted in, and slugging as well. Traded to New York in 1920, Ruth almost immediately became the most celebrated player in the game's history. He slugged a then-unthinkable 54 home runs, breaking existing records for runs, RBIs, bases on balls, and slugging percentage. To the public, Ruth was "the Sultan of Swat," "the Bazoo of Bang," "the Infant Swatigy," and "the Colossus of Clout." Batting averages and home run production rose league-wide as other players strove to imitate him. American League batters, who hit .248 with 136 home runs in 1917, raised those figures to .292 and 477 by 1921. In the National League, the increases for the same period were from .249 and 202 to .289 and 460. Part of that 150 to 200 percent increase in the home run count could be attributed to the banning—enforced gradually as of 1920—of the spitball and other so-called "doctored" pitches, part to improved craftsmanship on the part of the baseball makers, and part to the directive by league officials to replace soiled, scuffed balls with cleaner, whiter ones. But in large measure, the change was simply a strategic one: batters swung harder and tried to drive the ball farther than ever before. Once a poke-and-run contest, baseball had become—thanks in good measure to Ruth—a slugger's game. There is no question that the fans loved it: American League attendance soared from 1.7 million in 1918 (albeit in a season shortened by the owners because of World War I) to more than 5 million in 1920.

Unfortunately for pitchers, they proved less than capable of adapting to the new and more thrilling style. The rule change barring use of the spitball, emery ball, shine ball, and other similar pitches removed a potential weapon from all arsenals, save those of 17 men who were exempted from the ban. These 17 were permitted to continue throwing the pitch, which did not actually die out until the last of them, Burleigh Grimes, retired in 1934. Effective new pitches were not developed to fill the void, though a few toyed with a knuckleball. In the late 1920s George Blaeholder, a nondescript pitcher the St. Louis Browns, devised a pitch that eventually came to be known as the slider, but for years was derided by many as just a "nickel curve." For the most part, though, pitchers relied on the fastball, curve, and a very occasional changeup. With pitchers as with batters, raw power replaced guile and cunning as their chief weapon.

The result was predictable: for the better part of two decades, batting averages, home runs, and earned run averages soared. National League ERA skyrocketed from 3.13 in 1920 to 4.97 in 1930; in the American League, ERA increased from 3.79 in 1920 to 4.65 in 1930. National League home runs more than tripled, but strikeouts increased by only 6 percent. The differences in the American League were less dramatic, but still quite large. Pitchers reasserted their competitiveness somewhat in the 1930s, though by then bat-happy baseball society had been conditioned to view a 4.00 ERA as good.

The period between 1920 and 1960 produced some exceptional pitchers, but few changes in pitching style. In the mid-1930s, a rookie righthander in Detroit named Eldon Auker bothered batters with an underhanded delivery reminiscent of the style of the 1870s. Auker's so-called submarine pitch was necessitated by an arm injury that made it difficult for him to throw overhand. He won 130 games in a 10-year career, pitching on two pennant winners and one world champion. His style would be resurrected in the modern era by relievers like Ted Abernathy, Kent Tekulve, Dan Quisenberry, and Gene Garber. In the National League, the New York Giants' Carl Hubbell also reached back in time for a cudgel. Hubbell resurrected Mathewson's fadeaway, renaming it the screwball, and mystified opponents sufficiently to record five straight 20-win seasons between 1933 and 1937, leading the Giants to three pennants.

A more conventional, and more overpowering, form belonged to Lefty Grove, who pitched for 17 years for the Philadelphia Athletics and the Boston Red Sox. Grove's trademarks were a fastball that many have called the swiftest ever and a surly disposition. Four times a league leader in victories and nine times the ERA king, Grove was the only pitcher to win 300 games in the hot-hitting 1920s and 1930s, an achievement often cited by those who point to him as the best pitcher ever. His career ERA of 3.06 is more than one full run lower than the league average for the years (1925–1941) that he pitched.

Pitching rules, which had remained virtually untouched since 1920, underwent several adjustments between 1950 and 1969. The strike zone was tightened in 1950: the new upper limit being the armpit instead of the top of the shoulder (with the lower limit at bottom of the knees staying the same). After a decade of unprecedented home run hitting in the 1950s, both home runs and scoring increased in 1961–62, so the old strike zone was brought back in an attempt to help the beleaguered moundsmen. The result was in the intended direction, but of a magnitude unforeseen and undesired by everyone except pitchers: scoring plunged dramatically from 1963 through 1968. American League pitchers posted a post-1920 low ERA of 2.98 in 1968 as Denny McLain won 31 games and only one AL batter (Carl Yastrzemski, at .301) could top .300. In the National League, two hard-throwing righthanders who gave enemy hitters no quarter entranced fans: Bob Gibson posted an unbelievable 1.12 ERA while Don Drysdale set a then all-time record with 58 consecutive scoreless innings. Fully 21 percent of 1968 games resulted in shutouts. Rule makers quickly responded to that offensive nadir by lowering the mound several inches and restoring the strike zone to its 1950–1962 dimensions. Scoring and home runs climbed, aided further in the American League in 1973 when the designated hitter was introduced.

It would be overly simple and wrong to merely to point to the rule book as the fulcrum for all variations in pitching performance in the past five decades. Certainly, another very significant factor in the second half of the 20th century was the development of relief pitching. Beyond that, pitchers perfected pitches they had only toyed with before. The knuckleball was not new—it had been thrown since the early part of the century and, in the 1940s, the Washington Senators employed a foursome of flutterballing starters. No pitcher employed the erratic butterfly pitch as effectively, however, as the trio of Hoyt Wilhelm and Phil Niekro—both of whom rode the knuckler to the Hall of Fame—and Phil's younger brother, Joe Niekro. Wilhelm pitched in a then-unprecedented 1,070 games over 21 years and established what at the time was the all-time record for saves, 227. Phil Niekro won 318 games and, in tandem with Joe (who won 221), in 1987 set the record for most victories by members of one family.

A sort of variation on the knuckleball, also developed years before but resurrected recently, was the forkball or "split-fingered fastball." Credit for its development generally is given to 1940s New York Yankees pitcher Ernie Bonham, but the first famous exponent was Elroy Face, a relief pitcher for the Pittsburgh Pirates of the 1950s and 1960s. In 1959 Face compiled a sensational 18–1 record with 10 saves by the simple expedient of jamming the ball between his index and middle fingers before releasing it. This unusual grip caused the ball to have very little spin and gave it an unexpected dip as it crossed home plate; it also made it a devastating change-of-pace pitch. Face, who saved 20 games in 1958 and 24 in the Pirates' world championship year of 1960, is generally credited with ushering in the era of the modern relief ace or closer.

In the late 1970s another star reliever, Bruce Sutter of the Chicago Cubs, reinvented the same pitch with the help of his minor league pitching coach Fred Martin, though Sutter called it his "split-fingered fastball." Sutter saved 37 games for the fifth-place Cubs in 1979, and earned the Cy Young Award. In Sutter's wake, entire pitching staffs began learning what was quickly dubbed the "splitter." Roger Craig became a one-man traveling demonstration of the newly popular pitch's success. As Detroit pitching coach, he taught it to the Tigers staff in the early 1980s, and they responded by winning the world championship in 1984. Then Craig taught it to journeyman Houston righthander Mike Scott, and he blossomed into an 18-game winner capable of recording over 300 strikeouts while leading the Astros to a divisional flag in 1986. Craig returned to managing in San Francisco, where his staff of split-finger throwers helped the Giants win the NL West title in 1987.

The most widely used new pitch, however, was the one invented by Blaeholder 50 years before— the slider. Acting much like a fastball but with a sharp, late break, the slider supplemented and frequently supplanted the slower and bigger-breaking curveball in the repertoire of most big-league hurlers. Perhaps the pitch's most famous practitioner was Steve Carlton, who used it to become the second winningest lefthander of all time, behind only Warren Spahn. So disarming was Carlton's nasty slider that he became the first pitcher to win four Cy Young Awards; he also staged a dramatic contest in the mid-1980s with fastballer Nolan Ryan to see who would become the first pitcher in history to record 4,000 strikeouts.

If the evolution of pitching suggests anything, however, it is that no one style, no single delivery, no trick pitch, and no simple rules change can remain perpetually dominant. In the 1960s no two pitchers could have been more stylistically different than Juan Marichal, the high-kicking ace of the San Francisco Giants, and Sandy Koufax, the stylish lefthander of the Los Angeles Dodgers. Marichal employed seemingly every move, every trick, every pitch ever devised by professional pitchers.

He threw the fastball, the curveball, the slider, the changeup, and the screwball; he delivered them overhanded, three-quartered, or sidearmed whenever he chose, to the great consternation of most opposing hitters. Koufax relied on a fastball, a stunning curve, and (during his peak years after 1960) exemplary control. Yet in 1963, for instance, each won 25 games, each appeared among the league leaders in winning percentage, earned run average, strikeouts, complete games, and innings pitched. Between 1963 and 1966, Marichal averaged better than 23 victories; Koufax, 24.

One of the most frequently debated questions in baseball is whether modern pitchers throw harder than their predecessors. It is, of course, very difficult to answer that question. To the degree that today's pitchers are bigger and stronger than ever, to the degree that improved training and conditioning programs encourage greater speed, it is logical to assume that the fastest modern hurlers must be swifter than Cy Young or Walter Johnson or Lefty Grove. Consensus picks as to the hardest-throwing starting pitchers of the past two decades would probably be Nolan Ryan and Randy Johnson. Ryan's fastball was clocked in his prime on radar guns at about 100 miles per hour; Johnson has been routinely clocked at 100 or even higher in the late 1990s. (It is true that several relief pitchers—Rob Dibble, Roberto Hernandez, Mark Wohlers, Robb Nen, Troy Percival, and Billy Wagner—to name some of the more prominent—have been clocked as regularly throwing in the high 90s or around 100 miles per hour in recent years. However, it is like comparing apples and mangoes to talk about peak velocity for a pitcher that routinely pitches only one inning as contrasted with a starting pitcher.)

One of the biggest problems in discussing pitch velocity is changing standards. Prior to the advent of sports radar guns in the 1970s, various measures were used in an attempt to accurately time pitches. Some of the early radar guns used in the 1970s and 1980s sampled the speed of the pitch only a few times between the pitcher's release and when the ball crossed the plate. Because the pitch slows down more the farther it travels from the pitcher's hand—it can be traveling be as much as 10 m.p.h. slower at the plate than when released by the pitcher—the point at which the radar gun actually "clocked" the pitch could easily make a difference of multiple miles per hour. Therefore, earlier radar guns were best used to average the velocity of many pitches, not to give a definitive reading on one pitch. Newer, digital-technology radar guns can sample the speed of a pitch hundreds of times in the split-second it takes to travel from the mound to home plate, making individual pitch readings much more accurate. There is a four mile-per-hour difference between some of the old radar guns (which showed average big-league fastballs at 85–86 m.p.h.) and the current guns (which show average velocity at 89–90 m.p.h.). The effect of this difference is that a pitcher clocked at 100 miles per hour in the late 1990s would probably have been measured as throwing in the mid-to-high 90s with some of the old guns. The best that can be said is that changing measurement standards and changing technology over the decades, plus the lack of controlled tests and systematic records, make all of these discussions about peak velocity exercises in approximation, not precision.

Old-timers, of course, did not have the advantage, or disadvantage, of pitching to radar guns, so assessments of their speed are necessarily cruder. "Rapid Robert" Feller's fastball, for instance, once was clocked against a speeding motorcycle. The finding? About 100 miles per hour. The eyewitness testimony of old-timers varies. Many picked Walter Johnson, but Johnson himself picked Smoky Joe Wood. Billy Herman selected Van Lingle Mungo. Contemporaries like Wes Ferrell said Lefty Grove was faster than Feller, but numerous sportswriters sided with Feller as the fastest ever. Connie Mack, who played and managed across six decades, opted for Amos Rusie, the old-time "Hoosier Thunderbolt." Mack's opinion, however, could easily have been influenced by nostalgia: he batted against Rusie. Nolan Ryan was generally considered the fastest pitcher in the 1980s but, for a time, it was not universally presumed that he was the fastest on the Houston Astros! Until his crippling stroke, J.R. Richard was conceded that title by at least some that saw both.

Strategy Before 1920

There is no single "correct" way to win a pennant. If a club can hit the cover off the ball, it might have a chance. If it can field with the best, that might be enough. And if its pitchers are dominant, that, too, might do it. Then again, maybe not. If the history of major league baseball demonstrates anything, it is that the search for a single winning formula is as elusive as the search for a rainbow's end.

Since the National League of Professional Baseball Clubs first organized for play in 1876, through the 2000 season, there have been 238 recognized major league seasons played by the two currently operating leagues plus the handful of short-lived other major leagues. It stands to reason that if, over the years, ballclubs had found one strategy to be more successful than any other, that would be indicated by consistent adoption of that strategy by winning clubs.

Why do strategies change? Why don't the modern-day Mets approach the challenge of winning in the same fashion as the White Stockings of bygone days? Many of the reasons are obvious. Plainly, changing conditions and rules dictate some of the strategic adjustments. The White Stockings and their counterparts of the 1880s would, for instance, have considered it folly to pay more than one or two pitchers and an equal number of substitutes. Rules regulated the appearances of non-regulars and, in a time of 80-game schedules and underhanded deliveries, more bodies simply were not required. Night baseball and modern-day transcontinental travel demands place greater strains on players.

Changes in park sizes, styles and equipment contribute to strategic alterations as well. When, in the first quarter of the 20th century, improved manufacturing techniques made for a better grade of ball, managers eschewed the sacrifice in favor of swinging for the fences. The increasing popularity of artificial turf half a century later placed a renewed premium on defensive range and speed. Sociological adjustments played a part as well. The 1920 outlawing of the spitball and other pitches that defaced the ball—occasioned, at least in good measure, by sociological factors—plainly contributed to generally higher batting averages throughout the 1920s and 1930s.

The *de facto* banning of the beanball and its first cousin, the knockdown pitch, in recent years resulted in some degree from public complaints about the pitch's potential danger. But another, less obvious contributor to the constant ebb and flow of baseball strategy is simple managerial practice. If a particular team employs a new—or, more often, resurrected—strategy to success, the prospect is great that competitors will emulate it. Often, these strategic adjustments are of transitory duration but, in terms of their impact on individual pennant races, they can still be important.

It is overly simplistic to equate particular strategies with specific time periods: to suggest, for instance, that because earned run averages were lower during the first decade of the 1900s, the emphasis at that time was on pitching. Or to argue that teams stressed offense in the 1920s and 1930s because batting averages swelled, or to suggest that raw power has become the dominant force of the present-day game.

In fact, between 1900 and 1919—the commonly recognized Dead Ball Era—the league batting champion won 20 pennants, the slugging champion 19, and the earned run average champion only 16. Conversely, between 1920 and 1949—the period of unbridled hitting—32 pennants were won by clubs that led their league in ERA, only 24 by slugging leaders, and only 22 by batting average leaders.

Those numbers do not render the era labels meaningless, but they do suggest that successful managers of every generation may be following their own strategies, rather than the obvious ones. The art of strategy is as old as the game itself. When Candy Cummings discovered that he could make a baseball curve, he was developing a new strategy. So was the forgotten manager who, faced with the dilemma of none out in the ninth and the winning run at third, first brainstormed bringing both his infield and outfield in to a shallow depth, the better to cut off the run at home. When, in the 1880s, Chicago's legendarily innovative "King Kelly" apocryphally dashed from his seat on the bench, yelled "Kelly now substituting," then snagged a foul fly to save the game, he was enhancing strategy—at least until that particular practice was outlawed and substitutions permitted only during time-outs.

Perhaps the first recognized employer of what we might today consider as strategy on a prolonged basis was Ross Barnes, the second baseman of the champion Chicago White Stockings of the National League's inaugural season in 1876. The league at the time had a rule that stipulated that any ball landing in fair territory was considered a fair ball, irrespective of whether it subsequently rolled foul before passing a base. By that standard, many bunts and choppers of today would be fair balls. Barnes developed the skill of striking such "fair–foul" hits, and he did it so well that he led the league in batting that first season with a .429 average.

Alas for Barnes, as would be the case for some subsequent strategists of later ages, rulemakers reacted to his achievement by outlawing the strategy that he had perfected. When in 1877 the requirement was established that a groundball pass first or third base in fair territory to be legitimately fair, his average plummeted by over 150 points, to .272.

As would be expected, the development of strategy during the game's first decades occurred in very broad and general terms. There was, for instance, little thought given to the strategic advantages of relief pitchers, platooning, pinch hitting, pinch running, or defensive substitution, for the simple reason that, until the late 1880s, substitutions—save for injury—were not even permitted. Naturally, the growing awareness of the value of maintaining a group of reserve players first focused on the pitcher's box.

As early as 1876, managers employed diverse approaches to pitching strategy. Four of the eight teams, including the Chicago champions, stayed fundamentally with a single hurler. In the case of Chicago manager Al Spalding, that pitcher was Spalding himself, who pitched in 61 of the team's 66 games. But three other clubs divided the mound work roughly equally between two men of reasonably balanced skills. In the case of third-place Hartford, for instance, Tommy Bond pitched 408 innings with a 1.68 ERA, while old-timer Candy Cummings curved his way through 216 innings with a 1.67 ERA.

Fourth-place Boston went so far as to divide the work among three pitchers, each pitching between 170 and 220 innings. Boston manager Harry Wright might have seemed very much the trendsetter had he stuck with that notion. However, the very next year, Wright jettisoned all three of his 1876 arms and signed Bond away from Hartford to pitch 58 of the club's 61 games. Boston won the 1877 flag; Cincinnati employed a three-man staff and finished last.

If we define a pitching staff as consisting of at least four pitchers, each sharing a roughly equivalent part of the responsibility, then credit for devising the first one probably belongs to Jack Chapman, who directed the fortunes of several early-day National League teams. Chapman found himself in Detroit in 1884, surrounded by little offense and even less in the way of reliable pitching. The team's earned run average in 1883 had been 3.56, second worst in the league and considerably higher than the overall 3.13 average. This was still very much an era when a single hurler could carry a team's fortunes: In Providence, Old Hoss Radbourn would win 60 games and pitch 679 innings, the equivalent of 75 complete games.

Other mound stars included Pud Galvin (46–22) in Buffalo, Larry Corcoran (35–23) in Chicago, and Mickey Welch (39–21) in New York. Chapman had no one who could hope to match such standouts day after day, so he did not try. Instead, he rotated five men, none pitching more than 30 percent of the team's innings. The result wasn't much, as Detroit still finished last. Chapman took his approach to Buffalo in 1885, where the four-man pitching rotation lasted longer than Chapman himself, as he was dismissed after a 12–19 start.

From the mid-1880s, experiments with multi-pitcher staffs became more common, but no team won a pennant utilizing such an approach until Chapman's successor in Detroit, Bill Watkins, resurrected the notion in 1887. That club, too, featured five pitchers, none of whom did very much more than a third of the work. Like Chapman, Watkins plainly was trying to mask a weakness. His everyday lineup featured some of the game's greats: outfielder Sam Thompson won the batting (.372) and RBI (166) titles, and the team led the league in runs, doubles, triples, batting average, slugging, and fielding percentage.

But as usual, all of the great pitchers toiled for other teams: Tim Keefe and Welch in New York, John Clarkson in Chicago, Galvin in Pittsburgh. Watkins built a five-man staff based on his only two proven arms, Lady Baldwin (42–13 in 1886) and Charles Getzien (30–11), two lightly used reserves (Pete Conway and Larry Twitchell), and Stump Weidman, signed when Kansas City's team folded after the 1886 season. Suddenly the names of Detroit pitchers began showing up in the strangest of places, like among the league leaders in key pitching categories. Getzien led in percentage and was third in wins, Conway ranked second in ERA and allowed fewer hits per nine innings pitched than anyone.

The next season, a very funny thing happened: several teams ditched their reliance on a single pitcher in favor of a staff. There remained a few holdouts: Boston's John Clarkson pitched 483 innings in 1888, 620 in 1889, and 460 as late as 1891. Within a decade of the Detroit staff's accomplishment, though, Boston's Kid Nichols could lead the league in innings pitched with a comparatively modest 368. The era of a team asking one man to pitch as many as 400 innings was not quite dead yet—it would surface here and there through the first decade of the 20th century—but it was dying. The change to a multiple-pitcher staff may have been hastened by Detroit's inability to snare one of the league's stronger arms, but changing conditions and rules would have made it inevitable anyway.

Occasionally, a new strategy works so well that it must be legislated against. Ross Barnes's was one such. But the all-time champions, both in devising new strategies and in getting them banned, were the Baltimore Orioles teams that flourished under manager Ned Hanlon in the 1890s.

Hanlon's Orioles achieved that mastery by a singular combination of remarkable skill and superior innovative capacity. Among the strategies team members are credited with devising or popularizing:

The hit-and-run play. Stories as to the origin of the stratagem, whereby a runner breaks for the next base while the batter attempts to drive the ball through a hole vacated by the fielder covering the steal effort, are both numerous and hoary, and no definitive judgment can be rendered. Cap Anson, longtime manager of the Chicago White Stockings, is among those purported to have claimed this strategy as his own. But the best available evidence tends to support the claim of the Orioles' chief contemporary rivals, the Boston Beaneaters, and their manager, Frank Selee. John McGraw, the famous manager who played for the Orioles, insisted on the validity of Baltimore's claim. But even if Hanlon's Orioles cannot be established as the originators, they certainly brought the play to its first and lasting popularity. Typically, John McGraw, leading off, would reach base, and then Willie Keeler, a superlative hitter (lifetime .345 batting average) whose principal asset was his exquisite bat control, would direct the ball to the appropriate weak spot, often resulting in runners at first and third with none out.

The Baltimore chop. There is no question as to the origin of this play, which has waned in strategic significance with the ascension of the home run. Orioles' hitters mastered it and used that mastery to advantage. The chop was deceptively simple: a hitter would employ an exaggerated downward swing to drive the pitch almost directly into the ground in front of the plate. On the hard Baltimore dirt, the result would be an infield bouncer recoiling so high off the ground that there would be no defense—infielders could merely wait in vain for the ball to descend while the batter scampered to first unchallenged.

The bunt single. The sacrifice, of course, had been around for many years prior to the emergence of the Orioles. But Baltimore players like McGraw, Hughie Jennings, and Joe Kelley were among the first to use the bunt as a means for reaching base. Dickey Pearce and Tom Barlow of the old Brooklyn Atlantics pioneered in this regard, and Ross Barnes followed. McGraw especially was brash in his use of the bunt.

The Orioles weren't the only innovators of the 1890s. In Boston, the Beaneaters honed their skill at the double steal, wherein the runner at first broke for second and, when the catcher attempted to retire him, the runner on third tried to score. This rather daring technique required not only nerve and teamwork but superior speed. The Beaneaters had plenty of the latter commodity with the likes of Billy Hamilton, whose more than 900 career stolen bases represented the all-time record before Lou Brock shattered it. The Brooklyn club of the same era is generally credited with originating the cutoff play, when an infielder intercepts an outfielder's throw to the plate in an effort to retire the batter or another runner attempting to advance an extra base.

The Orioles devised other, less gentlemanly, strategies as well. Their first baseman, "Dirty Jack" Doyle got his nickname by tripping, jostling, or holding opposing runners by the belt; Jennings at shortstop or McGraw at third were equally as likely to obstruct a runner. Baltimore outfielders were known for hiding extra balls in the tall grass to be put in play in emergencies. It was said that catcher Wilbert Robinson always kept his pockets full of pebbles, which he dropped in the shoes of batters as he squatted behind them. On offense, the Orioles were by no means above cutting bases when an umpire's back was turned.

Baltimore could do all of those things because most games of the era were officiated by a single arbiter, who could not hope to watch everything taking place on the broad expanse. Ultimately, public disgust at the Orioles' open flaunting of rules caused league officials to authorize umpiring teams. Over time, the practice grew to using four umpires. The trend started with the rule-breaking Orioles.

Possibly the most convincing evidence of the prominent role played by Hanlon's Orioles in the development of baseball strategy is the fact that the two superior minds of the subsequent generation of baseball officials were former Orioles: McGraw and Jennings. It was they who, while piloting pennant winners in the first years of the 20th century, popularized strategic innovations that would eventually assume permanent, prominent roles in the planning of every major league franchise.

Jennings took over leadership of the American League's Detroit Tigers in 1907 following his retirement as an active player, and he became an immediate success. The Tigers, a 71–78 team the previous year under Bill Armour, leaped immediately to a 92–58 record and the pennant. They followed that up with pennants in 1908 and 1909 as well. Jennings' success was partially a product of being in the right place at the right time, as his managerial star ascended in almost precise concert with the development of Ty Cobb. Cobb came up as an 18-year-old rookie in 1905, winning batting titles in 12 of the 13 seasons from 1907 through 1919. Jennings deserves some credit as well, however, for analyzing his team's strengths and weaknesses and for inventing methods of overcoming the latter.

The prime example of that trait involved his handling of the Tigers' catchers. Even in their first two pennant-winning years, catching was a comparative liability for them. The regular, lefthanded batting Boss Schmidt, hit just .244 and .265, and he seemed especially bedazzled by lefthanded pitchers. Jennings had dealt summarily enough with other weak links by releasing them, but he did not want to dispatch Schmidt because of his still sharp defensive skills and above-average throwing arm. Instead, Jennings replaced Schmidt in the lineup against lefthanders, first with righthanded Ira Thomas and then with Oscar Stanage. By splitting time at the position between two players, Jennings was following the practice of his fired predecessor.

What Jennings was using was a platoon system, and it gradually caught on. New York Highlanders manager George Stallings applied the platoon with outfielders Willie Keeler and Birdie Cree in 1909, then took the idea with him to Boston when he assumed control of the Braves in 1914. There, his judicious mixing of a half dozen outfielders helped bring him a pennant. Although Jennings deserves the credit for popularizing platooning by demonstrating over a period of several seasons that it could work with a pennant contender, a solid case might also be made for manager Frank Bancroft as the father of platooning, way back in the 1880s.

McGraw pioneered strategy of a very different, but equally lasting, type. In 1908, 20-year-old rookie pitcher Otis "Doc" Crandall, who showed exceptional potential, came to the Giants. Crandall won 12 games, but he lacked stamina and overpowering speed, was hit hard in the later innings of games, and did his best work in relief of other pitchers. To minimize the weakness and take advantage of his strengths, McGraw in 1909 designated Crandall as the club's "relief" pitcher, chosen to enter in midgame if necessary and rescue a faltering teammate. In an era when starting pitchers were rarely removed—about two-thirds of all starts that were completed that year—the concept of a pitcher actually specializing in midgame appearances seemed demeaning. Yet that is exactly what Crandall did, making two-thirds of his appearances over the next three years in relief, winning 20 and saving 11.

As intriguing as it was, Crandall's success did not spur an immediate flood of imitators. Managers, who found quality starting pitching difficult enough to locate, could not bring themselves to isolate one or more of their better arms for emergency duty. One of the few mimics was Patsy Donovan of the Boston Red Sox who, in 1910, converted righthander Charley Hall from an ineffective occasional starter into a reliever of fairly consistent quality. Between 1910 and 1913, Hall made 136 pitching appearances for Boston, just 51 as a starter; in relief he won 20 of 24 decisions, saving 11 others. Fittingly, the 1912 World Series pitted Hall's Red Sox against Crandall's Giants. Hall saw more action, pitching 10⅔ innings in two games with a 3.38 ERA. Crandall saw action in just one game as the Giants eventually lost four games to three.

While McGraw and Jennings innovated, game strategy during the Dead Ball Era stressed strong pitching, aggressive baserunning, and playing for a single run. The game also featured an emphasis on standout players whose talents dwarfed their teammates. The most obvious example was Cobb, who batted .350 in 1907, .385 in 1910, .420 in 1911, and .410 in 1912. In 1910, for example, Cobb's batting average was nearly 100 points higher than any of his teammates, and his slugging average was 125 points superior. The Georgia Peach was not the only early 20th century player who could have been considered a one-man team. In Cleveland in 1911 outfielder Joe Jackson batted .408 and slugged .590 with 233 hits, 45 doubles, 19 triples, and 126 runs. The second highest totals on the team in each category were .304, .396, 142, 25, nine, and 89. In 1909 Pittsburgh's Honus Wagner led his team to the pennant with a .339 average. The second highest average among the club's regulars belonged to player-manager Fred Clarke, at .287.

With the home run not yet developed as a viable option, and with league earned run averages ranging between 2.30 and 2.70, managers often resorted to the sacrifice or the stolen base, mindful of the importance of every run. While it is not possible today to reconstruct sacrifice totals due to incomplete records, stolen base records rose higher and quicker than at any other period of the game until the 1970s. The evolution of individual and team stolen base records clearly indicates this. In 1898 the modern standard for counting steals was developed; prior to that, any extra-base advance—whether via a pitched or hit ball—had been counted as a steal. In 1900 Brooklyn led the majors with 274 steals, while Patsy Donovan of St. Louis and George Van Haltren of New York set the individual standard with 45. Then Frank Isbell of the new American League's Chicago team broke the modern individual record in 1901 with 52 as the White Sox stole 280. In 1903 Frank Chance of the Cubs and Jimmy Sheckard of the Dodgers upped the individual mark to 67 and, in 1904, the Giants raised the team record to 283. The Giants broke their own record in 1905, stealing 291, and Cobb shattered the modern individual record in 1909 with 76 steals.

Neither record lasted one season. In 1910 Eddie Collins of the Athletics stole 81 and the Reds purloined 310. Those new standards were erased within one year, Cobb stealing 83 and the Giants 347 in 1911. Clyde Milan of Washington broke Cobb's record with 88 in 1912; then Cobb broke Milan's mark in 1915, stealing 96. The individual record was thus broken seven times and the team record five times, all in a span of 15 seasons. Cobb's record did not fall for 47 years, until Maury Wills stole 104 bases for Los Angeles in 1962. The Giants' team record of 347 steals is unsurpassed to this day.

It might seem natural for a record in a newly established category to be broken several times in quick succession, then finally reach a comparatively unattainable plateau. It might, but consider that even the original team mark of 274 set by the 1900 Dodgers would have stood into the 1970s. The first 20 years of the century were not a case of a record gradually being raised beyond reach, they were a case of teams simply stressing the running game. The very worst basestealing team in the century's first decade, the 1906 Boston Braves (who stole 93), would have won either the American or National League stolen base championship 38 times between 1925 and 1960.

Night Ball

Baseball was invented before electric lights, so it originally was a game played largely in the afternoons. Thus, extra-inning affairs or late-starting games sometimes were called on account of darkness when the opposing nines had failed to complete their contest before twilight faded. That presented a distinct problem, as the decision about when to call a game on account of darkness affected the outcome. Hall of Famer Gabby Hartnett's fabled "Home run in the gloamin'" in 1938, which helped lead the Cubs to the pennant, is probably the most famous example. Hartnett was player–manager of Chicago, which was locked in a tight race with Pittsburgh in late September. In the second game of a three-game series, the Cubs tied the game at 5–5 in the bottom of the eighth as the light faded. The umpires decided to let play continue for one more inning before calling the game; the Bucs failed to score in the top of the ninth. Hartnett, 37 at the time, led off the home half of the inning, hitting a homer on an 0–2 curveball off Pirates reliever Mace Brown to put the Cubs into first place for good.

Of course, most working people couldn't afford to take an afternoon off to attend a weekday ballgame, leading to a high proportion of businessmen—yes, they were mostly men—among the relatively sparse crowds (by today's standards) of the early 20th century. Games played on weekends and holidays consequently drew much larger attendance.

By the early 1930s, however, major league games played under artificial lighting was nearing fruition. That the concept was feasible there could be no doubt: a baseball game had been played at night way back in 1880, only two years after the introduction of electric light, and the Des Moines, Iowa, club of the Western League installed lights in 1930. The idea, which caught on in a Depression era of dwindling attendance, was to stave off financial collapse by increasing weekday attendance.

Cincinnati executive Larry MacPhail finally advanced the notion of staging big-league games around the normal working fan's hours. MacPhail had good reason to lobby for the change; his Cincinnati franchise had drawn an anemic 206,000 fans in 1934, not even enough to offset expenses. MacPhail and club owner Powel Crosley petitioned the National League for the right to play seven 1935 games at night; the league reluctantly agreed, taking note of the extenuating circumstance of the depressed attendance in the Queen City.

The first of those games, played May 24, pitted Cincinnati against Philadelphia, and skeptics were moved to silence when it attracted an audience of better than 20,000 to what proved to be a 2–1 Reds victory. By 1941 night ball was an accepted fact in the majority of major league parks and, by shortly after the war's end, only Wrigley Field in Chicago still lacked lighting. Today, most major league games as well as virtually all minor league games are played under the lights. Even the traditional Cubs finally capitulated to the reality of night baseball in 1988 when lights were installed at Wrigley Field, despite vigorous opposition from traditionalists as well as neighborhood residents. (Without lights, the Cubs faced the prospect of removal of any postseason home games to another ballpark.)

Attendance figures partially reflect the reason: prior to the advent of night baseball, it was considered exceptional if a ballclub drew a half million fans for the season, and the entire National League schedule of 1933 attracted only about 3.1 million fans. In the 1960s, attendance of 1 million was considered a good year at the gate for most clubs. Today, the Cleveland Indians continue a six-year tradition of selling every seat at Jacobs Field *before* the season starts, while several clubs can anticipate drawing 3 million fans each season. Major League Baseball recorded a historic first in 1986 when all 26 ballclubs drew at least 1 million fans. The following season was the first in which MLB clubs averaged 2 million in home attendance. Seasonal attendance of less than seven figures is now considered a disgrace.

Scheduling a handful of weekday baseball games in the sunshine is still good business, as the popular "businesspersons' specials" attest, though most weekday afternoon games are mandated by the travel considerations of the modern schedule. Nevertheless, it is clear that night baseball is the normal paradigm of the national game today. Day games are a pleasant diversion, but the difference between when the game was played before 1935 and afterward is literally a difference of night and day.

Strategy After 1920

The reasons behind the switch that occurred about 1920 from a one-run strategy based on high batting average, the sacrifice, and stolen base to one focusing on power hitting are numerous and complex. Changes in rules, park design, equipment, and fan interest all played a part. The impact of those factors on the changed game is underscored in the dramatically altered statistics of the game in the 1920s and later. The numbers of runs being scored provides the clearest contrast.

Prior to the season of 1920, the major league record for runs scored in a season by an individual was 147, set by Ty Cobb in 1911. The highest total since the establishment of the 16-team, 154-game schedule, set in 1912, was 11,164 runs. But in 1920, New York's Babe Ruth easily broke Cobb's individual record by scoring 158. He broke it again in 1921 with 177, establishing the standard that still exists. In all, Cobb's former record was broken 13 times in the American League alone between 1920 and 1940. Meanwhile, total runs rose to 11,935 in 1921, then broke through the 12,000 barrier the following year to 12,059. It was broken again in 1925 (12,592), again in 1929 (12,747), and again in 1930 (13,695). And that record stood for more than three decades, until it was surpassed in 1962, by which time each major league had added two teams and eight more games to the playing schedule.

Power records similarly surged. Tris Speaker's Dead Ball Era record for doubles—53, set in 1912—fell to Speaker himself in 1923 (59), and was surpassed in eight more seasons during the 1920s and 1930s; in 1936 alone five players matched or bettered that pre-1920 record. The pre-1920 record for home runs—Ruth's 29 in 1919—bears no comparison, of course, with subsequent achievements. It had been raised three times by Ruth himself in 1927, and was bettered in every single American League season until the war year of 1944, when New York's Nick Etten led the league with only 22. League slugging percentage, which ranged between .310 and .340 during the Dead Ball Era, jumped by an average of more than 20 points in both leagues in 1920 alone, and by 30 more points the following year. The increase in the American League alone was nearly 14 percent between 1919 and 1921. Slugging soared to .421 by 1930 in the American League, and to .448 in the National.

With the increase in power came a concurrent acceptance of the intentional or semi-intentional base on balls as occasionally strategically prudent. Managers, operating on the theory that discretion might be the better part of valor, instructed or allowed pitchers to "work around" certain hitters like Ruth who were capable of doing far more damage with a home run than a walk. Previously, when pitchers looked on a walk as pariah, the Chicago Cubs' Jimmy Sheckard held the record by drawing 147 of them in 1911. That lasted only as long as it took Ruth to be walked 148 times in 1920. The Babe raised that standard to 170 in 1923. The league record of 4,282 walks issued in the National League in 1911 lasted until 1925, when American League pitchers walked 4,315 batters. The record was hiked biennially to 4,402, 4,611, 4,855 and 4,924 in the same league between 1932 and 1938.

Finally, in the 1920s and 1930s, the usage of relief pitchers first gained true prominence. In 1919 the St. Louis Cardinals' Oscar Tuero became the first relief pitcher to lead the league in appearances; he pitched in 45 games, 28 out of the bullpen. The achievement drew little notice, primarily because his team finished seventh. But in 1923 the pennant-winning Giants' Claude Jonnard and Rosy Ryan tied for the league lead in appearances, each with 45. Ryan started 15 games that season, Jonnard just one. The following season Firpo Marberry of the AL champion Washington Senators led the league with 50 appearances, only 15 of them starts. Marberry repeated as most-called upon in 1925 with 55 appearances, all in relief, in another pennant-winning year. Marberry's role was by no means yet established; he would lead the league three more times in appearances, twice as a reliever, once as a starter. Nevertheless, the idea of a specialist in quality relief pitching for first-rank teams had at last begun to gain acceptance.

When the 1927 New York Yankees blitzed the American League to win 110 games, their most frequently called upon pitcher was rookie Wilcy Moore, who won 19 games despite starting only 12. Moore pitched 38 times out of the bullpen. In 1901 National League pitchers had completed 976 games, representing nearly 90 percent of the schedule. By 1919 that figure had fallen to about 60 percent. In 1922, for the first time in history, National League pitchers completed fewer than half of all their starts. By 1930 the mark had fallen to 43 percent, and it held at roughly that level through the 1930s and 1940s.

As the perceived importance of the complete game waned, a temporary strategic miasma settled in. Managers, less unwilling to turn to the bullpen, still had not developed effective strategies for its use. That began to change in the early 1940s when Leo Durocher developed the notion of a bullpen "ace." The Brooklyn manager used his late-inning stopper both to give his team a chance to retake the lead as well as to try to hold the lead of a tiring starter through the final innings. For the first time, a manager appeared not to expect his starter to finish—or, at least, not to mind it if he didn't. Dodger starters completed only 66 games in 1941—one of the lowest totals ever by a pennant winner-and only 67 more the following season, while Durocher used hard-throwing Hugh Casey to win 14 games and save 20 those two years.

Others emulated Durocher's strategic development. Boston's Joe Cronin won the 1946 American League pennant, thanks in good measure to the relief pitching of Bob Klinger, who appeared 27 times in relief and saved a league-high nine games. The New York Yankees' Joe Page won 21 games and saved 33 in virtually exclusive bullpen action in 1947–1948. Slowly, the old concept of relievers merely as failed starters was eroding. As late as 1946 more than half the major league mound staffs were led in appearances by a starter, and it was still possible for Cleveland's Bob Feller to lead the league in that category. The trend was plain, however: in 1947, relievers led in appearances on 10 of the 16 staffs. By 1952, the figure was 13 of 16. In 1950 a relief pitcher, Jim Konstanty of the Phillies, won the Most Valuable Player Award by pitching in a then-record 74 games, saving 22 of them and leading his team to the National League pennant.

Joe Black won 15 games and saved 15 more for the pennant winning 1952 Dodgers. In 1954 Cleveland manager Al Lopez deployed a relief tandem of lefthander Don Mossi and righty Ray Narleski, who appeared in 82 games between them, saving 20. The major league save record, which had stood at 22 since being set by Marberry in 1926, was elevated to 27 by Page in 1949. Boston's Ellis Kinder matched that in 1953, and New York's Luis Arroyo topped it in 1961. Prior to 1949, only Marberry in all of baseball history had saved 20 games in a year. Between 1949 and 1961, 10 pitchers did it. All of this should be understood in the context that the concept of a "save" was unknown in the first half of the century, and the save was not adopted as an official statistic until 1969.

Player platooning, a dormant strategy after the early 1920s, was revived in the late 1940s, principally by Casey Stengel. A platoon player himself under John McGraw with the 1920s Giants, Stengel alternated lefthanded hitting third basemen Bobby Brown and righty Billy Johnson in his first two years as Yankees manager. In 1951 Gil McDougald supplanted Johnson as the righthanded half of the platoon as the Yankees won the world championship all three years. By 1955 Stengel had expanded his platoon system, alternating righthanded Bill Skowron with lefty Joe Collins at first base, and subbing righthanded Elston Howard for Irv Noren occasionally in the outfield. Howard and utility man Tony Kubek both were platooned at several positions in 1957 and 1958. Again, successful managers took their cues from Stengel. Fred Haney's use of the first base platoon of Joe Adcock and Frank Torre helped the Braves to the 1958 pennant.

The only manager to beat out Stengel for the AL pennant between 1949 and 1960, Al Lopez (who also managed Cleveland in 1954), used a platoon system to do so with the White Sox in 1959. Lopez alternated righty Bubba Phillips and lefty Billy Goodman at third base, and righty Jim McAnany and lefty Jim Rivera in right field. In 1960 Pittsburgh manager Danny Murtaugh often alternated at three positions: Hal Smith or Smoky Burgess at catcher, Dick Stuart or Rocky Nelson at first, and Gino Cimoli or Bill Virdon in center. But for Fred Hutchinson's use of platoons at three positions in 1961 (Jerry Zimmerman and John Edwards at catcher, Elio Chacon and Don Blasingame at second, Wally Post and Jerry Lynch in left), Cincinnati very possibly might not have held off the Dodgers to win by four games. By the mid-1960s, most teams were platooning at least one position.

The other significant change in strategy to evolve during the 1950s and early 1960s was a growing acceptance of the strikeout as an acceptable price to pay for home run power. In retrospect, that acceptance can clearly be seen as a delayed reaction, for home run totals had begun to mount sharply in 1953. For the past two decades, major league batters had averaged between 1,300 and 1,700 home runs; in 1953, they hit 2,076, a record 1,197 of them coming in the National League alone. That represented a 22 percent increase over the previous season. From 1953 through 1960, the record was raised only about 10 percent and, in fact, the raw numbers of home runs flattened and occasionally declined between 1956, the peak season for home runs in the decade, and 1960.

Strikeouts rose sharply during this period. In 1953 major league batters struck out 10,220 times; by 1960 that had risen steadily to more than 12,800, a climb of more than 25 percent. The strikeout explosion continued unabated through the 1960s, whether home runs rose (as they did in 1961 and 1962) or fell. In fact, between 1961 and 1966, home run totals remained virtually level in the major leagues, despite the addition of two expansion teams. But strikeouts rose by more than 25 percent over the same period. The increase (part of which was attributable to strategic concessions and part to the enlarged strike zone), showed itself in the individual strikeout totals as well. Until 1956 the record for most strikeouts in a season was Vince DiMaggio's 134, set in 1938. Washington's Jim Lemon broke it that season with 138. In 1961 Detroit's Jake Wood broke it again, fanning 141 times. Harmon Killebrew of Minnesota raised the mark to 142 the following season; then Dave Nicholson of the Chicago White Sox increased it to 175 in 1963.

San Francisco's Bobby Bonds whiffed 187 times in 1969, then followed with 189 strikeouts in 1970, setting the all-time record that still endures despite the homer-happy and K-happy decade of the 1990s. The rate of strikeouts dipped in the 1970s due to the smaller strike zone of 1969 and the designated hitter, then jumped in the 1980s. Batters willingness to swing for the fences, of course, has only increased in the past decade, and strikeouts per game are now higher than ever. Long gone is the ingrained prejudice against striking out, as contemporary hitters have increasingly focused on taking more pitches—and, therefore, walking more often—as well as hitting for power.

The game in the 1970s and 1980s featured several other changes: the regeneration of the running game, the implementation of the designated hitter, and the further specification of the role of the relief pitcher.

Stealing bases, as well as aggressive baserunning in general, were reinvigorated in the 1960s as runs became scarcer. It was in the 1970s and 1980s, however, that baserunning reached its post-1920 height of importance. Changing playing conditions, notably the wide use of artificial surfaces, certainly played a large part, as did the talent infusion from Latin America. Many of the new players who entered the major league ranks could run well and play defense well, but not hit with power. Managerial acumen certainly had something to do with it: Whitey Herzog and others found it easier to succeed in large ballparks by emphasizing speed over power. This two-way versatility and greater athleticism gave the Royals, Cardinals, and other similar teams both an important baserunning threat and a critical defensive boost, especially in the large outfields of the modern superstadiums. The resurrection of speed also essentially banished the lumbering, one-dimensional slugger to the American League and the good hitters' parks remaining in the NL.

If the reasons behind the stolen base's surge are complex, affixing the date of its arrival as a mainstream stratagem is less so. It clearly came from Venezuela by way of Chicago in the person of Luis Aparicio in 1956. Prior to Aparicio, there had not been a genuine basestealing threat—a player capable of swiping 50 or more bases in a season—in more than a decade. Moreover, the efforts of the comparative handful of fellows who had great speed in the decade prior to that (e.g., George Case in Washington and Snuffy Stirnweiss in New York) got lost in the glare of the home run. Stolen bases plummeted from more than one per team per game in the first two decades of the century to half that in the 1920s, then continued to decline to a low point of less than one every three games for the typical team in the 1950s!

Aparicio's debut sounded the call to speed. As a rookie he led the American League in steals in 1956. His total of 21 was certainly nothing special, even for the sluggish 1950s, but the notion of a baserunner as a weapon had not yet caught on. The following season Aparicio won the stolen base title again, this time with 28 before stealing an eye-opening and crowd-pleasing 56 in 1959 (Willie Mays, the National League champion, stole 27). Aparicio would go on to win the stolen base crown in nine successive seasons, topping 40 steals in four of the next five years.

By 1959 Aparicio was no longer the whole story. Stolen base totals had turned upward virtually league-wide. National Leaguers stole 439 bases that season, their highest total in nearly a decade. In 1960 Los Angeles shortstop Maury Wills joined Aparicio at the 50-steal plateau, then in 1962 Wills was successful 104 times, breaking Cobb's record of 96 that had stood since 1915. The Dodgers as a team stole 198 bases, the most by any major league club since 1918.

Baserunners became a critical part of most pennant winners in the National League. Wills was a key factor in the Dodgers' NL championships in 1963, 1965 and 1966. St. Louis obtained Lou Brock in midseason 1964 and promptly took off from mediocrity to the world championship as he stole 33 bases for the Cards. Brock helped St. Louis to another World Series title in 1967, and the Cards came within one game of repeating as world champions in 1968.

By 1966 stolen bases were up almost 50 percent from the depressed levels of the 1950s, and the rate of thefts in the 1970s more than doubled the slow-footed '50s. As was the case in the Dead Ball Era, every team had its "rabbit." In 1974 Brock broke Wills's single-season record by stealing 118 bases. In 1976 Chuck Tanner's Oakland A's stole 341 bases, falling just six steals short of the all-time record established in 1911. Bill North stole 75 that season, Bert Campaneris 54, and Don Baylor 52, as nine different Oakland players stole 20 or more. Yet the A's finished second behind Kansas City, which stole "only" 218.

In the last two decades, stolen bases records were almost rewritten routinely. In 1992 Rickey Henderson, who set the all-time single-season mark with 130 in Oakland in 1982, broke Brock's modern career mark of 938 in 1991, then became the first player to steal more than 1,000 bases in a career. Henderson stole 100 or more three times in the 1980s, a feat matched by St. Louis' swift Vince Coleman. What's more, the list of the top 10 basestealers of all-time in terms of success percentage includes eight players from the 1980s and 1990s.

The era of the designated hitter certainly has its strategic implications, but all of the game's deep thinkers of the ages couldn't have devised a way to use it had not rulemakers seen fit in 1973 to legalize it on a league-option basis. The premise of the DH is as simple as the realization that most pitchers are miserable batters. The rule allows one player to pinch hit repeatedly for the pitcher without requiring the pitcher's removal from the game.

The two major leagues split over the DH when it was adopted, and they have remained divided ever since. After the American League blazed the trail, the rule was also adopted by virtually every other college and professional league. It became part of the World Series after a compromise between the two major leagues, used from 1976 through 1985 in alternating years. Since 1986 the DH has been employed in games played in the home ballpark of the American League champion. That compromise has also been in effect for interleague games since their inception in 1997.

The designated hitter rule was adopted by the American League as an effort to increase offensive production and also spur fan interest. This radical move as made because AL scoring had fallen to a low of 3.41 in 1968; after a rebound in 1969–70, it then slumped again to only to 3.47 in 1972. National League scoring had fallen in the same way in the 1960s, but was almost half a run higher in 1972.

Concern about lower scoring among American League ownership was greatly heightened by the large gap in attendance between the two leagues at the time: from 1969 through 1972, the Senior Circuit outdrew its younger rival by 36 percent. Some of this had to do with the new ballparks being occupied by NL teams; nevertheless, it is clear that the large attendance deficit spurred AL owners to action. Apparently, the move worked as a way of drumming up more business; the AL had essentially achieved parity with the NL in per-team attendance by the early 1980s and eventually surpassed the NL in 1989.

The change also accomplished its goal of injecting more offense into the AL game. In 1973 the league scoring average jumped up 23 percent, one of the most dramatic one-season shifts in the game's history. Other statistics reflected the change as well: the league batting average rose from .239 to .259 as teams scored 29 percent more runs and hit 32 percent more home runs.

Most American League teams have used the DH position as a refuge for older (and frequently slower) power hitters who are no longer capable of playing daily in the field but who are still effective offensively. In that sense, the very first DH, the New York Yankees' Ron Blomberg, was an accurate precursor: Blomberg batted .293 over eight major league seasons but never carried a big-league reputation at either first base or left field. Blomberg's legacy has proved remarkably consistent in the quarter century-plus of the DH era.

Except for the common practice of using the DH to help players who are hobbled by minor injuries, or the similar stratagem of using an occasional game at DH as a semi-rest for regulars, most designated hitters have been defensive liabilities with power bats. Teams will sometimes use high-average hitters as regular DHs (usually they must have plus speed as well), but most often a lack of real power at DH indicates lack of a better choice, not a deliberate strategy. The best DHs, epitomized by Seattle's Edgar Martinez, would certainly play regularly despite their glove if the DH rule were repealed. However, many great DHs, especially those who can no longer physically play the field due to leg or knee injuries (e.g., Chili Davis and Harold Baines), would have had to retire years earlier if not for the DH rule.

Since the inception of the DH, the American League can be fairly characterized as a power-based offensive league, the National League as a league based on pitching and speed. Starting in 1973 the American League has seen more runs per game, more home runs per game, and higher batting and slugging averages than the National for almost every single season. Only in 1974 has the NL scored more runs; only in 1973 has it hit more home runs; only in 1976 did it outslug the AL by a tiny margin. While the difference between the leagues has waxed and waned somewhat, as one would expect due to random variation as well as shifting talent levels between the leagues, the gap was generally larger in the 1980s and 1990s than in the 1970s. (In the first 10 years of the DH, the AL outscored the NL by an average of 0.21 runs per game. The next 10 seasons saw that margin increase more than 80 percent to 0.38 runs per game.) These facts suggest AL teams took a few years to optimize DH strategy as well as to reorient their rosters to the new reality.

The principal points of debate concerning the effects of

DH on baseball strategy have been twofold. First, whether it inappropriately undermines one of baseball's appealing tenets, that all participants be complete athletes. Second, whether it diminishes in-game strategic moves by managers. Detractors argue that, logically, the DH must negatively impact on strategy by removing one of the questions a manager must repeatedly consider during the course of a game: whether to pinch hit for a reasonably effective pitcher when behind or tied. The fewer decisions the manager must make, the reasoning goes, the more muted become baseball's strategic nuances. As strategy dulls, so does the game according to this viewpoint.

Others argue, also logically, that the DH actually *enhances* strategy. The crux of this counterargument is that managers traditionally were forced into a series of very obvious pinch hit/relief pitcher moves that were almost always dictated by game circumstance. If the circumstances compel such moves, then they are not options at all and both brilliant and ordinary managers would make the same choices. A reasonably competent DH, by contrast, should give managers some discretion in the decision whether to bunt, steal, swing away, or hit and run. Most importantly, a manager must decide whether to remove his pitcher based on his estimate of how well he's likely to continue to pitch, not simply that he is due to bat in an obvious pinch-hitting situation.

The use of the bullpen as a strategic factor has progressed constantly from Luis Arroyo's days in New York until the present. Again, clear evidence is found in the record book. Arroyo's 29 saves were surpassed in 1965 when Ted Abernathy of the Chicago Cubs saved 31. Kansas City's Jack Aker broke the record again the following season with 32. That record lasted only until 1970, when Cincinnati's Wayne Granger saved 35 games. The Reds' Clay Carroll raised the record to 37 in 1972, and Detroit's John Hiller saved 38 in 1973. In 1983 Kansas City's Dan Quisenberry saved 46.

Since then, five pitchers have saved more than 50 games in one season, including Bobby Thigpen, whose 57 saves in 1990 established the current record. Discounting the strike year of 1981, Arroyo's remarkable 29 saves in 1961 would have led the major leagues in no season since 1976.

The primary role of the bullpen has changed from rescuing incompetent starters to a carefully worked-out and often rigid-strategy for victory. Modern relievers have much more clearly defined jobs. Today's ideal bullpen contains at least one lefthander whose primary job is to retire only lefthanded batters, plus a righthander who is especially tough on righty hitters, plus one or two setup pitchers (as well as "long man" to pitch the middle innings when necessary), and a closer. The closer's task has been narrowed greatly so that it now is rarely more than recording the final three outs of the game if his team has a one-to-three run lead.

Specialized setup pitchers evolved from the group of undifferentiated middle relievers in the late 1980s. Their job is to bridge the gap in the seventh and eighth innings of close games between the starter or middle reliever and the closer. Only in emergencies are pitchers used in roles that differ from their specialties. Many setup pitchers who distinguish themselves graduate to the premier role of closer; indeed, most closers now serve a *de facto* apprenticeship of one or more years as setup pitchers in the majors. Other setup pitchers are veterans whose stuff is good enough to be trusted in that secondary role, but not good enough to be trusted by contemporary managers with the job of racking up the save. Many sinker–slider pitchers and breaking-ball pitchers have become good setup relievers, but few pitchers without plus fastballs have been allowed to pitch in the ninth when the game is on the line.

With these changes have come additional recognition for the very best relievers. In 1974 Mike Marshall of the Los Angeles Dodgers became the first relief pitcher to win the Cy Young Award; his credentials included 15 victories, but also a league-leading 21 saves and a incredible record-setting 106 games. Three years later, New York's Sparky Lyle would win the AL award with 13 wins and 26 saves. By 1979 a reliever's victory total had become extraneous: Bruce Sutter was recognized as the National League's top pitcher that season despite winning just six games because he saved 37. Rollie Fingers did the same thing for Milwaukee in 1981, winning just six but saving 28; he was named both Cy Young Award winner and league MVP in the drastically strike-shortened season. Willie Hernandez won the 1984 Cy Young Award as well as the MVP for Detroit on the basis of only nine victories, but 32 saves.

Modern Strategy

The decade of the 1990s saw many wrenching changes in baseball, both on and off the field. Aside from the constant drumbeat of argument over economic issues, the biggest story of the final decade of the 20th century—a century of prosperity, stability, and popularity for baseball that is unparalleled among major team sports—was unquestionably the explosion of offense. In particular, the unprecedented barrage of home runs launched by major league hitters generated a huge amount of controversy, to the point where the owners were actively discussing making significant rules changes to help their shell-shocked pitchers.

On the mound, two major strategic changes helped to define the character of the 1990s. One, an increase in the size of pitching staffs, was a reaction to the dramatic increase in scoring. The other, the near-universal adoption of the Tony La Russa-style bullpen and its rigidly defined roles, was the climax of a long-running trend in relief strategy.

As scoring increased, the search by teams for pitchers who could stem the tide became almost frantic. Scouts were dispatched around the world to scour other countries for pitching talent, and many young pitchers—as well as a few veterans—came to North American from the Dominican Republic, Venezuela, Japan, Korea, Cuba, and elsewhere to play professional baseball. Young pitchers who were hit hard in their first few outings were quickly sent back to the minors. Veteran lefthanded pitchers found they had more professional lives than black cats. Typical pitching staffs ballooned from the previous nine pitchers in the American League and 10 in the National (due to the lack of the designated hitter, NL clubs pinch hit for their hurlers more often) to 11, and sometimes an even dozen!

More pitchers, each pitching fewer innings, trudged to the mound to face increasingly powerful lineups where virtually every hitter could hit a mistake over the fence.

Part of the reason for the procession of new pitchers was the decrease in workload among ace relievers and the specialization in the bullpen. Oakland's Dennis Eckersley attained the same double honor of Cy Young and MVP in 1992 as had Hernandez in 1984 and Fingers in 1981. The big difference between the three, however, was not in how many saves they compiled, but in how much each worked. Eckersley pitched just 80 innings and won just seven games while saving 51. Eight years earlier, Hernandez pitched 140⅓ innings while winning nine and saving 33. In strike-shortened 1981, Fingers had logged 78 innings while posting six wins and 28 saves in his team's 109 games; pro-rated to a full season, his 78 innings would equal 116.

By the time of Eckersley's ascendancy as the game's premier reliever, the narrowly defined role of one-inning closer—a pitcher who appeared only in the ninth inning and only to protect a three-run or smaller lead—had been adopted to a point of stridency. Managers almost never went to their best relievers except in ninth-inning or extra-inning "save situations," even if the game might hang in the balance in an earlier inning. This managerial reluctance to use the best pitcher in the bullpen until the game was already won was in stark contrast to earlier decades. The great ace relievers of the 1970s and 1980s—fearsome pitchers like Goose Gossage, Bruce Sutter, Rollie Fingers, Mike Marshall, and Sparky Lyle—could expect the bullpen phone to ring anytime after the sixth inning if the game was hanging in the balance. Moreover, they were expected to finish the game no matter what inning they entered. Great relievers prior to the 1990s didn't often enter the game when their team was behind, but it wasn't unheard of, either. They certainly weren't automatically held in reserve when the game was tied in the late innings, watching as their lesser bullpen compatriots tried to hold the line till their team took the lead. They frequently faced their first batter of the game with runners in scoring position, instead of almost always sauntering in from the bullpen with the bases empty.

Paradoxically, although the styles managers have employed to wrap up victories have changed over the last five decades—and although the salaries paid to relief pitchers have changed even more—the results have not. Major league teams today blow late-inning leads at almost the same frequency they did decades ago, when there was no such thing as a closer or setup man, when bullpens were commonly refuges for failed starters, and when managers signaled for relief help only at the moment of absolute peril.

That assertion will probably surprise a generation of fans brought up on the theories of Tony La Russa. His widely praised and highly-structured bullpens—a lefty specialist, a righty specialist, and a setup pitcher, all setting the stage for the closer who starts the ninth inning any time his team leads by three runs or less—became the model for virtually every major league team in the 1990s. A major league manager is now frequently second-guessed if he doesn't pull a starting pitcher after seven innings, even if he may be pitching a shutout.

A detailed study of every game played in the major leagues during seasons in which managers employed distinctly different bullpen usage patterns (originally published in the fourth edition of *Total Baseball*) defies widely held perceptions. In terms of victories—and winning or losing is what matters in baseball—the eighth-inning and ninth-inning strategies of the 1990s represent little if any advance whatsoever upon those of the 1970s or the 1950s.

YEAR	1R>7I	2R>7I	3R>7I	1R>8I	2R>8I	3R>8I
1952	.805	.901	.959	.894	.955	.950
1972	.771	.866	.930	.930	.853	.978
1992	.793	.897	.944	.891	.955	.975
1999–2000	.719	.856	.922	.825	.927	.962

KEY: 1R>7I=one-run lead after seventh inning; 2R>7I=two-run lead after seventh inning, etc.

The differences do not offer evidence that one usage pattern provides better results than another, that the modern concept of a specialized bullpen contributes to winning baseball games more frequently than other, older bullpen usage patterns. Contrary to accepted wisdom, a highly structured bullpen—one in which roles are defined and adhered to in a reasonably rigid fashion—appears to provide no advantage. As a general proposition, teams with a highly structured bullpen lose late-inning leads in roughly the same proportion as teams of previous eras. The evidence is substantial that a significant increase in the number of saves recorded in recent years is wholly reflexive and gratuitous, and provides little actual advantage in the standings.

The study was originally conducted by examining games played in 1992, 1972, and 1952, then updated for the past two seasons. These seasons provide contrast both across time and in the generally accepted patterns of bullpen use. In 1992 managers assumed that their starting pitchers would not finish games and had defined clear roles for their relief staff. In 1972 bullpen roles were evolving but not yet rigid; the concept of a closer (as opposed to the earlier "fireman," who was summoned in times of trouble) was in its early stages. Several teams did not even utilize closers. In 1972 a manager hoped that his starting pitcher would finish the game, but was willing to use his bullpen if necessary. In 1952 bullpen strategies had only begun to develop. Most teams still viewed relievers as failed starters or last-resort journeymen. Complete games were reasonably common, and only a few teams—the Yankees and Phillies being examples—had developed first-rate relief specialists. In 1952 a manager hoped his starting pitcher would finish the game and turned to his bullpen only when forced to do so.

Although managers did not derive greater benefit from their bullpen in 1992 than in previous seasons, they clearly relied on it to a far greater extent. Forty years earlier managers who led by one run after eight innings went to their bullpen only 17 percent of the time. By 1972, this figure had risen to 29 percent. In 1992, however, managers who led by one run after eight innings went to their bullpen a whopping 66 percent of the time while winning 4 percent less often. An even clearer example of this trend to reflexive bullpen use is seen in the category of games in which a team led by three runs after eight innings. In 1952 managers in that situation called for a reliever only 21.4 percent of the time; by 1972 that percentage had actually fallen fractionally, to 21.3 percent. In 1992, however, managers of teams that led by three runs after eight innings went to their bullpen 54.7 percent of the time. They could hardly have achieved a significantly greater winning percentage, since teams in that advantageous position won 95.1 percent of the time in 1952, and 95.5 percent of the time in 1972. In fact, in 1992 teams that led by three runs after eight innings also won 95.5 percent of the time.

For practical purposes, this two-generations-in-the-making shift in patterns of bullpen use can be compared to periodic and whimsical changes in dress hemlines: A lot of money is spent, but the gain is in the eye of the beholder.

This focus on improved pitching occurred in the context of a rapidly increasing advantage gained by big league hitters in the 1990s. Scoring had stabilized from the late 1970s through the mid-1980s at about 4.5 runs per team per game in the AL, with the DH-less NL generally about half a run per team less. Home run rates were also relatively static over that time span. Then, in 1987, in a summer of record hot weather throughout the east and Midwest, all hell broke loose from the pitchers' viewpoint.

"The Year of the Hitter," as 1987 quickly became known, caused the same kind of consternation among fans, the media, and those in the game that "The Year of the Pitcher" caused in 1968. While scoring rose less than 10 percent in both leagues, homers in the AL were clubbed at a pace of one per team per game, highest in AL history and only slightly below the NL record pace of 1955. In the NL homers jumped almost 20 percent to the highest rate since 1961.

As in 1968, a change in the strike zone definition was seized upon as the means to reverse the trend. Incongruously, the *de jure* strike zone was actually *reduced* from the "batter's armpits" to the "midpoint between the top of the shoulders and the top of the uniform pants." This was an attempt to *expand* the *de facto* strike zone, which many claimed had umpires calling balls on any pitch above the waist. Even though skeptics said that the besieged men in blue weren't following the new rules, both scoring and homers plummeted in 1988 to the levels of the early 1980s.

Runs and home runs in both leagues remained relatively stable from 1988 through 1992, and the controversy was muted. Then, on April 6, 1992, without an announcement or even any plan, baseball went back to the future.

On that day, Oriole Park at Camden Yards opened its gates in Baltimore for the first time. Instantly, every other ballpark in baseball became dated, and any multipurpose stadium was living on borrowed time as a baseball venue. As the first of what came to be called the "retro ballparks," Camden Yards received universal acclaim. Its old-time feel and old-fashioned attention to detail combined with its modern amenities to thrill fans and players alike. It succeeded beyond anyone's wildest dreams and spawned a legion of imitators in other cities.

One of the essential elements in creating the fan-friendly atmosphere at Camden Yards was keeping the fans close to the field. Not having to worry about configuring the park for football games, the architects placed the seats close to the action. This seemingly innocent detail automatically boosts offense, as the ability of the fielders to catch foul popups is curtailed, resulting in more swings for the hitters. Of course, more swings means more hits and more runs.

In 1993, 16 years after the AL, the NL finally expanded to 14 teams by placing new franchises in Colorado and Florida. The effect that playing baseball at a mile-high altitude has on the game can be seen in the statistics from Mile High Stadium, the temporary home of the Rockies for their first two seasons, and Coors Field, the Rockies' "retro" ballpark that opened in 1995. As in 1961, pumped-up offensive stats were seen in an expansion year. As in 1961, many blamed expansion for diluting the level of pitching talent, conveniently ignoring that expansion also dilutes the level of hitting talent. As in 1961, the engines fueling the offensive boom were the two new ballparks, both of which were exceedingly generous to hitters. In fact, Denver and Miami had the two best hitters' parks in the NL in both 1993 and 1994. (Note that the calculation for ballpark effect accounts for the performance of the home team, so having a bad pitching staff doesn't affect result.)

Playing in a converted football stadium in Denver in 1993–94 boosted runs by about 30–50 percent over league average—a very large effect, equal to or greater to the effect of the best hitters' parks (e.g., Wrigley and Fenway) in the most extreme years in their long history. Playing in Coors Field, a more intimate (even though its dimensions are spacious by normal standards) baseball-only park since 1995 has boosted scoring by 35–70 percent per year. This is a stupendous offensive inflation never seen since the advent of permanent concrete-and-steel ballparks in the early 20th century. The mile-high effect on home runs isn't quite as dramatic, but it's still huge.

After the big increase in offense and homers in 1993, the 1994 season saw another jump. All summer long, fans and the media were abuzz with speculation about whether anyone could reach the 61 home runs of Roger Maris in 1961. By then the record had stood for 33 years; Ruth's mark had stood for 34 years before it was toppled by Maris.

It was certainly not a coincidence that per-game attendance in 1994 was the highest ever seen in baseball, before or since. At the time play was tragically stopped by the players' strike after games of August 11, two players already had hit 40 home runs: Matt Williams of the Giants (43) and Ken Griffey Jr. of the Mariners (40). Williams was on a pace to hit 61 home runs, equal to Maris in 1961, with Griffey and others close behind.

The 1994 season—the first in major league history where more than one home run was hit per game by each team—set the stage for the rest of the decade. As the offense steadily increased, the frequency and the importance of baserunning diminished somewhat in the 1990s as scoring shot up to near-record levels. While the overall rate of stolen bases dropped less than 10 percent from the 1980s, it dropped more than twice as fast from 1996–2000 than from 1991–1995. Furthermore, the rate of stealing in 2000 (0.60 stolen bases per game) was the lowest since 1973, the first year of the DH era. Still, even at the relatively depressed rate in 2000, stolen bases were more frequent than the average for all five decades from the 1920s through the 1960s.

A little perspective on the magnitude of the offensive explosion of the 1990s is in order. As the table below shows, the past decade did not see the highest level of offense in baseball history, nor did it even see the second-highest level. Overall offense in the 1990s was below that of both the 1920s and the 1930s. Even the five runs-plus scored by each team in each game in the last two years—when it seemed like the sky was falling for all the wailing and gnashing of teeth in the sports media—fail to top the list of highest-scoring seasons of all-time.

DECADE	R/G	HR	HR/G	SO/G	BA	OPS	SB/G
1901–1910	3.92	3207	0.13	3.60	.252	.636	1.20
1911–1920	3.97	4256	0.18	3.59	.258	.665	1.11
1921–1930	4.93	10829	0.44	2.84	.287	.752	0.56
1931–1940	4.85	13448	0.55	3.36	.276	.735	0.39
1941–1950	4.32	13460	0.54	3.57	.260	.702	0.35
1951–1960	4.39	20915	0.85	4.53	.258	.721	0.31
1961–1970	4.06	27470	0.82	5.76	.249	.691	0.43
1971–1980	4.15	29201	0.73	5.05	.257	.703	0.65
1981–1990	4.30	33172	0.82	5.45	.258	.714	0.77
1991–2000	4.77	43725	1.00	6.23	.266	.754	0.71

Perspective, however, is not an explanation. Just what has caused the so-called collapse of the historic balance between pitching and hitting (if you ignore the 1920s and 1930s)? Boiling down the many, varied, and complex factors influencing baseball games is incredibly difficult. Multiply that by 162 and it boggles the mind. If it were simple to analyze baseball, predicting who would win each season would be a snap. Prognostications in baseball—whether for a season, a series, or an individual game—are by far the least accurate in all of team sports.

Stripping away all the hype in recent years about the offensive binge, the home run explosion, and the effects of repeated expansions, it's clear that the sky isn't falling in major league baseball. In 1930, generally considered to be smack in the middle of what is frequently called the "Golden Age" of baseball, fully 5.55 runs were scored by each team in the average game—8 percent more than in 2000! The golden years of 1929 and 1936 also saw runners cross the plate more frequently than in 2000. In fact, the slugger-happy 1990s saw only four of the top 10 scoring seasons of the century, and only five of the top 20.

Many trends, both intended and unintended, have combined to push scoring and homers up since the mid-1980s. The biggest reasons are the new ballparks, changes in existing ballparks, stronger hitters, and better bat selection. Putting them all together at the same time has produced the current big-offense climate in the major leagues.

Baseball fans crave intimacy, and intimacy helps hitters. The result: new baseball-only ballparks are usually better hitting venues than the parks they replace. Putting domes on ballparks in colder climates helps hitters as well. In the past two decades, teams have been constantly modifying parks to accommodate fans, and most of those modifications have directly or indirectly helped the hitters. Every time that premium seating is installed behind home plate and between the dugouts, foul pops that used to be caught fall into the stands. Outfield fences have been moved in more often than out, and fence height has been reduced in many parks. Some of the huge new scoreboards erected have helped block winds blowing in at the batter.

Three factors given far more play than they deserve for increased offense are expansion, the supposed shrinking of the strike zone, and the use of performance-enhancing drugs or supplements. Evidence of abuse of steroids in baseball is scant at best; brute strength is not a requirement in baseball as it is in football or several other sports. The effects of baseball players using legal, if controversial, supplements like creatine are completely unknown. It's entirely possible that creatine might make no difference in a ballplayer's performance—think of the placebo effect.

While the strike zone has clearly been compressed at the top, it has also been expanded at the bottom and on the outside. The unhittable sinker or splitter below the knees has replaced the "high, hard one" of bygone days as the pitcher's best pitch. The downward metamorphosis of the strike zone started with the change in umpire's chest protectors, then continued as pitchers were taught to keep the ball down and to view the high fastball just as if it were a hanging breaking ball—that is, a dangerous mistake.

The relentless "keep the ball down" coaching at all levels worked until good righthanded power hitters, who used to feast on high pitches and eschew low pitches, learned to reach down and lift any pitch above the knees. Once they developed that skill, their greatly increased arm and upper-body strength, courtesy of rigorous, year-round training, allowed them to hit those pitches with power. Improved strength and conditioning has also allowed smaller players, whose game often depends on their speed or their defense, to hit more home runs (think about how rarely the term "singles hitter" is used anymore). That's also why there's been such an increase in opposite-field home runs in recent years: power hitters with incredibly strong arms now stride into pitches on the outside part of the plate and literally muscle them 400 feet to the opposite power alley. When pitchers stopped busting hitters inside with high fastballs, hitters started crowding the plate and taking advantage of the increased reach it gave them.

There's nothing mysterious about all of this; left-handed batters have been known as low-ball hitters for decades. It just took an adjustment in hitting styles for righty swingers. That takes years of practice, but professionals can and will make that kind of adjustment when their livelihood depends on it—and those hitters that can't change are quickly replaced.

Another little-appreciated improvement in hitting has come from lighter bats. Bats weighing 30–34 ounces have replaced the 36–40-ounce shillelaghs wielded by the sluggers of yesteryear. Scientists studying the physics of hitting have found that the tradeoff in distance in hitting a ball with these lighter bats is very small, but lighter bats allow hitters to hit more pitches squarely because they can swing faster and have better bat control. A 425-foot homer is no better than a 410-foot homer, but hitting more pitches harder means more long flyballs—and that means more home runs.

Finally, while expansion has most certainly diluted the pitching, it has also diluted the hitting to a commensurate degree. This means that Pedro Martinez and Randy Johnson will be facing more inferior hitters, just the same as Alex Rodriguez and Barry Bonds will be facing more inferior pitchers. Thus, *individual* hitting and pitching records both become easier to break every time the league expands, but that doesn't mean overall offense must go up.

The upward trend in home runs has nothing to do with juicing the ball and everything to do with superb professional athletes reacting to changing circumstances. Hockey scoring has plummeted in the 1980s and 1990s, yet is anyone blaming the puck? If hockey scoring rebounds, as it surely will, will rumors spring up about the "lively puck"?

Baseball players, coaches, and managers are paid large sums of money to adjust successfully when their opponents are beating them. Scoring has risen and fallen throughout baseball history for many reasons, and home run rates have done the same. Major fluctuations can be due to seasonal variances in the weather, an especially talented crop of young players entering the league, and to the adoption of different playing, pitching, hitting and coaching strategies.

Right now, hitters have the upper hand. No doubt about it: power hitters are thriving. The beleaguered pitchers and their coaches haven't yet figured out how to counter the new generation of sluggers. But what's so bad about that? Fans *love* high-scoring games.

It's no exaggeration to say that Babe Ruth and his majestic home runs saved baseball in the 1920s. Mark McGwire and Sammy Sosa enchanted fans and non-fans with their home run heroics in 1998, lifting the game off its sickbed on the strength of their strong arms and powerful bats. Major League Baseball can put a damper on scoring anytime it wants by changing the rules in several ways. Whether it really wants to do so is another question.

One of the oldest baseball adages is that pitching and defense win games. Without bothering to analyze the validity of that old chestnut, it's plainly obvious that home runs and scoring win the hearts of the fans.

CHAPTER 5

The Top 100 Players

David Pietrusza, Matthew Silverman, Michael Gershman, and Mikhail Horowitz

Ranking the top baseball players of all time is a common exercise among fans, writers, and analysts. The recent end of the 20th century resulted in a significant increase in the publication of such lists as well as the election of Major League Baseball's own All-Century Team. As a result, the editors of *Total Baseball* have decided to present this book's own top 100 list, covering baseball from 1876 to the present, with biographies of each player that outline their achievements.

Total Baseball has presented a top 100 list before, but that list was a subjective one selected by a few individuals. The 100 players that follow have been determined exclusively by the statistical ranking system that is used in this book: Pete Palmer and John Thorn's Total Player Rating (TPR), and it should not be confused with Major League Baseball's 100 Greatest Players. Strictly speaking, this rating does not aim to rank the 100 best players; it has a more specific aim. Total Player Rating measures the number of extra wins (or losses) each player provided his teams compared to what an average player at the same position in his time would have produced. The list does not take into account data from leagues other than the major leagues (most notably the Negro Leagues) because of difficulty in verifying information.

Most of the players listed in our top 100 list will be no surprise to anyone. Babe Ruth is ranked first, with Willie Mays second. Walter Johnson is ranked highest among pitchers. But there are some inclusions that will come as a great surprise to many readers, while certain exclusions might be considered outrageous, if not downright sacrilegious. The important thing to remember, however, is that the rankings are all based on the TPR formula. TPR is based only on what each player achieved statistically in terms of creating and preventing runs compared to his peers. A player's raw numbers—especially his Triple Crown statistics—are not all that's important. The frequency of a hitter's outs makes a large difference, as does the era and the park he played in. Even though their raw numbers may be the same, a hitter whose home park was the Astrodome in the mid-1960s and a hitter playing half his games in Coors Field in the mid-1990s will be rated very differently. (A more technical explanation of TPR can be found in the Glossary.)

Also notable is that TPR's use of league-average player performance as a baseline credits significant periods of sustained excellence much more than a long career of average play or a brief period of total superiority. Thus you'll find neither Nolan Ryan—a pitching marvel who nonetheless had few significantly above average seasons—nor Sandy Koufax, who dominated for only a five-year period, in the top 100. Pete Rose is also not in the top 100 (though TPR's metrics do rank him as one of the top 50 hitters ever), primarily because of his indifferent fielding, a poor basestealing record, and the below average seasons he had at the beginning and end of his career.

On the other hand, there may be some players on this list that are unfamiliar to readers or are rarely considered all-time greats. George Davis, a shortstop whose career ended 92 years ago and who was elected to the Hall of Fame in 1998, ranks as the 32nd top player of all-time. Bill Dahlen, a superior defensive shortstop of the same era, ranks 31st. Bobby Grich, who received so few votes by the Baseball Writers Association of America that he was left off the Hall of Fame ballot after just one year, ranks 40th as a result of his superior defense and high walk totals. And the unheralded Jimmy Wynn squeaks into our top 100 as a result of his superior defense and the extremely low offensive context (a pitcher's park in a pitcher's era) within which he played most of his career.

Davis, Dahlen, Grich, and Wynn all played positions on the diamond that are considered relatively important defensively, and that's no coincidence. Total Player Rating ranks each player against his peers—shortstops are compared to other shortstops, first basemen are compared to other first basemen. This is important because the offensive expectations for each position vary widely. Alex Rodriguez and Edgar Martinez were similarly productive offensively in 2000, but Rodriguez was the more valuable Mariner by far because he played a key defensive position while Martinez didn't even play defense. If you don't take that type of variance into account, you'll end up with a top 100 consisting primarily of first basemen and corner outfielders. A list of the top 500 players, according to TPR, can be found in the All-Time Leaders section under the heading Total Baseball Ranking.

If you have quibbles about our rankings—as many readers no doubt will—just remember that all the player ratings are based on the same statistical criteria. Tim Raines is rated 36th by the exact same formula that ranks Ty Cobb fourth and Henry Aaron seventh. This is not to say that TPR should be the final word in determining which players are better or greater than other players—the concepts of "better" and "greater" are nebulous enough so that there can never really be an end to the discussions and debates. And TPR itself is constantly being improved and refined. But when you see Bobby Grich rated higher than Roberto Clemente on our list, before you take a Louisville Slugger to this hefty volume, we think it's reasonable to ask that you look at how those ratings are calculated instead of rejecting that analysis out of hand.

The Top 100 Players (followed by Total Player Rating):

1. Babe Ruth . . . 126.1
2. Willie Mays . . . 95.9
3. Nap Lajoie . . . 95.5
4. Ty Cobb . . . 92.1
5. Walter Johnson . . . 91.0
6. Barry Bonds . . . 89.4
7. Hank Aaron . . . 89.1
8. Tris Speaker . . . 88.2
9. Ted Williams . . . 83.0
10. Rogers Hornsby . . . 82.7
11. Honus Wagner . . . 82.0
12. Mike Schmidt . . . 79.6
13. Cy Young . . . 78.0
14. Mickey Mantle . . . 77.4
15. Rickey Henderson . . . 77.0
16. Eddie Collins . . . 73.3
17. Stan Musial . . . 71.5
18. Lou Gehrig . . . 68.9
19. Frank Robinson . . . 67.6
20. Grover Cleveland Alexander . . . 64.6
21. Christy Mathewson . . . 62.9
22. Mel Ott . . . 61.4
23. Greg Maddux . . . 60.0
24. Lefty Grove . . . 59.7
25. Roger Clemens . . . 57.5
    Kid Nichols . . . 57.5
27. Jimmie Foxx . . . 56.3
28. Joe Morgan . . . 54.8
29. Eddie Mathews . . . 52.2
30. Ken Griffey Jr. . . . 51.6
31. Bill Dahlen . . . 51.1
32. George Davis . . . 50.6
33. Warren Spahn . . . 50.2
    Joe DiMaggio . . . 50.2
35. Tom Seaver . . . 48.7
36. Tim Raines . . . 47.9
37. Carl Yastrzemski . . . 46.7
38. John Clarkson . . . 46.0
    Robin Yount . . . 46.0
40. Bobby Grich . . . 45.8
41. Tony Gwynn . . . 45.6
42. Jeff Bagwell . . . 45.2
    Al Kaline . . . 45.2
44. Charlie Gehringer . . . 45.0
45. Ed Walsh . . . 44.9
46. Wade Boggs . . . 44.4
47. Bob Gibson . . . 43.7
48. Roger Connor . . . 43.3
49. Ed Delahanty . . . 42.9
50. Lou Boudreau . . . 42.5
51. Luke Appling . . . 42.4
    Ozzie Smith . . . 42.4
53. Roberto Clemente . . . 42.2
    Reggie Jackson . . . 42.2
    Cal Ripken Jr. . . . 42.2
56. Dan Brouthers . . . 41.4
57. Barry Larkin . . . 41.2
58. Carl Hubbell . . . 41.1
59. Bid McPhee . . . 41.0
60. Ron Santo . . . 40.9
61. Hoyt Wilhelm . . . 40.8
62. Frank Thomas . . . 40.7
63. Bobby Doerr . . . 40.5
64. Gabby Hartnett . . . 40.3
65. George Brett . . . 40.0
66. Joe Cronin . . . 39.9
67. Amos Rusie . . . 39.8
68. Arky Vaughan . . . 39.7
69. Bobby Wallace . . . 39.4
70. Hal Newhouser . . . 39.3
71. Whitey Ford . . . 39.2
72. Joe Jackson . . . 39.0
73. Frankie Frisch . . . 38.6
74. Mark McGwire . . . 38.4
75. Tim Keefe . . . 38.1
76. Bob Lemon . . . 37.9
77. Dave Bancroft . . . 37.5
    Reggie Smith . . . 37.5
79. Yogi Berra . . . 37.4
80. Willie McCovey . . . 37.3
81. Ted Lyons . . . 37.1
82. Dave Winfield . . . 36.9
83. Carl Mays . . . 36.6
    Ryne Sandberg . . . 36.6
85. Bill Mazeroski . . . 36.3
86. Johnny Mize . . . 36.2
87. Mike Piazza . . . 36.0
88. Dick Allen . . . 35.9
    Jack Glasscock . . . 35.9
    Jimmy Wynn . . . 35.9
91. Edgar Martinez . . . 35.7
92. Craig Biggio . . . 35.6
93. Darrell Evans . . . 35.5
    Joe Sewell . . . 35.5
95. Bill Dickey . . . 35.4
96. Mordecai Brown . . . 35.3
97. Jim Palmer . . . 34.9
    Gaylord Perry . . . 34.9
    Bob Johnson . . . 34.9
100. Keith Hernandez . . . 34.8

BABE RUTH OF-P

Babe Ruth was not only the greatest baseball player who ever lived, but the most flamboyant. His gargantuan appetites and prodigious talents, ensconced in an oversized body with a face like that of a bloated Cupid, made him one of the most recognizable figures in American history. In the 1920s his name appeared in print more often than anyone except the president of the United States. In World War II, when American soldiers shouted "To hell with the Emperor!" at their Japanese counterparts, the Japanese hollered back, "To hell with Babe Ruth!"

Ruth was a presence of mythic proportions. While he was changing baseball and its economics forever, he was also defining a uniquely American kind of folk hero: a larger-than-life athlete with an even larger propensity for mischief and misbehavior, an intense love of children, and an irrepressible sense of fun. His career also typifies the classic "rags to riches" scenario, in that he rose from the harsh milieu of a Baltimore reform school to achieve wealth, celebrity, and lasting renown.

Ruth revolutionized the game with his unprecedented slugging, and in the wake of the "Black Sox Scandal" of 1919 he singlehandedly restored America's love of baseball. At his death in 1948 he owned 56 major league batting records, plus 10 American League marks. His record of 60 home runs in a single season was not surpassed until Roger Maris hit 61 in 1961. Ruth's lifetime tally of 714 home runs was not bested until 1974, when Henry Aaron hit No. 715 after nearly 3,000 more at bats than Ruth had needed to accomplish the feat. Ruth's average of one home run for every 11.76 at bats was for long the best in major league history—and may one day (as Mark McGwire plays through his career) be the best again.

In addition to his remarkable batting feats, Ruth was the best lefthanded pitcher of his era, and might have finished up as one of the best hurlers of all time had his hitting not necessitated his change to a position player. Pitching for the Boston Red Sox, he won more than 20 games in both 1917 and 1918; lifetime he was 94–46 for a winning percentage of .671. He led the AL with a 1.75 ERA in 1916; nine of his victories were shutouts, and opponents managed to bat only .201 against him. Over the five-year period from 1915 to 1919 Ruth had a 2.16 ERA. He threw 29⅔ consecutive scoreless innings in World Series play, another of his records that lasted until 1961.

His legacy went beyond baseball statistics. Because Ruth was well paid by the end of his career, he helped increase salaries for all players. In 1914, as a rookie with Baltimore in the Eastern League, he earned $600, and by 1930 he was up to $80,000. When someone pointed out to Ruth that he was earning $5,000 more than President Herbert Hoover's annual salary, the Babe supposedly replied, "So what? I had a better year than he did."

The Babe Ruth who was merely one of baseball's finest pitchers and the Babe Ruth who would soon become fabled as the game's greatest slugger began to diverge from one another in 1918. That was the season that Ruth's teammate Harry Hooper advised Red Sox manager Ed Barrow to move the Babe to the outfield full time. Barrow's compromise was to have Ruth pitch in 20 games, and play either the outfield or first base in 72 more. Ruth won 13 games, recorded a 2.22 ERA, and tied for the AL's home run crown with 11. The experiment was ruled a success. Ruth moved to the outfield for 111 games in 1919 and made only 17 pitching appearances. That year he exploded for 29 home runs, setting a new major league record. He also led the league in runs, RBIs, on-base percentage, and slugging average.

But the Red Sox finished sixth, and owner Harry Frazee, needing money to invest in a Broadway show, sold Ruth to the Yankees for $125,000 and a $300,000 loan. It's been known ever since as the "Curse of the Bambino." Boston, which had won the World Series with Ruth pitching in 1918 (the franchise's fifth since 1903), would not claim another world championship for the rest of the century; the Yankees, who had never captured a pennant prior to Ruth's arrival, would become the most successful franchise in baseball history.

In 1920 Ruth hit a mind-boggling 54 home runs, scored 158 runs, and drove in 137. He batted .376, and slugged an incredible .847, still a single-season record as of the year 2000. The Polo Grounds, which the Yankees shared with the New York Giants, was much more friendly to lefthanded longball hitters than Fenway Park, and Ruth fell in love with the place.

In September 1920 a Carl Mays pitch struck and killed Cleveland shortstop Ray Chapman. In response to Chapman's death, baseball changed its rules for 1921. Scuffed and dirty balls were removed from play, and pitchers were no longer allowed to tamper with the ball to gain an edge. Ruth took advantage of the white, undoctored baseballs to rip 59 homers, drive in 171 runs, and score 177 times. The Yankees won the pennant for the first of three straight seasons. Still only 26 years old, Ruth hit his 137th career homer, surpassing Roger Connors' previous lifetime record.

Ruth ushered in a new era of power in baseball, winning back the fans that had been soured by the Black Sox Scandal. But when the Babe tried to capitalize on his fame by organizing an all-star team for a postseason barnstorming tour, Commissioner Kenesaw Mountain Landis, who wanted to establish the World Series as the definitive postseason event, suspended Ruth and teammate Bob Meusel for the first six weeks of the 1922 season. It would prove the first season since 1917 that Ruth did not lead the league in homers; it would happen only once more in the next nine years.

In 1923 Yankee Stadium opened, and sportswriter Fred Lieb dubbed it "The House that Ruth Built." On Opening Day, before 74,200 fans, Ruth provided the Yankees' margin of victory with a three-run homer. That season he led the league in runs, homers, RBIs, walks, slugging, and on-base average, just as he had in 1920 and 1921. More importantly, in 1923 the Yankees claimed their first world championship, beating the Giants in the Series after losing the two previous years.

After missing much of the 1925 season due to what was diagnosed as an "intestinal abscess" and a suspension for carousing, the Bambino bounced back in 1926, a year that saw him teamed for the first time with Lou Gehrig. Ruth and Gehrig set off on a seven-year tear the likes of which the sport had never seen. During that span the duo averaged 84 homers and 303 RBIs a year. In 1927, when Ruth slugged his record 60 home runs, Gehrig added 47; the big first baseman finished second to the Babe in home runs each season from 1927 to 1931.

The Yanks won pennants in 1926, 1927, 1928, and 1932. They swept the World Series in three of those seasons, with Ruth batting .400, .625, and .333 and slugging .800, 1.375, and .733 in postseason play.

Game 3 of the 1932 World Series witnessed what has become the Babe's most legendary home run. With the Yankees down, 4–3, in the fifth inning, Ruth came to bat against Cubs pitcher Charlie Root. When Ruth took strike one, he held up one finger to indicate he knew the count. He repeated the gesture on the second strike. With one strike to go, Ruth held up his bat to indicate he had a single strike left—or, depending upon one's interpretation, he pointed to center field to signal where he would send Root's next offering. He then proceeded to slam the ball into the bleachers. The allegedly "called shot" has become an indelible part of baseball lore.

The Yankees did not sign Ruth for 1935. Instead, he was offered a contract with the Boston Braves as player, assistant manager, and vice president. The last two were a sham: Boston was only trying to beef up attendance by having the overweight, aging legend around. But Ruth's bat had one more display of fireworks on May 25, 1935, when he homered three times against the Pirates in Pittsburgh. The third blast, over the right field roof of Forbes Field, was his final major league run, and it was, typically, a monster shot.

Ruth was one of the five charter members inducted into the Hall of Fame in 1936. He spent the final 13 years of his life waiting for some club to offer him a managerial position; the closest he got was a coaching position with the Brooklyn Dodgers in 1938. When Ruth died of throat cancer in 1948, thousands paid their respects to the great slugger as his body lay in state at Yankee Stadium.

WILLIE MAYS OF

Willie Mays could do everything: hit for average, hit for power, run, field, and throw. There were better outfielders, players with better arms, batters with higher averages and more homers, and faster runners who stole more bases. But no one could combine all those things at Mays's skill level. On top of that, "Say Hey" added a dash of showmanship and childlike delight that made him a fan favorite for 22 years.

His lifetime stats only hint at his greatness. When he retired, no one except Babe Ruth had hit more home runs. Mays played in at least 150 games in a season 13 times, a major league record. He holds the National League record for most games with two or more homers, at 63. He hit 22 extra-inning home runs in his career; Ruth is second with 16. Mays also won a batting title, finished second three times, and third twice. He led the NL in home runs four times, twice hitting more than 50.

Mays was the league's Most Valuable Player twice, at age 23 and again at age 34. He had 300 or more total bases in 13 consecutive seasons. Only Lou Gehrig equaled that feat, and only Hank Aaron exceeded it. He ranks third all time in total bases, fourth in extra-base hits, sixth in runs scored, seventh in games played, eighth in RBIs, and 10th in hits. *The Sporting News* named Mays Player of the Decade for the 1960s.

Defensively, he was in a league of his own. Mays is the all-time leader in outfield putouts and total chances, but numbers don't even begin to tell the story. In 1951 Mays caught a drive by Rocky Nelson in Pittsburgh's Forbes Field with his bare hand, and did the same thing to Roberto Clemente a few years later in the same park. In the 1954 World Series Mays made a play that has gone down in baseball history as simply "the Catch." In Game 1 at the Polo Grounds, the score was tied, 2–2, in the eighth inning when two Indians reached base. Cleveland's Vic Wertz belted a long flyball to deep center field. Mays sprinted away with his back to home plate, turned at the last second, and snagged the ball over his shoulder at a dead run more than 440 feet from home. He then spun in one motion and let fly a perfect throw that allowed only one baserunner to tag up. The score remained tied. Then, in the 10th inning, Wertz led off with a line drive to left-center field that looked certain to reach the wall for a potential inside-the-park home run. Mays sped over to cut it off and held Wertz to a double. The two plays demoralized the Indians, and the Giants went on to sweep them in the Series.

For years, when baseball's best players met in the All-Star Game, Mays made it his personal show, demonstrating his incredible talents to the nation and intimidating American Leaguers in the process. Mays was an All-Star every year after he returned from the service in 1954, playing 24 games in 20 years. (From 1959 through 1962 the leagues played two games each year.) He set the all-time All-Star records for at bats, hits, runs, extra-base hits, triples, and stolen bases. In the first 1959 Midsummer Classic his ninth-inning triple drove in the winning run. In the first 1961 All-Star Game Mays drove in the tying run with a double in the last of the 10th inning; he scored the winning run moments later. In the 1963 All-Star Game he drove in two runs, scored two, swiped two bases, and made a superb grab in center. In 1965 he homered, walked twice, and scored the winning run.

At age 17, Mays signed his first professional contract, with the Birmingham Black Barons of the Negro National League. He was sold to the New York Giants in 1950 for $15,000, and came up to the big league club from Minneapolis in the American Association in 1951. Mays struggled through 24 plate appearances before getting his first major league hit, and the first of his 660 career home runs, off Warren Spahn. He was voted NL Rookie of the Year as the Giants won the pennant in a fabled three-game playoff with the Dodgers.

After returning from two years in the service in 1954, Mays lit up New York like a Roman candle. He led all NL hitters that year with a .345 average and 13 triples. He tied for third in home runs, with 41, drove in 110 runs, and scored 119.

In 1955 Mays slugged a league-leading 51 homers and 13 triples and also swiped 24 bases. It seemed that not a year went by without his leading the league in some category: triples in 1954, 1955, and 1957; home runs in 1954, 1962, 1965, and 1966; runs in 1958 and 1961; hits in 1960; slugging percentage in 1954, 1955, 1957, 1964, and 1965; and on-base percentage and walks in 1971.

On the streets of New York, Mays was considered a hometown hero. He would stop to play stickball with kids in Harlem, and his gleeful greeting, "Say hey," became his nickname. Although Mays didn't receive the same adulation on the West Coast, where the Giants followed the Dodgers in 1958, he continued to shine. He led the league with 49 homers in 1962 as San Francisco tied Los Angeles for the pennant. Mays clubbed two homers in the first game of the playoffs, and in the final game his bases-loaded line drive ignited the winning rally. San Francisco moved on to the World Series, which they lost to the Yankees in seven taut games. In the bottom of the ninth of Game 7, with two outs and Matty Alou on first, Mays cracked a double to right. But a super throw from Roger Maris held Alou at third and the Giants fell, 1–0.

In 1963 Mays homered in the last of the 16th to give Juan Marichal a complete-game, 1–0 victory over Warren Spahn, who had also gone the distance. In 1971 the 40-year-old Mays walked a league-best 112 times as Giants won their division, but the Pirates prevailed in the NLCS.

After 21 years in a Giants uniform, Mays was traded to the Mets in 1972. In his first game as a Met, Mays homered against San Francisco to give his new team a 5–4 win over his old. He reached base during his first 20 games in a Mets uniform.

By April 1973, however, aches and pains forced Mays to the bench. He played in only 66 games that season, but the Mets rallied to win the NL East. In Game 2 of that year's World Series, Mays delivered a 12th-inning single to put his club ahead to stay. It was his last major league hit. On his farewell night in Shea Stadium a sign read, "We who are about to cry salute you."

Mays was elected to the Baseball Hall of Fame in 1979, his first year of eligibility. One testimony to his legacy is the number of today's superstars who wear or have worn his No. 24 in tribute. They include outfielders Barry Bonds (while at Pittsburgh), Ken Griffey Jr., and Rickey Henderson.

NAP LAJOIE 2B

When fans debate the question of who was baseball's best hitter in the first decade of the 20th century, the two names most often mentioned are Nap Lajoie and Honus Wagner. Fellow Hall of Famer Kid Nichols called Lajoie "the hardest hitter I ever pitched to."

Hitting .338 for his career, Lajoie amassed three batting titles, four 200-hit seasons, and four 100-RBI seasons. His .426 in 1901 was the highest batting average of the century. A virtual artist at second base, he led the American League in double plays and putouts five times each, in fielding average seven times, and in chances per game—the best gauge of range—six times. The word "graceful," which appears on his Hall of Fame plaque, barely begins to describe his play.

Lajoie started his career at first base, hitting .326 for the Phillies in 1896. In his sophomore season he batted .361, hit 40 doubles and 23 triples, drove in 127 runs, and led the National League with a .569 slugging percentage. He also set a record with 13 total bases in a game.

In 1898 Lajoie was shifted to second base, where he'd camp for most of his career. He batted .324 and led the NL in doubles (43) and RBIs (127). Yet in 1900, the feisty Lajoie—who had suffered a broken thumb in a brawl with teammate Elmer Flick—jumped to the Philadelphia Athletics in the nascent American League.

Talent was thin in the new league, and Lajoie dominated. In 1901 he led the AL in eight major offensive categories. It was the Dead Ball Era, when seven or eight homers might top the league; Lajoie belted 14 that season, the third-highest total of the century's first decade.

A lawsuit had been filed to keep Lajoie from leaving the National League, however, and in February 1902 an appeal was finally heard before the Pennsylvania Supreme Court. Lajoie became, in effect, the first person to challenge baseball's reserve clause. The decision—that he be barred from playing for any team other than the Phillies—threw Organized Baseball into a tumult. The American League finally devised a solution whereby Lajoie would play for the Cleveland Blues, and that he'd absent himself from the lineup when the team played in Philadelphia.

Lajoie's presence and play rescued the Blues, who otherwise might have moved to Pittsburgh or Cincinnati. Later research showed that Lajoie hit .378 in 1902, two points higher than Ed Delahanty, but Major League Baseball maintained that Delahanty should retain his batting crown. The next season, the Cleveland club was renamed the Naps in honor of its captain. In 1904, a season in which he again dominated the league's hitters, Lajoie took over the managerial reins and kept the job for five years.

Blood poisoning from a spike wound ruined his 1905 season, and another spiking injury cost him five weeks in 1907. The next year Cleveland seriously contended for the pennant, but Lajoie committed errors in key games and the team finished half-a-game behind Detroit. He quit as the team's manager in 1909, but when the Cleveland press ran another contest to rename the team, the Naps won again.

Lajoie and Ty Cobb vied for the batting title in 1910, and it became the most scandalous batting race in baseball history. At the end of August, Lajoie and Cobb were only three points apart. But there was no unanimity on exactly what the averages were at any one time, and statements about "official" and "unofficial" figures added to the confusion. On October 6 one set of numbers said Cobb had an eight-point lead; another claimed Lajoie was out front by a point or so. Cobb, believing he'd already won the prize of a Chalmers 30 automobile, sat out his team's last two games. Lajoie, meanwhile, faced the Browns in a season-ending doubleheader. No one wanted Cobb to win; Lajoie, on the other hand, was very well liked. In his final two games Lajoie went 8 for 8; six of his safeties were bunts, with the Browns third baseman ordered to play deep. Another "hit" was very graciously awarded to Lajoie by the official scorer. After all the collusion Cobb won the title by .0007. Although both players were presented with cars, the fiasco prompted a policy change for awarding prizes to battling titlists.

More than 70 years later, research revealed that two hits had been mistakenly credited to Cobb. An attempt to have the "official" data changed and the title given to Lajoie, thereby breaking Cobb's incredible string of nine consecutive batting titles, was taken to Commissioner Bowie Kuhn. But he ruled against Lajoie, and the records stood.

Losing the batting title didn't diminish Lajoie's popularity. In 1912 Cleveland threw a "Nap Lajoie Day" that featured a huge floral horseshoe decorated with 1,009 silver dollars. In 1914 Lajoie reached 3,000 hits, joining Honus Wagner as the second player in the 20th century to attain the milestone. But he was sold to the A's before the

1915 season, and he retired after two mediocre years in Philadelphia.

Lifetime, Lajoie ranks sixth in doubles and 12th in hits, and his .338 batting average is second only to Rogers Hornsby among second basemen. He was elected to the Hall of Fame in 1937.

TY COBB OF

Ty Cobb, "the Georgia Peach," was a man possessed. Probably no other athlete has ever matched his furious desire to excel. In baseball legend he is the antithesis of Babe Ruth, the lazy, overweight hero to whom baseball excellence came easily and for whom life was fun. Cobb was the driven and bellicose adversary who fought desperately for everything he achieved.

A Detroit Tiger for 22 of his 24 seasons, Cobb was egotistical, brash, and thin-skinned; a brawler, a racist, and a bully. In short, he was a terrible person, but his greatness as a ballplayer is undisputed. His career total of 2,246 runs stood as the major league record through the end of the 20th century. Among his other marks are highest lifetime batting average, with .366; most years leading the league in both batting average and hits; and most games with five or more hits (14). Cobb's record of 4,189 hits stood for 56 years. He ranks among the top five players of all time in games, runs, hits, total bases, doubles, triples, RBIs, and stolen bases.

When it comes to batting records Cobb and Ruth stand together. When Cobb retired in 1928 he was the leader in 90 major league or American League offensive categories. Even some 70 years later, he still holds more than 30 records, including one for most consecutive years (three) leading the AL in RBIs, a mark he shares with Ruth and another Tiger, Cecil Fielder. Seven times Cobb had consecutive-game hitting streaks of 20 or more games.

To put Cobb's dominance during the Dead Ball Era into perspective, consider that current league-wide averages are regularly around .260, and a batter usually wins the batting title hitting 80 to 90 points higher than that. In eight of Cobb's first 11 years in the majors, the AL average was less than .250, yet Cobb put up marks of .324 to .420, typically batting 100 to 140 points higher than the league.

Cobb was also an expert on the basepaths. He would often try to stretch a single into a double in an unimportant game; the fielder might throw him out, but the next time Cobb tried it, when more was at stake, the same fielder could be pressured into a bobble or a bad throw. Cobb's single-season record of 96 stolen bases in 1915 wasn't broken until 1962. His 20th-century lifetime stolen base mark of 892 stood until 1977.

Cobb was famous for sharpening his spikes in the dugout in clear view of the opposition, but this was more of a psychological ploy than a real physical threat. Cobb was smart; he knew that intentional spiking would cause more trouble than it was worth. He preferred to slide away from the bag with a hook slide, offering just his toe to be tagged. But if the defense blocked the base or the baseline, he had no qualms about dumping a player on his backside. The fear Cobb could command from his opponents gave him the edge he desperately wanted.

He used the same intelligence in the field that he did at bat and on the bases. Cobb had 30 assists his first full major league season, and led the league with 23 the next year. He had 18 or more assists 13 times during his career.

Cobb came to the Tigers during the middle of the 1905 season. He didn't stand for the razzing that all rookies receive, and readily brawled with his teammates. In 1907 Cobb began his string of nine consecutive batting titles with a .350 average. He never hit below .323 again for his entire career.

On September 30, 1907, Cobb's Tigers held a slim lead over the Philadelphia Athletics in the standings. In a matchup between the clubs going into the top of the ninth, Philadelphia had a two-run lead. Then Cobb slugged a two-run homer. The teams played to a 17-inning, 9–9 tie that eliminated the A's from the race. Cobb said later that the game was one of the most satisfying moments of his career. He had propelled the Tigers to their first World Series, against the Cubs. After a 12-inning tie in the first game, however, the Tigers dropped four straight, and Cobb hit just .200.

Cobb led Detroit to two more pennants, in 1908 and 1909, but each time the world championship eluded his Tigers. His best World Series performance was in 1908, when he batted .368 against Chicago, including three hits in Game 3. In the 1909 Fall Classic he found himself outplayed by the Pittsburgh Pirates' Honus Wagner, his rival as the era's greatest player.

In 1909 Cobb became the second Triple Crown winner in the AL's young history, topping the league with a .377 batting average, 107 RBIs, and nine home runs. He also led the AL in runs, hits, on-base percentage, and slugging average. The following season witnessed the famous battle for the batting crown between Cobb and Nap Lajoie. Cobb was declared the winner, but both men were awarded the prize of a new Chalmers automobile; 70 years later, research established that Lajoie had the higher batting average.

In 1911 Cobb batted over .400 for the first of three times. Only Jesse Burkett and Rogers Hornsby achieved that mark as often. In addition, Cobb hit safely in 40 consecutive games to set an AL record and finished with a .420 average, the highest in league history. His 248 hits were a major league record (since broken), and he unanimously won the Chalmers Award as Most Valuable Player.

Cobb topped .400 again in 1912, but his wicked temper led him to assault a fan during a game in New York. AL president Ban Johnson suspended Cobb indefinitely for his actions. After Detroit's next game, sans Cobb, the entire team refused to continue the season unless their star was reinstated. On May 18 not one of them showed up, and a pickup team comprised of former coaches and collegians took the field wearing Detroit uniforms. The A's walloped them, 24–2. When Johnson threatened the striking Tigers with lifetime banishment from the game, they relented, with Cobb's approval and thanks. Cobb was suspended for 10 days and fined $50.

Cobb was named player-manager of the Tigers in 1921, but new responsibilities didn't calm him down. That year he nearly came to blows with Babe Ruth three times in one game, and he also slugged it out with umpire Billy Evans. Detroit never finished any better than second place with Cobb at the helm.

Before a game in 1925 a reporter asked Cobb about

Ruth and the art of slugging. Cobb said hitting home runs was no big deal. To prove it, he brought his hands together and quit choking up on the bat and slugged three homers that day. He added a double and two singles to set the AL record, since broken, for total bases in one game. The next day he hit two more homers, just to prove his performance was no fluke.

In 1926 the Tigers finished sixth and Cobb announced his resignation. After Cleveland manager Tris Speaker resigned one month later, rumors began to spread that the two had conspired to throw games several years earlier. Whatever the truth of the matter, the two stars were interviewed by Commissioner Kenesaw Mountain Landis and acquitted of all charges. They both subsequently signed with new teams, Speaker with the Washington Senators and Cobb with the A's. The 40-year-old Cobb played 134 games for Philadelphia in 1927, batting .357 and stealing 22 bases, which ranked third in the league. In his final year he hit .323.

Cobb was the first man elected to the Hall of Fame when it opened in 1936. He was also the game's first playing millionaire, having been an early stockholder in both Coca-Cola and General Motors. Seventy-two years after he hung up his spikes, he continues to haunt the imagination of fans, and his tempestuous career has been the subject of several plays and movies.

WALTER JOHNSON P

In his heyday with the Washington Senators, Walter Johnson was called the "Big Train." When his fastball came roaring down the tracks, American League batters knew they were facing the fastest pitcher they would ever see—or, more accurately, hear. As Frank "Ping" Bodie once said about Johnson's fastball, "You can't hit what you can't see."

In truth, Johnson may not have been quite as fast as he seemed. He had unusually long arms and threw with an easy sidearm motion. His arm movement seemed suited to easy lobs, but then his fastball exploded past batters. Even if some of Johnson's speed was illusory, it sparked a round of most of the well-worn "fast pitcher" stories. After one Johnson pitch, Joe Gedeon asked umpire Billy Evans if it had been a fastball or a curve, remarking, "I never saw it, I had to close my eyes." Said Evans later: "I knew the ballplayers couldn't second-guess me if they were closing their eyes, too."

During his career, which ran from 1907 through 1927, Johnson provided plenty of numbers to go with anecdotes. He won 30 or more games in consecutive seasons, including 36 in 1913. He won 20 or more games 12 times, including every season from 1910 through 1919 and again in 1924 and 1925. He pitched a major league record 110 shutouts, including 11 in 1913 when his ERA was 1.09. He also lost a record 65 shutouts, 26 of them by the score of 1–0. He won 416 games with the Senators, but his teammates played so poorly they were whitewashed in nearly a quarter of his defeats.

Several pitchers have now surpassed Johnson's career strikeout tally of 3,509, but in his day and long after it Johnson was regarded as indisputably the finest strikeout artist in baseball history. Relying solely on his fastball, Johnson led the American League in whiffs 12 times. Twice in his career, in situations with the bases loaded and none out, he struck out the side on just nine pitches: against Detroit's Ty Cobb, Sam Crawford, and Bobby Veach, and against Cleveland's Tris Speaker, Chick Gandil, and Elmer Smith.

The Senators signed Johnson in 1907 for $350 a month salary plus a $100 bonus. He had an up-and-down season in 1908, going 14–14 for seventh-place Washington. He heated up at season's end, pitching three shutouts in a four-day period in early September against the New York Highlanders. On September 4 he whitewashed them, 3–0, on four hits. The next day he tossed a three-hitter to win, 6–0. He might have pitched the next day, but Sunday baseball was still illegal in New York. On Monday, in the first game of a doubleheader, he delivered a two-hitter and won, 4–0.

The following season Johnson was dogged by a fever he contracted during spring training, and he lost a career-high 25 games. In 1910, however, he began the first of 10 consecutive 20-win seasons. That season he pitched 373 innings, hurled 38 complete games, and struck out 313 batters—all career highs.

From July 3 through August 23, 1912, Johnson won 16 straight games before losing in relief to the Browns. Through 2000, no AL pitcher has won more consecutive games in a single season, although three pitchers have tied the mark.

Johnson was at his best in 1913, when he was named American League Most Valuable Player. It was a storybook season, and few pitchers have put up similar numbers. His 1.09 ERA, 36 victories (against only seven losses), and 11 shutouts led the league. Johnson issued less than a walk an inning, recorded five one-hitters, and had streaks of 10, 11, and 14 consecutive wins. From the second inning on April 10 through the third inning on May 14 the Big Train did not surrender a single run. Those 56⅔ consecutive scoreless innings remain a league record.

Johnson's string of 20-win campaigns was snapped in 1920 when he suffered from a sore arm. He had pitched 11 straight seasons of 290 or more innings and had also taken the mound on preseason barnstorming tours. Yet it was on July 1, 1920, that Johnson recorded his only no-hitter, a 1–0, 10-strikeout victory over the Red Sox in Boston. It would have been a perfect game had it not been for a booted grounder by second baseman Bucky Harris. Ironically, Johnson had not expected to pitch that day, having been away from the ballclub until just before game time because his 5-year-old son was ill.

Despite his dominance on the mound, it appeared that Johnson would never appear in a World Series. But late in his career he pitched in two straight Fall Classics. In the 1924 Series against New York he started twice and lost both times. But in Game 7, manager Bucky Harris brought Johnson in as a reliever. In the 12th inning with the score tied, 3–3, Washington catcher Muddy Ruel came to the plate with one out and would have been retired on a foul pop had Giants catcher Hank Gowdy not tripped over his own mask. Given a reprieve, Ruel doubled to left. Johnson then reached on Travis Jackson's error. The next batter, Earl McNeely, hit a routine grounder to third baseman Freddie Lindstrom. The ball hit a pebble and skipped over Lindstrom's head for a hit, and Ruel raced home with the winning run. Johnson, who pitched four scoreless innings, picked up the victory as Washington captured its first and only world championship.

Johnson reversed his record in the following year's World Series, going 2–1. He won Games 1 and 4 but lost Game 7 to Pittsburgh's Ray Kremer. Johnson won 15 games the next season, slipped to 5–6 in 1927, and then retired. He went on to manage the Newark Bears of the International League for the second half of the 1928 season, and from 1929 to 1932 he piloted the Senators. In 1933 he briefly managed the Indians.

When the Baseball Hall of Fame was dedicated in 1936, Johnson was the one of the first five men elected. He died in 1946 in Washington, D.C.

BARRY BONDS OF

Both defensively and offensively, Barry Bonds was one of the preeminent players of the 1990s. Given his baseball pedigree, perhaps his stardom was only to be expected: he was the son of Bobby Bonds (332 career home runs), the godson of Willie Mays (660 home runs), and, through his mother, the cousin of Reggie Jackson (563 home runs).

Named Player of the Decade by *The Sporting News,* Bonds won the National League's Most Valuable Player Award in 1990 with the Pittsburgh Pirates, and earned back-to-back MVPs with the San Francisco Giants in 1992–93. That made Bonds the first player to win the award three times in four years. The only other National Leaguer to bag as many MVPs was Mike Schmidt.

Bonds was the first player to accumulate both 400 home runs and 400 stolen bases in a career; as of spring 2001, he remains the only player to have done so. He was also the first National Leaguer to hit 40 home runs and steal 40 bases in the same season, finishing with 42 homers and 40 thefts in 1996. Playing on a last-place team that season, Bonds walked 151 times, including 30 intentional passes.

Bonds captured a Gold Glove in every season of the 1990s except two. Even without the hardware, few could argue about his place as one of the greatest left fielders of all time. In his first 15 major league seasons, Bonds' single-season fielding percentage did not drop below .980, and his accurate arm notched 137 career assists.

An all-America outfielder at Arizona State University, Bonds signed with the Pittsburgh Pirates in 1985. He was a regular with the Bucs one year later, although he took a little time to develop. In his MVP campaign of 1990, however, Bonds hit .301 with 33 home runs, and his 114 RBIs nearly doubled his total from the previous season. He also stole 52 bases to become just the second player in baseball history to hit 30 home runs and steal 50 bases in the same season. Bonds helped lead the Pirates to the playoffs for the first time in 11 years that season. But he hit just .167 as Pittsburgh lost to the Reds in six games, the first of five postseason appearances in which he had less than stellar outings.

In 1992 Bonds batted .311 with 34 homers, 103 RBIs, and 39 stolen bases to win his second MVP. As in the previous season, though, the Bucs lost to the Braves in the NLCS—this time on a two-out, two-run single to left as Bonds's throw to the plate was just a shade too late to keep former teammate Sid Bream from scoring the winning run.

In 1993 Bonds returned to his hometown San Francisco. He made the Giants pay handsomely: more than $43 million over seven years. From the first pitch of the season, however, Bonds seemed intent to show that he deserved every penny. He batted .336 with 46 home runs, and he became the first player to lead the league in both on-base percentage and slugging percentage since Mike Schmidt in 1981.

Bonds pretty much owned the end of the decade. In four consecutive seasons, 1995–98, he scored more than 100 runs, drove in more than 100 runs, and walked more than 100 times. Despite playing in a career-low 102 games due to injuries in 1999, he hit 34 homers and scored 91 runs.

As the century turned, he showed no signs of slowing down. Bonds enjoyed another banner year in 2000, belting a career-best 49 homers and tying his career high for runs, with 129. His slugging average of .688 was second only to the .698 posted by Colorado's Todd Helton. Bonds finished second to his teammate Jeff Kent in the MVP balloting—the eighth time he had placed in the top five. It was the first 1–2 finish for a team in the NL MVP since Bonds and Bobby Bonilla did it for the Pirates in 1990.

Although he was instrumental in leading the Giants to the 2000 NL West title, Bonds once again bore the onus for his team's failure to advance. Despite hitting a key triple in Game 1 of the Division Series, Bonds made the Giants' last out twice in a four-game loss to the New York Mets.

HANK AARON OF

One of the greatest hitters ever to touch a bat, Hank Aaron combined strength, speed, and lightning-quick reflexes with a professorial study of opposing pitchers to break Babe Ruth's "unbreakable" record of 714 home runs. He finished up with 755, or about 51 miles worth of rounding the bases. At the start of the 21st century, he also leads the rest in RBIs (2,297), total bases (6,856), and extra base hits (1,477), and places in the top five in hits, runs, games, and at bats.

The African-American Aaron made waves well beyond baseball. The fact that he moved almost overnight from a segregated environment into the recently integrated major league world had a deep impact on Aaron. When he realized he could use his talents as a springboard to speak out effectively against racial intolerance and inequality, he became more than just a highly skilled athlete. He became a man with a mission.

Never in a rush, always quiet and dignified, Aaron played without the flash of Willie Mays or the fire of Roberto Clemente. Consistently excellent performance was Aaron's hallmark. He averaged 33 homers per year, hit more than 20 home runs in 20 consecutive years, and scored more than 100 runs 15 times—13 of them in a row, to tie Lou Gehrig's record. Not surprisingly, Aaron played in 21 consecutive All-Star Games. For his career he batted .305 and slugged .555.

As a hitter, Aaron's style was unique. Contrary to conventional baseball wisdom, he aggressively hit off his front foot; his incredibly strong wrists made this possible. The success of his relaxed style confounded many observers, and some misjudged him as lazy. As Lonnie Wheeler, Aaron's collaborator on his autobiography, *I*

Had a Hammer, reflected, "It was odd that Joe DiMaggio was also quiet and deliberate, and yet in DiMaggio's case these traits were perceived as dignity and grace, which translated into American heroism. In Aaron's case, the same qualities translated into comparative invisibility."

Aaron signed with the Negro League Indianapolis Clowns in 1952 for $200 a month, and the Milwaukee Braves bought his contract for $7,000 in 1952. He graduated to the Braves in 1954, replacing an injured Bobby Thomson. His rookie year was solid, if unspectacular, but the next year marked a new era for both Aaron and the Braves. It was the beginning of the two-decade run in which he would annually hit 20 or more homers. It was also the first season he batted .300, a mark that he would achieve 13 more times, and the first of his 11 seasons of 100-plus RBIs. In 1955 and 1956 the Braves finished second, and Aaron put up impressive numbers, leading the league in batting average with .328 in 1956. But 1957 was the real breakout year for Aaron and the Braves. He delivered a league-leading 44 homers and 132 RBIs, and batted .322, tying for third place in the NL with Frank Robinson.

With St. Louis challenging in late September, Aaron hit an 11th-inning home run that clinched the pennant for the Braves—the most satisfying, he later said, of his 755. Milwaukee set a league season attendance record, and Aaron was elected Most Valuable Player. The Braves went on to upset the mighty Yankees in a seven-game World Series as Aaron led all hitters in runs, hits, homers, batting average, and RBIs.

In 1958 Aaron batted .326 with 30 homers and 95 RBIs as the Braves easily won the pennant. Although he batted .333 in the Series, he drove in only two runs, and the Yanks prevailed in seven games. Aaron won his second batting title in 1959 and slugged for 400 total bases, a mark not reached again until 1978. The Braves lost two games of a best-of-three playoff and missed a third straight Series appearance; Aaron and his team would not see postseason action for 10 more years. Although Aaron maintained his standard of excellence, recording consecutive years of 39, 40, 34, 45, and 44 home runs from 1959 through 1963, Milwaukee's fortunes plummeted.

When the team moved to Atlanta in 1966 things changed forever for Aaron. He found the southern air to his liking, slugging 44 and 39 homers, respectively, in his first two years there. He was 34 years old and had 481 lifetime home runs, seemingly a universe away from Babe Ruth's mark. But after talking with baseball historian Lee Allen in 1969 spring training, Aaron became aware of the many records within his reach, and saw a chance not only to break them but also to make himself heard on social issues.

His first objective was to reach 3,000 hits. When Aaron smacked No. 3,000 in 1970 he joined Ty Cobb, Stan Musial, Eddie Collins, Tris Speaker, Honus Wagner, Nap Lajoie, Cap Anson, and Paul Waner. But lack of recognition still plagued him. When he sent the 3,000-hit ball to the Hall of Fame, they put it away in a back room.

The quest to match Ruth became an obsession. In 1971, at age 37, Aaron hit a career-best 47 homers. At the same time he hit .327 and drove in 118 runs. He signed a two-year contract that made him the first player to earn $200,000 a year, but because of financial problems he felt driven to break Ruth's record. He surpassed Musial for lifetime leadership in total bases in September 1972 and finished the year 41 homers behind Ruth's magical 714.

A quarter-century later, it is hard to comprehend the enmity that Hank Aaron inspired as he closed in on Ruth's sanctified record. Atlanta police had to assign a bodyguard to him; after telling sportswriters about the hate mail he'd received, he was flooded with supportive letters. At the end of the year he received a plaque from the U.S. Post Office for having received the most mail of any non-politician during the year—930,000 letters. Aaron finished 1973 with 40 homers, leaving him at 713, one behind Ruth.

The next year began with a minor brouhaha. The Braves wanted to hold Aaron out of the lineup for their first three road games so he could tie and break Ruth's record in Atlanta. The commissioner's office and many sportswriters felt that such maneuvering was a travesty. Ordered to play at least two of the games, Aaron hit homer No. 714 off Jack Billingham in his first at bat of the season. He sat out the second game, and went hitless in the third. His tie-breaking blast came at home against Al Downing of the Dodgers. Teammates, fans, and Aaron's mother met him at the plate. The game was halted for a brief ceremony, and the next time Aaron batted the stands had nearly emptied.

Soon after hitting his last 22 homers for the Milwaukee Brewers of the American League, Aaron became a vice president of the Braves and a leading spokesman for better opportunities for African-Americans in baseball. As of 2000, he sponsors the Hank Aaron Scholarship Program, and serves on the boards of many philanthropic and service foundations. The last player from the Negro Leagues to play in the majors, he left a legacy much greater than his remarkable statistics on the field. He was elected to the Hall of Fame in 1981, in his first year of eligibility.

TRIS SPEAKER OF

Tris Speaker played unusually shallow in center field, so shallow that he recorded 448 assists, more than any other outfielder in baseball history. In 1909 and 1912 he set the American League record with 35 assists in a season. In 1918 he played so close to second base that he made two unassisted double plays. On countless other occasions he turned probable hits into routine outs.

Some now consider Speaker's defensive mastery a by-product of the Dead Ball Era, when flyballs to deep center field were rare. They argue that Speaker could risk the chance of one or two balls a week sailing over his head because of the number of soft drives he'd catch by playing so shallow, a luxury that modern outfielders can't afford. Even Speaker, some say, would have to play much deeper today.

But the evidence is to the contrary. Speaker played the last nine years of his 22-year major league career after the lively ball was introduced in 1920. He continued to play within spitting distance of second base, and he continued to get away with it. His secret was a seemingly prescient ability to get a jump on a batted ball.

Perhaps the single greatest proof of his mastery of the outfield is that Speaker today is best remembered for his fielding even though he was one of the greatest hitters in baseball history. His career marks include a .345 batting average, seventh best overall, as well as 3,514 hits, 1,882 runs, 1,529 RBIs, and 434 stolen bases. He hit more doubles, 792, than anyone who ever played the game, and ranks sixth in triples, ninth in on-base percentage, ninth in extra base hits, and 11th in total bases.

After appearing in a handful of games with the Red Sox in 1907 and 1908, Speaker made the cut in 1909, batting .309 in his first full season. A lefthanded hitter, he sprayed the ball to all fields. Never a big home run hitter, of the four times he reached double figures in homers, three came in the 1920s after the lively ball arrived. His specialty was the line drive, and when coupled with his speed, a single often became a double or triple. Speaker led the AL in two-base hits eight times, topping 50 on five different occasions.

Speaker picked up the nickname "Spoke" from some dugout wag with an affinity for the past tense. But Speaker acted more like his other namesake, "the Grey Eagle," on the ballfield, even when pushing 40. He played in 100 or more games for 19 consecutive seasons and hit better than .300 in all but one.

When the Red Sox won the pennant in 1912, they did it with one of the finest outfields ever assembled. Flanking Speaker was left fielder Duffy Lewis, who drove in 109 runs, and right fielder Harry Hooper, who scored 98. Speaker won the Chalmers Award, a forerunner of the Most Valuable Player Award, that season. He hit .383, scored 136 runs and drove in 90, stole 52 bases, and led the league in doubles, with 53, and home runs, with 10. He finished off a great year by hitting .300 to lead the Red Sox to a World Series victory over the New York Giants. In 1915 Boston finished first again; Speaker hit .322 for the season and .294 in the Sox's World Series win over Philadelphia.

The Federal League was formed in 1914 and tried to lure established stars away from the majors with big salaries. To keep Speaker happy in Fenway Park, the Red Sox increased his wages to $18,000 a year, one of the highest salaries in baseball. When the Feds collapsed after the 1915 season, however, Red Sox owner Joe Lannin tried to cut Speaker's salary by half. When Speaker balked, Lannin traded him to Cleveland in April 1916. The Red Sox still managed to capture the flag, and Speaker won his only AL batting crown with a .386 average, also leading the league with 211 hits, 41 doubles, a .470 on-base percentage, and a .502 slugging average.

In 1920, as player-manager for the Indians, Speaker was brilliant. He coaxed outstanding years out of his pitchers, platooned half his lineup, and, after a pitched ball killed star shortstop Ray Chapman, inserted rookie Joe Sewell to fill the gap. Speaker was also fortunate to have a superb center fielder named Speaker, who hit .388 with 107 RBIs. Cleveland won its first AL pennant by edging the Yankees and White Sox. Then, in a World Series that produced the first Series grand slam, the first Series home run by a pitcher, and the first (and as of 2000 the only) unassisted triple play in Series history, the Tribe downed Brooklyn to become world champions. Speaker batted .320 in the Series, with six runs, two doubles, and a triple.

Speaker continued to manage Cleveland through 1926. Although he didn't win another pennant, he had only two losing seasons. Several of his best seasons with a bat came during this period. In 1923, at age 35, he hit .380 with a career-high 130 RBIs. In 1925 he recorded a career-best .389 average.

Following the 1926 season a former teammate accused Speaker and Ty Cobb of fixing a game back in 1919. Commissioner Kennesaw Mountain Landis investigated and gave both men a clean bill of health; in the meantime, however, both Speaker and Cobb, Detroit's player-manager, found themselves released by their clubs. Speaker signed with Washington and hit .327 in 1927. He finished his career the next year as a sub on Connie Mack's Philadelphia Athletics; Cobb also ended his career on Mack's bench that same season.

Speaker was elected to the Hall of Fame in 1937. His plaque states that he was "the greatest center fielder of his day." Many would change the last three words to "ever."

TED WILLIAMS OF

Ted Williams's one goal in life, he once said, was "to walk down the street and have people say, 'There goes the greatest hitter who ever lived.' " In a 19-year career that was interrupted by two stints in the military, Williams came very close to achieving his goal. If he's not the greatest hitter who ever lived, his competitors for the title are about as numerous as freestanding fingers on a catcher's mitt.

Williams, who spent his entire career with the Red Sox and was known to Boston fans as the "Kid," the "Splendid Splinter," and "Teddy Ballgame," retired with a host of records. Entering 2001, he remains the last player to bat in excess of .400 over the course of a full season. He won two Most Valuable Player Awards, six batting titles, led the American League in home runs and RBIs five times, and finished with a career batting average of .344. Only Babe Ruth and Rickey Henderson walked more times than Williams, and at the end of the 20th century he had the highest walk percentage, or walks per plate appearances, of anyone in baseball history.

From his rookie year of 1939 through 1949 (with three years lost to the Navy Air Corps in World War II), Williams scored and drove in more than 100 runs every season, while averaging 33 homers and 137 bases on balls per annum. During that span he led the league in on-base percentage for seven consecutive seasons and in slugging average for six consecutive seasons. On two occasions—1942 and 1947—he won the Triple Crown; no other American Leaguer has ever duplicated that feat, and only Rogers Hornsby accomplished it in the National League.

All arms, legs, and enthusiasm, the gangly Williams was purchased by the Red Sox from San Diego in the Pacific Coast League in 1937. As a rookie in 1939, the cocky Williams was a big hit with Boston fans, and he responded to their cheers by lifting his cap by its button and tipping it grandly. Things soon soured, however, when some fans and writers began to carp that he didn't work hard enough. Williams squared off with the press and the Fenway faithful for the remainder of his career, vowing never again to tip his cap.

Williams completed his rookie campaign with a .327 average, 31 home runs, and 145 RBIs. Seven of the homers landed in the right field bleachers at Fenway Park, an area reached previously by only five other players. The

Red Sox built bullpens in right field before the 1940 season, cutting the distance to the fence. The area was dubbed "Williamsburg."

The season of 1941 was a miraculous one for the Splinter and for baseball. On May 15 Williams began the longest hitting streak of his career, batting .488 in 23 games to raise his average to .430. Ironically, his feat was obscured by the performance of Joe DiMaggio, who had started his record-setting hitting streak on the same day. At the All-Star break Williams was hitting .405 with 16 home runs and 62 RBIs. DiMaggio had surpassed Willie Keeler's 44-game hitting streak and was about to make history. But at the All-Star Game in Detroit Williams briefly stole the spotlight from DiMaggio when his ninth-inning, three-run homer gave the AL a 7–5 win.

DiMaggio's streak stopped at 56 games, but Williams continued to hit and entered a season-ending doubleheader in Philadelphia batting .39955. It was speculated that he might sit out the final day, but instead Williams had six hits in the twinbill and finished at .406. Despite Williams' achievement, DiMaggio was voted the AL's MVP.

Williams returned to baseball in 1946 after three years as a Navy pilot. At the All-Star Game he delighted the crowd in Fenway Park by blasting Rip Sewell's "eephus" pitch into the bleachers. That season also saw Williams increasingly challenged by the "Boudreau Shift," when Cleveland manager Lou Boudreau crowded six of his fielders on the right side of second base and dared Williams to pull the ball. (Actually, Boudreau's old manager Roger Peckinpaugh had first sprung the shift against Williams in 1941.)

The Red Sox won the pennant and met the St. Louis Cardinals in the 1946 World Series. Williams had been plunked on the elbow by a pitch just before the Series and hit only .200 against the Cards, as Boston lost in seven games. It was little consolation that Williams was selected the AL's Most Valuable Player.

Williams never got another chance to shine in a World Series. He continued to put up big numbers, but the Red Sox always fell short. The team finished third in 1947, and despite winning his second Triple Crown, Williams again lost out in MVP balloting to DiMaggio.

When Williams was called back into the service because of the military action in Korea, the Red Sox held Ted Williams Day on April 30, 1952. For at least one day the Splinter's troubles with the press and the fans were forgotten. Most people thought it would be his final big league game, and the 34-year-old star homered off Dizzy Trout for his 324th home run. But after flying 39 missions, Williams returned to the Red Sox lineup on August 6, 1953. Despite the hiatus and without the benefit of spring training, he hit .407 in 91 at bats and smacked 13 home runs.

Although not quite the run-producer he had been before his stint in Korea, Williams remained a productive hitter. He briefly retired in 1955, and then returned to hit .356 with a .703 slugging average, his highest marks in either category since 1951.

His battles with the press and fans continued unabated. He spit at the crowd, flipped them the bird, and even threw a bat into the stands. When the Red Sox were no longer contenders, however, the fans warmed to Williams, and he enjoyed his greatest popularity since his rookie year. In 1957, at age 40, Williams flirted with .400 once again, finishing at .388. In 1958 he hit .328 to win his sixth, and last, batting crown.

After slumping in 1959, Williams bounced back in 1960 to hit .316 with 29 home runs, the last of which provided the most memorable moment of his career. A few days before the end of the season he had indicated his intention to retire. At his final home game Williams stepped up in the eighth inning against Jack Fisher of the Orioles. With the count 1-and-1, he drove the ball over the right-field fence for his 521st and last home run. He didn't look up, didn't smile, and didn't tip his cap.

When he was elected to the Baseball Hall of Fame in 1966 Williams surprised everyone by giving a memorable speech that contained a plea to include players from the Negro Leagues in the shrine. In 1969 he became manager of the Washington Senators, led them from the cellar to fourth place, and was named Manager of the Year. And on Ted Williams Day at Fenway Park in the summer of 1991, the Kid finally made peace with the fans and press of the city of Boston. He tipped his cap.

ROGERS HORNSBY 2B

Rogers Hornsby was nasty, rude, and mean. But he's not in the Hall of Fame for his disposition. His specialty was hitting, and there was no better righthanded batter in the history of the game. Standing straight up, deep in the batter's box, he would stride into the pitch to smash line drives all around the park with his perfectly level swing. In Les Bell's words, Hornsby "just didn't think anyone could get him out," and he was usually right.

Hornsby had the highest lifetime batting average (.358) and among the top three slugging percentages (.577) of any National Leaguer. His .424 batting average in 1924 was the NL's highest single-season mark of the 20th century. He led the senior circuit in slugging a record nine times, in on-base percentage eight times, and in batting seven times. He won two Triple Crowns, a feat duplicated only by Ted Williams, and only Babe Ruth ever had more total bases in a season than Hornsby's 450 in 1922.

Remarkably, Hornsby played second base, one of the least offense-oriented positions, and played it well, leading the league in putouts and assists twice each and double plays three times. His only weakness was pop flies hit over his head, because looking up could make him lose his balance.

Although scouting reports said Hornsby "couldn't hit a lick" as a minor league infielder, the Cardinals liked his glove and bought him from a Texas minor league team for $500. In 1915 he played in 18 games for St. Louis and batted only .246 as a "crouch and choke" hitter. Cardinals coach Bob Connery thought Hornsby could take advantage of his size and strength if he stood up straight. The next year he hit .313, and he would dip below .300 only once in the next 15 years.

From 1920 through 1925 Hornsby compiled the greatest six-year hitting streak in history. He averaged .397 over that span, including three seasons of topping .400, and set a league record with six consecutive batting titles. For good measure Hornsby added six consecutive slugging and on-base percentage titles as well. He led the league in homers twice, in runs scored three times, and in hits, doubles, and RBIs four times during that tear. In 1922 he walloped a then National League record 42 home runs; it remained a record for homers by a second baseman until broken by Davey Johnson in 1973. Combined with a .401 average and 152 RBIs, the package gave "the Rajah" the Triple Crown.

In 1924 Hornsby tacked on 43 doubles, 14 triples, and 25 home runs to go with his astronomical batting average. He hit .400 against five teams in the league; the Cubs managed to "hold" him to .387. Only two pitchers kept him hitless in more than two games. He played in 143 games, hit safely in 119 of them, and batted almost 50 points higher than the player who finished second that year. Amazingly, Hornsby was not chosen 1924 Most Valuable Player. He finished eight points behind Brooklyn's Dazzy Vance, who had won 28 games with a 2.16 ERA.

MVP or not, the Cardinals decided to make him their manager. With 115 games left in the 1925 season, they fired Branch Rickey and gave the job to Hornsby. The team was in last when he took over, and they climbed up to fourth, largely because manager Hornsby had player Hornsby to deliver a .403 average, 39 homers, 143 RBIs, and a second Triple Crown.

Although Hornsby "slumped" to .317 in 1926, the Cardinals won the pennant, and then beat the Yankees in the World Series, catching Babe Ruth on an attempted steal to give St. Louis its first championship. Years later Hornsby said his greatest thrill in baseball was "taking O'Farrell's throw, putting down the ball and letting that big monkey tag himself out, so we were world champions."

Hornsby and Cardinals owner Sam Breadon could not come to terms, however, on the slugging manager's contract for 1927. Breadon traded Hornsby to the New York Giants for Frank Frisch and Jimmy Ring. St. Louis fans didn't take well to the news. The mayor and the chamber of commerce filed official protests, and fans talked about a boycott of the team's games.

The trade began a bad time for Hornsby, who got into financial problems involving the thousand-plus shares of stock he owned in the Cardinals and legal problems when a gambling "partner" filed suit against him. It also began a period of migration. After single seasons with the Giants and Braves, the Cubs, smelling a chance for a pennant, made Hornsby the centerpiece of one of the largest deals ever up to that time. In November 1928 "the Rajah" went to Chicago for five players and $200,000. Hornsby had his last superlative season with the Cubs in 1929, and the North Siders won their first pennant in 11 years. As in 1926, however, Hornsby failed to shine in the postseason, hitting only .238 and striking out eight times as the Philadelphia Athletics won the World Series in five games.

Hornsby broke his ankle sliding during the 1930 season, and the injury greatly curtailed his playing time. Still bothered by the ankle, he played in only 100 games in 1931. The Cubs finished third, complaining all the while about Hornsby's draconian managing style. By the middle of the 1932 season he was gone, replaced by the easygoing Charlie Grimm, and the Cubs responded by winning the pennant by four games. The Cubs voted that Hornsby not receive one cent of World Series money.

By 1933 Hornsby's playing career was effectively over. He was fired after managing the Browns for a little more than three years, never finishing higher than sixth. Hornsby subsequently managed in the minors, briefly returned to manage the Browns and the Reds, and scouted and coached for the Cubs and the Mets. He was inducted into the Hall of Fame in 1942.

HONUS WAGNER SS

If a knowledgeable fan in 1910 had been asked to name baseball's all-time All-Star team, the shortstop would undoubtedly have been Honus Wagner. Ask any knowledgeable fan today the same question and their choice for shortstop would be the same. Every other player of Wagner's era has since been surpassed in overall excellence at his position. Only Wagner remains.

The reason for Wagner's longevity as baseball's most highly regarded shortstop is simple. No other shortstop has ever combined offensive and defensive excellence the way he did (although if Alex Rodriguez keeps it up for another decade, he may come close). Ungainly in appearance, Wagner was a superb fielder, with large, strong hands and a wicked arm. John McGraw once said, "The only way to get a ball past Honus is to hit it eight feet over his head."

Despite his legendary bowed legs, Wagner was extraordinarily fast on the basepaths, leading the National League in stolen bases five times. On three occasions he stole second, third, and home in a single inning. As a hitter, he ranks among the top 20 of all time in six different categories.

A genial and good-natured man, Wagner was adored wherever he went. The Pittsburgh Pirates, with whom he spent 18 of his 21 seasons, had days honoring him in 1902, 1903, 1908, and 1909. In his last season, 1917, these tributes were held all over the league. Once when a cigarette company put out baseball cards, Wagner sent back the check he had received and asked that the cards with his picture be destroyed. He didn't think encouraging children to smoke was a good idea. By doing so he inadvertently created the most valuable baseball card of all time, the T206 Honus Wagner—one of which sold at auction in 2000 for $1.2 million.

Breaking in with Louisville in 1897, Wagner was traded to the Pirates in 1900 in a blockbuster deal involving 18 players. (Louisville owner Barney Dreyfuss, aware that the National League was planning to drop his Colonels, traded his best players to Pittsburgh and subsequently bought the Pirates.) From that year through 1912 he led the National League in hitting seven times (with a high of .381, in 1900) and finished second once. Additionally, Wagner won six slugging titles and topped the competition in on-base percentage four times, RBIs five times, triples three times, doubles seven times (including four years in a row, from 1906–1909), and hits and runs twice each. In 1908 Wagner was only two home runs shy of a Triple Crown. *Total Baseball*'s Total Player Rating ranks him first every year from 1903 through 1909. Wagner's initial decade with Pittsburgh ranks with the performances of Rogers Hornsby and Babe Ruth during the 1920s as the greatest offensive 10-year spans in baseball history.

Wagner drove in six runs in the 1909 World Series against the Tigers of Ty Cobb, the first time that two batting champions faced each other in a Fall Classic. Wagner hit .333, Cobb .231, and the Pirates sent Detroit down to its third consecutive Series defeat. "The Flying Dutchman" played eight more years after 1909, although Pittsburgh never tasted a pennant again. He won his last batting title in 1911 and paced the senior circuit with 102 RBIs in 1912 at age 38, but his days of league leadership were over.

Wagner was the first player to have his name engraved on a Louisville Slugger bat, and the first player in the 20th century to accumulate 3,000 hits. He led the league in extra-base hits seven times, a major league record he shares with Ruth and Stan Musial. He ranks among the all-time top 15 in four categories: hits (sixth with 3,420), doubles (eighth with 643), stolen bases (10th with 723), and bats (13th with 10,439). Wagner is also in the top 20 in games played, total bases, runs batted in, and runs. His lifetime batting average of .328 is the highest ever tallied by a shortstop.

These achievements are all the more impressive, given the fearsome hurlers that Wagner faced. His lifetime average against Christy Mathewson was .324 in 327 at bats; against Kid Nichols it was .352 in 105 plate appearances. Against Cy Young, Wagner hit .343 in 70 at bats.

Baseball analyst Bill James states that Wagner "was the greatest athlete in baseball," and adds, "Acknowledging that there may have been one or two whose talents were greater, there is no one who has ever played the game that I would be more anxious to have on a baseball team." Such respected baseball people as John McGraw, Ed Barrow, Sam Crawford, Bill Klem, and Branch Rickey have seconded James' opinion.

Wagner was one of the first five men elected to the Hall of Fame in 1936, and one of the first three position players—along with Babe Ruth and Ty Cobb—to be immortalized. In 1955 the Pirates unveiled a huge bronze statue of the old shortstop in Schenley Park outside Forbes Field. In 1972 the statue was moved to Gate C at Three Rivers Stadium, and in 2001 it will grace the home plate entrance to the Pirates' new stadium, PNC Park. The words in the original statue dedication program summed up Wagner's character: "He played with the confidence born of exceptional natural talents and abilities and a consuming love of the game . . . Fighting heart and intense competitive spirit . . . and yet he maintained a sense of humor . . . a fine gentleman."

MIKE SCHMIDT 3B

Mike Schmidt was a great slugger, a record-setting fielder, a three-time National League Most Valuable Player, and the finest Philadelphia Phillie ever, according to a 1983 vote by Philadelphia fans. Schmidt hit 548 homers, placing him eighth all time. Only Babe Ruth, Harmon Killebrew, Jimmie Foxx, Mickey Mantle, and Mark McGwire scaled the 500-home run peak in fewer at bats.

Schmidt led the NL in home runs a record eight times; only Ruth led his league more often. He slugged 30 or more homers in a season 13 times, a figure surpassed only by Hank Aaron, and reached 35 homers 11 times, more often than anyone but Ruth. Schmidt and Ralph Kiner are the only players to homer in four consecutive at bats on two different occasions. The 18-year veteran of the Phillies hit 509 of his home runs as a third baseman, including 48 in 1980, both records for the position.

He was no slouch with the glove, either. Schmidt won 10 Gold Gloves, more than any third baseman except Brooks Robinson. His 2,212 games at the hot corner rank third all time, as do his number of assists; his 450 double plays at the position rank fourth.

Schmidt started slow—in 1973 he batted .196, the lowest average among major league regulars, and struck out 136 times in 367 at bats. But he found a swing while playing winter ball in Puerto Rico, and the improvement was dramatic. Schmidt led the NL with 36 homers in 1974, his first of three straight home run titles. He also enjoyed the first of nine 100-RBI seasons and won his first of five league slugging titles. Among his hits that season was perhaps the longest single ever, a drive off a speaker suspended from the roof of the Astrodome. He drew 106 bases on balls for the first of his seven 100-walk seasons, stole 23 bases, and received his first of 12 All-Star selections.

One of Schmidt's greatest days took place on April 17, 1976, at Wrigley Field, when he became the 10th major leaguer to hit four home runs in four consecutive at bats. The Phillies erased a 13–2 deficit and won, 18–16, on his 10th-inning homer. Schmidt finished the contest with eight RBIs and 17 total bases, one shy of the major league record. He went on to tie Willie Stargell's record with 11 home runs in April and won his third straight home run title.

Beginning in 1976 the Phillies won three straight NL East crowns but lost the National League Championship Series each time. Schmidt, who made some key errors and had a few dry spells at the plate, received much of the blame from Philadelphia fans, who have been known to boo Santa Claus as well as the best third baseman ever.

During the 1978 season Schmidt made a key change at the plate. Always a selective hitter, he started looking for pitches he could drive to any field instead of trying to pull every pitch. It paid off in 1979 when Schmidt hit 45 home runs, including four in a row over two games in July, and led the league with 120 walks. In 1980 he won the home run crown with 48 and the RBI title with 121, the first of four times in seven seasons that he would dominate both categories in the same season. He batted .286 and, at age 31, won his first MVP Award. It was also his final year playing with Greg Luzinski, with whom he combined for 503 home runs in nine years—the sixth-best home run total by two teammates in league history up to that point.

In 1980 the Phillies finally won the pennant, outlasting the Astros in four extra-inning games in the NLCS. In the World Series against Kansas City, Schmidt's double sparked a Phillies comeback in the eighth inning of Game 2. In Game 5 his two-run homer put Philadelphia on the board, and his single in the ninth ignited the rally that won the game. In Game 6 Schmidt singled in the Phillies' first two runs in the third inning. The Phils went on to win, 4–1, for the first world title in franchise history. Schmidt batted .381, scored six times, knocked in seven runs, and won Series MVP honors.

In the strike-shortened 1981 season Schmidt led the majors with 31 homers and 91 RBIs in 102 games. He batted a career-high .316, led the league in both slugging and on-base percentage, and won his second straight

MVP. In 1983 he topped the NL with 40 homers and also had the league's best on-base percentage for the third straight year. The Phillies' "Wheeze Kids" won the NL East that season and met the Dodgers in the playoffs. Schmidt's homer off Jerry Reuss was the only run of Game 1; he went on to bat .467 as the team advanced to the World Series against Baltimore. In the Series, however, he was a ghastly 1-for-20 with six strikeouts as the Orioles defeated the Phillies in five games.

Moved to first base in 1985, Schmidt returned to the hot corner in 1986, his third MVP season, when he again won the home run and RBI titles. He also won the slugging title, his 10th Gold Glove, and led league third basemen in fielding percentage for the only time in his career.

Schmidt suffered a torn right rotator cuff in 1987. He missed more than 50 games and broke his string of nine consecutive seasons with 30 or more homers. He tried to come back for the 1988 season at age 39, but retired on May 29 in a tearful ceremony. On January 10, 1995, Schmidt was voted into the Baseball Hall of Fame, becoming the 26th player to win election on his first ballot.

CY YOUNG P

How many Cy Youngs would Cy Young have won if the eponymous award had existed when he pitched? Various historians and statisticians have given estimates of three to six, but such assertions are based solely on numbers and ignore the human factor. Because Young was well liked, he might have been voted the award a couple of times even when he wasn't statistically the best pitcher in his league.

Young is significant not only because of how many seasons he was the best pitcher in his league, but also because of his consistency over a long career. While other pitchers came and went, Young turned in one very good year after another. He won 30 or more games five times, 25 or more 12 times, and 20 or more 15 times. His lifetime total of 511 victories remains, it seems reasonable to say, an unassailable record.

When Young first arrived in the major leagues John Clarkson, Tim Keefe, and Charley "Old Hoss" Radbourn were still star pitchers. When he retired, Walter Johnson and Christy Mathewson were well into their careers. Amos Rusie and Kid Nichols were among Young's contemporaries, yet Young was still pitching years after they retired. By the time he called it quits after 22 seasons Young had compiled a matchless record, and for this reason his name is on the modern award signifying pitching excellence.

Born on an Ohio farm in 1867, the husky Young always credited his durability to the chores he did as a youth. He picked up the nickname "Cy" early in his career. Some insist it was short for "Cyclone," because of the speed of his pitches. A more common suggestion is that "Cy" was a common name for a rube.

Young broke in with the National League's Cleveland Spiders in 1890, going 9–7 for the seventh-place team. The next season he won 27 and lost 22, the first of three times he'd register 20 losses. Young was still a bit wild, but in the next decade his control improved steadily, to the point where he became one of baseball's premiere "control artists," walking only slightly more than one batter per game. According to historian Lee Allen, "There have been faster pitchers . . . but his control was so unerring and he was so tireless that he just kept throwing as if he were systematically chopping down a tree."

The American Association folded after the 1891 campaign, and the National League, hoping to create a postseason moneymaker, divided the 1892 season into two halves, with the winner of the first half meeting the second-half winner in a so-called "World Series." Boston won the opening half, and Cleveland took the second part of the season behind Young. He finished 36–11, leading the league with a .766 winning percentage, nine shutouts, and an ERA of 1.93. Young opened the postseason by pitching an 11-inning scoreless tie against Boston's Jack Stivetts, but Boston won the next five games to take the Series.

In 1895 the Spiders and Orioles faced off in "the Temple Cup Series," another postseason championship. The Orioles didn't take the contest seriously and lost to the Spiders in five games. Young, a 35-game winner in the regular season, won three of the five postseason games.

On September 18, 1897, Young pitched a 6–0 no-hitter against Cincinnati. The Cleveland franchise was in trouble, however, and the burly righthander was sold to St. Louis in 1899. Young hated the town, and he also hated the NL's salary cap. When Ban Johnson offered him $3,000 to pitch for Boston in the new American League, Young jumped. His first three years in Boston were three of his very best. Young led the new league in victories all three seasons while compiling a 93–30 mark.

By the time Boston won the pennant in 1903, relations with the National League had improved to the point that a real World Series was staged between Boston and Pittsburgh. In the best-of-nine affair Young lost the opening game, then pitched seven innings of relief in another Boston loss in Game 3. He came back to beat Pittsburgh, 11–2 and 7–3, in Games 5 and 7, as Boston took the Series in eight games.

Young helped pitch Boston to another pennant in 1904, but the New York Giants refused to play the Pilgrims in a World Series. Young's 26 wins included a league-leading 10 shutouts. In one early-season stretch he threw 44 consecutive scoreless innings. During the streak, on May 5 against Philadelphia, he tossed a 3–0 perfect game.

When Boston slipped to fourth place the following year, Young suffered the first losing season of his career. Still, he completed 32 of 33 starts, lowered his ERA to 1.82, and struck out a personal-best 208 batters. In 1906, however, Young's record dropped to 13–21, and his ERA ballooned to 3.19.

The 39-year-old Young bounced back in 1907, winning 22 games with a 1.99 ERA for the seventh-place Red Sox. On June 30, 1908, at age 41, he pitched his third no-hitter, an 8–0 win over New York, and went on to compile his last 20-win season. On August 13 the *Boston Post* sponsored Cy Young Day. A crowd of 20,000 jammed the Huntington Avenue Grounds, and a grateful Young received a silver cup from the players, floral tributes, and $6,000.

Sold to Cleveland for $12,500 in 1909, Young went 19–15. He retired following the 1911 season, and in 1937 he was the third pitcher named to the Hall of Fame, after Walter Johnson and Christy Mathewson. Young died in 1955. The next year the award bearing his name was given for the first time.

In addition to his victory totals, Young lost 316 games—another mark that appears to be unreachable. Young also leads the pack in games started, complete games, and innings pitched. His 76 shutouts are fourth all time, and he tops all pitchers in wins above team (99.7) and wins above league (490.5).

MICKEY MANTLE OF

Mickey Mantle's awesome power and speed made him a rightful heir to the legacy of Babe Ruth, Lou Gehrig, and Joe DiMaggio. By the time he retired in 1968, after 18 big league seasons with the New York Yankees, Mantle ranked among the all-time leaders in home runs and home run percentage, had played in 12 World Series, and had won three Most Valuable Player awards, two of them back-to-back. Yet Mantle was hampered by injuries, and played in pain for most of his career. One can only speculate what his numbers would have been had he stayed healthy.

Named after legendary catcher Gordon "Mickey" Cochrane, Mantle was signed out of high school by Yankees scout Tom Greenwade. The scout later admitted, "The first time I saw Mantle I knew how Paul Krichell felt when he first saw Lou Gehrig. He knew that as a scout he'd never have another moment like it."

Mantle joined the Yankees in 1951 and, after a short slump and a return to the minors for seasoning, was back with the team for good in 1952. He hit .311 that year, starting in center field and scoring 105 runs—the first of nine consecutive seasons in which he topped the 100 mark. He led the American League in runs for six of those seasons, with highs of 132 in 1956 and 1961. Mantle also paced the circuit in bases on balls five times, in home runs and slugging average four times each, in on-base percentage three times, and in triples once. In 1956, his greatest season, he won the Triple Crown with a .353 batting average, 52 homers, and 130 RBIs. He belted three more home runs in the World Series, won the AL MVP, and was named Major League Player of the Year by *The Sporting News*.

Mantle specialized in monster home runs. One of his most famous was a 565-foot blast (according to the measurement of a Yankees publicity man) at Washington's Griffith Stadium in 1953. On May 15, 1955, Mantle hit three homers into the distant Yankee Stadium bleachers. Each cleared the 461-foot sign. On May 23, 1963, he struck the park's right field facade. It was estimated that—had it kept sailing—the ball would have traveled 602 feet.

Many of Mantle's pokes were scored as outs in Yankee Stadium's appropriately named "Death Valley," the deep left-center field portion of the park. Mantle hit 266 homers at home, four fewer than he blasted on the road. He slammed four consecutive home runs from July 4 to July 6, 1962.

In 1961 Mantle and teammate Roger Maris were both in pursuit of Babe Ruth's 60-home run single-season record. In September, Mantle developed a cold he couldn't shake, and soon after contracted an infection from a doctor's shot. In the end he played eight fewer games and had 76 fewer at bats than Maris, who eclipsed Ruth's record by a single homer. Nonetheless, Mantle wound up with a career-best 54 homers to go with 128 RBIs.

By the mid-1960s, however, it was apparent that Mantle's best days were over. His damaged shoulder caused him great pain, and he had difficulty throwing and even batting from the left side. He played first base the final two years of his career, retiring before the 1969 season.

Over the course of Mantle's career, his Yankees won 12 pennants and eight World Series. The Mick's bat was the Yanks' biggest, and it pounded opposing pitchers during the postseason. Entering 2000, Mantle still held the World Series records for home runs (18), RBIs (40), runs (42), and total bases (23). His 59 hits in the Fall Classic are second highest total ever amassed, trailing only his great teammate Yogi Berra.

Mantle's 536 home runs place ninth all time and are the most ever by a switch hitter. In every American League ballpark he appeared in, he hit home runs of at least 450 feet from both the left and right sides of the plate. He switch-hit homers in one game a record 10 times. Mantle was elected to the Hall of Fame in 1974, his first year of eligibility. He died of cancer on August 13, 1995, at the age of 63.

RICKEY HENDERSON OF

To assert that Rickey Henderson is the greatest leadoff hitter of all time is akin to asserting that the sky is blue, or that fire is hot; it seems to be self-evident, an objective reality that renders irrelevant any debate. Throughout his 22-year major league career, Henderson has consistently set the table with walks and hits, has advanced with stolen bases more often than anyone who has ever played the game, and has scored runs in numbers that border on the astronomical. By the end of the 2000 season, Henderson had scored 2,178 times, passing Babe Ruth and Hank Aaron and entrenching himself in second place behind Ty Cobb. He had also overtaken Ted Williams to assume second place in walks, with 2,060 to the Babe's 2,062.

Henderson stole 100 bases in his first full year in the American League, in 1980. He broke Lou Brock's single season stolen base record with 130 thefts in his third full year, and he snapped Brock's career stolen base mark in his 13th season in the major leagues. Henderson was the first player to achieve 1,000 steals; at the beginning of the 2001 season, the active player closest to his career total of 1,370 stolen bases was Barry Bonds, with 471. He's also the only American Leaguer to steal more than 100 bases in three seasons.

Henderson has played in 10 All-Star Games—six with the Oakland Athletics and four with the New York Yankees—and has seen action eight times in the postseason, most notably in his second tour of duty with the A's in 1989. In that year's American League Championship Series against the Blue Jays, Henderson hit .400, scored eight runs, stole eight bases, drew seven walks, and clubbed two homers in Oakland's five-game triumph. He was equally spectacular in the World Series against the cross-bay Giants, leading the A's to a sweep with a .474 average, nine hits, and three steals. Henderson led off the deciding Game 4 with a home run, one of his four extra base hits in the four-game Series.

The emergence of Henderson transformed the A's into one of the AL's top running clubs. Oakland won just 54 games in his rookie year; two years later the team played the Yankees in the ALCS. By 1985 Henderson was a Yankee, but he was never a fan favorite in the Bronx, where he feuded with manager Lou Piniella over the severity of his injuries. Despite the equivalent of four healthy seasons with the Yankees—averaging 149 games, 82 stolen bases, and 128 runs during his tenure—the insinuation was that Henderson was responsible for the Yankees not winning. In 1988 Henderson hit .305 and set a team record by stealing 93 bases; New York missed the AL East title by two games.

Back with Oakland in 1990, Henderson was named the AL's Most Valuable Player, hitting .325, scoring 119 runs (his fifth league-leading total), and pacing the junior circuit in stolen bases for a record 10th time. He was acquired by the Toronto Blue Jays for their pennant drive in 1993 and played for another World Series winner, although this time he didn't sparkle in postseason play. Henderson returned to Oakland in 1994, and two years later made his National League debut with San Diego. Although his batting average was slipping, Henderson, batting in his crouched style with his left leg extended straight out, continued to draw walks and steal bases. Back with the A's at age 39 in 1998, he led the AL in both categories.

Henderson signed with the Mets just shy of his 40th birthday in 1999. He batted .315 and was instrumental in New York's first postseason appearance in 12 years. While his antics—snatch catches, talking to fans during games, and going into home run trots on balls that hit the wall—aggravated some, he was still one of the game's clutch performers. He batted .400 and stole six bases in the Mets' four-game victory over Arizona in the Division Series. Mets manager Bobby Valentine summed up Henderson's season and career: "Every time someone thought we have seen it all, he turns it up and gives us more."

With Seattle in 2000, Henderson again appeared in postseason play, batting a combined .286 against the White Sox and the Yankees and scoring five times. The man with the most leadoff home runs in baseball history finished the year just 86 hits shy of 3,000, and 68 runs behind Ty Cobb's all-time mark.

EDDIE COLLINS 2B

A member of four world championship teams, Eddie "Cocky" Collins had an impressive .333 lifetime average and batted .300 or better every year from 1909 through 1916 and from 1919 through 1928. Had his contemporary Ty Cobb not been so dominant, Collins might have enjoyed even greater recognition. As it was, Collins hit .372, .365, and .360 without ever winning a batting title. He did lead the league in stolen bases four times (with a high of 81 in 1910), winding up with 744 career steals, seventh all-time.

Given his speed and his ability to draw walks, Collins was an ideal leadoff or number-two hitter. He led the American League with 119 bases on balls in 1915; over the course of his tenure in the majors he drew five walks for every time he struck out. For much of his career, however, Collins batted third, where his lack of power limited his runs batted in.

Defensively, Collins played more games (2,826) and had more putouts (6,526), assists (7,630), and total chances (14,591) than any other second baseman. He won eight fielding titles, and with the exception of 1918, when he missed 57 games because of injuries, he led the league in one fielding category or another from 1909 through 1922. He is usually named, along with Nap Lajoie and Rogers Hornsby, as one of the three finest second basemen of all time. Connie Mack, who managed both Collins and Lajoie and managed against Hornsby, ranked Eddie as the best.

In 1906 Collins debuted professionally under the alias "Edward T. Sullivan" and played until it was revealed that he was Columbia University's junior quarterback and infielder. He was allowed to continue for Columbia as nonplaying captain and joined the Philadelphia A's after graduation. Collins quickly became the anchor of the A's infield. When shortstop Jack Barry, third baseman Frank "Home Run" Baker, and first baseman John "Stuffy" McInnis joined the Athletics in 1909, together with Collins they became known as the "$100,000 infield." The A's proceeded to win four pennants in the next six years. For three of those years, 1912 through 1914, Collins led the AL in runs scored.

Collins was sold to the White Sox in 1915 the year after winning the Chalmers Award as the American League's Most Valuable Player. He hit .409 in the 1917 World Series and scored the deciding run by slipping out of a rundown between third and home to beat the Giants' pursuing third baseman, Heinie Zimmerman, to the plate.

Reportedly, Collins was the highest-paid player on the White Sox, and jealousy over his salary may have contributed to the decision by some Chicago players to take bribes from gamblers to throw the 1919 World Series. Dispirited by the play of his "Black Sox" teammates, Collins batted only .226 against the Reds; he did steal one base, which gave him 14 career World Series thefts.

In 1925 Collins became a manager, piloting the White Sox for two seasons before returning to the Athletics. In limited action, he batted .336 and led the league with 12 pinch hits in 34 pinch-hitting at bats. Elected to the Hall of Fame in 1939, Collins served as a Boston Red Sox executive from 1932 until his death in 1951.

STAN MUSIAL OF-1B

Although statistically Stan Musial is the equal of both Joe DiMaggio and Ted Williams, he lacked the Yankee Clipper's grace, the Kid's intense personality, and the media presence of both. As a result, Musial has suffered in comparison. There is no question, however, that he was one of the greatest players of his generation.

Musial's odd batting stance served him well in his 22 major league campaigns, all of them with the St. Louis Cardinals. He appeared in 24 All-Star Games, and retired at the end of the 1963 season as the major league leader in total bases and the National League leader in hits, games played, and runs (all of his marks have since been surpassed). Musial finished with a .331 lifetime batting average, 475 home runs, and 1,951 RBIs.

Dubbed "Stan the Man" by Brooklyn Dodgers fans, Musial was murder on NL pitchers. He won seven batting crowns, and led the league six times in hits, on-base percentage, and slugging average. One of only four players to amass more than 700 doubles in his career, Musial bested everyone in the NL eight times in this category. On six occasions he racked up more than 80 extra base hits.

On July 24, 1949, Musial hit for the cycle, and on May 2, 1954, against the New York Giants in St. Louis, he hit a major league-record five home runs in a doubleheader, the last against knuckleballer Hoyt Wilhelm. He slugged 20 home runs in the first 50 games of the '54 season before tailing off to finish with 35. In 1955 his 12th-inning home run in the All-Star Game gave the National League a 6–5 victory.

Musial was born in Donora, Pennsylvania, a hardscrabble mill town 28 miles east of Pittsburgh that also gave birth to Ken Griffey and Ken Griffey, Jr. He signed with St. Louis in 1937, and split his time between the outfield and the pitcher's mound in the minors. Nearly released by the Cardinals after he suffered a shoulder injury in 1940, Musial proved himself a hitter to be reckoned with at Class C Springfield and Triple-A Rochester, and was up with the Cards for good at the end of 1941.

In 1942, as the Cardinals' regular left fielder, Musial hit .315 and helped the team win 43 of its last 52 games to claim the pennant by two games over Brooklyn. Although he hit only .222 in the World Series, he made several fine plays in the field as the surprising Cards dumped the New York Yankees in five games.

St. Louis repeated as NL champs by 18 games in 1943, paced by Musial's league-best .357 batting average, 48 doubles, and 20 triples. This time the Yankees prevailed in a five-game World Series, as Musial hit .278. The Cards captured the flag again in 1944 and beat the crosstown Browns in the first and only all–St. Louis Series. Musial was named NL Most Valuable Player that year, and led all players in the World Series with seven hits.

After losing the 1945 season to military service, Musial returned to propel the Cards to their fourth pennant in five years in 1946. He won his second MVP Award, leading the senior circuit in batting (.365), runs, hits, doubles, triples, and slugging. During one three-game stretch he registered 12 hits. In midseason he replaced a slumping Dick Sisler and accepted a transfer to first base.

The Cardinals faced the Red Sox in the 1946 World Series. Although the press salivated over the showdown between Musial and the Red Sox's Ted Williams, arguably the two best hitters in the game, both disappointed. Williams, hampered by a sore elbow, hit only .200, and Musial was only marginally better, batting .222 in St. Louis' seven-game win. The Series was the last for both players.

Like Williams, Musial played much of the next two decades for teams that fell short in the pennant race. Despite this, his individual numbers got even better. From 1946 through 1955 Musial missed only 17 games. He developed into a longball threat, hitting a career-best 39 home runs in 1948, when he won his third and last MVP Award. His .373 batting average that season was 43 points better than his closest competitor, and he also topped the league with a career-high 131 RBIs.

On May 13, 1958, Musial doubled off Chicago right-hander Moe Drabowsky for his 3,000th career hit. But in 1959 when Musial slumped to only .255, many followers thought it was time for him to retire. He played on, refusing to accept part-time duty, and in 1962, at age 41, he hit .330 in 433 at bats, his best performance since 1954 and the third-highest average for a player over age 40. During the 1962 season Musial also tied a league record for most home runs in consecutive at bats with four.

Post-retirement, Musial opened a successful restaurant in St. Louis and worked for the Cardinals in the front office. His uniform number 6 was retired by the St. Louis organization. He was elected to the Hall of Fame in 1969, and in 1998 the Society for American Baseball Research (SABR) bestowed on Musial its fourth Hero of Baseball Award.

LOU GEHRIG 1B

His accomplishments on the field made him an authentic American hero, but Lou Gehrig's tragic early death made him a legend. He emerged from the shadow of Babe Ruth to become a superstar of the first magnitude, the "Iron Horse" who played in 2,130 consecutive games. Sportswriter Jim Murray once described him as "Gibraltar in cleats."

Gehrig's numbers are almost too impressive to believe. His lifetime batting average was .340, and he amassed more than 400 total bases on five occasions. Only 15 men have achieved that level in a season; Chuck Klein is the only other player to do it as many as three times. Gehrig is also one of only two players with more than 100 extra-base hits in more than one season.

In his 13 full seasons, Gehrig *averaged* 147 RBIs. His totals of 184 RBIs in 1931, 175 in 1927, and 174 in 1930 are three of the top six single-season marks of all time. More remarkable still, Gehrig accomplished all this, as historian Bill Curran pointed out, "while batting immediately behind two of history's greatest base-cleaners, Ruth and DiMaggio." Entering 2001, he still holds the record for career grand slams at 23. In 34 World Series games he batted .361 with 10 homers, eight doubles, and 35 RBIs.

The son of German immigrants, Gehrig was signed out of Columbia University by Yankees scout Paul Krichell in 1923. After a full season at Hartford, where he hit .369, he became a Yankee for good in 1925. On May 31 of that year he pinch-hit for Pee Wee Wanninger. The next day, Wally Pipp, New York's regular first baseman, took the day off with a headache. Gehrig's streak of consecutive games played began that afternoon and wouldn't end until 1939. It didn't come easily; he played every game for more than 13 years despite a broken thumb, a broken toe, and back spasms. Late in his career his hands were x-rayed, and doctors were able to spot 17 different fractures that had "healed" while Gehrig continued to play. The record stood for 56 years until broken by Cal Ripken Jr. in 1995.

After batting .295 in 1925, Gehrig erupted in 1926. He hit .313—the first of 12 consecutive years he would top .300—drove in 112 runs, and led the league with 20 triples. The Yanks won the pennant; Gehrig hit .348 in the World Series, but the Yankees lost to Rogers Hornsby's Cardinals in seven games.

Ruth and Gehrig began dominating the baseball headlines in 1927 in a way two players had never done before. That year Ruth hit 60 homers, breaking his old record of 59, and Gehrig clouted 47, more than anyone other than Ruth had ever hit. As late as August 10 Gehrig had more homers than the Babe, but Ruth's closing kick was spectacular. Together they outhomered every team in baseball except for the New York Giants. But homers were not

Gehrig's only contributions. He hit .373 and led the league with 52 doubles and 175 RBIs. He was named the American League's Most Valuable Player.

In 1928 Gehrig hit .374, again led the league with 47 doubles, and tied Ruth for the most RBIs with 142. In the World Series, despite being walked six times, he hit .545 and slugged a stunning 1.727.

By Gehrig's standard, 1929 was an off year. But he still finished second in the league in home runs, third in runs, and fourth in RBIs. He "bounced back" to bat .379 and top the AL with 174 RBIs in 1930. The following season he led the league in hits, runs, and RBIs, and tied Ruth for the lead with 46 home runs.

On June 3, 1932, Gehrig became the first American Leaguer to hit four home runs in a game. After his third homer to right field against Philadelphia, an upset Connie Mack removed pitcher George Earnshaw and demanded that Earnshaw stay with him to watch reliever Roy Mahaffey pitch to Gehrig. Gehrig's fourth homer was to left field, and only a great catch by Al Simmons kept him from hitting his fifth.

Ruth's dominance as a power hitter was slipping, and "Larrupin' Lou" was taking his place. Gehrig won the Triple Crown in 1934 with 49 home runs, 165 RBIs, and a .363 batting average. He came close to repeating two years later, when he topped the junior circuit in homers, runs, slugging average, and on-base percentage, while batting .354. He was named MVP for the second time after the Yankees regained the World Series title. For the next two years the tandem of DiMaggio and Gehrig dominated the AL the way Ruth and Gehrig had, with the Yankees in the midst of a four-season dynasty that included winning four straight World Series.

In 1938 Gehrig's batting average fell below .300 for the first time since 1925, and it was clear that something was wrong. He lacked his usual strength, and pitches he would have murdered were only flyouts. After a feeble start in 1939, Gehrig, the Yankees captain, presented the lineup card to the umpires for the ninth game of the season, but his own name wasn't penciled in. The game announcer stated, "Ladies and gentlemen, Lou Gehrig's consecutive streak of 2,130 games played has ended." Shortly thereafter, he was diagnosed as having a very rare degenerative disease: amyotrophic lateral sclerosis. He would never play baseball again.

New York honored Gehrig with a day on July 4, 1939. More than 62,000 attended, and Gehrig's teary words of thanks have become a part of baseball lore. The Hall of Fame inducted him that December. He died in 1941 at age 38, almost 16 years to the day after he had replaced Wally Pipp at first base for the Yanks.

FRANK ROBINSON OF

Few ballplayers have had as much impact on the game as Frank Robinson. He was the first and, through 2000, the only player to win the Most Valuable Player Award in both leagues—with the Cincinnati Reds in 1961, and with the Baltimore Orioles in 1966. In 1975 he brought the same fire and intensity he displayed on the field to his job as the first African-American manager in the major leagues.

Robinson collected 586 career home runs, clearing the fences in 33 different ballparks. But he was far more than just a slugger, finishing his career as a .294 hitter with 204 stolen bases in 281 attempts. Robinson also ranks third lifetime in most times hit by a pitch, with 204, a testimony to his aggressive style. Earl Weaver, who managed Robinson and the Orioles to three consecutive pennants from 1969 to 1971, marveled that the outfielder's batting stance in effect "dared pitchers to hit him."

Although Robinson played for five teams during his 21-year career, his main achievements came with the Reds from 1956 through 1965 and with the Orioles from 1966 through 1972. He won the Reds' left field job in spring training of 1956, and his great season earned him National League Rookie of the Year honors. Robinson's 38 home runs tied Wally Berger's NL rookie record, and he led the league with 122 runs scored.

In 1957 Robinson batted .322 and was the one of seven Reds voted to the All-Star Game through a ballot-stuffing effort by the club and its fans. He remained in the starting lineup even after angry Commissioner Ford Frick removed two of his Cincinnati teammates. It was the first of 11 All-Star Game appearances for Robinson as a player.

An arm injury in 1958 caused Robinson's batting average to drop to .269, but he still won a Gold Glove. He rebounded with another solid season in 1959, posting 36 home runs, 125 RBIs, and a .311 batting average. In 1960 he led the league with a .595 slugging average, the first of three consecutive slugging titles.

In 1961 Robinson was voted league MVP as the Reds won their first pennant since 1940. He stole 22 bases in 25 attempts that season to lead the league in stolen base efficiency. In 1962 Robinson put up even better numbers, with 39 homers, 136 RBIs, and a .342 average. He topped the NL in runs (134) and doubles (51), and missed winning the batting crown and total bases title when the Dodgers' Tommy Davis and the Giants' Willie Mays extended their respective numbers in a three-game postseason playoff.

At the end of the 1965 season Cincinnati traded Robinson to the Orioles. Refuting the charge that he was "an old 30," Robinson enjoyed a great second act in Baltimore, sparking the Orioles to four pennants and two World Series titles in the next six years.

In Robinson's first season in Baltimore he led the O's to the American League flag and a World Series sweep of the Dodgers. He won the Triple Crown with 49 home runs, 122 RBIs, and a .316 average, and was named 1966 American League MVP. In early May he also became the first player ever to hit a home run out of Baltimore's Memorial Stadium, connecting off Indians righthander Luis Tiant. Robinson's drive measured 451 feet on the fly and rolled to a stop 540 feet from home plate.

In 1969 the Orioles began a run of three straight pennants, with Robinson belting 32 homers, driving in 100 runs, and hitting .308. But despite his successes in the regular season, Robinson had his share of postseason woes. In three AL Championship Series he hit only .206 with two homers and five RBIs. In five World Series he hit .250 with eight home runs and 14 RBIs. But he had a knack for making his hits count. In the 1966 Series sweep of the Dodgers he hit two home runs off Don Drysdale, one of which was the only run scored in the Game 4 clincher. In the bottom of the ninth of Game 6 of the 1971 World Series, Robinson forced a Game 7 by scoring the winning run from third base on a short fly to the Pittsburgh outfield. The Orioles, however, lost the next day.

Robinson was traded to the Dodgers for the 1972 season. Following the trade, the Orioles retired his No. 20, making him the first Baltimore player so honored. He returned to the AL in 1973 with the California Angels, collecting 30 home runs and 97 RBIs. Sent to Cleveland in 1974, he hit only .200 in 15 games, but was named the Indians' player-manager for the following season. On Opening Day 1975 Robinson became the first African-American to manage in the major leagues. He also hit a home run in his first at bat to help register his first managerial victory.

In 1976 Robinson led the Indians to an 81–78 record, only their third winning season since 1959. But after a slow start in 1977, he became the first African-American manager to be fired. He later logged four years at the helm of the Giants, and resurfaced as manager of the Orioles after the Birds opened the 1988 season by going 0–6. Baltimore went on to lose 21 consecutive games, a major league record for dismal starts. The Orioles rebounded with a strong second-place finish in 1989, and Robinson was rewarded with the AL Manager of the Year Award. He eventually became assistant general manager in the Orioles front office.

Over time the fiery Robinson did mellow somewhat, but he remained an outspoken advocate of equal opportunity for African-Americans in baseball. In 1982, his first year of eligibility, he was voted into the Baseball Hall of Fame.

GROVER CLEVELAND ALEXANDER P

When he retired in 1930, Grover Cleveland Alexander was tied with Christy Mathewson for the most wins in National League history, with 373. Along with Mathewson, who pitched for better teams and in a much less hitter-friendly ballpark, he was the only NL pitcher of the 20th century to string together three consecutive 30-win seasons. "Old Pete," as he was known, threw 90 career shutouts, second only to Walter Johnson, and had a lifetime ERA of 2.56.

The Philadelphia Phillies bought Alexander from the Syracuse Stars of the Class B New York State League in 1910. The next year, in his first full major league season, Alexander broke in like few rookies before or since. He paced the league with 28 wins, 31 complete games, seven shutouts, and 367 innings pitched, while finishing second in strikeouts and fourth in ERA. Four of his shutouts were in succession, including a 12-inning, one-hit, 1–0 victory against Cy Young. Alexander's 28 wins remain the modern rookie record.

He was just getting started. From 1915 to 1917 Alexander enjoyed seasons as good as any ever posted, winning 31, 33, and 30 games, with ERAs of 1.22, 1.55, and 1.83, respectively. He became the only player ever to win the pitching Triple Crown—wins, ERA, and strikeouts—three years running. No pitcher since has equaled or exceeded the 38 complete games Alexander recorded in 1916; nor has anyone since surpassed his 33 victories that season. And only Bob Gibson in 1968 has since bettered Alexander's 1.22 ERA of 1915.

In 1915 Alexander led the Phils to their first pennant of the modern era. He threw four one-hitters that year, another record, all the while pitching in the tiny Baker Bowl, with its seemingly minuscule distance between first base and the right-field wall. As if to cap his awesome three-year display, Alexander won a September 1917 Labor Day doubleheader at Ebbets Field, defeating Brooklyn, 5–0 and 7–3.

His heroics on the mound, however, were offset by serious problems. Alexander spent most of the 1918 season in France, where he suffered shell shock as a sergeant in the artillery. He returned home with a partial loss of hearing, and his epilepsy, which may have originated with a beaning he sustained in the minors, became worse. Drinking was another problem, and it was even more severe after Armistice Day.

Nonetheless, Alexander was a more than reasonably effective hurler for his new team, the Chicago Cubs. Twice he won more than 20 games for Chicago, and in 1920 he achieved another Triple Crown, going 27–14 with a 1.91 ERA and 173 strikeouts. But the Cubs, tired of his bouts with the bottle and his perceived insubordination, sold Alexander to the Cardinals for the $4,000 waiver price during the 1926 season.

In St. Louis the 39-year-old Alexander proved he still had some pitching in him. His most dramatic moment came not long after the trade, in the seventh game of the 1926 World Series. He had already pitched complete game victories in Games 2 and 6. In Game 7 at Yankee Stadium, with the score 3–2 in favor of the Cards, Alexander was summoned from the bullpen to replace Jesse Haines. With the bases loaded and two men out, the shaky pitcher, still feeling the effects of a hangover, struck out Tony Lazzeri. Alexander made the score stand the next two innings and the Cardinals had their first world championship.

At age 40 in 1927, Alexander won 21 games for the Cardinals, but he continued to drink heavily and the club released him at the end of a mediocre 1929 season. He pitched a few games for the Phillies, had a brief stint in the Texas League, and then hooked up with the House of David, pitching for the barnstorming team until he was 51 years old. Debilitated by even worse bouts of alcoholism and epilepsy, his 1938 induction into Baseball's Hall of Fame brought him little solace.

CHRISTY MATHEWSON P

In a sport dominated by ruffians, Christy Mathewson exuded a sense of nobility. Not only was he a great pitcher—the co-holder of the National League record for career victories, with 373, and the league record-holder for most victories in a season, with 37—but he was a gentleman as well, a man of moral convictions who inspired an entire generation of fans.

Mathewson won 30 or more games in a season on four separate occasions. For 12 consecutive years he captured a minimum of 22 victories. In the 1905 World Series against the Philadelphia Athletics he pitched three complete-game shutouts. In 1908 he walked an average of less than one player per game. From June 13 through July 18, 1913, he pitched 68 consecutive innings without surrendering a single base on balls. His .665 lifetime winning percentage is the eighth highest ever notched, and his 2.13 career ERA is bested by only four pitchers.

A graduate of Bucknell College, Mathewson broke in with the New York Giants in 1900. He was ineffective as a rookie, but he began to experiment with a new pitch, the "fadeaway," which was basically a screwball. The freak delivery, in which the ball was thrown with the same motion that Mathewson threw his curve, only to drop and dart away as he turned his hand over and snapped his wrist, would baffle hitters for 14 years.

New York almost lost the big righthander to Cincinnati after his rookie season, when he returned to the Virginia League and was drafted by the Reds from the Norfolk roster. But the Giants had second thoughts, and traded Amos Rusie for Mathewson on December 15, 1900. Rusie, a fireballer who had already accumulated 245 big league victories, would not win another game. The deal was one of baseball's greatest steals.

Armed with his fadeaway, fastball, and curve, and possessed of preternatural control, Mathewson became the senior circuit's dominant pitcher in the early years of the 20th century. He led the league five times in strikeouts and ERA, and four times in victories and shutouts. He blanked his opponents on 79 occasions, a total surpassed only by Grover Cleveland Alexander and Walter Johnson. In 1908, Mathewson's greatest season, 11 of his 37 wins were shutouts; he also paced the NL with 34 complete games, 259 strikeouts, and five saves. Between 1905 and 1913, he pitched the Giants to five pennants and one world championship.

As successful as he was, Mathewson was, to some extent, a hard-luck pitcher. Bad things often happened to the Giants when he took the mound in big games. It was Mathewson who was pitching against the Cubs on September 23, 1908, when first baseman Fred Merkle forgot to touch second base after Al Bridwell singled in what appeared to be the winning run. Merkle headed into the clubhouse to join the celebration but was called out by umpire Hank O'Day. The game ended in a deadlock.

That tie had to be replayed on October 8, 1908. With the pennant at stake, "Big Six" Mathewson was once again on the mound. He sailed along until the third inning, when center fielder Cy Seymour, stubbornly ignoring Mathewson's entreaties to play deeper, saw a Joe Tinker flyball sail over his head for a triple. Four runs scored that inning, and the Giants lost the game, 4–2, as well as the pennant.

Mathewson was the victim again in the 1912 World Series when Fred Snodgrass muffed a routine fly in center field, and catcher Chief Meyers and Merkle subsequently let an easy foul pop drop between them. It cost the Giants the game and the Series.

In 1914 Mathewson started to wear out. He finished with a record of 24–13, but in the second half of the season he began to complain of pains in his left side. In 1915 he suffered his first losing season since 1902, and by 1916 he was being used out of the bullpen. On July 20, 1916, the Giants traded Mathewson to the Reds along with two other future Hall of Famers, outfielder Edd Roush and third baseman Bill McKechnie, for Reds manager Buck Herzog and outfielder Red Killefer. Although the deal was made to allow Mathewson to manage Cincinnati, Reds fans were probably relieved to get him off the Giants' mound. For New York, Mathewson's record against the Reds was 64–18, with 22 wins in a row at one point.

Mathewson's last pitching performance, his only one for the Reds, was a specially contrived matchup against another aging hurler, the Cubs' Mordecai Brown. In the second game of a Labor Day doubleheader, Mathewson outlasted Brown, 10–8. After several decades the significance of this game became apparent. The annals showed that when Mathewson retired he had accumulated 372 victories, a league record. Grover Alexander eventually won 373, erasing Matty's mark. But a statistician later discovered that a Mathewson victory over Pittsburgh in May 1902 had been erroneously entered as a loss. Mathewson's share of the record was restored.

Mathewson managed Cincinnati until midseason 1918, when he joined the army during World War I. He served as a captain, and was hit by a whiff of poison gas. Two years later he was diagnosed as having tuberculosis in both lungs; he succumbed to the disease in 1925. In 1936 Mathewson was among the first five players to be enshrined in the Hall of Fame.

MEL OTT OF

One of the greatest players ever to wear a Giants uniform, Mel Ott was the first National Leaguer to tally 500 homers. The small, soft-spoken Louisiana native knew how to take advantage of the Polo Grounds' short porch in right field, slugging 325 of his 511 home runs there—more than any other player has ever hit in one park. A superb outfielder, Ott also was well adapted to the idiosyncrasies of his home field, expertly playing the corners of the wall and erasing many a runner from the basepaths.

For most of his 22 seasons with the team, Ott was the center of the Giants' offense. The team was built on pitching and defense in his era, and Ott was the man who created the runs. From 1928 through 1945 he led the Giants in home runs every year, topping the league six times. He also led the Giants in RBIs nine times, exceeding the 100-mark nine times in a 10-year period.

In addition to the cozy confines of the Polo Grounds, another reason for Ott's success was his keen batting eye. He is one of only five players to hit 40 homers in a season without striking out more than 40 times. Moreover, he led the league in bases on balls six times, and he was walked five times in a game on four occasions—twice as often as anyone else. Often pitched around, he set the NL record with 10 seasons of 100 or more walks. When he retired his career total of 1,708 walks was the league record; it remained so for 35 years until broken by Joe Morgan.

Ott's batting style was dramatically different. As the pitch approached the plate he would step high with his forward (right) foot as he raised and lowered the bat vertically. As the ball neared the hitting zone he stepped forward with his right foot, shifting his weight for maximum leverage. By then his bat was low and almost horizontal, and he was in perfect hitting position to uncoil a smooth, level swing.

He brought that swing to the majors as a 17-year-old, having never played a day in the minors. Giants manager John McGraw brought Ott along carefully; he had only 60 at bats in 1926, his first season, but he batted .383. Ott was the youngest player in history to pinch-hit successfully and was 9 for 24 that season in that role. In 1927 he pinch-hit 46 times, more than anyone else in the league, and played 32 games in the outfield.

The following year Ott became a regular outfielder, and

he responded by batting .322 with 18 homers and 77 RBIs. In 1929 he exploded with his greatest all-around year, and one of the best years a player so young has ever had. Ott hit .328, slugged 42 homers, drove in 151 runs, scored 138, and led the league with 113 walks. He also participated in 12 double plays, most ever for an outfielder.

This was just the start, as Ott sustained a remarkably productive and consistent performance over the next 15 years. In 1932 he led the league in home runs, with 38. The next year, although his production dropped off a notch, he helped power the Giants to the World Series for the first time since 1924. There, against the Washington Senators, Ott provided big hits in two of the Giants' four victories. In Game 1 he went 4 for 4 and drove in three runs. In Game 5 he homered into Griffith Stadium's center field bleachers to win the game, and the Series, for New York.

In 1934 Ott led the league in homers and RBIs and was selected to the first of 11 consecutive All-Star Games. His Giants captured another flag in 1936, and Master Melvin paced the NL in home runs and slugging average while finishing in the top five in runs, total bases, RBIs, walks, and on-base percentage. But the Yankees battered the Giants in six games to win the world championship.

The 1937 season saw the Giants repeat as league champs, as Ott tied Joe Medwick for the home run title and led the league in walks. He managed only a .200 average with one home run, however, in the World Series loss to the Yankees. Ott won his third consecutive home run title in 1938, but the cracks were beginning to show on the team. During the next three seasons the Giants fell steadily from contention, and Ott replaced Bill Terry as the team's manager in 1942. He fared poorly in the role, and he and his Giants served as the inspiration for Leo Durocher's most memorable line, "Nice guys finish last."

Along with his impressive career numbers in home runs and walks, Ott garnered 5,041 total bases, 14th on the all-time list, and 1,859 runs, which places him 10th. He was voted into the Hall of Fame in 1951.

GREG MADDUX P

Greg Maddux's pitching is analogous to fine brushwork. One of the greatest control artists in the history of the game, he works from a palette of cut fastballs, curves, sliders, and changeups, and never throws a batter the same pitch in the same place twice. Indeed, Maddux has never had an overpowering fastball, but his combination of pinpoint control with exceptional movement has baffled hitters for more than a decade. He's also been a model of efficiency, throwing a lot of innings with remarkably low pitch counts.

It is hard to imagine that Maddux ever had a problem with major league hitters, yet the Atlanta Braves right-hander, who won four Cy Young awards before his 30th birthday and finished the 2000 season with a career total of 240 victories, was hit hard his first two seasons. In 1986 and 1987 he went a combined 8–18 with the Chicago Cubs and had an ERA over 5.00.

He followed with four solid seasons in Chicago. Recognition finally came to Maddux in 1992, when he pitched in the All-Star Game, led the National League in wins with 20, and earned his first Cy Young Award. His timing could not have been better, as he became a highly coveted free agent that winter. Maddux spurned the New York Yankees and their extra $6 million to come to Atlanta, where the Braves had appeared in back-to-back World Series.

Maddux won his second consecutive Cy Young Award with a 20–10 record, 267 strikeouts, and 2.36 ERA in his first year as a Brave. He was on pace to better those numbers in 1994 when the baseball strike ended his season with 16 wins and a minuscule 1.56 ERA. That was good enough for a third Cy Young, and the following year he won a fourth with a 19–2 season, 1.63 ERA, and 10 complete games to pace the NL in each category. Maddux then pitched a two-hitter against the Cleveland Indians in his first-ever World Series start.

The Cy Young streak ended in 1996, when Maddux's teammate John Smoltz had a Greg Maddux–like year, while Maddux's 15 wins seemed almost ordinary by his standards. Still, he was second in both innings (245) and ERA (2.72). He also won one game in each of the team's three postseason series, although he was the hard-luck loser in the Yankees' 3–2 World Series clinching victory in Game 6.

Maddux bounced back with a 19–4 record in 1997. His .826 won-lost percentage led the league, and he surrendered only 14 unintentional bases on balls in 232⅔ innings—a ratio of only .77 walks per nine innings of work. His 2.20 ERA trailed only Pedro Martinez's 1.90 among all major league pitchers. He had a complete game victory over the Astros, 2–1, in the Division Series, but lost two games to the eventual world champion Marlins despite a 1.38 ERA in NLCS. The following year Maddux won 18 games and surpassed 200 strikeouts for the first time. This time he beat the Cubs in Atlanta's Game 3 clincher of the Division Series, but lost Game 3 of the NLCS to the Padres, who went on defeat the Braves in six games.

Maddux showed signs of wear in 1999, as his ERA reached 3.57—still respectable in the high-offense environment of the late 1990s, but Maddux's first season over 3.00 since he joined Atlanta. Although he surrendered a career-worst 258 hits, he had enough support from teammates to go 19–9. He also captured his 10th consecutive Gold Glove Award, second all-time among pitchers to Jim Kaat's 14.

After a second straight 19–9 season in 2000, Maddux's career record stood at 240–135, for a .640 winning percentage. Unfortunately, his postseason record dropped to 10–11 following a loss to the Cardinals in Game 1 of the Division Series.

LEFTY GROVE P

Lefty Grove combined a blazing fastball and fiery competitiveness as few other pitchers ever have. During his peak years with the Philadelphia Athletics from 1927 to 1933, he was the dominant pitcher in the American League. And according to baseball analyst Bill James, Lefty Grove was "the greatest pitcher of all time, period."

Beginning in 1927, Grove rattled off seven straight seasons of 20 or more victories. Four times during that span he led the league in wins, and five times he led the league in won-lost percentage. Through 2000, no other pitcher has ever led the league in won-lost percentage more than three times. On nine occasions Grove's ERA was the lowest in the league. No other pitcher has accomplished that feat more than five times. And in his first seven seasons he also led the league in strikeouts.

Grove once struck out Babe Ruth, Lou Gehrig, and Tony Lazzeri on only 10 pitches. He equaled that 10-pitch, three-strikeout performance later in his career against the White Sox. Once, when the A's were playing an exhibition game against a decent semipro club, Connie Mack tabbed Grove to pitch the bottom of the ninth. When he completed his warm-ups, Grove looked back to make sure his outfielders were in place. Each one was standing just behind the infield, grinning broadly. Grove proceeded to strike out the three batters who faced him.

His temper was legendary. But as Ted Williams, Grove's teammate during the southpaw's years with the Boston Red Sox, has recalled, "When he punched a locker or something he always did it with his right hand. He was a careful tantrum thrower."

The son of a Maryland coal miner and a descendant of Betsy Ross, Grove graduated to the A's in 1925 after leading the International League in strikeouts four times. His one flaw when he joined the Athletics was a lack of control, but by 1927, having learned to take more time between pitches, he had pretty much licked his problem. That year saw Grove register his first of eight 20-victory seasons.

Grove's two biggest seasons came in 1930 and 1931, pennant-winning years for the A's. In 1930 he went 28–5 while leading the league not only in victories but also in saves, strikeouts, and ERA. In a fabled "hitter's year," when three teams in the AL batted over .300, no other pitcher in the league was as stingy to opponents—they hit only .247 against him, and their on-base average was .288. Grove won two World Series games and posted an ERA of 1.42 as the A's knocked off the St. Louis Cardinals in six.

His 1931 season was one of the finest in baseball annals. Grove finished at 31–4 with an ERA of only 2.06, in a year when the league's average was 4.38. His league-leading win total would not be equaled until 1968, when Denny McLain won 31 for the Detroit Tigers. Grove also led the AL in complete games, shutouts, and strikeouts, and won the Most Valuable Player Award over Babe Ruth (163 RBIs), Lou Gehrig (184 RBIs), and his teammate Al Simmons, who batted .390. Lefty then went 2–1 in the seven-game World Series loss to the Cardinals.

After posting records of 25–10 in 1932 and 24–8 in 1933, Grove was sent to the Boston Red Sox in a five-player trade by a financially strapped Connie Mack. Relying increasingly on his curveball, Grove spent eight productive years in Boston, once winning 20 games, once leading the league in winning percentage, four times leading in ERA, and five times being selected to the All-Star Game. In his last two seasons of note, 1938 and 1939, he went a combined 29–8.

Grove retired after the 1941 season, having recorded exactly 300 victories and having set the mark for highest winning percentage (.680) by any pitcher with that many wins. He often insisted that had he been pitching in an earlier era with a deader baseball and trick deliveries, he could have won 500 games. Grove's lifetime ERA of 3.06, when normalized to the league average and adjusted for home park, was the finest ever. He was elected to the Hall of Fame in 1947.

ROGER CLEMENS P

In addition to his record five Cy Young awards, Roger Clemens enjoys a distinction that practically no one knows about. Through 2000 Clemens won 260 games and lost just 142; a .647 percentage accumulated for teams (mostly the Boston Red Sox) with a combined winning percentage of .527. The .120 differential is the greatest pitcher-team differential in history for any player with 100 or more wins.

What is better known about Clemens is the blazing fastball that earned him the nickname "The Rocket." He became the first pitcher in major league history to fan 20 batters in a nine-inning game on April 29, 1986 against the Seattle Mariners; he repeated the feat on September 18, 1996 against the Detroit Tigers. At the end of the 2000 season, Clemens had 3,504 career strikeouts, eighth on the all-time list. Along the way he led the American League in strikeouts five times, in addition to winning six ERA titles and earning an invitation to seven All-Star Games.

Clemens won a total of 16 games in his first two years with the Boston Red Sox. Then he exploded. In 1986 he paced the AL with 24 wins, a startling .857 winning percentage, and a 2.48 ERA. Those numbers, and the fact that Boston won the pennant, allowed him to walk away with both the Cy Young and Most Valuable Player awards. Clemens won the deciding game of the AL Championship Series against the California Angels, and he left Game 6 of the 1986 World Series with a lead. It didn't hold up, as the Red Sox bowed to the New York Mets.

Clemens was again the Cy Young honoree in 1987, going 20–9 and leading the league with 18 complete games and seven shutouts. He claimed the award for a third time in a Red Sox uniform in 1990, winning 21 games against only six losses and posting an AL-leading and career-best 1.93 ERA.

After four mediocre seasons from 1993 through 1996—in which he still struck out nearly a batter per inning—Clemens left Boston to sign with Toronto as a free agent in December 1996. No one expected what followed. On a team that finished 76–86 in 1997 and 88–74 in 1998, Clemens was 21–7 and 20–6. In the process, he became only the second pitcher ever to reach 3,000 strikeouts without yet having issued 1,000 walks (Fergie Jenkins was the first). He also won the pitching Triple Crown both years and walked away with his fourth and record fifth Cy Young awards.

All that remained was for "The Rocket" to pitch for a World Series winner, and he got his chance with the New York Yankees in 1999. Although his season was hardly spectacular—he went 14–10 with an ERA of 4.60—Clemens won the deciding Game 4 of the World Series, 4–1, as the Yankees swept the Atlanta Braves. That same year a panel selected Clemens for Major League Baseball's All-Century Team, citing him as one of the 100 greatest players. He was subsequently chosen by fans as one of the six greatest pitchers of all time.

In 2000, the 38-year-old Clemens again took center stage in the postseason, after notching a 13–8 record for the Yankees during the year. He pitched a brilliant one-hit, complete-game shutout against the Seattle Mariners in Game 4 of the ALCS, striking out 15. Then, in Game 2 of the World Series against the Mets, Clemens throttled the Mets with two-hit pitching over eight scoreless innings before giving way to Mariano Rivera, who sealed his victory. The gem was tarnished, however, by an incident in the first inning, in which Clemens flung the barrel of Mike Piazza's bat, which had shattered on a fouled strike, in the direction of the Mets catcher. Both benches emptied, but no ejections were made. Clemens, however, was later fined $50,000 for the incident.

KID NICHOLS P

Kid Nichols is usually cited, along with Amos Rusie and Cy Young, as one of the three great pitchers of the 19th century. But while Rusie was the premier strikeout artist of the time and Young, who pitched for another decade, retired with untouchable career totals, Nichols was the winningest pitcher of the 1890s. Pitching for Boston in the National League, he collected 297 victories over that 10-year span—30 more than Young and 63 more than Rusie. Moreover, he was the only one of the three to pitch his team to a pennant during that decade, and he did it five times.

The slender righthander delivered a basic overhand fastball from a windup so simple it was almost nonexistent. But Nichols' real strength was his control. Batters knew a fastball was coming, but they had no idea where it would be placed.

Nicknamed "Kid" because of his youth and his slender build, Nichols went 27–19 and posted a 2.23 ERA in 1890, his first major league campaign. He completed all 47 of his starts and led the league with seven shutouts. In 1891 his Beaneaters took the NL pennant, with Nichols going 30–17 and finding the time to register a league-leading three saves. The Beaneaters won again in 1892 as Nichols improved his record to 35–16. That year the National League divided the season into halves, stipulating that the winners of each would meet at season's end in a "World Series." Boston, the first-half winner, knocked off Cleveland without a loss in the Series. Nichols pitched the final game, defeating Young.

In 1893 the pitching distance was increased from 50 feet to 60 feet 6 inches, adversely affecting many pitchers. Nichols' strikeout total was cut in half, from 187 to 94, and his ERA went up by more than half a run. Yet the Kid remained one of the league's most effective hurlers, going 34–14. Boston coasted to its third straight pennant.

Although his team began to falter, Nichols remained superb. From 1896 to 1898, he paced the NL each season in victories, with 30, 31, and 31, respectively. His 31–12 record in 1898 made it the seventh time in eight years that he had registered at least 30 wins. His opponents that season managed only a .221 batting average and a .272 on-base average against Nichols, giving him the league's best mark on both counts.

After winning the flag in 1897 and '98, the Beaneaters slumped, and so did Nichols. His slide continued in 1900, when he had his first losing season, going 13–16. But when many of his teammates jumped to the new American League in 1901, Nichols stuck it out and pitched well, earning 19 wins. Nevertheless, he was released at the end of the season, as the club tried to cut costs.

In 1904 Nichols returned to the National League and won 21 games as pitcher-manager for the St. Louis Cardinals. After one of the team's owners tried to humiliate him by ordering him to serve as gate attendant before a game, however, Nichols balked and was released. He won a few games for the Phillies and then retired.

In his career Nichols won 361 games, sixth best all-time, with an amazing 532 complete games in 562 starts. In 1949, four years before his death at age 83, he was inducted into the Hall of Fame.

JIMMIE FOXX 1B

Jimmie Foxx ranked second to Babe Ruth in career home runs until 1966, when Willie Mays passed his total of 534. Known as "Old Double-X" or simply "the Beast," he was the true successor to Ruth as baseball's preeminent slugger in the 1930s, walloping more home runs—415—during that decade than anyone else. Until the home run explosion of the late 1990s, Foxx was one of only five players to ever surpass 50 home runs in a season on two occasions.

He didn't just hit for distance, either. Foxx won the Triple Crown in 1933 after missing the batting title by only three percentage points the previous year. His .325 career batting average is the seventh best for a first baseman, and his .609 career slugging average trails only Ruth, Ted Williams, and Lou Gehrig. Foxx led the American League in homers four times, in RBIs three times, and in batting twice. He won back-to-back Most Valuable Player awards in 1932-33, and another MVP in 1938.

Foxx began as a catcher for Connie Mack's Philadelphia A's, but saw little action in his first few seasons behind the team's Hall of Fame backstop, Mickey Cochrane. As a 20-year-old in 1928 Foxx started to mature, hitting .328 with 13 homers and 79 RBIs in 400 at bats while playing 61 games at third, 30 at first, and 20 behind the plate. The following year, as the club's regular first baseman, he hit .354 with 33 homers and 118 RBIs as the A's won the pennant and World Series. He was even better in 1930, hitting .335 with 37 homers and 156 RBIs as the A's repeated.

Foxx's career hit a speed bump in 1931. His average fell to .291, his home run total to 30, and his RBIs to 120—an excellent season by almost any other player's standards. But his walk total dropped from 93 to 73, and he led the league in strikeouts for the third straight season (ultimately, he led the AL seven times in that category). He decided to cut down on his swing, and the result was immediate and spectacular. In 1932, five years after Ruth had hit 60 home runs, Foxx hit 58, and lost two more to rainouts. His league-leading slugging percentage was a phenomenal .749, and he also led the league with 169 RBIs and 151 runs scored.

Folks were impressed not only by the number of homers that Foxx hit, but also by how hard they were hit and how far they traveled. Many baseball people agreed with Yankees pitcher Lefty Gomez when he joked about Foxx, "He has muscles in his hair."

Like Ruth, Foxx was hardly a model of clean living. His drinking was no secret, and he was notorious for profligate spending. But while Foxx was throwing his money around during the Great Depression, Connie Mack was desperately trying to keep the A's afloat. In fact, after Foxx won the 1933 Triple Crown, Mack actually tried to cut his salary from $16,333 to $12,000. Foxx balked, but eventually took a token cut to $16,000.

Mack finally sold Foxx to the Red Sox after the 1935 season. With his salary now doubled, Foxx responded with 41 homers and 143 RBIs; he slumped in 1937, however, hitting a mere .285 with 36 homers and 127 RBIs. His last heroics came in 1938, when he drove in a career-best 175 runs (one every 3.2 at bats) and hit 50 homers to win his third MVP Award.

Nagged by injuries and increasingly enervated by the bottle, Foxx still had enough vigor left to produce 100-RBI seasons in 1940 and 1941, but he hit only 19 homers in 1941 and was waived to the Cubs on June 1, 1942. The fading slugger finished that season with a .226 average and eight homers at the relatively youthful age of 34.

He left baseball at the season's end, but rejoined the Cubs in 1944 for 20 at bats, with only one hit. After a minor league managing stint, he returned to the big leagues as a part-timer for the Phillies in 1945, where he hit .268 with seven homers. So desperate was wartime baseball for manpower that on August 19 Phillies manager Ben Chapman called on Foxx to pitch against the Cincinnati Reds. Foxx pitched six innings of no-hit ball. In the seventh inning his arm gave out, but it was nonetheless a remarkable accomplishment. He ended up going 1–0 with a 1.59 ERA in his final year in the majors. He was elected to the Hall of Fame in 1951.

JOE MORGAN 2B

When the Big Red Machine was operating in the 1970s, Joe Morgan was its generator. On a Cincinnati team laden with All Stars, Morgan was arguably the best between 1972 and 1977. During that six-year period he played in at least 141 games a season. He also walked more than 100 times each year and averaged 60 stolen bases, turning many of those walks into "doubles." Successful in nearly four out of every five steal attempts during his career, he stole 689 bases to rank among the all-time leaders.

Despite his small frame, Morgan had plenty of pop in his bat. From 1972 to 1977 he averaged 21 homers and 84 RBIs, generally batting second in the Reds lineup. In the field, he won Gold Gloves every year from 1973 through 1977. He was named National League Most Valuable Player in both 1975 and 1976, the first back-to-back MVP winner since Ernie Banks in 1958 and 1959.

Morgan was an All Star eight times, and helped his teammates win six division titles, four pennants, and two world championships. In Game 7 of the 1975 World Series, his bloop single with two out in the bottom of the ninth gave Cincinnati the championship over the Boston Red Sox.

In 1965, after cups of coffee with the Houston Colt .45s and having been named MVP of the Texas League, the lefthanded-hitting Morgan made it to the big leagues to stay. He got six hits in a 12-inning game on July 8, led the NL in walks with 97, and won *The Sporting News* Rookie of the Year Award. In 1968 injuries limited him to only 10 games, but from 1969 through 1977 he stole at least 40 bases every year and scored more than 100 runs seven times.

Despite twice being named to the All-Star team in Houston, Morgan was traded to Cincinnati in 1971. His new manager, Sparky Anderson, respected Morgan's intelligence so much that he never gave his second baseman a "take" sign in all their years together. Over the next five seasons Morgan led the league in on-base percentage four times, with a high of .471 in 1975.

Morgan's 1976 MVP season was a career best. He batted .320, hit 27 homers, drove in 111 runs and scored 113, stole 60 bases, and walked 114 times. It marked the third time in four years he hit at least 20 homers and stole more than 50 bases in the same season. During one 10-game stretch Morgan had at least one RBI in each game. In Cincinnati's four-game sweep of the New York Yankees in the 1976 World Series, Morgan homered in the first inning of the opener; tripled, singled, and stole a base in Game 2; doubled in a run in Game 3; and walked, stole a base, and scored the first run of Game 4.

In 1977 Morgan set a record for second basemen, making only five errors and handling 715 chances. He tailed off a bit offensively the next two seasons, however, and signed with the Astros as a free agent in 1980. Morgan led the league in bases on balls and helped his original team win the division title. After a couple of years with the Giants, he was reunited with former colleagues Pete Rose and Tony Perez in Philadelphia in 1983, hitting 16 homers and scoring 72 runs to help the "Wheeze Kid" Phillies win the pennant. He homered twice in the World Series loss to the Orioles.

Morgan made his 1984 farewell with Oakland memorable by replacing Rogers Hornsby as the most prolific homer-hitting second baseman of all time, with 268 (Ryne Sandberg later passed him). He was a first-year selection to the Hall of Fame in 1990.

EDDIE MATHEWS 3B

Prior to the coming of Mike Schmidt, Eddie Mathews was the greatest power-hitting third baseman in baseball history. He slugged 512 homers and smacked in 1,453 runs in his 17 seasons, most of them with the Braves in Boston and Milwaukee. No less an authority on hitting than Ty Cobb said of Mathews, "I've only known three or four perfect swings in my time. This lad has one of them."

The Texas-born Mathews spent several seasons in the minors before coming up to the Braves in 1952, the team's last season in Boston. Even though he led the league in strikeouts with 115, he slammed 25 homers, a very respectable mark for a rookie. The last three came at Ebbets Field on the next-to-last day of the season, which made him the first rookie ever to hit three homers in a single game.

In Milwaukee fans showered the Braves with adulation, which was not always welcome to the introverted and often sullen Mathews. In his first year there, he led the NL with 47 home runs while also driving in 135 runs; both marks were career highs. It was also the first of his three straight 40-homer, 100-RBI seasons.

Considering that he played in the same decade as Willie Mays, Mickey Mantle, Duke Snider, Ralph Kiner, and his great teammate Henry Aaron, it might surprise some people to learn that Mathews, from his rookie season of 1952 through 1959, led all major leaguers with 299 home runs. Overall, he topped 40 on four occasions—leading the league a second time, in 1959, with 46—and had 30 or more 10 times, nine of them in a row. He also led the NL in bases on balls four times, and in on-base percentage once during his 17-year major league career.

It wasn't a home run, however, that provided Mathews with his greatest moment in baseball. In 1957 Milwaukee won its only World Series, beating the Yankees in seven games. Mathews pulled out Game 4 with a 10th-inning homer off Bob Grim, and his dribbler of an infield single drove in the only run in Game 5. But the play that mattered most to him was his backhand stab of Bill Skowron's bases-loaded one-hopper for the last out of Game 7.

In 1962 Mathews tore his shoulder, and after that his career started heading downhill. He had one more high quality season left in 1965, hitting 32 homers with 95 RBIs in the Braves' last year in Milwaukee. Mathews moved with the Braves to Atlanta and hit only 16 homers in 1966. He was traded to Houston after the season, and then to Detroit, where he finished up with the Tigers in 1968. In 1978 he was elected to the Hall of Fame.

KEN GRIFFEY JR. OF

Having logged 12 seasons in the major leagues through 2000, Ken Griffey Jr. is the embodiment of the five-tool player that Leo Durocher referred to when speaking of Willie Mays. Griffey can hit, hit with power, run, field, and throw. The 6-foot-3-inch slugger commonly referred to as "Junior" finished the 2000 season with 438 career home runs, tied with Andre Dawson for 23rd on the all-time list. Barring injury, he seems a lock to challenge some of baseball's career slugging records.

Like Stan Musial, Griffey was born in Donora, Pennsylvania. His dad, Ken Griffey (another Donora native), played 19 seasons in the major leagues, finishing with the Seattle Mariners in 1991, where he played in 51 games over his last two seasons with his son. The Griffeys became the first father-son tandem to play in the same outfield in September 1990.

As good a player as his father was, the feats of Griffey Jr. have far surpassed those of the old man. Junior led the American League in home runs four times in his first 11 years, including back-to-back seasons with 56 homers. Indeed, Griffey is the player that Hank Aaron thinks has the best chance of breaking his record of 755 career home runs. While Griffey belts them with enough frequency (about one every 15 at bats, eighth best all time through 2000) and has youth on his side, he would need to play eight more seasons after 2000 and average nearly 40 home runs per year.

The 1997 American League Most Valuable Player, Griffey paced the junior circuit that season in homers (56), RBIs (147), runs (125), and slugging average (.646). As good he's been at the plate, Junior has also proved himself an outstanding fielder and baserunner. The winner of 10 consecutive Gold Gloves from 1990 to 1999, he's made numerous leaping catches in center field to rob opponents of home runs. Although not a prolific stealer, Griffey is nevertheless respected as a baserunner. He flew from first to home to score the most important run in Mariners' history, crossing the plate on Edgar Martinez's double in Game 5 of the 1995 Division Series to top the Yankees in 11 innings.

One of the game's most popular players, the personable Griffey was elected to the "All-Century Team" announced in July 1999. In a subsequent fans' vote he was named one of the top 25 players of the 20th century. Griffey was voted to start the All-Star Game in 10 consecutive seasons, and in 1992 joined his dad as an All-Star MVP, making them the first father-son duo to turn that trick.

After 11 seasons with the Mariners, Griffey was traded to the Cincinnati Reds in 2000, inking a nine-year, $116.5 million deal. Although his totals dropped in most offensive categories, Griffey had a productive, if not exceptional season by his standards, hitting 40 home runs with 118 RBIs and 100 runs scored. It was the fifth consecutive season in which he'd scored and driven in 100 or more runs.

BILL DAHLEN SS

Playing in an era when infields were littered with stones and pitted with craters, when scorekeepers regarded any ball touched as playable, and when gloves afforded hand protection but little help in spearing a ball, "Bad Bill" Dahlen made 975 errors at shortstop, more than any other player in history. Ironically, this proved that he was a wonderful fielder—had he not been so good at covering the toughest position on the diamond, his managers would never have penciled him in at shortstop 2,132 times.

In Dahlen's day, the batted ball sometimes arrived lopsided and was often covered with some slippery foreign substance that the pitcher had added. Dahlen got to more of these than most shortstops and, naturally, made more errors; nonetheless, he led the league in errors only once (in 1895), and that year was one of the four in which he led in assists. In fact, he ranks among the top three shortstops of all time in both putouts and assists. His nickname had nothing to do with his playing ability—it reflected the vehemence with which he argued with umpires, managers, and teammates.

Dahlen came to the National League with the Chicago White Stockings in 1891, and manager Cap Anson put him at third base to get his bat into the lineup. Usually batting fifth or sixth for Chicago, he hit less than .290 only once from 1892 through 1898, with highs of .359 (to go with 150 runs and 108 RBIs) in 1894 and .352 in 1896. In 1894 he set a record by hitting safely in 42 consecutive games, a mark since surpassed only by Willie Keeler, Pete Rose, and Joe DiMaggio.

Once Dahlen left the White Stockings after the 1898 season his batting average tumbled. He was fortunate to be dealt to Brooklyn in time to play shortstop for pennant winners in 1899 and 1900. Brooklyn had built a powerhouse team by acquiring most of the stars of the old Baltimore Orioles, renowned for their rough, no-holds-barred play, and Dahlen fit right in.

In 1904 former Oriole John McGraw brought Dahlen to the Giants, where he led the league in RBIs with only 80. Dahlen's statistics for the 1905 World Series were indicative of the way he played the game late in his career: despite going hitless in 15 at bats, he drew three walks, stole three bases, scored a run, knocked in another, and handled 28 fielding chances flawlessly. Dahlen finished his playing career with Boston in 1909, although he made a few pinch-hitting appearances while managing the Dodgers from 1910 through 1913.

As a manager, Dahlen's sharp tongue and irascible temper made him unpopular with his players and with reporters, but Brooklyn owner Charlie Ebbets liked him enough to keep him as skipper for four seasons, even though the club never finished higher than sixth.

GEORGE DAVIS SS

Stocky, powerful switch hitter George Davis began his career as a slightly erratic outfielder and went on to become a great shortstop. In 20 major league seasons he hit nearly .300, and ranks high in such lifetime statistics as hits, runs, and RBIs. He was a hero in one of the greatest upsets in World Series history. Yet it took nearly 90 years after his final at bat before he was finally elected to the Hall of Fame.

He started out with the National League's Cleveland Spiders in 1890. After three ordinary seasons as an outfielder and third baseman, Davis was traded to the New York Giants for Buck Ewing, considered one of the great players of the 19th century. His arrival in New York coincided with an increase in the pitching distance from 50 feet to 60 feet 6 inches, and his batting average subsequently jumped more than 100 points, to .355. Davis played with the Giants for nine seasons, hitting more than .300 each year. In each of four seasons he scored more than 100 runs and in three seasons collected more than 100 RBIs.

His best year offensively was 1897, when he batted .353, stole 65 bases, scored 112 runs, hit 31 doubles, 10 triples, and 10 home runs, and led the league with 136 RBIs. Davis also became New York's regular shortstop after several years of utility play. Two years later he led NL shortstops in fielding average, a feat he repeated in 1900.

Davis twice managed the Giants, once for 33 games in 1895 and again from mid-1900 through the 1901 season. The team, however, stayed near the bottom of the standings. The war between the National League and the new American League gave Davis his chance to escape the Giants' tight-fisted owner, Andrew Freedman, and in 1902 he became one of many NL players to jump to the AL, joining the Chicago White Sox. He hit .299 that year and led all league shortstops in fielding average. When John T. Brush bought the Giants, Davis tried to return to New York, but played only four games for his old team in 1903 before being declared the property of Chicago. Davis took his case to court but lost.

Davis returned to the White Sox in 1904. His average dropped to .252, still respectable in the Dead Ball Era, when batting averages plummeted throughout baseball. A better measure of his value was that the White Sox jumped from seventh place to third with him back at short. In 1905 they finished second as the 35-year-old Davis again led league shortstops in fielding.

The 1906 season capped his career. Chicago was engaged in a dogfight for the pennant with Cleveland and New York when a 19-game winning streak in August put the White Sox on top, and they pulled away in September. The Sox, dubbed "the Hitless Wonders," had a team batting average of .230, worst in the league. Davis hit .277, and led the team with 80 RBIs.

Few experts gave the White Sox a chance in the World Series against their crosstown rivals, the Cubs, who had won 116 games. But Davis led the way to a six-game victory, hitting .308 with three doubles and a Series-leading six RBIs. The Veterans Committee elected Davis to the Hall of Fall in 1998.

WARREN SPAHN P

The winningest lefthander in major league history, Warren Spahn won 20 or more games in 13 different seasons, a National League mark equaled only by Christy Mathewson. Few pitchers have been so good for so long. Spahn recorded 63 shutouts, the NL record for a lefthander, and produced a lifetime ERA of 3.09. His 363 victories are the fifth highest total ever notched, and he ranks eighth all time in innings pitched, 11th in games started, and 16th in strikeouts.

A consummate competitor, Spahn signed with the Braves in 1940 and started the 1942 season with the big league club. When he refused to throw a brushback pitch at Brooklyn shortstop Pee Wee Reese, Braves manager Casey Stengel demoted Spahn to Hartford of the Eastern League, where he went 17–12 with a 1.96 ERA. He didn't return to Boston in 1943. Drafted into the army, Spahn fought in the Battle of the Bulge and received a Bronze Star and a field commission for his role in taking the Remagen Bridge, as well as a Purple Heart for being hit with shrapnel. He lost more than three seasons to military service.

Spahn returned to Boston in July 1946 and quickly emerged as one of the top pitchers in the NL. In 1947 he won 21 games and led the league with a 2.33 ERA. In 1948 he comprised one-half of the Braves' famous "Spahn and [Johnny] Sain and Pray For Rain" pitching tandem. Some have pointed out that the duo's won-lost percentage was actually lower than the team's as a whole, .591 as compared with .595. This, however, fails to take into account the tremendous success the two pitchers enjoyed down the stretch. Beginning with a Labor Day doubleheader against the Dodgers in which Spahn won the first game on a five-hitter, 2–1, pitching 14 innings, and Sain tossed a 4–0 shutout in the nightcap, the two aces won eight games between them to help the Braves capture the flag. Exhausted from this stretch drive, Spahn started and lost Game 2 of the World Series against the Indians. He won Game 5 in relief, but surrendered a run in two innings of relief as Cleveland won Game 6 and the Series.

Although not remembered as a strikeout artist, Spahn led the league in that category from 1949 through 1952. On June 14, 1952, he struck out 18 batters in a 15-inning contest against the Cubs. After the Braves moved to Milwaukee in 1953 Spahn helped the club win two more pennants and a world championship. He won the Cy Young Award in 1957, and beat the Yankees twice in the 1958 World Series.

Spahn was a true craftsman on the mound, much more a pitcher than a thrower. Batters could take a "comfortable" 0 for 4 against Spahn—they would get around enough to hit the ball, but not well enough to do any real damage. They would be only slightly off.

Late in his career, Spahn cemented his reputation as an ageless wonder by pitching two no-hitters after his 39th birthday. At Milwaukee's County Stadium, he no-hit the Phillies for his 20th win of the 1960 season, the 11th time he had reached that number. He struck out 15 batters, his career high for nine innings. The following year he no-hit San Francisco, 1–0, just five days after his 40th birthday.

Later that season Spahn notched his 300th career victory, defeating the Cubs, 2–1, on a six-hitter.

One of baseball's better hitting pitchers, Spahn hit 35 lifetime home runs, the National League record for a hurler and fourth best on the all-time list. In 1958 he became one of the few pitchers to bat .300 and record 20 wins in the same season. He finished his career in 1965 with the last-place New York Mets—where he briefly served as a pitcher-coach under Casey Stengel and teamed up with fellow player-coach Yogi Berra to form a historic battery—and the San Francisco Giants. Spahn was elected to the Hall of Fame in 1973, his first year of eligibility.

JOE DIMAGGIO OF

Joe DiMaggio was one of those rare players who possessed a unique, inimitable style. His grace and elegance truly set him apart from his peers, as did his skills with a bat and a glove. Otherwise sober people have waxed effusively poetic about DiMaggio's play in center field, and he was as enthusiastically embraced on the road as he was in New York, where he spent his entire career with the Yankees. Although he lost three years to military service, DiMaggio finished with 2,214 hits, 361 home runs, 1,390 runs scored, 1,537 RBIs, and a .325 career batting average.

His 1941 record of hitting safely in 56 consecutive games might be called a freak statistic, but in some ways it is the perfect Joe DiMaggio stat. DiMaggio's creed was excellence, and he did whatever was needed for his team to win, without pomp or showmanship. He was both "the Yankee Clipper," a quiet, effortless batter who moved like a graceful sailing ship, and "Joltin' Joe," the potent slugger. But it was as a fielder and baserunner that DiMaggio's intelligent style of play was most obvious. Yankees manager Joe McCarthy said simply, "He was the best baserunner I ever saw."

After several seasons of tearing up the Pacific Coast League (including 1933, when he hit safely in 61 consecutive games, oddly foreshadowing his 1941 major league feat), DiMaggio made his big league debut with the Yankees on May 3, 1936. He set American League rookie records that season with 132 runs and 15 triples. He hit .323, belted 29 homers, and delivered 125 RBIs. His 22 assists led all AL outfielders. He had 21 assists the next season and had managed another 20 in 1938 before runners wised up.

Over his next seven years with the Yanks DiMaggio was a model of consistency. From 1936 through 1942 he batted over .300 every year, bettering .350 three times. He had more than 100 RBIs each season, including 167 in 1937—a year in which he led the league in homers (46, still the record for a Yankees righthanded hitter), runs (151), and slugging (.673). He won batting titles in 1939 and 1940, and topped the AL with 125 RBIs in 1941, the year he won his second Most Valuable Player Award. Between the day DiMaggio arrived at Yankee Stadium and the day in 1942 he shipped off to war, the Yankees won six pennants and five World Series, four of them in a row.

On May 15, 1941, DiMaggio started his streak of hitting safely in 56 consecutive games, during which he batted .408. The streak came to an end in Cleveland on July 17 in front of 67,468 fans, when Ken Keltner made two great plays and Lou Boudreau made another to keep the Clipper off the bases. DiMaggio's streak had lasted 15 games longer than George Sisler's 1922 mark and 12 games longer than Willie Keeler's 19th-century effort. The next day DiMaggio hit safely again, inaugurating a second streak of 16 games. Scratch only one of those three great plays by Cleveland's infielders, and he would have batted safely in 73 consecutive games.

When DiMaggio returned to baseball in 1946, a series of injuries hampered his effectiveness. He never won another batting title and only twice reached the 30-homer, 100-RBI level that he had topped in five of his first seven years. Yet despite undergoing surgery prior to the 1947 season, DiMaggio was again voted the AL MVP that year. In 1948 he almost single-handedly put the Yankees into another World Series, but despite his league-leading 39 home runs and 155 RBIs, New York finished second to Cleveland.

In November 1948 DiMaggio once again underwent surgery; this time his comeback was slow and painful, and he missed the first 65 games of the season. One day in June the pain suddenly disappeared, and he began an intense period of rehabilitation. He rejoined the lineup for a series in Boston, with the Yankees and Red Sox locked in a battle for first. DiMaggio belted four homers and drove in nine runs in the three-game Yankee sweep. He finished the season with a .346 batting average, including 14 homers and 67 RBIs in only 76 games. The Yankees went on to drub the Brooklyn Dodgers in the Series.

In 1950 DiMaggio's average fell to .301, but he still hit 32 homers, drove in 122 runs, and led the league in slugging average. That year he became the first player ever to homer three times in one game in Washington's mammoth Griffith Stadium. But his body was wearing out, and after struggling to play 116 games in 1951 he decided to retire. The Yankees offered him a full $100,000 salary if he would play in only home games during the 1952 season, but the great DiMaggio declined.

DiMaggio never left the American consciousness, even in retirement. In 1954 he married movie star Marilyn Monroe. Their marriage didn't last long, but the couple remained close friends for the rest of Monroe's life. In 1955 DiMaggio was inducted into the Baseball Hall of Fame, and in 1969 he was honored during baseball's centennial celebration as the greatest living ballplayer.

Any attempt to summarize DiMaggio's career must take into account the three years of prime playing time that he lost to World War II. Also worth consideration is that he played half of his games in a park especially detrimental to righthanded power, with fences in left and center field more than 400 feet from the plate. Of DiMaggio's 361 lifetime homers, 213 were hit on the road. Perhaps the most amazing statistic pertaining to DiMaggio is that he struck out only 369 times in his career. In his sensational 1941 season he hit 30 homers and struck out only 13 times.

TOM SEAVER P

Nicknamed "The Franchise" because of his value to the New York Mets in the late 1960s and early 1970s, Tom Seaver was that very rare player who, by sheer talent and shining example, was able to turn a struggling team into a winner. The stocky, muscular, Seaver harnessed considerable power from a leg drive that was so hard his right knee pounded the mound as he released the ball. He won three Cy Young Awards, led the National League in wins and ERA three times each, and struck out 3,640 batters—the fourth highest total of all time—en route to compiling a 311–205 record during 20 seasons.

Seaver broke in with the lowly Mets in 1967. The 23-year-old righthander won the NL Rookie of the Year Award, going 16–13 with a 2.76 ERA for a last-place team. By 1969 a staff of young pitchers that included Nolan Ryan, Jerry Koosman, Gary Gentry, and Seaver took the "Miracle" Mets to the world championship. Seaver was 25–7 with a 2.21 ERA that year, winning his first Cy Young Award, earning kudos as *The Sporting News* Pitcher of the Year, and narrowly losing the Most Valuable Player Award to Willie McCovey.

Fittingly, Seaver started and won the first postseason game in Mets history, which also happened to be the first-ever National League Championship Series game. The Mets swept the Braves in three games to take the pennant. Seaver went 1–1 with a 3.00 ERA to help defeat the favored Orioles four games to one in the World Series.

On April 22, 1970, Seaver struck out 19 San Diego Padres, including the last 10 batters he faced, for a 2–1 Mets win. The 10 consecutive strikeouts broke an 86-year-old record, and Seaver's mark remained unmatched through the end of the 20th century.

During his first 10½ seasons Seaver won 189 games and lost 110 for the Mets. His lowest ERA during that stretch came in 1971, when he recorded a league-leading 1.76 mark to accompany a career-best 289 strikeouts. "Tom Terrific" was 1–1 with a 1.62 ERA in the 1973 NLCS against the Cincinnati Reds, which New York won in five games. The Mets, whose 83 wins were the lowest ever for an NL champion, took the favored Oakland A's to seven games in the World Series before capitulating. Seaver was 0–1 in the Series, despite fanning 18 in his two starts.

In 1975 Seaver sparkled with a 22–9 record, a 2.38 ERA, and a league-leading 243 strikeouts. The following year he again led the NL in strikeouts, his ninth straight season with at least 200 Ks. But Seaver, a proud man, was feuding with Mets executive M. Donald Grant on a variety of issues. On June 15, 1977, Grant traded Seaver and Dave Kingman in separate deals. Seaver went to Cincinnati, finishing 14–3 for the Reds, 21–6 on the year.

Seaver pitched for the Reds until 1982, twice leading the league in winning percentage. On June 16, 1978, he notched the only no-hitter of his major league career, beating St. Louis, 4–0. In the strike-shortened 1981 season Seaver went 14–2 with a 2.55 ERA. But the following season he suffered the first losing season of his career, and in December he was traded back to the Mets.

Seaver was welcomed back by Mets fans, but the team offered him little support. He struggled to a 9–14 mark, and in January 1984 the White Sox claimed him in the compensation draft. He pitched two solid seasons for the White Sox, winning 15 games in 1984 and 16 in 1985. Ironically, Seaver won his 300th game in New York—at Yankee Stadium—as a member of the Chisox. On June 29, 1986, he was traded to the Red Sox, and when Boston faced the Mets in that year's World Series, Seaver was in the visitor's dugout at Shea Stadium, although he did not pitch in the Series. In fact, he did not pitch again.

In addition to his strikeout total, Seaver ranks high on the career list in several pitching categories—shutouts (tied for seventh with his former teammate Nolan Ryan), games started (12th), innings pitched (15th), wins (16th), and opponents' batting average (tied for 20th). His rating of 58.9 in the Wins Above Team category (how many wins a pitcher earned beyond what normally would have been expected of an average pitcher for his team or teams) is the sixth highest mark ever notched. Seaver was named to the Hall of Fame in 1992, his first year of eligibility. That same year the Mets retired his No. 41.

TIM RAINES OF

Tim Raines retired in 1999 following his 21st season in the major leagues. The man they called "Rock" because of his halfback-type build produced a solid career based almost entirely on his speed. At his peak, he was the National League equivalent of Rickey Henderson—batting for high averages, getting on base with walks, leading the league in stolen bases, and scoring runs.

By the time Raines hung up his spikes, he had pilfered 807 bases, trailing only Ty Cobb, Billy Hamilton, Lou Brock, and Rickey Henderson on the all-time list. Successful in 84.7 percent of his steals, he's second to none in that category; he was caught only 146 times in 953 attempts. At the plate, Raines was a compact switch hitter who relied on his dazzling speed, but was capable of mustering an occasional show of power, as demonstrated by his 18 homers in 1987.

In 1981, after being named Minor League Player of the Year by Topps and *The Sporting News,* Raines was ready to play on a regular basis with the Montreal Expos, with whom he'd had cups of coffee the two previous years. He set a rookie record by stealing 71 bases, despite playing in just 88 games due to the player strike and a September injury. Raines finished second in the National League Rookie of the Year balloting to Fernando Valenzuela.

Although his average fell from .304 to .277 in 1982, Raines continued to dominate on the basepaths, leading the league with 78 steals. Over his next four seasons he swiped 305 bases—including a career-best 90 in 1983—while his average steadily climbed. In 1986 he led the NL with a .334 average and a .415 on-base average. During that decade Raines also paced the senior circuit in runs twice, and in doubles once. He received 26 intentional walks in 1987, an Expos club record. On five occasions he stole four bases in one game. In 1993 he played 112 games in the outfield for the Chicago White Sox without making an error.

A seven-time All-Star, Raines also played for the 1996 and 1998 world champion New York Yankees. In 1999, after signing with Oakland, he was diagnosed with lupus. Raines played in 58 games with the A's and announced his retirement in March 2000. At age 41, however, he joined the Somerset Patriots of the independent Atlantic League, and tried out unsuccessfully for the U.S. Olympic baseball team.

CARL YASTRZEMSKI OF

Carl Yastrzemski had a tough task in 1961: replacing Boston Red Sox legend Ted Williams in Fenway Park's left field. After a slow start, he succeeded admirably, logging 23 seasons with the Red Sox. Only Brooks Robinson, with the Baltimore Orioles, had that many years of service with one team. By the time he retired after the 1983 season, Yastrzemski—known as "Yaz" to the Fenway faithful—had collected 3,419 hits, including 452 home runs. That put him in the rarefied company of Stan Musial, Willie Mays, and Hank Aaron, the only other players to tally 3,000 hits and 400 homers.

Yaz joined the Red Sox in 1961. He batted .266 as a rookie, and two years later he led the American League in five offensive categories with a .321 average, 183 hits, 40 doubles, 95 walks, and a .419 on-base percentage. In 1965 he batted .312 and led the league with 45 doubles and a .536 slugging average. On May 14 he hit for the cycle for the only time in his career.

Yastrzemski's biggest season was 1967. Boston had finished in ninth place the previous year, and neither Yaz nor the Sox were off to a good start. But the day after a slight from White Sox manager Eddie Stanky, who publicly commented that Yastrzemski was an All-Star "from the neck down," Yaz went 6 for 9 in a doubleheader, homering in his last at bat and tipping his cap to Stanky. He went on to record one of the best all-around seasons in baseball history, winning the Triple Crown with a .326 batting average, 44 home runs, and 121 RBIs, and also pacing the AL in runs, hits, on-base percentage, and slugging average—the latter a career-high .622. Yastrzemski's torrid hitting down the stretch helped rally the Red Sox to win the pennant over the Minnesota Twins.

In the 1967 World Series, the Red Sox split the first six games with the Cardinals. Yastrzemski homered twice in Game 2 in a 5–0 Boston victory, and fourth-inning home runs in Game 6 by Yaz, Reggie Smith, and Rico Petrocelli set a Series record and propelled the Red Sox to an 8–4 victory. The Cards' Bob Gibson, however, who had already won twice in the Series, allowed only three hits in the final game, striking out 10 as St. Louis prevailed. Nevertheless, Yastrzemski hit .400 in the Series.

Yaz led the league in batting in 1968 with the lowest average ever to win a major league crown: .301. No team in the American League batted over .240 in that "Year of the Pitcher"; had Yastrzemski not played that season, the league's batting crown would have been worn by Danny Cater, who hit .290. In 1969 Yastrzemski hit 40 homers and drove in 111 runs, and the following season he led the league in runs, slugging, and on-base percentage while slamming another 40 homers.

In 1975 Yastrzemski belted a three-run homer in the All-Star Game, but slumped to .269 with just 14 homers. Nonetheless, the Red Sox won the AL East and swept Oakland in the ALCS, as Yaz hit .455. In Game 3 he cracked two hits and made two defensive gems to lead the Red Sox into the World Series. Yastrzemski hit a respectable .310 in the Series against Cincinnati, with four RBIs and seven runs scored. But once again the Sox were done in seven games. Cincinnati beat Boston in the finale, 4–3, as Yaz made the final out.

On May 19, 1976, Yaz hit three home runs in one game and finished the season with 21 round-trippers and 102 RBIs. The following year he drove in more than 100 runs for his fifth and final time. In 1978 Yastrzemski experienced one of his biggest disappointments when he popped up with two men on for the final out of Boston's one-game playoff loss to the Yankees. He recorded his 3,000th hit on September 12, 1979, off New York's Jim Beattie.

All time, Yastrzemski ranks second in games, third in at bats, fifth in walks, seventh in hits, seventh in doubles, seventh in total bases, and 11th in RBIs. Opposing pitchers walked him intentionally 190 times, more than any other AL hitter since the statistic began to be kept in 1955. From his left field position at the base of Fenway's "Green Monster," Yaz led the league in assists six times, more than any outfielder in AL history. The Red Sox retired his uniform No. 8, and he joined the immortals in Cooperstown in 1989.

JOHN CLARKSON P

John Clarkson's "rubber arm" produced 328 wins in 12 major league seasons, including five consecutive 30-plus win seasons. In 1885 he won 53 games for the Chicago White Sox, the second highest season win total in major league history after Charley "Old Hoss" Radbourn's 59 in 1884.

"John Clarkson never had a superior as a pitcher and never will," infielder Fred Pfeffer said of his former teammate. "He was a master of control. I believe he could put a ball where he wanted it nine times out of 10. He had everything any pitcher ever had as well. His speed was something terrific, and he could throw any curve. However, his favorite pitch was a drop something like the spitball today, although he delivered it without the ointment necessary nowadays."

Discovered in 1884 by White Stockings player-manager Adrian "Cap" Anson while playing for Saginaw of the Northwestern League, Clarkson won 10 games for Chicago against three losses that season. Over the course of the next seven seasons, he *averaged* 38 wins a year.

Clarkson's 1885 numbers are almost superhuman. In addition to his 53–16 record and 1.85 ERA, he completed 68 games, pitched 623 innings, struck out 308, and tossed 10 shutouts and a no-hitter. In a battle of future Hall of Famers, Clarkson pitched a no-hitter against Providence and Radbourn, 4–0, on July 27. He gave up no walks and was denied a perfect game only because five batters reached base on errors.

After the 1887 season Clarkson demanded to be sold to Boston in order to be closer to home. The Boston Red Stockings bought him that winter from Chicago for $10,000. After winning 33 games in 1888, Clarkson was dazzling in 1889, posting a pitcher's Triple Crown by leading the league with 49 wins, 284 strikeouts, and a 2.73 ERA, to go with 620 innings pitched, eight shutouts, and 68 complete games. He was sent to the Cleveland Spiders in the middle of the 1892 season, and ended the year by facing his old teammates in the World Series. He lost both his starts to Boston, and pitched his last game for the Spiders two years later.

Through 2000, Clarkson's career totals ranked him eighth in complete games (485), 20th in innings pitched (4,536⅓), 33rd in games started (518), and 37th in shutouts (56).

"In knowing exactly what kind of ball a batter could not hit and in his ability to serve up just that kind of ball, I don't think I have ever seen the equal of Clarkson," said Cap Anson of his former star. Clarkson died of pneumonia on February 4, 1909. He was inducted into the Hall of Fame in 1963.

ROBIN YOUNT SS/OF

One of only three men in major league history ever to be named MVP at two different positions, Robin Yount played 20 years in the American League with a single team, the Milwaukee Brewers. An exuberant, hustling ballplayer, his dedication to the game, his all-around ability, and his loyalty to the often-mediocre Brewers franchise combined to make him a throwback to an earlier age.

Yount arrived in Milwaukee in 1974 after playing only a single season in the minors. At age 18, he was the youngest player in the majors; two seasons later, he became the youngest big leaguer ever to play in 161 games. That same year he led AL shortstops in double plays. In 1978, he teamed up with a new double play partner, second baseman Paul Molitor; the two would be teammates for the next 15 seasons.

The 1980 campaign was the first of Yount's three All-Star seasons. He collected 49 doubles and 82 extra-base hits to lead the league in both categories, and racked up 317 total bases—at that time the third-highest total ever by a shortstop. Following the strike-shortened season of 1981, Yount batted .316 in the division playoffs, which the Brewers lost to the Yankees.

In 1982 Yount engineered perhaps the best season ever by an AL shortstop to that point. He led the majors in slugging (.578), hits (210), doubles (46), and total bases (367). He finished second in the majors in batting at .331, and knocked in 114 runs—becoming the first shortstop in the history of the Junior Circuit to hit over .300 with at least 20 homers and 100 RBIs. He scored 129 runs, and led league shortstops in assists. Yount collected a plethora of postseason honors that year, including AL MVP, *The Sporting News* Player of the Year, and his first Gold Glove Award.

Yount cemented his reputation as a clutch hitter in Milwaukee's season-ending showdown with the Baltimore Orioles. In the game to determine the division champion, he tagged Jim Palmer for a home run in the top of the first and homered again in the third as Milwaukee took the AL East title. In the World Series against St. Louis, Yount hit .414 and homered to help win Game 5, but the Brewers came up short in Game 7.

Yount received more fan votes than any other player in 1983 All-Star balloting, but, ironically, it was his last appearance in the All-Star Game. The following year he began to suffer from the shoulder problems that would eventually drive him out of the infield. After the 1984 season, in which he scored over 100 runs for the third year in a row and narrowly missed his third consecutive .300 season, Yount underwent surgery twice in the next two years to repair damage in his right shoulder. Following the second surgery, however, he put together four consecutive .300 seasons, culminating in his second MVP year in 1989. His .997 fielding percentage in center field led the majors in 1986, making him the first player to lead the AL in fielding in both the outfield and the infield.

On September 6, 1986, at age 30, Yount notched his 2,000 hit, becoming one of the youngest players ever to reach that plateau. He hit for the cycle on June 12, 1988, and collected his 1,000th career RBI on August 27. He reached 2,500 hits on July 2, 1989, and after the season he captured his second MVP Award as the only player to appear on every ballot cast.

The 1992 season saw Yount achieve a number of important career milestones: 10,000 at bats, 1,500 runs, and, in the final month of the season, his 3,000th career hit. Only Ty Cobb and Henry Aaron were younger than Yount when he reached that total. The Milwaukee lifer retired following the 1993 season, and was voted into the Hall of Fame in his first year of eligibility in 1999.

BOBBY GRICH 2B

Until he injured his back, Bobby Grich was one of the best-fielding second basemen the game has ever seen. What made him even more special, however, was his bat. During his career he hit 224 homers, not a typical mark for Gold Glove second basemen.

The Orioles made Grich their top draft choice in the June 1967 amateur draft, signing him for $40,000. Playing regularly in 1972 and putting in time at short, second, first, and third, he fielded well, hit .278, and drove in 50 runs. Then followed four years of brilliance that would be hard to equal. Stationed at second base, Grich won four Gold Gloves and led the league in putouts, assists, double plays, and chances per game three times. In 1973 he committed only five errors and set a major league record with a .995 fielding percentage. While Jose Oquendo of the Cardinals subsequently topped that mark, Oquendo set it on an AstroTurf home field in a league filled with artificial surface infields. When Grich set his record, all 12 American League fields were grass, with far-less accommodating bounces.

During Grich's Gold Glove years he teamed with shortstop Mark Belanger to give the Orioles one of the greatest double play combinations the game has ever seen. At no time was their teamwork more important that in Baltimore's second-to-last game of the 1974 season, at which point the Orioles were one game ahead of the Yankees. Facing the Tigers, the Orioles were clinging to a one-run lead in the bottom of the ninth, with the bases loaded and one out. Detroit's Aurelio Rodriguez hit a one-hop bullet up the middle, but Grich came out of nowhere to make a diving stop and somehow flipped the ball to Belanger to start the game-ending double play.

Meanwhile, at the plate, Grich averaged 14 homers, 87 runs, and 98 walks a season. A free agent after the 1976 season, he signed a five-year contract with the Angels for $1.69 million. On Valentine's Day, 1977, however, Grich hurt his back trying to lift an air conditioner. He played only 52 games before undergoing surgery for a herniated disk. Post-surgery, he struggled in 1978, hitting only six homers.

He came back healthy in 1979, however, and had career highs with 30 homers, 101 RBIs, and 30 doubles as the Angels won their first division title. Two years later, in the strike-shortened 1981 season, Grich hit a career best .304 and led the AL with 22 homers. The next year, in which Grich was selected for his sixth All-Star Game, and his third as an Angel, California won the AL West a second time, but lost to the Brewers in the playoffs. In 1986 the Angels faced the Red Sox in the ALCS; they made it to within a strike of the World Series in Game 5, but were unable to close the game out. Grich had a particularly disappointing role in the loss. At 37 years old and in his last season, he had a chance to be the greatest hero in Angels' history in Game 5, but he lined out with two down in the bottom of the ninth, the score tied and the bases loaded.

Grich retired after the season with a career .984 fielding percentage, at the time a major league record. As of 2000, his participation in 1,302 double plays was the 10th-highest total for a second baseman.

TONY GWYNN OF

Tony Gwynn was one of the game's best pure hitters in two different decades. The likeable Padre won four batting titles each in the 1980s and 1990s; only Honus Wagner collected as many batting crowns in the National League. A true rarity for a modern athlete, Gwynn has spent his career through 2000 in one uniform and established himself as San Diego's all-time leader in nearly every offensive category except home runs.

Although his hitting got all the attention, Gwynn consistently ranked among the NL's best right fielders, winning five Gold Glove Awards. He could beat you on the basepaths, too. Despite his stocky build, Gwynn stole at least 10 bases in 11 seasons, including four seasons of 30 or more. In 1987 he stole 56 bases to finish second in the league.

Gwynn was selected by the Padres in the third round of the 1981 amateur draft out of San Diego State, where he lettered in both baseball and basketball. His first season, 1982, was the only one in which Gwynn failed to hit .300. His 18 consecutive years of attaining or bettering that mark is an NL record.

Despite missing almost the first three months of the 1983 season with an injury, Gwynn batted .309 and also had a 25-game hitting streak. The 1984 season was a breakout year for both Gwynn and the Padres. The outfielder won his first batting title with a .351 average, made the first of his 14 All-Star Game appearances, and helped lead San Diego to the pennant. Gwynn batted .368 in the 1984 National League Championship Series, scoring a Series-best six runs to lead the Padres to a come-from-behind win over the Cubs. He cooled off in the World Series, however, going 5-for-19 as Detroit topped San Diego in five games.

One year after Gwynn won his second batting title with a .370 mark, his .313 in 1988 set an NL record for lowest batting average by a leader. He won his third consecutive batting title the next season. Following a string of injuries he was back to his usual form in 1993, but expansion to the mile-high elevation of Denver provided some of his toughest competition for the batting crown. The only three batting titles Gwynn did not win from 1993 to 1999 were won by Colorado Rockies—Andres Galarraga (1993) and Larry Walker (1998–99).

Gwynn topped even himself in 1994. His .394 batting average was the highest in the major leagues since Ted Williams hit .406 in 1941, and the highest in the NL since Bill Terry of the New York Giants hit .401 in 1930. Gwynn had batted .433 (26 for 60) over his last 15 games when the baseball strike ended the season on August 11.

In 1996 Gwynn had the opportunity to play with his brother Chris. Tony won the batting title with a .353 average, and Chris singled in the winning run to clinch the NL West title on the final day of the season.

Gwynn won his fourth consecutive batting title in 1997, joining Ty Cobb, Rogers Hornsby, Rod Carew, and Wade Boggs as the only players to accomplish or better that feat. Although sometimes maligned for his lack of production, Gwynn also set career highs that season with 17 home runs, 119 RBIs, 220 hits, and 49 doubles. He appeared in his second World Series in 1998, but despite his .500 average with eight hits and a home run, San Diego dropped four straight to the Yankees.

On August 6, 1999, Gwynn became the 22nd member of the 3,000-hit club with a single against Montreal's Dan Smith. It was part of a "milestone weekend" for baseball—Gwynn and the Padres had surrendered Mark McGwire's 500th home run the previous night in St. Louis; Wade Boggs notched his 3,000th hit the night after Gwynn's milestone. Long known for his charitable nature and big heart, Gwynn was honored in 1999 with the Roberto Clemente Award as the player who best exemplified baseball on and off the field. He finished the 2000 season with 3,108 career hits, good for 17th on the all-time list.

JEFF BAGWELL 1B

If losing Babe Ruth wasn't bad enough, Boston Red Sox fans also bitterly lament the 1990 trade that sent Jeff Bagwell to the Houston Astros. The Sox dealt Bagwell for relief pitcher Larry Anderson, who appeared in only 15 games for a Red Sox team that was swept four straight by Oakland in the Championship Series. Bagwell went on to be National League Rookie of the Year; by 1994 he was the NL Most Valuable Player, a Gold Glove Award winner, and a four-time All-Star.

Through the 2000 season, Bagwell has wielded one of the NL's biggest bats for the better part of a decade. He has driven in more than 100 runs six times, four of them consecutive (1996–2000); over that same four-year span, he drew more than 100 bases on balls in each season. He has slammed more than 40 homers three times, and his lifetime batting average is over .300. He tied a major league record with four doubles against the San Francisco Giants on June 14, 1996; his 48 doubles that season led the league. He hit three homers and had 13 total bases against the Los Angeles Dodgers on June 24, 1994.

Originally a third baseman, Bagwell found the position already occupied in Houston by an established player, Ken Caminiti. Given the choice of playing third base in Triple A or first base in the majors he did not hesitate to change positions. He responded to the opportunity by hitting .294 with 15 home runs and 82 RBIs in his banner rookie year.

Bagwell steadily improved his game, transforming his body with weigh training and perfecting his unique batting stance. Feet planted wide apart, Bagwell bobs in a crouch until the pitch is delivered. Instead of striding forward he straightens his legs, uncoiling his body to generate a tremendous whip action with the bat. By 1994, his MVP season, Bagwell's swing was machine tooled. In only 110 games of a strike-shortened campaign he produced a .368 batting average and 39 home runs, while leading the league with 104 runs, 116 RBIs, a .461 on-base average, and an incredible .750 slugging percentage.

He also won a Gold Glove for his play at first base.

His penchant for crowding the plate, however, has cost Bagwell some playing time. Twice he broke his hand on pitched balls, prompting him to wear a padded brick on the back of his batting glove. After the 1995 season, when he appeared in only 114 games, Bagwell proved durable as he continued to improve his power game while leading the Astros to postseason play. He played in 162 games in each of the next two seasons, and again in 1999. In 1997 the Astros started a run of three straight division titles, but Bagwell's difficulties in the Division Series led to three straight early exits.

Bagwell also has shown surprising speed. In 1997 he became the first Astros player to hit 30 home runs and steal 30 bases in a season; he repeated the feat in 1999, with 42 homers and 30 thefts. His runs totals have steadily increased since 1998, when he scored 124 times. Bagwell's 152 runs in 2000 were the NL's highest total since Chuck Klein tallied the same number in 1932. His 295 runs over two consecutive seasons, 1999–2000, set a league record. Bagwell also slugged a career-best 47 homers in 2000 to go with 132 RBIs.

AL KALINE OF

Al Kaline never spent a minute in the minor leagues. Signed by the Detroit Tigers out of high school for $30,000 in 1953, he entered the lineup on June 25 of that year and remained in a Tigers uniform for the next 22 seasons. He retired in 1974 with 3,007 hits, 399 home runs, and a .297 batting average.

In 1955 Kaline opened the season with a bang on April 17, hitting three home runs in one game, including two in one inning. He was only the fourth player in American League history to hit two homers in a single inning, and the first since Joe DiMaggio did it 19 years earlier. At age 20, he became the youngest player to win a batting title when he finished the season at .340, leading the league with 200 hits and adding 27 homers, 121 runs, and 102 RBIs. In the outfield he was superb. Kaline quickly mastered the tricky caroms and bounces along the right field wall at Tiger Stadium, and baserunners soon learned not to challenge his arm.

For the next few seasons Kaline was the Motor City's answer to Willie Mays or Mickey Mantle. In 1956 he posted career highs in RBIs (128) and triples (10); he led the league with a .530 slugging average in 1959, the same year that he and Harvey Kuenn finished 1-2 in the American League batting race, becoming just the seventh pair of teammates in league history to do so. Kaline's 41 doubles paced the circuit in 1961. From 1955 to 1963 he hit at least .300 in all but two years.

Unfortunately, Kaline was dogged by injuries that kept him out of the lineup for 10 or 15 games a season. In a typical year, he would hit about 20 homers, knock in 80 or 90 runs, and throw out the occasional brazen baserunner. His performance was usually good enough to put him on the All-Star team and earn him a Gold Glove. But he never won another batting title, and he never led the league in homers or RBIs. Still, he was loved in Detroit, where fans appreciated his work ethic and modesty. Like many in the city, Kaline did his job, did it well, and did it without grumbling.

In 1962 Kaline appeared to be on his way to a career year when he broke his collarbone making a great game-ending catch against the Yankees. Despite missing nearly two months of play, he finished with a career-best 29 home runs, adding 94 RBIs in only 398 at bats.

Kaline had another 29-homer year in 1966, and was on pace to exceed that mark in 1967 when he broke his hand, missing a month of the season. Injured again in 1968, he finally made it into a World Series with the Tigers, bombing the Cardinals' pitching staff in a seven-game Detroit victory. Kaline batted .379 for the Series, slamming two home runs and leading both teams with eight RBIs; he also made several great plays in the field.

By 1973 Kaline had become a part-time player. Many thought he should retire, but he needed only 139 more hits to reach 3,000. In a controversial move, Detroit manager Ralph Houk removed Kaline from right field and made him the team's first designated hitter. In 1974 he hit a respectable .262, with 13 home runs, and his 64 RBIs were his best since 1970. On September 24, facing Baltimore's Dave McNally, Kaline stroked a double for his 3,000th career hit. He retired at the end of the season.

Kaline ranks third in major league history for the longest career spent with one team. He was a member of 15 All-Star teams and won 11 Gold Gloves. He was elected to the Hall of Fame in 1980 in his first year of eligibility.

CHARLIE GEHRINGER 2B

They called second baseman Charlie Gehringer "the Mechanical Man" because of the quiet, methodical way he went about his business. As outfielder Doc Cramer remarked, "You wind him up on opening day and forget about him." The finely tuned machine hit .320 lifetime, collected more than 200 hits in a season seven times, led American League second basemen in fielding average seven times, and twice had consecutive-game streaks that exceeded 500. During one 14-season span he fell under .300 only once, when he dropped to .298. He played in the All-Star Game, which was initiated midway through his career, the first six times it was held.

In 1925, after driving in 108 runs for Toronto of the International League, Gehringer came up to Ty Cobb's Detroit Tigers late in the season. He would spend his entire 19-year career with the team, seeing action in three World Series. Gehringer's first great season was 1929, when he batted .339 and led the league in hits, runs, doubles, and triples. He led the league again in hits and runs in Detroit's pennant-winning season of 1934, and also topped the AL a second time in doubles, belting 60 in 1936. However, his best year statistically was 1937, when Gehringer led the league with a .371 average, had a career-best .458 on-base percentage, and won Most Valuable Player honors.

Gehringer was spectacular in Detroit's back-to-back appearances (1934–35) in the World Series. In a losing effort against the St. Louis Cardinals in 1934, Gehringer hit .379 with 11 hits—one-shy of the Series record—and five runs. The following October, he batted .375 with three doubles as the Tigers triumphed in six games over the Cubs.

When 500 admirers from his hometown of Fowlerville honored Gehringer with his own "Day"—which, according to long-standing baseball tradition, jinxed a player—he hit the first pitch he saw for a home run, collected three other hits, and stole home to win the game.

Gehringer retired after 45 games in 1942, but played ball in the navy during the war as he rose to the rank of lieutenant commander. He was named to the Hall of Fame in 1949, and in 1951 the Tigers appointed him as their general manager and vice president; he served in the latter role through 1959.

Through 2000, Gehringer ranks 16th in runs and 15th in doubles on the all-time list. As a second baseman, he still has the fourth-highest career batting average (.320) for his position, and ranks second in assists, sixth in putouts, and seventh in double plays.

ED WALSH P

"Big Ed" Walsh, the greatest of the spitball pitchers, compiled a 1.82 ERA, still the lowest career mark of any hurler with more than 1,000 innings. Although he spent 14 years in the major leagues, most of his lifetime stats were accumulated in the seven seasons from 1906 through 1912. Walsh finished with a record of 195–126, and his 57 shutouts are tied for 11th best all time. He was also one of the game's great iron men, leading the American League four times in innings pitched, but his drive and guttiness eventually took a toll on his arm.

The son of a coal miner, Walsh worked in the mines and developed strong shoulders and arms on his generous frame. It was at the White Sox training camp in 1904 that he learned the secret to throwing a spitball. When, after a few seasons, Walsh was able to bring the spitter under control and combine it with his fastball, he became one of the dominant pitchers of the Dead Ball Era.

Walsh and his slippery pitch came into their own in 1906, when his 17 wins helped Chicago's legendary "Hitless Wonders" to the pennant. The White Sox team average of .230 was lowest in the league, but the club's big plus was a great pitching staff. Walsh led the AL with 10 shutouts and compiled a sparkling 1.88 ERA.

The Sox faced the Chicago Cubs that fall in the only all-Chicago World Series. The Cubs had racked up an all-time record 116 victories, and the Series looked like a mismatch. Yet the Sox won Game 1, and Walsh started Game 3 with the Series even. The spitball had rarely been seen in the National League, and Walsh whiffed 12 Cubs while surrendering only two hits. Then, in the crucial fifth game, Walsh survived a sloppy defense to leave in the seventh inning with an 8–6 lead, which held. The Chisox went on to win Game 6 and record a stunning upset.

In 1907 Walsh went 24–18. The team's poor hitting cost him, as he was shut out eight times. He completed a league-leading 37 of his 46 starts, and topped the AL with 422⅓ innings pitched and a 1.60 ERA. He also relieved in 10 games and, under modern rules, earned four saves.

That was merely a prelude to his remarkable season of 1908. In one of the finest performances of all time, Walsh led the league with 40 victories, 66 appearances, 42 complete games, 464 innings pitched (the modern record), 269 strikeouts, 11 shutouts, and six saves. His ERA was a skimpy 1.42. Detroit, Cleveland, and Chicago fought to the end for the pennant, and Walsh pitched seven of the last nine games. On September 27 he beat Boston, 3–0. Two days later he pitched a doubleheader against the Bosox and won, 5–1 and 2–0. On October 2 he pitched brilliantly in a losing effort against Cleveland, striking out 15 and allowing only an unearned run while the Indians' Addie Joss twirled a perfect game. Three days later Walsh held the Tigers to a single run to record his 40th victory. But the Sox finished third, a game and a half behind pennant-winning Detroit.

Walsh slipped to 15–11 in 1909, and critics speculated that he had been overworked the previous two years. That may have been true, but there was another reason for his ineffectiveness—hitters had caught on that Walsh was tipping off his spitter by tugging the bill of his cap. Despite that, Walsh still led the league with eight shutouts and lowered his ERA to 1.41.

After a 20–loss season in 1910, in which he still paced the AL with a career-low 1.27 ERA, Walsh was finally given some support by the White Sox. He responded by posting consecutive 27–win seasons. In both years, he led the league in games, innings pitched, and saves; in 1911, he also led the league in strikeouts for a second time. On August 27, 1911, he beat Boston, 5–0, on a no-hitter.

At the end of the 1912 season the White Sox and Cubs played a series of exhibitions in Chicago. Walsh, pitching nearly every day, hurled four complete games and relieved twice. The next spring his arm was shot. He struggled through another four seasons, and the White Sox released him in 1916. A comeback attempt with the Boston Braves ended after 18 innings.

In addition to his prowess on the mound, Walsh was also a superior fielder, a fair hitter, and the first American League pitcher to steal home twice. Walsh also had a hand in designing Comiskey Park—no surprise that it turned out to be one of the game's most friendly ballparks for pitchers. Walsh was elected to the Hall of Fame in 1946.

WADE BOGGS 3B

Though lacking in speed and power, Wade Boggs used a solid hitting stroke and keen eye to accumulate 3,010 career hits; only 20 players have ever had more. The red-haired, mustachioed third baseman batted .300 or better in each of his first 10 seasons, and won five batting titles in six years. He played in 12 consecutive All-Star Games.

After six years in the minors, Boggs earned a promotion to the Boston Red Sox in 1982. Used mostly at first base, he quickly established himself by batting .349, the best average by a rookie in American League history. Following a switch to third base, and long hours of practice with hitting coach Walt Hrniak, Boggs blossomed into a star. In 1983 he led the AL with a .361 batting average; two years later he batted a career-high .368, the best mark in either league.

In 1986 Boggs played in the postseason for the first time and batted a solid .290 in Boston's heartbreaking World Series loss to the New York Mets. The following season he again led the AL in batting, this time with a .363 average. More surprisingly, he hit 24 home runs, 16 better than his previous high.

Boggs won his fourth consecutive batting title in 1988, hitting over .360 for the fourth time as well. In 1989 he reached the 200-hit plateau for a record-setting seventh consecutive season.

As Boggs approached his 32nd birthday in 1990, his hitting began to fall off. He batted .302, by far the poorest mark of his career, and failed to lead the league in any major offensive category for the first time since 1984. He rebounded the following season, however, to hit .332 and play well at third base.

After slumping to a .259 batting average in 1992, Boggs was let go by the Red Sox and signed by the New York Yankees. The move rejuvenated Boggs, who proceeded to top the .300 mark in his first four seasons in pinstripes. His defensive play also improved, as he earned back-to-back Gold Gloves—the first of his career. More importantly, Boggs fulfilled a career-long goal in 1996 by playing on a World Series winner—and taking a memorable victory lap on horseback at Yankee Stadium.

Boggs signed with Tampa Bay, his hometown team, following the 1997 season. He batted .280 during the Devil Rays' inaugural season, and achieved one more moment of glory. On August 7, 1999, Boggs became the 23rd player to reach the 3,000-hit plateau—and, ironically, the first to reach the milestone with a home run. He retired after the season.

BOB GIBSON P

National League hitters of the 1960s and 1970s remember Bob Gibson as having been intimidating, aggressive, and sometimes downright mean. To historians of baseball, he is remembered as having enjoyed one of the greatest seasons any pitcher has ever recorded.

Gibson's 1.12 ERA in 1968 was the best since the introduction of the lively ball and the third best of the 20th century, behind only Dutch Leonard's 0.96 in 1914 and Mordecai Brown's 1.04 in 1906. During his sensational season with the St. Louis Cardinals, with whom he spent his entire career, Gibson pitched 13 shutouts. In one game he went 12 innings without surrendering an earned run. Five of his shutouts came consecutively; he lasted less than eight innings only twice and recorded 28 complete games in 34 starts. At one point Gibson pitched 47⅔ scoreless innings, ending his skein on a wild pitch against the Dodgers. He then pitched another 17⅓ scoreless innings. In one 95-inning stretch he surrendered a mere two earned runs.

Gibson won 22 games in 1968, including 15 in a row. The string would have been 16, except for an 11-inning no-decision against the Pirates. In three of his defeats the Cardinals were shut out. Gibson pitched a four-hitter against the Giants on September 17, but Gaylord Perry pitched a no-hitter and Gibson lost, 1–0.

Of course, 1968 was "the Year of the Pitcher." Seven pitchers that year had ERAs under 2.00, and the general lack of offense triggered a number of rule changes in 1969 designed to help hitters. Still, Gibson's figures were nothing short of amazing.

During the course of Gibson's 17-year career, his success was based on hard work, a fierce determination to win, control, and a willingness to back hitters off the plate. Although Gibson struck out more than 200 batters in a season nine times and led the league in strikeouts in 1968, he was not obsessed with fanning batters. "Believe me," he once contended, "I would much rather get three outs on three pitches than three outs on nine pitches, because that's going to make me that much stronger at the end of the game."

Most controversial was Gibson's habit of brushing hitters back from the plate, for which he earned a nasty reputation. But Gibson saw the intimidation of hitters as part of his job. He also claimed that a primary reason for pitching the way he did was to defend his teammate, Lou Brock, who was often the target of opposing pitchers who resented Brock stealing on them when the Cardinals were winning by big scores.

A sickly child who grew up in poverty in Omaha, Nebraska, Gibson signed with the Cardinals in 1957. He stuck with the team for good in 1961, tossing a shutout and hitting a home run in his first appearance as a member of the starting rotation. He won 13, and would improve his win total each season for the next five years.

In 1962 Gibson was selected to his first of eight All-Star Games. The following year he was 18–9, beginning a decade-long run in which he averaged 19 wins a season. In 1965, when Gibson was an All-Star for the second time, he enjoyed his first of five 20-victory campaigns. His only lapse came in 1967, when he missed a third of the season with a broken leg. But then he turned it on in the World Series, going 3–0 against the Red Sox and recording an ERA of 1.00.

After his phenomenal season of 1968, Gibson took up where he left off in the Series. In Game 1 he shut out Detroit, 4–0, while striking out a World Series record 17 batters. He came back in Game 4 to beat Denny McLain a second time, 10–1. But then the postseason magic ended, as it was Mickey Lolich who won a third time, beating Gibson, 4–1, in Game 7.

Gibson rolled off two more 20-win seasons, including a 23–7 mark in 1970. By 1974, however, he had lost his dominance, and suffered through his first losing season since 1960. He retired after going 3–10 in 1975.

As outstanding a moundsman as Gibson was, he was a complete athlete and offered the Cardinals a lot more than his pitching. An excellent fielder, he won nine consecutive Gold Glove Awards from 1965 to 1973. At the plate he hit 24 homers—including five in a season twice—and in 1963 he had 20 RBIs.

All told, opposing hitters managed only a .228 average against Gibson. His totals of 3,117 strikeouts (as the first National Leaguer to reach that plateau) and 56 shutouts rank 11th and 13th, respectively, on the all-time list. In 1981 Gibson became only the 11th man to be inducted into the Hall of Fame on the first ballot.

ROGER CONNOR 1B

Roger Connor was the most prolific longball hitter of the 19th century, and his 138 career home runs stood as the major league record until the advent of Babe Ruth. Oddly, he only once led his league in homers, which may explain in part why he was not named to the Hall of Fame until 1976, 45 years after his death.

At 6 feet 3 inches and 220 pounds, Connor was a giant for his time and required an oversize uniform. Signed by the National League's Troy Trojans in 1880, he committed 60 errors in only 83 games as a lefthanded third baseman, but he batted .332 and helped the Trojans leap from last to fourth place. After Connor shifted to first base in 1881, however, his fielding improved, and he eventually led the league's first basemen in fielding average four times.

On September 10, 1881, Connor blasted the first major league grand slam. In 1882 he began to show consistent longball power, hitting four home runs and leading the league with 18 triples. When Troy was expelled from the league that year, John B. Day's New York Gothams purchased Connor, who received a new contract for $1,800 with bonuses that increased his take to $2,100, one of the best salaries in the league. In his first season in New York, he earned the money by hitting .357, including one monstrous home run that so impressed the crowd that fans took up a collection and bought him a $500 gold watch.

In 1885, Connor's New York team—now called the Giants—battled Chicago down to the final days of the season before finishing two games behind. Connor led the league with 169 hits, a batting average of .371, and an on-base average of .435. In 1886 he paced the NL in triples for the second time with 20 and batted .355. In 1887 he smacked 17 home runs. Chicago's Ned Williamson had set the major league home run record with 27 a few years before, but he had played in a tiny ballpark with 180-foot foul lines. Four of Williamson's teammates had also topped 20 home runs that year. Apart from that single season, no other NL player had smacked more than 14 homers before 1887. But Connor missed out on the 1887 crown because Billy O'Brien of Washington hit 19. Connor also finished second in RBIs, with 104.

Contributing to the Giants' first pennant in 1888, Connor slammed 14 home runs, three of them in a May 9 game at Indianapolis. New York won a second pennant in 1889, paced by Connor's 13 homers and league-leading 130 RBIs. In the Series against the American Association's Brooklyn club, Connor hit .343 and drove in 12 runs to propel the Giants to a come-from-behind victory.

Deeply involved in the Brotherhood of Professional Base Ball Players, which sponsored the new Players League in 1890, Connor led the short-lived circuit with 14 homers—his only home run crown—and hit .349 with 103 RBIs. He returned to the Giants the following season, and after a year with Philadelphia, enjoyed his final 100-RBI season with the Giants in 1893. He completed his major league career with St. Louis in 1897. On June 1, 1895, Connor went 6 for 6 against his old New York team, with two doubles and a triple.

ED DELAHANTY OF

Big Ed Delahanty was one of the greatest hitters in baseball history, but his accomplishments have been overshadowed by the circumstances of his unusual death. Today, few fans are aware that he had a .346 career batting average, that he once hit four home runs in a single game, or that he is the only man ever to be credited with batting titles in both the National and American leagues. If they have heard of Delahanty at all, it is because he died by being swept over Niagara Falls.

Delahanty, whose four younger brothers followed him to the major leagues, started out with the Philadelphia Phillies in 1888. He struggled initially at the plate and in the field, but his hitting improved during the next three seasons—including one year with Cleveland in the Players' League in 1890—and his fielding followed suit when, in 1891, the Phillies stationed him permanently in the outfield.

In a preview of what was to come, Delahanty hit .306 in 1892 and led the NL with 21 triples. From 1893 through 1896 he hit .368, .404, .404, and .397. In an era of high batting averages, however, this performance earned him only a runner-up to the batting title in 1895 and third best the other three years. Over that same span, he was virtually a run-scoring machine, accumulating yearly totals of 145, 148, 149, and 131. In all, he scored 100 or more runs in a season 11 times, eight of them consecutive.

Delahanty led the league in doubles in 1895 and 1896, and in home runs and RBIs in 1893 and 1896. His total of 19 homers in 1893 was the second highest of the entire decade. In a loss to Chicago on July 13, 1896, Delahanty became the second man to hit four consecutive home runs in a single game, all inside the park. In a game on June 16, 1894, he went 6 for 6, a feat he had already achieved in the Players League on June 2, 1890.

During this period the Philadelphia outfield was one of the greatest of all time. Delahanty played left, "Sliding Billy" Hamilton patrolled center, and Sam Thompson was stationed in right. All three were eventually enshrined in the Hall of Fame. In 1894 each man batted more than .400. Unfortunately, Philadelphia's poor pitching prevented the club from winning any pennants.

In 1899, after several near misses, Delahanty finally topped the NL in hitting with a .410 batting average, his third time over .400. Only Ty Cobb and Rogers Hornsby have since matched this record. Also that season, Delahanty led the league with 238 hits, 55 doubles, and 137 RBIs. He hit well for the Phillies the next two seasons, leading the league in doubles for the fourth time in 1901 with 38.

Playing for Washington in the fledgling American League in 1902, Delahanty won his second batting crown with a .376 average (research has subsequently established that Nap Lajoie actually finished two points higher). He also paced the league in slugging (.590) and on-base percentage (.453). But the next summer saw Delahanty, in his 16th major league season, hitting the bottle even harder than he was hitting AL pitchers. When a deal that would have returned him to the New York Giants fell through, a sulking Delahanty began to drink yet more heavily.

On July 2, 1903, the slugger boarded a train in Detroit, apparently going to New York. While drinking on the train, he brandished a razor at several other passengers and caused a disturbance. Delahanty was put off the train at Niagara Falls, Ontario. When the train left the station to cross the bridge into the United States, he pushed past a guard and followed across the bridge on foot, ignoring a warning that the draw was open. One week later his body was discovered in the Niagara River some 20 miles below the falls.

Almost a century after his death in 1903, Delahanty's batting average remains the sixth best of all time. He ranks 13th with 186 triples, 29th with a .411 on-base average, and 30th with 522 doubles. He was elected to the Hall of Fame in 1945.

LOU BOUDREAU SS

Lou Boudreau had a long and highly successful career as both a playing manager and one of the outstanding shortstops of the 1940s. He ranks as one of the best defensive shortstops of all time and was also a feared hitter—through 2000 he ranked eighth among all shortstops in lifetime batting average. A confident and creative manager, he was elected to the Hall of Fame in 1970 for his talents on and off the field.

Boudreau started out with the Cleveland Indians as a third baseman, but was converted to shortstop. In 1940, his first full season in the majors, he hit .295 with 101 RBIs, 46 doubles, and 10 triples. He was also named to the All-Star team for the first of eight times.

Following the 1941 campaign, Boudreau applied for the club's managerial position. When the 1942 season opened, he was, at age 24, the youngest person to start a major league season as a manager. Although his Indians finished out of the running for the next six years, Boudreau was marvelous on the field. In 1944 he led the league with a .327 batting average and 45 doubles. He also set records (since broken) for shortstops with a .978 fielding percentage and 134 double plays.

On July 14, 1946, the Indians played the Red Sox in a doubleheader. In the first game Boudreau had four doubles and a homer, making him the only American Leaguer to ring up five extra-base hits in one game, a still-standing record as of 2000. Boston's Ted Williams went 5 for 5, however, and his three homers drove in eight runs. The Indians lost, 11–10, and Boudreau fumed. It was the impetus for his "Williams shift," in which Boudreau stationed six players to the right of second base the next time his team faced Williams, leaving only the left fielder on the left side. Over the years, Boudreau's charts indicated that his team was 37 percent more successful against Williams while using the shift.

After the Indians finished fourth in 1947, owner Bill Veeck wanted to swap Boudreau for Vern Stephens of the St. Louis Browns and several other players. Veeck received more than 4,000 letters from outraged fans demanding he keep Boudreau. When the *Cleveland News* ran a front-page ballot to elicit the fans' opinions, 100,000 responded, voting to retain Boudreau by a 10–1 margin. Veeck backed down.

Boudreau responded by bringing the fans a pennant. His own contribution to the team's success was a .355 batting average, an on-base percentage of .453, and a slugging percentage of .534. He hit 18 homers, drove in 106 runs, and scored 116. He also led AL shortstops in fielding percentage for the eighth time in nine years and was the club's emotional leader. A collision at second base in early August briefly took him out of the lineup. But in the first game of an August 8 doubleheader against the Yankees, with whom the Indians were tied for first place, Boudreau put himself in the game as a pinch hitter and tied the score with a bases-loaded single. The Tribe went on to win both games.

The 1948 season ended with the Indians and the Red Sox in a tie for first. Boudreau slammed two homers and added two singles to back Gene Bearden's five-hitter as Cleveland won the first postseason playoff in American League history. To cap the already incredible season, Boudreau hit four doubles as the Indians bested the Boston Braves in the World Series.

Boudreau ended his playing career with the Red Sox in 1952. He subsequently managed the Sox, the Kansas City Athletics, and the Chicago Cubs, and also became a Cubs broadcaster. But it was in Cleveland where Boudreau remained a hero. The street next to Cleveland Stadium was renamed Boudreau Boulevard in his honor.

LUKE APPLING SS

Luke Appling played every game of his 20-season major league career with the Chicago White Sox. Since his tenure at Comiskey Park fell precisely in the middle of Chicago's 40-year pennant drought, he belongs in that rare (and unfortunate) category of Hall of Famers who never played in a World Series.

As a young shortstop with the Southern Association's Atlanta Crackers in 1930, Appling showed an aptitude for hitting but not for dexterity afield. He joined the Chicago White Sox at the end of that year, and struggled over the next two seasons before breaking through in 1933, when he stopped swinging for the fences and started hitting to all fields. Appling finished the season batting .322, the first of nine consecutive .300-plus campaigns. His fielding improved, too—although he topped American League shortstops in errors five times, his range was excellent, and he led the league in assists seven times and in putouts twice. He always insisted that many of his errors were due to the uneven surface at Comiskey Park.

Appling was an excellent leadoff hitter, combining a high batting average, good speed, and a facility for drawing walks—he exceeded 100 free passes in a season on three occasions. Although he was anything but a slugger, he still drove in 1,116 runs during his long career.

Only once did Appling top 100 RBIs—during his career year of 1936, when he also set personal highs with 111 runs scored and 204 hits. At one point that season Appling had a club record 27-game hitting streak. On the season's final day he went 4 for 4 to finish with a .388 batting average and become the first AL shortstop to win a batting title. The mark is also the highest compiled by a shortstop in the 20th century. He won a second batting crown in 1943 with a .328 average.

Of all Appling's skills, the most legendary was his ability to foul off pitches until he got one he liked. According to a popular tale he once fouled off 14 unsatisfactory tosses before bashing a triple. He was also a notorious complainer, and his willingness to gripe about minor ailments earned him the sobriquet, "Old Aches and Pains."

Appling was 38 when he returned from military service in late 1945, but he picked up as though he had never been away, hitting .368 in his short season. In 1949, at age 42, he hit .301. But with the White Sox committed to a youth movement, the seven-time All-Star played only 50 games as a utility infielder in 1950 before retiring with a lifetime batting average of .310. At the time, he held the league career records for games played, assists, putouts, and chances accepted by a shortstop, all later eclipsed by another White Sox player, Luis Aparicio.

Appling was elected to the Hall of Fame in 1964. Still spry at age 75 in 1982, he appeared in the Cracker Jack All-Star Game in Washington, D.C., and hit an improbable home run off Warren Spahn.

OZZIE SMITH SS

Ozzie Smith was in a class by himself at shortstop. As Thomas Boswell of the *Washington Post* once wrote of him, "Instead of '1' his number should be '8,' but turned sideways because the possibilities he brings to his position are almost infinite."

The National League's career leader in Gold Gloves

and arguably the best-fielding shortstop of all time, Smith also made himself into an above-average hitter and high-average base-stealer. It was his glove, however, that made him a legend. Smith not only got to balls that other players could not even reach, he turned them into double plays; he retired having taken part in more twin killings than any shortstop in history. He also rarely missed games, appearing in 2,511—only 70 less than Luis Aparicio, the all-time leader at the position. In other fielding categories at short, Smith ranks first in assists, sixth in fielding average, and eighth in putouts.

"The Wizard of Oz" was adored in St. Louis, where he played his final 15 seasons. One of baseball's most popular players, Smith began each game by doing a backflip on the way to assuming his position. That was usually only a prelude to his acrobatics during the game, which helped earn him a berth on 15 All-Star teams.

Smith broke in with the San Diego Padres, who selected him in the fourth round of the 1977 free agent draft. After winning two Gold Gloves in San Diego and setting a record for assists with 621 in 1980, he was traded to the Cardinals for shortstop Garry Templeton after the 1981 season. In his debut season with St. Louis, Smith led the National League's shortstops in fielding, something he'd go on to achieve a record seven times. He also hit two home runs, doubling his four-year output in San Diego. In the NL Championship Series, Smith hit .556 with three doubles and three runs as the Cardinals swept the Braves. St. Louis went on to claim its first world championship in 15 years.

Learning to fit his talents to the spacious dimensions and artificial turf at Busch Stadium, the switch-hitting Smith became an expert bunter and hit-and-run specialist. He improved his batting average to .276 by 1985, when the Cardinals won their division again. Smith blossomed in the Championship Series against the Dodgers. With the game and the series tied, 2–2, in Game 5, he homered in the bottom of the ninth to win the game. It was the first lefthanded home run of his career. Smith batted .435 in the Cardinals' six-game victory and earned NLCS Most Valuable Player honors.

In 1987, for the fifth time in Smith's six years in St. Louis, the Cardinals led the league in team fielding. That year, Smith finally reached the .300 mark, won his accustomed Gold Glove, and finished second to Andre Dawson in Most Valuable Player voting. He also drove in 75 runs without hitting a single dinger, the best such showing since World War II.

In 1991 Smith set a record for NL shortstops, committing just eight errors in 150 games. The following season he won his 13th consecutive Gold Glove to break a tie with Willie Mays and Roberto Clemente for most in league history. At his retirement in 1996, he had amassed 580 stolen bases, 20th on the all-time list. After quitting the field, the affable Smith replaced the late Mel Allen as host on the long-running television show, *This Week in Baseball.*

ROBERTO CLEMENTE OF

Roberto Clemente was one of the true heroes American baseball has produced. His dedication on the field was unrivaled; off the field, his efforts on behalf of others were noble and inspiring. Proud and passionate, he played the game as if it were his and his alone.

Clemente won four batting titles and set a National League record for most years leading the league in outfield assists, with five. His marvelous arm made him legendary for the strength and accuracy of his throws. He won 12 Gold Gloves, tying him with Willie Mays for the most awarded an outfielder, and he retired as the all-time Pittsburgh Pirates leader in games played, at bats, hits, singles, and total bases.

Born in Puerto Rico, Clemente came up with the Pirates in 1955. During his first two seasons as the team's right fielder he gunned down 18 and 20 runners, respectively. In 1958 he led the league in outfield assists for the first time with 22.

Clemente, and all of Pittsburgh, had a terrific year in 1960. He batted .314, and his 94 RBIs led the team as they won the NL pennant and shocked baseball by beating the powerful Yankees in the World Series. Clemente hit .310 for the Series, batting safely in all seven games and driving in three runs.

In 1961 Clemente changed to a heavier bat to avoid overswinging on bad balls. He won his first batting title that year, hitting .351 with 23 homers, 10 triples, and 89 RBIs. In the first of two All-Star Games that season, he tripled for the NL's first hit off Whitey Ford, scored the game's first run, drove in the second run with a sacrifice fly, and singled in the bottom of the 10th to bring home Willie Mays with the winning run. From then on he wore his ring from that game, not his 1960 World Series ring.

Because of the aggressive way he played, Clemente suffered many injuries. He infuriated the Pirates' management by shunning medical experts in Pittsburgh and retaining a Puerto Rican chiropractor to deal with his physical problems. His constant complaining about aches and pains didn't sit well with sportswriters, who accused him of being a hypochondriac—overlooking the fact that Clemente played more than 140 games for eight seasons in a row.

Clemente won batting titles again in 1964 and 1965, and then enjoyed his best power year in 1966, belting 29 homers and driving in 119 runs. He had 15- and 17-game hitting streaks that season, along with four four-hit games. Defensively, he was still the best. In one game, in a bases-loaded situation, a batter lined an apparent single to right. The runner on third wasn't hustling, and Clemente fired a strike to the catcher for the forceout. He won the league's Most Valuable Player Award, and began taking the reins of leadership in the clubhouse.

Clemente hit .357 in 1967 to win his fourth batting title, adding 23 homers and 110 RBIs for good measure. In a loss to Cincinnati that season, he hit three homers and drove in all seven of his team's runs. When the Pirates honored him in 1970 at their new Three Rivers Stadium, fans delivered a scroll signed by 300,000 people in Puerto Rico (roughly 10 percent of the island's population). The Bucs won the game, 11–0, and Clemente had two hits and made two great catches—the second of them tearing up his knee.

His intensity and skill received their finest showcase in 1971. The Bucs knocked off the Giants in that year's NLCS, with Clemente hitting .333 and driving in four runs. In the World Series against the Baltimore Orioles, he torched the Birds for a .414 batting average, a .759

slugging average, 12 hits, and two homers, including a key shot off Mike Cuellar in the climactic seventh game. The Pirates won the Series, and Clemente was the Series MVP.

Nagged by injuries in 1972, Clemente still hit .312, and his double off the Mets' Jon Matlack on September 30 was his 3,000th hit. Tragically, it also proved to be his last. Working to gather, pack, and transport supplies to help the victims of an earthquake in Nicaragua, Clemente boarded a cargo plane for that country on New Year's Eve. The plane crashed into the ocean shortly after takeoff.

The Hall of Fame waived the five-year wait between last playing appearance and eligibility for Clemente, as it had done earlier for Lou Gehrig. In 1971 the Commissioner's Office had started an annual award to the player who best exemplified baseball on and off the field; in 1973 it was renamed the Roberto Clemente Award.

REGGIE JACKSON OF

Reggie Jackson, known to posterity as "Mr. October" for his postseason heroics, was the most electrifying hitter of the 1970s. He was at his best in the World Series, and his Series slugging average of .755 tops all other hitters. Jackson also ranks high with a career World Series batting average of .357, and his total of 10 Series home runs places him in a tie for fourth, with Lou Gehrig. Through 2000, Jackson and Sandy Koufax were the only two-time World Series Most Valuable Players, and Jackson remained the only player to do it with two different teams.

He walloped the ball in the regular season, too. Entering 2001, Jackson ranks sixth all-time with 563 home runs, 15th with 1,075 extra-base hits, and 17th with 1,702 RBIs. He also struck out a record 2,597 times—once in every four at-bats. But he considered the strikeouts as collateral damage for all the successful bombs he launched.

In 1968, his rookie year with the Oakland A's, Jackson hit 29 homers to go with a then record 171 strikeouts. The following year, he put together his finest all-around season at the plate, leading the American League with 123 runs and a .608 slugging average. Jackson also registered career highs with 47 homers, 118 RBIs, and 114 bases on balls.

In 1971 the A's romped through the AL West before falling to Baltimore in the League Championship Series. Jackson's 32 homers led the club, and he wowed the baseball world in that year's All-Star Game when he socked a home run off the light tower on the roof at Tiger Stadium. The following year the A's won the pennant and bested the Reds in the World Series, but Jackson missed the action, having torn a hamstring scoring the winning run in the A's five-game win over Detroit in the ALCS.

Jackson was named AL MVP in 1973, when he led the league in runs, home runs, RBIs, and slugging. He slumped in the playoffs before hitting .310 and leading the victorious A's with six RBIs against the Mets in the World Series. The A's won their third straight world championship in 1974, beating Los Angeles in five games as Jackson batted .286 and lent a homer and a double to the cause.

The A's won the West in 1975, but fell to Boston in the ALCS despite Jackson's .417 batting average. The following year the brash and outspoken slugger was dealt to the Orioles, and he responded with a fine all-around season that included a career-best 28 stolen bases. But it was merely a preliminary to his taking center stage with the New York Yankees, with whom he signed in 1977 for a then record $2.96 million over five years. Jackson bragged that they would name a candy bar after him in New York. They did.

Jackson and New York were made for each other. He craved the spotlight, and New York responded by bathing him in its glare. He alienated his new teammates, however, and over the next several years he was constantly at war—literally and figuratively—with Yankees manager Billy Martin. Nevertheless, Jackson earned his salary, hitting 32 home runs and leading the club with 110 RBIs in his first season with the team.

In the fifth game of the 1977 ALCS against Kansas City, Martin benched Jackson, who then returned to deliver a single in the climactic game. Yankees catcher Thurman Munson sarcastically dubbed the slugger "Mr. October." The sarcasm disappeared in the World Series against the Dodgers as Jackson slammed five homers, including a record-tying three in the championship-clinching Game 6. Along with his dinger in Game 5, Jackson had taken four swings at four consecutive pitches, and all had left the park.

Adding to his "Mr. October" luster, Jackson hit .462 with two home runs and six RBIs in the Yankees' four-game win over the Royals in the 1978 ALCS, then followed with two more homers and eight RBIs in the Series as the Yankees again defeated Los Angeles. His best year with the Yanks was 1980, when he shared the AL home run crown with 41, knocked in 111, and batted .300 for the only time in his career.

Picked up by California in 1982 after he had filed for free agency, Jackson surprised everyone by hitting 39 home runs, tying for the league lead. On April 27, 1982, in his first game back in New York, he smacked one into the seats. Jackson spent five productive seasons with the Angels, helping them win a division championship in 1982, and retired after a year with Oakland in 1987.

All told, Reggie Jackson finished with 17 home runs in postseason play, a record. In his 21-year career he was named to the All-Star team 14 times. Appropriately enough, Jackson, who rarely shared center stage on the field, was the only selection to the Hall of Fame in 1993.

CAL RIPKEN JR. SS-3B

Cal Ripken Jr. will be forever remembered for "the streak." Ripken became the most durable player to ever put on a major league uniform on September 6, 1995, when he appeared in his 2,131st consecutive game. He surpassed Lou Gehrig's "unbreakable record" (according to Gehrig's plaque at Yankee Stadium) at a time when baseball was still suffering the repercussions of the 1994 baseball strike. The national Ripken watch, as the Baltimore Orioles infielder approached the magic number, helped heal some of the wounds felt by many fans. The ovation at Camden Yards on that historic night lasted more than 20 minutes.

The following season Ripken would also break the world record of 2,216 consecutive games, a number reached by Sachio Kinugasa, a third baseman for the

Hiroshima Carp of Japan's Central League. The streak finally ended at 2,632 on September 19, 1998, when Ripken asked Baltimore manager Ray Miller to take him out of the lineup. He wasn't hurt; it was simply time, he decided, to put an end to a personal accomplishment that had begun to overshadow team goals.

Ripken was an Oriole practically from birth. He was born and raised in Maryland, the son of an Orioles minor league manager, Cal Ripken Sr. Baltimore drafted the young Ripken out of high school in 1978. He broke into the major leagues shortly after the close of the 1981 strike, debuting as a pinch runner on August 10 against Kansas City. Like Gehrig, once he stepped on the field, it was nearly impossible to get him off it.

In 1982 Ripken was named American League Rookie of the Year after leading first-year players in nearly every offensive category. He started the season at third base, but soon shifted to shortstop where he would play every game, and practically every inning, for the next 14 seasons before returning to third in 1997. During that span, Ripken became one of the game's best shortstops at bat and in the field. He won the AL MVP in 1983, posting career highs in hits (211), runs (121), and doubles (47), leading the league in all three categories. He also posted a .318 batting average, smacked 27 homers, and drove in 110 runs. Ripken led the Orioles to an AL Championship Series victory over the Chicago White Sox that season, hitting .400 and scoring five runs in the four games. His bat went flat in the World Series against the Phillies, but Baltimore won in five.

Although the Orioles finished sixth in 1991 Ripken became a two-time MVP, in acknowledgement of his 34 homers, 114 RBIs, .556 slugging average, and .323 batting average. In between MVPs, his father was hired to manage the club, but Cal Sr. was cashiered in the midst of a 21-game losing streak to start the 1988 season.

One of baseball's most popular players, Ripken appeared in 17 straight All-Star Games from 1983 to 1999 (he was voted to start the game in 2000 but was too injured to play). He set a major league record (since broken) with 95 consecutive errorless games at shortstop in 1990, and followed that with back-to-back Gold Glove Awards in 1991 and 1992. He also earned numerous honors for his work off the field, including the Bart Giamatti Caring Award (1989), Roberto Clemente Award (1992), and Lou Gehrig Award (1992).

In 1993 Ripken passed Ernie Banks as the all time home run leader for shortstops. The following year he hit his 300th home run. On September 2, 1999, he became the 29th player to hit 400 homers, but his season ended prematurely when he underwent back surgery. His .340 average in 332 at bats was the highest of his career, but it was the first time in 19 years that he failed to play in at least 99 percent of his team's games.

On April 16, 2000, Ripken tagged Hector Carrasco of the Minnesota Twins for his 3,000th career hit; he finished the season with 3,070, for 18th place on the all-time list. His 11,074 at bats rank sixth, and his 587 doubles rank 12th. Only two players, Luis Aparicio and Ozzie Smith, have played more games at shortstop than Ripken, and he places near the top at his position in fielding average, assists, and double plays. The 20-year veteran announced his intention to return to the Orioles in 2001.

DAN BROUTHERS 1B

"Big Dan" Brouthers was the first great slugger in baseball. The big first baseman not only led his league in batting average five times, but also connected for 106 homers, an amazing total for the Dead Ball Era.

After starting out with the National League's Troy Trojans, Brouthers became an overnight sensation with the Buffalo Bisons in 1881. He hit .319 and led the league with eight homers and a .541 slugging average. It was the first of six consecutive times he led the NL in slugging.

In 1882 Brouthers won the batting title by hitting .368, and then came back the following year to become the first player in major league history to win back-to-back titles, hitting .374 and leading the league with 17 triples and 97 RBIs. Despite an ankle injury in 1884, he still managed to hit 14 homers and to lead the league in slugging, at .563. Purchased (along with the entire Bisons roster) by the Detroit Wolverines in 1886, Brouthers had one of his best years, hitting .370 and topping the league with 11 homers and 40 doubles.

One of Brouthers' circuit clouts, at Washington's Capitol Park, was widely recognized as the longest home run in the game's short history. Various parks around the league commemorated some of his longest blows by placing flags at the spots where they landed. Brouthers also legged out 205 career triples, the eighth-highest total of all time.

Brouthers again won batting titles in 1889 with the Boston Beaneaters (.373), in 1891 with the Boston Red Stockings of the American Association (.350), and in 1892 with Brooklyn (.335, along with a league-leading 124 RBIs). His last hurrah was with Baltimore in 1894, where he hit .347 with 39 doubles, 23 triples, and a career-best 128 RBIs. After his big league days were through, he continued to play in the minors, hitting .415 for the Eastern League's Springfield Ponies in 1897 and, at age 46, leading the Class D Hudson River League's Poughkeepsie Colts to a pennant with his league-leading .373.

Post-retirement, Brouthers worked at the Polo Grounds as a press attendant for many years. He died in 1932 and was elected to the Hall of Fame in 1945. His lifetime batting average was .349, the highest career mark for a first baseman and tied for fourth on the all-time list.

BARRY LARKIN SS

In 1995 Barry Larkin batted .319, stole 51 bases, hit 15 home runs, and knocked in 66 runs for the Reds—good numbers, but trifling compared to the league leaders. Yet the Cincinnati shortstop was named the National League's Most Valuable Player because of a quality not measured by statistics—leadership. When the Reds began 1995 with a 1–8 record, Larkin held a closed-door meeting. The team responded by going on a 19–3 streak. Every time the Reds showed signs of a relapse, Larkin intervened on the field and, more importantly, in the dugout, leading the club to a division title.

The Reds coveted Larkin, a Cincinnati native, from the time he was teenager. He was chosen by the club in the second round of the 1982 free agent draft out of high school; after Larkin opted for the University of Michigan, where he became the Big Ten's first two-time MVP and played for the 1984 U.S. Olympic team, the Reds again drafted him, this time with the fourth overall pick. He spent only two years in the minors, winning MVP honors in the American Association for the Denver Zephyrs in 1986. His leadership skills were already in evidence: Larkin learned Spanish so he could build a better rapport with his Hispanic teammates.

Cincinnati quickly became dependent on Larkin, the team's success often hinging upon his health. After only one brief stint on the disabled list his first two years with the Reds, he missed nearly two months of the 1989 season; the Reds stumbled to fifth place. The following year, when Larkin established a career high with 185 hits while batting .301, his team won the World Series. Larkin batted .353 in the Series sweep of the heavily favored Oakland Athletics.

A consummate team player, Larkin has been no stranger to individual honors. Through 2000, he had been selected to 11 All-Star Games and won three Gold Gloves. In 1996 Larkin became the first shortstop to hit 30 home runs and steal 30 bases in the same season, adding 96 walks, 117 runs, and 89 RBIs. Statistically, it was a better year than his MVP season.

In 1997 Larkin was named the first Reds captain since 1988, but he only played 73 games due to injuries. He returned to health in 1998, belting 166 hits and recording a .309 average. Larkin, however, grew disillusioned with the course the franchise was taking. During and after the season, he requested a trade. The Reds found no suitable takers, and Larkin was in the lineup for 1999. As efficient as ever, he walked 93 times, scored 108 runs, and recorded 171 hits, leading the surprising Reds into playoff contention. The team missed the postseason by one game, but it was Cincinnati's finest year since Larkin's MVP campaign.

The 2000 season saw the Reds engineer a deal to send Larkin to the New York Mets. Larkin, however, nixed the trade, and his decision to stay with the team drew a standing ovation from 34,822 Reds fans. Less than 24 hours later, he signed a three-year contract with Cincinnati. Nevertheless, the joy in Redville was brief; Larkin dislocated his thumb a few days later, did the same to his middle finger in August, and also injured his knee. He batted .313 in 102 games, and the Reds, despite the acquisition of Ken Griffey Jr., finished out of the running for postseason glory.

CARL HUBBELL P

Carl Hubbell, the New York Giants' "Meal Ticket" for the decade of the 1930s, won 253 games and earned two Most Valuable Player Awards on the strength of a screwball that was supposed to be a sinker. He had five consecutive 20-plus-victory seasons from 1933 to 1937, but he's best remembered for his spectacular performance in the 1934 All-Star Game, during which he struck out future Hall of Fame sluggers Babe Ruth, Lou Gehrig, Jimmie Foxx, Al Simmons, and Joe Cronin in succession.

Hubbell learned his money pitch from an older hurler named Lefty Thomas in the Class A Western League. As he tinkered with the new delivery he kept turning his wrist farther and farther over, and as he did he developed an entirely new pitch—the screwball. Signed by the Detroit Tigers in 1925, Hubbell was discouraged from throwing the pitch and never got into a big league game until the Giants purchased him in 1928. He played with New York for his entire career, and his mastery over National League batters led eventually to his other sobriquet, "King Carl."

Over the course of his 16 years with the Giants, Hubbell led the NL in ERA three times, including a minuscule 1.66 in 1933. He also led the league in victories three times, with a high of 26 in 1936, and in won-lost percentage twice. His 159 strikeouts topped the league in 1937, and with his excellent control he walked less than two batters per nine innings of work. For seven seasons he enjoyed the lowest opponent on-base percentage in the league. He was named to nine All-Star teams. His success all came from the screwball, which Hubbell threw at the same speed as his fastball, thus giving him a real advantage over batters. He threw it so often that his left arm turned inward.

On May 8, 1929, Hubbell tossed a no-hitter against the Pittsburgh Pirates. In New York's pennant-winning year of 1933, he was virtually unhittable from July 13 to August 1, recording 46⅓ consecutive scoreless innings. Only Don Drysdale and Orel Hershiser topped that achievement in the National League during the 20th century. At the Polo Grounds on July 6, 1933, Hubbell defeated St. Louis, 1–0, in 18 innings, fanning 12. That season he was named the NL's Most Valuable Player.

In the 1933 World Series, Hubbell was awesome. He struck out the first three Washington Senators to face him and pitched 20 consecutive innings without allowing an earned run. He won Game 1, 4–2, and the 11-inning Game 4, 2–1.

Hubbell's feat in the 1934 All-Star Game began inauspiciously. He started the game by surrendering a hit to Charlie Gehringer and walking Heinie Manush. Then, employing the screwball, Hubbell bore down and struck out Ruth, Gehrig, and Foxx to end the inning. He picked up where he left off in the second, whiffing Simmons and Cronin before Bill Dickey reached him for a single. His dominance of the game's greats was, and remains, extraordinary.

Yet his All-Star heroics may not have been Hubbell's most amazing feat in baseball. Beginning on July 18 and extending through the end of the 1936 season, Hubbell recorded 16 straight victories en route to his second MVP Award. He then started off 1937 by notching eight more consecutive wins before losing to the Dodgers in the first game of a Memorial Day doubleheader.

During the late 1930s Hubbell began to wear down, but he still had one more remarkable game left in him. The game that Carl Hubbell regarded as his best was a one-hitter he recorded at Ebbets Field on Memorial Day, 1940. The only hit he allowed was a looper batted just over his head in the sixth; the runner, John Hudson, was erased when the next batter hit into a double play. He faced only 27 batters, made only 81 pitches, and only three balls were hit to the outfield.

After his playing days, Hubbell became a farm director for the Giants, and later a scout for the team. He was elected to the Hall of Fame in 1947.

BID MCPHEE 2B

Bid McPhee, who avoided using a glove until 1896, was the finest second baseman of the 19th century. Although others were occasionally more spectacular, no player was as consistent as McPhee. The man called "King Bid" was an innovator at his position, becoming one of the first second basemen to station himself to the left of the bag, ranging toward first. In 18 seasons with Cincinnati, he led league second basemen in putouts eight times, in assists six times, in double plays 11 times, and in fielding average eight times.

McPhee accomplished all this playing barehanded long after gloves were in common use. Each spring he soaked his hands in brine to toughen them for the season, ignoring suggestions that he put on a glove. Finally, on Opening Day 1896, hampered by a sore finger, McPhee gave in and donned a leather glove. The results were exceptional. Once more he led the league in fielding average, and his mark of .978 set a record that lasted 23 years.

At the plate, McPhee was a lifetime .277 hitter, but his batting steadily improved as his career progressed. He developed a knack for drawing bases on balls and was occasionally used as a leadoff man. In 1887, the first and only year bases on balls counted as hits, McPhee batted .355, which translates to .289 by today's standards. He topped .300 on two other occasions late in his career, and once more in 1897 in limited action. He scored more than 100 runs 10 times, with back-to-back highs of 139 and 137, respectively, in 1886 and 1887.

McPhee hit an astonishing number of triples for a player who lacked much power. In 1887 he led the American Association with 19; three years later he legged out 22. In one 1890 game he smacked three triples off Amos Rusie. In 1886 McPhee circled the bases seven times for inside-the-park home runs, and his eight-homer total led the league.

McPhee stole 568 bases during his career, but that figure is misleading. No stolen base records were kept during the American Association's first four seasons. Its totals from 1886 through 1898, and those for the National League, include other baserunning feats such as going from first to third on a single or advancing an extra base on an out. These calculations resulted in some spectacular numbers. When McPhee "stole" 95 bases in 1887, he finished only fifth in the league. Four other players were credited with more than 100 thefts.

Cincinnati fans and management knew they had a star at second base. In 1887, after major league owners decided to cap player salaries at $2,000, McPhee received a contract for that amount, but he also received an informal letter promising him $2,300. When he suffered an ankle injury in 1897, Cincinnati fans and sportswriters held a benefit and raised $3,500 for McPhee.

No second baseman has seriously challenged McPhee's single-season record of 529 putouts established in 1886. On the career list he remains first with 6,545 putouts at the keystone and fourth with 6,905 assists. In March 2000, 57 years after his death, he was elected to the Hall of Fame.

RON SANTO 3B

Ron Santo, who spent all but one season of his 15-year career with the Chicago Cubs, was often called the National League's version of Brooks Robinson. He won five Gold Gloves, 11 less than Robinson—but Santo more than made up for it in the hitting department, and often had to carry his team as well. The Cubs slugger was a durable player who played with a disability he kept hidden until he retired: diabetes. In fact, he once hit a grand slam while suffering the onset of a diabetic reaction.

Santo missed only 23 of a possible 1,595 games from 1961 through 1970. He established a major league record by leading the league nine times in total chances. Santo shares the NL record for most years leading the league in assists, with seven, and in double plays, with six. Offensively, he batted .277, with 342 home runs and 1,331 RBIs. His numbers compare favorably with those of other notable third baseman, including Robinson, Eddie Mathews, Mike Schmidt, and Pie Traynor.

A Seattle native, Santo was recruited out of high school by all 16 major league teams. He turned down better offers to sign with the Cubs, sensing that the franchise offered him a faster route to the majors, and joined the team in the spring of 1960. He took over at the third base the following year. By 1963, when he batted .297 and drove in 99 runs, he was a star.

From 1964 to 1970, Santo enjoyed four seasons in which he collected more than 100 RBIs, and four other seasons in which he just fell short of the mark. He hit 30 or more home runs for four consecutive years, 1964–67, with a high of 33 in 1965. In 1964, his best all-around campaign at the plate, Santo led the league in triples, bases on balls, and on-base percentage, while garnering 76 extra-base hits, batting .313, and driving in 114 runs. He had a 28-game hitting streak in 1966, and paced the circuit for a second time in on-base percentage, with a .417 mark. All told, Santo drew the most walks in the league on four occasions.

Santo's last season, 1974, was spent across town with the White Sox, where he clashed with Dick Allen. Even though he had another year left in his contract, he opted to retire at season's end, forfeiting $120,000 in salary. He joined the Cubs as a WGN radio color commentator in 1990. As of 2000, Santo remains the fourth-highest home run hitter among third basemen.

HOYT WILHELM P

Hoyt Wilhelm, the game's most famous knuckleballer, didn't make it to the majors until he was almost 29 years old and then pitched until he was almost 49. Although a starter for a few seasons in Baltimore, he was the first pitcher used primarily in relief to make it into the Hall of Fame.

When Wilhelm retired after the 1972 season, his 1,070 appearances were the most in baseball history. (Dennis Eckersley and Jesse Orosco later topped his record.) Arguably the most effective reliever of all time, Wilhelm ranks first on the career list in relief wins (124), first in relief innings pitched (1,871), second in relief appearances (1,018), eighth in opponent's batting average (.216), and 19th in saves (227).

Wilhelm, who learned how to throw the unpredictable knuckler as a child, had already had a lengthy, yet successful sojourn in the minors before the New York Giants signed him in 1952. Used in relief by Giants manager Leo Durocher, and instructed by coach Freddie Fitzsimmons to adopt a three-quarter delivery, Wilhelm had a sensational rookie season, going 15–3 with 11 saves. He became the first rookie to lead the National League in ERA, with 2.43, and winning percentage, with .833. Wilhelm pitched in a league-best 71 games, setting a since-broken rookie record, and worked 159⅓ innings. But perhaps the most remarkable event of his season came on April 23, the day he won his first game. In his first major league at bat he homered to the opposite field off Boston's Dick Hoover. Wilhelm had 431 more at bats in his career and never hit another homer. In fact, his .088 career batting average is one of the worst among pitchers with at least 100 at bats.

Wilhelm enjoyed another fine season in 1954, his 12–4 record and 2.10 ERA helping the Giants to the flag. Of course, Wilhelm's fluttering deliveries made life difficult for his catchers. With Wilhelm pitching in the eighth inning on September 10, 1954, Ray Katt set a modern record with four passed balls. But the good came with the bad. In the 1954 World Series, Wilhelm did not allow a run in two appearances and retired the last five batters in Game 3 to earn a save as the Giants swept the Indians in four games.

After that season Wilhelm slumped. He didn't save a single game in 1955 and his ERA ballooned to 3.83 in 1956. On February 26, 1957, the Giants traded him to the Cardinals, who in turn dealt him to Cleveland. Wilhelm was ineffective in his first career start for the Indians, and at age 35 he was released that August. But his career was just beginning.

The Baltimore Orioles were Wilhelm's next stop. Manager Paul Richards, who was known for rejuvenating older pitchers, decided to use Wilhelm as both a starter and reliever. On September 20, 1958, in only his third start for the Orioles, Wilhelm no-hit the Yankees. He threw only 99 pitches—87 of them knucklers—as Baltimore defeated New York, 1–0, on a home run by catcher Gus Triandos.

In 1959 Wilhelm won his first nine starts, but finished the season at just 15–11. Still, he led the American League with a 2.19 ERA, becoming the first pitcher to have led both leagues in that category. Traded to the White Sox in January 1963, Wilhelm saved 21 games for Chicago, beginning a string of three seasons in which he'd save 20 or more. In 1965, as he was saving 20 games and pitching 144 innings as a 42-year-old, J.C. Martin was scrambling after 33 passed balls to set a league record.

After a stint with California in 1969, Wilhelm was waived to Atlanta, and his clutch pitching down the stretch helped the Braves to an NL West title. He finished up with the Dodgers, who released him one month short of his 49th birthday. The Baseball Writers Association voted Wilhelm into the Hall of Fame in 1985.

FRANK THOMAS 1B-DH

From his earliest salvos against American League pitching, Frank Thomas was known as "The Big Hurt." The two-time American League Most Valuable Player became the first player in history to hit .300 with 20 home runs, 100 RBIs, 100 walks, and 100 runs scored in seven consecutive seasons. Remarkably, two of those years were shortened because of the players' strike.

The start of his career compared favorably with some of baseball's all-time greats. Thomas hit more homers over a comparable stretch than Ted Williams (not counting the two years Williams spent in military service in World War II), and also topped Williams's six-year run of driving in 100 runs and walking 100 times. Fittingly, Thomas was the first AL winner of the Ted Williams Award. The honor, presented by CNN/Sports Illustrated and *Total Baseball*, employs an adjusted formula combining on-base average and slugging average to measure the most productive hitters. Thomas finished the 1997 season with an adjusted production of .467.

Thomas played football and basketball as well as baseball at Columbus High School in Georgia, and was selected by the White Sox as the seventh overall pick in the 1989 draft. A year later, after only 180 minor league games, Thomas was playing at Comiskey Park. He batted .330 in 191 at bats in 1990, the highest average by a White Sox hitter with at least 200 plate appearances since 1942. In 1991, his first full season, Thomas hit 32 home runs while batting .318. Pitchers around the junior circuit quickly took notice and shied away from the powerful young hitter. He was walked an incredible 138 times to lead the AL. His resulting .454 on-base percentage also lead the league.

Thomas then began a string of seasons that in another era would have earned him Triple Crown honors. In 1993 he posted 41 home runs, 128 RBIs, and a .317 average and was named the American League MVP. He was a repeat winner the next year, this time recording 38 home runs, 101 RBIs, and a .353 average in a strike-shortened season. In the 1993 AL Championship Series, Thomas hit .353 with a record 10 walks, but despite his heroics the Sox lost to the eventual world champion Toronto Blue Jays in six games.

In 1997 Thomas added his first batting title, .347, to his list of accomplishments. He had such a commanding lead in the race that even though he went hitless in his last 10 at bats of the season, he still won the title by 17 points over Edgar Martinez. Thomas also finished with 35 home runs despite a poor start that saw him go without a homer for almost the first month of the season. Slowed by an injured right foot that eventually required surgery in September, his power numbers dropped off in 1999. He failed to drive in 100 runs for the first time since 1990, although he batted over .300 for the ninth time in 10 seasons.

The Big Hurt came back in a big way in 2000, finishing the season in the top five in seven offensive categories—homers (43), RBIs (143), total bases (364), slugging average (.625), on-base percentage (.436), walks (112), and doubles (44). He also tied for seventh in runs (115), and ranked ninth in both hits (191) and batting average (.328). The season was tainted for Thomas, however, when his White Sox, who finished atop the Central Division with the best record in the American League, lost in three games to the Seattle Mariners in the Division Series. Thomas was hitless in nine trips to the plate and, rightly or wrongly, assumed a great deal of the blame for Chicago's failure to advance.

BOBBY DOERR 2B

Bobby Doerr played every one of his 1,865 games for the Boston Red Sox, and save for a few pinch-hitting appearances, all of them were at second base. Baseball historian Bill James accurately summed up the career of this nine-time All-Star, calling him "an excellent offensive and defensive player from the day he reached the majors until the day that he left."

Installed as the regular Red Sox second baseman in 1938, Doerr hit well but without much power. He soon learned to pull the ball and take advantage of Fenway Park's left field wall, the Green Monster. He was the American League's Most Valuable Player in 1944, when he led the league with a .528 slugging average and was second in batting average, at .325. Doerr knocked in more than 100 runs six times in his career and ranks among the top second basemen in lifetime batting average, on-base percentage, slugging average, runs produced, fewest strikeouts, and home runs per season.

Doerr also was an exceptional fielder, especially adept at double plays. He helped turn 1,507 twin killings—fifth on the all-time list among second basemen—over the course of his career, and in 1950 he set a record by participating in eight double plays in a doubleheader. He led league second basemen in fielding average four times and tied for the lead on two other occasions. One of his many errorless strings deserves special notice. During the sizzling pennant race of 1948, Doerr handled 414 chances between June 24 and September 19 without an error.

Doerr was definitely a Fenway Park hitter. Lifetime, he batted .315 with 145 homers in the oddly shaped park, but only .261 with 78 home runs on the road. In his only postseason appearance, the 1946 World Series, he hit .409, drove in three runs, and handled 49 chances without an error as the Sox fell to the Cardinals in seven games.

He retired because of back trouble after the 1951 season, but later coached for the Red Sox and the Toronto Blue Jays. Doerr, who wore No. 1 for the Red Sox, was only the third player in team history to have his number retired. He was elected to the Hall of Fame in 1986.

GABBY HARTNETT C

Charles Leo "Gabby" Hartnett, whose nickname stemmed from a lack of loquaciousness in the presence of sportswriters during his rookie year, was one of the three great catchers of the 1930s. Along with Mickey Cochrane and Bill Dickey, Hartnett ushered in a new era of backstops who could hit, often with power. When he retired in 1941, he was the first catcher to have reached the 200-homer and 1,000-RBI plateaus.

He was first-rate behind the plate, too. Despite his small hands, which led one scout to proclaim he could never catch in the big leagues, Hartnett led National League catchers in fielding average six times, including three consecutive seasons from 1936 through 1938. He topped NL backstops in putouts on four occasions, and also shares the major league record for most years leading the league in assists, with six. No other NL catcher participated in more double plays than Hartnett, whose throwing arm was legendary. He handled pitchers well and they appreciated his catching smarts. Dizzy Dean once said of Hartnett, "If I had that guy to pitch to all the time, I'd never lose me a game."

Gabby spent only one season in the minors before the Cubs picked him up for $2,500 in 1922. He took charge behind the plate when Bob O'Farrell, Chicago's regular catcher, suffered a fractured skull in 1924. Hartnett held the post of No. 1 Cubs catcher for the next 15 years, with the exception of 1929, when early in spring training he damaged his arm and sat out most of the season.

Hartnett showed flashes of power during his first few years in the majors, slugging 16 homers in 1924 and 24 in 1925. But when major league bats went crazy in 1930, Gabby added his own artillery to the full-scale assault on pitching, batting .339 with career highs in homers (37) and RBIs (122).

Hartnett won his second pennant with the Cubs in 1932 and was stationed behind the plate for Game 3 of the World Series, when Babe Ruth allegedly "called his shot" off Charlie Root. In Chicago's four-game loss to the Yankees, Hartnett performed admirably, batting .313 with two doubles and a homer.

Gabby was the starting catcher for the National League in the first All-Star Game in 1933, an honor he merited for the next four All-Star Games as well. (He was named to the team for a fifth consecutive year in 1938, but didn't play.) He was catching Carl Hubbell in the 1934 All-Star Game when the first two American Leaguers reached base. Hartnett advised "King Carl" to go with his screwball, and Hubbell proceeded to fan Ruth, Lou Gehrig, Jimmie Foxx, Al Simmons, and Joe Cronin in order. Unable to restrain himself, Hartnett shouted to the AL bench, "We gotta look at that all season!"

After batting .344 in 1935 and leading his team to another flag, Hartnett was chosen the NL's Most Valuable Player. Although the Cubs once more ran true to form in the Series, this time against the Tigers, he was again a bright spot, hitting .292 with a home run. Hartnett batted a career-high .354 in 1937 while putting together a 26-game hitting streak. In the 1937 All-Star Game, he was again part of baseball history, catching Dizzy Dean when Earl Averill smashed a liner off Diz's left foot. The broken toe precipitated the end of Dean's career.

During the 1938 season, with the Cubs in third place, Hartnett took over the team from Charlie Grimm. Under their new manager, the Cubs went on a tear to challenge the league-leading Pirates. On September 28, with his team half a game out and playing Pittsburgh, Hartnett led off the bottom of the ninth with the score tied. Darkness was gathering, and the umpires had determined that the game would be called at the end of the inning. Hartnett walloped an 0–2 curveball from Mace Brown into the seats. The fabled "Home Run in the Gloamin' " put the Cubs in first place to stay.

Hartnett retired with the highest career slugging average by a catcher and the fifth-best batting average at his position. He was elected to the Hall of Fame in 1955.

GEORGE BRETT 3B

For two decades George Brett was one of the best hitters in the game. The most famous disciple of hitting coach Charlie Lau, Brett hit .300 or more 11 times during his major league career. He won a batting title in each of three decades—the 1970s, 1980s, and 1990s—a baseball first.

In 1974, his first full year in the majors, Brett batted .282 under Lau's tutelage. The next year he increased his average to .308, the first of nine times that he would pass .300 in an 11-year period. He was the American League's dominant third baseman in hitting, leading his position in every offensive category except homers, including league-leading totals of 195 hits and 13 triples.

In 1976 Brett was even better. He had six consecutive three-hit games early in the year, led the league with 215 hits and 14 triples, and won his first batting title, hitting .333. He was selected for his first of 11 consecutive All-Star Games and helped lead the Royals to their first division title.

Hampered by injuries in each of the next two years, Brett came back in 1979 to lead the league in both hits and triples while batting .329. He also drove in 107 runs, and his 42 doubles and 23 homers made him only the sixth player in history to exceed 20 doubles, triples, and homers in one season.

Somehow, in 1980 he improved his performance yet again. He batted close to .400 for most of the season, finishing at .390, the highest average by a third baseman in the 20th century, and the highest by any hitter since Ted Williams in 1941. Despite missing more than a month with a knee injury and a case of tendonitis, Brett had a 30-game hitting streak during the season. In 117 games he drove in 118 runs, the first year anyone had more RBIs than games played since Walt Dropo's 1950 season. Brett also had fewer strikeouts (22) than home runs (24), a feat not accomplished in 24 years. Not surprisingly, he was named AL Most Valuable Player.

When Kansas City took on the Yanks in the ALCS for the fourth time in five years, Brett avenged the Royals' previous defeats. In the seventh inning of Game 3, he homered off Goose Gossage to propel the franchise into its first World Series. Although Kansas City lost to the Philadelphia Phillies, Brett was one of four Royals to hit .375 or better.

The most famous single event of Brett's career occurred on July 24, 1983. Down 4–3 to the Yankees in the top of the ninth, Brett powered a two-run homer off Gossage. Yankees manager Billy Martin had been tipped off that Brett, who never wore batting gloves, had an illegal amount of pine tar on his bat. After determining Brett's bat to be in violation, plate umpire Tim McClelland called Brett out for an illegally batted ball. The usually mild-mannered Brett, celebrating his homer in the dugout, went crazy. He charged McClelland, and it took another umpire and two players to restrain him.

The Royals filed a protest that was upheld by AL president Lee MacPhail, who ordered that the game be completed from the point of Brett's home run. The continuation of the game began 25 days later, and the Royals won. The event has gone down in baseball lore as "the Pine Tar Incident."

In 1985 Brett led the Royals to another division title, hitting .335 with a league-leading slugging percentage of .585, which included his career high 30 home runs. He also won his only Gold Glove.

Brett moved to first base in 1987 and began spending more time as a designated hitter. In 1990 he surprised those who had written him off by claiming his third batting title. He hit .329 and led the league with 45 doubles, the same total as his league-leading mark a dozen years before.

On September 30, 1992, Brett needed one hit to become the 18th man to reach the 3,000-hit plateau. He got four. Moments after he reached that plateau, the still-dazed Brett was picked off first base. It was one of the few embarrassments of his career. In 1999, his first year of eligibility, he was elected to the Hall of Fame.

JOE CRONIN SS

In a career that spanned decades, Joe Cronin rose from backup shortstop to Most Valuable Player, pennant-winning manager, general manager, Hall of Famer, and finally president of the American League. His success story began when the Washington Senators purchased his contract from the Kansas City Blues of the American Association in 1927. After a few years of seasoning, Cronin exploded in 1930, hitting .346, driving in 126 runs, and leading American League shortstops in putouts, assists, double plays, and chances per game.

After the 1932 season Cronin replaced Walter Johnson as the Senators' manager. Determined to deliver a pennant at the age of 26, Cronin worked with Senators owner Clark Griffith to rebuild the team. With Cronin contributing his fourth straight 100-RBI season (he'd make it five straight in 1933, and eight in all over his career), the Senators won their last pennant as a Washington franchise that year before losing to the New York Giants in the World Series.

In 1935 Boston Red Sox general manager Eddie Collins obtained Cronin from the Senators for $250,000 plus shortstop Lyn Lary. The new player-manager soon became popular with Boston's large Irish population. Yet although Cronin continued to be a strong hitter (he had a .325 batting average with 73 extra-base hits in 1938, including a league-leading 51 doubles), he was no longer a capable shortstop. He inaugurated his Red Sox career with a series of embarrassing errors, and began to develop a case of "groundball jitters." He was also unpopular with his players—especially the erstwhile Philadelphia Athletics, Lefty Grove and Jimmie Foxx—and he annoyed his pitchers by calling pitches from the bench. Ted Williams, on the other hand, called Cronin "the easiest man in the world to play for" and dubbed him "a hitter's manager."

Cronin's last year as a regular player was 1941. He appeared in only 183 games during the next four seasons before a broken leg in 1945 brought his playing days to an end. "I used to send myself up to pinch hit whenever the wind was blowing out from home plate," he would joke. It must have been blowing at gale force in 1943 when he pinch hit five homers, including two grand slams.

After four second-place finishes during his tenure as Red Sox manager, Cronin finally delivered a pennant to Boston in 1946, although the Sox lost the World Series to St. Louis. He retired in 1947 and became Red Sox general manager the following year.

Cronin's .301 lifetime average is one of the best ever notched by a shortstop. As of 2001, he was ranked 31st in doubles and 48th in RBIs on the all-time list. Cronin was elected to the Hall of Fame in 1956. Three years later he became American League president, a post he held until 1974, when he was named chairman of the league, an honorary title.

AMOS RUSIE P

It's hard, if not impossible, to determine who was the fastest pitcher of all time. But the contemporaries of Amos Rusie, as well as many baseball historians, considered the New York Giants righthander the fastest pitcher of the 19th century. One piece of compelling evidence supports their claim: in 1893 the pitching distance was moved back from 50 feet to its present distance of 60 feet 6 inches to give batters a chance against Rusie's overpowering fastball.

Rusie pitched in the big leagues for only 10 years, but he won more than 20 games in eight of those seasons, and more than 30 in four of them, from 1891 to 1894. He led the National League in strikeouts five times, topping 300 in each of the three years leading up to the relocation of the mound. Yet even from the new pitching distance, Rusie remained a force to be reckoned with, striking out a league-high 208 batters in 1893. For one thing, his wicked curveball was more effective at the new distance.

Rusie started out with Indianapolis of the National League in 1889, posting an unspectacular 12–10 record and giving up 246 hits in 225 innings. He emerged as a star the following year with the sixth-place New York Giants, going 29–34 but leading the league with 341 strikeouts. When the stars who had skipped to the Players' League returned to the NL in 1891, Rusie kept pace and again led the league in strikeouts, with 337. His record improved to 33–20, and on July 31 he no-hit Brooklyn, 6–0, one of his league-best six shutouts. In 1892 Rusie collected his second 30-win season with a 32–31 mark, and his 288 strikeouts were second in the league. But he was as wild as he was fast. In his first three seasons in New York he gave up more than 260 walks each year. His wildness, combined with his speed, terrified batters.

The 1894 season was Rusie's finest. The "Hoosier Thunderbolt," as New York fans acclaimed him, won 36 games against 13 losses, leading the league in victories, ERA, shutouts, and strikeouts, while recording the NL's lowest opponent's batting and on-base averages. It remains one of the great years in the annals of pitching.

From that point on, though, Rusie's talents were undermined by problems with the Giants' duplicitous and penny-pinching owner, Andrew Freedman. After going 23–23 in 1895, Rusie held out for an entire season over a dispute involving the levying of capricious fines, and then sued Freedman for salary lost. Rusie won his suit, and enjoyed two more stellar seasons, 28–10 and 20–11. Late in 1898, however, he felt something pop in his shoulder. He took a two-year hiatus to rest his arm, after which the Giants traded him to the Cincinnati Reds for Christy Mathewson in 1901. Rusie aborted his comeback with the Reds after three games. All told he was 246–174, with 1,950 strikeouts and 1,707 walks. Of his 427 starts, he completed 392. He was elected posthumously to the Hall of Fame in 1977.

ARKY VAUGHAN SS

Shortstop Arky Vaughan was one of the National League's premier hitters in the 1930s. Never a flamboyant player, he left baseball at an early age and died young, virtually forgotten until his election to the Hall of Fame in 1985.

Vaughan spent 14 years in the NL with the Pittsburgh Pirates and Brooklyn Dodgers. A hard-hitting shortstop, his lifetime batting average of .318 is second only to Honus Wagner among all who have played the position. His league-leading .385 in 1935 is the 20th century record for a shortstop.

Born in the rural village of Clifty, Arkansas, and reared in northern California, Vaughan signed with the Pirates in 1930. With only one year of professional experience under his belt, he took over at short for the Bucs in 1932, hitting .318. Pittsburgh agreed with Vaughan. Playing in spacious Forbes Field, he paced the league in triples three times, and led all major leaguers in that category from 1932 to 1941. In that span he also placed fifth in batting average and doubles, and 11th in slugging percentage.

In 1935, in addition to his batting crown, Vaughan led the NL in slugging (.607), on-base percentage (.491), and bases on balls (97). The performance earned him *The Sporting News* Most Valuable Player Award. The following season Vaughan topped the league for a third consecutive year in on-base percentage with .453, while recording career bests in runs (122) and walks (118), both of which were good enough to pace the NL.

Not surprisingly, Vaughan had some monster individual performances. He's one of only a handful of players to hit for the cycle on two occasions. In the 1941 All-Star Game, he slammed a pair of home runs; only four other players have equaled the feat.

In 1940 Frankie Frisch took over the Pirates. He and Vaughan did not get along, and on December 12, 1941, Vaughan was traded to Brooklyn for four players. Despite bad knees, Vaughan hit .305 and led the league in runs scored and stolen bases in 1943, his last full season. He called it quits after that year, but the Dodgers coaxed him out of retirement, and he hit .325 in 64 games. He doubled and walked in three plate appearances in the 1947 World Series. After slumping to a career-worst .244 in 1948, however, he was unconditionally released by the Dodgers.

All told, Vaughan batted at least .300 in 12 seasons. He was one of the toughest players in the game to double up, hitting into a twin killing an average of once every 87.5 at bats. He drowned while trying to save his fishing companion after their boat capsized on August 30, 1952.

BOBBY WALLACE SS

Of all the players enshrined in the Hall of Fame, Roderick John "Bobby" Wallace is probably the most obscure. His name is not on any of the long lists of batting leaders in the record books. He never led his league in a single offensive category, and his career batting average is one of the lowest among position players ensconced in Cooperstown. He was not a World Series hero, he never played for a pennant-winning team, and he wasn't a colorful character.

What Wallace was, according to contemporary accounts, was a very good fielding shortstop, but the statistics are equivocal. Although he led American League shortstops in fielding percentage two times, he also led in errors twice. He spent 25 years in the major leagues, a very long career, but during nine of those seasons he played only part-time.

Nevertheless, in 1911 when Ty Cobb, Tris Speaker, and Nap Lajoie were the toast of the AL, Pittsburgh Pirates owner Barney Dreyfuss said, "The best player in the American League, the only man I would get if I could, plays on a tail-end team, and few people pay any attention to him. I mean Bobby Wallace of St. Louis. I wish I had him." At the time, Wallace was 37 and coming off a season in which he hit only .258. But Dreyfuss was a reliable judge of shortstops. On his own team was a fellow named Honus Wagner.

On September 15, 1894, Wallace made his major league debut for the Cleveland Spiders against Boston—as a pitcher. He was shelled, giving up 14 hits in six innings. By the next season, though, he was a regular starter, going 12–14. On July 21, 1896, Zeke Wilson and Wallace tossed back-to-back shutouts in a doubleheader against Washington. In that season's Temple Cup, the forerunner of the World Series, Wallace lost the second game, 7–2, as the Orioles beat the Spiders in four straight. Save for a two-inning stint in 1902, it was the last time he pitched.

In 1897 Wallace moved to third base and responded with the best offensive year of his career, batting .335, scoring 99 runs, and driving in 112. On July 14 he hit his only major league grand slam. He continued to hit well, and was shuttled over to shortstop in 1899. There he found his niche, logging 1,826 games at the position. Overall, Wallace ranks high on the career list for shortstops in many fielding categories, including chances accepted per game (eighth), putouts (10th), and assists per game (11th).

Playing for St. Louis in 1899, Wallace amassed 108 RBIs and smacked 12 homers, a high total for the Dead Ball Era. After accepting an offer to jump to the American League in 1901, he abrogated his contract over a salary dispute and returned to St. Louis, where he hit .324. On May 4 of that season he had 12 assists at shortstop in one game.

In 1902 the St. Louis Browns offered Wallace a $6,500 advance and a five-year, no-trade contract for $32,500, by all accounts making him the highest-paid player in baseball. He remained the club's regular shortstop through 1912, and stayed on in a substitute role for four more seasons. Wallace led AL shortstops in fielding in 1905 and 1908, but he hit poorly. In 1911, he had an unsuccessful term as the Browns' manager; he was replaced early the next season, with the team mired in eighth place. He suffered injuries in 1912 and 1914, and retired for good in 1918.

Although Wallace's career batting average was only .268, his cumulative statistics are fairly impressive: he collected 2,309 hits, scored 1,057 runs, knocked in 1,121 runs, and stole 201 bases. In 1953, seven years before his death, he was named to the Hall of Fame.

HAL NEWHOUSER P

Hal Newhouser is the only pitcher who ever won back-to-back Most Valuable Player Awards. His dominance of the American League—going 29–9 with a 2.22 ERA in 1944 and 25–9 with a 1.81 ERA in 1945, while leading the league in strikeouts both years—is sometimes unfairly attributed to the shortage of quality players caused by World War II. But that doesn't give enough credit to Newhouser, a seasoned professional with an excellent slider who was kept out of the military by a heart condition. No less a hitter than Ted Williams called Newhouser one of the three best pitchers he ever faced.

Newhouser was signed in 1938 by legendary Detroit Tigers scout Wish Egan, who called the 17-year-old hurler "the greatest lefthanded pitcher I ever saw." In his first four complete seasons with the Tigers, the young southpaw went a disappointing 34–51. But after Paul Richards helped him to develop a slider, Newhouser's improvement was staggering. In the following five seasons he went 118–46, pitched 25 shutouts, led the American League three times in wins, and twice each in strikeouts and ERA.

In 1945, Newhouser pitched the Tigers to a world championship, winning two of his three World Series decisions against the Cubs. Hammered in the opener, he yielded seven runs in less than three innings, but came back to win Game 5 and the decisive Game 7.

The war had thinned the talent in both leagues, but when the marquee players returned in 1946 there was no diminution of Newhouser's dominance. Along with his league-leading 26 wins and minuscule 1.94 ERA, he struck out 275 batters—second only to Bob Feller's 348—and recorded the AL's lowest opponents' batting average (.201) and lowest on-base average (.269). He became a 20-game winner for a fourth time in 1948, pacing the junior circuit with 21 victories.

Newhouser was selected to the All-Star Game seven consecutive times in the 1940s, but a sore shoulder took its toll on him by 1950. After several marginal seasons, the Tigers released the 32-year-old hurler in July of 1953. Newhouser signed on with Cleveland in 1954, and the Indians used him judiciously in relief. On a staff featuring three other future Hall-of-Famers—Feller, Early Wynn, and Bob Lemon—he went 7–2 for the Tribe, which steamrolled to the pennant with an AL record 111 wins.

Newhouser retired in 1955, having won 207 games, all but seven of them with the Tigers. He tried his hand at coaching and scouting before becoming a banker. The Veterans Committee elected him to the Hall of Fame in 1992.

WHITEY FORD P

Columnist Russell Baker once observed that the Yankees' Whitey Ford was "to lefthanded pitching what Edward G. Robinson was to the .45-caliber automatic." Ford's manager, Casey Stengel, put it another way: "If you had one game to win and your life depended on it, you'd want him to pitch it."

Ford—backed, of course, by an awesome lineup—was the toughest pitcher to beat in modern history. He enjoyed the highest winning percentage of the 20th century—.690—with 236 victories against only 106 losses. He was a dominant postseason pitcher, too; his 32 consecutive scoreless innings in World Series play broke Babe Ruth's long-standing record. Ford also holds World Series records for most victories (10), strikeouts (94), and innings pitched (146).

Ford started compiling his October records in his rookie season, 1950, winning the last game of the Yankees-Phillies World Series. After missing the next two Series because of military duty, he won Game 7 of the 1953 Fall Classic, holding Brooklyn to just one run in seven innings. In 1955 he beat the Dodgers in Games 1 and 6. In 1956, with the Yankees down two games to none, Ford won Game 3, and New York rallied to win the Series. Continuing his postseason dominance, Ford five-hit Milwaukee in Game 5 of the 1957 Series, and in Game 6 of the 1960 Series he shut out Pittsburgh on just three hits. He was World Series Most Valuable Player in 1961 when the Yankees bested the Reds.

Twice—in 1961 and 1963—Ford led the American League in wins, innings pitched, and won-lost percentage in the same season. In '63 he also won the Cy Young Award by posting 24 victories, including eight in the month of June. Catcher Elston Howard nicknamed Ford "the Chairman of the Board" in recognition of Whitey's masterly fashion of controlling a game and all the fielders around him.

As a rookie in 1950, Ford won nine consecutive games for the Yankees. After his two-year army stint, he rejoined the team in 1953 and posted 18 victories, the first of 13 straight seasons in which he recorded at least 11 wins. He did not register a losing record until the 1966 and 1967 seasons, his last two in the majors. Even then, his ERAs were 2.47 and 1.64, respectively.

Toward the end of his tenure in the big leagues Ford was dogged by accusations of doctoring the baseball. "I didn't cheat when I won the 25 games in 1961," he said, confessing to a bit of scuffing the ball with his wedding ring late in his career. "And I didn't cheat in 1963 when I won 24 games. Well, maybe just a little."

From 1942 to 1960, only Hoyt Wilhelm posted a lower ERA than Ford's 2.75. Over his career, opponents batted only .235 against Ford, and his 45 shutouts are tied for 28th on the all-time list. He was elected to the Baseball Hall of Fame in 1974, in his second year of eligibility.

JOE JACKSON OF

"Shoeless Joe" Jackson was the best of the eight ballplayers banned for life in 1920 for having conspired with gamblers to throw the 1919 World Series. Jackson, whose career batting average of .356 was bested only by Ty Cobb and Rogers Hornsby in the 20th century, is still considered one of the great natural hitters of all time. He twice led the American League in hits and three times led the league in triples. Even Babe Ruth admired and copied his batting stance. He fielded flawlessly and had a powerful throwing arm.

Jackson, who picked up his nickname by playing a Class D game in his stocking feet because the spikes on his shoes were causing him blisters, was signed by the Philadelphia Athletics in 1980. He got three hits in his major league debut, but only appeared in a handful of games with the A's that season and the next. It wasn't until he got to Cleveland in 1910 that his star began to blaze.

In 1911, his first full year with the Indians, Jackson batted .408. Cobb, however, registered a .420 average, which gave Jackson the curious distinction of topping .400 and not having a batting crown to show for it. (It happened to Cobb himself in 1921, when his .401 batting average was exceeded by George Sisler's .420.) Jackson did manage to lead the league with a .468 on-base percentage, and recorded career highs with 233 hits, 126 runs, and 45 doubles.

Jackson came close to .400 the following year, finishing at .395 and leading the AL with 226 hits and 26 triples. In 1913 he again topped the circuit with 197 hits, and also led the league-with 39 doubles and a .551 slugging average. In 1915, however, the financially strapped Indians traded Jackson to the White Sox for three players and $31,500. The Chicago club was a bad fit for the free-spending Jackson; the White Sox owner, Charles Comiskey, was a tightwad, and even meal money was less than what most teams gave players.

The talented White Sox won the 1917 World Series and the 1919 pennant, but bitter factionalism split the team. Jackson, who had hit .304 in the 1917 Fall Classic, was aligned with seven others teammates who had agreed to "fix" the Series in 1919. During Chicago's eight-game loss to the Cincinnati Reds, Jackson batted .375; nevertheless, when he appeared before a grand jury in 1920, he admitted to having failed to hustle after balls hit to left field, having made several weak throws, and to having struck out in key situations. He also owned to feeling pressure from his fellow conspirators, even to the point of receiving death threats.

Following the grand jury investigation, Jackson and his seven teammates were suspended from the game. In June 1921, with the exception of Fred McMullin, they were brought to trial regarding the fix. Although the jury brought back acquittals for all defendants, the newly installed Commissioner Kenesaw Mountain Landis ruled that Jackson and the other seven "Black Sox" were banned from baseball for life.

Ironically, Jackson had enjoyed what was perhaps his best all-around season at the plate in 1920. He batted .382 with a league-leading 20 triples, and established career highs in extra-base hits (74) and RBIs (121).

After his banishment Jackson played some semipro ball and ran a dry-cleaning establishment and a liquor store. In February 1951 the South Carolina Legislature petitioned Major League Baseball for Jackson's reinstatement, but its request was ignored. He died in December of that year.

FRANKIE FRISCH 2B

Second baseman Frankie Frisch was the key man on four straight pennant-winning New York Giants teams from 1921 through 1924, and the sparkplug on four St. Louis Cardinals pennant winners in 1928, 1930-31, and 1934. A slashing switch hitter, what he lacked in the way of home run power he more than made up for with singles, doubles, and triples. He led the National League with 223 hits in 1923, had 13 seasons of batting over .300, scored more than 100 runs on seven occasions, and knocked in 100 or more three times. His .316 lifetime average is the fifth-highest career mark for a second baseman.

Frisch joined the Giants in 1919 straight from Fordham University, where he starred in football, basketball, and track as well as baseball. As team captain, he scored more than 100 runs for each of New York's four consecutive pennant winners, including a league-leading 121 in 1924. He also led the NL with 49 stolen bases in 1921, the first of three times he'd top the league in steals. In four World Series with the Giants, he batted .300, .471, .400, and .333.

In 1927, after his relationship with Giants manager John McGraw became frayed, Frisch was traded to St. Louis along with pitcher Jimmy Ring for Rogers Hornsby. He responded magnificently, leading the Cards to a second-place finish with a .337 batting average and a league-best 48 stolen bases. And Frisch proved to be a demon in the field, setting NL records with 1,037 total chances and 641 assists. He finished just one vote behind

Paul Waner in Most Valuable Player balloting. "The greatest player I ever saw in one season was Frankie Frisch in 1927," Cardinals catcher and manager Bob O'Farrell said.

Frisch eventually did win the MVP, in the Cardinals' pennant-winning season of 1931. Three years later, after having replaced Gabby Street as St. Louis manager, Frisch and his rambunctious crew—known as the "Gas House Gang"—captured the flag and beat the Detroit Tigers in the 1934 World Series.

Throughout his career, Frisch was noted as being a tough guy to strike out. His 33.5 at bats per strikeout are seventh best on the all-time list. His 2,880 hits place him 33rd, and of all second basemen only Hughie Critz has exceeded his 3.42 assists per game.

Following his playing days, Frisch had a brief fling with managing the Pittsburgh Pirates, and broadcasted games for the Boston Braves and New York Giants. The "Fordham Flash" was inducted into the Hall of Fame in 1947.

MARK MCGWIRE 1B

Mark McGwire not only broke the most daunting record in baseball—most home runs in a single season—but he broke it with such authority and eclat that he set a whole new standard for longball hitting. When McGwire and Sammy Sosa staged their epic assault on the legacy of Roger Maris in 1998, they captured the hearts of millions of fans and even held non-fans spellbound as they chased the 37-year-old record. McGwire slammed No. 62 on the night of September 8, before his St. Louis Cardinals had played in 154 games, obviating the need for any Maris-like asterisk. He suffered no diminution in either his hitting or enthusiasm after the season-long, media-saturated slugfest, belting five homers in his last three games to finish the year with an unprecedented 70.

The genial McGwire—like another great slugger, Babe Ruth—was originally a pitcher, but he opted early on to concentrate on hitting with power. In his first six seasons with the Oakland A's, McGwire's cleanup hitting helped produce four division winners, three straight pennant winners, and one world champion.

When Oakland's Jose Canseco was the most feared hitter in the American League in the late 1980s, the imposing presence of the 6-foot-5-inch McGwire in the on-deck circle forced managers to pitch to Canseco. The two were known as the "Bash Brothers," and as teammates from 1986 to 1992 they combined for 446 home runs. McGwire set a rookie record with 49 homers in 1987, and hit more than 30 home runs in each of the next three seasons. In 1992 he had 42 dingers and 104 RBIs, and finished fourth in the AL Most Valuable Player balloting.

A strike-shortened season and two separate stints on the disabled list limited McGwire to just 104 games in 1995, but in his 317 at bats he put on one of the most prodigious power displays in major league history. He had more home runs than singles (39 to 35), and hit the most homers of anyone in history with so few at bats. Only Hank Aaron, who hit 40 homers in 392 at bats for the 1973 Braves, had ever come close.

McGwire's health permitted him to play 130 games in 1996, and he tied the record he set the season before with one home run every 8.13 at bats. He was the first to surpass 50 homers in less than 600 plate appearances. Along the way McGwire also reached the 300-home run plateau, which only Ruth had achieved in fewer at bats. Even more surprising was McGwire's career-high .312 average and 104 runs scored.

McGwire provided the few highlights of Oakland's 1997 season: a ninth-inning blast that spoiled the world championship flag raising at Yankee Stadium, an April 30 homer that dented the scoreboard at Jacobs Field, and a home run that led the Athletics past the Giants in the first-ever regular season game between the two Bay Area teams in interleague play. Still, it was clear that McGwire, who was eligible for free agency at the end of year, would not be in Oakland much longer.

In July 1997 McGwire was traded to the St. Louis Cardinals. He took some time to adjust to the senior league, but once he began launching balls the ovations at Busch Stadium were frequent and genuine. McGwire finished the season with 58 home runs—34 with Oakland, 24 with St. Louis—the highest total reached by any slugger since Maris in 1961. At the same time, McGwire became the first player to homer in 17 different parks in a season, the first to hit 20 or more homers with two different teams in the same season, and the first to lead the major leagues in homers and yet still not qualify as the home run champion in either league.

The following year witnessed a national obsession with McGwire and Sammy Sosa as they engaged in a friendly race to the home run summit. "Big Mac" connected twice on September 1 to surpass Hack Wilson's NL record of 56; on September 5 he hit his 60th to tie Ruth, and two days later he tied Maris. The next night, against Cubs pitcher Steve Trachsel, McGwire collected No. 62 by hitting a line drive just over the left field wall, his shortest blast of the year. His final home run ball, No. 70, fetched $3 million for the fan who caught it.

McGwire again surpassed the 60-home run mark in 1999, topping out at 65. He extended his own record with his fourth straight 50-homer season, and also drove in an NL-best 147 runs. An injured knee limited his playing time in 2000, but he finished the season with 554 career home runs to climb into the top seven all time.

TIM KEEFE P

An early master of the changeup, Tim Keefe compiled one of the great pitching records of the 19th century. For six straight years, 1883–1888, he won 32 games or more, twice exceeding 40 victories and on three occasions registering more than 300 strikeouts. Known as "Sir Timothy" in deference to his natty taste in sartorial matters, he ended his career with 342 wins, eighth on the all-time list.

It's true that Keefe enjoyed a distinct advantage over modern pitchers, in that for the entirety of his career he was throwing the ball to the plate from a distance of 50 feet. The year he retired, 1893, was the year the pitching distance was lengthened to 60 feet 6 inches. The shorter distance had allowed some fastball pitchers to rack up a huge number of strikeouts, making it difficult to judge the best pitchers of the 1880s by modern standards. But many historians believe that Keefe could not only have made the adjustment, but might actually have been even more successful had he pitched a decade or so later. They base this on the fact that Keefe, unlike many hurlers of his day, was a master of three pitches: a fastball, a curve, and a devastating changeup. He was perhaps the first pitcher to use the changeup as a major weapon; adding an extra 10 feet to the pitch may well have increased his effectiveness.

Keefe turned pro in 1878, and joined the Troy Haymakers of the National League in 1880. He lost 59 games during his three seasons with the team while winning only 41. When the league canceled the Troy franchise following the 1882 season, Keefe wound up with the American Association's Metropolitans, the original "Mets." He quickly established himself as one of AA's premier pitchers, compiling a 41–27 record in 1883 while leading the league with 68 complete games and 619 innings pitched. The following year he finished at 37–17 to account for more than half of the pennant-winning Mets' victories. In a series of postseason games regarded as the first World Series, Keefe lost two games to Charley "Old Hoss" Radbourn and the NL champion Providence Grays, then umpired as Radbourn defeated the Mets a third time to win the Series.

In 1885 the Mets' owner, John Day, transferred Keefe, several other Mets, and manager Jim Mutrie to his National League Gothams, who soon became known as the Giants. Keefe and Mickey Welch gave the Giants the most effective one-two pitching punch of the period. Keefe went 32–13 in his first season with the new club and led the league with an ERA of 1.58. In 1886 he topped the NL with 42 wins, 64 games pitched, 62 complete games, and 535 innings pitched.

Keefe's best season was 1888. His 35 victories led the NL, as did his .745 winning percentage. He also threw a league-high eight shutouts, finished with a league-leading 1.74 ERA, and reeled off a string of 19 straight wins. The rules crediting pitchers with wins were different then, but Keefe's amazing streak nevertheless remains the single-season record, although Rube Marquard later matched it.

The Giants won the 1888 pennant and disposed of the American Association's St. Louis Browns in an extended 10-game World Series, with Keefe winning four games while allowing only two earned runs. In 1889 New York took its second consecutive pennant and World Series, but Keefe, now the team's highest-paid player, slipped to only 28 regular-season wins and was 0–1 in two World Series appearances.

After baseball's club owners initiated a new salary policy in 1890, Keefe and many other players tried to establish a new circuit, the Players' League. Pitching for the league's New York team, Keefe went 17–11. He returned to the Giants when the Players' League folded, was dealt to Philadelphia, pitched for two more years, and then retired. During his 14 seasons, he had pitched 554 complete games and had a 2.62 ERA to go with his 342 victories. Keefe died in 1933; he was named to the Hall of Fame in 1964.

BOB LEMON P

Although he started as a position player, Bob Lemon became a 20-game winner seven times with the Cleveland Indians. On a pitching staff that featured such aces as Bob Feller, Mike Garcia, Early Wynn, and Herb Score, Lemon led the American League three times in wins, four times in innings pitched, and five times in complete games. An all-around talent, his career total of 37 homers places him second on the all-time list for pitchers, trailing only Wes Ferrell.

Lemon was converted to pitcher by Indians manager Lou Boudreau, who acted on advice from Ted Williams and other veterans who had batted against Lemon in service games during World War II. Lemon, convinced he was a major league hitter, fought the change every step of the way. For his first two seasons as a member of the Indians he refused to wear a toe plate, thinking he would return to being a position player at any time.

After two years mainly working as a reliever, Lemon moved into the regular rotation in 1948. On June 30, he pitched a no-hitter against the Detroit Tigers. That year he was named to the All-Star Game for the first of seven straight seasons, as he went on to notch 20 victories and lead the league in complete games, innings pitched, and shutouts. He also won Games 2 and 6 of the World Series against the Boston Braves.

Lemon won at least 20 games in five of the next six seasons, including American League highs of 23 in 1950 and again in 1954. In the former year he led the league in strikeouts, with 170; in the latter year he helped the Indians to a 111-win season and another flag. In the Series, however, Lemon lost in Game 1 and Game 4, as the New York Giants swept the Tribe.

Lemon again led the AL with 18 wins in 1955, although he completed only five—the only time in a nine-year period he had fewer than 17 complete games. The next year was his last 20-win season.

After injuring his leg in 1957, Lemon ended his playing days in the minors with San Diego. He went on to scout for the Indians, Royals, and Yankees, manage in the International and Pacific Coast leagues, coach in the majors, and manage the Royals, White Sox, and, most memorably, the Yankees.

In July 1978, two years after he was inducted into the Hall of Fame, Lemon replaced Billy Martin as manager of the dissension-ridden Bronx Bombers; his low-key style played a large role in New York's remarkable rally from fourth place in July to first place in October. The Yankees beat Boston in a one-game playoff for the AL East title, defeated the Kansas City Royals in the Championship Series, and beat the Los Angeles Dodgers in the World Series. Lemon took New York to another World Series against the Dodgers in 1981, but the Yanks lost the Series and Lemon, his job. He died in 2000.

DAVE BANCROFT SS

Dave "Beauty" Bancroft is generally deemed to be one of the three top fielding shortstops ever, along with Ozzie Smith and Art Fletcher. No shortstop ever handled more chances than Bancroft did in 1922 with the New York Giants—984. His 6.62 chances accepted per game in 1918 was the highest total for a shortstop in the 20th century, as was his average of 2.97 putouts per game that same season.

As a rookie with the Philadelphia Phillies in 1915, the slick-fielding shortstop was instrumental in his team's winning the National League pennant. It was while in Philly that Bancroft earned his nickname from his habit of yelling "Beauty!" whenever his pitcher made a good pitch.

In 1920 Giants manager John McGraw, convinced that

Bancroft was essential to New York's pennant hopes, asked Giants owner Charles Stoneham to offer the Phils $100,000, shortstop Art Fletcher, and pitcher Bill Hubbell for Bancroft. When the deal was consummated, it was the largest amount of cash that had ever been offered for a single player in National League history. Bancroft proved worthy of the expenditure. He was immediately named the captain of his new team, and he played a key role in the Giants winning three consecutive NL championships from 1921 through 1923. He also found his batting stroke—as a switch-hitting leadoff man who crowded the plate, Bancroft hit .318 in 1921, .321 in 1922, and .304 in 1923. Lifetime, he batted .279 and scored 1,048 runs.

A fiery team leader, Bancroft was as tough as they came. On one occasion in 1923, he showed up at the park with a high fever but insisted on playing. After the game he collapsed in the clubhouse; the doctor's diagnosis was pneumonia.

In November 1923, the Giants traded Bancroft to the Boston Braves, and he became the team's player-manager. Even though he hit better than .300 in two of his four seasons at Boston's helm, the Braves finished eighth, fifth, seventh, and seventh. Replaced by former catcher Jack Slattery following the 1927 season, Bancroft played two more seasons with the Brooklyn Dodgers and then returned to the Giants as a player-coach in 1930, retiring after the season. He remained with the Giants in a coaching capacity, often filling in for the ailing McGraw until the manager's retirement in 1932. According to Minneapolis sportswriter Charles Johnson, Bancroft knew "the technical side of the game up and down . . . As John McGraw's trusted assistant for three years, he rated with the best brains in the game."

As of 2001, Dave Bancroft was still ranked among the game's all-time leaders at his position in seven fielding categories—total chances per game (fourth), chances accepted per game (second), putouts (third), putouts per game (second), assists (10th), and assists per game (fifth). He was elected to the Hall of Fame by the Veterans Committee in 1971, a year before he died.

REGGIE SMITH OF

Outfielder Reggie Smith was one of the premier switch hitters in major league history, the first to record 100 or more homers in each league. With the Boston Red Sox he homered from both sides of the plate in a single game four times, and he repeated the feat twice with the St. Louis Cardinals.

Smith participated in seven All-Star Games (twice as an American Leaguer and five times as a National Leaguer), but he never really received the recognition he deserved as one of baseball's premier players—at least until injuries slowed him down. He played a deft center field, had a good arm, and hit for both average and power. In 1968, the "Year of the Pitcher," Smith led the AL in doubles with 37; his 33 doubles in 1971 also topped the league. On May 22, 1976, as a Cardinal, Smith hit three homers in a game against Philadelphia.

With the Los Angeles Dodgers in 1977, Smith was part of baseball's first-ever 30-homer quartet, slamming 32 to complement the efforts of his teammates Steve Garvey (33), Ron Cey (30), and Dusty Baker (30). He paced the NL that season with a .432 on-base percentage, while batting .307, scoring 104 runs, and knocking in the same number. Smith finished fourth in the MVP voting that year, and was a key factor in LA's winning the pennant.

In the World Series against the Yankees, Smith scored seven runs and drove in five in a losing cause. That wasn't the first time he acquitted himself well in the Fall Classic; in 1967, he homered twice for Boston, although the Red Sox lost to the Cards. All told, he connected for six homers in World Series competition.

In his final four major league seasons, knee, neck, and ankle problems beset Smith. When he retired in 1982 after a year with the San Francisco Giants, his total of 18 homers was at the time the second highest for a final season in NL history. Lifetime, he hit 314 homers, had 734 extra base hits, batted .287, and slugged for a .489 average. After leaving the majors Smith played in Japan with the Yomiuri Giants, hitting 45 home runs over 186 games in 1983 and 1984. He served as first base coach and hitting instructor for the Dodgers from 1995 to 1998.

YOGI BERRA C

Although Yogi Berra has achieved renown for his legendary (and often apocryphal) inversions and manglings of the English language, the abilities shown during his brilliant 19-year career were such that he was selected to the All-Century Team in 1999. As with Johnny Bench, the straight numbers—although impressive—do not begin to tell the whole story of the three-time American League Most Valuable Player.

A skilled receiver and a good handler of pitchers, Berra's most impressive marks were being selected for the All-Star Game 15 consecutive years, playing on 14 pennant-winning teams and 10 world champions, setting the World Series record for most hits (71), and going an entire season (1958) without an error. He was probably the key cog in the phenomenal success of the New York Yankees from 1949 to 1953, when the team won an unprecedented five consecutive World Series.

Berra, whose nickname was bestowed upon him by a childhood friend who noted his resemblance to a fakir in a movie, signed with the Yankees after being rejected by the Cardinals and the Browns. He broke in with the Yanks in 1946, sharing the catching duties and playing the outfield. When Casey Stengel took over the club in 1949, Berra assumed the first-string catcher's job. He responded with his greatest season at the plate in 1950, batting .322 and scoring 116 runs—both career highs—to go with 124 RBIs.

Those numbers were down a bit in 1951, but Berra was nonetheless voted the American League's Most Valuable Player. "I am lucky to have him and so are my pitchers," said Stengel. "He springs on a bunt like it was another dollar." Stengel also stated that he wouldn't trade Berra, his "assistant manager," for anyone, even Ted Williams.

A wild swinger, Berra was a notorious bad-ball hitter. Yet for all of Berra's free swinging, he was not easy to strike out. In 1950, for instance, he fanned just 12 times in 597 at bats. He also had a well-earned reputation as one of baseball's greatest-ever clutch hitters. Paul Richards praised him as "the toughest man in baseball in the last three innings."

Berra won back-to-back MVP awards in 1954–55,

making him the only catcher of the 20th century to have been so honored. From 1953 to 1956, he averaged 111 RBIs a season, with a high of 125 in 1954. All told, he slammed 358 homers, and his total of 313 as a catcher trails only Carlton Fisk and Johnny Bench. In World Series play, his special province, he holds the career records for games (75) and at bats (259) in addition to hits, and ranks second in runs, RBIs, and total bases, and third in home runs. And, of course, he was behind the plate for what was perhaps the greatest game ever pitched, Don Larsen's perfect game against the Brooklyn Dodgers in the 1956 World Series.

In 1964, at the end of his playing career, Stengel's erstwhile "assistant" rose to become the Yankees manager; he responded to the challenge by winning a pennant. But when New York fell to the Cardinals in a seven-game Series, Berra was fired. In a public relations coup, the rival Mets signed him as a player-coach, thereby reuniting him with Stengel. Berra played in only a few games, but in one of them he teamed up with Warren Spahn. "I don't know if we're the oldest battery, but we sure are the ugliest," admitted Spahn.

Berra later coached the Mets and, following the death of Gil Hodges in 1971, he was named manager. In 1973 his Amazin's came from last place in the final month of the season to capture the National League pennant with the lowest won-lost percentage of any league champion in history. It was the year of his famous coinage, "It ain't over 'til it's over." He also managed the Yankees and coached the Astros before calling it quits in 1992. At that time, Berra had been a member of the Hall of Fame for 20 years.

WILLIE MCCOVEY 1B-OF

An imposing 6 feet 4 inches and 210 pounds, Willie McCovey possessed a coiled and menacing lefthanded stance. He produced mammoth numbers during a 22-year career that climaxed with his enshrinement in the Hall of Fame in his first year of eligibility. McCovey's 521 home runs are the most by a lefthanded slugger in National League history. He homered every 15.73 at bats, which is more often than players such as Lou Gehrig, Hank Aaron, Willie Mays, and Reggie Jackson. His 18 career grand slams are second only to Gehrig's 23. From 1959 to 1971, McCovey and Mays combined for 800 homers, to rank as the NL's second-best longball duo of all time.

During the 1960s McCovey led the NL three times in home runs and twice in RBIs. A six-time NL All-Star, he hit two homers in the 1969 Midsummer Classic, driving in three runs and winning the Arch Ward Memorial Award as the game's Most Valuable Player.

McCovey broke into the majors with a flourish on July 30, 1959, slugging two triples and two singles against Philadelphia Phillies hurler Robin Roberts. Although he appeared in only 52 games with the Giants his first season, McCovey batted .354 with 13 home runs and 38 RBIs, and had a 23-game hitting streak. He was voted NL Rookie of the Year.

His sophomore slump was severe, and it took a couple of seasons for McCovey to get his groove back. Until 1965 he platooned in left field because Orlando Cepeda, the 1958 Rookie of the Year, was entrenched at first base. Bill James notes that McCovey was "probably the only truly great player to have been platooned for several years at the start of his career." From 1959 through 1964, he received at least 365 at bats only once, in 1963. That year he led the league with 44 homers and drove in 102 runs. Even as a platoon player, McCovey demonstrated All-Star potential. On June 12, 1960, he belted the first of his three major league pinch-hit grand slams. In the Giants' pennant-winning year of 1962, McCovey hit 20 home runs in only 229 at bats. On September 22, 1963, and April 22, 1964, he hit three consecutive home runs in a game.

In 1965, McCovey took over at first base for the Giants and remained there through 1973. He became a feared and productive power hitter, leading the league in slugging percentage for three consecutive seasons from 1968 through 1970. His finest year was 1969, during which he topped the NL with personal bests in homers (45) and RBIs (126), in addition to batting .320 and pacing the league in on-base percentage (.458)—numbers that won him the NL's MVP. The following year he again drove in 126 runs and led the league in bases on balls, with 137.

McCovey succumbed to multiple injuries and ailments in 1971 and '72, and was traded to the San Diego Padres in 1973. After 11 games with Oakland in August 1976, he was back with the Giants in 1977 and led the team with 28 home runs, 86 RBIs, and 15 game-winning hits. *The Sporting News* and United Press International named him Comeback Player of the Year. One of his biggest thrills of the season came on September 18—Willie McCovey Day at Candlestick Park—when he smashed a long two-out single to left-center in the ninth to knock home the game-winning run.

McCovey hit his 500th career home run off Jamie Easterly on July 1, 1978 at Atlanta. He got his 521st and final home run on May 3, 1980, a 385-foot shot off Montreal's Scott Sanderson, which moved McCovey into a tie on the all-time list with his boyhood idol, Ted Williams. His No. 44 is one of eight numbers that have been retired by the Giants organization.

TED LYONS P

Ted Lyons won 260 games for Chicago White Sox teams that were perennially pennant-impaired. In his 21-season career with the Chisox, the club finished in the second division 16 times. Only six players—Brooks Robinson, Carl Yastrzemski, Cap Anson, Stan Musial, Al Kaline, and Mel Ott—had longer careers with one team. Only two players—Phil Niekro and Gaylord Perry—played more seasons without appearing in a World Series.

The affable Lyons never complained, and quietly compiled a stellar record in spite of his surroundings. From the start he possessed an excellent fastball, and later added a fine curve. Never a strikeout artist, Lyons had good control, which improved nearly every year. In 1939 he tossed 42 consecutive innings without allowing a base on balls. As a result, he pitched fast games. One time he threw a complete game in only an hour and 18 minutes.

A baseball star at Baylor University, Lyons never pitched an inning of minor league ball. He signed with the White Sox in 1923 after spurning an offer from the Philadelphia Athletics. After a year split between starting and relief, he cracked the regular rotation for the White Sox in 1925 and quickly became a star. While pitching for a fifth-place team, Lyons led the American League with 21 wins and five shutouts. In September he was pitching a perfect game until Bobby Veach of the Washington Senators singled with two outs in the ninth inning.

In 1926 Lyons won 18 games, including a 6–0 no-hitter against the Boston Red Sox on August 21. The following year, he tied Waite Hoyt of the pennant-winning Yankees for most wins, 22, while leading the AL with 30 complete games and 307⅔ innings pitched.

Lyons lost 20 games in 1929 despite some heroic efforts. On May 24 he pitched 21 innings, the third-most in league history, giving up 24 hits but walking only two batters in a 6–5 loss to Detroit. The next year he rebounded with 22 wins, leading the league with 29 complete games and 297⅔ innings pitched.

In his first seven complete major league seasons, Lyons won 124 games. Then, on a damp night in Houston during spring training, he tried to break off a curve and injured his shoulder. He struggled through the 1931 season, winning only four games. With his fastball gone, a determined Lyons turned to a knuckleball and other junk pitches. He earned a starting position and won 31 games from 1932 through 1934, although he also lost 49. Then Chisox manager Jimmy Dykes had the idea of using Lyons only on Sundays. In 1939, the first year of the plan—when he went 14–6 with a 2.76 ERA—Lyons was selected to his only All-Star Game. These regular Sunday starts continued through 1942. During those four seasons Lyons pitched 85 times and posted a 52–30 record with 72 complete games.

The 1942 season was Lyons' 20th in a White Sox uniform. At age 41 he posted another 14–6 record with a league-leading, career-best 2.10 ERA. He seemed poised to tie Walter Johnson's record for the most years spent by a pitcher with one team, but he decided to enlist as a private in the U.S. Marines. After serving for three years and seeing combat in the South Pacific, he returned to Chicago in 1946 and tied Johnson's record. When he was named White Sox manager early that season, he retired as a pitcher with a career record of 260–230. Had he played on a contending team, he most likely would have won 300 games.

Lyons completed a remarkable 356 games in 484 starts, and his career ERA of 3.67 is impressive, considering the era in which he pitched. The White Sox retired his uniform number 16, and he was named to the Hall of Fame in 1955.

DAVE WINFIELD OF

A talented, durable player, Dave Winfield posted Hall of Fame-level offensive statistics and also won seven Gold Gloves. The 22-year veteran of six teams rapped 3,110 hits—16th on the all-time list—and 1,833 RBIs, which places him 13th, just behind Ted Williams. Winfield also ranks high in home runs (475), doubles (540), extra base hits (1,093), and total bases (5,221). He is perhaps most famous, however, for his fractious relationship with controversial Yankees owner George Steinbrenner.

The MVP of the 1973 College World Series, Winfield was signed by the San Diego Padres in June of that year and went immediately from the campus to the majors, singling off Jerry Reuss in his first at bat and hitting safely in his first six games. He became the star on the second-division Padres, hitting 34 homers and driving in a league-best 118 RBIs in 1979 and winning Gold Gloves in 1979 and 1980.

More prosperous clubs set their sights on Winfield, and he signed as free agent with the Yankees in 1981, netting a $1 million signing bonus and a 10-year contract at $1.4 million per year with a cost-of-living clause. As part of the agreement Steinbrenner personally agreed to contribute or cause to be contributed $300,000 to the David M. Winfield Foundation each year for the decade. That agreement would eventually become a key bone of contention between Winfield and Steinbrenner.

Winfield's first year with the Yankees was good but not spectacular. The next season, 1982, he delivered 37 homers—his career high—and knocked in 106 runs, his first of five consecutive years topping the 100-RBI mark. No Yankee had accomplished that since Joe DiMaggio had strung together seven straight 100-RBI seasons from 1936–1942. Winfield was selected to the American League All-Star team for the first eight seasons he played with the Yankees, continuing his string of four consecutive National League All-Star appearances with the Padres.

Few players in the majors were as productive as Winfield between 1982 and 1986. In addition to his RBI numbers he scored more than 100 runs in 1984 and 1985, and on the last day of the 1984 season, after a spirited race, he lost the batting title to teammate Don Mattingly (.343 to .340). Brilliant afield, Winfield won five Gold Glove Awards with the Yankees.

On August 4, 1983, while playing center field in Toronto, Winfield attempted to scare a seagull off the field by throwing a ball near it. The ball took a short bounce off the artificial turf at Exposition Stadium and killed the bird. Absurdly, the Toronto police booked Winfield on a charge of cruelty to animals, held him for 90 minutes and released him on $500 bail. Charges were dropped the following day.

Despite his play, a rift had arisen between Steinbrenner and Winfield, first sparked by the owner's miscalculations over the cost-of-living provisions of Winfield's contract. In 1989 the pair sued each other in regard to payments to the Winfield Foundation; the matter was settled out of court. Finally, Steinbrenner became entangled with a gambler who said he evidence that incriminated Winfield. The upshot of this imbroglio resulted in Commissioner Fay Vincent finding Steinbrenner's actions to be "not in the best interests of baseball." The Yankees owner was placed on the "permanently ineligible list," meaning he could retain ownership of the team but not participate in its business decisions.

Winfield missed the entire 1989 season due to a herniated disk, and started 1990 as the Yankees designated hitter. After another controversy regarding his contract, he was traded to the Angels. He led AL outfielders in fielding percentage that season and paced the team in RBIs, runs, and slugging percentage. *The Sporting News* named him its Comeback Player of the Year.

On April 13, 1991, Winfield hit three homers in one game against Minnesota. On June 24, 1991 versus Kansas City he hit for the cycle, becoming the oldest player to accomplish that feat. In 1992, with the Blue Jays, he became the oldest player to record 100 or more RBIs in a season, helped by a record 32 RBIs in August. His two-run double in the 11th inning of Game 6 of the 1992 World Series gave the Blue Jays a 4–3 win over Atlanta and the world championship.

With Minnesota in 1993, Winfield collected his 3,000th career hit on September 26 off Dennis Eckersley. He finished up as a DH for the Indians in 1995.

CARL MAYS P

Only once in the first 125 seasons of major league baseball did a pitch take the life of a batter. Carl Mays is remembered almost exclusively for throwing that pitch, but the record shows that the surly Kentuckian with the submarine delivery is also worth remembering for other things.

Mays, once described as having "the disposition of someone with a permanent toothache," was an excellent pitcher and a tough competitor. As a rookie he provoked a fight with Ty Cobb by throwing at him. He was a 20-game winner five times in his 15-year major league career, leading the American League in 1921 with 27 victories for the New York Yankees. On August 30, 1918, Mays pitched and won both games of a doubleheader to clinch the flag for the Boston Red Sox. In the World Series that year he started and won two games, allowing only 10 hits in a pair of complete-game victories.

The tragic moment that would permanently tar the name of Carl Mays took place during the 1920 AL pennant race. With his Yankees contending with the White Sox and the Indians, Mays got the starting assignment for the August 16 game with Cleveland. It was a muggy, drizzly day in New York, and the Indians were up, 3–0, as Cleveland shortstop Ray Chapman stepped in against Mays to lead off the fifth. Mays' first pitch, thrown in his characteristic submarine style, hit Chapman on the left temple, and the batter crumpled to the ground. The ball rolled toward third, and Mays picked it up and threw to first. Chapman got up, tried to walk, and fell again. He died the next day.

The outrage directed at Mays was enormous. His deceptive delivery and willingness to throw inside had earned him the league lead in hit batsmen in 1917, and he ranked second in 1918 and 1919. He denied throwing at Chapman and expressed regret over the incident, but some teams swore they would never play against him again.

The sad death of Ray Chapman led to a major change in the rules of the game. After that, umpires were encouraged to keep only new, white balls in the game and to throw out those that had been darkened by dirt and grass. It was the single most dramatic difference between the dead-ball game of the teens and the explosive home run era of the 1920s.

Although the antipathy directed against him was intense, Mays' performance wasn't hampered by the noise. He finished the year at 26–11, topping the AL with six shutouts. In 1921, he led the league in games and innings pitched to go with his 27 wins, and appeared in enough relief stints to be credited with seven saves. He won one game but took two tough losses in the Giants' victory over the Yankees in the 1921 World Series. After losing Game 4 of the 1922 World Series and spending the next season in New York manager Miller Huggins' doghouse, Mays was sold to Cincinnati in 1924.

National Leaguers were as fooled by his submarine delivery as their American League counterparts had been. Mays won 20 games with Cincinnati in 1924 and 19 in 1926. His major league career ended as a Giants reliever in 1929. Lifetime, he posted an excellent .623 winning percentage (208–126), and his 2.92 ERA was the third best recorded between the end of the Dead Ball Era and the advent of World War II.

RYNE SANDBERG 2B

Ryne Sandberg not only had incredible power for a second baseman, he was also one of the steadiest fielders to ever play the position. When he retired in 1997 he had the most career home runs (277) by a second baseman, and the highest fielding average (.989) of anyone that played more than 800 games at the keystone. An outstanding baserunner, Sandberg swiped 20 or more bases nine times (344 for his career), and scored 100 or more runs six times.

"Ryno," as he was known, was named after New York Yankees relief pitcher Ryne Duren. The Philadelphia Phillies selected him in the 20th round of the 1978 draft. The Phils projected Sandberg as a third baseman, and since the youngster had little chance of unseating All-Star Mike Schmidt, he was traded to the Chicago Cubs in January 1982. The Cubs shifted Sandberg to second base, and in 1983 he began a record nine-year run as the Gold Glove winner at that position. He played four full seasons without a throwing error.

In 1984, his third season in the majors, Sandberg and the Cubs enjoyed a fairy-tale year. He batted a career-high .314, stole 32 bases, led the majors with 114 runs scored, and tied for the major league lead with 19 triples (more than twice the number he'd ever again accumulate). He also continued his steady play in the field, notching a 61-game errorless streak and committing just six errors all season. He made the first of 10 consecutive trips to the All-Star Game, and his heroics propelled the Cubs into the postseason for the first time since 1945. Sandberg was named NL Most Valuable Player, becoming the first Cub to win the award since Hall of Fame shortstop Ernie Banks in 1959—the year Ryne Sandberg was born.

Eventually, Sandberg cultivated a home run swing. He hit 26 homers in 1985, 30 in 1989, and a league-leading 40 in 1990, becoming the first second baseman to lead the NL in home runs since Rogers Hornsby in 1925. That season Sandberg also set a record with 123 consecutive errorless games.

A protracted slump early in 1994 prompted Sandberg to announce that he was retiring. But after skipping the 1994 strike and the abbreviated 1995 season, he found that he missed baseball. He returned to the Cubs in 1996 and quickly regained his power stroke, hitting 25 homers and driving in 92 runs. While his range was not what it once was, he still committed just six errors in 1,234 innings. By the end of the 1997 season, however, he was no longer able to produce at the level he expected of himself. He bowed out amid a thunderous ovation at Wrigley Field.

BILL MAZEROSKI 2B

Bill Mazeroski will always be remembered for his October 1960 home run at Forbes Field, which brought a dramatic end to the World Series between his Pittsburgh Pirates and the New York Yankees. Unfortunately, that shining moment at the plate has overshadowed his brilliant 17-year career as one of the game's greatest defensive second basemen—indeed, as one of the all-time greatest defensive players at any position.

Mazeroski holds more defensive titles than any other player, ever, and his major league records as a second baseman include most lifetime double plays, most double plays in a season, and nine years leading his league in assists. His National League records include leading the league in chances eight times and in assists five consecutive years. He also led the NL in fielding percentage three times and was the Gold Glove second baseman eight times. His work on the double play—a lightning-fast sidestep and quick throw to first—earned him the nickname "No Touch" because he never seemed to touch the ball; he simply redirected it to first.

In Mazeroski's first of six All-Star Games, he received the ultimate compliment. During fielding practice, players on both teams, hardened major leaguers, stopped to watch Mazeroski field and throw. It was a tribute, the equivalent of stopping to watch Ted Williams hit.

Baseball analyst Bill James agrees that Mazeroski's defensive stats are the most impressive of any player at any position. Charles Faber, in his book, *Baseball Ratings,* awards points for percentage, assists, chances, and range factor to all players with 10 years' experience: Mazeroski leads every player from every era, regardless of position.

Mazeroski joined the Pirates, with whom he would spend his entire career, in 1956. He batted .283 and .275 in his first two full major league seasons, and he hit a career-best 19 homers the second year. In 1962, batting from the eighth spot all year, he drove in 81 runs to lead the team. In 1967, despite having pulled muscles in both his legs early in the season, Mazeroski set the NL record for games played in a season, with 163. His 138 career homers and lifetime .260 average compare favorably with such glove wizards as Ozzie Smith and Walter "Rabbit" Maranville.

It was the home run in Game 7 of the 1960 World Series, however, that earned the man called "Maz" an eternal niche in Pittsburgh's pantheon of heroes. The Pirates, who hadn't won a Series in 35 years, had clawed and sputtered to three victories against the Yankees by scores of 6–4, 5–2, and 3–2. The Yanks' wins had been laughers—16–3, 10–0, and 12–0. Yet at 3:36 P.M. on October 13, Mazeroski turned on a high Ralph Terry fastball to decide the outcome of the Fall Classic, 10–9 in favor of the Pirates. It was only the third World Series game to end on a homer, and it was the only Series determined by a dinger on the final pitch until 1993, when Toronto won the Series on Joe Carter's ninth-inning swat.

JOHNNY MIZE 1B

For most of his 15-year career, Johnny Mize was a power hitter to be feared. He was, in fact, that rarest of hitters—a genuine home run threat who hit for a high average and seldom struck out. Mize is the only man to hit 50 home runs in a season while fanning fewer than 50 times, and he hit three homers in a game a record six times. He also homered at least once in all 15 of the major league ballparks in use during his career.

Mize was a star for six years in the minor leagues, finally making it up to the St. Louis Cardinals in 1936 after surgery on both hips. He responded with an outstanding rookie performance, and he was nothing less than excellent in his next six years in St. Louis. Between 1937 and 1942, Mize drove in 100 runs or more every year, averaging 27 homers while hitting between .314 and .364. He won a batting title (.349 in 1939); paced the National League twice in home runs, once in doubles, and once in triples; won three slugging titles; and twice finished second in MVP voting. He was christened "the Big Cat" for the way he handled bad hops at first base. Stan Musial later used the nickname to describe Mize's graceful batting stance and the ease with which he casually avoided brushback pitches.

In 1942 Mize was traded to the Giants, and it was as a Giant that most people remember him. Mize led the league in RBIs (110) and slugging percentage (.521) his first year there and then spent three years in the navy. He returned to the team in 1946, hitting .357 and slugging .576 in limited action after breaking a bone in his hand. The 1947 campaign, however, was the Big Cat's biggest. Mize belted 51 home runs to become the only NL lefty in the 20th century to ever top 50 in a season. Even so, he garnered only a tie for the league lead as Ralph Kiner of the Pirates matched his total. But Mize captured league titles in RBIs (a career-best 138) and runs (137, another career high), and the Giants set a record (since broken) for most home runs by a team in a season.

In 1948 Mize slugged 40 homers to again tie Kiner for the league lead, and he knocked in 125 runs, but his average fell below .302 for the first time. After a slow start the following year he was sold to the Yankees. Though his playing time was curtailed due to an injury, Mize did manage to deliver a pinch single in the ninth inning of Game 3 of the 1949 World Series that won the game for New York.

For the next four years Mize served the Yankees well, providing power off the bench and occasionally starting. He led the league in pinch hits in 1951, 1952, and 1953. The 1952 World Series was the crowning achievement of his career. After making only one appearance in the first three games—a pinch-hit home run in a Yanks defeat in Game 3—Mize was installed at first in place of Joe Collins. His home run in Game 4 won a shutout for Allie Reynolds, and his three-run wallop in Game 5 marked the first time a player had ever homered in three consecutive Series games. In Game 7, Mize's single brought home the first run in the Yankees' 4–2 victory. He finished with three home runs and six RBIs while batting an even .400.

In May of 1953, his final season, Mize reached base in seven consecutive pinch-hit appearances with five hits. His 19 pinch hits for the season remains only one fewer than the league record; overall, he drove in 179 runs as a Yankee with only 230 hits.

Mize finished his career with 359 home runs and a batting average of .312. The Veterans Committee voted him into the Baseball Hall of Fame in 1981.

MIKE PIAZZA C

Only the legendary Negro Leaguer Josh Gibson rivals

Mike Piazza as the preeminent hitting catcher in baseball history. During the 1990s, Piazza rung up some truly frightening numbers for the Los Angeles Dodgers and the New York Mets, including seven seasons with more than 30 home runs (six of them consecutive), six seasons with more than 100 RBIs, and, entering 2001, a lifetime batting average of .328. His 1997 season with the Dodgers was arguably the best offensive performance ever staged by a backstop. Piazza batted .362, slugged 40 homers, and drove in 124 runs while scoring 104. He also tallied 201 hits, the most ever recorded by a catcher, while slugging for a .638 average. He won Silver Slugger Awards and appeared in the All-Star Game in each of his first seven full years in the majors.

The Dodgers selected Piazza in the 62nd round of the 1988 draft (manager Tommy Lasorda was a close friend of Piazza's father, and encouraged the team to draft the young ballplayer as a family favor). Lasorda decided to make him a catcher; after apprenticing his new craft in the Dominican Republic, the Mexican League, and several minor league towns, he joined the Dodgers in 1992.

Piazza was a unanimous choice for National League Rookie of the Year in 1993. Showing extraordinary opposite-field power, he batted .318 with 35 homers and 112 RBIs. Strike-shortened seasons in 1994 and 1995 curtailed his power numbers slightly, but he hit .346 in 1995 to finish second in the NL batting race.

In 1996, his first 162-game season since his rookie year, Piazza batted .336 with 36 home runs, 105 RBIs, and a .422 on base percentage. He was Most Valuable Player in the All-Star Game at Philadelphia's Veteran's Stadium, where he used to serve as batboy when the Dodgers came to town. He finished second to San Diego's Ken Caminiti for NL MVP.

Piazza's phenomenal 1997 season resulted in another second-place finish in the MVP race, this time to Larry Walker of the Colorado Rockies. Piazza beat out the rest of the NL, however, for the inaugural CNN/SI and *Total Baseball* Ted Williams Award, measuring production based on a formula devised by *Total Baseball*.

Following a salary dispute, the Dodgers traded Piazza to the Marlins in May 1998; he was sent to the Mets a week later. Despite a cool reception in Queens, the streaky Piazza finished the season batting .328. Speculation had him heading elsewhere as a free agent, but he signed a seven-year contract as one of the game's top paid players.

In 1999 the Mets survived a thrilling stretch drive to edge into the playoffs as the Wild Card, thanks largely to Piazza's 40 home runs, 124 RBIs, and 100 runs scored. Hampered by a thumb problem, Piazza missed two playoff games against Arizona, and had to leave two NLCS games early against Atlanta because of a slight concussion. He hit just .182 in the postseason, but he still managed 10 RBIs. He hit a game-tying home run in Game 6 of the NLCS, although he had to be removed shortly thereafter.

The Mets were back in the postseason in 2000, again spearheaded by Piazza (.324, 38 homers, 113 RBIs). Although he performed well, batting a combined .302 with four home runs for the Division Series, the NLCS, and the World Series, his team fell short against the Yankees in New York's first Subway Series in 44 years. Piazza hit a respectable .273 with two dingers in the Fall Classic, but attracted more notice for having his broken bat hurled back at him by Roger Clemens in Game 2.

The chief rap against Piazza concerns his defensive abilities. In 2000 opposing baserunners stole successfully against him in 88 percent of their attempts. Yet from 1995 to 1999 Piazza caught more games than any other National Leaguer at his position. Only Ivan Rodriguez of Texas caught more games during that span.

DICK ALLEN 1B-3B

Dick Allen feuded with writers, fans, managers, and teammates, earned many suspensions and behaved and fielded erratically. However, he certainly could hit, and, when he wanted to, he could carry a team. Signed by the Phillies for a $60,000 bonus, he quickly established himself as a star, winning National League Rookie of the Year honors in 1964 after hitting .318 and leading the league in runs and triples. The following year Allen—who was known as Richie during his early years with the Phillies—was selected to play in his first of seven All-Star Games. In 1966 he slammed a career-best 40 homers while driving in 110 runs.

Despite his ability with the bat, Allen did have a downside on the field. He struck out often, twice fanning five times in a single game and once whiffing seven times in a row. His fielding at third base also left a lot to be desired, but after a freak injury to his throwing hand in 1967, he was moved to first. Commenting on his turbulent relationship with Phillies fans and scribes, Allen remarked, "I'll play first, third, left. I'll play anywhere—except Philadelphia."

He got his wish in 1971, when the Phillies, after a long series of incidents both on and off the field involving their star slugger, shipped Allen and two other players to the Cardinals for Tim McCarver, Curt Flood, and two others from St. Louis. (Flood refused to report and sued baseball, paving the way for free agency.) But despite 34 homers and 101 RBIs, Allen soon wore out his welcome in St. Louis and was traded to the Dodgers. The next season, 1972, he was sent to the Chicago White Sox, a move that dramatically revived his career. Allen led the Sox to a division championship, pacing the American League with 37 homers, 113 RBIs, 99 walks, an on-base percentage of .422, and a slugging average of .603. Impressing even his harshest critics, he received 21 out of 24 first-place votes for AL MVP.

By 1974, however, Allen was feuding with teammates again, and on September 14 he walked out on the White Sox, even though he was leading the league in homers at the time with 32. The frustrated Sox sold his contract to the Braves for only $5,000 and a player to be named later, but Allen had no interest in ever playing in Dixie again. The Phillies, led by announcer Richie Ashburn, coaxed him out of retirement, but he was not the same player he had been. Granted free agency in November 1976, he called it quits in 1977 by storming off the Oakland A's.

Although his career was checkered by controversy, Allen was unquestionably one of the great sluggers of the 1960s and early 1970s. Perhaps his true ability was shown by a comment by Mike Schmidt. "When I was playing Legion ball in Ohio," Schmidt said, "I always pretended I was Dick Allen. He was my idol."

JACK GLASSCOCK SS

Jack Glasscock was the outstanding defensive shortstop of the 1880s and an above-average hitter. That he never enjoyed the wider fame achieved by some of his contemporaries may have been due to his colorless personality, or the fact that he never played for a championship team in his 17 major league seasons.

Appearing with nine different clubs over the course of his career, Glasscock was a team leader, but never an especially fiery one. His one verifiable idiosyncrasy was his penchant for landscaping his position. Critics said he found pebbles to throw away where none existed. Perhaps so, but "Pebbly Jack," playing without a glove until 1890, led National League shortstops in putouts twice, in double plays four times, and in fielding percentage and assists six times each. Meanwhile, less fastidious shortstops earned no nicknames and were charged with countless bad-hop errors.

Glasscock arrived in the NL with the Cleveland Spiders in 1879 as a good-field, no-hit third baseman. The next season he moved over to shortstop, where he stayed for the rest of his career. Glasscock's hitting steadily improved from awful to adequate to outstanding. In 1879 he hit .209; by 1883 it was up to .287, and in 1889 he led the league with 205 hits and batted a career-high .352 (he also scored 128 runs, another career high, and had 40 doubles). Glasscock took over as the Indianapolis manager for part of the 1889 season and some accounts say he discovered pitcher Amos Rusie.

Although he intended to jump to the Players League in 1890, Glasscock ended up instead with the National League's New York Giants. That season he again led the league in hits, and also in batting average, at .336. In a game on September 27, he went 6 for 6.

Glasscock played for four teams in his final three years, hitting .341 with Pittsburgh in 1893 (to go with a career-best 100 RBIs) and .338 with Louisville in 1895, his last year in the big leagues. After he left the majors, he played five more seasons in the minors, mostly as a first baseman. Entering 2001, he ranks 10th all time among shortstops with 3.46 assists per game, and his 242 fielding runs (a statistic that determines runs saved beyond what a league-average player at his position might have saved) places him just ahead of Ozzie Smith and second only to Bill Dahlen at shortstop.

JIMMY WYNN OF

Jimmy Wynn packed a lot of power into a relatively small frame. At 5 feet 9 inches and 170 pounds he didn't have the physique usually associated with a power hitter, but he belted 291 homers during a 15-year major league career. His power at the plate earned Wynn the nickname "the Toy Cannon." In a career that lasted from 1963 to 1977, he hit 20 or more homers in a season eight times and surpassed 30 homers in a year three times.

Wynn spent most of his career with the Houston Astros, playing 11 seasons for the club after being drafted in 1962. The Astrodome was notoriously hostile to power hitters; nevertheless, in his best season with the Astros, 1967, Wynn slugged 37 home runs, drove in 107, and scored 102 while playing in 158 games. It earned him a spot on *The Sporting News* NL All-Star team. In 1969 Wynn tied the National League record for walks with 148 (while striking out 142 times); he led the league in that category again with Atlanta, drawing 127 passes in 1976. Wynn drew more than 100 bases on balls in four other seasons, and his career total of 1,224 walks places him 38th on the all-time list.

A fine base runner and solid outfielder, Wynn twice led the NL in putouts and once in assists. He also stole 225 bases during his career, reaching a high of 43 in his first full season (1965).

Traded to the Los Angeles Dodgers in 1974, Wynn was a major factor in helping them win the pennant, slugging 32 homers and knocking in 108 runs. He played two seasons for the Dodgers before being dealt to the Braves. Sold to the Yankees in November of 1976, Wynn was used sparingly. He finished his career with the Milwaukee Brewers later that year.

EDGAR MARTINEZ DH-3B

Defensively, Edgar Martinez was no wiz at third base, and a knee injury in 1990 robbed him of whatever speed he once possessed. But with a bat in his hands, Martinez was a magician, one of the elite hitters of the 1990s. When, as a designated hitter, Martinez led the American League with a .356 average in 1995, he became the first right-handed hitter since Joe DiMaggio to notch two AL batting titles. He also led the league with a .482 on-base percentage that year, becoming only the fifth righty swinger in AL history to lead the league in both categories in the same season.

Martinez never went more than eight at bats without a hit in 1995. The Seattle Mariner slugger rang up a .433 average against lefties, and he tied Albert Belle for most runs scored (121) and most doubles (52). In 1996 he became the first player to hit 50 doubles in consecutive seasons since Joe Medwick of the Cardinals in 1936 and 1937. That year he combined with Alex Rodriguez to wallop 104 doubles, the fourth highest total by a pair of teammates in major league history. Martinez hit 369 doubles in the 1990s, more than anyone else in the game.

In Seattle's first-ever trip to the playoffs in 1995, Martinez showed he could hit in October as well. He mauled the New York Yankees with a .571 average that included 12 hits and 10 RBIs as the Mariners took the series in five games. In Game 4 Martinez set a postseason record with seven RBIs, the result of a three-run homer and a grand slam as the Mariners tied the series. He then delivered the final blow, a two-run, game- and series-ending double off Jack McDowell in Game 5.

From 1995 to 1998, Martinez collected at least 100 walks and 100 RBIs, becoming only the sixth major leaguer to post those numbers for four consecutive seasons. As the new century turned, he showed no sign of letting up on opposing pitchers. His 145 RBIs led the league in 2000, and he slugged a career-best 37 home runs. In Game 1 of the Division Series against the White Sox, his dramatic 10th-inning homer off Keith Foulke provided the go-ahead runs in the Mariners' victory. Against the Yankees in the AL Championship Series, Martinez cooled off, but still managed to drive in four runs in a losing cause.

Entering the 2001 season, Martinez's .320 lifetime batting average ranked eighth among active players; his .425 career on-base percentage was second only to Frank

Thomas' .439. He was also ranked ninth in walks, 12th in doubles, and 20th in slugging among current players.

CRAIG BIGGIO 2B

Craig Biggio, the premier National League second baseman of the 1990s, began his career as a catcher. In 1989, his first full season in the majors, Biggio won *The Sporting News* Silver Slugger Award as the top offensive backstop in baseball. He averaged 22 steals in his first three campaigns; only two catchers had previously reached that number in a single season. Although Biggio was voted to his first of seven All-Star teams in 1991, there was concern that regular catching duties would diminish his offensive contributions. The following year he switched to second base and didn't miss a beat.

In 1992 Biggio played in all 162 games for the Astros. Although he struggled at times to make the transition defensively, he was again named to the All-Star squad, making him the only player to earn the honor as both a catcher and a second baseman. In the strike-shortened 1994 season, Biggio led the NL in doubles, stolen bases, and fielding percentage. He won the first of four consecutive Gold Gloves and established himself as one of the elite all-around players in the major leagues.

Biggio added a new dimension to his offense in 1995. Wearing a baggy jersey and bulky arm pad, and employing a plate-crowding stance, he was hit by pitches 22 times, topping the NL in that category. Biggio led the majors in HBPs the next three seasons; he was plonked 34 times in 1997, the third highest total in the 20th century. By the end of the 2000 season, Biggio had been hit 169 times, ranking him fifth all-time.

Despite being a sitting duck at the plate, Biggio managed to avoid missing any serious playing time until a knee injury knocked him out of the lineup in 2000. He began a consecutive-game playing streak in 1995 that lasted more than three years and totaled 494 games. Batting at the top of the order with his "Killer B" teammates Derek Bell and Jeff Bagwell, Biggio helped to spur the Astros to three consecutive division titles from 1997 to 1999. He led the league with 146 runs in 1997, the highest total for an NL player since 1932. The following year Biggio joined Tris Speaker as the only other 20th-century player to collect 50 doubles and 50 steals in the same season. His 73 extra base hits (51 doubles, 20 homers, and a pair of triples) were the second most by a leadoff hitter in two decades. He also became the first Astros player to reach 200 hits in a season.

Biggio's total of 56 doubles in 1999 made him the first National Leaguer since Joe Medwick in 1937 to hit that many, and only the sixth player in major league history to hit 50 or more doubles in back-to-back seasons. His 123 runs scored that season gave him 1,042 for the decade, second only to the 1,091 accumulated by Barry Bonds. At the beginning of the 2001 campaign, he was seeking to return to form following knee surgery.

DARRELL EVANS 3B-1B-DH

Like fine wine, third baseman Darrell Evans seemed to get better with age. He became, at 38, the oldest player to win a home run title and the second oldest to hit 40 homers in a season. When he retired, only three players had exceeded his homer total (414) without having been inducted into the Hall of Fame—Mike Schmidt (selected in 1995), Dave Kingman, and Reggie Jackson (selected in 1993).

Oddly enough, when the Atlanta Braves drafted him after the 1968 season, Evans was not a longball hitter. But he worked at changing his batting style, and after hitting 19 home runs in 1972, he was ready for his breakout season. With Atlanta in 1973, Evans hit 41 home runs, while Hank Aaron slugged 40 and Davey Johnson added 43. It was the first time in major league history that three teammates hit 40 or more. Evans also weighed in with 104 RBIs and 114 runs that season, both career highs.

Evans hit for power but not for average, so he could easily be stereotyped as a free-swinging slugger. Actually, he was quite selective at the plate, and during the course of his career walked more times than he struck out, 1,605 versus 1,410. Twice—in 1973 and 1974—he led the National League in bases on balls.

Atlanta traded Evans to San Francisco in June 1976. Although the terms of his Giants contract were lucrative, Candlestick Park hurt his home run and RBI totals. In 8 years in San Francisco, he hit more than 20 homers in a season only once; that was in 1983, his final year with the Giants. Upon joining the Detroit Tigers in 1984, however, Evans shifted between first base and designated hitter, and he eventually regained his Atlanta-style power. In 1985 he rebounded, hitting an American League-leading 40 homers.

His renewed power continued. At age 40 in 1987 he hit 34 homers, topping Hank Sauer's previous record of 26 at that age. He hit 22 homers in 1988, and retired the next year after a season with his old Atlanta Braves.

JOE SEWELL SS-3B

Shortstop Joe Sewell was a smooth fielder and a lifetime .312 hitter. He was also, without question, the hardest man in the history of the game to strike out. Even considering the standards of his day, his bat control was remarkable, and by contemporary standards his strikeout ratio is unbelievable. Sewell fanned only once in every 62.6 at bats. Second on the all-time list is Lloyd Waner at 44.9. One of the very best of the post-expansion era was Felix Millan at 23.9.

In one year, during which Sewell struck out only four times, three of the whiffs occurred on called strikes; in only one case did Sewell swing and miss. And at least one of the called third strikes was highly questionable. "The ball was right at the bill of my cap," recalled Sewell. "[Umpire Bill McGowan] said, 'Strike three, you're out. Oh my God, I missed it, Joe.' But I didn't say a word. I just walked back to the bench. And the next day he came out and apologized and I said, 'Bill, don't worry about it. You were honest about it.'"

Sewell batted .312 for his career, with a high of .353 in 1923. He had almost no power—with the exception of one year with the Yankees, when he hit 11 homers, he never collected more than seven in a season—but he nevertheless drove in a lot of runs. In 1924, when he led the American League with 45 doubles, Sewell had four home runs and 106 RBIs. His ratio of dingers to runs batted in was even more impressive the previous season, when he homered only three times and drove in 109 of his Cleveland teammates.

Alabama-born Joseph Wheeler Sewell, named for a Confederate cavalry officer, was the son of a country doctor. His two brothers, Luke and Tommy, also became major league ballplayers. After graduating from the University of Alabama in 1920, Sewell signed with the New Orleans Pelicans of the Southern Association. He had only been there for 92 games when he was ordered to report to Cleveland. The Indians, who were battling the Yankees and the White Sox for the pennant, had lost their shortstop, Ray Chapman, to a lethal pitch by Carl Mays on August 16, 1920. The inexperienced Sewell tripled in his second at bat with the team; he finished the season hitting .329 as Cleveland captured the flag.

For a man of his size—5 feet 6 inches—Sewell was a remarkably durable player. He remembered once having run up a streak of "460 or so consecutive games" when he was spiked by St. Louis Browns pitcher Elam Van Gilder and missed the next game. He then proceeded to put together another streak of 1,103 straight contests.

Sewell hit at least .315 each season from 1923 through 1929. Converted to a third baseman in the late 1920s, he was released by Cleveland in January 1931 and signed with the Yankees. In the 1932 World Series against the Cubs he hit .333.

After hanging up his spikes, Sewell coached for the Yankees in 1934 and 1935, and then scouted for Cleveland for 11 seasons and the Mets for a year. He was inducted into the Hall of Fame in 1977.

BILL DICKEY C

One of the greatest catchers to ever play the game, Bill Dickey batted .300 or better 11 times, and was a major ingredient in the New York Yankees winning eight pennants and seven World Series during his tenure in pinstripes. "Dickey isn't just a catcher, he's a ballclub," Dan Daniels wrote. "He isn't just a player, he's an influence."

The Yankees promoted Dickey from Little Rock in 1928. He had an impressive first full season in 1929, batting .324—the first of six consecutive seasons he would top .300. By the mid-1930s, he had blossomed as a slugger without sacrificing his batting average. Over the four-year span from 1936 to 1939, the best-hitting catcher in baseball averaged 25 home runs, 115 RBIS, and .327 (with a high of .362 in 1936, to go with slugging average of .617). Lifetime, his .313 batting average as a backstop is surpassed only by Mike Piazza's .328 and Mickey Cochrane's .320.

Defensively, Dickey was just as good. He earned praise for his pitch selection and handling of pitchers, and he led American League catchers four times in fielding average.

Dickey's career had several highlights: hitting three homers in one game on July 6, 1939; catching 125 games without a passed ball during the 1931 season; being the first player to catch 100 or more games for 13 seasons; and being selected for 11 All-Star Games.

His biggest day in baseball, however, came in Game 5 of the 1943 World Series. With no score in the bottom of the sixth, left fielder Charlie "King Kong" Keller singled and Dickey, batting sixth, came to the plate against the Cardinals' Mort Cooper. His two-run homer gave the Yankees the game and the Series. In all, Dickey played in eight Series, hit five home runs, and had 24 RBIs—at the end of 2000, the eighth-highest total ever.

Dickey spent the 1944 and 1945 seasons in the navy. Returning to the Yankees in 1946, he replaced Joe McCarthy as manager in late May. The team never played well under him, and Dickey was let go on September 12. He later scouted and coached for the Yankees and was a sound judge of baseball talent, touting the young Mickey Mantle and helping to turn an unpolished Yogi Berra into a Hall of Fame receiver. He was elected to the Hall of Fame in 1954.

MORDECAI BROWN P

Mordecai Brown was a mainstay of the dominant Chicago Cubs teams of the early 1900s. His career ERA of 2.06 is the third best (after Ed Walsh and Addie Joss) in the history of major league baseball; for five seasons—1906 through 1910—he gave up less than two earned runs a game. What made the performance of "Three Finger" Brown truly amazing was that he achieved his remarkable record with a mangled pitching hand. The result of two farming accidents, his right index finger had been amputated just below the knuckle and the third and fourth fingers on the same hand were severely twisted.

Because his index finger was barely a stub, Brown had to exert extra pressure on the ball with his middle finger. Thanks to this unique grip, his curve dropped as if it had rolled off a table, like a modern forkball, and it baffled batters from both sides of the plate.

In 1906, when the Cubs won a record 116 games, Brown took 26 of them. He led the National League with nine shutouts, and his ERA of 1.04 was the second lowest recorded in the 20th century. In the opening game of the 1906 World Series against the Chicago White Sox, "the Hitless Wonders," Brown surrendered four hits but lost, 2–1, after committing an error in the seventh inning. He beat the Sox in Game 4 with a two-hit, 1–0 win, but was rushed back on one day's rest to absorb a six-run battering and the loss in the final Game 6. The next year, however, Brown won the clinching Game 5 of the 1907 World Series with a 2–0 whitewash of the Detroit Tigers.

On September 22, 1908, Brown won both ends of a doubleheader against the New York Giants, with whom the Cubs were contending for the pennant. The next day saw one of the most famous contests of all time, in which New York's Fred Merkle committed a baserunning error that erased a Giants victory, ending the contest with the teams tied. When the two teams finished in a dead heat at season's end, the tie was replayed to decide the pennant.

Jack Pfiester started the game for the Cubs, but when he got behind, 2–0, Brown walked to the mound and, without a word to manager Frank Chance, took the ball from the starter. He shut the Giants down the rest of the way, and the Cubs rallied against Christy Mathewson to win, 4–2. It was Brown's ninth straight win over Mathewson and his 29th victory of the season. In the World Series, Brown won twice—once with two scoreless innings of relief and once by pitching a shutout—as the Cubs again defeated the Tigers.

Brown had another remarkable season in 1909, leading the NL with 50 appearances, 27 victories, 32 complete games, and seven saves. The following year he won 25 and led the league in complete games, shutouts, and saves. In 1911 Brown's ERA went over 2.00 for the first time in six years, but he still won 21 games and set a major league record with 13 saves.

Following a two-year stint in the Federal League, Brown returned for a last try with the Cubs. On September 4, 1916, he and Mathewson, then the Cincinnati manager, pitched against each other for the last time. Mathewson staggered to a 10–8 victory.

After leaving the majors, Brown pitched and managed in the minors through 1920. He died in 1948, the year before he was elected to the Hall of Fame.

JIM PALMER P

Of the 18 pitchers who have won 20 or more games eight times, only three played in the American League, and only Jim Palmer of the Baltimore Orioles began his career after World War II. Palmer strung together those 20-win campaigns from 1970 through 1978, overcoming arm injuries to average 288 innings per season.

The Orioles won seven titles during Palmer's 19-year tenure, five of them highlighted by the amusing Mutt-and-Jeff feud between the elegant, well-bred pitcher and his pugnacious manager, Earl Weaver. The youngest pitcher ever to throw a World Series shutout, Palmer also was the only pitcher to win World Series games in three decades. He won three Cy Young Awards, and drew the third-highest plurality among pitchers elected to Cooperstown.

Through the 1970s Palmer mainly used a fastball, slider, and changeup, perfecting the curveball later in his career. He was a rare hurler who successfully pitched high in the strike zone but did not possess devastating stuff. Baltimore's old ballpark, with its spacious center field and short foul lines, encouraged outfielders to bunch towards center, and Palmer probably led the league every year in flyouts down the middle.

Part of the second tier of "Baby Bird" pitchers, Palmer hurled his first of four pennant clinchers in 1966. In Baltimore's sweep through the World Series, Palmer outdueled Sandy Koufax in Game 2 and shut out the Dodgers, 6–0.

In 1969 Palmer tossed "the ugliest no-hitter ever," by his own reckoning; he survived six walks and two errors to win, 8–0. Palmer completed the season with a league-high .800 winning percentage (16–4). He lost Game 3 of the 1969 World Series against the Mets. The following year he pitched a league-leading 305 innings, tied for most shutouts, was named to the first of six All-Star teams, and began a run of four straight 20-win seasons. Palmer beat Cincinnati in Game 1 of the World Series, won by Baltimore in five games.

With Palmer, Dave McNally, Mike Cuellar, and Pat Dobson, the Orioles featured a quartet of 20-game winners in 1971, a feat matched only by the 1920 Chicago White Sox. Palmer pitched his third straight pennant clincher in Baltimore's third straight sweep of the ALCS. He started and won Game 2 of the World Series, but the O's lost in seven to the Pirates.

Palmer registered 21 wins and a career-low 2.07 ERA in 1972. He upped the victory total to 22 in 1973, topping the AL with a 2.40 ERA and winning his first Cy Young Award. In the playoff opener against Oakland, Palmer dispatched the defending world champions with a five-hit shutout, fanning 12 and extending the O's ALCS winning streak to 10 games. His four playoff wins were unsurpassed by any pitcher until Dave Stewart collected his fifth ALCS win in 1990. In Game 3, though, Palmer was tagged for his only playoff loss when Oakland's Vida Blue shut out the O's, 1–0.

Palmer had his best year in 1975, setting career highs with 23 wins, 323 innings, and 10 shutouts—only the third time since 1914 that an AL pitcher reached double figures in that category. He won his second Cy Young Award, and led the league for a second time in ERA. In 1976 he won 22 and became the league's first pitcher to win back-to-back Cy Young Awards outright.

Palmer's 53 career shutouts tie him with Gaylord Perry for 16th place on the all-time list, and his .638 won-lost percentage ranks 23rd. Opponents managed only a .230 batting average against him, which puts Palmer in the all-time top 30 of pitchers who were stingiest with hits. He was inducted into the Hall of Fame in 1990.

GAYLORD PERRY P

Rule 8.02 of the Official Baseball Rules specifically prohibits a pitcher from either defacing the baseball or applying any foreign substance to it. Section E states that "the umpire shall be the sole judge on whether any portion of this rule has been violated." Gaylord Perry openly flaunted this rule for most of his career and was seldom caught. Although the spitball was banned in 1920 and last thrown legally in 1934 by Burleigh Grimes, Perry may have been baseball's most successful spitballer.

The first pitcher to win a Cy Young Award in both leagues, Perry won 314 games over 22 seasons divided among eight different teams. He struck out 3,534 batters, sixth on the all-time list, and also ranks among the career leaders in games started, innings pitched, and shutouts. His brother, Jim, was a major league pitcher for 17 seasons, and the 529 victories recorded by the Perry brothers are second only to the 539 registered by Phil and Joe Niekro.

Perry signed with the Giants in 1958. At the time, the illegal pitch was not yet part of his repertoire; he depended on a good fastball, curve, and changeup. In 1964, however, Perry learned the forbidden spitter from Bob Shaw, and he used it to pitch his way into the Giants' starting rotation.

The rules at the time made it easy to get away with using the spitball, and Perry became a master of deception. In 1966, with both his spitter and slider under control, he won 21 games and was the winning pitcher in the All-Star Game. On July 22 he struck out 15 Phillies. He finished the season with 201 strikeouts and walked only 40.

Perry was even better in 1967, lowering his ERA from 2.99 to 2.61. During one stretch he hurled 40 consecutive scoreless innings. But he lost 10 one-run decisions and finished the season with a 15–17 record. His spitball suddenly became a hot topic, and before the 1968 season, Rule 8.02 was amended to forbid the pitcher to put his hand to his mouth.

Perry adapted. He developed a similar pitch using grease instead of saliva, and became adept at decoying the batter and using the spitball as a psychological weapon. On September 17, 1968, he pitched a no-hitter against Bob Gibson and the Cardinals.

In 1970 Perry won 23 games, led the NL in shutouts and innings pitched, and finished second to Gibson in

CyYoung balloting. Brother Jim, meanwhile, won 24 games for the Twins, earning the AL's Cy Young Award. They were the first brothers to win 20 games apiece in the same season.

With the Indians in 1972, Perry enjoyed the best season of his career, winning his first Cy Young Award with a league-best 24 victories and a sparkling 1.92 ERA. The Perry brothers were united in Cleveland in 1974. Gaylord won 21 games, including 15 straight—one shy of the AL record—and Jim added 17. In 1978 with San Diego, at age 40, Perry won 21 games and his second Cy Young Award. He was selected to his fifth and final All-Star Game in 1979.

One of Perry's few disappointments was that he never appeared in a World Series. Only Phil Niekro played longer—24 seasons—without appearing in a Fall Classic. Perry published an entertaining biography, *Me and the Spitter,* in 1974. He was inducted into the Baseball Hall of Fame in 1991.

BOB JOHNSON OF

Bob Johnson was a seven-time All-Star outfielder with second-division American League clubs in the 1930s and early 1940s. Although he performed impressively, his name has slipped into baseball oblivion, in large part because none of his feats ever meant anything in a pennant race or World Series. He deserves to be remembered, however, for having one of the most consistent careers on record.

During 13 seasons, "Indian Bob" Johnson (so-called because he was part Cherokee) hit more than 20 homers nine times, drove in more than 100 runs eight times, scored more than 100 runs six times, and earned more than 75 bases on balls 10 times. He led the AL with a .431 on-base percentage in 1944 and tied the league record of six RBIs in a single inning. Columnist Red Smith noted that Johnson "was a first-rate outfielder with a powerful and accurate throwing arm. He was righthanded all the way, a flatfooted hitter with power."

In 1933 the Philadelphia A's sold veteran Al Simmons to the White Sox, and Johnson beat out Lou Finney for the center field job. In his rookie season, Johnson collected 69 extra-base hits, including 44 doubles. On June 16, 1934, he had his best single day at the plate. He went 6-for-6, with a double and two homers.

For several seasons when the Athletics were mired in the second division it seemed that on some days Johnson alone constituted the offense. On June 12, 1938, he drove in all eight runs in an A's win over the Browns.

Following the 1942 season, Johnson thought Philadelphia was underpaying him and demanded a trade. Owner Connie Mack complied and sent the valuable Johnson to Washington for another outfielder and cash. He was still an excellent hitter but no longer the power threat he was in his youth. After hitting only seven homers for Washington in 1943 he was sold to the Red Sox at the end of the season.

Aided by Fenway Park's short left field wall, Johnson enjoyed a brief resurgence in 1944. Although he hit only 17 homers, he smashed 40 doubles and had his eighth season of knocking in more than 100 runs (the first seven had been consecutive), in addition to leading the league in on-base percentage. He finished up with the Red Sox in 1945, retiring with a lifetime batting average of .296. In the span of years from the beginning of the lively ball era in 1920 to the advent of World War II in 1941, Johnson ranked 14th in RBIs, just behind Paul Waner. Everyone ahead him is in the Hall of Fame.

KEITH HERNANDEZ 1B

One of the best defensive first basemen in major league history, Keith Hernandez was also a savvy line drive hitter who won a batting title and world championships with two different teams. Co-winner of the National League's Most Valuable Player Award in 1979 as a member of the St. Louis Cardinals, Hernandez enjoyed a second act as a leader of the New York Mets following a controversial 1983 trade.

Neither a classic big target nor a hulking slugger at first base, the 6-foot, 200-pound displayed nimble footwork around the bag, exceptional range in both directions, and smooth, sure hands. His strong and accurate arm enabled him to gamble, usually successfully, on bunts and other force plays. He led the league in assists five times and set a career record for assists, which was later broken by Eddie Murray. Despite his high-risk play, he led the league in errors only once, while leading in fielding percentage twice and total chances four times. Hernandez also led the NL in double plays a record six times, mastering the 3–6–3 twin killing.

He was no slouch in the batter's box, either. Until his final two injury-plagued seasons, Hernandez was a career .300 hitter. He had a great eye at the plate, and was consistently among the league leaders in doubles. Hernandez won the 1979 NL batting crown at .344 and topped the circuit with 116 runs, 48 doubles, and a .421 on-base percentage. He also established career highs that year with 11 triples and 105 RBIs, and finished the season tied with Willie Stargell in the league MVP voting.

In 1980 Hernandez led the league with 111 runs scored and a .410 on-base percentage. He also batted .321, and went 2-for-2 in his second All-Star Game. He had his third straight season with a .300 average and a .400 on-base percentage in 1981, and he missed a fourth by batting .299 in 1982. Batting cleanup in the 1982 NLCS against the Atlanta Braves, Hernandez singled and scored in each of the Cardinals' first two wins, and started a four-run rally in the climactic Game 3. He led all players with eight RBIs in the World Series against the Milwaukee Brewers.

In 1983 the Cardinals traded Hernandez to the New York Mets. St. Louis manager Whitey Herzog hinted that Hernandez was using cocaine; the rumor became fact when the remorseful first baseman testified to heavy drug use during the 1985 Pittsburgh drug trials. Hernandez received a standing ovation from Shea Stadium fans after his testimony and averted a one-year suspension by donating 10 percent of his salary to drug rehabilitation programs, performing 100 hours of community service, and submitting to periodic drug tests.

Hernandez became co-captain (with Gary Carter) of the Mets, and was the team's best all-around batter. On July 4, 1985, he hit for the cycle off four different pitchers in a bizarre 19-inning, 16–13 win over Atlanta. A disciplined hitter, he holds the season and career records in the short-lived game-winning RBI statistic.

In 1986 Hernandez posted his third straight .300-plus average and led the league with 94 walks. In the playoffs against Houston, he tied for the team lead with seven hits. In the World Series against the Red Sox, his bases-loaded single in the sixth inning of Game 7 drove in two runs, and his sacrifice fly in the seventh extended the Mets' lead to 6–3 in an eventual 8–5 win.

Hernandez was an All-Star for the fifth time in 1987. When he finished up with the Cleveland Indians in 1990, only Brooks Robinson, Jim Kaat, Ozzie Smith, Willie Mays, and Roberto Clemente had exceeded his total of 11 Gold Gloves.

CHAPTER 6

Baseball Families

Larry Amman

Just as the Wright brothers were first in flight, so were Wright brothers first in baseball. In the National Association's inaugural season of 1871, the Boston team featured Harry Wright as manager and reserve outfielder, and George at shortstop. Brother Sam joined them on the bench for the 1876 season, after an apprenticeship in New Haven the year before.

Since then there have been 360 brother combinations in the majors. The only season in which there was not at least one such pair was 1899. There were three new ones in 2000 and one in 1999.

The first thing that strikes the eye as one reads the list is the large number who were teammates, however briefly—more than 25 percent.

Another observation one must make is how one-sided the big league performance was between so many of the combinations. For example, there are 25 members of the Hall of Fame who had brothers in the majors—plus the Negro Leagues' Foster brothers, Rube and Bill. Yet how many baseball fans have ever heard of the brothers of Bill Dickey, Christy Mathewson, or Honus Wagner? As another example, how many people remember the brothers of Steve Sax, Robin Yount, or Eddie Murray? These big names have brothers who played in the majors briefly.

Of course, being the brother of a major leaguer never guarantees success, nor even a shot at the big leagues. The five Delahantys, the three Boyers, and the two Ferrells all had other brothers who played minor league ball only. Because the combinations in which more than one brother excelled are so rare, we can limit the focus to the more outstanding ones.

In terms of balanced, outstanding achievement no group of three or more brothers can match the DiMaggios. The enduring folk hero status of Joe DiMaggio unfortunately has not done anything to keep alive the memory of his brothers, Vince and Dom. All three were gifted outfielders, good hitters, and fine all-around athletes. Vince, the oldest of these sons of a San Francisco fisherman, played for five different National League teams. In 1941 he had 21 homers and 100 RBIs for Pittsburgh. Four years later he hit four grand slams for the Phillies.

Dom DiMaggio was the youngest and smallest of the three brothers. Although lacking any of the power of the other two, he was the fastest on the bases and yielded nothing to his two brothers in the grace and skill he exhibited in the outfield. His lifetime batting average was just under .300.

In the 1941 All-Star Game, Dom went to right field as a late-inning substitute to play alongside Joe in center. This was a first in the Midsummer Classic. In the eighth inning, Joe doubled and Dom singled him home. In the 1949 All-Star Game, Joe drove in Dom with what proved to be the margin of victory for the junior circuit.

Dominic, or the "Little Professor" as he was called, started four different All-Star Games, including the 1946 contest. That year he was voted to start in center field ahead of his brother. On the season, Dom outhit Joe by 26 points (.316 to .290).

In the 1943 All-Star Game, Vince went 3-for-3, including a ninth-inning home run. While Joe and Dom were away in the military, Vince was "maintaining the family tradition of excellence in All-Star Games."

The first time two brothers played against each other in an All-Star Game was in 1969. Carlos May of the White Sox came to bat as a pinch hitter with brother Lee of the Reds playing first base. In the 1990 Midsummer Classic, television cameras showed Sandy Alomar Jr. at bat while Roberto Alomar set himself at second base, ready to field anything his brother might have hit his way. The Alomars have been teammates for the American League five times since then.

For the title of the best brother pitching combination (aside from the Fosters of the Negro Leagues), the competition is very close between the Niekros of Ohio and the Perrys of Williamston, North Carolina. In 1987 the ancient knuckleballing duo of Phil and Joe Niekro passed Jim and Gaylord Perry in wins. The two families remain very close in most statistical categories.

The Perry brothers had one full season as teammates—1974 with Cleveland, when the two combined for 39 victories, almost half of the team total. A year earlier, when Jim was with Detroit, the two made their only start against each other. Gaylord took the loss for Cleveland. Jim got a no-decision. In the 1970 All-Star Game the National League pitcher in the sixth and seventh innings was Gaylord Perry of the Giants. On the mound for the American League in the seventh and eighth innings was Jim Perry of the Twins. This is the only time two brothers were rival pitchers in the All-Star Game. Both have also won the Cy Young Award.

For Joe and Phil Niekro, pitching against each other was not that uncommon. It happened nine different times. The most noteworthy occasion came on September 26, 1978, in Atlanta. Before this, his last start of the season, Phil was 19–17 for the Braves; Joe was 12–14 for the Astros. Houston won, 2–0, much to the dismay of victor Joe. He loathed the idea of pitching against his brother in these circumstances.

Harry and Stan Coveleski of the coal-mining country in Pennsylvania were brother hurlers who refused to start games against each other. Stan, the younger, was in his first full season in the majors in 1916 at Cleveland while Harry was winning 20 for the third consecutive year at Detroit. Harry developed arm trouble and did not pitch another full season, but Stan went on to five 20-win seasons and a niche in the Hall of Fame.

Virtually every baseball fan has heard of the game on September 15, 1963, in which Felipe, Matty, and Jesus Alou formed the San Francisco outfield for one inning. A better story about this Dominican family, however, is the race for the 1966 National League batting title.

Going into the season, Felipe, with the Atlanta Braves, had established himself as a hitter of high average and respectable power. Younger brother Matty's career so far had been disappointing. With no power, his lifetime batting average was .260. In the off-season the Giants had traded him to Pittsburgh.

With the Bucs, Matty came under the special tutelage of manager Harry Walker. "Harry the Hat" taught his pupil to chop down on the ball and to hit to left field instead of trying to pull. This, plus over 20 bunt and 30 infield singles, propelled Matty to the top of the league batting race. Second or third to him almost all year was Atlanta leadoff man and first baseman Felipe Alou. Matty won the crown with a .342 average, while Felipe finished second at .327. The elder brother, however, led the circuit in runs, hits, and total bases.

It was only fitting that Harry Walker was the cause of the enormous jump in Matty's batting average. In 1947 Harry Walker the outfielder was traded from the Cardinals to the Phillies early in the season. There he won the batting title with an average 100 points higher than the year before. This was the second batting title in the family. In 1944 older brother Dixie had led the National League with a .357 mark at Brooklyn.

Brother rivalries and brother teammates come into very sharp focus under the media glare of the World Series. The Fall Classics from 1921 to 1923 featured Bob Meusel of the Yankees against older brother Emil or "Irish" of the Giants. These two outfielders were very similar in physical appearance and in capabilities.

Before the 1921 Series one writer summed up the pair:

Bob hits harder than Emil though he is not as consistent in garnering his hits. Bob also excels Emil as a thrower, but Emil is the more finished fielder. Bob is a left field hitter, and Emil often hits to right, so the play of "Meusel flied to Meusel" may be repeated frequently during the Series.

Indeed, it was so in all three Series. In Game 3 of the 1923 World Series, each brother robbed the other of an extra-base hit. Irish emerged superior to Bob in every category—even in extra-base hits. Bob, however, had the last laugh, driving in the go-ahead run in Game 6 of the 1923 World Series to give the Yankees their first world title.

For their entire careers, the Meusels startle the observer with the closeness of all their statistics. Irish averaged .310 to Bob's .309, both for 11 seasons. Bob leads in all other categories, but not by much. If Irish's totals were increased by prorating them based on his 100 fewer games, the two would look like clones. Each man led his league in RBIs one time.

Two brothers whose lifetime batting averages are identical are Bob and Roy Johnson. Both of these Oklahoma Indians hit .296 as American League outfielders in the 1930s. Bob amassed 2,000 hits and almost 300 home runs, playing mostly for Connie Mack. Elder brother Roy was a speedy singles and doubles hitter. He exceeded his brother only in stolen bases in his shorter career.

The 1927 World Series featured Lloyd Waner leading off and playing center field for Pittsburgh while older brother Paul hit third and patrolled right field. In just his second season, Paul had won the batting title. Rookie Lloyd finished second in hits and third in batting average. The two combined for 460 hits during the season and were 11-for-30 in the World Series as the Yankees swept the Pirates in four games. The Waners played parts of 16 seasons together, much longer than any other pair.

In 1934 Dizzy and Paul Dean had the greatest year any pitching brothers have ever enjoyed. "Me 'n' Paul" together won 49 games during the regular season and all four of the games the Cardinals won from the Tigers in the World Series (as Dizzy had predicted). In 1935 their combined victory total was 47. These two 19-win seasons were Paul's only full years in the majors.

An even more memorable year in St. Louis Cardinals history was 1942. In the last week of August, the Cards were five games behind the defending champion Brooklyn Dodgers. Five weeks later the Cardinals clinched first place with a record September rush. Winning five games in the last month for a total of 22 on the season was Mort Cooper. Catching him was younger brother Walker, in his first season as a regular. Mort won his September games with great flair. He was called the "fashion plate" for wearing the number on his back that equaled the victory he was seeking that day. The Cardinals beat the Yankees in a five-game World Series to shock all of baseball.

Mort also won 20 for the 1943 and 1944 pennant winners and had a victory in each of the World Series. Both brothers were named to *The Sporting News* All-Star team in 1944. Walker hit an even .300 for three Fall Classics.

The Coopers may have been the best of the 15 brother battery combinations, but Wes and Rick Ferrell have to be a close second. Rick caught his younger brother for five straight seasons. Wes won 20 their first two years together.

The next great brother act in the World Series was in 1964, when Ken and Clete Boyer were the opposing third basemen. Elder brother Ken was the National League's Most Valuable Player with a league-leading 119 RBIs for St. Louis. Clete had hit an anemic .219 for the Yankees. Still, this was his chance to show the baseball world he was Ken's equal in the field.

Although neither hit for a high average in the seven games, both did well with the glove. Ken gave his team all its runs in Game 4 with a grand slam as St. Louis won the contest, 4–3. In the seventh game, Ken scored the first run and later homered. Brother Clete helped make the finish exciting as he hit one of the two solo home runs off Bob Gibson in the ninth inning. Like the Coopers, the Boyers were born and raised in the "Show Me" state. Both parents were in the stands maintaining their strict neutrality and feeling great pride.

The integrity of play when brothers square off against each other has been taken for granted for many years. This wasn't always the case. In 1933 Joe Sewell, playing third base for the Yankees, and Luke Sewell, catching for Washington, found themselves on opposite sides of a hot pennant race. They had been teammates at Cleveland for a number of years.

Reporting on a crucial game in the 1933 AL race, Shirley Povich of the *Washington Post* wrote:

> *It was brother versus brother in the seventh when Joe Sewell made a whale of a stop and throw to cut down Luke. It's things like that help prove the honesty of baseball.*

There have been five brother shortstop–second base combinations in big league history: Granny and Garvin Hamner of the 1945 Phillies, Lou and Dino Chiozza of the 1935 Phillies, Milt and Frank Bolling of the 1958 Tigers, Eddie and Johnny O'Brien of the Pirates in the mid-1950s, and Cal and Bill Ripken of the Orioles from 1987 to 1992 and again in 1996. The O'Briens were one of seven sets of twins in the majors.

Certainly an infield comprised of only two families is something of note. The Cincinnati Reds had just that in a game at the end of the 1998 season. Newcomer Stephen Larkin was playing first. Bret Boone was stationed at the keystone. Barry Larkin was the shortstop and Aaron Boone held down the hot corner.

Josh Clarke with Louisville in the National League in 1898 and George "White Wings" Tebeau of Cleveland in 1894–1895 must have felt some sense of constraint in criticizing their managers. In both cases it was a brother: Fred Clarke and Patsy Tebeau. Both pilots were regular players those seasons as well. Ed Hengle, who never played in the majors, managed his brother Moxie in the Union Association for the entry that began the season in Chicago. By the end of the campaign, both Hengles were gone, and the club had moved to Pittsburgh.

Wes and Rick Ferrell have something in common with Jesse and Lee Tannehill. In each case the pitching brother—Wes and Jesse—had a higher career batting average and more home runs than the brother who played every day.

No, Henry and Tommie Aaron were not the first "soul-brother" brother combination in major league baseball. The game's first black siblings were Fleet and Welday Walker, who both played for Toledo of the American Association in 1884. That circuit was then considered a major league.

Fathers and Sons

Shortly after breaking into the majors, Dale Berra was asked about similarities between himself and his famous father, Yogi. The younger Berra replied, "Our similarities are different."

Like the many malapropisms of Yogi Berra, this one by his son may appear foolish on the surface, but it contains quite a bit of underlying wisdom. In fact, it can serve as a metaphor for father-son combinations in major league baseball.

Of the 153 combinations, only 52 feature both generations at the same position. There are 24 father-son pitcher combinations, five cases where both father and son caught, one where both played first, three where both played shortstop, and 19 where both father and son were outfielders. Very few fathers and sons at any position have career totals that are at all close. The only Hall of Fame father-son combination is a non-playing one, that of executives Larry and Lee MacPhail.

Another important generalization is the great increase in father-son combinations since World War II, especially in the last 20 years. The first son of a former big leaguer to break into the majors was Jack Doscher in 1903 as a pitcher for the Chicago Cubs—one of the three teams with whom his father, Herm, had toiled as a utility player years earlier. By 1945 the number of father-son combinations was 36. In 1965 the total was 66. Thus almost 40 percent of today's number has been added in the last two decades.

Is the son of a big league ballplayer more apt to develop into a major leaguer than the average boy? Some people think not. In the 1950s Hall of Famer George Sisler was asked this very question. The two-time .400 hitter shook his head over how two of his offspring had made the majors. He pointed out that baseball players are absentee fathers. They don't have much opportunity to teach their boys the fundamentals or to practice with them.

If not their fathers, perhaps other well-qualified professionals have instructed the second generation. A worthwhile study could be conducted to determine how many second-generation players who have broken in during the last two decades attended baseball camps as boys. If the number is significant, this could explain the big increase during this period.

Certainly, the Sisler family deserves special attention. Father George broke into the majors just before World War I as a pitcher for the St. Louis Browns. After being switched to first base, he spent 15 years as one of the greatest performers ever at that position. Accordingly, it is only fitting that he should have one son, Dick, who was a good hitter and another son, Dave, who pitched in the majors briefly. Dick's home run on the last day of the 1950 season, which gave the Philadelphia Whiz Kids the pennant, has given him an identity independent of his father. Also, these two men both managed in the majors for a short time. The Sislers and the Macks are the only families in which both father and son managed in the majors.

Baseball families fall into one of three categories: famous fathers only, famous sons only, and equals.

Let us consider the famous son category first. Another way of describing these men would be to call them "fathers of . . ." Two families stand out in this category. They are the Muellers and the Walkers.

Walter Mueller was a reserve outfielder for the Pirates for four seasons in the 1920s. His son, Don, hit .296 in 12 seasons as a National League outfielder. In 1954 Mueller and teammate Willie Mays battled all season for the batting title on the pennant-winning Giants. Mays finished first in hitting by three points, but Mueller led the league in hits with 212.

Dixie Walker was a pitcher for Washington from 1909 through 1912. His lifetime record was 24–30. Both his sons, Fred (or "Dixie") and Harry, won batting titles.

These two are the only clear cases of a son of All-Star quality who had a father whose career in the majors was forgettable. Other families with "fathers of . . . " are Coleman, Grimsley, and Smalley.

In contrast, the list of "sons of . . . " is a long one. There are eight playing baseball fathers in the Hall of Fame. Averill, Berra, Collins, Lindstrom, Mack, O'Rourke, and Walsh had offspring who fit this category. Four more families—Bagby, Camilli, Trosky, and Wood—had fathers of All-Star quality and sons who are footnotes to their careers. Hegan, Wills, and Trout are families where the sons had respectable careers similar to those of the fathers, but the older generation was clearly superior.

We must consider first whether some of the "sons of..." got to the majors, or second, stayed longer than they merited, because of the family name. Collins, Walsh, and Wood prove the former proposition, and Dale Berra and Marc Sullivan support the latter.

The younger Berra and Sullivan not only had the temerity to go into their father's business, but, like Bill and Cal Ripken Jr. of Baltimore, and Moises Alou of Montreal, they had dad for their boss. The Ripkens (in 1988) and Dale Berra (in 1985) saw their fathers dismissed as managers early in the season. Moises Alou, on the other hand, voluntarily left his father Felipe's side in Montreal to sign with Florida as a free agent after the 1996 season. Cal Ripken Sr. was not only the first father to manage two sons at once, but the first without major league playing experience to manage his sons.

Sullivan, whose father owned part of the Red Sox, traded his son to the Houston Astros before the 1988 season, where he could commiserate with the Berras on the difficulties of combining a baseball career with family obligations.

By far the most interesting category is that of the fathers and sons whose careers parallel each other.

The two Billy Sullivans caught for both the White Sox and the Tigers. Both played other positions as well as caught in one World Series. Sullivan Senior caught the older Ed Walsh; Junior caught the younger Ed Walsh—both at Chicago.

Jim and Mike Hegan were a father-son combination well known for defensive ability. Father Jim was a great handler of pitchers for Cleveland. Mike played first base and the outfield for several American League teams. Both appeared in two World Series. Mike broke into the majors just four seasons after his father's finale.

The father-son pitching combinations have few parallels. Both Thornton and Don Lee gave up home runs to Ted Williams. Only four families have had both father and son pitch in a World Series. Jim Bagby Sr. pitched for Cleveland in the 1920 Series and his son for the Red Sox in 1946. Mel Stottlemyre went 1–1 for the Yankees in the 1964 Series. Todd Stottlemyre pitched for Toronto in the 1992 and 1993 World Series. In the 1995 Fall Classic Pedro Borbon Jr. came in for Atlanta in relief. Pedro Senior pitched for the Reds in four World Series. Jason Grimsley pitched two innings for the Yankees in 1999. His father, Ross, was 2-1 for the Reds in 1972.

Joe Schultz Jr. received some unwanted publicity in Jim Bouton's book, *Ball Four,* for being Bouton's manager. Schultz and his father, Joe Senior, each spent almost a decade in the majors as reserve players. Senior was 46-for-170 as a pinch hitter. Junior went 43-for-160 in that same role.

It is only fitting that Buddy Bell spent a portion of his fine career with the Cincinnati Reds, the team on which his father Gus spent his best years. The two ended their careers with nearly identical batting averages and home run totals.

Ten father-son combinations have played in All-Star Games. Prior to 1990 only the Bell, Boone, Tresh, and Hegan families could have made that boast. Then Barry Bonds, Ken Griffey Jr., both Alomar sons, Todd Hundley, and Moises Alou made their debuts in the Midsummer Classic. The senior Tresh and the junior Hegan were named to the All-Star squads but did not play. The Bells and Boones have similar statistics. Gus was 2-for-6, hitting a home run his first time up; Buddy was 1-for-7, hitting a triple in his first plate appearance. Ray Boone went 1-for-5 in All-Star Games with a homer; Bob was 2-for-5 in three games.

Both Griffeys have been Most Valuable Player in an All-Star Game: Senior in 1980 and Junior in 1992. Currently the Cincinnati center fielder is 10-for-23 as an All Star. His father was 5-for-7 in three games. Each has a home run to his credit. Barry Bonds is now 5-for-20 in All-Star competition. His father, Bobby, went 2-for-6 in three contests and was MVP in 1972.

Felipe Alou may have had some feelings of regret mixed with the great pride he felt when his son Moises drove in the winning run in the 1994 All-Star Game. Felipe's one appearance was in 1968. He played one inning in left field and did not have an official time at bat. In the 1996 game Mets catcher Todd Hundley went 0-for-1 to become the 10th combination. His father, Randy, went 0-for-1 in the 1969 game.

In Game 2 of the 1984 World Series, a two-run double by San Diego catcher Terry Kennedy was noted by the television announcers as something significant. This was the first time in the history of the Fall Classic that both a father and son had a World Series RBI. Terry's father, Bob, knocked in a run for Cleveland as an outfielder in the 1948 Series. There have been 10 families in which the father and son both played in a World Series. Six have been mentioned already; there is also Ernie and Don Johnson. The father was a substitute infielder for the Yankees in the 1923 Series. Don was the regular second baseman for the Cubs in the 1945 Series. Stan Javier appeared in the 1988 and 1989 World Series for Oakland; his father, Julian, played in four World Series. In 1962, Felipe Alou played all seven games for the Giants, hitting .269. Son Moises hit three homers for Florida in the 1997 Fall Classic. Atlanta's poor performance in the 1999 Series made it easy to overlook Bret Boone going 7-for-13 as the second baseman for the Braves. Bret's father, Bob, was 7-for-17 for Philadelphia in 1980, and grandfather Ray was 0-for-1 for the Indians in 1948. Now we have a three-generation act in the World Series.

Career statistics for the Bonds family deserve special attention. Barry Bonds has now surpassed father Bobby in every significant category. Perhaps Bobby will be remembered as "the father of. . .".

The Bondses are not the first black father-son combination in major league history. That honor goes to the Hairstons. Father Sam played in two games for the Chicago White Sox in 1951. Son Jerry was a respected pinch hitter for that team for over a decade. Grandson Jerry made his major league debut with the Baltimore Orioles in 1998.

In September 1990 Ken Griffey Sr. took a place in the Seattle Mariners outfield next to his son. Late in the 1992 season, Bret Boone made his major league debut as the Seattle second baseman to give baseball its first three-generation family. In 1995 David Bell, son of Buddy and grandson of Gus, made his debut to give baseball its second three-generation family. The Hairston family makes three. Of less significance, but of great sentimental value for Cincinnati Reds fans, was an event that occurred in September 1997. Pete Rose Jr. played third base for a few games. More than once he threw out hitters at first base to Eduardo Perez. Pete Senior had done that many times with Tony Perez in the city's glory days in the 1970s.

Baseball Families

KEY

tm teammates
F-S also part of father-son combo

BROTHERS

AARON Henry & Tommie *tm*
ACOSTA Jose & Merito
ADAMS Bobby & Dick *F-S*
ALLEN Dick, Hank & Ron *tm*
ALLISON Art & Doug *tm*
ALOMAR Roberto & Sandy Jr. *tm F-S*
ALOU Felipe, Matty & Jesus *tm F-S*
ANDERSON Kent & Mike
ANDREWS Rob & Mike
ARMAS Tony & Marcos *F-S*
ASPROMONTE Bob & Ken

BAILEY Ed & Jim *tm*
BAKER Dave & Doug
BANDO Chris & Sal
BANNON Jimmy & Tom
BARNES Jesse & Virgil *tm*
BARRETT Marty & Tom
BAXES Jim & Mike
BELL Charlie & Frank
BELL George & Juan
BELL David & Mike *F-S*
BENES Alan & Andy *tm*
BENNETT Dave & Dennis *tm*
BERGEN Bill & Marty
BIGBEE Carson & Lyle *tm*
BLANKENSHIP Homer & Ted *tm*
BLUEGE Ossie & Otto
BOLLING Frank & Milt *tm*
BOONE Danny & Ike
BOONE Aaron & Bret *tm F-S*
BOYER Clete, Ken & Cloyd *tm*
BOYLE Buzz & Jim
BOYLE Eddie & Jack
BRASHEAR Kitty & Roy
BREEDEN Danny & Hal
BRETT George & Ken *tm*
BREWER Mike & Tony
BRINKMAN Chuck & Ed
BROWN Dick & Larry
BROWN Jackie & Paul
BROWN Oscar & Ollie
BROWN Curtis & Leon
BULLINGER Kirk & Jim
BUTLER Rich & Bob

CAMNITZ Harry & Howie *tm*
CAMP Kid & Llewellan *tm*
CAMPBELL Hugh & Mat *tm*
CANSECO Jose & Ozzie (twins) *tm*
CANTWELL Mike & Tom
CARLYLE Cleo & Roy
CASEY Dan & Dennis *tm*
CEDENO Andujar & Domingo
CHIOZZA Dino & Lou *tm*
CHRISTOPHER Lloyd & Russ
CLAPP Aaron & John
CLARK Jerald & Phil
CLARKE Fred & Josh *tm*
CLARKE Sumpter & Rufe
CLARKSON Dad, John & Walter *tm*
CLIBURN Stan & Stew (twins)
COFFMAN Dick & Slick
COHEN Andy & Syd
CONIGLIARO Billy & Tony
CONNELL Gene & Joe
CONNOR Joe & Roger
CONWAY Jim & Pete
CONWAY Bill & Dick *tm*
COONEY Jimmy & Johnny *tm F-S*
COOPER Mort & Walker *tm*
CORA Joey & Jose
CORCORAN Larry & Mike *tm*
COSCARART Joe & Pete

COVELESKI Harry & Stan
COVINGTON Sam & Tex
CROMER David & Tripp
CROSS Amos, Frank & Lave *tm*
CRUZ Hector, Jose & Tommy *tm F-S*
CUCCINELLO Al & Tony

DAILY Con & Ed
DALY Joe & Tom
DANNING Harry & Ike
DARINGER Cliff & Rolla
DARWIN Jeff & Danny
DAVALILLO Vic & Yo-Yo
DAVENPORT Claude & Dave
DAVIS Mark & Mike
DEAN Dizzy & Paul *tm*
DEASLEY John & Pat
DELAHANTY Ed, Frank, Jim, Joe & Tom *tm*
DEMONTREVILLE Gene & Lee
DICKEY Bill & George
DILLON Packy & John *tm*
DiMAGGIO Vince, Joe & Dom
DONAHUE Jiggs & Pat
DONNELLY Pete & John
DONOVAN Jerry & Tom
DORGAN Jerry & Mike
DOWNS Kelly & Dave
DOYLE Brian & Denny
DRAKE Sammy & Solly
DREW Tim & J.D.
DUGAN Bill & Ed *tm*

EDWARDS Dave, Marshall & Mike (twins)
ENS Jewel & Mutz
ERAUTT Eddie & Joe
EVERS Joe & Johnny
EWING Buck & John *tm*

FALK Bibb & Chet
FARMER Michael & Howard
FERRELL Rick & Wes *tm*
FERRY Cy & Jack
FINNEY Hal & Lou
FISHER Bob & Newt
FISHER Chauncey & Tom
FOGARTY Jim & Joe
FORD Gene & Russ
FOREMAN Brownie & Frank *tm*
FORSCH Bob & Ken
FOUTZ Dave & Frank
FOWLER Art & Jesse
FREESE Gene & George
FRIEL Bill & Pat
FULLER Harry & Shorty
FULMER Chick & Washington

GAGLIANO Phil & Ralph
GANZEL Charlie & John *F-S*
GARBARK Bob & Mike
GARDELLA Al & Danny *tm*
GARRETT Adrian & Wayne
GASTON Alex & Milt *tm*
GEISS Bill & Emil
GENTRY Harvey & Rufe
GIAMBI Jason & Jeremy
GILBERT Harry & John *tm*
GILBERT Charlie & Tookie *F-S*
GLEASON Bill & Jack *tm*
GLEASON Harry & Kid
GRABOWSKI Al & Reggie
GRAVES Joe & Sid
GREGG Dave & Vean
GRIMES Ray & Roy (twins) *F-S*
GRISSOM Lee & Marv
GROH Heine & Lew
GUERRERO Vladimir & Wilton *tm*
GUMBERT Ad & Billy
GWYNN Chris & Tony

HACKETT Mert & Walter *tm*

HAFEY Bud & Tom
HAIRSTON Jerry & John *F-S*
HAMNER Garvin & Granny *tm*
HAMMOND Chris & Steve
HANDLEY Gene & Lee
HARGRAVE Bubbles & Pinky
HATFIELD Gil & John
HAYWORTH Ray & Red
HEMPHILL Charlie & Frank
HERNANDEZ Livan & Orlando
HEVING Joe & Johnnie
HIGH Andy, Charlie & Hugh
HILL Hugh & Still Bill
HINCHMAN Bill & Harry *tm*
HITCHCOCK Billy & Jim
HOFFMAN Glenn & Trevor
HOGAN George & Happy
HOLBERT Aaron & Ray
HOLMAN Brian & Brad
HOVLIK Hick & Joe
HOWARD Del & Ivon
HUGHES Jim & Mickey
HUGHES Ed & Tom
HUNTER Bill & George (twins)

IGNASIAK Gary & Mike
IORG Dane & Garth
IRWIN Arthur & John

JEFFCOAT George & Hal
JIMENEZ Elvio & Manny
JOHNSON Bob & Roy
JOHNSON Chet & Earl
JOHNSTON Doc & Jimmy
JONES Darryl & Lynn
JONES Gary & Steve
JONNARD Bubber & Claude (twins)
JORGENS Arndt & Orville

KAPPEL Heinie & Joe
KELL George & Skeeter
KELLER Charlie & Hal
KELLNER Alex & Walt *tm*
KELLY George & Ren
KENNEDY Jim & Junior
KEOUGH Marty & Joe *F-S*
KIEFER Steve & Mark
KILLEFER Bill & Red
KILROY Matt & Mike *tm*
KLAUS Billy & Bobby
KLING Bill & Johnny
KNODE Mike & Ray
KNOTHE Fritz & George
KOPF Larry & Wally
KRSNICH Mike & Rocky

LACHEMANN Marcel & Rene
LANNING Johnny & Tom
LANSFORD Carney & Joe
LARKIN Barry & Stephen *tm*
LARY Al & Frank
LAWTON Matt & Mareus
LEITER Al & Mark
LELIVELT Bill & Jack
LILLARD Bill & Gene *tm*
LOBERT Frank & Hans
LOOK Bruce & Dean
LOWDERMILK Grover & Lou *tm*
LUSH Billy & Ernie

MACHA Ken & Mike
MACK Quinn & Shane
MADDUX Greg & Mike
MAHLER Mickey & Rick *tm*
MAISEL Fritz & George
MANCUSO Frank & Gus
MANGUAL Angel & Pepe
MANSELL John, Mike & Tom *tm*
MANUSH Frank & Heinie
MANZANILLO Josias & Ravelo
MARION Marty & Red
MARTINEZ Pedro & Ramon *tm*
MASKREY Harry & Leech *tm*
MATHEWSON Christy & Henry *tm*

MATTOX Cloy & Jim
MAY Carlos & Lee
MAYER Erskine & Sam
McDANIEL Lindy & Von *tm*
McFARLAN Alex & Dan
McFARLAND Lamont & Charles
McGEEHAN Connie & Dan
McLAUGHLIN Barney & Frank *tm*
MEUSEL Bob & Irish
MILAN Clyde & Horace *tm*
MILLER Jake & Russ
MILLER Bing & Ralph *tm*
MINOR Damon & Ryan
MITCHELL John & Charlie
MOFFETT Joe & Sam
MORIARTY Bill & George
MORRISON Johnny & Phil *tm*
MORRISSEY John & Tom
MOTA Andy & Jose *F-S*
MURRAY Eddie & Rich
MYERS Billy & Lynn

NETTLES Graig & Jim
NEWKIRK Floyd & Joel
NIEKRO Joe & Phil *tm*
NIXON Otis & Donnell
NYMAN Chris & Nyls

O'BRIEN Eddie & Johnny (twins) *tm*
OGDEN Curley & Jack
OLIVO Chi Chi & Diomedes *F-S*
O'NEILL Jack, Jim, Mike & Steve *tm*
ONSLOW Eddie & Jack
O'ROURKE Jim & John *F-S*
ORTIZ Baby & Roberto *tm*
O'TOOLE Denny & Jim
OWEN Dave & Spike

PACIOREK John, Tom & Jim
PARKER Jay & Doc
PARROTT Jiggs & Tom *tm*
PASCUAL Camilo & Carlos
PATTERSON Ham & Pat
PEITZ Heinie & Joe *tm*
PENA Ramon & Tony
PEPLOSKI Henry & Pepper
PEREZ Pascual, Melido & Carlos
PERRY Gaylord & Jim *tm*
PFEFFER Big Jeff & Jeff
PIERSON Dave & Dick
PIKE Jay & Lip
PIPGRAS Ed & George
POTTER Dykes & Squire

RAJSICH Dave & Gary
REACH Al & Bob
RECCIUS John & Phil *tm*
REUSCHEL Paul & Rick *tm*
REYNOLDS Harold & Don
RICKETTS Dick & Dave
RIDDLE Elmer & Johnny *tm*
RIPKEN Cal & Billy *tm*
ROBINSON Bruce & Dave
ROBINSON Fred & Wilbert
ROENICKE Gary & Ron
ROETTGER Oscar & Wally
ROMO Vicente & Romero Enrique
ROOF Gene & Phil
ROSENBERG Harry & Lou
ROTH Braggo & Frank
ROWE Dave & Jack
ROY Charlie & Luther
RUSSELL Allan & Lefty

SADOWSKI Bob, Eddie & Ted
SAUER Ed & Hank
SAX Dave & Steve *tm*
SAY Jimmie & Lou *tm*
SCANLAN Doc & Frank
SCHANG Bobby & Wally
SCHAREIN Art & George
SCHMIDT Boss & Walter
SCHULTE Herman & Leonard

SEWELL Luke, Joe & Tommie *tm*
SHAFFER Orator & Taylor *tm*
SHANNON Joe & Red (twins) *tm*
SHANTZ Billy & Bobby *tm*
SHERLOCK Monk & Vince
SHERRY Larry & Norm *tm*
SISLER Dave & Dick *F-S*
SMITH Charlie & Fred
SOWDERS Bill, John & Len
STAFFORD John & Jim
STANICEK Steve & Pete
STANLEY Buck & Joe
STOTTLEMYRE Mel, Jr. & Todd *F-S*
STOVALL George & Jessie
SURHOFF B.J. & Rick
SUTHERLAND Darrell & Gary

TANNEHILL Jesse & Lee
TEBEAU Patsy & White Wings *tm*
THIELMAN Henry & Jake
THOBE John & Thomas
THOMAS Bill & Roy *tm*
THOMPSON Homer & Tommy *tm*
THRONEBERRY Faye & Marv
TOBIN Jim & Johnny
TORRE Frank & Joe *tm*
TRAFFLEY Bill & John
TREACEY Fred & Pete *tm*
TREVINO Alex & Bobby
TWOMBLY Babe & George
TYLER Fred & Lefty *tm*
TYRONE Jim & Wayne

UNDERWOOD Pat & Tom
UPTON Bill & Tom

VALENTIN Jose Antonio & Jose Javier
VAN CUYK Chris & Johnny

WADE Ben & Jake
WAGNER Butts & Honus
WALKER Dixie Sr. & Ernie *F-S*
WALKER Dixie Jr. & Harry *F-S*
WALKER Gee & Hub *tm*
WALKER Fleet & Welday *tm*
WANER Lloyd & Paul *tm*
WATT Al & Frank
WEILAND Bob & Ed
WESTLAKE Jim & Wally
WEYHING Gus & John
WHEAT Mack & Zack
WHITE Deacon & Will *tm*
WHITNEY Art & Frank
WILLIAMS Gus & Harry
WILTSE Hooks & Snake
WINGO Al & Ivy
WOOD Fred & Pete *tm*
WORRELL Todd & Tim
WRIGHT George, Harry & Sam *tm*

YOCHIM Len & Ray
YOUNT Larry & Robin

ZIMMERMAN Jeff & Jordan

FATHERS-SONS

ADAMS Bobby-Mike
ALOMAR Sandy-Roberto & Sandy Jr.
ALOU Felipe-Moises
AMARO Ruben-Ruben Jr.
ARAGON Angel-Jack
ARMAS Tony-Antonio
AVERILL Earl-Earl

BAGBY Jim Sr. & Jr.
BARNHART Clyde-Vic
BEAMON Charlie-Charlie
BELL Buddy-David & Mike
BELL Gus-Buddy
BERRA Yogi-Dale
BERRY Charlie-Charlie
BERRY Joe-Joe
BONDS Bobby-Barry
BOONE Ray-Bob
BOONE Bob-Bret & Aaron
BORBON Pedro Sr. & Jr.
BRICKELL Fred-Fritzie
BRUCKER Earle Sr. & Jr.
BRUMLEY Mike-Mike
BUFORD Don-Damon

CAMILLI Dolf-Doug
CAMPANIS Alex-Jim
CARREON Camilo-Mark
COLEMAN Joe-Joe
COLLINS Ed Sr. & Jr.
CONNOLLY Ed Sr. & Jr.
COONEY Jimmy-Jimmy & John
CORRIDEN Red-John
CROUCH Bill-Wilmer
CRUZ Jose Sr. & Jr.

DAVANON Jerry-Jeffrey
DOSCHER Herm-Jack

ELLSWORTH Dick-Steve
ESCHEN Jim-Larry

FLETCHER Tom-Darrin
FRANCONA Tito-Terry

GABRIELSON Len-Len
GANZEL Charlie-Babe
GILBERT Larry-Charlie & Tookie
GRAHAM Peaches-Jack
GREEN Fred-Gary
GRIEVE Tom-Ben
GRIFFEY Ken Sr. & Jr. *tm*
GRILLI Steve-Jason
GRIMES Ray-Oscar
GRIMSLEY Ross-Ross

HAIRSTON Sam-Jerry & John
HAIRSTON Jerry Sr. & Jr.
HANEY Larry-Chris
HEGAN Jim-Mike
HEINTZELMAN Ken-Tom
HOOD Wally Sr. & Jr.
HOWARD Bruce-David
HUNDLEY Randy-Todd

JAVIER Julian-Stan
JETER Johnny-Shawn
JOHNSON Adam-Adam
JOHNSON Ernie-Don

KENDALL Fred-Jason
KENNEDY Bob-Terry
KEOUGH Marty-Matt
KESSINGER Don-Keith
KRAUSSE Lew Sr. & Jr.
KUNKEL Bill-Jeff

LANDRUM Joe-Bill
LANIER Max-Hal
LAW Vern-Vance
LEE Thornton-Don
LIEBHARDT Glenn-Glenn
LINDSTROM Fred-Charlie
LIVELY Jack-Bud

MACK Connie-Earle
MAGGERT Harl-Harl
MALAY Charlie-Joe
MARTIN Barney-Jerry
MATHEWS Nelson-T.J.
MATTHEWS Gary Sr. & Jr.
MATTICK Wally-Bobby
MAY Dave-Derrick
MAY Pinky-Milt
McANDREW Jim-Jamie
McKNIGHT Jim-Jeff
McRAE Hal-Brian
MEINKE Frank-Bob
MILLS Willie-Art
MONTEAGUDO Rene-Aurelio
MOORE Eugene Sr. & Jr.
MORTON Guy Sr. & Jr.
MOTA Manny-Andy & Jose
MUELLER Walter-Don

NARLESKI Bill-Ray
NAVARRO Julio-Jaime
NEN Dick-Robert
NICHOLS Chet Sr. & Jr.
NORTHEY Ron-Scott

O'DONOGHUE John Sr. & Jr.
OKRIE Frank-Len
OLIVARES Ed-Omar
OLIVER Bob-Darren
OLIVO Diomedes-Gilbert Rondon
O'ROURKE Patsy-Joe
O'ROURKE Jim-Queenie
OSBORNE Tiny-Bobo

PARTENHEIMER Steve-Stan
PEREZ Tony-Eduardo
PILLETTE Herman-Duane

QUEEN Mel-Mel

RATH Fred Sr. & Jr.
RIPLEY Walt-Allen
ROSE Pete Sr. & Jr.

SAVIDGE Ralph-Don
SCHOFIELD Ducky-Dick
SCHULTZ Joe Sr. & Jr.
SEGUI Diego-David
SHEELY Earl-Bud
SIEBERT Dick-Paul
SISLER George-Dick & Dave
SKINNER Bob-Joel
SMALLEY Roy Jr.-Roy III
SPEIER Chris-Justin
SPIEZIO Ed-Scott
SPRAGUE Ed Sr. & Jr.
ST. CLAIRE Ebba-Randy
STENHOUSE Dave-Mike
STEPHENSON Joe-Jerry
STILLWELL Ron-Kurt
STOTTLEMYRE Mel-Todd & Mel Jr.
SULLIVAN Billy Sr.-Jr.
SULLIVAN Haywood-Marc
SUSCE George-George

TANNER Chuck-Bruce
TARTABULL Jose-Danny
TORRES Ricardo-Gil
TRESH Mike-Tom
TROSKY Hal Sr. & Jr.
TROUT Paul-Steve

UNSER Al-Del

VIRGIL Ozzie Sr. & Jr.

WAKEFIELD Howard-Dick
WALKER Dixie-Dixie & Harry
WALSH Ed-Ed
WARD Gary-Daryle
WHITE JoJo-Mike
WILLS Maury-Bump
WINE Bobby-Robbie
WOOD Joe-Joe
WRIGHT Clyde-Jaret

YOUNG Del-Del

GREAT GRANDFATHER-GREAT GRANDSON

Jim Bluejacket & Bill Wilkinson

GRANDFATHER-GRANDSON

George Rooks-Lou Possehl
Shano Collins-Bob Gallagher
Bill Brubaker-Dennis Rasmussen
Marty & Ed Herrmann
Ben & Jim Spencer
Lennie & Matt Merullo
Ray & Bret & Aaron Boone
Bill & Roger Salkeld
Bobby Estalella-Robert Estalella
Gus, David & Mike Bell
Red & Brian Barkley
Sam & Jerry Hairston

GRANDFATHER-FATHER-SON

BELL Gus, Buddy, David & Mike
BOONE Ray, Bob, Bret & Aaron
HAIRSTON Sam, Jerry & Jerry

CHAPTER 7

Streaks and Feats

Lyle Spatz

Strikeouts indicate that a pitcher is dominating an opponent. An out, whether it comes on one pitch or nine, is just an out, but the strikeout is the primal right of the pitcher. Fans can anticipate it—clapping rhythmically when the home side's pitcher gets a two-strike count on an opponent, or by tacking up a "K" on a railing at the ballpark for each strikeout recorded. The strikeout has created excitement since 1884, the first year that overhand pitching was allowed. From Matt Kilroy, a rookie who in 1886 became the only pitcher to fan 500 batters in a season, to all-time strikeout king Nolan Ryan, the only pitcher to fan 5,000 batters in a career, the strikeout has been a source of pride for pitchers. Scouts search out strikeouts, too, paying extra for young men who can throw the ball past hitters, often ignoring pitchers with less speed but better control in the process.

On a given day, when the pitcher has his best "stuff," it can be like watching a magician as pitch after pitch flies past confused batters. The 1884 season was the first "Year of the Strikeout," as four pitchers had one-game totals of 18 or more: Charles Sweeney of the National League's Providence Grays and Hugh Daily of Chicago of the Union Association each fanned 19, while UA pitchers Dupee Shaw of Boston and Henry Porter of Milwaukee fanned 18 apiece. Seven of the highest single-season strikeout totals in history came over a three-year period, but strikeouts in general decreased dramatically when the modern mound distance of 60 feet, 6 inches was established in 1893. This rule was in place 45 years before anyone reached 18 strikeouts in a nine-inning game.

Cleveland's Bob Feller—still a month shy of his 20th birthday—fanned 18 Tigers on the last day of the 1938 season, breaking the major league record of 17 that he shared with Dizzy Dean of the Cardinals. Sandy Koufax of the Dodgers tied Feller's mark in 1959 and again in 1962, as did Houston's Don Wilson in 1968, but it was another National Leaguer—lefthander Steve Carlton—who became the first to fan 19 batters in a game. On September 15, 1969, Carlton struck out 19 but yielded two two-run homers to Ron Swoboda; his Cardinals lost the game to the New York Mets, 4–3. (Twenty-six seasons later another dominating lefthander, Randy Johnson, also fanned 19 in a loss; a few weeks later he reached 19 again in a win over the White Sox, becoming the first pitcher to hit that plateau twice in a season.)

In 1970 Tom Seaver tied Carlton's record with 19 strikeouts against fledgling San Diego. The Mets righthander also fanned the last 10 Padres he faced to set a major league mark. In 1974 Nolan Ryan became the first to strike out 19 in the American League, accomplishing the feat for the Angels against the Red Sox.

In 1986 Boston's Roger Clemens became the first pitcher to strike out 20 batters in a nine-inning game. In a late-April game against the Seattle Mariners, Clemens fanned Phil Bradley to register his record-setting 20th strikeout. He had a chance for 21, but Ken Phelps grounded out to end the game. Clemens duplicated the feat a decade later in front of 4,753 fans at Tiger stadium. In one of his final starts with the Red Sox, the 34-year-old Clemens struck out 20 Detroit Tigers on September 18, 1996. Two years later Clemens struck out 18 as a member of the Toronto Blue Jays.

In May 1998, Chicago Cubs rookie Kerry Wood, making only his fifth big league start, tied Clemens's major league mark and set the National League record by striking out 20 Houston Astros. Facing a Houston offense that went on to lead the league in runs that year, Wood was masterful. He allowed only two baserunners: a single to Ricky Gutierrez in the third inning and hitting Craig Biggio with a pitch in the sixth. Wood also became the second pitcher in major league history to strike out as many batters as his age; as a rookie, Bob Feller had fanned 17 Philadelphia Athletics on September 13, 1936.

Tom Cheney, a journeyman pitcher for the expansion Washington Senators, struck out 21 Baltimore Orioles in a 16-inning game in 1962. Cheney is the only major league pitcher to exceed 20 strikeouts in a single game of any length. Six other pitchers, including Ryan on three occasions, surpassed 18 strikeouts in an extra-inning game.

Pitchers With 18 or More Strikeouts in a Game (Since 1893)

Nine-Inning Game

20 Kerry Wood, Chicago (NL), May 6, 1998 vs. Houston
20 Roger Clemens, Boston (AL), September 18, 1996 at Detroit
20 Roger Clemens, Boston (AL), April 29, 1986 vs. Seattle
19 Randy Johnson, Seattle (AL), June 24, 1997 vs. Oakland
19 Randy Johnson, Seattle (AL), August 8, 1997 vs. Chicago
19 David Cone, New York (NL), October 6, 1991 at Philadelphia
19 Nolan Ryan, California (AL), August 12, 1974 vs. Boston
19 Tom Seaver, New York (NL), April 22, 1970 vs. San Diego
19 Steve Carlton, St. Louis (NL), September 15, 1969 vs. New York (NL)
18 Roger Clemens, Toronto (AL), August 25, 1998 vs. Kansas City
18 Randy Johnson, Seattle (AL), September 27, 1992 at Texas (8 innings)
18 Ramon Martinez, Los Angeles (NL), June 4, 1990 vs. Atlanta
18 Bill Gullickson, Montreal (NL), September 10, 1980 vs. Chicago
18 Ron Guidry, New York (AL), June 17, 1978 vs. California
18 Nolan Ryan, California (AL), September 10, 1976 at Chicago
18 Don Wilson, Houston (NL), July 14, 1968 at Cincinnati
18 Sandy Koufax, Los Angeles (NL), April 24, 1962 at Chicago
18 Sandy Koufax, Los Angeles (NL), August 31, 1959 vs. San Francisco
18 Bob Feller, Cleveland (AL), October 2, 1938 vs. Detroit

Extra-Inning Game

21 Tom Cheney, Washington (AL), September 12, 1962 at Baltimore, 16 innings
19 Luis Tiant, Cleveland (AL), July 3, 1968 vs. Minnesota, 10 innings
19 Nolan Ryan, California (AL), June 14, 1974 vs. Boston, 12 innings
19 Nolan Ryan, California (AL), August 20, 1974 vs. Detroit, 11 innings
19 Nolan Ryan, California (AL), June 8, 1977 vs. Toronto, 10 innings
18 Jack Coombs, Philadelphia (AL), September 1, 1906 at Boston, 24 innings
18 Warren Spahn, Boston (NL), June 14, 1952 vs. Chicago, 15 innings
18 Jim Maloney, Cincinnati (NL), June 14, 1965 vs. New York, 11 innings
18 Chris Short, Philadelphia (NL), October 2, 1965 at New York, 15 innings

Consecutive Games Played

In 1989, when the late Jack Kavanagh wrote this section for the first edition of *Total Baseball,* Orioles shortstop Cal Ripken Jr. had an active streak of 1,086 consecutive games played. Nevertheless, Jack dismissed the likelihood that Ripken, or anyone in the future, would ever seriously challenge Lou Gehrig's record of playing in 2,130 consecutive games.

"Lou Gehrig's legacy of stamina and determination reached such a length that all historians can do about the sturdy players who came after him is measure them for the role of runner-up," wrote Jack.

At the time, with Ripken barely past the halfway mark to Gehrig, it would have been difficult to find anyone who disagreed. Of course, back in 1925, when Everett Scott's consecutive games played streak reached a then record 1,307, many sportswriters had also deemed it an "unbreakable" record.

Everett Scott

While several late 19th- and early 20th-century players had played in more than 500 consecutive games, Everett Scott's consecutive-games-played streak was the first to gain attention throughout baseball. While he is now mostly remembered for that streak, Scott was an excellent shortstop, leading all American Leaguers in fielding at that position for eight straight years. He began his streak on June 20, 1916, as a member of the Boston Red Sox, and continued it after being traded to the Yankees in December 1921.

It was following the 1921 season—when Scott's consecutive-game streak had reached 832—that Al Munro Elias, one of baseball's early statisticians, first took note of it. Writing in the 1922 *Baseball Bat Bag,* Elias pointed out that during the 1920 season Scott had broken the record of George Pinkney, who had played in 577 consecutive games for Brooklyn (both in the American Association and the National League) between September 21, 1885 and May 2, 1890.

Scott continued to play every game after joining the Yankees, adding another 475 games to his streak and bringing his total of consecutive games played to 1,307. Although he played at a time when pitchers throwing at hitters and runners sliding hard into infielders were much more prevalent than they are today, it was not this rougher style of play that was responsible for the streak's ending. When manager Miller Huggins benched him on May 6, 1925, it was not because of any injury Scott had suffered, but simply because he was in a batting slump.

The next day, the New York newspapers noted that Scott's streak had ended but not one reporter complained about the way it had ended. There was no special ceremony to mark the streak's ending as there had been two years earlier, on May 2, 1923, at Washington, when Scott played in his 1,000th consecutive game. Prior to that game, American League President Ban Johnson and Secretary of the Navy Edwin Denby recognized the milestone by presenting Scott with a medal.

Lou Gehrig

Lou Gehrig's consecutive games played streak began on June 1, 1925, when he pinch hit for shortstop Pee Wee Wanninger. Coincidentally, it was Wanninger who was Scott's replacement at shortstop on the afternoon that manager Miller Huggins benched Scott, ending his streak. The day after pinch hitting for Wanninger, Gehrig started at first after regular first baseman Wally Pipp complained of a headache and was given the day off. At the time, of course, there was no suspicion that Gehrig had launched a string of 2,130 consecutive game appearances—a streak that would endure for 14 years despite injuries, illnesses, and accidents.

Little mention was made of the streak until June 1933, when Dan Daniel of the *New York World Telegram* wrote that Gehrig was within 60 games of breaking Scott's record. At the time, the record was only eight years old and not considered a very glamorous one. Nevertheless, as the Yankees began to look less and less like a pennant contender, Daniel and other reporters, seeking other things to write about, began to occasionally emphasize it in their stories.

On August 3, Lefty Grove of the A's defeated the Yankees, 7–0, ending New York's record streak of 308 consecutive games without being shut out. The next day Richards Vidmer, writing in the *New York Herald Tribune,* said in his notes following the game story that "at least Lou's streak remains intact, he needs only 12 more to pass Scott." However, there were no full stories about the streak; nor was it the topic of any columns. There was no "GEHRIG WATCH," no day-by-day detailing of how close he was getting to Scott's record.

On August 14, two days before what would be the record-tying game, Gehrig played left field (Babe Ruth played first base) in an exhibition game against the Pirates at Forbes Field. It was more than a token appearance for Babe and Lou, as each player batted three times.

A day later the Yanks began a four-game series against the Browns in St. Louis. This was a time before the current "show business" mentality had permeated baseball, so there had been no attempt by the Yankees to have this series moved to New York, nor had there been any attempt by the American League to have Gehrig set the record at Yankee Stadium. Even the beat writers covering the Yankees did not make the impending record the main focus of the stories they sent back from St. Louis. As usual, the writers considered Babe Ruth the major story. Ruth was struggling at the plate and had chosen to sit out the first two games.

On August 17, as Gehrig tied Scott's record by playing in his 1,307th consecutive game, his accomplishment generated no headlines. The following day, when Gehrig set the record, a ceremony honoring the achievement took place at home plate after New York pitcher Lefty Gomez retired the Browns in the first inning. Both teams gathered around American League President Will Harridge as he presented Lou with a silver statuette donated by *The Sporting News.* E.G. Brands, the editor of *The Sporting News,* posed for pictures with Gehrig, as did Joe Sewell. Sewell—a Yankee teammate—had once played in 1,103 consecutive games and at the time was thought to be the man most likely to break Scott's mark. Missing from the simple ceremony was Yankee manager Joe McCarthy, who was ill, and Scott, who had a business obligation in Fort Wayne, Indiana.

Although radio was at its peak, there was no nationwide hookup for the ceremony, and because the Yankees did not broadcast their games, even New Yorkers heard neither it nor the ceremony. A photograph of the presentation appeared in the *St. Louis Globe Democrat,* but not in any of the New York newspapers, nor did the New York papers headline the event. That evening Gehrig received a congratulatory phone call from Yankee owner Colonel Jacob Ruppert and was a guest at a dinner of the St. Louis Chamber of Commerce, where he received another statuette.

Exact attendance figures are difficult to find, but it's safe to say that the game was far from a sellout. In depression-plagued 1933, the Browns drew only 88,113 to Sportsman's Park for the entire season. Then again, there really wasn't much suspense involved. Everyone knew that Gehrig would show up and that he would play. Baseball was his job and he did it—every day. The fans, many of which had lost their own jobs because of the economic situation, understood that kind of work ethic and did not consider it particularly extraordinary.

Baseball's "Iron Horse" first began to show signs of wearing out in 1938. He batted .295 that year, the first time in his career he batted below .300. In spring training the next season it was evident that something was wrong, but manager Joe McCarthy left it to Gehrig to decide when to call it quits. That day came on May 2, 1939, at Detroit. After eight feebly played games had brought his string to 2,130, Lou Gehrig advised McCarthy to replace him.

Cal Ripken Jr.

Going into the 1989 season, Cal Ripken's streak—begun on May 30, 1982—had reached an impressive 1,068 games, sixth longest ever; but that was still less than half of Lou Gehrig's mark. It would take another seven seasons for Ripken to reach 2,130, a seemingly impossible task, especially for a shortstop.

But day after day and game after game, Ripken persevered, moving relentlessly toward Gehrig's place at the top. Moreover, he did it with a "grace under pressure" that brought glory to the game and stood in sharp contrast to many of the negative aspects of the national pastime. Ripken conducted his career in very much the same way Gehrig did his. He showed up every day and did his job in workmanlike fashion.

Like Gehrig, Ripken had the ability to shrug off those illnesses and little injuries that force most players to take an occasional day off. Yet, with the record in sight, forces beyond his control threatened to bring the streak to an end. It had reached 2,009 by August 1994 when the players' strike cost him half a season's worth of games. The strike led the major league owners to propose opening the 1995 season with replacement players. Of course, if the Baltimore Orioles were to begin the season with a replacement player at shortstop, Ripken would have surrendered his opportunity to break Gehrig's record. Nevertheless, he stood firm with the other members of the players union. Orioles' owner Peter Angelos added to the complications surrounding the start of the '95 season by refusing to sign replacement players and offering to forfeit games as a result.

Fortunately for Ripken, and more so for baseball, the strike was settled and a 144-game season was scheduled. Ripken first tied then broke Gehrig's longstanding record on September 5 and 6 against the California Angels at Baltimore's Camden Yards. Rising to the occasion, he had a combined five hits in nine at bats, with a home run in each game. But just as baseball is a different game now than it was in 1933, so is the attention the media pays to its record-breaking events. Contrary to the lack of attention when Gehrig passed Everett Scott, this was a national and even an international event, covered by newspapers, radio, and television, worldwide.

Ripken accepted the plaudits modestly, shared the moment with the fans by circling the ballpark to shake hands with those who crowded against the railings. He endlessly answered the same questions from reporters. Finally, when he had satisfied all demands, he dressed and went home to celebrate with his father, brother Bill, and wife and children. The next day he went to work as usual. By season's end the new record had reached 2,153 games.

Through 1996, 1997, and into 1998, Ripken continued to play every day, though now as a third baseman. Finally, on Sunday, September 20, 1998, with a week remaining in the 1998 season, Ripken without any fanfare took himself out of the lineup, ending his streak of consecutive games played at 2,632.

Ripken's pursuit of Gehrig's record generated a profusion of comparisons between the two "iron men." Much of what was said and written attempted to determine which player had the more difficult circumstances to overcome in recording such an amazing feat of endurance. Those who believe it was Gehrig point to numerous doubleheaders, long train trips, and summers without air conditioning. Ripken's defenders counter that Gehrig never had to play on artificial turf, or at night—Cleveland and Philadelphia played the first American League night game two weeks after Gehrig's streak had ended. And, they say, playing shortstop is a much more difficult and demanding task than playing first base.

However, whatever the advantages or disadvantages each man had, the fact remains that in both Gehrig's era and in Ripken's, every other major league player performed under the same conditions. Yet no one else—in any era—has come close to playing in 2,000 consecutive games. Gehrig was among the most admired players of his time and Ripken is among the most admired of his. Deservedly so, both were quiet men who preferred to let their play on the field define them, and each was perhaps the best American Leaguer at his position in the 20th century.

Other Noteworthy Streaks

Cal Ripken's rise to the top of the consecutive games played list in 1995 dropped Everett Scott, the No. 2 man since 1933, down to third place. Joe Sewell, with 1,103 consecutive games played for Cleveland between 1922 and 1930, had occupied that spot for many years, but Sewell's streak is now sixth all-time.

During the 1930s, Gus Suhr, a fine-fielding first baseman for the Pittsburgh Pirates, reached 822 consecutive games played. Suhr's streak was dwarfed, even as he made it, by Gehrig's string in progress, but he far exceeded earlier National League marks.

Cardinals great Stan Musial broke Suhr's National League record by playing in 895 straight games. Musial's streak—which ended in 1957 when he was 36 years old—stood as the NL mark until Billy Williams played in 1,117 games between September 1963 and September 1970.

Williams's record fell to Steve Garvey, who broke it while playing for Los Angeles and San Diego. Garvey's streak began in 1974 with the Dodgers, and ended in 1983, his first season with the Padres. A hand injury took him out of the lineup on July 29, 1983, a season after he had established the new record. Garvey's mark of 1,207 is still the National League record and is fourth all-time, exactly 100 games behind the No. 3 man, Scott.

The following table lists those men who have played in the most consecutive games:

2,316	Cal Ripken
2,130	Lou Gehrig
1,307	Everett Scott
1,207	Steve Garvey
1,117	Billy Williams
1,103	Joe Sewell
895	Stan Musial
829	Eddie Yost
822	Gus Suhr
798	Nellie Fox

Longest Hitting Streaks

Joe DiMaggio

Joe DiMaggio's death in March 1999 generated a huge outpouring of stories recalling the numerous exploits of the great Yankee. Paramount among them were the recollections of DiMaggio's 56-game hitting streak in 1941, a streak many believe will never be equaled. Perhaps not, but unlike some other records that changes in the game have rendered unbreakable, this one is attainable. That no one has come within a dozen games of it in 59 years attests to just how great an accomplishment it was.

DiMaggio, who'd won back-to-back American League batting championships in 1939 and 1940, picked right up in 1941. He hit safely in every spring training exhibition game and continued hitting well through the first eight games of the regular season. But he slumped off after that, and by mid-May his average was barely above .300.

DiMaggio, who held the minor league record with a 61-game streak with the 1933 San Francisco Seals of the Pacific Coast League, began his major league-record streak with a first-inning single off Ed Smith of the Chicago White Sox on May 15. It wouldn't end until two months later, when another pitcher named Smith, Al Smith, paired with Jim Bagby Jr. to hold DiMaggio hitless in a game against the Cleveland Indians. Yet in the streak's early days, as DiMaggio's average continued to rise, the fans focused less on it than they did on Joe's battle with Ted Williams for the batting title. He would, of course, never catch Williams, who was on his way to baseball's last .400 season.

The streak reached 19 on June 2, but it was overshadowed by the death of another Yankee immortal, Lou Gehrig. However, when it stretched into the 20s, reporters began checking into consecutive game hitting streaks that had been mostly unchallenged and unnoticed since 1922. That year, first baseman George Sisler of the St. Louis Browns hit in 41 straight to break Ty Cobb's American League record, but was stopped short of Willie Keeler's major league record of 44. (Denny Lyons had a 52-game hitting streak for Philadelphia of the American Association in 1887—the year that walks were counted as hits—with bases on balls twice extending the streak.)

Prior to DiMaggio, the only serious challenge to Sisler came in 1938, and it came from another lefthanded-hitting St. Louis Browns first baseman. George McQuinn ran off a string of 34 games, but McQuinn was playing in the anonymity of the second division, and his challenge drew minimal attention.

Because DiMaggio was a righthanded batter, his first target was deemed to be the record of Rogers Hornsby, who had hit in 33 straight games for the 1922 St. Louis Cardinals. On June 21, DiMaggio hit in his 34th consecutive game, passing Hornsby and putting Sisler's American League record within his grasp. Previously noted only by baseball fans, the streak now began to capture the attention of the general public. The national media soon followed. The wire services carried stories assuring newspaper readers that Joe had extended his string with front-page bulletins before they gave the account of the game in which he did it. Radio newscasts often began with bulletins about the progress of the streak before getting to the day's more sobering national and international events.

As they always did, rival managers juggled pitching rotations to bring their best to the mound when facing the Yankees. Despite that, and despite the growing distractions, DiMaggio continued his consistent, game-after-game pursuit of the next milestone: Sisler's league record. Even the official scorers around the league began to feel the pressure, fearful of making a scoring decision that would appear to unfairly favor DiMaggio. This was especially true for sportswriter Dan Daniel, the official scorer for games at Yankee Stadium, who was often besieged by fans seated nearby demanding a base hit no matter how glaring the error which allowed DiMaggio to reach base.

Years afterward, DiMaggio looked back on the 56 games and could find only one where he wished the play had not been as judgmental as it was. It came in the 30th game—the one that broke the club record held jointly by Roger Peckinpaugh and Earle Combs. The White Sox came to the Stadium, and Johnny Rigney was the pitcher. He had twice been DiMaggio's victim in earlier games in the streak, but on this day had stopped the Yankee Clipper until the seventh inning.

Then DiMaggio hit a routine grounder to shortstop Luke Appling. The future Hall of Famer moved for the ball, but it took a bad bounce, hitting him in the shoulder. In his rush to recover, Appling grabbed at the ball, dropped it, and then threw too late to first. The official scorer, Dan Daniel, ruled it a hit. Had he ruled it an error DiMaggio's streak would have ended that afternoon, because on his last time up, in the ninth, Taft Wright made a leaping catch to snatch a home run out of the right field stands.

The next day DiMaggio received another streak-extending break, in much the same way. This time the ball was hard hit and Appling could only knock it down. He couldn't make a throw. Scorer Daniel judged the ball too hard to handle and ruled it a hit. A few days later DiMaggio broke Hornsby's record for righthanded batters and took aim at Sisler's mark. Still, it took another break for DiMaggio to get there.

The streak was at 37 when the Yanks hosted the St. Louis Browns on June 26. Going into the home eighth, Browns pitcher Eldon Auker had held DiMaggio hitless, and with the Yankees ahead by two runs it did not appear there would be a bottom of the ninth. Unless one of the first three batters kept the inning alive, Joe—due up fourth—would not bat again.

First man up Johnny Sturm popped out, but Red Rolfe drew a walk. Tommy Henrich, the next batter, now had a dilemma. If he hit into a double play, it would deprive DiMaggio of a chance to bat. With manager Joe McCarthy's consent, Henrich bunted and moved Rolfe to second base. Now, with first base open, it was Auker who had a dilemma. He could walk DiMaggio, or pitch to him. He chose to pitch to him, and DiMaggio promptly smashed the first pitch into left field for a double.

Sisler's American League record fell in a June 29 doubleheader at Washington's Griffith Stadium. DiMaggio tied the record in the first game and broke it in the nightcap. The record-tying hit came against Washington's best pitcher, knuckleballer Dutch Leonard, and the record breaker was a last-chance single off the relatively unknown Arnold Anderson.

Two days later, in the second game of a July 1 doubleheader against the Red Sox, DiMaggio tied Keeler's 1897 record. The next day, again against the Red Sox, he hit a long home run off Boston's leading winner, Dick Newsome, giving him hits in 45 consecutive games and breaking Keeler's longstanding mark.

Although he was no longer faced with the pressure to produce at least one hit each game (or perhaps because of it) DiMaggio continued to add to his streak. He was at 53 on July 14 when the Yanks faced Johnny Rigney at Chicago. Rigney had come close to stopping the streak at 30; now he came close to stopping it at 53. DiMaggio's only hit came on a dribbler down the third base line. White Sox third baseman Bob Kennedy was playing deep, a precaution normally taken by rival third basemen when DiMaggio batted. It worked to Joe's advantage that day as he beat out the slowly hit ball; however, it would work to his disadvantage a few days later.

On July 16 the Yankees went from Chicago to Cleveland, where DiMaggio extended the streak to 56 games. The following day it finally ended, although when it did it was due more to the outstanding defense on the left side of the Indians' infield than it was to the pitching of starter Al Smith or reliever Jim Bagby Jr. Twice Ken Keltner, playing a very deep third base, took drives down the baseline and turned them into outs. Then in Joe's last at bat, he hit a ball up the middle that took an erratic hop, but shortstop Lou Boudreau grabbed it and flipped to second to start a double play.

After saying "I wish it could have gone on forever," DiMaggio immediately embarked on a new streak, hitting safely in the next 16 games. Had not Keltner and Boudreau pulled off outstanding defensive plays in game 57, the streak would have reached an incredible 73 games.

During his 56-game streak, Joe DiMaggio batted .408, scored 56 runs, and batted in 55. He hit 15 home runs—half his season's total—and had 35 extra-base hits among the 91 hits he collected in 223 at bats. He walked 21 times, was hit by a pitch twice, and struck out only seven times.

Joe DiMaggio's 1941 Hitting Streak

Game No.	Date	Club and Pitcher	AB	R	H
1	May 15	White Sox, Smith	4	0	1
2	May 16	White Sox, Lee	4	2	2
3	May 17	White Sox, Rigney	3	1	1
4	May 18	Browns, Harris, Niggeling	3	3	3
5	May 19	Browns, Galehouse	3	0	1
6	May 20	Browns, Auker	5	1	1
7	May 21	Tigers, Rowe, Benton	5	0	2
8	May 22	Tigers, McKain	4	0	1
9	May 23	Red Sox, Newsome	5	0	1
10	May 24	Red Sox, Johnson	4	2	1
11	May 25	Red Sox, Grove	4	0	1
12	May 27	Senators, Chase, Anderson, Carrasquel	5	3	4
13	May 28	Senators, Hudson	4	1	1
14	May 29	Senators, Sundra	3	1	1
15	May 30	Red Sox, Johnson	2	1	1
16	May 30	Red Sox, Harris	3	0	1
17	June 1	Indians, Milnar	4	1	1
18	June 1	Indians, Harder	4	0	1
19	June 2	Indians, Feller	4	2	2
20	June 3	Tigers, Trout	4	1	1
21	June 5	Tigers, Newhouser	5	1	1
22	June 7	Browns, Muncrief, Allen, Caster	5	2	3
23	June 8	Browns, Auker	4	3	2
24	June 8	Browns, Caster, Kramer	4	1	2
25	June 10	White Sox, Rigney	5	1	1
26	June 12	White Sox, Lee	4	1	2
27	June 14	Indians, Feller	2	0	1
28	June 15	Indians, Bagby	3	1	1
29	June 16	Indians, Milnar	5	0	1
30	June 17	White Sox, Rigney	4	1	1
31	June 18	White Sox, Lee	3	0	1
32	June 19	White Sox, Smith, Ross	3	2	3
33	June 20	Tigers, Newsom, McKain	5	3	4
34	June 21	Tigers, Trout	4	0	1
35	June 22	Tigers, Newhouser, Newsom	5	1	2
36	June 24	Browns, Muncrief	4	1	1
37	June 25	Browns, Galehouse	4	1	1
38	June 26	Browns, Auker	4	0	1
39	June 27	Athletics, Dean	3	1	2
40	June 28	Athletics, Babich, Harris	5	1	2
41	June 29	Senators, Leonard	4	1	1
42	June 29	Senators, Anderson	5	1	1
43	July 1	Red Sox, Harris, Ryba	4	0	2
44	July 1	Red Sox, Wilson	3	1	1
45	July 2	Red Sox, Newsome	5	1	1
46	July 5	Athletics, Marchildon	4	2	1
47	July 6	Athletics, Babich, Hadley	5	2	4
48	July 6	Athletics, Knott	4	0	2
49	July 10	Browns, Niggling	2	0	1
50	July 11	Browns, Harris, Kramer	5	1	4
51	July 12	Browns, Auker, Muncrief	5	1	2
52	July 13	White Sox, Lyons, Hallett	4	2	3
53	July 13	White Sox, Lee	4	0	1
54	July 14	White Sox, Rigney	3	0	1
55	July 15	White Sox, Smith	4	1	2
56	July 16	Indians, Milnar, Krakauskas	4	3	3
Totals			223	56	91

Other Consecutive Game Hitting Streaks

When Joe DiMaggio's 56-game hitting streak became a matter of national awareness in the summer of 1941, it forced baseball historians to look back at the streaks that had preceded his. Yet almost no mention was made of Bill Dahlen's 42-game streak of 1894, although it had been accomplished under the same rules as Willie Keeler's 1897 mark. Among the things they learned was that had Dahlen not had a most peculiar "off day" on August 7, 1894, even DiMaggio's streak would be just an American League record. In the game following the end of his 42-game streak, Dahlen had put together another one of 28 games. As it is, the 42 consecutive games in which Dahlen hit safely gives him—not Rogers Hornsby—the longest streak by a righthanded batter in National League history. Oddly, Dahlen was stopped by his own inability to fatten his record in a game in which almost everyone else did. While his team, the Chicago Colts, had 17 hits in a 10-inning win over the Reds, Cincinnati' pitchers Chauncey Fisher and Tom Parrott held Dahlen hitless in six at bats. The press did make note of the Dahlen streak when Keeler of the Baltimore Orioles eclipsed it three years later, although they did not recount it in the detail they paid to subsequent streaks.

A one-year change in scoring practices relegated Denny Lyons's 52-game hitting streak to obscurity. Lyons, a young third baseman for the Philadelphia Athletics of the American Association, hit safely in 52 games during the 1887 season, the only year in which walks were counted as hits. His streak was twice kept alive by games in which he only drew a base on balls.

Keeler's 44-game streak began on Opening Day, April 22, 1897, and continued until Frank Killen of Pittsburgh stopped him on June 19. Wee Willie's record still stands as the National League record, tied only by Pete Rose in 1978.

Ty Cobb hit in 20 or more games in a row seven times during his career and nearly equaled Keeler's mark in 1911, when he set an American League record with a 40-game streak. Then, in 1922, two St. Louis players—George Sisler of the Browns and Rogers Hornsby of the Cardinals—created new marks in hitting safely in consecutive games. Sisler hit in 41 straight to break Cobb's American League record, and Hornsby hit in 33 straight, which was hailed as a new record for righthanded batters, at least since 1900. Dahlen's 42 was dismissed as having been made before the turn of the century, despite his having done it under much the same rules in effect in 1922.

Sisler, a popular and widely admired player, began his string on July 27 and continued to get at least one base hit per game through August and past Labor Day. He was four short of tying Cobb's record when the Detroit Tigers, managed by Cobb, came to Sportsman's Park in St. Louis for a three-game series. Hits in the first two games raised the streak to 38, and on September 11 Sisler tried for game 39, one short of Cobb's record.

Early in the game, a generous scorer had granted Sisler a streak-extending single on a flyball that Bobby Veach had reached but couldn't hold. However, there were no message boards or public address systems to inform fans of scorer's decisions in 1922. So Cobb, playing center field, was too far away from the press box to see the scorer hold up one finger, the traditional sign of a safe hit. He didn't know Veach's muff had been ruled a hit. As far as he knew, Sisler—coming to bat in the bottom of the ninth with two out, a runner on first, and the score 4–3 in favor of Detroit—was hitless.

Manager Cobb had a choice. He could order Sisler, the Browns' most dangerous hitter, walked. Doing so would move the tying run into scoring position and put the winning run on base. Such a move would have been bad baseball and worse sportsmanship, and he chose not to do so. He did, however, take the precaution of removing Bob "Fatty" Fothergill, a slow-footed fielder, and replacing him in right with Ira Flagstead, a better defensive player. Then he signaled Howard Ehmke to pitch, whereupon Sisler lined a triple between Cobb and Flagstead, no doubt to the great relief of the official scorer.

Sisler had been playing the last few games with a very sore shoulder, which now ached so much he couldn't play the next four games against the last-place Boston Red Sox. But he was back in the lineup when the Yankees, a half-game ahead of the Browns in a torrid pennant race's final stages, came to St. Louis for a crucial three-game series. With his shoulder and right arm bandaged, Sisler had hits in each of the first two games to tie and then break Cobb's record. Trying for No. 42 in the September 18 series finale, Sisler went hitless in four plate appearances against Joe Bush, ending the streak.

Two days later Hornsby's streak ended at 33 when he failed to get a hit against Brooklyn's Burleigh Grimes. Hornsby's "post-1900" National League record fell in 1945 when Tommy Holmes of the Boston Braves hit in 37 consecutive games. Holmes fell seven games short of Willie Keeler's all-time NL record, and well behind Joe DiMaggio's major league high of 56. But in 1978, Pete Rose of the Cincinnati Reds mounted a serious challenge to both those marks.

Rose had gotten his 3,000th hit on May 5, but was batting just .267 when he got two hits in a game against the Cubs on June 14. He kept adding hits, and tied Holmes in a game at Shea Stadium on July 24, and passed him the next day with a hit off Mets pitcher Craig Swan. Following the record-breaker, Holmes—who was the Mets' community relations director and was at the game—came onto the field to shake the hand of the man who had erased him from the record books.

Rose now held the "modern" National League record and needed seven more games to break Keeler's mark of 44. He got six, tying Keeler on July 31 in Atlanta with a hit off knuckleballer Phil Niekro. The next night a rookie lefthander, Larry McWilliams, held Rose hitless through most of the game, and reliever Gene Garber struck him out in his final at bat.

Longest Hitting Streaks, NL

Player	Team	Year	G
Willie Keeler	BAL	1897	44
Pete Rose	CIN	1978	44
Bill Dahlen	CHI	1894	42
Tommy Holmes	BOS	1945	37
Billy Hamilton	PHI	1894	36
Fred Clarke	LOU	1895	35
Benito Santiago	SD	1987	34

Player	Team	Year	G
George Davis	NY	1893	33
Rogers Hornsby	STL	1922	33
Ed Delahanty	PHI	1899	31
Willie Davis	LA	1969	31
Rico Carty	ATL	1970	31
Vladimir Guerrero	MON	1999	31
Cal McVey	CHI	1876	30
Elmer Smith	CIN	1898	30
Stan Musial	STL	1950	30
Jerome Walton	CHI	1989	30
Luis Gonzalez	ARI	1999	30

Longest Hitting Streaks, AL

Player	Team	Year	G
Joe DiMaggio	NY	1941	56
George Sisler	STL	1922	41
Ty Cobb	DET	1911	40
Paul Molitor	MIL	1987	39
Ty Cobb	DET	1917	35
George Sisler	STL	1925	34
George McQuinn	STL	1938	34
Dom DiMaggio	BOS	1949	34
Hal Chase	NY	1907	33
Heinie Manush	WAS	1933	33
Nap Lajoie	CLE	1906	31
Sam Rice	WAS	1924	31
Ken Landreaux	MIN	1980	31
Tris Speaker	BOS	1912	30
Goose Goslin	DET	1934	30
Ron LeFlore	DET	1976	30
George Brett	KC	1980	30
Sandy Alomar Jr.	CLE	1997	30
Nomar Garciaparra	BOS	1997	30
Eric Davis	BAL	1998	30

Consecutive Base Hits

In all the years major league baseball has been played, only two players have had 12 consecutive base hits. Pinky Higgins of the Boston Red Sox did it in 1938, and Walt Dropo of the Detroit Tigers did it in 1952. Two other American Leaguers—Tris Speaker and Johnny Pesky—had 11 straight hits, but no National Leaguer has ever exceeded 10. Nine National Leaguers have reached that mark, beginning with Ed Delahanty and Jake Gettman in 1897. Delahanty was with Philadelphia, while Gettman (a rookie who appeared in only 36 games that season) was with Washington.

Speaker was the first to exceed 10 straight, getting 11 consecutive hits in 1920. The Indians player-manager had eclipsed Doc Johnston's American League total of nine, done in 1919, the same season Brooklyn's Ed Konetchy had joined Delahanty and Gettman with 10.

During the 1920s five players made a run at Speaker's record but none could get beyond 10 straight hits. Four of the five were future Hall of Famers: American Leaguers George Sisler in 1921 and Harry Heilmann in 1922, and National Leaguers Kiki Cuyler in 1925 and Chick Hafey in 1929. The other was Harry McCurdy, a reserve catcher with the White Sox, in 1926. All got up to 10 straight, as did another Hall of Famer—Joe Medwick—in 1936.

Two years later, in 1938, Boston Red Sox third baseman Mike "Pinky" Higgins put together a string of 12 consecutive hits to break Speaker's record. Higgins did it over three games, going 4 for 4 in each. He began the streak on June 19 with three singles and a double, plus a walk, in the second game of a doubleheader against the White Sox in Chicago. Following an off day, the Red Sox were in Detroit to play a doubleheader with the Tigers. In game one, Higgins again had three singles and a double, plus a walk.

After singling in his first two at bats of the second game, public address announcer Ty Tyson informed the crowd at Briggs Stadium that Higgins could tie Speaker's record if he got another hit the next time up. Higgins did so, and then broke Speaker's mark in his next at bat with a single off Tigers ace Tommy Bridges. The streak ended at 12 when Higgins struck out in his final at bat.

Slugging first baseman Walt Dropo of the Tigers tied that mark in 1952. Dropo had begun the season with Boston, but had been traded to Detroit in a multiplayer deal in June. Going with Dropo was Johnny Pesky, longtime shortstop for the Red Sox, who had made his own assault on the record when he had 11 consecutive hits back in 1946.

Dropo's streak began with a 5-for-5 day at Yankee Stadium on July 14. The next day, in the first game of a twi-night doubleheader in Washington's Griffith Stadium, he added four more hits. All nine hits had been singles, but in the first inning of the nightcap, Dropo tripled with the bases loaded. He had his 11th straight hit in the third inning—another single—and tied Higgins with a double off Lou Sleater in the fifth. Dropo's attempt to set a new record failed when he fouled out to catcher Mickey Grasso in the seventh.

Since Dropo tied Higgins's record in 1952, only three American Leaguers have gotten as many as 10 consecutive hits: Ken Singleton of Baltimore in 1981, Frank Thomas of the White Sox in 1997, and Joe Randa of Kansas City in 1999. Bip Roberts of Cincinnati had 10 in 1992, tying the National League record. Chris Stynes also had 10, splitting the streak them for two teams over two years in two leagues. He had the first three for the Kansas City Royals in 1996, and notched the final seven as a member of the Cincinnati Reds the following year.

Most Consecutive Hits

American League

Player	Team	Year	H
Pinky Higgins	BOS	1938	12
Walt Dropo	DET	1952	12
Tris Speaker	CLE	1920	11
Johnny Pesky	BOS	1946	11
George Sisler	STL	1921	10
Harry Heilmann	DET	1922	10
Harry McCurdy	CHI	1926	10
Rip Radcliff	CHI	1938	10
Ken Singleton	BAL	1981	10
Frank Thomas	CHI	1997	10
Joe Randa	KC	1999	10
Frank Catalanatto	TEX	2000	10
Doc Johnston	CLE	1919	9
Ty Cobb	DET	1925	9
Sam Rice	WAS	1925	9
Hal Trosky	CLE	1936	9
Ted Williams	BOS	1939	9
Tony Oliva	MIN	1967	9
Jorge Orta	CLE	1980	9
Mickey Hatcher	MIN	1985	9
Lance Johnson	CHI	1995	9
Todd Walker	MIN	1998	9
Charles Johnson	BAL	1999	9

National League

Player	Team	Year	H
Ed Delahanty	PHI	1897	10
Jake Gettman	WAS	1897	10
Ed Konetchy	BRO	1919	10
Kiki Cuyler	PIT	1925	10

National League

Player	Team	Year	H
Chick Hafey	STL	1929	10
Joe Medwick	STL	1936	10
Buddy Hassett	BOS	1940	10
Woody Williams	CIN	1943	10
Bip Roberts	CIN	1992	10
Chris Stynes*	CIN	1996–97	10
Joe Kelley	BAL	1894	9
Rogers Hornsby	STL	1924	9
Taylor Douthit	STL	1926	9
Babe Herman	BRO	1926	9
Bill Jurges	NY	1941	9
Terry Moore	STL	1947	9
Dick Sisler	PHI	1950	9
Eddie Waitkus	PHI	1950	9
Dave Philley	PHI	1958–59	9
Felipe Alou	SF	1962	9
Willie Stargell	PIT	1966	9
Rennie Stennett	PIT	1975	9
Ron Cey	LA	1977	9
Andres Galarraga	COL	1993	9
Sammy Sosa	CHI	1993	9
Jose Vizcaino	NY	1996	9
Barry Bonds	SF	1998	9
John Olerud	NY	1998	9
Jim Edmonds	STL	2000	9

** The first three hits of Stynes's streak were with the 1996 Kansas City Royals.*

Successive Pitching Victories One Season

When Tim Keefe of the 1888 New York Giants set the record for consecutive victories at 19 straight, he needed only seven weeks to do it. Between June 23 and August 10 Keefe won all 19 of his starts—17 of them complete games. The two he failed to finish included one in which he was hit on the arm by a line drive while leading 8–3 in the sixth inning; Ed Crane, his replacement, held on for a 9–6 victory, credited to Keefe. The other incomplete game would not have been added to his string by today's scoring rules. On July 16, the Giants were leading Chicago 9–0 after two innings and felt confident enough to give Keefe the rest of the day off. The scoring conventions of the time gave him the win.

Keefe began his great run with a 7–6 win over Philadelphia, after having lost his previous start to John Clarkson of Boston, himself a winner of 13 straight in 1885. Keefe's remarkable run came to an end on August 14, 1888, when his defense betrayed him and two unearned runs were the difference in a 4–2 loss to rookie lefthander Gus Krock of the Chicago White Stockings.

Considering the winning streaks his contemporaries had run off, it was probably thought at the time that Keefe's record was temporary. Until the 1890s, teams rarely used more than two principal pitchers. More open dates existed in the schedules, and two strong-armed men could carry the bulk of the work. A third pitcher, or a general substitute, could help out in doubleheaders. However, the regular duo met most occasions and had many more opportunities to reel off long strings of victories. In 1888 Keefe alternated on the mound with Mickey Welch, also the owner of an impressive winning streak. Welch had won 17 in a row in 1885, one less than the record set by Providence's Charles "Old Hoss" Radbourn in 1884. Another contemporary—Jim McCormick of Chicago—won 14 in a row in 1885 and 16 straight the next year.

Keefe's record, set when the pitching distance was 50 feet, was equaled in 1912 by Rube Marquard, also of the New York Giants, pitching at the present distance of 60 feet, 6 inches. Marquard had been a disappointment in his first two seasons in New York, but he benefited in 1911 when manager John McGraw brought Wilbert Robinson, an expert handler of pitchers, to spring training as a coach. Marquard responded with a 24-win season, then began his streak on Opening Day of the 1912 season. The crowd at Washington Park in Brooklyn was so large the afternoon of April 11 that fans were standing 15 feet from the baselines. The Giants won this ludicrous game, 18–3, with the umpires calling a halt after six innings.

Marquard continued winning, running his record to 19–0 with a 2–1 victory over Brooklyn's Nap Rucker on July 3. Five days later the streak ended with a 7–2 loss at Chicago. But whereas present scoring rules would have subtracted a win from Keefe's streak, they would have added one to Marquard's. Under today's rules, Marquard's record would total 20 consecutive victories. In an April 20 game at the Polo Grounds, he replaced starter Jeff Tesreau in the ninth inning with the Giants trailing Brooklyn, 3–2. The Giants rallied to win the game in the bottom of the ninth, but the rules of the day gave the victory to Tesreau, the starting pitcher. Still, even at 19, the record remains unmatched within the confines of a single season.

In addition to Marquard's equaling of Tim Keefe's National League record for successive victories, the 1912 season produced a new American League record, and then an immediate challenge to it. While Marquard was engaged in his run, Washington's Walter Johnson, almost concurrently, was setting the American League record at 16. And by the time Johnson was stopped another streak had been undertaken, this one by Smokey Joe Wood of the Boston Red Sox.

Johnson had a 13–7 record when he began his streak with a July 5 win over the Yankees. On August 20 he defeated Cleveland for his 15th straight, breaking the former American League record of 14 set by New York's Jack Chesbro in 1904. Johnson won his 16th straight against Detroit on August 23, and had his sights on Marquard's brand-new record. However, some bad luck—and a scoring rule that today would not have cost him a loss—prevented Johnson from catching Marquard.

He lost a game to St. Louis in relief after taking over in the seventh inning of a tie game. There were two runners on base, and before Johnson could get the side out one of them scored the winning run. Today the loss would be charged to the starting pitcher, Tom Hughes, who had allowed the runner to get on base. But at that time the loss was charged against whoever was pitching when the winning run scored. The press and sympathetic fans denounced the scorer's decision, but American League president Ban Johnson decreed the loss be placed against Johnson's record, and there it remains.

Meanwhile, Wood's streak—which had started on July 8, the day Marquard's ended—had grown to 13 by September 2. Although his next scheduled start (against Washington) was on September 7, the press called for it to be moved up a day so he could face Johnson. Red Sox manager Jake Stahl went along, and so on September 6 Johnson got his chance to prevent Wood from equaling or breaking his new record.

Whatever the capacity of Fenway Park was in 1912, it was far exceeded when, on a weekday, more than 30,000 baseball fans gained entrance. The crowd overflowed the stands. In fact, the players could not sit in their dugouts. Instead, they sat on chairs arranged in front of the throngs that stood just outside the baselines. Thousands more people stood in the outfield, behind ropes.

The game lived up to expectations. Great defensive plays snuffed out rallies, and both pitchers stopped scoring threats with clutch strikeouts. Boston broke a scoreless tie in the sixth inning when Tris Speaker's flyball reached the roped-back crowd for a ground-rule double and Duffy Lewis hit an opposite-field double down the right field foul line. It just eluded the grab of Danny Moeller, scoring Speaker. And that was it. The Red Sox won, 1–0.

Wood followed with a win against Chicago and then defeated St. Louis, 2–1, on September 15 to tie Johnson's mark. However, his effort to break it failed when he lost to Detroit on September 20. The final score was 6–4, with two of the Tigers' runs being unearned.

It wasn't until 1931 that anyone again challenged Marquard's 19 consecutive pitching victories, or even the lesser American League record of 16 straight. That challenge came from Lefty Grove of the Philadelphia Athletics, a team on its way to a third consecutive pennant.

Grove tied the American League record on August 19 and was expected to break it in his next start. That came four days later against the St. Louis Browns—a second-division team and perennial victim. Grove pitched with close to his usual brilliance, limiting the Browns to six hits, allowing only one run, and striking out six. However, the luck even the best pitchers must have to sustain a long streak deserted him. Unheralded Dick Coffman of the Browns shut out the Athletics, 1–0, allowing only three hits. Grove's streak came to an end at 16 straight victories, tying him with Johnson and Wood at the top of the American League list.

Never a gracious loser, Grove blamed the loss on the absence of Al Simmons from the lineup. Simmons was home in Milwaukee, seeing a doctor, and his replacement, Jim Moore, misjudged a flyball that became the game-winning hit. Grove fumed that Simmons would have caught the ball. What made the defeat even more bitter in retrospect was that Grove went on to win his next five starts. These victories would have put the record at 21, eclipsing not only the American League record but topping Keefe's and Marquard's all-time total of 19.

Three years after Grove reached 16, Schoolboy Rowe of Detroit mounted another assault on the record. Rowe had started slowly in 1934, splitting his first eight decisions, but with his fifth win embarked on what would be his record-equaling streak. He won his 16th straight game on August 26 against Washington before encountering the barrier that had blocked other American League pitchers. It was the second game of an August 29 doubleheader at Philadelphia, and Rowe was far off form. The by-now lowly A's knocked him out in the seventh inning and defeated him, 13–5. Like Lefty Grove before him, Rowe had to settle for sharing the record, which he now does with Walter Johnson, Joe Wood, and Grove.

Two Seasons

The record for consecutive wins beginning in one season and extending into the next belongs to Carl Hubbell of the New York Giants. Between July 17, 1936, and May 27, 1937, Hubbell won an amazing 24 games in a row. He won his last 16 decisions in 1936 and added eight more victories in 1937 before finally losing a game.

New York had started slowly in 1936. On July 17, the day Hubbell's winning streak began with a 6–0 shutout of Pittsburgh, they were in fifth place and 10 games behind the defending champion Chicago Cubs. Hubbell had lost his last start, 1–0, to the Cubs' Bill Lee on an unearned run.

Three times during the streak Hubbell's mound opponent was Dizzy Dean of the St. Louis Cardinals, his great rival for National League pitching supremacy during these years. In 1936 Hubbell defeated Dean twice by scores of 2–1. Dean was also the victim on May 19, 1937, the day the streak reached 22.

The end of Hubbell's streak came on May 31 at the hands of the team that considered any victory over the Giants compensation for an otherwise dismal season. The Brooklyn Dodgers invaded the Polo Grounds for a doubleheader that drew the second-largest crowd in the stadium's history.

Brooklyn had always been a tough team for Hubbell, yet he had beaten them five times during the streak, twice in relief. But in the opening game of the doubleheader, the Dodgers drove him out in the third inning on the way to a 10–3 victory, ending his run of consecutive wins at 24.

The most serious challenge to Hubbell's record came from Pittsburgh Pirates reliever Roy Face. After winning his final five decisions in 1958, Face won his first 17 in 1959, giving him 22 consecutive wins—all in relief. That, of course, also stands as the best achievement for a reliever.

Just as 1912 saw single-season record-setting streaks by Rube Marquard, Walter Johnson, and Joe Wood, 1936–37 saw both leagues produce record two-season streaks. In the same two seasons that Carl Hubbell was winning 24 straight in the National League, Cleveland's Johnny Allen was running off 17 consecutive wins to establish an American League record. Allen's record-tied by Baltimore's Dave McNally during the 1969–70 seasons-lasted until 1999.

The year before, Roger Clemens of the Toronto Blue Jays took a 15-game winning streak into his final start of the season. The Blue Jays won in 13 innings, but Clemens was not involved in the decision. Thwarted in his attempt to tie the American League single-season mark, he was still on track for the two-season records of Allen, McNally, and Hubbell.

While it is inconceivable that the Giants would have traded Carl Hubbell after the 1936 season, the reasons for player movements are much more complex in today's game, and in February 1999 Toronto traded the five-time Cy Young Award winner to the New York Yankees. Also inconceivable in Hubbel's time was the fact that a starting pitcher could be knocked out of several games only to have the team's bats and bullpen get the starter off the hook. Clemens managed to win his first five decisions as a Yankee, giving him 20 straight and establishing a new

American League mark for successive victories over two seasons. After the New York Mets stopped the streak in an interleague game, Clemens added another victory over an American League team. So while Clemens's two-year streak is officially 20 straight, it's actually 21 against American League opposition.

Pitchers with 12 or More Consecutive Victories in One Season

National League

Year	Pitcher	Won
1888	Tim Keefe, NY	19
1912	Rube Marquard, NY	19
1884	Charles Radbourn, PRO	18
1885	Mickey Welch, NY	17
1890	Pat Luby, CHI	17
1959	Roy Face, PIT	17
1886	Jim McCormick, CHI	16
1936	Carl Hubbell, NY	16
1947	Ewell Blackwell, CIN	16
1962	Jack Sanford, SF	16
1924	Dazzy Vance, BRO	15
1968	Bob Gibson, STL	15
1972	Steve Carlton, PHI	15
1885	Jim McCormick, CHI	14
1886	John Flynn, CHI	14
1904	Joe McGinnity, NY	14
1909	Ed Reulbach, CHI	14
1984	Rick Sutcliffe, CHI	14
1985	Dwight Gooden, NY	14
1996	John Smoltz, ATL	14
1880	Larry Corcoran, CHI	13
1884	Charlie Buffinton, BOS	13
1885	John Clarkson, CHI	13
1892	Cy Young, CLE	13
1893	Frank Killen, PIT	13
1896	Frank Dwyer, CIN	13
1897	Fred Klobededanz, BOS	13
1898	Ted Lewis, BOS	13
1909	Christy Mathewson, NY	13
1910	Deacon Phillippe PIT	13
1927	Burleigh Grimes, NY	13
1956	Brooks Lawrence, CIN	13
1966	Philip Regan, LA	13
1971	Dock Ellis, PIT	13
1992	Tom Glavine, Atl	13
1886	Charlie Ferguson, PHI	12
1902	Jack Chesbro, PIT	12
1904	Hooks Wiltse, NY	12
1906	Ed Reulbach, CHI	12
1975	Burt Hooton, LA	12
1992	Mark Portugal, HOU	12

American League

Year	Pitcher	Won
1912	Walter Johnson, WAS	16
1912	Joe Wood, BOS	16
1931	Lefty Grove, PHI	16
1934	Schoolboy Rowe, DET	16
1932	Alvin Crowder, WAS	15
1937	Johnny Allen, CLE	15
1969	Dave McNally, BAL	15
1974	Gaylord Perry, CLE	15
1998	Roger Clemens, TOR	15
1904	Jack Chesbro, NY	14
1913	Walter Johnson, WAS	14
1914	Chief Bender, PHI	14
1928	Lefty Grove, PHI	14
1961	Whitey Ford, NY	14
1980	Steve Stone, BAL	14
1986	Roger Clemens, BOS	14
1924	Walter Johnson, WAS	13
1925	Stan Coveleski, WAS	13
1930	Wes Ferrell, CLE	13
1940	Bobo Newsom, DET	13
1949	Ellis Kinder, BOS	13
1971	Dave McNally, BAL	13
1973	Jim Hunter, OAK	13
1978	Ron Guidry, NY	13
1983	LaMarr Hoyt, CHI	13
1901	Cy Young, BOS	12
1910	Russl Ford, NY	12
1914	"Dutch" Leonard, BOS	12
1929	Tom Zachary, NY	12
1931	George Earnshaw, PHI	12
1938	Johnny Allen, CLE	12
1939	Atley Donald, NY	12
1946	Dave Ferriss, BOS	12
1961	Luis Arroyo, NY	12
1963	Whitey Ford, NY	12
1968	Dave McNally, BAL	12
1971	Pat Dobson, BAL	12
1985	Ron Guidry, NY	12
1990	Bobby Witt, TEX	12
1991	Scott Erickson, MIN	12
1997	Brad Radke, MIN	12

Other Leagues

Year	League	Pitcher	Won
1890	AA	Scott Stratton, LOU	15
1884	AA	Jack Lynch, NY	14
1884	UA	Jim McCormick, CIN	14
1882	AA	Will White, CIN	12

Successive Pitching Victories Against One Team

A record for successive victories by a pitcher that has lasted even longer than Carl Hubbell's 24 against the National League is one held jointly by Christy Mathewson and Carl Mays. Mathewson, an earlier New York Giants great, had an equally long win streak that came against one team, the St. Louis Cardinals. After yielding five runs and lasting just one inning in a 14–1 loss at St. Louis on May 10, 1904, Mathewson defeated the Cardinals 24 consecutive times. The streak began on June 16, 1904 with a 4–3 win at the Polo Grounds and carried through to September 15, 1908 with a 5–4 win in relief, also at home. St. Louis ended the streak on May 24, 1909 in New York, when John Lush defeated Mathewson, 3–1.

Before Mathewson, Charley "Old Hoss" Radbourn of the Providence Grays held the major league record with 21 consecutive wins against the Detroit Wolverines. Radbourn had beaten Detroit 10 straight before losing to them on May 19, 1883. But he bested them again on June 14, which started the streak of 21 straight (and 31 of 32) against the Wolverines. Win number 21 came on September 18, 1884, with the streak ending when Radbourn was charged with the loss in the game of September 20.

Carl Mays set the American League record and tied Mathewson's major league mark by defeating the Philadelphia Athletics 24 straight times between August 30, 1918 and July 24, 1923. Unlike Mathewson, who won several games in relief, all of Mays's 24 wins were as a starter, and 23 were complete games. He launched the streak as a member of the Boston Red Sox by starting and winning both ends of the August 30, 1918 doubleheader. He had one more win against Philadelphia before Boston traded him to the New York Yankees on July 29, 1919. The change of uniform made no difference in his effectiveness against the Athletics. He defeated them 21 consecutive times as a Yankee, before the A's ended the streak in Mays's final AL appearance. The A's defeated him 7–6 on October 4, 1923.

Mathewson had come close to tying or breaking his own mark with 22 straight wins against Cincinnati (June 17, 1908 to August 16, 1911), and the Reds Pete Donohue made a run with a 20-game streak against the Phillies (September 22, 1921 to July 29, 1925). But since Donohue, only one National Leaguer has won as many as 19 straight against one team. Juan Marichal of the San Francisco Giants did so by winning his first nineteen decisions against the hapless New York Mets (June 3, 1962 to June 3, 1967).

Chief Bender of the Athletics had the American League's longest streak before Mays, winning 19 straight against the St. Louis Browns from August 15, 1908 to July 23, 1913. The longest AL streak since Mays belongs to Ellis Kinder of the Boston Red Sox. Between July 22, 1948 and June 1, 1952, Kinder defeated the Chicago White Sox 18 consecutive times.

The balanced scheduling of recent years, where most teams played each other far fewer times than the 22 games per season during Mathewson's and Mays's time, made it very difficult for modern day pitchers to challenge those streaks. That could change with the return to unbalanced schedules beginning in the 2001 season.

Christy Mathewson's 24-Game Winning Streak
Against the St. Louis Cardinals

1	June 16, 1904; 4–3 @ NY
2	August 6, 1904; 8–1 @ NY
3	August 8, 1904; 4–3 @ NY (relief)
4	August 27, 1904; 9–3 @ STL
5	October 3, 1904; 3–1 @ NY
6	May 11, 1905; 4–0 @ NY
7	June 17, 1905; 7–2 @ STL
8	July 21, 1905; 14–2 @ NY
9	August 28, 1905; 8–1 @ NY
10	September 29, 1905; 6–5 @ STL (11 innings)
11	May 26, 1906; 5–4 @ STL
12	June 15, 1906; 2–1 @ NY
13	July 14, 1906; 4–0 @ STL
14	September 28, 1906; 8–2 @ NY
15	May 17, 1907; 2–1 @ NY (12 innings)
16	June 11, 1907; 8–7 @ STL (relief)
17	July 9, 1907; 5–3 @ NY
18	July 29, 1907; 4–3 @ STL (11 innings)
19	August 27, 1907; 1–0 @ NY
20	June 6, 1908; 3–2 @ NY
21	July 21, 1908; 4–2 @ STL
22	July 29, 1908; 1–0 @ NY
23	August 17, 1908; 3–0 @ STL
24	September 15, 1908; 5–4 @ NY (relief)

Carl Mays's 24-Game Winning Streak
Against the Philadelphia Athletics

1	August 30, 1918; 12–0 @ BOS (1G)
2	August 30, 1918; 4–1 @ BOS (2G)
3	May 29, 1919; 7–1 @ PHI
4	August 31, 1919; 6–0 @ NY
5	September 26, 1919; 8–2 @ NY
6	April 24, 1920; 3–2 @ NY (10 innings)
7	June 6, 1920; 12–6 @ NY
8	July 3, 1920; 5–0 @ PHI (1G)
9	September 7, 1920; 2–0 @ NY
10	September 27, 1920; 3–0 @ PHI
11	April 13, 1921; 11–1 @ NY
12	April 21, 1921; 6–1 @ PHI
13	May 28, 1921; 5–1 @ NY (1G)
14	July 4, 1921; 14–4 @ NY (2G)
15	August 13, 1921; 7–2 @ PHI (1G)
16	September 10, 1921; 19–3 @ PHI
17	October 1, 1921; 5–3 @ NY (1G)
18	April 24, 1922; 6–4 @ NY (11 innings)
19	May 6, 1922; 2–0 @ PHI
20	May 29, 1922; 7–4 @ NY
21	June 4, 1922; 8–3 @ NY
22	July 3, 1922; 12–1 @ PHI
23	September 2, 1922; 11–6 @ PHI (1G)
24	July 24, 1923; 9–2 @ PHI

Longest Winning Streaks Against One Team

National League

24	Christy Mathewson NY vs. STL—June 16,1904 to September 15, 1908
22	Christy Mathewson NY vs. CIN—June 17,1908 to August 16, 1911
21	Old Hoss Radbourn PRO vs. DET—June 14,1883 to September 18, 1884
20	Pete Donohue CIN vs. PHI—September 22, 1921 to July 29, 1925
19	Juan Marichal SF vs. NY—June 3, 1962 to June 3, 1967 (1G)
19	Old Hoss Radbourn PRO vs. PHI—May 1, 1893 to July 17, 1885
17	John Clarkson CHI vs. STL—May 1, 1885 to August 14, 1886
17	Joe McGinnity NY vs. BOS—October 4, 1902 to May 5, 1905
17	Christy Mathewson NY vs. BRO—September 13, 1907 to June 24, 1911
17	Russ Meyer PHI/BRO vs. CHI—June 14, 1951 to April 30, 1955
16	Mickey Welch TRO vs. BUF—May 29, 1880 to July 4, 1881
16	Ed Reulbach CHI vs. CIN—July 15, 1906 to August 18,1909
16	Ed Reulbach CHI vs. BRO—July 30, 1907 to August 10, 1910
15	Charles Bufffinton BOS vs. PHI—May 4, 1883 to August 6, 1884
15	Tim Keefe NY vs. IND—May 16, 1887 to September 7, 1888
15	Kid Nichols BOS vs. NY—June 5, 1890 to May 15, 1893
15	Kid Nichols BOS vs. LOU—July 7, 1892 to June 3, 1896
15	Kid Nichols BOS vs. STL—May 6, 1895 to July 19, 1899
15	Christy Mathewson NY vs. BOS—June 24, 1908 to September 12, 1911
15	Robin Roberts PHI vs. PIT—May 20, 1951 to August 12, 1953

American League

24	Carl Mays BOS/NY vs. PHI—August 30, 1918 to July 24, 1923
19	Chief Bender PHI vs. STL—August 15, 1908 to July 23, 1913
18	Ellis Kinder BOS vs. CHI—July 22, 1948 (2G) to June 1, 1952
17	Mel Parnell BOS vs. WAS—July 8, 1948 to May 30, 1952 (2G)
16	Jack Chesbro NY vs. WAS—April 25, 1903 to September 5, 1905
16	Walter Johnson WAS vs. CHI—June 6, 1912 to May 12, 1914
16	Bob Lemon CLE vs. PHI/KC—June 14, 1951 to August 19,1956 (1G)
15	Joe Wood BOS vs. STL—May 25, 1911 to June 15, 1914
15	Walter Johnson WAS vs. STL—May 19, 1910 to August 11, 1912
15	Joe Bush NY vs. STL—July 11, 1922 to September 17, 1924
15	Hal Newhouser DET vs. STL—May 6, 1945 (1G) to June 29, 1947 (1G)

Team Winning Streaks

Harry Wright's Boston Red Stockings opened the 1875 National Association season with Al Spalding's 6–0 shutout of the New Haven Elm Citys. The victory was the first of 26 the Red Stockings would win before suffering their first loss, a 5–4 defeat by the St. Louis Browns on June 5. Boston's 26 consecutive wins established a major league record that has been equaled only once in the century and a quarter since it was set. However, unlike the Red Stockings who used the record to launch them to a fifth consecutive National Association title, John McGraw's 1916 New York Giants finished a mediocre fourth.

On September 7, when they began their record-tying streak, the New Yorkers were 13½ games out of first place. They won 12 in a row—all at home—and then paused for a rain-halted 1–1 tie with Pittsburgh. They then won their next 14, again all of them played at the Polo Grounds, before losing to the Boston Braves in the final home game of the season. The Giants had already had one significant winning streak in 1916, a 17-gamer in May (all of which, oddly enough, were won on the road).

Twice National League clubs from Chicago won 21 in a row, and both were pennant-winners. When the Chicago White Stockings did it under Cap Anson in 1880, it helped extend their lead from 3½ to 13½ games. They won the pennant by 15 games. However, when their descendants, the Chicago Cubs, won 21 in a row in September 1935, the streak capped a sensational stretch that allowed them to catch and then pass the St. Louis Cardinals. The Cubs were in third place, 2½ games behind St. Louis, when the streak began on September 4. They took the lead with their 11th consecutive win on September 14, and by the time it ended were six games ahead.

The Chicago White Sox and New York Yankees share the American League record for the most consecutive games won with 19. The 1906 White Sox, dubbed "the

Hitless Wonders" because of a .230 team batting average, were 7½ games behind and in fourth place on the second of August. Ahead of them were Philadelphia, New York, and Cleveland. By the time they had won their 19th straight, on August 23, they had a 5½-game lead. A week later the Yankees started a streak of their own, a 15-gamer that carried them past Chicago; but the Sox bounced back and won the pennant by three games.

In 1947 the Yanks used their 19-game win streak—13 of which were on the road—to all but end the pennant race. They had a 3½-game lead when it started, which climbed to 11½ games at its conclusion.

Brooklyn's 15-game streak in 1924, begun on August 25, took them from third place and 7½ games behind to a ½-game lead after their first-game victory on September 6. They failed to hold that lead, however, finishing 1½ games behind the Giants.

The Giants of 1936 also survived a 15-game streak, by the Cubs in June, to win a pennant. Of course, their own 15-game streak in August was the reason. It took them from third into the lead, which they held the rest of the way.

Then, of course, we have the 1951 Giants. On the morning of August 12 the Giants were 13 games behind their hated intra-city rivals, the Dodgers. The Giants won two that day, beginning a 16-game win streak that carried them into first place. The two finished tied for first, with the Giants winning the pennant on Bobby Thomson's ninth-inning home run in the third and deciding playoff game.

Remarkably, since 1900 New York teams have dominated both leagues in the amount of winning streaks of 15 games or more. The Yankees have five of the American League's 12, and the Giants have seven, and Brooklyn has one of the 13 National League streaks. The Yanks rode four of those five streaks to pennants, and the Giants accomplished this four times. Perhaps the poorest finish was by the 1907 Giants. When their 17-game win streak ended on May 18, they were on top of the National League by one game. But it was all downhill from there and they would finish fourth, 25½ games behind the first-place Cubs.

Team Winning Streaks of More Than 15 Games

Wins	H/A	Team	Lg.	Year	First Win	Last Win
26 (1 tie)	12/14	BOS	NA	1875	April 19*	June 3
26 (1 tie)	26/0	NY	NL	1916	September 7	September 30 (1G)
21 (1 tie)	11/10	CHI	NL	1880	June 2	July 8
21	18/3	CHI	NL	1935	September 4	September 27 (2G)
20	16/4	STL	UA	1884	April 20	May 22
20	16/4	PRO	NL	1884	August 7	September 6
19 (1 tie)	11/8	CHI	AL	1906	August 2	August 23
19	6/13	NY	AL	1947	June 29 (2G)	July 17 (2G)
18	14/4	CHI	NL	1885	June 1	June 24
18 (1 tie)	16/2	BOS	NL	1891	September 16	October 2
18	13/5	BAL	NL	1894	August 24	September 16 (1G)
18	13/5	NY	NL	1904	June 16	July 4 (2G)
18	3/15	NY	AL	1953	May 27	June 14 (2G)
17	14/3	STL	AA	1885	May 5	June 1
17	16/1	BOS	NL	1897	May 31	June 21
17	14/3	NY	NL	1907	April 25	May 18
17	1/16	WAS	AL	1912	May 30 (2G)	June 18
17	0/17	NY	NL	1916	May 9	May 29
17	5/12	PHI	AL	1931	May 5	May 25 (2G)
16	9/7	MUT	NA	1874	August 8	October 2
16	7/9	STL	UA	1884	August 26	September 17
16 (1 tie)	5/11	PHI	NL	1887	September 15	October 8**
16	14/2	PHI	NL	1890	July 8	July 26
16	11/5	PHI	NL	1892	June 11	June 28
16	12/4	PIT	NL	1909	September 9	September 27 (1G)
16	11/5	NY	NL	1912	June 19	July 3 (2G)
16	12/4	NY	AL	1926	May 10	May 26
16	13/3	NY	NL	1951	August 12 (1G)	August 27 (2G)
16	9/7	KC	AL	1977	August 31	September 15 (2G)
15	12/3	DET	NL	1886	May 8	May 29
15	15/0	STL	AA	1887	April 24	May 16
15	11/4	PIT	NL	1903	June 2	June 25 (1G)
15	12/3	NY	AL	1906	August 29	September 8
15	13/2	PHI	AL	1913	May 27 (1)	June 10
15	15/0	IND	FL	1914	June 11 (1G)	June 24
15	3/12	BRO	NL	1924	August 25	September 6 (1G)
15	11/4	CHI	NL	1936	June 4	June 21 (1G)
15	7/8	NY	NL	1936	August 11	August 28
15	11/4	BOS	AL	1946	April 25	May 10
15	9/6	NY	AL	1960	September 16	October 2**
15	10/5	MIN	AL	1991	June 1	June 16
15	9/6	ATL	NL	2000	April 16	May 2

* Beginning of season
** End of season

Home Runs

For many fans, baseball's most glamorous record is the single-season home run mark. Babe Ruth held that distinction for 42 years, beginning with his record-breaking 29-home run season in 1919, a record he himself broke with 54 in 1920, 59 in 1921, and 60 in 1927. Although Ruth had several challengers during those years—most notably Jimmie Foxx and Hank Greenberg with 58—the record endured until Roger Maris hit 61 home runs in 1961. Because it came during an expansion season with an extended schedule, and because he was not a player in the Ruthian mold, Maris's achievement was not a popular one. Still, it stood for 31 years before falling in spectacular fashion.

The season-long 1998 race between massive Mark McGwire and genial Sammy Sosa captured the nation's attention and did much to repair the damage baseball suffered after the 1994 players' strike. McGwire emerged the winner with a record-shattering 70 home runs, while Sosa finished with 66, the second-highest total ever. Maris's 61 remains the American League record. Below are lists of the men who held the single-season home run records in the National and American Leagues, and a game-by-game listing of the record-breaking seasons by Mark McGwire and Roger Maris.

Single-Season Home Run Record

National League	
George Hall, PHI 1876	5
Charley Jones, BOS 1879	9
Buck Ewing, NY 1883	10
Ned Williamson, CHI 1887	24
Rogers Hornsby, STL 1922	42
Chuck Klein, PHI 1929	43
Hack Wilson, CHI 1930	56
Mark McGwire, STL 1998	70
American League	
Nap Lajoie, PHI 1901	14
Socks Seybold, PHI 1902	16
Babe Ruth, BOS 1919	29
Babe Ruth, NY 1920	54
Babe Ruth, NY 1921	59
Babe Ruth, NY 1927	60
Roger Maris, NY 1961	61

Mark McGwire's 70-Home Run Season (1998)

HR	Game	Date	Opposing pitcher, Club	Place	On base
1	1	March 31	Ramon Martinez, Los Angeles	H	3
2	2	April 2	Frank Lankford, Los Angeles	H	2
3	3	April 3	Mark Langston, San Diego	H	1
4	4	April 4	Don Wengert, San Diego	H	2
5	13	April 14	Jeff Suppan, Arizona	H	1
6	13	April 14	Jeff Suppan, Arizona	H	0
7	13	April 14	Barry Manuel, Arizona	H	1
8	16	Apr 17	Matt Whiteside, Philadelphia	H	1
9	19	Apr 21	Trey Moore, Montreal	A	1
10	23	Apr 25	Jerry Spradlin, Philadelphia	A	1
11	27	Apr 30	Marc Pisciotta, Chicago(N)	A	1
12	28	May 1	Rod Beck, Chicago(N)	A	1
13	34	May 8	Rick Reed, New York(N)	A	1
14	36	May 12	Paul Wagner, Milwaukee	H	2
15	38	May 14	Kevin Millwood, Atlanta	H	0
16	40	May 16	Livan Hernandez, Florida	H	0
17	42	May 18	Jesus Sanchez, Florida	H	0
18	43	May 19	Tyler Green, Philadelphia	A	1
19	43	May 19	Tyler Green, Philadelphia	A	1
20	43	May 19	Wayne Gomes, Philadelphia	A	1
21	46	May 22	Mark Gardner, San Francisco	H	1
22	47	May 23	Rich Rodriguez, San Francisco	H	0
23	47	May 23	John Johnstone, San Francisco	H	2
24	48	May 24	Robb Nen, San Francisco	H	1
25	49	May 25	John Thomson, Colorado	H	0
26	52	May 29	Dan Miceli, San Diego	A	1
27	53	May 30	Andy Ashby, San Diego	A	0
28	59	June 5	Orel Hershiser, San Francisco	H	1
29	62	June 8	Jason Bere, Chicago(A)	A	1
30	64	June 10	Jim Parque, Chicago(A)	A	2
31	65	June 12	Andy Benes, Arizona	A	3
32	69	June 17	Jose Lima, Houston	A	0
33	70	June 18	Shane Reynolds, Houston	A	0
34	76	June 24	Jaret Wright, Cleveland	A	1
35	77	June 25	Dave Burba, Cleveland	A	0
36	79	June 27	Mike Trombley, Minnesota	A	1
37	81	June 30	Glendon Rusch, Kansas City	H	0
38	89	July 11	Billy Wagner, Houston	H	1
39	90	July 12	Sean Bergman, Houston	H	0
40	90	July 12	Scott Elarton, Houston	H	0
41	95	July 17	Brian Bohanon, Los Angeles	H	0
42	95	July 17	Antonio Osuna, Los Angeles	H	0
43	98	July 20	Brian Boehringer, San Diego	A	1
44	104	July 26	John Thomson, Colorado	A	0
45	105	July 28	Mike Myers, Milwaukee	H	0
46	115	August 8	Mark Clark, Chicago(N)	H	0
47	118	August 11	Bobby Jones, New York(N)	H	0
48	124	August 19	Matt Karchner, Chicago(N)	A	0
49	124	August 19	Terry Mulholland, Chicago(N)	A	0
50	125	August *20	Willie Blair, New York(N)	A	0
51	126	August +20	Rick Reed, New York(N)	A	0
52	129	August 22	Francisco Cordova, Pittsburgh	A	0
53	130	August 23	Ricardo Rincon, Pittsburgh	A	0
54	132	August 26	Justin Speier, Florida	H	1
55	136	August 30	Dennis Martinez, Atlanta	H	2
56	138	September 1	Livan Hernandez, Florida	A	0
57	138	September 1	Donn Pall, Florida	A	0
58	139	September 2	Brian Edmondson, Florida	A	1
59	139	September 2	Robby Stanifer, Florida	A	1
60	141	September 5	Dennis Reyes, Cincinnati	H	1
61	143	September 7	Mike Morgan, Chicago(N)	H	0
62	144	September 8	Steve Trachsel, Chicago(N)	H	0
63	151	September *15	Jason Christiansen, Pittsburgh	H	0
64	155	September 18	Rafael Roque, Milwaukee	A	1
65	157	September 20	Scott Karl, Milwaukee	A	1
66	161	September 25	Shayne Bennett, Montreal	H	1
67	162	September 26	Dustin Hermanson, Montreal	H	0
68	162	September 26	Kirk Bullinger, Montreal	H	1
69	163	September 27	Mike Thurman, Montreal	H	0
70	163	September 27	Carl Pavano, Montreal	H	2

**First game of doubleheader. +Second game of doubleheader. St. Louis played 163 games in 1998 (one tie on August 24). McGwire played in 155 games.*

Roger Maris's 61-Home Run Season (1961)

HR	Game	Date	Opposing pitcher, Club	Place	On base
1	11	April 26	Paul Foytack, Detroit	A	0
2	17	May 3	Pedro Ramos, Minnesota	A	2
3	20	May 6	Eli Grba, Los Angeles	A	0
4	29	May 17	Pete Burnside, Washington	H	1
5	30	May 19	Jim Perry, Cleveland	A	1
6	31	May 20	Gary Bell, Cleveland	A	0
7	32	May 21	Chuck Estrada, Baltimore	H	0
8	35	May 24	Gene Conley, Boston	H	1
9	38	May 28	Cal McLish, Chicago	H	1
10	40	May 30	Gene Conley, Boston	A	0
11	40	May 30	Mike Fornieles, Boston	A	2
12	41	May 31	Billy Muffett, Boston	A	0
13	43	June 2	Cal McLish, Chicago	A	2
14	44	June 3	Bob Shaw, Chicago	A	2
15	45	June 4	Russ Kemmerer, Chicago	A	0
16	48	June 6	Ed Palmquist, Minnesota	H	2
17	49	June 7	Pedro Ramos, Minnesota	H	2
18	52	June 9	Ray Herbert, Kansas City	H	1
19	55	June +11	Eli Grba, Los Angeles	H	0
20	55	June +11	Johnny James, Los Angeles	H	0
21	57	June 13	Jim Perry, Cleveland	A	0
22	58	June 14	Gary Bell, Cleveland	A	1
23	61	June 17	Don Mossi, Detroit	A	0
24	62	June 18	Jerry Casale, Detroit	A	1
25	63	June 19	Jim Archer, Kansas City	A	0
26	64	June 20	Joe Nuxhall, Kansas City	A	0
27	66	June 22	Norm Bass, Kansas City	A	1
28	74	July 1	Dave Sisler, Washington	H	1
29	75	July 2	Pete Burnside, Washington	H	2
30	75	July 2	Johnny Klippstein, Washington	H	1
31	77	July 4	Frank Lary, Detroit	H	1
32	78	July 5	Frank Funk, Cleveland	H	0
33	82	July *9	Bill Monbouquette, Boston	H	0
34	84	July 13	Early Wynn, Chicago	A	1
35	86	July 15	Ray Herbert, Chicago	A	0
36	92	July 21	Bill Monbouquette, Boston	A	0
37	95	July *25	Frank Baumann, Chicago	H	1
38	95	July *25	Don Larsen, Chicago	H	0
39	96	July +25	Russ Kemmerer, Chicago	H	0
40	96	July +25	Warren Hacker, Chicago	H	2
41	106	August 4	Camilo Pascual, Minnesota	H	2
42	114	August 11	Pete Burnside, Washington	A	0
43	115	August 12	Dick Donovan, Washington	A	0
44	116	August *13	Bennie Daniels, Washington	A	0
45	117	August +13	Marty Kutyna, Washington	A	1
46	118	August 15	Juan Pizarro, Chicago	H	0
47	119	August 16	Billy Pierce, Chicago	H	1
48	119	August 16	Billy Pierce, Chicago	H	1
49	124	August 20	Jim Perry, Cleveland	A	1
50	125	August 22	Ken McBride, Los Angeles	A	1
51	129	August 26	Jerry Walker, Kansas City	A	0
52	135	September 2	Frank Lary, Detroit	H	0
53	135	September 2	Hank Aguirre, Detroit	H	1
54	140	September 6	Tom Cheney, Washington	H	0
55	141	September 7	Dick Stigman, Cleveland	H	0
56	143	September 9	Mudcat Grant, Cleveland	H	0
57	151	September 16	Frank Lary, Detroit	A	1
58	152	September 17	Terry Fox, Detroit	A	1
59	155	September 20	Milt Pappas, Baltimore	A	0
60	159	September 26	Jack Fisher, Baltimore	H	0
61	163	October 1	Tracy Stallard, Boston	H	0

**First game of doubleheader. +Second game of doubleheader. New York played 163 games in 1961 (one tie on April 22). Maris played in 161 games.*

Four Home Runs in a Game

It is so rare a feat for a batter to hit four home runs in a game that in the long history of baseball only 12 men have accomplished it, and only nine did it in a nine-inning game. For greats such as Ed Delahanty, Lou Gehrig, Chuck Klein, Willie Mays, and Mike Schmidt, it was just one highlight of a Hall of Fame career. But for ordinary players like Pat Seerey and Mark Whiten, it was their one brief moment in the national spotlight.

Batters With Four Home Runs in One Game

Bobby Lowe, Boston, May 30, 1894 vs. Cincinnati (second game)
Ed Delahanty, Philadelphia, July 13, 1896 vs. Chicago (NL)
Lou Gehrig, New York (AL), June 3, 1932 at Philadelphia (AL)
Chuck Klein, Philadelphia (NL), July 10, 1936 at Pittsburgh (10-inning game)
Pat Seerey, Chicago (AL), July 18, 1948 at Philadelphia (AL) (11-inning game)
Gil Hodges, Brooklyn, August 31, 1950 vs. Boston (NL)
Joe Adcock, Milwaukee, July 31, 1954 at Brooklyn
Rocky Colavito, Cleveland, June 10, 1959 at Baltimore
Willie Mays, San Francisco, April 30, 1961 at Milwaukee
Mike Schmidt, Philadelphia, April 17, 1976 at Chicago (NL) (10-inning game)
Bob Horner, Atlanta, July 6, 1986 vs. Montreal
Mark Whiten, St Louis, September 7, 1993 at Cincinnati

Grand Slam Home Runs

Their frequency has increased dramatically in recent seasons, but few feats still electrify a crowd like the grand slam home run. Nap Lajoie hit two grand slams in 1901 and added one in 1902 and one in 1907 to hold the American League record in the league's early years. That mark held until 1922 when Babe Ruth hit his fifth grand slam. Ruth kept adding to his total, holding the record until 1934 when Lou Gehrig passed him by hitting his 17th. Gehrig retired with 23 grand slams, the major league record. However, in contrast to the American League, which has had only three lifetime record holders, the National League has had 12, including several players who have held it twice. The current NL leader is Willie McCovey, with 18 grand slams.

Although he holds neither league record, Eddie Murray, with 19, is second only to Gehrig in total grand slams. Murray had 16 in the American League and three in the National.

Lou Gehrig's 23 Grand Slam Home Runs

HR#	Date	Pitcher/Team
11	July 23, 1925	Frederick Marberry WAS
44	May 7, 1927	Ted Lyons CHI
65	July 4, 1927	Bobby Burke WAS
88	May 11, 1928	Joe Shaute CLE
142	September 10, 1929	Phil Page DET
145	September 18, 1929	Milt Shoffner CLE
154	May 22, 1930	Bill Shores PHI
179	July 31, 1930	Ed Durham BOS
223	August 29, 1931	Lefty Grove PHI
225	August 31, 1931	Lloyd Brown WAS
227	September 1, 1931	Ed Morris BOS
240	May 26, 1932	General Crowder WAS
265	September 9, 1932	Earl Whitehill DET
305	May 10, 1934	Lee Stine CHI
307	May 13, 1934	Lloyd Brown CLE
314	June 10, 1934	Bill Dietrich PHI
321	July 5, 1934	Lefty Stewart WAS
359	July 7, 1935	Bobo Newsom WAS
368	August 21, 1935	Jim Walkup STL
414	August 15, 1936	Randy Gumpert PHI
422	September 9, 1936	Oral Hildebrand CLE
458	August 31, 1937	Mel Harder CLE
488	August 20, 1938	Buck Ross PHI

Eddie Murray's 19 Grand Slam Home Runs

HR#	Date	Pitcher/Team
30	April 28, 1978	Lerrin LaGrow CHI (AL)
68	July 31, 1979	Reggie Cleveland MIL (AL)
122	August 16, 1981	Ross Baumgarten CHI (AL)
126	Sept 7, 1981	Wayne Garland CLE (AL)
134	April 5, 1982	Dennis Leonard KC (AL)
155	August 26, 1982	Ken Schrom TOR (AL)
193	September 18, 1983	Pete Ladd MIL (AL)
212	June 19, 1984	Bob Stanley BOS (AL)
215	July 7, 1984	Larry Gura KC (AL)
240	July 9, 1985	Curt Wardle MIN (AL)
243	July 25, 1985	Floyd Bannister CHI (AL)
251	August 26, 1985	Alan Fowlkes CAL (AL)
260	April 19, 1986	Dave Rozema TEX (AL)
265	May 18, 1986	Jose Rijo OAK (AL)
334	April 10, 1989	Mike LaCoss SF (NL)
404	June 2, 1992	Trevor Wilson SF (NL)
412	September 4, 1992	Tim Belcher CIN (NL)
495	August 10, 1996	Jeff Darwin CHI (AL)
501	September 21, 1996	Scott Brow TOR (AL)

Willie McCovey's 18 Grand Slam Home Runs

HR#	Date	Pitcher/Team
24	June 12, 1960	Carl Willey MIL
119	June 22, 1964	John Tsitouris CIN
160	September 10, 1965	Ted Abernathy CHI
166	April 27, 1966	Milt Pappas CIN
205	April 22, 1967	Ramon Hernandez ATL
229	September 23, 1967	Juan Pizarro PIT
231	September 27, 1967	Tug McGraw NY
238	May 4, 1968	Larry Jaster STL
292	June 28, 1969	Jack Fisher CIN
308	August 26, 1969	Jerry Johnson PHI
318	April 4, 1970	Bill Stoneman MON
322	May 10, 1970	Tug McGraw NY
364	July 21, 1971	Dave Giusti PIT
374	July 2, 1972	Don Sutton LA
416	May 19, 1974	Tom Bradley SF
440	May 30, 1975	Bob Apodaca NY
478	June 27, 1977	Joe Hoerner CIN
483	August 8, 1977	Wayne Twitchell MON

Ultimate Grand Slam Home Runs

The most dramatic of all grand slam home runs is the "ultimate grand slam," the one that comes in the home team's final at bat and carries them to a one-run victory. A relatively rare occurrence, only 21 ultimate grand slams have been hit in major league history.

Date	Batter	Team	Pitcher	Team	Score
Sept. 9, 1881	Roger Connor*	TRO-N	Lee Richmond	WOR	8–7
Sept. 24, 1925	Babe Ruth	NY-A	Sarge Connally	CHI	6–5 (10 innings)
May 23, 1936	Sam Byrd	CIN-N	Cy Blanton	PIT	4–3
July 8, 1950	Jack Phillips	PIT-N	Harry Brecheen	STL	7–6
June 16, 1952	Bobby Thomson	NY-N	Willard Schmidt	STL	8–7
July 15, 1952	Eddie Joost	PHI-A	Satchel Paige	STL	7–6
Sept. 11, 1955	Del Crandall*	MIL-N	Herm Wehmeier	PHI	5–4
May 11, 1956	Danny Kravitz	PIT-N	Jack Meyer	PHI	6–5
July 25, 1956	Roberto Clemente	PIT-N	Jim Brosnan	CHI	9–8
August 31, 1963	Ellis Burton*	CHI- N	Hal Woodeshick	HOU	6–5
August 2, 1970	Tony Taylor	PHI-N	Mike Davison	SF	7–6
August 11, 1970	Carl Taylor*	STL-N	Ron Herbel	SD	11–10
April 22, 1973	Ron Lolich*	CLE-A	Sonny Siebert	BOS	8–7 (11 innings)
May 1, 1979	Roger Freed*	STL-N	Joe Sambito	HOU	7–6
April 13, 1983	Bo Diaz*	PHI-N	Neil Allen	NY	10–9
August 31, 1984	Buddy Bell*	TEX-A	Pete Ladd	MIL	7–6
April 13, 1985	Phil Bradley*	SEA-A	Ron Davis	MIN	8–7
August 29, 1986	Dick Schofield*	CAL-A	Willie Hernandez	DET	13–12
June 21, 1988	Alan Trammell*	DET-A	Cecilio Guante	NY	7–6
May 17, 1996	Chris Hoiles*	BAL-A	Norm Charlton	SEA	14–13

** Home run came with two men out.*

(Chart courtesy of Herman Krabbenhoft, *Baseball Quarterly Review*)

Triple Crown Winners—Batting

For a batter to win the Triple Crown, he must be his league's season leader in batting average, home runs, and runs batted in. Back in 1878, Paul Hines of the Providence Grays led the National League in home runs and runs batted in, but finished second to Abner Dalrymple in batting. However, researchers later uncovered two tie games played by Hines and one by Dalrymple. Adding the stats from those games revealed that Hines's batting average was actually higher than Dalrymple's, .358 to .356.

In 1968, a special Baseball Records Committee approved this new information and retroactively awarded a Triple Crown to Paul Hines. Hines enjoyed the distinction of being the first Triple Crown winner from 1969, when Macmillan published the first edition of *The Baseball Encyclopedia,* through 1994, when Major League Baseball and *Total Baseball* adopted a new stance. Because the National League of 1878 did not count individual marks amassed in tie games, the ruling was that the championship should return to Dalrymple, despite his lower average under modern reconstruction.

Hines's ouster makes Tip O'Neill baseball's first Triple Crown winner. O'Neill, playing for the 1887 St. Louis Browns, led the American Association in batting (.485), home runs (14), and RBIs (123). Runs batted in, while known as a baseball statistic as early as 1879, did not become an official measure until 1920. They had to be reconstructed for earlier seasons, which allowed baseball historians to retroactively award Triple Crowns not only to O'Neill, but also to Nap Lajoie and Ty Cobb.

At one time, Hugh Duffy was included among the retroactive Triple Crown winners. In addition to his 18 home runs and 145 runs batted in, Duffy batted .440 for the 1894 Boston Beaneaters. However, the addition of individual statistics from protested games (in keeping with the National League practice of 1894) raised the RBI total of Philadelphia's Sam Thompson to 147.

Lajoie, who had jumped from the Philadelphia Phillies to the Philadelphia Athletics of the new American League, won his crown in 1901. The great second baseman's most sensational season ever—a .426 batting average, 14 home runs, and 145 runs batted in—brought instant respect to the new league. Lajoie would again win the batting and RBI titles with Cleveland in 1904, but fall short in the home run race.

Detroit's Cobb succeeded Lajoie as the American League's superstar, but despite 10 batting championships and four RBI titles won only one Triple Crown, in 1909. He did come close two other times, in 1907 and 1911, finishing second in home runs in each of those years.

Cobb's great rival was Honus Wagner of the National League's Pittsburgh Pirates. Wagner won eight batting titles, and combined them with RBI crowns in 1908 and 1909, but lost out in home runs (he was second in 1908).

Finishing with eight home runs (only one behind his Cincinnati teammate Fred Odwell) cost Cy Seymour a Triple Crown in 1905. The home run title was the most difficult for the stars of the Dead Ball Era to achieve, although it was a second-place finish to Jake Daubert in the batting race that kept the Phillies' Gavvy Cravath from a Triple Crown in 1913.

Rogers Hornsby of the St. Louis Cardinals just missed winning a Triple Crown in 1921, when his 21 home runs were two behind the Giants' George Kelly. But a year later Hornsby did lead in all three departments to become the first National Leaguer to win a Triple Crown. He repeated in 1925.

Babe Ruth, who got two legs up on the Triple Crown seven times without ever winning one, had many home run titles and frequently topped the league in RBIs. However, the competition for batting championships in the 1920s was intense. Cobb, George Sisler, and Harry Heilmann often topped .400, and Heilmann alone accounted for four batting titles. Ruth's second-place finishes to Heilmann and Heinie Manush in the 1923 and 1926 batting races, and to Goose Goslin in the 1924 RBI race cost him Triple Crown honors in each of those three years. The Babe won many honors in his illustrious career, but the Triple Crown was not among them.

In the 1930s the American League's two great first basemen—Jimmie Foxx and Lou Gehrig—were each a threat to claim the Crown every year. Gehrig won in 1934, but when Foxx narrowly failed on two occasions, it was not the Yankee great who stymied him. In 1932 Dale Alexander, who split the season between Detroit and Boston, edged Foxx out of the batting title. Alexander—the first player to win a batting title while appearing with two teams—barely qualified for the championship, but his .367 topped the .364 by Foxx. The following year, 1933, Foxx won his lone Triple Crown.

Foxx had moved from the Athletics to the Red Sox by 1938, when he had his second near miss of the Triple Crown. This time it was the home run lead that eluded him. Although Foxx hit 50 home runs while also winning batting and RBI honors, 1938 was the season Hank Greenberg hit 58 homers in his dramatic chase to equal Babe Ruth's record of 60.

The National League also produced two Triple Crown winners in the 1930s: Chuck Klein and Joe Medwick. Klein won as a member of the Phillies in 1933, the same season Jimmie Foxx was doing likewise for the A's. It was the only year that each league produced a Triple Crown winner. Medwick was with the St. Louis Cardinals in 1937 when he became the National League's last Triple Crown winner. Stan Musial narrowly missed his bid for a Triple Crown in 1948. Musial led the NL in batting and RBIs (and just about every other hitting category) but finished one home run behind Johnny Mize and Ralph Kiner, who tied for the title with 40.

Ted Williams added the home run title to his league-leading .406 batting average in 1941, but fell one leg short of the Triple Crown when Joe DiMaggio topped the RBI column. The next year Williams won all three titles for the first of his two Triple Crowns.

Several wartime players won two legs of the Triple Crown: Rudy York for the Detroit Tigers in 1943, and Bill Nicholson, a Chicago Cubs outfielder in 1943 and 1944. Both led in home runs and runs batted in, but both were far outdistanced in batting average.

Williams had gone off to serve in World War II after winning the Triple Crown in 1942. He returned in 1946 to finish second in each of the Triple Crown categories. Washington's Mickey Vernon beat him out for the batting title, and Hank Greenberg, who had blocked Jimmie Foxx in 1938, had his last hurrah with the Tigers, topping Williams in both home runs and runs batted in.

With Greenberg gone to the National League in 1947, Williams claimed his second Triple Crown. No one was close to him in any of the three prize categories, and despite three prime seasons lost to wartime service, the Red Sox star seemed most likely to be the first to win the Triple Crown three times. He would come agonizingly close in 1949. DiMaggio, winner of the home run and RBI titles in 1948, was injured much of the season and did not compete for individual honors. Williams's chief 1949 rival in those two categories was his Red Sox teammate Vern Stephens. He would edge Stephens in home runs and tie him for the RBI lead, but lose the batting race to the Tigers' George Kell on the season's final day. By going hitless as the Sox lost the pennant-deciding game in New York, Williams finished at .3427. Kell, meanwhile, had two hits to finish at. 3429. It was the closest any player ever came to a Triple Crown without actually winning it and the closest anyone has come to earning the honor three times.

Cleveland's Al Rosen had a similar near miss in 1953. Rosen won the home run and RBI titles, but Mickey Vernon edged him for the batting championship, .337 to .336. Mickey Mantle was at his peak in 1956 when he won the Triple Crown. Mantle won his only batting title with a .353 average, while leading the league with 52 home runs and 130 runs batted in.

In 1966, Frank Robinson of Baltimore won a Triple Crown in his first season in the American League. The former Cincinnati star won the home run and RBI titles comfortably, and while his .316 batting average wouldn't have made the top five in the National League in 1966, it was one of only two above .300 that year in the American League.

One year later, Carl Yastrzemski of the Red Sox made use of the second of his three batting titles to win the major leagues' most recent Triple Crown. Yastrzemski's RBI and home run titles (he tied Harmon Killebrew in home runs) were the only ones of his career.

Since Yaz won the last Triple Crown, many players have won two legs but failed on the third. Three National Leaguers—Joe Torre in 1971, Al Oliver in 1982, and Todd Helton in 2000—have won batting titles and the RBI championship, but not the home run race. Torre and Oliver were not serious threats to lead in home runs, but Helton's total of 42 was only eight behind leader Sammy Sosa.

Most of those who have won two titles in their Triple Crown quests have led the home run and RBI races, but lag far behind in the batting race. Among the players who have won home run and RBI titles (including several who have done it multiple times), are Frank Howard, Johnny Bench, Willie Stargell, George Foster, Andre Dawson, Eddie Murray, Tony Armas, Jose Canseco, Mike Schmidt, and Willie McCovey. Mark McGwire is the most recent member of that group, capturing the home run and RBI titles in 1999. Of all these sluggers, only McCovey came close to a batting title. His .320 mark in 1969 was fifth in the league behind Pete Rose's .348.

More recently, Barry Bonds lost the Triple Crown in 1993, his first year in San Francisco, because his excellent .336 batting average was only good for fourth place behind Andres Galarraga's .370 for the expansion Colorado Rockies. Galarraga was on the other side in 1996. He won the home run and RBI crowns, but batted only .304.

Dante Bichette—another Colorado slugger—lost out in 1995 because his .340 average was 28 points behind Tony Gwynn's winning mark. Gwynn also won batting titles in 1987, 1989, and 1996—years when Dawson, Kevin Mitchell, and Galarraga won the other two legs of the Triple Crown.

Rod Carew was Gwynn's counterpart In the American League. Carew's batting championships helped block five potential Triple Crown seasons: Harmon Killebrew in 1969, Dick Allen in 1972, Reggie Jackson in 1973, George Scott in 1975, and Jim Rice in 1978. In reality only Rice, who hit .315 to finish 15 points behind Carew, was a serious Triple Crown contender.

Sixty-three years have now elapsed since the last Triple Crown winner in the National League, and 33 in the American League. Obviously the proliferation of teams has made winning the Triple Crown much more difficult. The previous winners all played in an eight-team league except for Hugh Duffy (12 teams) and Carl Yastrzemski (10 teams), while current American Leaguers compete in a 14-team league and National Leaguers in a 16-team league.

Triple Crown Batters

American League

Player	Team	Year	HR	RBI	BA
Nap Lajoie	PHI	1901	14	125	.422
Ty Cobb	DET	1909	9	115	.377
Jimmie Foxx	PHI	1933	48	163	.356
Lou Gehrig	NY	1934	49	165	.363
Ted Williams	BOS	1942	36	137	.356
Ted Williams	BOS	1947	32	114	.343
Mickey Mantle	NY	1956	52	130	.353
Frank Robinson	BAL	1966	49	122	.316
Carl Yastrzemski	BOS	1967	44	121	.326

National League

Player	Team	Year	HR	RBI	BA
Rogers Hornsby	STL	1922	42	152	.401
Rogers Hornsby	STL	1925	39	143	.403
Chuck Klein	PHI	1933	28	120	.368
Joe Medwick	STL	1937	31	154	.374

American Association

Player	Team	Year	HR	RBI	BA
Tip O'Neill	STL	1887	14	123	.485

Triple Crown Winners—Pitching

The pitcher's equivalent of the Triple Crown requires that the pitcher lead the league in wins, strikeouts, and earned run average. But as was the case with runs batted in for hitters, earned run averages for pitchers was not an official statistic in the game's early years. It did not become so in the National League until 1912 and in the American League until 1913. When historians began reconstructing earned run averages for those early years, they discovered that Tommy Bond of Boston was the first pitcher to win a Triple Crown. Bond, the only 19th-century pitcher on the list of Triple Crown winners who is not in the Hall of Fame, led the National League in the three categories in 1877, the second year of the league's existence.

The next pitcher to retroactively claim the Triple Crown was Old Hoss Radbourn in 1884. Radbourn pitched the Providence Grays to the National League pennant almost single-handedly that season, after Charlie Sweeney's departure had left him as the team's only pitcher. Along with his 59 victories—the most ever by a pitcher in a season—and 441 strikeouts, Radbourn had a 1.38 ERA at a time when the league mark was 2.98.

Tim Keefe of the New York Giants achieved his Triple Crown in 1888 when his 35 victories edged out Boston's John Clarkson, who had 33. A year later, Clarkson raised his win total to 49 in winning the Triple Crown and leading his team to a pennant.

Amos Rusie was the most dominant pitcher of the 1890s, and his overwhelming fastball may have been the principal reason the distance of the pitcher's box was pushed back in 1893. But even at the new distance of 60 feet, 6 inches, Rusie continued to dominate. In 1894, along with again leading the league in strikeouts, he topped all pitchers with 36 wins and an ERA of 2.78. Rusie's earned run average was nearly a run lower than the No. 2 finisher, Jouett Meekin, and close to two and a half runs below the league ERA.

Boston's Cy Young brought prestige to the new American League by winning a Triple Crown in 1901, just as Nap Lajoie, another established star, had done by winning the batters' version.

Christy Mathewson of the New York Giants won two Triple Crowns: one in 1905 and one in 1908. In 1905 Matty won 31 games, struck out 206, and had an ERA of 1.28. That same year the eccentric Rube Waddell, in his last great year with the Philadelphia Athletics, also won a Triple Crown. Waddell produced 27 wins, 287 strikeouts, and an ERA of 1.48. The World Series, inaugurated in 1903 but boycotted by the Giants in 1904, was resumed in 1905. The Giants and A's had won their respective pennants, but the unpredictable Waddell injured his arm while wrestling with a teammate and couldn't pitch in the Series. The confrontation would have been the only one of its kind. Never since have two pennant winners also had pitching's Triple Crown winners.

Walter Johnson won three Triple Crowns, winning them at widely spaced intervals in his long career. The first came in 1913, the next in 1918, and the last in 1924, when he helped pitch the Senators to their first-ever American League pennant.

Grover Cleveland Alexander of the Philadelphia Phillies produced the most impressive reign ever enjoyed by a Triple Crown winner. A year after winning two legs of the crown (he missed on ERA), Alexander had three successive seasons with 30 or more victories, starting with the pennant-winning 1915 season; each time he led the NL in ERA and strikeouts as well. Alexander was in the U.S. Army in 1918, but the National League had its fourth straight Triple Crown winner—Jim "Hippo" Vaughn of the Chicago Cubs.

Ironically Alexander had served his military hitch as a member of the Chicago Cubs. Despite his three consecutive Triple Crowns, the Phillies sold him and his battery mate Bill Killefer to Chicago following the 1917 season. Alexander got into only three games in 1918 while Vaughn was in the star's role, but the two teammates competed for the Triple Crown in 1919. Alexander led the league in ERA and Vaughn in strikeouts; however, neither came close to topping the league in wins. The following year Alexander won another Triple Crown. It was his fourth, the most ever won by a pitcher.

Brooklyn's Dazzy Vance led the National League in wins twice, earned run average three times, and strikeouts seven times. But only in 1924 did he lead in all three—a feat that won him not only a Triple Crown, but also earned him the Chalmers Award as the National League's Most Valuable Player.

Lefty Grove won back-to-back Triple Crowns for the pennant-winning Philadelphia Athletics in 1930 and 1931, adding the first Baseball Writers Association Most Valuable Player Award in '31. They were Grove's only two Crowns—surprising for a pitcher who led the American League in individual Triple Crown categories 20 times. Another southpaw ace, the Yankees' Lefty Gomez, also won two Triple Crowns, although not consecutively. Gomez won in 1934, a season when the Yankees didn't win the pennant, and in 1937, when they did.

Converted third baseman Bucky Walters led Cincinnati to a pennant in 1939 by winning the National League's first Triple Crown in 15 years. The Reds repeated in 1940, but Walters missed doing so when he lost the strikeout title to Philadelphia's Kirby Higbe.

Cleveland's Bob Feller led the league in victories six times and strikeouts seven, and in five seasons he led in both. But only in 1940 did Feller add the ERA title necessary to give him the Triple Crown. (Ernie Bonham had a lower ERA, 1.90 to Feller's 2.62, but the Yankee rookie pitched only 99 innings.)

Hal Newhouser came close to winning back-to-back Triple Crowns in the last two years of World War II. He won two legs in 1944, but came in second to Detroit Tiger teammate Dizzy Trout for ERA honors. Newhouser won the crown in 1945, as the Tigers won the pennant, then won two legs again in 1946, this time against peacetime competition. However his 275 strikeouts—a total good enough to lead the league in most seasons—fell far below Bob Feller's 348.

Eighteen years passed between Newhouser's Triple Crown in 1945 and 1963, when Sandy Koufax won the first of his three. The honor eluded even Warren Spahn, who topped the National League in victories eight times, led in strikeouts four times, and took the ERA title three times, but could never achieve all three in a single season.

Koufax, who reached stardom after the Dodgers moved from Brooklyn to Los Angeles, won Triple Crowns again in 1965 and 1966. Unlike any previous winner, Koufax left the game following a Triple Crown season. An aching arthritic arm caused his early retirement after a 1966 season of 27 victories, 317 strikeouts, and an ERA of 1.73. Not surprisingly, all three of Koufax's Triple Crowns were achieved in pennant-winning years for the Dodgers. A Triple Crown-winning pitcher has not always meant a pennant for his team, but the two have gone together more often than not. Yet there has never been such a contrast in the success of a team's best pitcher and the rest of its staff as there was in 1972 when Steve Carlton took the honor despite pitching for a last-place team. The Phillies won 59 games, and Carlton won 27 of them. He also led—for the only time—in ERA, with 1.97, and struck out 310.

Another drought followed Carlton's success, despite the presence of such star pitchers as Tom Seaver, Fergie Jenkins, Jim Palmer, Gaylord Perry, Nolan Ryan, Phil Niekro, Don Sutton, and Catfish Hunter. Ron Guidry came the closest in 1978, when he had the most wins (25) and the lowest ERA (1.74), but had 12 fewer strikeouts than Ryan.

The drought ended in 1985 when 20-year-old Dwight Gooden of the New York Mets won the Triple Crown with a remarkable 24–4 record, 1.53 earned run average, and 268 strikeouts. A year later Roger Clemens, Gooden's American League contemporary, matched his 24–4 record of the previous year and also won the ERA title, but his 238 strikeouts were seven behind Seattle's Mark Langston.

Clemens would win two legs again in 1991, failing this time to lead the league in wins. (Not leading in victories also cost Seattle's Randy Johnson a Triple Crown in 1995.) Then, after 13 seasons with the Red Sox, Clemens signed as a free agent with Toronto in 1997 and won the American League's first Triple Crown in 52 years. Clemens repeated the feat in 1998, although he had to win his final 15 games to do it. (Clemens, Rick Helling, and David Cone all finished with 20 victories.)

In 1999 Pedro Martinez notched the American League's third consecutive Triple Crown with one of the greatest pitching seasons in baseball history. Martinez, who succeeded Clemens as the ace of the Red Sox staff, won 23 of 27 decisions, struck out 313 batters, and compiled an ERA that was less than half of the league average (2.07 to 4.86). Martinez missed repeating in 2000, despite winning the ERA and strikeout titles by large margins, because his 18 wins were two short of the league high.

Triple Crown Pitchers

American League

Player	Team	Year	W	L	SO	ERA
Cy Young	BOS	1901	33	10	158	1.62
Rube Waddell	PHI	1905	27	10	287	1.48
Walter Johnson	WAS	1913	36	7	243	1.14
Walter Johnson	WAS	1918	23	13	162	1.27
Walter Johnson	WAS	1924	23	7	158	2.72
Lefty Grove	PHI	1930	28	5	209	2.54
Lefty Grove	PHI	1931	31	4	175	2.06
Lefty Gomez	NY	1934	26	5	158	2.33
Lefty Gomez	NY	1937	21	11	194	2.33
Bob Feller	CLE	1940	27	11	261	2.61
Hal Newhouser	DET	1945	25	9	212	1.81
Roger Clemens	TOR	1997	21	7	292	2.05
Roger Clemens	TOR	1998	20	6	271	2.65
Pedro Martinez	BOS	1999	23	4	313	2.07

National League

Player	Team	Year	W	L	SO	ERA
Tommy Bond	BOS	1877	40	17	170	2.11
Old Hoss Radbourn	PRO	1884	59	12	441	1.38
Tim Keefe	NY	1888	35	12	333	1.74
John Clarkson	BOS	1889	49	19	284	2.73
Amos Rusie	NY	1894	36	13	195	2.78
Christy Mathewson	NY	1905	31	8	206	1.28
Christy Mathewson	NY	1908	37	11	259	1.43
Grover Alexander	PHI	1915	31	10	241	1.22
Grover Alexander	PHI	1916	33	12	167	1.55
Grover Alexander	PHI	1917	30	13	201	1.86
Hippo Vaughn	CHI	1918	22	10	148	1.74
Grover Alexander	CHI	1920	27	14	173	1.91
Dazzy Vance	BRO	1924	28	6	262	2.16
Bucky Walters	CIN	1939	27	11	137	2.29
Sandy Koufax	LA	1963	25	5	306	1.88
Sandy Koufax	LA	1965	26	8	382	2.04
Sandy Koufax	LA	1966	27	9	317	1.73
Steve Carlton	PHI	1972	27	10	310	1.97
Dwight Gooden	NY	1985	24	4	268	1.53

No Hitters

Of the more than 200 major league pitchers who have thrown no hitters, two deserve special mention: Johnny Vander Meer and Nolan Ryan.

In 1938, Vander Meer became the first pitcher in major league history to have two no hitters in one season, and he is still the only one to have thrown back-to-back no hitters. The Cincinnati lefthander no-hit the Boston Braves, 3–0, at Crosley Field on June 11, 1938, and in his next start, on June 15, he no-hit Brooklyn, 6–0, in the first night game ever played at Ebbets Field.

Nolan Ryan pitched the first four of his record seven no-hitters as a member of the California Angels. The first was on May 15 in Kansas City when he defeated the Royals, 3–0. Exactly two months later, on July 15, he got his second in a 6–0 win at Detroit.

Ryan tossed his third no-hitter—a 4–0 home victory against the Twins—on September 28, 1974, in his final start of the season. No-hitter No. 4—Ryan's 100th major league victory—was also at home: a gritty 1–0 win against Baltimore on June 1, 1975.

Ryan was with the National League's Houston Astros when he threw his fifth no-hitter, defeating Los Angeles 5–0 in the Astrodome on September 26, 1981. That one broke the record that he had previously shared with Sandy Koufax for most lifetime no-hitters.

Back in the American League with the Texas Rangers, Ryan tossed a 5–0 no-hitter at Oakland on June 11, 1990. His sixth no-hitter allowed the 43-year-old Ryan to replace Cy Young—who was 41 when he no-hit the New York Highlanders on June 30, 1908—as the oldest man ever to pitch a no-hitter.

On May 1, 1991, in Texas, Ryan no-hit the Toronto Blue Jays, 3–0, for the seventh and final no-hitter of his illustrious career. In doing so, he retained the record for oldest pitcher to have a no-hitter, but now it was as a 44-year-old.

No-hit games, nine or more innings

What follows is the traditional honor roll of the 200-plus pitchers who have tossed no-hitters from 1875 to present. The number to left is the career no-hitter total if greater than one. Notes on particular games follow in parentheses.

Joe Borden, Phi vs. Chi NA, 4–0; July 28, 1875
George Bradley, StL vs. Har NL, 2–0; July 15, 1876
Lee Richmond, Wor vs. Cle NL, 1–0; June 12, 1880 (perfect game)
John Ward, Pro vs. Buf NL, 5–0; June 17, 1880 (perfect game)
Larry Corcoran, Chi vs. Bos NL, 6–0; August 19, 1880
Jim Galvin, Buf at Wor NL, 1–0; August 20, 1880
Tony Mullane, Lou at Cin AA, 2–0; September 11, 1882
Guy Hecker, Lou at Pit AA, 3–1; September 19, 1882
2 Larry Corcoran, Chi vs. Wor NL, 5–0; September 20, 1882
Hoss Radbourn, Pro vs. Cle NL, 8–0; July 25, 1883
Hugh Daily, Cle at Phi NL, 1–0; September 13, 1883
Al Atkisson, Phi vs. Pit AA, 10–1; May 24, 1884
Ed Morris, Col at Pit AA, 5–0; May 29, 1884
Frank Mountain, Col at Was AA, 12–0; June 5, 1884
3 Larry Corcoran, Chi vs. Pro NL, 6–0; June 27, 1884
2 Jim Galvin, Buf at Det NL, 18–0; August 4, 1884
Dick Burns, Cin at KC UA, 3–1; August 26, 1884
Ed Cushman, Mil vs. Was UA, 5–0; September 28, 1884
Sam Kimber Bro vs. Tol AA, 0–0; October 4, 1884 (10 innings, tie)
John Clarkson, Chi at Pro NL, 4–0; July 27, 1885
Charlie Ferguson, Phi vs. Pro NL, 1–0; August 29, 1885
2 Al Atkisson, Phi vs. NY AA, 3–2; May 1, 1886
Adonis Terry, Bro vs. StL AA, 1–0; July 24, 1886
Matt Kilroy, Bal at Pit AA, 6–0; October 6, 1886
2 Adonis Terry, Bro vs. Lou AA, 4–0; May 27, 1888
Henry Porter, KC at Bal AA, 4–0; June 6, 1888
Ed Seward, Phi vs. Cin AA, 12–2; July 26, 1888
Gus Weyhing, Phi vs. KC AA, 4–0; July 31, 1888
Cannonball Titcomb, Roc at Syr AA, 7–0; September 15, 1890
Tom Lovett, Bro vs. NY NL, 4–0; June 22, 1891
Amos Rusie, NY vs. Bro NL, 6–0; July 31, 1891
Ted Breitenstein, StL vs. Lou AA, 8–0; October 4, 1891 (1st game) (first start in the major leagues)
Jack Stivetts, Bos vs. Bro NL, 11–0; August 6, 1892
Ben Sanders, Lou vs. Bal NL, 6–2; August 22, 1892
Bumpus Jones, Cin vs. Pit NL, 7–1; October 15, 1892 (first game in the major leagues)
Bill Hawke, Bal vs. Was NL, 5–0; August 16, 1893
Cy Young, Cle vs. Cin NL, 6–0; September 18, 1897 (1st game)
2 Ted Breitenstein, Cin vs. Pit NL, 11–0; April 22, 1898
Jim Hughes, Bal vs. Bos NL, 8–0; April 22, 1898
Red Donahue, Phi vs. Bos NL, 5–0; July 8, 1898
Walter Thornton, Chi vs. Bro NL, 2–0; August 21, 1898 (2nd game)
Deacon Phillippe, Lou vs. NY NL, 7–0; May 25, 1899
Noodles Hahn, Cin vs. Phi NL, 4–0; July 12, 1900
Christy Mathewson, NY at StL NL, 5–0; July 15, 1901
Jim Callahan, Chi vs. Det AL, 3–0; September 20, 1902 (1st game)
Chick Fraser, Phi at Chi NL, 10–0; September 18, 1903 (2nd game)
2 Cy Young, Bos vs. Phi AL, 3–0; May 5, 1904 (perfect game)

Jesse Tannehill, Bos at Chi AL, 6–0; August 17, 1904
2 Christy Mathewson, NY at Chi NL, 1–0; June 13, 1905
Weldon Henley, Phi at StL AL, 6–0; July 22, 1905 (1st game)
Frank Smith, Chi at Det AL, 15–0; September 6, 1905 (2nd game)
Bill Dinneen, Bos vs. Chi AL, 2–0; September 27, 1905 (1st game)
Johnny Lush, Phi at Bro NL, 6–0; May 1, 1906
Mal Eason, Bro at StL NL, 2–0; July 20, 1906
Jeff Pfeffer, Bos vs. Cin NL, 6–0; May 8, 1907
Nick Maddox, Pit vs. Bro NL, 2–1; September 20, 1907
3 Cy Young, Bos at NY AL, 8–0; June 30, 1908
Hooks Wiltse, NY vs. Phi NL, 1–0; July 4, 1908 (1st game, 10 innings)
Nap Rucker, Bro vs. Bos NL, 6–0; September 5, 1908 (2nd game)
Dusty Rhoades, Cle vs. Bos AL, 2–1; September 18, 1908
2 Frank Smith, Chi vs. Phi AL, 1–0; September 20, 1908
Addie Joss, Cle at Chi AL, 1–0; October 2, 1908 (perfect game)
2 Addie Joss, Cle vs. Chi AL, 1–0; April 20, 1910
Chief Bender, Phi vs. Cle AL, 4–0; May 12, 1910
Joe Wood, Bos vs StL AL, 5–0; July 29, 1911 (1st game)
Ed Walsh, Chi vs. Bos AL, 5–0; August 27, 1911
George Mullin, Det vs. StL AL, 7–0; July 4, 1912 (2nd game)
Earl Hamilton, StL at Det AL, 5–1; August 30, 1912
Jeff Tesreau, NY at Phi NL, 3–0; September 6, 1912 (1st game)
Joe Benz, Chi vs. Cle AL, 6–1; May 31, 1914
George Davis, Bos vs. Phi NL, 7–0; September 9, 1914 (2nd game)
Ed Lafitte, Bro vs. KC FL, 6–2; September 19, 1914
Rube Marquard, NY vs. Bro NL, 2–0; April 15, 1915
Frank Allen, Pit at StL FL, 2–0; April 24, 1915
Claude Hendrix, Chi at Pit FL, 10–0; May 15, 1915
Alex Main, KC at Buf FL, 5–0; August 16, 1915
Jimmy Lavender, Chi at NY NL, 2–0; August 31, 1915 (1st game)
Dave Davenport, StL vs. Chi FL, 3–0; September 7, 1915
2 Tom L. Hughes, Bos vs. Pit NL, 2–0; June 16, 1916
Rube Foster, Bos vs. NY AL, 2–0; June 16, 1916
Joe Bush, Phi vs. Cle AL, 5–0; August 26, 1916
Hubert (Dutch) Leonard, Bos vs. StL AL, 4–0; August 30, 1916
Eddie Cicotte, Chi at StL AL, 11–0; April 14, 1917
George Mogridge, NY at Bos AL, 2–1; April 24, 1917
Fred Toney, Cin at Chi NL, 1–0; May 2, 1917 (10 innings)
Ernie Koob, StL vs. Chi AL, 1–0; May 5, 1917
Bob Groom, StL vs. Chi AL, 3–0; May 6, 1917 (2nd game)
Babe Ruth (0 innings) and Ernie Shore (9 innings), Bos vs. Was AL, 4–0; June 23, 1917 (1st game). (Shore relieved Ruth after Ruth had been thrown out of the game for protesting a walk to the first batter. The runner was caught stealing and Shore retired the remaining 26 batters in order).
2 Hubert (Dutch) Leonard, Bos at Det AL, 5–0; June 3, 1918
Hod Eller, Cin vs. StL NL, 6–0; May 11, 1919
Ray Caldwell, Cle at NY AL, 3–0; September 10, 1919 (1st game)
Walter Johnson, Was at Bos AL, 1–0; July 1, 1920
Charlie Robertson, Chi at Det AL, 2–0; April 30, 1922 (perfect game)
Jesse Barnes, NY vs. Phi NL, 6–0; May 7, 1922
Sam Jones, NY at Phi AL, 2–0; September 4, 1923
Howard Ehmke, Bos at Phi AL, 4–0; September 7, 1923
Jesse Haines, StL vs Bos NL, 5–0; July 17, 1924
Dazzy Vance, Bro vs. Phi NL, 10–1; September 13, 1925 (1st game)
Ted Lyons, Chi at Bos AL, 6–0; August 21, 1926
Carl Hubbell, NY vs. Pit NL, 11–0; May 8, 1929
Wes Ferrell, Cle vs. StL AL, 9–0; April 29, 1931
Bobby Burke, Was vs. Bos AL, 5–0; August 8, 1931
Paul Dean, StL at Bro NL, 3–0; September 21, 1934 (2nd game)
Vern Kennedy, Chi vs. Cle AL, 5–0; August 31, 1935
Bill Dietrich, Chi vs. StL AL, 8–0; June 1, 1937
Johnny Vander Meer, Cin vs. Bos NL, 3–0; June 11, 1938
2 Johnny Vander Meer, Cin at Bro NL, 6–0; June 15, 1938 (next start after June 11)
Monte Pearson, NY vs. Cle AL, 13–0; August 27, 1938 (2nd game)
Bob Feller, Cle at Chi AL, 1–0; April 16, 1940 (Opening Day)
Tex Carleton, Bro at Cin NL, 3–0; April 30, 1940
Lon Warneke, StL at Cin NL, 2–0; August 30, 1941
Jim Tobin, Bos vs. Bro NL, 2–0; April 27, 1944
Clyde Shoun, Cin vs. Bos NL, 1–0; May 15, 1944
Dick Fowler, Phi vs. StL AL, 1–0; September 9, 1945 (2nd game)
Ed Head, Bro vs. Bos NL, 5–0; April 23, 1946
2 Bob Feller, Cle at NY AL, 1–0; April 30, 1946
Ewell Blackwell, Cin vs. Bos NL, 6–0; June 18, 1947
Don Black, Cle vs. Phi AL, 3–0; July 10, 1947 (1st game)
Bill McCahan, Phi vs. Was AL, 3–0; September 3, 1947
Bob Lemon, Cle at Det AL, 2–0; June 30, 1948
Rex Barney, Bro at NY NL, 2–0; September 9, 1948
Vern Bickford, Bos vs. Bro NL, 7–0; August 11, 1950
Cliff Chambers, Pit at Bos NL, 3–0; May 6, 1951 (2nd game)
3 Bob Feller, Cle vs. Det AL, 2–1; July 1, 1951 (1st game)
Allie Reynolds, NY at Cle AL, 1–0; July 12, 1951
2 Allie Reynolds, NY vs. Bos AL, 8–0; September 28, 1951 (1st game)
Virgil Trucks, Det vs. Was AL, 1–0; May 15, 1952
Carl Erskine, Bro vs. Chi NL, 5–0; June 19, 1952
2 Virgil Trucks, Det at NY AL, 1–0; August 25, 1952
Bobo Holloman, StL vs. Phi AL, 6–0; May 6, 1953 (first start in the major leagues)
Jim Wilson, Mil vs. Phi NL, 2–0; June 12, 1954
Sam Jones, Chi vs Pit NL, 4–0; May 12, 1955
2 Carl Erskine, Bro vs. NY NL, 3–0; May 12, 1956
Mel Parnell, Bos vs. Chi AL, 4–0; July 14, 1956
Sal Maglie, Bro vs. Phi NL, 5–0; September 25, 1956
Don Larsen, NY AL vs. Bro NL, 2–0; October 8, 1956 (World Series) (perfect game)
Bob Keegan, Chi vs. Was AL, 6–0; August 20, 1957 (2nd game)
Jim Bunning, Det at Bos AL, 3–0; July 20, 1958 (1st game)
Hoyt Wilhelm, Bal vs. NY AL, 1–0; September 20, 1958
Don Cardwell, Chi vs. StL NL, 4–0; May 15, 1960 (2nd game)
Lew Burdette, Mil vs. Phi NL, 1–0; August 18, 1960
Warren Spahn, Mil vs. Phi NL, 4–0; September 16, 1960
2 Warren Spahn, Mil vs. SF NL, 1–0; April 28, 1961
Bo Belinsky, LA vs. Bal AL, 2–0; May 5, 1962
Earl Wilson, Bos vs. LA Al, 2–0; June 26, 1962
Sandy Koufax, LA vs. NY NL, 5–0; June 30, 1962
Bill Monbouquette, Bos at Chi AL, 1–0; August 1, 1962
Jack Kralick, Min vs. KC AL, 1–0; August 26, 1962
2 Sandy Koufax, LA vs. SF NL, 8–0; May 11, 1963
Don Nottebart, Hou vs. Phi NL, 4–1; May 17, 1963
Juan Marichal, SF vs. Hou NL, 1–0; June 15, 1963
Ken T. Johnson, Hou vs. Cin NL, 0–1; April 23, 1964 (lost game)
3 Sandy Koufax, LA at Phi NL, 3–0; June 4, 1964
2 Jim Bunning, Phi at NY NL, 6–0; June 21, 1964 (1st game; perfect game)
Jim Maloney, Cin at Chi NL, 1–0; August 19, 1965 (1st game; 10 innings)
4 Sandy Koufax, LA vs. Chi NL, 1–0; September 9, 1965 (perfect game)
Dave Morehead, Bos vs. Cle AL, 2–0; September 16, 1965
Sonny Siebert, Cle vs. Was AL, 2–0; June 10, 1966
Steve Barber (8 2/3 innings). and Stu Miller (1/3 inning) Bal vs. Det AL, 1–2; April 30, 1967 (1st game; lost game)
Don Wilson, Hou vs. Atl NL, 2–0; June 18, 1967
Dean Chance, Min at Cle AL, 2–1; August 25, 1967 (2nd game)
Joe Horlen, Chi vs. Det AL, 6–0; September 10, 1967 (1st game)
Tom Phoebus, Bal vs. Bos AL, 6–0; April 27, 1968
Catfish Hunter, Oak vs. Min AL, 4–0; May 8, 1968 (perfect game)
George Culver, Cin at Phi NL, 6–1; July 29, 1968 (2nd game)
Gaylord Perry, SF vs. StL NL, 1–0; September 17, 1968
Ray Washburn, StL at SF NL, 2–0; September 18, 1968
Bill Stoneman, Mon at Phi NL, 7–0; April 17, 1969
2 Jim Maloney, Cin vs. Hou NL, 10–0; April 30, 1969
2 Don Wilson, Hou at Cin NL, 4–0; May 1, 1969
Jim Palmer, Bal vs. Oak AL, 8–0; August 13, 1969
Ken Holtzman, Chi vs. Atl NL, 3–0; August 19, 1969
Bob Moose, Pit at NY NL, 4–0; September 20, 1969
Dock Ellis, Pit at SD NL, 2–0; June 12, 1970 (1st game)
Clyde Wright, Cal vs. Oak AL, 4–0; July 3, 1970
Bill Singer, LA vs. Phi NL, 5–0; July 20, 1970
Vida Blue, Oak vs. Min AL, 6–0; September 21, 1970
2 Ken Holtzman, Chi at Cin NL, 1–0; June 3, 1971
Rick Wise, Phi at Cin NL, 4–0; June 23, 1971
Bob Gibson, StL at Pit NL, 11–0; August 14, 1971
Burt Hooton, Chi vs. Phi NL, 4–0; April 16, 1972
Milt Pappas, Chi vs. SD NL, 8–0; September 2, 1972
2 Bill Stoneman, Mon vs. NY NL, 7–0; October 2, 1972 (1st game)
Steve Busby, KC at Det AL, 3–0; April 27, 1973
Nolan Ryan, Cal at KC AL, 3–0; May 15, 1973
2 Nolan Ryan, Cal at Det AL, 6–0; July 15, 1973
Jim Bibby, Tex at Oak AL, 6–0; July 20, 1973
Phil Niekro, Atl vs. SD NL, 9–0; August 5, 1973
2 Steve Busby, KC at Mil AL, 2–0; June 19, 1974
Dick Bosman, Cle vs. Oak AL, 4–0; July 19, 1974
3 Nolan Ryan, Cal vs. Min AL, 4–0; September 28, 1974
4 Nolan Ryan, Cal vs. Bal AL, 1–0; June 1, 1975
Ed Halicki, SF vs. NY NL, 6–0; August 24, 1975 (2nd game)
Vida Blue (5 innings), Glenn Abbott (1 inning), Paul Lindblad (1 inning), and Rollie Fingers (2 innings), Oak vs. Cal AL, 5–0; September 28, 1975
Larry Dierker, Hou vs. Mon NL, 5–0; July 9, 1976
Blue Moon Odom (5 innings) and Francisco Barrios (4 innings), Chi at Oak AL, 6–0; July 28, 1976
John Candelaria, Pit vs. LA NL, 2–0; August 9, 1976
John Montefusco, SF at Atl NL, 9–0; September 29, 1976
Jim Colborn, KC vs. Tex AL, 6–0; May 14, 1977
Dennis Eckersley, Cle vs. Cal AL, 1–0; May 30, 1977
Bert Blyleven, Tex at Cal AL, 6–0; September 22, 1977
Bob Forsch, StL vs. Phi NL, 5–0; April 16, 1978
Tom Seaver, Cin vs. StL NL, 4–0; June 16, 1978
Ken Forsch, Hou vs. AtL NL, 6–0; April 7, 1979
Jerry Reuss, LA at SF NL, 8–0; June 27, 1980
Charlie Lea, Mon vs. SF NL, 4–0; May 10, 1981 (2nd game)
Len Barker, Cle vs. Tor AL, 3–0; May 15, 1981 (perfect game)
5 Nolan Ryan, Hou vs. LA NL, 5–0; September 26, 1981
Dave Righetti, NY vs. Bos AL, 4–0; July 4, 1983
2 Bob Forsch, StL vs. Mon NL, 3–0; September 26, 1983
Mike Warren, Oak vs. Chi AL, 3–0; September 29, 1983
Jack Morris, Det at Chi AL, 4–0; April 7, 1984
Mike Witt, Cal at Tex AL, 1–0; September 30, 1984 (perfect game)
Joe Cowley, Chi at Cal AL, 7–1; September 19, 1986
Mike Scott, Hou vs. SF NL, 2–0; September 25, 1986
Juan Nieves, Mil vs. Bal AL, 7–0; April 15, 1987
Tom Browning, Cin vs. LA NL, 1–0; September 16, 1988 (perfect game)
Mark Langston (7 innings) and Mike Witt (2 innings), Cal vs Sea AL, 1–0; April 11, 1990
Randy Johnson, Sea vs. Det AL, 2–0; June 2, 1990

6 Nolan Ryan, Tex at Oak AL, 5–0; June 11, 1990
Dave Stewart, Oak at Tor AL, 5–0; June 29, 1990
Fernando Valenzuela, LA vs. StL NL, 6–0; June 29, 1990
Terry Mulholland, Phi vs. SF NL, 6–0; August 15, 1990
Dave Stieb, Tor at Det AL, 3–0; September 2, 1990
7 Nolan Ryan, Tex vs. Tor AL. 3–0; May 1, 1991
Tommy Greene, Phi at Mon NL, 2–0; May 23, 1991
Bob Milacki (6 Innings), Mike Flanagan (1 Inning), Mark Williamson (1 Inning), Gregg Olson (1 inning) Bal at Oak AL, 2–0; July 13, 1991
Dennis Martinez, Mon at LA NL, 2–0; July 28, 1991 (perfect game)
Wilson Alvarez, Chi at Bal AL. 7–0; August 11, 1991
Bret Saberhagen, KC vs Chi AL, 7–0; August 26, 1991
Kent Mercker (6 innings), Mark Wohlers (2 innings), Alejandro Pena (1 inning), Atl at SD NL. 1–0; September 11, 1991
Kevin Gross, LA vs SF NL, 2–0; August 17, 1992
Chris Bosio, Sea vs. Bos AL, 7–0; April 22, 1993
Jim Abbott, NY vs. Cle AL, 4–0; September 4, 1993
Darryl Kile, Hou vs. NY NL, 7–1; September 8, 1993
Kent Mercker, Atl at LA NL, 6–0; April 8, 1994
Scott Erickson, Min vs. Mil AL, 6–0; April 27, 1994
Kenny Rogers, Tex vs. Cal AL, 4–0; July 29, 1994 (perfect game)
Ramon Martinez, LA vs. Fla. NL, 7–0, July 14, 1995
Al Leiter, Fla vs. Col NL, 11–0; May 11, 1996
Dwight Gooden, NY vs. Sea AL, 2–0; May 14, 1996
Hideo Nomo, LA at Col NL, 9–0, September 17, 1996
Kevin Brown, Fla at SF NL, 9–0; June 10, 1997
Francisco Cordova (10 innings) and Ricardo Rincon (1 inning), Pit vs. Hou NL, 3–0; July 12, 1997
David Wells, NY vs. Min AL, 4–0; May 17, 1998 (perfect game)
Jose Jiminez, STL at ARI NL, 1–0; June 25, 1999
David Cone, NY (AL) vs. MON (NL), 5–0; July 18, 1999 (interleague game) (perfect game)
Eric Milton, Min vs. Ana AL, 7–0; September 11, 1999

Perfect Games

Lee Richmond, Wor vs. Cle NL, 1–0; June 12, 1880
John Ward, Pro vs. Buf NL, 5–0; June 17, 1880
Cy Young, Bos vs. Phi AL, 3–0; May 5, 1904
Addie Joss, Cle at Chi AL, 1–0; October 2, 1908
Charlie Robertson, Chi at Det AL, 2–0; April 30, 1922
Don Larsen, NY AL vs. Bro NL, 2–0; October 8, 1956 (World Series)
Jim Bunning, Phi at NY NL, 6–0; June 21, 1964 (1st game)
Sandy Koufax, LA vs. Chi NL, 1–0; September 9, 1965
Catfish Hunter, Oak vs. Min AL, 4–0; May 8, 1968
Len Barker, Cle vs. Tor AL, 3–0; May 15, 1981
Mike Witt, Cal at Tex AL, 1–0; September 30, 1984
Tom Browning, Cin vs. LA NL, 1–0; September 16, 1988
Dennis Martinez, Mon at LA NL, 2–0; July 28, 1991
Kenny Rogers, Tex vs. Cal AL, 4–0; July 29, 1994
David Wells, NY vs. Min AL, 4–0; May 17, 1998
David Cone, NY (AL) vs. Mon (NL), 5–0; July 18, 1999 (interleague game)

No-hit games broken up in extra innings

Earl Moore, Cle vs. Chi AL, 2–4; May 9, 1901 (allowed first hit in 10th and lost in 10th)
Bob Wicker, Chi at NY NL, 1–0; June 11, 1904 (won in 12th after allowing first hit in 10th)
Harry McIntyre, Bro vs. Pit NL, 0–1; August 1, 1906 (lost in 13th after allowing first hit in 11th)
Red Ames, NY vs. Bro NL, 0–3; April 15, 1909 (lost in 13th after allowing first hit in 10th)
Tom Hughes, NY vs. Cle AL, 0–5; August 30, 1910 (2nd game) (lost in 11th after allowing first hit in 10th)
Jim Scott, Chi at Was AL, 0–1; May 14, 1914 (allowed first hit in 10th and lost in 10th)
Hippo Vaughn, Chi vs. Cin NL, 0–1; May 2, 1917 (allowed first hit in 10th and lost in 10th)
Bobo Newsom, StL vs Bos AL, 1–2; September 18, 1934 (allowed first hit in 10th and lost in 10th)
Johnny Klippstein (7 innings), Hershell Freeman (1 inning) and Joe Black (3 innings), Cin at Mil NL, 1–2; May 26, 1956 (lost in 11 innings after allowing first hit in 10th)
Harvey Haddix, Pit at Mil NL, 0–1; May 26, 1959 (allowed first hit in 13th after pitching 12 perfect innings, and lost in 13th)
Jim Maloney, Cin vs. NY NL, 0–1; June 14, 1965 (allowed first hit in 11th and lost in 11th)
Mark Gardner, Mon at LA NL, 0–1; July 26, 1991 (allowed first hit in 10th and lost in 10th)
Pedro Martinez (9 innings) and Mel Rojas (1 inning), Mon. vs. SD NL; 1–0; June 3, 1995 (Martinez pitched 9 perfect innings but allowed a hit in the 10th, Rojas relieved and finished the game)

The Unassisted Triple Play

On May 29, 2000, Oakland A's second baseman Randy Velarde executed the 11th unassisted triple play in major league history. As with the previous 10, it occurred with runners on first and second and was made by an infielder. Velarde made his unassisted triple play in the sixth inning of a game at Yankee Stadium. With Jorge Posada running from first (he got there on Velarde's error), and Tino Martinez running from second, Velarde caught a line drive hit by Shane Spencer. He tagged Posada and then ran over and stepped on second to retire Martinez.

The Cleveland Indians have been involved in five of the major leagues' 11 unassisted triple plays. Indians shortstop Neal Ball executed the first one during a July 19, 1909 doubleheader against the Red Sox at Cleveland's League Park. In the second inning of game one, Ball caught a liner hit by Boston's Amby McConnell, stepped on second base to retire Heinie Wagner before he could get back safely, and then tagged out Jake Stahl before he could return to first.

The most celebrated unassisted triple play, and the only one made in a World Series, was turned in by Cleveland second baseman Bill Wambsganss against Brooklyn in Game 5 of the 1920 Series. The Dodgers trailed 7–0, but their first two batters in the top of the fifth inning (Pete Kilduff and Otto Miller) reached base safely. When Clarence Mitchell—a very good-hitting pitcher—cracked a line drive that appeared to be heading to center field, they both took off running. But Wambsganss had been playing Mitchell perfectly. He made the catch, ran over and doubled Kilduff off second, then turned to find Miller standing in the baseline and tagged him out.

George Burns, playing for the Boston Red Sox (between stints as a member of the Indians), made Cleveland the victim in 1923. On September 14 at Fenway Park, first baseman Burns caught Frank Brower's second-inning liner, tagged Rube Lutzke off first, and ran to second to get Riggs Stephenson before he could return.

Three weeks later, on October 6, shortstop Ernie Padgett of the Boston Braves turned in the National League's first unassisted triple play. It came at Braves Field in the fourth inning of the second game of a season-ending doubleheader. Padgett, playing in only his fourth major league game, speared a liner by Philadelphia's Walter Holke, tagged second base to retire Cotton Tierney, then ran after and tagged Cliff Lee, the baserunner from first.

Pittsburgh shortstop Glenn Wright, playing at home, started his unassisted triple play in the usual manner, by catching a line drive. On May 7, 1925, Wright snared a ninth-inning liner off the bat of the Cardinals' Jim Bottomley, whereupon he doubled Jimmy Cooney off second and tagged out Rogers Hornsby coming from first.

Jimmy Cooney went from victim to perpetrator in 1927. Playing shortstop for the Cubs in a game at Pittsburgh on May 30, he became the only player to be involved in two unassisted triple plays. In the fourth inning, with Clyde Barnhart on first and Lloyd Waner on second both running on the pitch, Cooney caught Paul Waner's line drive. He stepped on second to retire Lloyd Waner and tagged out Barnhart when he reached the bag.

A day later, first baseman Johnny Neun of the Detroit Tigers duplicated the feat, executing the only game-ending unassisted triple play. In the top of the ninth Neun caught a line drive hit by Cleveland's Homer Summa, tagged Charlie Jamieson before he could get back to first, and ran to step on second to retire Glenn Myatt.

Following these back-to-back occurrences, the major leagues did not have another unassisted triple play for 41 years. In the bottom of the first inning of a July 30, 1968 game at Cleveland, the Indians had Dave Nelson on second and Russ Snyder on first. Joe Azcue lined one at Washington Senators shortstop Ron Hansen, who stepped on second to retire Nelson and tagged Snyder coming from first.

Second baseman Mickey Morandini of the Philadelphia Phillies completed the National League's most recent unassisted triple play at Pittsburgh on September 20, 1992. In the home sixth, Morandini made a diving catch of a line drive off the bat of Jeff King. He hustled to second base to double off Andy Van Slyke, and then tagged Barry Bonds who was running from first base. On July 8, 1994, Red Sox shortstop John Valentin became the last American Leaguer before Velarde to make an unassisted triple play. In the top of the sixth inning, the Seattle Mariners had Keith Mitchell on first and Mike Blowers on second. With the runners moving, Valentin caught Marc Newfield's line drive, stepped on second to erase Blowers, then tagged Mitchell who was about to run past him.

Total Baseball has eliminated the unassisted triple play purportedly made by Providence's Paul Hines and carried in previous editions. In the eighth inning of that May 8, 1878 game, Boston had Ezra Sutton at second and Jack Manning at third, when Jack Burdock hit a looping fly ball to short left-center field. Both runners took off, but Hines, the center fielder, caught the ball and stepped on third, retiring Manning and, presumably, Sutton. However, further research has determined that Sutton, the runner from second, had not yet reached third when Hines made the catch. Therefore, stepping on that base could not put him out. Sutton was not officially retired until Hines threw the ball to Providence second baseman Charlie Sweasy, who stepped on that base for the third out.

Unassisted Triple Plays

Player	Team	Pos	Date	OPP	At	Inn.	Batter
Neal Ball	CLE-A	SS	July 19, 1909	BOS	CLE	2 (1G)	Amby McConnell
Bill Wambsganss	CLE-A	2B	October 10, 1920	BRO (NL)	CLE	5	Clarence Mitchell
George Burns	BOS-A	1B	September 14, 1923	CLE	BOS	2	Frank Brower
Ernie Padgett	BOS-N	SS	October 6, 1923	PHI	BOS	4 (2G)	Walter Holke
Glenn Wright	PIT-N	SS	May 7, 1925	STL	PIT	9	Jim Bottomley
Jimmy Cooney	CHI-N	SS	May 30, 1927	PIT	PIT	4	Paul Waner
Johnny Neun	DET-A	1B	May 31, 1927	CLE	DET	9	Homer Summa
Ron Hansen	WAS-A	SS	July 30, 1968	CLE	CLE	1	Joe Azcue
Mickey Morandini	PHI-N	2B	September 20, 1992	PIT	PIT	6	Jeff King
John Valentin	BOS-A	SS	July 8, 1994	SEA	BOS	6	Marc Newfield
Randy Velarde	OAK-A	2B	May 29, 2000	NY	NY	6	Shane Spencer

CHAPTER 8

Awards and Honors

Bill Deane

This chapter presents the history and voting results of baseball's most prestigious awards and honors, including the complete balloting and current constituency of the Baseball Hall of Fame. We have included as complete a selection of results as you'll find anywhere. Our compilation ranges from some of the oldest and best known honors, such as Most Valuable Player, to some of the newest, like our own Ted Williams/*Total Baseball* Award, and some worthy but little-known prizes, such as the Fred Hutchinson Memorial Award. Included are awards for excellence in the regular season, heroics in the All-Star Game, leadership in the postseason, and character off the field. This material will be of interest to the fan who wonders how a player of the past was viewed by his contemporaries. I have ventured an additional section of "what if" awards: what if the Cy Young Award had been instituted long before its actual inception in 1956, or the Rookie of the Year before its real debut in 1947, and so on.

Balloting tables and lists of winners include each player's first initial, last name, and club city abbreviation (and point total, if applicable).

Most Valuable Player Award: History

The concept of most valuable player awards dates back more than a century. The first documented MVP-type honor in pro ball was bestowed upon James "Deacon" White of the 1875 Boston Red Stockings in the National Association. Catcher White sparked Boston to a remarkable 71-8 record that year, scoring 77 runs in 80 games and batting .355. An ardent Red Stockings' admirer presented Deacon with a silver tray, water pitcher, and loving cup inscribed with the words: WON BY JIM WHITE AS MOST VALUABLE PLAYER TO BOSTON TEAM, 1875.

The first official MVP honor was initiated some 35 years later. Prior to the 1910 season, baseball fan Hugh Chalmers, president and general manager of the Chalmers Motor Company, announced that he would present one of his company's automobiles—a Chalmers "30"—to the major league player who compiled the highest batting average. What appeared to be a harmless promotional gimmick was to soon turn into a public relations disaster.

The rules specified that players must accumulate a specific minimum number of times at bat, depending on position, to qualify for the award. For infielders and outfielders, it was a minimum of 350 at bats; for catchers, 250 at bats; and for pitchers, 100 at bats. Interest in the award was tremendous from the outset. Ty Cobb, who already owned a Chalmers "30" roadster, wrote: "I am glad that something besides medals and trophies is offered for the championship in batting. I think the offer of a Chalmers "30" is simply great and I hope to be lucky enough to own a new Chalmers next fall."

It developed into a two-man race, with Detroit's Cobb and Cleveland's Napoleon Lajoie, both American Leaguers, the only serious challengers for the coveted prize. Throughout the season there were charges and countercharges of favoritism by scorers in various cities. Furthermore, the general consensus of the press was that Cobb's selfish pursuit of this individual honor had cost his team the pennant. The controversy was capped by scandalous circumstances on the final day of the season.

Through games of September 16, Cobb held a solid lead over Lajoie, .368 to .357 (although, because of the era's sloppy record keeping, few actually knew the official figures at the time). From then through October 8, Cobb batted a torrid .532 (25-for-47) to seemingly lock up the crown with a .383 average. But Lajoie refused to surrender, going 30-for-54 (.556) in that same span to enter the final day, October 9, with a .376 mark. Cobb chose to sit out his final game, while Lajoie played the infamous doubleheader with the St. Louis Browns in which he went 8-for-8, including seven bunt hits—remarkable for a slow-footed slugger—to apparently edge out Cobb in the batting race. Browns' manager Jack O'Connor had instructed his rookie third baseman, Red Corriden, to play deep on Lajoie, advice with which Corriden complied. Lajoie took advantage of the strange defensive arrangement with the repeated safe bunts. Although neither Lajoie nor Corriden were implicated, there were charges of a Browns' frame-up to give the coveted batting title (and car) to the respected Lajoie over the disliked Cobb.

O'Connor lost his job due to his role in the alleged fix. Subsequently, AL president Ban Johnson announced that a "discrepancy" had been found in the official records, and that Cobb had actually won the batting crown after all (although this point is challenged by many current researchers, who have evidence that Cobb was credited wrongly for a 2-for-3 game). Meanwhile, Hugh Chalmers, attempting to divorce himself from the controversy, presented autos to both Cobb and Lajoie. It was generally acknowledged that this fiasco doomed the future of individual awards of any kind.

Hoping to salvage some goodwill out of the whole idea, Chalmers came up with a new proposal for the 1911 season. This time he would award an auto to one player in each league who "should prove himself as the most important and useful player to his club and to the league at large in point of deportment and value of services rendered." The decision for this honor was to be made by a committee of baseball writers, one writer from each club city in each league. Each writer was to make eight selections, with a first-place ballot scoring eight points, on down to an eighth-place vote counting one point. Thus was born the short-lived Chalmers Award, with Ty Cobb and Frank Schulte earning recognition in 1911. Both Cobb and Schulte voluntarily withdrew from the competition in 1912, although the former received 17 points anyway.

Interest in the award diminished within a few years. By 1914 the public was distracted by baseball's battles with the new Federal League and the escalation of the World War in Europe. The timing was right for the Chalmers Award to quietly disappear; it was noted that Mr. Chalmers had agreed to present vehicles for five years and that the 1914 awards marked the fifth presentations.

On July 15, 1922, the newly formed American League Trophy Committee adopted a set of rules governing the selection of an annual award-winner. The rules specified that "the purpose of the American League Trophy is to honor the baseball player who is of greatest all-round service to his club and credit to the sport during each season; to recognize and reward uncommon skill and ability when exercised by a player for the best interests of his team, and to perpetuate his memory." The rules further instructed voters to seek out the "winning ball player," reminding them that "combined offensive and defensive ability is not always indicated by any system of records."

Eight baseball writers, one from each AL city, were enfranchised, with each required to select exactly one player from each team, for a total of eight selections. Player-managers and previous winners were to be excluded from consideration. Points were distributed the same as in the Chalmers Award: eight for first place, down to one for eighth.

The intention of Ban Johnson was to have a monument to baseball erected in East Potomac Park, Washington, D.C., engraved with the names of winners of the AL Award. This proposal was introduced as a congressional resolution in 1924, and passed in the House of Representatives before dying on the Senate Floor.

The AL voting rules led to growing criticism for several reasons, one of which was the limitation on the number of vote-getters from each team. For example, when the Browns' George Sisler won the first AL Award in 1922, he was named on all eight ballots—thus disqualifying his teammates from receiving any votes. As a result, fellow Brownie Ken Williams, who led the league in home runs (39), RBIs (155), and total bases (367) and became the first player ever to have 30 homers and 30 stolen bases in the same season, was shut out in the voting. Secondly, the rule prohibiting player-managers from eligibility drew fire. In 1925, when this rule eliminated five solid candidates from consideration, *The New York Times* wrote, "to say that it is impossible or impractical to divorce a man's managerial skill from his talents purely as a player is to reflect on the intelligence of the committee that awards the prize."

The *Times* further editorialized on the fallacy of assuming that no player can be the "most valuable" more than one year: "the purpose, of course, is to pass the honor around, but the effect is to pass an empty honor around." This rule became increasingly ridiculous when it eliminated Babe Ruth (and his 60 home runs) from consideration in 1927; by the following year, both Ruth and teammate Lou Gehrig, who were in the process of finishing one-two in the AL home run derby in five consecutive seasons, were ineligible for the League Award.

In 1924 the National League instituted its own award, with radical differences in the selection method: each writer voted for 10 players rather than eight (with 10 points for first place, and so on); he was not bound to vote for a certain number of players from each team; he was free to select a player-manager; and, later, he was allowed to consider previous winners of the award. Additionally, the NL offered a cash "present" of $1,000 to the award-winner.

At various times between 1925 and 1951, writers were permitted to name "honorable mention" candidates, whose vote totals were listed but not counted in the balloting. Another feature of early voting reports was the listing of "cumulative vote leaders"—a forerunner to Bill James's "award shares"—over a period of years.

A number of factors led to the demise of the AL Award, including the award's loss of credibility due to the previously mentioned shortsighted voting rules. Secondly, Ban Johnson, having failed to secure the erection of his proposed monument, felt the award had fallen short of its aim. Finally, management was concerned with the efforts of award-winners to parlay their honors into substantial pay raises. The AL Award was officially voted out at a special league meeting on May 6, 1929.

The National League followed suit with the AL's decision, but agreed to continue its award through the 1929 season.

In October 1929 the Baseball Writers' Association of America (BBWAA) announced the results of an "unofficial" AL most valuable player poll, whose winner was Lew Fonseca of Cleveland.

Two months later, *The Sporting News* (TSN) conducted a poll of the eight writers who had previously voted on the League Award, thereby reporting Al Simmons as the "unofficial" AL Award-winner. Combining the results of these two unofficial polls gives Fonseca 77 points, followed by Heinie Manush (57), Simmons (56), Tony Lazzeri (55) and Charlie Gehringer (44).

In 1930, TSN chose Joe Cronin in the AL and Bill Terry in the NL. Earlier, the Associated Press also had a special committee of writers make an unofficial AL selection for 1930, while the BBWAA did the same for the NL (adding a check for $1,000 for the winner). The respective selections here were Cronin in the AL and Hack Wilson in the NL. Again combining the two sets of polls, the AL leaders were Cronin (100), Al Simmons (85), Lou Gehrig (68), Charlie Gehringer (67), and Ted Lyons (56). The NL pace-setters were Hack Wilson (111), Frankie Frisch (107), Bill Terry (105), Chuck Klein (57), and Floyd "Babe" Herman (52).

In an effort to standardize MVP voting, the BBWAA, in its annual winter meeting in New York on Dec. 11, 1930, decided to appoint two committees (one in each league) to elect Most Valuable Players, with the association to "award suitable emblems to the players selected." Thus was born what is considered the modern MVP Award, with most of the flaws of its forerunners eliminated.

TSN, however, continued to make its own selections in bitter competition with the BBWAA. Finally, beginning in 1938, TSN agreed to unify the award by abiding with BBWAA balloting, and presenting *The Sporting News* Trophy to the winner. Among the various prizes awarded to the winners were wristwatches and shotguns.

At a meeting during the 1944 World Series, the BBWAA decided to begin issuing its own trophy, the Kenesaw Mountain Landis Award, in honor of the ailing commissioner. Landis died a month later and the official MVP Award has born his name ever since. A plaque engraved with the names of the winners hangs in the National Baseball Library.

The Sporting News went back to naming its own MVPs in 1944 and '45. Then, at the request of the new commissioner, Happy Chandler, TSN "withdrew from the field to cooperate in making the Landis Awards, provided by the major leagues, the official designations of the year." In 1948, however, TSN went back to its own awards, selecting a Player of the Year and Pitcher of the Year in each league, as they have done ever since. For whatever reason, TSN awards have never received the public recognition that the BBWAA honors have.

Two major changes in the MVP voting began in 1938. The BBWAA began polling three writers in each major league city, rather than just one, which remained in effect until it was reduced to two writers per city, starting in 1961. Also in 1938, the process was initiated to award 14 points for each first-place vote, rather than 10.

"Split votes," which have since infiltrated all the major awards, first appeared in MVP Awards in 1959. The American League MVP race that year, by consensus, was between second baseman Nellie Fox and shortstop Luis Aparicio of the champion Chicago White Sox. Late in the season, the suggestion often arose that the two ought to share the award. When the votes were in, Fox had received 14 first-place votes, Aparicio had gotten six, and four writers had split their votes between the two. Tickled with the idea of a split vote, one NL writer also resorted to this option, dividing his first-place nomination between Ernie Banks and Eddie Mathews. The "cop-out vote," having been allowed in '59, has since surfaced in 16 more MVP Awards, 10 Rookie of the Year, and six Cy Young Award elections. The ultimate folly of this practice was best exemplified in 1979. One NL writer split his fourth-place vote between pitching brothers Phil and Joe Niekro, evidently convinced that the two were identical twins. But the writer was still permitted to make six more selections. That meant that his fifth-, sixth-, and seventh-place selections received more points (six, five and four, respectively) than his fourth-place co-selections, who were credited with just three and a half points apiece! The 1979 NL vote, incidentally, resulted in the only actual split MVP as sentimental favorite Willie Stargell of the Pittsburgh Pirates and batting champion Keith Hernandez of the St. Louis Cardinals each received 216 votes and were declared "co-MVP."

There has long been debate about the consideration of pitchers for the MVP Award, the theory (by some) that a man who plays every fourth game cannot be as valuable as a man who plays every day. The debate escalated after the inception of the Cy Young Award in 1956, giving pitchers their own exclusive honor, and the increasing practice of five-man rotations in the 1970s, giving starting pitchers even less of a chance to contribute.

As far as Jack Lang, assistant secretary of the BBWAA, is concerned, there is no room for controversy. "The rules that are sent out to the voters on the [MVP] committee state: 'Keep in mind that all players are eligible. That includes pitchers, starters and relievers,'" says Lang. "Anybody on the committee that feels they cannot vote for a pitcher, we replace them. In my 24 years running the elections, only two writers have said that to me." Since 1931 pitchers have won the award 10 times in the AL and nine times in the NL.

There have been 16 occasions in which one player received all of the available first-place MVP votes in his league. The AL players so honored are Ty Cobb (1911), Babe Ruth (1923), Hank Greenberg (1935), Al Rosen (1953), Mickey Mantle (1956), Frank Robinson (1966), Denny McLain (1968), Reggie Jackson (1973), Jose Canseco (1988), Frank Thomas (1993), and Ken Griffey Jr. (1997). The five unanimous NL selections are Carl Hubbell (1936), Orlando Cepeda (1967), Mike Schmidt (1980), Jeff Bagwell (1994), and Ken Caminiti (1996). Hubbell's distinction is disputable, as two of the eight writers did not submit ballots that year and were not replaced on the selection committee.

Following are the maximum possible point totals that could have been earned by an individual receiving the first-place nomination of every writer polled:

NATIONAL LEAGUE		AMERICAN LEAGUE	
1911–14	64	1911–14	64
1924–29	80	1922–28	64
1931–37	80	1931–37	80
1938–60	336	1938–60	336
1961	224	1961–68	280
1962–68	280	1969–76	336
1969–92	336	1977–present	392
1993–97	392		
1998–present	448		

There have been numerous cases in which the MVP vote point totals did not add up to the correct figure. Reasons for this include inaccuracies in tabulation, inaccuracies in reporting, and writers who failed to vote or to complete their ballots. However, the total impact of all these errors is a small fraction of 1 percent of the total voting over the years.

Following is a complete tabulation of all the recognized MVP elections since 1911:

MVP Award: Chalmers Award, 1911–14

1911 NATIONAL
F. Schulte, CHI 29
C. Mathewson, NY 25
L. Doyle, NY 23
H. Wagner, PIT 23
G. Alexander, PHI 23
M. Huggins, SL 21
F. Merkle, NY 19
R. Marquard, NY 19
J. Daubert, BRO 16
J. Tinker, CHI 11
C. Meyers, NY 11
J. Sheckard, CHI 9
M. Mitchell, CIN 9
M. Doolan, PHI 6
B. Harmon, SL 6
J. Archer, CHI 5
H. Lobert, PHI 4
G. Gibson, PIT 4
M. Brown, CHI 4
B. Bescher, CIN 4
B. Sweeney, BOS 3
O. Knabe, PHI 2
E. Konetchy, SL 2
D. Hoblitzell, CIN 2
J. Walsh, PHI 2
J. Devore, NY 2
F. Luderus, PHI 1
J. Kling, BOS 1
B. Adams, PIT 1
N. Rucker, BRO 1

1911 AMERICAN
T. Cobb, DET 64
E. Walsh, CHI 35
E. Collins, PHI 32
J. Jackson, CLE 28
W. Johnson, WAS 19
B. Cree, NY 16
T. Speaker, BOS 16
I. Thomas, PHI 12
C. Milan, WAS 10
V. Gregg, CLE 9
F. Baker, PHI 8
J. Coombs, PHI 6
N. Lajoie, CLE 5
J. Knight, NY 4
S. Crawford, DET 4
B. Lord, PHI 4
D. Bush, DET 4
R. Ford, NY 3
J. Barry, PHI 3
J. Austin, SL 2
F. LaPorte, SL 2
S. McInnis, PHI 1
G. McBride, WAS 1

1912 NATIONAL
L. Doyle, NY 48
H. Wagner, PIT 43
C. Meyers, NY 25
J. Tinker, CHI 22
B. Bescher, CIN 17
B. Sweeney, BOS 16
H. Zimmerman, CHI 16
R. Marquard, NY 13
O. Wilson, PIT 13
J. Daubert, BRO 13
O. Knabe, PHI 10
E. Konetchy, SL 8
C. Mathewson, NY 8
D. Paskert, PHI 6
J. Tesreau, NY 6
R. Murray, NY 5
M. Huggins, SL 5
A. Marsans, CIN 4
F. Merkle, NY 4
J. Evers, CHI 2
C. Hendrix, PIT 2
J. Archer, CHI 1
G. Alexander, PHI 1

1912 AMERICAN
T. Speaker, BOS 59
E. Walsh, CHI 30
W. Johnson, WAS 28
C. Milan, WAS 23
J. Wood, BOS 22
E. Collins, PHI 18
F. Baker, PHI 17
T. Cobb, DET 17
J. Jackson, CLE 16
H. Wagner, BOS 12
C. Gandil, WAS 7
B. Shotton, SL 6
D. Pratt, SL 5
E. Foster, WAS 4
L. Gardner, BOS 4
S. Crawford, DET 4
J. Barry, PHI 4
B. Carrigan, BOS 3
G. Moriarty, DET 3
J. Birmingham, CLE 2
D. Moeller, WAS 1
G. McBride, WAS 1
S. McInnis, PHI 1
B. Daniels, NY 1

1913 NATIONAL
J. Daubert, BRO 50
G. Cravath, PHI 40
R. Maranville, BOS 23
C. Mathewson, NY 21
C. Meyers, NY 20
V. Saier, CHI 15
L. Cheney, CHI 12
D. Miller, PIT 11
H. Wagner, PIT 11
J. Evers, CHI 10
T. Seaton, PHI 9
A. Fletcher, NY 7
J. Archer, CHI 6
M. Doolan, PHI 6
B. Sweeney, BOS 6
J. Viox, PIT 6
L. Doyle, NY 5
T. Shafer, NY 5
R. Murray, NY 4
H. Zimmerman, CHI 4
O. Knabe, PHI 4
B. Adams, PIT 3
G. Cutshaw, BRO 3
G. Burns, NY 2
A. Marsans, CIN 2
B. Humphries, CHI 2
M. Brown, CIN 1

1913 AMERICAN
W. Johnson, WAS 54
J. Jackson, CLE 43
E. Collins, PHI 30
T. Speaker, BOS 26
F. Baker, PHI 21
C. Gandil, WAS 14
S. McInnis, PHI 12
W. Schang, PHI 11
C. Milan, WAS 8
J. Barry, PHI 8
N. Lajoie, CLE 7
D. Bush, DET 6
H. Wagner, BOS 6
R. Russell, CHI 5
B. Shotton, SL 5
G. McBride, WAS 5
J. Scott, CHI 5
G. Stovall, SL 5
S. Crawford, DET 5
T. Cobb, DET 3
R. Schalk, CHI 3
C. Bender, PHI 2
T. Turner, CLE 2
S. O'Neill, CLE 1
H. Hooper, BOS 1

1914 NATIONAL
J. Evers, BOS 50
R. Maranville, BOS 44
B. James, BOS 33
G. Burns, NY 31
J. Miller, SL 18
J. Tesreau, NY 15
D. Rudolph, BOS 14
S. Magee, PHI 14
Z. Wheat, BRO 10
G. Alexander, PHI 9
R. Bresnahan, CHI 6
L. Magee, SL 6
B. Doak, SL 5
J. Viox, PIT 5
A. Fletcher, NY 5
C. Mathewson, NY 4
V. Saier, CHI 4
B. Schmidt, BOS 4
J. Daubert, BRO 4
L. McCarty, BRO 3
H. Groh, CIN 2
T. Clarke, CIN 1
G. Cravath, PHI 1

1914 AMERICAN
E. Collins, PHI 63
S. Crawford, DET 35
D. Bush, DET 17
F. Baker, PHI 17
J. Jackson, CLE 15
R. Schalk, CHI 13
E. Foster, WAS 11
B. Weaver, CHI 11
S. McInnis, PHI 11
D. Pratt, SL 10
W. Schang, PHI 10
T. Speaker, BOS 9
T. Walker, SL 9
T. Cobb, DET 7
E. Scott, BOS 7
J. Barry, PHI 6
D. Leonard, BOS 6
E. Plank, PHI 5
G. McBride, WAS 5
D. Lewis, BOS 4
H. Hooper, BOS 4
F. Maisel, NY 3
R. Peckinpaugh, NY 2
C. Milan, WAS 2
S. Agnew, SL 2
R. Hartzell, NY 2
E. Cicotte, CHI 1
G. Moriarty, DET 1

(No official awards, 1915–21)

MVP Award: League Awards, 1922–29

1922 AMERICAN
G. Sisler, SL 59
E. Rommel, PHI 31
R. Schalk, CHI 26
L. Bush, NY 19
E. Collins, CHI 18
J. Bassler, DET 13
S. O'Neill, CLE 13
J. Judge, WAS 12
W. Pipp, NY 12
L. Blue, DET 11
C. Galloway, PHI 10
H. Heilmann, DET 8
D. Pratt, BOS 7
W. Schang, NY 7
B. Meusel, NY 6
E. Scott, NY 6
W. Johnson, WAS 5
U. Shocker, SL 5
C. Jamieson, CLE 4
J. Sewell, CLE 4
G. Burns, BOS 2
J. Dykes, PHI 2
B. Harris, WAS 2
R. Peckinpaugh, WAS 2
B. Wambsganss, CLE 2
G. Cutshaw, DET 1
C. Perkins, PHI 1

1923 AMERICAN
B. Ruth, NY 64
E. Collins, CHI 37
H. Heilmann, DET 31
W. Gerber, SL 20
J. Sewell, CLE 20
C. Jamieson, CLE 19
J. Bassler, DET 17
C. Galloway, PHI 13
G. Uhle, CLE 13
G. Burns, BOS 8
H. Ehmke, BOS 7
M. Ruel, WAS 7
R. Peckinpaugh, WAS 6
U. Shocker, SL 5
J. Judge, WAS 4
M. McManus, SL 4
K. Williams, SL 4
J. Harris, BOS 3
B. Harris, WAS 3
J. Hauser, PHI 1
W. Johnson, WAS 1
C. Perkins, PHI 1

(No National League awards, 1922–23)

1924 NATIONAL
D. Vance, BRO 74
R. Hornsby, SL 62
F. Frisch, NY 40
Z. Wheat, BRO 40
R. Youngs, NY 35
G. Kelly, NY 34
R. Maranville, PIT 33
K. Cuyler, PIT 25
J. Fournier, BRO 21
E. Roush, CIN 12
G. Wright, PIT 10
A. High, BRO 9
B. Pinelli, CIN 7
R. Bressler, CIN 6
G. Hartnett, CHI 5
B. Grimes, BRO 5
J. Bottomley, SL 4
J. Johnston, BRO 3
M. Carey, PIT 3
T. Jackson, NY 3
E. Yde, PIT 2
C. Williams, PHI 1
E. Rixey, CIN 1
G. Alexander, CHI 1
H. DeBerry, BRO 1

1924 AMERICAN
W. Johnson, WAS 55
E. Collins, CHI 49
C. Jamieson, CLE 25
H. Pennock, NY 24
J. Bassler, DET 22
H. Severeid, SL 17
J. Hauser, PHI 13
W. Jacobson, SL 11
H. Heilmann, DET 9
J. Sewell, CLE 9
M. Ruel, WAS 7
W. Schang, NY 7
A. Simmons, PHI 7
W. Pipp, NY 6
H. Ehmke, BOS 5
I. Flagstead, BOS 5
W. Gerber, SL 4
E. Whitehill, DET 4
L. Blue, DET 3
I. Boone, BOS 2
J. Harris, BOS 2
C. Galloway, PHI 1
K. Williams, SL 1

1925 NATIONAL
R. Hornsby, SL 73
K. Cuyler, PIT 61
G. Kelly, NY 52
G. Wright, PIT 43
D. Vance, BRO 42
D. Bancroft, BOS 41
J. Bottomley, SL 28
P. Traynor, PIT 27
F. Frisch, NY 13
E. Roush, CIN 12
M. Carey, PIT 11
I. Meusel, NY 6
D. Luque, CIN 5
C. Grimm, CHI 5
Z. Wheat, BRO 4
P. Donohue, CIN 4
B. Hargrave, CIN 4
G. Harper, PHI 3
J. Sand, PHI 3
W. Gautreau, BOS 2
V. Aldridge, PIT 1

1925 AMERICAN
R. Peckinpaugh, WAS 45
A. Simmons, PHI 41
J. Sewell, CLE 21
H. Heilmann, DET 20
H. Rice, SL 18
E. Sheely, CHI 17
I. Flagstead, BOS 10
W. Jacobson, SL 10
J. Mostil, CHI 10
O. Bluege, WAS 8
M. Cochrane, PHI 8
L. Blue, DET 7
S. Coveleski, WAS 7
W. Kamm, CHI 7
E. Rommel, PHI 7
R. Schalk, CHI 7
A. Wingo, DET 7
E. Combs, NY 6
B. Meusel, NY 6
T. Lyons, CHI 5
G. Burns, CLE 4
M. McManus, SL 4
H. Pennock, NY 4
B. Bengough, NY 2
H. Ehmke, BOS 2
L. Gehrig, NY 2
I. Boone, BOS 1
J. Dugan, NY 1
P. Todt, BOS 1

1926 NATIONAL
B. O'Farrell, SL 79
H. Critz, CIN 60
R. Kremer, PIT 32
T. Thevenow, SL 30
H. Wilson, CHI 25
L. Bell, SL 24
B. Hargrave, CIN 24
F. Rhem, SL 20
F. Lindstrom, NY 17
D. Bancroft, BOS 17
H. Carlson, PHI 16
P. Waner, PIT 15
P. Traynor, PIT 14
W. Pipp, CIN 12
E. Brown, BOS 10
F. Herman, BRO 8
C. Root, CHI 8
R. Hornsby, SL 7
J. Butler, BRO 5
B. Southworth, NY-SL 5
G. Alexander, CHI-SL 5
C. Mays, CIN 4
G. Kelly, NY 2
C. Walker, CIN 1

1926 AMERICAN
G. Burns, CLE 63
J. Mostil, CHI 33
H. Pennock, NY 32
S. Rice, WAS 18
H. Heilmann, DET 16
H. Manush, DET 16
A. Simmons, PHI 16
L. Grove, PHI 12
G. Goslin, WAS 9
L. Gehrig, NY 7
T. Lazzeri, NY 7
B. Falk, CHI 6
F. Fothergill, DET 6
O. Melillo, SL 6
H. Rice, SL 6
O. Bluege, WAS 5
P. Todt, BOS 5
M. Cochrane, PHI 4
J. Judge, WAS 4
M. McManus, SL 4
B. Meusel, NY 3
E. Rigney, BOS 3
I. Flagstead, BOS 2
W. Gerber, SL 2
T. Zachary, SL 2
W. Jacobson, SL-BOS 1

1927 NATIONAL
P. Waner, PIT 72
F. Frisch, SL 66
R. Hornsby, NY 54
C. Root, CHI 46
T. Jackson, NY 42
L. Waner, PIT 25
P. Traynor, PIT 18
J. Haines, SL 16
R. Kremer, PIT 14
G. Hartnett, CHI 12
R. Lucas, CIN 10
H. Wilson, CHI 9
B. Terry, NY 6
J. Bottomley, SL 6
B. Hargrave, CIN 6
F. May, CIN 6
C. Williams, PHI 6
D. Farrell, NY-BOS 4
B. Grimes, NY 4
M. Carey, BRO 3
R. Stephenson, CHI 3
G. Alexander, SL 3
C. Hill, PIT 2
J. Petty, BRO 2
F. Ulrich, PHI 2
C. Hafey, SL 1

1927 AMERICAN
L. Gehrig, NY 56
H. Heilmann, DET 35
T. Lyons, CHI 34

M. Cochrane, PHI ... 18
A. Simmons, PHI ... 18
G. Goslin, WAS ... 15
M. Ruel, WAS ... 15
J. Dykes, PHI ... 14
L. Sewell, CLE ... 13
J. Sewell, CLE ... 9
T. Lazzeri, NY ... 8
R. Reeves, WAS ... 7
F. O'Rourke, SL ... 6
J. Tavener, DET ... 6
H. Lisenbee, WAS ... 5
E. Miller, SL ... 5
A. Metzler, CHI ... 4
I. Flagstead, BOS ... 3
C. Jamieson, CLE ... 3
W. Schang, SL ... 3
F. Schulte, SL ... 3
W. Hudlin, CLE ... 2
W. Regan, BOS ... 2
J. Rothrock, BOS ... 2
B. Harriss, BOS ... 1
P. Todt, BOS ... 1

1928 NATIONAL
J. Bottomley, SL ... 76
F. Lindstrom, NY ... 70
B. Grimes, PIT ... 53
L. Benton, NY ... 37
H. Critz, CIN ... 37
P. Traynor, PIT ... 28
H. Wilson, CHI ... 21
S. Hogan, NY ... 17
T. Jackson, NY ... 16
R. Maranville, SL ... 14
D. Vance, BRO ... 13
C. Hafey, SL ... 11
R. Hornsby, BOS ... 10
G. Hartnett, CHI ... 6
P. Waner, PIT ... 5
L. Richbourg, BOS ... 5
T. Douthit, SL ... 5
D. Bissonette, BRO ... 3
D. Flowers, BRO ... 3
J. Wilson, PHI-SL ... 3
A. Whitney, PHI ... 3
H. Ford, CIN ... 2
L. Thompson, PHI ... 1

1928 AMERICAN
M. Cochrane, PHI ... 53
H. Manush, SL ... 51
J. Judge, WAS ... 27
T. Lazzeri, NY ... 27
W. Kamm, CHI ... 15
G. Goslin, WAS ... 13
E. Combs, NY ... 13
C. Gehringer, DET ... 12
C. Myer, BOS ... 11
W. Hoyt, NY ... 8
J. Foxx, PHI ... 7
J. Sewell, CLE ... 6
L. Sewell, CLE ... 6
I. Flagstead, BOS ... 5
E. Morris, BOS ... 4
H. Heilmann, DET ... 4
C. Lind, CLE ... 4
W. Cissell, CHI ... 4
A. Thomas, CHI ... 4
O. Carroll, DET ... 3
H. Rice, DET ... 3
L. Fonseca, CLE ... 2
T. Lyons, CHI ... 2
J. Hodapp, CLE ... 2
A. Metzler, CHI ... 1
W. Regan, BOS ... 1

1929 NATIONAL
R. Hornsby, CHI ... 60
L. O'Doul, PHI ... 54
B. Terry, NY ... 48
B. Grimes, PIT ... 35
L. Waner, PIT ... 30
R. Lucas, CIN ... 29
P. Traynor, PIT ... 27
H. Wilson, CHI ... 24
F. Herman, BRO ... 24
G. Bush, CHI ... 16
C. Klein, PHI ... 15
M. Ott, NY ... 15
T. Douthit, SL ... 14
C. Grimm, CHI ... 13
T. Jackson, NY ... 8
R. Maranville, BOS ... 8
H. Critz, CIN ... 5
B. Friberg, PHI ... 4
P. Malone, CHI ... 3
F. Frisch, SL ... 2
P. Whitney, PHI ... 2
J. Frederick, BRO ... 2
R. Stephenson, CHI ... 1
Z. Taylor, BOS-CHI ... 1

(There were no official selections for the American League in 1929 or for either league in 1930.)

MVP Award:
Baseball Writers' Association of America Awards, 1931–Present

1931 NATIONAL
F. Frisch, SL ... 65
C. Klein, PHI ... 55
B. Terry, NY ... 53
W. English, CHI ... 30
C. Hafey, SL ... 29
J. Wilson, SL ... 28
T. Jackson, NY ... 24
C. Grimm, CHI ... 21
E. Adams, SL ... 18
E. Brandt, BOS ... 15
R. Maranville, BOS ... 15
K. Cuyler, CHI ... 14
P. Traynor, PIT ... 12
R. Lucas, CIN ... 10
L. Waner, PIT ... 8
J. Bottomley, SL ... 8
J. Elliott, PHI ... 6
J. Quinn, BRO ... 6
N. Finn, BRO ... 5
W. Clark, BRO ... 3
P. Derringer, SL ... 3
C. Root, CHI ... 3
D. Bartell, PHI ... 2
J. Vergez, NY ... 2
F. Fitzsimmons, NY ... 1
L. O'Doul, BRO ... 1
G. Wright, BRO ... 1
T. Cuccinello, CIN ... 1
C. Gelbert, SL ... 1

1931 AMERICAN
L. Grove, PHI ... 78
L. Gehrig, NY ... 59
A. Simmons, PHI ... 51
E. Averill, CLE ... 43
B. Ruth, NY ... 40
E. Webb, BOS ... 22
J. Cronin, WAS ... 18
O. Melillo, SL ... 17
S. West, WAS ... 16
M. Cochrane, PHI ... 16
G. Earnshaw, PHI ... 12
W. Ferrell, CLE ... 12
F. Marberry, WAS ... 11
H. Rhyne, BOS ... 10
B. Chapman, NY ... 7
J. Stone, DET ... 6
C. Gehringer, DET ... 4
L. Blue, CHI ... 4
R. Kress, SL ... 3
C. Reynolds, CHI ... 2
W. Stewart, SL ... 2
G. Goslin, SL ... 2
D. MacFayden, BOS ... 2
T. Oliver, BOS ... 2
J. Foxx, PHI ... 1

1932 NATIONAL
C. Klein, PHI ... 78
L. Warneke, CHI ... 68
L. O'Doul, BRO ... 58
P. Waner, PIT ... 37
R. Stephenson, CHI ... 32
B. Terry, NY ... 25
D. Hurst, PHI ... 24
P. Traynor, PIT ... 17
B. Herman, CHI ... 16
M. Ott, NY ... 15
R. Brown, BOS ... 10
F. Herman, CIN ... 8
L. Waner, PIT ... 6
W. Berger, BOS ... 6
H. Wilson, BRO ... 6
E. Orsatti, SL ... 6
R. Maranville, BOS ... 5
J. Wilson, SL ... 5
T. Cuccinello, BRO ... 4
J. Dean, SL ... 4
F. Frisch, SL ... 3
R. Collins, SL ... 3
A. Vaughan, PIT ... 1
G. Bush, CHI ... 1

1932 AMERICAN
J. Foxx, PHI ... 75
L. Gehrig, NY ... 55
H. Manush, WAS ... 41
E. Averill, CLE ... 37
L. Gomez, NY ... 27
J. Cronin, WAS ... 26
B. Ruth, NY ... 26
T. Lazzeri, NY ... 21
A. Simmons, PHI ... 13
C. Gehringer, DET ... 13
D. Alexander, DET-BOS ... 10
W. Cissell, CHI-CLE ... 10
R. Ferrell, SL ... 9
L. Grove, PHI ... 8
J. Allen, NY ... 8
B. Dickey, NY ... 8
G. Goslin, SL ... 7
M. Weaver, WAS ... 6
H. Davis, DET ... 5
D. Harris, WAS ... 5
W. Ferrell, CLE ... 5
J. Levey, SL ... 5
T. Lyons, CHI ... 5
B. Sullivan, CHI ... 3
E. McNair, PHI ... 3
S. Jolley, CHI-BOS ... 3
G. Crowder, WAS ... 2
M. McManus, BOS ... 2
G. Walker, DET ... 1
J. Sewell, NY ... 1

1933 NATIONAL
C. Hubbell, NY ... 77
C. Klein, PHI ... 48
W. Berger, BOS ... 44
B. Terry, NY ... 35
P. Martin, SL ... 31
G. Mancuso, NY ... 24
J. Dean, SL ... 23
P. Traynor, PIT ... 20
B. Ryan, NY ... 19
A. Lopez, BRO ... 18
B. Cantwell, BOS ... 18
H. Schumacher, NY ... 11
R. Maranville, BOS ... 11
G. Bush, CHI ... 11
L. French, PIT ... 10
F. Frisch, SL ... 7
J. Bottomley, CIN ... 6
J. Medwick, SL ... 5
G. Hartnett, CHI ... 5
L. Warneke, CHI ... 4
R. Lucas, CIN ... 3
D. Bartell, PHI ... 3
A. Vaughan, PIT ... 2
R. Moore, BOS ... 2
V. Davis, PHI ... 1
C. Hafey, CIN ... 1
D. Luque, NY ... 1

1933 AMERICAN
J. Foxx, PHI ... 74
J. Cronin, WAS ... 62
H. Manush, WAS ... 54
L. Gehrig, NY ... 39
L. Grove, PHI ... 35
C. Gehringer, DET ... 32
G. Crowder, WAS ... 28
A. Simmons, CHI ... 19
E. Whitehill, WAS ... 18
O. Melillo, SL ... 12
S. West, SL ... 11
R. Ferrell, SL-BOS ... 9
B. Dickey, NY ... 9
T. Lazzeri, NY ... 6
J. Kuhel, WAS ... 5
E. Averill, CLE ... 5
C. Myer, WAS ... 5
M. Cochrane, PHI ... 5
B. Johnson, PHI ... 5
B. Chapman, NY ... 4
M. Bishop, PHI ... 1
L. Appling, CHI ... 1
W. Kamm, CLE ... 1

1934 NATIONAL
J. Dean, SL ... 78
P. Waner, PIT ... 50
J. Moore, NY ... 42
T. Jackson, NY ... 39
M. Ott, NY ... 37
R. Collins, SL ... 32
B. Terry, NY ... 30
C. Davis, PHI ... 18
P. Dean, SL ... 16
H. Schumacher, NY ... 16
C. Hubbell, NY ... 16
W. Berger, BOS ... 13
L. Warneke, CHI ... 10
G. Hartnett, CHI ... 9
G. Slade, CIN ... 5
K. Cuyler, CHI ... 4
B. Frey, CIN ... 4
F. Frankhouse, BOS ... 4
R. Boyle, BRO ... 4
B. Herman, CHI ... 4
F. Frisch, SL ... 4
W. Hoyt, PIT ... 2
A. Lopez, BRO ... 1
V. Mungo, BRO ... 1
A. Vaughan, PIT ... 1

1934 AMERICAN
M. Cochrane, DET ... 67
C. Gehringer, DET ... 65
L. Gomez, NY ... 60
S. Rowe, DET ... 59
L. Gehrig, NY ... 54
H. Greenberg, DET ... 29
H. Trosky, CLE ... 18
W. Ferrell, BOS ... 16
M. Owen, DET ... 13
J. Foxx, PHI ... 11
A. Simmons, CHI ... 9
W. Werber, BOS ... 8
R. Johnson, BOS ... 8
G. Goslin, DET ... 6
S. West, SL ... 5
M. Harder, CLE ... 4
F. Higgins, PHI ... 3
E. Averill, CLE ... 3
B. Knickerbocker, CLE ... 2

1935 NATIONAL
G. Hartnett, CHI ... 75
J. Dean, SL ... 66
A. Vaughan, PIT ... 45
B. Herman, CHI ... 38
J. Medwick, SL ... 37
C. Hubbell, NY ... 20
W. Berger, BOS ... 20
B. Terry, NY ... 20
A. Galan, CHI ... 18
P. Martin, SL ... 16
H. Leiber, NY ... 11
L. Warneke, CHI ... 9
E. Lombardi, CIN ... 8
F. Frisch, SL ... 7
C. Blanton, PIT ... 5
J. Moore, PHI ... 5
E. Allen, PHI ... 4
G. Mancuso, NY ... 4
P. Derringer, CIN ... 4
M. Ott, NY ... 3
P. Dean, SL ... 2
R. Collins, SL ... 2
C. Davis, PHI ... 2
P. Waner, PIT ... 1
B. Lee, CHI ... 1
T. Jackson, NY ... 1
D. Camilli, PHI ... 1

1935 AMERICAN
H. Greenberg, DET ... 80
W. Ferrell, BOS ... 62
J. Vosmik, CLE ... 39
C. Myer, WAS ... 36
L. Gehrig, NY ... 29
C. Gehringer, DET ... 26
M. Cochrane, DET ... 24
R. Cramer, PHI ... 18
M. Solters, BOS-SL ... 16
R. Hemsley, SL ... 16
J. Foxx, PHI ... 11
T. Bridges, DET ... 11
T. Lyons, CHI ... 10
L. Grove, BOS ... 8
Z. Bonura, CHI ... 7
L. Appling, CHI ... 7
L. Sewell, CHI ... 7
J. Allen, NY ... 5
J. Whitehead, CHI ... 4
F. Higgins, PHI ... 3
J. Marcum, PHI ... 3
E. Auker, DET ... 2
M. Harder, CLE ... 2
L. Lary, WAS-SL ... 1

1936 NATIONAL
C. Hubbell, NY ... 60
J. Dean, SL ... 53
B. Herman, CHI ... 37
J. Medwick, SL ... 30
P. Waner, PIT ... 29
M. Ott, NY ... 28
F. Demaree, CHI ... 17
G. Mancuso, NY ... 13
D. MacFayden, BOS ... 12
L. Durocher, SL ... 8
P. Derringer, CIN ... 6
G. Hartnett, CHI ... 6
B. Whitehead, NY ... 6
A. Lopez, BOS ... 5
V. Mungo, BRO ... 5
W. Berger, BOS ... 4
D. Camilli, PHI ... 4
G. Phelps, BRO ... 3
D. Bartell, NY ... 2
E. Lombardi, CIN ... 1
T. Moore, SL ... 1

1936 AMERICAN
L. Gehrig, NY ... 73
L. Appling, CHI ... 65
E. Averill, CLE ... 48
C. Gehringer, DET ... 39
B. Dickey, NY ... 29
V. Kennedy, CHI ... 27
J. Kuhel, WAS ... 27
J. DiMaggio, NY ... 26
T. Bridges, DET ... 25
H. Trosky, CLE ... 19
J. Foxx, BOS ... 16
G. Walker, DET ... 14
B. Bell, SL ... 10
W. Moses, PHI ... 7
L. Grove, BOS ... 5
J. Dykes, CHI ... 3
R. Radcliff, CHI ... 3
S. West, SL ... 2
Z. Bonura, CHI ... 1
E. McNair, BOS ... 1

1937 NATIONAL
J. Medwick, SL ... 70
G. Hartnett, CHI ... 68
C. Hubbell, NY ... 52
J. Turner, BOS ... 30
L. Fette, BOS ... 29
D. Bartell, NY ... 26
M. Ott, NY ... 24
P. Waner, PIT ... 21
B. Herman, CHI ... 19
J. Mize, SL ... 18
C. Melton, NY ... 17
C. Root, CHI ... 15
P. Whitney, PHI ... 13
H. Danning, NY ... 10
F. Demaree, CHI ... 9
L. Warneke, SL ... 6
B. Jurges, CHI ... 4
J. Cooney, BRO ... 4
B. Myers, CIN ... 2
L. Grissom, CIN ... 2
H. Manush, BRO ... 1

1937 AMERICAN
C. Gehringer, DET ... 78
J. DiMaggio, NY ... 74
H. Greenberg, DET ... 48
L. Gehrig, NY ... 42
L. Sewell, CHI ... 22
B. Dickey, NY ... 22
J. Cronin, BOS ... 19
R. Ruffing, NY ... 18
L. Gomez, NY ... 14
M. Kreevich, CHI ... 13
C. Travis, WAS ... 12
W. Moses, PHI ... 12
J. Allen, CLE ... 11
H. Clift, SL ... 11
R. Radcliff, CHI ... 10
B. Lewis, WAS ... 7
L. Appling, CHI ... 5
B. Bell, SL ... 5
E. Averill, CLE ... 4
L. Lary, CLE ... 4
R. Lawson, DET ... 4
G. Walker, DET ... 3
R. York, DET ... 1
P. Fox, DET ... 1

1938 NATIONAL
E. Lombardi, CIN ... 229
B. Lee, CHI ... 166
A. Vaughan, PIT ... 163
M. Ott, NY ... 132
F. McCormick, CIN ... 130
J. Rizzo, PIT ... 96
S. Hack, CHI ... 87
P. Derringer, CIN ... 70
M. Brown, PIT ... 62
G. Hartnett, CHI ... 61
J. Medwick, SL ... 55
J. Mize, SL ... 28
T. Cuccinello, BOS ... 23
P. Young, PIT ... 19
C. Bryant, CHI ... 16
H. Danning, NY ... 13
I. Goodman, CIN ... 11
J. VanderMeer, CIN ... 6
L. Durocher, BRO ... 6
D. Coffman, NY ... 6
A. Lopez, BOS ... 5
L. Waner, PIT ... 5
D. Garms, BOS ... 5
D. Camilli, BRO ... 5
C. Root, CHI ... 3
J. Moore, NY ... 3
J. Hudson, BRO ... 3
H. Mulcahy, PHI ... 3
L. Handley, PIT ... 2
L. Warneke, SL ... 1
F. Fitzsimmons, BRO ... 1
H. Martin, PHI ... 1

1938 AMERICAN
J. Foxx, BOS ... 305
B. Dickey, NY ... 196
H. Greenberg, DET ... 162
R. Ruffing, NY ... 146
B. Newsom, SL ... 111
J. DiMaggio, NY ... 106
J. Cronin, BOS ... 92
E. Averill, CLE ... 34

C. Travis, WAS....... 33
C. Gehringer, DET ... 27
J. Heath, CLE........ 24
J. Gordon, NY 23
H. Trosky, CLE....... 22
K. Keltner, CLE 16
M. Stratton, CHI 15
M. Harder, CLE 14
B. Johnson, PHI 13
H. Clift, SL........... 11
L. Gehrig, NY 10
P. Fox, DET........... 9
J. Vosmik, BOS 7
G. McQuinn, SL 7
L. Grove, BOS 7
B. Lewis, WAS........ 5
R. Rolfe, NY 5
C. Myer, WAS 5
E. Brucker, PHI 5
J. Allen, CLE.......... 3
F. Crosetti, NY........ 2
L. Gomez, NY 1
D. Cramer, BOS 1

1939 NATIONAL
B. Walters, CIN 303
J. Mize, SL 178
P. Derringer, CIN ...174
F. McCormick, CIN 159
C. Davis, SL.........106
J. Brown, SL......... 99
J. Medwick, SL 81
L. Durocher, BRO.... 52
H. Danning, NY 33
L. Hamlin, BRO 32
M. Ott, NY............ 21
B. Jurges, NY......... 20
D. Camilli, BRO 20
W. Myers, CIN 18
S. Hack, CHI 17
A. Galan, CHI 15
T. Moore, SL......... 15
M. Arnovich, PHI 10
L. Frey, CIN........... 8
B. Lee, CHI 8
E. Slaughter, SL 8
W. Werber, CIN 6
M. West, BOS 5
G. Hartnett, CHI 5
I. Goodman, CIN...... 4
B. Hassett, BOS 4
P. Coscarart, BRO.... 4
E. Fletcher, BOS-PIT . 4
C. Lavagetto, BRO ... 3
R. Bowman, SL........ 2
E. Miller, BOS 1
B. Herman, CHI....... 1

1939 AMERICAN
J. DiMaggio, NY 280
J. Foxx, BOS 170
B. Feller, CLE.......155
T. Williams, BOS....126
R. Ruffing, NY 116
B. Dickey, NY........110
E. Leonard, WAS 71
B. Johnson, PHI 52
J. Gordon, NY 43
M. Kreevich, CHI 38
C. Brown, CHI 34
K. Keltner, CLE 26
G. McQuinn, SL 24
C. Gehringer, DET ... 21
L. Grove, BOS 17
J. Cronin, BOS 15
T. Lyons, CHI 13
H. Greenberg, DET ... 12
B. Newsom, SL-DET. 11
J. Rigney, CHI 9
J. Kuhel, CHI 8
C. Keller, NY.......... 7
J. Heath, CLE......... 7
G. Walker, CHI........ 7
F. Hayes, PHI......... 7
T. Bridges, DET....... 7
R. Rolfe, NY 6
B. McCosky, DET..... 6
E. McNair, CHI 5
H. Trosky, CLE....... 4
G. Case, WAS 3
M. Hoag, SL.......... 3
R. York, DET.......... 1
L. Appling, CHI 1

1940 NATIONAL
F. McCormick, CIN 274
J. Mize, SL 209
B. Walters, CIN 146
P. Derringer, CIN ...121
F. Fitzsimmons, BRO 84
D. Walker, BRO 71
H. Danning, NY 64
S. Hack, CHI 61
E. Lombardi, CIN 38
W. Werber, CIN 36
J. Cooney, BOS 31
D. Camilli, BRO 30
E. Miller, BOS 28
D. Garms, PIT 28
A. Vaughan, PIT 27
C. Passeau, CHI 26
J. Beggs, CIN........ 19
T. Moore, SL......... 18
E. Fletcher, PIT 16
B. Nicholson, CHI ... 12
K. Higbe, PHI 10
C. Rowell, BOS 10
A. Lopez, BOS-PIT ... 9
M. Van Robays, PIT... 8
R. Sewell, PIT......... 7
P. Reese, BRO 6
M. West, BOS 6
B. Young, NY 6
W. Wyatt, BRO 3
J. Rizzo, PHI 3
P. May, PHI........... 3
H. Mulcahy, PHI 3
J. Martin, SL.......... 2
F. Gustine, PIT........ 1

1940 AMERICAN
H. Greenberg, DET . 292
B. Feller, CLE.......222
J. DiMaggio, NY 151
B. Newsom, DET ...120
L. Boudreau, CLE....119
J. Foxx, BOS 110
S. Rowe, DET......... 62
R. York, DET.......... 61
R. Radcliff, SL........ 55
L. Appling, CHI 54
R. Weatherly, CLE ... 34
D. Bartell, DET 26
J. Kuhel, CHI 18
S. Hudson, WAS..... 16
T. Williams, BOS..... 16
B. McCosky, DET..... 11
E. Bonham, NY........ 8
W. Judnich, SL 6
J. Babich, PHI 5
M. Tresh, CHI......... 4
F. Hayes, PHI......... 4
R. Mack, CLE......... 4
J. Gordon, NY......... 3
C. Travis, WAS........ 3
B. Kennedy, CHI...... 3
C. Gehringer, DET 3
R. Hemsley, CLE 2
T. Lyons, CHI 2
L. Finney, BOS 1
E. Auker, SL 1

1941 NATIONAL
D. Camilli, BRO 300
P. Reiser, BRO 183
W. Wyatt, BRO 151
J. Brown, SL.........107
E. Riddle, CIN 98
E. White, SL 77
K. Higbe, BRO....... 64
J. Hopp, SL........... 61
J. Mize, SL 48
D. Walker, BRO...... 34
B. Herman, CHI-BRO 27
T. Moore, SL......... 26
S. Hack, CHI 26
E. Fletcher, PIT 22
J. Cooney, BOS 20
B. Nicholson, CHI ... 16
G. Mancuso, SL 14
F. Crespi, SL 13
M. Ott, NY 12
E. Slaughter, SL 12
B. Young, NY 10
V. DiMaggio, PIT..... 10
J. Tobin, BOS........ 10
A. Lopez, PIT 8
M. Marion, SL 8
M. Cooper, SL 8
L. Warneke, SL 7
N. Etten, PHI 6
B. Walters, CIN 6
B. Dahlgren, BOS-CHI 6
W. Werber, CIN 6
E. Crabtree, SL 5
J. Rucker, NY......... 4
D. Litwhiler, PHI 3
H. Danning, NY 2
C. Hubbell, NY 2
C. Lavagetto, BRO ... 2
A. Vaughan, PIT 2

1941 AMERICAN
J. DiMaggio, NY 291
T. Williams, BOS....254
B. Feller, CLE.......174
T. Lee, CHI 144
C. Keller, NY........126
C. Travis, WAS......101
J. Gordon, NY 60
J. Heath, CLE......... 37
H. Newsome, BOS ... 32
R. Cullenbine, SL 29
J. Cronin, BOS 26
S. Chapman, PHI 25
B. Dickey, NY......... 18
T. Henrich, NY....... 16
B. McCosky, DET.... 12
T. Lyons, CHI 12
D. Siebert, PHI....... 10
L. Boudreau, CLE.... 10
A. Benton, DET 8
P. Rizzuto, NY 7
E. Leonard, WAS 7
B. Campbell, DET..... 4
R. York, DET 3
F. Hayes, PHI......... 3
T. Wright, CHI 2
R. Ruffing, NY 2
E. Auker, SL 1
F. Higgins, DET 1
D. DiMaggio, BOS 1

1942 NATIONAL
M. Cooper, SL.......263
E. Slaughter, SL 200
M. Ott, NY...........190
A. Owen, BRO 103
J. Mize, NY 97
P. Reiser, BRO 91
M. Marion, SL 81
D. Camilli, BRO...... 42
R. Elliott, PIT......... 39
C. Passeau, CHI 33
W. Cooper, SL....... 28
S. Musial, SL 26
E. Lombardi, BOS ... 24
J. Beazley, SL 24
J. Brown, SL......... 24
W. Wyatt, BRO 22
J. Medwick, BRO 20
T. Moore, SL......... 15
B. Nicholson, CHI ... 14
S. Hack, CHI 11
J. VanderMeer, CIN .. 11
T. Hughes, PHI 10
R. Starr, CIN 9
L. French, BRO 7
P. Reese, BRO 6
W. Kurowski, SL 6
R. Lamanno, CIN 4
M. West, BOS 4
L. Frey, CIN........... 4
F. McCormick, CIN ... 4
A. Javery, BOS 3
E. Miller, BOS 1

1942 AMERICAN
J. Gordon, NY 270
T. Williams, BOS....249
J. Pesky, BOS 143
V. Stephens, SL 140
E. Bonham, NY.......102
T. Hughson, BOS.... 92
J. DiMaggio, NY...... 86
S. Spence, WAS 65
P. Marchildon, PHI... 39
L. Boudreau, CLE.... 34
B. Doerr, BOS 24
T. Lyons, CHI 23
G. Case, WAS 17
K. Keltner, CLE 15
C. Keller, NY......... 15
W. Judnich, SL 14
B. Dickey, NY......... 12
D. Gutteridge, SL 12
P. Rizzuto, NY 9
C. Laabs, SL.......... 9
R. Ferrell, SL.......... 8
H. Borowy, NY......... 8
J. Bagby, CLE 6
T. Wright, CHI 6
T. Lupien BOS......... 4
L. Fleming, CLE 4
S. Chandler, NY 3
R. York, DET 3
B. McCosky, DET...... 1

1943 NATIONAL
S. Musial, SL 267
W. Cooper, SL.......192
B. Nicholson, CHI ..181
B. Herman, BRO.....140
M. Cooper, SL.......130
R. Sewell, PIT.......127
E. Riddle, CIN 68
R. Elliott, PIT......... 52
F. McCormick, CIN ... 26
C. Shoun, CIN 24
E. Miller, CIN 24
M. Witek, NY......... 21
M. Marion, SL 20
S. Rowe, PHI 18
W. Wyatt, BRO 15
A. Vaughan, BRO 15
R. Mueller, CIN 12
A. Javery, BOS 12
S. Hack, CHI 10
M. Ott, NY............. 9
E. Fletcher, PIT 7
A. Adams, NY 7
L. Klein, SL 6
A. Galan, BRO 5
D. Walker, BRO 5
J. Tobin, BOS......... 5
D. Bartell, NY 5
P. Cavaretta, CHI 4
T. Holmes, BOS 2
R. Northey, PHI 2
B. Dahlgren, PHI 2
H. Bithorn, CHI 1
B. Walters, CIN 1
L. Frey, CIN............ 1

1943 AMERICAN
S. Chandler, NY 246
L. Appling, CHI 215
R. York, DET.........152
W. Johnson, NY 135
B. Johnson, WAS...116
D. Wakefield, DET ... 72
N. Etten, NY 61
B. Dickey, NY......... 58
V. Stephens, SL 49
L. Boudreau, CLE.... 40
D. Trout, DET 38
G. Case, WAS 37
C. Keller, NY......... 31
B. Doerr, BOS 21
A. Smith, CLE 19
G. Priddy, WAS...... 17
O. Hockett, CLE 14
D. Gutteridge, SL 13
E. Wynn, WAS 13
J. Bagby, CLE 11
R. Cramer, DET........ 8
F. Higgins, DET 8
C. Laabs, SL........... 6
J. Early, WAS 6
J. Gordon, NY 4
R. Wolff, PHI.......... 4
L. Newsome, BOS 3
J. Cronin, BOS 3
J. Flores, PHI 3
G. Maltzberger, CHI .. 3
F. Crosetti, NY........ 2
K. Keltner, CLE 2
P. Fox, BOS 1
R. Hodgin, CHI 1
J. Murphy, NY......... 1
D. Siebert, PHI........ 1
J. Tabor, BOS 1
H. Wagner, PHI....... 1

1944 NATIONAL
M. Marion, SL 190
B. Nicholson, CHI ..189
D. Walker, BRO 145
S. Musial, SL 136
B. Walters, CIN 107
B. Voiselle, NY......107
R. Mueller, CIN 85
W. Cooper, SL........ 72
M. Cooper, SL........ 63
R. Elliott, PIT......... 57
R. Sewell, PIT........ 49
B. Dahlgren, PIT 33
F. McCormick, CIN .. 32
P. Cavaretta, CHI 27
R. Sanders, SL 25
M. Ott, NY 20
J. Tobin, BOS 13
J. Hopp, SL.......... 10
R. Northey, PHI 10
J. Medwick, NY........ 9
J. Barrett, PIT......... 8
E. Miller, CIN 7
T. Holmes, BOS 6
T. Wilks, SL........... 4
T. Lupien, PHI 3
S. Hack, CHI 2
M. Lanier, SL 2
C. Ryan, BOS 2
A. Galan, BRO 1
W. Kurowski, SL 1
J. Russell, PIT 1

1944 AMERICAN
H. Newhouser, DET.236
D. Trout, DET 232
V. Stephens, SL 193
S. Stirnweiss, NY ...129
D. Wakefield, DET ..128
L. Boudreau, CLE.... 84
B. Doerr, BOS 75
S. Spence, WAS 56
N. Potter, SL......... 52
B. Johnson, BOS 51
M. Christman, SL..... 27
T. Hughson, BOS 22
D. Cramer, DET...... 14
F. Hayes, PHI........ 13
P. Fox, BOS 12
J. Kramer, SL.......... 9
J. Lindell, NY 8
P. Richards, DET 8
D. Gutteridge, SL 7
F. Higgins, DET 7
G. McQuinn, SL 7
G. Kell, PHI 6
R. Cullenbine, CLE ... 5
N. Etten, NY........... 5
R. York, DET 5
R. Hemsley, NY....... 4
M. Kreevich, SL 4
W. Moses, CHI 4
E. Mayo, DET.......... 3
D. Siebert, PHI........ 3
H. Borowy, NY........ 2
F. Crosetti, NY........ 2
R. Hodgin, CHI 2
B. Muncrief, SL........ 1

1945 NATIONAL
P. Cavaretta, CHI ...279
T. Holmes, BOS 175
C. Barrett, BOS-SL . 151
A. Pafko, CHI 131
W. Kurowski, SL...... 90
H. Borowy, CHI 84
H. Wyse, CHI 72
M. Marion, SL 69
D. Walker, BRO 66
G. Rosen, BRO 56
S. Hack, CHI 42
H. Brecheen, SL 31
M. Ott, NY 22
A. Galan, BRO 18
J. Hopp, SL.......... 17
R. Elliott, PIT......... 15
L. Olmo, BRO 13
B. Adams, PHI-SL ... 12
C. Passeau, CHI 9
J. Barrett, PIT......... 8
E. Heusser, CIN 7
D. Johnson, CHI 7
B. Kerr, NY 7
F. McCormick, CIN ... 6
B. Salkeld, PIT 6
P. Lowrey, CHI 5
A. Adams, NY 4
A. Karl, PHI 4
H. Gregg, BRO 2
A. Lopez, PIT 2
P. Masi, BOS 2
E. Miller, CIN 2
V. DiMaggio, PHI 1
E. Stanky, BRO 1

1945 AMERICAN
H. Newhouser, DET.236
E. Mayo, DET.........164
S. Stirnweiss, NY 161
B. Ferriss, BOS 148
G. Myatt, WAS........ 98
V. Stephens, SL 94
R. Wolff, WAS 78
L. Boudreau, CLE.... 70
G. Case, WAS 60
P. Richards, DET 35
M. Tresh, CHI........ 33
J. Kuhel, WAS 29
R. Cullenbine, DET .. 26
H. Greenberg, DET .. 25
N. Etten, NY 21
T. Cuccinello, CHI ... 18
D. Trout, DET 17
E. Leonard, WAS 16
R. Schalk, CHI 13
J. Heath, CLE......... 10
G. Binks, WAS 9
B. Muncrief, SL........ 8
A. Benton, DET 6
R. Ferrell, WAS 6
B. Johnson, BOS 6
M. Christman, SL..... 5
B. Estalella, PHI 5
F. Hayes, PHI-CLE.... 5
D. Cramer, DET........ 4
W. Moses, CHI 4
E. Lake, BOS 2
R. Christopher, PHI ... 1
L. Newsome, BOS 1
R. York, DET 1

1946 NATIONAL
S. Musial, SL 319
D. Walker, BRO 159
E. Slaughter, SL 144
H. Pollet, SL 116
J. Sain, BOS 95
P. Reese, BRO 79
E. Stanky, BRO 67
D. Ennis, PHI 61
P. Reiser, BRO 58
P. Cavaretta, CHI 49
B. Kerr, NY 37
J. Hopp, BOS 34
E. Waitkus, CHI 21
B. Edwards, BRO 20
K. Higbe, BRO....... 18
H. Brecheen, SL 14
J. Mize, NY 14
G. Hatton, CIN....... 12
T. Holmes, BOS 11
J. Tabor, PHI......... 10
E. Verban, SL-PHI ... 10
H. Walker, SL.......... 9
L. Rowe, PHI 8
P. Masi, BOS 8
J. VanderMeer, CIN ... 7
R. Schoendienst, SL .. 6
B. Cox, PIT 5
F. Gustine, PIT........ 4
M. Marion, SL 4
R. Kiner, PIT 3
W. Kurowski, SL 3
R. Mueller, CIN 3
J. Schmitz, CHI 3
P. Lowrey, CHI 2
F. McCormick, PHI ... 2
C. Furillo, BRO 1
O. Judd, PHI........... 1

1946 AMERICAN
T. Williams, BOS....224
H. Newhouser, DET. 197
B. Doerr, BOS 158
J. Pesky, BOS 141
M. Vernon, WAS 134
B. Feller, CLE.......105
B. Ferriss, BOS 94
H. Greenberg, DET .. 91
D. DiMaggio, BOS ... 56

L. Boudreau, CLE.... 37
R. York, BOS 28
L. Appling, CHI 26
T. Hughson, BOS 19
E. Caldwell, CHI 18
C. Keller, NY......... 17
G. Kell, PHI-DET 12
S. Chandler, NY 12
A. Robinson, NY...... 12
J. DiMaggio, NY 6
B. Newsom, PHI-WAS 6
V. Stephens, SL 6
P. Marchildon, PHI.... 5
B. Rosar, PHI 4
S. Spence, WAS 4
J. Berardino, SL 2
T. Henrich, NY......... 1
H. Wagner, BOS 1

1947 NATIONAL
R. Elliott, BOS 205
E. Blackwell, CIN ...175
J. Mize, NY..........144
B. Edwards, BRO ...140
J. Robinson, BRO ..106
R. Kiner, PIT 101
L. Jansen, NY 91
P. Reese, BRO 80
W. Kurowski, SL 45
H. Walker, SL-PHI ... 45
R. Branca, BRO 40
H. Casey, BRO 37
E. Leonard, PHI...... 32
E. Stanky, BRO 32
W. Spahn, BOS....... 26
W. Marshall, NY 20
J. Sain, BOS......... 20
W. Cooper, NY 19
D. Walker, BRO 14
E. Slaughter, SL 12
S. Musial, SL 12
E. Verban, PHI 9
P. Cavaretta, CHI...... 6
P. Lowrey, CHI 2
E. Miller, CIN 2
A. Pafko, CHI 1

1947 AMERICAN
J. DiMaggio, NY 202
T. Williams, BOS....201
L. Boudreau, CLE....168
J. Page, NY..........167
G. Kell, DET 132
G. McQuinn, NY 77
J. Gordon, CLE 59
B. Feller, CLE........ 58
P. Marchildon, PHI.... 47
L. Appling, CHI 43
E. Joost, PHI 35
B. McCosky, PHI 35
T. Henrich, NY........ 33
F. Shea, NY 23
Y. Berra, NY 18
A. Reynolds, NY 18
B. Dillinger, SL....... 13
J. Pesky, BOS 11
F. Fain, PHI........... 9
W. Johnson, NY 9
S. Spence, WAS....... 9
F. Hutchison, DET 8
E. Wynn, WAS 7
B. Doerr, BOS 6
B. Rosar, PHI.......... 6
M. Christman, WAS... 4
B. McCahan, PHI 4
D. Mitchell, CLE 4
R. Cullenbine, DET ... 3
J. Dobson, BOS 3
J. Heath, SL 1
E. Lopat, CHI 1
V. Stephens, SL 1
T. Wright, CHI 1

1948 NATIONAL
S. Musial, SL 303
J. Sain, BOS.........223
A. Dark, BOS 174
S. Gordon, NY 72
H. Brecheen, SL 61
P. Reese, BRO 60
R. Kiner, PIT.......... 55
E. Slaughter, SL 55
D. Murtaugh, PIT 52
S. Rojek, PIT 51
R. Ashburn, PHI 48
J. Schmitz, CHI 37
R. Elliott, BOS 33
W. Spahn, BOS 31
J. Robinson, BRO 30
A. Pafko, CHI 25
J. Mize, NY 22
R. Barney, BRO 15
J. VanderMeer, CIN.. 13
J. Wyrostek, CIN...... 9
R. Branca, BRO 8
R. Campanella, BRO.. 8
B. Chesnes, PIT 8
P. Cavaretta, CHI 6
E. Miller, PHI.......... 4
D. Ennis, PHI 3
G. Hatton, CIN......... 3
L. Jansen, NY 2
D. Walker, PIT 2
G. Hodges, BRO....... 1
W. Lockman, NY....... 1
H. Sauer, CIN.......... 1

1948 AMERICAN
L. Boudreau, CLE....324
J. DiMaggio, NY 213
T. Williams, BOS.....171
V. Stephens, BOS ..121
B. Lemon, CLE 101
J. Gordon, CLE 63
T. Henrich, NY........ 63
G. Bearden, CLE...... 52
H. Newhouser, DET.. 48
E. Joost, PHI 39
H. Majeski, PHI 23
B. Tebbetts, BOS 23
V. Raschi, NY......... 23
K. Keltner, CLE 18
J. Priddy, SL......... 16
G. Kell, DET 14
W. Evers, DET 13
A. Zarilla, SL......... 11
B. Doerr, BOS 10
B. Dillinger, SL....... 10
J. Hegan, CLE 10
L. Appling, CHI 8
B. Feller, CLE......... 6
L. Brissie, PHI 5
F. Fain, PHI........... 5
J. Dobson, BOS 5
B. Goodman, BOS..... 4
B. McCosky, PHI 4
Y. Berra, NY 3
D. DiMaggio, BOS 3
L. Doby, CLE 3
C. Fannin, SL 2
P. Mullin, DET 1
P. Rizzuto, NY 1

1949 NATIONAL
J. Robinson, BRO ..264
S. Musial, SL 226
E. Slaughter, SL 181
R. Kiner, PIT 133
P. Reese, BRO 118
C. Furillo, BRO 68
W. Spahn, BOS...... 60
D. Newcombe, BRO.. 55
K. Heintzelman, PHI . 48
R. Schoendienst, SL. 30
G. Hodges, BRO...... 29
H. Pollet, SL 29
D. Ennis, PHI 28
B. Thomson, NY...... 25
R. Campanella, BRO .. 22
P. Roe, BRO......... 21
G. Hamner, PHI......... 9
W. Lockman, NY 9
R. Meyer, PHI.......... 8
K. Raffensberger, CIN 8
H. Sauer, CIN-CHI 8
T. Wilks, SL............ 8
R. Ashburn, PHI 6
J. Schmitz, CHI 6
A. Dark, BOS 3
M. Marion, SL 3
W. Jones, PHI 2
W. Marshall, NY 2
E. Torgeson, BOS..... 2
S. Gordon, NY 1
D. Sisler, PHI 1

1949 AMERICAN
T. Williams, BOS....272
P. Rizzuto, NY 175
J. Page, NY..........166
M. Parnell, BOS 151
E. Kinder, BOS 122
T. Henrich, NY.......121
V. Stephens, BOS ..100
G. Kell, DET 80
B. Lemon, CLE 57
V. Wertz, DET........ 51
V. Raschi, NY 19
J. DiMaggio, NY 18
E. Joost, PHI 11
L. Boudreau, CLE.... 10
Y. Berra, NY 9
D. DiMaggio, BOS 7
D. Doerr, BOS 7
A. Kellner, PHI 6
E. Robinson, WAS 6
R. Sievers, SL 6
B. Tebbetts, BOS 6
L. Appling, CHI 3
A. Houtteman, DET ... 3
J. Priddy, SL........... 3
V. Trucks, DET 3
D. Mitchell, CLE 2
A. Reynolds, NY 2

1950 NATIONAL
J. Konstanty, PHI ...286
S. Musial, SL 158
E. Stanky, NY.......144
D. Ennis, PHI 104
R. Kiner, PIT 91
G. Hamner, PHI...... 79
R. Roberts, PHI 68
G. Hodges, BRO..... 55
D. Snider, BRO 53
S. Maglie, NY 51
E. Blackwell, CIN 41
A. Pafko, CHI 38
R. Campanella,
BRO 29
A. Seminick, PHI..... 25
J. Robinson, BRO ... 23
C. Simmons, PHI 22
P. Roe, BRO.......... 15
T. Kluszewski, CIN... 14
W. Spahn, BOS....... 14
D. Newcombe, BRO . 14
J. Sain, BOS......... 12
S. Gordon, BOS 11
J. Hearn, SL-NY 10
P. Reese, BRO 8
E. Waitkus, PHI 8
R. Elliott, BOS 8
E. Torgeson, BOS..... 6
S. Jethroe, BOS 6
H. Sauer, CHI.......... 5
V. Bickford, BOS 4
C. Furillo, BRO 4
W. Westrum, NY 3
D. Sisler, PHI 2
H. Thompson, NY 2
L. Jansen, NY 2
W. Jones, PHI 1

1950 AMERICAN
P. Rizzuto, NY 284
B. Goodman, BOS ..180
Y. Berra, NY 146
G. Kell, DET 127
B. Lemon, CLE 102
W. Dropo, BOS 75
V. Raschi, NY........ 63
L. Doby, CLE 57
J. DiMaggio, NY 54
V. Wertz, DET........ 50
W. Evers, DET 38
C. Carrasquel, CHI .. 21
D. Trout, DET 21
D. DiMaggio, BOS ... 17
I. Noren, WAS 16
B. Doerr, BOS 15
J. Mize, NY 11
J. Priddy, DET 11
A. Rosen, CLE 11
E. Yost, WAS 8
M. Parnell, BOS 7
W. Ford, NY 7
T. Williams, BOS....... 7
N. Garver, SL 6
V. Stephens, BOS 6
A. Houtteman, DET ... 6
S. Lollar, SL 4
E. Lopat, NY 3
K. Wood, SL............ 2
S. Dente, WAS......... 1
D. Philley, CHI 1

1951 NATIONAL
R. Campanella,
BRO 243
S. Musial, SL 191
M. Irvin, NY..........166
S. Maglie, NY........153
P. Roe, BRO..........138
J. Robinson, BRO ... 92
R. Ashburn, PHI 69
B. Thomson, NY 62
M. Dickson, PIT...... 59
R. Kiner, PIT 49
W. Spahn, BOS....... 45
A. Dark, NY.......... 30
R. Roberts, PHI 27
L. Jansen, NY 26
P. Reese, BRO 15
G. Hodges, BRO..... 10
S. Gordon, BOS 10
K. Raffensberger, CIN 8
J. Wyrostek, CIN...... 6
E. Blackwell, CIN 6
C. Furillo, BRO 6
D. Newcombe, BRO .. 3
P. Cavaretta, CHI 1
H. Sauer, CHI.......... 1

1951 AMERICAN
Y. Berra, NY 184
N. Garver, SL.......157
A. Reynolds, NY 125
M. Minoso,
CLE-CHI 120
B. Feller, CLE 118
F. Fain, PHI..........103
E. Kinder, BOS 66
V. Raschi, NY........ 64
G. McDougald, NY ... 63
B. Avila, CLE 49
P. Rizzuto, NY 47
E. Lopat, NY.......... 44
T. Williams, BOS..... 35
E. Joost, PHI 32
G. Kell, DET 30
E. Wynn, CLE........ 29
N. Fox, CHI.......... 25
B. Goodman, BOS... 21
D. DiMaggio, BOS ... 16
G. Zernial, CHI-PHI .. 15
B. Shantz, PHI 14
M. Garcia, CLE 11
G. Coan, WAS 8
M. Parnell, BOS 7
E. Robinson, CHI 7
G. Woodling, NY...... 5
J. Pesky, BOS 5
I. Noren, WAS 4
D. Mitchell, CLE 4
V. Trucks, DET 2
E. Yost, WAS 2
J. Busby, CHI.......... 2
J. Mize, NY 2

1952 NATIONAL
H. Sauer, CHI........226
R. Roberts, PHI.....211
J. Black, BRO 208
H. Wilhelm, NY 133
S. Musial, SL 127
E. Slaughter, SL 92
J. Robinson, BRO ... 31
P. Reese, BRO 29
D. Snider, BRO 29
R. Campanella, BRO. 25
R. Schoendienst, SL. 25
A. Dark, NY.......... 24
M. Dickson, PIT...... 22
D. Ennis, PHI 18
W. Lockman, NY 18
B. Thomson, NY...... 17
F. Baumholtz, CHI ... 16
T. Kluszewski, CIN... 16
G. Hodges, BRO..... 15
R. McMillan, CIN 15
E. Mathews, BOS.... 13
B. Adams, CIN......... 9
B. Cox, BRO............ 8
W. Hacker, CHI 8
R. Kiner, PIT........... 8
S. Maglie, NY........... 8
K. Raffensberger, CIN 8
W. Spahn, BOS........ 8
P. Roe, BRO............ 7
S. Gordon, BOS 6
G. Hamner, PHI......... 5
S. Hemus, SL........... 5
M. Irvin, NY............ 5
G. Shuba, BRO 5
E. Yuhas, SL........... 5
A. Brazle, SL........... 3
J. Logan, BOS 3
T. Atwell, CHI 2
C. Metkovich, PIT...... 2
W. Cooper, BOS 1

1952 AMERICAN
B. Shantz, PHI 280
A. Reynolds, NY 183
M. Mantle, NY 143
Y. Berra, NY 104
E. Wynn, CLE........ 99
F. Fain, PHI 66
N. Fox, CHI 59
B. Lemon, CLE 58
M. Garcia, CLE 52
A. Rosen, CLE 51
E. Robinson, CHI 47
L. Doby, CLE 46
L. Easter, CLE 40
P. Rizzuto, NY 33
E. Joost, PHI 20
B. Goodman, BOS... 18
J. Jensen, NY-WAS.. 12
S. Paige, SL 12
V. Raschi, NY........ 12
D. Mitchell, CLE 11
H. Bauer, NY 10
G. Woodling, NY...... 10
P. Runnels, WAS 8
C. Courtney, SL 7
D. Gernert, BOS 6
W. Dropo, BOS-DET .. 5
S. Rogovin, CHI 4
S. White, BOS 4
B. Avila, CLE 3
B. Pierce, CHI 3
J. Sain, NY 3
B. Young, SL........... 3
J. Collins, NY 2
C. Marrero, WAS....... 1
B. Porterfield, WAS ... 1

1953 NATIONAL
R. Campanella,
BRO 297
E. Mathews, MIL.....216
D. Snider, BRO 157
R. Schoendienst, SL 155
W. Spahn, MIL.......120
R. Roberts, PHI......106
T. Kluszewski, CIN.... 69
S. Musial, SL 62
C. Erskine, BRO 54
C. Furillo, BRO 54
P. Reese, BRO 27
J. Robinson, BRO ... 19
D. Ennis, PHI 14
G. Hodges, BRO..... 13
M. Irvin, NY.......... 11
D. O'Connell, PIT ... 10
H. Haddix, SL 9
F. Thomas, PIT 6
R. Ashburn, PHI 5
G. Bell, CIN............ 3
J. Logan, MIL.......... 3
R. Gomez, NY 2
G. Hamner, PHI........ 2
D. Crandall, MIL 1
H. Thompson, NY 1

1953 AMERICAN
A. Rosen, CLE.......336
Y. Berra, NY 167
M. Vernon, WAS.....162
M. Minoso, CHI.......100
V. Trucks, SL-CHI..... 81
P. Rizzuto, NY 76
B. Porterfield, WAS .. 64
R. Boone, CLE-DET . 59
J. Piersall, BOS 56
B. Pierce, CHI 55
E. Kinder, BOS 41
H. Bauer, NY 37
A. Reynolds, NY 37
M. Parnell, BOS 27
H. Kuenn, DET 23
B. Lemon, CLE 22
E. Lopat, NY.......... 18
G. Zernial, PHI 16
D. Philley, PHI 11
W. Ford, NY 8
B. Goodman, BOS.... 5
M. Mantle, NY 4
G. Woodling, NY 3
E. Yost, WAS 3
B. Martin, NY 2
C. Carrasquel, CHI ... 1
G. Kell, BOS 1
T. Williams, BOS....... 1

1954 NATIONAL
W. Mays, NY 283
T. Kluszewski, CIN..217
J. Antonelli, NY 154
D. Snider, BRO 135
A. Dark, NY...........110
S. Musial, SL 97
R. Roberts, PHI...... 70
J. Adcock, MIL 60
P. Reese, BRO 53
G. Hodges, BRO..... 40
W. Spahn, MIL....... 38
D. Mueller, NY 30
R. Schoendienst, SL . 24
F. Thomas, PIT 24
H. Wilhelm, NY 17
E. Banks, CHI 14
D. Crandall, MIL 13
J. Logan, MIL.......... 9
E. Mathews, MIL...... 5
G. Hamner, PHI........ 5
R. Ashburn, PHI 5
S. Maglie, NY 4
G. Conley, MIL 3
M. Grissom, NY 2
R. McMillan, CIN 2
D. Rhodes, NY......... 1
H. Sauer, CHI.......... 1

1954 AMERICAN
Y. Berra, NY 230
L. Doby, CLE 210
B. Avila, CLE 203
M. Minoso, CHI.....186
B. Lemon, CLE 179
E. Wynn, CLE....... 72
T. Williams, BOS.... 65
H. Kuenn, DET....... 37
M. Vernon, WAS 30
N. Fox, CHI.......... 30
B. Grim, NY 25
J. Finigan, PHI 19
V. Trucks, CHI 19
J. Jensen, BOS 17
M. Mantle, NY 16
I. Noren, NY 16
A. Rosen, CLE....... 16
J. Busby, WAS 7
J. Coleman, NY 6
B. Goodman, BOS..... 6
M. Garcia, CLE 6
J. Hegan, CLE 5
H. Bauer, NY 4
A. Kaline, DET 4
B. Turley, BAL 4
S. Gromek, DET 1
C. Abrams, BAL 1
R. Boone, DET......... 1
R. Sievers, WAS 1

1955 NATIONAL
R. Campanella,
BRO 226
D. Snider, BRO 221
E. Banks, CHI 195
W. Mays, NY 165
R. Roberts, PHI.....159
T. Kluszewski, CIN..111
D. Newcombe, BRO . 89
S. Musial, SL 46
H. Aaron, MIL........ 36
P. Reese, BRO 36
J. Logan, MIL........ 24
W. Post, CIN 23
D. Ennis, PHI 21
R. Ashburn, PHI 17
C. Labine, BRO...... 11

B. Friend, PIT ... 10
D. Crandall, MIL ... 8
E. Mathews, MIL ... 6
D. Long, PIT ... 3
J. Meyer, PHI ... 3
G. Baker, CHI ... 2
C. Furillo, BRO ... 2
V. Law, PIT ... 1
F. Thomas, PIT ... 1

1955 AMERICAN

Y. Berra, NY ... 218
A. Kaline, DET ... 201
A. Smith, CLE ... 200
T. Williams, BOS ... 143
M. Mantle, NY ... 113
R. Narleski, CLE ... 90
N. Fox, CHI ... 84
H. Bauer, NY ... 64
V. Power, KC ... 53
J. Jensen, BOS ... 39
S. Lollar, CHI ... 37
G. McDougald, NY ... 34
B. Klaus, BOS ... 27
T. Byrne, NY ... 24
W. Ford, NY ... 21
R. Boone, DET ... 16
R. Sievers, WAS ... 9
H. Kuenn, DET ... 8
B. Pierce, CHI ... 8
D. Philley, CLE-BAL ... 6
E. Wynn, CLE ... 6
E. Valo, KC ... 5
M. Vernon, WAS ... 4
B. Hoeft, DET ... 1
D. Mossi, CLE ... 1
F. Sullivan, BOS ... 1
G. Triandos, BAL ... 1
J. Valdivielso, WAS ... 1
S. White, BOS ... 1

1956 NATIONAL

D. Newcombe, BRO 223
S. Maglie, BRO ... 183
H. Aaron, MIL ... 146
W. Spahn, MIL ... 126
J. Gilliam, BRO ... 103
R. McMillan, CIN ... 96
F. Robinson, CIN ... 79
P. Reese, BRO ... 71
S. Musial, SL ... 62
D. Snider, BRO ... 55
J. Adcock, MIL ... 54
B. Friend, PIT ... 38
H. Freeman, CIN ... 25
J. Antonelli, NY ... 18
T. Kluszewski, CIN ... 18
J. Robinson, BRO ... 17
W. Mays, NY ... 14
E. Bailey, CIN ... 13
B. Virdon, SL-PIT ... 13
S. Lopata, PHI ... 11
C. Furillo, BRO ... 9
L. Burdette, MIL ... 8
B. Buhl, MIL ... 7
R. Roberts, PHI ... 7
B. Lawrence, CIN ... 6
D. Long, PIT ... 4
W. Moon, SL ... 3
E. Banks, CHI ... 2
K. Boyer, SL ... 2
C. Labine, BRO ... 1
J. Logan, MIL ... 1
R. Ashburn, PHI ... 1

1956 AMERICAN

M. Mantle, NY ... 336
Y. Berra, NY ... 186
A. Kaline, DET ... 142
H. Kuenn, DET ... 80
B. Pierce, CHI ... 75
T. Williams, BOS ... 70
B. Nieman, CHI-BAL ... 55
G. McDougald, NY ... 55
V. Wertz, CLE ... 45
B. Lemon, CLE ... 40
H. Simpson, KC ... 37
W. Ford, NY ... 33
E. Wynn, CLE ... 32
J. Piersall, BOS ... 28
N. Fox, CHI ... 28
S. Lollar, CHI ... 27
F. Lary, DET ... 24
P. Runnels, WAS ... 24
H. Score, CLE ... 18
J. Jensen, BOS ... 15
M. Vernon, BOS ... 14
T. Brewer, BOS ... 11
H. Bauer, NY ... 8
C. Maxwell, DET ... 8
L. Aparicio, CHI ... 7
G. Triandos, BAL ... 6
F. Bolling, DET ... 3
M. Minoso, CHI ... 3
V. Power, KC ... 3
J. Kucks, NY ... 2
R. Sievers, WAS ... 1

1957 NATIONAL

H. Aaron, MIL ... 239
S. Musial, SL ... 230
R. Schoendienst, NY-MIL ... 221
W. Mays, NY ... 174
W. Spahn, MIL ... 131
E. Banks, CHI ... 60
G. Hodges, BRO ... 54
E. Mathews, MIL ... 45
F. Robinson, CIN ... 42
J. Sanford, PHI ... 39
D. Hoak, CIN ... 31
D. Blasingame, SL ... 26
E. Bouchee, PHI ... 26
B. Buhl, MIL ... 15
D. Ennis, SL ... 13
D. Groat, PIT ... 13
A. Dark, SL ... 12
D. Snider, BRO ... 10
F. Thomas, PIT ... 8
D. Drysdale, BRO ... 8
R. McMillan, CIN ... 6
D. Drott, CHI ... 6
G. Hamner, PHI ... 3
L. Burdette, MIL ... 2
J. Logan, MIL ... 1
H. Anderson, PHI ... 1

1957 AMERICAN

M. Mantle, NY ... 233
T. Williams, BOS ... 209
R. Sievers, WAS ... 205
N. Fox, CHI ... 193
G. McDougald, NY ... 165
V. Wertz, CLE ... 61
F. Malzone, BOS ... 58
M. Minoso, CHI ... 55
J. Bunning, DET ... 46
A. Kaline, DET ... 40
B. Pierce, CHI ... 35
B. Gardner, BAL ... 22
D. Donovan, CHI ... 19
Y. Berra, NY ... 18
G. Woodling, CLE ... 13
B. Grim, NY ... 9
B. Boyd, BAL ... 9
C. Maxwell, DET ... 5
W. Held, NY-KC ... 4
W. Ford, NY ... 4
V. Power, KC ... 3
J. Piersall, BOS ... 2
B. Skowron, NY ... 2
H. Kuenn, DET ... 2
S. Lollar, CHI ... 2
T. Kubek, NY ... 1
B. Shantz, NY ... 1

1958 NATIONAL

E. Banks, CHI ... 283
W. Mays, SF ... 185
H. Aaron, MIL ... 166
F. Thomas, PIT ... 143
W. Spahn, MIL ... 108
B. Friend, PIT ... 98
R. Ashburn, PHI ... 62
B. Mazeroski, PIT ... 61
O. Cepeda, SF ... 57
D. Crandall, MIL ... 48
L. Burdette, MIL ... 47
S. Musial, SL ... 39
K. Boyer, SL ... 31
J. Temple, CIN ... 26
B. Skinner, PIT ... 18
W. Covington, MIL ... 16
E. Face, PIT ... 8
H. Anderson, PHI ... 5
J. Gilliam, LA ... 4
B. Purkey, CIN ... 4
F. Robinson, CIN ... 4
J. Adcock, MIL ... 2
C. Furillo, LA ... 1

1958 AMERICAN

J. Jensen, BOS ... 233
B. Turley, NY ... 191
R. Colavito, CLE ... 181
B. Cerv, KC ... 164
M. Mantle, NY ... 127
R. Sievers, WAS ... 95
T. Williams, BOS ... 89
N. Fox, CHI ... 88
S. Lollar, CHI ... 57
P. Runnels, BOS ... 29
G. Triandos, BAL ... 27
D. Hyde, WAS ... 26
H. Kuenn, DET ... 24
C. McLish, CLE ... 18
V. Power, KC-CLE ... 15
F. Bolling, DET ... 10
E. Howard, NY ... 9
Y. Berra, NY ... 6
M. Minoso, CLE ... 6
A. Kaline, DET ... 5
G. McDougald, NY ... 5
R. Duren, NY ... 4
F. Lary, DET ... 3
J. Harshman, BAL ... 2
D. Donovan, CHI ... 1
F. Malzone, BOS ... 1

1959 NATIONAL

E. Banks, CHI ... 232½
E. Mathews, MIL ... 189½
H. Aaron, MIL ... 174
W. Moon, LA ... 161
S. Jones, SF ... 130
W. Mays, SF ... 85
E. Face, PIT ... 67
C. Neal, LA ... 64
F. Robinson, CIN ... 52
K. Boyer, SL ... 37
D. Crandall, MIL ... 27
L. Burdette, MIL ... 14
R. Craig, LA ... 12
J. Cunningham, SL ... 12
V. Pinson, CIN ... 11
J. Temple, CIN ... 8
D. Hoak, PIT ... 6
G. Hodges, LA ... 4
O. Cepeda, SF ... 3
V. Law, PIT ... 3
W. Spahn, MIL ... 3
G. Conley, PHI ... 1
W. McCovey, SF ... 1
D. Snider, LA ... 1

1959 AMERICAN

N. Fox, CHI ... 295
L. Aparicio, CHI ... 255
E. Wynn, CHI ... 123
R. Colavito, CLE ... 117
T. Francona, CLE ... 102
A. Kaline, DET ... 84
J. Landis, CHI ... 66
H. Kuenn, DET ... 64
S. Lollar, CHI ... 44
J. Jensen, BOS ... 40
C. McLish, CLE ... 35
Y. Berra, NY ... 26
M. Minoso, CLE ... 26
F. Malzone, BOS ... 24
H. Killebrew, WAS ... 21
G. Woodling, BAL ... 18
M. Mantle, NY ... 13
B. Richardson, NY ... 11
C. Pascual, WAS ... 9
B. Shaw, CHI ... 8
G. Triandos, BAL ... 8
B. Daley, KC ... 7
V. Power, CLE ... 5
B. Tuttle, KC ... 5
J. Lemon, WAS ... 4
P. Runnels, BOS ... 2
T. Williams, BOS ... 2
B. Allison, WAS ... 1
G. Staley, CHI ... 1

1960 NATIONAL

D. Groat, PIT ... 276
D. Hoak, PIT ... 162
W. Mays, SF ... 155
E. Banks, CHI ... 100
L. McDaniel, SL ... 95
K. Boyer, SL ... 80
V. Law, PIT ... 80
R. Clemente, PIT ... 62
E. Broglio, SL ... 58
E. Mathews, MIL ... 52
H. Aaron, MIL ... 49
E. Face, PIT ... 47
D. Crandall, MIL ... 31
W. Spahn, MIL ... 27
N. Larker, LA ... 21
S. Musial, SL ... 18
M. Wills, LA ... 7
V. Pinson, CIN ... 6
J. Adcock, MIL ... 5
S. Burgess, PIT ... 2
F. Robinson, CIN ... 2
L. Sherry, LA ... 2
P. Herrera, PHI ... 1

1960 AMERICAN

R. Maris, NY ... 225
M. Mantle, NY ... 222
B. Robinson, BAL ... 211
M. Minoso, CHI ... 141
R. Hansen, BAL ... 110
A. Smith, CHI ... 73
R. Sievers, CHI ... 58
E. Battey, WAS ... 57
B. Skowron, NY ... 56
J. Lemon, WAS ... 36
T. Kubek, NY ... 29
C. Estrada, BAL ... 28
T. Williams, BOS ... 25
V. Wertz, BOS ... 22
Y. Berra, NY ... 21
J. Gentile, BAL ... 21
P. Runnels, BOS ... 18
N. Fox, CHI ... 11
V. Power, CLE ... 11
S. Barber, BAL ... 7
L. Aparicio, CHI ... 6
J. Perry, CLE ... 6
G. Staley, CHI ... 4
J. Bunning, DET ... 3
G. Woodling, BAL ... 3
H. Kuenn, CLE ... 3
B. Daley, KC ... 3
M. Fornieles, BOS ... 2
C. Maxwell, DET ... 2
J. Piersall, CLE ... 2

1961 NATIONAL

F. Robinson, CIN ... 219
O. Cepeda, SF ... 117
V. Pinson, CIN ... 104
R. Clemente, PIT ... 81
J. Jay, CIN ... 74
W. Mays, SF ... 70
K. Boyer, SL ... 43
H. Aaron, MIL ... 39
M. Wills, LA ... 36
J. O'Toole, CIN ... 31
W. Spahn, MIL ... 31
S. Miller, SF ... 26
W. Moon, LA ... 22
G. Altman, CHI ... 9
J. Podres, LA ... 9
R. McMillan, MIL ... 8
E. Mathews, MIL ... 7
S. Koufax, LA ... 5
J. Roseboro, LA ... 4
J. Brosnan, CIN ... 3
J. Torre, MIL ... 2
L. Jackson, SL ... 1
J. Lynch, CIN ... 1
B. Malkmus, PHI ... 1
D. Stuart, PIT ... 1

1961 AMERICAN

R. Maris, NY ... 202
M. Mantle, NY ... 198
J. Gentile, BAL ... 157
N. Cash, DET ... 151
W. Ford, NY ... 102
L. Arroyo, NY ... 95
F. Lary, DET ... 53
R. Colavito, DET ... 51
A. Kaline, DET ... 35
E. Howard, NY ... 30
H. Killebrew, MIN ... 29
L. Aparicio, CHI ... 16
J. Piersall, CLE ... 10
S. Barber, BAL ... 7
D. Schwall, BOS ... 7
N. Siebern, KC ... 7
D. Donovan, WAS ... 5
B. Phillips, CLE ... 5
B. Robinson, BAL ... 4
C. Schilling, BOS ... 4
T. Morgan, LA ... 3
A. Smith, CHI ... 3
Y. Berra, NY ... 2
B. Richardson, NY ... 1
J. Romano, CLE ... 1
L. Thomas, NY-LA ... 1
H. Wilhelm, BAL ... 1

1962 NATIONAL

M. Wills, LA ... 209
W. Mays, SF ... 202
T. Davis, LA ... 175
F. Robinson, CIN ... 164
D. Drysdale, LA ... 85
H. Aaron, MIL ... 72
J. Sanford, SF ... 62
B. Purkey, CIN ... 33
F. Howard, LA ... 32
S. Musial, SL ... 19
J. Pagan, SF ... 13
D. Demeter, PHI ... 12
F. Alou, SF ... 10
B. White, SL ... 10
O. Cepeda, SF ... 9
D. Groat, PIT ... 7
R. Clemente, PIT ... 6
E. Banks, CHI ... 5
K. Boyer, SL ... 5
J. Callison, PHI ... 5
H. Kuenn, SF ... 5
J. Marichal, SF ... 4
B. Skinner, PIT ... 4
J. Davenport, SF ... 3
S. Koufax, LA ... 3
D. Crandall, MIL ... 2
A. Mahaffey, PHI ... 2
E. Roebuck, LA ... 2
E. Kasko, CIN ... 1
E. Mathews, MIL ... 1

1962 AMERICAN

M. Mantle, NY ... 234
B. Richardson, NY ... 152
H. Killebrew, MIN ... 99
L. Wagner, LA ... 85
D. Donovan, CLE ... 64
A. Kaline, DET ... 58
N. Siebern, KC ... 53
R. Rollins, MIN ... 47
B. Robinson, BAL ... 41
F. Robinson, CHI ... 33
L. Thomas, LA ... 32
T. Tresh, NY ... 30
B. Moran, LA ... 28
R. Terry, NY ... 19
C. Pascual, MIN ... 14
R. Colavito, DET ... 13
H. Aguirre, DET ... 10
J. Cunningham, CHI ... 9
P. Runnels, BOS ... 9
C. Yastrzemski, BOS 9
V. Power, MIN ... 8
D. Radatz, BOS ... 8
J. Bunning, DET ... 8
Z. Versalles, MIN ... 8
J. Lumpe, KC ... 7
E. Bressoud, BOS ... 6
B. Rodgers, LA ... 6
W. Ford, NY ... 6
R. Herbert, CHI ... 5
C. Hinton, WAS ... 5
F. Malzone, BOS ... 3
N. Cash, DET ... 3
A. Smith, CHI ... 1

1963 NATIONAL

S. Koufax, LA ... 237
D. Groat, SL ... 190
H. Aaron, MIL ... 135
R. Perranoski, LA ... 130
W. Mays, SF ... 102
J. Gilliam, LA ... 62
B. White, SL ... 56
T. Davis, LA ... 41
R. Santo, CHI ... 41
V. Pinson, CIN ... 32
J. Marichal, SF ... 31
W. Spahn, MIL ... 30
K. Boyer, SL ... 19
R. Clemente, PIT ... 12
J. Callison, PHI ... 11
T. Taylor, PHI ... 10
W. McCovey, SF ... 9
M. Wills, LA ... 9
D. Ellsworth, CHI ... 7
J. Maloney, CIN ... 7
D. Demeter, PHI ... 3
D. Drysdale, LA ... 3
T. Gonzalez, PHI ... 2
C. Flood, SL ... 1

1963 AMERICAN

E. Howard, NY ... 248
A. Kaline, DET ... 148
W. Ford, NY ... 125
H. Killebrew, MIN ... 85
D. Radatz, BOS ... 84
C. Yastrzemski, BOS 81
E. Battey, MIN ... 57
G. Peters, CHI ... 55
P. Ward, CHI ... 52
B. Richardson, NY ... 43
T. Tresh, NY ... 38
C. Pascual, MIN ... 29
D. Stuart, BOS ... 25
A. Pearson, LA ... 22
B. Allison, MIN ... 15
J. Bouton, NY ... 11
M. Alvis, CLE ... 10
J. Pepitone, NY ... 10
L. Wagner, LA ... 9
S. Miller, BAL ... 9
W. Causey, KC ... 5
R. Rollins, MIN ... 5
L. Aparicio, BAL ... 3
B. Dailey, MIN ... 3
J. Fregosi, LA ... 3
N. Fox, CHI ... 2
T. Kubek, NY ... 1
F. Robinson, CHI ... 1
N. Siebern, KC ... 1

1964 NATIONAL

K. Boyer, SL ... 243
J. Callison, PHI ... 187
B. White, SL ... 106½
F. Robinson, CIN ... 98
J. Torre, MIL ... 85
W. Mays, SF ... 66
R. Allen, PHI ... 63
R. Santo, CHI ... 59
R. Clemente, PIT ... 56
L. Brock, CHI-SL ... 40
C. Flood, SL ... 38
L. Jackson, CHI ... 26
J. Bunning, PHI ... 23
H. Aaron, MIL ... 22
J. Marichal, SF ... 14
S. Ellis, CIN ... 13
S. Koufax, LA ... 7½
V. Pinson, CIN ... 6
J. Hart, SF ... 6
B. Williams, CHI ... 6
R. Amaro, PHI ... 5
T. Davis, LA ... 4
B. Gibson, SL ... 2
C. Short, PHI ... 2
R. Hunt, NY ... 1
B. Schultz, SL ... 1

1964 AMERICAN

B. Robinson, BAL ... 269
M. Mantle, NY ... 171
E. Howard, NY ... 124
T. Oliva, MIN ... 99
D. Chance, LA ... 97
P. Ward, CHI ... 67½
B. Freehan, DET ... 44
G. Peters, CHI ... 44
D. Radatz, BOS ... 37
H. Killebrew, MIN ... 31
B. Powell, BAL ... 28
W. Bunker, BAL ... 23
J. Fregosi, LA ... 21
A. Kaline, DET ... 17
F. Robinson, CHI ... 14
R. Hansen, CHI ... 10
B. Richardson, NY ... 9
L. Wagner, CLE ... 9
J. Pizarro, CHI ... 8
H. Wilhelm, CHI ... 8
J. Horlen, CHI ... 7
W. Ford, NY ... 7

B. Allison, MIN 5
R. Colavito, KC 5
M. Stottlemyre, NY 4
R. Maris, NY 4
W. Causey, KC 4
L. Aparicio, BAL 3½
D. Stuart, BOS 3
E. Bressoud, BOS 2
C. Osteen, WAS 2
D. Wickersham, DET 2
D. Lock, WAS 1

1965 NATIONAL
W. Mays, SF 224
S. Koufax, LA 177
M. Wills, LA 164
D. Johnson, CIN 108
D. Drysdale, LA 77
P. Rose, CIN 67
H. Aaron, MIL 58
R. Clemente, PIT 56
J. Marichal, SF 26
W. McCovey, SF 25
J. Torre, MIL 23
B. Williams, CHI 21
F. Linzy, SF 16
W. Stargell, PIT 15
C. Flood, SL 13
J. Hart, SF 13
V. Law, PIT 12
F. Robinson, CIN 11
R. Santo, CHI 11
E. Mathews, MIL 8
L. Cardenas, CIN 7
J. Maloney, CIN 7
L. Lefebvre, LA 7
J. Callison, PHI 6
L. Johnson, LA 6
C. Rojas, PHI 5
J. Roseboro, LA 5
R. Allen, PHI 4
T. Cloninger, MIL 4
J. Gilliam, LA 3
J. Morgan, HOU 1

1965 AMERICAN
Z. Versalles, MIN 275
T. Oliva, MIN 174
B. Robinson, BAL 150
E. Fisher, CHI 122
R. Colavito, CLE 89
J. Grant, MIN 74
S. Miller, BAL 45
W. Horton, DET 24
T. Tresh, NY 23
E. Battey, MIN 22
D. Wert, DET 22
C. Yastrzemski, BOS 22
J. Hall, MIN 19
M. Stottlemyre, NY 17
H. Killebrew, MIN 15
A. Kaline, DET 9
J. Adair, BAL 7
R. Hansen, CHI 7
S. McDowell, CLE 7
B. Richardson, NY 6
V. Davalillo, CLE 5
J. Fregosi, CAL 5
F. Whitfield, CLE 5
B. Knoop, CAL 4
D. Buford, CHI 3
M. Mantle, NY 3
P. Richert, WAS 3
F. Robinson, CHI 3
B. Campaneris, KC 2
F. Howard, WAS 2
R. Kline, WAS 2
F. Mantilla, BOS 2
N. Cash, DET 1
T. Conigliaro, BOS 1

1966 NATIONAL
R. Clemente, PIT 218
S. Koufax, LA 208
W. Mays, SF 111
R. Allen, PHI 107
F. Alou, ATL 83
J. Marichal, SF 74
P. Regan, LA 66
H. Aaron, ATL 57
M. Alou, PIT 36
P. Rose, CIN 31
G. Alley, PIT 24
R. Santo, CHI 23
J. Roseboro, LA 22
O. Cepeda, SF-SL 22
W. Stargell, PIT 19
J. Torre, ATL 18
W. McCovey, SF 12
J. Lefebvre, LA 8
G. Perry, SF 8
C. Flood, SL 7
M. Wills, LA 5
R. Staub, HOU 4
B. Mazeroski, PIT 3
G. Beckert, CHI 3
J. Maloney, CIN 3
B. White, PHI 3
L. Brock, SL 2
B. Shaw, SF-NY 1
C. Short, PHI 1
W. Davis, LA 1

1966 AMERICAN
F. Robinson, BAL 280
B. Robinson, BAL 153
B. Powell, BAL 122
H. Killebrew, MIN 96
J. Kaat, MIN 84
T. Oliva, MIN 71
A. Kaline, DET 66
T. Agee, CHI 63
L. Aparicio, BAL 51
B. Campaneris, KC 36
S. Miller, BAL 27
N. Cash, DET 23
J. Aker, KC 22
E. Wilson, BOS-DET 13
D. McLain, DET 12
B. Freehan, DET 9
A. Etchebarren, BAL 7
B. Knoop, CAL 6
M. Mantle, NY 5
T. Tresh, NY 5
J. Sanford, CAL 4
R. Reichardt, CAL 4
F. Valentine, WAS 4
W. Horton, DET 4
L. Wagner, CLE 4
P. Richert, WAS 3
J. Pepitone, NY 2
T. Conigliaro, BOS 1
S. Siebert, CLE 1
C. Yastrzemski, BOS 1
J. Fregosi, CAL 1

1967 NATIONAL
O. Cepeda, SL 280
T. McCarver, SL 136
R. Clemente, PIT 129
R. Santo, CHI 103
H. Aaron, ATL 79
M. McCormick, SF 73
L. Brock, SL 49
T. Perez, CIN 43
J. Javier, SL 41
P. Rose, CIN 40
J. Wynn, HOU 29
F. Jenkins, CHI 26
C. Flood, SL 24
E. Banks, CHI 22
N. Briles, SL 20
R. Staub, HOU 12
D. Hughes, SL 10
J. Hart, SF 10
R. Allen, PHI 9
T. Abernathy, CIN 8
C. Boyer, ATL 6
B. Gibson, SL 5
R. Hundley, CHI 5
J. Bunning, PHI 5
T. Seaver, NY 5
T. Davis, NY 3
G. Alley, PIT 3
T. Gonzalez, PHI 3
W. McCovey, SF 2

1967 AMERICAN
C. Yastrzemski, BOS 275
H. Killebrew, MIN 161
B. Freehan, DET 137
J. Horlen, CHI 91
A. Kaline, DET 88
J. Lonborg, BOS 82
C. Tovar, MIN 70
J. Fregosi, CAL 70
G. Peters, CHI 37
G. Scott, BOS 33
F. Robinson, BAL 31
E. Wilson, DET 20
D. Chance, MIN 19
R. Hansen, CHI 13
J. Adair, CHI-BOS 11
P. Blair, BAL 9
R. Petrocelli, BOS 7
E. Howard, NY-BOS 7
T. Oliva, MIN 6
J. Kaat, MIN 4
P. Casanova, WAS 3
D. Mincher, CAL 3
M. Lolich, DET 2
M. Rojas, CAL 1

1968 NATIONAL
B. Gibson, SL 242
P. Rose, CIN 205
W. McCovey, SF 135
C. Flood, SL 116
J. Marichal, SF 93
L. Brock, SL 73
M. Shannon, SL 55
B. Williams, CHI 48
G. Beckert, CHI 40
F. Alou, ATL 33
M. Alou, PIT 32
H. Aaron, ATL 19
W. Mays, SF 14
E. Banks, CHI 14
J. Koosman, NY 14
J. Bench, CIN 11
P. Regan, LA-CHI 7
F. Jenkins, CHI 6
T. Perez, CIN 5
N. Briles, SL 4
D. Maxvill, SL 4
S. Blass, PIT 3
T. Haller, LA 3
R. Santo, CHI 2
C. Carroll, ATL-CIN 1
T. Helms, CIN 1

1968 AMERICAN
D. McLain, DET 280
B. Freehan, DET 161
K. Harrelson, BOS 103
W. Horton, DET 102
D. McNally, BAL 78
L. Tiant, CLE 78
D. McAuliffe, DET 71
F. Howard, WAS 63
C. Yastrzemski, BOS 50
M. Stottlemyre, NY 43
B. Campaneris, OAK 39
R. White, NY 17
J. Northrup, DET 15
L. Aparicio, CHI 13
J. Fregosi, CAL 11
D. Buford, BAL 11
B. Robinson, BAL 8
R. Jackson, OAK 8
T. Oliva, MIN 5
D. Cater, OAK 5
M. Andrews, BOS 4
B. Powell, BAL 4
N. Cash, DET 3
C. Tovar, MIN 3
M. Stanley, DET 2
W. Wood, CHI 2
T. Uhlaender, MIN 1

1969 NATIONAL
W. McCovey, SF 265
T. Seaver, NY 243
H. Aaron, ATL 188
P. Rose, CIN 127
R. Santo, CHI 124
T. Agee, NY 89
C. Jones, NY 82
R. Clemente, PIT 51
P. Niekro, ATL 47
T. Perez, CIN 28
M. Wills, MON-LA 17
E. Banks, CHI 15
R. Carty, ATL 12
J. Bench, CIN 12
D. Kessinger, CHI 8
T. Gonzalez, SD-ATL 8
R. Hunt, SF 8
D. Menke, HOU 8
W. Granger, CIN 8
J. Wynn, HOU 8
W. Davis, LA 7
W. Stargell, PIT 7
J. Marichal, SF 6
B. Williams, CHI 6
J. Koosman, NY 6
J. Torre, SL 6
M. Alou, PIT 6
L. Dierker, HOU 6
T. Haller, LA 3
B. Gibson, SL 2
B. Bonds, SF 2
R. Hundley, CHI 2
L. May, CIN 2
T. Sizemore, LA 2
W. Parker, LA 2
J. Edwards, HOU 1
R. Staub, MON 1
O. Cepeda, ATL 1

1969 AMERICAN
H. Killebrew, MIN 294
B. Powell, BAL 227
F. Robinson, BAL 162
F. Howard, WAS 115
R. Jackson, OAK 110
D. McLain, DET 85
R. Petrocelli, BOS 71
M. Cuellar, BAL 55
J. Perry, MIN 40
R. Carew, MIN 30
P. Blair, BAL 28
L. Cardenas, MIN 27
R. Perranoski, MIN 25
D. McNally, BAL 25
T. Oliva, MIN 21
S. Bando, OAK 18
C. Tovar, MIN 9
M. Stottlemyre, NY 8
C. Yastrzemski, BOS 8
E. Brinkman, WAS 7
J. Fregosi, CAL 7
R. Smith, BOS 6
D. Unser, WAS 5
B. Robinson, BAL 5
M. Epstein, WAS 4
M. Andrews, BOS 3
D. Bosman, WAS 3
B. Freehan, DET 3
T. Harper, SEA 2
A. Messersmith, CAL 2
R. Reese, MIN 2
K. Tatum, CAL 2
R. White, NY 2
M. Belanger, BAL 2
D. Green, OAK 1
J. Northrup, DET 1
L. Piniella, KC 1

1970 NATIONAL
J. Bench, CIN 326
B. Williams, CHI 218
T. Perez, CIN 149
B. Gibson, SL 110
W. Parker, LA 91
D. Giusti, PIT 72
P. Rose, CIN 54
J. Hickman, CHI 52
W. McCovey, SF 47
R. Carty, ATL 43
M. Sanguillen, PIT 36
R. Clemente, PIT 33
D. Clendenon, NY 26
G. Perry, SF 24
W. Stargell, PIT 20
B. Tolan, CIN 17
H. Aaron, ATL 16
J. Torre, SL 15
T. Agee, NY 13
B. Harrelson, NY 10
F. Jenkins, CHI 8
J. Merritt, CIN 8
D. Kessinger, CHI 6
C. Gaston, SD 5
D. Johnson, PHI 4
L. Walker, PIT 4
C. Morton, MON 3
B. Robertson, PIT 3
T. Seaver, NY 2
W. Granger, CIN 1

1970 AMERICAN
B. Powell, BAL 234
T. Oliva, MIN 157
H. Killebrew, MIN 152
C. Yastrzemski, BOS 136
F. Howard, WAS 91
T. Harper, MIL 78
B. Robinson, BAL 75
A. Johnson, CAL 70
J. Perry, MIN 63
F. Robinson, BAL 60
M. Cuellar, BAL 45
R. Perranoski, MIN 35
J. Fregosi, CAL 35
L. Aparicio, CHI 35
R. White, NY 25
D. McNally, BAL 22
S. McDowell, CLE 22
C. Tovar, MIN 16
T. Munson, NY 15
D. Buford, BAL 12
C. Wright, CAL 8
L. McDaniel, NY 8
R. Fosse, CLE 7
B. Campaneris, OAK 5
J. Palmer, BAL 4
R. Smith, BOS 3
S. Bando, OAK 1
T. Horton, CLE 1
B. Oliver, KC 1

1971 NATIONAL
J. Torre, SL 318
W. Stargell, PIT 222
H. Aaron, ATL 180
B. Bonds, SF 139
R. Clemente, PIT 87
M. Wills, LA 74
F. Jenkins, CHI 71
M. Sanguillen, PIT 49
T. Seaver, NY 46
A. Downing, LA 36
G. Beckert, CHI 35
L. May, CIN 28
L. Brock, SL 20
D. Giusti, PIT 16
W. McCovey, SF 15
T. Simmons, SL 13
W. Davis, LA 13
J. Johnson, SF 12
W. Mays, SF 11
R. Staub, MON 11
B. Williams, CHI 10
B. Harrelson, NY 4
B. Gibson, SL 3
R. Garr, ATL 1
D. Roberts, SD 1
P. Rose, CIN 1

1971 AMERICAN
V. Blue, OAK 268
S. Bando, OAK 182
F. Robinson, BAL 170
B. Robinson, BAL 163
M. Lolich, DET 155
F. Patek, KC 77
B. Murcer, NY 72
A. Otis, KC 67
W. Wood, CHI 54
T. Oliva, MIN 36
D. McNally, BAL 26
N. Cash, DET 21
B. Melton, CHI 18
R. Jackson, OAK 15
C. Rojas, KC 15
K. Sanders, MIL 13
P. Dobson, BAL 9
R. Smith, BOS 9
D. Johnson, BAL 8
M. Rettenmund, BAL 8
H. Killebrew, MIN 5
J. Palmer, BAL 5
L. Cardenas, MIN 5
M. Cuellar, BAL 4
C. Tovar, MIN 4
G. Scott, BOS 3
D. Buford, BAL 2
J. Hunter, OAK 1
G. Nettles, CLE 1

1972 NATIONAL
J. Bench, CIN 263
B. Williams, CHI 211
W. Stargell, PIT 201
J. Morgan, CIN 197
S. Carlton, PHI 124
C. Cedeno, HOU 112
A. Oliver, PIT 52
N. Colbert, SD 45
L. May, HOU 30
T. Simmons, SL 22
M. Marshall, MON 22
P. Rose, CIN 19
R. Clemente, PIT 16
C. Carroll, CIN 16
L. Brock, SL 13
H. Aaron, ATL 12
M. Sanguillen, PIT 12
S. Blass, PIT 9
R. Garr, ATL 7
G. Clines, PIT 6
B. Tolan, CIN 6
D. Baker, ATL 5
M. Mota, LA 4
D. Kingman, SF 3
T. McGraw, NY 2
R. Staub, NY 2
T. Seaver, NY 2
J. Cardenal, CHI 1
F. Jenkins, CHI 1
C. Speier, SF 1

1972 AMERICAN
R. Allen, CHI 321
J. Rudi, OAK 164
S. Lyle, NY 158
C. Fisk, BOS 96
B. Murcer, NY 89
G. Perry, CLE 88
W. Wood, CHI 78
L. Tiant, BOS 70½
E. Brinkman, DET 62
M. Lolich, DET 60
J. Hunter, OAK 57
J. Mayberry, KC 27
J. Palmer, BAL 21
B. Grich, BAL 16
R. Carew, MIN 16
B. Campaneris, OAK 11
M. Epstein, OAK 11
L. Aparicio, BOS 9½
R. Petrocelli, BOS 9
R. Jackson, OAK 9
C. May, CHI 6
G. Scott, MIL 6
D. Thompson, MIN 5
T. Harper, BOS 4
A. Kaline, DET 4
B. Freehan, DET 3
K. McMullen, CAL 3
B. Robinson, BAL 3
R. Smith, BOS 3
S. Bando, OAK 2
N. Ryan, CAL 2
A. Otis, KC 1
L. Piniella, KC 1

1973 NATIONAL
P. Rose, CIN 274
W. Stargell, PIT 250
B. Bonds, SF 174
J. Morgan, CIN 102
M. Marshall, MON 93
L. Brock, SL 65
T. Perez, CIN 59
T. Seaver, NY 57
K. Singleton, MON 52
J. Bench, CIN 41
C. Cedeno, HOU 39
H. Aaron, ATL 35
D. Johnson, ATL 34
T. Simmons, SL 20
T. McGraw, NY 17
F. Millan, NY 12
W. Davis, LA 12
D. Evans, ATL 11
L. May, HOU 9
T. Fuentes, SF 8
B. Watson, HOU 7
J. Ferguson LA 7
J. Cardenal, CHI 6
J. Billingham, CIN 6
A. Oliver, PIT 6
R. Hunt, MON 5
R. Bryant, SF 5
G. Maddox, SF 3
B. Harrelson, NY 2
B. Williams, CHI 2
G. Luzinski, PHI 2
B. Russell, LA 1

1973 AMERICAN

R. Jackson, OAK ... 336
J. Palmer, BAL ... 172
A. Otis, KC ... 112
R. Carew, MIN ... 83
J. Hiller, DET ... 83
S. Bando, OAK ... 83
J. Mayberry, KC ... 76
D. May, MIL ... 65
B. Murcer, NY ... 53
T. Davis, BAL ... 47
J. Hunter, OAK ... 47
T. Munson, NY ... 43
T. Harper, BOS ... 33
G. Scott, MIL ... 25
O. Cepeda, BOS ... 21
F. Robinson, CAL ... 21
N. Ryan, CAL ... 20
C. Fisk, BOS ... 16
B. Grich, BAL ... 9
C. Yastrzemski, BOS ... 9
M. Belanger, BAL ... 8
D. Johnson, OAK ... 8
J. Briggs, MIL ... 6
J. Coleman, DET ... 6
C. Rojas, KC ... 5
B. Blyleven, MIN ... 4
G. Perry, CLE ... 4
B. Campaneris, OAK ... 4
V. Blue, OAK ... 3
C. May, CHI ... 3
W. Horton, DET ... 3
B. North, OAK ... 3
P. Blair, BAL ... 2
D. Nelson, TEX ... 2
R. Allen, CHI ... 1

1974 NATIONAL

S. Garvey, LA ... 270
L. Brock, SL ... 233
M. Marshall, LA ... 146
J. Bench, CIN ... 141
J. Wynn, LA ... 137
M. Schmidt, PHI ... 136
A. Oliver, PIT ... 87
J. Morgan, CIN ... 72
R. Zisk, PIT ... 54
W. Stargell, PIT ... 43
R. Smith, SL ... 39
R. Garr, ATL ... 11
T. Simmons, SL ... 7
D. Cash, PHI ... 6
D. Concepcion, CIN ... 5
J. Billingham, CIN ... 4
C. Cedeno, HOU ... 4
A. Hrabosky, SL ... 4
A. Messersmith, LA ... 4
B. Capra, ATL ... 3
L. McGlothen, SL ... 2
B. McBride, SL ... 2
R. Hebner, PIT ... 2
R. Stennett, PIT ... 2
B. Buckner, LA ... 1
R. Cey, LA ... 1

1974 AMERICAN

J. Burroughs, TEX ... 248
J. Rudi, OAK ... 161½
S. Bando, OAK ... 143½
R. Jackson, OAK ... 119
F. Jenkins, TEX ... 118
J. Hunter, OAK ... 107
R. Carew, MIN ... 70
E. Maddox, NY ... 59
B. Grich, BAL ... 49
M. Cuellar, BAL ... 42
L. Tiant, BOS ... 41
B. Robinson, BAL ... 30
P. Blair, BAL ... 27
N. Ryan, CAL ... 24
B. Campaneris, OAK ... 23
R. Fingers, OAK ... 21
G. Perry, CLE ... 18
C. Yastrzemski, BOS ... 14
K. Henderson, CHI ... 12
J. Hiller, DET ... 11
L. Randle, TEX ... 10
B. Murcer, NY ... 10
L. Piniella, NY ... 8
R. Allen, CHI ... 8
S. Lyle, NY ... 7
T. Munson, NY ... 6
T. Davis, BAL ... 6
M. Belanger, BAL ... 6
D. Money, MIL ... 5
T. Murphy, MIL ... 3
H. McRae, KC ... 3
S. Busby, KC ... 3
G. Scott, MIL ... 2
P. Dobson, NY ... 1

1975 NATIONAL

J. Morgan, CIN ... 321½
G. Luzinski, PHI ... 154
D. Parker, PIT ... 120
J. Bench, CIN ... 117
P. Rose, CIN ... 114
T. Simmons, SL ... 103
W. Stargell, PIT ... 69
A. Hrabosky, SL ... 66
T. Seaver, NY ... 65
R. Jones, SD ... 54
S. Garvey, LA ... 50
B. Madlock, CHI ... 45
D. Cash, PHI ... 26
R. Staub, NY ... 20
T. Perez, CIN ... 18
M. Schmidt, PHI ... 16
M. Sanguillen, PIT ... 16
R. Cey, LA ... 11½
D. Kingman, NY ... 9
B. Watson, HOU ... 8
L. Brock, SL ... 6
L. Bowa, PHI ... 3
J. Reuss, PIT ... 2
A. Messersmith, LA ... 1
W. Montanez, PHI-SF ... 1

1975 AMERICAN

F. Lynn, BOS ... 326
J. Mayberry, KC ... 157
J. Rice, BOS ... 154
R. Fingers, OAK ... 129
R. Jackson, OAK ... 118
J. Palmer, BAL ... 82
T. Munson, NY ... 69
G. Scott, MIL ... 64½
R. Carew, MIN ... 54½
K. Singleton, BAL ... 44
G. Brett, KC ... 37½
J. Hunter, NY ... 31
R. Burleson, BOS ... 28
C. Washington, OAK ... 22
T. Harrah, TEX ... 16
M. Torrez, BAL ... 12
R. Gossage, CHI ... 11
P. Lindblad, OAK ... 7
G. Tenace, OAK ... 7
B. Powell, CLE ... 6½
D. Baylor, BAL ... 6
B. Campaneris, OAK ... 6
B. Lee, BOS ... 5
J. Todd, OAK ... 5
D. Doyle, CAL-BOS ... 5
R. Wise, BOS ... 4
J. Rudi, OAK ... 3
J. Kaat, CHI ... 2
L. May, BAL ... 2
B. Bonds, NY ... 1
C. Yastrzemski, BOS ... 1

1976 NATIONAL

J. Morgan, CIN ... 311
G. Foster, CIN ... 221
M. Schmidt, PHI ... 179
P. Rose, CIN ... 131
G. Maddox, PHI ... 98
B. Madlock, CHI ... 51
S. Garvey, LA ... 51
G. Luzinski, PHI ... 49
K. Griffey, CIN ... 49
R. Jones, SD ... 48
B. Watson, HOU ... 38
A. Oliver, PIT ... 30
R. Eastwick, CIN ... 26
J. Koosman, NY ... 20
S. Carlton, PHI ... 16
D. Cash, PHI ... 15
J. Richard, HOU ... 12
R. Monday, CHI ... 11
D. Kingman, NY ... 11
D. Parker, PIT ... 10
B. Robinson, PIT ... 9
D. Sutton, LA ... 7
R. Cey, LA ... 6
W. Montanez, SF-ATL ... 4
L. Brock, SL ... 3
C. Cedeno, HOU ... 3
C. Geronimo, CIN ... 3
R. Zisk, PIT ... 3
L. Bowa, PHI ... 1

1976 AMERICAN

T. Munson, NY ... 304
G. Brett, KC ... 217
M. Rivers, NY ... 179½
H. McRae, KC ... 99
C. Chambliss, NY ... 71½
R. Carew, MIN ... 71
A. Otis, KC ... 58
B. Campbell, MIN ... 56
L. May, BAL ... 51
J. Palmer, BAL ... 47
M. Fidrych, DET ... 41
J. Rudi, OAK ... 35
S. Bando, OAK ... 31
C. Yastrzemski, BOS ... 26
F. Tanana, CAL ... 19
R. Jackson, BAL ... 17
G. Nettles, NY ... 17
G. Tenace, OAK ... 13
R. Fingers, OAK ... 12
V. Blue, OAK ... 10
E. Figueroa, NY ... 9
S. Lyle, NY ... 8
R. LeFlore, DET ... 6
M. Littell, KC ... 5
R. Carty, CLE ... 5
R. White, NY ... 3
L. Tiant, BOS ... 3
J. Mayberry, KC ... 1
B. Wynegar, MIN ... 1

1977 NATIONAL

G. Foster, CIN ... 291
G. Luzinski, PHI ... 255
D. Parker, PIT ... 156
R. Smith, LA ... 112
S. Carlton, PHI ... 100
S. Garvey, LA ... 98
B. Sutter, CHI ... 68
R. Cey, LA ... 60
T. Simmons, SL ... 58
M. Schmidt, PHI ... 48
B. Robinson, PIT ... 34
T. John, LA ... 33
G. Templeton, SL ... 20
R. Fingers, SD ... 17
P. Rose, CIN ... 15
J. Burroughs, ATL ... 9
A. Oliver, PIT ... 9
J. Candelaria, PIT ... 8
R. Stennett, PIT ... 7
W. McCovey, SF ... 5
J. Bench, CIN ... 3
R. Reuschel, CHI ... 3
E. Valentine, MON ... 3
T. McGraw, PHI ... 2
L. Bowa, PHI ... 1
T. Seaver, NY-CIN ... 1

1977 AMERICAN

R. Carew, MIN ... 273
A. Cowens, KC ... 217
K. Singleton, BAL ... 200
J. Rice, BOS ... 163
G. Nettles, NY ... 112
S. Lyle, NY ... 79
T. Munson, NY ... 70
R. Jackson, NY ... 67
C. Fisk, BOS ... 67
B. Campbell, BOS ... 65
M. Rivers, NY ... 59
L. Hisle, MIN ... 54
G. Brett, KC ... 51
R. Zisk, CHI ... 34
J. Sundberg, TEX ... 30
B. Bonds, CAL ... 28
C. Yastrzemski, BOS ... 25
R. Guidry, NY ... 11
J. Palmer, BAL ... 9
R. LeFlore, DET ... 7
J. Thompson, DET ... 6
R. Burleson, BOS ... 5
B. Hobson, BOS ... 4
N. Ryan, CAL ... 3
G. Scott, BOS ... 3
H. McRae, KC ... 3
L. Bostock, MIN ... 2
T. Johnson, MIN ... 2
C. Chambliss, NY ... 1
O. Gamble, CHI ... 1
D. Leonard, KC ... 1

1978 NATIONAL

D. Parker, PIT ... 320
S. Garvey, LA ... 194
L. Bowa, PHI ... 189
R. Smith, LA ... 164
J. Clark, SF ... 107
G. Foster, CIN ... 104
G. Luzinski, PHI ... 48
G. Perry, SD ... 45
W. Stargell, PIT ... 39
D. Winfield, SD ... 37
P. Rose, CIN ... 35
V. Blue, SF ... 33
K. Tekulve, PIT ... 23
R. Fingers, SD ... 16
B. Hooton, LA ... 15
D. Lopes, LA ... 12
P. Niekro, ATL ... 8
B. Buckner, CHI ... 8
J. Burroughs, ATL ... 7
B. Sutter, CHI ... 5
G. Maddox, PHI ... 4
E. Cabell, HOU ... 2
B. Boone, PHI ... 1

1978 AMERICAN

J. Rice, BOS ... 352
R. Guidry, NY ... 291
L. Hisle, MIL ... 201
A. Otis, KC ... 90
R. Staub, DET ... 88
G. Nettles, NY ... 86
D. Baylor, CAL ... 51
E. Murray, BAL ... 50
C. Fisk, BOS ... 49
D. Porter, KC ... 48
R. Carew, MIN ... 46
M. Caldwell, MIL ... 41
R. Gossage, NY ... 39
A. Oliver, TEX ... 26½
J. Sundberg, TEX ... 24
R. LeFlore, DET ... 21
R. Jackson, NY ... 18
C. Yastrzemski, BOS ... 17
G. Brett, KC ... 14
A. Thornton, CLE ... 12½
L. Piniella, NY ... 11
T. Munson, NY ... 9
L. Bostock, CAL ... 8
L. Gura, KC ... 8
F. Lynn, BOS ... 6
M. Rivers, NY ... 6
B. Stanley, BOS ... 6
D. LaRoche, CAL ... 6
D. Money, MIL ... 5
W. Randolph, NY ... 5
D. Eckersley, BOS ... 4
H. McRae, KC ... 4
L. Roberts, SEA ... 3
R. Gale, KC ... 2
K. Singleton, BAL ... 2
R. Burleson, BOS ... 1
F. Tanana, CAL ... 1

1979 NATIONAL

W. Stargell, PIT ... 216
K. Hernandez, SL ... 216
D. Winfield, SD ... 155
L. Parrish, MON ... 128
R. Knight, CIN ... 82
J. Niekro, HOU ... 75½
B. Sutter, CHI ... 69
K. Tekulve, PIT ... 64
D. Concepcion, CIN ... 63
D. Parker, PIT ... 56
D. Kingman, CHI ... 53
G. Foster, CIN ... 34
M. Schmidt, PHI ... 32
S. Garvey, LA ... 30
O. Moreno, PIT ... 23
P. Rose, PHI ... 23
G. Carter, MON ... 15
B. Madlock, SF-PIT ... 14
J. Richard, HOU ... 12
P. Niekro, ATL ... 11½
J. Sambito, HOU ... 9
T. Seaver, CIN ... 9
J. Bench, CIN ... 7
A. Dawson, MON ... 6
G. Templeton, SL ... 5
G. Matthews, ATL ... 4
D. Collins, CIN ... 3
B. Horner, ATL ... 1

1979 AMERICAN

D. Baylor, CAL ... 347
K. Singleton, BAL ... 241
G. Brett, KC ... 226
F. Lynn, BOS ... 160½
J. Rice, BOS ... 124
M. Flanagan, BAL ... 100
G. Thomas, MIL ... 87
B. Grich, CAL ... 58
D. Porter, KC ... 52
B. Bell, TEX ... 48
E. Murray, BAL ... 25½
J. Kern, TEX ... 25
M. Marshall, MIN ... 25
B. Downing, CAL ... 24
S. Lezcano, MIL ... 18
R. Smalley, MIN ... 16
W. Wilson, KC ... 15
S. Kemp, DET ... 15
M. Clear, CAL ... 12
P. Molitor, MIL ... 8
R. Burleson, BOS ... 7
T. John, NY ... 5
C. Cooper, MIL ... 4
R. Jackson, NY ... 3
W. Horton, SEA ... 3
D. Ford, CAL ... 1
R. Guidry, NY ... 1
M. Hargrove, CLE ... 1

1980 NATIONAL

M. Schmidt, PHI ... 336
G. Carter, MON ... 193
J. Cruz, HOU ... 166
D. Baker, LA ... 138
S. Carlton, PHI ... 134
S. Garvey, LA ... 131
A. Dawson, MON ... 72
G. Hendrick, SL ... 50
B. Horner, ATL ... 42
B. McBride, PHI ... 32
K. Hernandez, SL ... 29
D. Murphy, ATL ... 23
C. Cedeno, HOU ... 14
J. Bibby, PIT ... 11
B. Buckner, CHI ... 11
T. McGraw, PHI ... 10
J. Bench, CIN ... 7
J. Clark, SF ... 6
J. Niekro, HOU ... 3
M. Easler, PIT ... 2
J. Reuss, LA ... 2
K. Griffey, CIN ... 1
R. LeFlore, MON ... 1
G. Richards, SD ... 1
R. Scott, MON ... 1

1980 AMERICAN

G. Brett, KC ... 335
R. Jackson, NY ... 234
R. Gossage, NY ... 218
W. Wilson, KC ... 169
C. Cooper, MIL ... 160
E. Murray, BAL ... 106
R. Cerone, NY ... 77
D. Quisenberry, KC ... 76½
S. Stone, BAL ... 53
R. Henderson, OAK ... 51
A. Oliver, TEX ... 31½
T. Armas, OAK ... 29
A. Bumbry, BAL ... 27
B. Oglivie, MIL ... 27
W. Randolph, NY ... 10
M. Norris, OAK ... 10
R. Yount, MIL ... 8
M. Rivers, TEX ... 7
B. Bell, TEX ... 7
A. Trammell, DET ... 6
K. Singleton, BAL ... 4
T. Perez, BOS ... 2
M. Dilone, CLE ... 2
F. Lynn, BOS ... 1
J. Wathan, KC ... 1

1981 NATIONAL

M. Schmidt, PHI ... 321
A. Dawson, MON ... 215
G. Foster, CIN ... 146
D. Concepcion, CIN ... 108
F. Valenzuela, LA ... 90
G. Carter, MON ... 77
D. Baker, LA ... 65
B. Sutter, SL ... 59
S. Carlton, PHI ... 41
T. Seaver, CIN ... 35
P. Rose, PHI ... 35
B. Buckner, CHI ... 35
G. Matthews, PHI ... 31
J. Cruz, HOU ... 25
G. Hendrick, SL ... 25
N. Ryan, HOU ... 23
B. Madlock, PIT ... 20
A. Howe, HOU ... 16
T. Raines, MON ... 15
R. Camp, ATL ... 9
K. Hernandez, SL ... 9
T. Herr, SL ... 7
G. Minton, SF ... 4
W. Cromartie, MON ... 3
S. Garvey, LA ... 1
M. May, SF ... 1

1981 AMERICAN

R. Fingers, MIL ... 319
R. Henderson, OAK ... 308
D. Evans, BOS ... 140
T. Armas, OAK ... 139
E. Murray, BAL ... 137
C. Lansford, BOS ... 109
D. Winfield, NY ... 98
C. Cooper, MIL ... 96
R. Gossage, NY ... 62
T. Paciorek, SEA ... 46
D. Murphy, OAK ... 45
K. Gibson, DET ... 40
S. McCatty, OAK ... 22
B. Grich, CAL ... 19
J. Morris, DET ... 17
A. Oliver, TEX ... 8
R. Yount, MIL ... 7
B. Bell, TEX ... 7
B. Almon, CHI ... 6
J. Mumphrey, NY ... 5
M. Hargrove, CLE ... 4
A. Trammell, DET ... 4
K. Singleton, BAL ... 3
S. Kemp, DET ... 3
D. Martinez, BAL ... 3
G. Luzinski, CHI ... 3
D. Stieb, TOR ... 1
G. Brett, KC ... 1

1982 NATIONAL

D. Murphy, ATL ... 283
L. Smith, SL ... 218
P. Guerrero, LA ... 175
A. Oliver, MON ... 175
B. Sutter, SL ... 134
M. Schmidt, PHI ... 54
J. Clark, SF ... 53
G. Minton, SF ... 44
S. Carlton, PHI ... 41
B. Buckner, CHI ... 38
B. Madlock, PIT ... 37
G. Carter, MON ... 35
O. Smith, SL ... 25
G. Hendrick, SL ... 20
T. Kennedy, SD ... 20
J. Morgan, SF ... 17
K. Hernandez, SL ... 12
J. Thompson, PIT ... 12
G. Garber, ATL ... 6
J. Andujar, SL ... 6
F. Valenzuela, LA ... 3
A. Dawson, MON ... 3
C. Chambliss, ATL ... 2
G. Matthews, PHI ... 2
R. Knight, HOU ... 1

1982 AMERICAN

R. Yount, MIL ... 385
E. Murray, BAL ... 228
D. DeCinces, CAL ... 178
H. McRae, KC ... 175
C. Cooper, MIL ... 152
R. Jackson, CAL ... 107
D. Evans, BOS ... 57
G. Thomas, MIL ... 44½
D. Quisenberry, KC ... 39
R. Henderson, OAK ... 38
D. Winfield, NY ... 33
P. Molitor, MIL ... 29½
L. Parrish, DET ... 26
B. Downing, CAL ... 22
W. Wilson, KC ... 16
R. Fingers, MIL ... 12

B. Boone, CAL 12
P. Vuckovich, MIL 11
J. Rice, BOS 10
T. Harrah, CLE 9
H. Baines, CHI 9
G. Brett, KC 9
D. Baylor, CAL 8
A. Thornton, CLE 8
B. Stanley, BOS 6
J. Palmer, BAL 5
D. Garcia, TOR 5
R. Carew, CAL 5
B. Caudill, SEA 4
B. Bell, TEX 3
C. Ripken, BAL 3
C. Lansford, BOS 1
R. Sutcliffe, CLE 1
G. Ward, MIN 1

1983 NATIONAL
D. Murphy, ATL 318
A. Dawson, MON ...213
M. Schmidt, PHI 191
P. Guerrero, LA 182
T. Raines, MON 83
J. Cruz, HOU 76
D. Thon, HOU 67
B. Madlock, PIT 45
A. Holland, PHI 42
T. Kennedy, SD 37
G. Hendrick, SL 33
T. Pena, PIT 25
J. Denny, PHI 24
M. Soto, CIN 16
D. Evans, SF 16
R. Ramirez, ATL 15
J. Orosco, NY 14
L. Smith, CHI 8½
A. Oliver, MON 3
J. Leonard, SF 2
L. Smith, SL 1½
J. Davis, CHI 1
K. Hernandez, SL-NY . 1
B. Horner, ATL 1
O. Smith, SL 1

1983 AMERICAN
C. Ripken, BAL 322
E. Murray, BAL 290
C. Fisk, CHI 209
J. Rice, BOS 150
C. Cooper, MIL 123
D. Quisenberry, KC 107½
D. Winfield, NY 85
L. Whitaker, DET 84
L. Parrish, DET 66
H. Baines, CHI 49
W. Upshaw, TOR .. 41½
W. Boggs, BOS 25
L. Hoyt, CHI 24½
L. Moseby, TOR 21
B. Stanley, BOS 11½
A. Trammell, DET 11
G. Luzinski, CHI 9
R. Yount, MIL 6
T. Simmons, MIL 4
R. Dotson, CHI 3½
R. Law, CHI 2
R. Guidry, NY 2
J. Morris, DET 2
J. Cruz, SEA-CHI 1
R. Henderson, OAK ... 1
G. Wright, TEX 1
T. Martinez, BAL ...... ½

1984 NATIONAL
R. Sandberg, CHI ...326
K. Hernadez, NY 195
T. Gwynn, SD 184
R. Sutcliffe, CHI 151
G. Matthews, CHI ... 70
B. Sutter, SL 67
M. Schmidt, PHI ... 55½
J. Cruz, HOU 53
D. Murphy, ATL ... 52½
J. Davis, CHI 49
T. Raines, MON 41
L. Durham, CHI 38
R. Gossage, SD 34
G. Carter, MON 32
D. Gooden, NY 28
A. Wiggins, SD 14
R. Cey, CHI 6
K. McReynolds, SD ... 6
B. Dernier, CHI 6
S. Garvey, SD 5
B. Brenly, SF 1
J. Samuel, PHI 1
J. Leonard, SF 1

1984 AMERICAN
W. Hernandez, DET.306
K. Hrbek, MIN 247
D. Quisenberry, KC .235
E. Murray, BAL 197
D. Mattingly, NY 113
K. Gibson, DET 96
T. Armas, BOS 87½
D. Winfield, NY 83
A. Trammell, DET .. 76½
W. Wilson, KC 61
D. Evans, BOS 39
A. Davis, SEA 26
J. Rice, BOS 10
H. Baines, CHI 10
D. Kingman, OAK 10
L. Parrish, DET 8
W. Upshaw, TOR 8
B. Downing, CAL 6
S. Balboni, KC 5
A. Thornton, CLE 5
J. Bell, TOR 5
B. Bell, TEX 4
D. Stieb, TOR 4
L. Moseby, TOR 4
J. Beniquez, CAL 2
M. Boddicker, BAL ... 2
D. Alexander, TOR 1
C. Ripken, BAL 1

1985 NATIONAL
W. McGee, SL 280
D. Parker, CIN 220
P. Guerrero, LA 208
D. Gooden, NY 162
T. Herr, SL 119
G. Carter, NY 116
D. Murphy, ATL 63
K. Hernandez, NY 61
J. Tudor, SL 61
J. Clark, SL 20
V. Coleman, SL 16
T. Raines, MON 15
R. Sandberg, CHI 14
M. Marshall, LA 11
H. Brooks, MON 11
O. Hershiser, LA 9
K. Moreland, CHI 8
O. Smith, SL 5
M. Scioscia, LA 5
J. Reardon, MON 4
J. Cruz, HOU 2
B. Doran, HOU 2
M. Duncan, LA 1
T. Gwynn, SD 1
F. Valenzuela, LA 1
G. Wilson, PHI 1

1985 AMERICAN
D. Mattingly, NY 367
G. Brett, KC 274
R. Henderson, NY ...174
W. Boggs, BOS 159
E. Murray, BAL 130
D. Moore, CAL 96
J. Barfield, TOR 88
J. Bell, TOR 84
H. Baines, CHI 49
B. Saberhagen, KC .. 45
D. Quisenberry, KC .. 39
D. Winfield, NY 35
C. Fisk, CHI 29
Da. Evans, DET 17
R. Guidry, NY 15
P. Bradley, SEA 12
C. Ripken, BAL 9
K. Gibson, DET 7
S. Balboni, KC 6
T. Henke, TOR 5
D. Lamp, TOR 3
K. Puckett, MIN 3
D. Alexander, TOR 3
D. Garcia, TOR 2
R. Gedman, BOS 1

1986 NATIONAL
M. Schmidt, PHI 287
G. Davis, HOU 231
G. Carter, NY 181
K. Hernandez, NY ..179
D. Parker, CIN 144
T. Raines, MON 99
K. Bass, HOU 73
V. Hayes, PHI 41
T. Gwynn, SD 34
M. Scott, HOU 33
B. Doran, HOU 32
E. Davis, CIN 21
S. Sax, LA 13
R. Knight, NY 9
M. Krukow, SF 8
T. Worrell, SL 7
R. McDowell, NY 5
D. Smith, HOU 5
F. Valenzuela, LA 4
L. Dykstra, NY 4
B. Ojeda, NY 2
D. Murphy, ATL 2
C. Maldonado, SF 2

1986 AMERICAN
R. Clemens, BOS ...339
D. Mattingly, NY 258
J. Rice, BOS 241
J. Bell, TOR..........125
J. Barfield, TOR 107
K. Puckett, MIN 105
W. Boggs, BOS 87
W. Joyner, CAL 74
J. Carter, CLE 72
D. Righetti, NY 71
D. DeCinces, CAL ... 56
M. Witt, CAL 34
D. Baylor, BOS 32
T. Fernandez, TOR .. 17
T. Higuera, MIL 7
G. Gaetti, MIN 6
P. O'Brien, TEX 5
S. Fletcher, TEX 5
M. Barrett, BOS 5
J. Canseco, OAK 3
J. Presley, SEA 2
D. Schofield, CAL 1

1987 NATIONAL
A. Dawson, CHI 269
O. Smith, SL 193
J. Clark, SL 186
T. Wallach, MON 165
W. Clark, SF 128
D. Strawberry, NY ... 95
T. Raines, MON 80
T. Gwynn, SD 75
E. Davis, CIN 73
H. Johnson, NY 42
D. Murphy, ATL 34
V. Coleman, SL 20
J. Samuel, PHI 19
M. Schmidt, PHI 13
P. Guerrero, LA 12
S. Bedrosian, PHI 6
M. Thompson, PHI 4
B. Doran, HOU 1
T. Pendleton, SL 1

1987 AMERICAN
J. Bell, TOR 332
A. Trammell, DET ...311
K. Puckett, MIN 201
Dw. Evans, BOS 127
P. Molitor, MIL 125
M. McGwire, OAK ..109
D. Mattingly, NY 92
T. Fernandez, TOR .. 79
W. Boggs, BOS 64
G. Gaetti, MIN 47
J. Reardon, MIN 37
Da. Evans, DET 21
D. Alexander, DET ... 17
T. Henke, TOR 17
W. Joyner, CAL 17
K. Hrbek, MIN 11
D. Tartabull, KC 10
R. Yount, MIL 8
R. Clemens, BOS 7
J. Morris, DET 5
K. Seitzer, KC 5
R. Sierra, TEX 5
J. Canseco, OAK 4
M. Nokes, DET 1

1988 NATIONAL
K. Gibson, LA 272
D. Strawberry, NY ..236
K. McReynolds,NY . 162
A. Van Slyke, PIT ...160
W. Clark, SF 135
O. Hershiser, LA 111
A. Galarraga, MON . 105
G. Davis, HOU 72
D. Jackson, CIN 41
D. Cone, NY 37
T. Gwynn, SD 29
J. Franco, CIN 23
E. Davis, CIN 14
B. Bonilla, PIT 7
A. Dawson, CHI 6
R. Myers, NY 3
B. Butler, SF 2
S. Sax, LA 1

1988 AMERICAN
J. Canseco, OAK ...392
M. Greenwell, BOS .242
K. Puckett, MIN 219
D. Winfield, NY 164
D. Eckersley, OAK ..156
W. Boggs, BOS 107
A. Trammell, DET 62
P. Molitor, MIL 50
Dw. Evans, BOS 49
F. Viola, MIN 39
R. Yount, MIL 34
G. Brett, KC 29
D. Henderson, OAK .. 28
B. Hurst, BOS 15
D. Jones, CLE 11
J. Reardon, MIN 11
F. McGriff, TOR 9
R. Henderson, NY 8
M. McGwire, OAK 6
J. Carter, CLE 5
L. Smith, BOS 4
G. Gaetti, MIN 3
D. Plesac, MIL 3
D. Stewart, OAK 3
J. Franco, CLE 2
T. Fernandez, TOR ... 1

1989 NATIONAL
K. Mitchell, SF 314
W. Clark, SF 225
P. Guerrero. SL 190
R. Sandberg, CHI ...157
H. Johnson, NY 153
M. Davis, SD 76
G. Davis, HOU 64
T. Gwynn, SD 57
E. Davis, CIN 44
M. Williams, CHI 41
L. Smith, ATL 34
J. Clark, SD 16
J. Walton, CHI 14
M. Grace, CHI 9
M. Scott, HOU 6
B. Bonilla, PIT 5
B. Butler, SF 3
T. Raines, MON 3
M. Thompson, SL 3
S. Garrelts, SF 2

1989 AMERICAN
R. Yount, MIL 256
R. Sierra, TEX 228
C. Ripken, BAL 216
J. Bell, TOR 205
D. Eckersley, OAK ..116
F. McGriff, TOR 96
K. Puckett, MIN 84
B. Saberhagen, KC .. 82
R. Henderson, NY-OAK 67
B. Jackson, KC 46
D. Parker, OAK 44
G. Olson, BAL 35
B. Blyleven, CAL 32
D. Stewart, OAK 30
D. Mattingly, NY 25
J. Carter, CLE 23
C. Lansford, OAK 20
N. Esasky, BOS 19
T. Fernandez, TOR ... 9
M. Moore, OAK 6
W. Boggs, BOS 3
S. Sax, NY 3
A. Davis, SEA 2
N. Ryan, TEX 2
C. Davis, CAL 1
M. McGwire, OAK 1
M. Wilson, TOR 1

1990 NATIONAL
B. Bonds, PIT 331
B. Bonilla, PIT 212
D. Strawberry, NY .. 167
R. Sandberg, CHI ... 151
E. Murray, LA 123
M. Williams, SF 95
B. Larkin, CIN 82
D. Drabek, PIT 59
L. Dykstra, PHI 41
T. Wallach, MON 36
K. Mitchell, SF 20
E. Davis, CIN 12
C. Sabo, CIN 11
R. Gant, ATL 10
D. Gooden, NY 10
R. Martinez, LA 9
J. Carter, SD 7
R. Myers, CIN 7
P. O'Neill, CIN 6
J. Rijo, CIN 6
A. Dawson, CHI 6
D. Magadan, NY 4
B. Santiago, SD 3
B. Butler, SF 2
D. Justice, ATL 2
P. Guerrero, SL 2
K. Daniels, LA 1
A. Van Slyke, PIT 1

1990 AMERICAN
R. Henderson, OAK 317
C. Fielder, DET 286
R. Clemens, BOS ...212
K. Gruber, TOR 175
B. Thigpen, CHI 170
D. Eckersley, OAK ..112
G. Brett, KC 60
D. Stewart, OAK 56
B. Welch, OAK 54
F. McGriff, TOR 30
M. McGwire, OAK ... 29
J. Canseco, OAK 26
E. Burks, BOS 25
R. Palmeiro, TEX 22
C. Fisk, CHI 16
D. Parker, MIL 11
O. Guillen, CHI 10
J. Reed, BOS 9
K. Griffey, Jr., SEA 7
A. Trammell, DET 7
T. Pena, BOS 6
W. Boggs, BOS 5
D. Jones, CLE 3
C. Ripken, BAL 2
N. Ryan, TEX 1
D. Stieb, TOR 1

1991 NATIONAL
T. Pendleton, ATL ...274
B. Bonds, PIT 259
B. Bonilla, PIT 191
W. Clark, SF 118
H. Johnson, NY 112
R. Gant, ATL 110
B. Butler, LA 103
L. Smith, SL 89
D. Strawberry, LA 76
F. McGriff, SD 23
T. Glavine, ATL 16
D. Justice, ATL 11
J. Bell, PIT 11
A. Dawson, CHI 5
J. Smiley, PIT 5
T. Gwynn, SD 4
J. Kruk, PHI 2
R. Sandberg, CHI 2
B. Larkin, CIN 2
D. Martinez, MON 1
C. Sabo, CIN 1
O. Smith, SL 1

1991 AMERICAN
C. Ripken, BAL 318
C. Fielder, DET 286
F. Thomas, CHI 181
J. Canseco, OAK ...145
J. Carter, TOR 136
R. Alomar, TOR 128
K. Puckett, MIN 78
R. Sierra, TEX 63
K. Griffey, Jr., SEA ... 62
R. Clemens, BOS 57
P. Molitor, MIL 51
D. Tartabull, KC 32
J. Morris, MIN 29
C. Davis, MIN 21
J. Franco, TEX 17
D. White, TOR 15
S. Erickson, MIN 12
R. Aguilera, MIN 11
R. Palmeiro, TEX 6
R. Ventura, CHI 3
D. Henderson, OAK ... 1

1992 NATIONAL
B. Bonds, PIT 304
T. Pendleton, ATL ...232
G. Sheffield, SD 204
A. Van Slyke, PIT ...145
L. Walker, MON 111
D. Daulton, PHI 100
F. McGriff, SD 100
B. Roberts, CIN 64
M. Grissom, MON ... 54
T. Glavine, ATL 18
G. Maddux, CHI 14
R. Sandberg, CHI 12
B. Larkin, CIN 12
D. Jones, HOU 8
J. Kruk, PHI 8
M. Grace, PHI 6
D. DeShields, MON ... 6
R. Lankford, SL 5
J. Bagwell, HOU 4
D. Hollins, PHI 3
B. Butler, LA 2
O. Smith, SL 2
O. Nixon, ATL 1
J. Wetteland, MON ... 1

1992 AMERICAN
D. Eckersley, OAK ..306
K. Puckett, MIN 209
J. Carter, TOR 201
M. McGwire, OAK ..155
D. Winfield, TOR 141
R. Alomar, TOR 118
M. Devereaux, BAL 109
F. Thomas, CHI 108
C. Fielder, DET 83
P. Molitor, MIL 63
C. Baerga, CLE 31
E. Martinez, SEA 29
J. Morris, TOR 18
R. Clemens, BOS 16
B. Anderson, BAL ... 16
J. Gonzalez, TEX ... 15
K. Griffey, Jr., SEA ... 13
P. Listach, MIL 8
J. McDowell, CHI 5
J. Bell, CHI 3
M. Bordick, OAK 2
M. Mussina, BAL 2
A. Belle, CLE 1

1993 NATIONAL
B. Bonds, SF 372
L. Dykstra, PHI 267
D. Justice, ATL 183
F. McGriff, SD-ATL .177
R. Gant, ATL 176
M. Williams, SF 103
D. Daulton, PHI 79
M. Grissom, MON ... 66
M. Piazza, LA 49
A. Galarraga, COL .. 45
G. Jefferies, SL 28
R. Beck, SF 23
G. Maddux, ATL 17
B. Harvey, FLA 14
R. Thompson, SF 11
J. Blauser, ATL 9
J. Kruk, PHI 9
M. Grace, CHI 8
J. Bell, PIT 4
J. Bagwell, HOU 3
T. Gwynn, SD 2
R. Myers, CHI 2
J. Rijo, CIN 2
J. Burkett, SF 1
T. Glavine, ATL 1

J. Wetteland, MON ... 1

1993 AMERICAN
F. Thomas, CHI ... 392
P. Molitor, TOR ... 209
J. Olerud, TOR ... 198
J. Gonzalez, TEX ... 185
K. Griffey, Jr., SEA .. 182
R. Alomar, TOR ... 102
A. Belle, CLE ... 81
R. Palmeiro, TEX ... 52
J. McDowell, CHI ... 51
C. Baerga, CLE ... 50
J. Key, NY ... 29
J. Carter, TOR ... 25
M. Stanley, NY ... 15
J. Montgomery, KC .. 15
K. Lofton, CLE ... 11
T. Phillips, DET ... 10
C. Hoiles, BAL ... 10
M. Vaughn, BOS ... 8
D. Mattingly, NY ... 7
C. Ripken, BAL ... 7
A. Fernandez, CHI ... 4
D. Ward, TOR ... 3
G. Gagne, KC ... 3
K. Appier, KC ... 1
C. Fielder, DET ... 1
R. Johnson, SEA ... 1

1994 NATIONAL
J. Bagwell, HOU ... 392
M. Williams, SF ... 201
M. Alou, MON ... 183
B. Bonds, SF ... 144
G. Maddux, ATL ... 133
M. Piazza, LA ... 121
T. Gwynn, SD ... 112
F. McGriff, ATL ... 96
K. Mitchell, CIN ... 86
A. Galarraga, COL ... 42
L. Walker, MON ... 23
K. Hill, MON ... 22
M. Grissom, MON ... 22
D. Bichette, COL ... 19
H. Morris, CIN ... 18
C. Biggio, HOU ... 17
G. Jefferies, SL ... 5
J. Conine, FLA ... 4
T. Wallach, LA ... 4
J. Franco, NY ... 3
B. Boone, CIN ... 2
A. Benes, SD ... 1
B. Butler, LA ... 1
B. Saberhagen, NY ... 1

1994 AMERICAN
F. Thomas, CHI ... 372
K. Griffey, Jr., SEA .. 233
A. Belle, CLE ... 225
K. Lofton, CLE ... 181
P. O'Neill, NY ... 150
J. Key, NY ... 102
K. Puckett, MIN ... 100
J. Franco, CHI ... 49
D. Cone, KC ... 40
J. Carter, TOR ... 35
J. Canseco, TEX ... 27
C. Ripken, BAL ... 24
W. Boggs, NY ... 19
L. Smith, BAL ... 18
W. Clark, TEX ... 17
R. Palmeiro, BAL ... 11
M. Vaughn, BOS ... 10
D. Mattingly, NY ... 9
P. Molitor, TOR ... 9
C. Knoblauch, MIN ... 8
M. Mussina, BAL ... 8
C. Davis, CAL ... 3
J. Bere, CHI ... 1
R. Sierra, OAK ... 1

1995 NATIONAL
B. Larkin, CIN ... 281
D. Bichette, COL ... 251
G. Maddux, ATL ... 249
M. Piazza, LA ... 214
E. Karros, LA ... 135
R. Sanders, CIN ... 120
L. Walker, COL ... 88
S. Sosa, CHI ... 81
T. Gwynn, SD ... 72
C. Biggio, HOU ... 58
R. Gant, CIN ... 31
B. Bonds, SF ... 21
M. Grace, CHI ... 14
D. Bell, HOU ... 12
J. Bagwell, HOU ... 5
C. Hayes, PHI ... 4
A. Galarraga, COL ... 4
C. Jones, ATL ... 3
V. Castilla, COL ... 3
F. McGriff, ATL ... 2
P. Schourek, CIN ... 2
J. Conine, FLA ... 1
T. Henke, SL ... 1

1995 AMERICAN
M. Vaughn, BOS ... 308
A. Belle, CLE ... 300
E. Martinez, SEA ... 244
J. Mesa, CLE ... 130
J. Buhner, SEA ... 120
R. Johnson, SEA ... 111
T. Salmon, CAL ... 110
F. Thomas, CHI ... 86
J. Valentin, BOS ... 57
G. Gaetti, KC ... 45
R. Palmeiro, BAL ... 34
M. Ramirez, CLE ... 30
T. Wakefield, BOS ... 20
J. Edmonds, CAL ... 18
P. O'Neill, NY ... 14
M. McGwire, OAK ... 7
C. Knoblauch, MIN ... 5
W. Boggs, NY ... 5
G. DiSarcina, CAL ... 3
C. Ripken, BAL ... 3
K. Puckett, MIN ... 2

1996 NATIONAL
K. Caminiti, SD ... 392
M. Piazza, LA ... 237
E. Burks, COL ... 186
C. Jones, ATL ... 158
B. Bonds, SF ... 132
A. Galarraga, COL ... 112
G. Sheffield, FLA ... 112
B. Jordan, SL ... 69
J. Bagwell, HOU ... 59
S. Finley, SD ... 38
J. Smoltz, ATL ... 33
B. Larkin, CIN ... 29
M. Grissom, ATL ... 23
B. Gilkey, NY ... 13
S. Sosa, CHI ... 12
E. Karros, LA ... 10
H. Rodriguez, MON ... 9
T. Hundley, NY ... 7
L. Johnson, NY ... 7
D. Bichette, COL ... 6
T. Worrell, LA ... 3
K. Brown, FLA ... 2
T. Hoffman, SD ... 2
M. Alou, MON ... 1

1996 AMERICAN
J. Gonzalez, TEX ... 290
A. Rodriguez, SEA .. 228
A. Belle, CLE ... 228
K. Griffey, Jr., SEA .. 188
M. Vaughn, BOS ... 124
R. Palmeiro, BAL ... 104
M. McGwire, OAK ... 100
F. Thomas, CHI ... 88
B. Anderson, BAL ... 53
I. Rodriguez, TEX ... 52
K. Lofton, CLE ... 34
M. Duncan, NY ... 27
P. Molitor, MIN ... 19
A. Pettitte, NY ... 11
J. Thome, CLE ... 9
C. Knoblauch, MIN ... 8
J. Buhner, SEA ... 6
B. Williams, NY ... 4
J. Wetteland, NY ... 4
R. Alomar, BAL ... 3
T. Steinbach, OAK ... 1

1997 NATIONAL
L. Walker, COL ... 359
M. Piazza, LA ... 263
J. Bagwell, HOU ... 233
C. Biggio, HOU ... 157
B. Bonds, SF ... 123
T. Gwynn, SD ... 113
A. Galarraga, COL ... 85
J. Kent, SF ... 80
C. Jones, ATL ... 70
M. Alou, FLA ... 60
C. Johnson, FLA ... 22
G. Maddux, ATL ... 16
E. Alfonzo, NY ... 10
C. Schilling, PHI ... 9
R. Mondesi, LA ... 8
R. Lankford, SL ... 6
P. Martinez, MON ... 6
M. McGwire, SL ... 6
S. Sosa, CHI ... 5
K. Young, PIT ... 5
J. Blauser, ATL ... 4
V. Castilla, COL ... 3
D. Kile, HOU ... 3
R. Beck, SF ... 2
T. Womack, PIT ... 2
K. Lofton, ATL ... 1
J. Snow, SF ... 1

1997 AMERICAN
K. Griffey, Jr., SEA .. 392
T. Martinez, NY ... 248
F. Thomas, CHI ... 172
R. Myers, BAL ... 128
D. Justice, CLE ... 90
J. Thome, CLE ... 89
T. Salmon, ANA ... 84
N. Garciaparra, BOS . 83
J. Gonzalez, TEX ... 66
R. Clemens, TOR ... 56
R. Johnson, SEA ... 42
P. O'Neill, NY ... 37
R. Palmeiro, BAL ... 36
S. Alomar, CLE ... 22
E. Martinez, SEA ... 22
I. Rodriguez, TEX ... 16
B. Williams, NY ... 14
T. Clark, DET ... 13
J. Buhner, SEA ... 12
D. Jones, MIL ... 5
A. Rhodes, BAL ... 5
R. Alomar, BAL ... 4
R. Greer, TEX ... 4
D. Jeter, NY ... 3
D. Cruz, DET ... 2
B. Radke, MIN ... 2
M. Rivera, NY ... 2
M. Vaughn, BOS ... 2
J. Burnitz, MIL ... 1

1998 NATIONAL
S. Sosa, CHI ... 438
M. McGwire, SL ... 272
M. Alou, HOU ... 215
G. Vaughn, SD ... 185
C. Biggio, HOU ... 163
A. Galarraga, ATL ... 147
T. Hoffman, SD ... 117
B. Bonds, SF ... 66
C. Jones, ATL ... 56
J. Kent, SF ... 56
V. Castilla, COL ... 49
J. Olerud, NY ... 38
V. Guerrero, MON ... 25
M. Piazza, LA-FLA-NY ... 15
T. Gwynn, SD ... 11
K. Brown, SD ... 8
L. Walker, COL ... 7
R. Beck, CHI ... 5
J. Burnitz, MIL ... 4
S. Rolen, PHI ... 3
T. Glavine, ATL ... 2
R. Johnson, HOU ... 2
D. Bichette, COL ... 2
J. Lopez, ATL ... 1
M. Morandini, CHI ... 1

1998 AMERICAN
J. Gonzalez, TEX ... 357
N. Garciaparra, BOS ... 232
D. Jeter, NY ... 180
M. Vaughn, BOS ... 135
K. Griffey, Jr., SEA .. 135
M. Ramirez, CLE ... 127
B. Williams, NY ... 103
A. Belle, CHI ... 98
A. Rodriguez, SEA ... 92
I. Rodriguez, TEX ... 50
R. Clemens, TOR ... 49
P. O'Neill, NY ... 36
T. Gordon, BOS ... 27
D. Erstad, ANA ... 7
T. Salmon, ANA ... 7
D. Wells, NY ... 3
J. Wetteland, TEX ... 3
E. Davis, BAL ... 2
T. Fryman, CLE ... 2
R. Palmeiro, BAL ... 2
C. Delgado, TOR ... 1
R. Helling, TEX ... 1
M. Jackson, CLE ... 1
P. Martinez, BOS ... 1
J. Thome, CLE ... 1

1999 NATIONAL
C. Jones, ATL ... 432
J. Bagwell, HOU ... 276
M. Williams, ARI ... 269
G. Vaughn, CIN ... 121
M. McGwire, SL ... 115
R. Ventura, NY ... 113
M. Piazza, NY ... 109
E. Alfonzo, NY ... 88
S. Sosa, CHI ... 87
L. Walker, COL ... 35
V. Guerrero, MON ... 34
C. Biggio, HOU ... 32
J. Bell, ARI ... 31
S. Casey, CIN ... 23
R. Johnson, ARI ... 21
B. Wagner, HOU ... 19
C. Everett, HOU ... 15
L. Gonzalez, ARI ... 12
B. Jordan, ATL ... 11
B. Giles, PIT ... 11
M. Hampton, HOU ... 10
B. Larkin, CIN ... 7
B. Abreu, PHI ... 6
B. Bonds, SF ... 3
M. Mantei, ARI ... 3
J. Kent, SF ... 2
K. Millwood, ATL ... 2
T. Hoffman, SD ... 1

1999 AMERICAN
I. Rodriguez, TEX ... 252
P. Martinez, BOS ... 239
R. Alomar, CLE ... 226
M. Ramirez, CLE ... 226
R. Palmeiro, TEX ... 193
D. Jeter, NY ... 177
N. Garciaparra, BOS ... 137
J. Giambi, OAK ... 49
S. Green, TOR ... 44
K. Griffey, Jr., SEA ... 42
B. Williams, NY ... 21
C. Delgado, TOR ... 16
J. Gonzalez, TEX ... 10
M. Rivera, NY ... 9
A. Rodriguez, SEA ... 4
O. Vizquel, CLE ... 3
M. Stairs, OAK ... 2
J. Jaha, OAK ... 1
B. Surhoff, BAL ... 1

2000 NATIONAL
J. Kent, SF ... 392
B. Bonds, SF ... 279
M. Piazza, NY ... 271
J. Edmonds, SL ... 208
T. Helton, COL ... 198
V. Guerrero, MON .. 117
J. Bagwell, HOU ... 102
A. Jones, ATL ... 95
G. Sheffield, LA ... 71
S. Sosa, CHI ... 71
C. Jones, ATL ... 23
G. Maddux, ATL ... 12
R. Nen, SF ... 12
T. Glavine, ATL ... 8
E. Alfonzo, NY ... 6
E. Burks, SF ... 6
R. Johnson, ARI ... 5
D. Kile, SL ... 4
B. Giles, PIT ... 3
M. Alou, HOU ... 2
R. Hidalgo, HOU ... 2
A. Alfonseca, FLA ... 1

2000 AMERICAN
Ja. Giambi, OAK ... 317
F. Thomas, CHI ... 285
A. Rodriguez, SEA .. 218
C. Delgado, TOR ... 206
P. Martinez, BOS ... 103
E. Martinez, SEA ... 97
M. Ramirez, CLE ... 97
D. Erstad, ANA ... 94
N. Garciaparra, BOS . 66
D. Jeter, NY ... 44
M. Sweeney, KC ... 33
M. Ordoñez, CHI ... 28
D. Justice, CLE-NY .. 23
B. Williams, NY ... 23
T. Hudson, OAK ... 8
M. Tejada, OAK ... 5
T. Fryman, CLE ... 2
D. Wells, TOR ... 2
J. Damon, KC ... 1

Rookie of the Year Award: History

The Chicago chapter of the Baseball Writers' Association of America (BBWAA) established an award recognizing the major leagues' top rookie following the 1940 season, selecting Lou Boudreau for the honor. This procedure continued for six more years before going national. The subsequent winners of the Chicago chapter's award were Pete Reiser (1941), Johnny Beazley (1942), Bill Johnson (1943), Bill Voiselle (1944), Boo Ferriss (1945), and Eddie Waitkus (1946).

In 1947 a group of 39 baseball writers were asked to name five rookies in order of preference, with votes distributed on a 5-4-3-2-1 basis. Thus, Jackie Robinson became the first nationally recognized winner of the BBWAA Rookie of the Year Award, or the J. Louis Comiskey Memorial Award, as it was called. During the 1987 Hall of Fame induction ceremony, Commissioner Peter Ueberroth announced that, hereafter, the Rookie of the Year Award would be officially known as the Jackie Robinson Award.

In 1948 there were 48 writers taking part in the award, this time naming only a single candidate on each ballot. In 1949 the BBWAA began the process of choosing a top rookie in each league. Three writers from each league city, the same men who decided on the MVP Awards, participated in the voting. Voters were free to use their individual judgments as to the eligibility of rookie candidates, which created some problems, especially in 1950 when Al Rosen, and his league-leading 37 homers, was ignored by Rookie of the Year voters. Apparently they felt that Rosen's 58 previous major league at bats were tantamount to veteran status, while winner Walt Dropo's 41 previous at bats were not.

In 1957 formal guidelines were finally established for determining rookie status. A player could not have accumulated more than 75 at bats, 45 innings pitched, or have been on a major league roster between May 15 and September 1 of any previous season. Shortly after, the guidelines were changed to 90 at bats, 45 innings pitched or 45 days on a major league roster before September 1. Finally, in 1971, the guidelines were set at 130 at bats, 50 innings, or 45 days on a roster.

There were several instances, especially in the early days of the award, in which some Rookie of the Year voters didn't bother to exercise their franchise. In 1961, as with the MVP Award, the number of voters was reduced from three to two writers from each league city.

Following two tie votes in four years (1976 NL, 1979 AL), the writers adopted the system used in Cy Young Award balloting: naming three rookies on each ballot, in order of preference, with votes distributed on a 5-3-1 basis. This system began in 1980, although it had been scheduled to start a decade earlier.

The maximum possible point total available to Rookie of the Year Award candidates was 165 in 1947, 48 in 1948, and 24 in each league in 1949-1960. In the National League it was 16 in 1961, 20 in 1962-1968, 24 in 1969-1979, 120 in 1980-1992, 140 in 1993-97, and 160 from 1998 to the present. In the American League the maximum point total was 20 in 1961-1968, 24 in 1969-1976, 28 in 1977-1979, and 140 from 1980 to the present.

There have been 14 unanimous Rookie of the Year selections since 1947: Frank Robinson (NL, 1956), Orlando Cepeda (NL, 1958), Willie McCovey (NL, 1959), Carlton Fisk (AL, 1972), Vince Coleman (NL, 1985), Benito Santiago (NL, 1987), Mark McGwire (AL, 1987), Sandy Alomar (AL, 1990), Mike Piazza (NL, 1993), Tim Salmon (AL, 1993), Raul Mondesi (NL, 1994), Derek Jeter (AL, 1996), Scott Rolen (NL, 1997), and Nomar Garciaparra (AL, 1997). Technically, Tony Kubek's 1957 AL selection was also unanimous, as the lone dissenting vote went to an ineligible player.

Rookie of the Year Award

1947
J. Robinson, BRO (NL) 129
L. Jansen, NY (NL) 105
F. Shea, NY (AL) 67
F. Fain, PHI (AL) 43
F. Baumholtz, CIN (NL) 42
(Rest of voting unknown)

1948
A. Dark, BOS (NL) 27
G. Bearden, CLE (AL) 8
R. Ashburn, PHI (NL) 7
L. Brissie, PHI (AL) 3
B. Goodman, BOS (AL) 3

1949 NATIONAL
D. Newcombe, BRO 21
D. Crandall, BOS 3

1949 AMERICAN
R. Sievers, SL 10
A. Kellner, PHI 5
G. Coleman, NY 4
B. Kuzava, CHI 1
J. Groth, DET 1
M. Garcia, CLE 1

1950 NATIONAL
S. Jethroe, BOS 11
B. Miller, PHI 5
D. O' Connell, PIT 4
E. Church, PHI 2
B. Serena, CHI 1

1950 AMERICAN
W. Dropo, BOS 15
W. Ford, NY 6
C. Carrasquel, CHI 2

1951 NATIONAL
W. Mays, NY 18
C. Nichols, BOS 4
C. Labine, BRO 2

1951 AMERICAN
G. McDougald, NY 13
M. Minoso, CLE-CHI 11

1952 NATIONAL
J. Black, BRO 19
H. Wilhelm, NY 3
D. Groat, PIT 1
E. Mathews, BOS 1

1952 AMERICAN
H. Byrd, PHI 9
C. Courtney, SL 8
S. White, BOS 7

1953 NATIONAL
J. Gilliam, BRO 11
H. Haddix, SL 4
R. Jablonski, SL 3
R. Repulski, SL 2
B. Bruton, MIL 2
F. Baczewski, CIN 1
J. Greengrass, CIN 1

1953 AMERICAN
H. Kuenn, DET 23
T. Umphlett, BOS 1

1954 NATIONAL
W. Moon, SL 17
E. Banks, CHI 4
G. Conley, MIL 2
H. Aaron, MIL 1

1954 AMERICAN
B. Grim, NY 15
J. Finigan, PHI 8
A. Kaline, DET 1

1955 NATIONAL
B. Virdon, SL 15
J. Meyer, PHI 7
D. Bessent, BRO 2

1955 AMERICAN
H. Score, CLE 18
B. Klaus, BOS 5
N. Zauchin, BOS 1

1956 NATIONAL
F. Robinson, CIN 24

1956 AMERICAN
L. Aparicio, CHI 22
T. Francona, BAL 1
R. Colavito, CLE 1

1957 NATIONAL
J. Sanford, PHI 16
E. Bouchee, PHI 4
D. Drott, CHI 3
B. Hazle, MIL 1

1957 AMERICAN
T. Kubek, NY 23
F. Malzone, BOS 1

1958 NATIONAL
O. Cepeda, SF 21

1958 AMERICAN
A. Pearson, WAS 14
R. Duren, NY 7
G. Bell, CLE 3

1959 NATIONAL
W. McCovey, SF 24

1959 AMERICAN
B. Allison, WAS 18
J. Perry, CLE 5
R. Snyder, KC 1

1960 NATIONAL
F. Howard, LA 12
P. Herrera, PHI 4
A. Mahaffey, PHI 3
R. Santo, CHI 2
T. Davis, LA 1

1960 AMERICAN
R. Hansen, BAL 22
C. Estrada, BAL 1
J. Gentile, BAL 1

1961 NATIONAL
B. Williams, CHI 10
J. Torre, MIL 5
J. Curtis, CHI 1

1961 AMERICAN
D. Schwall, BOS 7
D. Howser, KC 6
Fl. Robinson, CHI 2
C. Schilling, BOS 2
L. Thomas, LA 2
J. Wood, DET 1

1962 NATIONAL
K. Hubbs, CHI 19
D. Clendenon, PIT 1

1962 AMERICAN
T. Tresh, NY 13
B. Rodgers, LA 4
B. Allen, MIN 1
D. Chance, LA 1
D. Radatz, BOS 1

1963 NATIONAL
P. Rose, CIN 17
R. Hunt, NY 2
R. Culp, PHI 1

1963 AMERICAN
G. Peters, CHI 10
P. Ward, CHI 6
J. Hall, MIN 4

1964 NATIONAL
R. Allen, PHI 18
R. Carty, MIL 1
J. Hart, SF 1

1964 AMERICAN
T. Oliva, MIN 19
W. Bunker, BAL 1

1965 NATIONAL
J. Lefebvre, LA 13
J. Morgan, HOU 4
F. Linzy, SF 3

1965 AMERICAN
C. Blefary, BAL 12
M. Lopez, CAL 8

1966 NATIONAL
T. Helms, CIN 12
S. Jackson, HOU 3
T. Fuentes, SF 2
R. Hundley, CHI 1
C. Jones, NY 1
L. Jaster, SL 1

1966 AMERICAN
T. Agee, CHI 16
J. Nash, KC 2
D. Johnson, BAL 1
G. Scott, BOS 1

1967 NATIONAL
T. Seaver, NY 11
D. Hughes, SL 6
G. Nolan, CIN 3

1967 AMERICAN
R. Carew, MIN 19
R. Smith, BOS 1

1968 NATIONAL
J. Bench, CIN 10½
J. Koosman, NY 9½

1968 AMERICAN
S. Bahnsen, NY 17
D. Unser, WAS 3

1969 NATIONAL
T. Sizemore, LA 14
C. Laboy, MON 3
A. Oliver, PIT 3
B. Didier, ATL 2
L. Hisle, PHI 2

1969 AMERICAN
L. Piniella, KC 9
M. Nagy, BOS 6
C. May, CHI 5
K. Tatum, CAL 4

1970 NATIONAL
C. Morton, MON 11
B. Carbo, CIN 8
L. Bowa, PHI 3
W. Simpson, CIN 1
C. Cedeno, HOU 1

1970 AMERICAN
T. Munson, NY 23
R. Foster, CLE 1

1971 NATIONAL
E. Williams, ATL 18
W. Montanez, PHI 6

1971 AMERICAN
C. Chambliss, CLE 11
B. Parsons, MIL 5
A. Mangual, OAK 4
D. Griffin, BOS 3
P. Splittorff, KC 1

1972 NATIONAL
J. Matlack, NY 19
Dv. Rader, SF 4
J. Milner, NY 1

1972 AMERICAN
C. Fisk, BOS 24

1973 NATIONAL
G. Matthews, SF 11
S. Rogers, MON 3½
B. Boone, PHI 2
E. Sosa, SF 2
D. Driessen, CIN 2
R. Cey, LA 1
D. Lopes, LA 1
J. Grubb, SD 1
R. Zisk, PIT ½

1973 AMERICAN
A. Bumbry, BAL 13½
P. Garcia, MIL 3
D. Porter, MIL 2
S. Busby, KC 2
D. Medich, NY 2
R. Coggins, BAL 1½

1974 NATIONAL
B. McBride, SL 16
G. Gross, HOU 7
B. Madlock CHI 1

1974 AMERICAN
M. Hargrove, TEX 16½
B. Dent, CHI 3
G. Brett, KC 2
R. Burleson, BOS 1½
J. Sundberg, TEX 1

1975 NATIONAL
J. Montefusco, SF 12
G. Carter, MON 9
Lr. Parrish, MON 1
R. Eastwick, CIN 1
M. Trillo, CHI 1

1975 AMERICAN
F. Lynn, BOS 23½
J. Rice, BOS ½

1976 NATIONAL
B. Metzger, SD 11
P. Zachry, CIN 11
H. Cruz, SL 2

1976 AMERICAN
M. Fidrych, DET 22
B. Wynegar, MIN 2

1977 NATIONAL
A. Dawson, MON 10
S. Henderson, NY 9
G. Richards, SD 4
F. Bannister, HOU 1

1977 AMERICAN
E. Murray, BAL 12½
M. Page, OAK 9½
B. Wills, TEX 4
D. Rozema, DET 2

1978 NATIONAL
B. Horner, ATL 12½
O. Smith, SD 8½
D. Robinson, PIT 3

1978 AMERICAN
L. Whitaker, DET 21
P. Molitor, MIL 3
C. Lansford, CAL 2
R. Gale, KC 1
A. Trammell, DET 1

1979 NATIONAL
R. Sutcliffe, LA 20
J. Leonard, HOU 3
S. Thompson, CHI 1

1979 AMERICAN
J. Castino, MIN 7
A. Griffin, TOR 7
M. Clear, CAL 5
R. Davis, NY 3
R. Baumgarten, CHI 3
P. Putnam, TEX 3

1980 NATIONAL
S. Howe, LA 80
B. Gullickson, MON 53
L. Smith, PHI 49
R. Oester, CIN 16
D. Smith, HOU 13
J. Reardon, NY 2
A. Holland, SF 1
L. Durham, SL 1
B. Walk, PHI 1

1980 AMERICAN
J. Charboneau, CLE 102
D. Stapleton, BOS ... 40
D. Corbett, MIN ... 38
D. Garcia, TOR ... 35
B. Burns, CHI ... 33
R. Peters, DET ... 3
R. Dotson, CHI ... 1

1981 NATIONAL
F. Valenzuela, LA ... 107
T. Raines, MON ... 85
H. Brooks, NY ... 8½
B. Berenyi, CIN ... 5
J. Bonilla, SD ... 5
T. Pena, PIT ... 4
M. Wilson, NY ... 1½

1981 AMERICAN
D. Righetti, NY ... 127
R. Gedman, BOS ... 64
B. Ojeda, BOS ... 36
M. Jones, KC ... 8
D. Engle, MIN ... 4½
M. Witt, CAL ... 4
S. Babitt, OAK ... 4
J. Bell, TOR ... 2
G. Ward, MIN ... 1½
B. Havens, MIN ... 1

1982 NATIONAL
S. Sax, LA ... 63
J. Ray, PIT ... 57
W. McGee, SL ... 39
C. Davis, SF ... 32
L. DeLeon, SD ... 10
R. Sandberg, CHI ... 9
S. Bedrosian, ATL ... 4
D. LaPoint, SL ... 1
E. Show, SD ... 1

1982 AMERICAN
C. Ripken, BAL ... 132
K. Hrbek, MIN ... 90
W. Boggs, BOS ... 10½
E. Vande Berg, SEA ... 9
G. Gaetti, MIN ... 4
D. Hostetler, TEX ... 3
V. Hayes, CLE ... 2
J. Barfield, TOR ... 1½

1983 NATIONAL
D. Strawberry, NY ... 106
C. McMurtry, ATL ... 49
M. Hall, CHI ... 32
G. Redus, CIN ... 8
B. Doran, HOU ... 7
F. DiPino, HOU ... 6
G. Brock, LA ... 3
J. DeLeon, PIT ... 3
M. Thurmond, SD ... 1
L. Tunnell, PIT ... 1

1983 AMERICAN
R. Kittle, CHI ... 104
J. Franco, CLE ... 78
M. Boddicker, BAL ... 70

1984 NATIONAL
D. Gooden, NY ... 118
J. Samuel, PHI ... 67
O. Hershiser, LA ... 15
G. Gladden, SF ... 14
R. Darling, NY ... 3
C. Martinez, SD ... 2
J. Stone, PHI ... 1
T. Pendleton, SL ... 1

1984 AMERICAN
A. Davis, SEA ... 134
M. Langston, SEA ... 82
K. Puckett, MIN ... 23
T. Teufel, MIN ... 5
M. Young, BAL ... 3
R. Clemens, BOS ... 2
M. Gubicza, KC ... 1
A. Nipper, BOS ... 1
R. Romanick, CAL ... 1

1985 NATIONAL
V. Coleman, SL ... 120
T. Browning, CIN ... 72
M. Duncan, LA ... 9
C. Brown, SF ... 7
G. Davis, HOU ... 3
R. McDowell, NY ... 2
J. Orsulak, PIT ... 2
J. Hesketh, MON ... 1

1985 AMERICAN
O. Guillen, CHI ... 101
T. Higuera, MIL ... 67
E. Riles, MIL ... 29
O. McDowell, TEX ... 25
S. Cliburn, CAL ... 16
B. Fisher, NY ... 7
T. Henke, TOR ... 5
M. Salas, MIN ... 2

1986 NATIONAL
T. Worrell, SL ... 118
R. Thompson, SF ... 46
K. Mitchell, NY ... 22
C. Kerfeld, HOU ... 17
W. Clark, SF ... 5
B. Bonds, PIT ... 4
J. Deshaies, HOU ... 1
B. Larkin, CIN ... 1
B. Ruffin, PHI ... 1
J. Kruk, SD ... 1

1986 AMERICAN
J. Canseco, OAK ... 110
W. Joyner, CAL ... 98
M. Eichhorn, TOR ... 23
C. Snyder, CLE ... 16
D. Tartabull, SEA ... 4
R. Sierra, TEX ... 1

1987 NATIONAL
B. Santiago, SD ... 120
M. Dunne, PIT ... 66
J. Magrane, SL ... 10
C. Candaele, MON ... 9
G. Young, HOU ... 7
C. James, PHI ... 1
L. Lancaster, CHI ... 1
G. Mathews, SL ... 1
R. Myers, NY ... 1

1987 AMERICAN
M. McGwire, OAK ... 140
K. Seitzer, KC ... 64
M. Nokes, DET ... 32
M. Greenwell, BOS ... 9
D. White, CAL ... 5
M. Henneman, DET ... 1
N. Liriano, TOR ... 1

1988 NATIONAL
C. Sabo, CIN ... 79
M. Grace, CHI ... 61
T. Belcher, LA ... 35
R. Gant, ATL ... 22
R. Alomar, SD ... 11
D. Berryhill, CHI ... 3
G. Jefferies, NY ... 3
R. Jordan, PHI ... 2

1988 AMERICAN
W. Weiss, OAK ... 103
B. Harvey, CAL ... 49
J. Reed, BOS ... 48
D. August, MIL ... 22
D. Gallagher, CHI ... 18
M. Perez, CHI ... 9
M. Schooler, SEA ... 2
C. Espy, TEX ... 1

1989 NATIONAL
J. Walton, CHI ... 116
D. Smith, CHI ... 68
G. Jefferies, NY ... 18
D. Lilliquist, ATL ... 6
A. Benes, SD ... 3
C. Hayes, PHI ... 3
G. Harris, SD ... 2

1989 AMERICAN
G. Olson, BAL ... 136
T. Gordon, KC ... 67
K. Griffey, SEA ... 21
C. Worthington, BAL ... 16
J. Abbott, CAL ... 10
K. Brown, TEX ... 2

1990 NATIONAL
D. Justice, ATL ... 118
D. DeShields, MON ... 60
H. Morris, CIN ... 13
J. Burkett, SF ... 12
M. Harkey, CHI ... 7
T. Zeile, SL ... 4
M. Grissom, MON ... 1
L. Walker, MON ... 1

1990 AMERICAN
S. Alomar, CLE ... 140
K. Maas, NY ... 47
K. Appier, KC ... 31
J. Olerud, TOR ... 13
K. Tapani, MIN ... 9
T. Fryman, DET ... 5
R. Ventura, CHI ... 3
B. McDonald, BAL ... 2
A. Cole, CLE ... 1
S. Radinsky, CHI ... 1

1991 NATIONAL
J. Bagwell, HOU ... 118
O. Merced, PIT ... 53
R. Lankford, SL ... 28
B. Hunter, ATL ... 7
B. Barberie, MON ... 3
W. Chamberlain, PHI ... 3
C. McElroy, CHI ... 3
M. Stanton, ATL ... 1

1991 AMERICAN
C. Knoblauch, MIN 136
J. Guzman, TOR ... 68
M. Cuyler, DET ... 22
I. Rodriguez, TEX ... 10
B. DeLucia, SEA ... 7
M. Timlin, TOR ... 2
M. Whiten, TOR-CLE ... 2
L. Gomez, BAL ... 1
D. Henry, MIL ... 1
B. Mayne, KC ... 1
C. Nagy, CLE ... 1
P. Plantier, BOS ... 1

1992 NATIONAL
E. Karros, LA ... 116
M. Alou, MON ... 30
T. Wakefield, PIT ... 29
R. Sanders, CIN ... 23
D. Osborne, SL ... 12
M. Perez, SL ... 2
B. Rivera, PHI ... 1
F. Seminara, SD ... 1
B. Williams, HOU ... 1
M. Wohlers, ATL ... 1

1992 AMERICAN
P. Listach, MIL ... 122
K. Lofton, CLE ... 85
D. Fleming, SEA ... 23
C. Eldred, MIL ... 22

1993 NATIONAL
M. Piazza, LA ... 140
G. McMicheal, ATL ... 40
J. Conine, FLA ... 31
C. Carr, FLA ... 18
A. Martin, PIT ... 6
K. Stocker, PHI ... 4
W. Cordero, MON ... 3
K. Rueter, MON ... 3
C. Garcia, PIT ... 2
P. Martinez, LA ... 2
S. Cooke, PIT ... 1
R. Guttierrez, SD ... 1
A. Reynoso, COL ... 1

1993 AMERICAN
T. Salmon, CAL ... 140
J. Bere, CHI ... 59
A. Sele, BOS ... 19
W. Kirby, CLE ... 12
R. Amaral, SEA ... 8
B. Gates, OAK ... 7
T. Neel, OAK ... 5
J. DiPoto, CLE ... 1
D. Hulse, TEX ... 1

1994 NATIONAL
R. Mondesi, LA ... 140
J. Hudek, HOU ... 27
R. Klesko, ATL ... 25
S. Trachsel, CHI ... 22
C. Floyd, MON ... 10
J. Hamilton, SD ... 10
W. Van Landingham, SF ... 9
H. Carrasco, CIN ... 3
B. Jones, NY ... 3
J. Lopez, ATL ... 2
S. Reynolds, HOU ... 1

1994 AMERICAN
B. Hamelin, KC ... 134
M. Ramirez, CLE ... 44
R. Greer, TEX ... 42
D. Hall, TOR ... 9
C. Gomez, DET ... 6
B. Risley, SEA ... 6
B. Anderson, CAL ... 4
J. Edmonds, CAL ... 2
J. Valentin, MIL ... 1

1995 NATIONAL
H. Nomo, LA ... 118
C. Jones, ATL ... 104
Q. Veras, FLA ... 14
J. Isringhausen, NY ... 4
J. Mabry, SL ... 4
C. Perez, MON ... 4
C. Fonville, LA ... 1
B. Hunter, HOU ... 1
C. Johnson, FLA ... 1
I. Valdes, LA ... 1

1995 AMERICAN
M. Cordova, MIN ... 105
G. Anderson, CAL ... 99
A. Pettitte, NY ... 16
T. Percival, CAL ... 13
S. Green, TOR ... 8
R. Durham, CHI ... 3
J. Tavarez, CLE ... 3
J. Nunnally, KC ... 2
T. Goodwin, KC ... 1
B. Radke, MIN ... 1
S. Sparks, MIL ... 1

1996 NATIONAL
T. Hollandsworth, LA ... 105
E. Renteria, FLA ... 84
J. Kendall, PIT ... 30
F. P. Santangelo, MON ... 15
R. Ordonez, NY ... 7
J. Dye, ATL ... 6
A. Benes, SL ... 5

1996 AMERICAN
D. Jeter, NY ... 140
J. Baldwin, CHI ... 64
T. Clark, DET ... 30
R. Coppinger, BAL ... 6
J. Rosado, KC ... 6
D. Erstad, CAL ... 3
T. Batista, OAK ... 1
T. Crabtree, TOR ... 1
J. D'Amico, MIL ... 1

1997 NATIONAL
S. Rolen, PHI ... 140
L. Hernandez, FLA ... 25
M. Morris, SL ... 25
R. Loiselle, PIT ... 22
A. Jones, ATL ... 15
V. Guerrero, MON ... 9
J. Guillen, PIT ... 4
B. Tomko, CIN ... 4
J. Gonzalez, CHI ... 3
T. Womack, PIT ... 3
K. Orie, CHI ... 1
N. Perez, COL ... 1

1997 AMERICAN
N. Garciaparra, BOS ... 140
J. Cruz, SEA-TOR ... 61
J. Dickson, ANA ... 27
D. Cruz, DET ... 12
J. Wright, CLE ... 7
M. Cameron, CHI ... 5

1998 NATIONAL
K. Wood, CHI ... 128
T. Helton, COL ... 119
T. Lee, ARI ... 21
K. Ligtenberg, ATL ... 18
B. Fullmer, MON ... 2

1998 AMERICAN
B. Grieve, OAK ... 130
R. Arrojo, TB ... 61
M. Caruso, CHI ... 34
O. Hernandez, NY ... 25
M. Ordoñez, CHI ... 1
S. Ponson, BAL ... 1

1999 NATIONAL
S. Williamson, CIN ... 118
P. Wilson, FLA ... 88
W. Morris, PIT ... 69
K. Benson, PIT ... 5
A. Gonzalez, FLA ... 4
J. McEwing, SL ... 3
K. McGlinchy, ATL ... 1

1999 AMERICAN
C. Beltran, KC ... 133
F. Garcia, SEA ... 45
J. Zimmerman, TEX ... 27
B. Daubach, BOS ... 16
T. Hudson, OAK ... 13
C. Singleton, CHI ... 9
C. Lee, CHI ... 4
B. Koch, TOR ... 4
T. Nixon, BOS ... 1

2000 NATIONAL
R. Furcal, ATL ... 144
R. Ankiel, SL ... 87
J. Payton, NY ... 37
P. Burrell, PHI ... 10
M. Meluskey, HOU ... 7
L. Berkman, HOU ... 1
J. Pierre, COL ... 1
C. Smith, FLA ... 1

2000 AMERICAN
K. Sasaki, SEA ... 104
T. Long, OAK ... 83
M. Quinn, KC ... 56
B. Molina, ANA ... 3
K. Wunsch, CHI ... 2
S. Cox, TB ... 1
A. Kennedy, ANA ... 1
M. Redman, MIN ... 1
B. Zito, OAK ... 1

Cy Young Award: History

Commissioner Ford Frick, troubled by pitchers' lack of representation in MVP voting, spearheaded the 1956 effort to initiate a "most valuable pitcher" award. Cy Young, baseball's winningest pitcher, who had died the previous November, was the logical choice to name the honor after. At a special meeting on July 9, 1956, the Baseball Writers' Association of America approved, by the slim margin of 14-12, the establishment of the Cy Young Memorial Award, designed to honor the major leagues' outstanding pitcher each year beginning in '56. Ironically, the first winner, Brooklyn's Don Newcombe, also won his league's MVP Award.

One writer from each major league city participated in the balloting. In case of a tie vote, a second balloting was to be taken between the deadlocked pitchers. Hurlers were not to be eligible to win the award more than once, a rule which was evidently scrapped within two years.

Frick was adamantly opposed to the commonly voiced idea to recognize a Cy Young winner in each league but, not long after his December 1965 retirement, the idea became a reality. On March 1, 1967, Frick's successor William Eckert approved the plan for dual awards, with two writers from each league city to select.

The system of having each writer make only one selection prevailed until 1969, when Detroit's Denny McLain and Baltimore's Mike Cuellar tied for the American

League Cy Young Award. Thereafter, writers were instructed to name three pitchers in each league, with five points for each first-place vote, three points for second, and one point for third.

The maximum number of points available for one pitcher was 16 from 1956-60, 18 in 1961, 20 in 1962-68, 24 in 1969, 120 in 1970-76 (AL), and 1970-92 (NL), 140 in 1977-present (AL), and 1993-97 (NL), and 160 in 1998-present (NL). As with every other major award, there have been a few instances in Cy Young voting where at least one writer failed to return a ballot.

Unanimous winners of the Cy Young Award are Sandy Koufax (NL, 1963, '65, and '66), Bob Gibson (NL, 1968), Denny McLain (AL, 1968), Steve Carlton (NL, 1972), Ron Guidry (AL, 1978), Rick Sutcliffe (NL, 1984), Dwight Gooden (NL, 1985), Roger Clemens (AL, 1986, 1998), Orel Hershiser (NL, 1988), and Greg Maddux (NL, 1994-95), and Pedro Martinez (AL, 1999-2000).

Relief pitchers, once overlooked in Cy Young balloting, have become strong candidates in recent years. Until 1970 only one reliever—Lindy McDaniel in 1960—had received even a single vote. The new voting system helped open opportunities for bullpen aces and in 1974 the Dodgers' Mike Marshall became the first reliever to win the Cy Young Award. He has been followed in that distinction by Sparky Lyle (AL, 1977), Bruce Sutter (NL, 1979), Rollie Fingers (AL, 1981), Willie Hernandez (AL, 1984), Steve Bedrosian (NL, 1987), Mark Davis (NL, 1989), and Dennis Eckersley (AL, 1992).

Cy Young Award

1956
D. Newcombe, BRO (NL) 10
S. Maglie, BRO (NL) .. 4
W. Spahn, MIL (NL) ... 1
W. Ford, NY (AL) 1

1957
W. Spahn, MIL (NL) .. 15
D. Donovan, CHI (AL) . 1

1958
B. Turley, NY (AL) 5
W. Spahn, MIL (NL) ... 4
B. Friend, PIT (NL) 3
L. Burdette, MIL (NL) .. 3

1959
E. Wynn, CHI (AL) 13
S. Jones, SF (NL) 2
B. Shaw, CHI (AL) 1

1960
V. Law, PIT (NL) 8
W. Spahn, MIL (NL) ... 4
E. Broglio, SL (NL) 1
L. McDaniel, SL (NL) .. 1

1961
W. Ford, NY (AL) 9
W. Spahn, MIL (NL) ... 6
F. Lary, DET (AL) 2

1962
D. Drysdale, LA (NL) . 14
J. Sanford, SF (NL) ... 4
B. Purkey, CIN (NL) ... 1
B. Pierce, SF (NL) 1

1963
S. Koufax, LA (NL) ... 20

1964
D. Chance, LA (AL) .. 17
L. Jackson, CHI (NL) .. 2
S. Koufax, LA (NL) 1

1965
S. Koufax, LA (NL) ... 20

1966
S. Koufax, LA (NL) ... 20

1967 NATIONAL
M. Mc Cormick, SF .. 18
F. Jenkins, CHI 1
J. Bunning, PHI 1

1967 AMERICAN
J. Lonborg, BOS 18
J. Horlen, CHI 2

1968 NATIONAL
B. Gibson, SL 20

1968 AMERICAN
D. McLain, DET 20

1969 NATIONAL
T. Seaver, NY 23
P. Niekro, ATL 1

1969 AMERICAN
M. Cuellar, BAL 10
D. McLain, DET 10
J. Perry, MIN 3
D. McNally, BAL 1

1970 NATIONAL
B. Gibson, SL 118
G. Perry, SF 51
F. Jenkins CHI 16
D. Giusti, PIT 8
J. Merritt, CIN 8
G. Nolan, CIN 5
T. Seaver, NY 4
W. Granger, CIN 3
C. Morton, MON 2
L. Walker, PIT 1

1970 AMERICAN
J. Perry, MIN 55
D. McNally, BAL 47
S. McDowell, CLE 45
M. Cuellar, BAL 44
J. Palmer, BAL 11
C. Wright, CAL 9
R. Perranoski, MIN 5

1971 NATIONAL
F. Jenkins, CHI 97
T. Seaver, NY 61
A. Downing, LA 40
D. Ellis, PIT 9
B. Gibson, SL 3
J. Johnson, SF 2
D. Roberts, SD 2
J. Marichal, SF 1
B. Stoneman, MON 1

1971 AMERICAN
V. Blue, OAK 98
M. Lolich, DET 85
W. Wood, CHI 23
D. McNally, BAL 8
D. Drago, KC 1
A. Messersmith, CAL ... 1

1972 NATIONAL
S. Carlton, PHI 120
S. Blass, PIT 35
F. Jenkins, CHI 23
M. Marshall, MON 8
G. Nolan, CIN 6
T. Seaver, NY 6
C. Carroll, CIN 6
D. Sutton, LA 6
B. Gibson, SL 3
M. Pappas, CHI 3

1972 AMERICAN
G. Perry, CLE 64
W. Wood, CHI 58
M. Lolich, DET 27
J. Hunter, OAK 26
J. Palmer, BAL 20
L. Tiant, BOS 16
S. Lyle, NY 3
N. Ryan, CAL 2

1973 NATIONAL
T. Seaver, NY 71
M. Marshall, MON 54
R. Bryant, SF 50
J. Billingham, CIN 30
D. Sutton, LA 7
F. Norman, SD-CIN 3
D. Giusti, PIT 1

1973 AMERICAN
J. Palmer, BAL 88
N. Ryan, CAL 62
J. Hunter, OAK 52
J. Hiller, DET 6
W. Wood, CHI 3
J. Colborn, MIL 2
V. Blue, OAK 1
B. Blyleven, MIN 1
G. Perry, CLE 1

1974 NATIONAL
M. Marshall, LA 96
A. Messersmith, LA .. 66
P. Niekro, ATL 15
D. Sutton, LA 12
A. Hrabosky, SL 9
J. Billingham, CIN 8
D. Gullett, CIN 5
C. Carroll, CIN 2
D. Giusti, PIT 1
B. Capra, ATL 1
L. McGlothen, SL 1

1974 AMERICAN
J. Hunter, OAK 90
F. Jenkins, TEX 75
N. Ryan, CAL 28
G. Perry, CLE 8
L. Tiant, BOS 8
M. Cuellar, BAL 6
J. Hiller, DET 1

1975 NATIONAL
T. Seaver, NY 98
R. Jones, SD 80
A. Hrabosky, SL 33
J. Montefusco, SF 2
D. Gullett, CIN 1
A. Messersmith, LA 1
D. Sutton, LA 1

1975 AMERICAN
J. Palmer, BAL 98
J. Hunter, NY 74
R. Fingers, OAK 25
F. Tanana, CAL 7
J. Kaat, CHI 7
V. Blue, OAK 2
R. Gossage, CHI 2
R. Wise, BOS 1

1976 NATIONAL
R. Jones, SD 96
J. Koosman, NY ... 69½
D. Sutton, LA 25½
S. Carlton, PHI 11
R. Eastwick, CIN 6
J. Matlack, NY 5
J. Richard, HOU 2
T. Seaver, NY 1

1976 AMERICAN
J. Palmer, BAL 108
M. Fidrych, DET 51
F. Tanana, CAL 18
E. Figueroa, NY 12
L. Tiant, BOS 10
V. Blue, OAK 8
B. Campbell, MIN 7
R. Fingers, OAK 1
W. Garland, BAL 1

1977 NATIONAL
S. Carlton, PHI 104
T. John, LA 54
T. Seaver, NY-CIN ... 18
R. Reuschel, CHI 18
J. Candelaria, PIT 17
B. Sutter, CHI 5

1977 AMERICAN
S. Lyle, NY 56½
J. Palmer, BAL 48
N. Ryan, CAL 46
D. Leonard, KC 45
B. Campbell, BOS . 25½
D. Goltz, MIN 19
R. Guidry, NY 5
D. Rozema, DET 4
F. Tanana, CAL 3

1978 NATIONAL
G. Perry, SD 116
B. Hooton, LA 38
V. Blue, SF 17
J. Richard, HOU 13
K. Tekulve, PIT 12
P. Niekro, ATL 10
R. Grimsley, MON 7
R. Fingers, SD 1
T. John, LA 1
D. Robinson, PIT 1

1978 AMERICAN
R. Guidry, NY 140
M. Caldwell, MIL 76
J. Palmer, BAL 14
D. Eckersley, BOS 10
R. Gossage, NY 4
F. Jenkins, TEX 2
E. Figueroa, NY 1
L. Gura, KC 1
D. Leonard, KC 1
M. Marshall, MIN 1
P. Splittorff, KC 1
B. Stanley, BOS 1

1979 NATIONAL
B. Sutter, CHI 72
J. Niekro, HOU 66
J. Richard, HOU 41
T. Seaver, CIN 20
K. Tekulve, PIT 14
P. Niekro, ATL 3

1979 AMERICAN
M. Flanagan, BAL ... 136
T. John, NY 51
R. Guidry, NY 26
J. Kern, TEX 25
M. Marshall, MIN 7
J. Koosman, MIN 5
D. Eckersley, BOS 1
A. Lopez, DET 1

1980 NATIONAL
S. Carlton, PHI 118
J. Reuss, LA 55
J. Bibby, PIT 28
J. Niekro, HOU 11
T. McGraw, PHI 1
S. Rogers, MON 1
J. Sambito, HOU 1
M. Soto, CIN 1

1980 AMERICAN
S. Stone, BAL 100
M. Norris, OAK 91
R. Gossage, NY ... 37½
T. John, NY 14
D. Quisenberry, KC .. 7½
L. Gura, KC 1
S. McGregor, BAL 1

1981 NATIONAL
F. Valenzuela, LA 70
T. Seaver, CIN 67
S. Carlton, PHI 50
N. Ryan, HOU 28
B. Sutter, SL 1

1981 AMERICAN
R. Fingers, MIL 126
S. McCatty, OAK .. 84½
J. Morris, DET 21
P. Vuckovich, MIL ... 8½
D. Martinez, BAL ... 3½
R. Gossage, NY 3
R. Guidry, NY 2½
B. Burns, CHI 2
L. Gura, KC 1

1982 NATIONAL
S. Carlton, PHI 112
S. Rogers, MON 29
F. Valenzuela, LA .. 25½
B. Sutter, SL 25
P. Niekro, ATL 18
G. Minton, SF 4
J. Andujar, SL 1
G. Garber, ATL 1
M. Soto, CIN .... ½

1982 AMERICAN
P. Vuckovich, MIL 87
J. Palmer, BAL 59
D. Quisenberry, KC .. 40
D. Stieb, TOR 36
R. Sutcliffe, CLE 14
G. Zahn, CAL 7
B. Stanley, BOS 4
B. Caudill, SEA 4
D. Petry, DET 1

1983 NATIONAL
J. Denny, PHI 103
M. Soto, CIN 61
J. Orosco, NY 19
S. Rogers, MON 15
L. McWilliams, PIT 7
A. Holland, PHI 4
C. McMurtry, ATL 3
B. Welch, LA 2
N. Ryan, HOU 1
L. Smith, CHI 1

1983 AMERICAN
L. Hoyt, CHI 116
D. Quisenberry, KC .. 81
J. Morris, DET 38
R. Dotson, CHI 9
R. Guidry, NY 5
S. McGregor, BAL 3

1984 NATIONAL
R. Sutcliffe, CHI 120
D. Gooden, NY 45
B. Sutter, SL 33½
J. Andujar, SL 12½
R. Gossage, SD 3
M. Soto, CIN 2

1984 AMERICAN
W. Hernandez, DET .. 88
D. Quisenberry, KC .. 71
B. Blyleven, CLE 45
M. Boddicker, BAL .. 41
D. Petry, DET 3
F. Viola, MIN 2
J. Morris, DET 1
D. Stieb, TOR 1

1985 NATIONAL
D. Gooden, NY 120
J. Tudor, SL 65
O. Hershiser, LA 17
J. Andujar, SL 6
F. Valenzuela, LA 4
T. Browning, CIN 3
J. Reardon, MON 1

1985 AMERICAN
B. Saberhagen, KC . 127
R. Guidry, NY 88
B. Blyleven, MIN 9
D. Quisenberry, KC ... 9
C. Leibrandt, KC 7
D. Alexander, TOR 5
B. Burns, CHI 2
D. Moore, CAL 2
D. Stieb, TOR 2
M. Moore, SEA 1

1986 NATIONAL
M. Scott, HOU 98
F. Valenzuela, LA 88
M. Krukow, SF 15
B. Ojeda, NY 9

R. Darling, NY 2
R. Rhoden, PIT 2
D. Gooden, NY 1
S. Fernandez, NY..... 1

1986 AMERICAN
R. Clemens, BOS ... 140
T. Higuera, MIL 42
M. Witt, CAL........... 35
D. Righetti, NY......... 20
J. Morris, DET 13
M. Eichhorn, TOR 2

1987 NATIONAL
S. Bedrosian, PHI.... 57
R. Sutcliffe, CHI 55
R. Reuschel, SF 54
O. Hershiser, LA 14
D. Gooden, NY 12
N. Ryan, HOU 12
M. Scott, HOU......... 9
B. Welch, LA........... 3

1987 AMERICAN
R. Clemens, BOS ... 124
J. Key, TOR 64
D. Stewart, OAK 32
D. Alexander, DET 8
M. Langston, SEA 7
T. Higuera, MIL 5
F. Viola, MIN 5
J. Reardon, MIN 4
J. Morris, DET 3

1988 NATIONAL
O. Hershisher, LA ... 120
D. Jackson, CIN 54
D. Cone, NY 42

1988 AMERICAN
F. Viola, MIN........ 138
D. Eckersley, OAK ... 52
M. Gubicza, KC...... 26
D. Stewart, OAK..... 16
B. Hurst, BOS 12

R. Clemens, BOS..... 8

1989 NATIONAL
M. Davis, SD 107
M. Scott, HOU....... 65
G. Maddux, CHI 17
O. Hershiser, LA 7
J. Magrane, SL 7
T. Belcher, LA 4
S. Garrelts, SF 4
R. Reuschel, SF 3
M. Bielecki, CHI 1
M. Williams, CHI....... 1

1989 AMERICAN
B. Saberhagen, KC . 138
D. Stewart, OAK 80
M. Moore, OAK 10
B. Blyleven, CAL...... 9
N. Ryan, TEX 5
J. Ballard, BAL......... 3
D. Eckersley, OAK 3
G. Olson, BAL 3
J. Russell, TEX 1

1990 NATIONAL
D. Drabek, PIT...... 118
R. Martinez, LA 70
F. Viola, NY.......... 19
D. Gooden, NY 8
R. Myers, CIN 1

1990 AMERICAN
B. Welch, OAK...... 107
R. Clemens, BOS.... 77
D. Stewart, OAK 43
B. Thigpen, CHI 20
D. Eckersley, OAK 2
D. Stieb, TOR.......... 2
C. Finley, CAL 1

1991 NATIONAL
T. Glavine, ATL 110
L. Smith, SL 60
J. Smiley, PIT........ 26

J. Rijo, CIN 13
D. Martinez, MON 4
S. Avery, ATL 1
A. Benes, SD 1
M. Williams, PHI 1

1991 AMERICAN
R. Clemens, BOS ... 119
S. Erickson, MIN..... 56
J. Abbott, CAL........ 26
J. Morris, MIN 17
B. Harvey, CAL 10
M. Langston, CAL 7
K. Tapani, MIN......... 6
B. Gullickson, DET.... 5
J. McDowell, CHI 3
D. Ward, TOR.......... 3

1992 NATIONAL
G. Maddux, CHI 112
T. Glavine, ATL 78
B. Tewksbury, SL 22
L. Smith, SL 3
D. Drabek, PIT 1

1992 AMERICAN
D. Eckersley, OAK .. 107
J. McDowell, CHI 51
R. Clemens, BOS ... 48
M. Mussina, BAL 26
J. Morris, TOR 10
K. Brown, TEX 9
C. Nagy, CLE........... 1

1993 NATIONAL
G. Maddux, ATL 119
B. Swift, SF.......... 61
T. Glavine, ATL 49
J. Burkett, SF......... 9
J. Rijo, CIN 8
T. Greene, PHI 2
M. Portugal, HOU..... 2
B. Harvey, FLA 1
R. Myers, CHI 1

1993 AMERICAN
J. McDowell, CHI ... 124
R. Johnson SEA 75
K. Appier, KC 30
J. Key, NY 14
D. Ward, TOR......... 5
P. Hentgen, TOR 3
J. Guzman, TOR 1

1994 NATIONAL
G. Maddux, ATL 140
K. Hill, MON 56
B. Saberhagen, NY .. 42
M. Freeman, COL.... 4
D. Drabek, HOU 4
D. Jackson, PHI 3
J. Franco, NY.......... 2
R. Beck, SF............ 1

1994 AMERICAN
D. Cone, KC 108
J. Key, NY 96
R. Johnson, SEA 24
M. Mussina, BAL 23
L. Smith, BAL......... 1

1995 NATIONAL
G. Maddux, ATL 140
P. Schourek, CIN 55
T. Glavine, ATL 30
H. Nomo, LA.......... 19
R. Martinez, LA 8

1995 AMERICAN
R. Johnson, SEA ... 136
J. Mesa, CLE 54
T. Wakefield, BOS ... 29
D. Cone, TOR-NY ... 18
M. Mussina, BAL 14
C. Nagy, CLE.......... 1

1996 NATIONAL
J. Smoltz, ATL 136
K. Brown, FLA 88
A. Benes, SL 9

H. Nomo, LA........... 5
T. Hoffman, SD 3
G. Maddux, ATL 3
T. Worrell, LA 3
D. Neagle, PIT-ATL ... 2
J. Fassero, MON...... 1
A. Leiter, FLA 1
S. Reynolds, HOU 1

1996 AMERICAN
P. Hentgen, TOR ... 110
A. Pettitte, NY 104
M. Rivera, NY......... 18
C. Nagy, CLE......... 12
M. Mussina, BAL 5
A. Fernandez, CHI 1
R. Fernandez, CHI 1
K. Hill, TEX 1

1997 NATIONAL
P. Martinez, MON .. 134
G. Maddux, ATL 75
D. Neagle, ATL....... 24
C. Schilling, PHI 12
D. Kile, HOU 7

1997 AMERICAN
R. Clemens, TOR ... 134
R. Johnson, SEA 77
B. Radke, MIN 17
R. Myers, BAL 14
A. Pettitte, NY 9
M. Mussina, BAL 1

1998 NATIONAL
T. Glavine, ATL 99
T. Hoffman, SD 88
K. Brown, SD 76
G. Maddux, ATL 10
J. Smoltz, ATL 10
A. Leiter, NY 3
R. Johnson, HOU 2

1998 AMERICAN
R. Clemens, TOR ... 140

P. Martinez, BOS ... 65
D. Wells, NY 31
D. Cone, NY 16

1999 NATIONAL
R. Johnson, ARI 134
M. Hampton, HOU .. 110
K. Millwood, ATL..... 36
J. Lima, HOU 3
B. Wagner, HOU...... 3
K. Brown, LA 1
T. Hoffman, SD 1

1999 AMERICAN
P. Martinez, BOS ... 140
M. Mussina, BAL 54
M. Rivera, NY......... 27
B. Colon, CLE 14
A. Sele, TEX 4
D. Cone, NY 3
J. Moyer, SEA 3
J. Wetteland, TEX..... 3
F. Garcia, SEA 2
K. Foulke, CHI......... 1
R. Hernandez, TB..... 1

2000 NATIONAL
R. Johnson, ARI 133
T. Glavine, ATL 64
G. Maddux, ATL 59
R. Nen, SF........... 20
D. Kile, SL............. 8
K. Brown, LA 4

2000 AMERICAN
P. Martinez, BOS ... 140
T. Hudson, OAK 54
D. Wells, TOR....... 46
A. Pettitte, NY 7
T. Jones, DET 3
R. Clemens, NY 1
M. Mussina, BAL 1

Hypothetical Awards

As the "expert" in baseball award-voting, I have been asked to make a set of hypothetical award selections for the years no official honors were given; i.e., pre-1956 Cy Young, pre-1947 Rookie of the Year, and pre-1911 MVP Awards, along with awards for any other "missing" years.

While this assignment gave me unusual freedom, I felt a certain responsibility to make my selections consistent with the perceptions and voting trends of a particular era. For example, although there were better NL players than Cincinnati's Edd Roush in 1919, he did two things which, combined, would have virtually guaranteed him the MVP Award: he won the batting crown, which was *the* individual title in the Dead Ball Era, and he played on a pennant-winner, which has always been a key factor in MVP voting.

Besides my own opinions and intuitions, several sources were instrumental in my selection process, including:

1. Society for American Baseball Research retroactive award surveys, which have been done for pre-1949 Rookie of the Year and pre-1967 Cy Young Awards. The ballots were tremendously helpful in screening candidates and the voting results were carefully compared to my own choices.

2. Linear Weights, an overall player rating system devised by Pete Palmer, first used in *The Hidden Game of Baseball* (Doubleday, 1984, 1985), and continued in *Total Baseball*.

3. MVP voting results, for comparing Cy Young and Rookie candidates. If rookie "A" receives 75 points in the MVP election, while comparable rookie "B" receives just 10, I am forced to conclude that the on-the-spot observers discerned some important difference that we can't see in the statistics and that "A" is probably the better choice.

4. Unofficial awards, including 1940-46 Rookie and 1929-30 MVP selections.

5. Cy Young (1956-66) and Rookie of the Year (1947-48) balloting, for years in which one league had no official winner.

The resulting selections are not necessarily ones the average reader will agree with, nor even that the writer agrees with; rather, they are the ones which can be best justified with the available evidence.

In comparison with the Palmer system, my selections concurred 54 percent with top player selections and 59 percent with top pitcher nominations. In comparison with the SABR surveys, my selections agreed 84 percent in the Rookie of the Year Award and 79 percent in the Cy Young Award.

The big winner in the hypothetical awards is Christy Mathewson, who picks up a Rookie of the Year, two MVPs, and eight Cy Young Awards. Other pitchers capturing at least three Cy Youngs are Walter Johnson (seven); Lefty Grove (six, consecutively); Warren Spahn (four, to add to the one he actually did win); Grover Cleveland Alexander (four); Burleigh Grimes, Carl Hubbell, Bob Feller, Bucky Walters, Bob Lemon, and appropriately, Cy Young himself (three each).

Notable Rookies of the Year include Grover Cleveland Alexander, Babe Ruth, Rogers Hornsby, Dizzy Dean, Joe DiMaggio, and Ted Williams.

Honus Wagner cops six MVP Awards, including four

in succession. Three-time MVPs are Nap Lajoie, Alexander, Ruth, and Hornsby. Ruth (once) and Hornsby (twice) also won official MVP Awards.

The following pages contain my hypothetical Cy Young (124), Rookie of the Year (97), and MVP (42) selections for this century.

Hypothetical Cy Young Award

American League Pitcher/Club	Year	American League Pitcher/Club	Year	American League Pitcher/Club	Year	National League Pitcher/Club	Year	National League Pitcher/Club	Year	National League Pitcher/Club	Year
C. Young, BOS	1901	E. Rommel, PHI	1922	S. Chandler, NY	1943	J. McGinnity, BRO	1900	B. Grimes, BRO	1921	M. Cooper, SL	1942
C. Young, BOS	1902	G. Uhle, CLE	1923	D. Trout, DET	1944	N. Hahn, CIN	1901	W. Cooper, PIT	1922	M. Cooper, SL	1943
C. Young, BOS	1903	W. Johnson, WAS	1924	H. Newhouser, DET	1945	J. Taylor, CHI	1902	D. Luque, CIN	1923	B. Walters, CIN	1944
J. Chesbro, NY	1904	S. Coveleski, WAS	1925	H. Newhouser, DET	1946	C. Mathewson, NY	1903	D. Vance, BRO	1924	C. Barrett, BOS-SL	1945
R. Waddell, PHI	1905	G. Uhle, CLE	1926	J. Page, NY	1947	J. McGinnity, NY	1904	D. Vance, BRO	1925	H. Pollet, SL	1946
A. Orth, NY	1906	W. Moore, NY	1927	B. Lemon, CLE	1948	Mathewson, NY	1905	R. Kremer, PIT	1926	E. Blackwell, CIN	1947
E. Walsh, CHI	1907	L. Grove, PHI	1928	M. Parnell, BOS	1949	M. Brown, CHI	1906	C. Root, CHI	1927	J. Sain, BOS	1948
E. Walsh, CHI	1908	L. Grove, PHI	1929	B. Lemon, CLE	1950	Mathewson, NY	1907	B. Grimes, PIT	1928	W. Spahn, BOS	1949
F. Smith, CHI	1909	L. Grove, PHI	1930	N. Garver, SL	1951	Mathewson, NY	1908	B. Grimes, PIT	1929	J. Konstanty, PHI	1950
J. Coombs, PHI	1910	L. Grove, PHI	1931	B. Shantz, PHI	1952	Mathewson, NY	1909	P. Malone, CHI	1930	S. Maglie, NY	1951
W. Johnson, WAS	1911	L. Grove, PHI	1932	B. Pierce, CHI	1953	Mathewson, NY	1910	E. Brandt, BOS	1931	R. Roberts, PHI	1952
J. Wood, BOS	1912	L. Grove, PHI	1933	B. Lemon, CLE	1954	Mathewson, NY	1911	L. Warneke, CHI	1932	W. Spahn, MIL	1953
W. Johnson, WAS	1913	L. Gomez, NY	1934	R. Narleski, CLE	1955	R. Marquard, NY	1912	C. Hubbell, NY	1933	J. Antonelli, NY	1954
W. Johnson, WAS	1914	W. Ferrell, BOS	1935	B. Pierce, CHI	1956	Mathewson, NY	1913	D. Dean, SL	1934	R. Roberts, PHI	1955
W. Johnson, WAS	1915	T. Bridges, DET	1936	J. Bunning, DET	1957	B. James, BOS	1914	D. Dean, SL	1935	W. Spahn, MIL	1958
B. Ruth, BOS	1916	L. Gomez, NY	1937	C. Estrada, BAL	1960	G. Alexander, PHI	1915	C. Hubbell, NY	1936	S. Jones, SF	1959
E. Cicotte, CHI	1917	R. Ruffing, NY	1938	D. Donovan, CLE	1962	G. Alexander, PHI	1916	C. Hubbell, NY	1937	W. Spahn, MIL	1961
W. Johnson, WAS	1918	B. Feller, CLE	1939	W. Ford, NY	1963	G. Alexander, PHI	1917	B. Lee, CHI	1938	L. Jackson, CHI	1964
W. Johnson, WAS	1919	B. Feller, CLE	1940	E. Fisher, CHI	1965	J. Vaughn, CHI	1918	B. Walters, CIN	1939		
J. Bagby, CLE	1920	B. Feller, CLE	1941	J. Kaat, MIN	1966	J. Vaughn, CHI	1919	B. Walters, CIN	1940		
R. Faber, CHI	1921	T. Hughson, BOS	1942			G. Alexander, CHI	1920	W. Wyatt, BRO	1941		

Hypothetical Federal League Awards

	1914	1915
Most Valuable Player	B. Kauff, IND	D. Zwilling, CHI
Cy Young	C. Hendrix, CHI	G. McConnell, CHI
Rookie of the Year	B. Kauff, IND	E. Johnson, SL

Hypothetical Rookie of the Year Award

American League Player/Club	Year	American League Player/Club	Year	American League Player/Club	Year	National League Player/Club	Year	National League Player/Club	Year	National League Player/Club	Year
S. Seybold, PHI	1901	A. Sothoron, SL	1917	B. Johnson, PHI	1933	E. Scott, CIN	1900	R. Hornsby, SL	1916	P. Derringer, SL	1931
A. Joss, CLE	1902	S. Perry, PHI	1918	H. Trosky, CLE	1934	C. Mathewson, NY	1901	L. Cadore, BRO	1917	D. Dean, SL	1932
C. Bender, PHI	1903	D. Kerr, CHI	1919	J. Powell, WAS	1935	H. Smoot, SL	1902	C. Hollocher, CHI	1918	F. Demaree, CHI	1933
F. Glade, SL	1904	B. Meusel, NY	1920	J. DiMaggio, NY	1936	J. Weimer, CHI	1903	O. Tuero, SL	1919	C. Davis, PHI	1934
G. Stone, SL	1905	J. Sewell, CLE	1921	R. York, DET	1937	H. Lumley, BRO	1904	J. Haines, SL	1920	C. Blanton, PIT	1935
C. Rossman, CLE	1906	H. Pillette, DET	1922	K. Keltner, DET	1938	E. Reulbach, CHI	1905	R. Grimes, CHI	1921	J. Mize, SL	1936
S. Nicholls, PHI	1907	H. Summa, CLE	1923	T. Williams, BOS	1939	J. Pfiester, CHI	1906	H. Miller, CHI	1922	J. Turner, BOS	1937
E. Summers, DET	1908	A. Simmons, PHI	1924	W. Judnich, SL	1940	N. Rucker, BRO	1907	G. Grantham, CHI	1923	J. Rizzo, PIT	1938
F. Baker, PHI	1909	E. Combs, NY	1925	P. Rizzuto, NY	1941	G. McQuillan, PHI	1908	K. Cuyler, PIT	1924	H. Casey, BRO	1939
R. Ford, NY	1910	T. Lazzeri, NY	1926	J. Pesky, BOS	1942	D. Miller, PIT	1909	J. Welsh, BOS	1925	B. Young, NY	1940
V. Gregg, CLE	1911	W. Moore, NY	1927	B. Johnson, NY	1943	K. Cole, CHI	1910	P. Waner, PIT	1926	E. Riddle, CIN	1941
D. Pratt, SL	1912	E. Morris, BOS	1928	J. Berry, PHI	1944	G. Alexander, PHI	1911	L. Waner, PIT	1927	J. Beazley, SL	1942
R. Russell, CHI	1913	D. Alexander, DET	1929	B. Ferriss, BOS	1945	L. Cheney, CHI	1912	D. Bissonette, BRO	1928	L. Klein, SL	1943
R. Bressler, PHI	1914	S. Jolley, CHI	1930	B. Lemon, CLE	1946	J. Viox, PIT	1913	J. Frederick, BRO	1929	B. Voiselle, NY	1944
B. Ruth, BOS	1915	J. Vosmik, CLE	1931	F. Shea, NY	1947	J. Pfeffer, BRO	1914	W. Berger, BOS	1930	K. Burkhart, SL	1945
J. Bagby, CLE	1916	J. Allen, NY	1932	G. Bearden, CLE	1948	T. Long, SL	1915			D. Ennis, PHI	1946

Hypothetical Most Valuable Player Award

American League Player/Club	Year	American League Player/Club	Year	American League Player/Club	Year	National League Player/Club	Year	National League Player/Club	Year	National League Player/Club	Year
N. Lajoie, PHI	1901	E. Walsh, CHI	1908	B. Ruth, BOS	1918	H. Wagner, PIT	1900	H. Wagner, PIT	1907	J. Vaughn, CHI	1918
C. Young, BOS	1902	T. Cobb, DET	1909	J. Jackson, CHI	1919	H. Wagner, PIT	1901	C. Mathewson, NY	1908	E. Roush, CIN	1919
N. Lajoie, CLE	1903	J. Coombs, PHI	1910	B. Ruth, NY	1920	H. Wagner, PIT	1902	H. Wagner, PIT	1909	R. Hornsby, SL	1920
J. Chesbro, NY	1904	E. Collins, CHI	1915	B. Ruth, NY	1921	H. Wagner, PIT	1903	S. Magee, PHI	1910	R. Hornsby, SL	1921
R. Waddell, PHI	1905	T. Speaker, CLE	1916	L. Fonseca, CLE	1929	J. McGinnity, NY	1904	G. Alexander, PHI	1915	R. Hornsby, SL	1922
N. Lajoie, CLE	1906	E. Cicotte, CHI	1917	J. Cronin, WAS	1930	C. Mathewson, NY	1905	G. Alexander, PHI	1916	D. Luque, CIN	1923
T. Cobb, DET	1907					F. Chance, CHI	1906	G. Alexander, PHI	1917	H. Wilson, CHI	1930

Gold Glove Award: History

In a 1956 spring training survey, Elmer A. Blasco—employed by Rawlings Sporting Goods as advertising, public relations and sales manager—found that 83 percent of the active regular major league players wore Rawlings gloves or mitts. Noting that Hillerich & Bradsby (the major leagues' leading baseball bat supplier) awarded Silver Bats to the leagues' top hitters, Blasco reasoned that Rawlings ought to sponsor some sort of fielding award. After his idea was accepted by Rawlings' management, Blasco contacted the Brown Shoe Company of St. Louis and obtained from them a hide of gold lame-tanned leather used to make ladies' formal slippers. A glove was crafted from this hide, laced and stamped as a regular fielder's glove, and attached to a metal fixture on a walnut base with an appropriate engraved plate.

Thus was born the Gold Glove Award.

The October 2, 1957, edition of *The Sporting News* featured a full-page advertisement/announcement that established the fielding award: "Recognizing the importance of superior individual fielding performance to the advancement of baseball as America's national game, Rawlings (Sporting Goods Company) has established Annual Gold Glove Awards beginning with the 1957 season.

"Each of the nine Major League players chosen for *The Sporting News* All-Star Fielding Team will be honored with a Rawlings Gold Glove Award. Selections will be made by a Committee named by *The Sporting News*. Awards will be Rawlings custom-built gloves or mitts hand-crafted of special metallic gold-finished leather, each mounted on a suitable hardwood stand bearing an engraved plate."

TSN publisher J.G. Taylor Spink appointed 19 noted sportswriters for the selection task. They included Shirley Povich, Edgar Munzel, Hy Hurwitz, Earl Lawson, Bob Broeg, Allen Lewis, and Hal Lebowitz. A contest to predict the winners, open to baseball-playing boys, was sponsored by Rawlings.

The first Gold Glove winners were announced with great pomp and circumstance in the December 18, 1957, issue of TSN. "Too long neglected, the magicians of the defense have had no real recognition," the article explained, adding that the selections were made "solely on the basis of their defensive ability."

Rawlings and TSN also joined forces that year in the establishment of the Silver Glove Award, given to the top minor league fielder at each position—based entirely on fielding averages.

In 1958 the Gold Glove selection privilege was turned over to the major league players and an All-Star Fielding Team was selected for each league (as it still is). In 1961 the method for selecting outfielders was changed. Rather than choosing a left fielder, center fielder, and right fielder for each league, each voter was instructed to name three outfielders regardless of position (still the practice today).

In 1965 the managers and coaches of each team took over the voting responsibility, which they have retained ever since. Voters are not permitted to select players on their own teams. In 1987, 139 different managers and coaches took part in the balloting.

Perhaps because of its originality, the Gold Glove is the one *Sporting News* award that has gained universal acceptance and prestige in the baseball world. However, as with any award, the selections often draw criticism. One complaint is that too much importance is given to fielding average. Most of us realize that fielding average is not always a reliable indicator of defensive ability, but how much does it influence the Gold Glove voters?

Of the 366 fielding average leaders at the various positions between 1957 and 1987 (discounting pitchers and counting only one outfielder per league each year), 118 (32 percent) also won their respective Gold Glove Awards (see Table 1). We can say, then, that if a player leads his league in fielding average he has about a one-in-three chance of winning the Gold Glove—not an overwhelming correlation, but about four times better than random chance.

This raises some interesting questions. Since official fielding statistics are not published until months after Gold Gloves (although unofficial stats are readily available) are voted on, any voter relying on fielding stats would probably have to consult (or remember) the previous year's data. Therefore, if fielding average itself really does impress voters, we should expect to see many players winning a Gold Glove the year after they lead in fielding average. Do they? Well, no (see Table 2). The percentage here is 25 percent or one-in-four—again, considerably better than chance, but less of a factor than leading in fielding average in the current year.

And what about the influence of Gold Gloves on fielding averages? Is an official scorer less likely to charge an error against a player simply because he won a Gold Glove the previous year? Apparently not (see Table 3). The percentage of Gold Glove recipients leading in fielding average the following year is 23 percent.

"It is my belief that a lot more is considered than fielding percentage," said TSN editor Tom Barnidge, citing "range, throwing arm, the headiness of the ballplayer." Pete Rose, a two-time Gold Glove winner and later a voter, concurred: "There are a lot of intangibles involved in voting for the Gold Glove. Take an outfielder. The coaches and managers watch these guys all the time. How they play the hitters, how strong their arms are, how often they hit the cutoff man, and all that is taken into consideration—things that do not show up in the statistics."

Another criticism of the Gold Glove is that batting performance plays a role in the selections, contrary to the award's philosophy. As USA Today baseball editor Hal Bodley put it, "A player who is outstanding on defense and respectable on offense has a much better chance of getting a Gold Glove than a counterpart whose forte is fielding alone."

Other factors can be distractions to the voters: flashiness, reputations, and the selection process itself. For insight on some of these and their effects, I consulted an expert on the Gold Glove: Wes Parker, a six-time winner of the award at first base. Parker, it should be noted, would seem to have no reason to gripe about the award. He grasped the honor from a seven-time winner; he won it even when he batted as low as .239; and he became one of only two nonpitchers (Roberto Clemente is the other) to win the award in his final major league season.

"I would say many, if not most, coaches and managers fail to take their voting responsibility seriously," said Parker. "They don't treat it as a vital act. They are usually much more concerned with their team and the pennant race and, as a result, tend to zip through the ballots (distributed in September). So they wind up voting for the most recognizable names."

Parker brought out another rarely discussed procedural problem: "Since players [when they were voting] and coaches are forbidden to vote for anyone on their own team, they often won't vote for the guy who is contending with their team's leading candidate for the same award. That increases their teammate's chances."

On the subject of reputation, Parker asserted that it "has a lot to do with it, absolutely. In 1966, Bill White won the award (for the seventh consecutive time), although even White admitted that I probably deserved it. It takes a couple of years for your reputation to catch up with you, but that can work to your advantage at the end of your career.

"Flashiness is a factor too," continued Parker. "It puts the player's name in the forefront of the voter's minds." Wes also concurred with the theory that a player's bat can be the difference in winning this "fielding' award.

"[Four-time Gold Glove winner Steve] Garvey is a good example of someone who won it with his bat and notoriety, a perfect example, in fact," opines Parker. "Garvey was vastly overrated defensively . . . he had no range, no arm, and no aggressiveness. He would hold the ball and allow opposing runners to take extra bases to avoid throwing errors. That's how he compiled his high [fielding] averages at first base. Remember, he was a terrible third baseman, worst I ever saw." (In 1972, Garvey's last season as a third-sacker, he led the NL with 28 errors in just 85 games, posting a woeful .902 percentage.)

"Amazingly, despite these prejudices," Parker concluded, "I think the Gold Glove choices have been excellent. At first base I think they have been perfect, with the exception of Garvey."

While the Gold Glove Award has adequately filled the need for a subjective fielding award, there is still something to be said about fielding statistics. It is fashionable to say that fielding stats are meaningless, but, as analyst Bill James said, "If a baseball statistic is meaningless to you, that is simply because you don't know what it means."

With the understanding of which fielding statistics are meaningful for each position, it is possible to make a pretty reliable judgment of a player's defensive skills based on stats alone. In recent years, several analysts have attempted to measure individual fielding performance on the basis of numbers.

One newer method is Linear Weights, Pete Palmer's translation of individual batting, pitching, and fielding statistics into runs gained and thus games won. The fielding portion of the system, Fielding or Defensive Wins, incorporates data (variously weighted according to position) on putouts, assists, errors, and double plays, comparing a player's totals against the league averages.

The formula first determines how many runs a player saves (or costs) his team as compared to an "average" player at the same position. Runs are then translated into wins, based on the league average of runs per win. For example, second baseman Glenn Hubbard was computed to have won about three and a half games for the Braves with his glove in 1986, the top Defensive Wins total in the majors.

Of the 60 players identified by the Palmer system as the best fielders in their leagues between 1957 and 1986, 28 also won their respective Gold Glove Awards.

Palmer has drawn criticism for comparing players with average, rather than replacement-level, players; for overemphasizing the double play; and for the use of arbitrary weighting schemes. It is particularly—and admittedly—inadequate in evaluating catchers.

Bill James has also presented a fielding measurement system, Defensive Won/Lost Percentage (DW/L%), although he hasn't used it since 1984. The formula varies from position to position, using four arbitrarily weighted components at each. These components range from readily available statistics (fielding average, assists per game, and so on) to abstruse estimations and calculations, using some data unavailable to the average researcher. The formula is not designed for cross-era comparisons.

The results of these calculations produce the DW/L%, which in turn is translated into defensive wins and losses, based on still more arbitrary assignments of defensive games at each position (ranging from three at first base to 11 at shortstop). Of the 32 players identified by DW/L% as the best at their positions and leagues for the 1983-84 seasons, 12 (38 percent) also won their respective Gold Gloves. The use of a series of arbitrary values is the glaring flaw of DW/L%. Criticism is also due for the complexity and lack of adaptability of the system(s).

The Elias Sports Bureau has demonstrated a simple and generally effective system for evaluating fielders: comparing the number of runs scored per nine innings while a player is on the field to the number scored when he isn't. For example, Elias calculated that the 1982-86 Cardinals averaged allowing 3.85 runs per nine innings with Ozzie Smith at shortstop, as compared to 4.04 per game with other shortstops.

There is nothing new or brilliant about this concept; the difference is that Elias has the data available to make this type of measurement, right down to thirds of an inning, at least since 1975. Since they generally choose not to share this data with the public, however, it is of no value at present.

So, when all is said and done about modern statistical fielding measurements, a subjective measurement—the Gold Glove—is probably still the best tool we have available to rate fielders.

The following pages list the winners of the Gold Glove at each position since 1957. Complete balloting for Gold Glove elections is, unfortunately, neither available nor researchable.

TABLE 1. Fielding Average Leaders Winning Gold Glove, 1957-87 (Maximum 61 Each Position).

POS.	NL	AL	TOT.	PCT.
C	7	7	14	23
1B	13	13	26	43
2B	14	5	19	31
3B	4	15	19	31
SS	14	12	26	43
OF	6	8	14	23
TOT.	58	60	118	32

TABLE 2. Fielding Average Leaders Winning Gold Glove in Following Season, 1956-86 (Maximum 61 Each Position).

POS.	NL	AL	TOT.	PCT.
C	7	7	14	23
1B	8	11	19	31
2B	9	6	15	25
3B	3	13	16	26
SS	11	9	20	33
OF	2	5	7	11
TOT.	40	51	91	25

TABLE 3. Fielding Average Leaders Who Won Gold Glove in Previous Season, 1958-87 (Maximum 59 Each Position).

POS.	NL	AL	TOT.	PCT.
C	3	7	10	17
1B	11	8	19	32
2B	8	2	10	17
3B	2	12	14	24
SS	10	9	19	32
OF	6	5	11	19
TOT.	40	43	83	23

Gold Glove Award

Pitchers

Year	National League	American League
1957	(No selection)	B. Shantz, NY
1958	H. Haddix, CIN	B. Shantz, NY
1959	H. Haddix, PIT	B. Shantz, NY
1960	H. Haddix, PIT	B. Shantz, NY
1961	B. Shantz, PIT	F. Lary, DET
1962	B. Shantz, SL	J. Kaat, MIN
1963	B. Shantz, SL	J. Kaat, MIN
1964	B. Shantz, PHI	J. Kaat, MIN
1965	B. Gibson, SL	J. Kaat, MIN
1966	B. Gibson, SL	J. Kaat, MIN
1967	B. Gibson, SL	J. Kaat, MIN
1968	B. Gibson, SL	J. Kaat, MIN
1969	B. Gibson, SL	J. Kaat, MIN
1970	B. Gibson, SL	J. Kaat, MIN
1971	B. Gibson, SL	J. Kaat, MIN
1972	B. Gibson, SL	J. Kaat, MIN
1973	B. Gibson, SL	J. Kaat, MIN
1974	A. Messersmith, LA	J. Kaat, CHI
1975	A. Messersmith, LA	J. Kaat, CHI
1976	J. Kaat, PHI	J. Palmer, BAL
1977	J. Kaat, PHI	J. Palmer, BAL
1978	P. Niekro, ATL	J. Palmer, BAL
1979	P. Niekro, ATL	J. Palmer, BAL
1980	P. Niekro, ATL	M. Norris, OAK
1981	S. Carlton, PHI	M. Norris, OAK
1982	P. Niekro, ATL	R. Guidry, NY
1983	P. Niekro, ATL	R. Guidry, NY
1984	J. Andujar, SL	R. Guidry, NY
1985	R. Reuschel, PIT	R. Guidry, NY
1986	F. Valenzuela, LA	R. Guidry, NY
1987	R. Reuschel, SF	M. Langston, SEA
1988	O. Hershiser, LA	M. Langston, SEA
1989	R. Darling, NY	B. Saberhagen, KC
1990	G. Maddux, CHI	M. Boddicker, BOS
1991	G. Maddux, CHI	M. Langston, CAL
1992	G. Maddux, CHI	M. Langston, CAL
1993	G. Maddux, ATL	M. Langston, CAL
1994	G. Maddux, ATL	M. Langston, CAL
1995	G. Maddux, ATL	M. Langston, CAL
1996	G. Maddux, ATL	M. Mussina, BAL
1997	G. Maddux, ATL	M. Mussina, BAL
1998	G. Maddux, ATL	M. Mussina, BAL
1999	G. Maddux, ATL	M. Mussina, BAL
2000	G. Maddux, ATL	K. Rogers, TEX

Catchers

Year	National League	American League
1957	(No selection)	S. Lollar, CHI
1958	D. Crandall, MIL	S. Lollar, CHI
1959	D. Crandall, MIL	S. Lollar, CHI
1960	D. Crandall, MIL	E. Battey, WAS
1961	J. Roseboro, LA	E. Battey, MIN
1962	D. Crandall, MIL	E. Battey, MIN
1963	J. Edwards, CIN	E. Howard, NY
1964	J. Edwards, CIN	E. Howard, NY
1965	J. Torre, MIL	B. Freehan, DET
1966	J. Roseboro, LA	B. Freehan, DET
1967	R. Hundley, CHI	B. Freehan, DET
1968	J. Bench, CIN	B. Freehan, DET
1969	J. Bench, CIN	B. Freehan, DET
1970	J. Bench, CIN	R. Fosse, CLE
1971	J. Bench, CIN	R. Fosse, CLE
1972	J. Bench, CIN	C. Fisk, BOS
1973	J. Bench, CIN	T. Munson, NY
1974	J. Bench, CIN	T. Munson, NY
1975	J. Bench, CIN	T. Munson, NY
1976	J. Bench, CIN	J. Sundberg, TEX
1977	J. Bench, CIN	J. Sundberg, TEX
1978	B. Boone, PHI	J. Sundberg, TEX
1979	B. Boone, PHI	J. Sundberg, TEX
1980	G. Carter, MON	J. Sundberg, TEX
1981	G. Carter, MON	J. Sundberg, TEX
1982	G. Carter, MON	B. Boone, CAL
1983	T. Pena, PIT	Lc. Parrish, DET
1984	T. Pena, PIT	Lc. Parrish, DET
1985	T. Pena, PIT	Lc. Parrish, DET
1986	J. Davis, CHI	B. Boone, CAL
1987	M. LaValliere, PIT	B. Boone, CAL
1988	B. Santiago, SD	B. Boone, CAL
1989	B. Santiago, SD	B. Boone, KC
1990	B. Santiago, SD	S. Alomar, CLE
1991	T. Pagnozzi, SL	T. Pena, BOS
1992	T. Pagnozzi, SL	I. Rodriguez, TEX
1993	K. Manwaring, SF	I. Rodriguez, TEX
1994	T. Pagnozzi, SL	I. Rodriguez, TEX
1995	C. Johnson, FLA	I. Rodriguez, TEX
1996	C. Johnson, FLA	I. Rodriguez, TEX
1997	C. Johnson, FLA	I. Rodriguez, TEX
1998	C. Johnson, FLA-LA	I. Rodriguez, TEX
1999	M. Lieberthal, PHI	I. Rodriguez, TEX
2000	M. Matheny, SL	I. Rodriguez, TEX

First Basemen

Year	National League	American League
1957	G. Hodges, BRO	(No selection)
1958	G. Hodges, LA	V. Power, CLE
1959	G. Hodges, LA	V. Power, CLE
1960	B. White, SL	V. Power, CLE
1961	B. White, SL	V. Power, CLE
1962	B. White, SL	V. Power, MIN
1963	B. White, SL	V. Power, MIN
1964	B. White, SL	V. Power, LA
1965	B. White, SL	J. Pepitone, NY
1966	B. White, PHI	J. Pepitone, NY
1967	W. Parker, LA	G. Scott, BOS
1968	W. Parker, LA	G. Scott, BOS
1969	W. Parker, LA	J. Pepitone, NY
1970	W. Parker, LA	J. Spencer, CAL
1971	W. Parker, LA	G. Scott, BOS
1972	W. Parker, LA	G. Scott, MIL
1973	M. Jorgensen, MON	G. Scott, MIL
1974	S. Garvey, LA	G. Scott, MIL
1975	S. Garvey, LA	G. Scott, MIL
1976	S. Garvey, LA	G. Scott, MIL
1977	S. Garvey, LA	J. Spencer, CHI
1978	K. Hernandez, SL	C. Chambliss, NY
1979	K. Hernandez, SL	C. Cooper, MIL
1980	K. Hernandez, SL	C. Cooper, MIL
1981	K. Hernandez, SL	M. Squires, CHI
1982	K. Hernandez, SL	E. Murray, BAL
1983	K. Hernandez, SL-NY	E. Murray, BAL
1984	K. Hernandez, NY	E. Murray, BAL
1985	K. Hernandez, NY	D. Mattingly, NY
1986	K. Hernandez, NY	D. Mattingly, NY
1987	K. Hernandez, NY	D. Mattingly, NY
1988	K. Hernandez, NY	D. Mattingly, NY
1989	A. Galarraga, MON	D. Mattingly, NY
1990	A. Galarraga, MON	M. McGwire, OAK
1991	W. Clark, SF	D. Mattingly, NY
1992	M. Grace, CHI	D. Mattingly, NY
1993	M. Grace, CHI	D. Mattingly, NY
1994	J. Bagwell, HOU	D. Mattingly, NY
1995	M. Grace, CHI	J. Snow, CAL
1996	M. Grace, CHI	J. Snow, CAL
1997	J. Snow, SF	R. Palmeiro, BAL
1998	J. Snow, SF	R. Palmeiro, BAL
1999	J. Snow, SF	R. Palmeiro, TEX
2000	J. Snow, SF	J. Olerud, SEA

Second Basemen

Year	National League	American League	Year	National League	American League
1957	(No selection)	N. Fox, CHI	1979	M. Trillo, PHI	F. White, KC
1958	B. Mazeroski, PIT	F. Bolling, DET	1980	D. Flynn, NY	F. White, KC
1959	C. Neal, LA	N. Fox, CHI	1981	M. Trillo, PHI	F. White, KC
1960	B. Mazeroski, PIT	N. Fox, CHI	1982	M. Trillo, PHI	F. White, KC
1961	B. Mazeroski, PIT	B. Richardson, NY	1983	R. Sandberg, CHI	L. Whitaker, DET
1962	K. Hubbs, CHI	B. Richardson, NY	1984	R. Sandberg, CHI	L. Whitaker, DET
1963	B. Mazeroski, PIT	B. Richardson, NY	1985	R. Sandberg, CHI	L. Whitaker, DET
1964	B. Mazeroski, PIT	B. Richardson, NY	1986	R. Sandberg, CHI	F. White, KC
1965	B. Mazeroski, PIT	B. Richardson, NY	1987	R. Sandberg, CHI	F. White, KC
1966	B. Mazeroski, PIT	B. Knoop, CAL	1988	R. Sandberg, CHI	H. Reynolds, SEA
1967	B. Mazeroski, PIT	B. Knoop, CAL	1989	R. Sandberg, CHI	H. Reynolds, SEA
1968	G. Beckert, CHI	B. Knoop, CAL	1990	R. Sandberg, CHI	H. Reynolds, SEA
1969	F. Millan, ATL	D. Johnson, BAL	1991	R. Sandberg, CHI	R. Alomar, TOR
1970	T. Helms, CIN	D. Johnson, BAL	1992	J. Lind, PIT	R. Alomar, TOR
1971	T. Helms, CIN	D. Johnson, BAL	1993	R. Thompson, SF	R. Alomar, TOR
1972	F. Millan, ATL	D. Griffin, BOS	1994	C. Biggio, HOU	R. Alomar, TOR
1973	J. Morgan, CIN	B. Grich, BAL	1995	C. Biggio, HOU	R. Alomar, TOR
1974	J. Morgan, CIN	B. Grich, BAL	1996	C. Biggio, HOU	R. Alomar, TOR
1975	J. Morgan, CIN	B. Grich, BAL	1997	C. Biggio, HOU	C. Knoblauch, MIN
1976	J. Morgan, CIN	B. Grich, BAL	1998	B. Boone, CIN	R. Alomar, BAL
1977	J. Morgan, CIN	F. White, KC	1999	P. Reese, CIN	R. Alomar, CLE
1978	D. Lopes, LA	F. White, KC	2000	P. Reese, CIN	R. Alomar, CLE

Third Basemen

Year	National League	American League	Year	National League	American League
1957	(No selection)	F. Malzone, BOS	1979	M. Schmidt, PHI	B. Bell, TEX
1958	K. Boyer, SL	F. Malzone, BOS	1980	M. Schmidt, PHI	B. Bell, TEX
1959	K. Boyer, SL	F. Malzone, BOS	1981	M. Schmidt, PHI	B. Bell, TEX
1960	K. Boyer, SL	B. Robinson, BAL	1982	M. Schmidt, PHI	B. Bell, TEX
1961	K. Boyer, SL	B. Robinson, BAL	1983	M. Schmidt, PHI	B. Bell, TEX
1962	J. Davenport, SF	B. Robinson, BAL	1984	M. Schmidt, PHI	B. Bell, TEX
1963	K. Boyer, SL	B. Robinson, BAL	1985	T. Wallach, MON	G. Brett, KC
1964	R. Santo, CHI	B. Robinson, BAL	1986	M. Schmidt, PHI	G. Gaetti, MIN
1965	R. Santo, CHI	B. Robinson, BAL	1987	T. Pendleton, SL	G. Gaetti, MIN
1966	R. Santo, CHI	B. Robinson, BAL	1988	T. Wallach, MON	G. Gaetti, MIN
1967	R. Santo, CHI	B. Robinson, BAL	1989	T. Pendleton, SL	G. Gaetti, MIN
1968	R. Santo, CHI	B. Robinson, BAL	1990	T. Wallach, MON	K. Gruber, TOR
1969	C. Boyer, ATL	B. Robinson, BAL	1991	M. Williams, SF	R. Ventura, CHI
1970	D. Rader, HOU	B. Robinson, BAL	1992	T. Pendleton, ATL	R. Ventura, CHI
1971	D. Rader, HOU	B. Robinson, BAL	1993	M. Williams, SF	R. Ventura, CHI
1972	D. Rader, HOU	B. Robinson, BAL	1994	M. Williams, SF	W. Boggs, NY
1973	D. Rader, HOU	B. Robinson, BAL	1995	K. Caminiti, SD	W. Boggs, NY
1974	D. Rader, HOU	B. Robinson, BAL	1996	K. Caminiti, SD	R. Ventura, CHI
1975	K. Reitz, SL	B. Robinson, BAL	1997	K. Caminiti, SD	M. Williams, CLE
1976	M. Schmidt, PHI	A. Rodriguez, DET	1998	S. Rolen, PHI	R. Ventura, CHI
1977	M. Schmidt, PHI	G. Nettles, NY	1999	R. Ventura, NY	S. Brosius, NY
1978	M. Schmidt, PHI	G. Nettles, NY	2000	S. Rolen, PHI	T. Fryman, CLE

Shortstops

Year	National League	American League	Year	National League	American League
1957	R. McMillan, CIN	(No selection)	1979	D. Concepcion, CIN	R. Burleson, BOS
1958	R. McMillan, CIN	L. Aparicio, CHI	1980	O. Smith, SD	A. Trammell, DET
1959	R. McMillan, CIN	L. Aparicio, CHI	1981	O. Smith, SD	A. Trammell, DET
1960	E. Banks, CHI	L. Aparicio, CHI	1982	O. Smith, SL	R. Yount, MIL
1961	M. Wills, LA	L. Aparicio, CHI	1983	O. Smith, SL	A. Trammell, DET
1962	M. Wills, LA	L. Aparicio, CHI	1984	O. Smith, SL	A. Trammell, DET
1963	B. Wine, PHI	Z. Versalles, MIN	1985	O. Smith, SL	A. Griffin, OAK
1964	R. Amaro, PHI	L. Aparicio, BAL	1986	O. Smith, SL	T. Fernandez, TOR
1965	L. Cardenas, CIN	Z. Versalles, MIN	1987	O. Smith, SL	T. Fernandez, TOR
1966	G. Alley, PIT	L. Aparicio, BAL	1988	O. Smith, SL	T. Fernandez, TOR
1967	G. Alley, PIT	J. Fregosi, CAL	1989	O. Smith, SL	T. Fernandez, TOR
1968	D. Maxvill, SL	L. Aparicio, CHI	1990	O. Smith, SL	O. Guillen, CHI
1969	D. Kessinger, CHI	M. Belanger, BAL	1991	O. Smith, SL	C. Ripken, BAL
1970	D. Kessinger, CHI	L. Aparicio, CHI	1992	O. Smith, SL	C. Ripken, BAL
1971	B. Harrelson, NY	M. Belanger, BAL	1993	J. Bell, PIT	O. Vizquel, SEA
1972	L. Bowa, PHI	E. Brinkman, DET	1994	B. Larkin, CIN	O. Vizquel, CLE
1973	R. Metzger, HOU	M. Belanger, BAL	1995	B. Larkin, CIN	O. Vizquel, CLE
1974	D. Concepcion, CIN	M. Belanger, BAL	1996	B. Larkin, CIN	O. Vizquel, CLE
1975	D. Concepcion, CIN	M. Belanger, BAL	1997	R. Ordoñez, NY	O. Vizquel, CLE
1976	D. Concepcion, CIN	M. Belanger, BAL	1998	R. Ordoñez, NY	O. Vizquel, CLE
1977	D. Concepcion, CIN	M. Belanger, BAL	1999	R. Ordoñez, NY	O. Vizquel, CLE
1978	L. Bowa, PHI	M. Belanger, BAL	2000	N. Perez, COL	O. Vizquel, CLE

National League Outfielders

YEAR	PLAYERS		
1957	W. Mays, NY (CF)	(No other selections)	
1958	F. Robinson, CIN (LF)	W. Mays, SF (CF)	H. Aaron, MIL (RF)
1959	J. Brandt, SF (LF)	W. Mays, SF (CF)	H. Aaron, MIL (RF)
1960	W. Moon, LA (LF)	W. Mays, SF (CF)	H. Aaron, MIL (RF)
1961	W. Mays, SF	R. Clemente, PIT	V. Pinson, CIN
1962	W. Mays, SF	R. Clemente, PIT	B. Virdon, PIT
1963	W. Mays, SF	R. Clemente, PIT	C. Flood, SL
1964	W. Mays, SF	R. Clemente, PIT	C. Flood, SL
1965	W. Mays, SF	R. Clemente, PIT	C. Flood, SL
1966	W. Mays, SF	C. Flood, SL	R. Clemente, PIT
1967	R. Clemente, PIT	C. Flood, SL	W. Mays, SF
1968	W. Mays, SF	R. Clemente, PIT	C. Flood, SL
1969	R. Clemente, PIT	C. Flood, SL	P. Rose, CIN
1970	R. Clemente, PIT	T. Agee, NY	P. Rose, CIN
1971	R. Clemente, PIT	B. Bonds, SF	W. Davis, LA
1972	R. Clemente, PIT	C. Cedeno, HOU	W. Davis, LA
1973	B. Bonds, SF	C. Cedeno, HOU	W. Davis, LA
1974	C. Cedeno, HOU	C. Geronimo, CIN	B. Bonds, SF
1975	C. Cedeno, HOU	C. Geronimo, CIN	G. Maddox, PHI
1976	C. Cedeno, HOU	C. Geronimo, CIN	G. Maddox, PHI
1977	C. Geronimo, CIN	G. Maddox, PHI	D. Parker, PIT
1978	G. Maddox, PHI	D. Parker, PIT	E. Valentine, MON

YEAR	PLAYERS		
1979	G. Maddox, PHI	D. Parker, PIT	D. Winfield, SD
1980	A. Dawson, MON	G. Maddox, PHI	D. Winfield, SD
1981	A. Dawson, MON	G. Maddox, PHI	D. Baker, LA
1982	A. Dawson, MON	D. Murphy, ATL	G. Maddox, PHI
1983	A. Dawson, MON	D. Murphy, ATL	W. McGee, SL
1984	D. Murphy, ATL	B. Dernier, CHI	A. Dawson, MON
1985	W. McGee, SL	D. Murphy, ATL	A. Dawson, MON
1986	T. Gwynn, SD	D. Murphy, ATL	W. McGee, SL
1987	E. Davis, CIN	T. Gwynn, SD	A. Dawson, CHI
1988	A. Van Slyke, PIT	E. Davis, CIN	A. Dawson, CHI
1989	A. Van Slyke, PIT	E. Davis, CIN	T. Gwynn, SD
1990	A. Van Slyke, PIT	T. Gwynn, SD	B. Bonds, PIT
1991	A. Van Slyke, PIT	T. Gwynn, SD	B. Bonds, PIT
1992	A. Van Slyke, PIT	L. Walker, MON	B. Bonds, PIT
1993	B. Bonds, SF	L. Walker, MON	M. Grissom, MON
1994	B. Bonds, SF	D. Lewis, SF	M. Grissom, MON
1995	R. Mondesi, LA	M. Grissom, ATL	S. Finley, SD
1996	B. Bonds, SF	M. Grissom, ATL	S. Finley, SD
1997	B. Bonds, SF	R. Mondesi, LA	L.Walker, COL
1998	B. Bonds, SF	A. Jones, ATL	L.Walker, COL
1999	S. Finley, ARI	A. Jones, ATL	L. Walker, COL
2000	S. Finley, ARI	A. Jones, ATL	J. Edmonds, SL

American League Outfielders

YEAR	PLAYERS		
1957	M. Minoso, CHI (LF)	A. Kaline, DET (RF)	(No other selection)
1958	N. Siebern, NY (LF)	J. Piersall, BOS (CF)	A. Kaline, DET (RF)
1959	M. Minoso, CLE (LF)	A. Kaline, DET (CF)	J. Jensen, BOS (RF)
1960	M. Minoso, CHI (LF)	J. Landis, CHI (CF)	R. Maris, NY (RF)
1961	A. Kaline, DET	J. Piersall, CLE	J. Landis, CHI
1962	J. Landis, CHI	M. Mantle, NY	A. Kaline, DET
1963	A. Kaline, DET	C. Yastrzemski, BOS	J. Landis, CHI
1964	A. Kaline, DET	J. Landis, CHI	V. Davalillo, CLE
1965	A. Kaline, DET	T. Tresh, NY	C. Yastrzemski, BOS
1966	A. Kaline, DET	T. Agee, CHI	T. Oliva, MIN
1967	C. Yastrzemski, BOS	P. Blair, BAL	A. Kaline, DET
1968	M. Stanley, DET	C. Yastrzemski, BOS	R. Smith, BOS
1969	P. Blair, BAL	M. Stanley, DET	C. Yastrzemski, BOS
1970	M. Stanley, DET	P. Blair, BAL	K. Berry, CHI
1971	P. Blair, BAL	A. Otis, KC	C. Yastrzemski, BOS
1972	P. Blair, BAL	B. Murcer, NY	K. Berry, CAL
1973	P. Blair, BAL	A. Otis, KC	M. Stanley, DET
1974	P. Blair, BAL	A. Otis, KC	J. Rudi, OAK
1975	P. Blair, BAL	J. Rudi, OAK	F. Lynn, BOS
1976	J. Rudi, OAK	Dw. Evans, BOS	R. Manning, CLE
1977	J. Beniquez, TEX	C. Yastrzemski, BOS	A. Cowens, KC
1978	F. Lynn, BOS	Dw. Evans, BOS	R. Miller, CAL
1979	Dw. Evans, BOS	S. Lezcano, MIL	F. Lynn, BOS

YEAR	PLAYERS		
1980	F. Lynn, BOS	D. Murphy, OAK	W. Wilson, KC
1981	D. Murphy, OAK	Dw. Evans, BOS	R. Henderson, OAK
1982	Dw. Evans, BOS	D. Winfield, NY	D. Murphy, OAK
1983	Dw. Evans, BOS	D. Winfield, NY	D. Murphy, OAK
1984	Dw. Evans, BOS	D. Winfield, NY	D. Murphy, OAK
1985	G. Pettis, CAL	D. Winfield, NY	Dw. Evans, BOS & D. Murphy, OAK
1986	G. Pettis, CAL	J. Barfield, TOR	K. Puckett, MIN
1987	J. Barfield, TOR	K. Puckett, MIN	D. Winfield, NY
1988	K. Puckett, MIN	D. White, CAL	G. Pettis, DET
1989	D. White, CAL	G. Pettis, DET	K. Puckett, MIN
1990	G. Pettis, TEX	K. Griffey, Jr., SEA	E. Burks, BOS
1991	K. Puckett, MIN	K. Griffey, Jr., SEA	D. White, TOR
1992	K. Puckett, MIN	K. Griffey, Jr., SEA	D. White, TOR
1993	K. Griffey, Jr., SEA	D. White, TOR	K. Lofton, CLE
1994	K. Griffey, Jr., SEA	D. White, TOR	K. Lofton, CLE
1995	K. Griffey, Jr., SEA	K. Lofton, CLE	D. White, TOR
1996	K. Griffey, Jr., SEA	K. Lofton, CLE	J. Buhner, SEA
1997	J. Edmonds, ANA	K. Griffey, Jr., SEA	B. Williams, NY
1998	J. Edmonds, ANA	K. Griffey, Jr., SEA	B. Williams, NY
1999	B. Williams, NY	K. Griffey, Jr., SEA	S. Green, TOR
2000	B. Williams, NY	D. Erstad, ANA	J. Dye, KC

Special MVP Awards

The All-Star Game

The All-Star Game MVP Award began in 1962, the last year in which two All-Star Games were played. It was called the Arch Ward Memorial Award, in honor of the late Chicago newspaper writer credited with conceiving the Mid-Summer Classic. Under Bowie Kuhn's regime (1970-84) the award was called the Commissioner's Trophy.

A committee of writers and executives in attendance votes on the recipient of the game's award. Only twice—Brooks Robinson in 1966 and Carl Yastrzemski in 1970—has a member of the losing team been honored. Two-time winners are Willie Mays, Steve Garvey, and Gary Carter.

Following are the winners of the All-Star Game MVP Awards. Complete voting breakdowns for the award are not available.

1962 Maury Wills, LA (NL) [Game 1]
Leon Wagner, LA (AL) [Game 2]
1963 Willie Mays, SF (NL)
1964 Johnny Callison, PHI (NL)
1965 Juan Marichal, SF (NL)
1966 Brooks Robinson, BAL (AL)
1967 Tony Perez, CIN (NL)
1968 Willie Mays, SF (NL)
1969 Willie McCovey, SF (NL)
1970 Carl Yastrzemski, BOS (AL)
1971 Frank Robinson, BAL (AL)
1972 Joe Morgan, CIN (NL)
1973 Bobby Bonds, SF (NL)
1974 Steve Garvey, LA (NL)
1975 Bill Madlock, CHI (NL)
Jon Matlack, NY (NL)
1976 George Foster, CIN (NL)
1977 Don Sutton, LA (NL)
1978 Steve Garvey, LA (NL)
1979 Dave Parker, PIT (NL)
1980 Ken Griffey, CIN (NL)
1981 Gary Carter, MON (NL)
1982 Dave Concepcion, CIN (NL)
1983 Fred Lynn, CAL (AL)
1984 Gary Carter, MON (NL)
1985 LaMarr Hoyt, SD (NL)
1986 Roger Clemens, BOS (AL)
1987 Tim Raines, MON (NL)
1988 Terry Steinbach, OAK (AL)
1989 Bo Jackson, KC (AL)
1990 Julio Franco, TEX (AL)
1991 Cal Ripken, BAL (AL)
1992 Ken Griffey, Jr., SEA (AL)
1993 Kirby Puckett, MIN (AL)
1994 Fred McGriff, ATL (NL)
1995 Jeff Conine, FLA (NL)
1996 Mike Piazza, LA (NL)
1997 Sandy Alomar, Jr., CLE (AL)
1998 Roberto Alomar, BAL (AL)
1999 Pedro Martinez, BOS (AL)
2000 Derek Jeter, NY (AL)

League Championship Series

MVP Awards for the League Championship Series were instituted by the National League in 1977, and in the American League three years later. A committee of writers and executives in attendance does the voting, which is announced at the conclusion of each series. Steve Garvey, Dave Stewart, and Orel Hershiser are the only two-time winners. Winners from losing teams are Fred Lynn (1982), Mike Scott (1986), and Jeffrey Leonard (1987).

Following are the winners of LCS MVP Awards. Complete voting breakdowns are not available.

Year	National League	American League
1977	Dusty Baker, LA	
1978	Steve Garvey, LA	
1979	Willie Stargell, PIT	
1980	Manny Trillo, PHI	Frank White, KC
1981	Burt Hooton, LA	Graig Nettles, NY
1982	Darrell Porter, SL	Fred Lynn, CAL
1983	Gary Matthews, PHI	Mike Boddicker, BAL
1984	Steve Garvey, SD	Kirk Gibson, DET
1985	Ozzie Smith, SL	George Brett, KC
1986	Mike Scott, HOU	Marty Barrett, BOS
1987	Jeffrey Leonard, SF	Gary Gaetti, MIN
1988	Orel Hershiser, LA	Dennis Eckersley, OAK
1989	Will Clark, SF	Rickey Henderson, OAK
1990	Rob Dibble, CIN Randy Myers, CIN	Dave Stewart, OAK
1991	Steve Avery, ATL	Kirby Puckett, MIN
1992	John Smoltz, ATL	Roberto Alomar, TOR
1993	Curt Schilling, PHI	Dave Stewart, TOR
1994	(No Series)	(No Series)
1995	Mike Devereaux, ATL	Orel Hershiser, CLE
1996	Javier Lopez, ATL	Bernie Williams, NY
1997	Livan Hernandez, FLA	Marquis Grissom, CLE
1998	Sterling Hitchcock, SD	David Wells, NY
1999	Eddie Perez, ATL	Orlando Hernandez, NY
2000	Mike Hampton, NY	David Justice, NY

World Series

There are two major World Series MVP Awards. The New York chapter of the Baseball Writers' Association of America established one in memory of Babe Ruth in 1949, the year after the Bambino's death. Six years later, *Sport* magazine introduced its version, presented in cooperation with the Chevrolet Motor Company (which typically presented a Corvette to the winner).

The winner of the *Sport* award was originally chosen by the magazine's editors, but the voting process eventually went to a committee of sports reporters and officials (and, since *Sport* folded in 2000, they are no longer involved with the award). The award is now sanctioned by Major League Baseball, and has eclipsed the Babe Ruth Award in prestige and public recognition. The *Sport* award is voted on during the final game of the Series and is presented immediately following its conclusion, whereas the Ruth Award is voted on during a local chapter meeting some time after the Series has concluded.

Following are the winners of the two World Series MVP Awards. Two-time winners of the *Sport* award are Sandy Koufax, Bob Gibson, and Reggie Jackson; double-winners of the Ruth award are Koufax and Jack Morris. Winners from losing teams are Bobby Richardson (*Sport*, 1960), and Luis Tiant (Ruth, 1975). Complete voting breakdowns on either award are not available.

Year	Babe Ruth Award	Sport Magazine Award
1949	Joe Page, NY (AL)	
1950	Jerry Coleman, NY (AL)	
1951	Phil Rizzuto, NY (AL)	
1952	Johnny Mize, NY (AL)	
1953	Billy Martin, NY (AL)	
1954	Dusty Rhodes, NY (NL)	
1955	Johnny Podres, BRO (NL)	Johnny Podres, BRO (NL)
1956	Don Larsen, NY (AL)	Don Larsen, NY (AL)
1957	Lew Burdette, MIL (NL)	Lew Burdette, MIL (NL)
1958	Elston Howard, NY (AL)	Bob Turley, NY (AL)
1959	Larry Sherry, LA (NL)	Larry Sherry, LA (NL)
1960	Bill Mazeroski, PIT (NL)	Bobby Richardson, NY (AL)
1961	Whitey Ford, NY (AL)	Whitey Ford, NY (AL)
1962	Ralph Terry, NY (AL)	Ralph Terry, NY (AL)
1963	Sandy Koufax, LA (NL)	Sandy Koufax, LA (NL)
1964	Bob Gibson, SL (NL)	Bob Gibson, SL (NL)
1965	Sandy Koufax, LA (NL)	Sandy Koufax, LA (NL)
1966	Frank Robinson, BAL (AL)	Frank Robinson, BAL (AL)
1967	Lou Brock, SL (NL)	Bob Gibson, SL (NL)
1968	Mickey Lolich, DET (AL)	Mickey Lolich, DET (AL)
1969	Al Weis, NY (NL)	Donn Clendenon, NY (NL)
1970	Brooks Robinson, BAL (AL)	Brooks Robinson, BAL (AL)
1971	Roberto Clemente, PIT (NL)	Roberto Clemente, PIT (NL)
1972	Gene Tenace, OAK (AL)	Gene Tenace, OAK (AL)
1973	Bert Campaneris, OAK (AL)	Reggie Jackson, OAK (AL)
1974	Dick Green, OAK (AL)	Rollie Fingers, OAK (AL)
1975	Luis Tiant, BOS (AL)	Pete Rose, CIN (NL)
1976	Johnny Bench, CIN (NL)	Johnny Bench, CIN (NL)
1977	Reggie Jackson, NY (AL)	Reggie Jackson, NY (AL)
1978	Bucky Dent, NY (AL)	Bucky Dent, NY (AL)
1979	Willie Stargell, PIT (NL)	Willie Stargell, PIT (NL)
1980	Tug McGraw, PHI (NL)	Mike Schmidt, PHI (NL)
1981	Ron Cey, LA (NL)	Ron Cey, LA (NL) Pedro Guerrero, LA (NL) Steve Yeager, LA (NL)
1982	Bruce Sutter, SL (NL)	Darrell Porter, SL (NL)
1983	Rick Dempsey, BAL (AL)	Rick Dempsey, BAL (AL)
1984	Jack Morris, DET (AL)	Alan Trammell, DET (AL)
1985	Bret Saberhagen, KC (AL)	Bret Saberhagen, KC (AL)
1986	Ray Knight, NY (NL)	Ray Knight, NY (NL)
1987	Frank Viola, MIN (AL)	Frank Viola, MIN (AL)
1988	Orel Hershiser, LA (NL)	Orel Hershiser, LA (NL)
1989	Dave Stewart, OAK (AL)	Dave Stewart, OAK (AL)
1990	Billy Hatcher, CIN (NL)	Jose Rijo, CIN (NL)
1991	Jack Morris, MIN (AL)	Jack Morris, MIN (AL)
1992	Dave Winfield, TOR (AL)	Pat Borders, TOR (AL)
1993	Paul Molitor, TOR (AL)	Paul Molitor, TOR (AL)
1994	(No Series)	(No Series)
1995	Tom Glavine, ATL (NL)	Tom Glavine, ATL (NL)
1996	Cecil Fielder, NY (AL)	John Wetteland, NY (AL)
1997	Moises Alou, FLA (NL)	Livan Hernandez, FLA (NL)
1998	Scott Brosius, NY (AL)	Scott Brosius, NY (AL)
1999	Mariano Rivera, NY (AL)	Mariano Rivera, NY (AL)
2000	Derek Jeter, NY (AL)	Derek Jeter, NY (AL)

The Player and Pitcher of the Month Awards

On June 4, 1958, NL president Warren Giles announced the very first winners of the Player of the Month Award: future Hall of Famers Stan Musial and Willie Mays, in a tie. Forty baseball writers and broadcasters—five from each NL city—had been polled to select the winners. Among the original voters were Bob Broeg, Harry Caray, Joe Garagiola, and Vin Scully.

Most winners have received a "handsome engraved desk set,"with timepieces and framed portrait photos also serving as trophies. In the early years of the award, none was given for April. The first month was considered too short a trial, featuring only about a dozen games per team in the days of a 154-game schedule. A September nomination was often bypassed, too, perhaps because the league and voters were too consumed by the pennant races and season-long awards. Since 1975, every month has been represented, except during the strike-shortened seasons of 1981, '94 and '95.

There was talk of establishing dual awards—one for everyday players, one for pitchers—as early as July 1958. Pitchers had been practically ignored in the first two POM polls (amassing just 13 of 79 votes), and there was a feeling that a hurler could not win the nomination. Joey Jay quieted the discussion by capturing the prize for that month, and Lew Burdette ended it by earning the August citation. The two Braves' pitchers unwittingly set back dual awards nearly two decades; it would be 1975 before the NL began separate awards for Players and Pitchers of the Month.

The American League waited until 1974 to establish its

version of the Player of the Month Award, and until 1979 to add the Pitcher of the Month. Through 2000, the two leagues had presented a total of 706 Player and Pitcher of the Month Awards, with 395 different winners (including 20 who won in both leagues). The most POM Awards received by any player is 13, by Roger Clemens. Frank Thomas leads non-pitchers with eight citations, while Barry Bonds and Greg Maddux are the NL leaders with seven.

The most POM Awards in one season is four, by Pedro Martinez in 1999; Mark McGwire won three in 1998, and dozens of others have won two. Tom Seaver won with two different teams in 1977: the Mets in April, the Reds (to whom he was traded June 15) in August. Not to be outdone, Fred McGriff won in July 1993 while splitting the month between two teams: he was swapped from the Padres to the Braves on the 18th of that month.

Winners have ranged in age from 19-year-old Robin Yount (April 1975), to 40-year-old Warren Spahn (August 1961). Eighteen rookies have won the award, including Marty Bystrom, the only man to win it in his very first month in the majors (September 1980). At the other end of the spectrum, Al Kaline won the award in his *last* month (September 1974) in the bigs.

A POM winner is typically either a great player having a good month, or a good player having a great month. Occasionally, it is a mediocre player—Jim Hughes and Otto Velez, to name two—who has stumbled into and out of "the zone" just long enough to be honored. On the other hand, winning a POM sometimes signals a player's transformation from mediocrity to superstardom. Two cases in point are Sandy Koufax (June 1962) and Ryne Sandberg (June 1984). Several all-time greats *never* won a POM Award during their careers. Examples include Ernie Banks, Johnny Bench, Bert Blyleven, Dennis Eckersley, Rollie Fingers, Carlton Fisk, Phil Niekro, and Ozzie Smith.

Following is a chart listing all of the Players and Pitchers of the Month since 1958:

National League Player & Pitcher of the Month Awards

YEAR	APRIL	MAY	JUNE	JULY	AUGUST	SEPTEMBER
1958		S. Musial/W. Mays	Frank Thomas	Joey Jay	Lew Burdette	Willie Mays
1959		Hank Aaron			Willie McCovey	
		Harvey Haddix	Elroy Face	Don Drysdale	Vern Law	Eddie Mathews
1960		Roberto Clemente	Lindy McDaniel	Don Drysdale	Warren Spahn	Ken Boyer
1961		Joey Jay	George Altman	Frank Robinson	Warren Spahn	Jim O'Toole
1962		Bob Purkey	Sandy Koufax	Frank Howard	Jack Sanford	
1963		Dick Ellsworth	Ron Santo	Willie McCovey	Willie Mays	
1964		Billy Williams	Jim Bunning	Ron Santo	Frank Robinson	Bob Gibson
1965			Willie Stargell			
		Joe Torre	Vern Law	Pete Rose	Willie Mays	
1966		Juan Marichal	Gaylord Perry	Mike Shannon	Pete Rose	
1967		Roberto Clemente	Hank Aaron	Jim Ray Hart	Orlando Cepeda	
1968		Don Drysdale	Bob Gibson	Bob Gibson	Pete Rose	Steve Blass
1969	Willie McCovey	Ken Holtzman	Ron Santo	Roberto Clemente	Willie Davis	
1970		Rico Carty	Tommie Agee	Bill Singer	Bob Gibson	
1971	Willie Stargell	Lou Brock	Willie Stargell	Fergie Jenkins	Joe Torre	
1972	Don Sutton	Bob Watson	Cesar Cedeño	Billy Williams	Ken Henderson	
1973	Jerry Koosman	Willie Crawford	Greg Luzinski	Pete Rose	Dave Johnson	
1974	Tommy John	Ralph Garr	Buzz Capra	Don Gullett	Lou Brock	
1975	Joe Morgan	Bob Watson	Joe Morgan	Dave Kingman	Tony Perez	Andre Thornton
	Don Sutton	Don Sutton	Tom Seaver	Al Hrabosky	Burt Hooton	Burt Hooton
1976	Mike Schmidt	George Foster	Al Oliver	George Foster	Joe Morgan	Steve Garvey
	Randy Jones	Randy Jones	Andy Messersmith	Jerry Koosman	Ray Burris	Don Sutton
1977	Ron Cey	Ken Reitz	George Foster	Greg Luzinski	George Foster	Cesar Cedeño
	Tom Seaver	Bruce Sutter	Rick Reuschel	Rick Reuschel	Tom Seaver	Larry Christenson
1978	Rick Monday	Jack Clark	Dave Winfield	Pete Rose	Dave Parker	Dave Parker
	Ross Grimsley	Bob Knepper	Vida Blue	J. R. Richard	Kent Tekulve	Gaylord Perry
1979	George Foster	Lou Brock	George Foster	Mike Schmidt	Keith Hernandez	Pete Rose
	Ken Forsch	Joe Niekro	Joaquin Andujar	Dick Tidrow	Rick Reuschel	J. R. Richard
1980	Dave Kingman	Mike Schmidt	Dusty Baker	Bob Horner	Dale Murphy	Gary Carter
	J. R. Richard	Steve Carlton	Jerry Reuss	Pat Zachry	Rick Reuschel	Marty Bystrom
1981	Dave Concepcion	Art Howe			Mike Schmidt	Gary Matthews
	F. Valenzuela	Charlie Lea			R.Camp/E.Whitson	Tom Seaver
1982	Dale Murphy	Tim Wallach	Al Oliver	Mike Schmidt	Bill Buckner	C. Washington
	Steve Rogers	Dick Ruthven	Steve Howe	John Candelaria	Nolan Ryan	Joaquin Andujar
1983	Terry Kennedy	Darrell Evans	Andre Dawson	Dusty Baker	Mel Hall	Dale Murphy
	Pascual Perez	Bill Laskey	Burt Hooton	Joe Price	Jesse Orosco	John Denny
1984	Tony Gwynn	Leon Durham	Ryne Sandberg	Jose Cruz	Keith Moreland	Dale Murphy
	Rick Honeycutt	Nolan Ryan	Ron Darling	Orel Hershiser	Rick Sutcliffe	Dwight Gooden
1985	Dale Murphy	Dave Parker	Pedro Guerrero	Keith Hernandez	Willie McGee	Gary Carter
	F. Valenzuela	Andy Hawkins	John Tudor	F. Valenzuela	Shane Rawley	Dwight Gooden
1986	Johnny Ray	Hubie Brooks	Kevin Bass	Eric Davis	Dale Murphy	Steve Sax
	Dwight Gooden	Jeff Reardon	Rick Rhoden	Todd Worrell	Bill Gullickson	Mike Krukow
1987	Eric Davis	Eric Davis	Tony Gwynn	Bo Diaz	Andre Dawson	Darryl Strawberry
	Sid Fernandez	Steve Bedrosian	Orel Hershiser	Floyd Youmans	Doug Drabek	Pascual Perez
1988	Bobby Bonilla	Bobby Bonilla	Will Clark	Tony Gwynn	Eric Davis	Kevin McReynolds
	Orel Hershiser	David Cone	Greg Maddux	John Franco	Danny Jackson	Orel Hershiser
1989	Von Hayes	Will Clark	Howard Johnson	Mark Grace	Pedro Guerrero	Bobby Bonilla
	Mark Davis	Rick Reuschel	Mike Scott	Mark Langston	Tom Browning	Tim Belcher
1990	Bobby Bonilla	Andre Dawson	Ryne Sandberg	Barry Bonds	David Justice	Kal Daniels
	John Tudor	Jack Armstrong	Ramon Martinez	D.Darwin/D.Drabek	Doug Drabek	Dwight Gooden
1991	Felix Jose	David Justice	Barry Larkin	Barry Bonds	Will Clark	Howard Johnson
	Lee Smith	Tom Glavine	Rob Dibble	Dennis Martinez	Mitch Williams	Chris Nabholz
1992	Barry Bonds	Felix Jose	Cory Snyder	Brett Butler	Gary Sheffield	Barry Bonds
	Billy Swift	Mike Morgan	Randy Tomlin	Tom Glavine	Dennis Martinez	Jose Rijo

YEAR	APRIL	MAY	JUNE	JULY	AUGUST	SEPTEMBER
1993	Barry Bonds	Jeff Bagwell	Andres Galarraga	Fred McGriff	Tony Gwynn	Andres Galarraga
	Ken Hill	Tommy Greene	D.Kile/C.Hammond	Billy Swift	Greg Maddux	John Wetteland
1994	Ellis Burks	L.Dykstra/M.Piazza	Jeff Bagwell	Jeff Bagwell		
	Bob Tewksbury	Doug Drabek	Bobby Muñoz	Bret Saberhagen		
1995		Matt Williams	Jeff Conine	Dante Bichette	Mike Piazza	Dante Bichette
		Heathcliff Slocumb	Hideo Nomo	Greg Maddux	Sid Fernandez	Greg Maddux
1996	Barry Bonds	Jeff Bagwell	Dante Bichette	Sammy Sosa	Ken Caminiti	Ken Caminiti
	John Smoltz	John Smoltz	Jeff Fassero	Jeff Fassero	Kevin Brown	Hideo Nomo
1997	Larry Walker	Tony Gwynn	Mike Piazza	Barry Bonds	Mike Piazza	Mark McGwire
	Tom Glavine	Bobby Jones	Kent Mercker	Darryl Kile	Pedro Martinez	Jeff Shaw
1998	Mark McGwire	Mark McGwire	Sammy Sosa	Vladimir Guerrero	Jeff Kent	Mark McGwire
	Tom Glavine	Orel Hershiser	Greg Maddux	Chan Ho Park	Randy Johnson	Randy Johnson
1999	Matt Williams	Sammy Sosa	Jeromy Burnitz	Mark McGwire	Vladimir Guerrero	Greg Vaughn
	John Smoltz	Curt Schilling	Al Leiter	Randy Johnson	Greg Maddux	Denny Neagle
2000	Vladimir Guerrero	Todd Helton	Jeff Kent	Sammy Sosa	Todd Helton	Richard Hidalgo
	Randy Johnson	Garrett Stephenson	Al Leiter	Jeff D'Amico	Russ Ortiz	Greg Maddux

American League Player & Pitcher of the Month Awards

YEAR	APRIL	MAY	JUNE	JULY	AUGUST	SEPTEMBER
1974	Graig Nettles	Rod Carew	Gaylord Perry	Doc Medich	Nolan Ryan	Al Kaline
1975	Robin Yount	Jim Hughes	Fred Lynn	John Mayberry	Jim Palmer	Gene Tenace
1976	Willie Horton	Ron LeFlore	Mark Fidrych	Reggie Jackson	Luis Tiant	N.Ryan/F.Tanana
1977	Otto Velez	Frank Tanana	Rod Carew	Jim Rice	Graig Nettles	Rod Carew
1978	Frank Tanana	Jim Rice	Ron Guidry	Doug DeCinces	Jim Rice	Ron Guidry
1979	Cecil Cooper	Don Baylor	Dan Meyer	Don Baylor	Fred Lynn	Alfredo Griffin
	Tommy John	Jim Kern	Mark Clear	Sid Monge	Rick Langford	Goose Gossage
1980	Lamar Johnson	Ben Oglivie	Rod Carew	G.Brett/R.Jackson	Cecil Cooper	E.Murray/J.Rice
	Dave Stieb	Chuck Rainey	Steve Stone	Larry Gura	Bob Stanley	Tim Stoddard
1981	Ken Singleton	Dwight Evans		Cecil Cooper	E.Murray/W.Wilson	
	Matt Keough	Mark Clear		Ron Guidry	L.Gura/D.Martinez	
1982	Eddie Murray	Hal McRae	George Brett	Robin Yount	Doug DeCinces	Dave Winfield
	Geoff Zahn	LaMarr Hoyt	Jim Beattie	Tippy Martinez	Jim Palmer	Rick Sutcliffe
1983	George Brett	Rod Carew	Lou Whitaker	Cecil Cooper	Lloyd Moseby	Cal Ripken
	Rick Honeycutt	Dave Stieb	Charlie Hough	Scott McGregor	Jack Morris	Rich Dotson
1984	Alan Trammell	Eddie Murray	Tony Armas	Kent Hrbek	Gary Ward	Greg Walker
	Jack Morris	Mike Boddicker	Charlie Hough	Willie Hernandez	Roger Clemens	Doyle Alexander
1985	Mike Davis	George Brett	Rickey Henderson	George Brett	Don Mattingly	Don Mattingly
	Charlie Leibrandt	Dave Stieb	Jay Howell	Bret Saberhagen	Dave Righetti	Charlie Leibrandt
1986	Kirby Puckett	Wade Boggs	Kent Hrbek	Scott Fletcher	Doug DeCinces	Don Mattingly
	Roger Clemens	Don Aase	Roger Clemens	Jack Morris	Mike Witt	Bruce Hurst
1987	Brian Downing	Larry Parrish	Wade Boggs	Don Mattingly	Dwight Evans	Alan Trammell
	Bret Saberhagen	Jim Clancy	Steve Ontiveros	Frank Viola	Mark Langston	Doyle Alexander
1988	Dave Winfield	Carney Lansford	Mike Greenwell	Chili Davis	Kent Hrbek	Jose Canseco
	Dave Stewart	Frank Viola	Mark Gubicza	Roger Clemens	Bruce Hurst	Mark Langston
1989	Fred McGriff	Ron Kittle	Ruben Sierra	Robin Yount	G.Bell/N.Esasky	Paul Molitor
	Jeff Ballard	Chuck Finley	Mark Gubicza	Mike Moore	Bret Saberhagen	Bret Saberhagen
1990	Ken Griffey, Jr.	Jose Canseco	Brook Jacoby	George Brett	Cecil Fielder	Kelly Gruber
	Dave Stewart	Bobby Thigpen	Randy Johnson	C.Finley/B.Witt	Roger Clemens	Dave Stewart
1991	Dave Henderson	Ruben Sierra	Joe Carter	Robin Ventura	Frank Thomas	Cal Ripken
	Roger Clemens	Scott Erickson	Jack Morris	Bill Krueger	Kevin Tapani	Roger Clemens
1992	Roberto Alomar	Kirby Puckett	Kirby Puckett	Edgar Martinez	Edgar Martinez	Frank Thomas
	Bill Krueger	Roger Clemens	John Smiley	Kevin Appier	Roger Clemens	Cal Eldred
1993	John Olerud	Paul Molitor	John Olerud	Rafael Palmeiro	Frank Thomas	Chris Hoiles
	Jimmy Key	Danny Darwin	Rick Aguilera	F. Valenzuela	Bill Gullickson	Wilson Alvarez
1994	Joe Carter	Frank Thomas	Albert Belle	Frank Thomas		
	Ben McDonald	David Cone	Cal Eldred	Alex Fernandez		
1995	Manny Ramirez	Edgar Martinez	Garret Anderson	Albert Belle	Albert Belle	
	Kenny Rogers	Kevin Appier	Tim Wakefield	Erik Hanson	Norm Charlton	
1996	Frank Thomas	Mo Vaughn	Mark McGwire	Juan Gonzalez	Alex Rodriguez	Frank Thomas
	Jose Guzman	Charles Nagy	Orel Hershiser	Pat Hentgen	Pat Hentgen	Charles Nagy
1997	Ken Griffey, Jr.	Frank Thomas	Jeff King	Tim Salmon	Bernie Williams	Juan Gonzalez
	Andy Pettitte	Roger Clemens	Randy Johnson	C. Finley/B. Radke	Roger Clemens	Jeff Fassero
1998	Ivan Rodriguez	Bernie Williams	Rafael Palmeiro	Albert Belle	Derek Jeter	Albert Belle
	Chuck Finley	Hideki Irabu	Bartolo Colon	David Cone	Roger Clemens	Rick Helling
1999	Manny Ramirez	Nomar Garciaparra	Rafael Palmeiro	Joe Randa	Palmeiro/I.Rodriguez	Albert Belle
	Pedro Martinez	Pedro Martinez	Pedro Martinez	Hideki Irabu	Mariano Rivera	Pedro Martinez
2000	Jermaine Dye	Edgar Martinez	Albert Belle	Johnny Damon	Glenallen Hill	Jason Giambi
	Pedro Martinez	James Baldwin	Cal Eldred	Roger Clemens	Steve Sparks	Tim Hudson

The Ted Williams/*Total Baseball* Award

The Ted Williams/*Total Baseball* Awards are presented to the most productive hitters and rookie hitters in the American League and National League each year by the Ted Williams Museum in Hernando, Florida. Adjusted production, a statistic originally formulated by Pete Palmer and John Thorn and listed in this edition of *Total Baseball* as Adjusted On-Base Plus Slugging (OPS+), is used to determine the annual winners. The Hall of Fame outfielder chose to use OPS+ as his standard because, as he wrote in his book Ted Williams' Hit List, that this "statistic most closely reflects my thinking on what makes up a superior hitter." The winners each year are the hitters with the highest level of productivity who have accumulated at least 3.1 plate appearances per team game.

Year	AL	NL	AL Rookie	NL Rookie
1997	Frank Thomas	Mike Piazza	Nomar Garciaparra	Scott Rolen
1998	Albert Belle	Mark McGwire	Ben Grieve	Todd Helton
1999	Manny Ramirez	Mark McGwire	Brian Daubach	Preston Wilson
2000	Jason Giambi	Barry Bonds	Mark Quinn	Rafael Furcal

The Fireman Of The Year Award

The 1950s saw the birth of a statistic called the "save." Chicago writer Jerome Holtzman has been called the inventor, or "father" of the stat, but he never felt he deserved either title. "Three people were keeping track of saves before I came along in 1957: Irving Kaze at Pittsburgh, Jim Toomey at St. Louis, and Allan Roth at Brooklyn. But, by their criteria, all a pitcher had to do was finish a winning game. What I did was develop a formula."

Holtzman's original definition of a save demanded that a reliever not only preserve someone else's victory, but face the potential tying or lead run during his tenure on the mound. Holtzman proposed to compile saves on a daily basis himself, reporting the results. He wrote to *The Sporting News* publisher J.G. Taylor Spink with his proposition, and was eventually rewarded with a "100 or 200 dollar bonus" and hired to keep track of the pen men. The result was the "Fireman of the Year Award," given annually since 1960, originally to the relief pitcher in each league with the highest combined total of wins and saves. The winner is now chosen by a consensus of TSN's editors.

Saves were considered "a very minor stat," said Holtzman. "Nobody paid much attention at first." But, by 1969, the save had grown in importance to the point that the Rules Committee felt obliged to make it an official statistic, the first new one in nearly a half-century.

Following are *The Sporting News*'s Firemen of the Year:

YEAR	NATIONAL LEAGUE
1960	Lindy McDaniel, SL
1961	Stu Miller, SF
1962	Elroy Face, PIT
1963	Lindy McDaniel, CHI
1964	Al McBean, PIT
1965	Ted Abernathy, CHI
1966	Phil Regan, LA
1967	Ted Abernathy, CIN
1968	Phil Regan, LA-CHI
1969	Wayne Granger, CIN
1970	Wayne Granger, CIN
1971	Dave Giusti, PIT
1972	Clay Carroll, CIN
1973	Mike Marshall, MON
1974	Mike Marshall, LA
1975	Al Hrabosky, SL
1976	Rawly Eastwick, CIN
1977	Rollie Fingers, SD
1978	Rollie Fingers, SD
1979	Bruce Sutter, CHI
1980	Rollie Fingers, SD
	Tom Hume, CIN

YEAR	NATIONAL LEAGUE
1981	Bruce Sutter, SL
1982	Bruce Sutter, SL
1983	Al Holland, PHI
	Lee Smith, CHI
1984	Bruce Sutter, SL
1985	Jeff Reardon, MON
1986	Todd Worrell, SL
1987	Steve Bedrosian, PHI
1988	John Franco, CIN
1989	Mark Davis, SD
1990	John Franco, NY
1991	Lee Smith, SL
1992	Doug Jones, HOU
	Lee Smith, SL
1993	Randy Myers, CHI
1994	John Franco, NY
1995	Randy Myers, CHI
1996	Trevor Hoffman, SD
1997	Jeff Shaw, CIN
1998	Trevor Hoffman, SD
1999	Ugueth Urbina, MON
2000	Antonio Alfonseca, FLA

YEAR	AMERICAN LEAGUE
1960	Mike Fornieles, BOS
1961	Luis Arroyo, NY
1962	Dick Radatz, BOS
1963	Stu Miller, BAL
1964	Dick Radatz, BOS
1965	Eddie Fisher, CHI
1966	Jack Aker, KC
1967	Minnie Rojas, CAL
1968	Wilbur Wood, CHI
1969	Ron Perranoski, MIN
1970	Ron Perranoski, MIN
1971	Ken Sanders, MIL
1972	Sparky Lyle, NY
1973	John Hiller, DET
1974	Terry Forster, CHI
1975	Goose Gossage, CHI
1976	Bill Campbell, MIN
1977	Bill Campbell, BOS
1978	Goose Gossage, NY
1979	Jim Kern, TEX
	Mike Marshall, MIN
1980	Dan Quisenberry, KC

YEAR	AMERICAN LEAGUE
1981	Rollie Fingers, MIL
1982	Dan Quisenberry, KC
1983	Dan Quisenberry, KC
1984	Dan Quisenberry, KC
1985	Dan Quisenberry, KC
1986	Dave Righetti, NY
1987	Jeff Reardon, MIN
	Dave Righetti, NY
1988	Dennis Eckersley, OAK
1989	Jeff Russell, TEX
1990	Bobby Thigpen, CHI
1991	Dennis Eckersley, OAK
	Bryan Harvey, CAL
1992	Dennis Eckersley, OAK
1993	Jeff Montgomery, KC
1994	Lee Smith, BAL
1995	Jose Mesa, CLE
1996	John Wetteland, NY
1997	Mariano Rivera, NY
1998	Tom Gordon, BOS
1999	Mariano Rivera, NY
2000	Todd Jones, DET

The Rolaids Relief Man Awards

New recognition for bullpen aces came in 1976, via a product that "spells relief." The American Chicle Group of the Warner-Lambert Company began sponsoring the "Rolaids Relief Man Awards" that year, identifying the top closers in each league with an arbitrary formula: double a pitcher's number of wins, plus double his number of saves, minus his loss total (algebraically, 2W + 2S - L). The formula would be amended in 1988, with the incorporation of "blown saves" (BS): 3S + 2W - 2L - 2 BS. The current formula adds what Rolaids calls "tough saves," awarding four points for each of those. Despite the cumbersome and seemingly random formulas, the first 36 winners of this award also earned *The Sporting News*'s "Fireman of the Year" (still based simply on W + S) citation.

The Rolaids people continue to expand the scope of their honors. In 1979 they named Hoyt Wilhelm for their first "Career Achievement Award"; Elroy Face (1980), Kent Tekulve (1989), and Jerome Holtzman (1993) followed in that distinction. In 1981 Rolaids began sponsoring awards for the National Association leagues, and a year later they started naming monthly winners at the big league level. In 1989 they presented their first "Reliever of the Decade" nomination to Jeff Reardon; and, in 1991 they recognized Reardon, Rollie Fingers, Lee Smith, Goose Gossage, and Bruce Sutter (since joined by several others) with the creation of the "Rolaids 300-Save Club."

Perhaps Rolaids' greatest contribution, besides the increased visibility and prestige they have provided bullpen stars, has been a new statistic. Talked about for years, "blown saves" in 1988 were finally defined and tabulated on a daily basis by the Rolaids statisticians. Whenever a reliever enters a game in a save situation, and leaves with that situation no longer in effect because he has given up the lead, he is charged with a blown save.

Rolaids selections which differed from the Firemen of the Year are Rod Beck (1994), Tom Henke (1995), Jeff Brantley (1996), and Billy Wagner (1999) in the National League, and Randy Myers (1997) in the American. Also, Jim Kern (AL, 1979), Rollie Fingers (NL, 1980), Al Holland (NL, 1983), Dave Righetti (AL, 1987), Bryan Harvey (AL, 1991), and Lee Smith (NL, 1992), who were co-winners of the Fireman award, were sole winners of the Rolaids version.

The Major League Executive Of The Year Award

The Major League Executive of the Year Award was instituted by *The Sporting News* in 1936. With one exception, winners have been affiliated with major league teams (1966 winner Lee MacPhail was an executive in the Office of the Commissioner). George Weiss won the award four times, Branch Rickey thrice and John Hart was the last executive to win it in consecutive years. Major league executives vote for the award.

YEAR	Winner, affiliation	YEAR	Winner, affiliation	YEAR	Winner, affiliation	YEAR	Winner, affiliation
1936	Branch Rickey, SL (N)	1953	Lou Perini, MIL (N)	1970	Harry Dalton, BAL (A)	1987	Al Rosen, SF (N)
1937	Ed Barrow, NY (A)	1954	H. Stoneham, NY (N)	1971	Cedric Tallis, KC (A)	1988	Fred Claire, LA (N)
1938	Warren Giles, CIN (N)	1955	W. O'Malley, BKN (N)	1972	R. Hemond, CHI (A)	1989	R. Hemond, BAL (A)
1939	La. MacPhail, BKN (N)	1956	Gabe Paul, CIN (N)	1973	Bob Howsam, CIN (N)	1990	Bob Quinn, CIN (N)
1940	W. Briggs Sr., DET (A)	1957	Frank Lane, SL (N)	1974	Gabe Paul, NY (A)	1991	A. MacPhail, MIN (A)
1941	Ed Barrow, NY (A)	1958	Joe Brown, PIT (N)	1975	D. O'Connell, BOS (A)	1992	D. Duquette, MON (N)
1942	Branch Rickey, SL (N)	1959	Buzzie Bavasi, LA (N)	1976	Joe Burke, KC (A)	1993	Lee Thomas, PHI (N)
1943	Cl. Griffith, WAS (A)	1960	George Weiss, NY (A)	1977	Bill Veeck, CHI (A)	1994	John Hart, CLE (A)
1944	Billy DeWitt, SL (A)	1961	Dan Topping, NY (A)	1978	S. Richardson, SF (N)	1995	John Hart, CLE (A)
1945	Phil Wrigley, CHI (N)	1962	Fred Haney, LA (A)	1979	Hank Peters, BAL (A)	1996	Doug Melvin, TEX (A)
1946	Tom Yawkey, BOS (A)	1963	Bing Devine, SL (N)	1980	Tal Smith, HOU (N)	1997	Cam Bonifay, PIT (N)
1947	B. Rickey, BKN (N)	1964	Bing Devine, SL (N)	1981	J. McHale, MON (N)	1998	G. Hunsicker, HOU (N)
1948	Bill Veeck, CLE (A)	1965	Cal. Griffith, MIN (A)	1982	Harry Dalton, MIL (A)	1999	Billy Beane, OAK (A)
1949	Bob Carpenter, PHI (N)	1966	Lee MacPhail*	1983	Hank Peters, BAL (A)	2000	Walt Jocketty, SL (N)
1950	George Weiss, NY (A)	1967	D. O'Connell, BOS (A)	1984	Dallas Green, CHI (A)		
1951	George Weiss, NY (A)	1968	Jim Campbell, DET (A)	1985	J. Schuerholz, KC (A)		
1952	George Weiss, NY (A)	1969	John Murphy, NY (N)	1986	Frank Cashen, NY (N)		

The Manager Of The Year Award

There are at least four different versions of the Manager of the Year Award, given by the Baseball Writers Association of America, *The Sporting News*, the Associated Press, and United Press International. Although it is the newest entry of the four, the BBWAA award (instituted in 1983) has come to be regarded as the most prestigious version. Following are the winners of the BBWAA Award for each league:

YEAR	NATIONAL LEAGUE	YEAR	NATIONAL LEAGUE	YEAR	AMERICAN LEAGUE	YEAR	AMERICAN LEAGUE
1983	Tommy Lasorda, LA	1993	Dusty Baker, SF	1983	Tony LaRussa, CHI	1993	Gene Lamont, CHI
1984	Jim Frey, CHI	1994	Felipe Alou, MON	1984	Sparky Anderson, DET	1994	Buck Showalter, NY
1985	Whitey Herzog, SL	1995	Don Baylor, COL	1985	Bobby Cox, TOR	1995	Lou Piniella, SEA
1986	Hal Lanier, HOU	1996	Bruce Bochy, SD	1986	John McNamara, BOS	1996	Johnny Oates, TEX
1987	Buck Rodgers, MON	1997	Dusty Baker, SF	1987	Sparky Anderson, DET		Joe Torre, NY
1988	Tommy Lasorda, LA	1998	Larry Dierker, HOU	1988	Tony LaRussa, OAK	1997	Davey Johnson, BAL
1989	Don Zimmer, CHI	1999	Jack McKeon, CIN	1989	Frank Robinson, BAL	1998	Joe Torre, NY
1990	Jim Leyland, PIT	2000	Dusty Baker, SF	1990	Jeff Torborg, CHI	1999	Jimy Williams, BOS
1991	Bobby Cox, ATL			1991	Tom Kelly, MIN	2000	Jerry Manuel, CHI
1992	Jim Leyland, PIT			1992	Tony La Russa, OAK		

The Player And Pitcher Of The Year Awards

The Sporting News first named a Most Valuable Player in 1929, filling a void left by the discontinuation of the American League Award, and polling the same voters as had participated in the 1928 version of that honor. After the National League Award was also discontinued a year later, TSN announced that, thereafter, they would take it upon themselves to conduct an annual poll to replace the League Awards. They originally retained the stipulation that each voter had to select just one player on each team.

TSN continued with its polls even after the Baseball Writers Association of America started the modern version of the MVP in 1931. Competition between the two awards became acrimonious, with *TSN* at first practically ignoring the BBWAA awards, and later publishing results with condescending statements like "merely confirming the choices made earlier by *The Sporting News*." Beginning in 1938, *TSN* agreed to unify the award, abiding by the BBWAA balloting and presenting "The Sporting News Trophy" to the winners. Among the various gifts awarded to the MVPs were wristwatches and shotguns.

The BBWAA and *TSN* went their separate ways again in 1944. After the 1945 elections, at the request of new Commissioner Happy Chandler, *TSN* "withdrew from the field to cooperate in making the Landis Awards, provided by the major leagues, the official designations of the year." In 1948, however, *TSN* resumed its own awards, selecting a Player of the Year and Pitcher of the Year in each league.

TSN had also been naming a Major League Player of the Year since 1936. In 1992 the NL and AL Player of the Year Awards were supplanted by this honor, though a Pitcher of the Year was still selected in each league. It should be noted that the Major League Player of the Year, since 1992, has been picked by a vote of players, whereas the leagues' Pitchers of the Year are still chosen by TSN's editors. Following are the winners of *The Sporting News*'s awards, with asterisks denoting the Major League Players of the Year:

YEAR	NL Player	NL Pitcher	AL Player	AL Pitcher
1929			Al Simmons, PHI	
1930	Bill Terry, NY		Joe Cronin, WAS	
1931	Chuck Klein, PHI		Lou Gehrig, NY	
1932	Chuck Klein, PHI		Jimmie Foxx, PHI	
1933		Carl Hubbell, NY	Jimmie Foxx, PHI	
1934		Dizzy Dean, SL	Lou Gehrig, NY	
1935	Arky Vaughan, PIT		H. Greenberg, DET	
1936		Carl Hubbell, NY*	Lou Gehrig, NY	

YEAR	NL Player	NL Pitcher	AL Player	AL Pitcher
1937	Joe Medwick, SL		C. Gehringer, DET	Johnny Allen, CLE*
1938	Ernie Lombardi, CIN	J. Vander Meer, CIN*	Jimmie Foxx, BOS	
1939		Bucky Walters, CIN	Joe DiMaggio, NY*	
1940	F. McCormick, CIN		H. Greenberg, DET	Bob Feller, CLE*
1941	Dolf Camilli, BKN		Joe DiMaggio, NY	
1942		Mort Cooper, SL	Joe Gordon, NY	
1943	Stan Musial, SL			Spud Chandler, NY*
1944	Marty Marion, SL*	Bill Voiselle, NY	Bobby Doerr, BOS	H. Newhouser, DET
1945	T. Holmes, BOS	Hank Borowy, CHI	Eddie Mayo, DET	H. Newhouser, DET*
1946	Stan Musial, SL*			
1947		Ted Williams, BOS*		
1948	Stan Musial, SL	Johnny Sain, BOS	Lou Boudreau, CLE*	Bob Lemon, CLE
1949	Enos Slaughter, SL	Howie Pollet, SL	Ted Williams, BOS*	Ellis Kinder, BOS
1950	Ralph Kiner, PIT	Jim Konstanty, PHI	Phil Rizzuto,NY*	Bob Lemon, CLE
1951	Stan Musial, SL*	Preacher Roe, BKN	Ferris Fain, PHI	Bob Feller, CLE
1952	Hank Sauer, CHI	Robin Roberts, PHI*	Luke Easter, CLE	Bobby Shantz, PHI
1953	R. Campanella, BKN	Warren Spahn, MIL	Al Rosen, CLE*	B. Porterfield, WAS
1954	Willie Mays, NY*	John Antonelli, NY	Bobby Avila, CLE	Bob Lemon, CLE
1955	Duke Snider, BKN*	Robin Roberts, PHI	Al Kaline, DET	Whitey Ford, NY
1956	Hank Aaron, MIL	D. Newcombe, BKN	Mickey Mantle, NY*	Billy Pierce, CHI
1957	Stan Musial, SL	Warren Spahn, MIL	Ted Williams, BOS*	Billy Pierce, CHI
1958	Ernie Banks, CHI	Warren Spahn, MIL	Jackie Jensen, BOS	Bob Turley, NY*
1959	Ernie Banks, CHI	Sam Jones, SF	Nellie Fox, CHI	Early Wynn, CHI*
1960	Dick Groat, PIT	Vern Law, PIT	Roger Maris, NY	Chuck Estrada, BAL
1961	Frank Robinson, CIN	Warren Spahn, MIL	Roger Maris, NY*	Whitey Ford, NY
1962	Maury Wills, LA*	Don Drysdale, LA*	Mickey Mantle, NY	Dick Donovan, CLE
1963	Hank Aaron, MIL	Sandy Koufax, LA*	Al Kaline, DET	Whitey Ford, NY
1964	Ken Boyer, SL*	Sandy Koufax, LA	B. Robinson, BAL	Dean Chance, LA
1965	Willie Mays, SF	Sandy Koufax, LA*	Tony Oliva, MIN	Mudcat Grant, MIN
1966	R. Clemente, PIT	Sandy Koufax, LA	F. Robinson, BAL*	Jim Kaat, MIN
1967	Orlando Cepeda, SL	Mike McCormick, SF	C.Yastrzemski,BOS*	Jim Lonborg, BOS
1968	Pete Rose, CIN	Bob Gibson, SL	Ken Harrelson, BOS	D. McLain, DET*
1969	Willie McCovey, SF*	Tom Seaver, NY	H. Killebrew, MIN	Denny McLain, DET
1970	Johnny Bench, CIN*	Bob Gibson, SL	H. Killebrew, MIN	Sam McDowell, CLE
1971	Joe Torre, SL*	Fergie Jenkins, CHI	Tony Oliva, MIN	Vida Blue, OAK
1972	Billy Williams, CHI*	Steve Carlton, PHI	Dick Allen, CHI	Wilbur Wood, CHI
1973	Bobby Bonds, SF	Ron Bryant, SF	R. Jackson, OAK*	Jim Palmer, BAL
1974	Lou Brock, SL*	Mike Marshall, LA	Jeff Burroughs, TEX	Catfish Hunter, OAK
1975	Joe Morgan, CIN*	Tom Seaver, NY	Fred Lynn, BOS	Jim Palmer, BAL
1976	George Foster, CIN	Randy Jones, SD	T. Munson, NY	Jim Palmer, BAL
1977	George Foster, CIN	Steve Carlton, PHI	Rod Carew, MIN*	Nolan Ryan, CAL
1978	Dave Parker, PIT	Vida Blue, SF	Jim Rice, BOS	Ron Guidry, NY*
1979	Keith Hernandez, SL	Joe Niekro, HOU	Don Baylor, CAL	Mike Flanagan, BAL
1980	Mike Schmidt, PHI	Steve Carlton, PHI	George Brett, KC*	Steve Stone, BAL
1981	A. Dawson, MON	F. Valenzuela, LA*	Tony Armas, OAK	Jack Morris, DET
1982	Dale Murphy, ATL	Steve Carlton, PHI	Robin Yount, MIL*	Dave Stieb, TOR
1983	Dale Murphy, ATL	John Denny, PHI	Cal Ripken, BAL*	LaMarr Hoyt, CHI
1984	R. Sandberg, CHI*	Rick Sutcliffe, CHI	Don Mattingly, NY	W. Hernandez, DET
1985	Willie McGee, SL	Dwight Gooden, NY	Don Mattingly, NY*	Bret Saberhagen, KC
1986	Mike Schmidt, PHI	Mike Scott, HOU	Don Mattingly, NY	R. Clemens, BOS*
1987	Andre Dawson, CHI	Rick Sutcliffe, CHI	George Bell, TOR*	Jimmy Key, TOR
1988	Andy Van Slyke, PIT	Orel Hershiser, LA*	Jose Canseco, OAK	Frank Viola, MIN
1989	Kevin Mitchell, SF*	Mark Davis, SD	Ruben Sierra, TEX	Bret Saberhagen, KC
1990	Barry Bonds, PIT*	Doug Drabek, PIT	Cecil Fielder, DET	Bob Welch, OAK
1991	Barry Bonds, PIT	Tom Glavine, ATL	Cal Ripken, BAL*	Roger Clemens, BOS
1992	Gary Sheffield, SD*	Greg Maddux, CHI		D. Eckersley, OAK
1993		Greg Maddux, ATL	Frank Thomas, CHI*	Jack McDowell, CHI
1994	Jeff Bagwell, HOU*	Greg Maddux, ATL		Jimmy Key, NY
1995		Greg Maddux, ATL	Albert Belle, CLE*	Randy Johnson, SEA
1996		John Smoltz, ATL	A. Rodriguez, SEA*	Pat Hentgen, TOR
1997		P. Martinez, MON	K. Griffey, Jr., SEA*	Roger Clemens, TOR
1998	Sammy Sosa, CHI*	Kevin Brown, SD		Roger Clemens, TOR
1999		Mike Hampton, HOU	R. Palmeiro, TEX*	Pedro Martinez, BOS
2000		Tom Glavine, ATL	C. Delgado, TOR*	Pedro Martinez, BOS

Note: The following players were named Major League Player of the Year although they did not receive nomination as their league's top player: Ted Williams (1941 and 1942), Bill Mazeroski (1960), Joe Morgan (1976), and Willie Stargell (1979).

The Rookie Player And Pitcher Of The Year Awards

The Sporting News instituted its Rookie of the Year Awards in 1946, a year before the BBWAA version went national. In 1949, *TSN* began recognizing a winner from each league, and in 1957 they started (sporadically, at first) selecting both a Rookie Player and a Rookie Pitcher of the Year in each league. TSN's editors select the honorees. Following are the winners:

YEAR	NL Player	NL Pitcher	AL Player	AL Pitcher
1946	Del Ennis, PHI			
1947	J. Robinson, BKN			
1948	Richie Ashburn, PHI			
1949		D. Newcombe, BKN	Roy Sievers, SL	
1950				Whitey Ford, NY
1951	Willie Mays, NY		Minnie Minoso, CHI	
1952		Joe Black, BKN	Clint Courtney, SL	
1953	Junior Gilliam, BKN		Harvey Kuenn, DET	
1954	Wally Moon, SL			Bob Grim, NY
1955	Bill Virdon, SL			Herb Score, CLE
1956	Frank Robinson, CIN		Luis Aparicio, CHI	
1957	Ed Bouchee, PHI	Jack Sanford, PHI	Tony Kubek, NY	
1958	Orlando Cepeda, SF	Carlton Willey, MIL	Albie Pearson, WAS	Ryne Duren, NY
1959	Willie McCovey, SF		Bob Allison, WAS	

YEAR	NL Player	NL Pitcher	AL Player	AL Pitcher
1960	Frank Howard, LA		Ron Hansen, BAL	
1961	Billy Williams, CHI	Ken Hunt, CIN	Dick Howser, KC	Don Schwall, BOS
1962	Ken Hubbs, CHI		Tom Tresh, NY	
1963	Pete Rose, CIN	Ray Culp, PHI	Pete Ward, CHI	Gary Peters, CHI
1964	Richie Allen, PHI	Bill McCool, CIN	Tony Oliva, MIN	Wally Bunker, BAL
1965	Joe Morgan, HOU	Frank Linzy, SF	Curt Blefary, BAL	M. Lopez, CAL
1966	Tommy Helms, CIN	Don Sutton, LA	Tommie Agee, CHI	Jim Nash, KC
1967	Lee May, CIN	Dick Hughes, SL	Rod Carew, MIN	Tom Phoebus, BAL
1968	Johnny Bench, CIN	Jerry Koosman, NY	Del Unser, WAS	Stan Bahnsen, NY
1969	Coco Laboy, MON	Tom Griffin, HOU	Carlos May, CHI	Mike Nagy, BOS
1970	Bernie Carbo, CIN	Carl Morton, MON	Roy Foster, CLE	Bert Blyleven, MIN
1971	Earl Williams, ATL	Reggie Cleveland, SL	C. Chambliss, CLE	Bill Parsons, MIL
1972	Dave Rader, SF	Jon Matlack, NY	Carlton Fisk, BOS	Dick Tidrow, CLE
1973	Gary Matthews, SF	Steve Rogers, MON	Al Bumbry, BAL	Steve Busby, KC
1974	Greg Gross, HOU	John D'Aquisto, SF	Mike Hargrove, TEX	Frank Tanana, CAL
1975	Gary Carter, MON	John Montefusco, SF	Fred Lynn, BOS	D. Eckersley, CLE
1976	Larry Herndon, SF	Butch Metzger, SD	Butch Wynegar, MIN	Mark Fidrych, DET
1977	A. Dawson, MON	Bob Owchinko, SD	Mitchell Page, OAK	Dave Rozema, DET
1978	Bob Horner, ATL	Don Robinson, PIT	Paul Molitor, MIL	Rich Gale, KC
1979	Jeff Leonard, HOU	Rick Sutcliffe, LA	Pat Putnam, TEX	Mark Clear, CAL
1980	Lonnie Smith, PHI	B. Gullickson, MON	J. Charboneau, CLE	Britt Burns, CHI
1981	Tim Raines, MON	F. Valenzuela, LA	Rich Gedman, BOS	Dave Righetti, NY
1982	Johnny Ray, PIT	S. Bedrosian, ATL	Cal Ripken, BAL	Ed Vande Berg, SEA
1983	D. Strawberry, NY	C. McMurtry, ATL	Ron Kittle, CHI	M. Boddicker, BAL
1984	Juan Samuel, PHI	Dwight Gooden, NY	Alvin Davis, SEA	Mark Langston, SEA
1985	Vince Coleman, SL	Tom Browning, CIN	Ozzie Guillen, CHI	Ted Higuera, MIL
1986	Robby Thompson, SF	Todd Worrell, SL	Jose Canseco, OAK	Mark Eichhorn, TOR
1987	Benito Santiago, SD	Mike Dunne, PIT	M. McGwire, OAK	M. Henneman, DET
1988	Mark Grace, CHI	Tim Belcher, LA	Walt Weiss, OAK	Bryan Harvey, CAL
1989	Jerome Walton, CHI	Andy Benes, SD	C.Worthington, BAL	Tom Gordon, KC
1990	Dave Justice, ATL	Mike Harkey, CHI	S. Alomar, Jr., CLE	Kevin Appier, KC
1991	Jeff Bagwell, HOU	Al Osuna, HOU	C. Knoblauch, MIN	Juan Guzman, TOR
1992	Eric Karros, LA	Tim Wakefield, PIT	Pat Listach, MIL	Cal Eldred, MIL
1993	Mike Piazza, LA	Kirk Rueter, MON	Tim Salmon, CAL	Aaron Sele, BOS
1994	Raul Mondesi, LA	Steve Trachsel, CHI	Bob Hamelin, KC	B. Anderson, CAL
1995	Chipper Jones, ATL	Hideo Nomo, LA	G. Anderson, CAL	Julian Tavarez, CLE
1996	Jason Kendall, PIT	Alan Benes, SL	Derek Jeter, NY	James Baldwin, CHI
1997	Scott Rolen, PHI	Matt Morris, SL	N. Garciaparra, BOS	Jason Dickson, ANA
1998	Todd Helton, COL	Kerry Wood, CHI	Ben Grieve, OAK	Rolando Arrojo, TB
1999	Preston Wilson, FLA	S. Williamson, CIN	Carlos Beltran, KC	Tim Hudson, OAK
2000	Rafael Furcal, ATL	Rick Ankiel, SL	Mark Quinn, KC	K. Sasaki, SEA

Other Awards

Of the awards not listed in this book, the one people most frequently ask about is the Comeback Player of the Year Award. Why don't we include it?

We would, if it were practical. There are at least four different decades-old versions of this award, given by the Baseball Writers Association of America, *The Sporting News*, the Associated Press, and United Press International (not to mention the Players' Choice Award). None has emerged as the "official" version, and our efforts to document the various versions have been mostly unsuccessful.

Off the Field Awards

The Associated Press Athlete of the Year Award

Associated Press sports editors have been naming male and female athletes of the year since 1931. Following are the baseball honorees, including two-time winner Sandy Koufax:

1931 Pepper Martin
1933 Carl Hubbell
1934 Dizzy Dean
1941 Joe DiMaggio
1948 Lou Boudreau
1950 Jim Konstanty
1954 Willie Mays
1956 Mickey Mantle
1957 Ted Williams
1961 Roger Maris
1962 Maury Wills
1963 Sandy Koufax
1965 Sandy Koufax
1966 Frank Robinson
1967 Carl Yastrzemski
1968 Denny McLain
1969 Tom Seaver
1975 Fred Lynn
1978 Ron Guidry
1979 Willie Stargell
1985 Dwight Gooden
1988 Orel Hershiser
1995 Cal Ripken Jr.

The Roberto Clemente Award

Under newcomer Bowie Kuhn in 1971, the Commissioner's Office created a new annual award—simply called the Commissioner's Award—honoring the player who best exemplified baseball on and off the field. Consideration was given to a player's sportsmanship, community involvement, and contribution to his team and baseball.

On March 12, 1973, the award was renamed for Roberto Clemente, the Pittsburgh star who had died 10 weeks earlier during a mercy mission.

This award is not to be confused with a host of others bearing the Hall of Famer's name, all of which appeared soon after his death. The Pittsburgh chapter of the BBWAA instituted the Roberto Clemente Memorial Award, given to the outstanding Pirate each year. The city of Hialeah, Florida created the Roberto Clemente Humanitarian Award, given to a private citizen in that community who best exemplified Clemente's humanitarian virtues. A third Clemente Award honored the top Latin-American player in the majors.

The Clemente Award given by the Commissioner's Office is selected by a panel of baseball executives and media personnel. It is currently sponsored by True Value, which presents some $175,000 to charities each year in conjunction with the award. Following is a list of the winners:

1971 Willie Mays
1972 Brooks Robinson
1973 Al Kaline
1974 Willie Stargell
1975 Lou Brock
1976 Pete Rose
1977 Rod Carew
1978 Greg Luzinski
1979 Andre Thornton
1980 Phil Niekro
1981 Steve Garvey
1982 Ken Singleton
1983 Cecil Cooper
1984 Ron Guidry
1985 Don Baylor
1986 Garry Maddox
1987 Rick Sutcliffe
1988 Dale Murphy
1989 Gary Carter
1990 Dave Stewart
1991 Harold Reynolds
1992 Cal Ripken
1993 Barry Larkin
1994 Dave Winfield
1995 Ozzie Smith
1996 Kirby Puckett
1997 Eric Davis
1998 Sammy Sosa
1999 Tony Gwynn
2000 Al Leiter

The Ford C. Frick Award

The Ford C. Frick Award was established in 1978, and goes to a broadcaster for "major contributions to Baseball." Frick, who died on April 8 of that year, had done some broadcasting early in his career, though he was better-known for his roles as NL president and baseball commissioner.

Winners of the Frick Award are selected by a panel of baseball executives and media personnel, and honored during the annual Hall of Fame induction ceremonies. Contrary to popular belief, however, the award-winners are *not* members of the Baseball Hall of Fame; there is no "Broadcasters' Wing" at the Hall. As with the Spink Award, a list of the Frick honorees is displayed in the Cooperstown museum's "Scribes and Mike-Men" exhibit.

Following are the winners of the Ford C. Frick Award:

1978 Mel Allen, Red Barber
1979 Bob Elson
1980 Russ Hodges
1981 Ernie Harwell
1982 Vin Scully
1983 Jack Brickhouse
1984 Curt Gowdy
1985 Buck Canel
1986 Bob Prince
1987 Jack Buck
1988 Lindsey Nelson
1989 Harry Caray
1990 By Saam
1991 Joe Garagiola
1992 Milo Hamilton
1993 Chuck Thompson
1994 Bob Murphy
1995 Bob Wolff
1996 Herb Carneal
1997 Jimmy Dudley
1998 Jaime Jarrin
1999 Arch McDonald
2000 Marty Brennaman

The Lou Gehrig Memorial Award

The Lou Gehrig Memorial Award was established by Gehrig's college fraternity in 1955. It is administered by the fraternity's national headquarters in Oxford, Ohio. Its plaque, which resides at the Baseball Hall of Fame in Cooperstown, N.Y., describes the award as follows:

"Presented annually to the major league baseball player who both on and off the field best exemplifies the character of Lou Gehrig, Columbia University '25, who played in 2164 games as a member of the New York American League Baseball Club. Dedicated by his brothers of Phi Delta Theta." The award is announced each spring.

Following are the winners of the Lou Gehrig Award:

1955 Alvin Dark
1956 Pee Wee Reese
1957 Stan Musial
1958 Gil McDougald
1959 Gil Hodges
1960 Dick Groat
1961 Warren Spahn
1962 Robin Roberts
1963 Bobby Richardson
1964 Ken Boyer
1965 Vernon Law
1966 Brooks Robinson
1967 Ernie Banks
1968 Al Kaline
1969 Pete Rose
1970 Hank Aaron
1971 Harmon Killebrew
1972 Wes Parker
1973 Ron Santo
1974 Willie Stargell
1975 Johnny Bench
1976 Don Sutton
1977 Lou Brock
1978 Don Kessinger
1979 Phil Niekro
1980 Tony Perez
1981 Tommy John
1982 Ron Cey
1983 Mike Schmidt
1984 Steve Garvey
1985 Dale Murphy
1986 George Brett
1987 Rick Sutcliffe
1988 Buddy Bell
1989 Ozzie Smith
1990 Glenn Davis
1991 Kent Hrbek
1992 Cal Ripken, Jr.
1993 Don Mattingly
1994 Barry Larkin
1995 Curt Schilling
1996 Brett Butler
1997 Paul Molitor
1998 Tony Gwynn
2000 Mark McGwire

The S. Rae Hickok Professional Athlete of the Year Award

The S. Rae Hickok Professional Athlete of the Year Award—better-known as the Hickok belt—was presented by the Kickik Manufacturing Company of Arlington, Texas, beginning in 1950. The trophy was a large belt of gold and jewelry, reportedly worth $30,000 in 1976, the last year the award was given.

Voting was done each month by several hundred newspaper sports editors nationwide. The 12 monthly winners then competed for the annual prize. Of the 27 annual winners, 15—including two-time winner Sandy Koufax—were from major league baseball. A list of those players follows:

1950 Phil Rizzuto
1951 Allie Reynolds
1954 Willie Mays
1956 Mickey Mantle
1958 Bob Turley
1961 Roger Maris
1962 Maury Wills
1963 Sandy Koufax
1965 Sandy Koufax
1966 Frank Robinson
1967 Carl Yastrzemski
1969 Tom Seaver
1970 Brooks Robinson
1972 Steve Carlton
1975 Pete Rose

The Fred Hutchinson Memorial Award

Reds' manager Fred Hutchinson died November 12, 1964, at age 45. He had been a well-respected major league pitcher and manager for most of a quarter-century, before losing a courageous battle with cancer (diagnosed by his brother, Dr. William B. Hutchinson). Five of Fred's friends in the media—Ritter Collett, Jim Enright, Joe McGuff, Ernie Harwell, and Bob Prince—sought to keep his name alive by creating the Fred Hutchinson Memorial Award. They raised money from various celebrities, mostly baseball executives and media personnel, and incorporated the project.

The Hutch Award is presented annually to a major leaguer who "best exemplifies the character, dedication and competitive spirit" of the late manager. Consideration is given to players who overcome major physical adversity, and show dedication to their team, community, and family. Winners receive a bronzed engraving of Hutchinson encased in a glass frame.

Concurrent with this presentation, a sister award is given—in the way of a scholarship—to a young medical student involved in cancer research. This selection was coordinated by Dr. Hutchinson from the Fred Hutchinson Cancer Center (established in 1975) in Seattle.

Ritter Collett ran the award's business operations from his home address in Dayton, Ohio, until 1994, by which time only three of its five founders were still alive. That year, the award's administration was turned over to the Seattle Mariners in conjunction with the *Seattle Post-Intelligencer* and the Hutchinson Cancer Center.

Voting for the prestigious Hutch Award is done by a panel of baseball writers and broadcasters. Following is a list of the winners:

1965 Mickey Mantle
1966 Sandy Koufax
1967 Carl Yastrzemski
1968 Pete Rose
1969 Al Kaline
1970 Tony Conigliaro
1971 Joe Torre
1972 Bobby Tolan
1973 John Hiller
1974 Danny Thompson
1975 Gary Nolan
1976 Tommy John
1977 Willie McCovey
1978 Willie Stargell
1979 Lou Brock
1980 George Brett
1981 Johnny Bench
1982 Andre Thornton
1983 Ray Knight
1984 Don Robinson
1985 Rick Reuschel
1986 Dennis Leonard
1987 Paul Molitor
1988 Ron Oester
1989 Dave Dravecky
1990 Sid Bream
1991 Bill Wegman
1992 Carney Lansford
1993 John Olerud
1994 Andre Dawson
1995 Jim Abbott
1996 Omar Vizquel
1997 Eric Davis
1998 David Cone
1999 Sean Casey

The Sid Mercer Memorial Award

Sid Mercer was a talented and beloved sportswriter in St. Louis and New York during the first half of the 20th century. He suggested and arranged for an "Outstanding Player of the Year" award to be presented at the New York BBWAA chapter's awards dinner each January, beginning in 1931. After Mercer's death in 1945, the award was renamed in his memory. The Sid Mercer Memorial Award honors "outstanding achievement and high contribution to (major league) baseball."

Don Mattingly won the Sid Mercer Award three times, while Joe DiMaggio, Ted Williams, Mickey Mantle, Sandy Koufax, George Brett, and Barry Bonds were honored twice each. Following are the annual winners of the award:

1930 Bill Terry
1931 Lou Gehrig
1932 Herb Pennock
1933 Carl Hubbell
1934 Dizzy Dean
1935 Hank Greenberg
1936 Tony Lazzeri
1937 Joe DiMaggio
1938 Jimmie Foxx
1939 Bucky Walters
1940 Bob Feller
1941 Joe DiMaggio
1942 Ted Williams
1943 Bill Dickey
1944 Dixie Walker
1945 Snuffy Stirnweiss
1946 Stan Musial
1947 Johnny Mize
1948 Lou Boudreau
1949 Phil Rizzuto
1950 Eddie Stanky
1951 Allie Reynolds
1952 Pee Wee Reese
1953 Roy Campanella
1954 Willie Mays
1955 Duke Snider
1956 Mickey Mantle
1957 Ted Williams
1958 Bob Turley
1959 Nellie Fox
1960 Warren Spahn
1961 M. Mantle/R. Maris
1962 Maury Wills
1963 Sandy Koufax
1964 Brooks Robinson
1965 Sandy Koufax
1966 Frank Robinson
1967 Carl Yastrzemski
1968 Denny McLain
1969 Tom Seaver
1970 Johnny Bench
1971 Joe Torre
1972 Steve Carlton
1973 Reggie Jackson
1974 Lou Brock
1975 Joe Morgan
1976 Mark Fidrych
1977 R. Carew/G. Foster
1978 Ron Guidry
1979 George Brett
1980 George Brett
1981 Mike Schmidt
1982 Robin Yount
1983 Dan Quisenberry
1984 Don Mattingly
1985 D. Gooden/D. Mattingly
1986 Don Mattingly
1987 Andre Dawson
1988 Jose Canseco
1989 Nolan Ryan
1990 Cecil Fielder
1991 Cal Ripken, Jr.
1992 Barry Bonds
1993 Barry Bonds
1994 Jeff Bagwell
1995 Randy Johnson
1996 Alex Rodriguez
1997 Larry Walker
1998 M. McGwire/S. Sosa
1999 Pedro Martinez
2000 Carlos Delgado

The J.G. Taylor Spink Award

As early as 1944, the Baseball Hall of Fame's administrators suggested that some sort of "Roll of Honor," distinct from actual Hall of Fame induction, be established for distinguished baseball writers. Following the December 7, 1962 death of *The Sporting News*'s long-time publisher, J. G. Taylor Spink, such an award was created. Spink was the first winner of the award bearing his name.

The Spink Award is given "for meritorious contributions to baseball writing." It is voted on by a committee of BBWAA members, and presented during the following year's Hall of Fame induction ceremony. Although the winners are often erroneously said to be "inducted into the Writers' Wing of the Hall of Fame," there is no such wing and these writers are not in fact members of the Hall. The museum's library does have an exhibit, called "Scribes and Mike-Men," which—among other things—lists winners of this award.

Following are winners of the Spink Award:

1962 J. G. Taylor Spink
1963 Ring Lardner
1964 Hugh Fullerton
1965 Charles Dryden
1966 Grantland Rice
1967 Damon Runyon
1968 H. G. Salsinger
1969 Sid Mercer
1970 Heywood C. Broun
1971 Frank Graham
Dan Daniel
1972 Fred Lieb
J. Roy Stockton
1973 Warren Brown
John Drebinger
John F. Kieran
1974 John Carmichael
James Isaminger
1975 Tom Meany
Shirley Povich
1976 Harold Kaese
Red Smith
1977 Gordon Cobbledick
Edgar Munzel
1978 Tim Murnane
Dick Young
1979 Bob Broeg
Tommy Holmes
1980 Joe Reichler
Milton Richman
1981 Bob Addie
Allen Lewis
1982 Si Burick
1983 Ken Smith
1984 Joe McGuff
1985 Earl Lawson
1986 Jack Lang
1987 Jim Murray
Leonard Koppett
1988 Bob Hunter
Ray Kelly
1989 Jerome Holtzman
1990 Phil Collier
1991 Ritter Collett
1992 Bus Saidt
1993 John Wendell Smith
1994 (No honoree)
1995 Joseph Durso
1996 Charlie Feeney
1997 Sam Lacy
1998 Bob Stevens
1999 Hal Lebovitz
2000 Ross Newhan

The Sports Illustrated *Sportsman of the Year Award*

The editors of *Sports Illustrated* have honored a "Sportsman of the Year" since 1954, the year the magazine started. The following is a list of baseball's representatives:

1955 Johnny Podres	1979 Willie Stargell (co-winner)
1957 Stan Musial	1987 Dale Murphy (co-winner)
1965 Sandy Koufax	1988 Orel Hershiser
1967 Carl Yastrzemski	1995 Cal Ripken Jr.
1969 Tom Seaver	1996 Joe Torre
1975 Pete Rose	1998 M. McGwire/S. Sosa

Hall of Fame Elections: History

In the 1930s plans were being made to celebrate baseball's 100th anniversary, based on the ill-advised findings of the Mills Commission three decades earlier: "The first scheme for playing baseball, according to the best evidence obtainable to date, was devised by Abner Doubleday at Cooperstown, New York, in 1839." A small-scale baseball museum was established in Cooperstown, and a Centennial Committee composed of six baseball bigwigs ordered the first Hall of Fame election. On January 29, 1936, the results of this election were announced, with five immortals qualifying for enshrinement (although actual induction was delayed until formal opening of the Hall on June 12, 1939).

Actually, there were two elections in 1936: one a poll of 226 members of the Baseball Writers' Association of America (BBWAA), and the other held by a special veterans' committee of 78 designed to choose from among "old-timers." No specific guidelines were set as to who was eligible for consideration (several active players received strong support), nor to which committee would consider whom (resulting in Cy Young's split vote: 49 percent in the writers' election, 41 percent in the veterans'). A 75 percent majority was necessary for election by either committee, a voting feature which survives.

Elections were held by both the BBWAA and an old-timers' committee for each of the next three years, resulting in a total of 26 inductees in 1939. After that, BBWAA elections were scheduled at three-year intervals, with only one player elected in 1942 and none in 1945. A decision was made to hold annual elections beginning in 1946. This continued through 1956, when it was decided to hold elections only every other year. Annual elections were resumed a decade later and continue to this day.

A nominating system was installed after the 1945 election, providing for the top 20 vote-getters in a preliminary balloting to be listed alphabetically on a second and final ballot. The preliminary election's vote totals were not to be divulged until after the final balloting (so as not to influence voters), nor would they assure anyone of automatic election. However, this system proved an utter failure in 1946 and was amended in December of that year. Thereafter, anyone receiving 75 percent of the votes on the nominating ballot would be automatically elected, eliminating the runoff election.

No runoff was required until 1949, when Charlie Gehringer was elected on the second ballot. The nominating system was discontinued after that year but revived from 1960-68 (providing for reconsideration of the top 30 vote-getters), being put into practice in 1964 and '67.

Currently, an eligible candidate must have played at least 10 seasons in the majors and been active at some point during a period beginning 20 years and ending five years before a given election (the former rule has been ignored in some recent cases). The five-year wait rule was first implemented in 1954 (excepting candidates who had already received 100 or more votes in a previous election); a one-year wait had been in effect from 1946–53, and no wait was specified before then (due to World War II, it was sometimes unclear who was still "active"). At the other end of the span, the 20-year rule has been in effect since 1962; the cutoff was 30 years in 1956-62, and 25 years in 1946-56.

Following Roberto Clemente's tragic death, a rule was passed in 1973 providing for the immediate consideration of an eligible candidate who dies while still active, or before the five-year waiting period has elapsed. Clemente was inducted overwhelmingly (393 of 424 votes) in a special election held that March. A few months later, the new rule was amended to allow consideration at least six months after a player's death (or five years after his retirement, whichever is less).

The "Pete Rose Rule" was added to the regulations in February 1991: "Any player on Baseball's ineligible list shall not be an eligible candidate." Many members of the BBWAA, in protest of the rule, cast write-in votes for Rose: 41 in 1992, and 14 in 1993. The BBWAA stopped reporting the scofflaw votes after that, but we know there were 19 in 1994 and 17 in 2000, and probably a like number in the intervening years. Of course, the votes didn't really count, since Rose was ineligible; thus, we don't list them in the charts that follow this chapter.

Ten-year active and honorary members of the BBWAA are eligible to vote in the annual election (the 10-year restriction was installed in 1947). About 450 writers submit ballots each year, voting for up to 10 eligible candidates apiece. At various times over the past three decades, it has been suggested that the enfranchisement be limited to a few dozen of the top baseball writers.

A candidate Screening Committee was first employed in 1968, limiting the ballot to forty candidates. Standards were relaxed somewhat after former pitcher Milt Pappas vociferously objected to his elimination by this committee (Pappas was allowed on the ballot in 1979, receiving five of 432 votes). Nomination by two of the six members of the Screening Committee now ensures a candidate at least one try on the BBWAA ballot; however, if he receives less than 5 percent of the vote, he is eliminated from future consideration. (Fortunately for many, this rule has not always been existent; more than 70 current Hall of Famers received less than 5 percent of the vote in their first tries!)

The Baseball Hall of Fame Committee on Baseball Veterans was established in July 1953. Previously, special old-timers' committees had elected new members in 1936–39, 1944–46, and 1949.

The new committee was composed of 11 members. This number was increased to 12 in 1960, 18 in 1979, and 20 in 1987; then it was reduced to 18 in 1988 and 15 in

1996. Elections were held every other year at first, but have been held annually since 1961.

In most years the committee has been limited to naming no more than two new inductees per election. Exceptions occurred in the elections of 1953 (six), 1963 (four), 1964 (six), 1970 (three), 1971 (seven), and 1972–77 (three each). Two additional slots opened for 1995-2001, one for 19th century players, the other for Negro Leaguers. Voting details are not released to the public.

Individuals considered by the Veterans Committee include managers, umpires, executives, and certain players no longer eligible through the BBWAA (except members of the committee). For eligibility under the former three groups, a person must have been retired five years, or six months if he has reached the age of 65 (a rule tailor-made for Casey Stengel's election in 1966). For players, the minimum wait is 23 years; previously, it was 25 years (1953–56, 1974–84), 30 years (1957–62), or 20 years (1963–73).

On June 10, 1971, a nine-member Baseball Hall of Fame Committee on Negro Baseball Leagues was established. Candidates were to have totaled at least ten years of service in the pre-1946 Negro Leagues and/or the major leagues, without being eligible for BBWAA election. A rule specified that the "Committee shall serve until it shall dissolve itself of its own motion or until further notice from the Board of Directors" of the Hall.

At least one new member was inducted by this committee in each year between 1971 and 1977, after which the committee dissolved and was absorbed into the Veterans Committee. Only two Negro League representatives were enshrined between 1978-94.

There have been a total of 249 men inducted into the National Baseball Hall of Fame and Museum through 2000, including 185 major league players, 23 classified as pioneers or executives, 17 Negro Leaguers, 16 managers, and eight umpires. (Many of the latter four groups also played in the majors or minors.)

What follows is, first, a roster of the 249 members of the Hall of Fame named between 1936 and early 2000; second, an index of every man who ever received so much as a single vote for the Hall of Fame, detailing each man's total for each year he received support; and third, the top ten finishers in the voting for each year of balloting since 1936. Men named to the Hall of Fame by special committee action, such as Alexander Cartwright or Josh Gibson, may not have received votes in an election, but they are included in this index as well. (There have been four such committee groupings: the Centennial Commission of 1937–1938, the Old Timers' Committee of 1939–1949, the Veterans Committee of 1953–present, and the Negro Leagues Committee of 1971–1977.)

Of special interest are some prominent players who were not elected or named to the Hall: Gil Hodges, who received the most votes for the Hall of Fame but remains outside it; Herman Long, who finished among the top ten vote-getters in the Veterans Ballot of 1936, which during later years produced 29 future Hall of Famers; Hank Gowdy, who in the 1950s experienced a fate similar to Long's; and Marty Marion and Allie Reynolds, other long-term vote-getters who were not able to bunch their support in a given year.

The 1936-88 Hall of Fame balloting results were researched and compiled by Pete Palmer.

Hall of Fame Roster

FIRST BASEMEN
Anson, Cap
Beckley, Jake
Bottomley, Jim
Brouthers, Dan
Cepeda, Orlando
Chance, Frank
Connor, Roger
Foxx, Jimmie
Gehrig, Lou
Greenberg, Hank
Kelly, George
Killebrew, Harmon
McCovey, Willie
Mize, Johnny
Perez, Tony
Sisler, George
Terry, Bill

SECOND BASEMEN
Carew, Rod
Collins, Eddie
Doerr, Bobby
Evers, Johnny
Fox, Nellie
Frisch, Frankie
Gehringer, Charlie
Herman, Billy
Hornsby, Rogers
Lajoie, Nap
Lazzeri, Tony
McPhee, Bid
Morgan, Joe
Robinson, Jackie
Schoendienst, Red

SHORTSTOPS
Aparicio, Luis
Appling, Luke
Bancroft, Dave
Banks, Ernie
Boudreau, Lou
Cronin, Joe
Davis, George
Jackson, Travis
Jennings, Hughie
Maranville, Rabbit
Reese, Pee Wee
Rizzuto, Phil
Sewell, Joe
Tinker, Joe
Vaughan, Arky
Wagner, Honus
Wallace, Bobby
Ward, Monte
Yount, Robin

THIRD BASEMEN
Baker, Frank
Brett, George
Collins, Jimmy
Kell, George
Lindstrom, Fred
Mathews, Eddie
Robinson, Brooks
Schmidt, Mike
Traynor, Pie

LEFT FIELDERS
Brock, Lou
Burkett, Jesse
Clarke, Fred
Delahanty, Ed
Goslin, Goose
Hafey, Chick
Kelley, Joe
Kiner, Ralph
Manush, Heinie
Medwick, Joe
Musial, Stan
O'Rourke, Jim
Simmons, Al
Stargell, Willie
Wheat, Zack
Williams, Billy
Williams, Ted
Yastrzemski, Carl

CENTER FIELDERS
Ashburn, Richie
Averill, Earl
Carey, Max
Cobb, Ty
Combs, Earle
DiMaggio, Joe
Doby, Larry
Duffy, Hugh
Hamilton, Billy
Mantle, Mickey
Mays, Willie
Roush, Edd
Snider, Duke
Speaker, Tris
Waner, Lloyd
Wilson, Hack

RIGHT FIELDERS
Aaron, Hank
Clemente, Roberto
Crawford, Sam
Cuyler, Kiki
Flick, Elmer
Heilmann, Harry
Hooper, Harry
Jackson, Reggie
Kaline, Al
Keeler, Willie
Kelly, King
Klein, Chuck
McCarthy, Tommy
Ott, Mel
Rice, Sam
Robinson, Frank
Ruth, Babe
Slaughter, Enos
Thompson, Sam
Waner, Paul
Youngs, Ross

CATCHERS
Bench, Johnny
Berra, Yogi
Bresnahan, Roger
Campanella, Roy
Cochrane, Mickey
Dickey, Bill
Ewing, Buck
Ferrell, Rick
Fisk, Carlton
Hartnett, Gabby
Lombardi, Ernie
Schalk, Ray

PITCHERS
Alexander, Grover
Bender, Chief
Brown, Mordecai
Bunning, Jim
Carlton, Steve
Chesbro, Jack
Clarkson, John
Coveleski, Stan
Dean, Dizzy
Drysdale, Don
Faber, Red
Feller, Bob
Fingers, Rollie
Ford, Whitey
Galvin, Pud
Gibson, Bob
Gomez, Lefty
Grimes, Burleigh
Grove, Lefty
Haines, Jess
Hoyt, Waite
Hubbell, Carl
Hunter, Catfish
Jenkins, Fergie
Johnson, Walter
Joss, Addie
Keefe, Tim
Koufax, Sandy
Lemon, Bob
Lyons, Ted
Marichal, Juan
Marquard, Rube
Mathewson, Christy
McGinnity, Joe
Newhouser, Hal
Nichols, Kid
Niekro, Phil
Palmer, Jim
Pennock, Herb
Perry, Gaylord
Plank, Eddie
Radbourn, Charles
Rixey, Eppa
Roberts, Robin
Ruffing, Red
Rusie, Amos
Ryan, Nolan
Seaver, Tom
Spahn, Warren
Sutton, Don
Vance, Dazzy
Waddell, Rube
Walsh, Ed
Welch, Mickey
Wilhelm, Hoyt
Willis, Vic
Wynn, Early
Young, Cy

FROM NEGRO LEAGUES
Bell, Cool Papa
Charleston, Oscar
Dandridge, Ray
Day, Leon
Dihigo, Martin
Foster, Bill
Foster, Rube
Gibson, Josh
Irvin, Monte
Johnson, Judy
Leonard, Buck
Lloyd, John Henry
Paige, Satchel
Rogan, Bullet Joe
Stearnes, Turkey
Wells, Willie
Williams, Smokey Joe

MANAGERS
Alston, Walter
Anderson, Sparky
Durocher, Leo
Hanlon, Ned
Harris, Bucky
Huggins, Miller
Lasorda, Tommy
Lopez, Al
Mack, Connie
McCarthy, Joe
McGraw, John
McKechnie, Bill
Robinson, Wilbert
Selee, Frank
Stengel, Casey
Weaver, Earl

UMPIRES
Barlick, Al
Chylak, Nestor
Conlan, Jocko
Connolly, Tom
Evans, Billy
Hubbard, Cal
Klem, Bill
McGowan, Bill

PIONEERS AND EXECUTIVES
Barrow, Ed
Bulkeley, Morgan
Cartwright, Alexander

Chadwick, Henry
Chandler, Happy
Comiskey, Charles
Cummings, Candy
Frick, Ford
Giles, Warren
Griffith, Clark
Harridge, Will
Hulbert, William
Johnson, Ban
Landis, Kenesaw
MacPhail, Larry
MacPhail, Lee
Rickey, Branch
Spalding, Al
Veeck, Bill
Weiss, George
Wright, George
Wright, Harry
Yawkey,Tom

Hall of Fame Balloting: Vote Totals of All Candidates

Hank Aaron
Inducted in 1982

1982 406

Babe Adams

1937 8
1938 11
1939 11
1942 11
1945 7
1946 NOM 6
1947 22
1948 4
1949 5
1950 6
1951 12
1952 9
1953 17
1954 13
1955 24

Sparky Adams

1958 1
1960 1

Bobby Adams

1966 1

Grover Alexander
Inducted in 1938

1936 55
1937 125
1938 212

Dick Allen

1983 14
1985 28
1986 41
1987 55
1988 52
1989 35
1990 58
1991 59
1992 69
1993 70
1994 66
1995 72
1996 89
1997 79

Johnny Allen

1955 1

Felipe Alou

1980 3

Jesus Alou

1985 1

Matty Alou

1980 5

Walter Alston
Inducted in 1983
Manager

1983 .... Vet. Com.

Nick Altrock

1937 3
1938 7
1939 6
1953 1
1954 2
1958 20
1960 18

Sparky Anderson
Inducted in 2000
Manager

2000 .... Vet. Com.

Cap Anson
Inducted in 1939

1936 V 40
1939 .... O/T Com.

Luis Aparicio
Inducted in 1984

1979 120
1980 124
1981 48
1982 174
1983 252
1984 341

Luke Appling
Inducted in 1964

1953 2
1955 3
1956 14
1958 77
1960 72
1962 48
1964 142
1964 RO 189

Jimmy Archer

1937 6
1938 7
1939 3

Richie Ashburn
Inducted in 1995

1968 6
1969 10
1970 11
1971 10
1972 11
1973 25
1974 56
1975 76
1976 85
1977 139
1978 158
1979 130
1980 134
1981 142
1982 126
1995 .... Vet. Comm.

Jimmy Austin

1958 1

Earl Averill
Inducted in 1975

1949 1
1952 2
1955 2
1956 3
1958 14
1960 11
1962 3
1975 .... Vet. Com.

Bob Bailey

1984 1

Frank Baker
Inducted in 1955

1936 1
1937 13
1938 32
1939 30
1942 39
1945 26
1946 NOM 39
1946 36
1947 49
1948 4
1950 4
1951 8
1955 .... Vet. Com.

Dusty Baker

1992 4

Dave Bancroft
Inducted in 1971

1937 3
1938 2
1939 1
1946 NOM 1
1948 4
1949 5
1950 9
1951 9
1952 11
1953 10
1954 10
1955 19
1956 15
1958 43
1960 30
1971 .... Vet. Com.

Sal Bando

1987 3

Ernie Banks
Inducted in 1977

1977 321

Al Barlick
Inducted in 1989
Umpire

1989 .... Vet. Com.

Ross Barnes

1936 V 3

Ed Barrow
Inducted in 1953
Executive

1953 .... Vet. Com.

Jack Barry

1938 3
1939 1

Dick Bartell

1948 1
1951 1
1958 1
1960 1

Joe Battin

1936 V 1

Hank Bauer

1967 23
1967 RO 9

Don Baylor

1994 12
1995 12

Ginger Beaumont

1938 1
1942 1
1945 1
1946 NOM 1

Glenn Beckert

1981 1

Jake Beckley
Inducted in 1971

1936 V 1
1942 1
1971 .... Vet. Com.

Mark Belanger

1988 16

Buddy Bell

1995 8

Cool Papa Bell
Inducted in 1974

1974 .... Neg. Com.

George Bell

1999 6

Johnny Bench
Inducted in 1989

1989 431

Chief Bender
Inducted in 1953

1936 2
1937 17
1938 33
1939 40
1942 55
1945 40
1946 NOM 39
1946 35
1947 72
1948 5
1949 2
1950 6
1951 35
1952 70
1953 104
1953 .... Vet. Com.

Charlie Bennett

1936 V 3

Larry Benton

1958 1

Moe Berg

1958 3
1960 5

Marty Bergen

1937 2
1938 1
1939 1

Wally Berger

1956 1
1958 2

Yogi Berra
Inducted in 1972

1971 242
1972 339

Charlie Berry

1955 1
1958 3

Jim Bibby

1990 1

Carson Bigbee

1948 1

Jack Billingham

1986 1

Max Bishop

1955 1
1956 1
1958 4
1960 5

Ewell Blackwell

1968 5
1969 11
1970 14

Ray Blades

1958 1
1960 1

Paul Blair

1986 8

Steve Blass

1980 2

Lu Blue

1954 1

Vida Blue

1992 23
1993 37
1994 14
1995 26

Ossie Bluege

1948 2
1949 1
1954 1
1956 2
1958 2
1960 3

Bert Blyleven

1998 83
1999 70
2000 87

Ping Bodie

1937 2
1949 1

Joe Boley

1942 1

Tommy Bond

1936 V 1

Bobby Bonds

1987 24
1988 27
1989 29
1990 30
1991 39
1992 40
1993 45
1994 37
1995 35
1996 24
1997 20

Bob Boone

1996 36
1997 28
1998 26
1999 27
2000 21

Jim Bottomley
Inducted in 1974

1948 4
1949 8
1950 8
1951 6
1952 7
1953 10
1954 16
1955 26
1956 42
1958 57
1960 89
1962 20
1974 .... Vet. Com.

Lou Boudreau
Inducted in 1970

1956 2
1958 64
1960 35
1962 12
1964 68
1964 RO 43
1966 115
1967 143
1967 RO 68
1968 146
1969 218
1970 232

Jim Bouton

1984 3

Larry Bowa

1991 11

Clete Boyer

1978 1
1979 3

Ken Boyer

1975 9
1976 15
1977 14
1978 18
1979 20
1985 68
1986 95
1987 96
1988 109
1989 62
1990 78
1991 58
1992 71
1993 69
1994 56

Bill Bradley

1936 1
1937 5
1938 2
1939 1
1942 1
1946 NOM 1

Harry Brecheen

1960 7
1968 3
1969 2
1970 3
1971 7
1972 5
1973 3

Ted Breitenstein

1937 1

Roger Bresnahan
Inducted in 1945

1936 ... 47
1937 ... 43
1938 ... 67
1939 ... 67
1942 ... 57
1945 ... 133
1945 ... O/T Com.

George Brett
Inducted in 1999

1999 ... 488

Jim Brewer

1982 ... 2

Tommy Bridges

1956 ... 3
1958 ... 11
1960 ... 4
1962 ... 1
1964 ... 15
1964 RO ... 1
1966 ... 16

Lou Brock
Inducted in 1985

1985 ... 315

Dan Brouthers
Inducted in 1945

1936 V ... 2
1945 ... O/T Com.

Gates Brown

1981 ... 1

Mordecai Brown
Inducted in 1949

1936 ... 6
1937 ... 31
1938 ... 54
1939 ... 54
1942 ... 63
1945 ... 46
1946 NOM ... 56
1946 ... 48
1949 ... O/T Com.

Bill Bruton

1971 ... 1

Bill Buckner

1996 ... 10

Morgan Bulkeley
Inducted in 1937
Executive

1937 ... Cen. Com.

Jim Bunning
Inducted in 1996

1977 ... 146
1978 ... 181
1979 ... 147
1980 ... 177
1981 ... 164
1982 ... 138
1983 ... 138
1984 ... 201
1985 ... 214
1986 ... 279
1987 ... 289
1988 ... 317
1989 ... 283
1990 ... 257
1991 ... 282
1996 ... Vet. Comm.

Lew Burdette

1973 ... 12
1974 ... 7
1975 ... 11
1976 ... 21
1977 ... 85
1978 ... 76
1979 ... 53
1980 ... 66
1981 ... 48
1982 ... 43
1983 ... 43
1984 ... 97
1985 ... 82
1986 ... 96
1987 ... 96

Smoky Burgess

1973 ... 1
1974 ... 2

Jesse Burkett
Inducted in 1946

1936 V ... 1
1937 ... 1
1938 ... 2
1942 ... 4
1945 ... 2
1946 NOM ... 2
1946 ... O/T Com.

George J. Burns

1937 ... 3
1938 ... 3
1939 ... 1
1949 ... 1
1950 ... 2

Jeff Burroughs

1991 ... 1

Guy Bush

1956 ... 2

Joe Bush

1958 ... 5

Donie Bush

1937 ... 1
1939 ... 2
1942 ... 2
1945 ... 1
1946 NOM ... 2
1953 ... 1

Leon Cadore

1948 ... 1

Johnny Callison

1979 ... 1

Dolf Camilli

1948 ... 1
1956 ... 1
1958 ... 4
1960 ... 3

Howie Camnitz

1945 ... 1

Roy Campanella
Inducted in 1969

1964 ... 115
1964 RO ... 138
1966 ... 197
1967 ... 204
1967 RO ... 170
1968 ... 205
1969 ... 270

Bert Campaneris

1989 ... 14

Bill Campbell

1993 ... 1

John Candelaria

1999 ... 1

Jose Cardenal

1986 ... 1

Leo Cardenas

1981 ... 1
1982 ... 1

Rod Carew
Inducted in 1991

1991 ... 401

Max Carey
Inducted in 1961

1937 ... 6
1938 ... 6
1939 ... 7
1945 ... 1
1948 ... 9
1949 ... 12
1950 ... 14
1951 ... 27
1952 ... 36
1953 ... 55
1954 ... 55
1955 ... 119
1956 ... 65
1958 ... 136
1961 ... Vet. Com.

Steve Carlton
Inducted in 1994

1994 ... 436

Chico Carrasquel

1966 ... 1

Bill Carrigan

1937 ... 5
1938 ... 4
1939 ... 2
1945 ... 3

Clay Carroll

1984 ... 1

Gary Carter

1998 ... 200
1999 ... 168
2000 ... 248

Rico Carty

1985 ... 1

Alexander Cartwright
Inducted in 1938
Pioneer

1938 ... Cen. Com.

George Case

1958 ... 1
1960 ... 1
1962 ... 1
1964 ... 2

Dave Cash

1986 ... 2

Norm Cash

1980 ... 6

Phil Cavaretta

1962 ... 2
1964 ... 22
1964 RO ... 1
1966 ... 9
1967 ... 15
1967 RO ... 4
1968 ... 23
1969 ... 37
1970 ... 51
1971 ... 83
1972 ... 61
1973 ... 73
1974 ... 61
1975 ... 129

Cesar Cedeno

1992 ... 2

Orlando Cepeda
Inducted in 1999

1980 ... 48
1981 ... 77
1982 ... 42
1983 ... 59
1984 ... 124
1985 ... 114
1986 ... 152
1987 ... 179
1988 ... 199
1989 ... 176
1990 ... 211
1991 ... 192
1992 ... 246
1993 ... 252
1994 ... 335
1999 ... Vet. Com.

Ron Cey

1993 ... 8

Henry Chadwick
Inducted in 1938
Pioneer

1938 ... Cen. Com.

Frank Chance
Inducted in 1946

1936 ... 5
1937 ... 49
1938 ... 133
1939 ... 158
1942 ... 136
1945 ... 179
1946 NOM ... 144
1946 ... 150
1946 ... O/T Com.

Happy Chandler
Inducted in 1982
Executive

1982 ... Vet. Com.

Spud Chandler

1950 ... 2
1951 ... 1
1956 ... 1
1962 ... 2
1964 ... 6

Ben Chapman

1949 ... 1
1952 ... 1

Ray Chapman

1938 ... 1

Sam Chapman

1958 ... 1

Oscar Charleston
Inducted in 1976

1976 ... Neg. Com.

Hal Chase

1936 ... 11
1937 ... 18

Jack Chesbro
Inducted in 1946

1937 ... 1
1938 ... 2
1939 ... 6
1946 NOM ... 1
1946 ... O/T Com.

Nestor Chylak
Inducted in 1999
Umpire

1999 ... Vet. Com.

Bill Cissell

1937 ... 1

Jack Clark

1998 ... 7

Watty Clark

1958 ... 1

Fred Clarke
Inducted in 1945

1936 V ... 9
1936 ... 1
1937 ... 22
1938 ... 63
1939 ... 59
1942 ... 58
1945 ... 53
1945 ... O/T Com.

John Clarkson
Inducted in 1963

1936 V ... 5
1946 NOM ... 1
1963 ... Vet. Com.

Roberto Clemente
Inducted in 1973

1973 ... Spec. El.

Andy Coakley

1938 ... 1

Ty Cobb
Inducted in 1936

1936 ... 222

Mickey Cochrane
Inducted in 1947

1936 ... 80
1939 ... 28
1942 ... 88
1945 ... 125
1946 NOM ... 80
1946 ... 65
1947 ... 128

Rocky Colavito

1974 ... 2
1975 ... 1

Eddie Collins
Inducted in 1939

1936 ... 60
1937 ... 115
1938 ... 175
1939 ... 213

Jimmy Collins
Inducted in 1945

1936 V ... 8
1936 ... 58
1937 ... 66
1938 ... 79
1939 ... 72
1942 ... 68
1945 ... 121
1945 ... O/T Com.

Shano Collins

1937 ... 1

Earle Combs
Inducted in 1970

1937 ... 4
1938 ... 7
1939 ... 3
1945 ... 1
1948 ... 6
1949 ... 6
1950 ... 3
1952 ... 1
1953 ... 3
1955 ... 1
1956 ... 14
1958 ... 34
1960 ... 43
1962 ... 6
1970 ... Vet. Com.

Charles Comiskey
Inducted in 1939
Executive

1936 V ... 6
1939 ... O/T Com.

Dave Concepcion

1994 ... 31
1995 ... 43
1996 ... 63
1997 ... 60
1998 ... 80
1999 ... 59
2000 ... 67

Jocko Conlan
Inducted in 1974
Umpire

1974 ... Vet. Com.

Tom Connolly
Inducted in 1953
Umpire

1953 ... Vet. Com.

Roger Connor
Inducted in 1976

1976 ... Vet. Com.

Wid Conroy

1945 ... 1

Jack Coombs

1937 ... 2
1938 ... 2
1946 NOM ... 2
1948 ... 2
1951 ... 1

Mort Cooper

1956 ... 2
1958 ... 3
1960 ... 1
1969 ... 3

Walker Cooper

1968 ... 8
1969 ... 5
1970 ... 9
1971 ... 7
1972 ... 8
1973 ... 8
1974 ... 9
1975 ... 13
1976 ... 56
1977 ... 45

Wilbur Cooper

1938 ... 1
1939 ... 1
1948 ... 2
1949 ... 4
1951 ... 1
1952 ... 2
1953 ... 9
1954 ... 7
1955 ... 11

Clint Courtney

1967 ... 1

Stan Coveleski
Inducted in 1969

1938 ... 1
1948 ... 2
1949 ... 3
1950 ... 1
1958 ... 34
1969 ... Vet. Com.

Billy Cox

1962 ... 1

Doc Cramer

1956 ... 4
1958 ... 2
1960 ... 1
1962 ... 1
1964 ... 12

Del Crandall

1976 ... 15
1977 ... 8
1978 ... 6

1979 ... 9

Doc Crandall

1938 ... 1

Gavvy Cravath

1937 ... 2
1938 ... 2
1939 ... 2
1946 NOM ... 1
1947 ... 2

Sam Crawford
Inducted in 1957

1936 ... 1
1937 ... 5
1938 ... 11
1939 ... 6
1942 ... 2
1945 ... 4
1946 NOM ... 9
1957 ... Vet. Com.

Lou Criger

1936 V ... 1
1936 ... 7
1937 ... 16
1938 ... 11
1939 ... 2
1946 NOM ... 6

Hughie Critz

1956 ... 2

Joe Cronin
Inducted in 1956

1947 ... 6
1948 ... 25
1949 ... 33
1949 RO ... 16
1950 ... 33
1951 ... 44
1952 ... 48
1953 ... 69
1954 ... 85
1955 ... 135
1956 ... 152

Frank Crosetti

1950 ... 1
1952 ... 1
1956 ... 1
1958 ... 5
1960 ... 8
1968 ... 15

Lave Cross

1939 ... 1
1942 ... 1

Al Crowder

1958 ... 1
1960 ... 1

Walt Cruise

1938 ... 1

Jose Cruz

1994 ... 2

Tony Cuccinello

1956 ... 1
1958 ... 3

Candy Cummings
Inducted in 1939
Pioneer

1939 ... O/T Com.

Kiki Cuyler
Inducted in 1968

1948 ... 3
1949 ... 4
1950 ... 11
1951 ... 8
1952 ... 10
1953 ... 18
1954 ... 20
1955 ... 35
1956 ... 55
1958 ... 90
1960 ... 72
1962 ... 31
1968 ... Vet. Com.

Bill Dahlen

1936 V ... 1
1938 ... 1

Ray Dandridge
Inducted in 1987

1987 ... Vet. Com.

Harry Danning

1958 ... 1
1960 ... 1

Alvin Dark

1966 ... 17
1967 ... 38
1967 RO ... 7
1968 ... 36
1969 ... 48
1970 ... 55
1971 ... 54
1972 ... 55
1973 ... 53
1974 ... 54
1975 ... 48
1976 ... 62
1977 ... 66
1978 ... 60
1979 ... 80
1980 ... 43

Jake Daubert

1936 V ... 1
1937 ... 2
1938 ... 1
1939 ... 1
1951 ... 1
1955 ... 1

Curt Davis

1958 ... 1

George Davis
Inducted in 1998

1998 ... Vet. Com.

Harry Davis

1945 ... 1
1946 NOM ... 2

Tommy Davis

1982 ... 5

Spud Davis

1948 ... 1
1949 ... 1

Leon Day
Inducted in 1995

1995 ... Vet. Comm.

Dizzy Dean
Inducted in 1953

1945 ... 17
1946 NOM ... 40
1946 ... 45
1947 ... 88
1948 ... 40
1949 ... 88
1949 RO ... 81
1950 ... 85
1951 ... 145
1952 ... 152
1953 ... 209

Doug DeCinces

1993 ... 2

Ed Delahanty
Inducted in 1945

1936 V ... 22
1936 ... 17
1937 ... 70
1938 ... 132
1939 ... 145
1942 ... 104
1945 ... 111
1945 ... O/T Com.

Rick Dempsey

1998 ... 1

Jerry Denny

1936 V ... 6

Bucky Dent

1990 ... 3

Paul Derringer

1948 ... 1
1950 ... 1
1951 ... 1
1955 ... 1
1956 ... 12
1958 ... 15
1960 ... 8

Bill Dickey
Inducted in 1954

1945 ... 17
1946 NOM ... 40
1946 ... 32
1948 ... 39
1949 ... 65
1949 RO ... 39
1950 ... 78
1951 ... 118
1952 ... 139
1953 ... 179
1954 ... 202

Martin Dihigo
Inducted in 1977

1977 ... Neg. Com.

Dom DiMaggio

1960 ... 4
1962 ... 2
1964 ... 12
1968 ... 8
1969 ... 13
1970 ... 15
1971 ... 15
1972 ... 36
1973 ... 43

Joe DiMaggio
Inducted in 1955

1945 ... 1
1953 ... 117
1954 ... 175
1955 ... 223

Bill Dinneen

1938 ... 4
1939 ... 7
1942 ... 1
1945 ... 1
1946 NOM ... 1

Bill Doak

1958 ... 3

Larry Doby
Inducted in 1998

1966 ... 7
1967 ... 10
1967 RO ... 1
1998 ... Vet. Com

Bobby Doerr
Inducted in 1986

1953 ... 2
1956 ... 5
1958 ... 25
1960 ... 15
1962 ... 10
1964 ... 24
1964 RO ... 5
1966 ... 30
1967 ... 35
1967 RO ... 15
1968 ... 48
1969 ... 62
1970 ... 75
1971 ... 78
1986 ... Vet. Com.

Mike Donlin

1937 ... 6
1938 ... 5
1939 ... 5
1945 ... 1

Bill Donovan

1937 ... 3
1938 ... 1
1939 ... 2
1945 ... 3
1946 NOM ... 4

Red Dooin

1937 ... 1
1938 ... 1

Brian Downing

1998 ... 2

Jack Doyle

1936 V ... 1

Larry Doyle

1937 ... 2
1938 ... 4
1939 ... 1

Walt Dropo

1967 ... 1

Don Drysdale
Inducted in 1984

1975 ... 76
1976 ... 114
1977 ... 197
1978 ... 219
1979 ... 233
1980 ... 238
1981 ... 243
1982 ... 233
1983 ... 242
1984 ... 316

Hugh Duffy
Inducted in 1945

1936 V ... 4
1937 ... 7
1938 ... 24
1939 ... 34
1942 ... 77
1945 ... 64
1945 ... O/T Com.

Joe Dugan

1937 ... 1
1938 ... 1
1948 ... 3
1949 ... 2
1956 ... 1
1958 ... 5
1960 ... 8

Fred Dunlap

1936 V ... 2

Jack Dunn

1942 ... 1
1945 ... 1
1946 NOM ... 1

Leo Durocher
Inducted in 1994
Manager

1948 ... 1
1949 ... 1
1952 ... 1
1956 ... 1
1958 ... 28
1960 ... 10
1962 ... 1
1964 ... 15
1964 RO ... 2
1994 ... Vet. Com.

Eddie Dyer

1947 ... 1

Jimmy Dykes

1948 ... 5
1949 ... 7
1950 ... 2
1951 ... 3
1952 ... 5
1953 ... 5
1955 ... 1
1956 ... 1
1958 ... 26
1960 ... 27
1962 ... 6

George Earnshaw

1948 ... 3
1949 ... 2
1950 ... 2
1955 ... 2
1956 ... 3

Hank Edwards

1960 ... 2

Howard Ehmke

1938 ... 1
1949 ... 1
1951 ... 1
1952 ... 1
1953 ... 3
1954 ... 1
1955 ... 8
1956 ... 8
1958 ... 7
1960 ... 12

Kid Elberfeld

1936 ... 1
1937 ... 1
1938 ... 2
1942 ... 1
1945 ... 2

Jumbo Elliott

1958 ... 1

Bob Elliott

1960 ... 2
1962 ... 1
1964 ... 4

Dock Ellis

1985 ... 1

Del Ennis

1966 ... 3
1967 ... 2

Jewel Ens

1950 ... 1

Carl Erskine

1966 ... 6
1968 ... 9
1969 ... 4
1970 ... 2
1971 ... 3
1972 ... 4
1973 ... 4
1974 ... 11

Billy Evans
Inducted in 1973
Umpire

1973 ... Vet. Com.

Darrell Evans

1995 ... 8

Dwight Evans

1997 ... 28
1998 ... 49
1999 ... 18

Johnny Evers
Inducted in 1946

1936 ... 6
1937 ... 44
1938 ... 91
1939 ... 107
1942 ... 91
1945 ... 134
1946 NOM ... 130
1946 ... 110
1946 ... O/T Com.

Buck Ewing
Inducted in 1939

1936 V ... 40
1939 ... 2
1939 ... O/T Com.

Red Faber
Inducted in 1964

1937 ... 3
1938 ... 1
1939 ... 3
1942 ... 1
1948 ... 3
1949 ... 6
1950 ... 9
1951 ... 8
1952 ... 9
1953 ... 9
1954 ... 12
1955 ... 27
1956 ... 34
1958 ... 68
1960 ... 83
1962 ... 30
1964 ... Vet. Com.

Elroy Face

1976 ... 23
1977 ... 33
1978 ... 27
1979 ... 35
1980 ... 21
1981 ... 23
1982 ... 22
1983 ... 32
1984 ... 65
1985 ... 62
1986 ... 74
1987 ... 78
1988 ... 79
1989 ... 47
1990 ... 50

Ron Fairly

1985 ... 3

Cy Falkenberg

1937 ... 1

Bob Feller
Inducted in 1962

1962 ... 150

Rick Ferrell
Inducted in 1984

1956 ... 1
1958 ... 1
1960 ... 1
1984 ... Vet. Com.

Wes Ferrell

1948 ... 1
1949 ... 1
1956 ... 7
1960 ... 8
1962 ... 1

Rollie Fingers
Inducted in 1992

1991 ... 291
1992 ... 349

Carlton Fisk
Inducted in 2000
1999 ... 330
2000 ... 397

Fred Fitzsimmons
1948 ... 2
1949 ... 2
1950 ... 1
1956 ... 3
1958 ... 16
1960 ... 13
1962 ... 1

Mike Flanagan
1998 ... 2

Art Fletcher
1937 ... 2
1938 ... 3
1939 ... 1
1947 ... 3
1948 ... 3
1949 ... 1
1950 ... 1
1951 ... 4

Elmer Flick
Inducted in 1963
1938 ... 1
1963 ... Vet. Com.

Curt Flood
1977 ... 16
1978 ... 8
1979 ... 14
1985 ... 28
1986 ... 45
1987 ... 50
1988 ... 48
1989 ... 27
1990 ... 35
1991 ... 23
1992 ... 42
1993 ... 36
1994 ... 40
1995 ... 59
1996 ... 71

Lew Fonseca
1948 ... 1
1950 ... 2
1956 ... 2
1958 ... 3
1960 ... 3

Whitey Ford
Inducted in 1974
1973 ... 255
1974 ... 284

Bob Forsch
1995 ... 2

Bill Foster
Inducted in 1996
1996 ... Vet. Com.

Eddie Foster
1938 ... 2

George Foster
1992 ... 24
1993 ... 29
1994 ... 16
1995 ... 19

Rube Foster
Inducted in 1981
Manager
1981 ... Vet. Com.

Nellie Fox
Inducted in 1997
1971 ... 39
1972 ... 64
1973 ... 73
1974 ... 79
1975 ... 76
1976 ... 174
1977 ... 152
1978 ... 149
1979 ... 174
1980 ... 161
1981 ... 168
1982 ... 127
1983 ... 173
1984 ... 246
1985 ... 295
1997 ... Vet. Com

Jimmie Foxx
Inducted in 1951
1936 ... 21
1946 NOM ... 26
1947 ... 10
1948 ... 50
1949 ... 85
1949 RO ... 89
1950 ... 103
1951 ... 179

Chick Fraser
1939 ... 1

Bill Freehan
1982 ... 2

Jim Fregosi
1984 ... 4

Ford Frick
Inducted in 1970
Executive
1970 ... Vet. Com.

Frankie Frisch
Inducted in 1947
1936 ... 14
1939 ... 26
1942 ... 84
1945 ... 101
1946 NOM ... 104
1946 ... 67
1947 ... 136

Carl Furillo
1966 ... 2
1967 ... 2
1970 ... 2
1971 ... 5
1972 ... 2

Augie Galan
1968 ... 2
1970 ... 3

Pud Galvin
Inducted in 1965
1965 ... Vet. Com.

Phil Garner
1994 ... 2

Ned Garver
1967 ... 1

Steve Garvey
1993 ... 176
1994 ... 166
1995 ... 196
1996 ... 175
1997 ... 167
1998 ... 195
1999 ... 150
2000 ... 160

Lou Gehrig
Inducted in 1939
1936 ... 51
1939 ... Spec. El.

Charlie Gehringer
Inducted in 1949
1945 ... 10
1946 NOM ... 43
1946 ... 23
1947 ... 105
1948 ... 52
1949 ... 102
1949 RO ... 159

Charlie Gelbert
1947 ... 1
1949 ... 2
1950 ... 1
1951 ... 1

Josh Gibson
Inducted in 1972
1972 ... Neg. Com.

Bob Gibson
Inducted in 1981
1981 ... 337

Warren Giles
Inducted in 1979
Executive
1979 ... Vet. Com.

Dave Giusti
1983 ... 1

Jack Glasscock
1936 V ... 2

Kid Gleason
1937 ... 1
1938 ... 1
1939 ... 1
1945 ... 1

Lefty Gomez
Inducted in 1972
1945 ... 7
1946 NOM ... 4
1947 ... 1
1948 ... 16
1949 ... 17
1950 ... 18
1951 ... 23
1952 ... 29
1953 ... 35
1954 ... 38
1955 ... 71
1956 ... 89
1958 ... 76
1960 ... 51
1962 ... 20
1972 ... Vet. Com.

Mike Gonzales
1950 ... 1
1952 ... 1
1953 ... 1
1958 ... 3
1960 ... 2

Joe Gordon
1945 ... 1
1955 ... 1
1956 ... 4
1958 ... 11
1960 ... 11
1962 ... 4
1964 ... 30
1964 RO ... 11
1966 ... 31
1967 ... 66
1967 RO ... 13
1968 ... 77
1969 ... 97
1970 ... 79

Goose Goslin
Inducted in 1968
1948 ... 1
1949 ... 4
1950 ... 2
1954 ... 1
1955 ... 7
1956 ... 26
1958 ... 26
1960 ... 30
1962 ... 14
1968 ... Vet. Com.

Goose Gossage
2000 ... 166

Hank Gowdy
1937 ... 2
1938 ... 8
1939 ... 4
1942 ... 8
1945 ... 3
1947 ... 1
1948 ... 3
1949 ... 10
1950 ... 6
1951 ... 26
1952 ... 34
1953 ... 58
1954 ... 51
1955 ... 90
1956 ... 49
1958 ... 45
1960 ... 38

Eddie Grant
1938 ... 1
1939 ... 2
1942 ... 3
1945 ... 2
1946 NOM ... 1

George Grantham
1958 ... 1

Hank Greenberg
Inducted in 1956
1945 ... 3
1949 ... 67
1949 RO ... 44
1950 ... 64
1951 ... 67
1952 ... 75
1953 ... 80
1954 ... 97
1955 ... 157
1956 ... 164

Bobby Grich
1992 ... 11

Ken Griffey, Sr.
1997 ... 22

Clark Griffith
Inducted in 1946
Executive
1937 ... 4
1938 ... 10
1939 ... 20
1942 ... 71
1945 ... 108
1946 NOM ... 73
1946 ... 82
1946 ... O/T Com.

Burleigh Grimes
Inducted in 1964
1937 ... 1
1938 ... 1
1939 ... 1
1948 ... 7
1949 ... 8
1950 ... 6
1951 ... 9
1952 ... 8
1953 ... 9
1955 ... 3
1956 ... 25
1958 ... 71
1960 ... 92
1962 ... 43
1964 ... Vet. Com.

Charlie Grimm
1939 ... 1
1945 ... 1
1946 NOM ... 1
1948 ... 6
1949 ... 10
1950 ... 13
1951 ... 9
1952 ... 6
1953 ... 9
1958 ... 26
1960 ... 13
1962 ... 2

Marv Grissom
1966 ... 2

Dick Groat
1973 ... 7
1974 ... 4
1975 ... 4
1976 ... 7
1977 ... 4
1978 ... 3

Heinie Groh
1937 ... 1
1938 ... 3
1945 ... 1
1948 ... 1
1950 ... 2
1954 ... 1
1955 ... 5
1960 ... 1

Steve Gromek
1964 ... 1

Orval Grove
1958 ... 5
1960 ... 7

Lefty Grove
Inducted in 1947
1936 ... 12
1945 ... 28
1946 NOM ... 71
1946 ... 61
1947 ... 123

Pedro Guerrero
1998 ... 6

Ron Guidry
1994 ... 24
1995 ... 25
1996 ... 37
1997 ... 31
1998 ... 37
1999 ... 31
2000 ... 44

Bill Gullickson
2000 ... 1

Frank Gustine
1958 ... 3

Mule Haas
1955 ... 1
1956 ... 1
1958 ... 1
1960 ... 1

Stan Hack
1948 ... 2
1949 ... 4
1950 ... 8
1951 ... 3
1956 ... 1
1958 ... 6
1960 ... 6

Harvey Haddix
1971 ... 10
1972 ... 9
1973 ... 1
1974 ... 8
1975 ... 8
1976 ... 8
1977 ... 7
1978 ... 7
1979 ... 8
1985 ... 15

Chick Hafey
Inducted in 1971
1948 ... 1
1949 ... 2
1950 ... 4
1951 ... 1
1952 ... 1
1953 ... 2
1954 ... 2
1955 ... 4
1956 ... 16
1958 ... 12
1960 ... 29
1962 ... 7
1971 ... Vet. Com.

Noodles Hahn
1939 ... 1

Jess Haines
Inducted in 1970
1939 ... 1
1947 ... 1
1948 ... 2
1949 ... 2
1950 ... 11
1953 ... 4
1954 ... 6
1955 ... 10
1956 ... 14
1958 ... 22
1960 ... 20
1962 ... 3
1970 ... Vet. Com.

Bill Hallahan
1948 ... 1
1956 ... 1
1958 ... 1
1960 ... 2

Billy Hamilton
Inducted in 1961
1936 V ... 2
1942 ... 1
1961 ... Vet. Com.

Ned Hanlon
Inducted in 1996
1996 ... Vet. Com.

Mel Harder
1949 ... 4
1950 ... 2
1951 ... 1
1952 ... 10
1953 ... 8
1958 ... 6
1960 ... 12
1962 ... 7
1964 ... 51
1964 RO ... 14
1966 ... 34
1967 ... 52
1967 RO ... 14

Bubbles Hargrave
1947 ... 1
1958 ... 1
1960 ... 1

Mike Hargrove
1991 ... 1

Toby Harrah
1992 ... 1

Bud Harrelson
1986 ... 1

Will Harridge
Inducted in 1972
Executive
1972 ... Vet. Com.

Bucky Harris
Inducted in 1975
Manager

1938 ... 1
1939 ... 1
1948 ... 3
1949 ... 11
1950 ... 4
1951 ... 9
1952 ... 12
1953 ... 21
1958 ... 45
1960 ... 31
1975 ... Vet. Com.

Gabby Hartnett
Inducted in 1955

1945 ... 2
1946 NOM ... 2
1947 ... 2
1948 ... 33
1949 ... 35
1949 RO ... 7
1950 ... 54
1951 ... 57
1952 ... 77
1953 ... 104
1954 ... 151
1955 ... 195

Grady Hatton

1966 ... 4
1967 ... 1

Jim Hearn

1966 ... 1
1967 ... 1

Richie Hebner

1991 ... 1

Jim Hegan

1966 ... 5
1967 ... 2

Harry Heilmann
Inducted in 1952

1937 ... 10
1938 ... 14
1939 ... 8
1942 ... 4
1945 ... 5
1946 NOM ... 23
1947 ... 65
1948 ... 40
1949 ... 59
1949 RO ... 52
1950 ... 87
1951 ... 153
1952 ... 203

Tommy Helms

1983 ... 1

Solly Hemus

1966 ... 1

Dave Henderson

2000 ... 2

Tommy Henrich

1952 ... 4
1953 ... 10
1956 ... 2
1958 ... 11
1960 ... 10
1962 ... 3
1964 ... 13
1968 ... 22
1969 ... 50
1970 ... 62

Babe Herman

1942 ... 1
1948 ... 2
1949 ... 5
1950 ... 2
1951 ... 1
1952 ... 3
1953 ... 2
1954 ... 1
1955 ... 5
1956 ... 11
1958 ... 13
1960 ... 7

Billy Herman
Inducted in 1975

1948 ... 1
1956 ... 2
1958 ... 7
1962 ... 4
1964 ... 26
1964 RO ... 9
1966 ... 28
1967 ... 59
1967 RO ... 14
1975 ... Vet. Com.

Keith Hernandez

1996 ... 24
1997 ... 45
1998 ... 51
1999 ... 34
2000 ... 52

Willie Hernandez

1995 ... 2

Buck Herzog

1938 ... 1

Jim Hickman

1980 ... 1

Mike Higgins

1950 ... 2
1951 ... 1
1958 ... 6
1960 ... 3

John Hiller

1986 ... 11

Bill Hinchman

1937 ... 1

Gil Hodges

1969 ... 82
1970 ... 145
1971 ... 180
1972 ... 161
1973 ... 218
1974 ... 198
1975 ... 188
1976 ... 233
1977 ... 224
1978 ... 226
1979 ... 242
1980 ... 230
1981 ... 241
1982 ... 205
1983 ... 237

Tommy Holmes

1958 ... 2
1960 ... 2

Ken Holtzman

1985 ... 4
1986 ... 5

Harry Hooper
Inducted in 1971

1937 ... 6
1938 ... 4
1939 ... 5
1948 ... 2
1950 ... 2
1951 ... 3
1971 ... Vet. Com.

Burt Hooton

1991 ... 1

Rogers Hornsby
Inducted in 1942

1936 ... 105
1937 ... 53
1938 ... 46
1939 ... 176
1942 ... 182

Willie Horton

1986 ... 4

Art Houtteman

1964 ... 2

Charlie Hough

2000 ... 4

Elston Howard

1974 ... 19
1975 ... 23
1976 ... 55
1977 ... 43
1978 ... 41
1979 ... 30
1980 ... 29
1981 ... 83
1982 ... 40
1983 ... 32
1984 ... 45
1985 ... 54
1986 ... 51
1987 ... 44
1988 ... 53

Frank Howard

1979 ... 6

Waite Hoyt
Inducted in 1969

1939 ... 1
1942 ... 1
1946 NOM ... 1
1948 ... 7
1949 ... 7
1950 ... 11
1951 ... 13
1952 ... 12
1953 ... 14
1954 ... 14
1955 ... 33
1956 ... 37
1958 ... 37
1960 ... 29
1962 ... 18
1969 ... Vet. Com.

Al Hrabosky

1988 ... 1

Kent Hrbek

2000 ... 5

Cal Hubbard
Inducted in 1976
Umpire

1976 ... Vet. Com.

Carl Hubbell
Inducted in 1947

1945 ... 24
1946 NOM ... 101
1946 ... 75
1947 ... 140

Miller Huggins
Inducted in 1964
Manager

1937 ... 5
1938 ... 48
1939 ... 97
1942 ... 111
1945 ... 133
1946 NOM ... 129
1946 ... 106
1948 ... 4
1950 ... 2
1964 ... Vet. Com.

William Hulbert
Inducted in 1995

1995 ... Vet. Com.

Catfish Hunter
Inducted in 1987

1985 ... 212
1986 ... 289
1987 ... 315

Bruce Hurst

2000 ... 1

Fred Hutchinson

1962 ... 1
1964 ... 10

Monte Irvin
Inducted in 1973

1973 ... Neg. Com.

Charlie Irwin

1938 ... 1
1939 ... 1

Joe Jackson

1936 ... 2
1946 NOM ... 2

Reggie Jackson
Inducted in 1993

1993 ... 396

Sonny Jackson

1980 ... 1

Travis Jackson
Inducted in 1982

1948 ... 5
1949 ... 6
1950 ... 6
1951 ... 4
1952 ... 1
1953 ... 2
1954 ... 1
1955 ... 5
1956 ... 14
1958 ... 11
1960 ... 11
1962 ... 1
1982 ... Vet. Com.

Fergie Jenkins
Inducted in 1991

1989 ... 234
1990 ... 296
1991 ... 334

Hughie Jennings
Inducted in 1945

1936 V ... 11
1937 ... 4
1938 ... 23
1939 ... 33
1942 ... 64
1945 ... 92
1945 ... O/T Com.

Jackie Jensen

1967 ... 3
1968 ... 3
1969 ... 1
1970 ... 1
1971 ... 2
1972 ... 1

Tommy John

1995 ... 98
1996 ... 102
1997 ... 97
1998 ... 129
1999 ... 93
2000 ... 135

Ban Johnson
Inducted in 1937
Executive

1937 ... Cen. Com.

Dave Johnson

1984 ... 3

Judy Johnson
Inducted in 1975

1975 ... Neg. Com.

Bob Johnson

1948 ... 1
1956 ... 1

Walter Johnson
Inducted in 1936

1936 ... 189

Fielder Jones

1946 NOM ... 1

Sam P. Jones

1939 ... 1
1955 ... 1
1956 ... 1

Tim Jordan

1951 ... 1

Mike Jorgensen

1991 ... 1

Addie Joss
Inducted in 1978

1937 ... 11
1938 ... 18
1939 ... 28
1942 ... 33
1945 ... 23
1946 NOM ... 14
1960 ... 1
1978 ... Vet. Com.

Joe Judge

1937 ... 1
1938 ... 2
1949 ... 1
1955 ... 2
1956 ... 2
1958 ... 9
1960 ... 15

Billy Jurges

1949 ... 2
1958 ... 1

Jim Kaat

1989 ... 87
1990 ... 79
1991 ... 62
1992 ... 114
1993 ... 125
1994 ... 98
1995 ... 100
1996 ... 91
1997 ... 107
1998 ... 129
1999 ... 100
2000 ... 125

Al Kaline
Inducted in 1980

1980 ... 340

Willie Kamm

1958 ... 3
1960 ... 1

Tim Keefe
Inducted in 1964

1936 V ... 1
1964 ... Vet. Com.

Willie Keeler
Inducted in 1939

1936 V ... 33
1936 ... 40
1937 ... 115
1938 ... 177
1939 ... 207

George Kell
Inducted in 1983

1964 ... 33
1964 RO ... 8
1966 ... 29
1967 ... 40
1967 RO ... 11
1968 ... 47
1969 ... 60
1970 ... 90
1971 ... 105
1972 ... 115
1973 ... 114
1974 ... 94
1975 ... 114
1976 ... 129
1977 ... 141
1983 ... Vet. Com.

Charlie Keller

1953 ... 1
1956 ... 2
1958 ... 9
1960 ... 7
1962 ... 1
1964 ... 12
1968 ... 11
1969 ... 14
1970 ... 7
1971 ... 14
1972 ... 24

Joe Kelley
Inducted in 1971

1939 ... 1
1942 ... 1
1971 ... Vet. Com.

George Kelly
Inducted in 1973

1947 ... 1
1948 ... 2
1949 ... 1
1956 ... 2
1958 ... 2
1960 ... 5
1962 ... 1
1973 ... Vet. Com.

King Kelly
Inducted in 1945

1936 V ... 15
1945 ... O/T Com.

Ken Keltner

1958 ... 1
1960 ... 1

Terry Kennedy

1997 ... 1

Dickie Kerr

1937 ... 1
1938 ... 3
1939 ... 5
1942 ... 1
1945 ... 1
1949 ... 1
1951 ... 3
1952 ... 9
1953 ... 13
1954 ... 13
1955 ... 25

Don Kessinger

1985 ... 2

Harmon Killebrew
Inducted in 1984

1981 ... 239
1982 ... 246

1983 269
1984 335

Bill Killefer

1946 NOM 1

Matt Kilroy

1936 V 1

Ellis Kinder

1964 3

Ralph Kiner
Inducted in 1975

1962 5
1964 31
1964 RO 3
1966 74
1967 124
1967 RO 41
1968 118
1969 137
1970 167
1971 212
1972 235
1973 235
1974 215
1975 273

Dave Kingman

1992 3

Chuck Klein
Inducted in 1980

1948 3
1949 9
1950 14
1951 15
1952 19
1954 11
1955 25
1956 44
1958 36
1960 37
1962 18
1964 56
1964 RO 18
1980 .... Vet. Com.

Bill Klem
Inducted in 1953
Umpire

1953 .... Vet. Com.

Johnny Kling

1936 8
1937 20
1938 26
1939 14
1942 15
1945 12
1946 NOM 20
1948 2
1953 1

Ted Kluszewski

1967 9
1968 14
1969 15
1970 8
1971 9
1972 10
1973 14
1974 28
1975 33
1976 50
1977 55
1978 51
1979 58
1980 50
1981 56

Otto Knabe

1939 1
1946 NOM 1

Ray Knight

1994 1

Jerry Koosman

1991 4

Sandy Koufax
Inducted in 1972

1972 344

Ray Kremer

1948 1
1958 2

Red Kress

1958 1
1960 3

Mike Krukow

1995 1

Harvey Kuenn

1977 57
1978 58
1979 63
1980 83
1981 93
1982 62
1983 77
1984 106
1985 125
1986 144
1987 144
1988 168
1989 115
1990 107
1991 100

Joe Kuhel

1956 1

Bob Kuzava

1964 1

Nap Lajoie
Inducted in 1937

1936 V 2
1936 146
1937 168

Kenesaw Landis
Inducted in 1944
Executive

1944 .... O/T Com.

Bill Lange

1936 V 6
1953 1

Hal Lanier

1979 1

Carney Lansford

1998 3

Don Larsen

1974 29
1975 23
1976 47
1977 39
1978 32
1979 53
1980 31
1981 33
1982 32
1983 22
1984 25
1985 32
1986 33
1987 30
1988 31

Tommy Lasorda
Inducted in 1997
Manager

1997 .... Vet. Com.

Arlie Latham

1936 V 1
1938 1
1942 1

Cookie Lavagetto

1958 4
1960 2

Vern Law

1973 9
1974 5
1975 6
1976 9
1977 5
1978 6
1979 9

Tony Lazzeri
Inducted in 1991

1945 1
1947 1
1948 21
1949 20
1949 RO 6
1950 21
1951 27
1952 29
1953 28
1954 30
1955 66
1956 64
1958 80
1960 59
1962 8
1991 .... Vet. Com.

Fred Leach

1958 2
1960 1

Tommy Leach

1937 1
1939 1

Bill Lee

1988 3

Sam Leever

1937 1

Bob Lemon
Inducted in 1976

1964 24
1964 RO 3
1966 21
1967 35
1967 RO 7
1968 47
1969 56
1970 70
1971 90
1972 117
1973 177
1974 190
1975 233
1976 305

Chet Lemon

1996 1

Buck Leonard
Inducted in 1972

1972 .... Neg. Com.

Dennis Leonard

1992 1

Emil Leonard

1960 2
1968 5
1969 4
1970 5
1971 3
1972 5
1973 6

Duffy Lewis

1937 3
1938 5
1939 6
1945 1
1951 2
1952 11
1953 20
1954 20
1955 34

Fred Lindstrom
Inducted in 1976

1949 1
1956 3
1958 5
1960 6
1962 7
1976 .... Vet. Com.

John Henry Lloyd
Inducted in 1977

1977 .... Neg. Com.

Hans Lobert

1937 2
1938 1
1939 2
1960 1

Whitey Lockman

1966 4

Mickey Lolich

1985 78
1986 86
1987 84
1988 109
1989 47
1990 27
1991 33
1992 45
1993 43
1994 23
1995 26
1996 33
1997 34
1998 39
1999 26

Ernie Lombardi
Inducted in 1986

1950 3
1951 3
1956 8
1958 4
1960 6
1962 5
1964 33
1964 RO 9
1966 34
1967 43
1967 RO 25
1986 .... Vet. Com.

Jim Lonborg

1985 3
1986 3

Herman Long

1936 V 16
1937 1
1938 1
1939 1
1945 1
1946 NOM 1

Ed Lopat

1968 2
1969 2
1970 1
1971 4
1972 2

Davey Lopes

1993 2

Al Lopez
Inducted in 1977
Manager

1949 1
1952 2
1953 2
1956 1
1958 34
1960 26
1962 11
1964 57
1964 RO 34
1966 109
1967 114
1967 RO 50
1977 .... Vet. Com.

Bobby Lowe

1936 V 2
1942 1
1945 2

John Lowenstein

1991 1

Red Lucas

1949 2
1950 1
1958 1

Dolph Luque

1937 1
1938 1
1939 1
1950 1
1952 1
1953 1
1956 1
1958 15
1960 4

Greg Luzinski

1990 1

Sparky Lyle

1988 56
1989 25
1990 25
1991 15

Fred Lynn

1996 26
1997 22

Ted Lyons
Inducted in 1955

1945 4
1946 NOM 3
1948 15
1949 29
1949 RO 14
1950 42
1951 71
1952 101
1953 139
1954 170
1955 217

Connie Mack
Inducted in 1937
Manager

1936 1
1937 .... Cen. Com.

Larry MacPhail
Inducted in 1978
Executive

1978 .... Vet. Com.

Lee MacPhail
Inducted in 1998
Executive

1998 .... Vet. Com.

Bill Madlock

1993 19

Sherry Magee

1937 2
1938 2
1939 1
1942 1
1945 1
1946 NOM 1
1950 1
1951 2

Sal Maglie

1964 13
1968 11

Jim Maloney

1978 2
1979 2

Gus Mancuso

1958 1

Mickey Mantle
Inducted in 1974

1974 322

Heinie Manush
Inducted in 1964

1948 1
1949 1
1956 13
1958 22
1960 20
1962 15
1964 .... Vet. Com.

Rabbit Maranville
Inducted in 1954

1937 25
1938 73
1939 82
1942 66
1945 51
1946 NOM 50
1946 29
1947 91
1948 38
1949 58
1949 RO 39
1950 66
1951 110
1952 133
1953 164
1954 209

Firpo Marberry

1938 1
1950 1
1958 5
1960 2
1962 2

Juan Marichal
Inducted in 1983

1981 233
1982 305
1983 313

Marty Marion

1956 1
1960 37
1962 16
1964 50
1964 RO 17
1966 86
1967 90
1967 RO 22
1968 89
1969 112
1970 120
1971 123
1972 120
1973 127

Roger Maris

1974 78
1975 70
1976 87
1977 72
1978 83
1979 127
1980 111
1981 94
1982 69
1983 69
1984 107
1985 128
1986 177

1987 ... 176
1988 ... 184

Rube Marquard
Inducted in 1971

1936 ... 1
1937 ... 13
1938 ... 10
1939 ... 4
1946 NOM ... 6
1947 ... 18
1948 ... 6
1949 ... 4
1951 ... 3
1952 ... 9
1953 ... 19
1954 ... 15
1955 ... 35
1971 ... Vet. Com.

Mike Marshall

1987 ... 6

Billy Martin

1967 ... 1

Pepper Martin

1942 ... 2
1945 ... 1
1946 NOM ... 1
1948 ... 7
1949 ... 16
1950 ... 7
1951 ... 19
1952 ... 31
1953 ... 43
1956 ... 7
1958 ... 46
1960 ... 29
1962 ... 6
1964 ... 19
1964 RO ... 5

Morrie Martin

1966 ... 2

Eddie Mathews
Inducted in 1978

1974 ... 118
1975 ... 148
1976 ... 189
1977 ... 239
1978 ... 301

Christy Mathewson
Inducted in 1936

1936 ... 205

Lee May

1988 ... 2

Carl Mays

1958 ... 6

Willie Mays
Inducted in 1979

1979 ... 409

Bill Mazeroski

1978 ... 23
1979 ... 36
1980 ... 33
1981 ... 38
1982 ... 28
1983 ... 48
1984 ... 74
1985 ... 87
1986 ... 100
1987 ... 125
1988 ... 143
1989 ... 134
1990 ... 131
1991 ... 142
1992 ... 182

Jim McAleer

1936 V ... 1

Joe McCarthy
Inducted in 1957
Manager

1939 ... 3
1947 ... 2
1951 ... 1
1953 ... 1
1958 ... 2
1957 ... Vet. Com.

Tommy McCarthy
Inducted in 1946

1936 V ... 1
1946 ... O/T Com.

Tim McCarver

1986 ... 16

Frank McCormick

1956 ... 3
1962 ... 1
1964 ... 6
1968 ... 3

Willie McCovey
Inducted in 1986

1986 ... 346

Lindy McDaniel

1981 ... 1
1982 ... 3

Gil McDougald

1966 ... 5
1967 ... 4
1968 ... 4
1969 ... 3
1970 ... 1
1971 ... 4
1972 ... 4
1973 ... 2
1974 ... 3

Joe McGinnity
Inducted in 1946

1937 ... 12
1938 ... 36
1939 ... 32
1942 ... 59
1945 ... 44
1946 NOM ... 53
1946 ... 47
1946 ... O/T Com.

Bill McGowan
Inducted in 1992
Umpire

1992 ... Vet. Com.

John McGraw
Inducted in 1937
Manager

1936 V ... 17
1936 ... 4
1937 ... 35
1937 ... Cen. Com.

Tug McGraw

1990 ... 6

Stuffy McInnis

1937 ... 1
1938 ... 4
1939 ... 4
1948 ... 5
1949 ... 8
1950 ... 1
1951 ... 3

Bill McKechnie
Inducted in 1962
Manager

1945 ... 2
1946 NOM ... 2
1950 ... 1
1951 ... 8
1962 ... Vet. Com.

Denny McLain

1978 ... 1
1979 ... 3
1985 ... 2

Larry McLean

1937 ... 1

Don McMahon

1980 ... 1

Marty McManus

1958 ... 2
1960 ... 2

Roy McMillan

1972 ... 9
1973 ... 5
1974 ... 4

Dave McNally

1981 ... 5
1982 ... 5
1985 ... 7
1986 ... 12

Bid McPhee
Inducted in 2000

2000 ... Vet. Com.

Cal McVey

1936 V ... 1

Lee Meadows

1958 ... 2

Joe Medwick
Inducted in 1968

1948 ... 1
1956 ... 31
1958 ... 50
1960 ... 38
1962 ... 34
1964 ... 108
1964 RO ... 130
1966 ... 187
1967 ... 212
1967 RO ... 248
1968 ... 240

Andy Messersmith

1985 ... 3
1986 ... 3

Bob Meusel

1937 ... 1
1938 ... 1
1945 ... 1
1948 ... 6
1949 ... 3
1950 ... 2
1952 ... 1
1955 ... 2
1956 ... 1
1958 ... 5
1960 ... 10

Eddie Miksis

1964 ... 1

Clyde Milan

1938 ... 1
1950 ... 1
1951 ... 1
1952 ... 1
1953 ... 1
1954 ... 3
1955 ... 6

Felix Millan

1983 ... 1

Bing Miller

1958 ... 1
1960 ... 6

Dots Miller

1948 ... 1

Hack Miller

1937 ... 1

Minnie Minoso

1969 ... 6
1986 ... 89
1987 ... 82
1988 ... 90
1989 ... 59
1990 ... 51
1991 ... 38
1992 ... 69
1993 ... 67
1994 ... 45
1995 ... 66
1996 ... 62
1997 ... 84
1998 ... 76
1999 ... 73

Johnny Mize
Inducted in 1981

1960 ... 45
1962 ... 14
1964 ... 54
1964 RO ... 12
1966 ... 81
1967 ... 89
1967 RO ... 14
1968 ... 103
1969 ... 116
1970 ... 126
1971 ... 157
1972 ... 157
1973 ... 157
1981 ... Vet. Com.

Rick Monday

1990 ... 2

Don Money

1989 ... 1

Wally Moon

1971 ... 2

Jo-Jo Moore

1950 ... 1

Terry Moore

1950 ... 1
1953 ... 1
1958 ... 12
1960 ... 7
1962 ... 1
1964 ... 14
1967 ... 3
1968 ... 33

Pat Moran

1937 ... 1
1938 ... 1
1939 ... 1
1945 ... 1

Jack Morris

2000 ... 111

Joe Morgan
Inducted in 1990

1990 ... 363

Wally Moses

1958 ... 1
1960 ... 1
1968 ... 4
1969 ... 4
1970 ... 5
1971 ... 7

Johnny Mostil

1956 ... 1
1958 ... 1

Manny Mota

1988 ... 18
1989 ... 9

Hugh Mulcahy

1948 ... 1

Van Mungo

1945 ... 1
1948 ... 1
1958 ... 2
1960 ... 2

Thurman Munson

1981 ... 62
1982 ... 26
1983 ... 18
1984 ... 29
1985 ... 32
1986 ... 35
1987 ... 28
1988 ... 32
1989 ... 31
1990 ... 33
1991 ... 28
1992 ... 32
1993 ... 40
1994 ... 31
1995 ... 30

Bobby Murcer

1989 ... 3

Dale Murphy

1999 ... 96
2000 ... 116

Danny Murphy

1937 ... 1
1945 ... 1

Red Murray

1937 ... 1
1938 ... 1

Stan Musial
Inducted in 1969

1969 ... 317

Buddy Myer

1949 ... 1

Art Nehf

1937 ... 3
1938 ... 5
1939 ... 1
1949 ... 1
1950 ... 2
1951 ... 4
1952 ... 3
1953 ... 4
1954 ... 7
1955 ... 7
1958 ... 13

Graig Nettles

1994 ... 38
1995 ... 28
1996 ... 37
1997 ... 22

Don Newcombe

1966 ... 7
1967 ... 18
1967 RO ... 2
1968 ... 9
1969 ... 3
1970 ... 5
1971 ... 8
1972 ... 7
1973 ... 11
1974 ... 7
1975 ... 11
1976 ... 21
1977 ... 43
1978 ... 48
1979 ... 52
1980 ... 59

Hal Newhouser
Inducted in 1992

1962 ... 4
1964 ... 26
1964 RO ... 3
1966 ... 32
1967 ... 62
1967 RO ... 13
1968 ... 67
1969 ... 82
1970 ... 80
1971 ... 94
1972 ... 92
1973 ... 79
1974 ... 73
1975 ... 155
1992 ... Vet. Com.

Bobo Newsom

1960 ... 6
1962 ... 3
1964 ... 17
1964 RO ... 1
1966 ... 25
1967 ... 19
1967 RO ... 6
1968 ... 22
1969 ... 32
1970 ... 12
1971 ... 17
1972 ... 31
1973 ... 33

Kid Nichols
Inducted in 1949

1936 V ... 3
1938 ... 3
1939 ... 7
1942 ... 5
1945 ... 5
1946 NOM ... 1
1949 ... O/T Com.

Bill Nicholson

1960 ... 1

Joe Niekro

1994 ... 6

Phil Niekro
Inducted in 1997

1993 ... 278
1994 ... 273
1995 ... 286
1996 ... 321
1997 ... 380

Ron Northey

1964 ... 1

Jim Northrup

1981 ... 1

Lefty O'Doul

1948 ... 4
1949 ... 4
1950 ... 9
1951 ... 13
1952 ... 19
1953 ... 11
1956 ... 5
1958 ... 27
1960 ... 45
1962 ... 13

Joe Oeschger

1948 ... 1

Bob O'Farrell

1950 ... 4
1958 ... 3
1960 ... 3

Charlie O'Leary

1953 ... 1
1958 ... 1
1960 ... 1

Tony Oliva
1982 ... 63
1983 ... 75
1984 ... 124
1985 ... 114
1986 ... 154
1987 ... 160
1988 ... 202
1989 ... 135
1990 ... 142
1991 ... 160
1992 ... 175
1993 ... 157
1994 ... 158
1995 ... 149
1996 ... 170

Al Oliver
1991 ... 19

Steve O'Neill
1948 ... 2
1949 ... 6
1950 ... 1
1951 ... 3
1952 ... 10
1953 ... 13
1958 ... 10

Jim O'Rourke
Inducted in 1945
1945 ... O/T Com.

Claude Osteen
1981 ... 2

Mel Ott
Inducted in 1951
1949 ... 94
1949 RO ... 128
1950 ... 115
1951 ... 197

Charlie Pabor
1936 V ... 1

Andy Pafko
1966 ... 2
1967 ... 1

Satchel Paige
Inducted in 1971
1951 ... 1
1971 ... Neg. Com.

Jim Palmer
Inducted in 1990
1990 ... 411

Milt Pappas
1979 ... 5

Dave Parker
1997 ... 83
1998 ... 116
1999 ... 80
2000 ... 104

Larry Parrish
1994 ... 2

Camilo Pascual
1977 ... 3
1978 ... 1

Dode Paskert
1937 ... 1

Monte Pearson
1958 ... 1

Roger Peckinpaugh
1937 ... 3
1938 ... 2
1939 ... 1
1942 ... 2
1949 ... 1
1952 ... 2
1953 ... 2
1954 ... 1
1955 ... 1

Heinie Peitz
1939 ... 1

Herb Pennock
Inducted in 1948
1937 ... 15
1938 ... 37
1939 ... 40
1942 ... 72
1945 ... 45
1946 NOM ... 41
1946 ... 16
1947 ... 86
1948 ... 94

Hub Perdue
1938 ... 1
1939 ... 1

Tony Perez
Inducted in 2000
1992 ... 215
1993 ... 233
1994 ... 263
1995 ... 259
1996 ... 309
1997 ... 312
1998 ... 321
1999 ... 302
2000 ... 385

Cy Perkins
1958 ... 2

Ron Perranoski
1979 ... 6

Gaylord Perry
Inducted in 1991
1989 ... 304
1990 ... 320
1991 ... 342

Jim Perry
1981 ... 6
1983 ... 7

Johnny Pesky
1960 ... 1

Rico Petrocelli
1982 ... 3

Deacon Phillippe
1939 ... 1
1942 ... 1
1945 ... 2
1946 NOM ... 1

Billy Pierce
1970 ... 5
1971 ... 7
1972 ... 6
1973 ... 4
1974 ... 4

Lip Pike
1936 V ... 1

Lou Piniella
1990 ... 2

Vada Pinson
1981 ... 18
1982 ... 6
1983 ... 12
1985 ... 19
1986 ... 43
1987 ... 48
1988 ... 67
1989 ... 33
1990 ... 36
1991 ... 30
1992 ... 36
1993 ... 38
1994 ... 46
1995 ... 32
1996 ... 51

Wally Pipp
1958 ... 1

Eddie Plank
Inducted in 1946
1937 ... 23
1938 ... 38
1939 ... 28
1942 ... 63
1945 ... 33
1946 NOM ... 34
1946 ... O/T Com.

Johnny Podres
1975 ... 3
1976 ... 2
1977 ... 3

Bob Porterfield
1966 ... 1

Boog Powell
1983 ... 5

Vic Power
1971 ... 2
1972 ... 3

Herb Pruett
1949 ... 1
1950 ... 1
1951 ... 1
1952 ... 1
1953 ... 1

Terry Puhl
1997 ... 1

Jack Quinn
1948 ... 2
1958 ... 9
1960 ... 2

Dan Quisenberry
1996 ... 18

Charles Radbourn
Inducted in 1939
1936 V ... 16
1939 ... O/T Com.

Willie Randolph
1998 ... 5

Vic Raschi
1962 ... 1
1964 ... 8
1968 ... 1
1969 ... 3
1971 ... 2
1972 ... 4
1973 ... 7
1974 ... 3
1975 ... 37

Bugs Raymond
1937 ... 1

Jeff Reardon
2000 ... 24

Pee Wee Reese
Inducted in 1984
1964 ... 73
1964 RO ... 47
1966 ... 95
1967 ... 89
1967 RO ... 16
1968 ... 81
1969 ... 89
1970 ... 97
1971 ... 127
1972 ... 129
1973 ... 126
1974 ... 141
1975 ... 154
1976 ... 186
1977 ... 163
1978 ... 169
1984 ... Vet. Com.

Pete Reiser
1958 ... 6
1960 ... 8

Jack Remsen
1936 V ... 1

Jerry Remy
1990 ... 1

Rick Reuschel
1997 ... 2

Jerry Reuss
1996 ... 2

Allie Reynolds
1956 ... 1
1960 ... 24
1962 ... 15
1964 ... 35
1964 RO ... 6
1966 ... 60
1967 ... 77
1967 RO ... 19
1968 ... 95
1969 ... 98
1970 ... 89
1971 ... 110
1972 ... 105
1973 ... 93
1974 ... 101

Del Rice
1966 ... 2

Jim Rice
1995 ... 137
1996 ... 166
1997 ... 178
1998 ... 203
1999 ... 146
2000 ... 257

Sam Rice
Inducted in 1963
1938 ... 1
1948 ... 1
1949 ... 3
1950 ... 1
1951 ... 1
1952 ... 1
1953 ... 3
1954 ... 9
1955 ... 28
1956 ... 45
1958 ... 90
1960 ... 143
1962 ... 81
1963 ... Vet. Com.

J. R. Richard
1986 ... 7

Hardy Richardson
1936 V ... 1

Bobby Richardson
1972 ... 8
1973 ... 2
1974 ... 5

Branch Rickey
Inducted in 1967
Executive
1942 ... 3
1945 ... 2
1967 ... Vet. Com.

Jimmy Ring
1949 ... 1

Claude Ritchey
1945 ... 1

Mickey Rivers
1990 ... 2

Eppa Rixey
Inducted in 1963
1937 ... 1
1938 ... 2
1945 ... 1
1947 ... 2
1948 ... 5
1949 ... 4
1950 ... 6
1951 ... 5
1952 ... 3
1953 ... 3
1954 ... 5
1955 ... 8
1956 ... 27
1958 ... 32
1960 ... 142
1962 ... 49
1963 ... Vet. Com.

Phil Rizzuto
Inducted in 1994
1956 ... 1
1962 ... 44
1964 ... 45
1964 RO ... 11
1966 ... 54
1967 ... 71
1967 RO ... 14
1968 ... 74
1969 ... 78
1970 ... 79
1971 ... 92
1972 ... 103
1973 ... 111
1974 ... 111
1975 ... 117
1976 ... 149
1994 ... Vet. Com.

Robin Roberts
Inducted in 1976
1973 ... 213
1974 ... 224
1975 ... 263
1976 ... 337

Dave Robertson
1953 ... 1

Brooks Robinson
Inducted in 1983
1983 ... 344

Frank Robinson
Inducted in 1982
1982 ... 370

Jackie Robinson
Inducted in 1962
1962 ... 124

Wilbert Robinson
Inducted in 1945
Manager
1936 V ... 6
1937 ... 5
1938 ... 17
1939 ... 46
1942 ... 89
1945 ... 81
1945 ... O/T Com.

Preacher Roe
1960 ... 1
1962 ... 1
1968 ... 2
1970 ... 1
1971 ... 3
1972 ... 2

Bullet Joe Rogan
Inducted in 1998
1998 ... Vet. Com.

Red Rolfe
1950 ... 7
1951 ... 6
1952 ... 4
1953 ... 5
1956 ... 3
1958 ... 13
1960 ... 10
1962 ... 1

Eddie Rommel
1948 ... 3
1949 ... 2
1950 ... 1
1951 ... 4
1952 ... 2
1953 ... 1
1958 ... 7
1960 ... 12

Charlie Root
1945 ... 1
1948 ... 3
1949 ... 1
1950 ... 1
1958 ... 6
1960 ... 2

Edd Roush
Inducted in 1962
1936 ... 2
1937 ... 10
1938 ... 9
1939 ... 8
1942 ... 1
1945 ... 5
1946 NOM ... 11
1947 ... 25
1948 ... 17
1949 ... 14
1950 ... 16
1951 ... 21
1952 ... 24
1953 ... 32
1954 ... 52
1955 ... 97
1956 ... 91
1958 ... 112
1960 ... 146
1962 ... Vet. Com.

Schoolboy Rowe
1958 ... 12
1960 ... 3
1968 ... 6
1969 ... 17

Nap Rucker
1936 ... 1
1937 ... 11
1938 ... 12
1939 ... 13
1942 ... 15
1945 ... 10
1946 NOM ... 13

Dick Rudolph
1937 ... 1
1951 ... 1

Muddy Ruel
1946 NOM ... 1
1950 ... 4
1951 ... 1
1952 ... 1
1953 ... 8
1954 ... 5
1955 ... 11
1956 ... 16
1958 ... 10
1960 ... 9

Red Ruffing
Inducted in 1967

1948 4
1949 22
1949 RO 4
1950 12
1951 9
1952 10
1953 24
1954 29
1955 60
1956 97
1958 99
1960 86
1962 72
1964 141
1964 RO 184
1966 208
1967 212
1967 RO 266

Amos Rusie
Inducted in 1977

1936 V 12
1937 1
1938 8
1939 6
1942 1
1945 1
1977 Vet. Com.

Bill Russell

1992 3

Babe Ruth
Inducted in 1936

1936 215

Nolan Ryan
Inducted in 1999

1999 491

Ray Sadecki

1983 2

Johnny Sain

1962 1
1964 3
1968 7
1969 8
1970 9
1971 11
1972 21
1973 47
1974 51
1975 123

Manny Sanguillen

1986 2

Ron Santo

1980 15
1985 53
1986 64
1987 78
1988 108
1989 75
1990 96
1991 116
1992 136
1993 155
1994 150
1995 139
1996 174
1997 186
1998 204

Hank Sauer

1966 4

Al Schacht

1939 1
1948 2
1951 4
1956 1

Germany Schaefer

1942 1
1953 1

Ray Schalk
Inducted in 1955

1936 4
1937 24
1938 45
1939 35
1942 53
1945 33
1946 NOM 36
1947 50
1948 22
1949 24
1949 RO 17
1950 16
1951 37
1952 44
1953 52
1954 54
1955 113
1955 Vet. Com.

Wally Schang

1948 1
1950 1
1956 1
1958 8
1960 11

Mike Schmidt
Inducted in 1995

1995 444

Red Schoendienst
Inducted in 1989

1969 65
1970 97
1971 123
1972 104
1973 96
1974 110
1975 94
1976 129
1977 105
1978 130
1979 159
1980 164
1981 166
1982 135
1983 146
1989 Vet. Com.

Ossie Schreckengost

1937 2
1938 2
1939 2

Frank Schulte

1937 1

Hal Schumacher

1948 1
1955 1
1956 2
1958 1
1960 11
1962 1
1964 10

Everett Scott

1937 2
1938 2
1939 1
1942 1
1947 1
1948 3
1949 3
1950 3
1951 2
1952 4
1953 5
1954 4
1955 8
1956 1

George Scott

1986 1

Jack Scott

1958 1

Mike Scott

1997 2

Tom Seaver
Inducted in 1992

1992 425

Frank Selee
Inducted in 1999
Manager

1999 Vet. Com.

George Selkirk

1948 1
1949 1
1950 1
1951 2
1952 1
1953 1

Hank Severeid

1948 1

Joe Sewell
Inducted in 1977

1937 1
1948 1
1954 1
1955 1
1956 3
1958 1
1960 23
1977 Vet. Com.

Luke Sewell

1948 1
1958 3
1960 3
1962 1

Rip Sewell

1958 1
1962 1
1964 1

Cy Seymour

1945 1

Bobby Shantz

1970 7
1971 5
1972 9
1973 5
1974 3

Jim Sheckard

1938 1
1945 1
1946 NOM 1

Bill Sherdel

1948 1
1949 1
1950 1
1951 1
1953 1
1955 1
1956 1
1958 2
1960 2

Urban Shocker

1938 1
1939 1
1948 1
1949 2
1958 4

Chris Short

1979 1

Sonny Siebert

1981 1

Roy Sievers

1971 4
1972 3

Al Simmons
Inducted in 1953

1936 4
1946 NOM 1
1947 6
1948 60
1949 89
1949 RO 76
1950 90
1951 116
1952 141
1953 199

Curt Simmons

1973 5
1974 3

Ted Simmons

1994 17

George Sisler
Inducted in 1939

1936 77
1937 106
1938 179
1939 235

Sibby Sisti

1960 1

Enos Slaughter
Inducted in 1985

1966 100
1967 123
1967 RO 48
1968 129
1969 128
1970 133
1971 165
1972 149
1973 145
1974 145
1975 177
1976 197
1977 222
1978 261
1979 297
1985 Vet. Com.

Roy Smalley

1964 1

Earl Smith

1948 1
1956 1

Lonnie Smith

2000 1

Reggie Smith

1988 3

Sherry Smith

1948 1

Duke Snider
Inducted in 1980

1970 51
1971 89
1972 84
1973 101
1974 111
1975 129
1976 159
1977 212
1978 254
1979 308
1980 333

Billy Southworth

1945 1
1946 NOM 1
1949 7
1950 1
1951 4
1952 1
1953 2
1958 18

Warren Spahn
Inducted in 1973

1973 316

Al Spalding
Inducted in 1939
Pioneer

1936 V 4
1939 O/T Com.

Tully Sparks

1946 NOM 1

Tris Speaker
Inducted in 1937

1936 133
1937 165

Chris Speier

1995 1

Jake Stahl

1938 1
1939 1

Eddie Stanky

1960 3

Mickey Stanley

1984 2

Willie Stargell
Inducted in 1988

1988 352

Rusty Staub

1991 28
1992 26
1993 32
1994 36
1995 23
1996 24
1997 18

Turkey Stearnes
Inducted in 2000

2000 Vet. Com.

Harry Steinfeldt

1937 1
1939 1
1942 1

Casey Stengel
Inducted in 1966
Manager

1938 2
1939 6
1945 2
1948 1
1949 3
1950 3
1951 8
1952 27
1953 61
1966 Vet. Com.

Riggs Stephenson

1956 2
1958 1
1960 4
1962 1

Mel Stottlemyre

1980 3

Harry Stovey

1936 V 6

Gabby Street

1937 1
1938 1
1953 1

Gus Suhr

1956 1
1958 1
1960 1

Clyde Sukeforth

1958 1

Billy Sullivan

1937 1
1946 NOM 1

Jim Sundberg

1995 1

Rick Sutcliffe

2000 9

Bruce Sutter

1994 109
1995 137
1996 137
1997 130
1998 147
1999 121
2000 192

Don Sutton
Inducted in 1998

1994 259
1995 264
1996 300
1997 346
1998 386

Bill Sweeney

1945 1

Jess Tannehill

1946 NOM 1

Birdie Tebbetts

1958 8
1960 1

Kent Tekulve

1995 6

Garry Templeton

1997 2

Gene Tenace

1989 1

Fred Tenney

1936 V 1
1937 5
1938 8
1939 3
1942 1
1946 NOM 1

Bill Terry
Inducted in 1954

1936 9
1938 7
1939 16
1942 36
1945 32
1946 NOM 31
1947 46
1948 52
1949 81
1949 RO 48
1950 105
1951 148
1952 155
1953 191
1954 195

Tommy Thevenow

1950 2

Ira Thomas

1938 1

Sam Thompson
Inducted in 1974
1974 Vet. Com.

Bobby Thomson
1966 12
1967 10
1967 RO 1
1968 13
1969 6
1970 4
1971 4
1972 10
1973 3
1974 6
1975 10
1976 9
1977 10
1978 5
1979 11

Andre Thornton
1993 2

Luis Tiant
1988 132
1989 47
1990 42
1991 32
1992 50
1993 62
1994 42
1995 45
1996 64
1997 53
1998 62
1999 53
2000 86

Joe Tinker
Inducted in 1946
1937 15
1938 16
1939 12
1942 36
1945 49
1946 NOM 55
1946 45
1946 O/T Com.

Jim Tobin
1956 2

Fred Toney
1949 1

Earl Torgeson
1967 2

Joe Torre
1983 20
1984 45
1985 44
1986 60
1987 47
1988 60
1989 40
1990 55
1991 41
1992 62
1993 63
1994 53
1995 50
1996 50
1997 105

Mike Torrez
1990 1

Pie Traynor
Inducted in 1948
1936 16
1938 3
1939 10
1942 45
1945 81
1946 NOM 65
1946 53
1947 119
1948 93

Dizzy Trout
1964 1

Virgil Trucks
1964 4

John Tudor
1996 2

Jim Turner
1956 1

Terry Turner
1947 2

George Uhle
1956 1
1958 4
1960 4

Ellis Valentine
1991 1

Elmer Valo
1967 2

Dazzy Vance
Inducted in 1955
1936 1
1937 10
1938 10
1939 15
1942 37
1945 18
1946 NOM 31
1947 50
1948 23
1949 33
1949 RO 15
1950 52
1951 70
1952 105
1953 150
1954 158
1955 205

Johnny Vander Meer
1945 1
1956 3
1958 35
1960 31
1962 5
1964 51
1964 RO 20
1966 72
1967 87
1967 RO 35
1968 79
1969 95
1970 88
1971 98

George Van Haltren
1936 V 1

Arky Vaughan
Inducted in 1985
1953 1
1954 2
1955 4
1956 9
1958 6
1960 10
1962 6
1964 17
1964 RO 6
1966 36
1967 46
1967 RO 19
1968 82
1985 Vet. Com.

Bobby Veach
1937 1

Bill Veeck
Inducted in 1991
Executive
1991 Vet. Com.

Mickey Vernon
1966 20
1967 14
1967 RO 2
1968 22
1969 21
1970 10
1971 12
1972 12
1973 23
1974 27
1975 22
1976 52
1977 52
1978 66
1979 88
1980 96

Bill Virdon
1974 3
1975 1

Rube Waddell
Inducted in 1946
1936 33
1937 67
1938 148
1939 179
1942 126
1945 154
1946 NOM 122
1946 87
1946 O/T Com.

Honus Wagner
Inducted in 1936
1936 V 5
1936 215

Rube Walberg
1958 1
1960 1

Dixie Walker
1962 1
1964 6
1968 6
1969 9

Harry Walker
1958 1

Bobby Wallace
Inducted in 1953
1936 V 1
1937 1
1938 7
1939 5
1942 2
1945 3
1953 Vet. Com.

Ed Walsh
Inducted in 1946
1936 20
1937 56
1938 110
1939 132
1942 113
1945 137
1946 NOM 115
1946 106
1946 O/T Com.

Bucky Walters
1950 4
1952 3
1953 10
1956 5
1958 33
1960 19
1962 5
1964 35
1964 RO 8
1966 56
1967 65
1967 RO 24
1968 67
1969 20
1970 29

Bill Wambsganss
1942 1
1950 1
1953 1
1954 4
1955 5
1956 3

Lloyd Waner
Inducted in 1967
1949 3
1950 1
1951 1
1952 2
1956 18
1958 39
1960 22
1962 5
1964 47
1964 RO 12
1967 Vet. Com.

Paul Waner
Inducted in 1952
1946 NOM 4
1948 51
1949 73
1949 RO 63
1950 95
1951 162
1952 195

Monte Ward
Inducted in 1964
1936 V 3
1964 Vet. Com.

Lon Warneke
1949 2
1958 2
1960 4
1962 2
1964 13

Bob Watson
1990 3

Earl Weaver
Inducted in 1996
1996 Vet. Com.

George Weiss
Inducted in 1971
Executive
1971 Vet. Com.

Bob Welch
2000 1

Mickey Welch
Inducted in 1973
1973 Vet. Com.

Willie Wells
Inducted in 1997
1997 Vet. Com.

Billy Werber
1949 1
1950 1
1952 1
1958 3

Vic Wertz
1970 2
1971 2
1972 4
1973 2
1974 2
1975 5
1976 5
1977 4
1978 4

Sam West
1948 1

Wes Westrum
1964 2

Zach Wheat
Inducted in 1959
1937 5
1938 7
1939 4
1942 3
1945 2
1946 NOM 6
1947 37
1948 15
1949 15
1950 17
1951 19
1952 30
1953 32
1954 33
1955 51
1956 26
1959 Vet. Com.

Deacon White
1936 V 1

Frank White
1996 18

Will White
1975 7
1976 7
1977 4

Burgess Whitehead
1956 1

Earl Whitehill
1956 1
1958 2
1960 3

Hoyt Wilhelm
Inducted in 1985
1978 158
1979 168
1980 209
1981 238
1982 236
1983 243
1984 290
1985 331

Billy Williams
Inducted in 1987
1982 97
1983 153
1984 202
1985 252
1986 315
1987 354

Fred Williams
1938 1
1945 1
1948 1
1949 2
1950 9
1951 7
1952 4
1953 4
1954 4
1955 3
1956 11
1958 6
1960 11

Ken Williams
1956 1
1958 1

Smokey Joe Williams
Inducted in 1999
1999 Vet. Com.

Ted Williams
Inducted in 1966
1966 282

Ned Williamson
1936 V 2

Vic Willis
Inducted in 1995
1995 Vet. Com.

Maury Wills
1978 115
1979 166
1980 146
1981 163
1982 91
1983 77
1984 104
1985 93
1986 124
1987 113
1988 127
1989 95
1990 95
1991 61
1992 110

Jimmie Wilson
1948 8
1949 6
1950 4
1951 2
1952 7
1953 10
1954 8
1955 13
1956 17
1958 3
1960 6
1962 4

Willie Wilson
2000 10

Jim Wilson
1964 2

Hack Wilson
Inducted in 1979
1937 1
1939 1
1942 1
1948 2
1949 24
1949 RO 12
1950 16
1951 21
1952 21
1953 43
1954 48
1955 81
1956 74
1958 94
1960 72
1962 39
1979 Vet. Com.

Whitey Witt
1949 1

Joe Wood
1937 13
1938 6
1939 2
1942 1
1946 NOM 5
1947 29
1948 5
1950 1
1951 5

Wilbur Wood
1984 14
1985 16

1986 23
1987 26
1988 30
1989 14

Glenn Wright

1948 2
1949 1
1950 2
1951 1
1952 1
1953 3
1954 1
1955 4
1956 3
1958 8
1960 18
1962 1

George Wright
Inducted in 1937
Pioneer

1936 V 6
1937 Cen. Com.

Harry Wright
Inducted in 1953
Pioneer

1953 Vet. Com.

Whit Wyatt

1958 1

Early Wynn
Inducted in 1972

1969 95
1970 140
1971 240
1972 301

Tom Yawkey
Inducted in 1980
Executive

1980 Vet. Com.

Carl Yastrzemski
Inducted in 1989

1989 423

Steve Yeager

1992 2

Steve Yerkes

1945 1

Rudy York

1962 1
1964 10

Cy Young
Inducted in 1937

1936 V 32
1936 111
1937 153

Pep Young

1958 1

Ross Youngs
Inducted in 1972

1936 10
1937 16
1938 40
1939 34
1942 44
1945 22
1946 NOM 25
1947 36
1948 19
1949 20
1949 RO 11
1950 17
1951 34
1952 34
1953 31
1954 34
1955 48
1956 19
1972 Vet. Com.

Robin Yount
Inducted in 1999

1999 385

Tom Zachary

1958 1
1960 1

Chief Zimmer

1938 1

Hall of Fame Balloting: Top 10 Candidates in Each Election

1936 Veterans
Needed to Elect: 59

Cap Anson 40
Buck Ewing 40
Willie Keeler 33
Cy Young 32
Ed Delahanty 22
John McGraw 17
Herman Long 16
Charlie Radbourn 16
Mike Kelly 15
Amos Rusie 12

1936
Needed to Elect: 170

Ty Cobb 222
Babe Ruth 215
Honus Wagner 215
Christy Mathewson 205
Walter Johnson 189
Nap Lajoie 146
Tris Speaker 133
Cy Young 111
Rogers Hornsby 105
Mickey Cochrane 80

1937
Needed to Elect: 151

Nap Lajoie 168
Tris Speaker 165
Cy Young 153
Grover Alexander 125
Eddie Collins 115
Willie Keeler 115
George Sisler 106
Ed Delahanty 70
Rube Waddell 67
Jimmy Collins 66

1938
Needed to Elect: 197

Grover Alexander 212
George Sisler 179
Willie Keeler 177
Eddie Collins 175
Rube Waddell 148
Frank Chance 133
Ed Delahanty 132
Ed Walsh 110
Johnny Evers 91
Jimmy Collins 79

1939
Needed to Elect: 206

George Sisler 235
Eddie Collins 213
Willie Keeler 207
Rube Waddell 179
Rogers Hornsby 176
Frank Chance 158
Ed Delahanty 145
Ed Walsh 132
Johnny Evers 107
Miller Huggins 97

1942
Needed to Elect: 175

Rogers Hornsby 182
Frank Chance 136
Rube Waddell 126
Ed Walsh 113
Miller Huggins 111
Ed Delahanty 104
Johnny Evers 91
Wilbert Robinson 89
Mickey Cochrane 88
Frankie Frisch 84

1945
Needed to Elect: 186

Frank Chance 179
Rube Waddell 154
Ed Walsh 137
Johnny Evers 134
Roger Bresnahan 133
Miller Huggins 133
Mickey Cochrane 125
Jimmy Collins 121
Ed Delahanty 111
Clark Griffith 108

1946 Nominating Total Voting: 202

Frank Chance 144
Johnny Evers 130
Miller Huggins 129
Rube Waddell 122
Ed Walsh 115
Frankie Frisch 104
Carl Hubbell 101
Mickey Cochrane 80
Clark Griffith 73
Lefty Grove 71

1946
Needed to Elect: 198

Frank Chance 150
Johnny Evers 110
Miller Huggins 106
Ed Walsh 106
Rube Waddell 87
Clark Griffith 82
Carl Hubbell 75
Frankie Frisch 67
Mickey Cochrane 65
Lefty Grove 61

1947
Needed to Elect: 121

Carl Hubbell 140
Frankie Frisch 136
Mickey Cochrane 128
Lefty Grove 123
Pie Traynor 119
Charlie Gehringer 105
Rabbit Maranville 91
Dizzy Dean 88
Herb Pennock 86
Chief Bender 72

1948
Needed to Elect: 91

Herb Pennock 94
Pie Traynor 93
Al Simmons 60
Charlie Gehringer 52
Bill Terry 52
Paul Waner 51
Jimmie Foxx 50
Dizzy Dean 40
Harry Heilmann 40
Bill Dickey 39

1949
Needed to Elect: 115

Charlie Gehringer 102
Mel Ott 94
Al Simmons 89
Dizzy Dean 88
Jimmie Foxx 85
Bill Terry 81
Paul Waner 73
Hank Greenberg 67
Bill Dickey 65
Harry Heilmann 59

1949 Run Off
Needed to Elect: 141
One Player Maximum

Charlie Gehringer 159
Mel Ott 128
Jimmie Foxx 89
Dizzy Dean 81
Al Simmons 76
Paul Waner 63
Harry Heilmann 52
Bill Terry 48
Hank Greenberg 44
Bill Dickey 39
Rabbit Maranville 39

1950
Needed to Elect: 126

Mel Ott 115
Bill Terry 105
Jimmie Foxx 103
Paul Waner 95
Al Simmons 90
Harry Heilmann 87
Dizzy Dean 85
Bill Dickey 78
Rabbit Maranville 66
Hank Greenberg 64

1951
Needed to Elect: 170

Mel Ott 197
Jimmie Foxx 179
Paul Waner 162
Harry Heilmann 153
Bill Terry 148
Dizzy Dean 145
Bill Dickey 118
Al Simmons 116
Rabbit Maranville 110
Ted Lyons 71

1952
Needed to Elect: 176

Harry Heilmann 203
Paul Waner 195
Bill Terry 155
Dizzy Dean 152
Al Simmons 141
Bill Dickey 139
Rabbit Maranville 133
Dazzy Vance 105
Ted Lyons 101
Gabby Hartnett 77

1953
Needed to Elect: 198

Dizzy Dean 209
Al Simmons 199
Bill Terry 191
Bill Dickey 179
Rabbit Maranville 164
Dazzy Vance 150
Ted Lyons 139
Joe DiMaggio 117
Chief Bender 104
Gabby Hartnett 104

1954
Needed to Elect: 189

Rabbit Maranville 209
Bill Dickey 202
Bill Terry 195
Joe DiMaggio 175
Ted Lyons 170
Dazzy Vance 158
Gabby Hartnett 151
Hank Greenberg 97
Joe Cronin 85
Max Carey 55

1955
Needed to Elect: 189

Joe DiMaggio 223
Ted Lyons 217
Dazzy Vance 205
Gabby Hartnett 195
Hank Greenberg 157
Joe Cronin 135
Max Carey 119
Ray Schalk 113
Edd Roush 97
Hank Gowdy 90

1956
Needed to Elect: 145

Hank Greenberg 164
Joe Cronin 152
Red Ruffing 97
Edd Roush 91
Lefty Gomez 89
Hack Wilson 74
Max Carey 65
Tony Lazzeri 64
Kiki Cuyler 55
Hank Gowdy 49

1958
Needed to Elect: 200

Max Carey 136
Edd Roush 112
Red Ruffing 99
Hack Wilson 94
Kiki Cuyler 90
Sam Rice 90
Tony Lazzeri 80
Luke Appling 77
Lefty Gomez 76
Burleigh Grimes 71

1960
Needed to Elect: 202

Edd Roush 146
Sam Rice 143
Eppa Rixey 142
Burleigh Grimes 92
Jim Bottomley 89
Red Ruffing 86
Red Faber 83
Luke Appling 72
Kiki Cuyler 72
Hack Wilson 72

1962
Needed to Elect: 120

Bob Feller 150
Jackie Robinson 124
Sam Rice 81
Red Ruffing 72
Eppa Rixey 49
Luke Appling 48
Phil Rizzuto 44
Burleigh Grimes 43
Hack Wilson 39
Ducky Medwick 34

1964
Needed to Elect: 151

Luke Appling 142
Red Ruffing 141
Roy Campanella 115
Ducky Medwick 108
Pee Wee Reese 73
Lou Boudreau 68
Al Lopez 57
Chuck Klein 56
Johnny Mize 54
Mel Harder 51
Johnny Vander Meer 51

1964 Run Off
Needed to Elect: 170
One Player Maximum

Luke Appling 189
Red Ruffing 184
Roy Campanella 138
Ducky Medwick 130
Pee Wee Reese 47
Lou Boudreau 43
Al Lopez 34
Johnny Vander Meer 20
Chuck Klein 18
Marty Marion 17

1966
Needed to Elect: 227

Ted Williams 282
Red Ruffing 208
Roy Campanella 197
Ducky Medwick 187
Lou Boudreau 115
Al Lopez 109
Enos Slaughter 100
Pee Wee Reese 95
Marty Marion 86
Johnny Mize 81

1967
Needed to Elect: 219

Ducky Medwick 212
Red Ruffing 212
Roy Campanella 204
Lou Boudreau 143
Ralph Kiner 124
Enos Slaughter 123
Al Lopez 114
Marty Marion 90
Johnny Mize 89
Pee Wee Reese 89

1967 Run Off
Needed to Elect: 230
One Player Maximum

- Red Ruffing ... 266
- Ducky Medwick ... 248
- Roy Campanella ... 170
- Lou Boudreau ... 68
- Al Lopez ... 50
- Enos Slaughter ... 48
- Ralph Kiner ... 41
- Johnny Vander Meer ... 35
- Ernie Lombardi ... 25
- Bucky Walters ... 24

1968
Needed to Elect: 213

- Ducky Medwick ... 240
- Roy Campanella ... 205
- Lou Boudreau ... 146
- Enos Slaughter ... 129
- Ralph Kiner ... 118
- Johnny Mize ... 103
- Allie Reynolds ... 95
- Marty Marion ... 89
- Arky Vaughan ... 82
- Pee Wee Reese ... 81

1969
Needed to Elect: 255

- Stan Musial ... 317
- Roy Campanella ... 270
- Lou Boudreau ... 218
- Ralph Kiner ... 137
- Enos Slaughter ... 128
- Johnny Mize ... 116
- Marty Marion ... 112
- Allie Reynolds ... 98
- Joe Gordon ... 97
- Johnny Vander Meer ... 95
- Early Wynn ... 95

1970
Needed to Elect: 225

- Lou Boudreau ... 232
- Ralph Kiner ... 167
- Gil Hodges ... 145
- Early Wynn ... 140
- Enos Slaughter ... 133
- Johnny Mize ... 126
- Marty Marion ... 120
- Pee Wee Reese ... 97
- Red Schoendienst ... 97
- George Kell ... 90

1971
Needed to Elect: 270

- Yogi Berra ... 242
- Early Wynn ... 240
- Ralph Kiner ... 212
- Gil Hodges ... 180
- Enos Slaughter ... 165
- Johnny Mize ... 157
- Pee Wee Reese ... 127
- Marty Marion ... 123
- Red Schoendienst ... 123
- Allie Reynolds ... 110

1972
Needed to Elect: 297

- Sandy Koufax ... 344
- Yogi Berra ... 339
- Early Wynn ... 301
- Ralph Kiner ... 235
- Gil Hodges ... 161
- Johnny Mize ... 157
- Enos Slaughter ... 149
- Pee Wee Reese ... 129
- Marty Marion ... 120
- Bob Lemon ... 117

1973
Needed to Elect: 285

- Warren Spahn ... 316
- Whitey Ford ... 255
- Ralph Kiner ... 235
- Gil Hodges ... 218
- Robin Roberts ... 213
- Bob Lemon ... 177
- Johnny Mize ... 157
- Enos Slaughter ... 145
- Marty Marion ... 127
- Pee Wee Reese ... 126

1974
Needed to Elect: 274

- Mickey Mantle ... 322
- Whitey Ford ... 284
- Robin Roberts ... 224
- Ralph Kiner ... 215
- Gil Hodges ... 198
- Bob Lemon ... 190
- Enos Slaughter ... 145
- Pee Wee Reese ... 141
- Eddie Mathews ... 118
- Phil Rizzuto ... 111
- Duke Snider ... 111

1975
Needed to Elect: 272

- Ralph Kiner ... 273
- Robin Roberts ... 263
- Bob Lemon ... 233
- Gil Hodges ... 188
- Enos Slaughter ... 177
- Hal Newhouser ... 155
- Pee Wee Reese ... 154
- Eddie Mathews ... 148
- Phil Cavaretta ... 129
- Duke Snider ... 129

1976
Needed to Elect: 291

- Robin Roberts ... 337
- Bob Lemon ... 305
- Gil Hodges ... 233
- Enos Slaughter ... 197
- Eddie Mathews ... 189
- Pee Wee Reese ... 186
- Nellie Fox ... 174
- Duke Snider ... 159
- Phil Rizzuto ... 149
- George Kell ... 129
- Red Schoendienst ... 129

1977
Needed to Elect: 288

- Ernie Banks ... 321
- Eddie Mathews ... 239
- Gil Hodges ... 224
- Enos Slaughter ... 222
- Duke Snider ... 212
- Don Drysdale ... 197
- Pee Wee Reese ... 163
- Nellie Fox ... 152
- Jim Bunning ... 146
- George Kell ... 141

1978
Needed to Elect: 285

- Eddie Mathews ... 301
- Enos Slaughter ... 261
- Duke Snider ... 254
- Gil Hodges ... 226
- Don Drysdale ... 219
- Jim Bunning ... 181
- Pee Wee Reese ... 169
- Richie Ashburn ... 158
- Hoyt Wilhelm ... 158
- Nellie Fox ... 149

1979
Needed to Elect: 324

- Willie Mays ... 409
- Duke Snider ... 308
- Enos Slaughter ... 297
- Gil Hodges ... 242
- Don Drysdale ... 233
- Nellie Fox ... 174
- Hoyt Wilhelm ... 168
- Maury Wills ... 166
- Red Schoendienst ... 159
- Jim Bunning ... 147

1980
Needed to Elect: 289

- Al Kaline ... 340
- Duke Snider ... 333
- Don Drysdale ... 238
- Gil Hodges ... 230
- Hoyt Wilhelm ... 209
- Jim Bunning ... 177
- Red Schoendienst ... 164
- Nellie Fox ... 161
- Maury Wills ... 146
- Richie Ashburn ... 134

1981
Needed to Elect: 301

- Bob Gibson ... 337
- Don Drysdale ... 243
- Gil Hodges ... 241
- Harmon Killebrew ... 239
- Hoyt Wilhelm ... 238
- Juan Marichal ... 233
- Nellie Fox ... 168
- Red Schoendienst ... 166
- Jim Bunning ... 164
- Maury Wills ... 163

1982
Needed to Elect: 312

- Hank Aaron ... 406
- Frank Robinson ... 370
- Juan Marichal ... 305
- Harmon Killebrew ... 246
- Hoyt Wilhelm ... 236
- Don Drysdale ... 233
- Gil Hodges ... 205
- Luis Aparicio ... 174
- Jim Bunning ... 138
- Red Schoendienst ... 135

1983
Needed to Elect: 281

- Brooks Robinson ... 344
- Juan Marichal ... 313
- Harmon Killebrew ... 269
- Luis Aparicio ... 252
- Hoyt Wilhelm ... 243
- Don Drysdale ... 242
- Gil Hodges ... 237
- Nellie Fox ... 173
- Billy Williams ... 153
- Red Schoendienst ... 146

1984
Needed to Elect: 303

- Luis Aparicio ... 341
- Harmon Killebrew ... 335
- Don Drysdale ... 316
- Hoyt Wilhelm ... 290
- Nellie Fox ... 246
- Billy Williams ... 202
- Jim Bunning ... 201
- Orlando Cepeda ... 124
- Tony Oliva ... 124
- Roger Maris ... 107

1985
Needed to Elect: 297

- Hoyt Wilhelm ... 331
- Lou Brock ... 315
- Nellie Fox ... 295
- Billy Williams ... 252
- Jim Bunning ... 214
- Catfish Hunter ... 212
- Roger Maris ... 128
- Harvey Kuenn ... 125
- Orlando Cepeda ... 114
- Tony Oliva ... 114

1986
Needed to Elect: 319

- Willie McCovey ... 346
- Billy Williams ... 315
- Catfish Hunter ... 289
- Jim Bunning ... 279
- Roger Maris ... 177
- Tony Oliva ... 154
- Orlando Cepeda ... 152
- Harvey Kuenn ... 144
- Maury Wills ... 124
- Bill Mazeroski ... 100

1987
Needed to Elect: 310

- Billy Williams ... 354
- Catfish Hunter ... 315
- Jim Bunning ... 289
- Orlando Cepeda ... 179
- Roger Maris ... 176
- Tony Oliva ... 160
- Harvey Kuenn ... 144
- Bill Mazeroski ... 125
- Maury Wills ... 113
- Ken Boyer ... 96
- Lew Burdette ... 96

1988
Needed to Elect: 321

- Willie Stargell ... 352
- Jim Bunning ... 317
- Tony Oliva ... 202
- Orlando Cepeda ... 199
- Roger Maris ... 184
- Harvey Kuenn ... 168
- Bill Mazeroski ... 143
- Luis Tiant ... 132
- Maury Wills ... 127
- Ken Boyer ... 109
- Mickey Lolich ... 109

1989
Needed to Elect: 336

- Johnny Bench ... 431
- Carl Yastrzemski ... 423
- Gaylord Perry ... 304
- Jim Bunning ... 283
- Fergie Jenkins ... 234
- Orlando Cepeda ... 176
- Tony Oliva ... 135
- Bill Mazeroski ... 134
- Harvey Kuenn ... 115
- Maury Wills ... 95

1990
Needed to Elect: 333

- Jim Palmer ... 411
- Joe Morgan ... 363
- Gaylord Perry ... 320
- Fergie Jenkins ... 296
- Jim Bunning ... 257
- Orlando Cepeda ... 211
- Tony Oliva ... 142
- Bill Mazeroski ... 131
- Harvey Kuenn ... 107
- Ron Santo ... 96

1991
Needed to Elect: 333

- Rod Carew ... 401
- Gaylord Perry ... 342
- Fergie Jenkins ... 334
- Rollie Fingers ... 291
- Jim Bunning ... 282
- Orlando Cepeda ... 192
- Tony Oliva ... 160
- Bill Mazeroski ... 142
- Ron Santo ... 116
- Harvey Kuenn ... 100

1992
Needed to Elect: 323

- Tom Seaver ... 425
- Rollie Fingers ... 349
- Orlando Cepeda ... 246
- Tony Perez ... 215
- Bill Mazeroski ... 182
- Tony Oliva ... 175
- Ron Santo ... 136
- Jim Kaat ... 114
- Maury Wills ... 110
- Ken Boyer ... 71

1993
Needed to Elect: 318

- Reggie Jackson ... 396
- Phil Niekro ... 278
- Orlando Cepeda ... 252
- Tony Perez ... 233
- Steve Garvey ... 176
- Tony Oliva ... 157
- Ron Santo ... 155
- Jim Kaat ... 125
- Dick Allen ... 70
- Ken Boyer ... 69

1994
Needed to Elect: 342

- Steve Carlton ... 436
- Orlando Cepeda ... 335
- Phil Niekro ... 273
- Tony Perez ... 263
- Don Sutton ... 259
- Steve Garvey ... 166
- Tony Oliva ... 158
- Ron Santo ... 150
- Bruce Sutter ... 109
- Jim Kaat ... 98

1995
Needed to Elect: 345

- Mike Schmidt ... 444
- Phil Niekro ... 286
- Don Sutton ... 264
- Tony Perez ... 259
- Steve Garvey ... 196
- Tony Oliva ... 149
- Ron Santo ... 139
- Jim Rice ... 137
- Bruce Sutter ... 137
- Jim Kaat ... 100

1996
Needed to Elect: 353

- Phil Niekro ... 321
- Tony Perez ... 309
- Don Sutton ... 300
- Steve Garvey ... 175
- Ron Santo ... 174
- Tony Oliva ... 170
- Jim Rice ... 166
- Bruce Sutter ... 137
- Tommy John ... 102
- Jim Kaat ... 91

1997
Needed to Elect: 355

- Phil Niekro ... 380
- Don Sutton ... 346
- Tony Perez ... 312
- Ron Santo ... 186
- Jim Rice ... 178
- Steve Garvey ... 167
- Bruce Sutter ... 130
- Jim Kaat ... 107
- Joe Torre ... 105
- Tommy John ... 97

1998
Needed to Elect: 355

- Don Sutton ... 386
- Tony Perez ... 321
- Ron Santo ... 204
- Jim Rice ... 203
- Gary Carter ... 200
- Steve Garvey ... 195
- Bruce Sutter ... 147
- Tommy John ... 129
- Jim Kaat ... 129
- Dave Parker ... 116

1999
Needed to Elect: 373

- Nolan Ryan ... 491
- George Brett ... 488
- Robin Yount ... 385
- Carlton Fisk ... 330
- Tony Perez ... 302
- Gary Carter ... 168
- Steve Garvey ... 150
- Jim Rice ... 146
- Bruce Sutter ... 121
- Jim Kaat ... 100

2000
Needed to Elect: 375

- Carlton Fisk ... 397
- Tony Perez ... 385
- Jim Rice ... 257
- Gary Carter ... 248
- Bruce Sutter ... 192
- Goose Gossage ... 166
- Steve Garvey ... 160
- Tommy John ... 135
- Jim Kaat ... 125
- Dale Murphy ... 116

CHAPTER 9

The All-Star Game

Frederick Ivor-Campbell

Although the tradition of All-Star Games in baseball dates back to an 1858 series between teams of stars from Brooklyn and New York (they were called "picked nines" in those days), the current All-Star series began when Arch Ward, sports editor of the *Chicago Tribune*, persuaded hesitant league owners to go along with his proposal for a game between stars from the American League and National League, to be played in Chicago during that city's Century of Progress Exposition in 1933.

All-Star managers (who, except for the first game, have been the pilots of the previous year's pennant winners) shared with fans the selection of players for the first two games. From 1935 through 1946 the manager selected his whole squad. Since 1947, he has chosen his pitchers and all other players except the eight members of the starting lineup. The fans chose the starters from 1947 to 1957; after an incident of ballot-box stuffing by Cincinnati partisans in 1957, the major league players, coaches, and managers made the choice from 1958 to 1969; in 1970 the selection of starting lineups was returned to the fans.

The American League dominated the early years of the series, winning the first three games, and extending their winning margin to eight games (12–4) by 1949. The National League cut the lead in half with four straight wins, and by 1964 had drawn even in the series as the two leagues stood at 17 wins apiece, plus one tie. From 1965 through 1985 the National Leaguers continued their drive, winning 19 All-Star Games while losing only two, to build a commanding 36–19 lead in the series. In recent years, though, the American Leaguers have started to come back, winning in 1993 their seventh game in eight years, and their sixth in a row. The National League won in 1994, though it took extra innings to break the American League streak. The National League won the next two All-Star Games, but the American League captured the next four games to cut the National League's overall advantage to 40–30.

GAME 1
Comiskey Park, Chicago
July 6, 1933
AL, 4–2

NL	000 002 000	2	8	0
AL	012 001 00X	4	9	1

Pitchers: HALLAHAN, Warneke (3), Hubbell (7) vs GOMEZ, Crowder (4), Grove (7)
Home Runs: Ruth-A, Frisch-N
Attendance: 49,200

Baseball's two grand old managers—Connie Mack and John McGraw—were chosen to lead the American and National League squads in the first All-Star Game, and American League starting pitcher Lefty Gomez of the Yankees took home honors both as the first All-Star winning pitcher and as the first player to drive in an All-Star run (singling in Jimmie Dykes in the second inning). But it was another "grand old man"—Babe Ruth—who made the game's headlines. At 38, in his next-to-last season as a Yankee, he lined a two-run homer in the third to make the score 3–0. In right field he robbed Chick Hafey of a hit with a remarkable running catch of Hafey's line drive in the eighth inning.

Frank Frisch homered for the Nationals, following up Pepper Martin's RBI with a solo shot in the National League's two-run sixth. But the American stars countered with an insurance run in the bottom of the sixth, as Earl Averill singled in Joe Cronin to end the scoring. Carl Hubbell for the Nationals and Lefty Grove for the Americans blanked the opposition through the final innings.

GAME 2
Polo Grounds, New York
July 10, 1934
AL, 9–7

AL	000 261 000	9	14	1
NL	103 030 000	7	8	1

Pitchers: Gomez, Ruffing (4), HARDER (5) vs Hubbell, Warneke (4), MUNGO (5), J.Dean (6), Frankhouse (9)
Home Runs: Frisch-N, Medwick-N
Attendance: 48,363

This was the game in which Carl Hubbell struck out Babe Ruth, Lou Gehrig, Jimmie Foxx, Al Simmons, and Joe Cronin in order in the first two innings. Hubbell also walked two and gave up two hits in his three innings of work, but allowed no run to score as his Nationals took a 4–0 lead on homers by Frank Frisch in the first and Joe Medwick (for three runs) in the third off American starter (and first-game winner) Lefty Gomez.

But with Hubbell gone, the Americans pounced on Lon Warneke and Van Lingle Mungo for four runs each in the fourth and fifth innings. The Nationals battled back for three off Red Ruffing in their half of the fifth, to come within a run of tying the game. But Mel Harder relieved Ruffing with none out and put out the fire, one-hitting the National stars over the final five innings. The Americans picked up an insurance run in the sixth off Dizzy Dean before Dean and Fred Frankhouse shut them down, too, through the final three frames.

GAME 3
Municipal Stadium, Cleveland
July 8, 1935
AL, 4–1

NL	000 100 000	1	4	1
AL	210 010 00X	4	8	0

Pitchers: WALKER, Schumacher (3), Derringer (7), J.Dean (8) vs GOMEZ, Harder (7)
Home Runs: Foxx-A
Attendance: 69,812

Lefty Gomez started his third All-Star Game, and pitched a record six innings to pick up his second All-Star win. For three innings he shut out the Nationals as the Americans built a lead behind him on Jimmie Foxx's two-run homer in the first, and Rollie Hemsley's triple and Joe Cronin's run-scoring fly in the second.

The National Leaguers tried to catch up in the fourth, when they put together two of their three hits off Gomez—a double by Arky Vaughan and a single by Bill Terry—and scored a run. But an inning later Foxx nullified the National run, singling Joe Vosmik home for his third RBI.

Gomez blanked the National stars through two more innings before yielding to Mel Harder, who came in to close his second All-Star Game. Harder had created an All-Star record the previous year with his five consecutive scoreless innings pitched, and extended the record to eight, with three more shutout innings to end the game.

GAME 4
Braves Field, Boston
July 7, 1936
NL, 4–3

AL	000 000 300	3	7	1
NL	020 020 00X	4	9	0

Pitchers: GROVE, Rowe (4), Harder (7) vs J.DEAN, Hubbell (4), C.Davis (7), Warneke (7)
Home Runs: Galan-N, Gehrig-A
Attendance: 25,534

The National League, which had not yet won an All-Star Game, scored first in the second when Gabby Hartnett tripled in a run off Lefty Grove—rookie Joe DiMaggio missing his try for a shoe-top catch of Hartnett's drive to right field. Pinky Whitney then singled in Hartnett. Augie Galan homered off Schoolboy Rowe (and the right field foul pole) in the fifth, and DiMaggio's bobble of Billy Herman's single a batter later put Herman in position to score an unearned fourth run, on Joe Medwick's single, that proved to be the margin of victory.

The Americans, shut out through six by Dizzy Dean and Carl Hubbell, nearly tied the game in the seventh off Curt Davis as Lou Gehrig homered and Luke Appling singled in two more. But Lon Warneke took over and, after loading the bases with a walk, escaped disaster as shortstop Leo Durocher snared DiMaggio's vicious line drive to his right for the third out. Warneke shut the Americans out over the final two innings to preserve the one-run lead and the National League's first All-Star win.

GAME 5
Griffith Stadium, Washington
July 7, 1937
AL, 8–3

NL	000 111 000	3	13	0
AL	002 312 00X	8	13	2

Pitchers: J.DEAN, Hubbell (4), Blanton (4), Grissom (5), Mungo (6), Walters (8) vs GOMEZ, Bridges (4), Harder (7)
Home Runs: Gehrig-A
Attendance: 31,391

President Franklin Roosevelt attended the game and saw the AL capture its fourth win in five tries. Lou Gehrig homered and doubled to drive in half the American League's eight runs in an easy American win. Lefty Gomez started his fourth All-Star Game in five years and earned his third win. And AL reliever Mel Harder pitched the final innings for the fourth All-Star Game in a row, pushing his record for consecutive All-Star shutout innings to 13. Yet the game is remembered not for any of these things, but for Earl Averill's line drive in the third inning which fractured Dizzy Dean's toe and led to the premature end of his spectacular career. (Dean recovered from the broken toe, but tried to resume his pitching too soon. In favoring the toe, he changed his delivery and irreparably injured his pitching arm.)

The Americans began their scoring when Gehrig, who preceded Averill in the batting order, homered off Dean in the third, with one aboard. They added to their score in each of the next three innings, so that although the Nationals countered with single runs in the three middle innings, they only fell farther behind.

GAME 6
Crosley Field, Cincinnati
July 6, 1938
NL, 4–1

AL	000 000 001	1	7	4
NL	100 100 20X	4	8	0

Pitchers: GOMEZ, Allen (4), Grove (7) vs VANDER MEER, Lee (4), Brown (7)
Attendance: 27,607

For the fifth (and final) time, Lefty Gomez started for the American League, and although he gave up only two hits and no earned runs in his three innings, he was saddled with the loss when an error by shortstop Joe Cronin paved the way for a National League run in the first.

The Nationals scored their only earned run in the fourth when Mel Ott tripled and Ernie Lombardi singled him home. But in the seventh they recorded two more unearned runs when Leo Durocher bunted to move Frank McCormick to second. Both McCormick and Durocher scored as third baseman Jimmie Foxx threw wildly to first and right fielder Joe DiMaggio (who chased the ball down) missed home plate with his throw.

In the ninth DiMaggio singled and Cronin doubled him home in partial atonement for their errors. But as Johnny Vander Meer and "Big Bill" Lee had each blanked the American stars on one hit in their three-inning stints, and some fine outfield catches had kept them from scoring more than this one run off Mace Brown, the Americans' errors cost them the game.

GAME 7
Yankee Stadium, New York
July 11, 1939
AL, 3–1

NL	001 000 000	1	7 1
AL	000 210 00X	3	6 1

Pitchers: Derringer, LEE (4), Fette (7) vs Ruffing, BRIDGES (4), Feller (6)
Home Runs: J.DiMaggio-A
Attendance: 62,892

Six Yankees started for the American League, and one of them—Joe DiMaggio—hit the game's only home run. But it was a young Cleveland pitcher—28-year-old Bob Feller, playing in his first All-Star Game—who turned in the most memorable performance.

The Nationals scored first, with a run in the third on three hits off the American League starter, Red Ruffing. But the Americans came back with two runs in the fourth on a walk, two singles, and a bobbled grounder by shortstop Arky Vaughan. DiMaggio hit his insurance homer an inning later.

In the top of the sixth, after two singles and an error had loaded the bases with National stars, with only one out, Feller replaced Tommy Bridges to face Vaughan (who had earlier singled and scored his team's only run). One pitch got Feller out of the inning as Vaughan grounded into a 4–6–3 double play. Feller shut out the National stars over the final three innings, striking out Johnny Mize and Stan Hack in the ninth to end the game and give the Americans their fifth All-Star victory.

GAME 8
Sportsman's Park, St. Louis
July 9, 1940
NL, 4–0

AL	000 000 000	0	3 1
NL	300 000 01X	4	7 0

Pitchers: RUFFING, Newsom (4), Feller (7) vs DERRINGER, Walters (3), Wyatt (5), French (7), Hubbell (9)
Home Runs: West-N
Attendance: 32,373

The National Leaguers made short work of the Americans, scoring three times in the first inning and holding the opposing stars to three hits for the All-Star Game's first shutout. Before American League starter Red Ruffing retired a single National batter in the bottom of the first inning, three of the game's four runs had been scored, on singles by Arky Vaughan and Billy Herman and Max West's home run to right center.

Ruffing then settled down, and he and Buck Newsom held the Nationals to just three additional hits through the seventh. Bob Feller gave up the Nationals' fourth run in the eighth, on a walk, a sacrifice, and Harry Danning's single.

Five National League pitchers combined for the shutout, permitting only five batters to reach base while striking out seven. Starter Paul Derringer, who struck out three men in his two innings, was awarded the win.

GAME 9
Briggs Stadium, Detroit
July 8, 1941
AL, 7–5

NL	000 001 220	5	10 2
AL	000 101 014	7	11 3

Pitchers: Wyatt, Derringer (3), Walters (5), PASSEAU (7) vs Feller, Lee (4), Hudson (7), SMITH (8)
Home Runs: Vaughan-N (2), Williams-A
Attendance: 54,674

The National Leaguers entered the last of the ninth with a 5–3 lead and hopes of nailing down their first back-to-back All-Star victories. The American stars had scored their first run in the fourth. The Nationals tied the score in the top of the sixth, but the Americans countered with a run later in the inning. The Nationals' Arky Vaughan then made a bid to be the game's hero, homering in the seventh off Sid Hudson with a man aboard to restore the National lead, and homering again an inning later off Edgar Smith for two more runs.

A double and single by the DiMaggio brothers Joe and Dom brought the Americans a run closer in the eighth, but they still needed two to tie as they faced Claude Passeau in the bottom of the ninth. Two one-out singles and a walk loaded the bases, and a force play at second (that just missed being a game-ending double play) scored Ken Keltner from third. With two men now out and the Americans still down a run, Ted Williams homered on a letter-high fastball against the upper parapet in right for three more runs and another American League victory.

GAME 10
Polo Grounds, New York
July 6, 1942
AL, 3–1

AL	300 000 000	3	7 0
NL	000 000 010	1	6 1

Pitchers: CHANDLER, Benton (5) vs M.COOPER, Vander Meer (4), Passeau (7), Walters (9)
Home Runs: Boudreau-A, York-A, Owen-N
Attendance: 33,694

Home runs accounted for all the scoring as the American League, in something of a reverse of the 1940 game, scored three times in the top of the first to defeat the Nationals. Lou Boudreau, leading off, hit the game winner off Mort Cooper's second pitch, into the upper deck in left field. A double and two outs later, Rudy York put one over the fence near the short right field foul line for two more runs.

The Americans hit safely only four more times, and scored no more runs, but they already had more than enough, as Spud Chandler and Al Benton combined to shut out the National League stars for seven innings, until Mickey Owen, pinch-hitting for pitcher Claude Passeau in the eighth, hit his only home run of the summer.

This was the second All-Star Game played in the Polo Grounds. It had been Brooklyn's turn to host the game at Ebbets Field, but because the proceeds were destined for the war effort, the site was shifted to the larger stadium. The game might as well have been held in Brooklyn, though, as a pregame rain held attendance to well below the Polo Grounds' capacity.

GAME 11
Shibe Park, Philadelphia
July 13, 1943
AL, 5–3

NL	100 000 101	3	10 3
AL	031 010 00X	5	8 1

Pitchers: M.COOPER, Vander Meer (3), Sewell (6), Javery (7) vs LEONARD, Newhouser (4), Hughson (7)
Home Runs: Doerr-A, V.DiMaggio-N
Attendance: 31,938

For the first time, the All-Star Game was played at night. And for the only time in All-Star history, no Yankee played—although six had been named to the American League squad. But Yankee Joe McCarthy (serving for the sixth time as American manager) was piqued by criticism that he favored his own players, and retaliated by keeping them all on the bench.

The only DiMaggio in this wartime game was Pittsburgh's Vince, and he provided most of the National League power—going 3-for-3 with eight total bases and two of his team's three runs. But after the Nationals had jumped to a one-run lead in the first, Bobby Doerr of the Americans homered off Mort Cooper with two aboard in the second to put the American stars ahead. They added to their lead with a run in the third and another in the fifth. DiMaggio scored in the seventh after tripling off Tex Hughson and added a homer against Hughson in the ninth, but his heroics were not enough to overcome the American League's march to its third win in a row, and its eighth in 11 tries.

GAME 12
Forbes Field, Pittsburgh
July 11, 1944
NL, 7–1

AL	010 000 000	1	6 3
NL	000 040 21X	7	12 1

Pitchers: Borowy, HUGHSON (4), Muncrief (5), Newhouser (7), Newsom (8) vs Walters, RAFFENSBERGER (4), Sewell (6), Tobin (9)
Attendance: 29,589

For the second time the game was played at night, and for the seventh time Joe McCarthy managed the American League team. But this time—unlike Game 11—he let his Yankees play. He started Yankees pitcher Hank Borowy, who not only shut out the Nationals in his three innings, but drove in a run in the second to give his team the lead.

That was all the American stars got. For the first four innings it was enough, but in the fifth a double, four singles, a walk, an error, and a stolen base brought in four National League runs. In the seventh, Whitey Kurowski doubled in two more National runs, and in the eighth a missed third strike, two walks, and a flyball produced a seventh and final tally.

No home runs were hit in the game, only the second time that had happened in All-Star play. But Phil Cavarretta of the Nationals tripled—and reached base four additional times on a single and three walks for a new All-Star on-base record.

GAME 13
Fenway Park, Boston
July 9, 1946
AL, 12–0

NL	000 000 000	0	3 0
AL	200 130 24X	12	14 1

Pitchers: PASSEAU, Higbe (4), Blackwell (5), Sewell (8) vs FELLER, Newhouser (4), Kramer (7)
Home Runs: Keller-A, Williams-A (2)
Attendance: 34,906

No All-Star Game was played in 1945 because of restrictions on wartime travel, but when the classic resumed in 1946 the American stars avenged their 1944 loss with the most decisive All-Star victory to date: 12–0. American pitchers Bob Feller, Hal Newhouser, and Jack Kramer combined to hold the National stars to three singles and a walk, as their teammates pounded National pitching for 14 hits, including two doubles and three home runs.

But the game belonged to Ted Williams. Back after three years at war, and playing before his hometown fans, he equaled Phil

Cavarretta's 1944 on-base record in spectacular fashion, with one walk, two singles, and two home runs: one a drive into the center field bleachers and the other the first homer ever hit off Rip Sewell's looping "eephus" pitch. He scored the game's first run in the first inning as Charlie Keller followed his walk with a homer, and went on to break an All-Star record by scoring three more times, while driving in a record five runs.

GAME 14
Wrigley Field, Chicago
July 8, 1947
AL, 2–1

		R	H	E
AL	000 001 100	2	8	0
NL	000 100 000	1	5	1

Pitchers: Newhouser, SHEA (4), Masterson (7), Page (8) vs Blackwell, Brecheen (4), SAIN (7), Spahn (8)
Home Runs: Mize-N
Attendance: 41,123

Johnny Mize homered for the National League off rookie Spec Shea in the fourth inning for the game's first run, following three one-hit innings by the two lanky starters, Ewell Blackwell of the Nationals and Hal Newhouser of the Americans. Mize's run remained the only score until the sixth inning, when the American Leaguers tied the game on two singles and a double-play grounder.

Sharp baserunning by Bobby Doerr—plus a little luck—led to the Americans' second run an inning later. Doerr singled, then stole second. He took third when pitcher Johnny Sain's pickoff throw bounced off Doerr's back into the outfield. Pinch hitter Stan Spence then singled Doerr home with what proved to be the game's final—and winning—run. The Nationals put men on first and third in the eighth, but shortstop Lou Boudreau's spectacular stop of a hot grounder and sharp throw to first retired the side and ended the threat.

GAME 15
Sportsman's Park, St. Louis
July 13, 1948
AL, 5–2

		R	H	E
NL	200 000 000	2	8	0
AL	011 300 00X	5	6	0

Pitchers: Branca, SCHMITZ (4), Sain (4), Blackwell (6) vs Masterson, RASCHI (4), Coleman (7)
Home Runs: Musial-N, Evers-A
Attendance: 34,009

Vic Raschi pitched three shutout innings for the American stars and drove in two go-ahead runs with a fourth-inning single. The 5-2 win marked the third time since the All-Star Game originated in 1933—won its third classic in a row that the American League had three straight wins.

The Nationals scored first on Stan Musial's two-run homer in the top of the first. But that was all they got, as starter Walt Masterson settled down and shut out the Nationals through the second and third innings. Raschi then came on for his shutout stint, and Joe Coleman stopped the Nationals without even a hit over the final three innings.

Meanwhile, the Americans scored a run in the second on Hoot Evers' homer, and tied the game with another run in the third on two walks, a double steal, and an outfield fly. Then in the fourth, when two walks and a single had loaded the bases, pitcher Raschi singled in the third and fourth American runs. Joe DiMaggio's pinch-hit sacrifice fly scored a fifth run. Johnny Sain and Ewell Blackwell shut out the Americans the rest of the way, but the damage had been done.

GAME 16
Ebbets Field, Brooklyn
July 12, 1949
AL, 11–7

		R	H	E
AL	400 202 300	11	13	1
NL	212 002 000	7	12	5

Pitchers: Parnell, TRUCKS (2), Brissie (4), Raschi (7) vs Spahn, NEWCOMBE (2), Munger (5), Bickford (6), Pollet (7), Blackwell (8), Roe (9)
Home Runs: Musial-N, Kiner-N
Attendance: 32,577

Each team scored seven earned runs in this game which saw a total of 25 hits, including seven doubles and two home runs. But two first-inning National League errors let in four unearned American runs to provide the margin for the American League's fourth consecutive All-Star win. Stan Musial and Ralph Kiner each drove in two National runs with homers, but Eddie Joost singled in two runs for the Americans and Joe DiMaggio singled and doubled in three more to lead the American attack. For the second year in a row, Vic Raschi shut out the National stars for three innings, this time holding the American lead over the final third of the game.

The game was notable as the first to include black players: three Dodgers (Jackie Robinson, Roy Campanella, and Don Newcombe) for the National League, and Larry Doby for the American. With the Americans now ahead 12-4 in the series, it also marked the farthest extent of American League domination of the midsummer classic.

GAME 17
Comiskey Park, Chicago
July 11, 1950
NL, 4–3

		R	H	E
NL	020 000 001 000 01	4	10	0
AL	001 020 000 000 00	3	8	1

Pitchers: Roberts, Newcombe (4), Konstanty (6), Jansen (7), BLACKWELL (12) vs Raschi, Lemon (4), Houtteman (7), Reynolds (10), GRAY (13), Feller (14)
Home Runs: Kiner-N, Schoendienst-N
Attendance: 46,127

For the first time, the All-Star Game went into extra innings, and for the first time the National League won a game as the visiting team. Three pitchers each hurled three innings of shutout ball: Bob Lemon and Allie Reynolds for the American League and Ewell Blackwell (who finished the game and got the win) for the Nationals. But top pitching honors were earned by National Leaguer Larry Jansen, who struck out six and gave up only one hit over five shutout innings.

The National stars scored first with two runs in the second. The Americans came back with one in the third, and tied and took the lead in the fifth on George Kell's run-scoring fly and an RBI single by Ted Williams (who, it was later learned, had broken his left elbow making an off-the-wall catch in the first inning). But in the top of the ninth, Ralph Kiner of the Nationals hit a game-tying homer, and 4½ scoreless innings later Red Schoendienst—on the first pitch of the 14th inning—homered off American Leaguer Ted Gray with what proved to be the game winner.

GAME 18
Briggs Stadium, Detroit
July 10, 1951
NL, 8–3

		R	H	E
NL	100 302 110	8	12	1
AL	010 110 000	3	10	2

Pitchers: Roberts, MAGLIE (3), Newcombe (6), Blackwell (9) vs Garver, LOPAT (4), Hutchinson (5), Parnell (8), Lemon (9)
Home Runs: Musial-N, Elliott-N, Wertz-A, Kell-A, Hodges-N, Kiner-N
Attendance: 52,075

In a game moved from Philadelphia to help Detroit celebrate its 250th birthday, hometowners Vic Wertz and George Kell of the Tigers hit solo homers in the fourth and fifth innings to bring the American stars within a run of the Nationals. But they came no closer, as the National Leaguers pulled away for a convincing 8-3 victory.

The Nationals, aided by six innings of shutout pitching (including three by Don Newcombe), produced four home runs of their own to drive in six of their eight runs. With the score tied 1-1 going into the fourth inning, Stan Musial greeted Ed Lopat's first pitch with a shot to the right field upper deck. Bob Elliott added two more runs later in the inning with a homer to left. Gil Hodges increased the National League lead to 6–3 with a two-run homer in the sixth, and Ralph Kiner concluded the Nationals' scoring with a solo upper-deck shot to left center in the eighth. For the first time in All-Star play, the National League had won two games in a row.

GAME 19
Shibe Park, Philadelphia
July 8, 1952
NL, 3–2

		R	H	E
AL	000 20	2	5	0
NL	100 20	3	3	0

Pitchers: Raschi, LEMON (3), Shantz (5) vs Simmons, RUSH (4)
Home Runs: J.Robinson-N, Sauer-N
Attendance: 32,785

No sun shone for this rain-shortened game, but two hometown pitchers did. Curt Simmons of the Phillies held the American stars to one hit as he shut them out over the first three innings. And the Athletics' Bobby Shantz—in the midst of an MVP season—struck out the side in the fifth for the Americans.

But home runs and rain determined the final outcome. Jackie Robinson opened the scoring with a homer off Vic Raschi in the bottom of the first to give the Nationals a 1–0 lead. In the fourth the Americans came back to take the lead briefly with two runs on a double, a walk, and two singles off eventual winner Bob Rush. In the bottom of the inning, Hank Sauer's home run off Bob Lemon with one aboard returned the lead to the National League. And there it stayed through a scoreless fifth, when the rain, which had fallen throughout the game, at last brought the soggy festivities to the All-Star series' first premature conclusion.

GAME 20
Crosley Field, Cincinnati
July 14, 1953
NL, 5–1

		R	H	E
AL	000 000 001	1	5	0
NL	000 020 12X	5	10	0

Pitchers: Pierce, REYNOLDS (4), Garcia (6) Paige (8) vs Roberts, SPAHN (4), Simmons (6), Dickson (8)
Attendance: 30,846

For the first 4½ innings, pitchers for both sides held the opposition scoreless, with one hit each. Then the National Leaguers got to Allie

Reynolds for two runs in the bottom of the fifth on a hit batsman, a walk, and two singles.

This proved margin enough for the National League's fourth consecutive victory, as four National pitchers held the Americans to just two hits through eight innings before three singles in the ninth gave the American Leaguers their only run. For good measure, though, the National stars added a run in the seventh, and two more in the eighth (with three singles and a walk off Satchel Paige in his only All-Star appearance).

Enos Slaughter of the Nationals provided much of the game's excitement. With two singles, a walk, and a stolen base, he drove in one run and scored two others, and defensively made a spectacular diving catch in right field. Pee Wee Reese's double in the seventh (scoring Slaughter) was the game's only extra-base hit.

GAME 21
Municipal Stadium, Cleveland
July 13, 1954
AL, 11–9

NL	000	520	020	9	14	0
AL	004	121	03X	11	17	1

Pitchers: Roberts, Antonelli (4), Spahn (6), Grissom (6), CONLEY (8), Erskine (8) vs Ford, Consuegra (4), Lemon (4), Porterfield (5), Keegan (8), STONE (8), Trucks (9)
Home Runs: Rosen-A (2), Boone-A, Kluszewski-N, Bell-N, Doby-A
Attendance: 68,751

American starter Whitey Ford gave up only one hit in three shutout innings, and National starter Robin Roberts shut out the American stars through two. But in the bottom of the third Al Rosen tagged Roberts for a three-run homer, and Ray Boone followed with a solo shot. By the end of the game new All-Star records had been set for hits (31), runs (20), and pitchers used (13), and the record of six home runs had been equaled.

The Nationals topped the American four-run third with five straight hits off Sandy Consuegra in the fourth, for five runs. The Americans tied the game with a run in their half of the fourth, but Ted Kluszewski homered in the fifth for two more National League runs. In the bottom of the fifth, Rosen homered again, for two, to bring the Americans even again.

A run in the sixth put the Americans ahead, but Gus Bell's two-run blast in the eighth returned the Nationals to the top by one. They were threatening to lengthen that lead when Dean Stone entered the contest in relief of Bob Keegan with two out and Red Schoendienst on third. Before Stone's first delivery, Schoendienst broke for home and was tagged out, setting the stage for Stone to become the winning pitcher without retiring a batter. Larry Doby tied it up for the American League later in the eighth with a home run, and Nellie Fox drove in the game's final two runs a few batters later with a bases-loaded single.

In the ninth, the Nationals' Stan Musial blasted two over the fence—both foul—with a man aboard. But Virgil Trucks retired him and Gil Hodges to preserve the American League's first victory in five games.

GAME 22
County Stadium, Milwaukee
July 12, 1955
NL, 6–5

AL	400	001	000	000	5	10	2
NL	000	000	230	001	6	13	1

Pitchers: Pierce, Wynn (4), Ford (7), SULLIVAN (8) vs Roberts, Haddix (4), Newcombe (7), Jones (8), Nuxhall (8), CONLEY (12)
Home Runs: Mantle-A, Musial-N
Attendance: 45,314

Down 5–0 in the seventh inning, the National Leaguers came back to tie the game and send it into extra innings. The Americans attacked early, scoring four runs off Robin Roberts (three of them on Mickey Mantle's home run to center) before the game's first out had been recorded. They added a fifth run in the sixth inning. Meanwhile, pitchers Billy Pierce and Early Wynn were shutting the Nationals down on four hits.

In the seventh, though, two singles, a walk, and an American error gave the Nationals two runs. In the eighth, four two-out singles and another error tied the game. Joe Nuxhall for the Nationals and the Americans' Frank Sullivan prevented further scoring through the 11th. In the top of the 12th, Gene Conley replaced Nuxhall and struck out the side: Al Kaline, Mickey Vernon, and Al Rosen. Sullivan returned for the Americans to face Stan Musial in the bottom of the 12th. Musial hit the first pitch—a fastball—over the screen in right and the game was over.

GAME 23
Griffith Stadium, Washington
July 10, 1956
NL, 7–3

NL	001	211	200	7	11	0
AL	000	003	000	3	11	0

Pitchers: FRIEND, Spahn (4), Antonelli (6) vs PIERCE, Ford (4), Wilson (5), Brewer (6), Score (8), Wynn (9)
Home Runs: Mays-N, Williams-A, Mantle-A, Musial-N
Attendance: 28,843

Four of the game's greatest sluggers—Willie Mays, Stan Musial, Ted Williams, and Mickey Mantle—hit home runs, three of them off two of the game's greatest pitchers—Whitey Ford and Warren Spahn. But the star of the game was National League third baseman Ken Boyer, who went 3-for-5, scoring one run and driving in another, while making three spectacular diving and leaping plays in the field.

The National stars scored five times—including twice in the fourth on Mays's homer off Ford—before the Americans put a run on the board. But in the bottom of the sixth, Williams homered for two runs off Spahn, and Mantle followed him with another homer to bring the Americans within two. But that was the end of their scoring, as Johnny Antonelli relieved Spahn to stop the American stars the rest of the way. The Nationals scored twice more in the seventh—one of the runs coming on Musial's homer—ensuring them a comfortable 7–3 victory.

GAME 24
Sportsman's Park, St. Louis
July 9, 1957
AL, 6–5

AL	020	001	003	6	10	0
NL	000	000	203	5	9	1

Pitchers: BUNNING, Loes (4), Wynn (7), Pierce (7), Mossi (9), Grim (9) vs SIMMONS, Burdette (2), Sanford (6), Jackson (7), Labine (9)
Attendance: 30,693

Cincinnati fans stuffed the ballot boxes and elected Reds to start everywhere but first base. Commissioner Ford Frick removed two elected starters, but left five Reds in the lineup. They could not bring the National League the victory, though.

The Americans scored twice in the second on singles and walks to take a lead they held to the finish. Although reliever Lew Burdette—after walking in the second run—stopped the American stars through the fifth, Jim Bunning and Billy Loes were combining to keep the Nationals from scoring through the first six innings. The Americans, meanwhile, added a third run in the top of the sixth on a double, a wild pitch, and a single.

The Nationals scored their first two in the seventh, on two singles and a double, to draw within a run of a tie. But in the top of the ninth the Americans combined two singles, an error, a sacrifice bunt, and Minnie Minoso's pinch double for three more runs. They needed them all because the Nationals responded in their half of the ninth with three runs of their own on a blend of walks, hits (including Willie Mays's triple), and a wild pitch. With two out and a runner at second, Gil Hodges lined one deep to left-center. But Minoso, now in left field, snared the drive on the run to end the game.

GAME 25
Memorial Stadium, Baltimore
July 8, 1958
AL, 4–3

NL	210	000	000	3	4	2
AL	110	011	00X	4	9	2

Pitchers: Spahn, FRIEND (4), Jackson (6), Farrell (7) vs Turley, Narleski (2), WYNN (6), O'Dell (7)
Attendance: 48,829

Although American League pitchers held the National Leaguers to only four hits (all singles), the Nationals took a quick lead, and held it for half the game before they were overtaken. Willie Mays and Stan Musial singled in the top of the first, both scoring as American starter Bob Turley proceeded to give up a sacrifice fly, hit a batter, walk a man, and unload a wild pitch.

The Americans came back with one run in their half of the first, but the Nationals drove Turley out with their third run as Mays (who had reached on a fielder's choice) worked his way around the bases on a steal, an error, and Bob Skinner's single. Once again the Americans answered with a run, but they didn't tie the game until Mickey Vernon scored on a bases-loaded ground out in the fifth. An inning later they took the lead when pinch hitter Gil McDougald singled home Frank Malzone.

Billy O'Dell set down the Nationals in order over the final three innings to preserve the lead and give the American Leaguers their second consecutive victory. It would take more than 30 years before the American League could again claim consecutive All-Star victories.

GAME 26
Forbes Field, Pittsburgh
July 7, 1959
NL, 5–4

AL	000	100	030	4	8	0
NL	100	000	22X	5	9	1

Pitchers: Wynn, Duren (4), Bunning (7), FORD (8), Daley (8) vs Drysdale, Burdette (4), Face (7), ANTONELLI (8), Elston (9)
Home Runs: Mathews-N, Kaline-A
Attendance: 35,277

For the third year in a row, the game was decided by one run, with the National League celebrating the city of Pittsburgh's bicentennial by breaking the American League's win streak at two.

Eddie Mathews homered for the Nationals in the bottom of the first for the only run in the first three innings, as Don Drysdale stopped the Americans without a hit or walk, fanning four. Al Kaline tied the game in the top of the fourth with an American home run for the only score of the middle three innings, as Ryne Duren one-hit the Nationals. Like Drysdale, Duren fanned four.

In the last of the seventh, though, a double and two singles off Jim Bunning put the Nationals ahead by two runs. The NL lead lasted only briefly, however, as the Americans moved back into the lead with three runs in the eighth off Roy Face, with two singles, a walk, and a double after Face had retired the first two men. But in their half of the eighth the Nationals hit Whitey Ford, tying the game with a single-sacrifice-single, and scoring the game winner on Willie Mays' triple to center.

GAME 27
Memorial Coliseum, Los Angeles
August 3, 1959
AL, 5–3

AL	012	000	110	5	6	0
NL	100	010	100	3	6	3

Pitchers: WALKER, Wynn (4), Wilhelm, (6), O'Dell (7), McLish (8) vs DRYSDALE, Conley (4), Jones (6), Face (8)
Home Runs: Malzone-A, Berra-A, F. Robinson-N, Gilliam-N, Colavito-A
Attendance: 55,105

To raise extra money for the players' pension fund and other causes, a second All-Star Game was scheduled for 1959, the first ever to be played in August, and the first on the West Coast. The American stars avenged their earlier defeat with a 5–3 win, out-homering the Nationals three to two.

The National Leaguers scored first on a first-inning double and sacrifice fly, but Frank Malzone tied the score with the game's first home run. Yogi Berra homered an inning later with one on for a 3–1 American lead, but Frank Robinson brought the Nationals back to within one with his homer in the fifth. The Americans replaced that run in the top of the seventh on a walk, two errors, and a single, but Junior Gilliam countered with a home run in the last of the inning. Rocky Colavito scored the game's final run for the Americans in the eighth with the game's final homer.

Don Drysdale, the pitching standout of the July game, struck out five this time, but also walked three and gave up three runs on homers to take the loss.

GAME 28
Municipal Stadium, Kansas City
July 11, 1960
NL, 5–3

NL	311	000	000	5	12	4
AL	000	001	020	3	6	1

Pitchers: FRIEND, McCormick (4), Face (6), Buhl (8), Law (9) vs MONBOUQUETTE, Estrada (3), Coates (4), Bell (6), Lary (8), Daley (9)
Home Runs: Banks-N, Crandall-N, Kaline-A
Attendance: 30,619

The day was hot—the temperature broke 100—and so were the National League bats. Willie Mays had three hits, including a leadoff triple and a double; Ernie Banks homered and doubled; Del Crandall homered and singled; and Joe Adcock doubled and singled for three-fourths of the Nationals' 12 hits. The National League scored five unanswered runs in the first three innings to take an unbeatable lead. Starter Bob Friend, meanwhile, blanked the Americans on one hit through three innings and Mike McCormick held them scoreless for two more before yielding the first American run in the sixth on Nellie Fox's bases-loaded single. Roy Face then came on to douse the fire, getting Luis Aparicio to ground into a double play.

Four American League pitchers stopped the National stars after the third inning, and Al Kaline homered for two more American runs in the eighth. In the ninth the Americans put men on first and second with one away. But their comeback fell short, as Vern Law came on to retire Brooks Robinson and Harvey Kuenn and preserve the National victory.

GAME 29
Yankee Stadium, New York
July 13, 1960
NL, 6–0

NL	021	000	102	6	10	0
AL	000	000	000	0	8	0

Pitchers: LAW, Podres (3), S.Williams (5), Jackson (7), Henry (8), McDaniel (9) vs FORD, Wynn (4), Staley (6), Lary (8), Bell (9)
Home Runs: Mathews-N, Mays-N, Musial-N, Boyer-N
Attendance: 38,362

Only two days after the first All-Star Game, the squads met a second time before fewer than 39,000 fans in capacious Yankee Stadium. It was no contest. Vern Law, who had completed and saved the first game, started and won this one. His two shutout innings set the pace for the five National pitchers who followed him to fashion the first National League shutout in 20 years. The American stars got only two fewer hits than the Nationals, but only one was for extra bases, whereas four of the National League hits were home runs.

Eddie Mathews began the scoring with a two-run homer in the second, and Willie Mays (on his way to a second straight 3-for-4 game) homered for the third National run an inning later. No one scored through the three middle innings, but in the seventh Stan Musial broke his own record with his sixth All-Star homer—a mighty shot three tiers up in right—and in the ninth Ken Boyer completed the rout with a two-run shot to left.

GAME 30
Candlestick Park, San Francisco
July 11, 1961
NL, 5–4

AL	000	001	002	1	4	4	2
NL	010	100	010	2	5	11	5

Pitchers: Ford, Lary (4), Donovan (4), Bunning (6), Fornieles (8), WILHELM (8) vs Spahn, Purkey (4), McCormick (6), Face (9), Koufax (9), MILLER (9)
Home Runs: Killebrew-A, Altman-N
Attendance: 44,115

National League pitchers began the game where they had left off the year before. For five innings Warren Spahn and Bob Purkey shut out the American stars without a hit or base on balls. In the sixth, Harmon Killebrew homered off Mike McCormick to end the American drought, but it was the only hit McCormick yielded through the eighth.

Meanwhile, the Nationals had taken a 3–1 lead with runs in the second and fourth innings and George Altman's homer in the eighth. But in the top of the ninth, Candlestick's notorious winds helped put the Americans back in the game. Their second and third hits of the game brought in one run, and their fourth (and last) hit put another man on base. The tying run came in when the wind blew pitcher Stu Miller off the mound for a balk to advance the runners, and then twisted a grounder out of third baseman Ken Boyer's grasp for a run-scoring error. In the 10th, the wind may have contributed to the Americans' go-ahead run as Boyer's throw to first sailed into the outfield, allowing Nellie Fox (who had walked) to score from first.

But in the last of the 10th the wind finally came to the aid of the Nationals, rendering useless the famous knuckleball of American reliever Hoyt Wilhelm, who gave up the tying run on hits by Hank Aaron and Willie Mays and lost the game when Roberto Clemente singled in Mays from second.

GAME 31
Fenway Park, Boston
July 31, 1961
Tie, 1–1

NL	000	001	000	1	5	1
AL	100	000	000	1	4	0

Pitchers: Purkey, Mahaffey (3), Koufax (5), Miller (7) vs Bunning, Schwall (4), Pascual (7)
Home Runs: Colavito-A
Attendance: 31,851

In the second All-Star Game of 1961, the weather again played a crucial role, as heavy rain at the end of the ninth inning forced the first (and, so far, only) All-Star tie.

Rocky Colavito's home run for the Americans in the first inning turned out to be his squad's only run, as four National League pitchers combined to shut out the American stars on only three singles the rest of the way. The American League pitching was just as effective, with starter Jim Bunning and finisher Camilo Pascual each pitching three no-hit innings. Don Schwall, who pitched the middle three innings, gave up all five National League hits and the Nationals' one run. But even that might have been prevented.

In the sixth, with two on and two out, American League shortstop Luis Aparicio waited for a slow grounder, failing to get the ball in time to throw the batter out and end the inning. The Nationals scored when Bill White followed with a hot ground single up the middle. Aparicio made a brilliant stop on White's ball to prevent more than one run from scoring, but it did drive in the game's tying—and final—run.

GAME 32
D.C. Stadium, Washington
July 10, 1962
NL, 3–1

NL	000 002 010	3	8	0
AL	000 001 000	1	4	0

MVP: Willis-N
Pitchers: Drysdale, MARICHAL (4), Purkey (6), Shaw (8) vs Bunning, PASCUAL (4), Donovan (7), Pappas (9)
Attendance: 45,480

The stadium was new, President John F. Kennedy threw out the first ball, and starters Don Drysdale of the Nationals and Jim Bunning of the Americans both pitched three innings of one-hit shutout ball. But Maury Wills stole the show. Entering the game in the sixth inning to run for 41-year-old Stan Musial, who had singled, Wills stole second, then scored on Dick Groat's single up the middle for the game's first run. Another single, a long fly out, and a ground out scored Groat with the second (and, as it turned out, winning) run.

Two singles and a fly out by Roger Maris brought in an American run in the bottom of the sixth off Bob Purkey. But that was all they got, as Purkey and Bob Shaw one-hit the American stars through the final three innings.

In the eighth inning Wills manufactured an insurance run for the Nationals. On first with a leadoff single, he somehow reached third on Jim Davenport's single to short left, racing from second to third as left fielder Rocky Colavito threw in to second. He scored after tagging on a foul out to right. Wills earned All-Star Most Valuable Player honors in the first year it was awarded.

GAME 33
Wrigley Field, Chicago
July 30, 1962
AL, 9–4

AL	001 201 302	9	10	0
NL	010 000 111	4	10	4

MVP: Wagner-A
Pitchers: Stenhouse, HERBERT (3), Aguirre (6), Pappas (9) vs Podres, MAHAFFEY (3), Gibson (5), Farrell (7), Marichal (8)
Home Runs: Runnels-A, Wagner-A. Colavito-A, Roseboro-N
Attendance: 38,359

With this second game of 1962, the leagues ended their four-year experiment of playing two All-Star games a year. The Americans out-homered the Nationals to spoil the National League's attempt to even the series at 16 wins apiece. But no matter—the American stars would win only once again in the next 20 years.

The National stars scored first on a double and single in the second, but Pete Runnels evened the score in the third with a solo homer, and Leon Wagner put the Americans ahead with a two-run shot an inning later. After Tom Tresh doubled home a fourth American run in the sixth, Rocky Colavito put the game out of reach with a three-run blast in the seventh.

The Nationals tried to come back with runs in the seventh and eighth, but the Americans neutralized them with two more of their own in the ninth (on two errors, two Juan Marichal wild pitches, a double, and a long fly out). With the score now 9-3, John Roseboro's solo homer in the last of the ninth put the Nationals in the home-run column, but that was all.

GAME 34
Municipal Stadium, Cleveland
July 9, 1963
NL, 5–3

NL	012 010 010	5	6	0
AL	012 000 000	3	11	1

MVP: Mays-N
Pitchers: O'Toole, JACKSON (3), Culp (5), Woodeshick (6), Drysdale (8) vs McBride, BUNNING (4), Bouton (6), Pizarro (7), Radatz (8)
Attendance: 44,160

Willie Mays sparked the National League to victory with his baserunning and timely hitting. Although he had only one hit—a single—he scored two runs and drove in two others in the Nationals' 5–3 win.

The National stars scored first when Mays walked in the second inning, stole second, and came in on a single by Dick Groat. The Americans tied the game in the last of the second, but in the top of the third Mays singled in one run, stole second again, and scored his second run on Ed Bailey's single.

Once again the Americans came back in the bottom of the third to tie the game on Albie Pearson's double, followed by two singles sandwiched around an infield out. But these were their last runs, as four National pitchers shut them out on four singles the rest of the way. Meanwhile, Mays drove in what proved to be the winning run with a ground out in the fifth. In the eighth the Nationals scored a final run when Ron Santo singled home Bill White, who had singled and stolen second.

GAME 35
Shea Stadium, New York
July 7, 1964
NL, 7–4

AL	100 002 100	4	9	1
NL	000 210 004	7	8	0

MVP: Callison-N
Pitchers: Chance, Wyatt (4), Pascual (5), RADATZ (7) vs Drysdale, Bunning (4), Short (6), Farrell (7), MARICHAL (9)
Home Runs: B.Williams-N, Boyer-N, Callison-N
Attendance: 50,850

A new stadium in the midst of a World's Fair was the venue for this game in which the National League at last drew even with the American at 17 wins apiece.

The American stars jumped into the lead with an unearned run in the first, but the Nationals (after Dean Chance had shut them out through three innings) overtook the Americans in the fourth, on home runs by Billy Williams and Ken Boyer, and Dick Groat doubled in a third run in the fifth. In the top of the sixth the Americans tied the score when Brooks Robinson tripled in a pair, and took the lead again an inning later on a sacrifice fly that barely scored Elston Howard ahead of Willie Mays's throw from center.

The Americans held their slim lead into the bottom of the ninth. But Mays walked (after fouling off five third strikes), stole second, and scored the tying run on a single to short right and an errant throw home. One intentional walk and two outs later, Johnny Callison hit Dick Radatz's fastball over the fence in right to win the game.

GAME 36
Metropolitan Stadium, Bloomington, Minnesota
July 13, 1965
NL, 6–5

NL	320 000 100	6	11	0
AL	000 140 000	5	8	0

MVP: Marichal-N
Pitchers: Marichal, Maloney (4), Drysdale (5), KOUFAX (6), Farrell (7), Gibson (8) vs Pappas, Grant (2), Richert (4), McDOWELL (6), Fisher (8)
Home Runs: Mays-N, Torre-N, Stargell-N, McAuliffe-A, Killebrew-A
Attendance: 46,706

For a while it looked as though the Nationals would run away with the game. Willie Mays led off with a home run in the first, and Joe Torre added two runs with a homer later in the inning. In the second Willie Stargell homered for two more runs to make the score 5-0. National starter Juan Marichal stopped the Americans on one hit through three innings.

But the American stars battled back. A single, a walk, and another single off Marichal's replacement, Jim Maloney, brought in one run in the fourth. Maloney retired the first two men in the fifth, but then he gave up a walk followed by a home run to Dick McAuliffe, and a scratch single followed by a Harmon Killebrew homer—and the score was tied at 5-5.

Only one more run was scored. In the seventh, Willie Mays, who had walked and gone to third on Hank Aaron's single, scored on Ron Santo's infield hit to short. The Nationals held off American threats in the eighth and ninth to take the All-Star series lead for the first time.

GAME 37
Busch Memorial Stadium, St. Louis
July 12, 1966
NL, 2–1

AL	010 000 000 0	1	6	0
NL	000 100 000 1	2	6	0

MVP: B. Robinson-A
Pitchers: McLain, Kaat (4), Stottlemyre (6), Siebert (8), RICHERT (10) vs Koufax, Bunning (4), Marichal (6), G.PERRY (9)
Attendance: 49,936

The celebration of another new stadium and the city's bicentennial—and a temperature of 106 degrees Fahrenheit—greeted participants in the 1966 classic. Pitching dominated: seven pitchers hurled two innings or more each of shutout ball. American starter Denny McLain threw three perfect innings, but the National League's Sandy Koufax gave the Americans a run in the second when he let loose a wild pitch after Brooks Robinson had tripled.

The Nationals tied the score in the fourth with three singles off Jim Kaat, but that ended the scoring for both sides through the regulation nine innings. Gaylord Perry stopped the American stars in the top of the 10th, but in the last half of the inning, National Leaguer Tim McCarver singled off Pete Richert, was sacrificed to second, and came across with the winning run on Maury Wills's single to right.

GAME 38
Anaheim Stadium, Anaheim, California
July 11, 1967
NL, 2–1

		R	H	E
NL	010 000 000 000 001	2	9	0
AL	000 001 000 000 000	1	8	0

MVP: Perez-N
Pitchers: Marichal, Jenkins (4), Gibson (7), Short (9), Cuellar (11), DRYSDALE (13), Seaver (15) vs Chance, McGlothlin (4), Peters (6), Downing (9), HUNTER (11)
Home Runs: Allen-N, B.Robinson-A, Perez-N
Attendance: 46,309

This was a game of strikeouts, home runs, and extra innings. Every one of the dozen pitchers used in the game struck out at least one batter. American Leaguers Gary Peters (who pitched three perfect middle innings) and Catfish Hunter struck out four apiece, while Ferguson Jenkins of the Nationals tied the All-Star record with six. The game total of 30 strikeouts shattered the previous record of 20 set in 1955.

Apart from the splendid pitching, three home runs provided the only excitement—and the only scoring—in this longest All-Star Game. Richie Allen of the Nationals scored first, homering to center off Dean Chance in the second inning. The Americans' Brooks Robinson tied the score in the sixth with a shot off Jenkins. And 8½ innings later, in the top of the 15th, National Leaguer Tony Perez homered off Hunter for the game's third and final run. Tom Seaver set down the Americans in the bottom of the inning, and the game—after a record three hours and 41 minutes—was history.

GAME 39
Astrodome, Houston
July 9, 1968
NL, 1–0

		R	H	E
AL	000 000 000	0	3	1
NL	100 000 00X	1	5	0

MVP: Mays-N
Pitchers: TIANT, Odom (3), McLain (5), McDowell (7), Stottlemyre (8), John (8) vs DRYSDALE, Marichal (4), Carlton (6), Seaver (7), Reed (9), Koosman (9)
Attendance: 48,321

This game could be described by what was missing: fresh air and real grass (it was the first All-Star Game held indoors), hitting (the eight hits were a new low for a nine-inning All-Star Game), and earned runs (the game's only run came with the help of an error). In fact, if it weren't for 37-year-old Willie Mays, the game might not have had any runs at all. Starting only because of an injury to Pete Rose, National Leaguer Mays led off the bottom of the first with a single, and took second when first baseman Harmon Killebrew mishandled pitcher Luis Tiant's pickoff throw for an error. Mays took third as the rattled Tiant threw a wild pitch to walk Curt Flood, and scored when Willie McCovey grounded into a double play. Mays became the first two-time All-Star MVP, having also won the award in 1963.

The pitching on both sides was superb, but the National Leaguers shone especially bright. Tom Seaver gave up two of the Americans' three hits (all of which were doubles), but struck out five in his two innings. Juan Marichal hurled two perfect innings, fanning three. And none of the six National pitchers walked a man. One American, Killebrew, couldn't walk. Stretching for a throw at first, the slugger tore a hamstring and missed the next two months, the most serious All-Star Game casualty since Ted Williams's broken elbow 18 years earlier.

GAME 40
R.F.K. Memorial Stadium, Washington, D.C.
July 23, 1969
NL, 9–3

		R	H	E
NL	125 100 000	9	11	0
AL	011 100 000	3	6	2

MVP: McCovey-N
Pitchers: CARLTON, Gibson (4), Singer (5), Koosman (7), Dierker (8), P.Niekro (9) vs STOTTLEMYRE, Odom (3), Knowles (3), McLain (4), McNally (5), McDowell (7), Culp (9)
Home Runs: Bench-N, Howard-A, McCovey-N (2), Freehan-A
Attendance: 45,259

After four one-run victories in a row, the National Leaguers finally broke loose, massing 10 of their 11 hits in the first four innings for nine runs and a crushing win. Scoring an unearned run in the first on a dropped outfield fly, and two in the second on Johnny Bench's home run, the Nationals erupted in the third for five runs off Blue Moon Odom before two outs had been recorded. Willie McCovey's two-run homer began the third-inning scoring, and an error, single, and two doubles added three more runs before Odom was mercifully relieved. McCovey homered again in the fourth for the Nationals' final tally.

The American bats were not wholly silent, but the solo homers by Frank Howard and Bill Freehan in the second and third, and a third run in the fourth, couldn't counter the Nationals' attack.

The final five innings of the game were as quiet as the opening four had been noisy. No runs scored, and the two teams together managed only three hits.

GAME 41
Riverfront Stadium, Cincinnati
July 14, 1970
NL, 5–4

		R	H	E
AL	000 001 120 000	4	12	0
NL	000 000 103 001	5	10	0

MVP: Yastrzemski-A
Pitchers: Palmer, McDowell (4), J.Perry (7), Hunter (9), Peterson (9), Stottlemyre (9), WRIGHT (11) vs Seaver, Merritt (4), G.Perry (6), Gibson (8), OSTEEN (10)
Home Runs: Dietz-N
Attendance: 51,838

In a new stadium opened only two weeks earlier, no one scored for the first five innings, as Jim Palmer and Sam McDowell of the Americans and Tom Seaver and Jim Merritt of the Nationals held the opposition to two hits per team. The Americans finally scored a run in the sixth, and another in the seventh. The Nationals got one back in the last of the seventh, but the Americans increased their lead to 4–1 in the eighth when Brooks Robinson tripled home two baserunners.

Fans had already begun to leave the park when the Nationals' Dick Dietz homered off Catfish Hunter to lead off the last of the ninth. Two pitchers, three singles, and a sacrifice fly later, the game was tied and headed for extra innings. Claude Osteen held the Americans scoreless from the 10th through the 12th, and the Nationals also failed to score in the 10th and 11th. But in the last of the 12th, with two out, Pete Rose, Billy Grabarkewitz, and Jim Hickman singled. Hometowner Rose, racing home from second on Hickman's hit, crashed into catcher Ray Fosse with a force that injured both players and still provokes controversy—but which also gave the National League its eighth straight victory.

GAME 42
Tiger Stadium, Detroit
July 13, 1971
AL, 6–4

		R	H	E
NL	021 000 010	4	5	0
AL	004 002 00X	6	7	0

MVP: F. Robinson-A
Pitchers: ELLIS, Marichal (4), Jenkins (6), Wilson (7) vs BLUE, Palmer (4), Cuellar (6), Lolich (8)
Home Runs: Bench-N, Aaron-N, Jackson-A, F.Robinson-A, Killebrew-A, Clemente-N
Attendance: 53,559

With an assist from a favorable wind, six all-time greats homered to account for all the scoring as the American League broke its eight-game All-Star drought with a 6-4 victory. Johnny Bench put the Nationals in front with a two-run homer in the second inning off Vida Blue, and Hank Aaron—with his first All-Star home run—added a third run off Blue an inning later. But the Americans, shut out by Dock Ellis through the first two innings, rocked him in the bottom of the third as Reggie Jackson and Frank Robinson wrested the lead from the Nationals with a pair of two-run homers. Robinson's blast made him the first player to hit an All-Star home run for both leagues and Jackson's memorable homer hit the light tower atop the second deck of the stadium in right-center.

Ferguson Jenkins yielded the game's fifth homer, Harmon Killebrew's two-run shot for the Americans in the sixth. Roberto Clemente brought the Nationals a run closer with his solo homer off Mickey Lolich in the eighth, but that ended the team's scoring, and (for a year, anyway) the National League's All-Star stranglehold.

GAME 43
Atlanta-Fulton County Stadium, Atlanta
July 25, 1972
NL, 4–3

		R	H	E
AL	001 000 020 0	3	6	0
NL	000 002 001 1	4	8	0

MVP: Morgan-N
Pitchers: Palmer, Lolich (4), G.Perry (6), Wood (8), McNALLY (10) vs Gibson, Blass (3), Sutton (4), Carlton (6), Stoneman (7), McGRAW (9)
Home Runs: Aaron-N, Rojas-A
Attendance: 53,107

The American Leaguers tried to extend their All-Star win streak to two games, and for a time it looked as though they might do it. In the third, they scored the only run of the first half of the game as Jim Palmer and Mickey Lolich held the Nationals to two hits through the first five innings. In the sixth Hank Aaron thrilled the hometown crowd with a two-run homer deep to left to shift the lead to the National League. But Cookie Rojas restored the American lead with his own two-run shot in the eighth.

The Americans held their lead into the bottom of the ninth, but after two singles and a force out, the score was tied. Tug McGraw set down the American stars in order in the 10th, but American reliever Dave McNally was not so fortunate. He walked leadoff batter Nate Colbert, who was sacrificed to second. Joe Morgan then sent the American Leaguers back into the ranks of losers with a sharp RBI single to right center. His single also gave the Nationals their seventh win in seven extra-inning games.

GAME 44
Royals Stadium, Kansas City
July 24, 1973
NL, 7–1

				R	H	E
NL	002	122	000	7	10	0
AL	010	000	000	1	5	0

MVP: Bonds-N
Pitchers: WISE, Osteen (3), Sutton (5), Twitchell (6), Giusti (7), Seaver (8), Brewer (9) vs Hunter, Holtzman (2), BLYLEVEN (3), Singer (4), Ryan (6), Lyle (8), Fingers (9)
Home Runs: Bench-N, Bonds-N, W.Davis-N
Attendance: 40,849

Once again a new stadium was chosen to host the All-Star Game, and once again the National League emerged victorious. The Americans scored first, with a run in the second when Reggie Jackson scored from second on a single after doubling off the center field wall. But that was the beginning and end of their offense, as six National pitchers shut them out on three hits the rest of the way.

Meanwhile the National League hitters came to life, producing seven runs in four innings. Two walks and two singles in the third brought in two runs, and Johnny Bench's homer in the fourth made the score 3–1. In the fifth, Bobby Bonds—in the midst of his finest season—homered for two more National runs. And in the sixth, Willie Davis' home run completed the game's scoring, bringing in the Nationals' sixth and seventh runs.

The final third of the game was anticlimactic, as only two hits were made after the sixth inning. But Bonds brought the crowd to life briefly in the seventh, stretching one of those hits into a double with some audacious baserunning (ensuring his selection as the game's MVP).

GAME 45
Three Rivers Stadium, Pittsburgh
July 23, 1974
NL, 7–2

				R	H	E
AL	002	000	000	2	4	1
NL	010	210	12X	7	10	1

MVP: Garvey-N
Pitchers: G.Perry, TIANT (4), Hunter (6), Fingers (8) vs Messersmith, BRETT (4), Matlack (6), McGlothen (7), Marshall (8)
Home Runs: R.Smith-N
Attendance: 50,706

Steve Garvey, who was elected to the National League starting lineup on write-in votes (his name was omitted from the fans' All-Star ballot), sparked the Nationals to yet another convincing win over the hapless American stars. After singling in the second inning, Garvey scored the game's first run on Ron Cey's double.

The Americans took the lead with two runs in the top of the third, capitalizing on two walks and an error sandwiched between Thurman Munson's leadoff double and Dick Allen's single. They might have scored more had not Garvey snared Bobby Murcer's hot grounder for an assist on the third out.

Garvey doubled in the tying run in the fourth, and Cey's RBI groundout restored the Nationals' lead. Lou Brock added a run in the fifth with a single and some inspired baserunning, and Reggie Smith homered in the seventh. Don Kessinger's triple and a wild pitch by Rollie Fingers in the eighth contributed to two final National League runs.

GAME 46
County Stadium, Milwaukee
July 15, 1975
NL, 6–3

				R	H	E
NL	021	000	003	6	13	1
AL	000	003	000	3	10	1

MVP: Matlack-N, Madlock-N
Pitchers: Reuss, Sutton (4), Seaver (6), MATLACK (7), R.Jones (9) vs Blue, Busby (3), Kaat (5), HUNTER (7), Gossage (9)
Home Runs: Garvey-N, Wynn-N, Yastrzemski-A
Attendance: 51,480

When National stars Steve Garvey and Jim Wynn led off the second with back-to-back homers and their teammates added another run in the third, it looked as if the National League might be on its way to another easy win. But the American pitchers shut down the National League offense for the next five innings, and Carl Yastrzemski made a contest of it with a three-run homer in the sixth off Tom Seaver to tie the score.

In the top of the ninth, though, the Americans all but gave the game away. Left fielder Claudell Washington dropped a fly on the run (it was scored a hit) and misplayed a line drive that went for a double. Goose Gossage came in to relieve Catfish Hunter on the mound and hit the next batter to load the bases. Bill Madlock then drove in two of the baserunners with a single through the drawn-in infield, and Pete Rose knocked in the third run of the inning with a sacrifice fly.

Randy Jones set the Americans down in order in the bottom of the ninth, and—*voilà!*—the National League had won again.

GAME 47
Veterans Stadium, Philadelphia
July 13, 1976
NL, 7–1

				R	H	E
AL	000	100	000	1	5	0
NL	202	000	03X	7	10	0

MVP: Foster-N
Pitchers: FIDRYCH, Hunter (3), Tiant (5), Tanana (7) vs R.JONES, Seaver (4), Montefusco (6), Rhoden (8), K.Forsch (9)
Home Runs: Foster-N, Lynn-A, Cedeno-N
Attendance: 63,974

Tom Seaver gave up a home run to Fred Lynn in the fourth inning, but that was the Americans' only score as the Nationals held the American stars to five hits while celebrating the nation's bicentennial with 10 hits and seven runs.

Rookie standout Mark Fidrych was chosen to start for the Americans and was promptly rapped for two runs. Pete Rose led off with a single and was tripled home by Steve Garvey, who scored himself on a groundout. The Nationals doubled their score in the third inning as George Foster tagged Catfish Hunter for two runs with a mighty home run to left center, and capped their assault with three more in the eighth off Frank Tanana, including a two-run homer by Cesar Cedeno.

The fans had elected five members of Cincinnati's "Big Red Machine" to the National League starting lineup, and Sparky Anderson, the Reds' and National squad's manager, added two more. They provided the bulk of the Nationals' offense, with seven hits, four RBIs, and four runs scored.

GAME 48
Yankee Stadium, New York
July 19, 1977
NL, 7–5

				R	H	E
NL	401	000	020	7	9	1
AL	000	002	102	5	8	0

MVP: Sutton-N
Pitchers: SUTTON, Lavelle (4), Seaver (6), R.Reuschel (8), Gossage (9) vs PALMER, Kern (3), Eckersley (4), LaRoche (6), Campbell (7), Lyle (8)
Home Runs: Morgan-N, Luzinski-N, Garvey-N, Scott-A
Attendance: 56,683

The Nationals' Joe Morgan homered off Jim Palmer to open the game, and before Palmer escaped the first inning three more National Leaguers had crossed the plate on a single, double, and Greg Luzinski's homer. Palmer got through the second inning without further damage, but before he was relieved in the third, Steve Garvey had homered to give the Nationals a 5–0 lead.

The Americans fought back against Tom Seaver in the sixth and seventh. Seaver retired two in the sixth, but then gave up two singles, and two runs as Richie Zisk doubled the runners home. Two more singles in the seventh produced a third American run.

But the Nationals—assisted by pitcher Sparky Lyle's wild pitch and hit batsman—put a sixth and seventh run on the board in the eighth with a double and single. The Americans added two final runs of their own in the bottom of the ninth on George Scott's homer off Goose Gossage, but fell short of victory once again.

GAME 49
San Diego Stadium,
July 11, 1978
NL, 7–3

				R	H	E
AL	201	000	000	3	8	1
NL	003	000	04X	7	10	0

MVP: Garvey-N
Pitchers: Palmer, Keough (3), Sorensen (4), Kern (7), Guidry (7), GOSSAGE (8) vs Blue, Rogers (4), Fingers (6), SUTTER (8), P. Niekro (9)
Attendance: 51,549

Rod Carew led off both the first and third innings with triples—an All-Star record—scoring both times as the Americans took a 3–0 lead into the bottom of the third. But then Jim Palmer, who had shut the Nationals out on one hit through the first two innings, lost his touch. After yielding a leadoff single, he retired two batters, but then issued three walks to force in a run, and when Steve Garvey singled past the shortstop two more runs scored to tie the game.

No one scored through the next 4½ innings, with Larry Sorensen turning in the game's top pitching performance as he shut the Nationals out on one hit through the three middle innings. But in the last of the eighth, Goose Gossage (the National League's closer the previous year) took the mound this year for the Americans. Garvey greeted him with a leadoff triple and scored what proved to be the winning run on a wild pitch. A walk and three singles added three insurance runs before the inning ended. Bruce Sutter and Phil Niekro blanked the Americans in the ninth, and the Nationals had extended their current win streak to seven.

GAME 50
Kingdome, Seattle
July 17, 1979
NL, 7–6

NL	211	001	011	7	10	0
AL	302	001	000	6	10	0

MVP: Parker-N
Pitchers: Carlton, Andujar (2), Rogers (4), G. Perry (6), Sambito (6), LaCoss (6), SUTTER (8) vs Ryan, Stanley (3), Clear (5), KERN (7), Guidry (9)
Home Runs: Lynn-A, Mazzilli-N
Attendance: 58,905

Mike Schmidt tripled and George Foster doubled to drive in the game's first runs as the Nationals began their scoring in the top of the first. The Americans fought back to take the lead later in the inning as Don Baylor doubled home one run and Fred Lynn homered for two more. The Nationals tied the score with a run in the second and went ahead again in the third when Schmidt scored after doubling. But the Americans recaptured the lead in the bottom of the third, scoring twice on a single, wild pitch, ground out, hit batsman, single, and error.

Three innings later the Nationals again tied the game, but the Americans went ahead for the third time with a run in their half of the sixth. Outstanding throws by right fielder Dave Parker, who notched two assists, helped to keep the Americans from pulling away. In the eighth the Nationals' Lee Mazzilli homered for yet another tie, and an inning later Ron Guidry walked Mazzilli with the bases loaded to force in the Nationals' go-ahead seventh run. When Bruce Sutter kept the Americans from scoring in the bottom of the ninth, the National Leaguers had for the second time defeated the Americans eight years in a row.

GAME 51
Dodger Stadium, Los Angeles
July 8, 1980
NL, 4–2

AL	000	020	000	2	7	1
NL	000	012	10X	4	7	0

MVP: Griffey-N
Pitchers: Stone, JOHN (4), Farmer (6), Stieb (7), Gossage (8) vs Richard, Welch (3), REUSS (6), Bibby (7), Sutter (8)
Home Runs: Lynn-A, Griffey-N
Attendance: 56,088

For 4⅔ innings J.R. Richard and Bob Welch held the American stars scoreless. But then Rod Carew singled and Fred Lynn drove in the game's first runs with his third All-Star homer.

The Americans' Steve Stone and Tommy John pitched even better, setting the Nationals down in order through four innings. John continued the perfect streak through the first two outs of the fifth, but then Ken Griffey homered, and the Americans' spell on the National Leaguers was broken.

While three National pitchers limited the Americans to a single and a walk over the final four innings, three singles and an error sent the Nationals into the lead in the sixth. A passed ball surrounded by two wild pitches moved Dave Concepcion around the bases in the seventh (he had reached on a fielder's choice) for the Nationals' fourth run. They didn't really need it, though, as Bruce Sutter—the winning pitcher in the two previous All-Star games—saved this one with two final innings of no-hit ball for the Nationals' ninth successive win.

GAME 52
Municipal Stadium, Cleveland
August 9, 1981
NL, 5–4

NL	000	011	120	5	9	1
AL	010	003	000	4	11	1

MVP: Carter
Pitchers: Valenzuela, Seaver (2), Knepper (3), Hooton (5), Ruthven (6), BLUE (7), Ryan (8), Sutter (9) vs Morris, Barker (3), K.Forsch (5), Norris (6), Davis (7), FINGERS (8), Stieb (8)
Home Runs: Singleton-A, Carter-N (2), Parker-N, Schmidt-N
Attendance: 72,086

The game, delayed until August by the midseason players' strike, drew an All-Star record crowd of more than 72,000 fans, and the managers set a new record by using 56 players. But the game itself followed a familiar pattern.

The Americans scored first in the second inning on Ken Singleton's home run off Tom Seaver, and held their slim lead into the fifth on Len Barker's two innings of perfect pitching. But Ken Forsch replaced Barker in the fifth and Gary Carter homered off his first pitch to tie the score. Dave Parker's homer off Mike Norris an inning later put the Nationals ahead for the first time, but the Americans came right back in the bottom of the inning, putting together four singles and a sacrifice fly for three runs and a two-run advantage.

Gary Carter's second home run of the game—this time off Ron Davis's first pitch—brought the Nationals within one in the seventh, and Mike Schmidt's two-run blast off Rollie Fingers in the eighth restored their lead. Three National pitchers shut out the Americans without a hit over the final three innings as closer Bruce Sutter picked up his second consecutive All-Star save and the National Leaguers had their 10th consecutive victory.

GAME 53
Olympic Stadium, Montreal
July 13, 1982
NL, 4–1

AL	100	000	000	1	8	2
NL	021	001	00X	4	8	1

MVP: Concepcion-N
Pitchers: ECKERSLEY, Clancy (4), Bannister (5), Quisenberry (6), Fingers (8) vs ROGERS, Carlton (4), Soto (6), Valenzuela (8), Minton (8), Howe (9), Hume (9)
Home Runs: Concepcion-N
Attendance: 59,057

In the first All-Star Game held outside the United States, the American League for the third year in a row put the first run on the board, but for the 11th year in a row the final score showed the National League the winner. Two singles, a wild pitch, and a sacrifice fly gave the Americans a run in the top of the first. But starter Steve Rogers of the host Expos held the Americans scoreless for the remainder of his three innings while the Nationals struck back for two runs in the second on Dave Concepcion's home run, and added another in the third when Ruppert Jones—who had tripled to open the inning—scored on a sacrifice fly.

Six National League pitchers (and shortstop Ozzie Smith's spectacular stop and throw to first with two on in the eighth) joined Rogers in holding the American stars scoreless after the first inning. Two hometowners put together the Nationals' final run in the sixth. Al Oliver, leading off, doubled down the line in left and took third as the ball got by left fielder Rickey Henderson. Two outs later Gary Carter lined a pitch to center, scoring Oliver as Willie Wilson's dive for the ball came up short.

GAME 54
Comiskey Park, Chicago
July 6, 1983
AL, 13–3

NL	100	110	000	3	8	3
AL	117	000	22X	13	15	2

MVP: Lynn-A
Pitchers: SOTO, Hammaker (3), Dawley (3), Dravecky (5), Perez (7), Orosco (7), L.Smith (8) vs STIEB, Honeycutt (4), Stanley (6), Young (8), Quisenberry (9)
Home Runs: Rice-A, Lynn-A
Attendance: 43,801

The game returned to the park where it had originated 50 years earlier, and the American League, after 11 years of All-Star losses, unleashed its pent-up fury to produce the greatest margin of victory in 37 years. The game began, though, as an embarrassment of errors. American starter Dave Stieb struck out the side in the first, but along the way two errors (one of them Stieb's) let in a run. An unearned run in the bottom of the first tied the score and another in the second put the American League ahead for good (making a loser out of the unfortunate National starter Mario Soto).

The hitting began in earnest in the last of the third as the Americans scored seven times for a new one-inning record. Among their six hits (also a record for an All-Star inning) were a homer by Jim Rice, a triple by George Brett, and a bases-loaded blast by Fred Lynn—his fourth All-Star home run and the first grand slam in All-Star history. With the score now 9–1, the National League's single runs in the fourth and fifth were exercises in futility, and the Americans' two each in the seventh and eighth served chiefly to boost the winning total to 13—another All-Star high.

GAME 55
Candlestick Park, San Francisco
July 10, 1984
NL, 3–1

AL	010	000	000	1	7	2
NL	110	000	01X	3	8	0

MVP: Carter-N
Pitchers: STIEB, Morris (3), Dotson (5), Caudill (7), Hernandez (8) vs LEA, Valenzuela (3), Gooden (5), Soto (7), Gossage (9)
Home Runs: Brett-A, Carter-N, Murphy-N
Attendance: 57,756

Only four times in the previous 54 All-Star Games had a pitcher struck out the side in order. In this game, three more pitchers did it. And, on this 50th anniversary of Carl Hubbell's five consecutive strikeouts, two of those pitchers combined to break Hubbell's record with six back-to-back whiffs. Hubbell, who threw out the first ball, also saw an All-Star nine-inning record set with 21 total Ks (11 by National League pitchers, 10 by American).

In the fourth inning, National star Fernando Valenzuela mowed down three of the game's premier sluggers: Dave Winfield, Reggie Jackson, and George Brett. The three men Dwight Gooden retired on strikes an inning later (Lance Parrish, Chet Lemon, and rookie Alvin Davis) were slightly less formidable, still, it was an impressive performance for a 19-year-old rookie (the youngest player in All-Star history). The three that American Leaguer Bill Caudill struck out in the seventh were no slouches either: Tim Raines, Ryne Sandberg (in the midst of an MVP season), and Keith Hernandez.

Three of the four runs scored in the game were homers. The National League's run in the first was unearned, but the Americans' George Brett homered to center to tie the game in the second, and the Nationals' go-ahead run later in the inning came on Gary Carter's blast to left. In the eighth, National Leaguer Dale Murphy also put one over the left field fence to end the scoring.

GAME 56
H. Humphrey Metrodome, Minneapolis
July 16, 1985
NL, 6–1

NL	011	020	002	6	9	1
AL	100	000	000	1	5	0

MVP: Hoyt-N
Pitchers: HOYT, Ryan (4), Valenzuela (7), Reardon (8), Gossage (9) vs MORRIS, Key (3), Blyleven (4), Stieb (6), Moore (7), Petry (9), W.Hernandez (9)
Attendance: 54,960

The American Leaguers scored first, as Rickey Henderson led off the bottom of the first with a single and circled the bases on a steal, error, and sacrifice fly. But the five National pitchers blanked the Americans the rest of the way on only four more singles.

Meanwhile, the National stars methodically dismantled the Americans for their 36th All-Star victory. In the top of the second, after Darryl Strawberry singled and stole second, Terry Kennedy, whose error had led to the American League run, redeemed himself by singling Strawberry home. An inning later, with two out, Tom Herr doubled and scored the go-ahead (and winning) run on Steve Garvey's single.

In the fifth the Nationals scored two more runs on a hit batsman, Tim Wallach's ground-rule double, and Ozzie Virgil's single, and finished their scoring in the ninth with another pair on three walks and Willie McGee's double—another ground-rule bounce out of play off the lively Metrodome surface. Goose Gossage struck out the final two American batters in the bottom of the ninth, and the Nationals had increased their winning margin in the series to a new high of 17 games.

GAME 57
Astrodome, Houston
July 15, 1986
AL, 3–2

AL	020	000	100	3	5	0
NL	000	000	020	2	5	1

MVP: Clemens-A
Pitchers: CLEMENS, Higuera (4), Hough (7), Righetti (8), Aase (9) vs GOODEN, Valenzuela (4), Scott (7), Fernandez (8), Krukow (9)
Home Runs: Whitaker-A, White-A
Attendance: 45,774

National League pitchers struck out 12 Americans, led by Fernando Valenzuela's five in a row, which matched the mark set by Carl Hubbell in 1934. (Two years earlier Valenzuela had helped set a multi-pitcher All-Star record of six consecutive strikeouts.) In the eighth inning Sid Fernandez, after walking two, struck out the next three.

Though the American Leaguers struck out fewer men, their pitching was more effective on the whole. Starter Roger Clemens hurled three perfect innings (three balls and 21 strikes), and Teddy Higuera one-hit the Nationals over the next three. Charlie Hough struck out three in the eighth after yielding the Nationals' only extra-base hit (a double) to Chris Brown. But catcher Rich Gedman couldn't handle Hough's knuckleball, and Brown advanced to third on the first strikeout (ruled a wild pitch) and scored on the second, a passed ball which also enabled batter Hubie Brooks to reach first safely. Brooks moved up on a balk and scored the Nationals' second run on Steve Sax's single.

But home runs had already undone the Nationals. With two gone in the second, Dave Winfield doubled off starter Dwight Gooden, and Lou Whitaker clubbed an 0–2 pitch over the fence in right. And in the seventh, Frank White (hitting for Whitaker) knocked Mike Scott's 0–2 pitch over the fence in left-center for what proved the margin of American League victory.

GAME 58
Oakland-Alameda County Coliseum, Oakland
July 14, 1987
NL, 2–0

NL	000	000	000	000	2	2	8	2
AL	000	000	000	000	0	0	6	1

MVP: Raines-N
Pitchers: Scott, Sutcliffe (3), Hershiser (5), R.Reuschel (7), Jo.Franco (8), Bedrosian (9), L.SMITH (10), S. Fernandez (13) vs Saberhagen, Morris (4), Langston (6), Plesac (8), Righetti (9), Henke (9), J.HOWELL (12)
Attendance: 49,671

None of the previous 57 All-Star Games had gone more than five innings without at least one run crossing the plate. But this game went more than twice that before National Leaguer Tim Raines tripled in two runs in the top of the 13th for the game's only scoring. It was the National League's eighth win in eight extra-inning All-Star games.

Both teams missed scoring opportunities in the ninth inning. Raines singled for the Nationals with only one out, and became the game's first runner to reach third when a throw from first on his attempted steal went into center field. But a fly to short right and a foul out left him stranded. In the bottom of the ninth, the Americans came close to winning the game as Dave Winfield headed for home from second on a missed 4-6-1 double play. But National pitcher Steve Bedrosian, covering first, snared the off-center throw from short and fired it home to catch Winfield for the third out.

The Americans again reached third in the 11th as Larry Parrish singled and moved around on a sacrifice and ground out. But pitcher Lee Smith (whose three shutout innings earned him the win) struck out Tony Fernandez to end the threat.

GAME 59
Riverfront Stadium, Cincinnati
July 12, 1988
AL, 2–1

AL	001	100	000	2	6	2
NL	000	100	000	1	5	0

MVP: Steinbach-A
Pitchers: VIOLA, Clemens (3), Gubicza (4), Stieb (6), Russell (7), Jones (8), Plesac (8), Eckersley (9) vs GOODEN, Knepper (4), Cone (5), Gross (6), Davis (7), Walk (7), Hershiser (8), Worrell (9)
Home Run: Steinbach-A
Attendance: 55,837

Oakland's Terry Steinbach was not among the 10 top American League catchers in batting; because of time lost to injuries, he was not even his club's leading catcher in games played. But the fans voted him to start in the All-Star Game, and he won it for the American Leaguers with a home run in his first trip to the plate and a sacrifice fly his next time up. Steinbach's homer—a drive off Dwight Gooden that led off the third inning—caromed off the glove of a leaping Darryl Strawberry over the wall in right for the game's first score. His sacrifice fly—high and deep to left in the fourth inning—scored Dave Winfield (aboard with his record seventh All-Star double) to give the American League a 2–0 lead.

Steinbach also contributed to the National League run later in the fourth. His throwing error on Vince Coleman's steal of second enabled Coleman to advance to third, whence he scored on a wild pitch by Mark Gubicza.

American starter Frank Viola, the midseason league leader in wins, was awarded the victory for his two perfect innings pitched. Dennis Eckersley, the majors' top reliever, preserved the win for the Americans with a perfect ninth inning.

GAME 60
Anaheim Stadium, Anaheim
July 11, 1989
AL, 5–3

NL	200	000	010	3	9	1
AL	212	000	00X	5	12	0

MVP: Jackson-A
Pitchers: Reuschel, SMOLTZ (2), Sutcliffe (3), Burke (4), M. Davis (6), Howell (7), Williams (8) vs Stewart, RYAN (2), Gubicza (4), Moore (5), Swindell (6), Russell (7), Plesac (8), Jones (8)
Home Runs: Jackson-A, Boggs-A
Attendance: 64,036

The National stars struck early with a pair of two-out runs in the top of the first inning, and a double steal put two more runners in scoring position. But left fielder Bo Jackson stifled the assault with a fine running catch, then opened the American half of the first with a massive home run to center field off Rick Reuschel. Wade Boggs, the next man up, added insult to the 40-year-old Reuschel's first All-Star start, tying the game with another homer.

In the second inning Jackson drove in the American League's go-ahead run with a slow grounder off young John Smoltz, and an inning later four American singles produced two more runs. A quartet of National League pitchers held the Americans scoreless on just three hits over the final six innings, and their teammates rallied for a third National run in the eighth. But Doug Jones (the majors' top reliever in 1989) came on to get the final out of the eighth, and in the ninth preserved the American lead to give the American Leaguers their first repeat All-Star victory in 31 years.

National League hurler Smoltz, at age 22 the youngest player in the lineup, took the loss. Nolan Ryan, back in the American League after nine National League seasons, earned the win with two shutout innings. Not only was he the oldest player on either side, he was the oldest All-Star winning pitcher ever.

GAME 61
Wrigley Field, Chicago
July 10, 1990
AL, 2–0

AL	000	000	200	2	7	0
NL	000	000	000	0	2	1

MVP: Ju. Franco-A
Pitchers: Welch, Stieb (3), SABERHAGEN (5), Thigpen (7), Finley (8), Eckersley (9) vs Armstrong, R. Martinez (3), D. Martinez (4), Viola (5), D. Smith (6), BRANTLEY (6), Dibble (7), Myers (8), Jo. Franco (9)
Attendance: 39,071

Back-to-back American League singles off Jeff Brantley had put men on third and first and brought Julio Franco to the plate in the seventh inning, when heavy rain halted the game for more than an hour. During the delay Brantley's side stiffened, so when Franco finally got his turn at bat he faced a new National pitcher, Rob Dibble. Franco lined Dibble's third pitch into the gap in right center for a double—the only extra-base hit of the game—driving in what proved to be the game's only runs.

Damp air and a stiff breeze in from left field helped tame the offense. American League batters managed to accumulate seven hits, but the Nationals were held to two—an All-Star all-time low. No runner advanced as far as third base until the sixth inning, when American stars Kelly Gruber and Jose Canseco pulled off a double steal. No National Leaguer reached that far, and if it weren't for Barry Larkin's third-inning steal, no National runner would even have stood on second base.

American League hurler Bret Saberhagen's two perfect middle innings earned him the win, and Dennis Eckersley, after yielding a leadoff hit in the ninth, retired the final three batters to record his second All-Star save in three years. The victory was the third in a row for the American Leaguers, the first time they had put together such a string of triumphs in 41 years.

GAME 62
SkyDome, Toronto
July 9, 1991
AL, 4–2

NL	100	100	000	2	10	1
AL	003	000	10X	4	8	0

MVP: Ripken-A
Pitchers: Glavine, MARTINEZ (3), Viola (5), Harnisch (6), Smiley (7), Dibble (7), Morgan (8) vs Morris, KEY (3), Clemens (4), McDowell (5), Reardon (7), Aguilera (7), Eckersley (9)
Home Runs: Ripken-A, Dawson-N
Attendance: 52,383

The National League took an early 1–0 lead on singles by Tony Gwynn, Will Clark, and Bobby Bonilla in the top of the first, and held it for two innings on Tom Glavine's strong pitching, which included three strikeouts. But Dennis Martinez yielded successive singles to Rickey Henderson and Wade Boggs in the third inning, and the next batter, Cal Ripken Jr., homered to center to give the Americans all the runs they would need for victory.

National Leaguer Andre Dawson led off the fourth inning with a massive home run to center off Roger Clemens. This brought the Nationals within a run of tying the game, but they scored no more, as a succession of American League pitchers shut them down on a walk and four singles the rest of the way. In the seventh inning the Americans added an insurance run when Joe Carter singled and moved around the bases on a call of catcher interference (the first in All-Star history), a sacrifice bunt, and Harold Baines' sacrifice liner to right.

Jimmy Key, the pitcher of record when Ripken's three-run homer put the American League ahead, was awarded the win. Dennis Eckersley, who pitched a perfect ninth, earned a record third All-Star save.

It was only the second time in All-Star history that the American League had won four games in a row.

GAME 63
Jack Murphy Stadium, San Diego
July 14, 1992
AL, 13–6

AL	411	004	030	13	19	1
NL	000	001	032	6	12	1

MVP: Griffey-A
Pitchers: BROWN, McDowell (2), Guzman (3), Clemens (4), Mussina (5), Langston (6), Nagy (7), Montgomery (8), Aguilera (8), Eckersley (9) vs GLAVINE, Maddux (2), Cone (4), Tewksbury (5), Smoltz (6), Martinez (7), Jones (8), Charlton (9)
Home Runs: Sierra-A, Griffey-A, Clark-N
Attendance: 59,372

By the time the National Leaguers pushed across their first run in the sixth inning, the Americans had already scored 10 times, and although National bats caught fire for five more runs in the eighth and ninth, they were powerless to prevent the American League from stretching its All-Star win streak to five games. National League starting pitcher Tom Glavine could not repeat his strong 1991 start: before his relief after $1\frac{2}{3}$ innings in 1992, he was tagged for nine singles and five runs. In the third inning, Ken Griffey Jr., who had driven in one of the first-inning runs, added the sixth American score with a homer off Greg Maddux. When he came up again to lead off the sixth inning, Griffey doubled to initiate a new American scoring spree, which included two-out doubles by Carlos Baerga and Robin Ventura, capped by Ruben Sierra's home run—all off Bob Tewksbury, who had set down the Americans 1–2–3 an inning earlier. Travis Fryman's RBI single and Roberto Kelly's two-run double in the eighth closed out the American League scoring.

Will Clark's two-out blast off Rick Aguilera in the last of the eighth was the National League's first three-run homer since 1964, but it was too little to make more than a dent in the American lead. With two men out in the ninth, a pair of singles off Dennis Eckersley loaded the bases, and Bip Roberts' single drove in two of the baserunners to bring the NL run total to six (enough to have defeated the AL in the seven previous All-Star Games).

Starter Kevin Brown was awarded the win; Glavine took the loss.

GAME 64
Oriole Park at Camden Yards, Baltimore
July 13, 1993
AL, 9–3

AL	011	033	10X	9	11	0
NL	200	001	000	3	7	2

MVP: Puckett-A
Pitchers: Mulholland, Benes (3), BURKETT (5), Avery (5), Smoltz (6), Beck (7), Harvey (8) vs Langston, Johnson (3), McDOWELL (5), Key (6), Montgomery (7), Aguilera (8), Ward (9)
Home Runs: Sheffield-N, Alomar-A, Puckett-A
Attendance: 48,147

Barry Bonds doubled off Mark Langston with one out in the first inning and Gary Sheffield followed with a home run to left that gave the National League two runs before the American Leaguers came to bat. In the bottom of the second inning, though, Kirby Puckett's solo shot over the center field wall off Terry Mulholland narrowed the gap, and an inning later Roberto Alomar led off with a homer to right off Andy Benes that evened the score.

The Americans pushed ahead in the last of the fifth when, with John Burkett pitching, Ivan Rodriguez lined a ground rule double to left and Albert Belle singled him home. Belle took second on an error, and scored on Ken Griffey Jr.'s single; Griffey scored on Puckett's double into the gap at left center. A half inning later, Barry Larkin drove Bonds home with a sacrifice fly to narrow the score to 5–3, but the Americans blew the game open in the sixth with a trio of unearned runs. After shortstop Jeff Blauser failed to field a grounder by Carlos Baerga—depriving pitcher Steve Avery of a 1–2–3 inning—Avery walked Belle and Devon White doubled, sending Baerga home and Bell to third. John Smoltz, who relieved Avery, unloaded a pair of wild pitches that enabled Belle and White to score.

In the bottom of the seventh inning, Terry Steinbach tagged Rod Beck for a double high off the wall in right to drive in the ninth—and final—AL run. The Nationals got runners to second and third in the eighth with just one out, but failed to score. Duane Ward retired the National Leaguers in order in the ninth to give the American League its sixth straight All-Star victory.

GAME 65
Three Rivers Stadium, Pittsburgh
July 12, 1994
NL, 8–7

AL 100 003 300 0 7 15 0
NL 103 001 002 1 8 12 1

MVP: McGriff-N
Pitchers: Key, Cone (3), Mussina (5), Johnson (6) Hentgen (7), Alvarez (8), L.Smith (9), BERE (10) vs Maddux, Hill (4), Drabek (6), Hudek (6), Jackson (7), Beck (7), Myers (9), JONES (10)
Home Runs: Grissom-N, McGriff-N
Attendance: 59,568

A blend of youth and experience enabled the National League to snap the American Leaguers' six-game winning streak with one of the tightest finishes in All-Star history. In the bottom of the 10th inning, with the score tied, 7–7, Tony Gwynn, a veteran of 10 All-Star games, led off by chopping a single to center off Jason Bere. He took off when novice All-Star Moises Alou drove Bere's second pitch to the base of the wall in left center. AL catcher Ivan Rodriguez received the ball—relayed sharply from the outfield—just as Gwynn slipped between the catcher's legs with the winning run.

It was a close game all the way. The teams traded single runs in the first inning. In the third, the National Leaguers grabbed the biggest lead of the evening when they sandwiched a hit batsman and Gwynn's double between a pair of singles to knock David Cone for three runs. In the top of the sixth the Americans evened the score again with a trio of runs off Doug Drabek. Then Marquis Grissom hit a home run off Randy Johnson a half inning later.

Once again the Americans knotted the game when Scott Cooper doubled home Ivan Rodriguez in the seventh and took their first (and, as it turned out, only) lead when Ken Lofton singled to score Chuck Knoblauch and Cooper. A fourth run would have scored in the seventh, however, if shortstop Ozzie Smith—39 years old and playing in his 13th All-Star contest—had not made a spectacular diving stop of Knoblauch's drive and recovered to force Mickey Tettleton at second.

The Americans maintained their 7–5 advantage into the last of the ninth. Pinch hitter Fred McGriff, after fouling off a third strike, brought National League fans to their feet with a game-tying home run. Doug Jones held the Americans scoreless in the top of the 10th, and the stage was set for the Gwynn–Alou finish.

GAME 66
The Ballpark at Arlington, Texas
July 11, 1995
NL, 3–2

NL 000 001 110 3 3 0
AL 000 200 000 2 8 0

MVP: Conine-N
Pitchers: Nomo, Smiley (3), Green (5), Neagle (6), Perez (7), SLOCUMB (7), Henke (8), Myers (9) vs Johnson, Appier (3), Martinez (5), Rogers (7), ONTIVEROS (8), Wells (8), Mesa (9)
Home Runs: Thomas-A, Biggio-N, Piazza-N, Conine-N
Attendance: 50,920

On a 96-degree evening at The Ballpark in Arlington, Texas, the National League made the most of just three hits (the lowest for a winning squad since 1952) in defeating the AL, 3-2. The key: all three hits were home runs.

After 5⅔ innings it certainly didn't appear the NL would triumph. AL pitchers Randy Johnson, Kevin Appier, and Dennis Martinez combined to no-hit senior circuit batters. Not until Craig Biggio homered off Martinez did the National Leaguers collect their first hit. That cut the AL's margin to 2-1, since Frank Thomas had delivered a monster two-run homer off John Smiley in the fourth. The ball landed in a left field luxury box and was eventually retrieved by Donald Fehr's 9-year-old nephew.

Mike Piazza tied the game an inning later by homering off Kenny Rogers. In the eighth inning Jeff Conine pinch-hit for Ron Gant. Facing Steve Ontiveros, who had also just entered the game, the 29-year-old Conine delivered a 410-foot homer to the lower deck in left. That was all the National League needed to win—and it earned Conine All-Star MVP honors.

Pregame excitement centered about the figure of Dodgers rookie Hideo Nomo. Nomo, the first Japanese national to appear in an All-Star Game, was also the first rookie to start since Fernando Valenzuela in 1981. Much of his native land stopped work (it was 9 a.m. in Japan) to watch—and cheer—Nomo's performance as he allowed just one hit in two innings and struck out Kenny Lofton, Edgar Martinez, and Albert Belle.

GAME 67
Veterans Stadium, Philadelphia
July 9, 1996
NL, 6–0

AL 000 000 000 0 7 0
NL 121 002 00X 6 12 1

MVP: Piazza-N
Pitchers: NAGY, Finley (3), Pavlik (5), Percival (7), Hernandez (8) vs. SMOLTZ, Brown (3), Glavine (4), Bottalico (5), Martinez (6), Trachsel (7), Worrell (8), Wohlers (9), Leiter (9)
Home Runs: Piazza-N, Caminiti-N
Attendance: 62,670

Mike Piazza a native of nearby Norristown, Pa., homered his first time up, doubled in his next at bat, and called the signals behind the plate as nine pitchers combined to shut out the potent AL lineup. Indians manager Mike Hargrove's power-packed AL lineup, which had Baltimore's Brady Anderson (who finished the year with 50 homers) batting eighth, managed only seven singles against the NL's parade of pitchers.

John Smoltz, like his counterpart Charles Nagy, was making his first All-Star start. Smoltz allowed only two hits and a walk in two innings to get the win. Nagy, on the other hand, was touched for four hits and three runs, including a 445-foot home run by Piazza leading off the second.

Center fielder Lance Johnson, who started and played the entire game in place of injured Tony Gwynn, had three hits and a stolen base. He set the tone for the game by legging out a double on the first pitch from Nagy, taking third on a groundout by Barry Larkin and scoring on a groundout by Barry Bonds. Following Piazza's homer, Chipper Jones singled and went to second on a groundout by Craig Biggio. Jones scored on a single by Henry Rodriguez. Piazza brought home the NL's fourth run with a double off Chuck Finley to score Larkin. Ken Caminiti homered to right off Roger Pavlik in the sixth and Craig Biggio delivered the final run later in the inning.

Ozzie Smith, playing his 15th and final All-Star Game, stole the show in the latter innings. Smith, who earlier announced that 1996 was his final season, received a long standing ovation when he came to bat in the seventh. He also started a double play at shortstop in the ninth.

GAME 68
Jacobs Field, Cleveland
July 8, 1997
AL, 3-1

NL 000 000 100 1 3 0
AL 010 000 20X 3 7 0

MVP: S. Alomar-A
Pitchers: Maddux, Schilling (3), Brown (5), Martinez (6), ESTES (7), B.Jones (8) vs. Johnson, Clemens (3), Cone (4), Thompson (5), Hentgen (6), ROSADO (7), Myers (8), Rivera (9)
Home Runs: E. Martinez-A, Lopez-N, S. Alomar-A
Attendance: 44,945

Sandy Alomar Jr. broke a seventh-inning tie and sent the Cleveland crowd into a frenzy with a two-out, two-run home run off Shawn Estes. Although there were three home runs hit at Jacobs Field, pitching was the name of the game. Eight American League pitchers limited the National League to just three hits to halt a three-year losing streak.

The most lasting image of game occurred in the top of the second inning with the long-awaited showdown between Randy Johnson and Larry Walker. The lefty-lefty matchup began with Johnson's first pitch sailing over the head of Walker—reminiscent of Johnson's memorable meeting with John Kruk in the 1993 All-Star Game—but Walker surprised everyone, by turning his helmet around and then stepping across the plate to bat right-handed. He took a pitch (another ball) before returning to bat from the left side and drawing a walk without taking the bat off his shoulder.

Edgar Martinez, the first designated hitter ever voted by the fans to start at the position in the All-Star Game, drilled a line drive over the fence in left field for a 1-0 American League lead in the second inning off Greg Maddux. Outstanding defensive plays by Roberto Alomar, Joey Cora, and Cal Ripken, who made his 14th consecutive All-Star start, but his first at third base, helped four American League pitchers nurse the 1-0 lead until the seventh inning. Javier Lopez, in his first All-Star at bat, pulled a pitch from Luis Rosado off the foul pole in left field to tie the game at 1-1. In the bottom of the seventh inning, Shawn Estes issued the only NL walk of the evening to Bernie Williams and Sandy Alomar, who entered the game having hit in his last 30 games of the first half of the season, homered to make it a 3-1 game. Randy Myers and Mariano Rivera each pitched perfect innings to give the AL its first win since 1993.

GAME 69
Coors Field, Denver
July 7, 1998
AL, 13-8

		R	H	E
AL	000 413 113	13	19	2
NL	002 130 020	8	12	1

MVP: R. Alomar-A
Pitchers: Wells, Clemens (3), Radke (4), COLON (5), Arrojo (6), Wetteland (7), Gordon (8), Percival (9) vs. Maddux, Glavine (3), Brown (4), Ashby (5), URBINA (6), Hoffman (7), Shaw (8), Nen (9)
Home Runs: A. Rodriguez-A, Bonds-N, R. Alomar-A
Attendance: 51,267

This Rocky Mountain version of the All-Star Game featured the most runs (21), but it was a defensive play that was the pivotal play of the game. With the National League having closed the gap to 10-8 with runners on first and second and none out in the eighth, Devon White singled to left and Fernando Vina was thrown out at the plate by Paul O'Neill. Had Vina held up, the bases would have been loaded with nobody out for Andres Galarraga, the NL RBI leader the past two years who had 72 RBI at the All-Star break, but his smash up the middle was turned into an inning-ending double play by Omar Vizquel.

Roberto Alomar was one of seven All-Stars to have a multiple-hit game, but the second baseman, who also had a walk, a stolen base, and a home run, was chosen as the game's Most Valuable Player a year after his brother, Sandy, was named MVP in the 1997 game. Roberto Alomar was one of just three players to homer in a game where longballs were expected to be plentiful in the thin air of Denver's high elevation. (The expectations were further heightened when 83 home runs were hit in the previous day's annual Home Run Derby, which was won by reluctant participant Ken Griffey.) The furthest ball hit in the All-Star Game came off the bat of Barry Bonds, a three-run shot that gave the NL a short-lived 6-5 lead after five innings.

A rocky sixth inning by both pitcher Ugueth Urbina and catcher Javier Lopez included three stolen bases, a wild pitch, a passed ball, and a run-scoring single by Ivan Rodriguez that gave the AL a lead it did not relinquish. The AL scored at least one run in every inning after the fourth. One of those runs came off Jeff Shaw, who spent the first half of the season pitching for the Reds, but he was traded to the Dodgers shortly before the All-Star break and became the first player to debut in a new uniform in the All-Star Game.

GAME 70
Fenway Park, Boston
July 13, 1999
AL, 4-1

		R	H	E
NL	001 000 000	1	7	1
AL	200 200 00X	4	6	2

MVP: Martinez-A
Pitchers: SCHILLING, Johnson (3), Bottenfield (4), Lima (5), Millwood (6), Ashby (7), Hampton (7), Hoffman (8), Wagner (8) VS MARTINEZ, Cone (3), Mussina (5), Rosado (6), Zimmerman (7), Hernandez (8), Wetteland (9)
Attendance: 34,187

The 70th All-Star Game was a thoroughly Boston affair. The 20th century's greatest players were honored prior to the game at Fenway Park, but Ted Williams, who threw out the first pitch, stole the show. The Red Sox Hall of Famer found himself surrounded by admiring All-Stars of both past and present. When Williams left the field, Pedro Martinez took over the show at his home ballpark.

Martinez struck out the first four batters he faced, the first time that had happened in All-Star competition; his feat called to mind Carl Hubbell's five straight strikeouts of American League sluggers in the 1934 game. Martinez retired all six batters he faced, striking out five of them. He set the tone for the American League's 4-1 win and walked away with Most Valuable Player honors. (The extra effort that night, however, briefly landed the Red Sox star on the disabled list.)

In all, the National League struck out 12 times and managed just seven hits and one run. The American League, on the other hand, scored twice in the first inning against Curt Schilling on two-out hits by Jim Thome and Cal Ripken. The National League scored its run in the third inning off David Cone as Barry Larkin singled home Jeromy Burnitz. The American League added two runs the following inning against Kent Bottenfield. Nine National League pitchers fanned 10 batters, setting an All-Star record with 22 strikeouts between the two squads.

GAME 71
Turner Field, Atlanta
July 11, 2000
AL, 6-3

		R	H	E
AL	001 200 003	6	10	2
NL	001 010 001	3	9	2

MVP: Jeter-A
Pitchers: Wells, BALDWIN (3), Sele (4), Isringhausen (5), Lowe (6), T. Jones (7), Hudson (8), Rivera (9), vs Johnson, Graves (2), Brown (3), LEITER (4), Glavine (5), Kile (6), Wickman (8), Hoffman (9)
Home Runs: C. Jones-N
Attendance: 51,323

The list of players who weren't at the 71st All-Star Game was practically a lineup of its own. Mark McGwire, Alex Rodriguez, Cal Ripken, Barry Bonds, Ken Griffey, Manny Ramirez, Mike Piazza, Pedro Martinez, and Greg Maddux were unavailable because of injuries, although Griffey did participate in the previous night's Home Run Derby. The game itself, however, was a tight, well-pitched 6-3 victory for the American League, with almost half the game's runs scored in the ninth inning.

Starters Randy Johnson and David Wells led a procession of eight pitchers for each All-Star squad. Kevin Brown surrendered the game's first run when he walked Carl Everett with the bases loaded in the third inning. Chipper Jones, who had three hits on the night, tied the game in the bottom of the inning with a home run off winning pitcher James Baldwin. Jones was heartily embraced by the hometown crowd at Turner Field, but the loudest ovation of the night was reserved for Andres Galarraga, who earned a trip to the All-Star Game after sitting out a season because of cancer.

Derek Jeter, the American League's starting shortstop in place of Alex Rodriguez, singled in the go-ahead runs in the fourth inning to earn Most Valuable Player honors. The American League put the game away with three runs in the ninth on RBIs by Matt Lawton and Magglio Ordonez, aided by an infield error. Manager Joe Torre, whose Yankees had beaten Bobby Cox's Braves in eight consecutive World Series games, won his second All-Star Game while paired against the Atlanta skipper. Of the American League's four straight All-Star wins, Torre was manager in three of the games.

CHAPTER 10

Tiebreakers: One-Game and Three-Game Playoffs

Bruce Markusen

Sometimes a 162-game schedule—or in the case of days gone by, a 154-game docket—is simply not enough to determine the best team in the league, the division, or even among the Wild Card contenders. Sometimes an extra game (or two, or even three) is needed to determine who should go to the postseason—and who should go home for a long winter of contemplation and regret. In those instances, the ultimate tiebreaking mechanism is required. For that, baseball calls upon a playoff.

Tiebreaker playoff games should not be confused with the term playoffs, which has long been used as an alternate name for the League Championship Series—and later the Division Series. League Championship Series have taken place since 1969, when both the American and National Leagues split into two divisions. In 1995 Major League Baseball initiated three divisions, a Wild Card qualifying team, and the corresponding Division Series, effectively creating another round of playoffs. These series, however, are on Major League Baseball's annual calendar; no one knows if a playoff will be required to break a tie until the last week—and usually the last day—of the regular season. Just in case, MLB always keeps the Monday after the season ends available for a playoff.

On 10 different occasions, extra games have been needed to break ties between teams that finished the regular season with identical records. Until the divisional format began, these playoffs were needed to determine the league champion. Since then the one-game format has been needed to decide divisional championships and Wild Card berths. While the games have the distinct feel of the postseason, these tiebreakers are considered regular-season games. All records accrued on these fateful days count toward the players' regular-season totals. Occasionally it has resulted in a home run crown (Eddie Mathews in 1959) or a 20th win (Joe Niekro in 1980), but winning is all that really matters when extra games are put on the schedule.

Sometimes the identity of playoff games can become confusing. For example, some might think that the season-ending 1908 game between the Chicago Cubs and New York Giants was a playoff game, but it was actually a *replaying* of an earlier game that had been suspended and declared a tie because of Fred Merkle's failure to touch second base on an apparent game-winning hit. The first tiebreaking playoff did not take place until 38 years later, when 154 games proved insufficient in determining superiority in the National League. That tie, between the St. Louis Cardinals and Brooklyn Dodgers, resulted in the first best-of-three playoff for the NL pennant. When the American League season ended in a tie between the Boston Red Sox and Cleveland Indians two years later, a one-game playoff was used to settle the score. The NL continued to use three-game playoffs to determine ties until the start of divisional play in 1969. In 1980 the first one-game playoff took place in the National League. That game, however, had one thing in common with the first four NL tiebreakers: It involved the Dodgers. And for the fourth time, the Dodgers lost.

Although there were no ties that needed to be broken during the 19th century or for most of the first half of the 20th century, 10 tiebreakers have been required to break deadlocks between pennant-contending teams: seven in the National League and three in the American League. What follows is a recap of those games, as well as the down-to-the-wire events that led to these unscheduled and unforgettable climaxes to the season.

1946: St. Louis vs. Brooklyn

Tiebreaking playoffs were unheard of for the first several decades of the game's history. That unusual trend did not end until 1946, when the Brooklyn Dodgers and St. Louis Cardinals staged one of most memorable races in National League history.

On August 21 the Cardinals tied the Dodgers in the standings, thanks to a doubleheader sweep of the Philadelphia Phillies coupled with Brooklyn's loss to the Cincinnati Reds. The two teams remained deadlocked for four days, until the Redbirds jumped ahead. The Cardinals fell back into a tie the following day, but regained the lead on August 28.

The Cardinals remained in first place until a mid-September series with the Dodgers. After a split of the first two games of the series, Brooklyn manager Leo Durocher surprisingly called upon rookie righthander Ralph Branca to pitch the rubber match. Under Durocher's original plan, Branca would pitch to only one batter before giving way to a lefthander, thus giving the Dodgers the platoon advantage.

Durocher altered his master plan after watching Branca pitch impressively to his first batter. "The Lip" allowed his rookie pitcher to remain in the game for another batter, and then another inning, and eventually the rest of the game. Branca finished with a three-hit shutout. His unexpected fortune brought the Dodgers within a half-game of the Cardinals.

On Friday, September 27, the Dodgers made up the half-game difference and moved into a first-place tie. Brooklyn won again on Saturday, as did St. Louis. With the pennant now resting on the final day of the regular season, both the Dodgers and the Cardinals lost, prompting the first tiebreaking playoff in major league history.

According to the National League's constitution at the time, the two teams would not be permitted to play a single game, but would have to play a *series* of games to determine the league's champion. Under the best two-out-of-three format, the Cardinals would host the first game at Sportsman's Park, followed by two games (if necessary) at Ebbets Field in Brooklyn.

Lefthander Howie Pollet pitched Game 1 for St. Louis despite a torn muscle in his throwing shoulder. Working in and out of trouble, he scattered eight hits and held the Dodgers to two runs. Pollet received ample offensive support from 20-year-old catcher Joe Garagiola, who had three hits and two RBIs. Veteran outfielder Terry Moore added three hits, as the Cardinals knocked Branca from the game in the third inning. Buoyed by Moore, Garagiola, and Pollet, the Cardinals claimed the first game of the playoff, 4–2.

In Game 2 the Cardinals erased an early 1–0 deficit by scoring a pair of runs in the top of the second. The Redbirds built up a 5–1 lead with a three-run rally in the fifth, then added three more runs in the seventh and eighth. With an 8–1 advantage and Murry Dickson efficiently striking down the Brooklyn offense, a sweep of the series seemed inevitable.

Then, in the bottom of the ninth, the Dodgers counterpunched. A three-run rally knocked Dickson from the game. With the bases loaded and only one out, the Dodgers brought the tying run to the plate. Relief pitcher Harry "The Cat" Brecheen fanned leadoff hitter Eddie Stanky and pinch hitter Howie Schultz to end the game. The 8–4 win gave the Cardinals a two-game sweep, launching them into the World Series. Furthermore, the tiebreaking playoff turned out to be a harbinger of good things to come, as the Cardinals defeated the Boston Red Sox on Slaughter's memorable "Mad Dash" in Game 7 of the World Series.

GAME 1 AT SPORTSMAN'S PARK, ST. LOUIS, OCTOBER 1, 1946

BROOKLYN	AB	R	H	2B	3B	HR	RBI
Stanky, 2B	3	0	1	0	0	0	0
Lavagetto, 3b	3	0	0	0	0	0	0
Medwick, lf	4	0	1	0	0	0	0
Tepsic, pr	0	0	0	0	0	0	0
Whitman, lf	0	0	0	0	0	0	0
F. Walker, rf	4	0	0	0	0	0	0
Furillo, cf	4	0	0	0	0	0	0
Reese, ss	4	1	2	0	0	0	0
Edwards, c	4	0	2	0	0	0	0
Schultz, 1b	3	1	2	0	0	1	2
Branca, p	1	0	0	0	0	0	0
Higbe, p	0	0	0	0	0	0	0
Rojek, ph	0	0	0	0	0	0	0
Gregg, p	0	0	0	0	0	0	0
Ramazzotti, ph	1	0	0	0	0	0	0
Lombardi, p	0	0	0	0	0	0	0
Melton, p	0	0	0	0	0	0	0

ST. LOUIS	AB	R	H	2B	3B	HR	RBI
Schoendienst, 2b	5	0	2	0	0	0	0
Moore, cf	5	1	3	0	0	0	0
Musial, 1b	4	2	1	0	1	0	0
Slaughter, rf	4	0	2	0	0	0	0
Kurowski, 3b	2	1	0	0	0	0	1
Garagiola, c	4	0	3	0	0	0	2
H. Walker, lf	3	0	1	0	0	0	1
Marion, ss	4	0	0	0	0	0	0
Pollet, p	4	0	0	0	0	0	0

BRO	001	000	100	2	8	0
STL	102	000	10x	4	12	1

Bases on balls—Kurowski 2, Musial, Rojek, Lavagetto, Stanky. Sacrifice hit—Schultz. Left on base—Brooklyn 6, St. Louis 11. Error—Pollet. Wild pitch—Melton. Umpires—Reardon, Pinelli, Goetz, Boggess. Time of game—2:48. Attendance—26,012.

PITCHING	IP	H	R	ER	BB	SO
BROOKLYN						
Branca (L, 3–1)	2.2	6	3	3	2	3
Higbe	1.1	1	0	0	0	0
Gregg	2	1	0	0	1	1
Lombardi	.1	1	1	1	0	0
Melton	1.2	3	0	0	1	0
ST. LOUIS						
Pollet (W, 21–10)	9	8	2	2	3	2

GAME 2 AT EBBETS FIELD, BROOKLYN, OCTOBER 3, 1946

ST. LOUIS	AB	R	H	2B	3B	HR	RBI
Schoendienst, 2b	5	1	1	0	0	0	0
Moore, cf	5	1	2	1	0	0	0
Musial, 1b	4	1	1	1	0	0	0
Kurowski, 3b	2	2	1	0	0	0	2
Slaughter, rf	3	1	1	0	1	0	2
Dusak, lf	3	1	2	0	1	0	1
H. Walker, ph-lf	1	0	0	0	0	0	0
Marion, ss	3	0	1	0	0	0	2
Dickson, p	5	0	2	0	1	0	1
Brecheen, p	0	0	0	0	0	0	0

BROOKLYN	AB	R	H	2B	3B	HR	RBI
Stanky, 2b	5	0	0	0	0	0	0
Whitman, lf	4	0	0	0	0	0	0
Schultz, ph	1	0	0	0	0	0	0
Galan, 3b	4	2	2	1	0	0	0
F. Walker, rf	3	0	0	0	0	0	0
Stevens, 1b	4	1	2	0	1	0	2
Furillo, cf	4	1	1	0	0	0	1
Reese, ss	2	0	0	0	0	0	0
Edwards, c	2	0	1	0	0	0	1
Hatten, p	1	0	0	0	0	0	0
Behrman, p	0	0	0	0	0	0	0
Hermanski, ph	1	0	0	0	0	0	0
Lombardi, p	0	0	0	0	0	0	0
Higbe, p	0	0	0	0	0	0	0
Melton, p	0	0	0	0	0	0	0
Medwick, ph	1	0	0	0	0	0	0
Taylor, p	0	0	0	0	0	0	0
Lavagetto, ph	0	0	0	0	0	0	0

STL	020	030	120	8	13	0
BRO	100	000	003	4	6	0

Bases on balls—F. Walker, Edwards 2, Reese 2, Kurowski 3, Marion, Musial, Slaughter, Lavagetto. Sacrifice hits—Schoendienst, Dusak, Marion. Left on base—St. Louis 11, Brooklyn 7. Wild pitch—Dickson. Umpires—Pinelli, Goetz, Boggess, Reardon. Time of game—2:44. Attendance—31,437.

PITCHING	IP	H	R	ER	BB	SO
ST. LOUIS						
Dickson (W, 15–6)	8.1	5	4	4	5	3
Brecheen	.2	1	0	0	1	2
BROOKLYN						
Hatten (L, 14–11)	4.2	7	5	5	3	0
Behrman	.1	1	0	0	0	0
Lombardi	1.1	1	1	1	2	0
Higbe	1	3	2	2	2	1
Melton	.2	0	0	0	0	0
Taylor	1	1	0	0	0	1

1948: Cleveland vs. Boston

With the Boston Red Sox, Cleveland Indians, and New York Yankees fighting for first place in the American League, a three-way tie at season's end was a distinct possibility. As the season moved into its second-to-last day, the Indians found themselves in first place, with the Red Sox and Yankees each a single game behind.

The Yankees were scheduled to continue a season-ending series against the Red Sox on Saturday, October 2. When the Red Sox defeated the Yankees to push them two games out, they officially eliminated New York from contention. Meanwhile, the Indians won their game against the Tigers to maintain a one-game lead. With Sunday the last day remaining on the regular-season schedule, the Indians needed only to win their final game to clinch the pennant.

That win did not figure to come easily, not with future Hall of Famer Hal Newhouser on the mound for the Tigers. Newhouser allowed only five hits and defeated another future Hall of Famer—Bob Feller—in a 7–1 Detroit win. Coupled with Boston's 10–5 pounding of the Yankees, the loss dropped the Indians into a first-place tie, each team sporting a record of 96–58.

In contrast to the National League's constitution, the American League's rules called for a one-game playoff to break any ties between teams at season's end. Since the Red Sox had won a coin flip conducted by American League president Will Harridge on September 24, Fenway Park would be the site of the AL's first playoff.

Both managers made surprising pitching choices. Indians player-manager Lou Boudreau tabbed rookie Gene Bearden, despite the fact that he had started only two days earlier and would be pitching on one day's rest. Red Sox skipper Joe McCarthy made an even more stunning choice: journeyman Denny Galehouse, a 36-year-old righthander who had posted a mediocre record of 8–7. Critics wondered why "Marse Joe" hadn't selected left-hander Mel Parnell, whose credentials seemed stronger than those of Galehouse.

Pitching in front of a capacity crowd of 33,957, Galehouse ran into immediate first-inning trouble. After retiring the first two batters, Galehouse surrendered a home run to Boudreau, who reached the screen atop Fenway's Green Monster in left field. The Red Sox countered quickly against Bearden. With one out in the bottom of the first, Johnny Pesky doubled to right-center field and came home on Vern Stephens' single to left. With the game tied in the top of the fourth, Boudreau singled, then moved up to second on Joe Gordon's hit. Ken Keltner followed with a three-run homer to knock Galehouse from the game. Veteran Ellis Kinder promptly allowed a double to Larry Doby, who eventually came around to score on Jim Hegan's infield grounder. The Indians now led by four runs.

The Indians scored another run in the fifth on Boudreau's second home run, but the Red Sox showed signs of life in the bottom of the sixth. After Joe Gordon mishandled a popup by Ted Williams, Bobby Doerr launched a two-out, two-run homer.

The Sox remained within striking distance until the eighth, when Larry Doby doubled against Kinder and scored on an error by Williams, who failed to handle a long flyball by Bearden. The Indians added another run in the top of the ninth and Bearden finished off the Red Sox for Cleveland's first pennant since 1920. It also set the stage for a championship performance in the World Series, something the Indians would not duplicate for the next half-century and beyond.

AT FENWAY PARK, BOSTON, OCTOBER 4, 1948

CLEVELAND	AB	R	H	2B	3B	HR	RBI
Mitchell, lf	5	0	1	0	0	0	0
Clark, 1b	2	0	0	0	0	0	0
Robinson, 1b	2	1	1	0	0	0	0
Boudreau, ss	4	3	4	0	0	2	2
Gordon, 2b	4	1	1	0	0	0	0
Keltner, 3b	5	1	3	1	0	1	3
Doby, cf	5	1	2	2	0	0	0
Kennedy, rf	2	0	0	0	0	0	0
Hegan, c	3	1	0	0	0	0	1
Bearden, p	3	0	1	0	0	0	0
BOSTON	**AB**	**R**	**H**	**2B**	**3B**	**HR**	**RBI**
DiMaggio, cf	4	0	0	0	0	0	0
Pesky, 3b	4	1	1	1	0	0	0
Williams, lf	4	1	1	0	0	0	0
Stephens, ss	4	0	1	0	0	0	1
Doerr, 2b	4	1	1	0	0	1	2
Spence, rf	1	0	0	0	0	0	0
Hitchcock, ph	0	0	0	0	0	0	0
Wright, pr	0	0	0	0	0	0	0
Goodman, 1b	3	0	0	0	0	0	0
Tebbetts, c	4	0	1	0	0	0	0
Galehouse, p	0	0	0	0	0	0	0
Kinder, p	2	0	0	0	0	0	0

				R	H	E
CLE	100	410	011	8	13	1
BOS	100	002	000	3	5	1

Bases on balls—Spence 2, Galehouse, Goodman, Hitchcock, Bearden, Boudreau, Hegan, Gordon. Sacrifice hits—Kennedy 2, Robinson. Left on base—Cleveland 7, Boston 5. Errors—Gordon, Williams. Wild pitch—Kinder. Umpires—McGowan, Summers, Rommel, Berry. Time of game—2:24. Attendance—33,957.

PITCHING	IP	H	R	ER	BB	SO
Cleveland						
Bearden (W, 20–7)	9	5	3	2	5	6
Boston						
Galehouse (L, 8–8)	3	5	4	4	1	1
Kinder	6	8	4	3	3	2

1951: Brooklyn vs. New York

By mid-August, the National League pennant race seemed like a foregone conclusion. With a 13½-game lead over the rival New York Giants, the Brooklyn Dodgers only needed to play a fair brand of ball over the season's final weeks to insure the National League pennant. Or so it seemed.

By September 20 the Giants had managed to cut the lead to a more manageable 4½ games. Still, New York trailed the Dodgers by six full games in the loss column. With only seven games remaining on the schedule, the prospect of catching the Dodgers could be classified as a pipe dream.

The Giants swept a three-game series with the Boston Braves while the Dodgers lost two of three to the Phillies. The sudden developments narrowed the margin to only 2½ games. On September 25 the Dodgers showed more signs of slippage by dropping a doubleheader to the Braves. In the meantime, the Giants took advantage of Brooklyn's woes by winning in Philadelphia. The lead, incredibly, was now down to a single game.

As the Giants took the next two days off, they gleefully watched the Dodgers stumble against Boston and then Philadelphia. Two more Brooklyn losses had left the

Dodgers in a flat-footed tie with the Giants for first place in the National League. Both teams sported identical records of 94–58.

The next day—the final Saturday of the regular season—both the Giants and the Dodgers won, courtesy of shutouts by Sal Maglie and Don Newcombe, respectively. Although the Dodgers had managed to break their losing streak, they remained tied with the Giants—with their regular-season finales scheduled for the next day.

On Sunday, September 30, the Giants posted a 3–2 victory over the Braves behind a five-hitter by Larry Jansen. The Dodgers, needing to win their game against the Phillies to force a tiebreaking playoff series, were in trouble early. Preacher Roe was out of the game and Philadelphia had a 6–1 lead after three innings. The Dodgers fought back over the next two innings, but still trailed, 8–5, as the game moved to the eighth inning.

Knowing that the Giants were on the verge of victory, the Dodgers promptly rallied to score three runs in the eighth to tie, eventually forcing extra innings. In the bottom of the 14th, an injured Jackie Robinson (who had hurt his elbow making a diving catch just two innings earlier) belted a solo home run against Robin Roberts. The blast gave the Dodgers a 9–8 win, preserving a share of first place with the Giants and setting up a best-of-three playoff.

The Dodgers took a 1–0 lead in Game 1 on Andy Pafko's home run in the second inning at Ebbets Field. The Giants retaliated in the fourth, as Bobby Thomson clubbed a two-run homer against Ralph Branca. Monte Irvin added a solo blast of his own in the eighth inning, increasing the advantage to 3–1. Jim Hearn pitched a complete-game five-hitter.

The second game, staged on an overcast day at the Polo Grounds, took on a more offensive-minded tone. The Dodgers reached Sam Jones for two runs on Jackie Robinson's first-inning home run. The Giants responded by putting early-game pressure on Clem Labine, picking up five hits in the first four innings. Labine worked his way out of several jams, stranding eight runners along the way.

The score remained 2–0 until the top of the fifth, when the Dodgers added another run. They scored three more in the sixth, highlighted by a Gil Hodges home run. Unfazed by a 41-minute rain delay in the sixth, Labine returned to the mound with a 6–0 lead in tow and continued to shut down the Giants' attack.

The Dodgers piled on additional runs in the seventh and ninth—spearheaded by Andy Pafko's second home run of the series. Rube Walker, filling in for an injured Roy Campanella behind the plate, added a homer in Brooklyn's 10–0 win.

Still, the Giants had the advantage of playing the final game at the Polo Grounds, giving them the tangible benefit of having the last at bat and the intangible help of a supportive crowd. Brooklyn struck first, however. Giants starter Sal Maglie walked two Dodgers and surrendered a single to Jackie Robinson to produce the first run of the day.

Twenty-game winner Don Newcombe shut out the Giants over the first six innings, but then had to face the middle of New York's order in the seventh. Monte Irvin pounded out a double and moved up to third on a sacrifice bunt by Whitey Lockman. With one out, Bobby Thomson lifted a sacrifice fly to score Irvin with the tying run. Maglie retired leadoff man Carl Furillo for the first out in the eighth, but then yielded singles to Pee Wee Reese and Duke Snider. With runners on first and third, an erratic Maglie uncorked a wild pitch, allowing Reese to score the go-ahead run. Maglie's wayward pitching continued when he walked Jackie Robinson, once again putting runners on first and third. Pafko and Billy Cox followed with singles, adding two more runs to Brooklyn's total and raising the Dodgers' lead to three runs.

Newcombe, who retired the Giants without incident in the eighth, still looked strong. He entered the ninth with a four-hitter and needed just three outs to put the Dodgers' late-season stumble behind them. The fateful inning began with an infield hit by Alvin Dark. Newk then surrendered a single to Don Mueller, putting runners on first and third while bringing the tying run to the plate in Monte Irvin. Irvin swung underneath a Newcombe delivery, popping it up on the infield for one out. Whitey Lockman followed with a double, bringing home one run and putting the potential tying runs in scoring position.

The game paused for several moments, as an injured Mueller left the game, the result of breaking his ankle during his run to third base. Leo Durocher inserted Clint Hartung as the pinch runner for Mueller. Brooklyn skipper Charlie Dressen also made a change, removing Newcombe. After calling down to the bullpen and conferring with coach Clyde Sukeforth, Dressen called on Ralph Branca, the starter in Game 1.

Branca jumped ahead in the count with a first-pitch strike to Bobby Thomson, who had been a part-time player earlier in the season before Durocher decided to convert him to third base. Since the move from the outfield to the infield, Thomson had batted a scalding .357; Thomson had also homered against Branca in the first game of the playoff series.

As Rookie of the Year Willie Mays waited his turn in the on-deck circle, Branca delivered his second pitch to the plate. Thomson swung and swung hard, prompting a breathless description from longtime Giants broadcaster Russ Hodges:

> There's a long drive! It's going to be, I believe. . . ! The Giants win the pennant! The Giants win the pennant! The Giants win the pennant! The Giants win the pennant! The Giants win the pennant! Bobby Thomson hits into the lower deck of the left field stands! The Giants win the pennant! And they're going crazy! They're going crazy! Oh-ho! . . . I don't believe it! I don't believe it! I do not believe it! Bobby Thomson . . . hit a line drive into the lower deck of the left field stands. And this whole place is going crazy!

This frenetic description conveyed, at least in part, the shocking drama of arguably the most famous home run in the history of the game. With one swing, Thomson had enabled the Giants to move on to the World Series, while crushing the hopes of the Dodgers. Unlike the other two playoffs that had occurred over the past five years, the 1951 tiebreaker produced one of the game's truly indelible moments. A half-century later it was still considered by some to be the greatest moment in New York sports history, even though both the Dodgers and Giants moved to California after the 1957 season.

GAME 1 AT EBBETS FIELD, BROOKLYN, OCTOBER 1, 1951

NEW YORK	AB	R	H	2B	3B	HR	RBI
Stanky, 3b	5	0	2	0	0	0	0
Dark, ss	4	0	1	1	0	0	0
Mueller, rf	5	0	0	0	0	0	0
Irvin, lf	4	2	1	0	0	1	1
Lockman, 1b	4	0	1	0	0	0	0
Thomson, 3b	2	1	1	0	0	1	2
Mays, cf	3	0	0	0	0	0	0
Westrum, c	2	0	0	0	0	0	0
Hearn, p	3	0	0	0	0	0	0

BROOKLYN	AB	R	H	2B	3B	HR	RBI
Furillo, rf	4	0	0	0	0	0	0
Reese, ss	3	0	1	0	0	0	0
Snider, cf	4	0	1	0	0	0	0
Robinson, 2b	3	0	1	0	0	0	0
Campanella, c	3	0	0	0	0	0	0
Pafko, lf	3	1	1	0	0	1	1
Hodges, 1b	2	0	0	0	0	0	0
Cox, 3b	3	0	1	0	0	0	0
Branca, p	2	0	0	0	0	0	0
Russell, ph	1	0	0	0	0	0	0
Podbielan, p	0	0	0	0	0	0	0

NY	000	200	010	3	6	1
BRO	010	000	000	1	5	1

Bases on balls—Mays, Thomson, Westrum 2, Dark, Hodges, Reese. Sacrifice hits—Hearn, Thomson. Left on base—New York 10, Brooklyn 2. Errors—Dark, Snider. Hit by pitcher—Branca (Irvin). Umpires—Stewart, Goetz, Jorda, Conlan. Time of game—2:39. Attendance—30,707.

PITCHING	IP	H	R	ER	BB	SO
NEW YORK						
Hearn (W, 17–9)	9	5	1	1	2	5
BROOKLYN						
Branca (L, 13–11)	8	5	3	3	5	5
Podbielan	1	1	0	0	0	0

GAME 2 AT POLO GROUNDS, NEW YORK, OCTOBER 2, 1951

BROOKLYN	AB	R	H	2B	3B	HR	RBI
Furillo, rf	5	0	0	0	0	0	0
Reese, ss	5	1	2	0	0	0	0
Snider, cf	4	1	2	1	0	0	1
Robinson, 2b	5	1	3	0	0	1	3
Pafko, lf	5	1	1	0	0	1	1
Hodges, 1b	4	2	2	0	0	1	1
Cox, 3b	3	2	0	0	0	0	0
Walker, c	5	1	3	0	0	1	2
Labine, p	4	1	0	0	0	0	0

NEW YORK	AB	R	H	2B	3B	HR	RBI
Stanky, 2b	5	0	1	0	0	0	0
Dark, ss	5	0	0	0	0	0	0
Mueller, rf	4	0	1	0	0	0	0
Irvin, lf	4	0	1	0	0	0	0
Lockman, 1b	3	0	0	0	0	0	0
Thomson, 3b	4	0	1	1	0	0	0
Mays, cf	4	0	1	0	0	0	0
Westrum, c	3	0	0	0	0	0	0
Williams, pr	0	0	0	0	0	0	0
Jones, p	1	0	0	0	0	0	0
Spencer, p	1	0	1	0	0	0	0
Rigney, ph	0	0	0	0	0	0	0
Corwin, p	0	0	0	0	0	0	0
Thompson, ph	1	0	0	0	0	0	0

BRO	200	013	202	10	13	2
NY	000	000	000	0	6	5

Bases on balls—Snider, Labine, Hodges, Cox, Lockman, Rigney, Westrum. Sacrifice hit—Cox. Left on base—New York 11, Brooklyn 8. Errors—Reese, Hodges, Thomson, Mays, Jones, Spencer 2. Umpires—Goetz, Jorda, Conlan, Stewart. Time of game—3:25. Attendance—38,609.

PITCHING	IP	H	R	ER	BB	SO
BROOKLYN						
Labine (W, 5–1)	9	6	0	0	3	3
NEW YORK						
Jones (L, 6–11)	2.1	4	2	2	1	2
Spencer	3.2	6	4	2	1	0
Corwin	3	3	4	3	2	2

GAME 3 AT POLO GROUNDS, NEW YORK, OCTOBER 3, 1951

BROOKLYN	AB	R	H	2B	3B	HR	RBI
Furillo, rf	5	0	0	0	0	0	0
Reese, ss	4	2	1	0	0	0	0
Snider, cf	3	1	2	0	0	0	0
Robinson, 2b	2	1	1	0	0	0	1
Pafko, lf	4	0	1	0	0	0	1
Hodges, 1b	4	0	0	0	0	0	0
Cox, 3b	4	0	2	0	0	0	1
Walker, c	4	0	1	0	0	0	0
Newcombe, p	4	0	0	0	0	0	0
Branca, p	0	0	0	0	0	0	0

NEW YORK	AB	R	H	2B	3B	HR	RBI
Stanky, 2b	4	0	0	0	0	0	0
Dark, ss	4	1	1	0	0	0	0
Mueller, rf	4	0	1	0	0	0	0
Hartung, pr	0	1	0	0	0	0	0
Irvin, lf	4	1	1	1	0	0	0
Lockman, 1b	3	1	2	1	0	0	1
*Thomson, 3b	4	1	3	1	0	1	4
Mays, cf	3	0	0	0	0	0	0
Westrum, c	0	0	0	0	0	0	0
Rigney, ph	1	0	0	0	0	0	0
Noble, c	0	0	0	0	0	0	0
Maglie, p	2	0	0	0	0	0	0
Thompson, ph	1	0	0	0	0	0	0
Jansen, p	0	0	0	0	0	0	0

BRO	100	000	030	4	8	0
NY	000	000	104	5	8	0

*One out when winning run scored on Thomson's home run. Bases on balls—Reese, Snider, Robinson 2, Westrum 2. Left on base—Brooklyn 7, New York 3. Wild pitch—Maglie. Umpires—Jorda, Conlan, Stewart, Goetz. Time of game—2:28. Attendance—34,320.

PITCHING	IP	H	R	ER	BB	SO
BROOKLYN						
Newcombe	8.1	7	4	4	2	2
Branca (L, 13–12)	0	1	1	1	0	0
New York						
Maglie	8	8	4	4	4	6
Jansen (W, 23–11)	1	0	0	0	0	0

1959: Los Angeles vs. Milwaukee

It was only fitting that the 1959 National League pennant race required a tiebreaking playoff game to decide its champion. After all, NL fans had enjoyed one of the most compelling races in the game's history that fall, with the league's lead changing hands seven times in the final nine days of the regular season. Three teams—the Los Angeles Dodgers, Milwaukee Braves, and San Francisco Giants—found themselves in a bizarre tangle over the final week and a half of the season and only narrowly avoided an unprecedented three-way tie at the top of the standings.

Heading into the final day of the regular season, the Braves and Dodgers stood tied for first place, with the Giants a game and a half back but still hopeful because of the potential of sweeping a doubleheader against the Cardinals. The Dodgers soon crushed San Francisco's pennant hopes by clubbing the Chicago Cubs, 7–1, behind the pitching of Roger Craig. That victory rendered the Giants' twinbill meaningless, but only tightened the pressure on the Braves, who were scheduled to host the Philadelphia Phillies. Bob Buhl—a 14-game winner—pitched Milwaukee to a 5–2 win, deadlocking the pennant race after 154 games.

The best-of-three-game playoff opened in Milwaukee the next day, but early-afternoon rain showers caused a 47-minute delay before the start of the game. The rain also damaged the Braves' home-field advantage by limiting the crowd to just over 18,000 at 50,000-seat County Stadium.

Both teams had used their best starting pitchers in the final days of the regular season, forcing managers Walter Alston and Fred Haney to rely on unappealing options in the opener. Alston tabbed lefthander Danny McDevitt, a 10-game winner for Los Angeles but a far less intimidating hurler than either Don Drysdale or Sandy Koufax, and less experienced than Roger Craig. Haney countered with an even more shadowy choice in Carlton Willey, who had won only five of 13 decisions and had not started a game since August 3.

The Dodgers touched Willey early, as Charlie Neal led off with a single, moved up to second on a infield grounder, and came home to score on Norm Larker's hit. After producing a scoreless bottom of the first, the Braves rallied for two runs in the second. McDevitt allowed a walk and two consecutive singles, which tied the game, and then missed badly with his first two pitches to Willey. The sudden ineffectiveness against the bottom of the Braves' order convinced Alston to make a change. He lifted Willey and replaced him with veteran reliever Larry Sherry. He induced a groundball, but shortstop Maury Wills bobbled it and all runners were safe. Bobby Avila plated the Braves' second run with an infield grounder. Sherry escaped further trouble, but the Braves now led, 2–1.

Willey immediately surrendered singles to Neal, Larker, and Gil Hodges in the top of the third to tie the game. Catcher John Roseboro, best known for his defense, hit his 10th home run of the year in the sixth inning to give the Dodgers a 3–2 lead. Sherry made the run stand up as he pitched scoreless ball from the third through the ninth inning.

While the first game had spotlighted the bottom end of each team's starting rotation, Game 2 at the Dodgers' new home at Los Angeles Memorial Coliseum offered a matchup of established aces: Lew Burdette for the Braves and Don Drysdale for the Dodgers. Now on the verge of elimination, the Braves handled Drysdale early, scoring two runs in the first inning. A walk, a double by Hank Aaron, and a single by Frank Torre accounted for the Braves' early rally.

The Dodgers cut the lead in half in the bottom of the first, but the Braves applied more pressure to Drysdale in the second. Johnny Logan singled and moved into scoring position on a base hit by Burdette. Duke Snider's errant throw from center field allowed Logan to score Milwaukee's third run.

Charlie Neal's solo home run in the fourth inning made it a one-run game, but Eddie Mathews countered with his 46th homer. His blast gave him the National League home run crown, breaking a tie with Chicago's Ernie Banks; more important, his homer boosted Milwaukee's advantage back to two runs. The Braves added another run in the top of the eighth. Given the pitching of Burdette, who had not permitted a Dodger past first base since Neal's fourth-inning blast, a 5–2 lead seemed nearly insurmountable.

Wally Moon opened the bottom of the ninth with a single, followed by a hit by Snider. Hodges then walked to load the bases and push a suddenly vulnerable Burdette from the game. With no one out, Haney called on veteran righthander Don McMahon.

Norm Larker, one of the heroes in Game 1, dented Milwaukee's lead with a two-run single to draw the Dodgers within one run and push the tying run to third base. McMahon then gave way to Warren Spahn, who surrendered a sacrifice fly to Carl Furillo that tied the game.

Alston turned the ball over to Stan Williams in the 10th. The hard-throwing righthander kept the Braves off the board for three innings. In the 12th, Bob Rush, Milwaukee's fifth pitcher of the day, retired the first two Dodgers. He then walked Hodges and allowed a single to Joe Pignatano. Furillo followed by hitting a high bouncer up the middle. Felix Mantilla, who had moved from second base to shortstop following a seventh-inning injury to Johnny Logan, fielded the ball behind the second base bag. Mantilla's off-balance throw short-hopped Frank Torre at first base. The ball took an unexpected hop to Torre's right and bounced past the first baseman, allowing Hodges to score the winning run.

GAME 1 AT COUNTY STADIUM, MILWAUKEE, SEPTEMBER 28, 1959

LOS ANGELES	AB	R	H	2B	3B	HR	RBI
Gilliam, 3b	4	0	0	0	0	0	0
Neal, 2b	5	1	3	0	0	0	0
Moon, lf	4	1	1	0	0	0	0
Larker, rf	4	0	3	0	0	0	1
Lillis, pr	0	0	0	0	0	0	0
Fairly, rf	0	0	0	0	0	0	0
Hodges, 1b	3	0	1	0	0	0	1
Demeter, cf	4	0	1	0	0	0	0
Roseboro, c	4	1	1	0	0	1	1
Wills, ss	4	0	0	0	0	0	0
McDevitt, p	1	0	0	0	0	0	0
L. Sherry, p	2	0	0	0	0	0	0

MILWAUKEE	AB	R	H	2B	3B	HR	RBI
Avila	5	0	0	0	0	0	1
Mathews	4	0	0	0	0	0	0
Aaron	2	0	0	0	0	0	0
Adcock	3	0	0	0	0	0	0
Pafko	2	0	0	0	0	0	0
Maye, ph-lf	2	0	1	0	0	0	0
Logan, ss	3	1	1	0	0	0	0
Crandall, c	4	1	2	0	0	0	0
Bruton, cf	4	0	1	0	0	0	1
Willey, p	2	0	1	0	0	0	0
Slaughter, ph	1	0	0	0	0	0	0
McMahon, p	0	0	0	0	0	0	0
Torre, ph	1	0	0	0	0	0	0

LA	101	001	000	3	10	1
MIL	020	000	000	2	6	0

Bases on balls—Aaron 2, Logan, Adcock, Hodges, L. Sherry, Gilliam. Left on base—Los Angeles 8, Milwaukee 8. Errors—Wills. Umpires—Conlan, Barlick, Boggess, Donatelli, Gorman, Jackowski. Time of game—2:40. Attendance—18,297.

PITCHING	IP	H	R	ER	BB	SO
LOS ANGELES						
McDevitt	1.1	2	2	2	2	2
L.Sherry (W, 7–2)	7.2	4	0	0	2	4
MILWAUKEE						
Willey (L, 5–9)	6	8	3	3	2	3
McMahon	3	2	0	0	1	2

GAME 2 AT MEMORIAL COLISEUM, LOS ANGELES, SEPTEMBER 29, 1959

MILWAUKEE	AB	R	H	2B	3B	HR	RBI
Bruton, cf	6	0	0	0	0	0	0
Mathews, 3b	4	2	2	0	0	1	1
Aaron, rf	4	1	2	1	0	0	0
Torre, 1b	3	0	1	0	0	0	2
Maye, lf	2	0	0	0	0	0	0
Pafko, ph-lf	1	0	0	0	0	0	0
Slaughter, ph	1	0	0	0	0	0	0
DeMerit, lf	0	0	0	0	0	0	0
Spangler, ph-lf	0	0	0	0	0	0	0
Logan, ss	3	1	2	0	0	0	0
Schoendienst, 2b	1	0	0	0	0	0	0
Vernon, ph	1	0	0	0	0	0	0
Cottier, 2b	0	0	0	0	0	0	0
Adcock, ph	1	0	0	0	0	0	0
Avila, 2b	0	0	0	0	0	0	0
Crandall, c	6	1	1	0	1	0	0

	AB	R	H	2B	3B	HR	RBI
Mantilla, 2b-ss	5	0	1	0	0	0	1
Burdette, p	4	0	1	0	0	0	0
McMahon, p	0	0	0	0	0	0	0
Spahn, p	0	0	0	0	0	0	0
Jay, p	1	0	0	0	0	0	0
Rush, p	1	0	0	0	0	0	0
LOS ANGELES	**AB**	**R**	**H**	**2B**	**3B**	**HR**	**RBI**
Gilliam, 3b	5	0	1	0	0	0	0
Neal, 2b	6	2	2	0	1	1	1
Moon, rf-lf	6	1	3	0	0	0	1
Snider, cf	4	0	1	0	0	0	0
Lillis, pr	0	1	0	0	0	0	0
Williams, p	2	0	0	0	0	0	0
Hodges, 1b	5	2	2	0	0	0	0
Larker, lf	4	0	2	0	0	0	2
Pignatano, pr-c	1	0	1	0	0	0	0
Roseboro, c	3	0	0	0	0	0	0
*Furillo, ph-rf	2	0	2	0	0	0	1
Wills, ss	5	0	1	0	0	0	0
Drysdale, p	1	0	0	0	0	0	0
Podres, p	1	0	0	0	0	0	0
Churn, p	0	0	0	0	0	0	0
Demeter, ph	1	0	0	0	0	0	0
Koufax, p	0	0	0	0	0	0	0
Labine, p	0	0	0	0	0	0	0
Essegian, ph	0	0	0	0	0	0	0
Fairly, ph	2	0	0	0	0	0	0

					R	H	E
MIL	210	010	010	000	5	10	0
LA	100	100	003	001	6	15	0

*Two out when winning run scored on Furillo's ground ball in the bottom of the 12th. Bases on balls—Mathews 2, Aaron 2, Torre 3, DeMerit, Spangler, Gilliam, Hodges. Hit by pitcher—By Jay (Pignatano). Wild pitch—Podres. Passed ball—Pignatano. Umpires—Barlick, Boggess, Donatelli, Conlan, Jackowski, Gorman. Time of game—4:06. Attendance—36,853.

PITCHING	IP	H	R	ER	BB	SO
MILWAUKEE						
Burdette	8	10	5	5	0	4
McMahon	0	1	0	0	0	0
Spahn	.1	1	0	0	0	0
Jay	2.1	1	0	0	1	1
Rush (L, 5–6)	1	2	1	0	1	0
LOS ANGELES						
Drysdale	4.1	6	4	3	2	3
Podres	2.1	3	0	0	1	1
Churn	1.1	1	1	1	0	0
Koufax	.2	0	0	0	3	1
Labine	.1	0	0	0	0	1
Williams (W, 5–5)	3	0	0	0	3	3

1962: San Francisco vs. Los Angeles

After playing outstanding baseball all summer, the Los Angeles Dodgers and San Francisco Giants both stumbled to the finish line. With only two weeks to go in the 1962 season, San Francisco won only six of their next 12 games, but received a major break when the rival Dodgers ran into a slump. Los Angeles went just 3–9 during the same stretch. As a result, the Dodgers held a mere one-game lead over the Giants going into the final day of the season.

With the National League pennant on the line, San Francisco manager Alvin Dark decided that star first baseman Orlando Cepeda didn't give the Giants their best chance of winning the last game. Dark felt Cepeda was exhausted from having played so many games during the regular season after another year of winter ball. As a result Dark benched Cepeda, the same player who had batted over .300 and belted 35 home runs for him during the season. Orlando cried in reaction to the news that he would not start. "That was the worst day of my life," he told Stan Isaacs of *Newsday*.

It wouldn't be a very good day for teammate Felipe Alou, either. San Francisco's starting right fielder also sat out the game—the result of another controversial decision by Dark. Yet the absence of both Cepeda and Alou did not stop the Giants from winning the game. Willie Mays hit a dramatic home run in the bottom of the eighth inning to give the Giants a 2–1 victory over the expansion Houston Colt .45s. With the Dodgers losing their game to the St. Louis Cardinals, the Giants tied Los Angeles atop the National League with a mark of 101–61. Eleven years earlier the same two teams had been forced to play a heart-stopping three-game playoff, but that was when the two clubs were based in New York; now the California clubs would battle it out again—and the series would again be decided by a ninth-inning rally.

Courtesy of a coin flip conducted by National League president Warren Giles, the series opened at San Francisco's Candlestick Park. The Dodgers actually won the flip, but opted to play the second and third games at home, rather than open the series with a single home game at Dodger Stadium. The Giants opened up an early 3–0 lead against a fatigued Sandy Koufax, who allowed a double to Felipe Alou and home runs to Mays and Jim Davenport before departing with no one out in the second.

In the bottom of the sixth inning, Mays and Cepeda hit back-to-back home runs against reliever Larry Sherry to put the game away. San Francisco southpaw Billy Pierce, meanwhile, continued his mastery by the Bay. Pierce's 8–0 complete game was his 12th consecutive win at Candlestick. For the Dodgers, it was their fifth consecutive loss—and their third straight shutout defeat.

Los Angeles hoped that the backdrop of Dodger Stadium would help the team in Game 2, but a disappointing crowd of only 25,321 and a heavy layer of smog hanging over the stadium greeted the club. The Giants scored four runs against Don Drysdale in the sixth to open up a five-run lead. San Francisco starter Jack Sanford blanked the Dodgers for the first five innings, extending the team's scoreless streak to 35 innings.

Without warning, the Dodgers awakened. Jim "Junior" Gilliam reached Sanford for a leadoff walk in the sixth, prompting Alvin Dark to remove his starter. Duke Snider rapped a double against Stu Miller, pushing Gilliam to third and marking the beginning of a hit parade that included three consecutive pinch hits—by Doug Camilli, Andy Carey, and Lee Walls. By the time the Giants employed their third reliever of the inning, the Dodgers had managed to score seven times to take a two-run lead.

The Giants rallied to tie the game with a pair of runs in the eighth, but Los Angeles reliever Stan Williams stopped that rally short. The game remained deadlocked until the bottom of the ninth, when Maury Wills and Gilliam both drew walks. With backup outfielder Daryl Spencer scheduled to bat in a clear-cut bunting situation, Dark summoned Gaylord Perry from the bullpen.

Spencer bunted the ball right to Perry, as Jose Pagan raced to cover third base from his regular position at shortstop. Perry appeared to have time to throw to Pagan and eliminate the lead runner, but opted to throw to first instead. With the game-winning run now standing on third, Dark replaced Perry with lefthander Mike McCormick.

McCormick intentionally walked Tommy Davis, loading the bases and bringing lefty Ron Fairly to the plate. A few moments later, Fairly lofted a flyball to short center field. Although the ball was not hit deep, the fleet Wills was able to score to give the Dodgers a thrilling 8–7 victory.

A much larger crowd of 45,693 fans showed up to watch the visiting Giants open up a 2–0 lead in Game 3. The Giants capitalized on shoddy fielding, which included three errors in the third inning behind starter Johnny Podres. As they had done in the second game, the Dodgers staged a comeback.

Los Angeles scored a run in the fourth and two more in the sixth on a home run by Tommy Davis, with Duke Snider picking up hits in the midst of each rally. The Dodgers added to the lead in the seventh, when Wills collected his fourth straight hit, stole second and third, and came home on Ed Bailey's wild throw down the left field line. The Dodgers took their 4–2 lead into the ninth inning, but pitching—the club's strength throughout the year—cost them the pennant.

Facing reliever Ed Roebuck, the slap-hitting Matty Alou led off the ninth with a pinch-hit single. With one out, Willie McCovey and Felipe Alou—Matty's brother—each drew walks, loading the bases. Willie Mays followed by hitting a ferocious line drive up the middle, off the hand of Roebuck. The infield hit brought home a run and knocked Roebuck from the game.

Los Angeles manager Walter Alston called on Stan Williams, his intimidating righthander who liked to throw inside pitches. Most scouts considered Williams one of the toughest pitchers—and perhaps the meanest—in the major leagues.

With the bases still loaded, Orlando Cepeda swung and missed at a rising fastball. Cepeda drove the next pitch deep toward right field. Frank Howard, the Dodgers' 6-foot-9 giant in the outfield, made a reaching stab of the drive, but it was far enough to score pinch runner Ernie Bowman from third base to tie the game.

The Giants then took the lead, scoring a run on a pair of walks (an intentional pass to Ed Bailey and an unintentional one to Jim Davenport). Jose Pagan followed by hitting a groundball that second baseman Larry Burright bobbled, allowing an insurance run to score.

Billy Pierce came on to retire the Dodgers in order in the bottom of the ninth, sealing an incredible 6–4 win and the first pennant for Horace Stoneham's Giants since 1954. With a dramatic comeback victory in their possession, the Giants were also headed to the World Series for the first time since moving to San Francisco.

GAME 1 AT CANDLESTICK PARK, SAN FRANCISCO, OCTOBER 1, 1962

LOS ANGELES	AB	R	H	2B	3B	HR	RBI
Wills, ss	4	0	0	0	0	0	0
Gilliam, 2b	3	0	0	0	0	0	0
T. Davis, lf	4	0	0	0	0	0	0
Howard, rf	4	0	0	0	0	0	0
Walls, 1b	3	0	0	0	0	0	0
Carey, 3b	3	0	1	0	0	0	0
W. Davis, cf	3	0	0	0	0	0	0
Koufax, p	0	0	0	0	0	0	0
Roebuck, p	1	0	0	0	0	0	0
McMullen, ph	1	0	1	0	0	0	0
Tracewski, pr	0	0	0	0	0	0	0
L. Sherry, p	0	0	0	0	0	0	0
Smith, p	0	0	0	0	0	0	0
Camilli, ph	1	0	1	1	0	0	0
Ortega, p	0	0	0	0	0	0	0
Perranoski, p	0	0	0	0	0	0	0

SAN FRANCISCO	AB	R	H	2B	3B	HR	RBI
Kuenn, lf	5	0	0	0	0	0	0
Hiller, 2b	4	0	1	0	0	0	0
F. Alou, rf	4	1	1	1	0	0	0
Mays, cf	3	3	3	0	0	2	3
Cepeda, 1b	4	1	1	0	0	1	1
Davenport, 3b	3	2	2	0	0	1	1
Bailey, c	2	1	1	0	0	0	0
Pagan, ss	3	0	1	1	0	0	2
Pierce, p	4	0	0	0	0	0	0

				R	H	E
LA	000	000	000	0	3	1
SF	210	002	03x	8	10	0

Bases on balls—Bailey 2, Mays, Davenport, Gilliam. Stolen base—Mays. Sacrifice hit—Pagan. Error—Howard. Umpires—Conlan, Boggess, Donatelli, Landes. Time of game—2:39. Attendance—32,652.

PITCHING	IP	H	R	ER	BB	SO
LOS ANGELES						
Koufax (L, 14–7)	1	4	3	3	0	0
Roebuck	4	1	0	0	0	2
L.Sherry	.1	3	2	2	1	0
Smith	1.2	1	0	0	0	2
Ortega	.1	0	2	2	2	0
Perranoski	.2	1	1	0	1	0
SAN FRANCISCO						
Pierce (W, 16–6)	9	3	0	0	1	6

GAME 2 AT DODGER STADIUM, LOS ANGELES, OCTOBER 2, 1962

SAN FRANCISCO	AB	R	H	2B	3B	HR	RBI
Hiller, 2b	3	1	1	0	0	0	1.
Nieman, ph	1	0	0	0	0	0	0
Bowman, 2b	1	0	0	0	0	0	0
Davenport, 3b	6	1	2	0	0	0	1
Mays, cf	5	0	1	0	0	0	0
McCovey, lf	2	0	1	0	0	0	1
Miller, p	0	0	0	0	0	0	0
O'Dell, p	0	0	0	0	0	0	0
Larsen, p	0	0	0	0	0	0	0
Bailey, ph	1	0	1	0	0	0	1
Boles, pr	0	1	0	0	0	0	0
Bolin, p	0	0	0	0	0	0	0
LeMay, p	0	0	0	0	0	0	0
Perry, p	0	0	0	0	0	0	0
McCormick, p	0	0	0	0	0	0	0
Cepeda, 1b	5	1	1	0	0	0	0
F. Alou, rf	4	0	2	1	0	0	1
Haller, c	1	1	0	0	0	0	0
Orsino, c	1	0	1	0	0	0	1
Pagan, ss	5	1	3	1	0	0	0
Sanford, p	3	1	0	0	0	0	0
M. Alou, lf	0	0	0	0	0	0	0
Kuenn, ph-lf	2	0	0	0	0	0	0

LOS ANGELES	AB	R	H	2B	3B	HR	RBI
Wills, ss	4	1	0	0	0	0	0
Gilliam, 2b-3b	3	1	0	0	0	0	0
Snider, lf	3	1	1	1	0	0	0
Spencer, ph	0	0	0	0	0	0	0
T. Davis, 3b-cf	3	0	1	0	0	0	1
Moon, 1b	2	1	1	0	0	0	0
Fairly, 1b	1	0	1	0	0	0	1
Howard, rf	3	1	1	0	0	0	1
Roseboro, c	2	0	0	0	0	0	0
Camilli, ph-c	2	1	1	0	0	0	0
W. Davis, cf	2	0	0	0	0	0	0
Carey, ph	0	0	0	0	0	0	1
Burright, pr-2b	0	1	0	0	0	0	0
Drysdale, p	2	0	0	0	0	0	0
Roebuck, p	0	0	0	0	0	0	0
Walls, ph	1	1	1	1	0	0	3
Perranoski, p	0	0	0	0	0	0	0
Smith, p	0	0	0	0	0	0	0
Williams, p	1	0	0	0	0	0	0

				R	H	E
SF	010	004	020	7	13	1
LA	000	007	001	8	7	2

Bases on balls—Snider, Howard, Gilliam 2, Moon, Burright, Wills, T. Davis, Haller 2, McCovey 2, F. Alou. Stolen base—Wills. Sacrifice hit—Spencer. Sacrifice flies—T. Davis, Orsino, Fairly. Left on base—San Francisco 13, Los Angeles 7. Errors—Haller, Howard, Drysdale. Hit by pitcher—By Drysdale (Hiller), by O'Dell (Carey). Umpires—Barlick, Boggess, Donatelli, Conlan. Time of game—4:18. Attendance—25,321.

PITCHING	IP	H	R	ER	BB	SO
SAN FRANCISCO						
Sanford	5	2	1	1	3	4
Miller	.1	2	3	3	1	0
O'Dell	0	2	3	2	0	0
Larsen	1.2	1	0	0	0	1
Bolin (L, 7–3)	1	0	1	1	2	2
LeMay	0	0	0	0	1	0

	IP	H	R	ER	BB	SO
Perry	.1	0	0	0	0	0
McCormick	.1	0	0	0	1	0
LOS ANGELES						
Drysdale	5.1	7	5	3	4	4
Roebuck	.2	1	0	0	0	0
Perranoski	1	4	1	1	0	0
Smith	.1	1	1	0	0	0
Williams (W, 14–12)	1.2	0	0	0	1	2

GAME 3 AT DODGER STADIUM, LOS ANGELES, OCTOBER 3, 1962

SAN FRANCISCO	**AB**	**R**	**H**	**2B**	**3B**	**HR**	**RBI**
Kuenn, lf	5	1	2	0	0	0	1
Hiller, 2b	3	0	1	1	0	0	0
McCovey, ph	0	0	0	0	0	0	0
Bowman, pr-2b	0	1	0	0	0	0	0
F. Alou, rf	4	1	1	0	0	0	0
Mays, cf	3	1	1	0	0	0	1
Cepeda, 1b	4	0	1	0	0	0	1
Bailey, c	4	0	2	0	0	0	0
Davenport, 3b	4	0	1	0	0	0	1
Pagan, ss	5	1	2	0	0	0	0
Marichal, p	2	1	1	0	0	0	0
Larsen, p	0	0	0	0	0	0	0
M. Alou, ph	1	0	1	0	0	0	0
Nieman, ph	1	0	0	0	0	0	0
Pierce, p	0	0	0	0	0	0	0

LOS ANGELES	**AB**	**R**	**H**	**2B**	**3B**	**HR**	**RBI**
Wills, ss	5	1	4	0	0	0	0
Gilliam, 2b-3b	5	0	0	0	0	0	0
Snider, lf	3	2	2	1	0	0	0
Burright, 2b	1	0	0	0	0	0	0
Walls, ph	1	0	0	0	0	0	0
T. Davis, 3b-lf	3	1	2	0	0	1	2
Moon, 1b	3	0	0	0	0	0	0
Fairly, 1b-rf	0	0	0	0	0	0	0
Howard, rf	4	0	0	0	0	0	1
Harkness, 1b	0	0	0	0	0	0	0
Roseboro, c	3	0	0	0	0	0	0
W. Davis, cf	3	0	0	0	0	0	0
Podres, p	2	0	0	0	0	0	0
Roebuck, p	2	0	0	0	0	0	0
Williams, p	0	0	0	0	0	0	0
Perranoski, p	0	0	0	0	0	0	0

SF	002	000	004	6	13	3
LA	000	102	100	4	8	4

Bases on balls—T. Davis, Roseboro, W. Davis, Mays 2, McCovey, F. Alou, Bailey, Davenport. Stolen bases—Wills 3, T. Davis. Sacrifice hits—Hiller, Marichal, Fairly. Sacrifice fly—Cepeda. Left on base—San Francisco 12, Los Angeles 8. Errors—Bailey, Pagan, Marichal, Gilliam, Burright, Roseboro, Podres. Wild pitch—Williams. Umpires—Boggess, Donatelli, Conlan, Barlick. Time of game—3:00. Attendance—45,693.

PITCHING	**IP**	**H**	**R**	**ER**	**BB**	**SO**
SAN FRANCISCO						
Marichal	7	8	4	3	1	2
Larsen (W, 5–4)	1	0	0	0	2	1
Pierce	1	0	0	0	0	0
LOS ANGELES						
Podres	5	9	2	1	1	0
Roebuck (L, 10–2)	3.1	4	4	3	3	0
Williams	.1	0	0	0	2	0
Perranoski	.1	0	0	0	0	1

1978: New York vs. Boston

Perhaps the most memorable one-game playoff took place in 1978, when the Boston Red Sox and New York Yankees met in Fenway Park's October twilight to decide the championship of the American League East. It was the culmination of one of baseball's greatest divisional races.

Riddled with injuries to key players like Rich Gossage, and laden with controversies involving the triumvirate of Reggie Jackson, Billy Martin, and George Steinbrenner, the Yankees had endured a miserable first half of the 1978 season. On July 19 the Yankees reached a low-water mark when they fell 14 games behind Boston. Martin's decision to resign four days later paved the way for the hiring of Bob Lemon, who had recently been fired by the White Sox. Lemon, a Hall of Fame pitcher during his playing days, quickly restored order by ignoring a tantrum thrown by Jackson and fining Mickey Rivers and Roy White for breaking team rules. Under Lemon's calming leadership, and aided by the continuing domination of ace lefthander Ron Guidry, the Yankees regrouped and slowly climbed back into contention in the East. (A New York City newspaper strike didn't hurt, either; beat writers were no longer around to fan the flames of controversy that had marked the first half of the season.)

By early September the Yankees moved within four games of the Red Sox, just in time for the start of a quartet of head-to-head games. Four days and one famed "Boston Massacre" later, there was a tie for first place in the AL East.

The Yankees eventually moved past the Red Sox, but Boston reeled off seven straight wins to close within one game of first place heading into the final day of the season. When Cleveland's Rick Waits blanked the Yankees in the Sunday finale, Boston found the door to the pennant ajar. The Red Sox shut out the Toronto Blue Jays, forcing a one-game playoff.

Having won a coin toss in September, the Red Sox enjoyed the advantage of hosting the matchup with the Yankees at Fenway Park. Red Sox manager Don Zimmer selected righthander Mike Torrez, who had won the final game of the previous season's World Series for the Yankees before departing as a free agent. Guidry, who had won 24 of 27 decisions, took the mound for New York.

Carl Yastrzemski started the scoring by driving one of Guidry's pitches inside the right field foul pole. In the sixth inning the Red Sox added to their lead. Leadoff batter Rick Burleson pounded a double and moved up to third on Jerry Remy's sacrifice bunt. Jim Rice, who would win the American League's Most Valuable Player Award over Guidry, followed with a single to center field. Rice's 139th RBI of the season gave the Sox a seemingly safe 2–0 lead.

Torrez still looked strong as he retired Graig Nettles to start the seventh inning, but Chris Chambliss and Roy White followed with back-to-back singles. Bob Lemon then sent veteran Jim Spencer to the plate as a pinch hitter for Brian Doyle, a light-hitting second baseman. Spencer failed to deliver, managing only a harmless flyball. With two on and two out, ninth-place hitter Bucky Dent stepped to the plate.

Second-guessers were already wondering why Lemon wasn't lifting Dent for a pinch hitter. The Yankees could have called on any one of three formidable veterans in the pinch: Jay Johnstone, Gary Thomasson, or Cliff Johnson. Since Lemon had already pinch hit for Doyle, and with Fred Stanley scheduled to come into the game to take his place at second base, Lemon had no other middle infielders at his disposal. The situation seemed to favor the Red Sox.

When Torrez delivered his second pitch, Dent fouled it directly off his left foot. Dent hobbled back to the dugout, changed his bat, and returned to the plate. On the next pitch he lifted a flyball toward left field. If Dent had hit a ball of such moderate depth at Yankee Stadium, it would have been caught well in front of the warning track. But at

Fenway Park the ball had plenty of depth to reach the park's famed left field fence. But did it have enough height to clear the wall and land in the netting above the Green Monster?

Fans watching the game on television back in New York struggled to see the ball against the October background of late afternoon sun and shadows. "Deep to left," cried Bill White, announcing the game on WPIX-TV in New York. "That ball is . . . gone! Home run!" It was just Dent's fifth home run of the year and the defining moment in his career—as well as Torrez's.

There were several critical moments still to come. Later that same inning, Thurman Munson provided an insurance run with an RBI double. In the top of the eighth, Jackson gave the Yankees a three-run lead with a monster home run to center field. The Red Sox rallied for two runs in the bottom of the eighth against Gossage and continued to apply pressure in the ninth. With Burleson on first, Jerry Remy lined a ball solidly toward right field. Draped and blinded by the Fenway sun, Lou Piniella had no idea of the ball's location. He didn't see the ball until it landed on the outfield grass, and then stabbed at it with his glove. Somehow Piniella fielded the ball cleanly, holding Burleson at second base. Instead of having the tying run on third with only one out, the Red Sox still needed to advance their lead runner two more bases to even the game.

Jim Rice followed with a flyball to right field, which would have scored Burleson easily had he already been on third base. As it was, Burleson had to settle for advancing from second to third. With two outs, Yastrzemski came to the plate. Gossage tried to throw his best pitch—a rising fastball—past the slowed swing of the aging Yaz. Down to his final strike, Yastrzemski swung late and lofted a popup down the third base line. Straddling the foul line, Graig Nettles cradled the ball with two hands, ending one of baseball's most classic pressure-filled games as well as one of its most thrilling races.

AT FENWAY PARK, BOSTON, OCTOBER 2, 1978

NEW YORK	AB	R	H	2B	3B	HR	RBI
Rivers, cf	2	1	1	1	0	0	0
Blair, ph-cf	1	0	1	0	0	0	0
Munson, c	5	0	1	1	0	0	1
Piniella, rf	4	0	1	0	0	0	0
Jackson, dh	4	1	1	0	0	1	1
Nettles, 3b	4	0	0	0	0	0	0
Chambliss, 1b	4	1	1	0	0	0	0
White, lf	3	1	1	0	0	0	0
Thomasson, lf	0	0	0	0	0	0	0
Doyle, 2b	2	0	0	0	0	0	0
Spencer, ph	1	0	0	0	0	0	0
F. Stanley, 2b	1	0	0	0	0	0	0
Dent, ss	4	1	1	0	0	1	3
Guidry, p	0	0	0	0	0	0	0
Gossage, p	0	0	0	0	0	0	0
BOSTON	**AB**	**R**	**H**	**2B**	**3B**	**HR**	**RBI**
Burleson, ss	4	1	1	1	0	0	0
Remy, 2b	4	1	2	1	0	0	0
Rice, rf	5	0	1	0	0	0	1
Yastrzemski, lf	5	2	2	0	0	1	2
Fisk, c	3	0	1	0	0	0	0
Lynn, cf	4	0	1	0	0	0	1
Hobson, dh	4	0	1	0	0	0	0
Scott, 1b	4	0	2	1	0	0	0
Brohamer, 3b	1	0	0	0	0	0	0
Bailey, ph	1	0	0	0	0	0	0
Duffy, 3b	0	0	0	0	0	0	0
Evans, ph	1	0	0	0	0	0	0
Torrez, p	0	0	0	0	0	0	0
B. Stanley, p	0	0	0	0	0	0	0
Hassler, p	0	0	0	0	0	0	0
Drago, p	0	0	0	0	0	0	0

				R	H	E
NY	000	000	410	5	8	0
BOS	010	001	020	4	11	0

Bases on balls—Rivers 2, White, Burleson, Fisk. Stolen bases—Rivers 2. Sacrifice hits—Brohamer, Remy. Left on base—New York 6, Boston 9. Passed ball—Munson. Umpires—Denkinger, Evans, Clark, Palermo. Time of game—2:52. Attendance—32,925.

PITCHING	IP	H	R	ER	BB	SO
NEW YORK						
Guidry (W, 25–3)	6.1	6	2	2	1	5
Gossage (Save 27)	2.2	5	2	2	1	2
BOSTON						
Torrez (L, 16–13)	6.2	5	4	4	3	4
Stanley	.1	2	1	1	0	0
Hassler	1.2	1	0	0	0	2
Drago	.1	0	0	0	0	0

1980: Houston vs. Los Angeles

The identity of the first-place finisher in the National League West seemed like a foregone conclusion. The Houston Astros held a three-game lead over the second-place Los Angeles Dodgers with only three games to play in the regular season. Of course, it helped the Dodgers that they were scheduled to play those three games against the Astros. Additionally, Los Angeles would have the comfort of playing at Dodger Stadium. Still, the Dodgers faced a daunting task; they would have to sweep the Astros in the weekend three-game set just to force a tiebreaking game on Monday afternoon.

The Dodgers won Friday's game in extra innings, thanks to a masterful pitching relief effort by recently recalled lefthander Fernando Valenzuela. Los Angeles also won Saturday's game, 2–1, as veteran southpaw Jerry Reuss outdueled Nolan Ryan. And then on Sunday, rookie Steve Howe notched a victory in relief as the Dodgers again scraped by the Astros, 4–3. Somehow, the Dodgers had won all three games—all by one-run margins. A one-game playoff would now be needed to determine the winner of the National League's crown—and an earlier coin flip had determined the game would be played in Los Angeles. Unlike the first four National League tiebreakers played before the start of divisional play in 1969, this would be the first one-game playoff—the others had all been best-of-three-game series. It would, however, be the same in one respect: For the fifth time it would involve the Dodgers.

In spite of having momentum and home field advantage in their favor, the Dodgers experienced moments of uncertainty early in the tiebreaking game. Second baseman Davey Lopes bobbled Terry Puhl's leadoff grounder for an error. Later in the inning, catcher Joe Ferguson dropped a throw at the plate, enabling Puhl to score the first run of the game. Cesar Cedeno followed with another run-scoring ground ball, giving the Astros a 2–0 jump.

Having capitalized on the Dodgers' unsettled defense, Astros hitters took on a more threatening pose in the third. Enos Cabell singled against starter Dave Goltz and then came home to score on an unlikely home run by Art Howe, Houston's singles-hitting first baseman. Houston continued to expand its lead in the fourth, knocking a wobbling Goltz from the game. Puhl led off with a single and then stole both second and third base. After walks to Cabell and Joe Morgan, Jose Cruz lofted a sacrifice fly to score Puhl. Two batters later, Howe added to his clutch-hitting resume by depositing a single into center field, increasing Houston's advantage to seven runs.

In the bottom of the fourth, veteran knuckleballer Joe Niekro showed small signs of cracking by allowing the Dodgers to score their first run of the afternoon on a single by Rick Monday. Niekro tossed scoreless ball over the final five innings. His complete-game six-hitter gave him his second consecutive 20-win season—and clinched the first division title in the history of the Houston franchise. The victory also set the stage for one of the league's most dramatic Championship Series: a taut five-game struggle between Houston and Philadelphia.

AT DODGER STADIUM, LOS ANGELES, OCTOBER 6, 1980

HOUSTON	AB	R	H	2B	3B	HR	RBI
Puhl, rf	5	2	1	0	0	0	0
Cabell, 3b	4	2	2	0	0	0	0
Bergman, 1b	0	0	0	0	0	0	0
Morgan, 2b	2	1	0	0	0	0	0
Landestoy, 2b	2	0	0	0	0	0	0
Cruz, lf	4	0	1	0	0	0	1
Cedeno, cf	4	1	1	0	0	0	1
A.Howe, 1b-3b	5	1	3	0	0	1	4
Ashby, c	4	0	1	0	0	0	0
Reynolds, ss	4	0	3	1	0	0	0
Niekro, p	2	0	0	0	0	0	0
LOS ANGELES	**AB**	**R**	**H**	**2B**	**3B**	**HR**	**RBI**
Lopes, 2b	4	0	0	0	0	0	0
S.Howe, p	0	0	0	0	0	0	0
Johnstone, rf	4	0	0	0	0	0	0
Baker, lf	4	1	1	0	0	0	0
Garvey, 1b	4	0	0	0	0	0	0
Monday, cf	3	0	1	0	0	0	1
Ferguson, c	4	0	1	0	0	0	0
Hatcher, 3b	3	0	1	0	0	0	0
Thomasson, ph	1	0	0	0	0	0	0
Thomas, ss	3	0	2	0	0	0	0
Goltz, p	0	0	0	0	0	0	0
Law, ph	1	0	0	0	0	0	0
Sutcliffe, p	0	0	0	0	0	0	0
Beckwith, p	0	0	0	0	0	0	0
Castillo, p	0	0	0	0	0	0	0
Davalillo, ph	1	0	0	0	0	0	0
Valenzuela, p	0	0	0	0	0	0	0
Perconte, ph-2b	2	0	0	0	0	0	0

				R	H	E
HOU	202	300	000	7	12	1
LA	000	100	000	1	6	2

Bases on balls—Cabell, Morgan, Cedeno, Ashby, Monday, Thomas. Stolen bases—Cabell, Cedeno, Puhl 2. Sacrifice hits—Niekro 2. Sacrifice flies—Cruz. Passed ball—Ashby. Umpires—Harvey, Colosi, Runge, Dale. Time of game—3:10. Attendance—51,127.

PITCHING	IP	H	R	ER	BB	SO
HOUSTON						
Niekro (W, 20–12)	9	6	1	0	2	6
LOS ANGELES						
Goltz (L, 7–11)	3	8	4	2	0	2
Sutcliffe	.1	1	3	3	2	0
Beckwith	.1	1	0	0	1	0
Castillo	1.1	1	0	0	1	2
Valenzuela	2	1	0	0	0	1
S.Howe	2	0	0	0	0	0

1995: Seattle vs. California

After tiebreaking playoff games had occurred twice in a three-year span, there were none for a decade and a half. And for most of the strike-shortened 1995 season, the possibility of a tiebreaking game seemed remote, at best, in the American League West. By August 9 the California Angels led the second-place Seattle Mariners by 11 games. By August 20 they had stretched their cushion to 12½ games—the largest lead in the team's checkered history.

Unfortunately for the Angels, the final two months of the regular season would reflect the futility of a franchise that had repeatedly failed in its quest to make beloved owner Gene Autry a World Series participant. From August 25 to September 26 the Angels won a grand total of six games. A pair of nine-game losing streaks contributed to California's collapse, which saw the Angels' lead completely disintegrate into a three-game deficit.

The Angels rallied to win their final five games, allowing them to draw into a deadlock with the Mariners at the end of the regular-season schedule. The Angels, however, faced two imposing obstacles in trying to win a tiebreaking playoff game. First, the club would have to play the elimination game at the Kingdome, where the Mariners had developed a powerful home field advantage thanks to their suddenly clamorous fans and an ear-numbing sound system. More important, the Angels would have to overcome the extraordinary pitching of Cy Young Award favorite Randy Johnson, winner of 17 of 19 decisions.

Ironically, the Angels countered with veteran left-hander Mark Langston, who had been the Mariners' ace during the late 1980s. From 1984 to mid-1989, Langston had won 79 games as one of the Mariners' few bright spots. Then came a trade to the pennant-contending Montreal Expos, whose return package featured three players, including a wild and uncertain prospect named Randy Johnson.

Over the first four innings, Langston matched Johnson in a scoreless duel. Seattle's offense finally broke through in the fifth, pushing across a single run against a stingy Langston. Given Johnson's domination during the regular season, a 1–0 lead seemed monumental. Still, the Angels had managed to keep the game close, giving their dangerous lineup (one of only two AL teams during the shortened 1995 season to score more than 800 runs) a reasonable chance to draw even.

The Angels needed only one swing of the bat to tie the game, but California could not even reach base against an impervious Johnson. The 6-foot-10 southpaw retired the first 17 batters he faced until California's ninth-place hitter, the pesky Rex Hudler, finally managed a two-out single. Hudler was left stranded when Johnson retired leadoff man Tony Phillips.

With their 1–0 lead still intact, Mike Blowers led off the bottom of the seventh with a single. Seattle manager Lou Piniella asked Tino Martinez to lay down a sacrifice bunt, but second baseman Hudler made a last-minute break in covering first, forcing a late throw by Langston. Dan Wilson followed with another sacrifice bunt, moving both runners up. After Langston hit Joey Cora with a pitch, Vince Coleman laced a line drive to right field, where Tim Salmon made the catch. To the surprise of some Mariners (especially an irate Coleman), Blowers did not tag. The bases remained loaded as the slap-hitting Luis Sojo waddled to the plate.

Just one out away from escaping what had seemed like a hopeless jam, Langston made a good pitch to Sojo, breaking his bat. Sojo fought off the pitch with his typical opposite-field swing, resulting in a line drive down the right field line. As the ball skirted into the bullpen, both Blowers and Martinez scored. Cora also rounded third and decided to challenge the arm of Langston, who had fielded the relay from Tim Salmon in right. Langston, a seven-time Gold Glove winner, double-pumped and then made a poor throw past catcher Andy Allanson. By the time Allanson had retrieved the ball and thrown to Langston at the plate, not only had Cora scored, but Sojo had raced home as well.

The Mariners added four more runs in the eighth, expanding their lead to 9–0. Johnson allowed a home run to Phillips in the ninth, but it mattered little, other than denying Johnson a shutout. The 9–1 victory put the Mariners in the postseason for the first time in the franchise's 19-year history and set the stage for a stunning five-game Division Series conquest of the New York Yankees.

As for the fallen Angels, they could not even console themselves with the newly created avenue to the postseason: the Wild Card. California's 76–67 record left the team 1½ games behind the Yankees. Gene Autry never saw his Angels reach the World Series; the club was sold the following year and the Hollywood legend died in 1998.

AT THE KINGDOME, SEATTLE, OCTOBER 2, 1995

CALIFORNIA	AB	R	H	2B	3B	HR	RBI
Phillips, 3b	4	1	1	0	0	1	1
DiSarcina, ss	3	0	0	0	0	0	0
Owen, ph	1	0	0	0	0	0	0
Edmonds, cf	3	0	0	0	0	0	0
Perez, ph	1	0	0	0	0	0	0
Salmon, rf	4	0	0	0	0	0	0
Davis, dh	2	0	0	0	0	0	0
Snow, 1b	3	0	0	0	0	0	0
Anderson, lf	2	0	0	0	0	0	0
Gallagher, ph-lf	1	0	0	0	0	0	0
Allanson, c	2	0	0	0	0	0	0
Gonzales, ph	1	0	1	1	0	0	0
Fabregas, c	0	0	0	0	0	0	0
Hudler, 2b	3	0	1	0	0	0	0
Langston, p	0	0	0	0	0	0	0
Patterson, p	0	0	0	0	0	0	0
James, p	0	0	0	0	0	0	0
Holzemer, p	0	0	0	0	0	0	0
Habyan, p	0	0	0	0	0	0	0

SEATTLE	AB	R	H	2B	3B	HR	RBI
Coleman, lf	5	0	2	0	0	0	1
Sojo, ss	3	1	2	1	0	0	3
Griffey, cf	3	0	0	0	0	0	0
E. Martinez, dh	3	1	2	0	0	0	0
Buhner, rf	4	1	1	0	0	0	0
Blowers, 3b	3	2	2	0	0	0	0
T. Martinez, 1b	2	2	1	0	0	0	1
Wilson, c	3	1	1	1	0	0	2
Cora, 2b	2	1	1	0	0	0	1
Johnson, p	0	0	0	0	0	0	0

CAL	000	000	001	1	3	1
SEA	000	010	44x	9	12	0

Bases on balls—Davis, Griffey, E. Martinez, Blowers, T. Martinez. Sacrifice hits—Sojo, T. Martinez, Wilson. Sacrifice fly—Cora. Left on base—California 3, Seattle 4. Error—Langston. Hit by pitch—By Langston (Cora). Umpires—Shulock, Evans, Young, Kosc, Johnson, Kaiser. Time of game—2:50. Attendance—52,356.

PITCHING	IP	H	R	ER	BB	SO
CALIFORNIA						
Langston (L, 15–7)	6.2	8	5	4	3	2
Patterson	.1	0	0	0	0	1
James	0	2	3	3	1	0
Holzemer	0	1	1	1	0	0
Habyan	1	1	0	0	0	1
SEATTLE						
Johnson (W, 18–2)	9	3	1	1	1	12

1998: Chicago vs. San Francisco

While tiebreaking playoff games had been needed to determine the winners of pennant races and divisional races, the 1998 season created the necessity for a different kind of tiebreaker: one that would determine the Wild Card, which had been introduced only three years earlier. Two surprising second-place teams, the Chicago Cubs from the Central Division and the San Francisco Giants from the Western Division, finished the regular season with identical records. The two teams arrived at that record in vastly different ways, as the Cubs dropped five of their last seven games, while the Giants won six of their last seven. Yet the Giants easily could have won the Wild Card without a tiebreaker, if only they had been able to maintain a 7–0 lead over Colorado in their 162nd game of the season. Instead, the Giants blew the lead and lost an 8–7 heartbreaker on a home run by Neifi Perez, mandating a one-game playoff against the Cubs. It could have been weirder—if the New York Mets had beaten the Atlanta Braves on the final day of the season, it would have created the first playoff involving three teams.

In addition to making history as the first Wild Card tiebreaker, the one-game matchup between the Cubs and Giants represented the first time that a tiebreaker would be played at night. Ironically, the backdrop would be provided by the historic presence of Wrigley Field, the last existing ballpark to install lights. Chicago's Steve Trachsel opposed San Francisco's Mark Gardner in a matchup of veteran righthanders.

During the regular season, Trachsel had gained unwanted notoriety by allowing Mark McGwire's record-breaking 62nd home run. Now, less than a month later, Trachsel was taking a no-hitter into the seventh inning. With one out in the top of the seventh, Giants catcher Brent Mayne broke through with a single, but was left stranded when Matt Karchner picked up the third out in relief of Trachsel.

By the time Trachsel's no-hit bid came to an end, the Cubs had built up a 4–0 lead. The ageless Gary Gaetti—who had been signed in midseason after being released by the Cardinals—had kick-started Chicago's offense with a two-run homer in the bottom of the fifth. The Cubs added to their advantage in the bottom of the sixth, when they loaded the bases and set the stage for a two-run single by pinch hitter Matt Mieske.

The offensive fireworks of supporting cast members like Mieske and Gaetti overshadowed the performance of Sammy Sosa, whose season-long pursuit with McGwire of the 37-year-old home run record of Roger Maris had helped rejuvenate the sport. Sosa did not homer in the tiebreaker against the Giants, leaving him with 66 home runs, four shy of McGwire's total but still the second-highest total ever. Sosa nonetheless had two hits in four at bats against San Francisco pitching.

With a 4–0 lead in tow, Cubs manager Jim Riggleman turned to his bullpen, but not his regular relievers. Lacking confidence in his usual corps of middle men, Riggleman called on a pair of starting pitchers—Kevin Tapani and Terry Mulholland—to pitch the seventh and eighth. The decision to use Mulholland was surprising, given that the veteran lefthander had thrown 121 pitches in an eight-inning stint the previous day.

Neither Tapani nor Mulholland pitched well, prompting Riggleman to call on another overworked pitcher, closer Rod Beck. With one out in the ninth inning and the Giants in the midst of a three-run rally, Beck retired the dangerous Jeff Kent. Beck would now have to face veteran slugger Joe Carter, who was hitless in three official at bats. Ironically, the 1993 World Series hero had started his career at Wrigley Field with the Cubs, only to be traded to the Indians as part of the famed 1984 deal that brought Rick Sutcliffe and his division-winning pitching to the Windy City. Now on the verge of retirement, Carter hoped he had enough bat speed left to hit a two-run homer, which would tie the game. Carter swung hard at a Beck delivery but popped the ball up meekly on the infield. Chicago's 5–3 victory earned the franchise its first trip to the postseason since 1989.

AT WRIGLEY FIELD, CHICAGO, SEPTEMBER 28, 1998

SAN FRANCISCO	AB	R	H	2B	3B	HR	RBI
Javier, cf	3	1	1	1	0	0	0
Aurilia, ss	3	0	0	0	0	0	0
Dunston, ph-ss	1	0	1	0	0	0	0
Burks, ph	0	0	0	0	0	0	0
Sanchez, pr	0	0	0	0	0	0	0
Bonds, lf	4	0	0	0	0	0	1
Kent, 2b	4	0	0	0	0	0	1
Carter, rf	4	0	0	0	0	0	0
Snow, 1b	3	0	1	0	1	0	0
Hayes, 3b	3	0	0	0	0	0	0
Mesa, p	0	0	0	0	0	0	0
B. Johnson, c	2	0	0	0	0	0	0
Mayne, ph-c	2	1	2	0	0	0	0
Gardner, p	2	0	0	0	0	0	0
Rodriguez, p	0	0	0	0	0	0	0
Johnstone, p	0	0	0	0	0	0	0
Rios, ph	0	0	0	0	0	0	0
Ortiz, p	0	0	0	0	0	0	0
Morman, p	0	0	0	0	0	0	0
Mueller, 3b	1	1	1	0	0	0	0
CHICAGO	**AB**	**R**	**H**	**2B**	**3B**	**HR**	**RBI**
L. Johnson, cf	4	1	1	0	0	0	0
Morandini, 2b	4	0	1	0	0	0	0
Sosa, rf	4	2	2	0	0	0	0
Grace, 1b	3	0	2	1	0	0	0
Rodriguez, lf	2	1	1	0	0	0	0
Mieske, ph-lf	1	0	1	0	0	0	2
Karchner, p	0	0	0	0	0	0	0
Heredia, p	0	0	0	0	0	0	0
Tapani, p	1	0	0	0	0	0	0
Mulholland, p	0	0	0	0	0	0	0
Beck, p	0	0	0	0	0	0	0
Gaetti, 3b	4	1	1	0	0	1	2
Houston, c	3	0	0	0	0	0	0
Hernandez, ss	2	0	1	0	0	0	0
Trachsel, p	1	0	0	0	0	0	0
Merced, lf	1	0	0	0	0	0	0

				R	H	E
SF	000	000	003	3	6	0
CHI	000	022	01X	5	10	0

Bases on balls—Javier 2, Burks, Carter, Snow, Hayes, Rios, Grace, Hernandez. Sacrifice—Trachsel. Sacrifice fly—Bonds. Stolen base—Hernandez. Left on base—San Francisco 11, Chicago 4. Umpires—Froemming, Rippley, Darling, Winters, Poncino, Vanover. Time of game—3:41. Attendance—39,556.

PITCHING	IP	H	R	ER	BB	SO
SAN FRANCISCO						
Gardner (L, 13–6)	5.1	6	4	4	1	2
R. Rodriguez	0	1	0	0	1	0
Johnstone	.2	0	0	0	0	0
Ortiz	.2	1	0	0	0	0
Morman	.2	0	0	0	0	1
Mesa	.2	2	1	1	0	0
CHICAGO						
Trachsel (W, 15–8)	6.1	1	0	0	6	6
Karchner	.1	1	0	0	0	0
Heredia	.1	0	0	0	0	0
Tapani	1.0	3	2	2	0	0
Mulholland	.1	1	1	1	1	0
Beck (Save 51)	.2	0	0	0	0	0

1999: New York vs. Cincinnati

On September 19, 1999, the New York Mets opened up a four-game lead over the Cincinnati Reds for the Wild Card berth in the National League playoff race. With only 10 days remaining in the regular season, the identity of the final playoff team in the NL seemed certain. Well, not quite so certain.

The Mets suddenly lost seven consecutive games, spurring rumors that embattled manager Bobby Valentine might be fired *before* the season came to an end. Just as the Mets reached the depths of depression, Valentine remained aboard and the team rebounded. After sweeping the final three regularly scheduled games against the Pittsburgh Pirates, the Mets insured themselves of at least a tie with the Cincinnati Reds.

In the meantime, the Reds experienced a rollercoaster conclusion to their season. They swept a four-game weekend series from the St. Louis Cardinals, but followed that up with a split of a two-game set with the Houston Astros. Cincinnati then lost the first two games of their final series to the lowly Milwaukee Brewers. On the final Sunday, the Reds had to wait out a 347-minute rain delay. By the time the rain had subsided and the game had been played to a 7–1 finish, an exhausted group of Reds prepared for a sudden-death winner-take-all match with the rejuvenated Mets.

As fortune would have it, the Mets could confidently hand the ball to their lefthanded ace, Al Leiter, who would pitch on his usual four days' rest. In contrast, the latest turn in Cincinnati's starting rotation fell upon journeyman Steve Parris. Although Parris had surprised observers by winning 11 of 14 decisions during the season, his pedigree lacked the impressiveness of Leiter, who had once started the seventh game of a World Series.

Playing in front of a capacity crowd of 54,621 at Cincinnati's Cinergy Field, the Mets took advantage of a shaky Parris from the opening pitch. After Rickey Henderson reached on a leadoff single, Edgardo Alfonzo clubbed the righthander's sixth pitch of the night over the left field wall. The two-run homer—Alfonzo's 27th of the season—placed immediate pressure on the Reds. The Mets added a single run in the third (knocking a wild Parris from the game in favor of Denny Neagle), then padded the lead further on Henderson's solo home run in the fifth. The Mets rounded out the scoring with a single run in the sixth.

Such ample run support proved more than enough for Leiter, who pitched his finest game of the season. Leiter allowed only two hits—a single to Jeffrey Hammonds and a double to Pokey Reese—in shutting down one of the National League's most prolific offensive lineups. When Dmitri Young hit Leiter's 133rd pitch right at Alfonzo, the lefthander's night—and Cincinnati's season—came to an official end.

The Mets poured onto the field to celebrate the 5–0 whitewash and the franchise's first trip to the postseason since 1988. No one had played as vital a role as Leiter, whose 13th win of the season seemed almost as momentous as his performance in Game 7 of the 1997 World Series.

AT CINERGY FIELD, CINCINNATI, OCTOBER 4, 1999

NEW YORK	AB	R	H	2B	3B	HR	RBI
Henderson, lf	5	2	2	0	0	1	1
Mora, lf	0	0	0	0	0	0	0
Alfonzo, 2b	4	2	2	1	0	1	3
Olerud, 1b	5	0	2	1	0	0	0
Piazza, c	2	0	0	0	0	0	0
Ventura, 3b	3	0	1	0	0	0	1
Hamilton, cf	4	0	1	0	0	0	0
Cedeno, rf	4	0	1	0	0	0	0
Ordonez, ss	3	1	0	0	0	0	0
Leiter, p	3	0	0	0	0	0	0
CINCINNATI	**AB**	**R**	**H**	**2B**	**3B**	**HR**	**RBI**
Reese, 2b	3	0	1	1	0	0	0
Larkin, ss	3	0	0	0	0	0	0
Casey, 1b	4	0	0	0	0	0	0
Vaughn, lf	3	0	0	0	0	0	0
Young, rf	4	0	0	0	0	0	0
Hammonds, cf	3	0	1	0	0	0	0
Taubensee, c	2	0	0	0	0	0	0
Boone, 3b	3	0	0	0	0	0	0
Parris, p	0	0	0	0	0	0	0
Neagle, p	1	0	0	0	0	0	0
Stynes, ph	1	0	0	0	0	0	0
Graves, p	0	0	0	0	0	0	0
Lewis, ph	1	0	0	0	0	0	0
Reyes, p	0	0	0	0	0	0	0

NY	201	011	000	5	9	0
CIN	000	000	000	0	2	0

Bases on balls—Alfonzo, Piazza 3, Ventura 2, Hamilton, Ordonez, Reese, Larkin, Vaughn, Taubensee. Sacrifice—Leiter. Left on base—New York 10, Cincinnati 5. Umpires—Froemming, G. Davis, M. Hirschbeck, Rapuano, Rieker, Nelson. Time of game—3:03. Attendance—54,621.

PITCHING	IP	H	R	ER	BB	SO
NEW YORK						
Leiter (W, 13–12)	9	2	0	0	4	7
CINCINNATI						
Parris (L, 11–4)	2.2	3	3	3	3	1
Neagle	2.1	2	1	1	3	2
Graves	3	2	1	1	2	2
Reyes	1	2	0	0	0	0

CHAPTER 11

Postseason Play

Frederick Ivor-Campbell and David Pietrusza

When Major League Baseball and the striking players were unable to work out a settlement of their dispute in 1994, they interrupted a tradition of major league postseason play that traced back to 1871, the first year there was a professional league. National Association teams in the 1870s typically followed the conclusion of their championship (regularly scheduled) season with exhibition games against amateur clubs. In the 1880s nearly every major league club played a couple of weeks of postseason games, generally against major and minor league teams they hadn't faced during the regular season. In the 20th century there had been a World Series every year for 90 years, prefaced since 1969 by League Championship Series to determine the American and National League pennant winners.

Before there was a World Series there were city and regional series. In 1882 Cleveland defeated Cincinnati for the championship of Ohio, and the next year teams in Philadelphia and New York played for the championships of those cities. These were informal series, arranged by the clubs themselves without official league sanction, and varied in the number of games scheduled according to the desires of the clubs involved.

The same held true for the early World Series, which had their beginnings in 1884. Two years earlier, the champions of the National League and the brand-new American Association played a pair of postseason contests (in which each team recorded a shutout against the other). Some would like to call these games the first World Series, but no one in 1882 saw them as more than exhibition games. In fact, because the NL didn't yet recognize the legitimacy of the AA and forbade its clubs to play those of the new league, the NL champion Chicago White Stockings had to release their players from their season contracts so they could face AA champion Cincinnati as technically independent players.

That winter the two major leagues made their peace, and although a proposed series between the 1883 NL and AA titlists was called off, the 1884 champion Providence Grays (NL) and the Metropolitan Club of New York (AA) played three games "for the championship of the United States." The winning Grays were acclaimed in the press as "champions of the world," and the World Series was born.

The brief 1884 Series set the stage for more elaborate World Series to follow. From 1885 through 1890 the NL and AA pennant-winners met in Series that ranged in length from six games to fifteen.

The demise of the AA after the 1891 season caused a one-year gap in postseason championship play. When the National League expanded from eight clubs to 12 the next year (by absorbing four teams from the defunct AA), it divided the regular season into two halves, with the first-half winner playing the winner of the second half for the title. Boston defeated Cleveland in the postseason championship series, but the unpopular divided season was not repeated (that is, until the strike year of 1981).

Two years later a new postseason scheme was devised when one William C. Temple offered a prize cup to the winner of a postseason series between the first- and second-place finishers in the NL. For four years these best-of-seven Temple Cup games served as the officially recognized world championship. But by the end of four lopsided Series (only one of which was won by the pennant-winning club), fan interest—never robust—had declined so much that the trophy was returned to its donor and the series abandoned.

In 1900, partisans of second-place Pittsburgh felt that their Pirates were the equal of pennant-winning Brooklyn, and a Pittsburgh newspaper, the *Chronicle-Telegraph*, offered a silver trophy cup to the winner of a best-of-five series between the clubs, to be played entirely in Pittsburgh. Described in the press as the "world's championship series," the games confirmed the superiority of Brooklyn's Superbas, who needed only four games to subdue the hometown Pirates.

The upgrading of the American League from minor to major league status in 1901 made a return to interleague World Series play theoretically possible, but it was not until after the NL and AL had made peace in 1903 that the first modern Series was contested. The owners of NL champion Pittsburgh and AL champion Boston arranged a best-of-nine postseason Series in 1903, which proved both popular and financially successful—a firm foundation for future Series. When the NL pennant-winning Giants refused to meet repeating AL titlist Boston in 1904, press and fan disappointment led baseball's National Commission to establish the World Series officially in 1905.

The end of the 1903 season saw not only the first modern World Series, but also a revival of city and regional series (which had lapsed when the AA folded) in Chicago, Philadelphia, St. Louis, and Ohio. In 1905 the National Commission offered to oversee these series, too, and give them the stability of official sanction. Until the manpower needs of the World War halted the 1918 season a month early (discouraging postseason play apart from the World Series), most of the city and regional series—and occasional series between other clubs, like Cleveland

and Pittsburgh, and the Boston Red Sox and New York Giants—were played under National Commission auspices.

After the war's end, only Chicago's Cubs and White Sox resumed a city series; they played 16 series between 1921 and 1942, when World War II intervened. For 26 years thereafter the World Series alone remained of the once multifaceted major league postseason—until the AL and NL split into two divisions each in 1969 and ushered in a new layer of playoffs: the League Championship Series. (In 1981, to recoup some of the money and fan interest lost during a midseason players' strike that split the season in half, a one-time third layer of postseason playoffs was added, pitting the first-half and second-half winners in each division against each other for the division titles—an aberration that made the divisional races even more surreal than the strike itself had done.) From 1969 through 1984 the LCS were played as best-of-five series, but in 1985 they were expanded to match the best-of-seven World Series.

In 1993, the club owners voted to realign each league into three divisions—East, Central, and West—and to install a preliminary layer of playoffs for each league. The three divisional champions and the second-place team with the best record would determine, through a pair of best-of-five Division Series, which two teams would compete for the pennant in the League Championship Series. The first Division Series games were held in 1995.

Key to the Statistics

The statistics in this section of *Total Baseball* are standard—there is little point in applying newer analytical measures to performances that run to seven games or fewer. We do offer, however, stats that were not standard at the time, such as earned run averages for years before 1912 and runs batted in before 1920 (which were determined from box scores and play-by-plays) and saves before 1969. Beyond our powers of reconstruction were the following: runs batted in, stolen bases, and batter strikeouts for the World Series of 1885.

The length of the World Series varied from three games in 1884 all the way up to 15 in 1887 and 10 the following year. The best-of-seven format came in with the Temple Cup Series of 1894 and has been the norm for World Series ever since (excepting 1900, 1903, and 1919–1921). In recent years this format has become the norm for League Championship Series as well. The rules of the day are used for scoring methods, so walks are counted as hits in the 1887 World Series.

If a player appeared at more than one position during the Series, the number of games he played at each is noted (for example, a man who divided seven games at shortstop and third base would carry the notation *ss-4, 3b-3*). Other abbreviations are as follows:

POS	Position	SB	Stolen Bases
AVG	Batting average	W	Wins
G	Games	L	Losses
AB	At bats	ERA	Earned run average
R	Runs	GS	Games started
H	Hits	CG	Complete games
2B	Doubles	SHO	Shutouts
3B	Triples	SV	Saves
HR	Home runs	IP	Innings pitched
RB	Runs batted in	ER	Earned runs
BB	Bases on Balls	SO	Strikeouts

After a flurry of boasts and challenges, Mets manager Jim Mutrie and the Grays' Frank Bancroft arranged a three-game series in New York to determine which team was the nation's best. These were not the first games between NL and AA pennant winners. In 1882, the AA's first season, champion Cincinnati met NL titlist Chicago twice as part of its postseason schedule, in games viewed simply as exhibition contests. (Each team won one). The next year a postseason series was proposed between champions Boston (NL) and the Athletics of Philadelphia (AA), but the Athletics fared so poorly in exhibitions against lesser NL teams that they refused to face Boston.

The 1884 Series was touted as "for the championship of the United States," but the influential weekly *Sporting Life* established precedent for future Series hype by naming victorious Providence "Champions of the World." The weather turned cold and windy as the Series got under way. A hardy opening game crowd of 2,500 saw the Grays' great Charlie "Old Hoss" Radbourn blank the Mets on two singles. Mets pitcher Tim Keefe, wild at the start, paved the way for two first-inning Providence runs by hitting the first two men to face him and assisted them around the bases with a pair of wild pitches. Paul Hines singled in the third for the Grays' first hit and scored as a passed ball and two more wild pitches brought him home. Keefe yielded only four other hits, but they came back to back in the seventh to produce the Grays' final three runs.

The 1,000 spectators at Game 2 witnessed the Series' closest contest. Keefe and Radbourn overwhelmed their opposition for four innings, but in the top of the fifth the Grays bunched three of their five hits for three two-out runs as Jerry Denny homered over the center field fence. The Mets responded with a run in the last of the fifth, but scored no more before darkness ended the game after seven innings.

The Grays had clinched the championship with their second win, and when they saw only a few hundred diehards in the stands for Game 3, they wanted to go home. The Mets must have regretted their insistence on playing the game. Although darkness halted it after only six innings, rookie New York pitcher Buck Becannon (replacing Keefe, who umpired) and awful Mets fielding gave Providence 11 or 12 runs (scorers disagreed), while Radbourn held the New Yorkers to a pair of unearned tallies.

Providence Grays (NL), 3; New York Mets (AA), 0

PRO (N)

PLAYER/POS	AVG	G	AB	R	H	2B	3B	HR	RB	BB	SO	SB
Cliff Carroll, of	.100	3	10	2	1	0	0	0	1	0	1	0
Jerry Denny, 3b	.444	3	9	3	4	0	1	1	2	0	3	0
Jack Farrell, 2b	.444	3	9	3	4	2	0	0	0	0	0	1
Barney Gilligan, c	.444	3	9	3	4	2	0	0	2	0	1	0
Paul Hines, of	.375	3	8	5	3	0	0	0	1	1	0	2
Arthur Irwin, ss	.333	3	9	3	3	0	1	0	2	0	2	0
Charlie Radbourn, p	.100	3	10	1	1	0	0	0	2	1	3	0
Paul Radford, of	.000	3	7	1	0	0	0	0	1	1	1	0
Joe Start, 1b	.100	3	10	0	1	0	0	0	1	0	2	0
TOTAL	.259		81	21	21	4	2	1	12	3	13	3

PITCHER	W	L	ERA	G	GS	CG	SV	SHO	IP	H	ER	BB	SO
Charlie Radbourn	3	0	0.00	3	3	3	0	1	22.0	11	0	0	16
TOTAL	3	0	0.00	3	3	3	0	1	22.0	11	0	0	16

NY (A)

PLAYER/POS	AVG	G	AB	R	H	2B	3B	HR	RB	BB	SO	SB
Buck Becannon, p	.500	1	2	0	1	0	0	0	0	0	0	0
Steve Brady, of	.000	3	10	1	0	0	0	0	0	0	1	0
Dude Esterbrook, 3b	.300	3	10	0	3	1	0	0	0	0	3	1
Tom Forster, 2b	.000	1	3	0	0	0	0	0	0	0	1	0
Bill Holbert, c	.000	1	2	0	0	0	0	0	0	0	1	0
Tim Keefe, p	.200	2	5	0	1	0	0	0	0	0	4	0
Ed Kennedy, of	.000	3	7	0	0	0	0	0	0	0	2	0
Candy Nelson, ss	.100	3	10	0	1	0	0	0	0	0	1	0
Dave Orr, 1b	.111	3	9	0	1	0	0	0	0	0	0	0
Charlie Reipschlager, c	.000	2	5	1	0	0	0	0	0	0	1	0
Chief Roseman, of	.333	3	9	1	3	0	0	0	1	0	1	0
Dasher Troy, 2b	.200	2	5	0	1	0	0	0	1	0	1	0
TOTAL	.143		77	3	11	1	0	0	2	0	16	1

PITCHER	W	L	ERA	G	GS	CG	SV	SHO	IP	H	ER	BB	SO
Buck Becannon	0	1	10.50	1	1	1	0	0	6.0	9	7	2	1
Tim Keefe	0	2	3.60	2	2	2	0	0	15.0	10	6	3	12
TOTAL	0	3	5.57	3	3	3	0	0	21.0	19	13	5	13

GAME 1 AT NY OCT 23

NY	000	000	000	0	2	1
PRO	201	000	30X	6	5	3

Pitchers: KEEFE vs RADBOURN
Attendance: 2,500

GAME 2 AT NY OCT 24

PRO	000	030	0	3	5	3
NY	000	010	0	1	3	0

Pitchers: RADBOURN vs KEEFE
Home Runs: Denny-PRO
Attendance: 1,000
(Game called at end of seventh, darkness)

GAME 3 AT NY OCT 25

PRO	120	144	12	11	4
NY	000	011	2	5	9

Pitchers: RADBOURN vs BECANNON
Attendance: 300
(Game called at end of sixth, darkness)

Before the start of the final game, the two clubs agreed to throw out Game 2, which had been forfeited to Chicago, leaving the Series tied at two wins apiece, plus the one tie. But after the Browns won the seventh game for their third victory, Chicago manager Cap Anson decided his club should retain its forfeit win after all, and a select committee agreed, leaving the Series in a tie instead of a White Stockings defeat.

Game 1, in Chicago, was called for darkness after eight innings, with the score tied 5–5. The Browns scored first with a run in the second and added four more in the top of the fourth. But Chicago came back with a run in the last of the fourth, and in the bottom of the eighth scored four more on a walk, two singles, and Fred Pfeffer's game-tying three-run homer.

The Series moved to St. Louis for the next three games. Chicago was leading 5–4 in the sixth inning of Game 2 when Browns manager Charlie Comiskey pulled his team off the field, objecting to the umpiring of David Sullivan. Umpire Sullivan later forfeited the game to the White Stockings; he worked no more in the Series. The Browns won Game 3, scoring five unearned runs with two out in the top of the first, and holding on for a 7–4 win. Chicago lost again the next day in a much closer game. The Browns scored first with a run in the third inning, but Abner Dalrymple's two-run homer in the fifth gave the White Stockings a 2–1 lead. In the bottom of the eighth, however, St. Louis scored twice and held on for the 3–2 win.

The Series took to the road for its final three games. In Pittsburgh for Game 5, Chicago overwhelmed the Browns 9–2, scoring four runs in the first inning, and their final three just before darkness ended the game after seven innings.

Game 6 and 7 were played in Cincinnati. The White Stockings won the sixth game by the same 9–2 score as Game 5. The Browns' two runs were unearned, as Chicago's Jim McCormick stopped St. Louis on just two hits, both singles. The Browns' victory in the finale was a runaway 13–4, called in the eighth for darkness. St. Louis' six-run fourth inning typified the game's sloppy play, the runs scoring on five hits, four errors, and two passed balls.

Chicago White Stockings (NL), 3; St. Louis Browns (AA), 3; tie, 1

CHI (N)

PLAYER/POS	AVG	G	AB	R	H	2B	3B	HR	RB	BB	SO	SB
Cap Anson, 1b	.423	7	26	8	11	1	1	0	7	2		
Tom Burns, ss-4,3b-3	.080	7	25	3	2	0	1	0	0	0		
John Clarkson, p-3,of-2	.125	5	16	1	2	1	0	0	1	0		
Abner Dalrymple, of	.269	7	26	4	7	2	0	1	3	2		
Silver Flint, c	.143	4	14	0	2	0	0	0	0	0		
George Gore, of	.000	1	3	1	0	0	0	0	0	1		
Bug Holliday, of	.000	1	4	0	0	0	0	0	0	0		
King Kelly, of-4,c-3	.346	7	26	9	9	3	1	0	4	2		
Jim McCormick, p	.214	4	14	1	3	0	0	0	2	0		
Fred Pfeffer, 2b	.407	7	27	5	11	2	0	1	7	0		
Billy Sunday, of	.273	6	22	5	6	2	0	0	1	2		
N. Williamson, 3b-4,ss-3	.087	7	23	1	2	0	0	0	3	4		
TOTAL	.243		226	38	55	11	3	2	28	13		

PITCHER	W	L	ERA	G	GS	CG	SV	SHO	IP	H	ER	BB	SO
John Clarkson	1	1	0.78	3	3	3	0	0	23.0	19	2	3	19
Jim McCormick	2	2	2.48	4	4	4	0	0	29.0	23	8	4	15
TOTAL	3	3	1.73	7	7	7	0	0	52.0	42	10	7	34

STL (A)

PLAYER/POS	AVG	G	AB	R	H	2B	3B	HR	RB	BB	SO	SB
Sam Barkley, 2b	.087	7	23	3	2	0	0	0	1	2		
Doc Bushong, c	.154	4	13	1	2	0	0	0	2	0		
Bob Caruthers, p-3,of-2	.200	5	15	1	3	0	1	0	6	1		
Charlie Comiskey, 1b	.292	7	24	6	7	0	0	0	1	0		
Dave Foutz, p	.167	4	12	1	2	0	0	0	0	0		
Bill Gleason, ss	.231	7	26	5	6	2	0	0	1	1		
Arlie Latham, 3b	.318	7	22	5	7	3	0	0	5	2		
Hugh Nicol, of	.000	1	2	0	0	0	0	0	0	0		
Tip O'Neill, of	.208	7	24	4	5	0	0	0	3	0		
Yank Robinson, of-4,c-3	.174	7	23	5	4	0	1	0	0	1		
Curt Welch, of	.148	7	27	5	4	1	1	0	2	0		
TOTAL	.199		211	36	42	6	3	0	21	7		

PITCHER	W	L	ERA	G	GS	CG	SV	SHO	IP	H	ER	BB	SO
Bob Caruthers	1	1	2.42	3	3	3	0	0	26.0	25	7	4	16
Dave Foutz	2	2	0.61	4	4	4	0	0	29.1	30	2	9	14
TOTAL	3	3	1.46	7	7	7	0	0	55.1	55	9	13	30

RBI totals include the following estimated RBIs: Anson 2, Kelly, Barkley, Gleason, Welch.

GAME 1 AT CHI OCT 14

		R	H	E
STL	010 400 00	5	7	2
CHI	000 100 04	5	5	10

Pitchers: Caruthers vs Clarkson
Home Runs: Pfeffer-CHI
Attendance: 2,000
(Game called at end of eighth, darkness)

GAME 2 AT STL OCT 15

		R	H	E
CHI	110 003	5	6	5
STL	300 10X	4	2	4

Pitchers: McCORMICK vs FOUTZ
Attendance: 2,000
(Game forfeited to Chicago in bottom of sixth)

GAME 3 AT STL OCT 16

		R	H	E
CHI	111 000 001	4	8	7
STL	500 002 00X	7	8	4

Pitchers: CLARKSON vs CARUTHERS
Attendance: 3,000

GAME 4 AT STL OCT 17

		R	H	E
CHI	000 020 000	2	8	3
STL	001 000 02X	3	6	7

Pitchers: McCORMICK vs FOUTZ
Home Runs: Dalrymple-CHI
Attendance: 3,000

GAME 5 AT PIT A OCT 22

		R	H	E
CHI	400 110 3	9	7	1
STL	010 000 1	2	4	7

Pitchers: CLARKSON vs FOUTZ
Attendance: 500
(Game called at end of seventh, darkness)

GAME 6 AT CIN A OCT 23

		R	H	E
CHI	200 111 040	9	11	7
STL	002 000 000	2	2	7

Pitchers: McCORMICK vs CARUTHERS
Attendance: 1,500

GAME 7 AT CIN A OCT 24

		R	H	E
CHI	200 020 00	4	9	9
STL	004 621 0X	13	13	5

Pitchers: McCORMICK vs FOUTZ
Attendance: 1,200
(Game called in eighth, darkness)

St. Louis Browns (AA), 4; Chicago White Stockings (NL), 2

It was a winner-take-all Series, with the club that won four games pocketing the entire proceeds. Attendance, very good for those days, averaged over 7,000 per game and brought the victorious Browns about $14,000.

The first three games were played in Chicago. The White Stockings won the opener on a sparkling five-hit shutout by their ace John Clarkson. But St. Louis's Bob Caruthers improved on Clarkson's performance the next day, blanking Chicago on just two singles as his Browns turned 13 hits and 13 Chicago errors into 12 runs (in a game shortened by darkness to eight innings). The White Stockings improved their fielding in the next game (which was also called after eight innings), and this time their bats came alive. With 11 hits (including home runs by Mike "King" Kelly and George Gore) combining with seven St. Louis errors, they regained the Series advantage with an easy 11–4 win.

When the venue shifted to St. Louis, though, the Browns battled back. In a back-and-forth battle in Game 4, Chicago tied the game at 5–5 with a pair of runs in the sixth, but St. Louis scored three final runs a half inning later, winning when darkness ended play in the middle of the seventh.

Game 5 repeated an innovation from the second game: two umpires (instead of the usual one), plus a "referee" who stood between the pitcher and second base. The umpiring satisfied everyone, but Chicago, handicapped by their scheduled pitcher's sore arm, lost when they sent shortstop Ned Williamson and right fielder Jimmy Ryan into the box. St. Louis got to Williamson and Ryan for 11 hits and 10 runs as their Nat Hudson held Chicago batters to three hits and three runs.

The finale proved to be the Series' best-played and closest game. Chicago's Clarkson shut out the Browns through seven innings as his mates built a three-run lead—one of them scored on Fred's Pfeffer's homer in the fourth. Rain (and a rowdy crowd which poured onto the field) halted play for a while in the fifth. But the game resumed and the rain subsided. In the last of the eighth, Charlie Comiskey scored the Browns' first run on a single, errant throw and run-scoring fly out, and Arlie Latham tripled home two more runners later in the inning to tie the game. The score remained 3–3 into the last of the tenth, when the Browns' Curt Welch singled (for only the fourth St. Louis hit), went to second on an infield hit, and took third on a sacrifice. Welch then attempted to steal home but catcher Kelly had smelled out the play and called for a pitchout. Clarkson's delivery was poor and bobbled by Kelly, allowing Welch to steal home with a "$15,000 slide" for the Browns' triumph.

STL (A)

PLAYER/POS	AVG	G	AB	R	H	2B	3B	HR	RB	BB	SO	SB
Doc Bushong, c	.188	6	16	4	3	1	0	0	2	4	5	0
Bob Caruthers, p-3,of-3	.250	6	24	6	6	1	2	0	5	1	4	1
Charlie Comiskey, 1b	.292	6	24	2	7	1	0	0	2	0	4	0
Dave Foutz, p-2,of-2	.200	4	15	2	3	1	1	0	3	0	3	0
Bill Gleason, ss	.208	6	24	3	5	0	0	0	5	1	3	0
Nat Hudson, p-1,of-1	.167	2	6	1	1	0	1	0	0	1	3	0
Arlie Latham, 3b-6,c-1	.174	6	23	4	4	0	1	0	3	3	4	2
Tip O'Neill, of	.400	6	20	4	8	0	2	2	5	4	5	2
Yank Robinson, 2b	.316	6	19	5	6	1	1	0	3	2	3	2
Curt Welch, of	.350	6	20	7	7	2	0	0	1	3	4	2
TOTAL	.262		191	38	50	7	8	2	29	19	38	9

PITCHER	W	L	ERA	G	GS	CG	SV	SHO	IP	H	ER	BB	SO
Bob Caruthers	2	1	2.42	3	3	3	0	1	26.0	18	7	6	12
Dave Foutz	1	1	3.60	2	2	2	0	0	15.0	16	6	6	7
Nat Hudson	1	0	2.57	1	1	1	0	0	7.0	3	2	3	3
TOTAL	4	2	2.81	6	6	6	0	1	48.0	37	15	15	22

CHI (N)

PLAYER/POS	AVG	G	AB	R	H	2B	3B	HR	RB	BB	SO	SB
Cap Anson, 1b-6,c-2	.238	6	21	3	5	1	0	0	1	4	0	1
Tom Burns, 3b-6,of-1	.286	6	21	2	6	2	1	0	1	0	2	0
John Clarkson, p-4,of-1	.067	4	15	0	1	0	0	0	1	0	2	1
Abner Dalrymple, of	.190	6	21	2	4	1	1	0	2	0	5	1
Silver Flint, c	.000	1	3	0	0	0	0	0	1	0	1	0
George Gore, of	.174	6	23	4	4	0	0	1	2	3	3	0
King Kelly, c-5,ss-2,1b-1,3b-1	.208	6	24	4	5	0	0	1	1	2	2	1
Jim McCormick, p	.000	1	3	0	0	0	0	0	0	0	0	0
Fred Pfeffer, 2b	.286	6	21	7	6	0	0	1	4	2	1	2
Jimmy Ryan, of-6,p-1,ss-1	.250	6	20	4	5	1	0	0	2	0	1	1
Ned Williamson, ss-6,p-2,c-1,of-1	.056	6	18	2	1	0	1	0	3	4	5	1
TOTAL	.195		190	28	37	5	3	3	18	15	22	8

PITCHER	W	L	ERA	G	GS	CG	SV	SHO	IP	H	ER	BB	SO
John Clarkson	2	2	2.01	4	4	3	0	1	31.1	25	7	12	28
Jim McCormick	0	1	6.75	1	1	1	0	0	8.0	13	6	2	4
Jimmy Ryan	0	0	9.00	1	0	0	0	0	5.0	8	5	4	4
Ned Williamson	0	1	4.50	2	1	0	0	0	2.0	4	1	1	2
TOTAL	2	4	3.69	8	6	4	0	1	46.1	50	19	19	38

GAME 1 AT CHI OCT 18

				R	H	E
STL	000	000	000	0	5	3
CHI	200	001	03X	6	10	4

Pitchers: FOUTZ vs CLARKSON
Attendance: 6,000

GAME 2 AT CHI OCT 19

				R	H	E
STL	200	230	50	12	13	2
CHI	000	000	00	0	2	10

Pitchers: CARUTHERS vs McCORMICK
Home Runs: O'Neill-STL (2)
Attendance: 8,000
(Game called at end of eighth, darkness)

GAME 3 AT CHI OCT 20

				R	H	E
CHI	200	112	32	11	11	2
STL	010	002	01	4	9	7

Pitchers: CLARKSON, Williamson (8) vs CARUTHERS
Home Runs: Kelly-CHI, Gore-CHI
Attendance: 6,000
(Game called at end of eighth, darkness)

GAME 4 AT STL OCT 21

				R	H	E
CHI	300	002	0	5	6	4
STL	011	033	X	8	7	4

Pitchers: CLARKSON vs FOUTZ
Attendance: 8,000
(Game called in seventh, darkness)

GAME 5 AT STL OCT 22

				R	H	E
CHI	011	100	00	3	3	3
STL	214	003	0X	10	11	3

Pitchers: WILLIAMSON, Ryan (2) vs HUDSON
Attendance: 10,000
(Game called in eighth, darkness)

GAME 6 AT STL OCT 23

					R	H	E
CHI	010	101	000	0	3	6	2
STL	000	000	030	1	4	5	3

Pitchers: CLARKSON vs CARUTHERS
Home Runs: Pfeffer-CHI
Attendance: 8,000

Even though their star slugger Dan Brouthers was sidelined for all but one game by a sprained ankle, the Wolverines—in baseball's longest World Series, played in 10 different cities—followed up their only pennant with an easy triumph over repeating AA champion St. Louis. The Browns won the opener at home, though, 6–1. They played errorless ball (rare in that era) as pitcher Bob Caruthers held Detroit scoreless until the ninth inning, and drove in the Browns' second run himself with a first-inning single.

The Wolverines came back to win the next three games. They took an early lead in Game 2 and held on for a 5–3 win in St. Louis to even the Series. Then, in the Series' tightest game (played in Detroit) the Wolverines defeated Caruthers 2–1 in the last of the 13th when their pitcher Charlie Getzien led off with a single, advanced to second and third on ground outs, and scored on an infield error. In Game 4 (in Pittsburgh) Detroit's Charles "Lady" Baldwin stopped the Browns on two hits.

Caruthers hurled a seven-hitter in Brooklyn for St. Louis's second win, but Detroit took the next four. Getzien contributed a two-hit shutout in New York, and Baldwin overcame Caruthers 3–1 in Philadelphia the next day. Getzien yielded eight hits the day after that in Boston, but Caruthers gave up thirteen, including two home runs to Sam Thompson, and Detroit took the game 9–2. Back in Philadelphia for Game 9, St. Louis broke a 1–1 tie with a run in the top of the sixth. But the Wolverines scored two in the seventh and a final run in the eighth. The win gave Detroit a 7–2 Series advantage.

Game 10, scheduled for the next day in Washington, was postponed because of rain until the following morning. Detroit's Hardy Richardson opened the game with a home run, but the Wolverines lost an opportunity to clinch the Series as the Browns overwhelmed Getzien with 16 hits for an 11–4 victory featuring a triple play. But that afternoon, in Baltimore, Detroit took the deciding game as decisively as they had lost in the morning, knocking the Browns' Dave Foutz for 14 hits (including four by Richardson and three—including a home run—by Larry Twitchell) as Baldwin held St. Louis to two hits in a 13–3 win.

The Browns and Wolverines split the final four meaningless games, played in Brooklyn, Detroit, Chicago, and St. Louis.

Detroit Wolverines (NL), 10; St. Louis Browns (AA), 5

DET (N)

PLAYER/POS	AVG	G	AB	R	H	2B	3B	HR	RB	BB	SO	SB
Lady Baldwin, p	.316	5	19	1	6	1	0	0	2	2	2	1
Charlie Bennett, c-10,1b-3	.311	11	45	6	14	2	1	0	9	3	5	5
Dan Brouthers, 1b	.667	1	3	0	2	0	0	0	0	0	0	0
Pete Conway, p	.000	4	12	0	0	0	0	0	0	0	2	0
Fred Dunlap, 2b	.150	11	40	5	6	0	1	0	1	0	4	4
Charlie Ganzel, 1b-10,c-7	.237	14	59	5	14	1	0	0	3	1	2	3
Charlie Getzien, p	.391	6	23	5	9	2	0	0	2	3	6	1
Ned Hanlon, of	.291	15	55	5	16	1	1	0	4	5	1	7
Hardy Richardson, of-10,2b-5,3b-1	.209	15	67	12	14	5	2	1	4	1	9	7
Jack Rowe, ss	.354	15	65	12	23	1	1	0	7	2	1	5
Cy Sutcliffe, 1b-3,c-1	.167	4	12	1	2	0	0	0	1	1	1	1
Sam Thompson, of	.393	15	61	8	24	2	0	2	8	3	3	5
Larry Twitchell, of	.250	6	20	5	5	1	0	1	3	0	1	1
Deacon White, 3b-14,1b-1	.233	15	60	8	14	1	1	0	5	2	0	2
TOTAL	.275		541	73	149	17	7	4	49	23	37	42

PITCHER	W	L	ERA	G	GS	CG	SV	SHO	IP	H	ER	BB	SO
Lady Baldwin	4	1	1.50	5	5	5	0	1	42.0	38	7	10	4
Pete Conway	2	2	3.00	4	4	4	0	0	33.0	37	11	6	10
Charlie Getzien	4	2	2.53	6	6	6	0	1	57.0	76	16	15	17
TOTAL	10	5	2.32	15	15	15	0	2	132.0	151	34	31	31

STL (A)

PLAYER/POS	AVG	G	AB	R	H	2B	3B	HR	RB	BB	SO	SB
Jack Boyle, c	.208	6	24	1	5	0	0	0	2	0	4	0
Doc Bushong, c	.333	9	33	3	11	0	0	0	1	4	1	0
Bob Caruthers, p-8,of-3	.255	10	47	2	12	0	0	0	3	1	1	3
Charlie Comiskey, 1b-14,of-1	.317	15	63	8	20	2	0	0	5	1	1	4
Dave Foutz, of-11,p-3,1b-1	.197	15	61	4	12	2	1	0	3	2	3	0
Bill Gleason, ss	.212	13	52	3	11	0	0	0	1	3	2	1
Silver King, p	.071	4	14	0	1	0	0	0	1	0	3	0
Arlie Latham, 3b	.388	15	67	12	26	1	0	1	2	9	2	15
Harry Lyons, ss	.375	2	8	3	3	0	0	0	2	1	0	0
Tip O'Neill, of	.200	15	65	7	13	2	1	1	9	0	2	0
Yank Robinson, 2b	.446	15	56	5	25	5	1	0	4	10	6	4
Curt Welch, of	.207	15	58	6	12	3	1	1	8	0	2	1
TOTAL	.276		548	54	151	15	4	3	41	31	27	28

PITCHER	W	L	ERA	G	GS	CG	SV	SHO	IP	H	ER	BB	SO
Bob Caruthers	4	4	2.13	8	8	8	0	0	71.2	76	17	12	19
Dave Foutz	0	3	3.46	3	3	3	0	0	26.0	45	10	9	6
Silver King	1	3	2.03	4	4	4	0	0	31.0	28	7	2	21
TOTAL	5	10	2.38	15	15	15	0	0	128.2	149	34	23	46

GAME 1 AT STL OCT 10

		R	H	E
STL	200 040 000	6	16	0
DET	000 000 001	1	5	5

Pitchers: CARUTHERS vs GETZIEN
Attendance: 4,208

GAME 2 AT STL OCT 11

		R	H	E
DET	022 000 100	5	12	2
STL	000 000 120	3	10	7

Pitchers: CONWAY vs FOUTZ
Attendance: 6,408

GAME 3 AT DET OCT 12

		R	H	E
STL	010 000 000 000 0	1	16	7
DET	000 000 010 000 1	2	7	1

Pitchers: CARUTHERS vs GETZIEN
Attendance: 4,509

GAME 4 AT PIT OCT 13

		R	H	E
DET	410 012 000	8	12	1
STL	000 000 000	0	5	6

Pitchers: BALDWIN vs KING
Attendance: 2,447

GAME 5 AT BRO OCT 14

		R	H	E
STL	200 002 100	5	7	4
DET	000 020 000	2	8	5

Pitchers: CARUTHERS vs CONWAY
Attendance: 6,796

GAME 6 AT NY OCT 15

		R	H	E
DET	330 000 003	9	15	1
STL	000 000 000	0	5	8

Pitchers: GETZIEN vs FOUTZ
Attendance: 5,797

GAME 7 AT PHI OCT 17

		R	H	E
STL	000 000 001	1	10	1
DET	030 000 00X	3	7	1

Pitchers: CARUTHERS vs BALDWIN
Home Runs: O'Neill-STL
Attendance: 6,478

GAME 8 AT BOS OCT 18

		R	H	E
DET	031 003 200	9	17	2
STL	100 001 000	2	10	5

Pitchers: GETZIEN vs CARUTHERS
Home Runs: Thompson-DET (2)
Attendance: 2,891

GAME 9 AT PHI OCT 19

		R	H	E
STL	000 101 000	2	9	2
DET	000 100 21X	4	6	3

Pitchers: KING vs CONWAY
Attendance: 2,389

GAME 10 AT WAS OCT 21 (AM)

		R	H	E
DET	200 010 001	4	9	3
STL	200 031 41X	11	19	5

Pitchers: GETZIEN vs CARUTHERS
Home Runs: Latham-STL, Welch-STL, Richardson-DET
Attendance: 1,261

GAME 11 AT BAL OCT 21 (PM)

		R	H	E
STL	110 010 000	3	4	7
DET	100 344 10X	13	18	7

Pitchers: FOUTZ vs BALDWIN
Home Runs: Twitchell-DET
Attendance: 2,707
(Detroit wins best of 15 series 8 to 3)

GAME 12 AT BRO OCT 22

		R	H	E
DET	000 100 0	1	6	3
STL	410 000 X	5	12	2

Pitchers: CONWAY vs KING
Attendance: 1,138
(Game called in seventh, darkness)

GAME 13 AT DET OCT 24

		R	H	E
DET	020 100 120	6	14	3
STL	100 010 001	3	5	5

Pitchers: BALDWIN vs CARUTHERS
Attendance: 3,389

GAME 14 AT CHI OCT 25

		R	H	E
STL	000 002 100	3	10	5
DET	300 010 00X	4	4	4

Pitchers: KING vs GETZIEN
Attendance: 378

GAME 15 AT STL OCT 26

		R	H	E
STL	340 110	9	13	5
DET	011 000	2	9	7

Pitchers: CARUTHERS vs BALDWIN
Attendance: 659
(Game called after sixth, cold)

St. Louis, AA champions for the fourth straight year, battled the Giants closely through several games, but blowout losses in Games 6 and 8 undid them. The first three games were played in New York. In a splendidly pitched opener, Browns ace Charles "Silver" King held New York to two hits and a walk while Giants ace Tim Keefe limited the Browns to three hits and a walk, striking out nine on his way to a narrow 2–1 win. St. Louis evened the Series in Game 2 behind the shutout pitching of Elton "Icebox" Chamberlain. Tommy McCarthy scored the Browns' first run in the second inning when, after singling, he moved around to third on two passed balls by Giants catcher Buck Ewing and came home on Ewing's failed attempt to throw out a runner stealing second. Two more runs in the ninth gave St. Louis more than enough insurance for the win.

The Giants scored twice in the first inning of Game 3, and increased their lead to 4–0 before allowing St. Louis a pair of harmless runs in the final innings. They also scored first and led all the way in Game 4 (played in Brooklyn). The Browns took a 4–1 lead into the bottom of the eighth in Game 5 (in New York), but a five-run Giants rally reversed the lead—and the outcome—as the game was called for darkness with St. Louis at bat in the ninth.

Mickey Welch hurled a three-hitter (in Philadelphia) two days later, but St. Louis, capitalizing on walks and a questionable "safe" call at home, carried a 4–1 lead into the sixth inning. New York exploded in the late innings for 11 runs.

The final four games were played in St. Louis. The Browns spoiled New York's hope of quick victory in Game 7, coming from behind to tie the score with three runs in the fourth, and—after New York had scored twice in the sixth—recovering again with a four-run eighth for a 7–5 lead before darkness again halted play after eight innings. But the Browns' win only delayed the inevitable. The Giants hammered Icebox Chamberlain for 12 hits in Game 8 (including home runs by Buck Ewing and Mike Tiernan) to clinch their first world championship with an 11–3 win.

The final two games meant nothing to the outcome, and both clubs used reserve pitchers in Game 9.

New York Giants (NL), 6; St. Louis Browns (AA), 4

NY (N)

PLAYER/POS	AVG	G	AB	R	H	2B	3B	HR	RB	BB	SO	SB
Willard Brown, c	.375	2	8	1	3	1	0	0	0	0	0	0
Roger Connor, 1b	.304	7	23	7	7	1	2	0	3	4	0	4
Ed Crane, p	.143	2	7	1	1	0	0	0	2	0	1	0
Buck Ewing, c-6,1b-1	.346	7	26	5	9	0	2	1	6	1	3	5
Bill George, p-1,1b-1	.333	2	9	2	3	1	0	1	4	0	2	0
George Gore, of-2,3b-1	.455	3	11	5	5	1	0	0	0	2	2	2
Gil Hatfield, p-1,2b-1,ss-1	.250	2	8	2	2	0	0	0	1	1	2	1
Tim Keefe, p	.091	4	11	2	1	0	0	0	0	2	2	1
Pat Murphy, c	.100	3	10	1	1	0	0	0	1	0	0	0
Jim O'Rourke, of-7,1b-2,ss-1	.222	10	36	4	8	0	0	0	1	4	2	3
Danny Richardson, 2b	.167	9	36	6	6	2	0	0	6	3	5	3
Mike Slattery, of-10,2b-1	.205	10	39	6	8	2	0	0	5	0	5	6
Mike Tiernan, of	.342	10	38	8	13	0	0	1	6	8	2	5
Ledell Titcomb, p-1,of-1	.500	1	4	1	2	1	0	0	1	0	0	0
Monte Ward, ss	.379	8	29	4	11	1	0	0	6	1	0	6
Mickey Welch, p	.286	2	7	2	2	0	0	0	1	0	0	0
Art Whitney, 3b-9,of-1	.324	10	37	7	12	0	1	0	12	1	4	2
TOTAL	.277		339	64	94	10	5	3	55	27	30	38

PITCHER	W	L	ERA	G	GS	CG	SV	SHO	IP	H	ER	BB	SO
Ed Crane	1	1	2.12	2	2	2	0	0	17.0	15	4	6	12
Bill George	0	1	7.20	1	1	1	0	0	10.0	15	8	3	4
Gil Hatfield	0	0	12.60	1	0	0	0	0	5.0	12	7	3	2
Tim Keefe	4	0	0.51	4	4	4	0	0	35.0	18	2	9	30
Ledell Titcomb	0	1	6.75	1	1	0	0	0	4.0	5	3	2	2
Mickey Welch	1	1	2.65	2	2	2	0	0	17.0	10	5	9	2
TOTAL	6	4	2.97	11	10	9	0	0	88.0	75	29	32	52

STL (A)

PLAYER/POS	AVG	G	AB	R	H	2B	3B	HR	RB	BB	SO	SB
Jack Boyle, c-4,of-1	.438	4	16	4	7	0	1	0	4	2	2	3
Icebox Chamberlain, p	.000	5	13	3	0	0	0	0	0	4	3	1
Charlie Comiskey, 1b-10,of-1	.268	10	41	6	11	1	1	0	3	1	1	4
Jim Devlin, p	.000	1	3	0	0	0	0	0	0	0	0	0
Ed Herr, of	.091	3	11	2	1	0	0	0	0	0	5	1
Silver King, p	.067	5	15	1	1	0	0	0	0	1	6	0
Arlie Latham, 3b	.250	10	40	10	10	0	0	0	3	5	6	11
Harry Lyons, of	.118	5	17	0	2	0	0	0	1	1	5	0
Tommy McCarthy, of	.244	10	41	10	10	1	0	1	9	0	0	6
Jocko Milligan, c-8,1b-1	.400	8	25	5	10	2	1	0	4	3	3	0
Tip O'Neill, of	.243	10	37	8	9	1	0	2	11	6	3	0
Yank Robinson, 2b	.250	10	36	7	9	2	1	0	7	6	12	2
Bill White, ss	.143	10	35	4	5	1	0	0	4	3	6	1
TOTAL	.227		330	60	75	8	4	3	46	32	52	29

PITCHER	W	L	ERA	G	GS	CG	SV	SHO	IP	H	ER	BB	SO
Icebox Chamberlain	2	3	5.32	5	5	5	0	1	44.0	52	26	16	13
Jim Devlin	1	0	2.57	1	0	0	0	0	7.0	5	2	2	5
Silver King	1	3	2.31	5	5	4	0	0	35.0	37	9	9	12
TOTAL	4	6	3.87	11	10	9	0	1	86.0	94	37	27	30

GAME 1 AT NY OCT 16

STL	001	000	000	1	3	5
NY	011	000	00X	2	2	4

Pitchers: KING vs KEEFE
Attendance: 4,876

GAME 2 AT NY OCT 17

STL	010	000	002	3	7	4
NY	000	000	000	0	6	1

Pitchers: CHAMBERLAIN vs WELCH
Attendance: 5,575

GAME 3 AT NY OCT 18

STL	000	000	011	2	5	5
NY	200	100	10X	4	5	2

Pitchers: KING vs KEEFE
Attendance: 5,780

GAME 4 AT BRO OCT 19

NY	104	010	000	6	8	2
STL	001	000	020	3	7	4

Pitchers: CRANE vs CHAMBERLAIN
Attendance: 3,062

GAME 5 AT NY OCT 20

STL	003	001	00	4	5	5
NY	100	000	05	6	9	2

Pitchers: KING vs KEEFE
Attendance: 9,124
(Game called at end of eighth, darkness)

GAME 6 AT PHI OCT 22

NY	000	103	35	12	13	5
STL	301	000	01	5	3	7

Pitchers: WELCH vs CHAMBERLAIN
Attendance: 3,281
(Game called at end of eighth, darkness)

GAME 7 AT STL OCT 24

NY	030	002	00	5	11	3
STL	000	300	04	7	8	3

Pitchers: CRANE vs KING
Attendance: 4,624
(Game called at end of eighth, darkness)

GAME 8 AT STL OCT 25

NY	103	100	006	11	12	2
STL	000	100	110	3	5	6

Pitchers: KEEFE vs CHAMBERLAIN
Home Runs: Ewing-NY, Tiernan-NY
Attendance: 4,865
(New York wins best of 10 series, 6 to 2)

GAME 9 AT STL OCT 26

STL	140	020	202	3	14	15	4
NY	035	000	120	0	11	14	5

Pitchers: King, DEVLIN (4) vs GEORGE
Home Runs: O'Neill-STL
Attendance: 711

GAME 10 AT STL OCT 27

STL	010	505	421	18	17	3
NY	310	000	021	7	13	8

Pitchers: CHAMBERLAIN vs TITCOMB, Hatfield (5)
Home Runs: George-NY, O'Neill-STL, McCarthy-STL
Attendance: 412

Six wins was the magic number this year, and it was agreed that—unlike most previous Series—play would not continue beyond the deciding game. The Giants wanted the opening game called for darkness after the seventh inning, when they led, 10–8. But the umpires held off until Brooklyn, in the deepening gloom, had scored four runs in the last of the eighth to go ahead, 12–10.

The next day, in Brooklyn before more than 16,000 spectators (by far the largest World Series crowd to that time), Ed "Cannonball" Crane held the Grooms to four hits as New York evened the Series. But Brooklyn won the next two for a 3–1 Series advantage. In Game 3, ahead 8–7 in the sixth inning, the Grooms began stalling, waiting for darkness to fall. The score was still 8–7 when the game was finally halted in the top of the ninth with one out and three Giants on base.

Darkness for a third time gave Brooklyn the victory in Game 4. New York overcame a 7–2 Bridegroom lead to tie the score with five runs in the top of the sixth, but in the bottom of the inning Brooklyn's Tom "Oyster" Burns homered in the dark for three runs. The umpires then halted the game.

The five remaining contests went the distance, and the Giants won them all. Crane in Game 5 gave up eight hits, but homered in his own behalf, driving in two runs in his Giants' 11–3 rout. In Game 6 the Grooms scored a run in the second inning, but New York tied the game with two outs in the last of the ninth (when Monte Ward singled, stole second and third, and scored on Roger Connor's single), and won it with two away in the 11th as Ward drove in Mike Slattery from second with an infield hit.

Back-to-back homers by Giants Dan Richardson and Jim O'Rourke highlighted an eight-run second inning in Game 7. The Giants' eventual 11–7 win gave them their first Series advantage. In Game 8 the Giants outscored the Grooms 12–2 over the first four innings and beat them, 16–7.

With their backs to the wall, the Bridegrooms scored first in Game 9 and held a 2–1 lead after five innings. But New York tied the score in the sixth and went ahead 3–2 on a passed ball in the seventh. Meanwhile pitcher Hank O'Day blanked the Grooms on just two hits after the first inning to bring New York its second straight world championship.

New York Giants (NL), 6; Brooklyn Bridegrooms (AA), 3

NY (N)

PLAYER/POS	AVG	G	AB	R	H	2B	3B	HR	RB	BB	SO	SB
Willard Brown, c	.600	1	5	3	3	0	0	1	2	0	0	0
Roger Connor, 1b	.343	9	35	9	12	2	2	0	12	3	2	8
Ed Crane, p	.278	5	18	3	5	1	1	1	5	1	2	0
Buck Ewing, c	.250	8	36	5	9	4	0	0	7	2	5	1
George Gore, of	.333	5	21	5	7	1	1	0	1	3	0	2
Tim Keefe, p	.500	2	4	1	2	1	0	0	0	1	1	0
Hank O'Day, p	.167	3	6	0	1	0	0	0	0	2	2	0
Jim O'Rourke, of	.389	9	36	7	14	2	2	2	7	2	2	3
Danny Richardson, 2b	.314	9	35	8	11	1	1	3	8	3	5	3
Mike Slattery, of	.188	4	16	6	3	0	0	0	1	3	1	1
Mike Tiernan, of	.289	9	38	12	11	1	1	1	5	5	3	3
Monte Ward, ss	.417	9	36	10	15	0	1	0	7	5	2	10
Mickey Welch, p	.333	1	3	0	1	1	0	0	0	0	1	0
Art Whitney, 3b	.229	9	35	4	8	2	1	0	3	1	0	0
TOTAL	.315		324	73	102	16	10	8	58	31	26	31

PITCHER	W	L	ERA	G	GS	CG	SV	SHO	IP	H	ER	BB	SO
Ed Crane	4	1	3.72	5	5	4	0	0	38.2	29	16	32	19
Tim Keefe	0	1	8.18	2	1	1	1	0	11.0	17	10	2	4
Hank O'Day	2	0	1.17	3	2	2	0	0	23.0	10	3	14	12
Mickey Welch	0	1	9.00	1	1	0	0	0	5.0	11	5	3	1
TOTAL	6	3	3.94	11	9	7	1	0	77.2	67	34	51	36

BRO (A)

PLAYER/POS	AVG	G	AB	R	H	2B	3B	HR	RB	BB	SO	SB
Oyster Burns, of	.229	9	35	8	8	3	0	2	11	5	6	0
Doc Bushong, c	.000	3	8	0	0	0	0	0	0	1	0	0
Bob Caruthers, p	.250	4	8	1	2	0	0	0	1	3	3	0
Bob Clark, c	.417	4	12	3	5	2	0	0	3	2	2	0
Hub Collins, 2b	.371	9	35	13	13	3	0	1	2	7	5	6
Pop Corkhill, of	.208	9	24	4	5	1	0	1	5	6	2	1
Jumbo Davis, ss	.000	1	4	0	0	0	0	0	0	0	0	0
Dave Foutz, 1b-9,p-1	.286	9	35	7	10	2	0	1	9	4	2	3
Mickey Hughes, p	.333	1	3	1	1	1	0	0	0	1	2	0
Tom Lovett, p	.000	1	1	0	0	0	0	0	0	0	0	0
Darby O'Brien, of	.161	9	31	8	5	0	1	0	4	12	6	6
George Pinckney, 3b	.258	9	31	2	8	2	0	0	3	4	2	2
Germany Smith, ss	.172	8	29	2	5	2	1	0	2	3	2	2
Adonis Terry, p-5,1b-1	.167	5	18	1	3	0	0	0	1	1	1	1
Joe Visner, c-3,of-2	.125	5	16	2	2	1	0	0	0	2	3	0
TOTAL	.231		290	52	67	17	2	5	41	51	36	21

PITCHER	W	L	ERA	G	GS	CG	SV	SHO	IP	H	ER	BB	SO
Bob Caruthers	0	2	3.75	4	2	2	1	0	24.0	28	10	6	6
Dave Foutz	0	0	7.20	1	0	0	0	0	5.0	5	4	2	2
Mickey Hughes	1	0	7.71	1	1	0	0	0	7.0	14	6	3	3
Tom Lovett	0	1	24.00	1	1	0	0	0	3.0	8	8	2	1
Adonis Terry	2	3	5.97	5	5	4	0	0	37.2	47	25	18	14
TOTAL	3	6	6.22	12	9	6	1	0	76.2	102	53	31	26

GAME 1 AT NY OCT 18

		R	H	E
NY	020 210 50	10	12	2
BRO	510 000 24	12	16	3

Pitchers: KEEFE vs TERRY
Home Runs: Collins-BRO, Richardson-NY
Attendance: 8,848
(Game called at end of eighth, darkness)

GAME 2 AT BRO OCT 19

		R	H	E
NY	111 120 000	6	10	4
BRO	110 000 000	2	4	8

Pitchers: CRANE vs CARUTHERS
Attendance: 16,172

GAME 3 AT NY OCT 22

		R	H	E
NY	200 032 00	7	15	2
BRO	023 120 00	8	12	3

Pitchers: WELCH, O'Day (6) vs HUGHES, Caruthers (8)
Home Runs: Corkhill-BRO, O'Rourke-NY
Attendance: 5,181
(Game called at end of eighth, darkness)

GAME 4 AT BRO OCT 23

		R	H	E
NY	001 105	7	9	8
BRO	202 033	10	7	1

Pitchers: CRANE vs TERRY
Home Runs: Burns-BRO
Attendance: 3,045
(Game called at end of sixth, darkness)

GAME 5 AT BRO OCT 24

		R	H	E
NY	004 040 021	11	12	2
BRO	000 111 000	3	8	2

Pitchers: CRANE vs CARUTHERS
Home Runs: Brown-NY, Richardson-NY, Crane-NY
Attendance: 2,901

GAME 6 AT NY OCT 25

		R	H	E
BRO	010 000 000 00	1	6	4
NY	000 000 001 01	2	7	1

Pitchers: TERRY vs O'DAY
Attendance: 2,556

GAME 7 AT NY OCT 26

		R	H	E
BRO	004 030 000	7	5	3
NY	180 001 10X	11	14	4

Pitchers: LOVETT, Caruthers (4) vs CRANE, Keefe (5)
Home Runs: Richardson-NY, O'Rourke-NY
Attendance: 3,312

GAME 8 AT BRO OCT 28

		R	H	E
NY	541 203 001	16	15	4
BRO	200 000 023	7	5	4

Pitchers: CRANE vs TERRY, Foutz (5)
Home Runs: Foutz-BRO, Tiernan-NY, Burns-BRO
Attendance: 2,584

GAME 9 AT NY OCT 29

		R	H	E
BRO	200 000 000	2	4	2
NY	100 001 10X	3	8	5

Pitchers: TERRY vs O'DAY
Attendance: 3,067

The Bridegrooms, AA pennant winners in 1889, switched to the NL and returned to World Series play as champions of their new league. Louisville, meanwhile, rose from a last-place finish in 1889 to replace Brooklyn at the top of the AA. The Series, though, seemed meaningless to many who believed that pennant-winning Boston of the outlaw Players League (which had drawn off many of the best NL and AA players) could beat both Louisville and Brooklyn if given the opportunity.

The first four games of the Series were played in Louisville before an ever decreasing number of spectators. The largest crowd—5,600—saw the Cyclones humiliated in the opener 9–0 as Brooklyn's Adonis Terry stopped them on two singles. The Grooms won the second game, too, breaking a 2–2 tie with a pair of runs in the fourth and holding on for a 5–3 win.

Louisville played catch-up throughout Game 3 and entered the last of the eighth still behind 7–4. But a walk, three hits, a sacrifice fly, and a passed ball tied the score before darkness ended the game. Only 1,050 spectators attended the final contest in Louisville, but they saw the first Louisville win. The Cyclones scored three runs in the first inning, but Brooklyn countered with three an inning later, and both teams scored single runs in the third. Louisville's Red Ehret blanked the Grooms the rest of the way, but Brooklyn's Tom Lovett yielded the Cyclones a winning run in the seventh when Tim Shinnick tripled and was sacrificed home.

Rain postponed the first game in Brooklyn for two days, but when it was played—on a cold, muddy day before a small crowd of 1,000—the Grooms took the lead on Oyster Burns's two-run homer in the first inning and held it all the way for their third win. As the weather grew colder, the crowds declined for the final two games. Louisville captured its second win by a 9–8 margin when a three-run Brooklyn rally in the eighth inning of Game 6 stalled one run short of a tie. Only abut 300 diehards saw the Cyclones even the Series in the finale, 6–2 behind Red Ehret's four-hitter. A tie-breaking eighth game seemed called for, but there was not enough interest in playing any further in the bitter cold.

Brooklyn Bridegrooms (NL), 3; Louisville Cyclones (AA), 3; tie, 1

BRO (N)

PLAYER/POS	AVG	G	AB	R	H	2B	3B	HR	RB	BB	SO	SB
Oyster Burns, of-4,3b-3	.222	7	27	6	6	2	0	1	5	3	4	0
Doc Bushong, c	.000	2	6	0	0	0	0	0	0	0	1	0
Bob Caruthers, of	.000	2	6	0	0	0	0	0	0	2	0	0
Bob Clark, c	.667	1	3	2	2	0	1	0	1	0	0	0
Hub Collins, 2b	.310	7	29	7	9	0	1	0	1	3	0	2
Tom Daly, c-6,1b-1	.182	6	22	1	4	2	0	0	3	0	4	2
Patsy Donovan, of	.471	5	17	5	8	1	0	0	3	2	1	3
Dave Foutz, 1b-7,of-1	.300	7	30	6	9	2	1	0	4	0	1	1
Tom Lovett, p-4,of-1	.067	5	15	0	1	0	0	0	0	0	4	0
Darby O'Brien, of	.125	6	24	3	3	0	1	0	3	1	5	3
George Pinkney, 3b	.357	4	14	4	5	0	2	0	3	2	1	1
Germany Smith, ss	.276	7	29	3	8	0	2	0	7	0	3	1
Adonis Terry, p-3,of-3	.050	6	20	5	1	1	0	0	0	6	3	1
TOTAL	.231		242	42	56	8	8	1	30	19	27	14

PITCHER	W	L	ERA	G	GS	CG	SV	SHO	IP	H	ER	BB	SO
Tom Lovett	2	2	2.83	4	4	4	0	0	35.0	29	11	6	14
Adonis Terry	1	1	3.60	3	3	3	0	1	25.0	25	10	10	8
TOTAL	3	3	3.15	7	7	7	0	1	60.0	54	21	16	22

LOU (A)

PLAYER/POS	AVG	G	AB	R	H	2B	3B	HR	RB	BB	SO	SB
Ned Bligh, c	.000	2	3	0	0	0	0	0	0	0	1	0
Ed Daily, of-4,p-2	.136	6	22	1	3	1	1	0	3	1	2	2
Red Ehret, p	.429	3	7	1	3	0	1	0	0	0	0	0
Charlie Hamburg, of	.269	7	26	3	7	1	0	0	2	0	3	0
George Meakim, p	.500	1	2	0	1	0	0	0	0	0	0	0
Harry Raymond, ss-5,ss-3	.148	7	27	5	4	1	1	0	1	2	5	1
John Ryan, c	.053	6	19	0	1	0	0	0	2	0	1	1
Tim Shinnick, 2b	.292	7	24	3	7	1	1	0	3	2	2	2
Scott Stratton, p-3,of-1	.222	4	9	4	2	1	0	0	0	2	1	3
Harry Taylor, 1b	.300	7	30	6	9	1	0	0	2	2	3	3
Phil Tomney, ss	.200	3	5	1	1	0	0	0	0	3	1	0
Farmer Weaver, of	.259	7	27	4	7	1	0	0	4	1	2	5
Pete Weckbecker, c	.000	1	4	0	0	0	0	0	0	0	1	0
Chicken Wolf, 3b-5,of-3	.360	7	25	4	9	3	1	0	8	3	0	2
TOTAL	.235		230	32	54	10	5	0	25	16	22	19

PITCHER	W	L	ERA	G	GS	CG	SV	SHO	IP	H	ER	BB	SO
Ed Daily	0	2	2.65	2	2	2	0	0	17.0	12	5	8	5
Red Ehret	2	0	1.35	3	2	2	1	0	20.0	12	3	6	13
George Meakim	0	0	0.00	1	0	0	0	0	4.0	6	0	1	1
Scott Stratton	1	1	2.37	3	3	1	0	0	19.0	26	5	4	8
TOTAL	3	3	1.95	9	7	5	1	0	60.0	56	13	19	27

GAME 1 AT LOU OCT 17

		R	H	E
BRO	300 030 30	9	11	1
LOU	000 000 00	0	2	6

Pitchers: TERRY vs STRATTON
Attendance: 5,600

GAME 2 AT LOU OCT 18

		R	H	E
BRO	020 201 000	5	5	3
LOU	101 000 001	3	6	5

Pitchers: LOVETT vs DAILY
Attendance: 2,860

GAME 3 AT LOU OCT 20

		R	H	E
BRO	020 130 10	7	10	2
LOU	001 012 03	7	11	3

Pitchers: Terry vs Stratton, Meakim (4)
Attendance: 2,500
(Game called at end of eighth, darkness)

GAME 4 AT LOU OCT 21

		R	H	E
BRO	031 000 000	4	7	2
LOU	301 000 10X	5	9	2

Pitchers: LOVETT vs EHRET
Attendance: 1,050

GAME 5 AT BRO OCT 25

		R	H	E
LOU	010 010 000	2	5	6
BRO	210 200 20X	7	7	0

Pitchers: DAILY vs LOVETT
Home Runs: Burns-BRO
Attendance: 1,000

GAME 6 AT BRO OCT 27

		R	H	E
LOU	012 101 220	9	13	3
BRO	100 004 030	8	12	3

Pitchers: STRATTON, Ehret (7) vs TERRY
Attendance: 600

GAME 7 AT BRO OCT 28

		R	H	E
LOU	103 000 020	6	8	3
BRO	200 000 000	2	4	1

Pitchers: EHRET vs LOVETT
Attendance: 300

Interleague squabbling prevented a World Series in 1891, and the AA folded before the next season. Four AA clubs were taken into the NL, expanding the NL to 12 teams. To create a postseason championship series, the regular season was divided in half, with first-half winner Boston meeting second-half victor Cleveland for both the league and world titles.

The first game, in Cleveland, was a pitching and fielding classic. Boston's Jack Stivetts and Cleveland's Cy Young blanked the opposition for 11 innings before darkness halted the game. Young yielded just six hits and Stivetts four—all singles. Just as remarkable in an era when errors were commonplace, Cleveland committed only one and Boston none; several outstanding plays were made in the field.

Boston center fielder Hugh Duffy was the offensive and defensive star of Game 2. He drove in three of the Beaneaters' four runs (with a fly out, a triple, and a double), and scored the fourth himself after tripling a second time. And in the bottom of the ninth he snared a leadoff liner with a great running catch. As it was, Cleveland scored once in the inning to pull within a run of a tie; Duffy's catch prevented a certain tie and a possible Cleveland win. Game 3 was just as close. Pitchers Stivetts and Young each gave up two early runs, but then blanked their foes until the seventh inning, when Boston's Tommy McCarthy singled in Stivetts (who had doubled) with what proved the winning run.

The Series moved to Boston for the next three games. In Game 4, Boston ace Kid Nichols shut out the Spiders, scattering seven hits and fanning eight. Cleveland's Nig Cuppy yielded only six hits, but one was a home run ball to Hugh Duffy for two runs in the third inning, and another was a two-run single to Joe Quinn in the sixth. Cleveland pitcher John Clarkson helped his own cause the next day with a three-run homer in a six-run second inning. But Boston pitcher Jack Stivetts—with the score now 7–5 Cleveland in the sixth—tripled in a run and scored the tying run. In the seventh, Stivetts scored Boston's twelfth (and final) run after singling, while holding Cleveland scoreless through the final four innings.

Two days later the Beaneaters brought the Series to an end with their fifth straight win. The Spiders scored first, with a three-run third, but pitcher Kid Nichols held them scoreless after that and singled home Boston's tying and go-ahead runs himself as the Beaneaters tagged Cy Young for eight runs over the final six innings.

Boston Beaneaters, 5; Cleveland Spiders, 0; tie, 1

BOS (N)

PLAYER/POS	AVG	G	AB	R	H	2B	3B	HR	RB	BB	SO	SB
Charlie Bennett, c	.286	2	7	2	2	0	0	1	1	0	2	1
Hugh Duffy, of	.462	6	26	3	12	3	2	1	9	1	0	3
Charlie Ganzel, c	.500	2	8	1	4	0	0	0	2	1	0	0
King Kelly, c	.000	2	8	0	0	0	0	0	0	0	2	1
Herman Long, ss	.222	6	27	4	6	0	0	0	1	0	0	2
Bobby Lowe, of	.130	6	23	8	3	0	0	0	0	1	2	1
Tommy McCarthy, of	.381	6	21	2	8	2	0	0	2	6	1	3
Billy Nash, 3b	.167	6	24	3	4	0	0	0	4	2	3	2
Kid Nichols, p	.286	2	7	1	2	0	0	0	2	0	1	1
Joe Quinn, 2b	.286	6	21	2	6	1	1	0	4	1	2	0
Harry Staley, p	.000	1	4	0	0	0	0	0	0	0	3	0
Jack Stivetts, p	.250	3	12	3	3	1	1	0	1	0	2	0
Tommy Tucker, 1b	.261	6	23	2	6	0	0	1	2	0	1	0
TOTAL	.265		211	31	56	7	4	3	28	12	19	14

PITCHER	W	L	ERA	G	GS	CG	SV	SHO	IP	H	ER	BB	SO
Kid Nichols	2	0	1.00	2	2	2	0	1	18.0	17	2	4	13
Harry Staley	1	0	3.00	1	1	1	0	0	9.0	10	3	1	0
Jack Stivetts	2	0	0.93	3	3	3	0	1	29.0	21	3	7	17
TOTAL	5	0	1.29	6	6	6	0	2	56.0	48	8	12	30

CLE (N)

PLAYER/POS	AVG	G	AB	R	H	2B	3B	HR	RB	BB	SO	SB
Jesse Burkett, of	.320	6	25	3	8	1	0	0	1	0	2	4
Cupid Childs, 2b	.409	6	22	3	9	0	2	0	0	5	1	0
John Clarkson, p	.250	2	8	1	2	0	0	1	3	0	1	0
Nig Cuppy, p	.000	1	3	0	0	0	0	0	0	0	2	0
George Davis, 3b-2	.167	3	6	0	1	0	0	0	0	0	1	0
Jimmy McAleer, of	.182	6	22	0	4	0	0	0	1	2	2	1
Ed McKean, ss	.440	6	25	2	11	0	0	0	6	1	3	0
Jack O'Connor, of	.136	6	22	1	3	0	0	0	0	2	3	0
Patsy Tebeau, 3b	.000	5	18	1	0	0	0	0	0	0	2	1
Jake Virtue, 1b	.125	6	24	1	3	0	0	0	0	2	5	1
Cy Young, p	.091	3	11	1	1	0	0	0	0	0	5	0
Chief Zimmer, c	.261	6	23	2	6	1	1	0	2	0	3	0
TOTAL	.230		209	15	48	2	3	1	13	12	30	7

PITCHER	W	L	ERA	G	GS	CG	SV	SHO	IP	H	ER	BB	SO
John Clarkson	0	2	5.29	2	2	2	0	0	17.0	24	10	5	9
Nig Cuppy	0	1	1.13	1	1	1	0	0	8.0	6	1	4	1
Cy Young	0	2	3.00	3	3	3	0	1	27.0	26	9	3	9
TOTAL	0	5	3.46	6	6	6	0	1	52.0	56	20	12	19

GAME 1 AT CLE OCT 17

		R	H	E
CLE	000 000 000 00	0	4	1
BOS	000 000 000 00	0	6	0

Pitchers: Young vs Stivetts
Attendance: 6,000
(Game called at end of eleventh, darkness)

GAME 2 AT CLE OCT 18

		R	H	E
BOS	101 010 010	4	10	2
CLE	001 100 001	3	10	2

Pitchers: STALEY vs CLARKSON
Attendance: 6,700

GAME 3 AT CLE OCT 19

		R	H	E
CLE	200 000 000	2	8	0
BOS	110 000 10X	3	9	2

Pitchers: YOUNG vs STIVETTS
Attendance: 5,000

GAME 4 AT BOS OCT 21

		R	H	E
CLE	000 000 000	0	7	3
BOS	002 002 00X	4	6	0

Pitchers: CUPPY vs NICHOLS
Home Runs: Duffy-BOS
Attendance: 6,547

GAME 5 AT BOS OCT 22

		R	H	E
CLE	060 010 000	7	9	4
BOS	000 324 30X	12	14	3

Pitchers: CLARKSON vs STIVETTS
Home Runs: Clarkson-CLE, Tucker-BOS
Attendance: 3,466

GAME 6 AT BOS OCT 24

		R	H	E
CLE	003 000 000	3	10	5
BOS	002 211 11X	8	11	5

Pitchers: YOUNG vs NICHOLS
Home Runs: Bennett-BOS
Attendance: 2,300

As the divided season of 1892 was not repeated, no postseason championship games were held in 1893. But in 1894 Pittsburgh sportsman William C. Temple offered an elegant trophy to the winner of a series between the NL's first- and second-place finishers. For four years the Temple Cup games determined the world championship. In this first matchup, second-place New York swept the feisty pennant-winning Orioles.

Game 1, in Baltimore, was a shutout through four innings as New York's Amos Rusie and Baltimore's Duke Esper held their opponents at bay. But New York's George Van Haltren tripled in the fifth inning and scored the game's first run on a fly to left. The Giants also scored single runs in the sixth, seventh, and eighth innings, while Rusie continued his shutout pitching through the eighth. In the ninth John McGraw singled, and he came around on a sacrifice, stolen base, and single to spoil the shutout. But the effort was too little to deprive Rusie of his win.

Some 200 policemen patrolled the second game the next day to protect the umpires and New York's players and fans from the abusive Orioles and the crowd. Baltimore scored first with two runs in the second and, after losing and regaining the lead, completed the eighth inning tied 5–5. But in the top of the ninth, the Giants put together their second four-run inning of the game. Once again the Orioles came up with a run in the last of the ninth, but once again came up short.

More than 22,000 spectators showed up for Game 3 as the Series shifted to New York—a huge crowd for that era, even for a Saturday. As in the first game, the Giants' Amos Rusie hurled a 4–1 victory. New York broke a 1–1 tie with a run in the fifth on a throwing error and a ground out, and scored the game's final runs an inning later. Threatening weather held down attendance at Game 4 to about 12,000. Baltimore jumped to a quick lead with two runs in the top of the first, but New York pitcher Jouett Meekin held the Orioles to just one run after that as the Giants piled up runs for a 16–3 advantage by the time darkness forced an end to play after eight innings. Meekin, in winning his second game of the Series, connected for three hits himself—half as many as he permitted the whole Baltimore team.

New York Giants, 4; Baltimore Orioles, 0

NY (N)

PLAYER/POS	AVG	G	AB	R	H	2B	3B	HR	RB	BB	SO	SB
Eddie Burke, of	.389	4	18	3	7	1	0	0	2	1	0	1
George Davis, 3b	.313	4	16	5	5	2	2	0	5	2	0	2
Jack Doyle, 1b	.588	4	17	4	10	1	1	0	6	1	1	6
Duke Farrell, c	.400	4	15	5	6	0	0	0	2	1	1	1
Shorty Fuller, ss	.286	4	14	4	4	0	0	0	2	2	0	1
Jouett Meekin, p	.556	2	9	2	5	0	0	0	3	0	1	0
Yale Murphy, of	.000	1	1	0	0	0	0	0	0	0	0	0
Amos Rusie, p	.429	2	7	1	3	1	0	0	1	0	1	0
Mike Tiernan, of	.294	4	17	5	5	0	1	0	3	2	2	0
George Van Haltren, of	.500	4	14	3	7	1	1	0	0	2	2	2
Monte Ward, 2b	.294	4	17	1	5	0	0	0	6	0	0	0
TOTAL	.393		145	33	57	6	5	0	30	11	8	13

PITCHER	W	L	ERA	G	GS	CG	SV	SHO	IP	H	ER	BB	SO
Jouett Meekin	2	0	1.59	2	2	2	0	0	17.0	13	3	8	6
Amos Rusie	2	0	0.50	2	2	2	0	0	18.0	14	1	3	9
TOTAL	4	0	1.03	4	4	4	0	0	35.0	27	4	11	15

BAL (N)

PLAYER/POS	AVG	G	AB	R	H	2B	3B	HR	RB	BB	SO	SB
Frank Bonner, ss-1,of-1	.000	2	5	0	0	0	0	0	0	0	2	0
Steve Brodie, of	.000	4	15	2	0	0	0	0	0	2	1	1
Dan Brouthers, 1b	.188	4	16	2	3	0	0	0	0	1	0	3
Duke Esper, p	.000	1	2	0	0	0	0	0	0	1	1	0
Kid Gleason, p	.200	2	5	0	1	0	1	0	1	0	1	0
Bill Hawke, p	.000	1	2	0	0	0	0	0	0	0	1	0
George Hemming, p	.000	1	3	0	0	0	0	0	0	1	1	0
Hughie Jennings, ss	.143	4	14	0	2	0	0	0	1	0	2	0
Willie Keeler, of	.250	3	12	1	3	0	0	0	1	1	0	0
Joe Kelley, of	.333	4	15	2	5	1	1	0	0	3	2	1
John McGraw, 3b	.250	4	16	2	4	0	0	0	2	0	0	1
Heinie Reitz, 2b	.333	4	15	1	5	0	0	0	4	1	3	1
Wilbert Robinson, c	.267	4	15	1	4	0	0	0	1	1	1	1
TOTAL	.200		135	11	27	1	2	0	10	11	15	8

PITCHER	W	L	ERA	G	GS	CG	SV	SHO	IP	H	ER	BB	SO
Duke Esper	0	1	4.00	1	1	1	0	0	9.0	13	4	1	3
Kid Gleason	0	1	9.69	2	1	1	0	0	13.0	25	14	6	3
Bill Hawke	0	1	9.00	1	1	0	0	0	4.0	9	4	1	0
George Hemming	0	1	1.13	1	1	1	0	0	8.0	10	1	3	2
TOTAL	0	4	6.09	5	4	3	0	0	34.0	57	23	11	8

GAME 1 AT BAL OCT 4

				R	H	E
NY	000	011	110	4	13	2
BAL	000	000	001	1	7	1

Pitchers: RUSIE vs ESPER
Attendance: 9,000

GAME 2 AT BAL OCT 5

				R	H	E
NY	004	000	014	9	14	3
BAL	022	000	101	6	7	2

Pitchers: MEEKIN vs GLEASON
Attendance: 11,000

GAME 3 AT NY OCT 6

				R	H	E
BAL	000	100	000	1	7	4
NY	100	012	00X	4	10	4

Pitchers: HEMMING vs RUSIE
Attendance: 22,000

GAME 4 AT NY OCT 8

				R	H	E
BAL	201	000	00	3	6	3
NY	101	351	50	16	20	4

Pitchers: HAWKE, Gleason (5) vs MEEKIN
Attendance: 12,000
(Game called at end of eighth, darkness)

Baltimore, repeating as NL pennant winner, returned to Temple Cup play against new runner-up Cleveland. The first half of the opener—played in Cleveland—featured a scoreless duel between Baltimore veteran John "Sadie" McMahon and the Spiders' great Cy Young. After Cleveland scored the game's first run in the last of the fifth, the teams traded runs and the lead, completing the eighth inning tied 3–3. In the top of the ninth, doubles by Wilbert Robinson and John McGraw restored the edge to Baltimore. But in the bottom of the inning, four straight Cleveland hits pushed across the tying run and filled the bases. One runner was forced at home for the first out, but a grounder that just missed being a double-play ball drove in the winning Cleveland run.

The next three games were not so closely contested. A large and enthusiastic Cleveland crowd watched its Spiders jump on Baltimore for three runs in the bottom of the first inning of Game 2 and coast to a 7–2 win behind the strong pitching of Nig Cuppy, who held the Orioles to five singles. Cleveland repeated itself in Game 3, again exploding for three runs in the bottom of the first on the way to a seven-run total. Cy Young was just as effective in the box as Cuppy had been, scattering four hits over seven shutout innings before Baltimore put together three singles in the eighth for their only run.

When the teams shifted to Baltimore for Game 4, the Orioles came to life. While their pitcher Duke Esper strangled the Spiders on just five singles—only two Cleveland runners advanced as far as second base—Baltimore batters tagged Nig Cuppy for five runs and their first Temple Cup win in two years of trying.

It proved to be their only win of the Series. The next day, in the first close struggle since the opener, Cy Young and Baltimore's rookie ace Bill Hoffer dueled scorelessly through six innings. But in the top of the seventh, Young doubled to start what became a three-run rally, and an inning later the Spiders scored twice more. Baltimore scored a single run in the last of the seventh, and, with two out in the ninth, loaded the bases on two walks and a hit batsman. A Cleveland error brought in the Orioles' second run as the bases remained full for Steve Brodie. But despite the pleas of Baltimore partisans to hit a homer or triple, Brodie didn't deliver and Cleveland copped the cup.

Cleveland Spiders, 4; Baltimore Orioles, 1

CLE (N)

PLAYER/POS	AVG	G	AB	R	H	2B	3B	HR	RB	BB	SO	SB
Harry Blake, of	.250	5	20	1	5	3	0	0	2	0	2	0
Jesse Burkett, of	.450	5	20	3	9	2	0	0	2	0	0	1
Cupid Childs, 2b	.190	5	21	4	4	1	0	0	2	1	0	1
Nig Cuppy, p	.167	2	6	1	1	1	0	0	1	0	0	0
Jimmy McAleer, of	.286	5	21	2	6	0	0	0	2	0	0	1
Chippy McGarr, 3b	.368	5	19	3	7	2	0	0	1	1	1	2
Ed McKean, ss	.300	5	20	2	6	1	1	0	4	3	0	1
Patsy Tebeau, 1b	.286	5	21	3	6	1	0	0	3	1	0	0
Cy Young, p	.250	3	12	3	3	1	0	0	1	0	1	0
Chief Zimmer, c	.333	4	18	2	6	2	0	0	3	3	5	0
TOTAL	.298		178	24	53	14	1	0	21	9	9*	6

PITCHER	W	L	ERA	G	GS	CG	SV	SHO	IP	H	ER	BB	SO
Nig Cuppy	1	1	3.18	2	2	2	0	0	17.0	14	6	4	6
Cy Young	3	0	2.33	3	3	3	0	0	27.0	28	7	4	2
TOTAL	4	1	2.66	5	5	5	0	0	44.0	42	13	8	8

BAL (N)

PLAYER/POS	AVG	G	AB	R	H	2B	3B	HR	RB	BB	SO	SB
Steve Brodie, of	.200	5	20	1	4	0	0	0	2	0	0	0
Scoops Carey, 1b	.263	5	19	0	5	1	0	0	1	0	0	0
Boileryard Clarke, c	.286	2	7	1	2	0	0	0	0	0	0	2
Duke Esper, p	.000	1	3	0	0	0	0	0	0	1	2	0
Kid Gleason, 2b	.105	5	19	0	2	0	0	0	0	0	1	0
Bill Hoffer, p	.000	2	7	0	0	0	0	0	0	0	2	0
Hughie Jennings, ss	.368	5	19	3	7	2	0	0	2	1	0	1
Willie Keeler, of	.235	5	17	3	4	0	0	0	1	3	1	0
Joe Kelley, of	.368	5	19	1	7	0	0	0	5	1	1	1
John McGraw, 3b	.400	5	20	4	8	2	0	0	1	2	0	2
Sadie McMahon, p	.000	2	7	0	0	0	0	0	0	0	0	0
Wilbert Robinson, c	.250	3	12	1	3	1	0	0	0	0	1	0
TOTAL	.249		169	14	42	6	0	0	12	8	8	6

PITCHER	W	L	ERA	G	GS	CG	SV	SHO	IP	H	ER	BB	SO
Duke Esper	1	0	0.00	1	1	1	0	1	9.0	5	0	0	3
Bill Hoffer	0	2	4.24	2	2	2	0	0	17.0	21	8	6	4
Sadie McMahon	0	2	5.94	2	2	2	0	0	16.2	27	11	3	2
TOTAL	1	4	4.01	5	5	5	0	1	42.2	53	19	9	9

GAME 1 AT CLE OCT 2

		R	H	E
BAL	000 001 021	4	12	0
CLE	000 011 012	5	14	3

Pitchers: McMAHON vs YOUNG
Attendance: 8,000

GAME 2 AT CLE OCT 3

		R	H	E
BAL	010 001 000	2	5	4
CLE	300 012 10X	7	10	5

Pitchers: HOFFER vs CUPPY
Attendance: 10,000

GAME 3 AT CLE OCT 5

		R	H	E
BAL	000 000 010	1	7	1
CLE	300 000 31X	7	13	1

Pitchers: McMAHON vs YOUNG
Attendance: 12,000

GAME 4 AT BAL OCT 7

		R	H	E
CLE	000 000 000	0	5	1
BAL	012 000 20X	5	9	1

Pitchers: CUPPY vs ESPER
Attendance: 9,100

GAME 5 AT BAL OCT 8

		R	H	E
CLE	000 000 320	5	11	3
BAL	000 000 101	2	9	5

Pitchers: YOUNG vs HOFFER
Attendance: 5,000

Baltimore captured its third consecutive pennant and for the second year in a row faced runner-up Cleveland in the Temple Cup games. But this time the Orioles emerged triumphant—with a sweep in which their margin of victory was never less than four runs.

Aces Bill Hoffer of Baltimore and the Spiders' Cy Young faced each other in the opener, in Baltimore. Hoffer walked four men, but gave up only five hits while the Orioles bombarded Young for 13. When the game ended, Hoffer and Baltimore had a 7–1 win.

Bobby Wallace (who had not yet discovered his role at shortstop that would propel him into the Hall of Fame) pitched for Cleveland in Game 2. He lost the game in the first inning when two Spider errors, a hit batsman, three hits, and a steal of home put four Baltimore runs on the board. The Orioles added two runs in the third and another in the fifth, while their promising 20-year-old pitcher Joe Corbett held the Spiders to two runs on seven hits.

The Orioles' Hoffer gave up 10 hits to Cleveland in Game 3—two more than the Birds made off Nig Cuppy. But all the hits off Hoffer were singles, and he walked only one. Half of Cleveland's hits went toward producing just two runs. Their second run tied the score in the fifth inning, but in the sixth Baltimore regained the lead as John McGraw singled, stole second, took third on an error, and came home on an outfield fly. In the eighth the Orioles bunched four of their eight hits for three insurance runs.

The Series moved to Cleveland for the fourth game. Young Joe Corbett was again sent into the box for Baltimore, this time to face Nig Cuppy. For six innings the game was a scoreless duel. Baltimore hit safely in every inning but the second, but failed to score until the seventh, when Joe Kelley's double and Jack Doyle's single scored the only run they would need. But the Orioles added a second run in that inning and three more in the eighth. Two of the four Cleveland hits against Corbett put men on base in the eighth inning, and Corbett walked two in the ninth to raise Cleveland's hopes. But no Spider scored, and with the 5–0 win the Orioles were world champions at last.

Baltimore Orioles, 4; Cleveland Spiders, 0

BAL (N)

PLAYER/POS	AVG	G	AB	R	H	2B	3B	HR	RB	BB	SO	SB
Steve Brodie, of	.067	4	15	1	1	0	0	0	3	0	0	1
Joe Corbett, p	.500	2	6	1	3	1	0	0	0	1	1	0
Jack Doyle, 1b	.294	4	17	3	5	1	0	0	4	0	0	2
Bill Hoffer, p	.286	2	7	1	2	0	2	0	0	0	1	0
Hughie Jennings, ss	.333	4	15	5	5	2	0	0	3	1	2	1
Willie Keeler, of	.471	4	17	4	8	1	2	0	4	0	0	1
Joe Kelley, of	.471	4	17	3	8	1	0	0	4	0	1	2
John McGraw, 3b	.267	4	15	4	4	0	0	0	1	0	0	4
Joe Quinn, 3b	.000	1	3	1	0	0	0	0	0	0	0	0
Heinie Reitz, 2b	.133	4	15	1	2	0	0	0	2	1	0	0
Wilbert Robinson, c	.267	4	15	1	4	1	0	0	2	0	3	0
TOTAL	.296		142	25	42	7	4	0	23	3	8	11

PITCHER	W	L	ERA	G	GS	CG	SV	SHO	IP	H	ER	BB	SO
Joe Corbett	2	0	0.50	2	2	2	0	1	18.0	11	1	7	10
Bill Hoffer	2	0	1.50	2	2	2	0	0	18.0	15	3	5	10
TOTAL	4	0	1.00	4	4	4	0	1	36.0	26	4	12	20

CLE (N)

PLAYER/POS	AVG	G	AB	R	H	2B	3B	HR	RB	BB	SO	SB
Harry Blake, of	.071	4	14	1	1	0	0	0	0	1	1	1
Jesse Burkett, of	.333	4	15	1	5	0	0	0	0	2	3	0
Cupid Childs, 2b	.231	4	13	2	3	0	0	0	0	4	0	1
Nig Cuppy, p	.143	2	7	0	1	0	0	0	0	0	1	0
Jimmy McAleer, of	.133	4	15	0	2	0	0	0	1	1	2	1
Chippy McGarr, 3b	.063	4	16	0	1	0	0	0	0	0	3	2
Ed McKean, ss	.313	4	16	0	5	1	1	0	1	1	2	1
Jack O'Connor, 1b	.286	4	14	1	4	0	0	0	1	1	2	0
Patsy Tebeau, 1b	.000	1	1	0	0	0	0	0	0	0	0	0
Bobby Wallace, p-1	.200	3	5	0	1	0	0	0	0	0	0	0
Cy Young, p	.000	1	3	0	0	0	0	0	0	0	0	0
Chief Zimmer, c	.214	4	14	0	3	1	0	0	1	2	6	0
TOTAL	.195		133	5	26	2	1	0	4	12	20	6

PITCHER	W	L	ERA	G	GS	CG	SV	SHO	IP	H	ER	BB	SO
Nig Cuppy	0	2	4.76	2	2	2	0	0	17.0	19	9	0	4
Bobby Wallace	0	1	4.50	1	1	1	0	0	8.0	10	4	2	4
Cy Young	0	1	6.00	1	1	1	0	0	9.0	13	6	1	0
TOTAL	0	4	5.03	4	4	4	0	0	34.0	42	19	3	8

GAME 1 AT BAL OCT 2

				R	H	E
BAL	002	001	310	7	13	1
CLE	000	001	000	1	5	4

Pitchers: HOFFER vs YOUNG
Attendance: 4,000

GAME 2 AT BAL OCT 3

				R	H	E
BAL	402	010	00	7	10	3
CLE	001	001	00	2	7	3

Pitchers: CORBETT vs WALLACE
Attendance: 3,100
(Game called at end of eighth, darkness)

GAME 3 AT BAL OCT 5

				R	H	E
BAL	011	001	030	6	8	2
CLE	001	010	000	2	10	2

Pitchers: HOFFER vs CUPPY
Attendance: 2,000

GAME 4 AT CLE OCT 8

				R	H	E
CLE	000	000	000	0	4	2
BAL	000	000	23X	5	11	1

Pitchers: CUPPY vs CORBETT
Attendance: 1,500

Boston had edged Baltimore in a close race for the NL pennant, but the Orioles turned the tables on the Beaneaters in Temple Cup play. The Series was a high-scoring affair with an average score of 11-8 for each game.

The opener, in Boston, set the tone for the games. Baltimore sent four runners across the plate in the top of the first inning, and Boston followed in its half with three. The Beaneaters recorded only 12 hits in the game to the Orioles' 20, but they also received seven walks from Baltimore hurler Jerry Nops, and five of those runners scored. The lead switched back and forth in the middle innings, but Boston scored two final runs in the eighth and hung on for a 13–12 win.

Baltimore's Joe Corbett gave up 16 hits (one a home run) and four walks in Game 2 as Boston scored 11 times. But Boston's two pitchers, Fred Klobedanz and Jack Stivetts, were even more generous, handing out 17 hits (including three homers—one of them to opposing pitcher Corbett, who also hit a double and two singles) and five walks as the Orioles evened the Series with their thirteen-run attack.

Game 3 was the Series' lowest in run production, with Baltimore scoring four in the second inning and another four in the third for an 8–3 win. But rain ended the game before Boston could complete its time at bat in the last of the eighth, which erased from the record four more Orioles runs scored earlier in the inning. Rather than waste the two free days before the Series resumed in Baltimore, the two clubs stayed in Massachusetts and played a pair of exhibition games in Worcester and Springfield. Baltimore won them both, 11–10, and 8–6.

The Orioles continued their roll in Series Game 4, with another close but high-scoring victory, 12–11. It looked at first like a blowout as Baltimore scored six runs in the first inning and five more in the second. But Ted Lewis relieved Boston starter Jack Stivetts and held Baltimore to just one further run as the Beaneaters fought back to within one run of a tie before faltering in the ninth.

Boston batters hit Bill Hoffer safely 15 times in Game Five, but only three Beaneaters scored. Baltimore, with two fewer hits, garnered six more runs than Boston and, with their fourth win, the right to hold the cup for another year. But attendance at the final game was so small the embarrassed Baltimore management refused to release the figures, and the league gave the cup back to Mr. Temple rather than sponsor another unprofitable Series. There was no postseason championship contest in 1898 or 1899.

Baltimore Orioles, 4; Boston Beaneaters, 1

BAL (N)

PLAYER/POS	AVG	G	AB	R	H	2B	3B	HR	RB	BB	SO	SB
Frank Bowerman, c-1,1b-1	.500	2	8	2	4	0	1	0	4	0	0	0
Boileryard Clarke, c	.563	4	16	5	9	1	1	1	4	1	0	0
Joe Corbett, p	.667	2	6	2	4	1	0	1	2	0	1	0
Jack Doyle, 1b	.526	5	19	7	10	2	0	0	9	0	1	2
Bill Hoffer, p	.250	2	8	2	2	1	0	0	0	0	0	0
Hughie Jennings, ss	.318	5	22	5	7	2	0	0	3	4	0	0
Willie Keeler, of	.391	5	23	5	9	2	0	0	2	4	0	0
Joe Kelley, of	.313	4	16	7	5	3	0	0	5	5	0	0
John McGraw, 3b	.300	5	20	6	6	1	1	0	6	7	0	0
Jerry Nops, p	.286	2	7	0	2	0	0	0	1	1	5	0
Tom O'Brien, of	.400	1	5	2	2	1	0	0	0	0	0	0
Heinie Reitz, 2b	.250	5	20	4	5	1	0	1	4	2	0	0
Jake Stenzel, of	.381	5	21	7	8	1	1	0	3	2	0	2
TOTAL	.382		191	54	73	16	4	3	43	26	7	4

PITCHER	W	L	ERA	G	GS	CG	SV	SHO	IP	H	ER	BB	SO
Joe Corbett	1	0	9.00	2	1	1	0	0	12.0	21	12	8	5
Bill Hoffer	2	0	3.38	2	2	2	0	0	16.0	25	6	4	2
Jerry Nops	1	1	12.86	2	2	1	0	0	14.0	23	20	9	3
TOTAL	4	1	8.14	6	5	4	0	0	42.0	69	38	21	10

BOS (N)

PLAYER/POS	AVG	G	AB	R	H	2B	3B	HR	RB	BB	SO	SB
Marty Bergen, c	.500	1	4	0	2	0	0	0	1	0	1	1
Jimmy Collins, 3b	.182	5	22	2	4	0	0	0	4	1	0	0
Hugh Duffy, of	.524	5	21	6	11	2	0	0	7	1	0	0
Billy Hamilton, of	.500	4	16	6	8	1	0	0	2	5	3	2
Charlie Hickman, p-1,of-1	.250	1	4	0	1	1	0	0	1	0	0	0
Fred Klobedanz, p	1.000	2	5	3	5	0	0	0	0	0	0	0
Fred Lake, c	.000	1	3	0	0	0	0	0	0	0	1	0
Ted Lewis, p	.500	3	6	1	3	1	0	0	1	1	0	0
Herman Long, ss	.286	5	21	4	6	1	1	1	5	2	2	1
Bobby Lowe, 2b	.391	5	23	6	9	2	0	0	6	1	0	1
Kid Nichols, p	.000	1	3	0	0	0	0	0	1	0	0	0
Chick Stahl, of	.381	5	21	6	8	1	0	0	6	3	2	2
Jack Stivetts, p-2,of-1	.000	3	7	1	0	0	0	0	0	1	0	1
Jim Sullivan, p	.000	1	1	0	0	0	0	0	0	0	0	0
Fred Tenney, 1b	.286	5	21	4	6	0	0	0	2	4	1	2
George Yeager, c	.500	3	12	2	6	1	1	0	2	2	0	0
TOTAL	.365		189	41	69	10	2	1	38	21	10	10

PITCHER	W	L	ERA	G	GS	CG	SV	SHO	IP	H	ER	BB	SO
Charlie Hickman	0	1	3.60	1	1	0	0	0	5.0	7	2	2	0
Fred Klobedanz	0	1	9.35	2	1	0	0	0	8.2	12	9	8	0
Ted Lewis	1	1	6.00	3	1	0	0	0	12	18	8	9	4
Kid Nichols	0	0	12.00	1	1	0	0	0	6.0	14	8	0	3
Jack Stivetts	0	1	18.47	2	1	0	0	0	6.1	16	13	7	0
Jim Sullivan	0	0	3.00	1	0	0	0	0	3.0	6	1	0	0
TOTAL	1	4	9.00	10	5	0	0	0	41.0	73	41	26	7

GAME 1 AT BOS OCT 4

				R	H	E
BAL	401	023	200	12	20	4
BOS	300	125	02X	13	12	4

Pitchers: NOPS vs Nichols, LEWIS (7)
Attendance: 9,600

GAME 2 AT BOS OCT 5

				R	H	E
BAL	130	160	110	13	17	2
BOS	002	620	100	11	16	3

Pitchers: CORBETT vs KLOBEDANZ, Stivetts (5)
Home Runs: Reitz-BAL, Clarke-BAL, Corbett-BAL, Long-BOS
Attendance: 6,500

GAME 3 AT BOS OCT 6

				R	H	E
BAL	044	000	0	8	9	2
BOS	003	000	0	3	10	2

Pitchers: HOFFER vs LEWIS, Klobedanz (3)
Attendance: 5,000
(Game called in eighth, rain)

GAME 4 AT BAL OCT 9

				R	H	E
BOS	000	024	320	11	16	3
BAL	650	001	00X	12	14	3

Pitchers: STIVETTS, Lewis (2) vs NOPS, Corbett (7)
Attendance: 2,500

GAME 5 AT BAL OCT 11

				R	H	E
BOS	020	000	001	3	15	3
BAL	023	000	22X	9	13	2

Pitchers: HICKMAN, Sullivan (7) vs HOFFER
Attendance: 700

Pennant-winning Brooklyn led the NL in hitting, but runner-up Pittsburgh claimed the best pitching. Honus Wagner was the only Pittsburgh regular to hit over .300, but he enjoyed what turned out to be his finest season offensively, leading the league with a .381 batting average. Pittsburghers believed their club superior to Brooklyn and a best-of-five "world championship" series was arranged, with all the games to be played in Pittsburgh for a silver cup donated by the *Pittsburgh Chronicle-Telegraph*. Brooklyn, however, proved that its pennant was no fluke.

Two of the game's best pitchers faced off in the opener: Pittsburgh's Rube Waddell, who had led the league in ERA, and Joe "Iron Man" McGinnity, whose 28 regular-season wins totaled eight more than those of the league's runners-up. McGinnity prevailed, shutting out the Pirates until two unearned runs came across in the top of the ninth. Pirates errors also gave Brooklyn a pair of unearned runs, but Waddell lost the game on hits—13 in all, including six in the Superbas' three-run third inning.

In Game 2, Brooklyn's Frank Kitson held Pittsburgh to four hits, and although his Superbas scored only one earned run, six Pirate errors gave them their second win, 4–2.

The Pirates staved off a Series sweep with sharp pitching and heavy hitting in Game 3. Deacon Phillippe shut out Brooklyn on six hits as the Pirates jumped on Harry Howell for 13. All Pittsburgh's hits were singles, but combined with Brooklyn errors they were good for ten runs, seven of them unearned.

Three Brooklyn singles and a fumble by Pirates pitcher Sam Leever in the fourth inning of Game 4 gave the Superbas three runs and a 4–0 lead the Pirates could not overcome. Brooklyn hurler McGinnity scattered nine hits and, supported by flawless fielding, held Pittsburgh to a single run to bring Brooklyn its first World Series triumph in three tries—and its last until 1955. The Brooklyn players voted to award their trophy to McGinnity for his fine pitching. The cup may be seen today—along with the Temple Cup and the current World Series trophy—at the Baseball Hall of Fame in Cooperstown.

Brooklyn Superbas, 3; Pittsburgh Pirates, 1

BRO (N)

PLAYER/POS	AVG	G	AB	R	H	2B	3B	HR	RB	BB	SO	SB
Lave Cross, 3b	.278	4	18	2	5	0	1	0	1	0	0	1
Bill Dahlen, ss	.176	4	17	3	3	0	1	0	2	0	3	1
Tom Daly, 2b	.154	4	13	2	2	1	0	0	1	3	1	0
Duke Farrell, c	.375	2	8	0	3	0	0	0	1	0	0	1
Harry Howell, p	.000	1	3	0	0	0	0	0	0	0	2	0
Hughie Jennings, 1b	.167	4	18	1	3	1	0	0	2	1	1	0
Fielder Jones, of	.278	4	18	3	5	0	0	0	4	1	1	1
Willie Keeler, of	.353	4	17	0	6	0	0	0	0	1	0	0
Joe Kelley, of	.176	4	17	2	3	0	0	0	1	2	3	0
Frank Kitson, p	.000	1	3	0	0	0	0	0	0	1	2	0
Joe McGinnity, p	.143	2	7	1	1	0	0	0	1	0	2	0
Deacon McGuire, c	.375	2	8	1	3	1	0	0	0	0	1	0
TOTAL	.231		147	15	34	3	2	0	13	9	16	4

PITCHER	W	L	ERA	G	GS	CG	SV	SHO	IP	H	ER	BB	SO
Harry Howell	0	1	3.38	1	1	1	0	0	8.0	13	3	2	3
Frank Kitson	1	0	1.00	1	1	1	0	0	9.0	4	1	1	2
Joe McGinnity	2	0	0.00	2	2	2	0	0	18.0	14	0	3	5
TOTAL	3	1	1.03	4	4	4	0	0	35.0	31	4	6	10

PIT (N)

PLAYER/POS	AVG	G	AB	R	H	2B	3B	HR	RB	BB	SO	SB
Ginger Beaumont, of	.267	4	15	2	4	0	0	0	1	1	0	1
Fred Ely, ss	.286	4	14	1	4	1	0	0	0	1	1	2
Tommy Leach, of	.176	4	17	4	3	0	0	0	1	1	2	0
Sam Leever, p	.250	2	4	0	1	0	0	0	0	0	1	1
Tom O'Brien, 1b	.125	4	16	1	2	1	0	0	2	0	1	0
Jack O'Connor, c	.250	2	4	0	1	0	0	0	1	1	0	0
Deacon Phillippe, p	.000	1	4	1	0	0	0	0	0	0	1	0
Claude Ritchey, 2b	.333	4	15	3	5	1	0	0	1	1	0	0
Pop Schriver, ph	.000	1	1	0	0	0	0	0	0	0	0	0
Rube Waddell, p	.200	2	5	0	1	0	0	0	0	0	1	0
Honus Wagner, of	.400	4	15	2	6	1	0	0	3	0	1	2
Jimmy Williams, 3b	.214	4	14	0	3	0	0	0	0	1	0	0
Chief Zimmer, c	.111	3	9	1	1	0	0	0	1	0	2	1
TOTAL	.233		133	15	31	4	0	0	10	6	10	7

PITCHER	W	L	ERA	G	GS	CG	SV	SHO	IP	H	ER	BB	SO
Sam Leever	0	2	1.38	2	2	1	0	0	13.0	13	2	4	4
Deacon Phillippe	1	0	0.00	1	1	1	0	1	9.0	6	0	2	5
Rube Waddell	0	1	1.93	2	1	1	0	0	14.0	15	3	3	7
TOTAL	1	3	1.25	5	4	3	0	1	36.0	34	5	9	16

GAME 1 AT PIT OCT 15

				R	H	E
BRO	003	101	000	5	13	1
PIT	000	000	002	2	5	4

Pitchers: McGINNITY vs WADDELL
Attendance: 4,000

GAME 2 AT PIT OCT 16

				R	H	E
BRO	010	003	000	4	7	0
PIT	000	100	100	2	4	6

Pitchers: KITSON vs LEEVER
Attendance: 1,800

GAME 3 AT PIT OCT 17

				R	H	E
BRO	000	000	000	0	6	3
PIT	310	020	13X	10	13	1

Pitchers: HOWELL vs PHILLIPPE
Attendance: 2,500

GAME 4 AT PIT OCT 18

				R	H	E
BRO	100	311	000	6	8	0
PIT	000	001	000	1	9	3

Pitchers: McGINNITY vs LEEVER, Waddell (5)
Attendance: 2,335

When the Boston Pilgrims of the young American League accepted a challenge from owner Barney Dreyfuss of the National League Pirates, the modern World Series was born. (In 1901 and 1902, the National and American Leagues were warring, and did not stage a postseason series.) Pittsburgh was favored to win but entered the Series weakened by injuries to pitching ace Sam Leever and shortstop Honus Wagner, and by the loss of pitcher Ed Doheny to mental illness.

Deacon Phillippe, the Pirates' one healthy starter, faced Cy Young in the opener, winning handily as the Pirates, with two out in the top of the first, jumped on Young (and a porous defense) for four runs. Right fielder Jimmy Sebring starred offensively for the Pirates, with four RBIs and the Series's first home run. Boston came back in Game 2 as Bill Dinneen shut out the Pirates on three hits. His teammates scored three runs off the sore-armed Leever and reliever Bucky Veil, two coming on homers by Patsy Dougherty. (They were the last World Series home runs for five years.)

Phillippe, with only a day's rest, started Game 3 and again pitched Pittsburgh into the Series lead, holding Boston to four hits. After a Sunday travel day to Pittsburgh and a day of rain, Phillippe defeated Boston a third time, though he yielded three ninth-inning runs before emerging with a 5–4 win.

The tide began to turn against the Pirates the next day, as Boston knocked five ground-rule triples into the overflow crowd, scoring 10 runs in the sixth and seventh innings to give Young an 11–2 victory. Dinneen bested Leever for a second time in Game 6, holding the Pirates scoreless in eight of their nine innings for a 6–3 win. And in Game 7, Phillippe finally lost and Young won.

After another travel Sunday and another rainout, Phillippe faced the Pilgrims for the fifth time. He pitched well, giving up three runs (only two of them earned). But Bill Dinneen pitched better, holding the Pirates to four hits as he shut them out for the second time to give Boston the Series.

Boston Pilgrims (AL), 5; Pittsburgh Pirates (NL), 3

BOS (A)

PLAYER/POS	AVG	G	AB	R	H	2B	3B	HR	RB	BB	SO	SB
Jimmy Collins, 3b	.250	8	36	5	9	1	2	0	1	1	1	3
Lou Criger, c	.231	8	26	1	6	0	0	0	4	2	3	0
Bill Dinneen, p	.250	4	12	1	3	0	0	0	0	2	2	0
Patsy Dougherty, of	.235	8	34	3	8	0	2	2	5	2	6	0
Duke Farrell, ph	.000	2	2	0	0	0	0	0	1	0	0	0
Hobe Ferris, 2b	.290	8	31	3	9	0	1	0	5	0	6	0
Buck Freeman, of	.281	8	32	6	9	0	3	0	4	2	2	0
Tom Hughes, p	.000	1	0	0	0	0	0	0	0	0	0	0
Candy La Chance, 1b	.222	8	27	5	6	2	1	0	4	3	2	0
Jack O'Ben, ph	.000	2	2	0	0	0	0	0	0	0	1	0
Freddy Parent, ss	.281	8	32	8	9	0	3	0	4	1	1	0
Chick Stahl, of	.303	8	33	6	10	1	3	0	3	1	2	2
Cy Young, p	.133	4	15	1	2	0	1	0	3	0	3	0
TOTAL	.252		282	39	71	4	16	2	34	14	29	5

PITCHER	W	L	ERA	G	GS	CG	SV	SHO	IP	H	ER	BB	SO
Bill Dinneen	3	1	2.06	4	4	4	0	2	35.0	29	8	8	28
Tom Hughes	0	1	9.00	1	1	0	0	0	2.0	4	2	2	0
Cy Young	2	1	1.85	4	3	3	0	0	34.0	31	7	4	17
TOTAL	5	3	2.15	9	8	7	0	2	71.0	64	17	14	45

PIT (N)

PLAYER/POS	AVG	G	AB	R	H	2B	3B	HR	RB	BB	SO	SB
Ginger Beaumont, of	.265	8	34	6	9	0	1	0	1	2	4	2
Kitty Bransfield, 1b	.207	8	29	3	6	0	2	0	1	1	6	1
Fred Clarke, of	.265	8	34	3	9	2	1	0	2	1	5	1
Brickyard Kennedy, p	.500	1	2	0	1	1	0	0	0	0	0	0
Tommy Leach, 3b	.273	8	33	3	9	0	4	0	7	1	4	1
Sam Leever, p	.000	2	4	0	0	0	0	0	0	0	0	0
Ed Phelps, c-7	.231	8	26	1	6	2	0	0	1	1	6	0
Deacon Phillippe, p	.222	5	18	1	4	0	0	0	1	0	3	0
Claude Ritchey, 2b	.111	8	27	2	3	1	0	0	2	4	7	1
Jimmy Sebring, of	.367	8	30	3	11	0	1	1	3	1	4	0
Harry Smith, c	.000	1	3	0	0	0	0	0	0	0	0	0
Gus Thompson, p	.000	1	1	0	0	0	0	0	0	0	0	0
Bucky Veil, p	.000	1	2	0	0	0	0	0	0	0	2	0
Honus Wagner, ss	.222	8	27	2	6	1	0	0	3	3	4	3
TOTAL	.237		270	24	64	7	9	1	21	14	45	9

PITCHER	W	L	ERA	G	GS	CG	SV	SHO	IP	H	ER	BB	SO
Brickyard Kennedy	0	1	5.14	1	1	0	0	0	7.0	11	4	3	3
Sam Leever	0	2	5.40	2	2	1	0	0	10.0	13	6	3	2
Deacon Phillippe	3	2	2.86	5	5	5	0	0	44.0	38	14	3	22
Gus Thompson	0	0	4.50	1	0	0	0	0	2.0	3	1	0	1
Bucky Veil	0	0	1.29	1	0	0	0	0	7.0	6	1	5	1
TOTAL	3	5	3.34	10	8	6	0	0	70.0	71	26	14	29

GAME 1 AT BOS OCT 1

		R	H	E
PIT	401 100 100	7	12	2
BOS	000 000 201	3	6	4

Pitchers: PHILLIPPE vs YOUNG
Home Runs: Sebring-PIT
Attendance: 16,242

GAME 2 AT BOS OCT 2

		R	H	E
PIT	000 000 000	0	3	2
BOS	200 001 00X	3	9	0

Pitchers: LEEVER, Veil (2) vs DINNEEN
Home Runs: Dougherty-BOS (2)
Attendance: 9,415

GAME 3 AT BOS OCT 3

		R	H	E
PIT	012 000 010	4	7	0
BOS	000 100 010	2	4	2

Pitchers: PHILLIPPE vs HUGHES, Young (3)
Attendance: 18,801

GAME 4 AT PIT OCT 6

		R	H	E
BOS	000 010 003	4	9	1
PIT	100 010 30X	5	12	1

Pitchers: DINNEEN vs PHILLIPPE
Attendance: 7,600

GAME 5 AT PIT OCT 7

		R	H	E
BOS	000 006 410	11	14	2
PIT	000 000 020	2	6	4

Pitchers: YOUNG vs KENNEDY, Thompson (8)
Attendance: 12,322

GAME 6 AT PIT OCT 8

		R	H	E
BOS	003 020 100	6	10	1
PIT	000 000 300	3	10	3

Pitchers: DINNEEN vs LEEVER
Attendance: 11,556

GAME 7 AT PIT OCT 10

		R	H	E
BOS	200 202 010	7	11	4
PIT	000 101 001	3	10	3

Pitchers: YOUNG vs PHILLIPPE
Attendance: 17,038

GAME 8 AT BOS OCT 13

		R	H	E
PIT	000 000 000	0	4	3
BOS	000 201 00X	3	8	0

Pitchers: PHILLIPPE vs DINNEEN
Attendance: 7,455

After a year's gap caused by the Giants' refusal to play the American League champion Boston Pilgrims, the World Series—now established on an official and permanent basis (and reduced to a best-of-seven format)—resumed with a pitching classic. Even though ERA league leader Rube Waddell had ostensibly injured his shoulder and could not pitch in the Series for the A's—rumor had it that gamblers had reached him—the Philadelphia staff recorded a Series ERA of only 1.47. But the Giants' staff—led by Christy Mathewson's three shutouts—registered a matchless ERA of 0.00, permitting only three unearned runs to score in their only Series loss. Every victory in the Series was a shutout.

Mathewson, a 31-game winner in the regular season, continued his winning ways in the Series opener. Though three of the four hits he yielded were doubles, he permitted no more than one hit in any inning, and stopped the only scoring threat, fielding a squeeze bunt to throw out the runner at the plate in the sixth inning.

The A's came back to tie the Series the next day. This time it was Chief Bender's turn to hurl a four-hit shutout. Joe McGinnity also pitched well for the Giants, but New York errors in the third and eighth innings let in three unearned runs—the only runs, as it turned out, to be scored against the Giants in the Series.

Mathewson, pitching with only two days' rest in Game 3, once again permitted only four hits (all singles this time), and Philadelphia's flawed fielding let in seven unearned runs to help give Matty an easy 9–0 win. In Game 4, McGinnity, the hard-luck loser of Game 2, tried again. This time the Giants supported him almost flawlessly, while he gave up only five singles on his way to victory in the Series' tightest game. An A's error led to a single Giants run, and a loss for Eddie Plank, who had pitched even better than McGinnity, giving up only four hits while fanning six.

Chief Bender, the A's winner in Game 2, pitched a five-hitter in Game 6, but he also yielded three walks, all of which contributed to the two New York runs. Mathewson, though he gave up six hits, walked none, retiring the final ten batters to conclude his record third shutout—and the Series.

New York Giants (NL), 4; Philadelphia Athletics (AL), 1

NY (N)

PLAYER/POS	AVG	G	AB	R	H	2B	3B	HR	RB	BB	SO	SB
Red Ames, p	.000	1	0	0	0	0	0	0	0	0	0	0
Roger Bresnahan, c	.313	5	16	3	5	2	0	0	1	4	0	1
George Browne, of	.182	5	22	2	4	0	0	0	1	0	2	2
Bill Dahlen, ss	.000	5	15	1	0	0	0	0	1	3	2	3
Art Devlin, 3b	.250	5	16	0	4	1	0	0	1	1	3	3
Mike Donlin, of	.263	5	19	4	5	1	0	0	1	2	1	2
Billy Gilbert, 2b	.235	5	17	1	4	0	0	0	2	0	2	1
Christy Mathewson, p	.250	3	8	1	2	0	0	0	0	1	1	0
Dan McGann, 1b	.235	5	17	1	4	2	0	0	4	2	7	0
Joe McGinnity, p	.000	2	5	0	0	0	0	0	0	0	2	0
Sam Mertes, of	.176	5	17	2	3	1	0	0	2	2	5	0
Sammy Strang, ph	.000	1	1	0	0	0	0	0	0	0	1	0
TOTAL	.203		153	15	31	7	0	0	13	15	26	12

PITCHER	W	L	ERA	G	GS	CG	SV	SHO	IP	H	ER	BB	SO
Red Ames	0	0	0.00	1	0	0	0	0	1.0	1	0	1	1
Christy Mathewson	3	0	0.00	3	3	3	0	3	27.0	14	0	1	18
Joe McGinnity	1	1	0.00	2	2	1	0	1	17.0	10	0	3	6
TOTAL	4	1	0.00	6	5	4	0	4	45.0	25	0	5	25

PHI (A)

PLAYER/POS	AVG	G	AB	R	H	2B	3B	HR	RB	BB	SO	SB
Chief Bender, p	.000	2	5	0	0	0	0	0	0	0	1	0
Andy Coakley, p	.000	1	2	0	0	0	0	0	0	0	1	0
Lave Cross, 3b	.105	5	19	0	2	0	0	0	0	1	1	0
Monte Cross, ss	.176	5	17	0	3	0	0	0	0	0	7	0
Harry Davis, 1b	.200	5	20	0	4	1	0	0	0	0	1	0
Topsy Hartsel, of	.294	5	17	1	5	1	0	0	0	2	1	2
Danny Hoffman, ph	.000	1	1	0	0	0	0	0	0	0	1	0
Bris Lord, of	.100	5	20	0	2	0	0	0	2	0	5	0
Danny Murphy, 2b	.188	5	16	0	3	1	0	0	0	0	2	0
Eddie Plank, p	.167	2	6	0	1	0	0	0	0	0	2	0
Mike Powers, c	.143	3	7	0	1	1	0	0	0	0	0	0
Ossee Schreckengost, c	.222	3	9	2	2	1	0	0	0	0	0	0
Socks Seybold, of	.125	5	16	0	2	0	0	0	0	2	3	0
TOTAL	.161		155	3	25	5	0	0	2	5	25	2

PITCHER	W	L	ERA	G	GS	CG	SV	SHO	IP	H	ER	BB	SO
Chief Bender	1	1	1.06	2	2	2	0	1	17.0	9	2	6	13
Andy Coakley	0	1	2.00	1	1	1	0	0	9.0	8	2	5	2
Eddie Plank	0	2	1.59	2	2	2	0	0	17.0	14	3	4	11
TOTAL	1	4	1.47	5	5	5	0	1	43.0	31	7	15	26

GAME 1 AT PHI OCT 9

		R	H	E
NY	000 020 001	3	10	1
PHI	000 000 000	0	4	0

Pitchers: MATHEWSON vs PLANK
Attendance: 17,955

GAME 2 AT NY OCT 10

		R	H	E
PHI	001 000 020	3	6	2
NY	000 000 000	0	4	2

Pitchers: BENDER vs McGINNITY, Ames (9)
Attendance: 24,992

GAME 3 AT PHI OCT 12

		R	H	E
NY	200 050 002	9	9	1
PHI	000 000 000	0	4	5

Pitchers: MATHEWSON vs COAKLEY
Attendance: 10,991

GAME 4 AT NY OCT 13

		R	H	E
PHI	000 000 000	0	5	2
NY	000 100 00X	1	4	1

Pitchers: PLANK vs McGINNITY
Attendance: 13,598

GAME 5 AT NY OCT 14

		R	H	E
PHI	000 000 000	0	6	0
NY	000 010 01X	2	5	1

Pitchers: BENDER vs MATHEWSON
Attendance: 24,187

Chicago White Sox (AL), 4; Chicago Cubs (NL), 2

The Cubs and White Sox have played more postseason City Series than any other clubs, but this was their only all-Chicago World Series. The Cubs were the clear favorites: league leaders in batting, fielding, and pitching (with a team ERA of only 1.76). They were one of baseball's greatest teams ever, with a still-record 116 wins, finishing 20 games ahead of the second-place Giants. The White Sox, by contrast, although their pitching and fielding were good enough to rank second in the American League, were the junior circuit's weakest hitters, batting as a team only .230, 32 points below the Cubs. But in the Series the "hitless wonders" prevailed. Though they hit only .198 and yielded eight unearned runs, the Sox bunched their hits for 20 earned runs—double the Cubs' total. Meanwhile, Sox pitchers held the Cubs to a .196 BA, and produced a team ERA less than half that of Cub pitchers.

Game 1 was a pitcher's duel as the Cubs' Mordecai "Three Finger" Brown and Nick Altrock traded four-hitters and one earned run apiece. But Brown lost the game when his error in the seventh led to the second run for the Sox. The Cubs snapped back to take Game 2 on Ed Reulbach's one-hit 7–1 win. Although Reulbach issued six walks, he didn't really need the five unearned runs handed his club by Sox errors.

In Game 3 the Sox regained the Series lead as Ed Walsh two-hit the Cubs, fanning 12 for the Series' first shutout. The Cubs' Jack Pfiester also pitched shutout ball in eight of his nine innings, but George Rohe's bases-loaded triple in the sixth gave the Sox more than enough to defeat him. Brown brought the Cubs back the next day, evening the Series with a two-hit shutout of his own, winning when Altrock yielded his only run on pairs of singles and sacrifice bunts in the seventh.

The rest of the Series belonged to the hitless wonders, who rocked three Cub pitchers for 12 hits and eight runs to take Game 5, and buried Brown and Orval Overall under 14 hits and another eight runs in Game 6 to capture their first world championship.

CHI (A)

PLAYER/POS	AVG	G	AB	R	H	2B	3B	HR	RB	BB	SO	SB
Nick Altrock, p	.250	2	4	0	1	0	0	0	0	1	1	0
George Davis, ss	.308	3	13	4	4	3	0	0	6	0	1	1
Jiggs Donahue, 1b	.333	6	18	0	6	2	1	0	4	3	3	0
Patsy Dougherty, of	.100	6	20	1	2	0	0	0	1	3	4	2
Eddie Hahn, of	.273	6	22	4	6	0	0	0	0	1	1	0
Frank Isbell, 2b	.308	6	26	4	8	4	0	0	4	0	6	1
Fielder Jones, of	.095	6	21	4	2	0	0	0	0	3	3	0
Ed McFarland, ph	.000	1	1	0	0	0	0	0	0	0	0	0
Bill O'Neill, of	.000	1	1	1	0	0	0	0	0	0	0	0
Frank Owen, p	.000	1	2	0	0	0	0	0	0	0	1	0
George Rohe, 3b	.333	6	21	2	7	1	2	0	4	3	1	2
Billy Sullivan, c	.000	6	21	0	0	0	0	0	0	0	9	0
Lee Tannehill, ss	.111	3	9	1	1	0	0	0	0	0	2	0
Babe Towne, ph	.000	1	1	0	0	0	0	0	0	0	0	0
Ed Walsh, p	.000	2	4	1	0	0	0	0	0	3	3	0
Doc White, p	.000	3	3	0	0	0	0	0	0	1	0	0
TOTAL	.198		187	22	37	10	3	0	19	18	35	6

PITCHER	W	L	ERA	G	GS	CG	SV	SHO	IP	H	ER	BB	SO
Nick Altrock	1	1	1.00	2	2	2	0	0	18.0	11	2	2	5
Frank Owen	0	0	3.00	1	0	0	0	0	6.0	6	2	3	2
Ed Walsh	2	0	1.20	2	2	1	0	1	15.0	7	2	6	17
Doc White	1	1	1.80	3	2	1	1	0	15.0	12	3	7	4
TOTAL	4	2	1.50	8	6	4	1	1	54.0	36	9	18	28

CHI (N)

PLAYER/POS	AVG	G	AB	R	H	2B	3B	HR	RB	BB	SO	SB
Mordecai Brown, p	.333	3	6	0	2	0	0	0	0	0	4	0
Frank Chance, 1b	.238	6	21	3	5	1	0	0	0	2	1	2
Johnny Evers, 2b	.150	6	20	2	3	1	0	0	1	1	3	2
Doc Gessler, ph	.000	2	1	0	0	0	0	0	0	1	0	0
Solly Hofman, of	.304	6	23	3	7	1	0	0	2	3	5	1
Johnny Kling, c	.176	6	17	2	3	1	0	0	0	4	3	0
Pat Moran, ph	.000	2	2	0	0	0	0	0	0	0	0	0
Orval Overall, p	.250	2	4	1	1	1	0	0	0	1	1	0
Jack Pfiester, p	.000	2	2	0	0	0	0	0	0	0	1	0
Ed Reulbach, p	.000	2	3	0	0	0	0	0	1	0	1	0
Frank Schulte, of	.269	6	26	1	7	3	0	0	3	1	3	0
Jimmy Sheckard, of	.000	6	21	0	0	0	0	0	1	2	4	1
Harry Steinfeldt, 3b	.250	6	20	2	5	1	0	0	2	1	0	0
Joe Tinker, ss	.167	6	18	4	3	0	0	0	1	2	2	3
TOTAL	.196		184	18	36	9	0	0	11	18	28	9

PITCHER	W	L	ERA	G	GS	CG	SV	SHO	IP	H	ER	BB	SO
Mordecai Brown	1	2	3.20	3	3	2	0	1	19.2	14	7	4	12
Orval Overall	0	0	2.25	2	0	0	0	0	12.0	10	3	3	8
Jack Pfiester	0	2	6.10	2	1	1	0	0	10.1	7	7	3	11
Ed Reulbach	1	0	2.45	2	2	1	0	0	11.0	6	3	8	4
TOTAL	2	4	3.40	9	6	4	0	1	53.0	37	20	18	35

GAME 1 AT CHI-N OCT 9

				R	H	E
CHI-A	000	011	000	2	4	1
CHI-N	000	001	000	1	4	2

Pitchers: ALTROCK vs BROWN
Attendance: 12,693

GAME 2 AT CHI-A OCT 10

				R	H	E
CHI-N	031	001	020	7	10	2
CHI-A	000	010	000	1	1	2

Pitchers: REULBACH vs WHITE, Owen (4)
Attendance: 12,595

GAME 3 AT CHI-N OCT 11

				R	H	E
CHI-A	000	003	000	3	4	1
CHI-N	000	000	000	0	2	2

Pitchers: WALSH vs PFIESTER
Attendance: 13,667

GAME 4 AT CHI-A OCT 12

				R	H	E
CHI-N	000	000	100	1	7	1
CHI-A	000	000	000	0	2	1

Pitchers: BROWN vs ALTROCK
Attendance: 18,385

GAME 5 AT CHI-N OCT 13

				R	H	E
CHI-A	102	401	000	8	12	6
CHI-N	300	102	000	6	6	0

Pitchers: WALSH, White (7) vs Reulbach, PFIESTER (3), Overall (4)
Attendance: 23,257

GAME 6 AT CHI-A OCT 14

				R	H	E
CHI-N	100	010	001	3	7	0
CHI-A	340	000	01X	8	14	3

Pitchers: BROWN, Overall (2) vs WHITE
Attendance: 19,249

The two-run lead that Detroit took into the bottom of the ninth inning of Game 1 proved to be its biggest of the Series. And it was short-lived, as Chicago—after Frank Chance's leadoff single—took advantage of a hit batsman, a fumble at third base, and a dropped third strike to even the score. Three scoreless extra innings later, darkness ended the game in a 3–3 tie.

The Tigers pitched well enough in the Series. Wild Bill Donovan and George Mullin, who provided more than 80 percent of Detroit's pitching, allowed only four earned runs each for a combined 1.89 ERA. But Cubs pitchers gave up only four earned runs *as a team,* suffocating the Tigers with a team ERA of 0.75. And while Tiger fielders made one less error than the Cubs, their misplays proved more costly, permitting eight unearned runs to the Cubs' two.

Detroit's three-run eighth in the opener provided half of their Series scoring. Nine Detroit hits in Game 2 produced only one run, while the Cubs bunched six of their nine hits into two innings for three runs and the Series' first win. In Games 3 and 4, while the Tigers were twice again limited to a single run, the Cubs increased their run production to five and six, clustering 40 percent of their hits into two three-run innings, one in each game. Mordecai "Three Finger" Brown wrapped up the Series for Chicago with a shutout, as his Cubs blended a hit in each of the first two innings with three stolen bases and a Detroit error for the game's only two runs.

Detroit's 20-year-old Ty Cobb, the American League batting, RBI, and stolen base leader in his first full big league season, hit an anemic .200 in the World Series, stealing no bases and driving in no runs. If there was an offensive hero, it was Cubs centerfielder Jimmy Slagle. At age 34, nearing the end of a 10-year major league career, he led both clubs with four RBIs (nearly quadruple his season's per-game output) and six stolen bases.

Chicago Cubs (NL), 4; Detroit Tigers (AL), 0; tie, 1

CHI (N)

PLAYER/POS	AVG	G	AB	R	H	2B	3B	HR	RB	BB	SO	SB
Mordecai Brown, p	.000	1	3	0	0	0	0	0	0	1	0	0
Frank Chance, 1b	.214	4	14	3	3	1	0	0	0	3	2	3
Johnny Evers, 2b-5,ss-1	.350	5	20	2	7	2	0	0	1	0	1	3
Del Howard, 1b-1	.200	2	5	0	1	0	0	0	0	0	2	1
Johnny Kling, c	.211	5	19	2	4	0	0	0	1	1	4	0
Pat Moran, ph	.000	1	0	0	0	0	0	0	0	0	0	0
Orval Overall, p	.200	2	5	0	1	0	0	0	2	0	1	0
Jack Pfiester, p	.000	1	2	0	0	0	0	0	0	0	1	0
Ed Reulbach, p	.200	2	5	0	1	0	0	0	1	0	0	0
Frank Schulte, of	.250	5	20	3	5	0	0	0	2	1	2	0
Jimmy Sheckard, of	.238	5	21	0	5	2	0	0	2	0	4	1
Jimmy Slagle, of	.273	5	22	3	6	0	0	0	4	2	3	6
Harry Steinfeldt, 3b	.471	5	17	2	8	1	1	0	2	1	2	1
Joe Tinker, ss	.154	5	13	4	2	0	0	0	1	3	3	1
Heinie Zimmerman, 2b	.000	1	1	0	0	0	0	0	0	0	1	0
TOTAL	.257		167	19	43	6	1	0	16	12	26	16

PITCHER	W	L	ERA	G	GS	CG	SV	SHO	IP	H	ER	BB	SO
Mordecai Brown	1	0	0.00	1	1	1	0	1	9.0	7	0	1	4
Orval Overall	1	0	1.00	2	2	1	0	0	18.0	14	2	4	11
Jack Pfiester	1	0	1.00	1	1	1	0	0	9.0	9	1	1	3
Ed Reulbach	1	0	0.75	2	1	1	0	0	12.0	6	1	3	4
TOTAL	4	0	0.75	6	5	4	0	1	48.0	36	4	9	22

DET (A)

PLAYER/POS	AVG	G	AB	R	H	2B	3B	HR	RB	BB	SO	SB
Jimmy Archer, c	.000	1	3	0	0	0	0	0	0	0	1	0
Ty Cobb, of	.200	5	20	1	4	0	1	0	0	0	3	0
Bill Coughlin, 3b	.250	5	20	0	5	0	0	0	0	1	4	1
Sam Crawford, of	.238	5	21	1	5	1	0	0	3	0	3	0
Bill Donovan, p	.000	2	8	0	0	0	0	0	0	0	3	0
Davy Jones, of	.353	5	17	1	6	0	0	0	0	4	0	3
Ed Killian, p	.500	1	2	1	1	0	0	0	0	0	0	0
George Mullin, p	.000	2	6	0	0	0	0	0	0	0	1	0
Charley O'Leary, ss	.059	5	17	0	1	0	0	0	0	1	3	0
Fred Payne, c-1	.250	2	4	0	1	0	0	0	1	0	0	1
Claude Rossman, 1b	.400	5	20	1	8	0	1	0	2	1	0	1
Germany Schaefer, 2b	.143	5	21	1	3	0	0	0	0	0	3	0
Boss Schmidt, c-3	.167	4	12	0	2	0	0	0	0	2	1	0
Ed Siever, p	.000	1	1	0	0	0	0	0	0	0	0	0
TOTAL	.209		172	6	36	1	2	0	6	9	22	6

PITCHER	W	L	ERA	G	GS	CG	SV	SHO	IP	H	ER	BB	SO
Bill Donovan	0	1	1.71	2	2	2	0	0	21.0	17	4	5	16
Ed Killian	0	0	2.25	1	0	0	0	0	4.0	3	1	1	1
George Mullin	0	2	2.12	2	2	2	0	0	17.0	16	4	6	8
Ed Siever	0	1	4.50	1	1	0	0	0	4.0	7	2	0	1
TOTAL	0	4	2.15	6	5	4	0	0	46.0	43	11	12	26

GAME 1 AT CHI OCT 8

		R	H	E
DET	000 000 030 000	3	9	3
CHI	000 100 002 000	3	10	5

Pitchers: Donovan vs Overall, Reulbach (10)
Attendance: 24,377
(Game called at end of twelfth, darkness)

GAME 2 AT CHI OCT 9

		R	H	E
DET	010 000 000	1	9	1
CHI	010 200 00X	3	9	1

Pitchers: MULLIN vs PFIESTER
Attendance: 21,901

GAME 3 AT CHI OCT 10

		R	H	E
DET	000 001 000	1	6	1
CHI	010 310 00X	5	10	1

Pitchers: SIEVER, Killian (5) vs REULBACH
Attendance: 13,114

GAME 4 AT DET OCT 11

		R	H	E
CHI	000 020 301	6	7	2
DET	000 100 000	1	5	2

Pitchers: OVERALL vs DONOVAN
Attendance: 11,306

GAME 5 AT DET OCT 12

		R	H	E
CHI	110 000 000	2	7	1
DET	000 000 000	0	7	2

Pitchers: BROWN vs MULLIN
Attendance: 7,370

The Tigers won their final game of the season to take their second straight pennant, and the Cubs won their third pennant in a row by defeating the Giants in a replay of an earlier tie. Ty Cobb and Detroit improved on their 1907 Series performance, as Cobb led his club in batting, hits, and RBIs, and the Tigers won a game. But the Cubs as a team hit 90 percentage points higher than Detroit, and outscored them 24–15, to take the Series with relative ease.

In Game 1, the Tigers took advantage of the Cubs' ragged fielding to score two runs in the eighth for a 6–5 lead. But in the top of the ninth the Cubs erupted for five runs on six consecutive singles and a double steal to win the game. The next day Chicago's Orval Overall held Detroit to four hits and one ninth-inning run. The Tigers' Wild Bill Donovan pitched even better for seven innings, holding Chicago to a single in the sixth. But in the eighth, Joe Tinker's two-run homer—the first in a World Series since 1903—began an assault that ended only after six Cubs had crossed the plate.

Detroit finally manufactured a Series win, pummeling Jack Pfiester in Game 3 for 10 hits (six of them in the sixth inning) and an 8–3 victory. But that was their last burst. As the Series moved to Detroit for Games 4 and 5, the Tiger offense collapsed. Three Finger Brown, the winner as a reliever in Game 1, won Game 4 as a starter, shutting out the Tigers on four hits. The Cubs needed only three of their 10 hits, combining them with a couple of walks and stolen bases, and a muffed fly ball, to score twice in the third inning and once in the ninth.

Only 6,210 spectators—the smallest World Series crowd of the century—saw Overall strike out four Tigers in the first inning of Game 5 (one reached first on a wild pitch) in what became a three-hit shutout. Meanwhile, his Cubs unloaded for 10 hits, defeating Donovan a second time, scoring runs in the first and fifth innings. Overall—after yielding a leadoff walk to Cobb in the fifth—retired Cobb on a force play and set down the final 11 men to face him.

Chicago Cubs (NL), 4; Detroit Tigers (AL), 1

CHI (N)

PLAYER/POS	AVG	G	AB	R	H	2B	3B	HR	RB	BB	SO	SB
Mordecai Brown, p	.000	2	4	0	0	0	0	0	0	0	2	0
Frank Chance, 1b	.421	5	19	4	8	0	0	0	2	3	1	5
Johnny Evers, 2b	.350	5	20	5	7	1	0	0	2	1	2	2
Solly Hofman, of	.316	5	19	2	6	0	1	0	4	1	4	2
Del Howard, ph	.000	1	1	0	0	0	0	0	0	0	0	0
Johnny Kling, c	.250	5	16	2	4	1	0	0	2	2	2	0
Orval Overall, p	.333	3	6	0	2	0	0	0	0	0	1	0
Jack Pfiester, p	.000	1	2	0	0	0	0	0	0	0	2	0
Ed Reulbach, p	.000	2	3	0	0	0	0	0	0	0	1	0
Frank Schulte, of	.389	5	18	4	7	0	1	0	2	2	1	2
Jimmy Sheckard, of	.238	5	21	2	5	2	0	0	1	2	3	1
Harry Steinfeldt, 3b	.250	5	16	3	4	0	0	0	3	2	5	1
Joe Tinker, ss	.263	5	19	2	5	0	0	1	4	0	2	2
TOTAL	.293		164	24	48	4	2	1	20	13	26	15

PITCHER	W	L	ERA	G	GS	CG	SV	SHO	IP	H	ER	BB	SO
Mordecai Brown	2	0	0.00	2	1	1	0	1	11.0	6	0	1	5
Orval Overall	2	0	0.98	3	2	2	0	1	18.1	7	2	7	15
Jack Pfiester	0	1	7.87	1	1	0	0	0	8.0	10	7	3	1
Ed Reulbach	0	0	4.70	2	1	0	0	0	7.2	9	4	1	5
TOTAL	4	1	2.60	8	5	3	0	2	45.0	32	13	12	26

DET (A)

PLAYER/POS	AVG	G	AB	R	H	2B	3B	HR	RB	BB	SO	SB
Ty Cobb, of	.368	5	19	3	7	1	0	0	4	1	2	2
Bill Coughlin, 3b	.125	3	8	0	1	0	0	0	1	0	1	0
Sam Crawford, of	.238	5	21	2	5	1	0	0	1	1	2	0
Bill Donovan, p	.000	2	4	0	0	0	0	0	0	1	1	1
Red Downs, 2b	.167	2	6	1	1	1	0	0	1	1	2	0
Davy Jones, ph	.000	3	2	1	0	0	0	0	0	1	1	0
Ed Killian, p	.000	1	0	0	0	0	0	0	0	0	0	0
Matty McIntyre, of	.222	5	18	2	4	1	0	0	0	3	2	1
George Mullin, p	.333	1	3	1	1	0	0	0	1	1	0	0
Charley O'Leary, ss	.158	5	19	2	3	0	0	0	0	0	3	0
Claude Rossman, 1b	.211	5	19	3	4	0	0	0	3	1	4	1
Germany Schaefer, 2b-3,3b-2	.125	5	16	0	2	0	0	0	0	1	4	1
Boss Schmidt, c	.071	4	14	0	1	0	0	0	1	0	2	0
Ed Summers, p	.200	2	5	0	1	0	0	0	1	0	2	0
Ira Thomas, c-1	.500	2	4	0	2	1	0	0	1	1	0	0
George Winter, p-1	.000	2	0	0	0	0	0	0	0	0	0	0
TOTAL	.203		158	15	32	5	0	0	14	12	26	6

PITCHER	W	L	ERA	G	GS	CG	SV	SHO	IP	H	ER	BB	SO
Bill Donovan	0	2	4.24	2	2	2	0	0	17.0	17	8	4	10
Ed Killian	0	0	11.57	1	1	0	0	0	2.1	5	3	3	1
George Mullin	1	0	0.00	1	1	1	0	0	9.0	7	0	1	8
Ed Summers	0	2	4.30	2	1	0	0	0	14.2	18	7	4	7
George Winter	0	0	0.00	1	0	0	0	0	1.0	1	0	1	0
TOTAL	1	4	3.68	7	5	3	0	0	44.0	48	18	13	26

GAME 1 AT DET OCT 10

				R	H	E
CHI	004	000	105	10	14	2
DET	100	000	320	6	10	4

Pitchers: Reulbach, Overall (7), BROWN (8) vs Killian, SUMMERS (3)
Attendance: 10,812

GAME 2 AT CHI OCT 11

				R	H	E
DET	000	000	001	1	4	1
CHI	000	000	06X	6	7	1

Pitchers: DONOVAN vs OVERALL
Home Runs: Tinker-CHI
Attendance: 17,760

GAME 3 AT CHI OCT 12

				R	H	E
DET	100	005	020	8	11	4
CHI	000	300	000	3	7	2

Pitchers: MULLIN vs PFIESTER, Reulbach (9)
Attendance: 14,543

GAME 4 AT DET OCT 13

				R	H	E
CHI	002	000	001	3	10	0
DET	000	000	000	0	4	1

Pitchers: BROWN vs SUMMERS, Winter (9)
Attendance: 12,907

GAME 5 AT DET OCT 14

				R	H	E
CHI	100	010	000	2	10	0
DET	000	000	000	0	3	0

Pitchers: OVERALL vs DONOVAN
Attendance: 6,210

Babe Adams, a 27-year-old rookie pitcher, was only the fifth biggest winner on the Pittsburgh staff. But his fine 12–3 record was supported by a team-best 1.11 ERA, and manager Fred Clarke started him in the Series opener against Detroit's ace George Mullin (who had led the American League with a career-high 29 wins). Mullin pitched well, giving up only one earned run—manager/outfielder Clarke's homer in the fourth inning. But four Tiger errors led to three Pittsburgh runs in the fifth and sixth. Meanwhile, Adams, after yielding a run in the first, pitched shutout ball the rest of the way for the win.

Detroit came back in Game 2 with seven runs (including Ty Cobb's theft of home) as Wild Bill Donovan held the Pirates to two runs on five hits. In Game 3 the Pirates took an early lead, which Detroit, despite rallies in the seventh and ninth innings, was unable to overcome. Errors determined most of the scoring, as only one of Detroit's six runs and two of Pittsburgh's eight were earned.

Mullin shut out the Pirates on five hits in Game 4, striking out 10 men as Detroit scored five runs (all earned, despite Pittsburgh's six errors) to drive out starter Lefty Leifield after four innings. The seesaw Series continued in Game 5, with Babe Adams winning his second game behind his Pirates' 10-hit, eight-run attack. Adams gave up leadoff homers to Davy Jones in the first and Sam Crawford in the eighth. But Pittsburgh's Clarke more than countered these with his three-run shot in the seventh. (All three homers were hit into temporary seats in center field.)

Back in Detroit for Game 6, the Tigers evened the Series for the third time, Mullin winning his second game in a close contest that saw Pittsburgh pull within a run of tying the game in the ninth before a runner thrown out at home and a game-ending double play cut their rally dead.

In the finale it was Babe Adams once again, scattering six hits for an easy 8–0 win, his third of the Series. Detroit had done better than ever, but still lost their third World Series in three consecutive attempts. A quarter century would pass before they would have a chance to try again.

Pittsburgh Pirates (NL), 4; Detroit Tigers (AL), 3

PIT (N)

PLAYER/POS	AVG	G	AB	R	H	2B	3B	HR	RB	BB	SO	SB
Ed Abbaticchio, ph	.000	1	1	0	0	0	0	0	0	0	0	0
Bill Abstein, 1b	.231	7	26	3	6	2	0	0	2	3	10	1
Babe Adams, p	.000	3	9	0	0	0	0	0	0	1	1	0
Bobby Byrne, 3b	.250	7	24	5	6	1	0	0	0	1	4	1
Howie Camnitz, p	.000	2	1	0	0	0	0	0	0	0	0	0
Fred Clarke, of	.211	7	19	7	4	0	0	2	7	5	3	3
George Gibson, c	.240	7	25	2	6	2	0	0	2	1	1	2
Ham Hyatt, of-1	.000	2	4	1	0	0	0	0	1	1	0	0
Tommy Leach, of-7,3b-1	.360	7	25	8	9	4	0	0	2	2	1	1
Lefty Leifield, p	.000	1	1	0	0	0	0	0	0	0	1	0
Nick Maddox, p	.000	1	4	0	0	0	0	0	0	0	1	0
Dots Miller, 2b	.250	7	28	2	7	1	0	0	4	2	5	3
Paddy O'Connor, ph	.000	1	1	0	0	0	0	0	0	0	1	0
Deacon Phillippe, p	.000	2	1	0	0	0	0	0	0	0	1	0
Honus Wagner, ss	.333	7	24	4	8	2	1	0	6	4	2	6
Vic Willis, p	.000	2	4	0	0	0	0	0	0	0	1	0
Chief Wilson, of	.154	7	26	2	4	1	0	0	1	0	2	1
TOTAL	.224		223	34	50	13	1	2	25	20	34	18

PITCHER	W	L	ERA	G	GS	CG	SV	SHO	IP	H	ER	BB	SO
Babe Adams	3	0	1.33	3	3	3	0	1	27.0	18	4	6	11
Howie Camnitz	0	1	9.82	2	1	0	0	0	3.2	8	4	2	2
Lefty Leifield	0	1	11.25	1	1	0	0	0	4.0	7	5	1	0
Nick Maddox	1	0	1.00	1	1	1	0	0	9.0	10	1	2	4
Deacon Phillippe	0	0	0.00	2	0	0	0	0	6.0	2	0	1	2
Vic Willis	0	1	3.97	2	1	0	0	0	11.1	10	5	8	3
TOTAL	4	3	2.80	11	7	4	0	1	61.0	55	19	20	22

DET (A)

PLAYER/POS	AVG	G	AB	R	H	2B	3B	HR	RB	BB	SO	SB
Donie Bush, ss	.261	7	23	5	6	1	0	0	3	5	3	1
Ty Cobb, of	.231	7	26	3	6	3	0	0	5	2	2	2
Sam Crawford, of-7,1b-1	.250	7	28	4	7	3	0	1	4	1	1	1
Jim Delahanty, 2b	.346	7	26	2	9	4	0	0	4	2	5	0
Bill Donovan, p	.000	2	4	0	0	0	0	0	0	0	1	0
Davy Jones, of	.233	7	30	6	7	0	0	1	1	2	1	1
Tom Jones, 1b	.250	7	24	3	6	1	0	0	2	2	0	1
Matty McIntyre, of-1	.000	4	3	0	0	0	0	0	0	0	1	0
George Moriarty, 3b	.273	7	22	4	6	1	0	0	1	3	1	0
George Mullin, p-4	.188	6	16	1	3	1	0	0	0	1	3	0
Charley O'Leary, 3b	.000	1	3	0	0	0	0	0	0	0	0	0
Boss Schmidt, c	.222	6	18	0	4	2	0	0	4	2	0	0
Oscar Stanage, c	.200	2	5	0	1	0	0	0	2	0	2	0
Ed Summers, p	.000	2	3	0	0	0	0	0	0	0	2	0
Ed Willett, p	.000	2	2	0	0	0	0	0	0	0	0	0
Ralph Works, p	.000	1	0	0	0	0	0	0	0	0	0	0
TOTAL	.236		233	28	55	16	0	2	26	20	22	6

PITCHER	W	L	ERA	G	GS	CG	SV	SHO	IP	H	ER	BB	SO
Bill Donovan	1	1	3.00	2	2	1	0	0	12.0	7	4	8	7
George Mullin	2	1	2.25	4	3	3	0	1	32.0	23	8	8	20
Ed Summers	0	2	8.59	2	2	0	0	0	7.1	13	7	4	4
Ed Willett	0	0	0.00	2	0	0	0	0	7.2	3	0	0	1
Ralph Works	0	0	9.00	1	0	0	0	0	2.0	4	2	0	2
TOTAL	3	4	3.10	11	7	4	0	1	61.0	50	21	20	34

GAME 1 AT PIT OCT 8

				R	H	E
DET	100	000	000	1	6	4
PIT	000	121	00X	4	5	0

Pitchers: MULLIN vs ADAMS
Home Runs: Clarke-PIT
Attendance: 29,264

GAME 2 AT PIT OCT 9

				R	H	E
DET	023	020	000	7	9	3
PIT	200	000	000	2	5	1

Pitchers: DONOVAN vs CAMNITZ, Willis (3)
Attendance: 30,915

GAME 3 AT DET OCT 11

				R	H	E
PIT	510	000	002	8	10	3
DET	000	000	402	6	10	5

Pitchers: MADDOX vs SUMMERS, Willett (1), Works (8)
Attendance: 18,277

GAME 4 AT DET OCT 12

				R	H	E
PIT	000	000	000	0	5	6
DET	020	300	00X	5	8	0

Pitchers: LEIFIELD, Phillippe (5) vs MULLIN
Attendance: 17,036

GAME 5 AT PIT OCT 13

				R	H	E
DET	100	002	010	4	6	1
PIT	111	000	41X	8	10	2

Pitchers: SUMMERS, Willett (8) vs ADAMS
Home Runs: D.Jones-DET, Crawford-DET, Clarke-PIT
Attendance: 21,706

GAME 6 AT DET OCT 14

				R	H	E
PIT	300	000	001	4	7	3
DET	100	211	00X	5	10	3

Pitchers: WILLIS, Camnitz (6), Phillippe (7) vs MULLIN
Attendance: 10,535

GAME 7 AT DET OCT 16

				R	H	E
PIT	020	203	010	8	7	0
DET	000	000	000	0	6	3

Pitchers: ADAMS vs DONOVAN, Mullin (4)
Attendance: 17,562

Pitcher Jack Coombs burst into stardom in 1910, emerging as the ace of a Philadelphia pitching staff which dominated the American League with an ERA of only 1.79. Coombs himself led league pitchers with 31 wins and 13 shutouts, and finished second to Chicago's Ed Walsh with an ERA of 1.30—all career bests. He continued his domination into the World Series, pitching three complete-game victories in the Athletics' surprisingly easy triumph over the Cubs.

The Series' finest pitching performance, though, was turned in by the A's Chief Bender in the opener. Only two batters reached base over the first eight innings—on a single and walk—and both of them were cut down trying to steal second. In the ninth, two Cubs singles and two A's errors produced an unearned run, but as the A's had scored four runs (Bender himself providing the margin of victory with the game's second RBI in the second inning), the Cubs' run did no damage.

Coombs started Game 2 and gave up a run in the top of the first inning. But Philadelphia bats were hot in the Series (their team .316 batting average stood as a Series record for 50 years), and their 14 hits in this game (including four doubles and six runs in the seventh) sank Three Finger Brown and gave Coombs an easy win. Connie Mack also started Coombs in Game 3, two days later, and again the result was a lopsided win. Coombs himself drove in three of his team's 12 runs, and right fielder Danny Murphy added three more with the Series' only home run.

Bender pitched Game 4 and suffered the A's only loss, as the Cubs tied the game at 3–3 with a run in the bottom of the ninth, and won it for reliever Three Finger Brown with a two-out RBI single an inning later.

Coombs faced Brown a second time in Game 5. Both clubs made nine hits, but the A's put four of them together with a walk, a wild pitch, and two stolen bases for five runs in the eighth to sink Brown as they had in Game 2, breaking a tight game wide open for Coombs's third win and the Athletics' first world championship.

Philadelphia Athletics (AL), 4; Chicago Cubs (NL), 1

PHI (A)

PLAYER/POS	AVG	G	AB	R	H	2B	3B	HR	RB	BB	SO	SB
Frank Baker, 3b	.409	5	22	6	9	3	0	0	4	2	1	0
Jack Barry, ss	.235	5	17	3	4	2	0	0	3	1	3	0
Chief Bender, p	.333	2	6	1	2	0	0	0	1	1	1	0
Eddie Collins, 2b	.429	5	21	5	9	4	0	0	3	2	0	4
Jack Coombs, p	.385	3	13	0	5	1	0	0	3	0	3	0
Harry Davis, 1b	.353	5	17	5	6	3	0	0	2	3	4	0
Topsy Hartsel, of	.200	1	5	2	1	0	0	0	0	0	1	2
Jack Lapp, c	.250	1	4	0	1	0	0	0	1	0	2	0
Bris Lord, of	.182	5	22	3	4	2	0	0	1	1	3	0
Danny Murphy, of	.350	5	20	6	7	3	0	1	9	1	0	1
Amos Strunk, of	.278	4	18	2	5	1	1	0	2	2	5	0
Ira Thomas, c	.250	4	12	2	3	0	0	0	1	4	1	0
TOTAL	.316		177	35	56	19	1	1	30	17	24	7

PITCHER	W	L	ERA	G	GS	CG	SV	SHO	IP	H	ER	BB	SO
Chief Bender	1	1	1.93	2	2	2	0	0	18.2	12	4	4	14
Jack Coombs	3	0	3.33	3	3	3	0	0	27.0	23	10	14	17
TOTAL	4	1	2.76	5	5	5	0	0	45.2	35	14	18	31

CHI (N)

PLAYER/POS	AVG	G	AB	R	H	2B	3B	HR	RB	BB	SO	SB
Jimmy Archer, c-2,1b-1	.182	3	11	1	2	1	0	0	0	0	3	0
Ginger Beaumont, ph	.000	3	2	1	0	0	0	0	0	1	1	0
Mordecai Brown, p	.000	3	7	0	0	0	0	0	0	0	1	0
Frank Chance, 1b	.353	5	17	1	6	1	1	0	4	0	3	0
King Cole, p	.000	1	2	0	0	0	0	0	0	0	2	0
Solly Hofman, of	.267	5	15	2	4	0	0	0	2	4	3	0
Johnny Kane, pr	.000	1	0	0	0	0	0	0	0	0	0	0
Johnny Kling, c-3	.077	5	13	0	1	0	0	0	1	1	2	0
Harry McIntire, p	.000	2	1	0	0	0	0	0	0	0	1	0
Tom Needham, ph	.000	1	1	0	0	0	0	0	0	0	0	0
Orval Ovall, p	.000	1	1	0	0	0	0	0	0	0	0	0
Jack Pfiester, p	.000	1	2	0	0	0	0	0	0	0	1	0
Ed Reulbach, p	.000	1	0	0	0	0	0	0	0	0	0	0
Lew Richie, p	.000	1	0	0	0	0	0	0	0	0	0	0
Frank Schulte, of	.353	5	17	3	6	3	0	0	2	2	3	0
Jimmy Sheckard, of	.286	5	14	5	4	2	0	0	1	7	2	1
Harry Steinfeldt, 3b	.100	5	20	0	2	1	0	0	1	0	4	0
Joe Tinker, ss	.333	5	18	2	6	2	0	0	0	2	2	1
Heinie Zimmerman, 2b	.235	5	17	0	4	1	0	0	2	1	3	1
TOTAL	.222		158	15	35	11	1	0	13	18	31	3

PITCHER	W	L	ERA	G	GS	CG	SV	SHO	IP	H	ER	BB	SO
Mordecai Brown	1	2	5.50	3	2	1	0	0	18.0	23	11	7	14
King Cole	0	0	3.38	1	1	0	0	0	8.0	10	3	3	5
Harry McIntire	0	1	6.75	2	0	0	0	0	5.1	4	4	3	3
Orval Overall	0	1	9.00	1	1	0	0	0	3.0	6	3	1	1
Jack Pfiester	0	0	0.00	1	0	0	0	0	6.2	9	0	1	1
Ed Reulbach	0	0	9.00	1	1	0	0	0	2.0	3	2	2	0
Lew Richie	0	0	0.00	1	0	0	0	0	1.0	1	0	0	0
TOTAL	1	4	4.70	10	5	1	0	0	44.0	56	23	17	24

GAME 1 AT PHI OCT 17

		R	H	E
CHI	000 000 001	1	3	1
PHI	021 000 01X	4	7	2

Pitchers: OVERALL, McIntire (4) vs BENDER
Attendance: 26,891

GAME 2 AT PHI OCT 18

		R	H	E
CHI	100 000 101	3	8	3
PHI	002 010 60X	9	14	4

Pitchers: BROWN, Richie (8) vs COOMBS
Attendance: 24,597

GAME 3 AT CHI OCT 20

		R	H	E
PHI	125 000 400	12	15	1
CHI	120 000 020	5	6	5

Pitchers: COOMBS vs Reulbach, McINTIRE (3), Pfiester (3)
Home Runs: Murphy-PHI
Attendance: 26,210

GAME 4 AT CHI OCT 22

		R	H	E
PHI	001 200 000 0	3	11	3
CHI	100 100 001 1	4	9	1

Pitchers: BENDER vs Cole, BROWN (9)
Attendance: 19,150

GAME 5 AT CHI OCT 23

		R	H	E
PHI	100 010 050	7	9	1
CHI	010 000 010	2	9	2

Pitchers: COOMBS vs BROWN
Attendance: 27,374

Connie Mack's pitching aces outdueled Christy Mathewson, and Frank Baker hit two crucial home runs to become "Home Run" Baker forever more, as the A's avenged their 1905 Series loss to the Giants. Game 1, though, belonged to Matty and New York. Philadelphia scored first, but the Giants tied the game with an unearned run in the fourth inning, and won it with two doubles in the seventh, setting at naught Chief Bender's otherwise splendid 11-strikeout performance.

The A's came back to take three in a row. In Game 2 Eddie Plank held the Giants to one run and Baker hit the first of his homers, breaking a tie in the sixth with a two-run blast off Rube Marquard. The next day, the A's and Jack Coombs handed Mathewson his first World Series loss. Both pitchers went the distance in an 11-inning duel that saw Matty hold the A's scoreless through eight, only to give up a game-tying home run to Baker in the ninth, and two unearned runs in the 11th. Coombs, meanwhile, pitched two-hit, one-run ball through 10 innings. In the last of the 11th, a third Giants hit and an A's error let in a second run, but the rally died when Beals Becker was cut down for the final out trying to steal second.

After a week of rain, Mathewson and Bender squared off in Game 4. The Giants jumped on Bender for two runs in the first, and held the lead until the fourth. But in the last of the fourth, three successive A's doubles and a run-scoring fly put the A's in front to stay as Bender held New York scoreless over the final eight innings.

In Game 5, a three-run homer by the A's Rube Oldring off Rube Marquard in the third provided the only scoring through 6½ innings. But the Giants crept back with one run in the seventh, and two more in the last of the ninth tied the score. Plank replaced Coombs for the A's in the 10th and took the loss as Larry Doyle led off with a double, took third on a missed force play, and scored on Fred Merkle's fly to deep right.

After five closely contested games, Game Six was a laugher. It, too, was close at first—tied 1-1 after 3½ innings. But the A's scored four runs in the fourth on singles and errors, once in the sixth, and seven times in the seventh on a barrage of hits, an error, and a two-run wild pitch. Chief Bender, who gave up only four hits and two unearned runs, was the beneficiary of this largesse, taking his second win of the Series and giving the A's their second consecutive world title.

Philadelphia Athletics (AL), 4; New York Giants (NL), 2

PHI (A)

PLAYER/POS	AVG	G	AB	R	H	2B	3B	HR	RB	BB	SO	SB
Frank Baker, 3b	.375	6	24	7	9	2	0	2	5	1	5	0
Jack Barry, ss	.368	6	19	2	7	4	0	0	2	0	2	2
Chief Bender, p	.091	3	11	0	1	0	0	0	0	0	1	0
Eddie Collins, 2b	.286	6	21	4	6	1	0	0	1	2	2	2
Jack Coombs, p	.250	2	8	1	2	0	0	0	0	0	0	0
Harry Davis, 1b	.208	6	24	3	5	1	0	0	5	0	3	0
Jack Lapp, c	.250	2	8	1	2	0	0	0	0	0	1	0
Bris Lord, of	.185	6	27	2	5	2	0	0	1	0	5	0
Stuffy McInnis, 1b	.000	1	0	0	0	0	0	0	0	0	0	0
Danny Murphy, of	.304	6	23	4	7	3	0	0	3	0	3	0
Rube Oldring, of	.200	6	25	2	5	2	0	1	3	0	5	0
Eddie Plank, p	.000	2	3	0	0	0	0	0	0	0	2	0
Amos Strunk, pr	.000	1	0	0	0	0	0	0	0	0	0	0
Ira Thomas, c	.083	4	12	1	1	0	0	0	1	1	2	0
TOTAL	.244		205	27	50	15	0	3	21	4	31	4

PITCHER	W	L	ERA	G	GS	CG	SV	SHO	IP	H	ER	BB	SO
Chief Bender	2	1	1.04	3	3	3	0	0	26.0	16	3	8	20
Jack Coombs	1	0	1.35	2	2	1	0	0	20.0	11	3	6	16
Eddie Plank	1	1	1.86	2	1	1	0	0	9.2	6	2	0	8
TOTAL	4	2	1.29	7	6	5	0	0	55.2	33	8	14	44

NY (N)

PLAYER/POS	AVG	G	AB	R	H	2B	3B	HR	RB	BB	SO	SB
Red Ames, p	.500	2	2	0	1	0	0	0	0	0	1	0
Beals Becker, ph	.000	3	3	0	0	0	0	0	0	0	0	0
Doc Crandall, p-2	.500	3	2	1	1	1	0	0	1	2	0	0
Josh Devore, of	.167	6	24	1	4	1	0	0	3	1	8	0
Larry Doyle, 2b	.304	6	23	3	7	3	1	0	1	2	1	2
Art Fletcher, ss	.130	6	23	1	3	1	0	0	1	0	4	0
Buck Herzog, 3b	.190	6	21	3	4	2	0	0	0	2	3	2
Rube Marquard, p	.000	3	2	0	0	0	0	0	0	0	2	0
Christy Mathewson, p	.286	3	7	0	2	0	0	0	0	1	3	0
Fred Merkle, 1b	.150	6	20	1	3	1	0	0	1	2	6	0
Chief Meyers, c	.300	6	20	2	6	2	0	0	2	0	3	0
Red Murray, of	.000	6	21	0	0	0	0	0	0	2	5	0
Fred Snodgrass, of	.105	6	19	1	2	0	0	0	1	2	7	0
Art Wilson, c	.000	1	1	0	0	0	0	0	0	0	0	0
Hooks Wiltse, p	.000	2	1	0	0	0	0	0	0	0	1	0
TOTAL	.175		189	13	33	11	1	0	10	14	44	4

PITCHER	W	L	ERA	G	GS	CG	SV	SHO	IP	H	ER	BB	SO
Red Ames	0	1	2.25	2	1	0	0	0	8.0	6	2	1	6
Doc Crandall	1	0	0.00	2	0	0	0	0	4.0	2	0	0	2
Rube Marquard	0	1	1.54	3	2	0	0	0	11.2	9	2	1	8
Christy Mathewson	1	2	2.00	3	3	2	0	0	27.0	25	6	2	13
Hooks Wiltse	0	0	18.90	2	0	0	0	0	3.1	8	7	0	2
TOTAL	2	4	2.83	12	6	2	0	0	54.0	50	17	4	31

GAME 1 AT NY OCT 14

		R	H	E
PHI	010 000 000	1	6	2
NY	000 100 10X	2	5	0

Pitchers: BENDER vs MATHEWSON
Attendance: 38,281

GAME 2 AT PHI OCT 16

		R	H	E
NY	010 000 000	1	5	3
PHI	100 002 00X	3	4	0

Pitchers: MARQUARD, Crandall (8) vs PLANK
Home Runs: Baker-PHI
Attendance: 26,286

GAME 3 AT NY OCT 17

		R	H	E
PHI	000 000 001 02	3	9	2
NY	001 000 000 01	2	3	5

Pitchers: COOMBS vs MATHEWSON
Home Runs: Baker-PHI
Attendance: 37,216

GAME 4 AT PHI OCT 24

		R	H	E
NY	200 000 000	2	7	3
PHI	000 310 00X	4	11	1

Pitchers: MATHEWSON, Wiltse (8) vs BENDER
Attendance: 24,355

GAME 5 AT NY OCT 25

		R	H	E
PHI	003 000 000 0	3	7	1
NY	000 000 102 1	4	9	2

Pitchers: Coombs, PLANK (10) vs Marquard, Ames (4), CRANDALL (8)
Home Runs: Oldring-PHI
Attendance: 33,228

GAME 6 AT PHI OCT 26

		R	H	E
NY	100 000 001	2	4	3
PHI	001 401 70X	13	13	5

Pitchers: AMES, Wiltse (5), Marquard (7) vs BENDER
Attendance: 20,485

The Giants outhit the Red Sox by 50 percentage points, and their pitchers let in one less earned run per game. But this was the Series in which Fred Snodgrass' famous muff of a routine fly to center in the 10th inning of the final game helped turn a slim Giants lead into a Red Sox world championship. In all fairness, it must be admitted that Snodgrass followed his muff with a brilliant catch off the next batter, and indecision by the catcher and first baseman permitted a pop foul to drop, keeping the Sox alive to score the tying and winning runs. For that matter, this final game might not have been needed at all if Snodgrass and Beals Becker hadn't both been cut down trying to steal second in the 11th inning of Game 2, which ended in a tie because of darkness. If either had gone on to score, the Giants would have won the Series in seven games.

Boston's Smokey Joe Wood followed up his spectacular 34–5 regular season with Series wins in Games 1 and 4, before being rocked for six runs in the first inning of Game 7 for a loss. Relieving in the eighth inning of the finale, he stopped the Giants for two innings, but gave up what would have been the losing run in the 10th had not the Giants' fielding in the last of the inning turned the game around, giving Wood the win and the Sox the Series.

Although Wood won three games, the best pitching of the Series was turned in by the Giants' Rube Marquard and Boston's Hugh Bedient. Marquard (who in the regular season had tied a major league record with 19 consecutive wins) won two of his club's three victories (Games 3 and 6), allowing three runs—only one of them earned. Bedient, in two starts and two relief appearances, matched Marquard's 0.50 earned run average, winning a duel with Christy Mathewson in Game 5, and hurling seven effective innings against Matty in the finale.

Mathewson was the Series' hard-luck pitcher: his one tie and two losses were all decided by unearned runs.

Boston Red Sox (AL), 4; New York Giants (NL), 3; tie, 1

BOS (A)

PLAYER/POS	AVG	G	AB	R	H	2B	3B	HR	RB	BB	SO	SB
Neal Ball, ph	.000	1	1	0	0	0	0	0	0	0	1	0
Hugh Bedient, p	.000	4	6	0	0	0	0	0	0	0	0	0
Hick Cady, c	.136	7	22	1	3	0	0	0	1	0	3	0
Bill Carrigan, c	.000	2	7	0	0	0	0	0	0	0	0	0
Ray Collins, p	.000	2	5	0	0	0	0	0	0	0	2	0
Clyde Engle, ph	.333	3	3	1	1	1	0	0	2	0	0	0
Larry Gardner, 3b	.179	8	28	4	5	2	1	1	5	2	5	0
Charley Hall, p	.750	2	4	0	3	1	0	0	0	1	0	0
Olaf Henricksen, ph	1.000	2	1	0	1	1	0	0	1	0	0	0
Harry Hooper, of	.290	8	31	3	9	2	1	0	1	4	4	2
Duffy Lewis, of	.156	8	32	4	5	3	0	0	2	2	2	0
Buck O'Brien, p	.000	2	2	0	0	0	0	0	0	0	2	0
Tris Speaker, of	.300	8	30	4	9	1	2	0	2	4	2	1
Jake Stahl, 1b	.281	8	32	3	9	2	0	0	2	0	6	2
Heinie Wagner, ss	.167	8	30	1	5	1	0	0	0	3	6	1
Joe Wood, p	.286	4	7	1	2	0	0	0	1	1	0	0
Steve Yerkes, 2b	.250	8	32	3	8	0	2	0	4	2	3	0
TOTAL	.220		273	25	60	14	6	1	21	19	36	6

PITCHER	W	L	ERA	G	GS	CG	SV	SHO	IP	H	ER	BB	SO
Hugh Bedient	1	0	0.50	4	2	1	0	0	18.0	10	1	7	7
Ray Collins	0	0	1.26	2	1	0	0	0	14.1	14	2	0	6
Charley Hall	0	0	3.38	2	0	0	0	0	10.2	11	4	9	1
Buck O'Brien	0	2	5.00	2	2	0	0	0	9.0	12	5	3	4
Joe Wood	3	1	3.68	4	3	2	0	0	22.0	27	9	3	21
TOTAL	4	3	2.55	14	8	3	0	0	74.0	74	21	22	39

NY (N)

PLAYER/POS	AVG	G	AB	R	H	2B	3B	HR	RB	BB	SO	SB
Red Ames, p	.000	1	0	0	0	0	0	0	0	0	0	0
Beals Becker, of-1	.000	2	4	1	0	0	0	0	0	2	0	0
Doc Crandall, p	.000	1	1	0	0	0	0	0	0	0	1	0
Josh Devore, of	.250	7	24	4	6	0	0	0	0	7	5	4
Larry Doyle, 2b	.242	8	33	5	8	1	0	1	2	3	2	2
Art Fletcher, ss	.179	8	28	1	5	1	0	0	3	1	4	1
Buck Herzog, 3b	.400	8	30	6	12	4	1	0	5	1	3	2
Rube Marquard, p	.000	2	4	0	0	0	0	0	0	1	0	0
Christy Mathewson, p	.167	3	12	0	2	0	0	0	0	0	4	0
Moose McCormick, ph	.250	5	4	0	1	0	0	0	1	0	0	0
Fred Merkle, 1b	.273	8	33	5	9	2	1	0	3	0	7	1
Chief Meyers, c	.357	8	28	2	10	0	1	0	3	2	3	1
Red Murray, of	.323	8	31	5	10	4	1	0	4	2	2	0
Tillie Shafer, ss	.000	3	0	0	0	0	0	0	0	0	0	0
Fred Snodgrass, of	.212	8	33	2	7	2	0	0	2	2	5	1
Jeff Tesreau, p	.375	3	8	0	3	0	0	0	2	1	3	0
Art Wilson, c	1.000	2	1	0	1	0	0	0	0	0	0	0
TOTAL	.270		274	31	74	14	4	1	25	22	39	12

PITCHER	W	L	ERA	G	GS	CG	SV	SHO	IP	H	ER	BB	SO
Red Ames	0	0	4.50	1	0	0	0	0	2.0	3	1	1	0
Doc Crandall	0	0	0.00	1	0	0	0	0	2.0	1	0	0	2
Rube Marquard	2	0	0.50	2	2	2	0	0	18.0	14	1	2	9
Christy Mathewson	0	2	1.26	3	3	3	0	0	28.2	23	4	5	10
Jeff Tesreau	1	2	3.13	3	3	1	0	0	23.0	19	8	11	15
TOTAL	3	4	1.71	10	8	6	0	0	73.2	60	14	19	36

GAME 1 AT NY OCT 8

BOS	000	001	300	4	6	1
NY	002	000	001	3	8	1

Pitchers: WOOD vs TESREAU, Crandall (8)
Attendance: 35,730

GAME 2 AT BOS OCT 9

NY	010	100	030	10	6	11	5
BOS	300	010	010	10	6	10	1

Pitchers: Mathewson vs Collins, Hall (8), Bedient (11)
Attendance: 30,148
(Game called at end of eleventh, darkness)

GAME 3 AT BOS OCT 10

NY	010	010	000	2	7	1
BOS	000	000	001	1	7	0

Pitchers: MARQUARD vs O'BRIEN, Bedient (9)
Attendance: 34,624

GAME 4 AT NY OCT 11

BOS	010	100	001	3	8	1
NY	000	000	100	1	9	1

Pitchers: WOOD vs TESREAU, Ames (8)
Attendance: 36,502

GAME 5 AT BOS OCT 12

NY	000	000	100	1	3	1
BOS	002	000	00X	2	5	1

Pitchers: MATHEWSON vs BEDIENT
Attendance: 34,683

GAME 6 AT NY OCT 14

BOS	020	000	000	2	7	2
NY	500	000	00X	5	11	2

Pitchers: O'BRIEN, Collins (2) vs MARQUARD
Attendance: 30,622

GAME 7 AT BOS OCT 15

NY	610	002	101	11	16	4
BOS	010	000	210	4	9	3

Pitchers: TESREAU vs WOOD, Hall (2)
Home Runs: Doyle-NY, Gardner-BOS
Attendance: 32,694

GAME 8 AT BOS OCT 16

NY	001	000	000	1	2	9	2
BOS	000	000	100	2	3	8	5

Pitchers: MATHEWSON vs Bedient, WOOD (8)
Attendance: 17,034

Third baseman Frank Baker and catcher Wally Schang drove in more than 60 percent of the Athletics' runs, as Philadelphia dispatched the Giants in five games. Chief Bender led A's pitchers with two wins, and rookie Bullet Joe Bush hurled a nifty five-hitter in Game 3, but the Series highlights were two duels between the A's Eddie Plank and Christy Mathewson of the Giants. The A's heavy hitting made Bender's wins possible and Bush's win easy, but pitching dominated the Plank-Matty games.

Bender yielded 11 hits in the opener, as did the Giants' pitchers. But five of the game's six extra-base hits belonged to the A's—including Baker's two-run homer and triples by Schang and Eddie Collins—and Bender emerged victorious. In Game 2, Plank and Mathewson pitched shutout ball through nine innings, but in the top of the 10th Matty himself singled in the game's first run and scored the second. Taking a 3–0 lead into the bottom of the inning, he set the A's down in order for New York's only Series win.

In Game 3, Schang's solo homer and Collins's three hits (including his second Series triple) and three RBIs led a 12-hit A's attack which, with Bush's fine pitching, put Philadelphia back into the Series lead. Bender won again in Game 4, shutting out the Giants through six innings as his A's scored six runs. But in the seventh, New York's Fred Merkle homered for three runs, and a single, double, and triple in the eighth brought in two more runs. With his lead cut to a single run, Bender bore down in the ninth and retired the side in order.

Plank avenged his earlier loss with a brilliant two-hitter in Game 5, facing the minimum three batters in eight of the nine innings. (His own error in the fifth—a dropped pop-up—led to the Giants' only run.) Mathewson pitched well, too, yielding only six singles. But four of them came in the first and third innings, combining with two sacrifice flies and an error for three runs. Only one Philadelphia batter reached base in the final six innings, but with Plank pitching as he was, the game and the title were in Philadelphia's pocket.

Philadelphia Athletics (AL), 4; New York Giants (NL), 1

PHI (A)

PLAYER/POS	AVG	G	AB	R	H	2B	3B	HR	RB	BB	SO	SB
Frank Baker, 3b	.450	5	20	2	9	0	0	1	7	0	2	1
Jack Barry, ss	.300	5	20	3	6	3	0	0	1	0	0	0
Chief Bender, p	.000	2	8	0	0	0	0	0	1	0	1	0
Joe Bush, p	.250	1	4	0	1	0	0	0	0	0	1	0
Eddie Collins, 2b	.421	5	19	5	8	0	2	0	3	1	2	3
Jack Lapp, c	.250	1	4	0	1	0	0	0	0	0	1	0
Stuffy McInnis, 1b	.118	5	17	1	2	1	0	0	2	0	2	0
Eddie Murphy, of	.227	5	22	2	5	0	0	0	0	2	0	0
Rube Oldring, of	.273	5	22	5	6	0	1	0	0	0	1	1
Eddie Plank, p	.143	2	7	0	1	0	0	0	0	0	0	0
Wally Schang, c	.357	4	14	2	5	0	1	1	7	2	4	0
Amos Strunk, of	.118	5	17	3	2	0	0	0	0	2	2	0
TOTAL	.264		174	23	46	4	4	2	21	7	16	5

PITCHER	W	L	ERA	G	GS	CG	SV	SHO	IP	H	ER	BB	SO
Chief Bender	2	0	4.00	2	2	2	0	0	18.0	19	8	1	9
Joe Bush	1	0	1.00	1	1	1	0	0	9.0	5	1	4	3
Eddie Plank	1	1	0.95	2	2	2	0	0	19.0	9	2	3	7
TOTAL	4	1	2.15	5	5	5	0	0	46.0	33	11	8	19

NY (N)

PLAYER/POS	AVG	G	AB	R	H	2B	3B	HR	RB	BB	SO	SB
George Burns, of	.158	5	19	2	3	2	0	0	2	1	5	1
Claude Cooper, pr	.000	2	0	0	0	0	0	0	0	0	0	1
Doc Crandall, p-2	.000	4	4	0	0	0	0	0	0	0	0	0
Al Demaree, p	.000	1	1	0	0	0	0	0	0	0	0	0
Larry Doyle, 2b	.150	5	20	1	3	0	0	0	2	0	1	0
Art Fletcher, ss	.278	5	18	1	5	0	0	0	3	1	1	1
Eddie Grant, ph	.000	2	1	1	0	0	0	0	0	0	0	0
Buck Herzog, 3b	.053	5	19	1	1	0	0	0	0	0	1	0
Rube Marquard, p	.000	2	1	0	0	0	0	0	0	0	0	0
Christy Mathewson, p	.600	2	5	1	3	0	0	0	1	1	0	0
Moose McCormick, ph	.500	2	2	1	1	0	0	0	0	0	0	0
Larry McLean, c-4	.500	5	12	0	6	0	0	0	2	0	0	0
Fred Merkle, 1b	.231	4	13	3	3	0	0	1	3	1	2	0
Chief Meyers, c	.000	1	4	0	0	0	0	0	0	0	0	0
Red Murray, of	.250	5	16	2	4	0	0	0	1	2	2	2
Tillie Shafer, of-5,3b-1	.158	5	19	2	3	1	1	0	1	2	3	0
Fred Snodgrass, 1b-1,of-1	.333	2	3	0	1	0	0	0	0	0	0	0
Jeff Tesreau, p	.000	2	2	0	0	0	0	0	0	0	1	0
Art Wilson, c	.000	3	3	0	0	0	0	0	0	0	2	0
Hooks Wiltse, 1b	.000	2	2	0	0	0	0	0	0	0	1	0
TOTAL	.201		164	15	33	3	1	1	15	8	19	5

PITCHER	W	L	ERA	G	GS	CG	SV	SHO	IP	H	ER	BB	SO
Doc Crandall	0	0	3.86	2	0	0	0	0	4.2	4	2	0	2
Al Demaree	0	1	4.50	1	1	0	0	0	4.0	7	2	1	0
Rube Marquard	0	1	7.00	2	1	0	0	0	9.0	10	7	3	3
Christy Mathewson	1	1	0.95	2	2	2	0	1	19.0	14	2	2	7
Jeff Tesreau	0	1	6.48	2	1	0	0	0	8.1	11	6	1	4
TOTAL	1	4	3.80	9	5	2	0	1	45.0	46	19	7	16

GAME 1 AT NY OCT 7

		R	H	E
PHI	000 320 010	6	11	1
NY	001 030 000	4	11	0

Pitchers: BENDER vs MARQUARD, Crandall (6), Tesreau (8)
Home Runs: Baker-PHI
Attendance: 36,291

GAME 2 AT PHI OCT 8

		R	H	E
NY	000 000 000 3	3	7	2
PHI	000 000 000 0	0	8	2

Pitchers: MATHEWSON vs PLANK
Attendance: 20,563

GAME 3 AT NY OCT 9

		R	H	E
PHI	320 000 210	8	12	1
NY	000 010 100	2	5	1

Pitchers: BUSH vs TESREAU, Crandall (7)
Home Runs: Schang-PHI
Attendance: 36,896

GAME 4 AT PHI OCT 10

		R	H	E
NY	000 000 320	5	8	2
PHI	010 320 00X	6	9	0

Pitchers: DEMAREE, Marquard (5) vs BENDER
Home Runs: Merkle-NY
Attendance: 20,568

GAME 5 AT NY OCT 11

		R	H	E
PHI	102 000 000	3	6	1
NY	000 010 000	1	2	2

Pitchers: PLANK vs MATHEWSON
Attendance: 36,682

The Athletics, easy winners of their fourth pennant in five years, were clear favorites over Boston. But the "Miracle Braves"—who moved from last place to first between July 18 and Aug. 25 and kept going to take the pennant by 10½ games—had the momentum and swept the Series.

Boston pitcher Dick Rudolph (who won 27 games during the season) limited the A's to five hits and an unearned run, to take the opener behind the Braves' heavy hitting, 7–1. But the rest of the games were not won so easily. Philadelphia's Eddie Plank held the Braves scoreless through eight innings of Game 2, and gave up only one run in the ninth. But the Braves' Bill James (26–7 during the season) allowed only two hits and no runs at all.

Game 3 was a seesaw affair not settled until the 12th inning. Through 10 innings, starters Lefty Tyler of Boston and Joe Bush of the A's traded runs. Philadelphia scored one in the top of the first, but Braves' catcher Hank Gowdy doubled in the tying run in the second. The teams traded runs again in the fourth, but no one else crossed the plate until the 10th, when Frank Baker's bases-loaded single drove in two. For the third time, the Braves came back to tie it up. Gowdy opened the last of the 10th with the Series' only home run, and after a walk and single, a sacrifice fly knotted the score. Bill James came on to pitch no-hit ball through the 11th and 12th. Bush remained in for the A's, retiring the side in the 11th. But an inning later Gowdy opened with his third crucial hit of the game, a double. Les Mann replaced him as runner, and after a walk, bunt, and wild throw to third, Mann scampered home with the winning run.

Two of Connie Mack's most promising young pitchers, Bob Shawkey and Herb Pennock (who would later find stardom as New York Yankees), shared the A's pitching in Game 4, and gave up only six hits between them. But a walk and an error led to a Boston run in the fourth, and although Shawkey himself doubled in the tying run a half inning later, two more Braves scored in the last of the fifth on Johnny Evers's single. Pennock came on to pitch three innings of shutout relief, but Rudolph held the A's hitless over the final four innings to preserve his second win and the Braves' crown.

Boston Braves (NL), 4; Philadelphia Athletics (AL), 0

BOS (N)

PLAYER/POS	AVG	G	AB	R	H	2B	3B	HR	RB	BB	SO	SB
Ted Cather, of	.000	1	5	0	0	0	0	0	0	0	1	0
Joe Connolly, of	.111	3	9	1	1	0	0	0	1	1	1	0
Charlie Deal, 3b	.125	4	16	1	2	2	0	0	0	0	0	2
Josh Devore, ph	.000	1	1	0	0	0	0	0	0	0	1	0
Johnny Evers, 2b	.438	4	16	2	7	0	0	0	2	2	2	1
Larry Gilbert, ph	.000	1	0	0	0	0	0	0	0	1	0	0
Hank Gowdy, c	.545	4	11	3	6	3	1	1	3	5	1	1
Bill James, p	.000	2	4	0	0	0	0	0	0	0	4	0
Les Mann, of-2	.286	3	7	1	2	0	0	0	1	0	1	0
Rabbit Maranville, ss	.308	4	13	1	4	0	0	0	3	1	1	2
Herbie Moran, of	.077	3	13	2	1	1	0	0	0	1	1	1
Dick Rudolph, p	.333	2	6	1	2	0	0	0	0	1	1	0
Butch Schmidt, 1b	.294	4	17	2	5	0	0	0	2	0	2	1
Lefty Tyler, p	.000	1	3	0	0	0	0	0	0	0	1	0
Possum Whitted, of	.214	4	14	2	3	0	1	0	2	3	1	1
TOTAL	.244		135	16	33	6	2	1	14	15	18	9

PITCHER	W	L	ERA	G	GS	CG	SV	SHO	IP	H	ER	BB	SO
Bill James	2	0	0.00	2	1	1	0	1	11.0	2	0	6	9
Dick Rudolph	2	0	0.50	2	2	2	0	0	18.0	12	1	4	15
Lefty Tyler	0	0	3.60	1	1	0	0	0	10.0	8	4	3	4
TOTAL	4	0	1.15	5	4	3	0	1	39.0	22	5	13	28

PHI (A)

PLAYER/POS	AVG	G	AB	R	H	2B	3B	HR	RB	BB	SO	SB
Frank Baker, 3b	.250	4	16	0	4	2	0	0	2	1	3	0
Jack Barry, ss	.071	4	14	1	1	0	0	0	0	1	3	1
Chief Bender, p	.000	1	2	0	0	0	0	0	0	0	0	0
Joe Bush, p	.000	1	5	0	0	0	0	0	0	0	2	0
Eddie Collins, 2b	.214	4	14	0	3	0	0	0	1	2	1	1
Jack Lapp, c	.000	1	1	0	0	0	0	0	0	0	0	0
Stuffy McInnis, 1b	.143	4	14	2	2	1	0	0	0	3	3	0
Eddie Murphy, of	.188	4	16	2	3	2	0	0	0	2	2	0
Rube Oldring, of	.067	4	15	0	1	0	0	0	0	0	5	0
Herb Pennock, p	.000	1	1	0	0	0	0	0	0	0	0	0
Eddie Plank, p	.000	1	2	0	0	0	0	0	0	0	1	0
Wally Schang, c	.167	4	12	1	2	1	0	0	0	1	4	0
Bob Shawkey, p	.500	1	2	0	1	1	0	0	1	0	1	0
Amos Strunk, of	.286	2	7	0	2	0	0	0	0	0	2	0
Jimmy Walsh, of-2	.333	3	6	0	2	1	0	0	1	3	1	0
Weldon Wyckoff, p	1.000	1	1	0	1	1	0	0	0	0	0	0
TOTAL	.172		128	6	22	9	0	0	5	13	28	2

PITCHER	W	L	ERA	G	GS	CG	SV	SHO	IP	H	ER	BB	SO
Chief Bender	0	1	10.13	1	1	0	0	0	5.1	8	6	2	3
Joe Bush	0	1	3.27	1	1	1	0	0	11.0	9	4	4	4
Herb Pennock	0	0	0.00	1	0	0	0	0	3.0	2	0	2	3
Eddie Plank	0	1	1.00	1	1	1	0	0	9.0	7	1	4	6
Bob Shawkey	0	1	3.60	1	1	0	0	0	5.0	4	2	2	0
Weldon Wyckoff	0	0	2.45	1	0	0	0	0	3.2	3	1	1	2
TOTAL	0	4	3.41	6	4	2	0	0	37.0	33	14	15	18

GAME 1 AT PHI OCT 9

BOS	020 013 010	7	11	2
PHI	010 000 000	1	5	0

Pitchers: RUDOLPH vs BENDER, Wyckoff (6)
Attendance: 20,562

GAME 2 AT PHI OCT 10

BOS	000 000 001	1	7	1
PHI	000 000 000	0	2	1

Pitchers: JAMES vs PLANK
Attendance: 20,562

GAME 3 AT BOS OCT 12

PHI	100 100 000 200	4	8	2
BOS	010 100 000 201	5	9	1

Pitchers: BUSH vs Tyler, JAMES (11)
Home Runs: Gowdy-BOS
Attendance: 35,520

GAME 4 AT BOS OCT 13

PHI	000 010 000	1	7	0
BOS	000 120 00X	3	6	0

Pitchers: SHAWKEY, Pennock (6) vs RUDOLPH
Attendance: 34,365

In a Series characterized by outstanding pitching, Boston's five runs in Game 5 were the most scored by either team. It was also one of the most closely contested Series: the deciding run was not scored until the ninth inning in three of the games, and only in Game 1 was the margin of victory as much as two runs.

Grover Cleveland Alexander pitched the opener for the Phillies, and while the Red Sox tagged him for eight hits, they were all singles, and not until the eighth inning did one manage to drive a runner home. Boston's Ernie Shore pitched just as well, giving up only five singles and four walks. But two Philadelphia hits produced a run in the fourth, and an alternating pair of walks and infield hits in the eighth broke the tie with two runs for the Phillies' only win.

The next three games were 2–1 Boston victories. Rube Foster held the Phillies to three hits in Game 2, and led his team at the bat, going 3-for-4, including a double in the fifth. But it was his single in the ninth with a man on second that produced what proved to be the winning run as he retired the side in the bottom of the ninth to preserve his win. Dutch Leonard duplicated Foster's three-hit pitching two days later as the Series moved to Boston's spacious new Braves Field for Game 3. Before a new Series record crowd of 42,300, Leonard defeated the great Alexander, as Boston's Duffy Lewis—with his third hit of the game—singled over second base to score Harry Hooper from third with two out in the bottom of the ninth.

Ernie Shore returned to the mound for Boston in Game 4, and although he gave up more hits (seven) than he had in Game 1, his Sox had scored their two runs before the Phillies put across their one in the eighth.

Rube Foster was not as effective in Game 5 as he had been in Game 2, twice giving the Phillies a two-run lead as Phillie first baseman Fred Luderus drove in three runs with a double and a home run. But from the fifth inning on, Foster held Philadelphia scoreless on two hits, while Duffy Lewis evened the score with a two-run homer in the eighth, and Harry Hooper (who had tied the score earlier with a home run in the third) won the game and the Series with a second homer in the top of the ninth.

Boston Red Sox (AL), 4; Philadelphia Phillies (NL), 1

BOS (A)

PLAYER/POS	AVG	G	AB	R	H	2B	3B	HR	RB	BB	SO	SB
Jack Barry, 2b	.176	5	17	1	3	0	0	0	1	1	2	0
Hick Cady, c	.333	4	6	0	2	0	0	0	0	1	2	0
Bill Carrigan, c	.000	1	2	0	0	0	0	0	0	1	1	0
Rube Foster, p	.500	2	8	0	4	1	0	0	1	0	2	0
Del Gainer, 1b	.333	1	3	1	1	0	0	0	0	0	0	0
Larry Gardner, 3b	.235	5	17	2	4	0	1	0	0	1	0	0
Olaf Henricksen, ph	.000	2	2	0	0	0	0	0	0	0	0	0
Dick Hoblitzel, 1b	.313	5	16	1	5	0	0	0	1	0	1	1
Harry Hooper, of	.350	5	20	4	7	0	0	2	3	2	4	0
Hal Janvrin, ss	.000	1	1	0	0	0	0	0	0	0	0	0
Dutch Leonard, p	.000	1	3	0	0	0	0	0	0	0	2	0
Duffy Lewis, of	.444	5	18	1	8	1	0	1	5	1	4	0
Babe Ruth, ph	.000	1	1	0	0	0	0	0	0	0	0	0
Everett Scott, ss	.056	5	18	0	1	0	0	0	0	0	3	0
Ernie Shore, p	.200	2	5	0	1	0	0	0	0	0	3	0
Tris Speaker, of	.294	5	17	2	5	0	1	0	0	4	1	0
Pinch Thomas, c	.200	2	5	0	1	0	0	0	0	0	0	0
TOTAL	.264		159	12	42	2	2	3	11	11	25	1

PITCHER	W	L	ERA	G	GS	CG	SV	SHO	IP	H	ER	BB	SO
Rube Foster	2	0	2.00	2	2	2	0	0	18.0	12	4	2	13
Dutch Leonard	1	0	1.00	1	1	1	0	0	9.0	3	1	0	6
Ernie Shore	1	1	2.12	2	2	2	0	0	17.0	12	4	8	6
TOTAL	4	1	1.84	5	5	5	0	0	44.0	27	9	10	25

PHI (N)

PLAYER/POS	AVG	G	AB	R	H	2B	3B	HR	RB	BB	SO	SB
Pete Alexander, p	.200	2	5	0	1	0	0	0	0	0	1	0
Dave Bancroft, ss	.294	5	17	2	5	0	0	0	1	2	2	0
Beals Becker, of	.000	2	0	0	0	0	0	0	0	0	0	0
Ed Burns, c	.188	5	16	1	3	0	0	0	0	1	2	0
Bobby Byrne, ph	.000	1	1	0	0	0	0	0	0	0	0	0
George Chalmers, p	.333	1	3	0	1	0	0	0	0	0	1	0
Gavvy Cravath, of	.125	5	16	2	2	1	1	0	1	2	6	0
Oscar Dugey, pr	.000	2	0	0	0	0	0	0	0	0	0	1
Bill Killefer, ph	.000	1	1	0	0	0	0	0	0	0	0	0
Fred Luderus, 1b	.438	5	16	1	7	2	0	1	6	1	4	0
Erskine Mayer, p	.000	2	4	0	0	0	0	0	0	0	2	0
Bert Niehoff, 2b	.063	5	16	1	1	0	0	0	0	1	5	0
Dode Paskert, of	.158	5	19	2	3	0	0	0	0	1	2	0
Eppa Rixey, p	.500	1	2	0	1	0	0	0	0	0	0	0
Milt Stock, 3b	.118	5	17	1	2	1	0	0	0	1	0	0
Possum Whitted, of-5,1b-1	.067	5	15	0	1	0	0	0	1	1	0	1
TOTAL	.182		148	10	27	4	1	1	9	10	25	2

PITCHER	W	L	ERA	G	GS	CG	SV	SHO	IP	H	ER	BB	SO
Pete Alexander	1	1	1.53	2	2	2	0	0	17.2	14	3	4	10
George Chalmers	0	1	2.25	1	1	1	0	0	8.0	8	2	3	6
Erskine Mayer	0	1	2.38	2	2	1	0	0	11.1	16	3	2	7
Eppa Rixey	0	1	4.05	1	0	0	0	0	6.2	4	3	2	2
TOTAL	1	4	2.27	6	5	4	0	0	43.2	42	11	11	25

GAME 1 AT PHI OCT 8

				R	H	E
BOS	000	000	010	1	8	1
PHI	000	100	02X	3	5	1

Pitchers: SHORE vs ALEXANDER
Attendance: 19,343

GAME 2 AT PHI OCT 9

				R	H	E
BOS	100	000	001	2	10	0
PHI	000	010	000	1	3	1

Pitchers: FOSTER vs MAYER
Attendance: 20,306

GAME 3 AT BOS OCT 11

				R	H	E
PHI	001	000	000	1	3	0
BOS	000	100	001	2	6	1

Pitchers: ALEXANDER vs LEONARD
Attendance: 42,300

GAME 4 AT BOS OCT 12

				R	H	E
PHI	000	000	010	1	7	0
BOS	001	001	00X	2	8	1

Pitchers: CHALMERS vs SHORE
Attendance: 41,096

GAME 5 AT PHI OCT 13

				R	H	E
BOS	011	000	021	5	10	1
PHI	200	200	000	4	9	1

Pitchers: FOSTER vs Mayer, RIXEY (3)
Home Runs: Hooper-BOS (2), Lewis-BOS, Luderus-PHI
Attendance: 20,306

Boston Red Sox (AL), 4; Brooklyn Robins (NL), 1

In close pennant races, the Red Sox repeated as league champions and Brooklyn won its first pennant since 1900. The first three games of the Series were tightly contested, and the outcomes were determined by only one run apiece. For 6½ innings in the opener, Brooklyn's Rube Marquard dueled Boston's Ernie Shore about equally. But in the last of the seventh the Sox capitalized on a double, some sloppy Brooklyn fielding, and a couple of sacrifice hits for three runs, adding another off reliever Jeff Pfeffer in the eighth for a 6–1 lead. The Robins fought back in the ninth, driving out Shore and drawing within one run of a tie before reliever Carl Mays retired the final man with the bases loaded.

Game 2 was even tighter. Boston starter Babe Ruth gave up a first-inning inside-the-park homer to Hy Myers, but in the third he drove in Everett Scott (who had tripled) to tie the game at 1–1. Then for the next 10 innings he and Robins pitcher Sherry Smith shut off all scoring. Ruth continued to blank Brooklyn in the 14th, and in the last of the inning a walk, sacrifice, and single over the head of the third baseman gave Boston and Ruth the victory.

Brooklyn veteran Jack Coombs took a 4–0 lead into the sixth inning of Game 3 before weakening. But after giving up a third Boston run on Larry Gardner's one-out homer in the seventh, he was relieved by Jeff Pfeffer, who set the Sox down in order the rest of the way. In saving what proved to be Coombs's last World Series appearance (as well as the Robins' only Series win), Pfeffer preserved Coombs's perfect Series won-lost record at 5–0.

Games 4 and 5 proved anticlimactic. In Game 4, Gardner's second homer of the Series—inside-the-park for three runs in the second inning—overcame the Robins' two runs in the first. The Sox added a run here and there to increase their lead, while Sox starter Dutch Leonard shut Brooklyn out through the final eight innings for a comfortable 6–2 win. And in what became the Series finale, Ernie Shore held the Robins to three singles and one unearned run as his Sox took advantage of a bad-hop triple in the second and two third-inning errors by Robin shortstop Ivy Olson to take the lead—and their fourth world championship.

BOS (A)

PLAYER/POS	AVG	G	AB	R	H	2B	3B	HR	RB	BB	SO	SB
Hick Cady, c	.250	2	4	1	1	0	0	0	0	3	0	0
Bill Carrigan, c	.667	1	3	0	2	0	0	0	1	0	1	0
Rube Foster, p	.000	1	1	0	0	0	0	0	0	0	1	0
Del Gainer, ph	1.000	1	1	0	1	0	0	0	1	0	0	0
Larry Gardner, 3b	.176	5	17	2	3	0	0	2	6	0	2	0
Olaf Henricksen, ph	.000	1	0	1	0	0	0	0	0	1	0	0
Dick Hoblitzel, 1b	.235	5	17	3	4	1	1	0	2	6	0	0
Harry Hooper, of	.333	5	21	6	7	1	1	0	1	3	1	1
Hal Janvrin, 2b	.217	5	23	2	5	3	0	0	1	0	6	0
Dutch Leonard, p	.000	1	3	0	0	0	0	0	0	1	3	0
Duffy Lewis, of	.353	5	17	3	6	2	1	0	1	2	1	0
Carl Mays, p	.000	2	1	0	0	0	0	0	0	0	1	0
Mike McNally, pr	.000	1	0	1	0	0	0	0	0	0	0	0
Babe Ruth, p	.000	1	5	0	0	0	0	0	1	0	2	0
Everett Scott, ss	.125	5	16	1	2	0	1	0	1	1	1	0
Ernie Shore, p	.000	2	7	0	0	0	0	0	0	0	2	0
Chick Shorten, of	.571	2	7	0	4	0	0	0	2	0	1	0
Pinch Thomas, c	.143	3	7	0	1	0	1	0	0	0	1	0
Tilly Walker, of	.273	3	11	1	3	0	1	0	1	1	2	0
Jimmy Walsh, of	.000	1	3	0	0	0	0	0	0	0	0	0
TOTAL	.238		164	21	39	7	6	2	18	18	25	1

PITCHER	W	L	ERA	G	GS	CG	SV	SHO	IP	H	ER	BB	SO
Rube Foster	0	0	0.00	1	0	0	0	0	3.0	3	0	0	1
Dutch Leonard	1	0	1.00	1	1	1	0	0	9.0	5	1	4	3
Carl Mays	0	1	5.06	2	1	0	1	0	5.1	8	3	3	2
Babe Ruth	1	0	0.64	1	1	1	0	0	14.0	6	1	3	4
Ernie Shore	2	0	1.53	2	2	1	0	0	17.2	12	3	4	9
TOTAL	4	1	1.47	7	5	3	1	0	49.0	34	8	14	19

BRO (N)

PLAYER/POS	AVG	G	AB	R	H	2B	3B	HR	RB	BB	SO	SB
Larry Cheney, p	.000	1	0	0	0	0	0	0	0	0	0	0
Jack Coombs, p	.333	1	3	0	1	0	0	0	1	0	0	0
George Cutshaw, 2b	.105	5	19	2	2	1	0	0	2	1	1	0
Jake Daubert, 1b	.176	4	17	1	3	0	1	0	0	2	3	0
Wheezer Dell, p	.000	1	0	0	0	0	0	0	0	0	0	0
Gus Getz, ph	.000	1	1	0	0	0	0	0	0	0	0	0
Jimmy Johnston, of-2	.300	3	10	1	3	0	1	0	0	1	0	0
Rube Marquard, p	.000	2	3	0	0	0	0	0	0	0	1	0
Fred Merkle, 1b-1	.250	3	4	0	1	0	0	0	1	2	0	0
Chief Meyers, c	.200	3	10	0	2	0	1	0	0	1	0	0
Otto Miller, c	.125	2	8	0	1	0	0	0	0	0	1	0
Harry Mowery, 3b	.176	5	17	2	3	0	0	0	1	3	2	0
Hy Myers, of	.182	5	22	2	4	0	0	1	3	0	3	0
Ivy Olson, ss	.250	5	16	1	4	0	1	0	2	2	2	0
Ollie O'Mara, ph	.000	1	1	0	0	0	0	0	0	0	1	0
Jeff Pfeffer, p-3	.250	4	4	0	1	0	0	0	0	0	2	0
Nap Rucker, p	.000	1	0	0	0	0	0	0	0	0	0	0
Sherry Smith, p	.200	1	5	0	1	1	0	0	0	0	0	0
Casey Stengel, of-3	.364	4	11	2	4	0	0	0	0	0	1	0
Zack Wheat, of	.211	5	19	2	4	0	1	0	1	2	2	1
TOTAL	.200		170	13	34	2	5	1	11	14	19	1

PITCHER	W	L	ERA	G	GS	CG	SV	SHO	IP	H	ER	BB	SO
Larry Cheney	0	0	3.00	1	0	0	0	0	3.0	4	1	1	5
Jack Coombs	1	0	4.26	1	1	0	0	0	6.1	7	3	1	1
Wheezer Dell	0	0	0.00	1	0	0	0	0	1.0	1	0	0	0
Rube Marquard	0	2	5.73	2	2	0	0	0	11.0	12	7	6	9
Jeff Pfeffer	0	1	1.69	3	1	0	1	0	10.2	7	2	4	5
Nap Rucker	0	0	0.00	1	0	0	0	0	2.0	1	0	0	3
Sherry Smith	0	1	1.35	1	1	1	0	0	13.1	7	2	6	2
TOTAL	1	4	2.85	10	5	1	1	0	47.1	39	15	18	25

GAME 1 AT BOS OCT 7

		R	H	E
BRO	000 100 004	5	10	4
BOS	001 010 31X	6	8	1

Pitchers: MARQUARD, Pfeffer (8) vs SHORE, Mays (9)
Attendance: 36,117

GAME 2 AT BOS OCT 9

		R	H	E
BRO	100 000 000 000 00	1	6	2
BOS	001 000 000 000 01	2	7	1

Pitchers: SMITH vs RUTH
Home Runs: H.Myers-BRO
Attendance: 41,373

GAME 3 AT BRO OCT 10

		R	H	E
BOS	000 002 100	3	7	1
BRO	001 120 00X	4	10	0

Pitchers: MAYS, Foster (6) vs COOMBS, Pfeffer (7)
Home Runs: Gardner-BOS
Attendance: 21,087

GAME 4 AT BRO OCT 11

		R	H	E
BOS	030 110 100	6	10	1
BRO	200 000 000	2	5	4

Pitchers: LEONARD vs MARQUARD, Cheney (5), Rucker (8)
Home Runs: Gardner-BOS
Attendance: 21,662

GAME 5 AT BOS OCT 12

		R	H	E
BRO	010 000 000	1	3	3
BOS	012 010 00X	4	7	2

Pitchers: PFEFFER, Dell (8) vs SHORE
Attendance: 42,620

Easy winners in their pennant races, the White Sox and Giants traded pairs of victories in the Series before the Sox came up with a second pair to take the title in six games. In the opener, Happy Felsch's solo homer in the fourth inning gave Sox starter Eddie Cicotte the margin he needed to defeat Slim Sallee, 2–1, and in Game 2 Red Faber went all the way, as his Sox broke a 2–2 tie in the fourth inning with five runs on six singles for Chicago's second win.

The clubs traveled to New York for Games 3 and 4, and Giants pitchers rewarded their fans with a pair of shutouts to even the Series. In Game 3, a triple, double, and single against the Sox' Cicotte in the fourth inning produced the only scoring, as Giant Rube Benton blanked the Sox on five hits, walking none. Giant ace Ferdie Schupp (a 21-game winner during the season) did the honors in Game 4, scattering seven hits, as teammate Benny Kauff, with his first Series hit in the fourth inning, homered inside the park to deep center against Red Faber for the deciding run. Two later runs against Faber and two more in the eighth (on Kauff's second homer) against reliever Dave Danforth made Schupp's win easy.

But Faber, the loser in Game 4, came in to pitch two innings of perfect relief two days later in Chicago for his second win, as the Sox rebounded from a 5–2 deficit with three runs in the bottom of the seventh to tie the game and three more an inning later to win it.

After a day of rest and a return to New York, Faber was given his third start. He pitched well enough, but his third win and the Series clincher was really the gift of some infamous Giants fielding. In the fourth inning, the first two Sox batters—Eddie Collins and Joe Jackson—reached on a high throw to first and a dropped fly. Happy Felsch, the third man up, reached on a fielder's choice as Giants third baseman Heinie Zimmerman chased Collins across the plate in a botched rundown. Jackson and Felsch scored the second and third unearned runs as Chick Gandil singled off the hapless Rube Benton. The Giants recovered to score two runs an inning later, but Faber shut them out the rest of the way to give his Sox the Series.

Chicago White Sox (AL), 4; New York Giants (NL), 2

CHI (A)

PLAYER/POS	AVG	G	AB	R	H	2B	3B	HR	RB	BB	SO	SB
Eddie Cicotte, p	.143	3	7	0	1	0	0	0	0	1	2	0
Eddie Collins, 2b	.409	6	22	4	9	1	0	0	2	2	3	3
Shano Collins, of	.286	6	21	2	6	1	0	0	0	0	2	0
Dave Danforth, p	.000	1	0	0	0	0	0	0	0	0	0	0
Red Faber, p	.143	4	7	0	1	0	0	0	0	2	3	0
Happy Felsch, of	.273	6	22	4	6	1	0	1	3	1	5	0
Chick Gandil, 1b	.261	6	23	1	6	1	0	0	5	0	2	1
Joe Jackson, of	.304	6	23	4	7	0	0	0	2	1	0	1
Nemo Leibold, of	.400	2	5	1	2	0	0	0	1	1	1	0
Byrd Lynn, ph	.000	1	1	0	0	0	0	0	0	0	1	0
Fred McMullin, 3b	.125	6	24	1	3	1	0	0	2	1	6	0
Swede Risberg, ph	.500	2	2	0	1	0	0	0	1	0	0	0
Reb Russell, p	.000	1	0	0	0	0	0	0	0	0	0	0
Ray Schalk, c	.263	6	19	1	5	0	0	0	0	2	1	1
Buck Weaver, ss	.333	6	21	3	7	1	0	0	1	0	2	0
Lefty Williams, p	.000	1	0	0	0	0	0	0	0	0	0	0
TOTAL	.274		197	21	54	6	0	1	17	11	28	6

PITCHER	W	L	ERA	G	GS	CG	SV	SHO	IP	H	ER	BB	SO
Eddie Cicotte	1	1	1.96	3	2	2	0	0	23.0	23	5	2	13
Dave Danforth	0	0	18.00	1	0	0	0	0	1.0	3	2	0	2
Red Faber	3	1	2.33	4	3	2	0	0	27.0	21	7	3	9
Reb Russell	0	0	∞	1	1	0	0	0	0.0	2	1	1	0
Lefty Williams	0	0	9.00	1	0	0	0	0	1.0	2	1	0	3
TOTAL	4	2	2.77	10	6	4	0	0	52.0	51	16	6	27

NY (N)

PLAYER/POS	AVG	G	AB	R	H	2B	3B	HR	RB	BB	SO	SB
Fred Anderson, p	.000	1	0	0	0	0	0	0	0	0	0	0
Rube Benton, p	.000	2	4	0	0	0	0	0	0	0	3	0
George Burns, of	.227	6	22	3	5	0	0	0	2	3	6	1
Art Fletcher, ss	.200	6	25	2	5	1	0	0	0	0	2	0
Buck Herzog, 2b	.250	6	24	1	6	0	1	0	2	0	4	0
Walter Holke, 1b	.286	6	21	2	6	2	0	0	1	0	6	0
Benny Kauff, of	.160	6	25	2	4	1	0	2	5	0	2	1
Lew McCarty, c-2	.400	3	5	1	2	0	1	0	1	0	0	0
Pol Perritt, p	1.000	3	2	0	2	0	0	0	0	0	0	0
Bill Rariden, c	.385	5	13	2	5	0	0	0	2	2	1	0
Dave Robertson, of	.500	6	22	3	11	1	1	0	1	0	0	2
Slim Sallee, p	.167	2	6	0	1	0	0	0	1	0	2	0
Ferdie Schupp, p	.250	2	4	0	1	0	0	0	1	0	1	0
Jeff Tesreau, p	.000	1	0	0	0	0	0	0	0	0	0	0
Jim Thorpe, of	.000	1	0	0	0	0	0	0	0	0	0	0
Joe Wilhoit, ph	.000	2	1	0	0	0	0	0	0	1	0	0
Heinie Zimmerman, 3b	.120	6	25	1	3	0	1	0	0	0	0	0
TOTAL	.256		199	17	51	5	4	2	16	6	27	4

PITCHER	W	L	ERA	G	GS	CG	SV	SHO	IP	H	ER	BB	SO
Fred Anderson	0	1	18.00	1	0	0	0	0	2.0	5	4	0	3
Rube Benton	1	1	0.00	2	2	1	0	1	14.0	9	0	1	8
Pol Perritt	0	0	1.08	3	0	0	0	0	8.1	9	1	3	3
Slim Sallee	0	2	5.28	2	2	1	0	0	15.1	20	9	4	4
Ferdie Schupp	1	0	1.74	2	2	1	0	1	10.1	11	2	2	9
Jeff Tesreau	0	0	0.00	1	0	0	0	0	1.0	0	0	1	1
TOTAL	2	4	2.82	11	6	3	0	2	51.0	54	16	11	28

GAME 1 AT CHI OCT 6

		R	H	E
NY	000 010 000	1	7	1
CHI	001 100 00X	2	7	1

Pitchers: SALLEE vs CICOTTE
Home Runs: Felsch-CHI
Attendance: 32,000

GAME 2 AT CHI OCT 7

		R	H	E
NY	020 000 000	2	8	1
CHI	020 500 00X	7	14	1

Pitchers: Schupp, ANDERSON (2), Perritt (4), Tesreau (8) vs FABER
Attendance: 32,000

GAME 3 AT NY OCT 10

		R	H	E
CHI	000 000 000	0	5	3
NY	000 200 00X	2	8	2

Pitchers: CICOTTE vs BENTON
Attendance: 33,616

GAME 4 AT NY OCT 11

		R	H	E
CHI	000 000 000	0	7	0
NY	000 110 12X	5	10	1

Pitchers: FABER, Danforth (8) vs SCHUPP
Home Runs: Kauff-NY (2)
Attendance: 27,746

GAME 5 AT CHI OCT 13

		R	H	E
NY	200 200 100	5	12	3
CHI	001 001 33X	8	14	6

Pitchers: SALLEE, Perritt (8) vs Russell, Cicotte (1), Williams (7), FABER (8)
Attendance: 27,323

GAME 6 AT NY OCT 15

		R	H	E
CHI	000 300 001	4	7	1
NY	000 020 000	2	6	3

Pitchers: FABER vs BENTON, Perritt (6)
Attendance: 33,969

Although both clubs had lost key players to military service, so had other major league teams, and after a season shortened by a month because of the war, the Red Sox and Cubs found themselves opponents in an early-September World Series.

In the opener, Babe Ruth pushed his string of consecutive scoreless World Series innings to 22, holding the Cubs to six singles as he went the distance. The Cubs' Hippo Vaughn pitched just as well, but two of the five singles he yielded followed a leadoff walk in the fourth and produced the game's only run. Chicago evened the Series in Game 2, bunching four of their seven hits after a walk in the second inning to take a 3–0 lead. Successive triples in Boston's ninth spoiled Lefty Tyler's shutout but not his victory.

Hippo Vaughn lost another close one in Game 3 when he gave up two runs in the fourth inning on a hit batsman and a succession of singles. The Cubs got him one run back in the fifth, but Boston's Carl Mays held Chicago to that one run as he hurled Boston back into the Series lead. Ruth pushed the Sox farther ahead in another squeaker in Game 4. As he continued his mastery over Cubs hitters, he drove Boston into the lead with a two-run triple in the fourth inning (his only Series hit). But in the eighth a run-scoring ground out ended his record setting string of scoreless innings at 29⅔, and a single drove in another run to tie the game. The Sox, though, scored a third run on a Chicago error in the last of the eighth, and reliever Bullet Joe Bush shut down a threat in the ninth to save Ruth's win.

Vaughn, in his third start, finally found what was needed for victory—a shutout, on five hits, as the Cubs added hits to walks from Boston's Sad Sam Jones in the third and eighth to push across their three runs. But in Game 6 the Sox scored two unearned runs on a dropped line drive to right in the third inning. It was their only scoring off Lefty Tyler, but Boston's Carl Mays was on his way to a one-run three-hitter that brought the Red Sox their fifth world championship in five tries. To date, although they have tried four more times, they have not won a sixth.

Boston Red Sox (AL), 4; Chicago Cubs (NL), 2

BOS (A)

PLAYER/POS	AVG	G	AB	R	H	2B	3B	HR	RB	BB	SO	SB
Sam Agnew, c	.000	4	9	0	0	0	0	0	0	0	0	0
Joe Bush, p	.000	2	2	0	0	0	0	0	0	1	0	0
Jean Dubuc, ph	.000	1	1	0	0	0	0	0	0	0	1	0
Harry Hooper, of	.200	6	20	0	4	0	0	0	0	2	2	0
Sam Jones, p	.000	1	1	0	0	0	0	0	0	1	0	0
Carl Mays, p	.200	2	5	1	1	0	0	0	0	1	0	0
Stuffy McInnis, 1b	.250	6	20	2	5	0	0	0	1	1	1	0
Hack Miller, ph	.000	1	1	0	0	0	0	0	0	0	0	0
Babe Ruth, p-2,of-2	.200	3	5	0	1	0	1	0	2	0	2	0
Wally Schang, c	.444	5	9	1	4	0	0	0	1	2	3	1
Everett Scott, ss	.100	6	20	0	2	0	0	0	1	1	1	0
Dave Shean, 2b	.211	6	19	2	4	1	0	0	0	4	3	1
Amos Strunk, of	.174	6	23	1	4	1	1	0	0	0	5	0
Fred Thomas, 3b	.118	6	17	0	2	0	0	0	0	1	2	0
George Whiteman, of	.250	6	20	2	5	0	1	0	1	2	1	1
TOTAL	.186		172	9	32	2	3	0	6	16	21	3

PITCHER	W	L	ERA	G	GS	CG	SV	SHO	IP	H	ER	BB	SO
Joe Bush	0	1	3.00	2	1	1	1	0	9.0	7	3	3	0
Sam Jones	0	1	3.00	1	1	1	0	0	9.0	7	3	5	5
Carl Mays	2	0	1.00	2	2	2	0	0	18.0	10	2	3	5
Babe Ruth	2	0	1.06	2	2	1	0	1	17.0	13	2	7	4
TOTAL	4	2	1.70	7	6	5	1	1	53.0	37	10	18	14

CHI (N)

PLAYER/POS	AVG	G	AB	R	H	2B	3B	HR	RB	BB	SO	SB
Turner Barber, ph	.000	3	2	0	0	0	0	0	0	0	0	0
Charlie Deal, 3b	.176	6	17	0	3	0	0	0	0	0	1	0
Phil Douglas, p	.000	1	0	0	0	0	0	0	0	0	0	0
Max Flack, of	.263	6	19	2	5	0	0	0	0	4	1	1
Claude Hendrix, p-1	1.000	2	1	0	1	0	0	0	0	0	0	0
Charlie Hollocher, ss	.190	6	21	2	4	0	1	0	1	1	1	1
Bill Killefer, c	.118	6	17	2	2	1	0	0	2	2	0	0
Les Mann, of	.227	6	22	0	5	2	0	0	2	0	0	0
Bill McCabe, ph	.000	3	1	1	0	0	0	0	0	0	0	0
Fred Merkle, 1b	.278	6	18	1	5	0	0	0	1	4	3	0
Bob O'Farrell, c-1	.000	3	3	0	0	0	0	0	0	0	0	0
Dode Paskert, of	.190	6	21	0	4	1	0	0	2	2	2	0
Charlie Pick, 2b	.389	6	18	2	7	1	0	0	0	1	1	1
Lefty Tyler, p	.200	3	5	0	1	0	0	0	2	2	0	0
Hippo Vaughn, p	.000	3	10	0	0	0	0	0	0	0	5	0
Chuck Wortman, 2b	.000	1	1	0	0	0	0	0	0	0	0	0
Rollie Zeider, 3b	.000	2	0	0	0	0	0	0	0	2	0	0
TOTAL	.210		176	10	37	5	1	0	10	18	14	3

PITCHER	W	L	ERA	G	GS	CG	SV	SHO	IP	H	ER	BB	SO
Phil Douglas	0	1	0.00	1	0	0	0	0	1.0	1	0	0	0
Claude Hendrix	0	0	0.00	1	0	0	0	0	1.0	0	0	0	0
Lefty Tyler	1	1	1.17	3	3	1	0	0	23.0	14	3	11	4
Hippo Vaughn	1	2	1.00	3	3	3	0	1	27.0	17	3	5	17
TOTAL	2	4	1.04	8	6	4	0	1	52.0	32	6	16	21

GAME 1 AT CHI SEPT 5

				R	H	E
BOS	000	100	000	1	5	0
CHI	000	000	000	0	6	0

Pitchers: RUTH vs VAUGHN
Attendance: 19,274

GAME 2 AT CHI SEPT 6

				R	H	E
BOS	000	000	001	1	6	1
CHI	030	000	00X	3	7	1

Pitchers: BUSH vs TYLER
Attendance: 20,040

GAME 3 AT CHI SEPT 7

				R	H	E
BOS	000	200	000	2	7	0
CHI	000	010	000	1	7	1

Pitchers: MAYS vs VAUGHN
Attendance: 27,054

GAME 4 AT BOS SEPT 9

				R	H	E
CHI	000	000	020	2	7	1
BOS	000	200	01X	3	4	0

Pitchers: Tyler, DOUGLAS (8) vs RUTH, Bush (9)
Attendance: 22,183

GAME 5 AT BOS SEPT 10

				R	H	E
CHI	001	000	002	3	7	0
BOS	000	000	000	0	5	0

Pitchers: VAUGHN vs JONES
Attendance: 24,694

GAME 6 AT BOS SEPT 11

				R	H	E
CHI	000	100	000	1	3	2
BOS	002	000	00X	2	5	0

Pitchers: TYLER, Hendrix (8) vs MAYS
Attendance: 15,238

In the bottom of the first inning of Game 1, White Sox pitcher Eddie Cicotte hit the first batter to face him, a prearranged signal to gamblers that "the fix was on"—that the Sox would throw the Series. The eight Chicago conspirators—pitching aces Cicotte and Lefty Williams, outfielders Joe Jackson and Happy Felsch, and infielders Chick Gandil, Buck Weaver, Fred McMullin and Swede Risberg—received no more than a fraction of the $100,000 promised them but "honored" their end of the deal. Cicotte (winner of 29 regular-season games, with a 1.82 ERA) gave up seven hits and six runs in the opening innings of Game 1 en route to a 9–1 loss. Williams, though he held the Reds to four hits in Game 2, uncharacteristically walked six and fanned only one, a performance bad enough for a 4–2 loss.

Dickie Kerr, Chicago's third-best pitcher and not in on the fix, won Game 3 with a three-hit shutout. But although Cicotte pitched well in Game 4, Chicago lost a third time as the Reds' Jimmy Ring hurled a three-hit shutout of his own (all three hits coming, ironically, off the bats of conspirators Jackson, Felsch, and Gandil).

Cincinnati's Hod Eller beat Chicago in Game 5 with the Series' third successive three-hit shutout. Loser Lefty Williams once again yielded only four hits, but three came in a four-run sixth inning which also saw a walk and a throwing error by Felsch. (The win, the Reds' fourth, did not decide the Series, which had been expanded to the best five of nine in the exuberance which followed the end of the Great War.)

Chicago exerted itself to win the next two games. In Game 6, Kerr's second win depended on crucial hits by Jackson and Gandil in the tenth inning; and in Game 7 Cicotte held the Reds to one run as Jackson and Felsch drove in all of Chicago's four runs.

But in Game 8, Williams gave up two singles and two doubles before being pulled with only one away in the first. Jackson homered in the third. And he doubled and Gandil tripled to drive in three Chicago runs in the eighth. But by then the Reds had scored 10 runs on their way to an easy win and their tainted world title.

Cincinnati Reds (NL), 5; Chicago White Sox (AL), 3

CIN (N)

PLAYER/POS	AVG	G	AB	R	H	2B	3B	HR	RB	BB	SO	SB
Jake Daubert, 1b	.241	8	29	4	7	0	1	0	1	1	2	1
Pat Duncan, of	.269	8	26	3	7	2	0	0	8	2	2	0
Hod Eller, p	.286	2	7	2	2	1	0	0	0	0	2	0
Ray Fisher, p	.500	2	2	0	1	0	0	0	0	0	0	0
Heinie Groh, 3b	.172	8	29	6	5	2	0	0	2	6	4	0
Larry Kopf, ss	.222	8	27	3	6	0	2	0	2	3	2	0
Dolf Luque, p	.000	2	1	0	0	0	0	0	0	0	1	0
Sherry Magee, ph	.500	2	2	0	1	0	0	0	0	0	0	0
Greasy Neale, of	.357	8	28	3	10	1	1	0	4	2	5	1
Bill Rariden, c	.211	5	19	0	4	0	0	0	2	0	0	1
Morrie Rath, 2b	.226	8	31	5	7	1	0	0	2	4	1	2
Jimmy Ring, p	.000	2	5	0	0	0	0	0	0	0	2	0
Edd Roush, of	.214	8	28	6	6	2	1	0	7	3	0	2
Dutch Ruether, p-2	.667	3	6	2	4	1	2	0	4	1	0	0
Slim Sallee, p	.000	2	4	0	0	0	0	0	0	0	0	0
Jimmy Smith, pr	.000	1	0	0	0	0	0	0	0	0	0	0
Ivey Wingo, c	.571	3	7	1	4	0	0	0	1	3	1	0
TOTAL	.255		251	35	64	10	7	0	33	25	22	7

PITCHER	W	L	ERA	G	GS	CG	SV	SHO	IP	H	ER	BB	SO
Hod Eller	2	0	2.00	2	2	2	0	1	18.0	13	4	2	15
Ray Fisher	0	1	2.35	2	1	0	0	0	7.2	7	2	2	2
Dolf Luque	0	0	0.00	2	0	0	0	0	5.0	1	0	0	6
Jimmy Ring	1	1	0.64	2	1	1	0	1	14.0	7	1	6	4
Dutch Ruether	1	0	2.57	2	2	1	0	0	14.0	12	4	4	1
Slim Sallee	1	1	1.35	2	2	1	0	0	13.1	19	2	1	2
TOTAL	5	3	1.63	12	8	5	0	2	72.0	59	13	15	30

CHI (A)

PLAYER/POS	AVG	G	AB	R	H	2B	3B	HR	RB	BB	SO	SB
Eddie Cicotte, p	.000	3	8	0	0	0	0	0	0	0	3	0
Eddie Collins, 2b	.226	8	31	2	7	1	0	0	1	1	2	1
Shano Collins, of	.250	4	16	2	4	1	0	0	0	0	0	0
Happy Felsch, of	.192	8	26	2	5	1	0	0	3	1	4	0
Chick Gandil, 1b	.233	8	30	1	7	0	1	0	5	1	3	1
Joe Jackson, of	.375	8	32	5	12	3	0	1	6	1	2	0
Bill James, p	.000	1	2	0	0	0	0	0	0	0	1	0
Dickie Kerr, p	.167	2	6	0	1	0	0	0	0	0	0	0
Nemo Leibold, of	.056	5	18	0	1	0	0	0	0	2	3	1
Grover Lowdermilk, p	.000	1	0	0	0	0	0	0	0	0	0	0
Byrd Lynn, c	.000	1	1	0	0	0	0	0	0	0	0	0
Erskine Mayer, p	.000	1	0	0	0	0	0	0	0	0	0	0
Fred McMullin, ph	.500	2	2	0	1	0	0	0	0	0	0	0
Eddie Murphy, ph	.000	3	2	0	0	0	0	0	0	0	1	0
Swede Risberg, ss	.080	8	25	3	2	0	1	0	0	5	3	1
Ray Schalk, c	.304	8	23	1	7	0	0	0	2	4	2	1
Buck Weaver, 3b	.324	8	34	4	11	4	1	0	0	0	2	0
Roy Wilkinson, p	.000	2	2	0	0	0	0	0	0	0	1	0
Lefty Williams, p	.200	3	5	0	1	0	0	0	0	0	3	0
TOTAL	.224		263	20	59	10	3	1	17	15	30	5

PITCHER	W	L	ERA	G	GS	CG	SV	SHO	IP	H	ER	BB	SO
Eddie Cicotte	1	2	2.91	3	3	2	0	0	21.2	19	7	5	7
Bill James	0	0	5.79	1	0	0	0	0	4.2	8	3	3	2
Dickie Kerr	2	0	1.42	2	2	2	0	1	19.0	14	3	3	6
Grover Lowdermilk	0	0	9.00	1	0	0	0	0	1.0	2	1	1	0
Erskine Mayer	0	0	0.00	1	0	0	0	0	1.0	0	0	1	0
Roy Wilkinson	0	0	1.23	2	0	0	0	0	7.1	9	1	4	3
Lefty Williams	0	3	6.61	3	3	1	0	0	16.1	12	12	8	4
TOTAL	3	5	3.42	13	8	5	0	1	71.0	64	27	25	22

GAME 1 AT CIN OCT 1

		R	H	E
CHI	010 000 000	1	6	1
CIN	100 500 21X	9	14	1

Pitchers: CICOTTE, Wilkinson (4), Lowdermilk (8) vs RUETHER
Attendance: 30,511

GAME 2 AT CIN OCT 2

		R	H	E
CHI	000 000 200	2	10	1
CIN	000 301 00X	4	4	2

Pitchers: WILLIAMS vs SALLEE
Attendance: 29,690

GAME 3 AT CHI OCT 3

		R	H	E
CIN	000 000 000	0	3	1
CHI	020 100 00X	3	7	0

Pitchers: FISHER, Luque (8) vs KERR
Attendance: 29,126

GAME 4 AT CHI OCT 4

		R	H	E
CIN	000 020 000	2	5	2
CHI	000 000 000	0	3	2

Pitchers: RING vs CICOTTE
Attendance: 34,363

GAME 5 AT CHI OCT 6

		R	H	E
CIN	000 004 001	5	4	0
CHI	000 000 000	0	3	3

Pitchers: ELLER vs WILLIAMS, Mayer (9)
Attendance: 34,379

GAME 6 AT CIN OCT 7

		R	H	E
CHI	000 013 000 1	5	10	3
CIN	002 200 000 0	4	11	0

Pitchers: KERR vs Ruether, RING (6)
Attendance: 32,006

GAME 7 AT CIN OCT 8

		R	H	E
CHI	101 020 000	4	10	1
CIN	000 001 000	1	7	4

Pitchers: CICOTTE vs SALLEE, Fisher (5), Luque (6)
Attendance: 13,923

GAME 8 AT CHI OCT 9

		R	H	E
CIN	410 013 010	10	16	2
CHI	001 000 040	5	10	1

Pitchers: ELLER vs WILLIAMS, James (1), Wilkinson (6)
Home Runs: Jackson-CHI
Attendance: 32,930

Cleveland Indians (AL), 5; Brooklyn Robins (NL), 2

The Indians outscored the Robins in the Series, 21-8. Yet after losing the opener in Brooklyn, the Robins fought back to take the next two, and held the Series lead as the teams traveled to Cleveland for the next four games.

Both clubs garnered five hits in Game 1, but an error, walk, single, and double gave the Indians two runs in the second and a lead they never yielded, as Stan Coveleski outlasted Rube Marquard for the win. In Game 2, both clubs increased their hit totals to seven, but the Robins bunched six of theirs into three innings for three runs, while Burleigh Grimes, only once yielding two hits in an inning, shut the Indians out. The two runs Brooklyn scored in the first inning of Game 3 were all Sherry Smith needed to give the Robins their second win behind his three-hit pitching. But Brooklyn scored only twice more in the Series as the Indians swept to the championship with four wins in Cleveland.

With the Indians scoring four runs in Game 4 before Brooklyn put its one run on the board, Coveleski breezed to his second five-hit Series run. Jim Bagby had it even easier the next day. The Robins tagged him for 13 hits, but not until the ninth inning were they able to put them together for a run. Meanwhile Bagby and his teammates were registering a couple of Series firsts as they moved to an eight-run lead. Right fielder Elmer Smith opened the scoring in the first inning with the first World Series grand slam, and Bagby himself homered for three more in the fourth—the first pitcher to hit a Series home run.

But the 1920 Series is best remembered for second baseman Bill Wambsganss' unassisted triple play in the fifth inning. With runners on first and second going on pitcher Clarence Mitchell's liner, Wambsganss snared the ball for the first out, stepped on second to force one runner, and tagged the runner coming in from first to retire the side.

In Game 6 Duster Mails, a late-season addition to the team, shut out Brooklyn on three hits in a 1–0 squeaker over Sherry Smith. Coveleski won the clincher the next day, also via the shutout, with his third five-hitter of the Series and his third Series win.

CLE (A)

PLAYER/POS	AVG	G	AB	R	H	2B	3B	HR	RB	BB	SO	SB
Jim Bagby, p	.333	2	6	1	2	0	0	1	3	0	0	0
George Burns, 1b-4	.300	5	10	1	3	1	0	0	3	3	3	0
Ray Caldwell, p	.000	1	0	0	0	0	0	0	0	0	0	0
Stan Coveleski, p	.100	3	10	2	1	0	0	0	0	0	4	0
Joe Evans, of	.308	4	13	0	4	0	0	0	0	1	0	0
Larry Gardner, 3b	.208	7	24	1	5	1	0	0	2	1	1	0
Jack Graney, of-2	.000	3	3	0	0	0	0	0	0	0	2	0
Charlie Jamieson, of-5	.333	6	15	2	5	1	0	0	1	1	0	1
Doc Johnston, 1b	.273	5	11	1	3	0	0	0	0	2	1	1
Harry Lunte, 2b	.000	1	0	0	0	0	0	0	0	0	0	0
Duster Mails, p	.000	2	5	0	0	0	0	0	0	0	1	0
Les Nunamaker, c-1	.500	2	2	0	1	0	0	0	0	0	0	0
Steve O'Neill, c	.333	7	21	1	7	3	0	0	2	4	3	0
Joe Sewell, ss	.174	7	23	0	4	0	0	0	0	2	1	0
Elmer Smith, of	.308	5	13	1	4	0	1	1	5	1	1	0
Tris Speaker, of	.320	7	25	6	8	2	1	0	1	3	1	0
Pinch Thomas, c	.000	1	0	0	0	0	0	0	0	0	0	0
George Uhle, p	.000	2	0	0	0	0	0	0	0	0	0	0
Bill Wambgsanss, 2b	.154	7	26	3	4	0	0	0	1	2	1	0
Joe Wood, of	.200	4	10	2	2	1	0	0	0	1	2	0
TOTAL	.244		217	21	53	9	2	2	18	21	21	2

PITCHER	W	L	ERA	G	GS	CG	SV	SHO	IP	H	ER	BB	SO
Jim Bagby	1	1	1.80	2	2	1	0	0	15.0	20	3	1	3
Ray Caldwell	0	1	27.00	1	1	0	0	0	0.1	2	1	1	0
Stan Coveleski	3	0	0.67	3	3	3	0	1	27.0	15	2	2	8
Duster Mails	1	0	0.00	2	1	1	0	1	15.2	6	0	6	6
George Uhle	0	0	0.00	2	0	0	0	0	3.0	1	0	0	3
TOTAL	5	2	0.89	10	7	5	0	2	61.0	44	6	10	20

BRO (N)

PLAYER/POS	AVG	G	AB	R	H	2B	3B	HR	RB	BB	SO	SB
Leon Cadore, p	.000	2	0	0	0	0	0	0	0	0	0	0
Tommy Griffith, of	.190	7	21	1	4	2	0	0	3	0	2	0
Burleigh Grimes, p	.333	3	6	1	2	0	0	0	0	0	0	0
Jimmy Johnston, 3b	.214	4	14	2	3	0	0	0	0	0	2	1
Pete Kilduff, 2b	.095	7	21	0	2	0	0	0	0	1	4	0
Ed Konetchy, 1b	.174	7	23	0	4	0	1	0	2	3	2	0
Ernie Krueger, c-3	.167	4	6	0	1	0	0	0	0	0	0	0
Bill Lamar, ph	.000	3	3	0	0	0	0	0	0	0	0	0
Al Mamaux, p	.000	3	1	0	0	0	0	0	0	0	1	0
Rube Marquard, p	.000	2	1	0	0	0	0	0	0	0	0	0
Bill McCabe, pr	.000	1	0	0	0	0	0	0	0	0	0	0
Otto Miller, c	.143	6	14	0	2	0	0	0	0	1	2	0
Clarence Mitchell, p-1	.333	2	3	0	1	0	0	0	0	0	0	0
Hy Myers, of	.231	7	26	0	6	0	0	0	1	0	1	0
Bernie Neis, of-2	.000	4	5	0	0	0	0	0	0	1	0	0
Ivy Olson, ss	.320	7	25	2	8	1	0	0	0	3	1	0
Jeff Pfeffer, p	.000	1	1	0	0	0	0	0	0	0	0	0
Ray Schmandt, ph	.000	1	1	0	0	0	0	0	0	0	0	0
Jack Sheehan, 3b	.182	3	11	0	2	0	0	0	0	0	1	0
Sherry Smith, p	.000	2	6	0	0	0	0	0	0	0	2	0
Zack Wheat, of	.333	7	27	2	9	2	0	0	2	1	2	0
TOTAL	.205		215	8	44	5	1	0	8	10	20	1

PITCHER	W	L	ERA	G	GS	CG	SV	SHO	IP	H	ER	BB	SO
Leon Cadore	0	1	9.00	2	1	0	0	0	2.0	4	2	1	1
Burleigh Grimes	1	2	4.19	3	3	1	0	1	19.1	23	9	9	4
Al Mamaux	0	0	4.50	3	0	0	0	0	4.0	2	2	0	5
Rube Marquard	0	1	3.00	2	1	0	0	0	9.0	7	3	3	6
Clarence Mitchell	0	0	0.00	1	0	0	0	0	4.2	3	0	3	1
Jeff Pfeffer	0	0	3.00	1	0	0	0	0	3.0	4	1	2	1
Sherry Smith	1	1	0.53	2	2	2	0	0	17.0	10	1	3	3
TOTAL	2	5	2.75	14	7	3	0	1	59.0	53	18	21	21

GAME 1 AT BRO OCT 5

		R	H	E
CLE	**020 100 000**	**3**	**5**	**0**
BRO	000 000 100	1	5	1

Pitchers: COVELESKI vs MARQUARD, Mamaux (7), Cadore (9)
Attendance: 23,753

GAME 2 AT BRO OCT 6

		R	H	E
CLE	000 000 000	0	7	1
BRO	**101 010 00X**	**3**	**7**	**0**

Pitchers: BAGBY, Uhle (7) vs GRIMES
Attendance: 22,559

GAME 3 AT BRO OCT 7

		R	H	E
CLE	000 100 000	1	3	1
BRO	**200 000 00X**	**2**	**6**	**1**

Pitchers: CALDWELL, Mails (1), Uhle (8) vs SMITH
Attendance: 25,088

GAME 4 AT CLE OCT 9

		R	H	E
BRO	000 100 000	1	5	1
CLE	**202 001 00X**	**5**	**12**	**2**

Pitchers: CADORE, Mamaux (2), Marquard (3), Pfeffer (6) vs COVELESKI
Attendance: 25,734

GAME 5 AT CLE OCT 10

		R	H	E
BRO	000 000 001	1	13	1
CLE	**400 310 00X**	**8**	**12**	**2**

Pitchers: GRIMES, Mitchell (4) vs BAGBY
Home Runs: E.Smith-CLE, Bagby-CLE
Attendance: 26,884

GAME 6 AT CLE OCT 11

		R	H	E
BRO	000 000 000	0	3	0
CLE	**000 001 00X**	**1**	**7**	**3**

Pitchers: SMITH vs MAILS
Attendance: 27,194

GAME 7 AT CLE OCT 12

		R	H	E
BRO	000 000 000	0	5	2
CLE	**000 110 10X**	**3**	**7**	**3**

Pitchers: GRIMES, Mamaux (8) vs COVELESKI
Attendance: 27,525

Since both the Giants and Yankees called the Polo Grounds home, all eight games were played there, with the two clubs alternating from game to game as the home team. Pitching dominated the first two games—especially Yankees pitching. In Game 1, Giant third baseman Frank Frisch went 4-for-4 against Carl Mays. But Mays gave up only one other hit and walked no one, to fashion a shutout. The next day Art Nehf of the Giants allowed the Yankees only three singles. But the Yankees capitalized on two of them, together with one of Nehf's seven walks, a couple of Giants errors, and Bob Meusel's steal of home to score three times, as pitcher Waite Hoyt shut out the Giants on two singles to put the Yanks two up in the Series.

In Game 3 the hitters finally came alive. With the score tied 4–4 in the last of the seventh, the Giants unloaded for eight hits which, with two walks and a sacrifice fly, produced eight runs and the first Giants win. They evened the Series the next day, scoring three runs in the eighth to take a 3–1 lead, adding another in the ninth. Babe Ruth's first World Series home run, a solo shot in the bottom of the ninth, thrilled the fans but had no effect on the game's outcome.

The Yankees regained the Series lead in Game 5. Waite Hoyt was not as sharp as he had been in the opener, yielding ten hits. But the only run scored against him came as the result of a first-inning error, a deficit his Yankees teammates overcame for a 3–1 win. In Game 6 the Yankees took a quick 3–0 lead in the first. The Giants tied it in the top of the second on home runs by Irish Meusel and Frank Snyder, but Chick Fewster hit a two-run shot a half inning later to restore the Yankees lead. In the fourth inning, though, the Giants parlayed four singles and an error into four runs and a lead that held up for a Series-tying win.

The Yankees scored only one run the rest of the way as the Giants took the final two games on unearned runs. In Game 7, Mays and the Giants' Phil Douglas dueled into the seventh tied 1–1. But in the last of the seventh, Frank Snyder's double drove in Johnny Rawlings, who had reached on an error, for the game's deciding run. In Game 8, Hoyt held the Giants to six hits and completed his third game without giving up an earned run. But a Giants runner had scored in the first inning when a grounder shot through the legs of shortstop Roger Peckinpaugh. It turned out to be the game's only run, as Art Nehf and his Giants' flawless fielding blanked the Yankees to give manager John McGraw his first world championship since 1905.

New York Giants (NL), 5; New York Yankees (AL), 3

NY (N)

PLAYER/POS	AVG	G	AB	R	H	2B	3B	HR	RB	BB	SO	SB
Dave Bancroft, ss	.152	8	33	3	5	1	0	0	3	1	5	0
Jesse Barnes, p	.444	3	9	3	4	0	0	0	0	0	0	0
George Burns, of	.333	8	33	2	11	4	1	0	2	3	5	1
Phil Douglas, p	.000	3	7	0	0	0	0	0	0	0	2	0
Frankie Frisch, 3b	.300	8	30	5	9	0	1	0	1	4	3	3
George Kelly, 1b	.233	8	30	3	7	1	0	0	4	3	10	0
Irish Meusel, of	.345	8	29	4	10	2	1	1	7	2	3	1
Art Nehf, p	.000	3	9	0	0	0	0	0	0	1	3	0
Johnny Rawlings, 2b	.333	8	30	2	10	3	0	0	4	0	3	0
Earl Smith, c-2	.000	3	7	0	0	0	0	0	0	1	0	0
Frank Snyder, c-6	.364	7	22	4	8	1	0	1	3	0	2	0
Fred Toney, p	.000	2	0	0	0	0	0	0	0	0	0	0
Ross Youngs, of	.280	8	25	3	7	1	1	0	4	7	2	2
TOTAL	.269		264	29	71	13	4	2	28	22	38	7

PITCHER	W	L	ERA	G	GS	CG	SV	SHO	IP	H	ER	BB	SO
Jesse Barnes	2	0	1.65	3	0	0	0	0	16.1	10	3	6	18
Phil Douglas	2	1	2.08	3	3	2	0	0	26.0	20	6	5	17
Art Nehf	1	2	1.38	3	3	3	0	1	26.0	13	4	13	8
Fred Toney	0	0	23.63	2	2	0	0	0	2.2	7	7	3	1
TOTAL	5	3	2.54	11	8	5	0	1	71.0	50	20	27	44

NY (A)

PLAYER/POS	AVG	G	AB	R	H	2B	3B	HR	RB	BB	SO	SB
Frank Baker, 3b-2	.250	4	8	0	2	0	0	0	0	1	0	0
Rip Collins, p	.000	1	0	0	0	0	0	0	0	0	0	0
Al DeVormer, c-1	.000	2	1	0	0	0	0	0	0	0	0	0
Chick Fewster, of	.200	4	10	3	2	0	0	1	2	3	3	0
Harry Harper, p	.000	1	0	0	0	0	0	0	0	0	0	0
Waite Hoyt, p	.222	3	9	0	2	0	0	0	1	0	1	0
Carl Mays, p	.111	3	9	0	1	0	0	0	0	0	1	0
Mike McNally, 3b	.200	7	20	3	4	1	0	0	1	1	3	2
Bob Meusel, of	.200	8	30	3	6	2	0	0	3	2	5	1
Elmer Miller, of	.161	8	31	3	5	1	0	0	2	2	5	0
Roger Peckinpaugh, ss	.179	8	28	2	5	1	0	0	0	4	3	0
Bill Piercy, p	.000	1	0	0	0	0	0	0	0	0	0	0
Wally Pipp, 1b	.154	8	26	1	4	1	0	0	2	2	3	1
Jack Quinn, p	.000	1	2	0	0	0	0	0	0	0	1	0
Tom Rogers, p	.000	1	0	0	0	0	0	0	0	0	0	0
Babe Ruth, of	.313	6	16	3	5	0	0	1	4	5	8	2
Wally Schang, c	.286	8	21	1	6	1	1	0	1	5	4	0
Bob Shawkey, p	.500	2	4	2	2	0	0	0	0	0	1	0
Aaron Ward, 2b	.231	8	26	1	6	0	0	0	4	2	6	0
TOTAL	.207		241	22	50	7	1	2	20	27	44	6

PITCHER	W	L	ERA	G	GS	CG	SV	SHO	IP	H	ER	BB	SO
Rip Collins	0	0	54.00	1	0	0	0	0	0.2	4	4	1	0
Harry Harper	0	0	20.25	1	1	0	0	0	1.1	3	3	2	1
Waite Hoyt	2	1	0.00	3	3	3	0	1	27.0	18	0	11	18
Carl Mays	1	2	1.73	3	3	3	0	1	26.0	20	5	0	9
Bill Piercy	0	0	0.00	1	0	0	0	0	1.0	2	0	0	2
Jack Quinn	0	1	9.82	1	0	0	0	0	3.2	8	4	2	2
Tom Rogers	0	0	6.75	1	0	0	0	0	1.1	3	1	0	1
Bob Shawkey	0	1	7.00	2	1	0	0	0	9.0	13	7	6	5
TOTAL	3	5	3.09	13	8	6	0	2	70.0	71	24	22	38

GAME 1 AT NY -N OCT 5

NY-A	100	011	000	3	7	0
NY-N	000	000	000	0	5	0

Pitchers: MAYS vs DOUGLAS, Barnes (9)
Attendance: 30,202

GAME 2 AT NY -A OCT 6

NY-N	000	000	000	0	2	3
NY-A	000	100	02X	3	3	0

Pitchers: NEHF vs HOYT
Attendance: 34,939

GAME 3 AT NY -N OCT 7

NY-A	004	000	010	5	8	0
NY-N	004	000	81X	13	20	0

Pitchers: Shawkey, QUINN (3), Collins (7), Rogers (8) vs Toney, BARNES (3)
Attendance: 36,509

GAME 4 AT NY -A OCT 9

NY-N	000	000	031	4	9	1
NY-A	000	010	001	2	7	1

Pitchers: DOUGLAS vs MAYS
Home Runs: Ruth-NY(A)
Attendance: 36,372

GAME 5 AT NY -N OCT 10

NY-A	001	200	000	3	6	1
NY-N	100	000	000	1	10	1

Pitchers: HOYT vs NEHF
Attendance: 35,758

GAME 6 AT NY -A OCT 11

NY-N	030	401	000	8	13	0
NY-A	320	000	000	5	7	2

Pitchers: Toney, BARNES (1) vs Harper, SHAWKEY (2), Piercy (9)
Home Runs: E.Meusel-NY(N), Snyder-NY(N), Fewster-NY(A)
Attendance: 34,283

GAME 7 AT NY -N OCT 12

NY-A	010	000	000	1	8	1
NY-N	000	100	10X	2	6	0

Pitchers: MAYS vs DOUGLAS
Attendance: 36,503

GAME 8 AT NY -A OCT 13

NY-N	100	000	000	1	6	0
NY-A	000	000	000	0	4	1

Pitchers: NEHF vs HOYT
Attendance: 25,410

New York Giants (NL), 4; New York Yankees (AL), 0; tie, 1

The Giants didn't quite sweep the Series—a tie in Game 2 interrupted their string of victories—but they shut down the Yankees offense, holding Yankees to three runs or less per game, and Babe Ruth to two hits and a .118 batting average. This Series restored the best-of-seven-games format after three years of best-of-nine.

The Giants had to come from behind to take Game 1. Bullet Joe Bush and Art Nehf hurled shutout ball through five innings before the Yankees scored single runs in the sixth and seventh innings (Ruth driving in the Series' first run for the second year in a row with his single in the sixth). But in the eighth, Bush gave up four straight singles and two runs before Waite Hoyt relieved him with the score tied and men on first and third. Hoyt set down all three men he faced, but the first out—Ross Youngs' fly to center—drove in what proved to be the Giants' winning run.

The Giants led off Game 2 with three first-inning runs on Irish Meusel's home run, but scored no more as Bob Shawkey stopped them for nine innings while his Yankees picked up runs in the first, fourth (on Aaron Ward's homer), and eighth to tie it all up. At the end of the 10th, with 45 minutes left before sundown, the umpires called the game for darkness and provoked a storm of seat cushions and bottles from the stands.

The Giants resumed their winning ways in Game 3 behind Jack Scott's shutout. Scott—picked up by the Giants in midseason—gave up only four hits, walking one, in the Series' top pitching performance. In Game 4 the Yankees scored twice in the first inning, but in the fifth the Giants pounced on Carl Mays for four hits and two runs before the first out was recorded. Before the inning ended, a ground out and another hit had brought two more Giants across the plate, enough to survive Aaron Ward's second Series home run for a 4–3 win.

Game 5, the clincher, showed Nehf the winner by two runs at game's end, but the game went back and forth before the outcome was decided. Nehf gave up only five hits—all singles—but all of them contributed toward scoring Yankees runs in the first, fifth, and seventh innings. The Giants took the lead in the second with a pair of runs, but again fell behind until four hits and a walk in the eighth undid pitcher Joe Bush's fine effort, giving the Giants three additional runs and John McGraw his third world title.

NY (N)

PLAYER/POS	AVG	G	AB	R	H	2B	3B	HR	RB	BB	SO	SB
Dave Bancroft, ss	.211	5	19	4	4	0	0	0	2	2	1	0
Jesse Barnes, p	.000	1	4	0	0	0	0	0	0	0	1	0
Bill Cunningham, of	.200	4	10	0	2	0	0	0	2	2	1	0
Frankie Frisch, 2b	.471	5	17	3	8	1	0	0	2	1	0	1
Heinie Groh, 3b	.474	5	19	4	9	0	1	0	0	2	1	0
George Kelly, 1b	.278	5	18	0	5	0	0	0	2	0	3	0
Lee King, of	1.000	2	1	0	1	0	0	0	1	0	0	0
Hugh McQuillan, p	.250	1	4	1	1	1	0	0	0	0	1	0
Irish Meusel, of	.250	5	20	3	5	0	0	1	7	0	1	0
Art Nehf, p	.000	2	3	0	0	0	0	0	0	2	0	0
Rosy Ryan, p	.000	1	0	0	0	0	0	0	0	0	0	0
Jack Scott, p	.250	1	4	0	1	0	0	0	0	0	1	0
Earl Smith, c-1	.143	4	7	0	1	0	0	0	0	0	2	0
Frank Snyder, c	.333	4	15	1	5	0	0	0	0	0	1	0
Casey Stengel, of	.400	2	5	0	2	0	0	0	0	0	1	0
Ross Youngs, of	.375	5	16	2	6	0	0	0	2	3	1	0
TOTAL	.309		162	18	50	2	1	1	18	12	15	1

PITCHER	W	L	ERA	G	GS	CG	SV	SHO	IP	H	ER	BB	SO
Jesse Barnes	0	0	1.80	1	1	1	0	0	10.0	8	2	2	6
Hugh McQuillan	1	0	3.00	1	1	1	0	0	9.0	8	3	2	4
Art Nehf	1	0	2.25	2	2	1	0	0	16.0	11	4	3	6
Rosy Ryan	1	0	0.00	1	0	0	0	0	2.0	1	0	0	2
Jack Scott	1	0	0.00	1	1	1	0	1	9.0	4	0	1	2
TOTAL	4	0	1.76	6	5	4	0	1	46.0	32	9	8	20

NY (A)

PLAYER/POS	AVG	G	AB	R	H	2B	3B	HR	RB	BB	SO	SB
Frank Baker, ph	.000	1	1	0	0	0	0	0	0	0	0	0
Joe Bush, p	.167	2	6	0	1	0	0	0	1	0	0	0
Joe Dugan, 3b	.250	5	20	4	5	1	0	0	0	0	1	0
Waite Hoyt, p	.500	2	2	0	1	0	0	0	0	0	0	0
Sam Jones, p	.000	2	0	0	0	0	0	0	0	0	0	0
Carl Mays, p	.000	1	2	0	0	0	0	0	0	0	0	0
Norm McMillan, of	.000	1	2	0	0	0	0	0	0	0	0	0
Mike McNally, 2b	.000	1	0	0	0	0	0	0	0	0	0	0
Bob Meusel, of	.300	5	20	2	6	1	0	0	2	1	3	1
Wally Pipp, 1b	.286	5	21	0	6	1	0	0	3	0	2	1
Babe Ruth, of	.118	5	17	1	2	1	0	0	1	2	3	0
Wally Schang, c	.188	5	16	0	3	1	0	0	0	0	3	0
Everett Scott, ss	.143	5	14	0	2	0	0	0	1	1	0	0
Bob Shawkey, p	.000	1	4	0	0	0	0	0	0	0	1	0
Elmer Smith, ph	.000	2	2	0	0	0	0	0	0	0	2	0
Aaron Ward, 2b	.154	5	13	3	2	0	0	2	3	3	3	0
Whitey Witt, of	.222	5	18	1	4	1	1	0	0	1	2	0
TOTAL	.203		158	11	32	6	1	2	11	8	20	2

PITCHER	W	L	ERA	G	GS	CG	SV	SHO	IP	H	ER	BB	SO
Joe Bush	0	2	4.80	2	2	1	0	0	15.0	21	8	5	6
Waite Hoyt	0	1	1.13	2	1	0	0	0	8.0	11	1	2	4
Sam Jones	0	0	0.00	2	0	0	0	0	2.0	1	0	1	0
Carl Mays	0	1	4.50	1	1	0	0	0	8.0	9	4	2	1
Bob Shawkey	0	0	2.70	1	1	1	0	0	10.0	8	3	2	4
TOTAL	0	4	3.35	8	5	2	0	0	43.0	50	16	12	15

GAME 1 AT NY -N OCT 4

NY-A	000 001 100		2	7	0
NY-N	**000 000 03X**		**3**	**11**	**3**

Pitchers: BUSH, Hoyt (8) vs Nehf, RYAN (8)
Attendance: 36,514

GAME 2 AT NY -A OCT 5

NY-N	300 000 000 0	3	8	1
NY-A	100 100 010 0	3	8	0

Pitchers: Barnes vs Shawkey
Home Runs: E.Meusel-NY(N), Ward-NY(A)
Attendance: 37,020

GAME 3 AT NY -N OCT 6

NY-A	000 000 000	0	4	1
NY-N	**002 000 10X**	**3**	**12**	**1**

Pitchers: HOYT, Jones (8) vs J.SCOTT
Attendance: 37,620

GAME 4 AT NY -A OCT 7

NY-N	**000 040 000**	**4**	**9**	**1**
NY-A	200 000 100	3	8	0

Pitchers: McQUILLAN vs MAYS, Jones (9)
Home Runs: Ward-NY(A)
Attendance: 36,242

GAME 5 AT NY -N OCT 8

NY-A	100 010 100	3	5	0
NY-N	**020 000 03X**	**5**	**10**	**0**

Pitchers: BUSH vs NEHF
Attendance: 38,551

After two Series played entirely in the Polo Grounds, the Giants and Yankees in 1923 had Yankee Stadium across the river to play alternate games in. Celebrating the opener in the new "house that Ruth built," the Yankees took an early three-run lead. In the third inning, though, the Giants drove out starter Waite Hoyt, emerging with four runs. Reliever Joe Bush prevented further scoring for several innings as the Yankees picked up a tying run in the seventh. But with the game still knotted in the top of the ninth, Casey Stengel legged out an inside-the-park homer to win it for the Giants.

Babe Ruth gave Herb Pennock his first World Series win with a pair of homers in Game 2. The first, a solo blast over the roof in right, broke a 1–1 tie in the fourth, and the second, an inning later, concluded the Yankees scoring in their 4–2 win that evened the Series. Stengel sent the Giants ahead in the seventh inning of Game 3, lifting a home run over the fence for the game's only score. The run gave Art Nehf the win in his duel with Sad Sam Jones, and again gave the Giants the Series lead.

Ross Youngs's fourth hit of Game 4, an inside-the-park homer into the Polo Grounds' deep outfield, gave the Giants a fourth run to lead off the bottom of the ninth, but as a rally it fell short; the Yankees, took the game to even the Series. In Game 5 Joe Bush gave up only three Giant hits—a single, double, and triple to Irish Meusel. Irish scored the only Giant run, but his Yankee brother Bob drove in three runs with his three hits—sharing RBI honors with Joe Dugan, whose four hits included the Series' third inside-the-park home run, a three-run shot in the second inning. Final score: 8–1.

In Game 6 Yankees starter Herb Pennock yielded four runs in his seven innings on the mound and seemed on the edge of defeat. But in the top of the eighth, Art Nehf (who had pitched one-hit ball since Ruth homered in the first) lost his stuff. With one out, two singles followed by two walks (on eight pitches) forced in a run. Rosy Ryan replaced Nehf and walked in another run. Ruth struck out, but Bob Meusel's single and a wild throw from center cleared the bases to put the Yankees ahead 6–4, where they remained to game's end for their first world championship.

New York Yankees (AL), 4; New York Giants (NL), 2

NY (A)

PLAYER/POS	AVG	G	AB	R	H	2B	3B	HR	RB	BB	SO	SB
Joe Bush, p-3	.429	4	7	2	3	1	0	0	1	1	1	0
Joe Dugan, 3b	.280	6	25	5	7	2	1	1	5	3	0	0
Hinky Haines, of	.000	2	1	1	0	0	0	0	0	0	0	0
Harvey Hendrick, ph	.000	1	1	0	0	0	0	0	0	0	0	0
Fred Hofmann, ph	.000	2	1	0	0	0	0	0	0	1	0	0
Waite Hoyt, p	.000	1	1	0	0	0	0	0	0	0	1	0
Ernie Johnson, ss-1	.000	2	0	1	0	0	0	0	0	0	0	0
Sam Jones, p	.000	2	2	0	0	0	0	0	0	0	1	0
Bob Meusel, of	.269	6	26	1	7	1	2	0	8	0	3	0
Herb Pennock, p	.000	3	6	0	0	0	0	0	0	0	2	0
Wally Pipp, 1b	.250	6	20	2	5	0	0	0	2	4	1	0
Babe Ruth, of-6,1b-1	.368	6	19	8	7	1	1	3	3	8	6	0
Wally Schang, c	.318	6	22	3	7	1	0	0	0	1	2	0
Everett Scott, ss	.318	6	22	2	7	0	0	0	3	0	1	0
Bob Shawkey, p	.333	1	3	0	1	0	0	0	1	0	0	0
Aaron Ward, 2b	.417	6	24	4	10	0	0	1	2	1	3	1
Whitey Witt, of	.240	6	25	1	6	2	0	0	4	1	1	0
TOTAL	.293		205	30	60	8	4	5	29	20	22	1

PITCHER	W	L	ERA	G	GS	CG	SV	SHO	IP	H	ER	BB	SO
Joe Bush	1	1	1.08	3	1	1	0	0	16.2	7	2	4	5
Waite Hoyt	0	0	15.43	1	1	0	0	0	2.1	4	4	1	0
Sam Jones	0	1	0.90	2	1	0	1	0	10.0	5	1	2	3
Herb Pennock	2	0	3.63	3	2	1	1	0	17.1	19	7	1	8
Bob Shawkey	1	0	3.52	1	1	0	0	0	7.2	12	3	4	2
TOTAL	4	2	2.83	10	6	2	2	0	54.0	47	17	12	18

NY (N)

PLAYER/POS	AVG	G	AB	R	H	2B	3B	HR	RB	BB	SO	SB
Dave Bancroft, ss	.083	6	24	1	2	0	0	0	1	1	2	1
Virgil Barnes, p	.000	2	1	0	0	0	0	0	0	0	1	0
Jack Bentley, p-2	.600	5	5	0	3	1	0	0	0	0	0	0
Bill Cunningham, of-3	.143	4	7	0	1	0	0	0	1	0	1	0
Frankie Frisch, 2b	.400	6	25	2	10	0	1	0	1	0	0	0
Dinty Gearin, pr	.000	1	0	0	0	0	0	0	0	0	0	0
Hank Gowdy, c-2	.000	3	4	0	0	0	0	0	0	1	0	0
Heinie Groh, 3b	.182	6	22	3	4	0	1	0	2	3	1	0
Travis Jackson, ph	.000	1	1	0	0	0	0	0	0	0	0	0
Claude Jonnard, p	.000	2	0	0	0	0	0	0	0	0	0	0
George Kelly, 1b	.182	6	22	1	4	0	0	0	1	1	2	0
Freddie Maguire, pr	.000	2	0	1	0	0	0	0	0	0	0	0
Hugh McQuillan, p	.000	2	3	0	0	0	0	0	0	0	1	0
Irish Meusel, of	.280	6	25	3	7	1	1	1	2	0	2	0
Art Nehf, p	.167	2	6	0	1	0	0	0	0	0	4	0
Jimmy O'Connell, ph	.000	2	1	0	0	0	0	0	0	0	1	0
Rosy Ryan, p	.000	3	2	0	0	0	0	0	0	0	1	0
Jack Scott, p	.000	2	1	0	0	0	0	0	0	0	0	0
Frank Snyder, c	.118	5	17	1	2	0	0	1	2	0	2	0
Casey Stengel, of	.417	6	12	3	5	0	0	2	4	4	0	0
Mule Watson, p	.000	1	0	0	0	0	0	0	0	0	0	0
Ross Youngs, of	.348	6	23	2	8	0	0	1	3	2	0	0
TOTAL	.234		201	17	47	2	3	5	17	12	18	1

PITCHER	W	L	ERA	G	GS	CG	SV	SHO	IP	H	ER	BB	SO
Virgil Barnes	0	0	0.00	2	0	0	0	0	4.2	4	0	0	4
Jack Bentley	0	1	9.45	2	1	0	0	0	6.2	10	7	4	1
Claude Jonnard	0	0	0.00	2	0	0	0	0	2.0	1	0	1	1
Hugh McQuillan	0	1	5.00	2	1	0	0	0	9.0	11	5	4	3
Art Nehf	1	1	2.76	2	2	1	0	1	16.1	10	5	6	7
Rosy Ryan	1	0	0.96	3	0	0	0	0	9.1	11	1	3	3
Jack Scott	0	1	12.00	2	1	0	0	0	3.0	9	4	1	2
Mule Watson	0	0	13.50	1	1	0	0	0	2.0	4	3	1	1
TOTAL	2	4	4.25	16	6	1	0	1	53.0	60	25	20	22

GAME 1 AT NY -A OCT 10

				R	H	E
NY-N	004	000	001	5	8	0
NY-A	120	000	100	4	12	1

Pitchers: Watson, RYAN (3) vs Hoyt, BUSH (3)
Home Runs: Stengel-NY(N)
Attendance: 55,307

GAME 2 AT NY -N OCT 11

				R	H	E
NY-A	010	210	000	4	10	0
NY-N	010	001	000	2	9	2

Pitchers: PENNOCK vs McQUILLAN, Bentley (4)
Home Runs: Ward-NY(A), E.Meusel-NY(N), Ruth-NY(A) (2)
Attendance: 40,402

GAME 3 AT NY -A OCT 12

				R	H	E
NY-N	000	000	100	1	4	0
NY-A	000	000	000	0	6	1

Pitchers: NEHF vs JONES, Bush (9)
Home Runs: Stengel-NY(N)
Attendance: 62,430

GAME 4 AT NY -N OCT 13

				R	H	E
NY-A	061	100	000	8	13	1
NY-N	000	000	031	4	13	1

Pitchers: SHAWKEY, Pennock (8) vs J.SCOTT, Ryan (2), McQuillan (2), Jonnard (8), Barnes (9)
Home Runs: Youngs-NY(N)
Attendance: 46,302

GAME 5 AT NY -A OCT 14

				R	H	E
NY-N	010	000	000	1	3	2
NY-A	340	100	00X	8	14	0

Pitchers: BENTLEY, J.Scott (2), Barnes (4), Jonnard (8) vs BUSH
Home Runs: Dugan-NY(A)
Attendance: 62,817

GAME 6 AT NY -N OCT 15

				R	H	E
NY-A	100	000	050	6	5	0
NY-N	100	111	000	4	10	1

Pitchers: PENNOCK, Jones (8) vs NEHF, Ryan (8)
Home Runs: Ruth-NY(A), Snyder-NY(N)
Attendance: 34,172

Washington Senators (AL), 4; New York Giants (NL), 3

Four of the seven games in this exciting Series were decided by one run—two of them after 12 innings. Pitcher Walter Johnson, in his first World Series after 18 big-league seasons and 376 victories, opened for Washington against the Giants' Art Nehf. Although 14 Giants reached base on hits or walks in the first nine innings, only two scored—George Kelly and Bill Terry, both of whom homered. In the bottom of the ninth, the Senators scored their second run to send the game into extra innings. Johnson shut out the Giants for two more frames, but in the top of the 12th, two walks and three singles put New York ahead by two. Washington came back with a run and had a man on third. But Kelly, making his only appearance at second base, stopped Goose Goslin's grounder with his bare hand, and Nehf had the Giants' first win.

Goslin and manager/second baseman Bucky Harris homered in Game 2 to give the Senators a 3–0 lead through six innings. The Giants scored once in the seventh and drove out starter Tom Zachary with two more in the ninth to tie the game, but in the last of the ninth Roger Peckinpaugh doubled in the tie breaker to even the Series.

The Giants took an early lead in Game 3 and held it to retake the Series lead, but Washington (led by Goslin's three-run homer in the third) unleashed a 13-hit, seven-run attack the next day to even the Series once more. In Game 5, though, New York pulled ahead again, defeating Johnson a second time as winning pitcher Jack Bentley put the Giants into the lead for good with a two-run homer in the fifth. In Game 6, Washington's two runs in the fifth inning overcame a first-inning Giant run and gave Tom Zachary all he needed for the Senators' third win, which set the stage for one of the most memorable games in Series history.

Washington scored first in Game 7 on manager Harris' homer in the fourth inning, but the Giants scored three runs in the sixth (two of them on Senator errors) to go ahead, 3–1. In the last of the eighth, though, Harris' grounder to third bounced over the head of rookie Freddie Lindstrom for two more runs and a 3–3 tie. Walter Johnson came in to face the Giants in the ninth, and shut them out through the 12th, fanning five. Then in the bottom of the 12th, with one out, Muddy Ruel (given a second chance after Giants catcher Hank Gowdy caught his foot in his mask and missed Ruel's pop foul) doubled to left. Pitcher Johnson then reached first when shortstop Travis Jackson bobbled what should have been a third-out grounder. With men on second and first, Earl McNeely bounced to Lindstrom at third. But again the ball bounded over Lindstrom's head, and Ruel raced home with Johnson's first Series win and Washington's only world championship.

WAS (A)

PLAYER/POS	AVG	G	AB	R	H	2B	3B	HR	RB	BB	SO	SB
Ossie Bluege, ss-5,3b-4	.192	7	26	2	5	0	0	0	3	3	4	1
Goose Goslin, of	.344	7	32	4	11	1	0	3	7	0	7	0
Bucky Harris, 2b	.333	7	33	5	11	0	0	2	7	1	4	0
Walter Johnson, p	.111	3	9	0	1	0	0	0	0	0	0	0
Joe Judge, 1b	.385	7	26	4	10	1	0	0	0	5	2	0
Nemo Leibold, of-1	.167	3	6	1	1	1	0	0	0	1	0	0
Firpo Marberry, p	.000	4	2	0	0	0	0	0	0	0	0	0
Joe Martina, p	.000	1	0	0	0	0	0	0	0	0	0	0
Earl McNeely, of	.222	7	27	4	6	3	0	0	1	4	4	1
Ralph Miller, 3b	.182	4	11	0	2	0	0	0	2	1	0	0
George Mogridge, p	.000	2	5	0	0	0	0	0	0	0	5	0
Curly Ogden, p	.000	1	0	0	0	0	0	0	0	0	0	0
Roger Peckinpaugh, ss	.417	4	12	1	5	2	0	0	2	1	0	1
Sam Rice, of	.207	7	29	2	6	0	0	0	1	3	2	2
Muddy Ruel, c	.095	7	21	2	2	1	0	0	0	6	1	0
Allan Russell, p	.000	1	0	0	0	0	0	0	0	0	0	0
Mule Shirley, ph	.500	3	2	1	1	0	0	0	1	0	0	0
By Speece, p	.000	1	0	0	0	0	0	0	0	0	0	0
Bennie Tate, ph	.000	3	0	0	0	0	0	0	1	3	0	0
Tommy Taylor, 3b	.000	3	2	0	0	0	0	0	0	0	2	0
Tom Zachary, p	.000	2	5	0	0	0	0	0	0	1	3	0
TOTAL	.246		248	26	61	9	0	5	25	29	34	5

PITCHER	W	L	ERA	G	GS	CG	SV	SHO	IP	H	ER	BB	SO
Walter Johnson	1	2	2.25	3	2	2	0	0	24.0	30	6	11	20
Firpo Marberry	0	1	1.13	4	1	0	2	0	8.0	9	1	4	10
Joe Martina	0	0	0.00	1	0	0	0	0	1.0	0	0	0	1
George Mogridge	1	0	2.25	2	1	0	0	0	12.0	7	3	6	5
Curly Ogden	0	0	0.00	1	1	0	0	0	0.1	0	0	1	1
Allan Russell	0	0	3.00	1	0	0	0	0	3.0	4	1	0	0
By Speece	0	0	9.00	1	0	0	0	0	1.0	3	1	0	0
Tom Zachary	2	0	2.04	2	2	1	0	0	17.2	13	4	3	3
TOTAL	4	3	2.15	15	7	3	2	0	67.0	66	16	25	40

NY (N)

PLAYER/POS	AVG	G	AB	R	H	2B	3B	HR	RB	BB	SO	SB
Harry Baldwin, p	.000	1	0	0	0	0	0	0	0	0	0	0
Virgil Barnes, p	.000	2	4	0	0	0	0	0	0	1	2	0
Jack Bentley, p-3	.286	5	7	1	2	0	0	1	2	1	1	0
Wayland Dean, p	.000	1	0	0	0	0	0	0	0	0	0	0
Frankie Frisch, 2b-7,3b-1	.333	7	30	1	10	4	1	0	0	4	1	1
Hank Gowdy, c	.259	7	27	4	7	0	0	0	1	2	2	0
Heinie Groh, ph	1.000	1	1	0	1	0	0	0	0	0	0	0
Travis Jackson, ss	.074	7	27	3	2	0	0	0	1	1	4	1
Claude Jonnard, p	.000	1	0	0	0	0	0	0	0	0	0	0
George Kelly, 1b-4,of-4,2b-1	.290	7	31	7	9	1	0	1	4	1	8	0
Fred Lindstrom, 3b	.333	7	30	1	10	2	0	0	4	3	6	0
Hugh McQuillan, p	1.000	3	1	0	1	0	0	0	1	1	0	0
Irish Meusel, of	.154	4	13	0	2	0	0	0	1	2	0	0
Art Nehf, p	.429	3	7	1	3	0	0	0	0	0	0	0
Rosy Ryan, p	.500	2	2	1	1	0	0	1	2	0	0	0
Frank Snyder, ph	.000	1	1	0	0	0	0	0	0	0	0	0
Billy Southworth, of-2	.000	5	1	1	0	0	0	0	0	0	0	0
Bill Terry, 1b-4	.429	5	14	3	6	0	1	1	1	3	1	0
Mule Watson, p	.000	1	0	0	0	0	0	0	0	0	0	0
Hack Wilson, of	.233	7	30	1	7	1	0	0	3	1	9	0
Ross Youngs, of	.185	7	27	3	5	1	0	0	1	5	6	1
TOTAL	.261		253	27	66	9	2	4	21	25	40	3

PITCHER	W	L	ERA	G	GS	CG	SV	SHO	IP	H	ER	BB	SO
Harry Baldwin	0	0	0.00	1	0	0	0	0	2.0	1	0	0	1
Virgil Barnes	0	1	5.68	2	2	0	0	0	12.2	15	8	1	9
Jack Bentley	1	2	3.18	3	2	1	0	0	17.0	18	6	8	10
Wayland Dean	0	0	4.50	1	0	0	0	0	2.0	3	1	0	2
Claude Jonnard	0	0	–	1	0	0	0	0	0.0	0	0	1	0
Hugh McQuillan	0	1	2.57	3	1	0	1	0	7.0	2	2	6	2
Art Nehf	1	1	1.83	3	2	1	0	0	19.2	15	4	9	7
Rosy Ryan	0	0	3.18	2	0	0	0	0	5.2	7	2	4	3
Mule Watson	0	0	0.00	1	0	0	1	0	0.2	0	0	0	0
TOTAL	3	4	3.10	17	7	2	2	0	66.2	61	23	29	34

GAME 1 AT WAS OCT 4

		R	H	E
NY	010 100 000 002	4	14	1
WAS	000 001 001 001	3	10	1

Pitchers: NEHF vs JOHNSON
Home Runs: Kelly-NY, Terry-NY
Attendance: 35,760

GAME 2 AT WAS OCT 5

		R	H	E
NY	000 000 102	3	6	0
WAS	200 010 001	4	6	1

Pitchers: BENTLEY vs ZACHARY, Marberry (9)
Home Runs: Goslin-WAS, Harris-WAS
Attendance: 35,922

GAME 3 AT NY OCT 6

		R	H	E
WAS	000 200 011	4	9	2
NY	021 101 01X	6	12	0

Pitchers: MARBERRY, Russell (4), Martina (7), Speece (8) vs McQUILLAN, Ryan (4), Jonnard (9), Watson (9)
Home Runs: Ryan-NY
Attendance: 47,608

GAME 4 AT NY OCT 7

		R	H	E
WAS	003 020 020	7	13	3
NY	100 001 011	4	6	1

Pitchers: MOGRIDGE, Marberry (8) vs BARNES, Baldwin (6), Dean (8)
Home Runs: Goslin-WAS
Attendance: 49,243

GAME 5 AT NY OCT 8

		R	H	E
WAS	000 100 010	2	9	1
NY	001 020 03X	6	13	0

Pitchers: JOHNSON vs BENTLEY, McQuillan (8)
Home Runs: Bentley-NY, Goslin-WAS
Attendance: 49,211

GAME 6 AT WAS OCT 9

		R	H	E
NY	100 000 000	1	7	1
WAS	000 020 00X	2	4	0

Pitchers: NEHF, Ryan (8) vs ZACHARY
Attendance: 34,254

GAME 7 AT WAS OCT 10

		R	H	E
NY	000 003 000 000	3	8	3
WAS	000 100 020 001	4	10	4

Pitchers: Barnes, McQuillan (8), Nehf (10), BENTLEY (11) vs Ogden, Mogridge (1), Marberry (6), JOHNSON (9)
Home Runs: Harris-WAS
Attendance: 31,667

Repeating as pennant winners, the Senators found themselves again locked in a tight Series, this time with the Pirates, who hadn't won a pennant since 1909. Again Walter Johnson pitched the Series opener, winning this time with a strong five-hit, 10-strikeout performance, giving up only one run on Pie Traynor's homer in the fifth. Home runs by Pirates Kiki Cuyler and Glenn Wright and Senator Joe Judge accounted for four of the five runs scored in Game 2, in which Vic Aldridge dueled Stan Coveleski to a narrow 3–2 Pittsburgh win, evening the Series.

Washington took Games 3 and 4, though, for a 3–1 Series advantage, Goose Goslin's solo homer in the sixth inning providing the margin of victory in Game 3, and homers by Goslin (for three runs) and Joe Harris the next day providing all the scoring as Johnson shut the Pirates out.

Harris hit his third Series homer in Game 5, but Pittsburgh overwhelmed Coveleski as he lost to Aldridge for a second time. And although Goslin's third homer gave the Senators an early lead in Game 6, Pittsburgh's Ray Kremer shut Washington out from the third inning on as his teammates pulled even with two runs in the bottom of the third, and Eddie Moore's homer in the fifth gave him the run he needed for a win that sent the Series into a seventh game.

Both clubs went with their best in the finale as Johnson, winner of Games 1 and 4, faced Aldridge, victor in Games 2 and 5. But Aldridge was wild, issuing three walks and two wild pitches in addition to two hits before being yanked with only one out in the top of the first. Johnson was hardly more effective: although he lasted the whole game, he gave up 15 hits and five earned runs. But if there was a Series goat, it would have to be Washington shortstop Roger Peckinpaugh, the American League MVP. Though he drove in a run in the first and homered for another in the eighth, his dropped pop fly in the seventh and wild throw in the eighth (his seventh and eighth errors of the Series) opened the way to four unearned runs and Pittsburgh's 9–7 triumph.

Pittsburgh Pirates (NL), 4; Washington Senators (AL), 3

PIT (N)

PLAYER/POS	AVG	G	AB	R	H	2B	3B	HR	RB	BB	SO	SB
Babe Adams, p	.000	1	0	0	0	0	0	0	0	0	0	0
Vic Aldridge, p	.000	3	7	0	0	0	0	0	0	0	0	0
Clyde Barnhart, of	.250	7	28	1	7	1	0	0	5	3	5	1
Carson Bigbee, of-1	.333	4	3	1	1	1	0	0	1	0	0	1
Max Carey, of	.458	7	24	6	11	4	0	0	2	2	3	3
Kiki Cuyler, of	.269	7	26	3	7	3	0	1	6	1	4	0
Johnny Gooch, c	.000	3	3	0	0	0	0	0	0	0	0	0
George Grantham, 1b-4	.133	5	15	0	2	0	0	0	0	0	3	1
Ray Kremer, p	.143	3	7	0	1	0	0	0	1	0	5	0
Stuffy McInnis, 1b-3	.286	4	14	0	4	0	0	0	1	0	2	0
Lee Meadows, p	.000	1	1	0	0	0	0	0	0	1	1	0
Eddie Moore, 2b	.231	7	26	7	6	1	0	1	2	5	2	0
Johnny Morrison, p	.500	3	2	1	1	0	0	0	0	0	0	0
Red Oldham, p	.000	1	0	0	0	0	0	0	0	0	0	0
Earl Smith, c	.350	6	20	0	7	1	0	0	0	1	2	0
Pie Traynor, 3b	.346	7	26	2	9	0	2	1	4	3	1	1
Glenn Wright, ss	.185	7	27	3	5	1	0	1	3	1	4	0
Emil Yde, p-1	.000	2	1	1	0	0	0	0	0	0	0	0
TOTAL	.265		230	25	61	12	2	4	25	17	32	7

PITCHER	W	L	ERA	G	GS	CG	SV	SHO	IP	H	ER	BB	SO
Babe Adams	0	0	0.00	1	0	0	0	0	1.0	2	0	0	0
Vic Aldridge	2	0	4.42	3	3	2	0	0	18.1	18	9	9	9
Ray Kremer	2	1	3.00	3	2	2	0	0	21.0	17	7	4	9
Lee Meadows	0	1	3.38	1	1	0	0	0	8.0	6	3	0	4
Johnny Morrison	0	0	2.89	3	0	0	0	0	9.1	11	3	1	7
Red Oldham	0	0	0.00	1	0	0	1	0	1.0	0	0	0	2
Emil Yde	0	1	11.57	1	1	0	0	0	2.1	5	3	3	1
TOTAL	4	1	3.69	13	7	4	1	0	61.0	59	25	17	32

WAS (A)

PLAYER/POS	AVG	G	AB	R	H	2B	3B	HR	RB	BB	SO	SB
Spencer Adams, 2b-1	.000	2	1	0	0	0	0	0	0	0	0	0
Win Ballou, p	.000	2	0	0	0	0	0	0	0	0	0	0
Ossie Bluege, 3b	.278	5	18	2	5	1	0	0	2	0	4	0
Stan Coveleski, p	.000	2	3	0	0	0	0	0	0	1	2	0
Alex Ferguson, p	.000	2	4	0	0	0	0	0	0	0	3	0
Goose Goslin, of	.308	7	26	6	8	1	0	3	6	3	3	0
Joe Harris, of	.440	7	25	5	11	2	0	3	6	3	4	0
Bucky Harris, 2b	.087	7	23	2	2	0	0	0	0	1	3	0
Walter Johnson, p	.091	3	11	0	1	0	0	0	0	0	3	0
Joe Judge, 1b	.174	7	23	2	4	1	0	1	4	3	2	0
Nemo Leibold, ph	.500	3	2	1	1	1	0	0	0	1	0	0
Firpo Marberry, p	.000	2	0	0	0	0	0	0	0	0	0	0
Earl McNeely, of-2	.000	4	0	2	0	0	0	0	0	0	0	1
Buddy Myer, 3b	.250	3	8	0	2	0	0	0	0	1	2	0
Roger Peckinpaugh, ss	.250	7	24	1	6	1	0	1	3	1	2	1
Sam Rice, of	.364	7	33	5	12	0	0	0	3	0	1	0
Muddy Ruel, c	.316	7	19	0	6	1	0	0	1	3	2	0
Dutch Ruether, ph	.000	1	1	0	0	0	0	0	0	0	1	0
Hank Severeid, c	.333	1	3	0	1	0	0	0	0	0	0	0
Bobby Veach, ph	.000	2	1	0	0	0	0	0	1	0	0	0
Tom Zachary, p	.000	1	0	0	0	0	0	0	0	0	0	0
TOTAL	.262		225	26	59	8	0	8	26	17	32	2

PITCHER	W	L	ERA	G	GS	CG	SV	SHO	IP	H	ER	BB	SO
Win Ballou	0	0	0.00	2	0	0	0	0	1.2	0	0	1	1
Stan Coveleski	0	2	3.77	2	2	1	0	0	14.1	16	6	5	3
Alex Ferguson	1	1	3.21	2	2	0	0	0	14.0	13	5	6	11
Walter Johnson	2	1	2.08	3	3	3	0	1	26.0	26	6	4	15
Firpo Marberry	0	0	0.00	2	0	0	1	0	2.1	3	0	0	2
Tom Zachary	0	0	10.80	1	0	0	0	0	1.2	3	2	1	0
TOTAL	3	4	2.85	12	7	4	1	1	60.0	61	19	17	32

GAME 1 AT PIT OCT 7

				R	H	E
WAS	010	020	001	4	8	1
PIT	000	010	000	1	5	0

Pitchers: JOHNSON vs MEADOWS, Morrison (9)
Home Runs: J.Harris-WAS, Traynor-PIT
Attendance: 41,723

GAME 2 AT PIT OCT 8

				R	H	E
WAS	010	000	001	2	8	2
PIT	000	100	02X	3	7	0

Pitchers: COVELESKI vs ALDRIDGE
Home Runs: Judge-WAS, Wright-PIT, Cuyler-PIT
Attendance: 43,364

GAME 3 AT WAS OCT 10

				R	H	E
PIT	010	101	000	3	8	3
WAS	001	001	20X	4	10	1

Pitchers: KREMER vs FERGUSON, Marberry (8)
Home Runs: Goslin-WAS
Attendance: 36,495

GAME 4 AT WAS OCT 11

				R	H	E
PIT	000	000	000	0	6	1
WAS	004	000	00X	4	12	0

Pitchers: YDE, Morrison (3), Adams (8) vs JOHNSON
Home Runs: Goslin-WAS, J.Harris-WAS
Attendance: 38,701

GAME 5 AT WAS OCT 12

				R	H	E
PIT	002	000	211	6	13	0
WAS	100	100	100	3	8	1

Pitchers: ALDRIDGE vs COVELESKI, Ballou (7), Zachary (8), Marberry (9)
Home Runs: J.Harris-WAS
Attendance: 35,899

GAME 6 AT PIT OCT 13

				R	H	E
WAS	110	000	000	2	6	2
PIT	002	010	00X	3	7	1

Pitchers: FERGUSON, Ballou (8) vs KREMER
Home Runs: Goslin-WAS, Moore-PIT
Attendance: 43,810

GAME 7 AT PIT OCT 15

				R	H	E
WAS	400	200	010	7	7	2
PIT	003	010	23X	9	15	2

Pitchers: JOHNSON vs Aldridge, Morrison (1), KREMER (5), Oldham (9)
Home Runs: Peckinpaugh-WAS
Attendance: 42,856

The Yankees, returning to the World Series after a two-year absence, faced the Cardinals, who had won their first pennant since joining the National League in 1892. Both clubs led their league in slugging and runs scored; this power erupted occasionally in the Series, but over all, pitching dominated as each staff bettered its regular-season earned run average by nearly a run per game.

Herb Pennock of the Yankees pitched a splendid three-hitter in the opener. After yielding two hits and a run in the first inning, he shut out the Cards the rest of the way, holding them hitless until the ninth. St. Louis starter Bill Sherdel also pitched effectively, but three walks in the first and a hit-sacrifice-hit sandwich in the sixth brought in enough runs to beat him.

In Game 2, the veteran Grover Cleveland Alexander evened the Series, striking out 10 and holding the Yankees to four singles (three of them in the two-run second) as Billy Southworth and Tommy Thevenow homered for four of St. Louis's six runs. Two days later Jesse Haines put the Cards into the lead, winning the game both ways with a five-hit shutout and a two-run homer.

New York's big bats finally awoke in Game 4. Five Yankees doubled, and Babe Ruth hit three home runs (a World Series record) in a 14-hit, 10-run assault. Yankees pitcher Waite Hoyt also gave up 14 hits, but 12 were singles and only five runs scored. In contrast, Game 5 was a pitchers' duel. Pennock and Sherdel again faced each other and held the opposition to two runs apiece through nine innings. But in the 10th, rookie Tony Lazzeri's sacrifice fly gave New York a 3–2 lead, which Pennock held in the last of the 10th for his second win.

With St. Louis down three games to two, the Series moved to hostile New York for the final games. This didn't seem to trouble the Cardinals, who erupted in Game 6 for their own 10-run game, four of them driven in by Les Bell's first-inning single and seventh-inning home run. Alexander pitched a complete game for his second Series win, and came back the next day to relieve Haines in the seventh with a 3–2 lead and the bases full. He struck out Lazzeri to end the inning and kept the Yankees off the bases until he issued Babe Ruth his 11th Series walk with two away in the ninth. But Ruth, trying to steal second, was caught, and the Cards were world champions.

St. Louis Cardinals (NL), 4; New York Yankees (AL), 3

STL (N)

PLAYER/POS	AVG	G	AB	R	H	2B	3B	HR	RB	BB	SO	SB
Pete Alexander, p	.000	3	7	1	0	0	0	0	0	0	2	0
Hi Bell, p	.000	1	0	0	0	0	0	0	0	0	0	0
Les Bell, 3b	.259	7	27	4	7	1	0	1	6	2	5	0
Jim Bottomley, 1b	.345	7	29	4	10	3	0	0	5	1	2	0
Taylor Douthit, of	.267	4	15	3	4	2	0	0	1	3	2	0
Jake Flowers, ph	.000	3	3	0	0	0	0	0	0	0	1	0
Chick Hafey, of	.185	7	27	2	5	2	0	0	0	0	7	0
Jesse Haines, p	.600	3	5	1	3	0	0	1	2	0	1	0
Bill Hallahan, p	.000	1	0	0	0	0	0	0	0	0	0	0
Wattie Holm, of-4	.125	5	16	1	2	0	0	0	1	1	2	0
Rogers Hornsby, 2b	.250	7	28	2	7	1	0	0	4	2	2	1
Vic Keen, p	.000	1	0	0	0	0	0	0	0	0	0	0
Bob O'Farrell, c	.304	7	23	2	7	1	0	0	2	2	2	0
Art Reinhart, p	.000	1	0	0	0	0	0	0	0	0	0	0
Flint Rhem, p	.000	1	1	0	0	0	0	0	0	0	1	0
Bill Sherdel, p	.000	2	5	0	0	0	0	0	0	0	2	0
Billy Southworth, of	.345	7	29	6	10	1	1	1	4	0	0	1
Tommy Thevenow, ss	.417	7	24	5	10	1	0	1	4	0	1	0
Specs Toporcer, ph	.000	1	0	0	0	0	0	0	1	0	0	0
TOTAL	.272		239	31	65	12	1	4	30	11	30	2

PITCHER	W	L	ERA	G	GS	CG	SV	SHO	IP	H	ER	BB	SO
Pete Alexander	2	0	1.33	3	2	2	1	0	20.1	12	3	4	17
Hi Bell	0	0	9.00	1	0	0	0	0	2.0	4	2	1	1
Jesse Haines	2	0	1.08	3	2	1	0	1	16.2	13	2	9	5
Bill Hallahan	0	0	4.50	1	0	0	0	0	2.0	2	1	3	1
Vic Keen	0	0	0.00	1	0	0	0	0	1.0	0	0	0	0
Art Reinhart	0	1	∞	1	0	0	0	0	0.0	1	4	4	0
Flint Rhem	0	0	6.75	1	1	0	0	0	4.0	7	3	2	4
Bill Sherdel	0	2	2.12	2	2	1	0	0	17.0	15	4	8	3
TOTAL	4	3	2.71	13	7	4	1	1	63.0	54	19	31	31

NY (A)

PLAYER/POS	AVG	G	AB	R	H	2B	3B	HR	RB	BB	SO	SB
Spencer Adams, ph	.000	2	0	0	0	0	0	0	0	0	0	0
Pat Collins, c	.000	3	2	0	0	0	0	0	0	0	1	0
Earle Combs, of	.357	7	28	3	10	2	0	0	2	5	2	0
Joe Dugan, 3b	.333	7	24	2	8	1	0	0	2	1	1	0
Mike Gazella, 3b	.000	1	0	0	0	0	0	0	0	0	0	0
Lou Gehrig, 1b	.348	7	23	1	8	2	0	0	4	5	4	0
Waite Hoyt, p	.000	2	6	0	0	0	0	0	0	0	1	0
Sam Jones, p	.000	1	0	0	0	0	0	0	0	0	0	0
Mark Koenig, ss	.125	7	32	2	4	1	0	0	2	0	6	0
Tony Lazzeri, 2b	.192	7	26	2	5	1	0	0	3	1	6	0
Bob Meusel, of	.238	7	21	3	5	1	1	0	0	6	1	0
Ben Paschal, ph	.250	5	4	0	1	0	0	0	1	1	2	0
Herb Pennock, p	.143	3	7	1	1	1	0	0	0	0	0	0
Dutch Ruether, p-1	.000	3	4	0	0	0	0	0	0	0	0	0
Babe Ruth, of	.300	7	20	6	6	0	0	4	5	11	2	1
Hank Severeid, c	.273	7	22	1	6	1	0	0	1	1	2	0
Bob Shawkey, p	.000	3	2	0	0	0	0	0	0	0	1	0
Urban Shocker, p	.000	2	2	0	0	0	0	0	0	0	2	0
Myles Thomas, p	.000	2	0	0	0	0	0	0	0	0	0	0
TOTAL	.242		223	21	54	10	1	4	20	31	31	1

PITCHER	W	L	ERA	G	GS	CG	SV	SHO	IP	H	ER	BB	SO
Waite Hoyt	1	1	1.20	2	2	1	0	0	15.0	19	2	1	10
Sam Jones	0	0	9.00	1	0	0	0	0	1.0	2	1	2	1
Herb Pennock	2	0	1.23	3	2	2	0	0	22.0	13	3	4	8
Dutch Ruether	0	1	8.31	1	1	0	0	0	4.1	7	4	2	1
Bob Shawkey	0	1	5.40	3	1	0	0	0	10.0	8	6	2	7
Urban Shocker	0	1	5.87	2	1	0	0	0	7.2	13	5	0	3
Myles Thomas	0	0	3.00	2	0	0	0	0	3.0	3	1	0	0
TOTAL	3	4	3.14	14	7	3	0	0	63.0	65	22	11	30

GAME 1 AT NY OCT 2

		R	H	E
STL	100 000 000	1	3	1
NY	100 001 00X	2	6	0

Pitchers: SHERDEL, Haines (8) vs PENNOCK
Attendance: 61,658

GAME 2 AT NY OCT 3

		R	H	E
STL	002 000 301	6	12	1
NY	020 000 000	2	4	0

Pitchers: ALEXANDER vs SHOCKER, Shawkey (8), Jones (9)
Home Runs: Southworth-STL, Thevenow-STL
Attendance: 63,600

GAME 3 AT STL OCT 5

		R	H	E
NY	000 000 000	0	5	1
STL	000 310 00X	4	8	0

Pitchers: RUETHER, Shawkey (5), Thomas (8) vs HAINES
Home Runs: Haines-STL
Attendance: 37,708

GAME 4 AT STL OCT 6

		R	H	E
NY	101 142 100	10	14	1
STL	100 300 001	5	14	0

Pitchers: HOYT vs Rhem, REINHART (5), H.Bell (5), Hallahan (7), Keen (9)
Home Runs: Ruth-NY (3)
Attendance: 38,825

GAME 5 AT STL OCT 7

		R	H	E
NY	000 001 001 1	3	9	1
STL	000 100 100 0	2	7	1

Pitchers: PENNOCK vs SHERDEL
Attendance: 39,552

GAME 6 AT NY OCT 9

		R	H	E
STL	300 010 501	10	13	2
NY	000 100 100	2	8	1

Pitchers: ALEXANDER vs SHAWKEY, Shocker (7), Thomas (8)
Home Runs: L.Bell-STL
Attendance: 48,615

GAME 7 AT NY OCT 10

		R	H	E
STL	000 300 000	3	8	0
NY	001 001 000	2	8	3

Pitchers: HAINES, Alexander (7) vs HOYT, Pennock (7)
Home Runs: Ruth-NY
Attendance: 38,093

New York Yankees (AL), 4; Pittsburgh Pirates (NL), 0

The Pirates, who struggled to a narrow pennant win in a four-team race, were no slouches at the bat. Their team batting average of .305 led the National League, and in the Waner brothers—Paul and Lloyd—and Pie Traynor they had three of the league's five top hitters. But in the World Series they came up against a Yankees team that is still widely regarded as the game's greatest ever. With 110 season victories and a 19-game margin over second-place Philadelphia, the Yankees led the American League in nearly every offensive category. Three Yankees—Earle Combs, Lou Gehrig, and Babe Ruth—hit over .350, and divided among them league crowns in runs, hits, doubles, triples, home runs (Ruth's 60), RBIs, and slugging average. The Yankees not only hit, but their pitching staff boasted the league's lowest earned run average.

In the Series, though, it was Pittsburgh's erratic play that brought about the first American League sweep. The Pirates scored four times off Waite Hoyt in Game 1, and might have won the game. But Paul Waner misplayed a Gehrig fly for a run-scoring triple in the first, and in the third, two Pirates errors led to three more runs. A final run in the fifth was all New York needed to win, 5–4.

The Yankees won the next two games more convincingly, with strong pitching and timely hitting. George Pipgras held Pittsburgh to two runs in Game 2 as his Yankees bunched seven of their 11 hits into the third and eighth innings (also taking advantage of two walks and a hit batsman in the eighth) for their six runs. And in Game 3—as Herb Pennock pitched perfectly into the eighth inning before yielding two hits and a run—the Yankees again bunched most of their hits into two innings, scoring two runs on Gehrig's first-inning triple and six more in the seventh, climaxed by Ruth's three-run homer.

Pittsburgh took advantage of two Yankees errors in the seventh inning of Game 4 to score two runs and tie the game at three-all. But in the last of the ninth, after the Pirates' Johnny Miljus had struck out Gehrig and Bob Meusel with the bases loaded, his second wild pitch of the inning undid him—Combs scored from third with the Series' winning run.

NY (A)

PLAYER/POS	AVG	G	AB	R	H	2B	3B	HR	RB	BB	SO	SB
Benny Bengough, c	.000	2	4	1	0	0	0	0	0	1	0	0
Pat Collins, c	.600	2	5	0	3	1	0	0	0	3	0	0
Earle Combs, of	.313	4	16	6	5	0	0	0	2	1	2	0
Joe Dugan, 3b	.200	4	15	2	3	0	0	0	0	0	0	0
Cedric Durst, ph	.000	1	1	0	0	0	0	0	0	0	0	0
Lou Gehrig, 1b	.308	4	13	2	4	2	2	0	4	3	3	0
Johnny Grabowski, c	.000	1	2	0	0	0	0	0	0	0	0	0
Waite Hoyt, p	.000	1	3	0	0	0	0	0	0	0	0	0
Mark Koenig, ss	.500	4	18	5	9	2	0	0	2	0	2	0
Tony Lazzeri, 2b	.267	4	15	1	4	1	0	0	2	1	4	0
Bob Meusel, of	.118	4	17	1	2	0	0	0	1	1	7	1
Wilcy Moore, p	.200	2	5	0	1	0	0	0	0	0	3	0
Herb Pennock, p	.000	1	4	1	0	0	0	0	1	0	1	0
George Pipgras, p	.333	1	3	0	1	0	0	0	0	1	1	0
Babe Ruth, of	.400	4	15	4	6	0	0	2	7	2	2	1
TOTAL	.279		136	23	38	6	2	2	19	13	25	2

PITCHER	W	L	ERA	G	GS	CG	SV	SHO	IP	H	ER	BB	SO
Waite Hoyt	1	0	4.91	1	1	0	0	0	7.1	8	4	1	2
Wilcy Moore	1	0	0.84	2	1	1	1	0	10.2	11	1	2	2
Herb Pennock	1	0	1.00	1	1	1	0	0	9.0	3	1	0	1
George Pipgras	1	0	2.00	1	1	1	0	0	9.0	7	2	1	2
TOTAL	4	0	2.00	5	4	3	1	0	36.0	29	8	4	7

PIT (N)

PLAYER/POS	AVG	G	AB	R	H	2B	3B	HR	RB	BB	SO	SB
Vic Aldridge, p	.000	1	2	0	0	0	0	0	0	0	0	0
Clyde Barnhart, of	.313	4	16	0	5	1	0	0	4	0	0	0
Fred Brickell, ph	.000	2	2	1	0	0	0	0	0	0	0	0
Mike Cvengros, p	.000	2	0	0	0	0	0	0	0	0	0	0
Joe Dawson, p	.000	1	0	0	0	0	0	0	0	0	0	0
Johnny Gooch, c	.000	3	5	0	0	0	0	0	0	1	1	0
George Grantham, 2b	.364	3	11	0	4	1	0	0	0	1	1	0
Heinie Groh, ph	.000	1	1	0	0	0	0	0	0	0	0	0
Joe Harris, 1b	.200	4	15	0	3	0	0	0	1	0	0	0
Carmen Hill, p	.000	1	1	0	0	0	0	0	0	1	0	0
Ray Kremer, p	.500	1	2	1	1	1	0	0	0	0	1	0
Lee Meadows, p	.000	1	2	0	0	0	0	0	0	0	0	0
Johnny Miljus, p	.000	2	2	0	0	0	0	0	0	0	2	0
Hal Rhyne, 2b	.000	1	4	0	0	0	0	0	0	0	0	0
Earl Smith, c-2	.000	3	8	0	0	0	0	0	0	0	0	0
Roy Spencer, c	.000	1	1	0	0	0	0	0	0	0	0	0
Pie Traynor, 3b	.200	4	15	1	3	1	0	0	0	0	1	0
Lloyd Waner, of	.400	4	15	5	6	1	1	0	0	1	0	0
Paul Waner, of	.333	4	15	0	5	1	0	0	3	0	1	0
Glenn Wright, ss	.154	4	13	1	2	0	0	0	2	0	0	0
Emil Yde, pr	.000	1	0	1	0	0	0	0	0	0	0	0
TOTAL	.223		130	10	29	6	1	0	10	4	7	0

PITCHER	W	L	ERA	G	GS	CG	SV	SHO	IP	H	ER	BB	SO
Vic Aldridge	0	1	7.36	1	1	0	0	0	7.1	10	6	4	4
Mike Cvengros	0	0	3.86	2	0	0	0	0	2.1	3	1	0	2
Joe Dawson	0	0	0.00	1	0	0	0	0	1.0	0	0	0	0
Carmen Hill	0	0	4.50	1	1	0	0	0	6.0	9	3	1	6
Ray Kremer	0	1	3.60	1	1	0	0	0	5.0	5	2	3	1
Lee Meadows	0	1	9.95	1	1	0	0	0	6.1	7	7	1	6
Johnny Miljus	0	1	1.35	2	0	0	0	0	6.2	4	1	4	6
TOTAL	0	4	5.19	9	4	0	0	0	34.2	38	20	13	25

GAME 1 AT PIT OCT 5

NY	103	010	000	5	6	1
PIT	101	010	010	4	9	2

Pitchers: HOYT, Moore (8) vs KREMER, Miljus (6)
Attendance: 41,467

GAME 2 AT PIT OCT 6

NY	003	000	030	6	11	0
PIT	100	000	010	2	7	2

Pitchers: PIPGRAS vs ALDRIDGE, Cvengros (8), Dawson (9)
Attendance: 41,634

GAME 3 AT NY OCT 7

PIT	000	000	010	1	3	1
NY	200	000	60X	8	9	0

Pitchers: MEADOWS, Cvengros (7) vs PENNOCK
Home Runs: Ruth-NY
Attendance: 60,695

GAME 4 AT NY OCT 8

PIT	100	000	200	3	10	1
NY	100	020	001	4	12	2

Pitchers: Hill, MILJUS (7) vs MOORE
Home Runs: Ruth-NY
Attendance: 57,909

After squandering a 13½-game lead and falling briefly behind the Athletics in early September, the Yankees recovered to meet the Cardinals—winners of another tight National League race—in the Series. With Herb Pennock lost to arm trouble, the Yankees made do with just three pitchers in extending their Series win streak to eight games.

The four games offered little suspense, but for Yankees fans there were thrills aplenty. The Bronx Bombers' nine home runs (including four by Lou Gehrig and three by Babe Ruth) nearly equalled St. Louis' total scoring (10 runs), and Gehrig himself drove in as many runs (nine) as the entire Cardinals offense. Ruth and Gehrig started things off with successive doubles and a run in the first inning of the opener, and when Bob Meusel followed Ruth's second double with a home run in the fourth, the Yanks had more than they would need to support Waite Hoyt's three-hitter. The Cardinals' Jim Bottomley homered off Hoyt in the seventh, but successive singles by Mark Koenig, Ruth, and Gehrig produced a fourth Yankee run and concluded the scoring.

Gehrig homered in the first inning of Game 2 to get New York off to a 3–0 lead against 41-year-old Grover Cleveland Alexander. The Cards snapped back to tie the game, but the Yankees retook the lead with a run in the last of the second and put together four hits, two walks, and a hit batsman for four more in the third. A final Yankees run in the seventh capped a 9–3 four-hit win for pitcher George Pipgras.

Jim Bottomley gave St. Louis its first lead of the Series with a two-run triple in the first inning of Game 3. But Tom Zachary gave up only one more run, taking the third Yankees win as Gehrig drove in three runs with homers in the second and fourth, and his teammates scored three more in the sixth (thanks in large part to two Cardinals errors and Meusel's steal of home) and a final (unearned) run an inning later.

New York completed its second straight Series sweep with another 7–3 win two days later. Waite Hoyt gained his second victory, mostly on the strength of five solo Yankees homers, including three by Babe Ruth.

New York Yankees (AL), 4; St. Louis Cardinals (NL), 0

NY (A)

PLAYER/POS	AVG	G	AB	R	H	2B	3B	HR	RB	BB	SO	SB
Benny Bengough, c	.231	4	13	1	3	0	0	0	1	1	1	0
Pat Collins, c	1.000	1	1	0	1	1	0	0	0	0	0	0
Earle Combs, ph	.000	1	0	0	0	0	0	0	1	0	0	0
Joe Dugan, 3b	.167	3	6	0	1	0	0	0	1	0	0	0
Leo Durocher, 2b	.000	4	2	0	0	0	0	0	0	0	1	0
Cedric Durst, of	.375	4	8	3	3	0	0	1	2	0	1	0
Lou Gehrig, 1b	.545	4	11	5	6	1	0	4	9	6	0	0
Waite Hoyt, p	.143	2	7	0	1	0	0	0	0	0	0	0
Mark Koenig, ss	.158	4	19	1	3	0	0	0	0	0	1	0
Tony Lazzeri, 2b	.250	4	12	2	3	1	0	0	0	1	0	2
Bob Meusel, of	.200	4	15	5	3	1	0	1	3	2	5	2
Ben Paschal, of	.200	3	10	0	2	0	0	0	1	1	0	0
George Pipgras, p	.000	1	2	0	0	0	0	0	1	0	1	0
Gene Robertson, 3b	.125	3	8	1	1	0	0	0	2	1	0	0
Babe Ruth, of	.625	4	16	9	10	3	0	3	4	1	2	0
Tom Zachary, p	.000	1	4	0	0	0	0	0	0	0	1	0
TOTAL	.276		134	27	37	7	0	9	25	13	13	4

PITCHER	W	L	ERA	G	GS	CG	SV	SHO	IP	H	ER	BB	SO
Waite Hoyt	2	0	1.50	2	2	2	0	0	18.0	14	3	6	14
George Pipgras	1	0	2.00	1	1	1	0	0	9.0	4	2	4	8
Tom Zachary	1	0	3.00	1	1	1	0	0	9.0	9	3	1	7
TOTAL	4	0	2.00	4	4	4	0	0	36.0	27	8	11	29

STL (N)

PLAYER/POS	AVG	G	AB	R	H	2B	3B	HR	RB	BB	SO	SB
Pete Alexander, p	.000	2	1	0	0	0	0	0	1	0	0	0
Ray Blades, ph	.000	1	1	0	0	0	0	0	0	0	1	0
Jim Bottomley, 1b	.214	4	14	1	3	0	1	1	3	2	6	0
Taylor Douthit, of	.091	3	11	1	1	0	0	0	1	1	1	0
Frankie Frisch, 2b	.231	4	13	1	3	0	0	0	1	2	2	2
Chick Hafey, of	.200	4	15	0	3	0	0	0	0	1	4	0
Jesse Haines, p	.000	1	2	0	0	0	0	0	0	0	0	0
George Harper, of	.111	3	9	1	1	0	0	0	0	2	2	0
Andy High, 3b	.294	4	17	1	5	2	0	0	1	1	3	0
Wattie Holm, of-1	.167	3	6	0	1	0	0	0	1	0	1	0
Syl Johnson, p	.000	2	0	0	0	0	0	0	0	0	0	0
Rabbit Maranville, ss	.308	4	13	2	4	1	0	0	0	1	1	1
Pepper Martin, pr	.000	1	0	1	0	0	0	0	0	0	0	0
Clarence Mitchell, p	.000	1	2	0	0	0	0	0	0	0	0	0
Ernie Orsatti, of-1	.286	4	7	1	2	1	0	0	0	1	3	0
Flint Rhem, p	.000	1	0	0	0	0	0	0	0	0	0	0
Bill Sherdel, p	.000	2	5	0	0	0	0	0	0	0	2	0
Earl Smith, c	.750	1	4	0	3	0	0	0	0	0	0	0
Tommy Thevenow, ss	.000	1	0	0	0	0	0	0	0	0	0	0
Jimmie Wilson, c	.091	3	11	1	1	1	0	0	1	0	3	0
TOTAL	.206		131	10	27	5	1	1	9	11	29	3

PITCHER	W	L	ERA	G	GS	CG	SV	SHO	IP	H	ER	BB	SO
Pete Alexander	0	1	19.80	2	1	0	0	0	5.0	10	11	4	2
Jesse Haines	0	1	4.50	1	1	0	0	0	6.0	6	3	3	3
Syl Johnson	0	0	4.50	2	0	0	0	0	2.0	4	1	1	1
Clarence Mitchell	0	0	1.59	1	0	0	0	0	5.2	2	1	2	3
Flint Rhem	0	0	0.00	1	0	0	0	0	2.0	0	0	0	1
Bill Sherdel	0	2	4.72	2	2	0	0	0	13.1	15	7	3	3
TOTAL	0	4	6.09	9	4	0	0	0	34.0	37	23	13	13

GAME 1 AT NY OCT 4

		R	H	E
STL	000 000 100	1	3	1
NY	100 200 01X	4	7	0

Pitchers: SHERDEL, Johnson (8) vs HOYT

Home Runs: Meusel-NY, Bottomley-STL

Attendance: 61,425

GAME 2 AT NY OCT 5

		R	H	E
STL	030 000 000	3	4	1
NY	314 000 10X	9	8	2

Pitchers: ALEXANDER, Mitchell (3) vs PIPGRAS

Home Runs: Gehrig-NY

Attendance: 60,714

GAME 3 AT STL OCT 7

		R	H	E
NY	010 203 100	7	7	2
STL	200 010 000	3	9	3

Pitchers: ZACHARY vs HAINES, Johnson (7), Rhem (8)

Home Runs: Gehrig-NY (2)

Attendance: 39,602

GAME 4 AT STL OCT 9

		R	H	E
NY	000 100 420	7	15	2
STL	001 100 001	3	11	0

Pitchers: HOYT vs SHERDEL, Alexander (7)

Home Runs: Ruth-NY (3), Durst-NY, Gehrig-NY

Attendance: 37,331

The surprising success of a surprise starter and the ultimate in big innings highlighted the return of the Athletics to World Series play after a gap of 15 years. In the opener, A's manager Connie Mack passed over the aces of his pitching staff in favor of Howard Ehmke, an aging journeyman who that season had started only eight times and pitched under 55 innings. But Ehmke, who (per Mack's instructions) had studied the Cubs' hitters in a series of late-season games, held the Cubs scoreless through the first eight innings of Game 1 (yielding an unearned run in the last of the ninth) while fanning 13 batters for a new Series record. Chicago's Charlie Root also pitched effectively until Jimmie Foxx's solo homer in the seventh gave the A's the game's first score. A pair of errors by Cubs shortstop Woody English in the ninth set up two unearned runs against reliever Guy Bush and gave Ehmke and the A's all the lead they needed.

Home runs by Foxx and Al Simmons drove in five of the A's nine runs in Game 2 as Philadelphia took a 2–0 Series lead. But Guy Bush held Mack's sluggers to nine singles and one run in Game 3 as his Cubs scored three runs in the sixth to take their first win.

The Cubs seemed well on their way to tying the Series in Game 4 as they entered the last of the seventh with an 8–0 lead. But Simmons led off with a homer to erase Charlie Root's shutout, and five of the next six batters singled. Art Nehf relieved Root, but the first batter to face him—Mule Haas—lofted a fly to center which Hack Wilson lost in the sun for a three-run inside-the-park homer, and the score was 8–7. After walking Mickey Cochrane, Nehf was replaced by Sheriff Blake, who gave up two singles and saw the tying run come home before Pat Malone took the mound with two men still on base and only one away. Malone struck out two in a row to end the inning—but not until he first hit a batter and gave up a double by Jimmy Dykes for the two runs that gave the A's a 10–8 win and a 3–1 Series advantage.

Game 5, although inevitably anticlimactic, was not decided until the final at bat. Chicago scored twice off Ehmke in the fourth as Malone shut out the A's with only two hits through eight. But in the last of the ninth a single and Haas' home run tied the score, and—with two men out—Simmons doubled, Foxx was walked intentionally, Bing Miller doubled, and the Series was history.

Philadelphia Athletics (AL), 4; Chicago Cubs (NL), 1

PHI (A)

PLAYER/POS	AVG	G	AB	R	H	2B	3B	HR	RB	BB	SO	SB
Max Bishop, 2b	.190	5	21	2	4	0	0	0	1	2	3	0
Joe Boley, ss	.235	5	17	1	4	0	0	0	1	0	3	0
George Burns, ph	.000	1	2	0	0	0	0	0	0	0	1	0
Mickey Cochrane, c	.400	5	15	5	6	1	0	0	0	7	0	0
Jimmy Dykes, 3b	.421	5	19	2	8	1	0	0	4	1	1	0
George Earnshaw, p	.000	2	5	1	0	0	0	0	0	0	4	0
Howard Ehmke, p	.200	2	5	0	1	0	0	0	0	0	0	0
Jimmie Foxx, 1b	.350	5	20	5	7	1	0	2	5	1	1	0
Walter French, ph	.000	1	1	0	0	0	0	0	0	0	1	0
Lefty Grove, p	.000	2	2	0	0	0	0	0	0	0	1	0
Mule Haas, of	.238	5	21	3	5	0	0	2	6	1	3	0
Bing Miller, of	.368	5	19	1	7	1	0	0	4	0	2	0
Jack Quinn, p	.000	1	2	0	0	0	0	0	0	0	2	0
Eddie Rommel, p	.000	1	0	0	0	0	0	0	0	0	0	0
Al Simmons, of	.300	5	20	6	6	1	0	2	5	1	4	0
Homer Summa, ph	.000	1	1	0	0	0	0	0	0	0	1	0
Rube Walberg, p	.000	2	1	0	0	0	0	0	0	0	0	0
TOTAL	.281		171	26	48	5	0	6	26	13	27	0

PITCHER	W	L	ERA	G	GS	CG	SV	SHO	IP	H	ER	BB	SO
George Earnshaw	1	1	2.63	2	2	1	0	0	13.2	14	4	6	17
Howard Ehmke	1	0	1.42	2	2	1	0	0	12.2	14	2	3	13
Lefty Grove	0	0	0.00	2	0	0	2	0	6.1	3	0	1	10
Jack Quinn	0	0	9.00	1	1	0	0	0	5.0	7	5	2	2
Eddie Rommel	1	0	9.00	1	0	0	0	0	1.0	2	1	1	0
Rube Walberg	1	0	0.00	2	0	0	0	0	6.1	3	0	0	8
TOTAL	4	1	2.40	10	5	2	2	0	45.0	43	12	13	50

CHI (N)

PLAYER/POS	AVG	G	AB	R	H	2B	3B	HR	RB	BB	SO	SB
Footsie Blair, ph	.000	1	1	0	0	0	0	0	0	0	0	0
Sheriff Blake, p	1.000	2	1	0	1	0	0	0	0	0	0	0
Guy Bush, p	.000	2	3	1	0	0	0	0	0	1	3	0
Hal Carlson, p	.000	2	0	0	0	0	0	0	0	0	0	0
Kiki Cuyler, of	.300	5	20	4	6	1	0	0	4	1	7	0
Woody English, ss	.190	5	21	1	4	2	0	0	0	1	6	0
Mike Gonzalez, c-1	.000	2	1	0	0	0	0	0	0	0	1	0
Charlie Grimm, 1b	.389	5	18	2	7	0	0	1	4	1	2	0
Gabby Hartnett, ph	.000	3	3	0	0	0	0	0	0	0	3	0
Cliff Heathcote, ph	.000	2	1	0	0	0	0	0	0	0	0	0
Rogers Hornsby, 2b	.238	5	21	4	5	1	1	0	1	1	8	0
Pat Malone, p	.250	3	4	0	1	1	0	0	0	0	2	0
Norm McMillan, 3b	.100	5	20	0	2	0	0	0	0	2	6	1
Art Nehf, p	.000	2	0	0	0	0	0	0	0	0	0	0
Charlie Root, p	.000	2	5	0	0	0	0	0	0	0	3	0
Riggs Stephenson, of	.316	5	19	3	6	1	0	0	3	2	2	0
Zack Taylor, c	.176	5	17	0	3	0	0	0	3	0	3	0
Chick Tolson, ph	.000	1	1	0	0	0	0	0	0	0	1	0
Hack Wilson, of	.471	5	17	2	8	0	1	0	0	4	3	0
TOTAL	.249		173	17	43	6	2	1	15	13	50	1

PITCHER	W	L	ERA	G	GS	CG	SV	SHO	IP	H	ER	BB	SO
Sheriff Blake	0	1	13.50	2	0	0	0	0	1.1	4	2	0	1
Guy Bush	1	0	0.82	2	1	1	0	0	11.0	12	1	2	4
Hal Carlson	0	0	6.75	2	0	0	0	0	4.0	7	3	1	3
Pat Malone	0	2	4.15	3	2	1	0	0	13.0	12	6	7	11
Art Nehf	0	0	18.00	2	0	0	0	0	1.0	1	2	1	0
Charlie Root	0	1	4.72	2	2	0	0	0	13.1	12	7	2	8
TOTAL	1	4	4.33	13	5	2	0	0	43.2	48	21	13	27

GAME 1 AT CHI OCT 8

		R	H	E
PHI	000 000 102	3	6	1
CHI	000 000 001	1	8	2

Pitchers: EHMKE vs ROOT, Bush (8)
Home Runs: Foxx-PHI
Attendance: 50,740

GAME 2 AT CHI OCT 9

		R	H	E
PHI	003 300 120	9	12	0
CHI	000 030 000	3	11	1

Pitchers: EARNSHAW, Grove (5) vs MALONE, Blake (4), Carlson (6), Nehf (9)
Home Runs: Simmons-PHI, Foxx-PHI
Attendance: 49,987

GAME 3 AT PHI OCT 11

		R	H	E
CHI	000 003 000	3	6	1
PHI	000 010 000	1	9	1

Pitchers: BUSH vs EARNSHAW
Attendance: 29,921

GAME 4 AT PHI OCT 12

		R	H	E
CHI	000 205 100	8	10	2
PHI	000 000 10 0 X	10	15	2

Pitchers: Root, Nehf (7), BLAKE (7), Malone (7), Carlson (8) vs Quinn, Walberg (6), ROMMEL (7), Grove (8)
Home Runs: Grimm-CHI, Haas-PHI, Simmons-PHI
Attendance: 29,921

GAME 5 AT PHI OCT 14

		R	H	E
CHI	002 000 000	2	8	1
PHI	000 000 003	3	6	0

Pitchers: MALONE vs Ehmke, WALBERG (4)
Home Runs: Haas-PHI
Attendance: 29,921

Pitching 85 percent of the Series with a combined ERA of 1.02, Philadelphia aces George Earnshaw and Lefty Grove chilled the hot Cardinals, who had hit .314 and averaged more than six runs per game during the season. The A's hit only .197 themselves in the Series, but more than half their hits went for extra bases as they outscored St. Louis 21–12 and took their second consecutive world championship in six games.

Grove faced Cardinals spitballer Burleigh Grimes in the opener, giving up nine hits, including four singles in the Cards' two-run third. The Athletics, for their part, touched Grimes for only five hits, all in separate innings. But every hit—a double, two triples, and home runs by Al Simmons and Mike Cochrane—resulted in a run, and Grove and the A's emerged 5–2 victors. In the first inning of Game 2, Cochrane again homered, sending Earnshaw on his way to Philadelphia's second win, 6–1.

When the Series moved to St. Louis, though, the Cards came alive. Wild Bill Hallahan (their leading winner during the season, with 15) spaced seven hits for a shutout. Taylor Douthit's fourth-inning home run off Rube Walberg was the first St. Louis hit, but the Cards knocked out nine more for four more runs before they were finished. A pair of unearned runs evened the Series the next day when A's third baseman Jimmy Dykes's wild throw to first in the fourth inning let in a tie-breaking run and led to a third against the ultimate loser Lefty Grove. Meanwhile, Cardinals veteran Jesse Haines, after yielding three Philadelphia hits and a run in the first inning, shut out the A's on one hit the rest of the way.

Earnshaw and Grove combined to restore the Series lead to the Athletics in Game 5 with a three-hit shutout. Grove, who took over when Earnshaw left for a pinch hitter in the eighth, garnered his second Series win as Jimmie Foxx homered off Grimes in the top of the ninth for the game's only runs. After a travel day to Philadelphia, Earnshaw pitched again for the A's in Game 6, and pushed the Cardinals' scoreless streak to 21 innings before allowing them a token run in the ninth. But by then seven A's had crossed the plate and the Series was theirs.

Philadelphia Athletics (AL), 4; St. Louis Cardinals (NL), 2

PHI (A)

PLAYER/POS	AVG	G	AB	R	H	2B	3B	HR	RB	BB	SO	SB
Max Bishop, 2b	.222	6	18	5	4	0	0	0	0	7	3	0
Joe Boley, ss	.095	6	21	1	2	0	0	0	1	0	1	0
Mickey Cochrane, c	.222	6	18	5	4	1	0	2	4	5	2	0
Jimmy Dykes, 3b	.222	6	18	2	4	3	0	1	5	5	3	0
George Earnshaw, p	.000	3	9	0	0	0	0	0	0	0	5	0
Jimmie Foxx, 1b	.333	6	21	3	7	2	1	1	3	2	4	0
Lefty Grove, p	.000	3	6	0	0	0	0	0	0	0	3	0
Mule Haas, of	.111	6	18	1	2	0	1	0	1	1	3	0
Eric McNair, ph	.000	1	1	0	0	0	0	0	0	0	0	0
Bing Miller, of	.143	6	21	0	3	2	0	0	3	0	4	0
Jim Moore, of-1	.333	3	3	0	1	0	0	0	0	1	1	0
Jack Quinn, p	.000	1	0	0	0	0	0	0	0	0	0	0
Bill Shores, p	.000	1	0	0	0	0	0	0	0	1	0	0
Al Simmons, of	.364	6	22	4	8	2	0	2	4	2	2	0
Rube Walberg, p	.000	1	2	0	0	0	0	0	0	0	1	0
TOTAL	.197		178	21	35	10	2	6	21	24	32	0

PITCHER	W	L	ERA	G	GS	CG	SV	SHO	IP	H	ER	BB	SO
George Earnshaw	2	0	0.72	3	3	2	0	0	25.0	13	2	7	19
Lefty Grove	2	1	1.42	3	2	2	0	0	19.0	15	3	3	10
Jack Quinn	0	0	4.50	1	0	0	0	0	2.0	3	1	0	1
Bill Shores	0	0	13.50	1	0	0	0	0	1.1	3	2	0	0
Rube Walberg	0	1	3.86	1	1	0	0	0	4.2	4	2	1	3
TOTAL	4	2	1.73	9	6	4	0	0	52.0	38	10	11	33

STL (N)

PLAYER/POS	AVG	G	AB	R	H	2B	3B	HR	RB	BB	SO	SB
Sparky Adams, 3b	.143	6	21	0	3	0	0	0	1	0	4	0
Hi Bell, p	.000	1	0	0	0	0	0	0	0	0	0	0
Ray Blades, of-3	.111	5	9	2	1	0	0	0	0	2	2	0
Jim Bottomley, 1b	.045	6	22	1	1	1	0	0	0	2	9	0
Taylor Douthit, of	.083	6	24	1	2	0	0	1	2	0	2	0
George Fisher, ph	.500	2	2	0	1	1	0	0	0	0	1	0
Frankie Frisch, 2b	.208	6	24	0	5	2	0	0	0	0	0	1
Charlie Gelbert, ss	.353	6	17	2	6	0	1	0	2	3	3	0
Burleigh Grimes, p	.400	2	5	0	2	0	0	0	0	0	1	0
Chick Hafey, of	.273	6	22	2	6	5	0	0	2	1	3	0
Jesse Haines, p	.500	1	2	0	1	0	0	0	1	0	0	0
Bill Hallahan, p	.000	2	2	0	0	0	0	0	0	1	1	0
Andy High, 3b	.500	1	2	1	1	0	0	0	0	0	0	0
Syl Johnson, p	.000	2	0	0	0	0	0	0	0	0	0	0
Jim Lindsey, p	1.000	2	1	0	1	0	0	0	0	0	0	0
Gus Mancuso, c	.286	2	7	1	2	0	0	0	0	1	2	0
Ernie Orsatti, ph	.000	1	1	0	0	0	0	0	0	0	0	0
George Puccinelli, ph	.000	1	1	0	0	0	0	0	0	0	0	0
Flint Rhem, p	.000	1	1	0	0	0	0	0	0	0	1	0
George Watkins, of	.167	4	12	2	2	0	0	1	1	1	3	0
Jimmie Wilson, c	.267	4	15	0	4	1	0	0	2	0	1	0
TOTAL	.200		190	12	38	10	1	2	11	11	33	1

PITCHER	W	L	ERA	G	GS	CG	SV	SHO	IP	H	ER	BB	SO
Hi Bell	0	0	0.00	1	0	0	0	0	1.0	0	0	0	0
Burleigh Grimes	0	2	3.71	2	2	2	0	0	17.0	10	7	6	13
Jesse Haines	1	0	1.00	1	1	1	0	0	9.0	4	1	4	2
Bill Hallahan	1	1	1.64	2	2	1	0	1	11.0	9	2	8	8
Syl Johnson	0	0	7.20	2	0	0	0	0	5.0	4	4	3	4
Jim Lindsey	0	0	1.93	2	0	0	0	0	4.2	1	1	1	2
Flint Rhem	0	1	10.80	1	1	0	0	0	3.1	7	4	2	3
TOTAL	2	4	3.35	11	6	4	0	1	51.0	35	19	24	32

GAME 1 AT PHI OCT 1

		R	H	E
STL	002 000 000	2	9	0
PHI	010 101 11X	5	5	0

Pitchers: GRIMES vs GROVE
Home Runs: Cochrane-PHI, Simmons-PHI
Attendance: 32,295

GAME 2 AT PHI OCT 2

		R	H	E
STL	010 000 000	1	6	2
PHI	202 200 00X	6	7	2

Pitchers: RHEM, Lindsey (4), Johnson (7) vs EARNSHAW
Home Runs: Cochrane-PHI, Watkins-STL
Attendance: 32,295

GAME 3 AT STL OCT 4

		R	H	E
PHI	000 000 000	0	7	0
STL	000 110 21X	5	10	0

Pitchers: WALBERG, Shores (5), Quinn (7) vs HALLAHAN
Home Runs: Douthit-STL
Attendance: 36,944

GAME 4 AT STL OCT 5

		R	H	E
PHI	100 000 000	1	4	1
STL	001 200 00X	3	5	1

Pitchers: GROVE vs HAINES
Attendance: 39,946

GAME 5 AT STL OCT 6

		R	H	E
PHI	000 000 002	2	5	0
STL	000 000 000	0	3	1

Pitchers: Earnshaw, GROVE (8) vs GRIMES
Home Runs: Foxx-PHI
Attendance: 38,844

GAME 6 AT PHI OCT 8

		R	H	E
STL	000 000 001	1	5	1
PHI	201 211 00X	7	7	0

Pitchers: HALLAHAN, Johnson (3), Lindsey (6), Bell (8) vs EARNSHAW
Home Runs: Dykes-PHI, Simmons-PHI
Attendance: 32,295

For the second year in a row, the A's met the Cardinals in the Series, and once again pitchers Lefty Grove and George Earnshaw provided more than 80 percent of the Athletics' pitching, performing splendidly and winning three games between them. But this time Cardinals pitchers Wild Bill Hallahan and Burleigh Grimes outshone them, winning two games apiece to bring St. Louis the world championship.

Grove gave up four hits and two runs in the first inning of the opener, but shut out the Cards the rest of the way as the A's scored six off Paul Derringer to take the Series lead. Earnshaw also held St. Louis to two runs the next day—both manufactured by Pepper Martin's daring baserunning. But they were more than enough for Hallahan, who shut out the A's on three singles.

The Cardinals took their first Series lead in Game 3, scoring five times off Grove and reliever Roy Mahaffey while Grimes held the A's hitless through seven innings and scoreless through eight before giving up a harmless two-run homer to Al Simmons in the bottom of the ninth. But the A's came back to even the Series the next day on Earnshaw's two-hit shutout.

Pepper Martin, hero of Game 2, homered for two runs in Game 5, and drove in two more of St. Louis' five runs with a sacrifice fly and a single. Meanwhile pitcher Hallahan held Philadelphia to a lone run, returning the Series lead to the Cardinals with his second win.

Game 6 pitted Grove and Derringer against each other again as in the opener, and again Grove emerged the victor, holding the Cardinals to one run and five hits. The Athletics scored four unearned runs in the fifth off the unfortunate Derringer. After an error put a runner on base to open the inning, he allowed two singles and walked four, including two with the bases full, before leaving the game. Four more Philadelphia runs in the seventh (two of them scoring on a dropped fly ball) gave the A's the Series' only lopsided win.

In the finale, Grimes once again held the A's scoreless through eight before giving up two runs in the ninth. And once again the runs proved harmless against an early Cardinals lead, as Hallahan came on to retire Max Bishop for the final out.

St. Louis Cardinals (NL), 4; Philadelphia Athletics (AL), 3

STL (N)

PLAYER/POS	AVG	G	AB	R	H	2B	3B	HR	RB	BB	SO	SB
Sparky Adams, 3b	.250	2	4	0	1	0	0	0	0	0	1	0
Ray Blades, ph	.000	2	2	0	0	0	0	0	0	0	2	0
Jim Bottomley, 1b	.160	7	25	2	4	1	0	0	2	2	5	0
Ripper Collins, ph	.000	2	2	0	0	0	0	0	0	0	1	0
Paul Derringer, p	.000	3	2	0	0	0	0	0	0	0	1	0
Jake Flowers, 3b-4	.091	5	11	1	1	1	0	0	0	1	0	0
Frankie Frisch, 2b	.259	7	27	2	7	2	0	0	1	1	2	1
Charlie Gelbert, ss	.261	7	23	0	6	1	0	0	3	0	4	0
Burleigh Grimes, p	.286	2	7	0	2	0	0	0	2	0	2	0
Chick Hafey, of	.167	6	24	1	4	0	0	0	0	0	5	1
Bill Hallahan, p	.000	3	6	0	0	0	0	0	0	0	3	0
Andy High, 3b	.267	4	15	3	4	0	0	0	0	0	2	0
Syl Johnson, p	.000	3	2	0	0	0	0	0	0	0	2	0
Jim Lindsey, p	.000	2	0	0	0	0	0	0	0	0	0	0
Gus Mancuso, c-1	.000	2	1	0	0	0	0	0	0	0	0	0
Pepper Martin, of	.500	7	24	5	12	4	0	1	5	2	3	5
Ernie Orsatti, of	.000	1	3	0	0	0	0	0	0	0	3	0
Flint Rhem, p	.000	1	0	0	0	0	0	0	0	0	0	0
Wally Roettger, of	.286	3	14	1	4	1	0	0	0	0	3	0
George Watkins, of	.286	5	14	4	4	1	0	1	2	2	1	1
Jimmie Wilson, c	.217	7	23	0	5	0	0	0	2	1	1	0
TOTAL	.236		229	19	54	11	0	2	17	9	41	8

PITCHER	W	L	ERA	G	GS	CG	SV	SHO	IP	H	ER	BB	SO
Paul Derringer	0	2	4.26	3	2	0	0	0	12.2	14	6	7	14
Burleigh Grimes	2	0	2.04	2	2	1	0	0	17.2	9	4	9	11
Bill Hallahan	2	0	0.49	3	2	2	1	1	18.1	12	1	8	12
Syl Johnson	0	1	3.00	3	1	0	0	0	9.0	10	3	1	6
Jim Lindsey	0	0	5.40	2	0	0	0	0	3.1	4	2	3	2
Flint Rhem	0	0	0.00	1	0	0	0	0	1.0	1	0	0	1
TOTAL	4	3	2.32	14	7	3	1	1	62.0	50	16	28	46

PHI (A)

PLAYER/POS	AVG	G	AB	R	H	2B	3B	HR	RB	BB	SO	SB
Max Bishop, 2b	.148	7	27	4	4	0	0	0	0	3	5	0
Joe Boley, ph	.000	1	1	0	0	0	0	0	0	0	1	0
Mickey Cochrane, c	.160	7	25	2	4	0	0	0	1	5	2	0
Doc Cramer, ph	.500	2	2	0	1	0	0	0	2	0	0	0
Jimmy Dykes, 3b	.227	7	22	2	5	0	0	0	2	5	1	0
George Earnshaw, p	.000	3	8	0	0	0	0	0	0	0	2	0
Jimmie Foxx, 1b	.348	7	23	3	8	0	0	1	3	6	5	0
Lefty Grove, p	.000	3	10	0	0	0	0	0	0	0	7	0
Mule Haas, of	.130	7	23	1	3	1	0	0	2	3	5	0
Johnnie Heving, ph	.000	1	1	0	0	0	0	0	0	0	0	0
Waite Hoyt, p	.000	1	2	0	0	0	0	0	0	0	0	0
Roy Mahaffey, p	.000	1	0	0	0	0	0	0	0	0	0	0
Eric McNair, 2b-1	.000	2	2	1	0	0	0	0	0	0	1	0
Bing Miller, of	.269	7	26	3	7	1	0	0	1	0	4	0
Jim Moore, of-1	.333	2	3	0	1	0	0	0	0	0	1	0
Eddie Rommel, p	.000	1	0	0	0	0	0	0	0	0	0	0
Al Simmons, of	.333	7	27	4	9	2	0	2	8	3	3	0
Phil Todt, ph	.000	1	0	0	0	0	0	0	0	1	0	0
Rube Walberg, p	.000	2	0	0	0	0	0	0	0	0	0	0
Dib Williams, ss	.320	7	25	2	8	1	0	0	1	2	9	0
TOTAL	.220		227	22	50	5	0	3	20	28	46	0

PITCHER	W	L	ERA	G	GS	CG	SV	SHO	IP	H	ER	BB	SO
George Earnshaw	1	2	1.88	3	3	2	0	1	24.0	12	5	4	20
Lefty Grove	2	1	2.42	3	3	2	0	0	26.0	28	7	2	16
Waite Hoyt	0	1	4.50	1	1	0	0	0	6.0	7	3	0	1
Roy Mahaffey	0	0	9.00	1	0	0	0	0	1.0	1	1	1	0
Eddie Rommel	0	0	9.00	1	0	0	0	0	1.0	3	1	0	0
Rube Walberg	0	0	3.00	2	0	0	0	0	3.0	3	1	2	4
TOTAL	3	4	2.66	11	7	4	0	1	61.0	54	18	9	41

GAME 1 AT STL OCT 1

				R	H	E
PHI	004	000	200	6	11	0
STL	200	000	000	2	12	0

Pitchers: GROVE vs DERRINGER, Johnson (8)
Home Runs: Simmons-PHI
Attendance: 38,529

GAME 2 AT STL OCT 2

				R	H	E
PHI	000	000	000	0	3	0
STL	010	000	10X	2	6	1

Pitchers: EARNSHAW vs HALLAHAN
Attendance: 35,947

GAME 3 AT PHI OCT 5

				R	H	E
STL	020	200	001	5	12	0
PHI	000	000	002	2	2	0

Pitchers: GRIMES vs GROVE, Mahaffey (9)
Home Runs: Simmons-PHI
Attendance: 32,295

GAME 4 AT PHI OCT 6

				R	H	E
STL	000	000	000	0	2	1
PHI	100	002	00X	3	10	0

Pitchers: JOHNSON, Lindsey (6), Derringer (8) vs EARNSHAW
Home Runs: Foxx-PHI
Attendance: 32,295

GAME 5 AT PHI OCT 7

				R	H	E
STL	100	002	011	5	12	0
PHI	000	000	100	1	9	0

Pitchers: HALLAHAN vs HOYT, Walberg (7), Rommel (9)
Home Runs: Martin-STL, Watkins-STL
Attendance: 32,295

GAME 6 AT STL OCT 9

				R	H	E
PHI	000	040	400	8	8	1
STL	000	001	000	1	5	2

Pitchers: GROVE vs DERRINGER, Johnson (5), Lindsey (7), Rhem (9)
Attendance: 39,401

GAME 7 AT STL OCT 10

				R	H	E
PHI	000	000	002	2	7	1
STL	202	000	00X	4	5	0

Pitchers: EARNSHAW, Walberg (8) vs GRIMES, Hallahan (9)
Attendance: 20,805

Lou Gehrig, who hit .529 and scored nearly a quarter of New York's runs, led both clubs in batting, slugging, hits, runs, and RBIs as the Yankees crushed the Cubs in four games. But the Series is best remembered for Babe Ruth's "called" shot in Game 3, when he pointed his bat at pitcher Charlie Root in the fifth inning and broke the game's 4–4 tie a moment later with a massive home run into the center field bleachers. Debate has raged ever since about whether Ruth intended his gesture as a home run prediction. Whether intended or not, it erased from public memory Gehrig's home run that followed Ruth's (and the homers both men had hit earlier in the game), and made memorable an otherwise undistinguished Series.

Chicago scored in the first inning of each game, taking early leads in three of the four, but held no lead beyond the sixth inning. In the opener the Cubs connected for ten hits to the Yankees' eight, but managed to score only half as many runs as the New Yorkers, who put what had been a close game out of reach with five runs in the sixth (on four walks, two singles, and a ground out) and three more in the seventh (a walk, two singles, a hit batsman, a sacrifice fly, and a wild pitch).

Chicago's Lon Warneke walked four batters in Game 2, and three of them went on to score as the Yankees countered single Chicago runs in the first and third with pairs of their own on two walks and two singles in each frame. (A fifth Yankees run—on two singles without bases on balls—concluded the scoring for the game.)

Game 3 featured not only the two homers each by Ruth and Gehrig, but home runs by the Cubs' Kiki Cuyler and Gabby Hartnett. Hartnett's solo shot in the last of the ninth brought Chicago to within two runs of New York for the Series' closest finish.

Four first-inning singles, Frank Demaree's three-run homer, and a Yankees error gave the Cubs a 4–1 advantage early in Game 4—their biggest lead of the Series. But by game's end, 19 Yankees hits (including two home runs by Tony Lazzeri and one by Earle Combs) had created 13 runs, and the world title belonged to the Yankees.

New York Yankees (AL), 4; Chicago Cubs (NL), 0

NY (A)

PLAYER/POS	AVG	G	AB	R	H	2B	3B	HR	RB	BB	SO	SB
Johnny Allen, p	.000	1	0	0	0	0	0	0	0	0	0	0
Sammy Byrd, of	.000	1	0	0	0	0	0	0	0	0	0	0
Ben Chapman, of	.294	4	17	1	5	2	0	0	6	2	4	0
Earle Combs, of	.375	4	16	8	6	1	0	1	4	4	3	0
Frankie Crosetti, ss	.133	4	15	2	2	1	0	0	0	2	3	0
Bill Dickey, c	.438	4	16	2	7	0	0	0	4	2	1	0
Lou Gehrig, 1b	.529	4	17	9	9	1	0	3	8	2	1	0
Lefty Gomez, p	.000	1	3	0	0	0	0	0	0	0	2	0
Myril Hoag, pr	.000	1	0	1	0	0	0	0	0	0	0	0
Tony Lazzeri, 2b	.294	4	17	4	5	0	0	2	5	2	1	0
Wilcy Moore, p	.333	1	3	0	1	0	0	0	0	0	2	0
Herb Pennock, p	.000	2	1	0	0	0	0	0	0	0	0	0
George Pipgras, p	.000	1	5	0	0	0	0	0	0	0	5	0
Red Ruffing, p-1	.000	2	4	0	0	0	0	0	0	1	1	0
Babe Ruth, of	.333	4	15	6	5	0	0	2	6	4	3	0
Joe Sewell, 3b	.333	4	15	4	5	1	0	0	3	4	0	0
TOTAL	.313		144	37	45	6	0	8	36	23	26	0

PITCHER	W	L	ERA	G	GS	CG	SV	SHO	IP	H	ER	BB	SO
Johnny Allen	0	0	40.50	1	1	0	0	0	0.2	5	3	0	0
Lefty Gomez	1	0	1.00	1	1	1	0	0	9.0	9	1	1	8
Wilcy Moore	1	0	0.00	1	0	0	0	0	5.1	2	0	0	1
Herb Pennock	0	0	2.25	2	0	0	2	0	4.0	2	1	1	4
George Pipgras	1	0	4.50	1	1	0	0	0	8.0	9	4	3	1
Red Ruffing	1	0	3.00	1	1	1	0	0	9.0	10	3	6	10
TOTAL	4	0	3.00	7	4	2	2	0	36.0	37	12	11	24

CHI (N)

PLAYER/POS	AVG	G	AB	R	H	2B	3B	HR	RB	BB	SO	SB
Guy Bush, p	.000	2	1	0	0	0	0	0	0	1	0	0
Kiki Cuyler, of	.278	4	18	2	5	1	1	1	2	0	3	1
Frank Demaree, of	.286	2	7	1	2	0	0	1	4	1	0	0
Woody English, 3b	.176	4	17	2	3	0	0	0	1	2	2	0
Burleigh Grimes, p	.000	2	1	0	0	0	0	0	0	0	1	0
Charlie Grimm, 1b	.333	4	15	2	5	2	0	0	1	2	2	0
Marv Gudat, ph	.000	2	2	0	0	0	0	0	0	0	1	0
Stan Hack, ph	.000	1	0	0	0	0	0	0	0	0	0	0
Gabby Hartnett, c	.313	4	16	2	5	2	0	1	1	1	3	0
Rollie Hemsley, c-1	.000	3	3	0	0	0	0	0	0	0	3	0
Billy Herman, 2b	.222	4	18	5	4	1	0	0	1	1	3	0
Billy Jurges, ss	.364	3	11	1	4	1	0	0	1	0	1	2
Mark Koenig, ss-1	.250	2	4	1	1	0	1	0	1	1	0	0
Pat Malone, p	.000	1	0	0	0	0	0	0	0	0	0	0
Jakie May, p	.000	2	2	0	0	0	0	0	0	0	0	0
Johnny Moore, of	.000	2	7	1	0	0	0	0	0	2	1	0
Charlie Root, p	.000	1	2	0	0	0	0	0	0	0	1	0
Bob Smith, p	.000	1	0	0	0	0	0	0	0	0	0	0
Riggs Stephenson, of	.444	4	18	2	8	1	0	0	4	0	0	0
Bud Tinning, p	.000	2	0	0	0	0	0	0	0	0	0	0
Lon Warneke, p	.000	2	4	0	0	0	0	0	0	0	3	0
TOTAL	.253		146	19	37	8	2	3	16	11	24	3

PITCHER	W	L	ERA	G	GS	CG	SV	SHO	IP	H	ER	BB	SO
Guy Bush	0	1	14.29	2	2	0	0	0	5.2	5	9	6	2
Burleigh Grimes	0	0	23.63	2	0	0	0	0	2.2	7	7	2	0
Pat Malone	0	0	0.00	1	0	0	0	0	2.2	1	0	4	4
Jakie May	0	1	11.57	2	0	0	0	0	4.2	9	6	3	4
Charlie Root	0	1	10.38	1	1	0	0	0	4.1	6	5	3	4
Bob Smith	0	0	9.00	1	0	0	0	0	1.0	2	1	0	1
Bud Tinning	0	0	0.00	2	0	0	0	0	2.1	0	0	0	3
Lon Warneke	0	1	5.91	2	1	1	0	0	10.2	15	7	5	8
TOTAL	0	4	9.26	13	4	1	0	0	34.0	45	35	23	26

GAME 1 AT NY SEPT 28

				R	H	E
CHI	200	000	220	6	10	1
NY	000	305	31X	12	8	2

Pitchers: BUSH, Grimes (6), Smith (8) vs RUFFING
Home Runs: Gehrig-NY
Attendance: 41,459

GAME 2 AT NY SEPT 29

				R	H	E
CHI	101	000	000	2	9	0
NY	202	010	00X	5	10	1

Pitchers: WARNEKE vs GOMEZ
Attendance: 50,709

GAME 3 AT CHI OCT 1

				R	H	E
NY	301	020	001	7	8	1
CHI	102	100	001	5	9	4

Pitchers: PIPGRAS, Pennock (9) vs ROOT, Malone (5), May (7), Tinning (9)
Home Runs: Ruth-NY (2), Gehrig-NY (2), Cuyler-CHI, Hartnett-CHI
Attendance: 49,986

GAME 4 AT CHI OCT 2

				R	H	E
NY	102	002	404	13	19	4
CHI	400	001	001	6	9	1

Pitchers: Allen, MOORE (1), Pennock (7) vs Bush, Warneke (1), MAY (4), Tinning (7), Grimes (9)
Home Runs: Demaree-CHI, Lazzeri-NY (2), Combs-NY
Attendance: 49,844

New York Giants (NL), 4; Washington Senators (AL), 1

Although John McGraw had retired from managing the Giants in 1932, he continued to regard them as "his" team. Led now by first baseman Bill Terry, the Giants faced a club also led by an active player, shortstop Joe Cronin in his rookie managerial season.

Giants ace Carl Hubbell dominated the first game, striking out 10 while limiting the Senators to five singles and a pair of unearned runs. Mel Ott set the tone for New York with a two-out two-run homer in the first inning, and singled home a third run in the third to build a lead Washington would not overcome. The next day the Senators scored first, on Goose Goslin's solo homer in the third. But that was the only run scored off Hal Schumacher, and when the Giants drove out Senators starter Alvin Crowder with six runs in the sixth they had their second win well in hand.

The Senators revived when the Series moved to Washington for Game 3. Each of second baseman Buddy Myer's three hits scored or drove in a run, providing a growing cushion for pitcher Earl Whitehill, who recorded the Series' only shutout.

Games 4 and 5 went to New York, but not without a struggle. In the fourth game, manager Terry's home run broke the ice in the fourth inning, but Hubbell muffed a bunt in the seventh which led to the tying run. Hubbell and Senators starter Monty Weaver dueled without further scoring until shortstop Blondy Ryan's single in the top of the 11th put New York up by one. Hubbell let men reach second and third with one out in the last of the 11th, but an intentional walk set up the hoped-for double play to end the game.

New York had built a three-run lead in Game 5 when Fred Schulte evened the score in the last of the sixth with a three-run homer. Relievers Jack Russell and Dolf Luque then dueled scorelessly into the 10th, when Mel Ott (whose homer had begun the Series' scoring in the first inning of Game One) homered once again for what proved the Series' final run. Luque shut down the Senators in their half of the 10th, and "McGraw's Giants" were for the fourth time the world's finest. But before the advent of another spring, McGraw was dead.

NY (N)

PLAYER/POS	AVG	G	AB	R	H	2B	3B	HR	RB	BB	SO	SB
Hi Bell, p	.000	1	0	0	0	0	0	0	0	0	0	0
Hughie Critz, 2b	.136	5	22	2	3	0	0	0	0	1	0	0
Kiddo Davis, of	.368	5	19	1	7	1	0	0	0	0	3	0
Freddie Fitzsimmons, p	.500	1	2	0	1	0	0	0	0	0	0	0
Carl Hubbell, p	.286	2	7	0	2	0	0	0	0	0	0	0
Travis Jackson, 3b	.222	5	18	3	4	1	0	0	2	1	3	0
Dolf Luque, p	1.000	1	1	0	1	0	0	0	0	0	0	0
Gus Mancuso, c	.118	5	17	2	2	1	0	0	2	3	0	0
Jo-Jo Moore, of	.227	5	22	1	5	1	0	0	1	1	3	0
Lefty O'Doul, ph	1.000	1	1	1	1	0	0	0	2	0	0	0
Mel Ott, of	.389	5	18	3	7	0	0	2	4	4	4	0
Homer Peel, of-1	.500	2	2	0	1	0	0	0	0	0	0	0
Blondy Ryan, ss	.278	5	18	0	5	0	0	0	1	1	5	0
Hal Schumacher, p	.286	2	7	0	2	0	0	0	3	0	3	0
Bill Terry, 1b	.273	5	22	3	6	1	0	1	1	0	0	0
TOTAL	.267		176	16	47	5	0	3	16	11	21	0

PITCHER	W	L	ERA	G	GS	CG	SV	SHO	IP	H	ER	BB	SO
Hi Bell	0	0	0.00	1	0	0	0	0	1.0	0	0	0	0
Freddie Fitzsimmons	0	1	5.14	1	1	0	0	0	7.0	9	4	0	2
Carl Hubbell	2	0	0.00	2	2	2	0	0	20.0	13	0	6	15
Dolf Luque	1	0	0.00	1	0	0	0	0	4.1	2	0	2	5
Hal Schumacher	1	0	2.45	2	2	1	0	0	14.2	13	4	5	3
TOTAL	4	1	1.53	7	5	3	0	0	47.0	37	8	13	25

WAS (A)

PLAYER/POS	AVG	G	AB	R	H	2B	3B	HR	RB	BB	SO	SB
Ossie Bluege, 3b	.125	5	16	1	2	1	0	0	0	1	6	0
Cliff Bolton, ph	.000	2	2	0	0	0	0	0	0	0	0	0
Joe Cronin, ss	.318	5	22	1	7	0	0	0	2	0	2	0
General Crowder, p	.250	2	4	0	1	0	0	0	0	0	0	0
Goose Goslin, of	.250	5	20	2	5	1	0	1	1	1	3	0
Dave Harris, of-1	.000	3	2	0	0	0	0	0	0	2	0	0
John Kerr, pr	.000	1	0	0	0	0	0	0	0	0	0	0
Joe Kuhel, 1b	.150	5	20	1	3	0	0	0	1	1	4	0
Heinie Manush, of	.111	5	18	2	2	0	0	0	0	2	1	0
Alex McColl, p	.000	1	0	0	0	0	0	0	0	0	0	0
Buddy Myer, 2b	.300	5	20	2	6	1	0	0	2	2	3	0
Sam Rice, ph	1.000	1	1	0	1	0	0	0	0	0	0	0
Jack Russell, p	.000	3	2	0	0	0	0	0	0	1	2	0
Fred Schulte, of	.333	5	21	1	7	1	0	1	4	1	1	0
Luke Sewell, c	.176	5	17	1	3	0	0	0	1	2	0	1
Lefty Stewart, p	.000	1	1	0	0	0	0	0	0	0	1	0
Tommy Thomas, p	.000	2	0	0	0	0	0	0	0	0	0	0
Monte Weaver, p	.000	1	4	0	0	0	0	0	0	0	2	0
Earl Whitehill, p	.000	1	3	0	0	0	0	0	0	0	0	0
TOTAL	.214		173	11	37	4	0	2	11	13	25	1

PITCHER	W	L	ERA	G	GS	CG	SV	SHO	IP	H	ER	BB	SO
General Crowder	0	1	7.36	2	2	0	0	0	11.0	16	9	5	7
Alex McColl	0	0	0.00	1	0	0	0	0	2.0	0	0	0	0
Jack Russell	0	1	0.87	3	0	0	0	0	10.1	8	1	0	7
Lefty Stewart	0	1	9.00	1	1	0	0	0	2.0	6	2	0	0
Tommy Thomas	0	0	0.00	2	0	0	0	0	1.1	1	0	0	2
Monte Weaver	0	1	1.74	1	1	0	0	0	10.1	11	2	4	3
Earl Whitehill	1	0	0.00	1	1	1	0	1	9.0	5	0	2	2
TOTAL	1	4	2.74	11	5	1	0	1	46.0	47	14	11	21

GAME 1 AT NY OCT 3

WAS	000	100	001	2	5	3
NY	202	000	00X	4	10	2

Pitchers: STEWART, Russell (3), Thomas (8) vs HUBBELL
Home Runs: Ott-NY
Attendance: 46,672

GAME 2 AT NY OCT 4

WAS	001	000	000	1	5	0
NY	000	006	00X	6	10	0

Pitchers: CROWDER, Thomas (6), McColl (7) vs SCHUMACHER
Home Runs: Goslin-WAS
Attendance: 35,461

GAME 3 AT WAS OCT 5

NY	000	000	000	0	5	0
WAS	210	000	10X	4	9	1

Pitchers: FITZSIMMONS, Bell (8) vs WHITEHILL
Attendance: 25,727

GAME 4 AT WAS OCT 6

NY	000	100	000	01	2	11	1
WAS	000	000	100	00	1	8	0

Pitchers: HUBBELL vs WEAVER, Russell (11)
Home Runs: Terry-NY
Attendance: 26,762

GAME 5 AT WAS OCT 7

NY	020	001	000	1	4	11	1
WAS	000	003	000	0	3	10	0

Pitchers: Schumacher, LUQUE (6) vs Crowder, RUSSELL (6)
Home Runs: Schulte-WAS, Ott-NY
Attendance: 28,454

Pitching brothers Dizzy and Paul Dean won seven games in 10 days to give the Cardinals the pennant on the final day of the season. In the Series they continued their winning ways, chalking up all four Cardinals victories. Dizzy pitched the opener in Detroit. Given a 3–0 lead, thanks to five Detroit errors in the first three innings, he breezed to an 8–3 win.

Detroit's Schoolboy Rowe brought the Tigers back with a pitching masterpiece in Game 2. After giving up single runs in the second and third innings, he allowed only one runner to reach base over the next nine as his Tigers tied the score in the ninth, and won it on two walks and a single in the 12th.

Paul Dean nearly pitched a shutout in Game 3, yielding a harmless run with two out in the ninth after the Cards had built him a 4–0 lead. Brother Diz figured in a curious and painful play in Game 4. Pinch-running in the fourth inning, he was beaned by a would-be double-play throw as he ran to second. The tying run scored from third on the play, but Detroit's pitcher Eldon Auker shut out the Cards through the final five innings, and his teammates scored six more runs to bury St. Louis 10–4, evening the Series at two apiece. Diz was rushed to the hospital, but as no damage was found he started Game 5 the next day. He pitched well enough, but Detroit's Tommy Bridges pitched better, giving the Cardinals only one run to the Tigers' three.

Paul Dean evened the Series again with a win against Rowe in a closely contested sixth game. A grounder through Dean's legs allowed the Tigers to tie the game in the sixth inning, but Paul redeemed his error in the seventh when he singled in the tie-breaking run. Dizzy came back after only a day's rest to hurl a six-hit shutout in the finale. He also scored the game's first run and drove in the sixth with a double and single in his team's seven-run third. Three innings later, frustrated Tigers fans, angered by Joe Medwick's rough slide into their third baseman, pelted Medwick with food and bottles, halting the game for 20 minutes until Commissioner Landis ordered St. Louis from the game. The delay only forestalled Detroit's defeat, as the Cards took the title game, 11–0.

St. Louis Cardinals (NL), 4; Detroit Tigers (AL), 3

STL (N)

PLAYER/POS	AVG	G	AB	R	H	2B	3B	HR	RB	BB	SO	SB
Tex Carleton, p	.000	2	1	0	0	0	0	0	0	0	0	0
Ripper Collins, 1b	.367	7	30	4	11	1	0	0	3	1	2	0
Pat Crawford, ph	.000	2	2	0	0	0	0	0	0	0	0	0
Spud Davis, ph	1.000	2	2	0	2	0	0	0	1	0	0	0
Dizzy Dean, p-3	.250	4	12	3	3	2	0	0	1	0	3	0
Paul Dean, p	.167	2	6	0	1	0	0	0	2	0	1	0
Bill DeLancey, c	.172	7	29	3	5	3	0	1	4	2	8	0
Leo Durocher, ss	.259	7	27	4	7	1	1	0	0	0	0	0
Frankie Frisch, 2b	.194	7	31	2	6	1	0	0	4	0	1	0
Chick Fullis, of	.400	3	5	0	2	0	0	0	0	0	0	0
Jesse Haines, p	.000	1	0	0	0	0	0	0	0	0	0	0
Bill Hallahan, p	.000	1	3	0	0	0	0	0	0	0	1	0
Pepper Martin, 3b	.355	7	31	8	11	3	1	0	4	3	3	2
Joe Medwick, of	.379	7	29	4	11	0	1	1	5	1	7	0
Jim Mooney, p	.000	1	0	0	0	0	0	0	0	0	0	0
Ernie Orsatti, of	.318	7	22	3	7	0	1	0	2	3	1	0
Jack Rothrock, of	.233	7	30	3	7	3	1	0	6	1	2	0
Dazzy Vance, p	.000	1	0	0	0	0	0	0	0	0	0	0
Bill Walker, p	.000	2	2	0	0	0	0	0	0	0	2	0
Burgess Whitehead, ss	.000	1	0	0	0	0	0	0	0	0	0	0
TOTAL	.279		262	34	73	14	5	2	32	11	31	2

PITCHER	W	L	ERA	G	GS	CG	SV	SHO	IP	H	ER	BB	SO
Tex Carleton	0	0	7.36	2	1	0	0	0	3.2	5	3	2	2
Dizzy Dean	2	1	1.73	3	3	2	0	1	26.0	20	5	5	17
Paul Dean	2	0	1.00	2	2	2	0	0	18.0	15	2	7	11
Jesse Haines	0	0	0.00	1	0	0	0	0	0.2	1	0	0	2
Bill Hallahan	0	0	2.16	1	1	0	0	0	8.1	6	2	4	6
Jim Mooney	0	0	0.00	1	0	0	0	0	1.0	1	0	0	0
Dazzy Vance	0	0	0.00	1	0	0	0	0	1.1	2	0	1	3
Bill Walker	0	2	7.11	2	0	0	0	0	6.1	6	5	6	2
TOTAL	4	3	2.34	13	7	4	0	1	65.1	56	17	25	43

DET (A)

PLAYER/POS	AVG	G	AB	R	H	2B	3B	HR	RB	BB	SO	SB
Eldon Auker, p	.000	2	4	0	0	0	0	0	0	0	2	0
Tommy Bridges, p	.143	3	7	0	1	0	0	0	0	1	4	0
Mickey Cochrane, c	.214	7	28	2	6	1	0	0	1	4	3	0
General Crowder, p	.000	2	1	0	0	0	0	0	0	0	0	0
Frank Doljack, of-1	.000	2	2	0	0	0	0	0	0	0	0	0
Pete Fox, of	.286	7	28	1	8	6	0	0	2	1	4	0
Charlie Gehringer, 2b	.379	7	29	5	11	1	0	1	2	3	0	1
Goose Goslin, of	.241	7	29	2	7	1	0	0	2	3	1	0
Hank Greenberg, 1b	.321	7	28	4	9	2	1	1	7	4	9	1
Ray Hayworth, c	.000	1	0	0	0	0	0	0	0	0	0	0
Chief Hogsett, p	.000	3	3	0	0	0	0	0	0	0	1	0
Firpo Marberry, p	.000	2	0	0	0	0	0	0	0	0	0	0
Marv Owen, 3b	.069	7	29	0	2	0	0	0	1	0	5	1
Billy Rogell, ss	.276	7	29	3	8	1	0	0	4	1	4	1
Schoolboy Rowe, p	.000	3	7	0	0	0	0	0	0	0	5	0
Gee Walker, ph	.333	3	3	0	1	0	0	0	1	0	1	0
Jo-Jo White, of	.130	7	23	6	3	0	0	0	0	8	4	1
TOTAL	.224		250	23	56	12	1	2	20	25	43	5

PITCHER	W	L	ERA	G	GS	CG	SV	SHO	IP	H	ER	BB	SO
Eldon Auker	1	1	5.56	2	2	1	0	0	11.1	16	7	5	2
Tommy Bridges	1	1	3.63	3	2	1	0	0	17.1	21	7	1	12
General Crowder	0	1	1.50	2	1	0	0	0	6.0	6	1	1	2
Chief Hogsett	0	0	1.23	3	0	0	0	0	7.1	6	1	3	3
Firpo Marberry	0	0	21.60	2	0	0	0	0	1.2	5	4	1	0
Schoolboy Rowe	1	1	2.95	3	2	2	0	0	21.1	19	7	0	12
TOTAL	3	4	3.74	15	7	4	0	0	65.0	73	27	11	31

GAME 1 AT DET OCT 3

STL	021 014 000	8 13	2
DET	001 001 010	3 8	5

Pitchers: J.DEAN vs CROWDER, Marberry (6), Hogsett (6)
Home Runs: Medwick-STL, Greenberg-DET
Attendance: 42,505

GAME 2 AT DET OCT 4

STL	011 000 000 000	2 7	3
DET	000 100 001 001	3 7	0

Pitchers: Hallahan, W.WALKER (9) vs ROWE
Attendance: 43,451

GAME 3 AT STL OCT 5

DET	000 000 001	1 8	2
STL	110 020 00X	4 9	1

Pitchers: BRIDGES, Hogsett (5) vs P.DEAN
Attendance: 34,073

GAME 4 AT STL OCT 6

DET	003 100 150	10 13	1
STL	011 200 000	4 10	5

Pitchers: AUKER vs Carleton, Vance (3), W.WALKER (5), Haines (8), Mooney (9)
Attendance: 37,492

GAME 5 AT STL OCT 7

DET	010 002 000	3 7	0
STL	000 000 100	1 7	1

Pitchers: BRIDGES vs J.DEAN, Carleton (9)
Home Runs: Gehringer-DET, DeLancey-STL
Attendance: 38,536

GAME 6 AT DET OCT 8

STL	100 020 100	4 10	2
DET	001 002 000	3 7	1

Pitchers: P.DEAN vs ROWE
Attendance: 44,551

GAME 7 AT DET OCT 9

STL	007 002 200	11 17	1
DET	000 000 000	0 6	3

Pitchers: J.DEAN vs AUKER, Rowe (3), Hogsett (3), Bridges (4), Marberry (8), Crowder (9)
Attendance: 40,902

With a 21-game September winning streak, the Cubs vaulted over the Giants and Cardinals to face Detroit in the Series, and for a moment it seemed as if their momentum might carry them past the Tigers as well. Chicago scored two runs off Schoolboy Rowe in the top of the first in the opener, and right fielder Frank Demaree homered to open the ninth as Lon Warneke blanked the Tigers on four hits. But Detroit retaliated quickly in Game 2, driving out starter Charlie Root in the first inning with four runs (including Hank Greenberg's two-run homer) before Root had had a chance to record even one out. Tigers pitcher Rocky Bridges gained an easy 8–3 win, but Greenberg broke a wrist and was finished for the Series.

In Game 3 the Cubs scored three times before Detroit countered with their first run in the sixth. But a walk and four Tiger hits in the eighth put the Bengals ahead, 4–3. Billy Rogell turned a foiled steal into a rundown to allow a fifth Tiger to cross the plate. Two Cubs runs in the last of the ninth tied the score, but Detroit pulled out the victory in the 11th as a pair of singles sandwiched Fred Lindstrom's error at third to give them an unearned run.

Detroit's Alvin "General" Crowder followed up the Tigers' advantage the next day with a neat five-hit 2–1 win. Once again the Cubs bobbled away the game, this time with two sixth-inning errors that enabled Detroit to score the winning run without a hit. Chuck Klein's two-run homer saved Chicago from elimination in Game Five as Lon Warneke and Bill Lee shut out the Tigers through eight before letting in a harmless run in the ninth.

Chicago's Larry French and Tiger Rocky Bridges yielded 12 hits apiece in Game 6. Cubs second baseman Billy Herman singled in a run in the third to tie the score, and homered for two more runs in the fifth to put the Cubs ahead. But the Tigers tied it up an inning later, and took their first world title ever when Goose Goslin singled in Mickey Cochrane with two out in the bottom of the ninth.

Detroit Tigers (AL), 4; Chicago Cubs (NL), 2

DET (A)

PLAYER/POS	AVG	G	AB	R	H	2B	3B	HR	RB	BB	SO	SB
Eldon Auker, p	.000	1	2	0	0	0	0	0	0	0	1	0
Tommy Bridges, p	.125	2	8	1	1	0	0	0	1	0	3	0
Flea Clifton, 3b	.000	4	16	1	0	0	0	0	0	2	4	0
Mickey Cochrane, c	.292	6	24	3	7	1	0	0	1	4	1	0
General Crowder, p	.333	1	3	1	1	0	0	0	0	1	0	0
Pete Fox, of	.385	6	26	1	10	3	1	0	4	0	1	0
Charlie Gehringer, 2b	.375	6	24	4	9	3	0	0	4	2	1	1
Goose Goslin, of	.273	6	22	2	6	1	0	0	3	5	0	0
Hank Greenberg, 1b	.167	2	6	1	1	0	0	1	2	1	0	0
Chief Hogsett, p	.000	1	0	0	0	0	0	0	0	0	0	0
Marv Owen, 1b-4,3b-2	.050	6	20	2	1	0	0	0	1	2	3	0
Billy Rogell, ss	.292	6	24	1	7	2	0	0	1	2	5	0
Schoolboy Rowe, p	.250	3	8	0	2	1	0	0	0	0	1	0
Gee Walker, of-1	.250	3	4	1	1	0	0	0	0	1	0	0
Jo-Jo White, of	.263	5	19	3	5	0	0	0	1	5	7	0
TOTAL	.248		206	21	51	11	1	1	18	25	27	1

PITCHER	W	L	ERA	G	GS	CG	SV	SHO	IP	H	ER	BB	SO
Eldon Auker	0	0	3.00	1	1	0	0	0	6.0	6	2	2	1
Tommy Bridges	2	0	2.50	2	2	2	0	0	18.0	18	5	4	9
General Crowder	1	0	1.00	1	1	1	0	0	9.0	5	1	3	5
Chief Hogsett	0	0	0.00	1	0	0	0	0	1.0	0	0	1	0
Schoolboy Rowe	1	2	2.57	3	2	2	0	0	21.0	19	6	1	14
TOTAL	4	2	2.29	8	6	5	0	0	55.0	48	14	11	29

CHI (N)

PLAYER/POS	AVG	G	AB	R	H	2B	3B	HR	RB	BB	SO	SB
Tex Carleton, p	.000	1	1	0	0	0	0	0	0	1	1	0
Phil Cavaretta, 1b	.125	6	24	1	3	0	0	0	0	0	5	0
Frank Demaree, of	.250	6	24	2	6	1	0	2	2	1	4	0
Larry French, p	.250	2	4	1	1	0	0	0	0	0	2	0
Augie Galan, of	.160	6	25	2	4	1	0	0	2	2	2	0
Stan Hack, 3b-6,ss-1	.227	6	22	2	5	1	1	0	0	2	2	1
Gabby Hartnett, c	.292	6	24	1	7	0	0	1	2	0	3	0
Roy Henshaw, p	.000	1	1	0	0	0	0	0	0	0	0	0
Billy Herman, 2b	.333	6	24	3	8	2	1	1	6	0	2	0
Billy Jurges, ss	.250	6	16	3	4	0	0	0	1	4	4	0
Chuck Klein, of-3	.333	5	12	2	4	0	0	1	2	0	2	0
Fabian Kowalik, p	.500	1	2	1	1	0	0	0	0	0	0	0
Bill Lee, p	.000	2	1	0	0	0	0	0	1	0	0	0
Fred Lindstrom, of-4,3b-1	.200	4	15	0	3	1	0	0	0	1	1	0
Ken O'Dea, ph	1.000	1	1	0	1	0	0	0	1	0	0	0
Charlie Root, p	.000	2	0	0	0	0	0	0	0	0	0	0
Walter Stephenson, ph	.000	1	1	0	0	0	0	0	0	0	1	0
Lon Warneke, p	.200	3	5	0	1	0	0	0	0	0	0	0
TOTAL	.238		202	18	48	6	2	5	17	11	29	1

PITCHER	W	L	ERA	G	GS	CG	SV	SHO	IP	H	ER	BB	SO
Tex Carleton	0	1	1.29	1	1	0	0	0	7.0	6	1	7	4
Larry French	0	2	3.38	2	1	1	0	0	10.2	15	4	2	8
Roy Henshaw	0	0	7.36	1	0	0	0	0	3.2	2	3	5	2
Fabian Kowalik	0	0	2.08	1	0	0	0	0	4.1	3	1	1	1
Bill Lee	0	0	4.35	2	1	0	1	0	10.1	11	5	5	5
Charlie Root	0	1	18.00	2	1	0	0	0	2.0	5	4	1	2
Lon Warneke	2	0	0.54	3	2	1	0	1	16.2	9	1	4	5
TOTAL	2	4	3.13	12	6	2	1	1	54.2	51	19	25	27

GAME 1 AT DET OCT 2

		R	H	E
CHI	200 000 001	3	7	0
DET	000 000 000	0	4	3

Pitchers: WARNEKE vs ROWE
Home Runs: Demaree-CHI
Attendance: 47,391

GAME 2 AT DET OCT 3

		R	H	E
CHI	000 010 200	3	6	1
DET	400 300 10X	8	9	2

Pitchers: ROOT, Henshaw (1), Kowalik (4) vs BRIDGES
Home Runs: Greenberg-DET
Attendance: 46,742

GAME 3 AT CHI OCT 4

		R	H	E
DET	000 001 040 01	6	12	2
CHI	020 010 002 00	5	10	3

Pitchers: Auker, Hogsett (7), ROWE (8) vs Lee, Warneke (8), FRENCH (10)
Home Runs: Demaree-CHI
Attendance: 45,532

GAME 4 AT CHI OCT 5

		R	H	E
DET	001 001 000	2	7	0
CHI	010 000 000	1	5	2

Pitchers: CROWDER vs CARLETON, Root (8)
Home Runs: Hartnett-CHI
Attendance: 49,350

GAME 5 AT CHI OCT 6

		R	H	E
DET	000 000 001	1	7	1
CHI	002 000 10X	3	8	0

Pitchers: ROWE vs WARNEKE, Lee (7)
Home Runs: Klein-CHI
Attendance: 49,237

GAME 6 AT DET OCT 7

		R	H	E
CHI	001 020 000	3	12	0
DET	100 101 001	4	12	1

Pitchers: FRENCH vs BRIDGES
Home Runs: Herman-CHI
Attendance: 48,420

The Giants managed to win two games, but this first Series between the cross-river rivals in 13 years was really no contest. Babe Ruth was gone, but Lou Gehrig was still there, and Joe DiMaggio had arrived. The Yankees outhit the Giants by 56 percentage points and outscored them by 20 runs.

Giants ace Carl Hubbell, who had won his final 16 decisions of the regular season, continued his streak in the Series opener. The Yankees scored first on George Selkirk's third-inning homer, but Giants shortstop Dick Bartell homered to even things in the fifth. Hubbell held the Yankees to that one run, but the Giants roughed up Red Ruffing for five more runs, to give the Polo Grounders a brief Series advantage.

Game 2 was a blowout, as the Yankees hammered five Giants pitchers for 18 runs—four of them on Tony Lazzeri's grand slam in the third—to give Lefty Gomez an easy win. By contrast, Game 3 was a pitchers' duel. Although the Giants touched Bump Hadley and Pat Malone for 11 hits, only Jimmy Ripple's fifth-inning homer produced a run. Freddie Fitzsimmons was much more stingy with hits, yielding only four. But one was Gehrig's home run in the second inning, and another was Frank Crosetti's game-winning RBI single in the eighth.

Gehrig homered again in the third inning of Game 4 to give the Yankees an insurmountable lead—and Hubbell his first loss in months. Down three games to one, the Giants struggled back in Game 5. They took a first-inning 3–0 lead, but the Yankees clawed their way back, and by the end of six the score was 4–4. There it stayed until the 10th, when a double, sacrifice, and fly to center put the Giants ahead by a run. Hal Schumacher, who had pitched the whole game, held the Yankees scoreless one more time for the win.

Fitzsimmons, who had pitched so well in his third-game loss, didn't last four innings in Game 6. Though the Giants scored first, Jake Powell (who led all Series hitters at .455) tied the game with a two-run homer in the top of the second for the Yankees. Two more runs in the fourth drove out Fitzsimmons, but the game stayed close until the top of the ninth, when five Yankees singles and three walks produced seven runs and a Series-ending 13–5 rout.

New York Yankees (AL), 4; New York Giants (NL), 2

NY (A)

PLAYER/POS	AVG	G	AB	R	H	2B	3B	HR	RB	BB	SO	SB
Frankie Crosetti, ss	.269	6	26	5	7	2	0	0	3	3	5	0
Bill Dickey, c	.120	6	25	5	3	0	0	1	5	3	4	0
Joe DiMaggio, of	.346	6	26	3	9	3	0	0	3	1	3	0
Lou Gehrig, 1b	.292	6	24	5	7	1	0	2	7	3	2	0
Lefty Gomez, p	.250	2	8	1	2	0	0	0	3	0	3	0
Bump Hadley, p	.000	1	2	0	0	0	0	0	0	0	1	0
Roy Johnson, ph	.000	2	1	0	0	0	0	0	0	0	1	0
Tony Lazzeri, 2b	.250	6	20	4	5	0	0	1	7	4	4	0
Pat Malone, p	1.000	2	1	0	1	0	0	0	0	0	0	0
Johnny Murphy, p	.500	1	2	1	1	0	0	0	1	0	1	0
Monte Pearson, p	.500	1	4	0	2	1	0	0	0	0	0	0
Jake Powell, of	.455	6	22	8	10	1	0	1	5	4	4	1
Red Rolfe, 3b	.400	6	25	5	10	0	0	0	4	3	1	0
Red Ruffing, p-2	.000	3	5	0	0	0	0	0	0	1	2	0
Bob Seeds, pr	.000	1	0	0	0	0	0	0	0	0	0	0
George Selkirk, of	.333	6	24	6	8	0	1	2	3	4	4	0
TOTAL	.302		215	43	65	8	1	7	41	26	35	1

PITCHER	W	L	ERA	G	GS	CG	SV	SHO	IP	H	ER	BB	SO
Lefty Gomez	2	0	4.70	2	2	1	0	0	15.1	14	8	11	9
Bump Hadley	1	0	1.13	1	1	0	0	0	8.0	10	1	1	2
Pat Malone	0	1	1.80	2	0	0	1	0	5.0	2	1	1	2
Johnny Murphy	0	0	3.38	1	0	0	1	0	2.2	1	1	1	1
Monte Pearson	1	0	2.00	1	1	1	0	0	9.0	7	2	2	7
Red Ruffing	0	1	5.14	2	2	1	0	0	14.0	16	8	5	12
TOTAL	4	2	3.50	9	6	3	2	0	54.0	50	21	21	33

NY (N)

PLAYER/POS	AVG	G	AB	R	H	2B	3B	HR	RB	BB	SO	SB
Dick Bartell, ss	.381	6	21	5	8	3	0	1	3	4	4	0
Slick Castleman, p	.500	1	2	0	1	0	0	0	0	0	0	0
Dick Coffman, p	.000	2	0	0	0	0	0	0	0	0	0	0
Harry Danning, c-1	.000	2	2	0	0	0	0	0	0	0	1	0
Kiddo Davis, ph	.500	4	2	2	1	0	0	0	0	0	0	0
Freddie Fitzsimmons, p	.500	2	4	0	2	0	0	0	0	0	1	0
Frank Gabler, p	.000	2	0	0	0	0	0	0	0	1	0	0
Harry Gumbert, p	.000	2	0	0	0	0	0	0	0	0	0	0
Carl Hubbell, p	.333	2	6	0	2	0	0	0	1	0	0	0
Travis Jackson, 3b	.190	6	21	1	4	0	0	0	1	1	3	0
Mark Koenig, 2b-1	.333	3	3	0	1	0	0	0	0	0	1	0
Hank Leiber, of	.000	2	6	0	0	0	0	0	0	2	2	0
Sam Leslie, ph	.667	3	3	0	2	0	0	0	0	0	0	0
Gus Mancuso, c	.263	6	19	3	5	2	0	0	1	3	3	0
Eddie Mayo, 3b	.000	1	1	0	0	0	0	0	0	0	0	0
Jo-Jo Moore, of	.214	6	28	4	6	2	0	1	1	1	4	0
Mel Ott, of	.304	6	23	4	7	2	0	1	3	3	1	0
Jimmy Ripple, of	.333	5	12	2	4	0	0	1	3	3	13	0
Hal Schumacher, p	.000	2	4	0	0	0	0	0	0	1	3	0
Al Smith, p	.000	1	0	0	0	0	0	0	0	0	0	0
Bill Terry, 1b	.240	6	25	1	6	0	0	0	5	1	4	0
Burgess Whitehead, 2b	.048	6	21	1	1	0	0	0	2	1	3	0
TOTAL	.246		203	23	50	9	0	4	20	21	33	0

PITCHER	W	L	ERA	G	GS	CG	SV	SHO	IP	H	ER	BB	SO
Slick Castleman	0	0	2.08	1	0	0	0	0	4.1	3	1	2	5
Dick Coffman	0	0	32.40	2	0	0	0	0	1.2	5	6	1	1
Freddie Fitzsimmons	0	2	5.40	2	2	1	0	0	11.2	13	7	2	6
Frank Gabler	0	0	7.20	2	0	0	0	0	5.0	7	4	4	0
Harry Gumbert	0	0	36.00	2	0	0	0	0	2.0	7	8	4	2
Carl Hubbell	1	1	2.25	2	2	1	0	0	16.0	15	4	2	10
Hal Schumacher	1	1	5.25	2	2	1	0	0	12.0	13	7	10	11
Al Smith	0	0	81.00	1	0	0	0	0	0.1	2	3	1	0
TOTAL	2	4	6.79	14	6	3	0	0	53.0	65	40	26	35

GAME 1 AT NY -N SEPT 30

		R	H	E
NY-A	001 000 000	1	7	2
NY-N	000 011 04X	6	9	1

Pitchers: RUFFING vs HUBBELL
Home Runs: Bartell-NY(N), Selkirk-NY(A)
Attendance: 39,419

GAME 2 AT NY -N OCT 2

		R	H	E
NY-A	207 001 206	18	17	0
NY-N	010 300 000	4	6	1

Pitchers: GOMEZ vs SCHUMACHER, Smith (3), Coffman (3), Gabler (5), Gumbert (9)
Home Runs: Dickey-NY(A), Lazzeri-NY(A)
Attendance: 43,543

GAME 3 AT NY -A OCT 3

		R	H	E
NY-N	000 010 000	1	11	0
NY-A	010 000 01X	2	4	0

Pitchers: FITZSIMMONS vs HADLEY, Malone (9)
Home Runs: Gehrig-NY(A), Ripple-NY(N)
Attendance: 64,842

GAME 4 AT NY -A OCT 4

		R	H	E
NY-N	000 100 010	2	7	1
NY-A	013 000 01X	5	10	1

Pitchers: HUBBELL, Gabler (8) vs PEARSON
Home Runs: Gehrig-NY(A)
Attendance: 66,669

GAME 5 AT NY -A OCT 5

		R	H	E
NY-N	300 001 000 1	5	8	3
NY-A	011 002 000 0	4	10	1

Pitchers: SCHUMACHER vs Ruffing, MALONE (7)
Home Runs: Selkirk-NY(A)
Attendance: 50,024

GAME 6 AT NY -N OCT 6

		R	H	E
NY-A	021 200 017	13	17	2
NY-N	200 010 110	5	9	1

Pitchers: GOMEZ, Murphy (7) vs FITZSIMMONS, Castleman (4), Coffman (9), Gumbert (9)
Home Runs: Moore-NY(N), Ott-NY(N), Powell-NY(A)
Attendance: 38,427

For the second year in a row, the Yankees overwhelmed the Giants, this time in just five games. Giants ace Carl Hubbell, who took the opener in 1936, was unable to repeat this time. For five innings he held the Yankees to one hit. But in the sixth everything fell apart. Before Hubbell was taken out, two walks, five singles, and an error had led in five runs. And the two runners Hubbell left on base scored later on a second Giants error and two walks by reliever Dick Coffman. The Yankees' Lefty Gomez also yielded six hits, but wider spacing and better field support held the Giants to one run in the fifth. Tony Lazzeri's homer in the eighth made the final score 8–1.

The Yankees spread their runs a bit more evenly in Game 2. For the second time the Giants gained a 1–0 lead. Rookie phenom Cliff Melton held the Yankees scoreless through four, but four straight hits for two runs at the start of the fifth drove him out. Reliever Ad Gumbert stopped the Yankees in the rest of the inning but gave up four more hits—and four more runs—in the sixth before Coffman stepped in to stop the assault. But Coffman gave up two final Yankees runs in the seventh, to complete a second straight 8–1 win, as Red Ruffing held the Giants scoreless through the final eight innings.

The Yankees had scored five times off Hal Schumacher in Game 3 before the Giants got their one run in the seventh. But Yankees starter Monte Pearson made the game tighter as he yielded a single and two walks to load the bases in the ninth before Johnny Murphy came on to record the final out.

The Giants' bats finally came alive in the second inning of Game 4. Seven singles, plus a walk and a missed play at the plate gave the club a 6–1 lead, which starter Hubbell protected for the only Giants win of the Series.

Solo homers by Myril Hoag and Joe DiMaggio in the second and the third gave the Yankees a 2–0 lead early in Game 5, but Giants slugger Mel Ott tied it up with a two-run shot off Lefty Gomez in the last of the third. But Gomez shut the Giants down the rest of the way, and singled in Lazzeri in the fifth with what proved the game winner (scoring himself on Lou Gehrig's double for the final run of the Series).

New York Yankees (AL), 4; New York Giants (NL), 1

NY (A)

PLAYER/POS	AVG	G	AB	R	H	2B	3B	HR	RB	BB	SO	SB
Ivy Andrews, p	.000	1	2	0	0	0	0	0	0	0	1	0
Frankie Crosetti, ss	.048	5	21	2	1	0	0	0	0	3	2	0
Bill Dickey, c	.211	5	19	3	4	0	1	0	3	2	2	0
Joe DiMaggio, of	.273	5	22	2	6	0	0	1	4	0	3	0
Lou Gehrig, 1b	.294	5	17	4	5	1	1	1	3	5	4	0
Lefty Gomez, p	.167	2	6	2	1	0	0	0	1	2	1	0
Bump Hadley, p	.000	1	0	0	0	0	0	0	0	0	0	0
Myril Hoag, of	.300	5	20	4	6	1	0	1	2	0	1	0
Tony Lazzeri, 2b	.400	5	15	3	6	0	1	1	2	3	3	0
Johnny Murphy, p	.000	1	0	0	0	0	0	0	0	0	0	0
Monte Pearson, p	.000	1	3	0	0	0	0	0	0	1	1	0
Jake Powell, ph	.000	1	1	0	0	0	0	0	0	0	1	0
Red Rolfe, 3b	.300	5	20	3	6	2	1	0	1	3	2	0
Red Ruffing, p	.500	1	4	0	2	1	0	0	3	0	0	0
George Selkirk, of	.263	5	19	5	5	1	0	0	6	2	0	0
Kemp Wicker, p	.000	1	0	0	0	0	0	0	0	0	0	0
TOTAL	.249		169	28	42	6	4	4	25	21	21	0

PITCHER	W	L	ERA	G	GS	CG	SV	SHO	IP	H	ER	BB	SO
Ivy Andrews	0	0	3.18	1	0	0	0	0	5.2	6	2	4	1
Lefty Gomez	2	0	1.50	2	2	2	0	0	18.0	16	3	2	8
Bump Hadley	0	1	33.75	1	1	0	0	0	1.1	6	5	0	0
Johnny Murphy	0	0	0.00	1	0	0	1	0	0.1	0	0	0	0
Monte Pearson	1	0	1.04	1	1	0	0	0	8.2	5	1	2	4
Red Ruffing	1	0	1.00	1	1	1	0	0	9.0	7	1	3	8
Kemp Wicker	0	0	0.00	1	0	0	0	0	1.0	0	0	0	0
TOTAL	4	1	2.45	8	5	3	1	0	44.0	40	12	11	21

NY (N)

PLAYER/POS	AVG	G	AB	R	H	2B	3B	HR	RB	BB	SO	SB
Dick Bartell, ss	.238	5	21	3	5	1	0	0	1	0	3	0
Wally Berger, ph	.000	3	3	0	0	0	0	0	0	0	1	0
Don Brennan, p	.000	2	0	0	0	0	0	0	0	0	0	0
Lou Chiozza, of	.286	2	7	0	2	0	0	0	0	1	1	0
Dick Coffman, p	.000	2	1	0	0	0	0	0	0	0	1	0
Harry Danning, c	.250	3	12	0	3	1	0	0	2	0	2	0
Harry Gumbert, p	.000	2	0	0	0	0	0	0	0	0	0	0
Carl Hubbell, p	.000	2	6	1	0	0	0	0	1	0	0	0
Hank Leiber, of	.364	3	11	2	4	0	0	0	2	1	1	0
Sam Leslie, ph	.000	2	1	0	0	0	0	0	0	1	0	0
Gus Mancuso, c-2	.000	3	8	0	0	0	0	0	1	0	1	0
Johnny McCarthy, 1b	.211	5	19	1	4	1	0	0	1	1	2	0
Cliff Melton, p	.000	3	2	0	0	0	0	0	0	1	1	0
Jo-Jo Moore, of	.391	5	23	1	9	1	0	0	1	0	1	0
Mel Ott, 3b	.200	5	20	1	4	0	0	1	3	1	4	0
Jimmy Ripple, of	.294	5	17	2	5	0	0	0	0	3	1	0
Blondy Ryan, ph	.000	1	1	0	0	0	0	0	0	0	1	0
Hal Schumacher, p	.000	1	1	0	0	0	0	0	0	0	1	0
Al Smith, p	.000	2	0	0	0	0	0	0	0	0	0	0
Burgess Whitehead, 2b	.250	5	16	1	4	2	0	0	0	2	0	1
TOTAL	.237		169	12	40	6	0	1	12	11	21	1

PITCHER	W	L	ERA	G	GS	CG	SV	SHO	IP	H	ER	BB	SO
Don Brennan	0	0	0.00	2	0	0	0	0	3.0	1	0	1	1
Dick Coffman	0	0	4.15	2	0	0	0	0	4.1	2	2	5	1
Harry Gumbert	0	0	27.00	2	0	0	0	0	1.1	4	4	1	1
Carl Hubbell	1	1	3.77	2	2	1	0	0	14.1	12	6	4	7
Cliff Melton	0	2	4.91	3	2	0	0	0	11.0	12	6	6	7
Hal Schumacher	0	1	6.00	1	1	0	0	0	6.0	9	4	4	3
Al Smith	0	0	3.00	2	0	0	0	0	3.0	2	1	0	1
TOTAL	1	4	4.81	14	5	1	0	0	43.0	42	23	21	21

GAME 1 AT NY -A OCT 6

		R	H	E
NY-N	000 010 000	1	6	2
NY-A	**000 007 01X**	**8**	**7**	**0**

Pitchers: HUBBELL, Gumbert (6), Coffman (6), Smith (8) vs GOMEZ
Home Runs: Lazzeri-NY(A)
Attendance: 60,573

GAME 2 AT NY -A OCT 7

		R	H	E
NY-N	100 000 000	1	7	0
NY-A	**000 024 20X**	**8**	**12**	**0**

Pitchers: MELTON, Gumbert (5), Coffman (6) vs RUFFING
Attendance: 57,675

GAME 3 AT NY -N OCT 8

		R	H	E
NY-A	**012 110 000**	**5**	**9**	**0**
NY-N	000 000 100	1	5	4

Pitchers: PEARSON, Murphy (9) vs SCHUMACHER, Melton (7), Brennan (9)
Attendance: 37,385

GAME 4 AT NY -N OCT 9

		R	H	E
NY-A	101 000 001	3	6	0
NY-N	**060 000 10X**	**7**	**12**	**3**

Pitchers: HADLEY, Andrews (2), Wicker (8) vs HUBBELL
Home Runs: Gehrig-NY(A)
Attendance: 44,293

GAME 5 AT NY -N OCT 10

		R	H	E
NY-A	**011 020 000**	**4**	**8**	**0**
NY-N	002 000 000	2	10	0

Pitchers: GOMEZ vs MELTON, Smith (6), Brennan (8)
Home Runs: DiMaggio-NY(A), Hoag-NY(A), Ott-NY(N)
Attendance: 38,216

As they had six years earlier, the Cubs faced the Yankees in the World Series, and as they had six years earlier, New York swept the Series in four games. Although Cubs batters made nearly as many hits as the Yankees, they did much less damage, driving in 13 fewer runs. In Game 1, Yankees ace Red Ruffing scattered nine hits, holding Chicago to a single run. The Cubs' Bill Lee was nearly as effective in scattering hits, but a base on balls in the second (the game's only walk) followed by a pair of singles sandwiched around an error accounted for two runs—all the Yankees would need for the win (though they scored once more in the sixth).

In Game 2 the Cubs outhit the Yankees 11 to 7, but scored only half as many runs as the New Yorkers. Chicago's Dizzy Dean, pitching on craft and guile with his fastball gone, managed to keep the game close until the final innings. With a 3–2 lead going into the eighth, though, he gave up a two-run homer to Frank Crosetti, and the same to Joe DiMaggio in the ninth before being relieved. Yankees fireman Johnny Murphy, meanwhile, held Chicago scoreless over the final two innings to preserve Lefty Gomez's win.

Utility outfielder Joe Marty drove in both Chicago runs in Game 3 with a grounder to third in the fifth and a homer in the eighth. (His .500 batting average was tops for both teams, and he drove in five of the Cubs' nine Series runs.) But again the Cubs fell short, as rookie second baseman Joe Gordon homered to tie the score in the bottom of the fifth with the first of what would be five Yankees runs by the time Bill Dickey's homer in the eighth ended the scoring for the day.

Cubs second baseman Billy Herman's wild throw with two out in the second inning of Game 4 led to three unearned runs, and a lead the Yankees would not relinquish. Though their lead was cut to one run (4–3) when Chicago scored twice in the top of the eighth, the Yankees took advantage of two wild pitches and two walks to turn their four hits into four runs that crushed Chicago hopes and gave the New Yorkers a record third consecutive world championship.

New York Yankees (AL), 4; Chicago Cubs (NL), 0

NY (A)

PLAYER/POS	AVG	G	AB	R	H	2B	3B	HR	RB	BB	SO	SB
Frankie Crosetti, ss	.250	4	16	1	4	2	1	1	6	2	4	0
Bill Dickey, c	.400	4	15	2	6	0	0	1	2	1	0	1
Joe DiMaggio, of	.267	4	15	4	4	0	0	1	2	1	1	0
Lou Gehrig, 1b	.286	4	14	4	4	0	0	0	0	2	3	0
Lefty Gomez, p	.000	1	2	0	0	0	0	0	0	0	0	0
Joe Gordon, 2b	.400	4	15	3	6	2	0	1	6	1	3	1
Tommy Henrich, of	.250	4	16	3	4	1	0	1	1	0	1	0
Myril Hoag, of-1	.400	2	5	3	2	1	0	0	1	0	0	0
Johnny Murphy, p	.000	1	0	0	0	0	0	0	0	0	0	0
Monte Pearson, p	.333	1	3	1	1	0	0	0	0	1	0	0
Jake Powell, of	.000	1	0	0	0	0	0	0	0	0	0	0
Red Rolfe, 3b	.167	4	18	0	3	0	0	0	1	0	3	1
Red Ruffing, p	.167	2	6	1	1	0	0	0	1	1	0	0
George Selkirk, of	.200	3	10	0	2	0	0	0	1	2	1	0
TOTAL	.274		135	22	37	6	1	5	21	11	16	3

PITCHER	W	L	ERA	G	GS	CG	SV	SHO	IP	H	ER	BB	SO
Lefty Gomez	1	0	3.86	1	1	0	0	0	7.0	9	3	1	5
Johnny Murphy	0	0	0.00	1	0	0	1	0	2.0	2	0	1	1
Monte Pearson	1	0	1.00	1	1	1	0	0	9.0	5	1	2	9
Red Ruffing	2	0	1.50	2	2	2	0	0	18.0	17	3	2	11
TOTAL	4	0	1.75	5	4	3	1	0	36.0	33	7	6	26

CHI (N)

PLAYER/POS	AVG	G	AB	R	H	2B	3B	HR	RB	BB	SO	SB
Clay Bryant, p	.000	1	2	0	0	0	0	0	0	0	1	0
Tex Carleton, p	.000	1	0	0	0	0	0	0	0	0	0	0
Phil Cavaretta, of-3	.462	4	13	1	6	1	0	0	0	0	1	0
Ripper Collins, 1b	.133	4	15	1	2	0	0	0	0	0	3	0
Dizzy Dean, p	.667	2	3	0	2	0	0	0	0	0	0	0
Frank Demaree, of	.100	3	10	1	1	0	0	0	0	1	2	0
Larry French, p	.000	3	0	0	0	0	0	0	0	0	0	0
Augie Galan, ph	.000	2	2	0	0	0	0	0	0	0	1	0
Stan Hack, 3b	.471	4	17	3	8	1	0	0	1	1	2	0
Gabby Hartnett, c	.091	3	11	0	1	0	1	0	0	0	2	0
Billy Herman, 2b	.188	4	16	1	3	0	0	0	0	1	4	0
Billy Jurges, ss	.231	4	13	0	3	1	0	0	0	1	3	0
Tony Lazzeri, ph	.000	2	2	0	0	0	0	0	0	0	1	0
Bill Lee, p	.000	2	3	0	0	0	0	0	0	0	1	0
Joe Marty, of	.500	3	12	1	6	1	0	1	5	0	2	0
Ken O'Dea, c-1	.200	3	5	1	1	0	0	1	2	1	0	0
Vance Page, p	.000	1	0	0	0	0	0	0	0	0	0	0
Carl Reynolds, of-3	.000	4	12	0	0	0	0	0	0	1	3	0
Charlie Root, p	.000	1	0	0	0	0	0	0	0	0	0	0
Jack Russell, p	.000	2	0	0	0	0	0	0	0	0	0	0
TOTAL	.243		136	9	33	4	1	2	8	6	26	0

PITCHER	W	L	ERA	G	GS	CG	SV	SHO	IP	H	ER	BB	SO
Clay Bryant	0	1	6.75	1	1	0	0	0	5.1	6	4	5	3
Tex Carleton	0	0	∞	1	0	0	0	0	0.0	1	2	2	0
Dizzy Dean	0	1	6.48	2	1	0	0	0	8.1	8	6	1	2
Larry French	0	0	2.70	3	0	0	0	0	3.1	1	1	1	2
Bill Lee	0	2	2.45	2	2	0	0	0	11.0	15	3	1	8
Vance Page	0	0	13.50	1	0	0	0	0	1.1	2	2	0	0
Charlie Root	0	0	3.00	1	0	0	0	0	3.0	3	1	0	1
Jack Russell	0	0	0.00	2	0	0	0	0	1.2	1	0	1	0
TOTAL	0	4	5.03	13	4	0	0	0	34.0	37	19	11	16

GAME 1 AT CHI OCT 5

				R	H	E
NY	020	000	100	3	12	1
CHI	001	000	000	1	9	1

Pitchers: RUFFING vs LEE, Russell (9)
Attendance: 43,642

GAME 2 AT CHI OCT 6

				R	H	E
NY	020	000	022	6	7	2
CHI	102	000	000	3	11	0

Pitchers: GOMEZ, Murphy (8) vs J.DEAN, French (9)
Home Runs: Crosetti-NY, DiMaggio-NY
Attendance: 42,108

GAME 3 AT NY OCT 8

				R	H	E
CHI	000	010	010	2	5	1
NY	000	022	01X	5	7	2

Pitchers: BRYANT, Russell (6), French (7) vs PEARSON
Home Runs: Dickey-NY, Gordon-NY, Marty-CHI
Attendance: 55,236

GAME 4 AT NY OCT 9

				R	H	E
CHI	000	100	020	3	8	1
NY	030	001	04X	8	11	1

Pitchers: LEE, Root (4), Page (7), French (8), Carleton (8), J.Dean (8) vs RUFFING
Home Runs: Henrich-NY, O'Dea-CHI
Attendance: 59,847

The Yankees won their fourth consecutive World Series with their second sweep in a row. This time the victim was Cincinnati, in the Series for the first time since their tainted triumph over the Black Sox two decades earlier. New York had lost the power of Lou Gehrig (whose illness forced his retirement early in the season), but in the Series rookie outfielder Charlie Keller took up the slack. He led both clubs in batting, slugging, home runs, RBIs, hits, and runs, and hit one of the Series' two triples. His eight runs scored equalled those of the whole Cincinnati team.

The Yankees' Red Ruffing and Cincinnati's Paul Derringer hurled matching four-hitters through eight innings of Game 1. With the score tied 1–1, Ruffing set the Reds down in order in the ninth. But in the bottom of the ninth Keller tripled off Derringer with one away, and scored the deciding run on catcher Bill Dickey's single.

Babe Dahlgren, Gehrig's replacement at first base, doubled in the third and later scored the Yankees' first run in Game 2, and homered in the next inning for New York's fourth and final run of the game. Reds starter Bucky Walters stopped the Yankees after that, but they had more than enough runs for the win, as Monte Pearson held the Reds hitless through seven and wound up with a two-hit shutout.

Keller provided the margin of victory with a pair of two-run homers in the first and fifth innings of Game 3. Joe DiMaggio's two-run homer in the third and Bill Dickey's solo shot that followed Keller's homer in the fifth accounted for the rest of New York's runs in their 7–3 win.

No one scored through six innings of Game 4. Keller and Dickey then homered in the top of the seventh, but Red Rolfe's error at third in the last of the inning opened the way for the Reds to go ahead with three unearned runs. They earned a fourth run an inning later, but the Yankees tied it up with two in the ninth (one unearned) and took the lead in the 10th with three more runs (two unearned) on a walk, a single, and three more Reds errors. Reliever Johnny Murphy held off a Cincinnati threat in the last of the 10th and the Series was over.

New York Yankees (AL), 4; Cincinnati Reds (NL), 0

NY (A)

PLAYER/POS	AVG	G	AB	R	H	2B	3B	HR	RB	BB	SO	SB
Frankie Crosetti, ss	.063	4	16	2	1	0	0	0	1	2	2	0
Babe Dahlgren, 1b	.214	4	14	2	3	2	0	1	2	0	4	0
Bill Dickey, c	.267	4	15	2	4	0	0	2	5	1	2	0
Joe DiMaggio, of	.313	4	16	3	5	0	0	1	3	1	1	0
Lefty Gomez, p	.000	1	1	0	0	0	0	0	0	0	1	0
Joe Gordon, 2b	.143	4	14	1	2	0	0	0	1	0	2	0
Bump Hadley, p	.000	1	3	0	0	0	0	0	0	0	0	0
Oral Hildebrand, p	.000	1	1	0	0	0	0	0	0	0	1	0
Charlie Keller, of	.438	4	16	8	7	1	1	3	6	1	2	0
Johnny Murphy, p	.000	1	2	0	0	0	0	0	0	0	1	0
Monte Pearson, p	.000	1	2	0	0	0	0	0	0	0	1	0
Red Rolfe, 3b	.125	4	16	2	2	0	0	0	0	0	0	0
Red Ruffing, p	.333	1	3	0	1	0	0	0	0	0	1	0
George Selkirk, of	.167	4	12	0	2	1	0	0	0	3	2	0
Steve Sundra, p	.000	1	0	0	0	0	0	0	0	1	0	0
TOTAL	.206		131	20	27	4	1	7	18	9	20	0

PITCHER	W	L	ERA	G	GS	CG	SV	SHO	IP	H	ER	BB	SO
Lefty Gomez	0	0	9.00	1	1	0	0	0	1.0	3	1	0	1
Bump Hadley	1	0	2.25	1	0	0	0	0	8.0	7	2	3	2
Oral Hildebrand	0	0	0.00	1	1	0	0	0	4.0	2	0	0	3
Johnny Murphy	1	0	2.70	1	0	0	0	0	3.1	5	1	0	2
Monte Pearson	1	0	0.00	1	1	1	0	1	9.0	2	0	1	8
Red Ruffing	1	0	1.00	1	1	1	0	0	9.0	4	1	1	4
Steve Sundra	0	0	0.00	1	0	0	0	0	2.2	4	0	1	2
TOTAL	4	0	1.22	7	4	2	0	1	37.0	27	5	6	22

CIN (N)

PLAYER/POS	AVG	G	AB	R	H	2B	3B	HR	RB	BB	SO	SB
Wally Berger, of	.000	4	15	0	0	0	0	0	1	0	4	0
Nino Bongiovanni, ph	.000	1	1	0	0	0	0	0	0	0	0	0
Frenchy Bordagaray, pr	.000	2	0	0	0	0	0	0	0	0	0	0
Harry Craft, of	.091	4	11	0	1	0	0	0	0	0	6	0
Paul Derringer, p	.200	2	5	0	1	0	0	0	0	0	0	0
Lonny Frey, 2b	.000	4	17	0	0	0	0	0	0	1	4	0
Lee Gamble, ph	.000	1	1	0	0	0	0	0	0	0	1	0
Ival Goodman, of	.333	4	15	3	5	1	0	0	1	1	2	1
Lee Grissom, p	.000	1	0	0	0	0	0	0	0	0	0	0
Willard Hershberger, c-2	.500	3	2	0	1	0	0	0	1	0	0	0
Ernie Lombardi, c	.214	4	14	0	3	0	0	0	2	0	1	0
Frank McCormick, 1b	.400	4	15	1	6	1	0	0	1	0	1	0
Whitey Moore, p	.000	1	1	0	0	0	0	0	0	0	0	0
Billy Myers, ss	.333	4	12	2	4	0	1	0	0	2	3	0
Al Simmons, of	.250	1	4	1	1	1	0	0	0	0	0	0
Junior Thompson, p	1.000	1	1	0	1	0	0	0	0	0	0	0
Bucky Walters, p	.000	2	3	0	0	0	0	0	0	0	0	0
Billy Werber, 3b	.250	4	16	1	4	0	0	0	2	2	0	0
TOTAL	.203		133	8	27	3	1	0	8	6	22	1

PITCHER	W	L	ERA	G	GS	CG	SV	SHO	IP	H	ER	BB	SO
Paul Derringer	0	1	2.35	2	2	1	0	0	15.1	9	4	3	9
Lee Grissom	0	0	0.00	1	0	0	0	0	1.1	0	0	1	0
Whitey Moore	0	0	0.00	1	0	0	0	0	3.0	0	0	0	2
Junior Thompson	0	1	13.50	1	1	0	0	0	4.2	5	7	4	3
Bucky Walters	0	2	4.91	2	1	1	0	0	11.0	13	6	1	6
TOTAL	0	4	4.33	7	4	2	0	0	35.1	27	17	9	20

GAME 1 AT NY OCT 4

				R	H	E
CIN	000	100	000	1	4	0
NY	000	010	001	2	6	0

Pitchers: DERRINGER vs RUFFING
Attendance: 58,541

GAME 2 AT NY OCT 5

				R	H	E
CIN	000	000	000	0	2	0
NY	003	100	00X	4	9	0

Pitchers: WALTERS vs PEARSON
Home Runs: Dahlgren-NY
Attendance: 59,791

GAME 3 AT CIN OCT 7

				R	H	E
NY	202	030	000	7	5	1
CIN	120	000	000	3	10	0

Pitchers: Gomez, HADLEY (2) vs THOMPSON, Grissom (5), Moore (7)
Home Runs: Keller-NY (2), DiMaggio-NY, Dickey-NY
Attendance: 32,723

GAME 4 AT CIN OCT 8

					R	H	E
NY	000	000	202	3	7	7	1
CIN	000	000	310	0	4	11	4

Pitchers: Hildebrand, Sundra (5), MURPHY (7) vs Derringer, WALTERS (8)
Home Runs: Keller-NY, Dickey-NY
Attendance: 32,794

The Tigers outpitched and outslugged the Reds, and scored six more runs than the Reds did. What they failed to do was win the Series.

Tigers ace Bobo Newsom, who had enjoyed what would be his finest season in a long career, carried his mastery into the Series opener. Detroit gave him an early lead, driving out Reds starter Paul Derringer with five runs in the second inning, and added a pair of runs in the fifth on Bruce Campbell's home run. Newsom, meanwhile, held the Reds to single runs in the fourth and eighth.

Cincinnati's Bucky Walters walked the first two Tigers he faced in Game 2, and both scored. But two Reds runs in the second tied the game, Jimmy Ripple's two-run homer an inning later gave them the lead, and pitcher Walters scored an insurance run in the fourth after doubling. Another Tigers walk in the sixth led to their third run, but Walters retired the remaining Tigers in order.

Detroit's Rocky Bridges yielded 10 hits and four runs in Game 3, but his teammates responded with 13 hits and seven runs, including a pair of two-run homers by Rudy York and Pinky Higgins in the seventh. Cincinnati again evened the Series the next day, though, with five runs to support Derringer's five-hit, two-run pitching. Although Newsom's father had suffered a fatal heart attack the day after seeing his son win the opener, the son pitched Game 5, and improved on his previous performance with a three-hit shutout. Hank Greenberg's homer in the third inning accounted for the first three of the Tigers' eight runs in their lopsided win.

The Reds returned home needing to win the final two games. Like Newsom, Bucky Walters bettered his earlier win with a shutout in Game 6, and drove in two of the Reds' four runs, one with a solo homer in the eighth. In the Series finale, Newsom and Derringer found themselves evenly matched. The Tigers scored a run in the third, while Newsom held Cincinnati scoreless through six. But in the seventh, leadoff doubles by Frank McCormick and Jimmy Ripple, plus a successful bunt and a fly to deep center, gave the Reds two runs—all they needed as Derringer stopped the Tigers through the final six innings for the victory.

Cincinnati Reds (NL), 4; Detroit Tigers (AL), 3

CIN (N)

PLAYER/POS	AVG	G	AB	R	H	2B	3B	HR	RB	BB	SO	SB
Morrie Arnovich, of	.000	1	1	0	0	0	0	0	0	0	0	0
Bill Baker, c	.250	3	4	1	1	0	0	0	0	0	1	0
Joe Beggs, p	.000	1	0	0	0	0	0	0	0	0	0	0
Harry Craft, ph	.000	1	1	0	0	0	0	0	0	0	0	0
Paul Derringer, p	.000	3	7	0	0	0	0	0	0	0	1	0
Lonny Frey, ph	.000	3	2	0	0	0	0	0	0	0	0	0
Ival Goodman, of	.276	7	29	5	8	2	0	0	5	0	3	0
Johnny Hutchings, p	.000	1	0	0	0	0	0	0	0	0	0	0
Eddie Joost, 2b	.200	7	25	0	5	0	0	0	2	1	2	0
Ernie Lombardi, c-1	.333	2	3	0	1	1	0	0	0	1	0	0
Frank McCormick, 1b	.214	7	28	2	6	1	0	0	0	1	1	0
Mike McCormick, of	.310	7	29	1	9	3	0	0	2	1	6	0
Whitey Moore, p	.000	3	2	0	0	0	0	0	0	0	1	0
Billy Myers, ss	.130	7	23	0	3	0	0	0	2	2	5	0
Elmer Riddle, p	.000	1	0	0	0	0	0	0	0	0	0	0
Lew Riggs, ph	.000	3	3	1	0	0	0	0	0	0	2	0
Jimmy Ripple, of	.333	7	21	3	7	2	0	1	6	4	2	0
Junior Thompson, p	.000	1	1	0	0	0	0	0	0	0	1	0
Jim Turner, p	.000	1	2	0	0	0	0	0	0	0	0	0
Johnny Vander Meer, p	.000	1	0	0	0	0	0	0	0	0	0	0
Bucky Walters, p	.286	2	7	2	2	1	0	1	2	0	1	0
Billy Werber, 3b	.370	7	27	5	10	4	0	0	2	4	2	0
Jimmie Wilson, c	.353	6	17	2	6	0	0	0	0	1	2	1
TOTAL	.250		232	22	58	14	0	2	21	15	30	1

PITCHER	W	L	ERA	G	GS	CG	SV	SHO	IP	H	ER	BB	SO
Joe Beggs	0	0	9.00	1	0	0	0	0	1.0	3	1	0	1
Paul Derringer	2	1	2.79	3	3	2	0	0	19.1	17	6	10	6
Johnny Hutchings	0	0	9.00	1	0	0	0	0	1.0	2	1	1	0
Whitey Moore	0	0	3.24	3	0	0	0	0	8.1	8	3	6	7
Elmer Riddle	0	0	0.00	1	0	0	0	0	1.0	0	0	0	2
Junior Thompson	0	1	16.20	1	1	0	0	0	3.1	8	6	4	2
Jim Turner	0	1	7.50	1	1	0	0	0	6.0	8	5	0	4
Johnny Vander Meer	0	0	0.00	1	0	0	0	0	3.0	2	0	3	2
Bucky Walters	2	0	1.50	2	2	2	0	1	18.0	8	3	6	6
TOTAL	4	3	3.69	14	7	4	0	1	61.0	56	25	30	30

DET (A)

PLAYER/POS	AVG	G	AB	R	H	2B	3B	HR	RB	BB	SO	SB
Earl Averill, ph	.000	3	3	0	0	0	0	0	0	0	0	0
Dick Bartell, ss	.269	7	26	2	7	2	0	0	3	3	3	0
Tommy Bridges, p	.000	1	3	0	0	0	0	0	0	0	1	0
Bruce Campbell, of	.360	7	25	4	9	1	0	1	5	4	4	0
Frank Croucher, ss	.000	1	0	0	0	0	0	0	0	0	0	0
Pete Fox, ph	.000	1	1	0	0	0	0	0	0	0	0	0
Charlie Gehringer, 2b	.214	7	28	3	6	0	0	0	1	2	0	0
Johnny Gorsica, p	.000	2	4	0	0	0	0	0	0	0	2	0
Hank Greenberg, of	.357	7	28	5	10	2	1	1	6	2	5	0
Pinky Higgins, 3b	.333	7	24	2	8	3	1	1	6	3	3	0
Fred Hutchinson, p	.000	1	0	0	0	0	0	0	0	0	0	0
Barney McCosky, of	.304	7	23	5	7	1	0	0	1	7	0	0
Archie McKain, p	.000	1	0	0	0	0	0	0	0	0	0	0
Bobo Newsom, p	.100	3	10	1	1	0	0	0	0	0	1	0
Schoolboy Rowe, p	.000	2	1	0	0	0	0	0	0	0	1	0
Clay Smith, p	.000	1	1	0	0	0	0	0	0	0	1	0
Billy Sullivan, c-4	.154	5	13	3	2	0	0	0	0	5	2	0
Birdie Tebbetts, c-3	.000	4	11	0	0	0	0	0	0	0	0	0
Dizzy Trout, p	.000	1	1	0	0	0	0	0	0	0	0	0
Rudy York, 1b	.231	7	26	3	6	0	1	1	2	4	7	0
TOTAL	.246		228	28	56	9	3	4	24	30	30	0

PITCHER	W	L	ERA	G	GS	CG	SV	SHO	IP	H	ER	BB	SO
Tommy Bridges	1	0	3.00	1	1	1	0	0	9.0	10	3	1	5
Johnny Gorsica	0	0	0.79	2	0	0	0	0	11.1	6	1	4	4
Fred Hutchinson	0	0	9.00	1	0	0	0	0	1.0	1	1	1	1
Archie McKain	0	0	3.00	1	0	0	0	0	3.0	4	1	0	0
Bobo Newsom	2	1	1.38	3	3	3	0	1	26.0	18	4	4	17
Schoolboy Rowe	0	2	17.18	2	2	0	0	0	3.2	12	7	1	1
Clay Smith	0	0	2.25	1	0	0	0	0	4.0	1	1	3	1
Dizzy Trout	0	1	9.00	1	1	0	0	0	2.0	6	2	1	1
TOTAL	3	4	3.00	12	7	4	0	1	60.0	58	20	15	30

GAME 1 AT CIN OCT 2

				R	H	E
DET	050	020	000	7	10	1
CIN	000	100	010	2	8	3

Pitchers: NEWSOM vs DERRINGER, Moore (2), Riddle (9)
Home Runs: Campbell-DET
Attendance: 31,793

GAME 2 AT CIN OCT 3

				R	H	E
DET	200	001	000	3	3	1
CIN	022	100	00X	5	9	0

Pitchers: ROWE, Gorsica (4) vs WALTERS
Home Runs: Ripple-CIN
Attendance: 30,640

GAME 3 AT DET OCT 4

				R	H	E
CIN	100	000	012	4	10	1
DET	000	100	42X	7	13	1

Pitchers: TURNER, Moore (7), Beggs (8) vs BRIDGES
Home Runs: York-DET, Higgins-DET
Attendance: 52,877

GAME 4 AT DET OCT 5

				R	H	E
CIN	201	100	010	5	11	1
DET	001	001	000	2	5	1

Pitchers: DERRINGER vs TROUT, Smith (3), McKain (7)
Attendance: 54,093

GAME 5 AT DET OCT 6

				R	H	E
CIN	000	000	000	0	3	0
DET	003	400	01X	8	13	0

Pitchers: THOMPSON, Moore (4), Vander Meer (5), Hutchings (8) vs NEWSOM
Home Runs: Greenberg-DET
Attendance: 55,189

GAME 6 AT CIN OCT 7

				R	H	E
DET	000	000	000	0	5	0
CIN	200	001	01X	4	10	2

Pitchers: ROWE, Gorsica (1), Hutchinson (8) vs WALTERS
Home Runs: Walters-CIN
Attendance: 30,481

GAME 7 AT CIN OCT 8

				R	H	E
DET	001	000	000	1	7	0
CIN	000	000	20X	2	7	1

Pitchers: NEWSOM vs DERRINGER
Attendance: 26,854

Dodgers catcher Mickey Owen's dropped third strike in Game 4 was the Series' memorable boner, but it was not the chief cause of Brooklyn's downfall. Yankees pitching was. Three Yankees hurled complete-game wins, with each giving the Dodgers only one earned run. And relief ace Johnny Murphy hurled two-hit shutout ball in six innings over two games, winning one.

Joe Gordon opened the Series scoring with a solo homer in the second inning for the Yankees in Game 1, and the Yankees added runs in the fourth and sixth. Owen tripled in the Dodgers' first run in the fifth, and pinch hitter Lew Riggs singled in an unearned run in the seventh. But Yankees starter Red Ruffing held on to his slim lead through the final two innings for the win.

Dodgers ace Whitlow Wyatt gave the Yankees single runs in the second and third innings of Game 2, but held them scoreless the rest of the way. Meanwhile, the Dodgers tied the game in the fifth, and scored an unearned run in the sixth to finish the scoring and give Brooklyn its only win of the Series.

Freddie Fitzsimmons, with the Dodgers' best pitching of the Series, dueled Marius Russo through seven scoreless innings in Game 3. But Fitzsimmons's final out of the seventh—a line drive by Russo that bounced off Fitzsimmons's leg into the glove of shortstop Pee Wee Reese—broke his kneecap. Hugh Casey, who replaced Fitzsimmons in the eighth, retired the first batter, but then gave up four straight singles for two runs before being removed. The Yankees scored no more, and Brooklyn came up with a run in the last of the eighth. But Russo stopped the Dodgers in order in the ninth to preserve his lead for the Yankees' second win.

In Game 4, for the first time in the Series, the margin of victory was more than one run, thanks to catcher Owen's famous boner. Brooklyn held the lead 4–3 with two out in the top of the ninth. Dodgers reliever Casey, who had shut out the Yankees since coming on in the fifth inning, then struck out Tommy Henrich for what should have been the game-ending out. But Owen let the ball get by him, and before the third out was recorded Casey had given up a single, two doubles, and two walks—and four runs, for Brooklyn's third loss.

The Yankees scored twice off Wyatt in the second inning of Game 5, and once more in the fifth (on Henrich's home run), as Tiny Bonham held Brooklyn to four hits and a single run to clinch the ninth Yankees world title.

New York Yankees (AL), 4; Brooklyn Dodgers (NL), 1

NY (A)

PLAYER/POS	AVG	G	AB	R	H	2B	3B	HR	RB	BB	SO	SB
Tiny Bonham, p	.000	1	4	0	0	0	0	0	0	0	4	0
Frenchy Bordagaray, pr	.000	1	0	0	0	0	0	0	0	0	0	0
Marv Breuer, p	.000	1	1	0	0	0	0	0	0	0	0	0
Spud Chandler, p	.500	1	2	0	1	0	0	0	1	0	0	0
Bill Dickey, c	.167	5	18	3	3	1	0	0	1	3	1	0
Joe DiMaggio, of	.263	5	19	1	5	0	0	0	1	2	2	0
Atley Donald, p	.000	1	2	0	0	0	0	0	0	0	1	0
Joe Gordon, 2b	.500	5	14	2	7	1	1	1	5	7	0	0
Tommy Henrich, of	.167	5	18	4	3	1	0	1	1	3	3	0
Charlie Keller, of	.389	5	18	5	7	2	0	0	5	3	1	0
Johnny Murphy, p	.000	2	2	0	0	0	0	0	0	0	1	0
Phil Rizzuto, ss	.111	5	18	0	2	0	0	0	0	3	1	1
Red Rolfe, 3b	.300	5	20	2	6	0	0	0	0	2	1	0
Buddy Rosar, c	.000	1	0	0	0	0	0	0	0	0	0	0
Red Ruffing, p	.000	1	3	0	0	0	0	0	0	0	0	0
Marius Russo, p	.000	1	4	0	0	0	0	0	0	0	1	0
George Selkirk, ph	.500	2	2	0	1	0	0	0	0	0	0	0
Johnny Sturm, 1b	.286	5	21	0	6	0	0	0	2	0	2	1
TOTAL	.247		166	17	41	5	1	2	16	23	18	2

PITCHER	W	L	ERA	G	GS	CG	SV	SHO	IP	H	ER	BB	SO
Tiny Bonham	1	0	1.00	1	1	1	0	0	9.0	4	1	2	2
Marv Breuer	0	0	0.00	1	0	0	0	0	3.0	3	0	1	2
Spud Chandler	0	1	3.60	1	1	0	0	0	5.0	4	2	2	2
Atley Donald	0	0	9.00	1	1	0	0	0	4.0	6	4	3	2
Johnny Murphy	1	0	0.00	2	0	0	0	0	6.0	2	0	1	3
Red Ruffing	1	0	1.00	1	1	1	0	0	9.0	6	1	3	5
Marius Russo	1	0	1.00	1	1	1	0	0	9.0	4	1	2	5
TOTAL	4	1	1.80	8	5	3	0	0	45.0	29	9	14	21

BRO (N)

PLAYER/POS	AVG	G	AB	R	H	2B	3B	HR	RB	BB	SO	SB
Johnny Allen, p	.000	3	0	0	0	0	0	0	0	0	0	0
Dolph Camilli, 1b	.167	5	18	1	3	1	0	0	1	1	6	0
Hugh Casey, p	.500	3	2	0	1	0	0	0	0	0	1	0
Pete Coscarart, 2b	.000	3	7	1	0	0	0	0	0	1	2	0
Curt Davis, p	.000	1	2	0	0	0	0	0	0	0	0	0
Freddie Fitzsimmons, p	.000	1	2	0	0	0	0	0	0	0	0	0
Herman Franks, c	.000	1	1	0	0	0	0	0	0	0	0	0
Larry French, p	.000	2	0	0	0	0	0	0	0	0	0	0
Augie Galan, ph	.000	2	2	0	0	0	0	0	0	0	1	0
Billy Herman, 2b	.125	4	8	0	1	0	0	0	0	2	0	0
Kirby Higbe, p	1.000	1	1	0	1	0	0	0	0	0	0	0
Cookie Lavagetto, 3b	.100	3	10	1	1	0	0	0	0	2	0	0
Joe Medwick, of	.235	5	17	1	4	1	0	0	0	1	2	0
Mickey Owen, c	.167	5	12	1	2	0	1	0	2	3	0	0
Pee Wee Reese, ss	.200	5	20	1	4	0	0	0	2	0	0	0
Pete Reiser, of	.200	5	20	1	4	1	1	1	3	1	6	0
Lew Riggs, 3b-2	.250	3	8	0	2	0	0	0	1	1	1	0
Dixie Walker, of	.222	5	18	3	4	2	0	0	0	2	1	0
Jimmy Wasdell, of-1	.200	3	5	0	1	1	0	0	2	0	0	0
Whit Wyatt, p	.167	2	6	1	1	1	0	0	0	0	1	0
TOTAL	.182		159	11	29	7	2	1	11	14	21	0

PITCHER	W	L	ERA	G	GS	CG	SV	SHO	IP	H	ER	BB	SO
Johnny Allen	0	0	0.00	3	0	0	0	0	3.2	1	0	3	0
Hugh Casey	0	2	3.38	3	0	0	0	0	5.1	9	2	2	1
Curt Davis	0	1	5.06	1	1	0	0	0	5.1	6	3	3	1
Freddie Fitzsimmons	0	0	0.00	1	1	0	0	0	7.0	4	0	3	1
Larry French	0	0	0.00	2	0	0	0	0	1.0	0	0	0	0
Kirby Higbe	0	0	7.36	1	1	0	0	0	3.2	6	3	2	1
Whit Wyatt	1	1	2.50	2	2	2	0	0	18.0	15	5	10	14
TOTAL	1	4	2.66	13	5	2	0	0	44.0	41	13	23	18

GAME 1 AT NY OCT 1

		R	H	E
BRO	000 010 100	2	6	0
NY	010 101 00X	3	6	1

Pitchers: DAVIS, Casey (6), Allen (7) vs RUFFING
Home Runs: Gordon-NY
Attendance: 68,540

GAME 2 AT NY OCT 2

		R	H	E
BRO	000 021 000	3	6	2
NY	011 000 000	2	9	1

Pitchers: WYATT vs CHANDLER, Murphy (6)
Attendance: 66,248

GAME 3 AT BRO OCT 4

		R	H	E
NY	000 000 020	2	8	0
BRO	000 000 010	1	4	0

Pitchers: RUSSO vs Fitzsimmons, CASEY (8), French (8), Allen (9)
Attendance: 33,100

GAME 4 AT BRO OCT 5

		R	H	E
NY	100 200 004	7	12	0
BRO	000 220 000	4	9	1

Pitchers: Donald, Breuer (5), MURPHY (8) vs Higbe, French (4), Allen (5), CASEY (5)
Home Runs: Reiser-BRO
Attendance: 33,813

GAME 5 AT BRO OCT 6

		R	H	E
NY	020 010 000	3	6	0
BRO	001 000 000	1	4	1

Pitchers: BONHAM vs WYATT
Home Runs: Henrich-NY
Attendance: 34,072

Rookies Stan Musial and Whitey Kurowski drove in game-winning runs for rookie-pitcher Johnny Beazley in Games 2 and 5 as the major leagues' youngest team upset the Yankees. New York won only the opener, building a seven-run lead for starter Red Ruffing, who shut out St. Louis on one hit through 8⅓ innings before giving up four hits and four harmless runs in the last of the ninth.

The Cardinals scored first in Game 2 on catcher Walker Cooper's two-run double in the first inning. Kurowski tripled in a third run in the seventh, but pitcher Beazley, after holding the Yankees scoreless through seven innings, gave up three runs in the eighth on two singles and Charlie Keller's two-run homer. St. Louis regained the lead a half inning later when Musial singled home Enos Slaughter (who had doubled), and stifled a threat in the ninth as Slaughter's great throw from right field nailed a runner at third.

Second-year Cardinals pitcher Ernie White turned in the Series' top mound performance with a six-single, no-walk shutout in Game 3 (aided by outfielders Musial and Slaughter, who hauled in a pair of potential home run blasts in the seventh inning). The Cards managed only five singles themselves, but they combined one with a walk, sacrifice, and ground out for a run in the third, and sandwiched a Yankees error with two hits in the ninth for an unearned insurance run.

Game 4 saw the Series' heaviest hitting. New York scored once in the first, but the Cards exploded in the fourth for six runs on six hits and two walks. The Yankees tied it up two innings later, with Keller's three-run homer the feature of the five-run inning. St. Louis took the lead for good with two runs in the seventh, and added a ninth run in the ninth.

Beazley and Ruffing tangled in Game 5. Phil Rizzuto's solo homer put New York ahead in the first inning. Slaughter's fourth-inning home run tied the score, but the Yankees regained the lead with a run later in the inning. The Cards tied the game again in the sixth, and took the final lead when Kurowski homered for two runs in the top of the ninth. The Yankees threatened in the last of the ninth, putting their first two men on with a single and error. But catcher Cooper picked a runner off second, second baseman Jimmy Brown redeemed his earlier error with a sparkling catch, then fielded a routine grounder for the final out.

St. Louis Cardinals (NL), 4; New York Yankees (AL), 1

STL (N)

PLAYER/POS	AVG	G	AB	R	H	2B	3B	HR	RB	BB	SO	SB
Johnny Beazley, p	.143	2	7	0	1	0	0	0	0	0	5	0
Jimmy Brown, 2b	.300	5	20	2	6	0	0	0	1	3	0	0
Mort Cooper, p	.200	2	5	1	1	0	0	0	2	0	1	0
Walker Cooper, c	.286	5	21	3	6	1	0	0	4	0	1	0
Creepy Crespi, pr	.000	1	0	1	0	0	0	0	0	0	0	0
Harry Gumbert, p	.000	2	0	0	0	0	0	0	0	0	0	0
Johnny Hopp, 1b	.176	5	17	3	3	0	0	0	0	1	1	0
Whitey Kurowski, 3b	.267	5	15	3	4	0	1	1	5	2	3	0
Max Lanier, p	1.000	2	1	0	1	0	0	0	1	0	0	0
Marty Marion, ss	.111	5	18	2	2	0	1	0	3	1	2	0
Terry Moore, of	.294	5	17	2	5	1	0	0	2	2	3	0
Stan Musial, of	.222	5	18	2	4	1	0	0	2	4	0	0
Ken O'Dea, ph	1.000	1	1	0	1	0	0	0	1	0	0	0
Howie Pollet, p	.000	1	0	0	0	0	0	0	0	0	0	0
Ray Sanders, ph	.000	2	1	1	0	0	0	0	0	1	0	0
Enos Slaughter, of	.263	5	19	3	5	1	0	1	2	3	2	0
Harry Walker, ph	.000	1	1	0	0	0	0	0	0	0	1	0
Ernie White, p	.000	1	2	0	0	0	0	0	0	0	0	0
TOTAL	.239		163	23	39	4	2	2	23	17	19	0

PITCHER	W	L	ERA	G	GS	CG	SV	SHO	IP	H	ER	BB	SO
Johnny Beazley	2	0	2.50	2	2	2	0	0	18.0	17	5	3	6
Mort Cooper	0	1	5.54	2	2	0	0	0	13.0	17	8	4	9
Harry Gumbert	0	0	0.00	2	0	0	0	0	0.2	1	0	0	0
Max Lanier	1	0	0.00	2	0	0	0	0	4.0	3	0	1	1
Howie Pollet	0	0	0.00	1	0	0	0	0	0.1	0	0	0	0
Ernie White	1	0	0.00	1	1	1	0	1	9.0	6	0	0	6
TOTAL	4	1	2.60	10	5	3	0	1	45.0	44	13	8	22

NY (A)

PLAYER/POS	AVG	G	AB	R	H	2B	3B	HR	RB	BB	SO	SB
Tiny Bonham, p	.000	2	2	0	0	0	0	0	0	1	0	0
Hank Borowy, p	.000	1	1	0	0	0	0	0	0	0	1	0
Marv Breuer, p	.000	1	0	0	0	0	0	0	0	0	0	0
Spud Chandler, p	.000	2	2	0	0	0	0	0	0	0	1	0
Frankie Crosetti, 3b	.000	1	3	0	0	0	0	0	0	0	1	0
Roy Cullenbine, of	.263	5	19	3	5	1	0	0	2	1	2	1
Bill Dickey, c	.263	5	19	1	5	0	0	0	0	1	0	0
Joe DiMaggio, of	.333	5	21	3	7	0	0	0	3	0	1	0
Atley Donald, p	.000	1	2	0	0	0	0	0	0	0	0	0
Joe Gordon, 2b	.095	5	21	1	2	1	0	0	0	0	7	0
Buddy Hassett, 1b	.333	3	9	1	3	1	0	0	2	0	1	0
Charlie Keller, of	.200	5	20	2	4	0	0	2	5	1	3	0
Jerry Priddy, 1b-3,3b-1	.100	3	10	0	1	1	0	0	1	1	0	0
Phil Rizzuto, ss	.381	5	21	2	8	0	0	1	1	2	1	2
Red Rolfe, 3b	.353	4	17	5	6	2	0	0	0	1	2	0
Buddy Rosar, ph	1.000	1	1	0	1	0	0	0	0	0	0	0
Red Ruffing, p-2	.222	4	9	0	2	0	0	0	0	0	2	0
George Selkirk, ph	.000	1	1	0	0	0	0	0	0	0	0	0
Tuck Stainback, pr	.000	2	0	0	0	0	0	0	0	0	0	0
Jim Turner, p	.000	1	0	0	0	0	0	0	0	0	0	0
TOTAL	.247		178	18	44	6	0	3	14	8	22	3

PITCHER	W	L	ERA	G	GS	CG	SV	SHO	IP	H	ER	BB	SO
Tiny Bonham	0	1	4.09	2	1	1	0	0	11.0	9	5	3	3
Hank Borowy	0	0	18.00	1	1	0	0	0	3.0	6	6	3	1
Marv Breuer	0	0	–	1	0	0	0	0	0.0	2	0	0	0
Spud Chandler	0	1	1.08	2	1	0	1	0	8.1	5	1	1	3
Atley Donald	0	1	6.00	1	0	0	0	0	3.0	3	2	2	1
Red Ruffing	1	1	4.08	2	2	1	0	0	17.2	14	8	7	11
Jim Turner	0	0	0.00	1	0	0	0	0	1.0	0	0	1	0
TOTAL	1	4	4.50	10	5	2	1	0	44.0	39	22	17	19

GAME 1 AT STL SEPT 30

				R	H	E
NY	000	110	032	7	11	0
STL	000	000	004	4	7	4

Pitchers: RUFFING, Chandler (9) vs M.COOPER, Gumbert (8), Lanier (9)
Attendance: 34,769

GAME 2 AT STL OCT 1

				R	H	E
NY	000	000	030	3	10	2
STL	200	000	11X	4	6	0

Pitchers: BONHAM vs BEAZLEY
Home Runs: Keller-NY
Attendance: 34,255

GAME 3 AT NY OCT 2

				R	H	E
STL	001	000	001	2	5	1
NY	000	000	000	0	6	1

Pitchers: WHITE vs CHANDLER, Breuer (9), Turner (9)
Attendance: 69,123

GAME 4 AT NY OCT 4

				R	H	E
STL	000	600	201	9	12	1
NY	100	005	000	6	10	1

Pitchers: M.Cooper, Gumbert (6), Pollet (6), LANIER (7) vs Borowy, DONALD (4), Bonham (7)
Home Runs: Keller-NY
Attendance: 69,902

GAME 5 AT NY OCT 5

				R	H	E
STL	000	101	002	4	9	4
NY	100	100	000	2	7	1

Pitchers: BEAZLEY vs RUFFING
Home Runs: Rizzuto-NY, Slaughter-STL, Kurowski-STL
Attendance: 69,052

Although both clubs had lost players to military service since the previous World Series, history seemed to be repeating itself. The Cardinals lost to the Yankees in the opener and won the second game, as they had the previous year. But this year it was the Yankees who took the next three games and the Series, as fine Cardinal pitching gave way to even finer mound work by New York.

Yankees pitcher Spurgeon (Spud) Chandler, coming off his finest season (20–4, 1.64 ERA), continued to overwhelm the opposition in the Series. He held the Cards to two runs (only one earned) in Game 1, and the Yankees took advantage of a wild pitch to score two runs of their own in the sixth inning, breaking a 2–2 tie for a 4–2 win. Cardinals shortstop Marty Marion homered in the third inning for the first run the next day, and first baseman Ray Sanders homered for two more runs in a three-run fourth. Cardinals ace Mort Cooper held New York to one run on four hits through eight innings, but he weakened in the last of the ninth, giving up a double and triple to the first two batters. But only two runs scored as he retired the next three men for St. Louis' only victory.

The Cardinals carried a 2–1 lead into the last of the eighth inning of Game 3, when a pair of errors, two walks, and five hits (including Billy Johnson's three-run triple) undid them. Yankees fireman Johnny Murphy retired the Cards in order in the ninth to save Hank Borowy's win. Max Lanier and Harry Brecheen held New York to just two runs (and six hits) in Game 4, but Yankees pitcher Marius Russo gave up only one run—and that was scored only because of two Yankees errors in the seventh inning.

In the fifth and (as it turned out) final game, St. Louis couldn't score, although they knocked Spud Chandler for 10 hits. But they were all singles and were spaced harmlessly over eight of the nine innings. Three St. Louis pitchers held the Yankees to just seven hits, six of them singles. But in the sixth inning Bill Dickey followed one of the singles with the game's only extra-base hit—a home run—to produce the game's only scoring, and bring the Yankees yet another world championship, their 10th.

New York Yankees (AL), 4; St. Louis Cardinals (NL), 1

NY (A)

PLAYER/POS	AVG	G	AB	R	H	2B	3B	HR	RB	BB	SO	SB
Tiny Bonham, p	.000	1	2	0	0	0	0	0	0	0	0	0
Hank Borowy, p	.500	1	2	1	1	1	0	0	0	0	1	0
Spud Chandler, p	.167	2	6	0	1	0	0	0	0	0	2	0
Frankie Crosetti, ss	.278	5	18	4	5	0	0	0	1	2	3	1
Bill Dickey, c	.278	5	18	1	5	0	0	1	4	2	2	0
Nick Etten, 1b	.105	5	19	0	2	0	0	0	2	1	2	0
Joe Gordon, 2b	.235	5	17	2	4	1	0	1	2	3	3	0
Billy Johnson, 3b	.300	5	20	3	6	1	1	0	3	0	3	0
Charlie Keller, of	.222	5	18	3	4	0	1	0	2	2	5	1
Johnny Lindell, of	.111	4	9	1	1	0	0	0	0	1	4	0
Bud Metheny, of	.125	2	8	0	1	0	0	0	0	0	2	0
Johnny Murphy, p	.000	2	0	0	0	0	0	0	0	0	0	0
Marius Russo, p	.667	1	3	1	2	2	0	0	0	1	1	0
Tuck Stainback, of	.176	5	17	0	3	0	0	0	0	0	2	0
Snuffy Stirnweiss, ph	.000	1	1	1	0	0	0	0	0	0	0	0
Roy Weatherly, ph	.000	1	1	0	0	0	0	0	0	0	0	0
TOTAL	.220		159	17	35	5	2	2	14	12	30	2

PITCHER	W	L	ERA	G	GS	CG	SV	SHO	IP	H	ER	BB	SO
Tiny Bonham	0	1	4.50	1	1	0	0	0	8.0	6	4	3	9
Hank Borowy	1	0	2.25	1	1	0	0	0	8.0	6	2	3	4
Spud Chandler	2	0	0.50	2	2	2	0	1	18.0	17	1	3	10
Johnny Murphy	0	0	0.00	2	0	0	1	0	2.0	1	0	1	1
Marius Russo	1	0	0.00	1	1	1	0	0	9.0	7	0	1	2
TOTAL	4	1	1.40	7	5	3	1	1	45.0	37	7	11	26

STL (N)

PLAYER/POS	AVG	G	AB	R	H	2B	3B	HR	RB	BB	SO	SB
Al Brazle, p	.000	1	3	0	0	0	0	0	0	0	1	0
Harry Brecheen, p	.000	3	0	0	0	0	0	0	0	0	0	0
Mort Cooper, p	.000	2	5	0	0	0	0	0	0	0	3	0
Walker Cooper, c	.294	5	17	1	5	0	0	0	0	0	1	0
Frank Demaree, ph	.000	1	1	0	0	0	0	0	0	0	0	0
Murry Dickson, p	.000	1	0	0	0	0	0	0	0	0	0	0
Debs Garms, of-1	.000	2	5	0	0	0	0	0	0	0	2	0
Johnny Hopp, of	.000	1	4	0	0	0	0	0	0	0	1	0
Lou Klein, 2b	.136	5	22	0	3	0	0	0	0	1	2	0
Howie Krist, p	.000	1	0	0	0	0	0	0	0	0	0	0
Whitey Kurowski, 3b	.222	5	18	2	4	1	0	0	1	0	3	0
Max Lanier, p	.250	3	4	0	1	0	0	0	1	0	0	0
Danny Litwhiler, of-4	.267	5	15	0	4	1	0	0	2	2	4	0
Marty Marion, ss	.357	5	14	1	5	2	0	1	2	3	1	1
Stan Musial, of	.278	5	18	2	5	0	0	0	0	2	2	0
Sam Narron, ph	.000	1	1	0	0	0	0	0	0	0	0	0
Ken O'Dea, c-1	.667	2	3	0	2	0	0	0	0	0	0	0
Ray Sanders, 1b	.294	5	17	3	5	0	0	1	2	3	4	0
Harry Walker, of	.167	5	18	0	3	1	0	0	0	0	2	0
Ernie White, pr	.000	1	0	0	0	0	0	0	0	0	0	0
TOTAL	.224		165	9	37	5	0	2	8	11	26	1

PITCHER	W	L	ERA	G	GS	CG	SV	SHO	IP	H	ER	BB	SO
Al Brazle	0	1	3.68	1	1	0	0	0	7.1	5	3	2	4
Harry Brecheen	0	1	2.45	3	0	0	0	0	3.2	5	1	3	3
Mort Cooper	1	1	2.81	2	2	1	0	0	16.0	11	5	3	10
Murry Dickson	0	0	0.00	1	0	0	0	0	0.2	0	0	1	0
Howie Krist	0	0	–	1	0	0	0	0	0.0	1	0	0	0
Max Lanier	0	1	1.76	3	2	0	0	0	15.1	13	3	3	13
TOTAL	1	4	2.51	11	5	1	0	0	43.0	35	12	12	30

GAME 1 AT NY OCT 5

				R	H	E
STL	010	010	000	2	7	2
NY	000	202	00X	4	8	2

Pitchers: LANIER, Brecheen (8) vs CHANDLER
Home Runs: Gordon-NY
Attendance: 68,676

GAME 2 AT NY OCT 6

				R	H	E
STL	001	300	000	4	7	2
NY	000	100	002	3	6	0

Pitchers: M.COOPER vs BONHAM, Murphy (9)
Home Runs: Marion-STL, Sanders-STL
Attendance: 68,578

GAME 3 AT NY OCT 7

				R	H	E
STL	000	200	000	2	6	4
NY	000	001	05X	6	8	0

Pitchers: BRAZLE, Krist (8), Brecheen (8) vs BOROWY, Murphy (9)
Attendance: 69,990

GAME 4 AT STL OCT 10

				R	H	E
NY	000	100	010	2	6	2
STL	000	000	100	1	7	1

Pitchers: RUSSO vs Lanier, BRECHEEN (8)
Attendance: 36,196

GAME 5 AT STL OCT 11

				R	H	E
NY	000	002	000	2	7	1
STL	000	000	000	0	10	1

Pitchers: CHANDLER vs M.COOPER, Lanier (8), Dickson (9)
Home Runs: Dickey-NY
Attendance: 33,872

The Cardinals entered the World Series as clear favorites against their landlord Browns (who owned Sportsman's Park, where both teams played). They won the Series in six games, but if the Browns' fielding had been as good as their pitching the outcome might have been different.

The Browns won the opener on Denny Galehouse's strong pitching. Galehouse gave up seven hits and four walks, but held the Cards scoreless before yielding a run in the ninth. Cardinals ace Mort Cooper also pitched well in six of his seven innings. He allowed the Browns only two hits, but they came back to back in the fourth inning—a single followed by George McQuinn's home run—to give the Browns all the scoring they needed.

Browns pitcher Nelson Potter's two errors (a fumble and a wild throw) on a bunt in the third inning of Game 2 led to an unearned run, and third baseman Mark Christman's bobble an inning later set up a second unearned run. The Browns tied the score with a pair of runs on three two-out hits in the seventh—enough to have won an error-free game—but lost when the Cardinals singled a run across in the last of the eleventh.

Two errors by the Browns led to a pair of unearned runs in Game 3, but Jack Kramer held the Cards scoreless apart from that, striking out 10. Meanwhile, the Browns tied together five singles with two out in the third inning for three runs, adding a fourth run on a wild pitch before the inning ended. In the seventh the Browns tacked on two more runs for a comfortable win and a 2–1 Series advantage.

The Cardinals came back to earn victory in Games 4 and 5, knocking three Browns pitchers for 12 hits in Game 4 (including Stan Musial's two-run homer in the first) and a 5–1 win for pitcher Harry Brecheen, then rapping Denny Galehouse for two solo homers in Game 5 (by Danny Litwhiler and Ray Sanders) for the game's only scoring as Mort Cooper fanned 12 Browns while shutting them out.

Two of the Cardinals' three runs in the fourth inning of Game 6 were made possible by Browns shortstop Vern Stephens's throwing error. They provided the margin of victory, as Cardinals pitchers Max Lanier and Ted Wilks held the Browns to three hits and a single run, and brought the Cards their second world title in three years.

St. Louis Cardinals (NL), 4; St. Louis Browns (AL), 2

STL (N)

PLAYER/POS	AVG	G	AB	R	H	2B	3B	HR	RB	BB	SO	SB
Augie Bergamo, of-2	.000	3	6	0	0	0	0	0	1	2	3	0
Harry Brecheen, p	.000	1	4	0	0	0	0	0	0	0	1	0
Bud Byerly, p	.000	1	0	0	0	0	0	0	0	0	0	0
Mort Cooper, p	.000	2	4	0	0	0	0	0	0	0	2	0
Walker Cooper, c	.318	6	22	1	7	2	1	0	2	3	2	0
Blix Donnelly, p	.000	2	1	0	0	0	0	0	0	0	1	0
George Fallon, 2b	.000	2	2	0	0	0	0	0	0	0	1	0
Debs Garms, ph	.000	2	2	0	0	0	0	0	0	0	0	0
Johnny Hopp, of	.185	6	27	2	5	0	0	0	0	0	8	0
Al Jurisich, p	.000	1	0	0	0	0	0	0	0	0	0	0
Whitey Kurowski, 3b	.217	6	23	2	5	1	0	0	1	1	4	0
Max Lanier, p	.500	2	4	0	2	0	0	0	1	0	0	0
Danny Litwhiler, of	.200	5	20	2	4	1	0	1	1	2	7	0
Marty Marion, ss	.227	6	22	1	5	3	0	0	2	2	3	0
Stan Musial, of	.304	6	23	2	7	2	0	1	2	2	0	0
Ken O'Dea, ph	.333	3	3	0	1	0	0	0	2	0	0	0
Ray Sanders, 1b	.286	6	21	5	6	0	0	1	1	5	8	0
Freddy Schmidt, p	.000	1	1	0	0	0	0	0	0	0	1	0
Emil Verban, 2b	.412	6	17	1	7	0	0	0	2	2	0	0
Ted Wilks, p	.000	2	2	0	0	0	0	0	0	0	2	0
TOTAL	.240		204	16	49	9	1	3	15	19	43	0

PITCHER	W	L	ERA	G	GS	CG	SV	SHO	IP	H	ER	BB	SO
Harry Brecheen	1	0	1.00	1	1	1	0	0	9.0	9	1	4	4
Bud Byerly	0	0	0.00	1	0	0	0	0	1.1	0	0	0	1
Mort Cooper	1	1	1.13	2	2	1	0	1	16.0	9	2	5	16
Blix Donnelly	1	0	0.00	2	0	0	0	0	6.0	2	0	1	9
Al Jurisich	0	0	27.00	1	0	0	0	0	0.2	2	2	1	0
Max Lanier	1	0	2.19	2	2	0	0	0	12.1	8	3	8	11
Freddy Schmidt	0	0	0.00	1	0	0	0	0	3.1	1	0	1	1
Ted Wilks	0	1	5.68	2	1	0	1	0	6.1	5	4	3	7
TOTAL	4	2	1.96	12	6	2	1	1	55.0	36	12	23	49

STL (A)

PLAYER/POS	AVG	G	AB	R	H	2B	3B	HR	RB	BB	SO	SB
Floyd Baker, 2b	.000	2	2	0	0	0	0	0	0	0	2	0
Milt Byrnes, ph	.000	3	2	0	0	0	0	0	0	1	2	0
Mike Chartak, ph	.000	2	2	0	0	0	0	0	0	0	2	0
Mark Christman, 3b	.091	6	22	0	2	0	0	0	1	0	6	0
Ellis Clary, ph	.000	1	1	0	0	0	0	0	0	0	0	0
Denny Galehouse, p	.200	2	5	0	1	0	0	0	0	1	1	0
Don Gutteridge, 2b	.143	6	21	1	3	1	0	0	0	3	5	0
Red Hayworth, c	.118	6	17	1	2	1	0	0	1	3	1	0
Al Hollingsworth, p	.000	1	1	0	0	0	0	0	0	0	0	0
Sig Jakucki, p	.000	1	0	0	0	0	0	0	0	0	0	0
Jack Kramer, p	.000	2	4	0	0	0	0	0	0	0	2	0
Mike Kreevich, of	.231	6	26	0	6	3	0	0	0	0	5	0
Chet Laabs, of-4	.200	5	15	1	3	1	1	0	0	2	6	0
Frank Mancuso, c-1	.667	2	3	0	2	0	0	0	1	0	0	0
George McQuinn, 1b	.438	6	16	2	7	2	0	1	5	7	2	0
Gene Moore, of	.182	6	22	4	4	0	0	0	0	3	6	0
Bob Muncrief, p	.000	2	1	0	0	0	0	0	0	0	1	0
Nelson Potter, p	.000	2	4	0	0	0	0	0	0	0	1	0
Tex Shirley, p-1	.000	2	0	0	0	0	0	0	0	0	0	0
Vern Stephens, ss	.227	6	22	2	5	1	0	0	0	3	3	0
Tom Turner, ph	.000	1	1	0	0	0	0	0	0	0	0	0
Al Zarilla, of-3	.100	4	10	1	1	0	0	0	1	0	4	0
TOTAL	.183		197	12	36	9	1	1	9	23	49	0

PITCHER	W	L	ERA	G	GS	CG	SV	SHO	IP	H	ER	BB	SO
Denny Galehouse	1	1	1.50	2	2	2	0	0	18.0	13	3	5	15
Al Hollingsworth	0	0	2.25	1	0	0	0	0	4.0	5	1	2	1
Sig Jakucki	0	1	9.00	1	1	0	0	0	3.0	5	3	0	4
Jack Kramer	1	0	0.00	2	1	1	0	0	11.0	9	0	4	12
Bob Muncrief	0	1	1.35	2	0	0	0	0	6.2	5	1	4	4
Nelson Potter	0	1	0.93	2	2	0	0	0	9.2	10	1	3	6
Tex Shirley	0	0	0.00	1	0	0	0	0	2.0	2	0	1	1
TOTAL	2	4	1.49	11	6	3	0	0	54.1	49	9	19	43

GAME 1 AT STL-N OCT 4

STL-A	000	200	000	2	2	0
STL-N	000	000	001	1	7	0

Pitchers: GALEHOUSE vs M.COOPER, Donnelly (8)
Home Runs: McQuinn-STL(A)
Attendance: 33,242

GAME 2 AT STL-N OCT 5

STL-A	000	000	200	00	2	7	4
STL-N	001	100	000	01	3	7	0

Pitchers: Potter, MUNCRIEF (7) vs Lanier, DONNELLY (8)
Attendance: 35,076

GAME 3 AT STL-A OCT 6

STL-N	100	000	100	2	7	0
STL-A	004	000	20X	6	8	2

Pitchers: WILKS, Schmidt (3), Jurisich (7), Byerly (7) vs KRAMER
Attendance: 34,737

GAME 4 AT STL-A OCT 7

STL-N	202	001	000	5	12	0
STL-A	000	000	010	1	9	1

Pitchers: BRECHEEN vs JAKUCKI, Hollingsworth (4), Shirley (8)
Home Runs: Musial-STL(N)
Attendance: 35,455

GAME 5 AT STL-A OCT 8

STL-N	000	001	010	2	6	1
STL-A	000	000	000	0	7	1

Pitchers: M.COOPER vs GALEHOUSE
Home Runs: Sanders-STL(N), Litwhiler-STL(N)
Attendance: 36,568

GAME 6 AT STL-N OCT 9

STL-A	010	000	000	1	3	2
STL-N	000	300	00X	3	10	0

Pitchers: POTTER, Muncrief (4), Kramer (7) vs LANIER, Wilks (6)
Attendance: 31,630

As World War II ended during the summer, military major leaguers began returning to their clubs. Hank Greenberg's return in July provided the spark needed for Detroit's narrow pennant victory, and his three-run homer in Game 2 of the World Series proved to be the decisive blow in the Tigers' successful struggle for the world title.

Chicago started strong as Cubs ace Hank Borowy shut out the Tigers on six singles while his teammates drove out Hal Newhouser with seven runs in the first three innings and won. Chicago continued its assault the next day with a run in the top of the fourth, but in the fifth inning Doc Cramer—with two out and two on—singled in the tying run, and Greenberg followed with his tie-breaking homer for three additional runs. Detroit pitcher Virgil Trucks (who had returned from the Navy in time to pitch in the regular-season finale) held the Cubs scoreless after the fourth inning for the win.

Chicago's Claude Passeau moved the Cubs back into the Series lead with a one-hit shutout in Game 3, but Dizzy Trout's five-hitter in Game 4 again evened the Series. The Tigers bunched four of their seven hits in the fourth inning for all four of their runs.

Detroit took the Series lead for the first time with an 8–4 win in Game 5. Borowy and Newhouser faced each other as they had in the opener, but this time Borowy was hit hard. Driven out when four Tigers opened the sixth inning with safe hits, he took the loss as Newhouser went the distance for the win.

In Game 6, Chicago concluded the seventh inning of a heavy-hitting game with a 7–3 lead. Detroit tied the score with four runs in the top of the eighth (capped by Greenberg's home run), but in the last of the 12th the Cubs' Stan Hack doubled home the winning run to keep Chicago's hopes alive.

Two days later in the finale, Cubs manager Charlie Grimm started Borowy, who had relieved for four shutout innings to win Game 6. But this third appearance in four days proved too much. Removed after the first three batters to face him singled, he took the loss, as the Tigers went on to score nine runs to win the World Series for the second time.

Detroit Tigers (AL), 4; Chicago Cubs (NL), 3

DET (A)

PLAYER/POS	AVG	G	AB	R	H	2B	3B	HR	RB	BB	SO	SB
Al Benton, p	.000	3	0	0	0	0	0	0	0	0	0	0
Red Borom, ph	.000	2	1	0	0	0	0	0	0	0	0	0
Tommy Bridges, p	.000	1	0	0	0	0	0	0	0	0	0	0
George Caster, p	.000	1	0	0	0	0	0	0	0	0	0	0
Doc Cramer, of	.379	7	29	7	11	0	0	0	4	1	0	1
Roy Cullenbine, of	.227	7	22	5	5	2	0	0	4	8	2	1
Zeb Eaton, ph	.000	1	1	0	0	0	0	0	0	0	1	0
Hank Greenberg, of	.304	7	23	7	7	3	0	2	7	6	5	0
Joe Hoover, ss	.333	1	3	1	1	0	0	0	1	0	0	0
Chuck Hostetler, ph	.000	3	3	0	0	0	0	0	0	0	0	0
Bob Maier, ph	1.000	1	1	0	1	0	0	0	0	0	0	0
Eddie Mayo, 2b	.250	7	28	4	7	1	0	0	2	3	2	0
John McHale, ph	.000	3	3	0	0	0	0	0	0	0	1	0
Ed Mierkowicz, of	.000	1	0	0	0	0	0	0	0	0	0	0
Les Mueller, p	.000	1	0	0	0	0	0	0	0	0	0	0
Hal Newhouser, p	.000	3	8	0	0	0	0	0	1	1	1	0
Jimmy Outlaw, 3b	.179	7	28	1	5	0	0	0	3	2	1	1
Stubby Overmire, p	.000	1	1	0	0	0	0	0	0	0	0	0
Paul Richards, c	.211	7	19	0	4	2	0	0	6	4	3	0
Bob Swift, c	.250	3	4	1	1	0	0	0	0	2	0	0
Jim Tobin, p	.000	1	1	0	0	0	0	0	0	0	0	0
Dizzy Trout, p	.167	2	6	0	1	0	0	0	0	0	0	0
Virgil Trucks, p	.000	2	4	0	0	0	0	0	0	1	1	0
Hub Walker, ph	.500	2	2	1	1	1	0	0	0	0	0	0
Skeeter Webb, ss	.185	7	27	4	5	0	0	0	1	2	1	0
Rudy York, 1b	.179	7	28	1	5	1	0	0	3	3	4	0
TOTAL	.223		242	32	54	10	0	2	32	33	22	3

PITCHER	W	L	ERA	G	GS	CG	SV	SHO	IP	H	ER	BB	SO
Al Benton	0	0	1.93	3	0	0	0	0	4.2	6	1	0	5
Tommy Bridges	0	0	16.20	1	0	0	0	0	1.2	3	3	3	1
George Caster	0	0	0.00	1	0	0	0	0	0.2	0	0	0	1
Les Mueller	0	0	0.00	1	0	0	0	0	2.0	0	0	1	1
Hal Newhouser	2	1	6.10	3	3	2	0	0	20.2	25	14	4	22
Stubby Overmire	0	1	3.00	1	1	0	0	0	6.0	4	2	2	2
Jim Tobin	0	0	6.00	1	0	0	0	0	3.0	4	2	1	0
Dizzy Trout	1	1	0.66	2	1	1	0	0	13.2	9	1	3	9
Virgil Trucks	1	0	3.38	2	2	1	0	0	13.1	14	5	5	7
TOTAL	4	3	3.84	15	7	4	0	0	65.2	65	28	19	48

CHI (N)

PLAYER/POS	AVG	G	AB	R	H	2B	3B	HR	RB	BB	SO	SB
Heinz Becker, ph	.500	3	2	0	1	0	0	0	0	1	1	0
Cy Block, pr	.000	1	0	0	0	0	0	0	0	0	0	0
Hank Borowy, p	.167	4	6	1	1	1	0	0	0	0	3	0
Phil Cavaretta, 1b	.423	7	26	7	11	2	0	1	5	4	3	0
Bob Chipman, p	.000	1	0	0	0	0	0	0	0	0	0	0
Paul Derringer, p	.000	3	0	0	0	0	0	0	0	0	0	0
Paul Erickson, p	.000	4	0	0	0	0	0	0	0	0	0	0
Paul Gillespie, c-1	.000	3	6	0	0	0	0	0	0	0	0	0
Stan Hack, 3b	.367	7	30	1	11	3	0	0	4	4	2	0
Roy Hughes, ss	.294	6	17	1	5	1	0	0	3	4	5	0
Don Johnson, 2b	.172	7	29	4	5	2	1	0	0	0	8	1
Mickey Livingston, c	.364	6	22	3	8	3	0	0	4	1	1	0
Peanuts Lowrey, of	.310	7	29	4	9	1	0	0	0	1	2	0
Clyde McCullough, ph	.000	1	1	0	0	0	0	0	0	0	1	0
Lennie Merullo, ss	.000	3	2	0	0	0	0	0	0	0	1	0
Bill Nicholson, of	.214	7	28	1	6	1	1	0	8	2	5	0
Andy Pafko, of	.214	7	28	5	6	2	1	0	2	2	5	1
Claude Passeau, p	.000	3	7	1	0	0	0	0	1	0	4	0
Ray Prim, p	.000	2	0	0	0	0	0	0	0	0	0	0
Ed Sauer, ph	.000	2	2	0	0	0	0	0	0	0	2	0
Bill Schuster, ss-1	.000	2	1	1	0	0	0	0	0	0	0	0
Frank Secory, ph	.400	5	5	0	2	0	0	0	0	0	2	0
Hy Vandenberg, p	.000	3	1	0	0	0	0	0	0	0	0	0
Dewey Williams, c-1	.000	2	2	0	0	0	0	0	0	0	1	0
Hank Wyse, p	.000	3	3	0	0	0	0	0	0	0	2	0
TOTAL	.263		247	29	65	16	3	1	27	19	48	2

PITCHER	W	L	ERA	G	GS	CG	SV	SHO	IP	H	ER	BB	SO
Hank Borowy	2	2	4.00	4	3	1	0	1	18.0	21	8	6	8
Bob Chipman	0	0	0.00	1	0	0	0	0	0.1	0	0	1	0
Paul Derringer	0	0	6.75	3	0	0	0	0	5.1	5	4	7	1
Paul Erickson	0	0	3.86	4	0	0	0	0	7.0	8	3	3	5
Claude Passeau	1	0	2.70	3	2	1	0	1	16.2	7	5	8	3
Ray Prim	0	1	9.00	2	1	0	0	0	4.0	4	4	1	1
Hy Vandenberg	0	0	0.00	3	0	0	0	0	6.0	1	0	3	3
Hank Wyse	0	1	7.04	3	1	0	0	0	7.2	8	6	4	1
TOTAL	3	4	4.15	23	7	2	0	2	65.0	54	30	33	22

GAME 1 AT DET OCT 3

				R	H	E
CHI	403	000	200	9	13	0
DET	000	000	000	0	6	0

Pitchers: BOROWY vs NEWHOUSER, Benton (3), Tobin (5), Mueller (8)
Home Runs: Cavarretta-CHI
Attendance: 54,637

GAME 2 AT DET OCT 4

				R	H	E
CHI	000	100	000	1	7	0
DET	000	040	00X	4	7	0

Pitchers: WYSE, Erickson (7) vs TRUCKS
Home Runs: Greenberg-DET
Attendance: 53,636

GAME 3 AT DET OCT 5

				R	H	E
CHI	000	200	100	3	8	0
DET	000	000	000	0	1	2

Pitchers: PASSEAU vs OVERMIRE, Benton (7)
Attendance: 55,500

GAME 4 AT CHI OCT 6

				R	H	E
DET	000	400	000	4	7	1
CHI	000	001	000	1	5	1

Pitchers: TROUT vs PRIM, Derringer (4), Vandenberg (6), Erickson (8)
Attendance: 42,923

GAME 5 AT CHI OCT 7

				R	H	E
DET	001	004	102	8	11	0
CHI	001	000	201	4	7	2

Pitchers: NEWHOUSER vs BOROWY, Vandenberg (6), Chipman (6), Derringer (7), Erickson (9)
Attendance: 43,463

GAME 6 AT CHI OCT 8

					R	H	E
DET	010	000	240	000	7	13	1
CHI	000	041	200	001	8	15	3

Pitchers: Trucks, Caster (5), Bridges (6), Benton (7), TROUT (8) vs Passeau, Wyse (7), Prim (8), BOROWY (9)
Home Runs: Greenberg-DET
Attendance: 41,708

GAME 7 AT CHI OCT 10

				R	H	E
DET	510	000	120	9	9	1
CHI	100	100	010	3	10	0

Pitchers: NEWHOUSER vs BOROWY, Derringer (1), Vandenberg (2), Erickson (6), Passeau (8), Wyse (9)
Attendance: 41,590

With World War II over, the majors were at full strength for the first time in five years. Boston's big bats were back, and the Sox ran away with the American League pennant. St. Louis had Stan Musial back, but they struggled to their pennant, finishing the regular schedule tied with Brooklyn, and defeating them in the first major league tie-breaker playoff, two games to none.

Favored Boston edged St. Louis in the opener, but it took a home run by Rudy York in the top of the 10th to spoil Howie Pollet's strong showing. Harry Brecheen brought the Cards back the next day with the first of his three Series wins—a four-hit shutout.

Boston regained the lead in Game 3. Sox ace Dave Ferriss spaced six hits and a walk, one per inning, in shutting out the Cardinals, and Rudy York hit his second game-winning homer, this time a three-run shot in the first inning. The next day, though, St. Louis exploded for a record-tying 20 hits—four apiece by Enos Slaughter, Joe Garagiola, and Whitey Kurowski—to give pitcher George Munger (who had completed only two of his seven regular-season starts) an easy complete-game 12–3 victory.

For the third time the Red Sox took the Series lead, winning Game 5 behind Joe Dobson's four-hit pitching (the Cards' three runs in the 6–3 loss were unearned), but St. Louis tied the Series for the third time with a win in Game 6. Brecheen, in his second start, again pitched splendidly, holding Boston to a single run in the seventh inning, long after the Cards had driven out Sox starter Mickey Harris with three runs in the third.

The final game, like the Series itself, was a seesaw battle. Boston scored the first run in the top of the first, but St. Louis tied the score an inning later. The Cards took a two-run lead on three hits in the fifth, but the Sox came back in the eighth to tie it up as Dom DiMaggio doubled off reliever Brecheen to drive in a pair of pinch hitters who had singled and doubled off starter Murry Dickson. The Series' final run came a half inning later. Slaughter opened with a single, but moved no farther as the next two batters were retired. Then Harry Walker hit a liner over short. Slaughter, off with the crack of the bat, never paused and beat the relay to the plate with what proved the winning run, as Brecheen held the Sox in the ninth for his third win of the Series to give the Cardinals their third world title in five seasons.

St. Louis Cardinals (NL), 4; Boston Red Sox (AL), 3

STL (N)

PLAYER/POS	AVG	G	AB	R	H	2B	3B	HR	RB	BB	SO	SB
Johnny Beazley, p	.000	1	0	0	0	0	0	0	0	0	0	0
Al Brazle, p	.000	1	2	0	0	0	0	0	0	0	0	0
Harry Brecheen, p	.125	3	8	2	1	0	0	0	1	0	1	0
Murry Dickson, p	.400	2	5	1	2	2	0	0	1	0	1	0
Erv Dusak, of	.250	4	4	0	1	1	0	0	0	2	2	0
Joe Garagiola, c	.316	5	19	2	6	2	0	0	4	0	3	0
Nippy Jones, ph	.000	1	1	0	0	0	0	0	0	0	1	0
Whitey Kurowski, 3b	.296	7	27	5	8	3	0	0	2	0	3	0
Marty Marion, ss	.250	7	24	1	6	2	0	0	4	1	1	0
Terry Moore, of	.148	7	27	1	4	0	0	0	2	2	6	0
Red Munger, p	.250	1	4	0	1	0	0	0	0	0	2	0
Stan Musial, 1b	.222	7	27	3	6	4	1	0	4	4	2	1
Howie Pollet, p	.000	2	4	0	0	0	0	0	0	0	1	0
Del Rice, c	.500	3	6	2	3	1	0	0	0	2	0	0
Red Schoendienst, 2b	.233	7	30	3	7	1	0	0	1	0	2	1
Dick Sisler, ph	.000	2	2	0	0	0	0	0	0	0	0	0
Enos Slaughter, of	.320	7	25	5	8	1	1	1	2	4	3	1
Harry Walker, of	.412	7	17	3	7	2	0	0	6	4	2	0
Ted Wilks, p	.000	1	0	0	0	0	0	0	0	0	0	0
TOTAL	.259		232	28	60	19	2	1	27	19	30	3

PITCHER	W	L	ERA	G	GS	CG	SV	SHO	IP	H	ER	BB	SO
Johnny Beazley	0	0	0.00	1	0	0	0	0	1.0	1	0	0	1
Al Brazle	0	1	5.40	1	0	0	0	0	6.2	7	4	6	4
Harry Brecheen	3	0	0.45	3	2	2	0	1	20.0	14	1	5	11
Murry Dickson	0	1	3.86	2	2	0	0	0	14.0	11	6	4	7
Red Munger	1	0	1.00	1	1	1	0	0	9.0	9	1	3	2
Howie Pollet	0	1	3.48	2	2	1	0	0	10.1	12	4	4	3
Ted Wilks	0	0	0.00	1	0	0	0	0	1.0	2	0	0	0
TOTAL	4	3	2.32	11	7	4	0	1	62.0	56	16	22	28

BOS (A)

PLAYER/POS	AVG	G	AB	R	H	2B	3B	HR	RB	BB	SO	SB
Jim Bagby, p	.000	1	1	0	0	0	0	0	0	0	0	0
Mace Brown, p	.000	1	0	0	0	0	0	0	0	0	0	0
Paul Campbell, pr	.000	1	0	0	0	0	0	0	0	0	0	0
Leon Culberson, of-3	.222	5	9	1	2	0	0	1	1	1	2	1
Dom DiMaggio, of	.259	7	27	2	7	3	0	0	3	2	2	0
Joe Dobson, p	.000	3	3	0	0	0	0	0	0	0	2	0
Bobby Doerr, 2b	.409	6	22	1	9	1	0	1	3	2	2	0
Clem Dreisewerd, p	.000	1	0	0	0	0	0	0	0	0	0	0
Dave Ferriss, p	.000	2	6	0	0	0	0	0	0	0	1	0
Don Gutteridge, 2b-2	.400	3	5	1	2	0	0	0	1	0	0	0
Mickey Harris, p	.333	2	3	0	1	0	0	0	0	0	1	0
Pinky Higgins, 3b	.208	7	24	1	5	1	0	0	2	2	0	0
Tex Hughson, p	.333	3	3	0	1	0	0	0	0	1	0	0
Earl Johnson, p	.000	3	1	0	0	0	0	0	0	0	0	0
Bob Klinger, p	.000	1	0	0	0	0	0	0	0	0	0	0
Tom McBride, of-2	.167	5	12	0	2	0	0	0	1	0	1	0
Catfish Metkovich, ph	.500	2	2	1	1	1	0	0	0	0	0	0
Wally Moses, of	.417	4	12	1	5	0	0	0	0	1	2	0
Roy Partee, c	.100	5	10	1	1	0	0	0	1	1	2	0
Johnny Pesky, ss	.233	7	30	2	7	0	0	0	0	1	3	1
Rip Russell, 3b-1	1.000	2	2	1	2	0	0	0	0	0	0	0
Mike Ryba, p	.000	1	0	0	0	0	0	0	0	0	0	0
Hal Wagner, c	.000	5	13	0	0	0	0	0	0	0	1	0
Ted Williams, of	.200	7	25	2	5	0	0	0	1	5	5	0
Rudy York, 1b	.261	7	23	6	6	1	1	2	5	6	4	0
Bill Zuber, p	.000	1	0	0	0	0	0	0	0	0	0	0
TOTAL	.240		233	20	56	7	1	4	18	22	28	2

PITCHER	W	L	ERA	G	GS	CG	SV	SHO	IP	H	ER	BB	SO
Jim Bagby	0	0	3.00	1	0	0	0	0	3.0	6	1	1	1
Mace Brown	0	0	27.00	1	0	0	0	0	1.0	4	3	1	0
Joe Dobson	1	0	0.00	3	1	1	0	0	12.2	4	0	3	10
Clem Dreisewerd	0	0	0.00	1	0	0	0	0	0.1	0	0	0	0
Dave Ferriss	1	0	2.03	2	2	1	0	1	13.1	13	3	2	4
Mickey Harris	0	2	3.72	2	2	0	0	0	9.2	11	4	4	5
Tex Hughson	0	1	3.14	3	2	0	0	0	14.1	14	5	3	8
Earl Johnson	1	0	2.70	3	0	0	0	0	3.1	1	1	2	1
Bob Klinger	0	1	13.50	1	0	0	0	0	0.2	2	1	1	0
Mike Ryba	0	0	13.50	1	0	0	0	0	0.2	2	1	1	0
Bill Zuber	0	0	4.50	1	0	0	0	0	2.0	3	1	1	1
TOTAL	3	4	2.95	19	7	2	0	1	61.0	60	20	19	30

GAME 1 AT STL OCT 6

					R	H	E
BOS	010	000	001	1	3	9	2
STL	000	001	010	0	2	7	0

Pitchers: Hughson, JOHNSON (9) vs POLLET
Home Runs: York-BOS
Attendance: 36,218

GAME 2 AT STL OCT 7

				R	H	E
BOS	000	000	000	0	4	1
STL	001	020	00X	3	6	0

Pitchers: HARRIS, Dobson (8) vs BRECHEEN
Attendance: 35,815

GAME 3 AT BOS OCT 9

				R	H	E
STL	000	000	000	0	6	1
BOS	300	000	01X	4	8	0

Pitchers: DICKSON, Wilks (8) vs FERRISS
Home Runs: York-BOS
Attendance: 34,500

GAME 4 AT BOS OCT 10

				R	H	E
STL	033	010	104	12	20	1
BOS	000	100	020	3	9	4

Pitchers: MUNGER vs HUGHSON, Bagby (3), Zuber (6), Brown (8), Ryba (9), Dreisewerd (9)
Home Runs: Slaughter-STL, Doerr-BOS
Attendance: 35,645

GAME 5 AT BOS OCT 11

				R	H	E
STL	010	000	002	3	4	1
BOS	110	001	30X	6	11	3

Pitchers: Pollet, BRAZLE (1), Beazley (8) vs DOBSON
Home Runs: Culberson-BOS
Attendance: 35,982

GAME 6 AT STL OCT 13

				R	H	E
BOS	000	000	100	1	7	0
STL	003	000	01X	4	8	0

Pitchers: HARRIS, Hughson (3), Johnson (8) vs BRECHEEN
Attendance: 35,768

GAME 7 AT STL OCT 15

				R	H	E
BOS	100	000	020	3	8	0
STL	010	020	01X	4	9	1

Pitchers: Ferriss, Dobson (5), KLINGER (8), Johnson (8) vs Dickson, BRECHEEN (8)
Attendance: 36,143

Two of the most memorable plays in World Series history brought Brooklyn victory in Games 4 and 6, but when the Series had ended the Yankees were world champions for the 11th time. Dodgers ace Ralph Branca set New York down in order through the first four innings of Game 1, but the first five batters to face him in the fifth inning reached base. Branca was lifted, but before the inning was over five Yankees had crossed the plate—more than enough for their first win.

The Yankees won again the next day, rocking four Brooklyn pitchers for 15 hits and an easy 10–3 win. Brooklyn finally made its presence felt in Game 3, another heavy-hitting affair, scoring six times in the second inning to establish a lead the Yankees could not overcome. Both teams recorded 13 hits, but Dodgers fireman Hugh Casey extinguished the last flame in the seventh inning, and preserved a narrow 9–8 Brooklyn lead the rest of the way.

Shortstop Pee Wee Reese's error and a bases-loaded walk gave the Yankees an unearned run in the first inning of Game 4, and they earned a second run in the fourth. Meanwhile, Yankees pitcher Bill Bevens, although he averaged a walk an inning, had allowed no hits and only one run as the game entered the last of the ninth. Bevens retired two in the ninth, but walked his ninth and 10th batters (one intentionally), then lost both his no-hitter and the game as Dodgers pinch hitter Cookie Lavagetto doubled home the two baserunners to even the Series.

Spec Shea (the winning pitcher in Game 1) held Brooklyn to four hits and one run in Game 5. Joe DiMaggio homered in the fifth inning for New York's second run, enough to put the Yankees back in the Series lead. The Dodgers rebounded in Game 6 to build an early 4–0 lead, but the Yankees tied the score in the last of the third and took a lead in the fourth. Brooklyn regained the lead in the sixth with four runs, but when DiMaggio hit a long fly to left with two on in the bottom half of the inning, it looked as if the score would be tied. But substitute left fielder Al Gionfriddo (in what turned out to be his last big league game) raced to the bullpen fence 415 feet out to rob DiMag of the home run. New York scored a run in the ninth, but thanks to Gionfriddo's catch it was not enough.

Brooklyn scored first in the finale with a pair of second-inning runs, but relievers Bill Bevens and Joe Page shut them out through the final seven innings as their teammates gradually built a Series-clinching 5–2 victory.

New York Yankees (AL), 4; Brooklyn Dodgers (NL), 3

NY (A)

PLAYER/POS	AVG	G	AB	R	H	2B	3B	HR	RB	BB	SO	SB
Yogi Berra, c-4,of-2	.158	6	19	2	3	0	0	1	2	1	2	0
Bill Bevens, p	.000	2	4	0	0	0	0	0	0	0	2	0
Bobby Brown, ph	1.000	4	3	2	3	2	0	0	3	1	0	0
Spud Chandler, p	.000	1	0	0	0	0	0	0	0	0	0	0
Allie Clark, of-1	.500	3	2	1	1	0	0	0	1	1	0	0
Joe DiMaggio, of	.231	7	26	4	6	0	0	2	5	6	2	0
Karl Drews, p	.000	2	2	0	0	0	0	0	0	0	2	0
Lonny Frey, ph	.000	1	1	0	0	0	0	0	1	0	0	0
Tommy Henrich, of	.323	7	31	2	10	2	0	1	5	2	3	0
Ralph Houk, ph	1.000	1	1	0	1	0	0	0	0	0	0	0
Billy Johnson, 3b	.269	7	26	8	7	0	3	0	2	3	4	0
Johnny Lindell, of	.500	6	18	3	9	3	1	0	7	5	2	0
Sherm Lollar, c	.750	2	4	3	3	2	0	0	1	0	0	0
George McQuinn, 1b	.130	7	23	3	3	0	0	0	1	5	8	0
Bobo Newsom, p	.000	2	0	0	0	0	0	0	0	0	0	0
Joe Page, p	.000	4	4	0	0	0	0	0	0	0	1	0
Jack Phillips, 1b-1	.000	2	2	0	0	0	0	0	0	0	0	0
Vic Raschi, p	.000	2	0	0	0	0	0	0	0	0	0	0
Allie Reynolds, p	.500	2	4	2	2	0	0	0	1	0	0	0
Phil Rizzuto, ss	.308	7	26	3	8	1	0	0	2	4	0	2
Aaron Robinson, c	.200	3	10	2	2	0	0	0	1	2	1	0
Spec Shea, p	.400	3	5	0	2	1	0	0	1	0	2	0
Snuffy Stirnweiss, 2b	.259	7	27	3	7	0	1	0	3	8	8	0
Butch Wensloff, p	.000	1	0	0	0	0	0	0	0	0	0	0
TOTAL	.282		238	38	67	11	5	4	36	38	37	2

PITCHER	W	L	ERA	G	GS	CG	SV	SHO	IP	H	ER	BB	SO
Bill Bevens	0	1	2.38	2	1	1	0	0	11.1	3	3	11	7
Spud Chandler	0	0	9.00	1	0	0	0	0	2.0	2	2	3	1
Karl Drews	0	0	3.00	2	0	0	0	0	3.0	2	1	1	0
Bobo Newsom	0	1	19.29	2	1	0	0	0	2.1	6	5	2	0
Joe Page	1	1	4.15	4	0	0	1	0	13.0	12	6	2	7
Vic Raschi	0	0	6.75	2	0	0	0	0	1.1	2	1	0	1
Allie Reynolds	1	0	4.76	2	2	1	0	0	11.1	15	6	3	6
Spec Shea	2	0	2.35	3	3	1	0	0	15.1	10	4	8	10
Butch Wensloff	0	0	0.00	1	0	0	0	0	2.0	0	0	0	0
TOTAL	4	3	4.09	19	7	3	1	0	61.2	52	28	30	32

BRO (N)

PLAYER/POS	AVG	G	AB	R	H	2B	3B	HR	RB	BB	SO	SB
Dan Bankhead, pr	.000	1	0	1	0	0	0	0	0	0	0	0
Rex Barney, p	.000	3	1	0	0	0	0	0	0	0	0	0
Hank Behrman, p	.000	5	0	0	0	0	0	0	0	0	0	0
Bobby Bragan, ph	1.000	1	1	0	1	1	0	0	1	0	0	0
Ralph Branca, p	.000	3	4	0	0	0	0	0	0	0	1	0
Hugh Casey, p	.000	6	1	0	0	0	0	0	0	0	1	0
Bruce Edwards, c	.222	7	27	3	6	1	0	0	2	2	7	0
Carl Furillo, of	.353	6	17	2	6	2	0	0	3	3	0	0
Al Gionfriddo, of-1	.000	4	3	2	0	0	0	0	0	1	0	1
Hal Gregg, p	.000	3	3	0	0	0	0	0	0	1	1	0
Joe Hatten, p	.333	4	3	1	1	0	0	0	0	0	0	0
Gene Hermanski, of	.158	7	19	4	3	0	1	0	1	3	3	0
Gil Hodges, ph	.000	1	1	0	0	0	0	0	0	0	1	0
Spider Jorgensen, 3b	.200	7	20	1	4	2	0	0	3	2	4	0
Cookie Lavagetto, 3b-3	.143	5	7	0	1	1	0	0	3	0	2	0
Vic Lombardi, p-2	.000	3	3	0	0	0	0	0	0	0	0	0
Eddie Miksis, 2b-1,of-1	.250	5	4	1	1	0	0	0	0	0	1	0
Pee Wee Reese, ss	.304	7	23	5	7	1	0	0	4	6	3	3
Pete Reiser, of-3	.250	5	8	1	2	0	0	0	0	3	1	0
Jackie Robinson, 1b	.259	7	27	3	7	2	0	0	3	2	4	2
Eddie Stanky, 2b	.240	7	25	4	6	1	0	0	2	3	2	0
Harry Taylor, p	.000	1	0	0	0	0	0	0	0	0	0	0
Arky Vaughan, ph	.500	3	2	0	1	1	0	0	0	1	0	0
Dixie Walker, of	.222	7	27	1	6	1	0	1	4	3	1	1
TOTAL	.230		226	29	52	13	1	1	26	30	32	7

PITCHER	W	L	ERA	G	GS	CG	SV	SHO	IP	H	ER	BB	SO
Rex Barney	0	1	2.70	3	1	0	0	0	6.2	4	2	10	3
Hank Behrman	0	0	7.11	5	0	0	0	0	6.1	9	5	5	3
Ralph Branca	1	1	8.64	3	1	0	0	0	8.1	12	8	5	8
Hugh Casey	2	0	0.87	6	0	0	1	0	10.1	5	1	1	3
Hal Gregg	0	1	3.55	3	1	0	0	0	12.2	9	5	8	10
Joe Hatten	0	0	7.00	4	1	0	0	0	9.0	12	7	7	5
Vic Lombardi	0	1	12.15	2	2	0	0	0	6.2	14	9	1	5
Harry Taylor	0	0	–	1	1	0	0	0	0.0	2	0	1	0
TOTAL	3	4	5.55	27	7	0	1	0	60.0	67	37	38	37

GAME 1 AT NY SEPT 30

BRO 100 001 100 3 6 0
NY 000 050 00X 5 4 0

Pitchers: BRANCA, Behrman (5), Casey (7) vs SHEA, Page (6)
Attendance: 73,365

GAME 2 AT NY OCT 1

BRO 001 100 001 3 9 2
NY 101 121 40X 10 15 1

Pitchers: LOMBARDI, Gregg (5), Behrman (7), Barney (7) vs REYNOLDS
Home Runs: Walker-BRO, Henrich-NY
Attendance: 69,865

GAME 3 AT BRO OCT 2

NY 002 221 100 8 13 0
BRO 061 200 00X 9 13 1

Pitchers: NEWSOM, Raschi (2), Drews (3), Chandler (4), Page (6) vs Hatten, Branca (5), CASEY (7)
Home Runs: DiMaggio-NY, Berra-NY
Attendance: 33,098

GAME 4 AT BRO OCT 3

NY 100 100 000 2 8 1
BRO 000 010 002 3 1 3

Pitchers: BEVENS vs Taylor, Gregg (1), Behrman (8), CASEY (9)
Attendance: 33,443

GAME 5 AT BRO OCT 4

NY 000 110 000 2 5 0
BRO 000 001 000 1 4 1

Pitchers: SHEA vs BARNEY, Hatten (5), Behrman (7), Casey (8)
Home Runs: DiMaggio-NY
Attendance: 34,379

GAME 6 AT NY OCT 5

BRO 202 004 000 8 12 1
NY 004 100 001 6 15 2

Pitchers: Lombardi, BRANCA (3), Hatten (6), Casey (9) vs Reynolds, Drews (3), PAGE (5), Newsom (6), Raschi (7), Wensloff (8)
Attendance: 74,065

GAME 7 AT NY OCT 6

BRO 020 000 000 2 7 0
NY 010 201 10X 5 7 0

Pitchers: GREGG, Behrman (4), Hatten (6), Barney (6), Casey (7) vs Shea, Bevens (2), PAGE (5)
Attendance: 71,548

Boston outpitched and outhit Cleveland, and the clubs tied in runs scored. But the Braves scored most of their runs in one game, and the Indians, spreading theirs more evenly, took the Series. Boston ace Johnny Sain dueled Bob Feller in the opener. Feller gave up only two singles, but one of them followed a walk and a sacrifice (and a controversial pickoff play at second, in which the Boston runner was ruled safe although photos later showed him clearly out). Both teams registered eight hits in Game 2, but Cleveland's led to four runs, while Indians hurler Bob Lemon held Boston to just one—and that was unearned.

Cleveland's rookie sensation Gene Bearden shut out the Braves on five hits in Game 3 as the Series moved to Cleveland's huge Municipal Stadium. Bearden himself, after doubling in the third, scored on a Boston error what proved to be the winning run. A record 81,897 fans saw Sain face Steve Gromek in Game 4. Only five Indians hit Sain safely, but a first-inning single and double put Cleveland on the board, and Larry Doby's home run two innings later made the score 2–0. Boston's Marv Rickert homered in the seventh to narrow Cleveland's lead, but that ended the scoring.

Another attendance record was set at Game 5 as 86,288 fans gathered to watch Bob Feller sew up the title for Cleveland. They went home disappointed. In a game that featured five of the Series' eight home runs, Boston jumped ahead on Bob Elliott's three-run blast in the first. Dale Mitchell opened Cleveland's half of the inning with a home run, but Elliott neutralized it in the third with his second homer. The Indians drove out Boston starter Nelson Potter with four runs in the fourth inning (three coming on Jim Hegan's homer). But Warren Spahn (who had lost Game 2) hurled one-hit shutout relief over the final five frames as his Braves tied the game on Bill Salkeld's homer in the sixth, and blew out Feller and two relievers with six runs in the seventh. The fourth Indians pitcher, Satchel Paige (in his only World Series appearance), retired two batters to end the inning, but the damage had been done.

A day later though, back in Boston, Cleveland edged the Braves 4–3 for the title. Gene Bearden's relief pitching allowed two inherited baserunners to score in the eighth, but halted Boston's rally one run short of a tie.

Cleveland Indians (AL), 4; Boston Braves (NL), 2

CLE (A)

PLAYER/POS	AVG	G	AB	R	H	2B	3B	HR	RB	BB	SO	SB
Gene Bearden, p	.500	2	4	1	2	1	0	0	0	0	1	0
Ray Boone, ph	.000	1	1	0	0	0	0	0	0	0	1	0
Lou Boudreau, ss	.273	6	22	1	6	4	0	0	3	1	1	0
Russ Christopher, p	.000	1	0	0	0	0	0	0	0	0	0	0
Allie Clark, of	.000	1	3	0	0	0	0	0	0	0	1	0
Larry Doby, of	.318	6	22	1	7	1	0	1	2	2	4	0
Bob Feller, p	.000	2	4	0	0	0	0	0	0	0	2	0
Joe Gordon, 2b	.182	6	22	3	4	0	0	1	2	1	2	1
Steve Gromek, p	.000	1	3	0	0	0	0	0	0	0	1	0
Jim Hegan, c	.211	6	19	2	4	0	0	1	5	1	4	1
Wally Judnich, of	.077	4	13	1	1	0	0	0	1	1	4	0
Ken Keltner, 3b	.095	6	21	3	2	0	0	0	0	2	3	0
Bob Kennedy, of	.500	3	2	0	1	0	0	0	1	0	1	0
Ed Klieman, p	.000	1	0	0	0	0	0	0	0	0	0	0
Bob Lemon, p	.000	2	7	0	0	0	0	0	0	0	0	0
Dale Mitchell, of	.174	6	23	4	4	1	0	1	1	2	0	0
Bob Muncrief, p	.000	1	0	0	0	0	0	0	0	0	0	0
Satchel Paige, p	.000	1	0	0	0	0	0	0	0	0	0	0
Hal Peck, of	.000	1	0	0	0	0	0	0	0	0	0	0
Eddie Robinson, 1b	.300	6	20	0	6	0	0	0	1	1	0	0
Al Rosen, ph	.000	1	1	0	0	0	0	0	0	0	0	0
Joe Tipton, ph	.000	1	1	0	0	0	0	0	0	0	1	0
Thurman Tucker, of	.333	1	3	1	1	0	0	0	0	1	0	0
TOTAL	.199		191	17	38	7	0	4	16	12	26	2

PITCHER	W	L	ERA	G	GS	CG	SV	SHO	IP	H	ER	BB	SO
Gene Bearden	1	0	0.00	2	1	1	1	1	10.2	6	0	1	4
Russ Christopher	0	0	∞	1	0	0	0	0	0.0	2	1	0	0
Bob Feller	0	2	5.02	2	2	1	0	0	14.1	10	8	5	7
Steve Gromek	1	0	1.00	1	1	1	0	0	9.0	7	1	1	2
Ed Klieman	0	0	∞	1	0	0	0	0	0.0	1	3	2	0
Bob Lemon	2	0	1.65	2	2	1	0	0	16.1	16	3	7	6
Bob Muncrief	0	0	0.00	1	0	0	0	0	2.0	1	0	0	0
Satchel Paige	0	0	0.00	1	0	0	0	0	0.2	0	0	0	0
TOTAL	4	2	2.72	11	6	4	1	1	53.0	43	16	16	19

BOS (N)

PLAYER/POS	AVG	G	AB	R	H	2B	3B	HR	RB	BB	SO	SB
Red Barrett, p	.000	2	0	0	0	0	0	0	0	0	0	0
Vern Bickford, p	.000	1	0	0	0	0	0	0	0	0	0	0
Clint Conatser, of	.000	2	4	0	0	0	0	0	1	0	0	0
Alvin Dark, ss	.167	6	24	2	4	1	0	0	0	0	2	0
Bob Elliott, 3b	.333	6	21	4	7	0	0	2	5	2	2	0
Tommy Holmes, of	.192	6	26	3	5	0	0	0	1	0	0	0
Phil Masi, c	.125	5	8	1	1	1	0	0	1	0	0	0
Frank McCormick, 1b-1	.200	3	5	0	1	0	0	0	0	0	2	0
Mike McCormick, of	.261	6	23	1	6	0	0	0	2	0	4	0
Nelson Potter, p	.500	2	2	0	1	0	0	0	0	0	1	0
Marv Rickert, of	.211	5	19	2	4	0	0	1	2	0	4	0
Connie Ryan, ph	.000	2	1	0	0	0	0	0	0	0	1	0
Johnny Sain, p	.200	2	5	0	1	0	0	0	0	0	0	0
Bill Salkeld, c	.222	5	9	2	2	0	0	1	1	5	1	0
Ray Sanders, ph	.000	1	1	0	0	0	0	0	0	0	0	0
Sibby Sisti, 2b	.000	2	1	0	0	0	0	0	0	0	0	0
Warren Spahn, p	.000	3	4	0	0	0	0	0	1	0	1	0
Eddie Stanky, 2b	.286	6	14	0	4	1	0	0	1	7	0	0
Earl Torgeson, 1b	.389	5	18	2	7	3	0	0	1	2	1	1
Bill Voiselle, p	.000	2	2	0	0	0	0	0	0	0	0	0
TOTAL	.230		187	17	43	6	0	4	16	16	19	1

PITCHER	W	L	ERA	G	GS	CG	SV	SHO	IP	H	ER	BB	SO
Red Barrett	0	0	0.00	2	0	0	0	0	3.2	1	0	0	1
Vern Bickford	0	1	2.70	1	1	0	0	0	3.1	4	1	5	1
Nelson Potter	0	0	8.44	2	1	0	0	0	5.1	6	5	2	1
Johnny Sain	1	1	1.06	2	2	2	0	1	17.0	9	2	0	9
Warren Spahn	1	1	3.00	3	1	0	0	0	12.0	10	4	3	12
Bill Voiselle	0	1	2.53	2	1	0	0	0	10.2	8	3	2	2
TOTAL	2	4	2.60	12	6	2	0	1	52.0	38	15	12	26

GAME 1 AT BOS OCT 6

				R	H	E
CLE	000	000	000	0	4	0
BOS	000	000	01X	1	2	2

Pitchers: FELLER vs SAIN
Attendance: 40,135

GAME 2 AT BOS OCT 7

				R	H	E
CLE	000	210	001	4	8	1
BOS	100	000	000	1	8	3

Pitchers: LEMON vs SPAHN, Barrett (5), Potter (8)
Attendance: 39,633

GAME 3 AT CLE OCT 8

				R	H	E
BOS	000	000	000	0	5	1
CLE	001	100	00X	2	5	0

Pitchers: BICKFORD, Voiselle (4), Barrett (8) vs BEARDEN
Attendance: 70,306

GAME 4 AT CLE OCT 9

				R	H	E
BOS	000	000	100	1	7	0
CLE	101	000	00X	2	5	0

Pitchers: SAIN vs GROMEK
Home Runs: Doby-CLE, Rickert-BOS
Attendance: 81,897

GAME 5 AT CLE OCT 10

				R	H	E
BOS	301	001	600	11	12	0
CLE	100	400	000	5	6	2

Pitchers: Potter, SPAHN (4) vs FELLER, Klieman (7), Christopher (7), Paige (7), Muncrief (8)
Home Runs: Elliott-BOS (2), Mitchell-CLE, Hegan-CLE, Salkeld-BOS
Attendance: 86,288

GAME 6 AT BOS OCT 11

				R	H	E
CLE	001	002	010	4	10	0
BOS	000	100	020	3	9	0

Pitchers: LEMON, Bearden (8) vs VOISELLE, Spahn (8)
Home Runs: Gordon-CLE
Attendance: 40,103

Casey Stengel, in the first of his 12 years as Yankees manager, edged his team past the Boston Red Sox for his first of 10 American League pennants, then past the Dodgers for his first of seven world championships. New York and Brooklyn traded 1–0 wins to begin the Series. In Game 1 Allie Reynolds dueled rookie Don Newcombe scorelessly through 8½ innings—until Tommy Henrich led off the last of the ninth with a home run to win the game for the Yankees. Jackie Robinson scored after doubling off Vic Raschi in the second inning of Game 2 for that game's only score, while Dodgers ace Preacher Roe permitted just six scattered hits—never more than one per inning.

The teams entered the ninth inning of Game 3 tied 1–1. But in the top of the ninth, Dodgers starter Ralph Branca, after loading the bases on two walks and a single, gave up another single to pinch hitter Johnny Mize for two runs. Jerry Coleman's single off reliever Jack Banta drove in another run before the third out was made. In the last of the ninth, Yankees fireman Joe Page (who had held Brooklyn scoreless since coming on with the bases loaded in the fourth) finally weakened. But after yielding solo homers to Luis Olmo and Roy Campanella, he struck out pinch hitter Bruce Edwards for New York's second win.

The Yankees' victory in Game 4 came a little easier. They scored first, driving out starter Don Newcombe with three runs in the fourth, and rapping reliever Joe Hatten for three more runs an inning later. Brooklyn retaliated in the sixth, sending Yankees starter Ed Lopat to the showers with seven singles for four runs. But Allie Reynolds came on for 3⅓ innings of no-hit relief to preserve the Yankees lead—and his Series 0.00 earned run average.

After four closely contested games, the Yankees erupted in Game 5 for 10 runs in the first six innings as Brooklyn was held to just two. In the last of the seventh, the Dodgers came back, driving out starter Vic Raschi with a four-run rally, capped by Gil Hodges' three-run homer. But Joe Page came on to get the final out of the seventh, and held the Dodgers scoreless over the final two innings to bring the Yankees' world titles to an even dozen.

New York Yankees (AL), 4; Brooklyn Dodgers (NL), 1

NY (A)

PLAYER/POS	AVG	G	AB	R	H	2B	3B	HR	RB	BB	SO	SB
Hank Bauer, of	.167	3	6	0	1	0	0	0	0	0	0	0
Yogi Berra, c	.063	4	16	2	1	0	0	0	1	1	3	0
Bobby Brown, 3b-3	.500	4	12	4	6	1	2	0	5	2	2	0
Tommy Byrne, p	1.000	1	1	0	1	0	0	0	0	0	0	0
Gerry Coleman, 2b	.250	5	20	0	5	3	0	0	4	0	4	0
Joe DiMaggio, of	.111	5	18	2	2	0	0	1	2	3	5	0
Tommy Henrich, 1b	.263	5	19	4	5	0	0	1	1	3	0	0
Billy Johnson, 3b	.143	2	7	0	1	0	0	0	0	0	2	1
Johnny Lindell, of	.143	2	7	0	1	0	0	0	0	0	2	0
Ed Lopat, p	.333	1	3	0	1	1	0	0	1	0	0	0
Cliff Mapes, of	.100	4	10	3	1	1	0	0	2	2	4	0
Johnny Mize, ph	1.000	2	2	0	2	0	0	0	2	0	0	0
Gus Niarhos, c	.000	1	0	0	0	0	0	0	0	0	0	0
Joe Page, p	.000	3	4	0	0	0	0	0	0	0	2	0
Vic Raschi, p	.200	2	5	0	1	0	0	0	1	1	1	0
Allie Reynolds, p	.500	2	4	0	2	1	0	0	0	0	1	0
Phil Rizzuto, ss	.167	5	18	2	3	0	0	0	1	3	1	1
Charlie Silvera, c	.000	1	2	0	0	0	0	0	0	0	0	0
Snuffy Stirnweiss, ph	.000	1	0	0	0	0	0	0	0	0	0	0
Gene Woodling, of	.400	3	10	4	4	3	0	0	0	3	0	0
TOTAL	.226		164	21	37	10	2	2	20	18	27	2

PITCHER	W	L	ERA	G	GS	CG	SV	SHO	IP	H	ER	BB	SO
Tommy Byrne	0	0	2.70	1	1	0	0	0	3.1	2	1	2	1
Ed Lopat	1	0	6.35	1	1	0	0	0	5.2	9	4	1	4
Joe Page	1	0	2.00	3	0	0	1	0	9.0	6	2	3	8
Vic Raschi	1	1	4.30	2	2	0	0	0	14.2	15	7	5	11
Allie Reynolds	1	0	0.00	2	1	1	1	1	12.1	2	0	4	14
TOTAL	4	1	2.80	9	5	1	2	1	45.0	34	14	15	38

BRO (N)

PLAYER/POS	AVG	G	AB	R	H	2B	3B	HR	RB	BB	SO	SB
Jack Banta, p	.000	3	1	0	0	0	0	0	0	0	0	0
Rex Barney, p	.000	1	0	0	0	0	0	0	0	0	0	0
Ralph Branca, p	.000	1	3	0	0	0	0	0	0	0	3	0
Tommy Brown, ph	.000	2	2	0	0	0	0	0	0	0	1	0
Roy Campanella, c	.267	5	15	2	4	1	0	1	2	3	1	0
Billy Cox, 3b-1	.333	2	3	0	1	0	0	0	0	0	1	0
Bruce Edwards, ph	.500	2	2	0	1	0	0	0	0	0	1	0
Carl Erskine, p	.000	2	0	0	0	0	0	0	0	0	0	0
Carl Furillo, of-2	.125	3	8	0	1	0	0	0	0	1	0	0
Joe Hatten, p	.000	2	0	0	0	0	0	0	0	0	0	0
Gene Hermanski, of	.308	4	13	1	4	0	1	0	2	3	3	0
Gil Hodges, 1b	.235	5	17	2	4	0	0	1	4	1	4	0
Spider Jorgensen, 3b-3	.182	4	11	1	2	2	0	0	0	2	2	0
Mike McCormick, of	.000	1	0	0	0	0	0	0	0	0	0	0
Eddie Miksis, 3b-2	.286	3	7	0	2	1	0	0	0	0	1	0
Paul Minner, p	.000	1	0	0	0	0	0	0	0	0	0	0
Don Newcombe, p	.000	2	4	0	0	0	0	0	0	0	3	0
Luis Olmo, of	.273	4	11	2	3	0	0	1	2	0	2	0
Erv Palica, p	.000	1	0	0	0	0	0	0	0	0	0	0
Marv Rackley, of	.000	2	5	0	0	0	0	0	0	0	2	0
Pee Wee Reese, ss	.316	5	19	2	6	1	0	1	2	1	0	1
Jackie Robinson, 2b	.188	5	16	2	3	1	0	0	2	4	2	0
Preacher Roe, p	.000	1	3	0	0	0	0	0	0	0	3	0
Duke Snider, of	.143	5	21	2	3	1	0	0	0	0	8	0
Dick Whitman, ph	.000	1	1	0	0	0	0	0	0	0	1	0
TOTAL	.210		162	14	34	7	1	4	14	15	38	1

PITCHER	W	L	ERA	G	GS	CG	SV	SHO	IP	H	ER	BB	SO
Jack Banta	0	0	3.18	3	0	0	0	0	5.2	5	2	1	4
Rex Barney	0	1	16.88	1	1	0	0	0	2.2	3	5	6	2
Ralph Branca	0	1	4.15	1	1	0	0	0	8.2	4	4	4	6
Carl Erskine	0	0	16.20	2	0	0	0	0	1.2	3	3	1	0
Joe Hatten	0	0	16.20	2	0	0	0	0	1.2	4	3	2	0
Paul Minner	0	0	0.00	1	0	0	0	0	1.0	1	0	0	0
Don Newcombe	0	2	3.09	2	2	1	0	0	11.2	10	4	3	11
Erv Palica	0	0	0.00	1	0	0	0	0	2.0	1	0	1	1
Preacher Roe	1	0	0.00	1	1	1	0	1	9.0	6	0	0	3
TOTAL	1	4	4.30	14	5	2	0	1	44.0	37	21	18	27

GAME 1 AT NY OCT 5

				R	H	E
BRO	000	000	000	0	2	0
NY	000	000	001	1	5	1

Pitchers: NEWCOMBE vs REYNOLDS
Home Runs: Henrich-NY
Attendance: 66,224

GAME 2 AT NY OCT 6

				R	H	E
BRO	010	000	000	1	7	2
NY	000	000	000	0	6	1

Pitchers: ROE vs RASCHI, Page (9)
Attendance: 70,053

GAME 3 AT BRO OCT 7

				R	H	E
NY	001	000	003	4	5	0
BRO	000	100	002	3	5	0

Pitchers: Byrne, PAGE (4) vs BRANCA, Banta (9)
Home Runs: Reese-BRO, Olmo-BRO, Campanella-BRO
Attendance: 32,788

GAME 4 AT BRO OCT 8

				R	H	E
NY	000	330	000	6	10	0
BRO	000	004	000	4	9	1

Pitchers: LOPAT, Reynolds (6) vs NEWCOMBE, Hatten (4), Erskine (6), Banta (7)
Attendance: 33,934

GAME 5 AT BRO OCT 9

				R	H	E
NY	203	113	000	10	11	1
BRO	001	001	400	6	11	2

Pitchers: RASCHI, Page (7) vs BARNEY, Banta (3), Erskine (6), Hatten (6), Palica (7), Minner (9)
Home Runs: DiMaggio-NY, Hodges-BRO
Attendance: 33,711

Philadelphia's Whiz Kids, who had capped an exciting pennant race with the Phillies' first flag in 35 years, carried the excitement into the World Series but couldn't quite catch up with the Yankees. New York scored only one run in the opener; Philadelphia didn't score any. The Phillies did score a run in the second game, but the Yankees scored two. In Game 3 the Phillies scored two runs, the Yankees three.

Jim Konstanty, the National League's ace reliever (and MVP), started his first major league game in four years to lead off the Series, and held the Yankees to just four hits in eight innings of work. But Bobby Brown's double in the fourth was followed by two long flies which moved Brown around to the plate—all the scoring New York needed as Vic Raschi held the Phillies to two singles and a walk.

Robin Roberts and Allie Reynolds dueled in Game 2. New York scored first with a run on a walk and two singles in the second inning, but two Philadelphia singles and a fly to left tied the game in the last of the fifth. There matters stood until the top of the tenth, when Joe DiMaggio led off with a home run to the upper deck in left. Reynolds held the Phillies in the bottom of the tenth for the second Yankees win.

The Phillies took a lead for the only time in the Series when they broke a 1–1 tie with a run in the seventh inning of Game 3. But New York scored on a Phillies error to tie the game again in the eighth, and in the last of the ninth—with two outs—Yankees Gene Woodling, Phil Rizzuto, and Jerry Coleman singled to produce the winning run.

Rookie sensation Whitey Ford started Game 4 and held Philadelphia scoreless into the ninth inning as his Yankees scored twice in the first and three more times in the sixth. He was taken out with two away in the ninth after two singles, a hit batsman, and a Yankee error had permitted two Phillies to score. But reliever Allie Reynolds struck out the final batter to secure a Series sweep for the Yankees.

New York Yankees (AL), 4; Philadelphia Phillies (NL), 0

NY (A)

PLAYER/POS	AVG	G	AB	R	H	2B	3B	HR	RB	BB	SO	SB
Hank Bauer, of	.133	4	15	0	2	0	0	0	1	0	0	0
Yogi Berra, c	.200	4	15	2	3	0	0	1	2	2	1	0
Bobby Brown, 3b	.333	4	12	2	4	1	1	0	1	0	0	0
Gerry Coleman, 2b	.286	4	14	2	4	1	0	0	3	2	0	0
Joe Collins, 1b	.000	1	0	0	0	0	0	0	0	0	0	0
Joe DiMaggio, of	.308	4	13	2	4	1	0	1	2	3	1	0
Tom Ferrick, p	.000	1	0	0	0	0	0	0	0	0	0	0
Whitey Ford, p	.000	1	3	0	0	0	0	0	0	0	2	0
Johnny Hopp, 1b	.000	3	2	0	0	0	0	0	0	0	0	0
Jackie Jensen, pr	.000	1	0	0	0	0	0	0	0	0	0	0
Billy Johnson, 3b	.000	4	6	0	0	0	0	0	0	0	3	0
Ed Lopat, p	.500	1	2	0	1	0	0	0	0	0	1	0
Cliff Mapes, of	.000	1	4	0	0	0	0	0	0	0	1	0
Johnny Mize, 1b	.133	4	15	0	2	0	0	0	0	0	1	0
Vic Raschi, p	.333	1	3	0	1	0	0	0	0	0	0	0
Allie Reynolds, p	.333	2	3	0	1	0	0	0	0	1	2	0
Phil Rizzuto, ss	.143	4	14	1	2	0	0	0	0	3	0	1
Gene Woodling, of	.429	4	14	2	6	0	0	0	1	2	0	0
TOTAL	.222		135	11	30	3	1	2	10	13	12	1

PITCHER	W	L	ERA	G	GS	CG	SV	SHO	IP	H	ER	BB	SO
Tom Ferrick	1	0	0.00	1	0	0	0	0	1.0	1	0	1	0
Whitey Ford	1	0	0.00	1	1	0	0	0	8.2	7	0	1	7
Ed Lopat	0	0	2.25	1	1	0	0	0	8.0	9	2	0	5
Vic Raschi	1	0	0.00	1	1	1	0	1	9.0	2	0	1	5
Allie Reynolds	1	0	0.87	2	1	1	1	0	10.1	7	1	4	7
TOTAL	4	0	0.73	6	4	2	1	1	37.0	26	3	7	24

PHI (N)

PLAYER/POS	AVG	G	AB	R	H	2B	3B	HR	RB	BB	SO	SB
Richie Ashburn, of	.176	4	17	0	3	1	0	0	1	0	4	0
Jimmy Bloodworth, 2b	.000	1	0	0	0	0	0	0	0	0	0	0
Putsy Caballero, ph	.000	3	1	0	0	0	0	0	0	0	1	0
Del Ennis, of	.143	4	14	1	2	1	0	0	0	0	1	0
Mike Goliat, 2b	.214	4	14	1	3	0	0	0	1	1	2	0
Granny Hamner, ss	.429	4	14	1	6	2	1	0	0	1	2	1
Ken Heintzelman, p	.000	1	2	0	0	0	0	0	0	0	0	0
Ken Johnson, pr	.000	1	0	1	0	0	0	0	0	0	0	0
Willie Jones, 3b	.286	4	14	1	4	1	0	0	0	0	3	0
Jim Konstanty, p	.250	3	4	0	1	0	0	0	0	0	1	0
Stan Lopata, c-1	.000	2	1	0	0	0	0	0	0	0	1	0
Jackie Mayo, of-1	.000	3	0	0	0	0	0	0	0	1	0	0
Russ Meyer, p	.000	2	0	0	0	0	0	0	0	0	0	0
Bob Miller, p	.000	1	0	0	0	0	0	0	0	0	0	0
Robin Roberts, p	.000	2	2	0	0	0	0	0	0	0	1	0
Andy Seminick, c	.182	4	11	0	2	0	0	0	0	1	3	0
Ken Silvestri, c	.000	1	0	0	0	0	0	0	0	0	0	0
Dick Sisler, of	.059	4	17	0	1	0	0	0	1	0	5	0
Eddie Waitkus, 1b	.267	4	15	0	4	1	0	0	0	2	0	0
Dick Whitman, ph	.000	3	2	0	0	0	0	0	0	1	0	0
TOTAL	.203		128	5	26	6	1	0	3	7	24	1

PITCHER	W	L	ERA	G	GS	CG	SV	SHO	IP	H	ER	BB	SO
Ken Heintzelman	0	0	1.17	1	1	0	0	0	7.2	4	1	6	3
Jim Konstanty	0	1	2.40	3	1	0	0	0	15.0	9	4	4	3
Russ Meyer	0	1	5.40	2	0	0	0	0	1.2	4	1	0	1
Bob Miller	0	1	27.00	1	1	0	0	0	0.1	2	1	0	0
Robin Roberts	0	1	1.64	2	1	1	0	0	11.0	11	2	3	5
TOTAL	0	4	2.27	9	4	1	0	0	35.2	30	9	13	12

GAME 1 AT PHI OCT 4

				R	H	E
NY	000	100	000	1	5	0
PHI	000	000	000	0	2	1

Pitchers: RASCHI vs KONSTANTY, Meyer (9)
Attendance: 30,746

GAME 2 AT PHI OCT 5

					R	H	E
NY	010	000	000	1	2	10	0
PHI	000	010	000	0	1	7	0

Pitchers: REYNOLDS vs ROBERTS
Home Runs: DiMaggio-NY
Attendance: 32,660

GAME 3 AT NY OCT 6

				R	H	E
PHI	000	001	100	2	10	2
NY	001	000	011	3	7	0

Pitchers: Heintzelman, Konstanty (8), MEYER (9) vs Lopat, FERRICK (9)
Attendance: 64,505

GAME 4 AT NY OCT 7

				R	H	E
PHI	000	000	002	2	7	1
NY	200	003	00X	5	8	2

Pitchers: MILLER, Konstanty (1), Roberts (8) vs FORD, Reynolds (9)
Home Runs: Berra-NY
Attendance: 68,098

The Giants—who caught Brooklyn with a tremendous late-season drive, then defeated them for the pennant on Bobby Thomson's ninth-inning home run in Game 3 of the tie-breaker playoff series—carried their momentum through Game 3 of the World Series before bowing to the Yankees. Dave Koslo (the only Giants starter not to see action in the playoff) pitched the Series opener and held the Yankees to one run. Monte Irvin's steal of home for the Giants' second run in the top of the first was enough for the win, but Alvin Dark made Koslo's lead more secure with a three-run homer in the sixth.

The Yankees evened the Series in Game 2, scoring two early runs (one of them Joe Collins' home run) off Larry Jansen, and holding on for the win behind Ed Lopat's five-hit pitching. But the Giants regained the lead in Game 3 with five unearned runs (three of them on Whitey Lockman's homer) in a fifth inning prolonged by two Yankees errors, as pitchers Jim Hearn and Sheldon Jones combined to hold the Bronx Bombers to five hits and a pair of runs (though Hearn issued eight walks).

But that was the end of the Giants' drive. Although they scored first in both Games 4 and 5 with first-inning runs, they couldn't hold the lead either time. In Game 4 Allie Reynolds held the Giants to two runs as his Yankees scored six—including a two-run homer by Joe DiMaggio in the fifth inning that proved to be the last home run of his career. DiMag drove in three more runs in Game 5, as did Phil Rizzuto, and rookie infielder Gil McDougald contributed a grand slam as the Bombers earned their nickname in obliterating Giants pitching with 13 runs. Ed Lopat, meanwhile, hurled his second five-hitter in four days to give the Yanks the Series lead.

Hank Bauer tripled with the bases full in the sixth inning of Game 6 to break a tie and give the Yankees a 4–1 lead. The Giants loaded the bases with three straight singles to open the top of the ninth, and scored two runners on successive flies to left, to come within one run of a tie. But pinch hitter Sal Yvars (in his only Series at bat) lined out to right and the Yankees had their 14th world title.

New York Yankees (AL), 4; New York Giants (NL), 2

NY (A)

PLAYER/POS	AVG	G	AB	R	H	2B	3B	HR	RB	BB	SO	SB
Hank Bauer, of	.167	6	18	0	3	0	1	0	3	1	1	0
Yogi Berra, c	.261	6	23	4	6	1	0	0	0	2	1	0
Bobby Brown, 3b-4	.357	5	14	1	5	1	0	0	0	2	1	0
Gerry Coleman, 2b	.250	5	8	2	2	0	0	0	0	1	2	0
Joe Collins, 1b-6,of-1	.222	6	18	2	4	0	0	1	3	2	1	0
Joe DiMaggio, of	.261	6	23	3	6	2	0	1	5	2	4	0
Bobby Hogue, p	.000	2	0	0	0	0	0	0	0	0	0	0
Johnny Hopp, ph	.000	1	0	0	0	0	0	0	0	1	0	0
Bob Kuzava, p	.000	1	0	0	0	0	0	0	0	0	0	0
Ed Lopat, p	.125	2	8	0	1	0	0	0	1	0	2	0
Mickey Mantle, of	.200	2	5	1	1	0	0	0	0	2	1	0
Billy Martin, pr	.000	1	0	1	0	0	0	0	0	0	0	0
Gil McDougald, 3b-5,2b-4	.261	6	23	2	6	1	0	1	7	2	2	0
Johnny Mize, 1b-2	.286	4	7	2	2	1	0	0	1	2	0	0
Tom Morgan, p	.000	1	0	0	0	0	0	0	0	0	0	0
Joe Ostrowski, p	.000	1	0	0	0	0	0	0	0	0	0	0
Vic Raschi, p	.000	2	2	0	0	0	0	0	0	2	1	0
Allie Reynolds, p	.333	2	6	0	2	0	0	0	1	0	1	0
Phil Rizzuto, ss	.320	6	25	5	8	0	0	1	3	2	3	0
Johnny Sain, p	.000	1	1	0	0	0	0	0	0	0	0	0
Gene Woodling, of-5	.167	6	18	6	3	1	1	1	1	5	3	0
TOTAL	.246		199	29	49	7	2	5	25	26	23	0

PITCHER	W	L	ERA	G	GS	CG	SV	SHO	IP	H	ER	BB	SO
Bobby Hogue	0	0	0.00	2	0	0	0	0	2.2	1	0	0	0
Bob Kuzava	0	0	0.00	1	0	0	1	0	1.0	0	0	0	0
Ed Lopat	2	0	0.50	2	2	2	0	0	18.0	10	1	3	4
Tom Morgan	0	0	0.00	1	0	0	0	0	2.0	2	0	1	3
Joe Ostrowski	0	0	0.00	1	0	0	0	0	2.0	1	0	0	1
Vic Raschi	1	1	0.87	2	2	0	0	0	10.1	12	1	8	4
Allie Reynolds	1	1	4.20	2	2	1	0	0	15.0	16	7	11	8
Johnny Sain	0	0	9.00	1	0	0	0	0	2.0	4	2	2	2
TOTAL	4	2	1.87	12	6	3	1	0	53.0	46	11	25	22

NY (N)

PLAYER/POS	AVG	G	AB	R	H	2B	3B	HR	RB	BB	SO	SB
Al Corwin, p	.000	1	0	0	0	0	0	0	0	0	0	0
Alvin Dark, ss	.417	6	24	5	10	3	0	1	4	2	3	0
Clint Hartung, of	.000	2	4	0	0	0	0	0	0	0	0	0
Jim Hearn, p	.000	2	3	0	0	0	0	0	0	0	1	0
Monte Irvin, of	.458	6	24	3	11	0	1	0	2	2	1	2
Larry Jansen, p	.000	3	2	0	0	0	0	0	0	0	0	0
Sheldon Jones, p	.000	2	0	0	0	0	0	0	0	0	0	0
Monte Kennedy, p	.000	2	0	0	0	0	0	0	0	0	0	0
Alex Konikowski, p	.000	1	0	0	0	0	0	0	0	0	0	0
Dave Koslo, p	.000	2	5	0	0	0	0	0	0	0	2	0
Whitey Lockman, 1b	.240	6	25	1	6	2	0	1	4	1	2	0
Jack Lohrke, ph	.000	2	2	0	0	0	0	0	0	0	1	0
Sal Maglie, p	.000	1	1	0	0	0	0	0	0	0	1	0
Willie Mays, of	.182	6	22	1	4	0	0	0	1	2	2	0
Ray Noble, c	.000	2	2	0	0	0	0	0	0	0	1	0
Bill Rigney, ph	.250	4	4	0	1	0	0	0	1	0	1	0
Hank Schenz, pr	.000	1	0	0	0	0	0	0	0	0	0	0
George Spencer, p	.000	2	0	0	0	0	0	0	0	0	0	0
Eddie Stanky, 2b	.136	6	22	3	3	0	0	0	1	3	2	0
Hank Thompson, of	.143	5	14	3	2	0	0	0	0	5	2	0
Bobby Thomson, 3b	.238	6	21	1	5	1	0	0	2	5	0	0
Wes Westrum, c	.235	6	17	1	4	1	0	0	0	5	3	0
Davey Williams, ph	.000	2	1	0	0	0	0	0	0	0	0	0
Sal Yvars, ph	.000	1	1	0	0	0	0	0	0	0	0	0
TOTAL	.237		194	18	46	7	1	2	15	25	22	2

PITCHER	W	L	ERA	G	GS	CG	SV	SHO	IP	H	ER	BB	SO
Al Corwin	0	0	0.00	1	0	0	0	0	1.2	1	0	0	1
Jim Hearn	1	0	1.04	2	1	0	0	0	8.2	5	1	8	1
Larry Jansen	0	2	6.30	3	2	0	0	0	10.0	8	7	4	6
Sheldon Jones	0	0	2.08	2	0	0	1	0	4.1	5	1	1	2
Monte Kennedy	0	0	6.00	2	0	0	0	0	3.0	3	2	1	4
Alex Konikowski	0	0	0.00	1	0	0	0	0	1.0	1	0	0	0
Dave Koslo	1	1	3.00	2	2	1	0	0	15.0	12	5	7	6
Sal Maglie	0	1	7.20	1	1	0	0	0	5.0	8	4	2	3
George Spencer	0	0	18.90	2	0	0	0	0	3.1	6	7	3	0
TOTAL	2	4	4.67	16	6	1	1	0	52.0	49	27	26	23

GAME 1 AT NY-A OCT 4

NY-N 200 003 000 5 10 1
NY-A 010 000 000 1 7 1

Pitchers: KOSLO vs REYNOLDS, Hogue (7), Morgan (8)
Home Runs: Dark-NY(N)
Attendance: 65,673

GAME 2 AT NY-A OCT 5

NY-N 000 000 100 1 5 1
NY-A 110 000 01X 3 6 0

Pitchers: JANSEN, Spencer (7) vs LOPAT
Home Runs: Collins-NY(A)
Attendance: 66,018

GAME 3 AT NY-N OCT 6

NY-A 000 000 011 2 5 2
NY-N 010 050 00X 6 7 2

Pitchers: RASCHI, Hogue (5), Ostrowski (7) vs HEARN, Jones (8)
Home Runs: Lockman-NY(N), Woodling-NY(A)
Attendance: 52,035

GAME 4 AT NY-N OCT 8

NY-A 010 120 200 6 12 0
NY-N 100 000 001 2 8 2

Pitchers: REYNOLDS vs MAGLIE, Jones (6), Kennedy (9)
Home Runs: DiMaggio-NY(A)
Attendance: 49,010

GAME 5 AT NY-N OCT 9

NY-A 005 202 400 13 12 1
NY-N 100 000 000 1 5 3

Pitchers: LOPAT vs JANSEN, Kennedy (4), Spencer (6), Corwin (7), Konikowski (9)
Home Runs: McDougald-NY(A), Rizzuto-NY(A)
Attendance: 47,530

GAME 6 AT NY-A OCT 10

NY-N 000 010 002 3 11 1
NY-A 100 003 00X 4 7 0

Pitchers: KOSLO, Hearn (7), Jansen (8) vs RASCHI, Sain (7), Kuzava (9)
Attendance: 61,711

In four of the seven games, home runs provided the margin of victory. Homers accounted for five of the six runs scored in the opener, with Duke Snider's two-run blast in the sixth putting Brooklyn ahead to stay. Star Dodgers reliever Joe Black, in only his third start of the year, held New York to six hits and two runs in defeating Yankees ace Allie Reynolds.

In Game 2 Billy Martin's three-run shot was the centerpiece. Vic Raschi tossed a three-hitter. Brooklyn needed no homers to regain the Series advantage in Game 3. In the top of the ninth, with the Dodgers leading by a run, Pee Wee Reese and Jackie Robinson singled (driving out starter Ed Lopat) and pulled a double steal. Both then scored on a passed ball. Yankees pinch hitter Johnny Mize homered in the last of the ninth, but Preacher Roe escaped without further scoring for a complete-game 5–3 win.

Black opposed Reynolds again in Game 4 and bettered his earlier performance, holding New York to three hits and one run (a Mize homer) in seven innings. But Reynolds improved even more, fanning 10 as he shut the Dodgers out.

Snider hit his second homer of the Series and Mize his third in the fifth inning of Game 5. Mize's shot put New York ahead, but Brooklyn tied the game in the seventh and took a 6–5 lead when Snider doubled home a run in the 11th. Right fielder Carl Furillo's leaping catch in the last of the 11th robbed Mize of another home run, and starter Carl Erskine held on for the win, giving Brooklyn a 3–2 Series lead.

Snider's home run in the last of the sixth ended Vic Raschi's shutout in Game 6, but Yogi Berra, the first Yankee up in the seventh, tied the game and spoiled Billy Loes's shutout with his home run, and pitcher Raschi singled home the go-ahead run two outs later. Mickey Mantle's blast in the eighth (the first of his record 18 World Series home runs) made the score 3–1. Snider's fourth homer of the Series gave the Dodgers a second run in the eighth, but Allie Reynolds relieved Raschi and prevented further scoring, sending the Series to a seventh game.

Joe Black traded three shutout innings with Ed Lopat in the finale before both clubs scored single runs in the fourth and fifth innings. Mantle homered off Black in the sixth for a third run that proved the Series winner, as three Yankees relievers held Brooklyn scoreless through the final four frames.

New York Yankees (AL), 4; Brooklyn Dodgers (NL), 3

NY (A)

PLAYER/POS	AVG	G	AB	R	H	2B	3B	HR	RB	BB	SO	SB
Hank Bauer, of	.056	7	18	2	1	0	0	0	1	4	3	0
Yogi Berra, c	.214	7	28	2	6	1	0	2	3	2	4	0
Ewell Blackwell, p	.000	1	1	0	0	0	0	0	0	0	0	0
Joe Collins, 1b	.000	6	12	1	0	0	0	0	0	1	3	0
Tom Gorman, p	.000	1	0	0	0	0	0	0	0	0	0	0
Ralph Houk, ph	.000	1	1	0	0	0	0	0	0	0	0	0
Bob Kuzava, p	.000	1	1	0	0	0	0	0	0	0	0	0
Ed Lopat, p	.333	2	3	0	1	0	0	0	1	1	1	0
Mickey Mantle, of	.345	7	29	5	10	1	1	2	3	3	4	0
Billy Martin, 2b	.217	7	23	2	5	0	0	1	4	2	2	0
Gil McDougald, 3b	.200	7	25	5	5	0	0	1	3	5	2	1
Johnny Mize, 1b-4	.400	5	15	3	6	1	0	3	6	3	1	0
Irv Noren, of-3	.300	4	10	0	3	0	0	0	1	1	3	0
Vic Raschi, p	.167	3	6	0	1	0	0	0	1	1	2	0
Allie Reynolds, p	.000	4	7	0	0	0	0	0	0	0	2	0
Phil Rizzuto, ss	.148	7	27	2	4	1	0	0	0	5	2	0
Johnny Sain, p-1	.000	2	3	0	0	0	0	0	0	0	0	0
Ray Scarborough, p	.000	1	0	0	0	0	0	0	0	0	0	0
Gene Woodling, of-6	.348	7	23	4	8	1	1	1	1	3	3	0
TOTAL	.216		232	26	50	5	2	10	24	31	32	1

PITCHER	W	L	ERA	G	GS	CG	SV	SHO	IP	H	ER	BB	SO
Ewell Blackwell	0	0	7.20	1	1	0	0	0	5.0	4	4	3	4
Tom Gorman	0	0	0.00	1	0	0	0	0	0.2	1	0	0	0
Bob Kuzava	0	0	0.00	1	0	0	1	0	2.2	0	0	0	2
Ed Lopat	0	1	4.76	2	2	0	0	0	11.1	14	6	4	3
Vic Raschi	2	0	1.59	3	2	1	0	0	17.0	12	3	8	18
Allie Reynolds	2	1	1.77	4	2	1	1	1	20.1	12	4	6	18
Johnny Sain	0	1	3.00	1	0	0	0	0	6.0	6	2	3	3
Ray Scarborough	0	0	9.00	1	0	0	0	0	1.0	1	1	0	1
TOTAL	4	3	2.81	14	7	2	2	1	64.0	50	20	24	49

BRO (N)

PLAYER/POS	AVG	G	AB	R	H	2B	3B	HR	RB	BB	SO	SB
Sandy Amoros, ph	.000	1	0	0	0	0	0	0	0	0	0	0
Joe Black, p	.000	3	6	0	0	0	0	0	0	1	6	0
Roy Campanella, c	.214	7	28	0	6	0	0	0	1	1	6	0
Billy Cox, 3b	.296	7	27	4	8	2	0	0	0	3	4	0
Carl Erskine, p	.000	3	6	1	0	0	0	0	0	0	1	0
Carl Furillo, of	.174	7	23	1	4	2	0	0	0	3	3	0
Gil Hodges, 1b	.000	7	21	1	0	0	0	0	1	5	6	0
Tommy Holmes, of	.000	3	1	0	0	0	0	0	0	0	0	0
Ken Lehman, p	.000	1	0	0	0	0	0	0	0	0	0	0
Billy Loes, p	.333	2	3	0	1	0	0	0	0	0	1	1
Bobby Morgan, 3b	.000	2	1	0	0	0	0	0	0	0	0	0
Rocky Nelson, ph	.000	4	3	0	0	0	0	0	0	1	2	0
Andy Pafko, of-5	.190	7	21	0	4	0	0	0	2	0	4	0
Pee Wee Reese, ss	.345	7	29	4	10	0	0	1	4	2	2	1
Jackie Robinson, 2b	.174	7	23	4	4	0	0	1	2	7	5	2
Preacher Roe, p	.000	3	2	0	0	0	0	0	0	0	0	0
Johnny Rutherford, p	.000	1	0	0	0	0	0	0	0	0	0	0
George Shuba, of-3	.300	4	10	0	3	1	0	0	0	0	4	0
Duke Snider, of	.345	7	29	5	10	2	0	4	8	1	5	1
TOTAL	.215		233	20	50	7	0	6	18	24	49	5

PITCHER	W	L	ERA	G	GS	CG	SV	SHO	IP	H	ER	BB	SO
Joe Black	1	2	2.53	3	3	1	0	0	21.1	15	6	8	9
Carl Erskine	1	1	4.50	3	2	1	0	0	18.0	12	9	10	10
Ken Lehman	0	0	0.00	1	0	0	0	0	2.0	2	0	1	0
Billy Loes	0	1	4.35	2	1	0	0	0	10.1	11	5	5	5
Preacher Roe	1	0	3.18	3	1	1	0	0	11.1	9	4	6	7
Johnny Rutherford	0	0	9.00	1	0	0	0	0	1.0	1	1	1	1
TOTAL	3	4	3.52	13	7	3	0	0	64.0	50	25	31	32

GAME 1 AT BRO OCT 1

		R	H	E
NY	010 000 010	2	6	2
BRO	010 002 01X	4	6	0

Pitchers: REYNOLDS, Scarborough (8) vs BLACK
Home Runs: Robinson-BRO, Snider-BRO, Reese-BRO, McDougald-NY
Attendance: 34,861

GAME 2 AT BRO OCT 2

		R	H	E
NY	000 115 000	7	10	0
BRO	001 000 000	1	3	1

Pitchers: RASCHI vs ERSKINE, Loes (6), Lehman (8)
Home Runs: Martin-NY
Attendance: 33,792

GAME 3 AT NY OCT 3

		R	H	E
BRO	001 010 012	5	11	0
NY	010 000 011	3	6	2

Pitchers: ROE vs LOPAT, Gorman (9)
Home Runs: Berra-NY, Mize-NY
Attendance: 66,698

GAME 4 AT NY OCT 4

		R	H	E
BRO	000 000 000	0	4	1
NY	000 100 01X	2	4	1

Pitchers: BLACK, Rutherford (8) vs REYNOLDS
Home Runs: Mize-NY
Attendance: 71,787

GAME 5 AT NY OCT 5

		R	H	E
BRO	010 030 100 01	6	10	0
NY	000 050 000 00	5	5	1

Pitchers: ERSKINE vs Blackwell, SAIN (6)
Home Runs: Snider-BRO, Mize-NY
Attendance: 70,536

GAME 6 AT BRO OCT 6

		R	H	E
NY	000 000 210	3	9	0
BRO	000 001 010	2	8	1

Pitchers: RASCHI, Reynolds (8) vs LOES, Roe (9)
Home Runs: Snider-BRO (2), Berra-NY, Mantle-NY
Attendance: 30,037

GAME 7 AT BRO OCT 7

		R	H	E
NY	000 111 100	4	10	4
BRO	000 110 000	2	8	1

Pitchers: Lopat, REYNOLDS (4), Raschi (7), Kuzava (7) vs BLACK, Roe (6), Erskine (8)
Home Runs: Woodling-NY, Mantle-NY
Attendance: 33,195

Although the Yankees easily won the American League pennant, the Dodgers seemed even more overwhelming, with a team batting average of .285 and a club-record 105 wins. But when the Series was over, the Yankees had added a record fifth straight world championship to their record fifth straight pennant.

Dodgers ace Carl Erskine lasted only one inning of the Series opener, giving up three walks and two triples for four runs. By the middle of the seventh inning, the Dodgers had tied the score at 5–5. But Joe Collins homered for the Yanks to break the tie in the last of the seventh, and reliever Johnny Sain ensured his own win with a two-run double an inning later. The Dodgers outhit New York in Game 2, and held a 2–1 lead entering the bottom of the seventh. Billy Martin (who hit .500 and slugged .958 in the Series) tied the game with a leadoff homer in the seventh, and Mickey Mantle won it with a two-run blast in the eighth.

Brooklyn evened the Series at home with victories in Games 3 and 4. Erskine redeemed his poor start in Game 1 with a record-setting 14-strikeout performance in Game 3. But it was a narrow win, settled only when Roy Campanella homered in the last of the eighth to break a 2–2 tie. In Game 4, Duke Snider made Billy Loes's three-run pitching a winning performance, driving in four of the Dodgers' seven runs with two doubles and a homer.

But Brooklyn never held the lead in the final two games. Four home runs (including a Mantle grand slam) rocked Dodgers pitching in Game 5 as the Bombers built a lead which Dodger home runs in the eighth and ninth were unable to overcome. In Game 6 the Yankees built a 3–0 lead over Erskine in the first two innings. Brooklyn fought back with a run in the sixth, and tied the game on Carl Furillo's two-run homer in the top of the ninth. But with men on first and second in the last of the ninth, Billy Martin singled in the game-ending, Series-winning run. It was Martin's 12th hit, a new record for a six-game Series.

New York Yankees (AL), 4; Brooklyn Dodgers (NL), 2

NY (A)

PLAYER/POS	AVG	G	AB	R	H	2B	3B	HR	RB	BB	SO	SB
Hank Bauer, of	.261	6	23	6	6	0	1	0	1	2	4	0
Yogi Berra, c	.429	6	21	3	9	1	0	1	4	3	3	0
Don Bollweg, 1b-1	.000	3	2	0	0	0	0	0	0	0	2	0
Joe Collins, 1b	.167	6	24	4	4	1	0	1	2	3	8	0
Whitey Ford, p	.333	2	3	0	1	0	0	0	0	0	0	0
Tom Gorman, p	.000	1	1	0	0	0	0	0	0	0	1	0
Bob Kuzava, p	.000	1	1	0	0	0	0	0	0	0	1	0
Ed Lopat, p	.000	1	3	0	0	0	0	0	0	0	2	0
Mickey Mantle, of	.208	6	24	3	5	0	0	2	7	3	8	0
Billy Martin, 2b	.500	6	24	5	12	1	2	2	8	1	2	1
Jim McDonald, p	.500	1	2	0	1	1	0	0	1	1	1	0
Gil McDougald, 3b	.167	6	24	2	4	0	1	2	4	1	3	0
Johnny Mize, ph	.000	3	3	0	0	0	0	0	0	0	1	0
Irv Noren, ph	.000	2	1	0	0	0	0	0	0	1	0	0
Vic Raschi, p	.000	1	2	0	0	0	0	0	0	0	1	0
Allie Reynolds, p	.500	3	2	0	1	0	0	0	0	1	1	0
Phil Rizzuto, ss	.316	6	19	4	6	1	0	0	0	3	2	1
Johnny Sain, p	.500	2	2	1	1	1	0	0	2	0	1	0
Art Schallock, p	.000	1	0	0	0	0	0	0	0	0	0	0
Gene Woodling, of	.300	6	20	5	6	0	0	1	3	6	2	0
TOTAL	.279		201	33	56	6	4	9	32	25	43	2

PITCHER	W	L	ERA	G	GS	CG	SV	SHO	IP	H	ER	BB	SO
Whitey Ford	0	1	4.50	2	2	0	0	0	8.0	9	4	2	7
Tom Gorman	0	0	3.00	1	0	0	0	0	3.0	4	1	0	1
Bob Kuzava	0	0	13.50	1	0	0	0	0	0.2	2	1	0	1
Ed Lopat	1	0	2.00	1	1	1	0	0	9.0	9	2	4	3
Jim McDonald	1	0	5.87	1	1	0	0	0	7.2	12	5	0	3
Vic Raschi	0	1	3.38	1	1	1	0	0	8.0	9	3	3	4
Allie Reynolds	1	0	6.75	3	1	0	1	0	8.0	9	6	4	9
Johnny Sain	1	0	4.76	2	0	0	0	0	5.2	8	3	1	1
Art Schallock	0	0	4.50	1	0	0	0	0	2.0	2	1	1	1
TOTAL	4	2	4.50	13	6	2	1	0	52.0	64	26	15	30

BRO (N)

PLAYER/POS	AVG	G	AB	R	H	2B	3B	HR	RB	BB	SO	SB
Wayne Belardi, ph	.000	2	2	0	0	0	0	0	0	0	1	0
Joe Black, p	.000	1	0	0	0	0	0	0	0	0	0	0
Roy Campanella, c	.273	6	22	6	6	0	0	1	2	2	3	0
Billy Cox, 3b	.304	6	23	3	7	3	0	1	6	1	4	0
Carl Erskine, p	.250	3	4	0	1	0	0	0	0	0	1	0
Carl Furillo, of	.333	6	24	4	8	2	0	1	4	1	3	0
Jim Gilliam, 2b	.296	6	27	4	8	3	0	2	4	0	2	0
Gil Hodges, 1b	.364	6	22	3	8	0	0	1	1	3	3	1
Jim Hughes, p	.000	1	1	0	0	0	0	0	0	0	1	0
Clem Labine, p	.000	3	2	0	0	0	0	0	0	0	1	0
Billy Loes, p	.667	1	3	0	2	0	0	0	0	0	0	0
Russ Meyer, p	.000	1	1	0	0	0	0	0	0	0	1	0
Bob Milliken, p	.000	1	0	0	0	0	0	0	0	0	0	0
Bobby Morgan, ph	.000	1	1	0	0	0	0	0	0	0	0	0
Johnny Podres, p	1.000	1	1	0	1	0	0	0	0	0	0	0
Pee Wee Reese, ss	.208	6	24	0	5	0	1	0	0	4	1	0
Jackie Robinson, of	.320	6	25	3	8	2	0	0	2	1	0	1
Preacher Roe, p	.000	1	3	0	0	0	0	0	0	0	2	0
George Shuba, ph	1.000	2	1	1	1	0	0	1	2	0	0	0
Duke Snider, of	.320	6	25	3	8	3	0	1	5	2	6	0
Don Thompson, of	.000	2	0	0	0	0	0	0	0	0	0	0
Ben Wade, p	.000	2	0	0	0	0	0	0	0	0	0	0
Dick Williams, ph	.500	3	2	0	1	0	0	0	0	1	1	0
TOTAL	.300		213	27	64	13	1	8	26	15	30	2

PITCHER	W	L	ERA	G	GS	CG	SV	SHO	IP	H	ER	BB	SO
Joe Black	0	0	9.00	1	0	0	0	0	1.0	1	1	0	2
Carl Erskine	1	0	5.79	3	3	1	0	0	14.0	14	9	9	16
Jim Hughes	0	0	2.25	1	0	0	0	0	4.0	3	1	1	3
Clem Labine	0	2	3.60	3	0	0	1	0	5.0	10	2	1	3
Billy Loes	1	0	3.38	1	1	0	0	0	8.0	8	3	2	8
Russ Meyer	0	0	6.23	1	0	0	0	0	4.1	8	3	4	5
Bob Milliken	0	0	0.00	1	0	0	0	0	2.0	2	0	1	0
Johnny Podres	0	1	3.38	1	1	0	0	0	2.2	1	1	2	0
Preacher Roe	0	1	4.50	1	1	1	0	0	8.0	5	4	4	4
Ben Wade	0	0	15.43	2	0	0	0	0	2.1	4	4	1	2
TOTAL	2	4	4.91	15	6	2	1	0	51.1	56	28	25	43

GAME 1 AT NY SEPT 30

				R	H	E
BRO	000	013	100	5	12	2
NY	400	010	13X	9	12	0

Pitchers: Erskine, Hughes (2), LABINE (6), Wade (8) vs Reynolds, SAIN (6)
Home Runs: Gilliam-BRO, Hodges-BRO, Shuba-BRO, Berra-NY, Collins-NY
Attendance: 69,374

GAME 2 AT NY OCT 1

				R	H	E
BRO	000	200	000	2	9	1
NY	100	000	12X	4	5	0

Pitchers: ROE vs LOPAT
Home Runs: Martin-NY, Mantle-NY
Attendance: 66,786

GAME 3 AT BRO OCT 2

				R	H	E
NY	000	010	010	2	6	0
BRO	000	011	01X	3	9	0

Pitchers: RASCHI vs ERSKINE
Home Runs: Campanella-BRO
Attendance: 35,270

GAME 4 AT BRO OCT 3

				R	H	E
NY	000	020	001	3	9	0
BRO	300	102	10X	7	12	0

Pitchers: FORD, Gorman (2), Sain (5), Schallock (7) vs LOES, Labine (9)
Home Runs: McDougald-NY, Snider-BRO
Attendance: 36,775

GAME 5 AT BRO OCT 4

				R	H	E
NY	105	000	311	11	11	1
BRO	010	010	041	7	14	1

Pitchers: McDONALD, Kuzava (8), Reynolds (9) vs PODRES, Meyer (3), Wade (8), Black (9)
Home Runs: Woodling-NY, Mantle-NY, Martin-NY, McDougald-NY, Cox-BRO, Gilliam-BRO
Attendance: 36,775

GAME 6 AT NY OCT 5

				R	H	E
BRO	000	001	002	3	8	3
NY	210	000	001	4	13	0

Pitchers: Erskine, Milliken (5), LABINE (7) vs Ford, REYNOLDS (8)
Home Runs: Furillo-BRO
Attendance: 62,370

The Indians, who had won a league-record 111 games to break the American League domination of the New York Yankees, entered the World Series as strong favorites to humble the Giants. It was not to be.

Cleveland would have won the opener had it not been played in New York's Polo Grounds, with their short foul lines and deep center field. Most of the game was a pitchers' duel. Vic Wertz (the only Indian to hit safely in all four games) tripled off Sal Maglie to give Cleveland a two-run lead in the top of the first, but three singles and a walk in the third off Bob Lemon tied the score. Lemon then settled down to hold New York scoreless through the ninth. Cleveland threatened in the eighth when the first two batters reached base, bringing Wertz to the plate. As Wertz had already hit Maglie safely three times, Don Liddle was brought in to pitch to him. Wertz responded with a fly to deep center that would have been a home run in Cleveland, but in New York turned into the most famous catch in World Series history as Willie Mays raced out and tracked down the ball about 425 feet from the plate. Marv Grissom replaced Liddle on the mound and issued a walk to load the bases, but he retired the next two batters and (despite Wertz's double in the top of the 10th) held Cleveland scoreless the rest of the way. In the last of the 10th, Lemon retired the first batter, but Mays walked and stole second, and Hank Thompson was walked intentionally to set up the double play. Pinch hitter Dusty Rhodes then entered the hall of heroes with a short fly to right that—though it would have been an out in Cleveland—fell into the Polo Grounds stands for three runs and a Giants victory.

The rest of the Series was anticlimax. In the second game Rhodes, with half the Giants' four hits, drove in two runs on a single and another homer, providing the margin of victory for ace Johnny Antonelli, who allowed only one of Cleveland's 14 baserunners to score. Game 3 was no contest. New York had scored all six of its runs before the Indians managed to come up with single runs in both the seventh and eighth. Pinch hitter Hank Majeski's three-run homer put Cleveland on the board in the fifth inning of Game 4. But as New York had already scored seven times, even a fourth Cleveland run in the seventh proved too little to prevent a shocking sweep by the Giants.

New York Giants (NL), 4; Cleveland Indians (AL), 0

NY (N)

PLAYER/POS	AVG	G	AB	R	H	2B	3B	HR	RB	BB	SO	SB
Johnny Antonelli, p	.000	2	3	0	0	0	0	0	1	0	0	0
Alvin Dark, ss	.412	4	17	2	7	0	0	0	0	1	1	0
Ruben Gomez, p	.000	1	4	0	0	0	0	0	0	0	2	0
Marv Grissom, p	.000	1	1	0	0	0	0	0	0	0	1	0
Monte Irvin, of	.222	4	9	1	2	1	0	0	2	0	3	0
Don Liddle, p	.000	2	3	0	0	0	0	0	0	0	2	0
Whitey Lockman, 1b	.111	4	18	2	2	0	0	0	0	1	2	0
Sal Maglie, p	.000	1	3	0	0	0	0	0	0	0	2	0
Willie Mays, of	.286	4	14	4	4	1	0	0	3	4	1	1
Don Mueller, of	.389	4	18	4	7	0	0	0	1	0	1	0
Dusty Rhodes, of-2	.667	3	6	2	4	0	0	2	7	1	2	0
Hank Thompson, 3b	.364	4	11	6	4	1	0	0	2	7	1	0
Wes Westrum, c	.273	4	11	0	3	0	0	0	3	1	3	0
Hoyt Wilhelm, p	.000	2	1	0	0	0	0	0	0	0	1	0
Davey Williams, 2b	.000	4	11	0	0	0	0	0	1	2	2	0
TOTAL	.254		130	21	33	3	0	2	20	17	24	1

PITCHER	W	L	ERA	G	GS	CG	SV	SHO	IP	H	ER	BB	SO
Johnny Antonelli	1	0	0.84	2	1	1	1	0	10.2	8	1	7	12
Ruben Gomez	1	0	2.45	1	1	0	0	0	7.1	4	2	3	2
Marv Grissom	1	0	0.00	1	0	0	0	0	2.2	1	0	3	2
Don Liddle	1	0	1.29	2	1	0	0	0	7.0	5	1	1	2
Sal Maglie	0	0	2.57	1	1	0	0	0	7.0	7	2	2	2
Hoyt Wilhelm	0	0	0.00	2	0	0	1	0	2.1	1	0	0	3
TOTAL	4	0	1.46	9	4	1	2	0	37.0	26	6	16	23

CLE (A)

PLAYER/POS	AVG	G	AB	R	H	2B	3B	HR	RB	BB	SO	SB
Bobby Avila, 2b	.133	4	15	1	2	0	0	0	0	2	1	0
Sam Dente, ss	.000	3	3	1	0	0	0	0	0	1	0	0
Larry Doby, of	.125	4	16	0	2	0	0	0	0	2	4	0
Mike Garcia, p	.000	2	0	0	0	0	0	0	0	0	0	0
Bill Glynn, 1b-1	.500	2	2	1	1	1	0	0	0	0	1	0
Mickey Grasso, c	.000	1	0	0	0	0	0	0	0	0	0	0
Jim Hegan, c	.154	4	13	1	2	1	0	0	0	1	1	0
Art Houtteman, p	.000	1	0	0	0	0	0	0	0	0	0	0
Bob Lemon, p-2	.000	3	6	0	0	0	0	0	0	1	1	0
Hank Majeski, 3b-1	.167	4	6	1	1	0	0	1	3	0	1	0
Dale Mitchell, ph	.000	3	2	0	0	0	0	0	0	1	0	0
Don Mossi, p	.000	3	0	0	0	0	0	0	0	0	0	0
Hal Naragon, c	.000	1	0	0	0	0	0	0	0	0	0	0
Ray Narleski, p	.000	2	0	0	0	0	0	0	0	0	0	0
Hal Newhouser, p	.000	1	0	0	0	0	0	0	0	0	0	0
Dave Philley, of-2	.125	4	8	0	1	0	0	0	0	1	3	0
Dave Pope, of-2	.000	3	3	0	0	0	0	0	0	1	1	0
Rudy Regalado, 3b-1	.333	4	3	0	1	0	0	0	1	0	0	0
Al Rosen, 3b	.250	3	12	0	3	0	0	0	0	1	0	0
Al Smith, of	.214	4	14	2	3	0	0	1	2	2	2	0
George Strickland, ss	.000	3	9	0	0	0	0	0	0	0	2	0
Vic Wertz, 1b	.500	4	16	2	8	2	1	1	3	2	2	0
Wally Westlake, of	.143	2	7	0	1	0	0	0	0	1	3	0
Early Wynn, p	.500	1	2	0	1	1	0	0	0	0	1	0
TOTAL	.190		137	9	26	5	1	3	9	16	23	0

PITCHER	W	L	ERA	G	GS	CG	SV	SHO	IP	H	ER	BB	SO
Mike Garcia	0	1	5.40	2	1	0	0	0	5.0	6	3	4	4
Art Houtteman	0	0	4.50	1	0	0	0	0	2.0	2	1	1	1
Bob Lemon	0	2	6.75	2	2	1	0	0	13.1	16	10	8	11
Don Mossi	0	0	0.00	3	0	0	0	0	4.0	3	0	0	1
Ray Narleski	0	0	2.25	2	0	0	0	0	4.0	1	1	1	2
Hal Newhouser	0	0	∞	1	0	0	0	0	0.0	1	1	1	0
Early Wynn	0	1	3.86	1	1	0	0	0	7.0	4	3	2	5
TOTAL	0	4	4.84	12	4	1	0	0	35.1	33	19	17	24

GAME 1 AT NY SEPT 29

					R	H	E
CLE	200	000	000	0	2	8	0
NY	002	000	000	3	5	9	3

Pitchers: LEMON vs Maglie, Liddle (8), GRISSOM (8)
Home Runs: Rhodes-NY
Attendance: 52,751

GAME 2 AT NY SEPT 30

				R	H	E
CLE	100	000	000	1	8	0
NY	000	020	10X	3	4	0

Pitchers: WYNN, Mossi (8) vs ANTONELLI
Home Runs: Smith-CLE, Rhodes-NY
Attendance: 49,099

GAME 3 AT CLE OCT 1

				R	H	E
NY	103	011	000	6	10	1
CLE	000	000	110	2	4	2

Pitchers: GOMEZ, Wilhelm (7) vs GARCIA, Houtteman (4), Narleski (6), Mossi (9)
Home Runs: Wertz-CLE
Attendance: 71,555

GAME 4 AT CLE OCT 2

				R	H	E
NY	021	040	000	7	10	3
CLE	000	030	100	4	6	2

Pitchers: LIDDLE, Wilhelm (7), Antonelli (8) vs LEMON, Newhouser (5), Narleski (5), Mossi (6), Garcia (8)
Home Runs: Majeski-CLE
Attendance: 78,102

The Dodgers and Yankees, after a year's absence, faced each other again in the World Series—their sixth Series confrontation in 15 years. And after Brooklyn had lost the first two games it began to look as though 1955 might also mark the Yankees' sixth Series triumph over the Dodgers. But this was Brooklyn's year.

The opener was a hitters' game, but closely contested. Both teams scored twice in the second inning and once in the third, but first baseman Joe Collins' leadoff homer in the last of the fourth gave New York its first lead of the game, and his two-run blast in the sixth made the score 6–3. Brooklyn clawed back in the eighth for two runs—including Jackie Robinson's steal of home—to pull within one run of a tie, but they came no closer. In Game 2, Tommy Byrne held the Dodgers to five hits and two runs, and won his own game at the bat with a two-run single that capped the Yankees' four-run fourth.

The Series turned around as the Dodgers captured the next three games in Brooklyn. Roy Campanella's two-run homer in the first inning of Game 3 gave Brooklyn a quick lead. New York tied the game with a pair of runs in the second (one of them a homer by Mickey Mantle, who appeared in only three Series games because of a leg injury). But two more runs in the last of the second drove out New York starter Bob Turley and put them ahead to stay as Dodgers hurler Johnny Podres held the Yankees to three runs. Home runs by Campanella, Gil Hodges, and Duke Snider accounted for six of Brooklyn's eight runs in Game 4 as the Dodgers evened the Series. Sandy Amoros' second-inning homer initiated the scoring in Game 5, and Snider's blasts in the third and fifth (which made him the first player to hit four home runs in two different Series) gave Brooklyn a 4–1 lead, which even late-inning Yankees homers by Bob Cerv and Yogi Berra could not overcome.

New York bounced back in Game 6, scoring all five of their runs in the first inning (including three on Bill Skowron's homer) to give Whitey Ford a comfortable lead, which he held with a one-run four-hitter. But in the finale, Gil Hodges drove in both Brooklyn runs with a single in the fourth and a sacrifice fly in the sixth. They were all Brooklyn got, but they proved more than enough to carry the Dodgers to their first world title in 55 years, as left fielder Sandy Amoros stifled New York's only real scoring threat with a spectacular running catch in the sixth that started a double play and preserved Johnny Podres' second Series win.

Brooklyn Dodgers (NL), 4; New York Yankees (AL), 3

BRO (N)

PLAYER/POS	AVG	G	AB	R	H	2B	3B	HR	RB	BB	SO	SB
Sandy Amoros, of	.333	5	12	3	4	0	0	1	3	4	4	0
Don Bessent, p	.000	3	1	0	0	0	0	0	0	0	1	0
Roy Campanella, c	.259	7	27	4	7	3	0	2	4	3	3	0
Roger Craig, p	.000	1	0	0	0	0	0	0	0	1	0	0
Carl Erskine, p	.000	1	1	0	0	0	0	0	0	0	0	0
Carl Furillo, of	.296	7	27	4	8	1	0	1	3	3	5	0
Jim Gilliam, 2b-5,of-4	.292	7	24	2	7	1	0	0	3	8	1	1
Don Hoak, 3b-1	.333	3	3	0	1	0	0	0	0	2	0	0
Gil Hodges, 1b	.292	7	24	2	7	0	0	1	5	3	2	0
Frank Kellert, ph	.333	3	3	0	1	0	0	0	0	0	0	0
Clem Labine, p	.000	4	4	0	0	0	0	0	0	0	3	0
Billy Loes, p	.000	1	1	0	0	0	0	0	0	0	0	0
Russ Meyer, p	.000	1	2	0	0	0	0	0	0	0	1	0
Don Newcombe, p	.000	1	3	0	0	0	0	0	0	0	0	0
Johnny Podres, p	.143	2	7	1	1	0	0	0	0	0	1	0
Pee Wee Reese, ss	.296	7	27	5	8	1	0	0	2	3	5	0
Jackie Robinson, 3b	.182	6	22	5	4	1	1	0	1	2	1	1
Ed Roebuck, p	.000	1	0	0	0	0	0	0	0	0	0	0
George Shuba, ph	.000	1	1	0	0	0	0	0	0	0	0	0
Duke Snider, of	.320	7	25	5	8	1	0	4	7	2	6	0
Karl Spooner, p	.000	2	0	0	0	0	0	0	0	0	0	0
Don Zimmer, 2b	.222	4	9	0	2	0	0	0	2	2	5	0
TOTAL	.260		223	31	58	8	1	9	30	33	38	2

PITCHER	W	L	ERA	G	GS	CG	SV	SHO	IP	H	ER	BB	SO
Don Bessent	0	0	0.00	3	0	0	0	0	3.1	3	0	1	1
Roger Craig	1	0	3.00	1	1	0	0	0	6.0	4	2	5	4
Carl Erskine	0	0	9.00	1	1	0	0	0	3.0	3	3	2	3
Clem Labine	1	0	2.89	4	0	0	1	0	9.1	6	3	2	2
Billy Loes	0	1	9.82	1	1	0	0	0	3.2	7	4	1	5
Russ Meyer	0	0	0.00	1	0	0	0	0	5.2	4	0	2	4
Don Newcombe	0	1	9.53	1	1	0	0	0	5.2	8	6	2	4
Johnny Podres	2	0	1.00	2	2	2	0	1	18.0	15	2	4	10
Ed Roebuck	0	0	0.00	1	0	0	0	0	2.0	1	0	0	0
Karl Spooner	0	1	13.50	2	1	0	0	0	3.1	4	5	3	6
TOTAL	4	3	3.75	17	7	2	1	1	60.0	55	25	22	39

NY (A)

PLAYER/POS	AVG	G	AB	R	H	2B	3B	HR	RB	BB	SO	SB
Hank Bauer, of-5	.429	6	14	1	6	0	0	0	1	0	1	0
Yogi Berra, c	.417	7	24	5	10	1	0	1	2	3	1	0
Tommy Byrne, p-2	.167	3	6	0	1	0	0	0	2	0	2	0
Andy Carey, ph	.500	2	2	0	1	0	1	0	1	0	0	0
Tom Carroll, pr	.000	2	0	0	0	0	0	0	0	0	0	0
Bob Cerv, of-4	.125	5	16	1	2	0	0	1	1	0	4	0
Gerry Coleman, ss	.000	3	3	0	0	0	0	0	0	0	1	0
Rip Coleman, p	.000	1	0	0	0	0	0	0	0	0	0	0
Joe Collins, 1b-5,of-1	.167	5	12	6	2	0	0	2	3	6	4	1
Whitey Ford, p	.000	2	6	1	0	0	0	0	0	1	1	0
Bob Grim, p	.000	3	2	0	0	0	0	0	0	0	0	0
Elston Howard, of	.192	7	26	3	5	0	0	1	3	1	8	0
Johnny Kucks, p	.000	2	0	0	0	0	0	0	0	0	0	0
Don Larsen, p	.000	1	2	0	0	0	0	0	0	0	0	0
Mickey Mantle, of-2	.200	3	10	1	2	0	0	1	1	0	2	0
Billy Martin, 2b	.320	7	25	2	8	1	1	0	4	1	5	0
Gil McDougald, 3b	.259	7	27	2	7	0	0	1	1	2	6	0
Tom Morgan, p	.000	2	0	0	0	0	0	0	0	0	0	0
Irv Noren, of	.063	5	16	0	1	0	0	0	1	1	1	0
Phil Rizzuto, ss	.267	7	15	2	4	0	0	0	1	5	1	2
Eddie Robinson, 1b-1	.667	4	3	0	2	0	0	0	1	2	1	0
Bill Skowron, 1b-3	.333	5	12	2	4	2	0	1	3	0	1	0
Tom Sturdivant, p	.000	2	0	0	0	0	0	0	0	0	0	0
Bob Turley, p	.000	3	1	0	0	0	0	0	0	0	0	0
TOTAL	.248		222	26	55	4	2	8	25	22	39	3

PITCHER	W	L	ERA	G	GS	CG	SV	SHO	IP	H	ER	BB	SO
Tommy Byrne	1	1	1.88	2	2	1	0	0	14.1	8	3	8	8
Rip Coleman	0	0	9.00	1	0	0	0	0	1.0	5	1	0	1
Whitey Ford	2	0	2.12	2	2	1	0	0	17.0	13	4	8	10
Bob Grim	0	1	4.15	3	1	0	1	0	8.2	8	4	5	8
Johnny Kucks	0	0	6.00	2	0	0	0	0	3.0	4	2	1	1
Don Larsen	0	1	11.25	1	1	0	0	0	4.0	5	5	2	2
Tom Morgan	0	0	4.91	2	0	0	0	0	3.2	3	2	3	1
Tom Sturdivant	0	0	6.00	2	0	0	0	0	3.0	5	2	2	0
Bob Turley	0	1	8.44	3	1	0	0	0	5.1	7	5	4	7
TOTAL	3	4	4.20	18	7	2	1	0	60.0	58	28	33	38

GAME 1 AT NY SEPT 28

				R	H	E
BRO	021	000	020	5	10	0
NY	021	102	00X	6	9	1

Pitchers: NEWCOMBE, Bessent (6), Labine (8) vs FORD, Grim (9)
Home Runs: Furillo-BRO, Snider-BRO, Howard-NY, Collins-NY (2)
Attendance: 63,869

GAME 2 AT NY SEPT 29

				R	H	E
BRO	000	110	000	2	5	2
NY	000	400	00X	4	8	0

Pitchers: LOES, Bessent (4), Spooner (5), Labine (8) vs BYRNE
Attendance: 64,707

GAME 3 AT BRO SEPT 30

				R	H	E
NY	020	000	100	3	7	0
BRO	220	200	20X	8	11	1

Pitchers: TURLEY, Morgan (2), Kucks (5), Sturdivant (7) vs PODRES
Home Runs: Campanella-BRO, Mantle-NY
Attendance: 34,209

GAME 4 AT BRO OCT 1

				R	H	E
NY	110	102	000	5	9	0
BRO	001	330	10X	8	14	0

Pitchers: LARSEN, Kucks (5), R.Coleman (6), Morgan (7), Sturdivant (8) vs Erskine, Bessent (4), LABINE (5)
Home Runs: McDougald-NY, Campanella-BRO, Hodges-BRO, Snider-BRO
Attendance: 36,242

GAME 5 AT BRO OCT 2

				R	H	E
NY	000	100	110	3	6	0
BRO	021	010	01X	5	9	2

Pitchers: GRIM, Turley (7) vs CRAIG, Labine (7)
Home Runs: Cerv-NY, Berra-NY, Amoros-BRO, Snider-BRO (2)
Attendance: 36,796

GAME 6 AT NY OCT 3

				R	H	E
BRO	000	100	000	1	4	1
NY	500	000	00X	5	8	0

Pitchers: SPOONER, Meyer (1), Roebuck (7) vs FORD
Home Runs: Skowron-NY
Attendance: 64,022

GAME 7 AT NY OCT 4

				R	H	E
BRO	000	101	000	2	5	0
NY	000	000	000	0	8	1

Pitchers: PODRES vs BYRNE, Grim (6), Turley (8)
Attendance: 62,465

With both teams repeaters as league champions, the Yankees followed Brooklyn's winning pattern of the previous Series: losing the first two games, winning the next three, then splitting the final pair.

Sal Maglie outlasted Yankees ace Whitey Ford in the opener. Maglie gave up nine hits and three runs (on homers by Mickey Mantle and Billy Martin), but struck out 10 and took the win as Jackie Robinson and Gil Hodges contributed homers for four of Brooklyn's six runs. Dodgers ace Don Newcombe was blown out by six Yankees runs (capped by Yogi Berra's grand slam) in the first two innings of Game 2. But Brooklyn came back with six unearned runs in their half of the second (three of them on Duke Snider's homer) and proceeded to run through seven Yankees pitchers for a 13–8 win and a two-game Series edge.

Whitey Ford tried again in Game 3, and this time held on for a complete-game 5–3 win, supported by Billy Martin's game-tying solo homer in the second and 40-year-old Enos Slaughter's go-ahead three-run shot in the sixth. Tom Sturdivant duplicated Ford's effectiveness and success the next day with a six-hit 6–2 win to even the Series.

Sal Maglie pitched Game 5 for Brooklyn and improved on his winning performance of Game 1, yielding only two runs and holding New York hitless until Mantle's two-out homer in the fourth inning. But no one was a match for Yankees pitcher Don Larsen that day. There was a close out on a deflected Dodger liner in the second inning, and center fielder Mantle made a fine running catch to prevent a hit in the fifth. But Larsen retired the rest routinely, and when Dale Mitchell fanned in the ninth Larsen had his perfect game—a feat still unique in World Series history.

Brooklyn reliever Clem Labine started in Game 6 against Bob Turley. No runner scored for either side until the last of the 10th inning when, with two out, Jackie Robinson lined a Turley pitch over the head of the left fielder, scoring Jim Gilliam from second and forcing New York into a seventh game.

The finale proved an anticlimactic disaster for Brooklyn. Once again Newcombe was driven out—this time by Yogi Berra's two two-run homers and Elston Howard's solo shot. By the time it was over, Bill Skowron had increased the Yankee run total to nine with a grand slam, and Johnny Kucks had shut Brooklyn out on three singles. For New York it was world title number 17.

New York Yankees (AL), 4; Brooklyn Dodgers (NL), 3

NY (A)

PLAYER/POS	AVG	G	AB	R	H	2B	3B	HR	RB	BB	SO	SB
Hank Bauer, of	.281	7	32	3	9	0	0	1	3	0	5	1
Yogi Berra, c	.360	7	25	5	9	2	0	3	10	4	1	0
Tommy Byrne, p-1	.000	2	1	0	0	0	0	0	0	0	0	0
Andy Carey, 3b	.158	7	19	2	3	0	0	0	0	1	6	0
Bob Cerv, ph	1.000	1	1	0	1	0	0	0	0	0	0	0
Gerry Coleman, 2b	.000	2	2	0	0	0	0	0	0	0	0	0
Joe Collins, 1b-5	.238	6	21	2	5	2	0	0	2	2	3	0
Whitey Ford, p	.000	2	4	0	0	0	0	0	0	0	3	0
Elston Howard, of	.400	1	5	1	2	1	0	1	1	0	0	0
Johnny Kucks, p	.000	3	3	0	0	0	0	0	0	0	1	0
Don Larsen, p	.333	2	3	1	1	0	0	0	1	0	1	0
Mickey Mantle, of	.250	7	24	6	6	1	0	3	4	6	5	1
Billy Martin, 2b-7,3b-1	.296	7	27	5	8	0	0	2	3	1	6	0
Maury McDermott, p	1.000	1	1	0	1	0	0	0	0	0	0	0
Gil McDougald, ss	.143	7	21	0	3	0	0	0	1	3	6	0
Tom Morgan, p	1.000	2	1	1	1	0	0	0	0	0	0	0
Norm Siebern, ph	.000	1	1	0	0	0	0	0	0	0	0	0
Bill Skowron, 1b-2	.100	3	10	1	1	0	0	1	4	0	3	0
Enos Slaughter, of	.350	6	20	6	7	0	0	1	4	4	0	0
Tom Sturdivant, p	.333	2	3	0	1	0	0	0	0	0	1	0
Bob Turley, p	.000	3	4	0	0	0	0	0	0	0	1	0
George Wilson, ph	.000	1	1	0	0	0	0	0	0	0	1	0
TOTAL	.253		229	33	58	6	0	12	33	21	43	2

PITCHER	W	L	ERA	G	GS	CG	SV	SHO	IP	H	ER	BB	SO
Tommy Byrne	0	0	0.00	1	0	0	0	0	0.1	1	0	0	1
Whitey Ford	1	1	5.25	2	2	1	0	0	12.0	14	7	2	8
Johnny Kucks	1	0	0.82	3	1	1	0	1	11.0	6	1	3	2
Don Larsen	1	0	0.00	2	2	1	0	1	10.2	1	0	4	7
Maury McDermott	0	0	3.00	1	0	0	0	0	3.0	2	1	3	3
Tom Morgan	0	1	9.00	2	0	0	0	0	4.0	6	4	4	3
Tom Sturdivant	1	0	2.79	2	1	1	0	0	9.2	8	3	8	9
Bob Turley	0	1	0.82	3	1	1	0	0	11.0	4	1	8	14
TOTAL	4	3	2.48	16	7	5	0	2	61.2	42	17	32	47

BRO (N)

PLAYER/POS	AVG	G	AB	R	H	2B	3B	HR	RB	BB	SO	SB
Sandy Amoros, of	.053	6	19	1	1	0	0	0	1	2	4	0
Don Bessent, p	.500	2	2	0	1	0	0	0	1	1	1	0
Roy Campanella, c	.182	7	22	2	4	1	0	0	3	3	7	0
Gino Cimoli, of	.000	1	0	0	0	0	0	0	0	0	0	0
Roger Craig, p	.500	2	2	0	1	0	0	0	0	0	0	0
Don Drysdale, p	.000	1	0	0	0	0	0	0	0	0	0	0
Carl Erskine, p	.000	2	1	0	0	0	0	0	0	0	1	0
Carl Furillo, of	.240	7	25	2	6	2	0	0	1	2	3	0
Jim Gilliam, 2b-6,of-1	.083	7	24	2	2	0	0	0	2	7	3	1
Gil Hodges, 1b	.304	7	23	5	7	2	0	1	8	4	4	0
Ransom Jackson, ph	.000	3	3	0	0	0	0	0	0	0	2	0
Clem Labine, p	.250	2	4	0	1	1	0	0	0	0	2	0
Sal Maglie, p	.000	2	5	0	0	0	0	0	0	0	2	0
Dale Mitchell, ph	.000	4	4	0	0	0	0	0	0	0	1	0
Charlie Neal, 2b	.000	1	4	0	0	0	0	0	0	0	1	0
Don Newcombe, p	.000	2	1	0	0	0	0	0	0	0	0	0
Pee Wee Reese, ss	.222	7	27	3	6	0	1	0	2	2	6	0
Jackie Robinson, 3b	.250	7	24	5	6	1	0	1	2	5	2	0
Ed Roebuck, p	.000	3	0	0	0	0	0	0	0	0	0	0
Duke Snider, of	.304	7	23	5	7	1	0	1	4	6	8	0
Rube Walker, ph	.000	2	2	0	0	0	0	0	0	0	0	0
TOTAL	.195		215	25	42	8	1	3	24	32	47	1

PITCHER	W	L	ERA	G	GS	CG	SV	SHO	IP	H	ER	BB	SO
Don Bessent	1	0	1.80	2	0	0	0	0	10.0	8	2	3	5
Roger Craig	0	1	12.00	2	1	0	0	0	6.0	10	8	3	4
Don Drysdale	0	0	9.00	1	0	0	0	0	2.0	2	2	1	1
Carl Erskine	0	1	5.40	2	1	0	0	0	5.0	4	3	2	2
Clem Labine	1	0	0.00	2	1	1	0	1	12.0	8	0	3	7
Sal Maglie	1	1	2.65	2	2	2	0	0	17.0	14	5	6	15
Don Newcombe	0	1	21.21	2	2	0	0	0	4.2	11	11	3	4
Ed Roebuck	0	0	2.08	3	0	0	0	0	4.1	1	1	0	5
TOTAL	3	4	4.72	16	7	3	0	1	61.0	58	32	21	43

GAME 1 AT BRO OCT 3

		R	H	E
NY	200 100 000	3	9	1
BRO	023 100 00X	6	9	0

Pitchers: FORD, Kucks (4), Morgan (6), Turley (8) vs MAGLIE
Home Runs: Mantle-NY, Robinson-BRO, Hodges-BRO, Martin-NY
Attendance: 34,479

GAME 2 AT BRO OCT 5

		R	H	E
NY	150 100 001	8	12	2
BRO	061 220 02X	13	12	0

Pitchers: Larsen, Kucks (2), Byrne (2), Sturdivant (3), MORGAN (3), Turley (5), McDermott (6) vs Newcombe, Roebuck (2), BESSENT (3)
Home Runs: Berra-NY, Snider-BRO
Attendance: 36,217

GAME 3 AT NY OCT 6

		R	H	E
BRO	010 001 100	3	8	1
NY	010 003 01X	5	8	1

Pitchers: CRAIG, Labine (7) vs FORD
Home Runs: Martin-NY, Slaughter-NY
Attendance: 73,977

GAME 4 AT NY OCT 7

		R	H	E
BRO	000 100 001	2	6	0
NY	100 201 20X	6	7	2

Pitchers: ERSKINE, Roebuck (5), Drysdale (7) vs STURDIVANT
Home Runs: Mantle-NY, Bauer-NY
Attendance: 69,705

GAME 5 AT NY OCT 8

		R	H	E
BRO	000 000 000	0	0	0
NY	000 101 00X	2	5	0

Pitchers: MAGLIE vs LARSEN
Home Runs: Mantle-NY
Attendance: 64,519

GAME 6 AT BRO OCT 9

		R	H	E
NY	000 000 000 0	0	7	0
BRO	000 000 000 1	1	4	0

Pitchers: TURLEY vs LABINE
Attendance: 33,224

GAME 7 AT BRO OCT 10

		R	H	E
NY	202 100 400	9	10	0
BRO	000 000 000	0	3	1

Pitchers: KUCKS vs NEWCOMBE, Bessent (4), Craig (7), Roebuck (7), Erskine (9)
Home Runs: Berra-NY (2), Howard-NY, Skowron-NY
Attendance: 33,782

Overall, the Yankees played better than the Braves, but the Braves had Lew Burdette, who was better than anybody in the Series.

The opener pitted the Braves' established great Warren Spahn against New York's Whitey Ford. Ford prevailed, with a five-hit 3–1 win as Spahn was chased in the sixth. Burdette, winner of 17 regular-season games, started Game 2 against veteran Bobby Shantz, the American League ERA leader. After a scoreless first inning, both pitchers gave up a run in the second and another in the third. Two go-ahead runs in the top of the fourth ended the Braves' scoring, but they were enough, as Burdette blanked New York through the final six innings to even the Series. Before he was finished, Burdette would stretch his consecutive scoreless innings streak to 24.

The Yankees exploded in Game 3, in Milwaukee, running through six Braves pitchers in a 12–3 rout. Braves fans even ended up cheering Yankees rookie Tony Kubek—a Milwaukee native—who opened the scoring with a solo homer in the first, scored again after singling in the fourth (on Mickey Mantle's home run), and concluded the Yankee scoring in the seventh with his second homer, with two aboard.

Warren Spahn carried a 4–1 Braves lead into the ninth inning of Game 4, but after retiring the first two batters in the ninth, he gave up singles to Yogi Berra and Gil McDougald, and a game-tying home run to Elston Howard. In the top of the 10th, Hank Bauer tripled in a go-ahead run, but Milwaukee's Johnny Logan doubled to tie it up in the last of the 10th, and Eddie Mathews homered to give Spahn a shaky victory.

Burdette faced Ford in Game 5. In the sixth inning the Braves put half their hits—three singles—back to back for a run. It was all they needed as Burdette spaced seven singles for the shutout. Back in New York two days later, all the scoring came on home runs. Each club hit a pair, but Berra's in the third was the only one with a man aboard. Braves blasts in the fifth (Frank Torre) and seventh (Hank Aaron) tied the score, but Bauer answered Aaron's homer in the last of the seventh with what proved the winning shot. Bob Turley, who yielded just four hits while fanning eight (the Series high) claimed the victory.

In the finale, Burdette, with only two days' rest, scattered four hits over the first eight innings as the Braves gave him a 5–0 lead. In the bottom of the ninth, though, three Yankees singles loaded the bases with two out. But third baseman Eddie Mathews snared Bill Skowron's sharp grounder and stepped on the bag for a force out that preserved Burdette's second shutout and gave Milwaukee its first world championship.

Milwaukee Braves (NL), 4; New York Yankees (AL), 3

MIL (N)

PLAYER/POS	AVG	G	AB	R	H	2B	3B	HR	RB	BB	SO	SB
Hank Aaron, of	.393	7	28	5	11	0	1	3	7	1	6	0
Joe Adcock, 1b	.200	5	15	1	3	0	0	0	2	0	2	0
Bob Buhl, p	.000	2	1	0	0	0	0	0	0	0	1	0
Lew Burdette, p	.000	3	8	0	0	0	0	0	0	1	2	0
Gene Conley, p	.000	1	0	0	0	0	0	0	0	0	0	0
Wes Covington, of	.208	7	24	1	5	1	0	0	1	2	6	1
Del Crandall, c	.211	6	19	1	4	0	0	1	1	1	1	0
John DeMerit, pr	.000	1	0	0	0	0	0	0	0	0	0	0
Bob Hazle, of	.154	4	13	2	2	0	0	0	0	1	2	0
Ernie Johnson, p	.000	3	1	0	0	0	0	0	0	0	1	0
Nippy Jones, ph	.000	3	2	0	0	0	0	0	0	0	0	0
Johnny Logan, ss	.185	7	27	5	5	1	0	1	2	3	6	0
Felix Mantilla, 2b-3	.000	4	10	1	0	0	0	0	0	1	0	0
Eddie Mathews, 3b	.227	7	22	4	5	3	0	1	4	8	5	0
Don McMahon, p	.000	3	0	0	0	0	0	0	0	0	0	0
Andy Pafko, of-5	.214	6	14	1	3	0	0	0	0	0	1	0
Juan Pizarro, p	.000	1	1	0	0	0	0	0	0	0	0	0
Del Rice, c	.167	2	6	0	1	0	0	0	0	1	2	0
Carl Sawatski, ph	.000	2	2	0	0	0	0	0	0	0	2	0
Red Schoendienst, 2b	.278	5	18	0	5	1	0	0	2	0	1	0
Warren Spahn, p	.000	2	4	0	0	0	0	0	0	1	2	0
Frank Torre, 1b	.300	7	10	2	3	0	0	2	3	2	0	0
Bob Trowbridge, p	.000	1	0	0	0	0	0	0	0	0	0	0
TOTAL	.209		225	23	47	6	1	8	22	22	40	1

PITCHER	W	L	ERA	G	GS	CG	SV	SHO	IP	H	ER	BB	SO
Bob Buhl	0	1	10.80	2	2	0	0	0	3.1	6	4	6	4
Lew Burdette	3	0	0.67	3	3	3	0	2	27.0	21	2	4	13
Gene Conley	0	0	10.80	1	0	0	0	0	1.2	2	2	1	0
Ernie Johnson	0	1	1.29	3	0	0	0	0	7.0	2	1	1	8
Don McMahon	0	0	0.00	3	0	0	0	0	5.0	3	0	3	5
Juan Pizarro	0	0	10.80	1	0	0	0	0	1.2	3	2	2	1
Warren Spahn	1	1	4.70	2	2	1	0	0	15.1	18	8	2	2
Bob Trowbridge	0	0	45.00	1	0	0	0	0	1.0	2	5	3	1
TOTAL	4	3	3.48	16	7	4	0	2	62.0	57	24	22	34

NY (A)

PLAYER/POS	AVG	G	AB	R	H	2B	3B	HR	RB	BB	SO	SB
Hank Bauer, of	.258	7	31	3	8	2	1	2	6	1	6	0
Yogi Berra, c	.320	7	25	5	8	1	0	1	2	4	0	0
Tommy Byrne, p	.500	2	2	0	1	0	0	0	0	0	1	0
Andy Carey, 3b	.286	2	7	0	2	1	0	0	1	1	0	0
Gerry Coleman, 2b	.364	7	22	2	8	2	0	0	2	3	1	0
Joe Collins, 1b-5	.000	6	5	0	0	0	0	0	0	0	3	0
Art Ditmar, p	.000	2	1	0	0	0	0	0	0	0	1	0
Whitey Ford, p	.000	2	5	0	0	0	0	0	0	0	1	0
Bob Grim, p	.000	2	0	0	0	0	0	0	0	0	0	0
Elston Howard, 1b-3	.273	6	11	2	3	0	0	1	3	1	3	0
Tony Kubek, of-5,3b-2	.286	7	28	4	8	0	0	2	4	0	4	0
Johnny Kucks, p	.000	1	0	0	0	0	0	0	0	0	0	0
Don Larsen, p	.000	2	2	1	0	0	0	0	0	2	1	0
Jerry Lumpe, 3b-3	.286	6	14	0	4	0	0	0	2	1	1	0
Mickey Mantle, of-5	.263	6	19	3	5	0	0	1	2	3	1	0
Gil McDougald, ss	.250	7	24	3	6	0	0	0	2	3	3	1
Bobby Richardson, 2b-1	.000	2	0	0	0	0	0	0	0	0	0	0
Bobby Shantz, p	.000	3	1	0	0	0	0	0	0	0	0	0
Harry Simpson, 1b-4	.083	5	12	0	1	0	0	0	1	0	4	0
Bill Skowron, 1b	.000	2	4	0	0	0	0	0	0	0	0	0
Enos Slaughter, of	.250	5	12	2	3	1	0	0	0	3	2	0
Tom Sturdivant, p	.000	2	1	0	0	0	0	0	0	0	0	0
Bob Turley, p	.000	3	4	0	0	0	0	0	0	0	2	0
TOTAL	.248		230	25	57	7	1	7	25	22	34	1

PITCHER	W	L	ERA	G	GS	CG	SV	SHO	IP	H	ER	BB	SO
Tommy Byrne	0	0	5.40	2	0	0	0	0	3.1	1	2	2	1
Art Ditmar	0	0	0.00	2	0	0	0	0	6.0	2	0	0	2
Whitey Ford	1	1	1.13	2	2	1	0	0	16.0	11	2	5	7
Bob Grim	0	1	7.71	2	0	0	0	0	2.1	3	2	0	2
Johnny Kucks	0	0	0.00	1	0	0	0	0	0.2	1	0	1	1
Don Larsen	1	1	3.72	2	1	0	0	0	9.2	8	4	5	6
Bobby Shantz	0	1	4.05	3	1	0	0	0	6.2	8	3	2	7
Tom Sturdivant	0	0	6.00	2	1	0	0	0	6.0	6	4	1	2
Bob Turley	1	0	2.31	3	2	1	0	0	11.2	7	3	6	12
TOTAL	3	4	2.89	19	7	2	0	0	62.1	47	20	22	40

GAME 1 AT NY OCT 2

				R	H	E
MIL	000	000	100	1	5	0
NY	000	012	00X	3	9	1

Pitchers: SPAHN, Johnson (6), McMahon (7) vs FORD
Attendance: 69,476

GAME 2 AT NY OCT 3

				R	H	E
MIL	011	200	000	4	8	0
NY	011	000	000	2	7	2

Pitchers: BURDETTE vs SHANTZ, Ditmar (4), Grim (8)
Home Runs: Logan-MIL, Bauer-NY
Attendance: 65,202

GAME 3 AT MIL OCT 5

				R	H	E
NY	302	200	500	12	9	0
MIL	010	020	000	3	8	1

Pitchers: Turley, LARSEN (2) vs BUHL, Pizarro (1), Conley (3), Johnson (5), Trowbridge (7), McMahon (8)
Home Runs: Kubek-NY (2), Mantle-NY, Aaron-MIL
Attendance: 45,804

GAME 4 AT MIL OCT 6

					R	H	E
NY	100	000	003	1	5	11	0
MIL	000	400	000	3	7	7	0

Pitchers: Sturdivant, Shantz (5), Kucks (8), Byrne (8), GRIM (10) vs SPAHN
Home Runs: Aaron-MIL, Torre-MIL, Howard-NY, Mathews-MIL
Attendance: 45,804

GAME 5 AT MIL OCT 7

				R	H	E
NY	000	000	000	0	7	0
MIL	000	001	00X	1	6	1

Pitchers: FORD, Turley (8) vs BURDETTE
Attendance: 45,811

GAME 6 AT NY OCT 9

				R	H	E
MIL	000	010	100	2	4	0
NY	002	000	10X	3	7	0

Pitchers: Buhl, JOHNSON (3), McMahon (8) vs TURLEY
Home Runs: Berra-NY, Torre-MIL, Aaron-MIL, Bauer-NY
Attendance: 61,408

GAME 7 AT NY OCT 10

				R	H	E
MIL	004	000	010	5	9	1
NY	000	000	000	0	7	3

Pitchers: BURDETTE vs LARSEN, Shantz (3), Ditmar (4), Sturdivant (6), Byrne (8)
Home Runs: Crandall-MIL
Attendance: 61,207

After four games, Milwaukee held a 3–1 Series advantage, but New York rebounded to take the final three games and avenge their loss to the Braves the year before. As in the previous series, Warren Spahn faced Whitey Ford in the opener. The durable Spahn emerged the victor when Bill Bruton singled home the Braves' winning run off reliever Ryne Duren in the last of the 10th. In Game 2, home runs by Bruton and pitcher Lew Burdette (for three runs) helped the Braves take a 7–1 lead in the first inning. Milwaukee scored off five Yankees hurlers in their eventual 13–5 win.

Don Larsen and Ryne Duren combined for a shutout in Game 3 to give New York its first victory. Hank Bauer drove in all four runs with a two-run single in the fifth and his third home run in three games in the seventh. Warren Spahn held Bauer hitless in Game 4, blanking New York on two hits to defeat Whitey Ford and bring Milwaukee within a win of the championship.

Bob Turley came up with a shutout of his own the next day, though, fanning 10 men along the way. Gil McDougald's solo homer in the third inning was all the offense Turley needed, but as insurance the Yankees bunched six of their 10 hits into the sixth inning for six more runs.

Spahn and Ford, with only two days' rest, confronted each other a third time in Game 6. Ford lasted less than two innings, but Spahn (despite Hank Bauer's fourth Series home run in the first inning) endured into extra innings, when McDougald put New York ahead with a leadoff homer in the 10th. Two outs and two hits later, Spahn was removed, and Bill Skowron's single off reliever Don McMahon drove home another Yankees run. Milwaukee scored once in the last of the 10th and threatened further damage with men on first and third. But Bob Turley came on to retire the final batter and send the Series to a seventh game.

In the sixth inning of the finale, the Braves' Del Crandall homered against Turley (who had relieved Don Larsen in the third) to tie the game 2–2. But four runs off starter Lew Burdette in the top of the eighth (including Skowron's three-run homer) made the score 6–2, where it remained, as Turley held on to bring Casey Stengel his seventh (and last) Series triumph—and the Yankees their 18th world title.

New York Yankees (AL), 4; Milwaukee Braves (NL), 3

NY (A)

PLAYER/POS	AVG	G	AB	R	H	2B	3B	HR	RB	BB	SO	SB
Hank Bauer, of	.323	7	31	6	10	0	0	4	8	0	5	0
Yogi Berra, c	.222	7	27	3	6	3	0	0	2	1	0	0
Andy Carey, 3b	.083	5	12	1	1	0	0	0	0	0	3	0
Murry Dickson, p	.000	2	0	0	0	0	0	0	0	0	0	0
Art Ditmar, p	.000	1	1	0	0	0	0	0	0	0	0	0
Ryne Duren, p	.000	3	3	0	0	0	0	0	0	0	2	0
Whitey Ford, p	.000	3	4	1	0	0	0	0	0	2	2	0
Elston Howard, of	.222	6	18	4	4	0	0	0	2	1	4	1
Tony Kubek, ss	.048	7	21	0	1	0	0	0	1	1	7	0
Johnny Kucks, p	1.000	2	1	0	1	0	0	0	0	0	0	0
Don Larsen, p	.000	2	2	0	0	0	0	0	0	1	0	0
Jerry Lumpe, 3b-3,ss-2	.167	6	12	0	2	0	0	0	0	1	2	0
Duke Maas, p	.000	1	0	0	0	0	0	0	0	0	0	0
Mickey Mantle, of	.250	7	24	4	6	0	1	2	3	7	4	0
Gil McDougald, 2b	.321	7	28	5	9	2	0	2	4	2	4	0
Zach Monroe, p	.000	1	0	0	0	0	0	0	0	0	0	0
Bobby Richardson, 3b	.000	4	5	0	0	0	0	0	0	0	0	0
Norm Siebern, of	.125	3	8	1	1	0	0	0	0	3	2	0
Bill Skowron, 1b	.259	7	27	3	7	0	0	2	7	1	4	0
Enos Slaughter, ph	.000	4	3	1	0	0	0	0	0	1	1	0
Marv Throneberry, ph	.000	1	1	0	0	0	0	0	0	0	1	0
Bob Turley, p	.200	4	5	0	1	0	0	0	2	0	1	0
TOTAL	.210		233	29	49	5	1	10	29	21	42	1

PITCHER	W	L	ERA	G	GS	CG	SV	SHO	IP	H	ER	BB	SO
Murry Dickson	0	0	4.50	2	0	0	0	0	4.0	4	2	0	1
Art Ditmar	0	0	0.00	1	0	0	0	0	3.2	2	0	0	2
Ryne Duren	1	1	1.93	3	0	0	1	0	9.1	7	2	6	14
Whitey Ford	0	1	4.11	3	3	0	0	0	15.1	19	7	5	16
Johnny Kucks	0	0	2.08	2	0	0	0	0	4.1	4	1	1	0
Don Larsen	1	0	0.96	2	2	0	0	0	9.1	9	1	6	9
Duke Maas	0	0	81.00	1	0	0	0	0	0.1	2	3	1	0
Zach Monroe	0	0	27.00	1	0	0	0	0	1.0	3	3	1	1
Bob Turley	2	1	2.76	4	2	1	1	1	16.1	10	5	7	13
TOTAL	4	3	3.39	19	7	1	2	1	63.2	60	24	27	56

MIL (N)

PLAYER/POS	AVG	G	AB	R	H	2B	3B	HR	RB	BB	SO	SB
Hank Aaron, of	.333	7	27	3	9	2	0	0	2	4	6	0
Joe Adcock, 1b	.308	4	13	1	4	0	0	0	0	1	3	0
Billy Bruton, of	.412	7	17	2	7	0	0	1	2	5	5	0
Lew Burdette, p	.111	3	9	1	1	0	0	1	3	0	3	0
Wes Covington, of	.269	7	26	2	7	0	0	0	4	2	4	0
Del Crandall, c	.240	7	25	4	6	0	0	1	3	3	10	0
Harry Hanebrink, ph	.000	2	2	0	0	0	0	0	0	0	0	0
Johnny Logan, ss	.120	7	25	3	3	2	0	0	2	2	4	0
Felix Mantilla, ss-1	.000	4	0	1	0	0	0	0	0	0	0	0
Eddie Mathews, 3b	.160	7	25	3	4	2	0	0	3	6	11	1
Don McMahon, p	.000	3	0	0	0	0	0	0	0	0	0	0
Andy Pafko, of	.333	4	9	0	3	1	0	0	1	0	0	0
Juan Pizarro, p	.000	1	0	0	0	0	0	0	0	0	0	0
Bob Rush, p	.000	1	2	0	0	0	0	0	0	0	2	0
Red Schoendienst, 2b	.300	7	30	5	9	3	1	0	0	2	1	0
Warren Spahn, p	.333	3	12	0	4	0	0	0	3	0	6	0
Frank Torre, 1b	.176	7	17	0	3	0	0	0	1	2	0	0
Carl Willey, p	.000	1	0	0	0	0	0	0	0	0	0	0
Casey Wise, ph	.000	2	1	0	0	0	0	0	0	0	1	0
TOTAL	.250		240	25	60	10	1	3	24	27	56	1

PITCHER	W	L	ERA	G	GS	CG	SV	SHO	IP	H	ER	BB	SO
Lew Burdette	1	2	5.64	3	3	1	0	0	22.1	22	14	4	12
Don McMahon	0	0	5.40	3	0	0	0	0	3.1	3	2	3	5
Juan Pizarro	0	0	5.40	1	0	0	0	0	1.2	2	1	1	3
Bob Rush	0	1	3.00	1	1	0	0	0	6.0	3	2	5	2
Warren Spahn	2	1	2.20	3	3	2	0	1	28.2	19	7	8	18
Carl Willey	0	0	0.00	1	0	0	0	0	1.0	0	0	0	2
TOTAL	3	4	3.71	12	7	3	0	1	63.0	49	26	21	42

GAME 1 AT MIL OCT 1

					R	H	E
NY	000	120	000	0	3	8	1
MIL	000	200	010	1	4	10	0

Pitchers: Ford, DUREN (8) vs SPAHN
Home Runs: Skowron-NY, Bauer-NY
Attendance: 46,367

GAME 2 AT MIL OCT 2

				R	H	E
NY	100	100	003	5	7	0
MIL	710	000	23X	13	15	1

Pitchers: TURLEY, Maas (1), Kucks (1), Dickson (5), Monroe (8) vs BURDETTE
Home Runs: Bruton-MIL, Burdette-MIL, Mantle-NY (2), Bauer-NY
Attendance: 46,367

GAME 3 AT NY OCT 4

				R	H	E
MIL	000	000	000	0	6	0
NY	000	020	20X	4	4	0

Pitchers: RUSH, McMahon (7) vs LARSEN, Duren (8)
Home Runs: Bauer-NY
Attendance: 71,599

GAME 4 AT NY OCT 5

				R	H	E
MIL	000	001	110	3	9	0
NY	000	000	000	0	2	1

Pitchers: SPAHN vs FORD, Kucks (8), Dickson (9)
Attendance: 71,563

GAME 5 AT NY OCT 6

				R	H	E
MIL	000	000	000	0	5	0
NY	001	006	00X	7	10	0

Pitchers: BURDETTE, Pizarro (6), Willey (8) vs TURLEY
Home Runs: McDougald-NY
Attendance: 65,279

GAME 6 AT MIL OCT 8

					R	H	E
NY	100	001	000	2	4	10	1
MIL	110	000	000	1	3	10	4

Pitchers: Ford, Ditmar (2), DUREN (6), Turley (10) vs SPAHN, McMahon (10)
Home Runs: Bauer-NY, McDougald-NY
Attendance: 46,367

GAME 7 AT MIL OCT 9

				R	H	E
NY	020	000	040	6	8	0
MIL	100	001	000	2	5	2

Pitchers: Larsen, TURLEY (3) vs BURDETTE, McMahon (8)
Home Runs: Crandall-MIL, Skowron-NY
Attendance: 46,367

It took a nosedive from first to third by San Francisco and a Dodgers playoff victory over Milwaukee (who had finished the season tied with the Dodgers), to bring Los Angeles the city's first major league pennant. But once they had made it to the Series, the Dodgers dispatched the White Sox in six games.

The opener, though, belonged to Chicago. In their first World Series in 40 years, the White Sox overwhelmed Los Angeles with 11 runs in the first four innings as pitchers Early Wynn and Gerry Staley combined to blank the Dodgers. Chicago's big gun was veteran slugger Ted Kluszewski (acquired from Pittsburgh in late August), whose single and two homers drove in five runs. Chicago scored twice in the first inning the next day, but Dodgers starter Johnny Podres settled down to blank the Sox over the next five innings as home runs by Charlie Neal in the fifth and pinch hitter Chuck Essegian and Neal (again) in the seventh put the Dodgers ahead by two. Rookie reliever Larry Sherry gave up a third Chicago run in the eighth on Al Smith's double, but a second runner was nailed at the plate, and Sherry set down the side in the ninth to save Podres's win.

When the Series moved to Los Angeles' cavernous Coliseum for the West Coast's first World Series games ever, fans turned out in record numbers, setting a new Series mark in each of the next three games. Dodgers starter Don Drysdale yielded 11 hits and four walks in Game 3, but the only run scored against him came on a double play after Larry Sherry had relieved him with two men on in the eighth. As Los Angeles had already scored twice, and added a third run in their half of the eighth, Drysdale emerged with the win and Sherry with his second save. In Game 4, the Sox's Sherm Lollar's three-run homer had tied the score by the time Sherry relieved Dodgers starter Roger Craig in the eighth, so Gil Hodges' solo homer in the last of the eighth gave Sherry the win this time—and Los Angeles a 3–1 Series advantage.

Chicago's Bob Shaw dueled Dodger Sandy Koufax through seven innings of Game 5 before 92,706 spectators (still a Series high). The Sox scored only once off Koufax, but one run was enough for their second win as a pair of Sox relievers continued Shaw's shutout through the final two innings.

Back in Chicago for Game 6, the Dodgers unloaded on Early Wynn and Dick Donovan for eight runs in the third and fourth innings. Ted Kluszewski's three-run homer in the last of the fourth led to Larry Sherry's fourth relief appearance—and his second Series win, as he held the Sox scoreless the rest of the game to bring the world championship to the West Coast for the first time.

Los Angeles Dodgers (NL), 4; Chicago White Sox (AL), 2

LA (N)

PLAYER/POS	AVG	G	AB	R	H	2B	3B	HR	RB	BB	SO	SB
Chuck Churn, p	.000	1	0	0	0	0	0	0	0	0	0	0
Roger Craig, p	.000	2	3	0	0	0	0	0	0	0	2	0
Don Demeter, of	.250	6	12	2	3	0	0	0	0	1	3	0
Don Drysdale, p	.000	1	2	0	0	0	0	0	0	0	2	0
Chuck Essegian, ph	.667	4	3	2	2	0	0	2	2	1	1	0
Ron Fairly, of-4	.000	6	3	0	0	0	0	0	0	0	1	0
Carl Furillo, of-1	.250	4	4	0	1	0	0	0	2	0	1	0
Jim Gilliam, 3b	.240	6	25	2	6	0	0	0	0	2	2	2
Gil Hodges, 1b	.391	6	23	2	9	0	1	1	2	1	2	0
Johnny Klippstein, p	.000	1	0	0	0	0	0	0	0	0	0	0
Sandy Koufax, p	.000	2	2	0	0	0	0	0	0	0	1	0
Clem Labine, p	.000	1	0	0	0	0	0	0	0	0	0	0
Norm Larker, of	.188	6	16	2	3	0	0	0	0	2	3	0
Wally Moon, of	.261	6	23	3	6	0	0	1	2	2	2	1
Charlie Neal, 2b	.370	6	27	4	10	2	0	2	6	0	1	1
Joe Pignatano, c	.000	1	0	0	0	0	0	0	0	0	0	0
Johnny Podres, p-2	.500	3	4	1	2	1	0	0	1	0	0	0
Rip Repulski, of	.000	1	0	0	0	0	0	0	0	1	0	0
Johnny Roseboro, c	.095	6	21	0	2	0	0	0	1	0	2	0
Larry Sherry, p-4	.500	5	4	0	2	0	0	0	0	0	1	0
Duke Snider, of-3	.200	4	10	1	2	0	0	1	2	2	0	0
Stan Williams, p	.000	1	0	0	0	0	0	0	0	0	0	0
Maury Wills, ss	.250	6	20	2	5	0	0	0	1	0	3	1
Don Zimmer, ss	.000	1	1	0	0	0	0	0	0	0	0	0
TOTAL	.261		203	21	53	3	1	7	19	12	27	5

PITCHER	W	L	ERA	G	GS	CG	SV	SHO	IP	H	ER	BB	SO
Chuck Churn	0	0	27.00	1	0	0	0	0	0.2	5	2	0	0
Roger Craig	0	1	8.68	2	2	0	0	0	9.1	15	9	5	8
Don Drysdale	1	0	1.29	1	1	0	0	0	7.0	11	1	4	5
Johnny Klippstein	0	0	0.00	1	0	0	0	0	2.0	1	0	0	2
Sandy Koufax	0	1	1.00	2	1	0	0	0	9.0	5	1	1	7
Clem Labine	0	0	0.00	1	0	0	0	0	1.0	0	0	0	1
Johnny Podres	1	0	4.82	2	2	0	0	0	9.1	7	5	6	4
Larry Sherry	2	0	0.71	4	0	0	2	0	12.2	8	1	2	5
Stan Williams	0	0	0.00	1	0	0	0	0	2.0	0	0	2	1
TOTAL	4	2	3.23	15	6	0	2	0	53.0	52	19	20	33

CHI (A)

PLAYER/POS	AVG	G	AB	R	H	2B	3B	HR	RB	BB	SO	SB
Luis Aparicio, ss	.308	6	26	1	8	1	0	0	0	2	3	1
Norm Cash, ph	.000	4	4	0	0	0	0	0	0	0	2	0
Dick Donovan, p	.333	3	3	0	1	0	0	0	0	0	1	0
Sammy Esposito, 3b	.000	2	2	0	0	0	0	0	0	0	1	0
Nellie Fox, 2b	.375	6	24	4	9	3	0	0	0	4	1	0
Billy Goodman, 3b	.231	5	13	1	3	0	0	0	1	0	5	0
Ted Kluszewski, 1b	.391	6	23	5	9	1	0	3	10	2	0	0
Jim Landis, of	.292	6	24	6	7	0	0	0	1	1	7	1
Sherm Lollar, c	.227	6	22	3	5	0	0	1	5	1	3	0
Turk Lown, p	.000	3	0	0	0	0	0	0	0	0	0	0
Jim McAnany, of	.000	3	5	0	0	0	0	0	0	1	0	0
Ray Moore, p	.000	1	0	0	0	0	0	0	0	0	0	0
Bubba Phillips, 3b-3,of-1	.300	3	10	0	3	1	0	0	0	0	0	0
Billy Pierce, p	.000	3	0	0	0	0	0	0	0	0	0	0
Jim Rivera, of	.000	5	11	1	0	0	0	0	0	3	1	0
Johnny Romano, ph	.000	1	1	0	0	0	0	0	0	0	0	0
Bob Shaw, p	.250	2	4	0	1	0	0	0	0	0	2	0
Al Smith, of	.250	6	20	1	5	3	0	0	1	4	4	0
Gerry Staley, p	.000	4	1	0	0	0	0	0	0	1	1	0
Earl Torgeson, 1b-1	.000	3	1	1	0	0	0	0	0	1	0	0
Early Wynn, p	.200	3	5	0	1	1	0	0	1	0	2	0
TOTAL	.261		199	23	52	10	0	4	19	20	33	2

PITCHER	W	L	ERA	G	GS	CG	SV	SHO	IP	H	ER	BB	SO
Dick Donovan	0	1	5.40	3	1	0	1	0	8.1	4	5	3	5
Turk Lown	0	0	0.00	3	0	0	0	0	3.1	2	0	1	3
Ray Moore	0	0	9.00	1	0	0	0	0	1.0	1	1	0	1
Billy Pierce	0	0	0.00	3	0	0	0	0	4.0	2	0	2	3
Bob Shaw	1	1	2.57	2	2	0	0	0	14.0	17	4	2	2
Gerry Staley	0	1	2.16	4	0	0	1	0	8.1	8	2	0	3
Early Wynn	1	1	5.54	3	3	0	0	0	13.0	19	8	4	10
TOTAL	2	4	3.46	19	6	0	2	0	52.0	53	20	12	27

GAME 1 AT CHI OCT 1

LA	000	000	000	0	8	3
CHI	207	200	00X	11	11	0

Pitchers: CRAIG, Churn (3), Labine (4), Koufax (5), Klippstein (7) vs WYNN, Staley (8)
Home Runs: Kluszewski-CHI (2)
Attendance: 48,013

GAME 2 AT CHI OCT 2

LA	000	010	300	4	9	1
CHI	200	000	010	3	8	0

Pitchers: PODRES, Sherry (7) vs SHAW, Lown (7)
Home Runs: Neal-LA (2), Essegian-LA
Attendance: 47,368

GAME 3 AT LA OCT 4

CHI	000	000	010	1	12	0
LA	000	000	21X	3	5	0

Pitchers: DONOVAN, Staley (7) vs DRYSDALE, Sherry (8)
Attendance: 92,394

GAME 4 AT LA OCT 5

CHI	000	000	400	4	10	3
LA	004	000	01X	5	9	0

Pitchers: Wynn, Lown (3), Pierce (4), STALEY (7) vs Craig, SHERRY (8)
Home Runs: Lollar-CHI, Hodges-LA
Attendance: 92,650

GAME 5 AT LA OCT 6

CHI	000	100	000	1	5	0
LA	000	000	000	0	9	0

Pitchers: SHAW, Pierce (7), Donovan (8) vs KOUFAX, Williams (8)
Attendance: 92,706

GAME 6 AT CHI OCT 8

LA	002	600	001	9	13	0
CHI	000	300	000	3	6	1

Pitchers: Podres, SHERRY (4) vs WYNN, Donovan (4), Lown (4), Staley (5), Pierce (8), Moore (9)
Home Runs: Snider-LA, Moon-LA, Kluszewski-CHI, Essegian-LA
Attendance: 47,653

Through six games and 8½ innings of the seventh, the Yankees had outscored the Pirates by 29 runs. But as Pirates second baseman Bill Mazeroski stepped to the plate to open the last of the ninth, the Series was even at three games apiece, and Game 7 was tied 9–9. The stage was set for Mazeroski to fulfill that ultimate baseball fantasy, and he did, on pitcher Ralph Terry's second pitch.

Roger Maris opened the Series scoring with a solo homer in the first inning of Game 1, and Elston Howard added two more runs with a homer in the ninth for the Yankees. But between the home runs New York scored only one run to the Pirates' six (including a two-run homer by Mazeroski in the fourth).

The Yankees avenged their first-game loss with a blowout in Game 2. Pittsburgh hit safely 13 times, but scored only three runs. New York, though, turned 19 hits (and a Pirates error) into 16 runs—five of them driven in by Mickey Mantle's two home runs. Continuing their assault in New York the next day, the Bronx Bombers scored six runs in the first inning and four in the fourth as Whitey Ford blanked the Pirates on four hits. Mantle homered again, and second baseman Bobby Richardson drove in a Series single-game record six runs with a grand slam and a single.

Pirates ace Vernon Law—the winner of Game 1—started Game 4 and, with relief help once again from Roy Face, held the Yankees to two runs to even the Series. Law's bat proved crucial, too, as he doubled in Pittsburgh's first run and scored the third in a three-run fifth that provided all the Pirate scoring. In Game 5, the Pirates' Mazeroski doubled in what proved the two decisive runs in a three-run second as Harvey Haddix and Roy Face (who recorded his third save of the Series) duplicated the previous day's achievement of limiting New York to two runs.

But once again the Yankees came back. Bobby Richardson drove in three of New York's 12 runs with two triples to establish a new Series record of 12 RBIs as the Yankees, behind Whitey Ford's second shutout, sent the Series into a seventh game.

Home runs dominated the finale. Rocky Nelson's two-run shot in the first opened the scoring, and homers by Bill Skowron in the fifth and Yogi Berra in the sixth contributed four of the five runs that put New York ahead 5–4. Hal Smith's three-run homer in the bottom of the eighth restored the lead to Pittsburgh, 9–7, and after the Yankees had tied the game in the top of the ninth (on three singles and a ground out), Mazeroski's immortal shot over the wall in left gave Pittsburgh its first world championship in 35 years.

Pittsburgh Pirates (NL), 4; New York Yankees (AL), 3

PIT (N)

PLAYER/POS	AVG	G	AB	R	H	2B	3B	HR	RB	BB	SO	SB
Gene Baker, ph	.000	3	3	0	0	0	0	0	0	0	1	0
Smoky Burgess, c	.333	5	18	2	6	1	0	0	0	2	1	0
Tom Cheney, p	.000	3	0	0	0	0	0	0	0	0	0	0
Joe Christopher, ph	.000	3	0	2	0	0	0	0	0	0	0	0
Gino Cimoli, of-6	.250	7	20	4	5	0	0	0	1	2	4	0
Roberto Clemente, of	.310	7	29	1	9	0	0	0	3	0	4	0
Roy Face, p	.000	4	3	0	0	0	0	0	0	0	2	0
Bob Friend, p	.000	3	1	0	0	0	0	0	0	0	0	0
Joe Gibbon, p	.000	2	0	0	0	0	0	0	0	0	0	0
Fred Green, p	.000	3	1	0	0	0	0	0	0	0	0	0
Dick Groat, ss	.214	7	28	3	6	2	0	0	2	0	1	0
Harvey Haddix, p	.333	2	3	0	1	0	0	0	0	0	1	0
Don Hoak, 3b	.217	7	23	3	5	2	0	0	3	4	1	0
Clem Labine, p	.000	3	0	0	0	0	0	0	0	0	0	0
Vern Law, p	.333	3	6	1	2	1	0	0	1	0	1	0
Bill Mazeroski, 2b	.320	7	25	4	8	2	0	2	5	0	3	0
Vinegar Bend Mizell, p	.000	2	0	0	0	0	0	0	0	0	0	0
Rocky Nelson, 1b-3	.333	4	9	2	3	0	0	1	2	1	1	0
Bob Oldis, c	.000	2	0	0	0	0	0	0	0	0	0	0
Dick Schofield, ss-2	.333	3	3	0	1	0	0	0	0	1	0	0
Bob Skinner, of	.200	2	5	2	1	0	0	0	1	1	0	1
Hal Smith, c	.375	3	8	1	3	0	0	1	3	0	0	0
Dick Stuart, 1b	.150	5	20	0	3	0	0	0	0	0	3	0
Bill Virdon, of	.241	7	29	2	7	3	0	0	5	1	3	1
George Witt, p	.000	3	0	0	0	0	0	0	0	0	0	0
TOTAL	.256		234	27	60	11	0	4	26	12	26	2

PITCHER	W	L	ERA	G	GS	CG	SV	SHO	IP	H	ER	BB	SO
Tom Cheney	0	0	4.50	3	0	0	0	0	4.0	4	2	1	6
Roy Face	0	0	5.23	4	0	0	3	0	10.1	9	6	2	4
Bob Friend	0	2	13.50	3	2	0	0	0	6.0	13	9	3	7
Joe Gibbon	0	0	9.00	2	0	0	0	0	3.0	4	3	1	2
Fred Green	0	0	22.50	3	0	0	0	0	4.0	11	10	1	3
Harvey Haddix	2	0	2.45	2	1	0	0	0	7.1	6	2	2	6
Clem Labine	0	0	13.50	3	0	0	0	0	4.0	13	6	1	2
Vern Law	2	0	3.44	3	3	0	0	0	18.1	22	7	3	8
Vinegar Bend Mizell	0	1	15.43	2	1	0	0	0	2.1	4	4	2	1
George Witt	0	0	0.00	3	0	0	0	0	2.2	5	0	2	1
TOTAL	4	3	7.11	28	7	0	3	0	62.0	91	49	18	40

NY (A)

PLAYER/POS	AVG	G	AB	R	H	2B	3B	HR	RB	BB	SO	SB
Luis Arroyo, p	.000	1	1	0	0	0	0	0	0	0	0	0
Yogi Berra, of-4,c-3	.318	7	22	6	7	0	0	1	8	2	0	0
Johnny Blanchard, c-2	.455	5	11	2	5	2	0	0	2	0	0	0
Clete Boyer, 3b-4,ss-1	.250	4	12	1	3	2	1	0	1	0	1	0
Bob Cerv, of-3	.357	4	14	1	5	0	0	0	0	0	3	0
Jim Coates, p	.000	3	1	0	0	0	0	0	0	0	1	0
Joe De Maestri, ss-3	.500	4	2	1	1	0	0	0	0	0	1	0
Art Ditmar, p	.000	2	0	0	0	0	0	0	0	0	0	0
Ryne Duren, p	.000	2	0	0	0	0	0	0	0	0	0	0
Whitey Ford, p	.250	2	8	1	2	0	0	0	2	0	2	0
Eli Grba, pr	.000	1	0	0	0	0	0	0	0	0	0	0
Elston Howard, c-4	.462	5	13	4	6	1	1	1	4	1	4	0
Tony Kubek, ss-7,of-2	.333	7	30	6	10	1	0	0	3	2	2	0
Dale Long, ph	.333	3	3	0	1	0	0	0	0	0	0	0
Hector Lopez, of-1	.429	3	7	0	3	0	0	0	0	0	0	0
Duke Maas, p	.000	1	0	0	0	0	0	0	0	0	0	0
Mickey Mantle, of	.400	7	25	8	10	1	0	3	11	8	9	0
Roger Maris, of	.267	7	30	6	8	1	0	2	2	2	4	0
Gil McDougald, 3b	.278	6	18	4	5	1	0	0	2	2	3	0
Bobby Richardson, 2b	.367	7	30	8	11	2	2	1	12	1	1	0
Bobby Shantz, p	.333	3	3	0	1	0	0	0	0	0	0	0
Bill Skowron, 1b	.375	7	32	7	12	2	0	2	6	0	6	0
Bill Stafford, p	.000	2	1	0	0	0	0	0	0	0	1	0
Ralph Terry, p	.000	2	2	0	0	0	0	0	0	0	1	0
Bob Turley, p	.250	2	4	0	1	0	0	0	1	0	1	0
TOTAL	.338		269	55	91	13	4	10	54	18	40	0

PITCHER	W	L	ERA	G	GS	CG	SV	SHO	IP	H	ER	BB	SO
Luis Arroyo	0	0	13.50	1	0	0	0	0	0.2	2	1	0	1
Jim Coates	0	0	5.68	3	0	0	0	0	6.1	6	4	1	3
Art Ditmar	0	2	21.60	2	2	0	0	0	1.2	6	4	1	0
Ryne Duren	0	0	2.25	2	0	0	0	0	4.0	2	1	1	5
Whitey Ford	2	0	0.00	2	2	2	0	2	18.0	11	0	2	8
Duke Maas	0	0	4.50	1	0	0	0	0	2.0	2	1	0	1
Bobby Shantz	0	0	4.26	3	0	0	1	0	6.1	4	3	1	1
Bill Stafford	0	0	1.50	2	0	0	0	0	6.0	5	1	1	2
Ralph Terry	0	2	5.40	2	1	0	0	0	6.2	7	4	1	5
Bob Turley	1	0	4.82	2	2	0	0	0	9.1	15	5	4	0
TOTAL	3	4	3.54	20	7	2	1	2	61.0	60	24	12	26

GAME 1 AT PIT OCT 5

		R	H	E
NY	100 100 002	4	13	2
PIT	**300 201 00X**	**6**	**8**	**0**

Pitchers: DITMAR, Coates (1), Maas (5), Duren (7) vs LAW, Face (8)
Home Runs: Maris-NY, Mazeroski-PIT, Howard-NY
Attendance: 36,676

GAME 2 AT PIT OCT 6

		R	H	E
NY	**002 127 301**	**16**	**19**	**1**
PIT	000 100 002	3	13	1

Pitchers: TURLEY, Shantz (9) vs FRIEND, Green (5), Labine (6), Witt (6), Gibbon (7), Cheney (9)
Home Runs: Mantle-NY (2)
Attendance: 37,308

GAME 3 AT NY OCT 8

		R	H	E
PIT	000 000 000	0	4	0
NY	**600 400 00X**	**10**	**16**	**1**

Pitchers: MIZELL, Labine (1), Green (1), Witt (4), Cheney (6), Gibbon (8) vs FORD
Home Runs: Richardson-NY, Mantle-NY
Attendance: 70,001

GAME 4 AT NY OCT 9

		R	H	E
PIT	**000 030 000**	**3**	**7**	**0**
NY	000 100 100	2	8	0

Pitchers: LAW, Face (7) vs TERRY, Shantz (7), Coates (8)
Home Runs: Skowron-NY
Attendance: 67,812

GAME 5 AT NY OCT 10

		R	H	E
PIT	**031 000 001**	**5**	**10**	**2**
NY	011 000 000	2	5	2

Pitchers: HADDIX, Face (7) vs DITMAR, Arroyo (2), Stafford (3), Duren (8)
Home Runs: Maris-NY
Attendance: 62,753

GAME 6 AT PIT OCT 12

		R	H	E
NY	**015 002 220**	**12**	**17**	**1**
PIT	000 000 000	0	7	1

Pitchers: FORD vs FRIEND, Cheney (3), Mizell (4), Green (6), Labine (6), Witt (9)
Attendance: 38,580

GAME 7 AT PIT OCT 13

		R	H	E
NY	000 014 022	9	13	1
PIT	**220 000 051**	**10**	**11**	**0**

Pitchers: Turley, Stafford (2), Shantz (3), Coates (8), TERRY (8) vs Law, Face (6), Friend (9), HADDIX (9)
Home Runs: Nelson-PIT, Skowron-NY, Berra-NY, Smith-PIT, Mazeroski-PIT
Attendance: 36,683

Slugger Mickey Mantle sat out most of the Series with a thigh infection, but rookie manager Ralph Houk enjoyed an otherwise splendid finish to a splendid season as his Yankees mauled the Reds, 27 runs to 13. Yankees ace Whitey Ford, coming off one of his finest seasons (25–4), carried his mound mastery into the Series opener, holding Cincinnati to two singles and a walk as he hurled his third straight World Series shutout. New York recorded only six hits, but two of them were home runs by Elston Howard and Bill Skowron.

Gordy Coleman's two-run homer the next day in the top of the fourth inning broke Cincinnati's scoring drought and gave the Reds a 2–0 lead. Yogi Berra tied the score half an inning later with a two-run blast for New York, but that was all they would get. Reds starter Joey Jay blanked the Yankees the rest of the way as his teammates put across four more runs to even the Series. Bob Purkey pitched for the Reds in Game 3 and blanked New York on one hit through the first six innings, taking a 1–0 lead into the top of the seventh. A pair of singles sandwiched around a passed ball evened the score, but the Reds regained the lead with a run in the last of the seventh. But pinch hitter Johnny Blanchard homered to retie the game in the eighth and—while Yankees relief ace Luis Arroyo stopped the Reds through the final two innings—Roger Maris, who set the major league record with 61 home runs during the season, added another to win the game and regain the Series lead for New York.

Cincinnati never again threatened. In Game 4, Whitey Ford held the Reds to four harmless singles until he was removed in the sixth because of an ankle injury. (In the third inning he passed Babe Ruth's World Series record of 29⅔ consecutive scoreless innings.) Reliever Jim Coates continued Ford's shutout as the Yankees scored seven runs for the decisive win. The fifth and final game also was no contest. Cincinnati did score five runs—three on Frank Robinson's third-inning home run and two on Wally Post's shot in the fifth. But the Yankees ran through eight Cincinnati pitchers, scoring 13 times. Seven of their 15 hits went for extra bases, including Johnny Blanchard's second home run of the Series, and a triple and homer by utility outfielder Hector Lopez.

New York Yankees (AL), 4; Cincinnati Reds (NL), 1

NY (A)

PLAYER/POS	AVG	G	AB	R	H	2B	3B	HR	RB	BB	SO	SB
Luis Arroyo, p	.000	2	0	0	0	0	0	0	0	0	0	0
Yogi Berra, of	.273	4	11	2	3	0	0	1	3	5	1	0
Johnny Blanchard, of-2	.400	4	10	4	4	1	0	2	3	2	0	0
Clete Boyer, 3b	.267	5	15	0	4	2	0	0	3	4	0	0
Jim Coates, p	.000	1	1	0	0	0	0	0	0	0	1	0
Buddy Daley, p	.000	2	1	0	0	0	0	0	1	0	0	0
Whitey Ford, p	.000	2	5	1	0	0	0	0	0	1	0	0
Billy Gardner, ph	.000	1	1	0	0	0	0	0	0	0	0	0
Elston Howard, c	.250	5	20	5	5	3	0	1	1	2	3	0
Tony Kubek, ss	.227	5	22	3	5	0	0	0	1	1	4	0
Hector Lopez, of-3	.333	4	9	3	3	0	1	1	7	2	3	0
Mickey Mantle, of	.167	2	6	0	1	0	0	0	0	0	2	0
Roger Maris, of	.105	5	19	4	2	1	0	1	2	4	6	0
Jack Reed, of	.000	3	0	0	0	0	0	0	0	0	0	0
Bobby Richardson, 2b	.391	5	23	2	9	1	0	0	0	0	0	1
Bill Skowron, 1b	.353	5	17	3	6	0	0	1	5	3	4	0
Bill Stafford, p	.000	1	2	0	0	0	0	0	0	0	0	0
Ralph Terry, p	.000	2	3	0	0	0	0	0	0	0	1	0
TOTAL	.255		165	27	42	8	1	7	26	24	25	1

PITCHER	W	L	ERA	G	GS	CG	SV	SHO	IP	H	ER	BB	SO
Luis Arroyo	1	0	2.25	2	0	0	0	0	4.0	4	1	2	3
Jim Coates	0	0	0.00	1	0	0	1	0	4.0	1	0	1	2
Buddy Daley	1	0	0.00	2	0	0	0	0	7.0	5	0	0	3
Whitey Ford	2	0	0.00	2	2	1	0	1	14.0	6	0	1	7
Bill Stafford	0	0	2.70	1	1	0	0	0	6.2	7	2	2	5
Ralph Terry	0	1	4.82	2	2	0	0	0	9.1	12	5	2	7
TOTAL	4	1	1.60	10	5	1	1	1	45.0	35	8	8	27

CIN (N)

PLAYER/POS	AVG	G	AB	R	H	2B	3B	HR	RB	BB	SO	SB
Gus Bell, ph	.000	3	3	0	0	0	0	0	0	0	0	0
Don Blasingame, 2b	.143	3	7	1	1	0	0	0	0	0	3	0
Jim Brosnan, p	.000	3	0	0	0	0	0	0	0	0	0	0
Leo Cardenas, ph	.333	3	3	0	1	1	0	0	0	0	1	0
Elio Chacon, 2b-3	.250	4	12	2	3	0	0	0	0	1	2	0
Gordie Coleman, 1b	.250	5	20	2	5	0	0	1	2	0	1	0
Johnny Edwards, c	.364	3	11	1	4	2	0	0	2	0	0	0
Gene Freese, 3b	.063	5	16	0	1	1	0	0	0	3	4	0
Dick Gernert, ph	.000	4	4	0	0	0	0	0	0	0	1	0
Bill Henry, p	.000	2	0	0	0	0	0	0	0	0	0	0
Ken Hunt, p	.000	1	0	0	0	0	0	0	0	0	0	0
Joey Jay, p	.000	2	4	0	0	0	0	0	0	0	2	0
Darrell Johnson, c	.500	2	4	0	2	0	0	0	0	0	0	0
Ken Johnson, p	.000	1	0	0	0	0	0	0	0	0	0	0
Sherman Jones, p	.000	1	0	0	0	0	0	0	0	0	0	0
Eddie Kasko, ss	.318	5	22	1	7	0	0	0	1	0	2	0
Jerry Lynch, ph	.000	4	3	0	0	0	0	0	0	1	1	0
Jim Maloney, p	.000	1	0	0	0	0	0	0	0	0	0	0
Jim O'Toole, p	.000	2	3	0	0	0	0	0	0	0	1	0
Vada Pinson, of	.091	5	22	0	2	1	0	0	0	0	1	0
Wally Post, of	.333	5	18	3	6	1	0	1	2	0	1	0
Bob Purkey, p	.000	2	3	0	0	0	0	0	0	0	3	0
Frank Robinson, of	.200	5	15	3	3	2	0	1	4	3	4	0
Jerry Zimmerman, c	.000	2	0	0	0	0	0	0	0	0	0	0
TOTAL	.206		170	13	35	8	0	3	11	8	27	0

PITCHER	W	L	ERA	G	GS	CG	SV	SHO	IP	H	ER	BB	SO
Jim Brosnan	0	0	7.50	3	0	0	0	0	6.0	9	5	4	5
Bill Henry	0	0	19.29	2	0	0	0	0	2.1	4	5	2	3
Ken Hunt	0	0	0.00	1	0	0	0	0	1.0	0	0	1	1
Joey Jay	1	1	5.59	2	2	1	0	0	9.2	8	6	6	6
Ken Johnson	0	0	0.00	1	0	0	0	0	0.2	0	0	0	0
Sherman Jones	0	0	0.00	1	0	0	0	0	0.2	0	0	0	0
Jim Maloney	0	0	27.00	1	0	0	0	0	0.2	4	2	1	1
Jim O'Toole	0	2	3.00	2	2	0	0	0	12.0	11	4	7	4
Bob Purkey	0	1	1.64	2	1	1	0	0	11.0	6	2	3	5
TOTAL	1	4	4.91	15	5	2	0	0	44.0	42	24	24	25

GAME 1 AT NY OCT 4

		R	H	E
CIN	000 000 000	0	2	0
NY	000 101 00X	2	6	0

Pitchers: O'TOOLE, Brosnan (8) vs FORD
Home Runs: Howard-NY, Skowron-NY
Attendance: 62,397

GAME 2 AT NY OCT 5

		R	H	E
CIN	000 211 020	6	9	0
NY	000 200 000	2	4	3

Pitchers: JAY vs TERRY, Arroyo (8)
Home Runs: Coleman-CIN, Berra-NY
Attendance: 63,083

GAME 3 AT CIN OCT 7

		R	H	E
NY	000 000 111	3	6	1
CIN	001 000 100	2	8	0

Pitchers: Stafford, Daley (7), ARROYO (8) vs PURKEY
Home Runs: Blanchard-NY, Maris-NY
Attendance: 32,589

GAME 4 AT CIN OCT 8

		R	H	E
NY	000 112 300	7	11	0
CIN	000 000 000	0	5	1

Pitchers: FORD, Coates (6) vs O'TOOLE, Brosnan (6), Henry (9)
Attendance: 32,589

GAME 5 AT CIN OCT 9

		R	H	E
NY	510 502 000	13	15	1
CIN	003 020 000	5	11	3

Pitchers: Terry, DALEY (3) vs JAY, Maloney (1), K.Johnson (2), Henry (3), Jones (4), Purkey (5), Brosnan (7), Hunt (9)
Home Runs: Blanchard-NY, Robinson-CIN, Lopez-NY, Post-CIN
Attendance: 32,589

New York Yankees (AL), 4; San Francisco Giants (NL), 3

After edging Los Angeles for the pennant in a three-game playoff to break a regular-season tie, San Francisco battled to the final out of Game 7 before falling to New York in the World Series. The teams alternated wins throughout the Series. In the opener Roger Maris doubled two runs home for a quick lead. Whitey Ford gave up a run in the second (ending his record streak for consecutive scoreless World Series innings pitched at 33⅔) and a tying run an inning later. But he blanked the Giants after that, and won the game on Clete Boyer's homer in the seventh.

Jack Sanford blanked the Yankees on three hits in Game 2, but in Game 3 Bill Stafford restored the Series edge to New York with a four-hit 3–2 win (a shutout until Ed Bailey's ninth-inning home run). Both clubs hit safely nine times in Game 4. But one of the Giants' hits was Chuck Hiller's tie-breaking grand slam in the seventh—more than enough for a Giants win and another Series tie. In Game 5 Sanford brought a three-hit 2–2 tie into the last of the eighth. But after he had notched his 10th strikeout, two singles and Tom Tresh's home run drove him out and gave Ralph Terry all the margin he needed to avenge his second-game loss to Sanford, and put the Yankees ahead in the Series for the third time.

When play resumed in San Francisco after several days of rain, Billy Pierce held New York to just three hits. One was Roger Maris' solo homer in the fifth, but Pierce's Giants unloaded on Whitey Ford for five runs, driving Ford out and keeping Giant hopes alive.

The finale pitted Terry against Sanford for the third time. Both pitched effectively, but Terry carried a 1–0 lead into the last of the ninth. Pinch hitter Matty Alou led off with a bunt single, but Terry fanned the next two batters. Then Willie Mays doubled to right, but Maris' slick fielding stopped Alou at third. As Terry faced Willie McCovey (who had homered off him in Game 2), he pondered the home run he had given up to Bill Mazeroski two years earlier to lose the 1960 World Series to Pittsburgh. McCovey lined Terry's third pitch toward right—but right at second baseman Bobby Richardson, who grabbed it for the Yankees' 20th world title. It would be 15 years before they saw another.

NY (A)

PLAYER/POS	AVG	G	AB	R	H	2B	3B	HR	RB	BB	SO	SB
Yogi Berra, c-1	.000	2	2	0	0	0	0	0	0	2	0	0
Johnny Blanchard, ph	.000	1	1	0	0	0	0	0	0	0	1	0
Clete Boyer, 3b	.318	7	22	2	7	1	0	1	4	1	3	0
Marshall Bridges, p	.000	2	0	0	0	0	0	0	0	0	0	0
Jim Coates, p	.000	2	0	0	0	0	0	0	0	0	0	0
Buddy Daley, p	.000	1	0	0	0	0	0	0	0	0	0	0
Whitey Ford, p	.000	3	7	0	0	0	0	0	0	1	3	0
Elston Howard, c	.143	6	21	1	3	1	0	0	1	1	4	0
Tony Kubek, ss	.276	7	29	2	8	1	0	0	1	1	3	0
Dale Long, 1b	.200	2	5	0	1	0	0	0	1	0	1	0
Hector Lopez, ph	.000	2	2	0	0	0	0	0	0	0	0	0
Mickey Mantle, of	.120	7	25	2	3	1	0	0	0	4	5	2
Roger Maris, of	.174	7	23	4	4	1	0	1	5	5	2	0
Bobby Richardson, 2b	.148	7	27	3	4	0	0	0	0	3	1	0
Bill Skowron, 1b	.222	6	18	1	4	0	1	0	1	1	5	0
Bill Stafford, p	.000	1	3	0	0	0	0	0	0	0	1	0
Ralph Terry, p	.125	3	8	0	1	0	0	0	0	1	6	0
Tom Tresh, of	.321	7	28	5	9	1	0	1	4	1	4	2
TOTAL	.199		221	20	44	6	1	3	17	21	39	4

PITCHER	W	L	ERA	G	GS	CG	SV	SHO	IP	H	ER	BB	SO
Marshall Bridges	0	0	4.91	2	0	0	0	0	3.2	4	2	2	3
Jim Coates	0	1	6.75	2	0	0	0	0	2.2	1	2	1	3
Buddy Daley	0	0	0.00	1	0	0	0	0	1.0	1	0	1	0
Whitey Ford	1	1	4.12	3	3	1	0	0	19.2	24	9	4	12
Bill Stafford	1	0	2.00	1	1	1	0	0	9.0	4	2	2	5
Ralph Terry	2	1	1.80	3	3	2	0	1	25.0	17	5	2	16
TOTAL	4	3	2.95	12	7	4	0	1	61.0	51	20	12	39

SF (N)

PLAYER/POS	AVG	G	AB	R	H	2B	3B	HR	RB	BB	SO	SB
Felipe Alou, of	.269	7	26	2	7	1	1	0	1	1	4	0
Matty Alou, of-4	.333	6	12	2	4	1	0	0	1	0	1	0
Ed Bailey, c-3	.071	6	14	1	1	0	0	1	2	0	3	0
Bobby Bolin, p	.000	2	0	0	0	0	0	0	0	0	0	0
Ernie Bowman, ss-1	.000	2	1	1	0	0	0	0	0	0	0	0
Orlando Cepeda, 1b	.158	5	19	1	3	1	0	0	2	0	4	0
Jim Davenport, 3b	.136	7	22	1	3	1	0	0	1	4	7	0
Tom Haller, c	.286	4	14	1	4	1	0	1	3	0	2	0
Chuck Hiller, 2b	.269	7	26	4	7	3	0	1	5	3	4	0
Harvey Kuenn, of	.083	3	12	1	1	0	0	0	0	1	1	0
Don Larsen, p	.000	3	0	0	0	0	0	0	0	0	0	0
Juan Marichal, p	.000	1	2	0	0	0	0	0	0	0	1	0
Willie Mays, of	.250	7	28	3	7	2	0	0	1	1	5	1
Willie McCovey, 1b-2,of-2	.200	4	15	2	3	0	1	1	1	1	3	0
Stu Miller, p	.000	2	0	0	0	0	0	0	0	0	0	0
Bob Nieman, ph	.000	1	0	0	0	0	0	0	0	1	0	0
Billy O'Dell, p	.333	3	3	0	1	0	0	0	0	0	0	0
John Orsino, c	.000	1	1	0	0	0	0	0	0	0	0	0
Jose Pagan, ss	.368	7	19	2	7	0	0	1	2	0	1	0
Billy Pierce, p	.000	2	5	0	0	0	0	0	0	0	1	0
Jack Sanford, p	.429	3	7	0	3	0	0	0	0	0	2	0
TOTAL	.226		226	21	51	10	2	5	19	12	39	1

PITCHER	W	L	ERA	G	GS	CG	SV	SHO	IP	H	ER	BB	SO
Bobby Bolin	0	0	6.75	2	0	0	0	0	2.2	4	2	2	2
Don Larsen	1	0	3.86	3	0	0	0	0	2.1	1	1	2	0
Juan Marichal	0	0	0.00	1	1	0	0	0	4.0	2	0	2	4
Stu Miller	0	0	0.00	2	0	0	0	0	1.1	1	0	2	0
Billy O'Dell	0	1	4.38	3	1	0	1	0	12.1	12	6	3	9
Billy Pierce	1	1	2.40	2	2	1	0	0	15.0	8	4	2	5
Jack Sanford	1	2	1.93	3	3	1	0	1	23.1	16	5	8	19
TOTAL	3	4	2.66	16	7	2	1	1	61.0	44	18	21	39

GAME 1 AT SF OCT 4

				R	H	E
NY	200	000	121	6	11	0
SF	011	000	000	2	10	0

Pitchers: FORD vs O'DELL, Larsen (7), Miller (9)
Home Runs: Boyer-NY
Attendance: 43,852

GAME 2 AT SF OCT 5

				R	H	E
NY	000	000	000	0	3	1
SF	100	000	10X	2	6	0

Pitchers: TERRY, Daley (8) vs SANFORD
Home Runs: McCovey-SF
Attendance: 43,910

GAME 3 AT NY OCT 7

				R	H	E
SF	000	000	002	2	4	3
NY	000	000	30X	3	5	1

Pitchers: PIERCE, Larsen (7), Bolin (8) vs STAFFORD
Home Runs: Bailey-SF
Attendance: 71,434

GAME 4 AT NY OCT 8

				R	H	E
SF	020	000	401	7	9	1
NY	000	002	001	3	9	1

Pitchers: Marichal, Bolin (5), LARSEN (6), O'Dell (7) vs Ford, COATES (7), Bridges (7)
Home Runs: Haller-SF, Hiller-SF
Attendance: 66,607

GAME 5 AT NY OCT 10

				R	H	E
SF	001	010	001	3	8	2
NY	000	101	03X	5	6	0

Pitchers: SANFORD, Miller (8) vs TERRY
Home Runs: Pagan-SF, Tresh-NY
Attendance: 63,165

GAME 6 AT SF OCT 15

				R	H	E
NY	000	010	010	2	3	2
SF	000	320	00X	5	10	1

Pitchers: FORD, Coates (5), Bridges (8) vs PIERCE
Home Runs: Maris-NY
Attendance: 43,948

GAME 7 AT SF OCT 16

				R	H	E
NY	000	100	000	1	7	0
SF	000	000	000	0	4	1

Pitchers: TERRY vs SANFORD, O'Dell (8)
Attendance: 43,948

The Yankees won the American League pennant by 10½ games, but in the Series they were overwhelmed by Dodgers pitching. The opener pitted two all-time greats against each other: Whitey Ford (24–7 that season) and Sandy Koufax (25–5). For an inning it was close. Ford fanned two of the first three batters to face him, and Koufax struck out the side. But in the top of the second the Dodgers' Frank Howard doubled with one out, and before Ford could record the second out, two singles and John Roseboro's home run had put four Dodgers across home plate. Koufax ran his consecutive Ks to five and had tied the Series single-game record of 14 by the time Tom Tresh tagged him for a two-run homer in the eighth. That was New York's only scoring, and Koufax ended the game with a new-record 15th strikeout an inning later.

Veteran Johnny Podres pitched shutout ball through 8⅓ innings of Game 2 as his Dodgers built him a four-run lead (one of the runs a homer by ex-Yankee Bill Skowron). New York scored a run in the last of the ninth, but it was not enough to keep the Dodgers from returning to Los Angeles with a 2–0 Series advantage.

A first-inning walk, a wild pitch, and a single moved Dodger Jim Gilliam around the bases for the only scoring in Game 3 as Jim Bouton hooked up in a duel with Don Drysdale. Bouton left after seven innings for Yankees relief ace Hal Reniff, who held Los Angeles hitless through the final frames. When Drysdale completed his shutout, only three singles had been hit against him, and he had struck out nine.

Ford and Koufax tangled again in the fourth game. Ford pitched much more impressively than he had in the opener, walking just one and yielding only two hits in seven innings. One of the hits was Frank Howard's solo homer in the fifth inning, but Mickey Mantle evened the score with a home run off Koufax in the seventh. In the last of the seventh, Yankee first baseman Joe Pepitone lost sight of a throw from the third baseman for an error that sent batter Jim Gilliam all the way to third, and Willie Davis followed with a fly to center that scored Gilliam with the go-ahead run. No one else scored against Ford (or Reniff, who relieved him in the eighth), but no other Yankee scored against Koufax either, and the Dodgers, with just two hits, captured the game and the Series.

Los Angeles Dodgers (NL), 4; New York Yankees (AL), 0

LA (N)

PLAYER/POS	AVG	G	AB	R	H	2B	3B	HR	RB	BB	SO	SB
Tommy Davis, of	.400	4	15	0	6	0	2	0	2	0	2	1
Willie Davis, of	.167	4	12	2	2	2	0	0	3	0	6	0
Don Drysdale, p	.000	1	1	0	0	0	0	0	0	2	0	0
Ron Fairly, of	.000	4	1	0	0	0	0	0	0	3	0	0
Jim Gilliam, 3b	.154	4	13	3	2	0	0	0	0	3	1	0
Frank Howard, of	.300	3	10	2	3	1	0	1	1	0	2	0
Sandy Koufax, p	.000	2	6	0	0	0	0	0	0	0	2	0
Ron Perranoski, p	.000	1	0	0	0	0	0	0	0	0	0	0
Johnny Podres, p	.250	1	4	0	1	0	0	0	0	0	0	0
Johnny Roseboro, c	.143	4	14	1	2	0	0	1	3	0	4	0
Bill Skowron, 1b	.385	4	13	2	5	0	0	1	3	1	3	0
Dick Tracewski, 2b	.154	4	13	1	2	0	0	0	0	1	2	0
Maury Wills, ss	.133	4	15	1	2	0	0	0	0	1	3	1
TOTAL	.214		117	12	25	3	2	3	12	11	25	2

PITCHER	W	L	ERA	G	GS	CG	SV	SHO	IP	H	ER	BB	SO
Don Drysdale	1	0	0.00	1	1	1	0	1	9.0	3	0	1	9
Sandy Koufax	2	0	1.50	2	2	2	0	0	18.0	12	3	3	23
Ron Perranoski	0	0	0.00	1	0	0	1	0	0.2	1	0	0	1
Johnny Podres	1	0	1.08	1	1	0	0	0	8.1	6	1	1	4
TOTAL	4	0	1.00	5	4	3	1	1	36.0	22	4	5	37

NY (A)

PLAYER/POS	AVG	G	AB	R	H	2B	3B	HR	RB	BB	SO	SB
Yogi Berra, ph	.000	1	1	0	0	0	0	0	0	0	0	0
Johnny Blanchard, of-1	.000	1	3	0	0	0	0	0	0	0	0	0
Jim Bouton, p	.000	1	2	0	0	0	0	0	0	0	2	0
Clete Boyer, 3b	.077	4	13	0	1	0	0	0	0	1	6	0
Harry Bright, ph	.000	2	2	0	0	0	0	0	0	0	2	0
Al Downing, p	.000	1	1	0	0	0	0	0	0	0	1	0
Whitey Ford, p	.000	2	3	0	0	0	0	0	0	0	0	0
Steve Hamilton, p	.000	1	0	0	0	0	0	0	0	0	0	0
Elston Howard, c	.333	4	15	0	5	0	0	0	1	0	3	0
Tony Kubek, ss	.188	4	16	1	3	0	0	0	0	0	3	0
Phil Linz, ph	.333	3	3	0	1	0	0	0	0	0	1	0
Hector Lopez, of-2	.250	3	8	1	2	2	0	0	0	0	1	0
Mickey Mantle, of	.133	4	15	1	2	0	0	1	1	1	5	0
Roger Maris, of	.000	2	5	0	0	0	0	0	0	0	1	0
Joe Pepitone, 1b	.154	4	13	0	2	0	0	0	0	1	3	0
Hal Reniff, p	.000	3	0	0	0	0	0	0	0	0	0	0
Bobby Richardson, 2b	.214	4	14	0	3	1	0	0	0	1	3	0
Ralph Terry, p	.000	1	0	0	0	0	0	0	0	0	0	0
Tom Tresh, of	.200	4	15	1	3	0	0	1	2	1	6	0
Stan Williams, p	.000	1	0	0	0	0	0	0	0	0	0	0
TOTAL	.171		129	4	22	3	0	2	4	5	37	0

PITCHER	W	L	ERA	G	GS	CG	SV	SHO	IP	H	ER	BB	SO
Jim Bouton	0	1	1.29	1	1	0	0	0	7.0	4	1	5	4
Al Downing	0	1	5.40	1	1	0	0	0	5.0	7	3	1	6
Whitey Ford	0	2	4.50	2	2	0	0	0	12.0	10	6	3	8
Steve Hamilton	0	0	0.00	1	0	0	0	0	1.0	0	0	0	1
Hal Reniff	0	0	0.00	3	0	0	0	0	3.0	0	0	1	1
Ralph Terry	0	0	3.00	1	0	0	0	0	3.0	3	1	1	0
Stan Williams	0	0	0.00	1	0	0	0	0	3.0	1	0	0	5
TOTAL	0	4	2.91	10	4	0	0	0	34.0	25	11	11	25

GAME 1 AT NY OCT 2

		R	H	E
LA	041 000 000	5	9	0
NY	000 000 020	2	6	0

Pitchers: KOUFAX vs FORD, Williams (6), Hamilton (9)
Home Runs: Roseboro-LA, Tresh-NY
Attendance: 69,000

GAME 2 AT NY OCT 3

		R	H	E
LA	200 100 010	4	10	1
NY	000 000 001	1	7	0

Pitchers: PODRES, Perranoski (9) vs DOWNING, Terry (6), Reniff (9)
Home Runs: Skowron-LA
Attendance: 66,455

GAME 3 AT LA OCT 5

		R	H	E
NY	000 000 000	0	3	0
LA	100 000 00X	1	4	1

Pitchers: BOUTON, Reniff (8) vs DRYSDALE
Attendance: 55,912

GAME 4 AT LA OCT 6

		R	H	E
NY	000 000 100	1	6	1
LA	000 010 10X	2	2	1

Pitchers: FORD, Reniff (8) vs KOUFAX
Home Runs: F.Howard-LA, Mantle-NY
Attendance: 55,912

St. Louis Cardinals (NL), 4; New York Yankees (AL), 3

With late-season spurts the Cardinals edged the Reds and Phillies for their first pennant in 18 years and the Yankees overtook the White Sox and Orioles for their 15th in 18 years and their 29th over all. But when the Series was over, the long era of Yankee dominance had come to an end.

St. Louis won the opener, a 24-hit slugfest in which Curt Flood's RBI triple in the sixth proved the decisive blow. But New York came back to take the next two games. Rookie Mel Stottlemyre won Game 2, holding the Cards to three runs as his Yankees scored eight. (Loser Bob Gibson struck out nine Yankees, though, on his way to a new Series record of 31.) Game 3, by contrast, featured a pitchers' duel between Jim Bouton and veteran Curt Simmons. Cardinals reliever Barney Schultz, who replaced Simmons for the last of the ninth with the score 1–1, lost the game on his first pitch when Mickey Mantle homered to deep right (his 16th World Series home run, which moved him ahead of Babe Ruth into the all-time Series lead).

Ray Sadecki (the winner in Game 1) left with one out in the first inning of Game 4 after four Yankees hit safely, but relievers Roger Craig and Ron Taylor stopped New York on just two singles the rest of the way. The Cards were also held to six hits, but one was Ken Boyer's grand slam in the sixth, which erased a 3–0 Yankees lead and gave St. Louis enough runs to even the Series at two games apiece.

Gibson and Stottlemyre faced off a second time in Game 5. Gibson carried a 2–0 lead into the last of the ninth, when with two out Tom Tresh tagged him for a game-tying home run. In the top of the 10th, though, the Cards regained the lead on Tim McCarver's three-run homer and held on for the win as Gibson notched his 13th K of the game.

Bouton and Simmons tangled again in Game 6. Another 1–1 duel was shattered, this time in the top of the sixth when Roger Maris and Mantle tagged Simmons for back-to-back home runs. New York put the game away in the eighth with five runs off Cardinals relievers—four of them on Joe Pepitone's grand slam.

With the series tied 3–3, Gibson and Stottlemyre were called upon to settle the title. Gibson pitched the whole game, striking out nine. Mantle touched him for a three-run homer in the sixth inning, and Clete Boyer and Phil Linz hit solo shots in the ninth. But as St. Louis had scored six times off Stottlemyre and his replacement Al Downing before the Yankees scored their first runs, the game ended with the Cards victors and world champions. Yogi Berra, New York's rookie manager, was fired the next day. The following season the Yankees finished sixth under Johnny Keane, who left St. Louis to manage New York.

STL (N)

PLAYER/POS	AVG	G	AB	R	H	2B	3B	HR	RB	BB	SO	SB
Ken Boyer, 3b	.222	7	27	5	6	1	0	2	6	1	5	0
Lou Brock, of	.300	7	30	2	9	2	0	1	5	0	3	0
Gerry Buchek, 2b	1.000	4	1	1	1	0	0	0	0	0	0	0
Roger Craig, p	.000	2	1	0	0	0	0	0	0	0	0	0
Curt Flood, of	.200	7	30	5	6	0	1	0	3	3	1	0
Bob Gibson, p	.222	3	9	1	2	0	0	0	0	0	3	0
Dick Groat, ss	.192	7	26	3	5	1	1	0	1	4	3	0
Bob Humphreys, p	.000	1	0	0	0	0	0	0	0	0	0	0
Charlie James, ph	.000	3	3	0	0	0	0	0	0	0	1	0
Julian Javier, 2b	.000	1	0	1	0	0	0	0	0	0	0	0
Dal Maxvill, 2b	.200	7	20	0	4	1	0	0	1	1	4	0
Tim McCarver, c	.478	7	23	4	11	1	1	1	5	5	1	1
Gordie Richardson, p	.000	2	0	0	0	0	0	0	0	0	0	0
Ray Sadecki, p	.500	2	2	0	1	0	0	0	1	0	1	0
Barney Schultz, p	.000	4	1	0	0	0	0	0	0	0	0	0
Mike Shannon, of	.214	7	28	6	6	0	0	1	2	0	9	1
Curt Simmons, p	.500	2	4	0	2	0	0	0	1	0	1	0
Bob Skinner, ph	.667	4	3	0	2	1	0	0	1	1	0	0
Ron Taylor, p	.000	2	1	0	0	0	0	0	0	0	1	0
Carl Warwick, ph	.750	5	4	2	3	0	0	0	1	1	0	0
Bill White, 1b	.111	7	27	2	3	1	0	0	2	2	6	1
TOTAL	.254		240	32	61	8	3	5	29	18	39	3

PITCHER	W	L	ERA	G	GS	CG	SV	SHO	IP	H	ER	BB	SO
Roger Craig	1	0	0.00	2	0	0	0	0	5.0	2	0	3	9
Bob Gibson	2	1	3.00	3	3	2	0	0	27.0	23	9	8	31
Bob Humphreys	0	0	0.00	1	0	0	0	0	1.0	0	0	0	1
Gordie Richardson	0	0	40.50	2	0	0	0	0	0.2	3	3	2	0
Ray Sadecki	1	0	8.53	2	2	0	0	0	6.1	12	6	5	2
Barney Schultz	0	1	18.00	4	0	0	1	0	4.0	9	8	3	1
Curt Simmons	0	1	2.51	2	2	0	0	0	14.1	11	4	3	8
Ron Taylor	0	0	0.00	2	0	0	1	0	4.2	0	0	1	2
TOTAL	4	3	4.29	18	7	2	2	0	63.0	60	30	25	54

NY (A)

PLAYER/POS	AVG	G	AB	R	H	2B	3B	HR	RB	BB	SO	SB
Johnny Blanchard, ph	.250	4	4	0	1	1	0	0	0	0	1	0
Jim Bouton, p	.143	2	7	0	1	0	0	0	1	0	2	0
Clete Boyer, 3b	.208	7	24	2	5	1	0	1	3	1	5	1
Al Downing, p	.000	3	2	0	0	0	0	0	0	0	2	0
Whitey Ford, p	1.000	1	1	0	1	0	0	0	1	2	0	0
Pedro Gonzalez, 3b	.000	1	1	0	0	0	0	0	0	0	0	0
Steve Hamilton, p	.000	2	0	0	0	0	0	0	0	0	0	0
Mike Hegan, ph	.000	3	1	1	0	0	0	0	0	1	1	0
Elston Howard, c	.292	7	24	5	7	1	0	0	2	4	6	0
Phil Linz, ss	.226	7	31	5	7	1	0	2	2	2	5	0
Hector Lopez, of-1	.000	3	2	0	0	0	0	0	0	0	2	0
Mickey Mantle, of	.333	7	24	8	8	2	0	3	8	6	8	0
Roger Maris, of	.200	7	30	4	6	0	0	1	1	1	4	0
Pete Mikkelsen, p	.000	4	0	0	0	0	0	0	0	0	0	0
Joe Pepitone, 1b	.154	7	26	1	4	1	0	1	5	2	3	0
Hal Reniff, p	.000	1	0	0	0	0	0	0	0	0	0	0
Bobby Richardson, 2b	.406	7	32	3	13	2	0	0	3	0	2	1
Rollie Sheldon, p	.000	2	0	0	0	0	0	0	0	0	0	0
Mel Stottlemyre, p	.125	3	8	0	1	0	0	0	0	0	6	0
Ralph Terry, p	.000	1	0	0	0	0	0	0	0	0	0	0
Tom Tresh, of	.273	7	22	4	6	2	0	2	7	6	7	0
TOTAL	.251		239	33	60	11	0	10	33	25	54	2

PITCHER	W	L	ERA	G	GS	CG	SV	SHO	IP	H	ER	BB	SO
Jim Bouton	2	0	1.56	2	2	1	0	0	17.1	15	3	5	7
Al Downing	0	1	8.22	3	1	0	0	0	7.2	9	7	2	5
Whitey Ford	0	1	8.44	1	1	0	0	0	5.1	8	5	1	4
Steve Hamilton	0	0	4.50	2	0	0	1	0	2.0	3	1	0	2
Pete Mikkelsen	0	1	5.79	4	0	0	0	0	4.2	4	3	2	4
Hal Reniff	0	0	0.00	1	0	0	0	0	0.1	2	0	0	0
Rollie Sheldon	0	0	0.00	2	0	0	0	0	2.2	0	0	2	2
Mel Stottlemyre	1	1	3.15	3	3	1	0	0	20.0	18	7	6	12
Ralph Terry	0	0	0.00	1	0	0	0	0	2.0	2	0	0	3
TOTAL	3	4	3.77	19	7	2	1	0	62.0	61	26	18	39

GAME 1 AT STL OCT 7

		R	H	E
NY	030 010 010	5	12	2
STL	110 004 03X	9	12	0

Pitchers: FORD, Downing (6), Sheldon (8), Mikkelsen (9) vs SADECKI, Schultz (7)
Home Runs: Tresh-NY, Shannon-STL
Attendance: 30,805

GAME 2 AT STL OCT 8

		R	H	E
NY	000 101 204	8	12	0
STL	001 000 011	3	7	0

Pitchers: STOTTLEMYRE vs GIBSON, Schultz (9), Craig (9), Richardson (9)
Home Runs: Linz-NY
Attendance: 30,805

GAME 3 AT NY OCT 10

		R	H	E
STL	000 010 000	1	6	0
NY	010 000 001	2	5	2

Pitchers: Simmons, SCHULTZ (9) vs BOUTON
Home Runs: Mantle-NY
Attendance: 67,101

GAME 4 AT NY OCT 11

		R	H	E
STL	000 004 000	4	6	1
NY	300 000 000	3	6	1

Pitchers: Sadecki, CRAIG (1), Taylor (6) vs DOWNING, Mikkelsen (7), Terry (8)
Home Runs: K.Boyer-STL
Attendance: 66,312

GAME 5 AT NY OCT 12

		R	H	E
STL	000 020 000 3	5	10	1
NY	000 000 002 0	2	6	2

Pitchers: GIBSON vs Stottlemyre, Reniff (8), MIKKELSEN (8)
Home Runs: Tresh-NY, McCarver-STL
Attendance: 65,633

GAME 6 AT STL OCT 14

		R	H	E
NY	000 012 050	8	10	0
STL	100 000 011	3	10	1

Pitchers: BOUTON, Hamilton (9) vs SIMMONS, Taylor (7), Schultz (8), Richardson (8), Humphreys (9)
Home Runs: Maris-NY, Mantle-NY, Pepitone-NY
Attendance: 30,805

GAME 7 AT STL OCT 15

		R	H	E
NY	000 003 002	5	9	2
STL	000 330 10X	7	10	1

Pitchers: STOTTLEMYRE, Downing (5), Sheldon (5), Hamilton (7), Mikkelsen (8) vs GIBSON
Home Runs: Brock-STL, Mantle-NY, K.Boyer-STL, C.Boyer-NY, Linz-NY
Attendance: 30,346

Los Angeles Dodgers (NL), 4; Minnesota Twins (AL), 3

The Twins (bringing the World Series to Minnesota for the first time ever) featured heavy hitting, while Dodgers hopes rested on great pitching and speed on the bases. For a while it looked as if power would triumph as the Twins took the first two games at home. They drove out starter Don Drysdale with seven runs in the first three innings of the opener—including home runs by Don Mincher and Zoilo Versalles—on the way to a convincing 8–2 win, and followed up with a 5–1 triumph the next day over Dodgers ace Sandy Koufax (who had declined to pitch Game 1 on Yom Kippur, the holiest day of the Jewish year) and star reliever Ron Perranoski, who was tagged for three of the Twins' runs.

But when the Series moved to Los Angeles, Dodgers pitching began to assert itself. Claude Osteen held Minnesota to five hits and no runs, while Los Angeles bunched seven of their 10 hits in the middle three innings for four runs. Drysdale evened the Series in Game 4, avenging his first-game pounding with a five-hitter. Twins Harmon Killebrew and Tony Oliva tagged him for a pair of solo homers, but that was Minnesota's only scoring—more than balanced by seven Dodgers runs, including homers by Wes Parker and Lou Johnson. In Game 5 the next day, Koufax avenged his earlier loss, carrying Los Angeles to its first Series lead with a shutout in which he allowed only four singles and a walk, while fanning 10 Twins. Speedster Willie Davis stole three bases and Maury Wills stole another as the Dodgers parlayed 14 hits into a 7–0 victory.

Back in Minnesota for Game 6, the Twins rallied, using the long ball to even the Series again with a 5–1 win. Bob Allison opened the scoring with a two-run shot off Claude Osteen in the fourth, and Minnesota pitcher Mudcat Grant insured his own win with a three-run blast two innings later.

In the finale, though, the visiting team won for the only time in the Series. Koufax again struck out 10, stopping the Twins on three hits for his second shutout. Lou Johnson's second Series homer (a fourth-inning solo shot to left off Twins starter Jim Kaat that was barely fair) was all the Dodgers needed for their fifth world championship, but Ron Fairly followed Johnson with a double and Wes Parker singled home an insurance run that drove Kaat from the game and concluded the Series scoring.

LA (N)

PLAYER/POS	AVG	G	AB	R	H	2B	3B	HR	RB	BB	SO	SB
Jim Brewer, p	.000	1	0	0	0	0	0	0	0	0	0	0
Willie Crawford, ph	.500	2	2	0	1	0	0	0	0	0	1	0
Willie Davis, of	.231	7	26	3	6	0	0	0	0	0	2	3
Don Drysdale, p-2	.000	3	5	0	0	0	0	0	0	0	4	0
Ron Fairly, of	.379	7	29	7	11	3	0	2	6	0	1	0
Jim Gilliam, 3b	.214	7	28	2	6	1	0	0	2	1	0	0
Lou Johnson, of	.296	7	27	3	8	2	0	2	4	1	3	0
John Kennedy, 3b	.000	4	1	0	0	0	0	0	0	0	0	0
Sandy Koufax, p	.111	3	9	0	1	0	0	0	1	1	5	0
Jim Lefebvre, 2b	.400	3	10	2	4	0	0	0	0	0	0	0
Don LeJohn, ph	.000	1	1	0	0	0	0	0	0	0	1	0
Bob Miller, p	.000	2	0	0	0	0	0	0	0	0	0	0
Wally Moon, ph	.000	2	2	0	0	0	0	0	0	0	0	0
Claude Osteen, p	.333	2	3	0	1	0	0	0	0	0	0	0
Wes Parker, 1b	.304	7	23	3	7	0	1	1	2	3	3	2
Ron Perranoski, p	.000	2	0	0	0	0	0	0	0	0	0	0
Howie Reed, p	.000	2	0	0	0	0	0	0	0	0	0	0
Johnny Roseboro, c	.286	7	21	1	6	1	0	0	3	5	3	1
Dick Tracewski, 2b	.118	6	17	0	2	0	0	0	0	1	5	0
Maury Wills, ss	.367	7	30	3	11	3	0	0	3	1	3	3
TOTAL	.274		234	24	64	10	1	5	21	13	31	9

PITCHER	W	L	ERA	G	GS	CG	SV	SHO	IP	H	ER	BB	SO
Jim Brewer	0	0	4.50	1	0	0	0	0	2.0	3	1	0	1
Don Drysdale	1	1	3.86	2	2	1	0	0	11.2	12	5	3	15
Sandy Koufax	2	1	0.38	3	3	2	0	2	24.0	13	1	5	29
Bob Miller	0	0	0.00	2	0	0	0	0	1.1	0	0	0	0
Claude Osteen	1	1	0.64	2	2	1	0	1	14.0	9	1	5	4
Ron Perranoski	0	0	7.36	2	0	0	0	0	3.2	3	3	4	1
Howie Reed	0	0	8.10	2	0	0	0	0	3.1	2	3	2	4
TOTAL	4	3	2.10	14	7	4	0	3	60.0	42	14	19	54

MIN (A)

PLAYER/POS	AVG	G	AB	R	H	2B	3B	HR	RB	BB	SO	SB
Bob Allison, of	.125	5	16	3	2	1	0	1	2	2	9	1
Earl Battey, c	.120	7	25	1	3	0	1	0	2	0	5	0
Dave Boswell, p	.000	1	0	0	0	0	0	0	0	0	0	0
Mudcat Grant, p	.250	3	8	3	2	1	0	1	3	0	1	0
Jimmie Hall, of	.143	2	7	0	1	0	0	0	0	1	5	0
Jim Kaat, p	.167	3	6	0	1	0	0	0	2	0	5	0
Harmon Killebrew, 3b	.286	7	21	2	6	0	0	1	2	6	4	0
Johnny Klippstein, p	.000	2	0	0	0	0	0	0	0	0	0	0
Jim Merritt, p	.000	2	0	0	0	0	0	0	0	0	0	0
Don Mincher, 1b	.130	7	23	3	3	0	0	1	1	2	7	0
Joe Nossek, of-5	.200	6	20	0	4	0	0	0	0	0	1	0
Tony Oliva, of	.192	7	26	2	5	1	0	1	2	1	6	0
Camilo Pascual, p	.000	1	1	0	0	0	0	0	0	0	0	0
Jim Perry, p	.000	2	0	0	0	0	0	0	0	0	0	0
Bill Pleis, p	.000	1	0	0	0	0	0	0	0	0	0	0
Frank Quilici, 2b	.200	7	20	2	4	2	0	0	1	4	3	0
Rich Rollins, ph	.000	3	2	0	0	0	0	0	0	1	0	0
Sandy Valdespino, of-2	.273	5	11	1	3	1	0	0	0	0	1	0
Zoilo Versalles, ss	.286	7	28	3	8	1	1	1	4	2	7	1
Al Worthington, p	.000	2	0	0	0	0	0	0	0	0	0	0
Jerry Zimmerman, c	.000	2	1	0	0	0	0	0	0	0	0	0
TOTAL	.195		215	20	42	7	2	6	19	19	54	2

PITCHER	W	L	ERA	G	GS	CG	SV	SHO	IP	H	ER	BB	SO
Dave Boswell	0	0	3.38	1	0	0	0	0	2.2	3	1	2	3
Mudcat Grant	2	1	2.74	3	3	2	0	0	23.0	22	7	2	12
Jim Kaat	1	2	3.77	3	3	1	0	0	14.1	18	6	2	6
Johnny Klippstein	0	0	0.00	2	0	0	0	0	2.2	2	0	2	3
Jim Merritt	0	0	2.70	2	0	0	0	0	3.1	2	1	0	1
Camilo Pascual	0	1	5.40	1	1	0	0	0	5.0	8	3	1	0
Jim Perry	0	0	4.50	2	0	0	0	0	4.0	5	2	2	4
Bill Pleis	0	0	9.00	1	0	0	0	0	1.0	2	1	0	0
Al Worthington	0	0	0.00	2	0	0	0	0	4.0	2	0	2	2
TOTAL	3	4	3.15	17	7	3	0	0	60.0	64	21	13	31

GAME 1 AT MIN OCT 6

				R	H	E
LA	010	000	001	2	10	1
MIN	016	001	00X	8	10	0

Pitchers: DRYSDALE, Reed (3), Brewer (5), Perranoski (7) vs GRANT
Home Runs: Fairly-LA, Mincher-MIN, Versalles-MIN
Attendance: 47,797

GAME 2 AT MIN OCT 7

				R	H	E
LA	000	000	100	1	7	3
MIN	000	002	12X	5	9	0

Pitchers: KOUFAX, Perranoski (7), Miller (8) vs KAAT
Attendance: 48,700

GAME 3 AT LA OCT 9

				R	H	E
MIN	000	000	000	0	5	0
LA	000	211	00X	4	10	1

Pitchers: PASCUAL, Merritt (6), Klippstein (8) vs OSTEEN
Attendance: 55,934

GAME 4 AT LA OCT 10

				R	H	E
MIN	000	101	000	2	5	2
LA	110	103	01X	7	10	0

Pitchers: GRANT, Worthington (6), Pleis (8) vs DRYSDALE
Home Runs: Killebrew-MIN, Parker-LA, Oliva-MIN, Johnson-LA
Attendance: 55,920

GAME 5 AT LA OCT 11

				R	H	E
MIN	000	000	000	0	4	1
LA	202	100	20X	7	14	0

Pitchers: KAAT, Boswell (3), Perry (6) vs KOUFAX
Attendance: 55,801

GAME 6 AT MIN OCT 13

				R	H	E
LA	000	000	100	1	6	1
MIN	000	203	00X	5	6	1

Pitchers: OSTEEN, Reed (6), Miller (8) vs GRANT
Home Runs: Allison-MIN, Grant-MIN, Fairly-LA
Attendance: 49,578

GAME 7 AT MIN OCT 14

				R	H	E
LA	000	200	000	2	7	0
MIN	000	000	000	0	3	1

Pitchers: KOUFAX vs KAAT, Worthington (4), Klippstein (6), Merritt (7), Perry (9)
Home Runs: Johnson-LA
Attendance: 50,596

The Orioles, with their first pennant since moving from St. Louis in 1954, won the franchise's first World Series ever, crushing NL repeater Los Angeles in four games. Back-to-back home runs by Frank and Brooks Robinson in the top of the first inning of the opener gave Baltimore a quick three-run lead, and the O's added a fourth run an inning later before the Dodgers attempted to come back with single runs in the second and third innings. But by then Orioles reliever Moe Drabowsky had come on to pitch, and he stopped the Dodgers on one hit the rest of the way, striking out 11 (including six in a row in the fourth and fifth innings). The Dodgers would not score again in the Series.

Sophomore Jim Palmer (a week shy of his 21st birthday) hurled a four-hit shutout at Los Angeles in Game 2, defeating the great—but critically sore-armed—Sandy Koufax, who, though only 30 years old, was pitching the final game of his career. Three errors by center fielder Willie Davis in the fifth (including a pair of flies lost in the sun) led to three unearned runs—the first scoring against Koufax. Frank Robinson's leadoff triple in the sixth and Boog Powell's single gave the Orioles an earned run before a double play ended the inning. Koufax was replaced after the inning by a succession of Dodgers relievers as Baltimore went on to win, 6–0.

Wally Bunker did the honors for the Orioles in Game 3, emerging the victor of a pitching duel with Claude Osteen on the strength of a fifth-inning home run by Paul Blair, a tremendous 430-foot shot to left. Osteen yielded only two other Orioles hits—both singles—in his seven innings, and Dodger reliever Phil Regan retired the side in the eighth. But one run was all Bunker needed for his shutout win.

Dave McNally, who had given up the Dodgers' only Series runs in Game 1, mended his ways with a four-hit shutout in Game 4. He needed the shutout for the sweep, for Don Drysdale was also in top form. Drysdale, too, gave up only four hits. But one of them was Frank Robinson's second home run of the Series, a fourth-inning solo shot to left for the game's only scoring.

Baltimore Orioles (AL), 4; Los Angeles Dodgers (NL), 0

BAL (A)

PLAYER/POS	AVG	G	AB	R	H	2B	3B	HR	RB	BB	SO	SB
Luis Aparicio, ss	.250	4	16	0	4	1	0	0	2	0	0	0
Paul Blair, of	.167	4	6	2	1	0	0	1	1	1	0	0
Curt Blefary, of	.077	4	13	0	1	0	0	0	0	2	3	0
Wally Bunker, p	.000	1	2	0	0	0	0	0	0	0	1	0
Moe Drabowsky, p	.000	1	2	0	0	0	0	0	0	1	1	0
Andy Etchebarren, c	.083	4	12	2	1	0	0	0	0	2	4	0
Davey Johnson, 2b	.286	4	14	1	4	1	0	0	1	0	1	0
Dave McNally, p	.000	2	3	0	0	0	0	0	0	0	1	0
Jim Palmer, p	.000	1	4	0	0	0	0	0	0	0	2	0
Boog Powell, 1b	.357	4	14	1	5	1	0	0	1	0	1	0
Brooks Robinson, 3b	.214	4	14	2	3	0	0	1	1	1	0	0
Frank Robinson, of	.286	4	14	4	4	0	1	2	3	2	3	0
Russ Snyder, of	.167	3	6	1	1	0	0	0	1	2	0	0
TOTAL	.200		120	13	24	3	1	4	10	11	17	0

PITCHER	W	L	ERA	G	GS	CG	SV	SHO	IP	H	ER	BB	SO
Wally Bunker	1	0	0.00	1	1	1	0	1	9.0	6	0	1	6
Moe Drabowsky	1	0	0.00	1	0	0	0	0	6.2	1	0	2	11
Dave McNally	1	0	1.59	2	2	1	0	1	11.1	6	2	7	5
Jim Palmer	1	0	0.00	1	1	1	0	1	9.0	4	0	3	6
TOTAL	4	0	0.50	5	4	3	0	3	36.0	17	2	13	28

LA (N)

PLAYER/POS	AVG	G	AB	R	H	2B	3B	HR	RB	BB	SO	SB
Jim Barbieri, ph	.000	1	1	0	0	0	0	0	0	0	1	0
Jim Brewer, p	.000	1	0	0	0	0	0	0	0	0	0	0
Wes Covington, ph	.000	1	1	0	0	0	0	0	0	0	1	0
Tommy Davis, of-3	.250	4	8	0	2	0	0	0	0	1	1	0
Willie Davis, of	.063	4	16	0	1	0	0	0	0	0	4	0
Don Drysdale, p	.000	2	2	0	0	0	0	0	0	0	1	0
Ron Fairly, of-2,1b-1	.143	3	7	0	1	0	0	0	0	2	4	0
Al Ferrara, ph	1.000	1	1	0	1	0	0	0	0	0	0	0
Jim Gilliam, 3b	.000	2	6	0	0	0	0	0	1	2	0	0
Lou Johnson, of	.267	4	15	1	4	1	0	0	0	1	1	0
John Kennedy, 3b	.200	2	5	0	1	0	0	0	0	0	0	0
Sandy Koufax, p	.000	1	2	0	0	0	0	0	0	0	0	0
Jim Lefebvre, 2b	.167	4	12	1	2	0	0	1	1	3	4	0
Bob Miller, p	.000	1	0	0	0	0	0	0	0	0	0	0
Joe Moeller, p	.000	1	0	0	0	0	0	0	0	0	0	0
Nate Oliver, pr	.000	1	0	0	0	0	0	0	0	0	0	0
Claude Osteen, p	.000	1	2	0	0	0	0	0	0	0	1	0
Wes Parker, 1b	.231	4	13	0	3	2	0	0	0	1	3	0
Ron Perranoski, p	.000	2	0	0	0	0	0	0	0	0	0	0
Phil Regan, p	.000	2	0	0	0	0	0	0	0	0	0	0
Johnny Roseboro, c	.071	4	14	0	1	0	0	0	0	0	3	0
Dick Stuart, ph	.000	2	2	0	0	0	0	0	0	0	1	0
Maury Wills, ss	.077	4	13	0	1	0	0	0	0	3	3	1
TOTAL	.142		120	2	17	3	0	1	2	13	28	1

PITCHER	W	L	ERA	G	GS	CG	SV	SHO	IP	H	ER	BB	SO
Jim Brewer	0	0	0.00	1	0	0	0	0	1.0	0	0	0	1
Don Drysdale	0	2	4.50	2	2	1	0	0	10.0	8	5	3	6
Sandy Koufax	0	1	1.50	1	1	0	0	0	6.0	6	1	2	2
Bob Miller	0	0	0.00	1	0	0	0	0	3.0	2	0	2	1
Joe Moeller	0	0	4.50	1	0	0	0	0	2.0	1	1	1	0
Claude Osteen	0	1	1.29	1	1	0	0	0	7.0	3	1	1	3
Ron Perranoski	0	0	5.40	2	0	0	0	0	3.1	4	2	1	2
Phil Regan	0	0	0.00	2	0	0	0	0	1.2	0	0	1	2
TOTAL	0	4	2.65	11	4	1	0	0	34.0	24	10	11	17

GAME 1 AT LA OCT 5

				R	H	E
BAL	310	100	000	5	9	0
LA	011	000	000	2	3	0

Pitchers: McNally, DRABOWSKY (3) vs DRYSDALE, Moeller (3), Miller (5), Perranoski (8)
Home Runs: F.Robinson-BAL, B.Robinson-BAL, Lefebvre-LA
Attendance: 55,941

GAME 2 AT LA OCT 6

				R	H	E
BAL	000	031	020	6	8	0
LA	000	000	000	0	4	6

Pitchers: PALMER vs KOUFAX, Perranoski (7), Regan (8), Brewer (9)
Attendance: 55,947

GAME 3 AT BAL OCT 8

				R	H	E
LA	000	000	000	0	6	0
BAL	000	010	00X	1	3	0

Pitchers: OSTEEN, Regan (8) vs BUNKER
Home Runs: Blair-BAL
Attendance: 54,445

GAME 4 AT BAL OCT 9

				R	H	E
LA	000	000	000	0	4	0
BAL	000	100	00X	1	4	0

Pitchers: DRYSDALE vs McNALLY
Home Runs: F.Robinson-BAL
Attendance: 54,458

The Cardinals cruised into the Series leading by 10½ games, whereas the Red Sox eked out their pennant over Minnesota and Detroit only by a dramatic win at season's end. The Sox continued to claw their way through six games of the Series before finally falling to superior pitching and hitting in the seventh game. Cardinals hurler Bob Gibson (who had missed a third of the season with a broken leg) edged Boston in the opener 2–1 with a six-hitter that included 10 strikeouts. The only run against him came on a solo homer by opposing pitcher Jose Santiago in the third that tied the game. But Santiago was undone when Lou Brock singled off him to open the seventh, then stole second, and moved around to score on a pair of ground outs.

Boston ace Jim Lonborg evened the Series the next day with a brilliant one-hit shutout. Triple Crown winner Carl Yastrzemski accounted for four of Boston's five runs with homers in the fourth and seventh innings. Cardinal Nelson Briles outlasted a succession of Boston pitchers for a go-ahead 5–2 win in Game 3, and Gibson, with a five-hit shutout in Game 4, put St. Louis up three games to one.

But Boston's Lonborg kept Red Sox hopes alive with another pitching gem—a three-hitter in which the only extra-base hit was Roger Maris' harmless home run in the last of the ninth, after the Sox had already scored three runs (two of them unearned). Boston's bats came alive as the Series moved to Boston for Game 6, and the Sox evened the Series with an 8–4 win. The Cards used eight pitchers in a futile effort to hold off the Boston assault. Boston's score would have been greater had not all four Boston homers (including three in the fourth inning by Yastrzemski, Reggie Smith, and Rico Petrocelli—his second of the game) been solo shots.

With the Series tied, the Series' two-game winners, Gibson and Lonborg, faced off in Game 7. It turned out to be no contest. Lonborg gave up 10 hits and seven runs (including a homer by pitcher Gibson in the fifth and a three-run blast by Julian Javier an inning later) in six innings. Four Boston relievers held the Cards scoreless the rest of the game, but it was too late. Gibson's three-hitter included 10 strikeouts and, as he had in 1964, Gibson walked off the mound a winner in the seventh game.

St. Louis Cardinals (NL), 4; Boston Red Sox (AL), 3

STL (N)

PLAYER/POS	AVG	G	AB	R	H	2B	3B	HR	RB	BB	SO	SB
Eddie Bressoud, ss	.000	2	0	0	0	0	0	0	0	0	0	0
Nelson Briles, p	.000	2	3	0	0	0	0	0	0	0	0	0
Lou Brock, of	.414	7	29	8	12	2	1	1	3	2	3	7
Steve Carlton, p	.000	1	1	0	0	0	0	0	0	0	0	0
Orlando Cepeda, 1b	.103	7	29	1	3	2	0	0	1	0	4	0
Curt Flood, of	.179	7	28	2	5	1	0	0	3	3	3	0
Phil Gagliano, ph	.000	1	1	0	0	0	0	0	0	0	0	0
Bob Gibson, p	.091	3	11	1	1	0	0	1	1	1	2	0
Joe Hoerner, p	.000	2	0	0	0	0	0	0	0	0	0	0
Dick Hughes, p	.000	2	3	0	0	0	0	0	0	0	3	0
Larry Jaster, p	.000	1	0	0	0	0	0	0	0	0	0	0
Julian Javier, 2b	.360	7	25	2	9	3	0	1	4	0	6	0
Jack Lamabe, p	.000	3	0	0	0	0	0	0	0	0	0	0
Roger Maris, of	.385	7	26	3	10	1	0	1	7	3	1	0
Dal Maxvill, ss	.158	7	19	1	3	0	1	0	1	4	1	0
Tim McCarver, c	.125	7	24	3	3	1	0	0	2	2	2	0
Dave Ricketts, ph	.000	3	3	0	0	0	0	0	0	0	0	0
Mike Shannon, 3b	.208	7	24	3	5	1	0	1	2	1	4	0
Ed Spiezio, ph	.000	1	1	0	0	0	0	0	0	0	0	0
Bobby Tolan, ph	.000	3	2	1	0	0	0	0	0	1	1	0
Ray Washburn, p	.000	2	0	0	0	0	0	0	0	0	0	0
Ron Willis, p	.000	3	0	0	0	0	0	0	0	0	0	0
Hal Woodeshick, p	.000	1	0	0	0	0	0	0	0	0	0	0
TOTAL	.223		229	25	51	11	2	5	24	17	30	7

PITCHER	W	L	ERA	G	GS	CG	SV	SHO	IP	H	ER	BB	SO
Nelson Briles	1	0	1.64	2	1	1	0	0	11.0	7	2	1	4
Steve Carlton	0	1	0.00	1	1	0	0	0	6.0	3	0	2	5
Bob Gibson	3	0	1.00	3	3	3	0	1	27.0	14	3	5	26
Joe Hoerner	0	0	40.50	2	0	0	0	0	0.2	4	3	1	0
Dick Hughes	0	1	5.00	2	2	0	0	0	9.0	9	5	3	7
Larry Jaster	0	0	0.00	1	0	0	0	0	0.1	2	0	0	0
Jack Lamabe	0	1	6.75	3	0	0	0	0	2.2	5	2	0	4
Ray Washburn	0	0	0.00	2	0	0	0	0	2.1	1	0	1	2
Ron Willis	0	0	27.00	3	0	0	0	0	1.0	2	3	4	1
Hal Woodeshick	0	0	0.00	1	0	0	0	0	1.0	1	0	0	0
TOTAL	4	3	2.66	20	7	4	0	1	61.0	48	18	17	49

BOS (A)

PLAYER/POS	AVG	G	AB	R	H	2B	3B	HR	RB	BB	SO	SB
Jerry Adair, 2b-4	.125	5	16	0	2	0	0	0	1	0	3	1
Mike Andrews, 2b-3	.308	5	13	2	4	0	0	0	1	0	1	0
Gary Bell, p	.000	3	0	0	0	0	0	0	0	0	0	0
Ken Brett, p	.000	2	0	0	0	0	0	0	0	0	0	0
Joe Foy, 3b-3	.133	6	15	2	2	1	0	0	1	1	5	0
Russ Gibson, c	.000	2	2	0	0	0	0	0	0	0	2	0
Ken Harrelson, of	.077	4	13	0	1	0	0	0	1	1	3	0
Elston Howard, c	.111	7	18	0	2	0	0	0	1	1	2	0
Dalton Jones, 3b-4	.389	6	18	2	7	0	0	0	1	1	3	0
Jim Lonborg, p	.000	3	9	0	0	0	0	0	0	0	7	0
Dave Morehead, p	.000	2	0	0	0	0	0	0	0	0	0	0
Dan Osinski, p	.000	2	0	0	0	0	0	0	0	0	0	0
Rico Petrocelli, ss	.200	7	20	3	4	1	0	2	3	3	8	0
Mike Ryan, c	.000	1	2	0	0	0	0	0	0	0	1	0
Jose Santiago, p	.500	3	2	1	1	0	0	1	1	0	1	0
George Scott, 1b	.231	7	26	3	6	1	1	0	0	3	6	0
Norm Siebern, of-1	.333	3	3	0	1	0	0	0	1	0	0	0
Reggie Smith, of	.250	7	24	3	6	1	0	2	3	2	2	0
Lee Stange, p	.000	1	0	0	0	0	0	0	0	0	0	0
Jerry Stephenson, p	.000	1	0	0	0	0	0	0	0	0	0	0
Jose Tartabull, of-6	.154	7	13	1	2	0	0	0	0	1	2	0
George Thomas, of-1	.000	2	2	0	0	0	0	0	0	0	1	0
Gary Waslewski, p	.000	2	1	0	0	0	0	0	0	0	1	0
John Wyatt, p	.000	2	0	0	0	0	0	0	0	0	0	0
Carl Yastrzemski, of	.400	7	25	4	10	2	0	3	5	4	1	0
TOTAL	.216		222	21	48	6	1	8	19	17	49	1

PITCHER	W	L	ERA	G	GS	CG	SV	SHO	IP	H	ER	BB	SO
Gary Bell	0	1	5.06	3	1	0	1	0	5.1	8	3	1	1
Ken Brett	0	0	0.00	2	0	0	0	0	1.1	0	0	1	1
Jim Lonborg	2	1	2.63	3	3	2	0	1	24.0	14	7	2	11
Dave Morehead	0	0	0.00	2	0	0	0	0	3.1	0	0	4	3
Dan Osinski	0	0	6.75	2	0	0	0	0	1.1	2	1	0	0
Jose Santiago	0	2	5.59	3	2	0	0	0	9.2	16	6	3	6
Lee Stange	0	0	0.00	1	0	0	0	0	2.0	3	0	0	0
Jerry Stephenson	0	0	9.00	1	0	0	0	0	2.0	3	2	1	0
Gary Waslewski	0	0	2.16	2	1	0	0	0	8.1	4	2	2	7
John Wyatt	1	0	4.91	2	0	0	0	0	3.2	1	2	3	1
TOTAL	3	4	3.39	21	7	2	1	1	61.0	51	23	17	30

GAME 1 AT BOS OCT 4

				R	H	E
STL	001	000	100	2	10	0
BOS	001	000	000	1	6	0

Pitchers: GIBSON vs SANTIAGO, Wyatt (8)
Home Runs: Santiago-BOS
Attendance: 34,796

GAME 2 AT BOS OCT 5

				R	H	E
STL	000	000	000	0	1	1
BOS	000	101	30X	5	9	0

Pitchers: HUGHES, Willis (6), Hoerner (7), Lamabe (7) vs LONBORG
Home Runs: Yastrzemski-BOS (2)
Attendance: 35,188

GAME 3 AT STL OCT 7

				R	H	E
BOS	000	001	100	2	7	1
STL	120	001	01X	5	10	0

Pitchers: BELL, Waslewski (3), Stange (6), Osinski (8) vs BRILES
Home Runs: Shannon-STL, Smith-BOS
Attendance: 54,575

GAME 4 AT STL OCT 8

				R	H	E
BOS	000	000	000	0	5	0
STL	402	000	00X	6	9	0

Pitchers: SANTIAGO, Bell (1), Stephenson (3), Morehead (5), Brett (8) vs GIBSON
Attendance: 54,575

GAME 5 AT STL OCT 9

				R	H	E
BOS	001	000	002	3	6	1
STL	000	000	001	1	3	2

Pitchers: LONBORG vs CARLTON, Washburn (7), Willis (9), Lamabe (9)
Home Runs: Maris-STL
Attendance: 54,575

GAME 6 AT BOS OCT 11

				R	H	E
STL	002	000	200	4	8	0
BOS	010	300	40X	8	12	1

Pitchers: Hughes, Willis (4), Briles (5), LAMABE (7), Hoerner (7), Jaster (7), Washburn (7), Woodeshick (8) vs Waslewski, WYATT (6), Bell (8)
Home Runs: Petrocelli-BOS (2), Yastrzemski-BOS, Smith-BOS, Brock-STL
Attendance: 35,188

GAME 7 AT BOS OCT 12

				R	H	E
STL	002	023	000	7	10	1
BOS	000	010	010	2	3	1

Pitchers: GIBSON vs LONBORG, Santiago (7), Morehead (9), Osinski (9), Brett (9)
Home Runs: Gibson-STL, Javier-STL
Attendance: 35,188

Detroit Tigers (AL), 4; St. Louis Cardinals (NL), 3

In this "year of the pitcher," Tiger Denny McLain's 31 wins were the most for a major leaguer in 37 years. Cardinal Bob Gibson's 1.12 ERA was the majors' best since Dutch Leonard's 1.01 in 1914, and his 13 season shutouts tied for third best of all time. In the Series, though, it was Detroit's second-best pitcher—Mickey Lolich—who emerged as the hero.

McLain came off second-best against Gibson in the opener. He yielded only three hits in his five innings, but two singles in the fourth combined with a pair of walks and an error accounted for three runs. Gibson, meanwhile, was in the process of striking out a Series-record 17 batters on the way to a five-hit shutout. But Lolich brought Detroit back in Game 2. He struck out nine, and his third-inning home run (the only one of his major league career) provided all the scoring needed for a Detroit victory, although the Tigers kept putting runs across for an eventual 8–1 win.

Home runs accounted for most of the scoring in Game 3. Veteran Al Kaline's two-run shot in the third opened the scoring, but Tim McCarver's three-run blast in the fifth put St. Louis ahead. Dick McAuliffe's solo shot later in the inning brought Detroit within one run of a tie, but the Cardinals put the game away on Orlando Cepeda's three-run homer in the seventh.

McLain faced Gibson again in Game 4, and again came off second-best. Lou Brock led off the game with a home run, and before the end of the third inning McLain was gone. Gibson gave up a solo homer to Jim Northrup in the fourth, but that was the only Detroit run he allowed. Gibson homered himself and struck out 10 in an easy 10–1 win.

Down three games to one, the Tigers were saved from elimination by Lolich's arm. Although three hits in the top of the first (including Orlando Cepeda's second homer of the Series) gave St. Louis a quick three runs, Lolich held the Cards scoreless the rest of the game as his Tigers fought back with two runs in the fourth and three more in the seventh (with a rally started by Lolich's single). McLain finally came through in Game 6, evening the Series with an easy 13–1 victory, in which Jim Northrup's grand slam provided the big blow of a 10-run third inning.

Lolich and Gibson—both 2–0 in the Series—faced off in the finale. Gibson broke his own World Series strikeout record in the third inning (finishing with 8 for the game and 35 for the Series), and both pitchers hurled shutout ball through six innings. But four two-out Tigers hits in the top of the seventh—including a misplayed flyball in center field—put three runs on the board, and another run in the ninth made the score 4–0. In the last of the ninth, Mike Shannon's solo homer spoiled Lolich's shutout, but not his third Series win—or the Tigers' comeback world title.

DET (A)

PLAYER/POS	AVG	G	AB	R	H	2B	3B	HR	RB	BB	SO	SB
Gates Brown, ph	.000	1	1	0	0	0	0	0	0	0	0	0
Norm Cash, 1b	.385	7	26	5	10	0	0	1	5	3	5	0
Wayne Comer, ph	1.000	1	1	0	1	0	0	0	0	0	0	0
Pat Dobson, p	.000	3	0	0	0	0	0	0	0	0	0	0
Bill Freehan, c	.083	7	24	0	2	1	0	0	2	4	8	0
John Hiller, p	.000	2	0	0	0	0	0	0	0	0	0	0
Willie Horton, of	.304	7	23	6	7	1	1	1	3	5	6	0
Al Kaline, of	.379	7	29	6	11	2	0	2	8	0	7	0
Fred Lasher, p	.000	1	0	0	0	0	0	0	0	0	0	0
Mickey Lolich, p	.250	3	12	2	3	0	0	1	2	1	5	0
Tom Matchick, ph	.000	3	3	0	0	0	0	0	0	0	1	0
Eddie Mathews, 3b-1	.333	2	3	0	1	0	0	0	0	1	1	0
Dick McAuliffe, 2b	.222	7	27	5	6	0	0	1	3	4	6	0
Denny McLain, p	.000	3	6	0	0	0	0	0	0	0	4	0
Don McMahon, p	.000	2	0	0	0	0	0	0	0	0	0	0
Jim Northrup, of	.250	7	28	4	7	0	1	2	8	1	5	0
Ray Oyler, ss	.000	4	0	0	0	0	0	0	0	0	0	0
Daryl Patterson, p	.000	2	0	0	0	0	0	0	0	0	0	0
Jim Price, ph	.000	2	2	0	0	0	0	0	0	0	1	0
Joe Sparma, p	.000	1	0	0	0	0	0	0	0	0	0	0
Mickey Stanley, ss-7,of-4	.214	7	28	4	6	0	1	0	0	2	4	0
Dick Tracewski, 3b-1	.000	2	0	1	0	0	0	0	0	0	0	0
Don Wert, 3b	.118	6	17	1	2	0	0	0	2	6	5	0
Earl Wilson, p	.000	1	1	0	0	0	0	0	0	0	1	0
TOTAL	.242		231	34	56	4	3	8	33	27	59	0

PITCHER	W	L	ERA	G	GS	CG	SV	SHO	IP	H	ER	BB	SO
Pat Dobson	0	0	3.86	3	0	0	0	0	4.2	5	2	1	0
John Hiller	0	0	13.50	2	0	0	0	0	2.0	6	3	3	1
Fred Lasher	0	0	0.00	1	0	0	0	0	2.0	1	0	0	1
Mickey Lolich	3	0	1.67	3	3	3	0	0	27.0	20	5	6	21
Denny McLain	1	2	3.24	3	3	1	0	0	16.2	18	6	4	13
Don McMahon	0	0	13.50	2	0	0	0	0	2.0	4	3	0	1
Daryl Patterson	0	0	0.00	2	0	0	0	0	3.0	1	0	1	0
Joe Sparma	0	0	54.00	1	0	0	0	0	0.1	2	2	0	0
Earl Wilson	0	1	6.23	1	1	0	0	0	4.1	4	3	6	3
TOTAL	4	3	3.48	18	7	4	0	0	62.0	61	24	21	40

STL (N)

PLAYER/POS	AVG	G	AB	R	H	2B	3B	HR	RB	BB	SO	SB
Nelson Briles, p	.000	2	4	0	0	0	0	0	0	0	4	0
Lou Brock, of	.464	7	28	6	13	3	1	2	5	3	4	7
Steve Carlton, p	.000	2	0	0	0	0	0	0	0	0	0	0
Orlando Cepeda, 1b	.250	7	28	2	7	0	0	2	6	2	3	0
Ron Davis, of	.000	2	7	0	0	0	0	0	0	0	2	0
Johnny Edwards, ph	.000	1	1	0	0	0	0	0	0	0	1	0
Curt Flood, of	.286	7	28	4	8	1	0	0	2	2	2	3
Phil Gagliano, ph	.000	3	3	0	0	0	0	0	0	0	0	0
Bob Gibson, p	.125	3	8	2	1	0	0	1	2	1	2	0
Wayne Granger, p	.000	1	0	0	0	0	0	0	0	0	0	0
Joe Hoerner, p	.500	3	2	0	1	0	0	0	0	0	1	0
Dick Hughes, p	.000	1	0	0	0	0	0	0	0	0	0	0
Larry Jaster, p	.000	1	0	0	0	0	0	0	0	0	0	0
Julian Javier, 2b	.333	7	27	1	9	1	0	0	3	3	4	1
Roger Maris, of-5	.158	6	19	5	3	1	0	0	1	3	3	0
Dal Maxvill, ss	.000	7	22	1	0	0	0	0	0	3	5	0
Tim McCarver, c	.333	7	27	3	9	0	2	1	4	3	2	0
Mel Nelson, p	.000	1	0	0	0	0	0	0	0	0	0	0
Dave Ricketts, ph	1.000	1	1	0	1	0	0	0	0	0	0	0
Dick Schofield, ss-1	.000	2	0	0	0	0	0	0	0	0	0	0
Mike Shannon, 3b	.276	7	29	3	8	1	0	1	4	1	5	0
Ed Spiezio, ph	1.000	1	1	0	1	0	0	0	0	0	0	0
Bobby Tolan, ph	.000	1	1	0	0	0	0	0	0	0	1	0
Ray Washburn, p	.000	2	3	0	0	0	0	0	0	0	1	0
Ron Willis, p	.000	3	0	0	0	0	0	0	0	0	0	0
TOTAL	.255		239	27	61	7	3	7	27	21	40	11

PITCHER	W	L	ERA	G	GS	CG	SV	SHO	IP	H	ER	BB	SO
Nelson Briles	0	1	5.56	2	2	0	0	0	11.1	13	7	4	7
Steve Carlton	0	0	6.75	2	0	0	0	0	4.0	7	3	1	3
Bob Gibson	2	1	1.67	3	3	3	0	1	27.0	18	5	4	35
Wayne Granger	0	0	0.00	1	0	0	0	0	2.0	0	0	1	1
Joe Hoerner	0	1	3.86	3	0	0	1	0	4.2	5	2	5	3
Dick Hughes	0	0	0.00	1	0	0	0	0	0.1	2	0	0	0
Larry Jaster	0	0	∞	1	0	0	0	0	0.0	2	3	1	0
Mel Nelson	0	0	0.00	1	0	0	0	0	1.0	0	0	0	1
Ray Washburn	1	1	9.82	2	2	0	0	0	7.1	7	8	7	6
Ron Willis	0	0	8.31	3	0	0	0	0	4.1	2	4	4	3
TOTAL	3	4	4.65	19	7	3	1	1	62.0	56	32	27	59

GAME 1 AT STL OCT 2

				R	H	E
DET	000	000	000	0	5	3
STL	000	300	10X	4	6	0

Pitchers: McLAIN, Dobson (6), McMahon (8) vs GIBSON
Home Runs: Brock-STL
Attendance: 54,692

GAME 2 AT STL OCT 3

				R	H	E
DET	011	003	102	8	13	1
STL	000	001	000	1	6	1

Pitchers: LOLICH vs BRILES, Carlton (6), Willis (7), Hoerner (9)
Home Runs: Horton-DET, Lolich-DET, Cash-DET
Attendance: 54,692

GAME 3 AT DET OCT 5

				R	H	E
STL	000	040	300	7	13	0
DET	002	010	000	3	4	0

Pitchers: WASHBURN, Hoerner (6) vs WILSON, Dobson (5), McMahon (6), Patterson (7), Hiller (8)
Home Runs: Kaline-DET, McCarver-STL, McAuliffe-DET, Cepeda-STL
Attendance: 53,634

GAME 4 AT DET OCT 6

				R	H	E
STL	202	200	040	10	13	0
DET	000	100	000	1	5	4

Pitchers: GIBSON vs McLAIN, Sparma (3), Patterson (4), Lasher (6), Hiller (8), Dobson (8)
Home Runs: Brock-STL, Gibson-STL, Northrup-DET
Attendance: 53,634

GAME 5 AT DET OCT 7

				R	H	E
STL	300	000	000	3	9	0
DET	000	200	30X	5	9	1

Pitchers: Briles, HOERNER (7), Willis (7) vs LOLICH
Home Runs: Cepeda-STL
Attendance: 53,634

GAME 6 AT STL OCT 9

				R	H	E
DET	0 2 10	0 1 0	0 0 0	13	12	1
STL	0 0 0	0 0 0	0 0 1	1	9	1

Pitchers: McLAIN vs WASHBURN, Jaster (3), Willis (3), Hughes (3), Carlton (4), Granger (7), Nelson (9)
Home Runs: Northrup-DET, Kaline-DET
Attendance: 54,692

GAME 7 AT STL OCT 10

				R	H	E
DET	000	000	301	4	8	1
STL	000	000	001	1	5	0

Pitchers: LOLICH vs GIBSON
Home Runs: Shannon-STL
Attendance: 54,692

Atlanta's Hank Aaron homered in each game and drove in a series-high seven runs. But the "Miracle Mets" as a team outhomered the Braves six to five, outhit them by 72 percentage points, and scored nearly twice as many runs.

Twice in the first game the Braves came from behind to lead by a run, but in the top of the eighth, five New York hits and poor Atlanta fielding buried starter Phil Niekro under five runs. In Game 2, home runs by Tommie Agee and Ken Boswell helped New York take an early 8–0 lead that even Aaron's three-run homer in the fifth couldn't threaten.

In the third game the lead changed hands three times on home runs. Aaron began the barrage with a two-run shot in the first inning. Agee's homer in the third followed by Boswell's for two runs in the fourth put the Mets ahead—until Orlando Cepeda's two-run homer in the fifth gave Atlanta another lead. But in the bottom of the fifth, Mets rookie Wayne Garrett's two-run blast reversed the lead one last time and, after four final shutout innings by 22-year-old reliever Nolan Ryan, the Mets had swept to their first pennant.

New York Mets (East), 3; Atlanta Braves (West), 0

NY (E)

PLAYER/POS	AVG	G	AB	R	H	2B	3B	HR	RB	BB	SO	SB
Tommie Agee, of	.357	3	14	4	5	1	0	2	4	2	5	2
Ken Boswell, 2b	.333	3	12	4	4	0	0	2	5	1	2	0
Wayne Garrett, 3b	.385	3	13	3	5	2	0	1	3	2	2	1
Rod Gaspar, of	.000	3	0	0	0	0	0	0	0	0	0	0
Gary Gentry, p	.000	1	0	0	0	0	0	0	0	0	0	0
Jerry Grote, c	.167	3	12	3	2	1	0	0	1	1	4	0
Bud Harrelson, ss	.182	3	11	2	2	1	1	0	3	1	2	0
Cleon Jones, of	.429	3	14	4	6	2	0	1	4	1	2	2
Jerry Koosman, p	.000	1	2	1	0	0	0	0	0	1	2	0
Ed Kranepool, 1b	.250	3	12	2	3	1	0	0	1	1	2	0
J. C. Martin, ph	.500	2	2	0	1	0	0	0	2	0	0	0
Tug McGraw, p	.000	1	0	0	0	0	0	0	0	0	0	0
Nolan Ryan, p	.500	1	4	1	2	0	0	0	0	0	1	0
Tom Seaver, p	.000	1	3	0	0	0	0	0	0	0	0	0
Art Shamsky, of	.538	3	13	3	7	0	0	0	1	0	3	0
Ron Taylor, p	.000	2	0	0	0	0	0	0	0	0	0	0
Al Weis, 2b	.000	3	1	0	0	0	0	0	0	0	0	0
TOTAL	.327		113	27	37	8	1	6	24	10	25	5

PITCHER	W	L	ERA	G	GS	CG	SV	SHO	IP	H	ER	BB	SO
Gary Gentry	0	0	9.00	1	1	0	0	0	2.0	5	2	1	1
Jerry Koosman	0	0	11.57	1	1	0	0	0	4.2	7	6	4	5
Tug McGraw	0	0	0.00	1	0	0	1	0	3.0	1	0	1	1
Nolan Ryan	1	0	2.57	1	0	0	0	0	7.0	3	2	2	7
Tom Seaver	1	0	6.43	1	1	0	0	0	7.0	8	5	3	2
Ron Taylor	1	0	0.00	2	0	0	1	0	3.1	3	0	0	4
TOTAL	3	0	5.00	7	3	0	2	0	27.0	27	15	11	20

ATL (W)

PLAYER/POS	AVG	G	AB	R	H	2B	3B	HR	RB	BB	SO	SB
Hank Aaron, of	.357	3	14	3	5	2	0	3	7	0	1	0
Tommie Aaron, ph	.000	1	1	0	0	0	0	0	0	0	0	0
Felipe Alou, ph	.000	1	1	0	0	0	0	0	0	0	0	0
Bob Aspromonte, ph	.000	3	3	0	0	0	0	0	0	0	0	0
Clete Boyer, 3b	.111	3	9	0	1	0	0	0	3	2	3	0
Jim Britton, p	.000	1	0	0	0	0	0	0	0	0	0	0
Rico Carty, of	.300	3	10	4	3	2	0	0	0	3	1	0
Orlando Cepeda, 1b	.455	3	11	2	5	2	0	1	3	1	2	1
Bob Didier, c	.000	3	11	0	0	0	0	0	0	0	2	0
Paul Doyle, p	.000	1	0	0	0	0	0	0	0	0	0	0
Gil Garrido, ss	.200	3	10	0	2	0	0	0	0	1	1	0
Tony Gonzalez, of	.357	3	14	4	5	1	0	1	2	1	4	0
Sonny Jackson, ss	.000	1	0	0	0	0	0	0	0	0	0	0
Pat Jarvis, p	.000	1	2	0	0	0	0	0	0	0	2	0
Mike Lum, of-1	1.000	2	2	0	2	1	0	0	0	0	0	0
Felix Millan, 2b	.333	3	12	2	4	1	0	0	0	3	0	0
Gary Neibauer, p	.000	1	0	0	0	0	0	0	0	0	0	0
Phil Niekro, p	.000	1	3	0	0	0	0	0	0	0	1	0
Milt Pappas, p	.000	1	1	0	0	0	0	0	0	0	1	0
Ron Reed, p	.000	1	0	0	0	0	0	0	0	0	0	0
George Stone, p	.000	1	1	0	0	0	0	0	0	0	1	0
Bob Tillman, c	.000	1	0	0	0	0	0	0	0	0	0	0
Cecil Upshaw, p	.000	3	1	0	0	0	0	0	0	0	1	0
TOTAL	.255		106	15	27	9	0	5	15	11	20	1

PITCHER	W	L	ERA	G	GS	CG	SV	SHO	IP	H	ER	BB	SO
Jim Britton	0	0	0.00	1	0	0	0	0	0.1	0	0	1	0
Paul Doyle	0	0	0.00	1	0	0	0	0	1.0	2	0	1	3
Pat Jarvis	0	1	12.46	1	1	0	0	0	4.1	10	6	0	6
Gary Neibauer	0	0	0.00	1	0	0	0	0	1.0	0	0	0	1
Phil Niekro	0	1	4.50	1	1	0	0	0	8.0	9	4	4	4
Milt Pappas	0	0	11.57	1	0	0	0	0	2.1	4	3	0	4
Ron Reed	0	1	21.60	1	1	0	0	0	1.2	5	4	3	3
George Stone	0	0	9.00	1	0	0	0	0	1.0	2	1	0	0
Cecil Upshaw	0	0	2.84	3	0	0	0	0	6.1	5	2	1	4
TOTAL	0	3	6.92	11	3	0	0	0	26.0	37	20	10	25

GAME 1 AT ATL OCT 4

NY	020	200	050	9	10	1
ATL	012	010	100	5	10	2

Pitchers: SEAVER, Taylor (8) vs NIEKRO, Upshaw (9)
Home Runs: Gonzalez-ATL, H.Aaron-ATL
Attendance: 50,122

GAME 2 AT ATL OCT 5

NY	132	210	200	11	13	1
ATL	000	150	000	6	9	3

Pitchers: Koosman, TAYLOR (5), McGraw (7) vs REED, Doyle (2), Pappas (3), Britton (6), Upshaw (6), Neibauer (9)
Home Runs: Agee-NY, Boswell-NY, H.Aaron-ATL, Jones-NY
Attendance: 50,270

GAME 3 AT NY OCT 6

ATL	200	020	000	4	8	1
NY	001	231	00X	7	14	0

Pitchers: JARVIS, Stone (5), Upshaw (6) vs Gentry, RYAN (3)
Home Runs: H.Aaron-ATL, Agee-NY, Boswell-NY, Cepeda-ATL, Garrett-NY
Attendance: 53,195

Minnesota led the league in batting, Baltimore in pitching. In the ALCS, pitching prevailed as the Twins were held to a series batting average 113 points below their season mark.

Still, Minnesota nearly won the first game with three runs on only four hits. But the Orioles tied the score on Boog Powell's homer in the bottom of the ninth and won the game three innings later on Paul Blair's suicide squeeze bunt with two away. In Game 2, Minnesota's Dave Boswell scattered seven Baltimore hits over 10⅔ scoreless innings before giving way to Ron Perranoski in the 11th. But Orioles pitcher Dave McNally was more than a match for Boswell. He gave up only three hits—none in the final 7⅔ innings of the 11 he pitched—and took the win when Baltimore pinch hitter Curt Motton lined a single off Perranoski to score Powell from second with the game's only run.

In the third game, the Twins fell apart as the Orioles battered seven Minnesota pitchers for 18 hits. Baltimore's Jim Palmer gave up more than a hit an inning himself, but coasted to the pennant 11–2.

Baltimore Orioles (East), 3; Minnesota Twins (West), 0

BAL (E)

PLAYER/POS	AVG	G	AB	R	H	2B	3B	HR	RB	BB	SO	SB
Mark Belanger, ss	.267	3	15	4	4	0	1	1	1	0	0	0
Paul Blair, of	.400	3	15	1	6	2	0	1	6	2	2	0
Don Buford, of	.286	3	14	3	4	1	0	0	1	3	0	0
Mike Cuellar, p	.000	1	2	0	0	0	0	0	0	0	1	0
Andy Etchebarren, c	.000	2	4	0	0	0	0	0	0	0	0	0
Dick Hall, p	.000	1	0	0	0	0	0	0	0	0	0	0
Elrod Hendricks, c	.250	3	8	2	2	2	0	0	3	1	2	0
Davey Johnson, 2b	.231	3	13	2	3	0	0	0	0	2	1	0
Marcelino Lopez, p	.000	1	0	0	0	0	0	0	0	0	0	0
Dave May, ph	.000	1	1	0	0	0	0	0	0	0	0	0
Dave McNally, p	.000	1	4	0	0	0	0	0	0	0	2	0
Curt Motton, ph	.500	2	2	0	1	0	0	0	1	0	0	0
Jim Palmer, p	.000	1	5	0	0	0	0	0	0	0	3	0
Boog Powell, 1b	.385	3	13	2	5	0	0	1	1	2	0	0
Merv Rettenmund, ph	.000	1	0	0	0	0	0	0	0	0	0	0
Pete Richert, p	.000	1	0	0	0	0	0	0	0	0	0	0
Brooks Robinson, 3b	.500	3	14	1	7	1	0	0	0	0	0	0
Frank Robinson, of	.333	3	12	1	4	2	0	1	2	3	3	0
Chico Salmon, ph	.000	1	1	0	0	0	0	0	0	0	0	0
Eddie Watt, p	.000	1	0	0	0	0	0	0	0	0	0	0
TOTAL	.293		123	16	36	8	1	4	15	13	14	0

PITCHER	W	L	ERA	G	GS	CG	SV	SHO	IP	H	ER	BB	SO
Mike Cuellar	0	0	2.25	1	1	0	0	0	8.0	3	2	1	7
Dick Hall	1	0	0.00	1	0	0	0	0	0.2	0	0	0	1
Marcelino Lopez	0	0	0.00	1	0	0	0	0	0.1	1	0	2	0
Dave McNally	1	0	0.00	1	1	1	0	1	11.0	3	0	5	11
Jim Palmer	1	0	2.00	1	1	1	0	0	9.0	10	2	2	4
Pete Richert	0	0	0.00	1	0	0	0	0	1.0	0	0	2	2
Eddie Watt	0	0	0.00	1	0	0	0	0	2.0	0	0	0	2
TOTAL	3	0	1.13	7	3	2	0	1	32.0	17	4	12	27

MIN (W)

PLAYER/POS	AVG	G	AB	R	H	2B	3B	HR	RB	BB	SO	SB
Bob Allison, of	.000	2	8	0	0	0	0	0	1	0	0	0
Dave Boswell, p	.000	1	4	0	0	0	0	0	0	0	4	0
Leo Cardenas, ss	.154	3	13	0	2	0	1	0	0	0	7	0
Rod Carew, 2b	.071	3	14	0	1	0	0	0	0	1	4	0
Dean Chance, p	.000	1	0	0	0	0	0	0	0	0	0	0
Joe Grzenda, p	.000	1	0	0	0	0	0	0	0	0	0	0
Tom Hall, p	.000	1	0	0	0	0	0	0	0	0	0	0
Harmon Killebrew, 3b	.125	3	8	2	1	1	0	0	0	6	2	0
Chuck Manuel, ph	.000	1	0	0	0	0	0	0	0	1	0	0
Bob Miller, p	.000	1	0	0	0	0	0	0	0	0	0	0
George Mitterwald, c	.143	2	7	0	1	0	0	0	0	1	3	0
Graig Nettles, ph	1.000	1	1	0	1	0	0	0	0	0	0	0
Tony Oliva, of	.385	3	13	3	5	2	0	1	2	1	3	1
Ron Perranoski, p	.000	3	1	0	0	0	0	0	0	0	1	0
Jim Perry, p	.000	1	3	0	0	0	0	0	0	0	0	0
Rich Reese, 1b	.167	3	12	0	2	0	0	0	2	1	1	0
Rich Renick, ph	.000	1	1	0	0	0	0	0	0	0	0	0
John Roseboro, c	.200	2	5	0	1	0	0	0	0	0	0	0
Cesar Tovar, of	.077	3	13	0	1	0	0	0	0	1	2	1
Ted Uhlaender, of	.167	2	6	0	1	0	0	0	0	0	0	0
Dick Woodson, p	1.000	1	1	0	1	0	0	0	0	0	0	0
Al Worthington, p	.000	1	0	0	0	0	0	0	0	0	0	0
TOTAL	.155		110	5	17	3	1	1	5	12	27	2

PITCHER	W	L	ERA	G	GS	CG	SV	SHO	IP	H	ER	BB	SO
Dave Boswell	0	1	0.84	1	1	0	0	0	10.2	7	1	7	4
Dean Chance	0	0	13.50	1	0	0	0	0	2.0	4	3	0	2
Joe Grzenda	0	0	0.00	1	0	0	0	0	0.2	0	0	0	0
Tom Hall	0	0	0.00	1	0	0	0	0	0.2	0	0	0	0
Bob Miller	0	1	5.40	1	1	0	0	0	1.2	5	1	0	0
Ron Perranoski	0	1	5.79	3	0	0	0	0	4.2	8	3	0	2
Jim Perry	0	0	3.38	1	1	0	0	0	8.0	6	3	3	3
Dick Woodson	0	0	10.80	1	0	0	0	0	1.2	3	2	3	2
Al Worthington	0	0	6.75	1	0	0	0	0	1.1	3	1	0	1
TOTAL	0	3	4.02	11	3	0	0	0	31.1	36	14	13	14

GAME 1 AT BAL OCT 4

		R	H	E
MIN	000 010 200 000	3	4	2
BAL	000 110 001 001	4	10	1

Pitchers: Perry, PERRANOSKI (9) vs Cuellar, Richert (9), Watt (10), Lopez (12), HALL (12)
Home Runs: F.Robinson-BAL, Belanger-BAL, Oliva-MIN, Powell-BAL
Attendance: 39,324

GAME 2 AT BAL OCT 5

		R	H	E
MIN	000 000 000 00	0	3	1
BAL	000 000 000 01	1	8	0

Pitchers: BOSWELL, Perranoski (11) vs McNALLY
Attendance: 41,704

GAME 3 AT MIN OCT 6

		R	H	E
BAL	030 201 023	11	18	0
MIN	100 010 000	2	10	2

Pitchers: PALMER vs MILLER, Woodson (2), Hall (4), Worthington (5), Grzenda (6), Chance (7), Perranoski (9)
Home Runs: Blair-BAL
Attendance: 32,735

The heavy-hitting, slick-fielding Orioles, who also boasted the majors' top pitching staff, entered the Series clear favorites against the upstart Mets. But the "Miracle Mets," after losing the opener, polished off Baltimore with four straight wins.

Tom Seaver (25–7) and Mike Cuellar (23–11) faced each other in the opener. Baltimore's leadoff batter, Don Buford, greeted Seaver with a home run, and a three-run rally with two out in the fourth made the score 4–0 before the Mets scored their first Series run in the seventh. Cuellar held New York to that one run for the victory.

No one scored for three innings of Game 2 off Oriole Dave McNally or even hit Met Jerry Koosman safely. But Donn Clendenon led off the fourth with a home run for the Mets as Koosman continued to no-hit Baltimore for three more innings. In the seventh, though, Baltimore's Paul Blair spoiled Koosman's no-hitter with a leadoff single, and after stealing second, scored the tying run on Brooks Robinson's single. But those were the only hits the O's would get, and in the top of the ninth three successive two-out singles produced what proved to be the winning run.

Mets pitchers Gary Gentry and Nolan Ryan (with the assist of two spectacular catches by center fielder Tommie Agee that saved a total of five runs) combined for a shutout in Game 3. Agee's leadoff homer against Jim Palmer in the first was all the scoring the Mets would need, but they added four more runs before the game ended. Game 4 was the Series' tightest. Seaver went the distance for the win, holding a 1–0 lead until a sacrifice fly scored the tying Baltimore run in the top of the ninth (Ron Swoboda's diving catch kept it from being an extra base hit). In the bottom of the 10th, the Mets finally won it as a bunt thrown to first hit the runner and bounded away, allowing pinch runner Rod Gaspar to score all the way from second.

Dave McNally and Jerry Koosman tangled a second time in Game 5, and again Koosman and the Mets emerged victorious. McNally's two-run homer in the third gave him a lead which Frank Robinson expanded with a solo shot. But in an eerie sixth inning reprise of Game 4 of the 1957 World Series featuring Nippy Jones, the Mets' Cleon Jones was struck by a pitch on the foot and awarded first base after inspection by the home plate umpire revealed tell-tale shoe polish on the ball. Similar to the episode of 12 years earlier, Cleon Jones scored a key run on Donn Clendenon's home run which followed immediately.

New York Mets (NL), 4; Baltimore Orioles (AL), 1

NY (N)

PLAYER/POS	AVG	G	AB	R	H	2B	3B	HR	RB	BB	SO	SB
Tommie Agee, of	.167	5	18	1	3	0	0	1	1	2	5	1
Ken Boswell, 2b	.333	1	3	1	1	0	0	0	0	0	0	0
Don Cardwell, p	.000	1	0	0	0	0	0	0	0	0	0	0
Ed Charles, 3b	.133	4	15	1	2	1	0	0	0	0	2	0
Donn Clendenon, 1b	.357	4	14	4	5	1	0	3	4	2	6	0
Duffy Dyer, ph	.000	1	1	0	0	0	0	0	0	0	0	0
Wayne Garrett, 3b	.000	2	1	0	0	0	0	0	0	2	1	0
Rod Gaspar, of-1	.000	3	2	1	0	0	0	0	0	0	0	0
Gary Gentry, p	.333	1	3	0	1	1	0	0	2	0	2	0
Jerry Grote, c	.211	5	19	1	4	2	0	0	1	1	3	0
Bud Harrelson, ss	.176	5	17	1	3	0	0	0	0	3	4	0
Cleon Jones, of	.158	5	19	2	3	1	0	0	0	0	1	0
Jerry Koosman, p	.143	2	7	0	1	1	0	0	0	0	4	0
Ed Kranepool, 1b	.250	1	4	1	1	0	0	1	1	0	0	0
J.C. Martin, ph	.000	1	0	0	0	0	0	0	0	0	0	0
Nolan Ryan, p	.000	1	0	0	0	0	0	0	0	0	0	0
Tom Seaver, p	.000	2	4	0	0	0	0	0	0	0	2	0
Art Shamsky, of-1	.000	3	6	0	0	0	0	0	0	0	0	0
Ron Swoboda, of	.400	4	15	1	6	1	0	0	1	1	3	0
Ron Taylor, p	.000	2	0	0	0	0	0	0	0	0	0	0
Al Weis, 2b	.455	5	11	1	5	0	0	1	3	4	2	0
TOTAL	.220		159	15	35	8	0	6	13	15	35	1

PITCHER	W	L	ERA	G	GS	CG	SV	SHO	IP	H	ER	BB	SO
Don Cardwell	0	0	0.00	1	0	0	0	0	1.0	0	0	0	0
Gary Gentry	1	0	0.00	1	1	0	0	0	6.2	3	0	5	4
Jerry Koosman	2	0	2.04	2	2	1	0	0	17.2	7	4	4	9
Nolan Ryan	0	0	0.00	1	0	0	1	0	2.1	1	0	2	3
Tom Seaver	1	1	3.00	2	2	1	0	0	15.0	12	5	3	9
Ron Taylor	0	0	0.00	2	0	0	1	0	2.1	0	0	1	3
TOTAL	4	1	1.80	9	5	2	2	0	45.0	23	9	15	28

BAL (A)

PLAYER/POS	AVG	G	AB	R	H	2B	3B	HR	RB	BB	SO	SB
Mark Belanger, ss	.200	5	15	2	3	0	0	0	1	2	1	0
Paul Blair, of	.100	5	20	1	2	0	0	0	0	2	5	1
Don Buford, of	.100	5	20	1	2	1	0	1	2	2	4	0
Mike Cuellar, p	.400	2	5	0	2	0	0	0	1	0	3	0
Clay Dalrymple, ph	1.000	2	2	0	2	0	0	0	0	0	0	0
Andy Etchebarren, c	.000	2	6	0	0	0	0	0	0	0	1	0
Dick Hall, p	.000	1	0	0	0	0	0	0	0	0	0	0
Elrod Hendricks, c	.100	3	10	1	1	0	0	0	0	1	0	0
Davey Johnson, 2b	.063	5	16	1	1	0	0	0	0	2	1	0
Dave Leonhard, p	.000	1	0	0	0	0	0	0	0	0	0	0
Dave May, ph	.000	2	1	0	0	0	0	0	0	1	1	0
Dave McNally, p	.200	2	5	1	1	0	0	1	2	0	2	0
Curt Motton, ph	.000	1	1	0	0	0	0	0	0	0	0	0
Jim Palmer, p	.000	1	2	0	0	0	0	0	0	0	0	0
Boog Powell, 1b	.263	5	19	0	5	0	0	0	0	1	4	0
Merv Rettenmund, pr	.000	1	0	0	0	0	0	0	0	0	0	0
Pete Richert, p	.000	1	0	0	0	0	0	0	0	0	0	0
Brooks Robinson, 3b	.053	5	19	0	1	0	0	0	2	0	3	0
Frank Robinson, of	.188	5	16	2	3	0	0	1	1	4	3	0
Chico Salmon, pr	.000	2	0	0	0	0	0	0	0	0	0	0
Eddie Watt, p	.000	2	0	0	0	0	0	0	0	0	0	0
TOTAL	.146		157	9	23	1	0	3	9	15	28	1

PITCHER	W	L	ERA	G	GS	CG	SV	SHO	IP	H	ER	BB	SO
Mike Cuellar	1	0	1.13	2	2	1	0	0	16.0	13	2	4	13
Dick Hall	0	1	–	1	0	0	0	0	0.0	1	0	1	0
Dave Leonhard	0	0	4.50	1	0	0	0	0	2.0	1	1	1	1
Dave McNally	0	1	2.81	2	2	1	0	0	16.0	11	5	5	13
Jim Palmer	0	1	6.00	1	1	0	0	0	6.0	5	4	4	5
Pete Richert	0	0	–	1	0	0	0	0	0.0	0	0	0	0
Eddie Watt	0	1	3.00	2	0	0	0	0	3.0	4	1	0	3
TOTAL	1	4	2.72	10	5	2	0	0	43.0	35	13	15	35

Al Weis homered in the seventh for a 3–3 tie. With McNally now gone, two doubles off Eddie Watt in the eighth brought in the go-ahead run, and a pair of errors let in a run for insurance. Koosman held Baltimore scoreless in the ninth and the Mets miracle was complete.

GAME 1 AT BAL OCT 11

		R	H	E
NY	000 000 100	1	6	1
BAL	100 300 00X	4	6	0

Pitchers: SEAVER, Cardwell (6), Taylor (7) vs CUELLAR
Home Runs: Buford-BAL
Attendance: 50,429

GAME 2 AT BAL OCT 12

		R	H	E
NY	000 100 001	2	6	0
BAL	000 000 100	1	2	0

Pitchers: KOOSMAN, Taylor (9) vs McNALLY
Home Runs: Clendenon-NY
Attendance: 50,850

GAME 3 AT NY OCT 14

		R	H	E
BAL	000 000 000	0	4	1
NY	120 001 01X	5	6	0

Pitchers: PALMER, Leonhard (7) vs GENTRY, Ryan (7)
Home Runs: Agee-NY, Kranepool-NY
Attendance: 56,335

GAME 4 AT NY OCT 15

		R	H	E
BAL	000 000 001 0	1	6	1
NY	010 000 000 1	2	10	1

Pitchers: Cuellar, Watt (8), HALL (10), Richert (10) vs SEAVER
Home Runs: Clendenon-NY
Attendance: 57,367

GAME 5 AT NY OCT 16

		R	H	E
BAL	003 000 000	3	5	2
NY	000 002 12X	5	7	0

Pitchers: McNally, WATT (8) vs KOOSMAN
Home Runs: McNally-BAL, F.Robinson-BAL, Clendenon-NY, Weis-NY
Attendance: 57,397

Pitching was the name of the game and three the magic number, as Cincinnati swept Pittsburgh, scoring three runs in each game while holding the Pirates to just three runs for the whole series.

Pirates pitcher Dock Ellis matched the Reds' Gary Nolan for nine scoreless innings in Game 1 before a pinch-hit triple, a single, and a double undid him for three runs in the top of the 10th. In Game Two Pittsburgh scored its first series run, but center fielder Bobby Tolan scored three for the Reds—including a home run—to give Cincinnati its second win.

The Pirates took a lead for the only time in the series with a run in the top of the first inning of Game 3. But Tony Perez and Johnny Bench homered in the bottom of the inning to put the Reds up 2–1. The Pirates tied the score in the fifth, but three Cincinnati relievers combined to shut them out over the final four innings. Tolan sank the Pirates ship with his second game-winner in two days: a single in the eighth that drove in Cincinnati's third—and final—run.

Cincinnati Reds (West), 3; Pittsburgh Pirates (East), 0

CIN (W)

PLAYER/POS	AVG	G	AB	R	H	2B	3B	HR	RB	BB	SO	SB
Johnny Bench, c	.222	3	9	2	2	0	0	1	1	3	1	0
Angel Bravo, ph	.000	1	1	0	0	0	0	0	0	0	0	0
Bernie Carbo, of	.000	2	6	0	0	0	0	0	0	1	2	0
Clay Carroll, p	.000	2	0	0	0	0	0	0	0	0	0	0
Ty Cline, of-1	1.000	2	1	2	1	0	1	0	0	1	0	0
Tony Cloninger, p	.000	1	1	0	0	0	0	0	0	0	0	0
Dave Concepcion, ss	.000	3	0	0	0	0	0	0	0	0	0	0
Wayne Granger, p	.000	1	0	0	0	0	0	0	0	0	0	0
Don Gullett, p	.000	2	1	0	0	0	0	0	0	0	0	0
Tommy Helms, 2b	.273	3	11	0	3	0	0	0	0	0	1	0
Lee May, 1b	.167	3	12	0	2	1	0	0	2	0	2	0
Hal McRae, of-1	.000	2	4	0	0	0	0	0	0	0	2	0
Jim Merritt, p	.000	1	2	0	0	0	0	0	0	0	2	0
Gary Nolan, p	.333	1	3	0	1	0	0	0	0	0	0	0
Tony Perez, 3b-3,1b-1	.333	3	12	1	4	2	0	1	2	1	1	0
Pete Rose, of	.231	3	13	1	3	0	0	0	1	0	0	0
Jimmy Stewart, of	.000	1	2	0	0	0	0	0	0	0	0	0
Bobby Tolan, of	.417	3	12	3	5	0	0	1	2	1	1	1
Milt Wilcox, p	.000	1	0	0	0	0	0	0	0	0	0	0
Woody Woodward, ss-3,3b-3	.100	3	10	0	1	0	0	0	0	1	0	0
TOTAL	.220		100	9	22	3	1	3	8	8	12	1

PITCHER	W	L	ERA	G	GS	CG	SV	SHO	IP	H	ER	BB	SO
Clay Carroll	0	0	0.00	2	0	0	1	0	1.1	2	0	0	2
Tony Cloninger	0	0	3.60	1	1	0	0	0	5.0	7	2	4	1
Wayne Granger	0	0	0.00	1	0	0	0	0	0.2	1	0	0	0
Don Gullett	0	0	0.00	2	0	0	1	0	3.2	1	0	2	3
Jim Merritt	1	0	1.69	1	1	0	0	0	5.1	3	1	0	2
Gary Nolan	1	0	0.00	1	1	0	0	0	9.0	8	0	4	6
Milt Wilcox	1	0	0.00	1	0	0	0	0	3.0	1	0	2	5
TOTAL	3	0	0.96	9	3	0	3	0	28.0	23	3	12	19

PIT (E)

PLAYER/POS	AVG	G	AB	R	H	2B	3B	HR	RB	BB	SO	SB
PLAYER, POS	AVG	G	AB	R	H	2B	3B	HR	RB	BB	SO	SB
Gene Alley, ss	.000	2	7	0	0	0	0	0	0	1	2	0
Matty Alou, of	.250	3	12	1	3	1	0	0	0	2	1	0
Dave Cash, 2b	.125	2	8	1	1	1	0	0	0	1	1	0
Roberto Clemente, of	.214	3	14	1	3	0	0	0	1	0	4	0
Dock Ellis, p	.000	1	2	0	0	0	0	0	0	0	1	0
Joe Gibbon, p	.000	2	0	0	0	0	0	0	0	0	0	0
Dave Giusti, p	.000	2	0	0	0	0	0	0	0	0	0	0
Richie Hebner, 3b	.667	2	6	0	4	2	0	0	0	2	1	0
Johnny Jeter, of-1	.000	3	2	0	0	0	0	0	0	0	2	0
Bill Mazeroski, 2b	.000	1	2	0	0	0	0	0	0	2	0	0
Bob Moose, p	.000	1	4	0	0	0	0	0	0	0	1	0
Al Oliver, 1b	.250	2	8	0	2	0	0	0	1	1	0	0
Jose Pagan, 3b	.333	1	3	0	1	0	0	0	0	1	1	0
Freddie Patek, ss	.000	1	3	0	0	0	0	0	0	1	2	0
Bob Robertson, 1b-1	.200	2	5	0	1	1	0	0	0	0	0	0
Manny Sanguillen, c	.167	3	12	0	2	0	0	0	0	0	1	0
Willie Stargell, of	.500	3	12	0	6	1	0	0	1	1	1	0
Luke Walker, p	.000	1	2	0	0	0	0	0	0	0	1	0
TOTAL	.225		102	3	23	6	0	0	3	12	19	0

PITCHER	W	L	ERA	G	GS	CG	SV	SHO	IP	H	ER	BB	SO
Dock Ellis	0	1	2.79	1	1	0	0	0	9.2	9	3	4	1
Joe Gibbon	0	0	0.00	2	0	0	0	0	0.1	1	0	0	1
Dave Giusti	0	0	3.86	2	0	0	0	0	2.1	3	1	1	1
Bob Moose	0	1	3.52	1	1	0	0	0	7.2	4	3	2	4
Luke Walker	0	1	1.29	1	1	0	0	0	7.0	5	1	1	5
TOTAL	0	3	2.67	7	3	0	0	0	27.0	22	8	8	12

GAME 1 AT PIT OCT 3

CIN	000 000 000 3	3	9	0
PIT	000 000 000 0	0	8	0

Pitchers: NOLAN, Carroll (10) vs ELLIS, Gibbon (10)
Attendance: 33,088

GAME 2 AT PIT OCT 4

CIN	001 010 010	3	8	1
PIT	000 001 000	1	5	2

Pitchers: MERRITT, Carroll (6), Gullett (6) vs WALKER, Giusti (8)
Home Runs: Tolan-CIN
Attendance: 39,317

GAME 3 AT CIN OCT 5

PIT	100 010 000	2	10	0
CIN	200 000 01X	3	5	0

Pitchers: MOOSE, Gibbon (8), Giusti (8) vs Cloninger, WILCOX (6), Granger (9), Gullett (9)
Home Runs: Perez-CIN, Bench-CIN
Attendance: 40,538

For the second year in a row, Baltimore swept Minnesota in the ALCS. In the first two games the Orioles' attack featured the big inning. The score was tied 2–2 in the first game as the Orioles came to bat in the top of the fourth. But by the time the Twins came to bat in the inning, they were seven runs behind—thanks in part to a grand slam by Baltimore pitcher Mike Cuellar. Harmon Killebrew's two-run homer in the fifth helped bring the Twins within three, but they came no closer.

Except for home runs to Killebrew and Tony Oliva in the fourth inning, Orioles pitcher Dave McNally stopped the Twins in Game 2, and Baltimore held a close 4–3 lead after eight. If they had been playing at home, they wouldn't have needed to bat at all in the ninth. But they did come to bat in the top of the ninth, and they once again buried Minnesota under a seven-run inning.

In the third game, for the second year in a row, pitcher Jim Palmer breezed through the series clincher. Baltimore scored five runs for him in the first three innings, and another in the eighth—four more than he needed to carry his club to another pennant.

Baltimore Orioles (East), 3; Minnesota Twins (West), 0

BAL (E)

PLAYER/POS	AVG	G	AB	R	H	2B	3B	HR	RB	BB	SO	SB
Mark Belanger, ss	.333	3	12	5	4	0	0	0	1	1	0	0
Paul Blair, of	.077	3	13	0	1	0	0	0	0	1	4	0
Don Buford, of	.429	2	7	2	3	1	0	1	3	2	0	0
Mike Cuellar, p	.500	1	2	1	1	0	0	1	4	0	1	0
Andy Etchebarren, c	.111	2	9	1	1	0	0	0	0	0	3	0
Dick Hall, p	.500	1	2	1	1	0	0	0	0	0	1	0
Elrod Hendricks, c	.400	1	5	2	2	0	0	0	0	0	1	0
Davey Johnson, 2b	.364	3	11	4	4	0	0	2	4	1	1	0
Dave McNally, p	.400	1	5	1	2	1	0	0	1	0	1	0
Jim Palmer, p	.250	1	4	1	1	1	0	0	1	0	0	0
Boog Powell, 1b	.429	3	14	2	6	2	0	1	6	0	3	0
Merv Rettenmund, of	.333	1	3	1	1	0	0	0	1	2	1	1
Brooks Robinson, 3b	.583	3	12	3	7	2	0	0	1	0	1	0
Frank Robinson, of	.200	3	10	3	2	0	0	1	2	5	2	0
TOTAL	.330		109	27	36	7	0	6	24	12	19	1

PITCHER	W	L	ERA	G	GS	CG	SV	SHO	IP	H	ER	BB	SO
Mike Cuellar	0	0	12.46	1	1	0	0	0	4.1	10	6	1	2
Dick Hall	1	0	0.00	1	0	0	0	0	4.2	1	0	0	3
Dave McNally	1	0	3.00	1	1	1	0	0	9.0	6	3	5	5
Jim Palmer	1	0	1.00	1	1	1	0	0	9.0	7	1	3	12
TOTAL	3	0	3.33	4	3	2	0	0	27.0	24	10	9	22

MIN (W)

PLAYER/POS	AVG	G	AB	R	H	2B	3B	HR	RB	BB	SO	SB
Bob Allison, ph	.000	3	2	0	0	0	0	0	0	1	1	0
Brant Alyea, of-2	.000	3	7	1	0	0	0	0	0	2	3	0
Bert Blyleven, p	.000	1	0	0	0	0	0	0	0	0	0	0
Leo Cardenas, ss	.182	3	11	1	2	0	0	0	1	1	1	0
Rod Carew, ph	.000	2	2	0	0	0	0	0	0	0	1	0
Tom Hall, p	.000	2	1	0	0	0	0	0	0	0	1	0
Jim Holt, of	.000	3	5	0	0	0	0	0	0	0	2	0
Jim Kaat, p	.000	1	1	0	0	0	0	0	0	0	1	0
Harmon Killebrew, 3b-2,1b-1	.273	3	11	2	3	0	0	2	4	2	4	0
Chuck Manuel, ph	.000	1	1	0	0	0	0	0	0	0	1	0
George Mitterwald, c	.500	2	8	2	4	1	0	0	2	0	2	0
Tony Oliva, of	.500	3	12	2	6	2	0	1	1	0	1	0
Ron Perranoski, p	.000	2	0	0	0	0	0	0	0	0	0	0
Jim Perry, p	.000	2	1	0	0	0	0	0	1	0	0	0
Frank Quilici, 2b-2	.000	3	2	0	0	0	0	0	0	0	1	0
Paul Ratliff, c	.250	1	4	0	1	0	0	0	0	0	1	0
Rich Reese, 1b	.143	2	7	0	1	0	0	0	0	1	1	0
Rich Renick, 3b-1	.200	2	5	0	1	0	0	0	0	0	1	0
Danny Thompson, 2b	.125	3	8	0	1	1	0	0	0	1	0	0
Luis Tiant, p-1, pr-1	.000	2	0	0	0	0	0	0	0	0	0	0
Cesar Tovar, of-3,2b-1	.385	3	13	2	5	0	1	0	1	0	0	0
Stan Williams, p	.000	2	0	0	0	0	0	0	0	1	0	0
Dick Woodson, p	.000	1	0	0	0	0	0	0	0	0	0	0
Bill Zepp, p	.000	2	0	0	0	0	0	0	0	0	0	0
TOTAL	.238		101	10	24	4	1	3	10	9	22	0

PITCHER	W	L	ERA	G	GS	CG	SV	SHO	IP	H	ER	BB	SO
Bert Blyleven	0	0	0.00	1	0	0	0	0	2.0	2	0	0	2
Tom Hall	0	1	6.75	2	1	0	0	0	5.1	6	4	4	6
Jim Kaat	0	1	9.00	1	1	0	0	0	2.0	6	2	2	1
Ron Perranoski	0	0	19.29	2	0	0	0	0	2.1	5	5	1	3
Jim Perry	0	1	13.50	2	1	0	0	0	5.1	10	8	1	3
Luis Tiant	0	0	13.50	1	0	0	0	0	0.2	1	1	0	0
Stan Williams	0	0	0.00	2	0	0	0	0	6.0	2	0	1	2
Dick Woodson	0	0	9.00	1	0	0	0	0	1.0	2	1	1	0
Bill Zepp	0	0	6.75	2	0	0	0	0	1.1	2	1	2	2
TOTAL	0	3	7.62	14	3	0	0	0	26.0	36	22	12	19

GAME 1 AT MIN OCT 3

				R	H	E
BAL	020	701	000	10	13	0
MIN	110	130	000	6	11	2

Pitchers: Cuellar, HALL (5) vs PERRY, Zepp (4), Woodson (5), Williams (6), Perranoski (9)
Home Runs: Cuellar-BAL, Buford-BAL, Powell-BAL, Killebrew-MIN
Attendance: 26,847

GAME 2 AT MIN OCT 4

				R	H	E
BAL	102	100	007	11	13	0
MIN	000	300	000	3	6	2

Pitchers: McNALLY vs HALL, Zepp (4), Williams (5), Perranoski (8), Tiant (9)
Home Runs: F.Robinson-BAL, Killebrew-MIN, Oliva-MIN, Johnson-BAL
Attendance: 27,490

GAME 3 AT BAL OCT 5

				R	H	E
MIN	000	010	000	1	7	2
BAL	113	000	10X	6	10	0

Pitchers: KAAT, Blyleven (3), Hall (5), Perry (7) vs PALMER
Home Runs: Johnson-BAL
Attendance: 27,608

With a near-sweep of Cincinnati, the Orioles helped Baltimore fans forget their 1969 Series humiliation by the New York Mets. Baltimore's first two wins, though, were closely contested. In the opener in Cincinnati (the first World Series game played on artificial grass), a run in the first inning and Lee May's third-inning two-run homer off Orioles starter Jim Palmer gave Cincinnati a 3–0 lead. But Orioles Boog Powell and Elrod Hendricks tagged Gary Nolan for home runs in the fourth and fifth that evened the score, and Brooks Robinson—whose other-worldly defense at third gave Reds righthanded hitters nightmares throughout the Series—homered in the seventh for a one-run Baltimore lead that held up as Palmer settled down to pitch one-hit ball from the fourth inning until he was relieved for the final out of the ninth.

Game 2 was just as close. The Reds scored four runs in the first three innings, but Baltimore came back with six in the fourth and fifth. Johnny Bench's leadoff homer in the last of the sixth brought the Reds within one, but that was the end of the scoring for either side. In Game 3 Dave McNally gave up nine hits and three runs. But he himself hit a grand slam in the sixth inning to cement what became a 9–3 Baltimore victory.

On the verge of a Series sweep, the Orioles scored three runs in the last of the third inning of Game 4 to take a 4–2 lead. But the Reds' Pete Rose homered in the fifth, and although Baltimore got the run back in the sixth, Lee May's three-run blast in the eighth overcame the Orioles lead and gave the Reds a narrow 6–5 win as Reds reliever Clay Carroll permitted only one Oriole to hit safely over the final 3⅔ innings.

Mike Cuellar, driven out of Game 2 in the third inning, hurled the complete game for Baltimore in Game 5, even though Cincinnati hammered him for four hits (three of them doubles) and three runs in the top of the first inning. But as Orioles home runs by Frank Robinson and Merv Rettenmund highlighted a Baltimore onslaught that produced 15 hits and nine runs, Cuellar settled down, holding Cincinnati to a walk and a pair of harmless singles over the final eight innings to bring Baltimore its second world title in five years.

Baltimore Orioles (AL), 4; Cincinnati Reds (NL), 1

BAL (A)

PLAYER/POS	AVG	G	AB	R	H	2B	3B	HR	RB	BB	SO	SB
Mark Belanger, ss	.105	5	19	0	2	0	0	0	1	1	2	0
Paul Blair, of	.474	5	19	5	9	1	0	0	3	2	4	0
Don Buford, of	.267	4	15	3	4	0	0	1	1	3	2	0
Terry Crowley, ph	.000	1	1	0	0	0	0	0	0	0	0	0
Mike Cuellar, p	.000	2	4	0	0	0	0	0	0	0	2	0
Moe Drabowsky, p	.000	2	1	0	0	0	0	0	0	0	1	0
Andy Etchebarren, c	.143	2	7	1	1	0	0	0	0	2	3	0
Dick Hall, p	.000	1	1	0	0	0	0	0	0	0	1	0
Elrod Hendricks, c	.364	3	11	1	4	1	0	1	4	1	2	0
Davey Johnson, 2b	.313	5	16	2	5	2	0	0	2	5	2	0
Marcelino Lopez, p	.000	1	0	0	0	0	0	0	0	0	0	0
Dave McNally, p	.250	1	4	1	1	0	0	1	4	0	2	0
Jim Palmer, p	.143	2	7	1	1	0	0	0	0	0	3	0
Tom Phoebus, p	.000	1	0	0	0	0	0	0	0	0	0	0
Boog Powell, 1b	.294	5	17	6	5	1	0	2	5	5	2	0
Merv Rettenmund, of-1	.400	2	5	2	2	0	0	1	2	1	0	0
Pete Richert, p	.000	1	0	0	0	0	0	0	0	0	0	0
Brooks Robinson, 3b	.429	5	21	5	9	2	0	2	6	0	2	0
Frank Robinson, of	.273	5	22	5	6	0	0	2	4	0	5	0
Chico Salmon, ph	1.000	1	1	1	1	0	0	0	0	0	0	0
Eddie Watt, p	.000	1	0	0	0	0	0	0	0	0	0	0
TOTAL	.292		171	33	50	7	0	10	32	20	33	0

PITCHER	W	L	ERA	G	GS	CG	SV	SHO	IP	H	ER	BB	SO
Mike Cuellar	1	0	3.18	2	2	1	0	0	11.1	10	4	2	5
Moe Drabowsky	0	0	2.70	2	0	0	0	0	3.1	2	1	1	1
Dick Hall	0	0	0.00	1	0	0	1	0	2.1	0	0	0	0
Marcelino Lopez	0	0	0.00	1	0	0	0	0	0.1	0	0	0	0
Dave McNally	1	0	3.00	1	1	1	0	0	9.0	9	3	2	5
Jim Palmer	1	0	4.60	2	2	0	0	0	15.2	11	8	9	9
Tom Phoebus	1	0	0.00	1	0	0	0	0	1.2	1	0	0	0
Pete Richert	0	0	0.00	1	0	0	1	0	0.1	0	0	0	0
Eddie Watt	0	1	9.00	1	0	0	0	0	1.0	2	1	1	3
TOTAL	4	1	3.40	12	5	2	2	0	45.0	35	17	15	23

CIN (N)

PLAYER/POS	AVG	G	AB	R	H	2B	3B	HR	RB	BB	SO	SB
Johnny Bench, c	.211	5	19	3	4	0	0	1	3	1	2	0
Angel Bravo, ph	.000	4	2	0	0	0	0	0	0	1	1	0
Bernie Carbo, of-2	.000	4	8	0	0	0	0	0	0	2	3	0
Clay Carroll, p	.000	4	1	0	0	0	0	0	0	0	1	0
Darrel Chaney, ss	.000	3	1	0	0	0	0	0	0	0	1	0
Ty Cline, ph	.333	3	3	0	1	0	0	0	0	0	0	0
Tony Cloninger, p	.000	2	2	0	0	0	0	0	0	0	1	0
Dave Concepcion, ss	.333	3	9	0	3	0	1	0	3	0	0	0
Pat Corrales, ph	.000	1	1	0	0	0	0	0	0	0	0	0
Wayne Granger, p	.000	2	0	0	0	0	0	0	0	0	0	0
Don Gullett, p	.000	3	1	0	0	0	0	0	0	0	1	0
Tommy Helms, 2b	.222	5	18	1	4	0	0	0	0	1	1	0
Lee May, 1b	.389	5	18	6	7	2	0	2	8	2	2	0
Jim McGlothlin, p	.000	1	2	0	0	0	0	0	0	0	1	0
Hal McRae, of	.455	3	11	1	5	2	0	0	3	0	1	0
Jim Merritt, p	.000	1	1	0	0	0	0	0	0	0	1	0
Gary Nolan, p	.000	2	3	0	0	0	0	0	0	0	0	0
Tony Perez, 3b	.056	5	18	2	1	0	0	0	0	3	4	0
Pete Rose, of	.250	5	20	2	5	1	0	1	2	2	0	0
Jimmy Stewart, ph	.000	2	2	0	0	0	0	0	0	0	1	0
Bobby Tolan, of	.211	5	19	5	4	1	0	1	1	3	2	1
Ray Washburn, p	.000	1	0	0	0	0	0	0	0	0	0	0
Milt Wilcox, p	.000	2	0	0	0	0	0	0	0	0	0	0
Woody Woodward, ss-3	.200	4	5	0	1	0	0	0	0	0	0	0
TOTAL	.213		164	20	35	6	1	5	20	15	23	1

PITCHER	W	L	ERA	G	GS	CG	SV	SHO	IP	H	ER	BB	SO
Clay Carroll	1	0	0.00	4	0	0	0	0	9.0	5	0	2	11
Tony Cloninger	0	1	7.36	2	1	0	0	0	7.1	10	6	5	4
Wayne Granger	0	0	33.75	2	0	0	0	0	1.1	7	5	1	1
Don Gullett	0	0	1.35	3	0	0	0	0	6.2	5	1	4	4
Jim McGlothlin	0	0	8.31	1	1	0	0	0	4.1	6	4	2	2
Jim Merritt	0	1	21.60	1	1	0	0	0	1.2	3	4	1	0
Gary Nolan	0	1	7.71	2	2	0	0	0	9.1	9	8	3	9
Ray Washburn	0	0	13.50	1	0	0	0	0	1.1	2	2	2	0
Milt Wilcox	0	1	9.00	2	0	0	0	0	2.0	3	2	0	2
TOTAL	1	4	6.70	18	5	0	0	0	43.0	50	32	20	33

GAME 1 AT CIN OCT 10

		R	H	E
BAL	000 210 100	4	7	2
CIN	102 000 000	3	5	0

Pitchers: PALMER, Richert (9) vs NOLAN, Carroll (7)
Home Runs: May-CIN, Powell-BAL, Hendricks-BAL, B.Robinson-BAL
Attendance: 51,531

GAME 2 AT CIN OCT 11

		R	H	E
BAL	000 150 000	6	10	2
CIN	301 001 000	5	7	0

Pitchers: Cuellar, PHOEBUS (3), Drabowsky (5), Lopez (7), Hall (7) vs McGlothlin, WILCOX (5), Carroll (5), Gullett (8)
Home Runs: Tolan-CIN, Powell-BAL, Bench-CIN
Attendance: 51,531

GAME 3 AT BAL OCT 13

		R	H	E
CIN	010 000 200	3	9	0
BAL	201 014 10X	9	10	1

Pitchers: CLONINGER, Granger (6), Gullett (7) vs McNALLY
Home Runs: F.Robinson-BAL, Buford-BAL, McNally-BAL
Attendance: 51,773

GAME 4 AT BAL OCT 14

		R	H	E
CIN	011 010 030	6	8	3
BAL	013 001 000	5	8	0

Pitchers: Nolan, Gullett (3), CARROLL (6) vs Palmer, WATT (8), Drabowsky (9)
Home Runs: B.Robinson-BAL, Rose-CIN, May-CIN
Attendance: 53,007

GAME 5 AT BAL OCT 15

		R	H	E
CIN	300 000 000	3	6	0
BAL	222 010 02X	9	15	0

Pitchers: MERRITT, Granger (2), Wilcox (3), Cloninger (5), Washburn (7), Carroll (8) vs CUELLAR
Home Runs: F.Robinson-BAL, Rettenmund-BAL
Attendance: 45,341

For the first time, an LCS went more than the minimum three games, as Pittsburgh rebounded from a loss in the opener to take the next three from San Francisco.

The Pirates scored first, with two runs in the third inning of Game 1, but the Giants came back with a run in the bottom of the inning and put the game away in the fifth as Tito Fuentes and Willie McCovey both hit two-out two-run homers. Pirates first baseman Bob Robertson avenged his club's opening-game defeat the next day, battering four of the Giants' six pitchers for three home runs and a double—and five RBIs—in the Pirates' 9–5 win. Robertson continued his assault in Game 3, homering off Juan Marichal in the second. The Giants came back with a run in the sixth, but third baseman Richie Hebner put the game away with a second Pirates home run off Marichal in the eighth.

Both clubs scored five times in the first two innings of Game 4. But Pirates relievers Bruce Kison and Dave Giusti then pinned the Giants down for the final seven innings, while Roberto Clemente and Al Oliver combined for four RBIs in the sixth to capture the flag.

Pittsburgh Pirates (East), 3; San Francisco Giants (West), 1

PIT (E)

PLAYER/POS	AVG	G	AB	R	H	2B	3B	HR	RB	BB	SO	SB
Gene Alley, ss	.500	1	2	1	1	0	0	0	0	0	0	0
Steve Blass, p	.000	2	1	0	0	0	0	0	0	0	1	0
Dave Cash, 2b	.421	4	19	5	8	2	0	0	1	0	1	1
Roberto Clemente, of	.333	4	18	2	6	0	0	0	4	1	6	0
Gene Clines, of	.333	1	3	1	1	0	0	1	1	0	1	0
Vic Davalillo, ph	.000	2	2	0	0	0	0	0	0	0	1	0
Dock Ellis, p	.000	1	3	0	0	0	0	0	0	0	2	0
Dave Giusti, p	.000	4	1	0	0	0	0	0	0	0	0	0
Richie Hebner, 3b	.294	4	17	3	5	1	0	2	4	0	4	0
Jackie Hernandez, ss	.231	4	13	2	3	0	0	0	1	0	4	0
Bob Johnson, p	.000	1	2	0	0	0	0	0	0	0	1	0
Bruce Kison, p	.000	1	2	0	0	0	0	0	0	0	0	0
Milt May, ph	.000	1	1	0	0	0	0	0	0	0	0	0
Bill Mazeroski, ph	1.000	1	1	1	1	0	0	0	0	0	0	0
Bob Miller, p	.000	1	1	0	0	0	0	0	0	0	0	0
Bob Moose, p	.000	1	0	0	0	0	0	0	0	0	0	0
Al Oliver, of	.250	4	12	2	3	0	0	1	5	1	3	0
Jose Pagan, 3b	.000	1	1	0	0	0	0	0	0	0	0	0
Bob Robertson, 1b	.438	4	16	5	7	1	0	4	6	0	2	0
Manny Sanguillen, c	.267	4	15	1	4	0	0	0	1	1	1	1
Willie Stargell, of	.000	4	14	1	0	0	0	0	0	2	6	0
TOTAL	.271		144	24	39	4	0	8	23	5	33	2

PITCHER	W	L	ERA	G	GS	CG	SV	SHO	IP	H	ER	BB	SO
Steve Blass	0	1	11.57	2	2	0	0	0	7.0	14	9	2	11
Dock Ellis	1	0	3.60	1	1	0	0	0	5.0	6	2	4	1
Dave Giusti	0	0	0.00	4	0	0	3	0	5.1	1	0	2	3
Bob Johnson	1	0	0.00	1	1	0	0	0	8.0	5	0	3	7
Bruce Kison	1	0	0.00	1	0	0	0	0	4.2	2	0	2	3
Bob Miller	0	0	6.00	1	0	0	0	0	3.0	3	2	3	3
Bob Moose	0	0	0.00	1	0	0	0	0	2.0	0	0	0	0
TOTAL	3	1	3.34	11	4	0	3	0	35.0	31	13	16	28

SF (W)

PLAYER/POS	AVG	G	AB	R	H	2B	3B	HR	RB	BB	SO	SB
Jim Barr, p	.000	1	1	0	0	0	0	0	0	0	0	0
Bobby Bonds, of	.250	3	8	0	2	0	0	0	0	2	4	0
Ron Bryant, p	.000	1	0	0	0	0	0	0	0	0	0	0
Don Carrithers, p	.000	1	0	0	0	0	0	0	0	0	0	0
John Cumberland, p	.000	1	0	0	0	0	0	0	0	0	0	0
Dick Dietz, c	.067	4	15	0	1	0	0	0	0	2	5	0
Frank Duffy, ph	.000	1	1	0	0	0	0	0	0	0	1	0
Tito Fuentes, 2b	.313	4	16	4	5	1	0	1	2	1	3	0
Alan Gallagher, 3b	.100	4	10	0	1	0	0	0	0	0	2	0
Steve Hamilton, p	.000	1	0	0	0	0	0	0	0	0	0	0
Jim Ray Hart, 3b-1	.000	3	5	0	0	0	0	0	0	0	2	0
Ken Henderson, of	.313	4	16	3	5	1	0	0	2	2	1	1
Jerry Johnson, p	.000	1	0	0	0	0	0	0	0	0	0	0
Dave Kingman, of-2	.111	4	9	0	1	0	0	0	0	1	3	0
Hal Lanier, 3b	.000	1	1	0	0	0	0	0	0	0	0	0
Juan Marichal, p	.000	1	3	0	0	0	0	0	0	0	1	0
Willie Mays, of	.267	4	15	2	4	2	0	1	3	3	3	1
Willie McCovey, 1b	.429	4	14	2	6	0	0	2	6	4	2	0
Don McMahon, p	.000	2	0	0	0	0	0	0	0	0	0	0
Gaylord Perry, p	.250	2	4	0	1	0	0	0	0	0	0	0
Jimmy Rosario, pr	.000	1	0	0	0	0	0	0	0	0	0	0
Chris Speier, ss	.357	4	14	4	5	1	0	1	1	1	1	0
TOTAL	.235		132	15	31	5	0	5	14	16	28	2

PITCHER	W	L	ERA	G	GS	CG	SV	SHO	IP	H	ER	BB	SO
Jim Barr	0	0	9.00	1	0	0	0	0	1.0	3	1	0	2
Ron Bryant	0	0	4.50	1	0	0	0	0	2.0	1	1	1	2
Don Carrithers	0	0	∞	1	0	0	0	0	0.0	3	3	0	0
John Cumberland	0	1	9.00	1	1	0	0	0	3.0	7	3	0	4
Steve Hamilton	0	0	9.00	1	0	0	0	0	1.0	1	1	0	3
Jerry Johnson	0	0	13.50	1	0	0	0	0	1.1	1	2	1	2
Juan Marichal	0	1	2.25	1	1	1	0	0	8.0	4	2	0	6
Don McMahon	0	0	0.00	2	0	0	0	0	3.0	0	0	0	3
Gaylord Perry	1	1	6.14	2	2	1	0	0	14.2	19	10	3	11
TOTAL	1	3	6.09	11	4	2	0	0	34.0	39	23	5	33

GAME 1 AT SF OCT 2

				R	H	E
PIT	002	000	200	4	9	0
SF	001	040	00X	5	7	2

Pitchers: BLASS, Moose (6), Giusti (8) vs PERRY
Home Runs: Fuentes-SF, McCovey-SF
Attendance: 40,977

GAME 2 AT SF OCT 3

				R	H	E
PIT	010	210	401	9	15	0
SF	110	000	002	4	9	0

Pitchers: ELLIS, Miller (6), Giusti (9) vs CUMBERLAND, Barr (4), McMahon (5), Carrithers (7), Bryant (7), Hamilton (9)
Home Runs: Robertson-PIT (3), Clines-PIT, Mays-SF
Attendance: 42,562

GAME 3 AT PIT OCT 5

				R	H	E
SF	000	001	000	1	5	2
PIT	010	000	01X	2	4	1

Pitchers: MARICHAL vs JOHNSON, Giusti (9)
Home Runs: Robertson-PIT, Hebner-PIT
Attendance: 38,322

GAME 4 AT PIT OCT 6

				R	H	E
SF	140	000	000	5	10	0
PIT	230	004	00X	9	11	2

Pitchers: PERRY, Johnson (6), McMahon (8) vs Blass, KISON (3), Giusti (7)
Home Runs: Speier-SF, McCovey-SF, Hebner-PIT, Oliver-PIT
Attendance: 35,487

Baltimore, dividing its 15 runs evenly among the three games, swept the ALCS for the third year in a row.

Oakland's Vida Blue took a 3–1 lead into the seventh inning of Game 1, but with two away and men on first and third, a single and two doubles pushed across four runs to beat him, 5–3. Orioles starter Dave McNally and reliever Eddie Watt held the A's scoreless from the fifth inning on. In the second game Oakland managed only one run off Mike Cuellar, while the Orioles hammered Catfish Hunter for five runs on four homers—two of them by Boog Powell, including one in the eighth with a man aboard.

Reggie Jackson retaliated for the A's in Game 3 with two home runs off Jim Palmer, and Sal Bando added a third. But Palmer permitted no other A's to score, and—supported by a Baltimore run in the first and two each in the fifth and seventh—preserved the lead throughout the game. For the third year in a row Palmer clinched the pennant for Baltimore with a complete-game victory.

Baltimore Orioles (East), 3; Oakland A's (West), 0

BAL (E)

PLAYER/POS	AVG	G	AB	R	H	2B	3B	HR	RB	BB	SO	SB
Mark Belanger, ss	.250	3	8	1	2	0	0	0	1	3	2	0
Paul Blair, of	.333	3	9	1	3	1	0	0	2	0	3	0
Don Buford, of	.429	2	7	1	3	0	1	0	0	2	1	0
Mike Cuellar, p	.333	1	3	0	1	0	0	0	0	0	2	0
Andy Etchebarren, c	.000	2	5	0	0	0	0	0	0	0	0	0
Elrod Hendricks, c	.500	2	4	1	2	0	0	1	2	1	1	0
Davey Johnson, 2b	.300	3	10	2	3	2	0	0	0	3	1	0
Dave McNally, p	.000	1	2	0	0	0	0	0	0	0	0	0
Curt Motton, ph	1.000	1	1	0	1	1	0	0	1	0	0	0
Jim Palmer, p-1	.200	2	5	1	1	0	0	0	0	0	1	0
Boog Powell, 1b	.300	3	10	4	3	0	0	2	3	3	3	0
Merv Rettenmund, of	.250	3	8	0	2	1	0	0	1	0	3	0
Brooks Robinson, 3b	.364	3	11	2	4	1	0	1	3	0	1	0
Frank Robinson, of	.083	3	12	2	1	1	0	0	1	1	4	0
Eddie Watt, p	.000	1	0	0	0	0	0	0	0	0	0	0
TOTAL	.274		95	15	26	7	1	4	14	13	22	0

PITCHER	W	L	ERA	G	GS	CG	SV	SHO	IP	H	ER	BB	SO
Mike Cuellar	1	0	1.00	1	1	1	0	0	9.0	6	1	1	2
Dave McNally	1	0	3.86	1	1	0	0	0	7.0	7	3	1	5
Jim Palmer	1	0	3.00	1	1	1	0	0	9.0	7	3	3	8
Eddie Watt	0	0	0.00	1	0	0	1	0	2.0	2	0	0	1
TOTAL	3	0	2.33	4	3	2	1	0	27.0	22	7	5	16

OAK (W)

PLAYER/POS	AVG	G	AB	R	H	2B	3B	HR	RB	BB	SO	SB
Sal Bando, 3b	.364	3	11	3	4	2	0	1	1	1	0	0
Curt Blefary, ph	.000	1	1	0	0	0	0	0	0	0	1	0
Vida Blue, p	.000	1	3	0	0	0	0	0	0	0	3	0
Bert Campaneris, ss	.167	3	12	0	2	1	0	0	0	0	1	0
Tommy Davis, 1b-2	.375	3	8	1	3	1	0	0	0	0	0	0
Dave Duncan, c	.500	2	6	0	3	1	0	0	2	0	0	0
Mike Epstein, 1b-1	.200	2	5	0	1	0	0	0	0	0	3	0
Rollie Fingers, p	.000	2	0	0	0	0	0	0	0	0	0	0
Mudcat Grant, p	.000	1	0	0	0	0	0	0	0	0	0	0
Dick Green, 2b	.286	3	7	0	2	0	0	0	0	1	1	0
Mike Hegan, ph	.000	1	1	0	0	0	0	0	0	0	1	0
Catfish Hunter, p	.000	1	3	0	0	0	0	0	0	0	1	0
Reggie Jackson, of	.333	3	12	2	4	1	0	2	2	0	1	0
Darold Knowles, p	.000	1	0	0	0	0	0	0	0	0	0	0
Bob Locker, p	.000	1	0	0	0	0	0	0	0	0	0	0
Angel Mangual, of	.167	3	12	1	2	1	1	0	2	0	1	0
Rick Monday, of	.000	1	3	0	0	0	0	0	0	1	2	0
Joe Rudi, of	.143	2	7	0	1	1	0	0	0	1	0	0
Diego Segui, p	.000	1	2	0	0	0	0	0	0	0	0	0
Gene Tenace, c	.000	1	3	0	0	0	0	0	0	1	1	0
TOTAL	.229		96	7	22	8	1	3	7	5	16	0

PITCHER	W	L	ERA	G	GS	CG	SV	SHO	IP	H	ER	BB	SO
Vida Blue	0	1	6.43	1	1	0	0	0	7.0	7	5	2	8
Rollie Fingers	0	0	7.71	2	0	0	0	0	2.1	2	2	1	2
Mudcat Grant	0	0	0.00	1	0	0	0	0	2.0	3	0	0	2
Catfish Hunter	0	1	5.63	1	1	1	0	0	8.0	7	5	2	6
Darold Knowles	0	0	0.00	1	0	0	0	0	0.1	1	0	0	0
Bob Locker	0	0	0.00	1	0	0	0	0	0.2	0	0	2	0
Diego Segui	0	1	5.79	1	1	0	0	0	4.2	6	3	6	4
TOTAL	0	3	5.40	8	3	1	0	0	25.0	26	15	13	22

GAME 1 AT BAL OCT 3

				R	H	E
OAK	020	100	000	3	9	0
BAL	000	100	40X	5	7	1

Pitchers: BLUE, Fingers (8) vs McNALLY, Watt (8)
Attendance: 42,621

GAME 2 AT BAL OCT 4

				R	H	E
OAK	000	100	000	1	6	0
BAL	011	000	12X	5	7	0

Pitchers: HUNTER vs CUELLAR
Home Runs: B.Robinson-BAL, Powell-BAL (2), Hendricks-BAL
Attendance: 35,003

GAME 3 AT OAK OCT 5

				R	H	E
BAL	100	020	200	5	12	0
OAK	001	001	010	3	7	0

Pitchers: PALMER vs SEGUI, Fingers (5), Knowles (7), Locker (7), Grant (8)
Home Runs: Jackson-OAK (2), Bando-OAK
Attendance: 33,176

In its third successive Series, Baltimore faced its third different opponent and beat the Pirates in the first two games. A walk, a wild pitch, two Baltimore errors, and a single in the second inning of the opener gave Pittsburgh an early 3–0 lead. But Dave McNally shut out the Pirates on two hits the rest of the game as Frank Robinson, Merv Rettenmund, and Don Buford homered to give Baltimore a 5–3 victory. Jim Palmer took the win in Game 2 as Baltimore hammered Pirates pitching for 14 hits and 11 runs before Palmer issued Richie Hebner a three-run homer—Pittsburgh's only scoring—in the eighth.

The Pirates overtook the Orioles when the Series moved to Pittsburgh. Steve Blass pitched a three-hitter in Game 3, and while Frank Robinson's solo homer in the seventh ended Blass' shutout, a three-run shot by Bob Robertson in the last of the inning cemented a 5–1 Pittsburgh win. The next evening (in the first World Series night game ever), Baltimore scored three times in the top of the first inning, but two Pirates runs later in the inning and another run in the third tied the game. It remained tied until Pirates pinch hitter Milt May singled home the game winner with two away in the seventh.

With the Series now even at two wins apiece, Pittsburgh's Nelson Briles stopped the Orioles in Game 5 on a pair of singles. Bob Robertson's leadoff homer in the second proved all the Pirates needed for the win, but Briles himself drove in an insurance run later in the inning and Pittsburgh went on to win, 4–0.

The Pirates tried to win it all in Game 6, scoring single runs against the O's Jim Palmer in the second inning and the third (Roberto Clemente's home run). But Pirates starter Bob Moose was replaced after giving up a solo homer to Don Buford in the sixth, and a tying Baltimore run came home an inning later. A ninth-inning pinch hitter for Palmer produced nothing, but Baltimore won in the last of the 10th, when Frank Robinson scored on Brooks Robinson's sacrifice fly to shallow center.

Steve Blass, who had defeated Mike Cuellar in Game 3, faced him again in the finale and again emerged the victor of a pitching duel. Clemente's two-out homer in the fourth inning provided the game's only run until the eighth, when both teams scored single runs. Blass retired Baltimore in order in the ninth and the Pirates were world champions.

Pittsburgh Pirates (NL), 4; Baltimore Orioles (AL), 3

PIT (N)

PLAYER/POS	AVG	G	AB	R	H	2B	3B	HR	RB	BB	SO	SB
Gene Alley, ss	.000	2	2	0	0	0	0	0	0	1	0	0
Steve Blass, p	.000	2	7	0	0	0	0	0	0	0	1	0
Nelson Briles, p	.500	1	2	0	1	0	0	0	1	0	1	0
Dave Cash, 2b	.133	7	30	2	4	1	0	0	1	3	1	1
Roberto Clemente, of	.414	7	29	3	12	2	1	2	4	2	2	0
Gene Clines, of	.091	3	11	2	1	0	1	0	0	1	1	1
Vic Davalillo, of-2	.333	3	3	1	1	0	0	0	0	0	0	0
Dock Ellis, p	.000	1	1	0	0	0	0	0	0	0	1	0
Dave Giusti, p	.000	3	0	0	0	0	0	0	0	0	0	0
Richie Hebner, 3b	.167	3	12	2	2	0	0	1	3	3	3	0
Jackie Hernandez, ss	.222	7	18	2	4	0	0	0	1	2	5	1
Bob Johnson, p	.000	2	3	0	0	0	0	0	0	0	2	0
Bruce Kison, p	.000	2	2	0	0	0	0	0	0	1	2	0
Milt May, ph	.500	2	2	0	1	0	0	0	1	0	0	0
Bill Mazeroski, ph	.000	1	1	0	0	0	0	0	0	0	0	0
Bob Miller, p	.000	3	0	0	0	0	0	0	0	0	0	0
Bob Moose, p	.000	3	2	0	0	0	0	0	0	0	1	0
Al Oliver, of-4	.211	5	19	1	4	2	0	0	2	2	5	0
Jose Pagan, 3b	.267	4	15	0	4	2	0	0	2	0	1	0
Bob Robertson, 1b	.240	7	25	4	6	0	0	2	5	4	8	0
Charlie Sands, ph	.000	1	1	0	0	0	0	0	0	0	1	0
Manny Sanguillen, c	.379	7	29	3	11	1	0	0	0	0	3	2
Willie Stargell, of	.208	7	24	3	5	1	0	0	1	7	9	0
Bob Veale, p	.000	1	0	0	0	0	0	0	0	0	0	0
Luke Walker, p	.000	1	0	0	0	0	0	0	0	0	0	0
TOTAL	.235		238	23	56	9	2	5	21	26	47	5

PITCHER	W	L	ERA	G	GS	CG	SV	SHO	IP	H	ER	BB	SO
Steve Blass	2	0	1.00	2	2	2	0	0	18.0	7	2	4	13
Nelson Briles	1	0	0.00	1	1	1	0	1	9.0	2	0	2	2
Dock Ellis	0	1	15.43	1	1	0	0	0	2.1	4	4	1	1
Dave Giusti	0	0	0.00	3	0	0	1	0	5.1	3	0	2	4
Bob Johnson	0	1	9.00	2	1	0	0	0	5.0	5	5	3	3
Bruce Kison	1	0	0.00	2	0	0	0	0	6.1	1	0	2	3
Bob Miller	0	1	3.86	3	0	0	0	0	4.2	7	2	1	2
Bob Moose	0	0	6.52	3	1	0	0	0	9.2	12	7	2	7
Bob Veale	0	0	13.50	1	0	0	0	0	0.2	1	1	2	0
Luke Walker	0	0	40.50	1	1	0	0	0	0.2	3	3	1	0
TOTAL	4	3	3.50	19	7	3	1	1	61.2	45	24	20	35

BAL (A)

PLAYER/POS	AVG	G	AB	R	H	2B	3B	HR	RB	BB	SO	SB
Mark Belanger, ss	.238	7	21	4	5	0	1	0	0	5	2	1
Paul Blair, of-3	.333	4	9	2	3	1	0	0	0	0	1	0
Don Buford, of	.261	6	23	3	6	1	0	2	4	3	3	0
Mike Cuellar, p	.000	2	3	0	0	0	0	0	0	1	2	0
Pat Dobson, p	.000	3	2	0	0	0	0	0	0	0	2	0
Tom Dukes, p	.000	2	0	0	0	0	0	0	0	0	0	0
Andy Etchebarren, c	.000	1	2	0	0	0	0	0	0	0	0	0
Dick Hall, p	.000	1	0	0	0	0	0	0	0	0	0	0
Elrod Hendricks, c	.263	6	19	3	5	1	0	0	1	3	3	0
Grant Jackson, p	.000	1	0	0	0	0	0	0	0	0	0	0
Davy Johnson, 2b	.148	7	27	1	4	0	0	0	3	0	1	0
Dave Leonhard, p	.000	1	0	0	0	0	0	0	0	0	0	0
Dave McNally, p	.000	4	4	0	0	0	0	0	0	0	3	0
Jim Palmer, p	.000	2	4	0	0	0	0	0	2	2	2	0
Boog Powell, 1b	.111	7	27	1	3	0	0	0	1	1	3	0
Merv Rettenmund, of-6	.185	7	27	3	5	0	0	1	4	0	4	0
Pete Richert, p	.000	1	0	0	0	0	0	0	0	0	0	0
Brooks Robinson, 3b	.318	7	22	2	7	0	0	0	5	3	1	0
Frank Robinson, of	.280	7	25	5	7	0	0	2	2	2	8	0
Tom Shopay, ph	.000	5	4	0	0	0	0	0	0	0	0	0
Eddie Watt, p	.000	2	0	0	0	0	0	0	0	0	0	0
TOTAL	.205		219	24	45	3	1	5	22	20	35	1

PITCHER	W	L	ERA	G	GS	CG	SV	SHO	IP	H	ER	BB	SO
Mike Cuellar	0	2	3.86	2	2	0	0	0	14.0	11	6	6	10
Pat Dobson	0	0	4.05	3	1	0	0	0	6.2	13	3	4	6
Tom Dukes	0	0	0.00	2	0	0	0	0	4.0	2	0	0	1
Dick Hall	0	0	0.00	1	0	0	1	0	1.0	1	0	0	0
Grant Jackson	0	0	0.00	1	0	0	0	0	0.2	0	0	1	0
Dave Leonhard	0	0	0.00	1	0	0	0	0	1.0	0	0	1	0
Dave McNally	2	1	1.98	4	2	1	0	0	13.2	10	3	5	12
Jim Palmer	1	0	2.65	2	2	0	0	0	17.0	15	5	9	15
Pete Richert	0	0	0.00	1	0	0	0	0	0.2	0	0	0	1
Eddie Watt	0	1	3.86	2	0	0	0	0	2.1	4	1	0	2
TOTAL	3	4	2.66	19	7	1	1	0	61.0	56	18	26	47

GAME 1 AT BAL OCT 9

PIT	030	000	000	3	3	0
BAL	013	010	00X	5	10	3

Pitchers: ELLIS, Moose (3), Miller (7) vs McNALLY
Home Runs: F.Robinson-BAL, Rettenmund-BAL, Buford-BAL
Attendance: 53,229

GAME 2 AT BAL OCT 11

PIT	000	000	030	3	8	1
BAL	010	361	00X	11	14	1

Pitchers: R.JOHNSON, Kison (4), Moose (4), Veale (5), Miller (6), Giusti (8) vs PALMER, Hall (9)
Home Runs: Hebner-PIT
Attendance: 53,239

GAME 3 AT PIT OCT 12

BAL	000	000	100	1	3	3
PIT	100	001	30X	5	7	0

Pitchers: CUELLAR, Dukes (7), Watt (8) vs BLASS
Home Runs: F.Robinson-BAL, Robertson-PIT
Attendance: 50,403

GAME 4 AT PIT OCT 13

BAL	300	000	000	3	4	1
PIT	201	000	10X	4	14	0

Pitchers: Dobson, Jackson (6), WATT (7), Richert (8) vs Walker, KISON (1), Giusti (8)
Attendance: 51,378

GAME 5 AT PIT OCT 14

BAL	000	000	000	0	2	1
PIT	021	010	00X	4	9	0

Pitchers: McNALLY, Leonhard (5), Dukes (6) vs BRILES
Home Runs: Robertson-PIT
Attendance: 51,377

GAME 6 AT BAL OCT 16

PIT	011	000	000	0	2	9	1
BAL	000	001	100	1	3	8	0

Pitchers: Moose, R.Johnson (6), Giusti (7), MILLER (10) vs Palmer, Dobson (10), McNALLY (10)
Home Runs: Clemente-PIT, Buford-BAL
Attendance: 44,174

GAME 7 AT BAL OCT 17

PIT	000	100	010	2	6	1
BAL	000	000	010	1	4	0

Pitchers: BLASS vs CUELLAR, Dobson (9), McNally (9)
Home Runs: Clemente-PIT
Attendance: 47,291

Pittsburgh traded wins with Cincinnati through the first four games—winning the first and third—and took a lead into the ninth inning of the fifth game before a home run and a wild pitch undid them.

Cincinnati got eight hits in each of the first two games. In the first game, though, only Joe Morgan's first-inning homer produced a run, and the Reds lost, 5–1. But the next day, five first-inning hits gave the Reds four runs and a lead the Pirates could not overcome.

Pirates catcher Manny Sanguillen brought Pittsburgh back in Game 3 with a home run in the fifth and the game-winning RBI in the eighth. But Reds pitcher Ross Grimsley evened the series for Cincinnati the next day with a two-hitter, in the series' only complete-game performance.

Game 5 was Pittsburgh's for 8½ innings. The Pirates scored first, and held the lead into the bottom of the ninth. But Johnny Bench opened the Reds' half of the ninth with a game-tying home run, and Tony Perez and Denis Menke followed him with singles. Bob Moose came in and retired the next two men, though George Foster (running for Perez) took third on a fly to right. Moose then threw away the pennant with a run-scoring, series-ending wild pitch.

Cincinnati Reds (West), 3; Pittsburgh Pirates (East), 2

CIN (W)

PLAYER/POS	AVG	G	AB	R	H	2B	3B	HR	RB	BB	SO	SB
Johnny Bench, c	.333	5	18	3	6	1	1	1	2	1	3	2
Jack Billingham, p	.000	1	2	0	0	0	0	0	0	0	1	0
Pedro Borbon, p	.000	3	0	0	0	0	0	0	0	0	0	0
Clay Carroll, p	.000	2	0	0	0	0	0	0	0	0	0	0
Darrel Chaney, ss	.188	5	16	3	3	0	0	0	1	1	1	1
Dave Concepcion, ss-1	.000	3	2	0	0	0	0	0	0	0	0	0
George Foster, pr	.000	1	0	1	0	0	0	0	0	0	0	0
Cesar Geronimo, of	.100	5	20	2	2	0	0	1	1	0	2	0
Ross Grimsley, p	.500	1	4	0	2	1	0	0	1	0	1	0
Don Gullett, p	.500	2	2	0	1	0	0	0	0	0	0	0
Joe Hague, ph	.000	3	1	0	0	0	0	0	0	2	1	0
Tom Hall, p	.000	2	1	0	0	0	0	0	0	0	0	0
Jim McGlothlin, p	.000	1	0	0	0	0	0	0	0	0	0	0
Hal McRae, ph	.000	1	0	0	0	0	0	0	0	0	0	0
Denis Menke, 3b	.250	5	16	1	4	1	0	0	0	4	3	0
Joe Morgan, 2b	.263	5	19	5	5	0	0	2	3	1	2	1
Gary Nolan, p	.000	1	2	0	0	0	0	0	0	0	1	0
Tony Perez, 1b	.200	5	20	0	4	1	0	0	2	0	7	0
Pete Rose, of	.450	5	20	1	9	4	0	0	2	1	2	0
Bobby Tolan, of	.238	5	21	3	5	1	1	0	4	0	4	0
Ted Uhlaender, ph	.500	2	2	0	1	0	0	0	0	0	0	0
TOTAL	.253		166	19	42	9	2	4	16	10	28	4

PITCHER	W	L	ERA	G	GS	CG	SV	SHO	IP	H	ER	BB	SO
Jack Billingham	0	0	3.86	1	1	0	0	0	4.2	5	2	2	4
Pedro Borbon	0	0	2.08	3	0	0	0	0	4.1	2	1	0	1
Clay Carroll	1	1	3.38	2	0	0	0	0	2.2	2	1	3	0
Ross Grimsley	1	0	1.00	1	1	1	0	0	9.0	2	1	0	5
Don Gullett	0	1	8.00	2	2	0	0	0	9.0	12	8	0	5
Tom Hall	1	0	1.23	2	0	0	0	0	7.1	3	1	3	8
Jim McGlothlin	0	0	0.00	1	0	0	0	0	1.0	0	0	0	0
Gary Nolan	0	0	1.50	1	1	0	0	0	6.0	4	1	1	4
TOTAL	3	2	3.07	13	5	1	0	0	44.0	30	15	9	27

PIT (E)

PLAYER/POS	AVG	G	AB	R	H	2B	3B	HR	RB	BB	SO	SB
Gene Alley, ss	.000	5	16	1	0	0	0	0	0	0	3	0
Steve Blass, p	.000	2	6	0	0	0	0	0	0	0	3	0
Nelson Briles, p	.000	1	2	0	0	0	0	0	0	0	1	0
Dave Cash, 2b	.211	5	19	0	4	0	0	0	3	0	0	0
Roberto Clemente, of	.235	5	17	1	4	1	0	1	2	3	5	0
Gene Clines, ph	.000	3	2	1	0	0	0	0	0	0	1	0
Vic Davalillo, ph	.000	1	0	0	0	0	0	0	0	1	0	0
Dock Ellis, p-1	.000	2	1	0	0	0	0	0	0	0	0	0
Dave Giusti, p	.000	3	1	0	0	0	0	0	0	0	0	0
Richie Hebner, 3b	.188	5	16	2	3	1	0	0	1	1	3	0
Ramon Hernandez, p	.000	3	0	0	0	0	0	0	0	0	0	0
Bob Johnson, p	.000	2	1	0	0	0	0	0	0	0	1	0
Bruce Kison, p	.000	2	0	0	0	0	0	0	0	0	0	0
Milt May, c	.500	1	2	0	1	0	0	0	1	0	0	0
Bill Mazeroski, ph	.500	2	2	0	1	0	0	0	0	0	1	0
Bob Miller, p	.000	1	0	0	0	0	0	0	0	0	0	0
Bob Moose, p	.000	2	0	0	0	0	0	0	0	0	0	0
Al Oliver, of	.250	5	20	3	5	2	1	1	3	0	4	0
Bob Robertson, 1b	.000	4	0	0	0	0	0	0	0	1	0	0
Manny Sanguillen, c	.313	5	16	4	5	1	0	1	2	0	0	0
Willie Stargell, 1b-5,of-1	.063	5	16	1	1	1	0	0	1	2	5	0
Rennie Stennett, of-5,2b-1	.286	5	21	2	6	0	0	0	1	1	0	0
Luke Walker, p	.000	1	0	0	0	0	0	0	0	0	0	0
TOTAL	.190		158	15	30	6	1	3	14	9	27	0

PITCHER	W	L	ERA	G	GS	CG	SV	SHO	IP	H	ER	BB	SO
Steve Blass	1	0	1.72	2	2	0	0	0	15.2	12	3	6	5
Nelson Briles	0	0	3.00	1	1	0	0	0	6.0	6	2	1	3
Dock Ellis	0	1	0.00	1	1	0	0	0	5.0	5	0	1	3
Dave Giusti	0	1	6.75	3	0	0	1	0	2.2	5	2	0	3
Ramon Hernandez	0	0	2.70	3	0	0	1	0	3.1	1	1	0	3
Bob Johnson	0	0	3.00	2	0	0	0	0	6.0	4	2	2	7
Bruce Kison	1	0	0.00	2	0	0	0	0	2.1	1	0	0	3
Bob Miller	0	0	0.00	1	0	0	0	0	1.0	0	0	0	1
Bob Moose	0	1	54.00	2	1	0	0	0	0.2	5	4	0	0
Luke Walker	0	0	18.00	1	0	0	0	0	1.0	3	2	0	0
TOTAL	2	3	3.30	18	5	0	2	0	43.2	42	16	10	28

GAME 1 AT PIT OCT 7

				R	H	E
CIN	100	000	000	1	8	0
PIT	300	020	00X	5	6	0

Pitchers: GULLETT, Borbon (7) vs BLASS, R.Hernandez (9)
Home Runs: Morgan-CIN, Oliver-PIT
Attendance: 50,476

GAME 2 AT PIT OCT 8

				R	H	E
CIN	400	000	010	5	8	1
PIT	000	111	000	3	7	1

Pitchers: Billingham, HALL (5) vs MOOSE, Johnson (1), Kison (6), R.Hernandez (7), Giusti (9)
Home Runs: Morgan-CIN
Attendance: 50,584

GAME 3 AT CIN OCT 9

				R	H	E
PIT	000	010	110	3	7	0
CIN	002	000	000	2	8	1

Pitchers: Briles, KISON (7), Giusti (8) vs Nolan, Borbon (7), CARROLL (7), McGlothlin (9)
Home Runs: Sanguillen-PIT
Attendance: 52,420

GAME 4 AT CIN OCT 10

				R	H	E
PIT	000	000	100	1	2	3
CIN	100	202	20X	7	11	1

Pitchers: ELLIS, Johnson (6), Walker (7), Miller (8) vs GRIMSLEY
Home Runs: Clemente-PIT
Attendance: 39,447

GAME 5 AT CIN OCT 11

				R	H	E
PIT	020	100	000	3	8	0
CIN	001	010	002	4	7	1

Pitchers: Blass, R.Hernandez (8), GIUSTI (9), Moose (9) vs Gullett, Borbon (4), Hall (6), CARROLL (9)
Home Runs: Geronimo-CIN, Bench-CIN
Attendance: 41,887

Oakland turned back the Tigers in the first two games, but Detroit evened the series before succumbing in the fifth game.

In Game 1 Al Kaline homered off Rollie Fingers in the 11th to give Detroit starter Mickey Lolich a 2–1 lead. But in the last of the inning, pinch hitter Gonzalo Marquez singled off Tigers reliever Chuck Seelbach with two on to drive in the tying run, and Gene Tenace scored to win it on the same play as right fielder Kaline threw the ball away. Blue Moon Odom increased the A's series lead with a three-hit shutout in Game 2, but Detroit's Joe Coleman retaliated with 14 strikeouts and a shutout of his own to save the Tigers from elimination in Game 3.

In Game 4 the A's pulled out of a 1–1 tie with two runs in the top of the 10th. But Detroit in its half of the inning went through three Oakland relievers for three runs and the win. In the finale, after Odom, the A's starter, had given Detroit a run and a brief lead in the first, he and Vida Blue divided eight shutout innings between them as the A's scored twice to capture their first pennant since Connie Mack won his last in Philadelphia 41 years earlier.

Oakland A's (West), 3; Detroit Tigers (East), 2

OAK (W)

PLAYER/POS	AVG	G	AB	R	H	2B	3B	HR	RB	BB	SO	SB
Matty Alou, of	.381	5	21	2	8	4	0	0	2	0	2	1
Sal Bando, 3b	.200	5	20	0	4	0	0	0	0	0	3	0
Vida Blue, p	.000	4	1	0	0	0	0	0	0	0	0	0
Bert Campaneris, ss	.429	2	7	3	3	0	0	0	0	1	0	2
Tim Cullen, ss	.000	2	1	0	0	0	0	0	0	0	0	0
Dave Duncan, c	.000	2	2	0	0	0	0	0	0	1	1	0
Mike Epstein, 1b	.188	5	16	1	3	0	0	1	1	4	5	1
Rollie Fingers, p	.000	3	1	0	0	0	0	0	0	0	0	0
Dick Green, 2b	.125	5	8	0	1	1	0	0	0	0	0	0
Dave Hamilton, p	.000	1	0	0	0	0	0	0	0	0	0	0
Mike Hegan, 1b-1	.000	3	1	1	0	0	0	0	0	0	0	0
George Hendrick, of-1	.143	5	7	2	1	0	0	0	0	0	1	0
Ken Holtzman, p	.000	1	1	0	0	0	0	0	0	0	1	0
Joe Horlen, p	.000	1	0	0	0	0	0	0	0	0	0	0
Catfish Hunter, p	.167	2	6	0	1	0	0	0	0	0	2	0
Reggie Jackson, of	.278	5	18	1	5	1	0	0	2	1	6	2
Ted Kubiak, 2b-3,ss-1	.500	4	4	0	2	0	0	0	1	0	0	0
Bob Locker, p	.000	2	0	0	0	0	0	0	0	0	0	0
Angel Mangual, ph	.000	3	3	0	0	0	0	0	0	0	1	0
Gonzalo Marquez, ph	.667	3	3	1	2	0	0	0	1	0	0	0
Dal Maxvill, ss-4,2b-1	.125	5	8	0	1	0	0	0	0	1	2	1
Don Mincher, ph	.000	1	1	0	0	0	0	0	0	0	1	0
Blue Moon Odom, p-2	.250	3	4	0	1	1	0	0	0	0	1	0
Joe Rudi, of	.250	5	20	1	5	1	0	0	2	1	4	0
Gene Tenace, c-5,2b-2	.059	5	17	1	1	0	0	0	1	3	5	0
TOTAL	.224		170	13	38	8	0	1	10	12	35	7

PITCHER	W	L	ERA	G	GS	CG	SV	SHO	IP	H	ER	BB	SO
Vida Blue	0	0	0.00	4	0	0	1	0	5.1	4	0	1	5
Rollie Fingers	1	0	1.69	3	0	0	0	0	5.1	4	1	1	3
Dave Hamilton	0	0	∞	1	0	0	0	0	0.0	1	0	1	0
Ken Holtzman	0	1	4.50	1	1	0	0	0	4.0	4	2	2	2
Joe Horlen	0	1	∞	1	0	0	0	0	0.0	0	1	1	0
Catfish Hunter	0	0	1.17	2	2	0	0	0	15.1	10	2	5	9
Bob Locker	0	0	13.50	2	0	0	0	0	2.0	4	3	0	1
Blue Moon Odom	2	0	0.00	2	2	1	0	1	14.0	5	0	2	5
TOTAL	3	2	1.76	16	5	1	1	1	46.0	32	9	13	25

DET (E)

PLAYER/POS	AVG	G	AB	R	H	2B	3B	HR	RB	BB	SO	SB
Ed Brinkman, ss	.250	1	4	0	1	1	0	0	0	0	0	0
Ike Brown, 1b	.500	1	2	0	1	0	0	0	2	0	1	0
Gates Brown, ph	.000	3	2	1	0	0	0	0	0	1	0	0
Norm Cash, 1b	.267	5	15	1	4	0	0	1	2	2	3	0
Joe Coleman, p	.500	1	2	0	1	0	0	0	0	1	0	0
Bill Freehan, c	.250	3	12	2	3	1	0	1	3	0	1	0
Woody Fryman, p	.000	2	3	0	0	0	0	0	0	0	0	0
Tom Haller, ph	.000	1	1	0	0	0	0	0	0	0	0	0
John Hiller, p	.000	3	0	0	0	0	0	0	0	0	0	0
Willie Horton, of-3	.100	5	10	0	1	0	0	0	0	1	3	0
Al Kaline, of	.263	5	19	3	5	0	0	1	1	2	2	0
John Knox, pr	.000	1	0	0	0	0	0	0	0	0	0	0
Lerrin LaGrow, p	.000	1	0	0	0	0	0	0	0	0	0	0
Mickey Lolich, p	.000	2	7	0	0	0	0	0	0	0	2	0
Dick McAuliffe, ss-4,2b-1	.200	5	20	3	4	0	0	1	1	1	4	0
Joe Niekro, pr	.000	1	0	0	0	0	0	0	0	0	0	0
Jim Northrup, of	.357	5	14	0	5	0	0	0	1	2	3	0
Aurelio Rodriguez, 3b	.000	5	16	0	0	0	0	0	0	2	2	0
Fred Scherman, p	.000	1	0	0	0	0	0	0	0	0	0	0
Chuck Seelbach, p	.000	2	0	0	0	0	0	0	0	0	0	0
Duke Sims, c-2,of-2	.214	4	14	0	3	2	1	0	0	1	2	0
Mickey Stanley, of-3	.333	4	6	0	2	0	0	0	0	0	0	0
Tony Taylor, 2b	.133	4	15	0	2	2	0	0	0	0	2	0
Chris Zachary, p	.000	1	0	0	0	0	0	0	0	0	0	0
TOTAL	.198		162	10	32	6	1	4	10	13	25	0

PITCHER	W	L	ERA	G	GS	CG	SV	SHO	IP	H	ER	BB	SO
Joe Coleman	1	0	0.00	1	1	1	0	1	9.0	7	0	3	14
Woody Fryman	0	2	3.65	2	2	0	0	0	12.1	11	5	2	8
John Hiller	1	0	0.00	3	0	0	0	0	3.1	1	0	1	1
Lerrin La Grow	0	0	0.00	1	0	0	0	0	1.0	0	0	0	1
Mickey Lolich	0	1	1.42	2	2	0	0	0	19.0	14	3	5	10
Fred Scherman	0	0	0.00	1	0	0	0	0	0.2	1	0	0	1
Chuck Seelbach	0	0	18.00	2	0	0	0	0	1.0	4	2	0	0
Chris Zachary	0	0	∞	1	0	0	0	0	0.0	0	1	1	0
TOTAL	2	3	2.14	13	5	1	0	1	46.1	38	11	12	35

GAME 1 AT OAK OCT 7

		R	H	E
DET	010 000 000 01	2	6	2
OAK	001 000 000 02	3	10	1

Pitchers: LOLICH, Seelbach (11) vs Hunter, Blue (9), FINGERS (9)
Home Runs: Cash-DET, Kaline-DET
Attendance: 29,536

GAME 2 AT OAK OCT 8

		R	H	E
DET	000 000 000	0	3	1
OAK	100 040 00X	5	8	0

Pitchers: FRYMAN, Zachary (5), Scherman (5), LaGrow (6), Hiller (7) vs ODOM
Attendance: 31,088

GAME 3 AT DET OCT 10

		R	H	E
OAK	000 000 000	0	7	0
DET	000 200 01X	3	8	1

Pitchers: HOLTZMAN, Fingers (5), Blue (6), Locker (7) vs COLEMAN
Home Runs: Freehan-DET
Attendance: 41,156

GAME 4 AT DET OCT 11

		R	H	E
OAK	000 000 100 2	3	9	2
DET	001 000 000 3	4	10	1

Pitchers: Hunter, Fingers (8), Blue (9), Locker (10), HORLEN (10), Hamilton (10) vs Lolich, Seelbach (10), HILLER (10)
Home Runs: McAuliffe-DET, Epstein-OAK
Attendance: 37,615

GAME 5 AT DET OCT 12

		R	H	E
OAK	010 100 000	2	4	0
DET	100 000 000	1	5	2

Pitchers: ODOM, Blue (6) vs FRYMAN, Hiller (9)
Attendance: 50,276

Oakland slugger Reggie Jackson missed the Series with a pulled hamstring, but Gene Tenace (the A's backup catcher during the season) took up the slack, hitting four of the club's five homers and driving in nine of their 16 runs.

Six of the seven games were decided by a single run. Oakland won the first two in Cincinnati, 3–2, and 2–1. Tenace made the difference in the opener, driving in all the A's runs with a two-run homer in the second inning and a solo shot in the fifth. In the second game, A's starting pitcher Catfish Hunter singled in a run in the second inning which proved the margin of his victory. His 8⅔-inning performance was the longest mound outing in a Series which saw the two clubs together use nearly seven pitchers per game.

Cincinnati took the first game in Oakland, 1–0. Blue Moon Odom held the Reds to one hit through six innings before giving up the game's only run on two singles and a sacrifice in the seventh. Cincinnati's Jack Billingham, too, yielded only three hits in eight-plus innings before yielding to ace reliever Clay Carroll, who retired the side in the ninth.

Game 4 went to Oakland, 3–2. Tenace opened the scoring with a solo homer in the fifth. The Reds' Bobby Tolan doubled in a pair in the eighth to put Cincinnati ahead, but in the last of the ninth four successive A's singles scored two runs, with Tenace scoring the game winner on pinch hitter Angel Mangual's hit. Tenace homered again in Game 5 for three runs, but it wasn't enough as the Reds tied the score in the eighth and won on Pete Rose's RBI single in the ninth.

The Reds produced the Series' only blowout with five runs in the seventh inning of Game 6 to make the score, 8–1. The finale saw Tenace drive in a run in the top of the first for a narrow Oakland lead which held until the Reds tied the game in the fifth. In the sixth the A's scored twice—Tenace doubling in the go-ahead run. Cincinnati scored once more in the eighth as a runner inherited by A's reliever Rollie Fingers came home on a sacrifice fly. But Fingers permitted no other runs to score, and the A's took the crown with their fourth one-run victory.

Oakland Athletics (AL), 4; Cincinnati Reds (NL), 3

OAK (A)

PLAYER/POS	AVG	G	AB	R	H	2B	3B	HR	RB	BB	SO	SB
Matty Alou, of	.042	7	24	0	1	0	0	0	0	3	0	1
Sal Bando, 3b	.269	7	26	2	7	1	0	0	1	2	5	0
Vida Blue, p	.000	4	1	0	0	0	0	0	0	2	1	0
Bert Campaneris, ss	.179	7	28	1	5	0	0	0	0	1	4	0
Dave Duncan, c-1	.200	3	5	0	1	0	0	0	0	1	3	0
Mike Epstein, 1b	.000	6	16	1	0	0	0	0	0	5	3	0
Rollie Fingers, p	.000	6	1	0	0	0	0	0	0	0	0	0
Dick Green, 2b	.333	7	18	0	6	2	0	0	1	0	4	0
Dave Hamilton, p	.000	2	0	0	0	0	0	0	0	0	0	0
Mike Hegan, 1b-5	.200	6	5	0	1	0	0	0	0	0	2	0
George Hendrick, of	.133	5	15	3	2	0	0	0	0	1	2	0
Ken Holtzman, p	.000	3	5	0	0	0	0	0	0	0	0	0
Joe Horlen, p	.000	1	0	0	0	0	0	0	0	0	0	0
Catfish Hunter, p	.200	3	5	0	1	0	0	0	1	2	1	0
Ted Kubiak, 2b	.333	4	3	0	1	0	0	0	0	0	0	0
Allan Lewis, pr	.000	6	0	2	0	0	0	0	0	0	0	0
Bob Locker, p	.000	1	0	0	0	0	0	0	0	0	0	0
Angel Mangual, of-2	.300	4	10	1	3	0	0	0	1	0	0	0
Gonzalo Marquez, ph	.600	5	5	0	3	0	0	0	1	0	0	0
Don Mincher, ph	1.000	3	1	0	1	0	0	0	1	0	0	0
Blue Moon Odom, p-2	.000	4	4	0	0	0	0	0	0	0	3	0
Joe Rudi, of	.240	7	25	1	6	0	0	1	1	2	5	0
Gene Tenace, c-6,1b-1	.348	7	23	5	8	1	0	4	9	2	4	0
TOTAL	.209		220	16	46	4	0	5	16	21	37	1

PITCHER	W	L	ERA	G	GS	CG	SV	SHO	IP	H	ER	BB	SO
Vida Blue	0	1	4.15	4	1	0	1	0	8.2	8	4	5	5
Rollie Fingers	1	1	1.74	6	0	0	2	0	10.1	4	2	4	11
Dave Hamilton	0	0	27.00	2	0	0	0	0	1.1	3	4	1	1
Ken Holtzman	1	0	2.13	3	2	0	0	0	12.2	11	3	3	4
Joe Horlen	0	0	6.75	1	0	0	0	0	1.1	2	1	2	1
Catfish Hunter	2	0	2.81	3	2	0	0	0	16.0	12	5	6	11
Bob Locker	0	0	0.00	1	0	0	0	0	0.1	1	0	0	0
Blue Moon Odom	0	1	1.59	2	2	0	0	0	11.1	5	2	6	13
TOTAL	4	3	3.05	22	7	0	3	0	62.0	46	21	27	46

CIN (N)

PLAYER/POS	AVG	G	AB	R	H	2B	3B	HR	RB	BB	SO	SB
Johnny Bench, c	.261	7	23	4	6	1	0	1	1	5	5	2
Jack Billingham, p	.000	3	5	0	0	0	0	0	0	0	4	0
Pedro Borbon, p	.000	6	0	0	0	0	0	0	0	0	0	0
Clay Carroll, p	.000	5	0	0	0	0	0	0	0	0	0	0
Darrel Chaney, ss-3	.000	4	7	0	0	0	0	0	0	2	2	0
Dave Concepcion, ss-5	.308	6	13	2	4	0	1	0	2	2	2	1
George Foster, of-1	.000	2	0	0	0	0	0	0	0	0	0	0
Cesar Geronimo, of	.158	7	19	1	3	0	0	0	3	1	4	1
Ross Grimsley, p	.000	4	2	0	0	0	0	0	0	0	2	0
Don Gullett, p	.000	1	2	0	0	0	0	0	0	0	0	0
Joe Hague, of-1	.000	3	3	0	0	0	0	0	0	0	0	0
Tom Hall, p	.000	4	2	0	0	0	0	0	0	0	1	0
Julian Javier, ph	.000	4	2	0	0	0	0	0	0	0	0	0
Jim McGlothlin, p	.000	1	1	0	0	0	0	0	0	0	0	0
Hal McRae, of-2	.444	5	9	1	4	1	0	0	2	0	1	0
Denis Menke, 3b	.083	7	24	1	2	0	0	1	2	2	6	0
Joe Morgan, 2b	.125	7	24	4	3	2	0	0	1	6	3	2
Gary Nolan, p	.000	2	3	0	0	0	0	0	0	0	3	0
Tony Perez, 1b	.435	7	23	3	10	2	0	0	2	4	4	0
Pete Rose, of	.214	7	28	3	6	0	0	1	2	4	4	1
Bobby Tolan, of	.269	7	26	2	7	1	0	0	6	1	4	5
Ted Uhlaender, ph	.250	4	4	0	1	1	0	0	0	0	1	0
TOTAL	.209		220	21	46	8	1	3	21	27	46	12

PITCHER	W	L	ERA	G	GS	CG	SV	SHO	IP	H	ER	BB	SO
Jack Billingham	1	0	0.00	3	2	0	1	0	13.2	6	0	4	11
Pedro Borbon	0	1	3.86	6	0	0	0	0	7.0	7	3	2	4
Clay Carroll	0	1	1.59	5	0	0	1	0	5.2	6	1	4	3
Ross Grimsley	2	1	2.57	4	1	0	0	0	7.0	7	2	3	2
Don Gullett	0	0	1.29	1	1	0	0	0	7.0	5	1	2	4
Tom Hall	0	0	0.00	4	0	0	1	0	8.1	6	0	2	7
Jim McGlothlin	0	0	12.00	1	1	0	0	0	3.0	2	4	2	3
Gary Nolan	0	1	3.38	2	2	0	0	0	10.2	7	4	2	3
TOTAL	3	4	2.17	26	7	0	3	0	62.1	46	15	21	37

GAME 1 AT CIN OCT 14

OAK	020	010	000	3	4	0
CIN	010	100	000	2	7	0

Pitchers: HOLTZMAN, Fingers (6), Blue (7) vs NOLAN, Borbon (7), Carroll (8)
Home Runs: Tenace-OAK (2)
Attendance: 52,918

GAME 2 AT CIN OCT 15

OAK	011	000	000	2	9	2
CIN	000	000	001	1	6	0

Pitchers: HUNTER, Fingers (9) vs GRIMSLEY, Borbon (6), Hall (8)
Home Runs: Rudi-OAK
Attendance: 53,224

GAME 3 AT OAK OCT 18

CIN	000	000	100	1	4	2
OAK	000	000	000	0	3	2

Pitchers: BILLINGHAM, Carroll (9) vs ODOM, Blue (8), Fingers (8)
Attendance: 49,410

GAME 4 AT OAK OCT 19

CIN	000	000	020	2	7	1
OAK	000	010	002	3	10	1

Pitchers: Gullett, Borbon (8), CARROLL (9) vs Holtzman, Blue (8), FINGERS (9)
Home Runs: Tenace-OAK
Attendance: 49,410

GAME 5 AT OAK OCT 20

CIN	100	110	011	5	8	0
OAK	030	100	000	4	7	2

Pitchers: McGlothlin, Borbon (4), Hall (5), Carroll (7), GRIMSLEY (8), Billingham (9) vs Hunter, FINGERS (5), Hamilton (9)
Home Runs: Rose-CIN, Tenace-OAK, Menke-CIN
Attendance: 49,410

GAME 6 AT CIN OCT 21

OAK	000	010	000	1	7	1
CIN	000	111	50X	8	10	0

Pitchers: BLUE, Locker (6), Hamilton (7), Horlen (7) vs Nolan, GRIMSLEY (5), Borbon (6), Hall (7)
Home Runs: Bench-CIN
Attendance: 52,737

GAME 7 AT CIN OCT 22

OAK	100	002	000	3	6	1
CIN	000	010	010	2	4	2

Pitchers: Odom, HUNTER (5), Holtzman (8), Fingers (8) vs Billingham, BORBON (6), Carroll (6), Grimsley (7), Hall (8)
Attendance: 56,040

The Mets received strong pitching throughout the series, and their offense came through just often enough to defeat Cincinnati in five games.

Though three Reds pitchers held New York to three hits in Game 1, the single Mets run in the second seemed for a time enough for a win. But Tom Seaver gave up a home run to Pete Rose in the eighth and lost the game in the ninth when Johnny Bench homered. Not wanting another last-inning loss in Game 2, the Mets unloaded for four runs in the top of the ninth to add to their one in the fourth. But this time one would have been enough as Jon Matlack blanked the Reds on two hits.

The Mets made it easy for Jerry Koosman in Game 3 in New York, scoring nine times in the first four innings. Things were more difficult for shortstop Bud Harrelson, who exchanged blows with Pete Rose following Rose's hard slide in the fifth inning. A bench-clearing melee ensued, and fans in the left field stands showered Rose with debris until a delegation of Tom Seaver, Willie Mays, and Rusty Staub visited the area to calm nerves and eliminate the threat of a forfeit. In Game 4, though, Mets bats were stifled once again as four Reds pitchers combined for a 12-inning three-hitter. The Reds won the game and tied the series on Rose's sweetly vengeful 12th-inning homer.

In the finale the Mets took a quick two-run lead. Cincinnati tied the game in the top of the fifth, but New York retaliated with four more in the bottom of the inning. Seaver—and Tug McGraw in the ninth—held the Reds scoreless the rest of the way.

New York Mets (East), 3; Cincinnati Reds (West), 2

NY (E)

PLAYER/POS	AVG	G	AB	R	H	2B	3B	HR	RB	BB	SO	SB
Ken Boswell, ph	.000	1	1	0	0	0	0	0	0	0	0	0
Wayne Garrett, 3b	.087	5	23	1	2	1	0	0	1	0	5	0
Jerry Grote, c	.211	5	19	2	4	0	0	0	2	1	3	0
Don Hahn, of	.235	5	17	2	4	0	0	0	1	2	4	0
Bud Harrelson, ss	.167	5	18	1	3	0	0	0	2	1	1	0
Cleon Jones, of	.300	5	20	3	6	2	0	0	3	2	4	0
Jerry Koosman, p	.500	1	4	1	2	0	0	0	1	0	0	0
Ed Kranepool, of	.500	1	2	0	1	0	0	0	2	0	0	0
Jon Matlack, p	.000	1	2	0	0	0	0	0	0	1	2	0
Willie Mays, of	.333	1	3	1	1	0	0	0	1	0	0	0
Tug McGraw, p	.000	2	1	0	0	0	0	0	0	0	1	0
Felix Millan, 2b	.316	5	19	5	6	0	0	0	2	2	1	0
John Milner, 1b	.176	5	17	2	3	0	0	0	1	5	3	0
Harry Parker, p	.000	1	0	0	0	0	0	0	0	0	0	0
Tom Seaver, p	.333	2	6	1	2	2	0	0	1	1	1	0
Rusty Staub, of	.200	4	15	4	3	0	0	3	5	3	2	0
George Stone, p	.000	1	1	0	0	0	0	0	0	1	1	0
TOTAL	.220		168	23	37	5	0	3	22	19	28	0

PITCHER	W	L	ERA	G	GS	CG	SV	SHO	IP	H	ER	BB	SO
Jerry Koosman	1	0	2.00	1	1	1	0	0	9.0	8	2	0	9
Jon Matlack	1	0	0.00	1	1	1	0	1	9.0	2	0	3	9
Tug McGraw	0	0	0.00	2	0	0	1	0	5.0	4	0	3	3
Harry Parker	0	1	9.00	1	0	0	0	0	1.0	1	1	0	0
Tom Seaver	1	1	1.62	2	2	1	0	0	16.2	13	3	5	17
George Stone	0	0	1.35	1	1	0	0	0	6.2	3	1	2	4
TOTAL	3	2	1.33	8	5	3	1	1	47.1	31	7	13	42

CIN (W)

PLAYER/POS	AVG	G	AB	R	H	2B	3B	HR	RB	BB	SO	SB
Ed Armbrister, of-1	.167	3	6	0	1	0	0	0	0	0	5	0
Johnny Bench, c	.263	5	19	1	5	2	0	1	1	2	3	0
Jack Billingham, p	.000	2	3	0	0	0	0	0	0	0	1	0
Pedro Borbon, p	.000	4	0	0	0	0	0	0	0	0	0	0
Clay Carroll, p	.000	3	0	0	0	0	0	0	0	0	0	0
Darrel Chaney, ph	.000	5	9	0	0	0	0	0	0	3	4	0
Ed Crosby, ss-2	.500	3	2	0	1	0	0	0	0	0	1	0
Dan Driessen, 3b	.167	4	12	0	2	1	0	0	1	0	2	0
Phil Gagliano, ph	.000	3	3	0	0	0	0	0	0	0	1	0
Cesar Geronimo, of	.067	4	15	0	1	0	0	0	0	0	7	0
Ken Griffey, of-2	.143	3	7	0	1	1	0	0	0	0	1	0
Ross Grimsley, p	.000	2	0	0	0	0	0	0	0	0	0	0
Don Gullett, p	.000	3	1	0	0	0	0	0	0	0	0	0
Tom Hall, p	.000	3	0	0	0	0	0	0	0	0	0	0
Hal King, ph	.500	3	2	0	1	0	0	0	0	1	1	0
Andy Kosco, of	.300	3	10	0	3	0	0	0	0	2	3	0
Denis Menke, ss-2,3b-2	.222	3	9	1	2	0	0	1	1	1	2	0
Joe Morgan, 2b	.100	5	20	1	2	1	0	0	1	2	2	0
Roger Nelson, p	.000	1	1	0	0	0	0	0	0	0	1	0
Fred Norman, p	.000	1	1	0	0	0	0	0	0	0	1	0
Tony Perez, 1b	.091	5	22	1	2	0	0	1	2	0	4	0
Pete Rose, of	.381	5	21	3	8	1	0	2	2	2	2	0
Larry Stahl, ph	.500	4	4	1	2	0	0	0	0	0	1	0
Dave Tomlin, p	.000	1	0	0	0	0	0	0	0	0	0	0
TOTAL	.186		167	8	31	6	0	5	8	13	42	0

PITCHER	W	L	ERA	G	GS	CG	SV	SHO	IP	H	ER	BB	SO
Jack Billingham	0	1	4.50	2	2	0	0	0	12.0	9	6	4	9
Pedro Borbon	1	0	0.00	4	0	0	1	0	4.2	3	0	0	3
Clay Carroll	1	0	1.29	3	0	0	0	0	7.0	5	1	1	2
Ross Grimsley	0	1	12.27	2	1	0	0	0	3.2	7	5	2	3
Don Gullett	0	1	2.00	3	1	0	0	0	9.0	4	2	3	6
Tom Hall	0	0	67.50	3	0	0	0	0	0.2	3	5	4	1
Roger Nelson	0	0	0.00	1	0	0	0	0	2.1	0	0	1	0
Fred Norman	0	0	1.80	1	1	0	0	0	5.0	1	1	3	3
Dave Tomlin	0	0	16.20	1	0	0	0	0	1.2	5	3	1	1
TOTAL	2	3	4.50	20	5	0	1	0	46.0	37	23	19	28

GAME 1 AT CIN OCT 6

NY	010	000	000	1	3	0
CIN	000	000	011	2	6	0

Pitchers: SEAVER vs Billingham, Hall (9), BORBON (9)
Home Runs: Rose-CIN, Bench-CIN
Attendance: 53,431

GAME 2 AT CIN OCT 7

NY	000	100	004	5	7	0
CIN	000	000	000	0	2	0

Pitchers: MATLACK vs GULLETT, Carroll (6), Hall (9), Borbon (9)
Home Runs: Staub-NY
Attendance: 54,041

GAME 3 AT NY OCT 8

CIN	002	000	000	2	8	1
NY	151	200	00X	9	11	1

Pitchers: GRIMSLEY, Hall (2), Tomlin (3), Nelson (4), Borbon (7) vs KOOSMAN
Home Runs: Staub-NY (2), Menke-CIN
Attendance: 53,967

GAME 4 AT NY OCT 9

CIN	000	000	100	001	2	8	0
NY	001	000	000	000	1	3	2

Pitchers: Norman, Gullett (6), CARROLL (10), Borbon (12) vs Stone, McGraw (7), PARKER (12)
Home Runs: Perez-CIN, Rose-CIN
Attendance: 50,786

GAME 5 AT NY OCT 10

CIN	001	010	000	2	7	1
NY	200	041	00X	7	13	1

Pitchers: BILLINGHAM, Gullett (5), Carroll (5), Grimsley (7) vs SEAVER, McGraw (9)
Attendance: 50,323

The Orioles finally met their match in an ALCS as Oakland took its second consecutive pennant. Baltimore started strong, chasing A's starter Vida Blue with four runs in the first inning as Jim Palmer—pitching the series opener for a change—blanked the A's on five hits. But Oakland snapped back in Game 2, with five of their six runs coming on homers by Sal Bando (two, for three runs), Joe Rudi, and Bert Campaneris.

Oriole Mike Cuellar and the A's Ken Holtzman cut down opposing batters for 10½ innings in Game 3 before Oakland's Campaneris broke the 1–1 tie in the bottom of the 11th with a leadoff home run. The next day Palmer was driven out in the second inning by three Oakland runs, and the A's added to their lead with another run in the sixth. But Andy Etchebarren led a four-run Orioles comeback in the seventh with a three-run homer, and Bobby Grich's solo shot in the next inning gave the Orioles the margin they needed to win the game and tie the series.

The A's took it all in the finale, though, needing only one of their three runs as Catfish Hunter stopped Baltimore cold on five scattered hits.

Oakland A's (West), 3; Baltimore Orioles (East), 2

OAK (W)

PLAYER/POS	AVG	G	AB	R	H	2B	3B	HR	RB	BB	SO	SB
Jesus Alou, dh-1	.333	4	6	0	2	0	0	0	1	0	1	0
Mike Andrews, 1b-1,dh-1	.000	2	1	0	0	0	0	0	0	0	0	0
Sal Bando, 3b	.167	5	18	2	3	0	0	2	3	3	6	0
Vida Blue, p	.000	2	0	0	0	0	0	0	0	0	0	0
Pat Bourque, dh	.000	2	1	0	0	0	0	0	0	2	1	0
Bert Campaneris, ss	.333	5	21	3	7	1	0	2	3	2	2	3
Billy Conigliaro, of	.000	1	4	0	0	0	0	0	0	0	2	0
Vic Davalillo, 1b-2,of-2	.625	4	8	2	5	1	1	0	1	1	0	0
Rollie Fingers, p	.000	3	0	0	0	0	0	0	0	0	0	0
Ray Fosse, c	.091	5	11	2	1	1	0	0	3	2	2	0
Dick Green, 2b	.077	5	13	0	1	1	0	0	1	0	4	0
Ken Holtzman, p	.000	1	0	0	0	0	0	0	0	0	0	0
Catfish Hunter, p	.000	2	0	0	0	0	0	0	0	0	0	0
Reggie Jackson, of	.143	5	21	0	3	0	0	0	0	0	6	0
Deron Johnson, dh	.100	4	10	0	1	0	0	0	0	2	6	0
Ted Kubiak, 2b	.000	3	2	0	0	0	0	0	0	0	1	0
Allan Lewis, pr	.000	2	0	1	0	0	0	0	0	0	0	0
Angel Mangual, of	.111	3	9	1	1	0	0	0	0	0	3	0
Blue Moon Odom, p	.000	1	0	0	0	0	0	0	0	0	0	0
Horacio Pina, p	.000	1	0	0	0	0	0	0	0	0	0	0
Joe Rudi, of	.222	5	18	1	4	0	0	1	3	3	1	0
Gene Tenace, 1b-5,c-3	.235	5	17	3	4	1	0	0	0	2	4	0
TOTAL	.200		160	15	32	5	1	5	15	17	39	3

PITCHER	W	L	ERA	G	GS	CG	SV	SHO	IP	H	ER	BB	SO
Vida Blue	0	1	10.29	2	2	0	0	0	7.0	8	8	5	3
Rollie Fingers	0	1	1.93	3	0	0	1	0	4.2	4	1	2	4
Ken Holtzman	1	0	0.82	1	1	1	0	0	11.0	3	1	1	7
Catfish Hunter	2	0	1.65	2	2	1	0	1	16.1	12	3	5	6
Blue Moon Odom	0	0	1.80	1	0	0	0	0	5.0	6	1	2	4
Horacio Pina	0	0	0.00	1	0	0	0	0	2.0	3	0	1	1
TOTAL	3	2	2.74	10	5	2	1	1	46.0	36	14	16	25

BAL (E)

PLAYER/POS	AVG	G	AB	R	H	2B	3B	HR	RB	BB	SO	SB
Doyle Alexander, p	.000	1	0	0	0	0	0	0	0	0	0	0
Frank Baker, ss	.000	2	0	0	0	0	0	0	0	0	0	0
Don Baylor, of-3	.273	4	11	3	3	0	0	0	1	3	5	0
Mark Belanger, ss	.125	5	16	0	2	0	0	0	1	1	1	0
Paul Blair, of	.167	5	18	2	3	0	0	0	0	1	5	0
Larry Brown, 3b	.000	1	0	0	0	0	0	0	0	0	0	0
Al Bumbry, of	.000	2	7	1	0	0	0	0	0	2	2	1
Rich Coggins, of	.444	2	9	1	4	1	0	0	0	0	0	0
Terry Crowley, of-1	.000	2	2	0	0	0	0	0	0	0	0	0
Mike Cuellar, p	.000	1	0	0	0	0	0	0	0	0	0	0
Tommy Davis, dh	.286	5	21	1	6	1	0	0	2	1	0	0
Andy Etchebarren, c	.357	4	14	1	5	1	0	1	4	0	1	0
Bobby Grich, 2b	.100	5	20	1	2	0	0	1	1	2	5	0
Don Hood, pr	.000	1	0	0	0	0	0	0	0	0	0	0
Grant Jackson, p	.000	2	0	0	0	0	0	0	0	0	0	0
Dave McNally, p	.000	1	0	0	0	0	0	0	0	0	0	0
Jim Palmer, p	.000	3	0	0	0	0	0	0	0	0	0	0
Boog Powell, 1b	.000	1	4	1	0	0	0	0	0	0	1	0
Merv Rettenmund, of	.091	3	11	1	1	0	0	0	0	3	2	0
Bob Reynolds, p	.000	2	0	0	0	0	0	0	0	0	0	0
Brooks Robinson, 3b	.250	5	20	1	5	2	0	0	2	1	1	0
Eddie Watt, p	.000	1	0	0	0	0	0	0	0	0	0	0
Earl Williams, 1b-4,c-1	.278	5	18	2	5	2	0	1	4	2	2	0
TOTAL	.211		171	15	36	7	0	3	15	16	25	1

PITCHER	W	L	ERA	G	GS	CG	SV	SHO	IP	H	ER	BB	SO
Doyle Alexander	0	1	4.91	1	1	0	0	0	3.2	5	2	0	1
Mike Cuellar	0	1	1.80	1	1	1	0	0	10.0	4	2	3	11
Grant Jackson	1	0	0.00	2	0	0	0	0	3.0	0	0	1	0
Dave McNally	0	1	5.87	1	1	0	0	0	7.2	7	5	2	7
Jim Palmer	1	0	1.84	3	2	1	0	1	14.2	11	3	8	15
Bob Reynolds	0	0	3.18	2	0	0	0	0	5.2	5	2	3	5
Eddie Watt	0	0	0.00	1	0	0	0	0	0.1	0	0	0	0
TOTAL	2	3	2.80	11	5	2	0	1	45.0	32	14	17	39

GAME 1 AT BAL OCT 6

		R	H	E
OAK	000 000 000	0	5	1
BAL	400 000 11X	6	12	0

Pitchers: BLUE, Pina (1), Odom (3), Fingers (8) vs PALMER
Attendance: 41,279

GAME 2 AT BAL OCT 7

		R	H	E
OAK	100 002 021	6	9	0
BAL	100 001 010	3	8	0

Pitchers: HUNTER, Fingers (8) vs McNALLY, Reynolds (8), G.Jackson (9)
Home Runs: Campaneris-OAK, Rudi-OAK, Bando-OAK (2)
Attendance: 48,425

GAME 3 AT OAK OCT 9

		R	H	E
BAL	010 000 000 00	1	3	0
OAK	000 000 010 01	2	4	3

Pitchers: CUELLAR vs HOLTZMAN
Home Runs: Williams-BAL, Campaneris-OAK
Attendance: 34,367

GAME 4 AT OAK OCT 10

		R	H	E
BAL	000 000 410	5	8	0
OAK	030 001 000	4	7	0

Pitchers: Palmer, Reynolds (2), Watt (7), G.JACKSON (7) vs Blue, FINGERS (7)
Home Runs: Etchebarren-BAL, Grich-BAL
Attendance: 27,497

GAME 5 AT OAK OCT 11

		R	H	E
BAL	000 000 000	0	5	2
OAK	001 200 00X	3	7	0

Pitchers: ALEXANDER, Palmer (4) vs HUNTER
Attendance: 24,265

For the second year in a row, the A's were outpitched and outscored by their Series opposition, and this time they were outhit as well. But again, when the dust of Game 7 had settled, they still wore the crown. A's starter Ken Holtzman, who because of the American League's new designated hitter rule had not batted all season, doubled for the A's first hit in the third inning of Game 1 and scored the first Oakland run on an error. The A's scored again in the inning, enough for the win as Holtzman and two relievers held New York to a single run.

The Mets evened things in a Game 2 that lasted a then-record 4 hours 13 minutes. New York scored four runs with two out in the top of the 12th inning for a lead the A's were not able to overcome. (Three of the runs scored on a pair of errors by second baseman Mike Andrews, prompting a flap that rocked the baseball world as A's owner Charlie Finley tried—unsuccessfully—to "fire" Andrews by declaring him injured.) Final score of the slugfest: 10–7.

In a somewhat more normal third game, the Mets grabbed an early lead on Wayne Garrett's lead-off homer in the bottom of the first and scored a second run on two singles and wild pitch for a 2–0 lead that held up until Oakland tied the game in the eighth. In the 11th, the A's Ted Kubiak worked his way around the bases on a walk, passed ball, and single for a lead that reliever Rollie Fingers held in the bottom of the inning.

New York evened the Series on Rusty Staub's three-run homer in the first inning of Game 4 (scoring three more times later for a 6–1 win). The Mets moved in front on a sparkling 2–0 three-hitter by Jerry Koosman and Tug McGraw in Game 5, but lost their edge as the Series returned to Oakland for Game 6, losing when Reggie Jackson's doubles in the first and third drove in two runs to give the A's a lead New York was unable to overtake.

Oakland made the finale look easy. Bert Campaneris and Jackson both hit two-run homers in the third inning, and Campaneris scored a fifth run two innings later before New York finally got on the board in the sixth. In the ninth inning the Mets scored a second run with two outs, but reliever Darold Knowles came on for a record seventh pitching appearance and retired the final batter for his second Series save.

Oakland Athletics (AL), 4; New York Mets (NL), 3

OAK (A)

PLAYER/POS	AVG	G	AB	R	H	2B	3B	HR	RB	BB	SO	SB
Jesus Alou, of-6	.158	7	19	0	3	1	0	0	3	0	0	0
Mike Andrews, 2b-1	.000	2	3	0	0	0	0	0	0	1	1	0
Sal Bando, 3b	.231	7	26	5	6	1	1	0	1	4	7	0
Vida Blue, p	.000	2	4	0	0	0	0	0	0	0	4	0
Pat Bourque, 1b	.500	2	2	0	1	0	0	0	0	0	0	0
Bert Campaneris, ss	.290	7	31	6	9	0	1	1	3	1	7	3
Billy Conigliaro, ph	.000	3	3	0	0	0	0	0	0	0	1	0
Vic Davalillo, of-4,1b-1	.091	6	11	0	1	0	0	0	0	2	1	0
Rollie Fingers, p	.333	6	3	0	1	0	0	0	0	0	1	0
Ray Fosse, c	.158	7	19	0	3	1	0	0	0	1	4	0
Dick Green, 2b	.063	7	16	0	1	0	0	0	0	1	6	0
Ken Holtzman, p	.667	3	3	2	2	2	0	0	0	0	0	0
Catfish Hunter, p	.000	2	5	0	0	0	0	0	0	0	3	0
Reggie Jackson, of	.310	7	29	3	9	3	1	1	6	2	7	0
Deron Johnson, 1b-2	.300	6	10	0	3	1	0	0	0	1	4	0
Darold Knowles, p	.000	7	0	0	0	0	0	0	0	0	0	0
Ted Kubiak, 2b	.000	4	3	1	0	0	0	0	0	1	1	0
Allan Lewis, pr	.000	3	0	1	0	0	0	0	0	0	0	0
Paul Lindblad, p	.000	3	1	0	0	0	0	0	0	0	0	0
Angel Mangual, of-1	.000	5	6	0	0	0	0	0	0	0	3	0
Blue Moon Odom, p-2	.000	3	1	0	0	0	0	0	0	0	1	0
Horacio Pina, p	.000	2	0	0	0	0	0	0	0	0	0	0
Joe Rudi, of	.333	7	27	3	9	2	0	0	4	3	4	0
Gene Tenace, 1b-7,c-3	.158	7	19	0	3	1	0	0	3	11	7	0
TOTAL	.212		241	21	51	12	3	2	20	28	62	3

PITCHER	W	L	ERA	G	GS	CG	SV	SHO	IP	H	ER	BB	SO
Vida Blue	0	1	4.91	2	2	0	0	0	11.0	10	6	3	8
Rollie Fingers	0	1	0.66	6	0	0	2	0	13.2	13	1	4	8
Ken Holtzman	2	1	4.22	3	3	0	0	0	10.2	13	5	5	6
Catfish Hunter	1	0	2.03	2	2	0	0	0	13.1	11	3	4	6
Darold Knowles	0	0	0.00	7	0	0	2	0	6.1	4	0	5	5
Paul Lindblad	1	0	0.00	3	0	0	0	0	3.1	4	0	1	1
Blue Moon Odom	0	0	3.86	2	0	0	0	0	4.2	5	2	2	2
Horacio Pina	0	0	0.00	2	0	0	0	0	3.0	6	0	2	0
TOTAL	4	3	2.32	27	7	0	4	0	66.0	66	17	26	36

NY (N)

PLAYER/POS	AVG	G	AB	R	H	2B	3B	HR	RB	BB	SO	SB
Jim Beauchamp, ph	.000	4	4	0	0	0	0	0	0	0	1	0
Ken Boswell, ph	1.000	3	3	1	3	0	0	0	0	0	0	0
Wayne Garrett, 3b	.167	7	30	4	5	0	0	2	2	5	11	0
Jerry Grote, c	.267	7	30	2	8	0	0	0	0	0	1	0
Don Hahn, of	.241	7	29	2	7	1	1	0	2	1	6	0
Bud Harrelson, ss	.250	7	24	2	6	1	0	0	1	5	3	0
Ron Hodges, ph	.000	1	0	0	0	0	0	0	0	1	0	0
Cleon Jones, of	.286	7	28	5	8	2	0	1	1	4	2	0
Jerry Koosman, p	.000	2	4	0	0	0	0	0	0	0	3	0
Ed Kranepool, ph	.000	4	3	0	0	0	0	0	0	0	0	0
Ted Martinez, pr	.000	2	0	0	0	0	0	0	0	0	0	0
Jon Matlack, p	.250	3	4	0	1	0	0	0	0	2	1	0
Willie Mays, of-2	.286	3	7	1	2	0	0	0	1	0	1	0
Tug McGraw, p	.333	5	3	1	1	0	0	0	0	0	1	0
Felix Millan, 2b	.188	7	32	3	6	1	1	0	1	1	1	0
John Milner, 1b	.296	7	27	2	8	0	0	0	2	5	1	0
Harry Parker, p	.000	3	0	0	0	0	0	0	0	0	0	0
Ray Sadecki, p	.000	4	0	0	0	0	0	0	0	0	0	0
Tom Seaver, p	.000	2	5	0	0	0	0	0	0	0	2	0
Rusty Staub, of	.423	7	26	1	11	2	0	1	6	2	2	0
George Stone, p	.000	2	0	0	0	0	0	0	0	0	0	0
George Theodore, of-1	.000	2	2	0	0	0	0	0	0	0	0	0
TOTAL	.253		261	24	66	7	2	4	16	26	36	0

PITCHER	W	L	ERA	G	GS	CG	SV	SHO	IP	H	ER	BB	SO
Jerry Koosman	1	0	3.12	2	2	0	0	0	8.2	9	3	7	8
Jon Matlack	1	2	2.16	3	3	0	0	0	16.2	10	4	5	11
Tug McGraw	1	0	2.63	5	0	0	1	0	13.2	8	4	9	14
Harry Parker	0	1	0.00	3	0	0	0	0	3.1	2	0	2	2
Ray Sadecki	0	0	1.93	4	0	0	1	0	4.2	5	1	1	6
Tom Seaver	0	1	2.40	2	2	0	0	0	15.0	13	4	3	18
George Stone	0	0	0.00	2	0	0	1	0	3.0	4	0	1	3
TOTAL	3	4	2.22	21	7	0	3	0	65.0	51	16	28	62

GAME 1 AT OAK OCT 13

NY	000	100	000	1	7	2
OAK	002	000	00X	2	4	0

Pitchers: MATLACK, McGraw (7) vs HOLTZMAN, Fingers (6), Knowles (9)
Attendance: 46,021

GAME 2 AT OAK OCT 14

NY	011	004	000	004	10	15	1
OAK	210	000	102	001	7	13	5

Pitchers: Koosman, Sadecki (3), Parker (5), McGRAW (6), Stone (12) vs Blue, Pina (6), Knowles (6), Odom (8), FINGERS (10), Lindblad (12)
Home Runs: Jones-NY, Garrett-NY
Attendance: 49,151

GAME 3 AT NY OCT 16

OAK	000	001	010	01	3	10	1
NY	200	000	000	00	2	10	2

Pitchers: Hunter, Knowles (7), LINDBLAD (9), Fingers (11) vs Seaver, Sadecki (9), McGraw (9), PARKER (11)
Home Runs: Garrett-NY
Attendance: 54,817

GAME 4 AT NY OCT 17

OAK	000	100	000	1	5	1
NY	300	300	00X	6	13	1

Pitchers: HOLTZMAN, Odom (1), Knowles (4), Pina (5), Lindblad (8) vs MATLACK, Sadecki (9)
Home Runs: Staub-NY
Attendance: 54,817

GAME 5 AT NY OCT 18

OAK	000	000	000	0	3	1
NY	010	001	00X	2	7	1

Pitchers: BLUE, Knowles (6), Fingers (7) vs KOOSMAN, McGraw (7)
Attendance: 54,817

GAME 6 AT OAK OCT 20

NY	000	000	010	1	6	2
OAK	101	000	01X	3	7	0

Pitchers: SEAVER, McGraw (8) vs HUNTER, Knowles (8), Fingers (8)
Attendance: 49,333

GAME 7 AT OAK OCT 21

NY	000	001	001	2	8	1
OAK	004	010	00X	5	9	1

Pitchers: MATLACK, Parker (3), Sadecki (5), Stone (7) vs HOLTZMAN, Fingers (6), Knowles (9)
Home Runs: Campaneris-OAK, Jackson-OAK
Attendance: 49,333

Dodgers pitcher Don Sutton—who had brought his won-lost record from 10–9 to 19–9 with a nine-game winning streak in the regular season—continued his winning ways in the NLCS, surrendering only seven hits and one run in 17 innings and taking both the opener and clincher of the four-game series. Los Angeles' Andy Messersmith followed up Sutton's opening-game shutout with six shutout innings of his own in Game 2 before Pittsburgh scored its first two runs of the series in the seventh. They tied the score, but the Dodgers countered with three more in the top of the eighth to assure their second win.

The Pirates captured their only victory in Game 3, as Richie Hebner and Willie Stargell homered for five of the Bucs' seven runs, while Bruce Kison and Ramon Hernandez shut out the Dodgers on four hits.

Pittsburgh finally got to Sutton for a run when Stargell homered in the seventh inning of Game 4. But it was too little, and too late to stem a 12-run attack led by Steve Garvey's four hits (two of them home runs) and four RBIs for the Dodgers.

Los Angeles Dodgers (West), 3; Pittsburgh Pirates (East), 1

LA (W)

PLAYER/POS	AVG	G	AB	R	H	2B	3B	HR	RB	BB	SO	SB
Rick Auerbach, ph	1.000	1	1	0	1	1	0	0	0	0	0	0
Bill Buckner, of	.167	4	18	0	3	1	0	0	0	0	2	0
Ron Cey, 3b	.313	4	16	2	5	3	0	1	1	3	2	0
Willie Crawford, of	.250	2	4	1	1	0	0	0	1	1	1	0
Al Downing, p	.000	1	1	0	0	0	0	0	0	0	0	0
Joe Ferguson, of-3,c-2	.231	4	13	3	3	0	0	0	2	5	1	0
Steve Garvey, 1b	.389	4	18	4	7	1	0	2	5	1	1	0
Charlie Hough, p	.000	1	0	0	0	0	0	0	0	0	0	0
Von Joshua, ph	.000	1	0	0	0	0	0	0	0	1	0	0
Lee Lacy, pr	.000	1	0	0	0	0	0	0	0	0	0	0
Davey Lopes, 2b	.267	4	15	4	4	0	1	0	3	5	1	3
Mike Marshall, p	.000	2	0	0	0	0	0	0	0	0	0	0
Ken McMullen, ph	.000	1	1	0	0	0	0	0	0	0	1	0
Andy Messersmith, p	.000	1	3	0	0	0	0	0	0	0	1	0
Manny Mota, of-1	.333	3	3	0	1	0	0	0	1	0	0	0
Tom Paciorek, of	1.000	1	1	0	1	0	0	0	0	0	0	0
Doug Rau, p	.000	1	0	0	0	0	0	0	0	0	0	0
Bill Russell, ss	.389	4	18	1	7	0	0	0	3	1	0	0
Eddie Solomon, p	.000	1	0	0	0	0	0	0	0	0	0	0
Don Sutton, p	.286	2	7	0	2	0	0	0	1	1	2	0
Jimmy Wynn, of	.200	4	10	4	2	2	0	0	2	9	1	1
Steve Yeager, c	.000	3	9	1	0	0	0	0	0	3	3	1
TOTAL	.268		138	20	37	8	1	3	19	30	16	5

PITCHER	W	L	ERA	G	GS	CG	SV	SHO	IP	H	ER	BB	SO
Al Downing	0	0	0.00	1	0	0	0	0	4.0	1	0	1	0
Charlie Hough	0	0	7.71	1	0	0	0	0	2.1	4	2	0	2
Mike Marshall	0	0	0.00	2	0	0	0	0	3.0	0	0	0	1
Andy Messersmith	1	0	2.57	1	1	0	0	0	7.0	8	2	3	0
Doug Rau	0	1	40.50	1	1	0	0	0	0.2	3	3	1	0
Eddie Solomon	0	0	0.00	1	0	0	0	0	2.0	2	0	1	1
Don Sutton	2	0	0.53	2	2	1	0	1	17.0	7	1	2	13
TOTAL	3	1	2.00	9	4	1	0	1	36.0	25	8	8	17

PIT (E)

PLAYER/POS	AVG	G	AB	R	H	2B	3B	HR	RB	BB	SO	SB
Ken Brett, p	.000	1	1	0	0	0	0	0	0	0	1	0
Gene Clines, of	.000	2	1	1	0	0	0	0	0	0	0	0
Larry Demery, p	.000	2	0	0	0	0	0	0	0	0	0	0
Dave Giusti, p	.000	3	0	0	0	0	0	0	0	0	0	0
Richie Hebner, 3b	.231	4	13	1	3	0	0	1	4	1	4	0
Ramon Hernandez, p	.000	2	1	0	0	0	0	0	0	0	1	0
Art Howe, ph	.000	1	1	0	0	0	0	0	0	0	0	0
Ed Kirkpatrick, 1b	.000	3	9	0	0	0	0	0	0	2	0	0
Bruce Kison, p	.000	1	3	0	0	0	0	0	0	0	2	0
Mario Mendoza, ss	.200	3	5	0	1	0	0	0	1	1	0	0
Al Oliver, of	.143	4	14	1	2	0	0	0	1	2	2	0
Dave Parker, of-2	.125	3	8	0	1	0	0	0	0	0	1	0
Juan Pizarro, p	.000	1	0	0	0	0	0	0	0	0	0	0
Paul Popovich, ss	.600	3	5	1	3	0	0	0	0	0	0	0
Jerry Reuss, p	.000	2	2	0	0	0	0	0	0	0	0	0
Bob Robertson, 1b	.000	1	5	1	0	0	0	0	0	0	0	0
Jim Rooker, p	.500	1	2	0	1	0	0	0	0	0	0	0
Manny Sanguillen, c	.250	4	16	0	4	1	0	0	0	0	0	0
Willie Stargell, of	.400	4	15	3	6	0	0	2	4	1	2	0
Rennie Stennett, 2b	.063	4	16	1	1	0	0	0	0	1	1	0
Frank Taveras, ss	.000	2	2	0	0	0	0	0	0	0	0	1
Richie Zisk, of-2	.300	3	10	1	3	0	0	0	0	0	3	0
TOTAL	.194		129	10	25	1	0	3	10	8	17	1

PITCHER	W	L	ERA	G	GS	CG	SV	SHO	IP	H	ER	BB	SO
Ken Brett	0	0	7.71	1	0	0	0	0	2.1	3	2	2	1
Larry Demery	0	0	36.00	2	0	0	0	0	1.0	3	4	2	0
Dave Giusti	0	1	21.60	3	0	0	0	0	3.1	13	8	5	1
Ramon Hernandez	0	0	0.00	2	0	0	0	0	4.1	3	0	1	2
Bruce Kison	1	0	0.00	1	1	0	0	0	6.2	2	0	6	5
Juan Pizarro	0	0	0.00	1	0	0	0	0	0.2	0	0	1	0
Jerry Reuss	0	2	3.72	2	2	0	0	0	9.2	7	4	8	3
Jim Rooker	0	0	2.57	1	1	0	0	0	7.0	6	2	5	4
TOTAL	1	3	5.14	13	4	0	0	0	35.0	37	20	30	16

GAME 1 AT PIT OCT 5

		R	H	E
LA	010 000 002	3	9	2
PIT	000 000 000	0	4	0

Pitchers: SUTTON vs REUSS, Giusti (8)
Attendance: 40,638

GAME 2 AT PIT OCT 6

		R	H	E
LA	100 100 030	5	12	0
PIT	000 000 200	2	8	3

Pitchers: MESSERSMITH, Marshall (8) vs Rooker, GIUSTI (8), Demery (8), Hernandez (8)
Home Runs: Cey-LA
Attendance: 49,247

GAME 3 AT LA OCT 8

		R	H	E
PIT	502 000 000	7	10	0
LA	000 000 000	0	4	5

Pitchers: KISON, Hernandez (7) vs RAU, Hough (1), Downing (4), Solomon (8)
Home Runs: Stargell-PIT, Hebner-PIT
Attendance: 55,953

GAME 4 AT LA OCT 9

		R	H	E
PIT	000 000 100	1	3	1
LA	102 022 23X	12	12	0

Pitchers: REUSS, Brett (3), Demery (6), Giusti (7), Pizarro (8) vs SUTTON, Marshall (9)
Home Runs: Garvey-LA (2), Stargell-PIT
Attendance: 54,424

Oakland A's (West), 3; Baltimore Orioles (East), 1

After spotting Baltimore a win in the opener, Oakland took the next three games and their third consecutive pennant. Although the A's got nine hits in Game 1—their series high—the Orioles hit harder, burying Oakland under home runs by Paul Blair, Brooks Robinson, and Bobby Grich. In Game 2, though, Ken Holtzman shut out Baltimore on five hits as Sal Bando and Ray Fosse homered. Bando homered again in the third game for the only Oakland run as Jim Palmer limited the A's to four hits. But one run was enough to defeat Baltimore, for Vida Blue shut them out on a masterful two-hitter.

Orioles starter Mike Cuellar walked nine men in 4⅔ innings of Game 4, including four in the fifth to force in Oakland's first run. Two innings later Reggie Jackson's double (the only Oakland hit of the game) off reliever Ross Grimsley drove in Oakland's second run, while starter Catfish Hunter was blanking the O's through seven-plus innings. After failing to score for 30 consecutive innings, the Orioles got to reliever Rollie Fingers for a run with two out in the bottom of the ninth. But Fingers then struck out Don Baylor, and the A's had their pennant.

OAK (W)

PLAYER/POS	AVG	G	AB	R	H	2B	3B	HR	RB	BB	SO	SB
Jesus Alou, ph	1.000	1	1	0	1	0	0	0	0	0	0	0
Sal Bando, 3b	.231	4	13	4	3	0	0	2	2	4	0	0
Vida Blue, p	.000	1	0	0	0	0	0	0	0	0	0	0
Bert Campaneris, ss	.176	4	17	0	3	0	0	0	3	0	3	1
Rollie Fingers, p	.000	2	0	0	0	0	0	0	0	0	0	0
Ray Fosse, c	.333	4	12	1	4	1	0	1	3	1	2	0
Dick Green, 2b	.222	4	9	0	2	0	0	0	0	2	1	0
Jim Holt, 1b-1	.000	2	0	0	0	0	0	0	0	1	0	0
Ken Holtzman, p	.000	1	0	0	0	0	0	0	0	0	0	0
Catfish Hunter, p	.000	2	0	0	0	0	0	0	0	0	0	0
Reggie Jackson, dh-3,of-1	.167	4	12	0	2	1	0	0	1	5	2	0
Angel Mangual, dh	.250	1	4	0	1	0	0	0	0	0	0	0
Dal Maxvill, 2b	.000	1	1	0	0	0	0	0	0	0	1	0
Billy North, of	.063	4	16	3	1	1	0	0	0	2	1	1
Blue Moon Odom, p-1	.000	3	0	0	0	0	0	0	0	0	0	0
Joe Rudi, of	.154	4	13	0	2	0	1	0	1	3	2	0
Gene Tenace, 1b	.000	4	11	1	0	0	0	0	1	4	4	1
Manny Trillo, pr	.000	1	0	1	0	0	0	0	0	0	0	0
Claudell Washington, of-3	.273	4	11	1	3	1	0	0	0	0	0	0
Herb Washington, pr	.000	2	0	0	0	0	0	0	0	0	0	0
TOTAL	.183		120	11	22	4	1	3	11	22	16	3

PITCHER	W	L	ERA	G	GS	CG	SV	SHO	IP	H	ER	BB	SO
Vida Blue	1	0	0.00	1	1	1	0	1	9.0	2	0	0	7
Rollie Fingers	0	0	3.00	2	0	0	1	0	3.0	3	1	1	3
Ken Holtzman	1	0	0.00	1	1	1	0	1	9.0	5	0	2	3
Catfish Hunter	1	1	4.63	2	2	0	0	0	11.2	11	6	2	6
Blue Moon Odom	0	0	0.00	1	0	0	0	0	3.1	1	0	0	1
TOTAL	3	1	1.75	7	4	2	1	2	36.0	22	7	5	20

BAL (E)

PLAYER/POS	AVG	G	AB	R	H	2B	3B	HR	RB	BB	SO	SB
Frank Baker, ss	.000	2	0	0	0	0	0	0	0	0	0	0
Don Baylor, of	.267	4	15	0	4	0	0	0	0	0	2	0
Mark Belanger, ss	.000	4	9	0	0	0	0	0	0	1	3	0
Paul Blair, of	.286	4	14	3	4	0	0	1	2	2	2	0
Al Bumbry, ph	.000	2	1	0	0	0	0	0	0	0	1	0
Enos Cabell, of-1	.250	3	4	0	1	0	0	0	0	0	2	0
Rich Coggins, of	.000	3	11	0	0	0	0	0	0	0	3	0
Mike Cuellar, p	.000	2	0	0	0	0	0	0	0	0	0	0
Tommy Davis, dh	.267	4	15	0	4	0	0	0	1	0	1	0
Andy Etchebarren, c	.333	2	6	0	2	0	0	0	0	0	0	0
Wayne Garland, p	.000	1	0	0	0	0	0	0	0	0	0	0
Bobby Grich, 2b	.250	4	16	2	4	1	0	1	2	0	1	0
Ross Grimsley, p	.000	2	0	0	0	0	0	0	0	0	0	0
Elrod Hendricks, c	.167	3	6	1	1	0	0	0	0	1	3	0
Grant Jackson, p	.000	1	0	0	0	0	0	0	0	0	0	0
Dave McNally, p	.000	1	0	0	0	0	0	0	0	0	0	0
Curt Motton, ph	.000	1	1	0	0	0	0	0	0	0	0	0
Jim Palmer, p-1	.000	2	0	0	0	0	0	0	0	0	0	0
Boog Powell, 1b	.125	2	8	0	1	0	0	0	1	0	0	0
Bob Reynolds, p	.000	1	0	0	0	0	0	0	0	0	0	0
Brooks Robinson, 3b	.083	4	12	1	1	0	0	1	1	1	0	0
Earl Williams, 1b	.000	2	6	0	0	0	0	0	0	0	2	0
TOTAL	.177		124	7	22	1	0	3	7	5	20	0

PITCHER	W	L	ERA	G	GS	CG	SV	SHO	IP	H	ER	BB	SO
Mike Cuellar	1	1	2.84	2	2	0	0	0	12.2	9	4	13	6
Wayne Garland	0	0	0.00	1	0	0	0	0	0.2	1	0	1	0
Ross Grimsley	0	0	1.69	2	0	0	0	0	5.1	1	1	2	2
Grant Jackson	0	0	0.00	1	0	0	0	0	0.1	1	0	0	1
Dave McNally	0	1	1.59	1	1	0	0	0	5.2	6	1	2	2
Jim Palmer	0	1	1.00	1	1	1	0	0	9.0	4	1	1	4
Bob Reynolds	0	0	0.00	1	0	0	0	0	1.1	0	0	3	1
TOTAL	1	3	1.80	9	4	1	0	0	35.0	22	7	22	16

GAME 1 AT OAK OCT 5

				R	H	E
BAL	100	140	000	6	10	0
OAK	001	010	001	3	9	0

Pitchers: CUELLAR, Grimsley (9) vs HUNTER, Odom (5), Fingers (9)
Home Runs: Blair-BAL, Robinson-BAL, Grich-BAL
Attendance: 41,609

GAME 2 AT OAK OCT 6

				R	H	E
BAL	000	000	000	0	5	2
OAK	000	101	03X	5	8	0

Pitchers: McNALLY, Garland (6), Reynolds (7), G.Jackson (8) vs HOLTZMAN
Home Runs: Bando-OAK, Fosse-OAK
Attendance: 42,810

GAME 3 AT BAL OCT 8

				R	H	E
OAK	000	100	000	1	4	2
BAL	000	000	000	0	2	1

Pitchers: BLUE vs PALMER
Home Runs: Bando-OAK
Attendance: 32,060

GAME 4 AT BAL OCT 9

				R	H	E
OAK	000	010	100	2	1	0
BAL	000	000	001	1	5	1

Pitchers: HUNTER, Fingers (8) vs CUELLAR, Grimsley (5)
Attendance: 28,136

Although the A's were in a turmoil of dislike for owner Charlie Finley—and for each other—they played well enough together to take their third consecutive world championship in just five games. Still, victory didn't come easily, as three of Oakland's wins came by identical 3–2 scores (as did the Dodgers' one victory), and their biggest winning margin was three runs in Game 4. It was the first World Series held entirely on the West Coast.

The A's and Dodgers split the first two games in Los Angeles. Oakland won the opener on the strength of Reggie Jackson's home run in the second inning, pitcher Ken Holtzman's double in the fifth (he moved around on a wild pitch and squeeze bunt), and a Dodgers throwing error in the eighth. The Dodgers evened the Series on Joe Ferguson's two-run homer in the sixth inning of the second game, which gave Los Angeles a 3–0 lead that an Oakland rally in the ninth failed to catch.

Los Angeles outhit Oakland in Game 3, but two of the A's runs were unearned, coming after Dodgers catcher Ferguson bobbled what should have been a third-out play in the third inning.

Pitcher Ken Holtzman, who had now gone two regular seasons without a time at bat, produced in Game 4 his second hit of the Series, this one a homer in the third inning for the game's first run. The Dodgers' Bill Russell tripled off him for two runs a half inning later, but in the last of the sixth inning Oakland regained the lead on three walks interspersed with a pair of singles and an RBI grounder to short. Four runs scored—more in this one inning than either team scored in any of the other four games.

Oakland took an early 2–0 lead in Game 5, with single runs in the first and second innings (the latter a Ray Fosse home run). The Dodgers put together a pinch-hit double, a walk, a pair of sacrifices (bunt and fly), and a single to tie the score in the sixth. But Joe Rudi hit the first pitch of Oakland's half of the seventh into the stands in left for the run that decided the game and the Series.

Oakland Athletics (AL), 4; Los Angeles Dodgers (NL), 1

OAK (A)

PLAYER/POS	AVG	G	AB	R	H	2B	3B	HR	RB	BB	SO	SB
Jesus Alou, ph	.000	1	1	0	0	0	0	0	0	0	1	0
Sal Bando, 3b	.063	5	16	3	1	0	0	0	2	2	5	0
Vida Blue, p	.000	2	4	0	0	0	0	0	0	0	4	0
Bert Campaneris, ss	.353	5	17	1	6	2	0	0	2	0	2	1
Rollie Fingers, p	.000	4	2	0	0	0	0	0	0	0	1	0
Ray Fosse, c	.143	5	14	1	2	0	0	1	1	1	5	0
Dick Green, 2b	.000	5	13	1	0	0	0	0	1	1	4	0
Larry Haney, c	.000	2	0	0	0	0	0	0	0	0	0	0
Jim Holt, 1b-1	.667	4	3	0	2	0	0	0	2	0	0	0
Ken Holtzman, p	.500	2	4	2	2	1	0	1	1	1	1	0
Catfish Hunter, p	.000	2	2	0	0	0	0	0	0	0	2	0
Reggie Jackson, of	.286	5	14	3	4	1	0	1	1	5	3	1
Angel Mangual, ph	.000	1	1	0	0	0	0	0	0	0	1	0
Dal Maxvill, 2b	.000	2	0	0	0	0	0	0	0	0	0	0
Billy North, of	.059	5	17	3	1	0	0	0	0	2	5	1
Blue Moon Odom, p	.000	2	0	0	0	0	0	0	0	0	0	0
Joe Rudi, of-5,1b-2	.333	5	18	1	6	0	0	1	4	0	3	0
Gene Tenace, 1b	.222	5	9	0	2	0	0	0	0	3	4	0
Claudell Washington, of	.571	5	7	1	4	0	0	0	0	1	1	0
Herb Washington, pr	.000	3	0	0	0	0	0	0	0	0	0	0
TOTAL	.211		142	16	30	4	0	4	14	16	42	3

PITCHER	W	L	ERA	G	GS	CG	SV	SHO	IP	H	ER	BB	SO
Vida Blue	0	1	3.29	2	2	0	0	0	13.2	10	5	7	9
Rollie Fingers	1	0	1.93	4	0	0	2	0	9.1	8	2	2	6
Ken Holtzman	1	0	1.50	2	2	0	0	0	12.0	13	2	4	10
Catfish Hunter	1	0	1.17	2	1	0	1	0	7.2	5	1	2	5
Blue Moon Odom	1	0	0.00	2	0	0	0	0	1.1	0	0	1	2
TOTAL	4	1	2.05	12	5	0	3	0	44.0	36	10	16	32

LA (N)

PLAYER/POS	AVG	G	AB	R	H	2B	3B	HR	RB	BB	SO	SB
Rick Auerbach, pr	.000	1	0	0	0	0	0	0	0	0	0	0
Jim Brewer, p	.000	1	0	0	0	0	0	0	0	0	0	0
Bill Buckner, of	.250	5	20	1	5	1	0	1	1	0	1	0
Ron Cey, 3b	.176	5	17	1	3	0	0	0	0	3	3	0
Willie Crawford, of-2	.333	3	6	1	2	0	0	1	1	0	0	0
Al Downing, p	.000	1	1	0	0	0	0	0	0	0	0	0
Joe Ferguson, of-4,c-2	.125	5	16	2	2	0	0	1	2	4	6	1
Steve Garvey, 1b	.381	5	21	2	8	0	0	0	1	0	3	0
Charlie Hough, p	.000	1	0	0	0	0	0	0	0	0	0	0
Von Joshua, ph	.000	4	4	0	0	0	0	0	0	0	0	0
Lee Lacy, ph	.000	1	1	0	0	0	0	0	0	0	1	0
Davey Lopes, 2b	.111	5	18	2	2	0	0	0	0	3	4	2
Mike Marshall, p	.000	5	0	0	0	0	0	0	0	1	0	0
Andy Messersmith, p	.500	2	4	0	2	0	0	0	0	0	2	0
Tom Paciorek, ph	.500	3	2	1	1	1	0	0	0	0	0	0
Bill Russell, ss	.222	5	18	0	4	0	1	0	2	0	2	0
Don Sutton, p	.000	2	3	0	0	0	0	0	0	0	2	0
Jimmy Wynn, of	.188	5	16	1	3	1	0	1	2	4	4	0
Steve Yeager, c	.364	4	11	0	4	1	0	0	1	1	4	0
TOTAL	.228		158	11	36	4	1	4	10	16	32	3

PITCHER	W	L	ERA	G	GS	CG	SV	SHO	IP	H	ER	BB	SO
Jim Brewer	0	0	0.00	1	0	0	0	0	0.1	0	0	0	1
Al Downing	0	1	2.45	1	1	0	0	0	3.2	4	1	4	3
Charlie Hough	0	0	0.00	1	0	0	0	0	2.0	0	0	1	4
Mike Marshall	0	1	1.00	5	0	0	1	0	9.0	6	1	1	10
Andy Messersmith	0	2	4.50	2	2	0	0	0	14.0	11	7	7	12
Don Sutton	1	0	2.77	2	2	0	0	0	13.0	9	4	3	12
TOTAL	1	4	2.79	12	5	0	1	0	42.0	30	13	16	42

GAME 1 AT LA OCT 12

				R	H	E
OAK	010	010	010	3	6	2
LA	000	010	001	2	11	1

Pitchers: Holtzman, FINGERS (5), Hunter (9) vs MESSERSMITH, Marshall (9)
Home Runs: Jackson-OAK, Wynn-LA
Attendance: 55,974

GAME 2 AT LA OCT 13

				R	H	E
OAK	000	000	002	2	6	0
LA	010	002	00X	3	6	1

Pitchers: BLUE, Odom (8) vs SUTTON, Marshall (9)
Home Runs: Ferguson-LA
Attendance: 55,989

GAME 3 AT OAK OCT 15

				R	H	E
LA	000	000	011	2	7	2
OAK	002	100	00X	3	5	2

Pitchers: DOWNING, Brewer (4), Hough (5), Marshall (7) vs HUNTER, Fingers (8)
Home Runs: Buckner-LA, Crawford-LA
Attendance: 49,347

GAME 4 AT OAK OCT 16

				R	H	E
LA	000	200	000	2	7	1
OAK	001	004	00X	5	7	0

Pitchers: MESSERSMITH, Marshall (7) vs HOLTZMAN, Fingers (8)
Home Runs: Holtzman-OAK
Attendance: 49,347

GAME 5 AT OAK OCT 17

				R	H	E
LA	000	002	000	2	5	1
OAK	110	000	10X	3	6	1

Pitchers: Sutton, MARSHALL (6) vs Blue, ODOM (7), Fingers (8)
Home Runs: Fosse-OAK, Rudi-OAK
Attendance: 49,347

The Reds, who had steamrolled the National League during the season, continued their roll in the NLCS. Reds pitcher Don Gullett gave up three Pirate runs in the first game, but he drove in three himself with a home run and a single. Pitching the series' only complete game, he won easily behind his club's 12-hit, eight-run attack. The Reds won just as handily in Game 2, with Fred Norman and reliever Rawley Eastwick holding the Pirates to one run as Tony Perez drove in half the Reds' six runs—two of them with a first-inning homer.

In Game 3 the Pirates struggled gamely against elimination. Cincinnati scored first in the second, but in the sixth Al Oliver put Pittsburgh ahead with a two-run homer. In the eighth, though, Pete Rose restored the Reds' lead (and nullified rookie John Candelaria's 14-strikeout effort over 7⅔ innings) with his two-run shot. The Pirates were granted a brief reprieve when Reds reliever Eastwick walked in the tying run in the bottom of the ninth. But in the 10th the Reds scored twice on three hits, and when Eastwick's replacement Pedro Borbon shut the Pirates down in the bottom of the tenth, Cincinnati had its series sweep.

Cincinnati Reds (West), 3; Pittsburgh Pirates (East), 0

CIN (W)

PLAYER/POS	AVG	G	AB	R	H	2B	3B	HR	RB	BB	SO	SB
Ed Armbrister, ph	.000	2	0	0	0	0	0	0	1	0	0	0
Johnny Bench, c	.077	3	13	1	1	0	0	0	0	1	6	1
Pedro Borbon, p	.000	1	0	0	0	0	0	0	0	0	0	0
Clay Carroll, p	.000	1	0	0	0	0	0	0	0	0	0	0
Dave Concepcion, ss	.455	3	11	2	5	0	0	1	1	1	2	2
Terry Crowley, ph	.000	1	0	0	0	0	0	0	0	0	0	0
Rawly Eastwick, p	.000	2	0	0	0	0	0	0	0	0	0	0
George Foster, of	.364	3	11	3	4	0	0	0	0	1	2	1
Cesar Geronimo, of	.000	3	10	0	0	0	0	0	1	1	7	0
Ken Griffey, of	.333	3	12	3	4	1	0	0	4	0	3	3
Don Gullett, p	.500	1	4	1	2	0	0	1	3	0	0	0
Will McEnaney, p	.000	1	0	0	0	0	0	0	0	0	0	0
Joe Morgan, 2b	.273	3	11	2	3	3	0	0	1	3	2	4
Gary Nolan, p	.000	1	2	0	0	0	0	0	0	0	2	0
Fred Norman, p	.000	1	1	0	0	0	0	0	1	0	0	0
Tony Perez, 1b	.417	3	12	3	5	0	0	1	4	1	2	0
Merv Rettenmund, ph	.000	2	1	1	0	0	0	0	0	1	0	0
Pete Rose, 3b	.357	3	14	3	5	0	0	1	2	0	2	0
TOTAL	.284		102	19	29	4	0	4	18	9	28	11

PITCHER	W	L	ERA	G	GS	CG	SV	SHO	IP	H	ER	BB	SO
Pedro Borbon	0	0	0.00	1	0	0	1	0	1.0	0	0	0	1
Clay Carroll	0	0	0.00	1	0	0	0	0	1.0	0	0	1	1
Rawly Eastwick	1	0	0.00	2	0	0	1	0	3.2	2	0	2	1
Don Gullett	1	0	3.00	1	1	1	0	0	9.0	8	3	2	5
Will McEnaney	0	0	6.75	1	0	0	0	0	1.1	1	1	0	1
Gary Nolan	0	0	3.00	1	1	0	0	0	6.0	5	2	0	5
Fred Norman	1	0	1.50	1	1	0	0	0	6.0	4	1	5	4
TOTAL	3	0	2.25	8	3	1	2	0	28.0	20	7	10	18

PIT (E)

PLAYER/POS	AVG	G	AB	R	H	2B	3B	HR	RB	BB	SO	SB
Ken Brett, p	.000	2	0	0	0	0	0	0	0	0	0	0
John Candelaria, p	.000	1	3	0	0	0	0	0	0	0	3	0
Larry Demery, p	.000	1	0	0	0	0	0	0	0	0	0	0
Duffy Dyer, ph	.000	1	0	0	0	0	0	0	1	1	0	0
Dock Ellis, p	.000	1	0	0	0	0	0	0	0	0	0	0
Dave Giusti, p	.000	1	0	0	0	0	0	0	0	0	0	0
Richie Hebner, 3b	.333	3	12	2	4	1	0	0	2	1	1	0
Ramon Hernandez, p	.000	1	0	0	0	0	0	0	0	0	0	0
Ed Kirkpatrick, ph	.000	2	2	0	0	0	0	0	0	0	0	0
Bruce Kison, p	.000	1	0	0	0	0	0	0	0	0	0	0
Al Oliver, of	.182	3	11	1	2	0	0	1	2	2	0	0
Dave Parker, of	.000	3	10	2	0	0	0	0	0	1	3	0
Willie Randolph, 2b-1	.000	2	2	1	0	0	0	0	0	0	1	0
Jerry Reuss, p	.000	1	1	0	0	0	0	0	0	0	0	0
Craig Reynolds, ss-1	.000	2	1	0	0	0	0	0	0	0	0	0
Bob Robertson, 1b-1	.500	3	2	0	1	0	0	0	1	1	0	0
Bill Robinson, ph	.000	2	2	0	0	0	0	0	0	0	1	0
Jim Rooker, p	.000	1	1	0	0	0	0	0	0	0	1	0
Manny Sanguillen, c	.167	3	12	0	2	0	0	0	0	0	0	0
Willie Stargell, 1b	.182	3	11	1	2	1	0	0	0	1	3	0
Rennie Stennett, 2b-3,ss-1	.214	3	14	0	3	0	0	0	0	0	1	0
Frank Taveras, ss	.143	3	7	0	1	0	0	0	1	1	2	0
Kent Tekulve, p	.000	2	0	0	0	0	0	0	0	0	0	0
Richie Zisk, of	.500	3	10	0	5	1	0	0	0	2	2	0
TOTAL	.198		101	7	20	3	0	1	7	10	18	0

PITCHER	W	L	ERA	G	GS	CG	SV	SHO	IP	H	ER	BB	SO
Ken Brett	0	0	0.00	2	0	0	0	0	2.1	1	0	0	1
John Candelaria	0	0	3.52	1	1	0	0	0	7.2	3	3	2	14
Larry Demery	0	0	18.00	1	0	0	0	0	2.0	4	4	1	1
Dock Ellis	0	0	0.00	1	0	0	0	0	2.0	2	0	0	2
Dave Giusti	0	0	0.00	1	0	0	0	0	1.1	0	0	0	1
Ramon Hernandez	0	1	27.00	1	0	0	0	0	0.2	3	2	0	0
Bruce Kison	0	0	4.50	1	0	0	0	0	2.0	2	1	1	1
Jerry Reuss	0	1	13.50	1	1	0	0	0	2.2	4	4	4	1
Jim Rooker	0	1	9.00	1	1	0	0	0	4.0	7	4	0	5
Kent Tekulve	0	0	6.75	2	0	0	0	0	1.1	3	1	1	2
TOTAL	0	3	6.58	12	3	0	0	0	26.0	29	19	9	28

GAME 1 AT CIN OCT 4

				R	H	E
PIT	020	000	001	3	8	0
CIN	013	040	00X	8	11	0

Pitchers: REUSS, Brett (3), Demery (5), Ellis (7) vs GULLETT
Home Runs: Gullett-CIN
Attendance: 54,633

GAME 2 AT CIN OCT 5

				R	H	E
PIT	000	100	000	1	5	0
CIN	200	201	10X	6	12	1

Pitchers: ROOKER, Tekulve (5), Brett (6), Kison (7) vs NORMAN, Eastwick (7)
Home Runs: Perez-CIN
Attendance: 54,752

GAME 3 AT PIT OCT 7

					R	H	E
CIN	010	000	020	2	5	6	0
PIT	000	002	001	0	3	7	2

Pitchers: Nolan, C.Carroll (7), McEnaney (8), EASTWICK (9), Borbon (10) vs Candelaria, Giusti (8), HERNANDEZ (10), Tekulve (10)
Home Runs: Concepcion-CIN, Oliver-PIT, Rose-CIN
Attendance: 46,355

The Oakland A's ran their domination of the American League West to five years, but an aroused Boston team stifled their try for a fourth straight pennant.

In the first game Luis Tiant held Oakland to three hits as his teammates—aided by four Oakland errors—scored seven times before giving the A's an unearned run in the eighth. Oakland scored first in Game 2 on Reggie Jackson's two-run homer in the first inning and added a run in the fourth. But Carl Yastrzemski's two-run shot in the last of the fourth, followed by a Carlton Fisk double and a Fred Lynn single, drove out A's starter Vida Blue, and the tying run scored on a double play. Single Boston runs in the sixth, seventh, and eighth put the game away.

The A's started Ken Holtzman for the second time in Game 3, after only two days of rest. He held the Sox scoreless for three innings, but was driven from the game in the fifth. Boston scored four times before Oakland put a run on the board, and retained the lead to the game's conclusion.

Boston Red Sox (East), 3; Oakland A's (West), 0

BOS (E)

PLAYER/POS	AVG	G	AB	R	H	2B	3B	HR	RB	BB	SO	SB
Juan Beniquez, dh	.250	3	12	2	3	0	0	0	1	0	1	2
Rick Burleson, ss	.444	3	9	2	4	2	0	0	1	1	0	0
Reggie Cleveland, p	.000	1	0	0	0	0	0	0	0	0	0	0
Cecil Cooper, 1b	.400	3	10	0	4	2	0	0	1	0	2	0
Denny Doyle, 2b	.273	3	11	3	3	0	0	0	1	0	1	0
Dick Drago, p	.000	2	0	0	0	0	0	0	0	0	0	0
Dwight Evans, of	.100	3	10	1	1	1	0	0	1	1	2	0
Carlton Fisk, c	.417	3	12	4	5	1	0	0	2	0	2	1
Fred Lynn, of	.364	3	11	1	4	1	0	0	3	0	0	0
Roger Moret, p	.000	1	0	0	0	0	0	0	0	0	0	0
Rico Petrocelli, 3b	.167	3	12	1	2	0	0	1	2	0	3	0
Luis Tiant, p	.000	1	0	0	0	0	0	0	0	0	0	0
Rick Wise, p	.000	1	0	0	0	0	0	0	0	0	0	0
Carl Yastrzemski, of	.455	3	11	4	5	1	0	1	2	1	1	0
TOTAL	.316		98	18	31	8	0	2	14	3	12	3

PITCHER	W	L	ERA	G	GS	CG	SV	SHO	IP	H	ER	BB	SO
Reggie Cleveland	0	0	5.40	1	1	0	0	0	5.0	7	3	1	2
Dick Drago	0	0	0.00	2	0	0	2	0	4.2	2	0	1	2
Roger Moret	1	0	0.00	1	0	0	0	0	1.0	1	0	1	0
Luis Tiant	1	0	0.00	1	1	1	0	0	9.0	3	0	3	8
Rick Wise	1	0	2.45	1	1	0	0	0	7.1	6	2	3	2
TOTAL	3	0	1.67	6	3	1	2	0	27.0	19	5	9	14

OAK (W)

PLAYER/POS	AVG	G	AB	R	H	2B	3B	HR	RB	BB	SO	SB
Glenn Abbott, p	.000	1	0	0	0	0	0	0	0	0	0	0
Sal Bando, 3b	.500	3	12	1	6	2	0	0	2	0	3	0
Vida Blue, p	.000	1	0	0	0	0	0	0	0	0	0	0
Dick Bosman, p	.000	1	0	0	0	0	0	0	0	0	0	0
Bert Campaneris, ss	.000	3	11	1	0	0	0	0	0	1	1	0
Rollie Fingers, p	.000	1	0	0	0	0	0	0	0	0	0	0
Ray Fosse, c	.000	1	2	0	0	0	0	0	0	0	1	0
Phil Garner, 2b	.000	3	5	0	0	0	0	0	0	0	1	0
Tommy Harper, ph	.000	1	0	0	0	0	0	0	0	1	0	0
Jim Holt, 1b-1	.333	3	3	0	1	1	0	0	0	0	0	0
Ken Holtzman, p	.000	2	0	0	0	0	0	0	0	0	0	0
Don Hopkins, dh	.000	1	0	0	0	0	0	0	0	0	0	0
Reggie Jackson, of	.417	3	12	1	5	0	0	1	3	0	2	0
Paul Lindblad, p	.000	2	0	0	0	0	0	0	0	0	0	0
Ted Martinez, 2b	.000	3	0	0	0	0	0	0	0	0	0	0
Billy North, of	.000	3	10	0	0	0	0	0	1	2	0	0
Joe Rudi, 1b-2,of-1	.250	3	12	1	3	2	0	0	0	0	1	0
Gene Tenace, c-3,1b-1	.000	3	9	0	0	0	0	0	0	3	2	0
Jim Todd, p	.000	3	0	0	0	0	0	0	0	0	0	0
Cesar Tovar, 2b-1	.500	2	2	2	1	0	0	0	0	1	0	0
Claudell Washington, of-2,dh-1	.250	3	12	1	3	1	0	0	1	0	2	0
Billy Williams, dh-2	.000	3	8	0	0	0	0	0	0	1	1	0
TOTAL	.194		98	7	19	6	0	1	7	9	14	0

PITCHER	W	L	ERA	G	GS	CG	SV	SHO	IP	H	ER	BB	SO
Glenn Abbott	0	0	0.00	1	0	0	0	0	1.0	0	0	0	0
Vida Blue	0	0	9.00	1	1	0	0	0	3.0	6	3	0	2
Dick Bosman	0	0	0.00	1	0	0	0	0	0.1	0	0	0	0
Rollie Fingers	0	1	6.75	1	0	0	0	0	4.0	5	3	1	3
Ken Holtzman	0	2	4.09	2	2	0	0	0	11.0	12	5	1	7
Paul Lindblad	0	0	0.00	2	0	0	0	0	4.2	5	0	1	0
Jim Todd	0	0	9.00	3	0	0	0	0	1.0	3	1	0	0
TOTAL	0	3	4.32	11	3	0	0	0	25.0	31	12	3	12

GAME 1 AT BOS OCT 4

				R	H	E
OAK	000	000	010	1	3	4
BOS	200	000	50X	7	8	3

Pitchers: HOLTZMAN, Todd (7), Lindblad (7), Bosman (7), Abbott (8) vs TIANT
Attendance: 35,578

GAME 2 AT BOS OCT 5

				R	H	E
OAK	200	100	000	3	10	0
BOS	000	301	11X	6	12	0

Pitchers: Blue, Todd (4), FINGERS (5) vs Cleveland, MORET (6), Drago (7)
Home Runs: Jackson-OAK, Yastrzemski-BOS, Petrocelli-BOS
Attendance: 35,578

GAME 3 AT OAK OCT 7

				R	H	E
BOS	000	130	010	5	11	1
OAK	000	001	020	3	6	2

Pitchers: WISE, Drago (8) vs HOLTZMAN, Todd (5), Lindblad (5)
Attendance: 49,358

The Red Sox entered the Series as underdogs to the mighty Reds, who had won 108 regular-season games. In the opening game, though, the Reds were surprised by veteran Sox starter Luis Tiant, who shut them out on five hits with the Series' first complete-game pitching effort in four years. Tiant also opened the Boston seventh with a single, starting a rally that ended only when he fouled out to end the inning after six runs had scored.

Boston took a 2–1 lead into the ninth inning of Game 2 before Johnny Bench doubled to drive out starter Bill Lee, and Dave Concepcion and Ken Griffey drove in runs off reliever Dick Drago to turn the tide for Cincinnati. The Reds moved ahead in the Series with a 10-inning victory in Game 3, a slugfest in which each club hit three home runs and used five pitchers. Boston tied the score on Dwight Evans's two-run homer in the ninth, but in the last of the 10th, the Reds' Joe Morgan drove one over the center fielder's head with the bases full to end the game.

Tiant pitched Game 4 for Boston. Four of the nine hits against him went for extra bases, and each drove in a run. But the Sox bunched six of their 11 hits in the fourth inning for five runs—their only scoring, but enough for the win. Tiant himself scored the fifth run after singling. The Reds moved nearer the title in Game 5, though, as Tony Perez homered twice for four runs in a 6–2 win for a 3–2 Series advantage.

A day of travel to Boston and three days of rain between Games 5 and 6 brought Tiant back to the mound for a third time. Rookie standout Fred Lynn gave Tiant a three-run lead with a first-inning homer, but Ken Griffey's triple and Johnny Bench's long single drove in the tying runs in the fifth. Two more runs in the seventh and Cesar Geronimo's leadoff homer in the eighth drove out Tiant, but Boston pinch hitter Bernie Carbo homered to center in the last of the eighth for three runs that tied the score again. After a trio of Boston relievers had held Cincinnati in check through the top of the 12th inning, the Sox leadoff hitter in the last of the 12th, Carlton Fisk, ended the game dramatically with a home run to left on the first pitch that came within inches of being foul.

After the pyrotechnics of Game 6 (ranked by some as the greatest World Series game ever), the seventh game, close as it was, came as an anticlimax. Boston scored three runs in the third inning, but the Reds began their comeback with Tony Perez's two-run homer in the sixth, tied the game an inning later, and took a 4–3 lead on Joe Morgan's bloop RBI single in the ninth. Reliever Will McEnaney came on to set the Sox down in order in the last of the ninth, and the Reds went home with their first world title in 35 years.

Cincinnati Reds (NL), 4; Boston Red Sox (AL), 3

CIN (N)

PLAYER/POS	AVG	G	AB	R	H	2B	3B	HR	RB	BB	SO	SB
Ed Armbrister, ph	.000	4	1	1	0	0	0	0	0	2	0	0
Johnny Bench, c	.207	7	29	5	6	2	0	1	4	2	4	0
Jack Billingham, p	.000	3	2	0	0	0	0	0	0	0	0	0
Pedro Borbon, p	.000	3	1	0	0	0	0	0	0	0	0	0
Clay Carroll, p	.000	5	0	0	0	0	0	0	0	0	0	0
Darrel Chaney, ph	.000	2	2	0	0	0	0	0	0	0	1	0
Dave Concepcion, ss	.179	7	28	3	5	1	0	1	4	0	1	3
Terry Crowley, ph	.500	2	2	0	1	0	0	0	0	0	1	0
Pat Darcy, p	.000	2	1	0	0	0	0	0	0	0	1	0
Dan Driessen, ph	.000	2	2	0	0	0	0	0	0	0	0	0
Rawly Eastwick, p	.000	5	1	0	0	0	0	0	0	0	0	0
George Foster, of	.276	7	29	1	8	1	0	0	2	1	1	1
Cesar Geronimo, of	.280	7	25	3	7	0	1	2	3	3	5	0
Ken Griffey, of	.269	7	26	4	7	3	1	0	4	4	2	2
Don Gullett, p	.286	3	7	1	2	0	0	0	0	0	2	0
Will McEnaney, p	1.000	5	1	0	1	0	0	0	0	0	0	0
Joe Morgan, 2b	.259	7	27	4	7	1	0	0	3	5	1	2
Gary Nolan, p	.000	2	1	0	0	0	0	0	0	0	0	0
Fred Norman, p	.000	2	1	0	0	0	0	0	0	0	0	0
Tony Perez, 1b	.179	7	28	4	5	0	0	3	7	3	9	1
Merv Rettenmund, ph	.000	3	3	0	0	0	0	0	0	0	1	0
Pete Rose, 3b	.370	7	27	3	10	1	1	0	2	5	1	0
TOTAL	.242		244	29	59	9	3	7	29	25	30	9

PITCHER	W	L	ERA	G	GS	CG	SV	SHO	IP	H	ER	BB	SO
Jack Billingham	0	0	1.00	3	1	0	0	0	9.0	8	1	5	7
Pedro Borbon	0	0	6.00	3	0	0	0	0	3.0	3	2	2	1
Clay Carroll	1	0	3.18	5	0	0	0	0	5.2	4	2	2	3
Pat Darcy	0	1	4.50	2	0	0	0	0	4.0	3	2	2	1
Rawly Eastwick	2	0	2.25	5	0	0	1	0	8.0	6	2	3	4
Don Gullett	1	1	4.34	3	3	0	0	0	18.2	19	9	10	15
Will McEnaney	0	0	2.70	5	0	0	1	0	6.2	3	2	2	5
Gary Nolan	0	0	6.00	2	2	0	0	0	6.0	6	4	1	2
Fred Norman	0	1	9.00	2	1	0	0	0	4.0	8	4	3	2
TOTAL	4	3	3.88	30	7	0	2	0	65.0	60	28	30	40

BOS (A)

PLAYER/POS	AVG	G	AB	R	H	2B	3B	HR	RB	BB	SO	SB
Juan Beniquez, of-2	.125	3	8	0	1	0	0	0	1	1	1	0
Rick Burleson, ss	.292	7	24	1	7	1	0	0	2	4	2	0
Jim Burton, p	.000	2	0	0	0	0	0	0	0	0	0	0
Bernie Carbo, of-2	.429	4	7	3	3	1	0	2	4	1	1	0
Reggie Cleveland, p	.000	3	2	0	0	0	0	0	0	0	2	0
Cecil Cooper, 1b	.053	5	19	0	1	1	0	0	1	0	3	0
Denny Doyle, 2b	.267	7	30	3	8	1	1	0	0	2	1	0
Dick Drago, p	.000	2	0	0	0	0	0	0	0	0	0	0
Dwight Evans, of	.292	7	24	3	7	1	1	1	5	3	4	0
Carlton Fisk, c	.240	7	25	5	6	0	0	2	4	7	7	0
Doug Griffin, ph	.000	1	1	0	0	0	0	0	0	0	0	0
Bill Lee, p	.167	2	6	0	1	0	0	0	0	0	3	0
Fred Lynn, of	.280	7	25	3	7	1	0	1	5	3	5	0
Rick Miller, of-2	.000	3	2	0	0	0	0	0	0	0	0	0
Bob Montgomery, ph	.000	1	1	0	0	0	0	0	0	0	0	0
Roger Moret, p	.000	3	0	0	0	0	0	0	0	0	0	0
Rico Petrocelli, 3b	.308	7	26	3	8	1	0	0	4	3	6	0
Dick Pole, p	.000	1	0	0	0	0	0	0	0	0	0	0
Diego Segui, p	.000	1	0	0	0	0	0	0	0	0	0	0
Luis Tiant, p	.250	3	8	2	2	0	0	0	0	2	4	0
Jim Willoughby, p	.000	3	0	0	0	0	0	0	0	0	0	0
Rick Wise, p	.000	2	2	0	0	0	0	0	0	0	0	0
Carl Yastrzemski, 1b-4,of-4	.310	7	29	7	9	0	0	0	4	4	1	0
TOTAL	.251		239	30	60	7	2	6	30	30	40	0

PITCHER	W	L	ERA	G	GS	CG	SV	SHO	IP	H	ER	BB	SO
Jim Burton	0	1	9.00	2	0	0	0	0	1.0	1	1	3	0
Reggie Cleveland	0	1	6.75	3	1	0	0	0	6.2	7	5	3	5
Dick Drago	0	1	2.25	2	0	0	0	0	4.0	3	1	1	1
Bill Lee	0	0	3.14	2	2	0	0	0	14.1	12	5	3	7
Roger Moret	0	0	0.00	3	0	0	0	0	1.2	2	0	3	1
Dick Pole	0	0	INF	1	0	0	0	0	0.0	0	1	2	0
Diego Segui	0	0	0.00	1	0	0	0	0	1.0	0	0	0	0
Luis Tiant	2	0	3.60	3	3	2	0	1	25.0	25	10	8	12
Jim Willoughby	0	1	0.00	3	0	0	0	0	6.1	3	0	0	2
Rick Wise	1	0	8.44	2	1	0	0	0	5.1	6	5	2	2
TOTAL	3	4	3.86	22	7	2	0	1	65.1	59	28	25	30

GAME 1 AT BOS OCT 11

				R	H	E
CIN	000	000	000	0	5	0
BOS	000	000	60X	6	12	0

Pitchers: GULLETT, Carroll (7), McEnaney (7) vs TIANT
Attendance: 35,205

GAME 2 AT BOS OCT 12

				R	H	E
CIN	000	100	002	3	7	1
BOS	100	001	000	2	7	0

Pitchers: Billingham, Borbon (6), McEnaney (7), EASTWICK (8) vs Lee, DRAGO (9)
Attendance: 35,205

GAME 3 AT CIN OCT 14

					R	H	E
BOS	010	001	102	0	5	10	2
CIN	000	230	000	1	6	7	0

Pitchers: Wise, Burton (5), Cleveland (5), WILLOUGHBY (7), Moret (10) vs Nolan, Darcy (5), Carroll (7), McEnaney (7), EASTWICK (9)
Home Runs: Fisk-BOS, Bench-CIN, Concepcion-CIN, Geronimo-CIN, Carbo-BOS, Evans-BOS
Attendance: 55,392

GAME 4 AT CIN OCT 15

				R	H	E
BOS	000	500	000	5	11	1
CIN	200	200	000	4	9	1

Pitchers: TIANT vs NORMAN, Borbon (4), Carroll (5), Eastwick (7)
Attendance: 55,667

GAME 5 AT CIN OCT 16

				R	H	E
BOS	100	000	001	2	5	0
CIN	000	113	01X	6	8	0

Pitchers: CLEVELAND, Willoughby (6), Pole (8), Segui (8) vs GULLETT, Eastwick (9)
Home Runs: Perez-CIN (2)
Attendance: 56,393

GAME 6 AT BOS OCT 21

					R	H	E
CIN	000	030	210	000	6	14	0
BOS	300	000	030	001	7	10	1

Pitchers: Nolan, Norman (3), Billingham (3), Carroll (5), Borbon (6), Eastwick (8), McEnaney (9), DARCY (10) vs Tiant, Moret (8), Drago (9), WISE (12)
Home Runs: Lynn-BOS, Geronimo-CIN, Carbo-BOS, Fisk-BOS
Attendance: 35,205

GAME 7 AT BOS OCT 22

				R	H	E
CIN	000	002	101	4	9	0
BOS	003	000	000	3	5	2

Pitchers: Gullett, Billingham (5), CARROLL (7), McEnaney (9) vs Lee, Moret (7), Willoughby (7), BURTON (9), Cleveland (9)
Home Runs: Perez-CIN
Attendance: 35,205

Philadelphia outhit Cincinnati in two of the three games, but couldn't turn enough hits into runs, as the Reds for the second year in a row swept the NLCS. The Phillies scored first in Game 1 with a run in the first inning. But pitcher Don Gullett held them scoreless for the next seven innings as his Reds caught up in the third, moved ahead in the sixth, and took a five-run lead into the last of the ninth. The Phillies scored twice in their half of the inning, but the rally fell short.

In the second game the Phillies outhit the Reds (10-6), scoring the game's first two runs while their starter Jim Lonborg threw a no-hitter for five innings. But in the sixth a walk and two singles drove Lonborg out and set the Reds off on a two-inning six-run spree for their second win.

Again in Game 3 the Phillies outhit the Reds, this time going into the last of the ninth ahead by two runs. But George Foster and Johnny Bench hit back-to-back homers off Ron Reed to tie the score, and two relievers (and a single and two walks) later, the Reds brought home another pennant as Ken Griffey's high-bouncing chop glanced off first baseman Bobby Tolan's outstretched glove.

Cincinnati Reds (West), 3; Philadelphia Phillies (East), 0

CIN (W)

PLAYER/POS	AVG	G	AB	R	H	2B	3B	HR	RB	BB	SO	SB
Ed Armbrister, ph	.000	1	0	0	0	0	0	0	0	0	0	0
Johnny Bench, c	.333	3	12	3	4	1	0	1	1	1	2	1
Pedro Borbon, p	.000	2	2	1	0	0	0	0	0	0	2	0
Dave Concepcion, ss	.200	3	10	4	2	1	0	0	0	2	1	0
Dan Driessen, ph	.000	1	1	0	0	0	0	0	0	0	0	0
Rawly Eastwick, p	.000	2	0	0	0	0	0	0	0	0	0	0
Doug Flynn, 2b	.000	1	0	0	0	0	0	0	0	0	0	0
George Foster, of	.167	3	12	2	2	0	0	2	4	0	4	0
Cesar Geronimo, of	.182	3	11	0	2	0	1	0	2	1	3	0
Ken Griffey, of	.385	3	13	2	5	0	1	0	2	2	1	2
Don Gullett, p	.500	1	4	1	2	1	0	0	3	0	0	0
Mike Lum, ph	.000	1	1	0	0	0	0	0	0	0	0	0
Joe Morgan, 2b	.000	3	7	2	0	0	0	0	0	6	1	2
Gary Nolan, p	.000	1	0	0	0	0	0	0	0	1	0	0
Tony Perez, 1b	.200	3	10	1	2	0	0	0	3	1	2	0
Pete Rose, 3b	.429	3	14	3	6	2	1	0	2	1	0	0
Manny Sarmiento, p	.000	1	1	0	0	0	0	0	0	0	0	0
Pat Zachry, p	.000	1	1	0	0	0	0	0	0	0	0	0
TOTAL	.253		99	19	25	5	3	3	17	15	16	5

PITCHER	W	L	ERA	G	GS	CG	SV	SHO	IP	H	ER	BB	SO
Pedro Borbon	0	0	0.00	2	0	0	1	0	4.1	4	0	1	0
Rawly Eastwick	1	0	12.00	2	0	0	0	0	3.0	7	4	2	1
Don Gullett	1	0	1.13	1	1	0	0	0	8.0	2	1	3	4
Gary Nolan	0	0	1.59	1	1	0	0	0	5.2	6	1	2	1
Manny Sarmiento	0	0	18.00	1	0	0	0	0	1.0	2	2	1	0
Pat Zachry	1	0	3.60	1	1	0	0	0	5.0	6	2	3	3
TOTAL	3	0	3.33	8	3	0	1	0	27.0	27	10	12	9

PHI (E)

PLAYER/POS	AVG	G	AB	R	H	2B	3B	HR	RB	BB	SO	SB
Richie Allen, 1b	.222	3	9	1	2	0	0	0	0	3	2	0
Bob Boone, c	.286	3	7	0	2	0	0	0	1	1	0	0
Larry Bowa, ss	.125	3	8	1	1	1	0	0	1	3	0	0
Ollie Brown, of	.000	1	2	0	0	0	0	0	0	1	1	0
Steve Carlton, p	.000	1	2	0	0	0	0	0	0	0	0	0
Dave Cash, 2b	.308	3	13	1	4	1	0	0	1	0	0	0
Gene Garber, p	.000	2	0	0	0	0	0	0	0	0	0	0
Terry Harmon, pr	.000	1	0	1	0	0	0	0	0	0	0	0
Tom Hutton, ph	.000	1	1	0	0	0	0	0	0	0	0	0
Jay Johnstone, of-2	.778	3	9	1	7	1	1	0	2	1	0	0
Jim Kaat, p	.500	1	2	0	1	0	0	0	0	0	0	0
Jim Lonborg, p	.000	1	1	0	0	0	0	0	0	0	0	0
Greg Luzinski, of	.273	3	11	2	3	2	0	1	3	1	4	0
Garry Maddox, of	.231	3	13	2	3	1	0	0	1	1	0	0
Jerry Martin, of	.000	1	1	1	0	0	0	0	0	0	0	0
Tim McCarver, c-1	.000	2	4	0	0	0	0	0	0	0	1	0
Tug McGraw, p	.000	2	0	0	0	0	0	0	0	0	0	0
Johnny Oates, c	.000	1	1	0	0	0	0	0	0	0	0	0
Ron Reed, p	.000	2	1	0	0	0	0	0	0	0	0	0
Mike Schmidt, 3b	.308	3	13	1	4	2	0	0	2	0	1	0
Bobby Tolan, 1b-1,of-1	.000	3	2	0	0	0	0	0	0	1	0	0
Tom Underwood, p	.000	1	0	0	0	0	0	0	0	0	0	0
TOTAL	.270		100	11	27	8	1	1	11	12	9	0

PITCHER	W	L	ERA	G	GS	CG	SV	SHO	IP	H	ER	BB	SO
Steve Carlton	0	1	5.14	1	1	0	0	0	7.0	8	4	5	6
Gene Garber	0	1	13.50	2	0	0	0	0	0.2	2	1	1	0
Jim Kaat	0	0	3.00	1	1	0	0	0	6.0	2	2	2	1
Jim Lonborg	0	1	1.69	1	1	0	0	0	5.1	2	1	2	2
Tug McGraw	0	0	11.57	2	0	0	0	0	2.1	4	3	1	5
Ron Reed	0	0	7.71	2	0	0	0	0	4.2	6	4	2	2
Tom Underwood	0	0	0.00	1	0	0	0	0	0.1	1	0	2	0
TOTAL	0	3	5.13	10	3	0	0	0	26.1	25	15	15	16

GAME 1 AT PHI OCT 9

				R	H	E
CIN	001	002	030	6	10	0
PHI	100	000	002	3	6	1

Pitchers: GULLETT, Eastwick (9) vs CARLTON, McGraw (8)
Home Runs: Foster-CIN
Attendance: 62,640

GAME 2 AT PHI OCT 10

				R	H	E
CIN	000	004	200	6	6	0
PHI	010	010	000	2	10	1

Pitchers: ZACHRY, Borbon (6) vs LONBORG, Garber (6), McGraw (7), Reed (7)
Home Runs: Luzinski-PHI
Attendance: 62,651

GAME 3 AT CIN OCT 12

				R	H	E
PHI	000	100	221	6	11	0
CIN	000	000	403	7	9	2

Pitchers: Kaat, Reed (7), GARBER (9), Underwood (9) vs Nolan, Sarmiento (6), Borbon (7), EASTWICK (8)
Home Runs: Foster-CIN, Bench-CIN
Attendance: 55,047

Returning to postseason play after a dozen years' absence, the Yankees found themselves evenly matched with the first-time-champion Royals. They didn't really need their two ninth-inning runs in the first game: the two they scored in the first inning proved cushion enough for Catfish Hunter's five-hitter. But Kansas City came back the next day, scoring first, losing the lead in the third, then regaining it for good in the sixth to gain a split in Kansas City.

The Royals again took a first-inning lead in Game 3, but this time the Yankees, once they went ahead in the sixth, didn't let go. Kansas City held on to its early lead in Game 4, building on it throughout the game for a second win, despite Graig Nettles' two home runs for New York.

But Game 5—like the series itself—was a seesaw affair. For the fourth time the Royals scored first, with a pair in the first on John Mayberry's home run. But the Yankees tied the game when they came to bat, and K.C. retook the lead in the second. New York went ahead again in the third and increased its lead to 6–3 in the sixth. But in the top of the eighth, George Brett's three-run homer tied the score once again, setting the stage for Chris Chambliss to win the 30th American League pennant for the Yankees with his first-pitch home run in the bottom of the ninth.

New York Yankees (East), 3; Kansas City Royals (West), 2

NY (E)

PLAYER/POS	AVG	G	AB	R	H	2B	3B	HR	RB	BB	SO	SB
Sandy Alomar, dh-1	.000	2	1	0	0	0	0	0	0	0	0	0
Chris Chambliss, 1b	.524	5	21	5	11	1	1	2	8	0	1	2
Dock Ellis, p	.000	1	0	0	0	0	0	0	0	0	0	0
Ed Figueroa, p	.000	2	0	0	0	0	0	0	0	0	0	0
Oscar Gamble, of	.250	3	8	1	2	1	0	0	1	1	1	0
Ron Guidry, pr	.000	1	0	0	0	0	0	0	0	0	0	0
Elrod Hendricks, ph	1.000	1	1	0	1	0	0	0	0	0	0	0
Catfish Hunter, p	.000	2	0	0	0	0	0	0	0	0	0	0
Grant Jackson, p	.000	2	0	0	0	0	0	0	0	0	0	0
Sparky Lyle, p	.000	1	0	0	0	0	0	0	0	0	0	0
Elliott Maddox, of	.222	3	9	0	2	1	0	0	1	0	1	0
Jim Mason, ss	.000	2	0	0	0	0	0	0	0	0	0	0
Carlos May, dh	.200	3	10	1	2	1	0	0	0	1	4	0
Thurman Munson, c	.435	5	23	3	10	2	0	0	3	0	1	0
Graig Nettles, 3b	.235	5	17	2	4	1	0	2	4	3	3	0
Lou Piniella, dh-3	.273	4	11	1	3	1	0	0	0	0	1	0
Willie Randolph, 2b	.118	5	17	0	2	0	0	0	1	3	1	1
Mickey Rivers, of	.348	5	23	5	8	0	1	0	0	1	1	0
Fred Stanley, ss	.333	5	15	1	5	2	0	0	0	2	0	0
Dick Tidrow, p	.000	3	0	0	0	0	0	0	0	0	0	0
Otto Velez, ph	.000	1	1	0	0	0	0	0	0	0	0	0
Roy White, of	.294	5	17	4	5	3	0	0	3	5	1	1
TOTAL	.316		174	23	55	13	2	4	21	16	15	4

PITCHER	W	L	ERA	G	GS	CG	SV	SHO	IP	H	ER	BB	SO
Dock Ellis	1	0	3.38	1	1	0	0	0	8.0	6	3	2	5
Ed Figueroa	0	1	5.84	2	2	0	0	0	12.1	14	8	2	5
Catfish Hunter	1	1	4.50	2	2	1	0	0	12.0	10	6	1	5
Grant Jackson	0	0	8.10	2	0	0	0	0	3.1	4	3	1	3
Sparky Lyle	0	0	0.00	1	0	0	1	0	1.0	0	0	1	0
Dick Tidrow	1	0	3.68	3	0	0	0	0	7.1	6	3	4	0
TOTAL	3	2	4.70	11	5	1	1	0	44.0	40	23	11	18

KC (W)

PLAYER/POS	AVG	G	AB	R	H	2B	3B	HR	RB	BB	SO	SB
Doug Bird, p	.000	1	0	0	0	0	0	0	0	0	0	0
George Brett, 3b	.444	5	18	4	8	1	1	1	5	2	1	0
Al Cowens, of	.190	5	21	3	4	0	1	0	0	1	1	2
Larry Gura, p	.000	2	0	0	0	0	0	0	0	0	0	0
Tom Hall, p	.000	1	0	0	0	0	0	0	0	0	0	0
Andy Hassler, p	.000	2	0	0	0	0	0	0	0	0	0	0
Dennis Leonard, p	.000	2	0	0	0	0	0	0	0	0	0	0
Mark Littell, p	.000	3	0	0	0	0	0	0	0	0	0	0
Buck Martinez, c	.333	5	15	0	5	0	0	0	4	1	3	0
John Mayberry, 1b	.222	5	18	4	4	0	0	1	3	1	0	0
Hal McRae, dh-3,of-2	.118	5	17	2	2	1	1	0	1	1	4	0
Steve Mingori, p	.000	3	0	0	0	0	0	0	0	0	0	0
Dave Nelson, dh-1	.000	2	2	0	0	0	0	0	0	0	1	0
Amos Otis, of	.000	1	1	0	0	0	0	0	0	0	0	0
Freddie Patek, ss	.389	5	18	2	7	2	0	0	4	0	1	0
Marty Pattin, p	.000	2	0	0	0	0	0	0	0	0	0	0
Tom Poquette, of	.188	5	16	1	3	2	0	0	4	2	3	0
Jamie Quirk, dh-2	.143	4	7	1	1	0	1	0	2	0	2	0
Cookie Rojas, 2b	.333	4	9	2	3	0	0	0	1	0	0	1
Paul Splittorff, p	.000	2	0	0	0	0	0	0	0	0	0	0
Bob Stinson, c-1	.000	2	1	0	0	0	0	0	0	0	0	0
John Wathan, c	.000	1	0	0	0	0	0	0	0	0	0	0
Frank White, 2b	.125	4	8	2	1	0	0	0	0	0	1	0
Jim Wohlford, of	.182	5	11	3	2	0	0	0	0	3	1	2
TOTAL	.247		162	24	40	6	4	2	24	11	18	5

PITCHER	W	L	ERA	G	GS	CG	SV	SHO	IP	H	ER	BB	SO
Doug Bird	1	0	1.93	1	0	0	0	0	4.2	4	1	0	1
Larry Gura	0	1	4.22	2	2	0	0	0	10.2	18	5	1	4
Tom Hall	0	0	0.00	1	0	0	0	0	0.1	1	0	0	0
Andy Hassler	0	1	6.14	2	1	0	0	0	7.1	8	5	6	4
Dennis Leonard	0	0	19.29	2	2	0	0	0	2.1	9	5	2	0
Mark Littell	0	1	1.93	3	0	0	0	0	4.2	4	1	1	3
Steve Mingori	0	0	2.70	3	0	0	1	0	3.1	4	1	0	1
Marty Pattin	0	0	27.00	2	0	0	0	0	0.1	0	1	1	0
Paul Splittorff	1	0	1.93	2	0	0	0	0	9.1	7	2	5	2
TOTAL	2	3	4.40	18	5	0	1	0	43.0	55	21	16	15

GAME 1 AT KC OCT 9

				R	H	E
NY	200	000	002	4	12	0
KC	000	000	010	1	5	2

Pitchers: HUNTER vs GURA, Littell (9)
Attendance: 41,077

GAME 2 AT KC OCT 10

				R	H	E
NY	012	000	000	3	12	5
KC	200	002	03X	7	9	0

Pitchers: FIGUEROA, Tidrow (6) vs Leonard, SPLITTORFF (3), Mingori (9)
Attendance: 41,091

GAME 3 AT NY OCT 12

				R	H	E
KC	300	000	000	3	6	0
NY	000	203	00X	5	9	0

Pitchers: HASSLER, Pattin (6), Hall (6), Mingori (6), Littell (6) vs ELLIS, Lyle (9)
Home Runs: Chambliss-NY
Attendance: 56,808

GAME 4 AT NY OCT 13

				R	H	E
KC	030	201	010	7	9	1
NY	020	000	101	4	11	0

Pitchers: Gura, BIRD (3), Mingori (7) vs HUNTER, Tidrow (4), Jackson (7)
Home Runs: Nettles-NY (2)
Attendance: 56,355

GAME 5 AT NY OCT 14

				R	H	E
KC	210	000	030	6	11	1
NY	202	002	001	7	11	1

Pitchers: Leonard, Splittorff (1), Pattin (4), Hassler (5), LITTELL (7) vs Figueroa, Jackson (8), TIDROW (9)
Home Runs: Mayberry-KC, Brett-KC, Chambliss-NY
Attendance: 56,821

The Reds led the National League in virtually every offensive category and in fielding as well. In the Series (which, incidentally, was the first to employ the designated hitter), the Big Red Machine continued its roll over the Yankees to become the first National League club in 54 years to repeat as world champions, as well as the first team to sweep both a League Championship and World Series. Reds catcher Johnny Bench led the attack with eight hits, half of them for extra bases, for a batting average of .533 and a 1.133 average in slugging.

Joe Morgan's home run for Cincinnati in the first inning of Game 1 was the first hit of the Series, but New York pushed across a tying run half an inning later on a sacrifice fly. Pitchers Don Gullett and Pedro Borbon held the Yankees scoreless after that as the Reds regained the lead with a run in the third and extended it in the sixth and seventh for a 5–1 win.

Game 2 turned out to be the Reds' only narrow victory. They scored first, with three runs in the second inning. In the fourth the Yankees scored their first run, and they tied the score with two more runs in the seventh. But with two men out in the last of the ninth, a throwing error by Yankee shortstop Fred Stanley allowed Ken Griffey to reach second. Griffey then scored the winning run on Tony Perez's line single to left.

In Game 3, four hits and a pair of stolen bases put Cincinnati ahead 3–0 in the second inning, and Dan Driessen homered in the fourth to make it 4–0 before the Yankees scored their first run. Another quartet of hits in the eighth gave the Reds two more runs and a 6–2 win.

New York took the lead for the only time in the Series when Chris Chambliss doubled in Thurman Munson in the first inning of Game 4. (Munson had singled with the third of what became six straight hits.) But the Reds' George Foster drove in a tying run in the fourth, and Johnny Bench followed him with a two-run homer. New York scored again an inning later to come close, but Bench's second home run, a three-run blast in the ninth, put the game out of reach, and a pair of ground-rule doubles touched by New York fans put a lid on Cincinnati's sweep.

Cincinnati Reds (NL), 4; New York Yankees (AL), 0

CIN (N)

PLAYER/POS	AVG	G	AB	R	H	2B	3B	HR	RB	BB	SO	SB
Johnny Bench, c	.533	4	15	4	8	1	1	2	6	0	1	0
Jack Billingham, p	.000	1	0	0	0	0	0	0	0	0	0	0
Pedro Borbon, p	.000	1	0	0	0	0	0	0	0	0	0	0
Dave Concepcion, ss	.357	4	14	1	5	1	1	0	3	1	3	1
Dan Driessen, dh	.357	4	14	4	5	2	0	1	1	2	0	1
George Foster, of	.429	4	14	3	6	1	0	0	4	2	3	0
Cesar Geronimo, of	.308	4	13	3	4	2	0	0	1	2	2	2
Ken Griffey, of	.059	4	17	2	1	0	0	0	1	0	1	1
Don Gullett, p	.000	1	0	0	0	0	0	0	0	0	0	0
Will McEnaney, p	.000	2	0	0	0	0	0	0	0	0	0	0
Joe Morgan, 2b	.333	4	15	3	5	1	1	1	2	2	2	2
Gary Nolan, p	.000	1	0	0	0	0	0	0	0	0	0	0
Fred Norman, p	.000	1	0	0	0	0	0	0	0	0	0	0
Tony Perez, 1b	.313	4	16	1	5	1	0	0	2	1	2	0
Pete Rose, 3b	.188	4	16	1	3	1	0	0	1	2	2	0
Pat Zachry, p	.000	1	0	0	0	0	0	0	0	0	0	0
TOTAL	.313		134	22	42	10	3	4	21	12	16	7

PITCHER	W	L	ERA	G	GS	CG	SV	SHO	IP	H	ER	BB	SO
Jack Billingham	1	0	0.00	1	0	0	0	0	2.2	0	0	0	1
Pedro Borbon	0	0	0.00	1	0	0	0	0	1.2	0	0	0	0
Don Gullett	1	0	1.23	1	1	0	0	0	7.1	5	1	3	4
Will McEnaney	0	0	0.00	2	0	0	2	0	4.2	2	0	1	2
Gary Nolan	1	0	2.70	1	1	0	0	0	6.2	8	2	1	1
Fred Norman	0	0	4.26	1	1	0	0	0	6.1	9	3	2	2
Pat Zachry	1	0	2.70	1	1	0	0	0	6.2	6	2	5	6
TOTAL	4	0	2.00	8	4	0	2	0	36.0	30	8	12	16

NY (A)

PLAYER/POS	AVG	G	AB	R	H	2B	3B	HR	RB	BB	SO	SB
Doyle Alexander, p	.000	1	0	0	0	0	0	0	0	0	0	0
Chris Chambliss, 1b	.313	4	16	1	5	1	0	0	1	0	2	0
Dock Ellis, p	.000	1	0	0	0	0	0	0	0	0	0	0
Ed Figueroa, p	.000	1	0	0	0	0	0	0	0	0	0	0
Oscar Gamble, of-2	.125	3	8	0	1	0	0	0	1	0	0	0
Elrod Hendricks, ph	.000	2	2	0	0	0	0	0	0	0	0	0
Catfish Hunter, p	.000	1	0	0	0	0	0	0	0	0	0	0
Grant Jackson, p	.000	1	0	0	0	0	0	0	0	0	0	0
Sparky Lyle, p	.000	2	0	0	0	0	0	0	0	0	0	0
Elliott Maddox, of-1,dh-1	.200	2	5	0	1	0	1	0	0	1	2	0
Jim Mason, ss	1.000	3	1	1	1	0	0	1	1	0	0	0
Carlos May, dh	.000	4	9	0	0	0	0	0	0	0	1	0
Thurman Munson, c	.529	4	17	2	9	0	0	0	2	0	1	0
Graig Nettles, 3b	.250	4	12	0	3	0	0	0	2	3	1	0
Lou Piniella, of-2,dh-2	.333	4	9	1	3	1	0	0	0	0	0	0
Willie Randolph, 2b	.071	4	14	1	1	0	0	0	0	1	3	0
Mickey Rivers, of	.167	4	18	1	3	0	0	0	0	1	2	1
Fred Stanley, ss	.167	4	6	1	1	1	0	0	1	3	1	0
Dick Tidrow, p	.000	2	0	0	0	0	0	0	0	0	0	0
Otto Velez, ph	.000	3	3	0	0	0	0	0	0	0	3	0
Roy White, of	.133	4	15	0	2	0	0	0	0	3	0	0
TOTAL	.222		135	8	30	3	1	1	8	12	16	1

PITCHER	W	L	ERA	G	GS	CG	SV	SHO	IP	H	ER	BB	SO
Doyle Alexander	0	1	7.50	1	1	0	0	0	6.0	9	5	2	1
Dock Ellis	0	1	10.80	1	1	0	0	0	3.1	7	4	0	1
Ed Figueroa	0	1	5.63	1	1	0	0	0	8.0	6	5	5	2
Catfish Hunter	0	1	3.12	1	1	1	0	0	8.2	10	3	4	5
Grant Jackson	0	0	4.91	1	0	0	0	0	3.2	4	2	0	3
Sparky Lyle	0	0	0.00	2	0	0	0	0	2.2	1	0	0	3
Dick Tidrow	0	0	7.71	2	0	0	0	0	2.1	5	2	1	1
TOTAL	0	4	5.45	9	4	1	0	0	34.2	42	21	12	16

GAME 1 AT CIN OCT 16

		R	H	E
NY	010 000 000	1	5	1
CIN	**101 001 20X**	**5**	**10**	**1**

Pitchers: ALEXANDER, Lyle (7) vs GULLETT, Borbon (8)
Home Runs: Morgan-CIN
Attendance: 54,826

GAME 2 AT CIN OCT 17

		R	H	E
NY	000 100 200	3	9	1
CIN	**030 000 001**	**4**	**10**	**0**

Pitchers: HUNTER vs Norman, BILLINGHAM (7)
Attendance: 54,816

GAME 3 AT NY OCT 19

		R	H	E
CIN	**030 100 020**	**6**	**13**	**2**
NY	000 100 100	2	8	0

Pitchers: ZACHRY, McEnaney (7) vs ELLIS, Jackson (4), Tidrow (8)
Home Runs: Driessen-CIN, Mason-NY
Attendance: 56,667

GAME 4 AT NY OCT 21

		R	H	E
CIN	**000 300 004**	**7**	**9**	**2**
NY	100 010 000	2	8	0

Pitchers: NOLAN, McEnaney (7) vs FIGUEROA, Tidrow (9), Lyle (9)
Home Runs: Bench-CIN (2)
Attendance: 56,700

The Phillies took the first game, but the Dodgers proved better at turning hits into runs and swept the next three. Philadelphia jumped ahead in the first inning of Game 1, and had built a 5–1 lead by the seventh, when Ron Cey tied the score with a grand slam. But the Phillies came back with two runs on three singles in the top of the ninth and held on for the win. As in Game 1, both clubs again got nine hits apiece in Game 2, but this time Dodgers pitcher Don Sutton scattered the Phillies' hits for a single run over nine innings, while Phillies starter Jim Lonborg—in the four innings he pitched—yielded five runs, including a grand slam to Dusty Baker.

In Game 3 Los Angeles outhit the Phillies, but the Dodgers were nearly undone when starter Burt Hooton walked in three Philadelphia runs in the second inning. The Phillies took a two-run lead into the ninth, but after two men were out the Dodgers rebounded, thanks largely to a couple of old pros. Pinch hitter Vic Davalillo, age 38, beat out a drag bunt on a disputed call, and 39-year-old Manny Mota doubled to deep left. Two more singles scored three runs that proved enough for the win.

The Dodgers didn't even need all of their five hits to take the final game behind Tommy John's one-run seven-hitter, for one of those hits was another Dusty Baker home run with a man aboard.

Los Angeles Dodgers (West), 3; Philadelphia Phillies (East), 1

LA (W)

PLAYER/POS	AVG	G	AB	R	H	2B	3B	HR	RB	BB	SO	SB
Dusty Baker, of	.357	4	14	4	5	1	0	2	8	2	3	0
Glenn Burke, of	.000	4	7	0	0	0	0	0	0	0	3	0
Ron Cey, 3b	.308	4	13	4	4	1	0	1	4	2	4	1
Vic Davalillo, ph	1.000	1	1	1	1	0	0	0	0	0	0	0
Mike Garman, p	.000	2	0	0	0	0	0	0	0	0	0	0
Steve Garvey, 1b	.308	4	13	2	4	0	0	0	0	2	1	1
Ed Goodson, ph	.000	1	1	0	0	0	0	0	0	0	0	0
Jerry Grote, c-1	.000	2	0	0	0	0	0	0	0	1	0	0
Burt Hooton, p	1.000	1	1	0	1	1	0	0	0	0	0	0
Charlie Hough, p	.000	1	0	0	0	0	0	0	0	0	0	0
Tommy John, p	.200	2	5	0	1	0	0	0	0	0	2	0
Lee Lacy, ph	1.000	1	1	1	1	0	0	0	0	0	0	0
Davey Lopes, 2b	.235	4	17	2	4	0	0	0	3	2	0	0
Rick Monday, of	.286	3	7	1	2	1	0	0	0	2	1	0
Manny Mota, ph	1.000	1	1	1	1	1	0	0	0	0	0	0
Doug Rau, p	.000	1	0	0	0	0	0	0	0	0	0	0
Lance Rautzhan, p	.000	1	0	0	0	0	0	0	0	0	0	0
Rick Rhoden, p	.000	1	1	0	0	0	0	0	0	0	0	0
Bill Russell, ss	.278	4	18	3	5	1	0	0	2	0	0	0
Reggie Smith, of	.188	4	16	2	3	0	1	0	1	2	5	1
Elias Sosa, p	.000	2	1	0	0	0	0	0	0	0	0	0
Don Sutton, p	.000	1	3	0	0	0	0	0	0	0	0	0
Steve Yeager, c	.231	4	13	1	3	0	0	0	2	1	3	0
TOTAL	.263		133	22	35	6	1	3	20	14	22	3

PITCHER	W	L	ERA	G	GS	CG	SV	SHO	IP	H	ER	BB	SO
Mike Garman	0	0	0.00	2	0	0	1	0	1.1	0	0	0	1
Burt Hooton	0	0	16.20	1	1	0	0	0	1.2	2	3	4	1
Charlie Hough	0	0	4.50	1	0	0	0	0	2.0	2	1	0	3
Tommy John	1	0	0.66	2	2	1	0	0	13.2	11	1	5	11
Doug Rau	0	0	0.00	1	0	0	0	0	1.0	0	0	0	1
Lance Rautzhan	1	0	0.00	1	0	0	0	0	0.1	0	0	0	0
Rick Rhoden	0	0	0.00	1	0	0	0	0	4.1	2	0	2	0
Elias Sosa	0	1	10.13	2	0	0	0	0	2.2	5	3	0	0
Don Sutton	1	0	1.00	1	1	1	0	0	9.0	9	1	0	4
TOTAL	3	1	2.25	12	4	2	1	0	36.0	31	9	11	21

PHI (E)

PLAYER/POS	AVG	G	AB	R	H	2B	3B	HR	RB	BB	SO	SB
Bob Boone, c	.400	4	10	1	4	0	0	0	0	0	0	0
Larry Bowa, ss	.118	4	17	2	2	0	0	0	1	1	0	0
Ollie Brown, ph	.000	2	2	0	0	0	0	0	0	0	1	0
Warren Brusstar, p	.000	2	0	0	0	0	0	0	0	0	0	0
Steve Carlton, p	.500	2	4	0	2	0	0	0	1	0	2	0
Larry Christenson, p	.000	1	0	0	0	0	0	0	1	1	0	0
Gene Garber, p	.000	3	0	0	0	0	0	0	0	0	0	0
Richie Hebner, 1b-3	.357	4	14	2	5	2	0	0	0	0	1	0
Tom Hutton, 1b-1	.000	3	3	0	0	0	0	0	0	0	0	0
Davey Johnson, 1b	.250	1	4	0	1	0	0	0	2	0	1	0
Jay Johnstone, of	.200	2	5	0	1	0	0	0	0	0	1	0
Jim Lonborg, p	.000	1	1	0	0	0	0	0	0	0	1	0
Greg Luzinski, of	.286	4	14	2	4	1	0	1	2	3	3	1
Garry Maddox, of	.429	2	7	1	3	0	0	0	2	0	1	0
Jerry Martin, of-1	.000	3	4	0	0	0	0	0	0	0	2	0
Bake McBride, of	.222	4	18	2	4	0	0	1	2	1	2	0
Tim McCarver, c-2	.167	3	6	1	1	0	0	0	0	1	3	0
Tug McGraw, p	.000	2	0	0	0	0	0	0	0	0	0	0
Ron Reed, p	.000	3	0	0	0	0	0	0	0	0	0	0
Mike Schmidt, 3b	.063	4	16	2	1	0	0	0	1	2	3	0
Ted Sizemore, 2b	.231	4	13	1	3	0	0	0	0	2	0	0
TOTAL	.225		138	14	31	3	0	2	12	11	21	1

PITCHER	W	L	ERA	G	GS	CG	SV	SHO	IP	H	ER	BB	SO
Warren Brusstar	0	0	3.38	2	0	0	0	0	2.2	2	1	1	2
Steve Carlton	0	1	6.94	2	2	0	0	0	11.2	13	9	8	6
Larry Christenson	0	0	8.10	1	1	0	0	0	3.1	7	3	0	2
Gene Garber	1	1	3.38	3	0	0	0	0	5.1	4	2	0	3
Jim Lonborg	0	1	11.25	1	1	0	0	0	4.0	5	5	1	1
Tug McGraw	0	0	0.00	2	0	0	1	0	3.0	1	0	2	3
Ron Reed	0	0	1.80	3	0	0	0	0	5.0	3	1	2	5
TOTAL	1	3	5.40	14	4	0	1	0	35.0	35	21	14	22

GAME 1 AT LA OCT 4

				R	H	E
PHI	200	021	002	7	9	0
LA	000	010	400	5	9	2

Pitchers: Carlton, GARBER (7), McGraw (9) vs John, Garman (5), Hough (6), SOSA (8)
Home Runs: Luzinski-PHI, Cey-LA
Attendance: 55,968

GAME 2 AT LA OCT 5

				R	H	E
PHI	001	000	000	1	9	1
LA	001	401	10X	7	9	1

Pitchers: LONBORG, Reed (5), Brusstar (7) vs SUTTON
Home Runs: McBride-PHI, Baker-LA
Attendance: 55,973

GAME 3 AT PHI OCT 7

				R	H	E
LA	020	100	003	6	12	2
PHI	030	000	020	5	6	2

Pitchers: Hooton, Rhoden (2), Rau (7), Sosa (8), RAUTZHAN (8), Garman (9) vs Christenson, Brusstar (4), Reed (5), GARBER (7)
Attendance: 63,719

GAME 4 AT PHI OCT 8

				R	H	E
LA	020	020	000	4	5	0
PHI	000	100	000	1	7	0

Pitchers: JOHN vs CARLTON, Reed (6), McGraw (7), Garber (9)
Home Runs: Baker-LA
Attendance: 64,924

As in 1976 the Royals met the Yankees in the ALCS, and as in 1976 the series went five games, with the Royals outscoring New York by a single run. But this time Kansas City won the first game, and as the teams traded victories through the first four games and K.C. took a lead into the ninth inning of Game 5, it began to look as though this year the Royals might take the pennant.

Royals hitters began things with a bang, scoring six of their seven runs in Game 1 in the first three innings for an insurmountable lead. New York came back to take the second game 6–2 behind Ron Guidry's three-hitter, but the Royals reversed the score the next day as Dennis Leonard limited the Yankees to four hits. Yankees reliever Sparky Lyle shut K.C. down over the final five innings of Game 4 after the Royals had drawn within a run of New York in the fourth inning, and the series was tied.

In the finale, Kansas City drew first blood with two runs in the bottom of the first and led by one run after eight. But with the pennant in sight, the Royals gave up three runs in the top of the ninth, scoring nothing themselves as reliever Lyle held them off to give the Yankees their thirty-first flag.

New York Yankees (East), 3; Kansas City Royals (West), 2

NY (E)

PLAYER/POS	AVG	G	AB	R	H	2B	3B	HR	RB	BB	SO	SB
Paul Blair, of	.400	3	5	1	2	0	0	0	0	0	0	0
Chris Chambliss, 1b	.059	5	17	0	1	0	0	0	0	3	4	0
Bucky Dent, ss	.214	5	14	1	3	1	0	0	2	1	0	0
Ed Figueroa, p	.000	1	0	0	0	0	0	0	0	0	0	0
Ron Guidry, p	.000	2	0	0	0	0	0	0	0	0	0	0
Don Gullett, p	.000	1	0	0	0	0	0	0	0	0	0	0
Reggie Jackson, of-4,dh-1	.125	5	16	1	2	0	0	0	1	2	2	1
Cliff Johnson, dh-4	.400	5	15	2	6	2	0	1	2	1	2	0
Sparky Lyle, p	.000	4	0	0	0	0	0	0	0	0	0	0
Thurman Munson, c	.286	5	21	3	6	1	0	1	5	0	2	0
Graig Nettles, 3b	.150	5	20	1	3	0	0	0	1	0	3	0
Lou Piniella, of-4,dh-1	.333	5	21	1	7	3	0	0	2	0	1	0
Willie Randolph, 2b	.278	5	18	4	5	1	0	0	2	1	0	0
Mickey Rivers, of	.391	5	23	5	9	2	0	0	2	0	2	1
Fred Stanley, ss	.000	2	0	0	0	0	0	0	0	0	0	0
Dick Tidrow, p	.000	2	0	0	0	0	0	0	0	0	0	0
Mike Torrez, p	.000	2	0	0	0	0	0	0	0	0	0	0
Roy White, of-1,dh-1	.400	4	5	2	2	2	0	0	0	1	0	0
TOTAL	.263		175	21	46	12	0	2	17	9	16	2

PITCHER	W	L	ERA	G	GS	CG	SV	SHO	IP	H	ER	BB	SO
Ed Figueroa	0	0	10.80	1	1	0	0	0	3.1	5	4	2	3
Ron Guidry	1	0	3.97	2	2	1	0	0	11.1	9	5	3	8
Don Gullett	0	1	18.00	1	1	0	0	0	2.0	4	4	2	0
Sparky Lyle	2	0	0.96	4	0	0	0	0	9.1	7	1	0	3
Dick Tidrow	0	0	3.86	2	0	0	0	0	7.0	6	3	3	3
Mike Torrez	0	1	4.09	2	1	0	0	0	11.0	11	5	5	5
TOTAL	3	2	4.50	12	5	1	0	0	44.0	42	22	15	22

KC (W)

PLAYER/POS	AVG	G	AB	R	H	2B	3B	HR	RB	BB	SO	SB
Doug Bird, p	.000	3	0	0	0	0	0	0	0	0	0	0
George Brett, 3b	.300	5	20	2	6	0	2	0	2	1	0	0
Al Cowens, of	.263	5	19	2	5	0	0	1	5	1	3	0
Larry Gura, p	.000	2	0	0	0	0	0	0	0	0	0	0
Andy Hassler, p	.000	1	0	0	0	0	0	0	0	0	0	0
Pete LaCock, 1b	.000	1	1	0	0	0	0	0	0	1	1	0
Joe Lahoud, dh	.000	1	1	2	0	0	0	0	0	2	0	0
Dennis Leonard, p	.000	2	0	0	0	0	0	0	0	0	0	0
Mark Littell, p	.000	2	0	0	0	0	0	0	0	0	0	0
John Mayberry, 1b	.167	4	12	1	2	1	0	1	3	1	2	0
Hal McRae, dh-3,of-2	.444	5	18	6	8	3	0	1	2	3	1	0
Steve Mingori, p	.000	3	0	0	0	0	0	0	0	0	0	0
Amos Otis, of	.125	5	16	1	2	1	0	0	2	2	3	2
Freddie Patek, ss	.389	5	18	4	7	3	1	0	5	1	2	0
Marty Pattin, p	.000	1	0	0	0	0	0	0	0	0	0	0
Tom Poquette, of	.167	2	6	0	1	0	0	0	0	0	0	0
Darrell Porter, c	.333	5	15	3	5	0	0	0	0	0	3	0
Cookie Rojas, dh	.250	1	4	0	1	0	0	0	0	0	1	1
Paul Splittorff, p	.000	2	0	0	0	0	0	0	0	0	0	0
John Wathan, 1b-2,c-1,dh-1	.000	4	6	0	0	0	0	0	0	0	3	0
Frank White, 2b	.278	5	18	1	5	1	0	0	2	0	4	1
Joe Zdeb, of	.000	4	9	0	0	0	0	0	0	0	2	1
TOTAL	.258		163	22	42	9	3	3	21	15	22	5

PITCHER	W	L	ERA	G	GS	CG	SV	SHO	IP	H	ER	BB	SO
Doug Bird	0	0	0.00	3	0	0	0	0	2.0	4	0	0	1
Larry Gura	0	1	18.00	2	1	0	0	0	2.0	7	4	1	2
Andy Hassler	0	1	4.76	1	1	0	0	0	5.2	5	3	0	3
Dennis Leonard	1	1	3.00	2	1	1	0	0	9.0	5	3	2	4
Mark Littell	0	0	3.00	2	0	0	0	0	3.0	5	1	3	1
Steve Mingori	0	0	0.00	3	0	0	0	0	1.1	0	0	0	1
Marty Pattin	0	0	1.50	1	0	0	0	0	6.0	6	1	0	0
Paul Splittorff	1	0	2.40	2	2	0	0	0	15.0	14	4	3	4
TOTAL	2	3	3.27	16	5	1	0	0	44.0	46	16	9	16

GAME 1 AT NY OCT 5

				R	H	E
KC	222	000	010	7	9	0
NY	002	000	000	2	9	0

Pitchers: SPLITTORFF, Bird (9) vs GULLETT, Tidrow (3), Lyle (9)
Home Runs: McRae-KC, Mayberry-KC, Munson-NY, Cowens-KC
Attendance: 54,930

GAME 2 AT NY OCT 6

				R	H	E
KC	001	001	000	2	3	1
NY	000	023	01X	6	10	1

Pitchers: HASSLER, Littell (6), Mingori (8) vs GUIDRY
Home Runs: Johnson-NY
Attendance: 56,230

GAME 3 AT KC OCT 7

				R	H	E
NY	000	010	001	2	4	1
KC	011	012	10X	6	12	1

Pitchers: TORREZ, Lyle (6) vs LEONARD
Attendance: 41,285

GAME 4 AT KC OCT 8

				R	H	E
NY	121	100	001	6	13	0
KC	002	200	000	4	8	2

Pitchers: Figueroa, Tidrow (4), LYLE (4) vs GURA, Pattin (3), Mingori (9), Bird (9)
Attendance: 41,135

GAME 5 AT KC OCT 9

				R	H	E
NY	001	000	013	5	10	0
KC	201	000	000	3	10	1

Pitchers: Guidry, Torrez (3), LYLE (8) vs Splittorff, Bird (8), Mingori (8), LEONARD (9), Gura (9), Littell (9)
Attendance: 41,133

This was the Series in which Reggie Jackson established his reputation as "Mr. October" with a record five home runs, including three in successive at bats in the final game, and the Yankees showed that after a decade or so of decline they were once again the world's best. Los Angeles scored first in the opening game with a pair of first-inning runs. But New York gained back half the ground in the bottom of the first and tied the game on Willie Randolph's leadoff homer in the sixth. The clubs traded runs in the eighth and ninth to take the game into extra innings. The impasse was not breached until the last of the 12th, when Randolph doubled and Paul Blair singled him home.

Game 2, by contrast, was a runaway Dodgers victory. Home runs in the first three innings by Ron Cey, Steve Yeager, and Reggie Smith made the score 5–0 before New York scored its lone run in the fourth. Burt Hooton got the win with a five-hitter, and for good measure, Steve Garvey homered in the ninth inning. The Yankees returned to form two days later in Los Angeles, though, scoring three runs in the top of the first on pairs of doubles and singles (and a Dodgers error). Dusty Baker's three-run homer tied the game in the third, but single runs in the next two innings provided Yankees pitcher Mike Torrez with runs enough for the win.

Two of the four hits yielded by emerging Yankees ace Ron Guidry in Game 4 were pitcher Rick Rhoden's double followed by Davey Lopes' home run in the third inning. But the Yankees had already scored three times in the second, and Reggie Jackson homered in the sixth as Guidry held Los Angeles scoreless after the third for a 4–2 win. New York's assault against pitcher Don Sutton in Game 5 included back-to-back home runs by Thurman Munson and Jackson in the eighth inning. But Los Angeles rocked Yankees pitching even harder, with homers by Steve Yeager and Reggie Smith producing five of the Dodgers' 10 runs as the club evaded elimination with its second win.

The Dodgers scored first in the sixth game when Steve Garvey's first-inning triple drove in two runners. Chris Chambliss matched that an inning later for the Yankees with a two-run homer. Smith restored the lead to Los Angeles with a solo shot in the third inning, but Jackson put the Yankees back in front with the first of his three home runs, a two-run blast in the fourth. By the time he had homered again for two in the fifth and for the third time in the eighth, the Yankees' 21st world title was well in hand.

New York Yankees (AL), 4; Los Angeles Dodgers (NL), 2

NY (A)

PLAYER/POS	AVG	G	AB	R	H	2B	3B	HR	RB	BB	SO	SB
Paul Blair, of-3	.250	4	4	0	1	0	0	0	1	0	0	0
Chris Chambliss, 1b	.292	6	24	4	7	2	0	1	4	0	2	0
Ken Clay, p	.000	2	0	0	0	0	0	0	0	0	0	0
Bucky Dent, ss	.263	6	19	0	5	0	0	0	2	2	1	0
Ron Guidry, p	.000	1	2	0	0	0	0	0	0	0	1	0
Don Gullett, p	.000	2	2	0	0	0	0	0	0	0	2	0
Catfish Hunter, p	.000	2	0	0	0	0	0	0	0	0	0	0
Reggie Jackson, of	.450	6	20	10	9	1	0	5	8	3	4	0
Cliff Johnson, c-1	.000	2	1	0	0	0	0	0	0	0	0	0
Sparky Lyle, p	.000	2	2	0	0	0	0	0	0	0	2	0
Thurman Munson, c	.320	6	25	4	8	2	0	1	3	2	8	0
Graig Nettles, 3b	.190	6	21	1	4	1	0	0	2	2	3	0
Lou Piniella, of	.273	6	22	1	6	0	0	0	3	0	3	0
Willie Randolph, 2b	.160	6	25	5	4	2	0	1	1	2	2	0
Mickey Rivers, of	.222	6	27	1	6	2	0	0	1	0	2	1
Fred Stanley, ss	.000	1	0	0	0	0	0	0	0	0	0	0
Dick Tidrow, p	.000	2	1	0	0	0	0	0	0	0	1	0
Mike Torrez, p	.000	2	6	0	0	0	0	0	0	0	4	0
Roy White, ph	.000	2	2	0	0	0	0	0	0	0	0	0
George Zeber, ph	.000	2	2	0	0	0	0	0	0	0	2	0
TOTAL	.244		205	26	50	10	0	8	25	11	37	1

PITCHER	W	L	ERA	G	GS	CG	SV	SHO	IP	H	ER	BB	SO
Ken Clay	0	0	2.45	2	0	0	0	0	3.2	2	1	1	0
Ron Guidry	1	0	2.00	1	1	1	0	0	9.0	4	2	3	7
Don Gullett	0	1	6.39	2	2	0	0	0	12.2	13	9	7	10
Catfish Hunter	0	1	10.38	2	1	0	0	0	4.1	6	5	0	1
Sparky Lyle	1	0	1.93	2	0	0	0	0	4.2	2	1	0	2
Dick Tidrow	0	0	4.91	2	0	0	0	0	3.2	5	2	0	1
Mike Torrez	2	0	2.50	2	2	2	0	0	18.0	16	5	5	15
TOTAL	4	2	4.02	13	6	3	0	0	56.0	48	25	16	36

LA (N)

PLAYER/POS	AVG	G	AB	R	H	2B	3B	HR	RB	BB	SO	SB
Dusty Baker, of	.292	6	24	4	7	0	0	1	5	0	2	0
Glenn Burke, of	.200	3	5	0	1	0	0	0	0	0	1	0
Ron Cey, 3b	.190	6	21	2	4	1	0	1	3	3	5	0
Vic Davalillo, ph	.333	3	3	0	1	0	0	0	1	0	0	0
Mike Garman, p	.000	2	0	0	0	0	0	0	0	0	0	0
Steve Garvey, 1b	.375	6	24	5	9	1	1	1	3	1	4	0
Ed Goodson, ph	.000	1	1	0	0	0	0	0	0	0	1	0
Jerry Grote, c	.000	1	1	0	0	0	0	0	0	0	0	0
Burt Hooton, p	.000	2	5	0	0	0	0	0	0	0	2	0
Charlie Hough, p	.000	2	0	0	0	0	0	0	0	0	0	0
Tommy John, p	.000	1	2	0	0	0	0	0	0	0	2	0
Lee Lacy, of-2	.429	4	7	1	3	0	0	0	2	1	1	0
Rafael Landestoy, pr	.000	1	0	0	0	0	0	0	0	0	0	0
Davey Lopes, 2b	.167	6	24	3	4	0	1	1	2	4	3	2
Rick Monday, of	.167	4	12	0	2	0	0	0	0	0	3	0
Manny Mota, ph	.000	3	3	0	0	0	0	0	0	0	1	0
Johnny Oates, c	.000	1	1	0	0	0	0	0	0	0	0	0
Doug Rau, p	.000	2	0	0	0	0	0	0	0	0	0	0
Lance Rautzhan, p	.000	1	0	0	0	0	0	0	0	0	0	0
Rick Rhoden, p	.500	2	2	1	1	1	0	0	0	0	0	0
Bill Russell, ss	.154	6	26	3	4	0	1	0	2	1	3	0
Reggie Smith, of	.273	6	22	7	6	1	0	3	5	4	3	0
Elias Sosa, p	.000	2	0	0	0	0	0	0	0	0	0	0
Don Sutton, p	.000	2	6	0	0	0	0	0	0	1	4	0
Steve Yeager, c	.316	6	19	2	6	1	0	2	5	1	1	0
TOTAL	.231		208	28	48	5	3	9	28	16	36	2

PITCHER	W	L	ERA	G	GS	CG	SV	SHO	IP	H	ER	BB	SO
Mike Garman	0	0	0.00	2	0	0	0	0	4.0	2	0	1	3
Burt Hooton	1	1	3.75	2	2	1	0	0	12.0	8	5	2	9
Charlie Hough	0	0	1.80	2	0	0	0	0	5.0	3	1	0	5
Tommy John	0	1	6.00	1	1	0	0	0	6.0	9	4	3	7
Doug Rau	0	1	11.57	2	1	0	0	0	2.1	4	3	0	1
Lance Rautzhan	0	0	0.00	1	0	0	0	0	0.1	0	0	2	0
Rick Rhoden	0	1	2.57	2	0	0	0	0	7.0	4	2	1	5
Elias Sosa	0	0	11.57	2	0	0	0	0	2.1	3	3	1	1
Don Sutton	1	0	3.94	2	2	1	0	0	16.0	17	7	1	6
TOTAL	2	4	4.09	16	6	2	0	0	55.0	50	25	11	37

GAME 1 AT NY OCT 11

LA	200	000	001	000	3	6	0
NY	100	001	010	001	4	11	0

Pitchers: Sutton, Rautzhan (8), Sosa (8), Garman (9), RHODEN (12) vs Gullett, LYLE (9)
Home Runs: Randolph-NY
Attendance: 56,668

GAME 2 AT NY OCT 12

LA	212	000	001	6	9	0
NY	000	100	000	1	5	0

Pitchers: HOOTON vs HUNTER, Tidrow (3), Clay (6), Lyle (9)
Home Runs: Cey-LA, Yeager-LA, Smith-LA, Garvey-LA
Attendance: 56,691

GAME 3 AT LA OCT 14

NY	300	110	000	5	10	0
LA	003	000	000	3	7	1

Pitchers: TORREZ vs JOHN, Hough (7)
Home Runs: Baker-LA
Attendance: 55,992

GAME 4 AT LA OCT 15

NY	030	001	000	4	7	0
LA	002	000	000	2	4	0

Pitchers: GUIDRY vs RAU, Rhoden (2), Garman (9)
Home Runs: Lopes-LA, Jackson-NY
Attendance: 55,995

GAME 5 AT LA OCT 16

NY	000	000	220	4	9	2
LA	100	432	00X	10	13	0

Pitchers: GULLETT, Clay (5), Tidrow (6), Hunter (7) vs SUTTON
Home Runs: Yeager-LA, Smith-LA, Munson-NY, Jackson-NY
Attendance: 55,955

GAME 6 AT NY OCT 18

LA	201	000	001	4	9	0
NY	020	320	01X	8	8	1

Pitchers: HOOTON, Sosa (4), Rau (5), Hough (7) vs TORREZ
Home Runs: Chambliss-NY, Smith-LA, Jackson-NY (3)
Attendance: 56,407

Steve Garvey hit half the Dodgers' eight home runs and Tommy John hurled the first LCS shutout in four years as Los Angeles, for the second year in a row, defeated the Phillies for the pennant in four games. Philadelphia's five runs in Game 1 would have been enough to win any of the other games, but not this one as the Dodgers outhomered the Phillies four to one (including two by Garvey) and scored nine times. Dodger Davey Lopes hit the game's only home run the next day (with a man aboard), but it was more than enough support for John's four-hit shutout.

The series' most decisive win went to the Phillies in Game 3. Steve Carlton allowed four runs to score, but he made up for it by driving four runs of his own on a homer and sacrifice fly. His teammates added five more, rendering futile Garvey's third series home run.

But Garvey's fourth homer, in Game 4, helped carry the Dodgers into the 10th inning, when Bill Russell—capitalizing on Gary Maddox's muff of Ron Cey's fly to center—singled home Cey with the Dodgers' unearned pennant winner.

Los Angeles Dodgers (West), 3; Philadelphia Phillies (East), 1

LA (W)

PLAYER/POS	AVG	G	AB	R	H	2B	3B	HR	RB	BB	SO	SB
Dusty Baker, of	.467	4	15	1	7	2	0	0	1	3	0	0
Ron Cey, 3b	.313	4	16	4	5	1	0	1	3	2	4	0
Joe Ferguson, ph	.000	2	2	0	0	0	0	0	0	0	1	0
Terry Forster, p	.000	1	0	0	0	0	0	0	0	0	0	0
Steve Garvey, 1b	.389	4	18	6	7	1	1	4	7	0	1	0
Jerry Grote, c	.000	1	0	0	0	0	0	0	0	0	0	0
Burt Hooton, p	.000	1	2	0	0	0	0	0	0	0	1	0
Charlie Hough, p	.000	1	0	0	0	0	0	0	0	0	0	0
Tommy John, p	.000	1	3	0	0	0	0	0	0	0	0	0
Lee Lacy, ph	.000	2	2	0	0	0	0	0	0	0	0	0
Davey Lopes, 2b	.389	4	18	3	7	1	1	2	5	0	1	1
Rick Monday, of	.200	3	10	2	2	0	1	0	0	1	5	0
Manny Mota, ph	1.000	2	1	0	1	1	0	0	0	0	0	0
Billy North, of	.000	4	8	0	0	0	0	0	0	0	1	0
Doug Rau, p	.000	1	1	0	0	0	0	0	0	0	0	0
Lance Rautzhan, p	.000	1	0	0	0	0	0	0	0	0	0	0
Rick Rhoden, p	.000	1	1	0	0	0	0	0	0	0	0	0
Bill Russell, ss	.412	4	17	1	7	1	0	0	2	1	1	0
Reggie Smith, of	.188	4	16	2	3	1	0	0	1	0	2	0
Don Sutton, p	.000	1	2	0	0	0	0	0	0	0	2	0
Bob Welch, p	.000	1	2	0	0	0	0	0	0	0	1	0
Steve Yeager, c	.231	4	13	2	3	0	0	1	2	2	2	1
TOTAL	.286		147	21	42	8	3	8	21	9	22	2

PITCHER	W	L	ERA	G	GS	CG	SV	SHO	IP	H	ER	BB	SO
Terry Forster	1	0	0.00	1	0	0	0	0	1.0	1	0	0	2
Burt Hooton	0	0	7.71	1	1	0	0	0	4.2	10	4	0	5
Charlie Hough	0	0	4.50	1	0	0	0	0	2.0	1	1	0	1
Tommy John	1	0	0.00	1	1	1	0	1	9.0	4	0	2	4
Doug Rau	0	0	3.60	1	1	0	0	0	5.0	5	2	2	1
Lance Rautzhan	0	0	6.75	1	0	0	0	0	1.1	3	1	2	0
Rick Rhoden	0	0	2.25	1	0	0	0	0	4.0	2	1	1	3
Don Sutton	0	1	6.35	1	1	0	0	0	5.2	7	4	2	0
Bob Welch	1	0	2.08	1	0	0	0	0	4.1	2	1	0	5
TOTAL	3	1	3.41	9	4	1	0	1	37.0	35	14	9	21

PHI (E)

PLAYER/POS	AVG	G	AB	R	H	2B	3B	HR	RB	BB	SO	SB
Bob Boone, c	.182	3	11	0	2	0	0	0	0	0	1	0
Larry Bowa, ss	.333	4	18	2	6	0	0	0	0	1	2	0
Warren Brusstar, p	.000	3	0	0	0	0	0	0	0	0	0	0
Jose Cardenal, 1b	.167	2	6	0	1	0	0	0	0	1	1	0
Steve Carlton, p	.500	1	4	2	2	0	0	1	4	0	0	0
Larry Christenson, p	.000	1	1	0	0	0	0	0	0	0	1	0
Rawly Eastwick, p	.000	1	0	0	0	0	0	0	0	0	0	0
Barry Foote, ph	.000	1	1	0	0	0	0	0	0	0	1	0
Orlando Gonzalez, ph	.000	1	1	0	0	0	0	0	0	0	1	0
Richie Hebner, 1b-2	.111	3	9	0	1	0	0	0	1	0	0	0
Randy Lerch, p	.000	1	2	0	0	0	0	0	0	0	0	0
Greg Luzinski, of	.375	4	16	3	6	0	1	2	3	1	2	0
Garry Maddox, of	.263	4	19	1	5	0	0	0	2	0	3	0
Jerry Martin, of-3	.222	4	9	1	2	1	0	1	2	1	3	0
Bake McBride, of-2	.222	3	9	2	2	0	0	1	1	0	2	0
Tim McCarver, c-1	.000	2	4	2	0	0	0	0	1	2	0	0
Tug McGraw, p	.000	3	0	0	0	0	0	0	0	0	0	0
Jim Morrison, ph	.000	1	1	0	0	0	0	0	0	0	1	0
Ron Reed, p	.000	2	0	0	0	0	0	0	0	0	0	0
Dick Ruthven, p	.000	1	1	0	0	0	0	0	0	0	1	0
Mike Schmidt, 3b	.200	4	15	1	3	2	0	0	1	2	2	0
Ted Sizemore, 2b	.385	4	13	3	5	0	1	0	1	1	0	0
TOTAL	.250		140	17	35	3	2	5	16	9	21	0

PITCHER	W	L	ERA	G	GS	CG	SV	SHO	IP	H	ER	BB	SO
Warren Brusstar	0	0	0.00	3	0	0	0	0	2.2	2	0	1	0
Steve Carlton	1	0	4.00	1	1	1	0	0	9.0	8	4	2	8
Larry Christenson	0	1	12.46	1	1	0	0	0	4.1	7	6	1	3
Rawly Eastwick	0	0	9.00	1	0	0	0	0	1.0	3	1	0	1
Randy Lerch	0	0	5.06	1	1	0	0	0	5.1	7	3	0	0
Tug McGraw	0	1	1.59	3	0	0	0	0	5.2	3	1	5	5
Ron Reed	0	0	2.25	2	0	0	0	0	4.0	6	1	0	2
Dick Ruthven	0	1	5.79	1	1	0	0	0	4.2	6	3	0	3
TOTAL	1	3	4.66	13	4	1	0	0	36.2	42	19	9	22

GAME 1 AT PHI OCT 4

LA	004	211	001	9	13	1
PHI	010	030	001	5	12	1

Pitchers: Hooton, WELCH (5) vs CHRISTENSON, Brusstar (5), Eastwick (6), McGraw (7)
Home Runs: Garvey-LA (2), Lopes-LA, Yeager-LA, Martin-PHI
Attendance: 63,460

GAME 2 AT PHI OCT 5

LA	000	120	100	4	8	0
PHI	000	000	000	0	4	0

Pitchers: JOHN vs RUTHVEN, Brusstar (5), Reed (7), McGraw (9)
Home Runs: Lopes-LA
Attendance: 60,642

GAME 3 AT LA OCT 6

PHI	040	003	101	9	11	1
LA	012	000	010	4	8	2

Pitchers: CARLTON vs SUTTON, Rautzhan (6), Hough (8)
Home Runs: Carlton-PHI, Luzinski-PHI, Garvey-LA
Attendance: 55,043

GAME 4 AT LA OCT 7

PHI	002	000	100	0	3	8	2
LA	010	101	000	1	4	13	0

Pitchers: Lerch, Brusstar (6), Reed (7), McGRAW (9) vs Rau, Rhoden (6), FORSTER (10)
Home Runs: Luzinski-PHI, Cey-LA, Garvey-LA, McBride-PHI
Attendance: 55,124

It took Bucky Dent's pop-fly home run against Boston in an Eastern Division tiebreaker to carry the Yankees into the ALCS. But once there they took the pennant, downing the Royals for the third year in a row. Reggie Jackson's three-run homer in the eighth inning of Game 1 capped a 16-hit attack that scored seven runs as pitchers Jim Beattie and Ken Clay combined to limit Kansas City to two hits and a single run. The Royals, though, made it look just as easy the next day as their own 16 hits and ten runs evened the series.

Twice in Game 3 George Brett gave the Royals a lead with a home run, and he tied the game with a third homer in the fifth. But Jackson's two-run homer in the fourth brought the Yankees back, and Thurman Munson's two-run shot in the eighth gave New York a close win. Game 4 was just as close, but more of a pitcher's duel. Dennis Leonard, who went the distance, gave up only four hits, but two of them were home runs to Graig Nettles and Roy White. Yankees starter Ron Guidry allowed a run in the first, but shut out the Royals for the next seven innings. Goose Gossage preserved Guidry's good work—and the pennant—in the ninth.

New York Yankees (East), 3; Kansas City Royals (West), 1

NY (E)

PLAYER/POS	AVG	G	AB	R	H	2B	3B	HR	RB	BB	SO	SB
Jim Beattie, p	.000	1	0	0	0	0	0	0	0	0	0	0
Paul Blair, of-3,2b-1	.000	4	6	1	0	0	0	0	0	0	1	0
Chris Chambliss, 1b	.400	4	15	1	6	0	0	0	2	0	4	0
Ken Clay, p	.000	1	0	0	0	0	0	0	0	0	0	0
Bucky Dent, ss	.200	4	15	0	3	0	0	0	4	0	0	0
Brian Doyle, 2b	.286	3	7	0	2	0	0	0	1	1	1	0
Ed Figueroa, p	.000	1	0	0	0	0	0	0	0	0	0	0
Rich Gossage, p	.000	2	0	0	0	0	0	0	0	0	0	0
Ron Guidry, p	.000	1	0	0	0	0	0	0	0	0	0	0
Catfish Hunter, p	.000	1	0	0	0	0	0	0	0	0	0	0
Reggie Jackson, dh-3,of-1	.462	4	13	5	6	1	0	2	6	3	4	0
Cliff Johnson, ph	.000	1	1	0	0	0	0	0	0	0	0	0
Sparky Lyle, p	.000	1	0	0	0	0	0	0	0	0	0	0
Thurman Munson, c	.278	4	18	2	5	1	0	1	2	0	0	0
Graig Nettles, 3b	.333	4	15	3	5	0	1	1	2	0	1	0
Lou Piniella, of	.235	4	17	2	4	0	0	0	0	0	3	0
Mickey Rivers, of	.455	4	11	0	5	0	0	0	0	2	0	0
Fred Stanley, 2b	.200	2	5	0	1	0	0	0	0	0	2	0
Gary Thomasson, of	.000	3	1	0	0	0	0	0	0	0	0	0
Dick Tidrow, p	.000	1	0	0	0	0	0	0	0	0	0	0
Roy White, of-3,dh-1	.313	4	16	5	5	1	0	1	1	1	2	0
TOTAL	.300		140	19	42	3	1	5	18	7	18	0

PITCHER	W	L	ERA	G	GS	CG	SV	SHO	IP	H	ER	BB	SO
Jim Beattie	1	0	1.69	1	1	0	0	0	5.1	2	1	5	3
Ken Clay	0	0	0.00	1	0	0	1	0	3.2	0	0	3	2
Ed Figueroa	0	1	27.00	1	1	0	0	0	1.0	5	3	0	0
Rich Gossage	1	0	4.50	2	0	0	1	0	4.0	3	2	0	3
Ron Guidry	1	0	1.13	1	1	0	0	0	8.0	7	1	1	7
Catfish Hunter	0	0	4.50	1	1	0	0	0	6.0	7	3	3	5
Sparky Lyle	0	0	13.50	1	0	0	0	0	1.1	3	2	0	0
Dick Tidrow	0	0	4.76	1	0	0	0	0	5.2	8	3	2	1
TOTAL	3	1	3.86	9	4	0	2	0	35.0	35	15	14	21

KC (W)

PLAYER/POS	AVG	G	AB	R	H	2B	3B	HR	RB	BB	SO	SB
Doug Bird, p	.000	2	0	0	0	0	0	0	0	0	0	0
Steve Braun, of-1	.000	2	5	0	0	0	0	0	0	1	1	0
George Brett, 3b	.389	4	18	7	7	1	1	3	3	0	1	0
Al Cowens, of	.133	4	15	2	2	0	0	0	1	0	2	0
Larry Gura, p	.000	1	0	0	0	0	0	0	0	0	0	0
Al Hrabosky, p	.000	3	0	0	0	0	0	0	0	0	0	0
Clint Hurdle, of-2	.375	4	8	1	3	0	1	0	1	2	3	0
Pete LaCock, 1b-3	.364	4	11	1	4	2	1	0	1	3	1	1
Dennis Leonard, p	.000	2	0	0	0	0	0	0	0	0	0	0
Hal McRae, dh	.214	4	14	0	3	0	0	0	2	2	2	1
Steve Mingori, p	.000	1	0	0	0	0	0	0	0	0	0	0
Amos Otis, of	.429	4	14	2	6	2	0	0	1	3	5	4
Freddie Patek, ss	.077	4	13	2	1	0	0	1	2	1	4	0
Marty Pattin, p	.000	1	0	0	0	0	0	0	0	0	0	0
Tom Poquette, ph	.000	1	1	0	0	0	0	0	0	0	0	0
Darrell Porter, c	.357	4	14	1	5	1	0	0	3	2	0	0
Paul Splittorff, p	.000	1	0	0	0	0	0	0	0	0	0	0
John Wathan, 1b	.000	1	3	0	0	0	0	0	0	0	0	0
Frank White, 2b	.231	4	13	1	3	0	0	0	2	0	0	0
Willie Wilson, of	.250	3	4	0	1	0	0	0	0	0	2	0
TOTAL	.263		133	17	35	6	3	4	16	14	21	6

PITCHER	W	L	ERA	G	GS	CG	SV	SHO	IP	H	ER	BB	SO
Doug Bird	0	1	9.00	2	0	0	0	0	1.0	2	1	0	1
Larry Gura	1	0	2.84	1	1	0	0	0	6.1	8	2	2	2
Al Hrabosky	0	0	3.00	3	0	0	0	0	3.0	3	1	0	2
Dennis Leonard	0	2	3.75	2	2	1	0	0	12.0	13	5	2	11
Steve Mingori	0	0	7.36	1	0	0	0	0	3.2	5	3	3	0
Marty Pattin	0	0	27.00	1	0	0	0	0	0.2	2	2	0	0
Paul Splittorff	0	0	4.91	1	1	0	0	0	7.1	9	4	0	2
TOTAL	1	3	4.76	11	4	1	0	0	34.0	42	18	7	18

GAME 1 AT KC OCT 3

				R	H	E
NY	011	020	030	7	16	0
KC	000	001	000	1	2	2

Pitchers: BEATTIE, Clay (6) vs LEONARD, Mingori (5), Hrabosky (8), Bird (9)
Home Runs: Jackson-NY
Attendance: 41,143

GAME 2 AT KC OCT 4

				R	H	E
NY	000	000	220	4	12	1
KC	140	000	32X	10	16	1

Pitchers: FIGUEROA, Tidrow (2), Lyle (7) vs GURA, Pattin (7), Hrabosky (8)
Home Runs: Patek-KC
Attendance: 41,158

GAME 3 AT NY OCT 6

				R	H	E
KC	101	010	020	5	10	1
NY	010	201	02X	6	10	0

Pitchers: Splittorff, BIRD (8), Hrabosky (8) vs Hunter, GOSSAGE (7)
Home Runs: Brett-KC (3), Jackson-NY, Munson-NY
Attendance: 55,535

GAME 4 AT NY OCT 7

				R	H	E
KC	100	000	000	1	7	0
NY	010	001	00X	2	4	0

Pitchers: LEONARD vs GUIDRY, Gossage (9)
Home Runs: Nettles-NY, R.White-NY
Attendance: 56,356

New York Yankees (AL), 4; Los Angeles Dodgers (NL), 2

The outcome was the same as in 1977: the Yankees over the Dodgers in six games. But this year New York overcame a two-game deficit by sweeping the next four, a feat never before achieved in a World Series.

Los Angeles overwhelmed New York in the opener. Home runs in the second and fourth innings by Dusty Baker and Davey Lopes (who had two homers and five RBIs) and another run in the fifth, gave the Dodgers a 7–0 lead before Reggie Jackson's leadoff homer in the seventh gave New York its first score. The Yankees scored four more times, but so did the Dodgers for an 11–5 win. Game 2 was closer. The Yankees scored first and held a lead through the top of the sixth, but Ron Cey's three-run homer in the bottom of the inning gave Los Angeles the runs they needed to win 4–3.

Ron Guidry, coming off a spectacular 25–3 regular season, gave up eight hits and issued seven walks. But only one baserunner scored, thanks in large part to several memorable stops and throws by third baseman Graig Nettles. Meanwhile, Roy White's home run in the first inning began the scoring in what would become a 5–1 Yankees' win.

It took 10 innings for New York to win Game 4. Starters Tommy John and Ed Figueroa hurled shutout ball until Reggie Smith tagged Figueroa for a three-run homer in the top of the fifth. The Yankees clawed back in the sixth. Reggie Jackson singled in one run, then—in a play that stirred great controversy—got in the way (the Dodgers claimed intentionally) of a throw from second on an attempted double play, deflecting the ball to the outfield and permitting a second run to score. In the eighth, Thurman Munson doubled home the tying run, and in the last of the 10th Lou Piniella's two-out drive to center scored baserunner Roy White with the game winner.

Game 5 was a blowout. No one hit home runs, but the Yankees hit 16 singles (a Series record) and two doubles for 12 runs (five of them driven in by Munson's three hits) to give Jim Beattie (nine hits, two runs) an easy win. Back in Los Angeles for the sixth game, the Yankees won the crown on the hitting of two men at the bottom of the batting order: Brian Doyle and Bucky Dent. With three hits each, they combined for five RBIs in the 7–2 win. For good measure, Reggie Jackson concluded the Series scoring with a mighty two-run homer in the seventh.

NY (A)

PLAYER/POS	AVG	G	AB	R	H	2B	3B	HR	RB	BB	SO	SB
Jim Beattie, p	.000	1	0	0	0	0	0	0	0	0	0	0
Paul Blair, of	.375	6	8	2	3	1	0	0	0	1	4	0
Chris Chambliss, 1b	.182	3	11	1	2	0	0	0	0	1	1	0
Ken Clay, p	.000	1	0	0	0	0	0	0	0	0	0	0
Bucky Dent, ss	.417	6	24	3	10	1	0	0	7	1	2	0
Brian Doyle, 2b	.438	6	16	4	7	1	0	0	2	0	0	0
Ed Figueroa, p	.000	2	0	0	0	0	0	0	0	0	0	0
Rich Gossage, p	.000	3	0	0	0	0	0	0	0	0	0	0
Ron Guidry, p	.000	1	0	0	0	0	0	0	0	0	0	0
Mike Heath, c	.000	1	0	0	0	0	0	0	0	0	0	0
Catfish Hunter, p	.000	2	0	0	0	0	0	0	0	0	0	0
Reggie Jackson, dh	.391	6	23	2	9	1	0	2	8	3	7	0
Cliff Johnson, ph	.000	2	2	0	0	0	0	0	0	0	1	0
Jay Johnstone, of	.000	2	0	0	0	0	0	0	0	0	0	0
Paul Lindblad, p	.000	1	0	0	0	0	0	0	0	0	0	0
Thurman Munson, c	.320	6	25	5	8	3	0	0	7	3	7	1
Graig Nettles, 3b	.160	6	25	2	4	0	0	0	1	0	6	0
Lou Piniella, of	.280	6	25	3	7	0	0	0	4	0	0	1
Mickey Rivers, of-4	.333	5	18	2	6	0	0	0	1	0	2	1
Jim Spencer, 1b-3	.167	4	12	3	2	0	0	0	0	2	4	0
Fred Stanley, 2b	.200	3	5	0	1	1	0	0	0	1	0	0
Gary Thomasson, of	.250	3	4	0	1	0	0	0	0	0	1	0
Dick Tidrow, p	.000	2	0	0	0	0	0	0	0	0	0	0
Roy White, of	.333	6	24	9	8	0	0	1	4	4	5	2
TOTAL	.306		222	36	68	8	0	3	34	16	40	5

PITCHER	W	L	ERA	G	GS	CG	SV	SHO	IP	H	ER	BB	SO
Jim Beattie	1	0	2.00	1	1	1	0	0	9.0	9	2	4	8
Ken Clay	0	0	11.57	1	0	0	0	0	2.1	4	3	2	2
Ed Figueroa	0	1	8.10	2	2	0	0	0	6.2	9	6	5	2
Rich Gossage	1	0	0.00	3	0	0	0	0	6.0	1	0	1	4
Ron Guidry	1	0	1.00	1	1	1	0	0	9.0	8	1	7	4
Catfish Hunter	1	1	4.15	2	2	0	0	0	13.0	13	6	1	5
Paul Lindblad	0	0	11.57	1	0	0	0	0	2.1	4	3	0	1
Dick Tidrow	0	0	1.93	2	0	0	0	0	4.2	4	1	0	5
TOTAL	4	2	3.74	13	6	2	0	0	53.0	52	22	20	31

LA (N)

PLAYER/POS	AVG	G	AB	R	H	2B	3B	HR	RB	BB	SO	SB
Dusty Baker, of	.238	6	21	2	5	0	0	1	1	1	3	0
Ron Cey, 3b	.286	6	21	2	6	0	0	1	4	3	3	0
Vic Davalillo, dh-1	.333	2	3	0	1	0	0	0	0	0	0	0
Joe Ferguson, c	.500	2	4	1	2	2	0	0	0	0	1	0
Terry Forster, p	.000	3	0	0	0	0	0	0	0	0	0	0
Steve Garvey, 1b	.208	6	24	1	5	1	0	0	0	1	7	1
Jerry Grote, c	.000	2	0	0	0	0	0	0	0	0	0	0
Burt Hooton, p	.000	2	0	0	0	0	0	0	0	0	0	0
Charlie Hough, p	.000	2	0	0	0	0	0	0	0	0	0	0
Tommy John, p	.000	2	0	0	0	0	0	0	0	0	0	0
Lee Lacy, dh	.143	4	14	0	2	0	0	0	1	1	3	0
Davey Lopes, 2b	.308	6	26	7	8	0	0	3	7	2	1	2
Rick Monday, of-4,dh-1	.154	5	13	2	2	1	0	0	0	4	3	0
Manny Mota, ph	.000	1	0	0	0	0	0	0	0	1	0	0
Billy North, of	.125	4	8	2	1	1	0	0	2	1	0	1
Johnny Oates, c	1.000	1	1	0	1	0	0	0	0	1	0	0
Doug Rau, p	.000	1	0	0	0	0	0	0	0	0	0	0
Lance Rautzhan, p	.000	2	0	0	0	0	0	0	0	0	0	0
Bill Russell, ss	.423	6	26	1	11	2	0	0	2	2	2	1
Reggie Smith, of	.200	6	25	3	5	0	0	1	5	2	6	0
Don Sutton, p	.000	2	0	0	0	0	0	0	0	0	0	0
Bob Welch, p	.000	3	0	0	0	0	0	0	0	0	0	0
Steve Yeager, c	.231	5	13	2	3	1	0	0	0	1	2	0
TOTAL	.261		199	23	52	8	0	6	22	20	31	5

PITCHER	W	L	ERA	G	GS	CG	SV	SHO	IP	H	ER	BB	SO
Terry Forster	0	0	0.00	3	0	0	0	0	4.0	5	0	1	6
Burt Hooton	1	1	6.48	2	2	0	0	0	8.1	13	6	3	6
Charlie Hough	0	0	8.44	2	0	0	0	0	5.1	10	5	2	5
Tommy John	1	0	3.07	2	2	0	0	0	14.2	14	5	4	6
Doug Rau	0	0	0.00	1	0	0	0	0	2.0	1	0	0	3
Lance Rautzhan	0	0	13.50	2	0	0	0	0	2.0	4	3	0	0
Don Sutton	0	2	7.50	2	2	0	0	0	12.0	17	10	4	8
Bob Welch	0	1	6.23	3	0	0	1	0	4.1	4	3	2	6
TOTAL	2	4	5.47	17	6	0	1	0	52.2	68	32	16	40

GAME 1 AT LA OCT 10

		R	H	E
NY	000 000 320	5	9	1
LA	030 310 31X	11	15	2

Pitchers: FIGUEROA, Clay (2), Lindblad (5), Tidrow (7) vs JOHN, Forster (8)
Home Runs: Baker-LA, Lopes-LA (2), Jackson-NY
Attendance: 55,997

GAME 2 AT LA OCT 11

		R	H	E
NY	002 000 100	3	11	0
LA	000 103 00X	4	7	0

Pitchers: HUNTER, Gossage (7) vs HOOTON, Forster (7), Welch (9)
Home Runs: Cey-LA
Attendance: 55,982

GAME 3 AT NY OCT 13

		R	H	E
LA	001 000 000	1	8	0
NY	110 000 30X	5	10	1

Pitchers: SUTTON, Rautzhan (7), Hough (8) vs GUIDRY
Home Runs: White-NY
Attendance: 56,447

GAME 4 AT NY OCT 14

		R	H	E
LA	000 030 000 0	3	6	1
NY	000 002 010 1	4	9	0

Pitchers: John, Forster (8), WELCH (8) vs Figueroa, Tidrow (6), GOSSAGE (9)
Home Runs: Smith-LA
Attendance: 56,445

GAME 5 AT NY OCT 15

		R	H	E
LA	101 000 000	2	9	3
NY	004 300 41X	12	18	0

Pitchers: HOOTON, Rautzhan (3), Hough (4) vs BEATTIE
Attendance: 56,448

GAME 6 AT LA OCT 17

		R	H	E
NY	030 002 200	7	11	0
LA	101 000 000	2	7	1

Pitchers: HUNTER, Gossage (8) vs SUTTON, Welch (7), Rau (8)
Home Runs: Lopes-LA, Jackson-NY
Attendance: 55,985

The Pirates—with a better season's record than Cincinnati and stronger hitting and pitching—proved their superiority in the NLCS as well, dominating the statistics and sweeping the series. Yet the games were closer than the stats alone would suggest. Pittsburgh won the first game by three runs—but they didn't come until Willie Stargell's homer in the 11th inning broke a 2–2 tie.

In Game 2, Cincinnati scored first. The Pirates tied the game with a run in the fourth and took a narrow lead with another in the fifth. But the Reds came back on a game-tying pair of doubles in the ninth, and it wasn't until the 10th that Pittsburgh eked out its victory with a run on two singles and Don Robinson's shutout relief.

Only in the third game did the Pirates take a commanding lead, with six runs in the first four innings (two of them on home runs by Stargell and Bill Madlock). The Reds outhit Pittsburgh, but only Johnny Bench's homer brought them a run, as Bert Blyleven overcame them in the series' only complete-game pitching performance. The Pirates, who had lost to the Reds three times in the NLCS in the 1970s, ended the decade by overcoming Cincinnati for the pennant.

Pittsburgh Pirates (East), 3; Cincinnati Reds (West), 0

PIT (E)

PLAYER/POS	AVG	G	AB	R	H	2B	3B	HR	RB	BB	SO	SB
Matt Alexander, pr	.000	1	0	1	0	0	0	0	0	0	0	0
Jim Bibby, p	.000	1	0	0	0	0	0	0	0	1	0	0
Bert Blyleven, p	.333	1	3	1	1	0	0	0	0	0	1	0
John Candelaria, p	.000	1	3	0	0	0	0	0	0	0	2	0
Mike Easler, ph	.000	1	1	0	0	0	0	0	0	0	0	0
Tim Foli, ss	.333	3	12	1	4	1	0	0	3	0	0	0
Phil Garner, 2b-3,ss-1	.417	3	12	4	5	0	1	1	1	1	0	0
Grant Jackson, p	.000	2	1	0	0	0	0	0	0	0	0	0
Bill Madlock, 3b	.250	3	12	1	3	0	0	1	2	2	0	2
John Milner, of	.000	3	9	0	0	0	0	0	0	2	0	0
Omar Moreno, of	.250	3	12	3	3	0	1	0	0	2	2	1
Ed Ott, c	.231	3	13	0	3	0	0	0	0	0	2	0
Dave Parker, of	.333	3	12	2	4	0	0	0	2	2	3	1
Dave Roberts, p	.000	1	0	0	0	0	0	0	0	0	0	0
Don Robinson, p	.000	2	0	0	0	0	0	0	0	0	0	0
Bill Robinson, of	.000	3	3	0	0	0	0	0	0	0	0	0
Enrique Romo, p	.000	2	0	0	0	0	0	0	0	0	0	0
Willie Stargell, 1b	.455	3	11	2	5	2	0	2	6	3	2	0
Rennie Stennett, 2b	.000	1	0	0	0	0	0	0	0	0	0	0
Kent Tekulve, p	.000	2	1	0	0	0	0	0	0	0	1	0
TOTAL	.267		105	15	28	3	2	4	14	13	13	4

PITCHER	W	L	ERA	G	GS	CG	SV	SHO	IP	H	ER	BB	SO
Jim Bibby	0	0	1.29	1	1	0	0	0	7.0	4	1	4	5
Bert Blyleven	1	0	1.00	1	1	1	0	0	9.0	8	1	0	9
John Candelaria	0	0	2.57	1	1	0	0	0	7.0	5	2	1	4
Grant Jackson	1	0	0.00	2	0	0	0	0	2.0	1	0	1	2
Dave Roberts	0	0	∞	1	0	0	0	0	0.0	0	0	1	0
Don Robinson	1	0	0.00	2	0	0	1	0	2.0	0	0	1	3
Enrique Romo	0	0	0.00	2	0	0	0	0	0.1	3	0	1	1
Kent Tekulve	0	0	3.38	2	0	0	0	0	2.2	2	1	2	2
TOTAL	3	0	1.50	12	3	1	1	0	30	23	5	11	26

CIN (W)

PLAYER/POS	AVG	G	AB	R	H	2B	3B	HR	RB	BB	SO	SB
Rick Auerbach, ph	.000	2	2	0	0	0	0	0	0	0	1	0
Doug Bair, p	.000	1	0	0	0	0	0	0	0	0	0	0
Johnny Bench, c	.250	3	12	1	3	0	1	1	1	2	2	0
Dave Collins, of	.357	3	14	0	5	1	0	0	1	0	2	2
Dave Concepcion, ss	.429	3	14	1	6	1	0	0	0	0	3	0
Hector Cruz, of-1	.200	2	5	1	1	1	0	0	0	0	1	0
Dan Driessen, 1b	.083	3	12	1	1	0	0	0	0	1	3	0
George Foster, of	.200	3	10	1	2	0	0	1	2	4	3	0
Cesar Geronimo, of	.143	2	7	0	1	0	0	0	0	0	5	0
Tom Hume, p	.000	3	1	0	0	0	0	0	0	0	1	0
Ray Knight, 3b	.286	3	14	0	4	1	0	0	0	0	2	1
Mike LaCoss, p	.000	1	0	0	0	0	0	0	0	0	0	0
Charlie Leibrandt, p	.000	1	0	0	0	0	0	0	0	0	0	0
Joe Morgan, 2b	.000	3	11	0	0	0	0	0	0	3	1	1
Fred Norman, p	.000	1	1	0	0	0	0	0	0	0	1	0
Frank Pastore, p	.000	1	0	0	0	0	0	0	1	1	0	0
Tom Seaver, p	.000	1	2	0	0	0	0	0	0	0	1	0
Mario Soto, p	.000	1	0	0	0	0	0	0	0	0	0	0
Harry Spilman, ph	.000	2	2	0	0	0	0	0	0	0	0	0
Dave Tomlin, p	.000	3	0	0	0	0	0	0	0	0	0	0
TOTAL	.215		107	5	23	4	1	2	5	11	26	4

PITCHER	W	L	ERA	G	GS	CG	SV	SHO	IP	H	ER	BB	SO
Doug Bair	0	1	9.00	1	0	0	0	0	1.0	2	1	1	0
Tom Hume	0	1	6.75	3	0	0	0	0	4.0	6	3	0	2
Mike LaCoss	0	1	10.80	1	1	0	0	0	1.2	1	2	4	0
Charlie Leibrandt	0	0	0.00	1	0	0	0	0	0.1	0	0	0	0
Fred Norman	0	0	18.00	1	0	0	0	0	2.0	4	4	1	1
Frank Pastore	0	0	2.57	1	1	0	0	0	7.0	7	2	3	1
Tom Seaver	0	0	2.25	1	1	0	0	0	8.0	5	2	2	5
Mario Soto	0	0	0.00	1	0	0	0	0	2.0	0	0	0	1
Dave Tomlin	0	0	0.00	3	0	0	0	0	3.0	3	0	2	3
TOTAL	0	3	4.34	13	3	0	0	0	29.0	28	14	13	13

GAME 1 AT CIN OCT 2

		R	H	E
PIT	002 000 000 03	5	10	0
CIN	000 200 000 00	2	7	0

Pitchers: Candelaria, Romo (8), Tekulve (8), JACKSON (10), D.Robinson (11) vs Seaver, HUME (9), Tomlin (11)
Home Runs: Garner-PIT, Foster-CIN, Stargell-PIT
Attendance: 55,006

GAME 2 AT CIN OCT 3

		R	H	E
PIT	000 110 000 1	3	11	0
CIN	010 000 001 0	2	8	0

Pitchers: Bibby, Jackson (8), Romo (8), Tekulve (8), Roberts (9), D.ROBINSON (9) vs Pastore, Tomlin (8), Hume (8), BAIR (10)
Attendance: 55,000

GAME 3 AT PIT OCT 5

		R	H	E
CIN	000 001 000	1	8	1
PIT	112 200 01X	7	7	0

Pitchers: LaCOSS, Norman (2), Leibrandt (4), Soto (5), Tomlin (7), Hume (8) vs BLYLEVEN
Home Runs: Stargell-PIT, Madlock-PIT, Bench-CIN
Attendance: 42,240

Baltimore, returning to postseason play after a four-year absence, struggled with first-timer California through three games before blowing them away in the fourth. Game 1 went into the last of the 10th tied 3–3, when Oriole pinch hitter John Lowenstein, up with two men on, ended it with a two-out, two-strike shot that just cleared the left field wall.

Game 2 looked like a blowout for Baltimore. Eddie Murray drove in four runs, and the rest of the team added five more to give the O's a 9–1 lead by the end of three. But California chipped away at the lead in the latter half of the game and drew within one in the ninth, before Brian Downing hit into a forceout with the bases full to end their scoring.

The Angels' late rally in Game 3 was more successful. Down by a run in the bottom of the ninth, they scored twice, on a walk, a dropped outfield fly, and Larry Harlow's game-winning double. The final game, though, was all Baltimore's, as Scott McGregor—pitching the series' only complete game—blanked the Angels on six hits. The Orioles scored two in the third and another in the fourth, before Pat Kelly put California pennant hopes out of reach with a three-run homer in the O's five-run seventh.

Baltimore Orioles (East), 3; California Angels (West), 1

BAL (E)

PLAYER/POS	AVG	G	AB	R	H	2B	3B	HR	RB	BB	SO	SB
Mark Belanger, ss	.200	3	5	0	1	0	0	0	1	0	2	0
Al Bumbry, of	.250	4	16	5	4	0	1	0	0	4	3	2
Terry Crowley, ph	.500	2	2	0	1	0	0	0	1	0	0	0
Rich Dauer, 2b	.182	4	11	0	2	0	0	0	0	0	1	0
Doug DeCinces, 3b	.308	4	13	4	4	1	0	0	3	1	1	0
Rick Dempsey, c	.400	3	10	3	4	2	0	0	2	1	0	1
Mike Flanagan, p	.000	1	0	0	0	0	0	0	0	0	0	0
Kiko Garcia, ss	.273	3	11	1	3	0	0	0	2	2	4	0
Pat Kelly, dh-2,of-1	.364	3	11	3	4	0	0	1	4	1	3	2
John Lowenstein, of-3	.167	4	6	2	1	0	0	1	3	2	2	0
Dennis Martinez, p	.000	1	0	0	0	0	0	0	0	0	0	0
Lee May, dh	.143	2	7	0	1	0	0	0	1	1	3	0
Scott McGregor, p	.000	1	0	0	0	0	0	0	0	0	0	0
Eddie Murray, 1b	.417	4	12	3	5	0	0	1	5	5	2	0
Jim Palmer, p	.000	1	0	0	0	0	0	0	0	0	0	0
Gary Roenicke, of	.200	2	5	1	1	0	0	0	1	0	0	0
Ken Singleton, of	.375	4	16	4	6	2	0	0	2	1	2	0
Dave Skaggs, c	.000	1	4	0	0	0	0	0	0	0	0	0
Billy Smith, 2b	.000	1	4	0	0	0	0	0	0	0	1	0
Don Stanhouse, p	.000	3	0	0	0	0	0	0	0	0	0	0
TOTAL	.278		133	26	37	5	1	3	25	18	24	5

PITCHER	W	L	ERA	G	GS	CG	SV	SHO	IP	H	ER	BB	SO
Mike Flanagan	1	0	5.14	1	1	0	0	0	7.0	6	4	1	2
Dennis Martinez	0	0	3.24	1	1	0	0	0	8.1	8	3	0	4
Scott McGregor	1	0	0.00	1	1	1	0	1	9.0	6	0	1	4
Jim Palmer	0	0	3.00	1	1	0	0	0	9.0	7	3	2	3
Don Stanhouse	1	1	6.00	3	0	0	0	0	3.0	5	2	3	0
TOTAL	3	1	2.97	7	4	1	0	1	36.1	32	12	7	13

CAL (W)

PLAYER/POS	AVG	G	AB	R	H	2B	3B	HR	RB	BB	SO	SB
Don Aase, p	.000	2	0	0	0	0	0	0	0	0	0	0
Jim Anderson, ss	.091	4	11	0	1	0	0	0	0	0	1	0
Mike Barlow, p	.000	1	0	0	0	0	0	0	0	0	0	0
Don Baylor, dh-3,of-1	.188	4	16	2	3	0	0	1	2	1	2	0
Bert Campaneris, ss	.000	1	0	0	0	0	0	0	0	0	0	0
Rod Carew, 1b	.412	4	17	4	7	3	0	0	1	0	0	1
Bobby Clark, of	.000	1	3	0	0	0	0	0	0	0	2	0
Mark Clear, p	.000	1	0	0	0	0	0	0	0	0	0	0
Willie Davis, ph	.500	2	2	1	1	1	0	0	0	0	0	0
Brian Downing, c	.200	4	15	1	3	0	0	0	1	1	1	0
Dan Ford, of	.294	4	17	2	5	1	0	2	4	0	0	0
Dave Frost, p	.000	2	0	0	0	0	0	0	0	0	0	0
Bobby Grich, 2b	.154	4	13	0	2	1	0	0	2	1	1	0
Larry Harlow, of-2	.125	3	8	0	1	1	0	0	1	1	2	0
Chris Knapp, p	.000	1	0	0	0	0	0	0	0	0	0	0
Carney Lansford, 3b	.294	4	17	2	5	0	0	0	3	1	2	1
Dave LaRoche, p	.000	1	0	0	0	0	0	0	0	0	0	0
Rick Miller, of	.250	4	16	2	4	0	0	0	0	0	1	0
John Montague, p	.000	2	0	0	0	0	0	0	0	0	0	0
Merv Rettenmund, dh	.000	2	2	0	0	0	0	0	0	2	1	0
Nolan Ryan, p	.000	1	0	0	0	0	0	0	0	0	0	0
Frank Tanana, p	.000	1	0	0	0	0	0	0	0	0	0	0
Dickie Thon, ss	.000	1	0	1	0	0	0	0	0	0	0	0
TOTAL	.234		137	15	32	7	0	3	14	7	13	2

PITCHER	W	L	ERA	G	GS	CG	SV	SHO	IP	H	ER	BB	SO
Don Aase	1	0	1.80	2	0	0	0	0	5.0	4	1	2	6
Mike Barlow	0	0	0.00	1	0	0	0	0	1.0	0	0	0	0
Mark Clear	0	0	4.76	1	0	0	0	0	5.2	4	3	2	3
Dave Frost	0	1	18.69	2	1	0	0	0	4.1	8	9	5	1
Chris Knapp	0	1	7.71	1	1	0	0	0	2.1	5	2	1	0
Dave LaRoche	0	0	6.75	1	0	0	0	0	1.1	2	1	1	1
John Montague	0	1	9.00	2	0	0	0	0	4.0	4	4	2	2
Nolan Ryan	0	0	1.29	1	1	0	0	0	7.0	4	1	3	8
Frank Tanana	0	0	3.60	1	1	0	0	0	5.0	6	2	2	3
TOTAL	1	3	5.80	12	4	0	0	0	35.2	37	23	18	24

GAME 1 AT BAL OCT 3

					R	H	E
CAL	101	001	000	0	3	7	1
BAL	002	100	000	3	6	6	0

Pitchers: Ryan, MONTAGUE (8) vs Palmer, STANHOUSE (10)
Home Runs: Ford-CAL, Lowenstein-BAL
Attendance: 52,787

GAME 2 AT BAL OCT 4

				R	H	E
CAL	100	001	132	8	10	1
BAL	441	000	00X	9	11	1

Pitchers: FROST, Clear (2), Aase (8) vs FLANAGAN, Stanhouse (8)
Home Runs: Ford-CAL, Murray-BAL
Attendance: 52,108

GAME 3 AT CAL OCT 5

				R	H	E
BAL	000	101	100	3	8	3
CAL	100	100	002	4	9	0

Pitchers: D.Martinez, STANHOUSE (9) vs Tanana, AASE (6)
Home Runs: Baylor-CAL
Attendance: 43,199

GAME 4 AT CAL OCT 6

				R	H	E
BAL	002	100	500	8	12	1
CAL	000	000	000	0	6	0

Pitchers: McGREGOR vs KNAPP, LaRoche (3), Frost (4), Montague (7), Barlow (9)
Home Runs: Kelly-BAL
Attendance: 43,199

Veteran Willie Stargell was "Pops," and in the Series he showed his Pirate "family" the way. Seven of his 12 hits went for extra bases, and he drove in a Series-high seven runs. What Stargell began, submarine reliever Kent Tekulve finished, appearing in five of the seven games and earning three saves.

Stargell drove in a pair of runs in the opener—one of them with an eighth-inning homer—but Pittsburgh's four runs fell short of the five Baltimore had scored in the first inning. The only extra-base hits in Game 2 came from the bat of Eddie Murray, who homered and doubled to drive in both Baltimore runs. But three singles and a sacrifice fly had already given Pittsburgh two runs in the second inning, and two more singles and a walk in the top of the ninth made the score 3–2. Tekulve came on in the last of the ninth to preserve the lead, fanning two as he retired the side in order.

Baltimore bounced back, though, to take the next two games in convincing fashion. The score favored the Orioles 8–4 when Tekulve came on to set the O's down in order over the final two innings. But Baltimore starter Scott McGregor had by then settled into his groove, retiring the final 11 Pirates with relative ease to preserve his lead and the win. It took four Orioles pitchers to hold the Pirates in Game 4. Stargell led the Bucs' 17-hit attack with a homer, double, and single, and the Pirates led 6–3 entering the eighth inning. But Baltimore loaded the bases in the top of the eighth, prompting Pirates manager Chuck Tanner to bring Tekulve in again. This one time the strategy failed, as Tekulve saw six runs score before he retired his first batter.

Down three games to one, the Pirates rebounded in Game 5, scoring seven times in the final three innings for a 7–1 victory. Baltimore starter Jim Palmer matched John Candelaria's shutout pitching through six innings of Game 6 before the Pirates tagged him for pairs of runs in the seventh and eighth. Tekulve, meanwhile, continued Candelaria's shutout through the final three innings, retiring the last seven men in order, four by strikeout. Baltimore scored first in the finale on Rich Dauer's leadoff home run in the third inning, but Stargell put the Pirates ahead with a two-run homer in the sixth. Tekulve came in with two Orioles on base in the eighth to stifle the threat, and (after the Pirates had scored a pair of insurance runs in the top of the ninth) set Baltimore down in order to complete the Pittsburgh's comeback.

Pittsburgh Pirates (NL), 4; Baltimore Orioles (AL), 3

PIT (N)

PLAYER/POS	AVG	G	AB	R	H	2B	3B	HR	RB	BB	SO	SB
Matt Alexander, of	.000	1	0	0	0	0	0	0	0	0	0	0
Jim Bibby, p	.000	2	4	0	0	0	0	0	0	0	1	0
Bert Blyleven, p	.000	2	3	0	0	0	0	0	0	0	0	0
John Candelaria, p	.333	2	3	0	1	0	0	0	0	0	2	0
Mike Easler, ph	.000	2	1	0	0	0	0	0	0	1	0	0
Tim Foli, ss	.333	7	30	6	10	1	1	0	3	2	0	0
Phil Garner, 2b	.500	7	24	4	12	4	0	0	5	3	1	0
Grant Jackson, p	.000	4	1	0	0	0	0	0	0	0	0	0
Bruce Kison, p	.000	1	0	0	0	0	0	0	0	0	0	0
Lee Lacy, ph	.250	4	4	0	1	0	0	0	0	0	1	0
Bill Madlock, 3b	.375	7	24	2	9	1	0	0	3	5	1	0
John Milner, of	.333	3	9	2	3	1	0	0	1	2	0	0
Omar Moreno, of	.333	7	33	4	11	2	0	0	3	1	7	0
Steve Nicosia, c	.063	4	16	1	1	0	0	0	0	0	2	0
Ed Ott, c	.333	3	12	2	4	1	0	0	3	0	2	0
Dave Parker, of	.345	7	29	2	10	3	0	0	4	2	7	0
Don Robinson, p	.000	4	0	0	0	0	0	0	0	0	0	0
Bill Robinson, of-6	.263	7	19	2	5	1	0	0	2	0	4	0
Enrique Romo, p	.000	2	1	0	0	0	0	0	0	0	0	0
Jim Rooker, p	.000	2	2	0	0	0	0	0	0	0	1	0
Manny Sanguillen, ph	.333	3	3	0	1	0	0	0	1	0	0	0
Willie Stargell, 1b	.400	7	30	7	12	4	0	3	7	0	6	0
Rennie Stennett, ph	1.000	1	1	0	1	0	0	0	0	0	0	0
Kent Tekulve, p	.000	5	2	0	0	0	0	0	0	0	0	0
TOTAL	.323		251	32	81	18	1	3	32	16	35	0

PITCHER	W	L	ERA	G	GS	CG	SV	SHO	IP	H	ER	BB	SO
Jim Bibby	0	0	2.61	2	2	0	0	0	10.1	10	3	2	10
Bert Blyleven	1	0	1.80	2	1	0	0	0	10.0	8	2	3	4
John Candelaria	1	1	5.00	2	2	0	0	0	9.0	14	5	2	4
Grant Jackson	1	0	0.00	4	0	0	0	0	4.2	1	0	2	2
Bruce Kison	0	1	108.00	1	1	0	0	0	0.1	3	4	2	0
Don Robinson	1	0	5.40	4	0	0	0	0	5.0	4	3	6	3
Enrique Romo	0	0	3.86	2	0	0	0	0	4.2	5	2	3	4
Jim Rooker	0	0	1.04	2	1	0	0	0	8.2	5	1	3	4
Kent Tekulve	0	1	2.89	5	0	0	3	0	9.1	4	3	3	10
TOTAL	4	3	3.34	24	7	0	3	0	62.0	54	23	26	41

BAL (A)

PLAYER/POS	AVG	G	AB	R	H	2B	3B	HR	RB	BB	SO	SB
Benny Ayala, of-3	.333	4	6	1	2	0	0	1	2	1	0	0
Mark Belanger, ss-4	.000	5	6	1	0	0	0	0	0	1	1	0
Al Bumbry, of	.143	7	21	3	3	0	0	0	1	2	1	0
Terry Crowley, ph	.250	5	4	0	1	1	0	0	2	1	0	0
Rich Dauer, 2b-5	.294	6	17	2	5	1	0	1	1	0	1	0
Doug DeCinces, 3b	.200	7	25	2	5	0	0	1	3	5	5	1
Rick Dempsey, c-6	.286	7	21	3	6	2	0	0	0	1	3	0
Mike Flanagan, p	.000	3	5	0	0	0	0	0	0	1	2	0
Kiko Garcia, ss	.400	6	20	4	8	2	1	0	6	1	3	0
Pat Kelly, ph	.250	5	4	0	1	0	0	0	0	1	1	0
John Lowenstein, of-3	.231	6	13	2	3	1	0	0	3	1	3	0
Tippy Martinez, p	.000	3	0	0	0	0	0	0	0	0	0	0
Dennis Martinez, p	.000	2	0	0	0	0	0	0	0	0	0	0
Lee May, ph	.000	2	1	0	0	0	0	0	0	1	1	0
Scott McGregor, p	.000	2	4	1	0	0	0	0	0	2	1	0
Eddie Murray, 1b	.154	7	26	3	4	1	0	1	2	4	4	1
Jim Palmer, p	.000	2	4	0	0	0	0	0	0	0	3	0
Gary Roenicke, of-5	.125	6	16	1	2	1	0	0	0	0	6	0
Ken Singleton, of	.357	7	28	1	10	1	0	0	2	2	5	0
Dave Skaggs, c	.333	1	3	1	1	0	0	0	0	0	0	0
Billy Smith, 2b-2	.286	4	7	1	2	0	0	0	0	2	0	0
Don Stanhouse, p	.000	3	0	0	0	0	0	0	0	0	0	0
Sammy Stewart, p	.000	1	1	0	0	0	0	0	0	0	1	0
Tim Stoddard, p	1.000	4	1	0	1	0	0	0	1	0	0	0
Steve Stone, p	.000	1	0	0	0	0	0	0	0	0	0	0
TOTAL	.232		233	26	54	10	1	4	23	26	41	2

PITCHER	W	L	ERA	G	GS	CG	SV	SHO	IP	H	ER	BB	SO
Mike Flanagan	1	1	3.00	3	2	1	0	0	15.0	18	5	2	13
Tippy Martinez	0	0	6.75	3	0	0	0	0	1.1	3	1	0	1
Dennis Martinez	0	0	18.00	2	1	0	0	0	2.0	6	4	0	0
Scott McGregor	1	1	3.18	2	2	1	0	0	17.0	16	6	2	8
Jim Palmer	0	1	3.60	2	2	0	0	0	15.0	18	6	5	8
Don Stanhouse	0	1	13.50	3	0	0	0	0	2.0	6	3	3	0
Sammy Stewart	0	0	0.00	1	0	0	0	0	2.2	4	0	1	0
Tim Stoddard	1	0	5.40	4	0	0	0	0	5.0	6	3	1	3
Steve Stone	0	0	9.00	1	0	0	0	0	2.0	4	2	2	2
TOTAL	3	4	4.35	21	7	2	0	0	62.0	81	30	16	35

GAME 1 AT BAL OCT 10

		R	H	E
PIT	000 102 010	4	11	3
BAL	500 000 000	5	6	3

Pitchers: KISON, Rooker (1), Romo (5), D.Robinson (6), Jackson (8) vs FLANAGAN
Home Runs: Stargell-PIT, DeCinces-BAL
Attendance: 53,735

GAME 2 AT BAL OCT 11

		R	H	E
PIT	020 000 001	3	11	2
BAL	010 001 000	2	6	1

Pitchers: Blyleven, D.ROBINSON (7), Tekulve (9) vs Palmer, T.Martinez (8), STANHOUSE (9)
Home Runs: Murray-BAL
Attendance: 53,739

GAME 3 AT PIT OCT 12

		R	H	E
BAL	002 500 100	8	13	0
PIT	120 001 000	4	9	2

Pitchers: McGREGOR vs CANDELARIA, Romo (4), Jackson (7), Tekulve (8)
Home Runs: Ayala-BAL
Attendance: 50,848

GAME 4 AT PIT OCT 13

		R	H	E
BAL	003 000 060	9	12	0
PIT	040 011 000	6	17	1

Pitchers: D.Martinez, Stewart (2), Stone (5), STODDARD (7) vs Bibby, Jackson (6), D.Robinson (8), TEKULVE (8)
Home Runs: Stargell-PIT
Attendance: 50,883

GAME 5 AT PIT OCT 14

		R	H	E
BAL	000 010 000	1	6	2
PIT	000 002 23X	7	13	1

Pitchers: FLANAGAN, Stoddard (7), T.Martinez (7), Stanhouse (8) vs Rooker, BLYLEVEN (6)
Attendance: 50,920

GAME 6 AT BAL OCT 16

		R	H	E
PIT	000 000 220	4	10	0
BAL	000 000 000	0	7	1

Pitchers: CANDELARIA, Tekulve (7) vs PALMER, Stoddard (9)
Attendance: 53,739

GAME 7 AT BAL OCT 17

		R	H	E
PIT	000 002 002	4	10	0
BAL	001 000 000	1	4	2

Pitchers: Bibby, D.Robinson (5), JACKSON (5), Tekulve (8) vs McGREGOR, Stoddard (9), Flanagan (9), Stanhouse (9), T.Martinez (9), D.Martinez (9)
Home Runs: Stargell-PIT, Dauer-BAL
Attendance: 53,733

In the tightest LCS yet, the Phillies took the opener 3–1 on the series' only home run—Greg Luzinski's two-run blast in the sixth inning. It was the only game not to go into extra innings.

The Astros evened the series in Game 2—demolishing a 3–3 tie with four runs in the 10th—and took the series lead in a Game 3 pitchers' duel that saw Joe Niekro hurl ten scoreless innings for Houston. Reliever Dave Smith continued the shutout and took the win as Joe Morgan's triple and Denny Walling's sacrifice fly off Phillies reliever Tug McGraw scored the game's only run in the bottom of the 11th.

The Phillies rebounded, though, with their own set of extra-inning victories. In Game 4, a single and two doubles pushed across two go-ahead runs in the top of the tenth, and McGraw preserved the edge for his second series save. And in the finale—which saw the lead change hands three times—after Del Unser scored on Gary Maddox's 10th-inning double, Dick Ruthven held off Houston to bring the Phillies their first pennant in 30 years.

Philadelphia Phillies (East), 3; Houston Astros (West), 2

PHI (E)

PLAYER/POS	AVG	G	AB	R	H	2B	3B	HR	RB	BB	SO	SB
Ramon Aviles, pr	.000	1	0	1	0	0	0	0	0	0	0	0
Bob Boone, c	.222	5	18	1	4	0	0	0	2	1	2	0
Larry Bowa, ss	.316	5	19	2	6	0	0	0	0	3	3	1
Warren Brusstar, p	.000	2	1	0	0	0	0	0	0	0	1	0
Marty Bystrom, p	.000	1	2	0	0	0	0	0	0	0	1	0
Steve Carlton, p	.000	2	4	0	0	0	0	0	0	0	1	0
Larry Christenson, p	.000	1	2	0	0	0	0	0	0	0	1	0
Greg Gross, of-1	.750	4	4	2	3	0	0	0	1	0	0	0
Greg Luzinski, of	.294	5	17	3	5	2	0	1	4	0	6	0
Garry Maddox, of	.300	5	20	2	6	2	0	0	3	2	2	2
Bake McBride, of	.238	5	21	0	5	0	0	0	0	1	5	2
Tug McGraw, p	.000	5	1	0	0	0	0	0	0	0	0	0
Keith Moreland, c-1	.000	2	1	0	0	0	0	0	1	0	0	0
Dickie Noles, p	.000	2	0	0	0	0	0	0	0	0	0	0
Ron Reed, p	.000	3	0	0	0	0	0	0	0	0	0	0
Pete Rose, 1b	.400	5	20	3	8	0	0	0	2	5	3	0
Dick Ruthven, p	.000	2	2	0	0	0	0	0	0	0	2	0
Kevin Saucier, p	.000	2	0	0	0	0	0	0	0	0	0	0
Mike Schmidt, 3b	.208	5	24	1	5	1	0	0	1	1	6	1
Lonnie Smith, of-2	.600	3	5	2	3	0	0	0	0	0	0	1
Manny Trillo, 2b	.381	5	21	1	8	2	1	0	4	0	2	0
Del Unser, of-2	.400	5	5	2	2	1	0	0	1	0	2	0
George Vukovich, of-1	.000	4	3	0	0	0	0	0	0	0	0	0
TOTAL	.289		190	20	55	8	1	1	19	13	37	7

PITCHER	W	L	ERA	G	GS	CG	SV	SHO	IP	H	ER	BB	SO
Warren Brusstar	1	0	3.38	2	0	0	0	0	2.2	1	1	1	0
Marty Bystrom	0	0	1.69	1	1	0	0	0	5.1	7	1	2	1
Steve Carlton	1	0	2.19	2	2	0	0	0	12.1	11	3	8	6
Larry Christenson	0	0	4.05	1	1	0	0	0	6.2	5	3	5	2
Tug McGraw	0	1	4.50	5	0	0	2	0	8.0	8	4	4	5
Dickie Noles	0	0	0.00	2	0	0	0	0	2.2	1	0	3	0
Ron Reed	0	1	18.00	3	0	0	0	0	2.0	3	4	1	1
Dick Ruthven	1	0	2.00	2	1	0	0	0	9.0	3	2	5	4
Kevin Saucier	0	0	0.00	2	0	0	0	0	0.2	1	0	2	0
TOTAL	3	2	3.28	20	5	0	2	0	49.1	40	18	31	19

HOU (W)

PLAYER/POS	AVG	G	AB	R	H	2B	3B	HR	RB	BB	SO	SB
Joaquin Andujar, p	.000	1	0	0	0	0	0	0	0	0	0	0
Alan Ashby, c	.125	2	8	0	1	0	0	0	1	0	0	0
Dave Bergman, 1b	.333	4	3	0	1	0	1	0	2	0	0	0
Bruce Bochy, c	.000	1	1	0	0	0	0	0	0	0	0	0
Enos Cabell, 3b	.238	5	21	1	5	1	0	0	0	1	3	0
Cesar Cedeno, of	.182	3	11	1	2	0	0	0	1	1	0	0
Jose Cruz, of	.400	5	15	3	6	1	1	0	4	8	1	0
Ken Forsch, p	1.000	2	2	0	2	0	0	0	0	0	0	0
Danny Heep, ph	.000	1	1	0	0	0	0	0	0	0	0	0
Art Howe, 1b-4	.200	5	15	0	3	1	1	0	2	2	2	0
Frank LaCorte, p	.000	2	1	0	0	0	0	0	0	0	0	0
Rafael Landestoy, 2b-3,ss-1	.222	5	9	3	2	0	0	0	2	1	0	1
Jeffrey Leonard, of-1	.000	3	3	0	0	0	0	0	0	0	2	0
Joe Morgan, 2b	.154	4	13	1	2	1	1	0	0	6	1	0
Joe Niekro, p	.000	1	3	0	0	0	0	0	0	0	1	0
Terry Puhl, of-4	.526	5	19	4	10	2	0	0	3	3	2	2
Luis Pujols, c	.100	4	10	1	1	0	1	0	0	3	0	0
Craig Reynolds, ss	.154	4	13	2	2	1	0	0	0	3	1	0
Vern Ruhle, p	.000	1	3	0	0	0	0	0	0	0	1	0
Nolan Ryan, p	.000	2	4	1	0	0	0	0	0	1	2	0
Joe Sambito, p	.000	3	0	0	0	0	0	0	0	0	0	0
Dave Smith, p	.000	3	0	0	0	0	0	0	0	0	0	0
Denny Walling, of-2,1b-1	.111	3	9	2	1	0	0	0	2	1	0	0
Gary Woods, of-3	.250	4	8	0	2	0	0	0	1	1	3	1
TOTAL	.233		172	19	40	7	5	0	18	31	19	4

PITCHER	W	L	ERA	G	GS	CG	SV	SHO	IP	H	ER	BB	SO
Joaquin Andujar	0	0	0.00	1	0	0	1	0	1.0	0	0	1	0
Ken Forsch	0	1	4.15	2	1	1	0	0	8.2	10	4	1	6
Frank LaCorte	1	1	3.00	2	0	0	0	0	3.0	7	1	2	2
Joe Niekro	0	0	0.00	1	1	0	0	0	10.0	6	0	1	2
Vern Ruhle	0	0	3.86	1	1	0	0	0	7.0	8	3	1	3
Nolan Ryan	0	0	5.40	2	2	0	0	0	13.1	16	8	3	14
Joe Sambito	0	1	4.91	3	0	0	0	0	3.2	4	2	2	6
Dave Smith	1	0	3.86	3	0	0	0	0	2.1	4	1	2	4
TOTAL	2	3	3.49	15	5	1	1	0	49.0	55	19	13	37

GAME 1 AT PHI OCT 7

				R	H	E
HOU	001	000	000	1	7	0
PHI	000	002	10X	3	8	1

Pitchers: FORSCH vs CARLTON, McGraw (8)
Home Runs: Luzinski-PHI
Attendance: 65,277

GAME 2 AT PHI OCT 8

					R	H	E
HOU	001	000	110	4	7	8	1
PHI	000	200	010	1	4	14	2

Pitchers: Ryan, Sambito (7), D.Smith (7), LaCORTE (9), Andujar (10) vs Ruthven, McGraw (8), REED (9), Saucier (10)
Attendance: 65,476

GAME 3 AT HOU OCT 10

					R	H	E
PHI	000	000	000	00	0	7	1
HOU	000	000	000	01	1	6	1

Pitchers: Christenson, Noles (7), McGRAW (8) vs Niekro, D.SMITH (11)
Attendance: 44,443

GAME 4 AT HOU OCT 11

					R	H	E
PHI	000	000	030	2	5	13	0
HOU	000	110	001	0	3	5	1

Pitchers: Carlton, Noles (6), Saucier (7), Reed (7), BRUSSTAR (8), McGraw (10) vs Ruhle, D.Smith (8), SAMBITO (8)
Attendance: 44,952

GAME 5 AT HOU OCT 12

					R	H	E
PHI	020	000	050	1	8	13	2
HOU	100	001	320	0	7	14	0

Pitchers: Bystrom, Brusstar (6), Christenson (7), Reed (7), McGraw (8), RUTHVEN (9) vs Ryan, Sambito (8), Forsch (8), LaCORTE (9)
Attendance: 44,802

Kansas City and New York met for the fourth time in the ALCS, and this time the Royals swept to their first pennant. In the first game the Yankees scored first, with second-inning home runs by Rick Cerone and Lou Piniella, but the Royals' Frank White doubled in a pair later in the inning to tie it, and Willie Aikens's hit in the third gave K.C. the lead. They held it to the end as Larry Gura shut out New York the rest of the way.

The Royals scored three runs in the third inning of Game 2, on Willie Wilson's two-run triple and an RBI double by U. L. Washington. Yankees starter Rudy May stopped K.C. after that, but the Royals already had enough for the win as Dennis Leonard held New York to two runs in eight innings. Dan Quisenberry kept the lid on in the ninth for the save.

Game 3 was decided by home runs. White scored first for the Royals with a solo shot in the fifth. New York took the lead briefly with a two-run sixth, but lost it—and the pennant—in the top of the seventh when Goose Gossage, relieving starter Tommy John with two outs and a man on, gave up an infield single to Washington and a home run to George Brett.

Kansas City Royals (West), 3; New York Yankees (East), 0

KC (W)

PLAYER/POS	AVG	G	AB	R	H	2B	3B	HR	RB	BB	SO	SB
Willie Aikens, 1b	.364	3	11	0	4	0	0	0	2	0	1	0
George Brett, 3b	.273	3	11	3	3	1	0	2	4	1	0	0
Larry Gura, p	.000	1	0	0	0	0	0	0	0	0	0	0
Clint Hurdle, of	.000	3	2	0	0	0	0	0	0	0	1	0
Pete LaCock, 1b	.000	1	0	0	0	0	0	0	0	0	0	0
Dennis Leonard, p	.000	1	0	0	0	0	0	0	0	0	0	0
Hal McRae, dh	.200	3	10	0	2	0	0	0	0	1	3	0
Amos Otis, of	.333	3	12	2	4	1	0	0	0	0	3	2
Darrell Porter, c	.100	3	10	2	1	0	0	0	0	1	0	0
Dan Quisenberry, p	.000	2	0	0	0	0	0	0	0	0	0	0
Paul Splittorff, p	.000	1	0	0	0	0	0	0	0	0	0	0
U. L. Washington, ss	.364	3	11	1	4	1	0	0	1	2	3	0
John Wathan, of	.000	3	6	1	0	0	0	0	0	3	1	0
Frank White, 2b	.545	3	11	3	6	1	0	1	3	0	1	1
Willie Wilson, of	.308	3	13	2	4	2	1	0	4	1	2	0
TOTAL	.289		97	14	28	6	1	3	14	9	15	3

PITCHER	W	L	ERA	G	GS	CG	SV	SHO	IP	H	ER	BB	SO
Larry Gura	1	0	2.00	1	1	1	0	0	9.0	10	2	1	4
Dennis Leonard	1	0	2.25	1	1	0	0	0	8.0	7	2	1	8
Dan Quisenberry	1	0	0.00	2	0	0	1	0	4.2	4	0	2	1
Paul Splittorff	0	0	1.69	1	1	0	0	0	5.1	5	1	2	3
TOTAL	3	0	1.67	5	3	1	1	0	27.0	26	5	6	16

NY (E)

PLAYER/POS	AVG	G	AB	R	H	2B	3B	HR	RB	BB	SO	SB
Bobby Brown, of	.000	3	10	1	0	0	0	0	0	1	2	0
Rick Cerone, c	.333	3	12	1	4	0	0	1	2	0	1	0
Ron Davis, p	.000	1	0	0	0	0	0	0	0	0	0	0
Bucky Dent, ss	.182	3	11	0	2	0	0	0	0	0	1	0
Oscar Gamble, of-1,dh-1	.200	2	5	1	1	0	0	0	0	1	1	0
Rich Gossage, p	.000	1	0	0	0	0	0	0	0	0	0	0
Ron Guidry, p	.000	1	0	0	0	0	0	0	0	0	0	0
Reggie Jackson, of	.273	3	11	1	3	1	0	0	0	1	4	0
Tommy John, p	.000	1	0	0	0	0	0	0	0	0	0	0
Joe Lefebvre, of	.000	1	0	0	0	0	0	0	0	0	0	0
Rudy May, p	.000	1	0	0	0	0	0	0	0	0	0	0
Bobby Murcer, dh	.000	1	4	0	0	0	0	0	0	0	2	0
Graig Nettles, 3b	.167	2	6	1	1	0	0	1	1	0	1	0
Lou Piniella, of	.200	2	5	1	1	0	0	1	1	2	1	0
Willie Randolph, 2b	.385	3	13	0	5	2	0	0	1	1	3	0
Aurelio Rodriguez, 3b	.333	2	6	0	2	1	0	0	0	0	0	0
Eric Soderholm, dh	.167	2	6	0	1	0	0	0	0	0	0	0
Jim Spencer, ph	.000	1	1	0	0	0	0	0	0	0	0	0
Tom Underwood, p	.000	2	0	0	0	0	0	0	0	0	0	0
Bob Watson, 1b	.500	3	12	0	6	3	1	0	0	0	0	0
TOTAL	.255		102	6	26	7	1	3	5	6	16	0

PITCHER	W	L	ERA	G	GS	CG	SV	SHO	IP	H	ER	BB	SO
Ron Davis	0	0	2.25	1	0	0	0	0	4.0	3	1	1	3
Rich Gossage	0	1	54.00	1	0	0	0	0	0.1	3	2	0	0
Ron Guidry	0	1	12.00	1	1	0	0	0	3.0	5	4	4	2
Tommy John	0	0	2.70	1	1	0	0	0	6.2	8	2	1	3
Rudy May	0	1	3.38	1	1	1	0	0	8.0	6	3	3	4
Tom Underwood	0	0	0.00	2	0	0	0	0	3.0	3	0	0	3
TOTAL	0	3	4.32	7	3	1	0	0	25.0	28	12	9	15

GAME 1 AT KC OCT 8

				R	H	E
NY	020	000	000	2	10	1
KC	022	000	12X	7	10	0

Pitchers: GUIDRY, Davis (4), Underwood (8) vs GURA
Home Runs: Cerone-NY, Piniella-NY, G.Brett-KC
Attendance: 42,598

GAME 2 AT KC OCT 9

				R	H	E
NY	000	020	000	2	8	0
KC	003	000	00X	3	6	0

Pitchers: MAY vs LEONARD, Quisenberry (9)
Home Runs: Nettles-NY
Attendance: 42,633

GAME 3 AT NY OCT 10

				R	H	E
KC	000	010	300	4	12	1
NY	000	002	000	2	8	0

Pitchers: Splittorff, QUISENBERRY (6) vs John, GOSSAGE (7), Underwood (8)
Home Runs: White-KC, G.Brett-KC
Attendance: 56,588

Both clubs had won divisional titles three years in a row—1976–1978—only to lose the League Championship Series. But both overcame the jinx in 1980 to face off in the World Series—the Phillies for the first time in 30 years, the Royals for the first time ever. Kansas City began with a rush in the opener, scoring two runs on Amos Otis' homer in the second inning and two more on Willie Aikens' blast an inning later. But the Phillies came back to take the lead in their half of the third with a five-run rally capped by Bake McBride's three-run homer. Single runs in each of the next two innings kept the Phillies out of reach of Aikens' second two-run shot in the eighth for a narrow 7–6 win. The Phillies extended their Series advantage with a 6–4 win in the second game, rebounding from a two-run deficit with four runs in the eighth inning.

The two clubs traded single runs throughout Game 3. George Brett's first-inning homer began the scoring. The Phillies got the run back in the second inning, the Royals took the lead back in the fourth, Mike Schmidt homered to tie it again in the fifth, Amos Otis countered with a homer in the seventh, and Pete Rose singled in another tying run for Philadelphia in the eighth. Phillies reliever Tug McGraw (who had a save in the opening game) came on to pitch the last of the 10th inning, but couldn't hold the tie, though two men were out before Aikens singled in the Royals' winning run. The Royals evened the Series with their second victory the next day, scoring four times in the first inning and once in the second (with Aikens for the second time in the Series hitting two home runs in a game), then holding on for a 5–3 win.

But the Phillies recovered to win the next two, and their first world crown. Mike Schmidt's fourth-inning two-run homer began the Phillies' scoring in Game 5. The Royals replied with one run in the fifth, and Amos Otis' home run an inning later tied the game. A second K.C. run in the inning put the Royals ahead until the top of the ninth, when pinch hitter Del Unser doubled home Schmidt to tie the game, and Manny Trillo drove home Unser with the go-ahead run. Tug McGraw, who had held K.C. scoreless through two innings of relief, loaded the bases in the last of the ninth with three walks, but at last fanned Jose Cardenal for the final out. In Game 6, with the Phillies ahead 4–0 in the eighth inning, McGraw relieved starter Steve Carlton with two men on, and loaded the bases with a walk. One Royal scored on a sacrifice fly before McGraw got his third out. In the ninth, another McGraw walk and two singles again loaded the bases with only one away. Frank White popped up in foul territory, and the ball bounced off Bob Boone's catcher's mitt into Pete Rose's hand. Willie Wilson then struck out for the 12th time to end the Series and give the Phillies their first world championship.

Philadelphia Phillies (NL), 4; Kansas City Royals (AL), 2

PHI (N)

PLAYER/POS	AVG	G	AB	R	H	2B	3B	HR	RB	BB	SO	SB
Bob Boone, c	.412	6	17	3	7	2	0	0	4	4	0	0
Larry Bowa, ss	.375	6	24	3	9	1	0	0	2	0	0	3
Warren Brusstar, p	.000	1	0	0	0	0	0	0	0	0	0	0
Marty Bystrom, p	.000	1	0	0	0	0	0	0	0	0	0	0
Steve Carlton, p	.000	2	0	0	0	0	0	0	0	0	0	0
Larry Christenson, p	.000	1	0	0	0	0	0	0	0	0	0	0
Greg Gross, of-3	.000	4	2	0	0	0	0	0	0	0	0	0
Greg Luzinski, dh-2,of-1	.000	3	9	0	0	0	0	0	0	1	5	0
Garry Maddox, of	.227	6	22	1	5	2	0	0	1	1	3	0
Bake McBride, of	.304	6	23	3	7	1	0	1	5	2	1	0
Tug McGraw, p	.000	4	0	0	0	0	0	0	0	0	0	0
Keith Moreland, dh	.333	3	12	1	4	0	0	0	1	0	1	0
Dickie Noles, p	.000	1	0	0	0	0	0	0	0	0	0	0
Ron Reed, p	.000	2	0	0	0	0	0	0	0	0	0	0
Pete Rose, 1b	.261	6	23	2	6	1	0	0	1	2	2	0
Dick Ruthven, p	.000	1	0	0	0	0	0	0	0	0	0	0
Kevin Saucier, p	.000	1	0	0	0	0	0	0	0	0	0	0
Mike Schmidt, 3b	.381	6	21	6	8	1	0	2	7	4	3	0
Lonnie Smith, of-5,dh-1	.263	6	19	2	5	1	0	0	1	1	1	0
Manny Trillo, 2b	.217	6	23	4	5	2	0	0	2	0	0	0
Del Unser, of	.500	3	6	2	3	2	0	0	2	0	1	0
Bob Walk, p	.000	1	0	0	0	0	0	0	0	0	0	0
TOTAL	.294		201	27	59	13	0	3	26	15	17	3

PITCHER	W	L	ERA	G	GS	CG	SV	SHO	IP	H	ER	BB	SO
Warren Brusstar	0	0	0.00	1	0	0	0	0	2.1	0	0	1	0
Marty Bystrom	0	0	5.40	1	1	0	0	0	5.0	10	3	1	4
Steve Carlton	2	0	2.40	2	2	0	0	0	15.0	14	4	9	17
Larry Christenson	0	1	108.00	1	1	0	0	0	0.1	5	4	0	0
Tug McGraw	1	1	1.17	4	0	0	2	0	7.2	7	1	8	10
Dickie Noles	0	0	1.93	1	0	0	0	0	4.2	5	1	2	6
Ron Reed	0	0	0.00	2	0	0	1	0	2.0	2	0	0	2
Dick Ruthven	0	0	3.00	1	1	0	0	0	9.0	9	3	0	7
Kevin Saucier	0	0	0.00	1	0	0	0	0	0.2	0	0	2	0
Bob Walk	1	0	7.71	1	1	0	0	0	7.0	8	6	3	3
TOTAL	4	2	3.69	15	6	0	3	0	53.2	60	22	26	49

KC (A)

PLAYER/POS	AVG	G	AB	R	H	2B	3B	HR	RB	BB	SO	SB
Willie Aikens, 1b	.400	6	20	5	8	0	1	4	8	6	8	0
George Brett, 3b	.375	6	24	3	9	2	1	1	3	2	4	1
Jose Cardenal, of	.200	4	10	0	2	0	0	0	0	0	3	0
Dave Chalk, 3b	.000	1	0	1	0	0	0	0	0	1	0	1
Onix Concepcion, pr	.000	3	0	0	0	0	0	0	0	0	0	0
Rich Gale, p	.000	2	0	0	0	0	0	0	0	0	0	0
Larry Gura, p	.000	2	0	0	0	0	0	0	0	0	0	0
Clint Hurdle, of	.417	4	12	1	5	1	0	0	0	2	1	1
Pete LaCock, 1b	.000	1	0	0	0	0	0	0	0	0	0	0
Dennis Leonard, p	.000	2	0	0	0	0	0	0	0	0	0	0
Renie Martin, p	.000	3	0	0	0	0	0	0	0	0	0	0
Hal McRae, dh	.375	6	24	3	9	3	0	0	1	2	2	0
Amos Otis, of	.478	6	23	4	11	2	0	3	7	3	3	0
Marty Pattin, p	.000	1	0	0	0	0	0	0	0	0	0	0
Darrell Porter, c-4	.143	5	14	1	2	0	0	0	0	3	4	0
Dan Quisenberry, p	.000	6	0	0	0	0	0	0	0	0	0	0
Paul Splittorff, p	.000	1	0	0	0	0	0	0	0	0	0	0
U L Washington, ss	.273	6	22	1	6	0	0	0	2	0	6	0
John Wathan, c-2,of-1	.286	3	7	1	2	0	0	0	1	2	1	0
Frank White, 2b	.080	6	25	0	2	0	0	0	0	1	5	1
Willie Wilson, of	.154	6	26	3	4	1	0	0	0	4	12	2
TOTAL	.290		207	23	60	9	2	8	22	26	49	6

PITCHER	W	L	ERA	G	GS	CG	SV	SHO	IP	H	ER	BB	SO
Rich Gale	0	1	4.26	2	2	0	0	0	6.1	11	3	4	4
Larry Gura	0	0	2.19	2	2	0	0	0	12.1	8	3	3	4
Dennis Leonard	1	1	6.75	2	2	0	0	0	10.2	15	8	2	5
Renie Martin	0	0	2.79	3	0	0	0	0	9.2	11	3	3	2
Marty Pattin	0	0	0.00	1	0	0	0	0	1.0	0	0	0	2
Dan Quisenberry	1	2	5.23	6	0	0	1	0	10.1	10	6	3	0
Paul Splittorff	0	0	5.40	1	0	0	0	0	1.2	4	1	0	0
TOTAL	2	4	4.15	17	6	0	1	0	52.0	59	24	15	17

GAME 1 AT PHI OCT 14

		R	H	E
KC	022 000 020	6	9	1
PHI	005 110 00X	7	11	0

Pitchers: LEONARD, Martin (4), Quisenberry (8) vs WALK, McGraw (8)
Home Runs: Otis-KC, Aikens-KC (2), McBride-PHI
Attendance: 65,791

GAME 2 AT PHI OCT 15

		R	H	E
KC	000 001 300	4	11	0
PHI	000 020 04X	6	8	1

Pitchers: Gura, QUISENBERRY (7) vs CARLTON, Reed (9)
Attendance: 65,775

GAME 3 AT KC OCT 17

		R	H	E
PHI	010 010 010 0	3	14	0
KC	100 100 100 1	4	11	0

Pitchers: Ruthven, McGRAW (10) vs Gale, Martin (5), QUISENBERRY (8)
Home Runs: Schmidt-PHI, G.Brett-KC, Otis-KC
Attendance: 42,380

GAME 4 AT KC OCT 18

		R	H	E
PHI	010 000 110	3	10	1
KC	410 000 00X	5	10	2

Pitchers: CHRISTENSON, Noles (1), Saucier (6), Brusstar (6) vs LEONARD, Quisenberry (8)
Home Runs: Aikens-KC (2)
Attendance: 42,363

GAME 5 AT KC OCT 19

		R	H	E
PHI	000 200 002	4	7	0
KC	000 012 000	3	12	2

Pitchers: Bystrom, Reed (6), McGRAW (7) vs Gura, QUISENBERRY (7)
Home Runs: Schmidt-PHI, Otis-KC
Attendance: 42,369

GAME 6 AT PHI OCT 21

		R	H	E
KC	000 000 010	1	7	2
PHI	002 011 00X	4	9	0

Pitchers: GALE, Martin (3), Splittorff (5), Pattin (7), Quisenberry (8) vs CARLTON, McGraw (8)
Attendance: 65,838

The Expos, who triumphed over the NL East in the second half of the season, won the first two playoff games at home by identical 3–1 scores over the first-half champion Phillies. In the first postseason game played in Canada the Phillies rapped Expos ace Steve Rogers for 10 hits in Game 1, but Keith Moreland's solo home run in the second was the only hit to produce a run. The homer tied the score briefly, but the Expos regained the lead in the last of the second inning on Chris Speier's double and increased it to 3–1 two innings later. The Expos scored their three runs early in Game 2 on Speier's second-inning single and Gary Carter's two-run homer an inning later. Expos starter Bill Gullickson blanked the Phillies on three hits through 7⅔ innings, but three two-out hits in the eighth scored a run and brought on reliever Jeff Reardon, who ended the threat for his second save in as many days.

When the Series moved to Philadelphia, the Phillies recovered to even things with a pair of wins. After an easy 13-hit 6–2 victory in Game 3, they took a 4–0 lead into the fourth inning of Game 4. Montreal fought back to tie the game, fell behind again, then re-tied the score at 5–5 in the top of the seventh. The final innings featured a duel between relievers Tug McGraw and Jeff Reardon. McGraw stopped the Expos on one hit through three innings, and took the win when Reardon, after retiring eight Phillies in a row, gave up a leadoff homer to pinch hitter George Vukovich in the bottom of the 10th.

Steve Rogers won the division title for Montreal in the finale, hurling a six-hit shutout against the Phillies and driving in the first two of Montreal's three runs with a bases-loaded single through the box in the fifth inning.

Montreal Expos, 3; Philadelphia Phillies, 2

MON (E)

PLAYER/POS	AVG	G	AB	R	H	2B	3B	HR	RB	BB	SO	SB
Stan Bahnsen, p	.000	1	0	0	0	0	0	0	0	0	0	0
Ray Burris, p	.000	1	2	0	0	0	0	0	0	0	2	0
Gary Carter, c	.421	5	19	3	8	3	0	2	6	1	1	0
Warren Cromartie, 1b	.227	5	22	1	5	2	0	0	1	0	9	0
Andre Dawson, of	.300	5	20	1	6	0	1	0	0	1	6	2
Terry Francona, of	.333	5	12	0	4	0	0	0	0	2	2	2
Woody Fryman, p	.000	1	0	0	0	0	0	0	0	0	0	0
Bill Gullickson, p	.000	1	3	0	0	0	0	0	0	0	1	0
Wallace Johnson, ph	.500	2	2	0	1	0	0	0	1	0	0	0
Bill Lee, p	.000	1	0	0	0	0	0	0	0	0	0	0
Jerry Manuel, 2b	.071	5	14	0	1	0	0	0	0	2	5	0
Brad Mills, ph	.000	1	0	0	0	0	0	0	0	1	0	0
John Milner, ph	.500	2	2	0	1	0	0	0	1	0	0	0
Larry Parrish, 3b	.150	5	20	3	3	1	0	0	1	1	3	0
Mike Phillips, 2b	.000	1	1	0	0	0	0	0	0	0	0	0
Jeff Reardon, p	.000	3	1	0	0	0	0	0	0	0	1	0
Steve Rogers, p	.400	2	5	0	2	0	0	0	2	0	1	0
Scott Sanderson, p	.000	1	1	0	0	0	0	0	0	0	1	0
Elias Sosa, p	.000	2	0	0	0	0	0	0	0	0	0	0
Chris Speier, ss	.400	5	15	4	6	2	0	0	3	4	2	0
Tim Wallach, of-3	.250	4	4	1	1	1	0	0	0	4	0	0
Jerry White, of	.167	5	18	3	3	1	0	0	1	2	2	3
TOTAL	.255		161	16	41	10	1	2	16	18	36	7

PITCHER	W	L	ERA	G	GS	CG	SV	SHO	IP	H	ER	BB	SO
Stan Bahnsen	0	0	0.00	1	0	0	0	0	1.1	1	0	1	1
Ray Burris	0	1	5.06	1	1	0	0	0	5.1	7	3	4	4
Woody Fryman	0	0	6.75	1	0	0	0	0	1.1	3	1	1	0
Bill Gullickson	1	0	1.17	1	1	0	0	0	7.2	6	1	1	3
Bill Lee	0	0	0.00	1	0	0	0	0	0.2	2	0	0	1
Jeff Reardon	0	1	2.08	3	0	0	2	0	4.1	1	1	1	2
Steve Rogers	2	0	0.51	2	2	1	0	1	17.2	16	1	3	5
Scott Sanderson	0	0	6.75	1	1	0	0	0	2.2	4	2	2	2
Elias Sosa	0	0	3.00	2	0	0	0	0	3.0	4	1	0	1
TOTAL	3	2	2.05	13	5	1	2	1	44.0	44	10	13	19

PHI (E)

PLAYER/POS	AVG	G	AB	R	H	2B	3B	HR	RB	BB	SO	SB
Luis Aguayo, pr	.000	2	0	1	0	0	0	0	0	0	0	0
Ramon Aviles, ph	.000	1	0	0	0	0	0	0	0	1	0	0
Bob Boone, c	.000	3	5	0	0	0	0	0	0	0	0	0
Larry Bowa, ss	.176	5	17	0	3	1	0	0	1	0	0	0
Warren Brusstar, p	.000	2	0	0	0	0	0	0	0	0	0	0
Steve Carlton, p	.250	2	4	0	1	0	0	0	0	0	0	0
Larry Christenson, p	.000	1	2	0	0	0	0	0	0	0	1	0
Dick Davis, of	.000	1	2	0	0	0	0	0	0	0	1	0
Greg Gross, of-2	.000	4	4	0	0	0	0	0	0	0	0	0
Sparky Lyle, p	.000	3	0	0	0	0	0	0	0	0	0	0
Garry Maddox, of	.333	2	3	0	1	1	0	0	0	0	0	0
Gary Matthews, of	.400	5	20	3	8	0	1	1	1	0	2	0
Bake McBride, of	.200	4	15	1	3	1	0	0	0	0	5	0
Tug McGraw, p	.000	2	0	0	0	0	0	0	0	0	0	0
Keith Moreland, c	.462	4	13	2	6	0	0	1	3	1	1	0
Dickie Noles, p	.000	1	0	0	0	0	0	0	0	1	0	0
Ron Reed, p	.000	4	0	0	0	0	0	0	0	0	0	0
Pete Rose, 1b	.300	5	20	1	6	1	0	0	2	2	0	0
Dick Ruthven, p	.000	1	1	0	0	0	0	0	0	0	0	0
Mike Schmidt, 3b	.250	5	16	3	4	1	0	1	2	4	2	0
Lonnie Smith, of	.263	5	19	1	5	1	0	0	0	0	4	0
Manny Trillo, 2b	.188	5	16	1	3	0	0	0	1	4	0	0
George Vukovich, of-3	.444	5	9	1	4	0	0	1	2	0	3	0
TOTAL	.265		166	14	44	6	1	4	12	13	19	0

PITCHER	W	L	ERA	G	GS	CG	SV	SHO	IP	H	ER	BB	SO
Warren Brusstar	0	0	4.91	2	0	0	0	0	3.2	5	2	1	3
Steve Carlton	0	2	3.86	2	2	0	0	0	14.0	14	6	8	13
Larry Christenson	1	0	1.50	1	1	0	0	0	6.0	4	1	1	8
Sparky Lyle	0	0	0.00	3	0	0	0	0	2.1	4	0	2	1
Tug McGraw	1	0	0.00	2	0	0	0	0	4.0	2	0	0	2
Dickie Noles	0	0	4.50	1	1	0	0	0	4.0	4	2	2	5
Ron Reed	0	0	3.00	4	0	0	0	0	6.0	5	2	3	4
Dick Ruthven	0	1	4.50	1	1	0	0	0	4.0	3	2	1	0
TOTAL	2	3	3.07	16	5	0	0	0	44.0	41	15	18	36

GAME 1 AT MON OCT 7

				R	H	E
PHI	010	000	000	1	10	1
MON	110	100	00X	3	8	0

Pitchers: CARLTON, R.Reed (7) vs ROGERS, Reardon (9)
Home Runs: Moreland-PHI
Attendance: 34,327

GAME 2 AT MON OCT 8

				R	H	E
PHI	000	000	010	1	6	2
MON	012	000	00X	3	7	0

Pitchers: RUTHVEN, Brusstar (5), Lyle (7), McGraw (8) vs GULLICKSON, Reardon (8)
Home Runs: Carter-MON
Attendance: 45,896

GAME 3 AT PHI OCT 9

				R	H	E
MON	010	000	010	2	8	4
PHI	020	002	20X	6	13	0

Pitchers: BURRIS, Lee (6), Sosa (7) vs CHRISTENSON, Lyle (7), R.Reed (8)
Attendance: 36,835

GAME 4 AT PHI OCT 10

					R	H	E
MON	000	112	100	0	5	10	1
PHI	202	001	000	1	6	9	0

Pitchers: Sanderson, Bahnsen (3), Sosa (5), Fryman (6), REARDON (7) vs Noles, Brusstar (5), Lyle (6), R.Reed (7), McGRAW (8)
Home Runs: Carter-MON, Schmidt-PHI, Matthews-PHI, G.Vukovich-PHI
Attendance: 38,818

GAME 5 AT PHI OCT 11

				R	H	E
MON	000	021	000	3	8	1
PHI	000	000	000	0	6	0

Pitchers: ROGERS vs CARLTON, R.Reed (9)
Attendance: 47,384

Cincinnati, with the league's best overall season record, failed to win either half season in the NL West, and watched from the sidelines as first-half winner Los Angeles, down two games to none, recovered to win the final three games—and the division title—from second-half victor Houston. In the opener, Alan Ashby's two-run homer in the last of the ninth broke a 1–1 tie and gave Nolan Ryan a two-hit victory. The next day, Denny Walling's two-out bases-loaded single in the last of the 11th scored Phil Garner with the game's only run.

When the clubs shifted to Los Angeles for the remainder of the series, the Dodgers came alive. In Game 3, a first-inning double by Dusty Baker and home run by Steve Garvey drove in three runs. Pitcher Burt Hooton and two relievers held Houston to three hits in what became a 6–1 Dodgers victory. The next day, Fernando Valenzuela and Vern Ruhle hurled matching four-hitters. But Pedro Guerrero's home run in the fifth inning and a pair of singles sandwiched around a sacrifice and intentional walk in the seventh gave Los Angeles two runs, while Valenzuela held Houston to a single run in the ninth. In the finale, Jerry Reuss blanked the Astros on five hits while his Dodgers blended three of their seven hits with a walk and an Astros error for three runs in the sixth. Two more hits produced a final run an inning later.

Los Angeles Dodgers, 3; Houston Astros, 2

LA (W)

PLAYER/POS	AVG	G	AB	R	H	2B	3B	HR	RB	BB	SO	SB
Dusty Baker, of	.167	5	18	2	3	1	0	0	1	2	0	0
Terry Forster, p	.000	1	0	0	0	0	0	0	0	0	0	0
Steve Garvey, 1b	.368	5	19	4	7	0	1	2	4	0	2	0
Pedro Guerrero, 3b	.176	5	17	1	3	1	0	1	1	2	4	1
Burt Hooton, p	.000	1	3	0	0	0	0	0	0	0	0	0
Steve Howe, p	.000	2	0	0	0	0	0	0	0	0	0	0
Jay Johnstone, ph	.000	1	1	0	0	0	0	0	0	0	0	0
Ken Landreaux, of	.200	5	20	1	4	1	0	0	1	0	1	0
Davey Lopes, 2b	.200	5	20	1	4	1	0	0	0	3	7	1
Mike Marshall, ph	.000	1	1	0	0	0	0	0	0	0	1	0
Rick Monday, of	.214	5	14	1	3	0	0	0	1	2	4	0
Tom Niedenfuer, p	.000	1	0	0	0	0	0	0	0	0	0	0
Jerry Reuss, p	.000	2	8	0	0	0	0	0	0	0	8	0
Bill Russell, ss	.250	5	16	1	4	1	0	0	2	3	1	0
Steve Sax, 2b	.000	1	0	0	0	0	0	0	0	0	0	0
Mike Scioscia, c	.154	4	13	0	2	0	0	0	1	1	2	0
Reggie Smith, ph	.000	2	1	0	0	0	0	0	1	0	1	0
Dave Stewart, p	.000	2	0	0	0	0	0	0	0	0	0	0
Derrel Thomas, of	.000	4	2	1	0	0	0	0	0	0	1	0
Fernando Valenzuela, p	.000	2	4	0	0	0	0	0	0	0	1	0
Bob Welch, p	.000	1	0	0	0	0	0	0	0	0	0	0
Steve Yeager, c	.400	2	5	1	2	1	0	0	0	0	1	0
TOTAL	.198		162	13	32	6	1	3	12	13	34	2

PITCHER	W	L	ERA	G	GS	CG	SV	SHO	IP	H	ER	BB	SO
Terry Forster	0	0	0.00	1	0	0	0	0	0.1	0	0	0	0
Burt Hooton	1	0	1.29	1	1	0	0	0	7.0	3	1	3	2
Steve Howe	0	0	0.00	2	0	0	0	0	2.0	1	0	0	2
Tom Niedenfuer	0	0	0.00	1	0	0	0	0	0.1	1	0	1	1
Jerry Reuss	1	0	0.00	2	2	1	0	1	18.0	10	0	5	7
Dave Stewart	0	2	40.50	2	0	0	0	0	0.2	4	3	0	1
Fernando Valenzuela	1	0	1.06	2	2	1	0	0	17.0	10	2	3	10
Bob Welch	0	0	0.00	1	0	0	0	0	1.0	0	0	1	1
TOTAL	3	2	1.17	12	5	2	0	1	46.1	29	6	13	24

HOU (W)

PLAYER/POS	AVG	G	AB	R	H	2B	3B	HR	RB	BB	SO	SB
Alan Ashby, c	.111	3	9	1	1	0	0	1	2	2	0	0
Cesar Cedeno, 1b	.231	4	13	0	3	1	0	0	0	2	2	2
Jose Cruz, of	.300	5	20	0	6	1	0	0	0	1	3	1
Kiko Garcia, ss-1	.000	2	4	0	0	0	0	0	0	0	1	0
Phil Garner, 2b	.111	5	18	1	2	0	0	0	0	3	3	0
Art Howe, 3b	.235	5	17	1	4	0	0	1	1	2	1	0
Bob Knepper, p	.000	1	1	0	0	0	0	0	0	0	0	0
Frank LaCorte, p	.000	2	0	0	0	0	0	0	0	0	0	0
Joe Niekro, p	.000	1	2	0	0	0	0	0	0	0	0	0
Joe Pittman, ph	.000	2	2	0	0	0	0	0	0	0	0	0
Terry Puhl, of	.190	5	21	2	4	1	0	0	0	0	1	1
Luis Pujols, c	.000	2	6	0	0	0	0	0	0	0	1	0
Craig Reynolds, ss-1	.333	2	3	1	1	0	0	0	0	0	1	0
Dave Roberts, ph	.000	1	1	0	0	0	0	0	0	0	1	0
Vern Ruhle, p	.000	1	1	0	0	0	0	0	0	0	1	0
Nolan Ryan, p	.250	2	4	0	1	0	0	0	0	1	1	0
Joe Sambito, p	.000	2	0	0	0	0	0	0	0	0	0	0
Tony Scott, of	.150	5	20	0	3	0	0	0	2	1	6	0
Billy Smith, p	.000	1	0	0	0	0	0	0	0	0	0	0
Dave Smith, p	.000	2	0	0	0	0	0	0	0	0	0	0
Harry Spilman, ph	.000	1	1	0	0	0	0	0	0	0	0	0
Dickie Thon, ss	.182	4	11	0	2	0	0	0	0	1	0	0
Denny Walling, 1b-2	.333	3	6	0	2	0	0	0	1	0	1	0
Gary Woods, ph	.000	2	2	0	0	0	0	0	0	0	1	0
TOTAL	.179		162	6	29	3	0	2	6	13	24	4

PITCHER	W	L	ERA	G	GS	CG	SV	SHO	IP	H	ER	BB	SO
Bob Knepper	0	1	5.40	1	1	0	0	0	5.0	6	3	2	4
Frank LaCorte	0	0	0.00	2	0	0	0	0	3.2	2	0	1	5
Joe Niekro	0	0	0.00	1	1	0	0	0	8.0	7	0	3	4
Vern Ruhle	0	1	2.25	1	1	1	0	0	8.0	4	2	2	1
Nolan Ryan	1	1	1.80	2	2	1	0	0	15.0	6	3	3	14
Joe Sambito	1	0	16.20	2	0	0	0	0	1.2	5	3	2	2
Billy Smith	0	0	0.00	1	0	0	0	0	0.1	0	0	0	0
Dave Smith	0	0	3.86	2	0	0	0	0	2.1	2	1	0	4
TOTAL	2	3	2.45	12	5	2	0	0	44.0	32	12	13	34

GAME 1 AT HOU OCT 6

				R	H	E
LA	000	000	100	1	2	0
HOU	000	001	002	3	8	0

Pitchers: Valenzuela, STEWART (9) vs RYAN
Home Runs: Garvey-LA, Ashby-HOU
Attendance: 44,836

GAME 2 AT HOU OCT 7

					R	H	E
LA	000	000	000	00	0	9	1
HOU	000	000	000	01	1	9	0

Pitchers: Reuss, S.Howe (10), STEWART (11), Forster (11), Niedenfuer (11) vs Niekro, D.Smith (9), SAMBITO (11)
Attendance: 42,398

GAME 3 AT LA OCT 9

				R	H	E
HOU	001	000	000	1	3	2
LA	300	000	03X	6	10	0

Pitchers: KNEPPER, LaCorte (6), Sambito (8), B.Smith (8) vs HOOTON, S.Howe (8), Welch (9)
Home Runs: Garvey-LA, A.Howe-HOU
Attendance: 46,820

GAME 4 AT LA OCT 10

				R	H	E
HOU	000	000	001	1	4	0
LA	000	010	10X	2	4	0

Pitchers: RUHLE vs VALENZUELA
Home Runs: Guerrero-LA
Attendance: 55,983

GAME 5 AT LA OCT 11

				R	H	E
HOU	000	000	000	0	5	3
LA	000	003	10X	4	7	2

Pitchers: RYAN, D.Smith (7), LaCorte (7) vs REUSS
Attendance: 55,979

The home field didn't seem to offer any advantage in this series. First-half winner New York captured both games played in Milwaukee, but when the Series moved to Yankee Stadium for the final three games, the second-half champion Brewers evened the series.

Milwaukee took a 2–0 lead early in the opener, but New York erupted for four runs in the fourth on Oscar Gamble's two-run homer and Rick Cerone's double, and held on to win, 5–3. In Game 2 rookie starter Dave Righetti fanned 10 Brewers in his six innings and Goose Gossage's brilliant relief earned him his second save in two days as the Yankees took a 3–0 win on homers by Lou Piniella and Reggie Jackson.

Milwaukee, struggling against elimination, took the lead in the seventh inning of Game 3 on Ted Simmons' two-run homer. New York tied the score at 3–3 in their half of the inning, but Paul Molitor broke the tie in the eighth with a solo homer. Simmons doubled home an insurance run later in the inning for a 5–3 Brewers win. The Brewers managed only four hits in Game 4, but three of them came in the fourth inning and combined with a sacrifice fly to produce the Brewers' two runs. New York scored once in the sixth, but base-running errors an inning later ended their only other scoring threat.

In the finale Milwaukee scored two early runs, but the Yankees (as they had done in the opener) took the lead with a four-run fourth—this time on home runs by Reggie Jackson and Oscar Gamble, and Rick Cerone's single. Cerone later hit an insurance homer, as the home team finally won a game—and captured the series.

New York Yankees, 3; Milwaukee Brewers, 2

NY (E)

PLAYER/POS	AVG	G	AB	R	H	2B	3B	HR	RB	BB	SO	SB
Bobby Brown, pr	.000	1	0	0	0	0	0	0	0	0	0	0
Rick Cerone, c	.333	5	18	1	6	2	0	1	5	0	2	0
Ron Davis, p	.000	3	0	0	0	0	0	0	0	0	0	0
Barry Foote, ph	.000	1	0	0	0	0	0	0	0	0	0	0
Oscar Gamble, dh	.556	4	9	2	5	1	0	2	3	1	2	0
Rich Gossage, p	.000	3	0	0	0	0	0	0	0	0	0	0
Ron Guidry, p	.000	2	0	0	0	0	0	0	0	0	0	0
Reggie Jackson, of	.300	5	20	4	6	0	0	2	4	1	5	0
Tommy John, p	.000	1	0	0	0	0	0	0	0	0	0	0
Rudy May, p	.000	1	0	0	0	0	0	0	0	0	0	0
Larry Milbourne, ss	.316	5	19	4	6	1	0	0	0	0	1	0
Jerry Mumphrey, of	.095	5	21	2	2	0	0	0	0	0	1	1
Bobby Murcer, ph	.000	2	1	0	0	0	0	0	0	1	0	0
Graig Nettles, 3b	.059	5	17	1	1	0	0	0	1	3	1	0
Lou Piniella, dh	.200	4	10	1	2	1	0	1	3	0	0	0
Willie Randolph, 2b	.200	5	20	0	4	0	0	0	1	1	4	0
Rick Reuschel, p	.000	1	0	0	0	0	0	0	0	0	0	0
Dave Revering, 1b	.000	2	0	0	0	0	0	0	0	0	0	0
Dave Righetti, p	.000	2	0	0	0	0	0	0	0	0	0	0
Bob Watson, 1b	.438	5	16	2	7	0	0	0	1	1	1	0
Dave Winfield, of	.350	5	20	2	7	3	0	0	0	1	5	0
TOTAL	.269		171	19	46	8	0	6	18	9	22	1

PITCHER	W	L	ERA	G	GS	CG	SV	SHO	IP	H	ER	BB	SO
Ron Davis	1	0	0.00	3	0	0	0	0	6.0	1	0	2	6
Rich Gossage	0	0	0.00	3	0	0	3	0	6.2	3	0	2	8
Ron Guidry	0	0	5.40	2	2	0	0	0	8.1	11	5	3	8
Tommy John	0	1	6.43	1	1	0	0	0	7.0	8	5	2	0
Rudy May	0	0	0.00	1	0	0	0	0	2.0	1	0	0	1
Rick Reuschel	0	1	3.00	1	1	0	0	0	6.0	4	2	1	3
Dave Righetti	2	0	1.00	2	1	0	0	0	9.0	8	1	3	13
TOTAL	3	2	2.60	13	5	0	3	0	45.0	36	13	13	39

MIL (E)

PLAYER/POS	AVG	G	AB	R	H	2B	3B	HR	RB	BB	SO	SB
Sal Bando, 3b	.294	5	17	1	5	3	0	0	1	2	3	0
Dwight Bernard, p	.000	2	0	0	0	0	0	0	0	0	0	0
Thad Bosley, dh	.000	1	0	0	0	0	0	0	0	0	0	0
Mike Caldwell, p	.000	2	0	0	0	0	0	0	0	0	0	0
Cecil Cooper, 1b	.222	5	18	1	4	0	0	0	3	1	3	0
Jamie Easterly, p	.000	2	0	0	0	0	0	0	0	0	0	0
Marshall Edwards, of	.000	2	1	0	0	0	0	0	0	0	1	0
Rollie Fingers, p	.000	3	0	0	0	0	0	0	0	0	0	0
Jim Gantner, 2b	.143	4	14	1	2	1	0	0	0	0	2	0
Moose Haas, p	.000	2	0	0	0	0	0	0	0	0	0	0
Roy Howell, dh-3	.400	4	5	0	2	0	0	0	0	2	2	0
Randy Lerch, p	.000	1	0	0	0	0	0	0	0	0	0	0
Bob McClure, p	.000	3	0	0	0	0	0	0	0	0	0	0
Paul Molitor, of	.250	5	20	2	5	0	0	1	1	2	5	0
Don Money, 2b-1,dh-1	.000	2	3	0	0	0	0	0	0	0	0	0
Charlie Moore, of-2,dh-2	.222	4	9	0	2	0	0	0	1	1	2	0
Ben Oglivie, of	.167	5	18	0	3	1	0	0	1	0	7	0
Ed Romero, 2b	.500	1	2	1	1	0	0	0	0	0	1	0
Ted Simmons, c	.222	5	18	1	4	1	0	1	4	2	2	0
Jim Slaton, p	.000	4	0	0	0	0	0	0	0	0	0	0
Gorman Thomas, of-3,dh-2	.111	5	18	2	2	0	0	1	1	1	9	0
Pete Vuckovich, p	.000	2	0	0	0	0	0	0	0	0	0	0
Robin Yount, ss	.316	5	19	4	6	0	1	0	1	2	2	1
TOTAL	.222		162	13	36	6	1	3	13	13	39	1

PITCHER	W	L	ERA	G	GS	CG	SV	SHO	IP	H	ER	BB	SO
Dwight Bernard	0	0	0.00	2	0	0	0	0	2.1	0	0	0	0
Mike Caldwell	0	1	4.32	2	1	0	0	0	8.1	9	4	0	4
Jamie Easterly	0	0	6.75	2	0	0	0	0	1.1	2	1	0	1
Rollie Fingers	1	0	3.86	3	0	0	1	0	4.2	7	2	1	5
Moose Haas	0	2	9.45	2	2	0	0	0	6.2	13	7	1	1
Randy Lerch	0	0	1.50	1	1	0	0	0	6.0	3	1	4	3
Bob McClure	0	0	0.00	3	0	0	0	0	3.1	4	0	0	2
Jim Slaton	0	0	3.00	4	0	0	0	0	6.0	6	2	0	2
Pete Vuckovich	1	0	0.00	2	1	0	0	0	5.1	2	0	3	4
TOTAL	2	3	3.48	21	5	0	1	0	44.0	46	17	9	22

GAME 1 AT MIL OCT 7

		R	H	E
NY	000 400 001	5	13	1
MIL	011 010 000	3	8	3

Pitchers: Guidry, DAVIS (5), Gossage (8) vs HAAS, Bernard (4), McClure (5), Slaton (6), Fingers (8)
Home Runs: Gamble-NY
Attendance: 35,064

GAME 2 AT MIL OCT 8

		R	H	E
NY	000 100 002	3	7	0
MIL	000 000 000	0	7	0

Pitchers: RIGHETTI, Davis (7), Gossage (7) vs CALDWELL, Slaton (9)
Home Runs: Piniella-NY, Jackson-NY
Attendance: 26,395

GAME 3 AT NY OCT 9

		R	H	E
MIL	000 000 320	5	9	0
NY	000 100 200	3	8	2

Pitchers: Lerch, FINGERS (7) vs JOHN, May (8)
Home Runs: Simmons-MIL, Molitor-MIL
Attendance: 56,411

GAME 4 AT NY OCT 10

		R	H	E
MIL	000 200 000	2	4	2
NY	000 001 000	1	5	0

Pitchers: VUCKOVICH, Easterly (6), Slaton (7), McClure (8), Fingers (9) vs REUSCHEL, Davis (7)
Attendance: 52,077

GAME 5 AT NY OCT 11

		R	H	E
MIL	011 000 100	3	8	0
NY	000 400 12X	7	13	0

Pitchers: HAAS, Caldwell (4), Bernard (4), McClure (6), Slaton (7), Easterly (8), Vuckovich (8) vs Guidry, RIGHETTI (5), Gossage (8)
Home Runs: Thomas-MIL, Jackson-NY, Gamble-NY, Cerone-NY
Attendance: 47,505

First-half winner Oakland, with the league's best win-loss record over the full season, swept the division title from second-half champ Kansas City (who, with a full-season record of 50–53, had become the only club in major-league history to qualify for postseason play with a losing record). Twice in the opener the Royals loaded the bases against Mike Norris with fewer than two outs, but both times failed to score. Meanwhile, after a Royals error had prolonged the A's fourth inning, Wayne Gross homered for three unearned Oakland runs. Dwayne Murphy's eighth-inning solo shot gave the A's a fourth run. The game ended with Norris possessor of a four-hit shutout.

Game 2 was closer. Oakland's Tony Armas doubled in a run in the top of the first, and doubled home another in the eighth (his fourth hit of the game) to break a 1–1 tie and provide the margin needed for pitcher Steve McCatty's six-hit win. Oakland's Rick Langford yielded 10 hits in Game 3 (including Kansas City's only extra-base hit of the series, a double), but only one Royal scored. The A's, meanwhile, were sending four runs across the plate—three of them by Rickey Henderson, who reached base four times on pairs of hits and walks.

Oakland Athletics, 3; Kansas City Royals, 0

KC (W)

PLAYER/POS	AVG	G	AB	R	H	2B	3B	HR	RB	BB	SO	SB
Willie Aikens, 1b	.333	3	9	0	3	0	0	0	0	3	2	0
George Brett, 3b	.167	3	12	0	2	0	0	0	0	0	0	0
Cesar Geronimo, pr	.000	1	0	0	0	0	0	0	0	0	0	0
Larry Gura, p	.000	1	0	0	0	0	0	0	0	0	0	0
Clint Hurdle, of	.273	3	11	0	3	0	0	0	0	1	1	0
Mike Jones, p	.000	1	0	0	0	0	0	0	0	0	0	0
Dennis Leonard, p	.000	1	0	0	0	0	0	0	0	0	0	0
Renie Martin, p	.000	2	0	0	0	0	0	0	0	0	0	0
Lee May, 1b	.000	1	0	0	0	0	0	0	0	0	0	0
Hal McRae, dh	.091	3	11	0	1	1	0	0	0	1	1	0
Amos Otis, of	.000	3	12	0	0	0	0	0	1	0	4	0
Dan Quisenberry, p	.000	1	0	0	0	0	0	0	0	0	0	0
U. L. Washington, ss	.222	3	9	0	2	0	0	0	0	0	1	0
John Wathan, c	.300	3	10	1	3	0	0	0	0	1	1	0
Frank White, 2b	.182	3	11	1	2	0	0	0	0	1	1	0
Willie Wilson, of	.308	3	13	0	4	0	0	0	1	0	0	0
TOTAL	.204		98	2	20	1	0	0	2	7	11	0

PITCHER	W	L	ERA	G	GS	CG	SV	SHO	IP	H	ER	BB	SO
Larry Gura	0	1	7.36	1	1	0	0	0	3.2	7	3	3	3
Mike Jones	0	1	2.25	1	1	0	0	0	8.0	9	2	0	2
Dennis Leonard	0	1	1.13	1	1	0	0	0	8.0	7	1	1	3
Renie Martin	0	0	0.00	2	0	0	0	0	5.1	1	0	2	2
Dan Quisenberry	0	0	0.00	1	0	0	0	0	1.0	1	0	0	0
TOTAL	0	3	2.08	6	3	0	0	0	26.0	25	6	6	10

OAK (W)

PLAYER/POS	AVG	G	AB	R	H	2B	3B	HR	RB	BB	SO	SB
Tony Armas, of	.545	3	11	1	6	2	0	0	3	1	1	0
Dave Beard, p	.000	1	0	0	0	0	0	0	0	0	0	0
Rick Bosetti, of	.000	1	0	0	0	0	0	0	0	0	0	0
Keith Drumright, dh	.250	1	4	0	1	0	0	0	0	0	0	0
Wayne Gross, 3b-1	.400	2	5	1	2	0	0	1	3	0	0	0
Mike Heath, c	.000	2	8	0	0	0	0	0	0	0	1	0
Rickey Henderson, of	.182	3	11	3	2	0	0	0	0	2	0	2
Cliff Johnson, dh	.286	2	7	0	2	1	0	0	0	0	1	0
Mickey Klutts, 3b	.143	2	7	0	1	0	0	0	0	0	1	0
Rick Langford, p	.000	1	0	0	0	0	0	0	0	0	0	0
Steve McCatty, p	.000	1	0	0	0	0	0	0	0	0	0	0
Dave McKay, 2b	.273	3	11	1	3	0	0	1	1	1	1	0
Kelvin Moore, 1b	.000	2	8	0	0	0	0	0	0	0	2	0
Dwayne Murphy, of	.545	3	11	4	6	1	0	1	2	1	1	0
Jeff Newman, c	.000	1	3	0	0	0	0	0	0	0	1	0
Mike Norris, p	.000	1	0	0	0	0	0	0	0	0	0	0
Rob Picciolo, ss	.333	1	3	0	1	0	0	0	0	0	0	0
Jim Spencer, 1b	.250	1	4	0	1	1	0	0	0	0	0	0
Fred Stanley, ss	.000	3	6	0	0	0	0	0	0	1	1	0
Tom Underwood, p	.000	1	0	0	0	0	0	0	0	0	0	0
TOTAL	.253		99	10	25	5	0	3	9	6	10	2

PITCHER	W	L	ERA	G	GS	CG	SV	SHO	IP	H	ER	BB	SO
Dave Beard	0	0	0.00	1	0	0	1	0	1.1	0	0	0	2
Rick Langford	1	0	1.23	1	1	0	0	0	7.1	10	1	0	3
Steve McCatty	1	0	1.00	1	1	1	0	0	9.0	6	1	4	3
Mike Norris	1	0	0.00	1	1	1	0	1	9.0	4	0	3	2
Tom Underwood	0	0	0.00	1	0	0	0	0	0.1	0	0	0	1
TOTAL	3	0	0.67	5	3	2	1	1	27.0	20	2	7	11

GAME 1 AT KC OCT 6

				R	H	E
OAK	000	300	010	4	8	2
KC	000	000	000	0	4	1

Pitchers: NORRIS vs LEONARD, Martin (9)
Home Runs: Gross-OAK, Murphy-OAK
Attendance: 40,592

GAME 2 AT KC OCT 7

				R	H	E
OAK	100	000	010	2	10	1
KC	000	010	000	1	6	0

Pitchers: McCATTY vs JONES, Quisenberry (9)
Attendance: 40,274

GAME 3 AT OAK OCT 9

				R	H	E
KC	000	100	000	1	10	3
OAK	101	200	00X	4	7	0

Pitchers: GURA, Martin (4) vs LANGFORD, Underwood (8), Beard (8)
Home Runs: McKay-OAK
Attendance: 40,002

Fine pitching characterized the series, with the losing team held to one run in four of the five games. In the exception Ray Burris hurled a shutout for the Expos.

Montreal put men on base in each inning of the opener. But the pitching of Burt Hooton and Bob Welch—plus some fine Dodgers fielding—kept the Expos from scoring until the ninth, when their one run was too little to overcome the Dodger's four-run cushion. Burris' shutout evened the series in Game 2 as the Expos scored three times against rookie sensation Fernando Valenzuela. The Expos took the series lead in Game 3, overcoming a 1–0 deficit with a two-out four-run burst in the sixth (capped by Jerry White's three-run homer).

In the end, though, the Dodgers prevailed. Through seven innings of Game 4, Hooton and the Expos' Bill Gullickson dueled at 1–1. But in the top of the eighth, Steve Garvey homered with a man aboard, and four more Dodger runs in the ninth put the game away. The finale—Burris vs. Valenzuela again—featured another 1–1 duel, this one reaching into the top of the ninth when, with two out, Rick Monday homered off Steve Rogers, who came on in relief of Burris. In the bottom of the ninth, Valenzuela walked two batters after retiring two, but Welch came on to save the game and the pennant.

Los Angeles Dodgers (West), 3; Montreal Expos (East), 2

LA (W)

PLAYER/POS	AVG	G	AB	R	H	2B	3B	HR	RB	BB	SO	SB
Dusty Baker, of	.316	5	19	3	6	1	0	0	3	1	0	0
Bobby Castillo, p	.000	1	0	0	0	0	0	0	0	0	0	0
Ron Cey, 3b	.278	5	18	1	5	1	0	0	3	3	2	0
Terry Forster, p	.000	1	0	0	0	0	0	0	0	0	0	0
Steve Garvey, 1b	.286	5	21	2	6	0	0	1	2	0	4	0
Pedro Guerrero, of	.105	5	19	1	2	0	0	1	2	1	4	0
Burt Hooton, p	.000	2	5	0	0	0	0	0	0	0	2	0
Steve Howe, p	.000	2	0	0	0	0	0	0	0	0	0	0
Jay Johnstone, ph	.000	2	2	0	0	0	0	0	0	0	0	0
Ken Landreaux, of-3	.100	5	10	0	1	1	0	0	0	3	2	0
Davey Lopes, 2b	.278	5	18	0	5	0	0	0	0	1	3	5
Rick Monday, of-2	.333	3	9	2	3	0	0	1	1	0	4	0
Tom Niedenfuer, p	.000	1	0	0	0	0	0	0	0	0	0	0
Alejandro Pena, p	.000	2	0	0	0	0	0	0	0	0	0	0
Jerry Reuss, p	.000	1	2	0	0	0	0	0	0	0	0	0
Bill Russell, ss	.313	5	16	2	5	0	1	0	1	1	1	0
Steve Sax, 2b	.000	1	0	0	0	0	0	0	0	0	0	0
Mike Scioscia, c	.133	5	15	1	2	0	0	1	1	2	1	0
Reggie Smith, ph	1.000	1	1	0	1	0	0	0	1	0	0	0
Derrel Thomas, 3b-1,of-1	1.000	2	1	2	1	0	0	0	0	0	0	0
Fernando Valenzuela, p	.000	2	5	0	0	0	0	0	1	0	0	0
Bob Welch, p	.000	3	0	0	0	0	0	0	0	0	0	0
Steve Yeager, c	.500	1	2	1	1	0	0	0	0	0	0	0
TOTAL	.233		163	15	38	3	1	4	15	12	23	5

PITCHER	W	L	ERA	G	GS	CG	SV	SHO	IP	H	ER	BB	SO
Bobby Castillo	0	0	0.00	1	0	0	0	0	1.0	0	0	0	1
Terry Forster	0	0	0.00	1	0	0	0	0	0.1	0	0	0	1
Burt Hooton	2	0	0.00	2	2	0	0	0	14.2	11	0	6	7
Steve Howe	0	0	0.00	2	0	0	0	0	2.0	1	0	0	2
Tom Niedenfuer	0	0	0.00	1	0	0	0	0	0.1	2	0	0	0
Alejandro Pena	0	0	0.00	2	0	0	0	0	2.1	1	0	0	0
Jerry Reuss	0	1	5.14	1	1	0	0	0	7.0	7	4	1	2
Fernando Valenzuela	1	1	2.45	2	2	0	0	0	14.2	10	4	5	10
Bob Welch	0	0	5.40	3	0	0	1	0	1.2	2	1	0	2
TOTAL	3	2	1.84	15	5	0	1	0	44.0	34	9	12	25

MON (E)

PLAYER/POS	AVG	G	AB	R	H	2B	3B	HR	RB	BB	SO	SB
Ray Burris, p	.000	2	6	0	0	0	0	0	0	0	4	0
Gary Carter, c	.438	5	16	3	7	1	0	0	0	4	2	0
Warren Cromartie, 1b	.167	5	18	0	3	1	0	0	2	0	2	0
Andre Dawson, of	.150	5	20	2	3	0	0	0	0	0	4	0
Terry Francona, of-1	.000	2	1	0	0	0	0	0	0	0	1	0
Woody Fryman, p	.000	1	0	0	0	0	0	0	0	0	0	0
Bill Gullickson, p	.000	2	3	0	0	0	0	0	0	1	2	0
Bill Lee, p	.000	1	0	0	0	0	0	0	0	0	0	0
Jerry Manuel, pr	.000	1	0	0	0	0	0	0	0	0	0	0
John Milner, ph	.000	1	1	0	0	0	0	0	0	0	1	0
Larry Parrish, 3b	.263	5	19	2	5	2	0	0	2	1	1	0
Tim Raines, of	.238	5	21	1	5	2	0	0	1	0	3	0
Jeff Reardon, p	.000	1	0	0	0	0	0	0	0	0	0	0
Steve Rogers, p	.000	2	2	0	0	0	0	0	0	0	1	0
Rodney Scott, 2b	.167	5	18	0	3	0	0	0	0	1	3	1
Elias Sosa, p	.000	1	0	0	0	0	0	0	0	0	0	0
Chris Speier, ss	.188	5	16	0	3	0	0	0	0	2	0	0
Tim Wallach, ph	.000	1	1	0	0	0	0	0	0	0	0	0
Jerry White, of	.313	5	16	2	5	1	0	1	3	3	1	1
TOTAL	.215		158	10	34	7	0	1	8	12	25	2

PITCHER	W	L	ERA	G	GS	CG	SV	SHO	IP	H	ER	BB	SO
Ray Burris	1	0	0.53	2	2	1	0	1	17.0	10	1	3	4
Woody Fryman	0	0	36.00	1	0	0	0	0	1.0	3	4	1	1
Bill Gullickson	0	2	2.51	2	2	0	0	0	14.1	12	4	6	12
Bill Lee	0	0	0.00	1	0	0	0	0	0.1	1	0	0	0
Jeff Reardon	0	0	27.00	1	0	0	0	0	1.0	3	3	0	0
Steve Rogers	1	1	1.80	2	1	1	0	0	10.0	8	2	1	6
Elias Sosa	0	0	0.00	1	0	0	0	0	0.1	1	0	1	0
TOTAL	2	3	2.86	10	5	2	0	1	44.0	38	14	12	23

GAME 1 AT LA OCT 13

MON	000	000	001	1	9	0
LA	020	000	03X	5	8	0

Pitchers: GULLICKSON, Reardon (8) vs HOOTON, Welch (8), Howe (9)
Home Runs: Guerrero-LA, Scioscia-LA
Attendance: 51,273

GAME 2 AT LA OCT 14

MON	020	001	000	3	10	1
LA	000	000	000	0	5	1

Pitchers: BURRIS vs VALENZUELA, Niedenfuer (7), Forster (7), Pena (7), Castillo (9)
Attendance: 53,463

GAME 3 AT MON OCT 16

LA	000	100	000	1	7	0
MON	000	004	00X	4	7	1

Pitchers: REUSS, Pena (8) vs ROGERS
Home Runs: White-MON
Attendance: 54,372

GAME 4 AT MON OCT 17

LA	001	000	024	7	12	1
MON	000	100	000	1	5	1

Pitchers: HOOTON, Welch (8), Howe (9) vs GULLICKSON, Fryman (8), Sosa (9), Lee (9)
Home Runs: Garvey-LA
Attendance: 54,499

GAME 5 AT MON OCT 19

LA	000	010	001	2	6	0
MON	100	000	000	1	3	1

Pitchers: VALENZUELA, Welch (9) vs Burris, ROGERS (9)
Home Runs: Monday-LA
Attendance: 36,491

The A's scored only four runs to their opponents' 20 as the Yankees swept the series. And only two of New York's six pitchers permitted an Oakland runner to score, while not one of Oakland's eight pitchers held New York scoreless. Even so, two of the three games were closely contested.

Oakland's Mike Norris gave up a bases-loaded double to Graig Nettles in the first inning of Game 1 before settling down to pitch shutout ball. But the three runs Nettles drove in were more than enough, as Tommy John and two relievers held the A's to a single run.

Game 2 was the series' only blowout, and even it remained close for three innings. But, led by a pair of three-run homers from Nettles and Lou Piniella, the Yankees parlayed 19 hits into 13 runs as Yankee reliever George Frazier held the A's scoreless over the final five frames.

Game 3 remained tight until the ninth. Through eight innings the only run came on Willie Randolph's homer off Oakland starter Matt Keough. But in the top of the ninth, Graig Nettles tagged reliever Tom Underwood for his second bases-clearing double of the series. The three runs weren't really needed, as Dave Righetti, Ron Davis, and Goose Gossage combined to shut out the A's for the full nine.

New York Yankees (East), 3; Oakland A's (West), 0

NY (E)

PLAYER/POS	AVG	G	AB	R	H	2B	3B	HR	RB	BB	SO	SB
Bobby Brown, of-2	1.000	3	1	2	1	0	0	0	0	0	0	0
Rick Cerone, c	.100	3	10	1	1	0	0	0	0	0	0	0
Ron Davis, p	.000	2	0	0	0	0	0	0	0	0	0	0
Barry Foote, c-1	1.000	2	1	0	1	0	0	0	0	0	0	0
George Frazier, p	.000	1	0	0	0	0	0	0	0	0	0	0
Oscar Gamble, dh-2,of-1	.167	3	6	2	1	0	0	0	1	5	3	0
Rich Gossage, p	.000	2	0	0	0	0	0	0	0	0	0	0
Reggie Jackson, of	.000	2	4	1	0	0	0	0	1	1	0	1
Tommy John, p	.000	1	0	0	0	0	0	0	0	0	0	0
Rudy May, p	.000	1	0	0	0	0	0	0	0	0	0	0
Larry Milbourne, ss	.462	3	13	4	6	0	0	0	1	0	0	0
Jerry Mumphrey, of	.500	3	12	2	6	1	0	0	0	3	2	0
Bobby Murcer, dh	.333	1	3	0	1	0	0	0	0	1	1	0
Graig Nettles, 3b	.500	3	12	2	6	2	0	1	9	1	0	0
Lou Piniella, dh-2,of-1	.600	3	5	2	3	0	0	1	3	0	0	0
Willie Randolph, 2b	.333	3	12	2	4	0	0	1	2	0	1	0
Dave Revering, 1b	.500	2	2	0	1	0	0	0	0	0	0	0
Dave Righetti, p	.000	1	0	0	0	0	0	0	0	0	0	0
Andre Robertson, ss	.000	1	1	0	0	0	0	0	0	0	0	0
Aurelio Rodriguez, 3b	.000	1	0	0	0	0	0	0	0	0	0	0
Bob Watson, 1b	.250	3	12	0	3	0	0	0	1	0	1	0
Dave Winfield, of	.154	3	13	2	2	1	0	0	2	2	2	1
TOTAL	.336		107	20	36	4	0	3	20	13	10	2

PITCHER	W	L	ERA	G	GS	CG	SV	SHO	IP	H	ER	BB	SO
Ron Davis	0	0	0.00	2	0	0	0	0	3.1	0	0	2	4
George Frazier	1	0	0.00	1	0	0	0	0	5.2	5	0	1	5
Rich Gossage	0	0	0.00	2	0	0	1	0	2.2	1	0	0	2
Tommy John	1	0	1.50	1	1	0	0	0	6.0	6	1	1	3
Rudy May	0	0	8.10	1	0	0	0	0	3.1	6	3	0	5
Dave Righetti	1	0	0.00	1	1	0	0	0	6.0	4	0	2	4
TOTAL	3	0	1.33	8	2	0	1	0	27.0	22	4	6	23

OAK (W)

PLAYER/POS	AVG	G	AB	R	H	2B	3B	HR	RB	BB	SO	SB
Tony Armas, of	.167	3	12	0	2	0	0	0	0	0	5	0
Dave Beard, p	.000	1	0	0	0	0	0	0	0	0	0	0
Rick Bosetti, of-1,dh-1	.250	2	4	1	1	1	0	0	0	0	1	0
Mike Davis, ph	1.000	1	1	0	1	0	0	0	0	0	0	0
Keith Drumright, dh-1	.000	3	4	0	0	0	0	0	0	1	0	0
Wayne Gross, 3b	.000	3	5	0	0	0	0	0	0	0	0	0
Mike Heath, c-2,of-1	.333	3	6	1	2	0	0	0	0	0	1	0
Rickey Henderson, of	.364	3	11	0	4	2	1	0	1	1	2	2
Cliff Johnson, dh	.000	2	6	0	0	0	0	0	0	2	2	0
Jeff Jones, p	.000	1	0	0	0	0	0	0	0	0	0	0
Matt Keough, p	.000	1	0	0	0	0	0	0	0	0	0	0
Brian Kingman, p	.000	1	0	0	0	0	0	0	0	0	0	0
Mickey Klutts, 3b	.429	3	7	1	3	0	0	0	0	0	1	0
Steve McCatty, p	.000	1	0	0	0	0	0	0	0	0	0	0
Dave McKay, 2b	.273	3	11	0	3	0	0	0	1	0	2	0
Kelvin Moore, 1b	.250	3	8	0	2	0	0	0	0	0	1	0
Dwayne Murphy, of	.250	3	8	0	2	1	0	0	1	2	3	0
Jeff Newman, c	.000	2	5	0	0	0	0	0	0	0	2	0
Mike Norris, p	.000	1	0	0	0	0	0	0	0	0	0	0
Bob Owchinko, p	.000	1	0	0	0	0	0	0	0	0	0	0
Rob Picciolo, ss	.200	2	5	1	1	0	0	0	0	0	2	0
Jim Spencer, 1b	.000	2	3	0	0	0	0	0	0	0	0	0
Fred Stanley, ss	.333	2	3	0	1	0	0	0	1	0	1	0
Tom Underwood, p	.000	2	0	0	0	0	0	0	0	0	0	0
TOTAL	.222		99	4	22	4	1	0	4	6	23	2

PITCHER	W	L	ERA	G	GS	CG	SV	SHO	IP	H	ER	BB	SO
Dave Beard	0	0	40.50	1	0	0	0	0	0.2	5	3	0	0
Jeff Jones	0	0	4.50	1	0	0	0	0	2.0	2	1	1	0
Matt Keough	0	1	1.08	1	1	0	0	0	8.1	7	1	6	4
Brian Kingman	0	0	81.00	1	0	0	0	0	0.1	3	3	0	0
Steve McCatty	0	1	13.50	1	1	0	0	0	3.1	6	5	2	2
Mike Norris	0	1	3.68	1	1	0	0	0	7.1	6	3	2	4
Bob Owchinko	0	0	5.40	1	0	0	0	0	1.2	3	1	0	0
Tom Underwood	0	0	13.50	2	0	0	0	0	1.1	4	2	2	0
TOTAL	0	3	6.84	9	3	0	0	0	25.0	36	19	13	10

GAME 1 AT NY OCT 13

OAK	000	010	000	1	6	1
NY	300	000	00X	3	7	1

Pitchers: NORRIS, Underwood (8) vs JOHN, Davis (7), Gossage (8)
Attendance: 55,740

GAME 2 AT NY OCT 14

OAK	001	200	000	3	11	1
NY	100	701	40X	13	19	0

Pitchers: McCATTY, Beard (4), Jones (5), Kingman (7), Owchinko (7) vs May, FRAZIER (4)
Home Runs: Piniella-NY, Nettles-NY
Attendance: 48,497

GAME 3 AT OAK OCT 15

NY	000	001	003	4	10	0
OAK	000	000	000	0	5	2

Pitchers: RIGHETTI, Davis (7), Gossage (9) vs KEOUGH, Underwood (9)
Home Runs: Randolph-NY
Attendance: 47,302

Los Angeles Dodgers (NL), 4; New York Yankees (AL), 2

What the Yankees had done to the Dodgers three years earlier, the Dodgers now did to the Yankees in this, their 11th meeting in the Series: they took the crown with four straight wins after losing the first two games. In the opener Bob Watson's first-inning three-run homer gave New York an insurmountable lead. Yankees starter Ron Guidry pitched seven strong innings, yielding just one run on a Steve Yeager homer, but two eighth-inning Dodgers runs charged to reliever Ron Davis made things exciting until Yankees third baseman Graig Nettles dampened the rally with a splendid diving catch of Steve Garvey's line drive. In Game 2, Tommy John (now a Yankee) shut out his old teammates on three hits for seven innings. Reliever Goose Gossage completed the shutout, earning his second save in two days in the 3–0 Yankees victory.

But as the Series moved to Los Angeles, the Dodgers took the upper hand. Rookie ace Fernando Valenzuela experienced rocky going in the early innings of Game 3, yielding six hits (including home runs to Bob Watson and Rick Cerone) and four runs in the second and third innings. But Ron Cey's first-inning home run had given Los Angeles three early runs, and the Dodgers added two more in the fifth as Valenzuela settled down to blank New York on three hits over the final six innings. The next day the Dodgers evened the Series with another close win. New York scored four times before the Dodgers got their first runs, but L.A. tied the game at 6–6 in the sixth and took an 8–6 lead an inning later. Reggie Jackson homered in the eighth to bring New York within one run of a tie, but they came no closer.

In Game 5, for the third day in a row, the Dodgers ovecame a Yankees lead to claim a one-run victory. Jerry Reuss gave the Yankees a run on two hits in the second inning, but shut them out on just three additional hits the rest of the way. Yankees starter Ron Guidry, meanwhile, stopped the Dodgers on two hits through the first six innings, but then gave up back-to-back homers to Pedro Guerrero and Steve Yeager in the seventh—runs enough for a 2–1 Dodgers win. The final game was close for four innings, but in the fifth and sixth the Dodgers broke it open with seven runs and coasted in on Steve Howe's 3⅔ innings of shutout relief to a 9–2 win and, including 1900, their sixth world championship.

LA (N)

PLAYER/POS	AVG	G	AB	R	H	2B	3B	HR	RB	BB	SO	SB
Dusty Baker, of	.167	6	24	3	4	0	0	0	1	1	6	0
Bobby Castillo, p	.000	1	0	0	0	0	0	0	0	0	0	0
Ron Cey, 3b	.350	6	20	3	7	0	0	1	6	3	3	0
Terry Forster, p	.000	2	0	0	0	0	0	0	0	0	0	0
Steve Garvey, 1b	.417	6	24	3	10	1	0	0	0	2	5	0
Dave Goltz, p	.000	2	0	0	0	0	0	0	0	0	0	0
Pedro Guerrero, of	.333	6	21	2	7	1	1	2	7	2	6	0
Burt Hooton, p	.000	2	4	1	0	0	0	0	0	1	3	0
Steve Howe, p	.000	3	2	0	0	0	0	0	0	0	2	0
Jay Johnstone, ph	.667	3	3	1	2	0	0	1	3	0	0	0
Ken Landreaux, of-3	.167	5	6	1	1	1	0	0	0	0	2	1
Davey Lopes, 2b	.227	6	22	6	5	1	0	0	2	4	3	4
Rick Monday, of-4	.231	5	13	1	3	1	0	0	0	3	6	0
Tom Niedenfuer, p	.000	2	0	0	0	0	0	0	0	0	0	0
Jerry Reuss, p	.000	2	3	0	0	0	0	0	0	1	2	0
Bill Russell, ss	.240	6	25	1	6	0	0	0	2	0	1	1
Steve Sax, 2b-1	.000	2	1	0	0	0	0	0	0	0	0	0
Mike Scioscia, c	.250	3	4	1	1	0	0	0	0	1	0	0
Reggie Smith, ph	.500	2	2	0	1	0	0	0	0	0	1	0
Dave Stewart, p	.000	2	0	0	0	0	0	0	0	0	0	0
Derrel Thomas, of-3,3b-2,ss-1	.000	5	7	2	0	0	0	0	1	1	2	0
Fernando Valenzuela, p	.000	1	3	0	0	0	0	0	0	1	0	0
Bob Welch, p	.000	1	0	0	0	0	0	0	0	0	0	0
Steve Yeager, c	.286	6	14	2	4	1	0	2	4	0	2	0
TOTAL	.258		198	27	51	6	1	6	26	20	44	6

PITCHER	W	L	ERA	G	GS	CG	SV	SHO	IP	H	ER	BB	SO
Bobby Castillo	0	0	9.00	1	0	0	0	0	1.0	0	1	5	0
Terry Forster	0	0	0.00	2	0	0	0	0	2.0	1	0	3	0
Dave Goltz	0	0	5.40	2	0	0	0	0	3.1	4	2	1	2
Burt Hooton	1	1	1.59	2	2	0	0	0	11.1	8	2	9	3
Steve Howe	1	0	3.86	3	0	0	1	0	7.0	7	3	1	4
Tom Niedenfuer	0	0	0.00	2	0	0	0	0	5.0	3	0	1	0
Jerry Reuss	1	1	3.86	2	2	1	0	0	11.2	10	5	3	8
Dave Stewart	0	0	0.00	2	0	0	0	0	1.2	1	0	2	1
Fernando Valenzuela	1	0	4.00	1	1	1	0	0	9.0	9	4	7	6
Bob Welch	0	0	∞	1	1	0	0	0	0.0	3	2	1	0
TOTAL	4	2	3.29	18	6	2	1	0	52.0	46	19	33	24

NY (A)

PLAYER/POS	AVG	G	AB	R	H	2B	3B	HR	RB	BB	SO	SB
Bobby Brown, of-2	.000	4	1	1	0	0	0	0	0	0	1	0
Rick Cerone, c	.190	6	21	2	4	1	0	1	3	4	2	0
Ron Davis, p	.000	4	0	0	0	0	0	0	0	0	0	0
Barry Foote, ph	.000	1	1	0	0	0	0	0	0	0	1	0
George Frazier, p	.000	3	2	0	0	0	0	0	0	0	1	0
Oscar Gamble, of-2	.333	3	6	1	2	0	0	0	1	1	0	0
Rich Gossage, p	.000	3	1	0	0	0	0	0	0	0	1	0
Ron Guidry, p	.000	2	5	0	0	0	0	0	0	0	3	0
Reggie Jackson, of	.333	3	12	3	4	1	0	1	1	2	3	0
Tommy John, p	.000	3	2	0	0	0	0	0	0	0	0	0
Dave LaRoche, p	.000	1	0	0	0	0	0	0	0	0	0	0
Rudy May, p	.000	3	1	0	0	0	0	0	0	0	0	0
Larry Milbourne, ss	.250	6	20	2	5	2	0	0	3	4	0	0
Jerry Mumphrey, of	.200	5	15	2	3	0	0	0	0	3	2	1
Bobby Murcer, ph	.000	4	3	0	0	0	0	0	0	0	0	0
Graig Nettles, 3b	.400	3	10	1	4	1	0	0	0	1	1	0
Lou Piniella, of-3	.438	6	16	2	7	1	0	0	3	0	1	1
Willie Randolph, 2b	.222	6	18	5	4	1	1	2	3	9	0	1
Rick Reuschel, p	.000	2	2	0	0	0	0	0	0	0	1	0
Dave Righetti, p	.000	1	1	0	0	0	0	0	0	0	1	0
Andre Robertson, pr	.000	1	0	0	0	0	0	0	0	0	0	0
Aurelio Rodriguez, 3b-3	.417	4	12	1	5	0	0	0	0	1	2	0
Bob Watson, 1b	.318	6	22	2	7	1	0	2	7	3	0	0
Dave Winfield, of	.045	6	22	0	1	0	0	0	1	5	4	1
TOTAL	.238		193	22	46	8	1	6	22	33	24	4

PITCHER	W	L	ERA	G	GS	CG	SV	SHO	IP	H	ER	BB	SO
Ron Davis	0	0	23.14	4	0	0	0	0	2.1	4	6	5	4
George Frazier	0	3	17.18	3	0	0	0	0	3.2	9	7	3	2
Rich Gossage	0	0	0.00	3	0	0	2	0	5.0	2	0	2	5
Ron Guidry	1	1	1.93	2	2	0	0	0	14.0	8	3	4	15
Tommy John	1	0	0.69	3	2	0	0	0	13.0	11	1	0	8
Dave LaRoche	0	0	0.00	1	0	0	0	0	1.0	0	0	0	2
Rudy May	0	0	2.84	3	0	0	0	0	6.1	5	2	1	5
Rick Reuschel	0	0	4.91	2	1	0	0	0	3.2	7	2	3	2
Dave Righetti	0	0	13.50	1	1	0	0	0	2.0	5	3	2	1
TOTAL	2	4	4.24	22	6	0	2	0	51.0	51	24	20	44

GAME 1 AT NY OCT 20

		R	H	E
LA	000 010 020	3	5	0
NY	301 100 00X	5	6	0

Pitchers: REUSS, Castillo (3), Goltz (4), Niedenfuer (5), Stewart (8) vs GUIDRY, Davis (8), Gossage (8)
Home Runs: Watson-NY, Yeager-LA
Attendance: 56,470

GAME 2 AT NY OCT 21

		R	H	E
LA	000 000 000	0	4	2
NY	000 010 02X	3	6	1

Pitchers: HOOTON, Forster (7), Howe (8), Stewart (8) vs JOHN, Gossage (8)
Attendance: 56,505

GAME 3 AT LA OCT 23

		R	H	E
NY	022 000 000	4	9	0
LA	300 020 00X	5	11	1

Pitchers: Righetti, FRAZIER (3), May (5), Davis (8) vs VALENZUELA
Home Runs: Cey-LA, Watson-NY, Cerone-NY
Attendance: 56,236

GAME 4 AT LA OCT 24

		R	H	E
NY	211 002 010	7	13	1
LA	002 013 20X	8	14	2

Pitchers: Reuschel, May (4), Davis (5), FRAZIER (5), John (7) vs Welch, Goltz (1), Forster (4), Niedenfuer (5), HOWE (7)
Home Runs: Johnstone-LA, Randolph-NY, Jackson-NY
Attendance: 56,242

GAME 5 AT LA OCT 25

		R	H	E
NY	010 000 000	1	5	0
LA	000 000 20X	2	4	3

Pitchers: GUIDRY, Gossage (8) vs REUSS
Home Runs: Guerrero-LA, Yeager-LA
Attendance: 56,115

GAME 6 AT NY OCT 28

		R	H	E
LA	000 134 010	9	13	1
NY	001 001 000	2	7	2

Pitchers: HOOTON, Howe (6) vs John, FRAZIER (5), Davis (6), Reuschel (6), May (7), LaRoche (9)
Home Runs: Guerrero-LA, Randolph-NY
Attendance: 56,513

The official records show Atlanta ahead only once in a three-game series swept by the Cardinals. But in the original Game 1, Phil Niekro held a slim 1–0 Atlanta lead in the fifth inning when rain wiped out the game just before it could become official.

In the first official game, the Braves scored nothing at all as Bob Forsch held them to three hits. Atlanta's Pascual Perez gave up only one run through the first five innings, but the Cardinals exploded for five runs in the sixth to put the game away. Following another rainout, Niekro tried again in Game 2. He gave up a run in the first, but Atlanta came back with three before he yielded a second run in the sixth. Gene Garber, who relieved Niekro, gave up the tying run in the eighth and lost the game in the bottom of the ninth on Ken Oberkfell's RBI liner over the center fielder's head.

Joaquin Andujar shut out the Braves through six innings of Game Three before giving up two runs in the seventh. But by then St. Louis had scored five times. Bruce Sutter retired the last seven Braves in relief of Andujar, and the Cardinals had their pennant.

St. Louis Cardinals (East), 3; Atlanta Braves (West), 0

STL (E)

PLAYER/POS	AVG	G	AB	R	H	2B	3B	HR	RB	BB	SO	SB
Joaquin Andujar, p	.000	1	1	0	0	0	0	0	0	0	1	0
Doug Bair, p	.000	1	0	0	0	0	0	0	0	0	0	0
Steve Braun, ph	.000	1	1	0	0	0	0	0	0	0	0	0
Bob Forsch, p	.667	1	3	1	2	0	0	0	1	0	0	0
David Green, of	1.000	2	1	1	1	0	0	0	0	0	0	0
George Hendrick, of	.308	3	13	2	4	0	0	0	2	1	2	0
Keith Hernandez, 1b	.333	3	12	3	4	0	0	0	1	2	3	0
Tommy Herr, 2b	.231	3	13	1	3	1	0	0	0	1	2	0
Willie McGee, of	.308	3	13	4	4	0	2	1	5	0	5	0
Ken Oberkfell, 3b	.200	3	15	1	3	0	0	0	2	0	0	0
Darrell Porter, c	.556	3	9	3	5	3	0	0	1	5	2	0
Lonnie Smith, of	.273	3	11	1	3	0	0	0	1	0	1	0
Ozzie Smith, ss	.556	3	9	0	5	0	0	0	3	3	0	1
John Stuper, p	.000	1	1	0	0	0	0	0	0	0	0	0
Bruce Sutter, p	.000	2	1	0	0	0	0	0	0	0	0	0
TOTAL	.330		103	17	34	4	2	1	16	12	16	1

PITCHER	W	L	ERA	G	GS	CG	SV	SHO	IP	H	ER	BB	SO
Joaquin Andujar	1	0	2.70	1	1	0	0	0	6.2	6	2	2	4
Doug Bair	0	0	0.00	1	0	0	0	0	1.0	2	0	3	0
Bob Forsch	1	0	0.00	1	1	1	0	1	9.0	3	0	0	6
John Stuper	0	0	3.00	1	1	0	0	0	6.0	4	2	1	4
Bruce Sutter	1	0	0.00	2	0	0	1	0	4.1	0	0	0	1
TOTAL	3	0	1.33	6	3	1	1	1	27.0	15	4	6	15

ATL (W)

PLAYER/POS	AVG	G	AB	R	H	2B	3B	HR	RB	BB	SO	SB
Steve Bedrosian, p	.000	2	0	0	0	0	0	0	0	0	0	0
Bruce Benedict, c	.250	3	8	1	2	1	0	0	0	2	1	0
Brett Butler, of-1	.000	2	1	0	0	0	0	0	0	0	0	0
Rick Camp, p	.000	1	0	0	0	0	0	0	0	0	0	0
Chris Chambliss, 1b	.000	3	10	0	0	0	0	0	0	1	0	0
Gene Garber, p	.000	2	1	0	0	0	0	0	0	0	0	0
Terry Harper, of	.000	1	1	1	0	0	0	0	0	0	0	0
Bob Horner, 3b	.091	3	11	0	1	0	0	0	0	0	2	0
Glenn Hubbard, 2b	.222	3	9	1	2	0	0	0	1	0	3	0
Rick Mahler, p	.000	1	0	0	0	0	0	0	0	0	0	0
Donnie Moore, p	.000	2	0	0	0	0	0	0	0	0	0	0
Dale Murphy, of	.273	3	11	1	3	0	0	0	0	0	2	1
Phil Niekro, p	.000	1	0	0	0	0	0	0	1	0	0	0
Pascual Perez, p	.000	2	3	0	0	0	0	0	0	0	1	0
Biff Pocoroba, ph	.000	1	1	0	0	0	0	0	0	0	0	0
Rafael Ramirez, ss	.182	3	11	1	2	0	0	0	1	1	1	0
Jerry Royster, of-3,3b-1	.182	3	11	0	2	0	0	0	0	0	2	0
Bob Walk, p	.000	1	0	0	0	0	0	0	0	0	0	0
Claudell Washington, of	.333	3	9	0	3	0	0	0	0	2	2	0
Larry Whisenton, ph	.000	2	2	0	0	0	0	0	0	0	1	0
TOTAL	.169		89	5	15	1	0	0	3	6	15	1

PITCHER	W	L	ERA	G	GS	CG	SV	SHO	IP	H	ER	BB	SO
Steve Bedrosian	0	0	18.00	2	0	0	0	0	1.0	3	2	1	2
Rick Camp	0	1	36.00	1	1	0	0	0	1.0	4	4	1	0
Gene Garber	0	1	8.10	2	0	0	0	0	3.1	4	3	1	3
Rick Mahler	0	0	0.00	1	0	0	0	0	1.2	3	0	2	0
Donnie Moore	0	0	0.00	2	0	0	0	0	2.2	2	0	0	1
Phil Niekro	0	0	3.00	1	1	0	0	0	6.0	6	2	4	5
Pascual Perez	0	1	5.19	2	1	0	0	0	8.2	10	5	2	4
Bob Walk	0	0	9.00	1	0	0	0	0	1.0	2	1	1	1
TOTAL	0	3	6.04	12	3	0	0	0	25.1	34	17	12	16

GAME 1 AT STL OCT 7

				R	H	E
ATL	000	000	000	0	3	0
STL	001	005	01X	7	13	1

Pitchers: PEREZ, Bedrosian (6), Moore (6), Walk (8) vs FORSCH

Attendance: 53,008

GAME 2 AT STL OCT 9

				R	H	E
ATL	002	010	000	3	6	0
STL	100	001	011	4	9	1

Pitchers: Niekro, GARBER (7) vs Stuper, Bair (7), SUTTER (8)

Attendance: 53,408

GAME 3 AT ATL OCT 10

				R	H	E
STL	040	010	001	6	12	0
ATL	000	000	200	2	6	1

Pitchers: ANDUJAR, Sutter (7) vs CAMP, Perez (2), Moore (5), Mahler (7), Bedrosian (8), Garber (9)

Home Runs: McGee-STL

Attendance: 52,173

For the first time in LCS play, a club won the first two games but lost the series. The Angels overcame a 3–1 deficit to take Game 1, with four runs in the third and three more later, while starter Tommy John settled down to stop the Brewers through the final six innings. In Game 2 Bruce Kison prevailed, as the Angels built a 4–0 lead over Milwaukee and Pete Vuckovich before Kison gave up what proved to be a harmless two-run homer to Paul Molitor in the fifth.

With three chances to clinch the pennant, California three times fell short. In the third game, their three eighth-inning runs couldn't catch the Brewers, who already had five. In Game 4, Don Baylor's eighth-inning grand slam completed California scoring at five runs, but Milwaukee had already scored seven, and they added two more. In the finale, Kison held a 3–2 lead when he was relieved after five innings. But Cecil Cooper singled off Luis Sanchez in the seventh (with two out and the bases loaded) for two runs and a Brewers lead. Bob McClure and Pete Ladd held off the Angels through the final two innings, and the Brewers were on their way to their first World Series.

Milwaukee Brewers (East), 3; California Angels (West), 2

MIL (E)

PLAYER/POS	AVG	G	AB	R	H	2B	3B	HR	RB	BB	SO	SB
Dwight Bernard, p	.000	1	0	0	0	0	0	0	0	0	0	0
Mark Brouhard, of	.750	1	4	4	3	1	0	1	3	0	0	0
Mike Caldwell, p	.000	1	0	0	0	0	0	0	0	0	0	0
Cecil Cooper, 1b	.150	5	20	1	3	2	0	0	4	0	6	0
Marshall Edwards, dh-2,of-1	.000	3	1	2	0	0	0	0	0	0	0	1
Jim Gantner, 2b	.188	5	16	1	3	0	0	0	2	1	1	0
Moose Haas, p	.000	1	0	0	0	0	0	0	0	0	0	0
Roy Howell, dh	.000	1	3	0	0	0	0	0	0	0	1	0
Pete Ladd, p	.000	3	0	0	0	0	0	0	0	0	0	0
Bob McClure, p	.000	1	0	0	0	0	0	0	0	0	0	0
Paul Molitor, 3b	.316	5	19	4	6	1	0	2	5	2	3	1
Don Money, dh	.182	4	11	2	2	0	0	0	1	3	1	0
Charlie Moore, of	.462	5	13	3	6	0	0	0	0	1	2	0
Ben Oglivie, of	.133	4	15	1	2	0	0	1	1	0	3	0
Ted Simmons, c	.167	5	18	3	3	0	0	0	1	1	4	0
Jim Slaton, p	.000	2	0	0	0	0	0	0	0	0	0	0
Don Sutton, p	.000	1	0	0	0	0	0	0	0	0	0	0
Gorman Thomas, of	.067	5	15	1	1	0	0	1	3	2	7	0
Pete Vuckovich, p	.000	2	0	0	0	0	0	0	0	0	0	0
Robin Yount, ss	.250	5	16	1	4	0	0	0	0	5	0	0
TOTAL	.219		151	23	33	4	0	5	20	15	28	2

PITCHER	W	L	ERA	G	GS	CG	SV	SHO	IP	H	ER	BB	SO
Dwight Bernard	0	0	0.00	1	0	0	0	0	1.0	0	0	0	0
Mike Caldwell	0	1	15.00	1	1	0	0	0	3.0	7	5	1	2
Moose Haas	1	0	4.91	1	1	0	0	0	7.1	5	4	5	7
Pete Ladd	0	0	0.00	3	0	0	2	0	3.1	0	0	0	5
Bob McClure	1	0	0.00	1	0	0	0	0	1.2	2	0	0	0
Jim Slaton	0	0	1.93	2	0	0	1	0	4.2	3	1	1	3
Don Sutton	1	0	3.52	1	1	0	0	0	7.2	8	3	2	9
Pete Vuckovich	0	1	4.40	2	2	1	0	0	14.1	15	7	7	8
TOTAL	3	2	4.19	12	5	1	3	0	43.0	40	20	16	34

CAL (W)

PLAYER/POS	AVG	G	AB	R	H	2B	3B	HR	RB	BB	SO	SB
Don Baylor, dh	.294	5	17	2	5	1	1	1	10	2	0	0
Juan Beniquez, of	.000	2	0	0	0	0	0	0	0	0	0	0
Bob Boone, c	.250	5	16	3	4	0	0	1	4	0	2	0
Rod Carew, 1b	.176	5	17	2	3	1	0	0	0	4	4	1
Bobby Clark, of	.000	2	0	0	0	0	0	0	0	0	0	0
Doug De Cinces, 3b	.316	5	19	5	6	2	0	0	0	1	5	0
Brian Downing, of	.158	5	19	4	3	1	0	0	0	3	2	0
Tim Foli, ss	.125	5	16	0	2	0	0	0	1	0	3	0
Dave Goltz, p	.000	1	0	0	0	0	0	0	0	0	0	0
Bobby Grich, 2b	.200	5	15	1	3	1	0	0	1	2	7	0
Andy Hassler, p	.000	2	0	0	0	0	0	0	0	0	0	0
Reggie Jackson, of	.111	5	18	2	2	0	0	1	2	2	7	0
Ron Jackson, ph	1.000	1	1	0	1	0	0	0	0	0	0	0
Tommy John, p	.000	2	0	0	0	0	0	0	0	0	0	0
Bruce Kison, p	.000	2	0	0	0	0	0	0	0	0	0	0
Fred Lynn, of	.611	5	18	4	11	2	0	1	5	2	3	0
Luis Sanchez, p	.000	2	0	0	0	0	0	0	0	0	0	0
Rob Wilfong, ph	.000	2	1	0	0	0	0	0	0	0	1	0
Mike Witt, p	.000	1	0	0	0	0	0	0	0	0	0	0
Geoff Zahn, p	.000	1	0	0	0	0	0	0	0	0	0	0
TOTAL	.255		157	23	40	8	1	4	23	16	34	1

PITCHER	W	L	ERA	G	GS	CG	SV	SHO	IP	H	ER	BB	SO
Dave Goltz	0	0	7.36	1	0	0	0	0	3.2	4	3	2	2
Andy Hassler	0	0	0.00	2	0	0	0	0	2.2	0	0	0	2
Tommy John	1	1	5.11	2	2	1	0	0	12.1	11	7	6	6
Bruce Kison	1	0	1.93	2	2	1	0	0	14.0	8	3	3	12
Luis Sanchez	0	1	6.75	2	0	0	0	0	2.2	4	2	1	1
Mike Witt	0	0	6.00	1	0	0	0	0	3.0	2	2	2	3
Geoff Zahn	0	1	7.36	1	1	0	0	0	3.2	4	3	1	2
TOTAL	2	3	4.29	11	5	2	0	0	42.0	33	20	15	28

GAME 1 AT CAL OCT 5

				R	H	E
MIL	021	000	000	3	7	2
CAL	104	210	00X	8	10	0

Pitchers: CALDWELL, Slaton (4), Ladd (7), Bernard (8) vs JOHN
Home Runs: Thomas-MIL, Lynn-CAL
Attendance: 64,406

GAME 2 AT CAL OCT 6

				R	H	E
MIL	000	020	000	2	5	0
CAL	021	100	00X	4	6	0

Pitchers: VUCKOVICH vs KISON
Home Runs: Re.Jackson-CAL, Molitor-MIL
Attendance: 64,179

GAME 3 AT MIL OCT 8

				R	H	E
CAL	000	000	030	3	8	0
MIL	000	300	20X	5	6	0

Pitchers: ZAHN, Witt (4), Hassler (7) vs SUTTON, Ladd (8)
Home Runs: Molitor-MIL, Boone-CAL
Attendance: 50,135

GAME 4 AT MIL OCT 9

				R	H	E
CAL	000	001	040	5	5	3
MIL	030	301	02X	9	9	2

Pitchers: JOHN, Goltz (4), Sanchez (8) vs HAAS, Slaton (8)
Home Runs: Baylor-CAL, Brouhard-MIL
Attendance: 51,003

GAME 5 AT MIL OCT 10

				R	H	E
CAL	101	100	000	3	11	1
MIL	100	100	20X	4	6	4

Pitchers: Kison, SANCHEZ (6), Hassler (7) vs Vuckovich, McCLURE (7), Ladd (9)
Home Runs: Oglivie-MIL
Attendance: 54,968

The Series was anticipated as a matchup of Cardinals speed and Brewers power. In the event, though, St. Louis outslugged the Brewers and wound up as world champions.

The Brewers, in their first World Series, looked unstoppable in the opening game. Hammering four Cardinals pitchers for 17 hits (including a record five for Paul Molitor), they scored 10 runs while pitcher Mike Caldwell was shutting out the Cards on three hits. In the second game Milwaukee continued the onslaught, building an early 3–0 lead. But St. Louis finally got on the scoreboard with two runs in the last of the third, and tied the game at 4–4 in the sixth on Darrell Porter's two-run double. And the Cards won the game on a bases-loaded walk in the eighth as relievers Doug Bair and Bruce Sutter held the Brewers scoreless over the final four innings.

St. Louis pushed into the Series lead in Game 3, thanks mostly to the $6\frac{1}{3}$ shutout innings of starter Joaquin Andujar and the fielding and batting of center fielder Willie McGee. McGee drove in four of the six Cardinal runs with a pair of homers and prevented an extra-base hit and a two-run Brewers homer with leaping catches in the first and final innings. The Cards pressed their advantage in Game 4 with four early runs. But in the last of the seventh (with the score now 5–1), an error by Cardinals pitcher Dave LaPoint opened the way for Milwaukee to win the game with six two-out runs on a barrage of hits (and the added assistance of a pair of walks and a wild pitch).

Mike Caldwell wasn't as effective in Game 5 as he had been in the opener, yielding 14 hits and four runs in $8\frac{1}{3}$ innings of work. But he was never behind in the game as his teammates, with 11 hits of their own (four of them by Robin Yount, including a home run) and several fielding gems put Milwaukee ahead again in the Series with a 6–4 win.

The Cards had their backs to the wall as the Series moved to St. Louis for the final games. But in Game 6 the Cards responded to their opening-game humiliation with a laugher of their own, 13–1, on John Stuper's four-hitter. And in the finale they rocked Brewers ace Pete Vuckovich and three relievers for 15 hits and a 6–3 victory that gave starter Joaquin Andujar his second Series win and reliever Bruce Sutter his second save.

St. Louis Cardinals (NL), 4; Milwaukee Brewers (AL), 3

STL (N)

PLAYER/POS	AVG	G	AB	R	H	2B	3B	HR	RB	BB	SO	SB
Joaquin Andujar, p	.000	2	0	0	0	0	0	0	0	0	0	0
Doug Bair, p	.000	3	0	0	0	0	0	0	0	0	0	0
Steve Braun, dh	.500	2	2	0	1	0	0	0	2	1	0	0
Glenn Brummer, c	.000	1	0	0	0	0	0	0	0	0	0	0
Bob Forsch, p	.000	2	0	0	0	0	0	0	0	0	0	0
David Green, of-4,dh-3	.200	7	10	3	2	1	1	0	0	1	3	0
George Hendrick, of	.321	7	28	5	9	0	0	0	5	2	2	0
Keith Hernandez, 1b	.259	7	27	4	7	2	0	1	8	4	2	0
Tommy Herr, 2b	.160	7	25	2	4	2	0	0	5	3	3	0
Dane Iorg, dh	.529	5	17	4	9	4	1	0	1	0	0	0
Jim Kaat, p	.000	4	0	0	0	0	0	0	0	0	0	0
Jeff Lahti, p	.000	2	0	0	0	0	0	0	0	0	0	0
Dave LaPoint, p	.000	2	0	0	0	0	0	0	0	0	0	0
Willie McGee, of	.240	6	25	6	6	0	0	2	5	1	3	2
Ken Oberkfell, 3b	.292	7	24	4	7	1	0	0	1	2	1	2
Darrell Porter, c	.286	7	28	1	8	2	0	1	5	1	4	0
Mike Ramsey, 3b-2	.000	3	1	1	0	0	0	0	0	0	1	0
Lonnie Smith, of-6,dh-1	.321	7	28	6	9	4	1	0	1	1	5	2
Ozzie Smith, ss	.208	7	24	3	5	0	0	0	1	3	0	1
John Stuper, p	.000	2	0	0	0	0	0	0	0	0	0	0
Bruce Sutter, p	.000	4	0	0	0	0	0	0	0	0	0	0
Gene Tenace, dh-1	.000	5	6	0	0	0	0	0	0	1	2	0
TOTAL	.273		245	39	67	16	3	4	34	20	26	7

PITCHER	W	L	ERA	G	GS	CG	SV	SHO	IP	H	ER	BB	SO
Joaquin Andujar	2	0	1.35	2	2	0	0	0	13.1	10	2	1	4
Doug Bair	0	1	9.00	3	0	0	0	0	2.0	2	2	2	3
Bob Forsch	0	2	4.97	2	2	0	0	0	12.2	18	7	3	4
Jim Kaat	0	0	3.86	4	0	0	0	0	2.1	4	1	2	2
Jeff Lahti	0	0	10.80	2	0	0	0	0	1.2	4	2	1	1
Dave LaPoint	0	0	3.24	2	1	0	0	0	8.1	10	3	2	3
John Stuper	1	0	3.46	2	2	1	0	0	13.0	10	5	5	5
Bruce Sutter	1	0	4.70	4	0	0	2	0	7.2	6	4	3	6
TOTAL	4	3	3.84	21	7	1	2	0	61.0	64	26	19	28

MIL (A)

PLAYER/POS	AVG	G	AB	R	H	2B	3B	HR	RB	BB	SO	SB
Dwight Bernard, p	.000	1	0	0	0	0	0	0	0	0	0	0
Mike Caldwell, p	.000	3	0	0	0	0	0	0	0	0	0	0
Cecil Cooper, 1b	.286	7	28	3	8	1	0	1	6	1	1	0
Marshall Edwards, of	.000	1	0	0	0	0	0	0	0	0	0	0
Jim Gantner, 2b	.333	7	24	5	8	4	1	0	4	1	1	0
Moose Haas, p	.000	2	0	0	0	0	0	0	0	0	0	0
Roy Howell, dh	.000	4	11	1	0	0	0	0	0	0	3	0
Pete Ladd, p	.000	1	0	0	0	0	0	0	0	0	0	0
Bob McClure, p	.000	5	0	0	0	0	0	0	0	0	0	0
Doc Medich, p	.000	1	0	0	0	0	0	0	0	0	0	0
Paul Molitor, 3b	.355	7	31	5	11	0	0	0	3	2	4	1
Don Money, dh-4	.231	5	13	4	3	1	0	0	1	2	3	0
Charlie Moore, of	.346	7	26	3	9	3	0	0	2	1	0	0
Ben Oglivie, of	.222	7	27	4	6	0	1	1	1	2	4	0
Ted Simmons, c	.174	7	23	2	4	0	0	2	3	5	3	0
Jim Slaton, p	.000	2	0	0	0	0	0	0	0	0	0	0
Don Sutton, p	.000	2	0	0	0	0	0	0	0	0	0	0
Gorman Thomas, of	.115	7	26	0	3	0	0	0	3	2	7	0
Pete Vuckovich, p	.000	2	0	0	0	0	0	0	0	0	0	0
Ned Yost, c	.000	1	0	0	0	0	0	0	0	1	0	0
Robin Yount, ss	.414	7	29	6	12	3	0	1	6	2	2	0
TOTAL	.269		238	33	64	12	2	5	29	19	28	1

PITCHER	W	L	ERA	G	GS	CG	SV	SHO	IP	H	ER	BB	SO
Dwight Bernard	0	0	0.00	1	0	0	0	0	1.0	0	0	0	1
Mike Caldwell	2	0	2.04	3	2	1	0	1	17.2	19	4	3	6
Moose Haas	0	0	7.36	2	1	0	0	0	7.1	8	6	3	4
Pete Ladd	0	0	0.00	1	0	0	0	0	0.2	1	0	2	0
Bob McClure	0	2	4.15	5	0	0	2	0	4.1	5	2	3	5
Doc Medich	0	0	18.00	1	0	0	0	0	2.0	5	4	1	0
Jim Slaton	1	0	0.00	2	0	0	0	0	2.2	1	0	2	1
Don Sutton	0	1	7.84	2	2	0	0	0	10.1	12	9	1	5
Pete Vuckovich	0	1	4.50	2	2	0	0	0	14.0	16	7	5	4
TOTAL	3	4	4.80	19	7	1	2	1	60.0	67	32	20	26

GAME 1 AT STL OCT 12

				R	H	E
MIL	200	112	004	10	17	0
STL	000	000	000	0	3	1

Pitchers: CALDWELL vs FORSCH, Kaat (6), LaPoint (8), Lahti (9)
Home Runs: Simmons-MIL
Attendance: 53,723

GAME 2 AT STL OCT 13

				R	H	E
MIL	012	010	000	4	10	1
STL	002	002	01X	5	8	0

Pitchers: Sutton, McCLURE (7), Ladd (8) vs Stuper, Kaat (5), Bair (5), SUTTER (7)
Home Runs: Simmons-MIL
Attendance: 53,723

GAME 3 AT MIL OCT 15

				R	H	E
STL	000	030	201	6	6	1
MIL	000	000	020	2	5	3

Pitchers: ANDUJAR, Kaat (7), Bair (7), Sutter (7) vs VUCKOVICH, McClure (9)
Home Runs: McGee-STL (2), Cooper-MIL
Attendance: 56,556

GAME 4 AT MIL OCT 16

				R	H	E
STL	130	001	000	5	8	1
MIL	000	010	60X	7	10	2

Pitchers: LaPoint, BAIR (7), Kaat (7), Lahti (7) vs Haas, SLATON (6), McClure (8)
Attendance: 56,560

GAME 5 AT MIL OCT 17

				R	H	E
STL	001	000	102	4	15	2
MIL	101	010	12X	6	11	1

Pitchers: FORSCH, Sutter (8) vs CALDWELL, McClure (9)
Home Runs: Yount-MIL
Attendance: 56,562

GAME 6 AT STL OCT 19

				R	H	E
MIL	000	000	001	1	4	4
STL	020	326	00X	13	12	1

Pitchers: SUTTON, Slaton (5), Medich (6), Bernard (8) vs STUPER
Home Runs: Porter-STL, Hernandez-STL
Attendance: 53,723

GAME 7 AT STL OCT 20

				R	H	E
MIL	000	012	000	3	7	0
STL	000	103	02X	6	15	1

Pitchers: Vuckovich, McCLURE (6), Haas (6), Caldwell (8) vs ANDUJAR, Sutter (8)
Home Runs: Oglivie-MIL
Attendance: 53,723

The Dodgers earned only four runs off Philadelphia pitching, and even though they doubled their run total to eight on unearned runs, the Phillies scored twice that number to take the pennant in four games.

Mike Schmidt homered off Jerry Reuss in the first inning of the opener for the game's only run. Phillies starter Steve Carlton loaded the bases in the eighth, but Al Holland came on to get the third out and preserve the shutout. The Phillies also scored only one run in the second game, on Gary Matthews' homer off Fernando Valenzuela in the second. But this time the run only tied the score, and in the fifth Pedro Guerrero tripled in two unearned runs to give Valenzuela the Dodgers' only win.

The Phillies' Charlie Hudson hurled the series' only complete game—a four-hitter—to win Game 3. Gary Matthews' four hits in Game 3 and 4 included his second and third series homers, and drove in half the Phillies' 14 runs as they took the two games by identical 7–2 scores.

Philadelphia Phillies (East), 3; Los Angeles Dodgers (West), 1

PHI (E)

PLAYER/POS	AVG	G	AB	R	H	2B	3B	HR	RB	BB	SO	SB
Steve Carlton, p	.200	2	5	0	1	0	0	0	0	0	3	0
Ivan DeJesus, ss	.250	4	12	0	3	0	0	0	1	3	3	0
John Denny, p	.000	1	1	0	0	0	0	0	0	0	0	0
Bob Dernier, of	.000	1	0	0	0	0	0	0	0	0	0	0
Bo Diaz, c	.154	4	13	0	2	1	0	0	0	2	1	0
Greg Gross, of-3	.000	4	5	1	0	0	0	0	0	2	2	0
Von Hayes, of-1	.000	2	2	0	0	0	0	0	0	0	0	0
Al Holland, p	.000	2	0	0	0	0	0	0	0	0	0	0
Charles Hudson, p	.000	1	4	0	0	0	0	0	0	0	3	0
Joe Lefebvre, of-1	.000	2	2	0	0	0	0	0	1	0	1	0
Sixto Lezcano, of	.308	4	13	2	4	0	0	1	2	1	1	0
Garry Maddox, of	.273	3	11	0	3	1	0	0	1	0	1	0
Gary Matthews, of	.429	4	14	4	6	0	0	3	8	2	1	1
Joe Morgan, 2b	.067	4	15	1	1	0	0	0	0	2	1	0
Tony Perez, ph	1.000	1	1	0	1	0	0	0	0	0	0	0
Ron Reed, p	.000	2	0	0	0	0	0	0	0	0	0	0
Pete Rose, 1b	.375	4	16	3	6	0	0	0	0	1	1	1
Juan Samuel, pr	.000	1	0	0	0	0	0	0	0	0	0	0
Mike Schmidt, 3b	.467	4	15	5	7	2	0	1	2	2	3	0
Ossie Virgil, ph	.000	1	1	0	0	0	0	0	0	0	1	0
TOTAL	.262		130	16	34	4	0	5	15	15	22	2

PITCHER	W	L	ERA	G	GS	CG	SV	SHO	IP	H	ER	BB	SO
Steve Carlton	2	0	0.66	2	2	0	0	0	13.2	13	1	5	13
John Denny	0	1	0.00	1	1	0	0	0	6.0	5	0	3	3
Al Holland	0	0	0.00	2	0	0	1	0	3.0	1	0	0	3
Charles Hudson	1	0	2.00	1	1	1	0	0	9.0	4	2	2	9
Ron Reed	0	0	2.70	2	0	0	0	0	3.1	4	1	1	3
TOTAL	3	1	1.03	8	4	1	1	0	35.0	27	4	11	31

LA (W)

PLAYER/POS	AVG	G	AB	R	H	2B	3B	HR	RB	BB	SO	SB
Dusty Baker, of	.357	4	14	4	5	1	0	1	1	2	0	0
Joe Beckwith, p	.000	2	0	0	0	0	0	0	0	0	0	0
Greg Brock, 1b	.000	3	9	1	0	0	0	0	0	0	3	0
Jack Fimple, c	.143	3	7	0	1	0	0	0	1	0	3	0
Pedro Guerrero, 3b	.250	4	12	1	3	1	1	0	2	3	3	0
Rick Honeycutt, p	.000	2	0	0	0	0	0	0	0	0	0	0
Rafael Landestoy, ph	.000	2	2	0	0	0	0	0	0	0	1	0
Ken Landreaux, of	.143	4	14	0	2	0	0	0	1	1	3	0
Candy Maldonado, ph	.000	2	2	0	0	0	0	0	0	0	1	0
Mike Marshall, 1b-3,of-2	.133	4	15	1	2	1	0	1	2	1	6	0
Rick Monday, ph	.000	1	0	0	0	0	0	0	0	0	0	0
Jose Morales, ph	.000	2	2	0	0	0	0	0	0	0	1	0
Tom Niedenfuer, p	.000	2	0	0	0	0	0	0	0	0	0	0
Alejandro Pena, p	1.000	1	1	0	1	0	0	0	0	0	0	0
Jerry Reuss, p	.000	2	3	0	0	0	0	0	0	0	3	0
Bill Russell, ss	.286	4	14	1	4	0	0	0	0	2	4	1
Steve Sax, 2b	.250	4	16	0	4	0	0	0	0	1	0	1
Derrel Thomas, of	.444	4	9	0	4	1	0	0	0	0	3	1
Fernando Valenzuela, p	.000	1	3	0	0	0	0	0	0	1	0	0
Bob Welch, p	.000	1	0	0	0	0	0	0	0	0	0	0
Steve Yeager, c	.167	2	6	0	1	1	0	0	0	0	0	0
Pat Zachry, p	.000	2	0	0	0	0	0	0	0	0	0	0
TOTAL	.209		129	8	27	5	1	2	7	11	31	3

PITCHER	W	L	ERA	G	GS	CG	SV	SHO	IP	H	ER	BB	SO
Joe Beckwith	0	0	0.00	2	0	0	0	0	2.1	1	0	2	3
Rick Honeycutt	0	0	21.60	2	0	0	0	0	1.2	4	4	0	2
Tom Niedenfuer	0	0	0.00	2	0	0	1	0	2.0	0	0	1	3
Alejandro Pena	0	0	6.75	1	0	0	0	0	2.2	4	2	1	3
Jerry Reuss	0	2	4.50	2	2	0	0	0	12.0	14	6	3	4
Fernando Valenzuela	1	0	1.13	1	1	0	0	0	8.0	7	1	4	5
Bob Welch	0	1	6.75	1	1	0	0	0	1.1	0	1	2	0
Pat Zachry	0	0	2.25	2	0	0	0	0	4.0	4	1	2	2
TOTAL	1	3	3.97	13	4	0	1	0	34.0	34	15	15	22

GAME 1 AT LA OCT 4

		R	H	E
PHI	100 000 000	1	5	1
LA	000 000 000	0	7	0

Pitchers: CARLTON, Holland (8) vs REUSS, Niedenfuer (9)
Home Runs: Schmidt-PHI
Attendance: 49,963

GAME 2 AT LA OCT 5

		R	H	E
PHI	010 000 000	1	7	2
LA	100 020 01X	4	6	1

Pitchers: DENNY, Reed (7) vs VALENZUELA, Niedenfuer (9)
Home Runs: Matthews-PHI
Attendance: 55,967

GAME 3 AT PHI OCT 7

		R	H	E
LA	000 200 000	2	4	0
PHI	021 120 10X	7	9	1

Pitchers: WELCH, Pena (2), Honeycutt (5), Beckwith (5), Zachry (7) vs HUDSON
Home Runs: Marshall-LA, Matthews-PHI
Attendance: 53,490

GAME 4 AT PHI OCT 8

		R	H	E
LA	000 100 010	2	10	0
PHI	300 022 00X	7	13	1

Pitchers: REUSS, Beckwith (5), Honeycutt (5), Zachry (7) vs CARLTON, Reed (7), Holland (8)
Home Runs: Matthews-PHI, Baker-LA, Lezcano-PHI
Attendance: 64,494

The White Sox and Orioles entered the ALCS evenly matched, with similar season's records and stats. But Baltimore all but shut down Chicago's run production in this quick four-game meeting. Both teams had 28 hits, but the Sox, held to four for extra bases, found themselves outslugged by 116 percentage points and outscored by 16 runs.

Chicago won the first game, scoring two of their three series runs as LaMarr Hoyt shut out Baltimore for eight innings before letting in a run in the ninth. But the White Sox had concluded their effective scoring. In Game 2, Orioles rookie Mike Boddicker shut them out on five hits, striking out 14. In Game 3 the Sox scored their final run. The Orioles got only two more hits than Chicago but blended them with nine walks, a hit batsman, and a Sox error to score 11 runs.

In the fourth game, Orioles pitchers Storm Davis and Tippy Martinez saw to it that ten Chicago hits scored no runs. Britt Burns held Baltimore scoreless, too, through nine innings. But Tito Landrum's solo homer in the top of the 10th drove Burns out, and two more Orioles runs provided more than enough scoring to win Baltimore the flag.

Baltimore Orioles (East), 3; Chicago White Sox (West), 1

BAL (E)

PLAYER/POS	AVG	G	AB	R	H	2B	3B	HR	RB	BB	SO	SB
Benny Ayala, dh	.000	1	0	0	0	0	0	0	1	0	0	0
Mike Boddicker, p	.000	1	0	0	0	0	0	0	0	0	0	0
Al Bumbry, of	.125	3	8	0	1	1	0	0	1	0	2	0
Todd Cruz, 3b	.133	4	15	0	2	0	0	0	1	0	5	0
Rich Dauer, 2b	.000	4	14	0	0	0	0	0	1	0	0	0
Storm Davis, p	.000	1	0	0	0	0	0	0	0	0	0	0
Rick Dempsey, c	.167	4	12	1	2	0	0	0	0	1	1	0
Jim Dwyer, of-1	.250	2	4	1	1	1	0	0	0	1	0	0
Mike Flanagan, p	.000	1	0	0	0	0	0	0	0	0	0	0
Dan Ford, of-1	.200	2	5	0	1	1	0	0	0	0	1	0
Tito Landrum, of-3	.200	4	10	2	2	0	0	1	1	0	2	0
John Lowenstein, of-2	.167	3	6	0	1	1	0	0	2	1	2	0
Tippy Martinez, p	.000	2	0	0	0	0	0	0	0	0	0	0
Scott McGregor, p	.000	1	0	0	0	0	0	0	0	0	0	0
Eddie Murray, 1b	.267	4	15	5	4	0	0	1	3	3	3	1
Joe Nolan, ph	.000	1	0	0	0	0	0	0	1	0	0	0
Jim Palmer, pr	.000	1	0	0	0	0	0	0	0	0	0	0
Cal Ripken, ss	.400	4	15	5	6	2	0	0	1	2	3	0
Gary Roenicke, of	.750	3	4	4	3	1	0	1	4	5	0	0
John Shelby, of-2	.222	3	9	1	2	0	0	0	0	1	3	1
Ken Singleton, dh	.250	4	12	0	3	2	0	0	1	2	2	0
Sammy Stewart, p	.000	2	0	0	0	0	0	0	0	0	0	0
TOTAL	.217		129	19	28	9	0	3	17	16	24	2

PITCHER	W	L	ERA	G	GS	CG	SV	SHO	IP	H	ER	BB	SO
Mike Boddicker	1	0	0.00	1	1	1	0	1	9.0	5	0	3	14
Storm Davis	0	0	0.00	1	1	0	0	0	6.0	5	0	2	2
Mike Flanagan	1	0	1.80	1	1	0	0	0	5.0	5	1	0	1
Tippy Martinez	1	0	0.00	2	0	0	0	0	6.0	5	0	3	5
Scott McGregor	0	1	1.35	1	1	0	0	0	6.2	6	1	3	2
Sammy Stewart	0	0	0.00	2	0	0	1	0	4.1	2	0	1	2
TOTAL	3	1	0.49	8	4	1	1	1	37.0	28	2	12	26

CHI (W)

PLAYER/POS	AVG	G	AB	R	H	2B	3B	HR	RB	BB	SO	SB
Juan Agosto, p	.000	1	0	0	0	0	0	0	0	0	0	0
Harold Baines, of	.125	4	16	0	2	0	0	0	0	1	3	0
Floyd Bannister, p	.000	1	0	0	0	0	0	0	0	0	0	0
Salome Barojas, p	.000	2	0	0	0	0	0	0	0	0	0	0
Britt Burns, p	.000	1	0	0	0	0	0	0	0	0	0	0
Julio Cruz, 2b	.333	4	12	0	4	0	0	0	0	3	4	2
Richard Dotson, p	.000	1	0	0	0	0	0	0	0	0	0	0
Jerry Dybzinski, ss	.250	2	4	0	1	0	0	0	0	0	0	0
Carlton Fisk, c	.176	4	17	0	3	1	0	0	0	1	3	0
Scott Fletcher, ss	.000	3	7	0	0	0	0	0	0	1	0	0
Jerry Hairston, of	.000	2	3	0	0	0	0	0	0	1	1	0
LaMarr Hoyt, p	.000	1	0	0	0	0	0	0	0	0	0	0
Ron Kittle, of	.286	3	7	1	2	1	0	0	0	1	2	0
Jerry Koosman, p	.000	1	0	0	0	0	0	0	0	0	0	0
Dennis Lamp, p	.000	3	0	0	0	0	0	0	0	0	0	0
Rudy Law, of	.389	4	18	1	7	1	0	0	0	0	1	2
Vance Law, 3b	.182	4	11	0	2	0	0	0	1	1	3	0
Greg Luzinski, dh	.133	4	15	0	2	1	0	0	0	1	5	0
Tom Paciorek, 1b-3,of-2	.250	4	16	1	4	0	0	0	1	1	2	0
Aurelio Rodriguez, 3b	.000	2	0	0	0	0	0	0	0	0	0	0
Mike Squires, 1b-3	.000	4	4	0	0	0	0	0	0	0	0	0
Dick Tidrow, p	.000	1	0	0	0	0	0	0	0	0	0	0
Greg Walker, 1b-1	.333	2	3	0	1	0	0	0	0	1	2	0
TOTAL	.211		133	3	28	4	0	0	2	12	26	4

PITCHER	W	L	ERA	G	GS	CG	SV	SHO	IP	H	ER	BB	SO
Juan Agosto	0	0	0.00	1	0	0	0	0	0.1	0	0	0	0
Floyd Bannister	0	1	4.50	1	1	0	0	0	6.0	5	3	1	5
Salome Barojas	0	0	18.00	2	0	0	0	0	1.0	4	2	0	0
Britt Burns	0	1	0.96	1	1	0	0	0	9.1	6	1	5	8
Richard Dotson	0	1	10.80	1	1	0	0	0	5.0	6	6	3	3
LaMarr Hoyt	1	0	1.00	1	1	1	0	0	9.0	5	1	0	4
Jerry Koosman	0	0	54.00	1	0	0	0	0	0.1	1	2	2	0
Dennis Lamp	0	0	0.00	3	0	0	0	0	2.0	0	0	2	1
Dick Tidrow	0	0	3.00	1	0	0	0	0	3.0	1	1	3	3
TOTAL	1	3	4.00	12	4	1	0	0	36.0	28	16	16	24

GAME 1 AT BAL OCT 5

CHI	001	001	000	2	7	0
BAL	000	000	001	1	5	1

Pitchers: HOYT vs McGREGOR, Stewart (7), T.Martinez (8)
Attendance: 51,289

GAME 2 AT BAL OCT 6

CHI	000	000	000	0	5	2
BAL	010	102	00X	4	6	0

Pitchers: BANNISTER, Barojas (7), Lamp (8) vs BODDICKER
Home Runs: Roenicke-BAL
Attendance: 52,347

GAME 3 AT CHI OCT 7

BAL	310	020	014	11	8	1
CHI	010	000	000	1	6	1

Pitchers: FLANAGAN, Stewart (6) vs DOTSON, Tidrow (6), Koosman (9), Lamp (9)
Home Runs: Murray-BAL
Attendance: 46,635

GAME 4 AT CHI OCT 8

BAL	000	000	000	3	3	9	0
CHI	000	000	000	0	0	10	0

Pitchers: Davis, T.MARTINEZ (7) vs BURNS, Barojas (10), Agosto (10), Lamp (10)
Home Runs: Landrum-BAL
Attendance: 45,477

Near neighbors Baltimore and Philadelphia met in a World Series for the first time. Both clubs were led by new managers: Baltimore by Joe Altobelli, who inherited a team built under longtime Orioles manager Earl Weaver, and the Phillies by general manager Paul Owens, who replaced Pat Corrales with himself in midseason.

Both started their top winners in the opener, and the result was a pitchers' duel, with all three runs scored on solo homers. John Denny gave up the first to Jim Dwyer in the first inning, but after that (with late-inning help from Al Holland) he blanked the Orioles, while Baltimore's Scott McGregor, after five and two thirds scoreless innings gave up home runs to Joe Morgan and (the deciding blast two innings later) to Garry Maddox.

The Orioles swept the next four games. In Game 2, Mike Boddicker yielded just three singles (and no walks) to Philadelphia. Though one of the singles led to a run in the fourth inning, giving the Phillies a 1–0 lead, John Lowenstein tied the score with a home run in the fifth. Three more hits in the inning and a sacrifice fly gave the Orioles the lead, 3–1, and three two-out singles in the seventh inning brought in a fourth Baltimore run.

Philadelphia again scored first in Game 3, on leadoff home runs in the second and third innings by Gary Matthews and Joe Morgan. But the Orioles finally got to veteran starter Steve Carlton in the sixth for one run and drove him out after a second run scored an inning later. Carlton suffered the loss when the baserunner he left scored the tie-breaking run from second on an error by shortstop Ivan DeJesus.

The Phillies also lost Game 4 by a single run. Baltimore scored first with two runs in the top of the fourth, but Philadelphia recovered with one run in the fourth and two an inning later. They would not lead again in the Series. Baltimore scored twice in the sixth to go ahead again, and once more in the seventh. The Phillies scored once more with two down in the last of the ninth to draw within one run of a tie, but Joe Morgan lined out to second to end the game.

Home runs by Rick Dempsey and Eddie Murray (who hit two) accounted for four of Baltimore's five runs in the final game—more than enough to support Scott McGregor's five-hit shutout pitching.

Baltimore Orioles (AL), 4; Philadelphia Phillies (NL), 1

BAL (A)

PLAYER/POS	AVG	G	AB	R	H	2B	3B	HR	RB	BB	SO	SB
Benny Ayala, ph	1.000	1	1	1	1	0	0	0	1	0	0	0
Mike Boddicker, p	.000	1	3	0	0	0	0	0	1	0	1	0
Al Bumbry, of	.091	4	11	0	1	1	0	0	1	0	1	0
Todd Cruz, 3b	.125	5	16	1	2	0	0	0	0	1	3	0
Rich Dauer, 2b	.211	5	19	2	4	1	0	0	3	0	3	0
Storm Davis, p	.000	1	2	0	0	0	0	0	0	0	2	0
Rick Dempsey, c	.385	5	13	3	5	4	0	1	2	2	2	0
Jim Dwyer, of	.375	2	8	3	3	1	0	1	1	0	0	0
Mike Flanagan, p	.000	1	1	0	0	0	0	0	0	0	1	0
Dan Ford, of-4	.167	5	12	1	2	0	0	1	1	1	5	0
Tito Landrum, of	.000	3	0	0	0	0	0	0	0	0	0	1
John Lowenstein, of	.385	4	13	2	5	1	0	1	1	0	3	0
Tippy Martinez, p	.000	3	0	0	0	0	0	0	0	0	0	0
Scott McGregor, p	.000	2	5	0	0	0	0	0	0	0	0	0
Eddie Murray, 1b	.250	5	20	2	5	0	0	2	3	1	4	0
Joe Nolan, c	.000	2	2	0	0	0	0	0	0	1	0	0
Jim Palmer, p	.000	1	0	0	0	0	0	0	0	0	0	0
Cal Ripken, ss	.167	5	18	2	3	0	0	0	1	3	4	0
Gary Roenicke, of-2	.000	3	7	0	0	0	0	0	0	0	2	0
Len Sakata, 2b	.000	1	1	0	0	0	0	0	0	0	0	0
John Shelby, of	.444	5	9	1	4	0	0	0	1	0	4	0
Ken Singleton, ph	.000	2	1	0	0	0	0	0	1	1	1	0
Sammy Stewart, p	.000	3	2	0	0	0	0	0	0	0	1	0
TOTAL	.213		164	18	35	8	0	6	17	10	37	1

PITCHER	W	L	ERA	G	GS	CG	SV	SHO	IP	H	ER	BB	SO
Mike Boddicker	1	0	0.00	1	1	1	0	0	9.0	3	0	0	6
Storm Davis	1	0	5.40	1	1	0	0	0	5.0	6	3	1	3
Mike Flanagan	0	0	4.50	1	1	0	0	0	4.0	6	2	1	1
Tippy Martinez	0	0	3.00	3	0	0	2	0	3.0	3	1	0	0
Scott McGregor	1	1	1.06	2	2	1	0	1	17.0	9	2	2	12
Jim Palmer	1	0	0.00	1	0	0	0	0	2.0	2	0	1	1
Sammy Stewart	0	0	0.00	3	0	0	0	0	5.0	2	0	2	6
TOTAL	4	1	1.60	12	5	2	2	1	45.0	31	8	7	29

PHI (N)

PLAYER/POS	AVG	G	AB	R	H	2B	3B	HR	RB	BB	SO	SB
Larry Andersen, p	.000	2	0	0	0	0	0	0	0	0	0	0
Marty Bystrom, p	.000	1	0	0	0	0	0	0	0	0	0	0
Steve Carlton, p	.000	1	3	0	0	0	0	0	0	0	1	0
Ivan DeJesus, ss	.125	5	16	0	2	0	0	0	0	1	2	0
John Denny, p	.200	2	5	1	1	0	0	0	1	0	1	0
Bob Dernier, pr	.000	1	0	1	0	0	0	0	0	0	0	0
Bo Diaz, c	.333	5	15	1	5	1	0	0	0	1	2	0
Greg Gross, of	.000	2	6	0	0	0	0	0	0	0	0	0
Von Hayes, of-1	.000	4	3	0	0	0	0	0	0	0	1	0
Willie Hernandez, p	.000	3	0	0	0	0	0	0	0	0	0	0
Al Holland, p	.000	2	0	0	0	0	0	0	0	0	0	0
Charles Hudson, p	.000	2	2	0	0	0	0	0	0	0	1	0
Joe Lefebvre, of-2	.200	3	5	0	1	1	0	0	2	0	1	0
Sixto Lezcano, of-3	.125	4	8	0	1	0	0	0	0	0	2	0
Garry Maddox, of-3	.250	4	12	1	3	1	0	1	1	0	2	0
Gary Matthews, of	.250	5	16	1	4	0	0	1	1	2	2	0
Joe Morgan, 2b	.263	5	19	3	5	0	1	2	2	2	3	1
Tony Perez, 1b-2	.200	4	10	0	2	0	0	0	0	0	2	0
Ron Reed, p	.000	3	0	0	0	0	0	0	0	0	0	0
Pete Rose, 1b-3,of-1	.313	5	16	1	5	1	0	0	1	1	3	0
Juan Samuel, ph	.000	3	1	0	0	0	0	0	0	0	0	0
Mike Schmidt, 3b	.050	5	20	0	1	0	0	0	0	0	6	0
Ossie Virgil, c-1	.500	3	2	0	1	0	0	0	1	0	0	0
TOTAL	.195		159	9	31	4	1	4	9	7	29	1

PITCHER	W	L	ERA	G	GS	CG	SV	SHO	IP	H	ER	BB	SO
Larry Andersen	0	0	2.25	2	0	0	0	0	4.0	4	1	0	1
Marty Bystrom	0	0	0.00	1	0	0	0	0	1.0	0	0	0	1
Steve Carlton	0	1	2.70	1	1	0	0	0	6.2	5	2	3	7
John Denny	1	1	3.46	2	2	0	0	0	13.0	12	5	3	9
Willie Hernandez	0	0	0.00	3	0	0	0	0	4.0	0	0	1	4
Al Holland	0	0	0.00	2	0	0	1	0	3.2	1	0	0	5
Charles Hudson	0	2	8.64	2	2	0	0	0	8.1	9	8	1	6
Ron Reed	0	0	2.70	3	0	0	0	0	3.1	4	1	2	4
TOTAL	1	4	3.48	16	5	0	1	0	44.0	35	17	10	37

GAME 1 AT BAL OCT 11

		R	H	E
PHI	000 001 010	2	5	0
BAL	100 000 000	1	5	1

Pitchers: DENNY, Holland (8) vs McGREGOR, Stewart (9), T.Martinez (9)
Home Runs: Morgan-PHI, Maddox-PHI, Dwyer-BAL
Attendance: 52,204

GAME 2 AT BAL OCT 12

		R	H	E
PHI	000 100 000	1	3	0
BAL	000 030 10X	4	9	1

Pitchers: HUDSON, Hernandez (5), Andersen (6), Reed (8) vs BODDICKER
Home Runs: Lowenstein-BAL
Attendance: 52,132

GAME 3 AT PHI OCT 14

		R	H	E
BAL	000 001 200	3	6	1
PHI	011 000 000	2	8	2

Pitchers: Flanagan, PALMER (5), Stewart (7), T.Martinez (9) vs CARLTON, Holland (7)
Home Runs: Matthews-PHI, Morgan-PHI, Ford-BAL
Attendance: 65,792

GAME 4 AT PHI OCT 15

		R	H	E
BAL	000 202 100	5	10	1
PHI	000 120 001	4	10	0

Pitchers: DAVIS, Stewart (6), T.Martinez (8) vs DENNY, Hernandez (6), Reed (6), Andersen (8)
Attendance: 66,947

GAME 5 AT PHI OCT 16

		R	H	E
BAL	011 210 000	5	5	0
PHI	000 000 000	0	5	1

Pitchers: McGREGOR vs HUDSON, Bystrom (5), Hernandez (6), Reed (9)
Home Runs: Murray-BAL (2), Dempsey-BAL
Attendance: 67,064

After two games in Chicago, the Cubs appeared headed for their first pennant in 39 years. Rick Sutcliffe and Warren Brusstar shut out the Padres, 13–0, in an opener enlivened by five Cubs home runs, including two homers by Gary Matthews and one by Sutcliffe. In a quieter second game, the Cubs built a 4–1 lead over the first four innings and held on for the win.

When the series moved to San Diego, though, the Padres came to life. In the fifth and sixth innings of Game 3, they obliterated a 1–0 Cubs lead with seven runs, as Ed Whitson and Goose Gossage held the Cubs scoreless after the second inning for what turned into an easy Padres win.

Game 4 was not so easy. San Diego scored first in the third inning, lost their lead in the fourth, tied it in the fifth, went ahead in the seventh, and fell back into a 5–5 tie in the eighth. But in the bottom of the ninth, Steve Garvey's two-run homer sent the series into a fifth game.

Leon Durham put the Cubs ahead with a two-run homer in the first inning of the finale, and Jody Davis added to the lead with a solo shot in the second. Rick Sutcliffe, meanwhile, was setting down Padres as he added five shutout innings to his seven from Game 1. But he gave up two runs in the sixth, and after first baseman Durham allowed a grounder go through his legs to let in the tying run in the seventh, the Cubs watched the pennant slip away as Tony Gwynn's double and Garvey's single drove in the game's final three runs.

San Diego Padres (West), 3; Chicago Cubs (East), 2

SD (W)

PLAYER/POS	AVG	G	AB	R	H	2B	3B	HR	RB	BB	SO	SB
Kurt Bevacqua, ph	.000	2	2	0	0	0	0	0	0	0	0	0
Greg Booker, p	.000	1	0	0	0	0	0	0	0	0	0	0
Bobby Brown, of	.000	3	4	1	0	0	0	0	0	1	2	1
Dave Dravecky, p	.000	3	0	0	0	0	0	0	0	0	0	0
Tim Flannery, ph	.500	3	2	2	1	0	0	0	0	0	0	0
Steve Garvey, 1b	.400	5	20	1	8	1	0	1	7	1	2	0
Rich Gossage, p	.000	3	0	0	0	0	0	0	0	0	0	0
Tony Gwynn, of	.368	5	19	6	7	3	0	0	3	1	2	0
Greg Harris, p	.000	1	0	0	0	0	0	0	0	0	0	0
Andy Hawkins, p	.000	3	0	0	0	0	0	0	0	0	0	0
Terry Kennedy, c	.222	5	18	2	4	0	0	0	1	1	3	0
Craig Lefferts, p	.000	3	0	0	0	0	0	0	0	0	0	0
Tim Lollar, p	.000	1	1	0	0	0	0	0	0	0	1	0
Carmelo Martinez, of	.176	5	17	1	3	0	0	0	0	2	4	0
Kevin McReynolds, of	.300	4	10	2	3	0	0	1	4	3	1	0
Graig Nettles, 3b	.143	4	14	1	2	0	0	0	2	1	1	0
Mario Ramirez, ph	.000	2	2	0	0	0	0	0	0	0	0	0
Luis Salazar, of-2,3b-1	.200	3	5	0	1	0	1	0	0	0	1	0
Eric Show, p	.000	2	1	0	0	0	0	0	0	0	1	0
Champ Summers, ph	.000	2	2	0	0	0	0	0	0	0	1	0
Garry Templeton, ss	.333	5	15	2	5	1	0	0	2	2	0	1
Mark Thurmond, p	1.000	1	1	0	1	0	0	0	0	0	0	0
Ed Whitson, p	.000	1	3	0	0	0	0	0	0	0	1	0
Alan Wiggins, 2b	.316	5	19	4	6	0	0	0	1	2	2	0
TOTAL	.265		155	22	41	5	1	2	20	14	22	2

PITCHER	W	L	ERA	G	GS	CG	SV	SHO	IP	H	ER	BB	SO
Greg Booker	0	0	0.00	1	0	0	0	0	2.0	2	0	1	2
Dave Dravecky	0	0	0.00	3	0	0	0	0	6.0	2	0	0	5
Rich Gossage	0	0	4.50	3	0	0	1	0	4.0	5	2	1	5
Greg Harris	0	0	31.50	1	0	0	0	0	2.0	9	7	3	2
Andy Hawkins	0	0	0.00	3	0	0	0	0	3.2	0	0	2	1
Craig Lefferts	2	0	0.00	3	0	0	0	0	4.0	1	0	1	1
Tim Lollar	0	0	6.23	1	1	0	0	0	4.1	3	3	4	3
Eric Show	0	1	13.50	2	2	0	0	0	5.1	8	8	4	2
Mark Thurmond	0	1	9.82	1	1	0	0	0	3.2	7	4	2	1
Ed Whitson	1	0	1.13	1	1	0	0	0	8.0	5	1	2	6
TOTAL	3	2	5.23	19	5	0	1	0	43.0	42	25	20	28

CHI (E)

PLAYER/POS	AVG	G	AB	R	H	2B	3B	HR	RB	BB	SO	SB
Thad Bosley, ph	.000	2	2	0	0	0	0	0	0	0	2	0
Larry Bowa, ss	.200	5	15	1	3	1	0	0	1	1	0	0
Warren Brusstar, p	.000	3	1	0	0	0	0	0	0	0	0	0
Ron Cey, 3b	.158	5	19	3	3	1	0	1	3	3	3	0
Henry Cotto, of	1.000	3	1	1	1	0	0	0	0	0	0	0
Jody Davis, c	.389	5	18	3	7	2	0	2	6	0	3	0
Bob Dernier, of	.235	5	17	5	4	2	0	1	1	5	4	2
Leon Durham, 1b	.150	5	20	2	3	0	0	2	4	1	4	0
Dennis Eckersley, p	.000	1	2	0	0	0	0	0	0	0	1	0
George Frazier, p	.000	1	0	0	0	0	0	0	0	0	0	0
Richie Hebner, ph	.000	2	1	0	0	0	0	0	0	0	0	0
Steve Lake, c	1.000	1	1	0	1	1	0	0	0	0	0	0
Davey Lopes, of-1	.000	2	1	0	0	0	0	0	0	0	0	0
Gary Matthews, of	.200	5	15	4	3	0	0	2	5	6	4	1
Keith Moreland, of	.333	5	18	3	6	2	0	0	2	1	1	0
Ryne Sandberg, 2b	.368	5	19	3	7	2	0	0	2	3	2	3
Scott Sanderson, p	.000	1	2	0	0	0	0	0	0	0	1	0
Lee Smith, p	.000	2	0	0	0	0	0	0	0	0	0	0
Tim Stoddard, p	.000	2	0	0	0	0	0	0	0	0	0	0
Rick Sutcliffe, p	.500	2	6	1	3	0	0	1	1	0	2	0
Steve Trout, p	.500	2	2	0	1	0	0	0	0	0	0	0
Tom Veryzer, ss-2,3b-1	.000	3	1	0	0	0	0	0	0	0	0	0
Gary Woods, of	.000	1	1	0	0	0	0	0	0	0	1	0
TOTAL	.259		162	26	42	11	0	9	25	20	28	6

PITCHER	W	L	ERA	G	GS	CG	SV	SHO	IP	H	ER	BB	SO
Warren Brusstar	0	0	0.00	3	0	0	0	0	4.1	6	0	0	1
Dennis Eckersley	0	1	8.44	1	1	0	0	0	5.1	9	5	0	0
George Frazier	0	0	10.80	1	0	0	0	0	1.2	2	2	0	1
Scott Sanderson	0	0	5.79	1	1	0	0	0	4.2	6	3	1	2
Lee Smith	0	1	9.00	2	0	0	1	0	2.0	3	2	0	3
Tim Stoddard	0	0	4.50	2	0	0	0	0	2.0	1	1	2	2
Rick Sutcliffe	1	1	3.38	2	2	0	0	0	13.1	9	5	8	10
Steve Trout	1	0	2.00	2	1	0	0	0	9.0	5	2	3	3
TOTAL	2	3	4.25	14	5	0	1	0	42.1	41	20	14	22

GAME 1 AT CHI OCT 2

				R	H	E
SD	000	000	000	0	6	1
CHI	203	062	00X	13	16	0

Pitchers: SHOW, Harris (5), Booker (7) vs SUTCLIFFE, Brusstar (8)
Home Runs: Dernier-CHI, Matthews-CHI (2), Sutcliffe-CHI, Cey-CHI
Attendance: 36,282

GAME 2 AT CHI OCT 3

				R	H	E
SD	000	101	000	2	5	0
CHI	102	100	00X	4	8	1

Pitchers: THURMOND, Hawkins (4), Dravecky (6), Lefferts (8) vs TROUT, Smith (9)
Attendance: 36,282

GAME 3 AT SD OCT 4

				R	H	E
CHI	010	000	000	1	5	0
SD	000	034	00X	7	11	0

Pitchers: ECKERSLEY, Frazier (6), Stoddard (8) vs WHITSON, Gossage (9)
Home Runs: McReynolds-SD
Attendance: 58,346

GAME 4 AT SD OCT 6

				R	H	E
CHI	000	300	020	5	8	1
SD	002	010	202	7	11	0

Pitchers: Sanderson, Brusstar (5), Stoddard (7), SMITH (8) vs Lollar, Hawkins (5), Dravecky (6), Gossage (8), LEFFERTS (9)
Home Runs: Davis-CHI, Durham-CHI,Garvey-SD
Attendance: 58,354

GAME 5 AT SD OCT 7

				R	H	E
CHI	210	000	000	3	5	1
SD	000	002	40X	6	8	0

Pitchers: SUTCLIFFE, Trout (7), Brusstar (8) vs Show, Hawkins (2), Dravecky (4), LEFFERTS (6), Gossage (8)
Home Runs: Durham-CHI, Davis-CHI
Attendance: 58,359

The heavily favored Tigers swept the series, but not without difficulty, despite a 14-hit, three-homer, 8–1 romp in the opener.

Games 2 and 3 were much tighter. In the second game, after Detroit had built a 3–0 lead over the first three innings, rookie starter Bret Saberhagen settled down and blanked the Tigers for the next five innings as K.C. inched its way to a tie with runs in the fourth, seventh, and eighth. Through the ninth and 10th innings, Tigers reliever Aurelio Lopez and Dan Quisenberry of the Royals dueled scorelessly, but in the top of the 11th Johnny Grubb doubled home two Tigers runs. Lopez struggled but held the Royals scoreless in the last of the 11th for the win.

In Game 3 the Royals' Charlie Leibrandt and Tigers' Milt Wilcox and Willie Hernandez hurled matching three-hitters. But the Tigers secured the game—and the pennant—when Chet Lemon scored on a broken double play in the second inning for the game's only run.

Detroit Tigers (East), 3; Kansas City Royals (West), 0

DET (E)

PLAYER/POS	AVG	G	AB	R	H	2B	3B	HR	RB	BB	SO	SB
Doug Baker, ss	.000	1	0	0	0	0	0	0	0	0	0	0
Dave Bergman, 1b-1	1.000	2	1	1	1	0	0	0	0	0	0	1
Tom Brookens, 2b-1,3b-1	.000	2	2	0	0	0	0	0	0	0	1	0
Marty Castillo, 3b	.250	3	8	0	2	0	0	0	2	0	3	1
Darrell Evans, 1b-3,3b-1	.300	3	10	1	3	1	0	0	1	1	0	1
Barbaro Garbey, dh-2	.333	3	9	1	3	0	0	0	0	0	1	0
Kirk Gibson, of	.417	3	12	2	5	1	0	1	2	2	1	1
Johnny Grubb, dh	.250	1	4	0	1	1	0	0	2	0	0	0
Willie Hernandez, p	.000	3	0	0	0	0	0	0	0	0	0	0
Larry Herndon, of	.200	2	5	1	1	0	0	1	1	1	2	0
Ruppert Jones, of	.000	2	5	1	0	0	0	0	0	1	1	0
Rusty Kuntz, of	.000	1	1	0	0	0	0	0	0	0	0	0
Chet Lemon, of	.000	3	13	1	0	0	0	0	0	0	1	0
Aurelio Lopez, p	.000	1	0	0	0	0	0	0	0	0	0	0
Jack Morris, p	.000	1	0	0	0	0	0	0	0	0	0	0
Lance Parrish, c	.250	3	12	1	3	1	0	1	3	0	3	0
Dan Petry, p	.000	1	0	0	0	0	0	0	0	0	0	0
Alan Trammell, ss	.364	3	11	2	4	0	1	1	3	3	1	0
Lou Whitaker, 2b	.143	3	14	3	2	0	0	0	0	0	3	0
Milt Wilcox, p	.000	1	0	0	0	0	0	0	0	0	0	0
TOTAL	.234		107	14	25	4	1	4	14	8	17	4

PITCHER	W	L	ERA	G	GS	CG	SV	SHO	IP	H	ER	BB	SO
Willie Hernandez	0	0	2.25	3	0	0	1	0	4.0	3	1	1	3
Aurelio Lopez	1	0	0.00	1	0	0	0	0	3.0	4	0	1	2
Jack Morris	1	0	1.29	1	1	0	0	0	7.0	5	1	1	4
Dan Petry	0	0	2.57	1	1	0	0	0	7.0	4	2	1	4
Milt Wilcox	1	0	0.00	1	1	0	0	0	8.0	2	0	2	8
TOTAL	3	0	1.24	7	3	0	1	0	29.0	18	4	6	21

KC (W)

PLAYER/POS	AVG	G	AB	R	H	2B	3B	HR	RB	BB	SO	SB
Steve Balboni, 1b	.091	3	11	0	1	0	0	0	0	1	4	0
Buddy Biancalana, ss	.000	2	1	0	0	0	0	0	0	0	1	0
Bud Black, p	.000	1	0	0	0	0	0	0	0	0	0	0
George Brett, 3b	.231	3	13	0	3	0	0	0	0	0	2	0
Onix Concepcion, ss	.000	3	7	0	0	0	0	0	0	0	0	0
Mark Huismann, p	.000	1	0	0	0	0	0	0	0	0	0	0
Dane Iorg, ph	.500	2	2	0	1	0	0	0	1	0	0	0
Lynn Jones, of-2	.200	3	5	1	1	0	0	0	0	0	0	0
Mike Jones, p	.000	1	0	0	0	0	0	0	0	0	0	0
Charlie Leibrandt, p	.000	1	0	0	0	0	0	0	0	0	0	0
Hal McRae, ph	1.000	2	2	0	2	1	0	0	1	0	0	0
Darryl Motley, of	.167	3	12	0	2	0	0	0	1	1	3	0
Jorge Orta, dh	.100	3	10	1	1	0	1	0	1	0	2	0
Greg Pryor, 3b	.000	1	0	0	0	0	0	0	0	0	0	0
Dan Quisenberry, p	.000	1	0	0	0	0	0	0	0	0	0	0
Bret Saberhagen, p	.000	1	0	0	0	0	0	0	0	0	0	0
Pat Sheridan, of	.000	3	6	1	0	0	0	0	0	3	3	0
Don Slaught, c	.364	3	11	0	4	0	0	0	0	0	0	0
U. L. Washington, ph	.000	2	1	0	0	0	0	0	0	0	1	0
John Wathan, dh	.000	1	1	0	0	0	0	0	0	0	0	0
Frank White, 2b	.091	3	11	1	1	0	0	0	0	0	3	0
Willie Wilson, of	.154	3	13	0	2	0	0	0	0	1	2	0
TOTAL	.170		106	4	18	1	1	0	4	6	21	0

PITCHER	W	L	ERA	G	GS	CG	SV	SHO	IP	H	ER	BB	SO
Bud Black	0	1	7.20	1	1	0	0	0	5.0	7	4	1	3
Mark Huismann	0	0	6.75	1	0	0	0	0	2.2	6	2	1	2
Mike Jones	0	0	6.75	1	0	0	0	0	1.1	1	1	0	0
Charlie Leibrandt	0	1	1.13	1	1	1	0	0	8.0	3	1	4	6
Dan Quisenberry	0	1	3.00	1	0	0	0	0	3.0	2	1	1	1
Bret Saberhagen	0	0	2.25	1	1	0	0	0	8.0	6	2	1	5
TOTAL	0	3	3.54	6	3	1	0	0	28.0	25	11	8	17

GAME 1 AT KC OCT 2

				R	H	E
DET	200	110	121	8	14	0
KC	000	000	100	1	5	1

Pitchers: MORRIS, Hernandez (8) vs BLACK, Huismann (6), M.Jones (8)
Home Runs: Herndon-DET, Trammell-DET, Parrish-DET
Attendance: 41,973

GAME 2 AT KC OCT 3

					R	H	E
DET	201	000	000	02	5	8	1
KC	000	100	110	00	3	10	3

Pitchers: Petry, Hernandez (8), LOPEZ (9) vs Saberhagen, QUISENBERRY (9)
Home Runs: Gibson-DET
Attendance: 42,019

GAME 3 AT DET OCT 5

				R	H	E
KC	000	000	000	0	3	3
DET	010	000	00X	1	3	0

Pitchers: LEIBRANDT vs WILCOX, Hernandez (9)
Attendance: 52,168

Few objective observers expected the Padres (playing in their first World Series) to best the mighty Tigers—and they didn't. Detroit's first two batters in Game 1 hit safely to produce the Series' first scoring before an out had been recorded. San Diego countered with three two-out hits in their half of the first to go ahead, 2–1. But Detroit starter Jack Morris settled down to shut out the Padres over the final eight innings, and his Tigers scored the tying and winning runs in the fifth on Larry Herndon's two-run homer.

The Tigers scored again in Game 2 before the first out was recorded and drove out Ed Whitson with three first-inning runs on five singles. But this time Detroit was shut out (by relievers Andy Hawkins and Craig Lefferts) over the final eight, while San Diego scored single runs in the first and fourth and the winning runs in the fifth on a three-run homer by the normally light-hitting Kurt Bevacqua.

The Tigers won Game 3 on walks—a Series-record 11—as the Series moved to Detroit. After scoring their first two runs in the second on a single and Marty Castillo's home run, they put across two more in the inning on a pair of hits alternated with three walks (the last with the bases full). Three more walks an inning later, followed by a hit batsman, gave Detroit its final run in what became a 5–2 win.

Alan Trammell's two-run homer in the first inning of Game 4 put the Tigers ahead to stay. Jack Morris gave up a solo home run to Terry Kennedy in the second, but Trammell swatted a second two-run shot an inning later for a 4–1 lead. Morris let a second run score on a wild pitch in the ninth, but then retired Kennedy for the third out and his second Series win.

Kirk Gibson's two home runs framed Detroit's scoring in the final game. His two-run shot in the first inning opened the game's scoring. San Diego tied it up with runs in the third and fourth, but Detroit took a 5–3 lead with runs in the fifth and seventh (the latter on Lance Parrish's homer). The unlikely Kurt Bevacqua brought the Padres within a run of tying the game with his second Series homer in the eighth (doubling his regular-season total), but Gibson ended the scoring—and Padres hopes—with a three-run blast half an inning later.

Detroit Tigers (AL), 4; San Diego Padres (NL), 1

DET (A)

PLAYER/POS	AVG	G	AB	R	H	2B	3B	HR	RB	BB	SO	SB
Doug Bair, p	.000	1	0	0	0	0	0	0	0	0	0	0
Dave Bergman, 1b	.000	5	5	0	0	0	0	0	0	0	1	0
Tom Brookens, 3b	.000	3	3	0	0	0	0	0	0	0	1	0
Marty Castillo, 3b	.333	3	9	2	3	0	0	1	2	2	1	0
Darrell Evans, 1b-4,3b-2	.067	5	15	1	1	0	0	0	1	4	4	0
Barbaro Garbey, dh-3	.000	4	12	0	0	0	0	0	0	0	2	0
Kirk Gibson, of	.333	5	18	4	6	0	0	2	7	4	4	3
Johnny Grubb, dh-2	.333	4	3	0	1	0	0	0	0	0	0	0
Willie Hernandez, p	.000	3	0	0	0	0	0	0	0	0	0	0
Larry Herndon, of	.333	5	15	1	5	0	0	1	3	3	2	0
Howard Johnson, ph	.000	1	1	0	0	0	0	0	0	0	0	0
Ruppert Jones, of	.000	2	3	0	0	0	0	0	0	0	1	0
Rusty Kuntz, ph	.000	2	1	0	0	0	0	0	1	0	1	0
Chet Lemon, of	.294	5	17	1	5	0	0	0	1	2	2	2
Aurelio Lopez, p	.000	2	0	0	0	0	0	0	0	0	0	0
Jack Morris, p	.000	2	0	0	0	0	0	0	0	0	0	0
Lance Parrish, c	.278	5	18	3	5	1	0	1	2	3	2	1
Dan Petry, p	.000	2	0	0	0	0	0	0	0	0	0	0
Bill Scherrer, p	.000	3	0	0	0	0	0	0	0	0	0	0
Alan Trammell, ss	.450	5	20	5	9	1	0	2	6	2	2	1
Lou Whitaker, 2b	.278	5	18	6	5	2	0	0	0	4	4	0
Milt Wilcox, p	.000	1	0	0	0	0	0	0	0	0	0	0
TOTAL	.253		158	23	40	4	0	7	23	24	27	7

PITCHER	W	L	ERA	G	GS	CG	SV	SHO	IP	H	ER	BB	SO
Doug Bair	0	0	0.00	1	0	0	0	0	0.2	0	0	0	1
Willie Hernandez	0	0	1.69	3	0	0	2	0	5.1	4	1	0	0
Aurelio Lopez	1	0	0.00	2	0	0	0	0	3.0	1	0	1	4
Jack Morris	2	0	2.00	2	2	2	0	0	18.0	13	4	3	13
Dan Petry	0	1	9.00	2	2	0	0	0	8.0	14	8	5	4
Bill Scherrer	0	0	3.00	3	0	0	0	0	3.0	5	1	0	0
Milt Wilcox	1	0	1.50	1	1	0	0	0	6.0	7	1	2	4
TOTAL	4	1	3.07	14	5	2	2	0	44.0	44	15	11	26

SD (N)

PLAYER/POS	AVG	G	AB	R	H	2B	3B	HR	RB	BB	SO	SB
Kurt Bevacqua, dh	.412	5	17	4	7	2	0	2	4	1	2	0
Bruce Bochy, ph	1.000	1	1	0	1	0	0	0	0	0	0	0
Greg Booker, p	.000	1	0	0	0	0	0	0	0	0	0	0
Bobby Brown, of	.067	5	15	1	1	0	0	0	2	0	4	0
Dave Dravecky, p	.000	2	0	0	0	0	0	0	0	0	0	0
Tim Flannery, 2b	1.000	1	1	0	1	0	0	0	0	0	0	0
Steve Garvey, 1b	.200	5	20	2	4	2	0	0	2	0	2	0
Rich Gossage, p	.000	2	0	0	0	0	0	0	0	0	0	0
Tony Gwynn, of	.263	5	19	1	5	0	0	0	0	3	2	1
Greg Harris, p	.000	1	0	0	0	0	0	0	0	0	0	0
Andy Hawkins, p	.000	3	0	0	0	0	0	0	0	0	0	0
Terry Kennedy, c	.211	5	19	2	4	1	0	1	3	1	1	0
Craig Lefferts, p	.000	3	0	0	0	0	0	0	0	0	0	0
Tim Lollar, p	.000	1	0	0	0	0	0	0	0	0	0	0
Carmelo Martinez, of	.176	5	17	0	3	0	0	0	0	1	9	0
Graig Nettles, 3b	.250	5	12	2	3	0	0	0	2	5	0	0
Ron Roenicke, of-1	.000	2	0	0	0	0	0	0	0	0	0	0
Luis Salazar, of-2,3b-1	.333	4	3	0	1	0	0	0	0	0	0	0
Eric Show, p	.000	1	0	0	0	0	0	0	0	0	0	0
Champ Summers, ph	.000	1	1	0	0	0	0	0	0	0	1	0
Garry Templeton, ss	.316	5	19	1	6	1	0	0	0	0	3	0
Mark Thurmond, p	.000	2	0	0	0	0	0	0	0	0	0	0
Ed Whitson, p	.000	1	0	0	0	0	0	0	0	0	0	0
Alan Wiggins, 2b	.364	5	22	2	8	1	0	0	1	0	2	1
TOTAL	.265		166	15	44	7	0	3	14	11	26	2

PITCHER	W	L	ERA	G	GS	CG	SV	SHO	IP	H	ER	BB	SO
Greg Booker	0	0	9.00	1	0	0	0	0	1.0	0	1	4	0
Dave Dravecky	0	0	0.00	2	0	0	0	0	4.2	3	0	1	5
Rich Gossage	0	0	13.50	2	0	0	0	0	2.2	3	4	1	2
Greg Harris	0	0	0.00	1	0	0	0	0	5.1	3	0	3	5
Andy Hawkins	1	1	0.75	3	0	0	0	0	12.0	4	1	6	4
Craig Lefferts	0	0	0.00	3	0	0	1	0	6.0	2	0	1	7
Tim Lollar	0	1	21.60	1	1	0	0	0	1.2	4	4	4	0
Eric Show	0	1	10.13	1	1	0	0	0	2.2	4	3	1	2
Mark Thurmond	0	1	10.13	2	2	0	0	0	5.1	12	6	3	2
Ed Whitson	0	0	40.50	1	1	0	0	0	0.2	5	3	0	0
TOTAL	1	4	4.71	17	5	0	1	0	42.0	40	22	24	27

GAME 1 AT SD OCT 9

				R	H	E
DET	100	020	000	3	8	0
SD	200	000	000	2	8	1

Pitchers: MORRIS vs THURMOND, Hawkins (6), Dravecky (8)
Home Runs: Herndon-DET
Attendance: 57,908

GAME 2 AT SD OCT 10

				R	H	E
DET	300	000	000	3	7	3
SD	100	130	00X	5	11	0

Pitchers: PETRY, Lopez (5), Scherrer (6), Bair (7), Hernandez (8) vs Whitson, HAWKINS (1), Lefferts (7)
Home Runs: Bevacqua-SD
Attendance: 57,911

GAME 3 AT DET OCT 12

				R	H	E
SD	001	000	100	2	5	0
DET	041	000	00X	5	7	0

Pitchers: LOLLAR, Booker (2), Harris (3) vs WILCOX, Scherrer (7), Hernandez (7)
Home Runs: Castillo-DET
Attendance: 51,970

GAME 4 AT DET OCT 13

				R	H	E
SD	010	000	001	2	10	2
DET	202	000	00X	4	7	0

Pitchers: SHOW, Dravecky (3), Lefferts (7), Gossage (8) vs MORRIS
Home Runs: Trammell-DET (2), Kennedy-SD
Attendance: 52,130

GAME 5 AT DET OCT 14

				R	H	E
SD	001	200	010	4	10	1
DET	300	010	13X	8	11	1

Pitchers: Thurmond, HAWKINS (1), Lefferts (5), Gossage (7) vs Petry, Scherrer (4), LOPEZ (5), Hernandez (8)
Home Runs: Gibson-DET (2), Parrish-DET, Bevacqua-SD
Attendance: 51,901

The Dodgers' league-leading pitchers held St. Louis to three runs over the first two games, even though the Cardinals recorded eight hits per game. But the Cards' league-leading hitters put their blows to better advantage in the next four games of the expanded NLCS, scoring 26 times for four wins and the pennant.

Fernando Valenzuela captured Game 1 for the Dodgers, thanks in part to some ragged fielding by the usually sharp Cardinals infield. And as Orel Hershiser was holding St. Louis to two runs in Game 2, an errant Cardinals pickoff throw and heavy Dodgers hitting gave him an increasingly comfortable lead.

When the series shifted to St. Louis for Game 3, the Cardinals revived, scoring twice in each of the first two innings for a quick lead, which they held for their first win. In Game 4 they unloaded for nine runs in the second inning, and in Game 5—with the game and series tied in the bottom of the ninth—Ozzie Smith hit his first left-handed home run ever to give St. Louis the series lead.

Back in Los Angeles, the Dodgers scored first in Game 6, and held a 4–1 lead after six innings. But three Cardinals scored on four hits in the seventh, and though Mike Marshall's eighth-inning home run restored the lead to Los Angeles, Jack Clark settled things for St. Louis with a three-run homer in the ninth.

St. Louis Cardinals (East), 4; Los Angeles Dodgers (West), 2

STL (E)

PLAYER/POS	AVG	G	AB	R	H	2B	3B	HR	RB	BB	SO	SB
Joaquin Andujar, p	.250	2	4	1	1	1	0	0	0	0	1	0
Steve Braun, ph	.000	2	2	0	0	0	0	0	0	0	0	0
Bill Campbell, p	.000	3	0	0	0	0	0	0	0	0	0	0
Cesar Cedeno, of-4	.167	5	12	2	2	1	0	0	0	2	3	0
Jack Clark, 1b	.381	6	21	4	8	0	0	1	4	5	5	0
Vince Coleman, of	.286	3	14	2	4	0	0	0	1	0	2	1
Danny Cox, p	.000	1	2	0	0	0	0	0	0	1	1	0
Ken Dayley, p	.500	5	2	0	1	0	0	0	0	0	0	0
Bob Forsch, p	.000	1	0	0	0	0	0	0	0	0	0	0
Brian Harper, ph	.000	1	1	0	0	0	0	0	0	0	0	0
Tommy Herr, 2b	.333	6	21	2	7	4	0	1	6	5	2	1
Rick Horton, p	.000	3	0	0	0	0	0	0	0	0	0	0
Mike Jorgensen, ph	.000	2	2	0	0	0	0	0	0	0	1	0
Jeff Lahti, p	.000	2	0	0	0	0	0	0	0	0	0	0
Tito Landrum, of-4	.429	5	14	2	6	0	0	0	4	1	1	1
Willie McGee, of	.269	6	26	6	7	1	0	0	3	3	6	2
Tom Nieto, c	.000	1	3	1	0	0	0	0	0	1	2	0
Terry Pendleton, 3b	.208	6	24	2	5	1	0	0	4	1	3	0
Darrell Porter, c	.267	5	15	1	4	1	0	0	0	5	4	0
Ozzie Smith, ss	.435	6	23	4	10	1	1	1	3	3	1	1
John Tudor, p	.000	2	4	1	0	0	0	0	0	1	1	0
Andy Van Slyke, of	.091	5	11	1	1	0	0	0	1	2	1	0
Todd Worrell, p	.000	4	0	0	0	0	0	0	0	0	0	0
TOTAL	.279		201	29	56	10	1	3	26	30	34	6

PITCHER	W	L	ERA	G	GS	CG	SV	SHO	IP	H	ER	BB	SO
Joaquin Andujar	0	1	6.97	2	2	0	0	0	10.1	14	8	4	9
Bill Campbell	0	0	0.00	3	0	0	0	0	2.1	3	0	0	2
Danny Cox	1	0	3.00	1	1	0	0	0	6.0	4	2	5	4
Ken Dayley	0	0	0.00	5	0	0	2	0	6.0	2	0	1	3
Bob Forsch	0	0	5.40	1	1	0	0	0	3.1	3	2	2	0
Rick Horton	0	0	9.00	3	0	0	0	0	3.0	4	3	2	1
Jeff Lahti	1	0	0.00	2	0	0	0	0	2.0	2	0	0	1
John Tudor	1	1	2.84	2	2	0	0	0	12.2	10	4	3	8
Todd Worrell	1	0	1.42	4	0	0	0	0	6.1	4	1	2	3
TOTAL	4	2	3.46	23	6	0	2	0	52.0	46	20	19	31

LA (W)

PLAYER/POS	AVG	G	AB	R	H	2B	3B	HR	RB	BB	SO	SB
Dave Anderson, ss-3,3b-1	.000	4	5	1	0	0	0	0	0	3	1	0
Bob Bailor, 3b	.000	2	1	0	0	0	0	0	0	0	0	0
Greg Brock, 1b-4	.083	5	12	2	1	0	0	1	2	2	2	0
Enos Cabell, 1b-3	.077	5	13	1	1	0	0	0	0	0	3	0
Bobby Castillo, p	.000	1	2	0	0	0	0	0	0	0	1	0
Carlos Diaz, p	.000	2	0	0	0	0	0	0	0	0	0	0
Mariano Duncan, ss	.222	5	18	2	4	2	1	0	1	1	3	1
Pedro Guerrero, of	.250	6	20	2	5	1	0	0	4	5	2	2
Orel Hershiser, p	.286	2	7	1	2	0	0	0	1	0	2	0
Rick Honeycutt, p	.000	2	0	0	0	0	0	0	0	0	0	0
Ken Howell, p	.000	1	0	0	0	0	0	0	0	0	0	0
Jay Johnstone, ph	.000	1	1	0	0	0	0	0	0	0	0	0
Ken Landreaux, of	.389	5	18	4	7	3	0	0	2	1	1	0
Bill Madlock, 3b	.333	6	24	5	8	1	0	3	7	0	2	1
Candy Maldonado, of-3	.143	4	7	0	1	0	0	0	1	0	3	0
Mike Marshall, of	.217	6	23	1	5	2	0	1	3	1	3	0
Len Matuszek, 1b-1,of-1	1.000	3	1	1	1	0	0	0	0	0	0	0
Tom Niedenfuer, p	.000	3	1	0	0	0	0	0	0	0	1	0
Jerry Reuss, p	.000	1	0	0	0	0	0	0	0	0	0	0
Steve Sax, 2b	.300	6	20	1	6	3	0	0	1	1	5	0
Mike Scioscia, c	.250	6	16	2	4	0	0	0	1	4	0	0
Fernando Valenzuela, p	.200	2	5	0	1	0	0	0	0	0	0	0
Bob Welch, p	.000	1	1	0	0	0	0	0	0	0	1	0
Terry Whitfield, ph	.000	1	0	0	0	0	0	0	0	0	0	0
Steve Yeager, c	.000	1	2	0	0	0	0	0	0	1	1	0
TOTAL	.234		197	23	46	12	1	5	23	19	31	4

PITCHER	W	L	ERA	G	GS	CG	SV	SHO	IP	H	ER	BB	SO
Bobby Castillo	0	0	3.38	1	0	0	0	0	5.1	4	2	2	4
Carlos Diaz	0	0	3.00	2	0	0	0	0	3.0	5	1	1	2
Orel Hershiser	1	0	3.52	2	2	1	0	0	15.1	17	6	6	5
Rick Honeycutt	0	0	13.50	2	0	0	0	0	1.1	4	2	2	1
Ken Howell	0	0	0.00	1	0	0	0	0	2.0	0	0	0	2
Tom Niedenfuer	0	2	6.35	3	0	0	1	0	5.2	5	4	2	5
Jerry Reuss	0	1	10.80	1	1	0	0	0	1.2	5	2	1	0
F. Valenzuela	1	0	1.88	2	2	0	0	0	14.1	11	3	10	13
Bob Welch	0	1	6.75	1	1	0	0	0	2.2	5	2	6	2
TOTAL	2	4	3.86	15	6	1	1	0	51.1	56	22	30	34

GAME 1 AT LA OCT 9

				R	H	E
STL	000	000	100	1	8	1
LA	000	103	00X	4	8	0

Pitchers: TUDOR, Dayley (6), Campbell (7), Worrell (8) vs VALENZUELA, Niedenfuer (7)
Attendance: 55,270

GAME 2 AT LA OCT 10

				R	H	E
STL	001	000	001	2	8	1
LA	003	212	00X	8	13	1

Pitchers: ANDUJAR, Horton (5), Campbell (6), Dayley (7), Lahti (8) vs HERSHISER
Home Runs: Brock-LA
Attendance: 55,222

GAME 3 AT STL OCT 12

				R	H	E
LA	000	100	100	2	7	2
STL	220	000	00X	4	8	0

Pitchers: WELCH, Honeycutt (3), Diaz (5), Howell (7) vs COX, Horton (7), Worrell (7), Dayley (9)
Home Runs: Herr-STL
Attendance: 53,708

GAME 4 AT STL OCT 13

				R	H	E
LA	000	000	110	2	5	2
STL	090	110	01X	12	15	0

Pitchers: REUSS, Honeycutt (2), Castillo (2), Diaz (8) vs TUDOR, Horton (8), Campbell (9)
Home Runs: Madlock-LA
Attendance: 53,708

GAME 5 AT STL OCT 14

				R	H	E
LA	000	200	000	2	5	1
STL	200	000	001	3	5	1

Pitchers: Valenzuela, NIEDENFUER (9) vs Forsch, Dayley (4), Worrell (7), LAHTI (9)
Home Runs: Madlock-LA, Smith-STL
Attendance: 53,708

GAME 6 AT LA OCT 16

				R	H	E
STL	001	000	303	7	12	1
LA	110	020	010	5	8	0

Pitchers: Andujar, WORRELL (7), Dayley (9) vs Hershiser, NIEDENFUER (7)
Home Runs: Madlock-LA, Marshall-LA, Clark-STL
Attendance: 55,208

Were it not for the expansion of the ALCS to a best-of-seven series, the Blue Jays would have won the pennant. But after winning three of the first four games, the Jays lost their steam, and K.C. swept to their second pennant.

The pitching of Toronto ace Dave Stieb proved a key to the club's fortunes. Three times he started for the Jays. In the opener he threw eight shutout innings as the Jays won easily. In Game 4 he continued to dominate batters, though three walks in the sixth helped the Royals score a go-ahead run before Toronto pulled it out (for reliever Tom Henke) with a three-run ninth.

Had the series ended there, Stieb would have been a hero. But it didn't, and he was called upon again for Game 7—perhaps with inadequate rest. This time he faltered. After giving up single runs in the second and fourth innings, he loaded the bases in the sixth with two walks and a hit batsman. Jim Sundberg unloaded them with a wind-blown triple, later scoring himself, and the Royals were on the road to victory.

George Brett keyed Kansas City's triumph. His four hits in Game 3 (including two home runs) gave the club its first victory, and his RBI ground out in Game 5 and go-ahead homer in Game 6 proved game-winners in contests the Royals had to win.

Kansas City Royals (West), 4; Toronto Blue Jays (East), 3

KC (W)

PLAYER/POS	AVG	G	AB	R	H	2B	3B	HR	RB	BB	SO	SB
Steve Balboni, 1b	.120	7	25	1	3	0	0	0	1	2	8	0
Buddy Biancalana, ss	.222	7	18	2	4	1	0	0	1	1	6	0
Bud Black, p	.000	3	0	0	0	0	0	0	0	0	0	0
George Brett, 3b	.348	7	23	6	8	2	0	3	5	7	5	0
Onix Concepcion, ss	.000	4	1	0	0	0	0	0	0	0	0	0
Steve Farr, p	.000	2	0	0	0	0	0	0	0	0	0	0
Mark Gubicza, p	.000	2	0	0	0	0	0	0	0	0	0	0
Dane Iorg, ph	.500	4	2	0	1	1	0	0	0	2	0	0
Danny Jackson, p	.000	2	0	0	0	0	0	0	0	0	0	0
Lynn Jones, of	.000	5	0	0	0	0	0	0	0	0	0	0
Charlie Leibrandt, p	.000	3	0	0	0	0	0	0	0	0	0	0
Hal McRae, dh	.261	6	23	1	6	2	0	0	3	1	6	0
Darryl Motley, of	.333	2	3	1	1	0	0	0	1	1	2	0
Jorge Orta, dh-1	.000	2	5	0	0	0	0	0	0	0	1	0
Jamie Quirk, ph	.000	1	1	0	0	0	0	0	0	0	0	0
Dan Quisenberry, p	.000	4	0	0	0	0	0	0	0	0	0	0
Bret Saberhagen, p	.000	2	0	0	0	0	0	0	0	0	0	0
Pat Sheridan, of	.150	7	20	4	3	0	0	2	3	2	3	0
Lonnie Smith, of	.250	7	28	2	7	2	0	0	1	3	6	1
Jim Sundberg, c	.167	7	24	3	4	1	1	1	6	1	7	0
Frank White, 2b	.200	7	25	1	5	0	0	0	3	1	2	0
Willie Wilson, of	.310	7	29	5	9	0	0	1	2	1	5	1
TOTAL	.225		227	26	51	9	1	7	26	22	51	2

PITCHER	W	L	ERA	G	GS	CG	SV	SHO	IP	H	ER	BB	SO
Bud Black	0	0	1.69	3	1	0	0	0	10.2	11	2	4	8
Steve Farr	1	0	1.42	2	0	0	0	0	6.1	4	1	1	3
Mark Gubicza	1	0	3.24	2	1	0	0	0	8.1	4	3	4	4
Danny Jackson	1	0	0.00	2	1	1	0	1	10.0	10	0	1	7
Charlie Leibrandt	1	2	5.28	3	2	0	0	0	15.1	17	9	4	6
Dan Quisenberry	0	1	3.86	4	0	0	1	0	4.2	7	2	0	3
Bret Saberhagen	0	0	6.14	2	2	0	0	0	7.1	12	5	2	6
TOTAL	4	3	3.16	18	7	1	1	1	62.2	65	22	16	37

TOR (E)

PLAYER/POS	AVG	G	AB	R	H	2B	3B	HR	RB	BB	SO	SB
Jim Acker, p	.000	2	0	0	0	0	0	0	0	0	0	0
Doyle Alexander, p	.000	2	0	0	0	0	0	0	0	0	0	0
Jesse Barfield, of	.280	7	25	3	7	1	0	1	4	3	7	1
George Bell, of	.321	7	28	4	9	3	0	0	1	0	4	0
Jeff Burroughs, ph	.000	1	1	0	0	0	0	0	0	0	0	0
Jim Clancy, p	.000	1	0	0	0	0	0	0	0	0	0	0
Tony Fernandez, ss	.333	7	24	2	8	2	0	0	2	1	2	0
Cecil Fielder, ph	.333	3	3	0	1	1	0	0	0	0	1	0
Damaso Garcia, 2b	.233	7	30	4	7	4	0	0	1	3	3	0
Jeff Hearron, c	.000	2	0	0	0	0	0	0	0	0	0	0
Tom Henke, p	.000	3	0	0	0	0	0	0	0	0	0	0
Garth Iorg, 3b	.133	6	15	1	2	0	0	0	0	1	3	0
Cliff Johnson, dh	.368	7	19	1	7	2	0	0	2	1	4	0
Jimmy Key, p	.000	2	0	0	0	0	0	0	0	0	0	0
Dennis Lamp, p	.000	3	0	0	0	0	0	0	0	0	0	0
Gary Lavelle, p	.000	1	0	0	0	0	0	0	0	0	0	0
Manny Lee, 2b	.000	1	0	0	0	0	0	0	0	0	0	0
Lloyd Moseby, of	.226	7	31	5	7	1	0	0	4	2	3	1
Rance Mulliniks, 3b	.364	5	11	1	4	1	0	1	3	2	2	0
Al Oliver, dh	.375	5	8	0	3	1	0	0	3	0	0	0
Dave Stieb, p	.000	3	0	0	0	0	0	0	0	0	0	0
Lou Thornton, pr	.000	2	0	1	0	0	0	0	0	0	0	0
Willie Upshaw, 1b	.231	7	26	2	6	2	0	0	1	1	4	0
Ernie Whitt, c	.190	7	21	1	4	1	0	0	2	2	4	0
TOTAL	.269		242	25	65	19	0	2	23	16	37	2

PITCHER	W	L	ERA	G	GS	CG	SV	SHO	IP	H	ER	BB	SO
Jim Acker	0	0	0.00	2	0	0	0	0	6.0	2	0	0	5
Doyle Alexander	0	1	8.71	2	2	0	0	0	10.1	14	10	3	9
Jim Clancy	0	1	9.00	1	0	0	0	0	1.0	2	1	1	0
Tom Henke	2	0	4.26	3	0	0	0	0	6.1	5	3	4	4
Jimmy Key	0	1	5.19	2	2	0	0	0	8.2	15	5	2	5
Dennis Lamp	0	0	0.00	3	0	0	0	0	9.1	2	0	1	10
Gary Lavelle	0	0	–	1	0	0	0	0	0.0	0	0	1	0
Dave Stieb	1	1	3.10	3	3	0	0	0	20.1	11	7	10	18
TOTAL	3	4	3.77	17	7	0	0	0	62.0	51	26	22	51

GAME 1 AT TOR OCT 8

		R	H	E
KC	000 000 001	1	5	1
TOR	023 100 00X	6	11	0

Pitchers: LEIBRANDT, Farr (3), Gubicza (5), Jackson (8) vs STIEB, Henke (9)
Attendance: 39,115

GAME 2 AT TOR OCT 9

		R	H	E
KC	002 100 001 1	5	10	3
TOR	000 102 010 2	6	10	0

Pitchers: Black, QUISENBERRY (8) vs Key, Lamp (4), Lavelle (8), HENKE (8)
Home Runs: Wilson-KC, Sheridan-KC
Attendance: 34,029

GAME 3 AT KC OCT 11

		R	H	E
TOR	000 050 000	5	13	1
KC	100 112 01X	6	10	1

Pitchers: Alexander, Lamp (6), CLANCY (8) vs Saberhagen, Black (5), FARR (5)
Home Runs: Brett-KC (2), Barfield-TOR, Mulliniks-TOR, Sundberg-KC
Attendance: 40,224

GAME 4 AT KC OCT 12

		R	H	E
TOR	000 000 003	3	7	0
KC	000 001 000	1	2	0

Pitchers: Stieb, HENKE (7) vs LEIBRANDT, Quisenberry (9)
Attendance: 41,112

GAME 5 AT KC OCT 13

		R	H	E
TOR	000 000 000	0	8	0
KC	110 000 00X	2	8	0

Pitchers: KEY, Acker (6) vs JACKSON
Attendance: 40,046

GAME 6 AT TOR OCT 15

		R	H	E
KC	101 012 000	5	8	1
TOR	101 001 000	3	8	2

Pitchers: GUBICZA, Black (6), Quisenberry (9) vs ALEXANDER, Lamp (6)
Home Runs: Brett-KC
Attendance: 37,557

GAME 7 AT TOR OCT 16

		R	H	E
KC	010 104 000	6	8	0
TOR	000 010 001	2	8	1

Pitchers: Saberhagen, LEIBRANDT (4), Quisenberry (9) vs STIEB, Acker (6)
Home Runs: Sheridan-KC
Attendance: 32,084

The underdog Royals surprised St. Louis with superior hitting and pitching and even outstole the speedy Cards, six bases to two. Still, had an umpire not muffed a call at first base in Game 6, St. Louis might have emerged from the game wearing the world crown.

The Cardinals broke a 1–1 tie in the fourth inning of the opener with back-to-back doubles off Danny Jackson and held on behind the strong pitching of John Tudor and reliever Todd Worrell for a 3–1 win. In Game 2, except for the fourth inning, when he yielded a single and two doubles (for two runs) before retiring his first batter, Cardinals starter Danny Cox held the Royals in check. Royals starter Charlie Leibrandt hurled even more effectively, holding St. Louis to two hits—until the ninth inning, when four hits (three of them doubles) produced four runs and a second Card victory.

Kansas City finally demonstrated its punch in Game 3. Frank White hit a two-run homer in the fifth, and the Royals scored four more times to win behind the six-hit hurling of sophomore sensation Bret Saberhagen. The next day, though, Royals bats died again against John Tudor, who shut them out on five hits. Three Royals pitchers yielded only six hits, but two were home runs to Tito Landrum and Willie McGee, and one was a triple to Terry Pendleton, who scored on a squeeze play.

Down three games to one, the Royals hammered 11 hits in Game 5 for six runs to win behind Danny Jackson's five-hitter. Seven hits in the first eight innings of Game 6, though, scored no runs against Cardinals starter Danny Cox and reliever Ken Dayley. But in the last of the ninth, with the Cards ahead, 1–0, and Todd Worrell now pitching, Royals pinch hitter Jorge Orta was ruled safe at first on what the cameras showed clearly as an out. This miscall, followed by a pop foul that first baseman Jack Clark should have caught but didn't, opened the door to disintegration by St. Louis. A single and passed ball put Royals at second and third, and, after an intentional walk to set up the double play, pinch hitter Dane Iorg singled home the tying and winning runs for the Royals.

The Cardinals threw seven pitchers at Kansas City in the finale in a vain attempt to halt the Royals' 14-hit, 11-run attack, while Bret Saberhagen stopped the Cards cold on five hits to bring the Royals their first world title.

Kansas City Royals (AL), 4; St. Louis Cardinals (NL), 3

KC (A)

PLAYER/POS	AVG	G	AB	R	H	2B	3B	HR	RB	BB	SO	SB
Steve Balboni, 1b	.320	7	25	2	8	0	0	0	3	5	4	0
Joe Beckwith, p	.000	1	0	0	0	0	0	0	0	0	0	0
Buddy Biancalana, ss	.278	7	18	2	5	0	0	0	2	5	4	0
Bud Black, p	.000	2	1	0	0	0	0	0	0	0	1	0
George Brett, 3b	.370	7	27	5	10	1	0	0	1	4	7	1
Onix Concepcion, ss-2	.000	3	0	1	0	0	0	0	0	0	0	0
Dane Iorg, ph	.500	2	2	0	1	0	0	0	2	0	0	0
Danny Jackson, p	.000	2	6	0	0	0	0	0	0	0	5	0
Lynn Jones, of-4	.667	6	3	0	2	1	1	0	0	0	0	0
Charlie Leibrandt, p	.000	2	4	0	0	0	0	0	0	0	2	0
Hal McRae, ph	.000	3	1	0	0	0	0	0	0	1	0	0
Darryl Motley, of-4	.364	5	11	1	4	0	0	1	3	0	1	0
Jorge Orta, ph	.333	3	3	0	1	0	0	0	0	0	0	0
Greg Pryor, 3b	.000	1	0	0	0	0	0	0	0	0	0	0
Dan Quisenberry, p	.000	4	0	0	0	0	0	0	0	0	0	0
Bret Saberhagen, p	.000	2	7	1	0	0	0	0	0	0	4	0
Pat Sheridan, of-4	.222	5	18	0	4	2	0	0	1	0	7	0
Lonnie Smith, of	.333	7	27	4	9	3	0	0	4	3	8	2
Jim Sundberg, c	.250	7	24	6	6	2	0	0	1	6	4	0
John Wathan, ph	.000	2	1	0	0	0	0	0	0	0	1	0
Frank White, 2b	.250	7	28	4	7	3	0	1	6	3	4	1
Willie Wilson, of	.367	7	30	2	11	0	1	0	3	1	4	3
TOTAL	.288		236	28	68	12	2	2	26	28	56	7

PITCHER	W	L	ERA	G	GS	CG	SV	SHO	IP	H	ER	BB	SO
Joe Beckwith	0	0	0.00	1	0	0	0	0	2.0	1	0	0	3
Bud Black	0	1	5.06	2	1	0	0	0	5.1	4	3	5	4
Danny Jackson	1	1	1.69	2	2	1	0	0	16.0	9	3	5	12
Charlie Leibrandt	0	1	2.76	2	2	0	0	0	16.1	10	5	4	10
Dan Quisenberry	1	0	2.08	4	0	0	0	0	4.1	5	1	3	3
Bret Saberhagen	2	0	0.50	2	2	2	0	1	18.0	11	1	1	10
TOTAL	4	3	1.89	13	7	3	0	1	62.0	40	13	18	42

STL (N)

PLAYER/POS	AVG	G	AB	R	H	2B	3B	HR	RB	BB	SO	SB
Joaquin Andujar, p	.000	2	1	0	0	0	0	0	0	0	1	0
Steve Braun, ph	.000	1	1	0	0	0	0	0	0	0	0	0
Bill Campbell, p	.000	3	0	0	0	0	0	0	0	0	0	0
Cesar Cedeno, of	.133	5	15	1	2	1	0	0	1	2	2	0
Jack Clark, 1b	.240	7	25	1	6	2	0	0	4	3	9	0
Danny Cox, p	.000	2	4	0	0	0	0	0	0	0	2	0
Ken Dayley, p	.000	4	0	0	0	0	0	0	0	0	0	0
Ivan DeJesus, ph	.000	1	1	0	0	0	0	0	0	0	0	0
Bob Forsch, p	.000	2	0	0	0	0	0	0	0	0	0	0
Brian Harper, ph	.250	4	4	0	1	0	0	0	1	0	1	0
Tommy Herr, 2b	.154	7	26	2	4	2	0	0	0	2	2	0
Rick Horton, p	.000	3	1	0	0	0	0	0	0	0	1	0
Mike Jorgensen, of-1	.000	2	3	0	0	0	0	0	0	0	0	0
Jeff Lahti, p	.000	3	0	0	0	0	0	0	0	0	0	0
Tito Landrum, of	.360	7	25	3	9	2	0	1	1	0	2	0
Tom Lawless, pr	.000	1	0	0	0	0	0	0	0	0	0	0
Willie McGee, of	.259	7	27	2	7	2	0	1	2	1	3	1
Tom Nieto, c	.000	2	5	0	0	0	0	0	1	1	2	0
Terry Pendleton, 3b	.261	7	23	3	6	1	1	0	3	3	2	0
Darrell Porter, c	.133	5	15	0	2	0	0	0	0	2	5	0
Ozzie Smith, ss	.087	7	23	1	2	0	0	0	0	4	0	1
John Tudor, p	.000	3	5	0	0	0	0	0	0	0	4	0
Andy Van Slyke, of	.091	6	11	0	1	0	0	0	0	0	5	0
Todd Worrell, p	.000	3	1	0	0	0	0	0	0	0	1	0
TOTAL	.185		216	13	40	10	1	2	13	18	42	2

PITCHER	W	L	ERA	G	GS	CG	SV	SHO	IP	H	ER	BB	SO
Joaquin Andujar	0	1	9.00	2	1	0	0	0	4.0	10	4	4	3
Bill Campbell	0	0	2.25	3	0	0	0	0	4.0	4	1	2	5
Danny Cox	0	0	1.29	2	2	0	0	0	14.0	14	2	4	13
Ken Dayley	1	0	0.00	4	0	0	0	0	6.0	1	0	3	5
Bob Forsch	0	1	12.00	2	1	0	0	0	3.0	6	4	1	3
Rick Horton	0	0	6.75	3	0	0	0	0	4.0	4	3	5	5
Jeff Lahti	0	0	12.27	3	0	0	1	0	3.2	10	5	0	2
John Tudor	2	1	3.00	3	3	1	0	1	18.0	15	6	7	14
Todd Worrell	0	1	3.86	3	0	0	1	0	4.2	4	2	2	6
TOTAL	3	4	3.96	25	7	1	2	1	61.1	68	27	28	56

GAME 1 AT KC OCT 19

				R	H	E
STL	001	100	001	3	7	1
KC	010	000	000	1	8	0

Pitchers: TUDOR, Worrell (7) vs JACKSON, Quisenberry (8), Black (9)
Attendance: 41,650

GAME 2 AT KC OCT 20

				R	H	E
STL	000	000	004	4	6	0
KC	000	200	000	2	9	0

Pitchers: Cox, DAYLEY (8), Lahti (9) vs LEIBRANDT, Quisenberry (9)
Attendance: 41,656

GAME 3 AT STL OCT 22

				R	H	E
KC	000	220	200	6	11	0
STL	000	001	000	1	6	0

Pitchers: SABERHAGEN vs ANDUJAR, Campbell (5), Horton (6), Dayley (8)
Home Runs: White-KC
Attendance: 53,634

GAME 4 AT STL OCT 23

				R	H	E
KC	000	000	000	0	5	1
STL	011	010	00X	3	6	0

Pitchers: BLACK, Beckwith (6), Quisenberry (8) vs TUDOR
Home Runs: Landrum-STL, McGee-STL
Attendance: 53,634

GAME 5 AT STL OCT 24

				R	H	E
KC	130	000	011	6	11	2
STL	100	000	000	1	5	1

Pitchers: JACKSON vs FORSCH, Horton (2), Campbell (4), Worrell (6), Lahti (8)
Attendance: 53,634

GAME 6 AT KC OCT 26

				R	H	E
STL	000	000	010	1	5	0
KC	000	000	002	2	10	0

Pitchers: Cox, Dayley (8), WORRELL (9) vs Leibrandt, QUISENBERRY (8)
Attendance: 41,628

GAME 7 AT KC OCT 27

				R	H	E
STL	000	000	000	0	5	0
KC	023	060	00X	11	14	0

Pitchers: TUDOR, Campbell (3), Lahti (5), Horton (5), Andujar (5), Forsch (5), Dayley (7) vs SABERHAGEN
Home Runs: Motley-KC
Attendance: 41,658

Houston pitcher Mike Scott overwhelmed the Mets in Games 1 and 4, and would have faced them a third time in Game 7 if the Astros had won Game 6. They tried, scoring three runs in the first as Bob Knepper shut out the Mets on two hits through eight innings of the sixth game. But in the top of the ninth New York tied the game and held on into extra innings. No one scored again until the Mets put a run across in the 14th. Billy Hatcher tied it up again later in the 14th with a home run just inside the left field foul pole. Two innings later the Mets (aided by a pair of wild pitches) scored three runs. Again the Astros came back, scoring twice, but fell just short as Jesse Orosco struck out Kevin Bass with two men on base to win his third game of the series and give New York the pennant.

In the series opener Houston scored just one run off Dwight Gooden, but it was enough, as Mike Scott, fanning 14, shut out the Mets on five hits. New York came back with five runs in Game 2 to win behind Bob Ojeda, who gave up 10 hits but only one run. In Game 3 the Astros held the lead into the last of the sixth, when New York tied the score with four runs. Houston retook the lead in the seventh with a run, but Len Dykstra won it for New York with a two-run homer in the bottom of the ninth.

The Astros' win in Game 4 evened the series. Houston had scored three runs by the time Scott (on his way to a three-hitter) gave the Mets their only run in the eighth. Houston's Nolan Ryan gave up only two hits in the first nine innings of Game 5 (one of them Darryl Strawberry's game-tying solo homer in the fifth), striking out 12. But New York's Gooden also yielded only one run in 10 innings of work. Charlie Kerfeld shut out the Mets in the 10th and 11th, and the Mets' Orosco stopped Houston in the 11th and 12th. But in the last of the 12th, Gary Carter singled home a run off Kerfeld to end the game (and his series-long batting slump)—setting the stage for the 16-inning marathon the next day.

New York Mets (East), 4; Houston Astros (West), 2

NY (E)

PLAYER/POS	AVG	G	AB	R	H	2B	3B	HR	RB	BB	SO	SB
Rick Aguilera, p	.000	2	0	0	0	0	0	0	0	0	0	0
Wally Backman, 2b	.238	6	21	5	5	0	0	0	2	2	4	1
Gary Carter, c	.148	6	27	1	4	1	0	0	2	2	5	0
Ron Darling, p	.000	1	1	0	0	0	0	0	0	0	0	0
Lenny Dykstra, of	.304	6	23	3	7	1	1	1	3	2	4	1
Kevin Elster, ss	.000	4	3	0	0	0	0	0	0	0	1	0
Sid Fernandez, p	.000	1	1	0	0	0	0	0	0	0	0	0
Dwight Gooden, p	.000	2	5	0	0	0	0	0	0	0	2	0
Danny Heep, of-1	.250	5	4	0	1	0	0	0	1	0	2	0
Keith Hernandez, 1b	.269	6	26	3	7	1	1	0	3	3	6	0
Howard Johnson, ph	.000	2	2	0	0	0	0	0	0	0	0	0
Ray Knight, 3b	.167	6	24	1	4	0	0	0	2	1	5	0
Lee Mazzilli, ph	.200	5	5	0	1	0	0	0	0	0	3	0
Roger McDowell, p	.000	2	1	0	0	0	0	0	0	0	0	0
Kevin Mitchell, of	.250	2	8	1	2	0	0	0	0	0	1	0
Bob Ojeda, p	.000	2	5	1	0	0	0	0	0	0	2	0
Jesse Orosco, p	.000	4	0	0	0	0	0	0	0	0	0	0
Rafael Santana, ss	.176	6	17	0	3	0	0	0	0	0	3	0
Doug Sisk, p	.000	1	0	0	0	0	0	0	0	0	0	0
Darryl Strawberry, of	.227	6	22	4	5	1	0	2	5	3	12	1
Tim Teufel, 2b	.167	2	6	0	1	0	0	0	0	0	0	0
Mookie Wilson, of	.115	6	26	2	3	0	0	0	1	1	7	1
TOTAL	.189		227	21	43	4	2	3	19	14	57	4

PITCHER	W	L	ERA	G	GS	CG	SV	SHO	IP	H	ER	BB	SO
Rick Aguilera	0	0	0.00	2	0	0	0	0	5.0	2	0	2	2
Ron Darling	0	0	7.20	1	1	0	0	0	5.0	6	4	2	5
Sid Fernandez	0	1	4.50	1	1	0	0	0	6.0	3	3	1	5
Dwight Gooden	0	1	1.06	2	2	0	0	0	17.0	16	2	5	9
Roger McDowell	0	0	0.00	2	0	0	0	0	7.0	1	0	0	3
Bob Ojeda	1	0	2.57	2	2	1	0	0	14.0	15	4	4	6
Jesse Orosco	3	0	3.38	4	0	0	0	0	8.0	5	3	2	10
Doug Sisk	0	0	0.00	1	0	0	0	0	1.0	1	0	1	0
TOTAL	4	2	2.29	15	6	1	0	0	63.0	49	16	17	40

HOU (W)

PLAYER/POS	AVG	G	AB	R	H	2B	3B	HR	RB	BB	SO	SB
Larry Andersen, p	.000	2	0	0	0	0	0	0	0	0	0	0
Alan Ashby, c	.130	6	23	2	3	1	0	1	2	2	1	0
Kevin Bass, of	.292	6	24	0	7	2	0	0	0	4	4	2
Jeff Calhoun, p	.000	1	0	0	0	0	0	0	0	0	0	0
Jose Cruz, of	.192	6	26	0	5	0	0	0	2	1	8	0
Glenn Davis, 1b	.269	6	26	3	7	1	0	1	3	1	3	0
Bill Doran, 2b	.222	6	27	3	6	0	0	1	3	2	2	2
Phil Garner, 3b	.222	3	9	1	2	1	0	0	2	1	2	0
Billy Hatcher, of	.280	6	25	4	7	0	0	1	2	3	2	3
Charlie Kerfeld, p	.000	3	0	0	0	0	0	0	0	0	0	0
Bob Knepper, p	.000	2	5	0	0	0	0	0	0	1	2	0
Davey Lopes, ph	.000	3	2	1	0	0	0	0	0	1	0	0
Aurelio Lopez, p	.000	2	0	0	0	0	0	0	0	0	0	0
Jim Pankovits, ph	.000	2	2	0	0	0	0	0	0	0	1	0
Terry Puhl, ph	.667	3	3	0	2	0	0	0	0	0	0	1
Craig Reynolds, ss	.333	4	12	1	4	0	0	0	0	1	3	0
Nolan Ryan, p	.000	2	4	0	0	0	0	0	0	0	2	0
Mike Scott, p	.000	2	6	0	0	0	0	0	0	0	5	0
Dave Smith, p	.000	2	0	0	0	0	0	0	0	0	0	0
Dickie Thon, ss	.250	6	12	1	3	0	0	1	1	0	1	0
Denny Walling, 3b	.158	5	19	1	3	1	0	0	2	0	4	0
TOTAL	.218		225	17	49	6	0	5	17	17	40	8

PITCHER	W	L	ERA	G	GS	CG	SV	SHO	IP	H	ER	BB	SO
Larry Andersen	0	0	0.00	2	0	0	0	0	5.0	1	0	2	3
Jeff Calhoun	0	0	9.00	1	0	0	0	0	1.0	1	1	1	0
Charlie Kerfeld	0	1	2.25	3	0	0	0	0	4.0	2	1	1	4
Bob Knepper	0	0	3.52	2	2	0	0	0	15.1	13	6	1	9
Aurelio Lopez	0	1	8.10	2	0	0	0	0	3.1	7	3	4	3
Nolan Ryan	0	1	3.86	2	2	0	0	0	14.0	9	6	1	17
Mike Scott	2	0	0.50	2	2	2	0	1	18.0	8	1	1	19
Dave Smith	0	1	9.00	2	0	0	0	0	2.0	2	2	3	2
TOTAL	2	4	2.87	16	6	2	0	1	62.2	43	20	14	57

GAME 1 AT HOU OCT 8

		R	H	E
NY	000 000 000	0	5	0
HOU	010 000 00X	1	7	1

Pitchers: GOODEN, Orosco (8) vs SCOTT
Home Runs: Davis-HOU
Attendance: 44,131

GAME 2 AT HOU OCT 9

		R	H	E
NY	000 230 000	5	10	0
HOU	000 000 100	1	10	2

Pitchers: OJEDA vs RYAN, Andersen (6), Lopez (8), Kerfeld (9)
Attendance: 44,391

GAME 3 AT NY OCT 11

		R	H	E
HOU	220 000 100	5	8	1
NY	000 004 002	6	10	1

Pitchers: Knepper, Kerfeld (8), SMITH (9) vs Darling, Aguilera (6), OROSCO (8)
Home Runs: Doran-HOU, Strawberry-NY, Dykstra-NY
Attendance: 55,052

GAME 4 AT NY OCT 12

		R	H	E
HOU	020 010 000	3	4	1
NY	000 000 010	1	3	0

Pitchers: SCOTT vs FERNANDEZ, McDowell (7), Sisk (9)
Home Runs: Ashby-HOU, Thon-HOU
Attendance: 55,038

GAME 5 AT NY OCT 14

		R	H	E
HOU	000 010 000 000	1	9	1
NY	000 010 000 001	2	4	0

Pitchers: Ryan, KERFELD (10) vs Gooden, OROSCO (11)
Home Runs: Strawberry-NY
Attendance: 54,986

GAME 6 AT HOU OCT 15

		R	H	E
NY	000 000 003 000 010 3	7	11	0
HOU	300 000 000 000 010 2	6	11	1

Pitchers: Ojeda, Aguilera (6), McDowell (9), OROSCO (14) vs Knepper, Smith (9), Andersen (11), LOPEZ (14), Calhoun (16)
Home Runs: Hatcher-HOU
Attendance: 45,718

For the second time in the two years of the expanded ALCS, a club that would have been eliminated in a five-game series came back to take the pennant in seven games. The first two games were one-sided. California scored five early runs off Roger Clemens and breezed to an easy 8–1 win in the opener. Boston retaliated in Game 2 with nine runs, breaking the game open with six unanswered runs in the seventh and eighth innings.

Game 3 was close until the Angels homered twice for three runs with two out in the seventh to break a 1–1 tie. In Game 4, the Angels were handed a tie in the last of the ninth when Boston reliever Calvin Schiraldi hit a batter with the bases loaded and won in the 11th on Bobby Grich's RBI single.

The Red Sox, down three games to one, were on the brink of elimination in Game Five, with two outs in the ninth, when Dave Henderson, after fouling off one third-strike pitch, hit the next for a two-run homer that gave Boston a one-run lead. The Angels tied the game in the last of the ninth, but Henderson's sacrifice fly in the 11th put the Sox ahead for good.

Boston needed two more wins and got them with surprising ease, 10–4 and 8–1, as Oil Can Boyd and Clemens redeemed their earlier losses.

Boston Red Sox (East), 4; California Angels (West), 3

BOS (E)

PLAYER/POS	AVG	G	AB	R	H	2B	3B	HR	RB	BB	SO	SB
Tony Armas, of	.125	5	16	1	2	1	0	0	0	0	2	0
Marty Barrett, 2b	.367	7	30	4	11	2	0	0	5	2	2	0
Don Baylor, dh	.346	7	26	6	9	3	0	1	2	4	5	0
Wade Boggs, 3b	.233	7	30	3	7	1	1	0	2	4	1	0
Oil Can Boyd, p	.000	2	0	0	0	0	0	0	0	0	0	0
Bill Buckner, 1b	.214	7	28	3	6	1	0	0	3	0	2	0
Roger Clemens, p	.000	3	0	0	0	0	0	0	0	0	0	0
Steve Crawford, p	.000	1	0	0	0	0	0	0	0	0	0	0
Dwight Evans, of	.214	7	28	2	6	1	0	1	4	3	3	0
Rich Gedman, c	.357	7	28	4	10	1	0	1	6	0	4	0
Mike Greenwell, ph	.500	2	2	0	1	0	0	0	0	0	0	0
Dave Henderson, of	.111	5	9	3	1	0	0	1	4	2	2	0
Bruce Hurst, p	.000	2	0	0	0	0	0	0	0	0	0	0
Spike Owen, ss	.429	7	21	5	9	0	1	0	3	2	2	1
Jim Rice, of	.161	7	31	8	5	1	0	2	6	1	8	0
Ed Romero, ss	.000	1	2	0	0	0	0	0	0	0	0	0
Joe Sambito, p	.000	3	0	0	0	0	0	0	0	0	0	0
Calvin Schiraldi, p	.000	4	0	0	0	0	0	0	0	0	0	0
Bob Stanley, p	.000	3	0	0	0	0	0	0	0	0	0	0
Dave Stapleton, 1b	.667	4	3	2	2	0	0	0	0	1	0	0
TOTAL	.272		254	41	69	11	2	6	35	19	31	1

PITCHER	W	L	ERA	G	GS	CG	SV	SHO	IP	H	ER	BB	SO
Oil Can Boyd	1	1	4.61	2	2	0	0	0	13.2	17	7	3	8
Roger Clemens	1	1	4.37	3	3	0	0	0	22.2	22	11	7	17
Steve Crawford	1	0	0.00	1	0	0	0	0	1.2	1	0	2	1
Bruce Hurst	1	0	2.40	2	2	1	0	0	15.0	18	4	1	8
Joe Sambito	0	0	0.00	3	0	0	0	0	0.2	1	0	1	0
Calvin Schiraldi	0	1	1.50	4	0	0	1	0	6.0	5	1	3	9
Bob Stanley	0	0	4.76	3	0	0	0	0	5.2	7	3	3	1
TOTAL	4	3	3.58	18	7	1	1	0	65.1	71	26	20	44

CAL (W)

PLAYER/POS	AVG	G	AB	R	H	2B	3B	HR	RB	BB	SO	SB
Bob Boone, c	.455	7	22	4	10	0	0	1	2	1	3	0
Rick Burleson, 2b-2,dh-1	.273	4	11	0	3	0	0	0	0	0	0	0
John Candelaria, p	.000	2	0	0	0	0	0	0	0	0	0	0
Doug Corbett, p	.000	3	0	0	0	0	0	0	0	0	0	0
Doug DeCinces, 3b	.281	7	32	2	9	3	0	1	3	0	2	0
Brian Downing, of	.222	7	27	2	6	0	0	1	7	4	5	0
Chuck Finley, p	.000	3	0	0	0	0	0	0	0	0	0	0
Bobby Grich, 2b-3,1b-3	.208	6	24	1	5	0	0	1	3	0	8	0
George Hendrick, of-2,1b-1	.083	3	12	0	1	0	0	0	0	0	2	0
Jack Howell, ph	.000	2	1	0	0	0	0	0	0	1	1	0
Reggie Jackson, dh	.192	6	26	2	5	2	0	0	2	2	7	0
Ruppert Jones, of-5	.176	6	17	4	3	1	0	0	2	5	2	0
Wally Joyner, 1b	.455	3	11	3	5	2	0	1	2	2	0	0
Gary Lucas, p	.000	4	0	0	0	0	0	0	0	0	0	0
Kirk McCaskill, p	.000	2	0	0	0	0	0	0	0	0	0	0
Donnie Moore, p	.000	3	0	0	0	0	0	0	0	0	0	0
Jerry Narron, c-3	.500	4	2	1	1	0	0	0	0	1	1	0
Gary Pettis, of	.346	7	26	4	9	1	0	1	4	3	5	0
Vern Ruhle, p	.000	1	0	0	0	0	0	0	0	0	0	0
Dick Schofield, ss	.300	7	30	4	9	1	0	1	2	1	5	1
Don Sutton, p	.000	2	0	0	0	0	0	0	0	0	0	0
Devon White, of-3	.500	4	2	2	1	0	0	0	0	0	1	0
Rob Wilfong, 2b	.308	4	13	1	4	1	0	0	2	0	2	0
Mike Witt, p	.000	2	0	0	0	0	0	0	0	0	0	0
TOTAL	.277		256	30	71	11	0	7	29	20	44	1

PITCHER	W	L	ERA	G	GS	CG	SV	SHO	IP	H	ER	BB	SO
John Candelaria	1	1	0.84	2	2	0	0	0	10.2	11	1	6	7
Doug Corbett	1	0	5.40	3	0	0	0	0	6.2	9	4	2	2
Chuck Finley	0	0	0.00	3	0	0	0	0	2.0	1	0	0	1
Gary Lucas	0	0	11.57	4	0	0	0	0	2.1	3	3	1	2
Kirk McCaskill	0	2	7.71	2	2	0	0	0	9.1	16	8	5	7
Donnie Moore	0	1	7.20	3	0	0	1	0	5.0	8	4	2	0
Vern Ruhle	0	0	13.50	1	0	0	0	0	0.2	2	1	0	0
Don Sutton	0	0	1.86	2	1	0	0	0	9.2	6	2	1	4
Mike Witt	1	0	2.55	2	2	1	0	0	17.2	13	5	2	8
TOTAL	3	4	3.94	22	7	1	1	0	64.0	69	28	19	31

GAME 1 AT BOS OCT 7

CAL	041 000 030	8	11	0
BOS	000 001 000	1	5	1

Pitchers: WITT vs CLEMENS, Sambito (8), Stanley (8)
Attendance: 32,993

GAME 2 AT BOS OCT 8

CAL	000 110 000	2	11	3
BOS	110 010 33X	9	13	2

Pitchers: McCASKILL, Lucas (8), Corbett (8) vs HURST
Home Runs: Joyner-CAL, Rice-BOS
Attendance: 32,786

GAME 3 AT CAL OCT 10

BOS	010 000 020	3	9	1
CAL	000 001 31X	5	8	0

Pitchers: BOYD, Sambito (7), Schiraldi (8) vs CANDELARIA, Moore (8)
Home Runs: Schofield-CAL, Pettis-CAL
Attendance: 64,206

GAME 4 AT CAL OCT 11

BOS	000 001 020 00	3	6	1
CAL	000 000 003 01	4	11	2

Pitchers: Clemens, SCHIRALDI (9) vs Sutton, Lucas (7), Ruhle (7), Finley (8), CORBETT (8)
Home Runs: DeCinces-CAL
Attendance: 64,223

GAME 5 AT CAL OCT 12

BOS	020 000 004 01	7	12	0
CAL	001 002 201 00	6	13	0

Pitchers: Hurst, Stanley (7), Sambito (9), CRAWFORD (9), Schiraldi (11) vs Witt, Lucas (9), MOORE (9), Finley (11)
Home Runs: Gedman-BOS, Boone-CAL, Grich-CAL, Baylor-BOS, Henderson-BOS
Attendance: 64,223

GAME 6 AT BOS OCT 14

CAL	200 000 110	4	11	1
BOS	205 010 20X	10	16	1

Pitchers: McCASKILL, Lucas (3), Corbett (4), Finley (7) vs BOYD, Stanley (8)
Home Runs: Downing-CAL
Attendance: 32,998

GAME 7 AT BOS OCT 15

CAL	000 000 010	1	6	2
BOS	030 400 10X	8	8	1

Pitchers: CANDELARIA, Sutton (4), Moore (8) vs CLEMENS, Schiraldi (8)
Home Runs: Rice-BOS, Evans-BOS
Attendance: 33,001

In their three most recent Series appearances—1946, 1967, and 1975—the Red Sox had battled to a seventh game, only to lose. This time they came within one strike of winning the crown in the sixth game—but wound up losing again in Game 7.

Boston surprised the favored Mets by taking the first two games in New York. Bruce Hurst (with relief from Calvin Schiraldi in the ninth) pitched a four-hitter. New York's Ron Darling hurled just as well but lost when a seventh-inning walk, a wild pitch, and an error by second baseman Tim Teufel moved Jim Rice around the bases with the game's only run. Game 2, close for three innings, turned into a 9–3 Boston blowout as the Sox racked New York pitching for 18 hits, including home runs by Dave Henderson and Dwight Evans.

When the Series moved to Boston, though, the Mets revived to rap Sox starter Oil Can Boyd and two relievers for 13 hits and seven runs (starting with Len Dykstra's lead-off home run in the first inning) as former Sox pitcher Bob Ojeda subdued his old teammates, giving up just one run on five hits in his seven innings of work. The next day Ron Darling redeemed his first-game loss with seven shutout innings as his teammates built him a 6–0 lead (five of the runs scoring on homers by Dykstra and a pair by Gary Carter). The game ended at 6–2, with the Series even at two wins apiece.

Boston recovered in its final home appearance, taking a 4–0 lead and holding it until Teufel spoiled Bruce Hurst's try for a second shutout by homering in the eighth inning. Hurst yielded a second run with two outs in the ninth, but struck out Len Dykstra on three pitches to seal his second win.

The ninth inning of Game 6 ended with the score tied, 3–3. Boston's Dave Henderson led off the 10th with a home run and two more Sox hits made the score, 5–3. Boston reliever Calvin Schiraldi retired the first two Mets in the last of the 10th on long flies, but then three Mets singled, driving in one run and driving out Schiraldi. Bob Stanley, his replacement, had two strikes on Mookie Wilson when a wild pitch let in the tying run, and then Wilson's grounder went through first baseman Bill Buckner's legs as the winning run bounded across the plate for the Mets.

The Red Sox nearly recovered in Game 7. Second-inning home runs by Dwight Evans and Rich Gedman, a walk, sacrifice, and single gave Boston a 3–0 lead which they held into the sixth inning. But then starter Bruce Hurst lost his touch: four hits and a walk later the score was tied. A succession of five Sox relievers tried to hold the line, but the Mets scored five runs to Boston's two in the final innings for an 8–5 triumph.

New York Mets (NL), 4; Boston Red Sox (AL), 3

NY (N)

PLAYER/POS	AVG	G	AB	R	H	2B	3B	HR	RB	BB	SO	SB
Rick Aguilera, p	.000	2	0	0	0	0	0	0	0	0	0	0
Wally Backman, 2b	.333	6	18	4	6	0	0	0	1	3	2	1
Gary Carter, c	.276	7	29	4	8	2	0	2	9	0	4	0
Ron Darling, p	.000	3	3	0	0	0	0	0	0	0	1	0
Lenny Dykstra, of	.296	7	27	4	8	0	0	2	3	2	7	0
Kevin Elster, ss	.000	1	1	0	0	0	0	0	0	0	0	0
Sid Fernandez, p	.000	3	0	0	0	0	0	0	0	0	0	0
Dwight Gooden, p	.500	2	2	1	1	0	0	0	0	0	0	0
Danny Heep, dh-2,of-1	.091	5	11	0	1	0	0	0	2	1	1	0
Keith Hernandez, 1b	.231	7	26	1	6	0	0	0	4	5	1	0
Howard Johnson, 3b-1,ss-1	.000	2	5	0	0	0	0	0	0	0	2	0
Ray Knight, 3b	.391	6	23	4	9	1	0	1	5	2	2	0
Lee Mazzilli, of-1	.400	4	5	2	2	0	0	0	0	0	0	0
Roger McDowell, p	.000	5	0	0	0	0	0	0	0	0	0	0
Kevin Mitchell, of-2,dh-1	.250	5	8	1	2	0	0	0	0	0	3	0
Bob Ojeda, p	.000	2	2	0	0	0	0	0	0	0	1	0
Jesse Orosco, p	1.000	4	1	0	1	0	0	0	1	0	0	0
Rafael Santana, ss	.250	7	20	3	5	0	0	0	2	2	5	0
Doug Sisk, p	.000	1	0	0	0	0	0	0	0	0	0	0
Darryl Strawberry, of	.208	7	24	4	5	1	0	1	1	4	6	3
Tim Teufel, 2b	.444	3	9	1	4	1	0	1	1	1	2	0
Mookie Wilson, of	.269	7	26	3	7	1	0	0	0	1	6	3
TOTAL	.271		240	32	65	6	0	7	29	21	43	7

PITCHER	W	L	ERA	G	GS	CG	SV	SHO	IP	H	ER	BB	SO
Rick Aguilera	1	0	12.00	2	0	0	0	0	3.0	8	4	1	4
Ron Darling	1	1	1.53	3	3	0	0	0	17.2	13	3	10	12
Sid Fernandez	0	0	1.35	3	0	0	0	0	6.2	6	1	1	10
Dwight Gooden	0	2	8.00	2	2	0	0	0	9.0	17	8	4	9
Roger McDowell	1	0	4.91	5	0	0	0	0	7.1	10	4	6	2
Bob Ojeda	1	0	2.08	2	2	0	0	0	13.0	13	3	5	9
Jesse Orosco	0	0	0.00	4	0	0	2	0	5.2	2	0	0	6
Doug Sisk	0	0	0.00	1	0	0	0	0	0.2	0	0	1	1
TOTAL	4	3	3.29	22	7	0	2	0	63.0	69	23	28	53

BOS (A)

PLAYER/POS	AVG	G	AB	R	H	2B	3B	HR	RB	BB	SO	SB
Tony Armas, ph	.000	1	1	0	0	0	0	0	0	0	1	0
Marty Barrett, 2b	.433	7	30	1	13	2	0	0	4	5	2	0
Don Baylor, dh-3	.182	4	11	1	2	1	0	0	1	1	3	0
Wade Boggs, 3b	.290	7	31	3	9	3	0	0	3	4	2	0
Oil Can Boyd, p	.000	1	0	0	0	0	0	0	0	0	0	0
Bill Buckner, 1b	.188	7	32	2	6	0	0	0	1	0	3	0
Roger Clemens, p	.000	2	4	1	0	0	0	0	0	0	1	0
Steve Crawford, p	.000	3	1	0	0	0	0	0	0	0	0	0
Dwight Evans, of	.308	7	26	4	8	2	0	2	9	4	3	0
Rich Gedman, c	.200	7	30	1	6	1	0	1	1	0	10	0
Mike Greenwell, ph	.000	4	3	0	0	0	0	0	0	1	2	0
Dave Henderson, of	.400	7	25	6	10	1	1	2	5	2	6	0
Bruce Hurst, p	.000	3	3	0	0	0	0	0	0	0	3	0
Al Nipper, p	.000	2	0	0	0	0	0	0	0	0	0	0
Spike Owen, ss	.300	7	20	2	6	0	0	0	2	5	6	0
Jim Rice, of	.333	7	27	6	9	1	1	0	0	6	9	0
Ed Romero, ss	.000	3	1	0	0	0	0	0	0	0	0	0
Joe Sambito, p	.000	2	0	0	0	0	0	0	0	0	0	0
Calvin Schiraldi, p	.000	3	1	0	0	0	0	0	0	0	1	0
Bob Stanley, p	.000	5	1	0	0	0	0	0	0	0	1	0
Dave Stapleton, 1b	.000	3	1	0	0	0	0	0	0	0	0	0
TOTAL	.278		248	27	69	11	2	5	26	28	53	0

PITCHER	W	L	ERA	G	GS	CG	SV	SHO	IP	H	ER	BB	SO
Oil Can Boyd	0	1	7.71	1	1	0	0	0	7.0	9	6	1	3
Roger Clemens	0	0	3.18	2	2	0	0	0	11.1	9	4	6	11
Steve Crawford	1	0	6.23	3	0	0	0	0	4.1	5	3	0	4
Bruce Hurst	2	0	1.96	3	3	1	0	0	23.0	18	5	6	17
Al Nipper	0	1	7.11	2	1	0	0	0	6.1	10	5	2	2
Joe Sambito	0	0	27.00	2	0	0	0	0	0.1	2	1	2	0
Calvin Schiraldi	0	2	13.50	3	0	0	1	0	4.0	7	6	3	2
Bob Stanley	0	0	0.00	5	0	0	1	0	6.1	5	0	1	4
TOTAL	3	4	4.31	21	7	1	2	0	62.2	65	30	21	43

GAME 1 AT NY OCT 18

		R	H	E
BOS	000 000 100	1	5	0
NY	000 000 000	0	4	1

Pitchers: HURST, Schiraldi (9) vs DARLING, McDowell (8)
Attendance: 55,076

GAME 2 AT NY OCT 19

		R	H	E
BOS	003 120 201	9	18	0
NY	002 010 000	3	8	1

Pitchers: Clemens, CRAWFORD (5), Stanley (7) vs GOODEN, Aguilera (6), Orosco (7), Fernandez (9), Sisk (9)
Home Runs: Henderson-BOS, Evans-BOS
Attendance: 55,063

GAME 3 AT BOS OCT 21

		R	H	E
NY	400 000 210	7	13	0
BOS	001 000 000	1	5	0

Pitchers: OJEDA, McDowell (8) vs BOYD, Sambito (8), Stanley (8)
Home Runs: Dykstra-NY
Attendance: 33,595

GAME 4 AT BOS OCT 22

		R	H	E
NY	000 300 210	6	12	0
BOS	000 000 020	2	7	1

Pitchers: DARLING, McDowell (7), Orosco (7) vs NIPPER, Crawford (7), Stanley (9)
Home Runs: Dykstra-NY, Carter-NY (2)
Attendance: 33,920

GAME 5 AT BOS OCT 23

		R	H	E
NY	000 000 011	2	10	1
BOS	011 020 00X	4	12	0

Pitchers: GOODEN, Fernandez (5) vs HURST
Home Runs: Teufel-NY
Attendance: 34,010

GAME 6 AT NY OCT 25

		R	H	E
BOS	110 000 100 2	5	13	3
NY	000 020 010 3	6	8	2

Pitchers: Clemens, SCHIRALDI (8), Stanley (10) vs Ojeda, McDowell (7), Orosco (8), AGUILERA (9)
Home Runs: Henderson-BOS
Attendance: 55,078

GAME 7 AT NY OCT 27

		R	H	E
BOS	030 000 020	5	9	0
NY	000 003 32X	8	10	0

Pitchers: Hurst, SCHIRALDI (7), Sambito (7), Stanley (7), Nipper (8), Crawford (8) vs Darling, Fernandez (4), McDOWELL (8), Orosco (9)
Home Runs: Evans-BOS, Gedman-BOS, Knight-NY, Strawberry-NY
Attendance: 55,032

The Giants scored four times in the fourth inning of Game 5, winning the game and taking a 3–2 series advantage. But Cardinals pitchers shut them out the rest of the series (an NLCS record 22 innings) to capture the flag.

St. Louis won the opener, 5–3, with pitcher Greg Mathews's two-run single in the sixth providing his margin of victory. The Giants came back in Game 2, supporting Dave Dravecky's two-hit shutout with home runs by Will Clark and Jeffrey Leonard. But the Cards retook the series lead in Game 3, overcoming a 4–0 deficit with two runs on Jim Lindeman's homer in the sixth and four more in the seventh (capped by Lindeman's sacrifice fly) for an eventual 6–5 win.

The Giants snapped back with a pair of wins, scoring four runs on three homers in Game 4 (including Leonard's fourth in successive games—an LCS record), and six runs in Game 5. But Dravecky and the Giants lost a heartbreaker in Game 6 when right fielder Candy Maldonado lost Tony Pena's fly in the lights for a triple. Pena scored on a sacrifice fly for the game's only run, as John Tudor and two late-inning relievers blanked the Giants. Danny Cox pitched an easier shutout in the finale as his Cardinals hammered seven San Francisco pitchers for 12 hits and six runs.

St. Louis Cardinals (East), 4; San Francisco Giants (West), 3

STL (E)

PLAYER/POS	AVG	G	AB	R	H	2B	3B	HR	RB	BB	SO	SB
Jack Clark, ph	.000	1	1	0	0	0	0	0	0	0	1	0
Vince Coleman, of	.269	7	26	3	7	1	0	0	4	4	6	1
Danny Cox, p	.333	2	6	0	2	0	0	0	1	0	2	0
Ken Dayley, p	.000	3	0	0	0	0	0	0	0	0	0	0
Dan Driessen, 1b-4	.250	5	12	1	3	2	0	0	1	1	1	0
Curt Ford, of	.333	4	9	2	3	0	0	0	0	1	1	0
Bob Forsch, p	.000	3	0	0	0	0	0	0	0	0	0	0
Tommy Herr, 2b	.222	7	27	0	6	0	0	0	3	0	1	1
Rick Horton, p	.000	1	0	0	0	0	0	0	0	0	0	0
Lance Johnson, pr	.000	1	0	1	0	0	0	0	0	0	0	1
Tom Lawless, 3b-2,of-1	.333	3	6	0	2	0	0	0	0	1	1	0
Jim Lindeman, 1b	.308	5	13	1	4	0	0	1	3	0	3	0
Joe Magrane, p	.000	1	1	0	0	0	0	0	0	0	0	0
Greg Mathews, p	1.000	2	2	0	2	0	0	0	2	0	0	0
Willie McGee, of	.308	7	26	2	8	1	1	0	2	0	5	0
John Morris, of	.000	2	3	0	0	0	0	0	0	0	0	0
Jose Oquendo, of-5,3b-1	.167	5	12	3	2	0	0	1	4	3	2	0
Tom Pagnozzi, ph	.000	1	1	0	0	0	0	0	0	0	0	0
Tony Pena, c	.381	7	21	5	8	0	1	0	0	3	4	1
Terry Pendleton, 3b	.211	6	19	3	4	0	1	0	1	0	6	0
Ozzie Smith, ss	.200	7	25	2	5	0	1	0	1	3	4	0
John Tudor, p	.000	2	4	0	0	0	0	0	0	0	4	0
Todd Worrell, p-3,of-1	.000	3	1	0	0	0	0	0	0	0	1	0
TOTAL	.260		215	23	56	4	4	2	22	16	42	4

PITCHER	W	L	ERA	G	GS	CG	SV	SHO	IP	H	ER	BB	SO
Danny Cox	1	1	2.12	2	2	2	0	1	17.0	17	4	3	11
Ken Dayley	0	0	0.00	3	0	0	2	0	4.0	1	0	2	4
Bob Forsch	1	1	12.00	3	0	0	0	0	3.0	4	4	1	3
Rick Horton	0	0	0.00	1	0	0	0	0	3.0	2	0	0	2
Joe Magrane	0	0	9.00	1	1	0	0	0	4.0	4	4	2	3
Greg Mathews	1	0	3.48	2	2	0	0	0	10.1	6	4	3	10
John Tudor	1	1	1.76	2	2	0	0	0	15.1	16	3	5	12
Todd Worrell	0	0	2.08	3	0	0	1	0	4.1	4	1	1	6
TOTAL	4	3	2.95	17	7	2	3	1	61.0	54	20	17	51

SF (W)

PLAYER/POS	AVG	G	AB	R	H	2B	3B	HR	RB	BB	SO	SB
Mike Aldrete, of-3	.100	5	10	0	1	0	0	0	1	0	2	0
Bob Brenly, c	.235	6	17	3	4	1	0	1	2	3	7	0
Will Clark, 1b	.360	7	25	3	9	2	0	1	3	3	6	1
Chili Davis, of	.150	6	20	2	3	1	0	0	0	1	4	0
Kelly Downs, p	.000	1	0	0	0	0	0	0	0	0	0	0
Dave Dravecky, p	.167	2	6	0	1	0	0	0	0	0	1	0
Scott Garrelts, p	.000	2	0	0	0	0	0	0	0	0	0	0
Atlee Hammaker, p	.000	2	3	0	0	0	0	0	0	0	2	0
Mike Krukow, p	.000	1	2	0	0	0	0	0	0	1	0	0
Mike LaCoss, p	.000	2	0	0	0	0	0	0	0	0	0	0
Craig Lefferts, p	.000	3	0	0	0	0	0	0	0	0	0	0
Jeffrey Leonard, of	.417	7	24	5	10	0	0	4	5	3	4	0
Candy Maldonado, of	.211	5	19	2	4	1	0	0	2	0	3	0
Bob Melvin, c-2	.429	3	7	0	3	0	0	0	0	1	1	0
Eddie Milner, of-4	.143	6	7	0	1	0	0	0	0	0	3	0
Kevin Mitchell, 3b	.267	7	30	2	8	1	0	1	2	0	3	1
Joe Price, p	.000	2	1	0	0	0	0	0	0	0	1	0
Rick Reuschel, p	.000	2	2	0	0	0	0	0	0	0	1	0
Don Robinson, p	.000	3	0	0	0	0	0	0	0	0	0	0
Chris Speier, 2b-1	.000	3	5	0	0	0	0	0	0	0	2	0
Harry Spilman, ph	.500	3	2	1	1	0	0	1	1	0	0	0
Rob Thompson, 2b-6	.100	7	20	4	2	0	1	1	2	5	7	2
Jose Uribe, ss	.269	7	26	1	7	1	0	0	2	0	4	1
TOTAL	.239		226	23	54	7	1	9	20	17	51	5

PITCHER	W	L	ERA	G	GS	CG	SV	SHO	IP	H	ER	BB	SO
Kelly Downs	0	0	0.00	1	0	0	0	0	1.1	1	0	0	0
Dave Dravecky	1	1	0.60	2	2	1	0	1	15.0	7	1	4	14
Scott Garrelts	0	0	6.75	2	0	0	0	0	2.2	2	2	4	4
Atlee Hammaker	0	1	7.87	2	2	0	0	0	8.0	12	7	0	7
Mike Krukow	1	0	2.00	1	1	1	0	0	9.0	9	2	1	3
Mike LaCoss	0	0	0.00	2	0	0	0	0	3.1	1	0	3	2
Craig Lefferts	0	0	0.00	3	0	0	0	0	2.0	3	0	1	0
Joe Price	1	0	0.00	2	0	0	0	0	5.2	3	0	1	7
Rick Reuschel	0	1	6.30	2	2	0	0	0	10.0	15	7	2	2
Don Robinson	0	1	9.00	3	0	0	0	0	3.0	3	3	0	3
TOTAL	3	4	3.30	20	7	2	0	1	60.0	56	22	16	42

GAME 1 AT STL OCT 6

		R	H	E
SF	100 100 010	3	7	1
STL	001 103 00X	5	10	1

Pitchers: REUSCHEL, Lefferts (7), Garrelts (8) vs MATHEWS, Worrell (8), Dayley (8)
Home Runs: Leonard-SF
Attendance: 55,331

GAME 2 AT STL OCT 7

		R	H	E
SF	020 100 020	5	10	0
STL	000 000 000	0	2	1

Pitchers: DRAVECKY vs TUDOR, Forsch (9)
Home Runs: Clark-SF, Leonard-SF
Attendance: 55,331

GAME 3 AT SF OCT 9

		R	H	E
STL	000 002 400	6	11	1
SF	031 000 001	5	7	1

Pitchers: Magrane, FORSCH (5), Worrell (7) vs Hammaker, D.ROBINSON (7), Lefferts (7), LaCoss (8)
Home Runs: Lindeman-STL, Leonard-SF, Spilman-SF
Attendance: 57,913

GAME 4 AT SF OCT 10

		R	H	E
STL	020 000 000	2	9	0
SF	000 120 01X	4	9	2

Pitchers: COX vs KRUKOW
Home Runs: Thompson-SF, Leonard-SF, Brenly-SF
Attendance: 57,997

GAME 5 AT SF OCT 11

		R	H	E
STL	101 100 000	3	7	0
SF	101 400 00X	6	7	1

Pitchers: Mathews, FORSCH (4), Horton (4), Dayley (7) vs Reuschel, PRICE (5)
Home Runs: Mitchell-SF
Attendance: 59,363

GAME 6 AT STL OCT 13

		R	H	E
SF	000 000 000	0	6	0
STL	010 000 00X	1	5	0

Pitchers: DRAVECKY, D.Robinson (7) vs TUDOR, Worrell (8), Dayley (9)
Attendance: 55,331

GAME 7 AT STL OCT 14

		R	H	E
SF	000 000 000	0	8	1
STL	040 002 00X	6	12	0

Pitchers: HAMMAKER, Price (3), Downs (3), Garrelts (5), Lefferts (6), LaCoss (6), D.Robinson (8) vs COX
Home Runs: Oquendo-STL
Attendance: 55,331

The Tigers, with the best overall won-lost record in the majors, were favored to defeat the Twins, whose record was the ninth best in baseball. Minnesota, however, held the home field advantage and the major leagues' best record at home. Tigers pitcher Doyle Alexander—he had been 9–0 since joining Detroit in mid-August—took a 5–4 lead into the last of the eighth in Game 1. But a single and double drove him out, and before the inning was over three more Twins had scored to sew up their first win. Detroit scored twice in the second inning the next day, but the Twins responded later in the inning with three runs, two on Tim Laudner's double off Tigers ace Jack Morris, and increased their lead in the fourth and fifth to seal Morris' first loss in Minnesota after 11 wins.

The Tigers won a game after the series moved to Detroit, when Pat Sheridan's two-run homer in the eighth inning of Game 3 restored a lead they had squandered in the middle innings. But that was it for Detroit, as the Twins surprised everyone by subduing the Tigers in their den. In Game 4 they took the lead for good on Greg Gagne's fourth-inning home run. And in Game 5, after initiating the scoring with four runs in the second, Minnesota pushed on to a 9–5 win and their first pennant in 22 years.

Minnesota Twins (West) 4; Detroit Tigers (East), 1

MIN (W)

PLAYER/POS	AVG	G	AB	R	H	2B	3B	HR	RB	BB	SO	SB
Keith Atherton, p	.000	1	0	0	0	0	0	0	0	0	0	0
Don Baylor, dh	.400	2	5	0	2	0	0	0	1	0	0	0
Juan Berenguer, p	.000	4	0	0	0	0	0	0	0	0	0	0
Bert Blyleven, p	.000	2	0	0	0	0	0	0	0	0	0	0
Tom Brunansky, of	.412	5	17	5	7	4	0	2	9	4	3	0
Randy Bush, dh	.250	4	12	4	3	0	1	0	2	3	2	3
Sal Butera, c	.667	1	3	0	2	0	0	0	0	0	0	0
Mark Davidson, pr	.000	1	0	0	0	0	0	0	0	0	0	0
Gary Gaetti, 3b	.300	5	20	5	6	1	0	2	5	1	3	0
Greg Gagne, ss	.278	5	18	5	5	3	0	2	3	3	4	0
Dan Gladden, of	.350	5	20	5	7	2	0	0	5	2	1	0
Kent Hrbek, 1b	.150	5	20	4	3	0	0	1	1	3	0	0
Gene Larkin, ph	1.000	1	1	0	1	1	0	0	1	0	0	0
Tim Laudner, c	.071	5	14	1	1	1	0	0	2	2	5	0
Steve Lombardozzi, 2b	.267	5	15	2	4	0	0	0	1	2	2	0
Al Newman, 2b	.000	1	2	0	0	0	0	0	0	0	0	0
Kirby Puckett, of	.208	5	24	3	5	1	0	1	3	0	5	1
Jeff Reardon, p	.000	4	0	0	0	0	0	0	0	0	0	0
Dan Schatzeder, p	.000	2	0	0	0	0	0	0	0	0	0	0
Les Straker, p	.000	1	0	0	0	0	0	0	0	0	0	0
Frank Viola, p	.000	2	0	0	0	0	0	0	0	0	0	0
TOTAL	.269		171	34	46	13	1	8	33	20	25	4

PITCHER	W	L	ERA	G	GS	CG	SV	SHO	IP	H	ER	BB	SO
Keith Atherton	0	0	0.00	1	0	0	0	0	0.1	1	0	0	0
Juan Berenguer	0	0	1.50	4	0	0	1	0	6.0	1	1	3	6
Bert Blyleven	2	0	4.05	2	2	0	0	0	13.1	12	6	3	9
Jeff Reardon	1	1	5.06	4	0	0	2	0	5.1	7	3	3	5
Dan Schatzeder	0	0	0.00	2	0	0	0	0	4.1	2	0	0	5
Les Straker	0	0	16.88	1	1	0	0	0	2.2	3	5	4	1
Frank Viola	1	0	5.25	2	2	0	0	0	12.0	14	7	5	9
TOTAL	4	1	4.50	16	5	0	3	0	44.0	40	22	18	35

DET (E)

PLAYER/POS	AVG	G	AB	R	H	2B	3B	HR	RB	BB	SO	SB
Doyle Alexander, p	.000	2	0	0	0	0	0	0	0	0	0	0
Dave Bergman, 1b-1,dh-1	.250	4	4	0	1	0	0	0	2	0	1	0
Tom Brookens, 3b	.000	5	13	0	0	0	0	0	0	0	3	0
Darrell Evans, 1b-5,3b-1	.294	5	17	0	5	0	0	0	0	4	2	0
Kirk Gibson, of	.286	5	21	4	6	1	0	1	4	3	8	3
Johnny Grubb, dh-1	.571	4	7	0	4	0	0	0	0	0	1	0
Mike Heath, c	.286	3	7	1	2	0	0	1	2	0	0	0
Mike Henneman, p	.000	3	0	0	0	0	0	0	0	0	0	0
Willie Hernandez, p	.000	1	0	0	0	0	0	0	0	0	0	0
Larry Herndon, of-2,dh-1	.333	3	9	1	3	1	0	0	2	1	1	0
Eric King, p	.000	2	0	0	0	0	0	0	0	0	0	0
Chet Lemon, of	.278	5	18	4	5	0	0	2	4	1	4	0
Bill Madlock, dh	.000	1	5	0	0	0	0	0	0	0	3	0
Jack Morris, p-1,dh-1	.000	2	0	1	0	0	0	0	0	0	0	0
Jim Morrison, 3b-1,dh-1	.400	2	5	1	2	0	0	0	0	0	1	0
Matt Nokes, c-3,dh-2	.143	5	14	2	2	0	0	1	2	1	4	0
Dan Petry, p	.000	1	0	0	0	0	0	0	0	0	0	0
Jeff Robinson, p	.000	1	0	0	0	0	0	0	0	0	0	0
Pat Sheridan, of-4	.300	5	10	2	3	1	0	1	2	0	2	1
Frank Tanana, p	.000	1	0	0	0	0	0	0	0	0	0	0
Walt Terrell, p	.000	1	0	0	0	0	0	0	0	0	0	0
Mark Thurmond, p	.000	1	0	0	0	0	0	0	0	0	0	0
Alan Trammell, ss	.200	5	20	3	4	1	0	0	2	1	2	0
Lou Whitaker, 2b	.176	5	17	4	3	0	0	1	1	7	3	1
TOTAL	.240		167	23	40	4	0	7	21	18	35	5

PITCHER	W	L	ERA	G	GS	CG	SV	SHO	IP	H	ER	BB	SO
Doyle Alexander	0	2	10.00	2	2	0	0	0	9.0	14	10	1	5
Mike Henneman	1	0	10.80	3	0	0	0	0	5.0	6	6	6	3
Willie Hernandez	0	0	0.00	1	0	0	0	0	0.1	2	0	0	0
Eric King	0	0	1.69	2	0	0	0	0	5.1	3	1	2	4
Jack Morris	0	1	6.75	1	1	1	0	0	8.0	6	6	3	7
Dan Petry	0	0	0.00	1	0	0	0	0	3.1	1	0	0	1
Jeff Robinson	0	0	0.00	1	0	0	0	0	0.1	1	0	0	0
Frank Tanana	0	1	5.06	1	1	0	0	0	5.1	6	3	4	1
Walt Terrell	0	0	9.00	1	1	0	0	0	6.0	7	6	4	4
Mark Thurmond	0	0	0.00	1	0	0	0	0	0.1	0	0	0	0
TOTAL	1	4	6.70	14	5	1	0	0	43.0	46	32	20	25

GAME 1 AT MIN OCT 7

				R	H	E
DET	001	001	120	5	10	0
MIN	010	030	04X	8	10	0

Pitchers: ALEXANDER, Henneman (8), Hernandez (8), King (8) vs Viola, REARDON (8)
Home Runs: Heath-DET, Gibson-DET, Gaetti-MIN (2)
Attendance: 53,269

GAME 2 AT MIN OCT 8

				R	H	E
DET	020	000	010	3	7	1
MIN	030	210	00X	6	6	0

Pitchers: MORRIS vs BLYLEVEN, Berenguer (8)
Home Runs: Lemon-DET, Whitaker-DET, Hrbek-MIN
Attendance: 55,245

GAME 3 AT DET OCT 10

				R	H	E
MIN	000	202	200	6	8	1
DET	005	000	02X	7	7	0

Pitchers: Straker, Schatzeder (3), Berenguer (7), REARDON (8) vs Terrell, HENNEMAN (7)
Home Runs: Gagne-MIN, Brunansky-MIN, Sheridan-DET
Attendance: 49,730

GAME 4 AT DET OCT 11

				R	H	E
MIN	001	111	010	5	7	1
DET	100	011	000	3	7	3

Pitchers: VIOLA, Atherton (6), Berenguer (6), Reardon (9) vs TANANA, Petry (6), Thurmond (9)
Home Runs: Puckett-MIN, Gagne-MIN
Attendance: 51,939

GAME 5 AT DET OCT 12

				R	H	E
MIN	040	000	113	9	15	1
DET	000	300	011	5	9	1

Pitchers: BLYLEVEN, Schatzeder (7), Berenguer (8), Reardon (8) vs ALEXANDER, King (2), Henneman (7), Robinson (9)
Home Runs: Brunansky-MIN, Nokes-DET, Lemon-DET
Attendance: 47,448

Minnesota Twins (AL) 4; St. Louis Cardinals (NL), 3

Although the Twins compiled a dismal record on the road during the season (29–52), their play at home (56–25) topped the majors. In postseason play they won all six games played in their Metrodome, including the four that won them the world championship. They overwhelmed St. Louis in the Series opener, the first World Series game ever played indoors. The Cardinals scored first, in the second inning, but Twins ace Frank Viola (with relief from Keith Atherton in the ninth) stopped them after that as his teammates unloaded for seven runs in the fourth inning (capped by Dan Gladden's grand slam) on their way to a 10–1 win. The Cardinals scored four runs in Game 2, but again the Twins enjoyed a big fourth inning—bunching six of their 10 hits together for six runs—and scored two other runs on homers by Gary Gaetti and Tim Laudner.

When the Series moved to St. Louis, the Cardinals grabbed the home advantage to post their three wins. In Game 3, Cardinal pitchers John Tudor and Todd Worrell combined for a five-hitter as the Cards came from behind with a three-run seventh to win, 3–1. The next day St. Louis broke a 1–1 tie with their own fourth-inning explosion, for six runs. The big blow was a three-run homer by utility infielder Tom Lawless—only the second home run of his big league career—as the Cards won, 7–2. After five scoreless innings in Game 5, St. Louis moved out to a 4–0 lead in the sixth and seventh innings. Gaetti's eighth-inning triple put two Minnesota runs across, but the Cards held on for a 4–2 win.

Back in Minneapolis, St. Louis built up a 5–2 lead in Game 6 before the Twins retaliated with four runs in the fifth inning (with Don Baylor's three-run homer providing the tying runs) and four more an inning later on Kent Hrbek's grand slam. A final Twins run in the eighth ended the scoring at 11–5.

The Cardinals scored first in Game 7, with a pair of runs in the second inning, but the Twins edged their way to a tie with single runs in the second and fifth, and an inning later took the lead on three walks and an infield single. As Twins starter Frank Viola held St. Louis scoreless on two hits after the second inning, Minnesota made the score 4–2 with a final run in the eighth, and ace reliever Jeff Reardon retired the Cards in order in the ninth to bring Minnesota its first world championship.

MIN (A)

PLAYER/POS	AVG	G	AB	R	H	2B	3B	HR	RB	BB	SO	SB
Keith Atherton, p	.000	2	0	0	0	0	0	0	0	0	0	0
Don Baylor, dh-3	.385	5	13	3	5	0	0	1	3	1	1	0
Juan Berenguer, p	.000	3	0	0	0	0	0	0	0	0	0	0
Bert Blyleven, p	.000	2	1	0	0	0	0	0	0	0	1	0
Tom Brunansky, of	.200	7	25	5	5	0	0	0	2	4	4	1
Randy Bush, dh-2	.167	4	6	1	1	1	0	0	2	0	1	0
Sal Butera, c	.000	1	0	0	0	0	0	0	0	0	0	0
Mark Davidson, of-1	.000	2	1	0	0	0	0	0	0	0	0	0
George Frazier, p	.000	1	0	0	0	0	0	0	0	0	0	0
Gary Gaetti, 3b	.259	7	27	4	7	2	1	1	4	2	5	2
Greg Gagne, ss	.200	7	30	5	6	1	0	1	3	1	6	0
Dan Gladden, of	.290	7	31	3	9	2	1	1	7	3	4	2
Kent Hrbek, 1b	.208	7	24	4	5	0	0	1	6	5	3	0
Gene Larkin, 1b-1,dh-1	.000	5	3	1	0	0	0	0	0	1	0	0
Tim Laudner, c	.318	7	22	4	7	1	0	1	4	5	4	0
Steve Lombardozzi, 2b	.412	6	17	3	7	1	0	1	4	2	2	0
Al Newman, 2b-3	.200	4	5	0	1	0	0	0	0	1	1	0
Joe Niekro, p	.000	1	0	0	0	0	0	0	0	0	0	0
Kirby Puckett, of	.357	7	28	5	10	1	1	0	3	2	1	1
Jeff Reardon, p	.000	4	0	0	0	0	0	0	0	0	0	0
Dan Schatzeder, p	.000	3	0	0	0	0	0	0	0	0	0	0
Roy Smalley, ph	.500	4	2	0	1	1	0	0	0	2	0	0
Les Straker, p	.000	2	2	0	0	0	0	0	0	0	2	0
Frank Viola, p	.000	3	1	0	0	0	0	0	0	0	1	0
TOTAL	.269		238	38	64	10	3	7	38	29	36	6

PITCHER	W	L	ERA	G	GS	CG	SV	SHO	IP	H	ER	BB	SO
Keith Atherton	0	0	6.75	2	0	0	0	0	1.1	0	1	1	0
Juan Berenguer	0	1	10.38	3	0	0	0	0	4.1	10	5	0	1
Bert Blyleven	1	1	2.77	2	2	0	0	0	13.0	13	4	2	12
George Frazier	0	0	0.00	1	0	0	0	0	2.0	1	0	0	2
Joe Niekro	0	0	0.00	1	0	0	0	0	2.0	1	0	1	1
Jeff Reardon	0	0	0.00	4	0	0	1	0	4.2	5	0	0	3
Dan Schatzeder	1	0	6.23	3	0	0	0	0	4.1	4	3	3	3
Les Straker	0	0	4.00	2	2	0	0	0	9.0	9	4	3	6
Frank Viola	2	1	3.72	3	3	0	0	0	19.1	17	8	3	16
TOTAL	4	3	3.75	21	7	0	1	0	60.0	60	25	13	44

STL (N)

PLAYER/POS	AVG	G	AB	R	H	2B	3B	HR	RB	BB	SO	SB
Vince Coleman, of	.143	7	28	5	4	2	0	0	2	2	10	6
Danny Cox, p	.000	3	2	0	0	0	0	0	0	0	1	0
Ken Dayley, p	.000	4	1	0	0	0	0	0	0	0	1	0
Dan Driessen, 1b	.231	4	13	3	3	2	0	0	1	1	1	0
Curt Ford, of-4	.308	5	13	1	4	0	0	0	2	1	1	0
Bob Forsch, p	.000	3	2	0	0	0	0	0	0	0	0	0
Tommy Herr, 2b	.250	7	28	2	7	0	0	1	1	2	2	0
Rick Horton, p	.000	2	0	0	0	0	0	0	0	0	0	0
Lance Johnson, pr	.000	1	0	0	0	0	0	0	0	0	0	1
Steve Lake, c	.333	3	3	0	1	0	0	0	1	0	0	0
Tom Lawless, 3b	.100	3	10	1	1	0	0	1	3	0	4	0
Jim Lindeman, 1b-6,of-1	.333	6	15	3	5	1	0	0	2	0	3	0
Joe Magrane, p	.000	2	0	0	0	0	0	0	0	0	0	0
Greg Mathews, p	.000	1	1	0	0	0	0	0	0	0	0	0
Willie McGee, of	.370	7	27	2	10	2	0	0	4	0	9	0
John Morris, of	.000	1	2	0	0	0	0	0	0	0	0	0
Jose Oquendo, 3b-4,of-3	.250	7	24	2	6	0	0	0	2	1	4	0
Tom Pagnozzi, dh-1	.250	2	4	0	1	0	0	0	0	0	0	0
Tony Pena, c-6,dh-1	.409	7	22	2	9	1	0	0	4	3	2	1
Terry Pendleton, dh-2	.429	3	7	2	3	0	0	0	1	1	1	2
Ozzie Smith, ss	.214	7	28	3	6	0	0	0	2	2	3	2
John Tudor, p	.000	2	2	0	0	0	0	0	0	0	2	0
Lee Tunnell, p	.000	2	0	0	0	0	0	0	0	0	0	0
Todd Worrell, p	.000	4	0	0	0	0	0	0	0	0	0	0
TOTAL	.259		232	26	60	8	0	2	25	13	44	12

PITCHER	W	L	ERA	G	GS	CG	SV	SHO	IP	H	ER	BB	SO
Danny Cox	1	2	7.71	3	2	0	0	0	11.2	13	10	8	9
Ken Dayley	0	0	1.93	4	0	0	1	0	4.2	2	1	0	3
Bob Forsch	1	0	9.95	3	0	0	0	0	6.1	8	7	5	3
Rick Horton	0	0	6.00	2	0	0	0	0	3.0	5	2	0	1
Joe Magrane	0	1	8.59	2	2	0	0	0	7.1	9	7	5	5
Greg Mathews	0	0	2.45	1	1	0	0	0	3.2	2	1	2	3
John Tudor	1	1	5.73	2	2	0	0	0	11.0	15	7	3	8
Lee Tunnell	0	0	2.08	2	0	0	0	0	4.1	4	1	2	1
Todd Worrell	0	0	1.29	4	0	0	2	0	7.0	6	1	4	3
TOTAL	3	4	5.64	23	7	0	3	0	59.0	64	37	29	36

GAME 1 AT MIN OCT 17

				R	H	E
STL	010	000	000	1	5	1
MIN	000	720	10X	10	11	0

Pitchers: MAGRANE, Forsch (4), Horton (7) vs VIOLA, Atherton (9)
Home Runs: Gladden-MIN, Lombardozzi-MIN
Attendance: 55,171

GAME 2 AT MIN OCT 18

				R	H	E
STL	000	010	120	4	9	0
MIN	010	601	00X	8	10	0

Pitchers: COX, Tunnell (4), Dayley (7), Worrell (8) vs BLYLEVEN, Berenguer (8), Reardon (9)
Home Runs: Gaetti-MIN, Laudner-MIN
Attendance: 55,257

GAME 3 AT STL OCT 20

				R	H	E
MIN	000	001	000	1	5	1
STL	000	000	30X	3	9	1

Pitchers: Straker, BERENGUER (7), Schatzeder (7) vs TUDOR, Worrell (8)
Attendance: 55,347

GAME 4 AT STL OCT 21

				R	H	E
MIN	001	010	000	2	7	1
STL	001	600	00X	7	10	1

Pitchers: VIOLA, Schatzeder (4), Niekro (5), Frazier (7) vs Mathews, FORSCH (4), Dayley (7)
Home Runs: Gagne-MIN, Lawless-STL
Attendance: 55,347

GAME 5 AT STL OCT 22

				R	H	E
MIN	000	000	020	2	6	1
STL	000	003	10X	4	10	0

Pitchers: BLYLEVEN, Atherton (7), Reardon (7) vs COX, Dayley (8), Worrell (8)
Attendance: 55,347

GAME 6 AT MIN OCT 24

				R	H	E
STL	110	210	000	5	11	2
MIN	200	044	01X	11	15	0

Pitchers: TUDOR, Horton (5), Forsch (6), Dayley (6), Tunnell (7) vs Straker, SCHATZEDER (4), Berenguer (6), Reardon (9)
Home Runs: Herr-STL, Baylor-MIN, Hrbek-MIN
Attendance: 55,293

GAME 7 AT MIN OCT 25

				R	H	E
STL	020	000	000	2	6	1
MIN	010	011	01X	4	10	0

Pitchers: Magrane, COX (5), Worrell (6) vs VIOLA, Reardon (9)
Attendance: 55,376

The Mets had defeated the Dodgers in 10 of 11 regular season games, but in the NLCS the pitching of Dodger ace Orel Hershiser and rookie Tim Belcher, and the timely hitting of Mike Scioscia and Kirk Gibson, propelled L.A. to the pennant. The Dodgers scored a first-inning run in the opener and carried a 2–0 lead into the ninth. But three Mets runs in the top of the ninth (the final two scoring with two outs on a fly to short center that bounced off the glove of a diving John Shelby) gave New York the victory.

Dodgers pitcher Tim Belcher singled with two away in the second inning of Game 2 to start a four-run rally—the margin of victory in Belcher's 6–3 win. In Game 3 (played in a steady downpour after a rainout the night before), the Mets overcame a 4–3 deficit, rapping four Dodgers pitchers for five runs in the last of the eighth to take the series lead.

Kirk Gibson's 12th-inning solo homer the next night put the Dodgers ahead, 5–4, after Mike Scioscia's ninth-inning home run had pulled them into a tie. In the last of the 12th, Orel Hershiser (who had pitched seven innings to no decision in the previous game) took the mound with two outs and the bases full, and saved the game as center fielder Shelby, on the run, snared Kevin McReynolds' looping fly.

Gibson homered again in Game 5—for three runs that provided the winning margin in a 7–4 Dodgers victory. One game from the pennant, as the series moved back to Los Angeles, the Dodgers for the first time failed to score first and saw the series evened a third time as David Cone held them to five hits and one run while the Mets scored five. But in the finale, the Dodgers unloaded on Ron Darling for six runs in the first two innings and Hershiser blanked the Mets on five hits.

Los Angeles Dodgers (West), 4; New York Mets (East), 3

LA (W)

PLAYER/POS	AVG	G	AB	R	H	2B	3B	HR	RB	BB	SO	SB
Tim Belcher, p	.125	2	8	1	1	0	0	0	0	0	3	0
Mike Davis, ph	.000	4	2	0	0	0	0	0	0	1	0	0
Rick Dempsey, c-3	.400	4	5	1	2	2	0	0	2	1	0	0
Kirk Gibson, of	.154	7	26	2	4	0	0	2	6	3	6	2
Jose Gonzalez, of-4	.000	5	0	2	0	0	0	0	0	0	0	0
Alfredo Griffin, ss	.160	7	25	1	4	1	0	0	3	0	5	0
Jeff Hamilton, 3b	.217	7	23	2	5	0	0	0	1	3	4	0
Mickey Hatcher, 1b-6,of-1	.238	6	21	4	5	2	0	0	3	3	0	0
Danny Heep, ph	.000	3	1	0	0	0	0	0	0	1	1	0
Orel Hershiser, p	.000	4	9	1	0	0	0	0	1	1	2	0
Brian Holton, p	1.000	3	1	1	1	0	0	0	0	0	0	0
Rick Horton, p	.000	4	0	0	0	0	0	0	0	0	0	0
Jay Howell, p	.000	2	0	0	0	0	0	0	0	0	0	0
Tim Leary, p	.000	2	1	0	0	0	0	0	0	0	0	0
Mike Marshall, of	.233	7	30	3	7	1	1	0	5	2	9	0
Jesse Orosco, p	.000	4	0	0	0	0	0	0	0	0	0	0
Alejandro Pena, p	.000	3	0	0	0	0	0	0	0	0	0	0
Steve Sax, 2b	.267	7	30	7	8	0	0	0	3	3	3	5
Mike Scioscia, c	.364	7	22	3	8	1	0	1	2	1	2	0
Mike Sharperson, ss-1,3b-1	.000	2	1	0	0	0	0	0	1	1	0	0
John Shelby, of	.167	7	24	3	4	0	0	0	3	5	12	2
Franklin Stubbs, 1b-3	.250	4	8	0	2	0	0	0	0	0	4	0
John Tudor, p	.000	1	2	0	0	0	0	0	0	0	2	0
Tracy Woodson, 1b	.250	3	4	0	1	0	0	0	0	0	1	0
TOTAL	.214		243	31	52	7	1	3	30	25	54	9

PITCHER	W	L	ERA	G	GS	CG	SV	SHO	IP	H	ER	BB	SO
Tim Belcher	2	0	4.11	2	2	0	0	0	15.1	12	7	4	16
Orel Hershiser	1	0	1.09	4	3	1	1	1	24.2	18	3	7	15
Brian Holton	0	0	2.25	3	0	0	1	0	4.0	2	1	1	2
Rick Horton	0	0	0.00	4	0	0	0	0	4.1	4	0	2	3
Jay Howell	0	1	27.00	2	0	0	0	0	0.2	1	2	2	1
Tim Leary	0	1	6.23	2	1	0	0	0	4.1	8	3	3	3
Jesse Orosco	0	0	7.71	4	0	0	0	0	2.1	4	2	3	0
Alejandro Pena	1	1	4.15	3	0	0	1	0	4.1	1	2	5	1
John Tudor	0	0	7.20	1	1	0	0	0	5.0	8	4	1	1
TOTAL	4	3	3.32	25	7	1	3	1	65.0	58	24	28	42

NY (E)

PLAYER/POS	AVG	G	AB	R	H	2B	3B	HR	RB	BB	SO	SB
Rick Aguilera, p	.000	3	1	0	0	0	0	0	0	0	1	0
Wally Backman, 2b	.273	7	22	2	6	1	0	0	2	2	5	1
Gary Carter, c	.222	7	27	0	6	1	1	0	4	1	3	0
David Cone, p	.000	3	4	0	0	0	0	0	0	0	0	0
Ron Darling, p-2	.000	2	3	0	0	0	0	0	0	0	2	0
Lennie Dykstra, of	.429	7	14	6	6	3	0	1	3	4	0	0
Kevin Elster, ss	.250	5	8	1	2	1	0	0	1	3	0	0
Sid Fernandez, p	.000	1	1	0	0	0	0	0	0	0	0	0
Dwight Gooden, p	.200	3	5	0	1	0	0	0	0	0	2	0
Keith Hernandez, 1b	.269	7	26	2	7	0	0	1	5	6	7	1
Gregg Jefferies, 3b	.333	7	27	2	9	2	0	0	1	4	0	0
Howard Johnson, ss-5,3b-1	.056	6	18	3	1	0	0	0	0	1	6	1
Terry Leach, p	.000	3	0	0	0	0	0	0	0	0	0	0
Dave Magadan, ph	.000	3	3	0	0	0	0	0	0	0	2	0
Lee Mazzilli, ph	.500	3	2	0	1	0	0	0	0	0	0	1
Roger McDowell, p	.000	4	0	0	0	0	0	0	0	0	0	0
Kevin McReynolds, of	.250	7	28	4	7	2	0	2	4	3	5	2
Randy Myers, p	.000	3	0	0	0	0	0	0	0	0	0	0
Mackey Sasser, c-1	.200	4	5	0	1	0	0	0	0	0	1	0
Darryl Strawberry, of	.300	7	30	5	9	2	0	1	6	2	5	0
Tim Teufel, 2b	.000	1	3	0	0	0	0	0	0	0	1	0
Mookie Wilson, of-3	.154	4	13	2	2	0	0	0	1	2	2	0
TOTAL	.242		240	27	58	12	1	5	27	28	42	6

PITCHER	W	L	ERA	G	GS	CG	SV	SHO	IP	H	ER	BB	SO
Rick Aguilera	0	0	1.29	3	0	0	0	0	7.0	3	1	2	4
David Cone	1	1	4.50	3	2	1	0	0	12.0	10	6	5	9
Ron Darling	0	1	7.71	2	2	0	0	0	7.0	11	6	4	7
Sid Fernandez	0	1	13.50	1	1	0	0	0	4.0	7	6	1	5
Dwight Gooden	0	0	2.95	3	2	0	0	0	18.1	10	6	8	20
Terry Leach	0	0	0.00	3	0	0	0	0	5.0	4	0	1	4
Roger McDowell	0	1	4.50	4	0	0	0	0	6.0	6	3	2	5
Randy Myers	2	0	0.00	3	0	0	0	0	4.2	1	0	2	0
TOTAL	3	4	3.94	22	7	1	0	0	64.0	52	28	25	54

GAME 1 AT LA OCT 4

				R	H	E
NY	000	000	003	3	8	1
LA	100	000	100	2	4	0

Pitchers: Gooden, MYERS (8) vs Hershiser, HOWELL (9)
Attendance: 55,582

GAME 2 AT LA OCT 5

				R	H	E
NY	000	200	001	3	6	0
LA	140	010	00X	6	7	0

Pitchers: CONE, Aguilera (3), Leach (6), McDowell (8) vs BELCHER, Orosco (9), Pena (9)
Home Runs: Hernandez-NY
Attendance: 55,780

GAME 3 AT NY OCT 8

				R	H	E
LA	021	000	010	4	7	2
NY	001	002	05X	8	9	2

Pitchers: Hershiser, Howell (8), PENA (8), Orosco (8), Horton (8) vs Darling, McDowell (7), MYERS (8), Cone (9)
Attendance: 44,672

GAME 4 AT NY OCT 9

					R	H	E
LA	200	000	002	001	5	7	1
NY	000	301	000	000	4	10	2

Pitchers: Tudor, Holton (6), Horton (7), PENA (9), Leary (12), Orosco (12), Hershiser (12) vs Gooden, Myers (9), McDOWELL (11)
Home Runs: Strawberry-NY, McReynolds-NY, Scioscia-LA, Gibson-LA
Attendance: 54,014

GAME 5 AT NY OCT 10

				R	H	E
LA	000	330	001	7	12	0
NY	000	030	010	4	9	1

Pitchers: BELCHER, Horton (8), Holton (8) vs FERNANDEZ, Leach (5), Aguilera (6), McDowell (8)
Home Runs: Gibson-LA, Dykstra-NY
Attendance: 52,069

GAME 6 AT LA OCT 11

				R	H	E
NY	101	021	000	5	11	0
LA	000	010	000	1	5	2

Pitchers: CONE vs LEARY, Holton (5), Horton (6), Orosco (8)
Home Runs: McReynolds-NY
Attendance: 55,885

GAME 7 AT LA OCT 12

				R	H	E
NY	000	000	000	0	5	2
LA	150	000	00X	6	10	0

Pitchers: DARLING, Gooden (2), Leach (5), Aguilera (7) vs HERSHISER
Attendance: 55,693

Jose Canseco's three home runs and Dennis Eckersley's sparkling relief pitching highlighted Oakland's sweep to the pennant. In his six shutout innings, Eckersley gave up just one hit and a pair of walks while fanning five, to record an ALCS record four saves.

Canseco's fourth-inning solo shot off Bruce Hurst put the A's out in front in Game 1. Boston tied it up in the seventh, but two former Boston players—Carney Lansford, who doubled, and Dave Henderson, who singled him home—put Oakland back in front in the eighth, and Eckersley (also an ex-Bostonian) held the Sox through the final two innings.

Oakland's Storm Davis and Boston's Roger Clemens dueled scorelessly through five innings of Game 2. The Sox took advantage of an Oakland error to score twice in the sixth, but four Oakland hits in the seventh (including a two-run homer by Canseco), a balk, and a wild pitch put the A's up, 3–2. Rich Gedman's home run for Boston in the last of the seventh tied the score, but in the ninth Oakland's rookie shortstop Walt Weiss singled home what proved the game winner off Sox ace reliever Lee Smith.

Boston unloaded for five runs in the first two innings of Game 3. But Weiss' double and home runs by Mark McGwire and Carney Lansford in the last of the second brought the A's within one run of a tie, and Ron Hassey's two-run homer an inning later gave the A's a lead that they held to the end. Dave Henderson's two-run blast in the eighth capped Oakland's 10–6 victory.

Canseco's first-inning homer in Game 4 put the A's ahead to stay, as starter Dave Stewart and relievers Rick Honeycutt and Eckersley combined for a four-hit, 4–1 pennant clincher.

Oakland Athletics (West), 4; Boston Red Sox (East), 0

OAK (W)

PLAYER/POS	AVG	G	AB	R	H	2B	3B	HR	RB	BB	SO	SB
Don Baylor, dh	.000	2	6	0	0	0	0	0	1	1	2	0
Greg Cadaret, p	.000	1	0	0	0	0	0	0	0	0	0	0
Jose Canseco, of	.313	4	16	4	5	1	0	3	4	1	2	1
Storm Davis, p	.000	1	0	0	0	0	0	0	0	0	0	0
Dennis Eckersley, p	.000	4	0	0	0	0	0	0	0	0	0	0
Mike Gallego, 2b	.083	4	12	1	1	0	0	0	0	0	3	0
Ron Hassey, c	.500	4	8	2	4	1	0	1	3	1	1	0
Dave Henderson, of	.375	4	16	2	6	1	0	1	4	1	7	0
Rick Honeycutt, p	.000	3	0	0	0	0	0	0	0	0	0	0
Stan Javier, of	.500	2	4	0	2	0	0	0	1	1	0	0
Carney Lansford, 3b	.294	4	17	4	5	1	0	1	2	0	2	0
Mark McGwire, 1b	.333	4	15	4	5	0	0	1	3	1	5	0
Gene Nelson, p	.000	2	0	0	0	0	0	0	0	0	0	0
Dave Parker, dh-2,of-1	.250	3	12	1	3	1	0	0	0	0	4	0
Tony Phillips, of-2,2b-1	.286	2	7	0	2	1	0	0	0	1	3	0
Eric Plunk, p	.000	1	0	0	0	0	0	0	0	0	0	0
Luis Polonia, of-1	.400	3	5	0	2	0	0	0	0	1	2	0
Terry Steinbach, c	.250	2	4	0	1	0	0	0	0	2	0	0
Dave Stewart, p	.000	2	0	0	0	0	0	0	0	0	0	0
Walt Weiss, ss	.333	4	15	2	5	2	0	0	2	0	4	0
Bob Welch, p	.000	1	0	0	0	0	0	0	0	0	0	0
Curt Young, p	.000	1	0	0	0	0	0	0	0	0	0	0
TOTAL	.299		137	20	41	8	0	7	20	10	35	1

PITCHER	W	L	ERA	G	GS	CG	SV	SHO	IP	H	ER	BB	SO
Greg Cadaret	0	0	27.00	1	0	0	0	0	0.1	1	1	0	0
Storm Davis	0	0	0.00	1	1	0	0	0	6.1	2	0	5	4
Dennis Eckersley	0	0	0.00	4	0	0	4	0	6.0	1	0	2	5
Rick Honeycutt	1	0	0.00	3	0	0	0	0	2.0	0	0	2	0
Gene Nelson	2	0	0.00	2	0	0	0	0	4.2	5	0	1	0
Eric Plunk	0	0	0.00	1	0	0	0	0	0.1	1	0	0	1
Dave Stewart	1	0	1.35	2	2	0	0	0	13.1	9	2	6	11
Bob Welch	0	0	27.00	1	1	0	0	0	1.2	6	5	2	0
Curt Young	0	0	0.00	1	0	0	0	0	1.1	1	0	0	2
TOTAL	4	0	2.00	16	4	0	4	0	36.0	26	8	18	23

BOS (E)

PLAYER/POS	AVG	G	AB	R	H	2B	3B	HR	RB	BB	SO	SB
Marty Barrett, 2b	.067	4	15	2	1	0	0	0	0	1	0	0
Todd Benzinger, 1b-3	.091	4	11	0	1	0	0	0	0	1	3	0
Mike Boddicker, p	.000	1	0	0	0	0	0	0	0	0	0	0
Wade Boggs, 3b	.385	4	13	2	5	0	0	0	3	3	4	0
Ellis Burks, of	.235	4	17	2	4	1	0	0	1	0	3	0
Roger Clemens, p	.000	1	0	0	0	0	0	0	0	0	0	0
Dwight Evans, of	.167	4	12	1	2	1	0	0	1	3	5	0
Wes Gardner, p	.000	1	0	0	0	0	0	0	0	0	0	0
Rich Gedman, c	.357	4	14	1	5	0	0	1	1	2	1	0
Mike Greenwell, of	.214	4	14	2	3	1	0	1	3	3	0	0
Bruce Hurst, p	.000	2	0	0	0	0	0	0	0	0	0	0
Spike Owen, dh	.000	1	0	0	0	0	0	0	0	1	0	0
Larry Parrish, 1b-2	.000	4	6	0	0	0	0	0	0	0	2	0
Jody Reed, ss	.273	4	11	0	3	1	0	0	0	2	1	0
Jim Rice, dh	.154	4	13	0	2	0	0	0	1	2	4	0
Ed Romero, pr	.000	1	0	0	0	0	0	0	0	0	0	0
Kevin Romine, pr	.000	2	0	1	0	0	0	0	0	0	0	0
Lee Smith, p	.000	2	0	0	0	0	0	0	0	0	0	0
Mike Smithson, p	.000	1	0	0	0	0	0	0	0	0	0	0
Bob Stanley, p	.000	2	0	0	0	0	0	0	0	0	0	0
TOTAL	.206		126	11	26	4	0	2	10	18	23	0

PITCHER	W	L	ERA	G	GS	CG	SV	SHO	IP	H	ER	BB	SO
Mike Boddicker	0	1	20.25	1	1	0	0	0	2.2	8	6	1	2
Roger Clemens	0	0	3.86	1	1	0	0	0	7.0	6	3	0	8
Wes Gardner	0	0	5.79	1	0	0	0	0	4.2	6	3	2	8
Bruce Hurst	0	2	2.77	2	2	1	0	0	13.0	10	4	5	12
Lee Smith	0	1	8.10	2	0	0	0	0	3.1	6	3	1	4
Mike Smithson	0	0	0.00	1	0	0	0	0	2.1	3	0	0	1
Bob Stanley	0	0	9.00	2	0	0	0	0	1.0	2	1	1	0
TOTAL	0	4	5.29	10	4	1	0	0	34.0	41	20	10	35

GAME 1 AT BOS OCT 5

OAK	000	100	010	2	6	0
BOS	000	000	100	1	6	0

Pitchers: Stewart, HONEYCUTT (7), Eckersley (8) vs HURST
Home Runs: Canseco-OAK
Attendance: 34,104

GAME 2 AT BOS OCT 6

OAK	000	000	301	4	10	1
BOS	000	002	100	3	4	1

Pitchers: Davis, Cadaret (7), NELSON (7), Eckersley (9) vs Clemens, Stanley (8), SMITH (8)
Home Runs: Canseco-OAK, Gedman-BOS
Attendance: 34,605

GAME 3 AT OAK OCT 8

BOS	320	000	100	6	12	0
OAK	042	010	12X	10	15	1

Pitchers: BODDICKER, Gardner (3), Stanley (8) vs Welch, NELSON (2), Young (6), Plunk (7), Honeycutt (7), Eckersley (8)
Home Runs: Greenwell-BOS, McGwire-OAK, Lansford-OAK, Hassey-OAK, Henderson-OAK
Attendance: 49,261

GAME 4 AT OAK OCT 9

BOS	000	001	000	1	4	0
OAK	101	000	02X	4	10	1

Pitchers: HURST, Smithson (5), Smith (7) vs STEWART, Honeycutt (8), Eckersley (9)
Home Runs: Canseco-OAK
Attendance: 49,406

Mickey Hatcher's home run in the first inning of Game 1 set the tone for the Dodgers' surprising triumph over Oakland's mighty A's. Hatcher, who homered only once during the season, initiated the Series scoring with a two-run blast to left center. Half an inning later the A's Jose Canseco—baseball's leading slugger, with 42 homers—erased the Dodger lead with his first career grand slam. But while Hatcher went on to hit safely six more times in the Series—including another home run—Canseco's first hit was also his last, as he went 0-for-19 the rest of the way. The Dodgers scored once in the sixth inning to draw within one run of a tie, but remained behind until the last of the ninth when, with two outs and one on, Kirk Gibson pinch hit for pitcher Alejandro Peña. Gibson, the Dodgers' top source of power during the season, was so hobbled by leg injuries that he had, till that moment, sat out the game in the training room. But with two strikes on him he belted a home run off baseball's premier reliever, Dennis Eckersley, to win the game. It was Gibson's only Series appearance.

Dodgers ace Orel Hershiser blanked the A's on three hits in Game 2 and led the offense with three hits of his own. His single in the third inning began a five-run rally (capped by Mike Marshall's three-run homer), and his fourth-inning double drove in the Dodgers' sixth and final run.

When the Series moved to Oakland, the A's recovered for a dramatic win in Game 3, as Mark McGwire (who had homered 32 times during the season) broke a 1–1 tie with his only Series hit, a solo homer in the last of the ninth. In Game 4, Dodgers reliever Jay Howell, who had yielded the losing home run the day before, got McGwire to pop up with the bases full to end the seventh inning, and blanked the A's the rest of the way to preserve a narrow 4–3 victory.

Hershiser returned to pitch Game 5. He allowed two runs in his four-hitter, but Mickey Hatcher had given the Dodgers the lead with a two-run homer in the first inning, and Mike Davis (who had homered just twice during the season) drove a 3–0 pitch into the stands for two more runs in the fourth. Veteran catcher Rick Dempsey (substituting for injured first-stringer Mike Scioscia) doubled home a fifth Los Angeles run in the sixth, and the Dodgers were on their way to a seventh world title.

Los Angeles Dodgers (NL), 4; Oakland Athletics (AL), 1

LA (N)

PLAYER/POS	AVG	G	AB	R	H	2B	3B	HR	RB	BB	SO	SB
Dave Anderson, dh	.000	1	1	0	0	0	0	0	0	0	1	0
Tim Belcher, p	.000	2	0	0	0	0	0	0	0	0	0	0
Mike Davis, dh-2,of-1	.143	4	7	3	1	0	0	1	2	4	0	2
Rick Dempsey, c	.200	2	5	0	1	1	0	0	1	1	2	0
Kirk Gibson, ph	1.000	1	1	1	1	0	0	1	2	0	0	0
Jose Gonzalez, of-3	.000	4	2	0	0	0	0	0	0	0	2	0
Alfredo Griffin, ss	.188	5	16	2	3	0	0	0	0	2	4	0
Jeff Hamilton, 3b	.105	5	19	1	2	0	0	0	0	1	4	0
Mickey Hatcher, of	.368	5	19	5	7	1	0	2	5	1	3	0
Danny Heep, of-1,dh-1	.250	3	8	0	2	1	0	0	0	0	2	0
Orel Hershiser, p	1.000	2	3	1	3	2	0	0	1	0	0	0
Brian Holton, p	.000	1	0	0	0	0	0	0	0	0	0	0
Jay Howell, p	.000	2	0	0	0	0	0	0	0	0	0	0
Tim Leary, p	.000	2	0	0	0	0	0	0	0	0	0	0
Mike Marshall, of	.231	5	13	2	3	0	1	1	3	0	5	0
Alejandro Pena, p	.000	2	0	0	0	0	0	0	0	0	0	0
Steve Sax, 2b	.300	5	20	3	6	0	0	0	0	1	1	1
Mike Scioscia, c	.214	4	14	0	3	0	0	0	1	0	2	0
John Shelby, of	.222	5	18	0	4	1	0	0	1	2	7	1
Franklin Stubbs, 1b	.294	5	17	3	5	2	0	0	2	1	3	0
John Tudor, p	.000	1	0	0	0	0	0	0	0	0	0	0
Tracy Woodson, 1b-3	.000	4	4	0	0	0	0	0	1	0	0	0
TOTAL	.246		167	21	41	8	1	5	19	13	36	4

PITCHER	W	L	ERA	G	GS	CG	SV	SHO	IP	H	ER	BB	SO
Tim Belcher	1	0	6.23	2	2	0	0	0	8.2	10	6	6	10
Orel Hershiser	2	0	1.00	2	2	2	0	1	18.0	7	2	6	17
Brian Holton	0	0	0.00	1	0	0	0	0	2.0	0	0	1	0
Jay Howell	0	1	3.38	2	0	0	1	0	2.2	3	1	1	2
Tim Leary	0	0	1.35	2	0	0	0	0	6.2	6	1	2	4
Alejandro Pena	1	0	0.00	2	0	0	0	0	5.0	2	0	1	7
John Tudor	0	0	0.00	1	1	0	0	0	1.1	0	0	0	1
TOTAL	4	1	2.03	12	5	2	1	1	44.1	28	10	17	41

OAK (A)

PLAYER/POS	AVG	G	AB	R	H	2B	3B	HR	RB	BB	SO	SB
Don Baylor, ph	.000	1	1	0	0	0	0	0	0	0	1	0
Todd Burns, p	.000	1	0	0	0	0	0	0	0	0	0	0
Greg Cadaret, p	.000	3	0	0	0	0	0	0	0	0	0	0
Jose Canseco, of	.053	5	19	1	1	0	0	1	5	2	5	1
Storm Davis, p	.000	2	1	0	0	0	0	0	0	0	1	0
Dennis Eckersley, p	.000	2	0	0	0	0	0	0	0	0	0	0
Mike Gallego, 2b	.000	1	0	0	0	0	0	0	0	0	0	0
Ron Hassey, c-4	.250	5	8	0	2	0	0	0	1	3	3	0
Dave Henderson, of	.300	5	20	1	6	2	0	0	1	2	7	0
Rick Honeycutt, p	.000	3	0	0	0	0	0	0	0	0	0	0
Glenn Hubbard, 2b	.250	4	12	2	3	0	0	0	0	1	2	1
Stan Javier, of-2	.500	3	4	0	2	0	0	0	2	0	1	0
Carney Lansford, 3b	.167	5	18	2	3	0	0	0	1	2	2	0
Mark McGwire, 1b	.059	5	17	1	1	0	0	1	1	3	4	0
Gene Nelson, p	.000	3	0	0	0	0	0	0	0	0	0	0
Dave Parker, of-2,dh-2	.200	4	15	0	3	0	0	0	0	2	4	0
Tony Phillips, 2b-1,of-1	.250	2	4	1	1	0	0	0	0	1	2	0
Eric Plunk, p	.000	2	0	0	0	0	0	0	0	0	0	0
Luis Polonia, of-2	.111	3	9	1	1	0	0	0	0	0	2	0
Terry Steinbach, c-2,dh-1	.364	3	11	0	4	1	0	0	0	0	2	0
Dave Stewart, p	.000	2	3	1	0	0	0	0	0	1	3	0
Walt Weiss, ss	.063	5	16	1	1	0	0	0	0	0	2	1
Bob Welch, p	.000	1	0	0	0	0	0	0	0	0	0	0
Curt Young, p	.000	1	0	0	0	0	0	0	0	0	0	0
TOTAL	.177		158	11	28	3	0	2	11	17	41	3

PITCHER	W	L	ERA	G	GS	CG	SV	SHO	IP	H	ER	BB	SO
Todd Burns	0	0	0.00	1	0	0	0	0	0.1	0	0	0	0
Greg Cadaret	0	0	0.00	3	0	0	0	0	2.0	2	0	0	3
Storm Davis	0	2	11.25	2	2	0	0	0	8.0	14	10	1	7
Dennis Eckersley	0	1	10.80	2	0	0	0	0	1.2	2	2	1	2
Rick Honeycutt	1	0	0.00	3	0	0	0	0	3.1	0	0	0	5
Gene Nelson	0	0	1.42	3	0	0	0	0	6.1	4	1	3	3
Eric Plunk	0	0	0.00	2	0	0	0	0	1.2	0	0	0	3
Dave Stewart	0	1	3.14	2	2	0	0	0	14.1	12	5	5	5
Bob Welch	0	0	1.80	1	1	0	0	0	5.0	6	1	3	8
Curt Young	0	0	0.00	1	0	0	0	0	1.0	1	0	0	0
TOTAL	1	4	3.92	20	5	0	0	0	43.2	41	19	13	36

GAME 1 AT LA OCT 15

				R	H	E
OAK	040	000	000	4	7	0
LA	200	001	002	5	7	0

Pitchers: Stewart, ECKERSLEY (9) vs Belcher, Leary (3), Holton (6), PENA (8) Home Runs: Hatcher-LA, Canseco-OAK, Gibson-LA
Attendance: 55,983

GAME 2 AT LA OCT 16

				R	H	E
OAK	000	000	000	0	3	0
LA	005	100	00X	6	10	1

Pitchers: DAVIS, Nelson (4), Young (6), Plunk (7), Honeycutt (8) vs HERSHISER
Home Runs: Marshall-LA
Attendance: 56,051

GAME 3 AT OAK OCT 18

				R	H	E
LA	000	010	000	1	8	1
OAK	001	000	001	2	5	0

Pitchers: Tudor, Leary (2), Pena (6), J.HOWELL (9) vs Welch, Cadaret (6), Nelson (6), HONEYCUTT (8)
Home Runs: McGwire-OAK
Attendance: 49,316

GAME 4 AT OAK OCT 19

				R	H	E
LA	201	000	100	4	8	1
OAK	100	001	100	3	9	2

Pitchers: BELCHER, J.Howell (7) vs STEWART, Cadaret (7), Eckersley (9)
Attendance: 49,317

GAME 5 AT OAK OCT 20

				R	H	E
LA	200	201	000	5	8	0
OAK	001	000	010	2	4	0

Pitchers: HERSHISER vs DAVIS, Cadaret (5), Nelson (5), Honeycutt (8), Plunk (9), Burns (9)
Home Runs: Hatcher-LA, Davis-LA
Attendance: 49,317

From the first inning of Game 1 when they drove in their teams' first runs, first basemen Will Clark of the Giants and Mark Grace of the Cubs dominated the offense, finishing with eight RBIs apiece and NLCS record-shattering batting average of .650 and .647, respectively. Although Grace homered for two Chicago runs in the opener, the game belonged to Clark, whose four hits—two of them home runs, one a grand slam—drove in six of the 11 San Francisco runs.

Grace led the Cubs' retaliation the next day with his second three-hit game, driving in four of Chicago's nine runs with doubles in the first and sixth innings. Kevin Mitchell, Matt Williams, and Robby Thompson—runners-up to Clark for Giants offensive honors in the series—all homered in the losing cause.

Chicago scored first in the next three games but lost them all narrowly. Thompson's two-run homer in the last of the seventh put the Giants ahead for good in Game 3. The next day, Williams's two-run single in the third inning overcame Chicago's lead, and his two-run homer in the fifth broke a 4–4 tie to conclude the scoring.

Cubs starter Mike Bielecki stopped San Francisco on a pair of singles through six innings of Game 5; he carried a 1–0 lead into the seventh, when Clark's triple and Mitchell's sacrifice fly tied the score. An inning later, after Bielecki loaded the bases with three two-out walks, relief ace Mitch Williams was called on to face Clark and got two strikes on him. But after fouling off a slider and fastball, Clark lined a single up the middle for two go-ahead runs. San Francisco closer Steve Bedrosian yielded Chicago a second run in the ninth on a trio of two-out singles, but Ryne Sandberg (until then batting .421 in the series) grounded out, and the Giants owned their first pennant in 27 years.

San Francisco Giants (West), 4; Chicago Cubs (East), 1

SF (W)

PLAYER/POS	AVG	G	AB	R	H	2B	3B	HR	RB	BB	SO	SB
Bill Bathe, ph	.000	2	1	0	0	0	0	0	0	0	1	0
Steve Bedrosian, p	.000	4	0	0	0	0	0	0	0	0	0	0
Jeff Brantley, p	.000	3	0	0	0	0	0	0	0	1	0	0
Brett Butler, of	.211	5	19	6	4	0	0	0	0	3	3	0
Will Clark, 1b	.650	5	20	8	13	3	1	2	8	2	2	0
Kelly Downs, p	.000	2	3	0	0	0	0	0	0	0	1	0
Scott Garrelts, p	.000	2	4	0	0	0	0	0	0	1	1	0
Atlee Hammaker, p	.000	1	0	0	0	0	0	0	0	0	0	0
Terry Kennedy, c	.188	5	16	0	3	1	0	0	0	1	4	0
Mike LaCoss, p	.000	1	1	0	0	0	0	0	0	0	0	0
Craig Lefferts, p	.000	2	0	0	0	0	0	0	0	0	0	0
Greg Litton, 3b	1.000	1	1	0	1	0	0	0	0	0	0	0
Candy Maldonado, of	.000	3	3	1	0	0	0	0	1	2	0	0
Kirt Manwaring, c	.000	3	2	0	0	0	0	0	0	0	0	0
Kevin Mitchell, of	.353	5	17	5	6	0	0	2	7	3	3	0
Donell Nixon, of-2	.000	3	3	0	0	0	0	0	0	0	1	1
Ken Oberkfell, 3b-1	.000	3	4	0	0	0	0	0	0	0	0	0
Rick Reuschel, p	.000	2	2	0	0	0	0	0	0	0	0	0
Ernest Riles, ph	.000	1	1	0	0	0	0	0	0	0	0	0
Don Robinson, p	.000	1	0	0	0	0	0	0	0	0	0	0
Pat Sheridan, of	.154	5	13	1	2	0	1	0	0	0	4	0
Robby Thompson, 2b	.278	5	18	5	5	0	0	2	3	3	2	0
Jose Uribe, ss	.235	5	17	2	4	1	0	0	1	1	5	1
Matt Williams, 3b-5,ss-1	.300	5	20	2	6	1	0	2	9	0	2	0
TOTAL	.267		165	30	44	6	2	8	29	17	29	2

PITCHER	W	L	ERA	G	GS	CG	SV	SHO	IP	H	ER	BB	SO
Steve Bedrosian	0	0	2.70	4	0	0	3	0	3.1	4	1	2	2
Jeff Brantley	0	0	0.00	3	0	0	0	0	5.0	1	0	2	3
Kelly Downs	1	0	3.12	2	0	0	0	0	8.2	8	3	6	6
Scott Garrelts	1	0	5.40	2	2	0	0	0	11.2	16	7	2	8
Atlee Hammaker	0	0	0.00	1	0	0	0	0	1.0	1	0	0	0
Mike LaCoss	0	0	9.00	1	1	0	0	0	3.0	7	3	0	2
Craig Lefferts	0	0	9.00	2	0	0	0	0	1.0	1	1	2	1
Rick Reuschel	1	1	5.19	2	2	0	0	0	8.2	12	5	2	5
Don Robinson	1	0	0.00	1	0	0	0	0	1.2	3	0	0	0
TOTAL	4	1	4.09	18	5	0	3	0	44.0	53	20	16	27

CHI (E)

PLAYER/POS	AVG	G	AB	R	H	2B	3B	HR	RB	BB	SO	SB
Paul Assenmacher, p	.000	2	0	0	0	0	0	0	0	0	0	0
Mike Bielecki, p	.200	2	5	0	1	0	0	0	2	0	2	0
Andre Dawson, of	.105	5	19	0	2	1	0	0	3	2	6	0
Shawon Dunston, ss	.316	5	19	2	6	0	0	0	0	1	1	1
Joe Girardi, c	.100	4	10	1	1	0	0	0	0	1	2	0
Mark Grace, 1b	.647	5	17	3	11	3	1	1	8	4	1	1
Paul Kilgus, p	.000	1	0	0	0	0	0	0	0	0	0	0
Lester Lancaster, p	.000	3	1	0	0	0	0	0	0	0	1	0
Vance Law, 3b-1	.000	2	3	0	0	0	0	0	0	0	3	0
Greg Maddux, p-2	.000	3	3	1	0	0	0	0	0	0	0	0
L. McClendon, c-2,of-1	.667	3	3	0	2	0	0	0	0	1	0	0
Domingo Ramos, ph	.000	1	1	0	0	0	0	0	0	0	0	0
Luis Salazar, 3b	.368	5	19	2	7	0	1	1	2	0	0	0
Ryne Sandberg, 2b	.400	5	20	6	8	3	1	1	4	3	4	0
Scott Sanderson, p	.000	1	0	0	0	0	0	0	0	0	0	0
Dwight Smith, of	.200	4	15	2	3	1	0	0	0	2	2	1
Rick Sutcliffe, p	.500	1	2	0	1	1	0	0	0	0	0	0
Jerome Walton, of	.364	5	22	4	8	0	0	0	2	2	2	0
Mitch Webster, of-2	.333	3	3	0	1	0	0	0	0	0	0	0
Curtis Wilkerson, 3b-1	.500	3	2	1	1	0	0	0	0	0	0	0
Mitch Williams, p	.000	2	0	0	0	0	0	0	0	0	0	0
Steve Wilson, p	.000	2	0	0	0	0	0	0	0	0	0	0
Rick Wrona, c	.000	2	5	0	0	0	0	0	0	0	3	0
Marvell Wynne, of-2	.167	4	6	0	1	0	0	0	0	0	0	0
TOTAL	.303		175	22	53	9	3	3	21	16	27	3

PITCHER	W	L	ERA	G	GS	CG	SV	SHO	IP	H	ER	BB	SO
P. Assenmacher	0	0	13.50	2	0	0	0	0	0.2	3	1	0	0
Mike Bielecki	0	1	3.65	2	2	0	0	0	12.1	7	5	6	11
Paul Kilgus	0	0	0.00	1	0	0	0	0	3.0	4	0	1	1
Lester Lancaster	1	1	6.00	3	0	0	0	0	6.0	6	4	1	3
Greg Maddux	0	1	13.50	2	2	0	0	0	7.1	13	11	4	5
Scott Sanderson	0	0	0.00	1	0	0	0	0	2.0	2	0	0	1
Rick Sutcliffe	0	0	4.50	1	1	0	0	0	6.0	5	3	4	2
Mitch Williams	0	0	0.00	2	0	0	0	0	1.0	1	0	0	2
Steve Wilson	0	1	4.91	2	0	0	0	0	3.2	3	2	1	4
TOTAL	1	4	5.57	16	5	0	0	0	42.0	44	26	17	29

GAME 1 AT CHI OCT 4

				R	H	E
SF	301	400	030	11	13	0
CHI	201	000	000	3	10	1

Pitchers: GARRELTS, Brantley (8), Hammaker (9) vs MADDUX, Kilgus (5), Wilson (8)
Home Runs: Grace-CHI, Clark-SF (2), Sandberg-CHI, Mitchell-SF
Attendance: 39,195

GAME 2 AT CHI OCT 5

				R	H	E
SF	000	200	021	5	10	0
CHI	600	003	00X	9	11	0

Pitchers: REUSCHEL, Downs (1), Lefferts (6), Brantley (7), Bedrosian (8) vs Bielecki, Assenmacher (5), LANCASTER (6)
Home Runs: Mitchell-SF, Williams-SF, Thompson-SF
Attendance: 39,195

GAME 3 AT SF OCT 7

				R	H	E
CHI	200	100	100	4	10	0
SF	300	000	20X	5	8	3

Pitchers: Sutcliffe, Assenmacher (7), LANCASTER (7) vs LaCoss, Brantley (4), ROBINSON (7), Lefferts (8), Bedrosian (9)
Home Runs: Thompson-SF
Attendance: 62,065

GAME 4 AT SF OCT 8

				R	H	E
CHI	110	020	000	4	12	1
SF	102	120	00X	6	9	1

Pitchers: Maddux, WILSON (4), Sanderson (6), Williams (8) vs Garrelts, DOWNS (5), Bedrosian (9)
Home Runs: Salazar-CHI, Williams-SF
Attendance: 62,078

GAME 5 AT SF OCT 9

				R	H	E
CHI	001	000	001	2	10	1
SF	000	000	12X	3	4	1

Pitchers: BIELECKI, Williams (8), Lancaster (8) vs REUSCHEL, Bedrosian (9)
Attendance: 62,084

The awesome A's produced their share of heroes. Jose Canseco powered a truly heroic home run into the top deck of Toronto's SkyDome in Game 4; Dave Parker, in his seventh postseason series, at last hit his first postseason homer (and later his second); closer Dennis Eckersley added three saves to his four from 1988 to establish a new LCS record; and Carney Lansford was batting .455, with four RBIs, when a hamstring pull in Game 3 ended his series play. But the hero of heroes was leadoff batter Rickey Henderson.

Oakland might have won the opener without Henderson, even though his hard slide into second in the sixth inning broke up a double play and forced a wide throw that gave the A's two runs and their first lead of the game. And the A's might also have won the next day even if Henderson had not rattled Toronto with four stolen bases. The A's suffered their loss in Game 3 despite an early 2–0 lead with Henderson scoring both runs—the first after walking, the second after a double and stolen base.

But in the final two games, Rickey Henderson's contribution made the difference between defeat and victory. A pair of two-run Henderson homers (together with Canseco's memorable blast and later RBI single) gave the A's their 6–5 win in Game 4. And in the first inning of Game 5, Henderson, after walking, stole his eighth base—a postseason series record—before Canseco singled him home with the A's first run. Two innings later Henderson tripled home the second Oakland run. The A's scored twice more in the seventh, but Toronto had narrowed Oakland's lead to one run when Eckersley fanned a final Blue Jay to secure the second straight Oakland pennant. Rickey Henderson was the unanimous choice for series MVP.

Oakland Athletics (West), 4;
Toronto Blue Jays (East), 1

OAK (W)

PLAYER/POS	AVG	G	AB	R	H	2B	3B	HR	RB	BB	SO	SB
Lance Blankenship, 2b	.000	1	0	0	0	0	0	0	0	0	0	0
Jose Canseco, of	.294	5	17	1	5	0	0	1	3	3	7	0
Storm Davis, p	.000	1	0	0	0	0	0	0	0	0	0	0
Dennis Eckersley, p	.000	4	0	0	0	0	0	0	0	0	0	0
Mike Gallego, 2b-2,ss-2	.273	4	11	3	3	1	0	0	1	0	2	0
Ron Hassey, c	.167	2	6	0	1	0	0	0	1	1	2	0
Dave Henderson, of	.263	5	19	4	5	3	0	1	1	2	5	0
Rickey Henderson, of	.400	5	15	8	6	1	1	2	5	7	0	8
Rick Honeycutt, p	.000	3	0	0	0	0	0	0	0	0	0	0
Stan Javier, of	.000	1	2	0	0	0	0	0	0	0	1	0
Carney Lansford, 3b	.455	3	11	2	5	0	0	0	4	2	1	2
Mark McGwire, 1b	.389	5	18	3	7	1	0	1	3	1	4	0
Mike Moore, p	.000	1	0	0	0	0	0	0	0	0	0	0
Gene Nelson, p	.000	1	0	0	0	0	0	0	0	0	0	0
Dave Parker, dh	.188	4	16	2	3	0	0	2	3	0	0	0
Ken Phelps, ph	1.000	1	1	0	1	1	0	0	0	0	0	0
Tony Phillips, 2b-3,3b-3	.167	5	18	1	3	1	0	0	1	2	4	2
Terry Steinbach, c-3,dh-1	.200	4	15	0	3	0	0	0	1	1	5	0
Dave Stewart, p	.000	2	0	0	0	0	0	0	0	0	0	0
Walt Weiss, ss	.111	4	9	2	1	1	0	0	0	1	1	1
Bob Welch, p	.000	1	0	0	0	0	0	0	0	0	0	0
Matt Young, p	.000	1	0	0	0	0	0	0	0	0	0	0
TOTAL	.272		158	26	43	9	1	7	23	20	32	13

PITCHER	W	L	ERA	G	GS	CG	SV	SHO	IP	H	ER	BB	SO
Storm Davis	0	1	7.11	1	1	0	0	0	6.1	5	5	2	3
Dennis Eckersley	0	0	1.59	4	0	0	3	0	5.2	4	1	0	2
Rick Honeycutt	0	0	32.40	3	0	0	0	0	1.2	6	6	5	1
Mike Moore	1	0	0.00	1	1	0	0	0	7.0	3	0	2	3
Gene Nelson	0	0	0.00	1	0	0	0	0	1.1	1	0	0	2
Dave Stewart	2	0	2.81	2	2	0	0	0	16.0	13	5	3	9
Bob Welch	1	0	3.18	1	1	0	0	0	5.2	8	2	1	4
Matt Young	0	0	0.00	1	0	0	0	0	0.1	0	0	2	0
TOTAL	4	1	3.89	14	5	0	3	0	44.0	40	19	15	24

TOR (E)

PLAYER/POS	AVG	G	AB	R	H	2B	3B	HR	RB	BB	SO	SB
Jim Acker, p	.000	5	0	0	0	0	0	0	0	0	0	0
George Bell, dh-3,of-2	.200	5	20	2	4	0	0	1	2	0	3	0
Pat Borders, c	1.000	1	1	0	1	0	0	0	1	0	0	0
John Cerutti, p	.000	2	0	0	0	0	0	0	0	0	0	0
Junior Felix, of	.273	3	11	0	3	1	0	0	3	0	2	0
Tony Fernandez, ss	.350	5	20	6	7	3	0	0	1	1	2	5
Mike Flanagan, p	.000	1	0	0	0	0	0	0	0	0	0	0
Kelly Gruber, 3b	.294	5	17	2	5	1	0	0	1	3	2	1
Tom Henke, p	.000	3	0	0	0	0	0	0	0	0	0	0
Jimmy Key, p	.000	1	0	0	0	0	0	0	0	0	0	0
Manny Lee, 2b	.250	2	8	2	2	0	0	0	0	0	1	0
Nelson Liriano, 2b	.429	3	7	1	3	0	0	0	1	2	0	3
Lee Mazzilli, dh-2	.000	3	8	0	0	0	0	0	0	0	2	0
Fred McGriff, 1b	.143	5	21	1	3	0	0	0	3	0	4	0
Lloyd Moseby, of	.313	5	16	4	5	0	0	1	2	5	2	1
Rance Mulliniks, ph	.000	1	1	0	0	0	0	0	0	0	1	0
Dave Stieb, p	.000	2	0	0	0	0	0	0	0	0	0	0
Todd Stottlemyre, p	.000	1	0	0	0	0	0	0	0	0	0	0
Duane Ward, p	.000	2	0	0	0	0	0	0	0	0	0	0
David Wells, p	.000	1	0	0	0	0	0	0	0	0	0	0
Ernie Whitt, c	.125	5	16	1	2	0	0	1	3	2	3	0
Mookie Wilson, of	.263	5	19	2	5	0	0	0	2	2	2	1
TOTAL	.242		165	21	40	5	0	3	19	15	24	11

PITCHER	W	L	ERA	G	GS	CG	SV	SHO	IP	H	ER	BB	SO
Jim Acker	0	0	1.42	5	0	0	0	0	6.1	4	1	1	4
John Cerutti	0	0	0.00	2	0	0	0	0	2.2	0	0	3	1
Mike Flanagan	0	1	10.38	1	1	0	0	0	4.1	7	5	1	3
Tom Henke	0	0	0.00	3	0	0	0	0	2.2	0	0	0	3
Jimmy Key	1	0	4.50	1	1	0	0	0	6.0	7	3	2	2
Dave Stieb	0	2	6.35	2	2	0	0	0	11.1	12	8	6	10
Todd Stottlemyre	0	1	7.20	1	1	0	0	0	5.0	7	4	2	3
Duane Ward	0	0	7.36	2	0	0	0	0	3.2	6	3	3	5
David Wells	0	0	0.00	1	0	0	0	0	1.0	0	0	2	1
TOTAL	1	4	5.02	18	5	0	0	0	43.0	43	24	20	32

GAME 1 AT OAK OCT 3

TOR	020	100	000	3	5	1
OAK	010	013	02X	7	11	0

Pitchers: STIEB, Acker (6), Ward (8) vs STEWART, Eckersley (9)
Home Runs: D.Henderson-OAK, Whitt-TOR, McGwire-OAK
Attendance: 49,435

GAME 2 AT OAK OCT 4

TOR	001	000	020	3	5	1
OAK	000	203	10X	6	9	1

Pitchers: STOTTLEMYRE, Acker (6), Wells (6), Henke (7), Cerutti (8) vs MOORE, Honeycutt (8), Eckersley (8)
Home Runs: Parker-OAK
Attendance: 49,444

GAME 3 AT TOR OCT 6

OAK	101	100	000	3	8	1
TOR	000	400	30X	7	8	0

Pitchers: DAVIS, Honeycutt (7), Nelson (7), M.Young (8) vs KEY, Acker (7), Henke (9)
Home Runs: Parker-OAK
Attendance: 50,268

GAME 4 AT TOR OCT 7

OAK	003	020	100	6	11	1
TOR	000	101	120	5	13	0

Pitchers: WELCH, Honeycutt (6), Eckersley (8) vs FLANAGAN, Ward (5), Cerutti (8), Acker (9)
Home Runs: R.Henderson-OAK (2), Canseco-OAK
Attendance: 50,076

GAME 5 AT TOR OCT 8

OAK	101	000	200	4	4	0
TOR	000	000	012	3	9	0

Pitchers: STEWART, Eckersley (9) vs STIEB, Acker (7), Henke (9)
Home Runs: Moseby-TOR, Bell-TOR
Attendance: 50,024

Not even the devastating earthquake that blindsided baseball's first San Francisco Bay World Series could halt the Oakland juggernaut. The A's scored first in every game and, except for an inning and a half of Game 2 in which the score stood at 1–1, held their lead to the finish.

A's ace Dave Stewart shut out the Giants on five hits in the opener. Three second-inning Oakland runs initiated the Series scoring, and Dave Parker and Walt Weiss expanded Stewart's margin of comfort with solo homers in the third and fourth. In Game 2, doubles by Carney Lansford in the first inning and Parker in the fourth drove home the two runs the A's would need for victory; Terry Steinbach's three-run blast later in the fourth added frosting to Oakland's cake. A's starter Mike Moore yielded a pair of singles and the first San Francisco run of the Series in the third inning but held the Giants to just two more singles in his seven-plus innings of work. Relievers Rick Honeycutt and Dennis Eckersley hurled perfect ball in the eighth and ninth.

After a day off, the Series shifted 11 miles across the Bay to San Francisco for Game 3. But just as fans were settling into their seats, the earthquake struck, knocking out power to Candlestick Park and (as gradually became known) killing 67 people in scattered pockets of destruction throughout the Bay Area. The fans were sent home, but despite the pleas of a few Eastern reporters that the rest of the Series be cancelled, the overwhelming desire of Bay Area residents prevailed, and Game 3 came off at last, 10 days late. Starter Dave Stewart gave up three runs in seven innings, but by the time he was relieved, his A's had sent nine men across the plate. Four more runs in the eighth completed the Oakland scoring. The Giants put together their first big inning of the Series, scoring four runs in the last of the ninth. Although the Giants' effort fell far short of what was needed, pinch hitter Bill Bathe's home run—the game's seventh, including five by the A's—set a new World Series record.

Oakland's Rickey Henderson led off Game 4 with a home run, and by the time Kevin Mitchell homered in San Francisco's first pair of runs in the sixth inning, the A's had scored eight times. The Giants struggled back, though, scoring four times in the seventh on a walk and a cycle of hits—home run, triple, double, and single—to draw within two runs of a tie. But they came no closer. Todd Burns and Eckersley hurled the Series to its conclusion.

Oakland Athletics (AL), 4; San Francisco Giants (NL), 0

OAK (A)

PLAYER/POS	AVG	G	AB	R	H	2B	3B	HR	RB	BB	SO	SB
Lance Blankenship, 2b	.500	1	2	1	1	0	0	0	0	0	0	0
Todd Burns, p	.000	2	0	0	0	0	0	0	0	0	0	0
Jose Canseco, of	.357	4	14	5	5	0	0	1	3	4	3	1
Dennis Eckersley, p	.000	2	0	0	0	0	0	0	0	0	0	0
Mike Gallego, 2b-1,3b-1	.000	2	1	0	0	0	0	0	0	0	0	0
Dave Henderson, of	.308	4	13	6	4	2	0	2	4	4	3	0
Rickey Henderson, of	.474	4	19	4	9	1	2	1	3	2	2	3
Rick Honeycutt, p	.000	3	0	0	0	0	0	0	0	0	0	0
Stan Javier, of	.000	1	0	0	0	0	0	0	0	0	0	0
Carney Lansford, 3b	.438	4	16	5	7	1	0	1	4	3	1	0
Mark McGwire, 1b	.294	4	17	0	5	1	0	0	1	1	3	0
Mike Moore, p	.333	2	3	1	1	1	0	0	2	0	1	0
Gene Nelson, p	.000	2	0	0	0	0	0	0	0	0	0	0
Dave Parker, dh-2	.222	3	9	2	2	1	0	1	2	0	2	0
Ken Phelps, ph	.000	1	1	0	0	0	0	0	0	0	0	0
Tony Phillips, 2b-3,3b-2,of-1	.235	4	17	2	4	1	0	1	3	0	3	0
Terry Steinbach, c	.250	4	16	3	4	0	1	1	7	2	1	0
Dave Stewart, p	.000	2	3	0	0	0	0	0	0	0	1	0
Walt Weiss, ss	.133	4	15	3	2	0	0	1	1	2	2	0
TOTAL	.301		146	32	44	8	3	9	30	18	22	4

PITCHER	W	L	ERA	G	GS	CG	SV	SHO	IP	H	ER	BB	SO
Todd Burns	0	0	0.00	2	0	0	0	0	1.2	1	0	1	0
Dennis Eckersley	0	0	0.00	2	0	0	1	0	1.2	0	0	0	0
Rick Honeycutt	0	0	6.75	3	0	0	0	0	2.2	4	2	0	2
Mike Moore	2	0	2.08	2	2	0	0	0	13.0	9	3	3	10
Gene Nelson	0	0	54.00	2	0	0	0	0	1.0	4	6	2	1
Dave Stewart	2	0	1.69	2	2	1	0	1	16.0	10	3	2	14
TOTAL	4	0	3.50	13	4	1	1	1	36.0	28	14	8	27

SF (N)

PLAYER/POS	AVG	G	AB	R	H	2B	3B	HR	RB	BB	SO	SB
Bill Bathe, ph	.500	2	2	1	1	0	0	1	3	0	0	0
Steve Bedrosian, p	.000	2	0	0	0	0	0	0	0	0	0	0
Jeff Brantley, p	.000	3	0	0	0	0	0	0	0	0	0	0
Brett Butler, of	.286	4	14	1	4	1	0	0	1	2	1	2
Will Clark, 1b	.250	4	16	2	4	1	0	0	0	1	3	0
Kelly Downs, p	.000	3	0	0	0	0	0	0	0	0	0	0
Scott Garrelts, p	.000	2	1	0	0	0	0	0	0	0	1	0
Atlee Hammaker, p	.000	2	0	0	0	0	0	0	0	0	0	0
Terry Kennedy, c	.167	4	12	1	2	0	0	0	2	1	3	0
Mike LaCoss, p	.000	2	1	0	0	0	0	0	0	0	0	0
Craig Lefferts, p	.000	3	0	0	0	0	0	0	0	0	0	0
Greg Litton, 2b-2,3b-1	.500	2	6	1	3	1	0	1	3	0	0	0
Candy Maldonado, of-3	.091	4	11	1	1	0	1	0	0	0	4	0
Kirt Manwaring, c	1.000	1	1	1	1	1	0	0	0	0	0	0
Kevin Mitchell, of	.294	4	17	2	5	0	0	1	2	0	3	0
Donell Nixon, of	.200	2	5	1	1	0	0	0	0	1	1	0
Ken Oberkfell, 3b	.333	4	6	1	2	0	0	0	0	3	0	0
Rick Reuschel, p	.000	1	0	0	0	0	0	0	0	0	0	0
Ernie Riles, dh-2	.000	4	8	0	0	0	0	0	0	0	1	0
Don Robinson, p	.000	1	0	0	0	0	0	0	0	0	0	0
Pat Sheridan, of	.000	1	2	0	0	0	0	0	0	0	0	0
Robby Thompson, 2b	.091	4	11	0	1	0	0	0	2	0	4	0
Jose Uribe, ss	.200	3	5	1	1	0	0	0	0	0	0	0
Matt Williams, ss-4,3b-3	.125	4	16	1	2	0	0	1	1	0	6	0
TOTAL	.209		134	14	28	4	1	4	14	8	27	2

PITCHER	W	L	ERA	G	GS	CG	SV	SHO	IP	H	ER	BB	SO
Steve Bedrosian	0	0	0.00	2	0	0	0	0	2.2	0	0	2	2
Jeff Brantley	0	0	4.15	3	0	0	0	0	4.1	5	2	3	1
Kelly Downs	0	0	7.71	3	0	0	0	0	4.2	3	4	2	4
Scott Garrelts	0	2	9.82	2	2	0	0	0	7.1	13	8	1	8
Atlee Hammaker	0	0	15.43	2	0	0	0	0	2.1	8	4	0	2
Mike LaCoss	0	0	6.23	2	0	0	0	0	4.1	4	3	3	2
Craig Lefferts	0	0	3.38	3	0	0	0	0	2.2	2	1	2	1
Rick Reuschel	0	1	11.25	1	1	0	0	0	4.0	5	5	4	2
Don Robinson	0	1	21.60	1	1	0	0	0	1.2	4	4	1	0
TOTAL	0	4	8.21	19	4	0	0	0	34.0	44	31	18	22

GAME 1 AT OAK OCT 14

				R	H	E
SF	000	000	000	0	5	1
OAK	031	100	00X	5	11	1

Pitchers: GARRELTS, Hammaker (5), Brantley (6), LaCoss (8) vs STEWART
Home Runs: Parker-OAK, Weiss-OAK
Attendance: 49,385

GAME 2 AT OAK OCT 15

				R	H	E
SF	001	000	000	1	4	0
OAK	100	400	00X	5	7	0

Pitchers: REUSCHEL, Downs (5), Lefferts (7), Bedrosian (8) vs MOORE, Honeycutt (8), Eckersley (9)
Home Runs: Steinbach-OAK
Attendance: 49,388

GAME 3 AT SF OCT 27

				R	H	E
OAK	200	241	040	13	14	0
SF	010	200	004	7	10	3

Pitchers: STEWART, Honeycutt (8), Nelson (9), Burns (9) vs GARRELTS, Downs (4), Brantley (5), Hammaker (8), Lefferts (9)
Home Runs: Williams-SF, D.Henderson-OAK (2), Phillips-OAK, Canseco-OAK, Lansford-OAK, Bathe-SF
Attendance: 62,038

GAME 4 AT SF OCT 28

				R	H	E
OAK	130	031	010	9	12	0
SF	000	002	400	6	9	0

Pitchers: MOORE, Nelson (7), Honeycutt (7), Burns (7), Eckersley (9) vs ROBINSON, LaCoss (2), Brantley (6), Downs (6), Lefferts (8), Bedrosian (8)
Home Runs: R.Henderson-OAK, Mitchell-SF, Litton-SF
Attendance: 62,032

Fielding plays and misplays provided some of the most crucial moments of the series. After the Pirates had overcome a three-run deficit to tie the score in Game 1, they won the game when Eric Davis misplayed Andy Van Slyke's fly to left field for a run-scoring double. Cincinnati right fielder Paul O'Neill evened the series in Game 2 by singling home the game's first run in the first inning, then (with the game tied 1–1 in the fifth) doubling in the go-ahead—and final—run on a fly Pirates left fielder Barry Bonds lost in the late afternoon sun. Finally, O'Neill gunned down Pittsburgh's potential tying run at third base when Van Slyke attempted to move up after Bonds's fly-out to right.

Two- and three-run homers by Reds Billy Hatcher and Mariano Duncan gave Cincinnati the series advantage in Game 3, and Chris Sabo's sacrifice fly and two-run blast proved the decisive blows a day later as the Reds pushed their series lead to 3–1. In that game left fielder Eric Davis, backing up Bobby Bonilla's double off the center field wall, prevented what would have become a game-tying run when, with a perfect throw to third, he nailed Bonilla trying for a triple.

The Pirates staved off elimination with a narrow 3–2 win in Game 5, a win preserved by a spectacular bases-loaded game-ending double play. But in Game 6, Pittsburgh's uncertain fielding in the first inning gave the Reds their first and, as it turned out, decisive run. In the ninth inning, with the Reds ahead 2–1, Reds right fielder Glen Braggs snared a deep fly with a leaping catch that prevented at least one, and perhaps two, Pirates runs from scoring. One strikeout later the Reds had snared the National League pennant.

Cincinnati Reds (West), 4; Pittsburgh Pirates (East), 2

CIN (W)

PLAYER/POS	AVG	G	AB	R	H	2B	3B	HR	RB	BB	SO	SB
Billy Bates, pr	.000	2	0	1	0	0	0	0	0	0	0	0
Todd Benzinger, 1b-2	.333	5	9	0	3	0	0	0	0	2	0	0
Glenn Braggs, of	.200	2	5	0	1	0	0	0	0	0	1	0
Tom Browning, p	.000	2	3	0	0	0	0	0	0	0	1	0
Norm Charlton, p	.000	4	0	0	0	0	0	0	0	0	0	0
Eric Davis, of	.174	6	23	2	4	1	0	0	2	1	9	0
Rob Dibble, p	.000	4	2	0	0	0	0	0	0	0	1	0
Mariano Duncan, 2b	.300	6	20	1	6	0	0	1	4	0	8	0
Billy Hatcher, of	.333	4	15	2	5	1	0	1	2	0	2	0
Danny Jackson, p	.000	2	3	0	0	0	0	0	0	0	2	0
Barry Larkin, ss	.261	6	23	5	6	2	0	0	1	3	1	3
Rick Mahler, p	.000	1	0	0	0	0	0	0	0	0	0	0
Hal Morris, 1b-4	.417	5	12	3	5	1	0	0	1	1	0	0
Randy Myers, p	.000	4	0	0	0	0	0	0	0	0	0	0
Ron Oester, 2b-2	.333	4	3	1	1	0	0	0	0	0	1	0
Joe Oliver, c	.143	5	14	1	2	0	0	0	0	0	2	0
Paul O'Neill, of	.471	5	17	1	8	3	0	1	4	1	1	1
Luis Quinones, ph	.500	3	2	1	1	0	0	0	2	0	0	1
Jeff Reed, c	.000	4	7	0	0	0	0	0	0	0	2	0
Jose Rijo, p	.000	2	5	0	0	0	0	0	0	0	1	0
Chris Sabo, 3b	.227	6	22	1	5	0	0	1	3	1	4	0
Scott Scudder, p	.000	1	0	0	0	0	0	0	0	0	0	0
Herm Winningham, of-2	.286	3	7	1	2	1	0	0	1	1	1	1
TOTAL	.255		192	20	49	9	0	4	20	10	37	6

PITCHER	W	L	ERA	G	GS	CG	SV	SHO	IP	H	ER	BB	SO
Tom Browning	1	1	3.27	2	2	0	0	0	11.0	9	4	6	5
Norm Charlton	1	1	1.80	4	0	0	0	0	5.0	4	1	3	3
Rob Dibble	0	0	0.00	4	0	0	1	0	5.0	0	0	1	10
Danny Jackson	1	0	2.38	2	2	0	0	0	11.1	8	3	7	8
Rick Mahler	0	0	0.00	1	0	0	0	0	1.2	2	0	0	0
Randy Myers	0	0	0.00	4	0	0	3	0	5.2	2	0	3	7
Jose Rijo	1	0	4.38	2	2	0	0	0	12.1	10	6	7	15
Scott Scudder	0	0	0.00	1	0	0	0	0	1.0	1	0	0	1
TOTAL	4	2	2.38	20	6	0	4	0	53.0	36	14	27	49

PIT (E)

PLAYER/POS	AVG	G	AB	R	H	2B	3B	HR	RB	BB	SO	SB
Wally Backman, 3b-2	.143	3	7	1	1	1	0	0	0	1	3	1
Stan Belinda, p	.000	3	0	0	0	0	0	0	0	0	0	0
Jay Bell, ss	.250	6	20	3	5	1	0	1	1	4	3	0
Barry Bonds, of	.167	6	18	4	3	0	0	0	1	6	5	2
Bobby Bonilla, of-5,3b-3	.190	6	21	0	4	1	0	0	1	3	1	0
Sid Bream, 1b	.500	4	8	1	4	1	0	1	3	2	3	0
Doug Drabek, p	.167	2	6	0	1	0	0	0	0	0	2	0
Jeff King, 3b-4	.100	5	10	0	1	0	0	0	0	1	5	0
Bill Landrum, p	.000	2	0	0	0	0	0	0	0	0	0	0
Mike LaValliere, c	.000	3	6	1	0	0	0	0	0	3	1	0
Jose Lind, 2b	.238	6	21	1	5	1	1	1	2	1	4	0
Carmelo Martinez, 1b	.250	2	8	0	2	2	0	0	2	0	1	0
Bob Patterson, p	.000	2	0	0	0	0	0	0	0	0	0	0
Ted Power, p	.000	3	1	0	0	0	0	0	0	0	1	0
Gary Redus, 1b-2	.250	5	8	1	2	0	0	0	0	1	3	1
R. J. Reynolds, of-3	.200	6	10	0	2	0	0	0	0	2	2	1
Don Slaught, c	.091	4	11	0	1	0	0	0	1	2	3	0
John Smiley, p	.000	1	0	0	0	0	0	0	0	0	0	0
Zane Smith, p	.000	2	3	0	0	0	0	0	0	0	1	0
Andy Van Slyke, of	.208	6	24	3	5	1	1	0	3	1	7	1
Bob Walk, p	.000	2	4	0	0	0	0	0	0	0	4	0
TOTAL	.194		186	15	36	9	2	3	14	27	49	6

PITCHER	W	L	ERA	G	GS	CG	SV	SHO	IP	H	ER	BB	SO
Stan Belinda	0	0	2.45	3	0	0	0	0	3.2	3	1	0	4
Doug Drabek	1	1	1.65	2	2	1	0	0	16.1	12	3	3	13
Bill Landrum	0	0	0.00	2	0	0	1	0	2.0	0	0	0	1
Bob Patterson	0	0	0.00	2	0	0	1	0	1.0	1	0	2	0
Ted Power	0	0	3.60	3	1	0	1	0	5.0	6	2	2	3
John Smiley	0	0	0.00	1	0	0	0	0	2.0	2	0	0	0
Zane Smith	0	2	6.00	2	1	0	0	0	9.0	14	6	1	8
Bob Walk	1	1	4.85	2	2	0	0	0	13.0	11	7	2	8
TOTAL	2	4	3.29	17	6	1	2	0	52.0	49	19	10	37

GAME 1 AT CIN OCT 4

		R	H	E
PIT	001 200 100	4	7	1
CIN	300 000 000	3	5	0

Pitchers: WALK, Belinda (7), Patterson (9), Power (9) vs Rijo, CHARLTON (6), Dibble (9)
Home Runs: Bream-PIT
Attendance: 55,700

GAME 2 AT CIN OCT 5

		R	H	E
PIT	000 010 000	1	6	0
CIN	100 010 00X	2	5	0

Pitchers: DRABEK vs BROWNING, Dibble (7), Myers (8)
Home Runs: Lind-PIT
Attendance: 54,456

GAME 3 AT PIT OCT 8

		R	H	E
CIN	020 030 001	6	13	1
PIT	000 200 010	3	8	0

Pitchers: JACKSON, Dibble (6), Charlton (8), Myers (9) vs SMITH, Landrum (6), Smiley (7), Belinda (9)
Home Runs: Duncan-CIN, Hatcher-CIN
Attendance: 45,611

GAME 4 AT PIT OCT 9

		R	H	E
CIN	000 200 201	5	10	1
PIT	100 100 010	3	8	0

Pitchers: RIJO, Myers (8), Dibble (9) vs WALK, Power (8)
Home Runs: O'Neill-CIN, Sabo-CIN, Bell-PIT
Attendance: 50,461

GAME 5 AT PIT OCT 10

		R	H	E
CIN	100 000 010	2	7	0
PIT	200 100 00X	3	6	1

Pitchers: BROWNING, Mahler (6), Charlton (7), Scudder (8) vs DRABEK, Patterson (9)
Attendance: 48,221

GAME 6 AT CIN OCT 12

		R	H	E
PIT	000 010 000	1	1	3
CIN	100 000 10X	2	9	0

Pitchers: Power, SMITH (3), Belinda (7), Landrum (8) vs Jackson, CHARLTON (7), Myers (8)
Attendance: 56,079

The ejection of Boston ace Roger Clemens from Game 4 for mouthing off to an umpire provided a moment of raucous counterpoint to the surgical precision with which Oakland dismembered the Red Sox. While the A's pitchers anesthetized Boston's hitters, parceling out just one run per game, their batters sliced up the Sox with singles, steals, and sacrifices.

In the fourth inning of Game 1, Boston's Wade Boggs interrupted a pitchers' duel between Clemens and Oakland's Dave Stewart with the series' only home run. But in the top of the seventh—after a tiring Clemens had been relieved—the A's evened the score with a walk, single, and sacrifice fly, took the lead an inning later with a pair of singles sandwiched around a bunt and stolen base, then buried the Sox with seven runs in the ninth. DH Harold Baines provided Oakland's most productive offense in the second game, singling home the tying run in the fourth inning, driving in the tiebreaker with a groundout in the seventh, and doubling home a third run in the ninth. In Game 3, a double steal by Baines and Jose Canseco set up the A's tying and tiebreaking runs, which scored on a sacrifice fly and a single.

The A's scored first for the only time in the series in Game 4, on a pair of singles and a grounder to short in the second inning. Following the shouting match between the Sox and umpires that erupted when pitcher Clemens was thrown out for disputing a walk, Mike Gallego doubled home two more Oakland runs. A trio of Boston relievers stopped the A's the rest of the way, and a pair of Red Sox hits in the ninth ended Dave Stewart's shutout bid. But Rick Honeycutt came on to preserve Stewart's second win of the series and sew up Oakland's third successive American League championship.

Oakland Athletics (West), 4; Boston Red Sox (East), 0

OAK (W)

PLAYER/POS	AVG	G	AB	R	H	2B	3B	HR	RB	BB	SO	SB
Harold Baines, dh	.357	4	14	2	5	1	0	0	3	2	1	1
Lance Blankenship, dh	.000	3	0	1	0	0	0	0	0	0	0	1
Jose Canseco, of	.182	4	11	3	2	0	0	0	1	5	5	2
Dennis Eckersley, p	.000	3	0	0	0	0	0	0	0	0	0	0
Mike Gallego, ss-3,2b-2	.400	4	10	1	4	1	0	0	2	1	1	0
Ron Hassey, c-1,dh-1	.333	2	3	0	1	0	0	0	0	2	0	0
Dave Henderson, of	.167	2	6	0	1	0	0	0	1	0	2	1
Rickey Henderson, of	.294	4	17	1	5	0	0	0	3	1	2	2
Rick Honeycutt, p	.000	3	0	0	0	0	0	0	0	0	0	0
Doug Jennings, of	.000	1	1	0	0	0	0	0	0	0	0	0
Carney Lansford, 3b	.438	4	16	2	7	1	0	0	2	0	1	0
Willie McGee, of-2,dh-1	.222	3	9	3	2	1	0	0	0	1	2	2
Mark McGwire, 1b	.154	4	13	2	2	0	0	0	2	3	3	0
Mike Moore, p	.000	1	0	0	0	0	0	0	0	0	0	0
Gene Nelson, p	.000	1	0	0	0	0	0	0	0	0	0	0
Jamie Quirk, ph	1.000	1	1	0	1	0	0	0	0	0	0	0
Willie Randolph, 2b	.375	4	8	1	3	0	0	0	3	1	0	0
Terry Steinbach, c	.455	3	11	2	5	0	0	0	1	1	2	0
Dave Stewart, p	.000	2	0	0	0	0	0	0	0	0	0	0
Walt Weiss, ss	.000	2	7	2	0	0	0	0	0	2	2	0
Bob Welch, p	.000	1	0	0	0	0	0	0	0	0	0	0
TOTAL	.299		127	20	38	4	0	0	18	19	21	9

PITCHER	W	L	ERA	G	GS	CG	SV	SHO	IP	H	ER	BB	SO
Dennis Eckersley	0	0	0.00	3	0	0	2	0	3.1	2	0	0	3
Rick Honeycutt	0	0	0.00	3	0	0	1	0	1.2	0	0	0	0
Mike Moore	1	0	1.50	1	1	0	0	0	6.0	4	1	1	5
Gene Nelson	0	0	0.00	1	0	0	0	0	1.2	3	0	0	0
Dave Stewart	2	0	1.13	2	2	0	0	0	16.0	8	2	2	4
Bob Welch	1	0	1.23	1	1	0	0	0	7.1	6	1	3	4
TOTAL	4	0	1.00	11	4	0	3	0	36.0	23	4	6	16

BOS (E)

PLAYER/POS	AVG	G	AB	R	H	2B	3B	HR	RB	BB	SO	SB
Larry Andersen, p	.000	3	0	0	0	0	0	0	0	0	0	0
Marty Barrett, 2b	.000	3	0	0	0	0	0	0	0	0	0	0
Mike Boddicker, p	.000	1	0	0	0	0	0	0	0	0	0	0
Wade Boggs, 3b	.438	4	16	1	7	1	0	1	1	0	3	0
Tom Bolton, p	.000	2	0	0	0	0	0	0	0	0	0	0
Tom Brunansky, of	.083	4	12	0	1	0	0	0	1	1	3	0
Ellis Burks, of	.267	4	15	1	4	2	0	0	0	1	1	1
Roger Clemens, p	.000	2	0	0	0	0	0	0	0	0	0	0
Dwight Evans, dh	.231	4	13	0	3	1	0	0	0	1	3	0
Jeff Gray, p	.000	2	0	0	0	0	0	0	0	0	0	0
Mike Greenwell, of	.000	4	14	1	0	0	0	0	0	2	2	0
Greg Harris, p	.000	1	0	0	0	0	0	0	0	0	0	0
Danny Heep, ph	.000	2	2	0	0	0	0	0	0	0	0	0
Dana Kiecker, p	.000	1	0	0	0	0	0	0	0	0	0	0
Randy Kutcher, pr	.000	2	0	0	0	0	0	0	0	0	0	0
Dennis Lamp, p	.000	1	0	0	0	0	0	0	0	0	0	0
Mike Marshall, ph	.333	3	3	0	1	0	0	0	0	0	0	0
Rob Murphy, p	.000	1	0	0	0	0	0	0	0	0	0	0
Tony Pena, c	.214	4	14	0	3	0	0	0	0	0	0	0
Carlos Quintana, 1b	.000	4	13	0	0	0	0	0	1	1	0	0
Jeff Reardon, p	.000	1	0	0	0	0	0	0	0	0	0	0
Jody Reed, 2b-4,ss-3	.133	4	15	0	2	0	0	0	1	0	2	0
Luis Rivera, ss	.222	4	9	1	2	1	0	0	0	0	2	0
TOTAL	.183		126	4	23	5	0	1	4	6	16	1

PITCHER	W	L	ERA	G	GS	CG	SV	SHO	IP	H	ER	BB	SO
Larry Andersen	0	1	6.00	3	0	0	0	0	3.0	3	2	3	3
Mike Boddicker	0	1	2.25	1	1	1	0	0	8.0	6	2	3	7
Tom Bolton	0	0	0.00	2	0	0	0	0	3.0	2	0	2	3
Roger Clemens	0	1	3.52	2	2	0	0	0	7.2	7	3	5	4
Jeff Gray	0	0	2.70	2	0	0	0	0	3.1	4	1	1	2
Greg Harris	0	1	27.00	1	0	0	0	0	0.1	3	1	0	0
Dana Kiecker	0	0	1.59	1	1	0	0	0	5.2	6	1	1	2
Dennis Lamp	0	0	108.00	1	0	0	0	0	0.1	2	4	2	0
Rob Murphy	0	0	13.50	1	0	0	0	0	0.2	2	1	1	0
Jeff Reardon	0	0	9.00	1	0	0	0	0	2.0	3	2	1	0
TOTAL	0	4	4.50	15	4	1	0	0	34.0	38	17	19	21

GAME 1 AT BOS OCT 6

				R	H	E
OAK	000	000	117	9	13	0
BOS	000	100	000	1	5	1

Pitchers: STEWART, Eckersley (9) vs Clemens, ANDERSEN (7), Bolton (8), Gray (8), Lamp (9), Murphy (9)
Home Runs: Boggs-BOS
Attendance: 35,192

GAME 2 AT BOS OCT 7

				R	H	E
OAK	000	100	102	4	13	1
BOS	001	000	000	1	6	0

Pitchers: WELCH, Honeycutt (8), Eckersley (8) vs Kiecker, HARRIS (6), Andersen (7), Reardon (8)
Attendance: 35,070

GAME 3 AT OAK OCT 9

				R	H	E
BOS	010	000	000	1	8	3
OAK	000	202	00X	4	6	0

Pitchers: BODDICKER vs MOORE, Nelson (7), Honeycutt (8), Eckersley (9)
Attendance: 49,026

GAME 4 AT OAK OCT 10

				R	H	E
BOS	000	000	001	1	4	1
OAK	030	000	00X	3	6	0

Pitchers: CLEMENS, Bolton (2), Gray (5), Andersen (8) vs STEWART, Honeycutt (9)
Attendance: 49,052

In the most stunning World Series sweep since 1954, Cincinnati's fired-up Reds roasted the team many were proclaiming baseball's newest dynasty. Reds left fielder Eric Davis, playing despite shoulder and knee injuries, provided the A's their first hint of what was to come when—on the first pitch thrown to him in the first inning—he homered over the center field wall for two runs. Billy Hatcher, on base with a walk, scored ahead of Davis, the first of his Series-high six runs. Hatcher would not be retired at the plate until Game 3. For Oakland starter Dave Stewart, the 7-0 loss in Game 1 ended a personal postseason six-game win streak. For the club, the loss ended a streak of 10 postseason wins in a row.

The A's put up their best fight of the Series in Game 2, scoring first, then overcoming a 2–1 deficit in the third inning with three more runs for a 4–2 lead. Cincinnati narrowed the gap with a run in the fourth and tied the score in the eighth when Hatcher tripled—setting a World Series record with his seventh straight hit—and came home on a grounder to short. The A's held on until the 10th inning, when ace reliever Dennis Eckersley gave up three straight hits to lose the game.

Game 3 was another Cincinnati blowout, an 8–3 contest in which all 11 runs were scored in the second and third innings. Chris Sabo led the Reds assault with two home runs, and handled a Series-record 10 chances at third base.

For seven innings of Game 4 the tide of battle seemed to be turning in Oakland's favor. Billy Hatcher—who was batting .750—left the game after a pitch hit his hand in the first inning. Later in the inning Eric Davis tore a kidney diving for a Willie McGee shot that went for a double. McGee went on to score, and Davis departed for the hospital. A renewed Dave Stewart, supported by sharp fielding, seemed capable of sustaining his 1–0 lead to the finish. But in the eighth the Reds, with just one solid hit, eked out the two runs they would need for victory. After loading the bases with a leadoff single, a third-strike bunt that went for a hit, and a sacrifice bunt that Stewart misplayed for an error, the Reds drove home the tying run with a grounder to short and took the lead on a sacrifice fly. Meanwhile Reds starter Jose Rijo held the A's hitless after the first inning, leveling 20 men in order from the second into the ninth, when ace closer Randy Myers relieved him for the final two outs of the sweep.

Cincinnati Reds (NL), 4; Oakland Athletics (AL), 0

CIN (N)

PLAYER/POS	AVG	G	AB	R	H	2B	3B	HR	RB	BB	SO	SB
Jack Armstrong, p	.000	1	0	0	0	0	0	0	0	0	0	0
Billy Bates, ph	1.000	1	1	1	1	0	0	0	0	0	0	0
Todd Benzinger, 1b-3	.182	4	11	1	2	0	0	0	0	0	0	0
Glenn Braggs, of-1	.000	2	4	0	0	0	0	0	2	1	0	0
Tom Browning, p	.000	1	0	0	0	0	0	0	0	0	0	0
Norm Charlton, p	.000	1	0	0	0	0	0	0	0	0	0	0
Eric Davis, of	.286	4	14	3	4	0	0	1	5	0	0	0
Rob Dibble, p	.000	3	0	0	0	0	0	0	0	0	0	0
Mariano Duncan, 2b	.143	4	14	1	2	0	0	0	1	2	2	1
Billy Hatcher, of	.750	4	12	6	9	4	1	0	2	2	0	0
Danny Jackson, p	.000	1	1	0	0	0	0	0	0	0	1	0
Barry Larkin, ss	.353	4	17	3	6	1	1	0	1	2	0	0
Hal Morris, 1b-2,dh-2	.071	4	14	0	1	0	0	0	2	1	1	0
Randy Myers, p	.000	3	0	0	0	0	0	0	0	0	0	0
Ron Oester, ph	1.000	1	1	0	1	0	0	0	1	0	0	0
Joe Oliver, c	.333	4	18	2	6	3	0	0	2	0	1	0
Paul O'Neill, of	.083	4	12	2	1	0	0	0	1	5	2	1
Jose Rijo, p	.333	2	3	0	1	0	0	0	0	0	0	0
Chris Sabo, 3b	.563	4	16	2	9	1	0	2	5	2	2	0
Scott Scudder, p	.000	1	0	0	0	0	0	0	0	0	0	0
Herm Winningham, of-1	.500	2	4	1	2	0	0	0	0	0	0	0
TOTAL	.317		142	22	45	9	2	3	22	15	9	2

PITCHER	W	L	ERA	G	GS	CG	SV	SHO	IP	H	ER	BB	SO
Jack Armstrong	0	0	0.00	1	0	0	0	0	3.0	1	0	0	3
Tom Browning	1	0	4.50	1	1	0	0	0	6.0	6	3	2	2
Norm Charlton	0	0	0.00	1	0	0	0	0	1.0	1	0	0	0
Rob Dibble	1	0	0.00	3	0	0	0	0	4.2	3	0	1	4
Danny Jackson	0	0	10.13	1	1	0	0	0	2.2	6	3	2	0
Randy Myers	0	0	0.00	3	0	0	1	0	3.0	2	0	0	3
Jose Rijo	2	0	0.59	2	2	0	0	0	15.1	9	1	5	14
Scott Scudder	0	0	0.00	1	0	0	0	0	1.1	0	0	2	2
TOTAL	4	0	1.70	13	4	0	1	0	37.0	28	7	12	28

OAK (A)

PLAYER/POS	AVG	G	AB	R	H	2B	3B	HR	RB	BB	SO	SB
Harold Baines, dh-2	.143	3	7	1	1	0	0	1	2	1	2	0
Lance Blankenship, ph	.000	1	1	0	0	0	0	0	0	0	1	0
Mike Bordick, ss	.000	3	0	0	0	0	0	0	0	0	0	0
Todd Burns, p	.000	2	0	0	0	0	0	0	0	0	0	0
Jose Canseco, of-3,dh-1	.083	4	12	1	1	0	0	1	2	2	3	0
Dennis Eckersley, p	.000	2	0	0	0	0	0	0	0	0	0	0
Mike Gallego, ss	.091	4	11	0	1	0	0	0	1	1	3	1
Ron Hassey, c-1	.333	3	6	0	2	0	0	0	1	0	0	0
Dave Henderson, of-3	.231	4	13	2	3	1	0	0	0	1	3	0
Rickey Henderson, of	.333	4	15	2	5	2	0	1	1	3	4	3
Rick Honeycutt, p	.000	1	0	0	0	0	0	0	0	0	0	0
Doug Jennings, ph	1.000	1	1	0	1	0	0	0	0	0	0	0
Joe Klink, p	.000	1	0	0	0	0	0	0	0	0	0	0
Carney Lansford, 3b	.267	4	15	0	4	0	0	0	1	1	0	1
Willie McGee, of-3	.200	4	10	1	2	1	0	0	0	0	2	1
Mark McGwire, 1b	.214	4	14	1	3	0	0	0	0	2	4	0
Mike Moore, p	.000	1	0	0	0	0	0	0	0	0	0	0
Gene Nelson, p	.000	2	0	0	0	0	0	0	0	0	0	0
Jamie Quirk, c	.000	1	3	0	0	0	0	0	0	0	2	0
Willie Randolph, 2b	.267	4	15	0	4	0	0	0	0	1	0	1
Scott Sanderson, p	.000	2	0	0	0	0	0	0	0	0	0	0
Terry Steinbach, c	.125	3	8	0	1	0	0	0	0	0	1	0
Dave Stewart, p	.000	2	1	0	0	0	0	0	0	0	1	0
Bob Welch, p	.000	1	3	0	0	0	0	0	0	0	2	0
Curt Young, p	.000	1	0	0	0	0	0	0	0	0	0	0
TOTAL	.207		135	8	28	4	0	3	8	12	28	7

PITCHER	W	L	ERA	G	GS	CG	SV	SHO	IP	H	ER	BB	SO
Todd Burns	0	0	16.20	2	0	0	0	0	1.2	5	3	2	0
Dennis Eckersley	0	1	6.75	2	0	0	0	0	1.1	3	1	0	1
Rick Honeycutt	0	0	0.00	1	0	0	0	0	1.2	2	0	1	0
Joe Klink	0	0	–	1	0	0	0	0	0.0	0	0	1	0
Mike Moore	0	1	6.75	1	1	0	0	0	2.2	8	2	0	1
Gene Nelson	0	0	0.00	2	0	0	0	0	5.0	3	0	2	0
Scott Sanderson	0	0	10.80	2	0	0	0	0	1.2	4	2	1	0
Dave Stewart	0	2	3.46	2	2	1	0	0	13.0	10	5	6	5
Bob Welch	0	0	4.91	1	1	0	0	0	7.1	9	4	2	2
Curt Young	0	0	0.00	1	0	0	0	0	1.0	1	0	0	0
TOTAL	0	4	4.33	15	4	1	0	0	35.1	45	17	15	9

GAME 1 AT CIN OCT 16

OAK	000	000	000		0	9	1
CIN	202	030	00X		7	10	0

Pitchers: STEWART, Burns (5), Nelson (5), Sanderson (7), Eckersley (8) vs RIJO, Dibble (8), Myers (9)
Home Runs: Davis-CIN
Attendance: 55,830

GAME 2 AT CIN OCT 17

OAK	103	000	000	0	4	10	2
CIN	200	100	010	1	5	14	2

Pitchers: Welch, Honeycutt (8), ECKERSLEY (10) vs Jackson, Scudder (3), Armstrong (5), Charlton (8), DIBBLE (9)
Home Runs: Canseco-OAK
Attendance: 55,832

GAME 3 AT OAK OCT 19

CIN	017	000	000		8	14	1
OAK	021	000	000		3	7	1

Pitchers: BROWNING, Dibble (7), Myers (8) vs MOORE, Sanderson (3), Klink (4), Nelson (4), Burns (8), Young (9)
Home Runs: Sabo-CIN (2), Baines-OAK, R.Henderson-OAK
Attendance: 48,269

GAME 4 AT OAK OCT 20

CIN	000	000	020		2	7	1
OAK	100	000	000		1	2	1

Pitchers: RIJO, Myers (9) vs STEWART
Attendance: 48,613

Atlanta Braves (West), 4; Pittsburgh Pirates (East), 3

Pitching dominated this back-and-forth series which featured four shutouts, including three 1–0 games. Three times Atlanta hurlers blanked Pittsburgh on the Pirates' home grounds. Andy Van Slyke opened the series scoring with a first-inning home run. Pirates starter Doug Drabek held the Braves scoreless through six innings of the opener, before injuring himself on the basepaths. By the time David Justice homered in the ninth for Atlanta's only score, the Pirates had the game well in hand.

Atlanta evened the series in Game 2 behind the pitching of Steve Avery and Alejandro Pena, and the bat and glove of Mark Lemke. The Braves' second baseman doubled home that game's only run in the sixth inning and prevented a Pittsburgh run from scoring in the eighth with a diving stop of a grounder up the middle. In Atlanta for Game 3, the Braves took the series lead with a 10–3 rout that featured home runs by Ron Gant, Greg Olson, and Sid Bream. (Orlando Merced and Jay Bell homered for Pittsburgh.)

Game 4 was much closer. The Braves took a quick lead with two first-inning runs, but Pittsburgh scored once in the second and tied the game in the fifth on a throwing error. In the top of the 10th, Andy Van Slyke led off with a walk. With two away he stole second, and then scored what proved the winning run on Don Slaught's double. With the series even again, Atlanta lost a run in Game 5 when David Justice was ruled out for missing third base as he dashed home from second. An inning later the Pirates parlayed a walk and a pair of singles into the only run they would need to carry the series advantage back to Pittsburgh.

In Game 6, though, the Braves returned the favor, tying the series once more with a gem of their own. Avery and Pena combined for their second 1–0 victory, while Drabek held the Braves scoreless into the ninth, when Olson doubled home the game's only run.

In the finale, John Smoltz enjoyed a three-run lead when he took the mound in the bottom of the first inning. Rookie first baseman Brian Hunter (who had homered for two of the first-inning runs) doubled in an additional Atlanta run in the fifth. Meanwhile Smoltz stopped the Pirates on six hits to bring the Braves their first pennant since their move to Atlanta in 1966.

ATL (W)

PLAYER/POS	AVG	G	AB	R	H	2B	3B	HR	RB	BB	SO	SB
Steve Avery, p	.143	2	7	0	1	0	0	0	0	0	4	0
Rafael Belliard, ss	.211	7	19	0	4	0	0	0	1	3	3	0
Jeff Blauser, ss	.000	2	2	0	0	0	0	0	0	0	0	0
Sid Bream, 1b	.300	4	10	1	3	0	0	1	3	0	1	0
Jim Clancy, p	.000	1	0	0	0	0	0	0	0	0	0	0
Ron Gant, of	.259	7	27	4	7	1	0	1	3	2	4	7
Tom Glavine, p	.250	2	4	0	1	0	0	0	0	0	2	0
Tommy Gregg, ph	.250	4	4	0	1	0	0	0	0	0	2	0
Brian Hunter, 1b	.333	5	18	2	6	2	0	1	4	0	2	0
David Justice, of	.200	7	25	4	5	1	0	1	2	3	7	0
Charlie Leibrandt, p	.000	1	1	0	0	0	0	0	0	0	0	0
Mark Lemke, 2b	.200	7	20	1	4	1	0	0	1	4	0	0
Kent Mercker, p	.000	1	0	0	0	0	0	0	0	0	0	0
Keith Mitchell, of	.000	5	4	0	0	0	0	0	0	0	1	0
Greg Olson, c	.333	7	24	3	8	1	0	1	4	4	3	1
Alejandro Pena, p	.000	4	0	0	0	0	0	0	0	0	0	0
Terry Pendleton, 3b	.167	7	30	1	5	1	1	0	1	1	3	0
Lonnie Smith, of	.250	7	24	3	6	3	0	0	0	4	5	1
John Smoltz, p	.200	2	5	0	1	0	0	0	0	1	4	1
Mike Stanton, p	.000	3	0	0	0	0	0	0	0	0	0	0
Jeff Treadway, 2b	.333	1	3	0	1	0	0	0	0	0	0	0
Jerry Willard, ph	.000	2	2	0	0	0	0	0	0	0	1	0
Mark Wohlers, p	.000	3	0	0	0	0	0	0	0	0	0	0
TOTAL	.231		229	19	53	10	1	5	19	22	42	10

PITCHER	W	L	ERA	G	GS	CG	SV	SHO	IP	H	ER	BB	SO
Steve Avery	2	0	0.00	2	2	0	0	0	16.1	9	0	4	17
Jim Clancy	0	0	0.00	1	0	0	0	0	0.1	0	0	0	0
Tom Glavine	0	2	3.21	2	2	0	0	0	14.0	12	5	6	11
Charlie Leibrandt	0	0	1.35	1	1	0	0	0	6.2	8	1	3	6
Kent Mercker	0	1	13.50	1	0	0	0	0	0.2	0	1	2	0
Alejandro Pena	0	0	0.00	4	0	0	3	0	4.1	1	0	0	4
John Smoltz	2	0	1.76	2	2	1	0	1	15.1	14	3	3	15
Mike Stanton	0	0	2.45	3	0	0	0	0	3.2	4	1	3	3
Mark Wohlers	0	0	0.00	3	0	0	0	0	1.2	3	0	1	1
TOTAL	4	3	1.57	19	7	1	3	1	63.0	51	11	22	57

PIT (E)

PLAYER/POS	AVG	G	AB	R	H	2B	3B	HR	RB	BB	SO	SB
Stan Belinda, p	.000	3	0	0	0	0	0	0	0	0	0	0
Jay Bell, ss	.414	7	29	2	12	2	0	1	1	0	10	0
Barry Bonds, of	.148	7	27	1	4	1	0	0	0	2	4	3
Bobby Bonilla, of	.304	7	23	2	7	2	0	0	1	6	2	0
Steve Buechele, 3b	.304	7	23	2	7	2	0	0	0	4	6	0
Doug Drabek, p	.200	2	5	0	1	1	0	0	1	0	2	0
Cecil Espy, ph	.000	2	2	0	0	0	0	0	0	0	2	0
Bob Kipper, p	.000	1	0	0	0	0	0	0	0	0	0	0
Bill Landrum, p	.000	1	0	0	0	0	0	0	0	0	0	0
Mike LaValliere, c	.333	3	6	0	2	0	0	0	1	2	0	0
Jose Lind, 2b	.160	7	25	0	4	0	0	0	3	0	6	0
Roger Mason, p	.000	3	1	0	0	0	0	0	0	0	1	0
Lloyd McClendon, 1b-1	.000	3	2	0	0	0	0	0	0	1	0	0
Orlando Merced, 1b-2	.222	3	9	1	2	0	0	1	1	0	1	0
Bob Patterson, p	.000	1	0	0	0	0	0	0	0	0	0	0
Gary Redus, 1b	.158	5	19	1	3	0	0	0	0	1	4	2
Rosario Rodriguez, p	.000	1	0	0	0	0	0	0	0	0	0	0
Don Slaught, c	.235	6	17	0	4	0	0	0	1	1	4	0
John Smiley, p	.000	2	0	0	0	0	0	0	0	0	0	0
Zane Smith, p	.000	2	5	0	0	0	0	0	0	0	4	0
Randy Tomlin, p	.000	1	2	0	0	0	0	0	0	0	0	0
Andy Van Slyke, of	.160	7	25	3	4	2	0	1	2	5	5	1
Gary Varsho, ph	.500	2	2	0	1	0	0	0	0	0	1	0
Bob Walk, p	.000	3	2	0	0	0	0	0	0	0	2	0
Curtis Wilkerson, ph	.000	4	4	0	0	0	0	0	0	0	3	0
TOTAL	.224		228	12	51	10	0	3	11	22	57	6

PITCHER	W	L	ERA	G	GS	CG	SV	SHO	IP	H	ER	BB	SO
Stan Belinda	1	0	0.00	3	0	0	0	0	5.0	0	0	3	4
Doug Drabek	1	1	0.60	2	2	1	0	0	15.0	10	1	5	10
Bob Kipper	0	0	4.50	1	0	0	0	0	2.0	2	1	0	1
Bill Landrum	0	0	9.00	1	0	0	0	0	1.0	2	1	2	2
Roger Mason	0	0	0.00	3	0	0	1	0	4.1	3	0	1	2
Bob Patterson	0	0	0.00	1	0	0	0	0	2.0	1	0	0	3
Rosario Rodriguez	0	0	27.00	1	0	0	0	0	1.0	1	3	2	1
John Smiley	0	2	23.63	2	2	0	0	0	2.2	8	7	1	3
Zane Smith	1	1	0.61	2	2	0	0	0	14.2	15	1	3	10
Randy Tomlin	0	0	3.00	1	1	0	0	0	6.0	6	2	2	1
Bob Walk	0	0	1.93	3	0	0	1	0	9.1	5	2	3	5
TOTAL	3	4	2.57	20	7	1	2	0	63.0	53	18	22	42

GAME 1 AT PIT OCT 9

				R	H	E
ATL	000	000	001	1	5	1
PIT	102	001	01X	5	8	1

Pitchers: GLAVINE, Wohlers (7), Stanton (8) vs DRABEK, Walk (7)
Home Runs: Van Slyke-PIT, Justice-ATL
Attendance: 57,347

GAME 2 AT PIT OCT 10

				R	H	E
ATL	000	001	000	1	8	0
PIT	000	000	000	0	6	0

Pitchers: AVERY, Pena (9) vs SMITH, Mason (8), Belinda (9)
Attendance: 57,533

GAME 3 AT ATL OCT 12

				R	H	E
PIT	100	100	100	3	10	2
ATL	411	000	13X	10	11	0

Pitchers: SMILEY, Landrum (3), Patterson (4), Kipper (6), Rodriguez (8) vs SMOLTZ, Stanton (7), Wohlers (8), Pena (8)
Home Runs: Merced-PIT, Bell-PIT, Gant-ATL, Olson-ATL, Bream-ATL
Attendance: 50,905

GAME 4 AT ATL OCT 13

					R	H	E
PIT	010	010	000	1	3	11	1
ATL	200	000	000	0	2	7	1

Pitchers: Tomlin, Walk (7), BELINDA (9) vs Leibrandt, Clancy (7), Stanton (8), MERCKER (10), Wohlers (10)
Attendance: 51,109

GAME 5 AT ATL OCT 14

				R	H	E
PIT	000	010	000	1	6	2
ATL	000	000	000	0	9	1

Pitchers: SMITH, Mason (8) vs GLAVINE, Pena (9)
Attendance: 51,109

GAME 6 AT PIT OCT 16

				R	H	E
ATL	000	000	001	1	7	0
PIT	000	000	000	0	4	0

Pitchers: AVERY, Pena (9) vs DRABEK
Attendance: 54,508

GAME 7 AT PIT OCT 17

				R	H	E
ATL	300	010	000	4	6	1
PIT	000	000	000	0	6	0

Pitchers: SMOLTZ vs SMILEY, Walk (1), Mason (6), Belinda (8)
Home Runs: Hunter-ATL
Attendance: 46,932

Minnesota struggled to achieve a 2–1 advantage in the first three games, then blew the Jays out of the SkyDome in the next two. Game 1 looked as though it would be an easy win for the Twins, who drove out starter Tom Candiotti with five runs on eight hits in the first two and two thirds innings. But Toronto scored once in the fourth and chased Twins starter Jack Morris in the sixth with five straight singles and three more runs. Relievers Carl Willis and Rick Aguilera, though, held Toronto to just one more single to preserve the victory for Minnesota.

The Jays scored three times in Game 2 before Minnesota put its first run across in the last of the third, and scored twice more in the seventh, taking their first—and, as it turned out, only—win behind the strong pitching of rookie Juan Guzman and relievers Tom Henke and Duane Ward. Toronto again scored early in Game 3, with a pair of two-out runs (one of them Joe Carter's homer) in the first inning. Jays starter Jimmy Key held the Twins scoreless until they got to him for a run in the fifth, and another in the sixth which evened the score. Meanwhile a string of Minnesota pitchers stifled the Blue Jays from the second inning on. In the 10th, pinch hitter Mike Pagliarulo won it for the Twins with a home run to right.

For the third game in a row, Toronto scored first, with a run in the second inning of Game 4. But Minnesota's Kirby Puckett homered in the fourth to tie the score, and by the time Toronto scored again two innings later, the Twins had upped its run total to six. Puckett's home run in the first inning of Game 5 gave the Twins the first of two early runs, but the Jays came back with three runs in the third and two more in the fourth to drive out starter Kevin Tapani. They scored no more, however, as three Twins relievers held them to one single in the final five frames. In the sixth inning, Minnesota reawakened to tie the game with a trio of runs, and salted it—and the pennant—away in the eighth: with two out, Puckett doubled home the go-ahead run, and Kent Hrbek singled in two more for insurance.

Minnesota Twins (West), 4; Toronto Blue Jays (East), 1

MIN (W)

PLAYER/POS	AVG	G	AB	R	H	2B	3B	HR	RB	BB	SO	SB
Rick Aguilera, p	.000	3	0	0	0	0	0	0	0	0	0	0
Steve Bedrosian, p	.000	2	0	0	0	0	0	0	0	0	0	0
Jarvis Brown, dh	.000	1	0	1	0	0	0	0	0	0	0	0
Chili Davis, dh	.294	5	17	3	5	2	0	0	2	5	8	1
Scott Erickson, p	.000	1	0	0	0	0	0	0	0	0	0	0
Greg Gagne, ss	.235	5	17	1	4	0	0	0	1	1	5	0
Dan Gladden, of	.261	5	23	4	6	0	0	0	3	1	3	3
Mark Guthrie, p	.000	2	0	0	0	0	0	0	0	0	0	0
Brian Harper, c	.278	5	18	1	5	2	0	0	1	0	2	0
Kent Hrbek, 1b	.143	5	21	0	3	0	0	0	3	1	3	0
Chuck Knoblauch, 2b	.350	5	20	5	7	2	0	0	3	3	3	2
Gene Larkin, ph	.000	3	3	0	0	0	0	0	0	0	1	0
Scott Leius, 3b	.000	3	4	0	0	0	0	0	0	1	1	0
Shane Mack, of	.333	5	18	4	6	1	1	0	3	2	4	2
Jack Morris, p	.000	2	0	0	0	0	0	0	0	0	0	0
Al Newman, 2b-1,3b-1	.000	2	0	0	0	0	0	0	0	0	0	0
Junior Ortiz, c	.000	3	3	0	0	0	0	0	0	0	0	0
Mike Pagliarulo, 3b	.333	5	15	4	5	1	0	1	3	0	2	0
Kirby Puckett, of	.429	5	21	4	9	1	0	2	6	1	4	0
Paul Sorrento, ph	.000	1	1	0	0	0	0	0	0	0	1	0
Kevin Tapani, p	.000	2	0	0	0	0	0	0	0	0	0	0
David West, p	.000	2	0	0	0	0	0	0	0	0	0	0
Carl Willis, p	.000	3	0	0	0	0	0	0	0	0	0	0
TOTAL	.276		181	27	50	9	1	3	25	15	37	8

PITCHER	W	L	ERA	G	GS	CG	SV	SHO	IP	H	ER	BB	SO
Rick Aguilera	0	0	0.00	3	0	0	3	0	3.1	1	0	0	3
Steve Bedrosian	0	0	0.00	2	0	0	0	0	1.1	3	0	2	2
Scott Erickson	0	0	4.50	1	1	0	0	0	4.0	3	2	5	2
Mark Guthrie	1	0	0.00	2	0	0	0	0	2.2	0	0	0	0
Jack Morris	2	0	4.05	2	2	0	0	0	13.1	17	6	1	7
Kevin Tapani	0	1	7.84	2	2	0	0	0	10.1	16	9	3	9
David West	1	0	0.00	2	0	0	0	0	5.2	1	0	4	4
Carl Willis	0	0	0.00	3	0	0	0	0	5.1	2	0	0	3
TOTAL	4	1	3.33	17	5	0	3	0	46.0	43	17	15	30

TOR (E)

PLAYER/POS	AVG	G	AB	R	H	2B	3B	HR	RB	BB	SO	SB
Jim Acker, p	.000	1	0	0	0	0	0	0	0	0	0	0
Roberto Alomar, 2b	.474	5	19	3	9	0	0	0	4	2	3	2
Pat Borders, c	.263	5	19	0	5	1	0	0	2	0	0	0
Tom Candiotti, p	.000	2	0	0	0	0	0	0	0	0	0	0
Joe Carter, of-3,dh-2	.263	5	19	3	5	2	0	1	4	1	5	0
Rob Ducey, of	.000	1	1	0	0	0	0	0	0	0	0	0
Rene Gonzales, 1b-1,ss-1	.000	2	0	0	0	0	0	0	0	0	0	0
Kelly Gruber, 3b	.286	5	21	1	6	1	0	0	4	0	4	1
Juan Guzman, p	.000	1	0	0	0	0	0	0	0	0	0	0
Tom Henke, p	.000	2	0	0	0	0	0	0	0	0	0	0
Jimmy Key, p	.000	1	0	0	0	0	0	0	0	0	0	0
Manuel Lee, ss	.125	5	16	3	2	0	0	0	0	1	5	0
Rob MacDonald, p	.000	1	0	0	0	0	0	0	0	0	0	0
Candy Maldonado, of	.100	5	20	1	2	1	0	0	1	1	6	0
Rance Mulliniks, dh-3	.125	5	8	1	1	0	0	0	0	3	0	0
John Olerud, 1b	.158	5	19	1	3	0	0	0	3	3	1	0
Todd Stottlemyre, p	.000	1	0	0	0	0	0	0	0	0	0	0
Pat Tabler, dh	.000	2	1	0	0	0	0	0	0	1	0	0
Mike Timlin, p	.000	4	0	0	0	0	0	0	0	0	0	0
Duane Ward, p	.000	2	0	0	0	0	0	0	0	0	0	0
David Wells, p	.000	4	0	0	0	0	0	0	0	0	0	0
Devon White, of	.364	5	22	5	8	1	0	0	0	2	3	3
Mookie Wilson, of-2	.250	3	8	1	2	0	0	0	0	1	3	1
TOTAL	.249		173	19	43	6	0	1	18	15	30	7

PITCHER	W	L	ERA	G	GS	CG	SV	SHO	IP	H	ER	BB	SO
Jim Acker	0	0	0.00	1	0	0	0	0	0.2	1	0	0	1
Tom Candiotti	0	1	8.22	2	2	0	0	0	7.2	17	7	2	5
Juan Guzman	1	0	3.18	1	1	0	0	0	5.2	4	2	4	2
Tom Henke	0	0	0.00	2	0	0	0	0	2.2	0	0	1	5
Jimmy Key	0	0	3.00	1	1	0	0	0	6.0	5	2	1	1
Rob MacDonald	0	0	9.00	1	0	0	0	0	1.0	1	1	1	0
Todd Stottlemyre	0	1	9.82	1	1	0	0	0	3.2	7	4	1	3
Mike Timlin	0	1	3.18	4	0	0	0	0	5.2	5	2	2	5
Duane Ward	0	1	6.23	2	0	0	1	0	4.1	4	3	1	6
David Wells	0	0	2.35	4	0	0	0	0	7.2	6	2	2	9
TOTAL	1	4	4.60	19	5	0	1	0	45.0	50	23	15	37

GAME 1 AT MIN OCT 8

		R	H	E
TOR	000 103 000	4	9	3
MIN	221 000 00X	5	11	0

Pitchers: CANDIOTTI, Wells (3), Timlin (6) vs MORRIS, Willis (6), Aguilera (8)
Attendance: 54,766

GAME 2 AT MIN OCT 9

		R	H	E
TOR	102 000 200	5	9	0
MIN	001 001 000	2	5	1

Pitchers: GUZMAN, Henke (6), Ward (8) vs TAPANI, Bedrosian (7), Guthrie (7)
Attendance: 54,816

GAME 3 AT TOR OCT 11

		R	H	E
MIN	000 011 000 1	3	7	0
TOR	200 000 000 0	2	5	1

Pitchers: Erickson, West (5), Willis (7), GUTHRIE (9), Aguilera (10) vs Key, Wells (7), Henke (8), TIMLIN (10)
Home Runs: Carter-TOR, Pagliarulo-MIN
Attendance: 51,454

GAME 4 AT TOR OCT 12

		R	H	E
MIN	000 402 111	9	13	1
TOR	010 001 001	3	11	2

Pitchers: MORRIS, Bedrosian (9) vs STOTTLEMYRE, Wells (4), Acker (6), Timlin (7), MacDonald (9)
Home Runs: Puckett-MIN
Attendance: 51,526

GAME 5 AT TOR OCT 13

		R	H	E
MIN	110 003 030	8	14	2
TOR	003 200 000	5	9	1

Pitchers: Tapani, WEST (5), Willis (8), Aguilera (9) vs Candiotti, Timlin (6), WARD (6), Wells (8)
Home Runs: Puckett-MIN
Attendance: 51,425

Minnesota Twins (AL), 4; Atlanta Braves (NL), 3

By any measure, this World Series was one of the great ones. Five of the seven games were decided by a single run, three of them—including Games 6 and 7—in extra innings. The opener in Minnesota gave no indication of the suspense to come, as the Twins opened up a 4–0 lead in the fifth inning en route to a 5–2 win. Game 2 proved more difficult. Chili Davis put the Twins in front with a two-run homer in the first inning, but in the fifth Atlanta tied the score. Braves hurler Tom Glavine lost the game when the Twins' Scott Leius lofted a homer to lead off the eighth.

Minnesota took a quick lead in Game 3, but Atlanta tied the game an inning later, and went ahead on solo homers by David Justice in the fourth inning and Lonnie Smith in the fifth. Home runs by Kirby Puckett and Chili Davis in the fifth and sixth re-tied the score, which remained at 4–4 into the last of the 11th inning, when Justice scored from second on Mark Lemke's two-out single. Lemke's heroics also made the difference in Game 4. Mike Pagliarulo drove in a pair of runs for Minnesota with a single in the second and a home run in the seventh, but Braves Terry Pendleton and Lonnie Smith neutralized the runs with solo homers in the third and seventh. Lemke came to bat in the bottom of the ninth with one out and the score still 2–2. He tripled, and scored in a tight play to even the Series.

In Game 5 the Braves assaulted five Minnesota pitchers for 14 runs and the Series lead, but when play returned to Minnesota for Game 6 the Twins revived with two first-inning runs. In the third inning Puckett prevented two Atlanta runs with a leaping catch above the wall, but in the fifth, Atlanta's Terry Pendleton evened the score with a two-run homer. Later in the inning the Twins regained the lead on Puckett's sacrifice fly. Atlanta knotted the score again in the seventh. In the last of the 11th, Puckett lined the ball over the wall near where he had earlier made his game-saving catch.

No one scored through 9½ innings of Game 7 as Minnesota's Jack Morris dueled John Smoltz, Mike Stanton, and Alejandro Pena. Lonnie Smith singled to lead off the 7th inning and could have come around on Terry Pendleton's double to the wall in left center. But, decoyed by the Twins' middle infielders into thinking there was a play at second, he paused just long enough after passing second to enable him to advance only to third. No one was out, but a grounder to first, an intentional walk to load the bases, and a smart 3–2–3 double play ended the Braves' threat.

Thus the game was still scoreless in the last of the 10th when Dan Gladden hustled his way into a broken-bat double and moved to third on Chuck Knoblauch's sacrifice bunt. Then, after the bases were loaded intentionally, pinch hitter Gene Larkin lobbed a hit over the head of the drawn-in left fielder. Gladden came home with the title for Minnesota.

MIN (A)

PLAYER/POS	AVG	G	AB	R	H	2B	3B	HR	RB	BB	SO	SB
Rick Aguilera, p	.000	4	1	0	0	0	0	0	0	0	0	0
Steve Bedrosian, p	.000	3	0	0	0	0	0	0	0	0	0	0
Jarvis Brown, of-2,dh-1	.000	3	2	0	0	0	0	0	0	0	0	0
Randy Bush, of-2	.250	3	4	0	1	0	0	0	0	0	1	0
Chili Davis, dh-4,of-1	.222	6	18	4	4	0	0	2	4	2	3	0
Scott Erickson, p	.000	2	1	0	0	0	0	0	0	0	1	0
Greg Gagne, ss	.167	7	24	1	4	1	0	1	3	0	7	0
Dan Gladden, of	.233	7	30	5	7	2	2	0	0	3	4	2
Mark Guthrie, p	.000	4	0	0	0	0	0	0	0	0	0	0
Brian Harper, c	.381	7	21	2	8	2	0	0	1	2	2	0
Kent Hrbek, 1b	.115	7	26	2	3	1	0	1	2	2	6	0
Chuck Knoblauch, 2b	.308	7	26	3	8	1	0	0	2	4	2	4
Gene Larkin, dh-1	.500	4	4	0	2	0	0	0	1	0	0	0
Terry Leach, p	.000	2	0	0	0	0	0	0	0	0	0	0
Scott Leius, 3b	.357	7	14	2	5	0	0	1	2	1	2	0
Shane Mack, of	.130	6	23	0	3	1	0	0	1	0	7	0
Jack Morris, p	.000	3	2	0	0	0	0	0	0	0	1	0
Al Newman, 3b-2,2b-1,ss-1	.500	4	2	0	1	0	1	0	1	0	0	0
Junior Ortiz, c	.200	3	5	0	1	0	0	0	1	0	1	0
Mike Pagliarulo, 3b	.273	6	11	1	3	0	0	1	2	1	2	0
Kirby Puckett, of	.250	7	24	4	6	0	1	2	4	5	7	1
Paul Sorrento, 1b-1	.000	3	2	0	0	0	0	0	0	1	2	0
Kevin Tapani, p	.000	2	1	0	0	0	0	0	0	0	0	0
David West, p	.000	2	0	0	0	0	0	0	0	0	0	0
Carl Willis, p	.000	4	0	0	0	0	0	0	0	0	0	0
TOTAL	.232		241	24	56	8	4	8	24	21	48	7

PITCHER	W	L	ERA	G	GS	CG	SV	SHO	IP	H	ER	BB	SO
Rick Aguilera	1	1	1.80	4	0	0	2	0	5.0	6	1	1	3
Steve Bedrosian	0	0	5.40	3	0	0	0	0	3.1	3	2	0	2
Scott Erickson	0	0	5.06	2	2	0	0	0	10.2	10	6	4	5
Mark Guthrie	0	1	2.25	4	0	0	0	0	4.0	3	1	4	3
Terry Leach	0	0	3.86	2	0	0	0	0	2.1	2	1	0	2
Jack Morris	2	0	1.17	3	3	1	0	1	23.0	18	3	9	15
Kevin Tapani	1	1	4.50	2	2	0	0	0	12.0	13	6	2	7
David West	0	0	∞	2	0	0	0	0	0.0	2	4	4	0
Carl Willis	0	0	5.14	4	0	0	0	0	7.0	6	4	2	2
TOTAL	4	3	3.74	26	7	1	2	1	67.1	63	28	26	39

ATL (N)

PLAYER/POS	AVG	G	AB	R	H	2B	3B	HR	RB	BB	SO	SB
Steve Avery, p	.000	2	3	0	0	0	0	0	0	0	2	0
Rafael Belliard, ss	.375	7	16	0	6	1	0	0	4	1	2	0
Jeff Blauser, ss	.167	5	6	0	1	0	0	0	0	1	1	0
Sid Bream, 1b	.125	7	24	0	3	2	0	0	0	3	4	0
Francisco Cabrera, c-1	.000	3	1	0	0	0	0	0	0	0	0	0
Jim Clancy, p	.000	3	1	0	0	0	0	0	0	0	1	0
Ron Gant, of	.267	7	30	3	8	0	1	0	4	2	3	1
Tom Glavine, p	.000	2	2	0	0	0	0	0	0	0	0	0
Tommy Gregg, ph	.000	4	3	0	0	0	0	0	0	0	2	0
Brian Hunter, 1b-4,of-4	.190	7	21	2	4	1	0	1	3	0	2	0
David Justice, of	.259	7	27	5	7	0	0	2	6	5	5	2
Charlie Leibrandt, p	.000	2	0	0	0	0	0	0	0	0	0	0
Mark Lemke, 2b	.417	6	24	4	10	1	3	0	4	2	4	0
Kent Mercker, p	.000	2	0	0	0	0	0	0	0	0	0	0
Keith Mitchell, of	.000	3	2	0	0	0	0	0	0	0	1	0
Greg Olson, c	.222	7	27	3	6	2	0	0	1	5	4	1
Alejandro Pena, p	.000	3	0	0	0	0	0	0	0	0	0	0
Terry Pendleton, 3b	.367	7	30	6	11	3	0	2	3	3	1	0
Randy St. Claire, p	.000	1	0	0	0	0	0	0	0	0	0	0
Lonnie Smith, dh-4,of-3	.231	7	26	5	6	0	0	3	3	3	4	1
John Smoltz, p	.000	2	2	0	0	0	0	0	0	0	1	0
Mike Stanton, p	.000	5	0	0	0	0	0	0	0	0	0	0
Jeff Treadway, 2b-1	.250	3	4	1	1	0	0	0	0	1	2	0
Jerry Willard, ph	.000	1	0	0	0	0	0	0	1	0	0	0
Mark Wohlers, p	.000	3	0	0	0	0	0	0	0	0	0	0
TOTAL	.253		249	29	63	10	4	8	29	26	39	5

PITCHER	W	L	ERA	G	GS	CG	SV	SHO	IP	H	ER	BB	SO
Steve Avery	0	0	3.46	2	2	0	0	0	13.0	10	5	1	8
Jim Clancy	1	0	4.15	3	0	0	0	0	4.1	3	2	4	2
Tom Glavine	1	1	2.70	2	2	1	0	0	13.1	8	4	7	8
Charlie Leibrandt	0	2	11.25	2	1	0	0	0	4.0	8	5	1	3
Kent Mercker	0	0	0.00	2	0	0	0	0	1.0	0	0	0	1
Alejandro Pena	0	1	3.38	3	0	0	0	0	5.1	6	2	3	7
Randy St. Claire	0	0	9.00	1	0	0	0	0	1.0	1	1	0	0
John Smoltz	0	0	1.26	2	2	0	0	0	14.1	13	2	1	11
Mike Stanton	1	0	0.00	5	0	0	0	0	7.1	5	0	2	7
Mark Wohlers	0	0	0.00	3	0	0	0	0	1.2	2	0	2	1
TOTAL	3	4	2.89	25	7	1	0	0	65.1	56	21	21	48

GAME 1 AT MIN OCT 19

				R	H	E
ATL	000	001	010	2	6	1
MIN	001	031	00X	5	9	1

Pitchers: LEIBRANDT, Clancy (5), Wohlers (7), Stanton (8) vs MORRIS, Guthrie (8), Aguilera (8)
Home Runs: Gagne-MIN, Hrbek-MIN
Attendance: 55,108

GAME 2 AT MIN OCT 20

				R	H	E
ATL	010	010	000	2	8	1
MIN	200	000	01X	3	4	1

Pitchers: GLAVINE vs TAPANI, Aguilera (9)
Home Runs: Davis-MIN, Leius-MIN
Attendance: 55,145

GAME 3 AT ATL OCT 22

					R	H	E
MIN	100	000	120	000	4	10	1
ATL	010	120	000	001	5	8	2

Pitchers: Erickson, West (5), Leach (5), Bedrosian (6), Willis (8), Guthrie (10), AGUILERA (12) vs Avery, Pena (8), Stanton (10), Wohlers (12), Mercker (12), CLANCY (12)
Home Runs: Justice-ATL, Smith-ATL, Puckett-MIN, Davis-MIN
Attendance: 50,878

GAME 4 AT ATL OCT 23

				R	H	E
MIN	010	000	100	2	7	0
ATL	001	000	101	3	8	0

Pitchers: Morris, Willis (7), GUTHRIE (8), Bedrosian (9) vs Smoltz, Wohlers (8), STANTON (8)
Home Runs: Pendleton-ATL, Pagliarulo-MIN, Smith-ATL
Attendance: 50,878

GAME 5 AT ATL OCT 24

				R	H	E
MIN	000	003	011	5	7	1
ATL	000	410	63X	14	17	1

Pitchers: TAPANI, Leach (5), West (7), Bedrosian (7), Willis (8) vs GLAVINE, Mercker (6), Clancy (7), St. Claire (9)
Home Runs: Justice-ATL, Smith-ATL, Hunter-ATL
Attendance: 50,878

GAME 6 AT MIN OCT 26

					R	H	E
ATL	000	020	100	00	3	9	1
MIN	200	010	000	01	4	9	0

Pitchers: Avery, Stanton (7), Pena (9), LEIBRANDT (11) vs Erickson, Guthrie (7), Willis (7), AGUILERA (10)
Home Runs: Pendleton-ATL, Puckett-MIN
Attendance: 55,155

GAME 7 AT MIN OCT 27

					R	H	E
ATL	000	000	000	0	0	7	0
MIN	000	000	000	1	1	10	0

Pitchers: Smoltz, Stanton (8), PENA (9) vs MORRIS
Attendance: 55,118

Atlanta opened the series with a pair of one-sided wins but Pittsburgh pulled out a close victory in Game 3. After a third loss, the Pirates pummelled the Braves for two wins even more lopsided than their losses in the first two games. With the series now even, the stage was set for what turned out to be one of the most dramatic finishes in postseason history.

Jose Lind spoiled John Smoltz's Game 1 shutout with his first home run of the season in the eighth inning. But by then the Braves had scored five times and held victory firmly in hand. Game 2 was even easier. By the time the Pirates came up with four runs in the seventh inning (ending Steve Avery's LCS-record streak of scoreless innings at 22⅓), Atlanta had already compiled two four-run innings of their own (one of them on Ron Gant's grand slam). The Braves added five more runs in the last of the seventh to put the game out of reach.

At home for Game 3, the Pirates pulled themselves together behind the five-hit pitching of rookie knuckleballer Tim Wakefield. Sid Bream's solo homer in the fourth inning gave Atlanta a 1–0 lead, but Don Slaught homered to even the score an inning later and a pair of sixth-inning doubles put the Pirates ahead. Ron Gant's homer for Atlanta in the top of the seventh tied the score again, but a single, double, and sacrifice fly in the bottom of the inning put Pittsburgh on top to stay.

A 6–4 loss in Game 4 brought the Pirates to the brink of elimination, but in Game 5 they counterattacked, driving out Atlanta starter Steve Avery in the first inning with five hits (four of them doubles) and four runs, on their way to a 7–1 victory. The Pirates unloaded on Atlanta's Tom Glavine for eight runs in the second inning of Game 6 before the first out was recorded, and pushed the assault to a 13–4 conclusion and a tied series.

While the Pirates scored single runs in the first and sixth innings of the final game, Pirates starter Doug Drabek (who had taken losses in Games 1 and 4) held Atlanta scoreless through eight innings. Then, in the last of the ninth, leadoff Brave Terry Pendleton doubled. He moved to third as David Justice reached on a grounder bobbled by the usually sure-handed second baseman Jose Lind. A walk to Sid Bream filled the bases. Stan Belinda replaced Drabek on the mound and retired Ron Gant on a fly to left, but Pendleton scored Atlanta's first run after the catch. Damon Berryhill walked to reload the bases, and pinch hitter Brian Hunter popped out. Had there been no error, the game would have been over, with Pittsburgh waving the pennant. Instead, little-used pinch hitter Francisco Cabrera lined the ball safely to left, scoring Justice and Bream for a repeat pennant in Atlanta.

Atlanta Braves (West), 4; Pittsburgh Pirates (East), 3

ATL (W)

PLAYER/POS	AVG	G	AB	R	H	2B	3B	HR	RB	BB	SO	SB
Steve Avery, p	.000	3	2	0	0	0	0	0	1	0	1	0
R. Belliard, ss-3,2b-1	.000	4	2	1	0	0	0	0	0	1	0	0
Damon Berryhill, c	.167	7	24	1	4	1	0	0	1	3	2	0
Jeff Blauser, ss	.208	7	24	3	5	0	1	1	4	3	2	0
Sid Bream, 1b	.273	7	22	5	6	3	0	1	2	3	0	0
Francisco Cabrera, ph	.500	2	2	0	1	0	0	0	2	0	0	0
Marvin Freeman, p	.000	3	0	0	0	0	0	0	0	0	0	0
Ron Gant, of	.182	7	22	5	4	0	0	2	6	4	4	1
Tom Glavine, p	.000	2	2	0	0	0	0	0	0	0	0	0
Brian Hunter, 1b-2	.200	3	5	1	1	0	0	0	0	0	1	0
David Justice, of	.280	7	25	5	7	1	0	2	6	6	2	0
Charlie Leibrandt, p	.000	2	1	0	0	0	0	0	0	0	1	0
Mark Lemke, 2b-7,3b-1	.333	7	21	2	7	1	0	0	2	5	3	0
Javier Lopez, c	.000	1	1	0	0	0	0	0	0	0	0	0
Kent Mercker, p	.000	2	0	0	0	0	0	0	0	0	0	0
Otis Nixon, of	.286	7	28	5	8	2	0	0	2	4	4	3
Terry Pendleton, 3b	.233	7	30	2	7	2	0	0	3	0	2	0
Jeff Reardon, p	.000	3	0	0	0	0	0	0	0	0	0	0
Deion Sanders, of-3	.000	4	5	0	0	0	0	0	0	0	3	0
Lonnie Smith, ph	.333	6	6	1	2	0	1	0	1	0	0	0
Pete Smith, p	.000	2	1	0	0	0	0	0	0	0	0	0
John Smoltz, p	.286	3	7	1	2	0	0	0	1	0	2	1
Mike Stanton, p	1.000	5	1	1	1	1	0	0	1	0	0	0
Jeff Treadway, 2b-1	.667	3	3	1	2	0	0	0	0	0	1	0
Mark Wohlers, p	.000	3	0	0	0	0	0	0	0	0	0	0
TOTAL	.244		234	34	57	11	2	6	32	29	28	5

PITCHER	W	L	ERA	G	GS	CG	SV	SHO	IP	H	ER	BB	SO
Steve Avery	1	1	9.00	3	2	0	0	0	8.0	13	8	2	3
Marvin Freeman	0	0	14.73	3	0	0	0	0	3.2	8	6	2	1
Tom Glavine	0	2	12.27	2	2	0	0	0	7.1	13	10	3	2
Charlie Leibrandt	0	0	1.93	2	0	0	0	0	4.2	4	1	3	3
Kent Mercker	0	0	0.00	2	0	0	0	0	3.0	1	0	1	1
Jeff Reardon	1	0	0.00	3	0	0	1	0	3.0	0	0	2	3
Pete Smith	0	0	2.45	2	0	0	0	0	3.2	2	1	3	3
John Smoltz	2	0	2.66	3	3	0	0	0	20.1	14	6	10	19
Mike Stanton	0	0	0.00	5	0	0	0	0	4.1	2	0	2	5
Mark Wohlers	0	0	0.00	3	0	0	0	0	3.0	2	0	1	2
TOTAL	4	3	4.72	28	7	0	1	0	61.0	59	32	29	42

PIT (E)

PLAYER/POS	AVG	G	AB	R	H	2B	3B	HR	RB	BB	SO	SB
Stan Belinda, p	.000	2	0	0	0	0	0	0	0	0	0	0
Jay Bell, ss	.172	7	29	3	5	2	0	1	4	3	4	0
Barry Bonds, of	.261	7	23	5	6	1	0	1	2	6	4	1
Alex Cole, of	.200	4	10	2	2	0	0	0	1	3	2	0
Danny Cox, p	.000	2	0	0	0	0	0	0	0	0	0	0
Doug Drabek, p	.000	3	6	0	0	0	0	0	0	1	4	0
Cecil Espy, of-2	.667	4	3	0	2	0	0	0	0	0	1	0
Carlos Garcia, 2b	.000	1	1	0	0	0	0	0	0	0	0	0
Danny Jackson, p	.000	1	0	0	0	0	0	0	0	0	0	0
Jeff King, 3b	.241	7	29	4	7	4	0	0	2	0	1	0
Mike LaValliere, c	.200	3	10	1	2	0	0	0	0	0	3	0
Jose Lind, 2b	.222	7	27	5	6	2	1	1	5	1	4	0
Roger Mason, p	.000	2	0	0	0	0	0	0	0	0	0	0
Lloyd McClendon, of	.727	5	11	4	8	2	0	1	4	4	1	0
Orlando Merced, 1b	.100	4	10	0	1	1	0	0	2	2	4	0
Denny Neagle, p	.000	2	0	0	0	0	0	0	0	0	0	0
Bob Patterson, p	.000	2	0	0	0	0	0	0	0	0	0	0
Gary Redus, 1b	.438	5	16	4	7	4	1	0	3	2	3	0
Don Slaught, c	.333	5	12	5	4	1	0	1	5	6	3	0
Randy Tomlin, p	.000	2	0	0	0	0	0	0	0	0	0	0
Andy Van Slyke, of	.276	7	29	1	8	3	1	0	4	1	5	0
Gary Varsho, of-1	.500	2	2	0	1	0	0	0	0	0	0	0
Tim Wakefield, p	.000	2	6	1	0	0	0	0	0	0	0	0
Bob Walk, p	.000	2	5	0	0	0	0	0	0	0	1	0
John Wehner, ph	.000	2	2	0	0	0	0	0	0	0	2	0
TOTAL	.255		231	35	59	20	3	5	32	29	42	1

PITCHER	W	L	ERA	G	GS	CG	SV	SHO	IP	H	ER	BB	SO
Stan Belinda	0	0	0.00	2	0	0	0	0	1.2	2	0	1	2
Danny Cox	0	0	0.00	2	0	0	0	0	1.1	1	0	1	1
Doug Drabek	0	3	3.71	3	3	0	0	0	17.0	18	7	6	10
Danny Jackson	0	1	21.60	1	1	0	0	0	1.2	4	4	2	0
Roger Mason	0	0	0.00	2	0	0	0	0	3.1	0	0	2	1
Denny Neagle	0	0	27.00	2	0	0	0	0	1.2	4	5	3	0
Bob Patterson	0	0	5.40	2	0	0	0	0	1.2	3	1	1	1
Randy Tomlin	0	0	6.75	2	0	0	0	0	2.2	5	2	1	0
Tim Wakefield	2	0	3.00	2	2	2	0	0	18.0	14	6	5	7
Bob Walk	1	0	3.86	2	1	1	0	0	11.2	6	5	7	6
TOTAL	3	4	4.45	20	7	3	0	0	60.2	57	30	29	28

GAME 1 AT ATL OCT 6

PIT	000	000	010	1	5	1
ATL	010	210	10X	5	8	0

Pitchers: DRABEK, Patterson (5), Neagle (7), Cox (8) vs SMOLTZ, Stanton (9)
Home Runs: Lind-PIT, Blauser-ATL
Attendance: 51,971

GAME 2 AT ATL OCT 7

PIT	000	000	410	5	7	0
ATL	040	040	50X	13	14	0

Pitchers: JACKSON, Mason (2), Walk (3), Tomlin (5), Neagle (7), Patterson (7), Belinda (8) vs AVERY, Freeman (7), Stanton (7), Wohlers (8), Reardon (9)
Home Runs: Gant-ATL
Attendance: 51,975

GAME 3 AT PIT OCT 9

ATL	000	100	100	2	5	0
PIT	000	011	10X	3	8	1

Pitchers: GLAVINE, Stanton (7), Wohlers (8) vs WAKEFIELD
Home Runs: Bream-ATL, Gant-ATL, Slaught-PIT
Attendance: 56,610

GAME 4 AT PIT OCT 10

ATL	020	022	000	6	11	1
PIT	021	000	100	4	6	1

Pitchers: SMOLTZ, Stanton (7), Reardon (9) vs DRABEK, Tomlin (5), Cox (6), Mason (7)
Attendance: 57,164

GAME 5 AT PIT OCT 11

ATL	000	000	010	1	3	0
PIT	401	001	10X	7	13	0

Pitchers: AVERY, Smith (1), Leibrandt (5), Freeman (6), Mercker (8) vs WALK
Attendance: 52,929

GAME 6 AT ATL OCT 13

PIT	080	041	000	13	13	1
ATL	000	100	102	4	9	1

Pitchers: WAKEFIELD vs GLAVINE, Leibrandt (2), Freeman (5), Mercker (7), Wohlers (9)
Home Runs: Bell-PIT, Bonds-PIT, McClendon-PIT, Justice-ATL (2)
Attendance: 51,975

GAME 7 AT ATL OCT 14

PIT	100	001	000	2	7	1
ATL	000	000	003	3	7	0

Pitchers: DRABEK, Belinda (9) vs Smoltz, Stanton (7), Smith (7), Avery (7), REARDON (9)
Attendance: 51,975

Oakland had competed in three ALCS in the previous four years and won them all. Toronto in its first 15 seasons of existence had competed three times in the ALCS and never won. In the first game of the 1992 matchup, the Athletics scored first on Mark McGwire's two-run homer and the next batter, Terry Steinbach, pushed the score to 3–0 with another home run. Toronto's Pat Borders and Dave Winfield retaliated with solo homers in the fifth and sixth innings to narrow the gap, and the Blue Jays tied the score in the eighth when Winfield, who had doubled with two outs, came home on John Olerud's single. But in the top of the ninth, Harold Baines led off with the game's fifth home run to put Oakland back into the lead, and A's reliever Dennis Eckersley preserved it for his 10th ALCS save.

After this encouraging beginning, though, the A's went into a three-game decline. In Game 2, fireballer David Cone held Oakland scoreless through eight innings while the Jays built a 3–0 lead on Kelly Gruber's two-run homer in the fifth inning and a third score two innings later. Oakland finally touched Cone for a run in the ninth, but reliever Tom Henke smothered the threat. The A's recovered from an early deficit in Game 3 to tie the score in the fourth inning, but fell behind on Candy Maldonado's leadoff homer in the sixth and never regained the lead. In Game 4 the A's rocked Toronto starter Jack Morris for five runs in the fifth, and added another in the sixth to take a 6–1 lead. But in the eighth, reliever Eckersley, who came on with one run in and two on, yielded singles on his first two pitches to let in two more runs, and in the ninth gave up a leadoff single and a game-tying home run to Roberto Alomar. Toronto finally took the lead in the eleventh as Derek Bell fouled off several pitches before drawing a walk, took third on Maldonado's single, and scored on Pat Borders' fly to left. Reliever Tom Henke held the lead.

Down three games to one, Oakland came out slugging in Game 5. Ruben Sierra homered for a pair of runs in the first inning and the A's added a third run two innings later. Dave Winfield homered in the Toronto fourth, but the A's took advantage of two Toronto errors to score three more runs an inning later. But they couldn't sustain their comeback. Joe Carter's two-run homer in the first inning of Game 6, and Candy Maldonado's three-run blast two innings later, highlighted a 9–2 Toronto romp that ended the team's string of failed opportunities and carried the American League pennant to Canada for the first time.

Toronto Blue Jays (East), 4
Oakland Athletics (West), 2

TOR (E)

PLAYER/POS	AVG	G	AB	R	H	2B	3B	HR	RB	BB	SO	SB
Roberto Alomar, 2b	.423	6	26	4	11	1	0	2	4	2	1	5
Derek Bell, of	.000	2	0	1	0	0	0	0	0	1	0	0
Pat Borders, c	.318	6	22	3	7	0	0	1	3	1	1	0
Joe Carter, of-6,1b-2	.192	6	26	2	5	0	0	1	3	2	4	2
David Cone, p	.000	2	0	0	0	0	0	0	0	0	0	0
Mark Eichhorn, p	.000	1	0	0	0	0	0	0	0	0	0	0
Alfredo Griffin, ss-1	.000	2	2	0	0	0	0	0	0	0	0	0
Kelly Gruber, 3b	.091	6	22	3	2	1	0	1	2	2	3	0
Juan Guzman, p	.000	2	0	0	0	0	0	0	0	0	0	0
Tom Henke, p	.000	4	0	0	0	0	0	0	0	0	0	0
Jimmy Key, p	.000	1	0	0	0	0	0	0	0	0	0	0
Manuel Lee, ss	.278	6	18	2	5	1	1	0	3	1	2	0
Candy Maldonado, of	.273	6	22	3	6	0	0	2	6	2	4	0
Jack Morris, p	.000	2	0	0	0	0	0	0	0	0	0	0
John Olerud, 1b	.348	6	23	4	8	2	0	1	4	2	5	0
Ed Sprague, ph	.500	2	2	0	1	0	0	0	0	0	1	0
Todd Stottlemyre, p	.000	1	0	0	0	0	0	0	0	0	0	0
Mike Timlin, p	.000	2	0	0	0	0	0	0	0	0	0	0
Duane Ward, p	.000	3	0	0	0	0	0	0	0	0	0	0
Devon White, of	.348	6	23	2	8	2	0	0	2	5	6	0
Dave Winfield, dh	.250	6	24	7	6	1	0	2	3	5	2	0
TOTAL	.281		210	31	59	8	1	10	30	23	29	7

PITCHER	W	L	ERA	G	GS	CG	SV	SHO	IP	H	ER	BB	SO
David Cone	1	1	3.00	2	2	0	0	0	12.0	11	4	5	9
Mark Eichhorn	0	0	0.00	1	0	0	0	0	1.0	0	0	0	0
Juan Guzman	2	0	2.08	2	2	0	0	0	13.0	12	3	5	11
Tom Henke	0	0	0.00	4	0	0	3	0	4.2	3	0	2	2
Jimmy Key	0	0	0.00	1	0	0	0	0	3.0	2	0	2	1
Jack Morris	0	1	6.57	2	2	1	0	0	12.1	11	9	9	6
Todd Stottlemyre	0	0	2.45	1	0	0	0	0	3.2	3	1	0	1
Mike Timlin	0	0	6.75	2	0	0	0	0	1.1	4	1	0	1
Duane Ward	1	0	6.75	3	0	0	0	0	4.0	6	3	1	2
TOTAL	4	2	3.44	18	6	1	3	0	55.0	52	21	24	33

OAK (W)

PLAYER/POS	AVG	G	AB	R	H	2B	3B	HR	RB	BB	SO	SB
Harold Baines, dh	.440	6	25	6	11	2	0	1	4	0	3	0
Lance Blankenship, 2b	.231	5	13	2	3	0	0	0	0	3	4	1
Mike Bordick, ss-4,2b-2	.053	6	19	1	1	0	0	0	0	1	2	1
Jerry Browne, 3b-2,of-1	.400	4	10	3	4	0	0	0	2	2	0	0
Jim Corsi, p	.000	3	0	0	0	0	0	0	0	0	0	0
Ron Darling, p	.000	1	0	0	0	0	0	0	0	0	0	0
Kelly Downs, p	.000	2	0	0	0	0	0	0	0	0	0	0
Dennis Eckersley, p	.000	3	0	0	0	0	0	0	0	0	0	0
Eric Fox, of-1,dh-1	.000	4	1	0	0	0	0	0	0	1	0	2
Rickey Henderson, of	.261	6	23	5	6	0	0	0	1	4	4	2
Rick Honeycutt, p	.000	2	0	0	0	0	0	0	0	0	0	0
Carney Lansford, 3b	.167	5	18	0	3	0	0	0	1	1	1	0
Mark McGwire, 1b	.150	6	20	1	3	0	0	1	3	5	4	0
Mike Moore, p	.000	2	0	0	0	0	0	0	0	0	0	0
Jeff Parrett, p	.000	3	0	0	0	0	0	0	0	0	0	0
Jamie Quirk, ph	.000	1	1	0	0	0	0	0	0	0	0	0
Randy Ready, ph	.000	1	1	0	0	0	0	0	0	0	1	0
Jeff Russell, p	.000	3	0	0	0	0	0	0	0	0	0	0
Ruben Sierra, of	.333	6	24	4	8	2	1	1	7	2	1	1
Terry Steinbach, c	.292	6	24	1	7	0	0	1	5	2	7	0
Dave Stewart, p	.000	2	0	0	0	0	0	0	0	0	0	0
Walt Weiss, ss	.167	3	6	1	1	0	0	0	0	2	1	2
Bob Welch, p	.000	1	0	0	0	0	0	0	0	0	0	0
Willie Wilson, of	.227	6	22	0	5	1	0	0	0	1	5	7
Bobby Witt, p	.000	1	0	0	0	0	0	0	0	0	0	0
TOTAL	.251		207	24	52	5	1	4	23	24	33	16

PITCHER	W	L	ERA	G	GS	CG	SV	SHO	IP	H	ER	BB	SO
Jim Corsi	0	0	0.00	3	0	0	0	0	2.0	2	0	3	0
Ron Darling	0	1	3.00	1	1	0	0	0	6.0	4	2	2	3
Kelly Downs	0	1	3.86	2	0	0	0	0	2.1	3	1	1	0
Dennis Eckersley	0	0	6.00	3	0	0	1	0	3.0	8	2	0	2
Rick Honeycutt	0	0	0.00	2	0	0	0	0	2.0	0	0	0	1
Mike Moore	0	2	7.45	2	2	0	0	0	9.2	11	8	5	7
Jeff Parrett	0	0	11.57	3	0	0	0	0	2.1	6	3	0	1
Jeff Russell	1	0	9.00	3	0	0	0	0	2.0	2	2	4	0
Dave Stewart	1	0	2.70	2	2	1	0	0	16.2	14	5	6	7
Bob Welch	0	0	2.57	1	1	0	0	0	7.0	7	2	1	7
Bobby Witt	0	0	18.00	1	0	0	0	0	1.0	2	2	1	1
TOTAL	2	4	4.50	23	6	1	1	0	54.0	59	27	23	29

GAME 1 AT TOR OCT 7

				R	H	E
OAK	030	000	001	4	6	1
TOR	000	011	010	3	9	0

Pitchers: Stewart, RUSSELL (8), Eckersley (9) vs MORRIS
Home Runs: Baines-OAK, McGwire-OAK, Steinbach-OAK, Winfield-TOR, Borders-TOR
Attendance: 51,039

GAME 2 AT TOR OCT 8

				R	H	E
OAK	000	000	001	1	6	0
TOR	000	020	10X	3	4	0

Pitchers: MOORE, Corsi (8), Parrett (8) vs CONE, Henke (9)
Home Runs: Gruber-TOR
Attendance: 51,114

GAME 3 AT OAK OCT 10

				R	H	E
TOR	010	110	211	7	9	1
OAK	000	200	210	5	13	3

Pitchers: GUZMAN, Ward (7), Timlin (8), Henke (8) vs DARLING, Downs (7), Corsi (8), Russell (8), Honeycutt (9), Eckersley (9)
Home Runs: Alomar-TOR, Maldonado-TOR
Attendance: 46,911

GAME 4 AT OAK OCT 11

					R	H	E
TOR	010	000	032	01	7	17	4
OAK	005	001	000	00	6	12	2

Pitchers: Morris, Stottlemyre (4), Timlin (8), WARD (9), Henke (11) vs Welch, Parrett (8), Eckersley (8), Corsi (9), DOWNS (10)
Home Runs: Alomar-TOR, Olerud-TOR
Attendance: 47,732

GAME 5 AT OAK OCT 12

				R	H	E
TOR	000	100	100	2	7	3
OAK	201	030	00X	6	8	0

Pitchers: CONE, Key (5), Eichhorn (8) vs STEWART
Home Runs: Winfield-TOR, Sierra-OAK
Attendance: 44,955

GAME 6 AT TOR OCT 14

				R	H	E
OAK	000	001	010	2	7	1
TOR	204	010	02X	9	13	0

Pitchers: MOORE, Parrett (3), Honeycutt (5), Russell (7), Witt (8) vs GUZMAN, Ward (8), Henke (9)
Home Runs: Carter-TOR, Maldonado-TOR
Attendance: 51,335

Atlanta outscored Toronto in the Series, 20 runs to 16, but the Blue Jays eked out four one-run victories to bring Canada its first baseball world championship.

In the fourth inning of Game 1, Atlanta's Tom Glavine gave up a leadoff homer to Joe Carter for the game's first run, but held the Jays to just one single the rest of the way. Meanwhile, Toronto starter Jack Morris shut out the Braves for five innings. But in the top of the sixth he gave up a deciding three-run homer to catcher Damon Berryhill. The next night, though, down 4–5 in the ninth inning, Toronto pinch hitter Derek Bell drew a walk from Braves closer Jeff Reardon, and pinch hitter Ed Sprague lined Reardon's first pitch over the left field wall.

Toronto moved ahead with another close victory in Game 3, the first World Series game ever played outside the United States. Atlanta threatened in the fourth inning when, with two on and none out, David Justice flied deep to center Devon White leaped high to snare it. Baserunner Terry Pendleton was ruled out for passing Deion Sanders on the basepath, and third baseman Kelly Gruber tagged Sanders, who was diving back into second base, to complete what seemed to be a triple play. The umpire didn't see the tag, however, and called Sanders safe. Still, no Braves scored, and Joe Carter homered for the game's first run in the last of the fourth. Atlanta tied the game in the sixth and took the lead in the top of the eighth. Gruber homered to re-tie it in the bottom of the inning, and after the Jays had filled the bases in the last of the ninth, Candy Maldonado tagged Reardon for a hit over the drawn-in outfield to bring home the winning run.

The Jays pushed their Series advantage to 3–1 in Game 4. Catcher Pat Borders opened the Toronto third with a home run, and Gruber scored from second on Devon White's seventh-inning single. The Braves got to Toronto starter Jimmy Key for a run in the eighth, but relievers Duane Ward and Tom Henke shut them out thereafter.

In the fifth game the Blue Jays twice came from one run down to even the score. But in the fifth inning, after the Braves had once again built a one-run lead, Lonnie Smith extended it with a grand slam that sent the Series back to Atlanta.

Toronto scored a run in the first inning of Game 6. Atlanta tied the game in the third, but Candy Maldonado's leadoff homer in the fourth restored the advantage to Toronto. In the bottom of the ninth, the Braves scrabbled back to tie it up again. The score was 2–2 until the top of the 11th, when Toronto's

Toronto Blue Jays (AL), 4; Atlanta Braves (NL), 2

TOR (A)

PLAYER/POS	AVG	G	AB	R	H	2B	3B	HR	RB	BB	SO	SB
Roberto Alomar, 2b	.208	6	24	3	5	1	0	0	0	3	3	3
Derek Bell, ph	.000	2	1	1	0	0	0	0	0	1	0	0
Pat Borders, c	.450	6	20	2	9	3	0	1	3	2	1	0
Joe Carter, of-4	.273	6	22	2	6	2	0	2	3	3	2	1
David Cone, p	.500	2	4	0	2	0	0	0	1	1	0	0
Mark Eichhorn, p	.000	1	0	0	0	0	0	0	0	0	0	0
Alfredo Griffin, ss	.000	2	0	0	0	0	0	0	0	0	0	0
Kelly Gruber, 3b	.105	6	19	2	2	0	0	1	1	2	5	1
Juan Guzman, p	.000	1	0	0	0	0	0	0	0	0	0	0
Tom Henke, p	.000	3	0	0	0	0	0	0	0	0	0	0
Jimmy Key, p	.000	2	1	0	0	0	0	0	0	0	0	0
Manuel Lee, ss	.105	6	19	1	2	0	0	0	0	1	2	0
Candy Maldonado, of-5	.158	6	19	1	3	0	0	1	2	2	5	0
Jack Morris, p	.000	2	2	0	0	0	0	0	0	0	2	0
John Olerud, 1b	.308	4	13	2	4	0	0	0	0	0	4	0
Ed Sprague, 1b-1	.500	3	2	1	1	0	0	1	2	1	0	0
Todd Stottlemyre, p	.000	4	0	0	0	0	0	0	0	0	0	0
Pat Tabler, ph	.000	2	2	0	0	0	0	0	0	0	0	0
Mike Timlin, p	.000	2	0	0	0	0	0	0	0	0	0	0
Duane Ward, p	.000	4	0	0	0	0	0	0	0	0	0	0
David Wells, p	.000	4	0	0	0	0	0	0	0	0	0	0
Devon White, of	.231	6	26	2	6	1	0	0	2	0	6	1
Dave Winfield, of-3,dh-3	.227	6	22	0	5	1	0	0	3	2	3	0
TOTAL	.230		196	17	45	8	0	6	17	18	33	6

PITCHER	W	L	ERA	G	GS	CG	SV	SHO	IP	H	ER	BB	SO
David Cone	0	0	3.48	2	2	0	0	0	10.1	9	4	8	8
Mark Eichhorn	0	0	0.00	1	0	0	0	0	1.0	0	0	0	1
Juan Guzman	0	0	1.13	1	1	0	0	0	8.0	8	1	1	7
Tom Henke	0	0	2.70	3	0	0	2	0	3.1	2	1	2	1
Jimmy Key	2	0	1.00	2	1	0	0	0	9.0	6	1	0	6
Jack Morris	0	2	8.44	2	2	0	0	0	10.2	13	10	6	12
Todd Stottlemyre	0	0	0.00	4	0	0	0	0	3.2	4	0	0	4
Mike Timlin	0	0	0.00	2	0	0	1	0	1.1	0	0	0	0
Duane Ward	2	0	0.00	4	0	0	0	0	3.1	1	0	1	6
David Wells	0	0	0.00	4	0	0	0	0	4.1	1	0	2	3
TOTAL	4	2	2.78	25	6	0	3	0	55.0	44	17	20	48

ATL (N)

PLAYER/POS	AVG	G	AB	R	H	2B	3B	HR	RB	BB	SO	SB
Steve Avery, p	.000	2	1	0	0	0	0	0	0	0	1	0
Rafael Belliard, ss-3, 2b-1	.000	4	0	0	0	0	0	0	0	0	0	0
Damon Berryhill, c	.091	6	22	1	2	0	0	1	3	1	11	0
Jeff Blauser, ss	.250	6	24	2	6	0	0	0	0	1	9	2
Sid Bream, 1b	.200	5	15	1	3	0	0	0	0	4	0	0
Francisco Cabrera, ph	.000	1	1	0	0	0	0	0	0	0	0	0
Ron Gant, of-3	.125	4	8	2	1	1	0	0	0	1	2	2
Tom Glavine, p	.000	2	2	0	0	0	0	0	0	1	0	0
Brian Hunter, 1b-3	.200	4	5	0	1	0	0	0	2	0	1	0
David Justice, of	.158	6	19	4	3	0	0	1	3	6	5	1
Charlie Leibrandt, p	.000	1	0	0	0	0	0	0	0	0	0	0
Mark Lemke, 2b	.211	6	19	0	4	0	0	0	2	1	3	0
Otis Nixon, of	.296	6	27	3	8	1	0	0	1	1	3	5
Terry Pendleton, 3b	.240	6	25	2	6	2	0	0	2	1	5	0
Jeff Reardon, p	.000	2	0	0	0	0	0	0	0	0	0	0
Deion Sanders, of	.533	4	15	4	8	2	0	0	1	2	1	5
Lonnie Smith, dh-3	.167	5	12	1	2	0	0	1	5	1	4	0
Pete Smith, p	.000	1	1	0	0	0	0	0	0	0	1	0
John Smoltz, p-2	.000	3	3	0	0	0	0	0	0	0	2	0
Mike Stanton, p	.000	4	0	0	0	0	0	0	0	0	0	0
Jeff Treadway, ph	.000	1	1	0	0	0	0	0	0	0	0	0
Mark Wohlers, p	.000	2	0	0	0	0	0	0	0	0	0	0
TOTAL	.220		200	20	44	6	0	3	19	20	48	15

PITCHER	W	L	ERA	G	GS	CG	SV	SHO	IP	H	ER	BB	SO
Steve Avery	0	1	3.75	2	2	0	0	0	12.0	11	5	3	11
Tom Glavine	1	1	1.59	2	2	2	0	0	17.0	10	3	4	8
Charlie Leibrandt	0	1	9.00	1	0	0	0	0	2.0	3	2	0	0
Jeff Reardon	0	1	13.50	2	0	0	0	0	1.1	2	2	1	1
Pete Smith	0	0	0.00	1	0	0	0	0	3.0	3	0	0	0
John Smoltz	1	0	2.70	2	2	0	0	0	13.1	13	4	7	12
Mike Stanton	0	0	0.00	4	0	0	1	0	5.0	3	0	2	1
Mark Wohlers	0	0	0.00	2	0	0	0	0	0.2	0	0	1	0
TOTAL	2	4	2.65	16	6	2	1	0	54.1	45	16	18	33

Dave Winfield delivered two runners with a two-out double into the left field corner. As it turned out, the Jays needed both runs, for Atlanta scored in the bottom of the 11th. But with two out and the potential tying run on third, Otis Nixon, was out at first attempting a bunt, and the Series was over.

GAME 1 AT ATL OCT 17

				R	H	E
TOR	000	100	000	1	4	0
ATL	**000**	**003**	**00X**	**3**	**4**	**0**

Pitchers: MORRIS, Stottlemyre (7), Wells (8) vs GLAVINE
Home Runs: Carter-TOR, Berryhill-ATL
Attendance: 51,763

GAME 2 AT ATL OCT 18

				R	H	E
TOR	**000**	**020**	**012**	**5**	**9**	**2**
ATL	010	120	000	4	5	1

Pitchers: Cone, Wells (5), Stottlemyre (7), WARD (8), Henke (9) vs Smoltz, Stanton (8), REARDON (8)
Home Runs: Sprague-TOR
Attendance: 51,763

GAME 3 AT TOR OCT 20

				R	H	E
ATL	000	001	010	2	9	0
TOR	**000**	**100**	**011**	**3**	**6**	**1**

Pitchers: AVERY, Wohlers (9), Stanton (9), Reardon (9) vs Guzman, WARD (9)
Home Runs: Carter-TOR, Gruber-TOR
Attendance: 51,813

GAME 4 AT TOR OCT 21

				R	H	E
ATL	000	000	010	1	5	0
TOR	**001**	**000**	**10X**	**2**	**6**	**0**

Pitchers: GLAVINE vs KEY, Ward (8), Henke (9)
Home Runs: Borders-TOR
Attendance: 52,090

GAME 5 AT TOR OCT 22

				R	H	E
ATL	**100**	**150**	**000**	**7**	**13**	**0**
TOR	010	100	000	2	6	0

Pitchers: SMOLTZ, Stanton (7) vs MORRIS, Wells (5), Timlin (7), Eichhorn (8), Stottlemyre (9)
Home Runs: Justice-ATL, L.Smith-ATL
Attendance: 52,268

GAME 6 AT ATL OCT 24

					R	H	E
TOR	**100**	**100**	**000**	**02**	**4**	**14**	**1**
ATL	001	000	001	01	3	8	1

Pitchers: Cone, Stottlemyre (7), Wells (7), Ward (8), Henke (9), KEY (10), Timlin (11) vs Avery, P.Smith (5), Stanton (8), Wohlers (9), LEIBRANDT (10)
Home Runs: Maldonado-TOR
Attendance: 51,763

Atlanta outhit the Phillies by 47 percentage points, outscored them by 10 runs, and yielded 1.6 fewer earned runs per game. But the Phillies won the pennant. In the opener, Philadelphia starter Curt Schilling fanned 10 batters—including the first five he faced—and left the game after eight innings with a 3–2 lead. An errant throw by Phillies third baseman Kim Batiste (who had just entered the game to strengthen the defense) set up an unearned tying run in the ninth inning. But in the last of the 10th, after John Kruk had doubled, Batiste redeemed himself with a game-winning hit down the left field line.

While the Philadelphia offense remained steady over the next two games, the Braves erupted for 23 runs. By the time Philadelphia scored its first runs in the fourth inning of Game 2, Atlanta had already sent eight men across the plate. In Game 3 the Phillies scored first, and held a 2–0 lead before the Braves destroyed them with five runs in the sixth inning and four more in the seventh.

Game 4 featured only four fewer hits than Game 3, but 10 fewer runs, as Philadelphia evened the series with its second close win. Phillies starter Danny Jackson yielded nine hits and a pair of walks, but only one second-inning run. In the top of the fourth, Darren Daulton, who had reached on an infield error, took third on Milt Thompson's double and scored on Kevin Stocker's two-out single. Pitcher Jackson then singled home Thompson with what proved the winning run.

In the fifth game, Curt Schilling held Atlanta to four hits through eight innings, and carried a 3–0 lead into the bottom of the ninth. But when a walk and infield error put the first two men on, Mitch Williams relieved Schilling and gave up a trio of singles which tied the game. In the top of the 10th inning, though, Lenny Dykstra's solo homer restored the Phillies' lead, and veteran reliever Larry Andersen blanked the Braves in the bottom of the 10th—striking out the final two batters—to preserve the win.

After their two narrow wins on the road, the Phillies clinched the pennant with relative ease when the series returned to Philadelphia for Game 6. Darren Daulton's two-out double in the third inning put the Phillies up 2–0. Atlanta scored once in the fifth, but Dave Hollins' two-run homer in the last of the fifth increased Philadelphia's lead to three runs, and Mickey Morandini's two-out, two-run triple an inning later pushed the score to 6–1. Atlanta's Jeff Blauser brought the score to 6–3 with a home run in the seventh inning, but Phillies relievers David West and Mitch Williams set the Braves down in order in the final two innings.

Philadelphia Phillies (East), 4; Atlanta Braves (West), 2

PHI (E)

PLAYER/POS	AVG	G	AB	R	H	2B	3B	HR	RB	BB	SO	SB
Larry Andersen, p	.000	3	0	0	0	0	0	0	0	0	0	0
Kim Batiste, 3b	1.000	4	1	0	1	0	0	0	1	0	0	0
Wes Chamberlain, of-2	.364	4	11	1	4	3	0	0	1	1	3	0
Darren Daulton, c	.263	6	19	2	5	1	0	1	3	6	3	0
Mariano Duncan, 2b	.267	3	15	3	4	0	2	0	0	0	5	0
Lenny Dykstra, of	.280	6	25	5	7	1	0	2	2	5	8	0
Jim Eisenreich, of-5	.133	6	15	0	2	1	0	0	1	0	2	0
Tommy Greene, p	.000	2	0	1	0	0	0	0	0	1	0	0
Dave Hollins, 3b	.200	6	20	2	4	1	0	2	4	5	4	1
Pete Incaviglia, of	.167	3	12	2	2	0	0	1	1	0	3	0
Danny Jackson, p	.250	1	4	0	1	0	0	0	1	0	3	0
Ricky Jordan, ph	.000	2	1	0	0	0	0	0	0	1	0	0
John Kruk, 1b	.250	6	24	4	6	2	1	1	5	4	5	0
Tony Longmire, ph	.000	1	1	0	0	0	0	0	0	0	1	0
Roger Mason, p	.000	2	0	0	0	0	0	0	0	0	0	0
Mickey Morandini, 2b	.250	4	16	1	4	0	1	0	2	0	3	1
Terry Mulholland, p	.000	1	2	0	0	0	0	0	0	0	1	0
Todd Pratt, c	.000	1	1	0	0	0	0	0	0	0	1	0
Ben Rivera, p	.000	1	0	0	0	0	0	0	0	0	0	0
Curt Schilling, p	.000	2	5	0	0	0	0	0	0	0	2	0
Kevin Stocker, ss	.182	6	22	0	4	1	0	0	1	2	5	0
Bobby Thigpen, p	.000	2	0	0	0	0	0	0	0	0	0	0
Milt Thompson, of-5	.231	6	13	2	3	1	0	0	0	1	2	0
David West, p	.000	3	0	0	0	0	0	0	0	0	0	0
Mitch Williams, p	.000	4	0	0	0	0	0	0	0	0	0	0
TOTAL	.227		207	23	47	11	4	7	22	26	51	2

PITCHER	W	L	ERA	G	GS	CG	SV	SHO	IP	H	ER	BB	SO
Larry Andersen	0	0	15.43	3	0	0	1	0	2.1	4	4	1	3
Tommy Greene	1	1	9.64	2	2	0	0	0	9.1	12	10	7	7
Danny Jackson	1	0	1.17	1	1	0	0	0	7.2	9	1	2	6
Roger Mason	0	0	0.00	2	0	0	0	0	3.0	1	0	0	2
Terry Mulholland	0	1	7.20	1	1	0	0	0	5.0	9	4	1	2
Ben Rivera	0	0	4.50	1	0	0	0	0	2.0	1	1	1	2
Curt Schilling	0	0	1.69	2	2	0	0	0	16.0	11	3	5	19
Bobby Thigpen	0	0	5.40	2	0	0	0	0	1.2	1	1	1	3
David West	0	0	13.50	3	0	0	0	0	2.2	5	4	2	5
Mitch Williams	2	0	1.69	4	0	0	2	0	5.1	6	1	2	5
TOTAL	4	2	4.75	21	6	0	3	0	55.0	59	29	22	54

ATL (W)

PLAYER/POS	AVG	G	AB	R	H	2B	3B	HR	RB	BB	SO	SB
Steve Avery, p	.500	2	4	1	2	1	0	0	0	0	1	0
Rafael Belliard, 2b-1,ss-1	.000	2	1	1	0	0	0	0	0	0	1	0
Damon Berryhill, c	.211	6	19	2	4	0	0	1	3	1	5	0
Jeff Blauser, ss	.280	6	25	5	7	1	0	2	4	4	7	0
Sid Bream, 1b	1.000	1	1	1	1	0	0	0	0	0	0	0
Francisco Cabrera, c-1	.667	3	3	0	2	0	0	0	1	0	1	0
Ron Gant, of	.185	6	27	4	5	3	0	0	3	2	9	0
Tom Glavine, p	.000	1	3	0	0	0	0	0	0	0	0	0
David Justice, of	.143	6	21	2	3	1	0	0	4	3	3	0
Mark Lemke, 2b	.208	6	24	2	5	2	0	0	4	1	6	0
Greg Maddux, p	.250	2	4	1	1	0	0	0	0	0	1	0
Fred McGriff, 1b	.435	6	23	6	10	2	0	1	4	4	7	0
Greg McMichael, p	.000	4	0	0	0	0	0	0	0	0	0	0
Kent Mercker, p	.000	5	0	0	0	0	0	0	0	0	0	0
Otis Nixon, of	.348	6	23	3	8	2	0	0	4	5	6	0
Greg Olson, c	.333	2	3	0	1	1	0	0	0	0	1	0
Bill Pecota, ph	.333	4	3	1	1	0	0	0	0	1	1	0
Terry Pendleton, 3b	.346	6	26	4	9	1	0	1	5	0	2	0
Deion Sanders, of-1	.000	5	3	0	0	0	0	0	0	0	1	0
John Smoltz, p	.000	1	1	0	0	0	0	0	0	1	1	0
Mike Stanton, p	.000	1	0	0	0	0	0	0	0	0	0	0
Tony Tarasco, of	.000	2	1	0	0	0	0	0	0	0	1	0
Mark Wohlers, p	.000	4	0	0	0	0	0	0	0	0	0	0
TOTAL	.274		215	33	59	14	0	5	32	22	54	0

PITCHER	W	L	ERA	G	GS	CG	SV	SHO	IP	H	ER	BB	SO
Steve Avery	0	0	2.77	2	2	0	0	0	13.0	9	4	6	10
Tom Glavine	1	0	2.57	1	1	0	0	0	7.0	6	2	0	5
Greg Maddux	1	1	4.97	2	2	0	0	0	12.2	11	7	7	11
Greg McMichael	0	1	6.75	4	0	0	0	0	4.0	7	3	2	1
Kent Mercker	0	0	1.80	5	0	0	0	0	5.0	3	1	2	4
John Smoltz	0	1	0.00	1	1	0	0	0	6.1	8	0	5	10
Mike Stanton	0	0	0.00	1	0	0	0	0	1.0	1	0	1	0
Mark Wohlers	0	1	3.38	4	0	0	0	0	5.1	2	2	3	10
TOTAL	2	4	3.15	20	6	0	0	0	54.1	47	19	26	51

GAME 1 AT PHI OCT 6

					R	H	E
ATL	001	100	001	0	3	9	0
PHI	100	101	000	1	4	9	1

Pitchers: Avery, Mercker (7), McMICHAEL (9) vs Schilling, WILLIAMS (9)
Home Runs: Incaviglia-PHI
Attendance: 62,012

GAME 2 AT PHI OCT 7

				R	H	E
ATL	206	010	041	14	16	0
PHI	000	200	001	3	7	2

Pitchers: MADDUX, Stanton (8), Wohlers (9) vs GREENE, Thigpen (3), Rivera (4), Mason (6), West (8), Andersen (9)
Home Runs: Blauser-ATL, McGriff-ATL, Pendleton-ATL, Berryhill-ATL, Dykstra-PHI, Hollins-PHI
Attendance: 62,436

GAME 3 AT ATL OCT 9

				R	H	E
PHI	000	101	011	4	10	1
ATL	000	005	40X	9	12	0

Pitchers: MULHOLLAND, Mason (6), Andersen (7), West (7), Thigpen (8) vs GLAVINE, Mercker (8), McMichael (9)
Home Runs: Kruk-PHI
Attendance: 52,032

GAME 4 AT ATL OCT 10

				R	H	E
PHI	000	200	000	2	8	1
ATL	010	000	000	1	10	1

Pitchers: JACKSON, Williams (8) vs SMOLTZ, Mercker (7), Wohlers (8)
Attendance: 52,032

GAME 5 AT ATL OCT 11

					R	H	E
PHI	100	100	001	1	4	6	1
ATL	000	000	003	0	3	7	1

Pitchers: Schilling, WILLIAMS (9), Andersen (10) vs Avery, Mercker (8), McMichael (9), WOHLERS (10)
Home Runs: Dykstra-PHI, Daulton-PHI
Attendance: 52,032

GAME 6 AT PHI OCT 13

				R	H	E
ATL	000	010	200	3	5	3
PHI	002	022	00X	6	7	1

Pitchers: MADDUX, Mercker (6), McMichael (7), Wohlers (7) vs GREENE, West (8), Williams (9)
Home Runs: Blauser-ATL, Hollins-PHI
Attendance: 62,502

Toronto Blue Jays (East), 4; Chicago White Sox (West), 2

The visiting team won the first four games of the series, but in Game 5, home team Toronto held off a ninth-inning White Sox rally to take a 3–2 series lead. Then, in Chicago two days later, the Jays put the Sox away.

In Chicago for the series opener, Toronto scored first when Ed Sprague tripled home a pair of runs in the fourth inning. The White Sox bounced ahead with three runs in the last of the fourth, but the Blue Jays regained the lead a half inning later on John Olerud's two-run double, then pulled away to a 17-hit, 7–3 win. Toronto also scored first in Game 2, with an unearned run in the first inning. But in the last of the inning, Dave Stewart walked the bases full, then handed Chicago the tying run with a wild pitch. With two out in the fourth inning, though, back-to-back doubles by Paul Molitor and Tony Fernandez restored the lead to Toronto, and a walk, an infield hit and an error increased the Jays' lead to 3–1. This ended the scoring, although the White Sox loaded the bases in the sixth before Stewart retired the next three batters.

The White Sox leaped to life when the series moved to Toronto for Game 3. After the first two men had been retired in the third inning, Sox batters combined five singles with a pair of walks for a 5–0 lead, which Chicago starter Wilson Alvarez held for a 6–1 complete game victory. Lance Johnson's two-run homer in the second inning of Game 4 put Chicago ahead. The Jays overtook them with three runs an inning later, but in the sixth inning Frank Thomas homered to even the score at 3–3, and after two batters walked, Johnson's two-out triple put the Sox ahead to stay.

The Blue Jays finally broke the visiting team's lock on victory, scoring single runs in each of the first four innings, and another in the seventh, while starter Juan Guzman held Chicago to three hits and a single run in his seven innings. Robin Ventura's two-run homer off Jays' reliever Duane Ward in the Chicago ninth narrowed Toronto's lead to 5–3, but Ward then retired Bo Jackson with his third strikeout.

Errors ended the White Sox season in Game 6. With the score tied 2–2 in the fourth inning, a bobble by Chicago third baseman Robin Ventura put Paul Molitor on base. Molitor subsequently scored the go-ahead run when second baseman Joey Cora threw a ball into the dugout. Devon White homered in the ninth inning to stretch Toronto's lead to 4–2, and an error by Sox reliever Scott Radinsky on what should have been the third out set the stage for Molitor to triple home a pair of baserunners. Warren Newson's leadoff homer against Toronto reliever Duane Ward in the bottom of the ninth narrowed the score to 6–3, but the White Sox came no closer. The win, starter Dave Stewart's second of the series, was his eighth triumph without a loss in LCS play.

GAME 1 AT CHI OCT 5

				R	H	E
TOR	000	230	200	7	17	1
CHI	000	300	000	3	6	1

Pitchers: GUZMAN, Cox (7), Ward (9) vs McDOWELL, DeLeon (7), Radinsky (8), McCaskill (9)
Home Runs: Molitor-TOR
Attendance: 46,246

GAME 2 AT CHI OCT 6

				R	H	E
TOR	100	200	000	3	8	0
CHI	100	000	000	1	7	2

Pitchers: STEWART, Leiter (7), Ward (9) vs FERNANDEZ, Hernandez (9)
Attendance: 46,101

GAME 3 AT TOR OCT 8

				R	H	E
CHI	005	100	000	6	12	0
TOR	001	000	000	1	7	1

Pitchers: ALVAREZ vs HENTGEN, Cox (4), Eichhorn (7), Castillo (9)
Attendance: 51,783

GAME 4 AT TOR OCT 9

				R	H	E
CHI	020	003	101	7	11	0
TOR	003	001	000	4	9	0

Pitchers: Bere, BELCHER (3), McCaskill (7), Radinsky (8), Hernandez (9) vs STOTTLEMYRE, Leiter (7), Timlin (7)
Home Runs: Thomas-CHI, Johnson-CHI
Attendance: 51,889

GAME 5 AT TOR OCT 10

				R	H	E
CHI	000	010	002	3	5	1
TOR	111	100	10X	5	14	0

Pitchers: McDOWELL, DeLeon (3), Radinsky (7), Hernandez (7) vs GUZMAN, Castillo (8), Ward (9)
Home Runs: Ventura-CHI, Burks-CHI
Attendance: 51,375

GAME 6 AT CHI OCT 12

				R	H	E
TOR	020	100	003	6	10	0
CHI	002	000	001	3	5	3

Pitchers: STEWART, Ward (8) vs FERNANDEZ, McCaskill (8), Radinsky (9), Hernandez (9)
Home Runs: White-TOR, Newson-CHI
Attendance: 45,527

TOR (E)

PLAYER/POS	AVG	G	AB	R	H	2B	3B	HR	RB	BB	SO	SB
Roberto Alomar, 2b	.292	6	24	3	7	1	0	0	4	4	3	4
Pat Borders, c	.250	6	24	1	6	1	0	0	3	0	6	1
Joe Carter, of	.259	6	27	2	7	0	0	0	2	1	5	0
Tony Castillo, p	.000	2	0	0	0	0	0	0	0	0	0	0
Danny Cox, p	.000	2	0	0	0	0	0	0	0	0	0	0
Mark Eichhorn, p	.000	1	0	0	0	0	0	0	0	0	0	0
Tony Fernandez, ss	.318	6	22	1	7	0	0	0	1	2	4	0
Juan Guzman, p	.000	2	0	0	0	0	0	0	0	0	0	0
Rickey Henderson, of	.120	6	25	4	3	2	0	0	0	4	5	2
Pat Hentgen, p	.000	1	0	0	0	0	0	0	0	0	0	0
Al Leiter, p	.000	2	0	0	0	0	0	0	0	0	0	0
Paul Molitor, dh	.391	6	23	7	9	2	1	1	5	3	3	0
John Olerud, 1b	.348	6	23	5	8	1	0	0	3	4	1	0
Ed Sprague, 3b	.286	6	21	0	6	0	1	0	4	2	4	0
Dave Stewart, p	.000	2	0	0	0	0	0	0	0	0	0	0
Todd Stottlemyre, p	.000	1	0	0	0	0	0	0	0	0	0	0
Mike Timlin, p	.000	1	0	0	0	0	0	0	0	0	0	0
Duane Ward, p	.000	4	0	0	0	0	0	0	0	0	0	0
Devon White, of	.444	6	27	3	12	1	1	1	2	1	5	0
TOTAL	.301		216	26	65	8	3	2	24	21	36	7

PITCHER	W	L	ERA	G	GS	CG	SV	SHO	IP	H	ER	BB	SO
Tony Castillo	0	0	0.00	2	0	0	0	0	2.0	0	0	1	1
Danny Cox	0	0	0.00	2	0	0	0	0	5.0	3	0	2	5
Mark Eichhorn	0	0	0.00	1	0	0	0	0	2.0	1	0	1	1
Juan Guzman	2	0	2.08	2	2	0	0	0	13.0	8	3	9	9
Pat Hentgen	0	1	18.00	1	1	0	0	0	3.0	9	6	2	3
Al Leiter	0	0	3.38	2	0	0	0	0	2.2	4	1	2	2
Dave Stewart	2	0	2.03	2	2	0	0	0	13.1	8	3	8	8
Todd Stottlemyre	0	1	7.50	1	1	0	0	0	6.0	6	5	4	4
Mike Timlin	0	0	3.86	1	0	0	0	0	2.1	3	1	0	2
Duane Ward	0	0	5.79	4	0	0	2	0	4.2	4	3	3	8
TOTAL	4	2	3.67	18	6	0	2	0	54.0	46	22	32	43

CHI (W)

PLAYER/POS	AVG	G	AB	R	H	2B	3B	HR	RB	BB	SO	SB
Wilson Alvarez, p	.000	1	0	0	0	0	0	0	0	0	0	0
Tim Belcher, p	.000	1	0	0	0	0	0	0	0	0	0	0
Jason Bere, p	.000	1	0	0	0	0	0	0	0	0	0	0
Ellis Burks, of	.304	6	23	4	7	1	0	1	3	3	5	0
Joey Cora, 2b	.136	6	22	1	3	0	0	0	1	3	6	0
Jose DeLeon, p	.000	2	0	0	0	0	0	0	0	0	0	0
Alex Fernandez, p	.000	2	0	0	0	0	0	0	0	0	0	0
Craig Grebeck, 3b	1.000	1	1	0	1	0	0	0	0	0	0	0
Ozzie Guillen, ss	.273	6	22	4	6	1	0	0	2	0	2	1
Roberto Hernandez, p	.000	4	0	0	0	0	0	0	0	0	0	0
Bo Jackson, dh	.000	3	10	1	0	0	0	0	0	3	6	0
Lance Johnson, of	.217	6	23	2	5	1	1	1	6	2	1	1
Ron Karkovice, c	.000	6	15	0	0	0	0	0	0	1	7	0
Mike LaValliere, c	.333	2	3	0	1	0	0	0	0	1	0	0
Kirk McCaskill, p	.000	3	0	0	0	0	0	0	0	0	0	0
Jack McDowell, p	.000	2	0	0	0	0	0	0	0	0	0	0
Warren Newson, dh-1	.200	2	5	1	1	0	0	1	1	0	1	0
Dan Pasqua, 1b	.000	2	6	1	0	0	0	0	0	1	2	0
Scott Radinsky, p	.000	4	0	0	0	0	0	0	0	0	0	0
Tim Raines, of	.444	6	27	5	12	3	0	0	1	2	2	1
Frank Thomas, 1b-4,dh-2	.353	6	17	2	6	0	0	1	3	10	5	0
Robin Ventura, 3b-6,1b-1	.200	6	20	2	4	0	0	1	5	6	6	0
TOTAL	.237		194	23	46	6	1	5	22	32	43	3

PITCHER	W	L	ERA	G	GS	CG	SV	SHO	IP	H	ER	BB	SO
Wilson Alvarez	1	0	1.00	1	1	1	0	0	9.0	7	1	2	6
Tim Belcher	1	0	2.45	1	0	0	0	0	3.2	3	1	3	1
Jason Bere	0	0	11.57	1	1	0	0	0	2.1	5	3	2	3
Jose DeLeon	0	0	1.93	2	0	0	0	0	4.2	7	1	1	6
Alex Fernandez	0	2	1.80	2	2	0	0	0	15.0	15	3	6	10
Roberto Hernandez	0	0	0.00	4	0	0	1	0	4.0	4	0	0	1
Kirk McCaskill	0	0	0.00	3	0	0	0	0	3.2	3	0	1	3
Jack McDowell	0	2	10.00	2	2	0	0	0	9.0	18	10	5	5
Scott Radinsky	0	0	10.80	4	0	0	0	0	1.2	3	2	1	1
TOTAL	1	4	3.57	20	6	1	1	0	53.0	65	21	21	36

The Phillies and Blue Jays split the first two games, played in Toronto. But the defending champions captured the lead when play moved to Philadelphia for Game 3. In a contest delayed more than an hour by rain, Paul Molitor tripled home two Blue Jay runs before the first out had been recorded, and the Jays pushed on from there to an easy 10–3 win.

By just about any measure except pitching effectiveness, Game 4—played in a steady drizzle that for a time increased to a downpour—was one of the great ones. At 4 hours 14 minutes, it was the longest in World Series history, and its 29 total runs scored established a new record for major league postseason championship play, as did Philadelphia's 14 runs for a losing team. Toronto scored three times after two men had been retired in the top of the first inning, but Philadelphia retaliated immediately with four two-out runs in the bottom of the inning, as Jays' starter Todd Stottlemyre walked four batters, and Milt Thompson tripled. Lenny Dykstra's two-run homer an inning later pushed the Phillies' lead to 6–3, but Toronto scrambled back to regain a 7–6 advantage in the third inning on two walks and four singles. Philadelphia scored a tying run in the fourth inning, then scored five times an inning later with a barrage of hits highlighted by Darren Daulton's two-run homer and Dykstra's second two-run blast of the game. Toronto scored twice in the sixth inning, but single runs in the sixth and seventh restored Philadelphia's five-run lead. Then, in the top of the eighth, the Blue Jays parlayed two walks, two singles and a two-base error (later changed by the official scorer to a double) into a pair of runs and a diamond full of baserunners. Mitch Williams fanned Ed Sprague for the second out of the inning, but Rickey Henderson lined a two-run single to center to bring the Jays within one run of a tie, and Devon White looped a triple to right center for the tying and go-ahead runs. Relievers Mike Timlin and Duane Ward retired the final seven Phillies on five strikeouts and a pair of pop flies.

The Phillies salvaged their final home game, scoring single runs in the first two innings as Curt Schilling shut out the Blue Jays and forced the Series back to Toronto for a sixth game. Paul Molitor's RBI triple gave the Jays a first-inning lead, and his solo homer in the fifth stretched it to 5–1. Lenny Dykstra's three-run shot in the seventh (his fourth home run of the Series) brought Philadelphia to within a run of Toronto and Mariano Duncan scored the tying run on Dave Hollins' single. Pinch hitter Pete Incaviglia's sacrifice fly gave the Phillies their first lead of the game, 6–5. In the bottom of the ninth, Mitch Williams walked Rickey Henderson and, with one away, gave up a single to Molitor (which raised his Series batting average to .500). Molitor scored the Series-winning run when Joe Carter, the next man up, lined Williams' would-be third strike over the left field fence for an 8–6 victory and Toronto's second straight world championship.

Toronto Blue Jays, 4; Philadelphia Phillies, 2

TOR (A)

PLAYER/POS	AVG	G	AB	R	H	2B	3B	HR	RB	BB	SO	SB
Roberto Alomar, 2b	.480	6	25	5	12	2	1	0	6	2	3	4
Pat Borders, c	.304	6	23	2	7	0	0	0	1	2	1	0
Rob Butler, ph	.500	2	2	1	1	0	0	0	0	0	0	0
Willie Canate, pr	.000	1	0	0	0	0	0	0	0	0	0	0
Joe Carter, of	.280	6	25	6	7	1	0	2	8	0	4	0
Tony Castillo, p	.000	2	1	0	0	0	0	0	0	0	1	0
Danny Cox, p	.000	3	1	0	0	0	0	0	0	0	0	0
Mark Eichhorn, p	.000	1	0	0	0	0	0	0	0	0	0	0
Tony Fernandez, ss	.333	6	21	2	7	1	0	0	9	3	3	0
Alfredo Griffin, 3b-2	.000	3	0	0	0	0	0	0	0	0	0	0
Juan Guzman, p	.000	2	2	0	0	0	0	0	0	0	1	0
Rickey Henderson, of	.227	6	22	6	5	2	0	0	2	5	2	1
Pat Hentgen, p	.000	1	3	0	0	0	0	0	0	0	1	0
Randy Knorr, c	.000	1	0	0	0	0	0	0	0	0	0	0
Al Leiter, p	1.000	3	1	0	1	1	0	0	0	0	0	0
Paul Molitor, dh-3	.500	6	24	10	12	2	2	2	8	3	0	1
John Olerud, 1b	.235	5	17	5	4	1	0	1	2	4	1	0
Ed Sprague, 3b-4,1b-1	.067	5	15	0	1	0	0	0	2	1	6	0
Dave Stewart, p	.000	2	0	0	0	0	0	0	0	0	0	0
Todd Stottlemyre, p	.000	1	0	0	0	0	0	0	0	1	0	0
Mike Timlin, p	.000	2	0	0	0	0	0	0	0	0	0	0
Duane Ward, p	.000	4	0	0	0	0	0	0	0	0	0	0
Devon White, of	.292	6	24	8	7	3	2	1	7	4	7	1
TOTAL	.311		206	45	64	13	5	6	45	25	30	7

PITCHER	W	L	ERA	G	GS	CG	SV	SHO	IP	H	ER	BB	SO
Tony Castillo	1	0	8.10	2	0	0	0	0	3.1	6	3	3	1
Danny Cox	0	0	8.10	3	0	0	0	0	3.1	6	3	5	6
Mark Eichhorn	0	0	0.00	1	0	0	0	0	0.1	1	0	1	0
Juan Guzman	0	1	3.75	2	2	0	0	0	12.0	10	5	8	12
Pat Hentgen	1	0	1.50	1	1	0	0	0	6.0	5	1	3	6
Al Leiter	1	0	7.71	3	0	0	0	0	7.0	12	6	2	5
Dave Stewart	0	1	6.75	2	2	0	0	0	12.0	10	9	8	8
Todd Stottlemyre	0	0	27.00	1	1	0	0	0	2.0	3	6	4	1
Mike Timlin	0	0	0.00	2	0	0	0	0	2.1	2	0	0	4
Duane Ward	1	0	1.93	4	0	0	2	0	4.2	3	1	0	7
TOTAL	4	2	5.77	21	6	0	2	0	53.0	58	34	34	50

PHI (N)

PLAYER/POS	AVG	G	AB	R	H	2B	3B	HR	RB	BB	SO	SB
PLAYER, POS	AVG	G	AB	R	H	2B	3B	HR	RB	BB	SO	SB
Larry Andersen, p	.000	4	0	0	0	0	0	0	0	0	0	0
Kim Batiste, 3b	.000	3	0	0	0	0	0	0	0	0	0	0
Wes Chamberlain, ph	.000	2	2	0	0	0	0	0	0	0	1	0
Darren Daulton, c	.217	6	23	4	5	2	0	1	4	4	5	0
Mariano Duncan, 2b-5,dh-1	.345	6	29	5	10	0	1	0	2	1	7	3
Lenny Dykstra, of	.348	6	23	9	8	1	0	4	8	7	4	4
Jim Eisenreich, of	.231	6	26	3	6	0	0	1	7	2	4	0
Tommy Greene, p	1.000	1	1	1	1	0	0	0	0	0	0	0
Dave Hollins, 3b	.261	6	23	5	6	1	0	0	2	6	5	0
Pete Incaviglia, of	.125	4	8	0	1	0	0	0	1	0	4	0
Danny Jackson, p	.000	1	1	0	0	0	0	0	0	0	1	0
Ricky Jordan, dh-2	.200	3	10	0	2	0	0	0	0	0	2	0
John Kruk, 1b	.348	6	23	4	8	1	0	0	4	7	7	0
Roger Mason, p	.000	4	1	0	0	0	0	0	0	0	0	0
Mickey Morandini, 2b-1	.200	3	5	1	1	0	0	0	0	1	2	0
Terry Mulholland, p	.000	2	0	0	0	0	0	0	0	0	0	0
Ben Rivera, p	.000	1	0	0	0	0	0	0	0	0	0	0
Curt Schilling, p	.500	2	2	0	1	0	0	0	0	0	1	0
Kevin Stocker, ss	.211	6	19	1	4	1	0	0	1	5	5	0
Bobby Thigpen, p	.000	2	0	0	0	0	0	0	0	0	0	0
Milt Thompson, of	.313	6	16	3	5	1	1	1	6	1	2	0
David West, p	.000	3	0	0	0	0	0	0	0	0	0	0
Mitch Williams, p	.000	3	0	0	0	0	0	0	0	0	0	0
TOTAL	.274		212	36	58	7	2	7	35	34	50	7

PITCHER	W	L	ERA	G	GS	CG	SV	SHO	IP	H	ER	BB	SO
Larry Andersen	0	0	12.27	4	0	0	0	0	3.2	5	5	3	3
Tommy Greene	0	0	27.00	1	1	0	0	0	2.1	7	7	4	1
Danny Jackson	0	1	7.20	1	1	0	0	0	5.0	6	4	1	1
Roger Mason	0	0	1.17	4	0	0	0	0	7.2	4	1	1	7
Terry Mulholland	1	0	6.75	2	2	0	0	0	10.2	14	8	3	5
Ben Rivera	0	0	27.00	1	0	0	0	0	1.1	4	4	2	3
Curt Schilling	1	1	3.52	2	2	1	0	1	15.1	13	6	5	9
Bobby Thigpen	0	0	0.00	2	0	0	0	0	2.2	1	0	1	0
David West	0	0	27.00	3	0	0	0	0	1.0	5	3	1	0
Mitch Williams	0	2	20.25	3	0	0	1	0	2.2	5	6	4	1
TOTAL	2	4	7.57	23	6	1	1	1	52.1	64	44	25	30

GAME 1 AT TOR OCT 16

				R	H	E
PHI	201	010	001	5	11	1
TOR	021	011	30X	8	10	3

Pitchers: SCHILLING, West (7), Andersen (7), Mason (8) vs Guzman, LEITER (6), Ward (8)
Home Runs: White-TOR, Olerud-TOR
Attendance: 52,011

GAME 2 AT TOR OCT 17

				R	H	E
PHI	005	000	100	6	12	0
TOR	000	201	010	4	8	0

Pitchers: MULHOLLAND, Mason (6), Williams (7) vs STEWART, Castillo (7), Eichhorn (8), Timlin (8)
Home Runs: Dykstra-PHI, Eisenreich-PHI, Carter-TOR
Attendance: 52,062

GAME 3 AT PHI OCT 19

				R	H	E
TOR	301	001	302	10	13	1
PHI	000	010	101	3	9	0

Pitchers: HENTGEN, Cox (7), Ward (9) vs JACKSON, Rivera (6), Thigpen (7), Andersen (9)
Home Runs: Molitor-TOR, Thompson-PHI
Attendance: 62,689

GAME 4 AT PHI OCT 20

				R	H	E
TOR	304	002	060	15	18	0
PHI	420	151	100	14	14	0

Pitchers: Stottlemyre, Leiter (3), CASTILLO (5), Timlin (8), Ward (8) vs Greene, Mason (3), West (6), Andersen (7), WILLIAMS (8), Thigpen (9)
Home Runs: Dykstra-PHI (2), Daulton-PHI
Attendance: 62,731

GAME 5 AT PHI OCT 21

				R	H	E
TOR	000	000	000	0	5	1
PHI	110	000	00X	2	5	1

Pitchers: GUZMAN, Cox (8) vs SCHILLING
Attendance: 62,706

GAME 6 AT TOR OCT 23

				R	H	E
PHI	000	100	500	6	7	0
TOR	300	110	003	8	10	2

Pitchers: Mulholland, Mason (6), West (8), Andersen (8), WILLIAMS (9) vs Stewart, Cox (7), Leiter (7), WARD (9)
Home Runs: Molitor-TOR, Dykstra-PHI, Carter-TOR
Attendance: 52,195

Pitching-rich Atlanta's appearance in the division playoffs surprised few, but the hard-hitting expansion Rockies made history by reaching the postseason in just their third year of existence.

Two individuals shared the spotlight in Game 1: Braves rookie third baseman Chipper Jones and Rockies manager Don Baylor, but for wildly different reasons. Jones collected two homers and made a spectacular stop to rob Andres Galarraga of a double. Baylor was less fortunate. He ran out of hitters in the bottom of the ninth—having to use pitcher Lance Painter as his last batter—after Jones homered with two outs in the top of the inning. Atlanta won, 5-4.

Atlanta trailed, 4-3, going into the top of the ninth in Game 2, but they came thundering back with four runs as Mike Mordecai pinch homered, and Rockies second baseman Eric Young botched a routine ground ball. The Braves triumphed, 7-4, taking a 2-0 lead in the series.

In Game 3 Atlanta came through in the ninth once more on pinch-hitter Luis Polonia's two-strike run-scoring single, and the game went into extra innings. But Colorado bounced back to score twice in the 10th on Dante Bichette's double down the left field line and run-scoring singles by Andres Galarraga and Vinny Castilla (who had homered in the sixth).

Cy Young Award winners battled in Game 4 as Greg Maddux and Bret Saberhagen started, but Saberhagen was ineffective and Atlanta eliminated the Rockies with a 10-4 win. Maddux struck out seven and walked none before leaving for a pinch hitter in the seventh inning. Not helping Saberhagen was a controversial "safe" call on a play in which he attempted to cover first. Fred McGriff followed with the first of his two homers in the contest.

Atlanta Braves (E), 3; Colorado Rockies (WC), 1

ATL (E)

PLAYER/POS	AVG	G	AB	R	H	2B	3B	HR	RB	BB	SO	SB
Steve Avery, p	.000	1	0	0	0	0	0	0	0	0	0	0
Rafael Belliard, ss	.000	4	5	1	0	0	0	0	0	0	1	0
Jeff Blauser, ss	.000	3	6	0	0	0	0	0	0	1	3	0
Pedro Borbon, p	.000	1	0	0	0	0	0	0	0	0	0	0
Brad Clontz, p	.000	1	0	0	0	0	0	0	0	0	0	0
Mike Devereaux, of-3	.200	4	5	1	1	0	0	0	0	0	0	0
Tom Glavine, p	.333	1	3	0	1	0	0	0	0	0	1	0
Marquis Grissom, of	.524	4	21	5	11	2	0	3	4	0	3	2
Chipper Jones, 3b	.389	4	18	4	7	2	0	2	4	2	2	0
David Justice, of	.231	4	13	2	3	0	0	0	0	5	2	0
Ryan Klesko, of	.467	4	15	5	7	1	0	0	1	0	3	0
Mark Lemke, 2b	.211	4	19	3	4	1	0	0	1	1	3	0
Javy Lopez, c	.444	3	9	0	4	0	0	0	3	0	3	0
Greg Maddux, p	.167	2	6	1	1	0	0	0	0	0	1	0
Fred McGriff, 1b	.333	4	18	4	6	0	0	2	6	2	3	0
Greg McMichael, p	.000	2	0	0	0	0	0	0	0	0	0	0
Kent Mercker, p	.000	1	0	0	0	0	0	0	0	0	0	0
Mike Mordecai, ss-1	.667	2	3	1	2	1	0	0	2	0	0	0
Charlie O'Brien, c	.200	2	5	0	1	0	0	0	0	1	1	0
Alejandro Pena, p	.000	3	0	0	0	0	0	0	0	0	0	0
Luis Polonia, ph	.333	3	3	0	1	0	0	0	2	0	1	1
Dwight Smith, ph	.667	4	3	0	2	1	0	0	1	0	0	0
John Smoltz, p	.000	1	2	0	0	0	0	0	0	0	0	0
Mark Wohlers, p	.000	3	0	0	0	0	0	0	0	0	0	0
TOTAL	.331		154	27	51	8	0	7	24	12	27	3

PITCHER	W	L	ERA	G	GS	CG	SV	SHO	IP	H	ER	BB	SO
Steve Avery	0	0	13.50	1	0	0	0	0	0.2	1	1	0	1
Pedro Borbon	0	0	0.00	1	0	0	0	0	1.0	1	0	0	3
Brad Clontz	0	0	0.00	1	0	0	0	0	1.1	0	0	0	2
Tom Glavine	0	0	2.57	1	1	0	0	0	7.0	5	2	1	3
Greg Maddux	1	0	4.50	2	2	0	0	0	14.0	19	7	2	7
Greg McMichael	0	0	6.75	2	0	0	0	0	1.1	1	1	2	1
Kent Mercker	0	0	0.00	1	0	0	0	0	0.1	0	0	0	0
Alejandro Pena	2	0	0.00	3	0	0	0	0	3.0	3	0	1	2
John Smoltz	0	0	7.94	1	1	0	0	0	5.2	5	5	1	6
Mark Wohlers	0	1	6.75	3	0	0	2	0	2.2	6	2	2	4
TOTAL	3	1	4.38	16	4	0	2	0	37.0	41	18	9	29

COL (W)

PLAYER/POS	AVG	G	AB	R	H	2B	3B	HR	RB	BB	SO	SB
Jason Bates, 2b-1,3b-1	.250	4	4	0	1	0	0	0	0	0	0	0
Dante Bichette, of	.588	4	17	6	10	3	0	1	3	1	3	0
Ellis Burks, of	.333	2	6	1	2	1	0	0	2	0	1	0
Vinny Castilla, 3b	.467	4	15	3	7	1	0	3	6	0	1	0
Andres Galarraga, 1b	.278	4	18	1	5	1	0	0	2	0	6	0
Joe Girardi, c	.125	4	16	0	2	0	0	0	0	0	2	0
Darren Holmes, p	.000	3	0	0	0	0	0	0	0	0	0	0
Trenidad Hubbard, ph	.000	3	2	0	0	0	0	0	0	0	0	0
Mike Kingery, of	.200	4	10	1	2	0	0	0	0	0	1	0
Curt Leskanic, p	.000	3	0	0	0	0	0	0	0	0	0	0
Mike Munoz, p	.000	4	0	0	0	0	0	0	0	0	0	0
J Owens, c	.000	1	1	0	0	0	0	0	0	0	1	0
Lance Painter, p-1	.000	2	2	0	0	0	0	0	0	0	1	0
Steve Reed, p	.000	3	0	0	0	0	0	0	0	0	0	0
Armando Reynoso, p	.000	1	0	0	0	0	0	0	0	0	0	0
Kevin Ritz, p	.000	2	2	0	0	0	0	0	0	0	0	0
Bruce Ruffin, p	.000	4	0	0	0	0	0	0	0	0	0	0
Bret Saberhagen, p	.000	1	1	0	0	0	0	0	0	0	0	0
Bill Swift, p	.000	1	3	0	0	0	0	0	0	0	2	0
Mark Thompson, p	.000	1	0	0	0	0	0	0	0	0	0	0
John Vander Wal, ph	.000	4	4	0	0	0	0	0	0	0	2	0
Larry Walker, of	.214	4	14	3	3	0	0	1	3	3	4	1
Walt Weiss, ss	.167	4	12	1	2	0	0	0	0	3	3	1
Eric Young, 2b	.438	4	16	3	7	1	0	1	2	2	2	1
TOTAL	.287		143	19	41	7	0	6	18	9	29	3

PITCHER	W	L	ERA	G	GS	CG	SV	SHO	IP	H	ER	BB	SO
Darren Holmes	1	0	0.00	3	0	0	0	0	1.2	6	0	0	2
Curt Leskanic	0	1	6.00	3	0	0	0	0	3.0	3	2	0	4
Mike Munoz	0	1	13.50	4	0	0	0	0	1.1	4	2	1	1
Lance Painter	0	0	5.40	1	1	0	0	0	5.0	5	3	2	4
Steve Reed	0	0	0.00	3	0	0	0	0	2.2	2	0	1	3
Armando Reynoso	0	0	0.00	1	0	0	0	0	1.0	2	0	0	0
Kevin Ritz	0	0	7.71	2	1	0	0	0	7.0	12	6	3	5
Bruce Ruffin	0	0	2.70	4	0	0	0	0	3.1	3	1	2	2
Bret Saberhagen	0	1	11.25	1	1	0	0	0	4.0	7	5	1	3
Bill Swift	0	0	6.00	1	1	0	0	0	6.0	7	4	2	3
Mark Thompson	0	0	0.00	1	0	0	1	0	1.0	0	0	0	0
TOTAL	1	3	5.75	24	4	0	1	0	36.0	51	23	12	27

GAME 1 AT COL OCT 3

				R	H	E
ATL	001	002	011	5	12	1
COL	000	300	010	4	13	4

Pitchers: Maddux, McMichael (8), PENA (8), Wohlers (9) vs Ritz, Reed (6), Ruffin (7), Munoz (8), Holmes (8), LESKANIC (9)
Home Runs: Grissom-ATL, Jones-ATL (2), Castilla-COL
Attendance: 50,040

GAME 2 AT COL OCT 4

				R	H	E
ATL	101	100	004	7	13	1
COL	000	003	010	4	8	2

Pitchers: Glavine, Avery (8), PENA (8), Wohlers (9) vs Painter, Reed (6), Ruffin (7), Leskanic (8), MUNOZ (9), Holmes (9)
Home Runs: Grissom-ATL (2), Walker-COL
Attendance: 50,040

GAME 3 AT ATL OCT 6

					R	H	E
COL	102	002	000	2	7	9	0
ATL	000	300	101	0	5	11	0

Pitchers: Swift, Reed] (7), Munoz (7), Leskanic (7), Ruffin (8), HOLMES (9), Thompson (10) vs Smoltz, Clontz (6), Borbon (8), McMichael (9), WOHLERS (10), Mercker (10)
Home Runs: Young-COL, Castilla-COL
Attendance: 51,300

GAME 4 AT ATL OCT 7

				R	H	E
COL	003	001	000	4	11	1
ATL	004	213	00X	10	15	0

Pitchers: SABERHAGEN, Ritz (5), Munoz (6), Reynoso (7), Ruffin (8) vs MADDUX, Pena (8)
Home Runs: Bichette-COL, Castilla-COL, McGriff-ATL (2)
Attendance: 50,027

Davey Johnson's Cincinnati Reds made short work of Tommy Lasorda's Los Angeles Dodgers in the 1995 NL division series, sweeping them, 3-0, and outscoring them, 22-7.

Game 1 saw the Reds score four times in the first inning as they walloped the Dodgers, 7-2. Los Angeles starter Ramon Martinez was ineffective, being cuffed for 10 hits and two walks in just four and a third innings.

Game 2 was a more even affair until the Los Angeles bullpen went to work. Barry Larkin's eighth-inning single to right broke open a 2-2 tie, and in the top of the ninth the Reds added two insurance runs.

The Reds wrapped up the series by humiliating the Dodgers 10-1 in Game 3. The Dodgers had their chances in the contest, but squandered their opportunities, leaving 11 runners on base. The Reds broke the game open in the sixth as pinch hitter Mark Lewis delivered a grand slam to left-center off Mark Guthrie.

Cincinnati Reds (C), 3; Los Angeles (W), 0

CIN (C)

PLAYER/POS	AVG	G	AB	R	H	2B	3B	HR	RB	BB	SO	SB
Bret Boone, 2b	.300	3	10	4	3	1	0	1	1	1	3	1
Jeff Branson, 3b	.286	3	7	0	2	1	0	0	2	2	0	0
Jeff Brantley, p	.000	3	0	0	0	0	0	0	0	0	0	0
Dave Burba, p	.000	1	0	0	0	0	0	0	0	0	0	0
Mariano Duncan, 2b-1	.667	2	3	1	2	0	0	0	1	0	0	1
Ron Gant, of	.231	3	13	3	3	0	0	1	2	0	3	0
Thomas Howard, of	.100	3	10	0	1	1	0	0	0	0	2	0
Mike Jackson, p	1.000	3	1	0	1	1	0	0	3	0	0	0
Barry Larkin, ss	.385	3	13	2	5	0	0	0	1	1	2	4
Darren Lewis, of	.000	3	3	0	0	0	0	0	0	0	1	0
Mark Lewis, 3b	.500	2	2	2	1	0	0	1	5	1	0	0
Hal Morris, 1b	.500	3	10	5	5	1	0	0	2	3	1	1
Reggie Sanders, of	.154	3	13	3	2	1	0	1	2	1	9	2
Benito Santiago, c	.333	3	9	2	3	0	0	1	3	3	3	0
Pete Schourek, p	.000	1	2	0	0	0	0	0	0	0	1	0
John Smiley, p	.000	1	2	0	0	0	0	0	0	0	1	0
Jerome Walton, of	.000	3	3	0	0	0	0	0	0	1	1	0
David Wells, p	.333	1	3	0	1	0	0	0	0	0	1	0
TOTAL	.279		104	22	29	6	0	5	22	13	28	9

PITCHER	W	L	ERA	G	GS	CG	SV	SHO	IP	H	ER	BB	SO
Jeff Brantley	0	0	6.00	3	0	0	1	0	3.0	5	2	0	2
Dave Burba	1	0	0.00	1	0	0	0	0	1.0	2	0	1	0
Mike Jackson	0	0	0.00	3	0	0	0	0	3.2	4	0	0	1
Pete Schourek	1	0	2.57	1	1	0	0	0	7.0	5	2	3	5
John Smiley	0	0	3.00	1	1	0	0	0	6.0	9	2	0	1
David Wells	1	0	0.00	1	1	0	0	0	6.1	6	0	1	8
TOTAL	3	0	2.00	10	3	0	1	0	27.0	31	6	5	17

LA (W)

PLAYER/POS	AVG	G	AB	R	H	2B	3B	HR	RB	BB	SO	SB
Billy Ashley, ph	.000	1	0	0	0	0	0	0	0	1	0	0
Pedro Astacio, p	.000	3	0	0	0	0	0	0	0	0	0	0
Brett Butler, of	.267	3	15	1	4	0	0	0	1	0	3	0
John Cummings, p	.000	2	0	0	0	0	0	0	0	0	0	0
Delino DeShields, 2b	.250	3	12	1	3	0	0	0	0	1	3	0
Chad Fonville, ss	.500	3	12	1	6	0	0	0	0	0	1	0
Mark Guthrie, p	.000	3	0	0	0	0	0	0	0	0	0	0
Chris Gwynn, ph	.000	1	1	0	0	0	0	0	0	0	1	0
Dave Hansen, ph	.667	3	3	0	2	0	0	0	0	0	0	0
Todd Hollandsworth, of	.000	2	2	0	0	0	0	0	0	0	0	0
Eric Karros, 1b	.500	3	12	3	6	1	0	2	4	1	0	0
Roberto Kelly, of	.364	3	11	0	4	0	0	0	0	1	0	0
Ramon Martinez, p	.000	1	1	0	0	0	0	0	0	0	0	0
Raul Mondesi, of	.222	3	9	0	2	0	0	0	1	0	2	0
Hideo Nomo, p	.000	1	2	0	0	0	0	0	0	0	2	0
Jose Offerman, pr	.000	1	0	0	0	0	0	0	0	0	0	0
Antonio Osuna, p	.000	3	0	0	0	0	0	0	0	0	0	0
Mike Piazza, c	.214	3	14	1	3	1	0	1	1	0	2	0
Kevin Tapani, p	.000	2	0	0	0	0	0	0	0	0	0	0
Ismael Valdes, p	.000	1	3	0	0	0	0	0	0	0	0	0
Tim Wallach, 3b	.083	3	12	0	1	0	0	0	0	1	3	0
Mitch Webster, ph	.000	2	2	0	0	0	0	0	0	0	0	0
TOTAL	.279		111	7	31	2	0	3	7	5	17	0

PITCHER	W	L	ERA	G	GS	CG	SV	SHO	IP	H	ER	BB	SO
Pedro Astacio	0	0	0.00	3	0	0	0	0	3.1	1	0	0	5
John Cummings	0	0	20.25	2	0	0	0	0	1.1	3	3	2	3
Mark Guthrie	0	0	6.75	3	0	0	0	0	1.1	2	1	1	1
Ramon Martinez	0	1	14.54	1	1	0	0	0	4.1	10	7	2	3
Hideo Nomo	0	1	9.00	1	1	0	0	0	5.0	7	5	2	6
Antonio Osuna	0	1	2.70	3	0	0	0	0	3.1	3	1	1	3
Kevin Tapani	0	0	81.00	2	0	0	0	0	0.1	0	3	4	1
Ismael Valdes	0	0	0.00	1	1	0	0	0	7.0	3	0	1	6
TOTAL	0	3	6.92	16	3	0	0	0	26.0	29	20	13	28

GAME 1 AT LA OCT 3

		R	H	E
CIN	400 030 000	7	12	0
LA	000 011 000	2	8	0

Pitchers: SCHOUREK, Jackson (8), Brantley (9) vs MARTINEZ, Cummings (5), Astacio (6), Guthrie (8), Osuna (9)
Home Runs: Santiago-CIN, Piazza-LA
Attendance: 44,199

GAME 2 AT LA OCT 4

		R	H	E
CIN	000 200 012	5	6	0
LA	100 100 002	4	14	2

Pitchers: Smiley, BURBA (7), Jackson (8), Brantley (9) vs Valdes, OSUNA (8), Tapani (9), Guthrie (9), Astacio (9)
Home Runs: Sanders-CIN, Karros-LA (2)
Attendance: 46,051

GAME 3 AT CIN OCT 6

		R	H	E
LA	000 100 000	1	9	1
CIN	002 104 30X	10	11	2

Pitchers: NOMO, Tapani (6), Guthrie (6), Astacio (6), Cummings (7), Osuna (7) vs WELLS, Jackson (7), Brantley (9)
Home Runs: Gant-CIN, Boone-CIN, M.Lewis-CIN
Attendance: 53,276

The Cleveland Indians had enjoyed a 100-44 record in the strike-shortened 1995 season and captured the AL's new Central Division by a record 30 games. Not surprisingly, they were heavily favored against the AL East champion Red Sox. And not surprisingly, the Curse of Rocky Colavito fell in three straight to the Curse of the Bambino—in other words, the Tribe won.

Yet there were moments of high drama in the series. Game 1 was a titanic struggle that had nearly everything: two rain delays (39 minutes at the start and 23 minutes in the eighth), three extra inning homers, and a controversial piece of lumber. The five-hour and one-minute game ended at 2:08 a.m. the next day. But no one in Cleveland was complaining.

Boston jumped off to a 2-0 lead on John Valentin's two-run homer, but Red Sox starter Roger Clemens surrendered three runs in the sixth. Boston's Luis Alicea evened the score up with a leadoff homer in the eighth. In the top of the 11th, Tim Naehring homered to give the Sox the lead, but Albert Belle retaliated in the bottom of the frame with a homer of his own. The next move was Boston's, which contended Belle's bat was corked. AL authorities confiscated it and sawed it in half but found no cork. In the 12th the Indians loaded the bases with one out but did not score. In the 13th former Red Sox catcher Tony Pena ended it all with an improbable homer off a 3-0 pitch from Zane Smith.

Game 2 was a much easier win as veteran Orel Hershiser faced Boston's Erik Hanson. Omar Vizquel doubled in two runs in the fifth. Eddie Murray added a two-run homer off Hanson in the eighth. That was more than Hershiser needed as he struck out seven in seven and a third innings while walking just two and allowing three hits.

Game 3 moved from Jacobs Field to Fenway Park, but the home field proved to be no advantage. Red Sox knuckleballer Tim Wakefield surrendered seven runs in five and a third innings as the Indians, behind Charles Nagy, eliminated Boston with an 8-2 win. Mo Vaughn and Jose Canseco went hitless, running their record to 0-for-27, with nine strikeouts in the series. But Boston's defeat was not the duo's fault entirely. Overall, Sox batters were 2-for-28 with runners in scoring position.

Cleveland Indians (C), 3; Boston Red Sox (E), 0

CLE (C)

PLAYER/POS	AVG	G	AB	R	H	2B	3B	HR	RB	BB	SO	SB
Sandy Alomar, c	.182	3	11	1	2	1	0	0	1	0	1	0
Paul Assenmacher, p	.000	3	0	0	0	0	0	0	0	0	0	0
Carlos Baerga, 2b	.286	3	14	2	4	1	0	0	1	0	1	0
Albert Belle, of	.273	3	11	3	3	1	0	1	3	4	3	0
Alvaro Espinoza, 3b	.000	1	1	0	0	0	0	0	0	0	0	0
Orel Hershiser, p	.000	1	0	0	0	0	0	0	0	0	0	0
Ken Hill, p	.000	1	0	0	0	0	0	0	0	0	0	0
Wayne Kirby, of-2	1.000	3	1	0	1	0	0	0	0	0	0	0
Kenny Lofton, of	.154	3	13	1	2	0	0	0	0	1	3	0
Dennis Martinez, p	.000	1	0	0	0	0	0	0	0	0	0	0
Jose Mesa, p	.000	2	0	0	0	0	0	0	0	0	0	0
Eddie Murray, dh	.385	3	13	3	5	0	1	1	3	2	1	0
Charles Nagy, p	.000	1	0	0	0	0	0	0	0	0	0	0
Tony Pena, c	.500	2	2	1	1	0	0	1	1	0	0	0
Herb Perry, ph	.000	1	1	0	0	0	0	0	0	0	0	0
Eric Plunk, p	.000	1	0	0	0	0	0	0	0	0	0	0
Jim Poole, p	.000	1	0	0	0	0	0	0	0	0	0	0
Manny Ramirez, of	.000	3	12	1	0	0	0	0	0	1	2	0
Paul Sorrento, 1b	.300	3	10	2	3	0	0	0	1	2	3	0
Julian Tavarez, p	.000	3	0	0	0	0	0	0	0	0	0	0
Jim Thome, 3b	.154	3	13	1	2	0	0	1	3	1	6	0
Omar Vizquel, ss	.167	3	12	2	2	1	0	0	4	2	2	1
TOTAL	.219		114	17	25	4	1	4	17	13	22	1

PITCHER	W	L	ERA	G	GS	CG	SV	SHO	IP	H	ER	BB	SO
Paul Assenmacher	0	0	0.00	3	0	0	0	0	1.2	0	0	0	3
Orel Hershiser	1	0	0.00	1	1	0	0	0	7.1	3	0	2	7
Ken Hill	1	0	0.00	1	0	0	0	0	1.1	1	0	0	2
Dennis Martinez	0	0	3.00	1	1	0	0	0	6.0	5	2	0	2
Jose Mesa	0	0	0.00	2	0	0	0	0	2.0	0	0	2	0
Charles Nagy	1	0	1.29	1	1	0	0	0	7.0	4	1	5	6
Eric Plunk	0	0	0.00	1	0	0	0	0	1.1	1	0	1	1
Jim Poole	0	0	5.40	1	0	0	0	0	1.2	2	1	1	2
Julian Tavarez	0	0	6.75	3	0	0	0	0	2.2	5	2	0	3
TOTAL	3	0	1.74	14	3	0	0	0	31.0	21	6	11	26

BOS (E)

PLAYER/POS	AVG	G	AB	R	H	2B	3B	HR	RB	BB	SO	SB
Rick Aguilera, p	.000	1	0	0	0	0	0	0	0	0	0	0
Luis Alicea, 2b	.600	3	10	1	6	1	0	1	1	2	2	1
Stan Belinda, p	.000	1	0	0	0	0	0	0	0	0	0	0
Jose Canseco, dh-2,of-1	.000	3	13	0	0	0	0	0	0	2	2	0
Roger Clemens, p	.000	1	0	0	0	0	0	0	0	0	0	0
Rheal Cormier, p	.000	2	0	0	0	0	0	0	0	0	0	0
Mike Greenwell, of	.200	3	15	0	3	0	0	0	0	0	1	0
Erik Hanson, p	.000	1	0	0	0	0	0	0	0	0	0	0
Bill Haselman, c	.000	1	2	0	0	0	0	0	0	0	0	0
Dwayne Hosey, of	.000	3	12	1	0	0	0	0	0	2	3	1
Joe Hudson, p	.000	1	0	0	0	0	0	0	0	0	0	0
Reggie Jefferson, dh	.250	1	4	1	1	0	0	0	0	0	1	0
Mike Macfarlane, c	.333	3	9	0	3	0	0	0	1	0	3	0
Mike Maddux, p	.000	2	0	0	0	0	0	0	0	0	0	0
Willie McGee, of	.250	2	4	0	1	0	0	0	1	0	2	0
Tim Naehring, 3b	.308	3	13	2	4	0	0	1	1	0	1	0
Zane Smith, p	.000	1	0	0	0	0	0	0	0	0	0	0
Matt Stairs, ph	.000	1	1	0	0	0	0	0	0	0	1	0
Mike Stanton, p	.000	1	0	0	0	0	0	0	0	0	0	0
Lee Tinsley, of	.000	1	5	0	0	0	0	0	0	1	2	0
John Valentin, ss	.250	3	12	1	3	1	0	1	2	3	1	0
Mo Vaughn, 1b	.000	3	14	0	0	0	0	0	0	1	7	0
Tim Wakefield, p	.000	1	0	0	0	0	0	0	0	0	0	0
TOTAL	.184		114	6	21	2	0	3	6	11	26	2

PITCHER	W	L	ERA	G	GS	CG	SV	SHO	IP	H	ER	BB	SO
Rick Aguilera	0	0	13.50	1	0	0	0	0	0.2	3	1	0	1
Stan Belinda	0	0	0.00	1	0	0	0	0	0.1	0	0	0	0
Roger Clemens	0	0	3.86	1	1	0	0	0	7.0	5	3	1	5
Rheal Cormier	0	0	13.50	2	0	0	0	0	0.2	2	1	1	2
Erik Hanson	0	1	4.50	1	1	1	0	0	8.0	4	4	4	5
Joe Hudson	0	0	0.00	1	0	0	0	0	1.0	2	0	1	0
Mike Maddux	0	0	0.00	2	0	0	0	0	3.0	2	0	1	1
Zane Smith	0	1	6.75	1	0	0	0	0	1.1	1	1	0	0
Mike Stanton	0	0	0.00	1	0	0	0	0	2.1	1	0	0	4
Tim Wakefield	0	1	11.81	1	1	0	0	0	5.1	5	7	5	4
TOTAL	0	3	5.16	12	3	1	0	0	29.2	25	17	13	22

GAME 1 AT CLE OCT 3

						R	H	E
BOS	002	000	010	010	0	4	11	2
CLE	000	003	000	010	1	5	10	2

Pitchers: Clemens, Cormier (8), Belinda (8), Stanton (8), Aguilera (11), Maddux (11), SMITH (12) vs Martinez, Tavarez (7), Assenmacher (8), Plunk (8), Mesa (10), Poole (11), HILL (12)
Home Runs: Valentin-BOS, Alicea-BOS, Naehring-BOS, Belle-CLE, Pena-CLE
Attendance: 44,218

GAME 2 AT CLE OCT 4

				R	H	E
BOS	000	000	000	0	3	1
CLE	000	020	02X	4	4	2

Pitchers: HANSON vs HERSHISER, Tavarez (8), Assenmacher (8), Mesa (9)
Home Runs: Murray-CLE
Attendance: 44,264

GAME 3 AT BOS OCT 6

				R	H	E
BOS	000	100	010	2	7	1
CLE	021	005	000	8	11	2

Pitchers: NAGY, Tavarez (8), Assenmacher (9) vs WAKEFIELD, Cormier (6), Maddux (6), Hudson (9)
Home Runs: Thome-CLE
Attendance: 34,211

The hitherto laughable Seattle Mariners shocked the New York Yankees in a gritty, exciting five-game division series that could only be likened to two prize fighters standing toe-to-toe and slugging it out.

Seattle found its rotation askew after being forced into a one-game playoff against California to determine the AL West championship. In Game 1 the Yankees' David Cone started against Seattle's Chris Bosio and triumphed 9-6 despite Ken Griffey, Jr.'s two homers. Ultimately, Griffey would hit five in the series.

The Yankees won Game 2 by breaking up a 5-5 marathon on a two-run Jim Leyritz homer in the bottom of the 15th. In the 12th Griffey had homered to right-center on a 3-1 pitch to give Seattle the lead, but New York evened it in the bottom of the inning on Ruben Sierra's run-scoring double to left.

Seattle's ace, Cy Young Award winner Randy Johnson, finally appeared in Game 3, striking out 10 as Seattle won, 7-6, before a delirious Kingdome crowd. New York jumped off to a 5-0 lead in Game 4, but Seattle battled back to even the series at 2-2. The big blow was Edgar Martinez's grand-slam to center in the Mariners' five-run eighth inning. The game went down to the last out as New York left runners on second and third in the ninth.

After Seattle scored twice in the eighth to deadlock deciding Game 5 at 4-4, Mariners manager Lou Piniella brought in Randy Johnson (who had pitched seven innings just two days before) to shut the door on New York. Not to be outdone, Yankees manager Buck Showalter countered with starter Jack McDowell. Once again, Edgar Martinez (series average of .571) came through in the clutch. hitting a two-run double down the left field line to end the game—and the series.

Seattle Mariners (W), 3; New York Yankees (WC), 2

SEA (W)

PLAYER/POS	AVG	G	AB	R	H	2B	3B	HR	RB	BB	SO	SB
Bobby Ayala, p	.000	2	0	0	0	0	0	0	0	0	0	0
Tim Belcher, p	.000	2	0	0	0	0	0	0	0	0	0	0
Andy Benes, p	.000	2	0	0	0	0	0	0	0	0	0	0
Mike Blowers, 3b-5,1b-1	.167	5	18	0	3	0	0	0	1	3	7	0
Chris Bosio, p	.000	2	0	0	0	0	0	0	0	0	0	0
Jay Buhner, of	.458	5	24	2	11	1	0	1	3	2	4	0
Norm Charlton, p	.000	4	0	0	0	0	0	0	0	0	0	0
Vince Coleman, of	.217	5	23	6	5	0	1	1	1	2	4	1
Joey Cora, 2b	.316	5	19	7	6	1	0	1	1	3	0	1
Alex Diaz, of-1	.333	2	3	0	1	0	0	0	0	1	1	0
Felix Fermin, ss-2,2b-1	.000	3	1	0	0	0	0	0	0	0	1	0
Ken Griffey, of	.391	5	23	9	9	0	0	5	7	2	4	1
Randy Johnson, p	.000	2	0	0	0	0	0	0	0	0	0	0
Tino Martinez, 1b	.409	5	22	4	9	1	0	1	5	3	4	0
Edgar Martinez, dh	.571	5	21	6	12	3	0	2	10	6	2	0
Jeff Nelson, p	.000	3	0	0	0	0	0	0	0	0	0	0
Warren Newson, ph	.000	1	1	0	0	0	0	0	0	0	1	0
Bill Risley, p	.000	4	0	0	0	0	0	0	0	0	0	0
Alex Rodriguez, ss	.000	1	1	1	0	0	0	0	0	0	0	0
Luis Sojo, ss	.250	5	20	0	5	0	0	0	3	0	3	0
Doug Strange, 3b	.000	2	4	0	0	0	0	0	1	1	1	0
Bob Wells, p	.000	1	0	0	0	0	0	0	0	0	0	0
Chris Widger, c	.000	2	3	0	0	0	0	0	0	0	3	0
Dan Wilson, c	.118	5	17	0	2	0	0	0	1	2	6	0
TOTAL	.315		200	35	63	6	1	11	33	25	41	3

PITCHER	W	L	ERA	G	GS	CG	SV	SHO	IP	H	ER	BB	SO
Bobby Ayala	0	0	54.00	2	0	0	0	0	0.2	6	4	1	0
Tim Belcher	0	1	6.23	2	0	0	0	0	4.1	4	3	5	0
Andy Benes	0	0	5.40	2	2	0	0	0	11.2	10	7	9	8
Chris Bosio	0	0	10.57	2	2	0	0	0	7.2	10	9	4	2
Norm Charlton	1	0	2.45	4	0	0	1	0	7.1	4	2	3	9
Randy Johnson	2	0	2.70	2	1	0	0	0	10.0	5	3	6	16
Jeff Nelson	0	1	3.18	3	0	0	0	0	5.2	7	2	3	7
Bill Risley	0	0	6.00	4	0	0	1	0	3.0	2	2	0	1
Bob Wells	0	0	9.00	1	0	0	0	0	1.0	2	1	1	0
TOTAL	3	2	5.79	22	5	0	2	0	51.1	50	33	32	43

NY (E)

PLAYER/POS	AVG	G	AB	R	H	2B	3B	HR	RB	BB	SO	SB
Wade Boggs, 3b	.263	4	19	4	5	2	0	1	3	3	5	0
David Cone, p	.000	2	0	0	0	0	0	0	0	0	0	0
Russ Davis, 3b	.200	2	5	0	1	0	0	0	0	0	2	0
Tony Fernandez, ss	.238	5	21	0	5	2	0	0	0	2	2	0
Sterling Hitchcock, p	.000	2	0	0	0	0	0	0	0	0	0	0
Steve Howe, p	.000	2	0	0	0	0	0	0	0	0	0	0
Dion James, of	.083	4	12	0	1	0	0	0	0	1	1	0
Scott Kamieniecki, p	.000	1	0	0	0	0	0	0	0	0	0	0
Pat Kelly, 2b-4	.000	5	3	3	0	0	0	0	1	1	3	0
Jim Leyritz, c	.143	2	7	1	1	0	0	1	2	0	1	0
Don Mattingly, 1b	.417	5	24	3	10	4	0	1	6	1	5	0
Jack McDowell, p	.000	2	0	0	0	0	0	0	0	0	0	0
Paul O'Neill, of	.333	5	18	5	6	0	0	3	6	5	5	0
Andy Pettitte, p	.000	1	0	0	0	0	0	0	0	0	0	0
Jorge Posada, pr	.000	1	0	1	0	0	0	0	0	0	0	0
Mariano Rivera, p	.000	3	0	0	0	0	0	0	0	0	0	0
Ruben Sierra, dh	.174	5	23	2	4	2	0	2	5	2	7	0
Mike Stanley, c	.313	5	16	2	5	0	0	1	3	2	1	0
Darryl Strawberry, ph	.000	2	2	0	0	0	0	0	0	0	1	0
Randy Velarde, 2b-4, 3b-2,of-2	.176	5	17	3	3	0	0	0	1	6	4	0
John Wetteland, p	.000	3	0	0	0	0	0	0	0	0	0	0
Bob Wickman, p	.000	3	0	0	0	0	0	0	0	0	0	0
Bernie Williams, of	.429	5	21	8	9	2	0	2	5	7	3	1
Gerald Williams, of	.000	5	5	1	0	0	0	0	0	2	3	0
TOTAL	.259		193	33	50	12	0	11	32	32	43	1

PITCHER	W	L	ERA	G	GS	CG	SV	SHO	IP	H	ER	BB	SO
David Cone	1	0	4.60	2	2	0	0	0	15.2	15	8	9	14
Sterling Hitchcock	0	0	5.40	2	0	0	0	0	1.2	2	1	2	1
Steve Howe	0	0	18.00	2	0	0	0	0	1.0	4	2	0	0
Scott Kamieniecki	0	0	7.20	1	1	0	0	0	5.0	9	4	4	4
Jack McDowell	0	2	9.00	2	1	0	0	0	7.0	8	7	4	6
Andy Pettitte	0	0	5.14	1	1	0	0	0	7.0	9	4	3	0
Mariano Rivera	1	0	0.00	3	0	0	0	0	5.1	3	0	1	8
John Wetteland	0	1	14.54	3	0	0	0	0	4.1	8	7	2	5
Bob Wickman	0	0	0.00	3	0	0	0	0	3.0	5	0	0	3
TOTAL	2	3	5.94	19	5	0	0	0	50.0	63	33	25	41

GAME 1 AT NY OCT 3

				R	H	E
SEA	000	101	202	6	9	0
NY	002	002	41X	9	13	0

Pitchers: Bosio, NELSON (6), Ayala (7), Risley (7), Wells (8) vs CONE, Wetteland (9)
Home Runs: Griffey-SEA (2), Boggs-NY, Sierra-NY
Attendance: 57,178

GAME 2 AT NY OCT 4

						R	H	E
SEA	001	001	200	001	000	5	16	2
NY	000	012	100	001	002	7	11	0

Pitchers: Benes, Risley (6), Charlton (7), Nelson (11), BELCHER (12) vs Pettitte, Wickman (8), Wetteland (9), RIVERA (12)
Home Runs: Coleman-SEA, Griffey-SEA, Sierra-NY, Mattingly-NY, O'Neill-NY, Leyritz-NY
Attendance: 57,126

GAME 3 AT SEA OCT 6

				R	H	E
NY	000	100	120	4	6	2
SEA	000	024	10X	7	7	0

Pitchers: McDOWELL, Howe (6), Wickman (6), Hitchcock (7), Rivera (7) vs JOHNSON, Risley (8), Charlton (8)
Home Runs: B.Williams-NY (2), Stanley-NY, T.Martinez-SEA
Attendance: 57,944

GAME 4 AT SEA OCT 7

				R	H	E
NY	302	000	012	8	14	1
SEA	004	011	05X	11	16	0

Pitchers: Kamieniecki, Hitchcock (6), Wickman (7), WETTELAND (8), Howe (8) vs Bosio, Nelson (3), Belcher (7), CHARLTON (8), Ayala (9), Risley (9)
Home Runs: O'Neill-NY, E.Martinez-SEA (2), Griffey-SEA, Buhner-SEA
Attendance: 57,180

GAME 5 AT SEA OCT 8

					R	H	E
NY	000	202	000	01	5	6	0
SEA	001	100	020	02	6	15	0

Pitchers: Cone, Rivera (8), McDOWELL (9) vs Benes, Charlton (7), JOHNSON (9)
Home Runs: O'Neill-NY, Cora-SEA, Griffey-SEA
Attendance: 57,411

Both the Braves and the Reds had moved through the National League's first-ever division series with ease, with Atlanta knocking off Colorado, 3-1, and Cincinnati sweeping the Dodgers in three games as the Reds made their first postseason appearance since 1990. The Braves, meanwhile, became the first team to play in the NLCS four straight times.

In Game 1 of the NLCS, a scant crowd of only 40,382 Riverfront Stadium patrons saw the Braves edge the Reds, 2-1. Atlanta prevailed despite failing to move a runner past second base until the ninth inning, as the Reds' Pete Schourek held the Braves to four singles through eight. Atlanta broke through in the 11th on Mike Devereaux's pinch-hit single, a feat which helped earn him NLCS MVP honors.

Game 2 was another extra inning affair as Atlanta cracked the game open with four in the 10th to triumph, 6-2. In that inning the Braves loaded the bases, scoring their first run on Mark Portugal's wild pitch. Javier Lopez followed with a three-run homer off the left-field foul screen. Game 3 remained scoreless until the sixth, when catcher Charlie O'Brien homered to left off David Wells, scoring Fred McGriff and Mike Devereaux. Chipper Jones followed with a two-run homer to complete the Braves' scoring.

Game 4 saw a 6-0 Atlanta win, completing the first sweep since 1982. Steve Avery allowed just three singles, two of which failed to make it out of the infield. Mike Devereaux delivered the key blow, a three-run homer to left in the seventh. Atlanta, seeking its first Series win since 1957, would now face Cleveland, making its first Fall Classic appearance since 1954.

Atlanta Braves (E), 4; Cincinnati Reds (C), 0

ATL (E)

PLAYER/POS	AVG	G	AB	R	H	2B	3B	HR	RB	BB	SO	SB
Steve Avery, p	.500	2	2	0	1	0	0	0	0	0	0	0
Rafael Belliard, ss	.273	4	11	1	3	0	0	0	0	0	3	0
Jeff Blauser, ss	.000	1	4	0	0	0	0	0	0	1	2	0
Brad Clontz, p	.000	1	0	0	0	0	0	0	0	0	0	0
Mike Devereaux, of	.308	4	13	2	4	1	0	1	5	1	2	0
Tom Glavine, p	.000	1	1	0	0	0	0	0	0	1	0	0
Marquis Grissom, of	.263	4	19	2	5	0	1	0	0	1	4	0
Chipper Jones, 3b	.438	4	16	3	7	0	0	1	3	3	1	1
David Justice, of	.273	3	11	1	3	0	0	0	1	2	1	0
Ryan Klesko, of-3	.000	4	7	0	0	0	0	0	0	3	4	0
Mark Lemke, 2b	.167	4	18	2	3	0	0	0	1	1	0	0
Javy Lopez, c	.357	3	14	2	5	1	0	1	3	0	1	0
Greg Maddux, p	.000	1	3	0	0	0	0	0	0	0	1	0
Fred McGriff, 1b	.438	4	16	5	7	4	0	0	0	3	0	0
Greg McMichael, p	.000	3	0	0	0	0	0	0	0	0	0	0
Mike Mordecai, ss-1	.000	2	2	0	0	0	0	0	0	0	1	0
Charlie O'Brien, c-1	.400	2	5	1	2	0	0	1	3	0	1	0
Alejandro Pena, p	.000	3	0	0	0	0	0	0	0	0	0	0
Luis Polonia, of-1	.500	3	2	0	1	0	0	0	1	0	0	0
Dwight Smith, ph	.000	2	2	0	0	0	0	0	0	0	0	0
John Smoltz, p	.333	1	3	0	1	0	0	0	0	0	1	1
Mark Wohlers, p	.000	4	0	0	0	0	0	0	0	0	0	0
TOTAL	.282		149	19	42	6	1	4	17	16	22	2

PITCHER	W	L	ERA	G	GS	CG	SV	SHO	IP	H	ER	BB	SO
Steve Avery	1	0	0.00	2	1	0	0	0	6.0	2	0	4	6
Brad Clontz	0	0	0.00	1	0	0	0	0	0.1	1	0	0	0
Tom Glavine	0	0	1.29	1	1	0	0	0	7.0	7	1	2	5
Greg Maddux	1	0	1.13	1	1	0	0	0	8.0	7	1	2	4
Greg McMichael	1	0	0.00	3	0	0	1	0	2.2	0	0	1	2
Alejandro Pena	0	0	0.00	3	0	0	0	0	3.0	2	0	1	4
John Smoltz	0	0	2.57	1	1	0	0	0	7.0	7	2	2	2
Mark Wohlers	1	0	1.80	4	0	0	0	0	5.0	2	1	0	8
TOTAL	4	0	1.15	16	4	0	1	0	39.0	28	5	12	31

CIN (C)

PLAYER/POS	AVG	G	AB	R	H	2B	3B	HR	RB	BB	SO	SB
Eric Anthony, ph	.000	2	1	0	0	0	0	0	0	1	1	0
Bret Boone, 2b	.214	4	14	1	3	0	0	0	0	1	2	0
Jeff Branson, 3b	.111	4	9	2	1	1	0	0	0	0	2	1
Jeff Brantley, p	.000	2	0	0	0	0	0	0	0	0	0	0
Dave Burba, p	.000	2	0	0	0	0	0	0	0	0	0	0
Hector Carrasco, p	.000	1	0	0	0	0	0	0	0	0	0	0
Mariano Duncan, 1b-1	.000	3	3	0	0	0	0	0	0	1	1	0
Ron Gant, of	.188	4	16	1	3	0	0	0	1	0	3	0
Lenny Harris, ph	1.000	3	2	0	2	0	0	0	1	0	0	1
Xavier Hernandez, p	.000	1	0	0	0	0	0	0	0	0	0	0
Thomas Howard, of-3	.250	4	8	0	2	1	0	0	1	2	0	0
Mike Jackson, p	.000	3	0	0	0	0	0	0	0	0	0	0
Barry Larkin, ss	.389	4	18	1	7	2	1	0	0	1	1	1
Darren Lewis, of	.000	2	1	0	0	0	0	0	0	0	0	0
Mark Lewis, 3b	.250	2	4	0	1	0	0	0	0	1	1	0
Hal Morris, 1b	.167	4	12	0	2	1	0	0	1	1	1	1
Mark Portugal, p	.000	1	0	0	0	0	0	0	0	0	0	0
Reggie Sanders, of	.125	4	16	0	2	0	0	0	0	2	10	0
Benito Santiago, c	.231	4	13	0	3	0	0	0	0	2	3	0
Pete Schourek, p	.000	2	5	0	0	0	0	0	0	0	4	0
John Smiley, p	.000	1	1	0	0	0	0	0	0	0	0	0
Eddie Taubensee, c-1	.500	2	2	0	1	0	0	0	0	0	0	0
Jerome Walton, of	.000	2	7	0	0	0	0	0	0	0	2	0
David Wells, p	.500	1	2	0	1	0	0	0	0	0	0	0
TOTAL	.209		134	5	28	5	1	0	4	12	31	4

PITCHER	W	L	ERA	G	GS	CG	SV	SHO	IP	H	ER	BB	SO
Jeff Brantley	0	0	0.00	2	0	0	0	0	2.2	0	0	2	1
Dave Burba	0	0	0.00	2	0	0	0	0	3.2	3	0	4	0
Hector Carrasco	0	0	0.00	1	0	0	0	0	1.1	1	0	0	3
Xavier Hernandez	0	0	27.00	1	0	0	0	0	0.2	3	2	0	0
Mike Jackson	0	1	23.14	3	0	0	0	0	2.1	5	6	4	1
Mark Portugal	0	1	36.00	1	0	0	0	0	1.0	3	4	1	0
Pete Schourek	0	1	1.26	2	2	0	0	0	14.1	14	2	3	13
John Smiley	0	0	3.60	1	1	0	0	0	5.0	5	2	0	1
David Wells	0	1	4.50	1	1	0	0	0	6.0	8	3	2	3
TOTAL	0	4	4.62	14	4	0	0	0	37.0	42	19	16	22

GAME 1 AT CIN OCT 10

		R	H	E
ATL	000 000 001 01	2	7	0
CIN	000 100 000 00	1	8	0

Pitchers: Glavine, Pena (8), WOHLERS (9), Clontz (11), Avery (11), McMichael (11) vs Schourek, Brantley (9), JACKSON (11)
Attendance: 40,382

GAME 2 AT CIN OCT 11

		R	H	E
ATL	100 100 000 4	6	11	1
CIN	000 020 000 0	2	9	1

Pitchers: Smoltz, Pena (8), MCMICHAEL (9), Wohlers (10) vs Smiley, Burba (6), Jackson (8), Brantley (9), PORTUGAL (10)
Home Runs: Lopez-ATL
Attendance: 44,624

GAME 3 AT ATL OCT 13

		R	H	E
CIN	000 000 011	2	8	0
ATL	000 003 20X	5	12	1

Pitchers: WELLS, Hernandez (7), Carrasco (7) vs MADDUX, Wohlers (9)
Home Runs: O'Brien-ATL, Jones-ATL
Attendance: 51,424

GAME 4 AT ATL OCT 14

		R	H	E
CIN	000 000 000	0	3	1
ATL	001 000 50X	6	12	1

Pitchers: SCHOUREK, Jackson (7), Burba (7) vs AVERY, McMichael (7), Pena (8), Wohlers (9)
Home Runs: Devereaux-ATL
Attendance: 52,067

Cleveland Indians (C), 4; Seattle Mariners (W), 2

Cleveland had romped in a three-game sweep of Boston. Seattle had engaged in a thrilling, exhausting five-game series against New York, fraying their pitching—and probably their nerves—in the process.

Most observers expected the Tribe to take Game 1. Seattle's rotation had been decimated in defeating the Yankees, and Mariners manager Lou Piniella had to start rookie Bob Wolcott rather than ace Randy Johnson. Wolcott gave up a game-tying seventh inning homer to Albert Belle, but otherwise Piniella had nothing to complain about. Seattle answered in the bottom of that frame and made the run hold up.

Cleveland stranded 10 runners in Game 2 (making a total of 22 left on in the first two contests) but still triumphed, 5-2. Manny Ramirez came into the game mired in a 1-for-16 postseason slump but went 4-for-4 with solo homers in the sixth and eighth innings.

Randy Johnson finally appeared in the series in Game 3 but wasn't around for a decision. The Mariners jumped off to a 2-0 lead thanks to two Cleveland errors, but at the end of eight the score was tied. In the top of the 11th an intentional walk to Tino Martinez backfired as Jay Buhner followed with a three-run homer.

In Game 4 Cleveland evened the series with a 7-0 triumph against an ineffective Andy Benes, aided by Eddie Murray's two-run first inning homer, Jim Thome's two-run third inning homer, and Omar Vizquel's run-scoring sixth inning double.

In Game 5 Orel Hershiser ran his career postseason record to 7-0 as he struck out eight and walked only two. He needed help, however, leaving the game with a 3-2 lead that Paul Assenmacher and Jose Mesa protected skillfully.

In the final game, the Indians' Dennis Martinez defeated Randy Johnson, 4-0. Through eight innings only one run had scored (an unearned one by Cleveland), but in that inning Mariners hopes unraveled. Johnson surrendered a leadoff double to Tony Pena, then an infield single to Kenny Lofton, who stole second. Next came a wild pitch. Ruben Amaro (running for Pena) scored, but so did Lofton, motoring all the way from second, embarrassing Mariners catcher Dan Wilson. That play sealed the Mariners' doom. Carlos Baerga then homered, and, two innings later, the Indians had their first AL pennant in 41 years.

CLE (C)

PLAYER/POS	AVG	G	AB	R	H	2B	3B	HR	RB	BB	SO	SB
Sandy Alomar, c	.267	5	15	0	4	1	1	0	1	1	1	0
Ruben Amaro, dh-1	.000	3	1	1	0	0	0	0	0	0	0	0
Paul Assenmacher, p	.000	3	0	0	0	0	0	0	0	0	0	0
Carlos Baerga, 2b	.400	6	25	3	10	0	0	1	4	2	3	0
Albert Belle, of	.222	5	18	1	4	1	0	1	1	3	5	0
Alan Embree, p	.000	1	0	0	0	0	0	0	0	0	0	0
Alvaro Espinoza, 3b	.125	4	8	1	1	0	0	0	0	0	3	0
Orel Hershiser, p	.000	2	0	0	0	0	0	0	0	0	0	0
Ken Hill, p	.000	1	0	0	0	0	0	0	0	0	0	0
Wayne Kirby, of	.200	5	5	2	1	0	0	0	0	0	0	1
Kenny Lofton, of	.458	6	24	4	11	0	2	0	3	4	6	5
Dennis Martinez, p	.000	2	0	0	0	0	0	0	0	0	0	0
Jose Mesa, p	.000	4	0	0	0	0	0	0	0	0	0	0
Eddie Murray, dh	.250	6	24	2	6	1	0	1	3	2	3	0
Charles Nagy, p	.000	1	0	0	0	0	0	0	0	0	0	0
Chad Ogea, p	.000	1	0	0	0	0	0	0	0	0	0	0
Tony Pena, c	.333	4	6	1	2	1	0	0	0	1	0	0
Herb Perry, 1b	.000	3	8	0	0	0	0	0	0	1	3	0
Eric Plunk, p	.000	3	0	0	0	0	0	0	0	0	0	0
Jim Poole, p	.000	1	0	0	0	0	0	0	0	0	0	0
Manny Ramirez, of	.286	6	21	2	6	0	0	2	2	2	5	0
Paul Sorrento, 1b	.154	4	13	2	2	1	0	0	0	2	3	0
Julian Tavarez, p	.000	4	0	0	0	0	0	0	0	0	0	0
Jim Thome, 3b	.267	5	15	2	4	0	0	2	5	2	3	0
Omar Vizquel, ss	.087	6	23	2	2	1	0	0	2	5	2	3
TOTAL	.257		206	23	53	6	3	7	21	25	37	9

PITCHER	W	L	ERA	G	GS	CG	SV	SHO	IP	H	ER	BB	SO
Paul Assenmacher	0	0	0.00	3	0	0	0	0	1.1	0	0	1	2
Alan Embree	0	0	0.00	1	0	0	0	0	0.1	0	0	0	1
Orel Hershiser	2	0	1.29	2	2	0	0	0	14.0	9	2	3	15
Ken Hill	1	0	0.00	1	1	0	0	0	7.0	5	0	3	6
Dennis Martinez	1	1	2.03	2	2	0	0	0	13.1	10	3	3	7
Jose Mesa	0	0	2.25	4	0	0	1	0	4.0	3	1	1	1
Charles Nagy	0	0	1.13	1	1	0	0	0	8.0	5	1	0	6
Chad Ogea	0	0	0.00	1	0	0	0	0	0.2	1	0	0	2
Eric Plunk	0	0	9.00	3	0	0	0	0	2.0	1	2	3	2
Jim Poole	0	0	0.00	1	0	0	0	0	1.0	0	0	0	2
Julian Tavarez	0	1	2.70	4	0	0	0	0	3.1	3	1	1	2
TOTAL	4	2	1.64	23	6	0	1	0	55.0	37	10	15	46

SEA (W)

PLAYER/POS	AVG	G	AB	R	H	2B	3B	HR	RB	BB	SO	SB
Rich Amaral, ph	.000	2	2	0	0	0	0	0	0	0	1	0
Bobby Ayala, p	.000	2	0	0	0	0	0	0	0	0	0	0
Tim Belcher, p	.000	1	0	0	0	0	0	0	0	0	0	0
Andy Benes, p	.000	1	0	0	0	0	0	0	0	0	0	0
Mike Blowers, 3b	.222	6	18	1	4	0	0	1	2	0	4	0
Chris Bosio, p	.000	1	0	0	0	0	0	0	0	0	0	0
Jay Buhner, of	.304	6	23	5	7	2	0	3	5	2	8	0
Norm Charlton, p	.000	3	0	0	0	0	0	0	0	0	0	0
Vince Coleman, of-5	.100	6	20	0	2	0	0	0	0	2	6	4
Joey Cora, 2b	.174	6	23	3	4	1	0	0	0	1	0	2
Alex Diaz, of-3	.429	4	7	0	3	1	0	0	0	1	1	0
Felix Fermin, 2b-1,ss-1	.000	2	0	0	0	0	0	0	0	0	0	0
Ken Griffey, of	.333	6	21	2	7	2	0	1	2	4	4	2
Randy Johnson, p	.000	2	0	0	0	0	0	0	0	0	0	0
Tino Martinez, 1b	.136	6	22	1	3	0	0	0	0	3	7	0
Edgar Martinez, dh	.087	6	23	0	2	0	0	0	0	2	5	1
Jeff Nelson, p	.000	3	0	0	0	0	0	0	0	0	0	0
Bill Risley, p	.000	3	0	0	0	0	0	0	0	0	0	0
Alex Rodriguez, ph	.000	1	1	0	0	0	0	0	0	0	1	0
Luis Sojo, ss	.250	6	20	0	5	2	0	0	1	0	2	0
Doug Strange, 3b-2	.000	4	4	0	0	0	0	0	0	0	2	0
Bob Wells, p	.000	1	0	0	0	0	0	0	0	0	0	0
Chris Widger, c	.000	3	1	0	0	0	0	0	0	0	1	0
Dan Wilson, c	.000	6	16	0	0	0	0	0	0	0	4	0
Bob Wolcott, p	.000	1	0	0	0	0	0	0	0	0	0	0
TOTAL	.184		201	12	37	8	0	5	10	15	46	9

PITCHER	W	L	ERA	G	GS	CG	SV	SHO	IP	H	ER	BB	SO
Bobby Ayala	0	0	2.45	2	0	0	0	0	3.2	3	1	3	3
Tim Belcher	0	1	6.35	1	1	0	0	0	5.2	9	4	2	1
Andy Benes	0	1	23.14	1	1	0	0	0	2.1	6	6	2	3
Chris Bosio	0	1	3.38	1	1	0	0	0	5.1	7	2	2	3
Norm Charlton	1	0	0.00	3	0	0	1	0	6.0	1	0	1	5
Randy Johnson	0	1	2.35	2	2	0	0	0	15.1	12	4	2	13
Jeff Nelson	0	0	0.00	3	0	0	0	0	3.0	3	0	5	3
Bill Risley	0	0	0.00	3	0	0	0	0	2.2	2	0	1	2
Bob Wells	0	0	3.00	1	0	0	0	0	3.0	2	1	2	2
Bob Wolcott	1	0	2.57	1	1	0	0	0	7.0	8	2	5	2
TOTAL	2	4	3.33	18	6	0	1	0	54.0	53	20	25	37

GAME 1 AT SEA OCT 10

				R	H	E
CLE	001	000	100	2	10	1
SEA	020	000	10X	3	7	0

Pitchers: MARTINEZ, Tavarez (7), Assenmacher (8), Plunk (8) vs WOLCOTT, Nelson (8), Charlton (8)
Home Runs: Belle-CLE, Blowers-SEA
Attendance: 57,065

GAME 2 AT SEA OCT 11

				R	H	E
CLE	000	022	010	5	12	0
SEA	000	001	001	2	6	1

Pitchers: HERSHISER, Mesa (9) vs BELCHER, Ayala (6), Risley (9)
Home Runs: Ramirez-CLE (2), Griffey-SEA, Buhner-SEA
Attendance: 58,144

GAME 3 AT CLE OCT 13

					R	H	E
SEA	011	000	000	03	5	9	1
CLE	000	100	010	00	2	4	2

Pitchers: Johnson, CHARLTON (9) vs Nagy, Mesa (9), TAVAREZ (10), Assenmacher (11), Plunk (11)
Home Runs: Buhner-SEA (2)
Attendance: 43,643

GAME 4 AT CLE OCT 14

				R	H	E
SEA	000	000	000	0	6	1
CLE	312	001	00X	7	9	0

Pitchers: BENES, Wells (3), Ayala (6), Nelson (7), Risley (8) vs HILL, Poole (8), Ogea (9), Embree (9)
Home Runs: Murray-CLE, Thome-CLE
Attendance: 43,686

GAME 5 AT CLE OCT 15

				R	H	E
SEA	001	010	000	2	5	2
CLE	100	002	00X	3	10	4

Pitchers: BOSIO, Nelson (6), Risley (7) vs HERSHISER, Tavarez (7), Assenmacher (7), Plunk (8), Mesa (9)
Home Runs: Thome-CLE
Attendance: 43,607

GAME 6 AT SEA OCT 17

				R	H	E
CLE	000	010	030	4	8	0
SEA	000	000	000	0	4	1

Pitchers: MARTINEZ, Tavarez (8), Mesa (9) vs JOHNSON, Charlton (8)
Home Runs: Baerga-CLE
Attendance: 58,489

The Indians and Braves met for a rematch of their tussle in the 1948 World Series, but this time the transplanted Braves went home with the honors. Game 1 quickly established that Atlanta's vaunted pitching staff was no myth. Perennial Cy Young Award winner Greg Maddux used just 95 pitches in shutting down the hard-hitting Indians. Only three runners reached against him, on opposite field singles by Kenny Lofton and Jim Thome, and on an error by Rafael Belliard. Cleveland starter Orel Hershiser tired in the seventh and walked two, leading to the second and third Atlanta runs and his first loss after seven straight postseason victories.

In Game 2 Atlanta took a 2-0 Series lead as catcher Javier Lopez anticipated a Dennis Martinez fastball on the outside part of the plate. He hammered it to straightaway center field for a two- run homer, shattering a 2-2 tie and providing the Braves with all the margin they would need for a 4-3 win.

The Indians bats finally came alive in Game 3. It looked like the Tribe would be facing a 3-0 deficit, as they trailed 6-5 in the bottom of the eighth. But in that inning Kenny Lofton (who reached base six times in the contest) scored the tying run on Sandy Alomar's first hit of the series. In the 11th Murray singled off Alejandro Pena's first pitch to score pinch-runner Alvaro Espinoza with the winning run.

Atlanta's Ryan Klesko and Cleveland's Albert Belle traded solo sixth-inning homers in Game 4 to set up a 1-1 tie going into the top of the seventh. Atlanta then scored three runs on Luis Polonia's run-scoring double and David Justice's two-out, two-run single to center to break the contest open and ultimately give Atlanta a 5-2 win.

The Tribe stayed alive in Game 5 as Jim Thome singled in the go-ahead run in the sixth and provided a crucial insurance run with an eighth inning homer. Ryan Klesko nicked Jose Mesa for a two-run homer in the ninth—the third straight game in which he'd homered—but it wasn't enough.

The keys to Game 6 were two players with something to prove: Tom Glavine, who had survived Atlanta's horrible days in the late 1980s, and David Justice, who was taking heat for comments he had made about Atlanta fans' lack of spirit. Glavine allowed only a sixth inning single to Tony Pena, walked three and struck out eight. Justice brought home the game's only run with a sixth inning homer off reliever Jim Poole. The Braves now had their first world championship since 1957 and had become the first franchise to win the crown in three different cities—Boston, Milwaukee, and Atlanta.

Atlanta Braves (N,) 4; Cleveland Indians (A), 2

ATL (N)

PLAYER/POS	AVG	G	AB	R	H	2B	3B	HR	RB	BB	SO	SB
Steve Avery, pn	.000	1	0	0	0	0	0	0	0	0	0	0
Rafael Belliard, ss	.000	6	16	0	0	0	0	0	1	0	4	0
Pedro Borbon, p	.000	1	0	0	0	0	0	0	0	0	0	0
Brad Clontz, p	.000	2	0	0	0	0	0	0	0	0	0	0
Mike Devereaux, of-4,dh-1	.250	5	4	0	1	0	0	0	1	2	1	0
Tom Glavine, p	.000	2	4	0	0	0	0	0	0	1	2	0
Marquis Grissom, of	.360	6	25	3	9	1	0	0	1	1	3	3
Chipper Jones, 3b	.286	6	21	3	6	3	0	0	1	4	3	0
David Justice, of	.250	6	20	3	5	1	0	1	5	5	1	0
Ryan Klesko, of-3,dh-3	.313	6	16	4	5	0	0	3	4	3	4	0
Mark Lemke, 2b	.273	6	22	1	6	0	0	0	0	3	2	0
Javy Lopez, c	.176	6	17	1	3	2	0	1	3	1	1	0
Greg Maddux, p	.000	2	3	0	0	0	0	0	0	0	1	0
Fred McGriff, 1b	.261	6	23	5	6	2	0	2	3	3	7	1
Greg McMichael, p	.000	3	0	0	0	0	0	0	0	0	0	0
Kent Mercker, p	.000	1	0	0	0	0	0	0	0	0	0	0
Mike Mordecai, ss-2, dh-1	.333	3	3	0	1	0	0	0	0	0	1	0
Charlie O'Brien, c	.000	2	3	0	0	0	0	0	0	0	1	0
Alejandro Pena, p	.000	2	0	0	0	0	0	0	0	0	0	0
Luis Polonia, of-4	.286	6	14	3	4	1	0	1	4	1	3	1
Dwight Smith, ph	.500	3	2	0	1	0	0	0	0	1	0	0
John Smoltz, p	.000	1	0	0	0	0	0	0	0	0	0	0
Mark Wohlers, p	.000	4	0	0	0	0	0	0	0	0	0	0
TOTAL	.244		193	23	47	10	0	8	23	25	34	5

PITCHER	W	L	ERA	G	GS	CG	SV	SHO	IP	H	ER	BB	SO
Steve Avery	1	0	1.50	1	1	0	0	0	6.0	3	1	5	3
Pedro Borbon	0	0	0.00	1	0	0	1	0	1.0	0	0	0	2
Brad Clontz	0	0	2.70	2	0	0	0	0	3.1	2	1	0	2
Tom Glavine	2	0	1.29	2	2	0	0	0	14.0	4	2	6	11
Greg Maddux	1	1	2.25	2	2	1	0	0	16.0	9	4	3	8
Greg McMichael	0	0	2.70	3	0	0	0	0	3.1	3	1	2	2
Kent Mercker	0	0	4.50	1	0	0	0	0	2.0	1	1	2	2
Alejandro Pena	0	1	9.00	2	0	0	0	0	1.0	3	1	2	0
John Smoltz	0	0	15.43	1	1	0	0	0	2.1	6	4	2	4
Mark Wohlers	0	0	1.80	4	0	0	2	0	5.0	4	1	3	3
TOTAL	4	2	2.67	19	6	1	3	0	54.0	35	16	25	37

CLE (A)

PLAYER/POS	AVG	G	AB	R	H	2B	3B	HR	RB	BB	SO	SB
Sandy Alomar, c	.200	5	15	0	3	2	0	0	1	0	2	0
Ruben Amaro, of-1	.000	2	2	0	0	0	0	0	0	0	1	0
Paul Assenmacher, p	.000	4	0	0	0	0	0	0	0	0	0	0
Carlos Baerga, 2b	.192	6	26	1	5	2	0	0	4	1	1	0
Albert Belle, of	.235	6	17	4	4	0	0	2	4	7	5	0
Alan Embree, p	.000	4	0	0	0	0	0	0	0	0	0	0
Alvaro Espinoza, 3b-1	.500	2	2	1	1	0	0	0	0	0	0	0
Orel Hershiser, p	.000	2	2	0	0	0	0	0	0	0	0	0
Ken Hill, p	.000	2	0	0	0	0	0	0	0	0	0	0
Wayne Kirby, of-2	.000	3	1	0	0	0	0	0	0	0	1	0
Kenny Lofton, of	.200	6	25	6	5	1	0	0	0	3	1	6
Dennis Martinez, p	.000	2	3	0	0	0	0	0	0	0	1	0
Jose Mesa, p	.000	2	0	0	0	0	0	0	0	0	0	0
Eddie Murray, 1b-3,dh-3	.105	6	19	1	2	0	0	1	3	5	4	0
Charles Nagy, p	.000	1	0	0	0	0	0	0	0	0	0	0
Tony Pena, c	.167	2	6	0	1	0	0	0	0	0	0	0
Herb Perry, 1b	.000	3	5	0	0	0	0	0	0	0	2	0
Jim Poole, p	.000	2	1	0	0	0	0	0	0	0	0	0
Manny Ramirez, of	.222	6	18	2	4	0	0	1	2	4	5	1
Paul Sorrento, 1b-3	.182	6	11	0	2	1	0	0	0	0	4	0
Julian Tavarez, p	.000	5	0	0	0	0	0	0	0	0	0	0
Jim Thome, 3b	.211	6	19	1	4	1	0	1	2	2	5	0
Omar Vizquel, ss	.174	6	23	3	4	0	1	0	1	3	5	1
TOTAL	.179		195	19	35	7	1	5	17	25	37	8

PITCHER	W	L	ERA	G	GS	CG	SV	SHO	IP	H	ER	BB	SO
Paul Assenmacher	0	0	6.75	4	0	0	0	0	1.1	1	1	3	3
Alan Embree	0	0	2.70	4	0	0	0	0	3.1	2	1	2	2
Orel Hershiser	1	1	2.57	2	2	0	0	0	14.0	8	4	4	13
Ken Hill	0	1	4.26	2	1	0	0	0	6.1	7	3	4	1
Dennis Martinez	0	1	3.48	2	2	0	0	0	10.1	12	4	8	5
Jose Mesa	1	0	4.50	2	0	0	1	0	4.0	5	2	1	4
Charles Nagy	0	0	6.43	1	1	0	0	0	7.0	8	5	1	4
Jim Poole	0	1	3.86	2	0	0	0	0	2.1	1	1	0	1
Julian Tavarez	0	0	0.00	5	0	0	0	0	4.1	3	0	2	1
TOTAL	2	4	3.57	24	6	0	1	0	53.0	47	21	25	34

GAME 1 AT ATL OCT 21

		R	H	E
CLE	100 000 001	2	2	0
ATL	010 000 20X	3	3	2

Pitchers: HERSHISER, Assenmacher (7), Tavarez (7), Embree (8) vs MADDUX
Home Runs: McGriff-ATL
Attendance: 51,876

GAME 2 AT ATL OCT 22

		R	H	E
CLE	020 000 100	3	6	2
ATL	002 002 00X	4	8	2

Pitchers: MARTINEZ, Embree (6), Poole (7), Tavarez (8) vs GLAVINE, McMichael (7), Pena (7), Wohlers (8)
Home Runs: Murray-CLE, Lopez-ATL
Attendance: 51,877

GAME 3 AT CLE OCT 24

		R	H	E
ATL	100 001 130 00	6	12	1
CLE	202 000 110 01	7	12	2

Pitchers: Smoltz, Clontz (3), Mercker (5), McMichael (7), Wohlers (8), PENA (11) vs Nagy, Assenmacher (8), Tavarez (8), MESA (9)
Home Runs: McGriff-ATL, Klesko-ATL
Attendance: 43,584

GAME 4 AT CLE OCT 25

		R	H	E
ATL	000 001 301	5	11	1
CLE	000 001 001	2	6	0

Pitchers: AVERY, McMichael (7), Wohlers (9), Borbon (9) vs HILL, Assenmacher (7), Tavarez (8), Embree (8)
Home Runs: Belle-CLE, Ramirez-CLE, Klesko-ATL
Attendance: 43,578

GAME 5 AT CLE OCT 26

		R	H	E
ATL	000 110 002	4	7	0
CLE	200 002 01X	5	8	1

Pitchers: MADDUX, Clontz (8) vs HERSHISER, Mesa (9)
Home Runs: Belle-CLE, Thome-CLE, Polonia-ATL, Klesko-ATL
Attendance: 43,595

GAME 6 AT ATL OCT 28

		R	H	E
CLE	000 000 000	0	1	1
ATL	000 001 00X	1	6	0

Pitchers: Martinez, POOLE (5), Hill (7), Embree (7), Tavarez (8), Assenmacher (8) vs GLAVINE, Wohlers (9)
Home Runs: Justice-ATL
Attendance: 51,875

Atlanta Braves (E), 3; Los Angeles Dodgers (WC), 0

The Braves became the first National League team to make five consecutive postseason appearances. The Braves struggled in mid-September, but their opponents in the Division Series, the Dodgers, had really stumbled into the postseason. Los Angeles lost its last four regular-season games, but still captured the Wild Card. Dodger Stadium was abuzz when the Division Series began and the two starting pitchers, LA's Ramon Martinez and Atlanta's John Smoltz, were equal to the task. Martinez allowed just one run and three hits through eight innings while Smoltz pitched nine innings with only one run and four hits against him. Smoltz and the Braves caught the break they needed in the 10th when Javier Lopez homered to right-center for a 2-1 lead. Reliever Mark Wohlers made it hold up with two strikeouts in the tenthth inning.

Pitching was the name of the game again the next night. While Greg Maddux's four-year streak of Cy Young Awards would end in 1996, he reminded the country that his trophy collection was well-deserved. Maddux, however, was touched for unearned runs in the first and fourth innings as the Dodgers took a 2-1 lead into the seventh inning despite just three hits. Dodgers starter Ismael Valdes limited the Braves to three hits as well through six innings, including a home run by Ryan Klesko, but that changed in a span of seven pitches in the seventh inning. Fred McGriff hit a line-drive home run to center field to tie the score. After Valdes recorded his fifth strikeout, Jermaine Dye hit the first pitch he saw over the left field wall for a 3-2 lead. Greg McMichael and Mark Wohlers each had a scoreless inning to close out the win.

A club-record crowd greeted the Braves at Fulton County Stadium for Game 3, but the fans fidgeted in their seats when Hideo Nomo struck out the first two Braves he faced. They were soon on their feet, however, when Chipper Jones singled and McGriff doubled him home. Nomo retired the first two batters he faced in the fourth inning, but he was on his way to the showers by the time the third out was recorded. Pitcher Tom Glavine started the rally with a double and Marquis Grissom walked before Mark Lemke doubled home both runners. Chipper Jones followed with a two-run home run to give Atlanta a 5-0 lead. To their credit, the Dodgers nicked Glavine for a run in the seventh inning and McMichael for another in the eighth, but Mike Bielecki and Mark Wohlers allowed nothing more and the Braves had another opportunity to celebrate.

ATL (E)

PLAYER/POS	AVG	G	AB	R	H	2B	3B	HR	RB	BB	SO	SB
Rafael Belliard, ss	.000	3	0	0	0	0	0	0	0	0	0	0
Mike Bielecki, p	.000	1	0	0	0	0	0	0	0	0	0	0
Jeff Blauser, ss	.111	3	9	0	1	0	0	0	0	1	3	0
Jermaine Dye, of	.182	3	11	1	2	0	0	1	1	0	6	1
Tom Glavine, p	.500	1	2	1	1	1	0	0	0	0	0	0
Marquis Grissom, of	.083	3	12	2	1	0	0	0	0	1	2	1
Andruw Jones, of	.000	3	0	0	0	0	0	0	0	1	0	0
Chipper Jones, 3b	.222	3	9	2	2	0	0	1	2	3	4	1
Ryan Klesko, of	.125	3	8	1	1	0	0	1	1	3	4	1
Mark Lemke, 2b	.167	3	12	1	2	1	0	0	2	0	1	0
Javy Lopez, c	.286	2	7	1	2	0	0	1	1	1	0	1
Greg Maddux, p	.000	1	2	0	0	0	0	0	0	0	1	0
Fred McGriff, 1b	.333	3	9	1	3	1	0	1	3	2	1	0
Greg McMichael, p	.000	2	0	0	0	0	0	0	0	0	0	0
Terry Pendleton, ph	.000	1	1	0	0	0	0	0	0	0	1	0
Eddie Perez, c	.333	1	3	0	1	0	0	0	0	0	0	0
Luis Polonia, ph	.000	2	2	0	0	0	0	0	0	0	1	0
John Smoltz, p	.000	1	2	0	0	0	0	0	0	0	0	0
Mark Wohlers, p	.000	3	0	0	0	0	0	0	0	0	0	0
TOTAL	.180		89	10	16	3	0	5	10	12	24	5

PITCHER	W	L	ERA	G	GS	CG	SV	SHO	IP	H	ER	BB	SO
Mike Bielecki	0	0	0.00	1	0	0	0	0	0.2	0	0	1	1
Tom Glavine	1	0	1.35	1	1	0	0	0	6.2	5	1	3	7
Greg Maddux	1	0	0.00	1	1	0	0	0	7.0	3	0	0	7
Greg McMichael	0	0	6.75	2	0	0	0	0	1.1	1	1	1	3
John Smoltz	1	0	1.00	1	1	0	0	0	9.0	4	1	2	7
Mark Wohlers	0	0	0.00	3	0	0	3	0	3.1	1	0	0	4
TOTAL	3	0	0.96	9	3	0	3	0	28.0	14	3	7	29

LA (W)

PLAYER/POS	AVG	G	AB	R	H	2B	3B	HR	RB	BB	SO	SB
Billy Ashley, ph	.000	2	2	0	0	0	0	0	0	0	2	0
Pedro Astacio, p	.000	1	0	0	0	0	0	0	0	0	0	0
Tom Candiotti, p	.000	1	0	0	0	0	0	0	0	0	0	0
Juan Castro, 2b	.200	2	5	0	1	1	0	0	1	1	1	0
Dave Clark, ph	.000	2	2	0	0	0	0	0	0	0	2	0
Chad Curtis, of	.000	1	2	0	0	0	0	0	0	1	1	0
Delino DeShields, 2b	.000	2	4	0	0	0	0	0	0	0	1	0
Darren Dreifort, p	.000	1	0	0	0	0	0	0	0	0	0	0
Greg Gagne, ss	.273	3	11	2	3	1	0	0	0	0	5	0
Mark Guthrie, p	.000	1	0	0	0	0	0	0	0	0	0	0
Dave Hansen, ph	.000	2	2	0	0	0	0	0	0	0	0	0
Todd Hollandsworth, of	.333	3	12	1	4	3	0	0	1	0	3	0
Eric Karros, 1b	.000	3	9	0	0	0	0	0	0	2	3	0
Wayne Kirby, of	.125	3	8	1	1	0	0	0	0	2	1	0
Ramon Martinez, p	.000	1	3	0	0	0	0	0	0	0	2	0
Raul Mondesi, of	.182	3	11	0	2	2	0	0	1	0	4	0
Hideo Nomo, p	.000	1	1	0	0	0	0	0	0	0	1	0
Antonio Osuna, p	.000	2	0	0	0	0	0	0	0	0	0	0
Mike Piazza, c	.300	3	10	1	3	0	0	0	2	1	2	0
Scott Radinsky, p	.000	2	0	0	0	0	0	0	0	0	0	0
Ismael Valdes, p	.000	1	2	0	0	0	0	0	0	0	0	0
Tim Wallach, 3b	.000	3	11	0	0	0	0	0	0	0	1	0
Todd Worrell, p	.000	1	0	0	0	0	0	0	0	0	0	0
TOTAL	.147		95	5	14	7	0	0	5	7	29	0

PITCHER	W	L	ERA	G	GS	CG	SV	SHO	IP	H	ER	BB	SO
Pedro Astacio	0	0	0.00	1	0	0	0	0	1.2	0	0	0	1
Tom Candiotti	0	0	0.00	1	0	0	0	0	2.0	0	0	0	1
Darren Dreifort	0	0	0.00	1	0	0	0	0	0.2	0	0	0	0
Mark Guthrie	0	0	0.00	1	0	0	0	0	0.1	0	0	1	1
Ramon Martinez	0	0	1.13	1	1	0	0	0	8.0	3	1	3	6
Hideo Nomo	0	1	12.27	1	1	0	0	0	3.2	5	5	5	3
Antonio Osuna	0	1	4.50	2	0	0	0	0	2.0	3	1	1	4
Scott Radinsky	0	0	0.00	2	0	0	0	0	1.1	0	0	1	2
Ismael Valdes	0	1	4.26	1	1	0	0	0	6.1	5	3	0	5
Todd Worrell	0	0	0.00	1	0	0	0	0	1.0	0	0	1	1
TOTAL	0	3	3.33	12	3	0	0	0	27.0	16	10	12	24

GAME ONE AT LA OCT 2

ATL	000 100 000 1	2	4	1
LA	000 010 000 0	1	5	0

Pitchers: SMOLTZ, Wohlers (10) vs Martinez, Radinsky (9), OSUNA (9)
Home Runs: Lopez-ATL
Attendance: 47,428

GAME TWO AT LA OCT 3

ATL	010 000 200	3	5	2
LA	100 100 000	2	3	0

Pitchers: MADDUX, McMichael (8), Wohlers (9) vs VALDES, Astacio (7), Worrell (9)
Home Runs: Klesko-ATL, McGriff-ATL, Dye-ATL
Attendance: 51,916

GAME THREE AT ATL OCT 5

LA	000 000 110	2	6	1
ATL	100 400 00X	5	7	0

Pitchers: NOMO, Guthrie (4), Candiotti (5), Radinsky (7), Osuna (8), Dreifort (8) vs GLAVINE, McMichael (7), Bielecki (8), Wohlers (8)
Home Runs: C.Jones-ATL
Attendance: 52,529

St. Louis finished 19 games under .500 in 1995, but with new manager Tony LaRussa and 14 new players, the Cards of 1996 won 88 games and captured the NL Central by six games. San Diego's storybook season ended with a three-game sweep over the Dodgers to claim the NL West title with a 91-71 mark. The Cardinals took control of the Division Series at Busch Stadium when Gary Gaetti hit a three-run home run, his only hit of the series, to give the Cards a first-inning lead against Joey Hamilton. St. Louis made it hold up. Todd Stottlemyre, who entered the game with a postseason ERA of 7.50, allowed only a Rickey Henderson home run in 6⅔ innings. Then LaRussa's veteran bullpen of Rick Honeycutt and Dennis Eckersley, with 40 years of major league experience between them, kept the Padres at bay.

Game 2 was another well-played contest as the two teams matched each other run for run through the first seven and a half innings in front of a record crowd in St. Louis. Willie McGee singled in the first run of the game for the Cards in the third, but Ken Caminiti answered back with a home run to right field to tie the score at 1-1 in the top of the fifth. St. Louis rallied for three runs in the bottom of the frame when Ron Gant hit a bases-clearing double. The Padres scored twice in the sixth when Tony Gwynn singled in one run and a throwing error allowed another run to score. San Diego tied the game in the top of the eighth on a groundout by Steve Finley, but Tom Pagnozzi's line drive in the bottom of the inning ticked off the glove of reliever Trevor Hoffman and brought home the winning run. Eckersley retired the side in order in the ninth to make a winner of Honeycutt.

In San Diego's only other playoff appearance in 1984, the Padres dropped the first two games in Chicago and then won the last three at home for the pennant. The Padres were looking for that magic again as they took a 4-1 lead after four innings against Cardinals starter Donovan Osborne. The Cards rallied to tie matters in the sixth. St. Louis pushed across a run in the seventh after the Padres misplayed a bunt, but Caminiti hit his second home run of the game—and third of the series—to tie the game in the eighth. San Diego had a chance to take the lead later in the inning, but right fielder Brian Jordan made a sensational diving catch to end the threat. With his shoulder still aching from the catch, Jordan crushed a home run to left off Hoffman for a 7-5 lead in the ninth. Eckersley made the sweep official by earning the save.

St. Louis Cardinals (C), 3; San Diego Padres (W), 0

STL (C)

PLAYER/POS	AVG	G	AB	R	H	2B	3B	HR	RB	BB	SO	SB
Luis Alicea, 2b	.182	3	11	1	2	2	0	0	0	1	4	0
Andy Benes, p	.500	1	2	1	1	0	0	0	0	0	1	0
Royce Clayton, ss	.333	2	6	1	2	0	0	0	0	3	1	0
Dennis Eckersley, p	.000	3	0	0	0	0	0	0	0	0	0	0
Gary Gaetti, 3b	.091	3	11	1	1	0	0	1	3	0	3	0
Mike Gallego, 2b-1,3b-1	.000	2	1	0	0	0	0	0	0	0	1	0
Ron Gant, of	.400	3	10	3	4	1	0	1	4	2	0	2
Rick Honeycutt, p	.000	3	1	0	0	0	0	0	0	0	1	0
Brian Jordan, of	.333	3	12	4	4	0	0	1	3	1	3	1
Ray Lankford, of	.500	1	2	1	1	0	0	0	0	1	0	0
John Mabry, 1b	.300	3	10	1	3	0	1	0	1	1	1	0
T. J. Mathews, p	.000	1	0	0	0	0	0	0	0	0	0	0
Willie McGee, of	.100	3	10	1	1	0	0	0	1	1	3	0
Miguel Mejia, pr	.000	1	0	0	0	0	0	0	0	0	0	0
Donovan Osborne, p	.000	1	1	0	0	0	0	0	0	0	0	0
Tom Pagnozzi, c	.273	3	11	0	3	0	0	0	2	1	3	0
Mark Petkovsek, p	.000	1	0	0	0	0	0	0	0	0	0	0
Ozzie Smith, ss-1	.333	2	3	1	1	0	0	0	0	2	0	0
Todd Stottlemyre, p	.000	1	2	0	0	0	0	0	0	0	2	0
Mark Sweeney, ph	1.000	1	1	0	1	0	0	0	0	0	0	0
TOTAL	.255		94	15	24	3	1	3	14	13	23	3

PITCHER	W	L	ERA	G	GS	CG	SV	SHO	IP	H	ER	BB	SO
Andy Benes	0	0	5.14	1	1	0	0	0	7.0	6	4	1	9
Dennis Eckersley	0	0	0.00	3	0	0	3	0	3.2	3	0	0	2
Rick Honeycutt	1	0	3.38	3	0	0	0	0	2.2	3	1	1	2
T. J. Mathews	1	0	0.00	1	0	0	0	0	1.0	1	0	0	2
Donovan Osborne	0	0	9.00	1	1	0	0	0	4.0	7	4	0	5
Mark Petkovsek	0	0	0.00	1	0	0	0	0	2.0	0	0	0	1
Todd Stottlemyre	1	0	1.35	1	1	0	0	0	6.2	5	1	2	7
TOTAL	3	0	3.33	11	3	0	3	0	27.0	25	10	4	28

SD (W)

PLAYER/POS	AVG	G	AB	R	H	2B	3B	HR	RB	BB	SO	SB
Andy Ashby, p	.000	1	1	0	0	0	0	0	0	0	1	0
Willie Blair, p.	000	1	0	0	0	0	0	0	0	0	0	0
Doug Bochtler, p	.000	1	0	0	0	0	0	0	0	0	0	0
Ken Caminiti, 3b	.300	3	10	3	3	0	0	3	3	2	5	0
Archi Cianfrocco, 1b	.333	3	3	1	1	0	0	0	0	0	1	0
Steve Finley, of	.083	3	12	0	1	0	0	0	1	0	4	1
John Flaherty, c	.000	2	4	0	0	0	0	0	0	0	1	0
Chris Gomez, ss	.167	3	12	0	2	0	0	0	1	0	4	0
Tony Gwynn, of	.308	3	13	0	4	1	0	0	1	0	2	1
Chris Gwynn, ph	1.000	2	2	1	2	0	0	0	0	0	0	0
Joey Hamilton, p	.000	1	2	0	0	0	0	0	0	0	2	0
Rickey Henderson, of	.333	3	12	2	4	0	0	1	1	2	3	0
Trevor Hoffman, p	.000	2	0	0	0	0	0	0	0	0	0	0
Brian Johnson, c	.375	2	8	2	3	1	0	0	0	0	1	0
Wally Joyner, 1b	.111	3	9	0	1	0	0	0	0	0	2	0
Scott Livingstone, ph	.500	2	2	1	1	0	0	0	0	0	0	0
Luis Lopez, pr	.000	1	0	0	0	0	0	0	0	0	0	0
Jody Reed, 2b	.273	3	11	0	3	1	0	0	2	0	1	0
Scott Sanders, p	.000	1	1	0	0	0	0	0	0	0	0	0
Fernando Valenzuela, p	.000	1	0	0	0	0	0	0	0	0	0	0
Greg Vaughn, ph	.000	3	3	0	0	0	0	0	0	0	1	0
Dario Veras, p	.000	2	0	0	0	0	0	0	0	0	0	0
Tim Worrell, p	.000	2	0	0	0	0	0	0	0	0	0	0
TOTAL	.238		105	10	25	3	0	4	9	4	28	2

PITCHER	W	L	ERA	G	GS	CG	SV	SHO	IP	H	ER	BB	SO
Andy Ashby	0	0	6.75	1	1	0	0	0	5.1	7	4	1	5
Willie Blair	0	0	0.00	1	0	0	0	0	2.0	1	0	2	3
Doug Bochtler	0	1	27.00	1	0	0	0	0	0.1	0	1	2	0
Joey Hamilton	0	1	4.50	1	1	0	0	0	6.0	5	3	0	6
Trevor Hoffman	0	1	10.80	2	0	0	0	0	1.2	3	2	1	2
Scott Sanders	0	0	8.31	1	1	0	0	0	4.1	3	4	4	4
Fernando Valenzuela	0	0	0.00	1	0	0	0	0	0.2	0	0	2	0
Dario Veras	0	0	0.00	2	0	0	0	0	1.0	1	0	0	1
Tim Worrell	0	0	2.45	2	0	0	0	0	3.2	4	1	1	2
TOTAL	0	3	5.40	12	3	0	0	0	25.0	24	15	13	23

GAME ONE AT STL OCT 1

				R	H	E
SD	000	001	000	1	8	1
STL	300	000	00X	3	6	0

Pitchers: HAMILTON, Blair (7) vs STOTTLEMYRE, Honeycutt (7), Eckersley (8)
Home Runs: Henderson-SD, Gaetti-STL
Attendance: 54,193

GAME TWO AT STL OCT 3

				R	H	E
SD	000	012	010	4	6	0
STL	001	030	01X	5	5	1

Pitchers: Sanders, Veras (5), Worrell (6), BOCHTLER (8), Hoffman (8) vs An.Benes, HONEYCUTT (8), Eckersley (9)
Home Runs: Caminiti-SD
Attendance: 56,752

GAME THREE AT SD OCT 5

				R	H	E
STL	100	003	102	7	13	1
SD	021	100	010	5	11	2

Pitchers: Osborne, Petkovsek (5), Honeycutt (7), MATHEWS (8), Eckersley (9) vs Ashby, Worrell (6), Valenzuela (8), Veras (8), HOFFMAN (9)
Home Runs: Gant-STL, Jordan-STL, Caminiti-SD (2)
Attendance: 53,899

The Rangers jumped out to a lead in all four games of the Division Series, but the difference was Yankees relief pitching—and Bernie Williams. The New York bullpen allowed just one earned run in 19⅔ innings of relief while Texas relievers failed to hold the lead in all three losses. Williams hit three home runs in the series, including two in decisive Game 4. Juan Gonzalez hit five home runs and drove in nine runs for the Rangers, but the Yankees won by corralling the rest of the Texas bats in the series.

John Burkett, a late-season acquisition, quieted the boisterous Yankee Stadium crowd with a complete-game effort in Game 1. Gonzalez and Dean Palmer both homered off David Cone in the fifth inning for a 6-2 Ranger win. Texas jumped out to a 4-1 lead in Game 2 against Andy Pettitte, courtesy of a pair of Gonzalez home runs, but the Rangers' failure to convert two tailor-made double-play grounders in the fourth inning gave the Yankees a key run. The Yankees tied it against the Texas bullpen and the Rangers defense gave New York the game when Palmer threw away Charlie Hayes' bunt in the 12th inning to score Derek Jeter with the winner.

In Game 3 Williams homered to the opposite field in the top of the first inning and then reached over the fence to rob Rusty Greer of a home run in the bottom of the inning. In the first home postseason game in the history of the franchise, Darren Oliver gave the crowd plenty to cheer about as he held the Yankees to four hits through eight innings. Texas scored two runs off Jimmy Key as Gonzalez provided the expected power with a fourth-inning home run and the other run was set up when no one covered second base on a steal. Rangers manager Johnny Oates knew the shaky state of his bullpen, so he let Oliver start the ninth and yanked him only after the first two runners reached base. Mike Henneman allowed a game-tying sacrifice fly and surrendered a single by Mariano Duncan for a 3-2 Yankees lead. John Wetteland retired the side in the ninth to give New York a two games to one lead.

The Rangers jumped out to a 4-0 lead the next afternoon in Game 4. Gonzalez, as usual, added a home run, but timely hits by Mickey Tettleton, Ivan Rodriguez, and Mark McLemore scored three more runs and ended the Yankees' streak of bullpen dominance. New York simply started a new streak. David Weathers pitched three scoreless innings of relief and wound up with the win when Mariano Rivera and Wetteland also pitched scoreless baseball. The Rangers, meanwhile, tried eight pitchers and still couldn't stop the Yankees. Cecil Fielder, Duncan, and Jeter each drove in runs in the fourth to cut the lead to 4-3. Switch-hitting Williams led off the fifth with a home run from the left side to tie the game and—after Fielder had given the Yankees the lead in the seventh—Williams clinched it with a homer from the right side in the ninth inning.

New York Yankees (E), 3; Texas Rangers (W), 1

NY (E)

PLAYER/POS	AVG	G	AB	R	H	2B	3B	HR	RB	BB	SO	SB
Brian Boehringer, p	.000	2	0	0	0	0	0	0	0	0	0	0
Wade Boggs, 3b	.083	3	12	0	1	1	0	0	0	0	2	0
David Cone, p	.000	1	0	0	0	0	0	0	0	0	0	0
Mariano Duncan, 2b	.313	4	16	0	5	0	0	0	3	0	4	0
Cecil Fielder, dh	.364	3	11	2	4	0	0	1	4	1	2	0
Andy Fox, dh-1	.000	2	0	0	0	0	0	0	0	0	0	0
Joe Girardi, c	.222	4	9	1	2	0	0	0	0	4	1	0
Charlie Hayes, 3b-2	.200	3	5	0	1	0	0	0	1	0	0	0
Derek Jeter, ss	.412	4	17	2	7	1	0	0	1	0	2	0
Jimmy Key, p	.000	1	0	0	0	0	0	0	0	0	0	0
Jim Leyritz, c-1	.000	2	3	0	0	0	0	0	1	0	1	0
Graeme Lloyd, p	.000	2	0	0	0	0	0	0	0	0	0	0
Tino Martinez, 1b	.267	4	15	3	4	2	0	0	0	3	1	0
Jeff Nelson, p	.000	2	0	0	0	0	0	0	0	0	0	0
Paul O'Neill, of	.133	4	15	0	2	0	0	0	0	0	2	0
Andy Pettitte, p	.000	1	0	0	0	0	0	0	0	0	0	0
Tim Raines, of	.250	4	16	3	4	0	0	0	0	3	1	0
Mariano Rivera, p	.000	2	0	0	0	0	0	0	0	0	0	0
Ruben Rivera, of	.000	2	1	0	0	0	0	0	0	0	1	0
Kenny Rogers, p	.000	2	0	0	0	0	0	0	0	0	0	0
Luis Sojo, 2b	.000	2	0	0	0	0	0	0	0	0	0	0
Darryl Strawberry, dh	.000	2	5	0	0	0	0	0	0	0	2	0
Dave Weathers, p	.000	2	0	0	0	0	0	0	0	0	0	0
John Wetteland, p	.000	3	0	0	0	0	0	0	0	0	0	0
Bernie Williams, of	.467	4	15	5	7	0	0	3	5	2	1	1
TOTAL	.264		140	16	37	4	0	4	15	13	20	1

PITCHER	W	L	ERA	G	GS	CG	SV	SHO	IP	H	ER	BB	SO
Brian Boehringer	1	0	6.75	2	0	0	0	0	1.1	3	1	2	0
David Cone	0	1	9.00	1	1	0	0	0	6.0	8	6	2	8
Jimmy Key	0	0	3.60	1	1	0	0	0	5.0	5	2	1	3
Graeme Lloyd	0	0	0.00	2	0	0	0	0	1.0	1	0	0	0
Jeff Nelson	1	0	0.00	2	0	0	0	0	3.2	2	0	2	5
Andy Pettitte	0	0	5.68	1	1	0	0	0	6.1	4	4	6	3
Mariano Rivera	0	0	0.00	2	0	0	0	0	4.2	0	0	1	1
Kenny Rogers	0	0	9.00	2	1	0	0	0	2.0	5	2	2	1
Dave Weathers	1	0	0.00	2	0	0	0	0	5.0	1	0	0	5
John Wetteland	0	0	0.00	3	0	0	2	0	4.0	2	0	4	4
TOTAL	3	1	3.46	18	4	0	2	0	39.0	31	15	20	30

TEX (W)

PLAYER/POS	AVG	G	AB	R	H	2B	3B	HR	RB	BB	SO	SB
Damon Buford, pr	.000	2	0	0	0	0	0	0	0	0	0	0
John Burkett, p	.000	1	0	0	0	0	0	0	0	0	0	0
Will Clark, 1b	.125	4	16	1	2	0	0	0	0	3	2	0
Dennis Cook, p	.000	2	0	0	0	0	0	0	0	0	0	0
Kevin Elster, ss	.333	4	12	2	4	2	0	0	0	3	2	1
Rene Gonzales, ss	.000	1	0	0	0	0	0	0	0	0	0	0
Juan Gonzalez, of	.438	4	16	5	7	0	0	5	9	3	2	0
Rusty Greer, of	.125	4	16	2	2	0	0	0	0	3	3	0
Darryl Hamilton, of	.158	4	19	0	3	0	0	0	0	0	2	0
Mike Henneman, p	.000	3	0	0	0	0	0	0	0	0	0	0
Ken Hill, p	.000	1	0	0	0	0	0	0	0	0	0	0
Mark McLemore, 2b	.133	4	15	1	2	0	0	0	2	0	4	0
Warren Newson, ph	.000	2	1	0	0	0	0	0	0	1	0	0
Darren Oliver, p	.000	1	0	0	0	0	0	0	0	0	0	0
Dean Palmer, 3b	.211	4	19	3	4	1	0	1	2	0	5	0
Danny Patterson, p	.000	1	0	0	0	0	0	0	0	0	0	0
Roger Pavlik, p	.000	1	0	0	0	0	0	0	0	0	0	0
Ivan Rodriguez, c	.375	4	16	1	6	1	0	0	2	2	3	0
Jeff Russell, p	.000	2	0	0	0	0	0	0	0	0	0	0
Mike Stanton, p	.000	3	0	0	0	0	0	0	0	0	0	0
Mickey Tettleton, dh	.083	4	12	1	1	0	0	0	1	5	7	0
Ed Vosberg, p	.000	1	0	0	0	0	0	0	0	0	0	0
Bobby Witt, p	.000	1	0	0	0	0	0	0	0	0	0	0
TOTAL	.218		142	16	31	4	0	6	16	20	30	1

PITCHER	W	L	ERA	G	GS	CG	SV	SHO	IP	H	ER	BB	SO
John Burkett	1	0	2.00	1	1	1	0	0	9.0	10	2	1	7
Dennis Cook	0	0	0.00	2	0	0	0	0	1.1	0	0	1	0
Mike Henneman	0	0	0.00	3	0	0	0	0	1.0	1	0	1	1
Ken Hill	0	0	4.50	1	1	0	0	0	6.0	5	3	3	1
Darren Oliver	0	1	3.38	1	1	0	0	0	8.0	6	3	2	3
Danny Patterson	0	0	0.00	1	0	0	0	0	0.1	1	0	0	0
Roger Pavlik	0	1	6.75	1	0	0	0	0	2.2	4	2	0	1
Jeff Russell	0	0	3.00	2	0	0	0	0	3.0	3	1	0	1
Mike Stanton	0	1	2.70	3	0	0	0	0	3.1	2	1	3	3
Ed Vosberg	0	0	INF	1	0	0	0	0	0.0	1	0	0	0
Bobby Witt	0	0	8.10	1	1	0	0	0	3.1	4	3	2	3
TOTAL	1	3	3.55	17	4	1	0	0	38.0	37	15	13	20

GAME ONE AT NY OCT 1

				R	H	E
TEX	000	501	000	6	8	0
NY	100	100	000	2	19	0

Pitchers: BURKETT vs CONE, Lloyd (7), Weathers (8)
Home Runs: Gonzalez-TEX, Palmer-TEX
Attendance: 57,205

GAME TWO AT NY OCT 2

					R	H	E
TEX	013	000	000	000	4	8	1
NY	010	100	110	001	5	8	0

Pitchers: Hill, Cook (7), Russell (8), STANTON (10), Henneman (12) vs Pettitte, Rivera (7), Wetteland (10), Lloyd (12), Nelson (12), Rogers (12), BOEHRINGER (12)
Home Runs: Gonzalez-TEX (2), Fielder-NY
Attendance: 57,156

GAME THREE AT TEX OCT 4

				R	H	E
NY	100	000	002	3	7	1
TEX	000	110	000	2	6	1

Pitchers: Key, NELSON (6), Wetteland (9) vs OLIVER, Henneman (9), Stanton (9)
Home Runs: Williams-NY, Gonzalez-TEX
Attendance: 50,860

GAME FOUR AT TEX OCT 5

				R	H	E
NY	000	310	101	6	12	1
TEX	022	000	000	4	9	0

Pitchers: Rogers, Boehringer (3), WEATHERS (4), Rivera (7), Wetteland (9) vs Witt, Patterson (4), Cook (4), PAVLIK (5), Vosberg (7), Russell (7), Stanton (8), Henneman (9)
Home Runs: Williams-NY (2), Gonzalez-TEX
Attendance: 50,066

Baltimore Orioles (WC), 3; Cleveland Indians (C), 1

An ugly spitting incident by Roberto Alomar overshadowed Baltimore's first trip to the postseason since 1983. Alomar spit at umpire John Hirschbeck during the last series of the regular season and that led the umpires to threaten to strike the postseason if Alomar was not suspended immediately. He was not suspended, the umpires (thanks to a court order) did not strike, and the fans both cheered Alomar (in Baltimore) and booed him (in Cleveland). But in the end, Alomar was the hero in the Orioles' unlikely win over the team with the best record in baseball.

Roberto Alomar was not the only player to come through with a big home run. Brady Anderson, the poster boy for "Year of the Home Run" with 50 regular-season clouts, started the series with a home run to lead off Game 1. The Orioles followed suit three more times, including a grand slam by Bobby Bonilla and two home runs by B.J. Surhoff, as the Orioles cruised to a 10-4 win. The Indians battled back from a 4-0 deficit to tie Game 2, but the difference was the way relief pitchers handled bases loaded situations in the eighth inning. In the top of the inning, the Indians had the bases loaded with no one out and the five-six-seven batters due up. Julio Franco hit a long sacrifice fly to tie the game, but reliever Armando Benitez came back to strike out Manny Ramirez and Sandy Alomar Jr. to end the threat. In the bottom of the eighth, the Orioles loaded the bases with none out and Indians reliever Paul Assenmacher got Surhoff to ground back to the mound. Assenmacher got the force out at home, but catcher Sandy Alomar's return throw to first bounced and could not be handled by Jeff Kent as Cal Ripken crossed the plate. The Indians argued that Surhoff ran on the inside route to the base and should have been ruled out automatically. This time, the umpires were on Baltimore's side and the O's went on to win, 7-4, to take a two games to none lead.

Relief pitching was again the difference in Game 3, but it was the Indians, not the Orioles who got the better of it at Jacobs Field. Jesse Orosco walked the bases loaded in the seventh inning and Benitez entered a 4-4 game with the chance to douse another Tribe rally. Albert Belle's grand slam broke the tie and shattered Baltimore's bid for a sweep. Game 4 was an uncharacteristic pitcher's duel. Charles Nagy, who had been hit hard by the O's in the opener, fanned 12 batters in six innings and four relievers held Baltimore to two runs through eight innings.

BAL (E)

PLAYER/POS	AVG	G	AB	R	H	2B	3B	HR	RB	BB	SO	SB
Manny Alexander, dh-1	.000	3	0	2	0	0	0	0	0	0	0	0
Roberto Alomar, 2b	.294	4	17	2	5	0	0	1	4	2	3	0
Brady Anderson, of	.294	4	17	3	5	0	0	2	4	2	3	0
Armando Benitez, p	.000	3	0	0	0	0	0	0	0	0	0	0
Bobby Bonilla, of	.200	4	15	4	3	0	0	2	5	4	6	0
Mike Devereaux, of-3	.000	4	1	0	0	0	0	0	0	0	0	0
Scott Erickson, p	.000	1	0	0	0	0	0	0	0	0	0	0
Chris Hoiles, c	.143	4	7	1	1	0	0	0	0	3	3	0
Pete Incaviglia, of	.200	2	5	1	1	0	0	0	0	0	4	0
Terry Mathews, p	.000	3	0	0	0	0	0	0	0	0	0	0
Eddie Murray, dh	.400	4	15	1	6	1	0	0	1	3	4	1
Mike Mussina, p	.000	1	0	0	0	0	0	0	0	0	0	0
Randy Myers, p	.000	3	0	0	0	0	0	0	0	0	0	0
Jesse Orosco, p	.000	4	0	0	0	0	0	0	0	0	0	0
Rafael Palmeiro, 1b	.176	4	17	4	3	1	0	1	2	1	6	0
Mark Parent, c	.200	4	5	0	1	0	0	0	0	0	2	0
Arthur Lee Rhodes, p	.000	2	0	0	0	0	0	0	0	0	0	0
Cal Ripken, ss	.444	4	18	2	8	3	0	0	2	0	3	0
B.J. Surhoff, of-3	.385	4	13	3	5	0	0	3	5	0	1	0
David Wells, p	.000	2	0	0	0	0	0	0	0	0	0	0
Todd Zeile, 3b	.263	4	19	2	5	1	0	0	0	2	5	0
TOTAL	.289		149	25	43	6	0	9	23	17	40	1

PITCHER	W	L	ERA	G	GS	CG	SV	SHO	IP	H	ER	BB	SO
Armando Benitez	2	0	2.25	3	0	0	0	0	4.0	1	1	2	6
Scott Erickson	0	0	4.05	1	1	0	0	0	6.2	6	3	2	6
Terry Mathews	0	0	0.00	3	0	0	0	0	2.2	3	0	1	2
Mike Mussina	0	0	4.50	1	1	0	0	0	6.0	7	3	2	6
Randy Myers	0	0	0.00	3	0	0	2	0	3.0	0	0	0	3
Jesse Orosco	0	1	36.00	4	0	0	0	0	1.0	2	4	3	2
Arthur Lee Rhodes	0	0	9.00	2	0	0	0	0	1.0	1	1	1	1
David Wells	1	0	4.61	2	2	0	0	0	13.2	15	7	4	6
TOTAL	3	1	4.50	19	4	0	2	0	38.0	35	19	15	32

CLE (C)

PLAYER/POS	AVG	G	AB	R	H	2B	3B	HR	RB	BB	SO	SB
Sandy Alomar, c	.125	4	16	0	2	0	0	0	3	0	2	0
Paul Assenmacher, p	.000	3	0	0	0	0	0	0	0	0	0	0
Albert Belle, of	.200	4	15	2	3	0	0	2	6	3	2	1
Casey Candaele, dh-1	.000	2	0	1	0	0	0	0	0	1	0	0
Alan Embree, p	.000	3	0	0	0	0	0	0	0	0	0	0
Julio Franco, 1b-3,dh-1	.133	4	15	1	2	0	0	0	1	1	6	0
Brian Giles, ph	.000	1	1	0	0	0	0	0	0	0	1	0
Orel Hershiser, p	.000	1	0	0	0	0	0	0	0	0	0	0
Jeff Kent, 3b-2,1b-1, 2b-1	.125	4	8	2	1	1	0	0	0	0	0	0
Kenny Lofton, of	.167	4	18	3	3	0	0	0	1	2	3	5
Jack McDowell, p	.000	1	0	0	0	0	0	0	0	0	0	0
Jose Mesa, p	.000	2	0	0	0	0	0	0	0	0	0	0
Charles Nagy, p	.000	2	0	0	0	0	0	0	0	0	0	0
Chad Ogea, p	.000	1	0	0	0	0	0	0	0	0	0	0
Tony Pena, c	.000	1	0	0	0	0	0	0	0	0	0	0
Eric Plunk, p	.000	3	0	0	0	0	0	0	0	0	0	0
Manny Ramirez, of	.375	4	16	4	6	2	0	2	2	1	4	0
Kevin Seitzer, dh-3,1b-1	.294	4	17	1	5	1	0	0	4	2	4	1
Paul Shuey, p	.000	3	0	0	0	0	0	0	0	0	0	0
Julian Tavarez, p	.000	2	0	0	0	0	0	0	0	0	0	0
Jim Thome, 3b	.300	4	10	1	3	0	0	0	0	1	5	0
Jose Vizcaino, 2b	.333	3	12	1	4	2	0	0	1	1	1	0
Omar Vizquel, ss	.429	4	14	4	6	1	0	0	2	3	4	4
Nigel Wilson, ph	.000	1	1	0	0	0	0	0	0	0	0	0
TOTAL	.245		143	20	35	7	0	4	20	15	32	11

PITCHER	W	L	ERA	G	GS	CG	SV	SHO	IP	H	ER	BB	SO
Paul Assenmacher	1	0	0.00	3	0	0	0	0	1.2	0	0	1	2
Alan Embree	0	0	9.00	3	0	0	0	0	1.0	0	1	0	1
Orel Hershiser	0	0	5.40	1	1	0	0	0	5.0	7	3	3	3
Jack McDowell	0	0	6.35	1	1	0	0	0	5.2	6	4	1	5
Jose Mesa	0	1	3.86	2	0	0	0	0	4.2	8	2	0	7
Charles Nagy	0	1	7.15	2	2	0	0	0	11.1	15	9	5	13
Chad Ogea	0	0	0.00	1	0	0	0	0	0.1	0	0	1	0
Eric Plunk	0	1	6.75	3	0	0	0	0	4.0	1	3	2	6
Paul Shuey	0	0	9.00	3	0	0	0	0	2.0	5	2	2	2
Julian Tavarez	0	0	0.00	2	0	0	0	0	1.1	1	0	2	1
TOTAL	1	3	5.84	21	4	0	0	0	37.0	43	24	17	40

Cleveland closer Jose Mesa had a 3-2 lead and a chance to force Game 5, but Roberto Alomar came through with a single to tie the game in the ninth. Mesa faced Alomar again in the 12th and he responded with a 402-foot home run to center for a 4-3 lead. Third baseman Todd Zeile, a converted catcher and a late-season pickup, made a great play on a bunt by Jose Vizcaino to get the first out in the bottom of the 12th and reliever Randy Myers did the rest. The Orioles, who struck out a postseason-record 23 times in the game, still found a way to get the bat on the ball when it counted.

GAME ONE AT BAL OCT 1

		R	H	E
CLE	010 200 100	4	10	0
BAL	112 005 10X	10	10	1

Pitchers: NAGY, Embree (6), Shuey (6), Tavarez (8) vs WELLS, Orosco (7), Mathews (7), Rhodes (8), Myers (9)
Home Runs: Ramirez-CLE, Anderson-BAL, Surhoff-BAL (2), Bonilla-BAL
Attendance: 47,644

GAME TWO AT BAL OCT 2

		R	H	E
CLE	000 003 010	4	8	2
BAL	100 030 03X	7	9	0

Pitchers: Hershiser, PLUNK (6), Assenmacher (8), Tavarez (8) vs Erickson, Orosco (7), BENITEZ (8), Myers (9)
Home Runs: Belle-CLE, Anderson-BAL
Attendance: 48,970

GAME THREE AT CLE OCT 4

		R	H	E
BAL	010 300 000	4	8	2
CLE	120 100 41X	9	10	0

Pitchers: Mussina, OROSCO (7), Benitez (7), Rhodes (8), Mathews (8) vs McDowell, Embree (6), Shuey (7), ASSENMACHER (7), Plunk (8), Mesa (9)
Home Runs: Surhoff-BAL, Ramirez-CLE, Belle-CLE
Attendance: 44,250

GAME FOUR AT CLE OCT 5

		R	H	E
BAL	020 000 001 001	4	14	1
CLE	000 210 000 000	3	7	1

Pitchers: Wells, Mathews (8), Orosco (9), BENITEZ (10), Myers (12) vs Nagy, Embree (7), Shuey (7), Assenmacher (7), Plunk (8), MESA (9), Ogea (12)
Home Runs: Palmeiro-BAL, Bonilla-BAL, R.Alomar-BAL
Attendance: 44,280

The Cards and Braves last met in the NLCS in 1982—a 3-0 Cardinals sweep. Fourteen years later, the Cardinals were just as tough, but John Smoltz beat the Cards in the opener in Atlanta, 4-2. In Game 2, St. Louis turned the tables. Four-time Cy Young winner Greg Maddux was touched for three runs in the first three innings, but the Braves rallied to tie the game on a two-run home run by Marquis Grissom and a single by Ryan Klesko. After the Cards took a 4-3 lead in the seventh on a Ray Lankford sacrifice fly, Maddux fanned Ron Gant and intentionally walked Brian Jordan to pitch to Gary Gaetti. Gaetti hit the first pitch for a grand slam and finished the scoring at 8-3.

The Cards kept the pressure on in St. Louis. Gant hit a pair of home runs off Tom Glavine and Cardinals starter Donovan Osborne pitched seven strong innings in Game 3. Dennis Eckersley came on in the ninth to earn his fourth save of the postseason in the 3-2 Cards win. The Braves handed Denny Neagle a 3-0 lead in Game 4 on home runs by Klesko and Mark Lemke plus an RBI single by Jermaine Dye. But the Cards came back. Neagle got the first two outs in the seventh, but John Mabry singled and Tom Pagnozzi walked. Dmitri Young greeted reliever Greg McMichael with triple that plated two runs. Luis Alicea, followed with a walk and the Cards evened the score on an infield hit by Royce Clayton. In the eighth, Jordan lined a 2-1 pitch over the wall for a 4-3 lead.

The series' second part commenced in Game 5—and it was all Atlanta. The Braves had a 5-0 lead after half an inning and that was more than enough for John Smoltz. But they kept on hitting, collecting 22 hits and sending Stottlemyre to the showers in the second. McGriff and Javier Lopez added home runs in the 14-0 rout to send the series back to Atlanta. In Game 6 the only run the Cards got came on a wild pitch by Mark Wohlers in relief of Greg Maddux.

The Cards never even had a chance to do any damage against Glavine in Game 7. Osborne allowed three runs on RBIs by McGriff, Dye, and Andruw Jones, but the crushing blow came off the bat of Glavine. His line drive to left went for a three-run triple and a 6-0 lead. Atlanta added nine more runs, including home runs by MVP Lopez and Andruw Jones, who, at 19, became the youngest player to hit a postseason round-tripper. The Braves also became the first team to come back from a three games to one deficit to win the NLCS. From Game 5 on, the Braves outscored the Cards, 32-1.

Atlanta Braves (E), 4; St. Louis Cardinals (C), 3

ATL (E)

PLAYER/POS	AVG	G	AB	R	H	2B	3B	HR	RB	BB	SO	SB
Steve Avery, p	.000	2	0	0	0	0	0	0	0	0	0	0
Rafael Belliard, ss	.667	4	6	0	4	0	0	0	2	0	0	0
Mike Bielecki, p	.000	3	0	0	0	0	0	0	0	0	0	0
Jeff Blauser, ss	.176	7	17	5	3	0	1	0	2	4	6	0
Brad Clontz, p	.000	1	0	0	0	0	0	0	0	0	0	0
Jermaine Dye, of	.214	7	28	2	6	1	0	0	4	1	7	0
Tom Glavine, p	.167	2	6	0	1	0	1	0	3	0	3	0
Marquis Grissom, of	.286	7	35	7	10	1	0	1	3	0	8	2
Andruw Jones, of	.222	5	9	3	2	0	0	1	3	3	2	0
Chipper Jones, 3b	.440	7	25	6	11	2	0	0	4	3	1	1
Ryan Klesko, of	.250	6	16	1	4	0	0	1	3	2	6	0
Mark Lemke, 2b	.444	7	27	4	12	2	0	1	5	4	2	0
Javy Lopez, c	.542	7	24	8	13	5	0	2	6	3	1	1
Greg Maddux, p	.000	2	4	0	0	0	0	0	0	0	2	0
Fred McGriff, 1b	.250	7	28	6	7	0	1	2	7	3	5	0
Greg McMichael, p	.000	3	0	0	0	0	0	0	0	0	0	0
Mike Mordecai, 2b-2, 3b-1	.250	4	4	1	1	0	0	0	0	0	1	0
Denny Neagle, p	.500	2	2	0	1	0	0	0	0	0	0	0
Terry Pendleton, 3b-2	.000	6	6	0	0	0	0	0	0	1	3	0
Eddie Perez, c	.000	4	1	0	0	0	0	0	0	1	0	0
Luis Polonia, ph	.000	3	3	0	0	0	0	0	0	0	0	0
John Smoltz, p	.286	2	7	1	2	0	0	0	1	0	3	0
Terrell Wade, p	.000	1	0	0	0	0	0	0	0	0	0	0
Mark Wohlers, p	.000	3	1	0	0	0	0	0	0	0	1	0
TOTAL	.309		249	44	77	11	3	8	43	25	51	4

PITCHER	W	L	ERA	G	GS	CG	SV	SHO	IP	H	ER	BB	SO
Steve Avery	0	0	0.00	2	0	0	0	0	2.0	2	0	1	1
Mike Bielecki	0	0	0.00	3	0	0	0	0	3.0	0	0	1	5
Brad Clontz	0	0	0.00	1	0	0	0	0	0.2	0	0	0	0
Tom Glavine	1	1	2.08	2	2	0	0	0	13.0	10	3	0	9
Greg Maddux	1	1	2.51	2	2	0	0	0	14.1	15	4	2	10
Greg McMichael	0	1	9.00	3	0	0	0	0	2.0	4	2	1	3
Denny Neagle	0	0	2.35	2	1	0	0	0	7.2	2	2	3	8
John Smoltz	2	0	1.20	2	2	0	0	0	15.0	12	2	3	12
Terrell Wade	0	0	0.00	1	0	0	0	0	0.1	0	0	0	1
Mark Wohlers	0	0	0.00	3	0	0	2	0	3.0	0	0	0	4
TOTAL	4	3	1.92	21	7	0	2	0	61.0	45	13	11	53

STL (C)

PLAYER/POS	AVG	G	AB	R	H	2B	3B	HR	RB	BB	SO	SB
Luis Alicea, 2b	.000	5	8	0	0	0	0	0	0	2	1	0
Alan Benes, p	.000	2	1	0	0	0	0	0	0	0	1	0
Andy Benes, p	.250	3	4	0	1	1	0	0	0	1	2	0
Royce Clayton, ss	.350	5	20	4	7	0	0	0	1	1	4	1
Dennis Eckersley, p	.000	3	0	0	0	0	0	0	0	0	0	0
Tony Fossas, p	.000	5	0	0	0	0	0	0	0	0	0	0
Gary Gaetti, 3b	.292	7	24	1	7	0	0	1	4	1	5	0
Mike Gallego, 2b-5,3b-2	.143	7	14	1	2	0	0	0	0	1	3	0
Ron Gant, of	.240	7	25	3	6	1	0	2	4	2	6	0
Rick Honeycutt, p	.000	5	0	0	0	0	0	0	0	0	0	0
Danny Jackson, p	.000	1	1	0	0	0	0	0	0	0	1	0
Brian Jordan, of	.240	7	25	3	6	1	1	1	2	1	3	0
Ray Lankford, of-3	.000	5	13	1	0	0	0	0	1	1	4	0
John Mabry, 1b-6,of-2	.261	7	23	1	6	0	0	0	0	0	6	0
T. J. Mathews, p	.000	2	0	0	0	0	0	0	0	0	0	0
Willie McGee, of-5	.333	6	15	0	5	0	0	0	0	0	3	0
Miguel Mejia, of-2	.000	3	1	1	0	0	0	0	0	0	1	0
Donovan Osborne, p	.000	2	3	0	0	0	0	0	0	0	3	0
Tom Pagnozzi, c	.158	7	19	1	3	1	0	0	1	1	4	0
Mark Petkovsek, p	.000	6	0	0	0	0	0	0	0	0	0	0
Danny Sheaffer, c	.000	2	3	0	0	0	0	0	0	0	1	0
Ozzie Smith, ss-2	.000	3	9	0	0	0	0	0	0	0	1	0
Todd Stottlemyre, p	.000	3	2	0	0	0	0	0	0	0	0	0
Mark Sweeney, of-2	.000	5	4	1	0	0	0	0	0	0	2	0
Dmitri Young, 1b-2	.286	4	7	1	2	0	1	0	2	0	2	0
TOTAL	.204		221	18	45	4	2	4	15	11	53	1

PITCHER	W	L	ERA	G	GS	CG	SV	SHO	IP	H	ER	BB	SO
Alan Benes	0	1	2.84	2	1	0	0	0	6.1	3	2	2	5
Andy Benes	0	0	5.28	3	2	0	0	0	15.1	19	9	3	9
Dennis Eckersley	1	0	0.00	3	0	0	1	0	3.1	2	0	0	4
Tony Fossas	0	0	2.08	5	0	0	0	0	4.1	1	1	3	1
Rick Honeycutt	0	0	9.00	5	0	0	0	0	4.0	5	4	3	3
Danny Jackson	0	0	9.00	1	0	0	0	0	3.0	7	3	3	3
T. J. Mathews	0	0	0.00	2	0	0	0	0	0.2	2	0	1	2
Donovan Osborne	1	1	9.39	2	2	0	0	0	7.2	12	8	4	6
Mark Petkovsek	0	1	7.36	6	0	0	0	0	7.1	11	6	3	7
Todd Stottlemyre	1	1	12.38	3	2	0	0	0	8.0	15	11	3	11
TOTAL	3	4	6.60	32	7	0	1	0	60.0	77	44	25	51

GAME ONE AT ATL OCT 9

				R	H	E
STL	010	000	100	2	5	1
ATL	000	020	02X	4	9	0

Pitchers: An.Benes, PETKOVSEK (7), Fossas (8), Mathews (8) vs SMOLTZ, Wohlers (9)
Attendance: 48,686

GAME TWO AT ATL OCT 10

				R	H	E
STL	102	000	500	8	11	2
ATL	002	001	000	3	5	2

Pitchers: STOTTLEMYRE, Petkovsek (7), Honeycutt (8), Eckersley (8) vs MADDUX, McMichael (7), Neagle (8), Avery (9)
Home Runs: Gaetti-STL, Grissom-ATL
Attendance: 52,067

GAME THREE AT STL OCT 12

				R	H	E
ATL	100	000	010	2	8	1
STL	200	001	00X	3	7	0

Pitchers: GLAVINE, Bielecki (7), McMichael (8) vs OSBORNE, Petkovsek (8), Honeycutt (9), Eckersley (9)
Home Runs: Gant-STL (2)
Attendance: 56,769

GAME FOUR AT STL OCT 13

				R	H	E
ATL	010	002	000	3	9	1
STL	000	000	31X	4	5	0

Pitchers: Neagle, McMICHAEL (7), Wohlers (8) vs An.Benes, Fossas (6), Mathews (6), Al.Benes (6), Honeycutt (8), ECKERSLEY (9)
Home Runs: Klesko-ATL, Lemke-ATL, Jordan-STL
Attendance: 56,764

GAME FIVE AT STL OCT 14

				R	H	E
ATL	520	310	012	14	22	0
STL	000	000	000	0	7	0

Pitchers: SMOLTZ, Bielecki (8), Wade (9), Clontz (9) vs STOTTLEMYRE, Jackson (2), Fossas (5), Petkovsek (7), Honeycutt (9)
Home Runs: Lopez-ATL, McGriff-ATL
Attendance: 56,782

GAME SIX AT ATL OCT 16

				R	H	E
STL	000	000	010	1	6	1
ATL	010	010	01X	3	7	0

Pitchers: Al.BENES, Fossas (6), Petkovsek (6), Stottlemyre (9) vs MADDUX, Wohlers (9)
Attendance: 52,067

GAME SEVEN AT ATL OCT 17

				R	H	E
STL	000	000	000	0	4	2
ATL	600	403	20X	15	17	0

Pitchers: OSBORNE, An.Benes (1), Petkovsek (6), Honeycutt (6), Fossas (8) vs GLAVINE, Bielecki (8), Avery (9)
Home Runs: Lopez-ATL, A.Jones-ATL, McGriff-ATL
Attendance: 52,067

The Yankees and the Orioles had gone a combined 28 years without a pennant, but that was going to change in 1996—for one team at least. The Orioles had the early advantage in Game 1 on home runs from Brady Anderson and Rafael Palmeiro, but the Yankees cut the lead to 4-3 after seven. Derek Jeter led off the eighth with a long fly to right that Tony Tarasco seemed to have lined up at the wall, but fate—in the form of a 12-year-old boy—intervened. Yankees fan Jeff Maier reached over the fence and knocked the ball into the stands. Right field umpire Rich Garcia ruled it a home run despite protests from several Orioles, including manager Davey Johnson, who was ejected. (Upon seeing a replay, Garcia admitted he made the wrong call, but AL president Gene Budig denied Baltimore's protest.) The Orioles got out of further trouble in the eighth, but Game 1 was tied at 4-4. With Randy Myers pitching in the bottom of the 11th, Bernie Williams hit a 1-1 pitch deep to left to give the Yanks the improbable win.

Baltimore bounced back in Game 2. Orioles southpaw David Wells spotted the Yanks a pair of first inning runs, but Wells improved to 10-1 at Yankee Stadium. Todd Zeile's two-run home run off David Cone tied the game in the third and Palmeiro's two-run shot off reliever Jeff Nelson gave Baltimore the lead in the seventh. The Orioles added a run in the eighth to go up 5-3, but Benitez retired Cecil Fielder and Tino Martinez with two on in the ninth to even the series at one game apiece.

The teams traveled to Camden Yards for the next three games, but the Yankees, who were 6-0 in Baltimore during the regular season, continued to treat the park like a home away from home. Zeile's two-run home run in the first looked like it might stand up as Mike Mussina was masterful through seven and two thirds innings. He never got that last out, though. The Yanks rallied to tie in the eighth then Martinez followed with a double to left field and Williams stopped at third; when Zeile's fake throw to second trickled away, Williams dashed home with the go-ahead run.

Darryl Strawberry took Game 4 of the ALCS into his own hands. His solo home run in the second gave the Yanks a 3-1 lead and his two-run blast in the eighth capped off New York's 8-4 victory. Mariano Rivera bailed New York out of a bases-loaded, no-out jam in the eighth and Wetteland retired the Orioles in order in the ninth.

Jim Leyritz started the decisive third-inning rally in Game 5 with a home run off Scott Erickson. Jeter singled and Wade Boggs ended an 0-for-23 playoff skid with an infield hit to set the stage for the rally that put the Birds away for good. Series MVP Bernie Williams sent a tailor-made double-play grounder to Roberto Alomar, but the second baseman let it go through his legs. One out later, Fielder cleared the basepaths with a three-run home run for a 5-0 lead. Strawberry followed with a 446-foot drive to tie the 1993 Blue Jays for the most home runs (10) in an LCS. Andy Pettitte and John Wetteland held off Baltimore to bring the World Series back to Yankee Stadium for the first time since 1981 and send manager Joe Torre to the Fall Classic for the first time after a record 4,272 games as a player and manager.

New York Yankees (E), 4; Baltimore Orioles (WC), 1

NY (E)

PLAYER/POS	AVG	G	AB	R	H	2B	3B	HR	RB	BB	SO	SB
Mike Aldrete, ph	.000	1	0	0	0	0	0	0	0	0	0	0
Wade Boggs, 3b	.133	3	15	1	2	0	0	0	0	1	3	0
David Cone, p	.000	1	0	0	0	0	0	0	0	0	0	0
Mariano Duncan, 2b	.200	4	15	0	3	2	0	0	0	0	3	0
Cecil Fielder, dh	.167	5	18	3	3	0	0	2	8	4	5	0
Andy Fox, dh	.000	2	0	0	0	0	0	0	0	0	0	0
Joe Girardi, c	.250	4	12	1	3	0	1	0	0	1	3	0
Charlie Hayes, 3b-2, dh-1	.143	4	7	0	1	0	0	0	0	2	2	0
Derek Jeter, ss	.417	5	24	5	10	2	0	1	1	0	5	2
Jimmy Key, p	.000	1	0	0	0	0	0	0	0	0	0	0
Jim Leyritz, c-2,of-1	.250	3	8	1	2	0	0	1	2	1	4	0
Graeme Lloyd, p	.000	2	0	0	0	0	0	0	0	0	0	0
Tino Martinez, 1b	.182	5	22	3	4	1	0	0	0	0	2	0
Jeff Nelson, p	.000	2	0	0	0	0	0	0	0	0	0	0
Paul O'Neill, of	.273	4	11	1	3	0	0	1	2	3	2	0
Andy Pettitte, p	.000	2	0	0	0	0	0	0	0	0	0	0
Tim Raines, of	.267	5	15	2	4	1	0	0	0	1	1	0
Mariano Rivera, p	.000	2	0	0	0	0	0	0	0	0	0	0
Kenny Rogers, p	.000	1	0	0	0	0	0	0	0	0	0	0
Luis Sojo, 2b	.200	3	5	0	1	0	0	0	0	0	1	0
Darryl Strawberry, of	.417	4	12	4	5	0	0	3	5	2	2	0
Dave Weathers, p	.000	2	0	0	0	0	0	0	0	0	0	0
John Wetteland, p	.000	4	0	0	0	0	0	0	0	0	0	0
Bernie Williams, of	.474	5	19	6	9	3	0	2	6	5	4	1
TOTAL	.273		183	27	50	9	1	10	24	20	37	3

PITCHER	W	L	ERA	G	GS	CG	SV	SHO	IP	H	ER	BB	SO
David Cone	0	0	3.00	1	1	0	0	0	6.0	5	2	5	5
Jimmy Key	1	0	2.25	1	1	0	0	0	8.0	3	2	1	5
Graeme Lloyd	0	0	0.00	2	0	0	0	0	1.2	0	0	0	1
Jeff Nelson	0	1	11.57	2	0	0	0	0	2.1	5	3	0	2
Andy Pettitte	1	0	3.60	2	2	0	0	0	15.0	10	6	5	7
Mariano Rivera	1	0	0.00	2	0	0	0	0	4.0	6	0	1	5
Kenny Rogers	0	0	12.00	1	1	0	0	0	3.0	5	4	2	3
Dave Weathers	1	0	0.00	2	0	0	0	0	3.0	3	0	0	0
John Wetteland	0	0	4.50	4	0	0	1	0	4.0	2	2	1	5
TOTAL	4	1	3.64	17	5	0	1	0	47.0	39	19	15	33

BAL (E)

PLAYER/POS	AVG	G	AB	R	H	2B	3B	HR	RB	BB	SO	SB
Roberto Alomar, 2b	.217	5	23	2	5	2	0	0	1	0	4	0
Brady Anderson, of	.190	5	21	5	4	1	0	1	1	3	5	0
Armando Benitez, p	.000	3	0	0	0	0	0	0	0	0	0	0
Bobby Bonilla, of	.050	5	20	1	1	0	0	1	2	1	4	0
Rocky Coppinger, p	.000	1	0	0	0	0	0	0	0	0	0	0
Mike Devereaux, of	.000	3	2	0	0	0	0	0	0	0	1	0
Scott Erickson, p	.000	2	0	0	0	0	0	0	0	0	0	0
Chris Hoiles, c	.167	4	12	1	2	0	0	1	2	1	3	0
Pete Incaviglia, dh	.500	1	2	1	1	0	0	0	0	0	0	0
Terry Mathews, p	.000	3	0	0	0	0	0	0	0	0	0	0
Alan Mills, p	.000	3	0	0	0	0	0	0	0	0	0	0
Eddie Murray, dh	.267	5	15	1	4	0	0	1	2	2	2	0
Mike Mussina, p	.000	1	0	0	0	0	0	0	0	0	0	0
Randy Myers, p	.000	3	0	0	0	0	0	0	0	0	0	0
Jesse Orosco, p	.000	4	0	0	0	0	0	0	0	0	0	0
Rafael Palmeiro, 1b	.235	5	17	4	4	0	0	2	4	4	4	0
Mark Parent, c	.167	2	6	0	1	0	0	0	0	0	2	0
Arthur Lee Rhodes, p	.000	3	0	0	0	0	0	0	0	0	0	0
Cal Ripken, ss	.250	5	20	1	5	1	0	0	0	1	4	0
B.J. Surhoff, of	.267	5	15	0	4	0	0	0	2	1	2	0
Tony Tarasco, of	.000	2	1	0	0	0	0	0	0	0	1	0
David Wells, p	.000	1	0	0	0	0	0	0	0	0	0	0
Todd Zeile, 3b	.364	5	22	3	8	0	0	3	5	2	1	0
TOTAL	.222		176	19	39	4	0	9	19	15	33	0

PITCHER	W	L	ERA	G	GS	CG	SV	SHO	IP	H	ER	BB	SO
Armando Benitez	0	0	7.71	3	0	0	1	0	2.1	3	2	3	2
Rocky Coppinger	0	1	8.44	1	1	0	0	0	5.1	6	5	1	3
Scott Erickson	0	1	2.38	2	2	0	0	0	11.1	14	3	4	8
Terry Mathews	0	0	0.00	3	0	0	0	0	2.1	0	0	2	3
Alan Mills	0	0	3.86	3	0	0	0	0	2.1	3	1	1	3
Mike Mussina	0	1	5.87	1	1	0	0	0	7.2	8	5	2	6
Randy Myers	0	1	2.25	3	0	0	0	0	4.0	4	1	3	2
Jesse Orosco	0	0	4.50	4	0	0	0	0	2.0	2	1	1	2
Arthur Lee Rhodes	0	0	0.00	3	0	0	0	0	2.0	2	0	0	2
David Wells	1	0	4.05	1	1	0	0	0	6.2	8	3	3	6
TOTAL	1	4	4.11	24	5	0	1	0	46.0	50	21	20	37

GAME ONE AT NY OCT 9

		R	H	E
BAL	011 101 000 00	4	11	1
NY	110 000 110 01	5	11	0

Pitchers: Erickson, Orosco (7), Benitez (7), Rhodes (8), Mathews (9), MYERS (9) vs Pettitte, Nelson (8), Wetteland (9), RIVERA (10)
Home Runs: Anderson-BAL, Palmeiro-BAL, Jeter-NY, Williams-NY
Attendance: 56,495

GAME TWO AT NY OCT 10

		R	H	E
BAL	002 000 210	5	10	0
NY	200 000 100	3	11	1

Pitchers: WELLS, Mills (7), Orosco (7), Myers (9), Benitez (9) vs Cone, NELSON (7), Lloyd (8), Weathers (9)
Home Runs: Zeile-BAL, Palmeiro-BAL
Attendance: 56,432

GAME THREE AT BAL OCT 11

		R	H	E
NY	000 100 040	5	8	0
BAL	200 000 000	2	3	2

Pitchers: KEY, Wetteland (9) vs MUSSINA, Orosco (8), Mathews (9)
Home Runs: Fielder-NY, Zeile-BAL
Attendance: 48,635

GAME FOUR AT BAL OCT 12

		R	H	E
NY	210 200 030	8	9	0
BAL	101 200 000	4	11	0

Pitchers: Rogers, WEATHERS (4), Lloyd (6), Rivera (7), Wetteland (9) vs COPPINGER, Rhodes (6), Mills (7), Orosco (8), Benitez (8), Mathews (9)
Home Runs: Williams-NY, Strawberry-NY (2), O'Neill-NY, Hoiles-BAL
Attendance: 48,974

GAME FIVE AT BAL OCT 13

		R	H	E
NY	006 000 000	6	11	0
BAL	000 001 012	4	4	1

Pitchers: PETTITTE, Wetteland (9) vs ERICKSON, Rhodes (6), Mills (7), Myers (8)
Home Runs: Leyritz-NY, Fielder-NY, Strawberry-NY, Zeile-BAL, Murray-BAL, Bonilla-BAL
Attendance: 48,718

New York Yankees (A), 4; Atlanta Braves (N), 2

New York looked disoriented in the opener, squandering opportunities early against John Smoltz, but it wasn't long before the Braves took advantage of Andy Pettitte. Andruw Jones, 19, became the youngest player in Series history to hit a homer in the second, and, an inning later, joined Gene Tenace as the second player to homer his first two times up in the Series. It was 9-0 before Wade Boggs broke up the no-hit bid by Smoltz in the fifth. Things didn't get much better for the Yanks the next night. Greg Maddux handcuffed New York on six hits in eight innings as Fred McGriff drove in three runs. The Braves steamrolled New York 16-1 in the first two games, and had outscored their postseason opposition 48-2 over their last five games.

Things changed in Atlanta. David Cone allowed just four hits through six, and RBI singles by Bernie Williams and Darryl Strawberry gave the Yankees a 2-1 lead against Tom Glavine. The Yankees got insurance in the form of a two-run home run by Williams and an RBI single by Luis Sojo in the eighth. The Braves battered Kenny Rogers for five runs in two-plus innings in Game 4 and Andruw Jones doubled off David Weathers for a 6-0 lead in the fifth. Right field umpire Tim Welke got in the way of Jermaine Dye and kept Derek Jeter's foul fly from being caught. Then Jeter singled; two hits, a walk and an error followed to cut Atlanta's lead in half. Closer Mark Wohlers came in to start the eighth and promptly gave up two hits. It looked like the Braves might escape when Mariano Duncan hit a double-play grounder to Rafael Belliard, but the shortstop botched it and only one out was recorded. Jim Leyritz then homered to tie the game. With runners on first and second in the 10th, Braves manager Bobby Cox opted to walk Williams to load the bases for Boggs. Steve Avery walked Boggs, to bring in the go-ahead run. The Yankees scored again and held on for the biggest comeback in the team's World Series history.

Things continued to go the Yankees' way in Game 5. New York's Andy Pettitte won the last game ever played at Fulton County Stadium because one of the game's best outfielders dropped a ball, and two gimpy outfielders made great catches to preserve the 1-0 victory. The only run Smoltz allowed was set up when a flyball bounced off Grissom's glove; Fielder plated the run with a double. Strawberry, playing despite a broken toe, crashed into the wall to take an extra-base hit away in the eighth, and Paul O'Neill, nursing a torn hamstring, reached to his right to snag Luis Polonia's line drive to end the game with the tying run at third.

The Yankees got good news on the only off-day of the Series. Manager Joe Torre's brother Frank, who won a World Series ring with the 1957 Braves, received a heart transplant after months of waiting for a donor. The good luck continued for Game 6. O'Neill doubled to start the third and Joe Girardi tripled him home; Jeter and Williams followed with RBI singles against Maddux. The Braves got a run when Dye walked with the bases loaded in the fourth, but Terry Pendleton grounded into a double play to end the threat. Key pitched into the sixth and Weathers, Lloyd, and Rivera got the Yanks to the ninth. Series MVP John Wetteland allowed a run but gained his fourth save of the Series when Mark Lemke popped up to Hayes in foul ground.

NY (A)

PLAYER/POS	AVG	G	AB	R	H	2B	3B	HR	RB	BB	SO	SB
Mike Aldrete, of-1	.000	2	1	0	0	0	0	0	0	0	0	0
Brian Boehringer, p	.000	2	0	0	0	0	0	0	0	0	0	0
Wade Boggs, 3b	.273	4	11	0	3	1	0	0	2	1	0	0
David Cone, p	.000	1	2	0	0	0	0	0	0	0	1	0
Mariano Duncan, 2b	.053	6	19	1	1	0	0	0	0	0	4	1
Cecil Fielder, 1b-3,dh-3	.391	6	23	1	9	2	0	0	2	2	2	0
Andy Fox, 2b-1,3b-1	.000	4	0	1	0	0	0	0	0	0	0	0
Joe Girardi, c	.200	4	10	1	2	0	1	0	1	1	2	0
Charlie Hayes, 3b-4, 1b-1	.188	5	16	2	3	0	0	0	1	1	5	0
Derek Jeter, ss	.250	6	20	5	5	0	0	0	1	4	6	1
Jimmy Key, p	.000	2	0	0	0	0	0	0	0	0	0	0
Jim Leyritz, c-3	.375	4	8	1	3	0	0	1	3	3	2	1
Graeme Lloyd, p	.000	4	1	0	0	0	0	0	0	0	0	0
Tino Martinez, 1b-5	.091	6	11	0	1	0	0	0	0	2	5	0
Jeff Nelson, p	.000	3	0	0	0	0	0	0	0	0	0	0
Paul O'Neill, of-4	.167	5	12	1	2	2	0	0	0	3	2	0
Andy Pettitte, p	.000	2	4	0	0	0	0	0	0	0	1	0
Tim Raines, of	.214	4	14	2	3	0	0	0	0	2	1	0
Mariano Rivera, p	.000	4	1	0	0	0	0	0	0	0	0	0
Kenny Rogers, p	1.000	1	1	0	1	0	0	0	0	0	0	0
Luis Sojo, 2b-3	.600	5	5	0	3	1	0	0	1	0	0	0
Darryl Strawberry, of	.188	5	16	0	3	0	0	0	1	4	6	0
Dave Weathers, p	.000	3	0	0	0	0	0	0	0	0	0	0
John Wetteland, p	.000	5	0	0	0	0	0	0	0	0	0	0
Bernie Williams, of	.167	6	24	3	4	0	0	1	4	3	6	1
TOTAL	.216		199	18	43	6	1	2	16	26	43	4

PITCHER	W	L	ERA	G	GS	CG	SV	SHO	IP	H	ER	BB	SO
Brian Boehringer	0	0	5.40	2	0	0	0	0	5.0	5	3	0	5
David Cone	1	0	1.50	1	1	0	0	0	6.0	4	1	4	3
Jimmy Key	1	1	3.97	2	2	0	0	0	11.1	15	5	5	1
Graeme Lloyd	1	0	0.00	4	0	0	0	0	2.2	0	0	0	4
Jeff Nelson	0	0	0.00	3	0	0	0	0	4.1	1	0	1	5
Andy Pettitte	1	1	5.91	2	2	0	0	0	10.2	11	7	4	5
Mariano Rivera	0	0	1.59	4	0	0	0	0	5.2	4	1	3	4
Kenny Rogers	0	0	22.50	1	1	0	0	0	2.0	5	5	2	0
Dave Weathers	0	0	3.00	3	0	0	0	0	3.0	2	1	3	3
John Wetteland	0	0	2.08	5	0	0	4	0	4.1	4	1	1	6
TOTAL	4	2	3.93	27	6	0	4	0	55.0	51	24	23	36

ATL (N)

PLAYER/POS	AVG	G	AB	R	H	2B	3B	HR	RB	BB	SO	SB
Steve Avery, p	.000	1	0	0	0	0	0	0	0	0	0	0
Rafael Belliard, ss-3	.000	4	0	0	0	0	0	0	0	0	0	0
Mike Bielecki, p	.000	2	1	0	0	0	0	0	0	0	1	0
Jeff Blauser, ss	.167	6	18	2	3	1	0	0	1	1	4	0
Brad Clontz, p	.000	3	0	0	0	0	0	0	0	0	0	0
Jermaine Dye, of	.118	5	17	0	2	0	0	0	1	1	1	0
Tom Glavine, p	.000	1	1	1	0	0	0	0	0	1	1	0
Marquis Grissom, of	.444	6	27	4	12	2	1	0	5	1	2	1
Andruw Jones, of	.400	6	20	4	8	1	0	2	6	3	6	1
Chipper Jones, 3b-6, ss-1	.286	6	21	3	6	3	0	0	3	4	2	1
Ryan Klesko, of-2, 1b-1,dh-1	.100	5	10	2	1	0	0	0	1	2	4	0
Mark Lemke, 2b	.231	6	26	2	6	1	0	0	2	0	3	0
Javy Lopez, c	.190	6	21	3	4	0	0	0	1	3	4	0
Greg Maddux, p	.000	2	0	0	0	0	0	0	0	0	0	0
Fred McGriff, 1b	.300	6	20	4	6	0	0	2	6	5	4	0
Greg McMichael, p	.000	2	0	0	0	0	0	0	0	0	0	0
Mike Mordecai, ph	.000	1	1	0	0	0	0	0	0	0	0	0
Denny Neagle, p	.000	2	1	0	0	0	0	0	0	0	1	0
Terry Pendleton, dh-2,3b-1	.222	4	9	1	2	1	0	0	0	1	1	0
Eddie Perez, c	.000	2	1	0	0	0	0	0	0	0	0	0
Luis Polonia, ph	.000	6	5	0	0	0	0	0	0	1	2	0
John Smoltz, p	.500	2	2	0	1	0	0	0	0	0	0	0
Terrell Wade, p	.000	2	0	0	0	0	0	0	0	0	0	0
Mark Wohlers, p	.000	4	0	0	0	0	0	0	0	0	0	0
TOTAL	.254		201	26	51	9	1	4	26	23	36	3

PITCHER	W	L	ERA	G	GS	CG	SV	SHO	IP	H	ER	BB	SO
Steve Avery	0	1	13.50	1	0	0	0	0	0.2	1	1	3	0
Mike Bielecki	0	0	0.00	2	0	0	0	0	3.0	0	0	3	6
Brad Clontz	0	0	0.00	3	0	0	0	0	1.2	1	0	1	2
Tom Glavine	0	1	1.29	1	1	0	0	0	7.0	4	1	3	8
Greg Maddux	1	1	1.72	2	2	0	0	0	15.2	14	3	1	5
Greg McMichael	0	0	27.00	2	0	0	0	0	1.0	5	3	0	1
Denny Neagle	0	0	3.00	2	1	0	0	0	6.0	5	2	4	3
John Smoltz	1	1	0.64	2	2	0	0	0	14.0	6	1	8	14
Terrell Wade	0	0	0.00	2	0	0	0	0	0.2	0	0	1	0
Mark Wohlers	0	0	6.23	4	0	0	0	0	4.1	7	3	2	4
TOTAL	2	4	2.33	21	6	0	0	0	54.0	43	14	26	43

GAME ONE AT NY OCT 20

				R	H	E
ATL	026	013	000	12	13	0
NY	000	010	000	1	4	1

Pitchers: SMOLTZ, McMichael (7), Neagle (8), Wade (9), Clontz (9) vs PETTITTE, Boehringer (3), Weathers (6), Nelson (8), Wetteland (9)
Home Runs: A.Jones-ATL (2), McGriff-ATL
Attendance: 56,365

GAME TWO AT NY OCT 21

				R	H	E
ATL	101	011	000	4	10	0
NY	000	000	000	0	7	1

Pitchers: MADDUX, Wohlers (9) vs KEY, Lloyd (7), Nelson (7), Rivera (9)
Attendance: 56,340

GAME THREE AT ATL OCT 22

				R	H	E
NY	100	100	030	5	8	1
ATL	000	001	010	2	6	1

Pitchers: CONE, Rivera (7), Lloyd (8), Wetteland (9) vs GLAVINE, McMichael (8), Clontz (8), Bielecki (9)
Home Runs: Williams-NY
Attendance: 51,843

GAME FOUR AT ATL OCT 23

					R	H	E
NY	000	003	030	2	8	12	0
ATL	041	010	000	0	6	9	2

Pitchers: Rogers, Boehringer (3), Weathers (5), Nelson (6), Rivera (8), LLOYD (9), Wetteland (10) vs Neagle, Wade (6), Bielecki (6), Wohlers (8), AVERY (10), Clontz (10)
Home Runs: Leyritz-NY, McGriff-ATL
Attendance: 51,881

GAME FIVE AT ATL OCT 24

				R	H	E
NY	000	100	000	1	4	1
ATL	000	000	000	0	5	1

Pitchers: PETTITTE, Wetteland (9) vs SMOLTZ, Wohlers (9)
Attendance: 51,881

GAME SIX AT NY OCT 26

				R	H	E
ATL	000	100	001	2	8	0
NY	003	000	00X	3	8	1

Pitchers: MADDUX, Wohlers (8) vs KEY, Weathers (6), Lloyd (6), Rivera (7), Wetteland (9)
Attendance: 56,375

The Giants went from last place in 1996 to first place in 1997, but Florida got the key hits late in each game to key a sweep of the division series. The Marlins became the first expansion team to win a postseason series, in their fifth year of existence. Kirk Reuter and Kevin Brown each threw seven innings of four-hit ball and each pitcher was nicked for a run in their last inning in Game 1. Bill Mueller homered for the Giants leading off the top of the seventh, and Charles Johnson answered with a home run in the bottom of the inning. In the last of the ninth, the Marlins loaded the bases with one out, but Devon White grounded into a force play at the plate. Reliever Roberto Hernandez fell behind Edgar Renteria and the Marlins shortstop grounded a single to right to win the game.

Game 2 was a battle of the bullpens; starters Shawn Estes and Al Leiter were both out of the game by the fifth inning. Stan Javier had four hits, and Barry Bonds, who had three RBIs in 21 career postseason games, drove home two runs. Bobby Bonilla's three RBIs and Gary Sheffield's home run gave the Marlins a 6-5 lead entering the ninth, but two errors and a broken-bat hit against Robb Nen tied the game. In the bottom of the ninth, Moises Alou singled with two runners on against Hernandez, and center fielder Dante Powell's strong throw hit the pitcher's mound and bounced straight up in the air, allowing Sheffield to score the winning run.

Wilson Alvarez, who came with Hernandez in a late season blockbuster deal with the White Sox, sailed through the first five and two thirds innings of Game 3, but then he filled the bases. Devon White, batting eighth, just missed getting hit by a pitch, then launched a grand slam to left field. Jeff Kent homered twice, the second coming just after Mueller was thrown out trying to steal, but Alex Fernandez, Dennis Cook, and Nen limited San Francisco to just five more hits.

Florida Marlins (E), 3; San Francisco Giants (W), 0

FLA (E)

PLAYER/POS	AVG	G	AB	R	H	2B	3B	HR	RB	BB	SO	SB
Kurt Abbott, 2b-2	.250	3	8	0	2	0	0	0	0	0	0	0
Moises Alou, of	.214	3	14	1	3	1	0	0	1	0	3	0
Alex Arias, ph	1.000	1	1	1	1	0	0	0	1	0	0	0
Bobby Bonilla, 3b	.333	3	12	1	4	0	0	1	3	2	1	0
Kevin Brown, p	.000	1	2	0	0	0	0	0	0	0	2	0
John Cangelosi, ph	.000	1	1	0	0	0	0	0	0	0	0	0
Jeff Conine, 1b	.364	3	11	3	4	1	0	0	0	1	0	0
Dennis Cook, p	.000	2	0	0	0	0	0	0	0	0	0	0
Craig Counsell, 2b	.400	3	5	0	2	1	0	0	1	1	0	0
Jim Eisenreich, ph	.000	2	0	0	0	0	0	0	0	2	0	0
Alex Fernandez, p	.000	1	2	0	0	0	0	0	0	1	1	0
Livan Hernandez, p	.000	1	1	0	0	0	0	0	0	0	0	0
Charles Johnson, c	.250	3	8	5	2	1	0	1	2	3	2	0
Al Leiter, p	.000	1	1	0	0	0	0	0	0	0	0	0
Robb Nen, p	.000	2	0	0	0	0	0	0	0	0	0	0
Edgar Renteria, ss	.154	3	13	1	2	0	0	0	1	2	4	0
Gary Sheffield, of	.556	3	9	2	5	1	0	1	1	5	0	1
John Wehner, of	.000	1	0	0	0	0	0	0	0	0	0	0
Devon White, of	.182	3	11	1	2	0	0	1	4	2	3	0
TOTAL	.273		99	15	27	5	0	4	14	19	16	1

PITCHER	W	L	ERA	G	GS	CG	SV	SHO	IP	H	ER	BB	SO
Kevin Brown	0	0	1.29	1	1	0	0	0	7.0	4	1	0	5
Dennis Cook	1	0	0.00	2	0	0	0	0	3.0	0	0	1	3
Alex Fernandez	1	0	2.57	1	1	0	0	0	7.0	7	2	0	5
Livan Hernandez	0	0	2.25	1	0	0	0	0	4.0	3	1	0	3
Al Leiter	0	0	9.00	1	1	0	0	0	4.0	7	4	3	3
Robb Nen	1	0	0.00	2	0	0	0	0	2.0	1	0	2	2
TOTAL	3	0	2.67	8	3	0	0	0	27.0	22	8	6	21

SF (W)

PLAYER/POS	AVG	G	AB	R	H	2B	3B	HR	RB	BB	SO	SB
Wilson Alvarez, p	.000	1	2	0	0	0	0	0	0	0	0	0
Rod Beck, p	.000	1	0	0	0	0	0	0	0	0	0	0
Marvin Benard, ph	.000	2	2	0	0	0	0	0	0	0	1	0
Damon Berryhill, ph	.000	1	1	0	0	0	0	0	0	0	0	0
Barry Bonds, of	.250	3	12	0	3	2	0	0	2	0	3	1
Shawn Estes, p	.000	1	1	0	0	0	0	0	0	0	1	0
Darryl Hamilton, of	.000	2	5	1	0	0	0	0	0	0	1	0
Doug Henry, p	.000	1	0	0	0	0	0	0	0	0	0	0
Roberto Hernandez, p	.000	3	0	0	0	0	0	0	0	0	0	0
Glenallen Hill, of-2	.000	3	7	0	0	0	0	0	0	2	2	0
Stan Javier, of	.417	3	12	2	5	1	0	0	1	0	2	1
Brian Johnson, c	.100	3	10	2	1	0	0	1	1	1	4	0
Jeff Kent, 2b-3,1b-1	.300	3	10	2	3	0	0	2	2	2	1	0
Mark Lewis, 2b	.600	1	5	0	3	0	0	0	1	0	0	0
Bill Mueller, 3b	.250	3	12	1	3	0	0	1	1	0	0	0
Dante Powell, of	.000	1	0	0	0	0	0	0	0	0	0	0
Rich Rodriguez, p	.000	2	0	0	0	0	0	0	0	0	0	0
Kirk Rueter, p	.500	1	2	0	1	0	0	0	0	0	0	0
J. T. Snow, 1b	.167	3	6	0	1	0	0	0	0	1	1	0
Julian Tavarez, p	.000	3	0	0	0	0	0	0	0	0	0	0
Jose Vizcaino, ss	.182	3	11	1	2	1	0	0	0	0	5	0
TOTAL	.224		98	9	22	4	0	4	8	6	21	2

PITCHER	W	L	ERA	G	GS	CG	SV	SHO	IP	H	ER	BB	SO
Wilson Alvarez	0	1	6.00	1	1	0	0	0	6.0	6	4	4	4
Rod Beck	0	0	0.00	1	0	0	0	0	1.1	1	0	0	1
Shawn Estes	0	0	15.00	1	1	0	0	0	3.0	5	5	4	3
Doug Henry	0	0	0.00	1	0	0	0	0	2.0	1	0	3	2
Roberto Hernandez	0	1	20.25	3	0	0	0	0	1.1	5	3	3	1
Rich Rodriguez	0	0	0.00	2	0	0	0	0	1.0	1	0	0	0
Kirk Rueter	0	0	1.29	1	1	0	0	0	7.0	4	1	3	5
Julian Tavarez	0	1	4.50	3	0	0	0	0	4.0	4	2	2	0
TOTAL	0	3	5.26	13	3	0	0	0	25.2	27	15	19	16

GAME 1 AT FLA SEPT 30

				R	H	E
SF	000	000	100	1	4	0
FLA	000	000	101	2	7	0

Pitchers: Rueter, TAVAREZ (8), Hernandez (9) vs Brown, COOK (8)
Home Runs: Mueller-SF, Johnson-FLA
Attendance: 42,167

GAME 2 AT FLA OCT 1

				R	H	E
SF	111	100	101	6	11	0
FLA	201	201	001	7	10	2

Pitchers: Estes, Henry (4), Tavarez (6), Rodriguez (8), HERNANDEZ (9) vs Leiter, Hernandez (5), NEN (9)
Home Runs: Bonilla-FLA, Johnson-SF, Sheffield-FLA
Attendance: 41,283

GAME 3 AT SF OCT 3

				R	H	E
FLA	000	004	020	6	10	2
SF	000	101	000	2	7	0

Pitchers: FERNANDEZ, Cook (8), Nen (8) vs ALVAREZ, Tavarez (7), Hernandez (8), Rodriguez (8), Beck (8)
Home Runs: Kent-SF (2), White-FLA
Attendance: 57,188

The Astros had the worst record of any team to reach the 1997 postseason while the Braves had the best record in baseball. It was a mismatch on paper, and it played out that way on the field, too. The Braves outscored the Astros, 19-5, and their pitching proved to be so dominant that 20-game winner Denny Neagle didn't even get a start in the series for Atlanta.

The handwriting was on the wall in Game 1 when Darryl Kile pitched a two-hitter and still lost, 2-1. Kile was also Houston's only hitter in the clutch, driving in the team's run. Kenny Lofton doubled to start the game and two fly outs brought him home. Ryan Klesko homered to lead off the second and that was it for the scoring and the hitting for the Braves, but Greg Maddux scattered seven hits for the complete-game victory.

Even in a 13-3 second game, the pitchers again had a lot to say about the outcome—although much of it was with their bats. Tom Glavine's single in the bottom of the third sparked a three-run Braves rally and Mike Hampton's single in the top of the fourth drove in the tying run. In the fifth inning Hampton got the first two outs, but then walked four straight batters. His replacement, Mike Magnante, allowed a two-run single to pinch hitter Greg Colrunn that gave the Braves a 6-3 lead. Glavine's single started a five-run rally in the sixth inning.

Game 3 belonged to John Smoltz, who pitched a three-hitter for his 10th career postseason victory. Shane Reynolds, starting the first postseason game in the Astrodome since 1986, had early chances to pitch out of trouble. He picked off Kenny Lofton in the first inning, then allowed a home run to Chipper Jones. In the second, he had a base open with Smoltz on deck, but he pitched instead to Jeff Blauser, who singled in the second run. Smoltz, meanwhile, struck out 11 Astros and silenced "The Killer B's." For the series, the top of the Astros order—Craig Biggio, Derek Bell, and Jeff Bagwell—batted a combined .054 (2-for-37).

Atlanta Braves (E), 3; Houston Astros (C), 0

ATL (E)

PLAYER/POS	AVG	G	AB	R	H	2B	3B	HR	RB	BB	SO	SB
Danny Bautista, of	.333	3	3	0	1	0	0	0	2	0	1	0
Jeff Blauser, ss	.300	3	10	2	3	0	0	1	4	2	2	0
Mike Cather, p	.000	1	1	0	0	0	0	0	0	0	1	0
Greg Colbrunn, ph	1.000	1	1	0	1	0	0	0	2	0	0	0
Tom Glavine, p	.667	1	3	2	2	0	0	0	0	0	0	0
Tony Graffanino, 2b	.000	3	3	0	0	0	0	0	0	2	1	0
Andruw Jones, of	.000	3	5	1	0	0	0	0	1	1	1	0
Chipper Jones, 3b	.500	3	8	3	4	0	0	1	2	3	2	1
Ryan Klesko, of	.250	3	8	2	2	1	0	1	1	0	2	0
Keith Lockhart, 2b	.000	2	6	0	0	0	0	0	0	0	1	0
Kenny Lofton, of	.154	3	13	2	2	1	0	0	0	1	2	0
Javy Lopez, c	.286	2	7	3	2	2	0	0	1	2	1	0
Greg Maddux, p	.000	1	2	0	0	0	0	0	0	1	1	0
Fred McGriff, 1b	.222	3	9	4	2	0	0	0	1	3	2	0
Eddie Perez, c	.000	1	3	0	0	0	0	0	0	0	1	0
John Smoltz, p	.000	1	4	0	0	0	0	0	0	0	1	0
Michael Tucker, of	.167	2	6	0	1	0	0	0	1	0	1	0
Mark Wohlers, p	.000	1	0	0	0	0	0	0	0	0	0	0
TOTAL	.217		92	19	20	4	0	3	15	15	20	1

PITCHER	W	L	ERA	G	GS	CG	SV	SHO	IP	H	ER	BB	SO
Mike Cather	0	0	0.00	1	0	0	0	0	2.0	0	0	1	2
Tom Glavine	1	0	4.50	1	1	0	0	0	6.0	5	3	5	4
Greg Maddux	1	0	1.00	1	1	1	0	0	9.0	7	1	1	6
John Smoltz	1	0	1.00	1	1	1	0	0	9.0	3	1	1	11
Mark Wohlers	0	0	0.00	1	0	0	0	0	1.0	1	0	0	1
TOTAL	3	0	1.67	5	3	2	0	0	27.0	16	5	8	24

HOU (C)

PLAYER/POS	AVG	G	AB	R	H	2B	3B	HR	RB	BB	SO	SB
Bob Abreu, ph	.333	3	3	0	1	0	0	0	0	0	2	1
Brad Ausmus, c	.400	2	5	1	2	1	0	0	2	0	1	0
Jeff Bagwell, 1b	.083	3	12	0	1	0	0	0	0	1	5	0
Derek Bell, of	.000	3	13	0	0	0	0	0	0	0	3	0
Sean Berry, ph	.000	1	1	0	0	0	0	0	0	0	0	0
Craig Biggio, 2b	.083	3	12	0	1	0	0	0	0	1	0	0
Chuck Carr, of	.250	2	4	1	1	0	0	1	1	1	3	0
Raul Eusebio, c	.667	1	3	1	2	0	0	0	0	0	1	1
Ramon Garcia, p	.000	2	0	0	0	0	0	0	0	0	0	0
Luis Gonzalez, of	.333	3	12	0	4	0	0	0	0	0	1	0
Ricky Gutierrez, ss	.125	3	8	0	1	0	0	0	0	2	1	0
Mike Hampton, p	.500	1	2	0	1	0	0	0	1	0	0	0
Richard Hidalgo, of	.000	2	5	1	0	0	0	0	0	1	2	0
Thomas Howard, ph	.000	2	1	0	0	0	0	0	0	1	1	0
Russ Johnson, ph	.000	1	1	0	0	0	0	0	0	0	1	0
Darryl Kile, p	1.000	1	2	0	2	0	0	0	1	0	0	0
Jose Lima, p	.000	1	0	0	0	0	0	0	0	0	0	0
Mike Magnante, p	.000	2	0	0	0	0	0	0	0	0	0	0
Tom Martin, p	.000	2	0	0	0	0	0	0	0	0	0	0
Tony Pena, c	.000	2	0	0	0	0	0	0	0	0	0	0
Shane Reynolds, p	.000	1	1	0	0	0	0	0	0	0	1	0
Bill Spiers, 3b	.000	3	11	1	0	0	0	0	0	1	2	0
Russ Springer, p	.000	2	0	0	0	0	0	0	0	0	0	0
Billy Wagner, p	.000	1	0	0	0	0	0	0	0	0	0	0
TOTAL	.167		96	5	16	1	0	1	5	8	24	2

PITCHER	W	L	ERA	G	GS	CG	SV	SHO	IP	H	ER	BB	SO
Ramon Garcia	0	0	0.00	2	0	0	0	0	1.0	1	0	1	1
Mike Hampton	0	1	11.57	1	1	0	0	0	4.2	2	6	8	2
Darryl Kile	0	1	2.57	1	1	0	0	0	7.0	2	2	2	4
Jose Lima	0	0	0.00	1	0	0	0	0	1.0	0	0	1	1
Mike Magnante	0	0	4.50	2	0	0	0	0	2.0	4	1	0	2
Tom Martin	0	0	0.00	2	0	0	0	0	0.2	1	0	1	0
Shane Reynolds	0	1	3.00	1	1	0	0	0	6.0	5	2	1	5
Russ Springer	0	0	5.40	2	0	0	0	0	1.2	2	1	1	3
Billy Wagner	0	0	18.00	1	0	0	0	0	1.0	3	2	0	2
TOTAL	0	3	5.04	13	3	0	0	0	25.0	20	14	15	20

GAME 1 AT ATL SEPT 30

		R	H	E
HOU	000 010 000	1	7	1
ATL	110 000 00X	2	2	0

Pitchers: KILE, Springer (8), Martin (8) vs MADDUX
Home Runs: Klesko-ATL
Attendance: 46,467

GAME 2 AT ATL OCT 1

		R	H	E
HOU	000 300 000	3	6	2
ATL	003 035 02X	13	10	1

Pitchers: HAMPTON, Magnante (5), Garcia (6), Lima (7), Wagner (8) vs GLAVINE, Cather (7), Wohlers (9)
Home Runs: Blauser-ATL
Attendance: 49,200

GAME 3 AT HOU OCT 3

		R	H	E
ATL	110 000 110	4	8	2
HOU	000 000 100	1	3	1

Pitchers: SMOLTZ vs REYNOLDS, Springer (7), Martin (8), Garcia (8), Magnante (9)
Home Runs: C.Jones-ATL, Carr-HOU
Attendance: 53,688

The predetermined postseason matchup seemed to favor the Wild Card Yankees, who drew the Indians in the Division Series while the AL East champion Orioles got the power-packed Mariners. The Indians had the worst record of any American League postseason club, but Cleveland got off to a 5-0 lead in the first inning of Game 1. Cleveland held a 6-1 lead by the time David Cone was chased from the mound, and Cone's injured shoulder made it his only appearance of the series. But Orel Hershiser, who came into the series with an 8-1 record with a 1.83 ERA in the postseason, didn't last through the fifth inning. In the sixth inning, Tim Raines, Derek Jeter, and Paul O'Neill hit successive home runs—a first in postseason history—to give the Yankees an 8-6 victory.

In Game 2 the Yankees couldn't hold the lead. New York reached 21-year-old rookie Jaret Wright for three runs in the first inning, but a two-out rally off Andy Pettitte in the fourth inning gave the Indians a 5-3 lead. Matt Williams homered in the fifth inning, and a trio of relievers held off a late Yankees comeback. David Wells pitched a five-hitter in Game 3 to win a Division Series game for the third straight year for his third different team. New York chased Cleveland starter Charles Nagy in the fourth inning, and Paul O'Neill greeted Chad Ogea with a grand slam. It was the last run the Indians bullpen would allow.

In Game 4 Orel Hershiser and Dwight Gooden looked a lot like they did when they faced each other in the 1988 playoffs. Hershiser was good for seven innings, but Gooden left with a 2-1 lead in the sixth. The Yankees were four outs from winning the series with their closer Mariano Rivera on the mound when Sandy Alomar hit an opposite-field home run to tie the game. In the ninth inning Omar Vizquel's hard grounder up the middle glanced off reliever Ramiro Mendoza and rolled into left field, allowing Marquis Grissom to score from second with the winning run.

Manny Ramirez stepped to the plate in the third inning of Game 5 batting .111 for the series, but he hit a ground-rule double on a two-strike pitch from Pettitte to score Grissom and Vizquel. The Indians took a 4-0 lead, but the Yankees made it a one-run game in the sixth inning against Wright. Jose Mesa snuffed a Yankees rally in the eighth, and, after a two-out double by O'Neill in the ninth, he retired Bernie Williams on a flyball to left to end the series.

Cleveland Indians (C), 3; New York Yankees (E), 2

CLE (C)

PLAYER/POS	AVG	G	AB	R	H	2B	3B	HR	RB	BB	SO	SB
Sandy Alomar, c	.316	5	19	4	6	1	0	2	5	0	2	0
Paul Assenmacher, p	.000	4	0	0	0	0	0	0	0	0	0	0
Tony Fernandez, 2b	.182	4	11	0	2	1	0	0	4	0	0	0
Brian Giles, of	.143	3	7	0	1	0	0	0	0	0	1	0
Marquis Grissom, of	.235	5	17	3	4	0	1	0	0	1	2	0
Orel Hershiser, p	.000	2	0	0	0	0	0	0	0	0	0	0
Mike Jackson, p	.000	4	0	0	0	0	0	0	0	0	0	0
David Justice, dh	.263	5	19	3	5	2	0	1	2	2	3	0
Jose Mesa, p	.000	2	0	0	0	0	0	0	0	0	0	0
Alvin Morman, p	.000	1	0	0	0	0	0	0	0	0	0	0
Charles Nagy, p	.000	1	0	0	0	0	0	0	0	0	0	0
Chad Ogea, p	.000	1	0	0	0	0	0	0	0	0	0	0
Eric Plunk, p	.000	1	0	0	0	0	0	0	0	0	0	0
Manny Ramirez, of	.143	5	21	2	3	1	0	0	3	0	3	0
Bip Roberts, of-4,2b-2	.316	5	19	1	6	0	0	0	1	2	2	2
Kevin Seitzer, 1b	.000	1	4	0	0	0	0	0	0	0	0	0
Jim Thome, 1b	.200	5	15	1	3	0	0	0	1	0	5	0
Omar Vizquel, ss	.500	5	18	3	9	0	0	0	1	2	1	4
Matt Williams, 3b	.235	5	17	4	4	1	0	1	3	3	3	0
Jaret Wright, p	.000	2	0	0	0	0	0	0	0	0	0	0
TOTAL	.257		167	21	43	6	1	4	20	10	22	6

PITCHER	W	L	ERA	G	GS	CG	SV	SHO	IP	H	ER	BB	SO
Paul Assenmacher	0	0	5.40	4	0	0	0	0	3.1	2	2	2	2
Orel Hershiser	0	0	3.97	2	2	0	0	0	11.1	14	5	2	4
Mike Jackson	1	0	0.00	4	0	0	0	0	4.1	3	0	1	5
Jose Mesa	0	0	2.70	2	0	0	1	0	3.1	5	1	1	2
Alvin Morman	0	0	INF	1	0	0	0	0	0.0	0	0	1	0
Charles Nagy	0	1	9.82	1	1	0	0	0	3.2	2	4	6	1
Chad Ogea	0	0	1.69	1	0	0	0	0	5.1	2	1	0	1
Eric Plunk	0	1	27.00	1	0	0	0	0	1.1	4	4	0	1
Jaret Wright	2	0	3.97	2	2	0	0	0	11.1	11	5	7	10
TOTAL	3	2	4.50	18	5	0	1	0	44.0	43	22	20	26

NY (E)

PLAYER/POS	AVG	G	AB	R	H	2B	3B	HR	RB	BB	SO	SB
Brian Boehringer, p	.000	1	0	0	0	0	0	0	0	0	0	0
Wade Boggs, 3b-2	.429	3	7	1	3	0	0	0	2	0	0	0
David Cone, p	.000	1	0	0	0	0	0	0	0	0	0	0
Chad Curtis, of	.167	4	6	0	1	0	0	0	0	3	1	0
Cecil Fielder, dh	.125	2	8	0	1	0	0	0	1	0	3	0
Andy Fox, 2b	.000	2	0	0	0	0	0	0	0	0	0	0
Joe Girardi, c	.133	5	15	2	2	0	0	0	0	1	3	0
Dwight Gooden, p	.000	1	0	0	0	0	0	0	0	0	0	0
Charlie Hayes, 3b-5,2b-1	.333	5	15	0	5	0	0	0	1	0	2	0
Derek Jeter, ss	.333	5	21	6	7	1	0	2	2	3	5	1
Graeme Lloyd, p	.000	2	0	0	0	0	0	0	0	0	0	0
Tino Martinez, 1b	.222	5	18	1	4	1	0	1	4	2	4	0
Ramiro Mendoza, p	.000	2	0	0	0	0	0	0	0	0	0	0
Jeff Nelson, p	.000	4	0	0	0	0	0	0	0	0	0	0
Paul O'Neill, of	.421	5	19	5	8	2	0	2	7	3	0	0
Andy Pettitte, p	.000	2	0	0	0	0	0	0	0	0	0	0
Jorge Posada, c	.000	2	2	0	0	0	0	0	0	0	1	0
Scott Pose, pr	.000	1	0	0	0	0	0	0	0	0	0	0
Tim Raines, of-3,dh-2	.211	5	19	4	4	0	0	1	3	3	1	2
Mariano Rivera, p	.000	2	0	0	0	0	0	0	0	0	0	0
Rey Sanchez, 2b	.200	5	15	1	3	1	0	0	1	1	2	0
Mike Stanley, dh-1	.750	2	4	1	3	1	0	0	1	0	1	0
Mike Stanton, p	.000	3	0	0	0	0	0	0	0	0	0	0
David Wells, p	.000	1	0	0	0	0	0	0	0	0	0	0
Bernie Williams, of	.118	5	17	3	2	1	0	0	1	4	3	0
TOTAL	.259		166	24	43	7	0	6	23	20	26	3

PITCHER	W	L	ERA	G	GS	CG	SV	SHO	IP	H	ER	BB	SO
Brian Boehringer	0	0	0.00	1	0	0	0	0	1.2	1	0	1	2
David Cone	0	0	16.20	1	1	0	0	0	3.1	7	6	2	2
Dwight Gooden	0	0	1.59	1	1	0	0	0	5.2	5	1	3	5
Graeme Lloyd	0	0	0.00	2	0	0	0	0	1.1	0	0	0	1
Ramiro Mendoza	1	1	2.45	2	0	0	0	0	3.2	3	1	0	2
Jeff Nelson	0	0	0.00	4	0	0	0	0	4.0	4	0	2	0
Andy Pettitte	0	2	8.49	2	2	0	0	0	11.2	15	11	1	5
Mariano Rivera	0	0	4.50	2	0	0	1	0	2.0	2	1	0	1
Mike Stanton	0	0	0.00	3	0	0	0	0	1.0	1	0	1	3
David Wells	1	0	1.00	1	1	1	0	0	9.0	5	1	0	1
TOTAL	2	3	4.36	19	5	1	1	0	43.1	43	21	10	22

GAME 1 AT NY SEPT 30

				R	H	E
CLE	500	100	000	6	11	0
NY	010	115	00X	8	11	0

Pitchers: Hershiser, Morman (5), PLUNK (5), Assenmacher (7), Jackson (7) vs Cone, MENDOZA (4), Nelson (7), Rivera (8)

Home Runs: Alomar-BAL, Martinez-NY, Raines-NY, Jeter-NY, O'Neill-NY

Attendance: 57,398

GAME 2 AT NY OCT 2

				R	H	E
CLE	000	520	000	7	11	1
NY	300	000	011	5	7	2

Pitchers: WRIGHT, Jackson (7), Assenmacher (7), Mesa (8) vs PETTITTE, Boehringer (6), Lloyd (7), Nelson (9)

Home Runs: Williams-CLE, Jeter-NY

Attendance: 57,360

GAME 3 AT CLE OCT 4

				R	H	E
NY	101	400	000	6	4	1
CLE	010	000	000	1	5	1

Pitchers: WELLS vs NAGY, Ogea (4)

Home Runs: O'Neill-NY

Attendance: 45,274

GAME 4 AT CLE OCT 5

				R	H	E
NY	200	000	000	2	9	1
CLE	010	000	011	3	9	0

Pitchers: Gooden, Lloyd (6), Nelson (6), Stanton (7), Rivera (8), MENDOZA (9) vs Hershiser, Assenmacher (8), JACKSON (8)

Home Runs: Justice-CLE, Alomar-CLE

Attendance: 45,231

GAME 5 AT CLE OCT 6

				R	H	E
NY	000	021	000	3	12	0
CLE	003	100	00X	4	7	2

Pitchers: PETTITTE, Nelson (7), Stanton (8) vs WRIGHT, Jackson (6), Assenmacher (7), Mesa (8)

Attendance: 45,203

The Orioles found an antidote to Randy Johnson, and they used it twice to beat the Mariners. Meanwhile, Mike Mussina found a way to silence Seattle's powerful lineup twice and that was the difference. Orioles manager Davey Johnson raised eyebrows when he rested Roberto Alomar, Rafael Palmeiro, and B.J. Surhoff against southpaw Randy Johnson, but their replacements and the rest of the Baltimore lineup had little trouble in Game 1. Johnson left in the fifth inning trailing 5-1, and the much-maligned Mariners bullpen lived up to its reputation as the Orioles coasted behind Mussina. Jamie Moyer had a 2-1 lead when he was forced to leave Game 2 with an injured left elbow in the fifth inning. Paul Spoljaric relieved and the next batter, Roberto Alomar, doubled off Ken Griffey's glove in center field to give the Orioles a 3-2 lead. Brady Anderson homered and doubled against two more Mariners relievers, and the Orioles left Seattle with their second straight 9-3 laugher.

Roberto Kelly doubled in a run in the first inning, and Griffey singled in a run in the fifth to stake Jeff Fassero to a 2-0 lead in Game 3. Fassero pitched a brilliant three-hitter for eight innings, but manager Lou Piniella brought in Heathcliff Slocumb to close the game when the Mariners took a 4-0 lead into the bottom of the ninth. Jeffrey Hammonds doubled home two runs, but Harold Baines popped out to end the game.

Mussina, who pitched a five-hitter for seven innings in the series opener, allowed just two hits in seven innings in Game 4. The Orioles helped him out by scoring twice in the first inning on a home run by Jeff Reboulet (Alomar's replacement in Davey Johnson's lineup against Randy Johnson) and a run-scoring single by Cal Ripken. Edgar Martinez led off the second inning with a home run, and Seattle followed that with a walk and a single. Mussina did not allow another hit and fanned seven.

Baltimore Orioles (E), 3; Seattle Mariners (W), 1

BAL (E)

PLAYER/POS	AVG	G	AB	R	H	2B	3B	HR	RB	BB	SO	SB
Roberto Alomar, 2b	.300	4	10	1	3	2	0	0	2	1	1	0
Brady Anderson, of	.353	4	17	3	6	1	0	1	4	1	4	1
Harold Baines, dh-1	.400	2	5	2	2	0	0	1	1	1	0	0
Armando Benitez, p	.000	3	0	0	0	0	0	0	0	0	0	0
Geronimo Berroa, dh-3,of-1	.385	4	13	4	5	1	0	2	2	2	2	0
Mike Bordick, ss	.400	4	10	4	4	1	0	0	4	4	2	0
Eric Davis, of	.222	3	9	0	2	0	0	0	2	0	5	0
Scott Erickson, p	.000	1	0	0	0	0	0	0	0	0	0	0
Jeffrey Hammonds, of	.100	4	10	3	1	1	0	0	2	2	2	1
Chris Hoiles, c	.143	3	7	1	1	0	0	1	1	2	1	0
Jimmy Key, p	.000	1	0	0	0	0	0	0	0	0	0	0
Terry Mathews, p	.000	1	0	0	0	0	0	0	0	0	0	0
Alan Mills, p	.000	1	0	0	0	0	0	0	0	0	0	0
Mike Mussina, p	.000	2	0	0	0	0	0	0	0	0	0	0
Randy Myers, p	.000	2	0	0	0	0	0	0	0	0	0	0
Jesse Orosco, p	.000	2	0	0	0	0	0	0	0	0	0	0
Rafael Palmeiro, 1b	.250	4	12	2	3	2	0	0	0	0	2	0
Jeff Reboulet, 2b	.200	2	5	1	1	0	0	1	1	0	2	0
Arthur Lee Rhodes, p	.000	1	0	0	0	0	0	0	0	0	0	0
Cal Ripken, 3b	.438	4	16	1	7	2	0	0	1	2	2	0
B.J. Surhoff, of	.273	3	11	0	3	1	0	0	2	0	2	0
Jerome Walton, 1b	.000	2	4	0	0	0	0	0	0	0	2	0
Lenny Webster, c	.167	3	6	1	1	0	0	0	1	1	0	0
TOTAL	.289		135	23	39	11	0	6	23	16	27	2

PITCHER	W	L	ERA	G	GS	CG	SV	SHO	IP	H	ER	BB	SO
Armando Benitez	0	0	3.00	3	0	0	0	0	3.0	3	1	2	4
Scott Erickson	1	0	4.05	1	1	0	0	0	6.2	7	3	2	6
Jimmy Key	0	1	3.86	1	1	0	0	0	4.2	8	2	0	4
Terry Mathews	0	0	18.00	1	0	0	0	0	1.0	2	2	0	1
Alan Mills	0	0	0.00	1	0	0	0	0	1.0	1	0	0	1
Mike Mussina	2	0	1.93	2	2	0	0	0	14.0	7	3	3	16
Randy Myers	0	0	0.00	2	0	0	1	0	2.0	0	0	0	5
Jesse Orosco	0	0	0.00	2	0	0	0	0	1.1	1	0	0	1
Arthur Lee Rhodes	0	0	0.00	1	0	0	0	0	2.1	0	0	0	4
TOTAL	3	1	2.75	14	4	0	1	0	36.0	29	11	7	42

SEA (W)

PLAYER/POS	AVG	G	AB	R	H	2B	3B	HR	RB	BB	SO	SB
Rich Amaral, 1b	.500	2	4	2	2	0	0	0	0	0	1	0
Bobby Ayala, p	.000	1	0	0	0	0	0	0	0	0	0	0
Mike Blowers, 3b	.200	3	5	0	1	0	0	0	0	0	3	0
Jay Buhner, of	.231	4	13	2	3	0	0	2	2	3	6	0
Norm Charlton, p	.000	2	0	0	0	0	0	0	0	0	0	0
Joey Cora, 2b	.176	4	17	1	3	0	0	0	0	0	4	0
Rob Ducey, of-1	.500	2	4	0	2	0	0	0	1	0	0	0
Jeff Fassero, p	.000	1	0	0	0	0	0	0	0	0	0	0
Brent Gates, 3b	.000	2	4	0	0	0	0	0	0	0	0	0
Ken Griffey, of	.133	4	15	0	2	0	0	0	2	1	3	2
Randy Johnson, p	.000	2	0	0	0	0	0	0	0	0	0	0
Roberto Kelly, of-3	.308	4	13	1	4	3	0	0	1	0	3	0
Edgar Martinez, dh	.188	4	16	2	3	0	0	2	3	0	3	0
Jamie Moyer, p	.000	1	0	0	0	0	0	0	0	0	0	0
Alex Rodriguez, ss	.313	4	16	1	5	1	0	1	1	0	5	0
Andy Sheets, 3b	.333	2	3	0	1	0	0	0	0	0	2	0
Heathcliff Slocumb, p	.000	2	0	0	0	0	0	0	0	0	0	0
Paul Sorrento, 1b	.300	4	10	2	3	1	0	1	1	2	3	0
Paul Spoljaric, p	.000	2	0	0	0	0	0	0	0	0	0	0
Mike Timlin, p	.000	1	0	0	0	0	0	0	0	0	0	0
Bob Wells, p	.000	1	0	0	0	0	0	0	0	0	0	0
Rick Wilkins, c	.000	1	0	0	0	0	0	0	0	1	0	0
Dan Wilson, c	.000	4	13	0	0	0	0	0	0	0	9	0
TOTAL	.218		133	11	29	5	0	6	11	7	42	2

PITCHER	W	L	ERA	G	GS	CG	SV	SHO	IP	H	ER	BB	SO
Bobby Ayala	0	0	40.50	1	0	0	0	0	1.1	4	6	1	3
Norm Charlton	0	0	0.00	2	0	0	0	0	2.1	2	0	0	1
Jeff Fassero	1	0	1.13	1	1	0	0	0	8.0	3	1	4	3
Randy Johnson	0	2	5.54	2	2	1	0	0	13.0	14	8	6	16
Jamie Moyer	0	1	5.79	1	1	0	0	0	4.2	5	3	1	2
Heathcliff Slocumb	0	0	4.50	2	0	0	0	0	2.0	3	1	1	0
Paul Spoljaric	0	0	0.00	2	0	0	0	0	1.2	4	0	0	1
Mike Timlin	0	0	54.00	1	0	0	0	0	0.2	3	4	1	1
Bob Wells	0	0	0.00	1	0	0	0	0	1.1	1	0	0	1
TOTAL	1	3	5.91	13	4	1	0	0	35.0	39	23	14	28

GAME 1 AT SEA OCT 1

				R	H	E
BAL	001	044	000	9	13	0
SEA	000	100	101	3	7	1

Pitchers: MUSSINA, Orosco (8), Benitez (9) vs JOHNSON, Timlin (6), Spoljaric (6), Wells (7), Charlton (8)

Home Runs: Martinez-SEA, Berroa-BAL, Hoiles-BAL, Buhner-SEA, Rodriguez-SEA

Attendance: 59,579

GAME 2 AT SEA OCT 2

				R	H	E
BAL	010	020	240	9	14	0
SEA	200	000	100	3	9	0

Pitchers: ERICKSON, Benitez (7), Orosco (8), Myers (9) vs MOYER, Spoljaric (5), Ayala (7), Charlton (8), Slocumb (9)

Home Runs: Baines-BAL, Anderson-BAL

Attendance: 59,309

GAME 3 AT BAL OCT 4

				R	H	E
SEA	001	010	002	4	11	0
BAL	000	000	002	2	5	0

Pitchers: FASSERO, Slocumb (9) vs KEY, Mills (5), Rhodes (6), Mathews (9)

Home Runs: Buhner-SEA, Sorrento-SEA

Attendance: 49,137

GAME 4 AT BAL OCT 5

				R	H	E
SEA	010	000	000	1	2	0
BAL	200	010	00X	3	7	0

Pitchers: JOHNSON vs MUSSINA, Benitez (8), Myers (9)

Home Runs: Reboulet-BAL, Martinez-SEA, Berroa-BAL

Attendance: 48,766

The Marlins didn't even exist the last time Jim Leyland led a team to the NLCS against the Braves; since then Atlanta had become the first team in history to win six straight division titles (minus the 1994 strike season). Leyland watched as his Pirates lost to the Braves in the bottom of the ninth in Game 7 of the 1992 NLCS in Fulton County Stadium, but now he was with a different team; the Braves had a different stadium (Turner Field), and the results were different, too.

The fifth-year Marlins struck for five unearned runs off Greg Maddux in the opener, and Kevin Brown and three relievers made it hold up. Charles Johnson, who was the first catcher in major league history to go through an entire season without an error, threw a ball into center field on a stolen base attempt by Kenny Lofton in the first inning of Game 2. Keith Lockhart tripled Lofton home and Ryan Klesko hit his second home run in as many nights. Lockhart singled in the third inning and Chipper Jones followed with his second home run in two games. Alex Fernandez left after two and two thirds innings; it was later revealed that he had a torn rotator cuff and would not pitch for a year.

Fernandez's replacement, Livan Hernandez, made his first appearance of the series in relief in Game 3 in Florida and picked up the win. This time poor defense and bad baserunning cost Atlanta. After Chipper Jones got caught in a rundown at second base with the bases loaded in the top of the sixth inning, Andruw Jones misplayed a flyball in right to tie the game. Johnson, who was hitless in 10 career at bats against John Smoltz, doubled in three runs and chased him from the game. Denny Neagle was masterful for the Braves in Game 4, pitching the first complete game in the NLCS since 1992. Series MVP Hernandez followed with an even more remarkable performance with 15 strikeouts, tying an LCS record set the day before by Baltimore's Mike Mussina in Cleveland. Maddux again pitched in bad luck. He allowed just four hits, but Jeff Conine's single in the seventh drove in Bobby Bonilla with the deciding run.

The Braves, who complained about umpire Eric Gregg's liberal strike zone in Game 5, could only complain about their inability to get timely hits in Game 6. The Marlins batted around and scored four runs in the first inning off Tom Glavine, but the Braves cut the lead to 4-3 by the second inning. Brown, whose start was pushed back three days because of a stomach virus, talked Leyland out of removing him after the sixth inning. He remained in the contest despite a two-out Braves rally in the ninth inning that brought the tying run to the plate. Chipper Jones grounded a ball up the middle but Craig Counsell went behind second base and flipped to Edgar Renteria for the force play to give the Marlins the pennant exactly five years after the Braves had rallied in the ninth to take the flag away from Leyland's Pirates.

Florida Marlins (WC), 4; Atlanta Braves (E), 2

FLA (E)

PLAYER/POS	AVG	G	AB	R	H	2B	3B	HR	RB	BB	SO	SB
Kurt Abbott, 2b	.375	2	8	0	3	1	0	0	0	0	2	0
Moises Alou, of-4	.067	5	15	0	1	1	0	0	5	1	3	0
Alex Arias, 3b-2	1.000	3	1	0	1	0	0	0	0	0	0	0
Bobby Bonilla, 3b	.261	6	23	3	6	1	0	0	4	1	6	0
Kevin Brown, p	.000	2	6	0	0	0	0	0	0	0	3	0
John Cangelosi, of-1	.200	3	5	0	1	0	0	0	0	1	0	0
Jeff Conine, 1b	.111	6	18	1	2	0	0	0	1	1	4	0
Dennis Cook, p	.000	2	0	0	0	0	0	0	0	0	0	0
Craig Counsell, 2b-4	.429	5	14	0	6	0	0	0	2	3	3	0
Darren Daulton, 1b-2	.250	3	4	1	1	1	0	0	1	1	2	0
Jim Eisenreich, of	.000	1	3	0	0	0	0	0	0	0	0	0
Alex Fernandez, p	.000	1	1	0	0	0	0	0	0	0	1	0
Felix Heredia, p	.000	2	0	0	0	0	0	0	0	0	0	0
Livan Hernandez, p	.000	2	3	0	0	0	0	0	0	0	1	0
Charles Johnson, c	.118	6	17	1	2	2	0	0	5	3	8	0
Al Leiter, p	.000	2	1	0	0	0	0	0	0	0	1	0
Robb Nen, p	.000	2	0	0	0	0	0	0	0	0	0	0
Jay Powell, p	.000	1	0	0	0	0	0	0	0	0	0	0
Edgar Renteria, ss	.227	6	22	4	5	1	0	0	0	3	6	1
Tony Saunders, p	.000	1	2	0	0	0	0	0	0	0	2	0
Gary Sheffield, of	.235	6	17	6	4	0	0	1	1	7	3	0
Ed Vosberg, p	.000	2	0	0	0	0	0	0	0	0	0	0
Devon White, of	.190	6	21	4	4	1	0	0	1	2	7	1
Greg Zaun, c	.000	1	0	0	0	0	0	0	0	0	0	0
TOTAL	.199		181	20	36	8	0	1	20	23	52	2

PITCHER	W	L	ERA	G	GS	CG	SV	SHO	IP	H	ER	BB	SO
Kevin Brown	2	0	4.20	2	2	1	0	0	15.0	16	7	5	11
Dennis Cook	0	0	0.00	2	0	0	0	0	2.1	0	0	0	2
Alex Fernandez	0	1	16.88	1	1	0	0	0	2.2	6	5	1	3
Felix Heredia	0	0	5.40	2	0	0	0	0	3.1	3	2	2	4
Livan Hernandez	2	0	0.84	2	1	1	0	0	10.2	5	1	2	16
Al Leiter	0	1	4.32	2	1	0	0	0	8.1	13	4	2	6
Robb Nen	0	0	0.00	2	0	0	2	0	2.0	0	0	0	1
Jay Powell	0	0	0.00	1	0	0	0	0	0.2	0	0	0	0
Tony Saunders	0	0	3.38	1	1	0	0	0	5.1	4	2	3	3
Ed Vosberg	0	0	0.00	2	0	0	0	0	2.2	2	0	1	3
TOTAL	4	2	3.57	17	6	2	2	0	53.0	49	21	16	49

ATL (E)

PLAYER/POS	AVG	G	AB	R	H	2B	3B	HR	RB	BB	SO	SB
Danny Bautista, of	.250	2	4	0	1	0	0	0	0	0	0	0
Jeff Blauser, ss	.300	6	20	5	6	0	0	1	1	3	6	0
Mike Cather, p	.000	4	0	0	0	0	0	0	0	0	0	0
Greg Colbrunn, ph	.667	3	3	0	2	0	0	0	0	0	0	0
Alan Embree, p	.000	1	0	0	0	0	0	0	0	0	0	0
Tom Glavine, p	.333	2	3	0	1	0	0	0	0	0	2	0
Tony Graffanino, 2b	.250	3	8	1	2	1	0	0	0	0	3	0
Tommy Gregg, ph	.000	4	4	0	0	0	0	0	0	0	1	0
Andruw Jones, of	.444	5	9	0	4	0	0	0	1	1	1	0
Chipper Jones, 3b	.292	6	24	5	7	1	0	2	4	2	3	0
Ryan Klesko, of	.235	5	17	2	4	0	0	2	4	2	3	0
Kerry Ligtenberg, p	.000	2	0	0	0	0	0	0	0	0	0	0
Keith Lockhart, 2b	.500	5	16	4	8	1	1	0	3	1	1	0
Kenny Lofton, of	.185	6	27	3	5	0	1	0	1	1	7	1
Javy Lopez, c	.059	5	17	0	1	1	0	0	2	1	7	0
Greg Maddux, p	.000	2	3	0	0	0	0	0	0	0	2	0
Fred McGriff, 1b	.333	6	21	0	7	1	0	0	4	2	7	0
Denny Neagle, p	.000	2	3	0	0	0	0	0	0	0	1	0
Eddie Perez, c	.000	2	3	0	0	0	0	0	0	0	0	0
John Smoltz, p	.000	1	2	0	0	0	0	0	0	0	1	0
Michael Tucker, of-4	.100	5	10	1	1	0	0	1	1	3	4	0
Mark Wohlers, p	.000	1	0	0	0	0	0	0	0	0	0	0
TOTAL	.253		194	21	49	5	2	6	21	16	49	1

PITCHER	W	L	ERA	G	GS	CG	SV	SHO	IP	H	ER	BB	SO
Mike Cather	0	0	0.00	4	0	0	0	0	2.2	3	0	0	3
Alan Embree	0	0	0.00	1	0	0	0	0	1.0	0	0	1	1
Tom Glavine	1	1	5.40	2	2	0	0	0	13.1	13	8	11	9
Kerry Ligtenberg	0	0	0.00	2	0	0	0	0	3.0	1	0	0	4
Greg Maddux	0	2	1.38	2	2	0	0	0	13.0	9	2	4	16
Denny Neagle	1	0	0.00	2	1	1	0	0	12.0	5	0	1	9
John Smoltz	0	1	7.50	1	1	0	0	0	6.0	5	5	5	9
Mark Wohlers	0	0	0.00	1	0	0	0	0	1.0	0	0	1	1
TOTAL	2	4	2.60	15	6	1	0	0	52.0	36	15	23	52

GAME 1 AT ATL OCT 7

		R	H	E
FLA	302 000 000	5	6	0
ATL	101 001 000	3	5	2

PITCHERS: BROWN, Cook (7), Powell (8), Nen(9) vs MADDUX, Neagle (7)
HOME RUNS: C.Jones-ATL, Klesko-ATL
ATTENDANCE: 49,244

GAME 2 AT ATL OCT 8

		R	H	E
FLA	000 000 010	1	3	1
ATL	302 000 20X	7	13	0

PITCHERS: FERNANDEZ, Leiter (3), Heredia (6), Vosberg (8) vs GLAVINE, Cather (8), Wohlers (9)
HOME RUNS: Klesko-ATL, C.Jones-ATL
ATTENDANCE: 48,933

GAME 3 AT FLA OCT 10

		R	H	E
ATL	000 101 000	2	6	1
FLA	000 104 00X	5	8	1

PITCHERS: SMOLTZ, Cather (7), Ligtenberg (8) vs Saunders, HERNANDEZ (6), Cook (8), Nen (9)
HOME RUNS: Sheffield-FLA
ATTENDANCE: 53,857

GAME 4 AT FLA OCT 11

		R	H	E
ATL	101 020 000	4	11	0
FLA	000 000 000	0	4	0

PITCHERS: NEAGLE vs LEITER, Heredia (7), Vosberg (9)
HOME RUNS: Blauser-ATL
ATTENDANCE: 54,890

GAME 5 AT FLA OCT 12

		R	H	E
ATL	010 000 000	1	3	0
FLA	100 000 10X	2	5	0

PITCHERS: MADDUX, Cather (8) vs HERNANDEZ
HOME RUNS: Tucker-ATL
ATTENDANCE: 51,982

GAME 6 AT ATL OCT 14

		R	H	E
FLA	400 003 000	7	10	1
ATL	120 000 001	4	11	1

PITCHERS: BROWN vs GLAVINE, Cather (6), Ligtenberg (7), Embree (9)
ATTENDANCE: 50,446

In a series dominated by pitching, Baltimore's starters were brilliant, but it was Cleveland's relief corps that won the day. Brady Anderson, who made a leaping catch at the wall to end the top of the first inning of Game 1, hit Chad Ogea's first pitch for a home run to lead off the bottom of the inning. Scott Erickson tossed a four-hitter for eight innings, and Randy Myers earned the save. The Indians got off to a solid start in Game 2 with a two-run home run by Manny Ramirez, but Cal Ripken matched it with a two-run homer in the second inning. Mike Bordick broke the tie with a two-run single in the sixth inning. Armando Benitez surrendered a three-run home run to ninth-place hitter Marquis Grissom in the eighth inning to even the series.

Game 3 was a bizarre contest played in the twilight of Jacobs Field that haunted batters and fielders alike. Baltimore's Mike Mussina struck out an LCS-record 15 batters, but a run-scoring single by Matt Williams gave Cleveland a 1-0 lead heading into the ninth. With a runner on second and one out, Grissom misplayed a fly ball to allow the tying run to score. The oddest play of the day was the one that finally ended the game in the 12th inning. On a suicide squeeze, Omar Vizquel missed the bunt attempt and catcher Lenny Webster missed the ball. Webster, thinking it was a foul ball, walked after it and ALCS MVP Grissom slid across the plate with the winning run.

A wild pitch resulted in two runs on one play in Game 4, one on a wild pitch by Arthur Rhodes and the second on Webster's throwing error. Rafael Palmeiro's single in the top of the ninth tied the game, but Sandy Alomar singled home Ramirez with the winning run in the bottom of the inning. The Orioles kept the series alive with a 4-2 win in Game 5, but the Indians had the tying runs on base left to end the game.

Mussina's performance in Game 6 was actually better than his Game 3 gem, but again the Orioles could not score for him. Charles Nagy was not as sharp for Cleveland, but 14 Baltimore baserunners were stranded. The play of the game was a perfectly-executed rotation play on Roberto Alomar's bunt in the seventh inning with Williams throwing to Vizquel for the out at third. Tony Fernandez, who got the start at second base because his batting practice line drive damaged the thumb of teammate Bip Roberts, homered to right field in the top of the 11th inning. The Indians bullpen earned all four wins in the series.

Cleveland Indians (C), 4; Baltimore Orioles (E), 2

CLE (C)

PLAYER/POS	AVG	G	AB	R	H	2B	3B	HR	RB	BB	SO	SB
Sandy Alomar, c	.125	6	24	3	3	0	0	1	4	1	3	0
Brian Anderson, p	.000	3	0	0	0	0	0	0	0	0	0	0
Paul Assenmacher, p	.000	5	0	0	0	0	0	0	0	0	0	0
Jeff Branson, dh	.000	1	2	0	0	0	0	0	0	0	2	0
Tony Fernandez, 2b	.357	5	14	1	5	1	0	1	2	1	2	0
Brian Giles, of	.188	6	16	1	3	3	0	0	0	2	6	0
Marquis Grissom, of	.261	6	23	2	6	0	0	1	4	1	9	3
Orel Hershiser, p	.000	1	0	0	0	0	0	0	0	0	0	0
Mike Jackson, p	.000	5	0	0	0	0	0	0	0	0	0	0
Jeff Juden, p	.000	3	0	0	0	0	0	0	0	0	0	0
David Justice, dh	.333	6	21	3	7	1	0	0	0	2	4	0
Jose Mesa, p	.000	4	0	0	0	0	0	0	0	0	0	0
Alvin Morman, p	.000	2	0	0	0	0	0	0	0	0	0	0
Charles Nagy, p	.000	2	0	0	0	0	0	0	0	0	0	0
Chad Ogea, p	.000	2	0	0	0	0	0	0	0	0	0	0
Eric Plunk, p	.000	1	0	0	0	0	0	0	0	0	0	0
Manny Ramirez, of	.286	6	21	3	6	1	0	2	3	5	5	0
Bip Roberts, 2b-4,of-2	.150	5	20	0	3	1	0	0	0	0	8	1
Kevin Seitzer, 1b-3	.000	4	4	0	0	0	0	0	0	1	2	0
Jim Thome, 1b	.071	6	14	3	1	0	0	0	0	5	4	0
Omar Vizquel, ss	.040	6	25	1	1	0	0	0	0	2	10	0
Matt Williams, 3b	.217	6	23	1	5	1	0	0	2	3	7	1
Jaret Wright, p	.000	1	0	0	0	0	0	0	0	0	0	0
TOTAL	.193		207	18	40	8	0	5	15	23	62	5

PITCHER	W	L	ERA	G	GS	CG	SV	SHO	IP	H	ER	BB	SO
Brian Anderson	1	0	1.42	3	0	0	0	0	6.1	1	1	3	7
Paul Assenmacher	1	0	9.00	5	0	0	0	0	2.0	5	2	1	3
Orel Hershiser	0	0	0.00	1	1	0	0	0	7.0	4	0	1	7
Mike Jackson	0	0	0.00	5	0	0	0	0	4.1	1	0	1	7
Jeff Juden	0	0	0.00	3	0	0	0	0	1.0	2	0	2	2
Jose Mesa	1	0	3.38	4	0	0	2	0	5.1	5	2	3	5
Alvin Morman	0	0	0.00	2	0	0	0	0	1.1	0	0	0	1
Charles Nagy	0	0	2.77	2	2	0	0	0	13.0	17	4	5	5
Chad Ogea	0	2	3.21	2	2	0	0	0	14.0	12	5	5	7
Eric Plunk	1	0	0.00	1	0	0	0	0	0.2	1	0	0	0
Jaret Wright	0	0	15.00	1	1	0	0	0	3.0	6	5	2	3
TOTAL	4	2	2.95	29	6	0	2	0	58.0	54	19	23	47

BAL (E)

PLAYER/POS	AVG	G	AB	R	H	2B	3B	HR	RB	BB	SO	SB
Roberto Alomar, 2b	.182	6	22	2	4	0	0	1	2	7	3	0
Brady Anderson, of	.360	6	25	5	9	2	0	2	3	4	4	2
Harold Baines, dh	.353	6	17	1	6	0	0	1	2	2	1	0
Armando Benitez, p	.000	4	0	0	0	0	0	0	0	0	0	0
Geronimo Berroa, of-4,dh-2	.286	6	21	1	6	2	0	0	3	0	3	0
Mike Bordick, ss	.158	6	19	0	3	1	0	0	2	0	6	0
Eric Davis, of-3,dh-3	.154	6	13	1	2	0	0	1	1	1	3	0
Scott Erickson, p	.000	2	0	0	0	0	0	0	0	0	0	0
Jeffrey Hammonds, of-4	.000	5	3	0	0	0	0	0	0	1	2	1
Chris Hoiles, c	.143	4	14	1	2	0	0	0	0	2	5	0
Scott Kamieniecki, p	.000	2	0	0	0	0	0	0	0	0	0	0
Jimmy Key, p	.000	2	0	0	0	0	0	0	0	0	0	0
Alan Mills, p	.000	3	0	0	0	0	0	0	0	0	0	0
Mike Mussina, p	.000	2	0	0	0	0	0	0	0	0	0	0
Randy Myers, p	.000	4	0	0	0	0	0	0	0	0	0	0
Jesse Orosco, p	.000	2	0	0	0	0	0	0	0	0	0	0
Rafael Palmeiro, 1b	.280	6	25	3	7	2	0	1	2	0	10	0
Jeff Reboulet, ss	.000	1	2	1	0	0	0	0	0	0	1	0
Arthur Lee Rhodes, p	.000	2	0	0	0	0	0	0	0	0	0	0
Cal Ripken, 3b	.348	6	23	3	8	2	0	1	3	4	6	0
B.J. Surhoff, of-6,1b-1	.200	6	25	1	5	2	0	0	1	2	2	0
Jerome Walton, of	.000	1	0	0	0	0	0	0	0	0	0	0
Lenny Webster, c-3	.222	4	9	0	2	0	0	0	0	0	1	0
TOTAL	.248		218	19	54	11	0	7	19	23	47	3

PITCHER	W	L	ERA	G	GS	CG	SV	SHO	IP	H	ER	BB	SO
Armando Benitez	0	2	12.00	4	0	0	0	0	3.0	3	4	4	6
Scott Erickson	1	0	4.26	2	2	0	0	0	12.2	15	6	1	6
Scott Kamieniecki	1	0	0.00	2	1	0	0	0	8.0	4	0	2	5
Jimmy Key	0	0	2.57	2	1	0	0	0	7.0	5	2	3	7
Alan Mills	0	1	2.70	3	0	0	0	0	3.1	1	1	2	3
Mike Mussina	0	0	0.60	2	2	0	0	0	15.0	4	1	4	25
Randy Myers	0	1	5.06	4	0	0	1	0	5.1	6	3	3	7
Jesse Orosco	0	0	0.00	2	0	0	0	0	1.1	0	0	1	1
Arthur Lee Rhodes	0	0	0.00	2	0	0	0	0	2.1	2	0	3	2
TOTAL	2	4	2.64	23	6	0	1	0	58.0	40	17	23	62

GAME 1 AT BAL OCT 8

				R	H	E
CLE	000	000	000	0	4	1
BAL	102	000	00X	3	6	1

Pitchers: OGEA, Anderson (7) vs ERICKSON, Myers (9)
Home Runs: Anderson-BAL, Alomar-BAL
Attendance: 49,029

GAME 2 AT BAL OCT 9

				R	H	E
CLE	200	000	030	5	6	3
BAL	020	002	000	4	8	1

Pitchers: Nagy, Morman (6), Juden (6), ASSENMACHER (6), Jackson (8), Mesa (9) vs Key, Kamieneicki (5), BENITEZ (8), Mills (9)
Home Runs: Ramirez-CLE, Ripken-BAL, Grissom-CLE
Attendance: 49,131

GAME 3 AT CLE OCT 11

					R	H	E
BAL	000	000	001	000	1	8	1
CLE	000	000	100	001	2	6	0

Pitchers: Mussina, Benitez (8), Orosco (9), Mills (9), Rhodes (10), MYERS (11) vs Hershiser, Assenmacher (8), Jackson (8), Mesa (9), Juden (11), Morman (11), PLUNK (12)
Attendance: 45,047

GAME 4 AT CLE OCT 12

				R	H	E
BAL	014	000	101	7	12	2
CLE	020	140	001	8	13	0

Pitchers: Erickson, Rhodes (5), MILLS (7), Orosco (9), Benitez (9) vs Wright, Anderson (4), Juden (7), Assenmacher (7), Jackson (7), MESA (8)
Home Runs: Alomar-CLE, Anderson-BAL, Baines-BAL, Palmiero-BAL, Ramirez-CLE
Attendance: 45,081

GAME 5 AT CLE OCT 13

				R	H	E
BAL	002	000	002	4	10	0
CLE	000	000	002	2	8	1

Pitchers: KAMIENIECKI, Key (6), Myers (9) vs OGEA, Assenmacher (9), Jackson (9)
Home Runs: Davis-BAL
Attendance: 45,068

GAME 6 AT BAL OCT 15

					R	H	E
CLE	000	000	000	01	1	3	0
BAL	000	000	000	00	0	10	0

Pitchers: Nagy, Assenmacher (8), Jackson (8), ANDERSON (10), Mesa (11) vs Mussina, Myers (9), BENITEZ (11)
Home Runs: Fernandez-CLE
Attendance: 49,075

Back-to-back home runs by Moises Alou and Charles Johnson in the fifth inning off Orel Hershiser helped the Marlins to a 7-4 win in Game 1 of the World Series. Florida starter Livan Hernandez didn't make it out of the sixth, but a trio of Marlins relievers finished off the Tribe before the first of four crowds of 67,000-plus in Miami. The home crowd didn't have much to cheer about in Game 2 as Bip Roberts and Sandy Alomar each drove in two runs and Chad Ogea pitched the Indians to a 6-1 win.

The temperature in Cleveland for Game 3 was 30 degrees lower and the wind blew almost 20 miles per hour harder than in Miami. The biggest change, though, was on the scorebook. The 25 combined runs and 17 walks were just shy of setting World Series marks, but a defensive play by the not-so slick-fielding Gary Sheffield was as crucial as any hit. The Marlins right fielder, who had five RBIs in the game, leaped to grab Jim Thome's seventh-inning drive at the wall to keep the score tied at 7-7. Cleveland's bullpen and defense collapsed in the ninth, resulting in seven runs. Marlins closer Rob Nen surrendered four runs in the bottom of the ninth, but Florida hung on for the ugly 14-11 win.

The 15-degree wind chill for Game 4 made it the coldest World Series in history, and home runs by Manny Ramirez and Matt Williams made it a long night for the Marlins. Jaret Wright outdistanced Tony Saunders amid snow flurries as the Indians evened the World Series with a 10-3 win. In Game 5 Alou hit his second three-run home run off Orel Hershiser, his third homer of the Series. Hernandez, who would be named Series MVP, pitched into the ninth inning of Florida's 8-7 win. In Game 6 Ogea had two hits, two RBIs, scored a run, and also earned the 4-1 win for the Indians to set the stage for a seventh game.

Starters Al Leiter and Jaret Wright both pitched well, but Game 7 came down to the bullpen. The Indians were within two outs of their first world championship since 1948 when Craig Counsell's sacrifice fly drove in the tying run in the ninth inning off Jose Mesa. Edgar Renteria ended the second-longest seventh game in World Series history with a bases-loaded single over the glove of Indians pitcher Charles Nagy with two outs in the 11th inning. Counsell crossed home plate with the deciding run in Florida's 3-2 win to make the Marlins the first Wild Card team to win the World Series. Tony Fernandez drove in both Cleveland runs, but his crucial error prolonged the deciding rally.

Florida Marlins (N), 4; Cleveland Indians (A), 3

FLA (N)

PLAYER/POS	AVG	G	AB	R	H	2B	3B	HR	RB	BB	SO	SB
Kurt Abbott, dh-1	.000	3	3	0	0	0	0	0	0	0	1	0
Antonio Alfonseca, p	.000	3	0	0	0	0	0	0	0	0	0	0
Moises Alou, of	.321	7	28	6	9	2	0	3	9	3	6	1
Alex Arias, 3b-1,dh-1	.000	2	1	1	0	0	0	0	0	0	0	0
Bobby Bonilla, 3b	.207	7	29	5	6	1	0	1	3	3	5	0
Kevin Brown, p	.000	2	3	0	0	0	0	0	0	0	1	0
John Cangelosi, ph	.333	3	3	0	1	0	0	0	0	0	2	0
Jeff Conine, 1b	.231	6	13	1	3	0	0	0	2	0	0	0
Dennis Cook, p	.000	3	0	0	0	0	0	0	0	0	0	0
Craig Counsell, 2b	.182	7	22	4	4	1	0	0	2	6	5	1
Darren Daulton, 1b-5,dh-1	.389	7	18	7	7	2	0	1	2	3	0	1
Jim Eisenreich, 1b-2,dh-2	.500	5	8	1	4	0	0	1	3	3	1	0
Cliff Floyd, dh-1	.000	4	2	1	0	0	0	0	0	1	1	0
Felix Heredia, p	.000	4	0	0	0	0	0	0	0	0	0	0
Livan Hernandez, p	.000	2	2	0	0	0	0	0	0	0	0	0
Charles Johnson, c	.357	7	28	4	10	0	0	1	3	1	6	0
Al Leiter, p	.000	2	0	0	0	0	0	0	0	2	0	0
Robb Nen, p	.000	4	0	0	0	0	0	0	0	0	0	0
Jay Powell, p	.000	4	0	0	0	0	0	0	0	0	0	0
Edgar Renteria, ss	.290	7	31	3	9	2	0	0	3	3	5	0
Tony Saunders, p	.000	1	0	0	0	0	0	0	0	0	0	0
Gary Sheffield, of	.292	7	24	4	7	1	0	1	5	8	5	0
Ed Vosberg, p	.000	2	0	0	0	0	0	0	0	0	0	0
Devon White, of	.242	7	33	0	8	3	1	0	2	3	10	1
Greg Zaun, c-1	.000	2	2	0	0	0	0	0	0	0	0	0
TOTAL	.272		250	37	68	12	1	8	34	36	48	4

PITCHER	W	L	ERA	G	GS	CG	SV	SHO	IP	H	ER	BB	SO
Antonio Alfonseca	0	0	0.00	3	0	0	0	0	6.1	6	0	1	5
Kevin Brown	0	2	8.18	2	2	0	0	0	11.0	15	10	5	6
Dennis Cook	1	0	0.00	3	0	0	0	0	3.2	1	0	1	5
Felix Heredia	0	0	0.00	4	0	0	0	0	5.1	2	0	1	5
Livan Hernandez	2	0	5.27	2	2	0	0	0	13.2	15	8	10	7
Al Leiter	0	0	5.06	2	2	0	0	0	10.2	10	6	10	10
Robb Nen	0	0	7.71	4	0	0	2	0	4.2	8	4	2	7
Jay Powell	1	0	7.36	4	0	0	0	0	3.2	5	3	4	2
Tony Saunders	0	1	27.00	1	1	0	0	0	2.0	7	6	3	2
Ed Vosberg	0	0	6.00	2	0	0	0	0	3.0	3	2	3	2
TOTAL	4	3	5.48	27	7	0	2	0	64.0	72	39	40	51

CLE (A)

PLAYER/POS	AVG	G	AB	R	H	2B	3B	HR	RB	BB	SO	SB
Sandy Alomar, c	.367	7	30	5	11	1	0	2	10	2	3	0
Brian Anderson, p	.000	3	0	0	0	0	0	0	0	0	0	0
Paul Assenmacher, p	.000	5	0	0	0	0	0	0	0	0	0	0
Jeff Branson, ph	.000	1	1	0	0	0	0	0	0	0	1	0
Tony Fernandez, 2b	.471	5	17	1	8	1	0	0	4	0	1	0
Brian Giles, of-2	.500	5	4	1	2	1	0	0	2	4	1	0
Marquis Grissom, of	.360	7	25	5	9	1	0	0	2	4	4	0
Orel Hershiser, p	.000	2	2	0	0	0	0	0	0	0	1	0
Mike Jackson, p	.000	4	2	0	0	0	0	0	0	0	1	0
Jeff Juden, p	.000	2	0	0	0	0	0	0	0	0	0	0
David Justice, of-4,dh-3	.185	7	27	4	5	0	0	0	4	6	8	0
Jose Mesa, p	.000	5	0	0	0	0	0	0	0	0	0	0
Alvin Morman, p	.000	2	0	0	0	0	0	0	0	0	0	0
Charles Nagy, p	.000	2	0	0	0	0	0	0	0	0	0	0
Chad Ogea, p	.500	2	4	1	2	1	0	0	2	0	1	0
Eric Plunk, p	.000	3	0	0	0	0	0	0	0	0	0	0
Manny Ramirez, of	.154	7	26	3	4	0	0	2	6	6	5	0
Bip Roberts, 2b-4,of-2	.273	6	22	3	6	4	0	0	4	3	5	0
Kevin Seitzer, ph	.000	1	1	0	0	0	0	0	0	0	0	0
Jim Thome, 1b	.286	7	28	8	8	0	1	2	4	5	7	0
Omar Vizquel, ss	.233	7	30	5	7	2	0	0	1	3	5	5
Matt Williams, 3b	.385	7	26	8	10	1	0	1	3	7	6	0
Jaret Wright, p	.000	2	2	0	0	0	0	0	0	0	2	0
TOTAL	.291		247	44	72	12	1	7	42	40	51	5

PITCHER	W	L	ERA	G	GS	CG	SV	SHO	IP	H	ER	BB	SO
Brian Anderson	0	0	2.45	3	0	0	1	0	3.2	2	1	0	2
Paul Assenmacher	0	0	0.00	5	0	0	0	0	4.0	5	0	0	6
Orel Hershiser	0	2	11.70	2	2	0	0	0	10.0	15	13	6	5
Mike Jackson	0	0	1.93	4	0	0	0	0	4.2	5	1	3	4
Jeff Juden	0	0	4.50	2	0	0	0	0	2.0	2	1	2	0
Jose Mesa	0	0	5.40	5	0	0	1	0	5.0	10	3	1	5
Alvin Morman	0	0	0.00	2	0	0	0	0	0.1	0	0	2	1
Charles Nagy	0	1	6.43	2	1	0	0	0	7.0	8	5	5	5
Chad Ogea	2	0	1.54	2	2	0	0	0	11.2	11	2	3	5
Eric Plunk	0	1	9.00	3	0	0	0	0	3.0	3	3	4	3
Jaret Wright	1	0	2.92	2	2	0	0	0	12.1	7	4	10	12
TOTAL	3	4	4.66	32	7	0	2	0	63.2	68	33	36	48

GAME 1 AT FLA OCT 18

				R	H	E
CLE	100	011	010	4	11	0
FLA	001	420	00X	7	7	1

Pitchers: HERSHISER, Juden (5), Plunk (6), Assenmacher (8) vs HERNANDEZ, Cook (6), Powell (8), Nen (9)
Home Runs: Alou-FLA, Johnson-FLA, Ramirez-CLE, Thome-CLE
Attendance: 67,245

GAME 2 AT FLA OCT 19

				R	H	E
CLE	100	032	000	6	14	0
FLA	100	000	000	1	8	0

Pitchers: OGEA, Jackson (7), Mesa (9) vs BROWN, Heredia (7), Alfonseca (8)
Home Runs: Alomar-CLE
Attendance: 67,025

GAME 3 AT CLE OCT 21

				R	H	E
FLA	101	102	207	14	16	3
CLE	200	320	004	11	10	3

Pitchers: Leiter, Heredia (5), COOK (8), Nen (9) vs Nagy, Anderson (7), Jackson (7), Assenmacher (8), PLUBK (8), Morman (9), Mesa (9)
Home Runs: Sheffield-FLA, Daulton-FLA, Thome-CLE, Esienreich-FLA
Attendance: 44,880

GAME 4 AT CLE OCT 22

				R	H	E
FLA	000	102	000	3	6	2
CLE	303	001	12X	10	15	0

Pitchers: SAUNDERS, Alfonseca (3), Vosberg (6), Powell (8) vs WRIGHT, Anderson (7)
Home Runs: Ramirez-CLE, Alou-FLA, Williams-CLE
Attendance: 44,877

GAME 5 AT CLE OCT 23

				R	H	E
FLA	020	004	011	8	15	2
CLE	013	000	003	7	9	0

Pitchers: HERNANDEZ, Nen (9) vs HERSHISER, Morman (6), Plunk (6), Juden (7), Assenmacher (8), Mesa (9)
Home Runs: Alomar-CLE, Alou-FLA
Attendance: 44,888

GAME 6 AT FLA OCT 25

				R	H	E
CLE	020	101	000	4	7	0
FLA	000	010	000	1	8	0

Pitchers: OGEA, Jackson (6), Assenmacher (8), Mesa (9) vs BROWN, Heredia (6), Powell (8), Vosberg (9)
Attendance: 67,498

GAME 7 AT FLA OCT 26

					R	H	E
CLE	002	000	000	00	2	6	2
FLA	000	000	101	01	3	8	0

Pitchers: Wright, Assenmacher (7), Jackson (8), Anderson (8), Mesa (9), NAGY (10) vs Leiter, Cook (7), Alfonseca (8), Heredia (9), Nen (9), POWELL (11)
Home Runs: Bonilla-FLA
Attendance: 67,204

The Astros and Padres had both won division titles by comfortable margins, but Houston was given the pre-series edge because they had won more games and held advantages in many offensive and defensive categories. Plus, the Astros had Randy Johnson, the 6-foot-10-inch left-hander obtained from Seattle who went 10-1 with a 1.28 ERA down the stretch. The Astros also had home-field advantage in the Division Series. Yet none of that prepared the Astros for Kevin Brown or Jim Leyritz. Brown struck out 16 and limited Houston to just two hits in eight innings in Game 1; Leyritz, who drove in at least one run in each game of the series, brought in the first run with a sacrifice fly in the sixth inning. Greg Vaughn added a home run off Johnson in the eighth and the Padres held on for the 2-1 win.

The Astros led Game 2 from the first inning as Jeff Bagwell drove in three runs and Derek Bell added a home run to take a 4-2 lead into the top of the ninth. Leyritz, who hit dramatic postseason home runs for the Yankees in 1995 and '96, lofted an opposite-field, two-run home run just inside the right-field foul pole to tie the game. Houston's Ricky Gutierrez stole third base in the bottom of the ninth and then scored when Bill Spiers singled to end the game and tie the series.

With an extra off day on the schedule, Padres manager Bruce Bochy moved Brown up in the rotation to pitch Game 3. Brown lowered his ERA for the series to 0.61 and reliever Dan Miceli came in with the bases loaded in the top of the seventh to strike out Spiers and keep the game tied at 1-1. Leyritz homered off Scott Elarton in the bottom of the seventh as the Padres took a 2-1 lead in the game and the series. The second consecutive crowd of more than 64,000 in San Diego watched Leyritz hit his third home run of the series in Game 4. Padres left-hander Sterling Hitchcock struck out 11 of the 21 batters he faced and earned the win when Sean Berry threw away Ken Caminiti's grounder to bring in the go-ahead run in the sixth. The Padres tacked on four insurance runs in the eighth on a two-run triple by John Vander Wal and a two-run homer by Wally Joyner. Trevor Hoffman, who pitched in all four games, set down the Astros in the ninth inning.

San Diego Padres (W), 3; Houston Astros (C), 1

SD (W)

PLAYER/POS	AVG	G	AB	R	H	2B	3B	HR	RB	BB	SO	SB
George Arias, ph	.000	1	1	0	0	0	0	0	0	0	1	0
Andy Ashby, p	.000	1	1	0	0	0	0	0	0	0	0	0
Kevin Brown, p	.000	2	3	0	0	0	0	0	0	0	2	0
Ken Caminiti, 3b	.143	4	14	2	2	0	0	0	0	1	3	0
Steve Finley, of	.100	4	10	2	1	1	0	0	1	1	4	0
Chris Gomez, ss	.273	4	11	1	3	0	0	0	0	4	1	0
Tony Gwynn, of	.200	4	15	1	3	2	0	0	2	0	2	0
Joey Hamilton, p	.000	2	0	0	0	0	0	0	0	0	0	0
Carlos Hernandez, c	.417	4	12	0	5	0	0	0	0	0	0	0
Sterling Hitchcock, p	.000	1	2	0	0	0	0	0	0	0	1	0
Trevor Hoffman, p	.000	4	0	0	0	0	0	0	0	0	0	0
Wally Joyner, 1b	.167	4	6	1	1	0	0	1	2	1	2	0
Jim Leyritz, 1b-3,c-1	.400	4	10	3	4	0	0	3	5	0	2	0
Dan Miceli, p	.000	3	0	0	0	0	0	0	0	0	0	0
Greg Myers, c	.000	1	0	0	0	0	0	0	0	0	0	0
Ruben Rivera, of	.000	3	6	0	0	0	0	0	0	0	3	0
Andy Sheets, 2b-1	.000	2	0	0	0	0	0	0	0	0	0	0
Mark Sweeney, ph	.000	2	1	0	0	0	0	0	0	1	0	0
John Vander Wal, ph	.333	3	3	1	1	0	1	0	2	0	1	0
Greg Vaughn, of	.333	4	15	2	5	1	0	1	1	0	4	0
Quilvio Veras, 2b	.133	4	15	1	2	0	0	0	0	1	6	0
Donne Wall, p	.000	1	0	0	0	0	0	0	0	0	0	0
TOTAL	.216		125	14	27	4	1	5	13	9	32	0

PITCHER	W	L	ERA	G	GS	CG	SV	SHO	IP	H	ER	BB	SO
Andy Ashby	0	0	6.75	1	1	0	0	0	4.0	6	3	1	4
Kevin Brown	1	0	0.61	2	2	0	0	0	14.2	5	1	7	21
Joey Hamilton	0	0	0.00	2	0	0	0	0	3.1	1	0	2	3
Sterling Hitchcock	1	0	1.50	1	1	0	0	0	6.0	3	1	0	11
Trevor Hoffman	0	0	0.00	4	0	0	2	0	3.0	3	0	1	4
Dan Miceli	1	1	2.70	3	0	0	0	0	3.1	2	1	0	4
Donne Wall	0	0	9.00	1	0	0	0	0	1.0	2	1	0	2
TOTAL	3	1	1.78	14	4	0	2	0	35.1	22	7	11	49

HOU (C)

PLAYER/POS	AVG	G	AB	R	H	2B	3B	HR	RB	BB	SO	SB
Moises Alou, of	.188	4	16	0	3	0	0	0	0	0	2	0
Brad Ausmus, c	.222	4	9	0	2	0	0	0	0	0	4	0
Jeff Bagwell, 1b	.143	4	14	0	2	0	0	0	4	1	6	0
Derek Bell, of	.125	4	16	1	2	0	0	1	1	0	7	0
Sean Berry, 3b	.000	1	2	0	0	0	0	0	0	0	1	0
Craig Biggio, 2b	.182	4	11	3	2	1	0	0	1	4	4	0
Dave Clark, ph	.000	2	0	0	0	0	0	0	0	2	0	0
Scott Elarton, p	.000	1	0	0	0	0	0	0	0	0	0	0
Raul Eusebio, c	.333	1	3	0	1	1	0	0	0	0	2	0
Carl Everett, of-3	.154	4	13	1	2	0	0	0	0	0	4	0
Ricky Gutierrez, ss	.300	4	10	1	3	0	0	0	0	3	7	1
Mike Hampton, p	.000	1	2	0	0	0	0	0	0	0	2	0
Doug Henry, p	.000	2	0	0	0	0	0	0	0	0	0	0
Richard Hidalgo, of	.250	1	4	0	1	0	0	0	0	0	1	0
Pete Incaviglia, ph	.000	1	1	0	0	0	0	0	0	0	1	0
Randy Johnson, p	.000	2	4	0	0	0	0	0	0	0	4	0
Trever Miller, p	.000	1	0	0	0	0	0	0	0	0	0	0
Jay Powell, p	.000	3	0	0	0	0	0	0	0	0	0	0
Shane Reynolds, p	.000	1	2	0	0	0	0	0	0	0	1	0
Bill Spiers, 3b	.286	4	14	2	4	3	0	0	1	1	3	0
Billy Wagner, p	.000	1	0	0	0	0	0	0	0	0	0	0
TOTAL	.182		121	8	22	5	0	1	7	11	49	1

PITCHER	W	L	ERA	G	GS	CG	SV	SHO	IP	H	ER	BB	SO
Scott Elarton	0	1	4.50	1	0	0	0	0	2.0	1	1	1	3
Mike Hampton	0	0	1.50	1	1	0	0	0	6.0	2	1	1	2
Doug Henry	0	0	5.40	2	0	0	0	0	1.2	2	1	0	1
Randy Johnson	0	2	1.93	2	2	0	0	0	14.0	12	3	2	17
Trever Miller	0	0	INF	1	0	0	0	0	0.0	0	0	1	0
Jay Powell	0	0	11.57	3	0	0	0	0	2.1	2	3	3	3
Shane Reynolds	0	0	2.57	1	1	0	0	0	7.0	4	2	1	5
Billy Wagner	1	0	18.00	1	0	0	0	0	1.0	4	2	0	1
TOTAL	1	3	3.44	12	4	0	0	0	34.0	27	13	9	32

GAME 1 AT HOU SEPT 29

				R	H	E
SD	000	001	010	2	9	1
HOU	000	000	001	1	4	0

Pitchers: BROWN, Hoffman (9) vs JOHNSON, Powell (9), Henry (9)
Home Runs: Vaughn-SD
Attendance: 50,080

GAME 2 AT HOU OCT 1

				R	H	E
SD	000	002	002	4	8	1
HOU	102	000	011	5	11	1

Pitchers: Ashby, Hamilton (5), Wall (8), MICELI (9), Hoffman (9) vs Reynolds, Powell (8), WAGNER (9)
Home Runs: Leyritz-SD, Bell-HOU
Attendance: 45,550

GAME 3 AT SD OCT 3

				R	H	E
HOU	000	000	100	1	4	0
SD	000	001	10X	2	3	0

Pitchers: Hampton, ELARTON (7) vs Brown, MICELI (7), Hoffman (9)
Home Runs: Leyritz-SD
Attendance: 65,235

GAME 4 AT SD OCT 4

				R	H	E
HOU	000	100	000	1	3	1
SD	010	001	04X	6	7	1

Pitchers: JOHNSON, Miller (7), Henry (7), Powell (8) vs HITCHCOCK, Hamilton (7), Miceli (7), Hoffman (9)
Home Runs: Leyritz-SD, Joyner-SD
Attendance: 64,898

The Cubs had just completed a remarkable season that included Sammy Sosa's home run chase with Mark McGwire and a three-way wild card race, while the Braves were just getting ready for business as usual in October. Atlanta, making its seventh consecutive trip to the postseason, was coming off a regular season that included a franchise-best 106 wins. By contrast, the Cubs had won 90 games, and they needed a one-game playoff victory over the Giants to secure a postseason berth for the first time in nine years.

The teams started even in Game 1, but the Braves still had great pitching. John Smoltz, who went 17-3 during the season, handcuffed the Cubs on five hits. Atlanta took the lead on Michael Tucker's home run in the second inning following a two-out error. A grand slam by Ryan Klesko in the seventh put the game out of reach.

Chicago's Kevin Tapani, a 19-game winner, outpitched 20-game winner Tom Glavine in Game 2. Tapani had a four-hit shutout through eight innings, and manager Jim Riggleman, hoping to save an exhausted bullpen, let the right-hander pitch the ninth inning with a 1-0 lead. Javier Lopez homered to left with one out to tie the game. Terry Mulholland relieved in the 10th, but he missed the first base bag on a bunt play to put runners on first and second for Chipper Jones. Jones hit a line drive that landed just inside the left field line to bring in the winning run.

Atlanta's Greg Maddux, who won the first of his four Cy Young Awards as a Cub in 1992, had the task of quieting the raucous crowd at Wrigley Field in Game 3. Maddux outdid Cubs phenom Kerry Wood on the mound and on the basepaths. A superb slide enabled Maddux to stretch a double in the third inning, and, after he crossed to third on a groundout, he scored on a passed ball. In the top of the eighth, Gerald Williams singled in Atlanta's second run, and Eddie Perez lifted a grand slam to left off Rod Beck. Maddux was charged with two runs in the eighth, but Kerry Ligtenberg relieved and finished off the Cubs. Atlanta pitching held Chicago to just three extra-base hits and four runs in the series, while Sosa, who clubbed 66 home runs during the season, was one of six Cubs regulars to bat under .200 in Atlanta's sweep.

Atlanta Braves (E), 3; Chicago Cubs (C), 0

ATL (E)

PLAYER/POS	AVG	G	AB	R	H	2B	3B	HR	RB	BB	SO	SB
Danny Bautista, of	.500	2	2	0	1	1	0	0	0	0	0	0
Greg Colbrunn, ph	.000	2	2	0	0	0	0	0	0	0	0	0
Andres Galarraga, 1b	.250	3	12	1	3	0	0	0	0	1	3	0
Tom Glavine, p	.000	1	1	0	0	0	0	0	0	0	0	0
Tony Graffanino, ph	.000	1	0	0	0	0	0	0	0	0	0	0
Ozzie Guillen, ph	.000	1	1	0	0	0	0	0	0	0	0	0
Andruw Jones, of	.000	3	9	2	0	0	0	0	1	3	2	2
Chipper Jones, 3b	.200	2	10	2	2	0	0	0	1	4	3	0
Ryan Klesko, of	.273	3	11	1	3	0	0	1	4	0	3	0
Kerry Ligtenberg, p	.000	3	0	0	0	0	0	0	0	0	0	0
Keith Lockhart, 2b	.333	3	12	2	4	0	0	0	0	1	0	0
Javy Lopez, c	.286	2	7	1	2	0	0	1	1	1	1	0
Greg Maddux, p	.250	1	4	1	1	1	0	0	0	0	1	0
Eddie Perez, c	.200	1	5	1	1	0	0	1	4	0	2	0
Odaliz Perez, p	.000	1	0	0	0	0	0	0	0	0	0	0
John Rocker, p	.000	2	0	0	0	0	0	0	0	0	0	0
Rudy Seanez, p	.000	1	0	0	0	0	0	0	0	0	0	0
John Smoltz, p	.500	1	2	0	1	0	0	0	0	1	1	0
Michael Tucker, of	.250	3	8	1	2	0	0	1	2	2	0	1
Walt Weiss, ss	.154	3	13	2	2	0	0	0	0	1	3	0
Gerald Williams, of	.500	2	2	1	1	0	0	0	1	0	1	0
TOTAL	.228		101	15	23	2	0	4	14	14	20	3

PITCHER	W	L	ERA	G	GS	CG	SV	SHO	IP	H	ER	BB	SO
Tom Glavine	0	0	1.29	1	1	0	0	0	7.0	3	1	1	8
Kerry Ligtenberg	0	0	0.00	3	0	0	0	0	3.1	1	0	4	3
Greg Maddux	1	0	2.57	1	1	0	0	0	7.0	7	2	0	4
Odaliz Perez	1	0	0.00	1	0	0	0	0	0.2	0	0	0	1
John Rocker	0	0	0.00	2	0	0	0	0	1.1	1	0	0	2
Rudy Seanez	0	0	0.00	1	0	0	0	0	1.0	0	0	0	0
John Smoltz	1	0	1.17	1	1	0	0	0	7.2	5	1	0	6
TOTAL	3	0	1.29	10	3	0	0	0	28.0	17	4	5	24

CHI (C)

PLAYER/POS	AVG	G	AB	R	H	2B	3B	HR	RB	BB	SO	SB
Manny Alexander, ss-1	.000	2	5	0	0	0	0	0	0	0	1	0
Rod Beck, p	.000	1	0	0	0	0	0	0	0	0	0	0
Jeff Blauser, ph	.000	2	2	0	0	0	0	0	0	0	1	0
Brant Brown, ph	.000	1	1	0	0	0	0	0	0	0	0	0
Mark Clark, p	.500	1	2	0	1	0	0	0	0	0	0	0
Gary Gaetti, 3b	.091	3	11	0	1	0	0	0	0	0	4	0
Mark Grace, 1b	.083	3	12	0	1	0	0	0	1	0	2	0
Felix Heredia, p	.000	1	0	0	0	0	0	0	0	0	0	0
Jose Hernandez, ss	.286	2	7	1	2	0	0	0	0	0	2	0
Glenallen Hill, of	.333	1	3	0	1	0	0	0	0	1	2	1
Tyler Houston, c	.167	3	6	1	1	0	0	1	1	0	3	0
Lance Johnson, of	.167	3	12	0	2	0	0	0	1	0	1	0
Matt Karchner, p	.000	1	0	0	0	0	0	0	0	0	0	0
Angel Martinez, c	1.000	1	1	1	1	0	0	0	0	0	0	0
Mickey Morandini, 2b	.222	3	9	1	2	0	0	0	1	2	2	0
Mike Morgan, p	.000	2	0	0	0	0	0	0	0	0	0	0
Terry Mulholland, p	.000	2	0	0	0	0	0	0	0	0	0	0
Henry Rodriguez, of-2	.143	3	7	0	1	1	0	0	0	1	2	0
Scott Servais, c	.667	1	3	0	2	0	0	0	0	0	0	0
Sammy Sosa, of	.182	3	11	0	2	1	0	0	0	1	4	0
Kevin Tapani, p	.000	1	1	0	0	0	0	0	0	0	0	0
Kerry Wood, p	.000	1	1	0	0	0	0	0	0	0	0	0
TOTAL	.181		94	4	17	2	0	1	4	5	24	1

PITCHER	W	L	ERA	G	GS	CG	SV	SHO	IP	H	ER	BB	SO
Rod Beck	0	0	16.20	1	0	0	0	0	1.2	5	3	2	1
Mark Clark	0	1	3.00	1	1	0	0	0	6.0	7	2	1	4
Felix Heredia	0	0	54.00	1	0	0	0	0	0.1	0	2	2	0
Matt Karchner	0	0	13.50	1	0	0	0	0	0.2	1	1	0	1
Mike Morgan	0	0	0.00	2	0	0	0	0	1.1	0	0	0	1
Terry Mulholland	0	1	11.57	2	0	0	0	0	2.1	2	3	2	2
Kevin Tapani	0	0	1.00	1	1	0	0	0	9.0	5	1	3	6
Kerry Wood	0	1	1.80	1	1	0	0	0	5.0	3	1	4	5
TOTAL	0	3	4.44	10	3	0	0	0	26.1	23	13	14	20

GAME 1 AT ATL SEPT 30

		R	H	E
CHI	000 000 010	1	5	1
ATL	020 001 40X	7	8	0

Pitchers: CLARK, Heredia (7), Karchner (7), Morgan (8) vs SMOLTZ, Rocker (8), Ligtenberg (9)

Home Runs: Tucker-ATL, Klesko-ATL, Houston-CHI

Attendance: 45,598

GAME 2 AT ATL OCT 1

		R	H	E
CHI	000 001 000 0	1	4	1
ATL	000 000 001 1	2	6	0

Pitchers: Tapani, MULHOLLAND (10) vs Glavine, Rocker (8), Seanez (9), Ligtenberg (10), O.PEREZ (10)

Home Runs: Lopez-ATL

Attendance: 51,713

GAME 3 AT CHI OCT 3

		R	H	E
ATL	001 000 050	6	9	0
CHI	000 000 020	2	8	2

Pitchers: MADDUX, Ligtenberg (8) vs WOOD, Mulholland (6), Beck (8), Morgan (9)

Home Runs: E.Perez-ATL

Attendance: 39,597

The Boston Red Sox had to go back to Game 5 of the 1986 World Series for the team's last postseason win, but they broke out of their postseason slump in a big way. Their string of 13 straight postseason losses (two World Series games, eight Championship Series games, and three Division Series games) ended quickly against the Indians in the opening game of the 1998 Division Series. Mo Vaughn launched a home run to left field with two men on in the first inning, then homered again with a runner on in the sixth, before he capped the day with a two-run double in the eighth. Nomar Garciaparra added a home run and a sacrifice fly as the two Boston sluggers drove in each run of their team's 11-3 win. For the series, the pair combined for 19 runs batted in, while the rest of the team drove in just one run.

The Red Sox jumped out to a quick 2-0 lead in the first inning of Game 2 as both Cleveland manager Mike Hargrove and starting pitcher Dwight Gooden were ejected after separate arguments with umpire Joe Brinkman. The Indians were a new team after that. They chased Boston starter Tim Wakefield in a five-run second inning, Dave Burba pitched five and a third innings of relief for the win, and Mike Jackson tossed the final two innings to even the series. In the third game the Indians managed just five hits, but four of those were solo home runs as Cleveland held on for a 4-3 win in Boston. The home run that wound up being the most important was Manny Ramirez's second of the game in the top of the ninth. Garciaparra's two-run home run in the bottom of the ninth cut the lead to 4-3, but two groundouts ended the game.

Both the fans and the press alike were critical of Boston manager Jimy Williams for not starting his ace, Pedro Martinez, on three day's rest in Game 4. Martinez, who won Game 1, watched as Pete Schourek pitched five and a third strong innings and left with a 1-0 lead supplied by Garciaparra's third home run of the series. Boston closer Tom Gordon had not blown a save since April 14, but he surrendered the lead in the eighth inning on a two-run double by left fielder David Justice, who had also thrown out John Valentin at the plate in the sixth inning. Jackson earned his third save in as many games as the Indians defeated the Red Sox in the postseason for the second time in three years.

Cleveland Indians (C), 3; Boston Red Sox (E), 1

CLE (C)

PLAYER/POS	AVG	G	AB	R	H	2B	3B	HR	RB	BB	SO	SB
Sandy Alomar, c	.231	4	13	2	3	3	0	0	2	1	4	0
Paul Assenmacher, p	.000	3	0	0	0	0	0	0	0	0	0	0
Dave Burba, p	.000	1	0	0	0	0	0	0	0	0	0	0
Bartolo Colon, p	.000	1	0	0	0	0	0	0	0	0	0	0
Joey Cora, 2b	.000	4	10	2	0	0	0	0	0	3	2	0
Travis Fryman, 3b	.154	4	13	1	2	1	0	0	0	3	4	1
Brian Giles, of-2,dh-1	.200	3	10	1	2	1	0	0	0	1	4	0
Dwight Gooden, p	.000	1	0	0	0	0	0	0	0	0	0	0
Mike Jackson, p	.000	3	0	0	0	0	0	0	0	0	0	0
Doug Jones, p	.000	1	0	0	0	0	0	0	0	0	0	0
David Justice, of-2,dh-2	.313	4	16	2	5	4	0	1	6	0	1	0
Kenny Lofton, of	.375	4	16	5	6	1	0	2	4	1	1	2
Charles Nagy, p	.000	1	0	0	0	0	0	0	0	0	0	0
Jim Poole, p	.000	2	0	0	0	0	0	0	0	0	0	0
Manny Ramirez, of	.357	4	14	2	5	2	0	2	3	1	4	0
Steve Reed, p	.000	2	0	0	0	0	0	0	0	0	0	0
Richie Sexson, 1b	.000	3	2	0	0	0	0	0	0	2	1	0
Paul Shuey, p	.000	3	0	0	0	0	0	0	0	0	0	0
Jim Thome, 1b-3,dh-1	.133	4	15	2	2	0	0	2	2	2	5	0
Omar Vizquel, ss	.067	4	15	1	1	0	0	0	0	1	0	0
Enrique Wilson, 2b	.000	1	2	0	0	0	0	0	0	0	0	0
Jaret Wright, p	.000	1	0	0	0	0	0	0	0	0	0	0
TOTAL	.206		126	18	26	12	0	7	17	15	26	3

PITCHER	W	L	ERA	G	GS	CG	SV	SHO	IP	H	ER	BB	SO
Paul Assenmacher	0	0	0.00	3	0	0	0	0	1.0	2	0	0	2
Dave Burba	1	0	5.06	1	0	0	0	0	5.1	4	3	2	4
Bartolo Colon	0	0	1.59	1	1	0	0	0	5.2	5	1	3	3
Dwight Gooden	0	0	54.00	1	1	0	0	0	0.1	1	2	2	1
Mike Jackson	0	0	4.50	3	0	0	3	0	4.0	3	2	1	1
Doug Jones	0	0	6.75	1	0	0	0	0	2.2	3	2	1	1
Charles Nagy	1	0	1.13	1	1	0	0	0	8.0	4	1	0	3
Jim Poole	0	0	0.00	2	0	0	0	0	1.0	1	0	1	2
Steve Reed	1	0	40.50	2	0	0	0	0	0.2	1	3	1	1
Paul Shuey	0	0	0.00	3	0	0	0	0	3.0	3	0	1	4
Jaret Wright	0	1	12.46	1	1	0	0	0	4.1	7	6	2	6
TOTAL	3	1	5.00	19	4	0	3	0	36.0	34	20	14	28

BOS (E)

PLAYER/POS	AVG	G	AB	R	H	2B	3B	HR	RB	BB	SO	SB
Mike Benjamin, 2b-4,1b-1	.091	4	11	1	1	0	0	0	0	1	3	0
Darren Bragg, of	.083	3	12	0	1	0	0	0	0	0	5	0
Damon Buford, of-1,dh-1	.000	3	1	2	0	0	0	0	0	0	0	0
Jim Corsi, p	.000	2	0	0	0	0	0	0	0	0	0	0
Midre Cummings, ph	.000	3	3	0	0	0	0	0	0	0	0	0
Dennis Eckersley, p	.000	1	0	0	0	0	0	0	0	0	0	0
Nomar Garciaparra, ss	.333	4	15	4	5	1	0	3	11	1	0	0
Tom Gordon, p	.000	2	0	0	0	0	0	0	0	0	0	0
Scott Hatteberg, c	.111	3	9	0	1	0	0	0	0	3	1	0
Darren Lewis, of	.357	4	14	4	5	2	0	0	0	1	3	1
Derek Lowe, p	.000	2	0	0	0	0	0	0	0	0	0	0
Pedro Martinez, p	.000	1	0	0	0	0	0	0	0	0	0	0
Trot Nixon, of	.333	2	3	0	1	0	0	0	0	1	0	0
Troy O'Leary, of	.063	4	16	0	1	0	0	0	0	1	4	0
Bret Saberhagen, p	.000	1	0	0	0	0	0	0	0	0	0	0
Donnie Sadler, 2b	.000	3	0	0	0	0	0	0	0	0	0	0
Pete Schourek, p	.000	1	0	0	0	0	0	0	0	0	0	0
Mike Stanley, dh	.267	4	15	1	4	0	0	0	0	2	5	0
Greg Swindell, p	.000	1	0	0	0	0	0	0	0	0	0	0
John Valentin, 3b	.467	4	15	5	7	1	0	0	0	3	1	0
Jason Varitek, c	.250	1	4	0	1	0	0	0	1	0	1	0
Mo Vaughn, 1b	.412	4	17	3	7	2	0	2	7	1	5	0
Tim Wakefield, p	.000	1	0	0	0	0	0	0	0	0	0	0
John Wasdin, p	.000	1	0	0	0	0	0	0	0	0	0	0
TOTAL	.252		135	20	34	6	0	5	19	14	28	1

PITCHER	W	L	ERA	G	GS	CG	SV	SHO	IP	H	ER	BB	SO
Jim Corsi	0	0	0.00	2	0	0	0	0	3.0	1	0	1	2
Dennis Eckersley	0	0	9.00	1	0	0	0	0	1.0	1	1	0	1
Tom Gordon	0	1	9.00	2	0	0	0	0	3.0	4	3	4	1
Derek Lowe	0	0	2.08	2	0	0	0	0	4.1	3	1	1	2
Pedro Martinez	1	0	3.86	1	1	0	0	0	7.0	6	3	0	8
Bret Saberhagen	0	1	3.86	1	1	0	0	0	7.0	4	3	1	7
Pete Schourek	0	0	0.00	1	1	0	0	0	5.1	2	0	4	1
Greg Swindell	0	0	0.00	1	0	0	0	0	1.1	0	0	1	1
Tim Wakefield	0	1	33.75	1	1	0	0	0	1.1	3	5	2	1
John Wasdin	0	0	10.80	1	0	0	0	0	1.2	2	2	1	2
TOTAL	1	3	4.63	13	4	0	0	0	35.0	26	18	15	26

GAME 1 AT CLE SEPT 29

				R	H	E
BOS	300	032	030	11	12	0
CLE	000	002	100	3	7	0

Pitchers: MARTINEZ, Corsi (8) vs WRIGHT, Jones (5), Reed (8), Assenmacher (8), Poole (8), Shuey (8), Assenmacher (9)

Home Runs: Vaughn-BOS (2), Garciaparra-BOS, Lofton-CLE, Thome-CLE

Attendance: 45,185

GAME 2 AT CLE SEPT 30

				R	H	E
BOS	201	002	000	5	10	0
CLE	151	001	01X	9	9	1

Pitchers: WAKEFIELD, Wasdin (2), Lowe (4), Swindell (6), Gordon (8) vs Gooden, BURBA (1), Shuey (6), Assenmacher (8), Jackson (8)

Home Runs: Justice-CLE

Attendance: 45,229

GAME 3 AT BOS OCT 2

				R	H	E
CLE	000	011	101	4	5	0
BOS	000	100	002	3	6	0

Pitchers: NAGY, Jackson (9) vs SABERHAGEN, Corsi (8), Eckersley (9)

Home Runs: Thome-CLE, Lofton-CLE, Ramirez-CLE (2), Garciaparra-BOS

Attendance: 33,114

GAME 4 AT BOS OCT 3

				R	H	E
CLE	000	000	020	2	5	0
BOS	000	100	000	1	6	0

Pitchers: Colon, Poole (6), REED (7), Shuey (8), Jackson (9) vs Schourek, Lowe (6), GORDON (8)

Home Runs: Garciaparra-BOS

Attendance: 33,537

Despite an AL-record 114 wins by the Yankees, the Rangers actually batted higher than New York during the regular season (.289 to .288). They were second in the league to New York in runs (965 to 940), but pitching stole the show in the Division Series. The Rangers received three good performances from their starters, but Texas scored just one run in three games and batted a meager .141. David Wells set the tone in Game 1 with a five-hitter through eight innings. Texas starter Todd Stottlemyre, son of Yankees pitching coach Mel Stottlemyre, nearly matched Wells with six hits in eight innings, but the two runs the Yankees scratched out in the second inning proved to be his downfall. With one out in the second, Jorge Posada walked and Chad Curtis doubled him to third. Scott Brosius singled in one run and then got in a rundown on an attempted steal of second while Curtis crossed the plate.

Shane Spencer, who hit 10 home runs in just 67 at bats in August and September for the Yankees, homered in the second inning off Rick Helling in Game 2. Spencer singled to start the fourth inning and Brosius followed with a home run. Andy Pettitte rose to the occasion—although he allowed the Rangers' lone run of the series—as he permitted just three hits in seven innings.

Not even a violent lightning storm and torrential rain could save the Rangers in Game 3. The Yankees scored four times in the sixth inning on homers by Paul O'Neill and Spencer before the weather forced a 3-hour, 16-minute delay in Texas. The Yankees, already drained from the news that teammate Darryl Strawberry had been diagnosed with colon cancer, showed no signs of fatigue when Game 3 finally resumed. The Rangers managed just three hits off four New York pitchers as the Yankees beat Texas in the Division Series for the second time in three years.

New York Yankees (E), 3; Texas Rangers (W), 0

NY (E)

PLAYER/POS	AVG	G	AB	R	H	2B	3B	HR	RB	BB	SO	SB
Scott Brosius, 3b	.400	3	10	1	4	0	0	1	3	0	3	0
Homer Bush, dh	.000	1	0	0	0	0	0	0	0	0	0	1
David Cone, p	.000	1	0	0	0	0	0	0	0	0	0	0
Chad Curtis, of	.667	3	3	1	2	1	0	0	0	1	1	1
Chili Davis, dh	.167	2	6	0	1	0	0	0	0	0	2	0
Joe Girardi, c	.429	2	7	0	3	0	0	0	0	0	1	0
Derek Jeter, ss	.111	3	9	0	1	0	0	0	0	2	2	0
Chuck Knoblauch, 2b	.091	3	11	0	1	0	0	0	0	0	4	0
Graeme Lloyd, p	.000	1	0	0	0	0	0	0	0	0	0	0
Tino Martinez, 1b	.273	3	11	1	3	2	0	0	0	0	2	0
Jeff Nelson, p	.000	2	0	0	0	0	0	0	0	0	0	0
Paul O'Neill, of	.364	3	11	1	4	2	0	1	1	1	1	0
Andy Pettitte, p	.000	1	0	0	0	0	0	0	0	0	0	0
Jorge Posada, c	.000	1	2	1	0	0	0	0	0	1	2	0
Tim Raines, dh-1	.250	2	4	1	1	1	0	0	0	1	1	0
Mariano Rivera, p	.000	3	0	0	0	0	0	0	0	0	0	0
Shane Spencer, of	.500	2	6	3	3	0	0	2	4	0	1	0
David Wells, p	.000	1	0	0	0	0	0	0	0	0	0	0
Bernie Williams, of	.000	3	11	0	0	0	0	0	0	1	4	0
TOTAL	.253		91	9	23	6	0	4	8	7	24	2

PITCHER	W	L	ERA	G	GS	CG	SV	SHO	IP	H	ER	BB	SO
David Cone	1	0	0.00	1	1	0	0	0	5.2	2	0	1	6
Graeme Lloyd	0	0	0.00	1	0	0	0	0	0.1	0	0	0	0
Jeff Nelson	0	0	0.00	2	0	0	0	0	2.2	2	0	1	2
Andy Pettitte	1	0	1.29	1	1	0	0	0	7.0	3	1	0	8
Mariano Rivera	0	0	0.00	3	0	0	2	0	3.1	1	0	1	2
David Wells	1	0	0.00	1	1	0	0	0	8.0	5	0	1	9
TOTAL	3	0	0.33	9	3	0	2	0	27.0	13	1	4	27

TEX (W)

PLAYER/POS	AVG	G	AB	R	H	2B	3B	HR	RB	BB	SO	SB
Luis Alicea, ph	.000	1	1	0	0	0	0	0	0	0	0	0
Will Clark, 1b	.091	3	11	0	1	0	0	0	0	1	2	0
Royce Clayton, ss	.222	3	9	0	2	0	0	0	0	0	4	0
Tim Crabtree, p	.000	2	0	0	0	0	0	0	0	0	0	0
Juan Gonzalez, of	.083	3	12	1	1	1	0	0	0	0	3	0
Tom Goodwin, of	.250	2	4	0	1	0	0	0	0	0	1	0
Rusty Greer, of	.091	3	11	0	1	0	0	0	0	1	2	0
Rick Helling, p	.000	1	0	0	0	0	0	0	0	0	0	0
Roberto Kelly, of	.143	1	7	0	1	1	0	0	0	0	2	0
Mark McLemore, 2b	.100	3	10	0	1	1	0	0	0	2	3	0
Ivan Rodriguez, c	.100	3	10	0	1	0	0	0	1	0	5	0
Aaron Sele, p	.000	1	0	0	0	0	0	0	0	0	0	0
Mike Simms, dh	.200	2	5	0	1	0	0	0	0	0	2	0
Lee Stevens, dh	.000	1	3	0	0	0	0	0	0	0	1	0
Todd Stottlemyre, p	.000	1	0	0	0	0	0	0	0	0	0	0
John Wetteland, p	.000	1	0	0	0	0	0	0	0	0	0	0
Todd Zeile, 3b	.333	3	9	0	3	0	0	0	0	0	2	0
TOTAL	.141		92	1	13	3	0	0	1	4	27	0

PITCHER	W	L	ERA	G	GS	CG	SV	SHO	IP	H	ER	BB	SO
Tim Crabtree	0	0	0.00	2	0	0	0	0	4.0	1	0	0	2
Rick Helling	0	1	4.50	1	1	0	0	0	6.0	8	3	1	9
Aaron Sele	0	1	6.00	1	1	0	0	0	6.0	8	4	1	4
Todd Stottlemyre	0	1	2.25	1	1	1	0	0	8.0	6	2	4	8
John Wetteland	0	0	0.00	1	0	0	0	0	1.0	0	0	1	1
TOTAL	0	3	3.24	6	3	1	0	0	25.0	23	9	7	24

GAME 1 AT NY SEPT 29

				R	H	E
TEX	000	000	000	0	5	0
NY	020	000	00X	2	6	0

Pitchers: STOTTLEMYRE vs WELLS, Rivera (9)

Attendance: 57,362

GAME 2 AT NY SEPT 30

				R	H	E
TEX	000	010	000	1	5	0
NY	010	200	00X	3	8	0

Pitchers: HELLING, Crabtree (7) vs PETTITTE, Nelson (8), Rivera (8)

Home Runs: Spencer-NY, Brosius-NY

Attendance: 57,360

GAME 3 AT TEX OCT 2

				R	H	E
NY	000	004	000	4	9	1
TEX	000	000	000	0	3	1

Pitchers: CONE, Lloyd (6), Nelson (7), Rivera (9) vs SELE, Crabtree (7), Wetteland (9)

Home Runs: O'Neill-NY, Spencer-NY

Attendance: 49,450

Good pitching and timely hitting sent the Padres to their first World Series in 14 years. The Braves, who were appearing in their seventh consecutive NLCS, missed the World Series after winning 100 games for the third time in five seasons. The first of four errors in the NLCS by normally reliable first baseman Andres Galarraga gave the Padres a 2-1 lead against John Smoltz in the seventh inning of Game 1. But Trevor Hoffman, who had 53 saves during the season, could not hold the lead as Andruw Jones drove in the tying run in the ninth. Ken Caminiti homered in the 10th, and the Padres held on for the 3-2 win. Game 2 was all Kevin Brown. Not only did he pitch a three-hit shutout, he also had two hits and hustled around the bases in the ninth for an important insurance run as the Padres left Atlanta up, two games to none.

The series shifted to the West Coast and the momentum stayed with the Padres. While Sterling Hitchcock labored through five innings, he trailed only 1-0 thanks to John Vander Wal, who started in left field in place of the injured Greg Vaughn. Vander Wal threw out Walt Weiss at the plate to end the third inning. Hitchcock singled to open the bottom of the fifth and he came around to score on Steve Finley's double. Finley then scored on a single by Tony Gwynn. The Braves threatened in the top of the sixth, but Donne Wall came out of the bullpen and struck out pinch-hitters Ryan Klesko and Michael Tucker with three men on—one of three innings in which Atlanta left the bases loaded. The Braves were down, 3-2, in the seventh inning of Game 4 and were looking at the wrong end of a sweep when they finally exploded. Javier Lopez homered off a tiring Joey Hamilton to tie the game, and Galarraga capped the six-run seventh with a grand slam.

The Padres had a 4-2 lead in Game 5 when manager Bruce Bochy brought in his scheduled Game 6 starter, Kevin Brown, to pitch out of a jam in the seventh inning. He retired all three batters that inning, but, in the eighth he surrendered a three-run home run to Michael Tucker, who drove in five runs in the game. Atlanta added two more runs in the inning, which turned out to be crucial when Jim Leyritz hit a two-run homer off Kerry Ligtenberg in the ninth to make it 7-6. Greg Maddux, with four Cy Young Awards but no saves in his 12-year career, got the last three outs. The Braves became the first team in postseason history to force a sixth game after trailing three games to none.

San Diego Padres (W), 4; Atlanta Braves (E), 2

SD (W)

PLAYER/POS	AVG	G	AB	R	H	2B	3B	HR	RB	BB	SO	SB
Andy Ashby, p	.000	2	4	0	0	0	0	0	0	0	4	0
Brian Boehringer, p	.000	3	0	0	0	0	0	0	0	0	0	0
Kevin Brown, p	.500	2	4	1	2	0	0	0	0	0	1	0
Ken Caminiti, 3b	.273	6	22	3	6	0	0	2	4	5	4	0
Steve Finley, of	.333	6	21	3	7	1	0	0	2	6	2	1
Chris Gomez, ss	.150	6	20	2	3	0	0	0	0	2	5	0
Tony Gwynn, of	.231	6	26	1	6	1	0	0	2	1	2	0
Joey Hamilton, p	.000	2	2	0	0	0	0	0	0	0	1	0
Carlos Hernandez, c	.333	6	18	2	6	2	0	0	0	1	5	0
Sterling Hitchcock, p	.200	2	5	1	1	0	0	0	0	0	0	0
Trevor Hoffman, p	.000	3	0	0	0	0	0	0	0	0	0	0
Wally Joyner, 1b	.313	6	16	3	5	0	0	0	2	4	3	0
Mark Langston, p	.000	3	0	0	0	0	0	0	0	0	0	0
Jim Leyritz, 1b-3,c-2	.167	5	12	1	2	0	0	1	4	0	2	0
Dan Miceli, p	.000	3	0	0	0	0	0	0	0	0	0	0
Greg Myers, ph	1.000	2	1	1	1	0	0	1	2	1	0	0
Randy Myers, p	.000	4	0	0	0	0	0	0	0	0	0	0
Ruben Rivera, of	.231	6	13	1	3	2	0	0	0	0	7	1
Andy Sheets, ss-2	.000	3	3	0	0	0	0	0	0	0	1	0
Mark Sweeney, ph	.000	3	2	1	0	0	0	0	0	1	1	0
John Vander Wal, of-2	.429	3	7	1	3	0	0	1	2	0	2	0
Greg Vaughn, of-2	.250	3	8	1	2	0	0	0	0	1	1	0
Quilvio Veras, 2b	.250	6	24	2	6	1	0	0	2	5	7	0
Donne Wall, p	.000	3	0	0	0	0	0	0	0	0	0	0
TOTAL	.255		208	24	53	7	0	5	20	27	48	2

PITCHER	W	L	ERA	G	GS	CG	SV	SHO	IP	H	ER	BB	SO
Andy Ashby	0	0	2.08	2	2	0	0	0	13.0	14	3	2	5
Brian Boehringer	0	0	0.00	3	0	0	0	0	3.0	3	0	1	1
Kevin Brown	1	1	2.61	2	1	1	0	0	10.1	5	3	4	12
Joey Hamilton	0	1	4.91	2	1	0	0	0	7.1	7	4	3	6
Sterling Hitchcock	2	0	0.90	2	2	0	0	0	10.0	5	1	8	14
Trevor Hoffman	1	0	2.08	3	0	0	1	0	4.1	2	1	2	7
Mark Langston	0	0	0.00	3	0	0	0	0	1.1	1	0	0	1
Dan Miceli	0	0	13.50	3	0	0	0	0	0.2	4	1	0	1
Randy Myers	0	0	13.50	4	0	0	0	0	2.0	3	3	2	3
Donne Wall	0	0	3.00	3	0	0	1	0	3.0	3	1	4	4
TOTAL	4	2	2.78	27	6	1	2	0	55.0	47	17	26	54

ATL (E)

PLAYER/POS	AVG	G	AB	R	H	2B	3B	HR	RB	BB	SO	SB
Danny Bautista, of-4	.000	5	5	0	0	0	0	0	0	0	1	0
Greg Colbrunn, ph	.333	6	6	0	2	0	0	0	0	0	2	0
Andres Galarraga, 1b	.095	6	21	1	2	0	0	1	4	6	6	0
Tom Glavine, p-2	.250	3	4	0	1	0	0	0	0	1	2	0
Tony Graffanino, 2b-3	.333	4	3	2	1	1	0	0	1	2	1	0
Ozzie Guillen, ss-3	.417	4	12	1	5	0	0	0	1	0	1	0
Andruw Jones, of	.273	6	22	3	6	0	0	1	2	1	4	1
Chipper Jones, 3b	.208	6	24	2	5	1	0	0	1	4	5	0
Ryan Klesko, of	.083	5	12	2	1	0	0	0	1	6	3	0
Kerry Ligtenberg, p	.000	4	0	0	0	0	0	0	0	0	0	0
Keith Lockhart, 2b	.235	6	17	2	4	1	1	0	0	0	4	0
Javy Lopez, c	.300	6	20	2	6	0	0	1	1	0	7	0
Greg Maddux, p	.000	2	1	0	0	0	0	0	0	0	0	0
Marty Malloy, 2b-1	.000	4	1	1	0	0	0	0	0	0	1	0
Dennis Martinez, p	.000	4	0	0	0	0	0	0	0	0	0	0
Denny Neagle, p	.000	2	2	0	0	0	0	0	0	0	0	0
Eddie Perez, c	.750	3	4	0	3	0	0	0	0	0	0	0
Odaliz Perez, p	.000	2	0	0	0	0	0	0	0	0	0	0
John Rocker, p	.000	6	0	1	0	0	0	0	0	1	0	0
Rudy Seanez, p	.000	4	0	0	0	0	0	0	0	0	0	0
John Smoltz, p	.200	2	5	0	1	0	0	0	0	0	1	0
Michael Tucker, of-5	.385	6	13	1	5	1	0	1	5	2	5	0
Walt Weiss, ss	.200	4	15	0	3	0	0	0	1	2	5	1
Gerald Williams, of	.154	5	13	0	2	0	0	0	0	1	6	1
TOTAL	.235		200	18	47	4	1	4	17	26	54	3

PITCHER	W	L	ERA	G	GS	CG	SV	SHO	IP	H	ER	BB	SO
Tom Glavine	0	2	2.31	2	2	0	0	0	11.2	13	3	9	8
Kerry Ligtenberg	0	1	7.36	4	0	0	0	0	3.2	3	3	2	5
Greg Maddux	0	1	3.00	2	1	0	0	0	6.0	5	2	3	4
Dennis Martinez	1	0	0.00	4	0	0	0	0	3.1	1	0	1	0
Denny Neagle	0	0	3.52	2	1	0	0	0	7.2	8	3	2	9
Odaliz Perez	0	0	54.00	2	0	0	0	0	0.1	5	2	2	0
John Rocker	1	0	0.00	6	0	0	0	0	4.2	3	0	1	5
Rudy Seanez	0	0	6.00	4	0	0	0	0	3.0	2	2	1	4
John Smoltz	0	0	3.95	2	2	0	0	0	13.2	13	6	6	13
TOTAL	2	4	3.50	28	6	0	0	0	54.0	53	21	27	48

Tom Glavine and Hitchcock were locked in a scoreless pitcher's duel when the Padres bunched six hits for five runs in the sixth inning. The decisive play, however, occurred when left fielder Danny Bautista dropped Hitchcock's sinking line drive allowing two runs to score. Hitchcock, who combined with four relievers for a two-hitter, earned series MVP. The Braves, meanwhile, missed the World Series after winning 100 games for the third time in five seasons.

GAME 1 AT ATL OCT 7

				R	H	E
SD	000	010	010	1	3	7 0
ATL	001	000	001	0	2	8 3

Pitchers: Ashby, R.Myers (8), Miceli (8), HOFFMAN (8), Wall (10) vs Smoltz, Rocker (8), Martinez (8), LIGTENBERG (9)

Home Runs: A.Jones-ATL, Caminiti-SD

Attendance: 42,117

GAME 2 AT ATL OCT 8

				R	H	E
SD	000	001	002	3	11	0
ATL	000	000	000	0	3	1

Pitchers: BROWN vs GLAVINE, Rocker (7), Seanez (8), O.Perez (9), Ligtenberg (9)

Attendance: 43,083

GAME 3 AT SD OCT 10

				R	H	E
ATL	001	000	000	1	8	2
SD	000	020	02X	4	7	0

Pitchers: MADDUX, Martinez (6), Rocker (7), Seanez (8) vs HITCHCOCK, Wall (6), Miceli (8), R.Myers (8), Hoffman (8)

Attendance: 62,799

GAME 4 AT SD OCT 11

				R	H	E
ATL	000	101	600	8	12	0
SD	002	001	000	3	8	0

Pitchers: Neagle, MARTINEZ (6), Rocker (7), O.Perez (8), Seanez (8), Ligtenberg (9) vs HAMILTON, Myers (7), Miceli (7), Boehringer (8), Langston (9)

Home Runs: Leyritz-SD, Lopez-ATL, Galarraga-ATL

Attendance: 65,042

GAME 5 AT SD OCT 12

				R	H	E
ATL	000	101	050	7	14	1
SD	200	002	002	6	10	1

Pitchers: Smoltz, ROCKER (7), Seanez (8), Ligtenberg (9), Maddux (9) vs Ashby, Langston (7), BROWN (7), Wall (8), Boehringer (9), R.Myers (9)

Home Runs: Caminiti-SD, Vander Wal-SD, Tucker-ATL, G.Myers-SD

Attendance: 58,988

GAME 6 AT ATL OCT 14

				R	H	E
SD	000	005	000	5	10	0
ATL	000	000	000	0	2	1

Pitchers: HITCHCOCK, Boehringer (6), Langston (7), Hamilton (7), Hoffman (9) vs GLAVINE, Rocker (6), Martinez (6), Neagle (8)

Attendance: 50,988

The Yankees, coming off a three-game sweep of Texas in the Division Series, handled the Indians easily to start the ALCS. New York scored five times in the first inning of Game 1 of the ALCS to knock out Indians starter Jaret Wright, who had been 2-0 against the Yankees in the 1997 Division Series. That was more than enough for David Wells, who pitched into the ninth inning of the 7-2 victory. Pitching and defense kept the Yankees and Indians tied at 1-1 through 11 innings the next afternoon, but it all fell apart for the Yankees in the top of the 12th. After a leadoff single by Jim Thome, Enrique Wilson came in to pinch run. Travis Fryman laid down a bunt that Tino Martinez errantly fired into Fryman's back. Chuck Knoblauch argued that Fryman had been out of the baseline and should be called out, but the Yankees second baseman made his protest while the play was still going on. By the time Knoblauch picked up the ball and threw home, Wilson had scored. The Indians won the argument and the game.

Bartolo Colon allowed just four hits in Game 3 to record the Tribe's first complete postseason game since the opening game of the 1954 World Series. Three home runs in the fifth inning (by Manny Ramirez, Jim Thome, and Mark Whiten) provided the power to give Cleveland a 2-1 series lead. The Yankees came back with a pitching gem of their own in Game 4 as rookie Orlando Hernandez teamed with two relievers to blank the Indians to even the ALCS. David Wells didn't have his best stuff and he wasn't in a good mood, but he still got the big outs when he needed to in Game 5. Angered by comments made by Cleveland fans as he warmed up, Wells shook off a rocky first inning to give the Yankees the lead in the series with a 5-3 win. Chili Davis drove in three runs in support of ALCS MVP Wells.

David Cone and Charles Nagy had both pitched splendidly in Game 2, but the hitters took charge in their rematch in Game 6. The Yankees grabbed a 6-0 lead after three innings as Cleveland played poor defense, and the Yankees took advantage of the wet grass to advance extra bases. The Indians nearly caught up with one swing on a grand slam by Thome, his fourth homer of the series, to make it 6-5 in the fifth inning. Omar Vizquel's wild throw after a record-tying 74 postseason games without an error set up a three-run sixth inning that put the game, and the Yankees' 35th AL pennant, on ice.

New York Yankees (E), 4; Cleveland Indians (C), 2

NY (E)

PLAYER/POS	AVG	G	AB	R	H	2B	3B	HR	RB	BB	SO	SB
Scott Brosius, 3b	.300	6	20	2	6	1	0	1	6	2	4	0
Homer Bush, dh-1	.000	2	0	1	0	0	0	0	0	0	0	1
David Cone, p	.000	2	0	0	0	0	0	0	0	0	0	0
Chad Curtis, of	.000	2	4	0	0	0	0	0	0	1	2	0
Chili Davis, dh	.286	5	14	2	4	1	0	1	5	2	3	0
Joe Girardi, c	.250	3	8	2	2	0	0	0	0	1	0	0
Orlando Hernandez, p	.000	1	0	0	0	0	0	0	0	0	0	0
Derek Jeter, ss	.200	6	25	3	5	1	1	0	2	2	5	3
Chuck Knoblauch, 2b	.200	6	25	4	5	1	0	0	0	4	2	0
Ricky Ledee, of-2,dh-1	.000	3	5	0	0	0	0	0	0	0	0	0
Graeme Lloyd, p	.000	1	0	0	0	0	0	0	0	0	0	0
Tino Martinez, 1b	.105	6	19	1	2	1	0	0	1	6	8	2
Ramiro Mendoza, p	.000	2	0	0	0	0	0	0	0	0	0	0
Jeff Nelson, p	.000	3	0	0	0	0	0	0	0	0	0	0
Paul O'Neill, of	.280	6	25	6	7	2	0	1	3	3	4	2
Andy Pettitte, p	.000	1	0	0	0	0	0	0	0	0	0	0
Jorge Posada, c	.182	5	11	1	2	0	0	1	2	4	2	0
Tim Raines, dh-2,of-1	.100	3	10	0	1	0	0	0	1	2	5	0
Mariano Rivera, p	.000	4	0	0	0	0	0	0	0	0	0	0
Luis Sojo, 1b	.000	1	0	0	0	0	0	0	0	0	0	0
Shane Spencer, of	.100	3	10	1	1	0	0	0	0	1	3	0
Mike Stanton, p	.000	3	0	0	0	0	0	0	0	0	0	0
David Wells, p	.000	2	0	0	0	0	0	0	0	0	0	0
Bernie Williams, of	.381	6	21	4	8	1	0	0	5	7	4	1
TOTAL	.218		197	27	43	8	1	4	25	35	42	9

PITCHER	W	L	ERA	G	GS	CG	SV	SHO	IP	H	ER	BB	SO
David Cone	1	0	4.15	2	2	0	0	0	13.0	12	6	6	13
Orlando Hernandez	1	0	0.00	1	1	0	0	0	7.0	3	0	2	6
Graeme Lloyd	0	0	0.00	1	0	0	0	0	0.2	1	0	0	0
Ramiro Mendoza	0	0	0.00	2	0	0	0	0	4.1	4	0	0	1
Jeff Nelson	0	1	20.25	3	0	0	0	0	1.1	3	3	1	3
Andy Pettitte	0	1	11.57	1	1	0	0	0	4.2	8	6	3	1
Mariano Rivera	0	0	0.00	4	0	0	1	0	5.2	0	0	1	5
Mike Stanton	0	0	0.00	3	0	0	0	0	3.2	2	0	1	4
David Wells	2	0	2.87	2	2	0	0	0	15.2	12	5	2	18
TOTAL	4	2	3.21	19	6	0	1	0	56.0	45	20	16	51

CLE (C)

PLAYER/POS	AVG	G	AB	R	H	2B	3B	HR	RB	BB	SO	SB
Sandy Alomar, c	.063	5	16	1	1	0	0	0	0	0	2	0
Paul Assenmacher, p	.000	3	0	0	0	0	0	0	0	0	0	0
Jeff Branson, ph	.000	1	1	0	0	0	0	0	0	0	0	0
Dave Burba, p	.000	3	0	0	0	0	0	0	0	0	0	0
Bartolo Colon, p	.000	1	0	0	0	0	0	0	0	0	0	0
Joey Cora, 2b	.143	2	7	1	1	0	0	0	0	2	1	0
Einar Diaz, c	.000	5	4	0	0	0	0	0	0	0	1	0
Travis Fryman, 3b	.174	6	23	2	4	0	0	0	0	1	5	1
Brian Giles, of-3	.083	4	12	0	1	0	0	0	0	1	3	0
Dwight Gooden, p	.000	1	0	0	0	0	0	0	0	0	0	0
Mike Jackson, p	.000	1	0	0	0	0	0	0	0	0	0	0
David Justice, dh-4,of-1	.158	6	19	2	3	0	0	1	2	3	3	0
Kenny Lofton, of	.185	6	27	2	5	1	0	1	3	1	7	1
Charles Nagy, p	.000	2	0	0	0	0	0	0	0	0	0	0
Chad Ogea, p	.000	2	0	0	0	0	0	0	0	0	0	0
Jim Poole, p	.000	4	0	0	0	0	0	0	0	0	0	0
Manny Ramirez, of	.333	6	21	2	7	1	0	2	4	4	9	0
Steve Reed, p	.000	3	0	0	0	0	0	0	0	0	0	0
Richie Sexson, 1b	.000	3	6	0	0	0	0	0	0	0	3	0
Paul Shuey, p	.000	5	0	0	0	0	0	0	0	0	0	0
Jim Thome, 1b-4,dh-2	.304	6	23	4	7	0	0	4	8	1	8	0
Omar Vizquel, ss	.440	6	25	2	11	0	1	0	0	1	3	4
Mark Whiten, of	.286	2	7	2	2	1	0	1	1	1	3	0
Enrique Wilson, 2b	.214	5	14	2	3	0	0	0	1	1	3	0
Jaret Wright, p	.000	2	0	0	0	0	0	0	0	0	0	0
TOTAL	.220		205	20	45	3	1	9	19	16	51	6

PITCHER	W	L	ERA	G	GS	CG	SV	SHO	IP	H	ER	BB	SO
Paul Assenmacher	0	0	0.00	3	0	0	0	0	2.0	0	0	0	3
Dave Burba	1	0	3.00	3	0	0	0	0	6.0	3	2	5	8
Bartolo Colon	1	0	1.00	1	1	1	0	0	9.0	4	1	4	3
Dwight Gooden	0	1	5.79	1	1	0	0	0	4.2	3	3	3	3
Mike Jackson	0	0	0.00	1	0	0	1	0	1.0	0	0	0	2
Charles Nagy	0	1	3.72	2	2	0	0	0	9.2	13	4	1	6
Chad Ogea	0	1	8.10	2	1	0	0	0	6.2	9	6	5	4
Jim Poole	0	0	0.00	4	0	0	0	0	1.1	0	0	1	2
Steve Reed	0	0	0.00	3	0	0	0	0	1.2	0	0	1	0
Paul Shuey	0	0	0.00	5	0	0	0	0	6.1	4	0	7	7
Jaret Wright	0	1	8.10	2	1	0	0	0	6.2	7	6	8	4
TOTAL	2	4	3.60	27	6	1	1	0	55.0	43	22	35	42

GAME 1 AT NY OCT 6

				R	H	E
CLE	000	000	002	2	5	0
NY	500	001	10X	7	11	0

Pitchers: WRIGHT, Ogea (1), Poole (7), Reed (7), Shuey (8) vs WELLS, Nelson (9)

Home Runs: Posada-NY, Ramirez-CLE

Attendance: 57,138

GAME 2 AT NY OCT 7

					R	H	E
CLE	000	100	000	003	4	8	1
NY	000	000	100	000	1	7	1

Pitchers: Nagy, Reed (7), Poole (8), Shuey (8), Assenmacher (10), BURBA (11), Jackson (12) vs Cone, Rivera (9), Stanton (11), NELSON (11), Lloyd (12)

Home Runs: Justice-CLE

Attendance: 57,128

GAME 3 AT CLE OCT 9

				R	H	E
NY	100	000	000	1	4	0
CLE	020	040	00X	6	12	0

Pitchers: PETTITTE, Mendoza (5), Stanton (7) vs COLON

Home Runs: Thome-CLE (2), Ramirez-CLE, Whiten-CLE

Attendance: 44,904

GAME 4 AT CLE OCT 10

				R	H	E
NY	100	200	001	4	4	0
CLE	000	000	000	0	4	3

Pitchers: HERNANDEZ, Stanton (8), Rivera (9) vs GOODEN, Poole (5), Burba (6), Shuey (9)

Home Runs: O'Neill-NY

Attendance: 44,981

GAME 5 AT CLE OCT 11

				R	H	E
NY	310	100	000	5	6	0
CLE	200	001	000	3	8	0

Pitchers: WELLS, Nelson (8), Rivera (8) vs OGEA, Wright (2), Reed (8), Assenmacher (8), Shuey (9)

Home Runs: Lofton-CLE, Davis-NY, Thome-CLE

Attendance: 44,966

GAME 6 AT NY OCT 13

				R	H	E
CLE	000	050	000	5	8	3
NY	213	003	00X	9	11	1

Pitchers: NAGY, Burba (4), Poole (6), Shuey (6), Assenmacher (8) vs CONE, Mendoza (6), Rivera (9)

Home Runs: Brosius-NY, Thome-CLE

Attendance: 57,142

New York Yankees (A), 4; San Diego Padres (N), 0

The World Series opened with the two hottest pitchers of the postseason facing each other, but neither New York's David Wells nor San Diego's Kevin Brown had their best stuff. The Yankees struck for two runs off Brown in the second inning, but three home runs—two by Greg Vaughn and one by Tony Gwynn—staked the Padres to a 5-2 lead. In the seventh Donne Wall relieved Brown with two runners on and Chuck Knoblauch promptly tied the game with a home run. A few batters later Tino Martinez launched a grand slam off Mark Langston to cap New York's seven-run seventh.

The Yankees jumped on the Padres for seven runs in the first three innings of Game 2. Paul O'Neill made a running catch to rob Wally Joyner of a hit with two runners on base in the top of the first, and a walk and a throwing error by San Diego set up New York for three runs in the bottom of the inning. Bernie Williams capped off a three-run second with a home run and Jorge Posada added a two-run shot of his own three innings later.

The Padres returned home and put the first three runs of the game across the plate in the sixth inning against David Cone. Padres pitcher Sterling Hitchcock started the rally with a single, and a throwing error by O'Neill kept it going. Scott Brosius led off the seventh with a home run, and a passed ball and an error made it a 3-2 game. With closer Trevor Hoffman pitching in the eighth with two runners aboard, Brosius hit his second homer in as many innings and the Yankees held on for a 5-4 win.

Andy Pettitte, pitching for the first time in 10 days, combined with Jeff Nelson and Mariano Rivera to blank the Padres on seven hits in Game 4. The Yankees, showing that they could win in a variety of ways, scored once on a groundout in the sixth and added two insurance runs off Brown on Brosius' sixth RBI in four games plus a sacrifice fly by Ricky Ledee. Mark Sweeney ended the game, fittingly, with a grounder to MVP Brosius, and the Yankees had their 24th world championship.

NY (A)

PLAYER/POS	AVG	G	AB	R	H	2B	3B	HR	RB	BB	SO	SB
Scott Brosius, 3b	.471	4	17	3	8	0	0	2	6	0	4	0
Homer Bush, dh-1	.000	2	0	0	0	0	0	0	0	0	0	0
David Cone, p	.500	1	2	0	1	0	0	0	0	0	0	0
Chili Davis, dh-2	.286	3	7	3	2	0	0	0	2	3	2	0
Joe Girardi, c	.000	2	6	0	0	0	0	0	0	0	2	0
Orlando Hernandez, p	.000	1	0	0	0	0	0	0	0	0	0	0
Derek Jeter, ss	.353	4	17	4	6	0	0	0	1	3	3	0
Chuck Knoblauch, 2b	.375	4	16	3	6	0	0	1	3	3	2	1
Ricky Ledee, of	.600	4	10	1	6	3	0	0	4	2	1	0
Graeme Lloyd, p	.000	1	0	0	0	0	0	0	0	0	0	0
Tino Martinez, 1b	.385	4	13	4	5	0	0	1	4	4	2	0
Ramiro Mendoza, p	.000	1	1	0	0	0	0	0	0	0	0	0
Jeff Nelson, p	.000	3	0	0	0	0	0	0	0	0	0	0
Paul O'Neill, of	.211	4	19	3	4	1	0	0	0	1	2	0
Andy Pettitte, p	.000	1	2	0	0	0	0	0	0	0	2	0
Jorge Posada, c	.333	3	9	2	3	0	0	1	2	2	2	0
Mariano Rivera, p	.000	3	1	0	0	0	0	0	0	0	0	0
Shane Spencer, of	.333	1	3	1	1	1	0	0	0	0	2	0
Mike Stanton, p	.000	1	0	0	0	0	0	0	0	0	0	0
David Wells, p	.000	1	0	0	0	0	0	0	0	0	0	0
Bernie Williams, of	.063	4	16	2	1	0	0	1	3	2	5	0
TOTAL	.309		139	26	43	5	0	6	25	20	29	1

PITCHER	W	L	ERA	G	GS	CG	SV	SHO	IP	H	ER	BB	SO
David Cone	0	0	3.00	1	1	0	0	0	6.0	2	2	3	4
Orlando Hernandez	1	0	1.29	1	1	0	0	0	7.0	6	1	3	7
Graeme Lloyd	0	0	0.00	1	0	0	0	0	0.1	0	0	0	0
Ramiro Mendoza	1	0	9.00	1	0	0	0	0	1.0	2	1	0	1
Jeff Nelson	0	0	0.00	3	0	0	0	0	2.1	2	0	1	4
Andy Pettitte	1	0	0.00	1	1	0	0	0	7.1	5	0	3	4
Mariano Rivera	0	0	0.00	3	0	0	3	0	4.1	5	0	0	4
Mike Stanton	0	0	27.00	1	0	0	0	0	0.2	3	2	0	1
David Wells	1	0	6.43	1	1	0	0	0	7.0	7	5	2	4
TOTAL	4	0	2.75	13	4	0	3	0	36.0	32	11	12	29

SD (N)

PLAYER/POS	AVG	G	AB	R	H	2B	3B	HR	RB	BB	SO	SB
Andy Ashby, p	.000	1	0	0	0	0	0	0	0	0	0	0
Brian Boehringer, p	.000	2	0	0	0	0	0	0	0	0	0	0
Kevin Brown, p	.500	2	2	0	1	0	0	0	0	0	0	0
Ken Caminiti, 3b	.143	4	14	1	2	1	0	0	1	2	7	0
Steve Finley, of	.083	3	12	0	1	1	0	0	0	0	2	1
Chris Gomez, ss	.364	4	11	2	4	0	1	0	0	1	1	0
Tony Gwynn, of	.500	4	16	2	8	0	0	1	3	1	0	0
Joey Hamilton, p	.000	1	0	0	0	0	0	0	0	0	0	0
Carlos Hernandez, c	.200	4	10	0	2	0	0	0	0	0	3	0
Sterling Hitchcock, p	.500	1	2	1	1	0	0	0	0	0	0	0
Trevor Hoffman, p	.000	1	0	0	0	0	0	0	0	0	0	0
Wally Joyner, 1b	.000	3	8	0	0	0	0	0	0	3	1	0
Mark Langston, p	.000	1	0	0	0	0	0	0	0	0	0	0
Jim Leyritz, 1b-2,c-1,dh-1	.000	4	10	0	0	0	0	0	0	1	4	0
Dan Miceli, p	.000	2	0	0	0	0	0	0	0	0	0	0
Greg Myers, c-1	.000	2	4	0	0	0	0	0	0	0	2	0
Randy Myers, p	.000	3	0	0	0	0	0	0	0	0	0	0
Ruben Rivera, of	.800	3	5	1	4	2	0	0	1	0	0	0
Andy Sheets, ss	.000	2	2	0	0	0	0	0	0	0	1	0
Mark Sweeney, ph	.667	3	3	0	2	0	0	0	1	0	0	0
John Vander Wal, of-1	.400	4	5	0	2	1	0	0	0	0	2	0
Greg Vaughn, of-3,dh-1	.133	4	15	3	2	0	0	2	4	1	2	0
Quilvio Veras, 2b	.200	4	15	3	3	2	0	0	1	3	4	0
Donne Wall, p	.000	2	0	0	0	0	0	0	0	0	0	0
TOTAL	.239		134	13	32	7	1	3	11	12	29	1

PITCHER	W	L	ERA	G	GS	CG	SV	SHO	IP	H	ER	BB	SO
Andy Ashby	0	1	13.50	1	1	0	0	0	2.2	10	4	1	1
Brian Boehringer	0	0	9.00	2	0	0	0	0	2.0	4	2	2	3
Kevin Brown	0	1	4.40	2	2	0	0	0	14.1	14	7	6	13
Joey Hamilton	0	0	0.00	1	0	0	0	0	1.0	0	0	1	1
Sterling Hitchcock	0	0	1.50	1	1	0	0	0	6.0	7	1	1	7
Trevor Hoffman	0	1	9.00	1	0	0	0	0	2.0	2	2	1	0
Mark Langston	0	0	40.50	1	0	0	0	0	0.2	1	3	2	0
Dan Miceli	0	0	0.00	2	0	0	0	0	1.2	2	0	2	1
Randy Myers	0	0	9.00	3	0	0	0	0	1.0	0	1	1	2
Donne Wall	0	1	6.75	2	0	0	0	0	2.2	3	2	3	1
TOTAL	0	4	5.82	16	4	0	0	0	34.0	43	22	20	29

GAME 1 AT NY OCT 17

SD	002	030	010	6	8	1
NY	020	000	70X	9	9	1

Pitchers: Brown, WALL (7), Langston (7), Boehringer (8), R.Myers (8) vs WELLS, Nelson (8), Rivera (8)

Home Runs: Vaughn-SD (2), Gwynn-SD, Knoblauch-NY, Martinez-NY

Attendance: 56,712

GAME 2 AT NY OCT 18

SD	000	010	020	3	10	1
NY	331	020	00X	9	16	0

Pitchers: ASHBY, Boehringer (3), Wall (5), Miceli (8) vs HERNANDEZ, Stanton (8), Nelson (8)

Home Runs: Williams-NY, Posada-NY

Attendance: 56,692

GAME 3 AT SD OCT 20

NY	000	000	230	5	9	1
SD	000	003	010	4	7	1

Pitchers: Cone, Lloyd (7), MENDOZA (7), Rivera (9) vs Hitchcock, Hamilton (7), R. Myers (8), HOFFMAN (8)

Home Runs: Brosius-NY (2)

Attendance: 64,667

GAME 4 AT SD OCT 21

NY	000	001	020	3	9	0
SD	000	000	000	0	7	0

Pitchers: PETTITTE, Nelson (8), Rivera (8) vs BROWN, Miceli (9), R. Myers (9)

Attendance: 65,427

The Atlanta Braves, with eight consecutive division titles to their credit, had won 10 consecutive Division Series games heading into Game 1 at Turner Field. Houston's Daryle Ward broke a 1-1 tie in the sixth inning with a home run off Greg Maddux, and Ken Caminiti's three-run homer in the ninth wrapped up the scoring. Shane Reynolds pitched out of several jams to earn the win for the Astros.

Caminiti homered in the second inning of Game 2; Kevin Millwood allowed nothing else. He struck out eight and walked none in his first postseason appearance. In contrast to Houston's one hit, the Braves had 11 hits, including three by Ryan Klesko.

In Game 3 the Braves wriggled out of trouble in inning after inning at the Astrodome. Starter Tom Glavine allowed an RBI-single to Caminiti and walked in a run in the first, but a line drive out ended the inning. The Astros tied it in the seventh on a single by Bill Spiers, but Mike Remlinger struck out Caminiti and Matt Mieske flied out to end the threat. The Astros loaded the bases on two hits and a walk with none out in the 10th. Reliever John Rocker induced Carl Everett to ground into a force play at home for the first out. With the infield in, Tony Eusebio hit a bullet up the middle that knocked Walt Weiss' glove off, but the shortstop grabbed the ball and threw home for a force play. Rocker fanned Ricky Gutierrez to end the inning. Brian Jordan doubled home two runs in the top of the 12th for a 5-3 lead. Millwood, like Maddux earlier in the game, made a rare bullpen appearance. He retired the side in order for the save.

The Braves scored five times on seven singles in the sixth inning in Game 5. Houston crawled back in the game on Eusebio's solo homer in the seventh and Caminiti's three-run shot in the eighth. Rocker came on to strike out Craig Biggio with a runner on third to end the threat. The Braves held on for the 7-5 win to take the series in the final game played at the Astrodome.

Atlanta Braves (W), 3; Houston Astros (C), 1

ATL (W)

PLAYER/POS	AVG	G	AB	R	H	2B	3B	HR	RB	BB	SO	SB
Howard Battle, ph	.000	1	1	0	0	0	0	0	0	0	0	0
Bret Boone, 2b	.474	4	19	3	9	1	0	0	1	0	4	1
Tom Glavine, p	.000	1	2	0	0	0	0	0	0	0	1	0
Ozzie Guillen, ph	.000	1	1	0	0	0	0	0	0	0	0	0
Jose Hernandez, ss	.091	4	11	1	1	0	0	0	0	1	3	1
Brian Hunter, 1b	.000	3	4	0	0	0	0	0	0	1	3	0
Andruw Jones, of	.222	4	18	1	4	1	0	0	2	1	3	0
Chipper Jones, 3b	.231	4	13	2	3	0	0	0	1	5	2	0
Brian Jordan, of	.471	4	17	2	8	1	0	1	7	1	2	0
Ryan Klesko, 1b	.333	4	12	3	4	0	0	0	1	1	4	0
Keith Lockhart, 2b-1	.000	3	1	0	0	0	0	0	0	0	1	0
Greg Maddux, p	.000	2	1	0	0	0	0	0	0	0	0	0
Kevin McGlinchy, p	.000	1	0	0	0	0	0	0	0	0	0	0
Kevin Millwood, p	.250	2	4	0	1	0	0	0	0	0	3	0
Terry Mulholland, p	.000	2	0	0	0	0	0	0	0	0	0	0
Otis Nixon, of	1.000	1	1	1	1	0	0	0	0	0	0	1
Eddie Perez, c	.250	0	16	1	4	0	0	0	3	0	3	0
Mike Remlinger, p	.000	2	0	0	0	0	0	0	0	0	0	0
John Rocker, p	.000	2	0	0	0	0	0	0	0	1	0	0
John Smoltz, p	.667	1	3	1	2	1	0	0	0	0	1	0
Russ Springer, p	.000	1	0	0	0	0	0	0	0	0	0	0
Walt Weiss, ss	.167	3	6	1	1	0	0	0	0	0	2	0
Gerald Williams, of	.389	4	18	2	7	1	0	0	3	0	3	1
TOTAL	.304		148	18	45	5	0	1	18	11	35	4

PITCHER	W	L	ERA	G	GS	CG	SV	SHO	IP	H	ER	BB	SO
Tom Glavine	0	0	3.00	1	1	0	0	0	6.0	5	2	3	6
Greg Maddux	0	1	2.57	2	1	0	0	0	7.0	10	2	5	5
Kevin McGlinchy	0	0	0.00	1	0	0	0	0	0.1	0	0	0	0
Kevin Millwood	1	0	0.90	2	1	1	1	0	10.0	1	1	0	9
Terry Mulholland	0	0	27.00	2	0	0	0	0	0.2	3	2	0	0
Mike Remlinger	0	0	9.82	2	0	0	0	0	3.2	4	4	3	4
John Rocker	1	0	0.00	2	0	0	1	0	3.1	0	0	2	5
John Smoltz	1	0	5.14	1	1	0	0	0	7.0	6	4	3	3
Russ Springer	0	0	0.00	1	0	0	0	0	1.0	2	0	1	1
TOTAL	3	1	3.46	14	4	1	2	0	39.0	31	15	17	33

HOU (C)

PLAYER/POS	AVG	G	AB	R	H	2B	3B	HR	RB	BB	SO	SB
Jeff Bagwell, 1b	.154	4	13	3	2	0	0	0	0	5	4	0
Glen Barker, of	.000	2	3	1	0	0	0	0	0	0	2	1
Derek Bell, of-1	.333	2	3	0	1	0	0	0	0	0	0	0
Craig Biggio, 2b	.105	4	19	1	2	0	0	0	0	1	5	0
Tim Bogar, ss-1	.750	2	4	0	3	1	0	0	1	1	0	0
Jose Cabrera, p	.000	1	0	0	0	0	0	0	0	0	0	0
Ken Caminiti, 3b	.471	4	17	3	8	0	0	3	8	2	1	0
Scott Elarton, p	.000	2	0	0	0	0	0	0	0	0	0	0
Tony Eusebio, c	.267	4	15	2	4	0	0	1	3	1	2	0
Carl Everett, of	.133	4	15	2	2	0	0	0	1	2	8	0
Ricky Gutierrez, ss	.000	3	10	0	0	0	0	0	0	2	5	0
Mike Hampton, p	.000	1	2	0	0	0	0	0	0	0	1	0
Doug Henry, p	.000	2	0	0	0	0	0	0	0	0	0	0
Chris Holt, p	.000	1	0	0	0	0	0	0	0	0	0	0
Stan Javier, of	.273	4	11	1	3	0	0	0	0	1	1	0
Russ Johnson, ph	1.000	2	1	0	1	1	0	0	0	1	0	0
Jose Lima, p	.000	1	2	0	0	0	0	0	0	0	1	0
Matt Mieske, of-1	.000	2	4	1	0	0	0	0	0	1	0	0
Trever Miller, p	.000	2	0	0	0	0	0	0	0	0	0	0
Jay Powell, p	.000	3	0	0	0	0	0	0	0	0	0	0
Shane Reynolds, p	.250	2	4	0	1	0	0	0	0	0	0	0
Bill Spiers, of-3	.273	4	11	0	3	0	0	0	1	0	1	1
Billy Wagner, p	.000	1	0	0	0	0	0	0	0	0	0	0
Daryle Ward, of-2	.143	3	7	1	1	0	0	1	1	0	2	0
TOTAL	.220		141	15	31	2	0	5	15	17	33	2

PITCHER	W	L	ERA	G	GS	CG	SV	SHO	IP	H	ER	BB	SO
Jose Cabrera	0	0	0.00	1	0	0	0	0	2.0	2	0	0	6
Scott Elarton	0	0	3.86	2	0	0	0	0	2.1	4	1	1	3
Mike Hampton	0	0	3.86	1	1	0	0	0	7.0	6	3	1	9
Doug Henry	0	0	0.00	2	0	0	0	0	3.2	1	0	3	2
Chris Holt	0	0	INF	1	0	0	0	0	0.0	3	3	0	0
Jose Lima	0	1	5.40	1	1	0	0	0	6.2	9	4	2	4
Trever Miller	0	0	0.00	2	0	0	0	0	1.1	1	0	0	2
Jay Powell	0	1	6.00	3	0	0	0	0	3.0	3	2	1	3
Shane Reynolds	1	1	4.09	2	2	0	0	0	11.0	16	5	3	5
Billy Wagner	0	0	0.00	1	0	0	0	0	1.0	0	0	0	1
TOTAL	1	3	4.26	16	4	0	0	0	38.0	45	18	11	35

GAME 1 AT ATL OCT 5

				R	H	E
HOU	010	001	004	6	13	0
ATL	000	010	000	1	7	0

Pitchers: REYNOLDS, Miller (7), Henry (7), Wagner (9) VS MADDUX, Remlinger (8)
Home Runs: Ward-HOU, Caminiti-HOU
Attendance: 39,119

GAME 2 AT ATL OCT 6

				R	H	E
HOU	010	000	000	1	1	1
ATL	100	001	30X	5	11	1

Pitchers: LIMA, Elarton (7), Powell (8) VS MILLWOOD
Home Runs: Caminiti-HOU
Attendance: 41,913

GAME 3 AT HOU OCT 8

					R	H	E
ATL	000	003	000	002	5	12	0
HOU	200	000	100	000	3	9	2

Pitchers: Glavine, Mulholland (7), Maddux (8), Remlinger (7), Springer (9), ROCKER (10), Millwood (12) VS Hampton, Cabrera (8), Henry (10), POWELL (12)
Home Runs: Jordan-ATL
Attendance: 48,625

GAME 4 AT HOU OCT 9

				R	H	E
ATL	101	005	000	7	15	1
HOU	000	000	140	5	8	1

Pitchers: SMOLTZ, Mulholland (8), McGlinchy (8), Rocker (8) VS REYNOLDS, Holt (6), Elarton (6), Miller (8), Powell (9)
Home Runs: Eusebio-HOU, Caminiti-HOU
Attendance: 48,553

The New York Mets had to win their last four games, including a one-game playoff in Cincinnati, to earn their first postseason berth since 1988. The Arizona Diamondbacks, only in their second year of existence, won 100 games and cruised to the National League West title.

Randy Johnson had early problems against the Mets in Game 1 of the Division Series, yet the Diamondbacks rallied to tie the score against Masato Yoshii. Johnson filled the bases in the ninth and left in favor of rookie Bobby Chouinard. Matt Williams made a diving stop and threw home for the force play for the second out, but Edgardo Alfonzo followed with his second home run of the game. Johnson suffered his sixth consecutive postseason loss.

Todd Stottlemyre, pitching with a 70 percent tear of his rotator cuff, allowed just four hits in 6 2/3 innings to win Game 2. Steve Finley drove in five runs and Matt Williams had three hits in Arizona's first postseason victory. Mike Piazza was on the bench in Game 3 because of a bad reaction to a cortisone shot to his left hand. The Mets made up for his absence with 11 hits and eight walks in a 9-2 victory. Rickey Henderson added his sixth stolen base in three games to set a Division Series record.

Al Leiter nursed a 2-1 lead into the eighth inning of Game 4. He left after Tony Womack's infield hit, and Jay Bell followed with a two-run double off Armando Benitez. The inning ended when defensive replacement Melvin Mora threw out Bell trying to score on a single. In the bottom of the inning, Womack, who had just moved from shortstop to right field, dropped a flyball. The Mets tied the game on Roger Cedeno's sacrifice fly. Piazza's replacement Todd Pratt homered off Matt Mantei in the bottom of the 10th inning to set off a raucous celebration at Shea Stadium.

New York Mets (E), 3; Arizona Diamondbacks (W), 1

NY (E)

PLAYER/POS	AVG	G	AB	R	H	2B	3B	HR	RB	BB	SO	SB
Benny Agbayani, of	.300	4	10	1	3	1	0	0	1	0	3	0
Edgardo Alfonzo, 2b	.250	4	16	6	4	1	0	3	6	3	2	0
Armando Benitez, p	.000	2	0	0	0	0	0	0	0	0	0	0
Bobby Bonilla, ph	.000	2	1	1	0	0	0	0	0	1	0	0
Roger Cedeno, of	.286	4	7	1	2	0	0	0	2	1	1	1
Dennis Cook, p	.000	1	0	0	0	0	0	0	0	0	0	0
Octavio Dotel, p	.000	1	0	0	0	0	0	0	0	0	0	0
Shawon Dunston, of-2	.167	4	6	0	1	0	0	0	0	0	1	0
John Franco, p	.000	3	0	0	0	0	0	0	0	0	0	0
Matt Franco, ph	.000	1	0	0	0	0	0	0	0	1	0	0
Darryl Hamilton, of	.125	4	8	0	1	0	0	0	2	2	0	0
Rickey Henderson, of	.400	4	15	5	6	0	0	0	1	3	1	6
Orel Hershiser, p	.000	1	0	0	0	0	0	0	0	0	0	0
Al Leiter, p	.000	1	3	0	0	0	0	0	0	0	2	0
Pat Mahomes, p	.000	1	0	0	0	0	0	0	0	0	0	0
Melvin Mora, of	.000	3	1	1	0	0	0	0	0	1	0	0
John Olerud, 1b	.438	4	16	3	7	0	0	1	6	3	2	0
Rey Ordonez, ss	.286	4	14	1	4	1	0	0	2	0	5	1
Mike Piazza, c	.222	2	9	0	2	0	0	0	0	0	4	0
Todd Pratt, c-2	.125	3	8	2	1	0	0	1	1	2	1	0
Rick Reed, p	.000	1	1	0	0	0	0	0	0	0	1	0
Kenny Rogers, p	.000	1	2	0	0	0	0	0	0	0	1	0
Robin Ventura, 3b	.214	4	14	1	3	2	0	0	1	4	2	0
Turk Wendell, p	.000	2	1	0	0	0	0	0	0	0	1	0
Masato Yoshii, p	.000	1	2	0	0	0	0	0	0	0	1	0
TOTAL	.254		134	22	34	5	0	5	22	21	28	8

PITCHER	W	L	ERA	G	GS	CG	SV	SHO	IP	H	ER	BB	SO
Armando Benitez	0	0	0.00	2	0	0	0	0	2.1	2	0	1	2
Dennis Cook	0	0	0.00	1	0	0	0	0	1.2	1	0	1	1
Octavio Dotel	0	0	54.00	1	0	0	0	0	0.1	1	2	2	0
John Franco	1	0	0.00	3	0	0	0	0	3.2	1	0	0	2
Orel Hershiser	0	0	0.00	1	0	0	0	0	1.0	0	0	0	1
Al Leiter	0	0	3.52	1	1	0	0	0	7.2	3	3	3	4
Pat Mahomes	0	0	5.40	1	0	0	0	0	1.2	3	1	0	1
Rick Reed	1	0	3.00	1	1	0	0	0	6.0	4	2	3	2
Kenny Rogers	0	1	8.31	1	1	0	0	0	4.1	5	4	2	6
Turk Wendell	1	0	0.00	2	0	0	0	0	2.0	0	0	2	0
Masato Yoshii	0	0	6.75	1	1	0	0	0	5.1	6	4	0	3
TOTAL	3	1	4.00	15	4	0	0	0	36.0	26	16	14	22

ARI (W)

PLAYER/POS	AVG	G	AB	R	H	2B	3B	HR	RB	BB	SO	SB
PLAYER, POS	AVG	G	AB	R	H	2B	3B	HR	RB	BB	SO	SB
Brian Anderson, p	.000	1	2	0	0	0	0	0	0	0	0	0
Jay Bell, 2b	.286	4	14	3	4	1	0	0	3	1	0	0
Bobby Chouinard, p	.000	2	0	0	0	0	0	0	0	0	0	0
Greg Colbrunn, 1b	.400	2	5	1	2	1	0	1	2	2	2	0
Omar Daal, p	.000	1	1	0	0	0	0	0	0	0	1	0
Erubiel Durazo, 1b	.143	2	7	1	1	0	0	1	1	1	0	0
Steve Finley, of	.385	4	13	0	5	1	0	0	5	3	1	0
Andy Fox, ss	.000	1	3	0	0	0	0	0	0	0	1	0
Hanley Frias, ss	.000	4	7	0	0	0	0	0	0	0	3	0
Bernard Gilkey, of	.000	2	6	0	0	0	0	0	0	0	0	0
Luis Gonzalez, of	.200	4	10	3	2	1	0	1	2	5	1	0
Lenny Harris, 3b-1	.000	2	2	0	0	0	0	0	0	0	0	0
Darren Holmes, p	.000	1	0	0	0	0	0	0	0	0	0	0
Randy Johnson, p	.333	1	3	0	1	1	0	0	0	0	1	0
Matt Mantei, p	.000	1	0	0	0	0	0	0	0	0	0	0
Gregg Olson, p	.000	2	0	0	0	0	0	0	0	0	0	0
Dan Plesac, p	.000	1	0	0	0	0	0	0	0	0	0	0
Kelly Stinnett, c	.143	4	14	1	2	1	0	0	0	1	4	0
Todd Stottlemyre, p	.000	1	3	0	0	0	0	0	0	0	1	0
Greg Swindell, p	.000	3	0	0	0	0	0	0	0	0	0	0
Turner Ward, ph	.500	3	2	2	1	0	0	1	3	1	0	0
Matt Williams, 3b	.375	4	16	3	6	1	0	0	0	0	1	0
Tony Womack, of-4,ss-2	.111	4	18	2	2	0	1	0	0	0	6	0
TOTAL	.206		126	16	26	7	1	4	16	14	22	0

PITCHER	W	L	ERA	G	GS	CG	SV	SHO	IP	H	ER	BB	SO
Brian Anderson	0	0	2.57	1	1	0	0	0	7.0	7	2	0	4
Bobby Chouinard	0	0	4.50	2	0	0	0	0	2.0	3	1	0	1
Omar Daal	0	1	6.75	1	1	0	0	0	4.0	6	3	3	4
Darren Holmes	0	0	27.00	1	0	0	0	0	1.1	1	4	3	0
Randy Johnson	0	1	7.56	1	1	0	0	0	8.1	8	7	3	11
Matt Mantei	0	1	4.50	1	0	0	0	0	2.0	1	1	3	1
Gregg Olson	0	0	0.00	2	0	0	0	0	0.1	0	0	1	0
Dan Plesac	0	0	54.00	1	0	0	0	0	0.1	3	2	0	0
Todd Stottlemyre	1	0	1.35	1	1	0	0	0	6.2	4	1	5	6
Greg Swindell	0	0	0.00	3	0	0	0	0	3.1	1	0	3	1
TOTAL	1	3	5.35	14	4	0	0	0	35.1	34	21	21	28

GAME 1 AT ARI OCT 5

				R	H	E
NY	102	100	004	8	10	0
ARI	001	102	000	4	7	0

Pitchers: Yoshii, Cook (6), WENDELL (8), Benitez (9) VS JOHNSON, Chouinard (9)
Home Runs: Alfonzo-NY (2), Olerud-NY, Durazo-ARI, Gonzalez-ARI
Attendance: 49,584

GAME 2 AT ARI OCT 6

				R	H	E
NY	001	000	000	1	5	0
ARI	003	020	20X	7	9	1

Pitchers: ROGERS, Mahomes (5), Dotel (7), J.Franco (7) VS STOTTLEMYRE, Olson (7), Swindell (8)
Attendance: 49,328

GAME 3 AT NY OCT 8

				R	H	E
ARI	000	020	000	2	5	3
NY	012	006	00X	9	11	0

Pitchers: DAAL, Holmes (5), Plesac (6), Chouinard (6), Swindell (8) VS REED, Wendell (7), J.Franco (8), Hershiser (9)
Home Runs: Ward-ARI
Attendance: 56,180

GAME 4 AT NY OCT 9

					R	H	E
ARI	000	010	020	0	3	5	1
NY	000	101	010	1	4	8	0

Pitchers: Anderson, Olson (8), Swindell (8), MANTEI (8) VS Leiter, Benitez (8), J.FRANCO (10)
Home Runs: Alfonzo-NY, Colbrunn-ARI, Pratt-NY
Attendance: 56,177

The New York Yankees limited the Texas Rangers to one run in three games for the second straight year. After losing their first Division Series game to Texas in 1996, the Yankees won nine consecutive postseason games against the Rangers. Orlando Hernandez made easy work of Texas in Game 1. He and two relievers combined on a two-hit shutout. Bernie Williams drove in six runs with three hits and added a sliding catch to stymie the Rangers.

Texas scored its lone run of the series in fourth inning of Game 2 on a home run by Juan Gonzalez. Scott Brosius tied the game with a double in the sixth, Ricky Ledee gave New York the lead with a seventh-inning double, and a bases-loaded walk added a third run in the eighth. Andy Pettitte survived seven hits to gain the victory.

Roger Clemens clinched the series for the Yankees in his native Texas. He allowed only three hits in seven innings, and Mariano Rivera pitched two scoreless innings for his second save of the series. Darryl Strawberry provided all the offensive support with a two-out, three-run home run in the first inning against Esteban Loaiza.

New York Yankees (E), 3; Texas Rangers (W), 0

NY (E)

PLAYER/POS	AVG	G	AB	R	H	2B	3B	HR	RB	BB	SO	SB
Clay Bellinger, dh	.000	1	0	0	0	0	0	0	0	0	0	0
Scott Brosius, 3b	.100	3	10	0	1	1	0	0	1	0	0	0
Roger Clemens, p	.000	1	0	0	0	0	0	0	0	0	0	0
Chad Curtis, of	.000	3	3	1	0	0	0	0	0	0	0	0
Chili Davis, dh	.333	1	3	0	1	0	0	0	0	0	2	0
Joe Girardi, c	.000	2	6	0	0	0	0	0	0	0	1	0
Orlando Hernandez, p	.000	1	0	0	0	0	0	0	0	0	0	0
Derek Jeter, ss	.455	3	11	3	5	1	1	0	0	2	3	0
Chuck Knoblauch, 2b	.167	3	12	1	2	0	0	0	0	1	3	0
Ricky Ledee, of	.273	3	11	1	3	2	0	0	2	1	5	0
Jim Leyritz, dh	.000	2	2	0	0	0	0	0	1	1	0	0
Tino Martinez, 1b	.182	3	11	2	2	0	0	0	0	2	2	0
Jeff Nelson, p	.000	3	0	0	0	0	0	0	0	0	0	0
Paul O'Neill, of	.250	3	8	2	2	0	0	0	0	1	1	0
Andy Pettitte, p	.000	1	0	0	0	0	0	0	0	0	0	0
Jorge Posada, c	.250	1	4	0	1	1	0	0	0	0	0	0
Mariano Rivera, p	.000	2	0	0	0	0	0	0	0	0	0	0
Darryl Strawberry, dh	.333	2	6	2	2	0	0	1	3	1	0	0
Bernie Williams, of	.364	3	11	2	4	1	0	1	6	1	2	0
TOTAL	.235		98	14	23	6	1	2	13	10	19	0

PITCHER	W	L	ERA	G	GS	CG	SV	SHO	IP	H	ER	BB	SO
Roger Clemens	1	0	0.00	1	1	0	0	0	7.0	3	0	2	2
Orlando Hernandez	1	0	0.00	1	1	0	0	0	8.0	2	0	6	4
Jeff Nelson	0	0	0.00	3	0	0	0	0	1.2	1	0	1	3
Andy Pettitte	1	0	1.23	1	1	0	0	0	7.1	7	1	0	5
Mariano Rivera	0	0	0.00	2	0	0	2	0	3.0	1	0	0	3
TOTAL	3	0	0.33	8	3	0	2	0	27.0	14	1	9	17

TEX (W)

PLAYER/POS	AVG	G	AB	R	H	2B	3B	HR	RB	BB	SO	SB
Royce Clayton, ss	.000	3	10	0	0	0	0	0	0	0	1	0
Tim Crabtree, p	.000	2	0	0	0	0	0	0	0	0	0	0
Jeff Fassero, p	.000	1	0	0	0	0	0	0	0	0	0	0
Juan Gonzalez, of	.182	3	11	1	2	0	0	1	1	1	3	0
Tom Goodwin, of	.143	3	7	0	1	0	0	0	0	0	1	0
Rusty Greer, of	.111	3	9	0	1	0	0	0	0	3	1	0
Rick Helling, p	.000	1	0	0	0	0	0	0	0	0	0	0
Roberto Kelly, of	.333	1	3	0	1	0	0	0	0	0	2	0
Esteban Loaiza, p	.000	1	0	0	0	0	0	0	0	0	0	0
Mark McLemore, 2b	.100	3	10	0	1	0	0	0	0	1	3	0
Rafael Palmeiro, dh	.273	3	11	0	3	0	0	0	0	1	1	0
Danny Patterson, p	.000	1	0	0	0	0	0	0	0	0	0	0
Ivan Rodriguez, c	.250	3	12	0	3	1	0	0	0	0	2	1
Aaron Sele, p	.000	1	0	0	0	0	0	0	0	0	0	0
Lee Stevens, 1b	.111	3	9	0	1	1	0	0	0	1	2	0
Mike Venafro, p	.000	2	0	0	0	0	0	0	0	0	0	0
John Wetteland, p	.000	1	0	0	0	0	0	0	0	0	0	0
Todd Zeile, 3b	.100	3	10	0	1	0	0	0	0	2	1	0
Jeff Zimmerman, p	.000	1	0	0	0	0	0	0	0	0	0	0
TOTAL	.152		92	1	14	2	0	1	1	9	17	1

PITCHER	W	L	ERA	G	GS	CG	SV	SHO	IP	H	ER	BB	SO
Tim Crabtree	0	0	5.40	2	0	0	0	0	1.2	1	1	1	1
Jeff Fassero	0	0	9.00	1	0	0	0	0	1.0	2	1	1	1
Rick Helling	0	1	2.84	1	1	0	0	0	6.1	5	2	1	8
Esteban Loaiza	0	1	3.86	1	1	0	0	0	7.0	5	3	1	4
Danny Patterson	0	0	0.00	1	0	0	0	0	1.0	1	0	0	0
Aaron Sele	0	1	5.40	1	1	0	0	0	5.0	6	3	5	3
Mike Venafro	0	0	0.00	2	0	0	0	0	1.0	2	0	1	0
John Wetteland	0	0	0.00	1	0	0	0	0	1.0	0	0	0	1
Jeff Zimmerman	0	0	0.00	1	0	0	0	0	1.0	1	0	0	1
TOTAL	0	3	3.60	11	3	0	0	0	25.0	23	10	10	19

GAME 1 AT NY OCT 5

		R	H	E
TEX	000 000 000	0	2	1
NY	010 024 01X	8	10	0

Pitchers: SELE, Crabtree (6), Venafro (6), Patterson (7), Fassero (8) VS HERNANDEZ, Nelson (9)
Home Runs: Williams-NY
Attendance: 57,099

GAME 2 AT NY OCT 7

		R	H	E
TEX	000 100 000	1	7	0
NY	000 010 11X	3	7	2

Pitchers: HELLING, Crabtree (7), Venafro (8) VS PETTITTE, Nelson (8), Rivera (9)
Home Runs: Gonzalez-TEX
Attendance: 57,485

GAME 3 AT TEX OCT 9

		R	H	E
NY	300 000 000	3	6	0
TEX	000 000 000	0	5	1

Pitchers: CLEMENS, Nelson (8), Rivera (8) VS LOAIZA, Zimmerman (8), Wetteland (9)
Home Runs: Strawberry-NY
Attendance: 50,269

Boston Red Sox (E), 3; Cleveland Indians (C), 2

The Boston Red Sox had lost 18 of their last 19 postseason games and were one game away from elimination when the club rallied to win the Division Series. From the seventh inning of Game 3 to the end of the series, Boston outscored the Cleveland Indians, 41-15.

Things looked bad for Boston after Pedro Martinez left Game 1 with a strained back muscle. Cleveland trailed 2-0, but John Valentin's throwing error kept the sixth inning alive and Jim Thome followed with a home run. Travis Fryman singled in the bottom of the ninth to win the game. The next afternoon the Indians scored six runs in the third inning and five runs in the fourth to walk away with an 11-1 win and two games to none lead.

The Red Sox led 3-2 after six innings in Game 3, but the Indians tied it in the seventh on Valentin's second throwing error of the series. After reliever Ricardo Rincon got two outs in the seventh inning, Valentin doubled to drive in two runs. Brian Daubach followed with a home run.

The fourth game of the series was the greatest scoring display in postseason history. Bartolo Colon, pitching on three days' rest, did not make it out of the second inning. The Red Sox scored multiple runs in seven of eight innings. Valentine homered twice and drove in seven runs, Mike Stanley had five hits, and Jason Varitek scored five times in the 23-7 shellacking.

The Indians and Red Sox traded longballs for the first three innings of Game 5 in Cleveland. Thome hit two mammoth home runs and Fryman added another, but the game took a decided turn after Boston forged an 8-all tie in the top of the fourth inning. Pedro Martinez came out of the bullpen and pitched six innings of no-hit relief. Sean DePaula, who pitched three innings of hitless relief for Cleveland, was removed in favor of Paul Shuey to start the seventh. Troy O'Leary, who had hit a grand slam earlier following an intentional walk to Nomar Garciaparra, ripped a three-run shot after another intentional pass to Garciaparra.

BOS (E)

PLAYER/POS	AVG	G	AB	R	H	2B	3B	HR	RB	BB	SO	SB
Rod Beck, p	.000	2	0	0	0	0	0	0	0	0	0	0
Damon Buford, of	.000	1	3	0	0	0	0	0	0	0	1	0
Rheal Cormier, p	.000	2	0	0	0	0	0	0	0	0	0	0
Brian Daubach, dh-4,1b-1	.250	4	16	3	4	2	0	1	3	0	7	0
Rich Garces, p	.000	2	0	0	0	0	0	0	0	0	0	0
Nomar Garciaparra, ss	.417	5	12	6	5	2	0	2	4	3	3	0
Tom Gordon, p	.000	2	0	0	0	0	0	0	0	0	0	0
Scott Hatteberg, c	1.000	1	1	1	1	0	0	0	1	0	0	0
Butch Huskey, dh	.200	2	5	0	1	0	0	0	0	0	1	0
Darren Lewis, of	.375	4	16	5	6	1	0	0	2	0	2	1
Derek Lowe, p	.000	3	0	0	0	0	0	0	0	0	0	0
Pedro Martinez, p	.000	2	0	0	0	0	0	0	0	0	0	0
Ramon Martinez, p	.000	1	0	0	0	0	0	0	0	0	0	0
Kent Mercker, p	.000	1	0	0	0	0	0	0	0	0	0	0
Lou Merloni, ss	.333	3	6	1	2	0	0	0	1	1	1	0
Trot Nixon, of	.214	5	14	5	3	3	0	0	6	4	5	0
Jose Offerman, 2b	.389	5	18	4	7	1	0	1	6	7	0	0
Troy O'Leary, of	.200	5	20	4	4	0	0	2	7	2	3	0
Bret Saberhagen, p	.000	2	0	0	0	0	0	0	0	0	0	0
Donnie Sadler, 3b-1,dh-1	.500	2	2	1	1	1	0	0	0	0	1	0
Mike Stanley, 1b	.500	5	20	4	10	2	1	0	2	2	3	0
John Valentin, 3b	.318	5	22	6	7	2	0	3	12	0	4	0
Jason Varitek, c	.238	5	21	7	5	3	0	1	3	0	4	0
Tim Wakefield, p	.000	2	0	0	0	0	0	0	0	0	0	0
John Wasdin, p	.000	2	0	0	0	0	0	0	0	0	0	0
TOTAL	.318		176	47	56	17	1	10	47	19	35	1

PITCHER	W	L	ERA	G	GS	CG	SV	SHO	IP	H	ER	BB	SO
Rod Beck	0	0	0.00	2	0	0	0	0	2.0	2	0	0	2
Rheal Cormier	0	0	0.00	2	0	0	0	0	4.0	2	0	1	4
Rich Garces	1	0	3.86	2	0	0	0	0	2.1	2	1	3	2
Tom Gordon	0	0	4.50	2	0	0	0	0	2.0	1	1	1	3
Derek Lowe	1	1	4.32	3	0	0	0	0	8.1	6	4	1	7
Pedro Martinez	1	0	0.00	2	1	0	0	0	10.0	3	0	4	11
Ramon Martinez	0	0	3.18	1	1	0	0	0	5.2	5	2	3	6
Kent Mercker	0	0	10.80	1	1	0	0	0	1.2	3	2	3	1
Bret Saberhagen	0	1	27.00	2	2	0	0	0	3.2	9	11	4	2
Tim Wakefield	0	0	13.50	2	0	0	0	0	2.0	3	3	4	4
John Wasdin	0	0	27.00	2	0	0	0	0	1.2	2	5	4	1
TOTAL	3	2	6.02	21	5	0	0	0	43.1	38	29	28	43

CLE (C)

PLAYER/POS	AVG	G	AB	R	H	2B	3B	HR	RB	BB	SO	SB
Roberto Alomar, 2b	.368	5	19	4	7	4	0	0	3	2	3	2
Sandy Alomar, c	.143	5	14	1	2	0	0	0	1	2	6	0
Paul Assenmacher, p	.000	1	0	0	0	0	0	0	0	0	0	0
Harold Baines, dh	.357	4	14	1	5	0	0	1	4	2	1	0
Dave Burba, p	.000	1	0	0	0	0	0	0	0	0	0	0
Bartolo Colon, p	.000	2	0	0	0	0	0	0	0	0	0	0
Wil Cordero, dh-2,of-1	.556	3	9	3	5	0	0	1	2	1	2	0
Sean DePaula, p	.000	3	0	0	0	0	0	0	0	0	0	0
Einar Diaz, c	.000	2	1	0	0	0	0	0	0	0	0	0
Travis Fryman, 3b	.267	5	15	2	4	0	0	1	4	3	2	1
Mike Jackson, p	.000	2	0	0	0	0	0	0	0	0	0	0
David Justice, of	.000	3	8	0	0	0	0	0	1	2	2	0
Steve Karsay, p	.000	2	0	0	0	0	0	0	0	0	0	0
Kenny Lofton, of	.125	5	16	5	2	1	0	0	1	5	6	2
Charles Nagy, p	.000	2	0	0	0	0	0	0	0	0	0	0
Manny Ramirez, of	.056	5	18	5	1	1	0	0	1	4	8	0
Steve Reed, p	.000	2	0	0	0	0	0	0	0	0	0	0
Ricardo Rincon, p	.000	1	0	0	0	0	0	0	0	0	0	0
Dave Roberts, of	.000	2	3	0	0	0	0	0	0	0	2	0
Richie Sexson, 1b-1,of-1	.167	3	6	1	1	0	0	0	1	1	3	0
Paul Shuey, p	.000	3	0	0	0	0	0	0	0	0	0	0
Jim Thome, 1b	.353	5	17	7	6	0	0	4	10	4	5	0
Omar Vizquel, ss	.238	5	21	3	5	1	1	0	3	2	3	0
Enrique Wilson, 2b-2	.000	3	2	0	0	0	0	0	0	0	0	0
Jaret Wright, p	.000	1	0	0	0	0	0	0	0	0	0	0
TOTAL	.233		163	32	38	7	1	7	31	28	43	5

PITCHER	W	L	ERA	G	GS	CG	SV	SHO	IP	H	ER	BB	SO
Paul Assenmacher	0	0	27.00	1	0	0	0	0	1.0	5	3	0	0
Dave Burba	0	0	0.00	1	1	0	0	0	4.0	1	0	1	0
Bartolo Colon	0	1	9.00	2	2	0	0	0	9.0	11	9	4	12
Sean DePaula	0	0	1.80	3	0	0	0	0	5.0	2	1	3	5
Mike Jackson	0	0	4.50	2	0	0	0	0	2.0	2	1	1	1
Steve Karsay	0	0	9.00	2	0	0	0	0	3.0	5	3	1	3
Charles Nagy	1	0	7.20	2	2	0	0	0	10.0	11	8	2	6
Steve Reed	0	0	30.86	2	0	0	0	0	2.1	9	8	1	1
Ricardo Rincon	0	0	40.50	1	0	0	0	0	0.2	2	3	1	1
Paul Shuey	1	1	11.25	3	0	0	0	0	4.0	4	5	4	5
Jaret Wright	0	1	22.50	1	0	0	0	0	2.0	4	5	1	1
TOTAL	2	3	9.63	20	5	0	0	0	43.0	56	46	19	35

GAME 1 AT CLE OCT 6

				R	H	E
BOS	010	100	000	2	5	1
CLE	000	002	001	3	6	1

Pitchers: P.Martinez, LOWE (5), Cormier (9), Garces (9) VS Colon, SHUEY (9)
Home Runs: Garciaparra-BOS, Thome-CLE
Attendance: 45,182

GAME 2 AT CLE OCT 7

				R	H	E
BOS	001	000	000	1	6	0
CLE	006	500	00X	11	8	0

Pitchers: SABERHAGEN, Wasdin (3), Wakefield (5), Gordon (7), Beck (8) VS NAGY, Karsay (8), Jackson (9)
Home Runs: Baines-CLE, Thome-CLE
Attendance: 45,184

GAME 3 AT BOS OCT 9

				R	H	E
CLE	000	101	100	3	9	1
BOS	000	021	60X	9	11	2

Pitchers: Burba, WRIGHT ((5), Rincon (7), DePaula (7), Reed (8) VS R.Martinez, LOWE (6), Beck (9)
Home Runs: Valentin-BOS, Daubach-BOS
Attendance: 33,539

GAME 4 AT BOS OCT 10

				R	H	E
CLE	110	040	001	7	8	0
BOS	253	530	32X	23	24	0

Pitchers: COLON, Karsay (2), Reed (4), DePaula (5), Assenmacher (7), Shuey (8) VS Mercker, GARCES (2), Wakefield (5), Wasdin (5), Cormier (5), Gordon (9)
Home Runs: Valentin-BOS (2), Offerman-BOS, Varitek-BOS, Cordero-CLE
Attendance: 33,898

GAME 5 AT CLE OCT 11

				R	H	E
BOS	205	100	301	12	10	0
CLE	323	000	000	8	7	1

Pitchers: Saberhagen, Lowe (2), P.MARTINEZ (4) VS Nagy, DePaula (4), SHUEY (7), Jackson (9)
Home Runs: Garciaparra-BOS, Thome-CLE (2), Fryman-CLE, O'Leary-BOS (2)
Attendance: 45,114

The Braves had beaten the Mets in 18 of their last 24 meetings and nearly knocked them out of the playoff picture in September, but New York rallied and made it to the Championship Series for the first time since 1988. Atlanta, playing in its eighth consecutive NLCS, rolled past the Mets in the opener as Greg Maddux outpitched Masato Yoshii. The next afternoon Kenny Rogers took a 2-0 lead into the bottom of the sixth, but two-run homers by Brian Jordan and Eddie Perez put the Braves in front. After closer John Rocker squashed a Mets rally in the eighth, John Smoltz, making his first major league relief appearance, earned the save. First-inning throwing errors by the Mets battery of Al Leiter and Mike Piazza allowed Atlanta to push across a first-inning run in Game 3. Tom Glavine and two relievers made it stand up in a 1-0 win at Shea Stadium.

The Mets grabbed a 1-0 lead in Game 4 on John Olerud's home run, but back-to-back homers by Jordan and Ryan Klesko in the eighth inning spoiled a brilliant outing by New York starter Rick Reed. In the bottom of the eighth, however, Olerud's grounder up the middle barley eluded replacement shortstop Ozzie Guillen to drive in the tying and go-ahead runs.

Olerud homered in the first inning of Game 5. The Braves tied it with consecutive hits by Jordan and Chipper Jones to chase Yoshii in the fourth. Orel Hershiser came on in relief and started a string of 10 straight scoreless innings by the Mets bullpen. Not to be outdone, the Braves blanked the Mets for 13 consecutive innings as a steady rain fell in New York. The Braves finally broke through in the 15th inning on a run-scoring triple by Keith Lockhart. Pinch hitter Shawon Dunston led off the bottom of the inning with a single to climax a 12-pitch at bat. Rookie Kevin McGlinchy walked three of the next four batters, including Todd Pratt to tie the game. Robin Ventura, in a 1-for-18 slump, cleared the fence in right for an apparent game-ending grand slam, but he was mobbed by teammates before he could get to second base. There was confusion over what the final score should be; after several minutes a 4-3 verdict was posted, and Ventura was credited with a game-winning single.

Leiter did not retire a batter in Game 6. The Braves took a 5-0 lead, highlighted by a two-run single by series Most Valuable Player Eddie Perez. Although Darryl Hamilton's two-run single in the sixth pulled the Mets within two runs, a pinch-hit single by Jose Hernandez upped Atlanta's lead to 7-3. Mike Piazza, who later left the game because of a slight concussion, slammed a home run in the seventh off Smoltz to tie the game. Melvin Mora singled in a run in the eighth to give the Mets the lead, but Brian Hunter's single in the bottom of the inning tied the game. After New York took another lead in the 10th, Guillen's single again knotted the score. When Jordan reached third with one out in the 11th, Kenny Rogers walked the next two batters intentionally. He then walked Andruw Jones to bring in the series-ending run.

Atlanta Braves (E), 4; New York Mets (E), 2

ATL (E)

PLAYER/POS	AVG	G	AB	R	H	2B	3B	HR	RB	BB	SO	SB
Howard Battle, 1b-1	.000	3	2	0	0	0	0	0	0	0	2	1
Bret Boone, 2b	.182	6	22	2	4	1	0	0	1	1	7	2
Jorge Fabregas, ph	.000	2	2	0	0	0	0	0	0	0	1	0
Tom Glavine, p	.000	1	2	0	0	0	0	0	0	0	1	0
Ozzie Guillen, ss-2	.333	3	3	0	1	0	0	0	1	0	0	0
Jose Hernandez, ph	.500	2	2	0	1	0	0	0	2	0	1	0
Brian Hunter, 1b	.100	6	10	1	1	0	0	0	2	5	2	1
Andruw Jones, of	.217	6	23	5	5	0	0	0	1	4	3	0
Chipper Jones, 3b	.263	6	19	3	5	2	0	0	1	9	7	3
Brian Jordan, of	.200	6	25	3	5	0	0	2	5	3	5	0
Ryan Klesko, 1b	.125	4	8	1	1	0	0	1	1	2	1	0
Keith Lockhart, 2b-1	.400	3	5	0	2	0	1	0	1	0	2	0
Greg Maddux, p	.000	2	5	0	0	0	0	0	0	0	4	0
Kevin McGlinchy, p	.000	1	1	0	0	0	0	0	0	0	1	0
Kevin Millwood, p	.000	2	4	0	0	0	0	0	0	1	0	0
Terry Mulholland, p	.000	2	0	0	0	0	0	0	0	0	0	0
Greg Myers, c	.000	2	2	0	0	0	0	0	0	1	1	0
Otis Nixon, pr	.000	2	0	1	0	0	0	0	0	0	0	2
Eddie Perez, c	.500	6	20	2	10	2	0	2	5	1	3	0
Mike Remlinger, p	.000	5	0	0	0	0	0	0	0	0	0	0
John Rocker, p	.000	6	0	0	0	0	0	0	0	0	0	0
John Smoltz, p	.000	3	2	0	0	0	0	0	0	0	0	0
Russ Springer, p	.000	2	0	0	0	0	0	0	0	0	0	0
Walt Weiss, ss	.286	6	21	2	6	2	0	0	1	2	4	2
Gerald Williams, of	.179	6	28	4	5	2	0	0	1	2	2	3
TOTAL	.223		206	24	46	9	1	5	22	31	47	14

PITCHER	W	L	ERA	G	GS	CG	SV	SHO	IP	H	ER	BB	SO
Tom Glavine	1	0	0.00	1	1	0	0	0	7.0	7	0	1	8
Greg Maddux	1	0	1.93	2	2	0	0	0	14.0	12	3	1	7
Kevin McGlinchy	0	1	18.00	1	0	0	0	0	1.0	2	2	4	1
Kevin Millwood	1	0	3.55	2	2	0	0	0	12.2	13	5	1	9
Terry Mulholland	0	0	0.00	2	0	0	0	0	2.2	1	0	1	2
Mike Remlinger	0	1	3.18	5	0	0	0	0	5.2	3	2	3	4
John Rocker	0	0	0.00	6	0	0	1	0	6.2	3	0	2	9
John Smoltz	0	0	6.23	3	1	0	1	0	8.2	8	6	0	8
Russ Springer	1	0	0.00	2	0	0	0	0	2.0	0	0	1	1
TOTAL	4	2	2.69	24	6	0	2	0	60.1	49	18	14	49

NY (E)

PLAYER/POS	AVG	G	AB	R	H	2B	3B	HR	RB	BB	SO	SB
Benny Agbayani, of-3	.143	4	7	2	1	0	0	0	0	4	2	1
Edgardo Alfonzo, 2b	.222	6	27	2	6	4	0	0	1	1	9	0
Armando Benitez, p	.000	5	0	0	0	0	0	0	0	0	0	0
Bobby Bonilla, ph	.333	3	3	0	1	0	0	0	0	0	2	0
Roger Cedeno, of-4	.500	5	12	2	6	1	0	0	1	0	1	2
Dennis Cook, p	.000	3	0	0	0	0	0	0	0	0	0	0
Octavio Dotel, p	.000	1	0	0	0	0	0	0	0	0	0	0
Shawon Dunston, of-1	.143	5	7	2	1	0	0	0	0	0	2	1
John Franco, p	.000	3	0	0	0	0	0	0	0	0	0	0
Matt Franco, ph	.500	5	2	1	1	1	0	0	0	1	0	0
Darryl Hamilton, of	.353	5	17	0	6	1	0	0	2	0	4	0
Rickey Henderson, of	.174	6	23	2	4	1	0	0	1	0	5	1
Orel Hershiser, p	.000	2	1	0	0	0	0	0	0	0	0	0
Al Leiter, p	.000	2	2	0	0	0	0	0	0	0	1	0
Pat Mahomes, p	.000	3	2	0	0	0	0	0	0	0	2	0
Melvin Mora, of-5	.429	6	14	3	6	0	0	1	2	2	2	2
John Olerud, 1b	.296	6	27	4	8	0	0	2	6	2	3	0
Rey Ordonez, ss	.042	6	24	0	1	0	0	0	0	0	2	0
Mike Piazza, c	.167	6	24	1	4	0	0	1	4	1	6	0
Todd Pratt, c-2	.500	4	2	0	1	0	0	0	3	1	1	0
Rick Reed, p	.000	1	2	0	0	0	0	0	0	0	0	0
Kenny Rogers, p	.000	3	1	0	0	0	0	0	0	0	1	0
Robin Ventura, 3b	.120	6	25	2	3	1	0	0	1	2	5	0
Turk Wendell, p	.000	5	0	0	0	0	0	0	0	0	0	0
Masato Yoshii, p	.000	2	3	0	0	0	0	0	0	0	1	0
TOTAL	.218		225	21	49	9	0	4	21	14	49	7

PITCHER	W	L	ERA	G	GS	CG	SV	SHO	IP	H	ER	BB	SO
Armando Benitez	0	0	1.35	5	0	0	1	0	6.2	3	1	2	9
Dennis Cook	0	0	0.00	3	0	0	0	0	1.1	1	0	2	1
Octavio Dotel	1	0	3.00	1	0	0	0	0	3.0	4	1	2	5
John Franco	0	0	3.38	3	0	0	0	0	2.2	3	1	1	3
Orel Hershiser	0	0	0.00	2	0	0	0	0	4.1	1	0	3	5
Al Leiter	0	1	6.43	2	2	0	0	0	7.0	5	5	4	5
Pat Mahomes	0	0	1.42	3	0	0	0	0	6.1	4	1	3	3
Rick Reed	0	0	2.57	1	1	0	0	0	7.0	3	2	0	5
Kenny Rogers	0	2	5.87	3	1	0	0	0	7.2	11	5	7	2
Turk Wendell	1	0	4.76	5	0	0	0	0	5.2	2	3	4	5
Masato Yoshii	0	1	4.70	2	2	0	0	0	7.2	9	4	3	4
TOTAL	2	4	3.49	30	6	0	1	0	59.1	46	23	31	47

GAME 1 AT ATL OCT 12

		R	H	E
NY	000 100 001	2	6	2
ATL	100 011 01X	4	8	2

Pitchers: YOSHII, Mahomes (5), Cook (7), Wendell (8) VS MADDUX, Remlinger (8), Rocker (8)
Home Runs: Perez-ATL
Attendance: 44,172

GAME 2 AT ATL OCT 13

		R	H	E
NY	010 010 010	3	5	1
ATL	000 004 00X	4	9	1

Pitchers: ROGERS, Wendell (6), Benitez (8) VS MILLWOOD, Rocker (8), Smoltz (9)
Home Runs: Mora-NY, Jordan-ATL, Perez-ATL
Attendance: 44,624

GAME 3 AT NY OCT 15

		R	H	E
ATL	100 000 000	1	3	1
NY	000 000 000	0	7	2

Pitchers: GLAVINE, Remlinger (8), Rocker (9) VS LEITER, J.Franco (8), Benitez (8)
Attendance: 55,911

GAME 4 AT NY OCT 16

		R	H	E
ATL	000 000 020	2	3	0
NY	000 001 02X	3	5	0

Pitchers: Smoltz, REMLINGER (8), Rocker (8) VS Reed, WENDELL (8), Benitez (9)
Home Runs: Olerud-NY, Jordan-ATL, Klesko-ATL
Attendance: 55,872

GAME 5 AT NY OCT 17

		R	H	E
ATL	000 200 000 000 001	3	13	2
NY	200 000 000 000 002	4	11	1

Pitchers: Maddux, Mulholland (8), Remlinger (10), Springer (12), Rocker (13), McGLINCHY (14) VS Yoshii, Hershiser (4), Wendell (7), Cook (7), Mahomes (7), J.Franco (8), Benitez (10), Rogers (11), DOTEL (13)
Home Runs: Olerud-NY
Attendance: 55,723

GAME 6 AT ATL OCT 19

		R	H	E
NY	000 003 410 10	9	15	2
ATL	500 002 010 11	10	10	1

Pitchers: Leiter, Mahomes (1), Wendell (5), Cook (6), Hershiser (7), J.Franco (8), Benitez (9), ROGERS (11) VS Millwood, Mulholland (6), Smoltz (7), Remlinger (7), Rocker (9), SPRINGER (10)
Home Runs: Piazza-NY
Attendance: 52,335

The only thing missing in the nearly century-long rivalry between the New York Yankees and Boston Red Sox was a postseason chapter. The addition of the Wild Card enabled the pair to meet in the 1999 Championship Series.

The Red Sox arrived in New York fresh off a dramatic win over the Cleveland Indians in the Division Series. Boston got off to a solid start in the ALCS by taking an early 3-0 lead over New York in Game 1. Scott Brosius homered off Kent Merker to cut the lead to 3-2, and New York tied the game on Derek Jeter's RBI-single in the seventh inning as Brosius jarred the ball from the grasp of catcher Jason Varitek. Bernie Williams homered off Rod Beck in the 10th to give the Yankees the win. Boston took an early lead again in Game 2, but the Yankees rallied in the seventh on two-out hits by Chuck Knoblauch and Paul O'Neill for the win. It was the Yanks' 12th consecutive postseason win, tying a their own record set between 1927 and 1932.

Fenway Park was not kind to the Yanks, or former favorite son Roger Clemens, in Game 3. The Sox rocked Clemens for five runs in two innings and he left to the hoots of the raucous Fenway crowd. Boston ace Pedro Martinez allowed just two hits in seven innings. John Valentin knocked in five runs and Nomar Garciaparra drove in three runs in a 13-1 rout. The Red Sox took an early lead for the fourth straight game the following night, but mistakes and blown chances cost Boston a chance to even the series. Two errors in the fourth inning allowed the Yanks to gain the lead. A Boston rally was snuffed in the eighth inning when umpire Tim Tschida called Jose Offerman out as part of a double play, even though Offerman was never tagged. Although Ricky Ledee's pinch-hit grand slam in the ninth inning put the game away, Fenway fans littered the field with debris and halted play following the ejection of manager Jimy Williams.

Jeter homered in the first inning of Game 5 to send the Yankees on their way to the pennant. Boston committed its LCS record 10th error and left 11 runners on bases against series Most Valuable Player Orlando Hernandez and four relievers.

New York Yankees (E), 4; Boston Red Sox (E), 1

NY (E)

PLAYER/POS	AVG	G	AB	R	H	2B	3B	HR	RB	BB	SO	SB
Clay Bellinger, dh-2,ss-1	.000	3	1	0	0	0	0	0	0	0	1	0
Scott Brosius, 3b	.222	5	18	3	4	0	1	2	3	1	4	0
Roger Clemens, p	.000	1	0	0	0	0	0	0	0	0	0	0
David Cone, p	.000	1	0	0	0	0	0	0	0	0	0	0
Chad Curtis, of-2,dh-1	.000	3	6	1	0	0	0	0	0	0	2	1
Chili Davis, dh	.091	5	11	0	1	0	0	0	1	3	4	0
Joe Girardi, c	.250	3	8	0	2	0	0	0	0	0	2	0
Orlando Hernandez, p	.000	2	0	0	0	0	0	0	0	0	0	0
Hideki Irabu, p	.000	1	0	0	0	0	0	0	0	0	0	0
Derek Jeter, ss	.350	5	20	3	7	1	0	1	3	2	3	0
Chuck Knoblauch, 2b	.333	5	18	3	6	1	0	0	1	3	0	1
Ricky Ledee, of-2	.250	3	8	2	2	0	0	1	4	1	4	0
Tino Martinez, 1b	.263	5	19	3	5	1	0	1	3	2	4	0
Ramiro Mendoza, p	.000	2	0	0	0	0	0	0	0	0	0	0
Jeff Nelson, p	.000	2	0	0	0	0	0	0	0	0	0	0
Paul O'Neill, of	.286	5	21	2	6	0	0	0	1	1	5	0
Andy Pettitte, p	.000	1	0	0	0	0	0	0	0	0	0	0
Jorge Posada, c	.100	3	10	1	1	0	0	1	2	1	2	0
Mariano Rivera, p	.000	3	0	0	0	0	0	0	0	0	0	0
Luis Sojo, 2b	.000	2	1	0	0	0	0	0	0	0	0	0
Shane Spencer, of	.111	3	9	1	1	0	0	0	0	1	6	0
Mike Stanton, p	.000	3	0	0	0	0	0	0	0	0	0	0
Darryl Strawberry, dh	.333	3	6	1	2	0	0	1	1	1	2	0
Allen Watson, p	.000	3	0	0	0	0	0	0	0	0	0	0
Bernie Williams, of	.250	5	20	3	5	1	0	1	2	2	5	1
TOTAL	.239		176	23	42	4	1	8	21	18	44	3

PITCHER	W	L	ERA	G	GS	CG	SV	SHO	IP	H	ER	BB	SO
Roger Clemens	0	1	22.50	1	1	0	0	0	2.0	6	5	2	2
David Cone	1	0	2.57	1	1	0	0	0	7.0	7	2	3	9
Orlando Hernandez	1	0	1.80	2	2	0	0	0	15.0	12	3	6	13
Hideki Irabu	0	0	13.50	1	0	0	0	0	4.2	13	7	0	3
Ramiro Mendoza	0	0	0.00	2	0	0	1	0	2.1	0	0	0	2
Jeff Nelson	0	0	0.00	2	0	0	0	0	0.2	0	0	0	0
Andy Pettitte	1	0	2.45	1	1	0	0	0	7.1	8	2	1	5
Mariano Rivera	1	0	0.00	3	0	0	2	0	4.2	5	0	0	3
Mike Stanton	0	0	0.00	3	0	0	0	0	0.1	1	0	1	0
Allen Watson	0	0	0.00	3	0	0	0	0	1.0	2	0	2	1
TOTAL	4	1	3.80	19	5	0	3	0	45.0	54	19	15	38

BOS (E)

PLAYER/POS	AVG	G	AB	R	H	2B	3B	HR	RB	BB	SO	SB
Rod Beck, p	.000	2	0	0	0	0	0	0	0	0	0	0
Damon Buford, of	.400	4	5	1	2	0	0	0	0	0	2	1
Rheal Cormier, p	.000	4	0	0	0	0	0	0	0	0	0	0
Brian Daubach, dh-5,1b-1	.176	5	17	2	3	1	0	1	3	1	4	0
Rich Garces, p	.000	2	0	0	0	0	0	0	0	0	0	0
Nomar Garciaparra, ss	.400	5	20	2	8	2	0	2	5	2	2	1
Tom Gordon, p	.000	3	0	0	0	0	0	0	0	0	0	0
Scott Hatteberg, c-1	.000	3	1	0	0	0	0	0	0	0	1	0
Butch Huskey, dh-3	.200	4	5	1	1	1	0	0	0	1	1	0
Darren Lewis, of	.118	5	17	2	2	1	0	0	1	1	3	1
Derek Lowe, p	.000	3	0	0	0	0	0	0	0	0	0	0
Pedro Martinez, p	.000	1	0	0	0	0	0	0	0	0	0	0
Ramon Martinez, p	.000	1	0	0	0	0	0	0	0	0	0	0
Kent Mercker, p	.000	2	0	0	0	0	0	0	0	0	0	0
Lou Merloni, ph	.000	1	0	0	0	0	0	0	0	1	0	0
Trot Nixon, of	.286	5	14	2	4	2	0	0	0	1	5	0
Jose Offerman, 2b	.458	5	24	4	11	0	1	0	2	1	3	1
Troy O'Leary, of	.350	5	20	2	7	3	0	0	1	2	5	0
Pat Rapp, p	.000	1	0	0	0	0	0	0	0	0	0	0
Bret Saberhagen, p	.000	1	0	0	0	0	0	0	0	0	0	0
Donnie Sadler, of-1,dh-1	.000	2	0	0	0	0	0	0	0	0	0	0
Mike Stanley, 1b	.222	5	18	1	4	0	0	0	1	2	4	0
John Valentin, 3b	.348	5	23	3	8	2	0	1	5	2	4	0
Jason Varitek, c	.200	5	20	1	4	1	1	1	1	1	4	0
TOTAL	.293		184	21	54	13	2	5	19	15	38	4

PITCHER	W	L	ERA	G	GS	CG	SV	SHO	IP	H	ER	BB	SO
Rod Beck	0	1	27.00	2	0	0	0	0	0.2	2	2	0	1
Rheal Cormier	0	0	0.00	4	0	0	0	0	3.2	3	0	3	4
Rich Garces	0	0	12.00	2	0	0	0	0	3.0	3	4	1	2
Tom Gordon	0	0	13.50	3	0	0	0	0	2.0	3	3	1	3
Derek Lowe	0	0	1.42	3	0	0	0	0	6.1	6	1	2	7
Pedro Martinez	1	0	0.00	1	1	0	0	0	7.0	2	0	2	12
Ramon Martinez	0	1	4.05	1	1	0	0	0	6.2	6	3	3	5
Kent Mercker	0	1	4.70	2	2	0	0	0	7.2	12	4	4	5
Pat Rapp	0	0	0.00	1	0	0	0	0	1.0	0	0	1	0
Bret Saberhagen	0	1	1.50	1	1	0	0	0	6.0	5	1	1	5
TOTAL	1	4	3.68	20	5	0	0	0	44.0	42	18	18	44

GAME 1 AT NY OCT 13

					R	H	E
BOS	210	000	000	0	3	8	2
NY	020	000	100	1	4	10	1

Pitchers: Mercker, Garces (5), Lowe (7), Cormier (9), BECK (10) VS Hernandez, RIVERA (9)
Home Runs: Brosius-NY, Williams-NY
Attendance: 57,181

GAME 2 AT NY OCT 14

				R	H	E
BOS	000	020	000	2	10	0
NY	000	100	20X	3	7	0

Pitchers: R.MARTINEZ, Gordon (7), Cormier (7) VS CONE, Stanton (8), Nelson (8), Watson (8), Mendoza (8), Rivera (9)
Home Runs: Martinez-NY, Garciaparra-BOS
Attendance: 57,180

GAME 3 AT BOS OCT 16

				R	H	E
NY	000	000	010	1	3	3
BOS	222	021	40X	13	21	1

Pitchers: CLEMENS, Irabu (3), Stanton (7), Watson (8) VS P.MARTINEZ, Gordon (8), Rapp (9)
Home Runs: Valentin-BOS, Daubach-BOS, Garciaparra-BOS, Brosius-NY
Attendance: 33,190

GAME 4 AT BOS OCT 17

				R	H	E
NY	010	200	006	9	11	0
BOS	011	000	000	2	10	3

Pitchers: PETTITTE, Rivera (8) VS SABERHAGEN, Lowe (7), Cormier (8), Garces (8), Beck (9)
Home Runs: Strawberry-NY, Ledee-NY
Attendance: 33,586

GAME 5 AT BOS OCT 18

				R	H	E
NY	200	000	202	6	11	1
BOS	000	000	010	1	5	2

Pitchers: HERNANDEZ, Stanton (8), Nelson (8), Watson (8), Mendoza (8) VS MERCKER, Lowe (4), Cormier (7), Gordon (9)
Home Runs: Jeter-NY, Varitek-BOS, Posada-NY
Attendance: 33,589

The Yankees steamrolled the Braves for their 25th world championship and second consecutive World Series sweep. Atlanta's only hit against Orlando Hernandez in Game 1 was a fourth-inning home run by Chipper Jones. Greg Maddux made that run stand up until a single, a walk, and an error loaded the bases with none out in the eighth inning. Derek Jeter singled to tie the game and force Maddux to the bench. Atlanta southpaw John Rocker came in to face Paul O'Neill, but the lefthanded-hitting outfielder grounded a single to bring in two runs. Yanks closer Mariano Rivera made the lead stand up. Atlanta got just one hit against New York's Game 2 starter, David Cone, and the Yanks knocked Braves starter Kevin Milwood from the game in the third inning at Turner Field.

The Braves jumped out to a 5-1 lead in Game 3 as Bret Boone had three doubles off starter Andy Pettitte. The Braves had 10 hits in less than four innings against Pettitte, and had several other chances to score throughout the game, but never got the hit that blew the game open. New York's bullpen blanked Atlanta for the final 6 1/3 innings. Meanwhile, solo home runs by Chad Curtis and Tino Martinez brought the Yankees within 5-3. With starter Tom Glavine still pitching in the bottom of the eighth inning, Chuck Knoblauch launched a flyball to right that tipped off right fielder Brian Jordan's glove for a game-tying two-run home run. Curtis, who hit just five home runs all season, led off the 10th inning with his second home run of the game to give the Yankees the victory.

Roger Clemens, who had struggled for much of the season, outdueled John Smoltz in Game 4. A single by Jeter followed an infield hit by Knoblauch in the decisive third inning. After Jeter stole second, Bernie Williams was intentionally walked, to set up a force with Tino Martinez at the plate. Smoltz induced a hard-hit grounder, but it caromed off first baseman Ryan Klesko into right field for a two-run single. With the Yanks leading 3-1 in the eighth inning, Jim Leyritz homered to left. Rivera, with two saves and a win in the sweep, retired the side in the ninth to earn Most Valuable Player honors.

New York Yankees (A), 4; Atlanta Braves (N), 0

NY (A)

PLAYER/POS	AVG	G	AB	R	H	2B	3B	HR	RB	BB	SO	SB
Scott Brosius, 3b	.375	4	16	2	6	1	0	0	1	0	5	0
Roger Clemens, p	.000	1	0	0	0	0	0	0	0	0	0	0
David Cone, p	.000	1	4	0	0	0	0	0	0	0	0	0
Chad Curtis, of	.333	3	6	3	2	0	0	2	2	0	0	0
Chili Davis, dh	.000	1	4	0	0	0	0	0	0	0	2	0
Joe Girardi, c	.286	2	7	1	2	0	0	0	0	0	1	0
Jason Grimsley, p	.000	1	0	0	0	0	0	0	0	0	0	0
Orlando Hernandez, p	.000	1	1	0	0	0	0	0	0	0	0	0
Derek Jeter, ss	.353	4	17	4	6	1	0	0	1	1	3	3
Chuck Knoblauch, 2b	.313	4	16	5	5	1	0	1	3	1	3	1
Ricky Ledee, of	.200	3	10	0	2	1	0	0	1	1	4	0
Jim Leyritz, dh-1	1.000	2	1	1	1	0	0	1	2	1	0	0
Tino Martinez, 1b	.267	4	15	3	4	0	0	1	5	2	4	0
Ramiro Mendoza, p	.000	1	1	0	0	0	0	0	0	0	0	0
Jeff Nelson, p	.000	4	0	0	0	0	0	0	0	0	0	0
Paul O'Neill, of	.200	4	15	0	3	0	0	0	4	2	2	0
Andy Pettitte, p	.000	1	0	0	0	0	0	0	0	0	0	0
Jorge Posada, c	.250	2	8	0	2	1	0	0	1	0	3	0
Mariano Rivera, p	.000	3	0	0	0	0	0	0	0	0	0	0
Luis Sojo, 2b	.000	1	0	0	0	0	0	0	0	0	0	0
Mike Stanton, p	.000	1	0	0	0	0	0	0	0	0	0	0
Darryl Strawberry, dh-1	.333	2	3	0	1	0	0	0	0	1	2	0
Bernie Williams, of	.231	4	13	2	3	0	0	0	0	4	2	1
TOTAL	.270		137	21	37	5	0	5	20	13	31	5

PITCHER	W	L	ERA	G	GS	CG	SV	SHO	IP	H	ER	BB	SO
Roger Clemens	1	0	1.17	1	1	0	0	0	7.2	4	1	2	4
David Cone	1	0	0.00	1	1	0	0	0	7.0	1	0	5	4
Jason Grimsley	0	0	0.00	1	0	0	0	0	2.1	2	0	2	0
Orlando Hernandez	1	0	1.29	1	1	0	0	0	7.0	1	1	2	10
Ramiro Mendoza	0	0	10.80	1	0	0	0	0	1.2	3	2	1	0
Jeff Nelson	0	0	0.00	4	0	0	0	0	2.2	2	0	1	3
Andy Pettitte	0	0	12.27	1	1	0	0	0	3.2	10	5	1	1
Mariano Rivera	1	0	0.00	3	0	0	2	0	4.2	3	0	1	3
Mike Stanton	0	0	0.00	1	0	0	0	0	0.1	0	0	0	1
TOTAL	4	0	2.19	14	4	0	2	0	37.0	26	9	15	26

ATL (N)

PLAYER/POS	AVG	G	AB	R	H	2B	3B	HR	RB	BB	SO	SB
Howard Battle, ph	.000	1	0	0	0	0	0	0	0	0	0	0
Bret Boone, 2b-3	.538	4	13	1	7	4	0	0	3	1	3	0
Jorge Fabregas, ph	.000	1	1	0	0	0	0	0	0	0	1	0
Tom Glavine, p	.000	1	0	0	0	0	0	0	0	0	0	0
Ozzie Guillen, ss-1,dh-1	.000	3	5	0	0	0	0	0	0	0	1	0
Jose Hernandez, ss-1,dh-1	.200	2	5	0	1	1	0	0	2	0	2	1
Brian Hunter, 1b	.250	2	4	0	1	0	0	0	0	0	1	0
Andruw Jones, of	.077	4	13	1	1	0	0	0	0	1	3	0
Chipper Jones, 3b	.231	4	13	2	3	0	0	1	2	4	2	0
Brian Jordan, of	.077	4	13	1	1	0	0	0	1	4	2	0
Ryan Klesko, 1b	.167	4	12	0	2	0	0	0	0	0	1	0
Keith Lockhart, 2b-2,dh-1	.143	4	7	1	1	0	0	0	0	2	0	0
Greg Maddux, p	.000	1	2	0	0	0	0	0	0	0	2	0
Kevin McGlinchy, p	.000	1	0	0	0	0	0	0	0	0	0	0
Kevin Millwood, p	.000	1	0	0	0	0	0	0	0	0	0	0
Terry Mulholland, p	.000	2	0	0	0	0	0	0	0	1	0	0
Greg Myers, c-3	.333	4	6	0	2	0	0	0	1	1	0	0
Otis Nixon, of-1	.500	2	2	0	1	0	0	0	0	0	0	0
Eddie Perez, c	.125	3	8	0	1	0	0	0	0	1	3	0
Mike Remlinger, p	.000	2	0	0	0	0	0	0	0	0	0	0
John Rocker, p	.000	2	0	0	0	0	0	0	0	0	0	0
John Smoltz, p	.000	1	0	0	0	0	0	0	0	0	0	0
Russ Springer, p	.000	2	0	0	0	0	0	0	0	0	0	0
Walt Weiss, ss	.222	3	9	1	2	0	0	0	0	0	1	0
Gerald Williams, of	.176	4	17	2	3	0	1	0	0	0	4	0
TOTAL	.200		130	9	26	5	1	1	9	15	26	1

PITCHER	W	L	ERA	G	GS	CG	SV	SHO	IP	H	ER	BB	SO
Tom Glavine	0	0	5.14	1	1	0	0	0	7.0	7	4	0	3
Greg Maddux	0	1	2.57	1	1	0	0	0	7.0	5	2	3	5
Kevin McGlinchy	0	0	0.00	1	0	0	0	0	2.0	2	0	1	2
Kevin Millwood	0	1	18.00	1	1	0	0	0	2.0	8	4	2	2
Terry Mulholland	0	0	7.36	2	0	0	0	0	3.2	5	3	1	3
Mike Remlinger	0	1	9.00	2	0	0	0	0	1.0	1	1	1	0
John Rocker	0	0	0.00	2	0	0	0	0	3.0	2	0	2	4
John Smoltz	0	1	3.86	1	1	0	0	0	7.0	6	3	3	11
Russ Springer	0	0	0.00	2	0	0	0	0	2.1	1	0	0	1
TOTAL	0	4	4.37	13	4	0	0	0	35.0	37	17	13	31

GAME 1 AT ATL OCT 23

NY	000	000	040	4	6	0
ATL	000	100	000	1	2	2

Pitchers: HERNANDEZ, Nelson (8), Stanton (8), Rivera (8) VS MADDUX, Rocker (8), Remlinger (9)
Home Runs: C.Jones-ATL
Attendance: 51,342

GAME 2 AT ATL OCT 24

NY	302	110	000	7	14	1
ATL	000	000	002	2	5	1

Pitchers: CONE, Mendoza (8), Nelson (9) VS MILLWOOD, Mulholland (3), Springer (6), McGlinchy (8)
Attendance: 51,226

GAME 3 AT NY OCT 26

ATL	103	100	000	0	5	14	1
NY	100	010	120	1	6	9	0

Pitchers: Glavine, Rocker (8), REMLINGER (10) VS Pettitte, Grimsley (4), Nelson (7), RIVERA (9)
Home Runs: Curtis-NY (2), Martinez-NY, Knoblauch-NY
Attendance: 56,794

GAME 4 AT NY OCT 27

ATL	000	000	010	1	5	0
NY	003	000	01X	4	8	0

Pitchers: SMOLTZ, Mulholland (8), Springer (8) VS CLEMENS, Nelson (8), Rivera (8)
Home Runs: Leyritz-NY
Attendance: 56,752

The Braves had lost just two Division Series games over the previous five seasons, including three sweeps, but this time it was Atlanta that was swept. The Cardinals, who had secured home-field advantage for the series on the last day of the season, made the most of it by scoring six times in the bottom of the first inning of the opener against Greg Maddux. Staked to a 6-0 lead, hard-throwing rookie Rick Ankiel suddenly-and disturbingly-fell apart. He issued a postseason-record five wild pitches in the third inning before being relieved. Mike James helped protect the 6-4 lead and earned the victory.

Atlanta scored twice in the top of the first inning in Game 2, but it was wiped out by a three-run home run by Will Clark. Ray Lankford's two-run double capped another outburst and forced Tom Glavine from the game. The 10-4 win marked the most runs scored in a postseason game against Atlanta since 1992.

Although the Braves managed to get out the first inning of Game 3 with a 1-1 tie, the Cards took the lead on a home run by Jim Edmonds in the third. When St. Louis starter Garrett Stephenson was forced to leave the game with elbow tendonitis, Britt Reames came out of the bullpen and combined with three relievers to keep Atlanta hitless for the rest of the game.

St. Louis Cardinals (C), 3; Atlanta Braves (E), 1

STL (C)

PLAYER/POS	AVG	G	AB	R	H	2B	3B	HR	RB	BB	SO	SB
Rick Ankiel, p	.000	1	1	0	0	0	0	0	0	0	0	0
Jason Christiansen, p	.000	1	0	0	0	0	0	0	0	0	0	0
Will Clark, 1b	.250	3	12	3	3	0	0	1	4	1	3	0
Eric Davis, of-1	.000	2	4	0	0	0	0	0	0	0	2	0
J.D. Drew, of	.167	2	6	1	1	0	0	0	0	2	1	2
Shawon Dunston, ph	1.000	1	1	0	1	0	0	0	0	0	0	0
Jim Edmonds, of	.571	3	14	5	8	4	0	2	7	1	2	1
Carlos Hernandez, c	.273	3	11	3	3	0	0	1	1	1	2	0
Mike James, p	.000	2	1	0	0	0	0	0	0	0	1	0
Darryl Kile, p-1	.000	2	3	0	0	0	0	0	0	0	1	0
Ray Lankford, of	.200	3	10	2	2	1	0	0	3	2	5	0
Mark McGwire, ph	.500	3	2	1	1	0	0	1	1	1	0	0
Matt Morris, p	.000	2	0	0	0	0	0	0	0	0	0	0
Craig Paquette, 3b-1,of-1	.000	2	2	0	0	0	0	0	0	0	0	0
Placido Polanco, 3b	.300	3	10	1	3	0	0	0	3	1	0	1
Britt Reames, p	.000	2	0	0	0	0	0	0	0	0	0	0
Edgar Renteria, ss	.200	3	10	5	2	0	0	0	0	4	1	2
Garrett Stephenson, p	.000	1	1	0	0	0	0	0	0	0	0	0
Mike Timlin, p	.000	2	0	0	0	0	0	0	0	0	0	0
Dave Veres, p	.000	2	0	0	0	0	0	0	0	0	0	0
Fernando Vina, 2b	.308	3	13	3	4	0	0	1	3	1	1	0
TOTAL	.277		101	24	28	5	0	6	22	14	19	6

PITCHER	W	L	ERA	G	GS	CG	SV	SHO	IP	H	ER	BB	SO
Rick Ankiel	0	0	13.50	1	1	0	0	0	2.2	4	4	6	3
Jason Christiansen	0	0	0.00	1	0	0	0	0	0.1	0	0	0	0
Mike James	1	0	0.00	2	0	0	0	0	4.1	1	0	1	1
Darryl Kile	1	0	2.57	1	1	0	0	0	7.0	4	2	2	6
Matt Morris	0	0	0.00	2	0	0	0	0	2.0	0	0	1	0
Britt Reames	1	0	0.00	2	0	0	0	0	3.1	0	0	3	2
Garrett Stephenson	0	0	2.45	1	1	0	0	0	3.2	3	1	2	2
Mike Timlin	0	0	10.80	2	0	0	0	0	1.2	5	2	1	2
Dave Veres	0	0	0.00	2	0	0	0	0	2.0	1	0	0	4
TOTAL	3	0	3.00	14	3	0	0	0	27.0	18	9	16	20

ATL (E)

PLAYER/POS	AVG	G	AB	R	H	2B	3B	HR	RB	BB	SO	SB
Andy Ashby, p	.000	2	0	0	0	0	0	0	0	0	0	0
Paul Bako, c	.000	2	1	0	0	0	0	0	0	0	1	0
Bobby Bonilla, of-1	.000	3	2	0	0	0	0	0	0	2	0	0
John Burkett, p	.000	1	0	0	0	0	0	0	0	0	0	0
Rafael Furcal, ss-3	.091	3	11	2	1	0	0	0	0	3	0	1
Andres Galarraga, 1b	.200	3	10	1	2	1	0	0	1	2	4	0
Tom Glavine, p	.000	1	1	0	0	0	0	0	0	0	1	0
Andruw Jones, of	.111	3	9	3	1	0	0	1	1	4	1	0
Chipper Jones, 3b	.333	3	12	2	4	1	0	0	1	1	4	0
Brian Jordan, of	.364	3	11	1	4	1	0	0	4	1	1	0
Wally Joyner, ph	.333	3	3	0	1	1	0	0	0	0	0	0
Kerry Ligtenberg, p	.000	3	0	0	0	0	0	0	0	0	0	0
Keith Lockhart, 2b	.125	3	8	0	1	0	0	0	0	0	1	0
Javy Lopez, c	.091	3	11	0	1	0	0	0	0	0	1	0
Greg Maddux, p-1	.000	2	1	1	0	0	0	0	0	1	0	0
Kevin Millwood, p	.000	1	1	0	0	0	0	0	0	0	1	0
Terry Mulholland, p	.000	3	0	0	0	0	0	0	0	0	0	0
Mike Remlinger, p	.000	3	0	0	0	0	0	0	0	0	0	0
John Rocker, p	.000	1	0	0	0	0	0	0	0	0	0	0
Reggie Sanders, of	.000	3	9	0	0	0	0	0	0	2	5	0
B.J. Surhoff, ph	.500	2	2	0	1	0	0	0	0	0	0	0
Walt Weiss, ss	.667	1	3	0	2	1	0	0	2	0	0	0
TOTAL	.189		95	10	18	5	0	1	9	16	20	1

PITCHER	W	L	ERA	G	GS	CG	SV	SHO	IP	H	ER	BB	SO
Andy Ashby	0	0	2.45	2	0	0	0	0	3.2	1	1	3	5
John Burkett	0	0	6.75	1	0	0	0	0	1.1	1	1	0	0
Tom Glavine	0	1	27.00	1	1	0	0	0	2.1	6	7	1	2
Kerry Ligtenberg	0	0	5.40	3	0	0	0	0	1.2	0	1	1	3
Greg Maddux	0	1	11.25	1	1	0	0	0	4.0	9	5	3	2
Kevin Millwood	0	1	7.71	1	1	0	0	0	4.2	4	4	3	3
Terry Mulholland	0	0	5.40	3	0	0	0	0	3.1	1	2	2	1
Mike Remlinger	0	0	2.70	3	0	0	0	0	3.1	6	1	0	3
John Rocker	0	0	0.00	1	0	0	0	0	0.2	0	0	1	0
TOTAL	0	3	7.92	16	3	0	0	0	25.0	28	22	14	19

GAME 1 AT STL OCT 3

				R	H	E
ATL	004	000	001	5	8	3
STL	600	100	00X	7	11	1

Pitchers: MADDUX, Remlinger (5), Mulholland (6), Rocker (8), Ligtenberg (8) VS Ankiel, JAMES (3), Timlin (6), Reames (7), Veres (9)
Home Runs: Edmonds-STL
Attendance: 52,378

GAME 2 AT STL OCT 5

				R	H	E
ATL	200	000	020	4	7	1
STL	313	101	01X	10	9	0

Pitchers: GLAVINE, Ashby (3), Burkett (5), Mulholland (6), Ligtenberg (7), Remlinger (8) VS KILE, Christiansen (8), Timlin (8), Morris (9)
Home Runs: Clark-STL, Hernandez-STL, A.Jones-ATL, McGwire-STL
Attendance: 52,389

GAME 3 AT ATL OCT 7

				R	H	E
STL	102	013	000	7	8	0
ATL	100	000	000	1	3	1

Pitchers: Stephenson, REAMES (4), James (6), Morris (8), Veres (9) VS MILLWOOD, Mulholland (5), Ligtenberg (6), Remlinger (6), Ashby (8)
Home Runs: Vina-STL, Edmonds-STL
Attendance: 49,898

The Giants, who had swept New York in a four-game series at Pac Bell Park in May, continued their dominance of the Mets in their new stadium in Game 1. A two-out triple by Barry Bonds in the fourth inning gave the Giants a 2-1 lead-and resulted in a season-ending injury to right fielder Derek Bell. Ellis Burks launched a three-run home run to cap the inning and the scoring.

Al Leiter allowed just one run and five hits in eight innings in Game 2, but he watched from the dugout as J.T. Snow's pinch-hit three-run homer off Armando Benitez tied the game in the ninth inning. In the top of the 10th, however, Felix Rodriguez surrendered a two-out single by Jay Payton to score Darryl Hamilton with the go ahead run. The game ended when Bonds was caught looking at a 3-2 changeup from John Franco.

Russ Ortiz kept the Mets hitless until the sixth inning of Game 3, but right fielder Timo Perez followed Hamilton's single with a run-scoring hit to make the score 2-1. Edgardo Alfonzo doubled home the tying run against closer Robb Nen in the eighth inning. Five innings later Benny Agbayani homered to left to win the game. The next day Robin Ventura smacked a two-run home run in the first inning and Bobby Jones had the Giants completely under control, except for one inning. Jeff Kent led off the fifth with a double for San Francisco's only hit of the day. Two outs and two walks followed but manager Dusty Baker sent pitcher Mark Gardner to bat. He popped up and Jones did not allow another baserunner.

New York Mets (E), 3; San Francisco Giants (W), 1

NY (E)

PLAYER/POS	AVG	G	AB	R	H	2B	3B	HR	RB	BB	SO	SB
Kurt Abbott, ss	.000	1	2	0	0	0	0	0	0	0	1	0
Benny Agbayani, of	.333	4	15	1	5	1	0	1	1	3	3	0
Edgardo Alfonzo, 2b	.278	4	18	1	5	2	0	1	5	1	2	0
Derek Bell, of	.000	1	1	0	0	0	0	0	0	0	0	0
Armando Benitez, p	.000	2	0	0	0	0	0	0	0	0	0	0
Mike Bordick, ss	.167	4	12	3	2	0	0	0	0	3	4	0
Dennis Cook, p	.000	2	0	0	0	0	0	0	0	0	0	0
John Franco, p	.000	2	0	0	0	0	0	0	0	0	0	0
Darryl Hamilton, of-2	.500	3	4	1	2	1	0	0	0	1	1	0
Mike Hampton, p	.500	1	2	0	1	0	0	0	0	0	1	0
Lenny Harris, ph	.000	2	2	1	0	0	0	0	0	0	0	1
Bobby J. Jones, p	.000	1	4	1	0	0	0	0	0	0	3	0
Al Leiter, p	.000	1	4	0	0	0	0	0	0	0	2	0
Joe McEwing, of-3,3b-1	1.000	4	1	0	1	0	0	0	0	0	0	0
Jay Payton, of	.176	4	17	1	3	0	0	0	2	0	4	1
Timo Perez, of	.294	4	17	2	5	1	0	0	3	0	2	1
Mike Piazza, c	.214	4	14	1	3	1	0	0	0	4	3	0
Todd Pratt, c	.000	1	1	0	0	0	0	0	0	0	0	0
Rick Reed, p	.000	1	1	0	0	0	0	0	0	0	0	0
Glendon Rusch, p	.000	1	0	0	0	0	0	0	0	0	0	0
Robin Ventura, 3b	.143	4	14	1	2	0	0	1	2	4	1	0
Turk Wendell, p	.000	2	0	0	0	0	0	0	0	0	0	0
Rick White, p	.000	2	0	0	0	0	0	0	0	0	0	0
Todd Zeile, 1b	.071	4	14	0	1	1	0	0	0	4	3	0
TOTAL	.210		143	13	30	7	0	3	13	20	30	3

PITCHER	W	L	ERA	G	GS	CG	SV	SHO	IP	H	ER	BB	SO
Armando Benitez	1	0	6.00	2	0	0	0	0	3.0	4	2	1	3
Dennis Cook	0	0	0.00	2	0	0	0	0	1.1	0	0	2	1
John Franco	0	0	0.00	2	0	0	1	0	2.0	1	0	0	2
Mike Hampton	0	1	8.44	1	1	0	0	0	5.1	6	5	3	2
Bobby J. Jones	1	0	0.00	1	1	1	0	1	9.0	1	0	2	5
Al Leiter	0	0	2.25	1	1	0	0	0	8.0	5	2	3	6
Rick Reed	0	0	3.00	1	1	0	0	0	6.0	7	2	2	6
Glendon Rusch	0	0	0.00	1	0	0	0	0	0.2	0	0	0	2
Turk Wendell	0	0	0.00	2	0	0	0	0	2.0	0	0	1	5
Rick White	1	0	0.00	2	0	0	0	0	2.2	6	0	2	4
TOTAL	3	1	2.48	15	4	1	1	1	40.0	30	11	16	36

SF (W)

PLAYER/POS	AVG	G	AB	R	H	2B	3B	HR	RB	BB	SO	SB
Rich Aurilia, ss	.133	4	15	0	2	1	0	0	0	0	3	0
Marvin Benard, of-3	.071	4	14	0	1	0	0	0	1	1	7	0
Barry Bonds, of	.176	4	17	2	3	1	1	0	1	3	4	1
Ellis Burks, of	.231	4	13	2	3	1	0	1	4	4	2	0
Felipe Crespo, ph	.250	4	4	0	1	0	0	0	0	0	0	0
Russ Davis, ph	.000	2	2	0	0	0	0	0	0	0	1	0
Miguel Del Toro, p	.000	1	0	0	0	0	0	0	0	0	0	0
Alan Embree, p	.000	2	0	0	0	0	0	0	0	0	0	0
Bobby Estalella, c	.083	4	12	1	1	0	0	0	1	0	2	0
Shawn Estes, p	.000	1	0	0	0	0	0	0	0	1	0	0
Aaron Fultz, p	.000	1	0	0	0	0	0	0	0	0	0	0
Mark Gardner, p	.000	1	2	0	0	0	0	0	0	0	1	0
Doug Henry, p	.000	3	0	0	0	0	0	0	0	0	0	0
Livan Hernandez, p	.000	1	3	0	0	0	0	0	0	0	1	0
Jeff Kent, 2b-4,1b-1	.375	4	16	3	6	1	0	0	1	1	3	1
Ramon Martinez, 2b-1,ss-1	.333	2	6	0	2	0	0	0	0	0	2	0
Doug Mirabelli, c	.000	1	2	0	0	0	0	0	0	1	1	0
Bill Mueller, 3b	.250	4	20	2	5	2	0	0	0	0	4	0
Calvin Murray, of	.200	3	5	0	1	0	0	0	0	0	3	0
Robb Nen, p	.000	2	0	0	0	0	0	0	0	0	0	0
Russ Ortiz, p	.000	1	3	0	0	0	0	0	0	0	1	0
Armando Rios, ph	.500	2	2	0	1	0	0	0	0	0	0	0
Felix Rodriguez, p	.000	3	0	0	0	0	0	0	0	0	0	0
Kirk Rueter, p	.000	1	0	0	0	0	0	0	0	1	0	0
J. T. Snow, 1b	.400	4	10	1	4	0	0	1	3	4	1	0
TOTAL	.205		146	11	30	6	1	2	11	16	36	2

PITCHER	W	L	ERA	G	GS	CG	SV	SHO	IP	H	ER	BB	SO
Miguel Del Toro	0	0	0.00	1	0	0	0	0	1.0	1	0	0	2
Alan Embree	0	0	0.00	2	0	0	0	0	1.2	0	0	0	0
Shawn Estes	0	0	6.00	1	1	0	0	0	3.0	3	2	3	3
Aaron Fultz	0	1	6.75	1	0	0	0	0	1.1	3	1	0	0
Mark Gardner	0	1	8.31	1	1	0	0	0	4.1	4	4	2	5
Doug Henry	0	0	2.25	3	0	0	0	0	4.0	1	1	3	1
Livan Hernandez	1	0	1.17	1	1	0	0	0	7.2	5	1	5	5
Robb Nen	0	0	0.00	2	0	0	0	0	2.1	2	0	1	3
Russ Ortiz	0	0	1.69	1	1	0	0	0	5.1	2	1	4	4
Felix Rodriguez	0	1	6.23	3	0	0	0	0	4.1	6	3	1	6
Kirk Rueter	0	0	0.00	1	0	0	0	0	4.1	3	0	1	1
TOTAL	1	3	2.97	17	4	0	0	0	39.1	30	13	20	30

GAME 1 AT SF OCT 4

		R	H	E
NY	001 000 000	1	5	0
SF	104 000 00X	5	10	0

Pitchers: HAMPTON, Wendell (6), Cook (7), White (7), Rusch (8) VS HERNANDEZ, Rodriguez (8), Nen (9)
Home Runs: Burks-SF
Attendance: 40,430

GAME 2 AT SF OCT 5

		R	H	E
NY	020 000 002 1	5	10	0
SF	010 000 003 0	4	8	0

Pitchers: Leiter, BENITEZ (9), J.Franco (10) VS Estes, Rueter (4), Henry (8), RODRIGUEZ (9)
Home Runs: Alfonzo-NY, Snow-SF
Attendance: 40,430

GAME 3 AT NY OCT 7

		R	H	E
SF	000 200 000 000 0	2	11	0
NY	000 001 010 000 1	3	9	0

Pitchers: Ortiz, Embree (6), Henry (7), Nen (8), Rodriguez (10), FULTZ (12) VS Reed, Cook (7), Wendell (7), J.Franco (9), Benitez (10), WHITE (12)
Home Runs: Agbayani-NY
Attendance: 56,270

GAME 4 AT NY OCT 8

		R	H	E
SF	000 000 000	0	1	1
NY	200 020 00X	4	6	0

Pitchers: GARDNER, Henry (5), Embree (7), Del Toro (8) VS B.J.JONES
Home Runs: Ventura-NY
Attendance: 52,888

Seattle clinched the Wild Card on the final day of the season, while the White Sox had wrapped up the American League Central Division several weeks earlier. The Mariners, however, twice received game-winning hits in their final at bat to gain the sweep.

Seattle took a 3-0 lead in the opener, but Chicago, keyed by RBI-triples in the second and third innings, forged a 4-3 lead. Mike Cameron tied the game in the seventh with a single against Chad Bradford. After Seattle squelched a Chicago rally in the bottom of the ninth, Edgar Martinez and John Olerud hit back-to-back home runs in the 10th inning. The Mariners won the next day behind Paul Abbott and three relievers to take a two-game advantage.

James Baldwin, pitching with a slight rotator cuff tear, held Seattle to one run in six innings in Game 3; Aaron Sele held Chicago to one run in 7 1/3 innings. Olerud led off the bottom of the ninth with a line drive that struck reliever Kelly Wunsch, whose wild throw allowed Olerud to reach second base. Stan Javier bunted pinch runner Rickey Henderson to third, and with the infield in, pinch hitter Carlos Guillen bunted past first baseman Frank Thomas to win the game and the series.

Seattle Mariners (W), 3; Chicago White Sox (C), 0

SEA (W)

PLAYER/POS	AVG	G	AB	R	H	2B	3B	HR	RB	BB	SO	SB
Paul Abbott, p	.000	1	0	0	0	0	0	0	0	0	0	0
David Bell, 3b	.364	3	11	0	4	1	0	0	1	2	2	0
Jay Buhner, of	.200	2	5	1	1	0	0	1	1	2	0	0
Mike Cameron, of	.250	3	12	2	3	0	0	0	2	0	0	1
Freddy Garcia, p	.000	1	0	0	0	0	0	0	0	0	0	0
Carlos Guillen, ph	1.000	1	1	0	1	0	0	0	1	0	0	0
Rickey Henderson, of-2	.400	3	5	3	2	0	0	0	0	1	0	1
Raul Ibanez, of	.375	3	8	2	3	0	0	0	0	0	0	0
Stan Javier, of	.167	3	6	0	1	0	0	0	1	0	3	0
Al Martin, ph	.000	1	1	0	0	0	0	0	0	0	0	0
Edgar Martinez, dh	.364	3	11	2	4	1	0	1	2	2	1	0
Mark McLemore, 2b	.111	3	9	1	1	0	0	0	0	2	1	0
Jose Mesa, p	.000	2	0	0	0	0	0	0	0	0	0	0
John Olerud, 1b	.300	3	10	2	3	0	0	1	2	2	1	0
Joe Oliver, c	.250	3	4	1	1	0	0	1	1	0	1	0
Jose Paniagua, p	.000	2	0	0	0	0	0	0	0	0	0	0
Arthur Lee Rhodes, p	.000	3	0	0	0	0	0	0	0	0	0	0
Alex Rodriguez, ss	.308	3	13	0	4	0	0	0	2	0	2	0
Kazuhiro Sasaki, p	.000	2	0	0	0	0	0	0	0	0	0	0
Aaron Sele, p	.000	1	0	0	0	0	0	0	0	0	0	0
Brett Tomko, p	.000	1	0	0	0	0	0	0	0	0	0	0
Dan Wilson, c	.000	2	3	0	0	0	0	0	1	1	2	0
TOTAL	.283		99	14	28	2	0	4	14	12	13	2

PITCHER	W	L	ERA	G	GS	CG	SV	SHO	IP	H	ER	BB	SO
Paul Abbott	1	0	1.59	1	1	0	0	0	5.2	5	1	3	1
Freddy Garcia	0	0	10.80	1	1	0	0	0	3.1	6	4	3	2
Jose Mesa	1	0	0.00	2	0	0	0	0	2.0	0	0	1	2
Jose Paniagua	1	0	0.00	2	0	0	0	0	2.1	1	0	2	3
Arthur Lee Rhodes	0	0	0.00	3	0	0	0	0	2.2	0	0	2	2
Kazuhiro Sasaki	0	0	0.00	2	0	0	2	0	2.0	1	0	0	5
Aaron Sele	0	0	1.23	1	1	0	0	0	7.1	3	1	3	1
Brett Tomko	0	0	0.00	1	0	0	0	0	2.2	1	0	1	0
TOTAL	3	0	1.93	13	3	0	2	0	28.0	17	6	15	16

CHI (C)

PLAYER/POS	AVG	G	AB	R	H	2B	3B	HR	RB	BB	SO	SB
Jeff Abbott, of	.000	1	1	0	0	0	0	0	0	0	0	0
Harold Baines, dh-1	.250	2	4	1	1	1	0	0	0	0	1	0
James Baldwin, p	.000	1	0	0	0	0	0	0	0	0	0	0
Lorenzo Barcelo, p	.000	1	0	0	0	0	0	0	0	0	0	0
Chad Bradford, p	.000	1	0	0	0	0	0	0	0	0	0	0
Mark Buehrle, p	.000	1	0	0	0	0	0	0	0	0	0	0
McKay Christensen, of	.000	1	0	0	0	0	0	0	0	0	0	0
Ray Durham, 2b	.200	3	10	2	2	1	0	1	1	3	3	0
Keith Foulke, p	.000	1	0	0	0	0	0	0	0	0	0	0
Tony Graffanino, 3b	.000	1	0	0	0	0	0	0	0	0	0	0
Bobby Howry, p	.000	1	0	0	0	0	0	0	0	0	0	0
Charles Johnson, c	.333	3	9	0	3	0	0	0	0	1	1	0
Paul Konerko, 1b-2	.000	3	9	1	0	0	0	0	0	1	1	0
Carlos Lee, of	.091	3	11	0	1	1	0	0	1	0	2	0
Magglio Ordonez, of	.182	3	11	0	2	0	1	0	1	2	2	1
Jim Parque, p	.000	1	0	0	0	0	0	0	0	0	0	0
Josh Paul, c	.000	1	0	0	0	0	0	0	0	0	0	0
Herb Perry, 3b	.444	3	9	0	4	1	0	0	1	2	2	0
Bill Simas, p	.000	2	0	0	0	0	0	0	0	0	0	0
Chris Singleton, of	.111	3	9	1	1	0	1	0	1	0	2	0
Mike Sirotka, p	.000	1	0	0	0	0	0	0	0	0	0	0
Frank Thomas, dh-2,1b-1	.000	3	9	0	0	0	0	0	0	4	0	0
Jose Valentin, ss	.300	3	10	2	3	2	0	0	1	2	2	3
Kelly Wunsch, p	.000	3	0	0	0	0	0	0	0	0	0	0
TOTAL	.185		92	7	17	6	2	1	6	15	16	4

PITCHER	W	L	ERA	G	GS	CG	SV	SHO	IP	H	ER	BB	SO
James Baldwin	0	0	1.50	1	1	0	0	0	6.0	3	1	3	2
Lorenzo Barcelo	0	0	0.00	1	0	0	0	0	1.2	0	0	1	0
Chad Bradford	0	0	0.00	1	0	0	0	0	0.2	2	0	0	0
Mark Buehrle	0	0	0.00	1	0	0	0	0	0.1	2	0	0	1
Keith Foulke	0	1	11.57	2	0	0	0	0	2.1	4	3	2	2
Bobby Howry	0	0	3.38	2	0	0	0	0	2.2	2	1	2	4
Jim Parque	0	0	4.50	1	0	0	0	0	6.0	6	3	1	2
Bill Simas	0	0	6.75	2	0	0	0	0	1.1	0	1	1	2
Mike Sirotka	0	1	4.76	1	0	0	0	0	5.2	7	3	2	0
Kelly Wunsch	0	1	0.00	3	0	0	0	0	0.2	2	0	0	0
TOTAL	0	3	3.95	15	1	0	0	0	27.1	28	12	12	13

GAME 1 AT CHI OCT 3

					R	H	E
SEA	210	000	100	3	7	13	0
CHI	022	000	000	0	4	9	0

Pitchers: Garcia, Tomko(4), Paniagua(7), Rhodes(9), MESA(9), Sasaki(10) VS Parque, Howry(7), Bradford(7), Wunsch(8), Simas(8), FOULKE(9)
Home Runs: Oliver-SEA, Durham-CHI, Martinez-SEA, Olerud-SEA
Attendance: 45,290

GAME 2 AT CHI OCT 4

				R	H	E
SEA	020	110	001	5	9	1
CHI	101	000	000	2	5	1

Pitchers: ABBOTT, Rhodes(6), Mesa(7), Sasaki(9) VS SIROTKA, Barcelo(6), Wunsch(8), Simas(8), Buehrle(9)
Home Runs: Buhner-SEA
Attendance: 45,383

GAME 3 AT SEA OCT 6

				R	H	E
CHI	010	000	000	1	3	1
SEA	000	100	001	2	6	0

Pitchers: Baldwin, Howry(7), WUNSCH(9), Foulke(9) VS Sele, Rhodes(8), PANIAGUA(9)
Attendance: 48,010

New York Yankees (E), 3; Oakland Athletics (C), 2

Oakland, playing its first postseason game since 1992, strung together three runs in the fifth inning of the opener to take a 3-2 lead against the two-time defending world champions. After New York tied the game in the top of the sixth, Ramon Hernandez doubled in his second run of the game to give Oakland back the lead. Jeff Tam, Jim Mecir, and Jason Isringhausen held the Yankees hitless over the last three innings in relief of Gil Heredia.

In Game 2 Glenallen Hill broke a scoreless tie with a single in the sixth inning. Paul O'Neill, who had been intentionally walked, scored along with Hill when Luis Sojo doubled. Andy Pettitte and Mariano Rivera combined on the shutout to even the series. The A's nicked Orlando Hernandez for a run in the second inning of Game 3, but the Yankees scored twice in the bottom of the inning on a fielder's choice and an infield single off Tim Hudson. Sojo, whose diving stop resulted in a key double play in the seventh inning, drove in an insurance run in the eighth.

Olmeda Saenz launched a three-run home run in the first inning of Game 4, and Oakland rolled to an 11-1 win. The second loss by Roger Clemens in four days resulted in an all-night flight back to Oakland for Game 5 the next afternoon. Leadoff hitter Chuck Knoblauch collected two hits in the first inning as New York exploded for six runs against Heredia. Pettitte could not make it out of the fourth inning, but four relievers-including Orlando Hernandez-held the A's scoreless the rest of the way.

NY (E)

PLAYER/POS	AVG	G	AB	R	H	2B	3B	HR	RB	BB	SO	SB
Clay Bellinger, of	1.000	2	1	0	1	1	0	0	1	0	0	0
Scott Brosius, 3b	.176	5	17	0	3	1	0	0	1	1	4	0
Randy Choate, p	.000	1	0	0	0	0	0	0	0	0	0	0
Roger Clemens, p	.000	2	0	0	0	0	0	0	0	0	0	0
Dwight Gooden, p	.000	1	0	0	0	0	0	0	0	0	0	0
Orlando Hernandez, p	.000	2	0	0	0	0	0	0	0	0	0	0
Glenallen Hill, dh-3	.083	4	12	1	1	0	0	0	2	1	5	0
Derek Jeter, ss	.211	5	19	1	4	0	0	0	2	2	3	0
David Justice, of	.222	5	18	2	4	0	0	1	1	3	4	0
Chuck Knoblauch, dh-2	.333	3	9	1	3	0	0	0	1	0	2	1
Tino Martinez, 1b	.421	5	19	2	8	2	0	0	4	1	3	0
Jeff Nelson, p	.000	2	0	0	0	0	0	0	0	0	0	0
Paul O'Neill, of	.211	5	19	4	4	1	0	0	0	2	4	0
Andy Pettitte, p	.000	2	0	0	0	0	0	0	0	0	0	0
Luis Polonia, ph	1.000	1	1	0	1	0	0	0	0	0	0	0
Jorge Posada, c	.235	5	17	2	4	2	0	0	1	3	5	0
Mariano Rivera, p	.000	3	0	0	0	0	0	0	0	0	0	0
Luis Sojo, 2b	.188	5	16	2	3	2	0	0	5	2	1	0
Mike Stanton, p	.000	3	0	0	0	0	0	0	0	0	0	0
Jose Vizcaino, 2b	.000	1	0	1	0	0	0	0	0	0	0	0
Bernie Williams, of	.250	5	20	3	5	3	0	0	1	1	4	0
TOTAL	.244		168	19	41	12	0	1	19	16	35	1

PITCHER	W	L	ERA	G	GS	CG	SV	SHO	IP	H	ER	BB	SO
Randy Choate	0	0	6.75	1	0	0	0	0	1.1	0	1	1	1
Roger Clemens	0	2	8.18	2	2	0	0	0	11.0	13	10	8	10
Dwight Gooden	0	0	21.60	1	0	0	0	0	1.2	4	4	1	1
Orlando Hernandez	1	0	2.45	2	1	0	0	0	7.1	5	2	5	5
Jeff Nelson	0	0	0.00	2	0	0	0	0	2.0	0	0	0	2
Andy Pettitte	1	0	3.97	2	2	0	0	0	11.1	15	5	3	7
Mariano Rivera	0	0	0.00	3	0	0	3	0	5.0	2	0	0	2
Mike Stanton	1	0	2.08	3	0	0	0	0	4.1	5	1	1	3
TOTAL	3	2	4.70	16	5	0	3	0	44.0	44	23	19	31

OAK (W)

PLAYER/POS	AVG	G	AB	R	H	2B	3B	HR	RB	BB	SO	SB
Kevin Appier, p	.000	2	0	0	0	0	0	0	0	0	0	0
Eric Chavez, 3b	.333	5	21	4	7	3	0	0	4	0	5	0
Ryan Christenson, of	.500	2	2	0	1	0	0	0	1	0	1	0
Sal Fasano, c	.000	1	0	0	0	0	0	0	0	0	0	0
Jason Giambi, 1b	.286	5	14	2	4	0	0	0	1	7	2	1
Jeremy Giambi, of-2,dh-2	.333	4	9	1	3	0	0	0	1	2	2	0
Ben Grieve, of	.118	5	17	1	2	0	0	0	2	3	7	0
Gil Heredia, p	.000	2	0	0	0	0	0	0	0	0	0	0
Ramon Hernandez, c	.375	5	16	3	6	2	0	0	3	0	3	0
Tim Hudson, p	.000	1	0	0	0	0	0	0	0	0	0	0
Jason Isringhausen, p	.000	1	0	0	0	0	0	0	0	0	0	0
Doug Jones, p	.000	2	0	0	0	0	0	0	0	0	0	0
Terrence Long, of	.158	5	19	2	3	0	0	1	1	3	2	0
Mike Magnante, p	.000	2	0	0	0	0	0	0	0	0	0	0
Jim Mecir, p	.000	3	0	0	0	0	0	0	0	0	0	0
Frank Menechino, 2b	.000	1	0	0	0	0	0	0	0	0	0	0
Adam Piatt, of-2	.167	3	6	2	1	0	0	0	0	0	1	0
Bo Porter, of	1.000	2	1	0	1	0	0	0	1	0	0	0
Olmedo Saenz, dh-3	.231	4	13	1	3	0	0	1	4	0	2	0
Matt Stairs, of-2	.111	3	9	0	1	1	0	0	0	0	1	0
Jeff Tam, p	.000	3	0	0	0	0	0	0	0	0	0	0
Miguel Tejada, ss	.350	5	20	5	7	2	0	0	1	2	2	1
Randy Velarde, 2b	.250	5	20	2	5	1	0	0	3	2	3	1
Barry Zito, p	.000	1	0	0	0	0	0	0	0	0	0	0
TOTAL	.263		167	23	44	9	0	2	22	19	31	3

PITCHER	W	L	ERA	G	GS	CG	SV	SHO	IP	H	ER	BB	SO
Kevin Appier	0	1	3.48	2	1	0	0	0	10.1	10	4	6	13
Gil Heredia	1	1	12.79	2	2	0	0	0	6.1	11	9	3	3
Tim Hudson	0	1	3.38	1	1	1	0	0	8.0	6	3	4	5
Jason Isringhausen	0	0	0.00	2	0	0	1	0	2.0	1	0	0	3
Doug Jones	0	0	0.00	2	0	0	0	0	1.1	1	0	0	1
Mike Magnante	0	0	0.00	2	0	0	0	0	3.0	1	0	0	2
Jim Mecir	0	0	0.00	3	0	0	0	0	5.1	1	0	0	2
Jeff Tam	0	0	0.00	3	0	0	0	0	2.0	3	0	1	1
Barry Zito	1	0	1.59	1	1	0	0	0	5.2	7	1	2	5
TOTAL	2	3	3.48	18	5	1	1	0	44.0	41	17	16	35

GAME 1 AT OAK OCT 3

				R	H	E
NY	020	001	000	3	7	0
OAK	000	031	01X	5	10	2

Pitchers: CLEMENS, Stanton (7), Nelson (8) VS HEREDIA, Tam (7), Mecir (7), Isringhausen (9)
Attendance: 47,360

GAME 2 AT OAK OCT 4

				R	H	E
NY	000	003	001	4	8	1
OAK	000	000	000	0	6	1

Pitchers: PETTITTE, Rivera (8) VS APPIER, Magnante (7), Tam (9), Jones (9)
Attendance: 47,860

GAME 3 AT NY OCT 6

				R	H	E
OAK	010	010	000	2	4	2
NY	020	100	01X	4	6	1

Pitchers: HUDSON VS HERNANDEZ, Rivera (8)
Home Runs: Long-OAK
Attendance: 56,606

GAME 4 AT NY OCT 7

				R	H	E
OAK	300	003	014	11	11	0
NY	000	001	000	1	8	0

Pitchers: ZITO, Mecir (6), Magnante (7), Jones (9) VS CLEMENS, Stanton (6), Choate (7), Gooden (8)
Home Runs: Saenz-OAK
Attendance: 56,915

GAME 5 AT OAK OCT 8

				R	H	E
NY	600	100	000	7	12	0
OAK	021	200	000	5	13	0

Pitchers: Pettitte, STANTON (4), Nelson (6), Hernandez (8), Rivera (8) VS HEREDIA, Tam (1), Appier (2), Mecir (6), Isringhausen (9)
Home Runs: Justice-NY
Attendance: 41,170

Some critics claimed the Cardinals did the Mets a favor by knocking the arch-rival Braves out of the postseason; New York returned the favor by defeating St. Louis in five games. The Mets scored in the first inning of each game and their pitching staff made the leads hold up.

Timo Perez, who had made his major league debut against the Cardinals just six weeks earlier, doubled to start the series and scored the first of his League Championship Series record-tying eight runs. Mike Hampton allowed just six hits in seven innings for the win. Rick Ankiel, who had been bafflingly wild in the Division Series, could not find the plate in Game 2. He walked three, threw two wild pitches, and was replaced by Britt Reames following a run-scoring double by Benny Agbayani in the first inning. The Cardinals rallied to tie the game in the fifth and again in the eighth, but Jay Payton singled in the go-ahead run in the ninth.

Jim Edmonds doubled in two runs in the first inning of Game 3, and Edgar Renteria scored twice and drove in two runs in an 8-2 win. Andy Benes allowed only six hits in eight innings, with both runs against him scoring on double plays. Darryl Kile, pitching on three days' rest, was drilled for seven runs in three innings in Game 4. The Cardinals pulled to within 10-6 and had two runners on base in the eighth, but manager Tony La Russa selected Craig Paquette to bat instead of All-Star Mark McGwire, who was relegated to pinch hitter because of knee tendonitis. Paquette grounded out to end the inning.

Pat Hentgen, who had not pitched in more than two weeks, surrendered three runs on four hits (plus two errors) in the first inning of Game 5. Todd Zeile drove Hentgen from the game with a three-run double in the fourth. Ankiel made another wobbly performance, issuing two walks and two wild pitches in two-thirds of an inning. A pitch from Dave Veres glanced off Payton's head in the eighth and caused both benches to empty, but order was restored quickly. NLCS Most Valuable Player Hampton retired the side in the ninth for the Mets' first National League pennant in 14 years.

New York Mets (E), 3; St. Louis Cardinals (C), 1

NY (E)

PLAYER/POS	AVG	G	AB	R	H	2B	3B	HR	RB	BB	SO	SB
Kurt Abbott, ss	.000	2	3	0	0	0	0	0	0	0	2	0
Benny Agbayani, of	.353	5	17	0	6	2	0	0	3	4	0	0
Edgardo Alfonzo, 2b	.444	5	18	5	8	1	1	0	4	4	1	0
Armando Benitez, p	.000	3	0	0	0	0	0	0	0	0	0	0
Mike Bordick, ss	.077	5	13	2	1	0	0	0	0	3	1	0
Dennis Cook, p	.000	1	0	0	0	0	0	0	0	0	0	0
John Franco, p	.000	3	0	0	0	0	0	0	0	0	0	0
Matt Franco, 1b-1	.000	2	3	0	0	0	0	0	0	0	1	0
Darryl Hamilton, ph	.000	3	2	0	0	0	0	0	0	0	0	0
Mike Hampton, p	.167	2	6	1	1	0	0	0	0	0	1	0
Lenny Harris, ph	.000	2	1	0	0	0	0	0	0	0	1	0
Bobby J. Jones, p	.000	1	2	0	0	0	0	0	0	0	1	0
Al Leiter, p	.000	1	3	0	0	0	0	0	0	0	2	0
Joe McEwing, of-3,3b-1	.000	4	0	2	0	0	0	0	0	0	0	0
Jay Payton, of	.158	5	19	1	3	0	0	1	3	2	5	0
Timo Perez, of	.304	5	23	8	7	2	0	0	0	1	3	2
Mike Piazza, c	.412	5	17	7	7	3	0	2	4	5	0	0
Rick Reed, p	.000	1	1	0	0	0	0	0	0	0	0	0
Glendon Rusch, p	.000	2	0	0	0	0	0	0	0	0	0	0
Bubba Trammell, ph	.000	3	3	0	0	0	0	0	0	0	2	0
Robin Ventura, 3b	.214	5	14	4	3	1	0	0	5	6	0	0
Turk Wendell, p	.000	2	0	0	0	0	0	0	0	0	0	0
Rick White, p	.000	1	0	0	0	0	0	0	0	0	0	0
Todd Zeile, 1b	.368	5	19	1	7	3	0	1	8	2	4	0
TOTAL	.262		164	31	43	12	1	4	27	27	24	2

PITCHER	W	L	ERA	G	GS	CG	SV	SHO	IP	H	ER	BB	SO
Armando Benitez	0	0	0.00	3	0	0	1	0	3.0	3	0	2	2
Dennis Cook	0	0	0.00	1	0	0	0	0	1.0	1	0	0	2
John Franco	0	0	6.75	3	0	0	0	0	2.2	3	2	2	2
Mike Hampton	2	0	0.00	2	2	1	0	1	16.0	9	0	4	12
Bobby J. Jones	0	0	13.50	1	1	0	0	0	4.0	6	6	0	2
Al Leiter	0	0	3.86	1	1	0	0	0	7.0	8	3	0	9
Rick Reed	0	1	10.80	1	1	0	0	0	3.1	8	4	1	4
Glendon Rusch	1	0	0.00	2	0	0	0	0	3.2	3	0	0	3
Turk Wendell	1	0	0.00	2	0	0	0	0	1.1	1	0	1	2
Rick White	0	0	9.00	1	0	0	0	0	3.0	5	3	1	1
TOTAL	4	1	3.60	17	5	1	1	1	45.0	47	18	11	39

STL (C)

PLAYER/POS	AVG	G	AB	R	H	2B	3B	HR	RB	BB	SO	SB
Rick Ankiel, p	.000	2	0	0	0	0	0	0	0	0	0	0
Alan Benes, p	.333	1	3	1	1	0	0	0	0	0	2	0
Jason Christiansen, p	.000	2	0	0	0	0	0	0	0	0	0	0
Will Clark, 1b	.412	5	17	3	7	2	0	1	1	2	1	0
Eric Davis, of-3	.200	4	10	1	2	1	0	0	1	0	2	0
J.D. Drew, of	.333	5	12	2	4	1	0	0	1	0	3	0
Shawon Dunston, of-2	.333	4	6	1	2	1	0	0	0	0	0	0
Jim Edmonds, of	.227	5	22	1	5	1	0	1	5	1	9	0
Pat Hentgen, p	1.000	1	1	0	1	0	0	0	0	0	0	0
Carlos Hernandez, c	.250	5	16	3	4	0	0	0	1	1	1	0
Mike James, p	.000	4	0	0	0	0	0	0	0	0	0	0
Darryl Kile, p-2	.000	3	2	0	0	0	0	0	0	1	0	0
Ray Lankford, of-4	.333	5	12	1	4	1	0	0	1	1	5	0
Eli Marrero, c-3	.000	4	4	0	0	0	0	0	1	0	1	0
Mark McGwire, ph	.000	3	2	0	0	0	0	0	0	1	0	0
Matt Morris, p	.000	2	0	0	0	0	0	0	0	0	0	0
Craig Paquette, of-2,3b-1	.167	4	6	0	1	0	0	0	0	0	2	0
Placido Polanco, 3b-2	.200	4	5	0	1	0	0	0	0	2	1	0
Britt Reames, p	.000	2	1	0	0	0	0	0	0	0	1	0
Edgar Renteria, ss	.300	5	20	4	6	1	0	0	4	0	2	3
Fernando Tatis, 3b-4	.231	5	13	1	3	2	0	0	2	1	5	0
Mike Timlin, p	.000	3	0	0	0	0	0	0	0	0	0	0
Dave Veres, p	.000	3	0	0	0	0	0	0	0	0	0	0
Fernando Vina, 2b	.261	5	23	3	6	1	0	0	1	1	4	0
Rick Wilkins, ph	.000	2	2	0	0	0	0	0	0	0	0	0
TOTAL	.266		177	21	47	11	0	2	18	11	39	3

PITCHER	W	L	ERA	G	GS	CG	SV	SHO	IP	H	ER	BB	SO
Rick Ankiel	0	0	20.25	2	1	0	0	0	1.1	1	3	5	2
Alan Benes	1	0	2.25	1	1	0	0	0	8.0	6	2	3	5
Jason Christiansen	0	0	0.00	2	0	0	0	0	2.0	0	0	0	1
Pat Hentgen	0	1	14.73	1	1	0	0	0	3.2	7	6	5	2
Mike James	0	0	15.43	4	0	0	0	0	2.1	5	4	1	0
Darryl Kile	0	2	9.00	2	2	0	0	0	10.0	13	10	5	3
Matt Morris	0	0	4.91	2	0	0	0	0	3.2	3	2	2	2
Britt Reames	0	0	1.42	2	0	0	0	0	6.1	5	1	4	6
Mike Timlin	0	1	0.00	3	0	0	0	0	3.1	1	0	2	0
Dave Veres	0	0	0.00	3	0	0	0	0	2.1	2	0	0	3
TOTAL	1	4	5.86	22	5	0	0	0	43.0	43	28	27	24

GAME 1 AT STL OCT 11

		R	H	E
NY	200 010 003	6	8	3
STL	000 000 002	2	9	0

Pitchers: HAMPTON, J.Franco (8), Benitez (9) VS KILE, James (8), Christiansen (9)
Home Runs: Zeile-NY, Payton-NY
Attendance: 52,255

GAME 2 AT STL OCT 12

		R	H	E
NY	201 000 021	6	9	0
STL	010 020 020	5	10	3

Pitchers: Leiter, J.Franco (8), WENDELL (8), Benitez (9) VS Ankiel, Reames (1), Morris (6), Veres (8), TIMLIN (9)
Home Runs: Piazza-NY
Attendance: 52,250

GAME 3 AT NY OCT 14

		R	H	E
STL	202 130 000	8	14	0
NY	100 100 000	2	7	1

Pitchers: AN.BENES, James (9), Veres (9) VS REED, Rusch (4), White (5), Cook (8), Wendell (9)
Attendance: 55,693

GAME 4 AT NY OCT 15

		R	H	E
STL	200 130 000	6	11	2
NY	430 102 00X	10	9	0

Pitchers: KILE, James (4), Timlin (5), Morris (7), Christiansen (8) VS B.J.Jones, RUSCH (5), J.Franco (8), Benitez (9)
Home Runs: Edmonds-STL, Clark-STL, Piazza-NY
Attendance: 55,665

GAME 5 AT NY OCT 16

		R	H	E
STL	000 000 000	0	3	2
NY	300 300 10X	7	10	0

Pitchers: HENTGEN, Timlin (4), Reames (5), Ankiel (7), James (7), Veres (8) VS HAMPTON
Attendance: 55,695

The Yankees entered the American League Championship Series in a batting slump, and Seattle's Freddy Garcia did not help matters with 6 2/3 shutout innings in Game 1. Denny Neagle, who had not pitched in the Division Series, allowed only an RBI-single by Rickey Henderson and a home run by Alex Rodriguez. Three relievers helped keep the Yanks off the scoreboard. New York did not score for the first seven innings of Game 2, but Bernie Williams plated the club's first run of the series with a game-tying single in the eighth. Six more hits followed, capped by Derek Jeter's home run.

The Yankees continued hitting when the series shifted to Seattle. Back-to-back home runs by Williams and Tino Martinez erased a 1-0 Mariners lead. Andy Pettitte allowed nine hits, but he got outs at key moments and helped New York nurse a 4-2 lead into the seventh. The Yankees assured victory with four runs in the ninth inning, led by a two-run double by David Justice.

New York needed little offense in Game 4, but Derek Jeter and Justice accounted for five runs with home runs in support of Roger Clemens. Clemens allowed only Al Martin's seventh-inning double, which glanced off Tino Martinez's glove, and two walks. His masterful 15-strikeout performance was the first complete-game shutout in the ALCS in 15 years. Neagle had a 2-1 lead when he was relieved with two runners on in the fifth inning of Game 5. Jeff Nelson surrendered a two-run single, followed by consecutive home runs by Edgar Martinez and John Olerud. Garcia beat the Yankees for the second time, again with shutout relief from Jose Paniagua, Arthur Rhodes, and Kazuhiro Sasaki.

Seattle's bullpen was its undoing in Game 6. The Mariners took a 4-0 lead on a pair of doubles in the first inning and a two-run home run by Carlos Guillen, but starter John Halama could not get out of the fourth inning. After Brett Tomko's 2 1/3 shutout innings in relief, the Yankees put together another big rally. Rhodes surrendered a three-run homer to Justice, the ALCS Most Valuable Player. Orlando Hernandez, who had benefited from a late rally in Game 2, earned the win again. Although Mariano Rivera's string of 34 consecutive scoreless postseason innings ended, he preserved the victory and assured New York of its first Subway Series since 1956.

New York Yankees (W), 4; Seattle Mariners (W), 2

NY (E)

PLAYER/POS	AVG	G	AB	R	H	2B	3B	HR	RB	BB	SO	SB
Clay Bellinger, of	.000	5	0	0	0	0	0	0	0	0	0	0
Scott Brosius, 3b	.222	6	18	2	4	0	0	0	0	2	3	0
Randy Choate, p	.000	1	0	0	0	0	0	0	0	0	0	0
Roger Clemens, p	.000	1	0	0	0	0	0	0	0	0	0	0
David Cone, p	.000	1	0	0	0	0	0	0	0	0	0	0
Dwight Gooden, p	.000	1	0	0	0	0	0	0	0	0	0	0
Jason Grimsley, p	.000	2	0	0	0	0	0	0	0	0	0	0
Orlando Hernandez, p	.000	2	0	0	0	0	0	0	0	0	0	0
Glenallen Hill, ph	.000	2	2	0	0	0	0	0	0	0	2	0
Derek Jeter, ss	.318	6	22	6	7	0	0	2	5	6	7	1
David Justice, of	.231	6	26	4	6	2	0	2	8	2	7	0
Chuck Knoblauch, dh	.261	6	23	3	6	2	0	0	2	3	4	0
Tino Martinez, 1b	.320	6	25	5	8	2	0	1	1	2	4	0
Denny Neagle, p	.000	2	0	0	0	0	0	0	0	0	0	0
Jeff Nelson, p	.000	3	0	0	0	0	0	0	0	0	0	0
Paul O'Neill, of	.250	6	20	0	5	0	0	0	5	1	2	0
Andy Pettitte, p	.000	1	0	0	0	0	0	0	0	0	0	0
Luis Polonia, ph	.000	1	1	0	0	0	0	0	0	0	1	0
Jorge Posada, c	.158	6	19	2	3	1	0	0	3	5	5	0
Mariano Rivera, p	.000	3	0	0	0	0	0	0	0	0	0	0
Luis Sojo, 2b-6,3b-2	.261	6	23	1	6	1	0	0	2	2	3	0
Jose Vizcaino, 2b-3	1.000	4	2	3	2	1	0	0	2	0	0	2
Bernie Williams, of	.435	6	23	5	10	1	0	1	3	2	3	1
TOTAL	.279		204	31	57	10	0	6	31	25	41	4

PITCHER	W	L	ERA	G	GS	CG	SV	SHO	IP	H	ER	BB	SO
Randy Choate	0	0	0.00	1	0	0	0	0	0.1	0	0	0	1
Roger Clemens	1	0	0.00	1	1	1	0	0	9.0	1	0	2	15
David Cone	0	0	0.00	1	0	0	0	0	1.0	0	0	0	0
Dwight Gooden	0	0	0.00	1	0	0	0	0	2.1	1	0	0	1
Jason Grimsley	0	0	0.00	2	0	0	0	0	1.0	2	0	3	1
Orlando Hernandez	2	0	4.20	2	2	0	0	0	15.0	13	7	8	14
Denny Neagle	0	2	4.50	2	2	0	0	0	10.0	6	5	7	7
Jeff Nelson	0	0	9.00	3	0	0	0	0	3.0	5	3	0	6
Andy Pettitte	1	0	2.70	1	1	0	0	0	6.2	9	2	1	2
Mariano Rivera	0	0	1.93	3	0	0	1	0	4.2	4	1	0	1
TOTAL	4	2	3.06	17	6	1	1	0	53.0	41	18	21	48

SEA (W)

PLAYER/POS	AVG	G	AB	R	H	2B	3B	HR	RB	BB	SO	SB
Paul Abbott, p	.000	1	0	0	0	0	0	0	0	0	0	0
David Bell, 3b-4,2b-1	.222	5	18	0	4	0	0	0	0	0	0	0
Jay Buhner, of-3	.182	4	11	0	2	0	0	0	0	1	6	0
Mike Cameron, of	.111	6	18	3	2	0	0	0	1	2	7	1
Freddy Garcia, p	.000	2	0	0	0	0	0	0	0	0	0	0
Charles Gipson, of	.000	2	0	0	0	0	0	0	0	0	0	0
Carlos Guillen, 3b	.200	2	5	1	1	0	0	1	2	2	2	0
John Halama, p	.000	2	0	0	0	0	0	0	0	0	0	0
Rickey Henderson, of	.222	3	9	2	2	1	0	0	1	2	2	0
Raul Ibanez, of-3	.000	6	9	0	0	0	0	0	0	0	2	0
Stan Javier, of	.071	4	14	0	1	0	0	0	1	0	4	0
Al Martin, of-3	.182	4	11	2	2	2	0	0	0	2	3	0
Edgar Martinez, dh	.238	6	21	2	5	1	0	1	4	3	5	0
Mark McLemore, 2b	.250	5	16	2	4	3	0	0	2	2	1	0
Jose Mesa, p	.000	3	0	0	0	0	0	0	0	0	0	0
John Olerud, 1b	.350	6	20	2	7	3	0	1	2	2	2	1
Joe Oliver, c	.167	4	6	0	1	0	0	0	0	1	1	0
Jose Paniagua, p	.000	5	0	0	0	0	0	0	0	0	0	0
Robert Ramsay, p	.000	2	0	0	0	0	0	0	0	0	0	0
Arthur Lee Rhodes, p	.000	4	0	0	0	0	0	0	0	0	0	0
Alex Rodriguez, ss	.409	6	22	4	9	2	0	2	5	3	8	1
Kazuhiro Sasaki, p	.000	2	0	0	0	0	0	0	0	0	0	0
Aaron Sele, p	.000	1	0	0	0	0	0	0	0	0	0	0
Brett Tomko, p	.000	2	0	0	0	0	0	0	0	0	0	0
Dan Wilson, c	.091	4	11	0	1	0	0	0	0	1	5	0
TOTAL	.215		191	18	41	12	0	5	18	21	48	3

PITCHER	W	L	ERA	G	GS	CG	SV	SHO	IP	H	ER	BB	SO
Paul Abbott	0	1	5.40	1	1	0	0	0	5.0	3	3	3	3
Freddy Garcia	2	0	1.54	2	2	0	0	0	11.2	10	2	4	11
John Halama	0	0	2.89	2	2	0	0	0	9.1	10	3	5	3
Jose Mesa	0	0	12.46	3	0	0	0	0	4.1	5	6	3	3
Jose Paniagua	0	1	4.15	5	0	0	0	0	4.1	4	2	1	4
Robert Ramsay	0	0	0.00	2	0	0	0	0	1.2	2	0	0	1
Arthur Lee Rhodes	0	1	31.50	4	0	0	0	0	2.0	8	7	4	5
Kazuhiro Sasaki	0	0	0.00	2	0	0	1	0	2.2	3	0	1	3
Aaron Sele	0	1	6.00	1	1	0	0	0	6.0	9	4	0	4
Brett Tomko	0	0	7.20	2	0	0	0	0	5.0	3	4	4	4
TOTAL	2	4	5.37	24	6	0	1	0	52.0	57	31	25	41

GAME 1 AT NY OCT 10

				R	H	E
SEA	000	011	000	2	5	0
NY	000	000	000	0	6	1

Pitchers: GARCIA, Paniagua (7), Rhodes (8), Sasaki (9) VS NEAGLE, Nelson (6), Choate (9), Grimsley (9)
Home Runs: Rodriguez-SEA
Attendance: 54,481

GAME 2 AT NY OCT 11

				R	H	E
SEA	001	000	000	1	7	2
NY	000	000	07X	7	14	0

Pitchers: Halama, Paniagua (7), RHODES (8), Mesa (8) VS HERNANDEZ, Rivera (9)
Home Runs: Jeter-NY
Attendance: 55,317

GAME 3 AT SEA OCT 13

				R	H	E
NY	021	001	004	8	13	0
SEA	100	010	000	2	10	1

Pitchers: PETTITTE, Nelson (7), Rivera (8) VS SELE, Tomko (7), Ramsay (9)
Home Runs: Williams-NY, Martinez-NY
Attendance: 47,827

GAME 4 AT SEA OCT 14

				R	H	E
NY	000	030	020	5	5	0
SEA	000	000	000	0	1	0

Pitchers: CLEMENS VS ABBOTT, Ramsay (6), Mesa (7), Paniagua (9)
Home Runs: Jeter-NY, Justice-NY
Attendance: 47,803

GAME 5 AT SEA OCT 15

				R	H	E
NY	000	200	000	2	8	0
SEA	100	050	00X	6	8	0

Pitchers: NEAGLE, Nelson (5), Grimsley (5), Gooden (5), Cone (8) VS GARCIA, Paniagua (6), Rhodes (7), Sasaki (8)
Home Runs: Martinez-SEA, Olerud-SEA
Attendance: 47,802

GAME 6 AT NY OCT 17

				R	H	E
SEA	200	200	030	7	10	0
NY	000	300	60X	9	11	0

Pitchers: Halama, Tomko (4), PANIAGUA (7), Rhodes (7), Mesa (7) VS HERNANDEZ, Rivera (8)
Home Runs: Guillen-SEA, Justice-NY, Rodriguez-SEA
Attendance: 56,598

Gripped by its first Subway Series in 44 years, New York was split in its favoritism for its two teams. The Mets made two key baserunning mistakes in the opener in the Bronx, but they still held a 3-2 lead heading into the bottom of the ninth inning thanks to a two-run pinch-hit single by Bubba Trammel and an infield hit by Edgardo Alfonzo. Paul O'Neill fouled off four two-strike offerings before walking against Armando Benitez with one out in the ninth. Two successive singles and Chuck Knoblauch's sacrifice fly tied the game. The Mets wriggled out of jams the next two innings, but Jose Vizcaino's fourth hit of the game plated the winning run for the Yanks in the 12th.

In the first inning of Game 2 Mike Piazza's bat shattered, hurling the sheared barrel at the feet of Roger Clemens. The pitcher threw the bat, nearly hitting Piazza and causing both benches to empty. When play resumed, Piazza grounded out and Clemens allowed just two hits over eight innings. By the time Piazza and Jay Payton homered in the ninth inning, the Yankees had built a large enough lead to hold on for the 6-5 win.

Game 3 was the highlight of the Series for Queens. In the bottom of the eighth inning of a tie game, Benny Agbayani doubled to score Todd Zeile. In the process the Mets handed Orlando Hernandez his first postseason loss after nine decisions, and John Franco earned his first World Series win after 17 major league seasons. The next night Series Most Valuable Player Derek Jeter homered on the first pitch of the game. Triples in the second and third innings provided two more runs. With two outs in the fifth and no one on, Yankees manager Joe Torre replaced Denny Neagle with David Cone. Piazza, who had homered in his last at bat, popped up. Jeff Nelson, Mike Stanton, and Mariano Rivera retired the Mets on two hits the rest of the way.

Al Leiter pitched brilliantly in Game 5, and his two-out bunt spurred his team's only rally. Home runs by Bernie Williams and Jeter kept the game even until two outs in the ninth when the Mets southpaw tired. Luis Sojo, whose grounder had plated the go-ahead run in Game 4, singled in Jorge Posada in the ninth inning. Another run scored when the throw was deflected out of play. After Piazza flied out to deep center field, the Yankees had become the first team since 1972-74 Oakland A's to win three straight world championships.

New York Yankees (A), 4; New York Mets (N), 1

NY (A)

PLAYER/POS	AVG	G	AB	R	H	2B	3B	HR	RB	BB	SO	SB
Clay Bellinger, of	.000	4	0	0	0	0	0	0	0	0	0	0
Scott Brosius, 3b	.308	5	13	2	4	0	0	1	3	2	2	0
Jose Canseco, ph	.000	1	1	0	0	0	0	0	0	0	1	0
Roger Clemens, p	.000	1	0	0	0	0	0	0	0	0	0	0
David Cone, p	.000	1	0	0	0	0	0	0	0	0	0	0
Orlando Hernandez, p	.000	1	2	0	0	0	0	0	0	0	2	0
Glenallen Hill, dh-of	.000	3	3	0	0	0	0	0	0	0	0	0
Derek Jeter, ss	.409	5	22	6	9	2	1	2	2	3	8	0
David Justice, of	.158	5	19	1	3	2	0	0	3	3	2	0
Chuck Knoblauch, dh-2	.100	4	10	1	1	0	0	0	1	2	1	0
Tino Martinez, 1b	.364	5	22	3	8	1	0	0	2	1	4	0
Denny Neagle, p	.000	1	2	0	0	0	0	0	0	0	1	0
Jeff Nelson, p	.000	3	0	0	0	0	0	0	0	0	0	0
Paul O'Neill, of	.474	5	19	2	9	2	2	0	2	3	4	0
Andy Pettitte, p	.000	2	3	0	0	0	0	0	0	0	1	0
Luis Polonia, ph	.500	2	2	0	1	0	0	0	0	0	0	0
Jorge Posada, c	.222	5	18	2	4	1	0	0	1	5	4	0
Mariano Rivera, p	.000	4	1	0	0	0	0	0	0	0	0	0
Luis Sojo, 2b-2,3b-2	.286	4	7	0	2	0	0	0	2	1	0	1
Mike Stanton, p	.000	4	0	0	0	0	0	0	0	0	0	0
Jose Vizcaino, 2b	.235	4	17	0	4	0	0	0	1	0	5	0
Bernie Williams, of	.111	5	18	2	2	0	0	1	1	5	5	0
TOTAL	.263		179	19	47	8	3	4	18	25	40	1

PITCHER	W	L	ERA	G	GS	CG	SV	SHO	IP	H	ER	BB	SO
Roger Clemens	1	0	0.00	1	1	0	0	0	8.0	2	0	0	9
David Cone	0	0	0.00	1	0	0	0	0	0.1	0	0	0	0
Orlando Hernandez	0	1	4.91	1	1	0	0	0	7.1	9	4	3	12
Denny Neagle	0	0	3.86	1	1	0	0	0	4.2	4	2	2	3
Jeff Nelson	1	0	10.13	3	0	0	0	0	2.2	5	3	1	1
Andy Pettitte	0	0	1.98	2	2	0	0	0	13.2	16	3	4	9
Mariano Rivera	0	0	3.00	4	0	0	2	0	6.0	4	2	1	7
Mike Stanton	2	0	0.00	4	0	0	0	0	4.1	0	0	0	7
TOTAL	4	1	2.68	17	5	0	2	0	47.0	40	14	11	48

NY (N)

PLAYER/POS	AVG	G	AB	R	H	2B	3B	HR	RB	BB	SO	SB
Kurt Abbott, ss	.250	5	8	0	2	1	0	0	0	1	3	0
Benny Agbayani, of	.278	5	18	2	5	2	0	0	2	3	6	0
Edgardo Alfonzo, 2b	.143	5	21	1	3	0	0	0	1	1	5	0
Armando Benitez, p	.000	3	0	0	0	0	0	0	0	0	0	0
Mike Bordick, ss	.125	4	8	0	1	0	0	0	0	0	3	0
Dennis Cook, p	.000	3	0	0	0	0	0	0	0	0	0	0
John Franco, p	.000	4	0	0	0	0	0	0	0	0	0	0
Matt Franco, 1b	.000	1	1	0	0	0	0	0	0	0	1	0
Darryl Hamilton, ph	.000	4	3	0	0	0	0	0	0	0	2	0
Mike Hampton, p	.000	1	0	0	0	0	0	0	0	0	0	0
Lenny Harris, dh-1	.000	3	4	1	0	0	0	0	0	1	1	0
Bobby Jones, p	.000	1	2	0	0	0	0	0	0	0	1	0
Al Leiter, p	.000	2	2	0	0	0	0	0	0	0	0	0
Joe McEwing, of-2	.000	3	1	1	0	0	0	0	0	0	0	0
Jay Payton, of	.333	5	21	3	7	0	0	1	3	0	5	0
Timo Perez, of	.125	5	16	1	2	0	0	0	0	1	4	0
Mike Piazza, c-4, dh	.273	5	22	3	6	2	0	2	4	0	4	0
Todd Pratt, c	.000	1	2	1	0	0	0	0	0	1	2	0
Rick Reed, p	1.000	1	1	0	1	0	0	0	0	0	0	0
Glendon Rusch, p	.000	3	0	0	0	0	0	0	0	0	0	0
Bubba Trammell, of-2	.400	4	5	1	2	0	0	0	3	1	1	0
Robin Ventura, 3b	.150	5	20	1	3	1	0	1	1	1	5	0
Turk Wendell, p	.000	2	0	0	0	0	0	0	0	0	0	0
Rick White, p	.000	1	0	0	0	0	0	0	0	0	0	0
Todd Zeile, 1b	.400	5	20	1	8	2	0	0	1	1	5	0
TOTAL	.229		175	16	40	8	0	4	15	11	48	0

PITCHER	W	L	ERA	G	GS	CG	SV	SHO	IP	H	ER	BB	SO
Armando Benitez	0	0	3.00	3	0	0	1	0	3.0	3	1	2	2
Dennis Cook	0	0	0.00	3	0	0	0	0	0.2	1	0	3	1
John Franco	1	0	0.00	4	0	0	0	0	3.1	3	0	0	1
Mike Hampton	0	1	6.00	1	1	0	0	0	6.0	8	4	5	4
Bobby Jones	0	1	5.40	1	1	0	0	0	5.0	4	3	3	3
Al Leiter	0	1	2.87	2	2	0	0	0	15.2	12	5	6	16
Rick Reed	0	0	3.00	1	1	0	0	0	6.0	6	2	1	8
Glendon Rusch	0	0	2.25	3	0	0	0	0	4.0	6	1	2	2
Turk Wendell	0	1	5.40	2	0	0	0	0	1.2	3	1	2	2
Rick White	0	0	6.75	1	0	0	0	0	1.1	1	1	1	1
TOTAL	1	4	3.47	21	5	0	1	0	46.2	47	18	25	40

GAME 1 AT NY-A OCT 21

					R	H	E
NY-N	000	000	300	000	3	10	0
NY-A	000	002	001	001	4	12	0

Pitchers: Leiter, J.Franco (8), Benitez (9), Cook (10), Rusch (10), WENDELL (11) VS Pettitte, Nelson (7), Rivera (9), STANTON (11)
Attendance: 55,913

GAME 2 AT NY-A OCT 22

				R	H	E
NY-N	000	000	005	5	7	3
NY-A	210	010	11X	6	12	1

Pitchers: HAMPTON, Rusch (7), White (7), Cook (8) VS CLEMENS, Nelson (9), Rivera (9)
Home Runs: Brosius-NY (A), Piazza-NY (N), Payton-NY (N)
Attendance: 56,059

GAME 3 AT NY-N OCT 24

				R	H	E
NY-A	001	100	000	2	8	0
NY-N	010	001	02X	4	9	0

Pitchers: HERNANDEZ, Stanton (8) VS Reed, Wendell (7), Cook (7), J.FRANCO (8), Benitez (9)
Home Runs: Ventura-NY (N)
Attendance: 55,299

GAME 4 AT NY-N OCT 25

				R	H	E
NY-A	111	000	000	3	8	0
NY-N	002	000	000	2	6	1

Pitchers: Neagle, Cone (5), NELSON (6), Stanton (7), Rivera (8) VS B.J.JONES, Rusch (6), J.Franco (8), Benitez (9)
Home Runs: Jeter-NY (A), Piazza-NY (N)
Attendance: 55,290

GAME 5 AT NY-N OCT 26

				R	H	E
NY-A	010	001	002	4	7	1
NY-N	020	000	000	2	8	1

Pitchers: Pettitte, STANTON (8), Rivera (9) VS LEITER, J.Franco (9)
Home Runs: Williams-NY (A), Jeter-NY (A)
Attendance: 55,292

CHAPTER 12

Black Ball

Jules Tygiel

More than 50 years have passed since what many have called the finest moment in the history of the national pastime—Jackie Robinson's shattering of the color barrier. Robinson's heroic triumph brought to an end six disgraceful decades of Jim Crow baseball. During that era, some of America's greatest ballplayers plied their trade on all-black teams, in Negro Leagues, on the playing fields of Latin America, and along the barnstorming frontier of the cities and towns of the United States, but never within the major and minor league realm of "organized baseball." When slowly and grudgingly given their chance in the years after 1947, blacks conclusively proved their competitive abilities on the diamond, but discrimination persisted as baseball executives continued to deny them the opportunity to display their talents in both managerial and front office positions.

Scattered evidence exists of blacks playing baseball in the antebellum period, but the first recorded black teams surfaced in northern cities in the aftermath of the Civil War. In October 1867 the Uniques of Brooklyn hosted the Excelsiors of Philadelphia in a contest billed as the "championship of colored clubs." Before a large crowd of black and white spectators, the Excelsiors marched around the field behind a fife and drum corps before defeating the Uniques, 37–24. Two months later, a second Philadelphia squad, the Pythians, dispatched a representative to the inaugural meetings of the National Association of Base Ball Players, the first organized league. The nominating committee unanimously rejected the Pythians' application, barring "any club which may be composed of one or more colored persons." Using the impeccable logic of a racist society, the committee proclaimed, "If colored clubs were admitted there would be in all probability some division of feeling, whereas, by excluding them no injury could result to anyone." The Philadelphia Pythians, however, continued their quest for interracial competition. In 1869 they became the first black team to face an all-white squad, defeating the cross-town City Items, 27–17.

In 1876 athletic entrepreneurs in the nation's metropolitan centers established the National League, which quickly came to represent the pinnacle of the sport. The new entity had no written policy regarding blacks, but precluded them nonetheless through a "gentleman's agreement" among the owners. In the smaller cities and towns of America, however, where under-funded teams and fragile minor league coalitions quickly appeared and faded, individual blacks found scattered opportunities to pursue baseball careers. During the next decade, at least two dozen black ballplayers sought to earn a living in this erratic professional baseball world.

Bud Fowler ranked among the best and most persistent of these trailblazers. Born John Jackson in upstate New York in 1858 and raised, ironically, in Cooperstown, Fowler first achieved recognition as a 20-year-old pitcher for a local team in Chelsea, Massachusetts. In April 1878, Fowler defeated the National League's Boston club, which included future Hall of Famers George Wright and Jim O' Rourke, 2–1, in an exhibition game, besting 40-game winner Tommy Bond. Later that season, Fowler hurled three games for the Lynn Live Oaks of the International Association, the nation's first minor league, and another for Worcester in the New England League. For the next six years, he toiled for a variety of independent and semi-professional teams in the United States and Canada. Despite a reputation as "one of the best pitchers on the continent," he failed to catch on with any major or minor league squads. In 1884, now appearing regularly as a second baseman, as well as a pitcher, Fowler joined Stillwater, Minnesota, in the Northwestern League. Over the next seven seasons, Fowler played for 14 teams in nine leagues, seldom batting less than .300 for a season. He led the Western League in triples in 1886. "He is one of the best general players in the country," reported *Sporting Life*, "and if he had a white face he would be playing with the best of them. . . Those who know, say there is no better second baseman in the country."

In 1886, however, a better second baseman did appear in the form of Frank Grant, perhaps the greatest black player of the 19th century. The light-skinned Grant, described as a "Spaniard" in the *Buffalo Express*, batted .325 for Meridien in the Eastern League. When that squad folded he joined Buffalo in the prestigious International Association and improved his average to .340, third best in the league.

Although not as talented as Fowler and Grant, barehanded catcher Moses Fleetwood Walker achieved the highest level of play of blacks of this era. The son of an Ohio physician, Fleet Walker had studied at Oberlin College, where in 1881 he and his younger brother Welday helped launch a varsity baseball team. For the next two years, the elder Walker played for the University of Michigan, and in 1883 he appeared in 60 games for the pennant-winning Toledo squad in the Northwestern League. In 1884, Toledo entered the American Association, the National League's primary rival, and Walker became the first black major leaguer. In an age when many catchers caught barehanded and lacked chest protectors, Walker suffered frequent injuries and played little after a foul tip broke his rib in mid-July. Nonetheless, he batted .263 and pitcher Tony Mullane later called him "the best catcher I ever worked with." In July, Toledo briefly signed Walker's brother, Welday, who appeared in six games batting .182. The following year, Toledo dropped from the league, ending the Walkers' major league careers.

These early black players found limited acceptance among teammates, fans, and opponents. In Ontario in 1881, Fowler's teammates forced him off the club. Walker found that Mullane and other pitchers preferred not to pitch to him. Although he acknowledged Walker's skills, Mullane confessed, "I disliked a Negro and whenever I had to pitch to him I used anything I wanted without looking at his signals." At Louisville in 1884, insults from Kentucky fans so rattled Walker that he made five errors in a game. In Richmond, after Walker had actually left the team due to injuries, the Toledo manager received a letter from "75 determined men" threatening "to mob Walker" and cause "much bloodshed" if the black catcher appeared. On August 10, 1883, Chicago White Stockings star and manager Cap Anson had threatened to cancel an exhibition game with Toledo if Walker played. The injured catcher had not been slated to start, but Toledo manager Charlie Morton defied Anson and inserted Walker into the lineup. The game proceeded without incident.

A Hopeful Start

In 1887 Walker, Fowler, Grant, Higgins, Stovey, and three other blacks converged on the International League, a newly reorganized circuit in Canada and upstate New York, one notch below the major league level. At the same time, a new six-team entity, the League of Colored Baseball Clubs, won recognition under baseball's National Agreement, a mutual pact to honor player contracts among team owners. Thus, an air of optimism pervaded the start of the season. But 1887 would prove a fateful year for the future of blacks in baseball.

On May 6 the Colored League made its debut in Pittsburgh with "a grand street parade and a brass band concert." Twelve hundred spectators watched the hometown Keystones lose to the Gorhams of New York, 11–8. Within days, however, the new league began to flounder. The Boston franchise disbanded in Louisville on May 8, stranding its players in the Southern city. Three weeks later, league founder Walter Brown formally announced the demise of the infant circuit.

Meanwhile, in the International League, black players found their numbers growing, but their status increasingly uncertain. Six of the 10 teams fielded blacks, prompting *Sporting Life* to wonder, "How far will this mania for engaging colored players go?" In Newark, fans marveled at the "colored battery" of Fleet Walker, dubbed the "coon catcher" by one Canadian newspaper, and "headstrong" pitcher George Stovey. Stovey, one of the greatest black pitchers of the 19th century, won 35 games, still an International League record. Frank Grant, in his second season as the Buffalo second baseman, led the league in batting average and home runs. Bud Fowler, one of two blacks on the Binghamton squad, compiled a .350 average through early July and stole 23 bases.

These athletes compiled their impressive statistics under the most adverse conditions. "I could not help pitying some of the poor black fellows that played in the International League," reported a white player. "Fowler used to play second base with the lower part of his legs encased in wooden guards. He knew that about every player that came down to second base on a steal had it in for him." Both Fowler and Grant, "would muff balls intentionally, so that [they] would not have to touch runners, fearing that they might injure [them]." In addition, "About half the pitchers try their best to hit these colored players when [they are] at bat." Grant, whose Buffalo teammates had refused to sit with him for a team portrait in 1886, reportedly saved himself from a "drubbing" at their hands in 1887, only by "the effective use of a club." In Toronto, fans chanted, "Kill the Nigger," at Grant, and a local newspaper headline declared, "THE COLORED PLAYERS DISTASTEFUL." In late June, Bud Fowler's Binghamton teammates refused to take the field unless the club removed him from the lineup. Soon after, on July 7, the Binghamton club submitted to the players' demands, releasing Fowler and a black teammate, a pitcher named Renfroe.

The most dramatic confrontations between black and white players occurred on the Syracuse squad, where a clique of refugees from the Southern League exacerbated racial tensions. In spring training, the club included a catcher named Dick Male, who, rumors had it, was a light-skinned black named Richard Johnson. Male charged "that the man calling him a Negro is himself a black liar," but when released after a poor preseason performance, he returned to his old club, Zanesville in the Ohio State League, and resumed his true identity as Richard Johnson. In May, Syracuse signed 19-year-old black pitcher Robert Higgins, angering the Southern clique. Higgins appeared in his first International League game in Toronto on May 25. "THE SYRACUSE PLOTTERS," as a *Sporting News* headline called his teammates, undermined his debut. According to one account, they "seemed to want the Toronto team to knock Higgins out of the box, and time and again they fielded so badly that the home team were enabled to secure many hits after the side had been retired."

"A disgusting exhibition," admonished the *Toronto World*. "They succeeded in running Male out of the club," reported a Newark paper, "and they will do the same with Higgins." One week later, two Syracuse players refused to pose for a team picture with Higgins. When manager "Ice Water" Joe Simmons suspended pitcher Doug Crothers for this incident, Crothers slugged the manager. Higgins miraculously recovered from his early travails and lack of support to post a 20–7 record.

On July 14, as the directors of the International League discussed the racial situation in Buffalo, the Newark Little Giants planned to send Stovey, their ace, to the mound in an exhibition game against the National League Chicago White Stockings. Once again manager Anson refused to field his squad if either Stovey or Walker appeared. Unlike 1883, Anson's will prevailed. On the same day, team owners, stating that "Many of the best players in the league are anxious to leave on account of the colored element," allowed current black players to remain, but voted by a 6–4 margin to reject all future contracts with blacks. The teams with black players all voted against the measure, but Binghamton, which had just released Fowler and Renfroe, swung the vote in favor of exclusion.

Events in 1887 continued to conspire against black players. On September 11 the St. Louis Browns of the American Association refused to play a scheduled contest against the all-black Cuban Giants. "We are only doing what is right," they proclaimed. In November, the Buffalo and Syracuse teams unsuccessfully attempted to lift the International League ban on blacks. The Ohio State League, which had fielded three black players, also adopted a rule barring additional contracts with blacks, prompting Welday Walker, who had appeared in the league, to protest, "The law is a disgrace to the present age. . . There should be some broader cause—such as lack of ability, behavior and intelligence—for barring a player, rather than his color."

Only a handful of blacks appeared on integrated squads after 1887. Grant and Higgins returned to their original teams in 1888. Walker jumped from Newark to Syracuse. The following year, only Walker remained for one final season, the last black in the International League until 1946. Richard Johnson, the erstwhile Dick Male, reappeared in the Ohio State League in 1888 and in 1889 joined Springfield in the Central Interstate League, where he hit 14 triples, stole 45 bases, and scored 100 runs in 100 games. In 1890, Harrisburg in the Eastern Interstate League fielded two blacks, while Jamestown in the New York-Penn League featured another. Bud Fowler and several other black players appeared in the Nebraska State League in 1892. Three years later, Adrian in the Michigan State League signed five blacks, including Fowler and pitcher George Wilson, who posted a 29–4 record. Meanwhile Sol White, who later chronicled these events in his 1906 book, *The History of Colored Baseball*, played for Fort Wayne in the Western State League. In 1896, pitcher-outfielder Bert Jones joined Atchison in the Kansas State League where he played for three seasons before being forced out in 1898. Almost 50 years would pass before another black would appear on an interracial club in organized baseball.

All-Black Teams

While integrated teams grew rare, several leagues allowed entry to all-black squads. In 1889 the Middle States League included the New York Gorhams and the Cuban Giants, the most famous black team of the age. The Giants posted a 55–17 record. A year later, the alliance reorganized as the Eastern Interstate League and again included the Cuban Giants. Giants star George Williams paced the circuit with a .391 batting average, while teammate Arthur Thomas slugged 26 doubles and 10 triples, both league-leading totals. The Eastern Interstate League folded in midseason, and in 1891 the Giants made one final minor league appearance in the Connecticut State League. When this circuit also disbanded, the brief entry of the Cuban Giants in organized baseball came to an end.

In the 1898 season a team calling itself the Acme Colored Giants affiliated with Pennsylvania's Iron and Oil League, but won only eight of 49 games before dropping out, marking an ignoble conclusion to these early experiments in interracial play.

Overall, at least 70 blacks appeared in organized baseball in the late 19th century. About half played for all-black teams, the remainder for integrated clubs. Few lasted more than one season with the same team. By the 1890s, the pattern for black baseball that would prevail for the next half century had emerged. Blacks were relegated to "colored" teams playing most of their games on the barnstorming circuit, outside of any organized league structure. While exhibition contests allowed them to pit their skills against whites, they remained on the outskirts of baseball's mainstream, unheralded and unknown to most Americans.

As early as the 1880s and 1890s several all-black traveling squads had gained national reputations. The Cuban Giants, formed among the waiters of the Argyle Hotel to entertain guests in 1885, set the pattern and provided the recurrent nickname for these teams. Passing as Cubans, so as not to offend their white clientele, the Giants toured the East in a private railroad car playing amateur and professional opponents. In the 1890s, rivals like the Lincoln Giants from Nebraska, the Page Fence Giants from Michigan, and the Cuban X Giants in New York emerged. From the beginning these teams combined entertainment with their baseball to attract crowds. The Page Fence Giants, founded by Bud Fowler in 1895, would ride through the streets on bicycles to attract attention. In 1899, Fowler organized the All-American Black Tourists, who would arrive in full dress suits with opera hats and silk umbrellas. Their showmanship notwithstanding, the black teams of the 1890s included some of the best players in the nation. The Page Fence Giants won 118 of 154 games in 1895, with two of their losses coming against the major league Cincinnati Reds.

During the early years of the 20th century many blacks still harbored hopes of regaining access to organized baseball. Sol White wrote in 1906 that baseball "should be taken seriously by the colored player. An honest effort of his great ability will open the avenue in the near future wherein he may walk hand-in-hand with the opposite race in the greatest of all American games—baseball." Rube Foster, the outstanding figure in black baseball from 1910 to 1926, stressed excellence because "we have to be ready when the time comes for integration."

But even clandestine efforts to bring in blacks met a harsh fate. In 1901 Baltimore Orioles manager John McGraw attempted to pass second baseman Charlie Grant of the Columbia Giants off as an Indian named Chief Tokohama, until Chicago White Sox president Charles Comiskey exposed the ruse.

In 1911 the Cincinnati Reds raised black hopes by signing two light-skinned Cubans, Armando Marsans and Rafael Almeida, prompting the *New York Age* to speculate, "Now that the first shock is over it would not be surprising to see a Cuban a few shades darker. . .breaking into the professional ranks. . .it would then be easier for colored players who are citizens of this country to get into fast company." But the Reds rushed to certify that Marsans and Almeida were "genuine Caucasians," and while light-skinned Cubans became a fixture in the majors, their darker brethren remained unwelcome. Over the years, tales circulated of United States blacks passing as Indians or Cubans, but no documented cases exist.

Although most blacks lived in the South, during the first two decades of the 20th century, the great black teams and players congregated in the metropolises and industrial cities of the North. Chicago emerged as the primary center of black baseball with teams like the Leland Giants and the Chicago American Giants. In New York, the Lincoln Giants, which boasted pitching stars Smokey Joe Williams and Cannonball Dick Redding, shortstop John Henry Lloyd and catcher Louis Santop, reigned supreme. Other top clubs of the era included the Philadelphia Giants, the Hilldale Club (also of Philadelphia), the Indianapolis ABCs, and the Bacharach Giants of Atlantic City. Player contracts were nonexistent or non-binding and stars jumped frequently from team to team. "Wherever the money was," recalled John Henry Lloyd, "that's where I was."

Fans and writers often compared the great black players of this era to their white counterparts. Lloyd, one of the outstanding shortstops and hitters of that or any era, came to be known as "The Black Wagner," after his white contemporary Honus Wagner, who called it an "honor" and a "privilege" to be compared to the gangling black infielder. A St. Louis sportswriter once said when asked who was the best player in baseball history, "If you mean in organized baseball, the answer would be Babe Ruth; but if you mean in all baseball. . .the answer would have to be a colored man named John Henry Lloyd." Pitcher "Rube" Foster earned his nickname by outpitching future Hall of Famer Rube Waddell, and Cuban Jose Mendez was called "The Black Matty" after Christy Mathewson.

The talents of Foster and Mendez notwithstanding, the greatest black pitcher of the early 20th century was 6-foot-5 "Smokey" Joe Williams. Born in 1886, Williams spent a good part of his career pitching in his native Texas, unheralded until he joined the Leland Giants in 1909 at the age of 24. From 1912 to 1923 he won renown as a strikeout artist for Harlem's Lincoln Giants. Against major league competition Williams won six games, lost four, and tied two, including a three-hit 1–0 victory over the National League champion Philadelphia Phillies in 1915. In 1925 he signed with the Homestead Grays and, although approaching his 40th birthday, starred for seven more seasons. A 1952 poll to name the outstanding black pitcher of the half-century placed Williams in first place, ahead of the legendary Satchel Paige.

Oscar Charleston ranks as the greatest outfielder of the 1910s and 1920s. With tremendous speed and a strong, accurate arm, Charleston was the quintessential centerfielder. During his 15-year career starting in 1915, Charleston hit for both power and average and may have been the most popular player of the 1920s. After he retired he managed the Philadelphia Stars, Brooklyn Brown Dodgers, and other clubs.

Several major stars of this era labored outside the usual channels of black baseball. In 1914, white Kansas City promoter J. L. Wilkinson organized the All-Nations team, which included whites, blacks, Indians, Asians, and Latin Americans. Pitchers John Donaldson, Jose Mendez, and Bill Drake and outfielder Cristobel Torriente played for the All-Nations team, described by one observer as "strong enough to give any major league team a nip-and-tuck battle." A black Army team from the 25th Infantry Unit in Nogales, Arizona, featured pitcher "Bullet" Joe Rogan and shortstop Dobie Moore. In 1920, when Wilkinson formed the famed Kansas City Monarchs, the players from the All-Nations and 25th Infantry teams formed the nucleus of his club. In 1921, the Monarchs challenged the minor league Kansas City Blues to a tournament for the city championship. The Blues won the series five games to three. In 1922, however, the Monarchs won five of six games to claim boasting honors in Kansas City. One week later, they swept a doubleheader from the touring Babe Ruth All-Stars.

Foster the Giant

In the years after 1910, Andrew "Rube" Foster emerged as the dominant figure in black baseball. Like many of his white contemporaries, Foster rose through the ranks of the national pastime from star player to field manager to club owner. Born in Texas in 1879, Foster accepted an invitation to pitch for Chicago's Union Giants in 1902. "If you play the best clubs in the land, white clubs as you say," he told owner Frank Leland, "it will be a case of Greek meeting Greek. I fear nobody." By 1903 he was hurling for the Cuban X Giants against the Philadelphia Giants in a series billed as the "Colored Championship of the World." His four victories in a best-of-nine series clinched the title.

The following year, he had switched sides and registered two of three wins for the Philadelphia Giants in a similar matchup, striking out 18 batters in one game and tossing a two-hitter in another. In 1907 he rejoined the Leland Giants and, in 1910, pitched for and managed a reconstituted team of that name to a 123–6 record.

As a pitcher, Foster had ranked among the nation's best; as a manager, his skills achieved legendary proportions. A master strategist and motivator, Foster's teams specialized in the bunt, the steal, and the hit-and-run, which came to characterize black baseball. Fans came to watch him sit on the bench giving signs with a wave of his ever-present pipe. He became the friend and confidant of major league managers like John McGraw. Over the years, Foster trained a generation of black managers, like Dave Malarcher, Biz Mackey, and Oscar Charleston in the subtleties of the game.

Foster entered the ownership ranks, uniting with white saloon keeper John Schorling (the son-in-law of White Sox owner Charles Comiskey) to form the Chicago American Giants in 1911. With Schorling's financial backing, Foster's managerial acumen, a regular home field in Chicago, and high salaries, the American Giants attracted the best black players in the nation. Throughout the decade, whether barnstorming or hosting opponents in Chicago, the American Giants came to represent the pinnacle of black baseball.

By World War I Foster dominated black baseball in Chicago and parts of the Midwest. In most other areas, however, white booking agents controlled access to stadiums, and as one newspaperman charged in 1917, "used circus methods to drag a bunch of our best citizens out, only to undergo humiliation . . . while [they sat] back and [grew] rich off a percentage of the proceeds." In the East, Nat Strong, the part owner of the Brooklyn Royal Giants, Philadelphia Giants, Cuban Stars, Cuban Giants, New

York Black Yankees, and the renowned white semi-pro team, the Bushwicks, held a stranglehold on black competition. To break this monopoly and place the game more firmly under black control, Foster created the National Association of Professional Baseball Clubs, better known as the Negro National League, in 1920.

Foster's new organization marked the third attempt of the century to meld black teams into a viable league. In 1906, the International League of Independent Baseball Clubs, which had four black and two white teams, struggled through one season characterized by shifting and collapsing franchises. Four years later, Beauregard Moseley, secretary of Chicago's Leland Giants, attempted to form a National Negro Baseball League, but the association folded before a single game had been played.

The new Negro National League, which included the top teams from Chicago, St. Louis, Detroit, and other Midwestern cities, fared far better. At Foster's insistence, all clubs, with the exception of the Kansas City Monarchs, whom Foster reluctantly accepted, were controlled by blacks. J. L. Wilkinson, who owned the Monarchs, a major drawing card, had won the respect of his fellow owners and soon overcame Foster's reservations. He became the league secretary and Foster's trusted ally. Operating under the able guidance of Foster and Wilkinson, the league flourished during its early years. In 1923, it attracted 400,000 fans and accumulated $200,000 in gate receipts.

The success of the Negro National League inspired competitors. In 1923 booking agent Nat Strong formed an Eastern Colored League, with teams in New York, Brooklyn, Baltimore, New Jersey, and Philadelphia. With four of the six teams owned by whites, and Strong controlling an erratic schedule, the league had somewhat less legitimacy than Foster's circuit. Playing in larger population centers, however, the more affluent Eastern clubs successfully raided some of the top players of the Negro National League before the circuits negotiated an uneasy truce in 1924. Throughout the remainder of the decade, however, acrimony rather than harmony characterized interleague relations. A third association emerged in the South, where the stronger independent teams in major cities formed the Southern Negro League. While this group became a breeding ground for top players, the impoverished nature of its clientele, and the inability of clubs to bolster revenues with games against white squads, rendered them unable to prevent their best players from jumping to the higher-paying Northern teams.

At their best the Negro Leagues of the 1920s were haphazard affairs. Since most clubs continued to rely on barnstorming for their primary livelihood, scheduling proved difficult. Teams played uneven numbers of games and especially in the Eastern circuit skipped official contests for more lucrative non-league matchups. Several of the stronger independent teams, like the Homestead Grays, remained unaffiliated. Umpires were often incompetent and lacked authority to control conditions. Finally, players frequently jumped from one franchise to another, peddling their services to the highest bidder. In 1926, Foster grew ill, stripping the Negro National League of his vital leadership. Two years later, the Eastern Colored League disbanded and in 1931, less than a year after Foster's death, the Negro National League departed the scene, once again leaving black baseball with no organized structure.

Two Holdovers Take Over

With the collapse of Foster's Negro National League and the onset of the Great Depression, the always-borderline economics of operating a black baseball club grew more precarious. White booking agents, like Philadelphia's Eddie Gottlieb or Abe Saperstein of the Midwest, again reigned supreme. In the early 1930s, only the stronger independent clubs like the Homestead Grays or Kansas City Monarchs, novelty acts like the Cincinnati Clowns, or those teams backed by the "numbers kings" of the black ghettos could survive.

The Kansas City Monarchs emerged as the healthiest holdover from the old Negro National League. In 1929 owner Wilkinson had commissioned an Omaha, Nebraska, company to design a portable lighting system for night games. The equipment, consisting of a 250-horsepower motor and a 100-kilowatt generator, which illuminated lights atop telescoping poles 50 feet above the field, took about two hours to assemble. To pay for the innovation, Wilkinson mortgaged everything he owned and took in Kansas City businessman Tom Baird as a partner. But the gamble paid off. The novelty of night baseball allowed the Monarchs to play two and three games a day and made them the most popular touring club in the nation.

Meanwhile, in Pittsburgh, former basketball star Cumberland Posey Jr. had forged the Homestead Grays into one of the best teams in America. Posey, the son of one of Pittsburgh's wealthiest black businessmen, had joined the Grays, then a sandlot team, as an outfielder in 1911. By the early 1920s he owned the club and began recruiting top national players to supplement local talent. In 1925 he signed 39-year-old Smokey Joe Williams, and the following year he lured Oscar Charleston, whom many consider the top black player of that era. Over the next several seasons Posey recruited Judy Johnson, Martin Dihigo, and James "Cool Papa" Bell. In 1930 he added a catcher from the Pittsburgh sandlots named Josh Gibson, and in 1934 brought in first baseman Buck Leonard from North Carolina. Unwilling to subject himself to outside control, Posey preferred to remain free from league affiliations. Yet for two decades, the Homestead Grays reigned as one of the strongest teams in black baseball.

In the 1930s Posey faced competition from crosstown rival Gus Greenlee, "Mr. Big" of Pittsburgh's North Side numbers rackets. Greenlee took over the Pittsburgh Crawfords, a local team, in 1930. Greenlee spent $100,000 to build a new stadium, and wooed established ballplayers with lavish salary offers. In 1931 he landed the colorful Satchel Paige, the hottest young pitcher in the land, and the following year raided the Grays, outbidding Posey for the services of Charleston, Johnson, and Gibson. In 1934 Cool Papa Bell jumped the St. Louis Stars and brought his legendary speed to the Crawfords. With five future Hall of Famers, Greenlee had assembled one of the great squads of baseball history.

The emergence of Gus Greenlee marked a new era for black baseball, the reign of the numbers men. In an age of limited opportunities for blacks, many of the most talented northern black entrepreneurs turned to gambling and other illegal operations for their livelihood. Novelist Richard Wright explained, "They would have been steel tycoons, Wall Street brokers, auto moguls, had they been white." Like the political bosses of 19th century urban America, numbers operators provided an informal assistance network for needy patrons in the impoverished black communities and represented a major source of capital for black businesses. In city after city, the numbers barons, seeking an element of respectability or an outlet to shield gambling profits from the Internal Revenue Service or merely the thrill of sports ownership, came to dominate black baseball. In Harlem second-generation Cuban immigrant Alex Pompez, a powerful figure in the Dutch Schultz mob, ran the Cuban Stars, while Ed "Soldier Boy" Semler controlled the Black Yankees. Abe Manley of the Newark Eagles, Ed Bolden of the Philadelphia Stars, and Tom Wilson of the Baltimore Elite Giants all garnered their fortunes from the numbers game. Even Cum Posey, who had no connection with the rackets, had to bring in Homestead numbers banker Rufus "Sonnyman" Jackson as a partner and financier to stave off Greenlee's challenge.

In 1933 Greenlee unified the franchises owned by the numbers kings into a rejuvenated Negro National League. Under his leadership, writes Donn Rogosin, "The Negro National League meetings were enclaves of the most powerful black gangsters in the nation." This "unholy alliance" sustained black baseball in the Northeast through depression and war. Even the collapse of the Crawfords and demolition of Greenlee Stadium in 1939 failed to weaken the league which survived until the onset of integration. In 1937 a second circuit, the Negro American League, was formed in the Midwest and South. Dominated by Wilkinson and the Kansas City Monarchs, the Negro American League relied less on numbers brokers, but more on white ownership for their financing.

The formation of the Negro American League encouraged the rejuvenation of an annual World Series, matching the champions of the two leagues. But the Negro League World Series never achieved the prominence of its white counterpart. The fact that league standings were often determined among teams playing uneven numbers of games diluted the notion of a champion. Furthermore, impoverished urban blacks could not sustain attendance at a prolonged series. As a result, the Negro League World Series always took a back seat to the annual East-West All-Star Game played in Chicago. The East-West Game, originated by Greenlee in 1933, quickly emerged as the centerpiece of black baseball. Fans chose the players in polls conducted by black newspapers. By 1939, leading candidates received as many as 500,000 votes. Large crowds of blacks and whites watched the finest Negro League stars, and the revenues divided among the teams often spelled the difference between profit and loss at the season's end.

By the 1930s and 1940s, black baseball had become an integral part of Northern ghetto life. With hundreds of employees and millions of dollars in revenue, the Negro Leagues, as Donn Rogosin notes, "may rank among the highest achievements of black enterprise during segregation." In addition, baseball provided an economic ripple effect, boosting business in hotels, cafes, restaurants, and bars. In Kansas City and other towns, games became social events, as black citizens, recalls manager Buck O'Neil, "wore their finery." The Monarch Booster Club was a leading civic organization and the "Miss Monarch Bathing Beauty" pageant a popular event.

Black baseball also represented a source of pride for the black community. "The Monarchs was Kansas City's team," boasted bartender Jesse Fisher. "They made Kansas City the talk of the town all over the world." In several cities, white politicians routinely appeared at Opening Day games to curry favor with their often neglected black constituents. When Greenlee Field launched its operations in Pittsburgh, the mayor, city council, and county commissioners lined the field boxes. Negro League owners also played a role in the fight against segregation. In Newark, Effa Manley, who ran the Eagles with her husband Abe, served as treasurer of the New Jersey NAACP and belonged to the Citizen's League for Fair Play which fought for black employment opportunities. Manley sponsored a "Stop Lynching" fundraiser at one Eagles home game.

The impact of the Negro Leagues, however, ranged beyond the communities whose names the teams bore. Throughout the age of Jim Crow baseball, even in those years when a substantial league structure existed, official league games accounted for a relatively small part of the black baseball experience. Black teams would typically play over 200 games a year, only a third of which counted in the league standings. The vast majority of contests occurred on the "barnstorming" circuit, pitting black athletes against a broad array of professional and semi-professional competition, white and black, throughout the nation. In the pre-television era, traveling teams brought a higher level of baseball to fans in the towns and cities of America and allowed local talent to test their skills against the professionals. While some all-white teams, like the "House of David" also trod the barnstorming trail, itinerancy was the key to survival for black squads. The capital needed to finance a Negro League team existed primarily in Northern cities, but the overwhelming majority of blacks lived in the South.

"The schedule was a rugged one," recalled Roy Campanella of the Baltimore Elite Giants. "Rarely were we in the same city two days in a row. Mostly we played by day and traveled by night." After the Monarchs introduced night baseball, teams played both day and night appearing in two and sometimes three different ballparks on the same day. Teams traveled in buses—"our home, dressing room, dining room, and hotel"—or sandwiched into touring cars. "We had little time to waste on the road," states Quincy Trouppe, "so it was a rare treat when the cars would stop at times to let us stretch out and exercise for a few minutes." Most major hotels barred black guests, so even when the schedule allowed overnight stays, the athletes found themselves in less than comfortable accommodations. Large cities usually had better black hotels where ballplayers, entertainers, and other members of the black bourgeoisie congregated. On the road, however, Negro Leaguers more frequently were relegated to Jim Crow roadhouses, "continually under attack by bedbugs."

The black baseball experience extended beyond the confines of the United States and into Central America and the Caribbean. Negro Leaguers appeared regularly in the Cuban, Puerto Rican, Venezuelan, and Dominican winter leagues where they competed against black and white Latin stars and major leaguers as well.

Some blacks, like Willie Wells and Ray Dandridge, jumped permanently to the Mexican League, where several also became successful managers of interracial teams. As Wells explained, "I am not faced by the racial problem. . . I've found freedom and democracy here, something I never found in the United States. . . In Mexico, I am a man."

Reluctant Clowns

In the United States, however, blacks often found themselves in more distasteful roles. To attract crowds throughout the nation and to keep fans interested in the frequently one-sided contests against amateur competition, some black clubs injected elements of clowning and showmanship into their pre-game and competitive performances. As early as the 1880s, comedy had characterized many barnstorming teams. Black baseball, even in its most serious form, tended to be flashier and less formal than white play. Against inferior teams, players often showboated and flaunted their superior skills. Pitcher Satchel Paige would call in his outfielders or guarantee to strike out the first six or nine batters to face him against semi-professional squads. In the late 1930s, Olympic star Jesse Owens traveled with the Monarchs, racing against horses in pre-game exhibitions.

Black teams, like the Tennessee Rats and Zulu Cannibals, thrived on their minstrel show reputations. The most famous of these franchises were the "Ethiopian Clowns." Originating in Miami in the 1930s, the Clowns later operated out of Cincinnati and then Indianapolis. Their antics included a "pepperball and shadowball" performance (later emulated by basketball's Harlem Globetrotters), and mid-game vaudeville routines by comics Spec Bebop, a dwarf, and King Tut. Players like Pepper Bassett, "the Rocking Chair Catcher," and "Goose" Tatum, a talented first baseman and natural comedian, enlivened the festivities. By the 1940s, the Clowns, through the effort of booking agent Syd Pollack, dominated the baseball comedy market. In 1943, their popularity won the Clowns entrance into the Negro Leagues, although other owners demanded they drop the demeaning "Ethiopian" nickname. Although never one of the better black teams, the Clowns greatly bolstered Negro League attendance.

Their popularity notwithstanding, the comedy teams reflected one of the worst elements of black baseball. The Clowns and Zulus perpetuated stereotypes drawn from Stepin Fetchit and Tarzan movies. "Negroes must realize the danger in insisting that ballplayers paint their faces and go through minstrel show revues before each ballgame," protested sportswriter Wendell Smith. Many black players resented the image that all were clowns. "Didn't nobody clown in our league but the Indianapolis Clowns," objected Piper Davis. "We played baseball."

Even without the clowning, black baseball offered a more freewheeling and, in many respects, more exciting brand of baseball than the major leagues. Since the 1920s, when Babe Ruth had revolutionized the game, the majors had pursued power strategies, emphasizing the home run above all else. Although the great sluggers of the Negro Leagues rivaled those in the National and American Leagues, they comprised but one element in the speed-dominated universe of "tricky baseball." Black teams emphasized the bunt, the stolen base, and the hit-and-run. "We played by the 'coonsbury' rules," boasted second baseman Newt Allen. "That's just any way you think you can win, any kind of play you think you could get by on."

In games between white and black all-star teams, this style of play often confounded the major leaguers. Center fielder Cool Papa Bell personified this approach. Bell was so fast, marveled rival third baseman Judy Johnson, "You couldn't play back in your regular position or you'd never throw him out." In one game against a major league all-star squad, Bell scored from first base on a sacrifice bunt! In center field, his great speed allowed him to lurk in the shallow reaches of the outfield, ranging great distances to make spectacular catches.

Negro League pitching also took on a peculiar caste. "Anything went in the Negro League," reported catcher Roy Campanella, "Spitballs, shineballs, emery balls; pitchers used any and all of them." Since league officials could not afford to replace the balls as frequently as in organized ball, scuffed and nicked baseballs remained in the game, giving pitchers great latitude for creative efforts. "I never knew what the ball would do once it left the pitcher's hand," recalled Campanella.

Since most rosters included only 14 to 18 men, Negro League players demonstrated a wide range of versatility. Each was required to fill in at a variety of positions. Star pitchers often found themselves in the outfield when not on the mound. Some won renown at more than one position. Ted "Double-Duty" Radcliffe often pitched in the first game of a doubleheader and caught in the second. Cuban Martin Dihigo, whom many rank as the greatest player of all time, excelled at every position. In 1938 he led all Mexican League pitchers with an 18–2 record and the league's hitters with a .387 average.

The manpower shortage offered opportunities for individuals to display their all-around talents, but it also limited the competitiveness of the black teams. While on a given day a Negro League franchise, featuring one of its top pitchers, might defeat a major league squad, most teams lacked the depth to compete on a regular basis. "The big leagues were strong in every position," remarks Radcliffe. "Most of the colored teams had a few stars but they weren't strong in every position."

While black teams may not have matched the top clubs in organized baseball, the individual stars of the 1930s and 1940s clearly ranked among the best of any age. Homestead Gray teammates Josh Gibson and Buck Leonard won renown as the Babe Ruth and Lou Gehrig of the Negro Leagues. The Grays discovered Gibson in 1929 as an 18-year-old catcher on the sandlots of Pittsburgh, where he had already earned a reputation for 500-foot home runs. For 17 years, he launched prodigious blasts off pitchers in the Negro Leagues, on the barnstorming tour, and in Latin America. As talented as any major league star, Gibson died in January 1947, at age 35, just three months before Jackie Robinson joined the Brooklyn Dodgers. Leonard, four years older than Gibson, starred in both the Negro and Mexican Leagues as a sure-handed, power-hitting first baseman. The Newark Eagles of the early 1940s boasted the "million dollar infield" of first baseman Mule Suttles, second baseman Dick Seay, shortstop Willie Wells, and third baseman Ray Dandridge. The acrobatic fielding skills of Seay, Wells, and Dandridge led Roy Campanella to call this the greatest infield he ever saw.

Paige Stands Alone

Amidst the many talented Negro Leaguers of the 1930s and 1940s, however, one long, lean figure came to personify black baseball to blacks and whites alike. Leroy "Satchel" Paige began his prolonged athletic odyssey in his hometown in 1924 as a 17-year-old pitcher with the semi-professional Mobile Tigers. He joined the Chattanooga Black Lookouts of the Negro Southern League in 1926. Two years later the Lookouts sold his contract to the Birmingham Black Barons. By 1930 his explosive fastball, impeccable control, and eccentric mannerisms had made him a legend in the South. In 1932 Gus Greenlee brought Paige to the Pittsburgh Crawfords where the colorful pitcher embellished his reputation by winning 54 games in his first two years. Greenlee also began the practice of hiring out Paige to semi-professional clubs that needed a one-day box office boost.

For seven years Paige feuded with Greenlee, jumping the club when a better offer appeared, being banished "for life," and then returning. In the mid-1930s, in addition to his stints with the Crawfords, Paige won fame by boosting Bismarck, North Dakota, to the national semi-professional championships, hurling for the Dominican Republic at the behest of dictator Rafael Trujillo, in the Mexican League, and especially on the postseason barnstorming trail pitted against Dizzy Dean's Major League All-Stars. "That skinny old Satchel Paige with those long arms is my idea of the pitcher with the greatest stuff I ever saw," claimed the unusually immodest Dean.

Paige's appeal stemmed as much from his unusual persona as his pitching prowess. A born showman, Paige's lanky, lackadaisical presence evoked popular racial stereotypes of the age. "As undependable as a pair of second-hand suspenders," Paige often arrived late or failed to show. His names for his pitches (the "bee ball" which buzzed and would all of a sudden, "be there"; the "jump ball"; and the "trouble ball") and his minstrel show one-liners enhanced the image. But on the mound, Paige invariably rose to the occasion against top competition or challenged inferior opponents by calling in the outfield or promising to strike out the side.

In 1938 a sore arm threatened to curtail Paige's career, but the Kansas City Monarchs, hoping his reputation alone would draw fans, signed him for their traveling second team. On the road, Paige perfected a repertoire of curves and off-speed pitches, including his famous "hesitation" pitch. When his fastball returned in 1939, he became a better pitcher than ever. Promoted to the main Monarch club, Paige pitched the team to four consecutive Negro American League pennants. From 1941–47, although officially still a Monarch, Paige spent far more time as an independent performer, hired out by Monarchs owner J. L. Wilkinson to semi-pro and Negro League clubs. "He kept our league going," recalls Othello Renfroe. "Anytime a team got into trouble, it sent for Satchel to pitch." Paige also continued to hurl against major league all-star teams. In the 1940s, the example of Satchel Paige, whose legend had spread into the white community, offered the most compelling argument for the desegregation of the national pastime.

Paige's exploits against white players revealed a fundamental irony about baseball in the Jim Crow era. While organized baseball rigidly enforced its ban on black players within the major and minor leagues, opportunities abounded for black athletes to prove themselves against white competition along the unpoliced boundaries of the national pastime. During the 1930s, Western promoters sponsored tournaments for the best semi-professional teams in the nation. These squads often featured former and future major leaguers as well as top local talent. In 1934 the *Denver Post* tourney, "the little World Series of the West," invited the Kansas City Monarchs to compete for the $7,500 first prize. The Monarchs fought their way into the finals against the House of David team (also owned by J. L. Wilkinson) only to find themselves confronted on the mound by Paige, rented out to pitch this one game. Paige outdueled Monarchs ace Chet Brewer, 2–1. Black teams became a fixture in the Post series, emerging victorious for several consecutive years.

In 1935, the National Baseball Congress began an annual tournament in Wichita, Kansas. The competition attracted community squads heartily bankrolled by local business leaders. Neil Churchill, an auto dealer from Bismarck, North Dakota, recruited a half-dozen black stars, including Paige and Brewer, to represent the town in the Wichita competition. Bismarck naturally swept the series, and thereafter teams that were either integrated or all black routinely appeared in the National Baseball Congress invitational each year.

In an age in which the major leagues were confined to the East and Midwest, and television had yet to bring baseball into people's homes, postseason tours by big league stars offered yet another opportunity for black players to prove their equality on the diamond. Games pitting blacks against whites were popular features of the barnstorming circuit. Until the late 1920s, when Commissioner Kenesaw Mountain Landis limited postseason play to all-star squads, black teams frequently met and defeated major league clubs in postseason competition. During the next decade, matchups between the Babe Ruth or Dizzy Dean "All-Stars" and black players became frequent. In the autumns of 1934 and 1935, Dean's team traveled the nation accompanied by the "Satchel Paige All-Stars." In one memorable 1934 game, called by baseball executive Bill Veeck, "the greatest pitching battle I have ever seen," Paige bested Dean, 1–0. Surviving records of interracial contests during the 1930s reveal that blacks won two-thirds of the games. "That's when we played the hardest," asserted Judy Johnson, "to let them know, and to let the public know, that we had the same talent they did and probably a little better at times."

The rivalries proved particularly keen on the West Coast where Monarchs co-owner Tom Baird organized the California Winter League, which included black teams, white major and minor league stars, and some of Mexico's top players. In 1940, pitcher Chet Brewer formed the Kansas City Royals, which each year fielded one of the best clubs on the coast. One year the Royals defeated the Hollywood Stars, who had won the Pacific Coast League championship, six straight times. In 1945, Brewer's team, including Jackie Robinson and Satchel Paige, regularly defeated major league competition.

The most famous of the interracial barnstorming tours occurred in 1946, when Cleveland Indians pitcher Bob Feller organized a major league All-Star Team, rented two Flying Tiger aircraft and hopped the nation accompanied by the Satchel Paige All-Stars. With Feller and Paige each pitching a few innings a day, the tour proved extremely lucrative for promoters and players alike and gave widespread publicity to the skills of the black athletes.

The World War II years marked the heyday of the Negro Leagues. With black and white workers flooding into Northern industrial centers, relatively full employment, and a scarcity of available consumer goods, attendance at all sorts of entertainment events increased dramatically. In 1942, three million fans saw Negro League teams play, while the East-West game in 1943 attracted over 51,000 fans. "Even the white folks was coming out big," recalled Satchel Paige.

Change in the Air

But World War II also generated forces that would challenge the foundations of Jim Crow baseball. In the armed forces, baseball teams like the Black Bluejackets of the Great Lakes Naval Station team posted outstanding records against teams featuring white major leaguers. In 1945, a well-publicized tournament of teams in the European theatre featured top black players like Leon Day, Joe Green, and Willard Brown in the championship round. More significantly, the hypocrisy of blacks fighting for their country but unable to participate in the national pastime grew steadily more apparent. As wartime manpower shortages forced major league teams to rely on a 15-year-old pitcher, over-the-hill veterans, and one-armed Pete Gray, their refusal to sign black players seemed increasingly irrational. "How do you think I felt when I saw a one-armed outfielder?" moaned Chet Brewer. Pitcher Nate Moreland protested, "I can play in Mexico, but I have to fight for America where I can't play." Pickets at Yankee Stadium carried placards asking, "If we are able to stop bullets, why not balls?"

Amidst this heightened awareness, organized baseball repeatedly walked to the precipice of integration, but always failed to take the final leap. In 1942, Moreland and All-American football star Jackie Robinson requested a tryout at a White Sox training camp in Pasadena, California. Robinson, in particular, impressed White Sox manager Jimmy Dykes but nothing came of the event. Brooklyn Dodgers manager Leo Durocher publicly stated his willingness to sign blacks, only to receive a stinging rebuke from Commissioner Landis. Landis again short-circuited integration talk the following year. At the annual baseball meetings, black leaders led by actor Paul Robeson gained the opportunity to address major league owners on the issue, but Landis ruled all further discussion out of order.

In 1943 several minor and major league teams were rumored close to signing black players. In California, where winter league play had demonstrated the potential of black players, several clubs considered integration. The Los Angeles Angels of the Pacific Coast League announced tryouts for three black players, but pressure from other league owners doomed the plan. Oakland owner Vince DeVicenzi ordered manager Johnny Vergez to consider pitcher Chet Brewer, the most popular black player on the West Coast. Vergez refused and the issue died. Two years later, Bakersfield, a Cleveland Indians farm team in the California League, offered Brewer a position as player-coach, but the parent club vetoed the plan.

At the major league level, Washington Senators owner Clark Griffith called sluggers Josh Gibson and Buck Leonard into his office and asked if they would like to play in the major leagues. They answered affirmatively, but never heard from Griffith again. In Pittsburgh, *Daily Worker* sports editor Nat Low pressured Pirates owner William Benswanger to arrange a tryout for catcher Roy Campanella and pitcher Dave Barnhill. At the last minute, Benswanger canceled the audition, citing "unnamed pressures."

For more than two decades, the imperial Landis had reigned over baseball as an implacable foe of integration. While hypocritically denying the existence of any "rule, formal or informal, or any understanding—unwritten, subterranean, or sub-anything—against the signing of Negro players," Landis had stringently policed the color line. His death in 1944 removed a major barrier for integration advocates.

In April 1945, with World War II entering its final months, the integration crusade gained momentum. On April 6, *People's Voice* sportswriter Joe Bostic appeared at the Brooklyn Dodger training camp at Bear Mountain, New York, with two Negro League players, Terris McDuffie and Dave "Showboat" Thomas, and demanded a tryout. Outraged, but outmaneuvered, Dodgers president Branch Rickey allowed the pair to work out with the club.

One week later, a more serious confrontation occurred in Boston. The Red Sox, under public pressure from popular columnist Dave Egan and city councilman Isidore Muchnick, agreed to audition Sam Jethroe, the Negro League's leading hitter in 1944, second baseman Marvin Williams, and Kansas City Monarchs shortstop Jackie Robinson, all top prospects in their mid-20s. The Fenway Park tryout, however, proved little more than a formality and the players never again heard from the Red Sox.

The publicity surrounding these events, however, forced the major leagues to address the issue at its April meetings. At the urging of black sportswriter Sam Lacy, Leslie O'Connor, Landis' interim successor, established a Major League Committee on Baseball Integration in April 1945, to review the problem. In addition, the racial views of the newly appointed commissioner, A. B. "Happy" Chandler, came under close scrutiny. A former governor of the segregated state of Kentucky, Chandler nonetheless offered at least verbal support to the entry of blacks into organized ball. "If a black boy can make it on Okinawa and Guadalcanal, hell, he can make it in baseball," Chandler told black reporter Rick Roberts. Whether Chandler, however, unlike Landis, would reinforce his rhetoric with positive actions remained uncertain.

Rickey Takes the First Step

Unbeknownst to the integration advocates, baseball officials, and local politicians sand-dancing around the race issue, Branch Rickey, the president of the Brooklyn Dodgers, had already set in motion the events which would lead to the historic breakthrough.

Raised in rural Ohio in a strict Methodist family, Rickey, nicknamed by sportwriters "The Deacon" and "The Mahatma," had financed his way through college and law school playing and coaching baseball. His skills as a catcher merited two years in the major leagues. In 1913 he abandoned a fledgling law career to manage the St. Louis Browns, and in 1917 he began a 25-year relationship with the St. Louis Cardinals. Rickey served as the field manager of the Cardinals from 1919 to 1925, after which he became the club's vice president and business manager. In the 1920s and 1930s, Rickey perfected the farm system, whereby a major league team controlled young, undeveloped players through a chain of minor league franchises. This innovation allowed the Cardinals to compete equally with richer teams in larger cities, generating pennants for the "Gashouse Gang" and allowing the team to profitably sell off surplus talent.

Although Rickey later claimed that his desire to integrate baseball dated from 1904, when an Indiana hotel had denied lodgings to a black player on his college squad, he gave no indication of any interest in the race issue during his years in St. Louis. Perhaps this stemmed from the fact that St. Louis was a southern city with firmly entrenched segregationist traditions. Throughout Rickey's reign with the Cardinals, blacks sat in Jim Crow sections at Sportsman's Park, a policy which he never openly challenged.

Nonetheless, in 1942, when Rickey left the Cardinals and assumed control of the Brooklyn Dodgers, he informed the Dodger ownership of his intentions to recruit black players in the near future. Rickey never clearly explained the motivations for this dramatic turnaround. At times Rickey cited moral considerations, stating, "I couldn't face my God much longer knowing that His black creatures are held separate and distinct from His white creatures in the game that has given me all I own." On other occasions, he eschewed the role of "crusader," proclaiming, "My selfish objective is to win baseball games. . .The Negroes will make us winners for years to come."

Some observers saw financial reasons behind Rickey's actions, citing the lure of the growing black population in northern cities and the prospects of increased attendance. Certainly, Brooklyn offered a more congenial atmosphere for integration than St. Louis. In all probability, a combination of these factors—geographic, moral, competitive, and financial—coupled with Rickey's desire for a broader role in history, impelled him to seek black players.

From 1942–45, Rickey, a conservative, cautious, and conspiratorial man, moved slowly, studying the philosophical and sociological ramifications of integration and taking few people into his confidence. During the spring and summer of 1945, under the guise of creating a new black baseball circuit, the United States League, Rickey's scouts combed the nation and the Caribbean for black players. Rickey sought one player who would spearhead the breakthrough and several other potential stars who would follow in his wake. By August 1945 scouting reports and Rickey's own investigations pointed to one man as the ideal candidate for the struggle ahead—Kansas City Monarchs shortstop Jackie Robinson.

In Robinson, Rickey had found a rare combination of athletic ability, competitive fire, intelligence, maturity, and poise. Born in Georgia and raised in Pasadena, California, Robinson had won fame at UCLA as the nation's greatest all-around athlete, earning All-America honors in football, establishing broad-jump records, and leading his basketball conference in scoring, all in addition to his baseball exploits. In 1942, he enlisted in the army where he attended officer's candidate school and became a lieutenant. Two years later, while stationed in Texas, Robinson's refusal to move to the back of a bus resulted in a court martial and ultimate acquittal. This incident demonstrated his commitment to the cause of equal rights. After his discharge from the army, Robinson joined the Monarchs and earned a starting spot in the 1945 East-West All-Star Game. Robinson's college education, experience in interracial athletics, and army career complemented his playing talents. But his fiery pride and temper seemed a potential obstacle to his success.

On August 28, 1945, Robinson met with Rickey at the latter's Brooklyn offices. Rickey revealed his bold plan to integrate organized baseball and challenged Robinson to accept the primary role. Rickey flamboyantly playacted, assuming the role of racist players, fans, and hotel clerks, impressing upon Robinson the need to "turn the other cheek" in the event of racial confrontations. By the end of the session, Robinson had signed a contract to play for the Montreal Royals in the International League, the top farm team in the Brooklyn system. Rickey promised that if Robinson's performance merited it, he would be promoted to the Dodgers.

Rickey intended to announce the Robinson signing along with that of several other black players, but political pressures stemming from the New York City fall elections forced him to abandon his original plans and, on October 23, 1945, to reveal the signing of Robinson alone. The announcement sent shock waves through the baseball establishment and placed Robinson into a spotlight that he would never relinquish. Numerous sports figures, from players to executives to reporters, predicted the ultimate failure of Rickey's "great experiment."

Robinson's first test came at spring training in Florida in 1946. Thrust into the deep South where Jim Crow reigned supreme, Robinson and black pitcher John Wright, whom Rickey had recruited to room with Robinson, were unable to room with their teammates and barred from playing in Jacksonville and other Florida cities. In addition, a shoulder injury hindered Robinson's performance, raising doubts about his abilities.

On April 18, 1946, at Roosevelt Stadium in Jersey City, Robinson became the first black to appear in modern organized baseball (excepting Jimmy Claxton, who passed as white in 1916 for the Oakland Oaks of the Pacific Coast League). In the process he staged one of the most remarkable performances under pressure in the history of the game. In Robinson's second at bat, he hit a three-run home run. He followed this with three singles and two stolen bases, scoring a total of four runs. As *The*

New York Times reported, "This would have been a big day for any man, but under the circumstances, it was a tremendous feat."

In many respects, 1946 proved a nightmare season for Robinson. Fans jeered him in Baltimore, and opposing players tormented him with insults. Pitchers made him a frequent target of brushback pitches and baserunners attempted to spike and maim him at second base. As the season drew to a close, Robinson hovered on the brink of a nervous breakdown. Through it all, however, Robinson remained a dominant force on the field. His .349 batting average and 113 runs scored led the league and paced the Royals to the International League pennant. His presence inspired new attendance records throughout the circuit. In the Little World Series, which pitted Montreal against the Louisville Colonels of the American Association, Robinson braved the hostility of Kentucky fans and stroked game-winning hits in the final two games to give the Royals the championship.

Rickey's initiative and Robinson's dramatic success failed to inspire other team owners. In August, major league executives debated a controversial report discussing the "race question" which argued that integration would "lessen the value of several major league franchises." No other clubs moved to sign black players. Only four blacks, all in the Brooklyn system, joined Robinson in organized baseball in 1946. At Nashua, New Hampshire, in the New England League, the Dodgers farm club fielded catcher Roy Campanella and pitcher Don Newcombe. The Nashua Dodgers won the league championship largely due to Campanella's hitting and Newcombe's hurling. In the small town of Trois Rivières in Quebec, pitchers John Wright and Roy Partlow, both of whom had appeared briefly with Robinson at Montreal, led a third Dodgers farm team to the Canadian-American League crown. Nonetheless, at the start of the 1947 season, no additional black players appeared on any major or minor league rosters.

The Big Leagues at Last

Although Robinson's performance at Montreal merited promotion to the Dodgers, Robinson remained a Royal when he reported to spring training in 1947. Rickey hoped that the Brooklyn players themselves, when exposed to Robinson's talents, would request his addition to the team. He switched Robinson to first base, a weak spot on the Dodgers, to make his case more compelling. Robinson compiled a .519 batting average against the major leaguers, but several Dodger players, instead of demanding his promotion, rebelled. Led by Fred "Dixie" Walker, a group of mostly southern Dodgers circulated a petition against Robinson. Rickey moved quickly to short-circuit the dissension, threatening to trade any athletes who opposed Robinson. In addition, the refusal of Pete Reiser, Pee Wee Reese and other Dodgers to support the protestors, effectively squelched the petition drive. Finally, on April 10, just five days before the start of the 1947 season, Rickey officially announced that Robinson would join the Dodgers.

Throughout the early months of the 1947 campaign Robinson stoically endured crises and challenges. The Philadelphia Phillies, led by manager Ben Chapman, unleashed a barrage of verbal abuse against Robinson, which horrified Dodgers players and fans. The Benjamin Franklin Hotel in Philadelphia refused lodgings for Robinson and death threats appeared among his voluminous daily mail. In early May, rumors that the St. Louis Cardinals planned to strike rather than compete against Robinson prompted National League President Ford Frick to warn the players, "If you do this you will be suspended from the league."

Opposing pitchers targeted Robinson's body at a record-setting pace and an early season 0-for-20 batting drought led many to question his qualifications as a professional baseball player. "But for the fact that he is the first acknowledged Negro in major league history," observed a Cincinnati sportswriter, "he would have been benched a week ago."

Yet, as the season unfolded, Robinson converted doubters and enemies into admirers. By the end of June, a 21-game hitting streak had raised his batting average to .315 and propelled the Dodgers into first place. Robinson's daring baserunning, typical of Negro League play, evoked images of an "Ebony Ty Cobb." In city after city, record crowds flocked to experience Robinson's charismatic dynamism as five teams set new all-time season attendance marks. While periodic controversies erupted over baserunners who used their spikes "to make a pincushion out of Robinson" at first base, Robinson won the acceptance and respect of teammates and opponents alike. In September, as the Dodgers coasted to the pennant, *The Sporting News* named Robinson the major league Rookie of the Year. To cap his triumphant season, Robinson became the first black player to appear in the World Series.

Robinson's success on the field and at the box office stimulated some movement on the part of other clubs to hire black players. In Cleveland, Bill Veeck recruited 23-year-old Larry Doby, who jumped straight from the Negro League Newark Eagles to the Indians in July. Used sparingly, Doby batted a meager .156, casting doubts upon his future. The St. Louis Browns, seeking to boost flagging attendance, signed Willard Brown and Hank Thompson of the Kansas City Monarchs. When the turnstiles failed to respond, the Browns released both Brown and Thompson, although the latter had established himself as a top prospect. In the National League, the Dodgers signed Dan Bankhead to bolster the club's pitching down the stretch. On August 25, Bankhead, the first black pitcher to appear in the major leagues, surrendered eight runs in three innings but also slammed a home run in his initial at bat.

In addition to the five athletes who appeared in the major leagues, a handful of blacks surfaced in the minors. Campanella succeeded Robinson at Montreal, earning accolades as "the best catcher in the business." Newcombe returned to Nashua where he won 19 games. The independent Stamford Bombers of the Colonial League fielded six black players, and two blacks, including future major leaguer Chuck Harmon, played in the Canadian-American League. Veteran Negro League hurler Nate Moreland won 20 games in California's Class C Sunset League. For the most part, however, organized baseball continued to ignore the treasure trove of black talent submerged in the Negro Leagues. A full year would pass before additional major league teams would add black players to their chains.

In 1948 the integration focus shifted from the Dodgers, where Robinson now reigned at second base, to the Cleveland Indians. In spring training, Larry Doby, who had performed so dismally in 1947, unexpectedly won a starting berth in the Cleveland outfield. After an erratic early season stretch in which Doby alternated errors and strikeouts with tape-measure home runs, he batted .301 and became a key performer for the American League champion Indians. In July, Cleveland owner Bill Veeck added the legendary Satchel Paige to the team. Amidst charges that his signing had been a publicity stunt, the 42-year-old Paige won six out of seven decisions, including back-to-back shutouts, and posted a 2.47 earned run average. Standing-room-only crowds greeted him in Washington, Chicago, Boston, and even in Cleveland's mammoth Municipal Stadium. The Indians, after defeating the Boston Red Sox in a pennant playoff, won the World Series in six games with Doby's .318 average leading the club.

In 1947 the Dodgers had integrated and reached the World Series; in 1948 the Indians had duplicated and surpassed this achievement. Both teams had set all-time attendance records. Remarkably, as the 1948 season drew to a close, no other franchise had followed their lead. In the minor leagues, Roy Campanella became the first black in the American Association, stopping at St. Paul before permanently joining Robinson on the Dodgers. Newcombe and Bankhead each won more than 20 games for Brooklyn affiliates. The Dodgers also added fleet-footed Sam Jethroe to the Montreal roster, where he batted .322. The Indians began to stockpile black talent as well, signing future major leaguers Al Smith, Dave Hoskins, and Orestes "Minnie" Minoso to minor league contracts. Several other blacks, including San Diego catcher John Ritchey, who broke the Pacific Coast League color line, played for independent teams.

In the interregnum between the 1948 and 1949 seasons four more teams—the Giants, Yankees, Braves, and Cubs—signed blacks to play in their farm systems, and 1949 would herald the beginning of widespread integration in the minor leagues. Blacks starred in all three Triple A leagues. In the Pacific Coast League, Luke Easter won acclaim as the "greatest natural hitter . . . since Ted Williams," amassing 25 home runs and 92 runs batted in in just 80 games before succumbing to a knee injury. Oakland's Artie Wilson led the league in hits, stolen bases, and batting average. In the International League, Jethroe scored 151 runs and stole 89 bases while Montreal teammate Dan Bankhead won 20 games for the second straight year. At Jersey City, Monte Irvin batted .373. The outstanding performer in the American Association was Ray Dandridge. Considered by many the greatest third baseman of all time, the acrobatic Dandridge, now in his late 30s, thrilled Minneapolis fans with his spectacular fielding, batting .364 in the process. Former Negro Leaguers turned in equally stellar performances at lower minor league levels as well.

In the major leagues, the spotlight again returned to Jackie Robinson. For three years, Robinson had honored his pledge to Branch Rickey "to turn the other cheek" and avoid confrontations. With his position in the majors firmly established, Robinson announced, "They better be prepared to be rough this year, because I'm going to be rough on them." The more combative Robinson produced his finest year, batting .342 and earning the Most Valuable Player Award. Complemented by teammates Newcombe and Campanella, Robinson led the Dodgers to another pennant.

Slow to Follow

By the end of the 1949 season integration had achieved spectacular success at both the major and minor league level, but most teams moved "with all deliberate speed" in signing black players. The New York Giants joined the interracial ranks in 1949 when they promoted Monte Irvin and Hank Thompson. The following year, the Boston Braves purchased Jethroe from the Dodgers for $100,000 and installed him in the starting lineup. In 1951, the Chicago White Sox acquired Minnie Minoso in a trade with Cleveland, and Bill Veeck, who had acquired the hapless St. Louis Browns, brought back Satchel Paige for another major league stint. Yet, as late as August 1953, out of 16 major league teams only these six fielded black players. Several teams displayed an interest in signing blacks but bypassed established Negro League stars who might have jumped directly to the majors, concentrating instead on younger prospects for the minor leagues. Still others like the Red Sox, Phillies, Cardinals, and Tigers continued to pursue a whites-only policy.

This failure to hire and promote blacks occurred amidst a continuing backdrop of outstanding performances by black players. The first generation of players from the Negro Leagues proved an extraordinary group. Jackie Robinson quickly established himself as one of the dominant stars in the national pastime, compiling a .311 batting average over his 10-year career while thrilling fans with his baserunning and clutch-hitting talents. Sportswriters called him, "the most dangerous man in baseball today." Campanella won accolades as the best catcher in the National League and won the Most Valuable Player Award in 1951, 1953, and 1955. Both Campanella and Robinson later won election to the Baseball Hall of Fame. Pitcher Don Newcombe averaged better than 20 wins a season during his first five full years with the Dodgers. In addition, from 1950 to 1953 Negro League graduates Sam Jethroe, Willie Mays, Joe Black, and Jim Gilliam each won the National League Rookie of the Year Award.

In the American League, where integration proceeded at a slower pace, several players compiled outstanding records. Larry Doby, while never achieving the superstar status many expected, nonetheless became a steady producer, twice leading the league in home runs and five times driving in more than 100 runs. He was elected to the Baseball Hall of Fame in 1998. Doby's Cleveland teammate Luke Easter, who reached the majors in his mid-30s, slugged 86 home runs and drove in 300 runs in his brief three-season career. Satchel Paige, after a two-year stint with the Indians, joined the hapless St. Louis Browns from 1951 to 1953 and became one of the American League's best relief pitchers. On the Chicago White Sox, Minnie Minoso proved himself a consistent .300 hitter.

Despite their relatively small numbers, teams with black players in both major leagues regularly finished high in the standings and only in 1950 did both pennant winners field all-white squads. In addition, the more aggressive stance of National League teams in recruiting black players gave that circuit a clear superiority in World Series and All-Star contests for more than two decades.

By the end of the 1953 season, the benefits of integration had grown apparent to all but the most recalcitrant of major league owners. In September, the Chicago Cubs purchased shortstop Ernie Banks from the Kansas City Monarchs and finally elevated longtime minor league standout Gene Baker. Connie Mack's Philadelphia Athletics ended their Jim Crow era by acquiring pitcher Bob Trice. At the start of the 1954 season, the Washington Senators, St. Louis Cardinals, Pittsburgh Pirates, and Cincinnati Reds all joined the interracial ranks. The sudden integration of six more clubs left only the Yankees, Tigers, Phillies, and Red Sox with all-white personnel. In addition, 1954 marked the debut of young Henry Aaron with the Braves and the return of Willie Mays, who had sparkled for the Giants in 1951, from military service.

The desegregation of organized baseball opened the way not only to blacks in the United States but to those in other parts of the Americas as well. Throughout the 20th century, baseball had imposed a curious double standard on Latin players, accepting those with light complexions but rejecting their darker countrymen. With the color barrier down, major league clubs found a wealth of talent in the Carribbean. Minnie Minoso, the "Cuban Comet" who integrated the Chicago White Sox, became the first of the great Latin stars. Over a 15-year career, Minoso compiled a .298 batting average. In 1954 slick-fielding Puerto Rican Vic Power launched his career with the Athletics. The following year, Roberto Clemente, the greatest of the Latin stars, debuted with the Pittsburgh Pirates. The proud Puerto Rican won four batting championships and amassed 3,000 hits en route to a .317 lifetime batting average. In the late 1950s the San Francisco Giants revealed the previously ignored treasure trove that existed in the Dominican Republic. In 1958 Felipe Alou became the first of three Alou brothers to play for the Giants, and in 1960 the Giants unveiled pitcher Juan Marichal, "the Dominican Dandy," who won 243 games en route to the Hall of Fame.

Among the early Latin players were two sons of stars of the Jim Crow age. Perucho Cepeda, who had won renown as "The Bull" in his native Puerto Rico, had refused to play in the segregated Negro leagues. His son Orlando, dubbed "The Baby Bull," went on to star for the Giants and Cardinals. Luis Tiant Sr., a standout performer in both Cuba and the Negro Leagues, lived to see Luis Jr. win over 200 major league games and excel in the 1975 World Series.

Major Changes in Minor Leagues

As the major leagues moved slowly toward complete desegregation, blacks invaded the minor leagues. In the Northern and Western states, these athletes, a combination of youthful prospects and Negro League veterans, were greeted by a storm of insults, beanballs, and discrimination. "I learned more names than I thought we had," states Piper Davis of his treatment by fans in the Pacific Coast League. At least a half-dozen blacks had to be carried off the field on stretchers after being hit by pitches between 1949 and 1951. In city after city, blacks found hotels and restaurants unwilling to serve them.

"At the same time when they signed blacks and Latins," argues John Roseboro about his Dodger employers, "they should have made sure they would be welcome." But neither the Dodgers nor other clubs provided any special assistance for their black farmhands. Despite these conditions, blacks compiled remarkable records in league after league. In the early 1950s, blacks overcame adversity and dominated the lists of batting leaders at the Triple A level and in many of the lower circuits as well.

In 1952, blacks began to appear on minor league clubs in the Jim Crow South. The Dallas Eagles of the Texas League, hoping to boost sagging attendance, signed former Homestead Gray pitcher Dave Hoskins to become the "Jackie Robinson of the Texas League." Hoskins took the Lone Star State by storm, attracting record crowds en route to a 22–10 record. The black pitcher posted a 2.12 earned run average and also finished third in the league in batting with a .328 mark. By 1955 every Texas League club except Shreveport fielded black players.

Hoskins' performance inspired other teams throughout the South to scramble for black players. In 1953 19-year-old Henry Aaron desegregated the South Atlantic League, which included clubs in Florida, Atlanta, and Georgia, while Bill White appeared in the Carolina League. Playing for Jacksonville (a city which seven years earlier had barred Jackie Robinson), Aaron "led the league in everything but hotel accommodations." By 1954 when the United States Supreme Court issued its historic *Brown* v. *Board of Education* decision ordering school desegregation, blacks had appeared in most Southern minor leagues.

The integration of the South, however, did not proceed without incidents. Black players recall these years as "an ordeal" or a "sentence" and described the South as "enemy country" or a "hellhole." In 1953 the Cotton States League barred brothers Jim and Leander Tugerson from competing.

The following year, Nat Peeples broke the color line in the Southern Association, but lasted only two weeks. For the remainder of the decade, the league adhered to a whites-only policy, a strategy which contributed to the collapse of the Southern Association in 1961. As resistance to the civil rights movement mounted in the 1950s, black players found themselves in increasingly hostile territory. Even in the pioneering Texas League, teams visiting Shreveport, Louisiana, in 1956 had to leave their black players at home due to stricter segregation laws.

In the face of these obstacles, young black stars like Aaron, Curt Flood, Frank Robinson, Bill White, and Leon Wagner overcame their frustrations "by taking it out on the ball." "What had started as a chance to test my baseball ability in a professional setting," wrote Curt Flood, "had become an obligation to test myself as a man." Throughout the 1950s, blacks appeared regularly among the league leaders of the Texas, South Atlantic, Carolina, and other circuits, advancing both their own careers and the cause of integration.

As these events unfolded in the South, the major leagues completed their long overdue integration process. The Yankees, after denying charges of racism for almost a decade, finally promoted Elston Howard to the parent club in 1955. Two more years passed before the Phillies integrated, and not until 1958 did a black player don a Tiger uniform. Thus, at the start of the 1959 season, only the Boston Red Sox, who had yet to hire either black scouts or representatives in the Caribbean, retained their Jim Crow heritage. A storm of protest arose when the Red Sox cut black infielder Elijah "Pumpsie" Green just before Opening Day, but on July 21, 1959, 12 years and 107 days after Jackie Robinson's Dodger debut, Green won promotion to the Boston club, completing the cycle of major league integration.

While integration became a reality in organized baseball, the Negro Leagues gradually faded into oblivion. As early as 1947, Negro League attendance, especially in cities close to National League parks, dropped precipitously. "People wanted to go Brooklynites," recalls Monarchs pitcher Hilton Smith. "Even if we were playing here in Kansas City, people wanted to go over to St. Louis to see Jackie." Negro League owners hoped to offset declining attendance by selling players to organized baseball, but major league teams paid what Effa Manley called "bargain basement" prices for all-star talent. In 1948 the Manleys' Newark Eagles and New York Black Yankees disbanded. The Homestead Grays severed all league connections and returned to its roots as a barnstorming unit. Without these teams the Negro National League collapsed. A reorganized 10-team Negro American League, most of whose franchises were located in minor league cities, vowed to go on, but the spread of integration quickly thinned its ranks. By 1951, the league had dwindled to six teams. Two years later, only the Birmingham Black Barons, Memphis Red Sox, Kansas City Monarchs, and Indianapolis Clowns remained.

For several years in the early 1950s, the Negro Leagues remained a breeding ground for young black talent. The New York Giants plucked Willie Mays from the roster of the Birmingham Black Barons, while the Boston Braves discovered Hank Aaron on the Indianapolis Clowns. The Kansas City Monarchs produced more than two dozen major leaguers, including Robinson, Paige, Banks, and Howard. But for most black players, the demise of the Negro Leagues had disastrous effects. "The livelihoods, the careers, the families of 400 Negro ballplayers are in jeopardy," complained Effa Manley in 1948, "because four players were successful in getting into the major leagues." The slow pace of integration left most in a state of limbo set adrift by their former teams, but still unwelcomed in organized baseball. Some players like Buck Leonard and Cool Papa Bell were too old to be considered, while others like Ray Dandridge and Piper Davis found themselves relegated to the minor leagues, where outstanding records failed to win them promotion.

Throughout the 1950s the Negro American League struggled to survive, recruiting teenagers and second-rate talent for the modest four-team loop. In 1963 Kansas City hosted the 30th and last East-West All-Star Game and the following year the famed Monarchs ceased touring the nation. By 1965 the Indianapolis Clowns remained as a last vestige of Jim Crow baseball. Utilizing white as well as black players, the Clowns continued for another decade. "We are all show now," explained their owner. "We clown, clown, clown."

But the legacy of the Negro Leagues remained. Robinson and other early black players introduced new elements of speed and "tricky baseball" into the major leagues, transforming and improving the quality of play. Since 1947 blacks have led the National League in stolen bases in all but two seasons. In the American League, a black or Latin baserunner has topped the league every year since 1951 with only two exceptions. Nor did this injection of speed come at the expense of power. In the 1950s and 1960s, Hank Aaron, Willie Mays, and Frank Robinson reigned as the greatest power hitters in baseball. Thus, by the 1960s, the national pastime more closely resembled the well-balanced offensive structure of the Negro Leagues than the one-dimensional power-oriented attack that had typified the all-white majors.

The demise of the Negro Leagues and the decline of segregation in the majors, however, did not end discrimination. Conditions on and off the field, in spring training and in the executive suites, repeatedly reminded the black athletes of their second-class status. In the early 1950s all-white teams taunted their black opponents with racial insults. Blacks like Jackie and Frank Robinson, Minnie Minoso and Luke Easter repeatedly appeared among the league leaders in being hit by pitches. While black superstars like Willie Mays had little difficulty ascending to the major leagues, players of only slightly above average talent found themselves buried for years in the minors. Many observers charged that teams had imposed quotas on the number of blacks they would field at one time.

In cities like St. Louis, Washington, D. C., and, later, Baltimore, black ballplayers could not stay at hotels with their teammates. In 1954 they achieved a breakthrough of sorts when the luxury Chase Hotel in St. Louis informed Jackie Robinson and other Dodger players that they could room there, but had to refrain from using the dining room or swimming pool or loitering in the lobby. Ten years later, the hotel had removed these restrictions, but still relegated black players, according to Hank Aaron, to rooms "looking out over some old building or some green pastures or a blank wall, so nobody can see us through a window."

Blacks faced even greater discrimination each year in spring training in Florida. While all spring training sites now accepted blacks, segregation statutes and local traditions forced them to live in all-black boarding houses far from the luxury air-conditioned hotels which accommodated white players. "The whole set-up is wrong," protested Jackie Robinson. "There is no reason why we shouldn't be able to live with our teammates." When teams traveled from place to place, blacks could not join their fellow players in restaurants. Instead they had to wait on the bus until someone brought their food out to them. Some teams attempted to reduce the problems faced by blacks. Several clubs moved to Arizona, where conditions were only moderately improved. The Dodgers built a special spring training camp at Vero Beach where players could live together. Most organizations, however, did very little to assist their black employees.

By the time that Jackie Robinson retired in 1956, conditions had barely improved. "After 10 years of traveling in the South," he charged, " I don't think advances have been fast enough. It's my belief that baseball itself hasn't done all it can to remedy the problems faced by . . . players." Over the next decade, a new generation of black players militantly demanded change. Cardinals stars Bill White, Curt Flood, and Bob Gibson protested against conditions in St. Petersburg, while Aaron and other black Braves demanded changes in Bradenton. In many instances, however, significant changes awaited passage of the Civil Rights Act of 1965 barring segregation in public facilities.

The Next Generation

By 1960 Robinson, Campanella, Doby, and the cadre of Negro League veterans who had formed the vanguard of baseball integration had retired. In their wake, a second generation of black players, most of whom had never appeared in the Negro Leagues, made most Americans forget that Jim Crow baseball had ever existed, as they shattered longstanding "unbreakable" records. In 1962 black shortstop Maury Wills stole 104 bases, eclipsing Ty Cobb's 47-year-old stolen base mark. Twelve years later, outfielder Lou Brock stole 118 bases en route to breaking Cobb's career stolen-base record as well.

In 1966 Frank Robinson, who had won the National League Most Valuable Player Award in 1961, became the first player to win that honor in both leagues when he led the Baltimore Orioles to the American League pennant. By the end of his career, Robinson had slugged 586 home runs. Both Ernie Banks and Willie McCovey also amassed more than 500 home runs during this era. On the pitcher's mound, the indomitable Bob Gibson proved himself one of the greatest strikeout pitchers in the game's history. Upon retirement, Gibson had amassed more strikeouts than anyone except Walter Johnson. Brock, Frank Robinson, Banks, McCovey, and Gibson all won election to the Hall of Fame in their first year of eligibility.

The greatness of these players notwithstanding, two other black players, Willie Mays and Hank Aaron, both of whom ironically had begun their careers in the Negro Leagues, reigned as the dominant stars of baseball in the 1950s and 1960s. Originally signed by the Birmingham Black Barons of the Negro American League, Mays had joined the New York Giants in midseason 1951, sparking their triumph in the most famous pennant race in history and winning the Rookie of the Year Award. After two years in the military, he returned in 1954 to bat a league-leading .345 and hit 41 home runs. The following year, he pounded 51 homers. A spectacular center fielder, Mays won widespread acclaim as the greatest all-around player in the history of the game. In 1969 he became only the second player in major league history to hit 600 home runs and took aim at Babe Ruth's legendary lifetime total of 714. Over the next four seasons, the aging Mays added 60 more homers before retiring, still well short of Ruth's record.

Unlike Mays, who had begun his career amidst the glare of the New York media, Hank Aaron had spent his career first in Milwaukee and later in Atlanta, far distant from the center of national publicity. Nonetheless, he steadily compiled record-threatening statistics in almost every offensive category. In 1972, at age 38, he surpassed Mays' home run total and set his sights on Ruth. Entering the 1973 season, he needed just 41 home runs to catch the Babe. Performing under tremendous pressure and fanfare, Aaron stroked 40 homers, leaving him just one shy of the record. He tied Ruth's mark with his first swing of the 1974 season. Three days later, on April 8, 1974, a nationwide television audience watched Aaron stroke home run number 715. Babe Ruth's "unreachable" record thus fell to a man whose career had started with the Indianapolis Clowns of the Negro Leagues. When Aaron retired in 1976, he boasted 755 home runs and held major league records for games played, at-bats, runs batted in and extra-base hits. He also ranked second to Ty Cobb in hits and runs scored.

By the 1970s black players had become an accepted part of the baseball scene and regularly ranked among the most well-known symbols of the sport. Reggie Jackson, Willie Stargell, and Joe Morgan had succeeded Aaron, Mays, and the Robinsons as Hall of Fame caliber superstars. Yet three decades after Jackie Robinson had broken the color barrier, racism and discrimination remained a persistent problem for baseball. Several studies demonstrated that baseball management channeled blacks into positions thought to require less thinking and fewer leadership qualities. In 1968 blacks accounted for more than half of the major league outfielders, but only 20 percent of other position players. Black catchers were rare and fewer than one in 10 pitchers were black. The disparity had grown greater by 1986. American-born blacks comprised 70 percent of all outfield positions but only 7 percent of all pitcher, second basemen, and third basemen positions. There were no American-born black catchers in the major leagues at the start of the 1986 season; the 1990s, however, saw some progress with the appearance of Charles Johnson and Lenny Webster.

While superior black players had open access to the major leagues, those of average or slightly above average skills often found their paths blocked. "The Negro player may have to be better qualified than a white player to win the same position," argued Aaron Rosenblatt in 1967. "The undistinguished Negro player is less likely to play in the major leagues than the equally undistinguished white player." Rosenblatt demonstrated that black major leaguers on the whole batted 20 points higher than whites. As batting averages dropped, so did the proportion of blacks. This trend continued into the 1980s. A 1982 study revealed that 70 percent of all black non-pitchers were everyday starters, indicating a substantial bias against blacks who filled utility or pinch-hitting roles. Statistics compiled in 1986 showed a strikingly similar pattern.

The subtle nature of this on-the-field discrimination obscured it from public controversy. The failure of baseball to provide jobs for blacks in managerial and front office positions, however, became an increasing embarrassment. In the early years of integration, baseball executives bypassed the substantial pool of experienced Negro Leaguers from consideration for managerial and coaching positions. A handful of blacks, including Sam Bankhead, Nate Moreland, Marvin Williams, and Chet Brewer managed independent, predominantly all-black teams in the minor leagues. The first generation of black major leaguers fared no better. "We bring dollars into club treasuries when we play," exclaimed Larry Doby, "but when we stop playing, our dollars stop." No major league organization hired a black pilot at any level until 1961 when the Pittsburgh Pirates placed Gene Baker at the helm of their Batavia franchise. By the mid-1960s no blacks had managed in the majors and only two had held full-time major league coaching positions. The first black umpire did not appear in the majors until 1966, when Emmett Ashford appeared in the American League.

In the final years of his life, Jackie Robinson made repeated pleas for baseball to eliminate these lingering vestiges of Jim Crow. "I'd like to live to see a black manager," he stated before a national television audience at the 1972 World Series. Nine days later he died, his dream unfulfilled. In 1975 the Cleveland Indians hired Frank Robinson to be the first black major league manager. This precedent, however, opened few new doors. Robinson lasted two-and-a-half seasons with the Indians, later managed the San Francisco Giants for four years, and piloted the Baltimore Orioles for three-and-a-half seasons before moving to the club's front office. Maury Wills and Larry Doby each had brief half-season stints as managers. After four decades of integration, only these three men had received major league managerial opportunities.

A similar situation existed in major league front offices. Only one black man, Bill Lucas of the Atlanta Braves, had served as a general manager. As late as 1982, a survey of 24 clubs (the Yankees and Red Sox refused to provide information) found that of 913 available white-collar baseball jobs, blacks held just 32 positions. Among 568 full-time major league scouts, only 15 were black. While many teams hired former players as announcers, few employed blacks in these roles. Five years later, conditions had not improved. Of the top 879 administrative positions in baseball only 17 were filled by blacks and 15 by Hispanics. Four teams in California—the Dodgers, Giants, Athletics, and Angels—accounted for almost two-thirds of the minority hiring. Ten out of 14 American League teams, and five of 12 National League franchises had no blacks in management positions.

These shortcomings came to haunt baseball in 1987. Commissioner Peter Ueberroth had dedicated the season to the commemoration of the 40th anniversary of Jackie Robinson's major league debut. As the celebration began, Los Angeles Dodgers general manager Al Campanis, who had played with Robinson at Montreal, appeared on ABC-TV's "Nightline." When asked about the dearth of black managers, Campanis explained that blacks "may not have some of the necessities to be, let's say, a field manager or general manager." Campanis' statement, which surely reflected the thinking of many baseball executives, evoked a storm of protest, and precipitated his resignation. An embarrassed Ueberroth pledged to take action to bring more blacks into leadership positions and hired University of California sociologist Harry Edwards to facilitate the process. Fifty blacks and Latins with past or present connections to baseball created their own Minority Baseball Network to apprise blacks of employment opportunities and to lobby clubs to recruit more minorities for front office jobs.

When the controversy of 1987 had subsided, few franchises had taken significant steps to increase minority hiring. Several clubs added blacks to administrative positions, but none offered field or general manager positions to nonwhite candidates (although Bill White was named National League president). In 1988 Frank Robinson received his third chance to manage in the major leagues, this time with the Baltimore Orioles. At midseason 1989 Cito Gaston assumed the reins of the Toronto Blue Jays. When the squads managed by Robinson and Gaston had their initial confrontation, it marked, after 40 years of integration, the first time that two teams managed by black men had competed in a major league game. Fittingly, on the final weekend of the season, the Orioles and Blue Jays met face-to-face in a series to decide the championship of the American League Eastern Division. The spectacle offered a resounding rebuke to the shortsightedness and discrimination that continue to plague the national pastime.

By the 1993 season baseball seemed to have finally made some real progress in including minorities in its managerial ranks. The season saw five black and Hispanic field managers: Gaston, who after five years at the helm of the Blue Jays ranked as one of the most successful managers in baseball history; Felipe Alou, who led the Montreal Expos to consecutive second place finishes; Dusty Baker, who became the winningest rookie manager ever when his San Francisco Giants won 103 games; Don Baylor, who would pilot the expansion Colorado Rockies into the playoffs in only their third year of existence in 1995; and Tony Perez, who started the season as the manager of the Cincinnati Reds.

Progress extended into other areas of hiring as well. In 1994 Leonard Coleman succeeded Bill White as National League vice-president. By 1995, 27 percent of all coaches were black or latino. Minority hiring in the front office expanded to 17 percent in 1992, a level which held steady through 1994. The Houston Astros named Bob Watson their general manager, making him only the second black man to assume these responsibilities. Watson assumed the same position with the New York Yankees in 1996 and under his stewardship the club won the world championship.

These undeniable gains, however, occurred against a backdrop of continuing racial controversy. The proportion of American-born black players in baseball's major leagues dropped from one in four in the late 1960s to only one in six in the late 1980s and 1990s. In minor league and college baseball, important sources of major league talent, the percentage of African-Americans was even lower. Surveys indicated that African-Americans, who had flocked to major league ballparks in the 1950s, now accounted for one out of every 14 fans. Allegations that Cincinnati Reds owner Marge Schott had repeatedly used racial slurs (and that other owners had ignored these offenses) led to her suspension in 1993.

There remained no American minority owners of major league clubs. All 30 chief executive officers are white. When Watson resigned after the 1997 season, there once again were no black general managers. The surge in the hiring of minority managers that had occurred in the early 1990s also seemed to have abated. Few African-American or Hispanic managers were hired after 1994.

During the early 1990s baseball undertook several initiatives to improve its image among minorities. The major leagues embraced John Young's RBI (Reviving Baseball in the Inner Cities) program, an effort to entice black youth away from other sports and back to the diamond. Attempts were also made to secure health benefits for surviving Negro League players. To achieve greater recognition for players from the Jim Crow era, the Hall of Fame instructed its Veterans Committee to honor one Negro League star a year for five years. As a result, Leon Day, Willie Wells, Bill Foster, Bullet Joe Rogan, and Turkey Stearnes were selected to enter the Hall. African-American reporter Wendell Smith was named to the writer's wing of the Hall of Fame. Nonetheless black athletes still remain woefully underrepresented at Cooperstown.

In 1997 baseball celebrated the 50th anniversary of what most consider its "finest moment"—Jackie Robinson's Brooklyn Dodgers debut—with extraordinary and unprecedented fanfare. Major League Baseball dedicated the season to Robinson's memory. Players wore arm patches honoring his achievements. Acting Commissioner Bud Selig announced that all teams would henceforth retire his number. On April 15 President Bill Clinton appeared between innings of a Los Angeles Dodgers–New York Mets game at Shea Stadium to address the nation about Robinson's legacy.

A year later the National Baseball Hall of Fame added Larry Doby, who broke the American League color line, and Baltimore Afro-American sportswriter Sam Lacy to its list of honorees. At times the commemorations threatened to be overwhelmed by nostalgia and commercialism. However the 1997 festivities reminded the nation once again of its past heritage—both the shameful and the heroic—and its ongoing obligations to seek greater equality in the future.

At the turn of the century, however, baseball continued to make incremental progress, at best, in alleviating the remnants of discrimination in managerial hiring. The paradoxical aftermath of the 2000 season amply illustrated the lingering problem. Only five of the 30 major league teams employed nonwhite managers in 2000. Two of them, Dusty Baker of the San Francisco Giants and Jerry Manuel of the Chicago White Sox, unexpectedly led their teams to division championships and the best records in their respective leagues. Baker and Manuel both won Manager of the Year Awards—Baker for the third time in nine years.

Yet only one of six teams with managerial vacancies—the Pittsburgh Pirates who hired Lloyd McClendon—offered a position to a minority candidate. When the White Sox named Kenny Williams as general manager, he became the first African American to hold that job in the major leagues since Bob Watson left the Yankees prior to the 1998 season, and only the third in major league history. Although parity seemed more evident on the playing field, the front office remained only a frontier, rather than a stronghold, of equality.

CHAPTER 13

The Minor Leagues

Bob Hoie

The International Association, founded in 1877, is frequently described as the first minor league. For two major reasons it shouldn't be so regarded. First, it was barely a league. Structurally it resembled the old National Association—there was virtually no central authority, no limitation on the number or location of member teams, no set schedule, and haphazard umpire selection. The league was so loosely assembled in fact that some member teams competed at the same time for the championships of other organizations like the New England Association and the League Alliance.

Second, the International Association was originally established as a rival to the National League and never officially recognized itself as being subordinate. It was generally acknowledged that several of its teams were as good as or better than some in the National League. Various off-the-field problems, administrative weaknesses, and a lack of solidarity and resolve on the part of the member clubs assured its subordinate status.

A strong case could be made for the 1879 Northwestern League as the first minor league—it had a preset schedule and had no pretensions of rivaling the National League, but the absence of league-appointed umpires led to frequent forfeits due to charges of biased "hometown" umpiring, and the league folded after only two months.

The Eastern Association was founded in 1881, but this was another loose alliance with no set schedule.

The first recognized minor league was another Northwestern League, this one organized on October 27, 1882. At that time they requested of the National League cooperation and reciprocity in protecting player contracts. This was necessary because independent clubs frequently lost their best players during the course of the season to the National League and later to the American Association clubs. In response to this request, the National League, American Association, and Northwestern League signed a "Tripartite Agreement" in March 1883. This agreement bound the clubs to honor the contracts of players on reserve lists, assured mutual recognition of expulsions and suspensions, established territorial rights, and created an arbitration committee to settle disputes. Minimum salaries were established and pegged at a higher level in the National League and American Association than in the Northwestern League or "any other parties to the agreement," thus by implication assigning a "major" and "minor" status to the leagues.

The Interstate Association was established early in 1883 and was quickly accepted as an "alliance" league by the American Association, becoming a junior partner of the Tripartite Agreement. Both the Northwestern and the Interstate opened their seasons on May 1, 1883. Each had a formal league organization, a schedule that was preset before the season opening, and a complement of umpires appointed and paid for by the league. Both leagues recognized and accepted their status as subordinate to the two "majors." In 1884 the Interstate Association reorganized as the Eastern League and became a fourth member of what now became known as the National Agreement.

In October 1885 a new National Agreement was adopted which made the National League and American Association the principal parties and removed from minor league clubs the protection of the reserve clause. Two years later the reserve clause was reinstated for the minors, but the major-minor league distinction had been formalized. Following the collapse of the American Association in 1892, another National Agreement for the first time established minor league classifications and gave major league clubs the right to draft minor league players at fixed prices.

While these events were taking place, organized baseball expanded dramatically, going from two minor leagues in 1883 to 17 by 1888. Baseball was played throughout the country, of course, but organized ball was confined to the northeast quadrant of the United States in 1884; it expanded to the South in 1885, to Colorado and the upper Midwest in 1886, California in 1887, Texas in 1888, and the Pacific Northwest in 1890. So in the year that the American frontier was officially declared closed, organized baseball had extended to all corners of the country.

In 1887 an organization called the Negro Baseball League, fearing player raids by the still moderately integrated minors, sought and received protection under the National Agreement. The league was to play in eight cities that also had major league teams, but it folded in less than two weeks. This was unfortunately characteristic of the era. Many teams and leagues were underfinanced and were ultrasensitive to changes in the national or local economy. In addition, being unable or unwilling to pay the required fees for reserving their players, they lost their better ones at the close of the season—and those teams that even managed to finish the season could usually consider themselves lucky. During the 19th century, more than 40 percent of the leagues that started a season failed to finish it. There was, however, a solid core of support for minor league baseball. Regardless of how many leagues started each season—usually about 15 but often as many as 20—only eight to 10 usually finished; the rest failed. The 1890s were not a period of expansion nor of stability as throughout the decade nearly half of the leagues that started a season failed to finish it. A depression in 1893 and the Spanish-American War in 1898 were significant factors, but a proliferation of "fly-by-night" operators played a role as well.

At the close of the 1900 season, the still minor American League withdrew from the National Agreement, announcing through that action its intention not to allow its players to be drafted and not to respect the reserve clause or territorial rights any longer.

In September 1901 the National League announced its intention to abrogate the National Agreement, contending that with the American League invading its cities and raiding its players the National League could not be expected to sit back and abide by restrictions which did not hinder its rival. Essentially this meant that the National, like the American, considered the players on minor league rosters "fair game."

In immediate reaction to this, the presidents of seven minor leagues met in Chicago on September 5, 1901, and in an act of self-protection they organized the National Association of Professional Baseball Leagues. On October 25 representatives of nine minor leagues met in New York and adopted a new "National Agreement." This new agreement established league classifications, roster and salary limits, and a draft system; it recognized reserve lists and created a Board of Arbitration which was given the power to suspend players, clubs, or officials for violations of the agreement. By the beginning of the 1902 season, the National Association included 15 member leagues.

The American and National Leagues ratified a peace agreement early in 1903, and in late August the presidents of the two major leagues and the National Association drafted a National Agreement which was initially rejected by the minors. After some concessions were made by the majors, such as a prohibition on "farming," the plan was adopted in September. The agreement formalized relations between the majors and minors and established a National Commission to serve as a Board of Arbitration.

These agreements were necessary because the majors and minors were mutually dependent on each other. The majors needed the minors as a reliable source of talent, while the minors, many of whom relied on player sales to stay in business, needed assurances from the majors that they would recognize their property rights in players.

Despite this mutual dependence there was a basic buyer-seller conflict. The majors wanted to acquire players as cheaply as possible, while the minors wanted to sell them for as much as possible. This same conflict existed within the minors as well, with the highest-classification clubs wanting to buy cheaply from the lower minors and sell at high prices to the majors. Thus the National Agreement, the major-minor agreement, and the National Association itself were uneasy alliances of clubs and leagues with competing and often conflicting objectives. Nearly annual revisions in draft rules and prices and limits on optional player assignments were required to maintain the equilibrium necessary to keep the alliance intact.

The majors favored an unlimited draft—i.e., any player on a minor league roster could be purchased for a fixed rate. As early as 1896, when Minneapolis of the Western League was decimated through what were in effect forced sales, it became clear that some limitations were necessary, so by 1905 only one player could be drafted from a club per year. The draft prices of top-classification minor leaguers went from $750 to $1,000 in 1905 and then to $2,500 in 1911. While these prices were not particularly low for average prospects in that era, they were well below the value of the best prospects in the minors; thus the draft or the threat of it served as an incentive for minor league clubs at all levels to sell their better players to major or higher-classification minor league clubs at competitive market prices. From the players' standpoint, the draft had the positive effect of allowing them eventually to advance to whatever levels their ability would take them. The lower-classification minor league clubs received lower draft prices for their players but seemed relatively satisfied with the system—after all, this was an era when the contracts of Tris Speaker, Rogers Hornsby, and Ty Cobb were sold to major league clubs for $400, $500, and $700, respectively.

On the other hand, many of the higher-classification minor league clubs had never really been satisfied with the draft. As early as 1908, this dissatisfaction nearly caused the two top minor leagues at that time—the American Association and the Eastern League—to go independent. Several of the top minor league clubs drew more fans annually than some major league clubs and represented substantial investments. As a result these owners were understandably not happy with a system that forced the sale of their top players for below-market prices to the majors; in addition to the challenge to club stability and autonomy caused by the draft, the gap between the market value of the top prospects and the draft price widened throughout the 1910s.

Despite the rumblings of discontent, the establishment of the National Association ushered in a period of minor league expansion to a fairly stable core of 30 leagues. While there were still leagues that failed to finish the season, the failure rate was down to 10–15 percent. For some reason, in 1910 the minors reached a level never to be topped until the post–World War II boom era—52 leagues started the season and 44 finished it. For the next five years more leagues folded, but each season generally closed with 40 leagues operating. Then, for reasons that ranged from the automobile, movies, the war in Europe, and the Federal League War, the bottom started to drop out. Forty-three leagues started in the 1914 season, and by the end of the 1918 season only one was operating (10 leagues had started that year—one folded and eight suspended operations due to the war).

After the 1918 season, with most of the lower minors driven out of business, the National Association, for the first time dominated by the higher minors, adopted a resolution demanding that the majors relinquish the right of the draft and end the practice of "farming out" players. When the majors rejected these demands, the National Association withdrew from the National Agreement. Pending a new major agreement, the majors and minors reached general agreement on property rights in players and territorial rights, and the National Commission ruled that the major league draft would be suspended.

In addition the minor leagues would not accept major league players on option, meaning that any players owned or controlled by major league clubs in excess of the active player roster limit would have to be sold or released to minor league clubs. A. R. Tierney, president of two minor leagues and a leader in the fight to end the draft, said, "This means that the minor leagues will be able to build fences for themselves instead of for the major leagues." He predicted expansion of the minors and higher sale prices for the players. He was correct on both counts. With no players on option, the majors needed to buy more players from the minors, some of whom they had been forced to sell but now had to buy back at higher prices, and without the draft the minor league clubs could virtually name their own price. The minors expanded, as the leagues that had been driven out of business during the war now reentered the fold.

A Minor Resurgence

The reappearance of the low minors again shifted the balance of power within the minors. The higher minors had never been happy with the one-league, one-vote system in the National Association. Club owners were wary of having their investments affected by the vote of what they perceived as little more than "fly-by-night" operators, and on occasion they tried to change the arrangement. But just as the majors needed the minors, so the high minors needed the low minors. Thus the high minors always stopped short of enacting any measures that might drive their underlings out of the National Association.

As noted previously, many of the low minors needed the revenues they received from the draft to survive. Although the minor league draft still existed, it had ceased to be a dependable source of revenue as the combination of numerous prewar minor league failures and returning military veterans yielded more than enough talent to fill the higher minors' rosters. In addition, many of the low-minor clubs did not have the resources to scout for and sign enough players to remain competitive on the field and/or at the box office; thus they were dependent on receiving some players on option.

So while most of the higher minor leagues were prospering as never before under the new independence, by 1920 the low minors were ready to withdraw from the National Association if a new agreement with the majors restoring the draft was not adopted. In addition, some of the higher minor league clubs were upset that the "no-farming" rules were being circumvented by "gentleman's agreements." These agreements enabled the major league clubs to "sell" a player to a minor league club and "buy" him back at the end of the season with little or no money actually changing hands.

On January 10, 1921, a new major-minor league agreement was signed. The new pact restored the major league draft with a top price of $5,000 but as a compromise gave individual minor leagues the right to be exempt from the draft; in addition major league clubs could option up to eight players for no more than two consecutive years, and a tax on player sales was instituted to help reduce the fake player transfers. Quickly the top three minors—the International League, Pacific Coast League, and the American Association—together with the Western and Three-I Leagues declared their exemption from the draft; this in turn prohibited them from drafting from the lower minors.

The prices the majors paid for top minor league players nearly doubled between 1919 and 1920, but they skyrocketed during the draft-exemption era. In 1921 the Giants paid $75,000 to San Francisco for Jimmy O'Connell; in 1922 the Giants paid $72,000 to Baltimore for Jack Bentley and the White Sox paid $100,000 to San Francisco for Willie Kamm. The majors clearly were not happy with this situation, and in 1922 they offered to raise the draft price to $7,500, but this failed to lure back the draft-exempt leagues. In early 1923 the majors, after considering but eventually rejecting the idea of a maximum purchase price of $25,000 for any minor league player and/or a boycott of draft-exempt leagues, declared that all players sent to the minors either by sale or option would be subject to the draft. The number of players who could be optioned was increased to 15. Western League clubs immediately began accepting players on option under these conditions.

The prices for ballplayers remained high in 1923. Baltimore of the International League was reportedly offered $100,000 by Brooklyn for Joe Boley and sold Max Bishop to the Philadelphia A's for $50,000. Salt Lake sold Paul Strand to the A's for a reported $70,000, Louisville sold Earle Combs to the Yankees for $50,000, Toronto sold Red Wingo to the Tigers for $50,000 and Rochester sold Maurice Archdeacon to the White Sox for $50,000, but these were isolated cases. Baltimore, aided by five years of draft exemption, had built a powerhouse, but many of the higher-classification minor league clubs had not been nearly as successful and found that they needed to receive players on option to fill holes and remain competitive. Therefore at the close of the 1923 season all exempt leagues but the International agreed to the modified draft which exempted only those players who had come up through the minors. In 1924, after Baltimore sold Lefty Grove to the A's for $100,000, the International League also fell into line.

The modified draft did nothing to reduce the prices paid for top minor league stars: Louisville sold Wayland Dean to the Giants for $72,000 in 1924, San Francisco sold Paul Waner and Hal Rhyne to Pittsburgh for $100,000 in 1925, and Baltimore continued selling star players to the majors for big prices—Tommy Thomas to the White Sox in 1925, Joe Boley to the A's in 1926, John Ogden to the Browns and George Earnshaw to the A's in 1927. Also in 1927 Portland (of the PCL) sold Billy Cissel to the White Sox for a package of cash and players worth over $100,000 and Oakland sold Lyn Lary and Jimmy Reese to the Yankees for $100,000. With prices like these, clubs could afford to lose an occasional Lefty O'Doul or Hack Wilson in the modified draft.

The major-minor agreement expired at the end of the 1927 season, with the National Association members deadlocked on the issue of the draft. The majors and minors were also at an impasse, so the modified draft continued and many of the higher minor league clubs continued to prosper, both through player sales and at the gate. The Pacific Coast League's Los Angeles franchise and ballpark were valued at $2 million, but in the lower minors all was not well through the 1920s. Leagues were operating that never should have been admitted to the National Association—for example, the West Arkansas, which operated in 1924, was comprised of six towns within a 750-square-mile area that had a combined population of 16,000 and played just a 60-game schedule.

In 1929 the rift between the high and low minors widened as the low minors, rebuffed in their efforts to nullify the modified draft agreement, now attempted to impose their own draft exemption—essentially exempting from the draft any player with fewer than two seasons of organized baseball.

Early in 1931 the majors and minors finally adopted a new National Agreement, including a provision which eliminated the modified draft and granted to major league clubs greater control of talent through revised option and draft rules. The higher minors had originally objected, but the majors told them to accept the universal draft or they would no longer have any relations with them. In other words, major league teams would not sell or option players to or buy players from the American Association, the International League, or the Pacific Coast League. While such threats had been taken relatively lightly by the minors in the early days of the draft-exempt leagues, they were now taken seriously enough that in less than a month the three recalcitrant leagues capitulated to the majors' terms. In exchange for all this and largely to secure the support of the low minors, the majors agreed to sign only collegian amateurs, leaving all high-schoolers and sandlotters to the minors. Of course, by this time farm systems had developed to the point that most major league clubs could still sign noncollegian amateurs through their farm clubs.

Milwaukee had sold Fred Schulte to the Browns for a reported $100,000 in 1928, but this was the end of an era. There would be no more $100,000 minor leaguers; in fact there would be few if any minor leaguers sold for as much as $50,000 again. At the 1928 National Association Convention, president Mike Sexton wondered when the majors would own enough clubs to control the National Association. The farm system, an old idea now in the process of being perfected by Branch Rickey, had clearly begun to alter the way the minors operated, and despite the efforts of some—most notably Judge Landis—the trend couldn't be reversed.

The Great Depression caused a contraction of the minors in the early 1930s, but even though a near-record low of 14 leagues opened the 1933 season, none of them folded. The minors then entered an era of unprecedented growth and stability, reaching 44 leagues in 1940, with only two leagues failing to finish the season between 1933 and 1941. This can be attributed in part to the substantial involvement of the major leagues through outright ownership or regular infusions of money through working agreements, but there were obviously other factors at work. Judge Bramham, on becoming president of the National Association, instituted a number of reforms, many of which were aimed at getting rid of "fly-by-night" or "shoestring" operators. Minor league baseball was better promoted—they had established a public relations department in 1934—and the advent of night baseball was of incalculable value in generating attendance, which reached 20 million in 1940. Interestingly, that year 54 percent of the minor league clubs were not affiliated with any major league clubs compared to just 37 percent that operated independently in 1936.

World War II caused the minors to drop to just 10 leagues in 1944, but in the first postwar year it was up to 43, increasing to an all-time high of 59 in 1949, and during that time no leagues folded. (In 1946 the Mexican National League, set up by organized baseball to compete with the outlaw Mexican League, is listed by the National Association as having folded during the season, but actually it only withdrew from the association and continued to operate independently.)

According to a general consensus, it was the coming of television that caused the minors to begin to disintegrate. Between 1949 and 1963 the number of minor leagues dropped from 59 to 18. Attendance decreased even more sharply, going from 40 million to less than 10 million over the same time period.

By 1963 the minors had become nothing more than a training ground for the majors—90 percent of the clubs were major league affiliates, and most of those that weren't affiliates were in the largely autonomous Mexican League. While television was commonly cited as the cause of the minors' contraction, some contended it was a natural response to overexpansion. Gerry Hirn, in an April 1954 *Baseball Digest* article, contended that while the number of minor leagues had dropped from 59 to 36, that was still too many and the minors would be stronger and more efficient if only 16 to 20 leagues operated. Interestingly, in 1954 three leagues failed to finish the season, the most failures in peacetime since 1932; they remain the last United States–based minor leagues that failed to finish a season (the Inter-American League, which had a team in Miami but was largely based in the Caribbean, failed to finish the 1979 season—the only year it operated).

An Unexpected But Welcome Boom

For reasons that aren't entirely clear, minor league baseball exploded in popularity in the 1980s. Attendance, which had remained stuck at 10–11 million through the 1960s and most of the 1970s, took off in the late 1970s, topping 20 million in 1987 for the first time since 1953. Louisville, which dropped out of organized ball after drawing just 116,000 in 1972, topped a million in 1983. Nashville, which dropped out in 1963 after drawing just 54,000 for the season, drew over half a million in 1980. Buffalo, which drew only 78,000 in 1969 and saw its franchise shifted to Winnipeg the following year, came back to set an all-time minor league attendance record with 1.1 million in 1988. The Louisville franchise, which didn't exist in 1981 (what became the Louisville franchise was at that time in Springfield, Illinois, drawing 120,000), sold for more than $4 million in 1987. In 1990 the far less successful Vancouver franchise sold to Japanese interests for $5.5 million. Minor league franchises that could be picked up in the early 1970s by anyone who would pay the outstanding debts were suddenly selling for several million dollars.

The high prices being paid for franchises may have precipitated the major-minor-league crisis of 1990, reminiscent of the battles earlier in the century. The Professional Baseball Agreement that binds the majors and minors was set to expire at the end of 1990. The majors, who under that agreement provided substantial financial support for the minors, proposed a reduction in those subsidies. The majors believed that the now financially healthy minor league clubs should assume a greater share of operational expenses.

In addition, the majors wanted the Commissioner's office to have greater control over minor league affairs. The minors felt the majors were trying to usurp their autonomy and, to add injury to insult, charge them for the privilege. If there was no agreement, the majors threatened to place their entire farm systems in spring training complexes in Arizona and Florida. Some minor league operators threatened to go independent and even form a third major league.

In the end, however, the majority of minor league clubs capitulated, believing that they could not afford to operate without players supplied by the major league clubs. The majors would still pick up most of the minor league operators' expenses, but the new agreement (a) eliminated the minors' share of big-league TV revenue, (b) required that the minors pay a share of their ticket revenues to the majors, and (c) established minimum standards that must be met by minor league facilities by 1994 (subsequently extended to 1995).

It was generally believed that these changes, by reducing minor league clubs' profits, might stabilize or reduce the value of franchises. However, in 1992 the Las Vegas franchise sold for a record $7 million and some unsuccessful Class A franchises were sold for well over $1 million each. And the fans kept coming—in 1993 minor league attendance topped 30 million for the first time since 1950, and in 1993 Buffalo went over 1 million in attendance for the sixth consecutive year. In 1994 the Bisons just missed a seventh million-fan season due to two rainouts. In 1998 minor league attendance went over the 35 million mark for the first time since 1949 (with 200 fewer clubs).

The positive trend of the past 20 years is unprecedented, but the minors have been riding a rollercoaster of success and failure over the past century—the Newark franchise which sold for a reported $600,000 during the depths of the Depression didn't even exist 20 years later. Even today the picture is not all positive: between 1987 and 1996 nearly 60 franchises were shifted, usually due to poor attendance. In the past few years these shifts have fueled large attendance increases as teams have moved from "dead" towns to virgin territories with spanking new state-of-the-art facilities. To illustrate this, from 1999 to 2000 attendance in the new U.S.-based leagues increased 1,854,000—better than 90 percent of which can be attributed to three franchise shifts: Vancouver to Sacramento; Jackson, Mississippi, to Round Rock, Texas; and Rockford, Illinois, to Dayton, Ohio. New parks in Louisville, Memphis, Chattanooga, and Knoxville contributed another 995,000 increase, so the combined attendance of all the remaining clubs was down 840,000.

The supply of new towns with new ballparks seems to be diminishing and the big success stories of the 1980s have seen their attendance decline. In 1999 Buffalo still drew a robust 684,000 to lead the minors for the 12th straight year but that was down nearly 440,000 from 1992; Louisville, once over a million, dropped to 361,000 in 1999, but demonstrating the value of a new ballpark saw their attendance climb to 686,000 in 2000. Some clubs still draw less than 1,000 fans per game; and it is generally believed that many clubs still substantially pad their attendance totals. So the current wave of success is somewhat deceptive and history tells us it won't last forever. However, regardless of fluctuations in popularity and economic viability, the minors have been and one can safely assume will continue to be the primary training ground for major league players.

The Players

Great players have passed through the minors, their careers frequently going in opposite directions and occasionally teaming up or crossing in unlikely locations. In 1924 in Easton, Maryland, Jimmie Foxx broke into organized baseball as a catcher on a team run by player-manager Frank "Home Run" Baker in his last season as an active player. There were many others: Rube Waddell and Red Faber with Minneapolis in 1911, young Waite Hoyt and ancient Jesse Burkett with Hartford in 1916, Dazzy Vance and Roger Bresnahan with Toledo in 1917, Chief Bender and Lefty Grove with Baltimore in 1923, and more recently Enos Slaughter and Billy Williams with Houston in 1960, and the unlikely battery of Satchel Paige and Johnny Bench for one game with Peninsula in 1966.

Two former Negro Leaguers, their careers going in opposite directions, Ray Dandridge and Willie Mays were teammates at Minneapolis in 1951 where another teammate was a seven-year minor league veteran, Hoyt Wilhelm. Wilhelm, a 28-year-old knuckleballer with a background that included three years in Class D ball and three more in the military service, at that time appeared to be a member of what in that era was a vast army of career minor leaguers, the best of whom held their own with the acknowledged major league greats passing through the minors, but who for a variety of reasons—some good, some not—would themselves spend the bulk of their careers in the minors.

For some of these players who were left behind, the designated hitter rule came 50 years too late, because while they could hit both for average and power, they generally lacked speed or had defensive shortcomings. For others it is less clear what, if any, deficiencies kept them in the minors, but from these groups a few players emerged as true minor league greats whose impact on fans in minor league cities—Buzz Arlett in Oakland, Joe Hauser in Minneapolis, and Bunny Brief in Kansas City, to name a few—was as great as that of more renowned players in major league cities.

The greatest of the minor league players is generally acknowledged to be Buzz Arlett.

Arlett started his career as a righthanded spitball pitcher with the hometown Oakland Oaks in 1918 and went on to win 108 games, twice going over 25 wins in a season. The Detroit Tigers looked at him, but without the spitball, which he wouldn't be able to use in the majors, they did not consider him a prospect. After suffering arm trouble early in 1923, Buzz switched to the outfield. Although he had been nothing more than a fair-hitting pitcher, once Arlett became a regular he annually averaged nearly .360 with 30 homers and 140 RBIs through the rest of the 1920s in the minor leagues.

Early in his career as an outfielder a Cardinals scout labeled him "good hit, no field," and it stuck. Finally in 1931 he was purchased by the Phillies. The 32-year-old switch-hitter batted .313 with 18 homers and 73 RBIs in a season when the National League introduced a "dead ball" in reaction to the hitting orgies of 1929–1930. However, at the end of the year Arlett was sent to Baltimore, where in 1932 he hit four home runs in a game twice within a five-week period and he led the league with 54 homers for the season, but he would never return to the majors. He spent another year with Baltimore, when he again won the home run title, a little over a month with Birmingham, and nearly three years with Minneapolis, where he had another home run championship. After a few games with Syracuse in 1937, Arlett's remarkable career was over.

In addition to his 108 wins, he hit 432 homers, a minor league record that held up until Hector Espino topped it in 1977. Arlett walked a lot, didn't strike out much, ran pretty well early in his career, had a .341 lifetime batting average—.350 after he became an outfielder—and was the only player to finish in the top five in home runs and slugging percentage in his only season in the majors. In addition, modern statistical analysis, including range factors, suggests he was nowhere near the defensive liability he was portrayed as being. He was big (6 feet 4 inches, 230) and gave the appearance of being lackadaisical, which apparently irritated some of his managers, but the evidence is strong that Arlett, despite nearly two decades spent in the minors, was a major league-caliber player.

Ike Boone was another player whose hitting feats were not limited to the minors. Boone was a college teammate (at the University of Alabama) of Joe Sewell and Riggs Stephenson; his lifetime major league batting average was .321, and in his only two full seasons in the majors—1924-1925 with the Boston Red Sox—he hit .337 and .330. Yet due to alleged defensive deficiencies most of his career was spent in the minors.

In 1929 with the Missions of San Francisco, Boone probably had the finest season any player has had in the minors. On the all-time minor league list of single-season accomplishments, his 553 total bases that year are first, his 323 hits are second, his 195 runs scored are tied for third, and his 218 RBIs are fourth. On the all-time Pacific Coast League list, his .407 average is second, and his 55 home runs are tied for fourth.

Boone's greatness wasn't confined to a single season; in four of his first eight years in the minors he hit over .400 (he was on his way to perhaps his greatest season in 1930, batting .448 with 22 homers and 96 RBIs when he was sold to Brooklyn in late June). His .402 average with San Antonio in 1923 is the highest in 20th-century Texas League history; his .389 with New Orleans in 1921 is the fifth highest in the Southern Association; he also led the International League in batting twice. His .370 lifetime average is the minor league record for players with ten or more seasons. He had an exceptional arm, but limited range in the outfield. Although he hit 77 home runs in a season and a half with the Missions, he was not generally regarded as a power hitter. He was, however, a great pure hitter; in 11 of his 14 seasons in the minors, he hit over .350, but while he hit very well in his two full seasons in the majors, it has been suggested he had a pronounced hitch in his swing—a weakness major league pitchers were able to exploit.

Smead Jolley was an atrocious outfielder. Stories of his defensive lapses are legion, and the statistical evidence suggests those stories are more than isolated anecdotes. Like Boone, Jolley had a powerful arm but no speed; like Arlett, he was big and awkward; and like both, he could hit—majors or minors. In the equivalent of three full major league seasons with the White Sox and Red Sox, he hit .305 and averaged 15 homers and 105 RBIs. He won six minor league batting championships—leading the Pacific Coast League in hitting three times (winning the Triple Crown with San Francisco in 1928) and the International League once. Twice he had over 300 hits in a season, and twice he drove in more than 180 runs. In the 13 minor league seasons in which he played over 100 games, he had this run: .370, .372, .346, .397, .404, .387, .360, .372, .373, .350, .309, .373, .345. Perhaps because he spent nearly six years in the low minors, the first four as a pitcher, and had a somewhat nomadic career (he was with 13 minor league teams), he has not always been ranked in the top echelon of minor league greats, yet he may have been the finest hitter of them all.

Minor league stars generally fit two stereotypes: one-dimensional players who could hit but could do nothing else well enough to stay in the majors—justly or not, Arlett, Boone, and Jolley were consigned to this group. Then there are those who excelled in the minors but couldn't produce in the majors. Perhaps the classic example is Bunny Brief.

Brief, born Antonio Bordetski, may have been the most dominant power hitter in the minor leagues. In major league trials with the Browns, White Sox, and Pirates between 1912 and 1917, he was consistently unimpressive—in a combined 569 at bats, he hit .223 with five homers, 59 RBIs, and nearly 100 strikeouts. In the minors, however, it was a different story. Although he hit 40 or more homers only twice and never had more than 42, he had eight league home run championships. Before going up to the majors, he led the Michigan State League twice; later he led the Pacific Coast League once and the American Association five times. He also led the Association in RBIs five times (four in succession), including a league-record 191 in 1921. He had a six-year stretch (1921–1926) with Kansas City and Milwaukee, where he averaged 90 extra-base hits, 151 RBIs, and a .351 average per season. Brief also drew a lot of walks. Early in his career he had excellent speed, and although he played most of his career at first base, he was the best defensive outfielder of the big minor league sluggers, with good range and an excellent arm. Still, for reasons that remain unclear, Brief never played in a major league game after his 25th birthday.

Nick Cullop was another minor league great who never produced in the majors. He, like many of the great minor league sluggers, began his career as a pitcher. In trials with the Yankees, Senators, Indians, Dodgers, and Reds between 1926 and 1931 he totaled 490 at bats, hit 11 homers, drove in 67 runs, hit .249, and struck out 128 times. He was the first farm-system minor league star, playing 1,450 games in the Cardinals chain from 1932 to 1944. In the minors, he hit 420 home runs and drove in

1,857 runs, 10 times exceeding 100 in a season.

Cullop had good speed early in his career and was a good enough outfielder to play center field into the late 1920s, but he slowed up considerably in the 1930s. While it is not clear why Brief never did well in the majors, Cullop struck out a lot even in the minors and didn't walk much—suggesting that he had holes which could be and were pitched to effectively in the majors.

Ox Eckhardt was a great football star at the University of Texas who after graduation signed with both Austin of the Texas Association and the Cleveland Indians. The resulting dispute delayed his real professional debut for three years until he was 26 years old. Ox quickly made up for lost time, hitting .376 with a league leading 27 triples for Wichita and Amarillo in the Western League in 1928. That fall he played for the New York Giants of the NFL. His baseball contract had been acquired by the Detroit Tigers and although he was on their 40-man roster in 1929, 1930, and 1931 he never got into a game with the big club. In 1929 he was sent to Seattle, where he hit .354 and again led the league in triples. In 1930 he went to Beaumont, where he led the Texas League with a .379 average. In 1931 he was sold to the Missions, for whom he led the PCL with a .369 average. In the spring of 1932 he was with the Boston Braves—he played eight games at the start of the season as a pinch hitter and was then sent back to the Missions, where over the next four seasons he hit .371, .414, .378, and .399, winning the batting title three times. He went to the Dodgers in 1936, lasted 16 games batting just .182, and was sent to Indianapolis, where he hit .353 and .341 over the next two years. He hit .321 with Toledo and Beaumont in 1938, .361 with Memphis in 1939, and after hitting .293 with Dallas in 1940, he retired with a minor league career batting average of .367 and the highest career average in organized baseball—.365. (Ty Cobb's minor league record drops his overall average to .3630; Ike Boone's major league record drops his organized-baseball average to .3629.) Eckhardt has the highest single-season and career batting average in the PCL, and 10 times he hit over .350.

Unlike many of the minor league stars, Eckhardt did not want for opportunities to play in the majors—counting a trial with the Indians in 1925, he had six shots, but they resulted in his playing in just 24 major league games. The reasons for his failure to make it in the majors are not obscure. Despite being an exceptional athlete with good speed early in his career, he was a poor fielder with a weak arm and no power. Reportedly managers tried to get him to pull the ball—an idea that should certainly have advanced his career in Detroit or Brooklyn—but it only served to foul up his swing, which he would rediscover after being returned to the minors.

A few minor league greats don't fit the stereotypes: Jigger Statz was the opposite of most—his strengths were speed and defense. Joe Hauser appeared to be on his way to a successful career in the majors, but he broke his leg, never regained his past form, and went to the minors, where he became the only player to have two 60-home run seasons. Hector Espino spent virtually his entire career in Mexico, and while major league scouts believed he could hit in the majors, he apparently had no desire to leave his homeland.

Of the great minor league stars, Statz spent the most time in the majors—683 games—and the most time with one club: all of his 18 minor league seasons were with Los Angeles. His 3,473 games in organized baseball were a record until broken by Hank Aaron in 1976.

Statz was a great fielder; virtually all of his contemporaries considered him the best or one of the best they had seen. Playing very shallow, he reminded many of Tris Speaker. The statistics offer strong support for his claim to greatness. In four full seasons in the majors, he led the league in chances-per-game once and was second the other three years. Between 1922 and 1932 in the majors and minors he had a stretch of 10 seasons in which he played in at least 100 games and never finished lower than second in chances-per-game. He had excellent speed, but during most of his career with the Angels they were a hard-hitting club that did not feature the running game, but that changed in the mid-1930s, and in the three seasons following his 36th birthday he stole 157 bases. His game was not just limited to speed and defense. A classic leadoff man of his era—a good contact hitter, small and fast—he hit .285 in the majors and .315 in the minors, collecting over 2,300 runs, 4,000 hits, 700 doubles, and 500 stolen bases in his organized-baseball career.

On April 7, 1925, the day of Babe Ruth's "big bellyache," Joe Hauser, a 26-year-old first baseman beginning his fourth season with the Athletics, broke his leg in a non-contact play while fielding during a preseason game against the Phillies at Baker Bowl. He had a .304 average for his first three major league seasons and had hit 27 homers with 115 RBIs in 1924. The injury kept him out for the entire 1925 season. In 1926 he tried to come back but hit only .192. After an excellent season with Kansas City, he went back to the majors but didn't do much in stints with the Philadelphia A's and Indians. Back in the minors, however, he was nothing short of remarkable. In 1930 with Baltimore he set a professional record with 63 homers; then he dropped to 31 in 1931 but still led the league. In 1932 he went to Minneapolis, where he led the American Association in homers with 49. In 1933 he broke his own home run record with 69, and he was off to a great start in 1934—33 homers, 88 RBIs in 82 games—when he broke his kneecap, knocking him out for the season. He continued to play until 1942 but never came close to achieving the success he had in the early 1930s.

Hauser did not hit for a high average, and it has been suggested that he took enormous advantage of short right field fences in Baltimore and Minneapolis—no one would argue that point, since 50 of his 69 homers in 1933 came at home. Yet many greats played in Oriole and Nicollet Parks, and none came close to Hauser's two record-breaking seasons, which remain the two highest home run seasons in the high minors.

Hector Espino holds the minor league career home run record with 484, and all but three of those were hit in Mexico. At the end of the 1964 Mexican League season, the 25-year-old first baseman, who had led the league with 46 homers and a .371 batting average, was sold by Monterrey to the St. Louis Cardinals' Jacksonville farm club. He hit .300 with those three home runs in 100 at bats and was invited to spring training by the Cards for 1965, but he never reported and was eventually returned to Monterrey. In the late 1960s the California Angels coveted Espino, who had led the Mexican League in hitting from 1966 to 1968, but they were never able to consummate a deal. Espino was a legend in Mexico, but it has never been clear why he didn't try the majors—he gave conflicting answers. Possibly he enjoyed being a big fish in a small pond—it wasn't the money, since he never made more than $18,000 a year in Mexico. He was notorious for marching to his own drummer, occasionally leaving clubs for a midseason vacation, and perhaps he was unwilling to sacrifice that independence.

Espino could hit for power and average—he led the Mexican League in batting five times and home runs four times—and scouts said he could have done the same in the majors, but like many players he played too long. His power started a sharp decline after his 33rd birthday, and he was virtually helpless at the plate during his last two or three seasons. Nevertheless he ranks as perhaps the greatest minor league player who never played in the majors.

Great players do not have to be distributed evenly among all positions or across all eras, but the emphasis being on great hitters, the result is a number of outfielder-first baseman-designated hitter types, most of whom played in the high-scoring 1920s and 1930s.

Ray French was perhaps the best middle infielder in the minors. He spent 28 years in the minors, most of it in the Pacific Coast League. He played 2,736 games at shortstop and was a brilliant fielder. In the 14 seasons that he played more than 100 games at short, he led the league in chances-per-game seven times. He was not an outstanding hitter, but his fielding kept him around long enough for him to collect 3,255 hits—seventh on the all-time minor league list.

The two best 19th-century minor leaguers were first baseman Perry Werden and pitcher Willie Mains. Werden had good speed and power. He had several good years in the majors (twice leading the league in triples), won six minor league home run titles, including two seasons when he went over 40, and his .341 lifetime average was exceptionally high for that era.

Mains was the first minor league pitcher to win 300 games, reaching that figure early in 1905. A seven-time 20-game winner, he was also an excellent hitter in an era when pitchers were frequently expected to take a shift in the outfield. Most of his career was in the New York State League, but in an interesting example of the mobility of players even in the game's early years, in 1892–1893 Mains had back-to-back seasons in Portland, Oregon, and Portland, Maine.

A highly productive but not great player who deserves mention is Spencer Harris, a little lefthanded-hitting outfielder who holds the minor league career records for runs, hits, doubles, total bases, and walks. He reached those levels primarily because he kept playing until he was 48 years old. He did lead the American Association in homers in 1928 while at Minneapolis, but he was aided enormously by the friendly right field fence at Nicollet Park. (He averaged 17 homers a year in 10 seasons with Minneapolis but only six per year in his 16 other minor league seasons.)

He was never thought of as the top player on his many minor league clubs—just as a good solid player of the type that formed the backbone of the minors for so many years.

The Pitchers

There have been few minor league pitching stars of the magnitude of the great hitters. Perhaps this is because pitching is a one-dimensional skill—no pitchers were kept in the minors because they couldn't hit or field. Many of the outstanding minor league pitchers stayed there because they didn't have great stuff. Bill Thomas, who won 383 games, and Hal Turpin, who won 271 without ever getting shots at the majors, had the same statistical profile—they struck out few, walked even less, and allowed a lot of hits.

Two pitchers that didn't fit that profile, however, were Joe Martina and Dick Barrett. Martina was a power pitcher who spent most of his career with Beaumont and with his hometown New Orleans Pelicans. He held the minor league career strikeout record until ageless George Brunet broke it while toiling in the Mexican League in 1981. Martina was a workhorse, pitching over 250 innings in 13 different seasons while winning 20 games seven times. He got his first and only big league opportunity at age 35 with the world champion Washington Senators in 1924.

"Kewpie" Dick Barrett didn't really find himself until he joined Seattle of the PCL in 1935, 10 years into his professional career. A little left hander with less than pinpoint control (he holds the minor league record for career bases on balls), he had good stuff and eight 20-win seasons.

Frank Shellenback is most frequently named as the greatest minor league pitcher. The Pacific Coast League career leader in wins with 295, Shellenback won nine games with the White Sox as a 19-year-old rookie spitballer in 1918. After a poor start the following season, he was sent to Minneapolis. In February 1920 the baseball rules committee outlawed the spitball and other trick pitches. Each major league team was allowed to designate two spitball pitchers who would be able to continue using the pitch in the majors. Unfortunately for Shellenback, he was on the Vernon roster by this time and at age 21 would be consigned forever to pitching in the minors if he couldn't get by without the spitball. Throughout much of his career, articles would be written that usually declared that Shellenback would be a major league star if he was eligible to play there. He did have a great six-year stretch with Hollywood (1928–1933) when he went 142–59. He was a very popular player with the Stars as well as Vernon and a fine hitter with good power, but a review of his record suggests he was never as good as everyone thought he was. He led the PCL in wins and won-loss percentage twice each but never led in another category. He had only five 20-win seasons.

Because of the spitball ban, Shellenback was viewed as a tragic figure, but he wasn't alone. Spitballer Paul Wachtel won 203 games in the Texas League after the ban, including five 20-win seasons. Rube Robinson won 148 games in the Southern Association, including two league-leading 26-win seasons. Wheeler Fuller, who never pitched in the majors, won 156 in the Eastern League after the ban.

Perhaps the greatest minor league pitcher was Tony Freitas, a little lefty who spent all or part of 15 seasons with Sacramento. He had great control, could get the strikeout, and had nine 20-win seasons (plus two 19-win seasons). If he hadn't lost three years to the military, he probably would have won 400 games in the minors. Freitas had an impressive major league debut, going 12–5 in less than a full season with the 1932 Philadelphia A's, but that was the last success he would have in the majors.

Four other pitchers worthy of mention are Sam Gibson, George Boehler, Bill Bailey, and George Brunet.

Gibson was an underappreciated pitcher who spent most of his career in the PCL, including 12 years with San Francisco. He didn't make his organized-baseball debut until he was 23 years old. After two promising seasons with Detroit, he never had much success in the majors, but he was extremely effective in the minors. He had six 20-win seasons (plus three 19-win seasons) and, pitching in a high-scoring era, he had eight seasons where his ERA was below 3.00.

Boehler was a hard-throwing workhorse who spent most of his career in the Western League. Twice he pitched over 400 innings, six times over 300. Unfortunately he was terribly inconsistent: with Tulsa from 1921-23 his season records were 4-20, 38-13, 7-9. He was consistently ineffective in a number of major league trials.

Bailey had seven league-leading strikeout seasons in four different leagues (International, Texas, Southern, Western), but only three 20-win seasons. After a promising September debut with the Browns in 1907, he pitched over 200 games in the majors with five teams spread over 15 years with no success.

Brunet pitched in organized ball for 33 years (1953-1985), and astonishingly he was a regular-rotation pitcher for all but the last year. When he was 48 years old, he had a 1.94 ERA pitching regularly in the Mexican League. He never won more than 17 games in a season, had only two 200-strikeout seasons (they were 21 years apart), but he had a credible major league career and holds the minor league career strikeout record.

The Teams

There have been a number of debates about the greatest minor league teams. The 1937 Newark Bears, the 1934 Los Angeles Angels, the 1920-1925 Ft. Worth Panthers, and the 1919-1925 Baltimore Orioles usually draw the most support. All were dominant teams with good players.

The Bears included Charlie Keller, Joe Gordon, George McQuinn, Atley Donald, and five other players who would go to the majors the following year. They won the International League pennant by 25½ games with a 109–41 record. The Angels included Frank Demaree, Jigger Statz, Gene Lillard, and Fay Thomas, and they compiled an astounding 137–50 record. The Panthers (or Cats) won six straight pennants and five Dixie Series. They were led by the home run hitting of Big Boy Kraft and a fine pitching staff that included spitballer Paul Wachtel and Joe Pate.

It is doubtful that any of the three could have competed successfully in the majors. It is occasionally claimed that the 1937 Newark Bears were the Yankees' B team and could have finished second in the American League, or at least in the first division. But that ignores the talent that was in the majors. The Red Sox finished fifth in 1937 with a club that included Jimmie Foxx, Joe Cronin, Lefty Grove, Pinky Higgins, Doc Cramer, Ben Chapman, Jack Wilson, and Bobo Newsom, all of whom, it is safe to say, would have started for the Bears. The same is true of the Angels, whose pitching staff chose 1934 to have career years, and of the Cats, who played well as a team but had few players that were even considered minor league standouts.

The Orioles were a different story. Thanks to the draft exemption, Jack Dunn was able to assemble a powerhouse comprised of players ready and capable of playing in the majors. The 1922 team was probably the best minor league club ever assembled. It had Jack Bentley, Max Bishop, Fritz Maisel, and Joe Boley in the infield, and Otis Lawry, Merwyn Jacobson, and Jimmy Walsh in the outfield. The catcher was Lena Styles, and the pitchers were Lefty Grove, John Ogden, Tommy Thomas, Rube Parnham, and Harry Frank with Bentley occasionally seeing action on the mound. Grove, Ogden, and Thomas combined for 60 wins and six years later would win a combined 56 games in the majors. Parnham, a free spirit who pitched when he wanted, was around long enough to win 16 (the following year he won 33). Frank won 22, but his career would soon be cut short by illness. Bentley hit .350 and won 13 games; he went to the Giants in 1923 as a pitcher but hit .427. Bishop and Boley, who hit .261 and .343 respectively, went on to become the double-play combo with the 1929-1930 world champion Philadelphia A's. Styles was just twenty-two years old and hit .315, but that was his peak. Maisel (.306), Walsh (.327), Jacobson (.304), and Lawry (.333) had all played briefly and/or ineffectively in the majors but would all go on to have great careers in the International League. A 20-year-old rookie utility player on the team was Dick Porter, who hit .279 and would have seven excellent seasons with the Orioles before going on to have several good years with the Indians.

As good as the Orioles were and as good as some of their players became, it is doubtful that even they could have finished in the first division of the American or National Leagues in 1922. Yet the strongest evidence of the attraction of minor league baseball and the hold it has long held on fans who were exposed to it is that those great Oriole, Bear, and Angel teams are far better known and more fondly remembered than hundreds of more talented second-division and higher major league clubs.

The Farm System

Farm teams are nearly as old as organized baseball. In 1884 the Boston Beaneaters of the National League owned a team called the Boston Reserves in the Massachusetts State Association. The Reserves, also called the Colts, were apparently intended to serve as a source of replacements for disabled members of the major league club. It has also been suggested that the farm team was a device to keep more players under contract and out of the hands of the Union Association that year. Whatever the origins of the idea, during the next decade a number of major league clubs operated such reserve teams, but they usually competed in local semipro leagues rather than in organized baseball and were viewed more as quick sources of replacements rather than as training grounds for players.

With John B. Day's joint ownership of the New York Gothams of the National League and the New York Metropolitans of the American Association as early as 1883 and with the proliferation of interlocking ownerships of major league clubs in the 1890s, it was only natural that some major and minor league clubs would come under joint ownership as well. The first instance of any significance, however, occurred when John T. Brush, owner of Cincinnati in the National League, entered the Indianapolis club in the newly formed Western League in 1894. While this was not the first case of joint major-minor league club ownership, Brush appears to have been the first to grasp the potential of such an arrangement. Indianapolis served as a place to develop talent that was not quite ready for the majors. The team gave Cincinnati an expanded roster as players were frequently shuffled to and from Indianapolis during the season. It also served as a source of profit because Indianapolis drew well at the gate, having become the dominant club in the Western League, with three pennants and two second-place finishes in five seasons (1895–1899). Indianapolis' success was aided in no small part by Brush's practice of drafting players from other Western League clubs and sending them to Indianapolis, thus simultaneously weakening the opposition and strengthening the Hoosiers. Efforts were made by the other Western League club owners to control "farming" or to modify the draft rules to stop Brush, but none were successful.

Perhaps copying Brush's strategy, in 1896 several National League clubs obtained minor league affiliates: Pittsburgh had Toronto, Boston had Wilkes-Barre, and Cleveland had Ft. Wayne. Philadelphia had a Philadelphia farm club in the Pennsylvania State League, and when that league folded, they shifted the junior club to the Atlantic Association. The New York Giants had the first farm "system," with the New York Mets in the Atlantic Association and Syracuse in the Eastern League.

When the National Agreement was adopted in 1903, it banned the "farming out" of players. Yet "farming" as defined in the agreement referred only to those efforts by major league clubs to exceed the limits on players who could be optioned through subterfuge—"fake transfers" such as loans or sell/buy-back arrangements with minor league clubs where title to a player was never surrendered.

The independent minor league operators saw farming as a curse for two reasons. First, it reduced their autonomy and potential revenue by placing more players under major league ownership, thus reducing the majors' need to buy or draft players from the minors. Second, clubs accepting players from the majors, either openly through options or secretly, might gain an unfair competitive advantage on the field. So while in 1905 the New York Giants' request to establish a working agreement with Bridgeport was validated by the National Commission, most of the legislation was focused on restricting farming, normally by limiting the number of players who could be optioned and the number of times each player could be optioned. For example, in 1904 a rule was adopted which required a player sent out on option to stay with the minor league club for the remainder of that season. In 1907 the rule was relaxed so that a major league club could option a player and recall him, but only once in a season. In 1911 a team could have no more than eight players out on option at one time.

Working agreements became quite common during this period. The major league club furnished the minor league club with its surplus players—youngsters in need of more experience or veterans past their prime who could still strengthen a minor league club—and/or cash. In return the major league club could obtain promising players from the minor league club. During this era the formal working agreement between major and minor league clubs was usually of short duration—a year or two at most—suggesting that major league clubs targeted certain minor league clubs that had two or three players they might be interested in and established a working agreement in order to get first claim on those that developed satisfactorily. There were also informal working agreements, generally based on friendships between major and minor league club operators, and it was usually through such arrangements that the "fake transfers" banned by the National Agreement took place. In the early 1900s there was substantial traffic in players between the White Sox and Milwaukee of the American Association and between the Dodgers and Baltimore in the Eastern League. (Brewers manager Joe Cantillon was a long-time friend of Charles Comiskey, and Brooklyn manager Ned Hanlon was also a minority owner of the Orioles.)

In the early teens E.S. Barnard, vice president and general manager of the Cleveland Indians (and future American League president), developed the first true farm system. Portland (PCL) became a Cleveland affiliate in 1910. Cleveland owner Charles W. Somers acquired Toledo (American Association) in 1912 and New Orleans (Southern Association) in 1913. In 1913 Cleveland also affiliated with Waterbury (Eastern Association) and Ironton (Ohio St.). So beginning in 1913 Cleveland had two Double-A clubs, plus clubs in A, B, and D, with players moving among the various classifications. But the system quickly collapsed. Ironton folded during the 1914 season and Waterbury folded at the end of the season (and their manager Lee Fohl moved up to become Cleveland pitching coach and later manager). In 1915 Somers suffered serious financial reverses, and when bankers took over his finances in late 1915 they sold the Indians and the former Toledo club (which had relocated to Cleveland during the Federal League war), but allowed him to retain the New Orleans club. New Orleans soon fell out of the Indians orbit and Cleveland severed its affiliation with Portland at the end of the 1916 season. The short-lived farm system had produced five members of the 1920 world championship team—Stan Coveleski, Jim Bagby, Guy Morton, Joe Evans, and the deceased Ray Chapman—and although Barnard remained with Cleveland after Somers was forced to sell, there was no effort to re-establish the farm system. This suggests that rather than being a carefully considered innovation it may have been something that "just happened". But if Barnard didn't appreciate the potential of his system, Branch Rickey certainly did.

In 1921 the Cardinals, who had already acquired an interest in Ft. Smith of the Western Association and Houston of the Texas League, acquired a half interest in Syracuse of the International League. This was the beginning of Branch Rickey's farm system, but initially it attracted little attention as it didn't appear to represent anything particularly new. It was less extensive than Cleveland's had been just a few years earlier. Major league clubs had been signing young talent directly off the sandlots and developing it in the minors. For example in1 910, before it had established its farm system, Cleveland signed Roger Peckinpaugh out of the Cleveland City League, gave him a brief trial, and then optioned him to New Haven and Portland in successive seasons before recalling him when he was deemed ready for the majors. This practice had developed to the point that Mike Sexton, president of the National Association, in 1921 spoke out against the fact that the majors and higher minors had preempted the low minors' traditional role of discovering and signing young talent.

As we have seen, major league clubs had occasionally owned minor league clubs, primarily to expand the number of players under their control, but these were generally higher-classification clubs, where talent was refined rather than developed. Initially Rickey's approach was much the same, but it didn't take long for the system to begin producing talent. The Cards, who had never finished higher than third in the 20th century, won the World Series in 1926 with a team that included future Hall of Famers Jim Bottomley and Chick Hafey as well as regulars Taylor Douthit, Tommy Thevenow, Les Bell, Ray Blades, Flint Rhem, and Art Reinhardt plus reserves Watty Holm, Jake Flowers, Spec Toporcher, Ernie Vick, and Bill Hallahan—but virtually all of these players were by way of Syracuse and Houston, the top two clubs in what was still only a three-club farm system. Then, using money earned by the Cardinals in winning the World Series, Rickey began adding lower-classification clubs to his system—Danville in 1927, Dayton in 1928, Laurel and Scottsdale in 1929. This gave the Cardinals one Double-A, one A, two B, two C, and one D-classification club and finally enabled Rickey to sign young talent and, through a hierarchy of minor league clubs, to develop and retain continuous title to a large number of players—his theory being that out of quantity comes quality.

During the 1920s when the Cardinals were discovering, signing, and developing players at little expense, the other major league clubs were essentially operating as they always had, signing some players out of the amateur ranks, optioning them out for seasoning, and buying top prospects from minor league clubs, even though the new draft rules were driving the prices of such players to unprecedented levels. For example, the Yankees team the Cardinals defeated in the 1926 World Series had just one home-grown player—Lou Gehrig, who was signed out of Columbia University in 1923 and optioned to Hartford until ready. Although this had been an inexpensive acquisition, the Yankees subsequently had purchased, for $50,000 each, Earle Combs from Louisville, Mark Koenig from St. Paul (with whom the Yankees had a working agreement), and Tony Lazzeri from Salt Lake. In 1925, the year the Pirates won the World Series, they acquired Paul Waner and Hal Rhyne from the San Francisco Seals for $100,000 and also signed Joe Cronin off the San Francisco sandlots for little more than train fare to his first assignment—Johnstown, Pennsylvania.

But the escalating prices of players and the success of the Cardinals finally encouraged other clubs to begin acquiring minor league clubs. Shortly after the Cardinals acquired the half interest in Syracuse in 1921, William Wrigley, owner of the Cubs, acquired Los Angeles of the Pacific Coast League, but he treated them virtually as separate investments. By 1927, however, major league acquisition of minor league clubs was causing concern in the minors. The first formal notice came late that year, when the American Association adopted a new Constitution which effectively prohibited major league ownership of its clubs (excluding Columbus, which was already owned by Cincinnati). At the National Association meeting in December 1928, Mike Sexton wondered aloud when the majors would own enough clubs to control the National Association. Early in 1929 major league clubs owned or controlled 27 minor league clubs. At that point Commissioner Landis, who until then had been remarkably quiet on the issue of farm systems, opened fire. He began granting free agency to minor leaguers "covered up" by various major league organizations. Later in 1929, Landis denounced the farm system, and announced his intention of destroying it. In response, Sam Breadon, owner of the Cardinals, cited letters from seven minor leagues saying the farm system was beneficial to them. Interestingly, in 1921 Landis had said, "The object of organized baseball is to facilitate the development of skill among ball players." No one could seriously argue that this wasn't the purpose of the farm system, but by 1929 Landis was accusing Rickey and Breadon of "raping the minors," robbing small-town America of its precious heritage of independent minor league baseball.

Landis tried to make good on his threat to destroy the farm system, but since it was not contrary to baseball law, he had to pick at the edges. Landis levied fines against teams having an interest in more than one team in a minor league or by granting free agency to players who were "covered up" through violations of the option rules or "secret agreements." Attracting much attention in this crusade was his granting of free agency to 74 St. Louis farmhands in 1938 and to 91 Detroit minor leaguers in 1940, but these shots were fired after the war was lost.

More important than the fireworks that erupted between Landis and Breadon at the 1929 major league meeting was Yankees owner Jacob Ruppert's declaration at the same meetings that no ballclub could afford the prices being paid for minor league players. Ruppert added that he was "going to be forced into owning minor league clubs, and so is every other major league owner in this room." At the time he spoke, the Yankees had already purchased the Chambersburg club of the Class D Blue Ridge League. In November 1931 Ruppert purchased Newark of the International League for a reported $600,000 and soon thereafter hired Baltimore general manager George Weiss to develop a farm system. Thus the farm system, a concept that had been created largely out of necessity by Branch Rickey because the Cardinals didn't have the financial resources to compete with other clubs for top minor league prospects, had in less than a decade been embraced by the wealthiest club in baseball as being the most efficient method of acquiring talent. There would still be an occasional Joe DiMaggio or Ted Williams, signed by a minor league club and sold to the majors, but the major league club that didn't establish a farm system did so at its own peril. Not coincidentally, the eight teams which were the slowest to get on the bandwagon and had the thinnest farm systems in the 1930s—the Phillies, Athletics, Senators, White Sox, Giants, Cubs, Braves, and Pirates—were, aside from the Browns, the eight least successful teams in the 1940s. (The Browns and Reds established extensive farm systems in the 1930s, and overall they were the two most improved clubs of the 1940s.)

While several clubs caught on to what the Cardinals were doing, none could catch up to the head start by St. Louis. The Depression had created a large pool of young men with few career options, and Rickey signed players by the hundreds at tryout camps. Whereas during the 1920s the Cardinals system had only increased from three clubs to five, by 1936 it had expanded to 28 teams—remarkable considering that there were only 26 minor leagues that year (the Cardinals had two teams each in the Nebraska State, Georgia-Florida, and Arkansas-Missouri Leagues). The Cardinal system finally topped out with 33 clubs in 1937—more than the two next-largest farm systems combined. Rickey's belief that out of quantity comes quality was proven on the field by the 1942 world champion Cardinals. Every player on the active roster, except for second-line pitchers Harry Gumbert and Whitey Moore, was a product of the St. Louis farm system, and Gumbert had been acquired in exchange for Cardinals farm graduate Bill McGee.

In addition, the sale of players developed by the Cardinals kept the coffers full—in 1940–1941 alone, Johnny Mize, Joe Medwick, and Mickey Owen were exchanged to other clubs for $240,000 and nine players.

Thus from the perspective of the majors the farm system was a success, and the minors seemed to be flourishing—going from 14 leagues in 1933 to 44 by 1940. Sam Breadon, responding to another barrage of attacks by Landis in the late 1930s, claimed that the farm system had brought stability and strength to the minors, but there were other factors at work—the proliferation of night games, better promotion, and an influx of good young talent resulted in a per-club increase in attendance of 40 percent from 1937 to 1940. During that same period the portion of minor league clubs affiliated with the majors actually dropped from 61 to 46 percent. Rickey's theory that out of quantity comes quality might have had practical merit during a depression, or again immediately following World War II when there was an influx of returning veterans. However, under normal circumstances huge farm systems were not cost-effective. While the minors were still expanding in the late 1930s, the Cardinals began pruning back their farm system of more than 30 teams. A decade later farm systems were contracting—in 1948 there were six farm systems of 20 or more teams; by 1951 there were none. The portion of minor league teams affiliated with major league teams dropped from 62 percent in 1946 to 47 percent in 1951 as major league farm systems collectively dropped from 280 to 175 clubs and outright major league ownership of minor league clubs dropped from 125 to 75.

In 1950 there were 232 minor league teams not affiliated with the majors. This was the highest number of independent teams in organized baseball in nearly 40 years. Nine of the 58 leagues had no teams with major league affiliations, and more than a dozen others had only one or two affiliates. These leagues operated virtually outside the player-development chain, existing much as a semipro team or league does—to provide entertainment and reflect civic pride. Their only source of revenue was through the turnstiles, and just as 40 years earlier automobiles and the movies helped drive out the marginal teams and leagues, now TV did the same. This can be clearly seen as the densely populated Northeast, the first region to be heavily penetrated by television, suffered the first wave of league failures.

Over the next few years, attendance declined sharply, most of the independent clubs folded, and farm systems continued to contract. In 1956 the majors established a "stabilization fund" of $500,000 to aid clubs and leagues in lower classifications, but the free-fall of leagues, clubs, and attendance continued. In 1959 the majors discontinued the stabilization fund and established a fund of $1 million to finance a player-development and promotional program for the minors. In 1962 the majors and minors adopted the Player Development Plan that, by requiring each major league club to have five farm teams, would guarantee the operation of at least 100 minor league teams, which the majors felt was adequate for their player-development purposes. The plan also included the Player Development Contract under the terms of which the parent major league club became responsible for all spring training costs and all or most of the salaries of players, managers, and coaches. After major league expansion in 1969, major league clubs were only required to support four farm clubs each, but their financial support of each was increased. By 1976 there were only 106 minor league teams with major league affiliations, the lowest peacetime total since 1935. American League expansion the following year created the need for additional minor league affiliates, and in subsequent years major league clubs expanded their farm systems—all of them back up to a minimum of five clubs by 1984. With the dramatic increase in minor league attendance and the resulting increase in the value of franchises in the 1980s, a new Professional Baseball Agreement was ratified by the majors and minors in 1990. The new agreement required the minors to assume a greater share of operational expenses but the majors continued to pay the salaries and meal money of all uniformed personnel. And farm systems continued to grow—by 1994 each major league club had at least six farm clubs and the number of minor league teams with major league affiliations was up to 194, the highest total since 1950. With further major league expansion and mass signings of Latin American players necessitating rookie leagues in the Dominican Republic and Venezuela, the number of major league affiliates reached 229 in 2000.

In 1928 Mike Sexton had asked how long it would be before the majors owned enough minor league clubs to control the National Association. Other than during World War II, when the minors were severely constricted, major league clubs never have "owned" more than 28 percent of the minor league clubs. Yet possibly as early as 1934, probably by 1935, and certainly by 1936, the majors through outright ownership, working agreements, or other interlocking devices "controlled" the National Association, and this situation was generally acknowledged throughout baseball by 1938. The majors ran the minors.

Until about 1960 there was still some room in the National Association for independent clubs and career minor leaguers. From 1961-1972 there were no U.S.-based independent clubs (Quincy did not have a major league affiliation in 1964 but received player help from major league organizations); but from 1973-1992 there were three or four independent clubs per season, in 1976-77 all the clubs in the Gulf States/Lone Star League were independent, and in the late 1970s the Northwest League had several independent clubs. Some of the independents were very good—Portland in the mid-1970s and Salt Lake in the late 1980s-early 1990s were both artistic and financial successes; Grays Harbor, Utica, and Helena won pennants but did not draw well at the gate. Most of the independents were very bad. In the late 1980s San Jose and Miami—initially using a number of former major leaguers, many with substance abuse problems—were both artistic and financial disasters. In 1980 Rocky Mount had one of the worst records in the history of the game, 24-114. The one thing the independents had in common was an inability to develop talent for the majors—Tom Candiotti was one of the few successful products, Greg (the original Boomer) Wells played briefly in the majors and went on to become a star in Japan. After that it might be a tossup as to the most famous graduate—actor Kurt Russell or Atlanta pitching guru Leo Mazzone.

The minors existed almost exclusively to develop talent for the majors and the independent clubs no longer fit. While this dismayed many minor league fans and traditionalists, it should be remembered that the principal role of the minors within organized baseball has always been to develop talent for the majors, and to receive money in exchange. The farm system, which owed its success in no small part to the greed of some minor league operators, was merely a different device by which talent moved to the majors and money moved to the minors.

Independent Leagues

At the end of the 1992 season the Salt Lake City Trappers, in their eight seasons in the Pioneer League, had won four pennants. In 1987 they set an organized baseball record with 29 consecutive wins, and in the last three seasons had an average attendance of 5,700 per game—better than any club had done in the Pacific Coast League. Although they were only in a rookie league, the Trappers were arguably the most successful independent club in the minors since Baltimore and Ft. Worth in the 1920s, but they had played their last game. Shortly before the start of the 1993 season their ballpark was torn down to make way for a new stadium to house the PCL Portland Beavers, who would be moving to Salt Lake in 1994. Even before the Trappers lost their park they had lost their director of player personnel, Van Schley, and their field manager to the new independent Northern League.

In 1993 the Northern League became the first U.S.-based independent league of any consequence in more than half a century. Its founder was Miles Wolff, publisher of Baseball America—a man with more than two decades of experience in the minor leagues and former owner of the Durham Bulls and several other clubs. After careful study Wolff had concluded that the upper Midwest might be a prime area for a new professional baseball league. He visited candidate cities where he generated enthusiasm and support from civic leaders for the new league, and during 1992 assembled a group of owners—most of whom had experience in minor league baseball, some with independent clubs within the context of organized baseball. Schley, who had owned—and supplied players for—independent clubs since 1977, was named director of baseball operations.

The Northern League began operations in 1993 with six clubs playing a 72-game schedule that began in mid-June and ended around Labor Day. Each team had a 22-man roster, of which six had to be rookies and no more than four could have more than four years playing experience. The league had a strict salary limit which would yield an average salary of about $1,000 a month; rookies would make $700 while some veterans might go as high as $2,000. The standard contract was for one year with a club option for an additional year, which enabled the clubs to sell their players to major league organizations rather than have the players simply walk away at the end of the season and make their own deals. The standard sale price was $3,000. The clubs followed the Portland/Salt Lake model of using generally unknown players who had been bypassed or jettisoned by major league organizations because they were not considered major league prospects and mixed in a few high-profile ex-major leaguers such as Pedro Guerrero and Leon Durham. In its first season the league generally drew well with St. Paul, operated by Mike Veeck, drawing near-capacity crowds every night. Rochester drew poorly and the following season the franchise was moved to Winnipeg where attendance quadrupled.

The success of the Northern League generated an explosion of independent leagues over the next few years. Most were failures. The Golden State lasted two weeks, the Atlantic Coast less than a month, the Great Central didn't finish its only season, and the Mid-American lasted a year. The Big South and North Atlantic opened with some promise but succumbed after two seasons when their best cities defected to other independent leagues. The Prairie and Heartland Leagues lasted three seasons each.

While all this was going on the Northern League continued to thrive, expanding, shifting its weaker franchises to better markets, and in 1999 absorbing the Northeast League, which had been operating for four years. The league, or more specifically its flagship franchise in St. Paul, was the subject of numerous articles, several books, and a cable television series.

Other leagues survived. The Frontier League began operations the same year as the Northern. It played mostly in small towns along the Ohio River, was virtually a rookie league with a lower salary scale than the Northern, and was beset with problems from the beginning—two teams folded early in the season, the league's founder was ousted in midseason, attendance was generally poor, and during the offseason there were suits and counter-suits between the founder and the owners—but it has survived. It has remained a league for players with limited professional experience, but it continued to upgrade its franchises, eventually moving to new parks in suburban

Chicago and St. Louis as well as abandoned organized baseball cities like Canton, Evansville, London, Ontario, and Springfield, Illinois.

The Texas-Louisiana—a centrally owned and operated league—started in 1994, and the Western in 1995. Both use slightly more experienced players than the Northern and many of their managers have been former major leaguers. Yet while the Northern has been a model of stability and growth, the Texas-Louisiana and Western Leagues have had teams in 36 cities, and in 1999 were drawing fewer fans than when they first started. Still, both remain in business and the Texas-Louisiana in particular seems to be getting into stronger markets.

The Atlantic League, after two years of planning, made its debut in 1998. It has a much higher salary limit than the other independents, which helped to attract a number of former major leaguers. It operates in a number of new markets—some with brand new ballparks—with more reportedly on the way. After three seasons of operation the Atlantic League was drawing nearly as well as the Northern League, while thriving in areas that had long been regarded as "major league" territory.

The independents didn't fit into organized baseball because they weren't developing major league players. Despite the occasional Kerry Ligtenberg, Jeff Zimmerman, or Kevin Millar, they still are not effective in developing major leaguers. Only 15 of the more than 1,000 men who played in the majors in 2000 had played in any of the independent leagues (and three of the 15—J.D. Drew, Rey Ordonez, and Ariel Prieto—had been there while awaiting or challenging the major league draft). By comparison in 2000, 35 major leaguers had played for Visalia, a club that plays in one of the worst parks in the minors and is perennially last in California League attendance.

But the purpose of independent leagues has never been to develop talent for the majors. When Miles Wolff started the Northern League in 1993 few expected that in seven years there would be five fairly stable independent leagues with 50 clubs drawing more than 5 million fans for the season, and the independents continue to thrive. Miles Wolff's dream has been fulfilled.

Minor League Attendance (since 1947)

Year	Number of Leagues	Number of Clubs	Regular Season Total Attendance
1947	52	388	37,815,753
1948	58	438	38,415,716
1949	59	448(6)	39,782,717
1950	58(1)	446(14)	32,960,733
1951	50(1)	371(13)	26,135,174
1952	43	324(5)	24,024,373
1953	38	292(4)	21,109,565
1954	36(3)	269(22)	18,674,503
1955	33	243(5)	18,203,889
1956	28	217(5)	16,402,953
1957	28	200(10)	14,875,346
1958	24	173	12,744,883
1959	21	150	11,622,581
1960	22	152	10,660,811
1961	22	147	9,766,505
1962	20	134	9,732,582
1963	18	130	9,749,381
1964	20	136	10,102,310
1965	19	136	10,029,518
1966	19	138	9,826,124
1967	19	141	9,940,660
1968	21	152	9,887,328
1969	21	155	9,993,615
1970	20	153	10,726,470
1971	20	155	11,134,084
1972	19	148	10,986,628
1973	18	147	10,828,828
1974	18	145	10,562,452
1975	18	137	11,021,848
1976	20	148(1)	11,324,947
1977	19	150	13,004,297
1978	18	156	13,012,727
1979	18(1)	155(6)	15,304,724
1980	17	155(14)	12,265,022
1981	17	152	16,178,790
1982	17	160	17,637,244
1983	17	162	18,599,190
1984	17	164	17,580,299
1985	17	168	18,380,000
1986	17	164	18,456,808
1987	18	176	20,215,564
1988	19	188	21,661,873
1989	19	197	23,103,593
1990	19	202	25,244,569
1991	19	207	26,590,096
1992	19	212	27,180,170
1993	19	214	30,022,761
1994	19	216	33,355,199
1995	19	216	33,126,934
1996	19	218	33,289,278
1997	21	236	34,721,716
1998	20	242	35,427,012
1999	19	241	35,179,471
2000	19	246	37,872,674

Independent Leagues (since 1993)

Year	Number of Leagues	Number of Clubs	Regular Season Total Attendance
1993	2	14(2)	734,667
1994	5	32	1,921,313
1995	11(3)	66(14)	3,077,955
1996	9	63(1)	3,453,897
1997	8	58	3,504,946
1998	7	51(2)	3,866,609
1999	5	45	4,871,797
2000	5	50	

( ) Did not finish season

Source: National Association of Professional Baseball Leagues

Minor Leagues

Year	Leagues Started	Didn't Finish	Year	Leagues Started	Didn't Finish	Year	Leagues Started	Didn't Finish	Year	Leagues Started	Didn't Finish	Year	Leagues Started	Didn't Finish	Year	Leagues Started	Didn't Finish
1883	2		1903	19		1923	31	2	1943	10	1	1963	18		1982	17	
1884	7	3	1904	23	3	1924	29	3	1944	10		1964	20		1983	17	
1885	8	3	1905	29	6	1925	25	1	1945	12		1965	19		1984	17	
1886	11	3	1906	33	5	1926	29	4	1946	43	1	1966	19		1985	18	
1887	15	6	1907	34	6	1927	24		1947	52		1967	19		1986	17	
1888	17	9	1908	39	8	1928	30	3	1948	58		1968	21		1987	18	
1889	15	5	1909	34	2	1929	26	3	1949	59		1969	21		1988	19	
1890	18	9	1910	52	8	1930	23	2	1950	58	1	1970	20		1989	19	
1891	13	5	1911	50	7	1931	18	2	1951	50	1	1971	20		1990	19	
1892	14	10	1912	45	6	1932	19	6	1952	43		1972	19		1991	19	
1893	7	4	1913	42	5	1933	14		1953	38		1973	18		1992	19	
1894	8	2	1914	43	7	1934	20	1	1954	36	3	1974	18		1993	19	
1895	17	9	1915	30	7	1935	21		1955	33		1975	18		1994	19	
1896	15	8	1916	25	3	1936	26		1956	28		1976	20		1995	19	
1897	20	8	1917	21	10	1937	37		1957	28		1977	19		1996	19	
1898	20	11	1918	10	9	1938	37		1958	24		1978	18		1997	21	
1899	14	5	1919	15	2	1939	41		1959	21		1979	18	1	1998	20	
1900	15	6	1920	22	1	1940	44	1	1960	22		1980	17		1999	19	
1901	13	2	1921	26	1	1941	41		1961	22		1981	17		2000	19	
1902	16	2	1922	30	2	1942	31	5	1962	20							

Minor League Clubs/Major League Affiliations

Year	Minor League Clubs	Affiliated with Majors	Owned by Majors	Year	Minor League Clubs	Affiliated with Majors	Owned by Majors	Year	Minor League Clubs	Affiliated with Majors	Owned by Majors
1936	184	116	38	1958	173	157	34	1980	155	125	
1937	251	154	39	1959	150	132	30	1981	152	133	
1938	267	162	49	1960	152	126	18	1982	160	136	
1939	292	152	48	1961	147	129	21	1983	162	139	
1940	310	146	61	1962	134	121	22	1984	164	140	
1941	304	147	62	1963	130	114	22	1985	168	140	
1942	206	116	46	1964	136	108	19	1986	164	143	
1943	66	42	23	1965	136	110	28	1987	176	149	
1944	70	57	21	1966	138	116	32	1988	188	168	
1945	85	68	33	1967	141	118	36	1989	197	179	
1946	316	197	79	1968	152	119	39	1990	202	183	
1947	388	247	103	1969	155	128	46	1991	207	184	
1948	438	280	125	1970	153	120	39	1992	212	192	
1949	448	243	116	1971	155	127	45	1993	214	193	
1950	446	210	99	1972	148	125	49	1994	216	195	
1951	371	172	75	1973	147	117	38	1995	216	193	
1952	324	166	65	1974	145	113	27	1996	218	198	
1953	292	152	50	1975	137	109	26	1997	236	214	
1954	269	156	49	1976	148	106	24	1998	242	225	
1955	243	155	40	1977	150	113	23	1999	241	224	
1956	217	150	33	1978	156	118	24	2000	246	229	
1957	200	153	32	1979	155	119					

Major League Farm Systems 1936–1969

	36	37	38	39	40	41	42	43	44	45	46	47	48	49	50	51	52	53	54	55	56	57	58	59	60	61	62	63	64	65	66	67	68	69
Boston, AL	9	10	7	8	6	7	6	3	5	4	12	13	15	11	8	8	6	6	6	6	5	7	7	6	6	6	6	5	5	5	6	5	6	6
Chicago, AL	5	4	10	8	6	5	5	0	0	0	17	12	15	9	8	8	6	8	6	6	5	6	6	6	6	6	6	5	5	5	6	6	6	6
Cleveland, AL	5	7	13	16	8	9	8	3	3	3	11	18	20	20	16	12	10	8	8	9	9	8	8	8	7	5	6	5	4	4	4	4	5	5
Detroit, AL	11	8	12	7	5	11	8	2	3	2	7	11	16	14	9	8	7	7	8	10	9	8	10	7	8	8	6	6	5	5	5	5	6	6
New York, AL	11	15	15	15	14	12	9	5	5	5	15	22	24	22	15	14	10	11	9	10	11	10	10	8	8	7	7	6	5	7	7	7	6	6
Phila.-K.C.-Oakland, AL	5	3	3	3	4	5	3	2	2	4	7	15	10	11	15	9	8	8	6	7	7	9	8	8	8	8	6	5	5	6	6	6	6	5
St. Louis-Baltimore, AL	3	15	16	12	11	11	6	1	3	3	11	15	20	18	13	10	12	10	12	8	9	8	9	7	7	9	6	6	6	7	6	6	6	6
Wash.-Minnesota, AL	1	5	2	8	4	6	3	1	2	2	5	7	12	9	10	6	8	7	8	7	6	8	8	7	6	7	7	7	6	8	8	8	8	8
Milwaukee-Atlanta, NL	4	6	6	6	5	4	4	1	1	2	13	15	15	11	8	8	12	11	10	10	12	15	14	12	10	9	8	7	6	5	6	7	5	4
Brklyn.-Los Angeles, NL	5	14	14	11	18	14	10	4	7	9	21	25	26	26	22	19	17	15	15	16	14	13	12	12	12	11	9	7	8	6	6	6	6	6
Chicago, NL	5	6	8	5	5	11	11	4	6	7	18	23	19	16	15	14	10	9	9	8	8	10	8	6	6	6	5	5	5	5	6	6	5	5
Cincinnati, NL	16	10	10	10	8	8	5	2	1	3	4	8	11	10	7	4	6	7	9	9	9	11	11	8	8	6	5	5	5	4	5	5	5	5
N.Y.-San Francisco, NL	2	11	4	5	6	7	7	3	5	8	16	19	22	19	18	14	13	9	9	10	10	10	12	9	8	9	8	7	7	6	6	6	6	5
Philadelphia, NL	1	2	3	3	8	3	2	1	3	5	9	11	15	14	12	11	11	9	9	8	8	9	9	7	10	8	7	6	6	6	7	7	6	6
Pittsburgh, NL	4	5	7	7	9	8	7	4	4	4	13	14	19	13	13	11	15	11	10	13	13	10	11	9	7	7	7	7	6	6	6	6	6	6
St. Louis, NL	28	33	32	28	29	25	22	6	7	7	18	19	22	20	21	16	15	16	22	18	15	11	14	12	9	8	6	5	5	6	6	7	7	7
L.A.-California, AL																										2	4	6	6	6	5	5	5	5
Washington, AL																										2	4	4	4	4	4	4	5	5
Houston, NL																										2	4	5	5	5	6	6	5	6
New York, NL																										3	4	5	4	4	5	6	6	5
Kansas City, AL																																		7
Seattle, AL																																		4
Montreal, NL																																		3
San Diego, NL																																		4

Annual Overall Minor League Pitching Percentage Leader (20 or more decisions)

Year	Player	Team (League)	W–L	Pct.	Overall W–L	Overall Pct.
1900	Christy Mathewson	Norfolk (Virginia)	20–2	.909		
1901	Henry Allemang	Little Rock (So. Assn.)	20–4	.833		
1902	Louis Bruce	Toronto (Eastern)	18–2	.900		
1903	Ernest Nichols	Spokane (Pac. Nat.)	20–4	.833		
1904	Ed Craig	Springfield (Mo. Valley)	19–4	.826		
1905	Bill Burns	Pittsburg (Mo. Valley)	21–3	.875		
1906	Frank Dick	Marshalltown (Iowa St.)	18–3	.857		
1907	Harley Young	Wichita (West. Assn.)	29–4	.879		
1908	Harry Gaspar	Waterloo (Cent. Assn.)	32–4	.889		
1909	Ray Fisher	Hartford (Conn.)	24–5	.828		
1910	Cyrus Dahlgren	Superior (Minn.-Wis.)	22–3	.880		
1911	Howard Northrop	Reading (Inter.-St.)	27–4	.871		
1912	Larue Kirby	Traverse City (Mich. St.)	18–3	.857		
1913	Ralph Bell	Winona (Northern)	28–6	.824		
1914	Joe Chabek	Harrisburg (Tri-St.)	28–3	.903		
1915	Booth Hopper	Minneapolis (A.A.)	18–3	.857		
1916	Howard Ehmke	Syracuse (N.Y. St.)	31–7	.816		
1917	John Verbout	Wilkes-Barre (N.Y. St.)	26–7	.788		
1918	John Beckvermit	Binghamton (Int.)	17–4	.810		
1919	C. A. "Chief" Bender	Richmond (Va.)	29–2	.935		
1920	George Carmen	London (Mich.,-Ont.)	26–2	.926		
1921	Earl Keiser	Mitchell (Dakota)	20–2			
		Oakland (PCL)	3–0		23–2	.920
1922	Byrd Hodges	Joplin (West. Assn.)	26–3	.897		
1923	Emil Levsen	Cedar Rapids (Miss. Val.)	19–4	.826		
1924	Carl Dunagan	Dyersburg (Kitty)	19–2	.905		
1925	Lloyd Brown	Ardmore-Western Assn.	17–1	.944*		
1926	Frank Tubbs	Port Huron (Mich.-Ont.)	8–1			
		Port Huron (Mich. St.)	8–0			
		Oklahoma City (Western)	9–2		25–3	.893
1927	Ben Cantwell	Jacksonville (So'east.)	25–5	.833		
1928	Paul Fittery	Carrollton (Ga.-Ala.)	21–2	.913		
1929	Andrew Bednar	McCook (Neb. St.)	21–4	.840		
1930	Jim Cameron	McCook (Neb. St.)	19–2	.905		
1931	Lyle "Bud" Tinning	Minneapolis (A.A.)	1–2			
		Des Moines (West. Assn.)	24–2		25–4	.862
1932	Marvin Duke	Erie (Central)	23–4	.852		
1933	Al Piechota	Davenport (Miss. Val.)	19–4	.826		
1934	Fay Thomas	Los Angeles (PCL)	28–4	.875		
1935	Lloyd Sterling	Winnipeg (Northern)	24–2	.923		
1936	Bill Yocke	Akron (Mid. Atl.)	1–2			
		Norfolk (Piedmont)	18–1		19–3	.864
1937	Joe Kohlman	Salisbury (E. Shore)	25–1	.962		
1938	Paige Dennis	Thomasville (N.C. St.)	28–2	.933		
1939	Charles Wensloff	Joplin (West. Assn.)	26–4	.867		
1940	Arthur Cyrolewski	Johnson City (App.)	20–3	.870		
	J. Merwin (Merv) Henley	La Crosse (Wis. St.)	20–3	.870		
1941	Frank Marino	Macon (Sally)	19–1	.950		
1942	Paul Minner	Elizabethton (App.)	18–2			
		Knoxville (So. Assn.)	1–0		19–2	.905
1943	Irvin Stein	Portsmouth (Piedmont)	24–6	.800		
1944	Pete Naktenis	Hartford (Eastern)	18–3	.857		
1945	Lewis Carpenter	Atlanta (So. Assn.)	22–2	.917		
1946	Bill Kennedy	Rocky Mount (C. Plain)	28–3	.903		
1947	Chris VanCuyk	Cambridge (E. Shore)	25–2	.926		
1948	Albert Tefft	Blackstone (Va.)	20–1	.952		
1949	Lynn Southworth	Thomasville (N.C. St.)	21–1	.955		
1950	Mike Hudak	Big Stone Gap (Mt. St.)	19–2	.905		
1951	Anderson Bush	Hagerstown (Int. St.)	22–3	.880		
1952	Russell Harris	Ozark (Ala-Fla.)	27–3	.900		
1953	Steve Kraly	Binghamton (Eastern)	19–2	.905		
1954	Don Vaughn	Merryville-Morristown (Mt. St.)	11–1			
		Highpoint-Thomasville (Carolina)	0–0			
		Vidalia (Ga. St.)	9–1		20–2	.909
1955	Jim Grant	Keokuk (I-I-I)	19–3	.864		
1956	Francisco Ramirez	Mexico City Reds (Mex.)	20–3	.870		
1957	Bob Riesner	Alexandria (Evang.)	20–0			
		New Orleans (So. Assn.)	0–2		20–2	.909
1958	Jerry Walker	Knoxville (Sally)	18–4	.818		
	Art Henriksen	St. Petersburg (Fla. St.)	17–3			
		New Orleans (So. Assn.)	0–1		18–4	.818
1959	Les Bass	Boise (Pioneer)	21–3	.875		
1960	Tom Haake	Grand Forks (Northern)	0–1			
		Dubuque (Midwest)	19–3		19–4	.826
1961	David Seeman	Selma (Ala.-Fla.)	17–3			
		Burlington (Carolina)	7–0		24–3	.889
1962	Bob Schmidt	Modesto (Calif.)	0–0			
		Jamestown (NYP)	17–3		17–3	.850
1963	Bob Lee	Batavia (NYP)	20–2			
		Asheville (Sally)	1–1		21–3	.875
1964	Ed Watt	Aberdeen (Northern)	14–1			
		Elmira (Eastern)	3–1		17–2	.895**
1965	Billy MacLeod	Pittsfield (Eastern)	18–0	1.000***		
1966	Bob Snow	Winston-Salem (Carolina)	20–2	.909		
1967	John Parker	Spartanburg (W. Car.)	17–3	.850		
1968	Pablo Montes De Oca	Campeche (Mex. S.E.)	21–4	.840		
1969	Don Eddy	Appleton (Midwest)	18–3	.857		
1970	Jim Flynn	Albuquerque (Texas)	19–4	.826		
1971	Rich Gossage	Appleton (Midwest)	18–2	.900		
1972	Andres Ayon	Saltillo (Mexican)	22–3	.880		
1973	Silvano Quezada	Tampico (Mexican)	22–2	.917		
1974	Bob Knepper	Fresno (Calif.)	20–5	.800		
1975	Jerry Garvin	Reno (Calif.)	17–5	.773		
1976	Enrique Romo	Mexico City Reds (Mexican)	20–4	.833		
1977	Mike Chris	Lakeland (Fla. St.)	18–5	.783		
1978	Tomas Armas	Saltillo (Mexican)	22–4	.846		
1979	Miguel Solis	Saltillo (Mexican)	25–5	.833		
1980	Gene Nelson	Ft. Lauderdale (Fla. St.)	20–3	.870		
1981	Ted Power	Albuquerque (PCL)	18–3	.857		
1982	Mike Warren	Stockton-Modesto (Calif.)	19–4	.826		
1983	Alfonso Pulido	Mexico City Reds (Mexican)	17–3	.850		
1984	Mike Bielecki	Hawaii (PCL)	19–3	.864		
1985	Eleazar Beltran	Tampico (Mexican)	18–3	.857		
1986	George Ferran	Shreveport (Texas)	16–1	.941		
1987	Bob Faron	Springfield (Midwest)	19–2	.905		
1988	Jimmy Rodgers	Myrtle Beach (So. Atl.)	18–4	.818		
1989	Royal Clayton	Albany (Eastern)	16–4	.800		
1989	Mercedes Esquer	Yucatan (Mexican)	16–4	.800		
1989	Walt Trice	Osceola (Fla. St.)	16–4	.800		
1990	Randy Marshall	Fayetteville (So. Atl.)	13–0			
		Lakeland (Fla. St.)	7–2			
1991	Jose Martinez	Columbus (So. Atl.)	20–4	.833		
1992	John Fritz	Quad Cities (Midwest)	20–4	.833		
1993	John Dettmer	Charlotte (Fla. St.)	16–3	.842		
	Ryan Karp	Albany (Eastern)	0–0			
		Prince William (Carolina)	3–2			
		Greensboro (So. Atl.)	13–1		16–3	.842****
1994	Francisco Montano	Monclova (Mexican)	19–1	.950		
1995	Rich Hunter	Piedmont (Sally)	10–2			
		Clearwater (Fla. St.)	6–0			
		Reading (Eastern)	3–0		19–2	.905
1996	Ted Silva	Charlotte (Fla. St.)	10–2			
		Tulsa (Texas)	7–2		17–4	.810
1997	Travis Smith	El Paso (Texas)	16–3	.842+		
1998	John Sneed	Hagerstown (Sally)	16–2	.889++		
	Narcisco Elvira	Monterrey (Mexican)	16–4	.800		
1999	Jose Navarro	Mexico City Tigers (Mex.)	16–4	.800		
2000	Bud Smith	Arkansas (Texas)	12–1			
		Memphis (PCL)	5–1		17–2	.895+++

*Adding two losses to Brown's record giving him 20 decisions yields a .850 percent, better than John Schmutte, Johnstown Middle Atlantic, 19–4, .822

**Adding one loss to Watt's record, giving him 20 decisions, yields an .850 percentage, better than Dave Leonhard, Aberdeen (Northern), 16–4 .800

***Adding two losses to MacLeod's record, giving him 20 decisions, yields a .900 percentage, better than Dave Leonhard, Elmira (Eastern), 20–5 .800

****Adding one loss to Dettmer's and Karp's records giving them 20 decisions yields an .800 percentage, better than Urbano Lugo, Jalisco (Mexican) 17–5 .773.

‡Adding three losses to Ferran's record, giving him 20 decisions, yields an .800 percentage, better than Kevin Armstrong, Columbia (Sally), 17–5 .773

+Adding one loss to Smith's record, giving him 20 decisions, yields an .800 percentage, better than Brian Rose, Pawtucket (International) 17–5. .773 and Reid Cornelius combined 17–5 .773 combined with Portland (Eastern) 5–0 and Charlotte (International) 12–5

++Adding two losses to Sneed's record giving him 20 decisions, yields a .800 percentage

+++Adding one loss to Smith's record, giving him 20 decisions, yields an .850 percentage.

Annual Overall Minor League Batting Leader (400 or more at bats)

Year	Player	Team (League)	G	AB	R	H	2B	3B	HR	RBI	SB	AVG.
1900	Kitty Bransfield	Worcester (Eastern)	122	501	115*	186*	30	8	17	—	40	.371*
1901	Frank Huelsman	Shreveport (So. Assn.)	121*	487	98	191*	31	10	9	—	15	.392*
1902	Emil Frisk	Denver (Western)	123	450	89	168	22	22	14*	—	20	.373*
1903	Frank Huelsman	Spokane (Pac. Int.)	98	418	89	160	35	11	6	—	14	.392*
1904	Billy Hamilton	Haverhill (New Eng.)	113	408	113*	168*	32	8	0	—	74*	412*
1905	Charlie Hemphill	St. Paul (A. A.)	145	560	122	204*	38	12	5	—	40	.364*
1906	Mike Welday	Des Moines (Western)	129	549	93	197	—	—	—	—	31	.359
1907	Ed Householder	Aberdeen (Northwest)	127	499	64	173	30*	19	9	—	19	.347*
1908	Ward Miller	Wausau (Wis.-Ill.)	124	408	91*	156*	—	—	—	—	—	.382*
1909	Harry Welch	Omaha (Western)	151	527	81	196*	41	15	7	—	51	.372*
1910	Dave Callahan	Eau Claire (Minn.-Wis.)	126	460	92*	168*	25	17*	2	—	52	.365*
1911	Frank Huelsman	Great Falls (U.A.)	135	516	117	212	48	15	17*	125*	25	.411*
1912	Charlie Johnson	Trenton (Tri-State)	109	400	86	161	31	5	14	—	22	.403*
1913	Frank Huelsman	Salt Lake City (U.A.)	122	473	123*	200*	36*	20*	22*	126*	16	.423*
1914	Joe Harris	Bay City (So. Michigan)	139	510	135	197*	39	22*	10	—	42	.386*
1915	Big Bill Kay	Binghamton (N.Y. St.)	125	447	98*	169*	22	25*	7	—	35	.378*
1916	Hank Butcher	Denver (Western)	145	541	116	204	31	20*	15	—	32	.377*
1917	Nap Lajoie	Toronto (Int.)	151	581	83	221*	39*	4	5	—	4	.380*
1918	Polly McLarry	Shreveport (Texas)	29	84	12	24	3	1	1	—	6	.286
		Binghamton (Int.)	103	335	51	129	26	7	4	—	15	.385*
											overall	.365
1919	Joe Wilhoit	Seattle (PCL)	17	67	8	11	1	0	0	—	3	.164
		Wichita (Western)	128	526	126*	222*	41	10	7	—	13	.422*
											overall	.393
1920	Merwyn Jacobson	Baltimore (Int.)	154*	581	161*	235*	35	16*	7	—	18	.404*
1921	Jack Lelivelt	Omaha (Western)	166	659	149	274*	70*	9	14	—	24	.416*
1922	Jack Schaefer	London (Mich.-Ont.)	100	407	79	167	27	21	9	—	9	.410*
1923	Moses Solomon	Hutchinson (So'west.)	134	527	143*	222*	40*	15	49*	—	12	.421*
1924	T. P. Osborne	Mt. Pleasant (E. Tex.)	101	396	93	171*	48	3	23	—	46*	.432*[1]
1925	Paul Waner	San Francisco (PCL)	174	699	167	280	75*	7	11	130	8	.401*
1926	Bill Diester	Salina (So'west.)	106	428	110*	190*	33*	4	27	—	10	.444*
		Tulsa (Western)	11	44	5	15	4	0	0	—	0	.341
											overall	.434
1927	Elton Langford	Des Moines (Western)	149	611	132	250	47	28*	8	—	31	.409*
1928	Danny Boone	High Point (Piedmont)	128	468	123	196*	40	11	38*	131*	11	.419*
1929	Ed Kallina	Midland(W. Tex.)	94	367	126	159	28	7	44*	—	16	.433*
		Sherman (Lone Star)	17	64	22	22	—	—	6	—	1	.344
											overall	.420
1930	Tony Antista	Bisbee (Arizona St.)	109*	444	127*	191*	36	16*	17	100	18	.430*
1931	Babe Phelps	Youngstown (Mid-Atl.)	115	436	71	178	29	9	15	88	9	.408*
1932	George Puccinelli	Rochester (Int.)	133	478	102	187	34	8	28	115	2	.391*
1933	Ox Eckhardt	Mission (PCL)	189*	760	145	315*	56	16	12	143	15	.414*
1934	Frank Demaree	Los Angeles (PCL)	186	702	190*	269*	51*	4	45*	173*	41	.383*
1935	Ox Eckhardt	Mission (PCL)	172	710	149	283*	40	11	2	114	8	.399*
1936	Cal Lahman	Jamestown (Northern)	127	466	154*	182*	30	9	48*	162*	20	.391*
1937	Earl "Red" Martin	Beckley (Mt. St.)	91	360	80	144	39*	14*	8	96*	7	.400*
		Scranton (NYP)	11	41	7	10	1	0	0	4	1	.244
											overall	.384
1938	Murray Franklin	Beckley (Mt. St.)	94	385	91	169	31	13*	26*	110	13	.439*[2]
1939	Joe Schmidt	Duluth (Northern)	120	440	114*	194*	29	9	31*	133*	17	.441*
1940	Ed Schweda	Lubbock (W. Tex.-N.M.)	114	469	142	198	39	15	11	118	7	.422*
1941	Lew Flick	Elizabethton (App.)	117	502*	127*	210*	37*	13	5	116*	20	.418*
1942	Don Manno	Welch (Mt. St.)	117	457	136*	174*	32	14*	34*	122*	23	.381*
1943	George Kell	Lancaster (Inter-St.)	138	555	120*	220*	33	23*	5	79	14	.396*
1944	Roland Gladu	Hartford (Eastern)	119	417	92	155	28	14	7	102	8	.372
1945	Arden "Cotton" McCaskey	Bristol (App.)	106	437	72	164*	26*	14*	2	96	5	.375*
1946	Walt Forwood	Carbondale (N. Atl.)	111	419	98	170*	43*	7	3	101	22	.406*
1947	Jim Prince	Midland (Longhorn)	108	415	111	178	31	6	34	141	4	.429*
		Lubbock (W. Tex.-N.M.)	12	37	7	10	3	0	1	12	0	.270
											overall	.416
1948	Hershel Martin	Albuquerque (W. Tex.-N.M.)	132	447	133	190	61*	6	18	128	5	.425*
1949	Bob Montag	Pawtucket (New Eng.)	125	454	139*	192*	36	18*	21*	91	43*	.423*
1950	Oscar Sierra	Hornell (Pony)	93	358	99	151	28	2	21	114	12	.422*
		Newport News (Piedmont)	15	45	5	13	1	0	0	5	0	.289
											overall	.407
1951	D. C. "Pud" Miller	Hickory (N.C. St.)	119	426	115	181	32	1	40*	136*	2	.425*
1952	Don Stafford	Salisbury (N.C. St.)	105	392	99	160	31	3	18	90	1	.408*[3]
1953	Russ Snyder	McAlester (Sooner St.)	138	556	137	240*	32	16	2	84	74*	.432*
1954	Neal Cobb	Crestview (Ala.-Fla.)	115	435	108	188	27	8	5	124	3	.432*
1955	Tom Jordan	Artesia (Longhorn)	136	543	116	221*	69*	2	28	159*	4	.407*
1956	Len Tucker	Pampa (So'west)	140	565	181*	228	40	13	51	181	47*	404*
1957	Fran Boniar	Reno (Calif.)	110	443	102	193	33	15	11	138*	4	.436*
		Pueblo (Western)	11	37	5	9	1	0	0	7	3	.243
											overall	.421
1958	Neb Wilson	Ft. Walton Beach-Pensacola (Ala.-Fla.)	119	409	102*	162	38*	3	24*	106*	3	.396*
1959	Tom Hamilton	St. Petersburg (Fla. St.)	125	401	109	155	20	3	20*	96	3	.387*
1960	Al Pinkston	Mexico City Reds (Mexican)	138	567	110	225*	41	11	26	144*	4	.397*
1961	Al Pinkston	Veracruz (Mexican)	109	406	79	152	26*	4	13	86	4	.374*
1962	Ramiro Caballero	Guanajuato (Mex. Center)	113	423	123	175*	25	0	59*	170	3	.414*
1963	Vinicio Garcia	Monterrey (Mexican)	122	475	107*	175	36*	5	21	88	3	.368*
1964	Ramiro Caballero	Leon (Mex. Center)	121	460	135*	175*	29	1	35*	145*	3	.380*
1965	Alfonso Peciado	Guanajuato (Mex. Center)	130	529	103	224*	48*	14*	11	147	11	.423*
1966	Heriberto Vargas	Veracruz (Mexican)	7	14	0	3	0	0	0	0	0	.214
		Guanajuato (Mex. Center)	127	481	168*	214	33	1	55*	174*	3	.445*
											overall	.438
1967	Hilario Pena	Campeche (Mex. S.E.)	102	404	60	159	61	3	1	49	9	.394*

Year	Player	Team (League)	G	AB	R	H	2B	3B	HR	RBI	SB	AVG.
1968	Jim Hicks	Tulsa (PCL)	117	407	100*	149	32	7	23	85	14	.366*
1969	Bernie Carbo	Indianapolis (A.A.)	111	404	83	145	37	2	21	76	7	.359*
1970	Miguel Suarez	Tampico (Mex. Center)	126	460	105	181*	37*	4	14	101	15	.393*
1971	Téolindo Acosta	Puebla (Mexican)	133	441	75	173	22	11	7	71	17	.392*
1972	Don Anderson	Jalisco (Mexican)	130	445	76	161	31	2	8	68	0	.362*
1973	Hector Espino	Tampico (Mexican)	116	422	82	159	20	2	22	107*	3	.377*
1974	Téolindo Acosta	Puebla (Mexican)	122	464	93*	170*	17	6	2	43	20	.366*
1975	Gene Richards	Reno (Calif.)	134	501*	148*	191*	29	10	12	58	85*	.381*
1976	Pat Putnam	Asheville (W. Car.)	138	538	100	194*	33*	3	24*	142*	8	.361*
1977	Rudy Law	Lodi (California)	122	451	124	174	22	5	9	88	37	.386*
1978	Champ Summers	Indianapolis (A.A.)	132	462	98	170*	25	5	34*	124*	11	.368
1979	Jimmie Collins	Chihuahua (Mexican)	124	470	95	206*	35	10	6	60	33	.438*
1980	Jimmie Collins	Chihuahua (Mex. #1)	91	346	62	131	19	13	4	52	19	.379
		Saltillo (Mex. #2)	39	137	25	52*	8	3*	2	31*	5	.380
											overall	.379
1981	Kent Hrbek	Visalia (Calif.)	121	462	119	175	25	5	27	111	12	.379*
1982	Randy Ready	El Paso (Texas)	132	475	122*	178*	33	5	20	99	13	.375*
1983	Chris Smith	Phoenix (PCL)	123	449	88	170	31	5	21	102	4	379*
1984	Jimmie Collins	Mexico City Reds-Cordoba (Mexican)	109	403	81	166	35	4	6	59	12	.412*
1985	Oswaldo Olivares	Aguas.-Campeche (Mexican)	110	441	85	175*	22	14*	5	49	20	.397*
1986	Willie Aikens	Puebla (Mexican)	129	445	134	202*	38	3	46	154*	0	.454*
1987	Orlando Sanchez	Puebla (Mexican)	123	439	95	182	34	1	25	115	6	.415*
1988	Nelson Barrera	Mexico City Reds (Mexican)	129	460	90	171	26	0	31	124*	7	.372
1989	Willie Aikens	León (Mexican)	128	423	108*	167	40	1	37	131*	1	.395*
1990	Trench Davis	Saltillo (Mexican)	127	498	84	189*	33	4	5	50	20	.380
1991	Rich Renteria	Jalisco (Mexican)	104	382	90	169	30	6	24	106	17	.442*
		Indianapolis (A.A.)	20	72	6	17	5	0	1	5	0	.236
											overall	.410
1992	Raul Perez Tovar	Monclova (Mexican)	129	483	83	201	32	5	8	93	14	.416*
1993	Nelson Simmons	Jalisco (Mexican)	109	369	81	141	27	0	34	95	1	.382
		Palm Springs (California)	20	76	13	25	8	0	5	23	0	.329
											overall	.373
1994	Brian Hunter	Tucson (PCL)	128	513	113*	191*	28	9	10	51	49*	.372*
1995	Adam Riggs	San Bernardino (Calif.)	134	542	111*	196*	39*	5	24	106	31	.362*
1996	Vladimir Guerrero	West Palm Beach (Fla. St.)	20	80	16	29	8	0	5	18	2	.363
		Harrisburg (Eastern)	118	417	84	150	32	8	19	78	17	.360*
											overall	.360
1997	Mike Kinkade	El Paso (Texas)	125	468	112	180	35	12	12	109	17	.385*
1998	Miguel Flores	Monterrey (Mexican)	100	399	87	152	32	4	4	67	32	.380
1999	Matias Carillo	Mexico City Tigers (Mexican)	112	421	107	175	27	2	20	98	3	.416
2000	Warren Newson	Union Laguna (Mexican)	112	417	104	161	2	1	39	121	3	.386*

*Led league in category

[1]If charged with 400 at bats, Osborne's average would be .428, higher than any player with 400 or more at bats. (George Rhinehardt, Greenville (Sally) G: 120, AB: 495, R: 110*, H: 200*, 2B: 45*, 3B: 18, HR: 8, RBI: 92, SB: 32*, AVG: .404*)

[2]If charged with 400 at bats, Franklin's average would be .423, higher than any player with 400 or more at bats. (Butch Moran, Rogers (Ark.-Mo.) G: 105, AB: 406, R: 107, H: 159, 2B: 43*, 3B: 12, HR: 22*, RBI: 114, SB: 8, AVG: .392*)

[3]If charged with 400 at bats, Stafford's average would be .400, higher than any player with 400 or more at bats. (Clint McCord, Clinton (Miss. Ohio Val.) G:119, AB: 482, R: 123, H: 189*, 2B: 40, 3B: 15, HR: 15, RBI: 109, SB: 20, AVG: .392*)

[4]If charged with 400 at bats, Flores average would be .380, higher than any player with 400 or more at bats. (Ramon Espinosa, Mexico City Reds (Mexican) G:121, AB: 533, R: 114, H: 202, 2B: 31, 3B: 5, HR: 7, RBI: 62, SB: 16, AVG: .379)

CHAPTER 14

College Baseball

Beau Riffenburgh

There are a lot of similarities in the way information about football and baseball players is recorded. If you compare all-time player registers for professional football and major league baseball, for example, you will see that they both include much of the same data for any particular player: full name, height, weight, birth and death dates, and sites, years played professionally and for which teams, and the appropriate statistics. But look at the register here in *Total Baseball.* See something missing that you would see in any football listing? There is no space for college attended.

That omission says a great deal about the historic significance of college baseball. It is a game that is almost a century and a half old, but one that was neglected until relatively recently not only by most sports fans but by scouts and personnel experts of the professional leagues. Oh, it has their attention now. If you don't believe it, go to Omaha, Nebraska, at the beginning of June, and you will think that you have stumbled into a scouting combine.

But it took a long time for the college version of the national pastime to really get going. After all, the first intercollegiate baseball game was played a dozen years before the National Association became America's first major professional sports league. On July 1, 1859, Amherst and Williams played a game at Pittsfield, Massachusetts. The score, 73–32 in favor of Amherst, was as different from those of today as was the field, which included a diamond only 60 feet per side and a pitcher 25 feet closer to the batter than in the current game. That day, Amherst and Williams actually played a version of the "Massachusetts Game," a contest a great deal closer to rounders than the "New York Game" that developed into modern baseball.

From the very beginning of professional baseball, there were ties to the college game. In 1871, the first year of the National Association, at least two of the new professionals had previously played college ball—Rockford's Denny Mack, who had attended Villanova, and Troy's Steve Bellan, who had played for Fordham, then known as Rose Hill. In the ensuing decades there was a continual trickle of players from the colleges into the major leagues, including, around the turn of the century, Christy Mathewson from Bucknell, Eddie Plank from Gettysburg, and Jack Coombs from Colby. Connie Mack's "$100,000 infield" included two "college boys": second baseman Jimmy Collins, who had played at Columbia, and shortstop Jack Barry, from Holy Cross.

Of course, college men were not always warmly received into the majors. There has always been a natural reluctance by veterans to accept new players who are trying to take their jobs or those of their friends. This was perhaps even more the case in days of smaller rosters, with only 18 men on each team. And that divide was even greater between many of the long-term professionals and the youngsters from college, who were seen as being not only more highly educated, better mannered, and more cultured, but from superior social and economic backgrounds.

Writing around the turn of the century, sportswriter George E. Stackhouse told the story of a catcher who became concerned when his manager began "to get the college baseball fever." The catcher approached a local college player and asked him if he wished to turn pro. Upon receiving an answer in the negative, the catcher said, "Now that's square, old man. You know Greek, Latin, and something about the world. You can make a good living anywhere. Don't interfere with us fellows, because you don't have to."

Early on, there were also many college players who simply were not interested in playing professionally. For every Lou Gehrig, who came to the Yankees from Columbia, there were numerous other college players who skipped a chance at a pro career because they could make more money in some other business, without having the unattractive travel conditions and long hours of a life in baseball. Nevertheless, by 1909 there were 57 major league players—approximately 14 percent of the players in the big leagues—who had college backgrounds. This figure soared to approximately one-third of the major leaguers by 1932.

Despite the obvious talent in it, the college game itself remained in the background. The colleges had to compete for attention not only with the professional leagues, but with semi-pro teams, town teams, and industrial league teams. In the early decades of the 20th century, the big-time university programs were all located in the east or midwest, where weather conditions prevented an early start to the season, which was therefore necessarily short in order to conform to term dates. Limited travel opportunities due to timing and cost, a short schedule of games, and competition from others sports within the athletic department also helped to hold down the popularity of college baseball.

The College World Series

The game took a major step forward after World War II, when the NCAA began its national championship tournament. Not only did this give the sport more exposure than it previously had received, national playoffs showed that the game had expanded beyond its early strongholds. In fact, it took six years before an eastern team actually won a national title.

In 1947 four teams participated in single-elimination regionals in both the east and west, and the two winners met in the initial College World Series, at Kalamazoo, Michigan. The first national championship was won by the University of California, which defeated Yale, 8–7. The champion Bears were led by All-America outfielders Jackie Jensen and John Fiscalini. The Elis' captain was a weak-hitting first baseman named George Bush, who would ultimately become President of the United States.

Yale lost in the championship game again the next year, as the University of Southern California won the first of its record dozen national titles. The Trojans had co-coaches that year, Sam Barry and Rod Dedeaux, the latter of whom had been a three-time letterman at USC before a two-game career with the Brooklyn Dodgers. Dedeaux was just the first of numerous college coaches to win national titles after having played professionally. The next two came along almost immediately.

In 1949 the College World Series was moved from Kalamazoo to Wichita, Kansas, where it was a four-team, double-elimination tournament. Texas, coached by long-time White Sox star Bibb Falk—a career .314 hitter who had been the successor to Shoeless Joe Jackson—won the title with a 10–3 victory over Wake Forest. The Deacons, led by second baseman Charles Teague, the first three-time All-America baseball player and the tournament's most valuable player, had reached the championship game by eliminating Southern California. The next year, Texas became the first team to repeat as national champions, as the Longhorns rolled through the newly expanded, eight-team tournament. But even more significantly, the College World Series itself, which played in a new site for the third time in four years, found a permanent home: Omaha, Nebraska. The CWS has now been in Omaha for more than half a century, and few sporting events have found venues with a local populace that has so totally embraced the event, the teams, and the athletes.

Two years after Falk's second title, another former professional star coached his team to a national championship. Jack Barry had been hired as coach at Holy Cross in 1921, shortly after he retired from the major leagues. In 1952 Barry's Crusaders defeated Missouri, 8–4, to bring the east its first national title and to give Barry his first World Series title since he had played for the Boston Red Sox in the "real World Series" in 1915. Almost 40 years after Barry retired, he still holds the NCAA career record for highest winning percentage (.806).

Throughout the rest of the 1950s and the early 1960s, college baseball was dominated by a handful of universities. At USC the story was Rod Dedeaux, who had become the coach on his own when Sam Barry died in 1950. Dedeaux's Trojans won national titles in 1958, 1961, and 1963, while just missing in 1960, when they lost 2–1 in 10 innings to Minnesota. The Gophers had become a power under the leadership of Dick Siebert, the former Philadelphia Athletics first baseman. Siebert led Minnesota to its first national title in 1956 and followed that with championships in 1960 and 1964. During the early 1950s, the Gophers had perhaps their greatest pitcher ever, Paul Giel. In 1953 Giel, who had been named second-team All-America the previous season and would be again the following year, had the unusual distinction of being named first team All-America by the Baseball Coaches Association the same calendar year he was a consensus All-America in football.

Meanwhile, Big Ten rival Michigan also managed two national titles during that span, despite changing coaches. Missouri won only one title—in 1954—but the Tigers reached the championship game three other times in that period, losing to teams coached by both Dedeaux and Siebert, a dubious distinction also held by Arizona, which also lost each of its three title appearances.

The Big Three Programs

The year after Arizona lost to USC in the 1963 national championship game, a new bully showed up on the scene, just down the road from the home of the Arizona Wildcats. Coached by Bobby Winkles, who was a master at recruiting talent and making disparate personalities work well together, Arizona State became a national contender almost overnight. In 1964 the Sun Devils finished ranked second in the nation.

The next year, with a team loaded with talent, Arizona State stormed to its first national title. Second baseman Luis Lagunas led the nation in RBIs, center fielder Rick Monday led in triples, and pitcher Jim Merrick led in victories. Meanwhile, Luganas, Monday, and pitcher John Pavilk were named All-America, as outfielder Reggie Jackson would be the next year. Sal Bando was selected the most valuable player in the 1965 CWS, which concluded with the Sun Devils' 2-1 victory over Ohio State. Monday then became the first player chosen in the first baseball amateur draft.

The draft not only helped change the face of major league baseball, it changed the way that college programs looked at players, and the way that coaches recruited them. Initially college players were eligible to be drafted if they had attained sophomore status or were 21 years old. Two years later the rule was changed so that players were eligible for the draft if they had attained junior status. The draft made it highly unlikely that many top-rated players would remain in a college program for four years. It also meant that players who transferred from a junior college might well leave after a single season at a major university, or, indeed, not attend a four-year college at all, since those completing junior college were also eligible for the draft.

Equally problematic for college coaches were the questions about freshman players. If drafted out of high school, a player remained eligible to be signed by the pro team until he had attended his first class. That meant a player signing a letter of intent with a university might well disregard his commitment at any moment, even once term was starting. The case of Richard Wortham, a high draft choice out of Odessa High School, who signed with the University of Texas, made many college coaches feel uncomfortable with the way major league teams interfered with their players. Before his freshman year in 1973, Wortham had to fight off the constant attentions of the professional representatives, who went so far as to walk with him to his first class, all the time attempting to sign him. Wortham attended class, however, and then stayed at Texas for four years, in the process becoming the first pitcher in NCAA history to win 50 games in his career.

Other players have not been so keen to stay in the college game. Alex Fernandez was selected in the first round of the 1988 draft, but chose rather to attend the University of Miami. His success there—he was named national Freshman of the Year in 1989 by *Baseball America*—led Fernandez to reconsider his choice. Fernandez transferred to Miami-Dade County Community College for his sophomore year. That season he went 12–2 with a 1.19 ERA and was named National Junior College Player of the Year. Fernandez was then selected by the White Sox fourth overall in the 1990 draft. By the end of the year, he was pitching in the major leagues.

A quarter of a century before Fernandez turned professional, the huge amounts of talent that Arizona State lost to the early drafts did not prevent the Sun Devils from becoming a regular national contender, in fact one of the three top teams of the mid-1960s to the mid-1970s. The Sun Devils won further titles in 1967 and 1969, and lost in the national championship games of 1972 and 1973. Winkles' teams had such success that in 1973 the California Angels hired him as manager, making him the first college coach to manage in the majors with no previous big league experience. Winkles had not been the entire story at Arizona State, of course. In each of these appearances by the Sun Devils in the title game, they featured a pitcher who both led the nation in victories and was named All-America: Gary Gentry in 1967, Larry Gura in 1969, Craig Swan in 1972, and Eddie Bane in 1973. Gura's 19 victories were an NCAA record at the time, as were Swan's 47 career wins, Gentry's 229 strikeouts in a season, and Bane's 505 K's in a career.

Since pitching was such a key to college baseball at the time, it is not surprising that Texas, like Arizona State, was one of the three dominating powers. In 1968 Cliff Gustafson succeeded Bibb Falk as head coach, and the Longhorns immediately established the greatest pitching dynasty in the history of the college game. From 1969 to 1971 Burt Hooton of the Longhorns became the first three-time All-America pitcher and probably the most dominant ever in college. Hooton's 35–3 career mark included a 1.14 ERA and an NCAA record 13 shutouts. "Hooton is easily the best college pitcher we've ever seen," Winkles later said. "He was never anything less than spectacular, never not at the height of his game."

Texas followed Hooton's stint with four All-America pitchers in five years, including two-timer Jim Gideon, who led the nation in victories in 1974 and 1975, tying the record of 19 the former year and setting a record with 17 without a loss the latter. At the time, only two pitchers per year were named All-America, meaning that seven times in eight years Texas had featured one of the two best pitchers in the country. Despite this, Texas won only one national title in a two decade span, in 1975 when Gideon and Wortham combined to go 32–1. The reason the Longhorns consistently came up short was simple: Southern California.

Starting in 1968, Rod Dedeaux's Trojans put together the most successful dynasty in college baseball history. USC won the national title that year, then, after surrendering it to Arizona State, the Trojans won a record five in a row. The Trojans did not always have the best record going into the playoffs, but there was something special about them—they just knew when they came to Omaha that they were going to win. Like in 1970, when, in a semi-final game against Texas, the last unbeaten team, the Trojans trailed 7–1 going into the seventh inning. But they managed to tie it up and the game went into extra innings. Then, in the 14th, they drove in a run to win, 8–7. USC followed that up with another marathon, defeating Florida State 2–1 in 15 innings for the championship.

Nothing, however, matched the Trojans' comeback against Minnesota in 1973. Trailing the Gophers and their star pitcher Dave Winfield 7–0 going into the bottom of the ninth, USC parlayed eight singles, a stolen base, a sacrifice fly, and several Minnesota errors into a stunning 8–7 victory that eliminated Minnesota and put the Trojans into the championship game. There, they defeated Arizona State, 4–3. That team, one of the greatest in college history, included future major leaguers Fred Lynn, Roy Smalley, Steve Kemp, Rich Dauer, Randy Scarbery, Pete Redfern, Dennis Littlejohn, and Ed Putnam.

The Aluminum Bat

The 1974 season not only marked the last year of USC's reign, it signaled two major changes in college baseball. First, the NCAA adopted the designated hitter rule. And second, it allowed the use of the aluminum bat. The new bats were a tremendous success in more ways than one. As a cost factor, they brought down bat budgets to approximately 10 percent of what they had previously been. As a weapon, they began to change the game dramatically. It was much easier to hit with the new bats. The entire surface of the bat was, more or less, a "sweet spot" and hits could be made as easily from the handle as from the meat of the bat. The ball traveled at a much greater rate coming off the bat—increasing home runs and hits to the outfield—and the "ping" sound did not help direct the fielders as did the typical crack of a bat. Runs and home runs both soared, and teams such as Arizona State, Wichita State, and Oklahoma State regularly began to average more than 10 runs per game.

When the new bats were combined with increasingly longer schedules, records began to fall with alarming frequency. The individual record of 17 home runs in a season was broken in 1974, and Bob Horner of Arizona State became the first player to hit 25 in a season in 1978. In 1982 Jeff Ledbetter of Florida State shattered the record with 42 homers, and three years later Pete Incaviglia of Oklahoma State had perhaps the greatest offensive season ever, when, in a 75-game season, he set NCAA records with 48 home runs, 143 RBIs, and a slugging percentage of 1.140.

For the fan who liked to see offense, it was wonderful. For purists, much less so. And it also began to have an effect on interactions with the pro game. Throughout the early 1970s, there had been a greater emphasis on taking college players in the draft. By 1977 more college players were being selected than high school players, and by 1981 five times as many college players were entering the major leagues as those drafted out of high school. But hitters were now forced to readjust to wooden bats, and quite a number struggled as they entered the minors. It was a problem that would not go away, because the universities could not return to wooden bats due to cost. The NCAA's attempts at adjusting the aluminum bats or using graphite bats have not solved the problem, and 25 years later it is still an issue. Many college players have tried to adjust to wooden bats in the summer leagues, such as the Cape Cod League, but this remains an inadequate solution.

Throughout the rest of the 1970s and during the 1980s, certain programs blossomed with the new bats, none more so than Wichita State and Oklahoma State. The Shockers—led by Joe Carter, Phil Stephenson, Jim Thomas, and Russ Mormon—simply wrecked the record book between 1979 and 1983, leading the nation in hits and doubles four times each, and runs and triples five times each, as well as recording team batting averages of .384 and .378 in 1979 and 1980, respectively. At the same time, Oklahoma State's Gary Ward, one of the great hitting instructors in the history of college baseball, made the Cowboys a regular in Omaha at the end of the season. Although Ward did not guide a team to a national title, his .753 winning percentage is the sixth best of all time, he led Oklahoma State to the NCAA championship game three times, and he coached two of the most productive players in college history, Incaviglia and Robin Ventura. One of only seven three-time All-Americas (according to recognized NCAA polls), Ventura was a career .428 hitter, who set a national record when he hit safely in 58 consecutive games.

Meanwhile, big numbers, and numerous records, were also put up regularly in the Rocky Mountains. The Western Athletic Conference teams tended to have small stadiums, which, in conjunction with the thin air, saw a lot of balls carry a long way. Brigham Young, Air Force, and New Mexico in particular showed a great deal of power, with Deacon Winters, Wally Joyner, Cory Snyder, Jim Fregosi, Mike Willis, and Gary Daniels each having big statistical seasons undoubtedly helped by where they played most of their games.

Despite the national trends in hitting, however, certain teams continued to emphasize—and win with—pitching. Texas won one national title and made the championship game three other times in the 1980s by continuing its tradition of dominating pitching. Ten times in a dozen-year period Texas had an All-America pitcher, including the second and third ones ever to be three-time All-Americas, Greg Swindell (1984-86) and Kirk Dressendorfer (1988-90). When the Longhorns won the 1983 national championship, Calvin Schiraldi was named national Pitcher of the Year, Kirk Killingsworth was honored as the nation's best relief pitcher, and Mike Capel had the best winning percentage on the team, while the other starter in the rotation was a guy named Roger Clemens.

On an individual level, the most successful pitcher was Derek Tatsuno of the University of Hawaii. Tatsuno led the nation in strikeouts three consecutive years (1977-79) and in that final year became the first pitcher to win 20 games in a season.

But, as usual, the teams that tended to win the most titles had, above all, outstanding coaching. There was not a better example of this than Jerry Kindall, who had been an All-America second baseman for Dick Siebert at Minnesota. Kindall led Arizona to three national championships—in 1976, 1980, and 1986—despite having only two All-Americas (Dave Stegman and Terry Francona) in those three years combined. Across the state Jim Brock succeeded Winkles and led Arizona State to two more national titles. The California teams also continued to be hugely successful. Dedeaux won another title in 1978 before retiring with a record 1,332 victories; Mark Marquess led Stanford to a pair of national championships; and Augie Garrido turned Cal State Fullerton into a power, winning national titles in three decades: 1979, 1984, and 1995.

ESPN and Growing Popularity

The single thing that increased national interest in college baseball more than any other happened off the field. ESPN's decisions to broadcast first the final stages of the College World Series, and then the entire series, gave national exposure to college baseball on a far-reaching level for the first time. People who didn't even know universities had baseball teams were able to watch Arizona State's 7–4 championship game victory over Oklahoma State in 1981. And the next year the entire CWS, with teams representing all sections of the country—including Miami, Wichita State, Texas, Maine, Oklahoma State, and Stanford—was broadcast nationally. Ratings were higher than many could have expected, leading the way within several years for ESPN to start showing a "game of the week" throughout the college season. Although this was later dropped, the College World Series gradually became such a popular commodity that by 1989 ESPN could no longer afford the national championship game.

The growing popularity of the CWS had one unfortunate effect. The scheduling of the national championship game on network television required a set date for the final contest. Thus, in 1989 the format of the World Series, which had been double elimination for 40 years, was changed so that the eight teams were divided into two four-team divisions. The winners of each division—based on double-elimination play—met for the national title in a single-elimination game. This set up the possibility that a team with one loss could defeat a team with no losses for the title, an eventuality that actually occurred the first season of the new format.

The increased popularity of college baseball in the 1980s was also assisted by its ever-closer relationship with the major leagues. Due to ESPN, fans could now, as they had always done in football, first get to see players in college, and then follow their progress as professionals. The juxtaposition of the draft with the College World Series allowed a chance to see the play of the top selections while they were still in college. In the early 1980s, much more than previously, the colleges came to be viewed as almost a minor league, particularly as players moved quickly through the minors to the big leagues.

There have always been the unusual players who have gone straight to the majors from college, skipping the minors. In 1973 Dave Winfield was one of the first of these. Winfield, a multi-talented athlete who had major league talent as both a pitcher and a hitter, was also selected in the National Football League and National Basketball Association drafts, but instead he went immediately from being the CWS Most Valuable Player to the San Diego Padres. He singled off Jerry Reuss in his first at bat, hit safely in his first six games, and went on to a long and successful career. Five years later, after leading the nation in home runs twice and winning the Golden Spikes Award as the best amateur baseball player, Arizona State's Bob Horner went straight to the Atlanta Braves. In his first game in the pros, Horner homered off Bert Blyleven, on his way to being named National League Rookie of the Year.

Neither Winfield nor Horner, however, attained the national reputation that Pete Incaviglia had at Oklahoma State, buoyed by his two appearances in the College World Series, which gave luster to his record-setting achievements and his status as College Player of the Year. Although drafted by Montreal in 1985, Incaviglia refused to sign and was traded to the Rangers, for whom he hit 30 homers as a rookie. In 1989 two other players leapt straight from the college ranks to the major leagues after being named Player of the Year by at least one of the growing number of organizations presenting that award: John Olerud of Washington State (the only All-America baseball player who was the son of an All-America baseball player) and Jim Abbott, the amazing one-handed pitcher from Michigan. Abbott had several successful professional seasons, while Olerud is still playing in the majors.

The Game of the Sun Belt

When Wichita State won the national title in 1989, it marked the first time since 1966, when Ohio State was national champion, that the title was won by a team out of the Sun Belt. Things have returned to normal since then. But whereas the CWS used to be dominated by teams from California, Arizona, and Texas, the deep south has now become the major player.

Miami won titles in 1982 and 1985 under Ron Fraser, and in 1999 under Jim Morris. The 6–5 victory against Florida State in 1999 marked the 18th appearance in the CWS for the Seminoles, although they have never won the national title. Georgia Tech, led by three-time All-America catcher Jason Varitek, reached the national championship game in 1994.

The past decade, however, has belonged to Louisiana State, winners of five national titles. The key to this success—like Dedeaux was at USC—has been coach Skip Bertman, who was widely considered to be the top assistant in the country when he was the pitching coach for Miami under Fraser. Bertman's initial contribution was made in the development of the pitching staff, including, in 1989, Ben McDonald, who was named College Player of the Year before being the number-one selection in the draft.

LSU's first national championship came two years later, on the heels of Georgia's 1990 title, the first ever for a Southeastern Conference team. In that championship run, the Tigers showed the offense that they have been known for ever since, setting or tying College World Series records for home runs, runs per game, and slugging percentage, as well as for fielding percentage. Two years later, LSU won again, defeating Wichita State in the title game for the second time.

In 1996 second baseman Warren Morris hit a two-out, two-run homer in the bottom of the ninth as the Tigers came from behind to defeat Miami 9–8, marking the first time that the national title was decided on a homer in the bottom of the ninth. The next year the Tigers had to outlast three other teams from the SEC—Alabama, Auburn, and Mississippi State—to win the championship. Such participation makes it clear that the SEC has at least equaled the quality of baseball in the Six Pac, the southern division of the Pacific 10 Conference, which was long considered the best conference in college baseball.

Not that the Six Pac isn't still a baseball power. USC won yet another national title in 1998, this time under Mike Gillespie, after losing in the championship game to Cal State Fullerton in 1995. And Arizona State and Stanford have both appeared in the title game in recent years.

Meanwhile, the Big 12 has become another center of excellence after joining teams from two strong baseball conferences, the Southwest and the Big 8. In the 1990s Oklahoma and Oklahoma State both reached the national championship game. Meanwhile, from 1991 to 1993 Texas fielded its fourth three-time All-America (more than the rest of the nation combined) in Brooks Kieschnick, the only player ever to win a major award (the Dick Howser Award) as the top amateur baseball player in America more than once. In 1996 Cliff Gustafson of the Longhorns retired after having broken Dedeaux's record by recording 1,427 victories, with a .792 winning percentage, second best of any coach ever with 500 victories.

The year 2000 showed that, despite its increasing popularity, some things never change and are seemingly carved in stone in college baseball. With one of its four-team divisions comprised of USC, Texas, LSU, and Florida State, the CWS not only fielded a flood of traditional powerhouses, but had a remarkably familiar feel among its eight teams from the Sun Belt. And then it came down to two teams that had never lost in a championship game before, and the two teams that were the last to have won back-to-back titles, LSU and Stanford.

With all the thrills that baseball can produce, Craig Thompson's grand slam in the fourth led Stanford to a 5–2 margin after seven innings. Then LSU's power showed up: first team captain Blair Barbier homered in the bottom of the eighth to cut it to 5–3, and then Jeremy Witten hit a two-out, two-run shot to tie it up. In the bottom of the ninth, Brad Cresse singled home the winning run for a 6–5 LSU victory. That temporarily scuttled Bertman's thoughts of retirement.

"What if I get another group like this one?" he said after the game. "Then I'd really be missing out. Because college baseball has a lot to offer."

Division I Baseball Championship Results

Year	Champion	Coach	Score	Runner-up
1947	California	Clint Evans	8–7	Yale
1948	Southern California	Sam Barry	9–2	Yale
1949	Texas	Bibb Falk	10–3	Wake Forest
1950	Texas	Bibb Falk	3–0	Washington State
1951	Oklahoma	Jack Baer	3–2	Tennessee
1952	Holy Cross	Jack Barry	8–4	Missouri
1953	Michigan	Ray Fisher	7–5	Texas
1954	Missouri	Hi Simmons	4–1	Rollins
1955	Wake Forest	Taylor Sanford	7–6	Western Michigan
1956	Minnesota	Dick Siebert	12–1	Arizona
1957	California	George Wolfman	1–0	Penn State
1958	Southern California	Rod Dedeaux	8–7	Missouri
1959	Oklahoma State	Toby Greene	5–3	Arizona
1960	Minnesota	Dick Siebert	2–1	Southern California
1961	Southern California	Rod Dedeaux	1–0	Oklahoma State
1962	Michigan	Don Lund	5–4	Santa Clara
1963	Southern California	Rod Dedeaux	5–2	Arizona
1964	Minnesota	Dick Siebert	5–1	Missouri
1965	Arizona State	Bobby Winkles	2–1	Ohio State
1966	Ohio State	Marty Karow	8–2	Oklahoma State
1967	Arizona State	Bobby Winkles	11–2	Houston
1968	Southern California	Rod Dedeaux	4–3	Southern Illinois
1969	Arizona State	Bobby Winkles	10–1	Tulsa
1970	Southern California	Rod Dedeaux	2–1	Florida State
1971	Southern California	Rod Dedeaux	7–2	Southern Illinois
1972	Southern California	Rod Dedeaux	1–0	Arizona State
1973	Southern California	Rod Dedeaux	4–3	Arizona State
1974	Southern California	Rod Dedeaux	7–3	Miami (Florida)
1975	Texas	Cliff Gustafson	5–1	South Carolina
1976	Arizona	Jerry Kindall	7–1	Eastern Michigan
1977	Arizona State	Jim Brock	2–1	South Carolina
1978	Southern California	Rod Dedeaux	10–3	Arizona State
1979	Cal State Fullerton	Augie Garrido	2–1	Arkansas
1980	Arizona	Jerry Kindall	5–3	Hawaii
1981	Arizona State	Jim Brock	7–4	Oklahoma State
1982	Miami (Florida)	Ron Fraser	9–3	Wichita State
1983	Texas	Cliff Gustafson	4–3	Alabama
1984	Cal State Fullerton	Augie Garrido	3–1	Texas
1985	Miami (Florida)	Ron Fraser	10–6	Texas
1986	Arizona	Jerry Kindall	10–2	Florida State
1987	Stanford	Mark Marquess	9–5	Oklahoma State
1988	Stanford	Mark Marquess	9–4	Arizona State
1989	Wichita State	Gene Stephenson	5–3	Texas
1990	Georgia	Steve Webber	2–1	Oklahoma State
1991	LSU	Skip Bertman	6–3	Wichita State
1992	Pepperdine	Andy Lopez	3–2	Cal State Fullerton
1993	LSU	Skip Bertman	8–0	Wichita State
1994	Oklahoma	Larry Cochell	13–5	Georgia Tech
1995	Cal State Fullerton	Augie Garrido	11–5	Southern California
1996	LSU	Skip Bertman	9–8	Miami (Florida)
1997	LSU	Skip Bertman	13–6	Alabama
1998	Southern California	Mike Gillespie	21–14	Arizona State
1999	Miami (Florida)	Jim Morris	6–5	Florida State
2000	LSU	Skip Bertman	6–5	Stanford

CHAPTER 15

Women in Baseball

Debra A. Shattuck

Women have been associated with baseball, either as players or spectators, since the game's dawn in the early 19th century. Even before baseball emerged in its final form, girls and young women sometimes played precursors of the game like One Old Cat, Town Ball, and Stoolball in Colonial America. As time passed, and the boys' amusement became serious business for grown men, baseball's reputation as a masculine domain was established. In 1865, one year before Charles Peverelly observed that baseball "has now become beyond question the leading feature of the outdoor sports of the United States," *Harper's Weekly* proclaimed: "There is no nobler or manlier game than base-ball."

During the latter half of the 19th century, women's presence as spectators at baseball games was tolerated and sometimes encouraged. Eventually promoters of the game hosted regular "Ladies Days" to attract female fans who would bring in added gate receipts and, hopefully, have a calming effect on the sometimes unruly crowds. Many women were content with their role as spectators and moral uplifters, but others yearned for the opportunity to try their hand at the national pastime. Those who lived out their fantasy often had to endure verbal and written derision from observers anxious to preserve the baseball status quo.

For the most part, the negative attitude toward women baseball players continues to this day. Many still share the opinion of an editorialist who noted in the *St. Louis Globe-Democrat* in 1885 that "The female has no place in base ball, except to the degradation of the game." The criticisms notwithstanding, uncounted women have pursued their own field of dreams, contributing their unique chapter to baseball's rich heritage.

Many of the first women baseball players were college students. The secluded atmosphere of all-girl schools enabled women to play the game without attracting too much attention. Students at Vassar College organized two baseball clubs as early as 1866. In 1879, according to Vassar alum Sophia Foster Richardson, the Vassar girls organized at least seven baseball clubs. The private grounds of college campuses did not always protect female players from public criticism, however. In a speech to an alumni association in 1896, Richardson recalled, "The public, so far as it knew of our playing, was shocked, but in our retired grounds, and protected from observation even in these grounds by sheltering trees, we continued to play in spite of a censorious public." Within a few years, however, the "censorious public" and "disapproving mothers" had succeeded in stifling the game at Vassar. But Vassar was not the only college where women tried their hand at baseball. In a letter to her former classmates at Smith College, Minnie Stephens (class of 1883) reminisced about the baseball clubs they had organized at the school in 1880. Stephens described the enthusiasm of the players and the keen competition at games. She also related how the Victorian-style clothing of the day, generally a hindrance to sporting endeavors, had actually benefited one of the players during a heated contest "One vicious batter drove a ball directly into the belt line of her opponent, and had it not been for the rigid steel corset clasp worn in those days, she would have been knocked out completely." Like the women at Vassar, baseball players at Smith College faced opposition that eventually forced them to give up the game for a number of years.

Women baseball players were not limited to college campuses. In Springfield, Illinois, three men organized a women's baseball club in 1875. They were confident that the novelty of women playing baseball would attract large crowds and fatten their bankroll. On September 11, 1875, the club's teams, labeled the "Blondes" and "Brunettes," played their first match. Newspapers heralded the event as the "first game of baseball ever played in public for gate money between feminine ball-tossers." The concept evidently caught on, for numerous other male entrepreneurs copied the idea and organized women's baseball teams. One group started the "Young Ladies' Baseball Club" in Philadelphia in 1883. These owners billed their team's games as entertainment spectacles, not serious competition, and they continually stressed the femininity and moral respectability of their players. A newspaper account of one of the club's first games relayed the management's claim that players were "selected with tender solicitude from 200 applicants, variety actresses and ballet girls being positively barred." Furthermore the article noted, "Only three of the lot had ever been on the stage, and they were in the strictly legitimate business."

The Young Ladies Baseball Club played its first game on August 18, 1883, at Pastime Park in Philadelphia. Despite the supposed "200 applicants," only 16 girls were mustered to form the two teams for the contest; two young men rounded out the rosters. The game was played on a regulation-size diamond, but, as one observer wrote, it was too large for the women. "A ball thrown from pitcher to second base almost invariably fell short and was stopped on the roll. The throw from first to third base was an utter impossibility." Five hundred spectators witnessed the club's debut and were caught up in "uncontrollable laughter" much of the time. From a financial standpoint, however, the venture was a success. More than 1,500 fans turned out for the club's match at the Manhattan Athletic Club on September 23, 1883, where they "laughed themselves hungry and thirsty." Though one observer conceded that "four of the girls had become expert—for girls," it is obvious that "novelty" and not "ability" was the hallmark of women's baseball at the time.

Bloomer Girls

Another novel group of women baseball players was the Bloomer Girls. Actually "Bloomer Girls" was a misnomer, since Bloomer Girls teams were composed of both men and women. Kansas City Bloomer Girls, New York Bloomer Girls, Texas Bloomer Girls, and Boston Bloomer Girls were just a few of the teams traveling from diamond to diamond in the late 19th and early 20th centuries in search of fame and fortune. Despite the number of Bloomer Girl teams, they did not play each other and no formal league was set up. Instead, they journeyed from town to town, challenging men's amateur and semiprofessional teams. The Bloomer Girls teams relied on sideshow-style appeal to draw fans and, not surprisingly, the bottom line was money. The manager of the Texas Bloomer Girls wrote to one prospective promoter in 1913, assuring him that the team's seven girls and four boys, "including the one-armed boy who plays center field," would draw enough fans to ensure the backer "three hundred dollars clear money" each week. A few of the male Bloomer Girls players like "Smoky Joe" Wood and Hall of Famer Rogers Hornsby went on to become successful big league ballplayers, but the future was not as bright for the female players who could not aspire to anything higher in the baseball world.

The Bloomer Girls teams were not the only option available to baseball-playing females around the turn of the century. Women's teams and mixed teams competed occasionally in "pickup" games. One such game took place in Kearsarge, New Hampshire, on August 7, 1903. An article in the *Boston Herald* the following day noted, "The teams were made up of young ladies gowned in white and young men decked out in girls' clothes, all New Englanders, guests at the hotel." On August 31, the newspaper announced an upcoming game at Forest Hills between the "Hickey and Clover clubs," each composed of five women and four men. One year later in Flat Rock, Indiana, a group of women organized two baseball clubs: one consisting only of married players, the other only of single players.

While some women played on all-female or coed teams, others challenged social constraints of the day by playing on otherwise all-male teams. On June 12, 1903, the *Cincinnati Enquirer* printed an article about the efforts of a local woman, Miss M. E. Phelan, to get a job as center fielder with the all-male Flora Baseball Club of Indiana. Phelan wrote to the club's manager informing him, "I have played with a number of lady ball clubs and am considered the equal of the average country player." Whether the Flora club took Phelan up on her offer to play for them for "$60 per month and expenses" is unknown, but only four years later another Ohioan, Alta Weiss, became an overnight female baseball-playing sensation and, as one article put it, "perhaps the only girl in the United States to obtain [a] college education through skill as a baseball player."

Weiss, a native of Ragersville, Ohio, became a celebrity in the Cleveland area when she made her pitching debut with the all-male, semiprofessional Vermilion Independents on September 2, 1907. More than 1,200 fans attended the game in which Weiss pitched five innings, giving up only four hits and one run. By the time Weiss made her second appearance on September 8, she was already being heralded as the "Girl Wonder" in the press. According to the *Vermilion News,* so many fans wanted to see Weiss play that special trains had to be run to Vermilion from Cleveland and surrounding towns.

Weiss pitched eight games for the Independents during their 1907 season. More than 13,000 fans saw the games, including a season high of 3,182, who witnessed her debut at Cleveland's League Park on October 2, 1907. At least a dozen newspapers covered her exploits. The following year her father bought a half-interest in a men's semiprofessional team which was known thereafter as the Weiss All-Stars. It was based in Cleveland and, with Alta as a drawing card, played for large crowds throughout Ohio and Kentucky.

Though Weiss was far and away the best-known woman baseball player in northern Ohio at this time, she was not the only one. On June 22, 1908, the *Cleveland Press* introduced 14-year-old Carita Masteller to the public. The paper reported that she had been playing baseball for eight or nine years and was as good as Weiss. That same month Weiss pitched against another female pitcher, Irma Gribble. The two dueled again in August. In another unique game, two sisters from Bellevue, Ohio, Irene and Ruth Basford, pitched for opposing men's teams.

Another well-known woman baseball player who played on men's teams was Rhode Islander Elizabeth Murphy. "Lizzie," as she liked to be called, played amateur and semiprofessional baseball from about 1915 to 1935 and was known as the "Queen of Baseball" throughout New England and eastern Canada. After playing for a number of amateur teams in Rhode Island, Murphy signed with the semiprofessional Providence Independents in 1918. A few years later she joined Ed Carr's All-Stars of Boston and earned quite a reputation for her skills as a first baseman.

In 1928, while Murphy was still impressing the fans in New England, 14-year-old Margaret Gisolo helped her Blanford, Indiana, American Legion boys' baseball team win county, district, sectional, and state championships. In seven tournament games she had nine hits in 21 at bats. She scored 10 putouts and 28 assists in the field, with no errors charged against her. A protest against her participation filed by opposing teams went all the way to the American Legion's National Americanism Commission, which referred it to the baseball commissioner, Judge Kenesaw Mountain Landis. Landis determined that American Legion rules did not specifically ban the participation of women and disallowed the protest.

Landis had to address a similar situation three years later when the "Barnum of Baseball," Chattanooga Lookouts manager Joe Engel, signed 17-year-old Jackie Mitchell to a contract with his Southern Association minor league team, thus making her the first female professional baseball player. Mitchell had been taught to pitch by major leaguer Dazzy Vance and had once struck out nine men in a row in an amateur game. She became an overnight celebrity on April 2, 1931, when she pitched in an exhibition game against the visiting New York Yankees—and struck out Babe Ruth and Lou Gehrig, back to back. Speculation continues as to whether Ruth and Gehrig were merely putting on a show or really trying to hit Mitchell's pitches. Mitchell contended that it was not a setup and that the only instructions to the players had been to try not to hit the ball straight through the pitcher's box. A number of Yankees confirmed her story. Unfortunately Mitchell never had a chance to repeat her performance as a professional baseball player. A few days after her debut, Landis informed Engel that he had disallowed Mitchell's contract on the grounds that life in baseball was too strenuous for women. Organized baseball formalized the ban against women signing professional baseball contracts with men's teams on June 21, 1952; the ruling still stands.

A League Is Born

The restriction on women playing professional baseball on men's teams did not prevent the formation of a women's professional baseball league, however. In 1943, with wartime manpower shortages threatening major league baseball, Chicago Cubs owner Philip K. Wrigley decided to form a women's professional softball league which would play its games in the major league stadiums while the men were away at war. Within a year of its founding, the league modified its rules and the All-American Girls Baseball League (AAGBL) was born. The AAGBL made its debut in 1943, when four teams—the Rockford (Illinois) Peaches, the South Bend (Indiana) Blue Sox, the Racine (Wisconsin) Belles, and the Kenosha (Wisconsin) Comets—squared off during the league's 108-game schedule. Attendance that year was 176,000 fans, which, according to one contemporary, meant that the league was "drawing a higher percentage of the population (in league cities) than major league baseball ever did in its greatest attendance years." Attendance figures continued to rise year after year, reaching a peak in 1948, when the league's 10 teams drew almost 1,000,000 fans. That same year, AAGBL teams drew more than 100,000 fans for a series of nine games in Puerto Rico.

Unlike women's teams of the past, the AAGBL relied on players' skills, not just their gender, to draw fans to the ballpark. The more than 500 women who played in the AAGBL during its 12-year existence were top-notch athletes. Many were veterans of championship school, community, or industrial softball teams, and a few had even played on boys' or men's baseball teams. In addition, many of the AAGBL managers were experienced professional baseball players—some, like Bill Wambsganss (the only player ever to achieve an unassisted triple play in a World Series), Max Carey, Jimmie Foxx, and Dave Bancroft, were legends.

The AAGBL represented one of the only times in history that women baseball players received widespread moral and financial support. Once World War II ended, however, social pressures for women to leave nontraditional jobs and return to household duties resumed. This fact, coupled with organizational problems and the rise of televised major league games, led to the demise of the AAGBL. Interest in the league all but disappeared until the 1980s, when a group of former players organized a players association and began lobbying to have the league honored in the National Baseball Hall of Fame. The popular media and serious scholars rediscovered the league and hundreds of articles about the AAGBL appeared in newspapers and magazines across the country. In October 1988 the Hall of Fame unveiled a permanent exhibit of AAGBL league memorabilia. In the summer of 1992, the AAGBL was further memorialized when it became the subject of the feature film, *A League of Their Own.*

Despite the newfound popularity of the AAGBL, modern-day women baseball players still face the same obstacles and criticisms endured by 19th century players. For the most part, organized teams and leagues remain closed to women. When Commissioner Ford Frick issued his ban against women players in 1952, his purpose was to prevent teams from using women players as publicity stunts. The end result of his edict was that even highly skilled women players (like those on the all-female team that tried, unsuccessfully, to gain admission to the men's Class A Florida State League in 1984) lost an important avenue for upward mobility and legitimacy in baseball. Women who challenge baseball's "men only" reputation rarely escape the experience unscathed. Julie Croteau, who gained notoriety in the late 1980s by playing first base for the St. Mary's (Maryland) College men's baseball team, earned school and conference honors yet still had to endure derisive comments from teammates. She left school in the middle of her junior year disillusioned with a system she believed treated women as inferior to men.

Thanks to a series of court battles in the 1970s, generations of young girls have had the opportunity to play baseball on Little League teams. The 1998 season marked the 25th season in which girls have participated in Little League baseball, and it was the first time a girl played in the championship game of the Little League World Series. A growing number of girls and women continue to find opportunities to play baseball in both female leagues and in co-educational leagues. Nearly 3 million girls and 300,000 women play amateur baseball, comprising 17.5 percent of baseball participants in the United States. Women's leagues also exist in Australia and Canada.

In 1994 the Colorado Silver Bullets began their inaugural season as the first, and only, all-female professional baseball team to be officially recognized by the National Association of Professional Baseball Leagues. Their existence was made possible by the sponsorship of the Coors Brewing Company. Competing against men's teams, the team struggled on the field during its first few seasons, but they attracted national attention.

The team improved its record in 1996 to 18-34, with pitcher Pam Davis (7–7) becoming the first Bullets pitcher to avoid a losing record. The team's third season also saw its offense improve dramatically, from a .183 team batting average in 1995 to .241 in 1996. And after failing to homer in their first two seasons, the Silver Bullets delivered five in 1996.

The Bullets finished with a winning record for the first

time in 1997, and their quality of play continued to improve. Three players hit above .300, and the pitching was impressive, led by Lee Anne Ketcham, who was 7–5 with a 3.35 ERA. As the season ended, though, Coors announced that they would not renew their sponsorship. Without a sponsor, the team folded after the 1997 season. "Everybody's put a lot of heart into it," founder Bob Hope said. "You've got little girls out there that had a glass ceiling in between them and the opportunity to play the game. The door's been opened, and we want to work hard to make sure it opens even wider."

Phil Niekro, a Hall of Fame pitcher and the only manager in Bullets history, said, "Women can play baseball. Someday a woman will play in the big leagues and I only hope I'm around to see it. I want to be sitting right there in the first row because I guarantee you that she will be standing in the batter's box and will be remembering the Silver Bullets. This is where we started."

The first steps towards that goal may have been taken in the past few years. Jodi Haller became the second woman to play college baseball, pitching for NAIA St. Vincent's (Pennsylvania) College in 1990. Then in the fall of 1994, Lee Anne Ketcham and Julie Croteau played for the Maui Stingrays in the Hawaiian Winter Baseball League, a developmental winter league for players at about the Class A level. Both were members of the Colorado Silver Bullets.

The most promising advances were made by Ila Borders, who became the first woman to win a college baseball game in 1994. The lefthanded pitcher posted a 2–4 record with a 2.92 ERA during her freshman year for Southern California College, finishing her college career with a 4–5 record at Whittier College in 1997. Later that year, Borders became the first woman to pitch in a men's professional baseball game as a member of the St. Paul Saints of the independent Northern League. She spent parts of four seasons with four different Northern League clubs, retiring midway through the 2000 season to pursue a broadcasting career with ESPN. "I'll look back and say I did something nobody ever did," Borders said. "I'm proud of that. I wasn't out to prove women's rights or anything. I just love baseball." Scores of young girls had found a role model, but it had never been easy for Borders. "I've been spit on, had beer thrown on me and been sworn at and was hit 11 times out of 11 at bats while in college,"she told the *Salt Lake Tribune*. "But the memories I have are the ovations when I would run in from the bullpen."

Borders and the Silver Bullets not only showed that women can play baseball, they also suggested that women's baseball could be economically viable. Ladies League Baseball debuted as a professional women's league in 1997 with four teams—two in Los Angeles and one each in San Jose and Phoenix. The 30-game season was a success, and the league expanded eastward in 1998. The league changed its name to Ladies League Baseball and added teams in Buffalo and New Jersey. The expanded league intended to play a 56-game schedule starting in July and ending in September. However, low attendance, and escalating costs forced LPB owners to abbreviate the first half, playing only 16 games in the first half and canceling the second half of the regular season. The popularity of the Silver Bullets, and the recent success of women athletes in soccer and professional basketball, suggest that this story is just beginning.

If girls and women continue to enjoy opportunities to play baseball, the sport will undoubtedly lose its masculine reputation. The question is whether or not current opportunities for female players will last. If they don't, today's female baseball players may find themselves sidelined, once again, with "a league of their own," watching rather than directly experiencing the national pastime.

CHAPTER 16

Baseball and the Civil War

Patricia Millen

Many writers and historians have argued that baseball's rise in popularity during the late 19th century was the result of the spread of the game by thousands of young men from all over the country during the American Civil War. Robert Weaver's thesis is typical of early baseball writers. In 1939 he extolled: "During this conflict . . . the game became nationalized. . . . When the soldiers were not fighting they played baseball; teams from different regiments frequently played games; soldiers from the North carried the game into Confederate prison camps." Sporting goods tycoon and former ballplayer Albert Spalding wrote in 1911, "For, during those years of unhappy conflict, on both sides of the line 'Yankees' and 'Johnnies' were playing ball and laying the foundation for the game which, when war's alarms cease, would be national in its spirit and national in its perpetuity."

Contemporary writers—even grammar and high school text books—continue to credit the Civil War for the dissemination of the game on the battlefield and in Southern prison camps. The singular print of Union prisoners playing baseball at the Confederate prison at Salisbury, North Carolina, is often used as evidence to exaggerate the progression of the game during the Civil War years.

Long before the first shot was fired at Fort Sumter, however, the game of baseball had already entrenched itself into American society and was well on its way to becoming "America's National Game." By examining available sources on the leisure time activities of Civil War soldiers in the Union and Confederate armies, it is clear that baseball was indeed played with great enthusiasm by Northern and Southern troops, though with far less regularity than other leisure-time pursuits. Baseball would have advanced throughout the 19th century as America's favorite sport even without the four-year interruption of the American Civil War. The game was not dramatically advanced by Northern soldiers moving south during the War, or by the sometime exchanges between Union and Confederate soldiers.

From colonization to the start of the American Civil War in 1861, primitive stick and ball games such as "one-old-cat," "two-old-cat," "stool ball," "rounders," "base," "fedder," and "town ball" were played for recreation in early America. "Base" or "goal ball" had been played in England in the early 18th century. By the late 18th and early 19th century, "base" and "base ball" were well known in the United States. Forms of these ball and bat games were often documented as being played in Colonial America in English and Dutch settlements. As one diarist recorded in his journal in 1753 while traveling through New York state, "Even at the celebration of the Lord's supper, (the Dutch boys) have been playing bat and ball the whole term around the house of God."

One of the earliest cited references to baseball in the colonies during a military campaign was at Valley Forge, Pennsylvania, during the American Revolution. On April 7, 1778, George Ewing, a Continental soldier, wrote in his diary of exercising in the afternoon and in the intervals he "playd at base." In the Ante-bellum South many primary source diaries, reminiscences, and travel accounts also mention ball as being played in the 17th, 18th, and early 19th centuries. According to a study done by Ruth Fink on the recreational activities in the "Old South," the author concluded that recreational pursuits of people living in the South were not even far removed from most Americans of the 20th century. Residents in the states of Virginia, Alabama, Louisiana, Georgia, and the Carolinas, for example, enjoyed dancing, hunting, fishing, barbecues, and playing games of bowling, tag, and games that were not unlike modern baseball.

Prior to the Civil War, baseball was played in the southern states in both the aristocratic setting of the plantation and in the areas reserved for people held as slaves. In *Baseball: The Early Years,* author Harold Seymour describes a scene of tents spread under the branches of giant oak trees for the protection of the ladies while "polite stewards of the clubs" waited on the delicate fans watching a game played by Southern whites in the Deep South in 1859. Ball play was also a source of entertainment among slave children living on small farms and on large plantations south of the Mason–Dixon Line during the 18th and 19th centuries.

Slave children used sticks to get a ball in a hole or a goal during games of "rolly hole" or "shinny"—a game that resembled hockey. And baseball was played, recalled a former slave in Kentucky, using a ball made out of yarn with a sock used as a cover. Most likely such ball games were variations of the games of rounders and town ball played by Southern whites. Henry Baker, a former slave from Alabama, recalled that players ran from one base to the other and were called out if they were hit with the ball.

According to one account, laws were even on the books as early as 1797 in the city of Fayetteville, North Carolina, to prohibit the organized play of baseball on Sundays by African-Americans. Organized athletic competition began in the 1820s with the increase of inter-collegiate sports and amateur and professional competition as the United States grew into an industrialized nation. By the 1840s the game of baseball had evolved into a game that any 20th century observer would have recognized. In 1856 *Porter's Spirit of the Times* reported: "This fine American game seems to be progressing in all parts of the United States with new spirit, while in New York and its neighborhood its revival seems to have been taken up almost as a matter of national pride. Matches are being made all around us, and games are being played on every available green plot within a 10-mile circuit of the city."

Foul lines, bleachers, stands, dressing rooms, gate receipts, and refreshment sales attracted more and more spectators to an organized sports arena. The game of baseball had developed from a simple children's game to a commercial sporting venture with newspapers carrying full column descriptions of games. In 1859, two years before the start of the Civil War, *Harper's Weekly* ran an article debating whether football or baseball was America's National Pastime.

Baseball games were played all along the eastern seaboard, in western territories, and in the South, hastened by strides in 19th century communication and transportation. The expanding railroad system promoted interstate rivalries and baseball tours. Ballclubs were formed in California by the start of the Civil War, where the "New York" game was the "only style of ball playing" at all encouraged in the Golden State as reported in December of 1860 by *Wilke's Spirit of the Times.*

Throughout the 19th century, the South was still very much an agrarian region with dispersed populations and therefore lagged behind the North in the organization of formal teams and baseball clubs. By 1860, however, at least seven teams were organized in New Orleans; cities such as Baltimore, Washington, D.C., and Louisville also had burgeoning baseball clubs. According to an 1859 news clipping, young men in Augusta, Georgia were encouraged to play the "noble and manly game of base ball . . . to toughen the muscles . . . and to stir the sluggish blood." Henry Chadwick, who came to be known as the "Father of Baseball" for his commentary on the game, even attempted to form a baseball team in Richmond, Virginia, but his efforts were interrupted by the start of the Civil War. Still, townball and baseball were routinely played in the states that would later become the Confederacy. When the call was made for troop enlistments by presidents Abraham Lincoln and Jefferson Davis at the start of the Civil War, many of the soon to be combatants knew how to play baseball.

Veteran Ballplayers as Army Veterans

Members of social clubs and sporting societies, farmers, professional men, journeymen, college men, and young boys in the North and South caught up in the excitement of the war, hurried into military service. Fear and anxiety gripped the country, as can be seen in the actions of leisure time participants. The New York Yacht Club canceled its regatta at the start of the war in fear of Confederate raiders, colleges with intercollegiate baseball teams postponed matches, and the National Association of Baseball Players cut short its season in 1861. By the second year of the war, "The great game of iron and lead ball, between the loyal and rebellious States," wrote the *New York Clipper,* was engrossing all attention. "We hope that the last innings will soon be played," and "the Union will be quickly and indissolubly restored—and that our fields may soon echo with shouts, 'How's that umpire?' and 'Foul!' as in the days that once were."

When the Civil War began, most people concluded that the conflict would be over quickly following a singular decisive battle. The war raged, however, until 1865 and cost America over half a million men. Many of these soldiers, whose median age was 24, first left for battle as if for a holiday. If the testimony of A.G. Mills (later president of the National League in 1882) and Albert Spalding is to be believed, many of these young men from the North and South went off to war with a baseball and bat tucked into their haversacks.

By the onset of the Civil War men living in the Union and Confederate states had grown up with a sporting heritage. The erratic demands of army life afforded both armies "down" time to engage in sport in between confrontations with the enemy and during long months spent in winter quarters. Both armies usually stood idle during the months of late November or early December until the spring thaw in April or May—waiting for passable roads and hospitable conditions for fighting. It was during these times that the monotony of drilling, drilling, and more drilling was broken by an occasional game of football or baseball.

There was certainly time available to play baseball. In Virginia Hughes Kaminsky's *A War to Petrify the Heart,* she describes a typical day in 1862 for Private Richard Van Wyck of the 150th New York Infantry: "At half-past five, the drums beat for us to get up." Van Wyck's company ate breakfast, drilled, had most of the day off with "exception of two hours between three and five, drill, we have leasure. Leasure is meant meal time or anything we choose to do."

There appears to be no substantial difference in how the two armies spent this leisure time. Documentation found in letters and accounts from Union and Confederate soldiers mentions a wide variety of leisure time activities that occupied a soldier's time in camp. Many waited anxiously for news from home or spent their spare time writing to family and friends. Soldiers in both armies also spent their quiet hours reading, playing cards, chuck-a luck (a dice game), chess, checkers, quoits, tenpins, and dominoes. Often bivouacked near a water source, soldiers reported fishing and swimming as a frequent pastime. A Confederate soldier wrote that his regiment looked "like so many puddle ducks in a barnyard stock pond" while he watched dozens of his comrades swim in a river during June of 1861.

Civil War doctors acknowledged the importance of physical exercises such as swimming to the health of their men. Doctor Julian Chisolm, a published surgeon in the Confederate Army, wrote that while in camp, "Temporary gymnasia might be established, and gymnastic exercise should be encouraged as conductive to health, strength, agility and address." The Southern doctor was also familiar with and recommended the "manly play of ball" as an important addition to a soldier's daily exercise regime. Such recommendations were made but soldiers, often lacking equipment and organization, made do with sport of a spontaneous nature by challenging each other to foot races, wheel barrow races, wrestling or boxing contests.

Athletic games, including baseball, became a way for soldiers in both armies to prove their manhood and to receive recognition in army circles. Team sports such as baseball and football played during the war demanded "physical courage and prowess" and often times guaranteed fame for a soldier that might not be found on the battlefield. Soldiers won accolades for their ability to run, swim, hunt, shoot, box, "snowball," or play baseball even though their soldiering might have been less than admirable. John Adams, a soldier in the Union 19th Massachusetts regiment, even came to view Confederate soldiers in a more favorable light after he witnessed their skill as baseball players.

Baseball games were played during camp and in between hostilities by both armies on many occasions. Confederate Corporal William Harding wrote while stationed in Georgia in 1863 that he "had a fine game of Town ball which gave me good exercise." James Hall of the 24th Alabama regiment observed his men playing baseball "just like school boys" while waiting for the advance of Union General William T. Sherman. The 13th Massachusetts played amongst themselves daily during April and May of 1862, while members of the 51st Pennsylvania played every evening on their drill field. The extensive documentation of such games in both armies strongly suggests that baseball was the most popular of sports engaged in by troops of both armies during the war. But many embellished accounts of great ball games include snowball battles, which reveal them as the most "pervasive" of activities in Union and Confederate camps during the winter months.

These ball games were played, however, not as a result of the war spreading the game, but because men in both armies went into the army with a history of playing baseball. Baseball may have been the most popular active pastime for Union and Confederate soldiers, but for men exhausted by drilling, forced marches, lack of proper nutrition and rest, documentation shows leisure hours were more often spent playing cards than any other activity. Soldiers who had the energy to play baseball more often than not played impromptu games with men in their own regiments and played by "home" regulations. One soldier remembered in his diary that he and the boys from his company played baseball with the 26th Regiment from Pennsylvania in a "new way" but he had already forgotten the different rules.

Although the times when Confederate and Union soldiers fraternized was not as common as Civil War myth would indicate, there are a few known instances when the meeting, or confrontation, did involve baseball. A game was played near Alexandria, Louisiana, for example, and was recounted in the writings of George Putnam. The men of the 114th New York were playing a game when Rebel skirmishers shot the right fielder, captured the center fielder, and ran off with Putnam's only ball!

In Albert Spalding's 1911 book, *America's National Game, Baseball,* he wrote "at periods when active hostilities were in abeyance, a series of games was played between picked nines from Federal and Confederate forces." This scenario, which he indicated as occurring during the long campaign outside Richmond, is possible but would have been a novelty. Even Spalding admittedly remarked, "I have heard rumors of this series repeatedly, but have not been able to trace them to any authoritative source."

Tyler's Farm in Virginia in May of 1862 became a playground for the Irish Brigade, which was attached to Union General George McClellan's army. Football and baseball were played, and one Union soldier insinuated that all the ruckus being made "must have aroused no small amount of curiosity in the rebels waiting across the Chickahominy." One Sunday morning a baseball game was played by members of the 57th New York and the 69th New York on the Tyler farm. As with many calm moments during the War, reality often interrupted. The blast of a Confederate cannon ended the game abruptly.

It was often on holidays that soldiers, Union and Confederate alike, had opportunities to relax and they indulged in sport as an alternative to their customary holiday celebrations. A wheelbarrow race and a contest to catch two greased pigs rounded out the Christmas Day festivities for a soldier from Maryland, for example, after he witnessed the officers of his company play three innings of baseball. Soldiers held foot races, boxing, and wrestling matches and marksmanship contests or challenged other regimental units to games of football or baseball to fill the day when most soldiers were especially homesick and lonely for family. Like all leisure time activities, baseball helped soldiers forget their troubles and endure terrible hardships. Most soldiers, however, because of the realities of life in the army, never played baseball with any regularity for any length of time, and only a handful actually ever played in prison camps.

Little Time for Play in Prison

A print "drawn from nature" by Otto Boetticher, an artist from New York City, depicts a bucolic scene with a baseball game taking place on the grounds of the Confederate prison camp in Salisbury, North Carolina. This popular image, published in 1863, is often used by modern day historians to underscore how baseball was frequently played in prison camps during the Civil War. Otto was a prisoner at Salisbury; he was Captain of Company G of the 68th New York Volunteers and was captured and sent to the camp during the summer of 1862. But the diaries and letters of several Union prisoners and writings of a Confederate chaplain who resided in the city of Salisbury give us a more accurate picture of the conditions of the camp and the baseball games played there.

Before the great influx of prisoners who were shipped to Salisbury in October of 1864, the prison population remained relatively low. The Confederate government renovated an old cotton factory and intended the prison to house about 2,500 men. Salisbury's buildings and grounds were relatively spacious and prisoners were allowed "liberty of the yard," according to a 1989 article by Jim Sumner. Some of the men enjoyed afternoon and evening games of baseball.

"Took a little walk in the evening and watched some of the officers play ball," wrote 23-year-old Charles Gray, who was captured and sent to the prison in May of 1862. Gray was a Union doctor who remained a spectator of the games at Salisbury and mentioned them frequently in his diary. "A good state of cheerfulness (sic), thanks to the open space is fairly prevailing," he wrote in a journal entry. "Ball play for those who like it and are able, walking, card playing as keep us in employment; but reading matter is about used up."

Josephus Clarkson, a ship chandler's apprentice from Boston before the war, recalled baseball games played at Salisbury with the prison guards. "Since many of the men were in a weakened condition, it was agreed," wrote Clarkson in his diary, "to play the faster but less harsh New York rules. . . . "The game of baseball had been played much in the South, but many of them (the guards) had never seen the sport devised by Mr. Cartwright." (This statement also adds further proof that Alexander Cartwright, not Union General Abner Doubleday, was credited as the inventor of baseball during the mid-1800s.)

One pitcher, a Confederate from Texas, was expelled from playing the game by widespread agreement for "badly laming" too many of the prisoner players. The Southerners kept forgetting that "plugging" the runner, or hitting the runner with the ball, was not allowed under the New York rules. Such fond memories of baseball games, for the majority of men imprisoned at Salisbury, are very few. As the population of prisoners soared in the fall of 1864, the conditions became unbearable. Baseball games would have been impossible as survival became paramount in a soldier's mind.

"For months Salisbury was the most endurable prison I had seen; there were 600 inmates," former prisoner Willard W. Glazier recalled in 1866. "They were exercised in the open air, comparatively well fed, and kindly treated. Early in October, 10,000 regular prisoners of war arrived. It immediately changed into a scene of cruelty and horror; it was densely crowded, rations were cut down and issued very irregularly." The prison, Glazier remembered, "became so notorious during the War as one of the most loathsome dungeons in rebeldom."

Rations at the Salisbury prison, toward the end of its existence, were intolerable and meager. They were not substantial enough to support most soldiers for very long, especially when the lack of food was compounded by the scarcity of shelter, heat and medical attention. In Louis Brown's *The Salisbury Prison, A Case Study of Confederate Military Prisons,* one soldier described the not always daily fare at the prison in 1864 as consisting of "coarse meal, cob, and all ground together, and so musty that a decent hog would not eat it." Starving soldiers ate anything they could get their hands on to stay alive, including roaming dogs, cats, and rats. The Confederate Army hadn't the means to feed its own men, let alone its prisoners of war.

When the Union Army marched into Salisbury on April 12, 1865, three days after Robert E. Lee surrendered at Appomattox Courthouse, Union General George Stoneman ordered the prison burned to the ground. The best estimate of the dead at Salisbury would tally almost 4,000 men, most of whom died during the last year of the prison's life.

It is easy for historians to surmise that the game of baseball spread as a result of the Civil War due to the many references to the game being played in the army, and because of its growth in popularity in America during the decades following the war. But, as research proves, the popularity of the game was well on its way before the start of the Civil War, when all leisure time activities were blossoming in the developing urbanized American society.

As author Harold Seymour confirmed, "by the time of the Civil War the rapid spread of the Knickerbockers style of baseball manifested itself in both the Union and Confederate armies." These rules, devised by the Knickerbocker Base Ball Club of New York in 1845, were no doubt taught to many soldiers during the course of the war, but whether it was townball, baseball, or rounders, men from the North and the South had already learned to play ball *before* they became soldiers. Regardless of the Civil War, baseball was already on its way to becoming the "National Game."

CHAPTER 17

How to Score a Game

David W. Smith

There are some things that almost all Americans, especially male Americans, think that they do well: drive a car, make love, barbecue steaks, and keep score of a baseball game, just to name a few. This article addresses only the last item on that list, but that is daunting enough, since anyone who has scored more than a handful of games has a unique style. These varied approaches—quite idiosyncratic—differ not only in the mechanical details of how the events of a game are recorded, but also more fundamentally on which parts of the action are seen as important enough to be recorded. Therefore, it is difficult to be authoritative when writing about scorekeeping, since there is no standard procedure to describe and it would be folly to attempt to define one.

Paul Dickson covered the history of this subject quite thoroughly in his book, *The Joy of Keeping Score*. The approach in the present discussion will not be to repeat Paul's work, or to be encyclopedic in all the nuances that are ultimately matters of individual taste. Rather, this brief essay will present a scoring system that illustrates one way to capture a lot of interesting detail in a concise form. This system is an amalgamation of examples gleaned from scoresheets obtained from over 150 different sources by Retrosheet, a group that collects these paper play-by-play accounts, converts them into a computer format, and distributes them free of charge.

Although many different scoresheet formats can be found, the one recognizable by almost all fans is the orderly display of gridded boxes in the center pages of a ballpark scorecard. As shown in the figure below, there is a separate row for the players in each batting order position and individual columns for the action of each inning. This figure presents the home half of the game played between the Brooklyn Dodgers and the New York Giants on October 3, 1951, arguably the most memorable game in baseball history. A few of the plays will be examined in detail to explain the basic features of the system; the reader will then be able to interpret the rest.

Most outs are recorded with the position code of the fielder or fielders involved, using the standard numbering system of 1 for pitcher, 2 for catcher, 3 for first base, and so on. Eddie Stanky flied to left to lead off the game, Alvin Dark popped to third base, and Bill Mueller lined to left. The inclusion of the "P" and "L" notations add more information. Monte Irvin led off the second with a groundout to shortstop. The first hit of the game was Whitey Lockman's single in the second, which went to right field, as indicated by "S9" in the lower right corner of the box.

Here is a major source of variation between different scorers: Some draw the advancement of the runners as though the box represents the view from behind home plate, as is done here, while others prefer the use of the corners of the box with no diagram of the bases. In this system, there is a dot at each base where the runner stops. For Lockman, he has one at first from his single and another at second where he advanced on Bobby Thomson's single to left. The "6" in Lockman's upper right-hand corner indicates his advance to second because of the action of the sixth batter, Thomson. Some scorers use the fielding position of the batter in place of batting order position and some use uniform numbers. Thomson also has a small "x" and 763 in his box. The "x" indicates he was out on the bases and "763" indicates that the play went from the left fielder to the shortstop to the first baseman. On this play, Thomson thought that Mueller would continue to third and was caught when the Dodgers threw behind him. At the bottom of each inning is a summary of runs and hits. Some scorers subdivide this box even more to record errors and runners left on base as well.

In the third inning there were two more outs on the bases. After Wes Westrum walked ("B" for "base on balls" in the first base corner of his box), he was retired at second—pitcher to shortstop—as the Dodgers turned Sal Maglie's bunt into a force play. Note the "FO" and "Bt" in Maglie's box. Maglie was then the first out in the double play ("DP") grounded into by Stanky. After Thomson's double in the fifth (note that there is no dot for him at first base since he did not stop there), Willie Mays struck out (the "K" has been the notation for the strikeout for well over a century) and Westrum was intentionally walked ("IB") to get to the pitcher. Lockman's play in the seventh is unusual in that he received credit for a sacrifice hit, but also reached base on a fielder's choice as the Dodgers tried to get Irvin advancing to third, but were too late. The "SF" which follows for Thomson indicates the sacrifice fly that scored Irvin.

The Giants used two pinch hitters in the eighth, with each substitution marked by a heavy vertical line before the appearance. The substitute players are marked under the men they replaced. Occasionally this can be difficult, especially when four or more players occupy the same batting order position other than the ninth spot. In those cases, the overflow players are usually written at the bottom of the scorecard with arrows indicating their correct lineup placement.

In the fateful ninth inning, Dark reached on an infield single and went to third on Mueller's single to right (note that there is no dot for Dark at second base). Many readers will recall that this hit was a groundball past first baseman Hodges that might very well have been fielded if the runner were not being held on. After Irvin fouled out (the "FL" indicates "foul"), Lockman doubled to score Dark and send Mueller to third. Mueller injured his ankle as he slid in and was replaced by pinch runner Clint Hartung. A short line marks the exact spot of his entry across the basepath just past third base. At this point the Dodgers changed pitchers, and this substitution is marked with a heavy horizontal line. To the everlasting sorrow of Brooklyn rooters, Thomson then ended the game with a homer to left, scoring Hartung and Lockman in front of him.

There are other plays that did not occur in this game but are frequent enough to deserve mention. There were no errors by Brooklyn on this day, but when they occur, they are simply marked as "E" followed by the position number of the fielder. A stolen base is marked as "SB" followed by a number indicating the batting order position of the batter at the time. This pattern is also used for caught stealing (with fielding credit), wild pitches, passed balls, and balks.

There is ample opportunity for individual modifications and embellishments, which make the scorekeeping more satisfying. Some like to indicate ground-ball hits with a wavy line under the "S7" and line-drive hits with an underline. There is usually space in adjacent boxes to note the count if desired, or this information can be marked in the center of the box. Keeping a running tally of strikeouts or walks by using small subscripted numbers with each one is also common, as is a backwards "K" to indicate a batter struck out looking. Codes are often used to indicate more precisely just where a fielding play was made or where a base hit landed.

Above all the scorecard is a very personal record of the game, akin to a diary. Keeping a detailed record can enhance enjoyment of the game by focusing attention on the action and can provide endless opportunities to relive exciting moments. Sometimes the memories can come even from an incomplete scorecard. For example, Retrosheet has the copies of the scorebooks and scorecards of nine different people who attended the game described here. Three of those do not have the final play of the game entered, since it was either too exciting or too painful for them to write down on their scorecard. Nonetheless, none of these men—all professional sportswriters and announcers—had any trouble recalling what happened, even decades later.

TEAM New York Giants

PLAYER	POS.	1	2	3	4	5	6	7	8	9
Stanky	2B	7		543 6DP			7		6FL	
Dark	SS	5P			4P		53			S3
Mueller / Hartung	RF / PR	7L			3L		3FL			S9
Irvin	LF		63		53			D7		3FL
Lockman	1B		S7			63		SH FC		D7
Thomson	3B		763x S7			D7		8SF		HT
Mays	CF		7L			K		643 DP		
Westrum / Rigney-PH/Noble	C / C			16x B		IB			K	
Maglie / Thompson / Jansen	P / PH / P			FO Bt		63			31	
	R	0	0	0	0	0	0	1	0	4
	H	0	2	0	0	1	0	1	0	4

The History of Major League Baseball Statistics

John Thorn, Pete Palmer, and Joseph M. Wayman

Part Two, the statistical section of *Total Baseball*, presents the record of major league contests played from 1871 through 2000—all 169,565 of them. It details the accomplishments of the game's 2,355 team seasons and 15,416 players so completely and accurately that Major League Baseball has authorized *Total Baseball* to be the official encyclopedia of the game, its authentic historical record.

Total Baseball won critical acclaim and a devoted following not only for its breadth and depth of information but also for its pioneering "sabermetric" stats that offered alternative, unofficial measures of player performance. Yet, for all its innovation, *Total Baseball* has stood squarely in the tradition of baseball record keeping; it is—like each new spring of our national pastime—a link in a long, long chain. As the New York Knickerbockers' game of 150 years ago lives on in the game of today, so is this volume enriched by the labors of statisticians from Henry Chadwick to Ernie Lanigan, from S.C. Thompson and Seymour Siwoff and the Hirdt brothers to David Neft and Bill James.

How we came from the Knickerbockers' primitive accounting of outs and runs to the vast array of statistics available today is an interesting process, in which Major League Baseball's role has been central. Through its evolving scoring rules and procedures, its judicious endorsement of new measures, and its continuing mission to set the record straight, the Commissioner's Office and its official scorers have provided fans with a wealth of statistical data unmatched by any other sport—perhaps any other human activity—on earth.

Here is how we who love baseball came to this fortunate estate, and how we at *Total Baseball* created what is now the official historical record.

The Origins, 1845-1875

Baseball and stats were a tandem from the very Eden of the game. The first box score appeared in the *New York Morning News* on October 22, 1845, less than a month after Alexander Cartwright and his Knickerbocker teammates codified the first set of rules. Why did these early players and scribes measure individual performance rather than simply count the score? In part to imitate the custom of cricket; yet the larger explanation is that the numbers served to legitimize men's concern with a boys' pastime. The pioneers of baseball reporting—William Cauldwell of the *Sunday Mercury*, William Porter of *Spirit of the Times*, an unknown annalist at the *News*, and later Henry Chadwick—may indeed have reflected that if they did not cloak the game in the "importance" of statistics, it might not seem worthwhile for adults to read about, let alone play. Statistics elevated baseball from other boys' field games of the 1840s and '50s to make it somehow systematic and serious, like business; despite baseball's essential simplicity, it was laced with intricate detail that suited it perfectly to quantification.

In the development of baseball statistics, no man is more important than Father Chadwick. Born in England in 1824, he came to these shores at age 13 steeped in the tradition of cricket. In his teens he played the English game and in his twenties he reported on it for a variety of newspapers, including the *Long Island Star* and the *New York Times*. In the early 1840s, before the Knickerbocker rules eliminated the practice of retiring a baserunner by throwing the ball at him rather than to the base, Chadwick occasionally played baseball too, but he was not favorably impressed, having received "some hard hits in the ribs." Not until 1856, by which time he had been a cricket reporter for a decade, were Chadwick's eyes opened to the possibilities in the American game, which had improved dramatically since his youth.

In 1868 he recalled, "On returning from the early close of a cricket match on Fox Hill, I chanced to go through the Elysian Fields during the progress of a contest between the noted Eagle and Gotham clubs. The game was being sharply played on both sides, and I watched it with deeper interest than any previous ball game between clubs that I had seen. It was not long before I was struck with the idea that baseball was just the game for a national sport for Americans . . . as much so as cricket in England. At the time I refer to I had been reporting cricket for years, and, in my method of taking notes of contests, I had a plan peculiarly my own. It was not long, therefore, after I had become interested in baseball, before I began to invent a method of giving detailed reports of leading contests at baseball . . . ."

Thus Chadwick's cricket background was largely the impetus to his method of scoring a baseball game, the format of his early box scores, and the copious if primitive statistics that appeared in his year-end summaries in the *New York Clipper*, Beadle's *Dime Base-Ball Player*, and other publications.

Actually, cricket had begun to shape baseball statistics even before Chadwick's conversion. The first box score reported on two categories, outs and runs: outs, or "hands out," counted both unsuccessful times at bat and outs run into on the basepaths; "runs" were runs scored, not those driven in. The reason for not recording hits in the early years, when coverage of baseball matches appeared alongside reports of cricket matches, was that, unlike baseball, cricket had no such category as the successful hit which did not produce a run. To reach "base" in cricket is to run to the opposite wicket, which tallies a run; if you hit the ball and do not score a run, you have been put out.

Cricket box scores were virtual play-by-plays, a fact made possible by the lesser number of possible events. This play-by-play aspect was applied to a baseball box score as early as 1856; interestingly, despite the abundance of detail, hits were not accounted, nor did they appear in Chadwick's own box scores until 1867. The batting champion as declared by Chadwick, whose computations were immediately and universally accepted as "official," was the man with the highest average of runs per game. An inverse though imprecise measure of batting quality was outs per game. After 1863, when a fair ball caught on one bounce was no longer an out, fielding leaders were those with the greatest total of fly catches, assists, and "foul bounds" (fouls caught on one bounce). Pitching effectiveness was based purely on control, with the leader recognized as the one whose delivery offered the most opportunities for outs at first base and led to the fewest passed balls.

In a sense, Chadwick's measuring of baseball as if it were cricket can be viewed as correct: when you strip the game to its basic elements, those that determine victory or defeat, outs and runs are indeed all that count in the end. No individual statistic is meaningful to the team unless it relates directly to the scoring of runs.

Early player stats were of the most primitive kind, the counting kind. They'd tell you how many runs, or outs, or fly catches had occurred—later, how many hits or total bases. Counting is the most basic of all statistical processes; the next step up is averaging, and Chadwick was the first to put this into practice.

As professionalism infiltrated the game, teams began to bid for star-caliber players. Stars were known not by their stats but by their style until 1865, when Chadwick began to record in the *Clipper* a form of batting average taken from the cricket pages—runs per game. Two years later, in his newly founded baseball weekly, *The Ball Players' Chronicle*, he began to record not only average runs and outs per game, but also home runs, total bases, total bases per game—and hits per game. The averages were expressed not with decimal places but in the standard cricket format of the "average and over." Thus a batter with 23 hits in six games would have an average expressed not as 3.83 but as "3–5"—an average of 3 with an overage, or remainder, of 5. Another innovation was to remove from the individual accounting all bases gained through errors. Runs scored by a team, beginning in 1867, were divided between those scored after a man reached base on a clean hit and those arising from a runner's having reached base on an error. This was a clear precursor of the modern earned run average.

By the end of the decade Chadwick was recording total bases and home runs, but he placed little stock in either, as conscious attempts at slugging violated his cricket-bred image of "form." Just as cricket aficionados watch the game for the many opportunities for fine fielding it affords, so was baseball from its inception perceived as a fielders' sport. The original Knickerbocker rules of 1845, in fact, specified that a ball hit out of the field—in fair territory or foul—was a foul ball! "Long hits are showy," Chadwick wrote in the *Clipper* in 1868, "but they do not pay in the long run. Sharp grounders insuring the first-base certain, and sometimes the second-base easily, are worth all the hits made for home-runs which players strive for."

Chadwick prevailed, and the batting average used from that year on is the same as that used today except in its denominator, where at bats replaced games in 1876. Moreover, Chadwick created a measure in the 1860s that divided total bases by games played; change that denominator to at bats and you have today's slugging average—which, incidentally, was not accepted by the National League as an official statistic until 1923 and by the American until 1946.

Chadwick's "total bases average" represent the game's first attempt at a weighted average—an average in which the elements collected together in the numerator or the denominator are recognized numerically as being unequal. In this instance, a single is the unweighted unit, the double is weighted by a factor of two, the triple by three, and the home run by four. Statistically, this is a distinct leap forward from, first, counting, and next, averaging. The weighted average is in fact the cornerstone of today's statistical innovations, or sabermetrics.

The 1870s gave rise to some new batting stats and to the first attempt to quantify thoroughly the other principal facets of the game, pitching and fielding. Although the *Clipper* recorded base hits and total bases as early as 1868, a significant wrinkle was added in 1870 when at bats were listed as well. This was a critical introduction because it permitted the improvement of the batting average, first introduced in its current form by H.A. Dobson of Washington, D.C., in the *Dime Base-Ball Player* of 1872, and first computed "officially"—that is, for the newly created National League—in 1876, the lone year in which bases on balls were figured as outs. Since then the batting average has not changed, except for 1887, when bases on balls were counted as *hits*.

The objections to the batting average are well known, but to date have not disturbed its place as the most popular measure of hitting ability. First of all, the batting average makes no distinction between the single, the double, the triple, and the home run, treating all as the same unit. This objection had been addressed in 1868 by Chadwick's total bases average. Second, the batting average gives no indication of the effect of that base hit—that is, its value to the team. Third, the batting average does not take into account those occasions when first base is reached via a walk, hit batsman, or error. This last point was addressed at a surprisingly early date, too: in 1879 the National League adopted as an official statistic a forerunner of the on base percentage; it was called "reached first base," which included times reached by error as well as base on balls and base hits. (Being hit by a pitch did not give the batter first base until the ensuing decade.)

The Flowering, 1876-1920

Ever since the Civil War, serial guides like *Beadle* and *DeWitt* and sporting columns like those in the *Clipper* had carried year-end tabulations of batting, fielding, and pitching exploits, varying from year to year with the brainstorms of Chadwick or other demon compilers like New York's M.J. Kelly or Philadelphia's Al Wright. But the year 1876 was special. It was significant not only for the founding of the National League and the official debut of the batting average in its current form, it was also the Centennial of the United States, which was marked by a giant exposition in Philadelphia celebrating the mechanical marvels of the day. American ingenuity reigned, and technology was seen as the new handmaiden of democracy. Baseball, that mirror of American life, reflected the fervor for things scientific with an explosion of statistics far more complex than those seen before, particularly in the previously neglected areas of pitching and fielding. The increasingly minute statistical examination of the game met a responsive audience, one primed to view complexity as a measure of worth.

In 1876 the number of "official" offensive stats tabulated at season's end—i.e., in any of the publications inspired by Chadwick or Albert Spalding—was six: games, at bats, runs, hits, runs per game, and batting average. (And as with all the various guides until 1941, the stats of men who played in fewer than a specified minimum number of games were not noted.) Of these six, only runs and runs per game were common in the 1860s, while that decade's tabulation of total bases vanished. The number of official offensive stats a hundred years later? Twenty. (Today the number is 21, with the addition of on base percentage).

The number of "official" pitching categories in 1876 was 11, and there were some modernistic surprises, such as earned run average, hits allowed, hits per game, and opponents' batting average. Strikeouts were not recorded, for Chadwick saw them strictly as a sign of poor batting rather than good pitching. (His view had such an impact that pitcher strikeouts were not kept officially until 1889.) The number of official pitching stats today? Twenty-four.

The number of fielding categories in 1876 was six. One hundred years later it was still six (with the exception of the catcher, who gets a seventh: passed balls), dramatizing how the game, which originated as a showcase for fielders, had changed. The fielding stats of 1876 lumped "battery errors" with fielding errors, so that wild pitches and passed balls—in some years, even walks—diminished one's fielding percentage. This practice continued until 1887, but in *Total Baseball* battery errors are not included in fielding stats. Battery-mates' fielding stats were boosted by the awarding of an assist to the pitcher on strikeouts. This practice lasted until 1889, but is not reflected in *Total Baseball*.

The custom in 1876, as it is now, was to combine putouts, assists, and errors to form a "percentage of chances accepted," or what is today known as fielding average or fielding percentage. A "missing link" variant, devised by Al Wright in 1875, was to form averages by dividing the putouts by the number of games to yield a "putout average"; dividing the assists similarly to arrive at an "assist average"; and dividing putouts plus assists by games to get "fielding average." These averages took no account of errors. (Wright's "fielding average" was reborn a century later as Bill James's "range factor.")

The public's appetite for new statistics was not sated by the outburst of 1876. New measures were introduced in dizzying profusion in the remaining years of the century. Some of these did not catch on and were soon dropped for all time, like the meaningless "total bases run," while others fizzled only to reappear with new vigor in the twentieth century. These include (a) the above-mentioned "reached first base," which resurfaced in the early 1950s in an unofficial, improved form called on base percentage and became an official stat more than thirty years later, and (b) an 1860s stat, earned run average, which was periodically revived before dropping from sight in the 1880s, only to return triumphant to the NL in 1912 and the AL in 1913. (In 1913 Ban Johnson not only proclaimed the ERA official but became so enamored with it that he also instructed American League scorers to compile no official won-lost records. This state of affairs lasted for seven years, 1913-1919, but *Total Baseball* does record wins and losses by pitchers in those years, in accordance with the understood scoring practices of the time.)

Another stat that was "sent back to the minors" before its eventual adoption as an official stat in 1920 was the run batted in. Introduced by a Buffalo newspaper in 1879, the stat was picked up the following year by the *Chicago Tribune* and even became an official NL stat for the opening months of 1891. By season's end it had faded as most NL scorers declined to account for it in their summaries. (The American Association, however, recorded it all year long.) Ernie Lanigan picked up the RBI baton with his reports to the *New York Press* from 1907 through 1919, and he did not figure RBI for men who played in fewer than ten games, or club totals for traded players.

For *Total Baseball* we have placed much reliance upon the source material donated by Information Concepts, Inc. (ICI) to the National Baseball Library in Cooperstown following publication of *The Baseball Encyclopedia,* which it developed for publication by Macmillan in 1969. David Neft also kindly supplied us with his unpublished RBI data for the previously missing National League seasons of 1880-1885. The John Tattersall collection of nineteenth century game accounts and box scores was valuable for uncovering RBI as well. (For a detailed accounting of the sources employed for this official historical record of Major League Baseball, see the conclusion of the essay.)

Other statistics introduced officially before the turn of the century were stolen bases (though not caught stealing); doubles, triples, and homers; and sacrifice bunts (though an at-bat was charged from 1889 through 1893). Pitcher strikeouts, bases on balls, and the hit-by-pitch also appeared before 1900, but hit-by-pitch stats were not kept for batters on a systematic basis until 1917 in the NL and 1920 in the AL. Through newspaper research, we have filled in HBP data from 1884 through 1916 in the National League; the Players League of 1890; the American Association of 1882-1891; from 1901 through 1919 in the American League, and the 1914-1915 Federal League.

Hit into double play—including line outs as well as an groundouts—was an erratically recorded stat in the nineteenth century, but separate stats for groundouts into double plays have been kept by the leagues only since 1933 in the NL and 1939 in the AL. Batters' strikeouts were reported unofficially in 1891, but not as a league stat until 1910 in the NL and 1913 in the AL. Innings pitched were not kept until 1908 in the AL and 1903 in the NL. You can see what a patchwork quilt the records of Major League Baseball were in its early years.

Stolen bases were awarded not only for clean steals but also for extra bases taken through daring, from the first year in which totals were kept, 1886, until 1898. Because the figures reported in the guides were grossly inflated (such as Harry Stovey's ostensible 156 steals in 1888), the figures in *Total Baseball* reflect game-by-game research and refiguring. Caught-stealing (CS) figures are available on a very sketchy basis in some of the later years of the century, as some newspapers carried the data in the box scores of hometown games. From 1912 on, Lanigan recorded CS in box scores of the *New York Press*, but the leagues did not keep the figure officially until 1920. The AL has tabulated CS from that year to the present, excepting 1927, which members of the Society for American Baseball Research reconstructed from newspaper box scores. National League caught-stealing data exists for 1920-1925, and for 1951 to the present.

The new century added little in the way of new official statistics—ERA, RBI, and slugging average are better regarded as revivals despite their respective adoption dates of 1912, 1920, and 1923. But back in 1908 there was a classic case of a statistic rushing in to fill a void, as Phillies' manager Billy Murray observed that his outfielder Sherry Magee had the happy facility of providing a long fly ball whenever presented with a situation of a man on third and fewer than two outs. Taking up the cudgels on his player's behalf, Murray protested to the National League office that it was unfair to charge Magee with an unsuccessful time at bat when he was in fact succeeding, doing precisely what the situation demanded. (More recent stats—the save and the short-lived game-winning run batted in, or GWRBI—have followed from this sort of perception that something important was occurring on the field yet had no verifiable reality because it was not being measured.)

A signal event took place in 1912: the publication by *Baseball Magazine* editor John Lawres of *Who's Who in Baseball,* a small book that became the first to provide career statistics and personal facts for a group of players. Although thoroughly inadequate by today's standards—its only tabulations were games, batting average, and fielding average (even for pitchers, who were given no pitching records!)—*Who's Who* was a groundbreaking work. It gave rise to a much-expanded format in 1916 and inspired two other significant encyclopedic works: in 1914, George Moreland's self-published opus called *Balldom* (grandiosely subtitled "The Britannica of Baseball,") and Ernest J. Lanigan's *Baseball Cyclopedia*, also sponsored by *Baseball Magazine*, which debuted in 1922 and was updated annually through 1933.

The Golden Age, 1920-1968

There have been other new statistical tabulations in this century, but generally of the counting sort: complete games (NL 1910, AL 1922), games started (AL 1926, NL 1938), games finished (NL 1920, AL 1926). And there were sacrifice bunts allowed (NL 1913, AL 1921), intentional bases on balls (only since 1955), and, in the next period, saves (1969) and game-winning RBI (1980). The only new average since slugging average was adopted in 1923 has been the on base percentage, adopted in 1985.

The ICI group computed saves for prior years. Another such stat that failed to survive, alas, was stolen bases off pitchers, which the American League recorded only in 1920-1924; it has been recorded on an unofficial basis since the 1980s by the Elias Sports Bureau and Baseball Workshop. The only new fielding measure was team double plays, added to the AL list in 1912 and the NL in 1919. Other new and more interesting stats appeared in the 1940s and '50s but have not yet gained the official stamp of approval, such as Ted Oliver's Weighted Rating System, Alfred P. Berry's Average Bases Allowed (opponents' slugging average), and Branch Rickey and Allan Roth's Isolated Power. (See the ensuing essay, "Sabermetrics" for more about these unorthodox measures, some of which have gained wide acceptance and may, like the on base percentage, one day be embraced by Major League Baseball.)

This period of baseball's history may have fielded its most dazzling array of stars, but strategically and statistically it was rather dim. There was some excitement, however, in baseball record keeping. First came *Daguerreotypes*, issued by *The Sporting News* in 1934, featuring the playing records of many retired players both celebrated and obscure; most if not all of these statistical and biographical profiles originally appeared in the pages of TSN. Although its number of statistical categories was fewer than one might have wished, *Daguerreotypes* was very useful and, through its several editions ably edited by Paul MacFarlane, long-lived.

In 1940 came *The Sporting News's Baseball Register*, which supplied full records for active players, managers, coaches, and umpires, plus a grab bag of former stars. Since the expansion of the major leagues from 16 teams to 30, the Register has only accommodated contemporary players and managers, but it remains a valuable source.

Then in 1951 came the first true encyclopedia of baseball, the claims of Moreland and Lanigan notwithstanding. Compiled by Hy Turkin and S.C. Thompson, *The Official Encyclopedia of Baseball* was published by the A.S. Barnes Company. Its 620 pages contained a wealth of features such as manager and umpire rosters, historical essays, playing tips, a bibliography, and much more. But the heart of the volume and the key to its subsequent success was a register of nearly nine thousand men who had played one or more games at the major league level from 1871 through 1949 (the 1950 record of players appearing in ten games or more was tacked on to the end). In this register, Turkin/Thompson also offered birth and death data and what today seems fairly limited statistical information but by previous standards was a veritable cornucopia: year, club, league, position, games, and batting average or won-lost record. A landmark volume that did much to inspire this one, the Barnes encyclopedia endured through ten revised editions, the last being published in 1979, 10 years after the initial appearance of

Macmillan's *The Baseball Encyclopedia.*

The Barnes encyclopedia went a long way toward making the study of baseball history and records a respectable pursuit, just as a century earlier the statistical accounting of a boys' game had helped to make baseball a sport for grown men. The researchers' ranks expanded to include such men as Bob Davids, who in 1971, aided by other experts like Cliff Kachline, Bill Haber, Ray Nemec, John Pardon, and Joe Simenic, would create SABR, the Society for American Baseball Research (pronounced "saber"). Formerly the lonely pursuit of a handful of "nuts" like S.C. Thompson, baseball research and sabermetrics—a neologism coined in honor of SABR, signifying the statistical analysis of the game's records—would become the pastime of thousands.

An article in *Life* magazine by Branch Rickey on August 2, 1954, gave further impetus to the study of baseball statistics, but not just to set the historical record straight. Indeed, this article may be viewed as the opening shot of the sabermetric assault of the 1980s. In "Goodby to Some Old Baseball Ideas," Rickey, with the aid of some new mathematical tools supplied by Dodger statistician Allan Roth, sought to puncture some long-held conceptions about how the game was divided among its elements (batting, baserunning, pitching, fielding), who was best at playing it, and what caused one team to win and another to lose. This is a pretty fair statement of what sabermetrics is about.

Rickey attacked the batting average and proposed in its place the on base percentage, but the most important thing Rickey did for baseball statistics was to strip the game and its stats to their pre-1876 essentials and start again, this time remembering that individual stats came into being as an attempt to apportion the players' contributions to achieving a team victory.

Rickey and Roth devised a formula to measure a team's efficiency in turning its offensive and defensive statistics into runs, and thus wins. They realized, and had confirmed for them by mathematicians at the Massachusetts Institute of Technology, that just as the team which scores more runs in a game gets the win, so a team which over the course of a season scores more runs than it allows should win more games than it loses—and by an extent correlated to its run differential.

From this startlingly simple (or rather, seemingly simple) observation of 1954 flowed: first, the trailblazing but little noted work of George Lindsey in the 1950s and early 1960s, when he developed a model for run-scoring probability from the 24 combinations of outs and bases occupied; the development of "percentage baseball" stats and strategies by Earnshaw Cook in the 1960s; the play-by-play analysis of complete seasons by the Mills brothers, Eldon and Harlan, in 1969-1970; the recording and analysis of situational statistics by the Elias Sports Bureau for use by Major League Baseball and its clubs; and, over the next two decades, the statistical and historical works of many sabermetricians.

The Computer Age, 1969-

Despite the death of Turkin in 1957 and Thompson 10 years later, their encyclopedia remained the dominant book of baseball statistics, although many fans were frustrated with the fragmentary records it presented. As Frank V. Phelps wrote in the 1987 edition of *The National Pastime*, "Gaps and obvious errors in official averages, the lack of many early records, difficulty in securing the records of players who appeared in only a few games, and frustrating discrepancies among existing guides and registers had long since created a desire for an ultimate, complete, correct set of major league records. But it wasn't until the mid-1960s that the development of sophisticated computers which could absorb, retain, order, and output huge amounts of data finally made a project feasible."

Beginning in 1967, a battalion of researchers commanded by David Neft foraged through the official records and newspaper box scores to provide freshly compiled figures for those who had no ERAs, RBI, slugging averages, saves, and all manner of wonderful things. The material which finally appeared in the tome was entered into a data bank, and the book was the first to be typeset entirely by computer, now a common practice. Published in 1969, *The Baseball Encyclopedia* was a milestone in computer technology, but as indispensable as the computer were the old-fashioned scrapbooks and files of Lee Allen and John Tattersall. The result was a mammoth ledger book of the major leagues more thorough than any that had ever appeared before.

The ICI group not only found new data to correct old inaccuracies but also applied new yardsticks to men who had gone to their graves never having heard of an RBI or a save. The ICI research that went into *The Baseball Encyclopedia* of 1969 created new stars, launching several previously underappreciated heroes of old into the Hall of Fame, such as Sam Thompson, Addie Joss, Roger Connor, and Amos Rusie. Their phenomenal level of play was hidden simply because statisticians back then were not recording the particular numbers which would show them off to best advantage. If sabermetrics consists of finding things in the existing data that were not seen before, or in collecting that data which makes possible the application of new statistics to old performances, the first edition of *The Baseball Encyclopedia* was a monument in the course of sabermetrics.

However, its subsequent editions declined from that standard, dropping valuable data, altering figures for star players in a misguided homage to tradition, and making a shambles of individual/team balance in the totals.

The seventh edition was issued in 1988 and, like the five that preceded it, was less accurate than the classic first issue. The eighth edition, published in 1990, corrected many of the errors in the seventh but retained many once-contested errors that historians had long since expunged from the record, while changing other statistics in a manner at variance with Major League Baseball's standards and with a rationale that remains unclear. For the ninth edition, Major League Baseball distanced itself from the both the product and its database.

Even when *The Baseball Encyclopedia* was being readied back in 1968-1969, the ICI findings raised the hackles of traditionalists, prompting the formation by Major League Baseball of a Special Baseball Records Committee. Its members ruled upon such matters as whether, for the historical record, bases on balls should be counted as hits (as they were in 1887), outs (as they were in 1876), or neither (as has been the practice in all other years); or whether "sudden-death" home runs—37 game-winning blows with men on base that they identified as having occurred in the bottom half of the ninth or an extra inning—would be credited as homers or, in the practice before 1920, would count for only as many bases as were needed to push across the winning run. In the latter controversy, committee members first decided to count the disputed blows as homers, but then, when complaints arose that Babe Ruth's famous total of 714 would change to 715, they reversed themselves. They also decided that the National Association of 1871-1875 was not a major league, while the Federal League, Union Association, and Players League were; and they ruled on several other issues, all of which were published in the Appendix to *The Baseball Encyclopedia*.

Because earlier editions of *Total Baseball* enjoyed neither the privilege nor the responsibility of official Major League Baseball status, the editors committed themselves to the *process* of history—its research, reporting, and interpretation—rather than to its product. History is not static and unchanging. Our course then as now seemed unassailable: publish the best-documented data and remain humbly amenable to subsequent revision in the light of new evidence. (This is not very different from the placard in the Baseball Hall of Fame, which states that although later studies have called into question the accuracy of information on the plaques, the facts as engraved were believed to be accurate at the time.)

However, it must be acknowledged that we paid little mind to the consequences of our findings and reasoned judgments, such as the stripping of a batting championship from Ty Cobb in 1910 or Bobby Avila in 1954. For the fourth, landmark edition of *Total Baseball*, our challenge was to devise a more historically sensitive framework that would permit us to incorporate the best modern research while continuing to honor the judgments of the past.

Total Baseball abided by the Special Baseball Records Committee's decision on game-ending homers—not to preserve Ruth's total, but because there were many more such homers before 1920 than the 37 the committee identified, and the disputes surrounding some of them are now beyond settling.

Like Turkin/Thompson and all previous record books, and in accordance with the view of most historians, we rejected the committee's position that the National Association was not a major league. We committed fully to the creation of a full statistical record of that trailblazing circuit, and hoped one day to integrate the NA and NL records of such players as Al Spalding, Cap Anson, George Wright, and all the others who played in the professional league between 1871 and 1875. For now, we provide NA stats within the Player and Pitcher Registers, but total them separately from those of the NL (or, in a rare case, the American Association, a major league from 1882 through 1891).

We also differed from the committee's ruling on awarding pitchers' wins and losses in the years before 1920. Not finding any official scoring rule or practice for that time, its members chose to apply 1950 guidelines to decisions awarded in 1876-1920. This well-intentioned decision produced substantial alterations in the records of such hurlers as Cy Young, Christy Mathewson, Grover Alexander, and others. In the ensuing years, the notable research of Frank Williams (reported in "All the Record Books Are Wrong," *The National Pastime*, 1982) revealed that there was indeed a pattern and a rationale for the way decisions were awarded in those days; the data in *Total Baseball* conforms with his meticulously substantiated findings.

More involved, and perhaps of most direct interest to fans and media, are the subjects of (a) statistical discrepancies between the official record presented in *Total Baseball* and the figures published in other reference works, or memorialized on Hall of Fame plaques, and (b) the implications of corrected data for the awarding of batting championships. We will address those questions, as well as the larger ones of transcription accuracy and ledger balance, in the "Issues and Answers" section of this essay.

Let's resume our chronicle of how Major League Baseball and others have kept the record of the game. Besides the debut of *The Baseball Encyclopedia* (and the Miracle Mets and the centennial of professional baseball), there were two other interesting baseball developments in 1969. The first and less celebrated was a research project launched by Eldon and Harlan Mills that, like the ICI effort, could not have been contemplated without the computer. The Mills brothers tracked the entire major league seasons of 1969 and 1970 on a play-by-play basis. Then they applied to that record the probabilities of winning which derived from each possible outcome of a plate appearance, as determined by a computer simulation incorporating nearly eight thousand possibilities. What, for example, was the visiting team's chance of winning the game before the first pitch was thrown? Fifty percent, if we are pitting two theoretical teams of equal or unknown ability on a neutral site. If the first man fails to get on base, the chances of the visiting team winning are reduced to 49.8 percent; should he hit a double, the visiting team's chance of victory is raised to 55.9 percent, as determined by the simulation. Every possible situation—combining half-inning, score, men on base, and men out—was tested by the simulator to arrive at "Win Points."

The Millses' purpose was to determine the clutch value of, say, hitting a homer with two men on and one man out in the bottom of the ninth, with the team trailing by two runs, the situation Bobby Thomson faced in the climactic National League game of 1951—oddly, the rookie year of the first modern computer. (That home run gained for him 1,472 Win Points; had it come with no one on in the eighth inning of a game in which his team led 4-0, the homer would have been worth only 12 Win Points.) What the Mills brothers were attempting to do was to evaluate not only the *what* of a performance, which traditional statistics indicate, but the *when*, or clutch factor, which no measure to that time could provide.

This project, detailed in a small book issued in 1970 called *Player Win Averages*, proceeded from the same impulse that led to other measures of clutch performance: the game-winning RBI, introduced as an official Major League Baseball stat in 1980 and scrapped in 1989; the measures of batting performance in late-inning and men-on-base situations first published by Seymour Siwoff,

Steve Hirdt, and Peter Hirdt of the Elias Sports Bureau in 1985; and the historically complete indexes of clutch hitting and clutch pitching developed for the first edition of this book.

The other noteworthy baseball event of 1969 was the official adoption by the major leagues of the save, the stat associated with relief pitching, the game's most significant strategic development since the advent of the gopher ball. Now shown in the papers on a daily basis, saves were not officially recorded at all until 1960. It was at the instigation of Jerome Holtzman of the *Chicago Sun-Times*, with the cooperation of *The Sporting News*, that this statistic was finally accepted (although Pat McDonough, a founding member of SABR, had developed a similar stat in 1924 which he called "games finished by relief hurlers"; its first appearance in print came in the *New York Telegram* three years later). The need for the save arose because relievers operated at a disadvantage when it came to picking up wins. The bullpen specialists were a new breed, and as their role increased, the need emerged to identify excellence, as it had long ago for batters, starting pitchers, and fielders.

The save's prime statistical drawback is that there is no negative to counteract the positive, no stat for saves blown (except, all too often, a victory for the "fireman"); unofficial attempts to develop such a stat have accelerated in recent years, and now are part of the formula for the Fireman of the Year award.

August 10, 1971, marked another milestone, the founding in Cooperstown of SABR, the group in whose annual publications most of today's sabermetricians cut their analytical teeth. Its statistical analysis research committee, headed for more than a decade by Pete Palmer, has served as a sounding board for the inventive approaches of such men as Dallas Adams, Dick Cramer, Steve Mann, Craig Wright, Gary Gillette, and Bill James.

Developments of the ensuing decade include the previously mentioned adoption of the game-winning RBI (GWRBI) in 1980; it rewarded the batter who drove in a run to give his club a lead that it never relinquished. This stat was pilloried in the press from its introduction; Major League Baseball finally gave up on it before the 1989 season. In 1985 on base percentage was made official, thirty-one years after its introduction to the general baseball public by Rickey and Roth.

Situational stats, unofficial but widely reported and employed, have been the specialty of the Elias Sports Bureau, the Baseball Workshop, and Stats, Inc.—performance in day games vs. night, grass vs. artificial turf, lefty vs. righty, day game following night, bases-loaded situations, and so on. When the data is drawn from a large enough sample, these stats can be provocative and meaningful; they represent the wave of the future in baseball, and are fast becoming useful analytical tools for review of the past. Elias has recorded situational data systematically since 1975, Baseball Workshop since 1984.

Total Baseball

The next major event in the history of baseball record keeping was *Total Baseball*. Founded upon a unique historical database that Pete Palmer has cultivated for decades—in the tradition of baseball archivists like S.C. Thompson, Bradshaw Swales, Leonard Gettelson, and John Tattersall—*Total Baseball* is the third-generation encyclopedia of the game. Just as the advent of the Macmillan/ICI encyclopedia supplanted Turkin/ Thompson, the standard for two decades, *Total Baseball* has taken advantage of new technology and new research, notably by members of the Society for American Baseball Research, to present data more accurate than ever before, and more of it.

There are, of course, the traditional stats one would expect in a baseball reference work; there are many of the more revealing sabermetric stats (discussed in detail in the essay that follows this); there are stats never published before their appearance in this book. And as you have seen in Part One, there is a recognition that baseball history and knowledge resides not only in its numbers.

Issues and Answers: Sources of Baseball Statistics

There are six major sources for baseball statistical research, and thus for the official statistics that comprise *Total Baseball*. By far the most significant one is the official Major League Baseball records kept by the leagues, published in the baseball guides, and maintained on microfilm at the Baseball Hall of Fame in Cooperstown and in the league offices. These records cover the years since 1903 for the National League and 1905 for the American League. Any official source data before these years were lost.

The second major source is the computer printouts prepared by ICI for *The Baseball Encyclopedia* in 1969. These cover the NL for 1891-1902, the AL for 1901-05, the Federal League for 1914-15, plus all the 19th-century major leagues (1882-91 American Association, 1884 Union Association, and the 1890 Players League). These records, obtained from newspaper box scores, were turned over to the Baseball Hall of Fame and made public by agreement with its resident historian Lee Allen, who permitted ICI to use his voluminous player demographic files.

The third source is John Tattersall's newspaper box-score research for the NL of 1876-90. Since Tattersall had done such careful work, day-by-day computer printouts were never generated for this period. Any day-by-day records created by Tattersall have been lost, but what has survived is a batting and fielding summary and a pitching summary for each club each year listing many categories. This collection, now owned by SABR, also includes the home run log, which lists every home run ever hit from 1871 to date, the date, teams, game location, batter, pitcher, inning, men on base, and other notes. John Tattersall, Bob McConnell, and Pete Palmer have discovered over a hundred errors in the homer data from the various accepted sources, either ICI research or guide data.

The fourth source for baseball statistics is a box score collection accumulated by Michael Stagno, covering the National Association of 1871-1875, which was also purchased by SABR. Preliminary basic data was calculated by Stagno. Bob Richardson of Boston and Bob Tiemann of St. Louis have accumulated complete totals in all categories from this data with the exception of caught stealing data.

The fifth source is additional work done by the ICI researchers for the 1969 edition, covering data that were not kept officially during the years since 1903 for the NL and 1905 for the AL. Examples of this data are runs batted in before 1920; extra base hits in the AL for 1905 and 1906, double plays by fielders before 1920 NL and 1923 AL; pitching data except wins and losses for the AL for 1905-07, earned runs for pitchers before 1912 NL and 1913 AL; complete games before 1913 NL and 1926 AL; games started before 1926 AL and 1938 NL; and saves before 1969. Any day-by-day records from this source have been lost, but the season totals have survived.

The sixth source is newspaper box score research to pick up additional categories not covered by the first five sources. Examples of this are hit by pitch for batters before 1917 NL and 1920 AL (by Alex Haas, Tattersall, Palmer, and many others), triple plays by fielders before 1928 AL and 1930 NL (mainly by Jim Smith), home runs allowed by pitchers before 1950 AL and 1952 NL (again by Tattersall). Frank Williams carefully researched AL pitching records for 1901-1919, when the league records were particularly sloppy. *Total Baseball* has day-by-day sheets for most of this data, with the rest residing in the Tattersall collection.

Issues and Answers: Discrepancies

The original data for record books and Hall of Fame plaques, before the 1969 ICI research, were mostly obtained from two sources, the Spalding and Reach annual guides and two *Sporting News* publications: the *Baseball Register* (published yearly 1940-date), which often contained records of oldtimers, and *Daguerreotypes* (published every so often from 1951 to date), which had records of all Hall of Famers and many other notable players. This research was done from guides and newspapers by Paul Rickart, Leonard Gettelson, and Paul MacFarlane.

When the 1969 encyclopedia came out, there were many small differences in player stats when compared to the traditional data. However, since any records used to generate guide data in the early years were lost, the new data appeared to be more reliable. In addition, many more categories were given, like extra-base hits, runs batted in, pitcher innings, hits and earned runs allowed, and fielder double plays. Also included in the new data were club splits for traded players and information on those who played in fewer than 15 games.

In addition to the previously mentioned retroactive scoring decisions of the Special Records Committee, it ruled to include in the averages many games that were thrown out before, particularly in 1877, 1879, and 1899. Also included were the NL's tie games of five or more innings in 1878 through 1884 (38 of them) previously uncounted. Before 1912 in the NL pinch hitters and defensive replacements were included in the official game sheets, but the players were not credited with a game played. The committee decided to add these in, too.

Our research has uncovered a great many small errors and a few major ones in the official statistics. This was done by comparing individual totals to team totals, and by rechecking the addition on the player sheets. Most of these errors were in the American League, particularly before 1920, for which the record keeping was very sloppy. The NL has been much better over the years. For example, from 1910 to date, they took the sum of all the batter and fielder stats for each team, compared them to the sum of the team stats, and resolved almost all the differences. The AL did not start doing this until 1973 when the record keeping was first computerized. The NL went to computers in 1981.

For example, up through 1935, most AL clubs are not in agreement in player sums and team figures for at bats and hits. The differences are usually small, less than 10. (We have corrected the larger discrepancies of those years, but the smaller ones are yet to be resolved.) For 1905 to 1920, the team totals are further removed from the sum of the players, so that *The Baseball Encyclopedia* and *Total Baseball* have replaced the team totals with the sum of the players. We corrected all the post-1935 cases of team at-bat and hit totals not agreeing, but have not yet begun work on the previous years.

An interesting quirk in the way records are kept—and another reminder, as if one needed it, that baseball record keeping remains subject to error and controversy—occurred as recently as the strike-shortened season of 1981. The American League rule was to round off the innings pitched at the end of the season, although the weekly reports showed thirds of innings. Baltimore's Sammy Stewart had 29 earned runs in 112⅓ innings, while Oakland's Steve McCatty had 48 in 185⅔ innings. This gave Stewart the ERA title, 2.323 to 2.327. But when the innings were rounded off, McCatty won, 2.32 to 2.33. McCatty got the title, but the next year both leagues decided to count thirds of innings.

Issues and Answers: Hall of Famers

The data reported by the ICI group in the first edition of *The Baseball Encyclopedia* upset many people in baseball, for their numbers were different from those traditionally accepted; in subsequent editions, many of the prominent players' statistics were fudged back to their traditional values. Yet 1969 had hardly been the first time corrections had been made to official data. In 1929 Grover Cleveland Alexander won his 373rd game, breaking Christy Mathewson's National League record, then thought to be 372. He never won another game. A number of years later, Joseph Reichler found a game in which, by the rules of that time, Matty should have gotten the win, this game taking place on May 21, 1902. The official record was changed and Matty pulled into a tie with Alex. The problem was that no one checked all of Mathewson's other games to see how many times he received a win under the old rules that wouldn't have been credited that way today. When ICI did its original research in 1968, it found Matty had only 367 wins total by today's rules, while Alexander had 374. (Further research, notably by Frank Williams, has restored Alexander and Mathewson to a tie at 373 wins.)

In another celebrated example of record-book flip-flops, when the American League was formed in 1901, Nap Lajoie was credited with a .422 average, with 220 hits in 543 at bats. After a number of years, someone noticed that if you take these at bats and hits, the average comes out only to .405, so his average was changed. (Turkin/Thompson gave Nap a mark of .409 in its first edition.) Later in the 1950s, John Tattersall had his doubts and decided to go through his newspaper collection of box scores. He found 229 hits for Lajoie, not 220—the error had been in the figure for hits, not in the figure for batting average. Thus his average was restored to .422, which happened to be the highest in American League history. Then ICI research in this area came up with a .426 mark (232 for 544, based on newspaper accounts), which was published in the first edition, then trimmed back to .422 in subsequent editions. The .426 figure is the one this book uses, because the day-by-day source data for the American League of 1901 has been lost.

Lajoie seemed to be involved in a number of controversies. ICI research found four more hits for him in 1902, raising his average from .369 to .378. Later editions of *The Baseball Encyclopedia* have changed Lajoie's stats back to the old values; we have not.

In 1910 there was a very close batting race between Cobb and Lajoie. At the end of the season, most people thought Nap had won, based on his getting seven hits in a doubleheader on the final day of the season. There was talk that the opposing Browns had let him get a number of bunts by playing back, so that the hated Cobb would lose. However, the AL office went over their figures and gave Cobb the title, .385 to .384. Nearly 80 years later, Palmer discovered a critical error: a game in which Cobb had two hits in three at bats had been entered twice. This was found because Sam Crawford had 14 games on his official sheet for the homestand yet the Tigers had only played 13. It turned out that Detroit played a doubleheader on September 24, but the second game inadvertently was inserted in the official sheets as being played on September 25. Later, this second game of the 24th, which appeared to have been missing, was put in the scoresheets again. The League Office discovered this mistake soon after its official announcement that Cobb had won the batting title, because the double entry was corrected for all the other Detroit players. However, Ban Johnson had made a big deal out of how carefully his people had checked the figures in order to settle the controversy, so the AL kept quiet about the gaffe, leaving Cobb the winner.

Appeals to Commissioner Kuhn in 1981 to set the matter straight officially were to no avail, because that would not only have changed the outcome of the 1910 batting race, it would also have altered Cobb's lifetime hit total, then being pursued to massive media attention by Pete Rose. Kuhn's statement read, in part, "The passage of seventy years, in our judgment . . . constitutes a certain statute of limitation as to recognizing any changes in the records with confidence of the accuracy of such changes . . . . Since a variety of questions have been raised through the years about the accuracy of the statistics of that period, the only way to make changes with confidence would be for a complete and thorough review of all team and individual statistics. That is not practical." It may not have not been practical, but we have embarked upon such a course, and Major League Baseball has dedicated itself to that ongoing process.

Asked at the time how we would have resolved the dispute over the 1910 batting race, we responded in this way: remove Cobb's two redundant hits and alter his batting average accordingly, effectively dropping it beneath Lajoie's, and correct his lifetime hit total as well; however, retain Cobb's batting championship, for two reasons—one, because Lajoie's flurry of bunt hits were highly suspect, and two, because Cobb was awarded the title *in his day*, and awards should be permanent, not contingent. Furthermore, a reasonable case can be made that Ban Johnson, if he had believed that Lajoie's tainted hits would have been sufficient to produce a batting championship, would have nullified them; after all, he did banish from baseball the Browns' manager who had instructed his rookie third baseman to play exceptionally deep.

It is this singular event in baseball history that supplied a model for how *Total Baseball* and Major League Baseball developed a policy for incorporating new research finds into the historical record without revoking long-held personal championships. Player records may be changed upon the evidence of historical error, but league awards and titles are forever.

Here is what happened in the now celebrated Honus Wagner case in the 1990 edition of *The Baseball Encyclopedia*, over which Major League Baseball and the Macmillan publishing firm became estranged. The Macmillan editor noticed that previous edition figures for Wagner did not agree with the data presented in the first edition in 1969. He assumed that the data had been corrupted over the years, and thus returned the 1897-1900 data to the original figures, costing Wagner 12 hits. However, the editor did not restore the 1901-02 data, which would have resulted in Wagner losing three more hits. The outcome was that Wagner had a total of 3415 hits in the 1969 edition, 3430 in the 1988 edition (the traditional figure) and 3418 in the 1990 edition (also in 1993). One of the problems with the Macmillan newspaper research was that it did not count protested games in the player data. Although the games were thrown out of the standings, the player stats *did* count in the league compilations at the time, which should be the criterion for inclusion. (Protested games were included in the official records through 1909, then omitted 1910-1919, and were made once again part of the official records in 1920. When our review of these protested games prior to 1909 is completed, the individual stats will be added to our figures.)

Wagner was involved in three of these protested games. There were about twenty-five of them altogether in the nineteenth century. However, the newspaper research did show up additional differences in player stats beyond those from the protested games.

When checking the plaques for the Hall of Fame players, we found about 40 players with differences from the *Total Baseball* data. Most were nineteenth century players with small differences due to discrepancies between the old guide figures and the later newspaper research. Some had to do with rule changes from the 1969 Special Records Committee. For the 20th century, there were a number of differences due to official errors, mostly in the area of pitcher won-lost marks in the 1901-1919 American League period. There were only a few outright errors on the plaques (see below for Anson, Clarkson, Hamilton, McCarthy, McGinnity, and Nichols). Exact differences can be found by comparing *Daguerreotypes* (which often agrees with the plaques) with *Total Baseball.*

Below is a guide to variances between the plaques and the official record of Major League Baseball embodied in *Total Baseball* (TB).

19th-Century Hall of Famers

Cap Anson ***Plaque**, four batting titles;* **TB**, *four**
In 1879, Anson appears to have been the beneficiary of 20 extra hits, either by error or, as is commonly believed, a civic-minded Chicago official scorer. This error was found by John Tattersall in his review of newspaper box scores. In addition he (and we) incorporated the player records of four Chicago tie games, of which Anson played in two. His traditional mark of .407 was really only .317, and is so recorded in this volume; however, although a modern accounting would result in an 1879 batting title for Paul Hines, with .357, we credit the *championship* that year to Anson, as an instance of the official Major League Baseball policy cited above.

*The singular season of 1887 presents a different case. Following the long-standing directive of the Special Baseball Records Committee, we did not, until this edition of *Total Baseball,* count walks as hits for this season, the practice which had been the sole basis of Anson's fourth batting championship. The modern computation revealed Sam Thompson to have had the highest batting average, with a mark of .372, and had prompted us to withdraw the fourth batting title from Anson; now, with this edition, the 1887 championship is restored to him with a mark of .421.

Jake Beckley ***Plaque**, .309 lifetime, also for fielding at first base, 2368 games, 23696 putouts, 25000 chances;* **TB**, *.308, 2380, 23709, 25024*
These are about as close as you can get when comparing several sources prior to 1900.

Dan Brouthers ***Plaque**, .419 average in 1887;* **TB**, *.420*
ICI research found an extra at bat and hit for Brouthers in 1887.

John Clarkson ***Plaque**, 175 losses, 2013 strikeouts, 4514 innings;* **TB**, *178, 1978, 4536⅓*
The major difference in strikeouts occurred in 1886, where the guide had 340 and we counted only 313. We recorded two additional losses in 1894, in accordance with the scoring rules of the day. Reviewing our sources, we counted 27 more innings in 1887. His plaque bore a clear error concerning his wins in 1888. He had 33 and did not lead the league, although the plaque says 49. This was a confusion with the 49 Clarkson did win in 1889, which was also listed.

Ed Delahanty ***Plaque**, hit. 408 in 1899;* **TB**, *.410*
The correction is a product of newspaper research.

Hugh Duffy ***Plaque**, hit .438 in 1894;* **TB**, *.440*
This was the highest average all-time. The 1895 guide has 236 hits while the newspaper count is 237; both had 539 at bats. Since no backup data has survived for the guide, there is no way to determine where the difference might be.

Jim Galvin ***Plaque**, 365-311 won-lost;* **TB**, *361-308*
The plaque data includes a 4-2 mark in the 1875 NA, which has been denied major league status by the Special Baseball Records Committee. There are other smaller differences.

Billy Hamilton ***Plaque**, 196 runs in 1894, 115 stolen bases and .338 batting average in 1891, 937 stolen bases total, 1893-1895 batting averages of .395,.399 .393, ten times scoring 100 runs;* **TB**, *198 runs in '94, 111 steals and .340 batting average in '91, 914 lifetime steals, 1893-1895 batting averages of .380, .403, .389, eleven times scoring 100 runs*
Whether Hamilton scored 196 runs or 192, he still holds the all-time record. There were small differences in stolen bases in several years. We speculate that when the folks at Cooperstown counted Hamilton's seasons of scoring 100 or more runs, they overlooked his 1889 A.A. accomplishment.

Hughie Jennings ***Plaque**, once hit .397;* **TB**, *.401 in 1896*
The guide had 208 hits in 523 at bats, which actually computes to .398, although .397 was shown. The newspaper research showed 209 for 521.

Tim Keefe ***Plaque**, 346 wins;* **TB**, *342*
Daguerreotypes currently also has 342.

Joe Kelley ***Plaque**, .391 in 1894;* **TB**, *.393*
Newspaper box score research pointed up discrepancies in the figures recorded in the guides.

King Kelly ***Plaque**, .394 average in 1887;* **TB**, *.391*
John Tattersall found several additional games that Kelly played in 1887 in which he went 4–for–14.

Tommy McCarthy ***Plaque**, 1268 games, 109 stolen bases in 1888, 53 assists in 1893;* **TB**, *1273 games, 93 steals, 28 assists*
Newspaper research found the early stolen base figures to be inflated, especially for the American Association. His 53 assists in 1893 included many at second base and shortstop. However, he did have 44 in the outfield in 1888, fourth best all-time.

Kid Nichols ***Plaque**, 360-202 won-lost, 30 wins in 1895;* **TB** *361-208, 26*
Daguerreotypes now has 361-208 as we do, including 26 wins in 1895. Nichols for years had been credited with winning 30 or more games from 1891 through 1897, but it has been conclusively shown that he had only 26 in 1895. The Spalding guide showed games pitched (which was usually interpreted to be decisions) and percentage. They had 44 and .681 which would give a mark of 30-14. The 1942 *Baseball Register* showed him 30-15. ICI's *The Baseball Encyclopedia* had him at 26-16 in 42 complete games and 0-0 in five relief appearances. Ironically, the corrected figures give him 30 wins in 1898, for seven seasons of 30 victories or more—total, but not consecutive.

Amos Rusie ***Plaque**, led in shutouts five times;* **TB**, *4*
Rusie pitched seven innings of a nine-inning shutout on July 5, 1897. Taking this shutout away, in accordance with current scoring rules (there were no official rules for crediting shutouts until 1951), gave him two shutouts instead of three that year.

Sam Thompson ***Plaque**, .336 lifetime;* **TB**, *.335, once*
Newspaper research found minor discrepancies in Thompson's statistics in the early 1890s.

John Ward ***Plaque**, 158-102 won-lost, 2151 hits;* **TB**, *164-103, 2136*
Eighteen "missing hits" came from the 1890 Players League, for which newspaper research offered a lower total than the league figures. Other minor discrepancies were spread out over several years. We spotted three extra wins in 1879 and again in 1883.

20th-Century Hall of Famers

Luke Appling ***Plaque**, 11,569 chances accepted at shortstop;* **TB**, *11,616*
There was an addition error for his putouts in 1940. He had 307, not 257. *Daguerreotypes* had 11,566, not 11,569.

Jack Chesbro ***Plaque***, 192-128 won-lost; **TB**, *198-132*
Daguerreotypes now has 198-128. The 1947 *Baseball Register*—only one year after Jack's election and the creation of his plaque—had 197-127. Still under review are two other games for which it has been argued that Chesbro should have received wins.

Ty Cobb ***Plaque**, 4191 hits;* **TB**, *4189*
See above for discussion of the doubly entered 2-for-3 game. But that is not the whole story of how Cobb's lifetime hit total fell by two, nor of how he comes to retain his twelve batting titles. Modern research of the official day-by-day sheets revealed that Cobb had two games in 1906—on April 22 and 23—in which he went 1-for-8 that were not entered on his sheet. Additionally, there was a game on July 12, 1912 (the first game of a doubleheader) in which Cobb had a run which was entered in his hit column. (If this had indeed been a hit, he would have had a 34-game hitting streak. It was really only 23 games.) Finally, under today's rules, Cobb would not have won the batting title in 1914, because he didn't have enough plate appearances (or at bats). However, he did win it under the rules of the day, as he won the 1910 title, and that is what counts.

Eddie Collins ***Plaque**, 3313 hits;* **TB**, *3315*
Collins picked up two hits in 1920 in a game for which his stats were switched with those of Buck Weaver.

Stan Coveleski ***Plaque***, 214-141 won-lost, 2.88 ERA; **TB**, 215-142, 2.89 *Daguerreotypes* has 215-141. The 1942 *Baseball Register* has 216-142. Our ERA includes 1912, when Stan had a 3.43 era in 21 innings. The beginning of official status for ERA in the AL was 1913.

Sam Crawford ***Plaque**, 2505 games, 2964 hits, 312 triples;* **TB**, *2517, 2961, 309*
Crawford's games played vary from the plaque largely because of the practice of not counting pinch-hit appearances as games played. His ICI sheets reveal five additional games in 1900 and seven in 1901. Also, he loses a triple in each of three seasons (1899, 1902, 1904) before the survival of official sheets; newspaper research does not support the Guide figures. And finally, Crawford lost three hits in 1900 through a recount of box score data, and five more in 1901. He gained back three in 1903 and two in 1904.

Red Faber ***Plaque**, 253-211 won-lost, 3.13 era;* **TB**, *254-213, 3.15.*
Faber was credited with one win less than he actually recorded in 1916, one of the years in which the American League, at Ban Johnson's behest, posted no official data in this category. For 1915, we add a loss that clearly was overlooked on the official AL sheet, and for 1926 we add another loss that somehow was not posted when the Guide figures were released. The ERA variance is purely mathematical; it had been computed incorrectly.

Elmer Flick ***Plaque**, .378 in 1900;* **TB**, *.367*
The guide had 207 hits in 547 at bats, while the newspaper research showed 200 in 545.

Harry Heilmann ***Plaque**, 2146 games;* **TB**, *2147*
Daguerreotypes has 2145 games. Heilmann appeared in 69 games in 1914, not 66. For 1912-14 the official AL averages did not count a game for any player who had all zeros in his entry. These would be pinch-runners or late-inning defensive replacements. There were a total of over 400 such uncounted appearances in this category altogether.

Walter Johnson ***Plaque**, 414 wins;* **TB**, *417*
This research was done by Frank Williams and detailed minutely in his previously cited essay in *The National Pastime* of 1982. Walter had a 16-game winning streak in 1912, but one of the games (August 5) was not marked as a win on his sheet. In 1911, wins were incorrectly marked as losses on June 27 and July 9. For the AL before 1920, there were about twenty or thirty errors in awarding wins and losses in the official statistics each year.

Heinie Manush ***Plaque**, 2009 games;* **TB**, *2008*
His games were added incorrectly on the 1927 American League official sheet.

Joe McGinnity ***Plaque**, won 20 seven times;* **TB**, *eight*
This looks like an error made by the Hall of Fame. He won 20 in 1902 between two leagues, as shown in the 1941 *Baseball Register* (McGinnity was elected in 1946).

Herb Pennock ***Plaque**, 161 losses;* **TB**, *162*
Daguerreotypes agrees with 162 losses. The 1941 *Baseball Register* had 161.

Eppa Rixey ***Plaque**, 4494 innings;* **TB**, *4494 2/3*
Official stats rounded innings pitched until 1982. *Total Baseball* records thirds of innings pitched in all seasons.

Red Ruffing ***Plaque**, led in shutouts 1938 and 1939;* **TB**, *1939 only*
Lefty Gomez had four shutouts in 1938, not three. This included a rain-shortened complete game on July 15. Ruffing had three. Also, the comment on the plaque about making the all-star team in 1937-38-39 applies to the *Sporting News* All-Star team, not the All-Star Game team.

Tris Speaker ***Plaque**, .344 lifetime;* **TB**, *.345*
There was an addition error on his official sheet for 1911. He had 500 at bats, not 510.

Pie Traynor ***Plaque**, one of few players with 200 hits in a season;* **TB**, *of course, many players have had 200 or more hits in a season*

Zack Wheat ***Plaque**, 2318 games for Brooklyn, 2406 total;* **TB**, *2322 for Brooklyn, 2410 total*
There were four unrecorded games in 1911 in which Wheat appeared only as a pinch hitter.

Issues and Answers: League Batting Leaders

Until the fourth edition of *Total Baseball*, Major League Baseball had established no official historical record, despite its product endorsement of several statistical compendiums over the years. As a result, writers, historians, statisticians, and fans were offered a choice amongst differing annual league batting leaders, depending on the major record book favored. Those most favored by recent chroniclers have been *Total Baseball* and *The Baseball Encyclopedia* because they contained all player and club records.

There are two recognized record summary tomes which feature leaders in various statistical categories, lifetime or single-season: *The Book of Baseball Records* (Elias Sports Bureau Inc.) and *The Complete Baseball Record Book* (*The Sporting News*). Though both are respected works, and both organizations have had long, and often official, relationships with Organized Baseball, neither record book enjoys official status, and discrepancies exist between the two.

There was *no* official batting championship rule until 1950. *Total Baseball* and *The Baseball Encyclopedia* remedied this oversight by formulating—independently—their own guidelines for the many years of omission, each based on their own concepts of fairness and equality.

In previous editions, *Total Baseball* established the following criteria for batting championships: 1876-1956, qualification by having plate appearances equal to 3.1 per game times the number of scheduled games, thus conforming to the Major League Baseball practice since 1957. The batting championship criteria for *The Baseball Encyclopedia* over the years have been: 1876-1919, games played equal to at least 60 percent of games the team scheduled; 1920-1949, at least 100 games played, based on acceptance of the unofficial but universally assumed rule requiring appearance in at least 100 games; and 1950-present, the various changing official rule definitions.

In a policy shift endorsed by Major League Baseball, *Total Baseball* identifies league batting champions according to the practice of the time, in each league, and each champion will have his seasonal batting average recorded in boldface in his entry in the Player Register. However, as noted above in the discussion of the 1910 AL batting race, in the Annual Record section of this volume, we record the highest batting averages in each league season as correctly calculated, although not necessarily in descending order.

The history of the official batting championship rule is as follows: (1) 1950-1951, 400 official times at bat; (2) 1952-1954, 400 official times at bat or, if less than 400 times at bat and by adding enough imaginary hitless at bats so as to total 400, "he still would have the highest batting average in his league, he shall be the champion batter"; (3) 1955-1956, 400 official times at bat; (4) 1957-1966, 3.1 plate appearances per game times number of scheduled games, equaling 477 in a 154-game schedule and 502 in a 162-game schedule; and it's 502 plate appearances; and (5) 1967-present, 3.1 plate appearances per scheduled game, except that "if there is any player whose average would be the highest if he were charged with the required number of plate appearances or official at bats, then that player shall be awarded the batting championship."

In the strike-shortened season of 1972, a 156-game standard prevailed instead of the 162 scheduled games. In the strike seasons of 1981 and 1994, the rule of 3.1 plate appearances per game was applied to the number of games played by each team, rather than to those scheduled.

The early record tomes, the *Spalding Record Book* and *The Sporting News Record Book*, placed Jake Stenzel (NL) in the lead for 1893 and Nap Lajoie (AL) on top in 1905. Both Stenzel and Lajoie were the leaders during the life of the Spalding volumes, 1908-1924, and in the *Sporting News* volume from its debut in 1921 until 1929, when Hugh Duffy replaced Stenzel and 1930, when Elmer Flick supplanted Lajoie. The reasoning behind the *Sporting News* switches was that both Stenzel and Lajoie failed to meet the unwritten criterion of a representative number of games—Stenzel had played in only 60 games and Lajoie in 65, not even half of their club's scheduled games. Otherwise the early record books' leaders were those endorsed by the leagues.

The Spalding Record Book in its 1917 edition made two important batting championship changes, both on the basis of mathematical errors which their editors had noted. To that time, Dan Brouthers had been tied with Cupid Childs for the highest batting average in 1892, but had been awarded the title based on his having played in more games, which was the tie-breaking guideline of the day. In 1917, however, Childs went to the front on the basis of extended batting average (calculating to extra decimal places beyond the thousandths that comprise conventional reporting of batting averages).

Next, Lajoie's average of .422 in 1901 was reduced in 1917 because of a *Reach Guide* typo in the hit column to a .405 figure. The Spalding management (the once independent Reach company had long since been acquired by Spalding) should have known that in 1892, the criterion for awarding a batting championship was indeed games played, not extended batting average, and that in 1901 they would have found Lajoie's correct (as then calculated) average in any number of newspapers. Lajoie's .422 average was restored in 1954 in response to John Tattersall's research, but Childs remained, until this writing, ahead of Brouthers in the NL's *Green Book.* (Since the fifth edition of *Total Baseball*, Brouthers has been credited as the champion because he played in more games, which was the criterion of the time—not because modern research has lowered Childs' batting average from .335 to .317.)

During its formative years, 1876-1919, the National League omitted any mention of batting championship criteria in its published rules. Certainly, this should have been addressed before 1920. Still, batting championships were tacitly acknowledged by the league, with guidelines drawn primarily from the comments of Henry Chadwick.

From 1876 to ca. 1888, the criterion was understood to be the best seasonal performance; as expressed by Chadwick in the *Spalding Guide* of 1887, "an average rating of a player should be on a season's work." Seasonal leadership may be deduced when the league's recognized champion was not listed first in the official averages. His preeminence was based on a representative number of games played over the season in which he excelled, as opposed to the nominal leader's handful of games.

The yardstick between 1889 and 1919 was playing in at least 100 games. In the 1890 *Spalding Guide* Chadwick wrote: "With the object in view of equalizing the averages and placing the names of the batsmen who have played in 100 games or over, are given the front rank, while those who have played in 50 games and over occupy second place, and those in 25 games and over third place, and so on."

The American League rules in its early years, 1901-1919, omitted any batting championship language. In honoring Cobb as its 1914 bat champ, the AL was undoubtedly proceeding from the guideline of best seasonal performance.

As discussed in the "Sources of Baseball Statistics" section of this essay, *Total Baseball* relies upon newspaper research and other data for the years before 1903 in the NL and 1905 in the AL. For subsequent seasons, the official league day-by-day sheets are available for study. The record summary books issued by Elias and *Sporting News* accept all the batting leaders recognized in the yearly Guides (Spalding, Reach, etc.). These champions are also accepted in today's league publications (AL *Red Book* and NL *Green Book*). Henceforward, *Total Baseball* recognizes the same champions, with the exception of 1892, discussed above.

For students of the game, Joe Wayman documented the variances among the record books and encyclopedias and highlighted particularly those traditional batting champions whom previous editions of *Total Baseball* had toppled from the pinnacle. Even though most of these champions have been rethroned, the following thumbnail account of the debatable batting leaders will serve to explain the seeming anomaly of a batting champion whose average is lower than that of a rival.

OFFICIAL							TB (eds. 1-5)				
			G	AB	H	BA		G	AB	H	BA
1878	NL	Dalrymple	60	267	95	.356	Hines	62	257	92	.358
1879	NL	Anson	49	221	90	.407	Hines	85	409	146	.357
1884	NL	O'Rourke	104	448	197	.350	Kelly	108	452	160	.354
1887	NL	Anson*	122	532	224	.421	Thompson	127	545	203	.372
1892	NL	Brouthers	152	588	197	.335	Brouthers	152	588	197	.335
1892	NL	Childs	144	552	185	.335					
1893	NL	Duffy	131	537	203	.378	Hamilton	82	355	135	.380
1902	AL	Delahanty	123	473	178	.376	Lajoie	87	352	133	.378
1910	AL	Cobb	140	509	196	.385	Lajoie	159	591	227	.384
1914	AL	Cobb	97	345	127	.368	Collins	152	526	181	.344
1926	NL	Hargrave	105	326	115	.353	Waner, P.	144	536	180	.336
1932	AL	Alexander	124	392	144	.367	Foxx	154	585	213	.364
1938	AL	Foxx	149	565	197	.349	Foxx	149	565	197	.349
1940	NL	Garms	103	358	127	.355	Hack	149	603	191	.317
1942	NL	Lombardi	105	309	102	.330	Slaughter	152	591	188	.318
1954	AL	Avila	143	555	189	.341	Williams	117	386	133	.345
1981	NL	Madlock	83	279	95	.341	Rose	107	431	140	.325

*Anson would be a .347 hitter without the benefit of his walks, which count as hits for only that year and make the difference in his winning the batting championship over Thompson.

1878: Abner Dalrymple captured the NL's batting title. Modern record tomes (*The Baseball Encyclopedia* and *Total Baseball*) list Paul Hines in the top spot. The NL in 1878 did not include tie games in its official averages, while today's record tomes count them. Thus, by counting tie games, Hines emerges with the higher average, but does not take away Dalrymple's championship.

1879: Cap Anson, the day's recognized batting champion, has been challenged by the moderns (*The Baseball Encyclopedia, Total Baseball, The Sports Encyclopedia: Baseball*, and *The National League Story*, Lee Allen) as to whether his .407 average is legitimate. In fact, the average was disputed as early as the 1880 DeWitt Guide, the averages for which were compiled by William Stevens of the *Boston Herald*, and *Balldom* (1914), compiled by George Moreland. *Total Baseball* keeps the title with Anson in recognition of the league action at the time, but reports his batting average correctly in the Player Register and in the Annual Record's listing of top batting averages in the 1879 NL.

1884: The official batting champion remains Orator Jim O'Rourke. Newspaper box scores, game accounts, and the results of tie games elevate King Kelly to a higher average. Tie games were not included in the official averages at the time, and how to handle them today remains a matter of controversy. No matter how we treat Kelly's 2-for-4 in his only tie-game appearance (August 11), his average is higher than O'Rourke's.

1887: In only this season, bases on balls counted as hits. One month into the season, the American Association wanted to scrap the rule, but the NL would not consent. *Total Baseball* now honors the rules of the day and thus recognizes Anson as the batting champion.

1892: Brouthers and Childs were honored as co-champions at .335, as discussed above. Childs had the higher extended average, .3351, against Brouthers' .3350 mark. By the day's reasoning, however, Brouthers is the leader. As Chadwick noted in the *Spalding Guide*, "the lead in all cases of tie scores in base hits belongs by right to the batsman who has played in the greatest number of games, and in this case Brouthers batted in 152 games to Child's 144." Childs's statistics, as compiled by ICI from newspapers, yield a batting average of .317, placing him third.

1893: Billy Hamilton's average was higher than Duffy's, and he would have met modern criteria for plate appearances. The NL, however, honored Duffy because he appeared in at least 100 games, which was expected of the leading players of that day. The title is thus accorded to him.

1902: The ICI sheets gave Lajoie four more hits than the guides had credited him with originally.

1910: Cobb is the champion, for reasons discussed amply above.

1914: Cobb, due to his proven hitting excellence, was awarded the championship because, in all reasoned probability, he would have been the leader over the full season. Consider, also, that the batting championship for the Chalmers car in 1910 for position players was based on 350 at bats. Cobb would have easily captured the hit crown on a mythical 100 game requirement, even though he was three games shy.

1926: Bubbles Hargrave topped three other questionable contenders—those not credited with at least 400 at bats. All qualified for the title, though, based on the period's acceptance of appearance in at least 100 games. In Hargrave's favor was his position—catcher. Over the years, catchers were considered somewhat differently when it came to handing out awards, because of the demands of their position. In fact, in order for a catcher to qualify for the fielding championship at his position, he need only have appeared in at least 77 games. Hargrave caught in 93 games.

1932: Dale Alexander had the games and at bats to satisfy the AL as to his claim. If the 400 at bat rule had been on the books, Alexander no doubt would have been inserted into the lineup until he secured eight additional at bats. If Jimmie Foxx were recognized as champion today, he would have the first of two consecutive Triple Crowns.

1938: Foxx was the AL leader—no ifs, ands, or buts about it. The AL had a rule in 1938 requiring the batting ". . . winner to be at least 400 times at bat." (*Reach Guide*, 1939) Taffy Wright is the trivia-question champion, batting .350 in 100 games.

1940: Debs Garms raised a few eyebrows as a come-from-nowhere champion. If enough imaginary at bats to reach 400 were to be added to Garms' total, his adjusted average would still be one point higher than that of Stan Hack, the runnerup.

1942: Ernie Lombardi was the recognized NL batting king. As a *Sporting News* headline advised, "Ernie's 105 contests suffice to qualify him for a second title." The announcement called attention to the "inquiries" which had been made regarding a Lombardi award since the AL had put in place a 400 at bat requirement. Bill James noted that the NL announced a "meritorious 400 at bat" requirement after the problematic Garms award two years earlier. NL President Frick, however, contended there was no specific bat rule and catchers, because of their demanding position, deserved special consideration. The catcher's fielding championship by this time was based on 100 games, lessening the Frick contention. Frick may have had in mind the prior, 77-game catching requirement for fielding leadership. Thus, Frick's reasoning could have been to create a proportion: 77 games for catchers is to 100 games for position players what 77 percent of 400 at bats (308) for catchers is to 400 at bats for position players.

1954: Ted Williams, the batter with the highest average in the AL, did not meet the official qualifications to claim the title. The 1954 official Rule 10.17 spelled out the champion as one who, with at least 400 at bats, or with fewer than 400 at bats plus enough imaginary ones to equal 400, has the higher average. Under the official rules definition, Bobby Avila is the batting leader. During the closing weeks of the campaign, Williams was aware of the rule but continued to be selective of pitches, rather than swing at those outside the strike zone simply in order to reach the required 400 at bats. Williams' extended average based on adding imaginary at bats to his 386 is a .331 figure.

1981: Bill Madlock is the official batting champion by the rules of the day. Due to the strike-shortened season, the games a team played, rather than the scheduled games, were the basis for individual championships. Pittsburgh, Madlock's club, played 103 games. Thus, $103 \times 3.1 = 319$ plate appearances to qualify for the batting championship. Madlock topped the required 319 PA's by one, with 279 at bats, four sacrifice flies, 34 bases on balls, three hit by pitch, and no sacrifice hits or interference calls. *Total Baseball* awarded the title to Pete Rose in editions 1 and 2, based on average games played per team, then corrected the procedure in its third edition.

The records of the four defunct major leagues show only the American Association had batting champions not agreeing with *Total Baseball* champions. This happened twice: in the 1884 AA, the official winner was Dude Esterbrook though his teammate Dave Orr actually batted 50 points higher; and in 1886 AA, the champ was officially Orr though Guy Hecker's recomputed average nips him by a point. (Pete Browning also surpassed Orr and was listed as champion in earlier editions of *Total Baseball*, for which a guideline of 3.1 plate appearances per game was employed throughout.)

A Little Help from Our Friends

The computer has made possible the rapid analysis of mountains of raw baseball data. But as invaluable as the computer has been in producing and cross-checking the statistical data for *Total Baseball*, the editors owe more to the people who have contributed their time, their expertise, their love of the game, and their passion for getting things right. These individuals are listed below, or in the Acknowledgements, or in the table at the end of the book that enumerates those readers of the earlier editions who helped us improve the accuracy of *Total Baseball* this time around. A collective debt is owed to the Society for American Baseball Research and the National Baseball Library.

The six principal sources of the statistics herein were discussed earlier. Supplemental sources were:

- For work on the Stagno Collection of NA data, 1871-75, SABR's 19th-century research committee, headed successively by John Thorn and Mark Rucker, Bob Tiemann, Bob Richardson, Fred Ivor-Campbell, and John Husman.
- For batters hit by pitch, 1884-1896 AA/NL/PL, 1909-1916 NL, 1909-1919 AL, research from newspapers by Alex Haas, Pete Palmer, John Schwartz, Bob Davids, John Tattersall, Lyle Spatz, Herb Goldman, Keith Carlson, Tom Chase, Ed Luteran, Frank Phelps, and others. (Note: research continues for the 1897-1908 period, but the data is, at this writing, about 95 percent complete.)
- For home runs allowed by pitchers, 1876-1950 AL/NL, the Tattersall Collection, aided by Bob McConnell.
- For runs batted in, 1903-1919 NL, 1905-1919 AL, ICI research.
- For runs batted in, 1880-1885 NL and 1882-87, 1890 AA, David Neft.
- For pitcher saves (except 1901-1919 AL) 1876-1968 NL/AA/UA/PL/AL, ICI research.
- For stolen bases, 1886 NL, Spalding *Baseball Guide*.
- For wins and losses for pitchers, 1876-1900 NL/AA/PL, and for wins, losses, games started, complete games, shutouts, saves, 1901-1919 AL, and complete pitching data, 1892, research from newspapers and official sheets by Frank Williams.
- For shutouts, 1876-1939, Joe Wayman.
- For biographical data, the biographical research committee of SABR, notably Richard Topp, Bill Carle.
- For caught-stealing data, 1914-1916 AL, 1915-1916 NL, Ernie Lanigan, courtesy of Bob Davids.
- For home/away data, 1876-1891 NL/AA/UA/PL, Bob McConnell.
- For game scores, 1876-1884 NL/AA/UA, Bob Tiemann.
- For game scores, 1885-1891 NL/AA/PL, Richard Topp.
- For runs and homers home/away, 1980s NL/AL, Bill Carr.

Missing data includes:

- Hit batters: 1897-1908, scattered data, especially for New York and Cincinnati.
- Caught stealing: 1886-1914, 1916 (players with fewer than 20 steals), 1917-1919, 1926-1950 NL; 1886-1891 AA; 1890 PL; 1901-1913, 1916 (players with fewer than 20 steals), 1917-1919, 1914-15 FL.
- Sacrifice hits: 1927-1930 (fly balls advancing runners to any base counted as sacrifice hits).
- Sacrifice flies: 1908-1930, 1939 (sacrifice flies are counted as sacrifice hits for these years).
- Runs batted in, 1882-1884 AA; 1884 UA. Partial data is shown for 1882-84. For 1885-87 and 1890, about 10 percent of the data is estimated.
- Strikeouts for batters: 1882-1888, 1890 AA; 1884 UA; 1897-1909 NL; 1901-1912 AL. (Team batting strikeouts are presented for 1897-1902 NL and 1901-1904 AL.)

Incomplete data for those years up to 1903 NL and 1905 AL are available from the ICI computer printouts at the National Baseball Library. Additional research could turn up more data. If your research or sharp eye should detect errors or gaps in *Total Baseball*, please write us in care of the publisher (or alternatively, simply e-mail us at jthorn@ts-pub.com) and we'll be delighted to improve our data and credit your catch in the next edition.

Sabermetrics

Pete Palmer and John Thorn

Sabermetrics may be a new coinage for the statistical analysis of baseball but it is not a new phenomenon. Henry Chadwick, in the antebellum period, was as much a sabermetrician as Allan Roth or Bill James: he saw as clearly as they did that, because the object of the game is to win, runs are the best measure of player performance, just as they are of team performance at the end of a game.

After many decades in which this fundamental truth was lost (amid the general worship of false idols like batting average and pitcher won-lost percentage), today's sabermetricians have come around full circle to the game as it was originally understood. And what's remarkable about this is that in order to return to the primordial simplicity of the 1840s, '50s, and '60s, when runs and outs were all that went into the box score, they have relied upon computer simulations and higher mathematics. In other words, with the new statistics, simplicity emerges from complexity; what baseball statistics have offered for the last hundred years or so has been, despite the appearance of simplicity, in fact extremely complex.

For the veteran fan as well as for Major League Baseball, new ideas, new statistics, and new discoveries that dispute long-held verities (Ty Cobb's hit total, Hoss Radbourn's number of victories in 1884, etc.) may represent a challenge to tradition and thus a threat to the very soul of baseball, its pride in anachronism. Bernard Malamud wrote, "The whole history of baseball has the quality of mythology." The editors of *Total Baseball* relish the game's myths, from Abner Doubleday to the sacrifice bunt, and believe that in setting the record straight or turning conventional wisdom on its head, they are adding to the fan's enjoyment of the rich texture of the game. If you are one of the skeptics—like Earl Weaver, who once said, "There's no such thing as a new statistic"—please permit us to make the case for sabermetrics. (Much of the material in this section is adapted from our 1984 study, *The Hidden Game of Baseball.*)

What's in a Number?

On April 27, 1983, the Montreal Expos came to bat in the bottom of the eighth inning trailing the Houston Astros, 4-2. First up to face pitcher Nolan Ryan was Tim Blackwell, a lifetime .228 hitter who had struck out in his first time at bat. At this routine juncture of this commonplace game, Ryan stared down at Blackwell, but his invisible—yet, for all that, more substantial—opponent was a man who had died the month before Ryan was born, a man about whom Ryan knew nothing, he confessed, except his statistical line. For at this moment of his glorious big-league career, Ryan had accumulated a total of 3,507 strikeouts, only one short of the mark Walter Johnson had set over 21 seasons, from 1907 to 1927. Long thought invulnerable, Johnson's record was in imminent danger of falling, in 1983, not only to Ryan but also to Steve Carlton and Gaylord Perry.

Ryan fanned Blackwell and then froze the next batter, pinch hitter Brad Mills, with a 1-and-2 curveball. The pinnacle was his. Johnson had been baseball's all-time strikeout leader since 1921, when he surpassed Cy Young. Ryan would hold that title for just a few weeks, then would be overtaken by Carlton, only to display an incredible finishing kick and finish at 5,714 in 1994. But at the time that Ryan topped Johnson, baseball savants scurried to assess the meaning of 3,509 for both the deposed King of K and the new.

In the aftermath of Ryan's feat, some writers pointed out that he only needed 16 full seasons, plus fractions of two others, in which to record 3,509 strikeouts while Johnson needed 21, or that Johnson pitched over 2,500 more innings than Ryan. Coming into the 1983 season, Ryan had fanned 9.44 men per nine innings, while Johnson was way down the list at 5.33. And Ryan had allowed fewer hits per nine innings than Johnson, or, for that matter, anyone in the history of the game. So, it would seem 3,509 was not just one batter better than Johnson, but rather was mere confirmation for the masses of a superiority that was clear to the cognoscenti years before.

However, other writers introduced mitigating factors on Johnson's behalf, much as Ruth found supporters as the home run king even after Aaron hit number 715. These champions of the old order cited Johnson's won-lost record of 417-279 and earned run average of 2.17 while scoffing at Ryan's mark, entering 1983, of 205-186 with an ERA of 3.11. This tack led to further argument in print, bringing in the quality of the teams each man pitched for and against, the resiliency of the ball, the attitudes of the batters in each era toward the strikeout, the advent of night ball, integration, expansion, the designated hitter, the overall talent pool, competition from other professional sports . . . and on down into the black hole of subjectivism.

Why were so many things dragged into that discussion? Because the underlying question about 3,509 was: does this total make Ryan better than Johnson, or even a better strikeout pitcher than Johnson? At the least, does it make him a great pitcher? In our drive to identify excellence on the baseball field (or off it), we inevitably look to the numbers as a means of encapsulating and comprehending experience. This quantifying habit is at the heart of baseball's hidden game, the one played by Ryan and Johnson and Ruth and Aaron—and, thanks to baseball's voluminous records, more than 15,000 other players—in a stadium bounded only by the imagination.

What's in a number? It's the answer to "How Many?" and sometimes a great deal more. In this case, 3,509 men had come to the plate against Ryan and failed to put the ball in play, one more man than Johnson had returned to the dugout, cursing. So what's the big deal? That Ryan was .0002849 faster, scarier, tougher—better—than Johnson? An absolute number like 3,509, or 714 (the home-run record once thought invulnerable, too), or 4,191 (the erroneous hit total of Ty Cobb that Pete Rose finally surpassed) does not resound with meaning unless it is placed into some context that will give it life.

Baseball statistics are not the instruments of vivisection, taking the life out of the game in order to examine it; rather, statistics are themselves the vital part of baseball, the only tangible and imperishable remains of contests played yesterday or a hundred years ago. Baseball may be loved without statistics, but it cannot be understood without them. As the statistics reflect more accurately the reality of what happened on the field, greater understanding leads to a deeper love and appreciation of this great game—which is, essentially, the case for sabermetrics and the reason for *Total Baseball.*

The Linear Weights System

In 1982 Milwaukee's Robin Yount had the year of his life, batting .331 with 29 homers, 114 RBIs and 129 runs scored; he led the American League in hits, doubles, total bases, and slugging percentage, while finishing just one point behind the league leader in batting average for the first of two times in his career, he was voted the Most Valuable Player in the American League, being named first on all but one of the 28 ballots cast by the baseball writers.

Over in the other league, Mike Schmidt of the Phillies was having an off year, batting only .280 with 35 homers and 87 RBIs; the previous year, when he was awarded the MVP, in only 102 games played he had totaled 31 homers and 91 RBIs. He did lead the league once again in 1982 in slugging percentage, and he did win the Gold Glove at third base for the seventh straight year, yet in the MVP balloting none of the ballots listed him higher than fourth; 10 ballots were cast without listing him at all.

For Yount, 1982 was a crowning achievement; for Schmidt, a disappointment: that was the verdict reached by the baseball writers and conventional baseball statistics. Yet in terms of actual performance, as determined by the number of runs contributed, Schmidt's "off year" was scarcely different from Yount's. With the bat, Yount accounted for 59 park-adjusted runs beyond what an average batter might have contributed; Schmidt, 45. Through base stealing, Yount added 2; Schmidt none. With the glove, Yount was four runs below league average at his position, shortstop; Schmidt was 19 above average at third base. Total runs contributed: Yount 57, Schmidt 64. (Because Yount's batting so far exceeded that of other shortstops, while third base provided several heavy hitters, Yount contributed 7.0 extra wins to his Brewers; Schmidt contributed 6.1 to the Phillies.) Both men had outstanding seasons, the best in their respective leagues, and both outstripped the second-best player by about the same margin.

Viewing player (and team) performance through this sort of prism frequently produces such illuminating results. Cecil Fielder had a wonderful year in 1990, with his 51 homers, 132 RBIs, and league-leading figures in slugging average and extra-base hits. But how did he convince any writer voting for MVP that he had a better year than Rickey Henderson? In *Total Baseball,* you could look it up: Fielder contributed 4.2 extra wins to his team (wins that an average player would not), which was the fourth-best figure in the American League that year; Henderson was responsible for a whopping 8.2, not only the top mark in 1990 but also, at the time, the second-best mark in the AL since Mickey Mantle's epic seasons of 1956-1957!

This is the kind of analysis of player performance possible with a variety of sabermetric measures, not just the Linear Weights System. The common ingredient of most of the new, as yet unofficial, statistics is their creators' recognition of the relationship between runs and wins. These newly calculated measures are not official statistics of Major League Baseball, but they are constructed from the raw data of the official record. Some of the new measures may one day be officially embraced, as the on-base percentage became an official stat three decades after its introduction. Because of fan interest, we include them in the Player and Pitcher Registers that follow, alongside the officially tabulated numbers.

Runs and Wins

George Lindsey, in an article in *Operations Research* in 1963, was the first to assign run values to the various offensive events which lead to runs: Runs = (.41)1B + (.82)2B + (1.06)3B + (1.42)HR. He based these values on recorded play-by-play data and basic probability theory. Unlike Earnshaw Cook, who in the following year assigned run values on the basis of the sum of the individual scoring probabilities—that is, the *direct* run potential of the hit or walk plus those of the baserunners set in motion—Lindsey recognized that a substantial part of the run value of any non-out is that it *brings another man to the plate.* This additional batter has a one-in-three chance of reaching base and thus bringing another man to the plate with the same chance, as do the batters to follow. The *indirect* run potential of these batters cannot be ignored.

Steve Mann's Run Productivity Average (RPA) assigned these values based on observation of some 12,000 plate appearances: RPA = (.51)1B + (.82)2B + (1.38)3B + (2.63)HR + (.25)BB + (.15)SB − (.25)CS, all divided by plate appearances, then plus .016. His values were denominated in terms of the number of runs and RBIs each event produced. Bill James, at about the same time, came up with a similar formula, since shunned, with values based on runs plus RBIs *minus home runs.* The drawbacks to the approaches of Mann and James were the drawbacks of the RBI, which gives the entire credit for producing a run to the man who plates it, and of the run scored, which gives credit only to the man who touches home, no matter how he came to do so. For example, with no outs, a man reaches first on an error; the next batter hits a double, placing runners on second and third; the following batter taps a roller to short and is thrown out at first, with the run scoring from third. The man who produced the out is given the credit for producing a run, while the man who started the sequence by reaching first on an error is likewise credited with a run. The man who hit the double, which is surely the key event in the sequence which produced the run, and the only one reflecting batting skill, receives no credit whatsoever. In this regard, any formula based on "Runs Produced" (whether R + RBI or R + RBI – HR) is philosophically inferior to the formula Lindsey proposed, despite his failure to account for walks, steals, and other events.

The run values in the Linear Weights formula for identifying batters' real contributions are derived from Pete Palmer's 1978 computer simulation of all major-league games played since 1901. All the data available concerning the frequencies of the various events was collected; following a test run, these were tabulated. Unmeasured quantities, such as the probability of a man going from first to third on a single vs. that of his advancing only one base, were assigned values based on play-by-play analysis of over 100 World Series contests. The goal was to get all the measured quantities very nearly equal to the league statistics; then the simulation would provide run values of each event in terms of net runs produced above average. Expressing the values in those terms would give a meaningful base line to individual performances, because if you are told that a player contributed 87 runs you don't know what that signifies unless you know the average level of run contribution in that year: 87 may sound like a lot, but if the norm was 80, then you know the player contributed only seven runs beyond average.

The values obtained from the simulation are remarkably similar from one era to the next, confounding expectations that the home run would prove more valuable today than in the dead-ball era, or that the steal was once a primary offensive weapon. These values are expressed in beyond-average runs.

Run Values of Various Events, by Periods

Event	Period			
	1901–20	1921–40	1941–60	1961–77
Home Run	1.36	1.40	1.42	1.42
Triple	1.02	1.05	1.03	1.00
Double	.82	.83	.80	.77
Single	.46	.50	.47	.45
Walk/HBP	.32	.35	.35	.33
Stolen Base	.20	.22	.19	.19
Caught Stealing	-.33	-.39	-.36	-.32
Out*	-.24	-.30	-.27	-.25

*An out is considered to be a hitless at bat and its value is set so that the sum of all events times their frequency is zero, thus establishing zero as the base line, or norm, for performance.

In the years since this simulation was conducted, statistician Dave Smith ("Maury Wills and the Value of the Stolen Base," *Baseball Research Journal,* 1980) convinced Pete to adjust the values of the stolen base and caught stealing because of their situation-dependent, elective nature: attempts are apt to occur more frequently in close games, where they would be worth more than if they were distributed randomly the way an event like a single or a home run would be. Pete revised the value for the steal upward to .30 runs, while for the caught stealing it becomes -.60 runs.

Just as these run values change marginally with changing conditions of play, they differ slightly up and down the batting order (a homer is not worth as much to the leadoff hitter as it is to the fifth-place batter; a walk is worth more for the man batting second than for the man batting eighth); however, these differences have been averaged out in the figures above. For evaluating runs contributed by any batter at any time, there is no better method than Batting Runs, the Linear Weights formula derived from the computer simulation which is the basis of the table above.

The Formula

Batting Runs = (.47)1B + (.78)2B + (1.09)3B + (1.40)HR + (.33)(BB + HB) + (.30)SB – (.60)CS – (.25)(AB – H) – .50(OOB).

The events not included in the formula that you might have thought to see are sacrifices, sacrifice hits, grounded into double plays, and reached on error. The last is not known for most years and in the official statistics is indistinguishable from outs on base (OOB).

The sacrifice has essentially canceling values, trading an out for an advanced base which, often as not, leaves the team in a situation with poorer run potential than it had before the sacrifice.

The sacrifice fly has dubious run value because it is entirely dependent upon a situation not under the batter's control: while a single or a walk always has a potential run value, a long fly does not, unless a man happens to be poised at third base (whether it is achieved by accident or design is open to question, as well, but that is beside the point—getting hit by a pitch is not a product of intent, either).

Last, the grounded into double play is to a far greater extent a function of one's place in the batting order than it is of poor speed or failure in the clutch, and thus it does not find a home in a formula applicable to all batters. It is no accident that Henry Aaron, who ran well for most of his long career and wasn't too bad in the clutch, hit into more DPs than anyone else, nor that Roberto Clemente, Al Kaline, and Frank Robinson, who fit the same description, are also among the 10 "worst" in this department. If a .230-hitting American League shortstop doesn't hit into many twin killings, it's not because of adept bat handling or blazing speed but because he bats ninth.

The Linear Weights formula for batters may be long, but it calls for only addition, subtraction, and multiplication and thus is as simple as the slugging average, whose incorrect weights (1, 2, 3, and 4) it revises and expands upon. Each event has a value and a frequency, just as in slugging average, yet—as in no batting statistic you have ever seen—outs are treated as offensive events with a run value of their own (albeit a negative one), a truth so obvious it somehow escaped notice. Just as the run potential for a team in a given half inning is boosted by a man reaching base, it is diminished by a man being retired; not only has he failed to change the situation on the bases but he has deprived his team of the services of a man further down the order who might have come up in this half inning, either with men on base and/or with scores already in.

What Batting Runs does is to take every offensive event and to treat it in terms of its impact upon the team—an average team, so that a man does not benefit in his individual record for having the good fortune to bat cleanup with the Giants or suffer for batting seventh with the Marlins. The relationship of individual performance to team play is stated poorly or not at all in conventional baseball statistics. In Batting Runs it is crystal clear: the linear progression, the sum of the various offensive events, when weighted by their accurately predicted run values, will total the runs contributed by that batter or that team beyond the league average.

Recognizing that some dedicated readers of *Total Baseball* will wish to keep track of batting performance by computing Batting Runs themselves over the course of a season, and that they may be frustrated by the difficulty of calculating the "At Bats-Hits" factor for the league, which is necessary to determine the negative value of an out, we advise that using a fixed value of -.25 for outs will tend to work quite well if you wish to include pitcher batting performance, and a fixed value of -.27 will serve if you wish to delete it. Actually, any fixed value will suffice in midseason; it's only when all the numbers are in and you care to compare this year's results with last year's (or with those of the 1927 Yankees) that more precision is desirable. At that point the value of the out may be calculated by the ambitious among you, but ideally, the sporting press will provide accurate Batting Runs figures. Who, after all, calculates ERA for himself?

Batting Runs and Production

For those to whom calculation is anathema, or at the least no pleasure, Batting Runs has a "shadow stat" that tracks its accuracy to a remarkable degree and is a breeze to calculate: Production, which consists simply of On-Base Percentage plus Slugging Average. (Hence it is referred to as OPS for On-Base Plus Slugging, and adjusted production is known as OPS+). While it is not expressed in runs and thus lacks the philosophical appeal of Batting Runs, the standard deviation of its most complete version is 20.4 runs compared to the 19.8 of Batting Runs. In other words, the correlation between Batting Runs and Production over the course of an average team season is 99.7 percent.

However, as an average or ratio, Production measures the *rate* of batting success (efficiency), while Batting Runs measures the *amount* of success. For example, a batter who goes 2-for-5 with a walk in one game, those 2 hits being doubles, will have an On-Base Percentage of .500 and a Slugging Average of .800; his Production will be 1.30 or, as stated for convenience in *Total Baseball,* 130. Another batter, who in 162 games gets 200 hits and 100 walks in 500 at bats, with 400 total bases, will have an identical OBP, SLG, and OPS. Which player has contributed more to his team? Clearly, longevity, or amount of production, is no less important than rate of production.

To cite a specific instance in which Production and Batting Runs differ, take George Brett's remarkable 1980 season in which he batted .390, had 298 total bases, 75 bases through walks or HBP, and 118 RBIs—all in only 117 games played. In the table of all-time single-season leaders in Production, the Kansas City third baseman ranks 57th when his OPS of 1.124 is normalized to the league average and adjusted for home-park effects. Yet in the table of park adjusted Batting Runs, Brett's season is not even included in the top 100 all-time because he missed 45 games, in which his team derived no benefit from his high rate of performance. (Had Brett played 162 games and continued to perform at the same level, his Batting Runs would have been not 64 but 88.6, the 23rd best mark in history.)

Because OPS is not expressed in runs, it is less versatile than Batting Runs. For just as runs are proportional to the events that form them, so are they proportional to wins and losses. This statement, a truism today, was a novelty in 1954 when Rickey and Roth first stated the correlation between run differentials and team standings. But they did not take the next step, to recognize that not only a team's standing but even its won-lost record could be predicted from the run totals.

"The initial published attempt on this subject," Palmer wrote in the 1982 issue of the SABR annual *The National Pastime,* "was Earnshaw Cook's *Percentage Baseball,* in 1964. Examining major-league results from 1950 through 1960 he found winning percentage equal to .484 times runs scored divided by runs allowed.... Arnold Soolman, in an unpublished paper which received some media attention, looked at results from 1901 through 1970 and came up with winning percentage equal to .102 times runs scored per game minus .103 times runs allowed per game plus .505.... Bill James, in the *Baseball Abstract,* developed winning percentage equal to runs scored raised to the power *x,* divided by the sum of runs scored and runs allowed, each raised to the power *x.* Originally, *x* was equal to two but then better results were obtained when a value of 1.83 was used....

"My work showed that as a rough rule of thumb, each additional 10 runs scored (or 10 less runs allowed) produced one extra win, essentially the same as the Soolman study. However, breaking the teams into groups showed that high-scoring teams needed more runs to produce a win. This runs-per-win factor I determined to be 10 times the square root of the average number of runs scored per inning by both teams. Thus in normal play, when 4.5 runs per game are scored by each club, each team scores .5 runs per inning—totaling one run, the square root of which is one, times 10."

Note that when we refer to the need for approximately 10 additional runs scored (or 10 fewer allowed) to provide a team with an additional win, we do not mean that it takes 10 runs to win any given game. Obviously, in a specific case, a one-run margin is all that is required; but statistics are designed for the long haul, not the short.

What does this have to do with Batting Runs? Remembering that Batting Runs are expressed not simply in runs but in beyond-average runs, the conversion from a batter's Linear Weights runs to his wins is a snap: simply divide

Batting Runs by the number of runs it takes to gain an extra win in a given year. Taking the exploits of Babe Ruth in 1927, we see that through batting alone he contributed 100.7 runs, or 9.56 wins, since in the American League in 1927 it took 10.53 runs to produce an additional win. If every other player on the Yankees had performed at the league average, the New York record should have been 87-67; if each of the seven other batters had performed only half as well as Ruth and had added five extra wins (discounting reserves, pitchers, fielders, and stealers, whom we shall presume for this discussion to have been average), the Yankees would have gained another 35 wins (7 × 5) to finish with a won-lost mark of 122-32.

Stolen Base Runs

The Linear Weights formula for batters contains a factor for base stealers, expressed in runs. How do you judge the effectiveness of a base stealer? Conventional baseball statistics will lead you to the conclusion that whoever has the most steals is the best thief; that is the sole criterion for *The Sporting News* annual "Golden Shoe Award" in each league. How often the man with the most steals may have been thrown out is of no concern.

An article in the 1981 *Baseball Research Journal* by Bob Davids offered something more sophisticated yet utterly simple: a stolen base percentage, which is simply stolen bases divided by attempts. The best stolen base average of all time, insofar as we know and based on a minimum of 30 attempts, is Max Carey's in 1922 when he stole 51 bases in 53 attempts. The most times caught stealing in the course of a season was Ty Cobb's 38 in 1915, until 1982 when Rickey Henderson was nabbed 42 times. But the best method yet devised, and the one that is pleasingly simple, is to apply the Linear Weights method to get Stolen Base Runs. One multiplies the steals by their run value of .22 and the failed attempts by -.35, and adds the two products. The implication for such men as Ty Cobb, Rickey Henderson, and Vince Coleman is clear: it takes a fabulous stealing performance to produce as many as ten extra runs—i.e., one extra win—for the team.

In 1915 Ty Cobb, when he established the modern stolen base record of 96, can be seen to have contributed to his team 21.1 runs, while his 38 foiled larcenies cost 13.3. Thus Cobb, for all his whirling-dervish activity, accounted for only 7.8 non-par runs—not even a single win. Whoa! You mean that not a single one of Cobb's steals produced a victory? That is not what is being said: the fact is that while the gain from the stolen base is entirely visible—an extra base which may be followed by a hit that would otherwise not have produced a run—the cost of the caught stealing is entirely invisible, or conjectural, except with the aid of statistics. How many big innings did Cobb run his team out of? How many batters reached base in ensuing innings who might, in an earlier inning, have had their contributions count for runs? What Stolen Base Runs indicate are that, on balance, not on a specific-case basis, the stolen base is at best a dubious method of increasing a team's run production.

Now let's take a look at what Henderson did. His record 130 stolen bases in 1982 produced 28.6 runs for his team. His 42 failed attempts took away 14.7 possible runs. Net effect: approximately 14 runs, or one and a half wins, a performance nearly three times as good as Cobb's. In 1983, stealing 22 fewer bases, he was even better, accounting for 17.1 runs. However, the all-time best stealing record is that of Maury Wills in 1962, when he stole 104 bases and was caught only 13 times. Wills' 104 stolen bases produced 22.9 runs; his 13 failed attempts cost only 4.5. So, his baserunning contribution was 18.4, or a little under two wins.

Fielding Runs

As mentioned earlier, in 1954 when Branch Rickey and Allan Roth came up with their "efficiency formula" for run scoring and run prevention, the defensive half of the equation was divided into five segments, the last of which was fielding, to which they assigned a mathematical value of zero. "There is nothing on earth," Rickey declared, "anyone can do with fielding."

Since then many have tried, with mixed results, to improve upon the mere toting up of raw data—putouts, assists, errors, double plays. In the second edition of *Total Baseball,* we improved upon the Fielding Runs formula by calculating innings played at each position, plate appearances for all players on the team, and then rating each fielder based on his chances per inning. Where previously all outfield positions had been grouped together, we now rate left fielders against left fielders, center fielders against center fielders, and right fielders against right fielders; we also revised thoroughly the formula for catchers, which retains the highest degree of subjectivism because their primary defensive contribution comes not with the glove but through calling the pitches.

More on this complex subject in the Glossary.

Pitching Runs

Determining the run contributions of pitchers is much easier than determining those of fielders or batters, though not quite so simple as that of base stealers. Actual runs allowed are known, as are innings pitched. Let's assume that a pitcher is responsible only for earned runs. Then why, we hear some of you asking, is the ERA not measure enough of his ability? Because it tells only the pitcher's *rate* of efficiency, not his actual benefit to the team. In a league with an ERA of 3.50, a starter who throws 300 innings with an ERA of 2.50 must be worth twice as much to his team as a starter with the same ERA who appears in only 150 innings. Through Pitching Runs, we seek to determine the number of beyond-average runs a pitcher saved—the number he prevented from scoring that an average pitcher would have allowed.

The formula for Earned Run Average is:

$$\text{ERA} = (\text{Earned Runs} \times 9)/\text{Innings Pitched}$$

The number of average, or par, runs for a pitcher, which is represented by a Pitching Runs figure of zero, is equal to:

$$(\text{League ERA} \times \text{IP})/9$$

If the league ERA is 4.21 (as the National League's was in 1994) and a pitcher's ERA is also 4.21, he will by definition have held batters in check at the league average no matter how many innings he pitched. If, however, his ERA was 1.56 and he hurled 202 innings (as Greg Maddux did for the Braves in '94), he will have saved a certain number of runs that an average pitcher might have allowed in his place; to find that number we employ the Pitching Runs formula:

Pitcher's Runs = Innings Pitched × (League ERA/9) − ER

This represents the difference between the number of earned runs allowed at the league average for the innings pitched and the actual earned runs allowed. For the case of Maddux, we get

$$\text{Runs} = 202 \times (4.21/9) - 35 = 59.5$$

Maddux was 59.5 runs better than the average National League pitcher in 1994, and had he been transported to an average NL team—that mythical entity that scores as many runs as it allows while winning 81 and losing 81—he would have made that team's mark 87-75. (Actually, in the strike shortened 112 game season of 1994, an average team would have been 56-56, and the addition of Maddux would have made that team's record 62-50.) An alternative way to calculate pitchers' Linear Weights, useful with oldtimers for whom you may have the ERA but not the number of earned runs allowed, is to use the pitcher's ERA, subtracted from the league's ERA, multiplying by the innings pitched, then dividing by nine. In Maddux's case, this approach would look like:

$$(4.21 - 1.56) \times 202/9 = 59.5$$

The two parts of performance—efficiency and durability—are incorporated into all Linear Weights measures. If you are performing at a better than average clip, the more regularly you do so, the more your team will benefit and thus the higher your Linear Weights measure. If you are stealing bases nine times out of 10, your team will benefit more from 60 attempts than from 40; if you are batting at an above average clip, it's better to play in 160 games than 110; if you're allowing one earned run per game less than the average pitcher, your LWTS will increase with innings pitched.

Linear Weights in Practice

Having formulas for pitching, fielding, baserunning, and batting, we can assess the run-scoring contribution of every individual who has ever played the game, and thus the number of wins that he has contributed in a given season or over his career. The number of runs required to produce an additional win has varied over the years between nine and 11 runs, with a very few league seasons outside those parameters.

Limited by conventional baseball statistics, one might, in 1990, have uttered something like, "Barry Bonds hit .293 with 33 homers and 114 RBIs—the guy must have been worth 10 extra wins to Pittsburgh all by himself!" Or: "The White Sox are only one pitcher away from winning the division." Or: "The Yankees are only three players away from being a contender." Or, "Letting Darryl Strawberry get away was the worst thing the Mets ever did; they'll be a second-division club for a decade." With Linear Weights, these statements, or rather the concerns they reflect, can be approached with some data and with some degree of objectivity. First: Barry Bonds had a fine year in 1990, but to have contributed 10 wins by himself he would have had to account for nearly 100 Linear Weights runs, a mark that up till then had been attained by only three men in major-league history. In fact, Bonds contributed 6.5 wins in '90, though he did post 9.0 wins in 1992.

As to the White Sox, they finished 94-68 in 1990, while their Linear Weights projected them to finish at 81-81. The Athletics, who won the AL West at 103-59, actually projected to finish 96-66. So, the Sox management might have asked, how to close ground on the Athletics? Could one pitcher—like Bob Welch, for whom they bid in the free-agent bazaar—make the difference? To do so, he would have to contribute about 150 Pitching Runs, a feat no pitcher has ever accomplished. In 1990, pitching for Oakland—and remember, the Linear Weights formula is divorced from considerations of batter support—Welch contributed 20.7 park-adjusted Pitching Runs. So presuming that he pitched as well for the White Sox as he did for the Athletics, or even slightly better, he would not be enough to "win" Chicago the flag on paper; Chicago would need help from other quarters.

Regarding the other statements, you get the picture: sabermetric analyses like the ones above will tend to puncture fantasies.

Park Factor

A central issue for sabermetricians is the network of illusion created by home-park dimensions, atmospheric conditions, and visibility for batters. How many home runs would Matt Williams hit if he played half his games in Fenway Park? Will the Boston Red Sox and Chicago Cubs keep "failing" to put together solid pitching staffs—or has their pitching been adequate all along? Why had the American League leaders in triples so often worn a Royals uniform? One's home park has a powerful effect on a player or pitcher's record, elevating some good players to greatness and denying the spotlight to some outstanding performers.

It should be understood that the average player does better at home regardless of the park—familiarity breeds success. Individuals bat and pitch at a rate 10 percent higher at home, on average. But parks don't create performance; they only affect it. For example, a left-handed hitter at Fenway can do very well indeed, as Wade Boggs did, by learning to take the outside pitch to left field. Likewise, a right-handed batter can make the friendly Green Monster into his nemesis by trying to pull every pitch.

For hard luck in some parks, it is tough to top the record of Mark McGwire, who for the first part of his career had the misfortune to call the Oakland Coliseum home. McGwire's prodigious and plentiful home run total in 1998 made him the single-season record holder, so it is natural to think of his record as a fair representation of his abilities. Yet he could have accomplished so much more if he played his home games almost anywhere else. Through 1996, his last full season in Oakland, McGwire's lifetime Production, normalized to league average but not adjusted for park effects, was 28th best on the all time list of those playing in 1,000 games. Had he played his home games instead in Fenway Park, his OPS would have projected to the eighth best of all time. Had he even played in an average hitters' park—which is what OPS+ measures—his record would show itself to be the 12th best ever. In 1998 McGwire hit 38 homers at Busch Stadium and 32 on the road.

If we desire to remove the silver spoon or the millstone that a home park can be, and measure individual ability alone, we must create a statistical balancer that diminishes the individual batting marks created in parks like Fenway and augments those created in Oakland. Pete Palmer developed an adjustment that enables us, for the first time, to measure a player's accomplishments apart from the influence of his home park.

Parks differ in so many ways that it may be hard to imagine how their differences can be quantified. The most obvious way in which they differ is in their dimensions, from home plate to the outfield walls, and from the base lines to the stands. The older arenas—Fenway Park, Wrigley Field, Tiger Stadium—tend to favor hitters in both regards, with reachable fences and little room to pursue a foul pop. Yet two parks can have nearly equal dimensions, like Pittsburgh's Three Rivers Stadium and Atlanta's Fulton County Stadium, yet have highly dissimilar impacts upon hitters because of climate (balls travel farther in hot weather), elevation (travel farther as altitude increases), and playing surface (travel faster and truer on artificial turf). Still another factor is how well batters think they see the ball; Shea Stadium is notorious as a cause of complaints.

And perhaps more important than any of the objective park characteristics, suggested Robert Kingsley in a 1980 study of why so many homers were hit at Fulton County Stadium in Atlanta, is the attitude of the players, the way that the park changes their view of how the game must be played in order to win. In their own home park the Astros might peck and scratch for runs, but playing at Fulton County Stadium in Atlanta they put the steal and hit-and-run in mothballs. Conversely, a team which comes into the Astrodome and plays for the big inning will generally get what it deserves—a loss. The successful team is one that can play its game at home—the game for which the team was constructed—yet is flexible enough to adapt when on the road.

Rather than try to assign a numerical value to each of the six or more variables that might go into establishing an estimator of home park impact, we looked to the single measure in which all these variables are reflected—runs. After all, why would we assign one value to dimensions, another to climate, and so on, except to identify their impact on scoring? If a stadium is a "hitters' park," it stands to reason that more runs would be scored there than in a park perceived as neutral, just as a "pitchers' park" could be expected to depress scoring.

The full and lengthy explanation for the computation of the Park Factor is left to the Glossary, where hardy readers might consider taking a peek right now. For most of us, though, it will be enough to understand that the Park Factor consists mainly of the team's home-road ratio of runs allowed, compared to the league's home-road ratio.

Relativity

Sabermetric statistics can be marvelous tools for cross-era comparisons, enabling us to determine if baseball's history is truly a seamless web or if its seams are real enough, but are camouflaged by traditional statistics.

If Batter A presented himself to you for approval with these statistics—.330 batting average, 16 home runs, 107 RBIs—what would your reaction be? You'd like to have him on your team, right? And what to make of Batter B, who presents these numbers—.257 batting average, 14 home runs, 53 RBIs? Not bad for a middle infielder with a good glove, you say, but otherwise undistinguished? In fact, the "impressive" figures of Batter A represent the average performance of a National League outfielder in 1930, while the "blah" figures of Batter B are those of the average American League outfielder of 1968: the former has more than twice the RBIs of the latter, along with a batting average 73 points higher, yet the two performed at identical levels, and an argument could be made that Batter B was superior.

In a similar comparison involving those two years of extremes, Bill Terry led the National League in 1930 with a batting average of .401, a mark surpassed by Ted Williams in 1941 but not equaled since; Carl Yastrzemski led the American League of 1968 with a performance that oldtimers held to be a disgrace, a lowly batting average of .301, the worst ever to win a batting championship. Terry's mark was achieved at a time when most pitchers had only two pitches, a fastball and a curve, and not enough confidence in the latter to throw it when behind in the count at 2-0 or 3-1. The parks were smaller; there was no night ball; the game was segregated racially; and a team played 22 games with each of its seven rivals, none farther west of the Mississippi than St. Louis. Moreover, 1930 was the year in which National League officials, attempting to match the popularity of the slugging American League, juiced the ball to such an extent that the entire league batted .312 (if you remove pitcher batting). In other words, the average nonpitcher in the NL of 1930 batted higher than the AL leader in 1968! When Yaz hit .301, pitchers dominated the game and the average American League nonpitcher hit .238. How to compare Terry and Yaz, who played under such different conditions 38 years apart?

You could view Terry's .401 in relation to his league's BA of .312, concluding that Memphis Bill was a better hitter (by BA alone, which despite its previously cited deficiencies remains the most comfortable stat by which to introduce this technique) by 28.5 percent. You could compare Yaz's .301 to his league's BA of .238 and conclude that he was a better than average hitter by 26.5 percent. A mere 2 percentage points separate the men—had they both played in the National League of 1983, when the league average was .255, the Terry of 1930 might have hit .328, the Yaz of 1968, .323. (A further refinement of this method would be to delete Terry's at bats and hits from his league's, and those of Yastrzemski from his league's, so that the batters are not in effect compared with themselves. This, however, necessitates the use of at bats and hits rather than simply the averages and does not significantly alter the results.)

Why do we need relative measures? Basically, for the same reason we need statistics altogether, to compare, to interpret, and to comprehend, but in a more reasonable and accurate manner when the disparity of the data sources makes the use of absolute, unadjusted numbers illogical. If the analysis involves data produced under widely varying conditions, such as a sample including performances 20, 50, or 100 years apart, any comparison will be meaningless without dragging in a series of rather complex historical understandings to modify the analysis—and in a highly subjective, unreliable manner.

Until the 1970s, when David Shoebotham ("Relative Batting Averages," *Baseball Research Journal,* 1976) and Merritt Clifton ("Relative Baseball," *Samisdat,* 1979) introduced the relativist approach, all baseball stats were absolute. And for cross-era comparison, that favorite Hot Stove League activity, absolute stats were absolutely useless, generating plenty of heat and precious little light.

What the theory of relativity, baseball-style, does beautifully is to eliminate the need for bringing historical baggage to statistical analysis. The normalized or relative versions of any statistic—batting average, Production, ERA, slugging average, you name it; even homers or strikeouts, though there are problems with these—will be greater than 1.00 for all above-average performers (1.41, for example, means 41 percent better than average in the given category) while relative statistics less than 1.00 will indicate a below average level of play (0.88 means 12 percent below the norm).

It is as simple as can be. So Early Wynn had a 3.20 ERA in 1950? What does that mean? Well, the league ERA was 4.58, so Wynn did very well indeed. His normalized ERA thus was 143, a mark better than that earned by Tom Seaver in 1968, when he had an absolute ERA a full run lower at 2.20.

We cannot employ a Relative Won-Lost record, for the league average is every year the same: .500. (A logical corollary is that one cannot fruitfully use relative measures of any sort for a single season's analysis, as all like figures will be compared to the same league average. The numbers may be changed into normalized form, but the players' rankings will be unchanged: the top 10 in batting average in 1990, for example, will retain their ranks in Relative Batting Average.)

Relativism in baseball echoes not only Einstein but also Shakespeare, whose words in *Hamlet* might be modified to read "There is nothing either good or bad, but context makes it so." No longer must we accept arbitrary assessments of performance or regard with awe such old-time figures as Hugh Duffy's BA of .440 in 1894 (not the accomplishment that Rod Carew's .388 was in 1977) or George Sisler's .407 in 1920 (not as good as Roberto Clemente's .357 in 1967). Conversely, a "mediocre" performance of recent years, such as Bobby Murcer's .292 of 1972, for instance, stacks up as the equal of Eddie Collins' .360 in 1923, while Charlie Grimm's seemingly solid .298 in 1929 compares unfavorably to Mike Cubbage's .260 in 1976.

Relativism redefines our understanding not only of particular accomplishments but also of baseball history itself. We see that the men who batted .400 with numbing regularity in the 1890s and 1920s were not supermen (would you swap Wade Boggs for Tuck Turner? Tony Gwynn for Tip O'Neill?) anymore than the sub-2.00 ERA pitchers of the late 1960s were superhuman (Gary Peters, Bob Bolin, Dave McNally, among other). Absolute figures lie. Are hitters today worse because none has hit .400 since 1941? Or are they superior because a Dave Kingman could average nearly 30 homers a year while Cap Anson only averaged four? Are infielders better today because they make fewer errors than their counterparts of 50, 75, or 100 years ago? Do modern outfielders have limp-noodle arms because their assist totals pale before those registered in the early decades of the 1900s? Is baseball improving or declining, and has its rise or fall been steady? One can spit absolute stats on the hot stove all winter long and get no closer to the answer, but with relative statistics, the issues are clarified.

Total Player Rating

Total Player Rating (TPR) and its sibling Total Pitcher Index (TPI) are the most important methods for evaluating player performance in *Total Baseball.* Each formula distills the detailed analysis of the different components of the game—batting, baserunning, fielding, and pitching—into a single number that describes how a particular player compares to the average major league player.

The standard chosen for this comparison is wins—the ultimate currency in the national pastime. TPR and TPI take each player's performance into account, place that performance in the proper context of the ballpark, the league, and the way the game is being played, and then translates it into how many games he won or lost for his team. For more detail, see the detailed discussions of how TPR and TPI are computed in the introductions to the Player Register and the Pitcher Register, respectively, as well as in the Glossary.

Total Player Rating and Total Pitcher Index are not fixed measures, graven in stone tablets handed down from Henry Chadwick. *The target for TPR and TPI is always the same—fairly and accurately measuring a player's contribution to his team's record. However, the methods used to make this measurement have changed over the years.* Despite all the hard work and exhaustive research that has gone into *Total Baseball* over the decades, every evaluation system can benefit from improvement, and TPR and TPI are no exceptions. Even the fundamental laws of physics change, and the last century saw the rules by which humanity understood the universe change from a Newtonian framework to a universe largely delineated by Einstein. Partly due to *Total Baseball,* the last decade saw substantial improvements in how the National Pastime is understood, yet there is no shame in admitting that more work remains to be done.

The biggest reason for the changes is that the information available to baseball scholars has been greatly expanded and somewhat improved since the first volume of *Total Baseball* went to press in 1989. These improvements in available data are primarily as a result of painstaking research by dozens of dedicated individuals, most of them amateurs who give their time for the love of the game. Along the way, a few minor mistakes—regrettable but inevitable—have been corrected as well.

The translation from the various performance statistics into the wins or losses of TPR and TPI is accomplished by comparing each player to an average player at his position for that season in that league. While the use of the average player as the baseline in computing TPR and TPI may not seem intuitive to everyone, it is the best way to tell who is helping his team win games and who is costing his team wins. If a player is no better than his average counterparts on other teams, he is by definition not conferring any advantage on his team. Thus, while he may help his team win some individual games during the season—just as he will also help lose some individual games—over the course of a season or a career, he isn't helping as much as his opponents are. Ultimately, a team full of worse-than-average players will lose more games than it wins.

The reason for using average performance as the standard is that it gives a truer picture of whether a player is helping or hurting his team. After all, almost every regular player is better than his replacement, and the members of the pool of replacement players available to a team are generally a lot worse than average regulars, for obvious reasons.

If Barry Bonds or Pedro Martinez is out of the lineup, the Giants or the Red Sox clearly don't have their equal waiting to substitute. The same is typically true for lesser mortals: when an average ballplayer cannot play, his team is not likely have an average big-league regular sitting on the bench, ready to take his place.

Choosing replacement-level performance as the baseline for measuring TPR and TPI would not be unreasonable, but it wouldn't give a clear picture of how the contributions of each player translate into wins or losses. Compared to replacement-level performance, all regulars would look like winners. Similarly, when compared to a group of their peers, many reserve players would have positive values, even though they would still be losing games for their teams. Only the worst reserves would have negative values if replacement level were chosen as the baseline.

The crux of the problem is that a team composed of replacement-level players (which would by definition be neither plus nor minus in the aggregate if replacement-level is the baseline) would lose the great majority of its games! A team of players who were somewhat better than replacement level—but still worse than their corresponding average regulars—would lose more games than it won, even though the player values (compared to a replacement-level baseline) would all be positive.

Refinements

For those readers who carefully examine the differences between the various editions of *Total Baseball,* here is a complete list of the changes that have been made in the way player ratings have been computed since the first edition of *Total Baseball* in 1989.

First, a note about a change that has affected the first four editions as batter hit by pitch data for 1897-1908 has been gradually filled in via persistent research. The first edition included most data for 1897-1899, no data for 1900-08, and no data for the Federal League. The second edition filled in most data for 1900-1902 as well as for the Federal League. The third edition was missing about 12 percent of the data for the whole 1897-1908 period; the fourth edition was missing only about 5 percent of the HBP data for these 12 seasons. Unfortunately, 5 percent of the data are still missing.

The second edition of *Total Baseball* in 1991 added caught stealing data for the American League in 1927 from newspaper accounts. The second edition also estimated innings played at each position for each player, based on total plate appearances and player games at each position for each team. Previously, each position was rated for each team, and each player given a fraction of that rating based on player putouts divided by team putouts. The final change was to add a team ERA factor to the catcher fielding rating, giving a catcher credit for 10 percent of the ERA difference between his team and league.

Several important changes were made for the third edition in 1993. Passed balls for American League catchers were added for 1910-1924 from newspaper accounts. Park factors were changed to include runs scored and runs allowed data for three years, instead of only runs-allowed data for one year. The intent of the original park factor calculation in not counting runs scored was to cancel out the effect of teams that built their lineups to match their parks. The new method has a bigger sample and, therefore, is more reliable.

Fielding ratings were also changed for the third edition of *Total Baseball.* Box score research by Pete Palmer added games played in left field, center field, and right field for all fielders and based their outfield ratings on this new information. Previously, regular center fielders were rated as one group, and all other outfielders as another group. This change raised regular center fielder ratings because they were now compared with substitutes as well as regulars, and it also raised the fielding ratings of left and right fielders because they were no longer being compared defensively to substitute center fielders. Finally, this change lowered the ratings for substitute center fielders.

The third edition marked the debut of a three-year, all-league average for positional adjustments, instead of the previous one-year, one-league adjustment. It also changed the weighting of positional adjustments for players based on estimated innings at each position, not games.

Finally, the third edition changed how batter and pitcher ratings were split for players who did both. Previously all batting stats were counted under the pitcher rating if half the player's games were as a pitcher and fielding at other positions was not counted. If less than half a player's games were at pitcher, all batting and non-pitching fielding was counted as in the batting rating. The new system counted all pitching and pitcher fielding under pitching, all fielding at other positions under batting, and split batting performance between the batting and pitching ratings based on the estimated total innings at all positions and the total innings pitched.

In 1995, the fourth edition, which had become the official encyclopedia of Major League Baseball, added a separate method for evaluating relief pitchers to account for the importance of closers. The new Relief Ranking formula modified pitching linear weight runs with a multiplier that added greater weight to decisions (including saves). The multiplier was 9 X (Wins+Losses+Saves/4)/ Innings Pitched. This factor is usually around 1 for starters, but it can approach 2 for a reliever with a lot of decisions.

Total Baseball, fourth edition, also downgraded performance in the Union Association by 20 percent and in the Federal League by 10 percent after careful research concluded that the level of competition in these short-lived leagues was demonstrably below that of the other major leagues. This change lowered the ratings of all players in these leagues.

The linear weights batting formula was changed in the fourth edition to apply the park factor to all runs, not just par runs. This caused player ratings to go down for players in good hitting parks and up for players in bad hitting parks. The pitching linear weights formula was unchanged.

The 1995 edition changed qualifications for batting titles for each season to the rules or customs in effect at that time instead of the modern 3.1 plate appearances per scheduled game. Finally, some minor mistakes were fixed: an error that caused players in two leagues in one season not to be shown in the all-time-best season records, some errors in games played, and an error in positional adjustments for designated hitters that caused anomalous results for a few players.

Total Baseball's fifth edition, published in 1997, featured a major improvement in 19th century records. This volume filled in the rest of the batting and pitching data for the National Association and introduced fielding data for the NA as well. It added batter strikeouts, runs batted in, stolen bases and incomplete caught stealing data for 1874-75. It replaced estimated earned runs (previously estimated at 40 percent of runs) with actual earned runs for pitchers for 1874-75. It added RBI data for the American Association for 1885-1887 and 1890. These data were complete on the ICI sheets for 25 or the 32 teams involved; newspaper research identified many of the missing RBI and the rest were estimated from player batting stats and position in the batting order. Last, known data was entered for some AA players in 1882-84.

Other changes in the fifth edition included changing the qualification for ERA leadership to the rules of the day, not the modern standard one inning per game; changing the Relief Ranking formula to use either 4 or 10 times league saves divided by league wins, whichever is greater, when dividing saves; and correcting an error in UA and FL team ratings made when downgrading those leagues in the fourth edition.

Changes in the Seventh Edition

There was no change in any analytical component in the sixth edition of *Total Baseball,* published in 1999. However, several improvements have been introduced for the current edition of *Total Baseball.* Positional adjustments for outfielders have been changed to show average offense for left field, center field and right field, not just the outfield as a whole. This will have the general effect of slightly adjusting most career center fielders upward somewhat and most career left fielders downward somewhat, with the magnitude of the effect depending on the era and whether they also played substantial numbers of games at other outfield positions.

TPR positional adjustments for all players will now be made by era rather than by a three-year moving average. For this purpose, 16 eras have been defined according to changes in the numbers of leagues (19th century), in the number of teams, or in the playing rules, with most "eras" for this purpose being around ten years in length. This will have the effect of making positional adjustments constant within each era, which makes sense since managerial and playing philosophies about the right mix of offense and defense at each position can be dramatically different between eras. It also means that positional adjustments will no longer be smoothed out by the moving average at the boundaries between eras.

The linear weights for stolen bases and times caught stealing have been changed in this edition from the previous 0.3 and -0.6, respectively, to 0.22 and -0.35. This downgrading of the importance of basestealing is a result of research that has shown that, while there are more stolen bases when the score is close, the excess at two to four runs ahead in the score cancels out the shortfall at two to four runs behind in the score. (Stolen bases are rare with a score difference of five runs or more in the score.) Though this change won't substantially affect very many players, it will, of course, negatively impact several high-profile players— especially Rickey Henderson.

The Relief Ranking formula has been changed to limit the multiplier for Factor F to a range of 0.5 to 2.0. Previously, there was no limit on Factor F, so pitchers with no decisions (including saves) would have a multiplier of zero. Most pitchers fall within this range, but pitchers who didn't have many decisions sometimes fell below this range and, thus, had some unnatural distortions in their pitching wins calculation. In addition, closers with a lot of saves but very few innings occasionally exceeded the range a little. By extension, this change also will affect Total Pitcher Index, though the change would not make a big difference for any pitcher who had a substantial career.

On the missing data front, the seventh edition adds in 15 protested games between 1894 and 1902 that originally weren't counted by ICI research. While team wins and losses for such protested games are not applicable, individual player stats (except, of course, for pitcher wins and losses) should have been counted by ICI. Two games in the American Association between Louisville and St. Louis from 1891 also were deleted. These games were later declared as exhibitions so that the two teams could play championship games in a doubleheader on October 4.

While the hits and walks for the years 1876 and 1887 could hardly be described as missing, they have been recategorized for this edition to conform with the scoring practices of the day (walks in 1876 are now recorded as outs, while walks in 1887 are recorded as hits). This change brings *Total Baseball's* (and Major League Baseball's) scoring practices for batting in line with the scoring practices for pitching wins and losses, which have for some time now been memorialized in accordance with contemporary practices rather than modern reconstructions. For more on this subject, see "The History of Major League Baseball Statistics."

The seventh edition further refines the adjusted batting and pitching run equations to park-adjust complete run totals, resulting in slightly better ratings for good hitters in bad hitting parks and worse ratings for good pitchers in bad hitting parks (and vice versa). This was the result of changing the park adjustment equation so that the park factor was applied *after* the adjustment was made to a player's batting or pitching runs, instead of before.

Finally, a small error in Total Pitcher Index that had introduced a random error of about 0.2 wins per season for AL pitchers in the DH era was fixed.

That's all for now, but the quest for more complete information is certainly ongoing, as is research that will result in refinements of Total Player Rating and Total Pitcher Index.

Evolution of Baseball Records

Marty Appel and Tom Ruane

Throughout baseball history, if a player was a league leader, his record would forever show an asterisk or boldface so we could readily remember the achievement. But, if the player set an *all-time* record that was later broken, his name would pass from the record books forever. Thus Roger Connor, who was baseball's all-time home run champion before Babe Ruth, is a forgotten man as far as statistical compilations go.

The following is a chronology of major batting, baserunning, and pitching records for a career and for a season. It is an attempt to honor those who set the standards of their times. After the player's name appears, we show the total he concluded with—before the mark was broken—followed by the years in which the record belonged to him. Records at the end of the season are the basis for establishing new leaders to avoid the daily leap-frogging that may have occurred in some cases. This does create the possibility of someone holding a record briefly within a season yet not being included here.

Changes in rules and scoring practices are worth mentioning. An asterisk marks the sections for single-season batting average, hits, at bats, and hitting streaks because of a change in scoring practice in 1887 that counted walks as hits. An asterisk marks the first post-1887 record holder on those lists; a similar note is made following a change in the definition of a stolen base after 1897 to exclude extra bases taken on teammates' hits. Likewise, single-season pitching records are given both before and after 1893, when the pitching distance was established at the current 60 feet, 6 inches. In records for strikeouts and hits per game, a game is defined as nine innings.

The authors extend special thanks to Pete Palmer for his assistance in compiling this section.

Career Batting and Baserunning

GAMES PLAYED

Players	Record	Years Held
Jack Manning, Jim O'Rourke Harry Schafer, George Wright	70	1876
Jim O'Rourke, George Wright	131	1877
Jim O'Rourke	191	1878
George Wright	275	1879
Jim O'Rourke	619	1880-84
Paul Hines	731	1884-85
John Morrill	1219	1885-89
Paul Hines	1327	1889-90
Cap Anson	2277	1890-1906
Jake Beckley	2389	1906-09
Bill Dahlen	2444	1909-15
Honus Wagner	2792	1915-26
Ty Cobb	2794	1926-74
Hank Aaron	3298	1974-83
Carl Yastrzemski	3308	1983-84
Pete Rose	3562	1984-present

CONSECUTIVE GAMES (incomplete for 19th century)

Players	Record	Years Held
George Pinkney	577	1889-1920
Everett Scott	1307	1920-33
Lou Gehrig	2130	1933-95
Cal Ripken Jr.	2632	1995-98

AT BATS

Players	Record	Years Held
George Wright	1288	1876-90
Paul Hines	6096	1880-91
Cap Anson	9176	1891-1906
Jake Beckley	9538	1906-15
Honus Wagner	10439	1915-26
Ty Cobb	11434	1926-74
Hank Aaron	12364	1974-82
Pete Rose	14053	1982-present

RUNS

Players	Record	Years Held
Ross Barnes	142	1876-78
Jim O'Rourke	173	1878-79
George Wright	244	1879-80
Jim O'Rourke	965	1880-88
King Kelly	1160	1888-90
Harry Stovey	1492	1890-94
Cap Anson	1722	1894-1916
Honus Wagner	1739	1916-23
Ty Cobb	2246	1923-present

HITS

Players	Record	Years Held
Ross Barnes	138	1876-77
Deacon White	207	1877-78
Deacon White, Cal McVey	288	1878-79
Paul Hines	1027	1879-85
Cap Anson	3056	1885-1914
Honus Wagner	3420	1914-23
Ty Cobb	4189	1923-85
Pete Rose	4256	1985-present

DOUBLES

Players	Record	Years Held
Ross Barnes, Dick Higham, Paul Hines	21	1876-77
George Wright	33	1877-78
Jim O'Rourke	48	1878-79
Tom York	72	1879-80
Paul Hines	213	1880-85
Cap Anson	529	1885-1911
Nap Lajoie	657	1911-25
Tris Speaker	792	1925-present

Players	Record	Years Held
TRIPLES		
Ross Barnes	14	1876-77
George Hall	21	1877-78
Tom York	24	1878-79
Charley Jones	31	1879-80
Charley Jones, Jim O'Rourke	34	1880-81
Jim O'Rourke	55	1881-84
Charley Jones	90	1884-87
Roger Connor	233	1887-1905
Jake Beckley	244	1905-13
Sam Crawford	309	1913-present
HOME RUNS		
George Hall	5	1876-77
Charley Jones	40	1877-85
Harry Stovey	57	1885-87
Dan Brouthers	74	1887-89
Harry Stovey	122	1889-95
Roger Connor	138	1895-1921
Babe Ruth	714	1921-74
Hank Aaron	755	1974-present
RBIs		
Deacon White	190	1876-80
Cap Anson	1880	1880-1927
Ty Cobb	1938	1927-32
Babe Ruth	2213	1932-75
Hank Aaron	2297	1975-present
STRIKEOUTS		
Johnny Ryan	23	1876-77
Lew Brown	120	1877-80
Will White	127	1880-81
Pud Galvin	418	1881-86
John Morrill	656	1886-95
Tom Brown	709	1895-1926
Babe Ruth	1330	1926-64
Mickey Mantle	1710	1964-78
Willie Stargell	1912	1978-82
Reggie Jackson	2597	1982-present
WALKS		
Ross Barnes	20	1876-77
Jim O'Rourke	40	1877-79
Charley Jones	55	1879-80
Jim O'Rourke	114	1880-83
Tom York	133	1883-84
George Gore	385	1884-88
Ned Williamson	447	1888-89
George Gore	650	1889-92
Roger Connor	1002	1892-99
Billy Hamilton	1189	1899-1923
Eddie Collins	1499	1923-30
Babe Ruth	2062	1930-present
HIT BY PITCH		
Ed Swartwood	15	1884-85
Bill Gleason	34	1885-87
Fred Mann	43	1887-88
Curt Welch	171	1888-93
Tommy Tucker	272	1893-1901
Hughie Jennings	287	1901-present
INTENTIONAL WALKS (since 1955)		
Ted Kluszewski	47	1955-57
Ted Williams	61	1957-58
Stan Musial	97	1958-61
Ernie Banks	183	1961-68
Hank Aaron	293	1968-99
Barry Bonds	319	1999-present

Players	Record	Years Held
STOLEN BASES		
Harry Stovey	68	1886-87
Arlie Latham	739	1887-97
Billy Hamilton	789	1897-98
*Ed Delahanty	58	1898-99
John McGraw	169	1899-1902
Sam Mertes	294	1902-05
Honus Wagner	723	1905-18
Ty Cobb	892	1918-77
Lou Brock	938	1977-91
Rickey Henderson	1370	1991-present
BATTING AVERAGE (3,000 at bat minimum)		
Jim O'Rourke	.316	1884-85
Cap Anson	.342	1885-87
Dan Brouthers	.362	1887-88
Pete Browning	.366	1888-89
Dan Brouthers	.356	1889-90
Pete Browning	.354	1890-92
Dan Brouthers	.349	1892-96
Billy Hamilton	.351	1896-97
Jesse Burkett	.352	1897-99
Willie Keeler	.364	1899-1905
Nap Lajoie	.350	1905-11
Ty Cobb	.366	1911-present
ON-BASE PERCENTAGE (3,000 at bat minimum)		
Jim O'Rourke	.351	1884-85
Cap Anson	.380	1885-87
Dan Brouthers	.423	1887-94
Billy Hamilton	.460	1894-99
John McGraw	.466	1899-1923
Babe Ruth	.474	1923-47
Ted Williams	.483	1947-present
SLUGGING PCT. (3,000 at bat minimum)		
Paul Hines	.434	1884-85
Cap Anson	.471	1885-87
Dan Brouthers	.520	1887-1903
Nap Lajoie	.529	1903-07
Dan Brouthers	.519	1907-16
Joe Jackson	.522	1916-17
Dan Brouthers	.519	1917-22
Rogers Hornsby	.536	1922-23
Babe Ruth	.690	1923-present
AT BATS PER HOME RUN (3,000 at bat minimum)		
Paul Hines	136.62	1884-85
Abner Dalrymple	84.35	1885-86
Charley Jones	64.10	1886-87
Dan Brouthers	50.59	1887-90
Harry Stovey	47.56	1890-92
Jimmy Ryan	47.25	1892-93
Mike Tiernan	47.09	1893-95
Sam Thompson	47.13	1895-1904
Buck Freeman	43.49	1904-05
Sam Thompson	47.13	1905-06
Bill Joyce	47.20	1906-17
Gavvy Cravath	33.20	1917-23
Babe Ruth	11.76	1923-98
Mark McGwire	10.63	1998-present

Career Pitching Records

Players	Record	Years Held
GAMES PITCHED		
Jim Devlin	129	1876-78
Tommy Bond	294	1878-83
Jim McCormick	386	1883-85
Pud Galvin	697	1885-1905
Cy Young	906	1905-68
Hoyt Wilhelm	1070	1968-1998

Players	Record	Years Held
Dennis Eckersley	1071	1998-9
Jesse Orosco	1096	1999-present

WINS

Players	Record	Years Held
Al Spalding	47	1876-77
Tommy Bond	180	1877-84
Will White	228	1884-86
Jim McCormick	252	1886-87
Pud Galvin	360	1887-1903
Cy Young	511	1903-present

LOSSES

Players	Record	Years Held
Jim Devlin	60	1876-79
George Bradley	82	1879-80
Tommy Bond	97	1880-81
Jim McCormick	173	1881-85
Pud Galvin	308	1885-1911
Cy Young	316	1911-present

INNINGS PITCHED

Players	Record	Years Held
Jim Devlin	1181	1876-78
Tommy Bond	2547.2	1878-83
Jim McCormick	3353.2	1883-85
Pud Galvin	5941.1	1885-1906
Cy Young	7356	1906-present

GAMES STARTED

Players	Record	Years Held
Jim Devlin	129	1876-78
Tommy Bond	288	1878-83
Jim McCormick	379	1883-85
Pud Galvin	682	1885-1907
Cy Young	815	1907-present

COMPLETE GAMES

Players	Record	Years Held
Jim Devlin	127	1876-78
Tommy Bond	270	1878-83
Will White	306	1883-84
Jim McCormick	392	1884-86
Pud Galvin	639	1886-1907
Cy Young	749	1907-present

STRIKEOUTS

Players	Record	Years Held
Jim Devlin	263	1876-78
Tommy Bond	715	1878-82
Jim McCormick	1704	1882-88
Tim Keefe	2545	1888-1908
Cy Young	2803	1908-21
Walter Johnson	3509	1921-83
Steve Carlton	3709	1983-84
Nolan Ryan	5714	1984-present

WALKS

Players	Record	Years Held
Joe Borden	51	1876-77
Jim Devlin	78	1877-78
Terry Larkin	84	1878-79
Will White	171	1879-81
Jim McCormick	565	1881-86
Mickey Welch	1297	1886-93
Tony Mullane	1408	1893-95
Amos Rusie	1707	1895-1952
Bobo Newsom	1732	1952-55
Bob Feller	1764	1955-63
Early Wynn	1775	1963-81
Nolan Ryan	2795	1981-present

HITS ALLOWED

Players	Record	Years Held
Bobby Mathews	693	1876-77
Jim Devlin	1183	1877-78
Tommy Bond	2610	1878-83
Pud Galvin	6419	1883-1908
Cy Young	7092	1908-present

HOME RUNS ALLOWED

Players	Record	Years Held
Bobby Mathews	8	1876-78
Tommy Bond	20	1878-80
Tommy Bond, George Bradley	21	1880-81
Tommy Bond	24	1881-82
George Bradley	28	1882-83
Will White	39	1883-84
Larry Corcoran	66	1884-86
Jim McCormick	84	1886-88
John Clarkson	88	1888-89
Pud Galvin	105	1889-90
John Clarkson	161	1890-1930
Grover Cleveland Alexander	164	1930-36
George Braeholder	173	1936-38
Earl Whitehill	184	1938-39
Red Ruffing	254	1939-56
Murry Dickson	269	1956-57
Robin Roberts	505	1957-present

SHUTOUTS

Players	Record	Years Held
George Bradley	18	1876-78
Tommy Bond	35	1878-84
Pud Galvin	56	1884-1904
Cy Young	76	1904-14
Christy Mathewson	77	1914-18
Christy Mathewson, Walter Johnson	79	1918-19
Walter Johnson	110	1919-present

SAVES

Players	Record	Years Held
Jack Manning	6	1876-89
Tony Mullane	15	1889-98
Tony Millane, Kid Nichols	15	1898-99
Kid Nichols	17	1899-1907
Joe McGinnity	24	1907-10
Mordecai Brown	49	1910-26
Firpo Marberry	101	1926-46
Johnny Murphy	107	1946-62
Roy Face	136	1962-64
Hoyt Wilhelm	227	1964-80
Rollie Ringers	341	1980-92
Jeff Reardon	357	1992-93
Lee Smith	478	1993-present

RUNS ALLOWED

Players	Record	Years Held
Bobby Mathews	395	1876-77
Jim Devlin	597	1877-78
Tommy Bond	634	1878-79
Terry Larkin	857	1879-80
Tommy Bond	1155	1880-82
Will White	1173	1882-83
Pud Galvin	3318	1883-present

EARNED RUNS ALLOWED

Players	Record	Years Held
Bobby Mathews	164	1876-77
Jim Devlin	248	1877-78
Tommy Bond	605	1878-83
Pud Galvin	1895	1883-1907
Cy Young	2146	1907-present

EARNED RUN AVERAGE (1,500 innings pitched minimum)

Players	Record	Years Held
Tommy Bond	1.97	1879-80
John Ward	1.90	1880-82
Will White	1.95	1882-84
Old Hoss Radbourn	1.95	1884-86
John Ward	2.10	1886-1905
Christy Mathewson	2.08	1905-06
John Ward	2.10	1906-07

Players	Record	Years Held
Addie Joss	1.89	1907-09
Mordecai Brown	1.63	1909-10
Ed Walsh	1.70	1910-12
Walter Johnson	1.80	1912-22
Ed Walsh	1.82	1922-present

WINNING PCT. (1,500 innings pitched minimum)

Players	Record	Years Held
Tommy Bond	.694	1879-80
John Ward	.659	1880-81
Tommy Bond	.641	1881-83
Larry Corcoran	.692	1883-84
Old Hoss Radbourn	.684	1884-86
Larry Corcoran	.670	1886-87
John Clarkson	.701	1887-88
Bob Caruthers	.708	1888-92
Dave Foutz	.690	1892-1911
Ed Ruelbach	.691	1911-12
Dave Foutz	.690	1912-31
Lefty Grove	.693	1931-36
Dave Foutz	.690	1936-39
Lefty Grove	.691	1939-40
Dave Foutz	.690	1940-53
Vic Raschi	.706	1953-54
Dave Foutz	.690	1954-59
Whitey Ford	.696	1959-67
Dave Foutz	.690	1967-83
Ron Guidry	.705	1983-84
Dave Foutz	.690	1984-85
Ron Guidry	.694	1984-86
Dave Foutz	.690	1986-90
Dwight Gooden	.714	1990-92
Dave Foutz	.690	1992-2000
Pedro Martinez	.691	2000-present

STRIKEOUTS PER GAME (1,500 innings pitched minimum)

Players	Record	Years Held
Tommy Bond	2.65	1879-80
John Ward	3.29	1880-83
Larry Corcoran	4.11	1883-84
Jim Whitney	4.60	1884-86
Ed Morris	5.32	1886-87
Charlie Buffinton	5.13	1887-88
Toad Ramsey	6.49	1888-1904
Rube Waddell	7.04	1904-45
Bob Feller	7.07	1945-50
Rube Waddell	7.04	1950-61
Sam Jones	7.55	1961-64
Sandy Koufax	9.28	1964-69
Sam McDowell	9.34	1969-71
Sandy Koufax	9.28	1971-75
Nolan Ryan	9.55	1975-96
Randy Johnson	10.95	1996-present

INTENTIONAL WALKS (since 1955)

Players	Record	Years Held
Hal Jeffcoat	12	1955-56
Bob Friend	115	1956-68
Don Drysdale	123	1968-73
Lindy McDaniel	136	1973-78
Gaylord Perry	164	1978-88
Kent Tekulve	179	1988-present

FEWEST HITS PER GAME (1,500 innings pitched minimum)

Players	Record	Years Held
Tommy Bond	8.92	1879-80
John Ward	8.33	1880-83
Larry Corcoran	7.91	1883-84
Tony Mullane	7.79	1884-85
Tim Keefe	7.72	1885-86
Ed Morris	8.10	1886-88
Tim Keefe	8.06	1888-92
Amos Rusie	8.08	1892-1902
Vic Willis	8.07	1902-04
Rube Waddell	7.44	1904-07
Addie Joss	7.26	1907-09
Ed Walsh	6.79	1909-11

Players	Record	Years Held
Ed Reulbach	6.99	1911-13
Walter Johnson	7.09	1913-22
Ed Walsh	7.12	1922-45
Bob Feller	7.01	1945-48
Ed Walsh	7.12	1948-61
Bob Turley	7.12	1961-63
Ed Walsh	7.12	1963-64
Sandy Koufax	6.79	1964-74
Andy Messersmith	6.71	1974-75
Nolan Ryan	6.56	1975-present

HIT BY PITCH

Players	Record	Years Held
Will White	68	1884-87
Tony Mullane	82	1887-92
Tim Keefe	98	1892-99
Kid Nichols	118	1899-1902
Chick Fraser	168	1902-07
Joe McGinnity	182	1907-14
Eddie Plank	196	1914-26
Eddie Plank, Walter Johnson	196	1926-27
Walter Johnson	203	1927-present

BALKS

Players	Record	Years Held
Fred Goldsmith, Jack Lynch, Lee Richmond, Jim Whitney	1	1881-82
Fred Goldsmith, Jack Lynch, Lee Richmond, Jim Whitney, Pud Galvin	1	1882-83
Fred Goldsmith	2	1883-84
Fred Goldsmith, John Henry	2	1884-85
Charlie Ferguson	3	1885-93
Charlie Ferguson, Al Maul	3	1893-97
Charlie Ferguson, Al Maul, Cy Seymour	3	1897-98
Cy Seymour	8	1898-1911
Cy Seymour, Ed Walsh	8	1911-12
Ed Walsh	14	1912-31
Ed Walsh, Tom Zachary	14	1931-35
Tom Zachary	15	1935-63
Jack Sanford	21	1963-77
Steve Carlton	90	1977-present

WILD PITCHES

Players	Record	Years Held
George Bradley	116	1876-80
Will White	141	1880-84
John Ward	144	1884-85
Will White	166	1885-86
Mickey Welch	274	1886-1992
Mickey Welch, Nolan Ryan	274	1992-93
Nolan Ryan	277	1993-present

Single Season Batting and Baserunning Records

GAMES

Players	Record	Years Held
Jack Manning, Jim O'Rourke, Harry Schafer, George Wright	70	1876-79
Paul Hines, Mike McGeary, George Wright	85	1879-80
Emil Gross	87	1880-83
Joe Farrell, Sadie Houck, Martin Powell	101	1883-84
Roger Connor, Billy Geer, Alex McKinnon	116	1884-86
Bill McClellan, Bill Phillips, George Pinkney	141	1886-88
George Pinkney	143	1888-92
Roger Connor	155	1892-98
George Van Haltren	156	1898-1904
Jimmy Barrett	162	1904-61
Rocky Colavito, Brooks Robinson	163	1961-62
Maury Wills	165	1962-present

AT BATS

Players	Record	Years Held
George Wright	343	1876-79
Paul Hines	409	1879-83
Jud Birchall	449	1883-84
Abner Dalrymple	521	1884-86
George Pinkney	597	1886-87
Arlie Latham	672	1887-92
*Tom Brown	660	1892-1921
Jack Tobin	671	1921-22
Rabbit Maranville	672	1922-31
Lloyd Waner	681	1931-35
Lloyd Waner, JoJo Moore	681	1935-36
Woody Jensen	696	1936-69
Matty Alou	698	1969-75
Dave Cash	699	1975-80
Willie Wilson	705	1980-present

RUNS

Players	Record	Years Held
Ross Barnes	126	1876-84
Fred Dunlap	160	1884-87
Tip O'Neill	167	1887-91
Tom Brown	177	1891-94
Billy Hamilton	198	1894-present

HITS

Players	Record	Years Held
Ross Barnes	138	1876-79
Paul Hines	146	1879-83
Dan Brouthers	159	1883-84
Fred Dunlap	185	1884-86
Dave Orr	193	1886-87
Tip O'Neill, Pete Browning	275	1887-94
*Hugh Duffy	237	1894-96
Jesse Burkett	240	1896-1911
Ty Cobb	248	1911-20
George Sisler	257	1920-present

DOUBLES

Players	Record	Years Held
Ross Barnes, Dick Higham, Paul Hines	21	1876-78
Dick Higham	22	1878-79
Charlie Eden	31	1879-82
King Kelly	37	1882-83
Ned Williamson	49	1883-87
Tip O'Neill	52	1887-99
Ed Delahanty	55	1899-1923
Tris Speaker	59	1923-26
George Burns	64	1926-31
Earl Webb	67	1931-present

TRIPLES

Players	Record	Years Held
Ross Barnes	14	1876-79
Ross Barnes, Buttercup Dickerson	14	1879-80
Ross Barnes, Buttercup Dickerson, Harry Stovey	14	1880-82
Roger Connor	18	1882-84
Harry Stovey	23	1884-86
Dave Orr	31	1886-94
Dave Orr, Heinie Reitz	31	1894-1912
Chief Wilson	36	1912-present

HOME RUNS

Players	Record	Years Held
George Hall	5	1876-79
Charley Jones	9	1879-83
Harry Stovey	14	1883-84
Ned Williamson	27	1884-1919
Babe Ruth	29	1919-21
Babe Ruth	59	1921-27
Babe Ruth	60	1927-61
Roger Maris	61	1961-98
Mark McGwire	70	1998-present

RBIs

Players	Record	Years Held
Deacon White	60	1876-79
Charley Jones, John O'Rourke	62	1879-80
Cap Anson	74	1880-82
Cap Anson	83	1882-83
Dan Brouthers	97	1883-84
Cap Anson	102	1884-86
Cap Anson	147	1886-87
Sam Thompson	166	1887-1921
Babe Ruth	171	1921-27
Lou Gehrig	175	1927-30
Hack Wilson	191	1930-present

STRIKEOUTS

Players	Record	Years Held
Johnny Ryan	23	1876-77
Lew Brown	33	1877-78
Will White	41	1878-79
Will White, Pud Galvin	41	1879-80
Pud Galvin	57	1880-81
Pud Galvin	70	1881-83
Pud Galvin	79	1883-84
Sam Wise	104	1884-1914
Gus Williams	120	1914-38
Vince DiMaggio	134	1938-56
Jim Lemon	138	1956-61
Jake Wood	141	1961-62
Harmon Killebrew	142	1962-63
Dave Nicholson	175	1963-69
Bobby Bonds	187	1969-70
Bobby Bonds	189	1970-present

WALKS

Players	Record	Years Held
Ross Barnes	20	1876-77
Ross Barnes, Jim O'Rourke	20	1877-79
Charley Jones	29	1879-81
John Clapp	35	1881-83
Tom York	37	1883-84
Candy Nelson	74	1884-85
Ned Williamson	75	1885-86
George Gore	102	1886-87
Paul Radford	106	1887-88
Yank Robinson	116	1888-89
Yank Robinson	118	1889-90
Bill Joyce	123	1890-92
Jack Crooks	136	1892-1911
Jimmy Sheckard	147	1911-20
Babe Ruth	150	1920-23
Babe Ruth	170	1923-present

HIT BY PITCH

Players	Record	Years Held
Ed Swartwood	15	1884-85
Bill Gleason, Ed Swartwood	15	1885-86
Frank Fennelly	18	1886-87
Tommy Tucker	29	1887-88
Tommy Tucker, Curt Welch	29	1888-89
Tommy Tucker	33	1889-90
Curt Welch	34	1890-91
Curt Welch	36	1891-96
Hughie Jennings	51	1896-present

STOLEN BASES

Players	Record	Years Held
Harry Stovey	68	1886-87
Hugh Nicol	138	1887-98
*Ed Delahanty	58	1898-99
Jimmy Sheckard	77	1899-1910
Eddie Collins	81	1910-11
Ty Cobb	83	1911-12
Clyde Milan	88	1912-15
Ty Cobb	96	1915-62
Maury Wills	104	1962-74
Lou Brock	118	1974-82
Rickey Henderson	130	1982-present

Players	Record	Years Held
BATTING AVERAGE		
Ross Barnes	.404	1876-84
Fred Dunlap	.412	1884-7
Tip O'Neill	.485	1887-94
*Hugh Duffy	.440	1894-present
SLUGGING PERCENTAGE		
Ross Barnes	.590	1876-84
Fred Dunlap	.621	1884-87
Tip O'Neill	.691	1887-94
Hugh Duffy	.694	1894-1921
Babe Ruth	.846	1921-present
ON-BASE PERCENTAGE		
Ross Barnes	.462	1876-86
King Kelly	.483	1886-87
Tip O'Neill	.4895	1887-93
Billy Hamilton	.4896	1893-94
Billy Hamilton	.522	1894-99
John McGraw	.547	1899-1941
Ted Williams	.551	1941-present
BATTING STREAKS		
Denny Lyons	52	1887-93
*George Davis	33	1893-94
Billy Hamilton	36	1894
Bill Dahlen	42	1894-97
Willie Keeler	44	1897-1941
Joe DiMaggio	56	1941-present
AT BATS PER HOME RUN		
George Hall	53.60	1876-79
Charley Jones	39.44	1879-81
Dan Brouthers	33.75	1881-83
Harry Stovey	30.07	1883-84
Ned Williamson	15.44	1884-1919
Babe Ruth	14.90	1919-20
Babe Ruth	8.48	1920-96
Mark McGwire	8.13	1996-98
Mark McGwire	7.27	1998-present

Single Season Pitching Records

(acknowledging 1893 change in pitching distance)

Players	Record	Years Held
GAMES PITCHED		
Jim Devlin	68	1876-79
Will White	76	1879-83
Will White, Pud Galvin, Old Hoss Radbourn	76	1883-93
Amos Rusie	56	1893-94
Amos Rusie, Ted Breitenstein	56	1894-95
Amos Rusie, Ted Breitenstein, Pink Hawley	56	1895-1907
Amos Rusie, Ted Breitenstein, Pink Hawley, Ed Walsh	56	1907-08
Ed Walsh	66	1908-43
Ace Adams	70	1943-50
Jim Konstanty	74	1950-64
John Wyatt	81	1964-65
Ted Abernathy	84	1965-68
Wilbur Wood	88	1968-69
Wayne Granger	90	1969-73
Mike Marshall	92	1973-74
Mike Marshall	106	1974-present

Players	Record	Years Held
WINS		
Al Spalding	47	1876-79
Al Spalding, John Ward	47	1879-83
Old Hoss Radbourn	48	1883-84
Old Hoss Radbourn	59	1884-93
Frank Killen	36	1893-94
Frank Killen, Amos Rusie	36	1894-1904
Jack Chesbro	41	1904-present
LOSSES		
Jim Devlin	35	1876-79
George Bradley, Jim McCormick	40	1879-80
Will White	42	1880-83
John Coleman	48	1883-93
Duke Esper	28	1893-95
Ted Breitenstein	30	1895-97
Red Donahue	35	1897-present
INNINGS PITCHED		
Jim Devlin	622	1876-79
Will White	680	1879-93
Amos Rusie	482	1893-present
GAMES STARTED		
Jim Devlin	68	1876-79
Will White	75	1879-83
Will White, Pud Galvin	75	1883-93
Amos Rusie	52	1893-present
COMPLETE GAMES		
Jim Devlin	66	1876-79
Will White	75	1879-93
Amos Rusie	50	1893-present
STRIKEOUTS		
Jim Devlin	122	1876-77
Tommy Bond	170	1877-78
Tommy Bond	182	1878-79
Monte Ward	239	1879-80
Larry Corcoran	268	1880-83
Tim Keefe	361	1883-84
Hugh Daily	483	1884-86
Matt Kilroy	513	1886-93
Amos Rusie	208	1893-98
Cy Seymour	239	1898-1901
Cy Seymour, Noodles Hahn	239	1901-03
Rube Waddell	302	1903-04
Rube Waddell	349	1904-65
Sandy Koufax	382	1965-73
Nolan Ryan	383	1973-present
STRIKEOUTS PER GAME		
Tommy Bond	1.94	1876-77
Bobby Mitchell	3.69	1877-78
Bobby Mitchell	5.74	1878-83
Jim Whitney	6.04	1883-84
Hugh Daily	8.68	1884-93
Amos Rusie	3.88	1893-94
Amos Rusie	3.95	1894-95
Amos Rusie	4.60	1895-97
Cy Seymour	4.83	1897-98
Cy Seymour	6.03	1898-1901
Tom Hughes	6.57	1901-02
Rube Waddell	6.84	1902-03
Rube Waddell	8.39	1903-46
Hal Newhouser	8.46	1946-55
Herb Score	9.70	1955-60
Sandy Koufax	10.13	1960-62
Sandy Koufax	10.55	1962-65
Sam McDowell	10.71	1965-84

Players	Record	Years Held
Dwight Gooden	11.39	1984-87
Nolan Ryan	11.48	1987-95
Randy Johnson	12.35	1995-98
Kerry Wood	12.58	1998-99
Pedro Martinez	13.20	1999-present

WALKS

Players	Record	Years Held
Joe Borden	51	1876-77
Terry Larkin, Tricky Nichols	53	1877-78
The Only Nolan	56	1878-79
Jim McCormick	74	1879-80
Larry Corcoran	99	1880-82
Jim McCormick	103	1882-83
Frank Mountain	123	1883-84
Mickey Welch	146	1884-86
Toad Ramsey	207	1886-89
Mark Baldwin	274	1889-90
Amos Rusie	289	1890-93
Amos Rusie	218	1893-present

INTENTIONAL WALKS (since 1955)

Players	Record	Years Held
Hal Jeffcoat	12	1955-56
Bob Friend	18	1956-64
Ron Perranoski	19	1964-65
Lindy McDaniel	20	1965-67
Lindy McDaniel, Jim Bunning, Ron Willis	20	1967-75
Mike Garman	23	1975-82
Mike Garman, Kent Tekulve	23	1982-present

HITS ALLOWED

Players	Record	Years Held
Bobby Mathews	693	1876-83
John Coleman	772	1883-93
Amos Rusie	451	1893-94
Ted Breitenstein	497	1894-present

FEWEST HITS PER GAME

Players	Record	Years Held
George Bradley	7.38	1876-80
Tim Keefe	6.09	1880-93
Amos Rusie	8.42	1893-96
Billy Rhines	8.06	1896-98
Kid Nichols	7.33	1898-99
Vic Willis	7.28	1899-1902
Bill Bernhard	7.01	1902-04
Mordecai Brown	6.57	1904-05
Rube Waddell	6.33	1905-06
Ed Reulbach	5.33	1906-68
Luis Tiant	5.30	1968-72
Nolan Ryan	5.26	1972-present

HOME RUNS ALLOWED

Players	Record	Years Held
Bobby Mathews	8	1876-79
George Bradley	12	1879-82
Jim McCormick	14	1882-83
John Coleman	17	1883-84
Larry Corcoran	35	1884-93
Harry Staley	22	1893-94
Frank Dwyer, Jack Stivetts	27	1894-1930
Ray Kremer	29	1930-34
Phil Collins	30	1934-37
Lon Warneke	32	1937-48
Murry Dickson	39	1948-55
Robin Roberts	41	1955-56
Robin Roberts	46	1956-86
Bert Blyleven	50	1986-present

SHUTOUTS

Players	Record	Years Held
George Bradley	16	1876-93
Red Ehret, Amos Rusie	4	1893-95
Red Ehret, Amos Rusie, Pink Hawley, Bill Hoffer, Sadie McMahon, Cy Young	4	1895-96
Frank Killen, Cy Young	5	1896-98
Jack Powell, Wiley Piatt	6	1898-1901
Jack Powell, Wiley Piatt, Jack Chesbro, Al Orth, Vic Willis	6	1901-02
Jack Chesbro, Christy Mathewson	8	1902-04
Cy Young	10	1904-06
Cy Young, Ed Walsh	10	1906-08
Christy Mathewson, Ed Walsh	11	1908-10
Jack Coombs	13	1910-16
Grover Cleveland Alexander	16	1916-present

SAVES

Players	Record	Years Held
Jack Manning	5	1876-89
Jack Manning, Tony Mullane	5	1889-93
Mark Baldwin, Tom Colcolough, Frank Donnelly, Frank Dwyer, Tony Mullane	2	1893-94
Tony Mullane	4	1894-98
Tony Mullane, Kid Nichols	4	1898-1900
Tony Mullane, Kid Nichols, Frank Kitson	4	1900-04
Joe McGinnity	5	1904-05
Claud Elliott	6	1905-06
George Ferguson	7	1906-09
Frank Arellanes	8	1909-11
Mordecai Brown	13	1911-13
Mordecai Brown, Chief Bender	13	1913-24
Firpo Marberry	15	1924-26
Firpo Marberry	22	1926-49
Joe Page	27	1949-53
Joe Page, Ellis Kinder	27	1953-61
Luis Arroyo	29	1961-64
Luis Arroyo, Dick Radatz	29	1964-65
Ted Abernathy	31	1965-66
Jack Aker	32	1966-70
Wayne Granger	35	1970-72
Clay Carroll	37	1972-73
John Hiller	38	1973-83
Dan Quisenberry	45	1983-84
Dan Quisenberry, Bruce Sutter	45	1984-86
Dave Righetti	46	1986-90
Bobby Thigpen	57	1990-present

RUNS ALLOWED

Players	Record	Years Held
Bobby Mathews	395	1876-79
Will White	404	1879-83
John Coleman	510	1883-93
Duke Esper	277	1893-94
Ted Breitenstein	320	1894-present

EARNED RUNS ALLOWED

Players	Record	Years Held
Bobby Mathews	164	1876-81
Lee Richmond	174	1881-83
John Coleman	291	1883-93
Scott Stratton	196	1893-94
Ted Breitenstein	238	1894-present

EARNED RUN AVERAGE

Players	Record	Years Held
George Bradley	1.23	1876-80
Tim Keefe	0.86	1880-93
Ted Breitenstein	3.18	1893-94
Amos Rusie	2.78	1894-95
Al Maul	2.45	1895-96
Billy Rhines	2.45	1896-98
Clark Griffith	1.88	1898-1901
Cy Young	1.62	1901-02
Jack Taylor	1.29	1902-05
Christy Mathewson	1.28	1905-06
Mordecai Brown	1.04	1906-14
Dutch Leonard	0.96	1914-present

Players	Record	Years Held
WINNING PERCENTAGE		
Al Spalding	.797	1876-80
Fred Goldsmith	.875	1880-84
Perry Werden	.923	1884-93
Hank Gastright	.750	1893-94
Jouett Meekin	.786	1894-95
Bill Hoffer	.838	1895-1907
Bill Donovan	.862	1907-12
Joe Wood	.872	1912-31
Lefty Grove	.886	1931-37
Johnny Allen	.938	1937-59
Roy Face	.947	1959-present
HIT BY PITCH		
Will White	35	1884-87
Gus Weyhing	37	1887-93
Kid Nichols	15	1893-97
Win Mercer, Jack Taylor	28	1897-98
Cy Seymour	32	1898-99
Ed Doheny	37	1899-1900
Joe McGinnity	40	1900-present
BALKS		
Fred Goldsmith, Jack Lynch, Lee Richmond, Jim Whitney	1	1881-82
Fred Goldsmith, Jack Lynch, Lee Richmond, Jim Whitney, Pud Galvin	1	1882-84

Players	Record	Years Held
John Henry	2	1884-85
Charlie Ferguson	3	1885-99
Bert Cunningham, Cy Seymour	4	1899-1909
Bert Cunningham, Cy Seymour, Al Mattern	4	1909-12
Ed Walsh	5	1912-15
Joe Boehling	6	1915-16
Joe Boehling, Al Mamaux	6	1916-50
Joe Boehling, Al Mamaux, Vic Raschi	6	1950-63
Bob Shaw	8	1963-74
Bob Shaw, Bill Bonham	8	1974-78
Bob Shaw, Bill Bonham, Frank Tanana	8	1978-79
Steve Carlton	11	1979-88
Dave Stewart	16	1988-present
WILD PITCHES		
George Bradley	34	1876-77
George Bradley	39	1877-78
Will White	40	1878-79
Will White	49	1879-85
Hardie Henderson	55	1885-86
Bill Stemmeyer	63	1886-93
Amos Rusie	26	1893-96
Chick Fraser	27	1896-1905
Red Ames	30	1905-present

An Important Change to the Official Record of Major League Baseball

Jerome Holtzman
Major League Baseball's Official Historian

Major League Baseball is pleased to announce that, beginning with this seventh edition of *Total Baseball,* all batting averages are recorded as they were at the time they were reported, and not in accordance with the decision of a 1968 Special Baseball Records Committee. For the sake of conformity, the committee ruled that the 1887 batting averages be recalculated and that walks not be counted as base hits (as they were that year) or as outs (as they were in 1876).

John Thorn, the eminent editor of *Total Baseball,* has described it as an attempt to normalize baseball's "gloriously messy" statistical history and bring the abnormal 1887 season in line with modern statistics. It was the only season when walks were considered hits and hence skewed the averages upwards.

For example, there were eleven .400 hitters, all properly listed in the 1888 Spalding and Reach guides, the official statistical compendiums of the time. (An arithmetic check has revealed that Paul Radford, the 11th and final such batsman, in fact batted "only" .397.) The acknowledged batting champions were Tip O'Neill, at .492, for the St. Louis Browns of the old American Association, and Cap Anson, .421, for the Chicago National League entry. (As with Radford, an arithmetic correction reduces O'Neill's average to .485, still the all-time record).

The special committee, in deciding walks were not hits, took 50 hits away from O'Neill, dropping his average to .435. Anson, stripped of 60 hits, fell to .347 and lost his batting title, fairly won. Worse, he no longer qualified for the 3,000 Hit Club of which he was the first member.

Revisionist history is admirable when new and undisputed evidence is brought forth. But this was an abomination, an absolute falsehood and twisting of the known facts for the singular purpose of regulating history to conform to previous and subsequent standards. It was a grievous corruption. If a walk was a hit in 1887 it should stand as a hit forevermore.

The committee was formed by General William Eckert, baseball's fourth commissioner. Eckert always had good intentions but was ill-equipped and didn't have a schoolboy's knowledge of the game. The day after he took office in 1965, during his first press unveiling, it was painfully apparent he was unaware the Los Angeles Dodgers had been transplanted from Brooklyn.

The committee was co-chaired by Dave Grote, public relations director of the National League and Robert Holbrook, his American League counterpart. Neither was qualified to rule on such matters. The other members were Jack Lang, secretary-treasurer of the Baseball Writers Association of America; Joseph Reichler, director of public relations of the Commissioner's Office, and Lee Allen, the historian of the Hall of Fame.

Why the committee was formed remains a puzzle. The general belief is that it was at the request of the Macmillan Company, which was preparing a new encyclopedia, trumpeted as better and more complete than any of its predecessors. It went on sale the next year.

To heighten the launch, the committee mostly reviewed statistics accumulated in the period before 1920, "a time that was somewhat chaotic for record-keeping procedures." Perhaps the encyclopedia's editors were eager to find previously published errors; adjustments would strengthen the authenticity and value of the new enterprise.

The only established historians on the committee were Joe Reichler, who had been the national baseball writer for the Associated Press, subsequently elected to the "writers' wing" of the Hall of Fame; and the distinguished Lee Allen, widely respected, the author of a half dozen noteworthy books, including delightful histories of the American and National Leagues.

Reichler knew his stuff. A stickler for accuracy at any cost, he had edited an earlier encyclopedia, published in 1962 by Ronald Press. Allen was a compulsive researcher and known for his fascinating player anecdotes of the late 19th and early 20th century. He also wrote a wonderful weekly column, "Cooperstown Corner," for *The Sporting News* and was not concerned with current events. They agreed to the changes. However, a year before he died, Allen admitted to historian David Voigt that "past records ought not to be tampered with."

The change in record-keeping procedure that commences with publication of this edition of *Total Baseball* should not be interpreted as a blanket damning of Macmillan's *The Baseball Encyclopedia.* In mid-life, it became known, fondly, as the "Big Mac," and was the final statistical authority, an enormous aid to sportswriters, book-writers, researchers, and super-fans. There were 10 editions. Sales may have approached a million copies.

Nor is this a total condemnation of Eckert's Special Baseball Records Committee. The committee voted on 17 thorny issues and responded with good reason, with two exceptions: the 1876 scoring of walks as an at bat (if a player drew four walks he was 0 for 4), a practice that has also been restored in this edition; and the 1887 statistical butchery. A listing of the significant 1887 batting averages restored to their proper dimension follows.

Batter	Team	Restored Avg.	Previous Avg. (1968–2000)
Tip O'Neill	St. Louis (AA)	.485	.435
Pete Browning	Louisville (AA)	.457	.402
Bob Caruthers	St. Louis (AA)	.456	.357
Yank Robinson	St. Louis (AA)	.427	.305
Cap Anson	Chicago (NL)	.421	.347
Dan Brouthers	Detroit (NL)	.420	.338
Denny Lyons	Philadelphia (AA)	.415	.367
Reddy Mack	Louisville (AA)	.410	.308
Oyster Burns	Baltimore (AA)	.409	.341
Sam Thompson	Detroit (NL)	.407	.372

The Player Register

The Player Register consists of the central batting, baserunning, and fielding statistics of every man who has batted in major league play since 1871, excepting those men who were primarily pitchers. A pitcher's complete batting record, however, is included for those pitchers who also, over the course of their careers, played in 100 or more games at another position—including pinch hitter—or played in more than half of their total major league games at a position other than pitcher, or played more games at a position other than pitcher in at least one year. (Pitcher batting is also expressed in Batting Wins in the Pitcher Batting column of the Pitcher Register.)

The players are listed alphabetically by surname and, when more than one player bears the name, alphabetically by *given* name—not by "use name," by which we mean the name that may have been applied to him during his playing career. This is the standard method of alphabetizing used in other biographical reference works, and in the case of baseball it makes it easier to find a lesser-known player with a common surname like Smith or Johnson. This method also jibes with that employed in the Annual Record where, for example, Charles "Old Hoss" Radbourn is shown not as the puzzling O. Radbourn or H. Radbourn, as some reference books have it, but as C. Radbourn. On the whole, we have been conservative in ascribing nicknames, doing so only when the player was in fact known by that name during his playing days.

Each page of the Player Register is topped at the corner by a finding aid: in capital letters, the surname of, first, the player whose entry heads up the page and, second, the player whose entry concludes it. Another finding aid is the use of boldface numerals to indicate a league-leading total in those categories in which a player is truly attempting to excel (no boldface is given to the "leaders" in batter strikeouts, times caught stealing, at bats, or games played). An additional finding aid is an asterisk alongside the team for which a player appeared in postseason competition. Additional symbols denote All-Star Game selection and/or play; these appear to the right of the team/league column. Condensed type appears occasionally throughout this section; it has no special significance but is designed simply to accommodate unusually wide figures, such as the 4.000 slugging average of a man who, in his only at bat of the year, hit a home run.

The record for each man who played in more than one season is given in a line for each season, plus a career total line. If he played for more than one team in a given year, his totals for each team are stated on separate lines. And if the teams for which he played in his "traded year" are in the same league, then his full record is stated in both separate and combined fashion. (In the odd case of a man playing for three or more clubs in one year, with some of these clubs being in the same league, the combined total line will reflect only his play in that one league.) Also in this edition, we include position data in the "Yr" line for traded players. A man who played in only one year will have no additional career total line, since it would be identical to his seasonal listing.

Batting records for the National Association are included in The Player Register because the editors, like most baseball historians, regard it as a major league, inasmuch as it was the only professional league of its day and supplied the National League of 1876 with most of its players. In this edition of *Total Baseball*, we benefit from the SABR research project referred to in the Introduction to the Annual Record—which to date has produced extra-base hits, corrected averages, walks, and some stolen bases, strikeouts, and other data heretofore unavailable. Unless Major League Baseball reverses the position it adopted in 1969 and restores the NA to offical major league status, we will continue the practice of carrying separate totals lines for the National Association years rather than integrating them into the career marks of those players whose major league tenures began before 1876 and concluded in that year or later.

Gaps remain elsewhere in the official record of baseball and in the ongoing process of sabermetric reconstruction. The reader will note occasional blank elements in biographical lines, or in single-season columns; these are not typographical lapses but signs that the information does not exist or has not yet been found. In the totals lines of many players, an underlined figure indicates that the total reflects partial data, such as caught stealing for a man whose career covers the National League of 1918–1930 (during which this data was available only for 1920–1925), or batter strikeouts for a man whose career spanned both sides of the year 1909.

For a discussion of which data is missing for particular years, see "The History of Major League Baseball Statistics." Here is a quick summation of the missing data:

Hit batters, 1897–1908 NL/AL, 5 percent missing;

Caught stealing, 1886–1914, 1916 for players with fewer than 20 stolen bases, 1917–1919, 1926–1950 NL; 1886–1891 AA; 1890 PL; 1901–1913, 1916 for players with fewer than 20 stolen bases, 1917–1919 AL (1927 data, missing from the first edition, is now 90 percent complete); 1914–1915 FL;

Sacrifice hit, 1908–1930, 1939 (in these years fly balls scoring runners counted as sacrifice hits, and in 1927–1930 fly balls advancing runners to any base counted as sacrifices);

Sacrifice fly, 1908–1930, 1939 (counted but inseparable from sacrifice hits), 1940–1953 (not counted);

Runs batted in, 1882–1884 AA; 1884 UA;

Strikeouts for batters, 1882–1888, 1890 AA; 1884 UA; 1897–1909 NL; 1901-1912 AL.

For a key to the team and league abbreviations used in the Player Register, flip to the last page of this volume. For a guide to the other procedures and abbreviations employed in the Player Register, review the comments on the prodigiously extended playing record below.

YEAR	TM/L	G	AB	R	H	2B	3B	HR	RBI	BB	SO	AVG	OBP	SLG	OPS	OPS+	BR+	SB	CS	SBR	FA	FR	G/POS	TPR
■ KID DE LEON		Ponce de Leon, Juan "Castilian Kid" (also played in 1874 as Kid Madrid)																						
		b: 3/13/1460, Madrid, Spain d: 2/25/1963, St. Augustine, Fl. BR/TR, 5'11", 173 lbs. Deb: 5/21/1874 FMUCH Career OF: (85-LF 10-CF 18-RF)																						
1874	Bos-n	52	277	73	94	7	4	1	14	2	4	.339	.342	.400	742	111	4	2	0	1	.892	3	*2-52	0.2
1875	Wes-n	2	3	1	1	0	0	0	1	0	0	.333	.333	.333	666	95	0	0	0	0	.500	0	/S-2	0.0
1883	Bal-a	28	121	12	33	2	1	1		8		.273	.318	.331	649	101	1				.901	0	C-16,O-10/S-2	0.0
1884	Was-U	86	371	75	107	12	5	1		11		.288	.309	.356	666	127	5	0			.913	0	0-86 (60-10-18)	0.9
	KC-U	1	4	1	0	0	0	0		0		.000	.000	.000	0	97	0				1.000	0	H	0.0
	Yr	87	375	76	107	12	5	1		11		.287	.308	.355	663	126	-0	0			.914	0	0-86 (60-10-18)	0.9
1890	Cin-P	1	1	1	1	0	0	1	1	0		1.000	1.000	4.000	5000	700	1	0			.000	0	/2-1	0.0
1908	Phi-N	1	0	0	0	0	0	0	0	0		—	—	—	—		0	0			.000	0	R	0.0
	Phi-A	9	31	5	9	3	0	0	2	0		.290	.290	.387	677	113	0	0			.899	-1	/3-8	0.0
1909	Phi-A	148	541	73	165	27	19	4	85	26		.305	.343	.447	790	146	26	20			.920	-5	*3-141	3.0
1910	Phi-A	146	561	83	159	25	15	2	74	34		.283	.329	.392	721	123	13	21			.934	3	*3-144	2.4
1911	Phi-A	148	592	96	198	40	4	11	115	50		.334	.379	.505	884	157	38	38			.912	-8	*3-147	3.3
1912	Phi-A	149	577	116	200	40	21	10	130	50		.347	.404	.541	945	171	50	40			.930	9	*3-149	5.4
1913	Phi-A	149	564	116	190	34	9	12	117	63	31	.337	.413	.493	906	171	48	34			.927	7	*3-148	6.1
1914	Phi-A	150	570	84	182	23	10	9	89	53	37	.319	.380	.442	822	151	33	19	20	-6	.929	8	*3-150	4.1
1915	Nwk-F	2	8	5	4	2	1	1	4	0	2	.500	.500	1.380	1380	304	3	0			.977	1	/3-2	0.1
1916	NY-A	100	360	46	97	23	2	10	52	36	30	.269	.344	.428	772	130	12	15			.931	3	3-98	2.1
1917	NY-A	146	553	57	156	24	2	6	71	48	27	.282	.345	.365	710	109	6	18			.940	11	*3-145	2.7
1918	NY-A	126	504	65	154	24	5	6	62	38	13	.306	.357	.409	766	138	20	8			.943	11	*3-122	3.4
1939	*NY-A☆	141	567	70	166	22	1	10	83	44	18	.293	.346	.388	734	100	-0	13			.944	-2	*3-140	0.9
1941	*NY-A★	94	330	46	97	16	2	9	71	26	12	.294	.353	.436	789	98	-2	8	5	-1	.955	13	3-92	1.6
1942	*NY-A†	69	234	30	65	12	3	7	36	15	14	.278	.327	.444	771	98	-2	1	3	-2	.940	-8	3-67	-0.4
Total	2 n	54	280	74	95	7	4	1	15	2	4	.339	.348	.404	752	110	4	/2	0	1	.892	3	*2-52/S-2	0.2
Total	17	1694	6489	981	1983	329	100	100	992	502	184	.306	.354	.446	800	130	246	235	28		.938	41	*3-1409,0-111/1SO2	45.1

Looking at the biographical line for any player, we see first his use name in full capitals, then his given name and nickname (and any other name he may have used or been born with, such as the matronymic of a Latin American player). His date and place of birth follow "b" and his date and place of death follow "d." Years through 1900 are expressed fully, in four digits, and years after 1900 are expressed in their last two digits.

Then comes the player's manner of batting and throwing, abbreviated for a lefthanded batter who throws right as BL/TR (a switch hitter would be shown as BB for "bats both" and a switch thrower as TB for "throws both"; dates are given for players who batted or threw both ways for part of a season or career).

Next, and for most players last, is the player's debut date in the major leagues, all of which are reported now.

Some players continue in major league baseball after their playing days are through, as managers, coaches, or even umpires. A player whose biographical line concludes with an M can be located in the Manager Roster; one whose line bears a C will be listed in the Coach Roster; and one with a U occupies a place in the Umpire Roster. (In the last case we have placed a U on the biographical line only for those players who umpired in at least six games in a year, for in the 19th century—and especially in the years of the National Association—literally hundreds of players were pressed into service as umpires for a game or two. It would be misleading to accord such players the same code we give to Bob Emslie or Babe Pinelli.) The select few who have been enshrined in the Baseball Hall of Fame at Cooperstown, New York, are noted with an H. They are also listed in the Hall of Fame Roster found toward the end of Bill Deane's "Awards and Honors" essay. Also in *Total Baseball* since the fourth edition is an F on this line to denote family connection—father-son-grandfather or brother.

The explanations for the statistical column heads follow; for more technical information about formulas and calculations, see the Glossary. The vertical rules in the column-header line separate the stats into seven logical groupings: year, team, league; fundamental counting stats for batters; hits and plate appearances broken out into their component counting stats; basic calculated averages; sabermetric figures of more complex calculation; baserunning stats; fielding stats and Total Player Rating.

Absent from the Player Register in recent editions are some statistics present in the original: Park Factor for batters (still available from the Annual Record); Clutch Hitting Index, newly developed for *Total Baseball* but which we have judged to be of lesser interest and value than the more established sabermetric measures (it is still present in the Annual Record and Leaders sections); and Total Average, a popular stat but one that is mirrored by Runs Created and Batting Runs, both of which are more accurate (TA is present in the Annual Record and Leaders sections). By deleting these statistics from the Register we have improved legibility, particularly by adding to the margin in the gutter of the book, and reduced some redundancy.

New to the fifth edition was additional hit-by-pitch data for batters in the 1897–1908 period, which is reflected in their on base percentages. We have also made an upward adjustment to overall league performance in the Federal League of 1914–15 and the Union Association of 1884 (thus lowering individual ratings), because while both leagues are regarded as major leagues, there can be no doubt that their caliber of play was not equivalent to that in the rival leagues of those years. Suffice it to say here that league at bats were reduced to 80 percent for the UA and 90 percent for the FL. A full explanation of the adjustment procedure may be found in the Glossary, under "League Performance."

New to the fifth edition were RBIs for the American Association for 1885–87 and 1890 with data for some players in 1882–1884. Also added were RBIs and strikeouts, stolen bases and caught stealing (incomplete) and fielding data for the National Association.

The seventh edition restores the raw Production figures of On-Base Percentage plus Slugging Average (OPS). The categories that follow it in the register have likewise been renamed: OPS+ for Adjusted Production and BR+ for Adjusted Batting Runs. New to this edition are 16 protested games from 1894–1902; this information will alter the season and career totals of some of the players from this era.

YEAR Year of play (when a space in the column is blank, this indicates that the man has played for two or more clubs in the last year stated in the column; if those clubs were in the same league, then the man will also have a combined total line, beginning with the abbreviation "Yr" placed in the TEAM/L column)

Yr Year's totals for play with two or more clubs in same league (see comments for YEAR)

* Denotes postseason play: World Series, League Championship Series, or Division Series

TM/L Team and League (see comments for YEAR)

★ Named to All-Star Game, played

☆ Named to All-Star Game, did not play

† Named to All-Star Game, replaced because of injury

G Games

AB At bats

R Runs

H Hits (Bases on balls were counted as hits by scorers in 1887.)

2B Doubles

3B Triples

HR Home Runs

RBI Runs Batted In

BB Bases on Balls (Bases on balls were counted as outs by scorers in 1876.)

SO Strikeouts

AVG Batting Average (Figured as hits over at bats; mathematically meaningless averages created through a division by zero are rendered as dashes; see Kid De Leon's entry for 1908 with Pit-N. League leaders in this category, as in others in the Player Register, are noted by bold type. However, some boldface leaders in batting average will have lower marks than other batters who are not credited with having won a championship; for a full explanation of the reasoning for this anomaly, see "The History of Major League Baseball Statistics."

OBP On Base Percentage (See comments for AVG)

SLG Slugging Average (See comments for AVG, and note the use of condensed type to express Kid De Leon's maximum SLG in 1890.)

OPS On Base Plus Slugging

OPS+ Production Plus, or Adjusted Production (On Base Percentage plus Slugging Average, normalized to league average and adjusted for home-park factor.) See comments for BR+.

BR+ Batting Runs (Linear Weights measure of runs contributed beyond what a league-average batter or team might have contributed, defined as zero. Occasionally the curious figure of -0 will appear in this column, or in the columns of other Linear Weights measures of batting, baserunning, fielding, and the TPR. This "negative zero" figure signifies a run contribution that falls below the league average, but to so small a degree that it cannot be said to have cost the team a run. The measure has been adjusted for home-park factor and normalized to league average. A mark of 100 is a league-average performance. Pitcher batting is removed from all league batting statistics before normalization, for a variety of reasons expanded upon in the Glossary. Three-year averages are employed for batting park factors. If a team moved or the park changed dramatically, then two-year averages are employed; if the park was used for only one year, then of course only that run-scoring data is used.)

SB Stolen Bases (for 1886 to the present, plus new data for the NA years, 1871–1875.)

CS Caught Stealing (Available 1915, 1916 for players with 20 or more stolen bases, 1920–1925, 1951–date NL; 1914–1915, 1916 for players with 20 or more stolen bases, 1920 to date AL with scattered data still missing from 1927.)

SBA Stolen Base Average (Stolen bases divided by attempts; availability dependent upon CS as shown above.)

SBR Stolen Base Runs (This is a Linear Weights measure of runs contributed *beyond* what a league-average base stealer might have gained, defined as zero and calculated on the basis of a 66.7 percent success rate, which computer simulations have shown to be the break-even point beyond which stolen bases have positive run value to the team; see the general introduction to Part Two and the Glossary. The presence of a figure in the SBR column in the Player Register is dependent upon the availability of CS as shown above. Lifetime Stolen Base Runs are not totaled where data is incomplete, but seasonal SBRs are reflected in the seasonal Total Player Ratings, which in turn are added to form the lifetime Total Player Rating.)

FA Fielding Average, often called Fielding Percentage as well (putouts plus assists divided by putouts plus assists plus errors, here calculated only for the position at which a man played the most games in a season or career.)

FR Fielding Runs (The Linear Weights measure of runs saved *beyond* what a league-average player at that position might have saved, defined as zero;

this stat is calculated to take account of the particular demands of the different positions; see Glossary for formulas, and note new method for the positional adjustment.)

G/POS Positions played (This is a ranking from left to right by frequency of the positions played in the field or at designated hitter. An asterisk to the left of the position indicates, generally, that in a given year the man played about two-thirds of his team's scheduled games at that position; more precisely, it is figured at 20 games in 1871, 30 in 1872, 35 in 1873, 40 in 1874, and 50 in 1875; two-thirds of the scheduled games in 1876–1900, and 100 or more games since. When a slash separates positions, the man played those positions listed to the left of the slash in 10 or more games and the positions to the right of the slash in fewer than 10 games. If there is no slash, he played all positions listed in 10 or more games. For the lifetime line, the asterisk signifies 1,000 games and the slash marks a dividing point of 100 games. A player's POS column will list him as a pinch runner or pinch hitter in only those years in which he appeared at no other position. New to this edition are games played by outfield positions. Players will still be listed by their total numbers of games in the outfield, but their games at various outfield positions will now be included. In the Kid De Leon entry, his total outfield information appears at the end of his biographical line: Career OF: (85-LF 10-CF 18-RF). His 1883 line reads O-10L, meaning he played most of his games that year in left field because of space taken up by other positions, the exact outfield positional data for that season will not fit on the line. Likewise, a C or R after a number indicates he played mostly center or right, respectively. The next year he played 86 games in the outfield, broken down as 60 in left field, 10 in center, and 18 in right. Where possible, a player's career outfield positional information will be displayed in the total column for G/POS. When players appeared as outfielders in both the National Association and subsequent leagues, separate NA career outfield appearances will be included.) The position abbreviations are:

1: First base	RF: Right Field
2: Second base	P: Pitcher
S: Shortstop	D: Designated hitter
3: Third base	R: Runner (pinch)
O: Outfield	H: Hitter (pinch)
LF: Left Field	M: Manager (playing)
CF: Center Field	C: Catcher

TPR Total Player Rating (This is the sum of a player's Adjusted Batting Runs, Fielding Runs, and Base Stealing Runs, minus his positional adjustment, all divided by the Runs Per Win factor for that year—generally around 10, historically in the 9–11 range. For more information on the formula and the Runs Per Win concept, see the general introduction to the statistical section and the Glossary. In the lifetime line, the TPR is the sum of the seasonal TPRs. For men who were primarily pitchers but whose extent of play at other positions warrants a listing in the Player Register as well as the Pitcher Register, the TPR may be listed as 0.0; this signifies that their batting records are summed up in the Total Pitcher Index [TPI] column of the Pitcher Register.) Note that the TPR (and the TPI, Total Pitcher Index) from the fourth edition on will differ from those in earlier volumes, for four reasons which are explained in greater detail in the Glossary. (1) A broader and more sophisticated computation of the positional adjustment to Batting Runs has improved the accuracy and reasonableness of the method, by which the TPR of those who play skill positions like shortstop and second base tend to be boosted and the TPR of the sluggers who customarily play first base and left field are generally diminished. (2) Because games in left, center, and right fields are now available for all outfielders, center fielders no longer need be compared to an average of the regular center fielders and now may be set against all the men who played center, thus tending to elevate their Fielding Runs. (3) Because new Hit Batsmen data is available (from 1884–1891 in the American Association, from 1887 on for the National League, for the 1890 Players League, and the Federal League in 1914–1915), men from that era who were frequently hit by pitches will increase their Batting Runs perceptibly. (4) And for players who were both batters and pitchers, the method of allocating Wins between TPR and TPI (Total Pitcher Index) was improved. Previously, if a pitcher pitched in over half his games, all his batting was included with his pitcher rating (TPI); if he pitched in less than half his games, his Batting Wins were thrown over to his batter rating (TPR), with his TPI including only his Pitching Wins and Pitcher Defense. The new method prorates batting proportionally with the number of games pitched. In addition, fielding ratings at nonpitching positions for players who pitched in over half their games, previously omitted, are now part of the Total Baseball Ranking.

Total For players whose careers include play in the National Association as well as other major leagues, two totals are given, as described above and as illustrated in Kid De Leon's record, where the record of his years in the National Association is shown alongside the notation "Total 2 n," where *2* stands for the number of years totaled and *n* stands for National Association. For players whose careers began in 1876 or later, the lifetime record is shown alongside the notation "Total x," where *x* stands for the number of post-1875 years totaled. Note the underlined entries in the record for Kid De Leon, reflecting the partial data for RBIs, batter strikeouts, stolen bases, and times caught stealing.

YEAR	TM/L	G	AB	R	H	2B	3B	HR	RBI	BB	SO	AVG	OBP	SLG	OPS	OPS+	BR+	SB	CS	SBR	FA	FR	G/POS	TPR
■ **HANK AARON** Aaron, Henry Louis "Hammerin' Hank" b: 2/5/34, Mobile, Ala. BR/TR, 6', 180 lbs. Deb: 4/13/54 FH Career OF: (313-LF 293-CF 2184-RF)																								
1954	Mil-N	122	468	58	131	27	6	13	69	28	39	.280	.325	.447	771	105	2	2	2	-0	.970	-2	*O-116(105-0-11)	-0.8
1955	Mil-N★	153	602	105	189	**37**	9	27	106	49	61	.314	.369	.540	908	144	36	3	1	0	.967	6	*O-126(26-0-105),2-27	3.8
1956	Mil-N★	153	609	106	**200**	**34**	14	26	92	37	54	**.328**	.369	.558	927	154	**43**	2	4	-1	.962	10	*O-152(0-0-152)	**4.7**
1957	*Mil-N★	151	615	**118**	198	27	6	**44**	**132**	57	58	.322	.379	.600	979	170	58	1	1	-0	.983	2	*O-150(1-69-83)	5.4
1958	*Mil-N★	153	601	109	196	34	4	30	95	59	49	.326	.387	.546	933	157	47	4	1	1	.984	2	*O-153(0-39-120)	4.3
1959	Mil-N★	154	629	116	**223**	46	7	39	123	51	54	**.355**	.406	**.636**	**1042**	**188**	**76**	8	0	2	.982	-2	*O-152(0-13-144)/3-5	**6.8**
1960	Mil-N★	153	590	102	172	20	11	40	**126**	60	63	.292	.359	.566	925	160	46	16	7	1	.982	9	*O-153(0-3-151)/2-2	5.1
1961	Mil-N★	155	603	115	197	**39**	10	34	120	56	64	.327	.386	.594	979	**165**	**54**	21	9	1	.982	12	*O-154(0-71-88)/3-2	**5.8**
1962	Mil-N★	156	592	127	191	28	6	45	128	66	73	.323	.393	.618	1012	171	58	15	7	1	.980	8	*O-153(0-83-71)/1-1	5.7
1963	Mil-N★	161	631	**121**	201	29	4	**44**	**130**	78	94	.319	.394	**.586**	**980**	**180**	**64**	31	5	**5**	.979	-1	*O-161(0-0-161)	6.0
1964	Mil-N★	145	570	103	187	30	2	24	95	62	46	.328	.394	.514	908	152	40	22	4	3	.983	11	*O-139(0-0-139),2-11	4.7
1965	Mil-N★	150	570	109	181	**40**	1	32	89	60	81	.318	.384	.560	943	161	45	24	4	4	.987	10	*O-148(0-0-148)	5.0
1966	Atl-N★	158	603	117	168	23	1	**44**	**127**	76	96	.279	.360	.539	899	144	35	21	3	4	.988	9	*O-158(0-4-158)/2-2	3.9
1967	Atl-N★	155	600	**113**	184	37	3	**39**	109	63	97	.307	.373	**.573**	946	169	**52**	17	6	2	.979	12	*O-152(0-11-141)/2-1	5.8
1968	Atl-N★	160	606	84	174	33	4	29	86	64	62	.287	.356	.498	855	154	39	28	5	4	.991	14	*O-151(0-0-151),1-14	**5.1**
1969	*Atl-N★	147	547	100	164	30	3	44	97	87	47	.300	.398	.607	1005	177	56	9	10	-2	.982	6	*O-144(0-0-144)/1-4	5.4
1970	Atl-N★	150	516	103	154	26	1	38	118	74	63	.298	.389	.574	962	146	33	9	0	2	.977	5	*O-125(0-0-125),1-11	3.2
1971	Atl-N★	139	495	95	162	22	3	47	118	71	58	.327	.414	**.669**	**1082**	**190**	58	1	1	-0	.996	-8	1-71,O-60(1-0-59)	4.3
1972	Atl-N★	129	449	75	119	10	0	34	77	92	55	.265	.391	.514	906	142	27	4	0	1	.987	1	*1-109,O-15(0-0-15)	2.0
1973	Atl-N★	120	392	84	118	12	1	40	96	68	51	.301	.406	.643	1048	173	39	1	1	-0	.977	2	*O-105(87-0-18)	3.6
1974	Atl-N★	112	340	47	91	16	0	20	69	39	29	.268	.343	.491	834	126	11	1	0	0	.986	-4	O-89(89-0-0)	0.2
1975	Mil-A★	137	465	45	109	16	2	12	60	70	51	.234	.336	.355	691	95	-2	0	1	-0	1.000	-1	*D-128/O-3(3-0-0)	-0.7
1976	Mil-A	85	271	22	62	8	0	10	35	35	38	.229	.317	.369	686	102	1	0	1	-0	1.000	-0	D-74/O-1(1-0-0)	-0.2
Total	23	3298	12364	2174	3771	624	98	755	2297	1402	1383	.305	.377	.555	932	156	919	240	73	27	.980	101	*O-2760R,1-210,D/23	89.1
■ **TOMMIE AARON** Aaron, Tommie Lee b: 8/5/39, Mobile, Ala. d: 8/16/84, Atlanta, Ga. BR/TR, 6'1", 200 lbs. Deb: 4/10/62 FC Career OF: (136-LF 1-CF 2-RF)																								
1962	Mil-N	141	334	54	77	20	2	8	38	41	58	.231	.315	.374	689	86	-7	6	0	1	.989	2	*1-110,O-42L/2-1,3	-0.8
1963	Mil-N	72	135	6	27	6	1	1	15	11	27	.200	.260	.281	542	57	-8	0	3	-1	1.000	-6	1-45,O-14L/2-6,3-1	-1.7
1965	Mil-N	8	16	1	3	0	0	0	1	1	2	.188	.235	.188	423	21	-2	0	0	0	.961	0	/1-6	-0.2
1968	Atl-N	98	283	21	69	10	3	1	25	21	37	.244	.296	.311	607	82	-6	3	4	-1	.942	-4	O-62(62-0-0),1-28/3-1	-1.7
1969	*Atl-N	49	60	13	15	2	0	1	5	6	6	.250	.318	.333	652	82	-1	0	1	-0	1.000	1	1-16/O-8(8-0-0)	-0.2
1970	Atl-N	44	63	3	13	2	0	2	7	3	10	.206	.242	.333	576	50	-5	0	0	0	.955	-2	1-16,O-12(10-0-2)	-0.8
1971	Atl-N	25	53	4	12	2	0	0	3	3	5	.226	.268	.264	532	48	-4	0	0	0	.974	2	1-11/3-7	-0.2
Total	7	437	944	102	216	42	6	13	94	86	145	.229	.293	.327	621	75	-31	9	8	-1	.990	-7	1-232,O-138L/3-10,2	-5.6
■ **JOHN ABADIE** Abadie, John b: 11/4/1854, Philadelphia, Pa. d: 5/17/05, Pemberton, N.J. BR/TR, 6', 192 lbs. Deb: 6/10/1875																								
1875	Cen-n	11	45	3	10	0	0	0	4	0	3	.222	.222	.222	444	60	-2	1	0	0	.912	-0	1-11	-0.1
	Atl-n	1	4	1	1	0	0	0	1	0	0	.250	.250	.250	500	85	-0	0	0	0	.875	-0	/1-1	0.0
	Yr	12	49	4	11	0	0	0	5	0	3	.224	.224	.224	449	62	-2	1	0	0	.910	-1	1-12	-0.1
■ **ED ABBATICCHIO** Abbaticchio, Edward James "Batty" b: 4/15/1877, Latrobe, Pa. d: 1/6/57, Ft.Lauderdale, Fla. BR/TR, 5'11", 170 lbs. Deb: 9/4/1897																								
1897	Phi-N	3	10	0	3	0	0	0	0	1		.300	.364	.300	664	78	-0	0			.875	-2	/2-3	-0.2
1898	Phi-N	25	92	9	21	4	0	0	14	7		.228	.290	.272	562	64	-4	4			.818	-13	3-20/2-4,O-1(0-0-1)	-1.6
1903	Bos-N	136	489	61	111	18	5	1	46	52		.227	.306	.290	597	73	-16	23			.934	3	*2-116,S-17	-1.1
1904	Bos-N	154	579	76	148	18	10	3	54	40		.256	.309	.337	646	103	2	24			.915	2	*S-154	1.0
1905	Bos-N	153	610	70	170	25	12	3	41	35		.279	.326	.374	700	111	7	30			.919	-12	*S-152/O-1(0-1-0)	0.0
1907	Pit-N	147	496	63	130	14	7	2	82	65		.262	.357	.331	687	114	10	35			.951	-23	*2-147	-1.3
1908	Pit-N	146	500	43	125	16	7	1	61	58		.250	.336	.316	652	108	7	22			**.969**	-12	*2-144	-0.5
1909	*Pit-N	36	87	13	20	0	0	1	16	19		.230	.368	.264	632	89	-0	2			.966	2	S-18/2-4,O-1(0-1-0)	0.3
1910	Pit-N	3	3	0	0	0	0	0	0	0	0	.000	.000	.000	0	-95	-1	0			.500	-0	/S-1	-0.1
	Bos-N	52	178	20	44	4	2	0	10	12	16	.247	.295	.292	587	68	-7	2			.910	-3	S-46/2-1	-1.0
	Yr	55	181	20	44	4	2	0	10	12	16	.243	.290	.287	577	66	-8	2			.907	-4	S-47/2-1	-1.1
Total	9	855	3044	355	772	99	43	11	324	289	16	.254	.325	.325	650	98	-3	142			.949	-59	2-419,S-388/3-20,O	-4.5
■ **CHARLIE ABBEY** Abbey, Charles S. b: 10/14/1866, Falls City, Neb. d: 4/27/26, San Francisco, Cal. BL/TL, 5'8.5", 169 lbs. Deb: 8/16/1893																								
1893	Was-N	31	116	11	30	1	4	0	12	12	6	.259	.333	.336	670	80	-3	9			.937	3	O-31(31-0-0)	-0.3
1894	Was-N	129	523	95	164	26	18	7	101	58	38	.314	.389	.472	862	110	9	31			.909	14	*O-129(54-74-0)	1.0
1895	Was-N	133	516	102	142	14	10	8	84	43	43	.275	.339	.388	727	88	-10	28			.902	11	*O-133(3-99-31)	-0.6
1896	Was-N	79	301	47	79	12	6	1	49	27	20	.262	.331	.352	683	80	-9	16			.879	-6	O-78(2-11-65)/P-1	-1.6
1897	Was-N	80	300	52	78	14	8	3	34	27		.260	.329	.390	719	90	-5	9			.946	2	O-80(2-1-77)	-0.6
Total	5	452	1756	307	493	67	46	19	280	167	107	.281	.351	.404	755	94	-18	93			.910	23	O-451(92-185-173)/P-1	-2.1
■ **FRED ABBOTT** Abbott, Harry Frederick (b: Harry Frederick Winbigler) b: 10/22/1874, Versailles, Ohio d: 6/11/35, Los Angeles, Cal. BR/TR, 5'10", 180 lbs. Deb: 4/25/03																								
1903	Cle-A	77	255	25	60	11	3	1	25	7		.235	.270	.314	583	76	-8	8			.958	9	C-71/1-3	0.8
1904	Cle-A	41	130	14	22	4	2	0	12	6		.169	.206	.231	437	38	-9	2			.953	-3	C-33/1-7	-1.0
1905	Phi-N	42	128	9	25	6	1	0	12	6		.195	.248	.258	506	53	-8	4			.954	-0	C-34/1-5	-0.5
Total	3	160	513	48	107	21	6	1	49	19		.209	.248	.279	527	61	-24	14			.956	6	C-138/1-15	-0.7
■ **JEFF ABBOTT** Abbott, Jeffrey William b: 8/17/72, Atlanta, Ga. BR/TL, 6'2", 190 lbs. Deb: 6/10/97																								
1997	Chi-A	19	38	8	10	1	0	1	2	0	6	.263	.263	.368	632	65	-2	0	0	0	1.000	-1	O-10(5-1-4)/D-3	-0.3
1998	Chi-A	89	244	33	68	14	1	12	41	9	28	.279	.304	.492	796	105	1	3	3	-0	.971	-13	O-76(20-38-27)/D-2	-1.3
1999	Chi-A	17	57	5	9	0	0	2	6	5	12	.158	.226	.263	489	24	-7	1	1	-0	.962	-2	O-17(17-0-0)	-0.9
2000	*Chi-A	80	215	31	59	15	1	3	29	21	38	.274	.345	.395	740	86	-4	2	1	0	.981	-9	O-65(20-33-16)/D-7	-1.3
Total	4	205	554	77	146	30	2	18	78	35	84	.264	.310	.422	732	86	-12	6	5	-0	.975	-26	O-168(62-72-47)/D-12	-3.8
■ **KURT ABBOTT** Abbott, Kurt Thomas b: 6/2/69, Zanesville, Ohio BR/TR, 6', 185 lbs. Deb: 9/8/93																								
1993	Oak-A	20	61	11	15	1	0	3	9	3	20	.246	.281	.410	691	89	-1	2	0	0	.971	1	O-13(13-0-0)/S-6,2-2	0.0
1994	Fla-N	101	345	41	86	17	3	9	33	16	98	.249	.292	.394	687	75	-13	3	0	1	.966	-8	S-99	-1.2
1995	Fla-N	120	420	60	107	18	7	17	60	36	110	.255	.321	.452	773	101	-1	4	3	-0	.959	-11	*S-115	-0.2
1996	Fla-N	109	320	37	81	18	7	8	33	22	99	.253	.307	.428	735	94	-4	3	3	-0	.969	2	S-44,3-33,2-20	0.3
1997	*Fla-N	94	252	35	69	18	2	6	30	14	68	.274	.315	.433	747	98	-2	3	1	0	.969	-3	2-54,O-10L/S-7,3D	-0.2
1998	Oak-A	35	123	17	33	7	1	2	9	10	34	.268	.328	.390	719	88	-2	2	1	0	.909	-11	S-28/O-5L,3-1,D-3	-1.0
	Col-N	42	71	9	18	6	0	3	15	2	19	.254	.284	.465	749	76	-3	0	0	0	.929	-0	/O-9R,2-7,S-7,3D	-0.2
1999	Col-N	96	286	41	78	17	2	8	41	16	69	.273	.311	.430	741	67	-14	3	2	-0	.989	-11	2-66/1-8,O-4C,S-3	-2.1
2000	*NY-N	79	157	22	34	7	1	6	12	14	51	.217	.285	.389	673	70	-8	1	1	-0	.953	-3	S-39,2-23/3-2,O-2C	-0.7
Total	8	696	2035	273	521	109	23	62	242	133	568	.256	.307	.424	731	85	-47	21	11	1	.958	-43	S-348,2-172/3-43,O1D	-5.3
■ **ODY ABBOTT** Abbott, Ody Cleon b: 9/5/1888, New Eagle, Pa. d: 4/13/33, Washington, D.C. BR/TR, 6'2", 180 lbs. Deb: 9/10/10																								
1910	StL-N	22	70	2	13	2	1	0	6	6	20	.186	.250	.243	493	46	-5	3			.982	1	O-21(0-21-0)	-0.5
■ **DAVE ABERCROMBIE** Abercrombie, David b: 5/6/1840, Falkirk, Scotland d: 9/2/16, Baltimore, Md. Deb: 10/21/1871																								
1871	Tro-n	1	4	0	0	0	0	0	0	0	0	.000	.000	.000	0	-99	-1	0	0	0	.667	-0	/S-1	-0.1
■ **CLIFF ABERSON** Aberson, Clifford Alexander "Kif" b: 8/28/21, Chicago, Ill. d: 6/23/73, Vallejo, Cal. BR/TR, 6', 200 lbs. Deb: 7/18/47																								
1947	Chi-N	47	140	24	39	6	3	4	20	20	32	.279	.369	.450	819	121	4	0			.920	-1	O-40(40-0-0)	0.0
1948	Chi-N	12	32	1	6	1	0	1	6	5	10	.188	.297	.313	610	68	-1	0			.867	-1	/O-8(8-0-0)	-0.3
1949	Chi-N	4	7	0	0	0	0	0	0	0	2	.000	.000	.000	0	-99	-2	0			1.000	0	/O-1(0-0-1)	-0.2
Total	3	63	179	25	45	7	3	5	26	25	44	.251	.343	.408	751	103	1	0			.913	-2	/O-49(48-0-1)	-0.5

YEAR	TM/L	G	AB	R	H	2B	3B	HR	RBI	BB	SO	AVG	OBP	SLG	OPS	OPS+	BR+	SB	CS	SBR	FA	FR	G/POS	TPR
■ **SHAWN ABNER**	Abner, Shawn Wesley b: 6/17/66, Hamilton, Ohio BR/TR, 6'1", 190 lbs. Deb: 9/8/87																							
1987	SD-N	16	47	5	13	3	1	2	7	2	8	.277	.306	.511	817	116	1	1	0	0	.926	1	O-14(6-2-6)	0.1
1988	SD-N	37	83	6	15	3	0	2	5	4	19	.181	.227	.289	516	48	-6	0	1	-0	.982	-4	O-35(10-11-17)	-1.2
1989	SD-N	57	102	13	18	4	0	2	14	5	20	.176	.215	.275	489	39	-8	1	0	0	1.000	-9	O-51(23-23-6)	-1.9
1990	SD-N	91	184	17	45	9	0	1	15	9	28	.245	.287	.310	597	64	-9	2	3	-1	.991	-7	O-62(23-35-6)	-1.8
1991	SD-N	53	115	15	19	4	1	1	5	7	25	.165	.220	.243	463	29	-11	0	0	0	1.000	1	O-39(0-36-3)	-1.1
	Cal-A	41	101	12	23	6	1	2	9	4	18	.228	.257	.366	623	71	-4	1	2	-0	1.000	-1	O-38(0-31-7)/D-3	-0.6
1992	Chi-A	97	208	21	58	10	1	1	16	12	35	.279	.327	.351	678	91	-2	1	2	-0	1.000	-13	O-94(12-14-75)/D-1	-1.8
Total	6	392	840	89	191	39	4	11	71	43	153	.227	.271	.323	593	65	-40	6	8	-1	.993	-32	O-333(74-152-120)/D-4	-8.3
■ **CAL ABRAMS**	Abrams, Calvin Ross b: 3/2/24, Philadelphia, Pa. d: 2/25/97, Ft.Lauderdale, Fla. BL/TL, 6', 185 lbs. Deb: 4/20/49																							
1949	Bro-N	8	24	6	2	1	0	0	0	7	6	.083	.290	.125	415	15	-3	1			.833	-1	/O-7(7-0-0)	-0.4
1950	Bro-N	38	44	5	9	1	0	0	4	9	13	.205	.340	.227	567	51	-3	0			1.000	-3	O-15(9-1-5)	-0.6
1951	Bro-N	67	150	27	42	8	0	3	19	36	26	.280	.419	.393	813	118	6	3	2	-0	.944	-1	O-34(34-0-0)	0.2
1952	Bro-N	10	10	1	2	0	0	0	0	2	4	.200	.333	.200	533	51	-1	0	0	0	.000	-0	/O-1(1-0-0)	-0.1
	Cin-N	71	158	23	44	9	2	2	13	19	25	.278	.356	.399	755	109	2	1	0	0	1.000	-5	O-46(31-18-0)	-0.4
	Yr	81	168	24	46	9	2	2	13	21	29	.274	.354	.387	741	106	2	1	0	0	1.000	-5	O-47(32-18-0)	-0.5
1953	Pit-N	119	448	66	128	10	6	15	43	58	70	.286	.368	.435	803	109	7	4	4	-1	.973	5	*O-112(0-0-112)	0.7
1954	Pit-N	17	42	6	6	1	1	0	2	10	9	.143	.308	.214	522	39	-4	0	0	0	1.000	0	O-13(5-3-5)	-0.4
	Bal-A	115	423	67	124	22	7	6	25	72	67	.293	.401	.421	822	135	23	1	4	-1	.977	4	*O-115(0-14-101)	2.2
1955	Bal-A	118	309	56	75	12	3	6	32	89	69	.243	.416	.359	776	118	14	2	8	-2	.985	-13	O-96(13-58-46)/1-4	-0.5
1956	Chi-A	4	3	0	1	0	0	0	0	2	1	.333	.600	.333	933	150	1	0	0	0	1.000	-0	/O-2(1-0-1)	0.0
Total	8	567	1611	257	433	64	19	32	138	304	290	.269	.387	.392	779	113	43	12	18		.977	-14	O-441(101-94-270)/1-4	0.7
■ **BOBBY ABREU**	Abreu, Bob Kelly b: 3/11/74, Aragua, Venez. BL/TR, 6', 160 lbs. Deb: 9/1/96																							
1996	Hou-N	15	22	1	5	1	0	0	1	2	3	.227	.292	.273	564	54	-1	0	0	0	1.000	-1	/O-7(6-0-1)	-0.3
1997	*Hou-N	59	188	22	47	10	2	3	26	21	48	.250	.329	.372	701	86	-4	7	2	1	.978	-0	O-53(10-1-43)	-0.5
1998	Phi-N	151	497	68	155	29	6	17	74	84	133	.312	.411	.497	908	136	28	19	10	1	.973	13	*O-146(0-0-146)	3.3
1999	Phi-N	152	546	118	183	35	**11**	20	93	109	113	.335	.448	.549	998	146	44	27	9	3	.989	0	*O-146(0-0-146)/D-5	3.7
2000	Phi-N	154	576	103	182	42	10	25	79	100	116	.316	.418	.554	972	140	38	28	8	3	.989	18	*O-152(0-0-152)	4.8
Total	5	531	1829	312	572	117	29	65	273	316	413	.313	.415	.515	930	135	105	81	29	8	.983	30	O-504(16-1-488)/D-5	11.0
■ **JOE ABREU**	Abreu, Joseph Lawrence b: 5/24/13, Oakland, Cal. d: 3/17/93, Hayward, Cal. BR/TR, 5'8", 160 lbs. Deb: 4/23/42																							
1942	Cin-N	9	28	4	6	1	0	1	3	4	4	.214	.313	.357	670	96	-0	0			.941	-1	/3-6,2-2	-0.1
■ **BILL ABSTEIN**	Abstein, William Henry "Big Bill" b: 2/2/1883, St.Louis, Mo. d: 4/8/40, St.Louis, Mo. BR/TR, 6', 185 lbs. Deb: 9/25/06																							
1906	Pit-N	8	20	2	4	0	0	0	3	0		.200	.200	.200	400	24	-2	2			.769	-2	/2-3,O-2(0-0-2)	-0.4
1909	*Pit-N	137	512	51	133	20	10	1	70	27		.260	.302	.344	646	93	-6	16			.982	-5	*1-135	-1.5
1910	StL-A	25	87	1	13	2	0	0	3	2		.149	.169	.172	341	7	-9	3			.963	2	1-23	-0.9
Total	3	170	619	54	150	22	10	1	76	29		.242	.281	.315	596	80	-17	21			.979	-5	1-158/2-3,O-2(0-0-2)	-2.8
■ **MERITO ACOSTA**	Acosta, Baldomero Pedro (Fernandez) b: 5/19/1896, Bauta, Cuba d: 11/17/63, Miami, Fla. BL/TL, 5'7", 140 lbs. Deb: 6/15/13 F																							
1913	Was-A	12	20	3	6	0	1	0	1	4	2	.300	.417	.400	817	136	1	2			.714	-3	/O-9(5-1-1)	-0.2
1914	Was-A	39	74	10	19	2	2	0	4	11	18	.257	.353	.338	691	104	1	3	4	-1	.857	-2	O-25(15-4-5)	-0.3
1915	Was-A	72	163	20	34	4	1	0	18	28	15	.209	.338	.245	584	73	-4	8	4	0	.963	-4	O-53(22-2-29)	-1.0
1916	Was-A	5	8	0	1	0	0	0	0	2	0	.125	.300	.125	425	28	-1	0			1.000	1	/O-4(4-0-0)	0.0
1918	Was-A	3	2	0	0	0	0	0	0	0	1	.000	.000	.000	0	-99	-0	0			.000	0	H	-0.1
	Phi-A	49	169	23	51	3	3	0	14	18	10	.302	.369	.355	724	117	4	4			.944	-3	O-45(5-20-21)	-0.2
	Yr	52	171	23	51	3	3	0	14	18	11	.298	.365	.351	716	115	3	4			.944	-3	O-45(5-20-21)	-0.3
Total	5	180	436	56	111	9	7	0	37	63	46	.255	.354	.307	661	97	0	17	8		.933	-11	O-136(51-27-56)	-1.8
■ **JIMMY ADAIR**	Adair, James Aubrey "Choppy" b: 1/25/07, Waxahachie, Tex. d: 12/9/82, Dallas, Tex. BR/TR, 5'10.5", 154 lbs. Deb: 8/24/31 C																							
1931	Chi-N	18	76	9	21	3	1	0	3	1	8	.276	.286	.342	628	67	-4	1			.948	-1	S-18	-0.3
■ **JERRY ADAIR**	Adair, Kenneth Jerry b: 12/17/36, Sand Springs, Okla. d: 5/31/87, Tulsa, Okla. BR/TR, 6', 175 lbs. Deb: 9/2/58 C																							
1958	Bal-A	11	19	1	2	0	0	0	0	1	7	.105	.150	.105	255	-30	-3	0	0	0	.967	2	S-10/2-1	-0.1
1959	Bal-A	12	35	3	11	0	1	0	2	1	5	.314	.333	.371	705	95	-0	0	0	0	.932	-4	2-11/S-1	-0.3
1960	Bal-A	3	5	1	1	0	0	1	1	0	0	.200	.200	.800	1000	159	0	0	0	0	1.000	0	/2-3	0.1
1961	Bal-A	133	386	41	102	21	1	9	37	35	51	.264	.329	.394	722	95	-3	5	2	0	.987	-1	*2-107,S-27/3-2	0.6
1962	Bal-A	139	538	67	153	29	4	11	48	27	77	.284	.321	.414	735	103	0	7	7	-1	.969	-10	*S-113,2-34/3-1	0.1
1963	Bal-A	109	382	34	87	21	3	6	30	9	51	.228	.249	.346	595	67	-18	3	3	-0	.985	-0	*2-103	-1.0
1964	Bal-A	155	569	56	141	20	3	9	47	28	72	.248	.284	.341	625	73	-21	3	2	-0	**.994**	9	*2-153	0.1
1965	Bal-A	157	582	51	151	26	3	7	66	35	65	.259	.304	.351	654	84	-13	6	4	-0	**.986**	12	*2-157	1.4
1966	Bal-A	17	52	3	15	1	0	0	3	4	8	.288	.339	.308	647	89	-1	0	0	0	.969	-1	2-13	0.0
	Chi-A	105	370	27	90	18	2	4	36	17	44	.243	.278	.335	613	81	-10	3	2	-0	.975	-2	S-75,2-50	-0.3
	Yr	122	422	30	105	19	2	4	39	21	52	.249	.286	.332	618	82	-11	3	2	-0	.975	-3	S-75,2-63	-0.3
1967	Chi-A	28	98	6	20	4	0	0	9	4	17	.204	.243	.245	488	46	-7	0	1	-0	.985	-0	2-27	-0.6
	*Bos-A	89	316	41	92	13	1	3	26	13	35	.291	.323	.367	690	96	-2	1	4	-1	.952	-8	3-35,S-30,2-23	-0.8
	Yr	117	414	47	112	17	1	3	35	17	52	.271	.304	.338	642	85	-8	1	5	-2	.976	-9	2-50,3-35,S-30	-1.4
1968	Bos-A	74	208	18	45	1	0	2	12	9	28	.216	.252	.250	502	49	-12	0	0	0	.976	-5	S-46,2-12/3-7,1-1	-1.6
1969	KC-A	126	432	29	108	9	1	5	48	20	36	.250	.288	.310	598	67	-20	1	3	-1	.984	-22	*2-109/S-8,3-1	-3.7
1970	KC-A	7	27	0	4	0	0	0	1	5	3	.148	.281	.148	429	22	-3	0	1	-0	1.000	2	/2-7	-0.1
Total	13	1165	4019	378	1022	163	19	57	366	208	499	.254	.294	.347	641	80	-112	29	29	-4	.985	-30	2-810,S-310/3-46,1	-6.2
■ **SPARKY ADAMS**	Adams, Earl John b: 8/26/1894, Zerbe, Pa. d: 2/24/89, Pottsville, Pa. BR/TR, 5'5.5", 151 lbs. Deb: 9/18/22																							
1922	Chi-N	11	44	5	11	0	1	0	3	4	3	.250	.313	.295	608	56	-3	1	2	-0	.914	-4	2-11	-0.7
1923	Chi-N	95	311	40	90	12	0	4	35	26	10	.289	.346	.367	713	88	-5	20	19	-2	.935	-6	S-79/O-1(0-0-1)	-0.5
1924	Chi-N	117	418	66	117	11	5	1	27	40	20	.280	.344	.337	682	83	-9	15	17	-3	.941	-8	S-88,2-19	-1.0
1925	Chi-N	149	627	95	180	29	8	2	48	44	15	.287	.341	.368	709	80	-18	26	12	2	**.983**	**28**	*2-144/S-5	1.5
1926	Chi-N	154	624	95	193	35	3	0	39	52	27	.309	.367	.375	742	99	1	27			.965	17	*2-136,3-19/S-2	2.2
1927	Chi-N	146	647	100	189	17	7	0	49	42	26	.292	.335	.340	675	81	-17	26			.994	-1	2-60,3-53,S-40	-0.8
1928	Pit-N	135	539	91	149	14	6	0	38	64	18	.276	.357	.325	682	76	-16	8			.971	-11	*2-107,S-27/O-1R	-2.1
1929	Pit-N	74	196	37	51	8	1	0	11	15	5	.260	.316	.311	627	55	-14	3			.901	-15	S-30,2-20,3-15,/O-2L	-2.3
1930	*StL-N	137	570	98	179	36	9	0	55	45	27	.314	.365	.409	774	84	-14	7			**.966**	-13	*3-104,2-25/S-7	-1.7
1931	*StL-N	143	608	97	178	**46**	5	1	40	42	24	.293	.340	.390	730	92	-6	16			**.963**	-12	*3-138/S-6	-1.3
1932	StL-N	31	127	22	35	3	1	0	13	14	5	.276	.352	.315	667	79	-3	0			.931	-4	3-30	-0.6
1933	StL-N	8	30	1	5	1	0	0	0	1	0	.167	.219	.200	419	19	-3	0			.955	-2	/S-5,3-3	-0.5
	Cin-N	137	538	59	141	21	1	1	22	44	30	.262	.320	.310	631	82	-12	3			.963	-3	*3-132/S-8	-1.0
	Yr	145	568	60	146	22	1	1	22	45	33	.257	.315	.305	620	78	-15	3			.959	-5	*3-135,S-13	-1.5
1934	Cin-N	87	278	38	70	16	1	0	14	20	10	.252	.307	.317	623	69	-12	2			.955	-3	3-38,2-29	-1.1
Total	13	1424	5557	844	1588	249	48	9	394	453	223	.286	.343	.353	695	82	-131	154	50		.974	-37	2-551,3-532,S-297,/O	-9.9
■ **BUSTER ADAMS**	Adams, Elvin Clark b: 6/24/15, Trinidad, Col. d: 9/1/90, Rancho Mirage, Cal. BR/TR, 6', 180 lbs. Deb: 4/27/39																							
1939	StL-N	2	1	1	0	0	0	0	0	0	0	.000	.000	.000	0	-94	-0	0			.000	0	H	0.0
1943	StL-N	8	11	1	1	1	0	0	1	4	4	.091	.333	.182	515	48	-1	0			1.000	-1	/O-6(0-6-0)	-0.2
	Phi-N	111	418	48	107	14	7	4	38	39	67	.256	.319	.352	671	98	-2	2			.984	3	*O-107(1-107-0)	-0.2
	Yr	119	429	49	108	15	7	4	39	43	71	.252	.320	.347	667	96	-3	2			.984	2	*O-113(1-113-0)	-0.4
1944	Phi-N	151	584	86	165	35	3	17	64	74	74	.283	.370	.440	810	132	25	2			.979	11	*O-151(0-151-0)	3.2
1945	Phi-N	14	56	6	13	3	1	2	8	5	5	.232	.295	.429	724	103	-0	0			1.000	-1	O-14(13-0-0)	-0.2
	StL-N	140	578	98	169	26	0	20	101	57	75	.292	.359	.441	800	119	14	3			.978	1	*O-140(14-126-0)	1.0
	Yr	154	634	104	182	29	1	22	109	62	80	.287	.353	.440	793	117	14	3			.979	0	*O-154(27-126-0)	0.8

YEAR	TM/L	G	AB	R	H	2B	3B	HR	RBI	BB	SO	AVG	OBP	SLG	OPS	OPS+	BR+	SB	CS	SBR	FA	FR	G/POS	TPR
1946	StL-N	81	173	21	32	6	0	5	22	29	27	.185	.312	.306	619	73	-6	3			.990	-9	O-58(24-35-0)	-1.8
1947	Phi-N	69	182	21	45	11	1	2	15	26	29	.247	.341	.352	693	88	-3	2			.954	-4	O-51(6-1-44)	-0.8
Total	6	576	2003	282	532	96	12	50	249	234	281	.266	.346	.400	747	110	27	12			.979	0	O-527(58-426-44)	1.0
■ **GEORGE ADAMS** Adams, George b: Grafton, Mass. BR/TR, 5'6", 175 lbs. Deb: 6/14/1879																								
1879	Syr-N	4	13	0	3	0	0	0	0	1	1	.231	.286	.231	516	82	-0				1.000	-1	/O-2(0-2-0),1-2	-0.1
■ **GLENN ADAMS** Adams, Glenn Charles b: 10/4/47, Northbridge, Mass. BL/TR, 6', 185 lbs. Deb: 5/4/75																								
1975	SF-N	61	90	10	27	2	1	4	15	11	25	.300	.382	.478	860	132	4	1	0	0	.941	-3	O-25(16-0-9)	0.0
1976	SF-N	69	74	2	18	4	0	0	3	1	12	.243	.253	.297	551	54	-5	1	0	0	1.000	-2	/O-6(4-0-2)	-0.7
1977	Min-A	95	269	32	91	17	0	6	49	18	30	.338	.380	.468	848	132	12	0	2	-1	.969	-4	D-47,O-44(16-0-28)	0.4
1978	Min-A	116	310	27	80	18	1	7	35	17	32	.258	.297	.390	687	90	-5	0	1	-0	1.000	-1	*D-101/O-5(2-0-3)	-1.0
1979	Min-A	119	326	34	98	13	1	8	50	25	27	.301	.356	.420	776	104	2	2	2	-0	.958	-8	D-55,O-53(45-0-8)	-0.9
1980	Min-A	99	262	32	75	11	2	6	38	15	26	.286	.325	.412	737	94	-3	2	4	-1	.947	-2	D-81,O-12(12-0-0)	-0.8
1981	Min-A	72	220	13	46	10	0	2	24	20	26	.209	.275	.282	557	57	-12	0	1	-0	.000	0	D-62	-1.5
1982	Tor-A	30	66	2	17	4	0	1	11	4	5	.258	.300	.364	664	74	-2	0	0	0	.000	0	D-27	-0.3
Total	8	661	1617	152	452	79	5	34	225	111	183	.280	.327	.398	725	96	-9	6	10	-2	.959	-20	D-373,O-145(95-0-50)	-4.8
■ **DOUG ADAMS** Adams, Harold Douglas b: 1/27/43, Blue River, Wis. BL/TR, 6'3", 185 lbs. Deb: 9/8/69																								
1969	Chi-A	8	14	1	3	0	0	0	1	1	3	.214	.267	.214	481	34	-1	0	0	0	1.000	-1	/C-4	-0.2
■ **HERB ADAMS** Adams, Herbert Loren b: 4/14/28, Hollywood, Cal. BL/TL, 5'9", 160 lbs. Deb: 9/17/48																								
1948	Chi-A	5	11	1	3	1	0	0	0	1	1	.273	.333	.364	697	88	-0	0	0	0	1.000	2	/O-4(0-2-2)	0.1
1949	Chi-A	56	208	26	61	5	3	0	16	9	16	.293	.323	.346	669	79	-7	1	2	-0	.975	-0	O-48(14-33-1)	-1.0
1950	Chi-A	34	118	12	24	2	3	0	2	12	7	.203	.288	.271	559	45	-10	3	0	1	.978	-1	O-33(0-33-0)	-1.0
Total	3	95	337	39	88	8	6	0	18	22	24	.261	.310	.320	631	67	-17	4	2	0	.978	0	/O-85(14-68-3)	-1.9
■ **JIM ADAMS** Adams, James J. b: 1868, E.St.Louis, Ill. TR, Deb: 4/21/1890																								
1890	StL-a	1	4	0	1	0	0	0	0	0		.250	.250	.250	500	42	-0	0			1.000	-1	/C-1	-0.1
■ **BERT ADAMS** Adams, John Bertram b: 6/21/1891, Wharton, Tex. d: 6/24/40, Los Angeles, Cal. BB/TR, 6'1", 185 lbs. Deb: 8/30/10																								
1910	Cle-A	5	13	1	3	0	0	0	0	0		.231	.231	.231	462	44	-1	0			.964	3	/C-5	0.3
1911	Cle-A	2	5	0	1	0	0	0	0	1		.200	.333	.200	533	50	-0	0			.900	-1	/C-2	-0.1
1912	Cle-A	20	54	5	11	2	1	0	6	4		.204	.259	.278	536	52	-4	0			.942	2	C-20	0.0
1915	Phi-N	24	27	1	3	0	0	0	2	2	3	.111	.172	.111	284	-13	-4	0			.974	-4	C-23/1-1	-0.8
1916	Phi-N	11	13	2	3	0	0	0	1	0	3	.231	.231	.231	462	40	-1	0			.929	1	C-11	0.0
1917	Phi-N	43	107	4	22	4	1	1	7	0	20	.206	.206	.290	495	49	-7	0			.994	1	C-38/1-1	-0.4
1918	Phi-N	84	227	10	40	4	0	0	12	10	26	.176	.214	.194	408	23	-20	5			.976	-1	C-76	-1.8
1919	Phi-N	78	232	14	54	7	2	1	17	6	27	.233	.252	.293	545	59	-12	4			.966	-2	C-73/1-1	-0.9
Total	8	267	678	37	137	17	4	2	45	23	79	.202	.229	.248	477	42	-48	9			.970	-2	C-248/1-3	-3.7
■ **DICK ADAMS** Adams, Richard Leroy b: 4/8/20, Tuolumne, Cal. BR/TL, 6', 185 lbs. Deb: 5/20/47 F																								
1947	Phi-A	37	89	9	18	2	3	2	11	2	18	.202	.220	.360	579	58	-6	0	0	0	.995	0	1-24/O-3(1-0-2)	-0.6
■ **RICKY ADAMS** Adams, Ricky Lee b: 1/21/59, Upland, Cal. BR/TR, 6'2", 180 lbs. Deb: 9/15/82																								
1982	Cal-A	8	14	1	2	0	0	0	0	0	2	.143	.200	.143	343	-4	-2	1	0	0	.947	-1	/S-8	-0.2
1983	Cal-A	58	112	22	28	2	0	2	6	5	12	.250	.300	.321	621	72	-4	1	1	-0	.960	22	S-38,3-16/2-4	2.0
1985	SF-N	54	121	12	23	3	1	2	10	5	23	.190	.228	.281	509	44	-9	1	1	-0	.964	3	S-25,3-16/2-6	-0.5
Total	3	120	247	35	53	5	1	4	16	10	37	.215	.260	.291	551	54	-16	3	2	-0	.961	24	/S-71,3-32,2-10	1.3
■ **BOBBY ADAMS** Adams, Robert Henry b: 12/14/21, Tuolumne, Cal. d: 2/13/97, Gig Harbor, Wash. BR/TR, 5'10", 170 lbs. Deb: 4/16/46 FC																								
1946	Cin-N	94	311	35	76	13	3	4	24	18	32	.244	.292	.344	636	83	-8	16			.967	24	2-74/O-2(0-0-2),3-1	2.1
1947	Cin-N	81	217	39	59	11	2	4	20	25	23	.272	.358	.396	754	101	1	9			.967	14	2-69	1.7
1948	Cin-N	87	262	33	78	20	3	1	21	25	23	.298	.361	.408	770	112	4	6			.965	-12	2-64/3-7	-0.4
1949	Cin-N	107	277	32	70	16	2	0	25	26	36	.253	.317	.325	642	72	-11	4			.984	-9	2-63,3-14	-1.6
1950	Cin-N	115	348	57	98	21	8	3	25	43	29	.282	.361	.414	774	103	2	7			.981	-9	2-53,3-42	-0.5
1951	Cin-N	125	403	57	107	12	5	5	24	43	40	.266	.338	.357	695	86	-7	4	10	-3	.956	-10	3-60,2-42/O-1(0-0-1)	-1.8
1952	Cin-N	154	637	85	180	25	4	6	48	49	67	.283	.334	.363	696	93	-6	11	9	-1	.962	9	*3-154	0.2
1953	Cin-N	150	607	99	167	14	6	8	49	58	67	.275	.338	.357	696	81	-16	3	2	-0	.951	8	*3-150	-0.8
1954	Cin-N	110	390	69	105	25	6	3	23	55	46	.269	.364	.387	751	93	-3	2	5	-1	.951	1	3-93/2-2	-0.3
1955	Cin-N	64	150	23	41	11	2	2	20	20	21	.273	.370	.413	783	102	1	2	0	0	.969	3	3-42/2-5	0.5
	Chi-A	28	21	8	2	0	1	0	3	4	4	.095	.240	.190	430	16	-3	0	0	0	.933	5	/3-9,2-1	0.3
1956	Bal-A	41	111	19	25	6	1	0	7	25	15	.225	.368	.297	665	84	-1	1	1	-0	.984	-6	3-24,2-18	-0.6
1957	Chi-N	60	187	21	47	10	2	1	10	17	28	.251	.320	.342	663	79	-5	0	3	-1	.949	-8	3-47/2-1	-1.5
1958	Chi-N	62	96	14	27	4	4	0	4	6	15	.281	.324	.406	730	93	-1	2	0	0	.961	-2	1-11/3-9,2-7	-0.3
1959	Chi-N	3	2	0	0	0	0	0	0	0	1	.000	.000	.000	0	-99	-1	0	0	0	.667	-0	/1-1	-0.1
Total	14	1281	4019	591	1082	188	49	37	303	414	447	.269	.340	.368	708	90	-54	67	30		.955	10	3-652,2-399/1-12,O	-3.1
■ **BOB ADAMS** Adams, Robert Melvin b: 1/6/52, Pittsburgh, Pa. BR/TR, 6'2", 200 lbs. Deb: 7/10/77																								
1977	Det-A	15	24	2	6	1	0	2	2	0	5	.250	.250	.542	792	103	-0	0	0	0	1.000	-0	/1-2,C-1	0.0
■ **MIKE ADAMS** Adams, Robert Michael b: 7/24/48, Cincinnati, Ohio BR/TR, 5'9", 180 lbs. Deb: 9/10/72 F Career OF: (27-LF 2-CF 2-RF)																								
1972	Min-A	3	6	0	2	0	0	0	0	0	1	.333	.333	.333	667	94	-0	0	0	0	1.000	-0	/O-1(1-0-0)	0.0
1973	Min-A	55	66	21	14	2	0	3	6	17	18	.212	.381	.379	760	110	2	2	1	0	.978	-1	O-24(23-1-0)/D-2	0.0
1976	Chi-N	25	29	1	4	2	0	0	2	8	7	.138	.342	.207	549	54	-1	0	0	0	1.000	-3	/O-4(2-0-2),3-3,2-1	-0.5
1977	Chi-N	2	2	0	0	0	0	0	0	0	1	.000	.000	.000	0	-90	-1	0	0	0	.000	-1	/O-2(1-1-0)	-0.1
1978	Oak-A	15	15	5	3	1	0	0	1	7	2	.200	.455	.267	721	113	1	0	0	0	1.000	-1	/2-6,3-3,D-3	0.0
Total	5	100	118	27	23	5	0	3	9	32	29	.195	.375	.314	689	93	1	2	1	0	.980	-5	/O-31L,2-7,3-6,D-5	-0.6
■ **SPENCER ADAMS** Adams, Spencer Dewey b: 6/21/1898, Layton, Utah d: 11/24/70, Salt Lake City, Ut BL/TR, 5'9", 158 lbs. Deb: 5/8/23																								
1923	Pit-N	25	56	11	14	0	1	0	4	6	6	.250	.323	.286	608	60	-3	2	1	0	.879	-6	2-11/S-6	-0.8
1925	*Was-A	39	55	11	15	4	1	0	4	5	4	.273	.333	.382	715	83	-2	1	1	-0	.941	-2	2-15/S-8,3-3	-0.3
1926	*NY-A	28	25	7	3	1	0	0	1	3	7	.120	.214	.160	374	-1	-4	1	0	0	1.000	4	/2-4,3-1	0.1
1927	StL-A	88	259	32	69	11	3	0	29	24	33	.266	.333	.332	665	71	-11	1	8	-3	.948	1	2-54,3-28	-0.9
Total	4	180	395	61	101	16	5	0	38	38	50	.256	.324	.322	646	66	-19	5	10	-2	.944	-3	/2-84,3-32,S-14	-1.9
■ **JOE ADCOCK** Adcock, Joseph Wilbur b: 10/30/27, Coushatta, La. d: 5/3/99, Coushatta, La. BR/TR, 6'4", 220 lbs. Deb: 4/23/50 M Career OF: (310-LF 0-CF 0-RF)																								
1950	Cin-N	102	372	46	109	16	1	8	55	24	24	.293	.336	.406	742	94	-4	2			.968	6	O-75(75-0-0),1-24	-0.4
1951	Cin-N	113	395	40	96	16	4	10	47	24	29	.243	.288	.380	668	77	-14	1	2	-0	.983	1	*O-107(107-0-0)	-2.2
1952	Cin-N	117	378	43	105	22	4	13	52	23	38	.278	.321	.460	781	115	6	1	4	-1	.985	4	O-85(85-0-0),1-17	0.2
1953	Mil-N	157	590	71	168	33	6	18	80	42	82	.285	.334	.453	787	110	6	3	2	-0	.991	-4	*1-157	-0.7
1954	Mil-N	133	500	73	154	27	5	23	87	44	58	.308	.367	.520	887	137	25	1	4	-1	.995	-11	*1-133	0.5
1955	Mil-N	84	288	40	76	14	0	15	45	31	44	.264	.340	.469	808	118	7	0	2	-1	.990	-5	1-78	-0.3
1956	Mil-N	137	454	76	132	23	1	38	103	32	86	.291	.339	.597	936	**154**	32	1	0	0	**.995**	-6	*1-129	1.9
1957	*Mil-N	65	209	31	60	13	2	12	38	20	51	.287	.352	.541	893	146	13	0	0	0	.996	-3	1-56	0.7
1958	*Mil-N	105	320	40	88	15	1	19	54	21	63	.275	.322	.506	828	125	10	0	0	0	.989	-1	1-71,O-22(22-0-0)	0.4
1959	Mil-N	115	404	53	118	19	2	25	76	32	77	.292	.344	.535	879	141	22	0	0	0	.998	10	1-89,O-21(21-0-0)	2.6
1960	Mil-N★	138	514	55	153	21	4	25	91	46	86	.298	.357	.500	857	142	28	2	2	-0	**.993**	3	*1-136	2.3
1961	Mil-N	152	562	77	160	20	0	35	108	59	94	.285	.355	.507	862	133	26	2	1	0	**.993**	-5	*1-148	1.2
1962	Mil-N	121	391	48	97	12	1	29	78	50	91	.248	.335	.506	841	126	13	2	0	0	**.997**	-4	*1-112	0.3
1963	Cle-A	97	283	28	71	7	1	13	49	30	53	.251	.323	.420	743	107	3	1	2	-0	.995	-4	1-78	-0.6
1964	LA-A	118	366	39	98	13	0	21	64	48	61	.268	.353	.475	828	142	20	0	2	-1	.993	-5	*1-105	0.9

YEAR	TM/L	G	AB	R	H	2B	3B	HR	RBI	BB	SO	AVG	OBP	SLG	OPS	OPS+	BR+	SB	CS	SBR	FA	FR	G/POS	TPR
1965	Cal-A	122	349	30	84	14	0	14	47	37	74	.241	.315	.401	716	104	2	2	2	-0	.996	-4	1-97	-0.9
1966	Cal-A	83	231	33	63	10	3	18	48	31	48	.273	.359	.576	935	168	20	2	2	-0	.997	-0	1-71	1.6
Total	17	1959	6606	823	1832	295	35	336	1122	594	1059	.277	.339	.485	824	125	213	20	25		.994	-28	*1-1501,O-310L	7.5
■ BOB ADDIS Addis, Robert Gordon b: 11/6/25, Mineral, Ohio BL/TR, 6′, 175 lbs. Deb: 9/1/50																								
1950	Bos-N	16	28	7	7	1	0	0	2	3	5	.250	.323	.286	608	66	-1	1			1.000	-2	/O-7(2-1-4)	-0.3
1951	Bos-N	85	199	23	55	7	0	1	24	9	10	.276	.308	.327	634	76	-7	3	2	-0	.982	-0	O-46(31-10-5)	-1.0
1952	Chi-N	93	292	38	86	13	2	1	20	23	30	.295	.346	.363	709	96	-1	4	4	-1	.988	-2	O-79(3-42-37)	-0.7
1953	Chi-N	10	12	2	2	1	0	0	1	2	0	.167	.286	.250	536	40	-1	0	0	0	1.000	1	/O-3(0-1-2)	0.0
	Pit-N	4	3	0	0	0	0	0	0	0	2	.000	.000	.000	0	-99	-1	0	0	0	.000	0	H	-0.1
	Yr	14	15	2	2	1	0	0	1	2	2	.133	.235	.200	435	15	-2	0	0	0	1.000	1	/O-3(0-1-2)	-0.1
Total	4	208	534	70	150	22	2	2	47	37	47	.281	.327	.341	668	84	-12	8	6		.986	-3	O-135(36-54-48)	-2.1
■ JIM ADDUCI Adduci, James David b: 8/9/59, Chicago, Ill. BL/TL, 6′5″, 200 lbs. Deb: 9/12/83 Career OF: (18-LF 0-CF 9-RF)																								
1983	StL-N	10	20	0	1	0	0	0	0	1	6	.050	.095	.050	145	-59	-4	0	0	0	1.000	0	/1-6,O-1(1-0-0)	-0.5
1986	Mil-A	3	11	2	1	1	0	0	0	1	2	.091	.167	.182	348	-5	-2	0	0	0	1.000	0	/1-3	-0.2
1988	Mil-A	44	94	8	25	6	1	1	15	0	15	.266	.266	.383	649	79	-3	0	1	-0	.969	-4	O-24(16-0-9),D-10/1-3	-0.8
1989	Phi-N	13	19	1	7	1	0	0	0	0	4	.368	.368	.421	789	125	1	0	0	0	1.000	0	/1-4,O-1(1-0-0)	0.1
Total	4	70	144	11	34	8	1	1	15	2	27	.236	.247	.326	573	58	-8	0	1	-0	.969	-3	/O-26L,1-16,D-10	-1.4
■ BOB ADDY Addy, Robert Edward "Magnet" b: 2/1845, Rochester, N.Y. d: 4/9/10, Pocatello, Idaho BL/TL, 5′8″, 160 lbs. Deb: 5/6/1871 M NA OF: (0-LF 1-CF 98-RF)																								
1871	Rok-n	25	118	30	32	6	0	0	13	4	0	.271	.295	.322	617	81	-2	8	1	1	.768	1	*2-22/S-3	-0.1
1873	Phi-n	10	51	12	16	1	0	0	10	2	0	.314	.340	.333	673	97	-0	0	1	-0	.855	-4	2-10	-0.3
	Bos-n	31	152	37	54	5	2	1	36	1	0	.355	.359	.434	794	124	3	2	3	-1	.750	-2	O-31(0-0-31)	0.2
	Yr	41	203	49	70	6	2	1	46	3	0	.345	.354	.409	763	118	3	2	4	-1	.750	-5	O-31(0-0-31),2-10	-0.1
1874	Har-n	50	213	25	51	9	2	0	22	1	1	.239	.243	.300	543	70	-8	4	2	0	.846	2	*2-45/3-5,S-1	-0.6
1875	Phi-n	69	310	60	80	8	4	0	43	0	2	.258	.258	.310	568	93	-3	16	8	1	.761	-0	*O-68(0-1-67)/2-2,M	0.1
1876	Chi-N	32	147	36	40	4	1	0	16	5	0	.272	.306	.324	630	98	-1				.800	0	O-32(3-0-29)	-0.1
1877	Cin-N	57	245	27	68	2	3	0	31	6	5	.278	.295	.310	605	102	2				.805	5	*O-57(0-1-56)/M	0.6
Total	4 n	185	844	164	233	29	8	1	124	8	3	.276	.283	.333	616	92	-10	30	15	1	.758	-2	/O-99R,2-79,3-5,S-4	-0.7
Total	2	89	392	63	108	6	4	0	47	11	5	.276	.299	.315	614	100	1				.803	5	/O-89(3-1-85)	0.5
■ MORRIE ADERHOLT Aderholt, Morris Woodroe b: 9/13/15, Mt.Olive, N.C. d: 3/18/55, Sarasota, Fla. BL/TR, 6′1″, 188 lbs. Deb: 9/13/39 Career OF: (42-LF 0-CF 3-RF)																								
1939	Was-A	7	25	5	5	0	0	1	4	2	6	.200	.259	.320	579	51	-2	0	1	-0	.872	0	/2-7	-0.2
1940	Was-A	1	2	0	0	0	0	0	0	0	0	.000	.000	.000	0	-99	-1	0	0	0	1.000	0	/2-1	0.0
1941	Was-A	11	14	3	2	0	0	0	1	1	3	.143	.200	.143	343	-8	-2	0	0	0	.818	0	/2-2,3-1	-0.2
1944	Bro-N	17	59	9	16	2	3	0	10	4	4	.271	.317	.407	724	105	0	0			.871	-1	O-13(11-0-2)	-0.2
1945	Bro-N	39	60	4	13	1	0	0	6	3	10	.217	.254	.233	487	36	-5	0			1.000	-2	/O-8(7-0-1)	-0.8
	Bos-N	31	102	15	34	4	0	2	11	9	6	.333	.387	.431	819	127	4	3			.984	0	O-24(24-0-0)/2-1	0.2
	Yr	70	162	19	47	5	0	2	17	12	16	.290	.339	.358	697	94	-1	3			.985	-2	O-32(31-0-1)/2-1	-0.6
Total	5	106	262	36	70	7	3	3	32	19	29	.267	.317	.351	668	85	-6	3	1		.949	-2	/O-45L,2-11,3-1	-1.2
■ DICK ADKINS Adkins, Richard Earl b: 3/3/20, Electra, Tex. d: 9/12/55, Electra, Tex. BR/TR, 5′10″, 165 lbs. Deb: 9/19/42																								
1942	Phi-A	3	7	2	1	0	0	0	0	2	2	.143	.333	.143	476	37	-0	0	0	0	.875	-1	/S-3	-0.2
■ HENRY ADKINSON Adkinson, Henry Magee b: 9/1/1874, Chicago, Ill. d: 5/1/23, Salt Lake City, Ut. Deb: 9/25/1895																								
1895	StL-N	1	5	1	2	0	0	0	0	0	2	.400	.400	.400	800	108	0	0			.667	-0	/O-1(1-0-0)	0.0
■ DAVE ADLESH Adlesh, David George b: 7/15/43, Long Beach, Cal. BR/TR, 6′, 187 lbs. Deb: 5/12/63																								
1963	Hou-N	6	8	0	0	0	0	0	0	0	4	.000	.000	.000	0	-99	-2	0	0	0	.889	-2	/C-6	-0.4
1964	Hou-N	3	10	0	2	0	0	0	0	0	5	.200	.200	.200	400	14	-1	0	0	0	1.000	-1	/C-3	-0.2
1965	Hou-N	15	34	2	5	1	0	0	3	2	12	.147	.216	.176	393	13	-4	0	0	0	1.000	-1	C-13	-0.5
1966	Hou-N	3	6	0	0	0	0	0	0	0	4	.000	.000	.000	0	-99	-2	0	0	0	1.000	1	/C-1	-0.1
1967	Hou-N	39	94	4	17	1	0	1	4	11	28	.181	.267	.223	490	43	-7	0	0	0	.995	-3	C-31	-0.9
1968	Hou-N	40	104	3	19	1	1	0	4	5	27	.183	.227	.212	439	33	-8	0	0	0	.990	-3	C-36	-1.1
Total	6	106	256	9	43	3	1	1	11	18	80	.168	.228	.199	427	26	-24	0	0	0	.992	-8	/C-90	-3.2
■ TROY AFENIR Afenir, Michael Troy b: 9/21/63, Escondido, Cal. BR/TR, 6′4″, 185 lbs. Deb: 9/14/87																								
1987	Hou-N	10	20	1	6	1	0	0	1	0	12	.300	.300	.350	650	74	-1	0	0	0	.974	-1	C-10	-0.1
1990	Oak-A	14	14	0	2	0	0	0	2	0	6	.143	.143	.143	286	-21	-2	0	0	0	1.000	-1	C-12/D-1	-0.3
1991	Oak-A	5	11	0	1	0	0	0	0	0	2	.091	.091	.091	182	-53	-2	0	0	0	1.000	1	/C-4,D-1	-0.1
1992	Cin-N	16	34	3	6	1	2	0	4	5	12	.176	.282	.324	606	69	-1	0	0	0	1.000	-3	C-15	-0.4
Total	4	45	79	4	15	2	2	0	7	5	32	.190	.238	.266	504	40	-7	0	0	0	.992	-4	/C-41,D-2	-0.9
■ BENNY AGBAYANI Agbayani, Benny Peter b: 12/28/71, Honolulu, Hawaii BR/TR, 6′, 225 lbs. Deb: 6/17/98																								
1998	NY-N	11	15	1	2	0	0	0	0	1	5	.133	.188	.133	321	-14	-2	0	2	-1	1.000	-2	/O-9(1-2-6)	-0.6
1999	*NY-N	101	276	42	79	18	3	14	42	32	60	.286	.367	.525	892	126	10	6	4	-0	.984	-10	O-80(47-4-45)/D-2	-0.2
2000	*NY-N	119	350	59	101	19	1	15	60	54	68	.289	.394	.477	871	123	14	5	5	-1	.975	-7	*O-110(102-2-12)/D-1	0.3
Total	3	231	641	102	182	37	4	29	102	87	133	.284	.378	.490	868	121	22	11	11	-1	.980	-19	O-199(150-8-63)/D-3	-0.5
■ TOMMIE AGEE Agee, Tommie Lee b: 8/9/42, Magnolia, Ala. BR/TR, 5′11″, 195 lbs. Deb: 9/14/62																								
1962	Cle-A	5	14	0	3	0	0	0	2	0	4	.214	.214	.214	429	16	-2	0	0	0	1.000	-0	/O-3(2-1-0)	-0.2
1963	Cle-A	13	27	3	4	1	0	1	3	2	9	.148	.207	.296	503	39	-2	0	0	0	1.000	-1	O-13(4-3-6)	-0.4
1964	Cle-A	13	12	0	2	0	0	0	0	0	3	.167	.167	.167	333	-7	-2	0	0	0	1.000	-4	O-12(0-3-10)	-0.6
1965	Chi-A	10	19	2	3	1	0	0	3	2	6	.158	.238	.211	449	30	-2	0	1	-0	1.000	-2	/O-9(0-5-6)	-0.5
1966	Chi-A★	160	629	98	172	27	8	22	86	41	127	.273	.328	.447	775	129	21	44	18	3	.982	11	*O-159(8-156-0)	3.3
1967	Chi-A★	158	529	73	124	26	2	14	52	44	129	.234	.303	.371	673	102	0	28	10	3	.969	2	*O-152(10-136-9)	0.0
1968	NY-N	132	368	30	80	12	3	5	17	15	103	.217	.256	.307	563	68	-15	13	8	0	.978	-10	*O-127(0-116-13)	-3.2
1969	*NY-N	149	565	97	153	23	4	26	76	59	137	.271	.343	.464	807	121	15	12	9	-1	.986	6	*O-146(0-143-7)	1.7
1970	NY-N	153	636	107	182	30	7	24	75	55	156	.286	.345	.469	813	115	12	31	15	2	.967	13	*O-150(0-149-2)	2.2
1971	NY-N	113	425	58	121	19	0	14	50	50	84	.285	.363	.428	791	125	14	28	6	4	.978	5	*O-107(0-94-32)	2.1
1972	NY-N	114	422	52	96	23	0	13	47	53	92	.227	.319	.374	694	99	-0	8	9	-1	.962	6	*O-109(6-91-20)	0.1
1973	Hou-N	83	204	30	48	5	2	8	15	16	55	.235	.294	.397	691	90	-3	2	5	-1	.983	-4	O-67(34-18-17)	-1.2
	StL-N	26	62	8	11	3	1	3	7	5	13	.177	.239	.403	642	75	-2	1	0	0	.981	1	O-19(0-19-2)	-0.2
	Yr	109	266	38	59	8	3	11	22	21	68	.222	.281	.398	680	87	-6	3	5	-1	.982	-3	O-86(34-37-19)	-1.4
Total	12	1129	3912	558	999	170	27	130	433	342	918	.255	.321	.412	733	108	35	167	81	8	.975	22	*O-1073(64-934-124)	3.1
■ HARRY AGGANIS Agganis, Harry "The Golden Greek" b: 4/20/29, Lynn, Mass. d: 6/27/55, Cambridge, Mass. BL/TL, 6′2″, 200 lbs. Deb: 4/13/54																								
1954	Bos-A	132	434	54	109	13	8	11	57	47	57	.251	.324	.394	718	86	-8	6	3	0	.990	7	*1-119	-0.8
1955	Bos-A	25	83	11	26	10	1	0	10	10	10	.313	.387	.458	845	116	2	2	0	0	.987	0	1-20	0.1
Total	2	157	517	65	135	23	9	11	67	57	67	.261	.334	.404	739	91	-6	8	3	1	.989	7	1-139	-0.7
■ JOE AGLER Agler, Joseph Abram b: 6/12/1887, Coshocton, Ohio d: 4/26/71, Massillon, Ohio BL/TL, 5′11″, 165 lbs. Deb: 10/1/12 Career OF: (52-LF 9-CF 18-RF)																								
1912	Was-A	2	1	0	0	0	0	0	0	0		.000	.000	.000	0	-99	-0	0			.000	0	/1-1	0.0
1914	Buf-F	135	463	82	126	17	6	0	20	77	78	.272	.376	.335	711	93	-8	21			.985	5	1-76,O-54(44-5-6)	-0.9
1915	Buf-F	25	73	11	13	1	2	0	2	20	14	.178	.355	.247	601	69	-3	2			.973	-2	O-20(6-3-11)/1-1	-0.7
	Bal-F	72	214	28	46	4	2	0	14	34	38	.215	.325	.252	578	62	-13	15			.981	5	1-58/O-4(2-1-1),2-3	-1.1
	Yr	97	287	39	59	5	4	0	16	54	52	.206	.333	.251	584	64	-16	17			.981	3	1-59,O-24(8-4-12)/2-3	-1.8
Total	3	234	751	121	185	22	10	0	36	131	130	.246	.359	.302	661	81	-25	38			.983	7	1-136/O-78L,2-3	-2.7
■ SAM AGNEW Agnew, Samuel Lester "Slam" b: 4/12/1887, Farmington, Mo. d: 7/19/51, Sonoma, Cal. BR/TR, 5′11″, 185 lbs. Deb: 4/10/13																								
1913	StL-A	105	307	27	64	9	5	2	24	20	49	.208	.272	.290	562	66	-14	11			.952	2	*C-103	-0.4

YEAR	TM/L	G	AB	R	H	2B	3B	HR	RBI	BB	SO	AVG	OBP	SLG	OPS	OPS+	BR+	SB	CS	SBR	FA	FR	G/POS	TPR
1914	StL-A	115	311	22	66	5	4	0	16	24	63	.212	.279	.254	533	63	-14	10	8	-1	.961	3	*C-115	-0.4
1915	StL-A	104	295	18	60	4	2	0	19	12	36	.203	.247	.231	477	45	-21	5	2	0	.934	5	*C-102	-0.7
1916	Bos-A	40	67	4	14	2	1	0	7	6	4	.209	.293	.269	562	69	-2	0			.952	8	C-38	0.8
1917	Bos-A	85	260	17	54	6	2	0	16	19	30	.208	.267	.246	513	57	-13	2			.965	-10	C-85	-1.9
1918	*Bos-A	72	199	11	33	8	0	0	6	11	26	.166	.221	.206	427	29	-17	0			.965	11	C-72	-0.2
1919	Was-A	42	98	6	23	7	0	0	10	10	8	.235	.312	.306	618	74	-3	1			.974	8	C-36	0.7
Total	7	563	1537	105	314	41	14	2	98	102	216	.204	.265	.253	518	56	-85	29	10		.955	26	C-551	-2.1

■ LUIS AGUAYO

Aguayo, Luis (Muriel) b: 3/13/59, Vega Baja, P.R. BR/TR, 5′9″, 185 lbs. Deb: 4/19/80

YEAR	TM/L	G	AB	R	H	2B	3B	HR	RBI	BB	SO	AVG	OBP	SLG	OPS	OPS+	BR+	SB	CS	SBR	FA	FR	G/POS	TPR
1980	Phi-N	20	47	7	13	1	2	1	8	2	3	.277	.306	.447	753	102	-0	1	1	-0	.962	1	2-14/S-5	0.2
1981	*Phi-N	45	84	11	18	4	0	1	7	6	15	.214	.283	.298	580	62	-4	1	0	0	.938	-4	2-21,S-21/3-3	-0.7
1982	Phi-N	50	56	11	15	1	2	3	7	5	7	.268	.339	.518	857	133	2	1	1	-0	.966	3	2-21,S-15/3-5	0.6
1983	Phi-N	2	4	1	1	0	0	0	0	1	2	.250	.400	.250	650	85	-0	0	0	0	1.000	-2	/S-2	-0.2
1984	Phi-N	58	72	15	20	4	0	3	11	8	16	.278	.350	.458	808	123	2	0	0	0	.909	8	3-14,2-12,S-10	1.1
1985	Phi-N	91	165	27	46	7	3	6	21	22	26	.279	.383	.467	850	133	8	1	0	0	.957	3	S-60,2-17/3-7	1.6
1986	Phi-N	62	133	17	28	6	1	4	13	8	26	.211	.271	.361	632	70	-6	1	1	-0	.967	-7	2-31,S-20/3-1	-1.0
1987	Phi-N	94	209	25	43	9	1	12	21	15	56	.206	.275	.431	706	81	-7	0	0	0	.971	-9	S-78/2-6,3-2	-1.0
1988	Phi-N	49	97	9	24	3	0	3	5	13	17	.247	.336	.371	707	101	0	2	0	0	.967	2	S-27,3-13/2-2	0.4
	NY-A	50	140	12	35	4	0	3	8	7	33	.250	.291	.343	633	77	-4	0	2	-1	.961	-2	3-33,2-13/S-6	-0.7
1989	Cle-A	47	97	7	17	4	1	1	8	7	19	.175	.245	.268	513	44	-7	0	0	0	.950	5	3-19,S-15,2-10,/D-2	-0.2
Total	10	568	1104	142	260	43	10	37	109	94	220	.236	.307	.393	700	91	-16	7	5	-0	.960	-2	S-259,2-147/3-97,D	0.1

■ CHARLIE AHEARN

Ahearn, Charles b: Troy, N.Y. Deb: 6/19/1880

YEAR	TM/L	G	AB	R	H	2B	3B	HR	RBI	BB	SO	AVG	OBP	SLG	OPS	OPS+	BR+	SB	CS	SBR	FA	FR	G/POS	TPR
1880	Tro-N	1	4	1	1	0	0	0	0	0	0	.250	.250	.250	500	67	-0				.778	-0	/C-1	0.0

■ WILLIE AIKENS

Aikens, Willie Mays b: 10/14/54, Seneca, S.C. BL/TR, 6′3″, 220 lbs. Deb: 5/17/77

YEAR	TM/L	G	AB	R	H	2B	3B	HR	RBI	BB	SO	AVG	OBP	SLG	OPS	OPS+	BR+	SB	CS	SBR	FA	FR	G/POS	TPR
1977	Cal-A	42	91	5	18	4	0	0	6	10	23	.198	.277	.242	519	45	-7	1	2	-0	.971	0	1-13,D-13	-0.8
1979	Cal-A	116	379	59	106	18	0	21	81	61	79	.280	.381	.493	874	138	21	1	3	-1	.996	-2	1-55,D-51	1.3
1980	*KC-A	151	543	70	151	24	0	20	98	64	88	.278	.362	.433	794	116	13	1	0	0	.990	-9	*1-138,D-13	-0.5
1981	*KC-A	101	349	45	93	16	0	17	53	62	47	.266	.382	.458	840	142	21	0	0	0	.992	-5	1-99	1.0
1982	KC-A	134	466	50	131	29	1	17	74	45	70	.281	.348	.457	805	119	12	0	1	-0	.994	-3	*1-128	0.0
1983	KC-A	125	410	49	124	26	1	23	72	45	75	.302	.374	.539	913	148	26	0	0	0	.989	-5	*1-112/D-6	1.5
1984	Tor-A	93	234	21	48	7	0	11	26	29	56	.205	.298	.376	674	82	-6	0	0	0	1.000	0	D-81/1-2	-0.8
1985	Tor-A	12	20	2	4	1	0	1	5	3	6	.200	.304	.400	704	89	-0	0	0	0	.000	0	D-11	-0.1
Total	8	774	2492	301	675	125	2	110	415	319	444	.271	.358	.455	813	123	80	3	6	-1	.991	-24	1-547,D-175	1.6

■ DANNY AINGE

Ainge, Daniel Ray b: 3/17/59, Eugene, Ore. BR/TR (BB 1979 (part), 1981 (1 GAME)), 6′4″, 175 lbs. Deb: 5/21/79 Career OF: (6-LF 25-CF 2-RF)

YEAR	TM/L	G	AB	R	H	2B	3B	HR	RBI	BB	SO	AVG	OBP	SLG	OPS	OPS+	BR+	SB	CS	SBR	FA	FR	G/POS	TPR
1979	Tor-A	87	308	26	73	7	1	2	19	12	58	.237	.270	.286	556	50	-22	1	0	0	.977	-4	2-86/D-1	-2.0
1980	Tor-A	38	111	11	27	6	1	0	4	2	29	.243	.263	.315	578	55	-7	3	0	1	.986	2	O-29C/3-3,2-1,D-2	-0.5
1981	Tor-A	86	246	20	46	6	2	0	14	23	41	.187	.259	.228	487	39	-19	8	5	0	.949	1	3-77/S-6,O-4C,2D	-2.0
Total	3	211	665	57	146	19	4	2	37	37	128	.220	.265	.269	534	47	-47	12	5	1	.977	-1	/2-89,3-80,O-33C,SD	-4.5

■ EDDIE AINSMITH

Ainsmith, Edward Wilbur “Dorf” b: 2/4/1892, Cambridge, Mass. d: 9/6/81, Ft.Lauderdale, Fla BR/TR, 5′11″, 180 lbs. Deb: 8/9/10

YEAR	TM/L	G	AB	R	H	2B	3B	HR	RBI	BB	SO	AVG	OBP	SLG	OPS	OPS+	BR+	SB	CS	SBR	FA	FR	G/POS	TPR
1910	Was-A	33	104	4	20	1	2	0	9	6		.192	.236	.240	477	52	-6	0			.963	-4	C-30	-0.8
1911	Was-A	61	149	12	33	2	3	0	14	10		.221	.275	.275	550	55	-9	5			.952	0	C-47	-0.5
1912	Was-A	61	186	22	42	7	2	0	22	14		.226	.280	.285	565	61	-10	4			.958	15	C-59	1.1
1913	Was-A	84	229	26	49	4	4	2	20	12	41	.214	.262	.293	555	61	-12	17			.967	6	C-79/P-1	0.0
1914	Was-A	62	151	11	34	7	0	0	13	9	28	.225	.273	.272	545	61	-7	8	5	0	.969	8	C-51	0.5
1915	Was-A	47	120	13	24	4	2	0	6	10	18	.200	.267	.267	534	59	-6	7	4	0	.988	6	C-42	0.3
1916	Was-A	51	100	11	17	4	0	0	8	8	14	.170	.231	.210	441	33	-8	3			.959	13	C-46	0.8
1917	Was-A	125	350	38	67	17	4	0	42	40	48	.191	.280	.263	543	66	-14	16			.971	15	*C-119	1.2
1918	Was-A	96	292	22	62	10	9	0	20	29	44	.212	.283	.308	592	80	-8	6			.975	8	C-89	0.8
1919	Det-A	114	364	42	99	17	12	3	32	45	30	.272	.354	.409	763	117	8	9			.962	-11	*C-106	0.7
1920	Det-A	69	186	19	43	5	3	1	19	14	19	.231	.285	.306	591	58	-11	4	3	-0	.955	-3	C-61/1-1	-1.0
1921	Det-A	35	98	6	27	5	2	0	12	13	7	.276	.360	.367	728	87	-2	1	0	0	.947	-4	C-34	-0.3
	StL-N	27	62	5	18	0	1	0	5	3	4	.290	.323	.323	646	73	-2	0	0	0	.956	1	C-23/1-1	0.0
1922	StL-N	119	379	46	111	14	4	13	59	28	43	.293	.343	.454	797	109	4	2	3	-1	.963	-2	*C-116	0.8
1923	StL-N	82	263	22	56	11	6	3	34	22	19	.213	.276	.335	611	62	-15	4	0	1	.980	-8	C-80	-1.7
	Bro-N	2	10	0	2	0	0	0	2	0	0	.200	.200	.200	400	6	-1	0	1	-0	1.000	1	/C-2	-0.1
	Yr	84	273	22	58	11	6	3	36	22	19	.212	.274	.330	603	60	-17	4	1	1	.981	-7	C-82	-1.8
1924	NY-N	10	5	0	3	0	0	0	0	0	0	.600	.600	.600	1200	229	1	0	0	0	1.000	-0	/C-9	0.1
Total	15	1078	3048	299	707	108	54	22	317	263	315	.232	.296	.324	620	76	-100	86	16		.966	41	C-993/1-2,P-1	1.9

■ GEORGE AITON

Aiton, George Wilson b: 12/29/1890, Kingman, Kan. d: 8/16/76, Van Nuys, Cal. BB/TR, 5′11.5″, 175 lbs. Deb: 6/29/12

YEAR	TM/L	G	AB	R	H	2B	3B	HR	RBI	BB	SO	AVG	OBP	SLG	OPS	OPS+	BR+	SB	CS	SBR	FA	FR	G/POS	TPR
1912	StL-A	10	17	1	4	0	0	0	1	4		.235	.381	.235	616	80	-0	0			.917	-0	/O-7(4-2-0)	-0.1

■ JOHN AKE

Ake, John Leckie b: 8/29/1861, Altoona, Pa. d: 5/11/1887, LaCrosse, Wis. BR/TR, 6′1″, 180 lbs. Deb: 5/12/1884

YEAR	TM/L	G	AB	R	H	2B	3B	HR	RBI	BB	SO	AVG	OBP	SLG	OPS	OPS+	BR+	SB	CS	SBR	FA	FR	G/POS	TPR
1884	Bal-a	13	52	1	10	0	1	0	2	0		.192	.208	.231	438	41	-3				.677	-3	/3-9,O-3(2-0-1),S-1	-0.6

■ BILL AKERS

Akers, William G. “Bump” b: 12/25/04, Chattanooga, Tenn. d: 4/13/62, Chattanooga, Tenn. BR/TR, 5′11″, 178 lbs. Deb: 9/8/29

YEAR	TM/L	G	AB	R	H	2B	3B	HR	RBI	BB	SO	AVG	OBP	SLG	OPS	OPS+	BR+	SB	CS	SBR	FA	FR	G/POS	TPR
1929	Det-A	24	83	15	22	4	1	1	9	10	9	.265	.351	.373	725	86	-2	2	0	0	.935	-9	S-24	-0.7
1930	Det-A	85	233	36	65	8	5	9	40	36	34	.279	.375	.472	848	111	4	5	5	-1	.944	9	S-49,3-26	1.7
1931	Det-A	29	66	5	13	2	2	0	3	7	6	.197	.274	.288	562	46	-5	0	1	-0	.935	-2	S-21/2-2	-0.6
1932	Bos-N	36	93	8	24	3	1	1	17	10	15	.258	.330	.344	674	85	-2	0			.927	-5	3-20/2-5,S-5	-0.5
Total	4	174	475	64	124	17	9	11	69	63	64	.261	.349	.404	753	93	-4	7	6		.936	-6	/S-99,3-46,2-7	-0.1

■ GUS ALBERTS

Alberts, Augustus Peter b: 1861, Reading, Pa. d: 5/7/12, Idaho Springs, Colo BR/TR, 5′6.5″, 180 lbs. Deb: 5/1/1884

YEAR	TM/L	G	AB	R	H	2B	3B	HR	RBI	BB	SO	AVG	OBP	SLG	OPS	OPS+	BR+	SB	CS	SBR	FA	FR	G/POS	TPR
1884	Pit-a	2	5	1	1	0	0	0		0		.200	.200	.200	400	31	-0				.500	-1	/S-2	-0.2
	Was-U	4	16	4	4	0	0	0		4		.250	.400	.250	650	105	-0				.870	2	/S-4	0.2
1888	Cle-a	102	364	51	75	10	6	1	48	41		.206	.299	.275	573	87	-4	26			.862	4	S-53,3-49	0.3
1891	Mil-a	12	41	6	4	0	0	0	2	7	5	.098	.260	.098	358	2	-5	1			.814	-3	3-12	-0.7
Total	3	120	426	62	84	10	6	1	50	52	5	.197	.298	.256	554	76	-9	27			.880	2	/3-61,S-59	-0.4

■ BUTCH ALBERTS

Alberts, Francis Burt b: 5/4/50, Williamsport, Pa. BR/TR, 6′2″, 205 lbs. Deb: 9/7/78

YEAR	TM/L	G	AB	R	H	2B	3B	HR	RBI	BB	SO	AVG	OBP	SLG	OPS	OPS+	BR+	SB	CS	SBR	FA	FR	G/POS	TPR
1978	Tor-A	6	18	1	5	1	0	0	0	0	2	.278	.278	.333	611	70	-1	0	0	0	.000	0	/D-4	-0.1

■ JACK ALBRIGHT

Albright, Harold John b: 6/30/21, St.Petersburg, Fla. d: 7/22/91, San Diego, Cal. BR/TR, 5′9″, 175 lbs. Deb: 5/19/47

YEAR	TM/L	G	AB	R	H	2B	3B	HR	RBI	BB	SO	AVG	OBP	SLG	OPS	OPS+	BR+	SB	CS	SBR	FA	FR	G/POS	TPR
1947	Phi-N	41	99	9	23	4	0	2	5	10	11	.232	.303	.333	636	71	-4	1			.943	3	S-33	0.0

■ ISRAEL ALCANTARA

Alcantara, Israel (Cristosomo) b: 5/6/73, Bani, D.R. BR/TR, 6′2″, 180 lbs. Deb: 6/25/2000

YEAR	TM/L	G	AB	R	H	2B	3B	HR	RBI	BB	SO	AVG	OBP	SLG	OPS	OPS+	BR+	SB	CS	SBR	FA	FR	G/POS	TPR
2000	Bos-A	21	45	9	13	1	0	4	7	3	7	.289	.333	.578	911	120	1	0	0	0	.889	-2	/O-7(1-0-7),1-5,D-8	-0.2

■ LUIS ALCARAZ

Alcaraz, Angel Luis (Acosta) b: 6/20/41, Humacao, P.R. BR/TR, 5′9″, 165 lbs. Deb: 9/13/67

YEAR	TM/L	G	AB	R	H	2B	3B	HR	RBI	BB	SO	AVG	OBP	SLG	OPS	OPS+	BR+	SB	CS	SBR	FA	FR	G/POS	TPR
1967	LA-N	17	60	1	14	1	0	0	3	1	13	.233	.246	.250	496	46	-4	1	1	-0	.990	9	2-17	0.6
1968	LA-N	41	106	4	16	1	0	2	5	9	23	.151	.217	.217	434	33	-9	1	1	-0	.979	3	2-20,3-13/S-1	-0.5
1969	KC-A	22	79	15	20	2	1	1	7	7	9	.253	.314	.342	656	83	-2	0	0	0	.988	-5	2-19/3-2,S-1	-0.6
1970	KC-A	35	120	10	20	5	1	1	14	4	13	.167	.194	.250	444	21	-13	0	0	0	.993	-8	2-31	-2.1
Total	4	115	365	30	70	9	2	4	29	21	58	.192	.236	.260	496	43	-28	2	2	-0	.988	-1	/2-87,3-15,S-2	-2.6

■ SCOTTY ALCOCK

Alcock, John Forbes b: 11/29/1885, Wooster, Ohio d: 1/30/73, Wooster, Ohio BR/TR, 5′9.5″, 160 lbs. Deb: 4/19/14

YEAR	TM/L	G	AB	R	H	2B	3B	HR	RBI	BB	SO	AVG	OBP	SLG	OPS	OPS+	BR+	SB	CS	SBR	FA	FR	G/POS	TPR
1914	Chi-A	54	156	12	27	4	2	0	7	7	14	.173	.213	.224	438	32	-13	4	2	0	.905	4	3-48/2-1	-0.9

■ MIKE ALDRETE
Aldrete, Michael Peter b: 1/29/61, Carmel, Cal. BL/TL, 5'11", 185 lbs. Deb: 5/28/86 Career OF: (278-LF 24-CF 135-RF)

YEAR	TM/L	G	AB	R	H	2B	3B	HR	RBI	BB	SO	AVG	OBP	SLG	OPS	OPS+	BR+	SB	CS	SBR	FA	FR	G/POS	TPR
1986	SF-N	84	216	27	54	18	3	2	25	33	34	.250	.355	.389	743	110	4	1	3	-1	1.000	3	1-37,O-31(30-0-2)	0.3
1987	*SF-N	126	357	50	116	18	2	9	51	43	50	.325	.398	.462	860	133	18	6	0	1	.986	-2	O-79(43-13-30),1-33	1.3
1988	SF-N	139	389	44	104	15	0	3	50	56	65	.267	.360	.329	689	103	4	6	5	-0	.982	-7	*O-115(83-7-40),1-10	-0.8
1989	Mon-N	76	136	12	30	8	1	1	12	19	30	.221	.321	.316	637	81	-3	1	3	-1	.980	-3	O-37(16-3-19),1-10	-0.8
1990	Mon-N	96	161	22	39	7	1	1	18	37	31	.242	.387	.317	704	100	2	1	2	-0	.982	-4	O-38(26-0-14),1-18	-0.4
1991	SD-N	12	15	2	0	0	0	0	1	3	4	.000	.167	.000	167	-48	-3	0	1	-0	1.000	0	/O-5(5-0-0)	-0.3
	Cle-A	85	183	22	48	6	1	1	19	36	37	.262	.384	.322	706	97	1	1	2	-0	.994	-3	1-47,O-16(16-0-0)/D-7	-0.5
1993	Oak-A	95	255	40	68	13	1	10	33	34	45	.267	.353	.443	796	120	7	1	1	-0	.995	-3	1-59,O-20(17-0-3)/D-6	-0.1
1994	Oak-A	76	178	23	43	5	0	4	18	20	35	.242	.318	.337	655	76	-6	2	0	0	1.000	-8	O-35L,1-27/D-1	-1.6
1995	Oak-A	60	125	18	34	8	0	4	21	19	23	.272	.372	.432	804	115	3	0	0	0	.989	-6	1-35,O-16(9-1-6)	-0.5
	Cal-A	18	24	1	6	0	0	0	3	0	8	.250	.250	.250	500	31	-2	0	0	0	1.000	1	/O-2(2-0-0),1-1,D-2	-0.2
	Yr	78	149	19	40	8	0	4	24	19	31	.268	.355	.403	758	101	1	0	0	0	.989	-5	1-36,O-18(11-1-6)/D-2	-0.7
1996	Cal-A	31	40	5	6	1	0	3	8	5	4	.150	.244	.400	644	59	-3	0	0	0	.750	-2	/O-6(4-0-2),1-1,D-6	-0.5
	*NY-A	32	68	11	17	5	0	3	12	9	15	.250	.338	.456	794	98	-0	0	1	-0	1.000	-4	/O-9L,1-8,P-1,D-9	-0.4
	Yr	63	108	16	23	6	0	6	20	14	19	.213	.303	.435	738	84	-3	0	1	-0	.909	-6	O-15L,D-15/1-9,P-1	-0.9
Total	10	930	2147	277	565	104	9	41	271	314	381	.263	.358	.377	736	104	21	19	18	-2	.983	-36	O-409L,1-286/D-31,P	-4.5

■ CHUCK ALENO
Aleno, Charles b: 2/19/17, St.Louis, Mo. BR/TR, 6'1.5", 215 lbs. Deb: 5/15/41

YEAR	TM/L	G	AB	R	H	2B	3B	HR	RBI	BB	SO	AVG	OBP	SLG	OPS	OPS+	BR+	SB	CS	SBR	FA	FR	G/POS	TPR
1941	Cin-N	54	169	23	41	7	3	1	18	11	16	.243	.289	.337	626	76	-6	3			.975	-4	3-40/1-2	-0.8
1942	Cin-N	7	14	1	2	1	0	0	0	3	3	.143	.294	.214	508	50	-1	0			.727	1	/3-2,2-1	0.1
1943	Cin-N	7	10	0	3	0	0	0	1	2	1	.300	.417	.300	717	110	0	0			1.000	-1	/O-2(2-0-0)	0.0
1944	Cin-N	50	127	10	21	3	0	1	15	15	15	.165	.259	.213	471	35	-11	0			.952	-4	3-42/1-3,S-3	-1.5
Total	4	118	320	34	67	11	3	2	34	31	35	.209	.281	.281	563	60	-17	3			.954	-7	/3-84,1-5,S-3,O2	-2.2

■ DALE ALEXANDER
Alexander, David Dale "Moose" b: 4/26/03, Greeneville, Tenn. d: 3/2/79, Greeneville, Tenn. BR/TR, 6'3", 210 lbs. Deb: 4/16/29

YEAR	TM/L	G	AB	R	H	2B	3B	HR	RBI	BB	SO	AVG	OBP	SLG	OPS	OPS+	BR+	SB	CS	SBR	FA	FR	G/POS	TPR
1929	Det-A	155	626	110	**215**	43	15	25	137	56	63	.343	.397	.580	977	148	42	5	9	-2	.988	-4	*1-155	2.4
1930	Det-A	154	602	86	196	33	8	20	135	42	56	.326	.372	.507	878	118	15	6	5	-0	.985	-7	*1-154	-0.2
1931	Det-A	135	517	75	168	47	3	3	87	64	35	.325	.401	.445	846	118	15	5	8	-2	.987	-8	*1-126/O-4(4-0-0)	-0.6
1932	Det-A	23	16	0	4	0	0	0	4	6	2	.250	.455	.250	705	84	0	0	0	0	1.000	-0	/1-2	0.0
	Bos-A	101	376	58	140	27	3	8	56	55	19	.372	.454	.524	978	157	34	4	5	-1	.992	2	*1-101	2.3
	Yr	124	392	58	144	27	3	8	60	61	21	**.367**	.454	.513	966	152	33	4	5	-1	.992	2	*1-103	2.3
1933	Bos-A	94	313	40	88	14	1	5	40	25	22	.281	.336	.380	716	90	-5	0	1	-0	.992	3	1-79	-0.9
Total	5	662	2450	369	811	164	30	61	459	248	197	.331	.394	.497	891	128	102	20	28	-5	.988	-14	1-617/O-4(4-0-0)	3.0

■ GARY ALEXANDER
Alexander, Gary Wayne b: 3/27/53, Los Angeles, Cal. BR/TR, 6'2", 200 lbs. Deb: 9/12/75 Career OF: (12-LF 0-CF 8-RF)

YEAR	TM/L	G	AB	R	H	2B	3B	HR	RBI	BB	SO	AVG	OBP	SLG	OPS	OPS+	BR+	SB	CS	SBR	FA	FR	G/POS	TPR
1975	SF-N	3	3	1	0	0	0	0	0	1	2	.000	.250	.000	250	-25	-0	0	0	0	1.000	-1	/C-2	-0.1
1976	SF-N	23	73	12	13	1	1	2	7	10	16	.178	.277	.301	578	62	-4	1	0	0	.964	-4	C-23	-0.6
1977	SF-N	51	119	17	36	4	2	5	20	20	33	.303	.411	.496	907	143	8	3	1	0	.968	-8	C-33/O-1(0-0-1)	0.2
1978	Oak-A	58	174	18	36	6	1	10	22	22	66	.207	.299	.425	725	107	1	0	3	-1	1.000	0	D-45/O-6L,C-1,1-1	-0.1
	Cle-A	90	324	39	76	14	3	17	62	35	100	.235	.311	.454	765	114	5	0	2	-1	.983	-9	C-66,D-25	-0.3
	Yr	148	498	57	112	20	4	27	84	57	166	.225	.307	.444	751	112	6	0	5	-2	.983	-9	D-70,C-67/O-6L,1-1	-0.4
1979	Cle-A	110	358	54	82	9	2	15	54	46	100	.229	.319	.391	710	90	-5	4	2	0	.961	-21	C-91,D-13/O-2(1-0-1)	-2.2
1980	Cle-A	76	178	22	40	7	1	5	31	17	52	.225	.292	.360	652	77	-6	0	4	-1	.971	-2	D-40,C-13/O-2(1-0-1)	-1.0
1981	Pit-N	21	47	6	10	4	1	1	6	3	12	.213	.260	.404	664	84	-1	0	0	0	.964	1	/1-9,O-8(7-0-2)	-0.1
Total	7	432	1276	169	293	45	11	55	202	154	381	.230	.315	.411	726	99	-2	8	12	-2	.969	-42	C-229,D-123/O-19L,1	-4.2

■ HUGH ALEXANDER
Alexander, Hugh b: 7/10/17, Buffalo, Mo. BR/TR, 6', 190 lbs. Deb: 8/15/37

YEAR	TM/L	G	AB	R	H	2B	3B	HR	RBI	BB	SO	AVG	OBP	SLG	OPS	OPS+	BR+	SB	CS	SBR	FA	FR	G/POS	TPR
1937	Cle-A	7	11	0	1	0	0	0	0	0	5	.091	.091	.091	182	-54	-3	1	0	0	.667	-2	/O-3(1-0-3)	-0.4

■ MANNY ALEXANDER
Alexander, Manuel De Jesus (b: Manuel De Jesus (Alexander))
b: 3/20/71, San Pedro De Macoris, D.R. BR/TR, 5'10", 165 lbs. Deb: 9/18/92 Career OF: (4-LF 0-CF 2-RF)

YEAR	TM/L	G	AB	R	H	2B	3B	HR	RBI	BB	SO	AVG	OBP	SLG	OPS	OPS+	BR+	SB	CS	SBR	FA	FR	G/POS	TPR
1992	Bal-A	4	5	1	1	0	0	0	0	0	3	.200	.200	.200	400	12	-1	0	0	0	1.000	1	/S-3	0.0
1993	Bal-A	3	0	1	0	0	0	0	0	0	0	—	—	—	—	—	0	0	0	0	.000	0	/R	0.0
1995	Bal-A	94	242	35	57	9	1	3	23	20	30	.236	.299	.318	617	60	-14	11	4	1	.971	-4	2-81/S-7,3-2,D-1	-1.3
1996	*Bal-A	54	68	6	7	0	0	0	4	3	27	.103	.141	.103	244	-37	-14	3	3	-0	.940	7	S-21/2-7,3-7,OPD	-0.6
1997	NY-N	54	149	26	37	9	3	2	15	9	38	.248	.296	.389	685	80	-5	11	0	2	.979	-1	2-31,S-26/3-1	-0.1
	Chi-N	33	99	11	29	3	1	1	7	8	16	.293	.358	.374	732	90	-1	2	1	0	.942	2	S-28/2-4	0.3
	Yr	87	248	37	66	12	4	3	22	17	54	.266	.321	.383	704	84	-6	13	1	3	.959	1	S-54,2-35/3-1	0.2
1998	*Chi-N	108	264	34	60	10	1	5	25	18	66	.227	.279	.330	609	57	-16	4	1	1	.964	-14	S-50,2-27,3-19,/OD	-2.6
1999	Chi-N	90	177	17	48	11	2	0	15	10	38	.271	.310	.356	666	69	-8	4	0	1	.988	-9	S-30,3-22,2-17,/O-2R	-1.4
2000	Bos-A	101	194	30	41	4	3	4	19	13	41	.211	.261	.325	586	45	-17	2	0	0	.944	6	3-63,S-20/2-7,D-2	-0.8
Total	8	541	1198	161	280	46	11	15	108	81	259	.234	.286	.328	614	57	-76	37	9	5	.968	-12	S-185,2-174,3/ODP	-6.5

■ MATT ALEXANDER
Alexander, Matthew b: 1/30/47, Shreveport, La. BB/TR, 5'11", 169 lbs. Deb: 8/23/73 Career OF: (25-LF 40-CF 31-RF)

YEAR	TM/L	G	AB	R	H	2B	3B	HR	RBI	BB	SO	AVG	OBP	SLG	OPS	OPS+	BR+	SB	CS	SBR	FA	FR	G/POS	TPR
1973	Chi-N	12	5	4	1	0	0	0	0	1	1	.200	.333	.200	533	48	-0	2	0	0	1.000	-1	/O-3(0-3-0)	-0.1
1974	Chi-N	45	54	15	11	2	1	0	0	12	12	.204	.358	.278	636	76	-1	8	4	0	.921	-2	3-19/O-4(0-2-1),2-2	-0.3
1975	Oak-A	63	10	16	1	0	0	0	0	1	1	.100	.182	.100	282	-19	-2	17	10	0	1.000	-3	D-17,O-11R/2-3,3-2	-0.5
1976	Oak-A	61	30	16	1	0	0	0	0	0	5	.033	.033	.033	67	-84	-7	20	7	2	1.000	-7	O-23(7-7-11),D-19	-1.4
1977	Oak-A	90	42	24	10	1	0	0	2	4	6	.238	.304	.262	566	57	-2	26	14	1	1.000	-11	O-31C,S-12/2-4,3D	-1.2
1978	Pit-N	7	0	2	0	0	0	0	0	0	0	—	—	—	—	—	0	4	1	1	.000	0	R	0.0
1979	*Pit-N	44	13	16	7	0	1	0	1	0	0	.538	.538	.692	1231	223	2	13	1	3	1.000	-3	O-11(6-3-3)/S-1	0.2
1980	Pit-N	37	3	13	1	1	0	0	0	0	0	.333	.333	.667	1000	170	0	10	3	1	1.000	-1	/O-4(2-2-0),2-1	0.0
1981	Pit-N	15	11	5	4	0	0	0	0	0	1	.364	.364	.364	727	104	0	3	2	-0	1.000	-1	/O-6(2-3-1)	-0.1
Total	9	374	168	111	36	4	2	0	4	18	26	.214	.294	.262	556	56	-10	103	42	8	1.000	-29	/O-93C,D-37,3-22,S2	-3.4

■ WALT ALEXANDER
Alexander, Walter Ernest b: 3/5/1891, Atlanta, Ga. d: 12/29/78, Fort Worth, Tex. BR/TR, 5'10.5", 165 lbs. Deb: 6/21/12

YEAR	TM/L	G	AB	R	H	2B	3B	HR	RBI	BB	SO	AVG	OBP	SLG	OPS	OPS+	BR+	SB	CS	SBR	FA	FR	G/POS	TPR
1912	StL-A	37	97	5	17	4	0	0	5	8		.175	.245	.216	462	34	-8	1			.969	-3	C-37	-0.9
1913	StL-A	43	110	5	15	2	1	0	7	4	36	.136	.174	.173	347	2	-14	1			.947	4	C-43	-0.8
1915	StL-A	1	1	0	0	0	0	0	0	0	0	.000	.000	.000	0	-99	-0	0			.000	0	/C-1	0.0
	NY-A	25	68	7	17	4	0	1	5	13	16	.250	.370	.353	723	117	2	2	1	0	.967	9	C-24	1.3
	Yr	26	69	7	17	4	0	1	5	13	16	.246	.366	.348	714	114	2	2	1	0	.967	9	C-25	1.3
1916	NY-A	36	78	8	20	6	1	0	3	13	20	.256	.376	.359	735	118	2	0			.960	2	C-27	0.6
1917	NY-A	20	51	1	7	2	1	0	4	4	11	.137	.200	.216	416	27	-5	1			.951	10	C-20	-0.4
Total	5	162	405	26	76	18	3	1	24	42	83	.188	.271	.254	525	56	-23	5	1		.959	11	C-152	-0.2

■ NIN ALEXANDER
Alexander, William Henry b: 11/24/1858, Pana, Ill. d: 12/22/33, Pana, Ill. BR/TR, 5'4.5", 163 lbs. Deb: 6/7/1884

YEAR	TM/L	G	AB	R	H	2B	3B	HR	RBI	BB	SO	AVG	OBP	SLG	OPS	OPS+	BR+	SB	CS	SBR	FA	FR	G/POS	TPR
1884	KC-U	19	65	2	9	0	0	0		1		.138	.152	.138	290	-13	-11				.907	-2	C-17/S-2,O-2(0-2-0)	-1.0
	StL-a	1	4	0	0	0	0	0		0		.000	.000	.000	0	-97	-1				.667	-0	/C-1,O-1(0-1-0)	-0.1
Total	1	20	69	2	9	0	0	0		1		.130	.143	.130	273	-19	-12				.895	-2	/C-18,O-3(0-3-0),S-2	-1.1

■ EDGARDO ALFONZO
Alfonzo, Edgardo Antonio b: 8/11/73, Santa Teresa, Venez. BR/TR, 5'11", 185 lbs. Deb: 4/26/95

YEAR	TM/L	G	AB	R	H	2B	3B	HR	RBI	BB	SO	AVG	OBP	SLG	OPS	OPS+	BR+	SB	CS	SBR	FA	FR	G/POS	TPR
1995	NY-N	101	335	26	93	13	5	4	41	12	37	.278	.305	.382	687	82	-9	1	1	-0	.962	-6	3-58,2-29/S-6	-1.3
1996	NY-N	123	368	36	96	15	2	4	40	25	56	.261	.308	.345	653	75	-13	2	0	0	.974	-2	2-66,3-36,S-15	-1.1
1997	NY-N	151	518	84	163	27	2	10	72	63	56	.315	.394	.432	827	121	18	11	6	0	.967	6	*3-143,S-12/2-3	2.5
1998	NY-N	144	557	94	155	28	2	17	78	65	77	.278	.357	.427	784	107	6	8	3	1	.976	-8	*3-144/S-1	0.0
1999	*NY-N	158	628	123	191	41	1	27	108	85	85	.304	.390	.502	891	127	27	9	2	1	**.993**	-13	*2-158	2.2
2000	*NY-N★	150	544	109	176	40	2	25	94	95	70	.324	.429	.542	971	149	44	3	2	-0	.985	-0	*2-146/D-2	4.7
Total	6	827	2950	472	874	164	14	87	433	345	381	.296	.373	.450	823	115	72	34	14	3	.987	-23	2-402,3-381/S-34,D	7.0

YEAR	TM/L	G	AB	R	H	2B	3B	HR	RBI	BB	SO	AVG	OBP	SLG	OPS	OPS+	BR+	SB	CS	SBR	FA	FR	G/POS	TPR
■ LUIS ALICEA	Alicea, Luis Rene (De Jesus) b: 7/29/65, Santurce, P.R. BB/TR, 5'9", 177 lbs. Deb: 4/23/88																							
1988	StL-N	93	297	20	63	10	4	1	24	25	32	.212	.278	.283	561	61	-15	1	1	-0	.970	4	2-91	-1.0
1991	StL-N	56	68	5	13	3	0	0	0	8	19	.191	.276	.235	512	45	-5	0	1	-0	1.000	-1	2-11/3-2,S-1	-0.7
1992	StL-N	85	265	26	65	9	11	2	32	27	40	.245	.324	.385	709	103	1	2	5	-1	.989	2	2-75/S-4	0.4
1993	StL-N	115	362	50	101	19	3	3	46	47	54	.279	.368	.373	741	101	2	11	1	2	.978	2	2-96/O-4(4-0-0),3-1	1.0
1994	StL-N	88	205	32	57	12	5	5	29	30	38	.278	.378	.459	837	119	6	4	5	-1	.986	4	2-53/O-2(2-0-0)	1.2
1995	*Bos-A	132	419	64	113	20	3	6	44	63	61	.270	.374	.375	749	93	-3	13	10	-1	.977	12	*2-132	1.5
1996	*StL-N	129	380	54	98	26	3	5	42	52	78	.258	.355	.382	736	95	-1	11	3	1	.957	-21	*2-125	-1.6
1997	Ana-A	128	388	59	98	16	7	5	37	69	65	.253	.376	.369	745	96	0	22	8	2	.978	-3	*2-105,3-12/D-6	0.4
1998	*Tex-A	101	259	51	71	15	3	6	33	37	40	.274	.375	.425	800	103	2	4	3	-0	.970	3	2-45,3-26,D-17,/O-2L	0.6
1999	Tex-A	68	164	33	33	10	0	3	17	28	32	.201	.318	.317	635	60	-10	2	1	0	.980	2	2-37,3-10/O-1L,D-7	-0.6
2000	Tex-A	139	540	85	159	25	8	6	63	59	75	.294	.369	.404	773	93	-5	1	3	-1	.978	-23	*2-130/3-8,S-2,D	-2.1
Total	11	1134	3347	479	871	165	47	42	367	445	534	.260	.354	.375	730	92	-26	71	41	1	.975	-21	2-900/3-59,D-34,OS	-0.9
■ ANDY ALLANSON	Allanson, Andrew Neal b: 12/22/61, Richmond, Va. BR/TR, 6'5", 225 lbs. Deb: 4/7/86																							
1986	Cle-A	101	293	30	66	7	3	1	29	14	36	.225	.263	.280	543	49	-21	10	1	2	.960	-7	C-99	-2.2
1987	Cle-A	50	154	17	41	6	0	3	16	9	30	.266	.307	.364	670	76	-5	1	1	-0	.986	-7	C-50	-1.0
1988	Cle-A	133	434	44	114	11	0	5	50	25	63	.263	.307	.323	630	75	-14	5	9	-2	.986	1	*C-133	-0.8
1989	Cle-A	111	323	30	75	9	1	3	17	23	47	.232	.291	.294	586	64	-15	4	4	-1	.986	3	*C-111	-0.6
1991	Det-A	60	151	10	35	10	0	1	16	7	31	.232	.266	.318	584	60	-8	0	1	-0	.979	6	C-56/1-2,D-1	-0.1
1992	Mil-A	9	25	6	8	1	0	0	0	1	2	.320	.346	.360	706	100	-0	3	1	0	.943	-2	/C-9	-0.1
1993	SF-N	13	24	3	4	1	0	0	2	1	2	.167	.200	.208	408	10	-3	0	0	0	1.000	-1	/C-8,1-2	-0.4
1995	Cal-A	35	82	5	14	3	0	3	10	7	12	.171	.244	.317	562	45	-7	0	1	-0	.994	5	C-35	0.0
Total	8	512	1486	145	357	48	4	16	140	87	223	.240	.286	.310	597	64	-74	23	18	-1	.980	-1	C-501/1-4,D-1	-5.2
■ NICK ALLEN	Allen, Artemus Ward b: 9/14/1888, Norton, Kan. d: 10/16/39, Hines, Ill. BR/TR, 6', 180 lbs. Deb: 5/1/14																							
1914	Buf-F	32	63	3	15	1	0	0	4	3	12	.238	.273	.254	527	43	-6	4			.969	2	C-26	-0.3
1915	Buf-F	84	215	14	44	7	1	0	17	18	34	.205	.269	.247	516	45	-19	4			.956	7	C-80	-0.7
1916	Chi-N	5	16	1	1	0	0	0	1	0	3	.063	.063	.063	125	-56	-3	0			.958	-1	/C-4	-0.4
1918	Cin-N	37	96	6	25	2	2	0	5	4	7	.260	.297	.323	620	91	-1	0			.950	8	C-31	0.9
1919	Cin-N	15	25	7	8	0	1	0	5	2	6	.320	.393	.400	793	142	1	0			.958	3	C-12	0.5
1920	Cin-N	43	85	10	23	3	1	0	4	6	11	.271	.340	.329	670	94	-0	0	0	0	.961	6	C-36	0.9
Total	6	216	500	41	116	13	5	0	36	33	73	.232	.288	.278	566	62	-28	8	0		.958	25	C-189	0.9
■ BERNIE ALLEN	Allen, Bernard Keith b: 4/16/39, E.Liverpool, O. BL/TR, 6', 185 lbs. Deb: 4/10/62																							
1962	Min-A	159	573	79	154	27	7	12	64	62	82	.269	.340	.403	743	96	-3	0	1	-0	.983	-17	*2-158	-0.7
1963	Min-A	139	421	52	101	20	1	9	43	38	52	.240	.304	.356	661	83	-10	0	0	0	.976	-24	*2-128	-2.6
1964	Min-A	74	243	28	52	8	1	6	20	33	30	.214	.310	.329	640	78	-7	1	2	-0	.979	-11	2-71	-1.3
1965	Min-A	19	39	2	9	2	0	0	6	6	8	.231	.333	.282	615	73	-1	0	0	0	1.000	-2	2-10/3-1	-0.2
1966	Min-A	101	319	34	76	18	1	5	30	26	40	.238	.300	.348	648	80	-8	2	3	-1	.974	-7	2-89/3-2	-0.8
1967	Was-A	87	254	13	49	5	1	3	18	18	43	.193	.246	.256	502	51	-16	1	2	-0	.990	19	2-75	0.9
1968	Was-A	120	373	31	90	12	4	6	40	28	35	.241	.301	.343	644	98	-1	2	0	0	**.991**	5	*2-110/3-2	1.4
1969	Was-A	122	365	33	90	17	4	9	45	50	35	.247	.337	.389	726	108	4	5	4	-0	.974	3	*2-110/3-6	1.4
1970	Was-A	104	261	31	61	7	1	8	29	43	21	.234	.342	.360	702	99	0	0	2	-1	.969	-0	2-80,3-12	0.4
1971	Was-A	97	229	18	61	11	1	4	22	33	27	.266	.359	.376	734	115	5	2	1	0	.961	-11	2-41,3-34	-0.4
1972	NY-A	84	220	26	50	9	0	9	21	23	42	.227	.300	.391	691	108	2	0	1	-0	.940	-0	3-44,2-20	0.2
1973	NY-A	17	57	5	13	3	0	0	4	5	5	.228	.290	.281	571	64	-3	0	0	0	.985	0	2-13/D-2	-0.2
	Mon-N	16	50	5	9	1	0	2	9	5	4	.180	.255	.320	575	56	-3	0	0	0	.970	-1	/2-9,3-8	-0.4
Total	12	1139	3404	357	815	140	21	73	351	370	424	.239	.315	.357	673	91	-41	13	16	-3	.980	-47	2-914,3-109/D-2	-2.3
■ JACK ALLEN	Allen, Cyrus Alban b: 10/2/1855, Woodstock, Ill. d: 4/21/15, Girard, Pa. BR/TR, 160 lbs. Deb: 5/1/1879																							
1879	Syr-N	11	48	7	9	2	1	0	3	1	5	.188	.204	.271	475	62	-2				.655	-6	/3-8,O-3(0-0-3)	-0.7
	Cle-N	16	60	7	7	1	1	0	4	1	9	.117	.131	.167	298	-3	-6				.845	3	3-14/O-2(0-2-0)	-0.3
	Yr	27	108	14	16	3	2	0	7	2	14	.148	.164	.213	377	24	-8				.790	-3	3-22/O-5(0-2-3)	-1.0
■ DUSTY ALLEN	Allen, Dustin R. b: 8/9/72, Oklahoma City, Okla. BR/TR, 6'4", 215 lbs. Deb: 7/1/2000 Career OF: (3-LF 0-CF 0-RF)																							
2000	SD-N	9	12	0	0	0	0	0	0	2	5	.000	.143	.000	143	-64	-3	0	0	0	1.000	-0	/O-2(2-0-0),1-1,D-1	-0.3
	Det-A	18	16	5	7	2	0	2	2	2	7	.438	.500	.938	1438	261	4	0	0	0	1.000	-1	1-17/3-1,O-1(1-0-0)	0.2
Total	1	27	28	5	7	2	0	2	2	4	12	.250	.344	.536	879	123	1	0	0	0	1.000	-1	/1-18,O-3L,3-1,D-1	-0.1
■ ETHAN ALLEN	Allen, Ethan Nathan b: 1/1/04, Cincinnati, Ohio d: 9/15/93, Brookings, Ore. BR/TR, 6'1", 180 lbs. Deb: 6/21/26																							
1926	Cin-N	18	13	3	4	1	0	0	0	0	3	.308	.308	.385	692	88	-0	0			1.000	-3	/O-9(5-0-4)	-0.3
1927	Cin-N	111	359	54	106	26	4	2	20	14	23	.295	.325	.407	732	98	-2	12			.988	-2	O-98(14-72-13)	-0.9
1928	Cin-N	129	485	55	148	30	7	1	62	27	29	.305	.343	.402	745	96	-4	6			.981	3	*O-129(1-128-0)	-0.7
1929	Cin-N	143	538	69	157	27	11	6	64	20	21	.292	.317	.416	734	84	-15	21			**.988**	-10	*O-137(24-134-10)	-3.0
1930	Cin-N	21	46	10	10	1	0	3	7	5	2	.217	.294	.435	729	77	-2	1			.969	-2	O-15(1-13-1)	-0.4
	NY-N	76	238	48	73	9	2	7	31	12	23	.307	.340	.450	790	91	-4	5			.985	-4	O-62(1-54-7)	-1.0
	Yr	97	284	58	83	10	2	10	38	17	25	.292	.332	.447	779	89	-6	6			.981	-6	O-77(2-67-8)	-1.4
1931	NY-N	94	298	58	98	18	2	5	43	15	15	.329	.363	.453	816	121	8	6			.975	-7	O-77(40-23-14)	-0.2
1932	NY-N	54	103	13	18	6	2	1	7	1	12	.175	.198	.301	499	33	-10	0			.957	-4	O-24(11-13-0)	-1.4
1933	StL-N	91	261	25	63	7	3	0	36	13	22	.241	.280	.291	571	60	-13	3			.984	8	O-67(0-46-21)	-0.8
1934	Phi-N	145	581	87	192	**42**	4	10	85	33	47	.330	.370	.468	838	108	7	6			.978	9	*O-145(87-47-16)	0.9
1935	Phi-N	156	645	90	198	46	1	8	63	43	54	.307	.351	.419	770	96	-3	5			.980	17	*O-156(19-136-1)	0.9
1936	Phi-N	30	125	21	37	3	1	1	9	4	8	.296	.318	.360	678	75	-4	4			.954	-0	O-30(11-16-6)	-0.6
	Chi-N	91	373	47	110	18	6	3	39	13	30	.295	.322	.399	722	91	-5	12			.980	-2	O-89(73-16-0)	-1.2
	Yr	121	498	68	147	21	7	4	48	17	38	.295	.321	.390	711	87	-10	16			.972	-3	*O-119(84-32-6)	-1.8
1937	StL-A	103	320	39	101	18	1	0	31	21	17	.316	.360	.378	738	86	-7	3	4	-1	.980	-1	O-78(12-54-14)	-1.0
1938	StL-A	19	33	4	10	3	1	0	4	2	4	.303	.343	.455	797	98	-0	0	0	0	1.000	-1	/O-7(2-5-0)	-0.2
Total	13	1281	4418	623	1325	255	45	47	501	223	310	.300	.336	.410	745	92	-55	84	4		.981	-0	*O-1123(301-757-107)	-9.9
■ SLED ALLEN	Allen, Fletcher Manson b: 8/23/1886, West Plains, Mo. d: 10/16/59, Lubbock, Tex. BR/TR, 6'1", 180 lbs. Deb: 5/4/10																							
1910	StL-A	14	23	3	3	1	0	0	1	1		.130	.231	.174	405	29	-2	0			.903	-6	C-12/1-1	-0.8
■ HANK ALLEN	Allen, Harold Andrew b: 7/23/40, Wampum, Pa. BR/TR, 6', 190 lbs. Deb: 9/9/66 F Career OF: (137-LF 95-CF 72-RF)																							
1966	Was-A	9	31	2	12	0	0	1	6	3	6	.387	.441	.484	925	167	3	0	0	0	.917	0	/O-9(8-0-3)	0.2
1967	Was-A	116	292	34	68	8	4	3	17	13	53	.233	.266	.318	584	75	-10	3	4	-1	.980	-21	O-99(59-65-1)	-3.9
1968	Was-A	68	128	16	28	2	2	1	9	7	16	.219	.265	.289	554	70	-5	0	0	0	.895	-8	O-25R,3-16,2-11	-1.5
1969	Was-A	109	271	42	75	9	3	1	17	13	28	.277	.312	.343	655	88	-5	12	3	2	.933	-17	O-91L/3-6,2-3	-2.5
1970	Was-A	22	38	3	8	2	0	0	4	5	9	.211	.302	.263	565	60	-2	0	0	0	1.000	-3	O-17(5-3-10)	-0.6
	Mil-A	28	61	4	14	4	0	0	4	7	5	.230	.309	.295	604	67	-3	0	1	-0	1.000	-1	O-14(1-11-2)/2-5,1-4	-0.5
	Yr	50	99	7	22	6	0	0	8	12	14	.222	.306	.283	589	65	-5	0	1	-0	1.000	-4	O-31(6-14-12)/2-5,1-4	-1.1
1972	Chi-A	9	21	1	3	0	0	0	0	0	2	.143	.143	.143	286	-15	-3	0	0	0	.905	3	/3-6	0.0
1973	Chi-A	28	39	2	4	2	0	0	0	1	9	.103	.125	.154	279	-21	-6	0	1	-0	1.000	-0	/3-9,1-8,O-5L,C2	-0.8
Total	7	389	881	104	212	27	9	6	57	49	128	.241	.282	.312	594	74	-31	15	9	0	.957	-48	O-260L/3-37,2-20,1C	-9.6
■ HEZEKIAH ALLEN	Allen, Hezekiah "Ki" b: 2/25/1863, Westport, Conn. d: 9/21/16, Saugatuck, Conn. 5'11", 160 lbs. Deb: 5/16/1884																							
1884	Phi-N	1	3	0	2	0	0	0	0	0	0	.667	.667	.667	1333	337	1				1.000	-1	/C-1	0.0
■ HAM ALLEN	Allen, Homer S. b: 8/1854, Hamden, Conn. d: 1/7/1892, Hamden, Conn. Deb: 4/27/1872																							
1872	Man-n	17	70	9	19	1	0	0	7	0	1	.271	.271	.286	557	76	-1	0	0	0	.811	7	/S-9,O-9(4-3-2)	0.4

YEAR	TM/L	G	AB	R	H	2B	3B	HR	RBI	BB	SO	AVG	OBP	SLG	OPS	OPS+	BR+	SB	CS	SBR	FA	FR	G/POS	TPR
■ HORACE ALLEN	Allen, Horace Tanner "Pug" b: 6/11/1899, DeLand, Fla. d: 7/5/81, Canton, N.C. BL/TR, 6', 187 lbs. Deb: 6/15/19																							
1919	Bro-N	4	7	0	0	0	0	0	0	0	2	.000	.000	.000	0	-98	-2	0			1.000	0	/O-2(1-1-0)	-0.2
■ JAMIE ALLEN	Allen, James Bradley b: 5/29/58, Yakima, Wash. BR/TR, 6', 205 lbs. Deb: 5/1/83																							
1983	Sea-A	86	273	23	61	10	0	4	21	33	52	.223	.309	.304	613	67	-12	6	5	-0	.959	-6	3-82/D-2	-1.9
■ PETE ALLEN	Allen, Jesse Hall b: 5/1/1868, Columbiana, Ohio d: 4/16/46, Philadelphia, Pa. BR/TR, 5'8.5", 185 lbs. Deb: 8/4/1893																							
1893	Cle-N	1	4	0	0	0	0	0	0	0	0	.000	.000	.000	0	-94	-1	0			1.000	-1	/C-1	-0.2
■ CHAD ALLEN	Allen, John Chad b: 2/6/75, Dallas, Tex. BR/TR, 6'1", 195 lbs. Deb: 4/6/99																							
1999	Min-A	137	481	69	133	21	3	10	46	37	89	.277	.331	.395	726	81	-14	14	7	1	.975	5	*O-133(133-0-1)/D-2	-1.1
2000	Min-A	15	50	2	15	3	0	0	7	3	14	.300	.352	.360	712	77	-2	0	2	-1	1.000	1	O-15(2-0-13)	-0.2
Total	2	152	531	71	148	24	3	10	53	40	103	.279	.333	.392	724	81	-15	14	9	-0	.977	6	O-148(135-0-14)/D-2	-1.3
■ KIM ALLEN	Allen, Kim Bryant b: 4/5/53, Fontana, Cal. BR/TR, 5'11", 175 lbs. Deb: 9/2/80 Career OF: (3-LF 2-CF 2-RF)																							
1980	Sea-A	23	51	9	12	3	0	0	3	8	3	.235	.350	.294	644	78	-1	10	3	1	.970	-2	2-15/O-4(3-0-2),S-1	-0.2
1981	Sea-A	19	3	1	0	0	0	0	0	0	2	.000	.000	.000	0	-96	-1	2	1	0	.000	-1	/2-2,O-2(0-2-0),D-2	-0.2
Total	2	42	54	10	12	3	0	0	3	8	5	.222	.333	.278	611	69	-2	12	4	1	.970	-4	/2-17,O-6L,D-2,S-1	-0.4
■ MYRON ALLEN	Allen, Myron Smith "Zeke" b: 3/22/1854, Kingston, N.Y. d: 3/8/24, Kingston, N.Y. BR/TR, 5'8", 150 lbs. Deb: 7/19/1883 Career OF: (106-LF 3-CF 41-RF)																							
1883	NY-N	1	4	0	0	0	0	0	1	0	2	.000	.000	.000	0	-99	-1				1.000	-0	/P-1	0.0
1886	Bos-N	1	3	0	0	0	0	0	0	0	1	.000	.000	.000	0	-99	-1	0			1.000	-0	/2-1	-0.1
1887	Cle-a	117	499	66	164	22	10	4	77	36		.329	.335	.393	728	106	4	26			.894	8	*O-115L/3-3,S-2,P-2	0.8
1888	KC-a	37	136	23	29	6	4	0	10	9		.213	.267	.316	583	81	-3	4			.931	7	O-35(33-2-0)/P-2	0.2
Total	4	156	642	89	193	28	14	4	88	45	3	.301	.317	.371	688	98	-1	30			.903	15	O-150L/P-5,3-3,S2	0.9
■ DICK ALLEN	Allen, Richard Anthony b: 3/8/42, Wampum, Pa. BR/TR, 5'11", 190 lbs. Deb: 9/3/63 F Career OF: (256-LF 1-CF 0-RF)																							
1963	Phi-N	10	24	6	7	2	1	0	2	0	5	.292	.292	.458	750	114	0	0	0	0	.833	-1	/O-7(7-0-0),3-1	-0.1
1964	Phi-N	162	632	**125**	201	38	**13**	29	91	67	138	.318	.383	.557	940	163	52	3	4	-1	.921	7	*3-162	6.0
1965	Phi-N★	161	619	93	187	31	14	20	85	74	150	.302	.378	.494	873	146	38	15	2	3	.943	-2	*3-160/S-2	4.0
1966	Phi-N★	141	524	112	166	25	10	40	110	68	136	.317	.398	**.632**	**1030**	**181**	**57**	10	6	0	.967	-8	3-91,O-47(47-0-0)	4.7
1967	Phi-N★	122	463	89	142	31	10	23	77	75	117	.307	**.404**	.566	**970**	**173**	45	20	5	3	.908	-6	*3-121/2-1,S-1	4.4
1968	Phi-N	152	521	87	137	17	9	33	90	74	161	.263	.356	.520	876	160	38	7	7	-1	.973	-5	*O-139(139-1-0),3-10	2.7
1969	Phi-N	118	438	79	126	23	3	32	89	64	144	.288	.378	.573	952	168	39	9	3	1	.985	-9	*1-117	2.2
1970	StL-N★	122	459	88	128	17	5	34	101	71	118	.279	.378	.560	938	145	28	5	4	-0	.993	-12	1-79,3-38/O-3(3-0-0)	1.0
1971	LA-N	155	549	82	162	24	1	23	90	93	113	.295	.398	.468	866	154	41	8	1	1	.918	-8	3-67,O-60L,1-28	3.1
1972	Chi-A★	148	506	90	156	28	5	**37**	**113**	**99**	126	.308	**.422**	**.603**	**1025**	**199**	**64**	19	8	1	.995	-4	*1-143/3-2	5.5
1973	Chi-A†	72	250	39	79	20	3	16	41	33	51	.316	.398	.612	1010	175	24	7	2	1	.994	0	1-67/2-2,D-1	2.0
1974	Chi-A★	128	462	84	139	23	1	**32**	88	57	89	.301	.379	**.563**	**942**	164	37	7	1	1	.986	-11	*1-125/2-1,D-1	1.8
1975	Phi-N	119	416	54	97	21	3	12	62	58	109	.233	.330	.385	714	94	-3	11	2	2	.982	-1	*1-113	-1.2
1976	*Phi-N	85	298	52	80	16	1	15	49	37	63	.268	.349	.480	829	130	11	11	4	1	.989	-3	1-85	0.2
1977	Oak-A	54	171	19	41	4	0	5	31	24	36	.240	.337	.351	688	89	-2	1	3	-1	.984	2	1-50/D-1	-0.4
Total	15	1749	6332	1099	1848	320	79	351	1119	894	1556	.292	.381	.534	914	156	470	133	52	11	.989	-62	1-807,3-652,O/2DS	35.9
■ BOB ALLEN	Allen, Robert (b: Alvah Charles Elliott) b: 10/13/1894, Muscoda, Wis. d: 12/18/75, Naperville, Ill. BR/TR, 5'10", 180 lbs. Deb: 8/20/19																							
1919	Phi-A	9	22	3	3	1	0	0	0	3	7	.136	.269	.182	451	27	-2	0			.889	-2	/O-6(0-6-0)	-0.5
■ BOB ALLEN	Allen, Robert Gilman b: 7/10/1867, Marion, Ohio d: 5/14/43, Little Rock, Ark. BR/TR, 5'11", 175 lbs. Deb: 4/19/1890 M																							
1890	Phi-N	133	456	69	103	15	11	2	57	87	54	.226	.356	.320	676	95	-0	13			.924	**39**	*S-133/M	3.7
1891	Phi-N	118	438	46	97	7	4	1	51	43	44	.221	.291	.263	554	60	-22	12			.896	13	*S-118	-0.5
1892	Phi-N	152	563	77	128	20	14	2	64	61	60	.227	.304	.323	627	90	-7	15			.919	18	*S-152	1.8
1893	Phi-N	124	471	86	126	19	12	8	90	71	40	.268	.369	.410	779	107	5	8			.919	19	*S-124	2.5
1894	Phi-N	41	154	27	40	10	4	0	19	17	11	.260	.337	.377	714	74	-7	4			.917	-0	S-41	-0.4
1897	Bos-N	34	119	33	38	5	0	1	24	18		.319	.409	.387	795	104	1	1			.924	8	S-32/O-1(0-1-0),2-1	0.9
1900	Cin-N	5	15	0	2	1	0	0	1	0		.133	.188	.200	388	7	-2	0			.864	-0	/S-5,M	-0.2
Total	7	607	2216	338	534	77	45	14	306	297	209	.241	.334	.335	669	88	-32	53			.915	96	S-605/2-1,O-1(0-1-0)	7.8
■ ROD ALLEN	Allen, Roderick Bernet b: 10/5/59, Los Angeles, Cal. BR/TR, 6'1", 185 lbs. Deb: 4/7/83																							
1983	Sea-A	11	12	1	2	0	0	0	0	0	1	.167	.167	.167	333	-8	-2	0	0	0	1.000	0	/O-2(0-0-2),D-3	-0.2
1984	Det-A	15	27	6	8	1	0	0	3	2	8	.296	.367	.333	700	96	-0	1	0	0	1.000	-0	D-11/O-2(2-0-0)	-0.1
1988	Cle-A	5	11	1	1	1	0	0	0	0	2	.091	.091	.182	273	-25	-2	0	0	0	.000	0	/D-4	-0.2
Total	3	31	50	8	11	2	0	0	3	2	11	.220	.264	.260	524	45	-4	1	0	0	1.000	-0	/D-18,O-4(2-0-2)	-0.5
■ RON ALLEN	Allen, Ronald Frederick b: 12/23/43, Wampum, Pa. BB/TR, 6'3", 205 lbs. Deb: 8/11/72 F																							
1972	StL-N	7	11	2	1	0	0	1	1	3	5	.091	.286	.364	649	84	-0	0	0	0	.968	-0	/1-5	-0.1
■ GARY ALLENSON	Allenson, Gary Martin b: 2/4/55, Culver City, Cal. BR/TR, 5'11", 185 lbs. Deb: 4/8/79 C																							
1979	Bos-A	108	241	27	49	10	2	3	22	20	42	.203	.267	.299	566	50	-17	1	1	-0	.980	9	*C-104/3-3	-0.5
1980	Bos-A	36	70	9	25	6	0	0	10	13	11	.357	.458	.443	901	141	5	2	2	-0	.981	4	C-24/3-5,D-6	0.9
1981	Bos-A	47	139	23	31	8	0	5	25	23	33	.223	.337	.388	726	102	1	0	0	0	.969	1	C-47	0.4
1982	Bos-A	92	264	25	54	11	0	6	33	38	39	.205	.307	.314	621	67	-11	0	3	-1	.992	8	C-91	-0.1
1983	Bos-A	84	230	19	53	11	0	3	30	27	43	.230	.317	.317	634	70	-9	0	1	-0	.984	4	C-84	-0.2
1984	Bos-A	35	83	9	19	2	0	2	8	9	14	.229	.304	.325	630	71	-3	0	0	0	.987	0	C-35	-0.2
1985	Tor-A	14	34	2	4	1	0	0	3	0	10	.118	.118	.147	265	-27	-6	0	0	0	1.000	-2	C-14	-0.7
Total	7	416	1061	114	235	49	2	19	131	130	192	.221	.309	.325	635	71	-41	3	7	-2	.984	25	C-399/3-8,D-6	-0.4
■ JERMAINE ALLENSWORTH	Allensworth, Jermaine Lamont b: 1/11/72, Anderson, Ind. BR/TR, 6', 189 lbs. Deb: 7/23/96																							
1996	Pit-N	61	229	32	60	9	3	4	31	23	50	.262	.340	.380	720	87	-4	11	6	0	.979	4	O-61(0-61-0)	0.1
1997	Pit-N	108	369	55	94	18	2	3	43	44	79	.255	.345	.339	684	79	-10	14	7	1	.980	-2	*O-104(0-104-0)	-1.1
1998	Pit-N	69	233	30	72	13	3	3	24	17	43	.309	.374	.429	803	109	4	8	4	0	.980	3	O-66(0-66-0)	0.7
	KC-A	30	73	15	15	5	0	0	3	9	17	.205	.326	.274	600	57	-4	7	0	2	.982	-3	O-27(1-24-2)	-0.5
	NY-N	34	54	9	11	2	0	2	4	2	16	.204	.246	.352	597	56	-4	0	2	-1	1.000	-8	O-31(4-4-25)	-1.3
1999	NY-N	40	73	14	16	2	0	3	9	9	23	.219	.313	.370	683	74	-3	2	1	0	1.000	-5	O-33(10-14-15)	-0.8
Total	4	342	1031	155	268	49	8	15	114	104	228	.260	.342	.367	708	84	-22	42	20	2	.982	-11	O-322(15-273-42)	-2.9
■ GENE ALLEY	Alley, Leonard Eugene b: 7/10/40, Richmond, Va. BR/TR, 6', 165 lbs. Deb: 9/4/63																							
1963	Pit-N	17	51	3	11	1	0	0	0	2	12	.216	.245	.235	481	39	-4	0	1	-0	.947	1	/3-7,2-4,S-4	-0.3
1964	Pit-N	81	209	30	44	3	1	6	13	21	56	.211	.289	.321	609	72	-8	0	1	-0	.966	24	S-61/3-3,2-1	2.1
1965	Pit-N	153	500	47	126	21	6	5	47	32	82	.252	.302	.348	650	82	-12	7	2	1	.968	**30**	*S-110,2-40/3-1	3.2
1966	Pit-N	147	579	88	173	28	10	7	43	27	83	.299	.336	.418	753	108	6	8	8	-1	.979	13	*S-143	3.1
1967	Pit-N★	152	550	59	158	25	7	6	55	36	70	.287	.339	.391	730	108	6	10	5	0	.967	8	*S-146	2.8
1968	Pit-N†	133	474	48	116	20	2	4	39	39	78	.245	.309	.321	630	91	-5	13	5	1	.974	26	*S-109,2-24	3.7
1969	Pit-N	82	285	28	70	3	2	8	32	19	48	.246	.295	.354	649	83	-7	4	0	1	.977	7	2-53,S-25/3-5	0.7
1970	*Pit-N	121	426	46	104	16	5	8	41	31	70	.244	.300	.362	662	78	-14	7	3	0	.975	34	*S-108/2-8,3-2	3.2
1971	*Pit-N	114	348	38	79	8	7	6	28	35	43	.227	.298	.342	640	81	-9	9	2	1	.958	-16	*S-108/3-1	-1.2
1972	*Pit-N	119	347	30	86	12	2	3	36	38	52	.248	.322	.320	642	85	-6	4	3	-0	.970	-5	*S-114/3-4	0.1
1973	Pit-N	76	158	25	32	3	2	2	8	20	28	.203	.292	.285	577	62	-8	1	0	0	.981	5	S-49/3-8	0.2
Total	11	1195	3927	442	999	140	44	55	342	300	622	.254	.312	.354	666	88	-62	63	30	3	.970	125	S-977,2-130/3-31	17.6
■ GAIR ALLIE	Allie, Gair Roosevelt b: 10/28/31, Statesville, N.C. BR/TR, 6'1", 190 lbs. Deb: 4/13/54																							
1954	Pit-N	121	418	38	83	8	6	3	30	56	84	.199	.296	.268	564	49	-31	1	1	-0	.952	-16	S-95,3-19	-3.9

YEAR	TM/L	G	AB	R	H	2B	3B	HR	RBI	BB	SO	AVG	OBP	SLG	OPS	OPS+	BR+	SB	CS	SBR	FA	FR	G/POS	TPR
■ **BOB ALLIETTA**	Allietta, Robert George b: 5/1/52, New Bedford, Mass. BR/TR, 6', 190 lbs. Deb: 5/6/75																							
1975	Cal-A	21	45	4	8	1	0	1	2	1	6	.178	.196	.267	462	32	-4	0	0	0	1.000	2	C-21	-0.2
■ **ANDY ALLISON**	Allison, Andrew K. b: 1848, New York, N.Y. 5'10", 150 lbs. Deb: 5/7/1872 M																							
1872	Eck-n	24	93	11	15	3	0	0	9	0	3	.161	.161	.194	355	10	-8	0	0	0	.913	-2	1-22/O-1(0-0-1),M	-0.6
■ **ART ALLISON**	Allison, Arthur Algernon b: 1/29/1849, Philadelphia, Pa. d: 2/25/16, Washington, D.C. 5'8", 150 lbs. Deb: 5/4/1871 F Career OF: (8-LF 56-CF 45-RF)																							
1871	Cle-n	29	137	28	40	4	5	0	19	2	5	.292	.302	.394	696	104	1	3	1	0	.885	1	*O-29(0-29-0)/2-2	0.2
1872	Cle-n	19	87	13	23	4	0	0	8	0	2	.264	.264	.310	575	80	-1	0	0	0	.804	0	O-19(0-17-2)	-0.1
1873	Res-n	23	99	12	32	2	0	0	11	0	0	.323	.323	.343	667	106	1	0	0	0	.848	-2	O-21(8-9-4)/1-3,C-1	0.0
1875	Was-n	26	112	18	24	3	1	0	3	1	2	.214	.221	.259	480	69	-3	6	0	1	.924	-3	1-23/O-3(0-1-2),C-1	-0.4
	Har-n	40	175	26	42	4	1	1	19	0	3	.240	.240	.291	531	80	-4	1	2	-0	.785	4	O-37R/2-2,C-1,1-1	0.1
	Yr	66	287	44	66	7	2	1	22	1	5	.230	.233	.279	511	76	-7	7	2	1	.800	1	O-40R,1-24/C-2,2-2	-0.3
1876	Lou-N	31	132	9	27	2	1	0	10	2	6	.205	.220	.238	458	45	-8				.789	6	O-23(0-0-23)/1-8	-0.3
Total	4 n	137	610	97	161	17	7	1	60	3	12	.264	.268	.320	587	88	-6	10	3	1	.833	1	O-109C/1-27,2-4,C-3	-0.2
■ **DOUG ALLISON**	Allison, Douglas L. b: 7/1845, Philadelphia, Pa. d: 12/19/16, Washington, D.C. BR/TR, 5'10.5", 160 lbs. Deb: 5/5/1871 FM NA OF: (0-LF 4-CF 49-RF)																							
1871	Oly-n	27	133	28	44	10	2	2	27	0	2	.331	.331	.481	812	137	7	1	1	-0	.806	-3	*C-27	0.2
1872	Tro-n	23	115	23	35	4	2	0	20	1	3	.304	.310	.374	684	108	1	1	1	-0	.897	6	C-22/S-1	0.5
	Eck-n	18	79	18	27	2	1	0	5	1	2	.342	.350	.392	742	151	6	0	0	0	.837	-8	C-18	-0.2
	Yr	41	194	41	62	6	3	0	25	2	5	.320	.327	.381	708	124	6	1	1	-0	.874	-2	C-40/S-1	0.3
1873	Res-n	19	83	11	24	5	0	0	8	0	0	.289	.289	.349	639	96	0	0	0	0	.810	-0	C-18/O-3(0-1-2),M	0.0
	Mut-n	11	48	6	10	0	0	0	3	1	0	.208	.224	.208	433	30	-4	0	0	0	.868	1	C-11/O-1(0-0-1)	-0.2
	Yr	30	131	17	34	5	0	0	11	1	0	.260	.265	.298	563	71	-4	0	0	0	.837	1	C-29/O-4(0-1-3)	-0.2
1874	Mut-n	65	318	68	90	7	5	0	28	6	5	.283	.296	.336	633	99	-1	1	0	0	.800	-4	*O-47R,C-34/2-1	-0.2
1875	Har-n	61	269	38	67	7	0	0	21	6	3	.249	.265	.275	541	84	-5	2	0	0	**.896**	17	*C-59/1-2,O-2(0-0-2)	1.1
1876	Har-N	44	166	19	43	4	0	0	15	3	9	.259	.277	.288	565	82	-4				**.881**	11	C-40/O-6(0-1-5)	0.7
1877	Har-N	29	115	14	17	2	0	0	6	3	7	.148	.169	.165	335	7	-11				.896	2	C-29	-0.8
1878	Pro-N	19	76	9	22	2	0	0	7	1	8	.289	.299	.316	614	102	0				.911	-0	C-19/P-1	0.1
1879	Pro-N	1	5	0	0	0	0	0	0	0	1	.000	.000	.000	0	-99	-1				.833	0	/C-1	-0.1
1883	Bal-a	1	3	2	2	0	0	0	0			.667	.667	.667	1333	321	1				.000	-1	/O-1(0-1-0),C-1	0.0
Total	5 n	224	1045	192	297	35	10	2	112	15	15	.284	.294	.343	637	101	4	5	2	0	.861	9	C-189/O-53R,1-2,2S	1.2
Total	5	94	365	44	84	8	0	0	28	7	25	.230	.247	.254	501	63	-15				.892	12	/C-90,O-7(0-2-5),P-1	-0.1
■ **MILO ALLISON**	Allison, Milo Henry b: 10/16/1889, Elk Rapids, Mich. d: 6/18/57, Kenosha, Wis. BL/TR, 5'10", 155 lbs. Deb: 9/26/13																							
1913	Chi-N	2	6	1	2	0	0	0	0	0	1	.333	.333	.333	667	91	-0	1			1.000	0	/O-1(0-1-0)	0.0
1914	Chi-N	1	1	0	1	0	0	0	0	0	0	1.000	1.000	1.000	2000	497	0	0			.000	0	H	0.0
1916	Cle-A	14	18	10	5	0	0	0	0	6	1	.278	.458	.278	736	115	1	0			1.000	-1	/O-5(1-0-4)	0.0
1917	Cle-A	32	35	4	5	0	0	0	0	9	7	.143	.318	.143	461	38	-2	3			1.000	-3	O-11(4-5-2)	-0.6
Total	4	49	60	15	13	0	0	0	0	15	9	.217	.373	.217	590	74	-1	4			1.000	-4	/O-17(5-6-6)	-0.6
■ **BILL ALLISON**	Allison, William Andrew b: 9/18/1848, Philadelphia, Pa. d: 6/12/23, Deb: 5/21/1872																							
1872	Eck-n	5	19	5	3	0	0	0	1	0	1	.158	.158	.158	316	-3	-2	0	0	0	.923	-2	/1-2,O-2(0-1-1),2-1	-0.2
■ **BOB ALLISON**	Allison, William Robert b: 7/11/34, Raytown, Mo. d: 4/9/95, Rio Verde, Ariz. BR/TR, 6'4", 220 lbs. Deb: 9/16/58 Career OF: (527-LF 187-CF 631-RF)																							
1958	Was-A	11	35	1	7	1	0	0	0	2	5	.200	.243	.229	472	31	-3	0	2	-1	1.000	-0	O-11(1-10-0)	-0.5
1959	Was-A☆	150	570	83	149	18	**9**	30	85	60	92	.261	.334	.482	816	122	15	13	8	0	.974	-2	*O-149(7-134-9)	0.6
1960	Was-A	144	501	79	126	30	3	15	69	92	94	.251	.370	.413	783	113	11	11	9	-1	.965	9	*O-140(0-4-139)/1-4	1.4
1961	Min-A	159	556	83	136	21	3	29	105	103	100	.245	.367	.450	817	111	10	2	7	-2	.975	7	*O-150(0-0-150),1-18	0.4
1962	Min-A	149	519	102	138	24	8	29	102	84	115	.266	.372	.511	883	130	23	8	5	0	.977	7	*O-147(2-0-146)	2.0
1963	Min-A★	148	527	**99**	143	25	4	35	91	90	109	.271	.381	.533	**914**	**150**	37	6	1	1	.971	11	*O-147(0-8-146)	4.0
1964	Min-A★	149	492	90	141	27	4	32	86	92	99	.287	.406	.553	959	163	44	10	1	2	.986	-4	1-93,O-61(27-28-16)	3.6
1965	*Min-A	135	438	71	102	14	5	23	78	73	114	.233	.345	.445	790	118	11	10	2	2	.972	11	*O-122(122-0-0)/1-3	1.7
1966	Min-A	70	168	34	37	6	1	8	19	30	34	.220	.348	.411	759	110	3	6	0	1	.967	-1	O-56(44-1-11)	0.1
1967	Min-A	153	496	73	128	21	6	24	75	74	114	.258	.357	.470	826	132	21	6	4	-0	.978	-1	*O-145(138-0-9)	1.2
1968	Min-A	145	469	63	116	16	8	22	52	52	98	.247	.325	.456	781	128	15	9	7	-0	.966	-4	*O-117(116-1-1),1-17	0.5
1969	*Min-A	81	189	18	43	8	2	8	27	29	39	.228	.333	.418	751	107	2	2	4	-1	1.000	-3	O-58(58-0-0)/1-3	-0.5
1970	*Min-A	47	72	15	15	5	0	1	7	14	20	.208	.345	.319	664	83	-1	1	0	0	1.000	-3	O-17(12-1-4)/1-7	-0.5
Total	13	1541	5032	811	1281	216	53	256	796	795	1033	.255	.360	.471	831	126	187	84	50	1	.975	27	*O-1320R,1-145	14.0
■ **BEAU ALLRED**	Allred, Dale Le Beau b: 6/4/65, Mesa, Ariz. BL/TL, 6', 190 lbs. Deb: 9/7/89																							
1989	Cle-A	13	24	0	6	3	0	0	1	2	10	.250	.308	.375	683	90	-0	0	0	0	1.000	1	/O-5(3-0-2),D-2	0.1
1990	Cle-A	4	16	2	3	1	0	1	2	2	3	.188	.278	.438	715	98	-0	0	0	0	.833	-1	/O-4(0-3-1)	-0.1
1991	Cle-A	48	125	17	29	3	0	3	12	25	35	.232	.364	.328	692	92	-0	2	2	-0	.972	2	O-42(20-0-27)/D-1	0.1
Total	3	65	165	19	38	7	0	4	15	29	48	.230	.349	.345	694	93	-1	2	2	-0	.969	2	/O-51(23-3-30),D-3	0.1
■ **MEL ALMADA**	Almada, Baldomero Melo (Quiros) b: 2/7/13, Huatabampo, Mexico d: 8/13/88, Hermosillo, Mexico BL/TL, 6', 170 lbs. Deb: 9/8/33																							
1933	Bos-A	14	44	11	15	0	0	1	3	11	3	.341	.473	.409	882	137	3	3	1	0	1.000	-0	O-13(7-6-0)	0.3
1934	Bos-A	23	90	7	21	2	1	0	10	6	8	.233	.281	.278	559	42	-8	3	2	-0	.985	4	O-23(0-16-7)	-0.5
1935	Bos-A	151	607	85	176	27	9	3	59	55	34	.290	.350	.379	729	83	-15	20	9	1	.968	-0	*O-149(0-126-25)/1-3	-1.8
1936	Bos-A	96	320	40	81	16	4	1	21	24	15	.253	.305	.338	643	55	-23	2	4	-1	.987	-2	O-81(11-3-69)	-2.7
1937	Bos-A	32	110	17	26	6	2	1	9	15	6	.236	.328	.355	683	69	-5	0	1	-0	.927	-6	O-27(4-2-21)/1-4	-1.2
	Was-A	100	433	74	134	21	4	4	33	38	21	.309	.365	.404	769	98	-1	12	4	1	.964	14	*O-100(0-97-3)	1.1
	Yr	132	543	91	160	27	6	5	42	53	27	.295	.357	.394	751	91	-7	12	5	1	.960	9	*O-127(4-99-24)/1-4	-0.1
1938	Was-A	47	197	24	48	7	4	1	15	8	16	.244	.277	.335	612	56	-14	4	1	1	.968	5	O-47(0-47-0)	-0.9
	StL-A	102	436	77	149	22	2	3	37	38	22	.342	.398	.422	820	106	5	9	5	0	.966	-1	*O-101(0-101-0)	0.2
	Yr	149	633	101	197	29	6	4	52	46	38	.311	.362	.395	757	92	-8	13	6	1	.967	4	*O-148(0-148-0)	-0.7
1939	StL-A	42	134	17	32	2	1	1	7	10	8	.239	.292	.291	583	48	-10	1	0	0	.987	-3	O-34(3-31-0)	-1.3
	Bro-N	39	112	11	24	4	0	0	3	9	17	.214	.273	.250	523	40	-9	2			.977	2	O-32(0-32-0)	-0.8
Total	7	646	2483	363	706	107	27	15	197	214	150	.284	.342	.367	710	79	-77	56	27		.970	13	O-607(25-461-125)/1-7	-7.6
■ **RAFAEL ALMEIDA**	Almeida, Rafael D. "Mike" b: 6/30/1887, Havana, Cuba d: 3/18/69, Havana, Cuba BR/TR, 5'9", 164 lbs. Deb: 7/4/11 Career OF: (0-LF 3-CF 0-RF)																							
1911	Cin-N	36	96	9	30	5	1	0	15	9	16	.313	.383	.385	769	120	3	3			.890	-2	3-27/2-1,S-1	0.2
1912	Cin-N	16	59	9	13	4	3	0	10	5	8	.220	.281	.390	671	85	-2	0			.891	-2	3-15	-0.3
1913	Cin-N	50	130	14	34	4	2	3	21	11	16	.262	.324	.392	716	104	0	4			.919	4	3-37/O-3C,S-2,2-1	0.6
Total	3	102	285	32	77	13	6	3	46	25	40	.270	.335	.389	725	106	2	7			.904	0	/3-79,O-3C,S-3,2-2	0.5
■ **BILL ALMON**	Almon, William Francis b: 11/21/52, Providence, R.I. BR/TR, 6'3", 190 lbs. Deb: 9/2/74 Career OF: (123-LF 8-CF 35-RF)																							
1974	SD-N	16	38	4	12	1	0	0	3	2	9	.316	.350	.342	692	98	-0	1	0	0	.915	-2	S-14	-0.1
1975	SD-N	6	10	0	4	0	0	0	0	0	1	.400	.400	.400	800	131	0	0	0	0	1.000	1	/S-2	0.1
1976	SD-N	14	57	6	14	3	0	1	6	2	9	.246	.271	.351	622	82	-2	3	1	0	.962	1	S-14	0.2
1977	SD-N	155	613	75	160	18	11	2	43	37	114	.261	.303	.336	639	79	-19	20	9	1	.954	18	*S-155	1.7
1978	SD-N	138	405	39	102	19	2	0	21	33	74	.252	.308	.309	617	79	-12	17	5	2	.933	0	*3-114,S-15/2-7	-1.1
1979	SD-N	100	198	20	45	3	0	1	8	21	48	.227	.301	.258	559	57	-11	6	5	-0	.985	16	2-61,S-25/O-1(0-1-0)	0.8
1980	Mon-N	18	38	2	10	1	1	0	3	1	5	.263	.282	.342	624	73	-1	0	0	0	.911	-2	S-12/2-1	-0.3
	NY-N	48	112	13	19	3	2	0	4	8	27	.170	.225	.232	457	29	-11	2	0	0	.967	9	S-22,2-18/3-9	0.1
	Yr	66	150	15	29	4	3	0	7	9	32	.193	.239	.260	499	40	-12	2	0	0	.948	6	S-34,2-19/3-9	-0.2
1981	Chi-A	103	349	46	105	10	2	4	41	21	60	.301	.344	.375	719	109	4	16	6	1	.969	14	*S-103	3.1
1982	Chi-A	111	308	40	79	10	4	4	26	25	49	.256	.314	.354	668	83	-7	10	8	-1	.949	20	*S-108/D-1	2.2
1983	Oak-A	143	451	45	120	29	1	4	63	26	67	.266	.309	.361	670	89	-7	26	8	3	.941	-31	S-52,3-40,1-38,O/2D	-3.5
1984	Oak-A	106	211	24	47	11	0	7	16	10	42	.223	.258	.374	632	78	-7	5	7	-1	1.000	-9	O-48L,1-44,D-12,/3CS	-2.1

YEAR	TM/L	G	AB	R	H	2B	3B	HR	RBI	BB	SO	AVG	OBP	SLG	OPS	OPS+	BR+	SB	CS	SBR	FA	FR	G/POS	TPR
1985	Pit-N	88	244	33	66	17	0	6	29	22	61	.270	.333	.414	747	109	3	10	7	-0	.987	-22	S-43,O-32L/1-7,3-7	-1.8
1986	Pit-N	102	196	29	43	7	2	7	27	30	38	.219	.323	.383	706	92	-2	11	4	1	.983	-13	O-54L,3-28,S-19,/1	-1.5
1987	Pit-N	19	20	5	4	1	0	0	1	1	5	.200	.238	.250	488	29	-2	0	0	0	.944	1	/S-4,O-2(2-0-0),3-1	-0.1
	NY-N	49	54	8	13	3	0	0	4	8	16	.241	.339	.296	635	74	-2	1	0	0	.972	-3	S-22,2-10/1-2,O-1R	-0.4
	Yr	68	74	13	17	4	0	0	5	9	21	.230	.313	.284	597	62	-4	1	0	0	.963	-2	S-26,2-10/O-3L,13	-0.5
1988	Phi-N	20	26	1	3	2	0	0	1	3	11	.115	.207	.192	399	15	-3	0	0	0	.944	1	/3-9,S-5,1-1	-0.2
Total	15	1236	3330	390	846	138	25	36	296	250	636	.254	.307	.343	650	83	-79	128	60	7	.956	-2	S-616,3-212,O2/1DC	-2.9

■ ROBERTO ALOMAR Alomar, Roberto (Velazquez) b: 2/5/68, Ponce, P.R. BB/TR, 6', 185 lbs. Deb: 4/22/88 F

YEAR	TM/L	G	AB	R	H	2B	3B	HR	RBI	BB	SO	AVG	OBP	SLG	OPS	OPS+	BR+	SB	CS	SBR	FA	FR	G/POS	TPR
1988	SD-N	143	545	84	145	24	6	9	41	47	83	.266	.328	.382	709	105	3	24	6	3	.980	17	*2-143	2.9
1989	SD-N	158	623	82	184	27	1	7	56	53	76	.295	.352	.376	727	108	7	42	17	3	.967	6	*2-157	2.1
1990	SD-N★	147	586	80	168	27	5	6	60	48	72	.287	.343	.381	723	98	-1	24	7	3	.976	-2	*2-137/S-5	0.4
1991	*Tor-A★	161	637	88	188	41	11	9	69	57	86	.295	.357	.436	793	114	12	53	11	**8**	.981	-22	*2-160	0.2
1992	*Tor-A★	152	571	105	177	27	8	8	76	87	52	.310	.406	.427	833	128	25	49	9	8	.993	-24	*2-150/D-1	1.2
1993	*Tor-A★	153	589	109	192	35	6	17	93	80	67	.326	.411	.492	903	141	36	55	15	7	.980	-7	*2-150	4.2
1994	Tor-A★	107	392	78	120	25	4	8	38	51	41	.306	.389	.452	840	115	10	19	8	1	.991	-4	*2-106	1.2
1995	Tor-A★	130	517	71	155	24	7	13	66	47	45	.300	.358	.449	807	109	7	30	3	6	**.994**	-5	*2-128	1.2
1996	*Bal-A★	153	588	132	193	43	4	22	94	90	65	.328	.418	.527	945	138	37	17	6	2	.985	13	*2-141,D-10	5.2
1997	*Bal-A★	112	412	64	137	23	2	14	60	40	43	.333	.396	.500	896	136	22	9	3	1	.988	4	*2-109/D-2	3.0
1998	Bal-A★	147	588	86	166	36	1	14	56	59	70	.282	.350	.418	768	100	1	18	5	2	.985	14	*2-144/D-3	2.2
1999	*Cle-A★	159	563	**138**	182	40	3	24	120	99	96	.323	.430	.533	963	138	35	37	6	6	**.992**	20	*2-156/D-3	**6.2**
2000	Cle-A★	155	610	111	189	40	2	19	89	64	82	.310	.381	.475	856	112	12	39	4	**7**	.980	16	*2-155	3.8
Total	13	1877	7221	1228	2196	412	60	170	918	822	878	.304	.378	.448	827	119	205	416	100	57	.983	24	*2-1836/D-19,S-5	33.8

■ SANDY ALOMAR Alomar, Santos Jr. (Velazquez) b: 6/18/66, Salinas, P.R. BR/TR, 6'5", 215 lbs. Deb: 9/30/88 F

YEAR	TM/L	G	AB	R	H	2B	3B	HR	RBI	BB	SO	AVG	OBP	SLG	OPS	OPS+	BR+	SB	CS	SBR	FA	FR	G/POS	TPR
1988	SD-N	1	1	0	0	0	0	0	0	0	1	.000	.000	.000	0	-99	-0	0	0	0	.000	0	H	0.0
1989	SD-N	7	19	1	4	1	0	1	6	3	3	.211	.318	.421	739	110	0	0	0	0	1.000	-0	/C-6	0.0
1990	Cle-A★	132	445	60	129	26	2	9	66	25	46	.290	.331	.418	748	109	4	4	1	1	.981	-13	*C-129	-0.1
1991	Cle-A★	51	184	10	40	9	0	0	7	8	24	.217	.265	.266	532	47	-13	0	4	-1	.987	2	C-46/D-4	-0.9
1992	Cle-A★	89	299	22	75	16	0	2	26	13	32	.251	.293	.324	618	74	-11	3	3	-0	.996	-4	C-88/D-1	-1.0
1993	Cle-A	64	215	24	58	7	1	6	32	11	28	.270	.323	.395	719	92	-3	3	1	0	.984	-12	C-64	-1.0
1994	Cle-A	80	292	44	84	15	1	14	43	25	31	.288	.348	.490	838	113	5	8	4	0	.996	-1	C-78	0.9
1995	*Cle-A	66	203	32	61	6	0	10	35	7	26	.300	.333	.478	811	106	1	3	1	0	.995	1	C-61	0.6
1996	*Cle-A★	127	418	53	110	23	0	11	50	19	42	.263	.300	.397	697	75	-17	1	0	0	.988	2	*C-124/1-1	-0.7
1997	*Cle-A★	125	451	63	146	37	0	21	83	19	48	.324	.355	.545	901	126	16	0	2	-1	.985	-15	*C-119/D-1	0.7
1998	*Cle-A★	117	409	45	96	26	2	6	44	18	45	.235	.272	.352	624	59	-25	0	3	-1	.992	3	*C-111/D-3	-1.6
1999	*Cle-A	37	137	19	42	13	0	6	25	4	23	.307	.326	.533	859	109	1	0	1	-0	.974	-2	C-35/D-1	0.1
2000	Cle-A	97	356	44	103	16	2	7	42	16	41	.289	.327	.404	732	82	-10	2	2	-0	.989	-11	C-95/D-1	-1.4
Total	13	993	3429	417	948	195	8	93	459	168	390	.276	.317	.419	736	91	-52	24	22	-2	.988	-49	C-956/D-11,1-1	-4.4

■ SANDY ALOMAR Alomar, Santos Sr. (Conde) b: 10/19/43, Salinas, P.R. BB/TR (BR 1964 (part), 65-66), 5'9", 155 lbs. Deb: 9/15/64 FC Career OF: (5-LF 0-CF 3-RF)

YEAR	TM/L	G	AB	R	H	2B	3B	HR	RBI	BB	SO	AVG	OBP	SLG	OPS	OPS+	BR+	SB	CS	SBR	FA	FR	G/POS	TPR
1964	Mil-N	19	53	3	13	1	0	0	6	0	11	.245	.245	.264	509	43	-4	1	0	0	.967	8	S-19	0.6
1965	Mil-N	67	108	16	26	1	1	0	8	4	12	.241	.268	.269	536	51	-7	12	5	1	.964	14	S-39,2-19	1.0
1966	Atl-N	31	44	4	4	1	0	0	2	1	10	.091	.111	.114	225	-37	-8	0	0	0	.981	3	2-21/S-5	-0.4
1967	NY-N	15	22	1	0	0	0	0	0	0	6	.000	.000	.000	0	-99	-6	0	0	0	1.000	2	S-10/3-3,2-2	-0.3
	Chi-A	12	15	4	3	0	0	0	0	2	0	.200	.294	.200	494	50	-1	2	0	0	.952	2	/S-8,2-2	0.2
1968	Chi-A	133	363	41	92	8	2	0	12	20	42	.253	.294	.287	581	76	-11	21	8	2	.958	-16	2-99,3-27/S-9,O-1L	-1.9
1969	Chi-A	22	58	8	13	2	0	0	4	4	6	.224	.274	.259	533	47	-4	2	0	0	.980	3	2-22	0.0
	Cal-A	134	559	60	140	10	2	1	30	36	48	.250	.296	.281	577	65	-26	18	3	3	.969	-10	*2-134	-2.5
	Yr	156	617	68	153	12	2	1	34	40	54	.248	.294	.279	573	63	-31	20	3	3	.970	-7	*2-156	-2.5
1970	Cal-A★	162	672	82	169	18	2	2	36	49	65	.251	.303	.293	596	68	-29	35	12	4	.979	9	*2-153,S-10/3-1	-0.6
1971	Cal-A	162	689	77	179	24	3	4	42	41	60	.260	.301	.321	622	82	-18	39	10	5	.989	21	*2-137,S-28	2.3
1972	Cal-A	155	610	65	146	20	3	1	25	47	55	.239	.294	.287	581	78	-17	20	12	0	.977	3	*2-154/S-4	-0.4
1973	Cal-A	136	470	45	112	7	1	0	28	34	44	.238	.290	.257	547	60	-25	25	10	2	.979	-8	*2-110,S-31	-2.1
1974	Cal-A	46	54	12	12	0	1	0	1	2	8	.222	.250	.259	509	49	-4	2	0	0	.977	9	S-19,2-15/3-5,OD	0.7
	NY-A	76	279	35	75	8	0	1	27	14	25	.269	.304	.308	612	78	-8	6	4	-0	.977	-12	2-76	-1.6
	Yr	122	333	47	87	8	1	1	28	16	33	.261	.295	.300	595	74	-11	8	4	0	.976	-3	2-91,S-19/3-5,OD	-0.9
1975	NY-A	151	489	61	117	18	4	2	39	26	58	.239	.278	.305	582	66	-23	28	6	4	**.985**	-12	*2-150/S-1	-2.2
1976	*NY-A	67	163	20	39	4	0	1	10	13	12	.239	.295	.282	578	70	-6	12	7	0	.970	-5	2-38/S-6,3-3,1-1,O	-0.9
1977	Tex-A	69	83	21	22	3	0	1	11	8	13	.265	.337	.337	674	84	-2	4	3	-0	.973	13	D-26,2-18/S-6,O13	1.0
1978	Tex-A	24	29	3	6	1	0	0	1	1	7	.207	.233	.241	475	34	-3	0	0	0	.975	5	/1-9,2-6,3-3,S-2,D	0.2
Total	15	1481	4760	558	1168	126	19	13	282	302	482	.245	.291	.288	579	68	-200	227	80	22	.977	31	*2-1156,S-197/3D1O	-6.9

■ FELIPE ALOU Alou, Felipe Rojas (b: Felipe Rojas (Alou)) b: 5/12/35, Haina, D.R. BR/TR, 6', 195 lbs. Deb: 6/8/58 FMC Career OF: (434-LF 484-CF 736-RF)

YEAR	TM/L	G	AB	R	H	2B	3B	HR	RBI	BB	SO	AVG	OBP	SLG	OPS	OPS+	BR+	SB	CS	SBR	FA	FR	G/POS	TPR
1958	SF-N	75	182	21	46	9	2	4	16	19	34	.253	.327	.390	717	91	-2	4	2	0	.985	-3	O-70(28-3-44)	-0.7
1959	SF-N	95	247	38	68	13	2	10	33	17	38	.275	.322	.466	788	109	2	5	3	0	.974	-6	O-69(0-10-64)	-0.6
1960	SF-N	106	322	48	85	17	3	8	44	16	42	.264	.303	.410	713	99	-2	10	2	2	.958	-4	O-95(68-7-24)	-0.9
1961	SF-N	132	415	59	120	19	0	18	52	26	41	.289	.334	.465	799	113	7	11	4	1	.990	-4	*O-122(42-6-87)	-0.3
1962	*SF-N★	154	561	96	177	30	3	25	98	33	66	.316	.359	.513	872	133	24	10	7	-0	.971	-2	*O-150(11-2-141)	1.3
1963	SF-N	157	565	75	159	31	9	20	82	27	87	.281	.321	.474	795	127	18	11	2	2	.986	0	*O-153(6-13-144)	1.1
1964	Mil-N	121	415	60	105	26	3	9	51	30	41	.253	.310	.395	705	96	-2	5	2	0	.975	-1	O-92(14-60-27),1-18	-0.9
1965	Mil-N	143	555	80	165	29	2	23	78	31	63	.297	.340	.481	821	128	19	8	4	0	.980	-4	O-91L,1-69/3-2,S-1	0.8
1966	Atl-N☆	154	666	**122**	**218**	32	6	31	74	24	51	.327	.362	.533	895	143	36	5	7	-1	.988	1	1-90,O-79L/3-3,S-1	2.9
1967	Atl-N	140	574	76	157	26	3	15	43	32	50	.274	.320	.408	727	108	5	6	5	-0	.993	-11	1-85,O-56(24-30-5)	-1.6
1968	Atl-N★	160	662	72	**210**	37	5	11	57	48	56	.317	.367	.438	805	140	32	12	11	-1	.980	8	*O-158(0-158-0)	3.8
1969	*Atl-N	123	476	54	134	13	1	5	32	23	23	.282	.320	.345	665	86	-9	4	6	-1	.989	3	*O-116(3-102-13)	-1.1
1970	Oak-A	154	575	70	156	25	3	8	55	32	31	.271	.311	.367	678	89	-10	10	5	0	.977	-3	*O-145(101-5-81)/1-1	-2.1
1971	Oak-A	2	8	0	2	1	0	0	0	0	1	.250	.250	.375	625	77	-0	0	0	0	1.000	1	/O-2(2-0-0)	0.0
	NY-A	131	461	52	133	20	6	8	69	32	24	.289	.337	.410	747	118	9	5	5	-1	.985	-12	O-80(7-20-56),1-42	-1.1
	Yr	133	469	52	135	21	6	8	69	32	25	.288	.336	.409	745	117	9	5	5	-1	.986	-11	O-82(9-20-56),1-42	-1.1
1972	NY-A	120	324	33	90	18	1	6	37	22	27	.278	.328	.395	723	118	6	1	0	0	.990	1	1-95,O-15(0-0-15)	0.2
1973	NY-A	93	280	25	66	12	0	4	27	9	25	.236	.260	.321	581	65	-14	0	1	-0	.988	-1	1-67,O-22(1-1-21)	-2.1
	Mon-N	19	48	4	10	1	0	1	4	2	4	.208	.240	.292	532	45	-4	0	1	-0	1.000	1	O-15(14-3-0)/1-1	-0.4
1974	Mil-A	3	3	0	0	0	0	0	0	0	2	.000	.000	.000	0	-99	-1	0	0	0	.000	-1	/O-1(0-0-1)	-0.2
Total	17	2082	7339	985	2101	359	49	206	852	423	706	.286	.330	.433	763	114	115	107	67	0	.979	-37	*O-1531R,1-468/3-5,S	-1.9

■ JESUS ALOU Alou, Jesus Maria Rojas (b: Jesus Maria Rojas (Alou)) b: 3/24/42, Haina, D.R. BR/TR, 6'2", 195 lbs. Deb: 9/10/63 FC Career OF: (445-LF 5-CF 655-RF)

YEAR	TM/L	G	AB	R	H	2B	3B	HR	RBI	BB	SO	AVG	OBP	SLG	OPS	OPS+	BR+	SB	CS	SBR	FA	FR	G/POS	TPR
1963	SF-N	16	24	3	6	1	0	0	5	0	3	.250	.280	.292	572	66	-1	0	1	-0	.875	-4	O-12(11-0-3)	-0.6
1964	SF-N	115	376	42	103	11	0	3	28	13	35	.274	.305	.327	632	77	-11	6	6	-1	.973	-1	*O-108(9-4-99)	-2.0
1965	SF-N	143	543	76	162	19	4	9	52	13	40	.298	.318	.398	716	98	-2	8	5	0	.980	1	*O-136(6-0-133)	-1.2
1966	SF-N	110	370	41	96	13	1	1	20	9	22	.259	.281	.308	589	62	-19	5	5	-1	.967	-5	*O-100(59-0-42)	-3.3
1967	SF-N	129	510	55	149	15	4	5	30	14	39	.292	.316	.367	683	96	-3	1	7	-2	.948	-6	*O-123(79-0-50)	-2.1
1968	SF-N	120	419	26	110	15	4	0	39	9	23	.263	.280	.317	597	79	-11	1	4	-1	.989	0	*O-105(49-0-65)	-2.2
1969	Hou-N	115	452	49	112	19	4	5	34	15	30	.248	.278	.341	619	74	-17	4	6	-1	.928	-0	*O-112(65-0-58)	-2.7
1970	Hou-N	117	458	59	140	27	3	1	44	21	15	.306	.338	.384	722	97	-3	3	2	-0	.962	-7	*O-108(30-0-88)	-1.5
1971	Hou-N	122	433	41	121	21	4	2	40	13	17	.279	.307	.360	667	91	-6	3	7	-2	.983	6	*O-109(52-0-63)	-0.8
1972	Hou-N	52	93	8	29	4	1	0	11	7	5	.312	.366	.376	743	114	2	0	2	-1	.970	-3	O-23(10-0-14)	-0.3
1973	Hou-N	28	55	7	13	2	0	1	8	1	6	.236	.276	.327	603	67	-3	0	0	0	.941	-3	O-14(1-0-13)	-0.6
	*Oak-A	36	108	10	33	3	0	1	11	2	6	.306	.318	.361	679	96	-1	0	0	0	1.000	-0	O-21(18-1-4)/D-6	-0.2
1974	*Oak-A	96	220	13	59	8	0	2	15	5	9	.268	.291	.332	623	84	-5	0	0	0	1.000	-1	D-41,O-25(9-0-16)	-0.8

YEAR	TM/L	G	AB	R	H	2B	3B	HR	RBI	BB	SO	AVG	OBP	SLG	OPS	OPS+	BR+	SB	CS	SBR	FA	FR	G/POS	TPR
1975	NY-N	62	102	8	27	3	0	0	11	4	5	.265	.299	.294	593	68	-4	0	1	-0	.963	-1	O-20(15-0-5)	-0.7
1978	Hou-N	77	139	7	45	5	1	2	19	6	5	.324	.352	.417	769	123	4	0	0	0	.976	-2	O-28(27-0-1)	0.1
1979	Hou-N	42	43	3	11	4	0	0	10	6	7	.256	.347	.349	696	96	-0	0	0	0	1.000	-1	/O-6(5-0-1),1-1	-0.1
Total	15	1380	4345	448	1216	170	26	32	377	138	267	.280	.307	.353	660	87	-82	31	46	-9	.968	-26	*O-1050R/D-47,1-1	-19.0

■ **MATTY ALOU** Alou, Mateo Rojas (b: Mateo Rojas (Alou)) b: 12/22/38, Haina, D.R. BL/TL, 5'9", 160 lbs. Deb: 9/26/60 F Career OF: (197-LF 844-CF 282-RF)

YEAR	TM/L	G	AB	R	H	2B	3B	HR	RBI	BB	SO	AVG	OBP	SLG	OPS	OPS+	BR+	SB	CS	SBR	FA	FR	G/POS	TPR
1960	SF-N	4	3	1	1	0	0	0	0	0	0	.333	.333	.333	667	88	-0	0	0	0	1.000	-0	/O-1(1-0-0)	0.0
1961	SF-N	81	200	38	62	7	2	6	24	15	18	.310	.358	.455	813	118	5	3	2	-0	.978	-4	O-58(16-3-40)	-0.2
1962	*SF-N	78	195	28	57	8	1	3	14	14	17	.292	.349	.390	739	100	0	3	1	0	.976	-6	O-57(35-9-21)	-0.8
1963	SF-N	63	76	4	11	1	0	0	2	2	13	.145	.177	.158	335	-3	-10	0	1	-0	.952	-3	O-20(13-2-7)	-1.6
1964	SF-N	110	250	28	66	4	2	1	14	11	25	.264	.303	.308	611	71	-9	5	3	0	.976	-9	O-80(42-18-35)	-2.2
1965	SF-N	117	324	37	75	12	2	2	18	17	28	.231	.274	.299	573	60	-17	10	2	2	.986	4	*O-103(72-11-3)/P-1	-1.7
1966	Pit-N	141	535	86	183	18	9	2	27	24	44	**.342**	.375	.421	795	121	15	23	15	-0	.972	-1	*O-136(1-135-0)	1.0
1967	Pit-N	139	550	87	186	21	7	2	28	24	42	.338	.372	.413	785	124	17	16	10	0	.989	-3	*O-134(0-134-0)/1-1	1.1
1968	Pit-N★	146	558	59	185	28	4	0	52	27	26	.332	.365	.396	761	130	20	18	10	0	.984	-2	*O-144(0-144-0)	1.6
1969	Pit-N★	162	698	105	**231**	**41**	6	1	48	42	35	.331	.371	.411	782	121	19	22	8	2	.977	5	*O-162(1-162-0)	2.3
1970	*Pit-N	155	677	97	201	21	8	1	47	30	18	.297	.331	.356	687	86	-14	19	11	0	.975	5	*O-153(0-152-1)	-1.3
1971	StL-N	149	609	85	192	28	6	7	74	34	27	.315	.355	.415	771	113	10	19	10	1	.981	-0	O-94(0-73-21),1-57	0.3
1972	StL-N	108	404	46	127	17	2	3	31	24	23	.314	.354	.389	743	112	6	11	4	1	.988	-2	1-66,O-39(1-0-38)	-0.2
	*Oak-A	32	121	11	34	5	0	1	16	11	12	.281	.346	.347	693	112	2	2	1	0	1.000	-2	O-32(2-0-31)/1-1	-0.2
1973	NY-A	123	497	59	147	22	1	2	28	30	43	.296	.340	.356	696	100	-0	5	2	0	.974	-4	O-85(0-0-85),1-40/D-1	-1.2
	StL-N	11	11	1	3	0	0	0	1	1	0	.273	.333	.273	606	70	-0	0	0	0	1.000	0	/1-1,O-1(0-1-0)	0.0
1974	SD-N	48	81	8	16	3	0	0	3	5	6	.198	.244	.235	479	36	-7	0	0	0	.947	-2	O-13(13-0-0)/1-2	-1.0
Total	15	1667	5789	780	1777	236	50	31	427	311	377	.307	.346	.381	727	105	36	156	80	6	.979	-23	*O-1312C,1-168/D-1,P	-4.1

■ **MOISES ALOU** Alou, Moises Rojas (b: Moises Rojas) b: 7/3/66, Atlanta, Ga. BR/TR, 6'3", 190 lbs. Deb: 7/26/90 F Career OF: (641-LF 99-CF 335-RF)

YEAR	TM/L	G	AB	R	H	2B	3B	HR	RBI	BB	SO	AVG	OBP	SLG	OPS	OPS+	BR+	SB	CS	SBR	FA	FR	G/POS	TPR
1990	Pit-N	2	5	0	1	0	0	0	0	0	0	.200	.200	.200	400	11	-1	0	0	0	1.000	-0	/O-2(2-0-0)	-0.1
	Mon-N	14	15	4	3	0	1	0	0	0	3	.200	.200	.333	533	46	-1	0	0	0	1.000	-0	/O-5(1-2-2)	-0.1
	Yr	16	20	4	4	0	1	0	0	0	3	.200	.200	.300	500	37	-2	0	0	0	1.000	-0	/O-7(3-2-2)	-0.2
1992	Mon-N	115	341	53	96	28	2	9	56	25	46	.282	.332	.455	787	122	9	16	2	3	.978	-3	*O-100(79-13-15)	0.7
1993	Mon-N	136	482	70	138	29	6	18	85	38	53	.286	.345	.483	828	114	9	17	6	2	.985	-1	*O-136(102-12-34)	0.5
1994	Mon-N★	107	422	81	143	31	5	22	78	42	63	.339	.401	.592	994	153	32	7	6	-1	.986	4	*O-106(63-0-45)	3.0
1995	Mon-N	93	344	48	94	22	0	14	58	29	56	.273	.346	.459	805	106	3	4	3	-0	.981	-0	O-92(61-4-30)	-0.1
1996	Mon-N	143	540	87	152	28	2	21	96	49	83	.281	.343	.457	801	106	4	9	4	1	.989	-1	*O-142(33-7-123)	-0.2
1997	*Fla-N★	150	538	88	157	29	5	23	115	70	85	.292	.377	.493	870	131	25	9	5	0	.988	-9	*O-150(89-55-22)	1.4
1998	*Hou-N★	159	584	104	182	34	5	38	124	84	87	.312	.403	.582	985	159	51	11	3	1	.980	2	*O-154(152-6-0)/D-1	4.8
2000	Hou-N	126	454	82	161	28	2	30	114	52	45	.355	.423	.623	1047	151	36	3	3	-0	.970	-4	*O-121(59-0-64)/D-1	2.5
Total	9	1045	3725	617	1127	229	28	175	726	389	521	.303	.373	.520	893	131	167	76	32	6	.983	-12	*O-1008L/D-2	12.4

■ **WHITEY ALPERMAN** Alperman, Charles Augustus b: 11/11/1879, Etna, Pa. d: 12/25/42, Pittsburgh, Pa. BR/TR, 5'10", 180 lbs. Deb: 4/13/06 Career OF: (0-LF 0-CF 5-RF)

YEAR	TM/L	G	AB	R	H	2B	3B	HR	RBI	BB	SO	AVG	OBP	SLG	OPS	OPS+	BR+	SB	CS	SBR	FA	FR	G/POS	TPR
1906	Bro-N	128	441	38	111	15	7	3	46	6		.252	.284	.338	622	102	-2	13			.940	2	*2-103,S-24/3-1	0.2
1907	Bro-N	141	558	44	130	23	**16**	2	39	13		.233	.266	.342	608	98	-5	5			.953	14	*2-115,3-14,S-12	1.2
1908	Bro-N	70	213	17	42	3	1	1	15	9		.197	.253	.235	488	58	-10	2			.934	-5	2-42/3-9,O-5R,S-2	-1.7
1909	Bro-N	111	420	35	104	19	12	1	41	2		.248	.262	.357	619	95	-6	7			.931	8	*2-108	0.4
Total	4	450	1632	134	387	60	36	7	141	30		.237	.268	.331	599	93	-22	27			.941	19	2-368/S-38,3-24,O-5R	0.1

■ **TOM ALSTON** Alston, Thomas Edison b: 1/31/26, Greensboro, N.C. d: 12/30/93, Winston-Salem, N.C. BL/TR, 6'5", 210 lbs. Deb: 4/13/54

YEAR	TM/L	G	AB	R	H	2B	3B	HR	RBI	BB	SO	AVG	OBP	SLG	OPS	OPS+	BR+	SB	CS	SBR	FA	FR	G/POS	TPR
1954	StL-N	66	244	28	60	14	2	4	34	24	41	.246	.319	.369	687	78	-8	3	5	-1	.989	10	1-65	-0.3
1955	StL-N	13	8	0	1	0	0	0	0	0	0	.125	.125	.125	250	-33	-2	0	0	0	1.000	0	/1-7	-0.1
1956	StL-N	3	2	0	0	0	0	0	0	0	0	.000	.000	.000	0	-99	-1	0	0	0	1.000	0	/1-3	0.0
1957	StL-N	9	17	2	5	1	0	0	2	1	5	.294	.333	.353	686	83	-0	0	0	0	.947	-1	/1-6	-0.2
Total	4	91	271	30	66	15	2	4	36	25	46	.244	.312	.358	670	74	-10	3	5	-1	.987	9	/1-81	-0.6

■ **WALTER ALSTON** Alston, Walter Emmons "Smokey" b: 12/1/11, Venice, Ohio d: 10/1/84, Oxford, Ohio BR/TR, 6'2", 195 lbs. Deb: 9/27/36 MH

YEAR	TM/L	G	AB	R	H	2B	3B	HR	RBI	BB	SO	AVG	OBP	SLG	OPS	OPS+	BR+	SB	CS	SBR	FA	FR	G/POS	TPR
1936	StL-N	1	1	0	0	0	0	0	0	0	1	.000	.000	.000	0	-99	-0	0			.500	-0	/1-1	-0.1

■ **DELL ALSTON** Alston, Wendell b: 9/22/52, Valhalla, N.Y. BL/TR, 6', 180 lbs. Deb: 5/17/77 Career OF: (52-LF 4-CF 54-RF)

YEAR	TM/L	G	AB	R	H	2B	3B	HR	RBI	BB	SO	AVG	OBP	SLG	OPS	OPS+	BR+	SB	CS	SBR	FA	FR	G/POS	TPR
1977	NY-A	22	40	10	13	4	0	1	4	3	4	.325	.372	.500	872	137	2	3	3	-0	1.000	0	D-10/O-2(0-0-2)	0.2
1978	NY-A	3	3	0	0	0	0	0	0	0	2	.000	.000	.000	0	-99	-1	0	0	0	.000	0	H	-0.1
	Oak-A	58	173	17	36	2	0	1	10	10	21	.208	.251	.237	488	40	-14	11	10	-1	.956	-5	O-50(22-0-29)/1-9,D-3	-2.4
	Yr	61	176	17	36	2	0	1	10	10	23	.205	.247	.233	480	38	-15	11	10	-1	.956	-5	O-50(22-0-29)/1-9,D-3	-2.5
1979	Cle-A	54	62	10	18	0	2	1	12	10	10	.290	.389	.403	792	114	2	4	4	-1	.969	-5	O-30(18-0-12)/D-7	-0.5
1980	Cle-A	52	54	11	12	1	2	0	9	5	7	.222	.311	.315	626	72	-2	2	4	-1	.947	-4	O-26(12-4-11)/D-6	-0.7
Total	4	189	332	48	79	7	4	3	35	28	44	.238	.301	.310	611	71	-13	20	21	-3	.957	-14	O-108R/D-26,1-9	-3.5

■ **JESSE ALTENBURG** Altenburg, Jesse Howard b: 1/2/1893, Ashley, Mich. d: 3/12/73, Lansing, Mich. BL/TR, 5'9", 158 lbs. Deb: 9/19/16

YEAR	TM/L	G	AB	R	H	2B	3B	HR	RBI	BB	SO	AVG	OBP	SLG	OPS	OPS+	BR+	SB	CS	SBR	FA	FR	G/POS	TPR
1916	Pit-N	8	14	2	6	1	1	0	0	1	1	.429	.467	.643	1110	237	2	0			1.000	-2	/O-8(4-2-0)	0.0
1917	Pit-N	11	17	1	3	0	0	0	3	0	4	.176	.176	.176	353	8	-2	0			1.000	-1	/O-4(1-0-3)	-0.3
Total	2	19	31	3	9	1	1	0	3	1	5	.290	.313	.387	700	112	0	0			1.000	-3	/O-12(5-2-3)	-0.3

■ **DAVE ALTIZER** Altizer, David Tilden "Filipino" b: 11/6/1876, Pearl, Ill. d: 5/14/64, Pleasant Hill, Ill BL/TR, 5'10.5", 160 lbs. Deb: 5/29/06 Career OF: (4-LF 53-CF 52-RF)

YEAR	TM/L	G	AB	R	H	2B	3B	HR	RBI	BB	SO	AVG	OBP	SLG	OPS	OPS+	BR+	SB	CS	SBR	FA	FR	G/POS	TPR
1906	Was-A	115	433	56	111	9	5	1	27	35		.256	.324	.307	631	103	2	37			.931	-20	*S-113/O-2(0-0-2)	-1.5
1907	Was-A	147	540	60	145	15	5	2	42	34		.269	.319	.326	645	115	9	38			.923	-2	S-80,1-50,O-17C	0.8
1908	Was-A	67	205	19	46	1	1	0	18	13		.224	.274	.239	513	73	-6	8			.959	-3	2-38,3-16/1-4,S-1	-0.9
	Cle-A	29	89	11	19	1	2	0	5	7		.213	.278	.270	548	78	-2	7			.952	4	O-24(0-20-4)/S-3	0.0
	Yr	96	294	30	65	2	3	0	23	20		.221	.275	.248	524	75	-8	15			.959	1	2-38,O-24C,3-16,/1S	-0.9
1909	Chi-A	116	382	47	89	6	7	1	20	39		.233	.330	.293	623	101	3	27			.949	8	O-61(4-14-45),1-46	0.8
1910	Cin-N	3	10	3	6	0	0	0	0	3	0	.600	.692	.600	1292	290	3	0			.933	-2	/S-3	0.2
1911	Cin-N	37	75	8	17	4	1	0	4	9	5	.227	.318	.307	624	78	-2	2			.907	1	S-23/1-1,2-1,O-1R	0.0
Total	6	514	1734	204	433	36	21	4	116	140	5	.250	.318	.302	619	101	6	119			.925	-14	S-223,O-105C,1/23	-0.6

■ **GEORGE ALTMAN** Altman, George Lee b: 3/20/33, Goldsboro, N.C. BL/TR, 6'4", 200 lbs. Deb: 4/11/59 Career OF: (222-LF 184-CF 396-RF)

YEAR	TM/L	G	AB	R	H	2B	3B	HR	RBI	BB	SO	AVG	OBP	SLG	OPS	OPS+	BR+	SB	CS	SBR	FA	FR	G/POS	TPR
1959	Chi-N	135	420	54	103	14	4	12	47	34	80	.245	.312	.383	696	85	-9	1	0	0	.990	4	*O-121(0-121-0)	-1.1
1960	Chi-N	119	334	50	89	16	4	13	51	32	67	.266	.332	.455	788	114	6	4	3	-0	.993	-5	O-79(26-32-23),1-21	-0.3
1961	Chi-N★	138	518	77	157	28	**12**	27	96	40	92	.303	.358	.560	917	137	26	6	2	1	.978	1	*O-130(1-25-115)/1-3	1.9
1962	Chi-N★	147	534	74	170	27	5	22	74	62	89	.318	.394	.511	906	136	28	19	7	2	.972	-0	*O-129(0-6-125),1-16	2.0
1963	StL-N	135	464	62	127	18	7	9	47	47	93	.274	.343	.401	744	104	3	13	4	1	.979	2	*O-124(12-0-116)	-0.2
1964	NY-N	124	422	48	97	14	1	9	47	18	70	.230	.263	.332	595	68	-19	4	2	0	.968	13	*O-109(95-0-14)	-1.3
1965	Chi-N	90	196	24	46	7	1	4	23	19	36	.235	.302	.342	644	79	-5	3	2	-0	.943	-3	O-45(44-0-1)/1-2	-1.1
1966	Chi-N	88	185	19	41	6	0	5	17	14	37	.222	.276	.335	612	68	-8	2	2	-0	.958	-3	O-42(41-0-1)/1-4	-1.4
1967	Chi-N	15	18	1	2	2	0	0	1	2	8	.111	.200	.222	422	20	-2	0	0	0	1.000	-1	/O-4(3-0-1),1-1	-0.4
Total	9	991	3091	409	832	132	34	101	403	268	572	.269	.331	.432	763	105	20	52	22	4	.977	7	O-783R/1-47	-1.9

■ **JOE ALTOBELLI** Altobelli, Joseph Salvatore b: 5/26/32, Detroit, Mich. BL/TL, 6', 185 lbs. Deb: 4/14/55 MC

YEAR	TM/L	G	AB	R	H	2B	3B	HR	RBI	BB	SO	AVG	OBP	SLG	OPS	OPS+	BR+	SB	CS	SBR	FA	FR	G/POS	TPR
1955	Cle-A	42	75	8	15	3	0	2	5	5	14	.200	.259	.320	579	53	-5	0	1	-0	.992	-1	1-40	-0.7
1957	Cle-A	83	87	9	18	3	2	0	9	5	14	.207	.258	.287	545	49	-6	3	2	-0	.994	-0	1-56/O-7(1-4-2)	-0.8
1961	Min-A	41	95	10	21	2	1	3	14	13	14	.221	.315	.358	673	75	-3	0	0	0	.951	-2	O-25(25-0-0)/1-2	-0.7
Total	3	166	257	27	54	8	3	5	28	23	42	.210	.280	.323	603	60	-15	3	3	-0	.993	-3	/1-98,O-32(26-4-2)	-2.2

■ **NICK ALTROCK** Altrock, Nicholas b: 9/15/1876, Cincinnati, Ohio d: 1/20/65, Washington, D.C. BB/TL, 5'10", 197 lbs. Deb: 7/14/1898 C

YEAR	TM/L	G	AB	R	H	2B	3B	HR	RBI	BB	SO	AVG	OBP	SLG	OPS	OPS+	BR+	SB	CS	SBR	FA	FR	G/POS	TPR
1898	Lou-N	11	29	4	7	0	0	0	2	2		.241	.313	.241	554	60	-1	1			1.000	2	P-11	0.0
1902	Bos-A	3	8	0	0	0	0	0	0	0		.000	.000	.000	0	-97	-2	0			.818	1	/P-3	0.0

YEAR	TM/L	G	AB	R	H	2B	3B	HR	RBI	BB	SO	AVG	OBP	SLG	OPS	OPS+	BR+	SB	CS	SBR	FA	FR	G/POS	TPR
1903	Bos-A	1	3	0	2	0	0	0	0	1		.667	.750	.667	1417	311	1	0			1.000	1	/P-1	0.0
	Chi-A	13	30	6	9	0	0	0	3	3		.300	.364	.300	664	105	0	1			.935	3	P-12	0.0
	Yr	14	33	6	11	0	0	0	3	4		.333	.405	.333	739	128	1	1			.944	4	P-13	0.0
1904	Chi-A	41	111	13	22	1	0	1	8	4		.198	.239	.234	474	52	-6	0			.969	4	P-38/1-1	0.0
1905	Chi-A	40	112	8	14	1	0	0	5	6		.125	.190	.134	324	3	-12	0			.988	8	P-38/1-1	0.0
1906	*Chi-A	38	100	4	16	2	0	0	3	8		.160	.222	.180	402	27	-8	2			.970	4	P-38/1-1	0.0
1907	Chi-A	30	72	7	13	3	0	0	2	3		.181	.234	.222	456	47	-4	0			.958	5	P-30	0.0
1908	Chi-A	23	49	6	10	2	0	0	3	0		.204	.235	.245	480	57	-2	1			.967	5	P-23	0.0
1909	Chi-A	1	3	0	0	0	0	0	0	0		.000	.000	.000	0	-99	-1	0			1.000	0	/P-1	0.0
	Was-A	12	19	2	1	0	0	0	0	1		.053	.143	.053	195	-40	-3	0			.905	-0	/P-9,O-3(2-0-1)	-0.2
	Yr	13	22	2	1	0	0	0	0	1		.045	.125	.045	170	-48	-4	0			.920	-0	P-10/O-3(2-0-1)	-0.2
1912	Was-A	1	1	0	0	0	0	0	0	0		.000	.000	.000	0	-99	-0	0			.000	-0	/P-1,1-1	0.0
1913	Was-A	4	1	0	0	0	0	0	0	0	0	.000	.000	.000	0	-98	-0	0			.833	-0	/P-4	0.0
1914	Was-A	1	0	0	0	0	0	0	0	0	0	—	—	—	—	—	0	0			.000	-0	/P-1	0.0
1915	Was-A	1	1	0	0	0	0	0	0	0	0	.000	.000	.000	0	-98	-0	0			.000	-0	/P-1	0.0
1918	Was-A	5	8	1	1	0	0	1	1	0	0	.125	.125	.500	625	90	-0	0			.917	0	/P-5,1-1	0.0
1919	Was-A	1	0	0	0	0	0	0	0	0	0	—	—	—	—	—	0	0			.000	0	/P-1	0.0
1924	Was-A	1	1	1	1	0	1	0	0	0	0	1.000	1.000	3.000	4000	935	1	0	0	0	.667	0	/P-1	0.0
1929	Was-A	1	1	0	1	0	0	0	0	0	0	1.000	1.000	1.000	2000	413	0	0	0	0	.000	-0	/O-1(0-0-1)	0.0
1931	Was-A	1	0	0	0	0	0	0	0	1	0	—	1.000	—	1000	182	0	0	1	-0	.000	0	H	0.0
1933	Was-A	1	1	0	0	0	0	0	0	0	0	.000	.000	.000	0	-99	-0	0	0	0	.000	0	H	0.0
Total	19	230	550	52	97	9	1	2	27	29	0	.176	.232	.207	439	39	-38	5	1		.964	33	P-218/1-5,O-4(2-0-2)	-0.2

■ GEORGE ALUSIK

Alusik, George Joseph b: 2/11/35, Ashley, Pa. BR/TR, 6′3.5″, 175 lbs. Deb: 9/11/58

YEAR	TM/L	G	AB	R	H	2B	3B	HR	RBI	BB	SO	AVG	OBP	SLG	OPS	OPS+	BR+	SB	CS	SBR	FA	FR	G/POS	TPR
1958	Det-A	2	2	0	0	0	0	0	0	0	1	.000	.000	.000	0	-93	-1	0	0	0	1.000	-0	/O-1(1-0-0)	-0.1
1961	Det-A	15	14	0	2	0	0	0	2	1	4	.143	.200	.143	343	-6	-2	0	0	0	.000	-0	/O-1(0-0-1)	-0.3
1962	Det-A	2	2	0	0	0	0	0	0	0	0	.000	.000	.000	0	-97	-1	0	0	0	.000	0	H	-0.1
	KC-A	90	209	29	57	10	1	11	35	16	29	.273	.327	.488	815	111	3	1	1	-0	.968	-3	O-50(35-0-22)/1-1	-0.3
	Yr	92	211	29	57	10	1	11	35	16	29	.270	.325	.483	808	109	2	1	1	-0	.968	-3	O-50(35-0-22)/1-1	-0.4
1963	KC-A	87	221	28	59	11	0	9	37	26	33	.267	.347	.439	786	112	4	0	1	-0	1.000	-3	O-63(30-1-36)	-0.3
1964	KC-A	102	204	18	49	10	1	3	19	30	36	.240	.343	.343	686	89	-2	0	0	0	.984	-4	O-44(43-0-3),1-12	-0.9
Total	5	298	652	75	167	31	2	23	93	73	103	.256	.335	.416	750	101	1	1	2	-0	.985	-10	O-159(109-1-62)/1-13	-2.0

■ LUIS ALVARADO

Alvarado, Luis Cesar (Martinez) b: 1/15/49, Lajas, P.R. BR/TR, 5′9″, 162 lbs. Deb: 9/13/68

YEAR	TM/L	G	AB	R	H	2B	3B	HR	RBI	BB	SO	AVG	OBP	SLG	OPS	OPS+	BR+	SB	CS	SBR	FA	FR	G/POS	TPR
1968	Bos-A	11	46	3	6	2	0	0	1	1	11	.130	.167	.174	341	3	-5	0	0	0	.976	-4	S-11	-0.9
1969	Bos-A	6	5	0	0	0	0	0	0	0	2	.000	.000	.000	0	-95	-1	0	1	-0	1.000	2	/S-5	0.1
1970	Bos-A	59	183	19	41	11	0	1	10	9	30	.224	.260	.301	561	51	-12	1	2	-0	.929	5	3-29,S-27	-0.6
1971	Chi-A	99	264	22	57	14	1	0	8	11	34	.216	.247	.277	524	47	-19	1	2	-0	.959	15	S-71,2-16	0.4
1972	Chi-A	103	254	30	54	4	1	4	29	13	36	.213	.254	.283	537	58	-13	2	2	-0	.957	2	S-81,2-16/3-2	-0.4
1973	Chi-A	80	203	21	47	7	2	0	20	4	20	.232	.250	.286	536	49	-14	6	2	1	.980	5	2-45,S-18,3-10,/D-1	-0.5
1974	Chi-A	8	10	1	1	0	0	0	0	0	1	.100	.100	.100	200	-41	-2	0	0	0	.667	-1	/S-4,2-1,3-1	-0.3
	StL-N	17	36	3	5	2	0	0	1	2	6	.139	.184	.194	379	6	-5	0	0	0	.980	-2	S-17	-0.6
	Cle-A	61	114	12	25	2	0	0	12	6	14	.219	.258	.237	495	44	-8	1	1	-0	.972	11	2-46/S-7,D-3	0.5
1976	StL-N	16	42	5	12	1	0	0	3	3	6	.286	.333	.310	643	82	-1	0	0	0	.936	-9	2-16	-1.0
1977	NY-N	1	2	0	0	0	0	0	0	0	0	.000	.000	.000	0	-99	-1	0	0	0	1.000	0	/2-1	0.0
	Det-A	2	1	0	0	0	0	0	0	0	0	.000	.000	.000	0	-95	-0	0	0	0	.000	0	/3-2	0.0
Total	9	463	1160	116	248	43	4	5	84	49	160	.214	.248	.271	518	47	-81	11	10	-1	.957	26	S-241,2-141/3-44,D	-3.3

■ CLEMENTE ALVAREZ

Alvarez, Clemente Rafael b: 5/18/68, Anzoategul, Venez. BR/TR, 5′11″, 180 lbs. Deb: 9/19/2000

YEAR	TM/L	G	AB	R	H	2B	3B	HR	RBI	BB	SO	AVG	OBP	SLG	OPS	OPS+	BR+	SB	CS	SBR	FA	FR	G/POS	TPR
2000	Phi-N	2	5	1	1	0	0	0	0	0	1	.200	.200	.200	400	1	-1	0	0	0	1.000	0	/C-2	-0.1

■ GABE ALVAREZ

Alvarez, Gabriel De Jesus b: 3/6/74, Navojoa, Mexico BR/TR, 6′1″, 205 lbs. Deb: 6/22/98

YEAR	TM/L	G	AB	R	H	2B	3B	HR	RBI	BB	SO	AVG	OBP	SLG	OPS	OPS+	BR+	SB	CS	SBR	FA	FR	G/POS	TPR
1998	Det-A	58	199	16	46	11	0	5	29	18	65	.231	.301	.362	663	71	-9	1	3	-1	.873	-3	3-55/D-2	-1.1
1999	Det-A	22	53	5	11	3	0	2	4	3	9	.208	.250	.377	627	57	-4	0	0	0	1.000	-2	D-12/O-5(0-0-5),3-2	-0.6
2000	Det-A	1	1	0	0	0	0	0	0	2	1	.000	.667	.000	667	92	0	0	1	-0	.000	0	/D-1	0.0
	SD-N	11	13	1	2	1	0	0	0	1	1	.154	.214	.231	445	13	-2	0	0	0	1.000	-1	/3-3,O-2(2-0-0)	-0.3
Total	3	92	266	22	59	15	0	7	33	24	76	.222	.291	.357	648	67	-14	1	4	-1	.875	-6	/3-60,D-15,O-7(2-0-5)	-2.0

■ ORLANDO ALVAREZ

Alvarez, Jesus Manuel Orlando (Monge) b: 2/28/52, Rio Grande, P.R. BR/TR, 6′, 165 lbs. Deb: 9/1/73

YEAR	TM/L	G	AB	R	H	2B	3B	HR	RBI	BB	SO	AVG	OBP	SLG	OPS	OPS+	BR+	SB	CS	SBR	FA	FR	G/POS	TPR
1973	LA-N	4	4	0	1	1	0	0	0	0	1	.250	.250	.500	750	108	0	0	0	0	.000	0	H	0.0
1974	LA-N	2	1	0	0	0	0	0	0	0	0	.000	.000	.000	0	-99	-0	0	0	0	1.000	-0	/O-1(1-0-0)	0.0
1975	LA-N	4	4	0	0	0	0	0	0	0	1	.000	.000	.000	0	-99	-1	0	0	0	.000	0	H	-0.1
1976	Cal-A	15	42	4	7	1	0	2	8	0	3	.167	.167	.333	500	47	-3	0	0	0	1.000	-1	O-11(10-1-0)/D-2	-0.5
Total	4	25	51	4	8	2	0	2	8	0	5	.157	.157	.314	471	36	-4	0	0	0	1.000	-2	/O-12(11-1-0),D-2	-0.6

■ OSSIE ALVAREZ

Alvarez, Oswaldo (Gonzalez) b: 10/19/33, Bolondron, Cuba BR/TR, 5′10″, 165 lbs. Deb: 4/19/58

YEAR	TM/L	G	AB	R	H	2B	3B	HR	RBI	BB	SO	AVG	OBP	SLG	OPS	OPS+	BR+	SB	CS	SBR	FA	FR	G/POS	TPR
1958	Was-A	87	196	20	41	3	0	0	5	16	26	.209	.269	.224	493	38	-16	1	1	-0	.968	12	S-64,2-14/3-3	0.1
1959	Det-A	8	2	0	1	0	0	0	0	0	1	.500	.500	.500	1000	166	0	0	0	0	.000	0	H	0.0
Total	2	95	198	20	42	3	0	0	5	16	27	.212	.271	.227	498	39	-16	1	1	-0	.968	12	/S-64,2-14,3-3	0.1

■ ROGELIO ALVAREZ

Alvarez, Rogelio (Hernandez) b: 4/18/38, Pinar Del Rio, Cuba BR/TR, 5′11″, 183 lbs. Deb: 9/18/60

YEAR	TM/L	G	AB	R	H	2B	3B	HR	RBI	BB	SO	AVG	OBP	SLG	OPS	OPS+	BR+	SB	CS	SBR	FA	FR	G/POS	TPR
1960	Cin-N	3	9	1	1	0	0	0	0	0	3	.111	.111	.111	222	-38	-2	0	0	0	1.000	-1	/1-2	-0.3
1962	Cin-N	14	28	1	6	0	0	0	2	1	10	.214	.241	.214	456	23	-3	0	0	0	.973	-1	1-13	-0.4
Total	2	17	37	2	7	0	0	0	2	1	13	.189	.211	.189	400	8	-5	0	0	0	.979	-1	/1-15	-0.7

■ MAX ALVIS

Alvis, Roy Maxwell b: 2/2/38, Jasper, Tex. BR/TR, 5′11″, 187 lbs. Deb: 9/11/62

YEAR	TM/L	G	AB	R	H	2B	3B	HR	RBI	BB	SO	AVG	OBP	SLG	OPS	OPS+	BR+	SB	CS	SBR	FA	FR	G/POS	TPR
1962	Cle-A	12	51	1	11	2	0	0	3	2	13	.216	.245	.255	500	36	-5	3	1	0	.935	-4	3-12	-0.8
1963	Cle-A	158	602	81	165	32	7	22	67	36	109	.274	.326	.460	786	118	13	9	7	-0	.942	-5	*3-158	0.7
1964	Cle-A	107	381	51	96	14	3	18	53	29	77	.252	.315	.446	761	110	4	5	5	-1	.955	-7	*3-105	-0.4
1965	Cle-A★	159	604	88	149	24	2	21	61	47	121	.247	.311	.397	708	99	-2	12	8	-0	.958	-19	*3-156	-2.3
1966	Cle-A	157	596	67	146	22	3	17	55	50	98	.245	.306	.378	683	95	-4	4	7	-2	.958	-6	*3-157	-1.3
1967	Cle-A★	161	637	66	163	23	4	21	70	38	107	.256	.302	.403	705	106	3	3	10	-3	.965	-8	*3-161	-0.9
1968	Cle-A	131	452	38	101	17	3	8	37	41	91	.223	.294	.327	621	89	-6	5	5	-1	.960	-17	*3-128	-2.8
1969	Cle-A	66	191	13	43	6	0	1	15	14	26	.225	.278	.272	550	53	-12	1	1	-0	.973	-2	3-58/S-1	-1.5
1970	Mil-A	62	115	16	21	2	0	3	12	5	20	.183	.217	.278	495	35	-10	1	2	-0	.909	2	3-36	-0.9
Total	9	1013	3629	421	895	142	22	111	373	262	662	.247	.304	.390	693	97	-19	43	46	-7	.956	-64	3-971/S-1	-10.2

■ BILLY ALVORD

Alvord, William Charles "Uncle Bill" b: 8/1863, St.Louis, Mo. 5′10″, 187 lbs. Deb: 4/30/1885

YEAR	TM/L	G	AB	R	H	2B	3B	HR	RBI	BB	SO	AVG	OBP	SLG	OPS	OPS+	BR+	SB	CS	SBR	FA	FR	G/POS	TPR
1885	StL-N	2	5	0	0	0	0	0	0	1	2	.000	.167	.000	167	-45	-1				.714	-1	/3-2	-0.1
1889	KC-a	50	186	23	43	8	9	0	18	10	35	.231	.270	.371	641	77	-7	3			.877	5	3-34/S-8,2-8	-0.1
1890	Tol-a	116	495	69	135	13	16	2	52	22		.273	.304	.376	679	97	-5	21			.872	4	*3-116	0.1
1891	Cle-N	13	59	7	17	2	2	1	7	0	7	.288	.300	.441	741	110	0	0			.814	-2	3-13	-0.1
	Was-a	81	312	28	73	8	3	0	30	11	38	.234	.260	.279	539	57	-18	3			.862	17	3-81	0.0
1893	Cle-N	3	12	2	2	0	0	0	2	0	1	.167	.167	.167	333	-11	-2	0			.875	-2	/3-3	-0.3
Total	5	265	1069	129	270	31	30	3	109	44	83	.253	.283	.346	629	81	-33	27			.865	22	3-249/2-8,S-8	-0.5

■ BRANT ALYEA

Alyea, Garrabrant Ryerson b: 12/8/40, Passaic, N.J. BR/TR, 6′3″, 215 lbs. Deb: 9/11/65

YEAR	TM/L	G	AB	R	H	2B	3B	HR	RBI	BB	SO	AVG	OBP	SLG	OPS	OPS+	BR+	SB	CS	SBR	FA	FR	G/POS	TPR
1965	Was-A	8	13	3	3	0	0	2	6	1	4	.231	.286	.692	978	171	1	0	0	0	1.000	-1	/1-3,O-1(1-0-0)	0.0
1968	Was-A	53	150	18	40	11	1	6	23	10	39	.267	.317	.473	790	141	7	0	0	0	1.000	1	O-39(16-0-24)	0.6
1969	Was-A	104	237	29	59	4	0	11	40	34	67	.249	.346	.405	751	115	5	1	3	-1	.938	-7	O-69(36-0-36)/1-3	-0.7
1970	*Min-A	94	258	34	75	12	1	16	61	28	51	.291	.367	.531	898	143	14	3	3	-0	.980	-5	O-75(73-0-2)	0.5
1971	Min-A	79	158	13	28	4	0	2	15	24	38	.177	.290	.241	530	50	-10	1	1	-0	.962	-6	O-48(47-0-1)	-2.0

YEAR	TM/L	G	AB	R	H	2B	3B	HR	RBI	BB	SO	AVG	OBP	SLG	OPS	OPS+	BR+	SB	CS	SBR	FA	FR	G/POS	TPR
1972	Oak-A	20	31	3	6	1	0	1	2	3	5	.194	.265	.323	587	78	-1	0	0	0	1.000	3	/O-8(2-0-6)	0.2
	StL-N	13	19	0	3	1	0	0	1	0	6	.158	.158	.211	368	4	-2	0	0	0	1.000	1	/O-3(1-0-2)	-0.2
Total	6	371	866	100	214	33	2	38	148	100	210	.247	.329	.421	751	113	14	5	7	-1	.972	-15	O-243(176-0-71)/1-6	-1.6
■ JOEY AMALFITANO Amalfitano, John Joseph b: 1/23/34, San Pedro, Cal. BR/TR, 5'11", 180 lbs. Deb: 5/3/54 MC Career OF: (1-LF 0-CF 0-RF)																								
1954	NY-N	9	5	2	0	0	0	0	0	0	4	.000	.000	.000	0	-99	-1	0	0	0	1.000	2	/3-4,2-1	0.1
1955	NY-N	36	22	8	5	1	1	0	1	2	2	.227	.292	.364	655	72	-1	0	0	0	.957	10	/S-5,3-2	0.9
1960	SF-N	106	328	47	91	15	3	1	27	26	31	.277	.336	.351	687	94	-3	2	3	-1	.935	3	3-63,2-33/S-3,O-1L	0.2
1961	SF-N	109	384	64	98	11	4	2	23	44	59	.255	.332	.320	652	77	-12	7	4	0	.970	-22	2-95/3-6	-2.6
1962	Hou-N	117	380	44	90	12	5	1	27	45	43	.237	.319	.303	622	73	-13	4	4	-1	.967	2	*2-110/3-5	-0.4
1963	SF-N	54	137	11	24	3	0	1	7	12	18	.175	.247	.219	466	36	-11	2	6	-2	.980	-3	2-37/3-7	-1.5
1964	Chi-N	100	324	51	78	19	6	4	27	40	42	.241	.333	.373	707	95	-1	2	7	-2	.964	2	2-86/1-1,S-1	0.6
1965	Chi-N	67	96	13	26	4	0	0	8	12	14	.271	.364	.313	676	90	-1	2	2	-0	.989	5	2-24/S-4	0.6
1966	Chi-N	41	38	8	6	2	0	0	3	4	10	.158	.238	.211	449	26	-4	0	0	0	.977	1	2-12/3-3,S-2	-0.2
1967	Chi-N	4	1	0	0	0	0	0	0	0	1	.000	.000	.000	0	-96	-0	0	0	0	.000	0	H	0.0
Total	10	643	1715	248	418	67	19	9	123	185	224	.244	.322	.321	642	78	-47	19	26	-5	.970	0	2-398/3-90,S-15,1O	-2.3
■ RICH AMARAL Amaral, Richard Louis b: 4/1/62, Visalia, Cal. BR/TR, 6', 175 lbs. Deb: 5/27/91 Career OF: (232-LF 101-CF 52-RF)																								
1991	Sea-A	14	16	2	1	0	0	0	0	1	5	.063	.167	.063	229	-34	-3	0	0	0	1.000	4	/2-5,3-2,S-2,1-1,D	0.1
1992	Sea-A	35	100	9	24	3	0	1	7	5	16	.240	.276	.300	576	61	-5	4	2	0	.955	2	3-17,S-17/O-3L,12	-0.3
1993	Sea-A	110	373	53	108	24	1	1	44	33	54	.290	.352	.367	719	92	-3	19	11	0	.975	10	2-77,3-19,S-14,/1D	1.1
1994	Sea-A	77	228	37	60	10	2	4	18	24	28	.263	.336	.377	713	82	-6	5	1	1	.943	-12	2-42,O-16L/S-7,1D	-1.4
1995	*Sea-A	90	238	45	67	14	2	2	19	21	33	.282	.342	.382	725	87	-4	21	2	4	.992	-7	O-73(53-29-8)/D-1	-0.8
1996	Sea-A	118	312	69	91	11	3	1	29	47	55	.292	.393	.356	749	91	-2	25	6	3	1.000	-5	O-91L,2-15,1-10,/3D	-0.4
1997	*Sea-A	89	190	34	54	5	0	1	21	10	34	.284	.330	.326	656	73	-7	12	8	-0	1.000	-9	O-52L,1-14,2-11,/3SD	-1.6
1998	Sea-A	73	134	25	37	6	0	1	4	13	24	.276	.345	.343	688	80	-4	11	1	2	1.000	-9	O-52L,2-11/1-7,3D	-1.1
1999	Bal-A	91	137	21	38	8	1	0	11	15	20	.277	.353	.350	703	83	-3	9	6	-0	1.000	-11	O-50R,D-18/1-2,23	-1.5
2000	Bal-A	30	60	10	13	1	1	0	6	7	8	.217	.299	.267	565	46	-5	6	2	1	1.000	3	O-19(3-12-4)/1-1,D-5	-0.2
Total	10	727	1788	305	493	82	10	11	159	176	277	.276	.346	.351	697	82	-42	112	39	11	.996	-35	O-356L,2-164/D13S	-6.1
■ RUBEN AMARO Amaro, Ruben Jr. b: 2/12/65, Philadelphia, Pa. BB/TR, 5'10", 175 lbs. Deb: 6/8/91 F Career OF: (108-LF 106-CF 132-RF)																								
1991	Cal-A	10	23	0	5	1	0	0	2	3	3	.217	.308	.261	569	59	-1	0	0	0	1.000	-2	/O-5(3-0-2),2-4,D-1	-0.4
1992	Phi-N	126	374	43	82	15	6	7	34	37	54	.219	.305	.348	652	85	-7	11	5	1	.992	0	*O-113(27-27-68)	-1.0
1993	Phi-N	25	48	7	16	2	2	1	6	6	5	.333	.407	.521	928	149	3	0	0	0	.963	-2	O-16(3-8-6)	0.2
1994	Cle-A	26	23	5	5	1	0	2	5	2	3	.217	.280	.522	802	100	-0	2	1	0	.909	-4	O-12(1-10-1)/D-3	-0.4
1995	*Cle-A	28	60	5	12	3	0	1	7	4	6	.200	.273	.300	573	48	-5	1	3	-1	1.000	-4	O-22(5-14-6)/D-3	-0.9
1996	Phi-N	61	117	14	37	10	0	2	15	9	18	.316	.380	.453	833	117	3	0	0	0	1.000	-4	O-35(0-7-28)/1-1	-0.2
1997	Phi-N	117	175	18	41	6	1	2	21	21	24	.234	.323	.314	638	68	-8	1	1	-0	.987	-12	O-72(26-37-15)/1-1	-2.1
1998	Phi-N	92	107	7	20	5	0	1	10	6	15	.187	.230	.262	492	29	-11	0	0	0	1.000	-10	O-51(43-3-6)	-2.2
Total	8	485	927	99	218	43	9	16	100	88	128	.235	.312	.353	665	80	-26	15	10	-0	.989	-38	O-326R/D-7,2-4,1-2	-7.0
■ RUBEN AMARO Amaro, Ruben Sr. (Mora) b: 1/6/36, Veracruz, Mexico BR/TR, 5'11", 170 lbs. Deb: 6/29/58 FC Career OF: (1-LF 0-CF 0-RF)																								
1958	StL-N	40	76	8	17	2	1	0	0	5	8	.224	.272	.276	548	44	-6	0	1	-0	.948	3	S-36/2-1	-0.2
1960	Phi-N	92	264	25	61	9	1	0	16	21	32	.231	.293	.273	565	56	-16	0	1	-0	.965	-8	S-92	-1.8
1961	Phi-N	135	381	34	98	14	9	1	32	53	59	.257	.351	.349	700	88	-5	1	0	0	.970	14	*S-132/1-3,2-1	1.9
1962	Phi-N	79	226	24	55	10	0	0	19	30	28	.243	.335	.288	622	71	-8	5	2	0	.968	6	S-78/1-1	0.5
1963	Phi-N	115	217	25	47	9	2	2	19	19	31	.217	.280	.304	584	69	-9	0	1	-0	.950	2	S-63,3-45/1-5	-0.4
1964	Phi-N	129	299	31	79	11	0	4	34	16	37	.264	.308	.341	649	84	-6	1	6	-2	.971	-4	S-79,1-58/2-3,3O	-0.8
1965	Phi-N	118	184	26	39	7	0	0	15	27	22	.212	.316	.250	566	63	-8	1	1	-0	.990	-3	1-60,S-60/2-6	-0.8
1966	NY-A	14	23	0	5	0	0	0	3	0	2	.217	.217	.217	435	26	-2	0	0	0	.977	5	S-14	0.4
1967	NY-A	130	417	31	93	12	0	1	17	43	49	.223	.297	.259	556	68	-16	3	2	-0	.973	9	*S-123/3-3,1-2	0.4
1968	NY-A	47	41	3	5	1	0	0	0	9	6	.122	.280	.146	426	33	-3	0	0	0	.962	-0	S-23,1-22	-0.3
1969	Cal-A	41	27	4	6	0	0	0	1	4	6	.222	.323	.222	545	58	-1	0	0	0	1.000	0	1-18/2-9,S-5,3-2	-0.1
Total	11	940	2155	211	505	75	13	8	156	227	280	.234	.310	.292	603	70	-80	11	14	-2	.967	24	S-705,1-169/3-53,2O	-1.2
■ WAYNE AMBLER Ambler, Wayne Harper b: 11/8/15, Abington, Pa. d: 1/3/98, Ponte Vedra Beach, Fla. BR/TR, 5'8.5", 165 lbs. Deb: 6/4/37																								
1937	Phi-A	56	162	3	35	5	0	0	11	13	8	.216	.274	.247	521	33	-17	1	0	0	.955	-4	2-56	-1.6
1938	Phi-A	120	393	42	92	21	2	0	38	48	31	.234	.317	.298	615	56	-26	2	1	0	.942	-19	*S-116/2-4	-3.4
1939	Phi-A	95	227	15	48	13	0	0	24	22	25	.211	.281	.269	550	42	-20	1	0	0	.954	-3	S-77,2-19	-1.6
Total	3	271	782	60	175	39	2	0	73	83	64	.224	.298	.279	577	47	-63	4	1	1	.946	-26	S-193/2-79	-6.6
■ ED AMELUNG Amelung, Edward Allen b: 4/13/59, Fullerton, Cal. BL/TL, 5'11", 180 lbs. Deb: 7/28/84																								
1984	LA-N	34	46	7	10	0	0	0	4	2	4	.217	.250	.217	467	33	-4	3	2	-0	1.000	-3	O-23(9-4-11)	-0.8
1986	LA-N	8	11	0	1	0	0	0	0	0	4	.091	.091	.091	182	-53	-2	0	0	0	1.000	-1	/O-4(0-2-2)	-0.3
Total	2	42	57	7	11	0	0	0	4	2	8	.193	.220	.193	413	17	-6	3	2	-0	1.000	-4	/O-27(9-6-13)	-1.1
■ SANDY AMOROS Amoros, Edmundo (Isasi) b: 1/30/30, Havana, Cuba d: 6/27/92, Miami, Fla. BL/TL, 5'7.5", 170 lbs. Deb: 8/22/52																								
1952	*Bro-N	20	44	10	11	3	1	0	3	5	14	.250	.327	.364	690	90	-1	1	0	0	1.000	-3	O-10(3-4-7)	-0.4
1954	Bro-N	79	263	44	72	18	6	9	34	31	24	.274	.353	.490	843	113	5	1	4	-1	.987	5	O-70(68-1-2)	0.4
1955	*Bro-N	119	388	59	96	16	7	10	51	55	45	.247	.350	.402	752	96	-1	10	5	0	.972	-1	*O-109(102-8-5)	-0.8
1956	*Bro-N	114	292	53	76	11	8	16	58	59	51	.260	.386	.517	903	130	14	3	4	-1	.955	-10	O-86(79-5-10)	-0.3
1957	Bro-N	106	238	40	66	7	1	7	26	46	42	.277	.401	.403	804	107	4	3	2	-0	.984	-1	O-66(65-1-2)	0.0
1959	LA-N	5	5	1	1	0	0	0	1	0	1	.200	.200	.200	400	6	-1	0	0	0	.000	0	H	-0.1
1960	LA-N	9	14	1	2	0	0	0	0	3	2	.143	.294	.143	437	23	-1	0	0	0	1.000	0	/O-3(0-1-3)	-0.1
	Det-A	65	67	7	10	0	0	1	7	12	10	.149	.278	.194	473	29	-6	0	0	0	1.000	-1	O-10(1-9-0)	-0.8
Total	7	517	1311	215	334	55	23	43	180	211	189	.255	.363	.430	793	105	12	18	15	-1	.976	-11	O-354(318-29-29)	-2.1
■ ALF ANDERSON Anderson, Alfred Walton b: 1/28/14, Gainesville, Ga. d: 6/23/85, Albany, Ga. BR/TR, 5'11", 165 lbs. Deb: 4/20/41																								
1941	Pit-N	70	223	32	48	7	2	1	10	14	30	.215	.265	.278	543	53	-14	2			.931	-6	S-58	-1.7
1942	Pit-N	54	166	24	45	4	1	0	7	18	19	.271	.342	.307	650	89	-2	4			.942	-15	S-48	-1.5
1946	Pit-N	2	1	0	0	0	0	0	0	1	0	.000	.500	.000	500	47	0	0			.000	0	H	0.0
Total	3	126	390	56	93	11	3	1	17	33	49	.238	.300	.290	589	68	-16	6			.936	-21	S-106	-3.2
■ ANDY ANDERSON Anderson, Andy Holm b: 11/13/22, Bremerton, Wash. d: 7/18/82, Seattle, Wash. BR/TR, 5'11", 172 lbs. Deb: 5/10/48																								
1948	StL-A	51	87	13	24	5	1	1	12	8	15	.276	.337	.391	728	91	-1	0	0	0	.917	-2	2-21,S-10/1-2	-0.2
1949	StL-A	71	136	10	17	3	0	1	5	14	21	.125	.207	.169	376	-0	-20	0	1	-0	.957	-7	S-44/2-8,3-8	-2.5
Total	2	122	223	23	41	8	1	2	17	22	36	.184	.257	.256	513	35	-21	0	1	-0	.946	-9	/S-54,2-29,3-8,1-2	-2.7
■ BRADY ANDERSON Anderson, Brady Kevin b: 1/18/64, Silver Spring, Md. BL/TL, 6'1", 185 lbs. Deb: 4/4/88 Career OF: (628-LF 905-CF 71-RF)																								
1988	Bos-A	41	148	14	34	5	3	0	12	15	35	.230	.317	.304	621	72	-5	4	2	0	.989	2	O-41(0-17-25)	-0.4
	Bal-A	53	177	17	35	8	1	1	9	8	40	.198	.232	.271	504	42	-14	6	4	-0	.981	5	O-49(0-49-0)	-0.9
	Yr	94	325	31	69	13	4	1	21	23	75	.212	.273	.286	559	57	-19	10	6	0	.984	7	O-90(0-66-25)	-1.3
1989	Bal-A	94	266	44	55	12	2	4	16	43	45	.207	.324	.312	636	82	-5	16	4	2	.985	-2	O-79(3-75-1)/D-8	-0.6
1990	Bal-A	89	234	24	54	5	2	3	24	31	46	.231	.333	.308	641	83	-4	15	2	3	.987	2	O-63(44-21-1),D-11	-0.1
1991	Bal-A	113	256	40	59	12	3	2	27	38	44	.230	.341	.324	665	89	-3	12	5	1	.981	-15	*O-101(75-26-9)/D-2	-1.9
1992	Bal-A★	159	623	100	169	28	10	21	80	98	98	.271	.378	.449	828	128	25	53	16	6	.980	14	*O-158(148-7-3)	4.0
1993	Bal-A	142	560	87	147	36	8	13	66	82	99	.262	.367	.425	792	108	8	24	12	1	.993	2	*O-140(126-18-3)/D-2	0.7
1994	Bal-A	111	453	78	119	25	5	12	48	57	75	.263	.358	.419	777	95	-3	31	1	6	.996	-0	*O-109(76-38-5)	0.1
1995	Bal-A	143	554	108	145	33	10	16	64	87	111	.262	.372	.444	816	109	9	26	7	3	.989	-16	*O-142(131-40-0)	-0.6
1996	*Bal-A★	149	579	117	172	37	5	50	110	76	106	.297	.399	.637	1036	157	50	21	8	2	.992	6	*O-143(0-143-0)/D-2	5.3
1997	*Bal-A★	151	590	97	170	39	7	18	73	84	105	.288	.394	.469	863	128	27	18	12	-0	.989	-2	*O-124(0-124-0),D-25	2.3
1998	Bal-A	133	479	84	113	28	3	18	51	75	78	.236	.357	.420	776	103	3	21	7	2	.985	-9	*O-130(0-130-0)	-0.2

YEAR	TM/L	G	AB	R	H	2B	3B	HR	RBI	BB	SO	AVG	OBP	SLG	OPS	OPS+	BR+	SB	CS	SBR	FA	FR	G/POS	TPR
1999	Bal-A	150	564	109	159	28	5	24	81	96	105	.282	.408	.477	885	130	30	36	7	5	.997	-4	*O-136(9-129-0),D-10	2.9
2000	Bal-A	141	506	89	130	26	0	19	50	92	103	.257	.380	.421	800	106	7	16	9	0	.997	2	*O-127(16-88-24),D-11	0.8
Total	13	1669	5989	1008	1561	322	64	201	711	882	1090	.261	.369	.436	805	112	126	299	96	32	.989	-15	*O-1542C/D-71	11.4

■ DAVE ANDERSON

Anderson, David Carter b: 8/1/60, Louisville, Ky. BR/TR, 6'2", 185 lbs. Deb: 5/8/83

YEAR	TM/L	G	AB	R	H	2B	3B	HR	RBI	BB	SO	AVG	OBP	SLG	OPS	OPS+	BR+	SB	CS	SBR	FA	FR	G/POS	TPR
1983	LA-N	61	115	12	19	4	2	1	2	12	15	.165	.244	.261	505	40	-9	6	3	0	.969	3	S-53/3-1	-0.3
1984	LA-N	121	374	51	94	16	2	3	34	45	55	.251	.335	.329	664	88	-5	15	5	2	.965	19	*S-111,3-11	2.7
1985	*LA-N	77	221	24	44	6	0	4	18	35	42	.199	.311	.281	592	69	-8	5	4	-0	.957	17	3-51,S-25/2-2	1.0
1986	LA-N	92	216	31	53	9	0	1	15	22	39	.245	.315	.301	616	76	-7	5	1	1	.976	9	3-51,S-34/2-5	0.6
1987	LA-N	108	265	32	62	12	3	1	13	24	43	.234	.300	.313	613	64	-13	9	5	0	.977	6	S-65,3-35/2-5	-0.2
1988	*LA-N	116	285	31	71	10	2	2	20	32	45	.249	.327	.319	646	89	-3	4	2	0	.986	14	S-82,3-12,2-11	1.7
1989	LA-N	87	140	15	32	2	0	1	14	17	26	.229	.312	.264	576	67	-5	2	0	0	.990	0	S-33,3-18/2-7	-0.3
1990	SF-N	60	100	14	35	5	1	1	6	3	20	.350	.369	.450	819	129	4	1	2	-0	1.000	-6	S-29,2-13/1-3,3-2	-0.1
1991	SF-N	100	226	24	56	5	2	2	13	12	35	.248	.286	.314	600	71	-9	2	4	-1	.956	-10	S-63,1-16,3-11,/2-6	-1.8
1992	LA-N	51	84	10	24	4	0	3	8	4	11	.286	.318	.440	759	115	1	0	4	-1	.974	2	3-26/S-7	0.2
Total	10	873	2026	244	490	73	12	19	143	206	331	.242	.313	.318	631	79	-56	49	30	0	.970	54	S-502,3-218/2-49,1	3.5

■ DWAIN ANDERSON

Anderson, Dwain Cleaven b: 11/23/47, Oakland, Cal. BR/TR, 5'11", 165 lbs. Deb: 9/3/71 Career OF: (0-LF 2-CF 0-RF)

YEAR	TM/L	G	AB	R	H	2B	3B	HR	RBI	BB	SO	AVG	OBP	SLG	OPS	OPS+	BR+	SB	CS	SBR	FA	FR	G/POS	TPR
1971	Oak-A	16	37	3	10	2	1	0	3	5	9	.270	.372	.378	750	115	1	0	1	-0	.968	-1	S-10/2-5,3-1	0.1
1972	Oak-A	3	7	2	0	0	0	0	0	1	4	.000	.125	.000	125	-64	-1	0	0	0	1.000	-0	/S-1,3-1	-0.2
	StL-N	57	135	12	36	4	1	1	8	8	23	.267	.313	.333	646	85	-3	0	1	-0	.952	-3	S-43,3-13/2-1	-0.3
1973	StL-N	18	17	5	2	0	0	0	0	4	4	.118	.286	.118	403	16	-2	0	0	0	.500	-3	/S-3,O-2(0-2-0)	-0.4
	SD-N	53	107	11	13	0	0	0	3	14	29	.121	.223	.121	345	-2	-15	2	0	0	.932	3	S-39/3-6	-0.8
	Yr	71	124	16	15	0	0	0	3	18	33	.121	.232	.121	353	1	-16	2	0	0	.919	1	S-42/3-6,O-2(0-2-0)	-1.2
1974	Cle-A	2	3	0	1	0	0	0	0	0	1	.333	.333	.333	667	93	-0	0	0	0	1.000	-1	/2-1	-0.1
Total	4	149	306	33	62	6	2	1	14	32	70	.203	.282	.245	527	52	-20	2	2	-0	.940	-4	/S-96,3-21,2-7,O-2C	-1.7

■ GOAT ANDERSON

Anderson, Edward John b: 1/13/1880, Cleveland, Ohio d: 3/15/23, South Bend, Ind. BL/TR, Deb: 4/11/07

YEAR	TM/L	G	AB	R	H	2B	3B	HR	RBI	BB	SO	AVG	OBP	SLG	OPS	OPS+	BR+	SB	CS	SBR	FA	FR	G/POS	TPR
1907	Pit-N	127	413	73	85	3	1	1	12	80		.206	.343	.225	568	77	-6	27			.953	-1	*O-117(2-24-91)/2-5	-1.4

■ FERRELL ANDERSON

Anderson, Ferrell Jack "Andy" b: 1/9/18, Maple City, Kan. d: 3/12/78, Joplin, Mo. BR/TR, 6'1", 200 lbs. Deb: 4/16/46

YEAR	TM/L	G	AB	R	H	2B	3B	HR	RBI	BB	SO	AVG	OBP	SLG	OPS	OPS+	BR+	SB	CS	SBR	FA	FR	G/POS	TPR
1946	Bro-N	79	199	19	51	10	0	2	14	18	21	.256	.330	.337	667	89	-3	1			.964	-2	C-70	-0.2
1953	StL-N	18	35	1	10	2	0	0	1	0	4	.286	.286	.343	629	63	-2	0	0	0	1.000	-1	C-12	-0.3
Total	2	97	234	20	61	12	0	2	15	18	25	.261	.324	.338	662	85	-5	1	0		.968	-3	/C-82	-0.5

■ GARRET ANDERSON

Anderson, Garret Joseph b: 6/30/72, Los Angeles, Cal. BL/TL, 6'3", 190 lbs. Deb: 7/27/94 Career OF: (444-LF 284-CF 154-RF)

YEAR	TM/L	G	AB	R	H	2B	3B	HR	RBI	BB	SO	AVG	OBP	SLG	OPS	OPS+	BR+	SB	CS	SBR	FA	FR	G/POS	TPR
1994	Cal-A	5	13	0	5	0	0	0	1	0	2	.385	.385	.385	769	98	-0	0	0	0	1.000	0	/O-4(4-0-0)	0.0
1995	Cal-A	106	374	50	120	19	1	16	69	19	65	.321	.355	.505	861	122	11	6	2	1	.978	7	*O-100(99-1-1)/D-1	1.5
1996	Cal-A	150	607	79	173	33	2	12	72	27	84	.285	.315	.405	721	80	-19	7	9	-2	.979	6	*O-146(140-3-6)/D-1	-1.8
1997	Ana-A	154	624	76	189	36	3	8	92	30	70	.303	.337	.409	746	94	-6	10	4	1	.992	13	*O-148(130-27-4)/D-4	0.3
1998	Ana-A	156	622	62	183	41	7	15	79	29	80	.294	.327	.455	782	100	-2	8	3	1	.983	8	*O-155(39-0-122)	0.0
1999	Ana-A	157	620	88	188	36	2	21	80	34	81	.303	.339	.469	809	104	2	3	4	-1	.993	11	*O-153(32-116-6)/D-4	1.2
2000	Ana-A	159	647	92	185	40	3	35	117	24	87	.286	.311	.519	831	105	1	7	6	-1	.990	2	*O-148(0-137-15),D-10	0.2
Total	7	887	3507	447	1043	205	18	107	510	163	469	.297	.329	.458	787	99	-12	41	28	-1	.986	47	O-854L/D-20	1.4

■ GEORGE ANDERSON

Anderson, George Jendrus "Andy" (Born George Andrew Jendrus)
b: 9/26/1889, Cleveland, Ohio d: 5/28/62, Cleveland, Ohio BL/TR, 5'8", 160 lbs. Deb: 5/26/14

YEAR	TM/L	G	AB	R	H	2B	3B	HR	RBI	BB	SO	AVG	OBP	SLG	OPS	OPS+	BR+	SB	CS	SBR	FA	FR	G/POS	TPR
1914	Bro-F	98	364	58	115	13	3	3	24	31	50	.316	.376	.393	769	110	1	16			.946	4	O-92(70-21-1)	0.0
1915	Bro-F	136	511	70	135	23	9	2	39	52	54	.264	.342	.356	698	97	-9	20			.956	-8	*O-134(40-12-82)	-2.6
1918	StL-N	35	132	20	39	4	5	0	6	15	7	.295	.380	.402	782	143	7	0			.956	-1	O-35(0-0-35)	0.4
Total	3	269	1007	148	289	40	17	5	69	98	111	.287	.359	.375	734	108	-1	36			.952	-5	O-261(110-33-118)	-2.2

■ SPARKY ANDERSON

Anderson, George Lee b: 2/22/34, Bridgewater, S.Dak BR/TR, 5'9", 170 lbs. Deb: 4/10/59 MCH

YEAR	TM/L	G	AB	R	H	2B	3B	HR	RBI	BB	SO	AVG	OBP	SLG	OPS	OPS+	BR+	SB	CS	SBR	FA	FR	G/POS	TPR
1959	Phi-N	152	477	42	104	9	3	0	34	42	53	.218	.283	.249	532	43	-38	6	9	-2	.984	3	*2-152	-2.7

■ HAL ANDERSON

Anderson, Harold b: 2/10/04, St.Louis, Mo. d: 5/1/74, St.Louis, Mo. BR/TR, 5'11", 160 lbs. Deb: 4/12/32

YEAR	TM/L	G	AB	R	H	2B	3B	HR	RBI	BB	SO	AVG	OBP	SLG	OPS	OPS+	BR+	SB	CS	SBR	FA	FR	G/POS	TPR
1932	Chi-A	9	32	4	8	0	0	0	2	0	1	.250	.250	.250	500	32	-3	0	1	-0	1.000	0	/O-9(0-9-0)	-0.4

■ HARRY ANDERSON

Anderson, Harry Walter b: 9/10/31, North East, Md. d: 6/11/98, Greenville, Del. BL/TR, 6'3", 210 lbs. Deb: 4/18/57

YEAR	TM/L	G	AB	R	H	2B	3B	HR	RBI	BB	SO	AVG	OBP	SLG	OPS	OPS+	BR+	SB	CS	SBR	FA	FR	G/POS	TPR
1957	Phi-N	118	400	53	107	15	4	17	61	36	61	.268	.337	.452	790	113	7	2	3	-1	.986	4	*O-109(107-0-2)	0.4
1958	Phi-N	140	515	80	155	34	6	23	97	59	95	.301	.376	.524	900	137	27	0	2	-1	.975	-2	O-87(87-0-0),1-49	1.7
1959	Phi-N	142	508	50	122	28	6	14	63	43	95	.240	.306	.402	707	85	-12	1	1	-0	.980	18	*O-137(137-0-0)	-0.2
1960	Phi-N	38	93	10	23	2	0	5	12	10	19	.247	.333	.430	763	107	1	0	0	0	1.000	-1	O-16(16-0-0),1-12	-0.2
	Cin-N	42	66	6	11	3	0	1	9	11	20	.167	.286	.258	543	49	-4	0	0	0	.990	-1	1-15/O-4(2-0-2)	-0.7
	Yr	80	159	16	34	5	0	6	21	21	39	.214	.313	.358	672	82	-4	0	0	0	.989	-2	1-27,O-20(18-0-2)	-0.9
1961	Cin-N	4	4	0	1	0	0	0	0	0	1	.250	.250	.250	500	33	-0	0	0	0	.000	0	H	0.0
Total	5	484	1586	199	419	82	16	60	242	159	291	.264	.337	.450	787	109	19	3	6	-1	.982	19	O-353(349-0-4)/1-76	1.0

■ JIM ANDERSON

Anderson, James Lea b: 2/23/57, Los Angeles, Cal. BR/TR, 6', 170 lbs. Deb: 7/2/78 Career OF: (2-LF 0-CF 1-RF)

YEAR	TM/L	G	AB	R	H	2B	3B	HR	RBI	BB	SO	AVG	OBP	SLG	OPS	OPS+	BR+	SB	CS	SBR	FA	FR	G/POS	TPR
1978	Cal-A	48	108	6	21	7	0	0	7	11	16	.194	.269	.259	528	51	-7	0	0	0	.955	3	S-47/2-1	-0.1
1979	*Cal-A	96	234	33	58	13	1	3	23	17	31	.248	.302	.350	652	78	-7	3	2	-0	.949	-1	S-82,3-10/2-6,C-3	-0.2
1980	Sea-A	116	317	46	72	7	0	8	30	27	39	.227	.294	.325	619	69	-14	2	4	-1	.958	3	S-65,3-33/2-2,CD	-0.6
1981	Sea-A	70	162	12	33	7	0	2	19	17	29	.204	.283	.284	567	61	-8	3	5	-1	.947	4	S-68/3-2	0.0
1983	Tex-A	50	102	8	22	1	1	0	6	5	8	.216	.252	.245	497	38	-9	1	2	-0	.962	6	S-27,2-17/3-3,OCD	-0.1
1984	Tex-A	39	47	2	5	0	0	0	1	4	7	.106	.176	.106	283	-19	-8	0	0	0	.989	10	S-31/3-6,2-1	0.4
Total	6	419	970	107	211	35	2	13	86	81	130	.218	.281	.298	579	60	-52	9	13	-3	.955	24	S-320/3-54,2-27,DCO	-0.6

■ JOHN ANDERSON

Anderson, John Joseph "Honest John" b: 12/14/1873, Sarpsborg, Norway
d: 7/23/49, Worcester, Mass. BB/TR, 6'2", 180 lbs. Deb: 9/8/1894 Career OF: (561-LF 229-CF 219-RF)

YEAR	TM/L	G	AB	R	H	2B	3B	HR	RBI	BB	SO	AVG	OBP	SLG	OPS	OPS+	BR+	SB	CS	SBR	FA	FR	G/POS	TPR
1894	Bro-N	17	63	14	19	1	3	1	19	3	3	.302	.333	.460	794	96	-1	7			.778	-5	O-16(15-1-0)/3-1	-0.6
1895	Bro-N	103	423	77	122	11	14	10	87	12	29	.288	.316	.452	767	105	1	24			.882	-6	*O-102(90-0-12)	-1.1
1896	Bro-N	108	430	70	135	23	17	1	55	18	23	.314	.344	.453	798	116	8	37			.942	-3	O-68(33-9-26),1-42	0.0
1897	Bro-N	117	492	93	160	28	12	4	85	17		.325	.357	.455	812	120	12	29			.936	0	*O-115(115-0-0)/1-3	0.2
1898	Bro-N	6	21	1	3	2	0	0	2	1		.143	.217	.238	455	31	-2	0			1.000	0	/O-5(2-1-2)	-0.2
	Was-N	110	430	70	131	28	18	9	71	23		.305	.357	.516	873	150	24	18			.948	9	O-93(13-78-2),1-17	2.4
	Bro-N	19	69	11	19	3	4	0	8	5		.275	.333	.435	768	120	1	2			.966	-1	O-17(17-0-0)/1-2	-0.1
	Yr	135	520	82	153	33	**22**	9	81	29		.294	.348	**.494**	842	141	24	20			.952	8	*O-115(32-79-4),1-19	2.1
1899	Bro-N	117	439	65	118	18	7	4	92	27		.269	.317	.369	686	86	-10	25			.933	-4	O-76(7-61-8),1-41	-1.7
1901	Mil-A	138	576	90	190	46	7	8	99	24		.330	.360	.476	836	137	26	35			**.982**	5	*1-125,O-13(12-0-1)	2.5
1902	StL-A	126	524	60	149	29	6	4	85	21		.284	.316	.385	701	95	-5	15			.985	-9	*1-126/O-3(2-0-1)	-1.6
1903	StL-A	138	550	65	156	34	8	2	78	23		.284	.312	.385	698	111	6	16			.986	4	*1-133/O-7(2-3-2)	0.8
1904	NY-A	143	558	62	155	27	12	3	82	23		.278	.313	.385	699	115	8	20			.956	-0	*O-112(46-52-13),1-33	0.2
1905	NY-A	32	99	12	23	3	1	0	14	8		.232	.296	.283	579	75	-3	9			.900	-2	O-22(1-19-2)/1-3	-0.6
	Was-A	101	400	50	116	21	6	1	38	22		.290	.330	.380	710	130	12	22			.960	0	O-97(16-3-78)/1-4	0.8
	Yr	133	499	62	139	24	7	1	52	30		.279	.323	.361	684	117	9	31			.949	-2	*O-119(17-22-80)/1-7	0.2
1906	Was-A	151	583	62	158	25	4	3	70	19		.271	.296	.343	639	105	1	**39**			.953	5	*O-151(151-0-0)	-0.3
1907	Was-A	87	333	33	96	12	4	0	44	34		.288	.359	.348	708	136	15	19			.983	-1	1-61,O-26(26-0-0)	1.3
1908	Chi-A	123	355	36	93	17	1	0	47	30		.262	.321	.315	637	109	4	21			.963	-6	O-87(13-2-72)/1-9	-0.7
Total	14	1636	6345	871	1843	328	124	50	976	310	55	.290	.329	.405	734	115	99	338			.939	-14	*O-1010L,1-599/3-1	1.3

■ KENT ANDERSON

Anderson, Kent McKay b: 8/12/63, Florence, S.C. BR/TR, 6'1", 180 lbs. Deb: 4/15/89 F

YEAR	TM/L	G	AB	R	H	2B	3B	HR	RBI	BB	SO	AVG	OBP	SLG	OPS	OPS+	BR+	SB	CS	SBR	FA	FR	G/POS	TPR
1989	Cal-A	86	223	27	51	6	1	0	17	17	42	.229	.286	.265	551	57	-12	1	2	-0	.972	14	S-70/2-7,3-5,O-2R,D	0.6

YEAR	TM/L	G	AB	R	H	2B	3B	HR	RBI	BB	SO	AVG	OBP	SLG	OPS	OPS+	BR+	SB	CS	SBR	FA	FR	G/POS	TPR
1990	Cal-A	49	143	16	44	6	1	1	5	13	19	.308	.369	.385	754	113	3	0	2	-1	.964	13	S-28,3-16/2-5	1.7
Total	2	135	366	43	95	12	2	1	22	30	61	.260	.319	.311	631	79	-9	1	4	-1	.969	27	/S-98,3-21,2-12,OD	2.3
■ **MARLON ANDERSON**	Anderson, Marlon Ordell b: 1/6/74, Montgomery, Ala. BL/TR, 5'11", 190 lbs. Deb: 9/8/98																							
1998	Phi-N	17	43	4	14	3	0	1	4	1	6	.326	.341	.465	806	108	0	2	0	0	.978	1	/2-9	0.3
1999	Phi-N	129	452	48	114	26	4	5	54	24	61	.252	.293	.361	654	62	-26	13	2	2	.979	-6	*2-121	-2.4
2000	Phi-N	41	162	10	37	8	1	1	15	12	22	.228	.282	.309	590	48	-13	2	2	-0	.989	-3	2-41	-1.3
Total	3	187	657	62	165	37	5	7	73	37	89	.251	.293	.355	648	62	-39	17	4	2	.982	-7	2-171	-3.4
■ **MIKE ANDERSON**	Anderson, Michael Allen b: 6/22/51, Florence, S.C. BR/TR, 6'2", 200 lbs. Deb: 9/2/71 F Career OF: (115-LF 78-CF 443-RF)																							
1971	Phi-N	26	89	11	22	5	1	2	5	13	28	.247	.343	.393	736	108	1	0	0	0	.986	2	O-26(0-26-0)	0.2
1972	Phi-N	36	103	8	20	5	1	2	5	19	36	.194	.320	.320	640	80	-2	1	0	0	.987	4	O-35(0-3-34)	0.0
1973	Phi-N	87	193	32	49	9	1	9	28	19	53	.254	.324	.451	775	110	2	0	3	-1	.981	-6	O-67(0-12-57)	-0.8
1974	Phi-N	145	395	35	99	22	2	5	34	37	75	.251	.315	.354	669	83	-9	2	1	0	.980	4	*O-133(1-2-131)/1-1	-1.1
1975	Phi-N	115	247	24	64	10	3	4	28	17	66	.259	.312	.372	684	86	-5	1	2	-0	.977	-10	*O-105(0-24-88)/1-3	-1.9
1976	StL-N	86	199	17	58	8	1	1	12	26	30	.291	.376	.357	733	108	3	1	1	-0	.982	0	O-58(24-2-33)/1-5	0.0
1977	StL-N	94	154	18	34	4	1	4	17	14	31	.221	.286	.338	623	68	-7	2	3	-1	.980	-10	O-77(2-1-74)	-2.0
1978	Bal-A	53	32	2	3	0	1	0	3	3	10	.094	.171	.156	328	-8	-5	0	0	0	.962	-15	O-47(41-2-6)	-2.1
1979	Phi-N	79	78	12	18	4	0	1	2	13	14	.231	.341	.321	661	79	-2	1	2	-0	.973	-13	O-70(47-6-20)/P-1	-1.7
Total	9	721	1490	159	367	67	11	28	134	161	343	.246	.321	.362	684	88	-24	8	12	-2	.980	-44	O-618R/1-9,P-1	-9.4
■ **ERNIE ANDRES**	Andres, Ernest Henry "Junie" b: 1/11/18, Jeffersonville, Ind. BR/TR, 6'1", 200 lbs. Deb: 4/16/46																							
1946	Bos-A	15	41	0	4	2	0	0	1	3	5	.098	.159	.146	305	-14	-6	0	0	0	1.000	1	3-15	-0.6
■ **KIM ANDREW**	Andrew, Kim Darrell b: 11/14/53, Glendale, Cal. BR/TR, 5'10", 160 lbs. Deb: 4/16/75																							
1975	Bos-A	2	2	0	1	0	0	0	0	0	0	.500	.500	.500	1000	169	0	0	0	0	1.000	-0	/2-2	0.0
■ **SHANE ANDREWS**	Andrews, Darrell Shane b: 8/28/71, Dallas, Tex. BR/TR, 6'1", 215 lbs. Deb: 4/26/95																							
1995	Mon-N	84	220	27	47	10	1	8	31	17	68	.214	.273	.377	650	67	-11	1	1	-0	.973	2	3-51,1-29	-1.1
1996	Mon-N	127	375	43	85	15	2	19	64	35	119	.227	.296	.429	725	86	-9	3	1	0	.955	21	*3-123	1.3
1997	Mon-N	18	64	10	13	3	0	4	9	3	20	.203	.239	.438	676	73	-3	0	0	0	.895	3	3-18	0.0
1998	Mon-N	150	492	48	117	30	1	25	69	58	137	.238	.318	.455	773	102	0	1	6	-2	.954	20	*3-147	1.8
1999	Mon-N	98	281	28	51	8	0	11	37	43	88	.181	.290	.327	618	57	-19	1	0	0	.932	-5	3-82,1-18/D-1	-2.3
	Chi-N	19	67	13	17	4	0	5	14	7	21	.254	.333	.537	871	117	1	0	1	-0	.955	-1	3-19/1-1	0.0
	Yr	117	348	41	68	12	0	16	51	50	109	.195	.298	.368	666	69	-17	1	1	-0	.936	-6	*3-101,1-19/D-1	-2.3
2000	Chi-N	66	192	25	44	5	0	14	39	27	59	.229	.330	.474	804	102	0	1	1	-0	.907	1	3-58/1-6	0.1
Total	6	562	1691	194	374	75	4	86	263	190	512	.221	.302	.423	725	86	-40	7	10	-2	.946	41	3-498/1-54,D-1	-0.2
■ **FRED ANDREWS**	Andrews, Fred b: 5/4/52, Lafayette, La. BR/TR, 5'8", 163 lbs. Deb: 9/26/76																							
1976	Phi-N	4	6	1	4	0	0	0	0	2	0	.667	.778	.667	1444	304	2	1	1	-0	1.000	-1	/2-4	0.2
1977	Phi-N	12	23	3	4	0	1	0	2	1	5	.174	.208	.261	469	24	-2	1	0	0	1.000	3	/2-7	0.1
Total	2	16	29	4	8	0	1	0	2	3	5	.276	.364	.345	708	90	-0	2	1	0	1.000	2	/2-11	0.3
■ **ED ANDREWS**	Andrews, George Edward b: 4/5/1859, Painesville, Ohio d: 8/12/34, W.Palm Beach, Fla. BR/TR, 5'8", 160 lbs. Deb: 5/1/1884 U Career OF: (192-LF 455-CF 5-RF)																							
1884	Phi-N	109	420	74	93	21	2	0	23	9	42	.221	.238	.281	519	66	-16				.891	-22	*2-109	-3.1
1885	Phi-N	103	421	77	112	15	3	0	23	32	25	.266	.318	.316	634	108	5				.921	0	*O-99(99-0-0)/2-5	0.2
1886	Phi-N	107	437	93	109	15	4	2	28	31	35	.249	.299	.316	615	86	-7	**56**			.903	4	*O-104(1-103-0)/2-3	-0.6
1887	Phi-N	104	485	110	172	19	7	4	67	21	21	.355	.359	.422	781	110	5	57			.902	-4	*O-99(0-99-0)/2-7,1-1	-0.2
1888	Phi-N	124	528	75	126	14	4	3	44	21	41	.239	.272	.297	569	77	-14	35			.903	-4	*O-124(0-124-0)	-2.2
1889	Phi-N	10	39	10	11	1	0	0	7	2	4	.282	.317	.308	625	69	-2	7			.808	-1	/O-9(8-0-1),2-1	-0.2
	Ind-N	40	173	32	53	11	0	0	22	5	10	.306	.330	.370	700	94	-2	7			.885	-3	O-40(0-40-0)/2-1	-0.6
	Yr	50	212	42	64	12	0	0	29	7	14	.302	.327	.358	686	89	-4	14			.867	-4	O-49(8-40-1)/2-2	-0.8
1890	Bro-P	94	395	84	100	14	2	3	38	40	32	.253	.323	.322	645	68	-19	21			.912	1	*O-94(1-89-4)	-1.7
1891	Cin-a	83	356	47	75	7	4	0	26	33	35	.211	.279	.253	532	48	-25	22			.961	17	O-83(83-0-0)	-0.9
Total	8	774	3254	602	851	117	26	12	278	194	245	.262	.301	.320	621	82	-75	205			.912	-12	O-652C,2-126/1-1	-9.3
■ **JIM ANDREWS**	Andrews, James Pratt b: 6/5/1865, Shelburne Falls, Mass. d: 12/27/07, Chicago, Ill. Deb: 4/19/1890																							
1890	Chi-N	53	202	32	38	4	2	3	17	23	41	.188	.278	.272	550	58	-11	11			.900	1	O-53(0-0-54)	-1.0
■ **MIKE ANDREWS**	Andrews, Michael Jay b: 7/9/43, Los Angeles, Cal. BR/TR, 6'3", 195 lbs. Deb: 9/18/66 F																							
1966	Bos-A	5	18	1	3	0	0	0	0	0	2	.167	.167	.167	333	-4	-2	0	0	0	1.000	2	/2-5	0.0
1967	*Bos-A	142	494	79	130	20	0	8	40	62	72	.263	.348	.352	700	99	1	7	7	-1	.976	-6	*2-139/S-6	0.7
1968	Bos-A	147	536	77	145	22	1	7	45	81	57	.271	.369	.354	724	113	12	3	8	-2	.976	1	*2-139/S-4,3-1	2.6
1969	Bos-A★	121	464	79	136	26	2	15	59	71	53	.293	.393	.455	847	129	20	1	1	-0	.972	5	*2-120	3.4
1970	Bos-A	151	589	91	149	28	1	17	65	81	63	.253	.346	.390	737	96	-2	2	1	0	.973	-30	*2-148	-2.3
1971	Chi-A	109	330	45	93	16	0	12	47	67	36	.282	.405	.439	844	135	18	3	5	-1	.956	-3	2-76,1-25	1.8
1972	Chi-A	148	505	58	111	18	0	7	50	70	78	.220	.317	.297	614	82	-9	2	2	-0	.973	-14	*2-145/1-5	-1.7
1973	Chi-A	52	159	10	32	9	0	0	10	23	28	.201	.302	.258	560	57	-8	0	1	-0	1.000	-3	D-30/1-9,2-6,3-5	-1.3
	*Oak-A	18	21	1	4	1	0	0	0	3	1	.190	.292	.238	530	53	-1	0	0	0	.944	-1	/2-9,D-2	-0.2
	Yr	70	180	11	36	10	0	0	10	26	29	.200	.301	.256	557	57	-10	0	1	-0	.974	-4	D-32,2-15/1-9,3-5	-1.5
Total	8	893	3116	441	803	140	4	66	316	458	390	.258	.356	.369	724	104	28	18	25	-5	.973	-49	2-787/1-39,D-32,S3	3.0
■ **ROB ANDREWS**	Andrews, Robert Patrick b: 12/11/52, Santa Monica, Cal. BR/TR, 6', 185 lbs. Deb: 4/7/75 F																							
1975	Hou-N	103	277	29	66	5	4	0	19	31	34	.238	.315	.285	600	73	-10	12	5	1	.982	7	2-94/S-6	0.3
1976	Hou-N	109	410	42	105	8	5	0	23	33	27	.256	.312	.300	612	81	-10	7	3	0	.977	8	*2-107/S-3	0.6
1977	SF-N	127	436	60	115	11	3	0	25	56	33	.264	.348	.303	650	76	-12	5	6	-1	.964	-12	*2-115	-2.0
1978	SF-N	79	177	21	39	3	3	1	11	20	18	.220	.299	.288	588	67	-8	5	1	1	.977	9	2-62/S-1	0.5
1979	SF-N	75	154	22	40	3	0	2	13	8	9	.260	.296	.318	614	73	-6	4	1	1	.956	4	2-53/3-3	0.0
Total	5	493	1454	174	365	30	15	3	91	148	121	.251	.320	.298	619	76	-46	33	16	2	.972	15	2-431/S-10,3-3	-0.6
■ **STAN ANDREWS**	Andrews, Stanley Joseph "Polo" (b: Stanley Joseph Andruskewicz) b: 4/17/17, Lynn, Mass. d: 6/10/95, Bradenton, Fla. BR/TR, 5'11", 178 lbs. Deb: 6/11/39																							
1939	Bos-N	13	26	1	6	0	0	0	1	1	2	.231	.259	.231	490	35	-2	0			.857	-2	C-10	-0.4
1940	Bos-N	19	33	1	6	0	0	0	2	0	3	.182	.182	.182	364	1	-4	1			.944	-1	C-14	-0.5
1944	Bro-N	4	8	1	1	0	0	0	1	1	2	.125	.222	.125	347	-1	-1	0			1.000	-0	/C-4	-0.1
1945	Bro-N	21	49	5	8	0	1	0	2	5	4	.163	.255	.204	459	29	-5	0			.948	2	C-21	-0.2
	Phi-N	13	33	3	11	2	0	1	6	1	5	.333	.353	.485	838	135	1	1			.950	-1	C-12	0.1
	Yr	34	82	8	19	2	1	1	8	6	9	.232	.292	.317	609	70	-3	1			.949	1	C-33	-0.1
Total	4	70	149	11	32	2	1	1	12	8	16	.215	.259	.262	521	46	-11	2			.938	-1	/C-61	-1.1
■ **WALLY ANDREWS**	Andrews, William Walter b: 9/18/1859, Philadelphia, Pa. d: 1/20/40, Indianapolis, Ind. BR/TR, 6'3", 170 lbs. Deb: 5/22/1884 Career OF: (1-LF 0-CF 0-RF)																							
1884	Lou-a	14	49	10	10	5	1	0	8	4		.204	.264	.347	611	102	0				.950	-1	/1-9,3-3,O-1L,S-1	-0.1
1888	Lou-a	26	93	12	18	6	3	0	6	13		.194	.292	.323	615	99	0	5			.997	2	1-26	-0.1
Total	2	40	142	22	28	11	4	0	14	17		.197	.283	.331	614	100	0	5			.985	1	/1-35,3-3,S-1,O-1L	-0.2
■ **FRED ANDRUS**	Andrus, Frederick Hotham b: 8/23/1850, Washington, Mich. d: 11/10/37, Detroit, Mich. BR/TR, 6'2", 185 lbs. Deb: 7/25/1876																							
1876	Chi-N	8	36	6	11	3	0	0	2	0	5	.306	.306	.389	694	116	0				.714	-3	/O-8(1-3-5)	-0.3
1884	Chi-N	1	5	3	1	0	0	0	0	1	0	.200	.333	.200	533	67	-0				1.000	0	/P-1	0.0
Total	2	9	41	9	12	3	0	0	2	1	5	.293	.310	.366	675	110	0				.714	-3	/O-8(1-3-5),P-1	-0.3
■ **BILL ANDRUS**	Andrus, William Morgan "Andy" b: 7/25/07, Beaumont, Tex. d: 3/12/82, Washington, D.C. BR/TR, 6', 185 lbs. Deb: 9/19/31																							
1931	Was-A	3	7	0	0	0	0	0	1	0	1	.000	.000	.000	0	-99	-2	0	0	0	.750	-0	/3-2	-0.2

YEAR	TM/L	G	AB	R	H	2B	3B	HR	RBI	BB	SO	AVG	OBP	SLG	OPS	OPS+	BR+	SB	CS	SBR	FA	FR	G/POS	TPR
1937	Phi-N	3	2	0	0	0	0	0	0	0	2	.000	.000	.000	0	-93	-1	0			.000	0	/3-1	-0.1
Total	2	6	9	0	0	0	0	0	1	0	3	.000	.000	.000	0	-98	-3	0	0		.750	-0	/3-3	-0.3
■ WIMAN ANDRUS Andrus, William Wiman b: 10/14/1858, Orono, Ontario, Can d: 6/17/35, Miles City, Mont. 5'6.5", 155 lbs. Deb: 9/15/1885																								
1885	Pro-N	1	4	0	0	0	0	0	0	0	1	.000	.000	.000	0	-99	-1				1.000	1	/3-1	0.0
■ TOM ANGLEY Angley, Thomas Samuel b: 10/2/04, Baltimore, Md. d: 10/26/52, Wichita, Kan. BL/TR, 5'8", 190 lbs. Deb: 4/23/29																								
1929	Chi-N	5	16	1	4	1	0	0	6	2	2	.250	.333	.313	646	61	-1	0			.968	1	/C-5	0.1
■ PAT ANKENMAN Ankenman, Frederick Norman b: 12/23/12, Houston, Tex. d: 1/13/89, Houston, Tex. BR/TR, 5'4", 125 lbs. Deb: 4/16/36																								
1936	StL-N	1	3	0	0	0	0	0	0	0	3	.000	.000	.000	0	-99	-1	0			.600	-1	/S-1	-0.2
1943	Bro-N	1	2	1	1	0	0	0	0	0	0	.500	.500	.500	1000	189	0	0			1.000	1	/S-1	0.1
1944	Bro-N	13	24	1	6	1	0	0	3	0	2	.250	.250	.292	542	53	-2	0			.971	0	2-11/S-2	-0.1
Total	3	15	29	2	7	1	0	0	3	0	5	.241	.241	.276	517	46	-2	0			.800	-1	/2-11,S-4	-0.2
■ BILL ANNIS Annis, William Perley b: 3/8/1857, Stoneham, Mass. d: 6/10/23, Kennebunkport, Me BR, 5'7", 150 lbs. Deb: 5/1/1884																								
1884	Bos-N	27	96	17	17	2	0	0	3	0	8	.177	.177	.198	375	18	-9				.897	-3	O-27(4-15-8)	-1.2
■ CAP ANSON Anson, Adrian Constantine b: 4/11/1852, Marshalltown, Iowa d: 4/14/22, Chicago, Ill. BR/TR, 6', 227 lbs. Deb: 5/6/1871 MH NA OF: (1-LF 5-CF 31-RF) Career OF: (45-LF 3-CF 1-RF)																								
1871	Rok-n	25	120	29	39	**11**	3	0	16	2	1	.325	.336	.467	803	134	6	6	2	1	.763	2	*3-20/C-5,2-2,1O	0.5
1872	Ath-n	46	217	60	90	10	7	0	50	16	3	.415	**.455**	.525	980	200	26	6	6	-1	.752	-10	*3-46	1.0
1873	Ath-n	52	254	53	101	9	2	0	36	5	1	.398	.409	.449	858	144	12	0	2	-1	.923	-4	*1-36,3-11/C-3,2O	0.5
1874	Ath-n	55	260	51	87	8	3	0	37	4	1	.335	.345	.388	733	124	5	6	0	1	.936	-6	1-24,3-20/O-8R,SC	0.1
1875	Ath-n	69	326	84	106	15	3	0	58	4	2	.325	.333	.390	723	135	9	11	6	0	.922	12	1-32,O-25R,C-13,/3M	1.9
1876	Chi-N	66	321	63	110	9	7	2	59	12	8	.343	.380	.450	830	157	17				.849	13	*3-66/C-2	2.7
1877	Chi-N	59	255	52	86	**19**	1	0	32	9	3	.337	.360	.420	779	129	7				**.883**	8	*3-40,C-31	1.5
1878	Chi-N	60	261	55	89	12	2	0	40	13	1	.341	.372	.402	775	145	12				.825	-8	*O-48L/2-9,3-3,C-3	0.2
1879	Chi-N	51	227	40	72	20	1	0	34	2	2	**.317**	.323	.414	737	133	7				.975	0	1-51/M	0.5
1880	Chi-N	86	356	54	120	24	1	1	**74**	14	12	.337	.362	.419	781	154	19				**.978**	0	*1-81/3-9,S-1,2M	1.6
1881	Chi-N	84	343	67	**137**	21	7	1	**82**	26	4	**.399**	**.442**	.510	**952**	**189**	**35**				**.975**	7	*1-84/C-2,S-1,M	**3.5**
1882	Chi-N	82	348	69	126	29	8	1	**83**	20	7	.362	.397	.500	897	177	29				.949	-1	*1-82/C-1,M	1.9
1883	Chi-N	98	413	70	127	36	5	0	68	18	9	.308	.336	.419	755	118	8				.964	3	*1-98/P-2,O-1R,CM	0.1
1884	Chi-N	112	475	108	159	30	3	21	**102**	29	13	.335	.373	.543	916	170	36				.956	-0	*1-112/C-3,S-1,PM	2.2
1885	*Chi-N	112	464	100	144	**35**	7	7	**108**	34	13	.310	.357	.461	819	143	20				.958	-2	*1-112/C-1,M	0.7
1886	*Chi-N	125	504	117	187	35	11	10	**147**	55	19	.371	.433	.544	977	171	41	29			.963	8	*1-125,C-12,M	3.4
1887	Chi-N	122	532	107	224	33	13	7	102	60	18	**.421**	.422	.517	939	141	25	27			.973	10	*1-122/C-1,M	2.0
1888	Chi-N	134	515	101	177	20	12	12	**84**	47	24	**.344**	**.400**	.499	**899**	173	41	28			**.986**	9	*1-134,M	3.7
1889	Chi-N	134	518	100	161	32	7	7	117	86	19	.311	.414	.440	854	132	24	27			**.982**	9	*1-134,M	1.8
1890	Chi-N	139	504	95	157	14	5	7	107	**113**	23	.312	**.443**	.401	844	141	33	29			.978	0	*1-135/C-3,2-2,M	1.9
1891	Chi-N	136	540	81	157	24	8	8	**120**	75	29	.291	.378	.409	788	129	21	17			.981	8	*1-136/C-2,M	1.5
1892	Chi-N	146	559	62	152	25	9	1	74	67	30	.272	.354	.354	708	113	10	13			.973	-5	*1-146/M	0.4
1893	Chi-N	103	398	70	125	24	2	0	91	68	12	.314	.415	.384	800	115	12	13			.981	-4	*1-101/M	0.6
1894	Chi-N	84	343	85	133	29	4	5	100	41	15	.388	.457	.539	997	132	19	17			.990	3	1-83/2-1,M	1.6
1895	Chi-N	122	474	87	159	23	6	2	91	55	23	.335	.408	.422	830	107	6	12			.985	-1	*1-122/M	0.4
1896	Chi-N	108	402	72	133	18	2	2	90	49	10	.331	.407	.400	808	109	7	24			.983	-1	*1-98,C-10,M	0.5
1897	Chi-N	114	424	67	121	17	3	3	75	60		.285	.379	.361	740	92	-3	11			.975	1	*1-103,C-11,M	-0.1
Total	5 n	247	1177	277	423	53	18	0	197	31	8	.359	.376	.435	811	146	57	29	16	1	.765	-6	3-102/1-93,O-37R,CS2	4.0
Total	22	2277	9176	1722	3056	529	124	97	1880	953	294	.333	.395	.446	841	138	425	247			.974	59	*1-2059,3-118/CO2PS	32.6
■ ERIC ANTHONY Anthony, Eric Todd b: 11/8/67, San Diego, Cal. BL/TL, 6'2", 195 lbs. Deb: 7/29/89 Career OF: (114-LF 40-CF 416-RF)																								
1989	Hou-N	25	61	7	11	2	0	4	7	9	16	.180	.286	.410	696	100	-0	0	0	0	1.000	-1	O-21(3-0-18)	-0.1
1990	Hou-N	84	239	26	46	8	0	10	29	29	78	.192	.285	.351	637	76	-8	5	0	1	.970	-2	O-71(13-0-59)	-1.2
1991	Hou-N	39	118	11	18	6	0	1	7	12	41	.153	.231	.229	460	31	-11	1	0	0	.986	3	O-37(0-0-37)	-1.0
1992	Hou-N	137	440	45	105	15	1	19	80	38	98	.239	.301	.407	707	103	0	5	4	-0	.973	-6	*O-115(1-2-113)	-1.1
1993	Hou-N	145	486	70	121	19	4	15	66	49	88	.249	.320	.397	717	94	-5	3	5	-1	.988	-7	*O-131(0-23-121)	-1.9
1994	Sea-A	79	262	31	62	14	1	10	30	23	66	.237	.298	.412	710	79	-9	6	2	1	.985	-2	O-71(62-5-10)/D-4	-1.2
1995	*Cin-N	47	134	19	36	6	0	5	23	13	30	.269	.333	.425	759	99	-0	2	1	0	1.000	-1	O-24(4-1-20),1-17	-0.3
1996	Cin-N	47	123	22	30	6	0	8	13	22	36	.244	.359	.488	846	120	4	0	1	-0	.949	-5	O-37(13-0-24)	-0.3
	Col-N	32	62	10	15	2	0	4	9	10	20	.242	.347	.468	815	91	-1	0	1	-0	1.000	-3	O-19(1-9-10)	-0.4
	Yr	79	185	32	45	8	0	12	22	32	56	.243	.355	.481	836	107	2	0	2	-1	.967	-8	O-56(14-9-34)	-0.7
1997	LA-N	47	74	8	18	3	2	2	5	12	18	.243	.349	.419	768	108	1	2	0	0	.966	-1	O-21(17-0-4)	0.0
Total	9	682	1999	249	462	81	8	78	269	217	491	.231	.308	.397	705	91	-29	24	14	0	.981	-25	O-547R/1-17,D-4	-7.5
■ JOE ANTOLICK Antolick, Joseph b: 4/11/16, Hokendauqua, Pa. BR/TR, 6', 185 lbs. Deb: 9/20/44																								
1944	Phi-N	4	6	1	2	0	0	0	0	1	0	.333	.429	.333	762	120	0	0			1.000	1	/C-3	0.1
■ JOHN ANTONELLI Antonelli, John Lawrence b: 7/15/15, Memphis, Tenn. d: 4/18/90, Memphis, Tenn. BR/TR, 5'10.5", 165 lbs. Deb: 9/16/44																								
1944	StL-N	8	21	0	4	1	0	0	1	0	4	.190	.190	.238	429	20	-2	0			1.000	1	/1-3,3-3,2-2	-0.1
1945	StL-N	2	3	0	0	0	0	0	0	0	1	.000	.000	.000	0	-98	-1	0			.667	-0	/3-1	-0.1
	Phi-N	125	504	50	129	27	2	1	28	24	24	.256	.292	.323	616	73	-19	1			.959	-9	*3-108,2-23/1-1,S-1	-2.6
	Yr	127	507	50	129	27	2	1	28	24	25	.254	.291	.321	612	72	-20	1			.957	-9	*3-109,2-23/1-1,S-1	-2.7
Total	2	135	528	50	133	28	2	1	29	24	29	.252	.287	.318	605	70	-22	1			.958	-8	3-112/2-25,1-4,S-1	-2.8
■ BILL ANTONELLO Antonello, William James b: 5/19/27, Brooklyn, N.Y. d: 3/4/93, Fridley, Minn. BR/TR, 5'11", 185 lbs. Deb: 4/30/53																								
1953	Bro-N	40	43	9	7	1	1	1	4	2	11	.163	.200	.302	502	28	-5	0	0	0	.964	-6	O-25(20-2-4)	-1.0
■ LUIS APARICIO Aparicio, Luis Ernesto (Montiel) b: 4/29/34, Maracaibo, Venez. BR/TR, 5'9", 160 lbs. Deb: 4/17/56 H																								
1956	Chi-A	152	533	69	142	19	6	3	56	34	63	.266	.312	.341	653	71	-23	**21**	4	**3**	.954	0	*S-152	-0.7
1957	Chi-A	143	575	82	148	22	6	3	41	52	55	.257	.319	.332	651	78	-17	**28**	8	**3**	.972	-13	*S-142	-1.6
1958	Chi-A★	145	557	76	148	20	9	2	40	35	38	.266	.310	.345	655	82	-14	**29**	6	**4**	.973	9	*S-145	1.2
1959	*Chi-A★	152	612	98	157	18	5	6	51	53	40	.257	.319	.332	651	80	-16	**56**	13	**8**	.970	-4	*S-152	0.0
1960	Chi-A★	153	600	86	166	20	7	2	61	43	39	.277	.326	.343	669	82	-15	**51**	8	**8**	**.979**	**30**	*S-153	3.7
1961	Chi-A★	156	625	90	170	24	4	6	45	38	33	.272	.315	.352	667	79	-19	**53**	13	**7**	**.962**	6	*S-156	0.8
1962	Chi-A★	153	581	72	140	23	5	7	40	32	36	.241	.282	.334	616	65	-29	**31**	12	3	**.973**	10	*S-152	-0.4
1963	Bal-A★	146	601	73	150	18	8	5	45	36	35	.250	.294	.331	625	78	-18	**40**	6	**7**	**.983**	-5	*S-145	-0.5
1964	Bal-A†	146	578	93	154	20	3	10	37	49	51	.266	.327	.363	690	92	-6	**57**	17	**7**	**.979**	3	*S-145	1.7
1965	Bal-A	144	564	67	127	20	10	8	40	46	56	.225	.287	.339	626	76	-18	26	7	3	**.971**	3	*S-141	0.1
1966	*Bal-A	151	659	97	182	25	8	6	41	33	42	.276	.312	.366	677	95	-5	25	11	2	**.978**	10	*S-151	2.2
1967	Bal-A	134	546	55	127	22	5	4	31	29	44	.233	.273	.313	586	73	-19	18	5	2	.957	-20	*S-131	-2.8
1968	Chi-A	155	622	55	164	24	4	4	36	33	43	.264	.303	.334	637	92	-7	17	11	-0	.977	25	*S-154	3.5
1969	Chi-A	156	599	77	168	24	5	5	51	66	29	.280	.354	.362	716	96	-2	24	4	4	.976	29	*S-154	5.1
1970	Chi-A★	146	552	86	173	29	3	5	43	53	34	.313	.375	.404	779	110	9	8	3	1	.976	18	*S-146	4.6
1971	Bos-A★	125	491	56	114	23	0	4	45	35	43	.232	.286	.303	589	63	-24	6	4	-0	.971	-18	*S-121	-3.0
1972	Bos-A†	110	436	47	112	26	3	3	39	26	28	.257	.302	.351	653	89	-6	3	3	-0	.968	-17	*S-109	-1.2
1973	Bos-A	132	499	56	135	17	1	0	49	43	33	.271	.328	.309	637	76	-15	13	1	3	.966	-17	*S-132	-1.4
Total	18	2599	10230	1335	2677	394	92	83	791	736	742	.262	.313	.343	655	82	-244	506	136	64	.972	51	*S-2581	11.3
■ LUKE APPLING Appling, Lucius Benjamin b: 4/2/07, High Point, N.C. d: 1/3/91, Cumming, Ga. BR/TR, 5'10", 183 lbs. Deb: 9/10/30 MCH																								
1930	Chi-A	6	26	2	8	2	0	0	2	0	0	.308	.308	.385	692	77	-1	2	0	0	.879	-1	/S-6	-0.1
1931	Chi-A	96	297	36	69	13	4	1	28	29	27	.232	.303	.313	616	66	-15	9	2	1	.900	-6	S-76/2-1	-1.3
1932	Chi-A	139	489	66	134	20	10	3	63	40	36	.274	.329	.374	703	87	-10	9	8	-1	.929	18	S-85,2-30,3-14	1.5

YEAR	TM/L	G	AB	R	H	2B	3B	HR	RBI	BB	SO	AVG	OBP	SLG	OPS	OPS+	BR+	SB	CS	SBR	FA	FR	G/POS	TPR
1933	Chi-A	151	612	90	197	36	10	6	85	56	29	.322	.379	.443	822	122	19	6	11	-3	.939	11	*S-151	3.6
1934	Chi-A	118	452	75	137	28	6	2	61	59	27	.303	.384	.405	788	100	2	3	1	0	.945	-9	*S-110/2-8	0.1
1935	Chi-A	153	525	94	161	28	6	1	71	122	40	.307	.437	.389	826	112	17	12	6	1	.958	**21**	*S-153	4.6
1936	Chi-A★	138	526	111	204	31	7	6	128	85	25	**.388**	.474	.508	981	137	36	10	6	0	.951	15	*S-137	5.3
1937	Chi-A	154	574	98	182	42	8	4	77	86	28	.317	.407	.439	846	113	15	18	10	0	.944	14	*S-154	3.7
1938	Chi-A	81	294	41	89	14	0	0	44	42	17	.303	.392	.350	742	85	-5	1	3	-1	.953	1	S-78	0.1
1939	Chi-A☆	148	516	82	162	16	6	0	56	105	37	.314	.430	.368	798	103	9	16	9	0	.951	-2	*S-148	1.7
1940	Chi-A★	150	566	96	197	27	13	0	79	69	35	.348	.420	.442	862	122	22	3	5	-1	.953	-2	*S-150	2.8
1941	Chi-A☆	154	592	93	186	26	8	1	57	82	32	.314	.399	.390	789	111	13	12	8	-0	.948	0	*S-154	2.3
1942	Chi-A	142	543	78	142	26	4	3	53	63	23	.262	.342	.341	682	94	-3	17	5	2	.948	-7	*S-141	0.3
1943	Chi-A☆	155	585	63	192	33	2	3	80	90	29	**.328**	**.419**	.407	825	142	35	27	8	3	.957	7	*S-155	6.1
1945	Chi-A	18	57	12	21	2	2	1	10	12	7	.368	.478	.526	1005	197	8	1	0	0	.930	-1	S-17	0.9
1946	Chi-A★	149	582	59	180	27	5	1	55	71	41	.309	.384	.378	762	118	16	6	4	-0	.951	7	*S-149	3.4
1947	Chi-A★	139	503	67	154	29	0	8	49	64	28	.306	.386	.412	797	126	19	8	6	-0	.949	-7	*S-129/3-2	2.1
1948	Chi-A	139	497	63	156	16	2	0	47	94	35	.314	.423	.354	777	112	14	10	4	1	.943	12	3-72,S-64	3.0
1949	Chi-A	142	492	82	148	21	5	5	58	121	24	.301	.439	.394	833	125	25	7	12	-3	.964	-1	*S-141	2.9
1950	Chi-A	50	128	11	30	3	4	0	13	12	8	.234	.300	.320	620	61	-8	2	0	0	.967	0	S-20,1-13/2-1	-0.6
Total	20	2422	8856	1319	2749	440	102	45	1116	1302	528	.310	.399	.398	798	113	208	179	108	2	.948	73	*S-2218/3-88,2-40,1	42.4

■ ANGEL ARAGON Aragon, Angel (Valdes) "Pete" b: 8/2/1890, Havana, Cuba d: 1/24/52, New York, N.Y. BR/TR, 5'5", 150 lbs. Deb: 8/20/14 F

YEAR	TM/L	G	AB	R	H	2B	3B	HR	RBI	BB	SO	AVG	OBP	SLG	OPS	OPS+	BR+	SB	CS	SBR	FA	FR	G/POS	TPR
1914	NY-A	6	7	1	1	0	0	0	0	1	2	.143	.333	.143	476	44	-0	0			.000	-1	/O-1(0-1-0)	-0.1
1916	NY-A	12	24	1	5	0	0	0	3	2	2	.208	.269	.208	478	43	-2	2			.864	1	/3-8,O-2(1-0-1)	0.0
1917	NY-A	14	45	2	3	1	0	0	2	2	2	.067	.106	.089	195	-40	-8	0			.933	1	/O-6(4-2-0),3-4,S-2	-0.8
Total	3	32	76	4	9	1	0	0	5	5	6	.118	.183	.132	315	-4	-10	2			.921	2	/3-12,O-9(5-3-1),S-2	-0.9

■ JACK ARAGON Aragon, Angel Valdes (Reyes) b: 11/20/15, Havana, Cuba d: 4/4/88, Clearwater, Fla. BR/TR, 5'10", 176 lbs. Deb: 8/13/41 F

YEAR	TM/L	G	AB	R	H	2B	3B	HR	RBI	BB	SO	AVG	OBP	SLG	OPS	OPS+	BR+	SB	CS	SBR	FA	FR	G/POS	TPR
1941	NY-N	1	0	0	0	0	0	0	0	0	0	—	—	—	—	—	0	0			.000	0	R	0.0

■ MAURICE ARCHDEACON Archdeacon, Maurice John "Flash" b: 12/14/1897, St.Louis, Mo. d: 9/5/54, St.Louis, Mo. BL/TL, 5'8", 153 lbs. Deb: 9/17/23

YEAR	TM/L	G	AB	R	H	2B	3B	HR	RBI	BB	SO	AVG	OBP	SLG	OPS	OPS+	BR+	SB	CS	SBR	FA	FR	G/POS	TPR
1923	Chi-A	22	87	23	35	5	1	0	4	6	8	.402	.441	.483	924	145	6	2	3	-1	.918	-2	O-20(0-18-2)	0.2
1924	Chi-A	95	288	59	92	9	3	0	25	40	30	.319	.410	.372	781	106	5	11	7	-0	.958	-5	O-77(0-77-0)	-0.3
1925	Chi-A	10	9	2	1	0	0	0	0	2	1	.111	.273	.111	384	0	-1	0	0	0	1.000	-0	/O-1(1-0-0)	-0.1
Total	3	127	384	84	128	14	4	0	29	48	39	.333	.413	.391	803	112	9	13	10	-1	.950	-7	/O-98(1-95-2)	-0.2

■ JIMMY ARCHER Archer, James Patrick b: 5/13/1883, Dublin, Ireland d: 3/29/58, Milwaukee, Wis. BR/TR, 5'10", 168 lbs. Deb: 9/6/04 Career OF: (1-LF 0-CF 0-RF)

YEAR	TM/L	G	AB	R	H	2B	3B	HR	RBI	BB	SO	AVG	OBP	SLG	OPS	OPS+	BR+	SB	CS	SBR	FA	FR	G/POS	TPR
1904	Pit-N	7	20	1	3	0	0	0	1	0		.150	.150	.150	300	-7	-2	0			.919	0	/C-7,O-1(1-0-0)	-0.2
1907	*Det-A	18	42	6	5	0	0	0	0	4		.119	.196	.119	315	1	-5	0			.975	2	C-17/2-1	-0.1
1909	Chi-N	80	261	31	60	9	2	1	30	12		.230	.266	.291	558	71	-9	5			.960	-4	C-80	-0.6
1910	*Chi-N	98	313	36	81	17	6	2	41	14	49	.259	.293	.371	663	94	-4	6			.970	3	C-49,1-40	0.3
1911	Chi-N	116	387	41	98	18	5	4	41	18	43	.253	.288	.357	645	80	-12	5			.977	-1	*C-102,1-10/2-1	-0.4
1912	Chi-N	120	385	35	109	20	2	5	58	22	36	.283	.330	.384	715	95	-3	7			.966	-5	*C-118	0.1
1913	Chi-N	111	368	38	98	14	7	2	44	19	27	.266	.311	.359	670	91	-5	4			.969	-3	*C-103/1-8	0.1
1914	Chi-N	79	248	17	64	9	2	0	19	9	9	.258	.284	.310	595	77	-8	1			.973	5	C-76	0.4
1915	Chi-N	97	309	21	75	11	5	1	27	11	38	.243	.273	.320	594	79	-9	5	6	-1	.977	-2	C-88/1-4	-0.4
1916	Chi-N	77	205	11	45	6	2	1	30	12	24	.220	.269	.283	552	63	-9	3			.979	-3	C-61/3-1	-0.8
1917	Chi-N	2	2	0	0	0	0	0	0	0	1	.000	.000	.000	0	-93	-0	0			.000	0	H	-0.1
1918	Pit-N	24	58	4	9	1	2	0	3	1	6	.155	.197	.241	438	32	-5	0			.989	5	C-21/1-1	0.2
	Bro-N	9	22	3	6	0	1	0	0	1	5	.273	.304	.364	668	104	0	0			.968	1	/C-7	0.1
	Cin-N	9	26	2	7	1	0	0	2	1	3	.269	.296	.308	604	86	-0	0			1.000	1	/C-7,1-1	0.1
	Yr	42	106	9	22	2	3	0	5	3	14	.208	.243	.283	526	59	-5	0			.987	7	C-35/1-2	0.4
Total	12	847	2646	246	660	106	34	16	296	124	241	.249	.288	.333	621	80	-72	36	6		.971	-0	C-736/1-64,2-2,3O	-1.3

■ GEORGE ARCHIE Archie, George Albert b: 4/27/14, Nashville, Tenn. BR/TR, 6', 170 lbs. Deb: 9/14/38

YEAR	TM/L	G	AB	R	H	2B	3B	HR	RBI	BB	SO	AVG	OBP	SLG	OPS	OPS+	BR+	SB	CS	SBR	FA	FR	G/POS	TPR
1938	Det-A	3	2	1	0	0	0	0	0	0	1	.000	.000	.000	0	-95	-1	0	0	0	.000	0	H	-0.1
1941	Was-A	105	379	45	102	20	4	3	48	30	42	.269	.324	.367	691	87	-8	8	4	0	.936	-4	3-73,1-23	-1.1
	StL-A	9	29	3	11	3	0	0	5	7	3	.379	.500	.483	983	156	3	2	0	0	.975	0	/1-8	0.3
	Yr	114	408	48	113	23	4	3	53	37	45	.277	.339	.375	714	92	-5	10	4	1	.936	-4	3-73,1-31	-0.8
1946	StL-A	4	11	1	2	1	0	0	0	0	1	.182	.182	.273	455	25	-1	0	0	0	1.000	2	/1-3	0.1
Total	3	121	421	50	115	24	4	3	53	37	47	.273	.333	.371	704	90	-7	10	4	1	.988	-2	/3-73,1-34	-0.8

■ JOSE ARCIA Arcia, Jose Raimundo (Orta) b: 8/22/43, Havana, Cuba BR/TR, 6'3", 170 lbs. Deb: 4/10/68 Career OF: (16-LF 13-CF 0-RF)

YEAR	TM/L	G	AB	R	H	2B	3B	HR	RBI	BB	SO	AVG	OBP	SLG	OPS	OPS+	BR+	SB	CS	SBR	FA	FR	G/POS	TPR
1968	Chi-N	59	84	15	16	4	0	1	8	3	24	.190	.218	.274	492	44	-6	0	0	0	1.000	-2	O-17C,2-10/S-7,3-1	-0.8
1969	SD-N	120	302	35	65	11	3	0	10	14	47	.215	.255	.272	526	49	-21	14	7	1	.977	5	2-68,S-37/3-8,O1	-1.0
1970	SD-N	114	229	28	51	9	3	0	17	12	36	.223	.282	.288	570	55	-15	3	6	-1	.955	10	S-67,2-20/3-9,O-7L	0.0
Total	3	293	615	78	132	24	6	1	35	29	107	.215	.260	.278	538	51	-41	17	13	-1	.950	13	S-111/2-98,O-28L,31	-1.8

■ DAN ARDELL Ardell, Daniel Miers b: 5/27/41, Seattle, Wash. BL/TL, 6'2", 190 lbs. Deb: 9/14/61

YEAR	TM/L	G	AB	R	H	2B	3B	HR	RBI	BB	SO	AVG	OBP	SLG	OPS	OPS+	BR+	SB	CS	SBR	FA	FR	G/POS	TPR
1961	LA-A	7	4	1	1	0	0	0	0	1	2	.250	.400	.250	650	70	-0	0	0	0	1.000	-0	/1-1	0.0

■ JOE ARDNER Ardner, Joseph A. "Old Hoss" b: 2/27/1858, Mt.Vernon, Ohio d: 9/15/35, Cleveland, Ohio BR/TR, 160 lbs. Deb: 5/1/1884

YEAR	TM/L	G	AB	R	H	2B	3B	HR	RBI	BB	SO	AVG	OBP	SLG	OPS	OPS+	BR+	SB	CS	SBR	FA	FR	G/POS	TPR
1884	Cle-N	26	92	6	16	1	1	0	4	1	24	.174	.183	.207	389	21	-8				.866	-5	2-25/3-1	-1.1
1890	Cle-N	84	323	28	72	13	1	0	35	17	40	.223	.266	.269	535	57	-18	9			.920	-6	2-84	-1.9
Total	2	110	415	34	88	14	2	0	39	18	64	.212	.248	.255	504	50	-26	9			.908	-11	2-109/3-1	-3.0

■ DANNY ARDOIN Ardoin, Daniel Wayne b: 7/8/74, Mamou, La. BR/TR, 6', 205 lbs. Deb: 8/2/2000

YEAR	TM/L	G	AB	R	H	2B	3B	HR	RBI	BB	SO	AVG	OBP	SLG	OPS	OPS+	BR+	SB	CS	SBR	FA	FR	G/POS	TPR
2000	Min-A	15	32	4	4	1	0	1	5	8	10	.125	.300	.250	550	39	-3	0	0	0	.989	3	C-15	0.0

■ HANK ARFT Arft, Henry Irven "Bow Wow" b: 1/28/22, Manchester, Mo. BL/TL, 5'10.5", 190 lbs. Deb: 7/27/48

YEAR	TM/L	G	AB	R	H	2B	3B	HR	RBI	BB	SO	AVG	OBP	SLG	OPS	OPS+	BR+	SB	CS	SBR	FA	FR	G/POS	TPR
1948	StL-A	69	248	25	59	10	3	5	38	45	43	.238	.355	.363	718	89	-3	1	2	-0	.995	-1	1-69	-0.7
1949	StL-A	6	5	1	1	1	0	0	2	0	1	.200	.200	.400	600	55	-0	0	0	0	.000	0	H	0.0
1950	StL-A	98	280	45	75	16	4	1	32	46	48	.268	.375	.364	739	87	-4	3	2	-0	.995	2	1-84	-0.5
1951	StL-A	112	345	44	90	16	5	7	42	41	34	.261	.339	.397	736	96	-2	4	6	-1	.989	8	1-97	0.1
1952	StL-A	15	28	1	4	3	1	0	4	5	7	.143	.273	.321	594	63	-1	0	0	0	.985	-0	1-10	-0.2
Total	5	300	906	116	229	46	13	13	118	137	133	.253	.352	.375	727	90	-12	8	10	-2	.992	8	1-260	-1.3

■ ALEX ARIAS Arias, Alejandro b: 11/20/67, New York, N.Y. BR/TR, 6'3", 185 lbs. Deb: 5/12/92

YEAR	TM/L	G	AB	R	H	2B	3B	HR	RBI	BB	SO	AVG	OBP	SLG	OPS	OPS+	BR+	SB	CS	SBR	FA	FR	G/POS	TPR
1992	Chi-N	32	99	14	29	6	0	0	7	11	13	.293	.375	.354	729	105	1	0	0	0	.967	-4	S-30	-0.1
1993	Fla-N	96	249	27	67	5	1	2	20	27	18	.269	.348	.321	669	76	-7	1	1	-0	.987	-9	2-30,3-22,S-18	-1.3
1994	Fla-N	59	113	4	27	5	0	0	15	9	19	.239	.301	.283	584	52	-8	0	1	-0	.985	-5	S-20,3-15	-1.1
1995	Fla-N	94	216	22	58	9	2	3	26	22	20	.269	.342	.370	712	87	-4	1	0	0	.947	-5	S-36,3-21/2-6	-0.5
1996	Fla-N	100	224	27	62	11	2	3	26	17	28	.277	.336	.384	720	92	-2	2	0	0	.956	1	3-59,S-20/1-1,2-1	0.1
1997	*Fla-N	74	93	13	23	2	0	1	11	12	12	.247	.352	.301	653	76	-3	0	1	-0	.971	1	3-37,S-11	-0.2
1998	Phi-N	56	133	17	39	8	0	1	16	13	18	.293	.361	.376	736	93	-1	2	0	0	.985	-5	S-38/3-5,2-1	-0.2
1999	Phi-N	118	347	43	105	20	1	4	48	36	31	.303	.375	.401	775	94	-2	2	2	-0	.988	-25	S-95/3-2,2-1	-1.9
2000	Phi-N	70	155	17	29	9	0	2	15	16	28	.187	.276	.284	560	41	-14	1	0	0	.963	-5	S-39,3-10/2-1	-1.6
Total	9	699	1629	184	439	75	6	16	184	163	187	.269	.344	.352	696	81	-40	9	5	0	.973	-56	S-307,3-171/2-40,1	-6.8

■ GEORGE ARIAS Arias, George Alberto b: 3/12/72, Tucson, Ariz. BR/TR, 5'11", 190 lbs. Deb: 4/2/96

YEAR	TM/L	G	AB	R	H	2B	3B	HR	RBI	BB	SO	AVG	OBP	SLG	OPS	OPS+	BR+	SB	CS	SBR	FA	FR	G/POS	TPR
1996	Cal-A	84	252	19	60	8	1	6	28	16	50	.238	.284	.349	633	59	-16	2	0	0	.960	28	3-83/D-1	1.2
1997	Ana-A	3	6	1	2	0	0	0	1	0	0	.333	.333	.333	667	75	-0	0	0	0	1.000	1	/3-1,D-1	0.0
	SD-N	11	22	2	5	1	0	0	2	0	1	.227	.227	.273	500	33	-2	0	0	0	.941	2	/3-8	-0.1
1998	*SD-N	20	36	4	7	1	1	1	4	3	16	.194	.293	.361	654	77	-1	0	0	0	.933	3	3-14/1-1	0.2

YEAR	TM/L	G	AB	R	H	2B	3B	HR	RBI	BB	SO	AVG	OBP	SLG	OPS	OPS+	BR+	SB	CS	SBR	FA	FR	G/POS	TPR
1999	SD-N	55	164	20	40	8	0	7	20	6	54	.244	.271	.421	691	77	-7	0	0	0	.941	6	3-50	0.0
Total	4	173	480	46	114	18	2	14	55	25	121	.237	.278	.371	649	65	-27	2	0	0	.952	40	3-156/D-2,1-1	1.3
■ BUZZ ARLETT Arlett, Russell Loris b: 1/3/1899, Elmhurst, Cal. d: 5/16/64, Minneapolis, Minn. BB/TR, 6'2", 210 lbs. Deb: 4/14/31																								
1931	Phi-N	121	418	65	131	26	7	18	72	45	39	.313	.387	.538	925	135	21	3			.955	1	O-94(0-0-94),1-13	1.5
■ TONY ARMAS Armas, Antonio Rafael (Machado) b: 7/2/53, Anzoategui, Venez. BR/TR, 6'1", 200 lbs. Deb: 9/6/76 F Career OF: (124-LF 615-CF 623-RF)																								
1976	Pit-N	4	6	0	2	0	0	0	1	0	2	.333	.333	.333	667	89	-0	0	0	0	1.000	-0	/O-2(1-1-0)	0.0
1977	Oak-A	118	363	26	87	8	2	13	53	20	99	.240	.279	.380	660	79	-12	1	2	-0	.981	9	*O-112(3-84-30)/S-1	-0.5
1978	Oak-A	91	239	17	51	6	1	2	13	10	62	.213	.251	.272	523	50	-16	1	2	-0	.991	3	O-85(2-40-47)/D-3	-1.7
1979	Oak-A	80	278	29	69	9	3	11	34	16	67	.248	.292	.421	712	95	-3	1	0	0	.976	7	O-80(12-17-53)	0.1
1980	Oak-A	158	628	87	175	18	8	35	109	29	128	.279	.313	.500	813	128	20	5	3	0	.975	18	*O-158(0-10-152)	3.0
1981	*Oak-A★	109	440	51	115	24	3	**22**	76	19	115	.261	.295	.480	775	126	11	5	1	1	.993	12	*O-109(0-2-108)	1.9
1982	Oak-A	138	536	58	125	19	2	28	89	33	128	.233	.279	.433	712	96	-5	2	2	-0	.983	12	*O-135(0-5-133)/D-1	-0.1
1983	Bos-A	145	574	77	125	23	2	36	107	29	131	.218	.258	.453	711	85	-14	0	1	-0	.985	7	*O-116(0-116-0)/D-27	-1.0
1984	Bos-A☆	157	639	107	171	29	5	**43**	**123**	32	156	.268	.304	.531	834	120	14	1	3	-1	.974	2	*O-126(0-126-1)/D-31	1.3
1985	Bos-A	103	385	50	102	17	5	23	64	18	90	.265	.301	.514	816	114	5	0	0	0	.983	-7	O-79(16-69-2)/D-19	-0.3
1986	*Bos-A	121	425	40	112	21	4	11	58	24	77	.264	.306	.409	715	92	-5	0	3	-1	.969	-13	*O-117(9-108-19)/D-1	-2.1
1987	Cal-A	28	81	8	16	3	1	3	9	1	11	.198	.207	.370	578	51	-6	1	0	0	1.000	-4	O-27(2-0-26)	-1.1
1988	Cal-A	120	368	42	100	20	2	13	49	22	87	.272	.313	.443	756	112	5	1	3	-1	.986	-9	*O-113(74-36-10)/D-5	-0.7
1989	Cal-A	60	202	22	52	7	1	11	30	7	48	.257	.282	.465	748	109	1	0	0	0	.990	2	O-47(5-1-42)/1-2,D-6	0.2
Total	14	1432	5164	614	1302	204	39	251	815	260	1201	.252	.290	.453	742	103	-6	18	20	-3	.981	38	*O-1306R/D-93,1-2,S	-1.0
■ MARCOS ARMAS Armas, Marcos Rafael (Ruiz) b: 8/5/69, Puerto Piritu, Venez. BR/TR, 6'5", 195 lbs. Deb: 5/25/93 F																								
1993	Oak-A	15	31	7	6	2	0	1	1	1	12	.194	.242	.355	597	62	-2	1	0	0	1.000	0	1-12/O-1(0-0-1),D-2	-0.2
■ ED ARMBRISTER Armbrister, Edison Rosanda b: 7/4/48, Nassau, Bahamas BR/TR, 5'11", 160 lbs. Deb: 8/31/73																								
1973	*Cin-N	18	37	5	8	3	1	1	5	2	8	.216	.256	.432	689	92	-1	0	0	0	.917	-2	O-14(3-4-7)	-0.3
1974	Cin-N	9	7	0	2	0	0	0	0	1	1	.286	.375	.286	661	88	-0	0	0	0	1.000	-1	/O-4(2-0-2)	-0.2
1975	*Cin-N	59	65	9	12	1	0	0	2	5	19	.185	.254	.200	454	27	-6	3	1	0	.867	-7	O-19(10-4-7)	-1.4
1976	*Cin-N	73	78	20	23	3	2	2	7	6	22	.295	.345	.462	807	124	2	7	3	0	.972	-4	O-32(20-0-13)	-0.2
1977	Cin-N	65	78	12	20	4	3	1	5	10	21	.256	.341	.423	764	102	0	5	6	-1	.903	-3	O-27(20-0-7)	-0.4
Total	5	224	265	46	65	11	6	4	19	24	71	.245	.310	.377	688	88	-5	15	10	-0	.925	-17	/O-96(55-8-36)	-2.5
■ CHARLIE ARMBRUSTER Armbruster, Charles A. b: 8/30/1880, Cincinnati, Ohio d: 10/7/64, Grants Pass, Ore. BR/TR, 5'9", 180 lbs. Deb: 7/17/05																								
1905	Bos-A	35	91	13	18	4	0	0	6	18		.198	.336	.242	578	83	-1	3			.944	-6	C-35	-0.4
1906	Bos-A	72	201	9	29	6	1	0	6	25		.144	.242	.184	426	34	-15	2			.955	1	C-66/1-1	-0.8
1907	Bos-A	23	60	2	6	1	0	0	0	8		.100	.206	.117	323	3	-6	1			.935	2	C-21	-0.2
	Chi-A	1	3	0	0	0	0	0	0	1		.000	.250	.000	250	-20	-0	0			1.000	1	/C-1	0.0
	Yr	24	63	2	6	1	0	0	0	9		.095	.208	.111	319	2	-7	1			.940	3	C-22	-0.2
Total	3	131	355	24	53	11	1	0	12	52		.149	.262	.186	448	42	-22	6			.949	-2	C-123/1-1	-1.4
■ HARRY ARMBRUSTER Armbruster, Henry "Army" b: 3/20/1882, Cincinnati, Ohio d: 12/10/53, Cincinnati, Ohio BL/TL, 5'10", 190 lbs. Deb: 4/30/06																								
1906	Phi-A	91	265	40	63	6	3	2	24	43		.238	.353	.306	658	103	3	13			.971	0	O-74(0-40-34)	0.0
■ GEORGE ARMSTRONG Armstrong, Noble George "Dodo" b: 6/3/24, Orange, N.J. d: 7/24/93, Orange, N.J. BR/TR, 5'10", 190 lbs. Deb: 4/26/46																								
1946	Phi-A	8	6	0	1	1	0	0	0	1	1	.167	.286	.333	619	73	-0	0	0	0	1.000	1	/C-4	0.0
■ BOB ARMSTRONG Armstrong, Robert b: 1850, Baltimore, Md. 6'2", 160 lbs. Deb: 6/26/1871																								
1871	Kek-n	12	49	9	11	2	1	0	5	0	1	.224	.224	.306	531	50	-3	0	1	-0	.816	2	O-12(0-11-1)	-0.1
■ HARRY ARNDT Arndt, Harry J. b: 2/12/1879, South Bend, Ind. d: 3/25/21, South Bend, Ind. TR, Deb: 7/2/02 Career OF: (8-LF 0-CF 74-RF)																								
1902	Det-A	10	34	4	5	0	1	0	7	6		.147	.275	.206	481	34	-3	0			.958	0	O-10(7-0-3)/1-1	-0.3
	Bal-A	68	248	41	63	7	4	2	28	35		.254	.355	.339	694	89	-3	9			.872	1	O-62R/2-4,3-2,S-1	-0.4
	Yr	78	282	45	68	7	5	2	35	41		.241	.346	.323	668	83	-5	9			.885	1	O-72R/2-4,3-2,1S	-0.7
1905	StL-N	113	415	40	101	11	6	2	36	24		.243	.290	.313	603	82	-10	13			.951	-14	2-90/O-9R,3-7,S-5	-2.4
1906	StL-N	69	256	30	69	7	9	2	26	19		.270	.320	.391	711	127	7	5			.965	12	3-65/1-1,O-1(0-0-1)	2.2
1907	StL-N	11	32	3	6	1	0	0	2	1		.188	.212	.219	431	36	-2	0			1.000	0	/1-4,3-3	-0.3
Total	4	271	985	118	244	26	20	6	99	85		.248	.312	.333	645	91	-11	27			.952	-1	/2-94,O-82R,3-77,S1	-1.2
■ LARRY ARNDT Arndt, Larry Wayne b: 2/25/63, Fremont, Ohio BR/TR, 6'1", 195 lbs. Deb: 6/6/89																								
1989	Oak-A	2	6	1	1	0	0	0	0	0	1	.167	.167	.167	333	-6	-1	0	0	0	1.000	0	/1-1,3-1	-0.1
■ CHRIS ARNOLD Arnold, Christopher Paul b: 11/6/47, Long Beach, Cal. BR/TR, 5'10", 160 lbs. Deb: 9/7/71 Career OF: (3-LF 0-CF 1-RF)																								
1971	SF-N	6	13	2	3	0	0	1	3	1	2	.231	.286	.462	747	110	0	0	0	0	.917	-1	/2-3	-0.1
1972	SF-N	51	84	8	19	3	1	1	4	8	12	.226	.293	.321	615	74	-3	0	1	-0	.970	3	3-17/2-7,S-4	0.0
1973	SF-N	49	54	7	16	2	0	1	13	8	11	.296	.387	.389	776	111	1	0	0	0	.944	-5	/C-9,2-1,3-1	-0.4
1974	SF-N	78	174	22	42	7	3	1	26	15	27	.241	.305	.333	639	75	-6	1	1	-0	.974	-6	2-31/3-7,S-1	-1.0
1975	SF-N	29	41	4	8	0	0	0	0	4	8	.195	.267	.195	462	28	-4	0	0	0	.923	1	/2-4,O-4(3-0-1)	-0.4
1976	SF-N	60	69	4	15	0	1	0	5	6	16	.217	.280	.246	526	49	-4	0	0	0	1.000	3	/2-8,3-4,1-1,S-1	-0.1
Total	6	273	435	47	103	12	5	4	51	42	76	.237	.305	.315	620	72	-16	1	2	-0	.971	-5	/2-54,3-29,C-9,SO1	-2.0
■ BILLY ARNOLD Arnold, Willis S. b: 3/2/1851, Middletown, Conn. d: 1/17/1899, Albany, N.Y. Deb: 4/26/1872																								
1872	Man-n	2	7	2	1	0	0	0	0	0	0	.143	.143	.143	286	-13	-1	0	0	0	1.000	-0	/O-2(0-0-2)	-0.1
■ MORRIE ARNOVICH Arnovich, Morris "Snooker" b: 11/16/10, Superior, Wis. d: 7/20/59, Superior, Wis. BR/TR, 5'10", 168 lbs. Deb: 9/14/36																								
1936	Phi-N	13	48	4	15	3	0	1	7	1	3	.313	.353	.438	790	102	0	0			1.000	2	O-13(13-0-0)	0.2
1937	Phi-N	117	410	60	119	27	4	10	60	34	32	.290	.349	.449	798	107	3	5			.972	7	*O-107(97-9-1)	0.5
1938	Phi-N	139	502	47	138	29	0	4	72	42	37	.275	.333	.357	690	92	-5	2			.983	17	*O-133(130-1-3)	0.4
1939	Phi-N☆	134	491	68	159	25	2	5	67	58	28	.324	.397	.413	811	122	17	7			.983	15	*O-132(131-2-0)	2.4
1940	Phi-N	39	141	13	28	2	1	0	12	14	15	.199	.276	.227	503	42	-11	0			.959	3	O-37(36-0-1)	-1.0
	*Cin-N	62	211	17	60	10	2	0	21	13	10	.284	.326	.351	677	86	-4	1			1.000	2	O-60(57-0-3)	-0.5
	Yr	101	352	30	88	12	3	0	33	27	25	.250	.305	.301	606	68	-15	1			.983	5	O-97(93-0-4)	-1.5
1941	NY-N	85	207	25	58	8	3	2	22	23	14	.280	.352	.377	729	103	1	2			.982	-4	O-61(61-0-0)	-0.6
1946	NY-N	1	3	0	0	0	0	0	0	0	0	.000	.000	.000	0	-99	-1	0			1.000	-0	/O-1(1-0-0)	-0.1
Total	7	590	2013	234	577	104	12	22	261	185	139	.287	.350	.383	733	100	1	17			.981	42	O-544(526-12-8)	1.3
■ TUG ARUNDEL Arundel, John Thomas b: 6/30/1862, Romulus, N.Y. d: 9/5/12, Auburn, N.Y. Deb: 5/23/1882																								
1882	Phi-a	1	5	0	0	0	0	0		0		.000	.000	.000	0	-90	-1				.800	-0	/C-1	-0.1
1884	Tol-a	15	47	6	4	0	0	0		3		.085	.140	.085	225	-24	-6				.946	8	C-15	0.3
1887	Ind-N	43	165	13	39	4	0	0	13	8	12	.236	.241	.223	464	31	-14	8			.865	-5	C-42/O-2(0-0-2),1-1	-1.4
1888	Was-N	17	51	2	10	0	1	0	3	5	10	.196	.268	.235	503	65	-2	1			.840	-7	C-17	-0.8
Total	4	76	268	21	53	4	1	0	16	16	22	.198	.224	.196	420	25	-23	9			.882	-4	/C-75,O-2(0-0-2),1-1	-2.0
■ RANDY ASADOOR Asadoor, Randall Carl b: 10/20/62, Fresno, Cal. BR/TR, 6'1", 185 lbs. Deb: 9/14/86																								
1986	SD-N	15	55	9	20	5	0	0	7	3	13	.364	.397	.455	851	137	3	1	2	-0	.889	0	3-15/2-2	0.2
■ JIM ASBELL Asbell, James Marion "Big Train" b: 6/22/14, Dallas, Tex. d: 7/6/67, San Mateo, Cal. BR/TR, 6', 195 lbs. Deb: 5/8/38																								
1938	Chi-N	17	33	6	6	2	0	0	3	3	9	.182	.250	.242	492	35	-3	0			1.000	-1	O-10(7-0-3)	-0.4
■ CASPER ASBJORNSON Asbjornson, Robert Anthony (Name Changed To Asby) b: 6/19/09, Concord, Mass. d: 1/21/70, Williamsport, Pa. BR/TR, 6'1", 196 lbs. Deb: 9/17/28																								
1928	Bos-A	6	16	0	3	1	0	0	1	1	1	.188	.235	.250	485	28	-2	0	0	0	.917	-2	/C-6	-0.3

YEAR	TM/L	G	AB	R	H	2B	3B	HR	RBI	BB	SO	AVG	OBP	SLG	OPS	OPS+	BR+	SB	CS	SBR	FA	FR	G/POS	TPR
1929	Bos-A	17	29	1	3	0	0	0	0	1	6	.103	.133	.103	237	-39	-6	0	0	0	.897	-3	C-15	-0.8
1931	Cin-N	45	118	13	36	7	1	0	22	7	23	.305	.349	.381	731	102	0	0			.981	-0	C-31	0.2
1932	Cin-N	29	58	5	10	2	0	1	4	0	15	.172	.186	.259	445	19	-7	0			.961	0	C-16	-0.6
Total	4	97	221	19	52	10	1	1	27	9	45	.235	.272	.303	575	56	-14	0	0		.960	-5	/C-68	-1.5
■ **RICHIE ASHBURN** Ashburn, Don Richard "Whitey" b: 3/19/27, Tilden, Neb. d: 9/9/97, New York, N.Y. BL/TR, 5'10", 170 lbs. Deb: 4/20/48 H Career OF: (84-LF 1995-CF 43-RF)																								
1948	Phi-N★	117	463	78	154	17	4	2	40	60	22	.333	.410	.400	810	122	17	**32**			.981	**18**	*O-116(15-102-0)	3.1
1949	Phi-N	154	662	84	188	18	11	1	37	58	38	.284	.343	.349	692	88	-10	9			.980	**25**	*O-154(0-154-0)	1.0
1950	*Phi-N	151	594	84	180	25	**14**	2	41	63	32	.303	.372	.402	774	105	6	14			.988	8	*O-147(0-147-0)	1.0
1951	Phi-N★	154	643	92	**221**	31	5	4	63	50	37	.344	.393	.426	819	122	21	29	6	4	.988	**32**	*O-154(0-154-0)	5.2
1952	Phi-N	154	613	93	173	31	6	1	42	75	30	.282	.362	.357	720	101	3	16	11	-0	.980	15	*O-154(0-154-0)	1.4
1953	Phi-N★	156	622	110	**205**	25	9	2	57	61	35	.330	.394	.408	802	110	12	14	6	1	.990	**26**	*O-156(0-156-0)	3.0
1954	Phi-N	153	559	111	175	16	8	1	41	**125**	46	.313	**.442**	.376	818	116	22	11	8	-0	.984	17	*O-153(0-153-0)	3.1
1955	Phi-N	140	533	91	180	32	9	3	42	105	36	**.338**	**.449**	.448	898	142	39	12	10	-1	.983	11	*O-140(0-140-0)	4.2
1956	Phi-N	154	628	94	190	26	8	3	50	79	45	.303	.385	.384	769	110	12	10	1	2	.983	25	*O-154(0-154-0)	3.2
1957	Phi-N	156	626	93	186	26	8	0	33	**94**	44	.297	.392	.364	756	108	12	13	10	-1	.987	**32**	*O-156(0-156-1)	3.6
1958	Phi-N☆	152	615	98	**215**	24	**13**	2	33	**97**	48	**.350**	**.441**	.441	882	136	38	30	12	2	.984	22	*O-152(0-152-0)	5.5
1959	Phi-N	153	564	86	150	16	2	1	20	79	42	.266	.362	.307	669	79	-13	9	11	-2	.971	5	*O-149(0-149-0)	-1.8
1960	Chi-N	151	547	99	159	16	5	0	40	**116**	50	.291	**.416**	.338	754	110	15	16	4	2	.976	1	*O-146(45-106-0)	1.1
1961	Chi-N	109	307	49	79	7	4	0	19	55	27	.257	.375	.306	682	83	-5	7	6	-1	.978	-7	O-76(14-62-0)	-1.5
1962	NY-N★	135	389	60	119	7	3	7	28	81	39	.306	.426	.393	819	119	15	12	7	0	.975	-4	O-97(10-56-42)/2-2	0.7
Total	15	2189	8365	1322	2574	317	109	29	586	1198	571	.308	.397	.382	779	111	184	234	92		.983	227	*O-2104C/2-2	32.8
■ **ALAN ASHBY** Ashby, Alan Dean b: 7/8/51, Long Beach, Cal. BB/TR (BL 1976), 6'2", 190 lbs. Deb: 7/3/73 C																								
1973	Cle-A	11	29	4	5	1	0	1	3	2	11	.172	.226	.310	536	49	-2	0	0	0	.978	-2	C-11	-0.4
1974	Cle-A	10	7	1	1	0	0	0	0	1	2	.143	.250	.143	393	15	-1	0	0	0	1.000	0	/C-9	0.0
1975	Cle-A	90	254	32	57	10	1	5	32	30	42	.224	.309	.331	639	81	-6	3	2	-0	.990	3	C-87/1-2,3-1,D-1	0.1
1976	Cle-A	89	247	26	59	5	1	4	32	27	49	.239	.314	.316	630	86	-4	0	2	-1	.987	6	C-86/1-2,3-1	0.5
1977	Tor-A	124	396	25	83	16	3	2	29	50	51	.210	.301	.280	582	59	-22	0	2	-1	.984	-7	*C-124	-2.4
1978	Tor-A	81	264	27	69	15	0	9	29	28	32	.261	.334	.420	755	109	3	1	1	-0	.986	-7	C-81	-0.1
1979	Hou-N	108	336	25	68	15	2	2	35	26	70	.202	.264	.277	541	51	-23	0	0	0	.987	-1	*C-105	-2.1
1980	*Hou-N	116	352	30	90	19	2	3	48	35	40	.256	.323	.347	670	94	-3	0	0	0	.991	2	*C-114	0.4
1981	*Hou-N	83	255	20	69	13	0	4	33	35	33	.271	.359	.369	727	112	5	0	2	-1	.982	7	C-81	1.6
1982	Hou-N	100	339	40	87	14	2	12	49	27	53	.257	.313	.416	729	111	4	2	0	0	.977	-5	C-95	0.3
1983	Hou-N	87	275	31	63	18	1	8	34	31	38	.229	.307	.389	696	98	-2	0	0	0	.974	-13	C-85	-1.1
1984	Hou-N	66	191	16	50	7	0	4	27	20	22	.262	.335	.361	696	103	1	0	0	0	.986	-3	C-63	0.0
1985	Hou-N	65	189	20	53	8	0	8	25	24	27	.280	.364	.450	814	130	8	0	0	0	.978	-0	C-60	1.1
1986	*Hou-N	120	315	24	81	15	0	7	38	39	56	.257	.339	.371	710	98	-0	1	0	0	.985	-4	*C-103	0.0
1987	Hou-N	125	386	53	111	16	0	14	63	50	52	.288	.371	.438	809	118	11	0	1	-0	**.993**	-4	*C-110	1.1
1988	Hou-N	73	227	19	54	10	0	7	33	29	36	.238	.324	.374	699	104	1	0	0	0	.991	-10	C-66	-0.5
1989	Hou-N	22	61	4	10	1	1	0	3	7	8	.164	.261	.213	474	38	-5	0	0	0	1.000	-3	C-19	-0.7
Total	17	1370	4123	397	1010	183	13	90	513	461	622	.245	.323	.361	684	93	-36	7	10	-2	.986	-41	*C-1299/1-4,3-2,D-1	-2.2
■ **TUCKER ASHFORD** Ashford, Thomas Steven b: 12/4/54, Memphis, Tenn. BR/TR, 6'1", 195 lbs. Deb: 9/21/76																								
1976	SD-N	4	5	0	3	1	0	0	0	1	0	.600	.667	.800	1467	343	2	2	0	0	1.000	0	/3-1	0.2
1977	SD-N	81	249	25	54	18	0	3	24	21	35	.217	.280	.325	606	69	-12	2	3	-1	.937	2	3-74,S-10/2-4	-1.0
1978	SD-N	75	155	11	38	11	0	3	26	14	31	.245	.308	.374	682	97	-1	1	0	0	.917	-16	3-32,2-18,1-14	-1.8
1980	Tex-A	15	32	2	4	0	0	0	3	3	3	.125	.200	.125	325	-9	-5	0	0	0	.943	3	3-12/S-2	-0.2
1981	NY-A	3	0	0	0	0	0	0	0	0	0	—	—	—	—	—	0	0	0	0	.000	0	/2-2	0.0
1983	NY-N	35	56	3	10	0	1	0	2	7	4	.179	.270	.214	484	36	-5	0	0	0	.957	-1	3-15,2-13/C-1	-0.6
1984	KC-A	9	13	1	2	1	0	0	0	1	2	.154	.214	.231	445	23	-1	0	0	0	.909	0	/3-9	-0.1
Total	7	222	510	42	111	31	1	6	55	47	75	.218	.285	.318	603	70	-22	5	3	0	.936	-12	3-143/2-37,1-14,SC	-3.5
■ **BILLY ASHLEY** Ashley, Billy Manual b: 7/11/70, Trenton, Mich. BR/TR, 6'7", 227 lbs. Deb: 9/1/92 Career OF: (158-LF 0-CF 26-RF)																								
1992	LA-N	29	95	6	21	5	0	2	6	5	34	.221	.260	.337	597	69	-4	0	0	0	.857	-3	O-27(1-0-26)	-0.9
1993	LA-N	14	37	0	9	0	0	0	0	2	11	.243	.282	.243	525	45	-3	0	0	0	1.000	0	O-11(11-0-0)	-0.3
1994	LA-N	2	6	0	2	1	0	0	0	0	2	.333	.333	.500	833	121	0	0	0	0	1.000	-0	/O-2(2-0-0)	0.0
1995	*LA-N	81	215	17	51	5	0	8	27	25	88	.237	.322	.372	694	91	-3	0	0	0	.972	-1	O-69(69-0-0)	-0.5
1996	*LA-N	71	110	18	22	2	1	9	25	21	44	.200	.333	.482	815	121	3	0	0	0	.952	-4	O-38(38-0-0)	-0.1
1997	LA-N	71	131	12	32	7	0	6	19	8	46	.244	.293	.435	728	95	-2	0	0	0	.911	-3	O-35(35-0-0)	-0.6
1998	Bos-A	13	24	3	7	3	0	3	7	2	11	.292	.346	.792	1138	180	3	0	0	0	.857	-0	/1-2,O-2(2-0-0),D-5	0.2
Total	7	281	618	56	144	23	1	28	84	63	236	.233	.308	.409	717	95	-6	0	0	0	.941	-11	O-184L/D-5,1-2	-2.2
■ **TOM ASMUSSEN** Asmussen, Thomas William b: 9/26/1876, Chicago, Ill. d: 8/21/63, Arlington Heights, Ill. TR, Deb: 8/10/07																								
1907	Bos-N	2	5	0	0	0	0	0	0	0		.000	.000	.000	0	-99	-1	0			1.000	-1	/C-2	-0.3
■ **KEN ASPROMONTE** Aspromonte, Kenneth Joseph b: 9/22/31, Brooklyn, N.Y. BR/TR, 6', 180 lbs. Deb: 9/2/57 FM Career OF: (1-LF 0-CF 0-RF)																								
1957	Bos-A	24	78	9	21	5	0	0	4	17	10	.269	.400	.333	733	97	1	0	1	-0	.965	-3	2-24	-0.1
1958	Bos-A	6	16	0	2	0	0	0	0	3	1	.125	.263	.125	388	10	-2	0	0	0	.952	-3	/2-6	-0.5
	Was-A	92	253	15	57	9	1	5	27	25	28	.225	.297	.328	626	73	-9	1	1	-0	.964	3	2-72,3-11/S-1	-0.2
	Yr	98	269	15	59	9	1	5	27	28	29	.219	.295	.316	611	69	-11	1	1	-0	.963	-0	2-78,3-11/S-1	-0.7
1959	Was-A	70	225	31	55	12	0	2	14	26	39	.244	.323	.324	647	79	-6	2	1	0	.960	-10	2-52,S-12/1-1,O-1L	-1.1
1960	Was-A	4	3	0	0	0	0	0	0	0	1	.000	.000	.000	0	-99	-1	0	0	0	.000	0	H	-0.1
	Cle-A	117	459	65	133	20	1	10	48	53	32	.290	.366	.403	769	111	8	4	1	1	.976	-12	2-80,3-36	0.2
	Yr	121	462	65	133	20	1	10	48	53	33	.288	.364	.400	764	110	7	4	1	1	.976	-12	2-80,3-36	0.1
1961	LA-A	66	238	29	53	10	0	2	14	33	21	.223	.322	.290	612	58	-13	0	0	0	.970	18	2-62	1.0
	Cle-A	22	70	5	16	6	1	0	5	6	3	.229	.289	.343	632	70	-3	0	0	0	.963	-2	2-21	-0.3
	Yr	88	308	34	69	16	1	2	19	39	24	.224	.315	.302	617	61	-16	0	0	0	.969	17	2-83	0.7
1962	Cle-A	20	28	4	4	2	0	0	1	6	5	.143	.294	.214	508	41	-2	0	0	0	1.000	-1	/2-6,3-3	-0.3
	Mil-N	34	79	11	23	2	0	0	7	6	5	.291	.349	.316	665	82	-2	0	1	-0	1.000	-0	2-12/3-6	-0.1
1963	Chi-N	20	34	2	5	3	0	0	4	4	4	.147	.237	.235	472	35	-3	0	0	0	.951	3	/2-7,1-2	0.1
Total	7	475	1483	171	369	69	3	19	124	179	149	.249	.332	.338	670	82	-33	7	5	-0	.969	-7	2-342/3-56,S-13,1O	-1.4
■ **BOB ASPROMONTE** Aspromonte, Robert Thomas b: 6/19/38, Brooklyn, N.Y. BR/TR, 6'2", 185 lbs. Deb: 9/19/56 F Career OF: (60-LF 0-CF 2-RF)																								
1956	Bro-N	1	1	0	0	0	0	0	0	0	1	.000	.000	.000	0	-93	-0	0	0	0	.000	0	H	0.0
1960	LA-N	21	55	1	10	1	0	1	6	0	6	.182	.196	.255	451	21	-6	1	0	0	.933	-2	S-15/3-4	-0.7
1961	LA-N	47	58	7	14	3	0	0	2	4	12	.241	.290	.293	583	51	-4	0	0	0	.917	0	/3-9,S-4,2-2	-0.3
1962	Hou-N	149	534	59	142	18	4	11	59	46	54	.266	.333	.376	710	97	-2	4	5	-1	.967	1	*3-142,S-11/2-1	-0.2
1963	Hou-N	136	468	42	100	9	5	8	49	40	57	.214	.277	.306	583	72	-17	3	1	0	.938	-16	*3-131/1-1	-3.7
1964	Hou-N	157	553	51	155	20	3	12	69	35	54	.280	.332	.392	725	109	6	6	7	-1	**.973**	-15	*3-155	-1.1
1965	Hou-N	152	578	53	152	15	2	5	52	38	54	.263	.312	.322	634	85	-12	2	2	-0	.962	0	*3-146/1-6,S-4	-1.3
1966	Hou-N	152	560	55	141	16	3	8	52	35	63	.252	.298	.334	632	81	-15	0	4	-1	**.962**	-11	*3-149/1-2,S-2	-2.9
1967	Hou-N	137	486	51	143	24	5	6	58	45	44	.294	.356	.401	758	121	13	2	2	-0	.963	-4	*3-133	0.9
1968	Hou-N	124	409	25	92	9	2	1	46	35	57	.225	.289	.264	553	68	-15	1	0	0	.973	0	3-75,O-36L/1-1,S-1	-1.9
1969	*Atl-N	82	198	16	50	8	1	3	24	13	19	.253	.305	.348	654	82	-5	0	1	-0	.975	-6	O-24L,3-23,S-18,/2	-1.3
1970	Atl-N	62	127	5	27	3	0	0	7	13	13	.213	.286	.236	522	39	-11	0	0	0	.938	-1	3-30/S-4,1-1,O-1L	-1.1
1971	NY-N	104	342	21	77	9	1	5	33	29	25	.225	.286	.301	587	67	-15	0	2	-1	.965	-5	3-97	-2.2
Total	13	1324	4369	386	1103	135	26	60	457	333	459	.252	.310	.336	646	86	-82	19	24	-4	.960	-57	*3-1094/O-61L,S12	-15.8

YEAR	TM/L	G	AB	R	H	2B	3B	HR	RBI	BB	SO	AVG	OBP	SLG	OPS	OPS+	BR+	SB	CS	SBR	FA	FR	G/POS	TPR
■ **BRIAN ASSELSTINE**	Asselstine, Brian Hanly b: 9/23/53, Santa Barbara, Cal BL/TR, 6'1", 175 lbs. Deb: 9/14/76																							
1976	Atl-N	11	33	2	7	0	0	1	3	1	2	.212	.235	.303	538	49	-2	0	0	0	1.000	-1	/O-9(0-7-2)	-0.3
1977	Atl-N	83	124	12	26	6	0	4	17	9	10	.210	.263	.355	618	57	-8	1	0	0	.983	-2	O-35(9-13-13)	-1.1
1978	Atl-N	39	103	11	28	3	3	2	13	11	16	.272	.353	.417	771	103	1	2	1	0	.968	-5	O-35(0-11-31)	-0.6
1979	Atl-N	8	10	1	1	0	0	0	0	1	2	.100	.182	.100	282	-20	-2	0	0	0	1.000	-0	/O-1(1-0-0)	-0.2
1980	Atl-N	87	218	18	62	13	1	3	25	11	37	.284	.322	.394	716	96	-2	1	3	-1	.962	-9	O-61(29-32-2)	-1.3
1981	Atl-N	56	86	8	22	5	0	2	10	5	7	.256	.297	.384	680	90	-1	1	0	0	.958	-1	O-16(4-0-12)	-0.3
Total	6	284	574	52	146	27	4	12	68	38	74	.254	.304	.378	682	83	-14	5	4	-0	.971	-19	O-157(43-63-60)	-3.8
■ **JOE ASTROTH**	Astroth, Joseph Henry b: 9/1/22, East Alton, Ill. BR/TR, 5'9", 187 lbs. Deb: 8/13/45																							
1945	Phi-A	10	17	1	1	0	0	0	1	0	1	.059	.111	.059	170	-50	-3	0	0	0	.857	0	/C-8	-0.3
1946	Phi-A	4	7	0	1	0	0	0	0	0	2	.143	.143	.143	286	-20	-1	0	0	0	.889	-0	/C-4	-0.1
1949	Phi-A	55	148	18	36	4	1	0	12	21	13	.243	.337	.284	621	67	-6	1	0	0	.979	2	C-44	-0.2
1950	Phi-A	39	110	11	36	3	1	1	18	18	3	.327	.422	.400	822	113	3	0	0	0	.985	-6	C-38	-0.1
1951	Phi-A	64	187	30	46	10	2	2	19	18	13	.246	.312	.353	665	78	-6	0	1	-0	.992	4	C-57	0.0
1952	Phi-A	104	337	24	84	7	2	1	36	25	27	.249	.305	.291	596	62	-17	2	2	-0	.992	-5	*C-102	-1.7
1953	Phi-A	82	260	28	77	15	2	3	24	27	12	.296	.367	.404	771	104	2	1	0	0	.987	7	C-79	1.3
1954	Phi-A	77	226	22	50	8	1	1	23	21	19	.221	.296	.279	575	58	-13	0	0	0	.988	-2	C-71	-1.2
1955	KC-A	101	274	29	69	4	1	5	23	47	33	.252	.373	.328	702	89	-2	2	3	-1	.989	-4	*C-100	-0.2
1956	KC-A	8	13	0	1	0	0	0	0	0	1	.077	.077	.077	154	-59	-3	0	0	0	1.000	2	/C-8	-0.1
Total	10	544	1579	163	401	51	10	13	156	177	124	.254	.334	.324	658	77	-47	6	6	-1	.987	-2	C-511	-2.6
■ **CHARLIE ATHERTON**	Atherton, Charles Morgan Herbert "Prexy" b: 11/19/1874, New Brunswick, N.J d: 12/19/35, Vienna, Austria BR/TR, 5'10", 160 lbs. Deb: 5/30/1899																							
1899	Was-N	65	242	28	60	5	6	0	23	21		.248	.313	.318	631	74	-9	2			.890	-6	3-63/O-1(0-0-1)	-1.3
■ **ED ATKINSON**	Atkinson, Edward b: 1851, Baltimore, Md. Deb: 10/22/1873																							
1873	Was-n	2	8	2	0	0	0	0	0	0	0	.000	.000	.000	0	-99	-2	0	0	0	1.000	-0	/O-2(0-0-2)	-0.2
■ **LEFTY ATKINSON**	Atkinson, Hubert Berley b: 6/2/06, Chicago, Ill. d: 2/12/61, Chicago, Ill. BL/TL, 5'6.5", 149 lbs. Deb: 8/5/27																							
1927	Was-A	1	1	1	0	0	0	0	0	0	0	.000	.000	.000	0	-99	-0	0	0	0	.000	0	H	0.0
■ **DICK ATTREAU**	Attreau, Richard Gilbert b: 4/8/1897, Chicago, Ill. d: 7/5/64, Chicago, Ill. BL/TL, 6', 160 lbs. Deb: 9/14/26																							
1926	Phi-N	17	61	9	14	1	1	0	5	6	5	.230	.299	.279	577	53	-4	0			.989	-1	1-17	-0.6
1927	Phi-N	44	83	17	17	1	1	1	11	14	18	.205	.320	.277	597	60	-4	1			.989	-2	1-26	-0.7
Total	2	61	144	26	31	2	2	1	16	20	23	.215	.311	.278	589	57	-8	1			.989	-3	/1-43	-1.3
■ **TOBY ATWELL**	Atwell, Maurice Dailey b: 3/8/24, Leesburg, Va. BL/TR, 5'9.5", 185 lbs. Deb: 4/15/52																							
1952	Chi-N☆	107	362	36	105	16	3	2	31	40	22	.290	.362	.367	730	102	2	2	1	0	.977	-7	*C-101	0.1
1953	Chi-N	24	74	10	17	2	0	1	8	13	7	.230	.345	.297	642	68	-3	0	0	0	.940	1	C-24	-0.1
	Pit-N	53	139	11	34	6	0	0	17	20	12	.245	.352	.288	640	70	-5	0	0	0	.967	-3	C-45	-0.6
	Yr	77	213	21	51	8	0	1	25	33	19	.239	.349	.291	640	69	-8	0	0	0	.957	-2	C-69	-0.7
1954	Pit-N	96	287	36	83	8	4	3	26	43	21	.289	.387	.376	764	101	2	2	3	-1	.990	-2	C-88	0.4
1955	Pit-N	71	207	21	44	8	0	1	18	40	16	.213	.343	.266	608	65	-9	0	1	-0	.992	6	C-67	-0.1
1956	Pit-N	12	18	0	2	0	0	0	3	1	5	.111	.158	.111	269	-27	-3	0	0	0	1.000	1	/C-9	-0.2
	Mil-N	15	30	2	5	1	0	2	7	4	1	.167	.265	.400	665	80	-1	0	0	0	1.000	-1	C-10	-0.1
	Yr	27	48	2	7	1	0	2	10	5	6	.146	.226	.292	518	40	-4	0	0	0	1.000	0	C-19	-0.3
Total	5	378	1117	116	290	41	7	9	110	161	84	.260	.357	.333	690	86	-17	4	5	-1	.980	-5	C-344	-0.6
■ **BILL ATWOOD**	Atwood, William Franklin b: 9/25/11, Rome, Ga. d: 9/14/93, Snyder, Tex. BR/TR, 5'11.5", 190 lbs. Deb: 4/15/36																							
1936	Phi-N	71	192	21	58	9	2	2	29	11	15	.302	.346	.401	747	92	-2	0			.972	-1	C-53	0.0
1937	Phi-N	87	279	27	68	15	1	2	32	30	27	.244	.317	.326	643	69	-11	3			.968	-15	C-80	-2.1
1938	Phi-N	102	281	27	55	8	1	3	28	25	26	.196	.261	.263	525	46	-21	0			.969	0	C-94	-1.6
1939	Phi-N	4	6	0	0	0	0	0	1	2	3	.000	.250	.000	250	-29	-1	1			1.000	-0	/C-2	-0.1
1940	Phi-N	78	203	7	39	9	0	0	22	25	18	.192	.284	.236	520	47	-14	0			.989	1	C-69	-1.0
Total	5	342	961	82	220	41	4	7	112	93	89	.229	.299	.302	601	63	-50	4			.974	-14	C-298	-4.8
■ **JAKE ATZ**	Atz, John Jacob (b: Jacob Henry Atz) b: 7/1/1879, Washington, D.C. d: 5/22/45, New Orleans, La. BR/TR, 5'9", 150 lbs. Deb: 9/24/02 Career OF: (0-LF 1-CF 3-RF)																							
1902	Was-A	3	10	1	1	0	0	0	0	0		.100	.100	.100	200	-44	-2	0			1.000	0	/2-3	-0.1
1907	Chi-A	4	8	0	1	0	0	0	0	0		.125	.125	.125	250	-21	-1	0			1.000	1	/3-2,O-1(0-1-0)	0.0
1908	Chi-A	83	206	24	40	3	0	0	27	31		.194	.311	.209	520	71	-5	9			.936	-3	2-46,S-18/3-1	-0.8
1909	Chi-A	119	381	39	90	18	3	0	22	38		.236	.309	.299	608	96	-1	14			.954	-7	*2-114/O-3(0-0-3),S-1	-0.8
Total	4	209	605	64	132	21	3	0	49	69		.218	.304	.263	567	83	-9	23			.949	-8	2-163/S-19,O-4R,3-3	-1.7
■ **HARRY AUBREY**	Aubrey, Harry Herbert "Chub" b: 7/5/1880, St.Joseph, Mo. d: 9/18/53, Baltimore, Md. TR, Deb: 4/22/03																							
1903	Bos-N	96	325	26	69	8	2	0	27	18		.212	.264	.249	514	49	-22	7			.868	-10	S-94/2-1,O-1(1-0-0)	-2.8
■ **RICH AUDE**	Aude, Richard Thomas b: 7/13/71, Van Nuys, Cal. BR/TR, 6'5", 180 lbs. Deb: 9/9/93																							
1993	Pit-N	13	26	1	3	1	0	0	4	1	7	.115	.148	.154	302	-19	-4	0	0	0	1.000	-1	/1-7,O-1(1-0-0)	-0.6
1995	Pit-N	42	109	10	27	8	0	2	19	6	20	.248	.287	.376	663	72	-5	1	2	-0	.996	-3	1-32	-1.0
1996	Pit-N	7	16	0	4	0	0	0	1	0	8	.250	.250	.250	500	32	-2	0	0	0	.969	0	/1-4	-0.2
Total	3	62	151	11	34	9	0	2	24	7	35	.225	.259	.325	584	52	-11	1	2	-0	.994	-3	/1-43,O-1(1-0-0)	-1.8
■ **RICK AUERBACH**	Auerbach, Frederick Steven b: 2/15/50, Woodland Hills, Cal BR/TR, 6', 165 lbs. Deb: 4/13/71																							
1971	Mil-A	79	236	22	48	10	0	1	9	20	40	.203	.271	.258	530	51	-15	3	2	-0	.963	-10	S-78	-1.8
1972	Mil-A	153	554	50	121	16	3	2	30	43	62	.218	.277	.269	546	64	-24	24	8	2	.959	-21	*S-153	-2.8
1973	Mil-A	6	10	2	1	1	0	0	0	0	1	.100	.100	.200	300	-18	-2	0	1	-0	.833	0	/S-2	-0.2
1974	*LA-N	45	73	12	25	0	0	1	4	8	9	.342	.407	.384	791	127	3	4	2	0	.950	2	S-19,2-16/3-3	0.7
1975	LA-N	85	170	18	38	9	0	0	12	18	22	.224	.298	.276	574	63	-8	3	2	-0	.960	-17	S-81/2-1,3-1	-2.0
1976	LA-N	36	47	7	6	0	0	0	1	6	6	.128	.226	.128	354	2	-6	0	1	-0	.943	11	S-12/3-8,2-7	0.6
1977	Cin-N	33	45	5	7	2	0	0	3	4	7	.156	.224	.200	424	15	-5	0	0	0	.976	6	2-19,S-12	0.2
1978	Cin-N	63	55	17	18	6	0	2	5	7	12	.327	.413	.545	958	166	5	1	0	0	.971	10	S-26,2-10/3-3	1.7
1979	*Cin-N	62	100	17	21	8	1	1	12	14	19	.210	.307	.340	647	76	-3	0	1	-0	.933	-1	3-18,S-16/2-3	-0.3
1980	Cin-N	24	33	5	11	1	1	1	4	3	5	.333	.389	.515	904	150	2	0	3	-1	1.000	-1	/S-3,3-3,2-1	0.1
1981	Sea-A	38	84	12	13	3	0	1	6	4	15	.155	.202	.226	428	22	-8	1	1	-0	.979	3	S-38	-0.3
Total	11	624	1407	167	309	56	5	9	86	127	198	.220	.287	.286	573	65	-62	36	21	1	.960	-16	S-440/2-57,3-36	-4.1
■ **DAVE AUGUSTINE**	Augustine, David Ralph b: 11/28/49, Follansbee, W.Va. BR/TR, 6'2", 174 lbs. Deb: 9/3/73																							
1973	Pit-N	11	7	1	2	1	0	0	0	0	1	.286	.286	.429	714	98	-0	0	0	0	1.000	-2	/O-9(4-4-1)	-0.2
1974	Pit-N	18	22	3	4	0	0	0	0	0	5	.182	.182	.182	364	2	-3	0	1	-0	1.000	1	O-11(1-6-4)	-0.3
Total	2	29	29	4	6	1	0	0	0	0	6	.207	.207	.241	448	26	-3	0	1	-0	1.000	-2	/O-20(5-10-5)	-0.5
■ **LESLIE AULDS**	Aulds, Leycester Doyle "Tex" b: 12/28/20, Farmerville, La. BR/TR, 6'2", 185 lbs. Deb: 5/25/47																							
1947	Bos-A	3	4	0	1	0	0	0	0	0	1	.250	.250	.250	500	37	-0	0	0	0	1.000	0	/C-3	0.0
■ **DOUG AULT**	Ault, Douglas Reagan b: 3/9/50, Beaumont, Tex. BR/TL, 6'3", 200 lbs. Deb: 9/9/76																							
1976	Tex-A	9	20	0	6	1	0	0	0	1	3	.300	.333	.350	683	98	-0	0	0	0	1.000	-1	/1-4,D-3	-0.1
1977	Tor-A	129	445	44	109	22	3	11	64	39	68	.245	.311	.382	693	87	-8	4	4	-1	.987	7	*1-122/D-4	-0.9
1978	Tor-A	54	104	10	25	1	1	3	7	17	14	.240	.352	.356	708	98	0	0	0	0	.979	-2	1-25/O-7(6-0-1),D-5	-0.3
1980	Tor-A	64	144	12	28	5	1	3	15	14	23	.194	.275	.306	581	56	-9	0	1	-0	1.000	3	1-32,D-21/O-1(1-0-0)	-0.8
Total	4	256	713	66	168	29	5	17	86	71	108	.236	.311	.362	673	82	-17	4	5	-1	.988	8	1-183/D-33,O-8(7-0-1)	-2.1

YEAR	TM/L	G	AB	R	H	2B	3B	HR	RBI	BB	SO	AVG	OBP	SLG	OPS	OPS+	BR+	SB	CS	SBR	FA	FR	G/POS	TPR
■ RICH AURILIA	Aurilia, Richard Santo b: 9/2/71, Brooklyn, N.Y. BR/TR, 6', 170 lbs. Deb: 9/6/95																							
1995	SF-N	9	19	4	9	3	0	2	4	1	2	.474	.500	.947	1447	280	5	1	0	0	1.000	1	/S-6	0.6
1996	SF-N	105	318	27	76	7	1	3	26	25	52	.239	.297	.296	592	59	-19	4	1	1	.973	-4	S-93,2-11	-1.4
1997	SF-N	46	102	16	28	8	0	5	19	8	15	.275	.327	.500	827	116	2	1	1	-0	.979	11	S-36	1.5
1998	SF-N	122	413	54	110	27	2	9	49	31	62	.266	.321	.407	727	95	-4	3	3	-0	.979	0	*S-120	0.5
1999	SF-N	152	558	68	157	23	1	22	80	43	71	.281	.338	.444	783	103	1	2	3	-1	.957	-0	*S-150	1.2
2000	*SF-N	141	509	67	138	24	2	20	79	54	90	.271	.341	.444	785	103	2	1	2	-0	.967	10	*S-140	2.1
Total	6	575	1919	236	518	92	6	61	257	162	292	.270	.329	.419	749	97	-13	12	10	-1	.969	19	S-545/2-11	4.5
■ BRAD AUSMUS	Ausmus, Bradley David b: 4/14/69, New Haven, Conn. BR/TR, 5'11", 195 lbs. Deb: 7/28/93																							
1993	SD-N	49	160	18	41	8	1	5	12	6	28	.256	.283	.412	696	82	-5	2	0	0	.975	5	C-49	0.4
1994	SD-N	101	327	45	82	12	1	7	24	30	63	.251	.316	.358	673	77	-11	5	1	1	.991	2	C-99/1-1	-0.3
1995	SD-N	103	328	44	96	16	4	5	34	31	56	.293	.357	.412	769	106	3	16	5	2	.992	1	*C-100/1-1	1.1
1996	SD-N	50	149	16	27	4	0	1	13	13	27	.181	.261	.228	489	32	-15	1	4	-1	.982	2	C-46	-1.1
	Det-A	75	226	30	56	12	0	4	22	26	45	.248	.331	.354	685	73	-9	3	4	-1	.992	1	C-73	-0.4
1997	*Hou-N	130	425	45	113	25	1	4	44	38	78	.266	.330	.358	688	83	-10	14	6	1	.992	4	*C-129	0.2
1998	*Hou-N	128	412	62	111	10	4	6	45	53	60	.269	.357	.357	714	91	-4	10	3	1	.992	6	*C-124	1.0
1999	Det-A★	127	458	62	126	25	6	9	54	51	71	.275	.365	.415	780	99	1	12	9	-1	**.998**	-15	*C-127	-0.6
2000	Det-A	150	523	75	139	25	3	7	51	69	79	.266	.358	.365	723	86	-9	11	5	1	.992	6	*C-150/1-1,2-1,3-1	0.6
Total	8	913	3008	397	791	137	20	48	299	317	507	.263	.340	.370	710	86	-58	74	37	3	.991	11	C-897/1-3,3-1,2-1	0.9
■ HENRY AUSTIN	Austin, Henry C. b: 1844, Brooklyn, N.Y. d: 9/3/1895, Amityville, N.Y. Deb: 4/28/1873																							
1873	Res-n	23	101	10	25	3	3	0	11	0	4	.248	.248	.337	584	78	-2	0	0	0	.722	-0	O-23(0-14-9)	-0.1
■ JIMMY AUSTIN	Austin, James Philip "Pepper" b: 12/8/1879, Swansea, Wales d: 3/6/65, Laguna Beach, Cal. BB/TR, 5'7.5", 155 lbs. Deb: 4/19/09 MC																							
1909	NY-A	136	437	37	101	11	5	1	39	32		.231	.285	.286	571	80	-10	30			.928	13	*3-111,S-23/2-1	0.7
1910	NY-A	133	432	46	94	11	4	2	36	47		.218	.305	.275	580	77	-10	22			.942	3	*3-133	-0.4
1911	StL-A	148	541	84	141	25	11	2	45	69		.261	.351	.359	709	102	3	26			.931	16	*3-148	2.3
1912	StL-A	149	536	57	135	14	8	2	44	38		.252	.306	.319	625	82	-13	28			.911	-1	*3-149	-1.1
1913	StL-A	142	489	56	130	18	6	2	42	45	51	.266	.338	.339	677	101	1	37			**.944**	7	*3-142,M	1.2
1914	StL-A	130	466	55	111	16	4	0	30	40	59	.238	.300	.290	590	80	-11	20	23	-4	.935	1	*3-127	-1.2
1915	StL-A	141	477	61	127	6	6	1	30	64	60	.266	.355	.310	666	103	4	18	15	-1	.917	10	*3-141	1.7
1916	StL-A	129	411	55	85	15	6	1	28	74	59	.207	.333	.280	613	89	-3	19			.939	-7	*3-124	-0.7
1917	StL-A	127	455	61	109	18	8	0	19	50	46	.240	.319	.314	633	97	-1	13			.947	3	*3-121/S-6	0.6
1918	StL-A	110	367	42	97	14	4	0	20	53	32	.264	.359	.324	683	109	6	18			.939	-17	S-57,3-48,M	-0.6
1919	StL-A	106	396	54	94	9	9	1	21	42	31	.237	.314	.313	627	74	-13	8			.939	7	3-98	-0.4
1920	StL-A	83	280	38	76	11	3	1	32	31	15	.271	.352	.343	695	82	-6	2	4	-1	.943	2	3-75	-0.3
1921	StL-A	27	66	8	18	2	1	0	2	4	7	.273	.324	.333	657	64	-4	2	1	0	.938	-3	S-14/2-6,3-2	-0.5
1922	StL-A	15	31	6	9	3	1	0	1	3	2	.290	.353	.452	805	105	0	0	0	0	.957	-3	/3-9,2-2	-0.2
1923	StL-A	1	0	0	0	0	0	0	0	0	0	—	—	—	—	—	0	0	0	0	.000	0	/M	0.0
1925	StL-A	1	1	0	0	0	0	0	0	0	0	.000	.000	.000	0	-95	-0	0	0	0	1.000	0	/3-1	0.0
1926	StL-A	1	2	1	1	1	0	0	1	0	0	.500	.500	1.000	1500	272	0	1	0	0	1.000	0	/3-1	0.1
1929	StL-A	1	1	0	0	0	0	0	0	0	1	.000	.000	.000	0	-96	-0	0	0	0	1.000	1	/3-1	0.0
Total	18	1580	5388	661	1328	174	76	13	390	592	363	.246	.326	.314	640	90	-59	244	43		.933	32	*3-1431,S-100/2-9	1.2
■ CHICK AUTRY	Autry, Martin Gordon b: 3/5/03, Martindale, Tex. d: 1/26/50, Savannah, Ga. BR/TR, 6', 180 lbs. Deb: 4/20/24																							
1924	NY-A	2	0	1	0	0	0	0	0	0	0	—	1.000	—	1000	172	0	0	0	0	1.000	-0	/C-2	0.0
1926	Cle-A	3	7	1	1	0	0	0	0	1	0	.143	.250	.143	393	4	-1	0	0	0	1.000	-0	/C-3	-0.1
1927	Cle-A	16	43	5	11	4	1	0	7	0	6	.256	.256	.395	651	66	-2	0	0	0	.933	2	C-14	0.0
1928	Cle-A	22	60	6	18	6	1	1	9	1	7	.300	.311	.483	795	105	0	0	0	0	.972	0	C-18	0.1
1929	Chi-A	43	96	7	20	6	0	1	12	1	8	.208	.224	.302	527	35	-10	0	0	0	.940	-4	C-30	-1.2
1930	Chi-A	34	71	1	18	1	1	0	5	4	8	.254	.293	.296	589	52	-5	0	0	0	.992	8	C-29	0.3
Total	6	120	277	21	68	17	3	2	33	7	29	.245	.269	.350	619	59	-18	0	0	0	.965	5	/C-96	-0.9
■ CHICK AUTRY	Autry, William Askew b: 1/2/1885, Humboldt, Tenn. d: 1/16/76, Santa Rosa, Cal. BL/TL, 5'11", 168 lbs. Deb: 9/18/07																							
1907	Cin-N	7	25	3	5	0	0	0	0	1		.200	.231	.200	431	34	-2	0			.929	-1	/O-7(4-3-0)	-0.4
1909	Cin-N	9	33	3	6	2	0	0	4	2		.182	.229	.242	471	46	-2	1			.956	0	/1-9	-0.2
	Bos-N	65	199	16	39	4	0	0	13	21		.196	.279	.216	495	51	-11	5			.994	5	1-61/O-4(4-1-0)	-0.8
	Yr	74	232	19	45	6	0	0	17	23		.194	.272	.220	492	51	-13	6			.989	5	1-70/O-4(4-1-0)	-1.0
Total	2	81	257	22	50	6	0	0	17	24		.195	.269	.218	486	49	-15	6			.968	4	/1-70,O-11(8-4-0)	-1.4
■ BRUCE AVEN	Aven, David Bruce b: 3/4/72, Orange, Tex. BR/TR, 5'9", 180 lbs. Deb: 8/27/97																							
1997	Cle-A	13	19	4	4	1	0	0	2	1	5	.211	.250	.263	513	33	-2	0	1	-0	1.000	-1	O-13(10-1-2)	-0.4
1999	Fla-N	137	381	57	110	19	2	12	70	44	82	.289	.376	.444	819	113	8	3	0	1	.984	-3	*O-102(78-9-24)/D-6	0.2
2000	Pit-N	72	148	18	37	11	0	5	25	5	31	.250	.275	.426	700	74	-7	2	3	-1	.980	-8	O-41(17-8-20)	-1.5
	LA-N	9	20	2	5	0	0	2	4	3	8	.250	.348	.550	898	128	1	0	0	0	1.000	-1	/O-9(9-0-0)	0.0
	Yr	81	168	20	42	11	0	7	29	8	39	.250	.284	.440	725	80	-6	2	3	-1	.984	-9	O-50(26-8-20)	-1.5
Total	3	231	568	81	156	31	2	19	101	53	126	.275	.346	.437	783	101	1	5	4	-0	.985	-13	O-165(114-18-46)/D-6	-1.7
■ EARL AVERILL	Averill, Earl Douglas b: 9/9/31, Cleveland, Ohio BR/TR, 5'10", 190 lbs. Deb: 4/19/56 F Career OF: (72-LF 0-CF 0-RF)																							
1956	Cle-A	42	93	12	22	6	0	3	14	14	25	.237	.343	.398	740	93	-1	0	1	-0	.994	3	C-34	0.3
1958	Cle-A	17	55	2	10	1	0	2	7	4	7	.182	.250	.309	559	54	-4	1	0	0	.863	0	3-17	-0.3
1959	Chi-N	74	186	22	44	10	0	10	34	15	39	.237	.300	.452	752	98	-1	0	1	-0	.963	3	C-32,3-13/O-5L,2-2	0.3
1960	Chi-N	52	102	14	24	4	0	1	13	11	16	.235	.316	.304	620	71	-4	1	1	-0	.979	-9	C-34/3-1,O-1(1-0-0)	-1.2
	Chi-A	10	14	2	3	0	0	0	2	4	2	.214	.389	.214	603	68	-0	0	0	0	1.000	2	/C-5	0.2
1961	LA-A	115	323	56	86	9	0	21	59	62	70	.266	.388	.489	877	119	10	1	0	0	.991	-7	C-88/O-9(9-0-0),2-1	0.8
1962	LA-A	92	187	21	41	9	0	4	22	43	47	.219	.368	.332	700	93	-0	0	0	0	1.000	-4	O-49(49-0-0)/C-6	-0.6
1963	Phi-N	47	71	8	19	2	0	3	8	9	14	.268	.350	.423	773	123	2	0	0	0	.966	1	C-20/O-8L,1-1,3-1	0.4
Total	7	449	1031	137	249	41	0	44	159	162	220	.242	.349	.409	758	101	2	3	3	-0	.984	-11	C-219/O-72L,3-32,21	-0.1
■ EARL AVERILL	Averill, Howard Earl "Rock" b: 5/21/02, Snohomish, Wash. d: 8/16/83, Everett, Wash. BL/TR, 5'9.5", 172 lbs. Deb: 4/16/29 FH																							
1929	Cle-A	151	597	110	198	43	13	18	96	63	53	.332	.398	.538	936	134	29	13	13	-2	.966	-4	*O-151(0-151-0)	1.6
1930	Cle-A	139	534	102	181	33	8	19	119	56	48	.339	.404	.537	941	131	25	10	7	-0	.949	2	*O-134(0-132-2)	1.9
1931	Cle-A	155	627	140	209	36	10	32	143	68	38	.333	.404	.576	979	147	41	9	9	-1	.976	0	*O-155(0-155-0)	3.3
1932	Cle-A	153	631	116	198	37	14	32	124	75	40	.314	.392	.569	961	137	33	5	8	-2	.964	2	*O-153(0-153-0)	2.6
1933	Cle-A★	151	599	83	180	39	16	11	92	54	29	.301	.363	.474	837	115	12	3	1	0	.971	2	*O-149(0-149-0)	1.0
1934	Cle-A★	154	598	128	187	48	6	31	113	99	44	.313	.414	.569	982	149	44	5	3	0	.970	9	*O-154(0-154-0)	4.4
1935	Cle-A†	140	563	109	162	34	13	19	79	70	58	.288	.368	.496	863	119	15	8	4	0	.982	-2	*O-139(0-139-0)	0.9
1936	Cle-A★	152	614	136	**232**	39	**15**	28	126	65	35	.378	.438	.627	1065	159	55	3	3	-0	.969	-4	*O-150(0-150-0)	4.1
1937	Cle-A★	156	609	121	182	33	11	21	92	88	65	.299	.387	.493	880	119	18	5	4	-0	.976	-8	*O-156(0-156-0)	0.6
1938	Cle-A★	134	482	101	159	27	15	14	93	81	48	.330	.429	.535	965	143	34	5	2	0	.975	5	*O-131(0-118-13)	3.2
1939	Cle-A	24	55	8	15	8	0	1	7	6	12	.273	.344	.473	817	111	1	0	1	-0	1.000	-2	O-11(0-0-11)	-0.3
	Det-A	87	309	58	81	20	6	10	58	43	30	.262	.354	.463	817	100	-1	4	2	0	.976	-5	O-80(75-5-0)	-0.9
	Yr	111	364	66	96	28	6	11	65	49	42	.264	.353	.464	817	102	0	4	3	-0	.977	-7	O-91(75-5-11)	-1.2
1940	*Det-A	64	118	10	33	4	1	2	20	5	14	.280	.309	.381	690	71	-5	0	0	0	.962	-5	O-22(7-11-5)	-1.1
1941	Bos-N	8	17	2	2	0	0	0	2	1	4	.118	.211	.118	328	-6	-2	0			1.000	1	/O-4(1-3-0)	-0.2
Total	13	1668	6353	1224	2019	401	128	238	1164	774	518	.318	.395	.534	928	132	298	70	57		.970	-8	*O-1589(83-1476-31)	21.1
■ BOBBY AVILA	Avila, Roberto Francisco (Gonzales) b: 4/2/24, Veracruz, Mexico BR/TR, 5'10", 175 lbs. Deb: 4/30/49 Career OF: (1-LF 0-CF 9-RF)																							
1949	Cle-A	31	14	3	3	0	0	0	3	1	3	.214	.267	.214	481	29	-1	0	0	0	1.000	4	/2-5	0.2
1950	Cle-A	80	201	39	60	10	2	1	21	29	17	.299	.390	.383	773	102	2	5	0	1	.983	-5	2-62/S-2	0.0

YEAR	TM/L	G	AB	R	H	2B	3B	HR	RBI	BB	SO	AVG	OBP	SLG	OPS	OPS+	BR+	SB	CS	SBR	FA	FR	G/POS	TPR
1951	Cle-A	141	542	76	165	21	3	10	58	60	31	.304	.374	.410	783	118	14	14	8	0	.982	-1	*2-136	2.1
1952	Cle-A★	150	597	102	179	26	**11**	7	45	67	36	.300	.371	.415	787	127	22	12	10	-1	.966	-18	*2-149	1.2
1953	Cle-A	141	559	85	160	22	3	8	55	58	27	.286	.355	.379	735	101	1	10	8	-1	**.986**	13	*2-140	2.5
1954	*Cle-A★	143	555	112	189	27	2	15	67	59	31	**.341**	.405	.477	882	139	30	9	7	-0	.976	8	*2-141/S-7	**4.9**
1955	Cle-A★	141	537	83	146	22	4	13	61	82	47	.272	.370	.400	771	103	4	1	4	-1	.982	-3	*2-141	1.1
1956	Cle-A	138	513	74	115	14	2	10	54	70	68	.224	.323	.318	641	68	-23	17	4	2	.977	-10	*2-135	-2.0
1957	Cle-A	129	463	60	124	19	3	5	48	46	47	.268	.335	.354	690	89	-6	2	4	-1	.983	-15	*2-107,3-16	-1.5
1958	Cle-A	113	375	54	95	21	3	5	30	55	45	.253	.350	.365	716	100	1	5	7	-1	.986	-21	2-82,3-33	-1.6
1959	Bal-A	20	47	1	8	0	0	0	0	4	5	.170	.235	.170	406	14	-5	0	0	0	1.000	-4	O-10(1-0-9)/2-8,3-1	-1.0
	Bos-A	22	45	7	11	0	0	3	6	6	11	.244	.333	.444	778	107	0	0	0	0	.975	-2	2-11	-0.1
	Yr	42	92	8	19	0	0	3	6	10	16	.207	.284	.304	589	61	-5	0	0	0	.967	-6	2-19,O-10(1-0-9)/3-1	-1.1
	Mil-N	51	172	29	41	3	2	3	19	24	31	.238	.332	.331	663	84	-3	3	0	1	.967	-12	2-51	-1.1
Total	11	1300	4620	725	1296	185	35	80	467	561	399	.281	.360	.388	748	104	35	78	52	-1	.979	-64	*2-1168/3-50,O-10R,S	4.7

■ **RAMON AVILES** Aviles, Ramon Antonio (Miranda) b: 1/22/52, Manati, P.R. BR/TR, 5'9", 155 lbs. Deb: 7/10/77

YEAR	TM/L	G	AB	R	H	2B	3B	HR	RBI	BB	SO	AVG	OBP	SLG	OPS	OPS+	BR+	SB	CS	SBR	FA	FR	G/POS	TPR
1977	Bos-A	1	0	0	0	0	0	0	0	0	0	—	—	—	—	—	-0	0	0	0	1.000	0	/2-1	0.0
1979	Phi-N	27	61	7	17	2	0	0	12	8	8	.279	.371	.311	683	86	-1	0	0	0	.977	-7	2-27	-0.7
1980	*Phi-N	51	101	12	28	6	0	2	9	10	9	.277	.342	.396	738	100	0	0	0	0	.944	-7	S-29,2-15	-0.5
1981	*Phi-N	38	28	2	6	1	0	0	3	3	5	.214	.290	.250	540	52	-2	0	0	0	1.000	4	2-20,3-13/S-5	0.3
Total	4	117	190	21	51	9	0	2	24	21	22	.268	.344	.347	692	88	-2	0	0	0	.971	-10	/2-63,S-34,3-13	-0.9

■ **BENNY AYALA** Ayala, Benigno (Felix) b: 2/7/51, Yauco, P.R. BR/TR, 6'1", 185 lbs. Deb: 8/27/74 Career OF: (140-LF 2-CF 16-RF)

YEAR	TM/L	G	AB	R	H	2B	3B	HR	RBI	BB	SO	AVG	OBP	SLG	OPS	OPS+	BR+	SB	CS	SBR	FA	FR	G/POS	TPR
1974	NY-N	23	68	9	16	1	0	2	8	7	17	.235	.316	.338	654	84	-1	0	0	0	.927	0	O-20(18-0-2)	-0.2
1976	NY-N	22	26	2	3	0	0	1	2	2	6	.115	.179	.231	409	16	-3	0	1	-0	.889	-1	/O-7(4-0-3)	-0.4
1977	StL-N	1	3	0	1	0	0	0	0	0	1	.333	.333	.333	667	81	-0	0	0	0	1.000	2	/O-1(0-0-1)	0.2
1979	*Bal-A	42	86	15	22	5	0	6	13	6	9	.256	.304	.523	828	123	2	0	0	0	.974	-3	O-24(23-1-1),D-10	-0.2
1980	Bal-A	76	170	28	45	8	1	10	33	19	21	.265	.339	.500	839	128	6	0	0	0	1.000	-2	D-41,O-19(16-1-2)	0.2
1981	Bal-A	44	86	12	24	2	0	3	13	11	9	.279	.367	.407	774	123	3	0	1	-0	1.000	0	D-27/O-4(4-0-0)	0.2
1982	Bal-A	64	128	17	39	6	0	6	24	5	14	.305	.331	.492	823	123	3	1	1	-0	.972	-5	O-25(25-0-0),D-17/1-3	-0.3
1983	*Bal-A	47	104	12	23	7	0	4	13	9	18	.221	.283	.404	687	88	-2	0	0	0	.953	-3	O-24(19-0-5),D-11	-0.6
1984	Bal-A	60	118	9	25	6	0	4	24	8	24	.212	.262	.364	626	73	-5	1	1	-0	1.000	-4	D-34,O-13(11-0-2)	-1.0
1985	Cle-A	46	76	10	19	7	0	2	15	4	17	.250	.287	.421	709	92	-1	0	0	0	.917	-4	O-20(20-0-0)/D-3	-0.5
Total	10	425	865	114	217	42	1	38	145	71	136	.251	.309	.434	743	104	2	2	4	-1	.958	-19	O-157L,D-143/1-3	-2.6

■ **DICK AYLWARD** Aylward, Richard John "Dandy" b: 6/4/25, Baltimore, Md. d: 6/11/83, Spring Valley, Cal. BR/TR, 6', 190 lbs. Deb: 5/1/53

YEAR	TM/L	G	AB	R	H	2B	3B	HR	RBI	BB	SO	AVG	OBP	SLG	OPS	OPS+	BR+	SB	CS	SBR	FA	FR	G/POS	TPR
1953	Cle-A	4	3	0	0	0	0	0	0	0	1	.000	.000	.000	0	-99	-1	0	0	0	1.000	-0	/C-4	-0.1

■ **JOE AYRAULT** Ayrault, Joseph Allen b: 10/8/71, Rochester, Mich. BR/TR, 6'3", 190 lbs. Deb: 9/1/96

YEAR	TM/L	G	AB	R	H	2B	3B	HR	RBI	BB	SO	AVG	OBP	SLG	OPS	OPS+	BR+	SB	CS	SBR	FA	FR	G/POS	TPR
1996	Atl-N	7	5	0	1	0	0	0	0	0	1	.200	.333	.200	533	43	-0	0	0	0	1.000	0	/C-7	0.0

■ **JOE AZCUE** Azcue, Jose Joaquin (Lopez) b: 8/18/39, Cienfuegos, Cuba BR/TR, 6', 200 lbs. Deb: 8/3/60

YEAR	TM/L	G	AB	R	H	2B	3B	HR	RBI	BB	SO	AVG	OBP	SLG	OPS	OPS+	BR+	SB	CS	SBR	FA	FR	G/POS	TPR
1960	Cin-N	14	31	1	3	0	0	0	3	2	6	.097	.152	.097	248	-30	-5	0	1	-0	1.000	5	C-14	0.0
1962	KC-A	72	223	18	51	9	1	2	25	17	27	.229	.292	.305	597	58	-13	1	0	0	.985	3	C-70	-0.6
1963	KC-A	2	4	0	0	0	0	0	0	0	1	.000	.000	.000	0	-95	-1	0	0	0	1.000	0	/C-1	-0.1
	Cle-A	94	320	26	91	16	0	14	46	15	46	.284	.316	.466	782	117	6	1	1	-0	.992	5	C-91	1.5
	Yr	96	324	26	91	16	0	14	46	15	47	.281	.313	.460	773	114	5	1	1	-0	.992	5	C-92	1.4
1964	Cle-A	83	271	20	74	9	1	4	34	16	38	.273	.318	.358	676	88	-4	0	2	-1	.993	-0	C-76	-0.2
1965	Cle-A	111	335	16	77	7	0	2	35	27	54	.230	.293	.269	562	60	-17	2	1	0	.994	-1	*C-108	-1.4
1966	Cle-A	98	302	22	83	10	1	9	37	20	22	.275	.324	.404	728	108	3	0	2	-1	.989	-8	C-97	-0.2
1967	Cle-A	86	295	33	74	12	5	11	34	22	35	.251	.309	.437	747	117	5	0	3	-1	**.999**	5	C-86	1.5
1968	Cle-A★	115	357	23	100	10	0	4	42	28	33	.280	.332	.342	674	106	3	1	1	-0	**.996**	11	C-97	2.1
1969	Cle-A	7	24	1	7	0	0	1	1	4	3	.292	.393	.417	810	122	1	0	0	0	.980	2	/C-6	0.3
	Bos-A	19	51	7	11	2	0	0	3	4	5	.216	.273	.255	528	46	-4	0	0	0	.981	3	C-19	0.0
	Cal-A	80	248	15	54	6	0	1	19	27	28	.218	.300	.254	554	59	-13	0	1	-0	.992	5	C-80	-0.6
	Yr	106	323	23	72	8	0	2	23	35	36	.223	.303	.266	569	62	-16	0	1	-0	.989	9	*C-105	-0.3
1970	Cal-A	114	351	19	85	13	1	2	25	24	40	.242	.294	.302	596	67	-16	0	0	0	.991	-5	*C-112	-1.7
1972	Cal-A	3	2	0	0	0	0	0	0	0	1	.000	.000	.000	0	-99	-1	0	0	0	1.000	1	/C-2	0.0
	Mil-A	11	14	0	2	0	0	0	0	1	5	.143	.200	.143	343	3	-2	0	0	0	1.000	2	/C-9	0.0
	Yr	14	16	0	2	0	0	0	0	1	6	.125	.176	.125	301	-10	-2	0	0	0	1.000	2	C-11	0.0
Total	11	909	2828	201	712	94	9	50	304	207	344	.252	.307	.344	651	85	-58	5	12	-3	.992	26	C-868	0.6

■ **OSCAR AZOCAR** Azocar, Oscar Gregorio (Azocar) b: 2/21/65, Soro, Venez. BL/TL, 6'1", 170 lbs. Deb: 7/17/90 Career OF: (90-LF 0-CF 19-RF)

YEAR	TM/L	G	AB	R	H	2B	3B	HR	RBI	BB	SO	AVG	OBP	SLG	OPS	OPS+	BR+	SB	CS	SBR	FA	FR	G/POS	TPR
1990	NY-A	65	214	18	53	8	0	5	19	2	15	.248	.258	.355	613	70	-9	7	0	2	.991	0	O-57(47-0-12)/D-1	-0.9
1991	SD-N	38	57	5	14	2	0	0	9	1	9	.246	.271	.281	552	54	-3	2	0	0	.875	-3	O-13(12-0-1)/1-1	-0.7
1992	SD-N	99	168	15	32	6	0	0	8	9	12	.190	.232	.226	458	30	-15	1	0	0	.942	-1	O-37(31-0-6)	-1.9
Total	3	202	439	38	99	16	0	5	36	12	36	.226	.249	.296	546	52	-28	10	0	2	.964	-4	O-107L/1-1,D-1	-3.5

■ **CHARLIE BABB** Babb, Charles Amos b: 2/20/1873, Milwaukie, Ore. d: 3/20/54, Portland, Ore. BB/TR, 5'10", 165 lbs. Deb: 4/17/03

YEAR	TM/L	G	AB	R	H	2B	3B	HR	RBI	BB	SO	AVG	OBP	SLG	OPS	OPS+	BR+	SB	CS	SBR	FA	FR	G/POS	TPR
1903	NY-N	121	424	68	105	15	8	0	46	45		.248	.350	.321	671	88	-5	22			.912	-2	*S-113/3-8	-0.2
1904	Bro-N	151	521	49	138	18	3	0	53	53		.265	.345	.311	656	106	6	34			.927	-3	*S-151	0.8
1905	Bro-N	75	235	27	44	8	2	0	17	27		.187	.303	.238	541	67	-8	10			.923	-2	S-36,1-31/3-5,2-2	-1.0
Total	3	347	1180	144	287	41	13	0	116	125		.243	.339	.300	639	92	-7	66			.921	-7	S-300/1-31,3-13,2-2	-0.4

■ **LOREN BABE** Babe, Loren Rolland "Bee Bee" b: 1/11/28, Pisgah, Iowa d: 2/14/84, Omaha, Neb. BL/TR, 5'10", 180 lbs. Deb: 8/19/52 C

YEAR	TM/L	G	AB	R	H	2B	3B	HR	RBI	BB	SO	AVG	OBP	SLG	OPS	OPS+	BR+	SB	CS	SBR	FA	FR	G/POS	TPR
1952	NY-A	12	21	1	2	1	0	0	0	4	4	.095	.240	.143	383	9	-3	1	0	0	.909	2	/3-9	-0.1
1953	NY-A	5	18	2	6	1	0	2	6	0	2	.333	.333	.722	1056	185	2	0	0	0	.920	3	/3-5	0.5
	Phi-A	103	343	34	77	16	2	0	20	35	20	.224	.300	.283	583	56	-21	0	1	-0	.950	1	3-93/S-1	-2.0
	Yr	108	361	36	83	17	2	2	26	35	22	.230	.302	.305	606	62	-19	0	1	-0	.948	5	3-98/S-1	-1.5
Total	2	120	382	37	85	18	2	2	26	39	26	.223	.298	.296	594	59	-21	1	1	-0	.946	6	3-107/S-1	-1.6

■ **CHARLIE BABINGTON** Babington, Charles Percy b: 5/4/1895, Cranston, R.I. d: 3/22/57, Providence, R.I. BR/TR, 6', 170 lbs. Deb: 7/20/15

YEAR	TM/L	G	AB	R	H	2B	3B	HR	RBI	BB	SO	AVG	OBP	SLG	OPS	OPS+	BR+	SB	CS	SBR	FA	FR	G/POS	TPR
1915	NY-N	28	33	5	8	3	1	0	2	0	4	.242	.265	.394	659	104	-0	1			.909	-5	O-12(2-11-1)/1-1	-0.6

■ **SHOOTY BABITT** Babitt, Mack Neal b: 3/9/59, Oakland, Cal. BR/TR, 5'8", 174 lbs. Deb: 4/9/81

YEAR	TM/L	G	AB	R	H	2B	3B	HR	RBI	BB	SO	AVG	OBP	SLG	OPS	OPS+	BR+	SB	CS	SBR	FA	FR	G/POS	TPR
1981	Oak-A	54	156	10	40	1	3	0	14	13	13	.256	.314	.301	615	82	-3	5	4	-0	.972	-17	2-52	-1.9

■ **WALLY BACKMAN** Backman, Walter Wayne b: 9/22/59, Hillsboro, Ore. BB/TR, 5'9", 160 lbs. Deb: 9/2/80

YEAR	TM/L	G	AB	R	H	2B	3B	HR	RBI	BB	SO	AVG	OBP	SLG	OPS	OPS+	BR+	SB	CS	SBR	FA	FR	G/POS	TPR
1980	NY-N	27	93	12	30	1	1	0	9	11	14	.323	.400	.355	755	115	3	2	3	-1	1.000	-10	2-20/S-8	-0.7
1981	NY-N	26	36	5	10	2	0	0	0	4	7	.278	.350	.333	683	96	-0	1	0	0	.946	-3	2-11/3-1	-0.3
1982	NY-N	96	261	37	71	13	2	3	22	49	47	.272	.387	.372	759	114	7	8	7	-1	.964	-13	2-88/3-6,S-1	-0.3
1983	NY-N	26	42	6	7	0	1	0	3	2	8	.167	.205	.214	419	16	-5	0	0	0	1.000	-2	2-14/3-2	-0.7
1984	NY-N	128	436	68	122	19	2	1	26	56	63	.280	.362	.339	701	99	2	32	9	4	.981	-12	*2-115/S-8	0.0
1985	NY-N	145	520	77	142	24	5	1	38	36	72	.273	.321	.344	666	88	-8	30	12	2	**.989**	-9	*2-140/S-1	-0.8
1986	*NY-N	124	387	67	124	18	2	1	27	36	32	.320	.378	.385	763	114	8	13	7	0	.966	-3	*2-113	1.1
1987	NY-N	94	300	43	75	6	1	1	23	25	43	.250	.308	.287	594	62	-16	11	3	1	.983	-7	2-87	-1.7
1988	*NY-N	99	294	44	89	12	0	0	17	41	49	.303	.390	.344	733	118	9	9	5	0	.989	-9	2-92	0.3
1989	Min-A	87	299	33	69	9	2	1	26	32	45	.231	.307	.284	592	63	-14	1	1	-0	.982	-22	2-84/D-1	-3.5
1990	*Pit-N	104	315	62	92	21	3	2	28	42	53	.292	.377	.397	774	118	9	6	3	0	.920	-19	3-71,2-15	-0.9
1991	Phi-N	94	185	20	45	12	0	0	15	30	30	.243	.349	.308	657	87	-2	3	2	-0	.981	-15	2-36,3-20	-1.7
1992	Phi-N	42	48	6	13	1	0	0	6	6	9	.271	.352	.292	644	84	-1	1	0	0	.968	0	2-10/3-2	0.0
1993	Sea-A	10	29	2	4	0	0	0	0	1	8	.138	.167	.138	305	-17	-5	0	0	0	.857	-1	/3-9,2-1	-0.5
Total	14	1102	3245	482	893	138	19	10	240	371	480	.275	.350	.339	689	94	-13	117	52	8	.980	-125	2-826,3-111/S-18,D	-9.7

YEAR	TM/L	G	AB	R	H	2B	3B	HR	RBI	BB	SO	AVG	OBP	SLG	OPS	OPS+	BR+	SB	CS	SBR	FA	FR	G/POS	TPR
■ **EDDIE BACON**	Bacon, Edgar Suter b: 4/8/1895, Franklin Co., Ky. d: 10/2/63, Louisville, Ky. Deb: 8/13/17																							
1917	Phi-A	4	6	1	3	1	0	0	2	0	0	.500	.500	.667	1167	259	1	0			1.000	1	/P-1	0.0
■ **ART BADER**	Bader, Arthur Herman b: 9/21/1886, St.Louis, Mo. d: 4/5/57, St.Louis, Mo. BR/TR, 5'9", 160 lbs. Deb: 8/2/04																							
1904	StL-A	2	3	0	0	0	0	0	0	1		.000	.250	.000	250	-19	-0	0			1.000	1	/O-1(1-0-0)	0.0
■ **RED BADGRO**	Badgro, Morris Hiram b: 12/1/02, Orillia, Wash. d: 7/13/98, Kent, Wash. BL/TR, 6', 190 lbs. Deb: 6/20/29																							
1929	StL-A	54	148	27	42	12	0	1	18	11	15	.284	.342	.385	727	84	-4	1	0	0	.983	-4	O-37(0-0-37)	-1.0
1930	StL-A	89	234	30	56	18	3	1	27	13	27	.239	.285	.355	640	59	-15	3	5	-1	.952	0	O-61(4-14-43)	-1.8
Total	2	143	382	57	98	30	3	2	45	24	42	.257	.307	.366	674	69	-19	4	5	-1	.962	-4	/O-98(4-14-80)	-2.8
■ **CARLOS BAERGA**	Baerga, Carlos Obed (Ortiz) b: 11/4/68, Santurce, P.R. BB/TR, 5'11", 200 lbs. Deb: 4/14/90																							
1990	Cle-A	108	312	46	81	17	2	7	47	16	57	.260	.304	.394	698	94	-3	0	2	-1	.944	-9	3-50,S-48/2-8	-1.1
1991	Cle-A	158	593	80	171	28	2	11	69	48	74	.288	.348	.398	746	105	4	3	2	-0	.944	11	3-89,2-75/S-2	1.7
1992	Cle-A★	161	657	92	205	32	1	20	105	35	76	.312	.359	.455	814	129	24	10	2	2	.979	8	*2-160/D-1	3.8
1993	Cle-A★	154	624	105	200	28	6	21	114	34	68	.321	.361	.486	847	126	21	15	4	2	.979	8	*2-150/D-4	3.7
1994	Cle-A	103	442	81	139	32	2	19	80	10	45	.314	.338	.525	863	118	10	8	2	1	.973	9	*2-102/D-1	2.3
1995	*Cle-A★	135	557	87	175	28	2	15	90	35	31	.314	.358	.452	810	108	6	11	2	2	.973	12	*2-134/D-1	2.4
1996	Cle-A	100	424	54	113	25	0	10	55	16	25	.267	.304	.396	700	76	-17	1	1	-0	.971	-3	*2-100	-1.3
	NY-N	26	83	5	16	3	0	2	11	5	2	.193	.256	.301	557	48	-6	0	0	0	.990	-5	1-16/3-6,2-1	-1.2
1997	NY-N	133	467	53	131	25	1	9	52	20	54	.281	.314	.396	710	88	-10	2	6	-2	.978	4	*2-131	-0.1
1998	NY-N	147	511	46	136	27	1	7	53	24	55	.266	.307	.364	671	77	-18	0	1	-0	.986	-10	*2-144	-2.1
1999	SD-N	33	80	6	20	1	0	2	5	6	14	.250	.318	.338	656	72	-3	1	0	0	1.000	-8	2-13,3-13/1-2,D-1	-1.0
	Cle-A	22	57	4	13	0	0	1	5	4	10	.228	.279	.281	559	41	-5	1	1	-0	.964	-1	3-15/2-6,D-1	-0.5
Total	10	1280	4807	659	1400	246	17	124	686	253	511	.291	.334	.427	761	102	3	52	23	3	.976	19	*2-1024,3-173/S1D	6.6
■ **JOSE BAEZ**	Baez, Jose Antonio (b: Jose Antonio Mota (Baez)) b: 12/31/53, San Cristobal, D.R. BR/TR, 5'8", 160 lbs. Deb: 4/6/77																							
1977	Sea-A	91	305	39	79	14	1	1	17	19	20	.259	.305	.321	626	71	-12	6	1	1	.973	9	2-77/3-1,D-3	0.2
1978	Sea-A	23	50	8	8	0	1	0	2	6	7	.160	.250	.200	450	28	-5	1	0	0	.978	12	2-14/3-3,D-1	0.8
Total	2	114	355	47	87	14	2	1	19	25	27	.245	.297	.304	601	65	-17	7	1	1	.974	21	/2-91,D-4,3-4	1.0
■ **KEVIN BAEZ**	Baez, Kevin Richard b: 1/10/67, Brooklyn, N.Y. BR/TR, 6', 160 lbs. Deb: 9/3/90																							
1990	NY-N	5	12	0	2	1	0	0	0	0	0	.167	.167	.250	417	13	-1	0	0	0	1.000	0	/S-4	-0.1
1992	NY-N	6	13	0	2	0	0	0	0	0	0	.154	.154	.154	308	-13	-2	0	0	0	.889	1	/S-5	-0.1
1993	NY-N	52	126	10	23	9	0	0	7	13	17	.183	.259	.254	513	38	-11	0	0	0	.967	-5	S-52	-1.2
Total	3	63	151	10	27	10	0	0	7	13	17	.179	.244	.245	489	33	-14	0	0	0	.962	-4	/S-61	-1.4
■ **JEFF BAGWELL**	Bagwell, Jeffery Robert b: 5/27/68, Boston, Mass. BR/TR, 6', 195 lbs. Deb: 4/8/91 Career OF: (0-LF 0-CF 1-RF)																							
1991	Hou-N	156	554	79	163	26	4	15	82	75	116	.294	.391	.437	828	141	33	7	4	0	.991	-1	*1-155	2.1
1992	Hou-N	162	586	87	160	34	6	18	96	84	97	.273	.375	.444	819	137	31	10	6	0	.995	7	*1-159	2.8
1993	Hou-N	142	535	76	171	37	4	20	88	62	73	.320	.393	.516	909	146	36	13	4	1	.993	6	*1-140	2.9
1994	Hou-N★	110	400	**104**	147	32	2	39	**116**	65	65	.368	**.461**	**.750**	**1211**	**220**	**71**	15	4	2	.991	17	*1-109/O-1(0-0-1)	**7.6**
1995	Hou-N	114	448	88	130	29	0	21	87	79	102	.290	.403	.496	899	145	32	12	5	1	.994	18	*1-114	3.8
1996	Hou-N★	162	568	111	179	**48**	2	31	120	135	114	.315	.454	.570	1025	182	76	21	7	2	.989	8	*1-162	6.7
1997	*Hou-N★	162	566	109	162	40	2	43	135	127	122	.286	.430	.592	1022	171	64	31	10	3	.993	7	*1-159/D-1	5.7
1998	*Hou-N	147	540	124	164	33	1	34	111	109	90	.304	.427	.557	984	161	52	19	7	2	.995	9	*1-147	4.6
1999	*Hou-N★	162	562	**143**	171	35	0	42	126	**149**	127	.304	.458	.591	1049	165	**64**	30	11	3	.994	4	*1-161/D-2	**5.2**
2000	Hou-N	159	590	**152**	183	37	1	47	132	107	116	.310	.428	.615	1044	151	49	9	6	-0	.994	6	*1-158/D-1	3.8
Total	10	1476	5349	1073	1630	351	22	310	1093	992	1022	.305	.422	.552	975	161	506	167	64	14	.993	80	*1-1464/D-4,O-1R	45.2
■ **BILL BAGWELL**	Bagwell, William Mallory "Big Bill" b: 2/24/1896, Choudrant, La. d: 10/5/76, Choudrant, La. BL/TL, 6'1", 175 lbs. Deb: 4/17/23																							
1923	Bos-N	56	93	8	27	4	2	2	10	6	12	.290	.333	.441	774	107	1	0	0	0	1.000	-3	O-22(22-0-0)	-0.3
1925	Phi-A	36	50	4	15	2	1	0	10	2	2	.300	.327	.380	707	74	-2	0	0	0	.667	-2	/O-4(4-0-0)	-0.4
Total	2	92	143	12	42	6	3	2	20	8	14	.294	.331	.420	751	95	-1	0	0	0	.973	-5	/O-26(26-0-0)	-0.7
■ **FRANK BAHRET**	Bahret, Frank F. b: 1858, Poughkeepsie, N.Y. d: 3/30/1888, Poughkeepsie, N.Y. 6'1", 184 lbs. Deb: 4/17/1884																							
1884	Bal-U	2	8	0	0	0	0	0		0		.000	.000	.000	0	-91	-2				1.000	0	/O-2(0-1-1)	-0.2
■ **GENE BAILEY**	Bailey, Arthur Eugene b: 11/25/1893, Pearsall, Tex. d: 11/14/73, Houston, Tex. BR/TR, 5'8", 160 lbs. Deb: 9/10/17																							
1917	Phi-A	5	12	1	1	0	0	0	0	1	1	.083	.154	.083	237	-28	-2	0			.833	-1	/O-4(4-0-0)	-0.4
1919	Bos-N	4	6	0	2	0	0	0	1	0	2	.333	.333	.333	667	105	0	1			1.000	0	/O-3(0-1-1)	0.0
1920	Bos-N	13	24	2	2	0	0	0	0	3	3	.083	.185	.083	269	-22	-4	0	1	-0	.929	-2	/O-8(5-4-1)	-0.7
	Bos-A	46	135	14	31	2	0	0	5	9	15	.230	.283	.244	527	42	-11	2	7	-2	.986	-4	O-40(9-16-15)	-1.9
1923	Bro-N	127	411	71	109	11	7	1	42	43	34	.265	.343	.333	677	81	-10	9	7	-0	.959	2	*O-100(25-60-17)/1-5	-1.3
1924	Bro-N	18	46	7	11	3	0	1	4	7	6	.239	.340	.370	709	93	-0	1	0	0	1.000	1	O-17(0-10-8)	0.0
Total	5	213	634	95	156	16	7	2	52	63	61	.246	.321	.303	624	69	-27	13	15		.965	-5	O-172(43-91-42)/1-5	-4.3
■ **FRED BAILEY**	Bailey, Frederick Middleton "Penny" b: 8/16/1895, Mt.Hope, W.Va. d: 8/16/72, Huntington, W.Va. BL/TL, 5'11", 150 lbs. Deb: 8/19/16																							
1916	Bos-N	6	10	0	1	0	0	0	1	0	3	.100	.100	.100	200	-40	-2	0			1.000	-0	/O-2(1-0-0)	-0.2
1917	Bos-N	50	110	9	21	2	1	1	5	9	25	.191	.270	.255	525	65	-4	3			.962	-1	O-27(9-15-4)	-0.8
1918	Bos-N	4	4	1	1	0	0	0	0	0	1	.250	.250	.250	500	55	-0	0			.000	0	H	0.0
Total	3	60	124	10	23	2	1	1	6	9	29	.185	.257	.242	499	57	-6	3			.963	-2	/O-29(10-15-4)	-1.0
■ **BILL BAILEY**	Bailey, Harry Lewis b: 11/19/1881, Shawnee, Ohio d: 10/27/67, Seattle, Wash. BL/TR, 5'10.5", 170 lbs. Deb: 4/21/11																							
1911	NY-A	5	9	1	1	0	0	0	0	0		.111	.111	.111	222	-36	-2	0			.000	0	/O-2,3-1	-0.1
■ **MARK BAILEY**	Bailey, John Mark b: 11/4/61, Springfield, Mo. BB/TR, 6'5", 195 lbs. Deb: 4/27/84																							
1984	Hou-N	108	344	38	73	16	1	9	34	53	71	.212	.321	.343	664	93	-2	0	1	-0	.983	-2	*C-108	0.0
1985	Hou-N	114	332	47	88	14	0	10	45	67	70	.265	.390	.398	788	124	14	0	2	-1	.979	-10	*C-110/1-2	0.7
1986	Hou-N	57	153	9	27	5	0	4	15	28	45	.176	.304	.288	591	66	-7	1	1	-0	.989	2	C-53/1-1	-0.3
1987	Hou-N	35	64	5	13	1	0	0	3	10	21	.203	.311	.219	530	45	-5	1	0	0	.985	-0	C-27	-0.4
1988	Hou-N	8	23	1	3	0	0	0	0	5	6	.130	.286	.130	416	24	-2	0	1	-0	.981	-1	/C-8	-0.3
1990	SF-N	5	7	1	1	0	0	1	3	0	2	.143	.143	.571	714	90	-0	0	0	0	1.000	-0	/C-1	-0.1
1992	SF-N	13	26	0	4	1	0	0	1	3	7	.154	.241	.192	434	26	-3	0	0	0	1.000	-1	/C-7	-0.3
Total	7	340	949	101	209	37	1	24	101	166	222	.220	.338	.337	675	93	-5	2	5	-1	.983	-13	C-314/1-3	-0.7
■ **ED BAILEY**	Bailey, Lonas Edgar b: 4/15/31, Strawberry Plains, Tenn. BL/TR, 6'2", 205 lbs. Deb: 9/26/53 F Career OF: (1-LF 0-CF 0-RF)																							
1953	Cin-N	2	8	1	3	1	0	0	1	1	3	.375	.444	.500	944	145	1	0	0	0	1.000	-1	/C-2	0.0
1954	Cin-N	73	183	21	36	2	3	9	20	35	34	.197	.326	.388	714	83	-5	1	0	0	.973	-12	C-61	-1.4
1955	Cin-N	21	39	3	8	1	1	1	4	4	10	.205	.326	.359	685	77	-1	0	0	0	.962	3	C-11	0.2
1956	Cin-N★	118	383	59	115	8	2	28	75	52	50	.300	.388	.551	939	140	22	2	0	0	.984	4	*C-106	3.2
1957	Cin-N★	122	391	54	102	15	2	20	48	73	69	.261	.380	.463	843	117	11	5	3	0	.991	-12	*C-115	0.5
1958	Cin-N	112	360	39	90	23	1	11	59	47	61	.250	.338	.411	749	92	-4	2	2	-0	.988	-4	C-99	-0.3
1959	Cin-N	121	379	43	100	13	0	12	40	62	53	.264	.370	.393	763	101	2	2	0	0	.990	2	*C-117	1.0
1960	Cin-N★	133	441	52	115	19	3	13	67	59	70	.261	.351	.406	756	105	4	1	0	0	.990	-13	*C-129	-0.2
1961	Cin-N	12	43	4	13	4	0	0	2	3	5	.302	.348	.395	743	95	-0	0	0	0	.967	-4	C-12	-0.4
	SF-N☆	107	340	39	81	9	1	13	51	42	41	.238	.329	.385	714	92	-4	1	5	-2	.985	-1	*C-103/O-1(1-0-0)	-0.1
	Yr	119	383	43	94	13	1	13	53	45	46	.245	.331	.386	717	93	-4	1	5	-2	.984	-5	*C-115/O-1(1-0-0)	-0.5
1962	*SF-N	96	254	32	59	9	1	17	45	42	42	.232	.354	.476	831	123	8	1	1	-0	.987	-5	C-75	0.7
1963	SF-N★	105	308	41	81	8	0	21	68	50	64	.263	.368	.494	861	147	19	0	6	-2	.987	-0	C-88	2.3
1964	Mil-N	95	271	30	71	10	1	5	34	34	39	.262	.346	.362	708	99	1	2	0	0	.982	-10	C-80	-0.5
1965	SF-N	24	28	1	3	0	0	0	3	6	7	.107	.265	.107	372	9	-3	0	0	0	1.000	3	C-12/1-2	0.0

YEAR	TM/L	G	AB	R	H	2B	3B	HR	RBI	BB	SO	AVG	OBP	SLG	OPS	OPS+	BR+	SB	CS	SBR	FA	FR	G/POS	TPR
	Chi-N	66	150	13	38	6	0	5	23	34	28	.253	.391	.393	785	119	5	0	1	-0	.981	-5	C-54/1-3	0.2
	Yr	90	178	14	41	6	0	5	26	40	35	.230	.372	.348	720	102	2	0	1	-0	.984	-2	C-66/1-5	0.2
1966	Cal-A	5	3	0	0	0	0	0	0	1	1	.000	.250	.000	250	-22	-0	0	0	0	.000	0	H	0.0
Total	14	1212	3581	432	915	128	15	155	540	545	577	.256	.358	.429	787	110	56	17	18	-3	.986	-54	*C-1064/1-5,O-1L	5.2

■ BOB BAILEY

Bailey, Robert Sherwood b: 10/13/42, Long Beach, Cal. BR/TR, 6', 188 lbs. Deb: 9/14/62 Career OF: (399-LF 2-CF 3-RF)

YEAR	TM/L	G	AB	R	H	2B	3B	HR	RBI	BB	SO	AVG	OBP	SLG	OPS	OPS+	BR+	SB	CS	SBR	FA	FR	G/POS	TPR
1962	Pit-N	14	42	6	7	2	1	0	6	6	10	.167	.271	.262	533	44	-3	1	1	-0	.921	0	3-12	-0.3
1963	Pit-N	154	570	60	130	15	3	12	45	58	98	.228	.305	.328	633	82	-13	10	9	-1	.933	6	*3-153/S-3	-0.9
1964	Pit-N	143	530	73	149	26	3	11	51	44	78	.281	.337	.404	741	108	6	10	8	-1	.943	6	*3-105,O-35L/S-2	1.0
1965	Pit-N	159	626	87	160	28	3	11	49	70	93	.256	.330	.363	693	95	-3	10	14	-3	.939	-18	*3-142,O-28(28-0-0)	-2.7
1966	Pit-N	126	380	51	106	19	3	13	46	47	65	.279	.361	.447	809	123	13	5	3	0	.956	-0	3-96,O-20(20-0-0)	1.2
1967	LA-N	116	322	21	73	8	2	4	28	40	50	.227	.314	.301	615	84	-6	5	5	-1	.941	0	3-65,O-27L/1-4,S-1	-0.9
1968	LA-N	105	322	24	73	9	3	8	39	38	69	.227	.310	.348	658	105	2	1	2	-0	.953	-3	3-90/S-1,O-1(1-0-0)	-0.2
1969	Mon-N	111	358	46	95	16	6	9	53	40	76	.265	.341	.419	760	111	5	3	3	-0	.992	4	1-85,O-12(12-0-0)/3-1	0.2
1970	Mon-N	131	352	77	101	19	3	28	84	72	70	.287	.409	.597	1006	166	34	5	3	0	.953	-13	3-48,O-44L,1-18	1.7
1971	Mon-N	157	545	65	137	21	4	14	83	97	105	.251	.364	.382	746	111	11	13	7	0	**.960**	-15	*3-120,O-51L/1-9	-0.7
1972	Mon-N	143	489	55	114	10	4	16	57	59	112	.233	.317	.368	685	92	-5	6	7	-1	.938	-8	*3-134/O-5(5-0-0),1-3	-1.5
1973	Mon-N	151	513	77	140	25	4	26	86	88	99	.273	.380	.489	870	134	25	5	8	-2	.956	-5	*3-146/O-2(2-0-0)	1.8
1974	Mon-N	152	507	69	142	20	2	20	73	100	107	.280	.400	.446	845	129	23	4	7	-2	.974	-16	O-78(78-0-0),3-68	0.1
1975	Mon-N	106	227	23	62	5	0	5	30	46	38	.273	.398	.361	759	107	4	4	4	-1	.979	-5	O-61(61-0-0)/3-3	-0.4
1976	Cin-N	69	124	17	37	6	1	6	23	16	26	.298	.379	.508	887	146	7	0	0	0	.974	-5	O-31(31-0-0),3-10	0.2
1977	Cin-N	49	79	9	20	2	1	2	11	12	10	.253	.352	.380	731	94	-0	1	1	-0	.975	-1	1-19/O-3(4-0-0)	-0.2
	Bos-A	2	2	0	0	0	0	0	0	0	1	.000	.000	.000	0	-90	-1	0	0	0	.000	0	H	-0.1
1978	Bos-A	43	94	12	18	3	0	4	9	19	19	.191	.333	.351	684	84	-2	2	1	0	1.000	0	D-34/3-1,O-1(1-0-0)	-0.2
Total	17	1931	6082	772	1564	234	43	189	773	852	1126	.257	.350	.403	753	111	98	85	83	-10	.946	-71	*3-1194,O-399L,1/DS	-1.9

■ BOB BAILOR

Bailor, Robert Michael b: 7/10/51, Connellsville, Pa. BR/TR, 5'11", 170 lbs. Deb: 9/6/75 C Career OF: (79-LF 105-CF 254-RF)

YEAR	TM/L	G	AB	R	H	2B	3B	HR	RBI	BB	SO	AVG	OBP	SLG	OPS	OPS+	BR+	SB	CS	SBR	FA	FR	G/POS	TPR
1975	Bal-A	5	7	0	1	0	0	0	0	1	0	.143	.250	.143	393	14	-1	0	0	0	1.000	2	/S-2,2-1	0.1
1976	Bal-A	9	6	2	2	0	1	0	0	0	0	.333	.333	.667	1000	200	1	0	1	-0	.000	-0	/S-1,D-1	0.0
1977	Tor-A	122	496	62	154	21	5	5	32	17	26	.310	.336	.403	739	99	-1	15	6	1	.988	1	O-63C,S-53/D-7	0.5
1978	Tor-A	154	621	74	164	29	7	1	52	38	21	.264	.312	.338	650	81	-16	5	6	-1	.964	15	*O-125R,3-28/S-4	-0.8
1979	Tor-A	130	414	50	95	11	5	1	38	36	27	.229	.300	.287	588	59	-23	14	8	0	.987	1	*O-118R/3-9,D-1	-2.7
1980	Tor-A	117	347	44	82	14	2	1	16	36	33	.236	.312	.297	609	65	-16	12	8	-0	.991	12	O-98L,S-12,3-11,/P2D	-0.6
1981	NY-N	51	81	11	23	3	1	0	8	8	11	.284	.356	.346	701	101	0	2	0	0	.955	-5	S-22,2-13,O-13L,/3	-0.2
1982	NY-N	110	376	44	104	14	1	0	31	20	17	.277	.317	.319	636	79	-10	20	3	3	.984	-19	S-60,2-56,3-21,/O-4L	-2.1
1983	NY-N	118	340	33	85	8	0	1	30	20	23	.250	.294	.282	576	61	-18	18	3	3	.969	-6	S-75,2-50,3-11,/O-3L	-1.4
1984	LA-N	65	131	11	36	4	0	0	8	8	1	.275	.317	.305	622	76	-4	3	1	0	.944	10	2-23,3-17,S-16	0.8
1985	*LA-N	74	118	8	29	3	1	0	7	3	5	.246	.270	.288	559	58	-7	1	0	0	.962	15	3-45,2-16/S-5,O-1L	0.9
Total	11	955	2937	339	775	107	23	9	222	187	164	.264	.312	.325	638	76	-95	90	36	7	.980	26	O-425R,S-250,23/DP	-5.5

■ HAROLD BAINES

Baines, Harold Douglass b: 3/15/59, Easton, Md. BL/TL, 6'2", 195 lbs. Deb: 4/10/80 Career OF: (9-LF 30-CF 1039-RF)

YEAR	TM/L	G	AB	R	H	2B	3B	HR	RBI	BB	SO	AVG	OBP	SLG	OPS	OPS+	BR+	SB	CS	SBR	FA	FR	G/POS	TPR
1980	Chi-A	141	491	55	125	23	6	13	49	19	65	.255	.284	.405	689	87	-11	2	4	-1	.963	-7	*O-137(0-0-137)/D-1	-2.5
1981	Chi-A	82	280	42	80	11	7	10	41	12	41	.286	.320	.482	802	131	10	6	2	1	.985	-0	O-80(0-0-80)/D-1	0.6
1982	Chi-A	161	608	89	165	29	8	25	105	49	95	.271	.326	.469	794	115	11	10	3	1	.980	2	*O-161(1-3-160)	0.6
1983	*Chi-A	156	596	76	167	33	2	20	99	49	85	.280	.336	.443	779	108	6	7	5	-0	.973	0	*O-155(1-20-142)	-0.1
1984	Chi-A	147	569	72	173	28	10	29	94	54	75	.304	.364	**.541**	906	141	30	1	2	-0	.981	0	*O-147(0-7-147)	2.2
1985	Chi-A★	160	640	86	198	29	3	22	113	42	89	.309	.353	.467	820	118	15	1	1	-0	.994	7	*O-159(0-0-159)/D-1	1.3
1986	Chi-A★	145	570	72	169	29	2	21	88	38	89	.296	.343	.465	808	114	10	2	1	0	.984	12	*O-141(0-0-141)/D-3	1.4
1987	Chi-A★	132	505	59	148	26	4	20	93	46	82	.293	.353	.479	832	115	11	0	0	0	1.000	-1	*D-117/O-8(0-0-8)	0.6
1988	Chi-A	158	599	55	166	39	1	13	81	67	109	.277	.351	.411	762	113	11	0	0	0	.882	-1	*D-147/O-9(0-0-10)	0.5
1989	Chi-A★	96	333	55	107	20	1	13	56	60	52	.321	.426	.505	931	165	31	0	1	-0	.981	-0	D-70,O-25(0-0-24)	2.8
	Tex-A	50	172	18	49	9	0	3	16	13	27	.285	.335	.390	725	102	0	0	2	-1	.667	-0	D-46/O-1(0-0-1)	-0.2
	Yr	146	505	73	156	29	1	16	72	73	79	.309	.397	.465	863	144	31	0	3	-1	.964	-1	*D-116,O-26(0-0-25)	2.6
1990	Tex-A	103	321	41	93	10	1	13	44	47	63	.290	.380	.449	829	131	14	0	1	-0	.833	0	D-95/O-2(0-0-2)	1.1
	*Oak-A	32	94	11	25	5	0	3	21	20	17	.266	.395	.415	810	132	5	0	2	-1	.000	0	D-30	0.3
	Yr	135	415	52	118	15	1	16	65	67	80	.284	.384	.441	825	131	19	0	3	-1	.855	0	*D-125/O-2(0-0-2)	1.4
1991	Oak-A★	141	488	76	144	25	1	20	90	72	67	.295	.387	.473	860	145	31	0	1	-0	.923	-2	*D-125,O-12(1-0-10)	2.5
1992	*Oak-A	140	478	58	121	18	0	16	76	59	61	.253	.335	.391	726	109	6	1	3	-1	.964	-5	*D-116,O-23(6-0-17)	-0.4
1993	Bal-A	118	416	64	130	22	0	20	78	57	52	.313	.395	.510	905	136	22	0	0	0	.000	0	*D-116	1.4
1994	Bal-A	94	326	44	96	12	1	16	54	30	49	.294	.356	.485	840	109	4	0	0	0	.000	0	D-91	-0.1
1995	Bal-A	127	385	60	115	19	1	24	63	70	45	.299	.407	.540	947	142	25	0	2	-1	.000	0	*D-122	1.6
1996	Chi-A	143	495	80	154	29	0	22	95	73	62	.311	.401	.503	904	133	27	3	1	0	.000	0	*D-141	1.7
1997	Chi-A	93	318	40	97	18	0	12	52	41	47	.305	.384	.475	859	128	14	0	1	-0	.000	0	D-86	0.8
	*Bal-A	44	134	15	39	5	0	4	15	14	15	.291	.358	.418	776	105	1	0	0	0	.000	-0	D-35/O-1(0-0-1)	-0.1
	Yr	137	452	55	136	23	0	16	67	55	62	.301	.377	.458	835	121	15	0	1	-0	.885	-0	*D-121/O-1(0-0-1)	0.7
1998	Bal-A	104	293	40	88	17	0	9	57	32	40	.300	.371	.451	822	114	7	0	0	0	.000	0	D-80	0.2
1999	Bal-A★	107	345	57	111	16	1	24	81	43	38	.322	.397	.583	980	151	26	1	2	-0	.000	0	D-96	1.9
	*Cle-A	28	85	5	23	2	0	1	22	11	10	.271	.354	.329	684	73	-3	0	0	0	.000	0	D-33	-0.5
	Yr	135	430	62	134	18	1	25	103	54	48	.312	.388	.533	921	134	23	1	2	-0	.000	0	*D-129	1.4
2000	Bal-A	72	222	24	59	8	0	10	30	29	39	.266	.351	.437	788	101	0	0	0	0	.000	0	D-62	-0.3
	*Chi-A	24	61	2	13	5	0	1	9	7	11	.213	.294	.344	638	60	-4	0	0	0	.000	0	D-16	-0.4
	Yr	96	283	26	72	13	0	11	39	36	50	.254	.339	.417	756	92	-4	0	0	0	.000	0	D-78	-0.7
Total	21	2798	9824	1296	2855	487	49	384	1622	1054	1425	.291	.360	.467	828	122	298	34	34	-4	.978	6	*D-1630,O-1061R	16.9

■ AL BAIRD

Baird, Albert Wells b: 6/2/1895, Cleburne, Tex. d: 11/27/76, Shreveport, La. BR/TR, 5'9", 160 lbs. Deb: 9/10/17

YEAR	TM/L	G	AB	R	H	2B	3B	HR	RBI	BB	SO	AVG	OBP	SLG	OPS	OPS+	BR+	SB	CS	SBR	FA	FR	G/POS	TPR
1917	NY-N	10	24	1	7	0	0	0	4	2	2	.292	.346	.292	638	100	0	2			1.000	2	/2-7,S-3	0.2
1919	NY-N	38	83	8	20	1	0	0	5	5	9	.241	.284	.253	537	63	-4	3			.898	8	2-24/S-9,3-5	0.5
Total	2	48	107	9	27	1	0	0	9	7	11	.252	.298	.262	560	71	-4	5			.921	10	/2-31,S-12,3-5	0.7

■ DOUG BAIRD

Baird, Howard Douglas b: 9/27/1891, St.Charles, Mo. d: 6/13/67, Thomasville, Ga. BR/TR, 5'9.5", 148 lbs. Deb: 4/18/15 Career OF: (10-LF 27-CF 3-RF)

YEAR	TM/L	G	AB	R	H	2B	3B	HR	RBI	BB	SO	AVG	OBP	SLG	OPS	OPS+	BR+	SB	CS	SBR	FA	FR	G/POS	TPR
1915	Pit-N	145	512	49	112	26	12	1	53	37	88	.219	.277	.322	599	82	-12	29	12	2	.939	-3	*3-120,O-20C/2-3	-1.2
1916	Pit-N	128	430	41	93	10	7	1	28	24	49	.216	.263	.279	542	66	-18	20	16	-1	.933	-5	3-80,2-29,O-16L	-2.5
1917	Pit-N	43	135	17	35	6	1	0	18	20	19	.259	.355	.319	673	104	1	8			.935	-4	3-41/2-2	-0.2
	StL-N	104	364	38	92	19	12	0	24	23	52	.253	.301	.371	672	108	3	18			.941	13	*3-103/O-2(0-2-0)	2.1
	Yr	147	499	55	127	25	13	0	42	43	71	.255	.316	.357	673	107	4	26			.940	9	*3-144/2-2,O-2(0-2-0)	1.9
1918	StL-N	82	316	41	78	12	8	2	25	25	42	.247	.304	.354	659	104	1	25			.967	16	3-81/S-1,O-1(0-0-1)	2.1
1919	Phi-N	66	242	33	61	13	3	2	30	22	28	.252	.317	.355	672	95	-1	13			.950	11	3-66	1.3
	StL-N	16	33	4	7	0	1	0	4	2	3	.212	.257	.273	530	63	-2	2			.773	-4	/3-8,2-1,O-1(0-0-1)	-0.6
	Bro-N	20	60	6	11	0	1	0	8	1	10	.183	.197	.217	413	24	-6	3			1.000	1	3-17	-0.5
	Yr	102	335	43	79	13	5	2	42	25	41	.236	.291	.322	613	81	-8	18			.946	8	3-91/2-1,O-1(0-0-1)	0.2
1920	Bro-N	6	6	1	2	0	0	0	1	2	1	.333	.556	.333	889	154	1	0	0	0	.800	-0	/3-2	0.1
	NY-N	7	8	0	1	0	0	0	0	1	3	.125	.222	.125	347	1	-1	0	0	0	1.000	2	/3-4	0.1
	Yr	13	14	1	3	0	0	0	1	3	4	.214	.389	.214	603	76	-0	0	0	0	.929	1	/3-6	0.2
Total	6	617	2106	230	492	86	45	6	191	157	295	.234	.291	.326	616	88	-33	118	28		.944	27	3-522/O-40C,2-35,S	0.7

■ CHARLIE BAKER

Baker, Charles A. b: 1/15/1856, W.Boylston, Mass. d: 1/15/37, Manchester, N.H. BR/TR, 5'4", 140 lbs. Deb: 8/1/1884

YEAR	TM/L	G	AB	R	H	2B	3B	HR	RBI	BB	SO	AVG	OBP	SLG	OPS	OPS+	BR+	SB	CS	SBR	FA	FR	G/POS	TPR
1884	CP-U	15	57	5	8	2	0	1		0		.140	.140	.228	368	10	-8				.722	-1	O-11(0-0-11)/S-3,2-1	-0.8

■ CHUCK BAKER

Baker, Charles Joseph b: 12/6/52, Seattle, Wash. BR/TR, 5'11", 180 lbs. Deb: 4/7/78

YEAR	TM/L	G	AB	R	H	2B	3B	HR	RBI	BB	SO	AVG	OBP	SLG	OPS	OPS+	BR+	SB	CS	SBR	FA	FR	G/POS	TPR
1978	SD-N	44	58	8	12	1	0	0	3	2	15	.207	.233	.224	457	31	-5	0	0	0	.952	14	2-24,S-12	0.9
1980	SD-N	9	22	0	3	1	0	0	0	0	4	.136	.136	.182	318	-13	-3	0	0	0	.963	2	/S-8	-0.1

YEAR	TM/L	G	AB	R	H	2B	3B	HR	RBI	BB	SO	AVG	OBP	SLG	OPS	OPS+	BR+	SB	CS	SBR	FA	FR	G/POS	TPR
1981	Min-A	40	66	6	12	0	3	0	6	1	8	.182	.194	.273	467	31	-6	0	0	0	.969	7	S-31/2-3,3-1,D-1	0.3
Total	3	93	146	14	27	2	3	0	9	3	27	.185	.201	.240	441	25	-15	0	0	0	.962	22	/S-51,2-27,D-1,3-1	1.1
■ **DAVE BAKER**	Baker, David Glenn b: 11/25/57, Lacona, Iowa BL/TR, 6′, 185 lbs. Deb: 9/12/82 F																							
1982	Tor-A	9	20	3	5	1	0	0	2	3	3	.250	.400	.300	700	88	-0	0	0	0	.808	1	/3-8	0.0
■ **DEL BAKER**	Baker, Delmer David b: 5/3/1892, Sherwood, Ore. d: 9/11/73, San Antonio, Tex. BR/TR, 5′11.5″, 176 lbs. Deb: 4/16/14 MC																							
1914	Det-A	44	70	4	15	2	1	0	1	6	9	.214	.276	.271	548	63	-3	0	2	-1	.920	-6	C-38	-0.9
1915	Det-A	68	134	16	33	3	3	0	15	15	15	.246	.327	.313	640	87	-2	3	1	0	.940	-5	C-61	-0.3
1916	Det-A	61	98	7	15	4	0	0	6	11	8	.153	.245	.194	439	31	-8	2			.975	-2	C-59	-0.8
Total	3	173	302	27	63	9	4	0	22	32	32	.209	.289	.265	554	63	-13	5	3		.948	-12	C-158	-2.0
■ **DOUG BAKER**	Baker, Douglas Lee b: 4/3/61, Fullerton, Cal. BB/TR, 5′9″, 165 lbs. Deb: 7/2/84 F																							
1984	*Det-A	43	108	15	20	4	1	0	12	7	22	.185	.241	.241	482	34	-10	3	0	1	.969	2	S-39/2-5,D-1	-0.4
1985	Det-A	15	27	4	5	1	0	0	1	0	9	.185	.185	.222	407	11	-3	0	0	0	.960	-3	S-12/2-1	-0.5
1986	Det-A	13	24	1	3	1	0	0	0	2	7	.125	.192	.167	359	-1	-3	0	0	0	.970	2	S-10/2-2,D-1	0.0
1987	Det-A	8	1	0	0	0	0	0	0	0	1	.000	.000	.000	0	-99	-0	0	0	0	1.000	3	/S-6,2-1,3-1	0.2
1988	Min-A	11	7	1	0	0	0	0	0	0	5	.000	.000	.000	0	-97	-2	0	0	0	1.000	1	/S-9,2-1,3-1	0.0
1989	Min-A	43	78	17	23	5	1	0	9	9	18	.295	.382	.385	767	109	1	0	0	0	.982	-2	2-25,S-19/D-1	0.1
1990	Min-A	3	1	0	0	0	0	0	0	0	0	.000	.000	.000	0	-94	-0	0	0	0	1.000	1	/2-3	0.0
Total	7	136	246	38	51	11	2	0	22	18	62	.207	.270	.268	538	49	-17	3	0	1	.973	5	/S-95,2-38,D-3,3-2	-0.6
■ **GENE BAKER**	Baker, Eugene Walter b: 6/15/25, Davenport, Iowa d: 12/1/99, Davenport, Iowa BR/TR, 6′1″, 170 lbs. Deb: 9/20/53 C																							
1953	Chi-N	7	22	1	5	1	0	0	0	1	4	.227	.261	.273	534	39	-2	1	0	0	.917	-3	/2-6	-0.4
1954	Chi-N	135	541	68	149	32	5	13	61	47	55	.275	.336	.425	761	96	-4	4	5	-1	.967	-3	*2-134	0.2
1955	Chi-N★	154	609	82	163	29	7	11	52	49	57	.268	.324	.392	717	89	-10	9	7	-0	.967	7	*2-154	0.8
1956	Chi-N	140	546	65	141	23	3	12	57	39	54	.258	.311	.377	689	85	-12	4	3	-0	.969	17	*2-140	1.6
1957	Chi-N	12	44	4	11	3	1	1	10	6	3	.250	.353	.432	785	111	1	0	0	0	.867	-4	3-12	-0.3
	Pit-N	111	365	36	97	19	4	2	36	29	29	.266	.322	.356	678	84	-8	3	2	-0	.955	-4	3-60,S-28,2-13	-0.9
	Yr	123	409	40	108	22	5	3	46	35	32	.264	.325	.364	689	87	-7	3	2	-0	.942	-7	3-72,S-28,2-13	-1.2
1958	Pit-N	29	56	3	14	2	1	0	7	8	6	.250	.344	.321	665	80	-1	0	0	0	1.000	-1	3-11/2-3	-0.2
1960	*Pit-N	33	37	5	9	0	0	0	4	2	9	.243	.282	.243	525	45	-3	0	0	0	1.000	2	/3-7,2-1	-0.1
1961	Pit-N	9	10	1	1	0	0	0	0	3	2	.100	.308	.100	408	15	-1	0	0	0	1.000	1	/3-3	0.0
Total	8	630	2230	265	590	109	21	39	227	184	219	.265	.323	.385	708	88	-40	21	17	-1	.968	12	2-451/3-93,S-28	0.7
■ **FLOYD BAKER**	Baker, Floyd Wilson b: 10/10/16, Luray, Va. BL/TR, 5′9″, 160 lbs. Deb: 5/4/43 C																							
1943	StL-A	22	46	5	8	2	0	0	4	6	4	.174	.269	.217	487	42	-3	0	1	-0	.961	0	S-10/3-1	-0.3
1944	*StL-A	44	97	10	17	3	0	0	5	11	5	.175	.259	.206	465	32	-8	2	0	0	.979	-3	2-17,S-16	-1.0
1945	Chi-A	82	208	22	52	8	0	0	19	23	12	.250	.325	.288	613	81	-5	3	2	-0	.971	2	3-58,2-11	-0.2
1946	Chi-A	9	24	2	6	1	0	0	3	2	3	.250	.308	.292	599	71	-1	0	0	0	.962	1	/3-6	0.0
1947	Chi-A	105	371	61	98	12	3	0	22	66	28	.264	.375	.313	688	96	1	9	7	-0	.980	18	*3-101/2-1,S-1	1.9
1948	Chi-A	104	335	47	72	8	3	0	18	73	26	.215	.359	.257	615	68	-12	4	10	-3	.961	13	3-71,2-18/S-1	-0.1
1949	Chi-A	125	388	38	101	15	4	1	40	84	32	.260	.392	.327	719	94	1	3	1	0	**.977**	12	*3-122/S-3,2-1	1.2
1950	Chi-A	83	186	26	59	7	0	0	11	32	10	.317	.417	.355	772	102	3	1	1	-0	.987	3	3-53/2-3,O-2(2-0-0)	0.5
1951	Chi-A	82	133	24	35	6	1	0	14	25	12	.263	.380	.323	703	93	-0	0	1	-0	.924	-1	3-44/2-5,S-3	-0.1
1952	Was-A	79	263	27	69	8	0	0	33	30	17	.262	.342	.293	635	81	-6	1	0	0	.994	-16	2-68/S-7,3-1	-1.9
1953	Was-A	9	7	0	0	0	0	0	0	1	0	.000	.222	.000	222	-37	-1	0	0	0	.000	-0	/3-1	-0.2
	Bos-A	81	172	22	47	4	2	0	24	24	10	.273	.365	.320	685	82	-3	0	2	-1	.963	1	3-37,2-16	-0.2
	Yr	90	179	22	47	4	2	0	24	25	10	.263	.359	.307	666	78	-4	0	2	-1	.952	0	3-38,2-16	-0.4
1954	Bos-A	21	20	1	4	2	0	0	3	0	1	.200	.200	.300	500	32	-2	0	0	0	.889	1	/3-7,2-1	-0.1
	Phi-N	23	22	0	5	0	0	0	0	5	4	.227	.370	.227	598	60	-1	0	0	0	1.000	4	/3-7,2-2	0.3
1955	Phi-N	5	8	0	0	0	0	0	0	0	1	.000	.000	.000	0	-99	-2	0	0	0	1.000	1	/3-1	-0.1
Total	13	874	2280	285	573	76	13	1	196	382	165	.251	.360	.297	658	82	-41	23	25	-4	.971	34	3-510,2-143/S-41,O	-0.3
■ **FRANK BAKER**	Baker, Frank b: 1/11/44, Bartow, Fla. BL/TR, 5′10″, 180 lbs. Deb: 7/27/69																							
1969	Cle-A	52	172	21	44	5	3	3	15	14	34	.256	.316	.372	688	89	-3	2	1	0	.950	1	O-46(46-0-0)	-0.5
1971	Cle-A	73	181	18	38	12	1	1	23	12	34	.210	.263	.304	567	55	-11	1	3	-1	.985	-6	O-51(17-6-30)	-2.2
Total	2	125	353	39	82	17	4	4	38	26	68	.232	.289	.337	626	71	-13	3	4	-1	.966	-6	/O-97(63-6-30)	-2.7
■ **FRANK BAKER**	Baker, Frank Watts b: 10/29/46, Meridian, Miss. BL/TR, 6′2″, 178 lbs. Deb: 8/9/70																							
1970	NY-A	35	117	6	27	4	1	0	11	14	26	.231	.323	.282	605	72	-4	1	2	-0	.973	4	S-35	0.4
1971	NY-A	43	79	9	11	2	0	0	2	16	22	.139	.284	.165	449	32	-7	3	0	1	.949	11	S-38	0.8
1973	*Bal-A	44	63	10	12	1	2	1	11	7	7	.190	.271	.317	589	66	-3	0	0	0	.964	4	S-32/2-7,1-1,3-1	0.3
1974	*Bal-A	24	29	3	5	1	0	0	0	3	5	.172	.250	.207	457	34	-2	0	0	0	.842	2	S-17/2-3,3-1	0.0
Total	4	146	288	28	55	8	3	1	24	40	60	.191	.294	.250	544	56	-16	4	2	0	.953	20	S-122/2-10,3-2,1-1	1.5
■ **GEORGE BAKER**	Baker, George F. b: 1859, St.Louis, Mo. Deb: 5/24/1883 Career OF: (3-LF 2-CF 3-RF)																							
1883	Bal-a	7	22	0	5	0	0	0		0		.227	.227	.227	455	45	-1				.667	-3	/S-4,C-3,O-1(0-0-1)	-0.3
1884	StL-U	80	317	39	52	6	0	0		5		.164	.177	.183	360	9	-44				**.897**	16	C-68/2-4,O-4L,3S	-1.9
1885	StL-N	38	131	5	16	0	0	0	5	9	28	.122	.179	.122	301	-1	-14				.865	-11	C-32/3-3,O-2L,2-1	-2.1
1886	KC-N	1	4	1	1	0	0	0	0	0	1	.250	.250	.250	500	49	-0	0			.889	-0	/C-1	0.0
Total	4	126	474	45	74	6	0	0	5	14	29	.156	.180	.169	349	8	-60	0			.887	3	C-104/O-7L,3-6,S2	-4.3
■ **HOWARD BAKER**	Baker, Howard Francis b: 3/1/1888, Bridgeport, Conn. d: 1/16/64, Bridgeport, Conn. BR/TR, 5′11″, 175 lbs. Deb: 8/11/12																							
1912	Cle-A	11	30	1	5	0	0	0	2	5		.167	.286	.167	452	29	-3	0			.964	-1	3-10	-0.4
1914	Chi-A	15	47	4	13	1	1	0	5	3	8	.277	.320	.340	660	100	-0	2	1	0	.879	-4	3-15	-0.5
1915	Chi-A	2	2	0	0	0	0	0	0	0	2	.000	.000	.000	0	-97	-0	0			.000	0	H	-0.1
	NY-N	1	3	0	0	0	0	0	0	0	0	.000	.000	.000	0	-99	-1	0			1.000	0	/3-1	-0.1
Total	3	29	82	5	18	1	1	0	7	8	10	.220	.289	.256	545	61	-4	2	1		.922	-6	/3-26	-1.1
■ **JACK BAKER**	Baker, Jack Edward b: 5/4/50, Birmingham, Ala. BR/TR, 6′5″, 225 lbs. Deb: 9/11/76																							
1976	Bos-A	12	23	1	3	0	0	1	2	1	5	.130	.167	.261	428	21	-2	0	0	0	.981	-0	/1-8,D-1	-0.3
1977	Bos-A	2	3	0	0	0	0	0	0	0	1	.000	.000	.000	0	-90	-1	0	0	0	.857	0	/1-1	-0.1
Total	2	14	26	1	3	0	0	1	2	1	6	.115	.148	.231	379	8	-3	0	0	0	.966	-0	/1-9,D-1	-0.4
■ **JESSE BAKER**	Baker, Jesse (b: Michael Myron Silverman) b: 3/4/1895, Cleveland, Ohio d: 7/29/76, W.Los Angeles, Cal. BR/TR, 5′4″, 140 lbs. Deb: 9/14/19																							
1919	Was-A	1	0	0	0	0	0	0	1	0	0	—	—	—	—	—	0	0			1.000	0	/S-1	0.0
■ **FRANK BAKER**	Baker, John Franklin "Home Run" b: 3/13/1886, Trappe, Md. d: 6/28/63, Trappe, Md. BL/TR, 5′11″, 173 lbs. Deb: 9/21/08 H																							
1908	Phi-A	9	31	5	9	3	0	0	2	0		.290	.290	.387	677	112	0	0			1.000	2	/3-9	0.3
1909	Phi-A	148	541	73	165	27	**19**	4	85	26		.305	.343	.447	790	146	25	20			.920	-9	*3-146	2.3
1910	*Phi-A	146	561	83	159	25	15	2	74	34		.283	.329	.392	721	127	15	21			.920	6	*3-146	2.7
1911	*Phi-A	148	592	96	198	42	14	**11**	115	40		.334	.379	.508	887	149	35	38			**.942**	-1	*3-148	3.8
1912	Phi-A	149	577	116	200	40	21	**10**	**130**	50		.347	.404	.541	945	176	54	40			.941	10	*3-149	6.6
1913	*Phi-A	149	564	116	190	34	9	**12**	**117**	63	31	.337	.413	.493	906	169	49	34			.921	8	*3-149	6.3
1914	*Phi-A	150	570	84	182	23	10	**9**	89	53	37	.319	.380	.442	822	153	35	19	20	-3	.955	10	*3-149	5.0
1916	NY-A	100	360	46	97	23	2	10	52	36	30	.269	.344	.428	772	129	11	15			.940	2	3-96	1.8
1917	NY-A	146	553	57	156	24	2	6	71	48	27	.282	.345	.365	710	116	10	18			.949	11	*3-146	2.7
1918	NY-A	126	504	65	154	24	5	6	62	38	13	.306	.357	.409	765	128	15	8			**.972**	11	*3-126	3.3
1919	NY-A	141	567	70	166	22	1	10	83	44	18	.293	.346	.388	734	105	3	13			.955	-2	*3-141	0.5
1921	*NY-A	94	330	46	97	16	2	9	71	26	12	.294	.353	.436	789	98	-2	8	5	0	.959	-2	3-83	0.2

YEAR	TM/L	G	AB	R	H	2B	3B	HR	RBI	BB	SO	AVG	OBP	SLG	OPS	OPS+	BR+	SB	CS	SBR	FA	FR	G/POS	TPR
1922	*NY-A	69	234	30	65	12	3	7	36	15	14	.278	.327	.444	771	97	-2	1	3	-1	.962	-10	3-60	-0.9
Total	13	1575	5984	887	1838	315	103	96	987	473	182	.307	.363	.442	805	136	250	235	28		.943	36	*3-1548	34.6

■ **DUSTY BAKER** Baker, Johnnie B b: 6/15/49, Riverside, Cal. BR/TR, 6'2", 187 lbs. Deb: 9/7/68 MC Career OF: (1117-LF 490-CF 348-RF)

YEAR	TM/L	G	AB	R	H	2B	3B	HR	RBI	BB	SO	AVG	OBP	SLG	OPS	OPS+	BR+	SB	CS	SBR	FA	FR	G/POS	TPR
1968	Atl-N	6	5	0	2	0	0	0	0	0	1	.400	.400	.400	800	140	0	0	0	0	.000	-1	/O-3(0-3-0)	-0.1
1969	Atl-N	3	7	0	0	0	0	0	0	0	3	.000	.000	.000	0	-99	-2	0	0	0	1.000	-1	/O-3(0-3-0)	-0.3
1970	Atl-N	13	24	3	7	0	0	0	4	2	4	.292	.346	.292	638	69	-1	0	0	0	.800	-2	O-11(5-4-2)	-0.3
1971	Atl-N	29	62	2	14	2	0	0	4	1	14	.226	.238	.258	496	38	-5	0	1	-0	1.000	-2	O-18(1-4-16)	-0.9
1972	Atl-N	127	446	62	143	27	2	17	76	45	68	.321	.388	.504	892	139	23	4	7	-2	.989	2	*O-123(30-121-3)	2.1
1973	Atl-N	159	604	101	174	29	4	21	99	67	72	.288	.364	.454	818	116	14	24	3	4	.983	10	*O-156(0-156-0)	2.5
1974	Atl-N	149	574	80	147	35	0	20	69	71	87	.256	.339	.422	761	107	5	18	7	2	.981	-18	*O-148(0-102-112)	-1.8
1975	Atl-N	142	494	63	129	18	2	19	72	67	57	.261	.349	.421	770	109	6	12	7	0	.990	7	*O-136(0-12-129)	0.6
1976	LA-N	112	384	36	93	13	0	4	39	31	54	.242	.300	.307	608	74	-13	2	4	-1	.996	-1	*O-106(0-83-24)	-1.9
1977	*LA-N	153	533	86	155	26	1	30	86	58	89	.291	.367	.512	879	134	25	2	6	-2	.987	-4	*O-152(150-1-2)	1.3
1978	*LA-N	149	522	62	137	24	1	11	66	47	66	.262	.327	.375	702	96	-3	12	3	2	.985	5	*O-145(145-0-0)	-0.3
1979	LA-N	151	554	86	152	29	1	23	88	56	70	.274	.342	.455	797	117	12	11	4	1	.990	13	*O-150(150-0-0)	2.0
1980	LA-N	153	579	80	170	26	4	29	97	43	66	.294	.346	.503	848	137	26	12	10	-1	.991	6	*O-151(151-1-1)	2.6
1981	*LA-N★	103	400	48	128	17	3	9	49	29	43	.320	.367	.445	812	134	17	10	7	-0	.990	1	*O-101(101-0-0)	1.5
1982	LA-N★	147	570	80	171	19	1	23	88	56	62	.300	.366	.458	824	132	24	17	10	0	.975	-7	*O-144(144-0-1)	1.2
1983	*LA-N	149	531	71	138	25	1	15	73	72	59	.260	.350	.395	746	107	6	7	1	1	.981	-1	*O-143(143-0-0)	-0.1
1984	SF-N	100	243	31	71	7	2	3	32	40	27	.292	.392	.374	767	120	8	4	1	1	.974	-1	O-62(29-0-33)	0.5
1985	Oak-A	111	343	48	92	15	1	14	52	50	47	.268	.361	.440	802	128	14	2	1	0	.993	-5	1-58,O-35L,D-13	0.4
1986	Oak-A	83	242	25	58	8	0	4	19	27	37	.240	.316	.322	638	80	-6	0	1	-0	1.000	-3	O-55L,D-15/1-3	-1.3
Total	19	2039	7117	964	1981	320	23	242	1013	762	926	.278	.351	.432	782	116	151	137	73	5	.985	-2	*O-1842L/1-61,D-28	7.7

■ **KIRTLEY BAKER** Baker, Kirtley "Whitey" b: 6/24/1869, Aurora, Ind. d: 4/15/27, Covington, Ky. BR/TR, 5'9", 160 lbs. Deb: 5/7/1890

YEAR	TM/L	G	AB	R	H	2B	3B	HR	RBI	BB	SO	AVG	OBP	SLG	OPS	OPS+	BR+	SB	CS	SBR	FA	FR	G/POS	TPR
1890	Pit-N	26	68	6	10	0	0	0	0	10	6	.147	.275	.147	422	27	-5	1			.878	-0	P-25	0.0
1893	Bal-N	19	57	9	17	1	1	0	6	8	6	.298	.385	.351	735	94	-0	1			.930	5	P-15/O-3(3-0-0)	0.2
1894	Bal-N	2	4	0	0	0	0	0	0	0	1	.000	.000	.000	0	-96	-1	0			1.000	1	/O-1(0-0-1),P-1	0.0
1898	Was-N	6	18	3	5	0	1	0	3	3		.278	.381	.389	770	121	1	0			1.000	-1	/P-6	0.0
1899	Was-N	12	19	1	3	0	0	0	1	1		.158	.200	.158	358	-1	-3	0			.862	2	P-11	0.0
Total	5	65	166	19	35	1	2	0	10	22	13	.211	.311	.241	551	57	-9	2			.895	7	/P-58,O-4(3-0-1)	0.2

■ **PHIL BAKER** Baker, Philip b: 9/19/1856, Philadelphia, Pa. d: 6/4/40, Washington, D.C. BL/TL, 5'8", 152 lbs. Deb: 5/1/1883 Career OF: (2-LF 40-CF 26-RF)

YEAR	TM/L	G	AB	R	H	2B	3B	HR	RBI	BB	SO	AVG	OBP	SLG	OPS	OPS+	BR+	SB	CS	SBR	FA	FR	G/POS	TPR
1883	Bal-a	28	121	22	33	2	1	1		8		.273	.318	.331	648	106	1				.883	-7	C-19,O-14(1-1-12)/S-1	-0.4
1884	Was-U	86	371	75	107	12	5	1		11		.288	.309	.356	665	104	-9				.955	-10	1-39,O-32C,C-27	-1.8
1886	Was-N	81	325	37	72	6	5	1	34	20	32	.222	.267	.280	547	70	-11	16			.967	-7	1-56,O-21(1-7-14)/C-4	-2.1
Total	3	195	817	134	212	20	11	3	34	39	32	.259	.293	.322	615	91	-18	16			.963	-23	/1-95,O-67C,C-50,S	-4.3

■ **TRACY BAKER** Baker, Tracy Lee b: 11/7/1891, Pendleton, Ore. d: 3/14/75, Placerville, Cal. BR/TR, 6'1", 180 lbs. Deb: 6/19/11

YEAR	TM/L	G	AB	R	H	2B	3B	HR	RBI	BB	SO	AVG	OBP	SLG	OPS	OPS+	BR+	SB	CS	SBR	FA	FR	G/POS	TPR
1911	Bos-A	1	0	0	0	0	0	0	0	0		—	—	—	—	—	0	0			1.000	-0	/1-1	0.0

■ **BILL BAKER** Baker, William Presley b: 2/22/11, Paw Creek, N.C. BR/TR, 6', 200 lbs. Deb: 5/4/40 C

YEAR	TM/L	G	AB	R	H	2B	3B	HR	RBI	BB	SO	AVG	OBP	SLG	OPS	OPS+	BR+	SB	CS	SBR	FA	FR	G/POS	TPR
1940	*Cin-N	27	69	5	15	1	1	0	7	4	8	.217	.260	.261	521	44	-5	2			1.000	4	C-24	-0.1
1941	Cin-N	2	0	0	0	0	0	0	0	1	0	.000	.500	.000	500	49	0	0			1.000	0	/C-1	0.0
	Pit-N	35	67	5	15	3	0	0	6	11	0	.224	.333	.269	602	71	-2	0			.967	0	C-33	-0.1
	Yr	37	68	5	15	3	0	0	6	12	1	.221	.338	.265	602	71	-2	0			.967	0	C-34	-0.1
1942	Pit-N	18	17	1	2	0	0	0	2	1	0	.118	.167	.118	284	-16	-2	0			1.000	1	C-11	-0.1
1943	Pit-N	63	172	12	47	6	3	1	26	22	6	.273	.365	.360	726	106	2	3			.979	0	C-56	0.6
1946	Pit-N	53	113	7	27	4	0	1	8	12	6	.239	.312	.301	613	72	-4	0			.965	-6	C-41/1-1	-0.9
1948	StL-N	45	119	13	35	10	1	0	15	15	7	.294	.373	.395	768	102	1	1			.994	-1	C-36	0.2
1949	StL-N	20	30	2	4	1	0	0	4	2	2	.133	.188	.167	354	-4	-4	0			1.000	-2	C-10	-0.6
Total	7	263	588	45	145	25	5	2	68	68	30	.247	.328	.316	644	79	-15	6			.983	-3	C-212/1-1	-1.0

■ **PAUL BAKO** Bako, Gabor Paul b: 6/20/72, Lafayette, La. BL/TR, 6'2", 205 lbs. Deb: 4/30/98

YEAR	TM/L	G	AB	R	H	2B	3B	HR	RBI	BB	SO	AVG	OBP	SLG	OPS	OPS+	BR+	SB	CS	SBR	FA	FR	G/POS	TPR
1998	Det-A	96	305	23	83	12	1	3	30	23	82	.272	.323	.348	671	74	-11	1	1	-0	.989	-7	C-94	-1.2
1999	Hou-N	73	215	16	55	14	1	2	17	26	57	.256	.336	.358	694	77	-7	1	1	-0	.988	8	C-71	0.4
2000	Hou-N	1	2	0	0	0	0	0	0	0	1	.000	.000	.000	0	-95	-1	0	0	0	1.000	0	/C-1	0.0
	Fla-N	56	161	10	39	6	1	0	14	22	48	.242	.337	.292	629	64	-8	0	0	0	.991	-7	C-56	-1.1
	*Atl-N	24	58	8	11	4	0	2	6	5	15	.190	.254	.362	616	54	-4	0	0	0	.992	4	C-23/1-1	0.1
	Yr	81	221	18	50	10	1	2	20	27	64	.226	.313	.308	621	60	-13	0	0	0	.992	-3	C-80/1-1	-1.0
Total	3	250	741	57	188	36	3	7	67	76	203	.254	.324	.339	663	71	-32	2	2	-0	.989	-1	C-245/1-1	-1.8

■ **JOHN BALAZ** Balaz, John Lawrence b: 11/24/50, Toronto, Ont., Can. BR/TR, 6'3", 180 lbs. Deb: 9/10/74

YEAR	TM/L	G	AB	R	H	2B	3B	HR	RBI	BB	SO	AVG	OBP	SLG	OPS	OPS+	BR+	SB	CS	SBR	FA	FR	G/POS	TPR
1974	Cal-A	14	42	4	10	0	0	1	5	2	10	.238	.289	.310	598	76	-1	0	0	0	1.000	-1	O-12(12-0-0)	-0.3
1975	Cal-A	45	120	10	29	8	1	1	10	5	25	.242	.272	.350	622	80	-4	0	0	0	1.000	-0	O-27(19-0-8),D-11	-0.5
Total	2	59	162	14	39	8	1	2	15	7	35	.241	.276	.340	616	79	-5	0	0	0	1.000	-1	/O-39(31-0-8),D-11	-0.8

■ **STEVE BALBONI** Balboni, Stephen Charles b: 1/16/57, Brockton, Mass. BR/TR, 6'3", 225 lbs. Deb: 4/22/81

YEAR	TM/L	G	AB	R	H	2B	3B	HR	RBI	BB	SO	AVG	OBP	SLG	OPS	OPS+	BR+	SB	CS	SBR	FA	FR	G/POS	TPR
1981	NY-A	4	7	2	2	1	1	0	2	1	4	.286	.375	.714	1089	211	1	0	0	0	1.000	0	/1-3,D-1	0.1
1982	NY-A	33	107	8	20	2	1	2	4	6	34	.187	.230	.280	510	40	-9	0	0	0	.990	-1	1-26/D-5	-1.1
1983	NY-A	32	86	8	20	2	0	5	17	8	23	.233	.298	.430	728	101	-0	0	0	0	.984	-1	1-23/D-4	-0.3
1984	*KC-A	126	438	58	107	23	2	28	77	45	139	.244	.320	.498	818	122	11	0	0	0	.987	-5	*1-125/D-1	-0.1
1985	*KC-A	160	600	74	146	28	2	36	88	52	166	.243	.309	.477	786	111	7	1	1	-0	.993	-8	*1-160	-1.1
1986	KC-A	138	512	54	117	25	1	29	88	43	146	.229	.290	.451	741	96	-5	0	0	0	.987	-6	*1-137	-1.9
1987	KC-A	121	386	44	80	11	1	24	60	34	97	.207	.275	.427	702	80	-12	0	0	0	.989	1	1-55,D-52	-1.5
1988	KC-A	21	63	2	9	2	0	2	5	1	20	.143	.156	.270	426	17	-7	0	0	0	.980	-1	1-13/D-6	-0.9
	Sea-A	97	350	44	88	15	1	21	61	23	67	.251	.299	.480	779	110	3	0	1	-0	.994	-1	D-56,1-40	-0.3
	Yr	118	413	46	97	17	1	23	66	24	87	.235	.279	.448	726	96	-4	0	1	-0	.991	-2	D-62,1-53	-1.2
1989	NY-A	110	300	33	71	12	2	17	59	25	67	.237	.302	.460	762	113	4	0	0	0	.994	-2	D-82,1-20	-0.2
1990	NY-A	116	266	24	51	6	0	17	34	35	91	.192	.293	.406	699	93	-3	0	0	0	.984	-3	D-72,1-28	-1.0
1993	Tex-A	2	5	0	3	0	0	0	0	0	2	.600	.600	.600	1200	233	1	0	0	0	.000	0	/D-2	0.1
Total	11	960	3120	351	714	127	11	181	495	273	856	.229	.295	.451	745	100	-9	1	2	-0	.989	-26	1-630,D-281	-8.2

■ **BOBBY BALCENA** Balcena, Robert Rudolph b: 8/1/25, San Pedro, Cal. d: 1/4/90, San Pedro, Cal. BR/TL, 5'7", 160 lbs. Deb: 9/16/56

YEAR	TM/L	G	AB	R	H	2B	3B	HR	RBI	BB	SO	AVG	OBP	SLG	OPS	OPS+	BR+	SB	CS	SBR	FA	FR	G/POS	TPR
1956	Cin-N	7	2	2	0	0	0	0	0	0	1	.000	.000	.000	0	-94	-1	0	0	0	1.000	-1	/O-2(2-0-0)	-0.1

■ **LADY BALDWIN** Baldwin, Charles Busted b: 4/8/1859, Oramel, N.Y. d: 3/7/37, Hastings, Mich. BR/TL, 5'11", 160 lbs. Deb: 9/30/1884

YEAR	TM/L	G	AB	R	H	2B	3B	HR	RBI	BB	SO	AVG	OBP	SLG	OPS	OPS+	BR+	SB	CS	SBR	FA	FR	G/POS	TPR
1884	Mil-U	7	27	6	6	3	0	0		0		.222	.222	.333	556	122	-0				.778	0	/O-5(0-5-0),P-2	0.0
1885	Det-N	31	124	12	30	6	3	0	18	6	22	.242	.277	.339	616	98	-0				.879	1	P-21,O-12(10-0-2)	-0.1
1886	Det-N	57	204	25	41	6	3	0	25	18	44	.201	.266	.260	526	59	-10	3			.969	3	P-56/O-2(2-0-0)	0.0
1887	*Det-N	24	95	15	33	0	1	0	7	10	6	.347	.354	.294	648	79	-2	4			.926	1	P-24	0.0
1888	Det-N	6	23	5	6	0	0	0	3	3	3	.261	.346	.261	607	96	0	0			1.000	-0	/P-6,O-1(1-0-0)	0.0
1890	Bro-N	2	3	1	0	0	0	0	0	1	1	.000	.250	.000	250	-25	-0	0			.625	0	/P-2	0.0
	Buf-P	7	28	4	8	1	0	0	2	2	1	.286	.333	.321	655	82	-1	0			1.000	-0	/P-7	0.0
Total	6	134	504	68	124	16	7	0	55	40	77	.246	.290	.291	581	76	-13	7			.934	6	P-118/O-20(13-5-2)	-0.1

■ **KID BALDWIN** Baldwin, Clarence Geoghan b: 11/1/1864, Newport, Ky. d: 7/10/1897, Cincinnati, Ohio BR/TR, 5'6", 147 lbs. Deb: 7/27/1884 Career OF: (11-LF 13-CF 8-RF)

YEAR	TM/L	G	AB	R	H	2B	3B	HR	RBI	BB	SO	AVG	OBP	SLG	OPS	OPS+	BR+	SB	CS	SBR	FA	FR	G/POS	TPR
1884	KC-U	50	191	19	37	6	3	0		4		.194	.210	.257	467	47	-18				.885	1	C-44,O-10L/2-1,3-1	-1.2
	CP-U	1	1	0	1	0	0	0		0		1.000	1.000	1.000	2000	511	0				1.000	-0	/C-1	0.0
	Yr	51	192	19	38	6	3	0		4		.198	.214	.260	475	49	-17				.885	0	C-45,O-10L/2-1,3-1	-1.2
1885	Cin-a	34	126	9	17	1	0	1	8	3		.135	.155	.167	322	2	-14				.863	-2	C-25/O-6C,2-2,P3	-1.3

YEAR	TM/L	G	AB	R	H	2B	3B	HR	RBI	BB	SO	AVG	OBP	SLG	OPS	OPS+	BR+	SB	CS	SBR	FA	FR	G/POS	TPR
1886	Cin-a	87	315	41	72	8	7	3	32	8		.229	.252	.327	579	78	-9	12			.891	-6	C-71,3-13/O-6(0-5-1)	-0.8
1887	Cin-a	96	394	46	104	15	10	1	57	6		.264	.271	.351	622	71	-17	13			.874	-2	*C-96/O-2(2-0-0)	-0.9
1888	Cin-a	67	271	27	59	11	3	1	25	3		.218	.235	.292	526	65	-12	4			.918	-2	C-65/O-2(0-0-2),1-1	-0.7
1889	Cin-a	60	223	34	55	14	2	1	34	5	32	.247	.273	.341	614	72	-9	7			.912	2	C-55/O-4R,3-1,1-1	-0.3
1890	Cin-N	22	72	5	11	0	0	0	10	3	6	.153	.187	.153	339	-1	-9	2			.902	3	C-20/O-2(0-0-2)	-0.4
	Phi-a	24	90	5	21	1	2	0	12	4		.233	.274	.289	563	66	-4	2			.887	1	C-19/3-5	-0.1
Total	7	441	1683	186	377	56	27	7	178	36	38	.224	.243	.299	543	61	-92	40			.893	-6	C-396/O-32C,3-21,21P	-5.7
■ FRANK BALDWIN	Baldwin, Frank De Witt b: 12/25/28, High Bridge, N.J. BR/TR, 5′11″, 195 lbs. Deb: 4/22/53																							
1953	Cin-N	16	20	0	2	0	0	0	0	1	9	.100	.143	.100	243	-35	-4	0	0	0	1.000	-1	/C-6	-0.5
■ HENRY BALDWIN	Baldwin, Henry Clay "Ted" b: 6/13/1894, Chadds Ford, Pa. d: 2/24/64, West Chester, Pa. BR/TR, 5′11″, 180 lbs. Deb: 5/22/27																							
1927	Phi-N	6	16	1	5	0	0	0	1	1	2	.313	.353	.313	665	78	-0	0			.857	-2	/S-3,3-2	-0.2
■ JEFF BALDWIN	Baldwin, Jeffrey Allen b: 9/5/65, Milford, Del. BL/TL, 6′1″, 180 lbs. Deb: 5/22/90																							
1990	Hou-N	7	8	1	0	0	0	0	0	1	2	.000	.111	.000	111	-69	-2	0	0	0	1.000	-1	/O-3(2-0-1)	-0.3
■ REGGIE BALDWIN	Baldwin, Reginald Conrad b: 8/19/54, River Rouge, Mich. BR/TR, 6′1″, 195 lbs. Deb: 5/25/78																							
1978	Hou-N	38	67	5	17	5	0	1	11	3	3	.254	.286	.373	659	89	-1	0	0	0	.955	-1	C-17	-0.2
1979	Hou-N	14	20	0	4	1	0	0	1	0	1	.200	.200	.250	450	23	-2	0	0	0	1.000	-1	/C-3,1-1	-0.3
Total	2	52	87	5	21	6	0	1	12	3	4	.241	.267	.345	611	74	-3	0	0	0	.956	-2	/C-20,1-1	-0.5
■ BILLY BALDWIN	Baldwin, Robert Harvey b: 6/9/51, Tazewell, Va. BL/TL, 6′, 175 lbs. Deb: 7/29/75																							
1975	Det-A	30	95	8	21	3	0	4	8	5	14	.221	.260	.379	639	75	-3	2	1	0	.983	2	O-25(0-13-13)/D-1	-0.3
1976	NY-N	9	22	4	6	1	1	1	5	1	2	.273	.304	.545	850	146	1	0	0	0	.929	1	/O-5(3-0-2)	0.2
Total	2	39	117	12	27	4	1	5	13	6	16	.231	.268	.410	679	87	-2	2	1	0	.972	3	/O-30(3-13-15),D-1	-0.1
■ MIKE BALENTI	Balenti, Michael Richard b: 7/3/1886, Calumet, Okla. d: 8/4/55, Altus, Okla. BR/TR, 5′11″, 175 lbs. Deb: 7/19/11																							
1911	Cin-N	8	8	2	2	0	0	0	0	0	1	.250	.250	.250	500	42	-1	3			.857	0	/S-2,O-1(0-1-0)	0.0
1913	StL-A	70	211	17	38	2	4	0	11	6	32	.180	.206	.227	434	28	-20	3			.923	1	S-56/O-8(8-0-0)	-1.7
Total	2	78	219	19	40	2	4	0	11	6	33	.183	.208	.228	436	28	-21	6			.922	1	/S-58,O-9(8-1-0)	-1.7
■ LEE BALES	Bales, Wesley Owen b: 12/4/44, Los Angeles, Cal. BB/TR, 5′10.5″, 165 lbs. Deb: 8/7/66																							
1966	Atl-N	12	16	4	1	0	0	0	0	0	5	.063	.063	.063	125	-64	-3	0	0	0	1.000	3	/2-7,3-3	0.0
1967	Hou-N	19	27	4	3	0	0	0	2	8	7	.111	.314	.111	425	28	-2	1	1	-0	.944	-2	/2-6,S-1	-0.4
Total	2	31	43	8	4	0	0	0	2	8	12	.093	.235	.093	328	-3	-6	1	1	-0	.978	1	/2-13,3-3,S-1	-0.4
■ ART BALL	Ball, Arthur Clark b: 4/1876, Kentucky d: 12/26/15, Chicago, Ill. TR, 168 lbs. Deb: 8/1/1894 Career OF: (0-LF 1-CF 0-RF)																							
1894	StL-N	1	3	0	1	0	0	0	0	0	1	.333	.333	.333	667	61	-0	0			.667	-1	/2-1	-0.1
1898	Bal-N	32	81	7	15	2	0	0	8	7		.185	.258	.210	468	34	-7	2			.906	9	3-15,S-14/2-2,O-1C	0.3
Total	2	33	84	7	16	2	0	0	8	7	1	.190	.261	.214	475	35	-7	2			.929	8	/3-15,S-14,2-3,O-1C	0.2
■ NEAL BALL	Ball, Cornelius b: 4/22/1881, Grand Haven, Mich. d: 10/15/57, Bridgeport, Conn. BR/TR, 5′7″, 145 lbs. Deb: 9/12/07																							
1907	NY-A	15	44	5	9	1	1	0	4	1		.205	.222	.273	495	53	-2	1			.817	-3	S-11/2-5	-0.6
1908	NY-A	132	446	35	110	16	2	0	38	21		.247	.284	.291	575	86	-7	32			.898	-6	*S-130/2-1	-1.1
1909	NY-A	8	29	5	6	1	1	0	3	3		.207	.281	.310	592	86	-0	2			.917	-3	/2-8	-0.5
	Cle-A	96	324	29	83	13	2	1	25	17		.256	.295	.318	613	90	-4	17			.914	-11	S-95	-1.4
	Yr	104	353	34	89	14	3	1	28	20		.252	.294	.317	611	90	-5	19			.914	-14	S-95/2-8	-1.9
1910	Cle-A	54	123	13	25	3	1	0	12	9		.203	.258	.244	501	56	-6	4			.927	-1	S-27/2-7,O-6C,3-3	-0.7
1911	Cle-A	116	412	45	122	14	9	3	45	27		.296	.339	.396	735	104	1	21			.945	6	2-94,3-17/S-1	0.8
1912	Cle-A	40	132	12	30	4	1	0	14	9		.227	.277	.273	549	55	-8	7			.938	0	2-37	-0.7
	*Bos-A	18	45	10	9	2	0	0	6	3		.200	.250	.244	494	40	-4	5			.927	-4	2-17	-0.7
	Yr	58	177	22	39	6	1	0	20	12		.220	.270	.266	535	51	-11	12			.936	-3	2-54	-1.4
1913	Bos-A	23	58	9	10	2	0	0	4	9	13	.172	.294	.207	501	46	-4	3			.902	-2	2-10/S-7,3-1	-0.5
Total	7	502	1613	163	404	56	17	4	151	99	13	.250	.295	.314	609	83	-35	92			.902	-25	S-271,2-179/3-21,O	-5.4
■ JIM BALL	Ball, James Chandler b: 2/22/1884, Harford Co., Md. d: 4/7/63, Glendale, Cal. BR/TR, 5′11″, 175 lbs. Deb: 9/21/07																							
1907	Bos-N	10	36	3	6	2	0	0	3	2		.167	.211	.222	433	36	-3	0			.963	-2	C-10	-0.4
1908	Bos-N	6	15	1	1	0	0	0	0	1		.067	.125	.067	192	-39	-2	0			.917	-1	/C-6	-0.3
Total	2	16	51	4	7	2	0	0	3	3		.137	.185	.176	362	14	-5	0			.949	-2	/C-16	-0.7
■ JEFF BALL	Ball, Jeffery D. b: 4/17/69, Merced, Cal. BR/TR, 5′10″, 185 lbs. Deb: 6/10/98																							
1998	SF-N	2	4	0	1	0	0	0	0	0	0	.250	.250	.250	500	34	-0	0	0	0	1.000	-0	/1-1	-0.1
■ PELHAM BALLENGER	Ballenger, Pelham Ashby b: 2/6/1894, Gilreath Mill, S.C. d: 12/8/48, Greenville, S.C. BR/TR, 5′11″, 160 lbs. Deb: 5/7/28																							
1928	Was-A	3	9	0	1	0	0	0	0	0	1	.111	.111	.111	222	-42	-2	0	0	0	1.000	1	/3-3	0.0
■ HAL BAMBERGER	Bamberger, Harold Earl "Dutch" b: 10/29/24, Lebanon, Pa. BL/TR, 6′, 173 lbs. Deb: 9/15/48																							
1948	NY-N	7	12	0	1	0	0	0	0	1	2	.083	.154	.083	237	-34	-2	0			1.000	-0	/O-3(0-1-2)	-0.3
■ STUD BANCKER	Bancker, John b: Philadelphia, Pa. Deb: 4/21/1875																							
1875	NH-n	19	72	3	11	0	0	0	2	0	3	.153	.153	.153	306	7	-6	1	0	0	.796	-4	C-14/2-4,3-3,S-1,1	-0.9
■ DAVE BANCROFT	Bancroft, David James "Beauty" b: 4/20/1891, Sioux City, Iowa d: 10/9/72, Superior, Wis. BB/TR, 5′9.5″, 160 lbs. Deb: 4/14/15 MCH																							
1915	*Phi-N	153	563	85	143	18	2	7	30	77	62	.254	.346	.330	676	104	5	15	27	-6	.928	5	*S-153	1.6
1916	Phi-N	142	477	53	101	10	0	3	33	74	57	.212	.323	.252	574	75	-11	15			.933	25	*S-142	2.7
1917	Phi-N	127	478	56	116	22	5	4	43	44	42	.243	.307	.335	641	93	-4	14			.936	**28**	*S-120/2-3,O-2(2-0-0)	3.6
1918	Phi-N	125	499	69	132	19	4	0	26	54	36	.265	.338	.319	656	94	-2	11			.928	18	*S-125	2.7
1919	Phi-N	92	335	45	91	13	7	0	25	31	30	.272	.333	.352	686	99	0	8			.951	10	S-88	1.8
1920	Phi-N	42	171	23	51	7	2	0	5	9	12	.298	.337	.363	700	96	-1	1	7	-2	.981	9	S-42	1.0
	NY-N	108	442	79	132	29	7	0	31	33	32	.299	.349	.396	745	115	8	7	5	-0	.946	30	*S-108	4.7
	Yr	150	613	102	183	36	9	0	36	42	44	.299	.346	.387	732	109	7	8	12	-2	**.955**	**39**	*S-150	5.7
1921	*NY-N	153	606	121	193	26	15	6	67	66	23	.318	.389	.441	830	119	18	17	10	0	.960	17	*S-153	5.1
1922	*NY-N	156	651	117	209	41	5	4	60	79	27	.321	.397	.418	815	109	12	16	11	-0	.941	22	*S-156	4.7
1923	*NY-N	107	444	80	135	33	3	1	31	62	23	.304	.391	.399	789	110	9	8	7	-1	.936	21	S-96,2-11	3.8
1924	Bos-N	79	319	49	89	11	1	2	21	37	24	.279	.356	.339	694	91	-3	4	4	-1	.961	-5	S-79,M	0.0
1925	Bos-N	128	479	75	153	29	8	2	49	64	22	.319	.400	.426	826	122	18	7	4	0	**.945**	10	*S-125,M	3.9
1926	Bos-N	127	453	70	141	18	6	1	44	64	29	.311	.399	.384	783	122	18	3			.956	-3	*S-123/3-2,M	2.8
1927	Bos-N	111	375	44	91	13	4	1	31	43	36	.243	.322	.307	629	75	-12	5			.939	5	*S-104/3-1,M	0.4
1928	Bro-N	149	515	47	127	19	5	0	51	59	20	.247	.326	.303	629	66	-24	7			.948	4	*S-149	-0.4
1929	Bro-N	104	358	35	99	11	3	1	44	29	11	.277	.331	.332	663	66	-18	7			.955	-0	*S-102	-0.7
1930	NY-N	10	17	0	1	1	0	0	0	2	1	.059	.158	.118	276	-33	-4	0			.966	1	/S-8	-0.2
Total	16	1913	7182	1048	2004	320	77	32	591	827	487	.279	.355	.358	714	98	10	145	75		.944	197	*S-1873/2-14,3-3,O	37.5
■ CHRIS BANDO	Bando, Christopher Michael b: 2/4/56, Cleveland, Ohio BB/TR, 6′, 195 lbs. Deb: 8/13/81 FC																							
1981	Cle-A	21	47	3	10	3	0	0	6	2	2	.213	.245	.277	521	51	-3	0	0	0	.967	-2	C-15/D-2	-0.4
1982	Cle-A	66	184	13	39	6	1	3	16	24	30	.212	.303	.304	607	68	-8	0	0	0	.990	-6	C-63/3-2	-1.2
1983	Cle-A	48	121	15	31	3	0	4	15	15	19	.256	.338	.380	718	94	-1	0	1	-0	.995	-2	C-43	-0.1
1984	Cle-A	75	220	38	64	11	0	12	41	33	35	.291	.383	.505	888	141	13	1	2	-0	.982	-4	C-63/1-1,3-1,D-1	1.1
1985	Cle-A	73	173	11	24	4	1	0	13	22	21	.139	.236	.173	409	14	-20	0	1	-0	.986	-3	C-67	-2.1
1986	Cle-A	92	254	28	68	9	0	2	26	22	49	.268	.329	.327	655	81	-6	0	1	-0	.990	-10	C-86	-1.3
1987	Cle-A	89	211	20	46	9	0	5	16	12	28	.218	.260	.332	592	55	-14	0	0	0	.990	-2	C-86	-1.3
1988	Cle-A	32	72	6	9	1	0	1	8	8	12	.125	.222	.181	403	14	-8	0	0	0	.979	1	C-32	-0.6

YEAR	TM/L	G	AB	R	H	2B	3B	HR	RBI	BB	SO	AVG	OBP	SLG	OPS	OPS+	BR+	SB	CS	SBR	FA	FR	G/POS	TPR
	Det-A	1	0	0	0	0	0	0	0	0	0	—	—	—	—	—	0	0	0	0	.000	0	/C-1	0.0
	Yr	33	72	6	9	1	0	1	8	8	12	.125	.222	.181	403	14	-8	0	0	0	.979	1	C-33	-0.6
1989	Oak-A	1	2	0	1	0	0	0	1	0	1	.500	.500	.500	1000	189	0	0	0	0	1.000	1	/C-1	0.1
Total	9	498	1284	134	292	46	2	27	142	138	197	.227	.303	.329	633	73	-47	1	5	-2	.987	-28	C-457/3-3,D-3,1-1	-5.8
■ SAL BANDO Bando, Salvatore Leonard b: 2/13/44, Cleveland, O. BR/TR, 6', 205 lbs. Deb: 9/3/66 FC Career OF: (1-LF 0-CF 0-RF)																								
1966	KC-A	11	24	1	7	1	1	0	1	1	3	.292	.320	.417	737	113	0	0	0	0	.933	4	/3-7	0.5
1967	KC-A	47	130	11	25	3	2	0	6	16	24	.192	.295	.246	541	64	-5	1	0	0	.959	8	3-44	0.3
1968	Oak-A	162	605	67	152	25	5	9	67	51	78	.251	.317	.354	670	108	5	13	4	1	.964	-12	*3-162/O-1(1-0-0)	-0.6
1969	Oak-A★	162	609	106	171	25	3	31	113	111	82	.281	.401	.484	885	153	47	1	4	-1	.954	-13	*3-162	3.3
1970	Oak-A	155	502	93	132	20	2	20	75	118	88	.263	.409	.430	839	137	31	6	10	-2	.954	-22	*3-152	0.6
1971	*Oak-A	153	538	75	146	23	1	24	94	86	55	.271	.380	.452	831	137	28	3	7	-2	.971	-17	*3-153	1.0
1972	*Oak-A★	152	535	64	126	20	3	15	77	78	55	.236	.342	.368	711	118	13	3	1	0	.960	6	*3-151/2-1	2.1
1973	*Oak-A★	162	592	97	170	**32**	3	29	98	82	84	.287	.378	.498	876	153	42	4	2	0	.949	-23	*3-159/D-3	1.8
1974	*Oak-A†	146	498	84	121	21	2	22	103	86	79	.243	.360	.426	786	134	24	2	3	-1	.946	-13	*3-141/D-3	1.0
1975	*Oak-A	160	562	64	129	24	1	15	78	87	80	.230	.338	.356	694	98	1	7	1	1	.967	-16	*3-160	-1.5
1976	Oak-A	158	550	75	132	18	2	27	84	76	74	.240	.337	.427	764	128	19	20	6	2	.962	-5	*3-155/S-5,D-2	1.7
1977	Mil-A	159	580	65	145	27	3	17	82	75	89	.250	.339	.395	734	99	0	4	2	0	.966	-2	*3-135,D-24/2-1,S-1	-0.4
1978	Mil-A	152	540	85	154	20	6	17	78	72	52	.285	.375	.439	814	128	22	3	2	-0	.968	12	*3-134,D-12/1-5	3.1
1979	Mil-A	130	476	57	117	14	3	9	43	57	42	.246	.330	.345	675	82	-11	2	0	0	.963	-9	*3-109,D-19/1-4,P2	-2.1
1980	Mil-A	78	254	28	50	12	1	5	31	29	35	.197	.282	.311	593	64	-13	5	3	0	.934	-4	3-57,D-15/1-7	-1.8
1981	*Mil-A	32	65	10	13	4	0	2	9	6	3	.200	.268	.354	621	82	-2	1	1	-0	.967	0	3-15/1-9,D-2	-0.2
Total	16	2019	7060	982	1790	289	38	242	1039	1031	923	.254	.355	.408	763	120	202	75	46	0	.959	-104	*3-1896/D-80,1S2PO	8.8
■ JEFF BANISTER Banister, Jeffery Todd b: 1/15/65, Weatherford, Okla. BR/TR, 6'2", 200 lbs. Deb: 7/23/91																								
1991	Pit-N	1	1	0	1	0	0	0	0	0	0	1.000	1.000	1.000	2000	471	0	0	0	0	.000	0	/H	0.0
■ BRIAN BANKS Banks, Brian Glen b: 9/28/70, Mesa, Ariz. BB/TR, 6'3", 200 lbs. Deb: 9/9/96 Career OF: (23-LF 0-CF 2-RF)																								
1996	Mil-A	4	7	2	4	2	0	1	2	1	2	.571	.625	1.286	1911	353	3	0	0	0	1.000	-1	/O-3(3-0-0),1-1	0.1
1997	Mil-A	28	68	9	14	1	0	1	8	6	17	.206	.270	.265	535	40	-6	0	0	-0	.950	-1	O-15L/1-5,3-1,D-1	-0.8
1998	Mil-N	24	24	3	7	2	0	1	5	4	7	.292	.393	.500	893	133	1	0	0	0	1.000	-2	/C-5,1-2,3-1,O-1L	-0.1
1999	Mil-N	105	219	34	53	7	1	5	22	25	59	.242	.320	.352	671	70	-10	6	1	1	.992	-4	1-44,C-40/O-5(4-0-1)	-1.3
Total	4	161	318	48	78	12	1	8	37	36	85	.245	.322	.365	687	75	-12	6	2	1	.989	-8	/1-52,C-45,O-24L,3D	-2.1
■ ERNIE BANKS Banks, Ernest "Mr. Cub" b: 1/31/31, Dallas, Tex. BR/TR, 6'1", 180 lbs. Deb: 9/17/53 CH																								
1953	Chi-N	10	35	3	11	1	1	2	6	4	5	.314	.385	.571	956	142	2	0	0	0	.981	3	S-10	0.5
1954	Chi-N	154	593	70	163	19	7	19	79	40	50	.275	.328	.427	755	94	-6	6	10	-2	.959	-1	*S-154	0.3
1955	Chi-N★	154	596	98	176	29	9	44	117	45	72	.295	.347	.596	942	145	35	9	3	1	**.972**	5	*S-154	5.3
1956	Chi-N☆	139	538	82	160	25	8	28	85	52	62	.297	.359	.530	889	137	27	6	9	-2	.962	-16	*S-139	2.2
1957	Chi-N★	156	594	113	169	34	6	43	102	70	85	.285	.363	.579	942	150	40	8	4	0	.975	-17	*S-100,3-58	3.2
1958	Chi-N★	154	617	119	193	23	11	**47**	**129**	52	87	.313	.370	**.614**	984	157	48	4	4	-1	.960	-2	*S-154	5.8
1959	Chi-N★	155	589	97	179	25	6	45	**143**	64	72	.304	.379	.596	975	156	46	2	4	-1	**.985**	6	*S-154	6.3
1960	Chi-N★	156	597	94	162	32	7	**41**	117	71	69	.271	.353	.554	907	145	36	1	3	-1	**.977**	11	*S-156	5.9
1961	Chi-N★	138	511	75	142	22	4	29	80	54	75	.278	.349	.507	856	122	15	1	2	-0	.965	13	*S-104,O-23L/1-7	3.4
1962	Chi-N★	154	610	87	164	20	6	37	104	30	71	.269	.311	.503	814	110	6	5	1	1	.993	0	*1-149/3-3	-0.2
1963	Chi-N	130	432	41	98	20	1	18	64	39	73	.227	.297	.403	700	94	-3	0	3	-1	.993	-2	*1-125	-1.5
1964	Chi-N	157	591	67	156	29	6	23	95	36	84	.264	.310	.450	760	107	4	1	2	-0	.994	11	*1-157	0.6
1965	Chi-N★	163	612	79	162	25	3	28	106	55	64	.265	.331	.453	784	116	12	3	5	-1	.992	-7	*1-162	-0.7
1966	Chi-N	141	511	52	139	23	7	15	75	29	59	.272	.317	.432	750	105	3	0	1	-0	.992	2	*1-130/3-8	-0.4
1967	Chi-N★	151	573	68	158	26	4	23	95	27	93	.276	.312	.455	767	112	7	2	2	-0	.993	1	*1-147	-0.2
1968	Chi-N	150	552	71	136	27	0	32	83	27	67	.246	.288	.469	757	116	9	2	0	0	.996	-1	*1-147	-0.1
1969	Chi-N★	155	565	60	143	19	2	23	106	42	101	.253	.313	.416	729	91	-7	0	0	0	**.997**	1	*1-153	-2.0
1970	Chi-N	72	222	25	56	6	2	12	44	20	33	.252	.317	.459	776	94	-2	0	0	0	.993	-2	1-62	-0.9
1971	Chi-N	39	83	4	16	2	0	3	6	6	14	.193	.247	.325	572	53	-5	0	0	0	1.000	1	1-20	-0.6
Total	19	2528	9421	1305	2583	407	90	512	1636	763	1236	.274	.333	.500	833	122	264	50	53	-8	.994	4	*1-1259,S-1125/3-69,O	26.9
■ GEORGE BANKS Banks, George Edward b: 9/24/38, Pacolet Mills, S.C. d: 3/1/85, Spartanburg, S.C. BR/TR, 5'11", 185 lbs. Deb: 4/15/62 Career OF: (10-LF 0-CF 12-RF)																								
1962	Min-A	63	103	22	26	0	2	4	15	21	27	.252	.384	.408	792	109	2	0	0	0	.962	-3	O-17(7-0-11)/3-6	-0.1
1963	Min-A	25	71	5	11	4	0	3	8	9	21	.155	.259	.338	597	65	-3	0	0	0	.910	2	3-21	-0.2
1964	Min-A	1	1	0	0	0	0	0	0	0	1	.000	.000	.000	0	-99	-0	0	0	0	.000	0	H	0.0
	Cle-A	9	17	6	5	1	0	2	3	6	6	.294	.478	.706	1184	226	3	0	0	0	1.000	-1	/O-3(3-0-1),2-1,3-1	0.3
	Yr	10	18	6	5	1	0	2	3	6	7	.278	.458	.667	1125	210	3	0	0	0	1.000	-1	/O-3(3-0-1),2-1,3-1	0.3
1965	Cle-A	4	5	0	1	1	0	0	0	1	3	.200	.333	.400	733	107	0	0	1	-0	1.000	0	/3-1	0.0
1966	Cle-A	4	4	0	1	0	0	0	1	0	1	.250	.250	.250	500	44	-0	0	0	0	.000	0	H	0.0
Total	5	106	201	33	44	6	2	9	27	37	59	.219	.346	.403	749	102	1	0	1	-0	.919	-1	/3-29,O-20R,2-1	0.0
■ EVERETT BANKSTON Bankston, Wilborn Everett b: 5/25/1893, Barnesville, Ga. d: 2/26/70, Griffin, Ga. BL/TR, 5'11", 180 lbs. Deb: 8/15/15																								
1915	Phi-A	11	36	6	5	1	1	1	2	2	5	.139	.205	.306	511	55	-2	1			.882	-1	/O-8(4-4-0)	-0.4
■ JIM BANNING Banning, James M. b: 1866, New York, N.Y. BL/TR, 5'6", 150 lbs. Deb: 9/27/1888																								
1888	Was-N	1	0	0	0	0	0	0	0	0	0	—	—	—	—	—	0	0			1.000	-0	/C-1	0.0
1889	Was-N	2	1	0	0	0	0	0	0	0	0	.000	.000	.000	0	-99	-0	0			1.000	1	/C-2	0.1
Total	2	3	1	0	0	0	0	0	0	0	0	.000	.000	.000	0	-99	-0	0			1.000	1	/C-3	0.1
■ ALAN BANNISTER Bannister, Alan b: 9/3/51, Montebello, Cal. BR/TR, 5'11", 175 lbs. Deb: 7/13/74 Career OF: (254-LF 72-CF 100-RF)																								
1974	Phi-N	26	25	4	3	0	0	0	1	3	7	.120	.241	.120	361	3	-3	0	0	0	1.000	-2	/O-8(0-8-0),S-2	-0.6
1975	Phi-N	24	61	10	16	3	1	0	0	1	9	.262	.274	.344	618	68	-3	2	2	-0	1.000	1	O-18(4-14-1)/2-1,S-1	-0.3
1976	Chi-A	73	145	19	36	6	2	0	8	14	21	.248	.319	.317	636	86	-2	12	4	1	.988	-2	O-43L,S-14/2-4,3D	-0.4
1977	Chi-A	139	560	87	154	20	3	3	57	54	49	.275	.341	.338	678	86	-10	4	3	-0	.936	-34	*S-133/2-3,O-3(2-2-0)	-2.9
1978	Chi-A	49	107	16	24	3	2	0	8	11	12	.224	.303	.290	592	67	-5	3	3	-0	1.000	-3	D-19,O-15L/S-8,2-2	-0.9
1979	Chi-A	136	506	71	144	28	8	2	55	43	40	.285	.344	.383	728	96	-2	22	6	3	.963	-24	2-65,O-47L,3-12,/1D	-2.2
1980	Chi-A	45	130	16	25	6	0	0	9	12	16	.192	.261	.238	499	38	-11	5	2	0	1.000	-2	O-23(22-0-1),3-17	-1.4
	Cle-A	81	262	41	86	17	4	1	32	28	25	.328	.393	.435	828	126	10	9	2	1	.968	-17	2-41,O-40R/3-3,S-2	-0.5
	Yr	126	392	57	111	23	4	1	41	40	41	.283	.350	.370	719	97	-1	14	4	2	.981	-19	O-63L,2-41,3-20,/S	-1.9
1981	Cle-A	68	232	36	61	11	1	1	17	16	19	.263	.310	.332	642	86	-4	16	2	3	.986	-14	O-35L,2-30/1-2,S-1	-1.6
1982	Cle-A	101	348	40	93	16	1	4	41	42	41	.267	.348	.353	701	94	-2	18	5	2	.991	-11	O-55L,2-48/S-2,3D	-1.1
1983	Cle-A	117	377	51	100	25	4	5	45	31	43	.265	.326	.393	719	93	-3	6	6	-1	.969	-14	O-91L,2-27/1-3,D-3	-2.1
1984	Hou-N	9	20	2	4	2	0	0	0	2	2	.200	.273	.300	573	65	-1	0	0	0	.947	-1	/S-4,O-1(1-0-0)	-0.2
	Tex-A	47	112	20	33	2	1	2	9	21	17	.295	.410	.384	794	118	4	3	0	1	.959	-12	2-25/O-3L,1-1,3D	-0.7
1985	Tex-A	57	122	17	32	4	1	1	6	14	17	.262	.338	.336	674	84	-2	8	2	1	1.000	-2	D-21,O-14L,2-10,/31	-0.4
Total	12	972	3007	430	811	143	28	19	288	292	318	.270	.337	.355	692	90	-34	108	37	11	.983	-138	O-396L,2-256,S/D31	-15.3
■ JIMMY BANNON Bannon, James Henry "Foxy Grandpa" b: 5/5/1871, Amesbury, Mass. d: 3/24/48, Glen Rock, N.J. BR/TR, 5'5", 160 lbs. Deb: 6/15/1893 F Career OF: (4-LF 1-CF 346-RF)																								
1893	StL-N	26	107	9	36	3	4	0	15	4	5	.336	.366	.439	805	113	2	8			.795	-6	O-24(1-0-23)/S-2,P-1	-0.4
1894	Bos-N	128	494	130	166	29	10	13	114	62	42	.336	.414	.514	928	114	9	47			.873	19	*O-128(0-0-128)/P-1	1.6
1895	Bos-N	124	493	101	171	35	5	6	74	54	31	.347	.417	.475	891	120	14	28			.879	11	*O-123(1-0-122)/P-1	1.5
1896	Bos-N	89	344	53	87	9	5	0	50	32	23	.253	.318	.308	626	62	-19	16			.901	-1	O-76R/2-6,S-5,3-3	-2.0
Total	4	367	1438	293	460	76	24	19	253	152	101	.320	.389	.446	835	104	6	99			.877	23	O-351R/S-7,2-6,3P	0.7
■ TOM BANNON Bannon, Thomas Edward "Ward Six" b: 5/8/1869, Amesbury, Mass. d: 1/26/50, Lynn, Mass. BR/TR, 5'8", 175 lbs. Deb: 5/10/1895 F																								
1895	NY-N	37	159	33	43	6	2	0	8	7	8	.270	.301	.333	635	65	-9	20			.894	2	O-21(13-0-8),1-16	-0.7

YEAR	TM/L	G	AB	R	H	2B	3B	HR	RBI	BB	SO	AVG	OBP	SLG	OPS	OPS+	BR+	SB	CS	SBR	FA	FR	G/POS	TPR
1896	NY-N	2	7	1	1	1	0	0	0	1	1	.143	.250	.286	536	42	-1	0			.500	-1	/O-2(1-1-0)	-0.2
Total	2	39	166	34	44	7	2	0	8	8	9	.265	.299	.331	630	64	-9	20			.878	1	/O-23(14-1-8),1-16	-0.9

■ ROD BARAJAS

Barajas, Rodrigo Richard b: 9/5/75, Ontario, Cal. BR/TR, 6'2", 220 lbs. Deb: 9/25/99

YEAR	TM/L	G	AB	R	H	2B	3B	HR	RBI	BB	SO	AVG	OBP	SLG	OPS	OPS+	BR+	SB	CS	SBR	FA	FR	G/POS	TPR
1999	Ari-N	5	16	3	4	1	0	1	3	1	1	.250	.294	.500	794	95	-0	0	0	0	1.000	-1	/C-5	-0.1
2000	Ari-N	5	13	1	3	0	0	1	3	0	4	.231	.231	.462	692	68	-1	0	0	0	1.000	-1	/C-5	-0.1
Total	2	10	29	4	7	1	0	2	6	1	5	.241	.267	.483	749	83	-1	0	0	0	1.000	-2	/C-10	-0.2

■ WALTER BARBARE

Barbare, Walter Lawrence "Dinty" b: 8/11/1891, Greenville, S.C. d: 10/28/65, Greenville, S.C. BR/TR, 6', 162 lbs. Deb: 9/17/14

YEAR	TM/L	G	AB	R	H	2B	3B	HR	RBI	BB	SO	AVG	OBP	SLG	OPS	OPS+	BR+	SB	CS	SBR	FA	FR	G/POS	TPR
1914	Cle-A	15	52	6	16	2	2	0	5	2	5	.308	.345	.423	769	126	1	1	4	-1	.933	0	3-14/S-1	0.1
1915	Cle-A	77	246	15	47	3	1	0	11	10	27	.191	.235	.211	446	33	-21	6	5	-0	.960	7	3-68/1-1	-1.3
1916	Cle-A	13	48	3	11	1	0	0	3	4	9	.229	.288	.250	538	58	-2	0			.977	1	3-12	-0.1
1918	Bos-A	13	29	2	5	3	0	0	2	0	1	.172	.172	.276	448	36	-2	1			.826	-4	3-11/S-1	-0.7
1919	Pit-N	85	293	34	80	11	5	1	34	18	18	.273	.317	.355	672	98	-1	11			.961	-7	3-80/2-1	-0.6
1920	Pit-N	57	186	9	51	5	2	0	12	9	11	.274	.308	.323	630	79	-5	5	3	0	.923	-5	S-34,2-12/3-5	-0.8
1921	Bos-N	134	550	66	166	22	7	0	49	24	28	.302	.331	.367	698	89	-9	11	4	1	.957	-17	*S-121/2-8,3-2	-1.0
1922	Bos-N	106	373	38	86	5	4	0	40	21	22	.231	.272	.265	537	41	-33	2	0	0	.966	2	2-45,3-38,1-14	-2.6
Total	8	500	1777	173	462	52	21	1	156	88	121	.260	.297	.315	612	71	-71	37	16		.959	-21	3-230,S-157/2-66,1	-7.0

■ RED BARBARY

Barbary, Donald Odell b: 6/20/20, Simpsonville, S.C BR/TR, 6'2", 195 lbs. Deb: 5/22/43

YEAR	TM/L	G	AB	R	H	2B	3B	HR	RBI	BB	SO	AVG	OBP	SLG	OPS	OPS+	BR+	SB	CS	SBR	FA	FR	G/POS	TPR
1943	Was-A	1	1	0	0	0	0	0	0	0	0	.000	.000	.000	0	-99	-0	0	0	0	.000	0	H	0.0

■ JAP BARBEAU

Barbeau, William Joseph b: 6/10/1882, New York, N.Y. d: 9/10/69, Milwaukee, Wis. BR/TR, 5'5", 140 lbs. Deb: 9/27/05

YEAR	TM/L	G	AB	R	H	2B	3B	HR	RBI	BB	SO	AVG	OBP	SLG	OPS	OPS+	BR+	SB	CS	SBR	FA	FR	G/POS	TPR
1905	Cle-A	11	37	1	10	1	1	0	2	1		.270	.289	.351	641	102	-0	1			.905	1	2-11	0.1
1906	Cle-A	42	129	8	25	5	3	0	12	9		.194	.257	.279	536	69	-5	5			.830	-7	3-32/S-6	-1.2
1909	Pit-N	91	350	60	77	16	3	0	25	37		.220	.302	.283	585	75	-10	19			.891	-19	3-85	-3.0
	StL-N	48	175	23	44	3	0	0	5	28		.251	.370	.269	639	105	3	14			.901	-10	3-47	-0.6
	Yr	139	525	83	121	19	3	0	30	65		.230	.326	.278	604	85	-7	33			.895	-29	*3-132	-3.6
1910	StL-N	7	21	4	4	0	1	0	2	3	3	.190	.292	.286	577	71	-1	0			.917	2	/3-6,2-1	0.2
Total	4	199	712	96	160	25	8	0	46	78	3	.225	.311	.282	593	82	-12	39			.884	-33	3-170/2-12,S-6	-4.5

■ DAVE BARBEE

Barbee, David Monroe b: 5/7/05, Greensboro, N.C. d: 7/1/68, Albemarle, N.C. BR/TR, 5'11.5", 178 lbs. Deb: 7/29/26

YEAR	TM/L	G	AB	R	H	2B	3B	HR	RBI	BB	SO	AVG	OBP	SLG	OPS	OPS+	BR+	SB	CS	SBR	FA	FR	G/POS	TPR
1926	Phi-A	19	47	7	8	1	1	1	5	2	4	.170	.220	.298	518	32	-5	0	0	0	1.000	0	O-10(0-0-10)	-0.6
1932	Pit-N	97	327	37	84	22	6	5	55	18	38	.257	.300	.407	706	89	-6	1			.975	4	O-78(77-1-0)	-0.6
Total	2	116	374	44	92	23	7	6	60	20	42	.246	.290	.393	683	82	-10	1	0		.977	4	/O-88(77-1-10)	-1.2

■ CHARLIE BARBER

Barber, Charles D. b: 1854, Philadelphia, Pa. d: 11/23/10, Philadelphia, Pa. BR/TR, Deb: 4/17/1884

YEAR	TM/L	G	AB	R	H	2B	3B	HR	RBI	BB	SO	AVG	OBP	SLG	OPS	OPS+	BR+	SB	CS	SBR	FA	FR	G/POS	TPR
1884	Cin-U	55	204	38	41	1	4	0		11		.201	.242	.245	487	44	-20				.837	4	3-55	-1.4

■ TURNER BARBER

Barber, Tyrus Turner b: 7/9/1893, Lavinia, Tenn. d: 10/20/68, Milan, Tenn. BL/TR, 5'11", 170 lbs. Deb: 8/19/15 Career OF: (194-LF 76-CF 70-RF)

YEAR	TM/L	G	AB	R	H	2B	3B	HR	RBI	BB	SO	AVG	OBP	SLG	OPS	OPS+	BR+	SB	CS	SBR	FA	FR	G/POS	TPR
1915	Was-A	20	53	9	16	1	1	0	6	6	7	.302	.383	.358	742	120	1	0	3	-1	.952	-2	O-19(3-0-16)	-0.2
1916	Was-A	15	33	3	7	0	1	1	5	2	3	.212	.257	.364	621	87	-1	0			.833	-3	O-10(6-0-4)	-0.4
1917	Chi-N	7	28	2	6	1	0	0	2	2	8	.214	.267	.250	517	54	-1	1			1.000	1	/O-7(1-6-0)	-0.2
1918	*Chi-N	55	123	11	29	3	2	0	10	9	16	.236	.293	.293	586	77	-3	3			.940	-8	O-27(4-17-15)/1-4	-1.4
1919	Chi-N	76	230	26	72	9	4	0	21	14	17	.313	.355	.387	742	122	6	7			.949	-4	O-68(53-13-2)	-0.1
1920	Chi-N	94	340	27	90	10	5	0	50	9	26	.265	.290	.324	613	74	-11	5	6	-1	.988	-7	1-69,O-17(6-8-3)/2-2	-2.4
1921	Chi-N	127	452	73	142	14	4	1	54	41	24	.314	.379	.369	748	99	1	5	9	-2	.970	2	*O-123(90-20-14)	-0.8
1922	Chi-N	84	226	35	70	7	4	0	29	30	9	.310	.391	.376	767	97	0	7	4	0	.953	-6	O-47(31-0-16),1-16	-0.9
1923	Bro-N	13	46	3	10	2	0	0	8	2	2	.217	.250	.261	511	36	-4	0	1	-0	1.000	-2	O-12(0-12-0)	-0.7
Total	9	491	1531	189	442	47	21	2	185	115	112	.289	.343	.351	694	93	-12	28	23		.959	-29	O-330L/1-89,2-2	-7.1

■ BRET BARBERIE

Barberie, Bret Edward b: 8/16/67, Long Beach, Cal. BB/TR, 5'11", 180 lbs. Deb: 6/16/91

YEAR	TM/L	G	AB	R	H	2B	3B	HR	RBI	BB	SO	AVG	OBP	SLG	OPS	OPS+	BR+	SB	CS	SBR	FA	FR	G/POS	TPR
1991	Mon-N	57	136	16	48	12	2	2	18	20	22	.353	.443	.515	958	171	14	0	0	0	.931	-2	S-19,2-10,3-10,/1-1	1.4
1992	Mon-N	111	285	26	66	11	0	1	24	47	62	.232	.356	.281	637	83	-4	9	5	0	.932	5	3-63,2-26/S-1	0.3
1993	Fla-N	99	375	45	104	16	2	5	33	33	58	.277	.347	.371	718	87	-6	2	4	-1	.982	11	2-97	0.9
1994	Fla-N	107	372	40	112	20	2	5	31	23	65	.301	.356	.406	762	95	-2	2	0	0	.975	10	*2-106	1.3
1995	Bal-A	90	237	32	57	14	0	2	25	36	50	.241	.355	.325	680	77	-7	3	3	-0	.977	-4	2-74/3-3,D-5	-0.8
1996	Chi-N	15	29	4	1	0	0	1	2	5	11	.034	.176	.138	314	-15	-5	0	1	-0	1.000	-3	/2-6,3-2,S-1	-0.8
Total	6	479	1434	163	388	73	6	16	133	164	268	.271	.358	.363	722	92	-10	16	13	-1	.980	17	2-319/3-78,S-21,D1	2.3

■ JIM BARBIERI

Barbieri, James Patrick b: 9/15/41, Schenectady, N.Y. BL/TR, 5'7", 155 lbs. Deb: 7/5/66

YEAR	TM/L	G	AB	R	H	2B	3B	HR	RBI	BB	SO	AVG	OBP	SLG	OPS	OPS+	BR+	SB	CS	SBR	FA	FR	G/POS	TPR
1966	*LA-N	39	82	9	23	5	0	0	3	9	7	.280	.352	.341	693	102	0	2	0	0	.939	0	O-20(9-0-11)	0.0

■ GEORGE BARCLAY

Barclay, George Oliver "Deerfoot" b: 5/16/1876, Millville, Pa. d: 4/3/09, Philadelphia, Pa. BR/TR, 5'10", 162 lbs. Deb: 4/17/02

YEAR	TM/L	G	AB	R	H	2B	3B	HR	RBI	BB	SO	AVG	OBP	SLG	OPS	OPS+	BR+	SB	CS	SBR	FA	FR	G/POS	TPR
1902	StL-N	137	543	79	163	14	2	3	53	31		.300	.345	.350	695	119	12	30			.904	-7	*O-137(137-0-0)	-0.4
1903	StL-N	108	419	37	104	10	8	0	42	15		.248	.278	.310	588	70	-18	12			.901	-8	*O-107(107-0-0)	-3.1
1904	StL-N	103	375	41	75	7	4	1	28	12		.200	.237	.248	485	52	-21	14			.947	-6	*O-103(103-0-0)	-3.6
	Bos-N	24	93	5	21	3	1	0	10	2		.226	.258	.280	537	68	-4	3			.935	-3	O-24(6-1-17)	-0.8
	Yr	127	468	46	96	10	5	1	38	14		.205	.241	.254	495	55	-25	17			.945	-9	*O-127(109-1-17)	-4.4
1905	Bos-N	29	108	5	19	1	0	0	7	2		.176	.205	.185	391	17	-11	2			.854	-5	O-28(28-0-0)	-1.8
Total	4	401	1538	167	382	35	15	4	140	62		.248	.286	.298	584	79	-42	61			.911	-28	O-399(381-1-17)	-9.7

■ JESSE BARFIELD

Barfield, Jesse Lee b: 10/29/59, Joliet, Ill. BR/TR, 6'1", 205 lbs. Deb: 9/3/81 Career OF: (3-LF 87-CF 1340-RF)

YEAR	TM/L	G	AB	R	H	2B	3B	HR	RBI	BB	SO	AVG	OBP	SLG	OPS	OPS+	BR+	SB	CS	SBR	FA	FR	G/POS	TPR
1981	Tor-A	25	95	7	22	3	2	2	9	4	19	.232	.270	.368	638	77	-3	4	3	-0	1.000	5	O-25(0-0-25)	0.1
1982	Tor-A	139	394	54	97	13	2	18	58	42	79	.246	.323	.426	750	95	-3	1	4	-1	.963	-6	*O-137(1-3-136)/D-1	-1.6
1983	Tor-A	128	388	58	98	13	3	27	68	22	110	.253	.300	.510	810	111	4	2	5	-1	.966	4	*O-120(0-1-120)/D-5	0.2
1984	Tor-A	110	320	51	91	14	1	14	49	35	81	.284	.359	.466	824	122	10	8	2	1	.952	6	O-88(0-9-79)/D-9	1.3
1985	*Tor-A	155	539	94	156	34	9	27	84	66	143	.289	.371	.536	907	141	30	22	8	2	.989	22	*O-154(0-8-147)	4.5
1986	Tor-A★	158	589	107	170	35	2	**40**	108	69	146	.289	.371	.559	929	145	36	8	8	-1	.992	21	*O-157(0-18-147)	**4.6**
1987	Tor-A	159	590	89	155	25	3	28	84	58	141	.263	.332	.458	789	104	3	3	5	-1	.992	16	*O-158(0-13-152)	1.0
1988	Tor-A	137	468	62	114	21	5	18	56	41	108	.244	.306	.425	731	102	0	7	3	0	.988	13	*O-136(0-13-132)/D-1	0.9
1989	Tor-A	21	80	8	16	4	0	5	11	5	28	.200	.256	.438	693	94	-1	0	2	-1	.979	3	O-21(1-0-20)	0.0
	NY-A	129	441	71	106	19	1	18	56	82	122	.240	.362	.410	772	119	13	5	3	0	.972	9	*O-129(0-18-120)	1.9
	Yr	150	521	79	122	23	1	23	67	87	150	.234	.347	.415	762	115	12	5	5	-1	.973	12	*O-150(1-18-140)	1.9
1990	NY-A	153	476	69	117	21	2	25	78	82	150	.246	.362	.456	818	127	18	4	3	-0	.973	9	*O-151(0-4-151)	2.3
1991	NY-A	84	284	37	64	12	0	17	48	36	80	.225	.313	.447	760	107	2	1	0	0	1.000	11	O-81(1-0-81)	1.1
1992	NY-A	30	95	8	13	2	0	2	7	9	27	.137	.212	.221	433	21	-10	1	1	-0	.966	0	O-30(0-0-30)	-1.1
Total	12	1428	4759	715	1219	216	30	241	716	551	1234	.256	.338	.466	804	116	100	66	47	-2	.980	114	*O-1387R/D-16	15.2

■ AL BARKER

Barker, Alfred L b: 1/18/1839, Rockford, Ill. d: 9/15/12, Rockford, Ill. Deb: 6/1/1871

YEAR	TM/L	G	AB	R	H	2B	3B	HR	RBI	BB	SO	AVG	OBP	SLG	OPS	OPS+	BR+	SB	CS	SBR	FA	FR	G/POS	TPR
1871	Rok-n	1	4	0	1	0	0	0	2	1	0	.250	.400	.250	650	97	0	0	0	0	1.000	-0	/O-1(1-0-0)	0.0

■ GLEN BARKER

Barker, Glen F. b: 5/10/71, Albany, N.Y. BB/TR, 5'10", 180 lbs. Deb: 4/7/99

YEAR	TM/L	G	AB	R	H	2B	3B	HR	RBI	BB	SO	AVG	OBP	SLG	OPS	OPS+	BR+	SB	CS	SBR	FA	FR	G/POS	TPR
1999	*Hou-N	81	73	23	21	2	0	1	11	11	19	.288	.388	.356	744	91	-0	17	6	2	.981	-13	O-57(3-47-8)/D-1	-1.1
2000	Hou-N	84	67	18	15	2	1	2	6	7	23	.224	.307	.373	680	67	-3	9	6	-0	.985	-18	O-69(2-63-4)	-2.1
Total	2	165	140	41	36	4	1	3	17	18	42	.257	.350	.364	714	80	-4	26	12	2	.983	-31	O-126(5-110-12)/D-1	-3.2

■ KEVIN BARKER

Barker, Kevin Stewart b: 7/26/75, Bristol, Va. BL/TL, 6'3", 205 lbs. Deb: 8/19/99

YEAR	TM/L	G	AB	R	H	2B	3B	HR	RBI	BB	SO	AVG	OBP	SLG	OPS	OPS+	BR+	SB	CS	SBR	FA	FR	G/POS	TPR
1999	Mil-N	38	117	13	33	3	0	3	23	9	19	.282	.333	.385	718	82	-3	1	0	0	.996	0	1-31	-0.5
2000	Mil-N	40	100	14	22	5	0	2	9	20	21	.220	.355	.330	685	76	-3	1	0	0	.993	-1	1-32	-0.7
Total	2	78	217	27	55	8	0	5	32	29	40	.253	.344	.359	704	79	-6	2	0	0	.994	-1	/1-63	-1.2

YEAR	TM/L	G	AB	R	H	2B	3B	HR	RBI	BB	SO	AVG	OBP	SLG	OPS	OPS+	BR+	SB	CS	SBR	FA	FR	G/POS	TPR
■ RAY BARKER Barker, Raymond Herrell "Buddy" b: 3/12/36, Martinsburg, W.Va. BL/TR, 6', 192 lbs. Deb: 9/13/60																								
1960	Bal-A	5	6	0	0	0	0	0	0	0	3	.000	.000	.000	0	-99	-2	0	0	0	.000	-0	/O-1(1-0-0)	-0.2
1965	Cle-A	11	6	0	0	0	0	0	0	2	2	.000	.250	.000	250	-22	-1	0	0	0	1.000	-0	/1-3	-0.1
	NY-A	98	205	21	52	11	0	7	31	20	46	.254	.329	.410	739	109	2	1	0	0	.991	6	1-61/3-3	0.7
	Yr	109	211	21	52	11	0	7	31	22	48	.246	.326	.398	724	105	1	1	0	0	.991	6	1-64/3-3	0.6
1966	NY-A	61	75	11	14	5	0	3	13	4	20	.187	.228	.373	601	72	-3	0	0	0	.987	5	1-47	0.1
1967	NY-A	17	26	2	2	0	0	0	0	3	5	.077	.172	.077	249	-25	-4	0	0	0	.961	1	1-13	-0.4
Total	4	192	318	34	68	16	0	10	44	29	76	.214	.286	.358	644	84	-7	1	0	0	.987	12	1-124/3-3,O-1(1-0-0)	0.1
■ RED BARKLEY Barkley, John Duncan b: 9/19/13, Childress, Tex. BR/TR, 5'11", 160 lbs. Deb: 9/2/37																								
1937	StL-A	31	101	9	27	6	0	0	14	14	17	.267	.357	.327	683	73	-4	1	0	0	.969	-4	2-31	-0.6
1939	Bos-N	12	11	1	0	0	0	0	0	1	2	.000	.083	.000	83	-82	-3	0			.842	4	/S-7,3-4	0.1
1943	Bro-N	20	51	6	16	3	0	0	7	4	7	.314	.364	.373	736	113	1	1			.894	-3	S-18	-0.1
Total	3	63	163	16	43	9	0	0	21	19	26	.264	.341	.319	660	75	-6	2	0		.882	-3	/2-31,S-25,3-4	-0.6
■ SAM BARKLEY Barkley, Samuel E b: 5/24/1858, Wheeling, W.Va. d: 4/20/12, Wheeling, W.Va. BR/TR, 5'11.5", 180 lbs. Deb: 5/1/1884 M Career OF: (8-LF 0-CF 0-RF)																								
1884	Tol-a	104	435	71	133	**39**	9	1		22		.306	.342	.444	786	149	22				.930	25	*2-103/C-2	**4.5**
1885	*StL-a	106	418	67	112	18	10	3	53	25		.268	.312	.380	693	113	5				.921	15	*2-96,1-11	2.0
1886	Pit-a	122	478	77	127	31	8	1	69	58		.266	.345	.370	715	125	15	22			.936	-4	*2-112/O-8(8-0-0),1-2	1.3
1887	Pit-N	89	370	44	106	10	4	1	35	30	24	.286	.294	.285	579	66	-14	6			.979	-5	1-53,2-36	-1.9
1888	KC-a	116	482	67	104	21	6	4	51	26		.216	.262	.309	571	78	-14	15			.938	-7	*2-116/M	-1.6
1889	KC-a	45	176	36	50	6	2	0	23	15	20	.284	.340	.341	681	89	-3	8			.923	-12	2-41/1-4	-1.1
Total	6	582	2359	362	632	125	39	10	231	176	44	.268	.314	.359	672	105	11	51			.929	12	2-504/1-70,O-8L,C-2	3.2
■ TOM BARLOW Barlow, Thomas H. Deb: 5/2/1872																								
1872	Atl-n	37	171	34	53	1	0	0	10	3	2	.310	.322	.316	638	83	-6	7	5	-0	.761	-8	*C-36/S-4,3-1	-1.0
1873	Atl-n	55	271	48	74	0	2	1	14	4	0	.273	.284	.299	583	82	-3	3	3	-0	.762	-15	*C-55/2-1,S-1	-1.3
1874	Har-n	32	155	37	46	5	1	0	12	2	2	.297	.306	.342	648	102	-0	**17**	4	**2**	.820	9	S-32	0.8
1875	NH-n	1	5	1	1	0	0	0	0	0	0	.200	.200	.200	400	45	-0	0	0	0	.800	0	/S-1	0.0
	Atl-n	1	4	0	0	0	0	0	0	0	0	.000	.000	.000	0	-99	-1	0	0	0	.500	-2	/2-1	-0.2
	Yr	2	9	1	1	0	0	0	0	0	0	.111	.111	.111	222	-26	-1	0	0	0	.800	-1	/S-1,2-1	-0.2
Total	4 n	126	606	120	174	6	3	1	36	9	4	.287	.298	.312	609	86	-10	27	12	2	.762	-16	/C-91,S-38,2-2,3-1	-1.7
■ BRUCE BARMES Barmes, Bruce Raymond "Squeaky" b: 10/23/29, Vincennes, Ind. BL/TR, 5'8", 165 lbs. Deb: 9/13/53																								
1953	Was-A	5	5	1	1	0	0	0	0	0	0	.200	.200	.200	400	8	-1	0	0	0	1.000	0	/O-1(0-0-1)	-0.1
■ BABE BARNA Barna, Herbert Paul b: 3/2/15, Clarksburg, W.Va. d: 5/18/72, Charleston, W.Va. BL/TR, 6'2", 210 lbs. Deb: 9/16/37																								
1937	Phi-A	14	36	10	14	2	0	2	9	2	6	.389	.421	.611	1032	159	3	1	0	0	.800	-2	/O-9(9-0-0),1-1	0.0
1938	Phi-A	9	30	4	4	0	0	0	2	3	5	.133	.212	.133	345	-12	-5	0	0	0	.917	-1	/O-7(4-0-3)	-0.6
1941	NY-N	10	42	5	9	3	0	1	5	2	6	.214	.250	.357	607	68	-2	0			1.000	1	O-10(2-0-8)	-0.2
1942	NY-N	104	331	39	85	8	7	6	58	38	48	.257	.333	.378	711	107	3	3			.983	-5	O-89(88-0-1)	-0.7
1943	NY-N	40	113	11	23	5	1	1	12	16	9	.204	.302	.292	594	72	-4	3			.984	-1	O-31(31-0-0)	-0.8
	Bos-A	30	112	19	19	4	1	2	10	15	24	.170	.268	.277	545	58	-6	2	1	0	.940	-4	O-29(29-0-0)	-1.3
Total	5	207	664	88	154	22	9	12	96	76	98	.232	.311	.346	657	88	-11	9	1		.969	-13	O-175(163-0-12)/1-1	-3.6
■ RED BARNES Barnes, Emile b: 12/25/04, Suggsville, Ala. d: 7/3/59, Mobile, Ala. BL/TR, 5'10.5", 158 lbs. Deb: 9/29/27																								
1927	Was-A	3	11	5	4	1	0	0	0	1	3	.364	.417	.455	871	127	0	0	0	0	1.000	0	/O-3(0-1-2)	0.0
1928	Was-A	114	417	82	127	22	15	6	51	55	38	.305	.391	.472	863	127	17	7	3	0	.978	4	*O-104(8-96-1)	1.6
1929	Was-A	72	130	16	26	5	2	1	15	13	12	.200	.273	.292	565	45	-11	1	0	0	.877	-6	O-30(8-14-9)	-1.7
1930	Was-A	12	12	1	2	1	0	0	0	0	3	.167	.167	.250	417	4	-2	0	0	0	.000	0	H	-0.2
	Chi-A	85	266	48	66	12	7	1	31	26	20	.248	.317	.357	675	73	-11	4	2	0	.939	-0	O-72(1-71-0)	-1.3
	Yr	97	278	49	68	13	7	1	31	26	23	.245	.311	.353	664	70	-13	4	2	0	.939	-0	O-72(1-71-0)	-1.5
Total	4	286	836	152	225	41	24	8	97	95	76	.269	.347	.404	752	95	-6	12	5	1	.953	-2	O-209(17-182-12)	-1.6
■ EPPIE BARNES Barnes, Everett Duane b: 12/1/1900, Ossining, N.Y. d: 11/17/80, Mineola, N.Y. BL/TL, 5'9", 175 lbs. Deb: 9/25/23																								
1923	Pit-N	2	2	0	1	0	0	0	0	0	1	.500	.500	.500	1000	161	0	0	0	0	1.000	0	/1-1	0.0
1924	Pit-N	2	5	0	0	0	0	0	0	0	1	.000	.000	.000	0	-98	-1	0	0	0	1.000	0	/1-1	-0.1
Total	2	4	7	0	1	0	0	0	0	0	2	.143	.143	.143	286	-23	-1	0	0	0	1.000	1	/1-2	-0.1
■ JOHN BARNES Barnes, John Delbert b: 4/24/76, San Diego, Cal. BR/TR, 6'2", 176 lbs. Deb: 9/16/2000																								
2000	Min-A	11	37	5	13	4	0	0	2	2	6	.351	.415	.459	874	115	1	0	1	-0	1.000	3	O-11(2-2-8)	0.3
■ HONEY BARNES Barnes, John Francis b: 1/31/1900, Fulton, N.Y. d: 6/18/81, Lockport, N.Y. BL/TR, 5'10", 175 lbs. Deb: 4/20/26																								
1926	NY-A	1	0	0	0	0	0	0	0	1	0	—	1.000	—	1000	179	0	0	0	0	.000	0	/C-1	0.0
■ LUTE BARNES Barnes, Luther Owens b: 4/28/47, Forest City, Iowa BR/TR, 5'10", 160 lbs. Deb: 8/6/72																								
1972	NY-N	24	72	5	17	2	2	0	6	6	4	.236	.295	.319	614	76	-2	0	1	-0	.959	1	2-14/S-6	-0.1
1973	NY-N	3	2	2	1	0	0	0	1	0	1	.500	.500	.500	1000	181	0	0	0	0	.000	0	H	0.0
Total	2	27	74	7	18	2	2	0	7	6	5	.243	.300	.324	624	79	-2	0	1	-0	.959	1	/2-14,S-6	-0.1
■ ROSS BARNES Barnes, Roscoe Charles b: 5/8/1850, Mount Morris, N.Y. d: 2/5/15, Chicago, Ill. BR/TR, 5'8.5", 145 lbs. Deb: 5/5/1871 U NA OF: (1-LF 0-CF 0-RF)																								
1871	Bos-n	31	157	**66**	63	10	9	0	34	13	1	.401	.447	.580	1027	186	17	11	6	0	.873	13	2-16,S-15	**1.9**
1872	Bos-n	45	229	81	**99**	**28**	2	1	44	9	4	**.432**	.454	**.585**	**1039**	**206**	**27**	12	2	2	**.901**	25	*2-45	**3.5**
1873	Bos-n	60	322	**125**	**137**	**29**	8	2	62	**18**	2	**.425**	**.456**	**.584**	**1040**	**191**	**33**	**13**	4	1	.852	20	*2-47,3-13	**3.5**
1874	Bos-n	51	259	72	88	12	4	0	39	8	2	.340	.360	.417	777	140	10	8	7	-1	**.856**	19	*2-51/O-1(1-0-0)	1.9
1875	Bos-n	78	393	**115**	**143**	20	4	1	58	7	3	.364	**.375**	.443	818	177	28	29	6	**4**	.877	**19**	*2-76/O-3,S-2	**3.9**
1876	Chi-N	66	342	**126**	**138**	**21**	**14**	1	59	**20**	8	**.404**	**.462**	**.590**	**1052**	**222**	**39**				**.910**	5	*2-66/P-1	**4.0**
1877	Chi-N	22	92	16	25	1	0	0	5	7	4	.272	.323	.283	606	83	-2				.838	-8	2-22	-0.8
1879	Cin-N	77	323	55	86	9	2	1	30	16	25	.266	.301	.316	617	109	4				.864	-1	*S-61,2-16	0.6
1881	Bos-N	69	295	42	80	14	1	0	17	16	16	.271	.309	.325	634	104	2				.854	-0	*S-63/2-7	0.5
Total	5 n	265	1360	459	530	99	27	4	237	55	12	.390	.413	.511	924	180	116	73	25	7	.871	97	2-235/S-17,3-13,O-4L	14.7
Total	4	234	1052	239	329	45	17	2	111	59	53	.313	.356	.401	757	142	44				.859	-5	S-124,2-111/P-1	4.3
■ SAM BARNES Barnes, Samuel Thomas b: 12/18/1899, Suggsville, Ala. d: 2/19/81, Montgomery, Ala. BL/TR, 5'8", 150 lbs. Deb: 9/14/21																								
1921	Det-A	7	11	2	2	1	0	0	0	2	1	.182	.357	.273	630	63	-1	0	0	0	.944	2	/2-2	0.1
■ BILL BARNES Barnes, William H. b: Indianapolis, Ind. Deb: 9/27/1884																								
1884	StP-U	8	30	2	6	1	0	0		0		.200	.200	.233	433	57	-2				.727	-2	/O-8(0-8-0)	-0.4
■ SKEETER BARNES Barnes, William Henry b: 3/3/57, Cincinnati, Ohio BR/TR, 5'10", 180 lbs. Deb: 9/6/83 Career OF: (37-LF 11-CF 30-RF)																								
1983	Cin-N	15	34	5	7	0	0	1	4	7	3	.206	.372	.294	666	84	-0	2	2	-0	1.000	-0	/1-7,3-7	-0.1
1984	Cin-N	32	42	5	5	0	0	1	3	4	6	.119	.196	.190	386	8	-5	0	0	0	1.000	0	3-11/O-3(3-0-0)	-0.5
1985	Mon-N	19	26	0	4	1	0	0	0	0	2	.154	.154	.192	346	-4	-4	0	1	-0	1.000	1	/3-4,O-3(1-0-2),1-1	-0.3
1987	StL-N	4	4	1	1	0	0	1	3	0	0	.250	.250	1.000	1250	208	1	0	0	0	.000	0	/3-1	0.1
1989	Cin-N	5	3	1	0	0	0	0	0	0	0	.000	.000	.000	0	-97	-1	0	1	-0	.000	0	H	-0.1
1991	Det-A	75	159	28	46	13	2	5	17	9	24	.289	.327	.491	818	121	4	10	7	-0	1.000	-1	O-33R,3-17/1-9,2D	0.2
1992	Det-A	95	165	27	45	8	1	3	25	10	18	.273	.322	.388	710	97	-1	3	1	0	.919	2	3-39,1-17,O-15C,/2D	0.1
1993	Det-A	84	160	24	45	8	1	2	27	11	19	.281	.327	.381	709	90	-2	5	5	-1	.984	-0	1-27,O-18L,3-13,D2/S	-0.5
1994	Det-A	24	21	4	6	0	0	1	4	0	2	.286	.286	.429	714	81	-1	0	1	-0	1.000	-1	1-15/O-4(4-0-0),D-1	-0.2
Total	9	353	614	95	159	30	4	14	83	41	74	.259	.310	.389	699	90	-9	20	18	-2	.938	1	/3-92,O-76L,1-76,D2S	-1.3

YEAR	TM/L	G	AB	R	H	2B	3B	HR	RBI	BB	SO	AVG	OBP	SLG	OPS	OPS+	BR+	SB	CS	SBR	FA	FR	G/POS	TPR
■ ED BARNEY Barney, Edmund J. b: 1/23/1890, Amery, Wis. d: 10/4/67, Rice Lake, Wis. BL/TR, 5'10.5", 178 lbs. Deb: 7/22/15																								
1915	NY-A	11	36	1	7	0	0	0	0	8	3	6	.194	.256	.194	451	35	-3	2	1	0	1.000	-0	O-10(3-7-0)	-0.4
	Pit-N	32	99	16	27	1	2	0	5	11	12	.273	.363	.323	686	110	2	7	3	0	.972	2	O-26(3-22-1)	0.3
1916	Pit-N	45	137	16	27	4	0	0	9	23	15	.197	.313	.226	539	66	-4	8			.964	5	O-40(20-20-0)	-0.2
Total	2	88	272	33	61	5	2	0	22	37	33	.224	.324	.257	581	78	-5	17	4		.971	7	/O-76(26-49-1)	-0.3
■ CLYDE BARNHART Barnhart, Clyde Lee "Pooch" b: 12/29/1895, Buck Valley, Pa. d: 1/21/80, Hagerstown, Md. BR/TR, 5'10", 155 lbs. Deb: 9/22/20 F Career OF: (336-LF 0-CF 213-RF)																								
1920	Pit-N	12	46	5	15	4	2	0	5	1	2	.326	.340	.500	840	135	2	1	0	0	.971	0	3-12	0.2
1921	Pit-N	124	449	66	116	15	13	3	62	32	36	.258	.312	.370	682	78	-15	3	3	-0	.956	-19	*3-118	-2.6
1922	Pit-N	75	209	30	69	7	5	1	38	25	7	.330	.402	.426	828	112	5	3	2	-0	.918	-12	3-30,O-26(5-0-21)	-0.7
1923	Pit-N	114	327	60	106	25	13	9	72	47	21	.324	.409	.563	972	151	24	5	7	-1	.985	3	O-92(0-0-92)	1.8
1924	Pit-N	102	344	49	95	6	11	3	51	30	17	.276	.338	.384	721	91	-4	8	4	0	.970	2	O-88(0-0-88)	-0.9
1925	*Pit-N	142	539	85	175	32	11	4	114	59	25	.325	.391	.447	838	106	6	9	5	0	.962	1	*O-138(138-0-0)	-0.3
1926	Pit-N	76	203	26	39	3	0	0	10	23	13	.192	.278	.207	484	30	-19	2	0	0	.991	-4	O-61(54-0-8)	-2.8
1927	*Pit-N	108	360	65	115	23	4	3	54	37	19	.319	.384	.431	815	110	6	2			.978	4	O-94(94-0-0)	0.3
1928	Pit-N	61	196	18	58	6	2	4	30	11	9	.296	.333	.408	741	89	-3	3			.971	-2	O-48(45-0-4)/3-1	-0.9
Total	9	814	2673	404	788	121	61	27	436	265	149	.295	.360	.416	776	100	2	35	21		.973	-27	O-547L,3-161	-5.9
■ VIC BARNHART Barnhart, Victor Dee b: 9/1/22, Hagerstown, Md. BR/TR, 6', 188 lbs. Deb: 10/1/44 F																								
1944	Pit-N	1	2	0	1	0	0	0	0	1	1	.500	.667	.500	1167	222	0	0			.889	1	/S-1	0.2
1945	Pit-N	71	201	21	54	7	0	0	19	9	11	.269	.300	.303	603	65	-9	2			.928	8	S-60/3-4	0.2
1946	Pit-N	2	1	0	0	0	0	0	0	0	0	.000	.000	.000	0	-98	-0	0			.000	0	H	0.0
Total	3	74	204	21	55	7	0	0	19	10	12	.270	.304	.304	608	67	-9	2			.927	9	/S-61,3-4	0.4
■ BILLY BARNIE Barnie, William Harrison "Bald Billy" b: 1/26/1853, New York, N.Y. d: 7/15/1900, Hartford, Conn. TR, 5'7", 157 lbs. Deb: 5/7/1874 MU NA OF: (0-LF 8-CF 31-RF)																								
1874	Har-n	45	190	21	35	4	2	0	20	1	13	.184	.188	.226	415	31	-15	2	2	-0	.733	-6	C-30,O-29(0-4-25)/S-1	-1.6
1875	Wes-n	10	36	3	4	1	0	0	2	0	3	.111	.111	.139	250	-13	-4	0	0	0	.889	1	/O-7(0-3-4),C-3	-0.2
	Mut-n	9	34	1	5	0	0	0	1	1	0	.147	.171	.147	318	11	-3	0	0	0	.750	-4	/C-6,O-3(0-1-2)	-0.6
	Yr	19	70	4	9	1	0	0	3	1	3	.129	.141	.143	284	-1	-7	0	0	0	.857	-3	O-10(0-4-6)/C-9	-0.8
1883	Bal-a	17	55	7	11	0	0	0		2		.200	.228	.200	428	38	-4				.846	-2	C-13/O-6(0-0-6),S-1,M	-0.4
1886	Bal-a	2	6	0	0	0	0	0	0	1		.000	.143	.000	143	-55	-1	0			.000	-1	/O-1(0-1-0),C-1	-0.2
Total	2 n	64	260	25	44	5	2	0	23	2	16	.169	.176	.204	379	23	-22	2	2	-0	.690	-9	/O-39R,C-39,S-1	-2.4
Total	2	19	61	7	11	0	0	0	0	3		.180	.219	.180	399	29	-5	0			.848	-3	/C-14,O-7(0-1-6),S-1	-0.6
■ DICK BARONE Barone, Richard Anthony b: 10/13/32, San Jose, Cal. BR/TR, 5'9", 165 lbs. Deb: 9/22/60																								
1960	Pit-N	3	6	0	0	0	0	0	0	0	1	.000	.000	.000	0	-99	-2	0	0	0	.875	-0	/S-2	-0.2
■ SCOTTY BARR Barr, Hyder Edward b: 10/6/1886, Bristol, Tenn. d: 12/2/34, Ft.Worth, Tex. BR/TR, 6', 175 lbs. Deb: 8/22/08 Career OF: (2-LF 15-CF 0-RF)																								
1908	Phi-A	19	56	4	8	2	0	0	1	3		.143	.200	.179	379	22	-5	0			.923	-7	2-11/3-4,1-2,O-2L	-1.4
1909	Phi-A	22	51	5	4	1	0	0	1	11		.078	.254	.098	352	12	-5	2			.947	-1	O-15(1-14-0)/1-7	-0.8
Total	2	41	107	9	12	3	0	0	2	14		.112	.228	.140	368	17	-9	2			.947	-8	/O-17C,2-11,1-9,3-4	-2.2
■ CUNO BARRAGAN Barragan, Facundo Anthony b: 6/20/32, Sacramento, Cal. BR/TR, 5'11", 180 lbs. Deb: 9/1/61																								
1961	Chi-N	10	28	3	6	0	0	1	2	2	7	.214	.267	.321	588	54	-2	0	0	0	1.000	-1	C-10	-0.3
1962	Chi-N	58	134	11	27	6	1	0	12	21	28	.201	.310	.261	571	53	-8	0	2	-1	.971	-7	C-55	-1.4
1963	Chi-N	1	1	0	0	0	0	0	0	0	1	.000	.000	.000	0	-95	-0	0	0	0	1.000	-0	/C-1	0.0
Total	3	69	163	14	33	6	1	1	14	23	36	.202	.301	.270	571	53	-11	0	2	-1	.975	-8	/C-66	-1.7
■ GERMAN BARRANCA Barranca, German (Costales) b: 10/19/56, Veracruz, Mex. BL/TR, 6', 160 lbs. Deb: 9/2/79																								
1979	KC-A	5	5	3	3	1	0	0	0	0	0	.600	.600	.800	1400	269	1	3	1	0	1.000	3	/2-1,3-1,D-1	0.4
1980	KC-A	7	0	3	0	0	0	0	0	0	0	—	—	—	—	—	0	0	0	0	.000	0	/R	0.0
1981	Cin-N	9	6	2	2	0	0	0	1	0	0	.333	.333	.333	667	88	-0	0	0	0	.000	0	/H	0.0
1982	Cin-N	46	51	11	13	1	3	0	2	2	9	.255	.283	.392	675	85	-1	2	0	0	.824	-1	/2-6	-0.2
Total	4	67	62	19	18	2	3	0	3	2	9	.290	.313	.419	732	101	-0	5	1	1	.893	2	/2-7,D-1,3-1	0.2
■ JIMMY BARRETT Barrett, James Erigena b: 3/28/1875, Athol, Mass. d: 10/24/21, Detroit, Mich. BL/TR, 5'9", 170 lbs. Deb: 9/13/1899																								
1899	Cin-N	26	92	30	34	2	4	0	10	18		.370	.477	.478	956	159	9	4			.936	-2	O-26(3-0-23)	0.5
1900	Cin-N	137	545	114	172	11	7	5	42	72		.316	.400	.389	789	121	19	44			.929	4	*O-137(0-115-22)	1.3
1901	Det-A	135	542	110	159	16	9	4	65	76		.293	.385	.378	763	107	8	26			.940	15	*O-135(0-135-0)	1.4
1902	Det-A	136	509	93	154	19	6	4	44	74		.303	.397	.387	784	116	14	24			.961	8	*O-136(0-136-0)	1.4
1903	Det-A	136	517	95	163	13	10	2	31	**74**		.315	**.407**	.391	798	144	33	27			.955	7	*O-136(0-136-0)	3.4
1904	Det-A	162	624	83	167	10	5	0	31	**79**		.268	.353	.300	652	111	12	15			.971	12	*O-162(0-162-0)	1.8
1905	Det-A	20	67	2	17	1	0	0	3	6		.254	.324	.269	593	88	-1	0			1.000	-3	O-18(0-18-0)	-0.5
1906	Cin-N	5	12	1	0	0	0	0	0	2		.000	.143	.000	143	-53	-2	0			1.000	0	/O-4(0-0-4)	-0.3
1907	Bos-A	106	390	52	95	11	6	1	28	38		.244	.314	.310	624	100	1	3			.966	4	O-99(96-3-0)	-0.1
1908	Bos-A	3	8	0	1	0	0	0	1	1		.125	.222	.125	347	13	-1	0			1.000	-1	/O-2(0-2-0)	-0.2
Total	10	866	3306	580	962	83	47	16	255	440		.291	.379	.359	738	117	92	143			.954	44	O-855(99-707-49)	8.7
■ JOHN BARRETT Barrett, John b: Brooklyn, N.Y. Deb: 9/18/1872																								
1872	Atl-n	8	34	7	7	1	0	0	2	0	1	.206	.206	.235	441	30	-3	1	0	0	.808	-0	/O-8(8-0-0)	-0.2
■ JOHNNY BARRETT Barrett, John Joseph "Jack" b: 12/18/15, Lowell, Mass. d: 8/17/74, Seabrook Beach, N.H. BL/TL, 5'10.5", 170 lbs. Deb: 4/14/42																								
1942	Pit-N	111	332	56	82	11	6	0	26	48	42	.247	.347	.316	664	92	-1	10			.973	6	O-94(15-5-74)	-0.1
1943	Pit-N	130	290	41	67	12	3	1	32	32	23	.231	.316	.303	619	77	-8	5			.988	-11	O-99(4-3-92)	-2.6
1944	Pit-N	149	568	99	153	24	**19**	7	83	86	56	.269	.366	.415	782	115	13	**28**			.972	-1	*O-147(1-67-92)	0.4
1945	Pit-N	142	507	97	130	29	4	15	67	79	68	.256	.357	.418	775	111	8	25			.976	-2	*O-132(0-75-57)	0.0
1946	Pit-N	32	71	7	12	3	0	0	6	8	11	.169	.253	.211	464	32	-6	1			.919	-3	O-21(0-12-9)	-1.1
	Bos-N	24	43	3	10	3	0	0	6	12	1	.233	.400	.302	702	100	1	0			.962	-3	O-17(2-11-4)	-0.3
	Yr	56	114	10	22	6	0	0	12	20	12	.193	.313	.246	559	59	-6	1			.937	-6	O-38(2-23-13)	-1.4
Total	5	588	1811	303	454	82	32	23	220	265	201	.251	.349	.369	718	100	5	69			.974	-15	O-510(22-173-328)	-3.7
■ MARTY BARRETT Barrett, Martin F. b: 11/1860, Port Henry, N.Y. d: 1/29/10, Holyoke, Mass. BR/TR, 5'9", 170 lbs. Deb: 6/24/1884																								
1884	Bos-N	3	6	0	0	0	0	0	0	0	4	.000	.000	.000	0	-99	-1				.900	-1	/C-3	-0.2
	Ind-a	5	13	1	1	1	0	0		1		.077	.143	.154	297	-3	-1				.808	-3	/C-4,O-1(0-0-2)	-0.4
Total	1	8	19	1	1	1	0	0	0	1	4	.053	.100	.105	205	-34	-3				.833	-4	/C-7,O-1(0-0-2)	-0.6
■ MARTY BARRETT Barrett, Martin Glenn b: 6/23/58, Arcadia, Cal. BR/TR, 5'10", 176 lbs. Deb: 9/6/82 F																								
1982	Bos-A	8	18	0	1	0	0	0	0	0	1	.056	.056	.056	111	-66	-4	0	0	0	1.000	5	/2-7	0.1
1983	Bos-A	33	44	7	10	1	1	0	2	3	1	.227	.277	.295	572	54	-3	0	0	0	.984	4	2-23/D-5	0.2
1984	Bos-A	139	475	56	144	23	3	3	45	42	25	.303	.361	.383	744	101	2	5	3	0	**.987**	0	*2-136	0.9
1985	Bos-A	156	534	59	142	26	0	5	56	56	50	.266	.338	.343	681	84	-11	7	5	-0	.987	15	*2-155	1.2
1986	*Bos-A	158	625	94	179	39	4	4	60	65	31	.286	.355	.381	735	100	1	15	7	1	.982	-3	*2-158	0.8
1987	Bos-A	137	559	72	164	23	0	3	43	51	38	.293	.354	.351	704	85	-10	15	2	3	**.988**	**32**	*2-137	3.0
1988	*Bos-A	150	612	83	173	28	1	1	65	40	35	.283	.334	.337	670	85	-12	7	3	0	.990	2	*2-150	-0.5
1989	Bos-A	86	336	31	86	18	0	1	27	32	12	.256	.324	.318	643	77	-10	4	1	1	.975	1	2-80/D-4	-0.6
1990	*Bos-A	62	159	15	36	4	0	0	13	15	13	.226	.297	.252	549	53	-10	4	0	1	.992	9	2-60/3-1,D-1	0.1
1991	SD-N	12	16	1	3	1	0	1	3	0	3	.188	.235	.438	673	83	-0	0	0	0	1.000	1	/2-2,3-2	0.0
Total	10	941	3378	418	938	163	9	18	314	304	209	.278	.340	.347	687	86	-56	57	21	5	.986	66	2-908/D-10,3-3	5.2

YEAR	TM/L	G	AB	R	H	2B	3B	HR	RBI	BB	SO	AVG	OBP	SLG	OPS	OPS+	BR+	SB	CS	SBR	FA	FR	G/POS	TPR
■ MICHAEL BARRETT	Barrett, Michael Patrick b: 10/22/76, Atlanta, Ga. BR/TR, 6'3", 185 lbs. Deb: 9/19/98																							
1998	Mon-N	8	23	3	7	2	0	1	2	3	6	.304	.407	.522	929	144	2	0	0	0	.963	-1	/C-3,3-3	0.1
1999	Mon-N	126	433	53	127	32	3	8	52	32	39	.293	.346	.436	783	99	-1	0	2	-1	.943	-15	3-66,C-59/S-2	-1.3
2000	Mon-N	89	271	28	58	15	1	1	22	23	35	.214	.278	.288	566	43	-24	0	1	-0	.891	-9	3-55,C-28	-3.0
Total	3	223	727	84	192	49	4	10	76	58	80	.264	.323	.384	707	79	-23	0	3	-1	.915	-24	3-124/C-90,S-2	-4.2
■ BOB BARRETT	Barrett, Robert Schley "Jumbo" b: 1/27/1899, Atlanta, Ga. d: 1/18/82, Atlanta, Ga. BR/TR, 5'11", 175 lbs. Deb: 4/30/23 Career OF: (1-LF 0-CF 0-RF)																							
1923	Chi-N	3	3	0	1	0	0	0	0	0	0	.333	.333	.333	667	76	-0	0	0	0	.000	0	H	0.0
1924	Chi-N	54	133	12	32	2	3	5	21	7	29	.241	.279	.414	692	82	-4	1	0	0	.943	-1	2-25,1-10/3-8	-0.4
1925	Chi-N	14	32	1	10	1	0	0	7	1	4	.313	.333	.344	677	72	-1	1	2	-0	1.000	-3	/3-6,2-4	-0.4
	Bro-N	1	1	0	0	0	0	0	1	0	0	.000	.000	.000	0	-99	-0	0	0	0	.000	0	H	0.0
	Yr	15	33	1	10	1	0	0	8	1	4	.303	.324	.333	657	67	-2	1	2	-0	1.000	-3	/3-6,2-4	-0.4
1927	Bro-N	99	355	29	92	10	2	5	38	14	22	.259	.289	.341	630	68	-17	1			.920	-8	3-96	-1.8
1929	Bos-A	68	126	15	34	10	0	0	19	10	6	.270	.324	.349	673	75	-5	3	1	0	.938	6	3-34/1-4,2-2,O-1L	0.2
Total	5	239	650	57	169	23	5	10	86	32	61	.260	.296	.357	653	72	-27	6	3		.924	-6	3-144/2-31,1-14,O-1L	-2.4
■ TOM BARRETT	Barrett, Thomas Loren b: 4/2/60, San Fernando, Cal. BB/TR, 5'9", 157 lbs. Deb: 7/2/88 F																							
1988	Phi-N	36	54	5	11	1	0	0	3	7	8	.204	.306	.222	529	53	-3	0	0	0	.959	2	2-10	-0.1
1989	Phi-N	14	27	3	6	0	0	0	1	1	7	.222	.250	.222	472	36	-2	0	0	0	.978	4	/2-9	0.2
1992	Bos-A	4	3	1	0	0	0	0	0	2	0	.000	.400	.000	400	19	-0	0	0	0	1.000	1	/2-2	0.0
Total	3	54	84	9	17	1	0	0	4	10	15	.202	.295	.214	509	47	-5	0	0	0	.970	7	/2-21	0.1
■ BILL BARRETT	Barrett, William b: Washington, D.C. Deb: 7/8/1871 Career OF: (0-LF 0-CF 1-RF)																							
1871	Kek-n	1	5	1	1	1	0	0	1	0	0	.200	.200	.400	600	66	-0	0	0	0	1.000	1	/C-1,3-1	0.0
1872	Oly-n	1	4	0	0	0	0	0	0	0	0	.000	.000	.000	0	-99	-1	0	0	0	.400	-1	/C-1	-0.2
1873	Bal-n	1	4	0	1	0	0	0	0	0	0	.250	.250	.250	500	49	-0	0	1	-0	.667	-1	/S-1,O-1(0-0-1)	-0.1
Total	3 n	3	13	1	2	1	0	0	1	0	0	.154	.154	.231	385	12	-1	0	1	-0	.769	-1	/C-2,O-1R,S-1,3-1	-0.3
■ BILL BARRETT	Barrett, William Joseph "Whispering Bill" b: 5/28/1900, Cambridge, Mass. d: 1/26/51, Cambridge, Mass. BR/TR, 6', 175 lbs. Deb: 5/13/21 Career OF: (74-LF 28-CF 400-RF)																							
1921	Phi-A	14	30	3	7	2	1	0	3	0	5	.233	.233	.367	600	51	-2	0	0	0	.925	2	/S-8,P-4,3-2,1-1	0.1
1923	Chi-A	44	162	17	44	7	2	2	23	9	24	.272	.310	.377	686	81	-5	12	3	2	.940	0	O-40(40-1-0)/3-1	-0.6
1924	Chi-A	119	406	52	110	18	5	2	56	30	38	.271	.326	.355	680	78	-14	15	10	-0	.904	-15	S-77,O-28(25-3-0)/3-8	-2.1
1925	Chi-A	81	245	44	89	23	3	3	40	24	27	.363	.420	.518	938	145	16	5	6	-1	.943	-7	2-41,O-27R/S-4,3-4	0.8
1926	Chi-A	111	368	46	113	31	4	6	61	25	26	.307	.353	.462	815	115	6	9	7	-0	.969	-6	*O-102(1-0-102)/1-2	-0.7
1927	Chi-A	147	556	62	159	35	9	4	83	52	46	.286	.347	.403	750	96	-4	20	13	-0	.963	7	*O-147(0-12-136)	-0.8
1928	Chi-A	76	235	34	65	11	2	3	26	14	30	.277	.320	.379	699	84	-6	8	3	1	.988	-5	O-37(4-1-32),2-25	-1.2
1929	Chi-A	3	1	0	0	0	0	0	0	2	0	.000	.667	.000	667	87	0	0	0	0	.000	0	H	0.0
	Bos-A	111	370	57	100	23	4	3	35	51	38	.270	.363	.378	742	93	-2	11	8	-0	.974	4	*O-109(1-10-101)/3-1	-0.7
	Yr	114	371	57	100	23	4	3	35	53	38	.270	.365	.377	743	94	-2	11	8	-0	.974	4	*O-109(1-10-101)/3-1	-0.7
1930	Bos-A	6	18	3	3	1	0	0	1	1	3	.167	.211	.222	433	10	-2	0	0	0	1.000	-1	/O-5(0-0-5)	-0.4
	Was-A	6	4	0	0	0	0	0	0	1	2	.000	.200	.000	200	-44	-1	0	0	0	1.000	-0	/O-1(0-0-1)	-0.1
	Yr	12	22	3	3	1	0	0	1	2	5	.136	.208	.182	390	-0	-3	0	0	0	1.000	-1	/O-6(0-0-6)	-0.5
Total	9	718	2395	318	690	151	30	23	328	209	239	.288	.347	.405	752	97	-13	80	50	0	.964	-21	O-496R/S-89,2-66,3P1	-5.7
■ JOSE BARRIOS	Barrios, Jose Manuel b: 6/26/57, New York, N.Y. BR/TR, 6'4", 195 lbs. Deb: 4/23/82																							
1982	SF-N	10	19	2	3	0	0	0	0	1	4	.158	.200	.158	358	1	-2	0	0	0	1.000	-1	/1-7	-0.4
■ TONY BARRON	Barron, Anthony Dirk b: 8/17/66, Portland, Ore. BR/TR, 6', 185 lbs. Deb: 6/2/96																							
1996	Mon-N	1	1	0	0	0	0	0	0	0	1	.000	.000	.000	0	-98	-0	0	0	0	.000	0	/H	0.0
1997	Phi-N	57	189	22	54	12	1	4	24	12	38	.286	.335	.423	758	97	-1	0	1	-0	.983	6	O-53(0-0-53)	0.2
Total	2	58	190	22	54	12	1	4	24	12	39	.284	.333	.421	754	96	-1	0	1	-0	.983	6	/O-53(0-0-53)	0.2
■ RED BARRON	Barron, David Irenus b: 6/21/1900, Clarksville, Ga. d: 10/4/82, Atlanta, Ga. BR/TR, 5'11.5", 185 lbs. Deb: 6/10/29																							
1929	Bos-N	10	21	3	4	1	0	0	1	1	4	.190	.227	.238	465	16	-3	2			.929	1	/O-6(6-0-0)	-0.2
■ FRANK BARROWS	Barrows, Franklin L. b: 10/22/1846, Hudson, Ohio d: 2/6/22, Fitchburg, Mass. Deb: 5/20/1871																							
1871	Bos-n	18	86	13	13	2	1	0	11	0	0	.151	.151	.198	349	-1	-11	1	0	0	.829	-2	O-17(13-0-4)/2-1	-0.8
■ CUKE BARROWS	Barrows, Roland b: 10/20/1883, Gray, Maine d: 2/10/55, Gorham, Maine BL/TR, 5'8", 158 lbs. Deb: 9/18/09																							
1909	Chi-A	5	20	1	3	0	0	0	2	0		.150	.190	.150	340	8	-2	0			.923	2	/O-5(5-0-0)	-0.1
1910	Chi-A	6	20	0	4	0	0	0	1	3		.200	.304	.200	504	61	-1	0			.875	-1	/O-6(6-0-0)	-0.3
1911	Chi-A	13	46	5	9	2	0	0	4	7		.196	.315	.239	554	57	-2	2			1.000	-2	O-13(0-0-13)	-0.5
1912	Chi-A	8	13	0	3	0	0	0	2	2		.231	.333	.231	564	64	-0	1			1.000	-0	/O-3(0-0-3)	-0.1
Total	4	32	99	6	19	2	0	0	9	12		.192	.292	.212	504	50	-6	3			.950	-2	/O-27(11-0-16)	-1.0
■ JEFF BARRY	Barry, Jeffrey Finas b: 9/22/69, Medford, Ore. BB/TR, 6'1", 190 lbs. Deb: 6/9/95																							
1995	NY-N	15	15	2	2	1	0	0	0	1	8	.133	.188	.200	388	2	-2	0	0	0	1.000	-0	/O-2(1-0-1)	-0.3
1998	Col-N	15	34	4	6	1	0	0	2	2	11	.176	.222	.206	428	11	-4	0	0	0	1.000	-1	O-10(1-8-5)	-0.6
1999	Col-N	74	168	19	45	16	0	5	26	19	29	.268	.349	.452	802	79	-5	0	4	-1	1.000	-4	O-56(14-32-15)	-1.1
Total	3	104	217	25	53	18	0	5	28	22	48	.244	.320	.396	716	65	-12	0	4	-1	1.000	-5	/O-68(16-40-21)	-2.0
■ SHAD BARRY	Barry, John C. b: 10/27/1878, Newburgh, N.Y. d: 11/27/36, Los Angeles, Cal. BR/TR, Deb: 5/30/1899 Career OF: (214-LF 39-CF 371-RF)																							
1899	Was-N	78	247	31	71	7	5	1	33	12		.287	.328	.368	697	92	-3	11			.946	-16	O-23L,1-22,S-13,3/2	-1.8
1900	Bos-N	81	254	40	66	10	7	1	37	13		.260	.301	.366	667	74	-10	9			.956	-16	O-24L,S-18,2-16,1/3	-2.5
1901	Bos-N	11	40	3	7	2	0	0	6	2		.175	.233	.225	458	30	-4	1			.926	-0	O-11(11-0-0)	-0.4
	Phi-N	67	252	35	62	10	0	1	22	15		.246	.294	.298	591	70	-10	13			.903	-13	2-35,3-16,O-13C,/S	-2.2
	Yr	78	292	38	69	12	0	1	28	17		.236	.285	.288	573	64	-13	14			.903	-13	2-35,O-24L,3-16,/S	-2.6
1902	Phi-N	138	543	65	156	20	6	3	58	44		.287	.343	.363	706	118	11	14			.939	-5	*O-137(7-0-130)/1-1	-0.1
1903	Phi-N	138	550	75	152	24	5	1	60	30		.276	.321	.344	664	92	-6	26			.970	-2	*O-107L,1-30/3-1	-1.4
1904	Phi-N	35	122	15	25	2	0	0	3	11		.205	.281	.221	503	58	-6	2			.979	13	O-32(11-6-15)/3-1	0.6
	Chi-N	73	263	29	69	7	2	1	26	17		.262	.310	.316	625	93	-2	12			.917	-1	O-30R,1-18,3-16,/S2	-0.5
	Yr	108	385	44	94	9	2	1	29	28		.244	.300	.286	586	82	-8	14			.955	12	O-62R,1-18,3-17,/S2	0.1
1905	Chi-N	27	104	10	22	2	0	0	10	5		.212	.255	.231	485	43	-7	5			.982	1	1-26	-0.8
	Cin-N	125	494	90	160	11	12	1	56	33		.324	.372	.401	773	118	10	16			.982	-7	*1-124/O-2(1-1-0)	0.1
	Yr	152	598	100	182	13	12	1	66	38		.304	.352	.371	723	105	3	21			.982	-7	*1-150/O-2(1-1-0)	-0.7
1906	Cin-N	73	279	38	80	10	5	1	33	26		.287	.354	.369	723	120	7	11			.993	1	1-43,O-30(14-7-9)	0.6
	StL-N	62	237	26	59	9	1	0	12	15		.249	.299	.295	595	89	-3	6			.930	-7	O-35(0-0-35),1-21/3-6	-1.3
	Yr	135	516	64	139	19	6	1	45	41		.269	.329	.335	664	107	4	17			.922	-6	O-65R,1-64/3-6	-0.7
1907	StL-N	81	294	30	73	5	2	0	19	28		.248	.320	.279	599	91	-2	4			.963	-6	O-81(0-0-81)	-1.4
1908	StL-N	74	268	24	61	8	1	0	11	19		.228	.286	.265	551	80	-6	9			.967	-1	O-69(0-0-69)/S-2	-1.1
	NY-N	37	67	5	10	1	1	0	5	9		.149	.260	.194	454	43	-4	1			.971	-6	O-31(20-0-10)	-1.3
	Yr	111	335	29	71	9	2	0	16	28		.212	.281	.251	531	71	-10	10			.968	-7	*O-100(20-0-79)/S-2	-2.4
Total	10	1100	4014	516	1073	128	47	10	391	279		.267	.321	.330	651	94	-35	140			.955	-65	O-625R,1-295/2-60,3S	-13.5
■ JACK BARRY	Barry, John Joseph b: 4/26/1887, Meriden, Conn. d: 4/23/61, Shrewsbury, Mass. BR/TR, 5'9", 158 lbs. Deb: 7/13/08 M																							
1908	Phi-A	40	135	13	30	4	3	0	8	10		.222	.291	.296	587	85	-2	5			.966	-11	2-20,S-14/3-3	-1.4
1909	Phi-A	124	409	56	88	11	2	1	23	44		.215	.307	.259	566	77	-9	17			.927	-31	*S-124	-4.1
1910	*Phi-A	145	487	64	126	19	5	3	60	52		.259	.336	.337	673	112	8	14			.916	-22	*S-145	-1.1
1911	*Phi-A	127	442	73	117	18	7	1	63	38		.265	.333	.344	677	90	-6	30			**.944**	-7	*S-127	-0.3
1912	Phi-A	140	483	75	126	19	9	0	55	47		.261	.335	.337	673	96	-2	22			.925	-6	*S-139	0.1
1913	*Phi-A	134	455	62	125	20	6	3	85	44	32	.275	.349	.365	714	111	7	15			.953	-8	*S-134	0.9

YEAR	TM/L	G	AB	R	H	2B	3B	HR	RBI	BB	SO	AVG	OBP	SLG	OPS	OPS+	BR+	SB	CS	SBR	FA	FR	G/POS	TPR
1914	*Phi-A	140	467	57	113	12	0	0	42	53	34	.242	.324	.268	592	81	-9	22	13	0	.947	5	*S-140	0.6
1915	Phi-A	54	194	16	43	6	2	0	15	15	9	.222	.284	.273	558	69	-8	6	5	-0	.952	-4	S-54	-0.9
	*Bos-A	78	248	30	65	13	2	0	26	24	11	.262	.342	.331	672	104	2	0			.962	-4	2-78	-0.1
	Yr	132	442	46	108	19	4	0	41	39	20	.244	.317	.305	622	89	-6	6	5	-0	.962	-9	2-78,S-54	-1.0
1916	Bos-A	94	330	28	67	6	1	0	20	17	24	.203	.277	.227	505	52	-19	8			.974	2	2-94	-1.8
1917	Bos-A	116	388	45	83	9	0	2	30	47	27	.214	.305	.253	558	71	-12	12			**.974**	-11	*2-116,M	-2.3
1919	Bos-A	31	108	13	26	5	1	0	2	5	5	.241	.293	.306	599	72	-4	2			.922	-7	2-31	-1.1
Total	11	1223	4146	532	1009	142	38	10	429	396	142	.243	.321	.303	624	88	-54	153	18		.935	-104	S-877,2-339/3-3	-11.5
■ **RICH BARRY**	Barry, Richard Donovan b: 9/12/40, Berkeley, Cal. BR/TR, 6'4", 205 lbs. Deb: 7/4/69																							
1969	Phi-N	20	32	4	6	1	0	0	0	5	6	.188	.316	.219	535	54	-2	0	0	0	.938	-0	/O-9(9-0-0)	-0.2
■ **KIMERA BARTEE**	Bartee, Kimera Anotchi b: 7/21/72, Omaha, Neb. BR/TR (BB 1998), 6', 175 lbs. Deb: 4/3/96																							
1996	Det-A	110	217	32	55	6	1	1	14	17	77	.253	.308	.304	612	56	-14	20	10	1	.991	-5	O-99(4-95-2)/D-2	-1.7
1997	Det-A	12	5	4	1	0	0	0	0	2	2	.200	.500	.200	700	93	0	3	1	0	1.000	-0	/O-6(3-3-0),D-3	-0.1
1998	Det-A	57	98	20	19	5	1	3	15	6	35	.194	.240	.357	598	52	-7	9	5	0	.964	-2	O-29(11-18-1),D-10	-0.9
1999	Det-A	41	77	11	15	1	3	0	3	9	20	.195	.279	.286	565	45	-6	3	3	-0	.985	-6	O-38(0-38-0)/D-1	-1.1
2000	Cin-N	11	4	2	0	0	0	0	0	0	2	.000	.200	.000	200	-42	-1	1	0	0	1.000	-1	/O-3(2-1-0)	-0.2
Total	5	231	401	69	90	12	5	4	32	34	136	.224	.288	.309	598	53	-29	36	19	1	.986	-16	O-175(20-155-3)/D-16	-4.0
■ **DICK BARTELL**	Bartell, Richard William "Rowdy Richard" b: 11/22/07, Chicago, Ill. d: 8/4/95, Alameda, Cal. BR/TR, 5'9", 160 lbs. Deb: 10/2/27 C																							
1927	Pit-N	1	2	0	0	0	0	0	0	2	0	.000	.500	.000	500	41	0	0			1.000	0	/S-1	0.0
1928	Pit-N	72	233	27	71	8	4	1	36	21	18	.305	.377	.386	763	96	-1	4			.974	2	2-39,S-27/3-1	0.5
1929	Pit-N	143	610	101	184	40	13	2	57	40	29	.302	.347	.420	766	87	-13	11			.953	4	S-74,2-70	0.1
1930	Pit-N	129	475	69	152	32	13	4	75	39	34	.320	.378	.467	845	102	2	8			.941	6	*S-126	1.9
1931	Phi-N	135	554	88	160	43	7	0	34	27	38	.289	.325	.392	717	85	-12	6			.948	3	*S-133/2-3	0.2
1932	Phi-N	154	614	118	189	48	7	1	53	64	47	.308	.379	.414	792	101	3	8			.963	10	*S-154	2.4
1933	Phi-N★	152	587	78	159	25	5	1	37	56	46	.271	.340	.336	675	83	-11	6			.951	9	*S-152	0.9
1934	Phi-N	146	604	102	187	30	4	0	37	64	59	.310	.384	.373	757	91	-4	13			.954	14	*S-146	2.0
1935	NY-N	137	539	60	141	28	4	14	53	37	52	.262	.316	.406	722	94	-5	5			.954	10	*S-137	1.4
1936	*NY-N	145	510	71	152	31	3	8	42	40	36	.298	.355	.418	773	109	6	6			.956	**45**	*S-144	**5.9**
1937	*NY-N★	128	516	91	158	38	2	14	62	40	38	.306	.362	.469	836	124	17	5			.958	**38**	*S-128	**6.2**
1938	NY-N	127	481	67	126	26	1	9	49	55	60	.262	.347	.376	724	98	-0	4			.952	22	*S-127	3.1
1939	Chi-N	105	336	37	80	24	2	3	34	42	25	.238	.335	.348	683	82	-8	6			.943	-5	*S-101/3-1	-0.5
1940	*Det-A	139	528	76	123	24	3	7	53	76	53	.233	.335	.330	665	67	-25	12	2	2	.953	12	*S-139	-0.1
1941	Det-A	5	12	0	2	1	0	0	1	2	2	.167	.333	.250	583	51	-1	0	1	-0	.920	1	/S-5	0.0
	NY-N	104	373	44	113	20	0	5	35	52	29	.303	.394	.397	791	121	12	6			.959	-10	3-84,S-21	0.6
1942	NY-N	90	316	53	77	10	3	5	24	44	34	.244	.351	.342	692	102	2	4			.965	1	3-52,S-31	0.8
1943	NY-N	99	337	48	91	14	0	5	28	47	27	.270	.371	.356	727	110	6	5			.980	18	3-54,S-33	2.9
1946	NY-N	5	2	0	0	0	0	0	0	0	0	.000	.000	.000	0	-99	-1	0			1.000	1	/3-4,2-2	0.0
Total	18	2016	7629	1130	2165	442	71	79	710	748	627	.284	.355	.391	747	96	-31	109	3		.953	178	*S-1679,3-196,2-114	28.3
■ **TONY BARTIROME**	Bartirome, Anthony Joseph b: 5/9/32, Pittsburgh, Pa. BL/TL, 5'10", 155 lbs. Deb: 4/19/52 C																							
1952	Pit-N	124	355	32	78	10	3	0	16	26	37	.220	.273	.265	538	48	-24	3	3	-0	.989	2	*1-118	-2.7
■ **BOYD BARTLEY**	Bartley, Boyd Owen b: 2/11/20, Chicago, Ill. BR/TR, 5'8.5", 165 lbs. Deb: 5/30/43																							
1943	Bro-N	9	21	0	1	0	0	0	1	1	3	.048	.091	.048	139	-59	-4	0			.897	2	/S-9	-0.2
■ **IRV BARTLING**	Bartling, Henry Irving b: 6/27/14, Bay City, Mich. d: 6/12/73, Westland, Mich. BR/TR, 6', 175 lbs. Deb: 9/8/38																							
1938	Phi-A	14	46	5	8	1	1	0	5	3	7	.174	.224	.239	464	17	-6	0	0	0	.914	-3	S-13/3-1	-0.7
■ **HARRY BARTON**	Barton, Harry Lamb b: 1/20/1875, Chester, Pa. d: 1/25/55, Upland, Pa. BB/TR, 5'6.5", 155 lbs. Deb: 4/15/05																							
1905	Phi-A	29	60	5	10	2	1	0	3	3		.167	.206	.233	440	39	-4	2			.954	-5	C-13/1-2,3-2,O-1R	-1.0
■ **BOB BARTON**	Barton, Robert Wilbur b: 7/30/41, Norwood, O. BR/TR, 6', 175 lbs. Deb: 9/17/65																							
1965	SF-N	4	7	1	4	0	0	0	1	0	0	.571	.571	.571	1143	217	1	0	0	0	1.000	1	/C-2	0.2
1966	SF-N	43	91	1	16	2	1	0	3	5	4	.176	.219	.220	439	22	-9	0	0	0	.994	-7	C-39	-0.1
1967	SF-N	7	19	0	4	0	0	0	1	0	2	.211	.250	.211	461	34	-2	0	0	0	1.000	-1	/C-7	-0.1
1968	SF-N	46	92	4	24	2	0	0	5	7	18	.261	.313	.283	596	80	-2	0	0	0	.995	12	C-45	1.2
1969	SF-N	49	106	5	18	2	0	0	1	9	19	.170	.241	.189	430	22	-11	0	0	0	.985	1	C-49	-1.0
1970	SD-N	61	188	15	41	6	0	4	16	15	37	.218	.279	.314	593	61	-11	1	1	-0	.995	7	C-59	-0.1
1971	SD-N	121	376	23	94	17	2	5	23	35	49	.250	.317	.346	663	94	-3	0	5	-2	.981	14	*C-119	1.5
1972	SD-N	29	88	1	17	1	0	0	9	2	19	.193	.211	.205	416	20	-9	2	0	0	.989	-0	C-29	-0.7
1973	Cin-N	3	1	0	0	0	0	0	0	1	0	.000	.500	.000	500	52	0	0	0	0	1.000	1	/C-2	0.1
1974	SD-N	30	81	4	19	1	0	0	7	13	19	.235	.340	.247	587	69	-3	0	0	0	.981	10	C-29	0.8
Total	10	393	1049	54	237	31	3	9	66	87	168	.226	.288	.287	575	65	-49	3	6	-1	.987	53	C-380	1.8
■ **VINCE BARTON**	Barton, Vincent David b: 2/1/08, Edmonton, Alberta, Canada d: 9/13/73, Toronto, Ont., Can BL/TR, 6', 180 lbs. Deb: 7/17/31																							
1931	Chi-N	66	239	45	57	10	1	13	50	21	40	.238	.323	.452	775	104	1	1			.964	-4	O-61(0-0-61)	-0.7
1932	Chi-N	36	134	19	30	2	3	3	15	8	22	.224	.273	.351	623	67	-6	0			1.000	-2	O-34(0-0-34)	-1.0
Total	2	102	373	64	87	12	4	16	65	29	62	.233	.306	.416	721	91	-6	1			.976	-6	/O-95(0-0-95)	-1.7
■ **DAVE BARTOSCH**	Bartosch, David Robert b: 3/24/17, St.Louis, Mo. BR/TR, 6'1", 190 lbs. Deb: 4/28/45																							
1945	StL-N	24	47	9	12	1	0	0	1	6	3	.255	.340	.277	616	71	-2	0			.964	1	O-11(4-0-7)	-0.2
■ **MONTY BASGALL**	Basgall, Romanus b: 2/8/22, Pfeifer, Kan. BR/TR, 5'10.5", 175 lbs. Deb: 4/19/48 C																							
1948	Pit-N	38	51	12	11	1	0	2	6	3	5	.216	.259	.353	612	63	-3	0			1.000	6	2-22	-0.3
1949	Pit-N	107	308	25	67	9	1	2	26	31	32	.218	.291	.273	564	51	-21	1			.972	-7	2-98/3-3	-2.4
1951	Pit-N	55	153	15	32	5	2	0	9	12	14	.209	.271	.268	539	44	-12	0	0		.969	11	2-55	0.1
Total	3	200	512	52	110	15	3	4	41	46	51	.215	.282	.279	561	50	-36	1	0		.973	9	2-175/3-3	-2.0
■ **AL BASHANG**	Bashang, Albert C. b: 8/22/1888, Cincinnati, Ohio d: 6/23/67, Cincinnati, Ohio BB/TR, 5'8", 150 lbs. Deb: 7/30/12																							
1912	Det-A	6	12	3	1	0	0	0	0	3		.083	.267	.083	350	2	-1	0			1.000	-1	/O-6(5-0-0)	-0.3
1918	Bro-N	2	5	0	1	0	0	0	0	0	0	.200	.200	.200	400	22	-0	0			1.000	0	/O-1	0.0
Total	2	8	17	3	2	0	0	0	0	3	0	.118	.250	.118	368	8	-2	0			1.000	-1	/O-7(5-0-0)	-0.3
■ **WALT BASHORE**	Bashore, Walter Franklin (b: Walter Franklin Beshore) b: 10/6/09, Harrisburg, Pa. d: 9/26/84, Sebring, Fla. BR/TR, 6', 170 lbs. Deb: 7/14/36																							
1936	Phi-N	10	10	1	2	0	0	0	0	1	3	.200	.273	.200	473	26	-1	0			1.000	-3	/O-6(0-6-0),3-1	-0.4
■ **EDDIE BASINSKI**	Basinski, Edwin Frank "Bazooka" or "Fiddler" b: 11/4/22, Buffalo, N.Y. BR/TR, 6'1", 172 lbs. Deb: 5/20/44																							
1944	Bro-N	39	105	13	27	4	1	0	9	6	10	.257	.310	.314	624	77	-3	1			.960	-2	2-37/S-3	-0.3
1945	Bro-N	108	336	30	88	9	4	0	33	11	33	.262	.293	.313	606	69	-15	0			.926	-10	*S-101/2-6	-1.7
1947	Pit-N	56	161	15	32	6	2	4	17	18	27	.199	.279	.335	615	61	-9	0			.972	-1	2-56	-0.8
Total	3	203	602	58	147	19	7	4	59	35	70	.244	.292	.319	611	68	-27	1			.925	-13	S-104/2-99	-2.8
■ **JOHN BASS**	Bass, John E. b: 1850, Baltimore, Md. 5'6", 150 lbs. Deb: 5/4/1871																							
1871	Cle-n	22	89	18	27	1	**10**	3	18	3	4	.303	.326	.640	967	179	9	0	1	-0	.779	-6	*S-22/C-1	0.1
1872	Atl-n	2	7	0	1	1	0	0	1	0	0	.143	.143	.286	429	24	-1	0	0	0	.500	-1	/O-2(0-0-2)	-0.1
1877	Har-N	1	4	1	1	0	0	0	0	0	0	.250	.250	.250	500	65	-0				.000	-1	/O-1(1-0-0)	0.0
Total	2 n	24	96	18	28	2	10	3	19	3	4	.292	.313	.615	928	166	8	0	1	-0	.779	-7	/S-22,O-2(0-0-2),C-1	0.0
■ **KEVIN BASS**	Bass, Kevin Charles b: 5/12/59, Redwood City, Cal. BB/TR, 6', 183 lbs. Deb: 4/9/82 Career OF: (209-LF 194-CF 953-RF)																							
1982	Mil-A	18	9	4	0	0	0	0	0	1	1	.000	.100	.000	100	-74	-2	0	0	0	1.000	-5	O-14(0-6-8)/D-2	-0.8

YEAR	TM/L	G	AB	R	H	2B	3B	HR	RBI	BB	SO	AVG	OBP	SLG	OPS	OPS+	BR+	SB	CS	SBR	FA	FR	G/POS	TPR
	Hou-N	12	24	2	1	0	0	0	1	0	8	.042	.042	.042	83	-83	-6	0	0	0	.917	-1	/O-7(4-4-0)	-0.8
1983	Hou-N	88	195	25	46	7	3	2	18	6	27	.236	.259	.333	592	67	-9	2	2	-0	.945	-6	O-52(0-5-47)	-1.9
1984	Hou-N	121	331	33	86	17	5	2	29	6	57	.260	.279	.360	639	84	-8	5	5	-1	.975	-2	O-81(0-31-52)	-1.5
1985	Hou-N	150	539	72	145	27	5	16	68	31	63	.269	.316	.427	743	109	5	19	8	1	**.997**	6	*O-141(10-105-39)	1.0
1986	*Hou-N★	157	591	83	184	33	5	20	79	38	72	.311	.359	.486	845	134	26	22	13	0	.984	4	*O-155(2-41-133)	2.4
1987	Hou-N	157	592	83	168	31	5	19	85	53	77	.284	.347	.449	796	113	10	21	8	2	.987	10	*O-155(0-0-155)	1.4
1988	Hou-N	157	541	57	138	27	2	14	72	42	65	.255	.316	.390	706	106	3	31	6	5	.979	2	*O-147(0-0-147)	0.6
1989	Hou-N	87	313	42	94	19	4	5	44	29	44	.300	.362	.435	796	131	12	11	4	1	.985	9	O-84(31-0-53)	2.1
1990	SF-N	61	214	25	54	9	1	7	32	14	26	.252	.304	.402	706	96	-2	2	2	-0	.968	-5	O-55(0-0-55)	-0.9
1991	SF-N	124	361	43	84	10	4	10	40	36	56	.233	.309	.366	675	92	-4	7	4	0	.977	-1	*O-101(23-0-79)	-0.9
1992	SF-N	89	265	25	71	11	3	7	30	16	53	.268	.312	.411	723	109	2	7	7	-1	.983	-5	O-72(56-0-21)	-0.7
	NY-N	46	137	15	37	12	2	2	9	7	17	.270	.306	.431	736	108	1	7	2	1	.987	1	O-39(28-0-13)	0.1
	Yr	135	402	40	108	23	5	9	39	23	70	.269	.310	.418	728	109	3	14	9	-0	.985	-5	*O-111(84-0-34)	-0.6
1993	Hou-N	111	229	31	65	18	0	3	37	26	31	.284	.359	.402	761	107	3	7	1	1	.989	-7	O-64(12-2-51)	-0.5
1994	Hou-N	82	203	37	63	15	1	6	35	28	24	.310	.397	.483	879	135	11	2	3	-1	.977	-4	O-57(11-0-47)	0.4
1995	Bal-A	111	295	32	72	12	0	5	32	24	47	.244	.305	.336	641	66	-15	8	8	-1	.984	-5	O-77(32-0-53),D-19	-2.4
Total	14	1571	4839	609	1308	248	40	118	611	357	668	.270	.325	.411	736	106	26	151	73	8	.982	-10	*O-1301R/D-21	-2.4

■ RANDY BASS Bass, Randy William b: 3/13/54, Lawton, Okla. BL/TR, 6′1″, 210 lbs. Deb: 9/3/77

YEAR	TM/L	G	AB	R	H	2B	3B	HR	RBI	BB	SO	AVG	OBP	SLG	OPS	OPS+	BR+	SB	CS	SBR	FA	FR	G/POS	TPR
1977	Min-A	9	19	0	2	0	0	0	0	0	5	.105	.105	.105	211	-43	-4	0	0	0	.000	0	/D-6	-0.4
1978	KC-A	2	2	0	0	0	0	0	0	0	0	.000	.000	.000	0	-97	-1	0	0	0	.000	0	H	-0.1
1979	Mon-N	2	1	0	0	0	0	0	0	0	0	.000	.000	.000	0	-99	-0	0	0	0	1.000	-0	/1-1	0.0
1980	SD-N	19	49	5	14	0	1	3	8	7	7	.286	.386	.510	896	157	4	0	0	0	.985	-1	1-15	0.2
1981	SD-N	69	176	13	37	4	1	4	20	20	28	.210	.294	.313	607	78	-5	0	1	-0	.993	2	1-50	-0.7
1982	SD-N	13	30	1	6	0	0	1	8	2	4	.200	.273	.300	573	63	-2	0	0	0	1.000	-1	/1-9	-0.3
	Tex-A	16	48	5	10	2	0	1	6	1	7	.208	.240	.313	553	53	-3	0	0	0	1.000	-0	/1-6,D-7	-0.4
Total	6	130	325	24	69	6	2	9	42	30	51	.212	.287	.326	613	76	-11	0	1	-0	.993	-0	/1-81,D-13	-1.7

■ DOC BASS Bass, William Capers (also played one game in 1918 under name of Johnson)
b: 12/4/1899, Macon, Ga. d: 1/12/70, Macon, Ga. BL/TL, 5′10″, 165 lbs. Deb: 7/29/18

YEAR	TM/L	G	AB	R	H	2B	3B	HR	RBI	BB	SO	AVG	OBP	SLG	OPS	OPS+	BR+	SB	CS	SBR	FA	FR	G/POS	TPR
1918	Bos-N	2	1	1	1	0	0	0	0	0	0	1.000	1.000	1.000	2000	533	0	1			.000	0	/H	0.1

■ CHARLEY BASSETT Bassett, Charles Edwin b: 2/9/1863, Central Falls, R.I. d: 5/28/42, Pawtucket, R.I. BR/TR, 5′10″, 150 lbs. Deb: 7/22/1884 Career OF: (1-LF 1-CF 0-RF)

YEAR	TM/L	G	AB	R	H	2B	3B	HR	RBI	BB	SO	AVG	OBP	SLG	OPS	OPS+	BR+	SB	CS	SBR	FA	FR	G/POS	TPR
1884	Pro-N	27	79	10	11	2	1	0	6	4	15	.139	.181	.190	371	17	-7				.815	0	3-13/S-7,O-2L,2-1	-0.6
1885	Pro-N	82	285	21	41	8	2	0	16	19	60	.144	.197	.186	383	25	-23				.900	5	2-39,S-23,3-20,/C-1	-1.4
1886	KC-N	90	342	41	89	19	8	2	32	36	43	.260	.331	.380	711	109	3	6			.886	8	S-82/3-8	1.2
1887	Ind-N	119	477	41	129	14	6	1	47	25	31	.270	.278	.294	572	61	-23	25			**.931**	16	*2-119	-0.2
1888	Ind-N	128	481	58	116	20	3	2	60	32	41	.241	.297	.308	604	91	-4	24			.922	-16	*2-128	-1.5
1889	Ind-N	127	477	64	117	12	5	4	68	37	38	.245	.304	.317	620	72	-18	15			.937	11	*2-127	-0.3
1890	NY-N	100	410	52	98	13	8	0	54	29	25	.239	.300	.310	610	78	-12	14			**.952**	12	*2-100	0.3
1891	NY-N	130	524	60	136	19	8	4	68	36	29	.260	.312	.349	661	96	-3	16			**.908**	8	*3-121/2-9	0.7
1892	NY-N	35	130	9	27	2	3	0	16	6	11	.208	.254	.269	523	59	-7	0			.938	9	2-30/3-5	0.4
	Lou-N	79	313	36	67	5	5	2	35	15	19	.214	.250	.281	531	66	-14	16			.861	-0	3-73/2-6	-1.2
	Yr	114	443	45	94	7	8	2	51	21	30	.212	.251	.278	529	64	-20	16			.858	9	3-78,2-36	-0.8
Total	9	917	3518	392	831	114	49	15	402	239	312	.236	.285	.304	590	75	-108	116			.932	53	2-559,3-240,S/OC	-2.6

■ JOHNNY BASSLER Bassler, John Landis b: 6/3/1895, Mechanics Grove, Pa. d: 6/29/79, Santa Monica, Cal BL/TR, 5′9″, 170 lbs. Deb: 7/11/13 C

YEAR	TM/L	G	AB	R	H	2B	3B	HR	RBI	BB	SO	AVG	OBP	SLG	OPS	OPS+	BR+	SB	CS	SBR	FA	FR	G/POS	TPR
1913	Cle-A	1	2	0	0	0	0	0	0	0	0	.000	.000	.000	0	-97	-0	0			.500	-1	/C-1	-0.2
1914	Cle-A	43	77	5	14	1	1	0	6	15	8	.182	.323	.221	543	61	-3	3	2	-0	.946	-1	C-25/3-1,O-1(0-0-1)	-0.2
1921	Det-A	119	388	37	119	18	5	0	56	58	16	.307	.401	.379	780	101	3	2	1	0	.975	2	*C-114	1.2
1922	Det-A	121	372	41	120	14	0	0	41	62	12	.323	.422	.360	782	109	9	2	1	0	.980	-3	*C-118	1.4
1923	Det-A	135	383	45	114	12	3	0	49	76	13	.298	.414	.345	759	103	7	2	2	-0	.988	12	*C-128	2.5
1924	Det-A	124	379	43	131	20	3	1	68	62	11	.346	.441	.422	864	125	18	2	1	0	.979	-4	*C-122	2.1
1925	Det-A	121	344	40	96	19	3	0	52	74	6	.279	.408	.352	760	96	2	1	1	-0	.983	-8	*C-118	0.1
1926	Det-A	66	174	20	53	8	1	0	22	45	6	.305	.447	.362	810	111	6	0	0	0	1.000	2	C-63	1.2
1927	Det-A	81	200	19	57	7	0	0	24	45	9	.285	.416	.320	736	92	0	1	0	0	.974	-2	C-67	0.3
Total	9	811	2319	250	704	99	16	1	318	437	81	.304	.416	.361	777	104	42	13	8		.980	-1	C-756/O-1(0-0-1),3-1	8.4

■ CHARLIE BASTIAN Bastian, Charles J. b: 7/4/1860, Philadelphia, Pa. d: 1/18/32, Pennsauken, N.J. BR/TR, 5′6.5″, 145 lbs. Deb: 8/18/1884

YEAR	TM/L	G	AB	R	H	2B	3B	HR	RBI	BB	SO	AVG	OBP	SLG	OPS	OPS+	BR+	SB	CS	SBR	FA	FR	G/POS	TPR
1884	Wil-U	17	60	6	12	1	3	2		3		.200	.238	.417	655	92	-3				.907	10	2-16/P-1,S-1	0.7
	KC-U	11	46	6	9	3	0	1		4		.196	.260	.326	586	88	-2				.950	-1	2-11	-0.2
	Yr	28	106	12	21	4	3	3		7		.198	.248	.377	625	90	-5				.923	10	2-27/P-1,S-1	0.5
1885	Phi-N	103	389	63	65	11	5	4	29	35	82	.167	.236	.252	488	59	-17				.890	6	*S-103	-0.7
1886	Phi-N	105	373	46	81	9	11	2	38	33	73	.217	.281	.316	597	81	-9	29			**.945**	-5	*2-87,S-10/3-8	-0.9
1887	Phi-N	60	240	33	66	11	1	1	21	19	29	.275	.284	.285	569	55	-14	11			.921	-13	2-39,S-18/3-4	-2.1
1888	Phi-N	80	275	30	53	4	1	1	17	27	41	.193	.282	.225	507	60	-11	12			.945	12	2-65,3-14/S-1	0.3
1889	Chi-N	46	155	19	21	0	0	0	10	25	46	.135	.256	.135	391	10	-18	1			.919	6	S-45/2-1	-1.0
1890	Chi-P	80	283	38	54	10	5	0	29	33	37	.191	.287	.261	548	45	-23	4			.880	-10	S-64,2-12/3-4	-2.4
1891	Cin-a	1	4	0	0	0	0	0	0	0	0	.000	.000	.000	0	-92	-1	0			1.000	1	/2-1	0.0
	Phi-N	1	0	0	0	0	0	0	0	0	0	—	—	—	—	—	0	0			1.000	0	/S-1	0.0
Total	8	504	1825	241	361	49	26	11	144	179	308	.198	.268	.264	532	57	-97	57			.892	7	S-243,2-232/3-30,P	-6.3

■ EMIL BATCH Batch, Emil "Heinie" or "Ace" b: 1/21/1880, Brooklyn, N.Y. d: 8/23/26, Brooklyn, N.Y. BR/TR, 5′7″, 170 lbs. Deb: 9/13/04 Career OF: (128-LF 1-CF 23-RF)

YEAR	TM/L	G	AB	R	H	2B	3B	HR	RBI	BB	SO	AVG	OBP	SLG	OPS	OPS+	BR+	SB	CS	SBR	FA	FR	G/POS	TPR
1904	Bro-N	28	94	9	24	1	2	2	7	1		.255	.271	.372	643	100	-1	6			.880	-2	3-28	-0.2
1905	Bro-N	145	568	64	143	20	11	5	49	26		.252	.285	.352	637	96	-5	21			.887	-8	*3-145	-1.0
1906	Bro-N	59	203	23	52	7	6	0	11	15		.256	.311	.350	660	115	3	3			.964	1	O-50(47-0-3)/3-2	0.1
1907	Bro-N	116	388	38	96	10	3	0	31	23		.247	.291	.289	580	89	-6	7			.937	-3	*O-102L/3-2,2-1,S-1	-1.6
Total	4	348	1253	134	315	38	22	7	98	65		.251	.290	.334	624	98	-8	37			.886	-12	3-177,O-152L/S-1,2	-2.7

■ JOHN BATEMAN Bateman, John Alvin b: 7/21/40, Killeen, Tex. d: 12/3/96, Sand Springs, Tex. BR/TR, 6′3″, 220 lbs. Deb: 4/19/63

YEAR	TM/L	G	AB	R	H	2B	3B	HR	RBI	BB	SO	AVG	OBP	SLG	OPS	OPS+	BR+	SB	CS	SBR	FA	FR	G/POS	TPR
1963	Hou-N	128	404	23	85	8	6	10	59	13	103	.210	.251	.334	585	71	-16	0	0	0	.971	2	*C-115	-0.9
1964	Hou-N	74	221	18	42	8	0	5	19	17	48	.190	.251	.294	545	56	-13	0	1	-0	.987	6	C-72	-0.4
1965	Hou-N	45	142	15	28	3	1	7	14	12	37	.197	.260	.380	640	83	-4	0	1	-0	.985	0	C-39	-0.2
1966	Hou-N	131	433	39	121	24	3	17	70	20	74	.279	.319	.467	785	123	12	0	0	0	.981	1	*C-121	2.0
1967	Hou-N	76	252	16	48	9	0	2	17	17	53	.190	.247	.250	497	44	-18	0	0	0	.989	1	C-71	-1.5
1968	Hou-N	111	350	28	87	19	0	4	33	23	46	.249	.301	.337	638	93	-3	1	1	-0	.985	-2	*C-108	-0.1
1969	Mon-N	74	235	16	49	4	0	8	19	12	44	.209	.250	.328	578	60	-13	0	2	-1	.985	-0	C-66	-1.2
1970	Mon-N	139	520	51	123	21	5	15	68	28	75	.237	.277	.383	660	75	-20	8	4	0	.983	-2	*C-137	-1.5
1971	Mon-N	139	492	34	119	17	3	10	56	19	87	.242	.276	.350	625	76	-17	1	1	0	.985	-9	*C-137	-2.0
1972	Mon-N	18	29	0	7	1	0	0	3	3	4	.241	.313	.276	588	67	-1	0	0	0	1.000	-2	/C-7	-0.3
	Phi-N	82	252	10	56	9	0	3	17	8	39	.222	.249	.294	543	52	-16	0	1	-0	.972	1	C-80	-1.3
	Yr	100	281	10	63	10	0	3	20	11	43	.224	.256	.292	548	54	-17	0	1	-0	.973	-1	C-87	-1.6
Total	10	1017	3330	250	765	123	18	81	375	172	610	.230	.273	.350	624	77	-110	10	10	-1	.982	-2	C-953	-7.4

■ CHARLIE BATES Bates, Charles William b: 9/17/07, Philadelphia, Pa. d: 1/29/80, Topeka, Kan. BR/TR, 5′10″, 165 lbs. Deb: 9/22/27

YEAR	TM/L	G	AB	R	H	2B	3B	HR	RBI	BB	SO	AVG	OBP	SLG	OPS	OPS+	BR+	SB	CS	SBR	FA	FR	G/POS	TPR
1927	Phi-A	9	38	5	9	2	2	0	2	3	5	.237	.293	.395	687	73	-2	3	1	0	.857	-0	/O-9(0-1-8)	-0.2

■ DEL BATES Bates, Delbert Oakley b: 6/12/40, Seattle, Wash. BL/TR, 6′2″, 195 lbs. Deb: 5/6/70

YEAR	TM/L	G	AB	R	H	2B	3B	HR	RBI	BB	SO	AVG	OBP	SLG	OPS	OPS+	BR+	SB	CS	SBR	FA	FR	G/POS	TPR
1970	Phi-N	22	60	1	8	2	0	0	1	6	15	.133	.257	.167	424	16	-7	0	1	-0	.992	-4	C-20	-1.0

■ BUD BATES Bates, Hubert Edgar b: 3/16/12, Los Angeles, Cal. d: 4/29/87, Long Beach, Cal. BR/TR, 6′, 165 lbs. Deb: 9/16/39

YEAR	TM/L	G	AB	R	H	2B	3B	HR	RBI	BB	SO	AVG	OBP	SLG	OPS	OPS+	BR+	SB	CS	SBR	FA	FR	G/POS	TPR
1939	Phi-N	15	58	8	15	2	0	1	2	2	8	.259	.283	.345	628	70	-3	1			.978	3	O-14(1-13-0)	0.0

YEAR	TM/L	G	AB	R	H	2B	3B	HR	RBI	BB	SO	AVG	OBP	SLG	OPS	OPS+	BR+	SB	CS	SBR	FA	FR	G/POS	TPR
■ **JASON BATES** Bates, Jason Charles b: 1/5/71, Downey, Cal. BB/TR, 5'11", 170 lbs. Deb: 4/26/95																								
1995	*Col-N	116	322	42	86	17	4	8	46	42	70	.267	.355	.419	774	80	-8	3	6	-1	.991	10	2-82,S-20,3-15	0.4
1996	Col-N	88	160	19	33	8	1	1	9	23	34	.206	.314	.287	601	48	-12	2	1	0	.978	0	2-37,S-18,3-12	-0.9
1997	Col-N	62	121	17	29	10	0	3	11	15	27	.240	.338	.397	735	74	-4	0	1	-0	1.000	-5	2-22,S-16/3-6	-0.7
1998	Col-N	53	74	10	14	3	0	0	3	8	21	.189	.268	.230	498	27	-8	0	0	0	.974	-5	2-17/3-3,S-3	-1.2
Total	4	319	677	88	162	38	5	12	69	88	152	.239	.333	.363	696	66	-32	5	8	-2	.987	1	2-158/S-57,3-36	-2.4
■ **JOHNNY BATES** Bates, John William b: 1/10/1884, Steubenville, Ohio d: 2/10/49, Steubenville, Ohio BL/TL, 5'7", 168 lbs. Deb: 4/12/06																								
1906	Bos-N	140	504	52	127	21	5	6	54	36		.252	.315	.349	664	110	5	9			.958	-10	*O-140(7-133-0)	-1.4
1907	Bos-N	126	447	52	116	18	12	2	49	39		.260	.329	.367	695	118	9	11			.979	-2	*O-120(1-1-118)	0.1
1908	Bos-N	127	445	48	115	14	6	1	29	35		.258	.315	.324	639	106	3	25			.948	-4	*O-117(101-8-8)	-0.8
1909	Bos-N	63	236	27	68	15	3	1	23	20		.288	.354	.390	744	125	7	15			.945	5	O-60(60-0-0)	0.9
	Phi-N	77	266	43	78	11	1	1	15	28		.293	.365	.353	718	122	7	22			.959	-2	O-73(11-62-0)	0.2
	Yr	140	502	70	146	26	4	2	38	48		.291	.360	.371	730	123	14	37			.952	3	*O-133(71-62-0)	1.1
1910	Phi-N	135	498	91	152	26	11	3	61	61	49	.305	.385	.420	805	130	20	31			.954	12	*O-131(25-103-3)	2.6
1911	Cin-N	148	518	89	151	24	13	1	61	103	59	.292	.415	.394	808	131	28	33			.966	5	*O-147(0-145-2)	2.3
1912	Cin-N	81	239	45	69	12	7	1	29	47	16	.289	.406	.410	816	127	11	10			.950	7	O-65(1-64-0)	1.3
1913	Cin-N	131	407	63	113	13	7	6	51	67	30	.278	.387	.388	776	122	15	21			.946	4	*O-111(0-24-88)	1.3
1914	Cin-N	58	155	29	39	7	5	2	15	28	17	.252	.380	.400	780	128	6	4			.913	-6	O-54(0-54-0)	-0.3
	Chi-N	9	8	2	1	0	0	0	1	1	1	.125	.300	.125	425	28	-1	0			1.000	-0	/O-3(0-2-1)	-0.1
	Yr	67	163	31	40	7	5	2	16	29	18	.245	.376	.387	762	124	6	4			.917	-6	O-57(0-56-1)	-0.4
	Bal-F	59	190	24	58	6	3	1	29	38	18	.305	.429	.384	813	119	5	6			.950	-1	O-59(12-48-0)	0.0
Total	9	1154	3913	565	1087	167	73	25	417	503	190	.278	.367	.377	744	121	114	187			.955	9	*O-1080(218-644-220)	6.1
■ **RAY BATES** Bates, Raymond b: 2/8/1890, Paterson, N.J. d: 8/15/70, Tucson, Ariz. BR/TR, 6', 165 lbs. Deb: 5/31/13																								
1913	Cle-A	27	30	4	5	0	2	0	4	3	9	.167	.265	.300	565	63	-1	3			.905	-0	3-12/O-2(0-2-0)	-0.1
1917	Phi-A	127	485	47	115	20	7	2	66	21	39	.237	.277	.320	597	83	-12	12			.933	6	*3-124	-0.2
Total	2	154	515	51	120	20	9	2	70	24	48	.233	.277	.318	595	82	-13	15			.932	6	3-136/O-2(0-2-0)	-0.3
■ **BILLY BATES** Bates, William Derrick b: 12/7/63, Houston, Tex. BL/TR, 5'7", 155 lbs. Deb: 8/17/89																								
1989	Mil-A	7	14	3	3	0	0	0	0	0	1	.214	.214	.214	429	21	-1	2	0	0	.938	4	/2-7	0.3
1990	Mil-A	14	29	6	3	1	0	0	2	4	7	.103	.212	.138	350	-0	-4	4	0	1	.962	3	2-14	0.0
	*Cin-N	8	5	2	0	0	0	0	0	0	2	.000	.000	.000	0	-96	-1	2	1	0	1.000	0	/2-1	-0.1
Total	2	29	48	11	6	1	0	0	2	4	10	.125	.192	.146	338	-4	-7	8	1	1	.953	7	/2-22	0.2
■ **BILL BATHE** Bathe, William David b: 10/14/60, Downey, Cal. BR/TR, 6'2", 200 lbs. Deb: 4/12/86																								
1986	Oak-A	39	103	9	19	3	0	5	11	2	20	.184	.208	.359	567	55	-7	0	0	0	.991	1	C-39	-0.5
1989	*SF-N	30	32	3	9	1	0	0	6	0	7	.281	.281	.313	594	72	-1	0	0	0	1.000	-1	/C-7	-0.2
1990	SF-N	52	48	3	11	0	1	3	12	7	12	.229	.327	.458	786	118	1	0	0	0	1.000	-1	/C-8	0.0
Total	3	121	183	15	39	4	1	8	29	9	39	.213	.254	.377	631	75	-7	0	0	0	.992	-1	/C-54	-0.7
■ **TONY BATISTA** Batista, Leocadio Francisco b: 12/9/73, Puerto Plata, D.R. BR/TR, 6', 180 lbs. Deb: 6/3/96																								
1996	Oak-A	74	238	38	71	10	2	6	25	19	49	.298	.353	.433	785	99	-0	7	3	0	.988	10	2-52,3-18/S-4,D-4	1.2
1997	Oak-A	68	188	22	38	10	1	4	18	14	31	.202	.265	.330	594	55	-13	2	2	-0	.970	11	S-61/3-4,2-1,D-1	0.2
1998	Ari-N	106	293	46	80	16	1	18	41	18	52	.273	.322	.519	840	117	6	1	1	-0	.994	1	2-41,S-34,3-15	1.1
1999	Ari-N	44	144	16	37	5	0	5	21	16	17	.257	.340	.396	735	85	-3	2	0	0	.979	10	S-43	0.9
	Tor-A	98	375	61	107	25	1	26	79	22	79	.285	.332	.565	897	121	10	2	0	0	.975	9	S-98	2.5
2000	Tor-A★	154	620	96	163	32	2	41	114	35	121	.263	.309	.519	828	103	-0	5	4	-0	.963	13	*3-154	1.2
Total	5	544	1858	279	496	98	7	100	298	124	349	.267	.319	.489	808	102	-1	19	10	1	.975	54	S-240,3-191/2-94,D	7.1
■ **RAFAEL BATISTA** Batista, Rafael (Sanchez) b: 10/20/47, San Pedro De Macoris, D.R. BL/TL, 6'1", 195 lbs. Deb: 6/17/73																								
1973	Hou-N	12	15	2	4	0	0	0	2	1	6	.267	.313	.267	579	62	-1	0	0	0	1.000	-0	/1-8	-0.1
1975	Hou-N	10	10	0	3	1	0	0	0	0	4	.300	.300	.400	700	100	-0	0	0	0	.000	0	H	0.0
Total	2	22	25	2	7	1	0	0	2	1	10	.280	.308	.320	628	76	-1	0	0	0	1.000	-0	/1-8	-0.1
■ **KEVIN BATISTE** Batiste, Kevin Wade b: 10/21/66, Galveston, Tex. BR/TR, 6'2", 175 lbs. Deb: 6/13/89																								
1989	Tor-A	6	8	1	2	0	0	0	0	0	5	.250	.250	.250	500	42	-1	0	0	0	1.000	-1	/O-5(2-0-3)	-0.2
■ **KIM BATISTE** Batiste, Kimothy Emil b: 3/15/68, New Orleans, La. BR/TR, 6', 193 lbs. Deb: 9/8/91																								
1991	Phi-N	10	27	2	6	0	0	0	1	1	8	.222	.250	.222	472	34	-2	0	1	-0	.970	1	/S-7	-0.1
1992	Phi-N	44	136	9	28	4	0	1	10	4	18	.206	.229	.257	486	37	-11	0	0	0	.922	-8	S-41	-1.8
1993	*Phi-N	79	156	14	44	7	1	5	29	3	29	.282	.300	.436	736	95	-2	0	1	-0	.956	13	3-58,S-24	1.2
1994	Phi-N	64	209	17	49	6	0	1	13	1	32	.234	.242	.278	519	34	-20	1	1	-0	.919	2	3-42,S-17	-1.7
1996	SF-N	54	130	17	27	6	0	3	11	5	33	.208	.237	.323	560	48	-10	3	3	-0	.847	-3	3-25/S-7	-1.3
Total	5	251	658	59	154	23	1	10	64	14	120	.234	.252	.318	570	52	-45	4	6	-1	.908	5	3-125/S-96	-3.7
■ **BILL BATSCH** Batsch, William McKinley b: 5/18/1892, Mingo Junction, O. d: 12/31/63, Canton, Ohio BR/TR, 5'10.5", 168 lbs. Deb: 9/9/16																								
1916	Pit-N	1	0	0	0	0	0	0	0	1	0	—	1.000	—	1000	218	0	0			.000	0	H	0.0
■ **LARRY BATTAM** Battam, Lawrence J. b: 5/1/1878, Brooklyn, N.Y. d: 1/27/38, Brooklyn, N.Y. 5'11", Deb: 9/28/1895																								
1895	NY-N	2	4	0	1	0	0	0	0	2	1	.250	.500	.250	750	99	0	0			.667	-1	/3-2	0.0
■ **GEORGE BATTEN** Batten, George Burnett b: 10/7/1891, Haddonfield, N.J. d: 8/4/72, New Port Richey, Fla. BR/TR, 5'11", 165 lbs. Deb: 9/28/12																								
1912	NY-A	1	3	0	0	0	0	0	0	0		.000	.000	.000	0	-94	-1	0			1.000	-1	/2-1	-0.1
■ **EARL BATTEY** Battey, Earl Jesse b: 1/5/35, Los Angeles, Cal. BR/TR, 6'1", 205 lbs. Deb: 9/10/55																								
1955	Chi-A	5	7	1	2	0	0	0	0	1	1	.286	.444	.286	730	97	0	0	0	0	1.000	2	/C-5	0.2
1956	Chi-A	4	4	1	1	0	0	0	0	1	1	.250	.400	.250	650	74	-0	0	0	0	.800	-1	/C-3	-0.1
1957	Chi-A	48	115	12	20	2	3	3	6	11	38	.174	.246	.322	568	54	-8	0	2	-1	.989	6	C-43	-0.1
1958	Chi-A	68	168	24	38	8	0	8	26	24	34	.226	.330	.417	747	106	1	0	0	0	.988	2	C-49	0.6
1959	Chi-A	26	64	9	14	1	2	2	7	8	13	.219	.306	.391	696	91	-1	0	0	0	.990	4	C-20	0.3
1960	Was-A	137	466	49	126	24	2	15	60	48	68	.270	.349	.427	776	110	6	4	5	-1	.982	5	*C-136	1.8
1961	Min-A	133	460	70	139	24	1	17	55	53	66	.302	.378	.470	847	118	13	3	3	-0	.993	7	*C-131	2.5
1962	Min-A★	148	522	58	146	20	3	11	57	57	48	.280	.351	.393	743	96	-2	0	0	0	.991	6	*C-147	1.2
1963	Min-A★	147	508	64	145	17	1	26	84	61	75	.285	.371	.476	847	133	23	0	0	0	.994	1	*C-146	3.2
1964	Min-A	131	405	33	110	17	1	12	52	51	49	.272	.354	.407	762	111	7	1	1	-0	.990	-5	*C-125	0.8
1965	*Min-A★	131	394	36	117	22	2	6	60	50	23	.297	.379	.409	788	119	11	0	0	0	.986	-8	*C-128	1.0
1966	Min-A★	115	364	30	93	12	1	4	34	43	30	.255	.339	.327	666	87	-5	4	1	1	.995	6	*C-113	0.7
1967	Min-A	48	109	6	18	3	1	0	8	13	24	.165	.254	.211	465	36	-8	0	0	0	.987	-2	C-41	-1.0
Total	13	1141	3586	393	969	150	17	104	449	421	470	.270	.351	.409	760	106	38	13	12	-1	.990	23	*C-1087	11.1
■ **JOE BATTIN** Battin, Joseph V. b: 11/11/1851, Philadelphia, Pa. d: 12/10/37, Akron, Ohio BR/TR, Deb: 8/11/1871 MU NA OF: (0-LF 4-CF 6-RF) Career OF: (0-LF 5-CF 0-RF)																								
1871	Cle-n	1	3	0	0	0	0	0	0	1	0	.000	.250	.000	250	-21	-0	0	0	0	1.000	-0	/O-1(0-0-1)	0.0
1873	Ath-n	1	5	4	3	0	0	0	2	1	0	.600	.667	.600	1267	260	1	0	0	0	.667	0	/O-1(0-1-0)	0.1
1874	Ath-n	51	226	40	52	11	1	0	27	1	7	.230	.233	.288	521	61	-11	3	2	-0	.813	5	*2-41/O-7(0-2-5),S-5	-0.6
1875	StL-n	67	284	31	71	6	3	0	33	0	6	.250	.250	.292	542	97	1	15	3	2	.861	14	*2-62/3-6,C-2,O-1C	1.1
1876	StL-N	64	289	34	85	11	4	0	46	6	6	.294	.315	.367	682	134	11				**.867**	14	*3-63/2-1	2.3
1877	StL-N	57	226	28	45	3	7	1	22	6	17	.199	.220	.288	507	62	-9				.823	-3	3-32,2-21/O-5C,P-1	-0.9
1882	Pit-a	34	133	13	28	5	1	1		3		.211	.228	.286	514	76	-3				.876	21	3-34	1.7
1883	Pit-a	98	388	42	83	9	6	1		11		.214	.236	.276	511	67	-13				**.891**	29	*3-98/P-2,M	1.5
1884	Pit-a	43	158	10	28	1	2	0		3		.177	.198	.209	406	33	-11				.919	8	3-43,M	-0.2

YEAR	TM/L	G	AB	R	H	2B	3B	HR	RBI	BB	SO	AVG	OBP	SLG	OPS	OPS+	BR+	SB	CS	SBR	FA	FR	G/POS	TPR
	CP-U	18	69	8	13	2	0	0		0		.188	.188	.217	406	23	-8				.908	11	3-18,M	0.3
	Bal-U	17	59	3	6	1	0	0		0		.102	.102	.119	220	-30	-11				.813	2	3-17	-0.8
	Yr	35	128	11	19	3	0	0		0		.148	.148	.172	320	-3	-20				.868	13	3-35	-0.5
1890	Syr-a	29	119	15	25	2	1	0	13	8		.210	.260	.244	504	54	-7	8			.794	-4	3-29	-0.9
Total	4 n	120	518	75	126	17	4	0	62	3	13	.243	.248	.292	539	80	-10	18	5	2	.842	19	2-103/O-10R,3-6,SC	0.6
Total	6	360	1441	153	313	34	21	3	81	37	23	.217	.238	.277	516	67	-52	8			.870	77	3-334/2-22,O-5C,P-3	3.0
■ ALLEN BATTLE	Battle, Allen Zelmo b: 11/29/68, Grantham, N.C. BR/TR, 6', 170 lbs. Deb: 4/26/95																							
1995	StL-N	61	118	13	32	5	0	0	2	15	26	.271	.358	.314	672	79	-3	3	3	-0	.984	-2	O-32(15-7-14)	-0.6
1996	Oak-A	47	130	20	25	3	0	1	5	17	26	.192	.295	.238	534	38	-12	10	2	2	.988	-6	O-47(24-27-0)	-1.6
Total	2	108	248	33	57	8	0	1	7	32	52	.230	.325	.274	599	57	-15	13	5	1	.986	-8	/O-79(39-34-14)	-2.2
■ HOWARD BATTLE	Battle, Howard Dion b: 3/25/72, Biloxi, Miss. BR/TR, 6', 210 lbs. Deb: 9/5/95																							
1995	Tor-A	9	15	3	3	0	0	0	0	4	8	.200	.368	.200	568	53	-1	1	0	0	1.000	0	/3-6,D-1	0.0
1996	Phi-N	5	5	0	0	0	0	0	0	0	2	.000	.000	.000	0	-99	-1	0	0	0	.000	0	/3-1	-0.1
1999	*Atl-N	15	17	2	6	0	0	1	5	2	3	.353	.421	.529	950	138	1	0	0	0	1.000	0	/3-6	0.1
Total	3	29	37	5	9	0	0	1	5	6	13	.243	.349	.324	673	75	-1	1	0	0	1.000	0	/3-13,D-1	0.0
■ JIM BATTLE	Battle, James Milton b: 3/26/01, Bailey, Tex. d: 9/30/65, Chico, Cal. BR/TR, 6'1", 170 lbs. Deb: 9/9/27																							
1927	Chi-A	6	8	1	3	0	1	0	0	0	1	.375	.375	.625	1000	160	1	0	0	0	1.000	-1	/3-4,S-2	0.0
■ MATT BATTS	Batts, Matthew Daniel b: 10/16/21, San Antonio, Tex. BR/TR, 5'11", 200 lbs. Deb: 9/10/47																							
1947	Bos-A	7	16	3	8	1	0	1	5	1	1	.500	.529	.750	1279	236	3	0	0	0	1.000	-1	/C-6	0.2
1948	Bos-A	46	118	13	37	12	0	1	24	15	9	.314	.391	.441	832	115	3	0	0	0	.986	-1	C-41	0.3
1949	Bos-A	60	157	23	38	9	1	3	31	25	22	.242	.350	.369	719	84	-3	1	0	0	.977	2	C-50	0.1
1950	Bos-A	75	238	27	65	15	3	4	34	18	19	.273	.327	.412	739	80	-8	0	0	0	.994	3	C-73	-0.1
1951	Bos-A	11	29	1	4	1	0	0	2	1	2	.138	.167	.172	339	-8	-4	0	0	0	.975	-0	C-11	-0.4
	StL-A	79	248	26	75	17	1	5	31	21	21	.302	.357	.440	796	111	3	2	0	0	.960	-8	C-64	-0.1
	Yr	90	277	27	79	18	1	5	33	22	23	.285	.338	.412	749	98	-1	2	0	0	.962	-9	C-75	-0.5
1952	Det-A	56	173	11	41	4	1	3	13	14	22	.237	.298	.324	622	72	-7	1	0	0	.983	3	C-55	-0.1
1953	Det-A	116	374	38	104	24	3	6	42	24	36	.278	.322	.406	728	97	-3	2	3	-1	.986	-14	*C-103	-1.3
1954	Det-A	12	21	1	6	1	0	0	5	2	4	.286	.348	.333	681	89	-0	0	0	0	.967	1	/C-8	0.1
	Chi-A	55	158	16	36	7	1	3	19	17	15	.228	.303	.342	645	74	-6	0	1	-0	.992	7	C-42	0.2
	Yr	67	179	17	42	8	1	3	24	19	19	.235	.308	.341	649	76	-6	0	1	-0	.989	8	C-50	0.3
1955	Cin-N	26	71	4	18	4	1	0	13	4	11	.254	.293	.338	631	63	-4	0	0	0	.986	-1	C-21	-0.4
1956	Cin-N	3	2	0	0	0	0	0	0	1	1	.000	.333	.000	333	0	-0	0	0	0	.000	0	H	0.0
Total	10	546	1605	163	432	95	11	26	219	143	163	.269	.330	.391	721	89	-26	6	4	-0	.983	-10	C-474	-1.5
■ HANK BAUER	Bauer, Henry Albert b: 7/31/22, E.St.Louis, Ill. BR/TR, 6', 192 lbs. Deb: 9/6/48 MC Career OF: (177-LF 29-CF 1292-RF)																							
1948	NY-A	19	50	6	9	1	1	1	9	6	13	.180	.268	.300	568	51	-4	1	0	0	.964	-1	O-14(8-0-7)	-0.5
1949	*NY-A	103	301	56	82	6	6	10	45	37	42	.272	.354	.432	786	107	2	2	2	-0	.977	-9	O-95(21-25-60)	-1.0
1950	*NY-A	113	415	72	133	16	2	13	70	35	41	.320	.380	.463	843	118	11	2	3	-1	.987	-1	*O-110(36-0-82)	0.4
1951	*NY-A	118	348	53	103	19	3	10	54	42	39	.296	.373	.454	827	128	13	5	2	0	.990	-5	*O-107(51-1-62)	0.4
1952	*NY-A★	141	553	86	162	31	6	17	74	50	61	.293	.355	.463	818	134	23	6	7	-1	.984	3	*O-139(18-0-122)	2.0
1953	*NY-A★	133	437	77	133	20	6	10	57	59	45	.304	.394	.446	841	131	20	2	3	-1	.992	0	*O-126(3-1-124)	1.6
1954	NY-A★	114	377	73	111	16	5	12	54	40	42	.294	.362	.459	821	128	14	4	4	-1	.989	-6	*O-108(8-0-104)	0.3
1955	*NY-A	139	492	97	137	20	5	20	53	56	65	.278	.362	.461	823	122	14	8	4	0	.981	4	*O-133(5-0-131)/C-1	1.4
1956	*NY-A	147	539	96	130	18	7	26	84	59	72	.241	.318	.445	764	103	-1	4	2	0	.969	-8	*O-146(7-0-143)	-1.4
1957	*NY-A	137	479	70	124	22	**9**	18	65	42	64	.259	.324	.455	779	112	6	7	2	1	.986	-7	*O-135(3-0-134)	-0.5
1958	*NY-A	128	452	62	121	22	6	12	50	32	56	.268	.318	.423	740	106	2	3	2	-0	.980	-9	*O-123(2-0-121)	-1.1
1959	NY-A	114	341	44	81	20	0	9	39	33	54	.238	.309	.375	684	90	-5	4	2	0	.972	-13	*O-111(4-0-108)	-2.2
1960	KC-A	95	255	30	70	15	0	3	31	21	36	.275	.332	.369	701	89	-4	1	0	0	.978	-6	O-67(0-0-67)	-1.2
1961	KC-A	43	106	11	28	3	1	3	18	9	8	.264	.322	.396	718	89	-2	1	0	0	.958	-7	O-35(11-2-27),M	-1.0
Total	14	1544	5145	833	1424	229	57	164	703	521	638	.277	.347	.439	786	114	90	50	33	-1	.982	-65	*O-1449R/C-1	-2.8
■ JUSTIN BAUGHMAN	Baughman, Justin Reis b: 8/1/74, Mountain View, Cal. BR/TR, 5'11", 175 lbs. Deb: 5/17/98																							
1998	Ana-A	63	196	24	50	9	1	1	20	6	36	.255	.281	.327	607	57	-12	10	4	1	.977	-1	2-59/S-3,D-1	-0.9
2000	Ana-A	16	22	4	5	2	0	0	0	1	2	.227	.261	.318	579	45	-2	3	0	1	.958	3	/2-5,S-5,D-4	0.2
Total	2	79	218	28	55	11	1	1	20	7	38	.252	.279	.326	604	56	-14	13	4	1	.976	2	/2-64,S-8,D-5	-0.7
■ PADDY BAUMANN	Baumann, Charles John b: 12/20/1885, Indianapolis, Ind. d: 11/20/69, Indianapolis, Ind. BR/TR, 5'9", 160 lbs. Deb: 8/10/11 Career OF: (16-LF 4-CF 20-RF)																							
1911	Det-A	26	94	8	24	2	4	0	11	6		.255	.307	.362	669	82	-3	1			.956	6	2-23/O-3(0-0-3)	0.3
1912	Det-A	16	42	3	11	1	0	0	7	6		.262	.354	.286	640	86	-0	4			.786	-2	/3-6,2-5,O-2(0-1-0)	-0.2
1913	Det-A	50	191	31	57	7	4	1	22	16	18	.298	.353	.393	745	120	4	4			.943	-7	2-49	-0.2
1914	Det-A	3	11	1	0	0	0	0	0	2	1	.000	.154	.000	154	-52	-2	0			1.000	-1	/2-3	-0.3
1915	NY-A	76	219	30	64	13	1	2	28	28	32	.292	.380	.388	768	130	9	9	10	-2	.978	-2	2-43,3-19/O-1(0-1-0)	0.7
1916	NY-A	79	237	35	68	5	3	1	25	19	16	.287	.352	.346	698	108	2	10			.958	-7	O-28R,3-26/2-9	-0.6
1917	NY-A	49	110	10	24	2	1	0	8	4	9	.218	.246	.255	500	52	-7	2			.941	-12	2-18/O-7(4-1-2),3-1	-2.1
Total	7	299	904	118	248	30	13	4	101	81	76	.274	.340	.350	690	103	4	30	10		.953	-26	2-150/3-52,O-41R	-2.4
■ JIM BAUMER	Baumer, James Sloan b: 1/29/31, Tulsa, Okla. d: 7/8/96, Paoli, Pa. BR/TR, 6'2", 185 lbs. Deb: 9/14/49																							
1949	Chi-A	8	10	2	4	1	1	0	2	2	1	.400	.571	.700	1271	243	2	0	0	0	.938	1	/S-7	0.3
1961	Cin-N	10	24	0	3	0	0	0	0	0	9	.125	.125	.125	250	-33	-4	0	0	0	1.000	-0	/2-9	-0.4
Total	2	18	34	2	7	1	1	0	2	2	10	.206	.289	.294	584	55	-2	0	0	0	1.000	1	/2-9,S-7	-0.1
■ JOHN BAUMGARTNER	Baumgartner, John Edward b: 5/29/31, Birmingham, Ala. BR/TR, 6'1", 190 lbs. Deb: 4/14/53																							
1953	Det-A	7	27	3	5	0	0	0	2	0	5	.185	.185	.185	370	0	-4	0	0	0	.913	-1	/3-7	-0.4
■ FRANK BAUMHOLTZ	Baumholtz, Frank Conrad b: 10/7/18, Midvale, Ohio d: 12/14/97, Winter Springs, Fla. BL/TL (BR 1952 (1 GAME)), 5'10.5", 175 lbs. Deb: 4/15/47																							
1947	Cin-N	151	643	96	182	32	9	5	45	56	53	.283	.341	.384	726	93	-7	6			.977	-5	*O-150(0-29-136)	-1.6
1948	Cin-N	128	415	57	123	19	5	4	30	27	32	.296	.344	.395	739	103	1	8			.987	3	*O-110(20-23-67)	0.0
1949	Cin-N	27	81	12	19	5	3	1	8	6	8	.235	.295	.407	703	86	-2	0			.964	2	O-20(13-0-7)	-0.2
	Chi-N	58	164	15	37	4	2	1	15	9	21	.226	.270	.293	563	52	-11	2			.986	-4	O-43(0-7-38)	-1.7
	Yr	85	245	27	56	9	5	2	23	15	29	.229	.279	.331	609	64	-13	2			.976	-3	O-63(13-7-45)	-1.9
1951	Chi-N	146	560	62	159	28	10	2	50	49	36	.284	.346	.380	726	94	-5	5	4	-0	.975	-7	*O-140(17-64-60)	-1.6
1952	Chi-N	103	409	59	133	17	4	4	35	27	27	.325	.371	.416	787	116	9	5	7	-1	.974	3	*O-101(0-47-65)	0.7
1953	Chi-N	133	520	75	159	36	7	3	25	42	36	.306	.359	.419	778	100	0	3	3	-0	.980	-3	*O-130(0-69-64)	-0.8
1954	Chi-N	90	303	38	90	12	6	4	28	20	15	.297	.343	.416	758	95	-2	1	3	-1	.988	-10	O-71(10-61-13)	-1.6
1955	Chi-N	105	280	23	81	12	5	1	27	16	24	.289	.330	.379	709	88	-5	0	1	-0	.993	2	O-63(40-0-23)	-0.7
1956	Phi-N	76	100	13	27	0	0	0	9	6	6	.270	.318	.270	588	61	-5	0	2	-1	.962	-0	O-15(0-1-14)	-0.7
1957	Phi-N	2	2	0	0	0	0	0	0	0	0	.000	.000	.000	0	-99	-1	0	0	0	.000	0	H	-0.1
Total	10	1019	3477	450	1010	165	51	25	272	258	258	.290	.342	.389	731	95	-27	30	20		.980	-20	O-843(100-301-487)	-8.3
■ DANNY BAUTISTA	Bautista, Daniel (Alcantara) b: 5/24/72, Santo Domingo, D.R. BR/TR, 5'11", 170 lbs. Deb: 9/15/93																							
1993	Det-A	17	61	6	19	3	0	1	9	1	10	.311	.323	.410	732	96	-1	3	1	0	1.000	1	O-16(0-9-8)/D-1	0.1
1994	Det-A	31	99	12	23	4	1	4	15	3	18	.232	.255	.414	669	68	-5	1	2	-0	1.000	-1	O-30(0-14-16)/D-1	-0.7
1995	Det-A	89	271	28	55	9	0	7	27	12	68	.203	.237	.314	550	42	-24	4	1	1	.988	1	O-86(2-0-84)/D-1	-2.5
1996	Det-A	25	64	12	16	2	0	2	8	9	15	.250	.342	.375	717	81	-2	1	2	-0	.974	-2	O-22(12-0-12)/D-1	-0.5
	Atl-N	17	20	1	3	0	0	0	1	2	5	.150	.261	.150	411	11	-3	0	0	0	1.000	-3	O-14(2-2-10)	-0.6
1997	*Atl-N	64	103	14	25	3	2	3	9	5	24	.243	.284	.398	682	75	-4	2	0	0	.984	-8	O-57(48-1-10)	-1.3

YEAR	TM/L	G	AB	R	H	2B	3B	HR	RBI	BB	SO	AVG	OBP	SLG	OPS	OPS+	BR+	SB	CS	SBR	FA	FR	G/POS	TPR
1998	*Atl-N	82	144	17	36	11	0	3	17	7	21	.250	.285	.389	674	75	-6	1	0	0	.959	-9	O-58(53-1-4)/D-1	-1.6
1999	Fla-N	70	205	32	59	10	1	5	24	4	30	.288	.305	.420	724	86	-5	3	0	1	.979	1	O-60(22-18-31)	-0.5
2000	Fla-N	44	89	9	17	4	0	4	12	5	20	.191	.234	.371	605	52	-7	1	0	0	.980	-7	O-38(25-5-17)	-1.4
	Ari-N	87	262	45	83	16	7	7	47	20	30	.317	.372	.511	883	119	7	5	2	0	.987	-3	O-82(2-21-67)	0.2
	Yr	131	351	54	100	20	7	11	59	25	50	.285	.338	.476	814	104	1	6	2	1	.985	-9	*O-120(27-26-84)	-1.2
Total	8	526	1318	176	336	62	11	36	169	68	241	.255	.295	.401	695	77	-48	21	8	2	.985	-31	O-463(166-71-259)/D-5	-8.8

■ JIM BAXES

Baxes, Dimitrios Speros b: 7/5/28, San Francisco, Cal d: 11/14/96, Garden Grove, Cal. BR/TR, 6'1", 190 lbs. Deb: 4/11/59 F

YEAR	TM/L	G	AB	R	H	2B	3B	HR	RBI	BB	SO	AVG	OBP	SLG	OPS	OPS+	BR+	SB	CS	SBR	FA	FR	G/POS	TPR
1959	LA-N	11	33	4	10	1	0	2	5	4	7	.303	.395	.515	910	130	2	1	0	0	.952	7	3-10	0.8
	Cle-A	77	247	35	59	11	0	15	34	21	47	.239	.299	.466	764	111	2	0	1	-0	.956	-13	2-48,3-22	-0.8
Total	1	88	280	39	69	12	0	17	39	25	54	.246	.310	.471	782	113	4	1	1	-0	.931	-7	/2-48,3-32	0.0

■ MIKE BAXES

Baxes, Michael b: 12/18/30, San Francisco, Cal BR/TR, 5'10", 175 lbs. Deb: 4/17/56 F

YEAR	TM/L	G	AB	R	H	2B	3B	HR	RBI	BB	SO	AVG	OBP	SLG	OPS	OPS+	BR+	SB	CS	SBR	FA	FR	G/POS	TPR
1956	KC-A	73	106	9	24	3	1	1	5	18	15	.226	.339	.302	641	70	-4	0	1	-0	.944	4	S-62/2-1	0.2
1958	KC-A	73	231	31	49	10	1	0	8	21	24	.212	.286	.264	550	52	-15	1	6	-2	.969	-4	2-61/S-4	-1.7
Total	2	146	337	40	73	13	2	1	13	39	39	.217	.303	.276	579	58	-19	1	7	-2	.946	-0	/S-66,2-62	-1.5

■ MOOSE BAXTER

Baxter, John Morris b: 7/27/1876, Chippewa Falls, Wis. d: 8/7/26, Portland, Ore. BL/TR, 6'2", 200 lbs. Deb: 4/19/07

YEAR	TM/L	G	AB	R	H	2B	3B	HR	RBI	BB	SO	AVG	OBP	SLG	OPS	OPS+	BR+	SB	CS	SBR	FA	FR	G/POS	TPR
1907	StL-N	6	21	1	4	0	0	0	0	0		.190	.190	.190	381	20	-2	0			.921	-1	/1-6	-0.3

■ HARRY BAY

Bay, Harry Elbert "Deerfoot" b: 1/17/1878, Pontiac, Ill. d: 3/20/52, Peoria, Ill. BL/TL, 5'8", 138 lbs. Deb: 7/23/01

YEAR	TM/L	G	AB	R	H	2B	3B	HR	RBI	BB	SO	AVG	OBP	SLG	OPS	OPS+	BR+	SB	CS	SBR	FA	FR	G/POS	TPR
1901	Cin-N	41	157	25	33	1	2	1	3	13		.210	.275	.261	536	60	-8	4			.953	-1	O-40(0-25-15)	-1.0
1902	Cin-N	6	16	3	6	0	0	0	1	2		.375	.474	.375	849	148	1	0			.778	0	/O-3(3-0-0)	0.1
	Cle-A	108	455	71	132	10	5	0	23	36		.290	.343	.334	678	92	-4	22			**.973**	4	*O-107(24-79-4)	-0.5
1903	Cle-A	140	579	94	169	15	12	1	35	29		.292	.329	.364	693	110	7	**45**			.950	-3	*O-140(26-114-0)	-0.4
1904	Cle-A	132	506	69	122	12	9	3	36	43		.241	.307	.318	625	99	-0	**38**			**.987**	7	*O-132(5-127-0)	0.1
1905	Cle-A	144	552	90	166	18	10	0	22	36		.301	.349	.370	719	126	16	36			.970	0	*O-144(0-144-0)	1.0
1906	Cle-A	68	280	47	77	8	3	0	14	26		.275	.337	.325	662	109	3	17			.979	-3	O-68(0-68-0)	-0.3
1907	Cle-A	34	95	14	17	1	1	0	7	10		.179	.271	.211	482	53	-5	7			.968	1	O-31(7-23-1)	-0.6
1908	Cle-A	2	0	0	0	0	0	0	0	0		—	—	—	—	—	0	0			.000	0	R	0.0
Total	8	675	2640	413	722	65	42	5	141	195		.273	.328	.336	663	103	11	169			.968	6	O-665(65-580-20)	-1.6

■ DICK BAYLESS

Bayless, Harry Owen b: 9/6/1883, Joplin, Mo. d: 12/16/20, Santa Rita, N.Mex. BL/TR, 5'9", 178 lbs. Deb: 9/9/08

YEAR	TM/L	G	AB	R	H	2B	3B	HR	RBI	BB	SO	AVG	OBP	SLG	OPS	OPS+	BR+	SB	CS	SBR	FA	FR	G/POS	TPR
1908	Cin-N	19	71	7	16	1	0	1	3	6		.225	.304	.282	585	90	-1	0			.946	3	O-19(0-2-17)	0.1

■ DON BAYLOR

Baylor, Don Edward b: 6/28/49, Austin, Tex. BR/TR, 6'1", 195 lbs. Deb: 9/18/70 MC Career OF: (623-LF 37-CF 195-RF)

YEAR	TM/L	G	AB	R	H	2B	3B	HR	RBI	BB	SO	AVG	OBP	SLG	OPS	OPS+	BR+	SB	CS	SBR	FA	FR	G/POS	TPR
1970	Bal-A	8	17	4	4	0	0	0	4	2	3	.235	.316	.235	551	54	-1	1	1	-0	1.000	0	/O-6(3-4-0)	-0.1
1971	Bal-A	1	2	0	0	0	0	0	1	2	1	.000	.600	.000	600	83	0	0	0	0	1.000	0	/O-1(0-0-1)	0.1
1972	Bal-A	102	320	33	81	13	3	11	38	29	50	.253	.332	.416	748	118	7	24	2	5	.975	-9	O-84(35-13-48)/1-9	-0.2
1973	*Bal-A	118	405	64	116	20	4	11	51	35	48	.286	.362	.437	799	125	14	32	9	4	.981	-1	*O-110L/1-6,D-1	1.1
1974	*Bal-A	137	489	66	133	22	1	10	59	43	56	.272	.343	.382	726	112	8	29	12	2	.978	-17	*O-129L/1-8,D-1	-1.6
1975	Bal-A	145	524	79	148	21	6	25	76	53	64	.282	.363	.489	851	148	32	32	17	1	.982	-2	*O-135L/1-2,D-7	2.4
1976	Oak-A	157	595	85	147	25	1	15	68	58	72	.247	.334	.368	702	110	8	52	12	7	.981	-9	O-76R,1-69,D-23	-0.3
1977	Cal-A	154	561	87	141	27	0	25	75	62	76	.251	.339	.433	772	113	10	26	12	2	.966	-1	O-77L,D-61,1-18	0.4
1978	Cal-A	158	591	103	151	26	0	34	99	56	71	.255	.338	.472	810	131	23	22	9	2	.974	-2	*D-102,O-39L,1-17	1.7
1979	*Cal-A★	162	628	**120**	186	33	3	36	**139**	71	51	.296	.377	.530	908	147	41	22	12	1	.976	2	O-97L,D-65/1-1	3.5
1980	Cal-A	90	340	39	85	12	2	5	51	24	32	.250	.320	.341	661	83	-7	6	6	-1	.969	3	O-54(37-0-18),D-36	-0.9
1981	Cal-A	103	377	52	90	18	1	17	66	42	51	.239	.326	.427	753	116	7	3	3	-0	1.000	1	D-97/1-4,O-1(1-0-0)	0.5
1982	*Cal-A	157	608	80	160	24	1	24	93	57	69	.263	.333	.424	758	106	5	10	4	1	.000	0	*D-155	0.1
1983	NY-A	144	534	82	162	33	3	21	85	40	53	.303	.366	.494	861	139	28	17	7	1	1.000	-0	*D-136/O-5(2-0-4),1-1	2.5
1984	NY-A	134	493	84	129	29	1	27	89	38	68	.262	.343	.489	832	132	21	1	1	-0	.889	-1	*D-127/O-5(1-0-4)	1.6
1985	NY-A	142	477	70	110	24	1	23	91	52	90	.231	.336	.430	766	111	8	0	4	-1	.000	0	*D-140	0.2
1986	*Bos-A	160	585	93	139	23	1	31	94	62	111	.238	.346	.439	785	112	10	3	5	-1	.986	-1	*D-143,1-13/O-3L	0.3
1987	Bos-A	108	339	64	81	8	0	16	57	40	47	.239	.360	.404	764	100	1	5	2	0	.000	0	D-97	-0.1
	*Min-A	20	49	3	14	1	0	0	6	5	12	.286	.397	.306	703	87	-0	0	1	-0	.000	0	D-14	-0.1
	Yr	128	388	67	95	9	0	16	63	45	59	.245	.364	.392	756	98	1	5	3	0	.000	0	*D-111	-0.2
1988	*Oak-A	92	264	28	58	7	0	7	34	34	44	.220	.335	.326	661	89	-3	0	1	-0	.000	0	D-80	-0.5
Total	19	2292	8198	1236	2135	366	28	338	1276	805	1069	.260	.346	.436	782	119	213	285	120	21	.977	-37	*D-1285,O-822L,1-148	10.6

■ JACK BEACH

Beach, Stonewall Jackson b: 1862, Alexandria, Va. d: 7/23/1896, Alexandria, Va. Deb: 5/1/1884

YEAR	TM/L	G	AB	R	H	2B	3B	HR	RBI	BB	SO	AVG	OBP	SLG	OPS	OPS+	BR+	SB	CS	SBR	FA	FR	G/POS	TPR
1884	Was-a	8	31	3	3	2	0	0		0		.097	.097	.161	258	-20	-4				.667	-1	/O-8(1-0-7)	-0.4

■ JOHNNY BEALL

Beall, John Woolf b: 3/12/1882, Beltsville, Md. d: 6/13/26, Beltsville, Md. BL/TR, 6', 180 lbs. Deb: 4/17/13

YEAR	TM/L	G	AB	R	H	2B	3B	HR	RBI	BB	SO	AVG	OBP	SLG	OPS	OPS+	BR+	SB	CS	SBR	FA	FR	G/POS	TPR
1913	Cle-A	6	6	0	1	0	0	0	1	0	2	.167	.167	.167	333	-2	-1	0			.000	0	H	-0.1
	Chi-A	17	60	10	16	0	1	2	3	0	0	.267	.279	.400	679	99	-1	1			.953	1	O-17(0-17-0)	-0.1
	Yr	23	66	10	17	0	1	2	4	0	2	.258	.269	.379	647	89	-1	1			.953	1	O-17(0-17-0)	-0.2
1915	Cin-N	10	34	3	8	1	0	0	3	5	10	.235	.350	.265	615	86	-0	0	1	-0	.960	1	O-10(9-1-0)	0.0
1916	Cin-N	6	21	3	7	2	0	1	4	3	7	.333	.417	.571	988	207	3	1			1.000	1	/O-6(5-0-0)	0.4
1918	StL-N	19	49	2	11	1	0	0	6	3	6	.224	.269	.245	514	59	-2	0			1.000	-1	O-18(0-0-18)	-0.5
Total	4	58	170	18	43	4	1	3	17	11	25	.253	.306	.341	647	95	-1	2	1		.972	2	/O-51(14-18-18)	-0.3

■ BOB BEALL

Beall, Robert Brooks b: 4/24/48, Portland, Ore. BB/TL, 5'11", 180 lbs. Deb: 5/12/75

YEAR	TM/L	G	AB	R	H	2B	3B	HR	RBI	BB	SO	AVG	OBP	SLG	OPS	OPS+	BR+	SB	CS	SBR	FA	FR	G/POS	TPR
1975	Atl-N	20	31	2	7	2	0	0	1	6	9	.226	.351	.290	642	77	-1	0	0	0	.984	-0	/1-8	-0.2
1978	Atl-N	108	185	29	45	8	0	1	16	36	27	.243	.369	.303	672	81	-3	4	5	-1	.987	-1	1-40/O-8(6-2-0)	-0.8
1979	Atl-N	17	15	1	2	2	0	0	1	3	4	.133	.278	.267	544	46	-1	0	0	0	1.000	0	/1-3	-0.1
1980	Pit-N	3	3	0	0	0	0	0	0	0	1	.000	.000	.000	0	-99	-1	0	0	0	.000	0	/H	-0.1
Total	4	148	234	32	54	12	0	1	18	45	41	.231	.357	.295	652	76	-6	4	5	-1	.987	-1	/1-51,O-8(6-2-0)	-1.2

■ TOMMY BEALS

Beals, Thomas L. (a.k.a. W.Thomas In 1871-1873) b: 8/1850, New York
d: 10/2/15, San Francisco, Cal. BR, 5'5", 144 lbs. Deb: 7/27/1871 Career OF: (9-LF 23-CF 18-RF)

YEAR	TM/L	G	AB	R	H	2B	3B	HR	RBI	BB	SO	AVG	OBP	SLG	OPS	OPS+	BR+	SB	CS	SBR	FA	FR	G/POS	TPR
1871	Oly-n	10	36	6	7	0	0	0	1	2	0	.194	.237	.194	431	27	-3	2	0	0	.778	3	/O-8(4-0-4),2-2	0.0
1872	Oly-n	9	36	6	11	1	1	0	5	1	1	.306	.324	.389	713	125	1	0	0	0	.853	1	/2-5,S-2,O-2(0-2-0)	0.1
1873	Was-n	37	169	35	46	9	5	0	24	1	1	.272	.276	.385	661	97	-0	1	0	0	.871	7	2-26,C-13/O-1(1-0-0)	0.4
1874	Bos-n	19	97	20	19	3	4	0	17	0	2	.196	.196	.309	505	56	-5	0	1	-0	.849	-2	2-12/O-9(1-2-6)	-0.6
1875	Bos-n	35	155	38	41	2	6	0	16	3	1	.265	.278	.355	633	114	2	1	0	0	.867	1	O-30(3-19-8)/2-8	0.3
1880	Chi-N	13	46	4	7	0	0	0	3	1	6	.152	.170	.152	322	10	-4				.889	-6	O-10(0-0-10)/2-3	-1.0
Total	5 n	110	493	105	124	15	16	0	63	7	5	.252	.262	.347	609	90	-5	4	1	1	.864	10	/2-53,O-50C,C-13,S	0.2

■ CHARLIE BEAMON

Beamon, Charles Alfonzo Jr. b: 12/4/53, Oakland, Cal. BL/TL, 6'1", 183 lbs. Deb: 9/11/78 F

YEAR	TM/L	G	AB	R	H	2B	3B	HR	RBI	BB	SO	AVG	OBP	SLG	OPS	OPS+	BR+	SB	CS	SBR	FA	FR	G/POS	TPR
1978	Sea-A	10	11	2	2	0	0	0	0	1	1	.182	.250	.182	432	23	-1	0	0	0	1.000	1	/1-2,D-6	0.0
1979	Sea-A	27	25	5	5	1	0	0	0	0	5	.200	.200	.240	440	18	-3	1	0	0	1.000	0	/1-7,O-2(2-0-0),D-5	-0.3
1981	Tor-A	8	15	1	3	1	0	0	0	2	2	.200	.294	.267	561	59	-1	0	0	0	1.000	-0	/D-4,1-1	-0.1
Total	3	45	51	8	10	2	0	0	0	3	8	.196	.241	.235	476	32	-5	1	0	0	1.000	1	/D-15,1-10,O-2(2-0-0)	-0.4

■ TREY BEAMON

Beamon, Clifford b: 2/11/74, Dallas, Tex. BL/TR, 6'3", 195 lbs. Deb: 8/4/96

YEAR	TM/L	G	AB	R	H	2B	3B	HR	RBI	BB	SO	AVG	OBP	SLG	OPS	OPS+	BR+	SB	CS	SBR	FA	FR	G/POS	TPR
1996	Pit-N	24	51	7	11	2	0	0	6	4	6	.216	.273	.255	528	39	-4	1	1	-0	.960	-1	O-14(5-0-10)	-0.6
1997	SD-N	43	65	5	18	3	0	0	7	2	17	.277	.309	.323	632	71	-3	1	2	-0	.909	-2	O-20(15-0-5)	-0.5
1998	Det-A	28	42	4	11	4	0	0	2	5	13	.262	.340	.357	698	81	-1	1	0	0	1.000	-0	D-11/O-4(2-0-2)	-0.2
Total	3	95	158	16	40	9	0	0	15	11	36	.253	.306	.310	616	63	-8	3	3	-0	.944	-3	/O-38(22-0-17),D-11	-1.3

■ JOE BEAN

Bean, Joseph William b: 3/18/1874, Boston, Mass. d: 2/15/61, Atlanta, Ga. BR/TR, 5'8", 138 lbs. Deb: 4/28/02

YEAR	TM/L	G	AB	R	H	2B	3B	HR	RBI	BB	SO	AVG	OBP	SLG	OPS	OPS+	BR+	SB	CS	SBR	FA	FR	G/POS	TPR
1902	NY-N	50	182	13	40	2	1	0	5	5		.220	.249	.242	490	52	-10	9			.880	-7	S-50	-1.7

■ **BILL BEAN** Bean, William Daro b: 5/11/64, Santa Ana, Cal. BL/TL, 6'1", 185 lbs. Deb: 4/25/87 Career OF: (69-LF 55-CF 62-RF)

YEAR	TM/L	G	AB	R	H	2B	3B	HR	RBI	BB	SO	AVG	OBP	SLG	OPS	OPS+	BR+	SB	CS	SBR	FA	FR	G/POS	TPR
1987	Det-A	26	66	6	17	2	0	0	4	5	11	.258	.310	.288	598	63	-3	1	1	-0	1.000	0	O-24(5-17-3)	-0.4
1988	Det-A	10	11	2	2	0	1	0	0	0	2	.182	.182	.364	545	51	-1	0	0	0	1.000	-1	/O-4(0-2-3),1-2,D-1	-0.2
1989	Det-A	9	11	0	0	0	0	0	0	2	3	.000	.214	.000	214	-36	-2	0	0	0	.833	-3	/O-6(4-1-2),1-2	-0.5
	LA-N	51	71	7	14	4	0	0	3	4	10	.197	.250	.254	504	45	-5	0	2	-1	1.000	-9	O-44(28-11-7)	-1.6
1993	SD-N	88	177	19	46	9	0	5	32	6	29	.260	.292	.395	687	81	-5	2	4	-1	.987	-7	O-54(11-17-32),1-12	-1.5
1994	SD-N	84	135	7	29	5	1	0	14	7	25	.215	.254	.267	520	37	-13	0	1	-0	1.000	-5	O-39(17-7-15),1-16	-1.9
1995	SD-N	4	7	1	0	0	0	0	0	1	4	.000	.125	.000	125	-66	-2	0	0	0	.750	-1	/O-4(4-0-0)	-0.3
Total	6	272	478	42	108	20	2	5	53	25	84	.226	.270	.308	578	55	-31	3	8	-2	.988	-25	O-175L/1-32,D-1	-6.4

■ **BILLY BEANE** Beane, William Lamar b: 3/29/62, Orlando, Fla. BR/TR, 6'4", 195 lbs. Deb: 9/13/84 Career OF: (75-LF 7-CF 33-RF)

YEAR	TM/L	G	AB	R	H	2B	3B	HR	RBI	BB	SO	AVG	OBP	SLG	OPS	OPS+	BR+	SB	CS	SBR	FA	FR	G/POS	TPR
1984	NY-N	5	10	0	1	0	0	0	0	0	2	.100	.100	.100	200	-44	-2	0	1	-0	1.000	-2	/O-5(2-1-2)	-0.4
1985	NY-N	8	8	0	2	1	0	0	1	0	3	.250	.250	.375	625	74	-0	0	0	0	1.000	-1	/O-2(1-0-1)	-0.1
1986	Min-A	80	183	20	39	6	0	3	15	11	54	.213	.258	.295	553	49	-13	2	3	-1	1.000	-5	O-67(64-5-1)/D-5	-2.0
1987	Min-A	12	15	1	4	2	0	0	1	0	6	.267	.267	.400	667	71	-1	0	0	0	1.000	-1	/O-7(0-0-7)	-0.2
1988	Det-A	6	6	1	1	0	0	0	1	0	2	.167	.167	.167	333	-7	-1	0	0	0	1.000	-2	/O-6(4-1-1)	-0.3
1989	Oak-A	37	79	8	19	5	0	0	11	0	13	.241	.241	.304	544	54	-5	3	1	0	1.000	-2	O-25R/1-4,C-1,3D	-0.7
Total	6	148	301	30	66	14	0	3	29	11	80	.219	.247	.296	542	48	-22	5	5	-1	1.000	-11	O-112L/D-9,1-4,3C	-3.7

■ **TED BEARD** Beard, Cramer Theodore b: 1/7/21, Woodsboro, Md. BL/TL, 5'8", 165 lbs. Deb: 9/5/48

YEAR	TM/L	G	AB	R	H	2B	3B	HR	RBI	BB	SO	AVG	OBP	SLG	OPS	OPS+	BR+	SB	CS	SBR	FA	FR	G/POS	TPR
1948	Pit-N	25	81	15	16	1	3	0	7	12	18	.198	.316	.284	600	62	-4	5			1.000	2	O-22(0-22-0)	-0.3
1949	Pit-N	14	24	1	2	0	0	0	1	2	2	.083	.154	.083	237	-34	-5	0			.900	-3	O-10(0-0-10)	-0.8
1950	Pit-N	61	177	32	41	6	2	4	12	27	45	.232	.333	.356	689	79	-5	3			.983	2	O-49(1-21-27)	-0.4
1951	Pit-N	22	48	7	9	1	0	1	3	6	14	.188	.291	.271	562	51	-3	0	0	0	1.000	-2	O-15(12-4-0)	-0.6
1952	Pit-N	15	44	5	8	2	1	0	3	7	9	.182	.294	.273	567	57	-2	2	0	0	1.000	0	O-13(0-3-10)	-0.2
1957	Chi-A	38	78	15	16	1	0	0	7	18	14	.205	.354	.218	572	59	-3	3	2	-0	.974	-1	O-28(0-3-25)	-0.6
1958	Chi-A	19	22	5	2	0	0	1	2	6	5	.091	.286	.227	513	44	-2	3	0	1	1.000	-4	O-15(10-6-1)	-0.6
Total	7	194	474	80	94	11	6	6	35	78	107	.198	.315	.285	600	61	-25	16	2		.987	-5	O-152(23-59-73)	-3.5

■ **OLLIE BEARD** Beard, Oliver Perry b: 5/2/1862, Lexington, Ky. d: 5/28/29, Cincinnati, Ohio BR/TR, 5'11", 180 lbs. Deb: 4/17/1889

YEAR	TM/L	G	AB	R	H	2B	3B	HR	RBI	BB	SO	AVG	OBP	SLG	OPS	OPS+	BR+	SB	CS	SBR	FA	FR	G/POS	TPR
1889	Cin-a	141	558	96	159	13	14	1	77	35	39	.285	.328	.364	692	94	-6	36			.896	20	*S-141	1.5
1890	Cin-N	122	492	64	132	17	15	3	72	44	13	.268	.331	.382	713	108	4	30			.897	1	*S-113/3-9	0.7
1891	Lou-a	68	257	35	62	4	5	0	24	33	9	.241	.330	.296	626	80	-6	7			.879	7	3-61/S-7	0.2
Total	3	331	1307	195	353	34	34	4	173	112	61	.270	.330	.357	687	97	-8	73			.896	28	S-261/3-70	2.4

■ **LEW BEASLEY** Beasley, Lewis Paige b: 8/27/48, Sparta, Va. BL/TR, 5'10", 172 lbs. Deb: 5/21/77

YEAR	TM/L	G	AB	R	H	2B	3B	HR	RBI	BB	SO	AVG	OBP	SLG	OPS	OPS+	BR+	SB	CS	SBR	FA	FR	G/POS	TPR
1977	Tex-A	25	32	5	7	1	0	0	3	2	2	.219	.265	.250	515	41	-3	1	1	-0	.833	-6	O-18(14-0-4)/S-1,D-1	-0.9

■ **DAVE BEATLE** Beatle, David b: 1861, New York, N.Y. 6'2", 200 lbs. Deb: 6/17/1884

YEAR	TM/L	G	AB	R	H	2B	3B	HR	RBI	BB	SO	AVG	OBP	SLG	OPS	OPS+	BR+	SB	CS	SBR	FA	FR	G/POS	TPR
1884	Det-N	1	3	0	0	0	0	0	0	0	2	.000	.000	.000	0	-99	-1				.500	-1	/O-1(1-0-1),C-1	-0.1

■ **DESMOND BEATTY** Beatty, Aloysius Desmond "Desperate" b: 4/7/1893, Baltimore, Md. d: 10/6/69, Norway, Maine BR/TR, 5'8.5", 158 lbs. Deb: 9/28/14

YEAR	TM/L	G	AB	R	H	2B	3B	HR	RBI	BB	SO	AVG	OBP	SLG	OPS	OPS+	BR+	SB	CS	SBR	FA	FR	G/POS	TPR
1914	NY-N	2	3	0	0	0	0	0	1	0	0	.000	.000	.000	0	-99	-1	0			.400	-1	/S-1,3-1	-0.1

■ **JIM BEAUCHAMP** Beauchamp, James Edward b: 8/21/39, Vinita, Okla. BR/TR, 6'2", 205 lbs. Deb: 9/22/63 C

YEAR	TM/L	G	AB	R	H	2B	3B	HR	RBI	BB	SO	AVG	OBP	SLG	OPS	OPS+	BR+	SB	CS	SBR	FA	FR	G/POS	TPR
1963	StL-N	4	3	0	0	0	0	0	0	0	2	.000	.000	.000	0	-91	-1	0	0	0	.000	0	H	-0.1
1964	Hou-N	23	55	6	9	2	0	2	4	5	16	.164	.246	.309	555	58	-3	0	0	0	.913	-1	O-15(11-4-0)/1-2	-0.5
1965	Hou-N	24	53	5	10	1	0	0	4	5	11	.189	.259	.208	466	36	-4	0	2	-1	1.000	2	/O-9(9-0-0),1-3	-0.5
	Mil-N	4	3	0	0	0	0	0	0	1	1	.000	.250	.000	250	-23	-0	0	1	-0	1.000	-0	/1-2	-0.1
	Yr	28	56	5	10	1	0	0	4	6	12	.179	.258	.196	454	32	-5	0	3	-1	1.000	1	/O-9(9-0-0),1-5	-0.6
1967	Atl-N	4	3	0	0	0	0	0	1	0	0	.000	.000	.000	0	-99	-1	0	0	0	.000	0	H	-0.1
1968	Cin-N	31	57	10	15	2	0	2	14	4	19	.263	.311	.404	715	107	0	0	0	0	1.000	-0	O-13(1-11-1)/1-1	0.0
1969	Cin-N	43	60	8	15	1	0	1	8	5	13	.250	.308	.317	624	71	-2	0	0	0	1.000	-2	/O-9(5-4-0),1-3	-0.5
1970	Hou-N	31	26	3	5	0	0	1	4	3	7	.192	.276	.308	584	59	-2	0	1	-0	1.000	-4	O-16(13-3-0)	-0.6
	StL-N	44	58	8	15	2	0	1	6	8	11	.259	.348	.345	693	85	-1	2	0	0	1.000	1	O-10(2-6-2)/1-5	-0.1
	Yr	75	84	11	20	2	0	2	10	11	18	.238	.326	.333	660	78	-3	2	1	0	1.000	-4	O-26(15-9-2)/1-5	-0.7
1971	StL-N	77	162	24	38	8	3	2	16	9	26	.235	.279	.358	637	76	-5	3	1	0	.982	-2	1-44/O-1(1-0-0)	-1.1
1972	NY-N	58	120	10	29	1	0	5	19	7	33	.242	.289	.375	664	90	-2	0	0	0	.979	-3	1-35/O-5(5-0-0)	-0.7
1973	*NY-N	50	61	5	17	1	1	0	14	7	11	.279	.353	.328	681	91	-1	1	0	0	.969	-1	1-11	-0.2
Total	10	393	661	79	153	18	4	14	90	54	150	.231	.292	.334	627	76	-22	6	5	-0	.980	-11	1-106/O-78(47-28-3)	-4.5

■ **GINGER BEAUMONT** Beaumont, Clarence Howeth b: 7/23/1876, Rochester, Wis. d: 4/10/56, Burlington, Wis. BL/TR, 5'8", 190 lbs. Deb: 4/21/1899 Career OF: (18-LF 1380-CF 8-RF)

YEAR	TM/L	G	AB	R	H	2B	3B	HR	RBI	BB	SO	AVG	OBP	SLG	OPS	OPS+	BR+	SB	CS	SBR	FA	FR	G/POS	TPR
1899	Pit-N	111	437	90	154	15	8	3	38	41		.352	.416	.444	860	136	23	31			.924	6	*O-100(3-96-1)/1-2	2.0
1900	*Pit-N	138	567	105	158	14	9	5	50	40		.279	.331	.362	692	90	-8	27			.944	-12	*O-138(0-138-0)	-2.7
1901	Pit-N	133	558	120	185	14	5	8	72	44		.332	.382	.418	800	128	20	36			.943	-5	*O-133(0-133-0)	0.9
1902	Pit-N	130	541	100	**193**	21	6	0	67	39		**.357**	.404	.418	822	148	31	33			.975	0	*O-130(0-130-0)	2.5
1903	*Pit-N	141	613	**137**	**209**	30	6	7	68	44		.341	.390	.444	833	133	25	23			.948	-7	*O-141(0-141-0)	1.1
1904	Pit-N	153	615	97	**185**	12	12	3	54	34		.301	.338	.374	712	117	11	28			.968	-4	*O-153(0-153-0)	-0.1
1905	Pit-N	103	384	60	126	12	8	3	40	22		.328	.365	.424	789	131	14	21			.972	-0	O-97(0-96-0)	0.9
1906	Pit-N	80	310	48	82	9	3	2	32	19		.265	.311	.332	643	96	-2	1			.945	-5	O-78(0-78-0)	-1.2
1907	Bos-N	150	580	67	**187**	19	14	4	62	37		.322	.366	.424	790	148	30	25			.962	5	*O-149(0-149-0)	3.1
1908	Bos-N	125	476	66	127	20	6	2	52	42		.267	.328	.347	674	117	9	13			.965	-1	*O-121(0-121-0)	0.3
1909	Bos-N	123	407	35	107	11	4	0	60	35		.263	.321	.310	631	92	-4	12			.969	1	*O-111(0-111-0)	-0.9
1910	*Chi-N	76	172	30	46	5	1	2	22	28	14	.267	.373	.343	716	110	3	4			.957	-4	O-56(15-34-7)	-0.3
Total	12	1463	5660	955	1759	182	82	39	617	425	14	.311	.362	.393	755	122	152	254			.956	-25	*O-1407C/1-2	5.6

■ **ED BEAVENS** Beavens, Edward P. (a.k.a. Edward P. Bevens) b: 1848, Troy, N.Y. TR, 5'8", 138 lbs. Deb: 5/9/1871

YEAR	TM/L	G	AB	R	H	2B	3B	HR	RBI	BB	SO	AVG	OBP	SLG	OPS	OPS+	BR+	SB	CS	SBR	FA	FR	G/POS	TPR
1871	Tro-n	3	15	7	6	0	0	0	5	0	0	.400	.400	.400	800	129	1	2	0	0	.818	1	/2-3	0.1
1872	Atl-n	10	43	6	9	2	0	0	2	1	0	.209	.227	.256	483	41	-4	0	0	0	.683	-5	2-10/S-1,O-1(1-0-0)	-0.6
Total	2 n	13	58	13	15	2	0	0	7	1	0	.259	.271	.293	564	62	-3	2	0	0	.720	-4	/2-13,O-1(1-0-0),S-1	-0.5

■ **BUCK BECANNON** Becannon, James Melvin b: 8/22/1859, New York, N.Y. d: 11/5/23, New York, N.Y. 5'10", 165 lbs. Deb: 10/15/1884

YEAR	TM/L	G	AB	R	H	2B	3B	HR	RBI	BB	SO	AVG	OBP	SLG	OPS	OPS+	BR+	SB	CS	SBR	FA	FR	G/POS	TPR
1884	*NY-a	1	3	0	0	0	0	0		0		.000	.000	.000	0	-99	-1				1.000	0	/P-1	0.0
1885	NY-a	10	33	3	10	0	0	0	2	1		.303	.343	.303	646	114	1				.947	0	P-10	0.0
1887	NY-N	1	5	0	0	0	0	0	0	0	2	.000	.000	.000	0	-99	-1	0			.667	-0	/3-1	-0.2
Total	3	12	41	3	10	0	0	0	2	1	2	.244	.279	.244	523	69	-1	0			.952	0	/P-11,3-1	-0.2

■ **GEORGE BECHTEL** Bechtel, George A. b: 1848, Philadelphia, Pa. 5'11", 165 lbs. Deb: 5/20/1871 NA OF: (15-LF 7-CF 156-RF)

YEAR	TM/L	G	AB	R	H	2B	3B	HR	RBI	BB	SO	AVG	OBP	SLG	OPS	OPS+	BR+	SB	CS	SBR	FA	FR	G/POS	TPR
1871	Ath-n	20	94	24	33	9	1	1	21	2	2	.351	.365	.500	865	147	6	4	0	1	.821	0	O-15(1-3-11)/P-3,3-3	0.4
1872	Mut-n	51	248	60	74	11	2	0	41	6	3	.298	.315	.359	674	114	6	9	1	2	.823	-0	*O-50(13-0-37)/1-1	0.7
1873	Phi-n	53	258	53	63	12	1	1	40	9	1	.244	.270	.310	580	69	-10	2	1	0	.853	8	*O-52(0-1-51)/P-3	0.1
1874	Phi-n	32	151	29	42	4	5	1	34	2	1	.278	.288	.391	678	111	1	0	0	0	.731	-4	O-28(1-0-28)/P-6	0.0
1875	Cen-n	14	61	12	17	5	0	0	7	1	1	.279	.290	.361	651	136	2	0	0	0	.791	-1	P-14	0.0
	Ath-n	35	164	33	46	6	2	0	20	1	3	.280	.285	.341	626	105	-0	2	0	0	.810	1	O-31(0-3-29)/P-4	0.3
	Yr	49	225	45	63	11	2	0	27	2	4	.280	.286	.347	633	113	2	2	0	0	.810	0	O-31(0-3-29),P-18	0.3
1876	Lou-N	14	55	2	10	1	0	0	2	0	1	.182	.182	.200	382	23	-5				.882	-2	O-14(0-0-14)	-0.6
	NY-N	2	10	2	3	0	0	0	0	0	0	.300	.300	.300	600	115	0				.429	-1	/O-2(0-2-0)	-0.1
	Yr	16	65	4	13	1	0	0	2	0	1	.200	.200	.215	415	34	-5				.750	-3	O-16(0-2-14)	-0.7
Total	5 n	205	976	211	275	47	11	3	163	21	11	.282	.297	.362	659	104	5	17	2	3	.816	5	O-176R/P-30,3-3,1-1	1.5

YEAR	TM/L	G	AB	R	H	2B	3B	HR	RBI	BB	SO	AVG	OBP	SLG	OPS	OPS+	BR+	SB	CS	SBR	FA	FR	G/POS	TPR
■ **CLYDE BECK**	Beck, Clyde Eugene "Jersey" b: 1/6/1900, Bassett, Cal. d: 7/15/88, Temple City, Cal. BR/TR, 5'10", 176 lbs. Deb: 5/19/26																							
1926	Chi-N	30	81	10	16	0	0	1	4	7	15	.198	.261	.235	496	34	-7	0			.993	12	2-30	0.5
1927	Chi-N	117	391	44	101	20	5	2	44	43	37	.258	.332	.350	682	83	-9	0			.969	22	2-99,3-17/S-1	1.6
1928	Chi-N	131	483	72	124	18	4	3	52	58	58	.257	.341	.329	670	77	-15	3			.958	-1	3-87,S-47/2-1	-0.6
1929	Chi-N	54	190	28	40	7	0	0	9	19	24	.211	.282	.247	530	32	-20	3			.978	5	3-33,S-14	-1.0
1930	Chi-N	83	244	32	52	7	0	6	34	36	32	.213	.314	.316	630	53	-19	2			.953	0	S-57,2-24/3-2	-1.1
1931	Cin-N	53	136	17	21	4	2	0	19	21	14	.154	.272	.213	485	34	-12	1			.960	-2	3-38/S-6	-1.3
Total	6	468	1525	203	354	56	11	12	162	184	180	.232	.317	.307	624	63	-83	9			.959	36	3-177,2-154,S-125	-1.9
■ **ERVE BECK**	Beck, Ervin Thomas "Dutch" b: 7/19/1878, Toledo, Ohio d: 12/23/16, Toledo, Ohio BR/TR, 5'10", 168 lbs. Deb: 9/19/1899 Career OF: (3-LF 0-CF 8-RF)																							
1899	Bro-N	8	24	2	4	2	0	0	2	0		.167	.167	.250	417	13	-3	0			.931	-2	/2-6,S-2	-0.4
1901	Cle-A	135	539	78	156	26	8	6	79	23		.289	.320	.401	720	103	1	7			.927	-11	*2-132	-0.8
1902	Cin-N	48	187	19	57	10	3	1	20	3		.305	.319	.406	726	113	2	2			.936	-5	2-32/1-6,O-6(3-0-3)	-0.4
	Det-A	41	162	23	48	4	0	2	22	4		.296	.313	.358	671	84	-4	3			.971	1	1-36/O-5(0-0-5)	-0.3
Total	3	232	912	122	265	42	11	9	123	30		.291	.315	.390	705	99	-4	12			.929	-16	2-170/1-42,O-11R,S	-1.9
■ **FRANK BECK**	Beck, Frank J. (b: Frank J. Hengstebeck) b: 4/29/1860, Poughkeepsie, N.Y. d: 2/8/41, Detroit, Mich. TR, 5'9", 141 lbs. Deb: 5/2/1884																							
1884	Pit-a	3	12	1	4	1	0	0		0		.333	.333	.417	750	145	1				1.000	0	/P-3	0.0
	Bal-U	5	20	1	2	1	0	0		0		.100	.100	.150	250	-23	-4				.500	-1	/O-4(0-0-4),P-2	-0.4
Total	1	8	32	2	6	2	0	0		0		.188	.188	.250	438	33	-3				1.000	-1	/P-5,O-4(0-0-4)	-0.4
■ **FRED BECK**	Beck, Frederick Thomas b: 11/17/1886, Havana, Ill. d: 3/12/62, Havana, Ill. BL/TL, 6'1", 180 lbs. Deb: 4/14/09 Career OF: (29-LF 173-CF 66-RF)																							
1909	Bos-N	96	334	20	66	5	6	2	27	17		.198	.245	.266	512	56	-18	5			.966	4	O-57(12-42-2),1-33	-1.9
1910	Bos-N	154	571	52	157	32	9	**10**	64	19	55	.275	.307	.415	722	105	-0	8			.963	2	*O-134(2-125-7),1-19	-0.5
1911	Cin-N	41	87	7	16	1	2	2	20	1	13	.184	.193	.310	504	41	-7	2			1.000	-2	O-16(4-5-7)/1-6	-1.0
	Phi-N	66	210	26	59	8	3	3	25	17	21	.281	.346	.390	737	105	1	3			.957	-5	O-61(11-1-50)	-0.7
	Yr	107	297	33	75	9	5	5	45	18	34	.253	.304	.367	671	88	-6	5			.966	-7	O-77(15-6-57)/1-6	-1.7
1914	Chi-F	157	555	51	155	23	4	11	77	44	66	.279	.341	.395	736	106	-5	9			.982	-13	*1-157	-2.3
1915	Chi-F	121	373	35	83	9	3	5	38	24	38	.223	.277	.303	580	67	-23	4			.992	-6	*1-117	-3.5
Total	5	635	2130	191	536	78	27	33	251	122	193	.252	.301	.360	661	89	-53	31			.984	-20	1-332,O-268C	-9.9
■ **ZINN BECK**	Beck, Zinn Bertram b: 9/30/1885, Steubenville, O. d: 3/19/81, W.Palm Beach, Fla. BR/TR, 5'10.5", 160 lbs. Deb: 9/14/13																							
1913	StL-N	10	30	4	5	1	0	0	2	4	10	.167	.265	.200	465	34	-2	1			.833	1	/S-5,3-5	-0.2
1914	StL-N	137	457	42	106	15	11	3	45	28	32	.232	.282	.333	615	84	-11	14			.935	10	*3-122,S-16	0.4
1915	StL-N	70	223	21	52	9	4	0	15	12	31	.233	.282	.309	591	79	-6	3	10	-3	.935	-0	3-62/S-4,2-2	-0.8
1916	StL-N	62	184	8	41	7	1	0	10	14	21	.223	.281	.272	553	71	-6	3			.910	-6	3-52/1-1,2-1	-1.3
1918	NY-A	11	8	0	0	0	0	0	1	0	1	.000	.000	.000	0	-98	-2	0			1.000	0	/1-5,3-1	-0.2
Total	5	290	902	75	204	32	16	3	73	58	95	.226	.279	.307	586	76	-27	21	10		.932	4	3-242/S-25,1-6,2-3	-2.1
■ **HEINIE BECKENDORF**	Beckendorf, Henry Ward b: 6/15/1884, New York, N.Y. d: 9/15/49, Jackson Heights, N.Y. BR/TR, 5'9", 174 lbs. Deb: 4/16/09																							
1909	Det-A	15	27	1	7	1	0	0	1	2		.259	.310	.296	607	88	-0	0			.957	-0	C-15	0.0
1910	Det-A	3	7	0	3	0	0	0	2	1		.429	.500	.429	929	179	1	0			.909	-1	/C-2	0.0
	Was-A	37	103	8	15	1	0	0	10	5		.146	.207	.155	363	14	-10	0			.991	0	C-36	-0.7
	Yr	40	110	8	18	1	0	0	12	6		.164	.227	.173	400	26	-9	0			.988	-0	C-38	-0.7
Total	2	55	137	9	25	2	0	0	13	8		.182	.243	.197	440	39	-10	0			.983	-1	/C-53	-0.7
■ **BEALS BECKER**	Becker, David Beals b: 7/5/1886, ElDorado, Kan. d: 8/16/43, Huntington Park, Cal. BL/TL, 5'9", 170 lbs. Deb: 4/19/08 Career OF: (252-LF 199-CF 313-RF)																							
1908	Pit-N	20	65	4	10	0	1	0	0	2		.154	.191	.185	376	20	-6	2			1.000	-1	O-17(0-0-17)	-0.9
	Bos-N	43	171	13	47	3	1	0	7	7		.275	.303	.304	607	96	-1	7			.941	-4	O-43(0-1-42)	-0.9
	Yr	63	236	17	57	3	2	0	7	9		.242	.272	.271	544	74	-7	9			.958	-5	O-60(0-1-59)	-1.8
1909	Bos-N	152	562	60	138	15	6	6	24	47		.246	.305	.326	631	91	-6	21			.932	-2	*O-152(0-0-152)	-1.7
1910	NY-N	80	126	18	36	2	4	3	24	14	25	.286	.357	.437	794	131	5	11			.972	-3	O-45(6-23-14)/1-1	0.1
1911	*NY-N	88	172	28	45	11	1	1	20	26	22	.262	.359	.355	713	97	-0	19			.975	-5	O-55(17-6-33)	-0.7
1912	*NY-N	125	402	66	106	18	8	6	58	54	35	.264	.354	.393	747	101	1	30			.958	-1	*O-117(1-93-26)	-0.7
1913	Cin-N	30	108	11	32	5	3	0	14	6	12	.296	.333	.398	731	109	1	0			.971	2	O-28(9-8-11)	0.2
	Phi-N	88	306	53	99	19	10	9	44	22	30	.324	.369	.539	908	151	19	11			.983	-2	O-77(42-36-2)/1-1	1.3
	Yr	118	414	64	131	24	13	9	58	28	42	.316	.360	.502	862	140	20	11			.980	0	*O-105(51-44-13)/1-1	1.5
1914	Phi-N	138	514	76	167	25	5	9	66	37	59	.325	.370	.446	816	133	20	16			.947	9	*O-126(87-32-8)	2.3
1915	*Phi-N	112	338	38	83	16	4	11	35	26	48	.246	.301	.414	716	114	4	12	15	-3	.943	-7	O-98(90-0-8)	-1.1
Total	8	876	2764	367	763	114	43	45	292	241	231	.276	.335	.397	732	112	35	129	15		.955	-13	O-758R/1-2	-2.1
■ **HEINZ BECKER**	Becker, Heinz Reinhard "Dutch" b: 8/26/15, Berlin, Germany d: 11/11/91, Dallas, Tex. BB/TR (BL 1946), 6'2", 200 lbs. Deb: 4/21/43																							
1943	Chi-N	24	69	5	10	0	0	0	2	9	6	.145	.244	.145	389	14	-7	0			.983	1	1-18	-0.7
1945	*Chi-N	67	133	25	38	8	2	2	27	17	16	.286	.375	.421	796	124	5	0			1.000	-2	1-28	0.2
1946	Chi-N	9	7	0	2	0	0	0	1	1	1	.286	.375	.286	661	91	-0	0			.000	0	H	0.0
	Cle-A	50	147	15	44	10	1	0	17	23	18	.299	.401	.381	782	127	7	1	0	0	.995	0	1-44	0.6
1947	Cle-A	2	2	0	0	0	0	0	0	0	1	.000	.000	.000	0	-99	-1	0	0	0	.000	0	H	-0.1
Total	4	152	358	45	94	18	3	2	47	50	42	.263	.359	.346	706	102	3	1	0		.994	0	/1-90	0.0
■ **JOE BECKER**	Becker, Joseph Edward b: 6/25/08, St.Louis, Mo. d: 1/11/98, Sunset Hills, Mo. BR/TR, 6'1", 180 lbs. Deb: 5/10/36 C																							
1936	Cle-A	22	50	5	9	3	1	1	11	5	4	.180	.255	.340	595	45	-5	0	0	0	.977	-4	C-15	-0.7
1937	Cle-A	18	33	3	11	2	1	0	2	3	4	.333	.405	.455	860	116	1	0	0	0	.949	-1	C-12	0.1
Total	2	40	83	8	20	5	2	1	13	8	8	.241	.315	.386	701	73	-4	0	0	0	.964	-5	/C-27	-0.6
■ **MARTY BECKER**	Becker, Martin Henry b: 12/25/1893, Tiffin, Ohio d: 9/25/57, Cincinnati, Ohio BB/TL, 5'8.5", 155 lbs. Deb: 9/8/15																							
1915	NY-N	17	52	5	13	2	0	0	3	2	9	.250	.278	.288	566	76	-2	3			.917	0	O-16(0-16-1)	-0.2
■ **RICH BECKER**	Becker, Richard Godhard b: 2/1/72, Aurora, Ill. BL/TL (BB 1993-95), 5'10", 199 lbs. Deb: 9/10/93 Career OF: (104-LF 476-CF 160-RF)																							
1993	Min-A	3	7	3	2	2	0	0	0	5	4	.286	.583	.571	1155	211	2	1	1	-0	.875	-0	/O-3(0-3-0)	0.1
1994	Min-A	28	98	12	26	3	0	1	8	13	25	.265	.351	.327	678	76	-3	6	1	1	.989	5	O-26(1-23-2)/D-1	0.3
1995	Min-A	106	392	45	93	15	1	2	33	34	95	.237	.305	.296	601	57	-24	8	9	-1	.986	13	*O-105(2-99-5)	-1.2
1996	Min-A	148	525	92	153	31	4	12	71	68	118	.291	.375	.434	809	102	3	19	5	2	.993	**24**	*O-146(15-121-10)	2.7
1997	Min-A	132	443	61	117	22	3	10	45	62	130	.264	.356	.395	751	94	-2	17	5	2	.985	1	*O-128(9-114-14)	0.0
1998	NY-N	49	100	15	19	4	2	3	10	21	42	.190	.331	.360	691	83	-2	3	1	0	.984	-3	O-41(17-14-13)	-0.5
	Bal-A	79	113	22	23	1	0	3	11	22	34	.204	.343	.292	635	69	-5	2	0	0	.984	-13	O-60(5-13-43)D-1	-1.8
1999	Mil-N	89	139	15	35	5	2	5	16	33	38	.252	.395	.424	820	109	3	5	0	1	.970	-7	O-50(16-19-17)/D-2	-0.3
	Oak-A	40	125	21	33	3	0	1	10	25	43	.264	.395	.312	707	87	-1	3	2	-0	.986	-10	O-39(17-32-8)	-1.1
2000	Oak-A	23	47	11	11	2	0	1	5	11	17	.234	.390	.340	730	89	-0	1	1	-0	.949	-2	O-19(8-14-1)/D-2	-0.2
	Det-A	92	238	48	58	12	0	7	34	56	70	.244	.388	.382	770	99	2	1	2	-0	.956	-9	O-80(14-24-47)/D-3	-0.9
	Yr	115	285	59	69	14	0	8	39	67	87	.242	.388	.375	764	98	2	2	2	-0	.954	-11	O-99(22-38-48)/D-5	-1.1
Total	8	789	2227	345	570	100	12	45	243	350	616	.256	.360	.372	732	89	-28	66	26	5	.983	-2	O-697C/D-9	-2.9
■ **GLENN BECKERT**	Beckert, Glenn Alfred b: 10/12/40, Pittsburgh, Pa. BR/TR, 6'1", 190 lbs. Deb: 4/12/65 Career OF: (0-LF 1-CF 0-RF)																							
1965	Chi-N	154	614	73	147	21	3	3	30	28	52	.239	.276	.298	574	60	-32	6	8	-1	.973	9	*2-153	-1.2
1966	Chi-N	153	656	73	188	23	7	1	59	26	36	.287	.318	.348	665	84	-14	10	4	1	.970	-20	*2-152/S-1	-2.1
1967	Chi-N	146	597	91	167	32	3	5	40	30	25	.280	.314	.369	683	91	-7	10	3	1	.968	4	*2-144	1.1
1968	Chi-N	155	643	**98**	189	28	4	4	37	31	20	.294	.328	.369	697	102	2	8	4	0	.977	6	*2-155	2.5
1969	Chi-N★	131	543	69	158	22	1	1	37	24	24	.291	.328	.341	669	78	-15	6	0	1	.965	6	*2-129	0.1
1970	Chi-N★	143	591	99	170	15	6	3	36	32	22	.288	.324	.349	673	72	-23	4	1	1	.970	10	*2-138/O-1(0-1-0)	-0.3
1971	Chi-N★	131	530	80	181	18	5	2	42	24	24	.342	.370	.406	776	104	4	3	2	-0	.986	-3	*2-129	1.0
1972	Chi-N★	120	474	51	128	22	2	3	43	23	17	.270	.307	.344	650	76	-14	2	1	0	.976	11	*2-118	0.5

YEAR	TM/L	G	AB	R	H	2B	3B	HR	RBI	BB	SO	AVG	OBP	SLG	OPS	OPS+	BR+	SB	CS	SBR	FA	FR	G/POS	TPR
1973	Chi-N	114	372	38	95	13	0	0	29	30	15	.255	.314	.290	605	64	-17	0	2	-1	.984	-12	2-88	-2.6
1974	SD-N	64	172	11	44	1	0	0	7	11	8	.256	.301	.262	562	61	-9	0	0	0	.938	-17	2-36/3-1	-2.5
1975	SD-N	9	16	2	6	1	0	0	0	1	0	.375	.412	.438	849	145	1	0	0	0	1.000	-1	/3-4	0.0
Total	11	1320	5208	685	1473	196	31	22	360	260	243	.283	.319	.345	664	81	-125	49	25	2	.973	-7	*2-1242/3-5,O-1C,S	-3.5

■ JAKE BECKLEY Beckley, Jacob Peter "Eagle Eye" b: 8/4/1867, Hannibal, Mo. d: 6/25/18, Kansas City, Mo. BL/TL, 5'10", 200 lbs. Deb: 6/20/1888 H Career OF: (2-LF 3-CF 1-RF)

YEAR	TM/L	G	AB	R	H	2B	3B	HR	RBI	BB	SO	AVG	OBP	SLG	OPS	OPS+	BR+	SB	CS	SBR	FA	FR	G/POS	TPR
1888	Pit-N	71	283	35	97	15	3	0	27	7	22	.343	.363	.417	780	160	19	20			.979	-3	1-71	0.9
1889	Pit-N	123	522	91	157	24	10	9	97	29	29	.301	.345	.437	781	130	20	11			.982	2	*1-122/O-1(0-0-1)	0.9
1890	Pit-P	121	516	109	167	38	**22**	9	120	42	32	.324	.381	.535	916	156	39	18			.976	-0	*1-121	2.2
1891	Pit-N	133	554	94	162	20	19	4	73	44	46	.292	.353	.419	772	128	18	13			.982	13	*1-133	1.7
1892	Pit-N	151	614	102	145	21	19	10	96	31	44	.236	.288	.381	669	102	-2	30			.978	21	*1-151	1.6
1893	Pit-N	131	542	108	164	32	19	5	106	54	26	.303	.386	.459	846	127	21	15			.986	11	*1-131	2.5
1894	Pit-N	132	537	123	185	36	19	7	122	43	16	.345	.412	.521	934	125	21	21			.978	5	*1-132	2.0
1895	Pit-N	130	534	104	175	31	19	5	110	24	20	.328	.380	.485	865	129	22	20			.978	-7	*1-130	1.2
1896	Pit-N	59	217	44	55	7	5	3	32	22	28	.253	.349	.373	723	94	-1	8			.982	-1	1-56/O-3(0-3-0),2-1	-0.2
	NY-N	46	182	37	55	8	4	6	38	9	7	.302	.352	.489	841	124	5	11			.982	-1	1-45/O-2(2-0-0)	0.3
	Yr	105	399	81	110	15	9	9	70	31	35	.276	.351	.426	777	108	4	19			.982	-2	*1-101/O-5(2-3-0),2-1	0.1
1897	NY-N	17	68	8	17	2	3	1	11	2		.250	.301	.412	713	90	-1	2			.973	2	1-17	0.0
	Cin-N	97	365	76	126	17	9	7	76	18		.345	.395	.499	894	127	12	23			.979	-4	*1-97	0.7
	Yr	114	433	84	143	19	12	8	87	20		.330	.380	.485	865	121	11	25			.978	-2	*1-114	0.7
1898	Cin-N	118	459	86	135	20	12	4	72	28		.294	.348	.416	764	111	5	6			.983	-1	*1-118	0.3
1899	Cin-N	135	517	87	172	27	16	3	99	40		.333	.392	.464	856	132	22	20			.986	5	*1-135	2.4
1900	Cin-N	141	558	98	190	26	10	2	94	40		.341	.389	.434	822	130	23	23			.980	6	*1-140	2.5
1901	Cin-N	140	580	78	178	36	13	3	79	28		.307	.346	.429	776	133	23	4			.977	-4	*1-140	1.6
1902	Cin-N	129	531	82	175	23	7	5	69	34		.330	.377	.427	804	135	21	15			.983	-3	*1-129/P-1	1.5
1903	Cin-N	120	459	85	150	29	10	2	81	42		.327	.384	.447	831	123	13	23			.976	4	*1-119	1.3
1904	StL-N	142	551	72	179	22	9	1	67	35		.325	.375	.403	778	147	30	17			.988	-12	*1-142	1.7
1905	StL-N	134	514	48	147	20	10	1	57	30		.286	.333	.370	702	113	7	12			.982	-8	*1-134	-0.3
1906	StL-N	87	320	29	79	16	6	0	44	13		.247	.283	.334	617	96	-3	3			.987	-4	1-85	-1.0
1907	StL-N	32	115	6	24	3	0	0	7	1		.209	.222	.235	457	45	-8	0			.988	-2	1-32	-1.2
Total	20	2389	9538	1602	2934	473	244	87	1577	616	270	.308	.361	.436	797	126	305	315			.981	19	*1-2380/O-6C,P-1,2	22.6

■ JULIO BECQUER Becquer, Julio (Villegas) b: 12/20/31, Havana, Cuba BL/TL, 5'11.5", 178 lbs. Deb: 9/13/55

YEAR	TM/L	G	AB	R	H	2B	3B	HR	RBI	BB	SO	AVG	OBP	SLG	OPS	OPS+	BR+	SB	CS	SBR	FA	FR	G/POS	TPR
1955	Was-A	10	14	1	3	0	0	0	1	0	1	.214	.214	.214	429	16	-2	0	0	0	1.000	1	/1-2	-0.1
1957	Was-A	105	186	14	42	6	2	2	22	10	29	.226	.269	.312	581	59	-11	3	3	-0	1.000	-0	1-43	-1.4
1958	Was-A	86	164	10	39	3	0	0	12	8	21	.238	.273	.256	529	47	-12	1	2	-0	.994	6	1-42/O-1(1-0-0)	-0.9
1959	Was-A	108	220	20	59	12	5	1	26	8	17	.268	.297	.382	679	85	-5	3	2	-0	.990	2	1-53	-0.6
1960	Was-A	110	298	41	75	15	7	4	35	12	35	.252	.283	.389	672	81	-9	1	3	-1	.989	-3	1-77/P-1	-1.7
1961	LA-A	11	8	0	0	0	0	0	0	1	5	.000	.111	.000	111	-61	-2	0	0	0	1.000	0	/1-5	-0.2
	Min-A	57	84	13	20	1	2	5	18	2	12	.238	.256	.476	732	86	-2	0	1	-0	1.000	-1	1-18/O-5(5-0-0),P-1	-0.4
	Yr	68	92	13	20	1	2	5	18	3	17	.217	.242	.435	677	72	-4	0	1	-0	1.000	-0	1-23/O-5(5-0-0),P-1	-0.6
1963	Min-A	1	0	1	0	0	0	0	0	0	0	—	—	—	—	—	0	0	0	0	.000	0	H	0.0
Total	7	488	974	100	238	37	16	12	114	41	120	.244	.277	.352	629	70	-42	8	11	-2	.993	5	1-240/O-6(6-0-0),P-2	-5.3

■ HOWIE BEDELL Bedell, Howard William b: 9/29/35, Clearfield, Pa. BL/TR, 6'1", 185 lbs. Deb: 4/10/62 C

YEAR	TM/L	G	AB	R	H	2B	3B	HR	RBI	BB	SO	AVG	OBP	SLG	OPS	OPS+	BR+	SB	CS	SBR	FA	FR	G/POS	TPR
1962	Mil-N	58	138	15	27	1	2	0	2	11	22	.196	.255	.232	487	33	-13	1	0	0	.955	-3	O-45(44-2-0)	-1.8
1968	Phi-N	9	7	0	1	0	0	0	1	1	0	.143	.250	.143	393	20	-1	0	0	0	.000	0	H	-0.1
Total	2	67	145	15	28	1	2	0	3	12	22	.193	.255	.228	482	32	-14	1	0	0	.955	-3	/O-45(44-2-0)	-1.9

■ GENE BEDFORD Bedford, William Eugene b: 12/2/1896, Dallas, Tex. d: 10/6/77, San Antonio, Tex. BB/TR, 5'8", 170 lbs. Deb: 6/25/25

YEAR	TM/L	G	AB	R	H	2B	3B	HR	RBI	BB	SO	AVG	OBP	SLG	OPS	OPS+	BR+	SB	CS	SBR	FA	FR	G/POS	TPR
1925	Cle-A	2	3	1	0	0	0	0	0	0	1	.000	.000	.000	0	-99	-1	0	0	0	1.000	-1	/2-2	-0.2

■ ED BEECHER Beecher, Edward "Scrap Iron" b: 5/1876, Indiana Deb: 9/26/1897

YEAR	TM/L	G	AB	R	H	2B	3B	HR	RBI	BB	SO	AVG	OBP	SLG	OPS	OPS+	BR+	SB	CS	SBR	FA	FR	G/POS	TPR
1897	StL-N	3	12	1	4	0	0	0	1	0		.333	.333	.333	667	78	-0	1			1.000	-0	/O-3(3-0-0)	-0.1
1898	Cle-N	8	25	1	5	2	0	0	0	0		.200	.200	.280	480	38	-2	0			.846	-2	/O-8(0-8-0)	-0.4
Total	2	11	37	2	9	2	0	0	1	0		.243	.243	.297	541	51	-3	1			.895	-2	/O-11(3-8-0)	-0.5

■ ED BEECHER Beecher, Edward Harry b: 7/2/1860, Guilford, Conn. d: 9/12/35, Hartford, Conn. BL/TL, 5'10", 185 lbs. Deb: 6/28/1887 Career OF: (190-LF 28-CF 62-RF)

YEAR	TM/L	G	AB	R	H	2B	3B	HR	RBI	BB	SO	AVG	OBP	SLG	OPS	OPS+	BR+	SB	CS	SBR	FA	FR	G/POS	TPR
1887	Pit-N	41	176	15	48	8	0	2	22	7	8	.273	.281	.325	606	72	-6	8			.915	5	O-41(18-22-1)	-0.2
1889	Was-N	42	179	20	53	9	0	0	30	5	4	.296	.319	.346	665	91	-2	3			.861	-1	O-39(1-0-38)/1-3	-0.4
1890	Buf-P	126	536	69	159	22	10	3	90	29	23	.297	.341	.392	733	104	3	14			.810	-5	*O-126(119-0-7)/P-1	-0.3
1891	Was-a	58	235	35	57	11	3	2	28	27	9	.243	.333	.340	674	97	-0	17			.824	3	O-58(52-6-0)	0.1
	Phi-a	16	71	9	15	2	4	0	7	3	4	.211	.243	.352	595	70	-3	7			1.000	-1	O-16(0-0-16)	-0.4
	Yr	74	306	44	72	13	7	2	35	30	13	.235	.314	.343	657	91	-4	24			.845	2	O-74(52-6-16)	-0.3
Total	4	283	1197	148	332	52	17	7	177	71	48	.277	.322	.363	685	94	-9	49			.843	1	O-280L/1-3,P-1	-1.2

■ JODIE BEELER Beeler, Joseph Sam b: 11/26/21, Dallas, Tex. BR/TR, 6', 170 lbs. Deb: 9/21/44

YEAR	TM/L	G	AB	R	H	2B	3B	HR	RBI	BB	SO	AVG	OBP	SLG	OPS	OPS+	BR+	SB	CS	SBR	FA	FR	G/POS	TPR
1944	Cin-N	3	3	0	0	0	0	0	0	0	2	.000	.000	.000	0	-99	-1	0			.000	-1	/2-1,3-1	-0.2

■ GENE BEGLEY Begley, Eugene T. b: 6/7/1861, Brooklyn, N.Y. Deb: 9/11/1886

YEAR	TM/L	G	AB	R	H	2B	3B	HR	RBI	BB	SO	AVG	OBP	SLG	OPS	OPS+	BR+	SB	CS	SBR	FA	FR	G/POS	TPR
1886	NY-N	5	16	1	2	0	0	0	1	1	3	.125	.176	.125	301	-7	-2	1			.864	-1	/C-3,O-2(0-0-2)	-0.2

■ JIM BEGLEY Begley, James Lawrence "Imp" b: 9/19/02, San Francisco, Cal. d: 2/20/57, San Francisco, Cal BR/TR, 5'6", 145 lbs. Deb: 5/28/24

YEAR	TM/L	G	AB	R	H	2B	3B	HR	RBI	BB	SO	AVG	OBP	SLG	OPS	OPS+	BR+	SB	CS	SBR	FA	FR	G/POS	TPR
1924	Cin-N	2	5	1	1	0	0	0	0	2	0	.200	.429	.200	629	75	-0	0	0	0	.933	1	/2-2	0.1

■ STEVE BEHEL Behel, Stephen Arnold Douglas b: 11/6/1860, Earlville, Ill. d: 2/15/45, Los Angeles, Cal. Deb: 9/27/1884

YEAR	TM/L	G	AB	R	H	2B	3B	HR	RBI	BB	SO	AVG	OBP	SLG	OPS	OPS+	BR+	SB	CS	SBR	FA	FR	G/POS	TPR
1884	Mil-U	9	33	5	8	1	0	0		3		.242	.306	.273	578	141	1				1.000	-1	/O-9(9-0-0)	0.0
1886	NY-a	59	224	32	46	5	2	0	17	22		.205	.279	.246	525	68	-7	16			.858	-4	O-59(26-33-0)	-1.2
Total	2	68	257	37	54	6	2	0	17	25		.210	.283	.249	532	73	-6	16			.865	-5	/O-68(35-33-0)	-1.2

■ OLLIE BEJMA Bejma, Alojzy Frank b: 9/12/07, South Bend, Ind. d: 1/3/95, South Bend, Ind. BR/TR, 5'10", 165 lbs. Deb: 4/24/34 Career OF: (0-LF 0-CF 9-RF)

YEAR	TM/L	G	AB	R	H	2B	3B	HR	RBI	BB	SO	AVG	OBP	SLG	OPS	OPS+	BR+	SB	CS	SBR	FA	FR	G/POS	TPR
1934	StL-A	95	262	39	71	16	3	2	29	40	36	.271	.376	.378	754	87	-4	3	2	-0	.952	-12	S-32,2-14,3-13,/O-9R	-1.2
1935	StL-A	64	198	18	38	8	2	2	26	27	21	.192	.289	.283	572	46	-16	1	0	0	.952	-4	2-47/S-8,3-2	-1.6
1936	StL-A	67	139	19	36	2	3	2	18	27	21	.259	.380	.360	739	81	-3	0	0	0	.963	-12	2-32/3-7,S-1	-1.2
1939	Chi-A	90	307	52	77	9	3	8	44	36	27	.251	.331	.378	709	79	-10	1	3	-1	.981	-14	2-81/S-1,3-1	-1.8
Total	4	316	906	128	222	35	11	14	117	130	105	.245	.343	.354	697	75	-33	5	5	-1	.967	-42	2-174/S-42,3-23,O-9R	-5.8

■ MARK BELANGER Belanger, Mark Henry b: 6/8/44, Pittsfield, Mass. d: 10/6/98, New York, N.Y. BR/TR, 6'1", 170 lbs. Deb: 8/7/65

YEAR	TM/L	G	AB	R	H	2B	3B	HR	RBI	BB	SO	AVG	OBP	SLG	OPS	OPS+	BR+	SB	CS	SBR	FA	FR	G/POS	TPR
1965	Bal-A	11	3	1	1	0	0	0	0	0	1	.333	.333	.333	667	88	-0	0	1	-0	1.000	1	/S-4	0.1
1966	Bal-A	8	19	2	3	1	0	0	0	0	3	.158	.158	.211	368	5	-2	0	0	0	1.000	4	/S-6	0.2
1967	Bal-A	69	184	19	32	5	0	1	10	12	46	.174	.224	.217	442	31	-16	6	1	1	.952	7	S-38,2-26/3-2	-0.5
1968	Bal-A	145	472	40	98	13	0	2	21	40	114	.208	.275	.248	523	59	-22	10	1	2	.969	12	*S-145	0.5
1969	*Bal-A	150	530	76	152	17	4	2	50	53	54	.287	.354	.345	699	95	-2	14	6	1	.968	-10	*S-148	0.7
1970	*Bal-A	145	459	53	100	6	5	1	36	52	65	.218	.304	.259	564	56	-26	13	2	2	.970	8	*S-143	-0.1
1971	*Bal-A	150	500	67	133	19	4	0	35	73	48	.266	.367	.320	687	97	1	10	8	-1	.978	-0	*S-149	1.9
1972	Bal-A	113	285	36	53	9	1	2	16	18	53	.186	.239	.246	485	43	-20	6	3	0	.975	21	*S-105	1.2
1973	*Bal-A	154	470	60	106	15	1	0	27	49	54	.226	.305	.262	567	61	-23	13	6	1	.971	-3	*S-154	-0.1
1974	*Bal-A	155	493	54	111	14	4	5	36	51	69	.225	.300	.300	601	75	-15	17	7	1	**.984**	9	*S-155	1.5
1975	Bal-A	152	442	44	100	11	1	3	27	36	53	.226	.286	.276	562	63	-21	16	4	2	.978	**28**	*S-152	2.7
1976	Bal-A★	153	522	66	141	22	2	1	40	51	64	.270	.337	.326	663	101	2	27	17	-0	.982	16	*S-153	3.8
1977	Bal-A	144	402	39	83	13	4	2	30	43	68	.206	.288	.274	562	58	-23	15	8	1	**.985**	21	*S-142	1.1

YEAR	TM/L	G	AB	R	H	2B	3B	HR	RBI	BB	SO	AVG	OBP	SLG	OPS	OPS+	BR+	SB	CS	SBR	FA	FR	G/POS	TPR
1978	Bal-A	135	348	39	74	13	0	0	16	40	55	.213	.305	.250	555	61	-17	6	6	-1	**.985**	**34**	*S-134	2.9
1979	*Bal-A	101	198	28	33	6	2	0	9	29	33	.167	.276	.217	493	36	-17	5	1	1	.990	3	S-98	-0.7
1980	Bal-A	113	268	37	61	7	3	0	22	12	25	.228	.261	.276	537	48	-19	6	3	0	.975	-1	*S-109	-1.1
1981	Bal-A	64	139	9	23	3	2	1	10	12	25	.165	.242	.237	479	39	-11	2	1	0	.973	5	S-63	-0.1
1982	LA-N	54	50	6	12	1	0	0	4	5	10	.240	.309	.260	569	62	-2	1	0	0	.953	8	S-44/2-1	0.7
Total	18	2016	5784	676	1316	175	33	20	389	576	839	.228	.302	.280	582	68	-233	167	75	10	.977	167	*S-1942/2-27,3-2	14.7
■ **WAYNE BELARDI**	Belardi, Carroll Wayne b: 9/5/30, St.Helena, Cal. d: 10/21/93, Santa Cruz, Cal. BL/TL, 6'1", 185 lbs. Deb: 4/18/50																							
1950	Bro-N	10	10	0	0	0	0	0	0	0	4	.000	.000	.000	0	-98	-3	0			1.000	-0	/1-1	-0.3
1951	Bro-N	3	3	1	1	0	1	0	0	0	2	.333	.333	1.000	1333	240	1	0	0	0	.000	0	H	0.1
1953	*Bro-N	69	163	19	39	3	2	11	34	16	40	.239	.311	.485	796	101	-0	0	0	0	.984	-0	1-38	-0.3
1954	Bro-N	11	9	0	2	0	0	0	1	2	3	.222	.364	.222	586	55	-0	0	0	0	.000	0	H	0.0
	Det-A	88	250	27	58	7	1	11	24	33	34	.232	.333	.400	733	102	0	1	0	0	.988	2	1-79	-0.2
1955	Det-A	3	3	0	0	0	0	0	0	0	1	.000	.000	.000	0	-99	-1	0	0	0	.000	0	H	-0.1
1956	Det-A	79	154	24	43	3	1	6	15	15	13	.279	.373	.429	801	111	3	0	0	0	.988	-1	1-31/O-2(2-0-1)	0.0
Total	6	263	592	71	143	13	5	28	74	66	97	.242	.332	.422	754	100	-1	1	0	0	.987	0	1-149/O-2(2-0-1)	-0.8
■ **KEVIN BELCHER**	Belcher, Kevin Donnell b: 8/8/67, Waco, Tex. BR/TR, 6', 170 lbs. Deb: 9/3/90																							
1990	Tex-A	16	15	4	2	1	0	0	0	2	6	.133	.235	.200	435	23	-2	0	0	0	1.000	-2	/O-9(2-5-2)	-0.3
■ **IRA BELDEN**	Belden, Ira Allison b: 4/16/1874, Cleveland, Ohio d: 7/15/16, Lakewood, Ohio BL/TR, 5'11", 175 lbs. Deb: 9/17/1897																							
1897	Cle-N	8	30	5	8	0	2	0	4	2		.267	.333	.400	733	88	-1	0			1.000	2	/O-8(0-0-8)	0.1
■ **TIM BELK**	Belk, Timothy William b: 4/6/70, Cincinnati, Ohio BR/TR, 6'3", 200 lbs. Deb: 6/25/96																							
1996	Cin-N	7	15	2	3	0	0	0	0	1	2	.200	.250	.200	450	20	-2	0	0	0	1.000	-1	/1-6	-0.3
■ **CHARLIE BELL**	Bell, Charles C. b: 8/12/1868, Cincinnati, Ohio d: 2/7/37, Cincinnati, Ohio TR, Deb: 10/13/1889 F																							
1889	KC-a	2	6	1	1	1	0	0	3	2	2	.167	.375	.333	708	97	0	0			.000	-0	/O-1(1-0-0),P-1	-0.1
1891	Lou-a	10	28	3	1	0	0	0	0	6	8	.036	.206	.036	242	-31	-5	0			.783	-2	P-10	0.0
	Cin-a	1	4	1	2	0	0	0	1	0	0	.500	.500	.500	1000	171	0	0			1.000	0	/P-1	0.0
	Yr	11	32	4	3	0	0	0	1	6	8	.094	.237	.094	331	-5	-4	0			.815	-1	P-11	0.0
Total	2	13	38	5	4	1	0	0	4	8	10	.105	.261	.132	392	13	-4	0			.844	-1	/P-12,O-1(1-0-0)	-0.1
■ **BUDDY BELL**	Bell, David Gus b: 8/27/51, Pittsburgh, Pa. BR/TR, 6'2", 185 lbs. Deb: 4/15/72 FMC Career OF: (11-LF 64-CF 66-RF)																							
1972	Cle-A	132	466	49	119	21	1	9	36	34	29	.255	.310	.363	673	96	-2	5	6	-1	.990	7	*O-123(0-63-65)/3-6	-0.1
1973	Cle-A★	156	631	86	169	23	7	14	59	49	47	.268	.327	.393	720	100	-1	7	15	-4	.958	24	*3-154/O-2(0-1-1)	1.9
1974	Cle-A	116	423	51	111	15	1	7	46	35	29	.262	.323	.352	675	95	-3	1	3	-1	.963	4	*3-115/D-1	0.0
1975	Cle-A	153	553	66	150	20	4	10	59	51	72	.271	.334	.376	710	100	0	6	5	-0	.950	-3	*3-153	-0.4
1976	Cle-A	159	604	75	170	26	2	7	60	44	49	.281	.332	.366	698	105	4	3	8	-2	.956	5	*3-158/1-2	0.6
1977	Cle-A	129	479	64	140	23	4	11	64	45	63	.292	.354	.426	780	115	10	1	8	-3	.960	13	*3-118,O-11(11-0-0)	1.8
1978	Cle-A	142	556	71	157	27	8	6	62	39	43	.282	.329	.392	721	103	2	1	3	-1	.970	28	*3-139/D-1	2.7
1979	Tex-A	162	670	89	200	42	3	18	101	30	45	.299	.331	.451	782	110	7	5	4	-0	.969	12	*3-147,S-33	1.9
1980	Tex-A★	129	490	76	161	24	4	17	83	40	39	.329	.379	.498	877	143	28	3	1	0	**.981**	22	*3-120/S-3	4.7
1981	Tex-A★	97	360	44	106	16	1	10	64	42	30	.294	.373	.428	801	137	18	3	3	-0	.961	**30**	3-96/S-1	4.7
1982	Tex-A★	148	537	62	159	27	2	13	67	70	50	.296	.379	.426	806	127	22	5	4	-0	**.976**	**34**	*3-145/S-4	5.3
1983	Tex-A	156	618	75	171	35	3	14	66	50	48	.277	.335	.411	746	106	5	3	5	-1	.967	16	*3-154	1.7
1984	Tex-A★	148	553	88	174	36	5	11	83	63	54	.315	.388	.458	845	129	23	2	1	0	.958	21	*3-147	4.1
1985	Tex-A	84	313	33	74	13	3	4	32	33	21	.236	.311	.335	647	76	-10	3	2	-0	.942	13	3-83	0.2
	Cin-N	67	247	28	54	15	2	6	36	34	27	.219	.313	.368	682	86	-5	0	1	-0	.946	-9	3-67	-1.6
1986	Cin-N	155	568	89	158	29	3	20	75	73	49	.278	.365	.445	811	117	14	2	8	-2	.975	1	*3-151/2-1	1.1
1987	Cin-N	143	522	74	148	19	2	17	70	71	39	.284	.370	.425	796	105	6	4	1	1	**.979**	-17	*3-142	-1.3
1988	Cin-N	21	54	3	10	0	0	0	3	7	3	.185	.279	.185	464	34	-4	0	0	0	.968	0	3-13/1-2	-0.5
	Hou-N	74	269	24	68	10	1	7	37	19	29	.253	.302	.375	678	97	-2	1	1	-0	.924	-11	3-66/1-7	-1.5
	Yr	95	323	27	78	10	1	7	40	26	32	.241	.298	.344	642	86	-6	1	1	-0	.931	-11	3-79/1-9	-2.0
1989	Tex-A	34	82	4	15	4	0	0	3	7	10	.183	.247	.232	479	35	-7	0	0	0	1.000	1	D-22/3-9,1-1	-0.7
Total	18	2405	8995	1151	2514	425	56	201	1106	836	776	.279	.343	.406	750	108	106	55	79	-16	.964	191	*3-2183,O-136R/SD12	24.6
■ **DAVID BELL**	Bell, David Michael b: 9/14/72, Cincinnati, Ohio BR/TR, 5'10", 170 lbs. Deb: 5/3/95 F Career OF: (1-LF 0-CF 0-RF)																							
1995	Cle-A	2	2	0	0	0	0	0	0	0	0	.000	.000	.000	0	-99	-1	0	0	0	1.000	0	/3-2	0.0
	StL-N	39	144	13	36	7	2	2	19	4	25	.250	.280	.368	648	69	-7	1	2	-0	.967	-3	2-37/3-3	-0.8
1996	StL-N	62	145	12	31	6	0	1	9	10	22	.214	.269	.276	545	45	-12	1	1	-0	.953	9	3-45,2-20/S-1	-0.2
1997	StL-N	66	142	9	30	7	2	1	12	10	28	.211	.263	.310	573	50	-11	1	0	0	.913	3	3-35,2-23,S-13	-0.6
1998	StL-N	4	9	0	2	1	0	0	0	0	3	.222	.222	.333	556	44	-1	0	0	0	1.000	-1	/3-4,2-1	-0.1
	Cle-A	107	340	37	89	21	2	10	41	22	54	.262	.310	.424	734	86	-8	0	4	-1	.982	23	*2-101/3-6,1-1,S-1	1.7
	Sea-A	21	80	11	26	8	0	0	8	5	8	.325	.365	.425	790	105	1	0	0	0	.984	3	2-14/1-5,3-5,O-1L	0.3
	Yr	128	420	48	115	29	2	10	49	27	62	.274	.321	.424	745	89	-7	0	4	-1	.982	**26**	*2-115,3-11/1-6,SO	2.0
1999	Sea-A	157	597	92	160	31	2	21	78	58	90	.268	.335	.432	767	96	-4	7	4	0	.978	-12	*2-154/1-4,S-1	-0.8
2000	*Sea-A	133	454	57	112	24	2	11	47	42	66	.247	.319	.381	700	78	-15	2	3	-1	.944	-14	3-93,2-48/1-2,S-1	-2.5
Total	6	591	1913	231	486	105	10	46	214	151	296	.254	.313	.392	704	81	-57	12	14	-2	.979	9	2-398,3-193/S-17,1O	-3.0
■ **GUS BELL**	Bell, David Russell b: 11/15/28, Louisville, Ky. d: 5/7/95, Montgomery, Ohio BL/TR, 6'2", 196 lbs. Deb: 5/30/50 F																							
1950	Pit-N	111	422	62	119	22	11	8	53	28	46	.282	.333	.443	776	99	-2	4			.977	6	*O-104(0-0-104)	0.1
1951	Pit-N	149	600	80	167	27	**12**	16	89	42	41	.278	.330	.443	773	103	1	1	4	-1	.986	3	*O-145(0-0-145)	-0.2
1952	Pit-N	131	468	53	117	21	5	16	59	36	72	.250	.306	.419	725	97	-4	1	4	-1	.972	-7	*O-123(0-0-123)	-1.7
1953	Cin-N★	151	610	102	183	37	5	30	105	48	72	.300	.354	.525	879	124	20	0	2	-1	.977	14	*O-151(0-145-6)	2.5
1954	Cin-N★	153	619	104	185	38	7	17	101	48	58	.299	.353	.465	818	108	7	5	3	0	.986	2	*O-153(0-153-0)	0.1
1955	Cin-N	154	610	88	188	30	6	27	104	54	57	.308	.364	.510	874	122	18	4	4	-1	.987	-8	*O-154(0-154-0)	0.3
1956	Cin-N★	150	603	82	176	31	4	29	84	50	66	.292	.349	.501	850	117	14	6	2	1	.986	-7	*O-149(0-149-0)	0.0
1957	Cin-N★	121	510	65	149	20	3	13	61	30	54	.292	.335	.420	755	95	-4	0	1	-0	.988	0	*O-121(0-121-0)	-1.0
1958	Cin-N	112	385	42	97	16	2	10	46	36	40	.252	.318	.382	699	80	-11	2	3	-1	**.996**	-2	*O-107(20-87-0)	-1.9
1959	Cin-N	148	580	59	170	27	2	19	115	29	44	.293	.329	.445	774	101	-0	2	3	-1	**.996**	7	*O-145(6-0-141)	0.1
1960	Cin-N	143	515	65	135	19	5	12	62	29	40	.262	.303	.388	691	86	-11	4	3	-0	.988	0	*O-131(41-0-97)	-1.6
1961	*Cin-N	103	235	27	60	10	1	3	33	18	21	.255	.308	.345	653	72	-9	1	1	-0	.991	-6	O-75(43-1-33)	-1.9
1962	NY-N	30	101	8	15	2	0	1	6	10	7	.149	.225	.198	423	14	-12	0	1	-0	.979	4	O-26(0-0-26)	-1.1
	Mil-N	79	214	28	61	11	3	5	24	12	17	.285	.323	.435	758	104	1	0	0	0	.987	-3	O-58(52-1-8)	-0.6
	Yr	109	315	36	76	13	3	6	30	22	24	.241	.291	.359	650	74	-12	0	1	-0	.984	0	O-84(52-1-34)	-1.7
1963	Mil-N	3	3	0	1	0	0	0	0	0	0	.333	.333	.333	667	94	-0	0	0	0	.000	0	H	0.0
1964	Mil-N	3	3	0	0	0	0	0	0	0	1	.000	.000	.000	0	-99	-1	0	0	0	.000	0	H	-0.1
Total	15	1741	6478	865	1823	311	66	206	942	470	636	.281	.333	.445	778	102	8	30	31		.985	2	*O-1642(162-811-683)	-7.0
■ **DEREK BELL**	Bell, Derek Nathaniel b: 12/11/68, Tampa, Fla. BR/TR, 6'2", 215 lbs. Deb: 6/28/91 Career OF: (32-LF 324-CF 771-RF)																							
1991	Tor-A	18	28	5	4	0	0	0	1	6	5	.143	.314	.143	457	30	-2	3	2	-0	.889	-3	O-13(7-6-0)	-0.6
1992	*Tor-A	61	161	23	39	6	3	2	15	15	34	.242	.326	.354	680	86	-3	7	2	1	1.000	-1	O-56(24-18-15)/D-1	-0.4
1993	SD-N	150	542	73	142	19	1	21	72	23	122	.262	.307	.417	724	90	-9	26	5	4	.976	6	*O-125(1-119-6),3-19	0.2
1994	SD-N	108	434	54	135	20	0	14	54	29	88	.311	.356	.454	810	112	7	24	8	2	.962	-0	*O-108(0-108-0)	1.1
1995	Hou-N	112	452	63	151	21	2	8	86	33	71	.334	.389	.442	832	128	19	27	9	3	.963	1	*O-110(0-30-82)	1.8
1996	Hou-N	158	627	84	165	40	3	17	113	40	123	.263	.316	.418	733	99	-3	29	3	5	.977	9	*O-157(0-2-157)	0.3
1997	*Hou-N	129	493	67	136	29	3	15	71	40	94	.276	.345	.438	783	107	5	15	7	1	.967	-0	*O-125(0-36-89)/D-1	0.1
1998	*Hou-N	156	630	111	198	41	2	22	108	51	126	.314	.369	.490	860	127	24	13	3	2	.973	5	*O-154(0-0-154)	2.1
1999	*Hou-N	128	509	61	120	22	0	12	66	50	129	.236	.309	.350	659	67	-26	18	6	2	.985	-7	*O-126(0-0-126)	-3.6

YEAR	TM/L	G	AB	R	H	2B	3B	HR	RBI	BB	SO	AVG	OBP	SLG	OPS	OPS+	BR+	SB	CS	SBR	FA	FR	G/POS	TPR
2000	*NY-N	144	546	87	145	31	1	18	69	65	125	.266	.350	.425	775	98	-1	8	4	0	.988	-3	*O-143(0-5-142)/P-1	-1.1
Total	10	1164	4422	628	1235	229	15	129	655	352	917	.279	.341	.425	766	102	11	170	49	20	.975	7	*O-1117R/3-19,D-2,P	-0.1

■ FERN BELL Bell, Fernando Jerome Lee (b: Fern Oran Bell) "Danny" b: 1/21/13, Ada, Okla. BR/TR, 6', 180 lbs. Deb: 4/17/39

YEAR	TM/L	G	AB	R	H	2B	3B	HR	RBI	BB	SO	AVG	OBP	SLG	OPS	OPS+	BR+	SB	CS	SBR	FA	FR	G/POS	TPR
1939	Pit-N	83	262	44	75	5	8	2	34	42	18	.286	.385	.389	774	110	5	2			.975	0	O-67(15-46-7)/3-1	0.3
1940	Pit-N	6	3	0	0	0	0	0	1	1	1	.000	.250	.000	250	-26	-0	0			.000	0	H	-0.1
Total	2	89	265	44	75	5	8	2	35	43	19	.283	.383	.385	768	109	5	2			.975	0	/O-67(15-46-7),3-1	0.2

■ FRANK BELL Bell, Frank Gustav b: 1863, Cincinnati, Ohio d: 4/14/1891, Cincinnati, Ohio 6', Deb: 7/7/1885 F

YEAR	TM/L	G	AB	R	H	2B	3B	HR	RBI	BB	SO	AVG	OBP	SLG	OPS	OPS+	BR+	SB	CS	SBR	FA	FR	G/POS	TPR
1885	Bro-a	10	29	5	5	0	1	0	2	0		.172	.200	.241	441	39	-2				.739	-2	/C-5,O-4(0-3-1),3-2	-0.3

■ GEORGE BELL Bell, George Antonio (Mathey) b: 10/21/59, San Pedro De Macoris, D.R. BR/TR, 6'1", 190 lbs. Deb: 4/9/81 F Career OF: (1123-LF 0-CF 114-RF)

YEAR	TM/L	G	AB	R	H	2B	3B	HR	RBI	BB	SO	AVG	OBP	SLG	OPS	OPS+	BR+	SB	CS	SBR	FA	FR	G/POS	TPR
1981	Tor-A	60	163	19	38	2	1	5	12	5	27	.233	.256	.350	606	69	-7	3	2	-0	.969	1	O-44(26-0-18)/D-8	-0.8
1983	Tor-A	39	112	5	30	5	4	2	17	4	17	.268	.305	.438	743	96	-1	1	1	-0	.954	-2	O-34(28-0-6)/D-2	-0.5
1984	Tor-A	159	606	85	177	39	4	26	87	24	86	.292	.328	.498	826	121	15	11	2	2	.971	-1	*O-147R/3-3,D-7	0.8
1985	*Tor-A	157	607	87	167	28	6	28	95	43	90	.275	.331	.479	811	116	12	21	6	3	.968	8	*O-157(157-0-0)/3-2	1.5
1986	Tor-A	159	641	101	198	38	6	31	108	41	62	.309	.352	.532	884	133	27	7	8	-1	.966	7	*O-147L,D-11/3-2	2.5
1987	Tor-A★	156	610	111	188	32	4	47	**134**	39	75	.308	.357	.605	962	146	37	5	1	1	.960	0	*O-148L/2-1,3-1,D-7	3.0
1988	Tor-A	156	614	78	165	27	5	24	97	34	66	.269	.308	.446	754	108	4	4	2	0	.946	-7	*O-149(149-0-0)/D-7	-0.8
1989	*Tor-A	153	613	88	182	41	2	18	104	33	60	.297	.337	.458	795	124	18	4	3	-0	.963	-4	*O-134(134-0-0),D-19	0.8
1990	Tor-A★	142	562	67	149	25	0	21	86	32	80	.265	.308	.422	730	100	-1	3	2	-0	.979	4	*O-106(106-0-0),D-36	-0.2
1991	Chi-N★	149	558	63	159	27	0	25	86	32	62	.285	.328	.468	796	116	10	2	6	-2	.962	-5	*O-146(146-0-0)	-0.1
1992	Chi-A	155	627	74	160	27	0	25	112	31	97	.255	.297	.418	715	99	-3	5	2	0	.964	-2	*D-140,O-15(15-0-0)	-0.9
1993	Chi-A	102	410	36	89	17	2	13	64	13	49	.217	.248	.363	612	64	-23	1	1	-0	.000	0	*D-102	-2.8
Total	12	1587	6123	814	1702	308	34	265	1002	331	771	.278	.320	.469	789	113	88	67	36	2	.964	-0	*O-1227L,D-339/3-8,2	2.5

■ JAY BELL Bell, Jay Stuart b: 12/11/65, Eglin A.F.B., Fla. BR/TR, 6'1", 185 lbs. Deb: 9/29/86

YEAR	TM/L	G	AB	R	H	2B	3B	HR	RBI	BB	SO	AVG	OBP	SLG	OPS	OPS+	BR+	SB	CS	SBR	FA	FR	G/POS	TPR
1986	Cle-A	5	14	3	5	2	0	1	4	2	3	.357	.438	.714	1152	211	2	0	0	0	.778	-0	/2-2,D-2	0.2
1987	Cle-A	38	125	14	27	9	1	2	13	8	31	.216	.269	.352	621	62	-7	2	0	0	.947	3	S-38	0.0
1988	Cle-A	73	211	23	46	5	1	2	21	21	53	.218	.292	.280	571	59	-11	4	2	0	.965	-13	S-72/D-1	-1.9
1989	Pit-N	78	271	33	70	13	3	2	27	19	47	.258	.309	.351	660	91	-3	5	3	0	.968	-15	S-78	-1.3
1990	*Pit-N	159	583	93	148	28	7	7	52	65	109	.254	.332	.362	694	94	-4	10	6	0	.970	-3	*S-159	0.6
1991	*Pit-N	157	608	96	164	32	8	16	67	52	99	.270	.331	.428	759	114	10	10	6	0	.968	8	*S-156	3.1
1992	*Pit-N	159	632	87	167	36	6	9	55	55	103	.264	.327	.383	710	102	1	7	5	-0	.973	17	*S-159	3.1
1993	Pit-N★	154	604	102	187	32	9	9	51	77	122	.310	.393	.437	830	122	22	16	10	0	**.986**	**26**	*S-154	5.9
1994	Pit-N	110	424	68	117	35	4	9	45	49	82	.276	.355	.441	796	105	3	2	0	0	.973	19	*S-110	3.1
1995	Pit-N	138	530	79	139	28	4	13	55	55	110	.262	.336	.404	740	92	-6	2	5	-1	.978	7	*S-136/3-3	1.1
1996	Pit-N	151	527	65	132	29	3	13	71	54	108	.250	.326	.391	717	86	-11	6	4	-0	**.986**	13	*S-151	1.4
1997	KC-A	153	573	89	167	28	3	21	92	71	101	.291	.373	.461	834	113	12	10	6	0	.985	2	*S-149/3-4	2.6
1998	Ari-N	155	549	79	138	29	5	20	67	81	129	.251	.355	.432	786	106	6	3	5	-1	.971	-16	*S-138,2-15	0.1
1999	*Ari-N★	151	589	132	170	32	6	38	112	82	132	.289	.379	.557	936	132	28	7	4	0	.968	-20	*2-148/S-1,D-2	1.5
2000	Ari-N	149	565	87	151	30	6	18	68	70	88	.267	.351	.437	788	97	-3	7	3	0	.988	-8	*2-145/D-1	-0.3
Total	15	1830	6805	1050	1828	368	66	180	800	761	1317	.269	.347	.421	768	104	40	91	59	-1	.975	20	*S-1501,2-310/3-7,D	19.2

■ RUDY BELL Bell, John (b: Rudolph Fred Baerwald) b: 1/1/1881, Wausau, Wis. d: 7/28/55, Albuquerque, N.Mex. BR/TR, 5'8.5", 158 lbs. Deb: 9/16/07

YEAR	TM/L	G	AB	R	H	2B	3B	HR	RBI	BB	SO	AVG	OBP	SLG	OPS	OPS+	BR+	SB	CS	SBR	FA	FR	G/POS	TPR
1907	NY-A	17	52	4	11	2	1	0	3	3		.212	.268	.288	556	72	-2	4			.897	-1	O-17(12-0-5)	-0.4

■ JUAN BELL Bell, Juan (Mathey) b: 3/29/68, San Pedro De Macoris, D.R. BR/TR, 5'11", 176 lbs. Deb: 9/6/89 F Career OF: (1-LF 1-CF 2-RF)

YEAR	TM/L	G	AB	R	H	2B	3B	HR	RBI	BB	SO	AVG	OBP	SLG	OPS	OPS+	BR+	SB	CS	SBR	FA	FR	G/POS	TPR
1989	Bal-A	8	4	2	0	0	0	0	0	0	1	.000	.000	.000	0	-99	-1	1	0	0	1.000	2	/2-2,S-2,D-4	0.1
1990	Bal-A	5	2	1	0	0	0	0	0	0	1	.000	.000	.000	0	-99	-1	0	0	0	1.000	0	/S-1,D-1	0.0
1991	Bal-A	100	209	26	36	9	2	1	15	8	51	.172	.203	.249	452	25	-22	0	0	0	.973	-1	2-77,S-15/O-1L,D-4	-2.1
1992	Phi-N	46	147	12	30	3	1	1	8	18	29	.204	.295	.259	554	58	-8	5	0	1	.972	4	S-46	0.1
1993	Phi-N	24	65	5	13	6	1	0	7	5	12	.200	.268	.323	591	58	-4	0	1	-0	.909	3	S-22	0.0
	Mil-A	91	286	42	67	6	2	5	29	36	64	.234	.322	.322	644	75	-10	6	6	-1	.983	2	2-47,S-40/O-3R,D-2	-0.3
1994	Mon-N	38	97	12	27	4	0	2	10	15	21	.278	.375	.381	756	97	0	4	0	1	.991	-2	2-25/3-3,S-1	0.1
1995	Bos-A	17	26	7	4	2	0	1	2	2	10	.154	.214	.346	560	41	-2	0	0	0	.857	4	/S-6,2-5,3-1	0.2
Total	7	329	836	107	177	30	6	10	71	84	189	.212	.286	.298	584	60	-47	16	7	1	.981	13	2-156,S-133/D-11,3O	-1.9

■ KEVIN BELL Bell, Kevin Robert b: 7/13/55, Los Angeles, Cal. BR/TR, 6', 195 lbs. Deb: 6/16/76 Career OF: (1-LF 0-CF 0-RF)

YEAR	TM/L	G	AB	R	H	2B	3B	HR	RBI	BB	SO	AVG	OBP	SLG	OPS	OPS+	BR+	SB	CS	SBR	FA	FR	G/POS	TPR
1976	Chi-A	68	230	24	57	7	6	5	20	18	56	.248	.305	.396	701	104	0	2	1	0	.970	3	3-67/D-1	0.3
1977	Chi-A	9	28	4	5	1	0	1	6	3	8	.179	.258	.321	579	57	-2	0	0	0	.909	0	/S-5,3-4,O-1(1-0-0)	-0.1
1978	Chi-A	54	68	9	13	0	0	2	5	5	19	.191	.257	.279	536	50	-5	1	0	0	.946	11	3-52/D-1	0.7
1979	Chi-A	70	200	20	49	8	1	4	22	15	43	.245	.298	.355	653	75	-7	2	4	-1	.923	12	3-68/S-2	0.3
1980	Chi-A	92	191	16	34	5	2	1	11	29	37	.178	.286	.241	527	46	-14	0	0	0	.925	7	3-83/S-3,D-3	-0.8
1982	Oak-A	4	9	1	3	1	0	0	0	0	2	.333	.333	.444	778	117	0	0	0	0	.857	0	/3-3,D-1	0.0
Total	6	297	726	74	161	22	9	13	64	70	165	.222	.292	.331	623	73	-26	5	5	-1	.940	33	3-277/S-10,D-6,O-1L	0.4

■ LES BELL Bell, Lester Rowland b: 12/14/01, Harrisburg, Pa. d: 12/26/85, Hershey, Pa. BR/TR, 5'11", 165 lbs. Deb: 9/18/23

YEAR	TM/L	G	AB	R	H	2B	3B	HR	RBI	BB	SO	AVG	OBP	SLG	OPS	OPS+	BR+	SB	CS	SBR	FA	FR	G/POS	TPR
1923	StL-N	15	51	5	19	2	1	0	9	9	7	.373	.467	.451	918	146	4	1	0	0	.917	-1	S-15	0.4
1924	StL-N	17	57	5	14	3	2	1	5	3	7	.246	.295	.421	716	91	-1	0	0	0	.905	-4	S-17	-0.3
1925	StL-N	153	586	80	167	29	9	11	88	43	47	.285	.334	.422	755	89	-10	4	5	-1	.924	-1	*3-153/S-1	-0.2
1926	*StL-N	155	581	85	189	33	14	17	100	54	62	.325	.383	.518	901	135	27	9			.950	-22	*3-155	1.5
1927	StL-N	115	390	48	101	26	6	9	65	34	63	.259	.320	.426	746	95	-4	5			.904	-14	*3-100,S-10	-1.1
1928	Bos-N	153	591	58	164	36	7	10	91	40	45	.277	.323	.413	736	96	-5	1			.948	5	*3-153	0.9
1929	Bos-N	139	483	58	144	23	5	9	72	50	42	.298	.364	.422	786	98	-1	4			.953	-20	*3-127/2-1,S-1	-1.2
1930	Chi-N	74	248	35	69	15	4	5	47	24	27	.278	.342	.431	773	85	-6	1			.948	-0	3-70/1-2	-0.3
1931	Chi-N	75	252	30	71	17	1	4	32	19	22	.282	.332	.405	737	95	-2	0			.944	4	3-70	0.4
Total	9	896	3239	404	938	184	49	66	509	276	322	.290	.346	.438	784	102	2	25	5		.939	-53	3-828/S-44,1-2,2-1	0.1

■ MIKE BELL Bell, Michael Allen b: 4/22/68, Lewiston, N.Y. BL/TL, 6'1", 175 lbs. Deb: 5/2/90

YEAR	TM/L	G	AB	R	H	2B	3B	HR	RBI	BB	SO	AVG	OBP	SLG	OPS	OPS+	BR+	SB	CS	SBR	FA	FR	G/POS	TPR
1990	Atl-N	36	45	8	11	5	1	1	5	2	9	.244	.292	.467	758	99	-0	0	1	-0	.981	1	1-24	0.0
1991	Atl-N	17	30	4	4	0	0	1	1	2	7	.133	.188	.233	421	17	-3	1	0	0	.975	-0	1-14	-0.4
Total	2	53	75	12	15	5	1	2	6	4	16	.200	.250	.373	623	67	-4	1	1	-0	.979	1	/1-38	-0.4

■ MIKE BELL Bell, Michael John b: 12/7/74, Cincinnati, Ohio BR/TR, 6'2", 195 lbs. Deb: 7/20/2000 F

YEAR	TM/L	G	AB	R	H	2B	3B	HR	RBI	BB	SO	AVG	OBP	SLG	OPS	OPS+	BR+	SB	CS	SBR	FA	FR	G/POS	TPR
2000	Cin-N	19	27	5	6	0	0	2	4	4	7	.222	.323	.444	767	87	-1	0	0	0	.900	1	3-13	0.1

■ BEAU BELL Bell, Roy Chester b: 8/20/07, Bellville, Tex. d: 9/14/77, College Station, Tex. BR/TR, 6'2", 185 lbs. Deb: 4/16/35 Career OF: (68-LF 0-CF 534-RF)

YEAR	TM/L	G	AB	R	H	2B	3B	HR	RBI	BB	SO	AVG	OBP	SLG	OPS	OPS+	BR+	SB	CS	SBR	FA	FR	G/POS	TPR
1935	StL-A	76	220	20	55	8	2	3	17	16	16	.250	.304	.345	649	65	-12	1	1	-0	.918	-5	O-37R,1-15/3-3	-1.9
1936	StL-A	155	616	100	212	40	12	11	123	60	55	.344	.403	.502	905	119	18	4	1	1	.974	-2	*O-142(12-0-133),1-17	0.6
1937	StL-A☆	156	642	82	**218**	**51**	8	14	117	53	54	.340	.391	.509	900	124	23	2	2	-0	.984	3	*O-131R,1-26/3-2	1.4
1938	StL-A	147	526	91	138	35	3	13	84	71	46	.262	.350	.414	765	91	-8	1	3	-1	.979	4	*O-132(0-0-132)/1-4	-1.2
1939	StL-A	11	32	4	7	1	0	1	5	4	3	.219	.324	.344	668	69	-1	0	0	0	1.000	0	/O-9(9-0-0)	-0.2
	Det-A	54	134	14	32	4	2	0	24	24	16	.239	.358	.299	657	65	-6	0	1	-0	1.000	-0	O-37(37-0-0)	-0.7
	Yr	65	166	18	39	5	2	1	29	28	19	.235	.352	.307	659	66	-8	0	1	-0	1.000	1	O-46(46-0-0)	-0.9
1940	Cle-A	120	444	55	124	22	2	4	58	34	41	.279	.332	.365	697	83	-11	2	2	-0	.971	-2	O-97(0-0-97),1-14	-1.9
1941	Cle-A	48	104	12	20	4	3	0	9	10	8	.192	.270	.288	558	50	-8	1	2	-0	1.000	-3	O-14(0-0-14),1-10	-1.3
Total	7	767	2718	378	806	165	32	46	437	272	239	.297	.362	.432	794	99	-6	11	12	-2	.976	-5	O-599R/1-86,3-5	-5.2

■ TERRY BELL Bell, Terence William b: 10/27/62, Dayton, Ohio BR/TR, 6', 195 lbs. Deb: 9/3/86

YEAR	TM/L	G	AB	R	H	2B	3B	HR	RBI	BB	SO	AVG	OBP	SLG	OPS	OPS+	BR+	SB	CS	SBR	FA	FR	G/POS	TPR
1986	KC-A	8	3	0	0	0	0	0	0	2	1	.000	.400	.000	400	20	-0	0	0	0	1.000	-0	/C-8	0.0

YEAR	TM/L	G	AB	R	H	2B	3B	HR	RBI	BB	SO	AVG	OBP	SLG	OPS	OPS+	BR+	SB	CS	SBR	FA	FR	G/POS	TPR
1987	Atl-N	1	1	0	0	0	0	0	0	0	1	.000	.000	.000	0	-95	-0	0	0	0	.000	0	/H	0.0
Total	2	9	4	0	0	0	0	0	0	2	2	.000	.333	.000	333	-0	-0	0	0	0	1.000	-0	/C-8	0.0
■ **ZEKE BELLA**	Bella, John b: 8/23/30, Greenwich, Conn. BR/TL, 5'11", 185 lbs. Deb: 9/11/57																							
1957	NY-A	5	10	0	1	0	0	0	0	1	2	.100	.182	.100	282	-21	-2	0	0	0	1.000	1	/O-4(1-0-3)	-0.1
1959	KC-A	47	82	10	17	2	1	1	9	9	14	.207	.293	.293	586	60	-4	0	0	0	1.000	-3	O-25(11-0-14)/1-1	-0.9
Total	2	52	92	10	18	2	1	1	9	10	16	.196	.282	.272	553	52	-6	0	0	0	1.000	-3	/O-29(12-0-17),1-1	-1.0
■ **STEVE BELLAN**	Bellan, Esteban Enrique b: 1850, Cuba d: 8/8/32, Havana, Cuba 5'6", 154 lbs. Deb: 5/9/1871 Career OF: (0-LF 6-CF 0-RF)																							
1871	Tro-n	29	128	26	32	3	3	0	23	9	2	.250	.299	.320	620	77	-4	4	4	-1	.713	-2	*3-28/S-1	-0.5
1872	Tro-n	23	114	22	30	4	0	0	16	0	0	.263	.263	.298	561	71	-4	1	0	0	.673	-6	/S-9,3-8,O-6(0-6-0)	-0.7
1873	Mut-n	8	32	4	7	2	0	0	3	2	0	.219	.265	.281	546	63	-1	0	0	0	.488	-5	/3-7,2-3	-0.5
Total	3 n	60	274	52	69	9	3	0	42	11	2	.252	.281	.307	587	73	-9	5	4	-0	.671	-14	/3-43,S-10,O-6C,2-3	-1.7
■ **ALBERT BELLE**	Belle, Albert Jojuan "Joey" b: 8/25/66, Shreveport, La. BR/TR, 6'2", 210 lbs. Deb: 7/15/89 Career OF: (1017-LF 0-CF 297-RF)																							
1989	Cle-A	62	218	22	49	8	4	7	37	12	55	.225	.272	.394	666	84	-5	2	2	-0	.979	1	O-44(15-0-31),D-17	-0.7
1990	Cle-A	9	23	1	4	0	0	1	3	1	6	.174	.208	.304	513	42	-2	0	0	0	.000	-0	/O-1(1-0-0),D-6	-0.2
1991	Cle-A	123	461	60	130	31	2	28	95	25	99	.282	.326	.540	866	134	19	3	1	0	.952	3	O-89(88-0-2),D-32	1.9
1992	Cle-A	153	585	81	152	23	1	34	112	52	128	.260	.324	.477	801	124	16	8	2	1	.969	-4	*D-100,O-52(52-0-0)	0.9
1993	Cle-A★	159	594	93	172	36	3	38	**129**	76	96	.290	.378	.552	930	147	39	23	12	-1	.986	19	*O-150(150-0-0)/D-9	5.1
1994	Cle-A★	106	412	90	147	35	2	36	101	58	71	.357	.442	.714	1156	191	56	9	6	-0	.973	3	*O-104(104-0-0)/D-2	5.0
1995	*Cle-A★	143	546	**121**	173	**52**	1	**50**	**126**	73	80	.317	.403	**.690**	1094	175	59	5	2	0	.981	8	*O-142(142-0-0)/D-1	**5.8**
1996	*Cle-A★	158	602	124	187	38	3	48	**148**	99	87	.311	.414	.623	1037	158	54	11	0	2	.970	7	*O-152(152-0-0)/D-6	5.2
1997	Chi-A☆	161	634	90	174	45	1	30	116	53	105	.274	.336	.491	827	117	14	4	4	-1	.972	7	*O-154(154-0-0)/D-7	1.5
1998	Chi-A	163	609	113	200	48	2	49	152	81	84	.328	.408	**.655**	**1063**	**175**	**67**	6	4	-0	.976	7	*O-159(159-0-0)/D-4	**6.3**
1999	Bal-A	161	610	108	181	36	1	37	117	101	82	.297	.403	.541	943	143	42	17	3	3	.985	-0	*O-154(0-0-154)/D-7	3.3
2000	Bal-A	141	559	71	157	37	1	23	103	52	68	.281	.346	.474	820	108	6	0	5	-2	.986	5	*O-110(0-0-110),D-31	0.2
Total	12	1539	5853	974	1726	389	21	381	1239	683	961	.295	.374	.564	938	144	364	88	41	5	.976	55	*O-1311L,D-222	34.3
■ **MARK BELLHORN**	Bellhorn, Mark Christian b: 8/23/74, Boston, Mass. BB/TR, 6'1", 195 lbs. Deb: 6/10/97																							
1997	Oak-A	68	224	33	51	9	1	6	19	32	70	.228	.324	.357	681	79	-7	7	1	1	.951	6	3-40,2-17/S-1,D-3	0.1
1998	Oak-A	11	12	1	1	1	0	0	1	3	4	.083	.313	.167	479	30	-1	2	0	0	1.000	1	/3-5,S-2,2-1,D-2	0.0
2000	Oak-A	9	13	2	2	0	0	0	0	2	6	.154	.267	.154	421	11	-2	0	0	0	1.000	-1	/2-2,3-2,S-1	-0.3
Total	3	88	249	36	54	10	1	6	20	37	80	.217	.321	.337	658	73	-10	9	1	2	.957	5	/3-47,2-20,D-5,S-4	-0.2
■ **RAFAEL BELLIARD**	Belliard, Rafael Leonidas (Matias) b: 10/24/61, Pueblo Nuevo, D.R. BR/TR (BB 1982), 5'6", 150 lbs. Deb: 9/6/82																							
1982	Pit-N	9	2	3	1	0	0	0	0	0	0	.500	.500	.500	1000	175	0	1	0	0	1.000	1	/S-4	0.2
1983	Pit-N	4	1	1	0	0	0	0	0	0	1	.000	.000	.000	0	-98	-0	0	0	0	1.000	1	/S-3	0.1
1984	Pit-N	20	22	3	5	0	0	0	0	0	1	.227	.227	.227	455	28	-2	4	1	1	.889	1	S-12/2-1	0.0
1985	Pit-N	17	20	1	4	0	0	0	1	0	5	.200	.200	.200	400	12	-2	0	0	0	.947	6	S-12	0.4
1986	Pit-N	117	309	33	72	5	2	0	31	26	54	.233	.299	.262	561	55	-18	12	2	2	.970	13	S-96,2-23	0.6
1987	Pit-N	81	203	26	42	4	3	1	15	20	25	.207	.288	.271	559	49	-15	5	1	1	.979	6	S-71/2-7	-0.2
1988	Pit-N	122	286	28	61	0	4	0	11	26	47	.213	.288	.241	529	54	-16	7	1	1	**.977**	-12	*S-117/2-3	-2.1
1989	Pit-N	67	154	10	33	4	0	0	8	8	22	.214	.253	.240	493	43	-11	5	2	0	.978	7	S-40,2-20/3-6	-0.2
1990	Pit-N	47	54	10	11	3	0	0	6	5	13	.204	.283	.259	543	52	-3	1	2	-0	1.000	5	2-21,S-10/3-5	0.1
1991	*Atl-N	149	353	36	88	9	2	0	27	22	63	.249	.297	.286	583	61	-18	3	1	0	.967	26	*S-145	1.7
1992	*Atl-N	144	285	20	60	6	1	0	14	14	43	.211	.255	.239	494	38	-23	0	1	-0	.969	**27**	*S-139/2-1	1.0
1993	*Atl-N	91	79	6	18	5	0	0	6	4	13	.228	.291	.291	582	56	-5	0	0	0	1.000	20	S-58,2-24	1.6
1994	Atl-N	46	120	9	29	7	1	0	9	2	29	.242	.266	.317	583	50	-9	0	2	-1	.984	-5	S-26,2-18	-1.2
1995	*Atl-N	75	180	12	40	2	1	0	7	6	28	.222	.255	.244	500	32	-18	2	2	-0	.992	13	S-40,2-32	-0.1
1996	*Atl-N	87	142	9	24	7	0	0	3	2	22	.169	.181	.218	399	4	-19	3	1	0	.983	23	S-63,2-15	0.6
1997	Atl-N	72	71	9	15	3	0	1	3	1	17	.211	.222	.296	518	33	-7	0	1	-0	.990	13	S-53/2-7	0.7
1998	Atl-N	7	20	1	5	0	0	0	1	0	1	.250	.250	.250	500	32	-2	0	0	0	.952	1	/S-7	-0.1
Total	17	1155	2301	217	508	55	14	2	142	136	384	.221	.271	.259	531	46	-168	43	17	4	.974	146	S-896,2-172/3-11	3.1
■ **RON BELLIARD**	Belliard, Ronald b: 4/7/75, Bronx, N.Y. BR/TR, 5'8", 180 lbs. Deb: 9/12/98																							
1998	Mil-N	8	5	1	1	0	0	0	0	0	0	.200	.200	.200	400	6	-1	0	0	0	.000	0	/2-1	-0.1
1999	Mil-N	124	457	60	135	29	4	8	58	64	59	.295	.382	.429	811	106	6	4	5	-1	.978	6	*2-119/3-1,S-1	1.6
2000	Mil-N	152	571	83	150	30	9	8	54	82	84	.263	.358	.389	747	90	-7	7	5	-0	.976	8	*2-151	0.8
Total	3	284	1033	144	286	59	13	16	112	146	143	.277	.368	.406	774	97	-2	11	10	-1	.977	14	2-271/S-1,3-1	2.3
■ **CLAY BELLINGER**	Bellinger, Clayton Daniel b: 11/18/68, Oneonta, N.Y. BR/TR, 6'3", 195 lbs. Deb: 4/9/99 Career OF: (19-LF 26-CF 5-RF)																							
1999	*NY-A	32	45	12	9	2	0	1	2	1	10	.200	.217	.311	529	33	-5	1	0	0	1.000	3	3-16/1-8,O-2L,2SD	-0.2
2000	*NY-A	98	184	33	38	8	2	6	21	17	48	.207	.291	.370	661	67	-10	5	0	1	.968	2	O-46C,2-21,3-18,1/S	-0.6
Total	2	130	229	45	47	10	2	7	23	18	58	.205	.278	.358	636	61	-14	6	0	1	.969	5	/O-48C,3-34,2-22,1SD	-0.8
■ **JACK BELLMAN**	Bellman, John Hutchins "Happy Jack" b: 3/4/1864, Taylorsville, Ky. d: 12/8/31, Louisville, Ky. Deb: 4/23/1889																							
1889	StL-a	1	2	1	1	0	0	0	0	1	0	.500	.667	.500	1167	207	0	0			1.000	-0	/C-1	0.0
■ **ROB BELLOIR**	Belloir, Robert Edward b: 7/13/48, Heidelberg, W.Ger. BR/TR, 5'10", 155 lbs. Deb: 8/2/75																							
1975	Atl-N	43	105	11	23	2	1	0	9	7	8	.219	.268	.257	525	45	-8	0	0	0	.922	-2	S-38/2-1	-0.7
1976	Atl-N	30	60	5	12	2	0	0	4	5	7	.200	.262	.233	495	39	-5	0	0	0	.929	-1	S-12,3-10/2-5	-0.5
1977	Atl-N	6	1	2	0	0	0	0	0	0	0	.000	.000	.000	0	-89	-0	0	0	0	1.000	1	/S-3	0.1
1978	Atl-N	2	1	0	1	1	0	0	0	0	0	1.000	1.000	2.000	3000	647	1	0	0	0	1.000	-0	/S-1,3-1	0.1
Total	4	81	167	18	36	5	1	0	13	12	15	.216	.268	.257	526	45	-12	0	0	0	.924	-3	/S-54,3-11,2-6	-1.0
■ **CARLOS BELTRAN**	Beltran, Carlos Ivan b: 4/24/77, Manati, P.R. BB/TR, 6', 175 lbs. Deb: 9/14/98																							
1998	KC-A	14	58	12	16	5	3	0	7	3	12	.276	.323	.466	788	99	-0	3	0	1	.978	2	O-14(0-14-0)	0.2
1999	KC-A	156	663	112	194	27	7	22	108	46	123	.293	.342	.454	796	99	-2	27	8	3	.972	11	*O-154(0-154-0)/D-2	1.2
2000	KC-A	98	372	49	92	15	4	7	44	35	69	.247	.312	.366	678	70	-17	13	0	3	.975	6	O-88(2-83-3)/D-7	-0.7
Total	3	268	1093	173	302	47	14	29	159	84	204	.276	.331	.425	755	89	-20	43	8	7	.973	18	O-256(2-251-3)/D-9	0.7
■ **ADRIAN BELTRE**	Beltre, Adrian (Perez) b: 4/7/79, Santo Domingo, D.R. BR/TR, 5'11", 200 lbs. Deb: 6/24/98																							
1998	LA-N	77	195	18	42	9	0	7	22	14	37	.215	.278	.369	648	73	-8	3	1	0	.925	10	3-74/S-2	0.2
1999	LA-N	152	538	84	148	27	5	15	67	61	105	.275	.355	.428	783	103	3	18	7	2	.932	-5	*3-152	0.0
2000	LA-N	138	510	71	148	30	2	20	85	56	80	.290	.363	.475	837	115	11	12	5	1	.944	10	*3-138/S-1	2.2
Total	3	367	1243	173	338	66	7	42	174	131	222	.272	.347	.438	784	103	5	33	13	3	.936	15	3-364/S-3	2.4
■ **ESTEBAN BELTRE**	Beltre, Esteban (Valera) b: 12/26/67, Ingenio Quisquella, D.R. BR/TR, 5'10", 172 lbs. Deb: 9/3/91																							
1991	Chi-A	8	6	0	1	0	0	0	0	1	1	.167	.286	.167	452	29	-1	1	0	0	1.000	-1	/S-8	-0.1
1992	Chi-A	49	110	21	21	2	0	1	10	3	18	.191	.212	.236	449	26	-11	1	0	0	.924	-1	S-43/D-4	-0.9
1994	Tex-A	48	131	12	37	5	0	0	12	16	25	.282	.361	.321	681	78	-4	2	5	-1	.961	8	S-41/3-5,2-1	0.6
1995	Tex-A	54	92	7	20	8	0	0	7	4	15	.217	.250	.304	554	42	-8	0	0	0	.969	3	S-36,2-15/3-1	-0.3
1996	Bos-A	27	62	6	16	2	0	0	6	4	14	.258	.303	.290	593	50	-5	1	0	0	1.000	-1	3-13/2-8,S-6,D-1	-0.4
Total	5	186	401	46	95	17	0	1	35	28	73	.237	.287	.287	573	51	-28	5	5	-1	.951	9	S-134/2-24,3-19,D-5	-1.1
■ **HARRY BEMIS**	Bemis, Harry Parker b: 2/1/1874, Farmington, N.H. d: 5/23/47, Cleveland, Ohio BR/TR, 5'7.5", 175 lbs. Deb: 4/23/02 Career OF: (0-LF 0-CF 2-RF)																							
1902	Cle-A	93	317	42	99	12	7	1	29	19		.312	.366	.404	770	118	8	3			.964	6	C-87/O-2(0-0-2),2-1	2.2
1903	Cle-A	92	314	31	82	20	3	1	41	8		.261	.295	.354	648	96	-2	5			**.988**	-7	C-74,1-10/2-1	-0.2
1904	Cle-A	97	336	35	76	11	6	0	25	8		.226	.259	.295	554	76	-10	6			.958	-3	C-79,1-13/2-1	-0.5
1905	Cle-A	70	226	27	66	13	3	0	28	13		.292	.344	.376	720	127	7	3			.972	-6	C-58/2-4,3-2,1-1	0.7
1906	Cle-A	93	297	28	82	13	5	2	30	12		.276	.311	.374	685	116	4	8			.963	-10	C-81	0.3

YEAR	TM/L	G	AB	R	H	2B	3B	HR	RBI	BB	SO	AVG	OBP	SLG	OPS	OPS+	BR+	SB	CS	SBR	FA	FR	G/POS	TPR
1907	Cle-A	65	172	12	43	7	0	0	19	7		.250	.283	.291	574	82	-4	5			.957	-2	C-51/1-2	-0.8
1908	Cle-A	91	277	23	62	9	1	0	33	7		.224	.253	.264	517	68	-10	14			.964	-6	C-76/1-2	-1.1
1909	Cle-A	42	123	4	23	2	3	0	13	0		.187	.194	.252	446	39	-9	2			.971	-0	C-36	-0.7
1910	Cle-A	61	167	12	36	5	1	1	16	5		.216	.238	.275	514	60	-8	3			.961	-4	C-46	-0.9
Total	9	704	2229	214	569	92	29	5	234	79		.255	.292	.329	621	92	-24	49			.966	-37	C-588/1-28,2-7,3O	-1.0

■ MARVIN BENARD

Benard, Marvin Larry b: 1/20/71, Bluefields, Nic. BL/TL, 5'10", 180 lbs. Deb: 9/5/95

YEAR	TM/L	G	AB	R	H	2B	3B	HR	RBI	BB	SO	AVG	OBP	SLG	OPS	OPS+	BR+	SB	CS	SBR	FA	FR	G/POS	TPR
1995	SF-N	13	34	5	13	2	0	1	4	1	7	.382	.400	.529	929	147	2	1	0	0	1.000	1	/O-7(0-7-0)	0.3
1996	SF-N	135	488	89	121	17	4	5	27	59	84	.248	.334	.330	664	79	-14	25	11	2	.984	5	*O-132(5-102-38)	-0.8
1997	*SF-N	84	114	13	26	4	0	1	13	13	29	.228	.318	.289	607	62	-6	3	1	0	.967	-8	O-36(14-6-18)/D-1	-1.4
1998	SF-N	121	286	41	92	21	1	3	36	34	39	.322	.398	.434	831	126	12	11	4	1	.982	-10	O-79(12-9-64)/D-2	0.0
1999	SF-N	149	562	100	163	36	5	16	64	55	97	.290	.360	.457	817	113	11	27	14	1	.988	3	*O-142(4-123-20)	1.4
2000	*SF-N	149	560	102	147	27	6	12	55	63	97	.262	.343	.396	740	93	-6	22	7	2	.997	-9	*O-141(21-128-38)	-1.3
Total	6	651	2044	350	562	107	16	38	199	225	353	.275	.353	.399	751	99	-1	89	37	7	.989	-19	O-537(56-375-178)/D-3	-1.8

■ FREDDIE BENAVIDES

Benavides, Alfredo b: 4/7/66, Laredo, Tex. BR/TR, 6'2", 180 lbs. Deb: 5/14/91

YEAR	TM/L	G	AB	R	H	2B	3B	HR	RBI	BB	SO	AVG	OBP	SLG	OPS	OPS+	BR+	SB	CS	SBR	FA	FR	G/POS	TPR
1991	Cin-N	24	63	11	18	1	0	0	3	1	15	.286	.308	.302	609	69	-3	1	0	0	.974	3	S-20/2-3	0.2
1992	Cin-N	74	173	14	40	10	1	1	17	10	34	.231	.277	.318	595	66	-8	0	1	-0	1.000	4	2-37,S-34/3-1	-0.2
1993	Col-N	74	213	20	61	10	3	3	26	6	27	.286	.306	.404	710	76	-7	3	2	-0	.937	-3	S-48,2-19/3-5,1-1	-0.6
1994	Mon-N	47	85	8	16	5	1	0	6	3	15	.188	.225	.271	495	28	-9	0	0	0	.976	-5	2-36/3-5,1-3,S-3	-1.3
Total	4	219	534	53	135	26	5	4	52	20	91	.253	.284	.343	626	65	-26	4	3	-0	.948	-0	S-105/2-95,3-11,1-4	-1.9

■ JOHNNY BENCH

Bench, Johnny Lee b: 12/7/47, Oklahoma City, Okla. BR/TR, 6'1", 208 lbs. Deb: 8/28/67 H Career OF: (55-LF 2-CF 54-RF)

YEAR	TM/L	G	AB	R	H	2B	3B	HR	RBI	BB	SO	AVG	OBP	SLG	OPS	OPS+	BR+	SB	CS	SBR	FA	FR	G/POS	TPR
1967	Cin-N	26	86	7	14	3	1	1	6	5	19	.163	.209	.256	465	29	-8	0	1	-1	.995	5	C-26	-0.2
1968	Cin-N★	154	564	67	155	40	2	15	82	31	96	.275	.315	.433	748	115	9	1	5	-2	.991	7	*C-154	2.5
1969	Cin-N★	148	532	83	156	23	1	26	90	49	86	.293	.357	.487	844	128	19	6	6	-1	.992	-3	*C-147	2.3
1970	*Cin-N★	158	605	97	177	35	4	**45**	**148**	54	102	.293	.351	.587	937	146	35	5	2	0	.986	4	*C-139,O-24L,1-12,/3	4.4
1971	Cin-N★	149	562	80	134	19	2	27	61	49	83	.238	.300	.423	723	105	1	2	1	0	.988	-4	*C-141,1-12,O-12L,/3	0.4
1972	*Cin-N★	147	538	87	145	22	2	**40**	**125**	100	84	.270	.386	.541	927	**171**	**51**	6	6	-1	.992	-5	*C-129,O-17R/1-7,3	5.3
1973	*Cin-N★	152	557	83	141	17	3	25	104	83	83	.253	.350	.429	779	121	16	4	1	1	.995	-3	*C-134,O-23R/1-4,3	2.0
1974	Cin-N★	160	621	108	174	38	2	33	**129**	80	90	.280	.365	.507	872	144	35	5	4	-0	.993	-5	*C-137,3-36/1-5	3.7
1975	*Cin-N★	142	530	83	150	39	1	28	110	65	108	.283	.363	.519	882	140	27	11	0	2	.989	3	*C-121,O-19L/1-9	3.8
1976	*Cin-N★	135	465	62	109	24	1	16	74	81	95	.234	.350	.394	744	108	7	13	2	2	**.997**	-3	*C-128/O-5(5-0-0),1-1	1.2
1977	Cin-N★	142	494	67	136	34	2	31	109	58	95	.275	.353	.540	893	133	22	2	4	-1	.987	-13	*C-135/O-8L,1-4,3-1	1.3
1978	Cin-N†	120	393	52	102	17	1	23	73	50	83	.260	.345	.483	828	129	14	4	2	0	.989	-9	*C-107,1-11/O-2L	1.0
1979	*Cin-N†	130	464	73	128	19	0	22	80	67	73	.276	.367	.459	826	123	16	4	2	0	.986	-7	*C-126/1-2	1.5
1980	Cin-N★	114	360	52	90	12	0	24	68	41	64	.250	.330	.483	813	124	11	4	2	0	.991	-17	*C-105	-0.2
1981	Cin-N	52	178	14	55	8	0	8	25	17	21	.309	.369	.489	858	139	9	0	2	-1	.983	-2	1-38/C-7	0.5
1982	Cin-N	119	399	44	103	16	0	13	38	37	58	.258	.321	.396	717	98	-2	1	2	-0	.917	-17	*3-107/1-8,C-1	-2.2
1983	Cin-N★	110	310	32	79	15	2	12	54	24	38	.255	.308	.432	741	100	-1	0	1	-0	.933	-12	3-42,1-32/C-5,O-1L	-1.7
Total	17	2158	7658	1091	2048	381	24	389	1376	891	1278	.267	.345	.476	821	127	262	68	43	-0	.990	-80	*C-1742,3-195,1O	25.6

■ ART BENEDICT

Benedict, Arthur Melville b: 3/31/1862, Cornwall, Ill. d: 1/20/48, Denver, Colo. BR/TR, Deb: 5/14/1883

YEAR	TM/L	G	AB	R	H	2B	3B	HR	RBI	BB	SO	AVG	OBP	SLG	OPS	OPS+	BR+	SB	CS	SBR	FA	FR	G/POS	TPR
1883	Phi-N	3	15	3	4	1	0	0	4	0	4	.267	.267	.333	600	89	-0				.571	-5	/2-3	-0.4

■ BRUCE BENEDICT

Benedict, Bruce Edwin b: 8/18/55, Birmingham, Ala. BR/TR, 6'1", 190 lbs. Deb: 8/18/78 C

YEAR	TM/L	G	AB	R	H	2B	3B	HR	RBI	BB	SO	AVG	OBP	SLG	OPS	OPS+	BR+	SB	CS	SBR	FA	FR	G/POS	TPR
1978	Atl-N	22	52	3	13	2	0	0	1	6	6	.250	.328	.288	616	66	-2	0	0	0	.990	2	C-22	0.1
1979	Atl-N	76	204	14	46	11	0	0	15	33	18	.225	.333	.279	613	64	-9	1	3	-1	.984	1	C-76	-0.6
1980	Atl-N	120	359	18	91	14	1	2	34	28	36	.253	.309	.315	624	72	-13	3	3	-0	.988	3	*C-120	-0.6
1981	Atl-N★	90	295	26	78	12	1	5	35	33	21	.264	.344	.363	707	98	-0	1	1	-0	.986	6	C-90	1.1
1982	*Atl-N	118	386	34	95	11	1	3	44	37	40	.246	.317	.303	620	71	-14	4	4	-1	**.993**	2	*C-118	-0.7
1983	Atl-N★	134	423	43	126	13	1	2	43	61	24	.298	.388	.348	735	98	2	1	3	-1	.992	9	*C-134	1.6
1984	Atl-N	95	300	26	67	8	1	4	25	34	25	.223	.304	.297	601	65	-13	1	2	-0	.991	1	C-95	-0.9
1985	Atl-N	70	208	12	42	6	0	0	20	22	12	.202	.281	.231	512	42	-15	0	1	-0	.989	-2	C-70	-1.6
1986	Atl-N	64	160	11	36	10	1	0	13	15	10	.225	.299	.300	599	62	-8	1	0	0	.993	-3	C-57	-0.9
1987	Atl-N	37	95	4	14	1	0	1	5	17	15	.147	.277	.189	466	25	-10	0	1	-0	.989	4	C-35	-0.5
1988	Atl-N	90	236	11	57	7	0	0	19	19	26	.242	.298	.271	569	61	-11	0	2	-1	.989	8	C-89	0.0
1989	Atl-N	66	160	12	31	3	0	1	6	23	18	.194	.299	.231	530	52	-9	0	0	0	.995	16	C-65	1.0
Total	12	982	2878	214	696	98	6	18	260	328	251	.242	.322	.299	621	71	-103	12	20	-4	.990	47	C-971	-2.0

■ JOE BENES

Benes, Joseph Anthony "Bananas" b: 1/8/01, Long Island City, N.Y. d: 3/7/75, Elmhurst, N.Y. BR/TR, 5'8.5", 158 lbs. Deb: 5/9/31

YEAR	TM/L	G	AB	R	H	2B	3B	HR	RBI	BB	SO	AVG	OBP	SLG	OPS	OPS+	BR+	SB	CS	SBR	FA	FR	G/POS	TPR
1931	StL-N	10	12	1	2	0	0	0	0	2	1	.167	.333	.167	500	37	-1	0			1.000	1	/S-6,2-2,3-1	0.0

■ BENNY BENGOUGH

Bengough, Bernard Oliver b: 7/27/1898, Niagara Falls, N.Y. d: 12/22/68, Philadelphia, Pa. BR/TR, 5'7.5", 168 lbs. Deb: 5/18/23 C

YEAR	TM/L	G	AB	R	H	2B	3B	HR	RBI	BB	SO	AVG	OBP	SLG	OPS	OPS+	BR+	SB	CS	SBR	FA	FR	G/POS	TPR
1923	NY-A	19	53	1	7	2	0	0	3	4	2	.132	.193	.170	363	-4	-8	0	0	0	.973	1	C-19	-0.6
1924	NY-A	11	16	4	5	1	1	0	3	2	0	.313	.389	.500	889	128	1	0	0	0	1.000	3	C-11	0.4
1925	NY-A	95	283	17	73	14	2	0	23	19	9	.258	.305	.322	626	60	-18	0	2	-1	**.993**	6	C-94	-0.6
1926	NY-A	36	84	9	32	6	0	0	14	7	4	.381	.435	.452	887	134	4	1	0	0	.973	8	C-35	1.4
1927	*NY-A	31	85	6	21	3	3	0	10	4	4	.247	.281	.353	634	66	-5	0	3	-1	.986	12	C-30	0.7
1928	*NY-A	58	161	12	43	3	1	0	9	7	8	.267	.302	.298	600	60	-9	0	0	0	.992	6	C-58	0.0
1929	NY-A	23	62	5	12	2	1	0	7	0	2	.194	.194	.258	452	16	-8	0	0	0	.982	-5	C-23	-1.1
1930	NY-A	44	102	10	24	4	2	0	12	3	8	.235	.257	.314	571	46	-9	1	0	0	.990	9	C-44	0.2
1931	StL-A	40	140	6	35	4	1	0	12	4	4	.250	.271	.293	564	46	-11	0	3	-1	.986	-1	C-37	-1.0
1932	StL-A	54	139	13	35	7	1	0	15	12	4	.252	.311	.317	628	60	-8	0	1	-0	.989	6	C-47	0.0
Total	10	411	1125	83	287	46	12	0	108	62	45	.255	.295	.317	613	59	-70	2	9	-3	.988	45	C-398	-0.6

■ JUAN BENIQUEZ

Beniquez, Juan Jose (Torres) b: 5/13/50, San Sebastian, P.R. BR/TR, 5'11", 165 lbs. Deb: 9/4/71 Career OF: (295-LF 735-CF 184-RF)

YEAR	TM/L	G	AB	R	H	2B	3B	HR	RBI	BB	SO	AVG	OBP	SLG	OPS	OPS+	BR+	SB	CS	SBR	FA	FR	G/POS	TPR
1971	Bos-A	16	57	8	17	2	0	0	4	3	4	.298	.333	.333	667	83	-1	3	1	0	.895	-8	S-15	-0.8
1972	Bos-A	33	99	10	24	4	1	1	8	7	11	.242	.292	.333	626	81	-2	2	0	0	.900	5	S-27	0.6
1974	Bos-A	106	389	60	104	14	3	5	33	25	61	.267	.313	.357	671	86	-7	19	11	0	.978	2	O-97(7-91-0)/D-4	-0.8
1975	*Bos-A	78	254	43	74	14	4	2	17	25	26	.291	.359	.402	761	106	2	7	10	-2	.991	1	O-44L,D-20,3-14	-0.1
1976	Tex-A	145	478	49	122	14	4	0	33	39	56	.255	.315	.301	617	79	-12	17	6	2	.986	20	*O-141(0-141-0)/2-1	0.7
1977	Tex-A	123	424	56	114	19	6	10	50	43	43	.269	.338	.413	750	102	1	26	18	-1	.988	7	*O-123(0-123-0)	0.6
1978	Tex-A	127	473	61	123	17	3	11	50	20	59	.260	.294	.378	673	88	-9	10	12	-2	.972	-0	*O-126(0-126-0)	-1.3
1979	NY-A	62	142	19	36	6	1	4	17	9	17	.254	.307	.394	702	90	-2	3	3	-0	.981	-6	O-60(18-38-4)/3-3	-0.9
1980	Sea-A	70	237	26	54	10	0	6	21	17	25	.228	.280	.346	626	70	-10	2	3	-1	.957	1	O-65(2-63-0)/D-1	-1.1
1981	Cal-A	58	166	18	30	5	0	3	13	15	16	.181	.253	.265	518	49	-11	2	1	0	.959	-7	O-55(15-36-7)/D-1	-2.0
1982	*Cal-A	112	196	25	52	11	2	3	24	15	21	.265	.321	.388	709	93	-2	3	0	1	.983	-27	*O-107(37-25-51)	-3.0
1983	Cal-A	92	315	44	96	15	0	3	34	15	29	.305	.344	.381	725	100	0	4	2	0	.968	-8	O-84(38-30-31)/D-6	-1.1
1984	Cal-A	110	354	60	119	17	0	8	39	18	43	.336	.373	.452	825	128	13	0	3	-1	.971	-12	O-98(64-8-50)	-0.4
1985	Cal-A	132	411	54	125	13	5	8	42	34	46	.304	.364	.418	783	114	9	4	3	-0	1.000	-15	O-71C,1-46,D-14,/3S	-1.1
1986	Bal-A	113	343	48	103	15	0	6	36	40	49	.300	.378	.397	775	113	7	2	3	-1	.963	-6	O-54L,3-25,D-16,1	-0.3
1987	KC-A	57	174	14	41	7	0	3	26	11	26	.236	.285	.328	613	60	-10	0	0	0	1.000	-4	O-22L,D-15/1-6,3-6	-1.5
	Tor-A	39	81	6	23	5	1	5	21	5	13	.284	.333	.556	889	127	3	0	0	0	.875	-2	D-15/O-7(3-0-4),1-2	0.0
	Yr	96	255	20	64	12	1	8	47	16	39	.251	.300	.400	700	82	-7	0	0	0	.976	-6	D-30,O-29L/1-8,3-6	-1.5
1988	Tor-A	27	58	9	17	2	0	1	8	8	6	.293	.379	.379	758	112	1	0	0	0	.000	-0	D-19/O-1(1-0-0)	0.0
Total	17	1500	4651	610	1274	190	30	79	476	349	551	.274	.329	.379	707	95	-29	104	76	-4	.977	-60	*O-1155C,D-111/13S2	-12.5

■ YAMIL BENITEZ

Benitez, Yamil Antonio b: 10/5/72, San Juan, P.R. BR/TR, 6'2", 180 lbs. Deb: 9/16/95

YEAR	TM/L	G	AB	R	H	2B	3B	HR	RBI	BB	SO	AVG	OBP	SLG	OPS	OPS+	BR+	SB	CS	SBR	FA	FR	G/POS	TPR
1995	Mon-N	14	39	8	15	2	1	2	7	1	7	.385	.400	.641	1041	163	3	0	2	-1	.950	-2	O-14(3-4-8)	0.1
1996	Mon-N	11	12	0	2	0	0	0	2	0	4	.167	.167	.167	333	-11	-2	0	0	0	.500	-1	/O-4(3-0-1)	-0.3

YEAR	TM/L	G	AB	R	H	2B	3B	HR	RBI	BB	SO	AVG	OBP	SLG	OPS	OPS+	BR+	SB	CS	SBR	FA	FR	G/POS	TPR
1997	KC-A	53	191	22	51	7	1	8	21	10	49	.267	.307	.440	747	90	-3	2	2	-0	.965	-1	O-52(31-0-22)	-0.6
1998	Ari-N	91	206	17	41	7	1	9	30	14	46	.199	.263	.374	637	65	-11	2	2	-0	.972	1	O-62(49-0-13)/D-2	-1.2
Total	4	169	448	47	109	16	3	19	60	25	106	.243	.291	.420	710	82	-13	4	6	-1	.963	-2	O-132(86-4-44)/D-2	-2.0
■ **STAN BENJAMIN**	Benjamin, Alfred Stanley b: 5/20/14, Framingham, Mass. BR/TR, 6′2″, 194 lbs. Deb: 9/16/39 Career OF: (9-LF 53-CF 112-RF)																							
1939	Phi-N	12	50	4	7	2	1	0	2	1	6	.140	.157	.220	377	0	-7	1			.867	-0	/O-7(4-2-2),3-5	-0.8
1940	Phi-N	8	9	1	2	0	0	0	1	1	1	.222	.300	.222	522	48	-1	0			1.000	1	/O-2(0-0-2)	0.0
1941	Phi-N	129	480	47	113	20	7	3	27	20	81	.235	.266	.325	591	68	-22	17			.980	-4	*O-110R/1-8,2-2,3-1	-3.4
1942	Phi-N	78	210	24	47	8	3	2	8	10	27	.224	.262	.319	581	73	-8	5			.976	-3	O-45(0-25-21),1-15	-1.4
1945	Cle-A	14	21	1	7	2	0	0	3	0	0	.333	.333	.429	762	126	1	0	1	-0	1.000	2	/O-4(3-0-1)	0.2
Total	5	241	770	77	176	32	11	5	41	32	115	.229	.260	.318	578	66	-37	23	1		.975	-5	O-168R/1-23,3-6,2-2	-5.4
■ **MIKE BENJAMIN**	Benjamin, Michael Paul b: 11/22/65, Euclid, Ohio BR/TR, 6′, 169 lbs. Deb: 7/7/89																							
1989	SF-N	14	6	6	1	0	0	0	0	0	1	.167	.167	.167	333	-5	-1	0	0	0	1.000	2	/S-8	0.1
1990	SF-N	22	56	7	12	3	1	2	3	3	10	.214	.254	.411	665	83	-2	1	0	0	.988	5	S-21	0.5
1991	SF-N	54	106	12	13	3	0	2	8	7	26	.123	.191	.208	399	13	-13	3	0	1	.984	16	S-51/3-1	0.6
1992	SF-N	40	75	4	13	2	1	1	3	4	15	.173	.215	.267	482	38	-6	1	0	0	.991	5	S-33/3-2	0.0
1993	SF-N	63	146	22	29	7	0	4	16	9	23	.199	.264	.329	593	59	-9	0	0	0	.991	20	2-23,S-23,3-16	1.3
1994	SF-N	38	62	9	16	5	1	1	9	5	16	.258	.343	.419	762	102	0	5	0	1	.968	9	S-18,2-10/3-5	1.1
1995	SF-N	68	186	19	41	6	0	3	12	8	51	.220	.256	.301	557	48	-14	11	1	2	.964	3	3-43,S-16/2-8	-0.8
1996	Phi-N	35	103	13	23	5	1	4	13	12	21	.223	.316	.408	724	88	-2	3	1	0	.954	-2	S-31/2-1	-0.1
1997	Bos-A	49	116	12	27	9	1	0	7	4	27	.233	.264	.328	592	52	-8	2	3	-1	.929	9	3-19,S-16/2-5,1PD	0.1
1998	*Bos-A	124	349	46	95	23	0	4	39	15	73	.272	.314	.372	686	76	-12	3	0	1	.994	4	2-87,S-20,3-11,1/D	-0.3
1999	Pit-N	110	368	42	91	26	7	1	37	20	90	.247	.290	.364	654	64	-21	10	1	2	.982	**36**	S-93,2-12/3-6	2.3
2000	Pit-N	93	233	28	63	18	2	2	19	12	45	.270	.315	.391	705	77	-8	5	4	-0	.974	30	3-34,S-30,2-27,/1-1	2.2
Total	12	710	1806	220	424	107	14	24	166	99	398	.235	.284	.349	633	65	-96	44	10	6	.980	135	S-360,2-173,3/1DP	7.0
■ **IKE BENNERS**	Benners, Isaac B. b: 6/7/1856, Philadelphia, Pa. d: 4/18/32, Philadelphia, Pa. BL, 175 lbs. Deb: 5/1/1884																							
1884	Bro-a	49	189	25	38	11	5	1		7		.201	.237	.328	565	82	-4				.815	-5	O-49(49-0-0)	-0.9
	Wil-U	6	22	0	1	0	0	0		1		.045	.087	.045	132	-57	-5				.750	0	/O-6(0-3-3)	-0.5
Total	1	55	211	25	39	11	5	1		8		.185	.222	.299	520	66	-9				.806	-5	/O-55(49-3-3)	-1.4
■ **CHARLIE BENNETT**	Bennett, Charles Wesley b: 11/21/1854, New Castle, Pa. d: 2/24/27, Detroit, Mich. BR/TR, 5′11″, 180 lbs. Deb: 5/1/1878 Career OF: (25-LF 25-CF 20-RF)																							
1878	Mil-N	49	184	16	45	9	0	1	12	10	26	.245	.284	.310	593	89	-2				.831	-13	C-35,O-20(0-16-4)	-1.4
1880	Wor-N	51	193	20	44	9	3	0	18	10	30	.228	.266	.306	572	86	-3				.913	-0	C-46/O-6(0-3-3)	-0.2
1881	Det-N	76	299	44	90	18	7	7	64	18	37	.301	.341	.478	819	149	16				**.962**	18	*C-70/3-5,O-3(1-2-0)	3.3
1882	Det-N	84	342	43	103	16	10	5	51	20	33	.301	.340	.450	790	151	19				.945	7	*C-65,3-11/2-7,S1	2.8
1883	Det-N	92	371	56	113	34	7	5	55	26	59	.305	.350	.474	825	155	25				**.944**	-3	*C-72,2-15,O-12R	2.5
1884	Det-N	90	341	37	90	18	6	3	40	36	40	.264	.334	.378	713	132	14				.917	-5	*C-80/O-5R,S-4,321	1.4
1885	Det-N	91	349	49	94	24	13	5	60	47	37	.269	.356	.456	812	161	24				.919	-1	C-62,O-19L,3-10	2.7
1886	Det-N	72	235	37	57	13	5	4	34	48	29	.243	.371	.391	763	128	10	4			**.955**	12	C-69/O-4(3-0-1),S-1	2.4
1887	*Det-N	46	190	26	69	6	5	3	20	30	22	.363	.363	.400	763	108	2	7			.951	2	C-45/O-1(1-0-0),1-1	0.7
1888	Det-N	74	258	32	68	12	4	5	29	31	40	.264	.347	.399	746	138	12	4			**.966**	7	C-73/1-1	2.4
1889	Bos-N	82	247	42	57	8	2	4	28	21	43	.231	.296	.328	624	70	-11	7			**.955**	12	C-82	0.6
1890	Bos-N	85	281	59	60	17	2	3	40	72	56	.214	.377	.320	698	96	1	6			**.959**	10	C-85	1.6
1891	Bos-N	75	256	35	55	9	3	5	39	42	61	.215	.332	.332	664	84	-6	3			**.960**	14	C-75	1.3
1892	*Bos-N	35	114	19	23	4	0	1	16	27	23	.202	.355	.263	618	80	-2	6			.948	1	C-35	0.2
1893	Bos-N	60	191	34	40	6	0	4	27	40	36	.209	.352	.304	656	69	-8	5			.953	-3	C-60	-0.5
Total	15	1062	3851	549	1008	203	67	55	533	478	572	.262	.340	.387	728	118	92	42			.942	57	C-954/O-70L,3-27,2S1	19.8
■ **GARY BENNETT**	Bennett, Gary David b: 4/17/72, Waukegan, Ill. BR/TR, 6′, 190 lbs. Deb: 9/24/95																							
1995	Phi-N	1	1	0	0	0	0	0	0	0	1	.000	.000	.000	0	-99	-0	0	0	0	.000	0	-0,-0	0.0
1996	Phi-N	6	16	0	4	0	0	0	1	2	6	.250	.333	.250	583	56	-1	0	0	0	1.000	3	/C-5	0.2
1998	Phi-N	9	31	4	9	0	0	0	3	5	5	.290	.389	.290	679	81	-1	0	0	0	1.000	-4	/C-9	-0.4
1999	Phi-N	36	88	7	24	4	0	1	21	4	11	.273	.304	.352	657	64	-5	0	0	0	.971	-5	C-32	-0.8
2000	Phi-N	31	74	8	18	5	0	2	5	13	15	.243	.371	.392	763	91	-1	0	0	0	.995	4	C-31	0.5
Total	5	83	210	19	55	9	0	3	30	24	38	.262	.343	.348	691	75	-7	0	0	0	.988	-3	/C-77	-0.5
■ **HERSCHEL BENNETT**	Bennett, Herschel Emmett b: 9/21/1896, Elwood, Mo. d: 9/9/64, Springfield, Mo. BL/TR, 5′9.5″, 160 lbs. Deb: 4/19/23																							
1923	StL-A	5	4	0	0	0	0	0	0	1	1	.000	.200	.000	200	-42	-1	0	0	0	1.000	-0	/O-1(0-1-0)	-0.1
1924	StL-A	41	94	16	31	4	3	1	11	3	6	.330	.364	.468	832	107	1	1	0	0	.966	-4	O-21(12-0-9)	-0.4
1925	StL-A	93	298	46	83	11	6	2	37	18	16	.279	.324	.376	700	73	-13	4	10	-3	.916	-2	O-73(41-12-21)	-2.1
1926	StL-A	80	225	33	60	14	2	1	26	22	21	.267	.337	.360	697	78	-7	2	1	0	.950	3	O-50(36-6-9)	-0.8
1927	StL-A	93	256	40	68	12	2	3	30	14	21	.266	.311	.363	675	72	-11	6	2	1	.946	1	O-55(12-2-42)	-1.3
Total	5	312	877	135	242	41	13	7	104	58	65	.276	.327	.376	704	77	-31	13	13	-2	.937	-1	O-200(101-21-81)	-4.7
■ **FRED BENNETT**	Bennett, James Fred "Red" b: 3/15/02, Atkins, Ark. d: 5/12/57, Atkins, Ark. BR/TR, 5′9″, 185 lbs. Deb: 4/13/28																							
1928	StL-A	7	8	0	2	1	0	0	0	0	2	.250	.250	.375	625	60	-0	0	0	0	1.000	0	/O-1(0-0-1)	-0.1
1931	Pit-N	32	89	6	25	5	0	1	7	7	4	.281	.333	.371	704	90	-1	0			.951	-2	O-21(3-0-18)	-0.4
Total	2	39	97	6	27	6	0	1	7	7	6	.278	.327	.371	698	87	-2	0	0		.953	-2	/O-22(3-0-19)	-0.5
■ **JOE BENNETT**	Bennett, Joseph Rosenblum b: 7/2/1900, New York, N.Y. d: 7/11/87, Morro Bay, Cal. BR/TR, 5′9″, 168 lbs. Deb: 7/5/23																							
1923	Phi-N	1	0	0	0	0	0	0	0	0	0	—	—	—	—	—	0	0	0	0	1.000	0	/3-1	0.0
■ **PUG BENNETT**	Bennett, Justin Titus b: 2/20/1874, Ponca, Neb. d: 9/12/35, Kirkland, Wash. BR/TR, 5′11″, 165 lbs. Deb: 4/12/06																							
1906	StL-N	153	595	66	156	16	7	1	34	56		.262	.334	.318	651	108	6	20			.948	-7	*2-153	0.1
1907	StL-N	87	324	20	72	8	2	0	21	21		.222	.272	.259	531	69	-12	7			.939	-16	2-83/3-3	-3.2
Total	2	240	919	86	228	24	9	1	55	77		.248	.312	.297	609	94	-6	27			.945	-23	2-236/3-3	-3.1
■ **VERN BENSON**	Benson, Vernon Adair b: 9/19/24, Granite Quarry, N.C. BL/TR, 5′11″, 180 lbs. Deb: 7/31/43 MC																							
1943	Phi-A	2	2	0	0	0	0	0	0	0	0	.000	.000	.000	0	-99	-0	0	0	0	.000	0	H	-0.1
1946	Phi-A	7	5	1	0	0	0	0	0	1	3	.000	.167	.000	167	-51	-1	0	0	0	1.000	-0	/O-2(2-0-0)	-0.1
1951	StL-N	13	46	8	12	3	1	1	7	6	8	.261	.346	.435	781	108	1	0	0	0	.950	0	/3-9,O-4(4-0-0)	0.0
1952	StL-N	20	47	6	9	2	0	2	5	5	9	.191	.269	.362	631	73	-2	0	0	0	.889	-1	3-15	-0.3
1953	StL-N	13	4	2	0	0	0	0	0	1	2	.000	.200	.000	200	-42	-1	0	0	0	.000	0	H	-0.1
Total	5	55	104	17	21	5	1	3	12	13	22	.202	.291	.356	646	75	-4	0	0	0	.911	-0	/3-24,O-6(6-0-0)	-0.6
■ **JACK BENTLEY**	Bentley, John Needles b: 3/8/1895, Sandy Spring, Md. d: 10/24/69, Olney, Md. BL/TL, 5′11.5″, 200 lbs. Deb: 9/6/13																							
1913	Was-A	3	3	0	0	0	0	0	0	0	0	.000	.000	.000	0	-98	-1	0			1.000	0	/P-3	0.0
1914	Was-A	30	40	7	11	2	0	0	4	0	5	.275	.275	.325	600	77	-1	0			.930	-1	P-30	0.0
1915	Was-A	4	2	0	0	0	0	0	0	0	1	.000	.000	.000	0	-98	-0	0			.750	-0	/P-4	0.0
1916	Was-A	2	0	0	0	0	0	0	0	0	0	—	—	—	—	—	0	0			1.000	0	/P-2	0.0
1923	*NY-N	52	89	9	38	6	2	1	14	3	4	.427	.446	.573	1019	169	9	0	0	0	.977	-1	P-31	0.0
1924	*NY-N	46	98	12	26	5	1	0	6	3	13	.265	.287	.337	624	68	-5	0	0	0	.979	-1	P-28	0.0
1925	NY-N	64	99	10	30	5	2	3	18	9	11	.303	.361	.485	846	119	3	0	0	0	.930	-2	P-28/O-3(0-0-3),1-1	-0.1
1926	Phi-N	75	240	19	62	12	3	2	27	5	4	.258	.273	.358	632	66	-12	0			.993	-2	1-56/P-7	-1.7
	NY-N	3	4	0	1	0	0	0	0	0	0	.250	.250	.250	500	35	-0	0			.000	-0	/P-1	0.0
	Yr	78	244	19	63	12	3	2	27	5	4	.258	.273	.357	630	65	-12	0			.993	-2	1-56/P-8	-1.7
1927	NY-N	8	9	1	2	0	0	1	2	1	1	.222	.300	.556	856	125	0	0			.750	-0	/P-4,1-2	0.0
Total	9	287	584	58	170	30	8	7	71	21	39	.291	.316	.406	722	91	-8	0	0		.949	-6	P-138/1-59,O-3(0-0-3)	-1.8

■ BUTCH BENTON Benton, Alfred Lee b: 8/24/57, Tampa, Fla. BR/TR, 6′1″, 190 lbs. Deb: 9/14/78

YEAR	TM/L	G	AB	R	H	2B	3B	HR	RBI	BB	SO	AVG	OBP	SLG	OPS	OPS+	BR+	SB	CS	SBR	FA	FR	G/POS	TPR
1978	NY-N	4	4	1	2	0	0	0	2	0	0	.500	.600	.500	1100	218	1	0	0	0	1.000	0	/C-1	0.1
1980	NY-N	12	21	0	1	0	0	0	0	2	4	.048	.167	.048	214	-39	-4	0	0	0	.935	-1	/C-8	-0.5
1982	Chi-N	4	7	0	1	0	0	0	1	0	1	.143	.143	.143	286	-19	-1	0	0	0	1.000	2	/C-4	0.1
1985	Cle-A	31	67	5	12	4	0	0	7	3	9	.179	.214	.239	453	24	-7	0	0	0	.957	-3	C-26	-0.9
Total	4	51	99	6	16	4	0	0	10	5	14	.162	.217	.202	419	16	-11	0	0	0	.959	-2	/C-39	-1.2

■ RABBIT BENTON Benton, Stanley W. "Stan" b: 9/29/01, Cannel City, Ky. d: 6/7/84, Mesquite, Tex. BR/TR, 5′7″, 150 lbs. Deb: 9/13/22

YEAR	TM/L	G	AB	R	H	2B	3B	HR	RBI	BB	SO	AVG	OBP	SLG	OPS	OPS+	BR+	SB	CS	SBR	FA	FR	G/POS	TPR
1922	Phi-N	6	19	1	4	1	0	0	3	2	1	.211	.286	.263	549	39	-2	0	0	0	.889	0	/2-5	-0.1

■ TODD BENZINGER Benzinger, Todd Eric b: 2/11/63, Dayton, Ky. BB/TR, 6′1″, 190 lbs. Deb: 6/21/87 Career OF: (69-LF 5-CF 123-RF)

YEAR	TM/L	G	AB	R	H	2B	3B	HR	RBI	BB	SO	AVG	OBP	SLG	OPS	OPS+	BR+	SB	CS	SBR	FA	FR	G/POS	TPR
1987	Bos-A	73	223	36	62	11	1	8	43	22	41	.278	.348	.444	792	105	2	5	4	-0	.987	8	O-61(14-5-47)/1-2	0.6
1988	*Bos-A	120	405	47	103	28	1	13	70	22	80	.254	.294	.425	719	95	-4	2	3	-1	.991	-4	1-85,O-48(5-0-43)/D-1	-1.5
1989	Cin-N	161	628	79	154	28	3	17	76	44	120	.245	.297	.381	677	89	-10	3	7	-2	.995	-13	*1-158	-3.9
1990	*Cin-N	118	376	35	95	14	2	5	46	19	69	.253	.296	.340	636	71	-15	3	4	-1	.992	-2	1-95,O-10(10-0-0)	-2.5
1991	Cin-N	51	123	7	23	3	2	1	11	10	20	.187	.248	.268	516	43	-9	2	0	0	.986	-1	1-21,O-15(15-0-0)	-1.2
	KC-A	78	293	29	86	15	3	2	40	17	46	.294	.339	.386	724	99	-0	2	6	-2	.996	-5	1-75/D-1	-1.2
1992	LA-N	121	293	24	70	16	2	4	31	15	54	.239	.276	.348	624	77	-10	2	4	-1	.989	0	O-51(18-0-33),1-42	-1.5
1993	SF-N	86	177	25	51	7	2	6	26	13	35	.288	.337	.452	789	112	3	0	0	0	1.000	-4	1-40/O-7(7-0-0),3-1	-0.4
1994	SF-N	107	328	32	87	13	2	9	31	17	84	.265	.305	.399	705	86	-8	2	1	0	.994	-4	1-99	-2.0
1995	SF-N	9	10	2	2	0	0	1	2	2	3	.200	.333	.500	833	120	0	0	0	0	1.000	-1	/1-5	-0.1
Total	9	924	2856	316	733	135	18	66	376	181	552	.257	.304	.386	690	88	-51	21	29	-6	.994	-25	1-622,O-192R/D-2,3	-13.7

■ JOHNNY BERARDINO Berardino, John "Bernie" b: 5/1/17, Los Angeles, Cal. d: 5/19/96, Los Angeles, Cal. BR/TR, 6′, 180 lbs. Deb: 4/22/39 Career OF: (1-LF 0-CF 0-RF)

YEAR	TM/L	G	AB	R	H	2B	3B	HR	RBI	BB	SO	AVG	OBP	SLG	OPS	OPS+	BR+	SB	CS	SBR	FA	FR	G/POS	TPR
1939	StL-A	126	468	42	120	24	5	5	58	37	36	.256	.314	.361	675	71	-21	6	2	1	.958	4	*2-114/3-8,S-2	-0.9
1940	StL-A	142	523	71	135	31	4	16	85	32	46	.258	.301	.424	725	84	-14	6	8	-1	.939	13	*S-112,2-13/3-9	0.6
1941	StL-A	128	469	48	127	30	4	5	89	41	27	.271	.332	.384	716	86	-10	3	5	-1	.954	-14	*S-123/3-1	-1.6
1942	StL-A	29	74	11	21	6	0	1	10	4	2	.284	.329	.405	735	104	0	3	1	0	.950	0	/S-6,3-6,1-5,2-4	0.1
1946	StL-A	144	582	70	154	29	5	5	68	34	58	.265	.306	.357	664	81	-16	2	4	-1	.972	-2	*2-143	-1.1
1947	StL-A	90	306	29	80	22	1	1	20	44	26	.261	.358	.350	708	95	-1	6	5	-0	.977	-9	2-86	-0.5
1948	Cle-A	66	147	19	28	5	1	2	10	27	16	.190	.328	.279	607	64	-7	0	1	-0	.988	4	2-20,1-18,S-12,/3-3	-0.3
1949	Cle-A	50	116	11	23	6	1	0	13	14	14	.198	.295	.267	563	50	-8	0	1	-0	.935	-1	3-25/2-8,S-3	-0.9
1950	Cle-A	4	5	1	2	0	0	0	3	1	0	.400	.500	.400	900	137	0	0	0	0	1.000	1	/2-1,3-1	0.1
	Pit-N	40	131	12	27	3	1	1	12	19	11	.206	.307	.267	574	51	-9	0	0	0	.964	3	2-36/3-3	-0.4
1951	StL-A	39	119	13	27	7	1	0	13	17	18	.227	.324	.303	626	68	-5	1	1	-0	.917	-7	3-31/2-2,1-1,O-1L	-1.2
1952	Cle-A	35	32	5	3	0	0	0	2	10	8	.094	.310	.094	403	17	-3	0	1	-0	.960	2	/2-8,S-8,3-4,1-2	-0.2
	Pit-N	19	56	2	8	4	0	0	4	4	6	.143	.200	.214	414	14	-7	0	0	0	.960	6	2-18	0.1
Total	11	912	3028	334	755	167	23	36	387	284	268	.249	.316	.355	672	77	-101	27	29	1	.968	1	2-453,S-266/3-91,1O	-6.2

■ LOU BERBERET Berberet, Louis Joseph b: 11/20/29, Long Beach, Cal. BL/TR, 5′11″, 212 lbs. Deb: 9/17/54

YEAR	TM/L	G	AB	R	H	2B	3B	HR	RBI	BB	SO	AVG	OBP	SLG	OPS	OPS+	BR+	SB	CS	SBR	FA	FR	G/POS	TPR
1954	NY-A	5	5	1	2	0	0	0	3	1	1	.400	.500	.400	900	154	0	0	0	0	1.000	1	/C-3	0.2
1955	NY-A	2	5	1	2	0	0	0	2	1	0	.400	.500	.400	900	147	0	0	0	0	1.000	1	/C-1	0.1
1956	Was-A	95	207	25	54	6	3	4	27	46	33	.261	.402	.377	779	107	4	0	0	0	.997	-1	C-59	0.6
1957	Was-A	99	264	24	69	11	2	7	36	41	38	.261	.365	.398	763	110	4	0	1	-0	**1.000**	-3	C-77	0.5
1958	Was-A	5	6	0	1	0	0	0	0	4	1	.167	.500	.167	667	94	0	0	0	0	.917	1	/C-2	0.1
	Bos-A	57	167	11	35	5	3	2	18	31	32	.210	.337	.311	648	74	-5	0	2	-1	.984	-6	C-49	-0.9
	Yr	62	173	11	36	5	3	2	18	35	33	.208	.344	.306	651	76	-5	0	2	-1	.981	-5	C-51	-0.8
1959	Det-A	100	338	38	73	8	2	13	44	35	59	.216	.290	.367	656	75	-12	0	0	0	.989	-11	C-95	-1.9
1960	Det-A	85	232	18	45	4	0	5	23	41	31	.194	.318	.276	593	60	-12	2	0	0	.993	-0	C-81	-0.8
Total	7	448	1224	118	281	34	10	31	153	200	195	.230	.341	.350	691	86	-19	2	3	-1	.992	-17	C-367	-2.1

■ JEFF BERBLINGER Berblinger, Jeffrey James b: 11/19/70, Wichita, Kan. BR/TR, 6′, 190 lbs. Deb: 9/7/97

YEAR	TM/L	G	AB	R	H	2B	3B	HR	RBI	BB	SO	AVG	OBP	SLG	OPS	OPS+	BR+	SB	CS	SBR	FA	FR	G/POS	TPR
1997	StL-N	7	5	1	0	0	0	0	0	0	1	.000	.000	.000	0	-99	-1	0	0	0	1.000	2	/2-4	0.0

■ DAVE BERG Berg, David Scott b: 9/3/70, Roseville, Cal. BR/TR, 5′11″, 185 lbs. Deb: 4/2/98 Career OF: (3-LF 0-CF 0-RF)

YEAR	TM/L	G	AB	R	H	2B	3B	HR	RBI	BB	SO	AVG	OBP	SLG	OPS	OPS+	BR+	SB	CS	SBR	FA	FR	G/POS	TPR
1998	Fla-N	81	182	18	57	11	0	2	21	26	46	.313	.399	.407	806	119	6	3	0	1	1.000	4	2-27,3-25,S-17	1.2
1999	Fla-N	109	304	42	87	18	1	3	25	27	59	.286	.348	.382	730	90	-5	2	2	-0	.969	1	S-37,2-29,3-19,/O-3L	0.0
2000	Fla-N	82	210	23	53	14	1	1	21	25	46	.252	.346	.343	689	79	-6	3	0	1	.957	-11	S-49,3-13,2-11	-1.2
Total	3	272	696	83	197	43	2	6	67	78	151	.283	.361	.376	738	94	-5	8	2	1	.958	-6	S-103/2-67,3-57,O-3L	0.0

■ MOE BERG Berg, Morris b: 3/2/02, New York, N.Y. d: 5/29/72, Belleville, N.J. BR/TR, 6′1″, 185 lbs. Deb: 6/27/23 C

YEAR	TM/L	G	AB	R	H	2B	3B	HR	RBI	BB	SO	AVG	OBP	SLG	OPS	OPS+	BR+	SB	CS	SBR	FA	FR	G/POS	TPR
1923	Bro-N	49	129	9	24	3	2	0	6	2	5	.186	.198	.240	439	16	-16	1	0	0	.906	-6	S-47/2-1	-1.7
1926	Chi-A	41	113	4	25	6	0	0	7	6	9	.221	.261	.274	535	41	-10	0	2	-1	.948	6	S-31/2-2,3-1	-0.2
1927	Chi-A	35	69	4	17	4	0	0	4	4	10	.246	.288	.304	592	55	-5	0	0	0	.952	-4	2-11,C-10/S-6,3-3	-0.7
1928	Chi-A	76	224	25	55	16	0	0	29	14	25	.246	.302	.317	619	64	-12	2	1	0	.990	5	C-73	-0.2
1929	Chi-A	107	352	32	101	7	0	0	47	17	16	.287	.323	.307	630	64	-18	5	1	1	.982	-3	*C-106	-1.3
1930	Chi-A	20	61	4	7	3	0	0	7	1	5	.115	.129	.164	293	-27	-12	0	0	0	.986	-1	C-20	-1.1
1931	Cle-A	10	13	1	1	1	0	0	0	1	1	.077	.143	.154	297	-21	-2	0	0	0	.889	0	/C-8	-0.2
1932	Was-A	75	195	16	46	8	1	1	26	8	13	.236	.266	.303	569	48	-15	1	1	-0	1.000	7	C-75	-0.5
1933	Was-A	40	65	8	12	3	0	2	9	4	5	.185	.232	.323	555	46	-5	0	0	0	1.000	3	C-35	-0.2
1934	Was-A	33	86	5	21	4	0	0	6	6	4	.244	.301	.291	592	55	-6	2	0	0	.988	-4	C-31	-0.7
	Cle-A	29	97	4	25	3	1	0	9	1	7	.258	.265	.309	575	47	-8	0	0	0	.980	5	C-28	-0.1
	Yr	62	183	9	46	7	1	0	15	7	11	.251	.283	.301	583	51	-13	2	0	0	.983	1	C-59	-0.8
1935	Bos-A	38	98	13	28	5	0	2	12	5	3	.286	.320	.398	718	79	-3	0	0	0	.991	2	C-37	0.1
1936	Bos-A	39	125	9	30	4	1	0	19	2	6	.240	.264	.288	552	34	-13	0	0	0	.986	12	C-39	0.1
1937	Bos-A	47	141	13	36	3	1	0	20	5	4	.255	.281	.291	572	43	-12	0	0	0	.979	3	C-47	-0.7
1938	Bos-A	10	12	0	4	0	0	0	0	0	1	.333	.333	.333	667	64	-1	0	0	0	1.000	1	/C-7,1-1	0.0
1939	Bos-A	14	33	3	9	1	0	1	5	2	3	.273	.314	.394	708	77	-1	0	0	0	.965	4	C-13	0.3
Total	15	663	1813	150	441	71	6	6	206	78	117	.243	.278	.299	577	49	-140	11	5	1	.986	29	C-529/S-84,2-14,31	-7.1

■ AUGIE BERGAMO Bergamo, August Samuel b: 2/14/17, Detroit, Mich. d: 8/19/74, Grosse Pointe, Mich. BL/TL, 5′9″, 165 lbs. Deb: 4/25/44

YEAR	TM/L	G	AB	R	H	2B	3B	HR	RBI	BB	SO	AVG	OBP	SLG	OPS	OPS+	BR+	SB	CS	SBR	FA	FR	G/POS	TPR
1944	*StL-N	80	192	35	55	6	3	2	19	35	23	.286	.399	.380	779	118	6	0			.988	-7	O-50(31-1-19)/1-2	-0.4
1945	StL-N	94	304	51	96	17	2	3	44	43	21	.316	.401	.414	815	124	11	0			.969	-1	O-77(7-0-70)/1-2	0.5
Total	2	174	496	86	151	23	5	5	63	78	44	.304	.400	.401	801	122	17	0			.975	-9	O-127(38-1-89)/1-4	0.1

■ MARTY BERGEN Bergen, Martin b: 10/25/1871, N.Brookfield, Mass d: 1/19/1900, N.Brookfield, Mass TR, 5′10″, 170 lbs. Deb: 4/17/1896 F

YEAR	TM/L	G	AB	R	H	2B	3B	HR	RBI	BB	SO	AVG	OBP	SLG	OPS	OPS+	BR+	SB	CS	SBR	FA	FR	G/POS	TPR
1896	Bos-N	65	245	39	66	6	4	4	37	11	22	.269	.309	.376	684	75	-10	6			.920	6	C-63/1-1	0.1
1897	*Bos-N	87	327	47	81	11	3	2	45	18		.248	.295	.318	613	58	-21	5			.963	4	C-85/O-1(0-1-0)	-0.7
1898	Bos-N	120	446	62	125	16	5	3	60	13		.280	.302	.359	661	85	-11	9			.962	2	*C-117/1-2	0.2
1899	Bos-N	72	260	32	67	11	3	1	34	10		.258	.290	.335	625	65	-13	4			.955	3	C-72	-0.3
Total	4	344	1278	180	339	44	15	10	176	52	22	.265	.299	.347	646	72	-55	24			.954	15	C-337/1-3,O-1(0-1-0)	-0.7

■ BILL BERGEN Bergen, William Aloysius b: 6/13/1878, N.Brookfield, Mass. d: 12/19/43, Worcester, Mass. BR/TR, 6′, 184 lbs. Deb: 5/6/01 F

YEAR	TM/L	G	AB	R	H	2B	3B	HR	RBI	BB	SO	AVG	OBP	SLG	OPS	OPS+	BR+	SB	CS	SBR	FA	FR	G/POS	TPR
1901	Cin-N	87	308	15	55	6	4	1	17	8		.179	.199	.234	433	27	-29	2			.970	-4	C-87	-2.4
1902	Cin-N	89	322	19	58	8	3	0	36	14		.180	.214	.224	438	32	-26	2			.959	17	C-89	0.0
1903	Cin-N	58	207	21	47	4	2	0	19	7		.227	.252	.266	518	43	-16	2			.980	2	C-58	-0.8
1904	Bro-N	96	329	17	60	4	2	0	12	9		.182	.204	.207	411	28	-28	3			.959	14	C-93/1-1	-0.5
1905	Bro-N	79	247	12	47	3	2	0	22	7		.190	.213	.219	431	31	-21	4			.954	12	C-76	-0.3
1906	Bro-N	103	353	9	56	3	3	0	19	7		.159	.175	.184	359	13	-36	2			.977	6	*C-103	-2.3
1907	Bro-N	51	138	2	22	3	0	0	14	1		.159	.165	.181	347	9	-15	1			.968	3	C-51	-0.9
1908	Bro-N	99	302	8	53	8	2	0	15	5		.175	.189	.215	404	30	-24	1			**.989**	16	C-99	0.1

YEAR	TM/L	G	AB	R	H	2B	3B	HR	RBI	BB	SO	AVG	OBP	SLG	OPS	OPS+	BR+	SB	CS	SBR	FA	FR	G/POS	TPR
1909	Bro-N	112	346	16	48	1	1	1	15	10		.139	.163	.156	319	-1	-41	4			.976	22	*C-112	-1.0
1910	Bro-N	89	249	11	40	2	1	0	14	6	39	.161	.180	.177	357	4	-31	0			.981	18	C-89	-0.5
1911	Bro-N	84	227	8	30	3	1	0	10	14	42	.132	.183	.154	337	-6	-32	2			**.981**	15	C-84	-1.1
Total	11	947	3028	138	516	45	21	2	193	88	81	.170	.194	.201	395	20	-299	23			.972	119	C-941/1-1	-9.7
■ CLARENCE BERGER Berger, Clarence Edward b: 11/1/1894, E.Cleveland, Ohio d: 6/30/59, Washington, D.C. BL/TR, 6′, 185 lbs. Deb: 9/23/14																								
1914	Pit-N	6	13	2	1	0	0	0	0	1	4	.077	.143	.077	220	-36	-2	0			1.000	-2	/O-5(0-0-5)	-0.5
■ JOHNNY BERGER Berger, John Henne b: 8/27/01, Philadelphia, Pa. d: 5/7/79, Lake Charles, La. BR/TR, 5′9″, 165 lbs. Deb: 4/20/22																								
1922	Phi-A	2	1	0	1	0	0	0	0	0	0	1.000	1.000	1.000	2000	412	0	1	0	0	1.000	1	/C-2	0.1
1927	Was-A	9	15	1	4	0	0	0	1	2	3	.267	.353	.267	620	63	-1	0	0	0	.926	0	/C-9	0.0
Total	2	11	16	1	5	0	0	0	1	2	3	.313	.389	.313	701	85	-0	1	0	0	.935	1	/C-11	0.1
■ TUN BERGER Berger, John Henry b: 12/6/1867, Pittsburgh, Pa. d: 6/10/07, Pittsburgh, Pa. TR, 204 lbs. Deb: 5/9/1890 Career OF: (4-LF 4-CF 37-RF)																								
1890	Pit-N	104	391	64	104	18	4	0	40	35	23	.266	.337	.332	670	108	6	11			.912	-7	O-41R,S-33,C-21,/23	0.1
1891	Pit-N	43	134	15	32	2	1	1	14	12	10	.239	.315	.291	606	79	-3	4			.920	-13	C-18,2-17/S-6,O-2C	-1.2
1892	Was-N	26	97	9	14	2	1	0	3	7	9	.144	.210	.186	395	20	-9	3			.872	-11	S-18/C-9	-1.8
Total	3	173	622	88	150	22	6	1	57	54	42	.241	.313	.301	614	87	-7	18			.837	-30	/S-57,C-48,O-43R,23	-2.9
■ JOE BERGER Berger, Joseph August "Fats" b: 12/20/1886, St.Louis, Mo. d: 3/5/56, Rock Island, Ill. BR/TR, 5′10.5″, 170 lbs. Deb: 4/11/13																								
1913	Chi-A	79	223	27	48	6	2	2	20	36	28	.215	.330	.287	616	82	-4	5			.959	3	2-71/S-4,3-1	0.0
1914	Chi-A	48	148	11	23	3	1	0	3	13	9	.155	.224	.189	413	25	-14	2	8	-2	.922	-2	S-28,2-12/3-7	-1.8
Total	2	127	371	38	71	9	3	2	23	49	37	.191	.289	.248	537	60	-18	7	8		.956	1	/2-83,S-32,3-8	-1.8
■ BOZE BERGER Berger, Louis William b: 5/13/10, Baltimore, Md. d: 11/3/92, Bethesda, Md. BR/TR, 6′2″, 180 lbs. Deb: 8/17/32																								
1932	Cle-A	1	1	0	0	0	0	0	0	0	1	.000	.000	.000	0	-94	-0	0	0	0	1.000	1	/S-1	0.1
1935	Cle-A	124	461	62	119	27	5	5	43	34	97	.258	.310	.371	681	74	-19	7	5	-0	.964	13	*2-120/S-3,1-2,3-1	0.2
1936	Cle-A	28	52	1	9	2	0	0	3	1	14	.173	.189	.212	400	-1	-8	0	0	0	.959	4	/1-8,2-8,3-7,S-2	-0.4
1937	Chi-A	52	130	19	31	5	0	5	13	15	24	.238	.322	.392	714	79	-5	1	1	-0	.931	-1	3-40/2-1,S-1	-0.4
1938	Chi-A	118	470	60	102	15	3	3	36	43	80	.217	.284	.281	565	41	-43	4	1	1	.946	-10	S-67,2-42/3-9	-4.1
1939	Bos-A	20	30	4	9	2	0	0	2	1	10	.300	.323	.367	689	73	-1	0	0	0	.947	1	S-10/3-5,2-2	0.0
Total	6	343	1144	146	270	51	8	13	97	94	226	.236	.296	.329	624	57	-77	12	7	0	.954	9	2-173/S-84,3-62,1	-4.6
■ WALLY BERGER Berger, Walter Antone b: 10/10/05, Chicago, Ill. d: 11/30/88, Redondo Beach, Cal BR/TR, 6′2″, 198 lbs. Deb: 4/15/30 Career OF: (344-LF 943-CF 9-RF)																								
1930	Bos-N	151	555	98	172	27	14	38	119	54	69	.310	.375	.614	990	139	32	3			.966	4	*O-145(145-0-0)	2.1
1931	Bos-N	156	617	94	199	44	8	19	84	55	70	.323	.380	.512	892	143	36	13			.977	11	*O-156(0-156-0)/1-1	**4.2**
1932	Bos-N	145	602	90	185	34	6	17	73	33	66	.307	.346	.468	815	121	17	5			**.993**	5	*O-134(0-134-0),1-11	1.7
1933	Bos-N★	137	528	84	165	37	8	27	106	41	77	.313	.365	.566	932	**177**	49	2			.977	4	*O-136(0-136-0)	5.1
1934	Bos-N★	150	615	92	183	35	8	34	121	49	65	.298	.352	.546	899	148	38	2			.978	1	*O-150(0-150-0)	3.4
1935	Bos-N★	150	589	91	174	39	4	**34**	**130**	50	80	.295	.355	.548	903	151	39	3			.965	9	*O-149(0-149-0)	4.3
1936	Bos-N☆	138	534	88	154	23	3	25	91	53	84	.288	.361	.483	844	134	25	1			.966	7	*O-133(0-133-0)	2.7
1937	Bos-N	30	113	14	31	9	1	5	22	11	33	.274	.344	.504	848	140	6	0			1.000	-2	O-28(28-0-0)	0.2
	*NY-N	59	199	40	58	11	2	12	43	18	30	.291	.359	.548	907	141	11	3			.965	-2	O-52(3-46-3)	0.7
	Yr	89	312	54	89	20	3	17	65	29	63	.285	.354	.532	886	141	16	3			.976	-4	O-80(31-46-3)	0.9
1938	NY-N	16	32	5	6	0	0	0	4	2	4	.188	.235	.188	423	17	-4	0			1.000	1	/O-9(0-8-1)	-0.3
	Cin-N	99	407	74	125	23	4	16	56	29	44	.307	.356	.501	857	137	19	2			.966	-3	O-98(98-0-0)	1.0
	Yr	115	439	79	131	23	4	16	60	31	48	.298	.347	.478	826	128	15	2			.970	-2	*O-107(98-8-1)	0.7
1939	*Cin-N	97	329	36	85	15	1	14	44	36	63	.258	.341	.438	778	107	3	1			.970	-8	O-95(66-29-0)	-0.9
1940	Cin-N	2	2	0	0	0	0	0	0	0	1	.000	.000	.000	0	-99	-1	0			.000	0	H	-0.1
	Phi-N	20	41	3	13	2	0	1	5	4	7	.317	.378	.439	817	130	2	1			.947	-2	O-11(4-2-5)/1-1	-0.1
	Yr	22	43	3	13	2	0	1	5	4	8	.302	.362	.419	780	119	1	1			.947	-2	O-11(4-2-5)/1-1	-0.2
Total	11	1350	5163	809	1550	299	59	242	898	435	693	.300	.359	.522	881	140	271	36			.974	26	*O-1296C/1-13	24.0
■ PETER BERGERON Bergeron, Peter Francis b: 11/9/77, Greenfield, Mass. BL/TR, 6′2″, 185 lbs. Deb: 9/7/99																								
1999	Mon-N	16	45	12	11	2	0	0	1	9	5	.244	.370	.289	659	72	-2	0	0	0	.967	1	O-13(13-3-0)	-0.1
2000	Mon-N	148	518	80	127	25	7	5	31	58	100	.245	.321	.349	671	69	-25	11	13	-2	.985	7	*O-146(32-117-0)	-1.8
Total	2	164	563	92	138	27	7	5	32	67	105	.245	.325	.345	670	69	-26	11	13	-2	.983	8	O-159(45-120-0)	-1.9
■ JOHN BERGH Bergh, John Baptist b: 10/8/1857, Boston, Mass. d: 4/17/1883, Boston, Mass. Deb: 8/5/1876																								
1876	Phi-N	1	4	0	0	0	0	0	0	0	2	.000	.000	.000	0	-99	-1				1.000	-0	/O-1(0-1-0),C-1	-0.1
1880	Bos-N	11	40	2	8	3	0	0	0	2	5	.200	.238	.275	513	76	-1				.844	-3	C-11	-0.4
Total	2	12	44	2	8	3	0	0	0	2	7	.182	.217	.250	467	59	-2				.841	-4	/C-12,O-1(0-1-0)	-0.5
■ MARTY BERGHAMMER Berghammer, Martin Andrew "Pepper" b: 6/18/1888, Elliott, Pa. d: 12/21/57, Pittsburgh, Pa. BL/TR, 5′9″, 172 lbs. Deb: 9/8/11																								
1911	Chi-A	2	5	0	0	0	0	0	0	0		.000	.167	.000	167	-54	-1	0			1.000	-0	/2-2	-0.1
1913	Cin-N	74	188	25	41	4	1	1	13	10	29	.218	.269	.266	535	53	-11	16			.909	5	S-54,2-13	-0.4
1914	Cin-N	77	112	15	25	2	0	0	6	10	18	.223	.287	.241	528	56	-6	4			.906	7	S-33,2-13	0.2
1915	Pit-F	132	469	96	114	10	6	0	33	83	44	.243	.371	.290	661	88	-10	26			**.943**	-16	*S-132	-1.7
Total	4	285	774	136	180	16	7	1	52	103	91	.233	.335	.275	610	75	-28	46			.931	-5	S-219/2-28	-2.0
■ AL BERGMAN Bergman, Alfred Henry "Dutch" b: 9/27/1890, Peru, Ind. d: 6/20/61, Fort Wayne, Ind. BR/TR, 5′7″, 155 lbs. Deb: 8/29/16																								
1916	Cle-A	8	14	2	3	0	1	0	0	2	4	.214	.313	.357	670	95	-0	0			.889	-2	/2-3	-0.2
■ DAVE BERGMAN Bergman, David Bruce b: 6/6/53, Evanston, Ill. BL/TL, 6′1.5″, 185 lbs. Deb: 8/26/75 Career OF: (88-LF 1-CF 18-RF)																								
1975	NY-A	7	17	0	0	0	0	0	0	2	4	.000	.105	.000	105	-69	-4	0	0	0	.917	0	/O-6(0-0-6)	-0.4
1977	NY-A	5	4	1	1	0	0	0	1	0	0	.250	.250	.250	500	37	-0	0	0	0	1.000	-1	/O-3(1-1-1),1-2	-0.1
1978	Hou-N	104	186	15	43	5	1	0	12	39	32	.231	.364	.269	633	86	-1	2	0	0	.993	-2	1-66,O-29(29-0-0)	-0.7
1979	Hou-N	13	15	4	6	0	0	1	2	0	3	.400	.400	.600	1000	179	1	0	0	0	1.000	-0	/1-4	0.1
1980	*Hou-N	90	78	12	20	6	1	0	3	10	10	.256	.341	.359	700	104	1	1	0	0	.995	2	1-59/O-5(3-0-2)	0.2
1981	Hou-N	6	6	1	1	0	0	1	1	0	0	.167	.167	.667	833	134	0	0	0	0	1.000	0	/1-1	0.1
	SF-N	63	145	16	37	9	0	3	13	19	18	.255	.341	.379	721	106	1	2	0	0	.992	0	1-33,O-15(15-0-0)	0.0
	Yr	69	151	17	38	9	0	4	14	19	18	.252	.335	.391	726	108	2	2	0	0	.992	1	1-34,O-15(15-0-0)	0.1
1982	SF-N	100	121	22	33	3	1	4	14	18	11	.273	.367	.413	780	118	3	3	0	1	.991	1	1-69/O-6(4-0-3)	0.3
1983	SF-N	90	140	16	40	4	1	6	24	24	21	.286	.394	.457	851	140	8	2	1	0	.994	2	1-50/O-6(6-0-0)	0.8
1984	*Det-A	120	271	42	74	8	5	7	44	33	40	.273	.358	.417	775	115	6	3	4	-1	.989	8	*1-114/O-2(1-0-1)	0.9
1985	Det-A	69	140	8	25	2	0	3	7	14	15	.179	.253	.257	510	41	-11	0	0	0	.991	1	1-44/O-1(1-0-0),D-5	-1.2
1986	Det-A	65	130	14	30	6	1	1	9	21	16	.231	.338	.315	653	79	-3	0	0	0	.986	2	1-41/O-2(1-0-1),D-8	-0.3
1987	*Det-A	91	172	25	47	7	3	6	22	30	23	.273	.384	.453	838	127	8	0	1	-0	.992	-1	1-65/O-7(3-0-4),D-7	0.3
1988	Det-A	116	289	37	85	14	0	5	35	38	34	.294	.376	.394	771	121	9	0	2	-1	.990	-0	1-64,D-30,O-13L	0.4
1989	Det-A	137	385	38	103	13	1	7	37	44	44	.268	.346	.361	707	102	2	1	3	-1	.993	5	*1-123/O-1(1-0-0),D-7	-0.2
1990	Det-A	100	205	21	57	10	1	2	26	33	17	.278	.378	.366	744	108	4	3	2	-0	.995	-3	D-51,1-27/O-5(5-0-0)	-0.2
1991	Det-A	86	194	23	46	10	1	7	29	35	40	.237	.354	.407	761	108	3	1	1	-0	.997	-1	1-49,D-13/O-4(4-0-0)	-0.1
1992	Det-A	87	181	17	42	3	0	1	10	20	19	.232	.308	.265	574	62	-9	1	0	0	.986	-2	1-55,D-12/O-1(1-0-0)	-1.4
Total	17	1349	2679	312	690	100	16	54	289	380	347	.258	.351	.367	719	102	17	19	14	-1	.992	10	1-866,D-133,O-106L	-1.5
■ NATE BERKENSTOCK Berkenstock, Nathan b: 1831, Pennsylvania d: 2/23/1900, Philadelphia, Pa. Deb: 10/30/1871																								
1871	Ath-n	1	4	0	0	0	0	0	0	0	3	.000	.000	.000	0	-99	-1	0	0	0	1.000	0	/O-1(0-0-1)	0.0
■ LANCE BERKMAN Berkman, William Lance b: 2/10/76, Waco, Tex. BB/TL, 6′1″, 205 lbs. Deb: 7/16/99																								
1999	Hou-N	34	93	10	22	2	0	4	15	12	21	.237	.324	.387	711	80	-3	5	1	1	.955	-3	O-27(22-0-8)/1-1	-0.6
2000	Hou-N	114	353	76	105	28	1	21	67	56	73	.297	.395	.561	956	130	17	6	2	1	.968	-0	O-96(40-0-63)/1-2	1.2
Total	2	148	446	86	127	30	1	25	82	68	94	.285	.381	.525	905	121	14	11	3	1	.965	-3	O-123(62-0-71)/1-3	0.6

YEAR	TM/L	G	AB	R	H	2B	3B	HR	RBI	BB	SO	AVG	OBP	SLG	OPS	OPS+	BR+	SB	CS	SBR	FA	FR	G/POS	TPR
■ BOB BERMAN	Berman, Robert Leon b: 1/24/1899, New York, N.Y. d: 8/2/88, Bridgeport, Conn. BR/TR, 5'7.5", 158 lbs. Deb: 6/4/18																							
1918	Was-A	2	0	0	0	0	0	0	0	0	0	—	—	—	—	—	0	0			1.000	0	/C-1	0.0
■ CURT BERNARD	Bernard, Curtis Henry b: 2/18/1878, Parkersburg, W.Va. d: 4/10/55, Culver City, Cal. BL/TR, 5'10", 150 lbs. Deb: 9/17/00 Career OF: (0-LF 8-CF 26-RF)																							
1900	NY-N	20	71	9	18	2	0	0	8	6		.254	.329	.282	611	73	-2	1			.929	-2	O-19(0-0-19)/S-1	-0.5
1901	NY-N	23	76	11	17	0	2	0	6	7		.224	.289	.276	565	67	-3	2			.800	-1	O-15C/2-4,S-2,3-1	-0.4
Total	2	43	147	20	35	2	2	0	14	13		.238	.309	.279	588	70	-5	3			.857	-3	/O-34R,2-4,S-3,3-1	-0.9
■ TONY BERNAZARD	Bernazard, Antonio (Garcia) b: 8/24/56, Caguas, P.R. BB/TR, 5'9", 160 lbs. Deb: 7/13/79																							
1979	Mon-N	22	40	11	12	2	0	1	8	15	12	.300	.500	.425	925	156	5	1	2	-0	.982	-1	2-14	0.4
1980	Mon-N	82	183	26	41	7	1	5	18	17	41	.224	.290	.355	645	79	-5	9	2	1	.976	2	2-39,S-22	0.1
1981	Chi-A	106	384	53	106	14	4	6	34	54	66	.276	.368	.380	748	118	11	4	4	-1	.987	-1	*2-104/S-1	1.6
1982	Chi-A	137	540	90	138	25	9	11	56	67	88	.256	.340	.396	736	101	2	11	0	2	.985	25	*2-137	3.6
1983	Chi-A	59	233	30	61	16	2	2	26	17	45	.262	.312	.373	685	85	-5	2	1	0	.976	-2	2-59	-0.3
	Sea-A	80	300	35	80	18	1	6	30	38	52	.267	.353	.393	746	101	1	21	8	2	.971	1	2-79	0.8
	Yr	139	533	65	141	34	3	8	56	55	97	.265	.336	.385	720	94	-4	23	9	2	.973	-1	*2-138	0.5
1984	Cle-A	140	439	44	97	15	4	2	38	43	70	.221	.293	.287	580	60	-23	20	13	-0	.971	-11	*2-136/D-1	-2.7
1985	Cle-A	153	500	73	137	26	3	11	59	69	72	.274	.363	.404	767	111	9	17	9	1	.978	-29	*2-147/S-1	-1.1
1986	Cle-A	146	562	88	169	28	4	17	73	53	77	.301	.367	.456	823	125	19	17	8	1	.979	1	*2-146	2.9
1987	Cle-A	79	293	39	70	12	1	11	30	25	49	.239	.301	.399	700	83	-8	7	4	0	.983	-16	2-78	-1.8
	Oak-A	61	214	34	57	14	1	3	19	30	30	.266	.357	.383	740	103	2	4	4	-1	.953	-18	2-59/D-3	-1.4
	Yr	140	507	73	127	26	2	14	49	55	79	.250	.325	.393	718	91	-6	11	8	-0	.971	-34	*2-137/D-3	-3.2
1991	Det-A	6	12	0	2	0	0	0	0	0	4	.167	.167	.167	333	-7	-2	0	0	0	.900	1	/2-2,D-2	0.0
Total	10	1071	3700	523	970	177	30	75	391	428	606	.262	.341	.387	728	100	6	113	55	6	.978	-48	2-1000/S-24,D-6	2.1
■ JUAN BERNHARDT	Bernhardt, Juan Ramon (Coradin) b: 8/31/53, San Pedro De Macoris, D.R. BR/TR, 5'11", 160 lbs. Deb: 7/10/76 Career OF: (1-LF 0-CF 3-RF)																							
1976	NY-A	10	21	1	4	1	0	0	1	0	4	.190	.190	.238	429	25	-2	0	0	0	.800	-1	/O-4(1-0-3),3-1,D-2	-0.3
1977	Sea-A	89	305	32	74	9	2	7	30	5	26	.243	.260	.354	614	66	-15	2	3	-1	.982	-1	D-54,3-21/1-8	-1.9
1978	Sea-A	54	165	13	38	9	0	2	12	9	10	.230	.274	.321	595	67	-7	1	1	-0	.989	-0	1-25,3-22/D-2	-1.0
1979	Sea-A	1	1	0	1	0	0	0	0	0	0	1.000	1.000	1.000	2000	434	0	0	0	0	.000	0	/H	0.0
Total	4	154	492	46	117	19	2	9	43	14	40	.238	.263	.339	603	66	-24	3	4	-1	.965	-2	/D-58,3-44,1-33,O-4R	-3.2
■ CARLOS BERNIER	Bernier, Carlos (Rodriguez) b: 1/28/27, Juana Diaz, P.R. d: 4/6/89, Juana Diaz, P.R. BR/TR, 5'9", 180 lbs. Deb: 4/22/53																							
1953	Pit-N	105	310	48	66	7	8	3	31	51	53	.213	.332	.316	648	70	-12	15	14	-2	.970	5	O-86(11-57-18)	-1.3
■ JOHNNY BERO	Bero, John George b: 12/22/22, Gary, W.Va. d: 5/11/85, Gardena, Cal. BL/TR, 6', 170 lbs. Deb: 9/26/48																							
1948	Det-A	4	9	2	0	0	0	0	0	1	1	.000	.100	.000	100	-70	-2	0	0	0	1.000	-1	/2-2	-0.3
1951	StL-A	61	160	24	34	5	0	5	17	26	30	.213	.323	.338	660	76	-5	1	1	-0	.954	-9	S-55/2-1	-1.1
Total	2	65	169	26	34	5	0	5	17	27	31	.201	.311	.320	631	69	-7	1	1	-0	1.000	-10	/S-55,2-3	-1.4
■ DALE BERRA	Berra, Dale Anthony b: 12/13/56, Ridgewood, N.J. BR/TR, 6', 190 lbs. Deb: 8/22/77 F																							
1977	Pit-N	17	40	0	7	1	0	0	3	1	8	.175	.195	.200	395	6	-5	0	0	0	.973	3	3-14	-0.3
1978	Pit-N	56	135	16	28	2	0	6	14	13	20	.207	.287	.356	642	75	-5	3	0	1	.908	1	3-55/S-2	-0.4
1979	Pit-N	44	123	11	26	5	0	3	15	11	17	.211	.276	.325	601	61	-7	0	0	0	.940	1	S-22,3-22	-0.5
1980	Pit-N	93	245	21	54	8	2	6	31	16	52	.220	.271	.343	614	69	-11	2	0	0	.968	2	3-48,S-45/2-4	-0.6
1981	Pit-N	81	232	21	56	12	0	2	27	17	34	.241	.302	.319	621	74	-8	11	2	2	.976	2	3-42,S-30,2-18	-0.1
1982	Pit-N	156	529	64	139	25	5	10	61	33	83	.263	.311	.386	697	91	-7	6	6	-1	.961	-2	*S-153/3-6	0.6
1983	Pit-N	161	537	51	135	25	1	10	52	61	84	.251	.328	.358	685	88	-8	8	5	0	.963	16	*S-161	2.5
1984	Pit-N	136	450	31	100	16	0	9	52	34	78	.222	.278	.318	596	67	-20	1	3	-1	.955	-2	*S-135/3-1	-0.9
1985	NY-A	48	109	8	25	5	1	1	8	7	20	.229	.276	.321	597	64	-5	1	1	-0	.917	4	3-41/S-6	-0.1
1986	NY-A	42	108	10	25	7	0	2	13	9	14	.231	.297	.352	648	77	-4	0	0	0	.972	-1	S-19,3-18/D-4	-0.3
1987	Hou-N	19	45	3	8	3	0	0	2	8	12	.178	.302	.244	546	49	-3	0	0	0	.963	-3	S-18/2-3	-0.4
Total	11	853	2553	236	603	109	9	49	278	210	422	.236	.297	.344	641	76	-83	32	17	1	.959	21	S-591,3-247/2-25,D	-0.5
■ YOGI BERRA	Berra, Lawrence Peter b: 5/12/25, St.Louis, Mo. BL/TR, 5'8", 194 lbs. Deb: 9/22/46 FMCH Career OF: (148-LF 0-CF 115-RF)																							
1946	NY-A	7	22	3	8	1	0	2	4	1	1	.364	.391	.682	1073	193	2	0	0	0	1.000	2	/C-6	0.5
1947	*NY-A	83	293	41	82	15	3	11	54	13	12	.280	.310	.464	775	115	3	0	1	-0	.972	-6	C-51,O-24(12-0-12)	-0.2
1948	NY-A☆	125	469	70	143	24	10	14	98	25	24	.305	.341	.488	830	120	10	3	3	-0	.979	-9	C-71,O-50(0-0-50)	0.3
1949	*NY-A★	116	415	59	115	20	2	20	91	22	25	.277	.323	.480	802	111	2	2	1	0	.989	11	*C-109	1.9
1950	*NY-A★	151	597	116	192	30	6	28	124	55	12	.322	.383	.533	915	136	29	4	2	0	.985	1	*C-148	3.6
1951	*NY-A★	141	547	92	161	19	4	27	88	44	20	.294	.350	.492	842	131	20	5	4	-0	.984	9	*C-141	3.5
1952	*NY-A★	142	534	97	146	17	1	30	98	66	24	.273	.358	.478	835	139	26	2	3	-1	.992	2	*C-140	3.7
1953	*NY-A★	137	503	80	149	23	5	27	108	50	32	.296	.363	.523	886	142	27	0	3	-1	.986	3	*C-133	3.5
1954	NY-A★	151	584	88	179	28	6	22	125	56	29	.307	.371	.488	859	139	29	0	1	-0	.990	-0	*C-149/3-1	3.7
1955	*NY-A★	147	541	84	147	20	3	27	108	60	20	.272	.352	.470	821	121	14	1	0	0	.984	-0	*C-145	2.1
1956	*NY-A★	140	521	93	155	29	2	30	105	65	29	.298	.381	.534	914	144	31	3	2	-0	.986	7	*C-135/O-1(1-0-0)	4.4
1957	*NY-A★	134	482	74	121	14	2	24	82	57	24	.251	.331	.438	769	110	6	1	2	-0	.995	16	*C-121/O-6(5-0-1)	2.7
1958	*NY-A★	122	433	60	115	17	3	22	90	35	35	.266	.323	.471	795	120	10	3	0	1	**1.000**	6	C-88,O-21(0-0-21)/1-2	2.1
1959	NY-A★	131	472	64	134	25	1	19	69	43	38	.284	.349	.462	811	125	15	1	2	-0	**.997**	7	*C-116/O-7(1-0-6)	2.7
1960	*NY-A★	120	359	46	99	14	1	15	62	38	23	.276	.350	.446	796	120	10	2	1	0	.989	-10	C-63,O-36(20-0-17)	0.1
1961	*NY-A★	119	395	62	107	11	0	22	61	35	28	.271	.333	.466	799	117	8	2	0	1	.988	3	O-87(81-0-8),C-15	0.7
1962	*NY-A★	86	232	25	52	8	0	10	35	24	18	.224	.302	.388	690	87	-5	0	0	0	.990	8	C-31,O-28(28-0-0)	0.3
1963	*NY-A	64	147	20	43	6	0	8	28	15	17	.293	.362	.497	859	139	8	1	0	0	.988	8	C-35	1.8
1965	NY-N	4	9	1	2	0	0	0	0	0	3	.222	.222	.222	444	27	-1	0	0	0	.941	1	/C-2	0.0
Total	19	2120	7555	1175	2150	321	49	358	1430	704	414	.285	.350	.482	832	126	246	30	26	-2	.989	57	*C-1699,O-260L/1-2,3	37.4
■ DENNIS BERRAN	Berran, Dennis Martin b: 10/8/1887, Merrimac, Mass. d: 4/28/43, Boston, Mass. BL/TL, Deb: 8/11/12																							
1912	Chi-A	2	4	1	1	0	0	0	0	0		.250	.250	.250	500	44	-0	0			1.000	-1	/O-2(2-0-0)	-0.1
■ RAY BERRES	Berres, Raymond Frederick b: 8/31/07, Kenosha, Wis. BR/TR, 5'9", 170 lbs. Deb: 4/24/34 C																							
1934	Bro-N	39	79	7	17	4	0	0	3	1	16	.215	.225	.266	491	32	-8	0			.969	-2	C-37	-0.8
1936	Bro-N	105	267	16	64	10	1	1	13	14	35	.240	.280	.296	576	55	-17	1			.988	23	*C-105	1.0
1937	Pit-N	2	6	0	1	0	0	0	0	0	0	.167	.167	.167	333	-9	-1	0			1.000	1	/C-2	0.0
1938	Pit-N	40	100	7	23	2	0	0	6	8	10	.230	.287	.250	537	48	-7	0			.993	4	C-40	-0.1
1939	Pit-N	81	231	22	53	6	1	0	16	11	25	.229	.267	.264	532	44	-18	1			.993	-2	C-80	-1.6
1940	Pit-N	21	32	2	6	0	0	0	2	1	1	.188	.212	.188	400	11	-4	0			.980	3	C-21	-0.1
	Bos-N	85	229	12	44	4	1	0	14	18	19	.192	.251	.218	469	32	-21	0			.981	1	C-85	-1.6
	Yr	106	261	14	50	4	1	0	16	19	20	.192	.246	.215	461	29	-25	0			.981	3	*C-106	-1.7
1941	Bos-N	120	279	21	56	10	0	1	19	17	20	.201	.247	.247	494	41	-22	2			**.995**	9	*C-120	-0.8
1942	NY-N	12	32	0	6	0	0	0	1	2	3	.188	.235	.188	423	24	-3	0			.973	-2	C-12	-0.4
1943	NY-N	20	28	1	4	1	0	0	0	1	2	.143	.172	.179	351	1	-4	0			.981	4	C-17	0.1
1944	NY-N	16	17	4	8	0	0	1	2	1	0	.471	.526	.647	1173	230	3	0			1.000	0	C-12	0.4
1945	NY-N	20	30	4	5	0	0	0	2	2	3	.167	.219	.167	385	8	-4	0			1.000	1	C-20	-0.2
Total	11	561	1330	96	287	37	3	3	78	76	134	.216	.260	.255	515	43	-105	4			.989	40	C-551	-4.1
■ GERONIMO BERROA	Berroa, Geronimo Emiliano Letta (b: Geronimo Emiliano Letta (Berroa)) b: 3/18/65, Santo Domingo, D.R. BR/TR, 6', 195 lbs. Deb: 4/5/89 Career OF: (100-LF 0-CF 243-RF)																							
1989	Atl-N	81	136	7	36	4	0	2	9	7	32	.265	.301	.338	639	80	-4	0	1	-0	.971	1	O-34(1-0-33)	-0.4
1990	Atl-N	7	4	0	0	0	0	0	0	1	1	.000	.200	.000	200	-38	-1	0	0	0	1.000	-1	/O-3(3-0-0)	-0.2
1992	Cin-N	13	15	2	4	1	0	0	0	2	1	.267	.389	.333	722	103	0	0	1	-0	1.000	0	/O-3(3-0-0)	0.0
1993	Fla-N	14	34	3	4	1	0	0	0	2	7	.118	.167	.147	314	-14	-5	0	0	0	.833	-1	/O-9(1-0-8)	-0.7

YEAR	TM/L	G	AB	R	H	2B	3B	HR	RBI	BB	SO	AVG	OBP	SLG	OPS	OPS+	BR+	SB	CS	SBR	FA	FR	G/POS	TPR
1994	Oak-A	96	340	55	104	18	2	13	65	41	62	.306	.385	.485	871	134	18	7	2	1	1.000	1	D-44,O-42(36-0-7)/1-9	1.4
1995	Oak-A	141	546	87	152	22	3	22	88	63	98	.278	.354	.451	805	114	11	7	4	0	.971	2	D-72,O-71(17-0-54)	0.6
1996	Oak-A	153	586	101	170	32	1	36	106	47	122	.290	.347	.532	879	120	16	0	3	-1	.980	-7	D-91,O-61(17-0-54)	0.0
1997	Oak-A	73	261	40	81	12	0	16	42	36	58	.310	.396	.540	936	144	17	3	2	-0	.986	-3	O-43(0-0-43),D-32	0.9
	*Bal-A	83	300	48	78	13	0	10	48	40	62	.260	.353	.403	756	100	1	1	2	-0	.959	-2	D-42,O-40(0-0-40)	-0.6
	Yr	156	561	88	159	25	0	26	90	76	120	.283	.373	.467	840	120	18	4	4	-1	.939	-5	O-83(0-0-83),D-74	0.3
1998	Cle-A	20	65	6	13	3	1	0	3	7	17	.200	.278	.277	555	44	-5	1	0	0	1.000	1	O-14(14-0-0)/D-5	-0.5
	Det-A	52	126	17	30	4	1	1	10	17	27	.238	.338	.310	647	70	-5	0	1	-0	1.000	-1	D-37/O-4(2-0-2)	-0.8
	Yr	72	191	23	43	7	2	1	13	24	44	.225	.318	.298	616	61	-11	1	1	-0	1.000	-0	D-42,O-18(16-0-2)	-1.3
1999	Tor-A	22	62	11	12	3	0	1	6	9	15	.194	.315	.290	605	55	-4	0	0	0	1.000	0	D-17/O-2(2-0-0)	-0.5
2000	LA-N	24	31	2	8	0	1	0	5	4	8	.258	.343	.323	665	73	-1	0	0	0	1.000	-0	/O-6(4-0-2),1-2	-0.2
Total	11	779	2506	379	692	113	9	101	382	276	510	.276	.352	.449	801	109	37	19	16	-1	.977	-11	D-340,O-332R/1-11	-1.0
■ **KEN BERRY**	Berry, Allen Kent b: 5/10/41, Kansas City, Mo. BR/TR, 5′11″, 180 lbs. Deb: 9/9/62 Career OF: (202-LF 1018-CF 141-RF)																							
1962	Chi-A	3	6	2	2	0	0	0	0	0	0	.333	.333	.333	667	80	-0	0	0	0	1.000	1	/O-2(1-1-1)	0.0
1963	Chi-A	4	5	2	1	0	0	0	0	1	1	.200	.333	.200	533	55	-0	0	0	0	.857	-0	/O-2(2-0-0),2-1	0.0
1964	Chi-A	12	32	4	12	1	0	1	4	5	3	.375	.459	.500	959	171	3	0	1	-0	1.000	-3	O-12(0-12-0)	0.0
1965	Chi-A	157	472	51	103	17	4	12	42	28	96	.218	.269	.347	617	79	-15	4	2	0	.980	3	*O-156(0-156-0)	-1.6
1966	Chi-A	147	443	50	120	20	2	8	34	28	63	.271	.317	.379	696	106	3	7	10	-2	.991	-9	*O-141(101-13-41)	-1.7
1967	Chi-A★	147	485	49	117	14	4	7	41	46	68	.241	.311	.330	641	93	-4	9	8	-1	.992	-15	*O-143(50-38-86)	-3.0
1968	Chi-A	153	504	49	127	21	2	7	32	25	64	.252	.289	.343	632	90	-7	6	6	-1	.981	3	*O-151(0-149-2)	-1.1
1969	Chi-A	130	297	25	69	12	2	4	18	24	50	.232	.296	.327	623	71	-12	1	2	-0	**1.000**	-5	*O-120(2-116-2)	-2.0
1970	Chi-A	141	463	45	128	12	2	7	50	43	61	.276	.346	.356	702	90	-5	6	4	-0	.988	6	*O-138(0-138-0)	-0.2
1971	Cal-A	111	298	29	66	17	0	3	22	18	33	.221	.273	.309	581	69	-13	3	2	-0	.988	2	*O-101(8-94-0)	-1.4
1972	Cal-A	119	409	41	118	15	3	5	39	35	47	.289	.348	.377	724	122	11	5	3	0	**1.000**	14	*O-116(0-116-0)	2.5
1973	Cal-A	136	415	48	118	11	2	3	36	26	50	.284	.328	.342	670	96	-2	1	6	-2	**.997**	3	*O-129(15-111-4)	-0.5
1974	Mil-A	98	267	21	64	9	2	1	24	18	26	.240	.295	.300	595	72	-10	3	1	0	.995	-3	O-82(5-74-5),D-13	-1.6
1975	Cle-A	25	40	6	8	1	0	0	1	1	7	.200	.238	.225	463	31	-4	0	1	-0	.926	-2	O-18(18-0-0)/D-5	-0.7
Total	14	1383	4136	422	1053	150	23	58	343	298	569	.255	.309	.344	653	90	-54	45	46	-6	.989	-5	*O-1311C/D-18,2-1	-11.3
■ **CHARLIE BERRY**	Berry, Charles Francis b: 10/18/02, Phillipsburg, N.J. d: 9/6/72, Evanston, Ill. BR/TR, 6′, 185 lbs. Deb: 6/15/25 FUC																							
1925	Phi-A	10	14	1	3	1	0	0	3	0	2	.214	.214	.286	500	24	-2	0	0	0	.900	-1	/C-4	-0.2
1928	Bos-A	80	177	18	46	7	3	1	19	21	19	.260	.342	.350	692	84	-4	1	1	-0	.959	-9	C-63	-0.9
1929	Bos-A	77	207	19	50	11	4	1	21	15	29	.242	.302	.348	650	69	-10	2	4	-1	.983	3	C-72	-0.4
1930	Bos-A	88	256	31	74	9	6	6	35	16	22	.289	.331	.441	772	98	-2	2	0	0	.988	7	C-85	1.0
1931	Bos-A	111	357	41	101	16	2	6	49	29	38	.283	.337	.389	726	96	-3	4	0	1	.985	-3	*C-102	0.1
1932	Bos-A	10	32	0	6	3	0	0	6	3	2	.188	.257	.281	538	40	-3	0	0	0	.944	-1	C-10	-0.3
	Chi-A	72	226	33	69	15	6	4	31	21	23	.305	.364	.478	842	124	8	3	0	1	.981	-2	C-70	1.0
	Yr	82	258	33	75	18	6	4	37	24	25	.291	.351	.453	805	114	5	3	0	1	.977	-2	C-80	0.7
1933	Chi-A	86	271	25	69	8	3	2	28	17	16	.255	.301	.328	629	70	-12	0	0	0	.987	-8	C-83	-1.5
1934	Phi-A	99	269	14	72	10	2	0	34	22	23	.268	.323	.320	643	69	-12	1	0	0	.987	-0	C-99	-0.7
1935	Phi-A	62	190	14	48	7	3	3	29	10	20	.253	.290	.368	658	70	-9	0	0	0	.987	-1	C-56	-0.6
1936	Phi-A	13	17	0	1	1	0	0	1	6	2	.059	.304	.118	422	8	-2	0	0	0	.971	1	C-12	-0.1
1938	Phi-A	1	2	0	0	0	0	0	0	0	0	.000	.000	.000	0	-99	-1	0	0	0	1.000	0	/C-1	0.0
Total	11	709	2018	196	539	88	29	23	256	160	196	.267	.322	.374	696	83	-52	13	5	1	.982	-12	C-657	-2.6
■ **CHARLIE BERRY**	Berry, Charles Joseph b: 9/6/1860, Elizabeth, N.J. d: 1/22/40, Phillipsburg, N.J. BR/TR, 5′11″, 175 lbs. Deb: 4/30/1884 F																							
1884	Alt-U	7	25	2	6	0	0	0		0		.240	.240	.240	480	45	-2				.862	-6	/2-7	-0.8
	KC-U	29	118	15	29	6	1	1		1		.246	.252	.339	591	89	-5				.887	3	2-22/O-8(1-7-0),3-1	-0.1
	CP-U	7	27	4	3	2	0	0		0		.111	.111	.185	296	-12	-4				.833	1	/2-7	-0.3
	Yr	43	170	21	38	8	1	1		1		.224	.228	.300	528	64	-12				.871	-3	2-36/O-8(1-7-0),3-1	-1.2
■ **CLAUDE BERRY**	Berry, Claude Elzy "Admiral" b: 2/14/1880, Losantville, Ind. d: 2/1/74, Richmond, Ind. BR/TR, 5′7″, 165 lbs. Deb: 4/22/04																							
1904	Chi-A	3	1	1	0	0	0	0	0	1		.000	.500	.000	500	68	0	0			1.000	1	/C-3	0.1
1906	Phi-A	10	30	2	7	0	0	0	2	2		.233	.281	.233	515	60	-1	1			.938	6	C-10	0.5
1907	Phi-A	8	19	2	4	2	0	0	1	2		.211	.286	.316	602	90	-0	0			.944	-2	/C-8	-0.2
1914	Pit-F	124	411	35	98	18	9	2	36	26	50	.238	.284	.341	624	70	-25	6			.970	1	*C-122	-1.4
1915	Pit-F	100	292	32	56	11	1	1	26	29	42	.192	.269	.247	516	46	-25	7			.980	-0	C-99	-1.9
Total	5	245	753	72	165	31	10	3	65	60	92	.219	.279	.299	577	61	-52	14			.971	4	C-242	-2.9
■ **NEIL BERRY**	Berry, Cornelius John b: 1/11/22, Kalamazoo, Mich. BR/TR, 5′10″, 170 lbs. Deb: 4/20/48																							
1948	Det-A	87	256	46	68	8	1	0	16	37	23	.266	.358	.305	663	75	-8	1	3	-1	.930	4	S-41,2-26	-0.1
1949	Det-A	109	329	38	78	9	1	0	18	27	24	.237	.299	.271	569	51	-23	4	2	0	.970	-0	2-95/S-4	-1.8
1950	Det-A	39	40	9	10	1	0	0	7	6	11	.250	.348	.275	623	59	-2	0	0	0	.944	2	S-12/2-2,3-1	0.1
1951	Det-A	67	157	17	36	5	2	0	9	10	15	.229	.275	.287	562	52	-11	4	2	0	.944	8	S-38,2-10/3-7	0.0
1952	Det-A	73	189	22	43	4	3	0	13	22	19	.228	.311	.280	592	65	-9	1	3	-1	.965	4	S-66/3-2	-0.3
1953	StL-A	57	99	14	28	1	2	0	11	9	10	.283	.343	.333	676	82	-2	1	2	-0	.825	-1	3-18,2-15/S-6	-0.3
	Chi-A	5	8	1	1	0	0	0	0	1	1	.125	.222	.125	347	-4	-1	0	0	0	1.000	2	/2-3	0.1
	Yr	62	107	15	29	1	2	0	11	10	11	.271	.333	.318	651	75	-4	1	2	-0	.825	1	3-18,2-18/S-6	-0.2
1954	Bal-A	5	9	1	1	0	0	0	0	1	2	.111	.200	.111	311	-14	-1	0	0	0	1.000	0	/S-5	-0.1
Total	7	442	1087	148	265	28	9	0	74	113	105	.244	.317	.286	603	62	-57	11	12	-2	.949	19	S-172,2-151/3-28	-2.4
■ **JOE BERRY**	Berry, Joseph Howard Jr. "Nig" b: 12/31/1894, Philadelphia, Pa. d: 4/29/76, Philadelphia, Pa. BB/TR, 5′10.5″, 159 lbs. Deb: 7/18/21 F																							
1921	NY-N	9	6	0	2	0	1	0	2	1	1	.333	.429	.667	1095	185	1	0	0	0	.875	0	/2-7	0.1
1922	NY-N	6	0	0	0	0	0	0	0	0	0	—	—	—	—	—	0	0	0	0	.000	0	R	0.0
Total	2	15	6	0	2	0	1	0	2	1	1	.333	.429	.667	1095	185	1	0	0	0	.875	0	/2-7	0.1
■ **JOE BERRY**	Berry, Joseph Howard Sr. "Hodge" b: 9/10/1872, Wheeling, W.Va. d: 3/13/61, Allenwood, N.J. BB/TR, 5′9″, 172 lbs. Deb: 9/4/02 F																							
1902	Phi-N	1	4	0	1	0	0	0	1	1		.250	.400	.250	650	101	0	1			1.000	-1	/C-1	-0.1
■ **SEAN BERRY**	Berry, Sean Robert b: 3/22/66, Santa Monica, Cal. BR/TR, 5′11″, 210 lbs. Deb: 9/17/90																							
1990	KC-A	8	23	2	5	1	1	0	4	2	5	.217	.280	.348	628	76	-1	0	0	0	.944	1	/3-8	0.0
1991	KC-A	31	60	5	8	3	0	0	1	5	23	.133	.212	.183	395	10	-7	0	0	0	.970	8	3-30	0.1
1992	Mon-N	24	57	5	19	1	0	1	4	1	11	.333	.345	.404	748	112	1	2	1	0	.879	-3	3-20	-0.2
1993	Mon-N	122	299	50	78	15	2	14	49	41	70	.261	.354	.465	819	112	5	12	2	2	.936	5	3-96	1.3
1994	Mon-N	103	320	43	89	19	2	11	41	32	50	.278	.349	.453	802	106	3	14	0	3	.938	-2	*3-100	0.4
1995	Mon-N	103	314	38	100	22	1	14	55	25	53	.318	.372	.529	901	130	13	3	8	-2	.947	6	3-83/1-3	1.7
1996	Hou-N	132	431	55	121	38	1	17	95	23	58	.281	.330	.492	822	123	12	12	6	1	.922	-5	*3-110	0.8
1997	*Hou-N	96	301	37	77	24	1	8	43	25	53	.256	.323	.422	745	97	-2	1	5	-2	.921	-2	3-85/D-3	-0.4
1998	*Hou-N	102	299	48	94	17	1	13	52	31	50	.314	.392	.508	900	138	17	3	1	0	.953	3	3-87/D-1	2.0
1999	Mil-N	106	259	26	59	11	1	2	23	17	50	.228	.283	.301	584	49	-20	0	0	0	.989	-4	1-64	-2.8
2000	Mil-N	32	46	1	7	2	0	1	2	4	13	.152	.220	.261	481	21	-6	0	1	-0	1.000	-4	/3-9	-0.9
	Bos-A	1	4	0	0	0	0	0	0	0	2	.000	.000	.000	0	-96	-1	0	0	0	.000	-1	/3-1	-0.2
Total	11	860	2413	310	657	153	10	81	369	206	438	.272	.338	.445	782	105	13	47	24	2	.937	2	3-629/1-67,D-4	1.8
■ **TOM BERRY**	Berry, Thomas Haney b: 12/31/1842, Chester, Pa. d: 6/6/15, Chester, Pa. 5′6″, 140 lbs. Deb: 9/2/1871																							
1871	Ath-n	1	4	0	1	0	0	0	0	0	0	.250	.250	.250	500	45	-0	0	0	0	.000	-1	/O-1(0-0-1)	0.0
■ **DAMON BERRYHILL**	Berryhill, Damon Scott b: 12/3/63, South Laguna, Cal. BB/TR, 6′, 205 lbs. Deb: 9/5/87																							
1987	Chi-N	12	28	2	5	1	0	0	1	3	5	.179	.258	.214	472	26	-3	0	1	-0	.909	-4	C-11	-0.7
1988	Chi-N	95	309	19	80	19	1	7	38	17	56	.259	.298	.395	692	93	-3	1	0	0	.982	-3	C-90	-0.1
1989	Chi-N	91	334	37	86	13	0	5	41	16	54	.257	.295	.341	637	76	-10	1	0	0	.992	-12	C-89	-1.8

YEAR	TM/L	G	AB	R	H	2B	3B	HR	RBI	BB	SO	AVG	OBP	SLG	OPS	OPS+	BR+	SB	CS	SBR	FA	FR	G/POS	TPR
1990	Chi-N	17	53	6	10	4	0	1	9	5	14	.189	.259	.321	579	54	-3	0	0	0	.978	-3	C-15	-0.5
1991	Chi-N	62	159	13	30	7	0	5	14	11	41	.189	.246	.327	573	57	-9	1	2	-0	.967	-6	C-48	-1.5
	Atl-N	1	1	0	0	0	0	0	0	0	1	.000	.000	.000	0	-94	-0	0	0	0	1.000	0	/C-1	0.0
	Yr	63	160	13	30	7	0	5	14	11	42	.188	.244	.325	569	56	-10	1	2	-0	.967	-6	C-49	-1.5
1992	*Atl-N	101	307	21	70	16	1	10	43	17	67	.228	.271	.384	655	79	-9	0	2	-1	.998	-8	C-84	-1.5
1993	*Atl-N	115	335	24	82	18	2	8	43	21	64	.245	.293	.382	675	78	-11	0	0	0	.990	8	*C-105	0.3
1994	Bos-A	82	255	30	67	17	2	6	34	19	59	.263	.314	.416	730	82	-7	0	1	-0	.995	-1	C-67/D-6	-0.4
1995	Cin-N	34	82	6	15	3	0	2	11	10	19	.183	.272	.293	564	49	-6	0	0	0	.988	2	C-29/1-1	-0.3
1997	*SF-N	73	167	17	43	8	0	3	23	20	29	.257	.337	.359	696	85	-3	0	0	0	.990	1	C-51/1-1	0.0
Total	10	683	2030	175	488	106	6	47	257	139	409	.240	.291	.368	659	77	-67	3	6	-1	.988	-25	C-590/D-6,1-2	-6.5
■ HARRY BERTE	Berte, Harry Thomas b: 5/10/1872, Covington, Ky. d: 5/6/52, Los Angeles, Cal. TR, Deb: 9/17/03																							
1903	StL-N	4	15	1	5	0	0	0	1	1		.333	.375	.333	708	106	0	0			.778	-4	/2-3,S-1	-0.4
■ DICK BERTELL	Bertell, Richard George b: 11/21/35, Oak Park, Ill. d: 12/20/99, Mission Viejo, Cal. BR/TR, 6'0.5", 200 lbs. Deb: 9/22/60																							
1960	Chi-N	5	15	0	2	0	0	0	2	3	1	.133	.278	.133	411	17	-2	0	0	0	1.000	-1	/C-5	-0.3
1961	Chi-N	92	267	20	73	7	1	2	33	15	33	.273	.312	.330	642	70	-11	0	0	0	.982	4	C-90	-0.4
1962	Chi-N	77	215	19	65	6	2	2	18	13	30	.302	.345	.377	722	90	-3	0	1	-0	.986	-13	C-76	-1.3
1963	Chi-N	100	322	15	75	7	2	2	14	24	41	.233	.286	.286	572	62	-15	0	2	-1	.988	16	C-99	0.6
1964	Chi-N	112	353	29	84	11	3	4	35	33	67	.238	.307	.320	627	74	-12	2	1	0	.981	-5	*C-110	-1.1
1965	Chi-N	34	84	6	18	2	0	0	7	11	10	.214	.305	.238	543	54	-5	0	0	0	.981	3	C-34	-0.1
	SF-N	22	48	1	9	1	0	0	3	7	5	.188	.291	.208	499	42	-3	0	0	0	.992	2	C-22	-0.1
	Yr	56	132	7	27	3	0	0	10	18	15	.205	.300	.227	527	50	-8	0	0	0	.986	5	C-56	-0.2
1967	Chi-N	2	6	1	1	0	1	0	0	0	1	.167	.167	.500	667	80	-0	0	0	0	1.000	0	/C-2	0.0
Total	7	444	1310	91	327	34	9	10	112	106	188	.250	.307	.312	619	70	-51	2	4	-1	.985	7	C-438	-2.7
■ HARRY BERTHRONG	Berthrong, Henry W. b: 1/1/1844, Mumford, N.Y. d: 4/28/28, Chelsea, Mass. TR, 5'6.5", 140 lbs. Deb: 5/5/1871																							
1871	Oly-n	17	73	17	17	1	1	0	8	4	2	.233	.273	.274	547	61	-3	3	1	0	.806	-3	O-12(11-1-0)/2-5,C-1	-0.4
■ FRANK BERTLEBACK	Bertleback, Francis P. b: Philadelphia, Pa. 6', 182 lbs. Deb: 7/4/1884																							
1884	Cin-a	6	25	3	6	0	1	0	3	0		.240	.296	.320	616	96	-0				.667	-2	/O-6(6-0-0)	-0.2
■ RENO BERTOIA	Bertoia, Reno Peter b: 1/8/35, St.Vito Udine, Italy BR/TR, 5'11.5", 185 lbs. Deb: 9/22/53																							
1953	Det-A	1	1	0	0	0	0	0	0	0	1	.000	.000	.000	0	-99	-0	0	0	0	.500	-0	/2-1	-0.1
1954	Det-A	54	37	13	6	2	0	1	2	5	9	.162	.262	.297	559	54	-2	1	0	0	.969	17	2-15/3-8,S-3	1.5
1955	Det-A	38	68	13	14	2	1	1	10	5	11	.206	.260	.309	569	54	-5	0	0	0	.923	7	3-14/2-6,S-5	0.2
1956	Det-A	22	66	7	12	2	0	1	5	6	12	.182	.260	.258	518	37	-6	0	0	0	.982	10	2-18/3-2	0.5
1957	Det-A	97	295	28	81	16	2	4	28	19	43	.275	.327	.383	710	91	-4	2	3	-1	.953	-19	3-83/S-7,2-2	-2.4
1958	Det-A	86	240	28	56	6	0	6	27	20	35	.233	.298	.333	631	68	-10	5	2	0	.950	4	3-68/S-5,O-1(1-0-0)	-0.6
1959	Was-A	90	308	33	73	10	0	8	29	29	48	.237	.305	.347	652	79	-9	2	5	-1	.971	-11	2-71/3-5,S-1	-1.6
1960	Was-A	121	460	44	122	17	7	4	45	26	58	.265	.316	.359	674	83	-11	3	5	-1	.961	-0	*3-112,2-21	-1.3
1961	Min-A	35	104	17	22	2	0	1	8	20	12	.212	.339	.260	598	59	-5	0	0	0	.900	-5	3-32	-1.1
	KC-A	39	120	12	29	2	0	0	13	9	15	.242	.295	.258	553	48	-9	1	0	0	.942	5	3-29/2-6	-0.3
	Det-A	24	46	6	10	1	0	1	4	3	8	.217	.265	.304	570	50	-3	2	0	0	.931	0	3-13/2-7,S-1	-0.3
	Yr	98	270	35	61	5	0	2	25	32	35	.226	.308	.267	575	53	-17	3	0	1	.923	-1	3-74,2-13/S-1	-1.7
1962	Det-A	5	0	3	0	0	0	0	0	0	0	—	—	—	—	—	0	0	0	0	1.000	0	/2-1,S-1,3-1	0.0
Total	10	612	1745	204	425	60	10	27	171	142	252	.244	.306	.336	642	73	-65	16	15	-2	.949	7	3-367,2-148/S-23,O	-5.5
■ BOB BESCHER	Bescher, Robert Henry b: 2/25/1884, London, Ohio d: 11/29/42, London, Ohio BB/TL, 6'1", 200 lbs. Deb: 9/5/08																							
1908	Cin-N	32	114	16	31	5	5	0	17	9		.272	.336	.404	740	140	5	10			1.000	4	O-32(32-0-0)	0.8
1909	Cin-N	124	446	73	107	17	6	1	34	56		.240	.335	.312	647	102	3	**54**			.953	-0	*O-117(115-0-2)	-0.5
1910	Cin-N	150	589	95	147	20	10	4	48	81	75	.250	.344	.338	682	104	4	**70**			.947	2	*O-150(150-0-0)	-0.3
1911	Cin-N	153	599	106	165	32	10	1	45	102	78	.275	.385	.367	753	115	16	**81**			.954	-8	*O-153(153-0-0)	0.2
1912	Cin-N	145	548	**120**	154	29	11	4	38	83	61	.281	.381	.396	777	116	15	**67**			.963	4	*O-143(143-0-0)	1.2
1913	Cin-N	141	511	86	132	22	11	1	37	**94**	68	.258	.377	.350	727	109	10	38			.968	4	*O-138(138-0-0)	0.8
1914	NY-N	135	512	82	138	23	4	6	35	45	48	.270	.336	.365	701	112	7	36			.960	9	*O-126(15-111-0)	0.8
1915	StL-N	130	486	71	128	15	7	4	34	52	53	.263	.342	.348	690	109	6	27	19	-1	.971	-2	*O-129(128-0-1)	-0.2
1916	StL-N	151	561	78	132	24	8	6	43	60	50	.235	.316	.339	654	102	2	39	12	4	.953	0	*O-151(151-2-1)	0.0
1917	StL-N	42	110	10	17	1	1	1	8	20	13	.155	.290	.209	499	56	-5	3			.984	-3	O-32(27-4-0)	-1.1
1918	Cle-A	25	60	12	20	2	1	0	6	17	5	.333	.487	.400	887	153	5	3			.969	-0	O-17(0-3-14)	0.5
Total	11	1228	4536	749	1171	190	74	28	345	619	451	.258	.353	.351	704	109	69	428	31		.960	9	*O-1188(1052-120-18)	2.2
■ WILLIAM BESTICK	Bestick, William b: New York, N.Y. Deb: 6/10/1872																							
1872	Eck-n	4	14	0	4	0	0	0	1	0	0	.286	.286	.286	571	90	0	0	0	0	.773	-2	/C-4	-0.1
■ JIM BESWICK	Beswick, James William b: 2/12/58, Wilkinsburg, Pa. BB/TR, 6'1", 180 lbs. Deb: 8/9/78																							
1978	SD-N	17	20	2	1	0	0	0	0	1	7	.050	.095	.050	145	-63	-4	0	0	0	1.000	-1	/O-6(0-2-4)	-0.6
■ FRANK BETCHER	Betcher, Franklin Lyle (b: Franklin Lyle Bettger) b: 2/15/1888, Philadelphia, Pa. d: 11/27/81, Wynnewood, Pa. BB/TR, 5'11", 173 lbs. Deb: 5/21/10																							
1910	StL-N	35	89	7	18	2	0	0	6	7	14	.202	.276	.225	500	48	-6	1			.928	0	S-12/3-7,2-6,O-2L	-0.5
■ BILL BETHEA	Bethea, William Lamar "Spot" b: 1/1/42, Houston, Tex. BR/TR, 6', 175 lbs. Deb: 9/13/64																							
1964	Min-A	10	30	4	5	1	0	0	2	4	4	.167	.265	.200	465	31	-3	0	0	0	1.000	-1	/2-7,S-3	-0.3
■ LARRY BETTENCOURT	Bettencourt, Lawrence Joseph b: 9/22/05, Newark, Cal. d: 9/15/78, New Orleans, La. BR/TR, 5'11", 195 lbs. Deb: 6/2/28 Career OF: (4-LF 0-CF 61-RF)																							
1928	StL-A	67	159	30	45	9	4	4	24	22	19	.283	.377	.465	842	117	4	2	1	0	.946	-11	3-41/O-2(0-0-2),C-1	-0.4
1931	StL-A	74	206	27	53	9	2	3	26	31	35	.257	.357	.364	721	87	-3	4	3	-0	.963	-2	O-58(2-0-56)	-0.8
1932	StL-A	27	30	4	4	1	0	1	3	7	6	.133	.297	.267	564	45	-2	1	0	0	1.000	-0	/O-4(2-0-3),3-2	-0.3
Total	3	168	395	61	102	19	6	8	53	60	60	.258	.360	.397	758	95	-2	7	4	0	.966	-13	/O-64R,3-43,C-1	-1.5
■ BRUNO BETZEL	Betzel, Christian Frederick Albert John Henry David b: 12/6/1894, Chattanooga, Ohio d: 2/7/65, W.Hollywood, Fla. BR/TR, 5'9", 158 lbs. Deb: 9/3/14 Career OF: (14-LF 10-CF 28-RF)																							
1914	StL-N	7	9	2	0	0	0	0	0	1	1	.000	.100	.000	100	-70	-2	0			1.000	2	/2-4,3-1	0.0
1915	StL-N	117	367	42	92	12	4	0	27	18	48	.251	.291	.305	596	80	-9	10	13	-2	.937	4	*3-105/2-3,S-2	-0.5
1916	StL-N	142	510	49	119	15	11	1	37	39	77	.233	.288	.312	600	85	-10	22	16	-1	.960	28	*2-113,3-33/O-7R	2.3
1917	StL-N	106	328	24	71	4	3	1	17	20	47	.216	.266	.256	522	62	-15	9			.962	12	2-75,O-23(12-1-9)/3-4	-0.3
1918	StL-N	76	230	18	51	6	7	0	13	12	16	.222	.260	.309	569	76	-7	8			.914	-2	3-34,O-21R,2-10	-1.0
Total	5	448	1444	135	333	37	25	2	94	90	189	.231	.278	.295	573	76	-42	49	29		.956	45	2-205,3-177/O-51R,S	0.5
■ KURT BEVACQUA	Bevacqua, Kurt Anthony b: 1/23/47, Miami Beach, Fla. BR/TR, 6'1", 185 lbs. Deb: 6/22/71 Career OF: (47-LF 0-CF 25-RF)																							
1971	Cle-A	55	137	9	28	3	1	3	13	4	28	.204	.227	.307	534	46	-10	0	0	0	.971	-9	2-36/O-5R,3-3,S-2	-1.8
1972	Cle-A	19	35	2	4	0	0	1	1	3	10	.114	.184	.200	384	14	-4	0	0	0	.900	-1	O-11(8-0-3)/3-1	-0.6
1973	KC-A	99	276	39	71	8	3	2	40	25	42	.257	.321	.330	651	78	-8	2	3	-1	.935	-11	3-40,2-16,D-16,O/1	-2.1
1974	Pit-N	18	35	1	4	1	0	0	0	2	10	.114	.162	.143	305	-15	-5	0	0	0	.955	-1	/3-8,O-1(1-0-0)	-0.6
	KC-A	39	90	10	19	0	0	0	3	9	20	.211	.290	.211	501	43	-6	1	1	-0	.987	-4	1-14,3-13/2-7,SD	-1.1
1975	Mil-A	104	258	30	59	14	0	2	24	26	45	.229	.302	.306	608	72	-9	3	4	-1	.948	1	3-60,2-32/S-5,1D	-0.7
1976	Mil-A	12	7	3	1	0	0	0	0	0	0	.143	.143	.143	286	-17	-1	0	0	0	1.000	2	/2-2,D-3	0.1
1977	Tex-A	39	96	13	32	7	2	5	28	6	13	.333	.373	.604	977	159	7	0	1	-0	1.000	-7	O-14R,3-11/1-5,2D	0.0
1978	Tex-A	90	248	21	55	12	0	6	30	18	31	.222	.274	.343	617	72	-10	1	2	-0	.877	-4	3-49,D-16,2-13,/1-1	-1.5
1979	SD-N	114	297	23	75	12	4	1	34	38	25	.253	.337	.330	667	88	-4	2	5	-1	.954	-5	3-64,2-16/1-8,O-8L	-1.2
1980	SD-N	62	71	4	19	6	1	0	12	6	1	.268	.325	.380	705	102	0	1	1	-0	.929	-3	3-13/O-4L,2-2,1-1	-0.4

YEAR	TM/L	G	AB	R	H	2B	3B	HR	RBI	BB	SO	AVG	OBP	SLG	OPS	OPS+	BR+	SB	CS	SBR	FA	FR	G/POS	TPR
	Pit-N	22	43	1	7	1	0	0	4	6	7	.163	.280	.186	466	32	-4	0	0	0	.958	0	/3-9,1-2	-0.4
	Yr	84	114	5	26	7	1	0	16	12	8	.228	.307	.307	614	75	-4	1	1	-0	.947	-3	3-22/O-4L,1-3,2-2	-0.8
1981	Pit-N	29	27	2	7	1	0	1	4	4	6	.259	.355	.407	762	112	0	0	0	0	.941	1	/2-4,3-2	0.2
1982	SD-N	64	123	15	31	9	0	0	24	17	22	.252	.343	.325	668	93	-1	2	0	0	.989	-3	1-30/O-3(2-0-1),3-1	-0.5
1983	SD-N	74	156	17	38	7	0	2	24	18	33	.244	.322	.327	649	83	-3	0	3	-1	.995	-1	1-27,3-12,O-12(9-0-3)	-0.7
1984	*SD-N	59	80	7	16	3	0	1	9	14	19	.200	.326	.275	601	71	-3	0	0	0	1.000	-2	1-20,3-10/O-3(1-0-2)	-0.5
1985	SD-N	71	138	17	33	6	0	3	25	25	17	.239	.356	.348	704	99	1	0	0	0	.946	-2	3-33/1-9,O-1(1-0-0)	-0.2
Total	15	970	2117	214	499	90	11	27	275	221	329	.236	.309	.327	636	78	-59	12	20	-4	.938	-46	3-329,2-133,1/ODS	-12.0
■ HAL BEVAN	Bevan, Harold Joseph b: 11/15/30, New Orleans, La. d: 10/5/68, New Orleans, La. BR/TR, 6′2″, 198 lbs. Deb: 4/24/52																							
1952	Bos-A	1	1	0	0	0	0	0	0	0	0	.000	.000	.000	0	-93	-0	0	0	0	.000	0	/3-1	0.0
	Phi-A	8	17	1	6	0	0	0	4	0	1	.353	.353	.353	706	91	-0	2	0	0	1.000	1	/3-6	0.1
	Yr	9	18	1	6	0	0	0	4	0	1	.333	.333	.333	667	81	-0	2	0	0	1.000	1	/3-7	0.1
1955	KC-A	3	3	0	0	0	0	0	0	0	0	.000	.000	.000	0	-99	-1	0	0	0	1.000	0	/3-1	-0.1
1961	Cin-N	3	3	1	1	0	0	1	1	0	2	.333	.333	1.333	1667	311	1	0	0	0	.000	0	H	0.1
Total	3	15	24	2	7	0	0	1	5	0	3	.292	.292	.417	708	89	-0	2	0	0	1.000	1	/3-8	0.1
■ MONTE BEVILLE	Beville, Henry Monte b: 2/24/1875, Dublin, Ind. d: 1/24/55, Grand Rapids, Mich BL/TR, 5′11″, 180 lbs. Deb: 4/24/03																							
1903	NY-A	82	258	23	50	14	1	0	29	16		.194	.252	.256	508	49	-16	4			.960	-11	C-75/1-3	-2.1
1904	NY-A	9	22	2	6	2	0	0	2	2		.273	.333	.364	697	115	0	0			.906	-2	/1-4,C-3	-0.1
	Det-A	54	174	14	36	5	1	0	13	8		.207	.250	.247	497	59	-8	2			.957	-3	C-30,1-24	-1.0
	Yr	63	196	16	42	7	1	0	15	10		.214	.260	.260	520	66	-8	2			.950	-5	C-33,1-28	-1.1
Total	2	145	454	39	92	21	2	0	44	26		.203	.255	.258	513	56	-23	6			.957	-16	C-108/1-31	-3.2
■ BUDDY BIANCALANA	Biancalana, Roland Americo b: 2/2/60, Larkspur, Cal. BB/TR, 5′11″, 160 lbs. Deb: 9/12/82																							
1982	KC-A	3	2	0	1	0	1	0	0	1	0	.500	.667	1.500	2167	474	1	0	0	0	1.000	3	/S-3	0.3
1983	KC-A	6	15	2	3	0	0	0	0	0	7	.200	.200	.200	400	10	-2	1	0	0	.914	4	/S-6	0.3
1984	*KC-A	66	134	18	26	6	1	2	9	6	44	.194	.229	.299	527	44	-10	1	2	-0	.946	6	S-33,2-29/D-1	-0.1
1985	*KC-A	81	138	21	26	5	1	1	6	17	34	.188	.277	.261	538	48	-10	1	4	-1	.961	11	S-74/2-4,D-2	0.5
1986	KC-A	100	190	24	46	4	4	2	8	15	50	.242	.298	.337	634	71	-8	5	1	1	.946	2	S-89,2-12	0.2
1987	KC-A	37	47	4	10	1	0	1	7	1	10	.213	.229	.298	527	37	-4	0	0	0	.886	4	S-22,2-12/D-1	0.1
	Hou-N	18	24	1	1	0	0	0	0	1	12	.042	.080	.042	122	-69	-6	0	0	0	.889	-1	S-16/2-3	-0.6
Total	6	311	550	70	113	16	7	6	30	41	157	.205	.261	.293	553	50	-38	8	7	-1	.945	28	S-243/2-60,D-4	0.7
■ TOMMY BIANCO	Bianco, Thomas Anthony b: 12/16/52, Rockville Centre, N.Y. BB/TR, 5′11″, 190 lbs. Deb: 5/28/75																							
1975	Mil-A	18	34	6	6	1	0	0	0	3	7	.176	.263	.206	469	34	-3	0	0	0	.941	-1	/3-7,1-5,D-2	-0.4
■ HANK BIASATTI	Biasatti, Henry Arcado b: 1/14/22, Beano, Italy d: 4/20/96, Dearborn, Mich. BL/TL, 5′11″, 175 lbs. Deb: 4/23/49																							
1949	Phi-A	21	24	6	2	2	0	0	2	8	5	.083	.313	.167	479	30	-2	0	0	0	.979	-1	/1-8	-0.3
■ DANTE BICHETTE	Bichette, Alphonse Dante b: 11/18/63, W.Palm Beach, Fla. BR/TR, 6′3″, 225 lbs. Deb: 9/5/88 Career OF: (612-LF 56-CF 891-RF)																							
1988	Cal-A	21	46	1	12	2	0	0	8	0	7	.261	.261	.304	565	59	-3	0	0	0	.979	-2	O-21(3-17-5)	-0.5
1989	Cal-A	48	138	13	29	7	0	3	15	6	24	.210	.243	.326	569	60	-8	3	0	1	.990	6	O-40(12-6-23)/D-1	-0.2
1990	Cal-A	109	349	40	89	15	1	15	53	16	79	.255	.293	.433	726	103	-0	5	2	0	.965	-4	*O-105(51-16-53)	-0.7
1991	Mil-A	134	445	53	106	18	3	15	59	22	107	.238	.276	.393	669	85	-11	14	8	0	.976	11	*O-127(1-7-120)/3-1	-0.3
1992	Mil-A	112	387	37	111	27	2	5	41	16	74	.287	.320	.406	726	104	1	18	7	2	.990	-2	*O-101(0-1-101)/D-4	-0.2
1993	Col-N	141	538	93	167	43	5	21	89	28	99	.310	.353	.526	879	113	9	14	8	0	.973	13	*O-137(0-9-134)	1.5
1994	Col-N★	116	484	74	147	33	2	27	95	19	70	.304	.335	.548	883	107	5	21	8	2	.991	4	*O-116(0-0-116)	0.4
1995	*Col-N★	139	579	102	**197**	38	2	**40**	**128**	22	96	.340	.369	**.620**	989	120	16	13	9	-0	.986	-6	*O-136(120-0-35)	0.5
1996	Col-N★	159	633	114	198	39	3	31	141	45	105	.313	.364	.531	895	107	6	31	12	3	.967	-7	*O-156(19-0-138)	-0.6
1997	Col-N	151	561	81	173	31	2	26	118	30	90	.308	.347	.510	857	98	-1	6	5	-0	.987	-6	*O-139(128-0-16)/D-5	-1.2
1998	Col-N★	161	662	97	**219**	48	2	22	122	28	76	.331	.359	.509	868	103	3	14	4	2	.965	11	*O-156(134-0-29)/D-1	1.0
1999	Col-N	151	593	104	177	38	2	34	133	54	84	.298	.359	.541	900	97	-3	6	6	-1	.951	8	*O-144(144-0-0)/D-2	0.0
2000	Cin-N	125	461	67	136	27	2	16	76	41	69	.295	.358	.466	824	102	1	5	2	0	.969	6	*O-121(0-0-121)	0.1
	Bos-A	30	114	13	33	5	0	7	14	8	22	.289	.336	.518	854	107	1	0	0	0	.000	0	D-30	-0.1
Total	13	1597	5990	889	1794	371	26	262	1092	335	1002	.299	.341	.501	842	104	17	150	71	8	.974	30	*O-1499R/D-43,3-1	-0.3
■ OSCAR BIELASKI	Bielaski, Oscar b: 3/21/1847, Washington, D.C. d: 11/8/11, Washington, D.C. BR/TR, 5′10.5″, 170 lbs. Deb: 4/24/1872																							
1872	Nat-n	10	46	13	9	0	0	0	3	0	0	.196	.196	.196	391	18	-5	0	0	0	.737	-1	O-10(0-0-10)	-0.3
1873	Was-n	38	173	35	49	3	2	0	23	4	5	.283	.299	.324	623	88	-2	0	1	-0	.772	4	*O-38(2-0-36)	0.3
1874	Bal-n	43	187	24	45	0	0	0	8	2	4	.241	.249	.241	489	58	-8	3	1	0	.806	6	*O-43(0-1-43)/1-1	0.1
1875	Chi-n	51	201	21	48	1	0	0	11	2	5	.239	.246	.244	490	70	-6	5	5	-1	.748	0	*O-51(4-0-48)	-0.3
1876	Chi-N	32	141	24	29	3	0	0	10	2	3	.206	.220	.230	450	45	-9				.763	-2	O-32(0-0-32)	-1.0
Total	4 n	142	607	93	151	4	2	0	45	8	14	.249	.259	.262	520	67	-21	8	7	-1	.772	10	O-142(6-1-137)/1-1	-0.2
■ LOU BIERBAUER	Bierbauer, Louis W. b: 9/28/1865, Erie, Pa. d: 1/31/26, Erie, Pa. BL/TR, 5′8″, 140 lbs. Deb: 4/17/1886																							
1886	Phi-a	137	522	56	118	17	5	2	47	21		.226	.256	.289	545	70	-19	19			.910	-3	*2-133/C-4,S-2,P-2	-1.5
1887	Phi-a	126	543	74	157	19	7	1	82	13		.289	.289	.340	629	75	-19	40			.921	-8	*2-126/P-1	-1.9
1888	Phi-a	134	535	83	143	20	9	0	80	25		.267	.301	.338	640	105	2	34			.916	22	*2-121,3-13/P-1	2.6
1889	Phi-a	130	549	80	167	27	7	7	105	29	30	.304	.344	.417	761	118	11	17			.941	37	*2-130/C-1	4.3
1890	Bro-P	133	589	128	180	31	11	7	99	40	15	.306	.350	.431	781	102	-2	16			.931	25	*2-133	2.2
1891	Pit-N	121	500	60	103	13	6	1	47	28	19	.206	.252	.262	514	51	-32	12			.929	-2	*2-121	-2.6
1892	Pit-N	152	649	81	153	20	9	8	65	25	29	.236	.264	.331	595	79	-19	11			.950	32	*2-152	1.8
1893	Pit-N	128	528	84	150	19	11	4	94	36	12	.284	.335	.384	719	93	-7	11			**.959**	16	*2-128	1.2
1894	Pit-N	131	528	87	160	20	13	3	109	26	10	.303	.338	.407	745	80	-19	19			.939	12	*2-131	-0.1
1895	Pit-N	118	470	54	122	13	11	1	69	19	8	.260	.291	.340	632	66	-25	18			.947	16	*2-118	-0.2
1896	Pit-N	59	258	33	74	10	6	0	39	5	7	.287	.300	.372	672	80	-9	7			.966	12	2-59	0.6
1897	StL-N	12	46	1	10	0	0	0	1	0		.217	.217	.217	435	15	-6	2			.921	-2	2-12	-0.7
1898	StL-N	4	9	0	0	0	0	0	0	1		.000	.100	.000	100	-69	-2	0			.429	-1	/2-2,S-1,3-1	-0.3
Total	13	1385	5726	821	1537	209	95	34	837	268	130	.268	.301	.354	656	84	-146	206			.935	154	*2-1366/3-14,C-5,PS	5.4
■ CHARLIE BIERMAN	Bierman, Charles S. b: 1845, Hoboken, N.J. d: 8/4/1879, Hoboken, N.J. 6′, 180 lbs. Deb: 6/21/1871																							
1871	Kek-n	1	2	0	0	0	0	0	0	1	0	.000	.333	.000	333	6	-0	0	0	0	.818	-0	/1-1	0.0
■ STEVE BIESER	Bieser, Steven Ray b: 8/4/67, Perryville, Mo. BL/TR, 5′10″, 170 lbs. Deb: 4/1/97																							
1997	NY-N	47	69	16	17	3	0	0	4	7	20	.246	.350	.290	640	72	-2	2	3	-1	1.000	-2	O-21(9-13-1)/C-2	-0.5
1998	Pit-N	13	11	2	3	1	0	0	1	2	2	.273	.385	.364	748	97	0	0	0	0	.000	-0	/O-1(1-0-0)	0.0
Total	2	60	80	18	20	4	0	0	5	9	22	.250	.355	.300	655	76	-2	2	3	-1	1.000	-2	/O-22(10-13-1),C-2	-0.5
■ CARSON BIGBEE	Bigbee, Carson Lee "Skeeter" b: 3/31/1895, Waterloo, Ore. d: 10/17/64, Portland, Ore. BL/TR, 5′9″, 157 lbs. Deb: 8/25/16 F Career OF: (892-LF 109-CF 32-RF)																							
1916	Pit-N	43	164	17	41	3	6	0	3	7	14	.250	.285	.341	626	91	-2	8			.946	-5	2-23,O-19(19-0-0)/3-1	-0.8
1917	Pit-N	133	469	46	112	11	6	0	21	37	16	.239	.301	.288	589	79	-11	19			.961	-3	*O-107L,2-16/S-2	-2.2
1918	Pit-N	92	310	47	79	11	3	1	19	42	10	.255	.344	.319	663	99	1	19			.958	0	O-92(87-0-5)	-0.3
1919	Pit-N	125	478	61	132	11	4	2	27	37	26	.276	.332	.328	660	95	-2	31			.971	18	*O-124(50-75-0)	1.0
1920	Pit-N	137	550	78	154	19	15	4	32	45	28	.280	.341	.391	732	106	5	31	15	2	.971	6	*O-133(128-6-0)	0.6
1921	Pit-N	147	632	100	204	23	17	3	42	41	19	.323	.364	.427	791	106	6	21	20	-2	.977	16	*O-146(133-13-0)	0.8
1922	Pit-N	150	614	113	215	29	15	5	99	56	13	.350	.405	.471	876	124	23	24	15	0	.956	17	*O-150(146-4-0)	2.6
1923	Pit-N	123	499	79	149	18	7	0	54	43	15	.299	.355	.363	718	88	-8	10	9	-1	.990	10	*O-122(122-0-0)	-0.8
1924	Pit-N	89	282	42	74	4	1	0	15	26	12	.262	.331	.284	615	65	-13	15	7	1	.943	0	O-75(75-0-0)	-1.7
1925	*Pit-N	66	126	31	30	7	0	0	8	7	8	.238	.278	.294	572	43	-11	2	2	-0	.942	-6	O-42(30-2-10)	-1.8

YEAR	TM/L	G	AB	R	H	2B	3B	HR	RBI	BB	SO	AVG	OBP	SLG	OPS	OPS+	BR+	SB	CS	SBR	FA	FR	G/POS	TPR
1926	Pit-N	42	68	15	15	3	1	2	4	3	0	.221	.264	.382	646	69	-3	2			.966	-3	O-21(17-4-0)	-0.7
Total	11	1147	4192	629	1205	139	75	17	324	344	161	.287	.345	.369	713	96	-15	182	68		.966	50	*O-1031L/2-39,S-2,3	-3.3
■ **LYLE BIGBEE**	Bigbee, Lyle Randolph "Al" b: 8/22/1893, Sweet Home, Ore. d: 8/5/42, Portland, Ore. BL/TR, 6', 180 lbs. Deb: 4/15/20 F																							
1920	Phi-A	38	75	5	14	2	0	1	8	9	12	.187	.282	.253	536	42	-6	1	0	0	.857	-2	O-13(11-0-1),P-12	-0.7
1921	Pit-N	5	2	0	0	0	0	0	0	0	1	.000	.000	.000	0	-97	-1	0	0	0	1.000	-0	/P-5	0.0
Total	2	43	77	5	14	2	0	1	8	9	13	.182	.276	.247	523	39	-7	1	0	0	1.000	-2	/P-17,O-13(11-0-1)	-0.7
■ **ELLIOT BIGELOW**	Bigelow, Elliot Allardice "Babe" or "Gilly" b: 10/13/1897, Tarpon Springs, Fla. d: 8/10/33, Tampa, Fla. BL/TL, 5'11", 185 lbs. Deb: 4/18/29																							
1929	Bos-A	100	211	23	60	16	0	1	26	23	18	.284	.357	.374	732	91	-2	1	4	-1	.944	-10	O-59(2-2-55)	-1.7
■ **CRAIG BIGGIO**	Biggio, Craig Alan b: 12/14/65, Smithtown, N.Y. BR/TR, 5'11", 180 lbs. Deb: 6/26/88 Career OF: (25-LF 39-CF 2-RF)																							
1988	Hou-N	50	123	14	26	6	1	3	5	7	29	.211	.254	.350	603	74	-5	6	1	1	.991	16	C-50	1.5
1989	Hou-N	134	443	64	114	21	2	13	60	49	64	.257	.339	.402	741	115	9	21	3	4	.990	-6	*C-125/O-5(1-4-0)	1.4
1990	Hou-N	150	555	53	153	24	2	4	42	53	79	.276	.342	.348	690	93	-4	25	11	2	.985	-7	*C-113,O-50(17-34-2)	-0.5
1991	Hou-N★	149	546	79	161	23	4	4	46	53	71	.295	.359	.374	733	113	10	19	6	2	.990	-14	*C-139/2-3,O-2(1-1-0)	0.7
1992	Hou-N★	162	613	96	170	32	3	6	39	94	95	.277	.380	.369	748	118	19	38	15	3	.984	-21	*2-161	0.5
1993	Hou-N	155	610	98	175	41	5	21	64	77	93	.287	.376	.474	850	130	27	15	17	-3	.982	-2	*2-155	3.0
1994	Hou-N★	114	437	88	139	**44**	5	6	56	62	58	.318	.412	.483	895	139	28	**39**	4	**7**	.988	-5	*2-113	3.5
1995	Hou-N★	141	553	**123**	167	30	2	22	77	80	85	.302	.411	.483	894	145	39	33	8	4	.986	-4	*2-141	4.6
1996	Hou-N★	162	605	113	174	24	4	15	75	75	72	.288	.390	.415	805	122	23	25	7	3	.988	-1	*2-162	3.2
1997	*Hou-N★	162	619	**146**	191	37	8	22	81	84	107	.309	.419	.501	920	145	45	47	10	7	.979	**24**	*2-160/D-1	**8.0**
1998	*Hou-N★	160	646	123	210	**51**	2	20	88	64	113	.325	.405	.503	908	141	40	50	8	8	.980	-3	*2-159/D-1	5.1
1999	*Hou-N	160	639	123	188	**56**	0	16	73	88	107	.294	.389	.457	846	115	17	28	14	1	.985	23	*2-155/O-6(6-0-0),D-2	4.5
2000	Hou-N	101	377	67	101	13	5	8	35	61	73	.268	.392	.393	785	94	-1	12	2	2	.987	-5	*2-100	0.1
Total	13	1800	6766	1187	1969	402	43	160	741	847	1046	.291	.384	.434	818	123	248	358	106	42	.984	-6	*2-1309,C-427/O-63C,D	35.6
■ **PETE BIGLER**	Bigler, Ivan Edward b: 12/13/1892, Bradford, Ohio d: 4/1/75, Coldwater, Mich. BR/TR, 5'9", 150 lbs. Deb: 5/6/17																							
1917	StL-A	1	0	0	0	0	0	0	0	0	0	—	—	—	—	—	0	0			.000	0	/R	0.0
■ **GEORGE BIGNELL**	Bignell, George William b: 7/18/1858, Taunton, Mass. d: 1/16/25, Providence, R.I. 5'9", 160 lbs. Deb: 9/27/1884																							
1884	Mil-U	4	9	4	2	0	0	0		1		.222	.300	.222	522	112	0				.951	3	/C-4	0.3
■ **LARRY BIITTNER**	Biittner, Lawrence David b: 7/27/45, Pocahontas, Ia. BL/TL, 6'2", 205 lbs. Deb: 7/17/70 Career OF: (268-LF 15-CF 219-RF)																							
1970	Was-A	2	2	0	0	0	0	0	0	0	0	.000	.000	.000	0	-99	-1	0	0	0	.000	0	H	-0.1
1971	Was-A	66	171	12	44	4	1	0	16	16	20	.257	.324	.292	617	80	-4	1	0	0	.940	-0	O-41(7-0-38)/1-3	-0.7
1972	Tex-A	137	382	34	99	18	1	3	31	29	37	.259	.315	.335	650	98	-2	1	3	-1	.991	-1	1-65,O-65(28-8-32)	-1.1
1973	Tex-A	83	258	19	65	8	2	1	12	20	21	.252	.308	.310	618	78	-8	1	0	0	.980	1	O-57R,1-20/D-3	-1.1
1974	Mon-N	18	26	2	7	1	0	0	3	0	2	.269	.269	.308	577	58	-1	0	0	0	1.000	1	/O-4(4-0-0)	-0.1
1975	Mon-N	121	346	34	109	13	5	3	28	34	33	.315	.376	.408	784	113	7	2	1	0	.972	0	O-93(35-4-55)	0.2
1976	Mon-N	11	32	2	6	1	0	0	1	0	3	.188	.188	.219	406	14	-4	0	0	0	.947	1	/O-7(3-0-4)	-0.3
	Chi-N	78	192	21	47	13	1	0	17	10	6	.245	.286	.323	609	66	-8	0	2	-1	.985	4	1-33,O-24(22-0-3)	-0.9
	Yr	89	224	23	53	14	1	0	18	10	9	.237	.272	.308	580	59	-12	0	2	-1	.985	5	1-33,O-31(25-0-7)	-1.2
1977	Chi-N	138	493	74	147	28	1	12	62	35	36	.298	.346	.432	778	97	-2	2	1	0	.987	6	1-80,O-52(52-0-0)/P-1	-0.3
1978	Chi-N	120	343	32	88	15	1	4	50	23	37	.257	.305	.341	646	72	-13	0	1	-0	.987	5	1-62,O-29(29-0-0)	-1.3
1979	Chi-N	111	272	35	79	13	3	3	50	21	23	.290	.341	.393	735	91	-3	1	1	-0	.925	-6	O-44(23-1-21),1-32	-1.2
1980	Chi-N	127	273	21	68	12	2	1	34	18	33	.249	.300	.319	619	68	-11	1	3	-1	.996	1	1-41,O-38(20-0-17)	-1.5
1981	Cin-N	42	61	1	13	4	0	0	8	4	4	.213	.262	.279	540	52	-4	0	0	0	1.000	1	/1-8,O-3(0-0-3)	-0.3
1982	Cin-N	97	184	18	57	9	2	2	24	17	16	.310	.374	.413	787	118	5	1	0	0	.978	-2	O-31(26-0-6),1-15	0.1
1983	Tex-A	66	116	5	32	5	1	0	18	9	16	.276	.328	.336	664	85	-2	0	0	0	.987	2	1-22/O-2(0-0-2),D-9	-0.1
Total	14	1217	3151	310	861	144	20	29	354	236	287	.273	.326	.359	685	87	-51	10	12	-2	.970	14	O-490L,1-381/D-12,P	-8.7
■ **DANN BILARDELLO**	Bilardello, Dann James b: 5/26/59, Santa Cruz, Cal. BR/TR, 6', 190 lbs. Deb: 4/11/83																							
1983	Cin-N	109	298	27	71	18	0	9	38	15	49	.238	.277	.389	666	80	-9	2	1	0	.991	-1	*C-105	-0.7
1984	Cin-N	68	182	16	38	7	0	2	10	19	34	.209	.287	.280	567	57	-10	0	1	-0	.992	1	C-68	-0.7
1985	Cin-N	42	102	6	17	0	0	1	9	4	15	.167	.206	.196	402	12	-12	0	0	0	.986	8	C-42	-0.3
1986	Mon-N	79	191	12	37	5	0	4	17	14	32	.194	.249	.283	532	47	-14	1	0	0	.982	2	C-77	-1.0
1989	Pit-N	33	80	11	18	6	0	2	8	2	18	.225	.244	.375	619	77	-3	1	2	-0	.970	5	C-33	0.3
1990	Pit-N	19	37	1	2	0	0	0	3	4	10	.054	.146	.054	200	-44	-7	0	0	0	1.000	3	C-19	-0.4
1991	SD-N	15	26	4	7	2	1	0	5	3	4	.269	.345	.423	768	111	0	0	0	0	1.000	5	C-13	0.6
1992	SD-N	17	33	2	4	1	0	0	1	4	8	.121	.216	.152	368	6	-4	0	0	0	1.000	5	C-14	0.2
Total	8	382	949	79	194	39	1	18	91	65	170	.204	.258	.305	562	55	-59	4	4	-1	.988	28	C-371	-2.0
■ **STEVE BILKO**	Bilko, Stephen Thomas b: 11/13/28, Nanticoke, Pa. d: 3/7/78, Wilkes-Barre, Pa. BR/TR, 6'1", 230 lbs. Deb: 9/22/49																							
1949	StL-N	6	17	3	5	2	0	0	2	5	6	.294	.455	.412	866	128	1	0			1.000	0	/1-5	0.1
1950	StL-N	10	33	1	6	1	0	0	2	4	10	.182	.270	.212	482	27	-3	0			.989	0	/1-9	-0.3
1951	StL-N	21	72	5	16	4	0	2	12	9	10	.222	.309	.361	670	79	-2	0	0	0	.984	-0	1-19	-0.3
1952	StL-N	20	72	7	19	6	1	1	6	4	15	.264	.303	.417	719	97	-1	0	0	0	.995	4	1-20	0.3
1953	StL-N	154	570	72	143	23	3	21	84	70	125	.251	.334	.412	746	93	-6	0	1	-0	.991	7	*1-154	-0.8
1954	StL-N	8	14	1	2	0	0	0	1	3	1	.143	.294	.143	437	18	-2	0	0	0	1.000	2	/1-6	0.0
	Chi-N	47	92	11	22	8	1	4	12	11	24	.239	.320	.478	799	104	0	0	0	0	1.000	6	1-22	0.5
	Yr	55	106	12	24	8	1	4	13	14	25	.226	.317	.434	751	92	-1	0	0	0	1.000	8	1-28	0.5
1958	Cin-N	31	87	12	23	4	2	4	17	10	20	.264	.340	.494	834	111	1	0	0	0	.995	-1	1-21	-0.1
	LA-N	47	101	13	21	1	2	7	18	8	37	.208	.266	.465	731	86	-3	0	0	0	.995	2	1-25	-0.2
	Yr	78	188	25	44	5	4	11	35	18	57	.234	.301	.479	780	98	-1	0	0	0	.995	0	1-46	-0.3
1960	Det-A	78	222	20	46	11	2	9	25	27	31	.207	.293	.396	690	82	-6	0	1	-0	.991	0	1-62	-1.0
1961	LA-A	114	294	49	82	16	1	20	59	58	81	.279	.398	.544	942	134	15	1	1	-0	.989	3	1-86/O-3(0-0-3)	1.3
1962	LA-A	64	164	26	47	9	1	8	38	25	35	.287	.387	.500	887	141	10	1	1	-0	.995	-1	1-50	0.6
Total	10	600	1738	220	432	85	13	76	276	234	395	.249	.339	.444	782	103	5	2	4		.992	22	1-479/O-3(0-0-3)	0.1
■ **JOSH BILLINGS**	Billings, John Augustus b: 11/30/1892, Grantville, Kan. d: 12/30/81, Santa Monica, Cal. BR/TR, 5'11", 165 lbs. Deb: 9/9/13																							
1913	Cle-A	1	3	0	0	0	0	0	0	0	3	.000	.000	.000	0	-97	-1	0			.857	0	/C-1	0.0
1914	Cle-A	11	8	3	2	1	0	0	0	1	1	.250	.333	.375	708	109	0	1			.813	2	/C-3	0.3
1915	Cle-A	8	21	2	4	1	0	0	0	0	6	.190	.190	.238	429	28	-2	1			1.000	-1	/C-7,O-1(0-1-0)	-0.3
1916	Cle-A	22	31	2	5	0	0	0	1	2	11	.161	.212	.161	373	12	-3	0			.981	3	C-12	0.0
1917	Cle-A	66	129	8	23	3	2	0	9	8	21	.178	.243	.233	475	42	-9	2			.974	2	C-48	-0.4
1918	Cle-A	2	3	0	1	0	0	0	0	0	0	.333	.333	.333	667	92	-0	0			1.000	-0	/C-1	0.0
1919	StL-A	38	76	9	15	1	1	0	3	1	12	.197	.218	.237	455	27	-7	0			.982	5	C-26/1-1	-0.1
1920	StL-A	66	155	19	43	5	2	0	11	11	10	.277	.353	.335	688	81	-4	1	0	0	.967	-5	C-40	-0.5
1921	StL-A	20	46	2	10	0	0	0	4	0	7	.217	.217	.217	435	11	-6	0	0	0	.982	2	C-12	-0.4
1922	StL-A	5	7	0	3	1	0	0	1	0	0	.429	.429	.571	1000	153	1	0	0	0	1.000	0	/C-3	0.1
1923	StL-A	4	9	0	0	0	0	0	0	0	2	.000	.000	.000	0	-95	-3	0	0	0	.917	0	/C-4	-0.2
Total	11	243	488	45	106	12	5	0	29	23	73	.217	.268	.262	530	47	-34	5	0		.970	7	C-157/1-1,O-1(0-1-0)	-1.5
■ **DICK BILLINGS**	Billings, Richard Arlin b: 12/4/42, Detroit, Mich. BR/TR, 6'1", 195 lbs. Deb: 9/11/68 Career OF: (78-LF 1-CF 15-RF)																							
1968	Was-A	12	33	3	6	1	0	1	3	5	13	.182	.289	.303	593	82	-1	0	0	0	.929	0	/O-8(8-0-0),3-4	-0.1
1969	Was-A	27	37	3	5	0	0	0	0	6	8	.135	.256	.135	391	13	-4	0	1	-0	1.000	0	/O-6(5-1-0),3-1	-0.5
1970	Was-A	11	24	3	6	2	0	1	1	2	3	.250	.308	.458	766	114	0	0	0	0	1.000	-2	/C-8	-0.1
1971	Was-A	116	349	32	86	14	0	6	48	21	54	.246	.299	.338	637	85	-8	2	5	-1	.992	-3	C-62,O-32L/3-2	-1.1
1972	Tex-A	133	469	41	119	15	1	5	58	29	77	.254	.300	.322	622	89	-7	1	5	-2	.981	-5	C-92,O-41L/3-5,1-1	-1.3
1973	Tex-A	81	280	17	50	11	0	3	32	20	43	.179	.238	.250	488	39	-23	1	1	-0	.975	-19	C-72/O-4L,1-3,D-2	-4.1

YEAR	TM/L	G	AB	R	H	2B	3B	HR	RBI	BB	SO	AVG	OBP	SLG	OPS	OPS+	BR+	SB	CS	SBR	FA	FR	G/POS	TPR
1974	Tex-A	16	31	2	7	1	0	0	0	4	6	.226	.314	.258	572	68	-1	2	0	0	1.000	1	C-13/O-1(1-0-0),D-1	0.1
	StL-N	1	5	0	1	0	0	0	0	0	1	.200	.200	.200	400	12	-1	0	0	0	1.000	0	/C-1	0.0
1975	StL-N	3	3	0	0	0	0	0	0	0	2	.000	.000	.000	0	-97	-1	0	0	0	.000	0	H	-0.1
Total	8	400	1231	101	280	44	1	16	142	87	207	.227	.283	.304	587	73	-45	6	12	-3	.984	-27	C-248/O-92L,3-12,1D	-7.2
■ GEORGE BINKS Binks, George Alvin "Bingo" (b: George Alvin Binkowski) b: 7/11/16, Chicago, Ill. BL/TL, 6', 175 lbs. Deb: 9/23/44																								
1944	Was-A	5	12	0	3	0	0	0	0	0	1	.250	.250	.250	500	45	-1	0	0	0	1.000	-1	/O-3(0-0-3)	-0.2
1945	Was-A	145	550	62	153	32	6	6	81	34	52	.278	.324	.391	715	117	9	11	7	-0	.977	4	*O-128(27-79-26),1-20	0.7
1946	Was-A	65	134	13	26	3	0	0	12	6	16	.194	.229	.216	445	26	-13	1	0	0	1.000	-0	O-28(15-9-5)	-1.6
1947	Phi-A	104	333	33	86	19	4	2	34	23	36	.258	.308	.357	665	83	-8	8	2	1	.965	1	O-75(25-0-51),1-13	-1.0
1948	Phi-A	17	41	2	4	1	0	0	2	2	2	.098	.140	.122	261	-30	-8	1	0	0	1.000	-2	O-14(2-0-12)	-1.0
	StL-A	15	23	2	5	0	0	0	1	2	1	.217	.280	.217	497	32	-2	0	0	0	1.000	-1	/O-5(2-0-3),1-4	-0.4
	Yr	32	64	4	9	1	0	0	3	4	3	.141	.191	.156	347	-7	-10	1	0	0	1.000	-3	O-19(4-0-15)/1-4	-1.4
Total	5	351	1093	112	277	55	10	8	130	67	108	.253	.299	.344	643	86	-24	21	9	1	.977	1	O-253(71-88-100)/1-37	-3.5
■ STEVE BIRAS Biras, Stephen Alexander b: 2/26/22, E.St.Louis, Ill. d: 4/21/65, St.Louis, Mo. BR/TR, 5'11", 185 lbs. Deb: 9/15/44																								
1944	Cle-A	2	2	0	2	0	0	0	2	0	0	1.000	1.000	1.000	2000	491	1	0	0	0	.667	0	/2-1	0.1
■ JUD BIRCHALL Birchall, Adoniram Judson b: 1858, Germantown, Pa. d: 12/22/1887, Philadelphia, Pa. Deb: 5/2/1882 Career OF: (221-LF 0-CF 1-RF)																								
1882	Phi-a	75	338	65	89	12	1	0	27	8		.263	.280	.305	585	87	-6				.860	0	*O-74(74-0-0)/2-1	-0.7
1883	Phi-a	96	448	95	108	10	1	1	24	20		.241	.274	.275	548	70	-16				.809	6	*O-96(96-0-0)	-1.1
1884	Phi-a	54	221	36	57	2	2	0		4		.258	.287	.285	572	82	-5				.838	3	O-52(51-0-1)/3-2	-0.2
Total	3	225	1007	196	254	24	4	1	51	32		.252	.279	.287	566	78	-27				.832	9	O-222L/3-2,2-1	-2.0
■ FRANK BIRD Bird, Frank Zepherin "Dodo" b: 3/10/1869, Spencer, Mass. d: 5/20/58, Worcester, Mass. BR/TR, 5'10", 195 lbs. Deb: 4/16/1892																								
1892	StL-N	17	50	9	10	3	1	1	1	6	11	.200	.286	.360	646	100	-0	2			.920	-4	C-17	-0.3
■ GEORGE BIRD Bird, George Raymond b: 6/23/1850, Stillman Valley, Ill. d: 11/9/40, Rockford, Ill. BR/TR, 5'9", 150 lbs. Deb: 5/6/1871																								
1871	Rok-n	25	106	19	28	2	5	0	13	3	2	.264	.284	.377	662	92	-1	1	0	0	.756	-5	*O-25(1-25-0)	-0.3
■ DAVE BIRDSALL Birdsall, David Solomon b: 7/16/1838, New York, N.Y. d: 12/30/1896, Boston, Mass. BR/TR, 5'9", 126 lbs. Deb: 5/5/1871																								
1871	Bos-n	29	152	51	46	3	3	0	24	4	4	.303	.321	.362	682	93	-2	6	0	1	.769	-1	*O-27(0-0-27)/C-7	0.0
1872	Bos-n	16	76	11	16	3	0	0	15	1	0	.211	.221	.250	471	42	-5	0	2	-1	.838	1	C-12/O-8(4-0-4)	-0.3
1873	Bos-n	3	12	4	1	0	0	0	1	0	0	.083	.083	.083	167	-46	-2	0	0	0	.200	-1	/O-3(0-0-3)	-0.2
Total	3 n	48	240	66	63	6	3	0	40	5	4	.262	.278	.313	590	70	-9	6	2	1	.720	-1	/O-38(4-0-34),C-19	-0.5
■ JOE BIRMINGHAM Birmingham, Joseph Leo "Dode" b: 8/6/1884, Elmira, N.Y. d: 4/24/46, Tampico, Mexico BR/TR, 5'10", 185 lbs. Deb: 9/12/06 M Career OF: (38-LF 647-CF 28-RF)																								
1906	Cle-A	10	40	5	11	2	1	0	6	1		.275	.293	.375	668	110	0	2			1.000	1	/O-9(9-0-0),3-1	0.1
1907	Cle-A	137	476	55	112	10	9	1	33	16		.235	.265	.300	565	79	-12	23			.949	13	*O-133(17-101-16)/S-3	-0.6
1908	Cle-A	122	413	32	88	10	1	2	38	19		.213	.253	.257	510	65	-16	15			.957	6	*O-121(1-119-1)/S-1	-1.8
1909	Cle-A	100	343	29	99	10	5	1	38	19		.289	.333	.356	689	113	5	12			.948	4	O-98(0-98-0)	0.5
1910	Cle-A	104	367	41	84	11	2	0	35	23		.229	.284	.270	553	72	-12	18			.961	14	*O-103(1-102-0)/3-1	-0.3
1911	Cle-A	125	447	55	136	18	5	2	51	15		.304	.334	.380	714	98	-3	16			.973	8	*O-102(3-96-3),3-16	-0.1
1912	Cle-A	107	369	49	94	19	3	1	45	26		.255	.311	.331	641	81	-10	15			.952	5	O-96(3-93-0)/1-9,M	-1.1
1913	Cle-A	47	131	16	37	9	1	0	15	8	22	.282	.324	.366	690	99	-1	7			.974	-3	O-36(4-32-0),M	-0.6
1914	Cle-A	19	47	2	6	0	0	0	4	2	5	.128	.163	.128	291	-12	-6	0	1	-0	1.000	-2	O-14(0-6-8),M	-1.1
Total	9	771	2633	284	667	89	27	7	265	129	27	.253	.294	.316	610	84	-54	108	1		.958	46	O-712C/3-18,1-9,S-4	-5.0
■ JOHN BISCHOFF Bischoff, John George "Smiley" b: 10/28/1894, Granite City, Ill. d: 12/28/81, Granite City, Ill. BR/TR, 5'7", 165 lbs. Deb: 4/18/25																								
1925	Chi-A	7	11	1	1	0	0	0	0	1	5	.091	.167	.091	258	-35	-2	0	0	0	1.000	-0	/C-4	-0.2
	Bos-A	41	133	13	37	9	1	1	16	6	11	.278	.309	.383	693	75	-6	1	2	-0	.952	-3	C-40	-0.6
	Yr	48	144	14	38	9	1	1	16	7	16	.264	.298	.361	659	67	-8	1	2	-0	.955	-3	C-44	-0.8
1926	Bos-A	59	127	6	33	11	2	0	19	15	16	.260	.343	.378	721	91	-2	1	3	-1	.974	-1	C-46	-0.1
Total	2	107	271	20	71	20	3	1	35	22	32	.262	.320	.369	689	78	-10	2	5	-1	.964	-4	/C-90	-0.9
■ FRANK BISHOP Bishop, Frank H. b: 9/21/1860, Belvidere, Ill. d: 6/18/29, Chicago, Ill. Deb: 5/27/1884																								
1884	CP-U	4	16	1	3	1	0	0		0		.188	.188	.250	438	32	-2				.667	-2	/3-3,S-1	-0.3
■ MAX BISHOP Bishop, Max Frederick "Tilly" or "Camera Eye" b: 9/5/1899, Waynesboro, Pa. d: 2/24/62, Waynesboro, Pa. BL/TR, 5'8.5", 165 lbs. Deb: 4/15/24																								
1924	Phi-A	91	294	52	75	13	2	2	21	54	30	.255	.380	.333	713	84	-5	4	3	-0	.969	6	2-80	0.3
1925	Phi-A	105	368	66	103	18	4	4	27	87	37	.280	.420	.383	803	98	3	5	9	-2	.957	5	*2-104	0.8
1926	Phi-A	122	400	77	106	20	2	0	33	116	41	.265	.431	.325	756	94	4	4	5	-1	**.987**	0	*2-119	0.6
1927	Phi-A	117	372	80	103	15	1	0	22	105	28	.277	.442	.323	764	95	5	8	6	-0	.967	3	*2-106	1.0
1928	Phi-A	126	472	104	149	27	5	6	50	97	36	.316	.435	.432	868	125	23	9	9	-1	**.978**	-11	*2-125	1.4
1929	*Phi-A	129	475	102	110	19	6	3	36	**128**	44	.232	.398	.316	713	83	-6	1	4	-1	.970	-26	*2-129	-2.8
1930	*Phi-A	130	441	117	111	27	6	10	38	128	60	.252	.426	.408	834	108	11	3	2	-0	.976	-6	*2-127	0.8
1931	*Phi-A	130	497	115	146	30	4	5	37	112	51	.294	.426	.400	826	111	14	3	1	0	.984	-0	*2-130	2.1
1932	Phi-A	114	409	89	104	24	2	5	37	110	43	.254	.412	.359	772	98	4	2	2	-0	**.988**	-9	*2-106	0.1
1933	Phi-A	117	391	80	115	27	1	4	42	106	46	.294	.446	.399	845	124	21	1	5	-2	.975	-13	*2-113	1.2
1934	Bos-A	97	253	65	66	13	1	1	22	82	22	.261	.445	.332	777	96	4	3	2	-0	.990	0	2-57,1-15	0.5
1935	Bos-A	60	122	19	28	3	1	1	14	28	14	.230	.377	.295	673	71	-4	0	2	-1	.978	-5	2-34,1-11/S-2	-0.8
Total	12	1338	4494	966	1216	236	35	41	379	1153	452	.271	.423	.366	789	102	74	43	50	-8	.976	-56	*2-1230/1-26,S-2	5.2
■ MIKE BISHOP Bishop, Michael David b: 11/5/58, Santa Maria, Cal. BR/TR, 6'2", 188 lbs. Deb: 4/16/83																								
1983	NY-N	3	8	2	1	1	0	0	0	3	4	.125	.364	.250	614	74	-0	0	0	0	.944	-0	/C-3	0.0
■ RIVINGTON BISLAND Bisland, Rivington Martin b: 2/17/1890, New York, N.Y. d: 1/11/73, Salzburg, Austria BR/TR, 5'9", 155 lbs. Deb: 9/13/12																								
1912	Pit-N	1	1	0	0	0	0	0	0	0	0	.000	.000	.000	0	-99	-0	0			.000	0	H	0.0
1913	StL-A	12	44	3	6	0	0	0	3	2	5	.136	.191	.136	328	-4	-6	0			.963	-5	S-12	-1.1
1914	Cle-A	18	57	9	6	1	0	0	2	6	2	.105	.190	.123	313	-5	-7	2	5	-1	.962	-0	S-15/3-1	-0.9
Total	3	31	102	12	12	1	0	0	5	8	7	.118	.189	.127	317	-6	-13	2	5		.962	-5	/S-27,3-1	-2.0
■ DEL BISSONETTE Bissonette, Delphia Louis b: 9/6/1899, Winthrop, Me. d: 6/9/72, Augusta, Maine BL/TL, 5'11", 180 lbs. Deb: 4/11/28 MC																								
1928	Bro-N	155	587	90	188	30	13	25	106	70	75	.320	.396	.543	940	145	38	5			.987	-4	*1-155	2.3
1929	Bro-N	116	431	68	121	28	10	12	75	46	58	.281	.351	.476	827	105	2	2			.987	-9	*1-113	-1.3
1930	Bro-N	146	572	102	192	33	13	16	113	56	66	.336	.396	.523	919	121	20	4			.987	-9	*1-146	0.1
1931	Bro-N	152	587	90	170	19	14	12	87	59	53	.290	.354	.431	785	111	9	4			.990	-7	*1-152	-1.2
1933	Bro-N	35	114	9	28	7	0	1	10	2	17	.246	.259	.333	592	71	-5	2			.988	0	1-32	-0.8
Total	5	604	2291	359	699	117	50	66	391	233	269	.305	.371	.486	857	119	64	17			.988	-28	1-598	-0.9
■ RED BITTMAN Bittman, Henry Peter b: 7/22/1862, Cincinnati, Ohio d: 11/8/29, Cincinnati, Ohio Deb: 10/10/1889																								
1889	KC-a	4	14	2	4	0	0	0	2	1	1	.286	.333	.286	619	73	-0	1			1.000	1	/2-4	0.1
■ GEORGE BJORKMAN Bjorkman, George Anton b: 8/26/56, Ontario, Cal. BR/TR, 6'2", 190 lbs. Deb: 7/10/83																								
1983	Hou-N	29	75	8	17	4	0	2	14	16	29	.227	.370	.360	730	110	2	0	0	0	.993	-3	C-29	0.0
■ JOHN BLACK Black, John Falcnor "Jack" (b: John Falcnor Haddow) b: 2/23/1890, Covington, Ky. d: 3/20/62, Rutherford, N.J. BR/TR, 6'1", 185 lbs. Deb: 6/20/11																								
1911	StL-A	54	186	13	28	4	0	0	7	10		.151	.202	.172	374	5	-24	4			.972	0	1-54	-2.5
■ BILL BLACK Black, John William "Jigger" b: 8/12/1899, Philadelphia, Pa. d: 1/14/68, Philadelphia, Pa. BL/TR, 5'11", 168 lbs. Deb: 5/4/24																								
1924	Chi-A	6	5	0	1	0	0	0	0	0	0	.200	.200	.200	400	3	-1	0	0	0	.000	0	/2-1	-0.1

■ **BOB BLACK** Black, Robert Benjamin b: 12/10/1862, Cincinnati, Ohio d: 3/21/33, Sioux City, Iowa 5'5.5", 155 lbs. Deb: 8/19/1884

YEAR	TM/L	G	AB	R	H	2B	3B	HR	RBI	BB	SO	AVG	OBP	SLG	OPS	OPS+	BR+	SB	CS	SBR	FA	FR	G/POS	TPR
1884	KC-U	38	146	25	36	14	2	1		10		.247	.295	.390	685	122	-0				.784	-1	O-19C,P-16/2-6,S-1	-0.3

■ **ETHAN BLACKABY** Blackaby, Ethan Allen b: 7/24/40, Cincinnati, O. BL/TL, 5'11", 190 lbs. Deb: 9/6/62

YEAR	TM/L	G	AB	R	H	2B	3B	HR	RBI	BB	SO	AVG	OBP	SLG	OPS	OPS+	BR+	SB	CS	SBR	FA	FR	G/POS	TPR
1962	Mil-N	6	13	0	2	1	0	0	0	1	8	.154	.214	.231	445	20	-1	0	0	0	1.000	-1	/O-3(2-1-0)	-0.2
1964	Mil-N	9	12	0	1	0	0	0	1	1	2	.083	.154	.083	237	-31	-2	0	0	0	.500	-2	/O-5(2-0-3)	-0.4
Total	2	15	25	0	3	1	0	0	1	2	10	.120	.185	.160	345	-4	-4	0	0	0	.800	-2	/O-8(4-1-3)	-0.6

■ **EARL BLACKBURN** Blackburn, Earl Stuart b: 11/1/1892, Leesville, Ohio d: 8/3/66, Mansfield, Ohio BR/TR, 5'11", 180 lbs. Deb: 9/17/12

YEAR	TM/L	G	AB	R	H	2B	3B	HR	RBI	BB	SO	AVG	OBP	SLG	OPS	OPS+	BR+	SB	CS	SBR	FA	FR	G/POS	TPR
1912	Pit-N	1	0	0	0	0	0	0	0	0	0	—	—	—	—	—	0	0			1.000	0	/C-1	0.0
	Cin-N	1	0	0	0	0	0	0	0	1	0	—	1.000	—	1000	191	0	0			1.000	0	/C-1	0.1
	Yr	2	0	0	0	0	0	0	0	1	0	—	1.000	—	1000	190	0	0			1.000	0	/C-2	0.1
1913	Cin-N	17	27	1	7	0	0	0	3	2	5	.259	.310	.259	570	64	-1	2			.848	-1	C-12	-0.2
1915	Bos-N	3	6	0	1	0	0	0	0	2	1	.167	.375	.167	542	70	-0	0			1.000	-0	/C-3	0.0
1916	Bos-N	47	110	12	30	4	4	0	7	9	21	.273	.328	.382	710	123	3	2			.972	-1	C-44	0.5
1917	Chi-N	2	2	0	0	0	0	0	0	0	0	.000	.000	.000	0	-93	-0	0			.000	0	H	-0.1
Total	5	71	145	13	38	4	4	0	10	14	27	.262	.327	.345	672	107	1	4			.954	-2	/C-61	0.3

■ **LENA BLACKBURNE** Blackburne, Russell Aubrey "Slats"
b: 10/23/1886, Clifton Heights, Pa. d: 2/29/68, Riverside, N.J. BR/TR, 5'11", 160 lbs. Deb: 4/14/10 MC

YEAR	TM/L	G	AB	R	H	2B	3B	HR	RBI	BB	SO	AVG	OBP	SLG	OPS	OPS+	BR+	SB	CS	SBR	FA	FR	G/POS	TPR
1910	Chi-A	75	242	16	42	3	1	0	10	19		.174	.245	.194	439	39	-16	4			.911	19	S-74	0.6
1912	Chi-A	5	1	0	0	0	0	0	0	1		.000	.500	.000	500	48	0	1			.800	1	/S-4,3-1	0.1
1914	Chi-A	144	474	52	105	10	5	1	35	66	58	.222	.324	.270	594	80	-9	25	15	0	.963	1	*2-143	-0.6
1915	Chi-A	96	283	33	61	5	1	0	25	35	34	.216	.304	.240	544	61	-13	13	11	-1	.949	-10	3-83/S-9	-2.3
1918	Cin-N	125	435	34	99	8	10	1	45	25	30	.228	.271	.299	570	75	-14	6			.938	10	*S-125	0.5
1919	Bos-N	31	80	5	21	3	1	0	4	6	7	.262	.322	.325	647	99	-0	3			.948	3	3-24/1-1,2-1,S-1	0.4
	Phi-N	72	291	32	58	10	5	2	19	10	22	.199	.228	.289	517	51	-18	2			.933	6	3-72/1-1	-1.0
	Yr	103	371	37	79	13	6	2	23	16	29	.213	.249	.296	546	61	-18	5			.937	10	3-96/1-2,2-1,S-1	-0.6
1927	Chi-A	1	1	1	1	0	0	0	1	0	0	1.000	1.000	1.000	2000	431	0	0	0	0	.000	0	H	0.0
1929	Chi-A	1	0	0	0	0	0	0	0	0	0	—	—	—	—	—	0	0	0	0	.000	0	/P-1,M	0.0
Total	8	550	1807	173	387	39	23	4	139	162	151	.214	.284	.268	552	67	-69	54	26		.927	30	S-213,3-180,2/1P	-2.3

■ **GEORGE BLACKERBY** Blackerby, George Franklin b: 11/10/03, Luther, Okla. d: 5/30/87, Wichita Falls, Tex. BR/TR, 6'1", 176 lbs. Deb: 8/10/28

YEAR	TM/L	G	AB	R	H	2B	3B	HR	RBI	BB	SO	AVG	OBP	SLG	OPS	OPS+	BR+	SB	CS	SBR	FA	FR	G/POS	TPR
1928	Chi-A	30	83	8	21	0	0	0	12	4	10	.253	.287	.253	540	44	-7	2	1	0	.953	-1	O-20(20-0-0)	-0.9

■ **FRED BLACKWELL** Blackwell, Fredrick William "Blacky" b: 9/7/1891, Bowling Green, Ky. d: 12/8/75, Morgantown, Ky. BL/TR, 5'11.5", 160 lbs. Deb: 9/25/17

YEAR	TM/L	G	AB	R	H	2B	3B	HR	RBI	BB	SO	AVG	OBP	SLG	OPS	OPS+	BR+	SB	CS	SBR	FA	FR	G/POS	TPR
1917	Pit-N	3	10	1	2	0	0	0	2	0	3	.200	.200	.200	400	22	-1	0			1.000	0	/C-3	-0.1
1918	Pit-N	8	13	1	2	0	0	0	4	3	4	.154	.313	.154	466	42	-1	0			.926	0	/C-8	0.0
1919	Pit-N	24	65	3	14	3	0	0	4	3	9	.215	.261	.262	522	55	-3	0			.964	-0	C-22	-0.2
Total	3	35	88	5	18	3	0	0	10	6	16	.205	.263	.239	502	50	-5	0			.961	0	/C-33	-0.3

■ **TIM BLACKWELL** Blackwell, Timothy P b: 8/19/52, San Diego, Cal. BB/TR, 5'11", 180 lbs. Deb: 7/3/74

YEAR	TM/L	G	AB	R	H	2B	3B	HR	RBI	BB	SO	AVG	OBP	SLG	OPS	OPS+	BR+	SB	CS	SBR	FA	FR	G/POS	TPR
1974	Bos-A	44	122	9	30	1	1	0	8	10	21	.246	.308	.270	579	63	-5	1	1	-0	.971	2	C-44	-0.2
1975	Bos-A	59	132	15	26	3	2	0	6	19	13	.197	.303	.250	553	53	-8	0	0	0	.984	8	C-57/D-2	0.2
1976	Phi-N	4	8	0	2	0	0	0	1	0	1	.250	.250	.250	500	41	-1	0	0	0	1.000	1	/C-4	0.0
1977	Phi-N	1	0	1	0	0	0	0	0	0	0	—	—	—	—	—	0	0	0	0	1.000	0	/C-1	0.0
	Mon-N	16	22	3	2	1	0	0	0	2	7	.091	.167	.136	303	-18	-4	0	0	0	.925	-1	C-14	-0.4
	Yr	17	22	4	2	1	0	0	0	2	7	.091	.167	.136	303	-18	-4	0	0	0	.929	-1	C-15	-0.4
1978	Chi-N	49	103	8	23	3	0	0	7	23	17	.223	.370	.252	623	68	-3	0	0	0	.987	7	C-49	0.6
1979	Chi-N	63	122	8	20	3	1	0	12	32	25	.164	.342	.205	547	48	-7	0	0	0	.975	1	C-63	-0.5
1980	Chi-N	103	320	24	87	16	4	5	30	41	62	.272	.355	.394	748	101	1	0	1	-0	.982	17	*C-103	2.3
1981	Chi-N	58	158	21	37	10	2	1	11	23	23	.234	.331	.342	673	87	-2	2	1	0	.993	2	C-56	0.2
1982	Mon-N	23	42	2	8	2	1	0	3	3	11	.190	.244	.286	530	47	-3	0	0	0	.985	2	C-18	-0.1
1983	Mon-N	6	15	0	3	1	0	0	2	1	3	.200	.250	.267	517	43	-1	0	0	0	.935	1	/C-5	-0.1
Total	10	426	1044	91	238	40	11	6	80	154	183	.228	.329	.305	634	73	-33	3	3	-0	.981	40	C-414/D-2	2.0

■ **RAY BLADES** Blades, Francis Raymond b: 8/6/1896, Mt.Vernon, Ill. d: 5/18/79, Lincoln, Ill. BR/TR, 5'7.5", 163 lbs. Deb: 8/19/22 MC Career OF: (500-LF 4-CF 124-RF)

YEAR	TM/L	G	AB	R	H	2B	3B	HR	RBI	BB	SO	AVG	OBP	SLG	OPS	OPS+	BR+	SB	CS	SBR	FA	FR	G/POS	TPR
1922	StL-N	37	130	27	39	2	4	3	21	25	21	.300	.428	.446	874	132	8	3	3	-0	.931	-1	O-29(28-0-1)/S-4,3-1	0.4
1923	StL-N	98	317	48	78	21	5	5	44	37	46	.246	.342	.391	733	95	-2	4	2	0	.967	6	O-83(81-1-3)/3-4	-0.2
1924	StL-N	131	456	86	142	21	13	11	68	35	38	.311	.373	.487	860	131	19	7	9	-2	.956	-3	*O-109L/2-7,3-7	0.7
1925	StL-N	122	462	112	158	37	8	12	57	59	47	.342	.423	.535	958	140	29	6	8	-1	.979	11	*O-114(114-0-0)/3-1	2.7
1926	StL-N	107	416	81	127	17	12	8	43	62	57	.305	.409	.462	871	129	19	6			.980	4	*O-105(105-0-0)	1.5
1927	StL-N	61	180	33	57	8	5	2	29	28	22	.317	.414	.450	864	127	8	3			.914	-13	O-50(29-0-21)	-0.8
1928	*StL-N	51	85	9	20	7	1	1	19	20	26	.235	.393	.376	769	100	1	0			.972	-2	O-19(4-0-15)	-0.2
1930	*StL-N	45	101	26	40	6	2	4	25	21	15	.396	.504	.614	1118	163	12	1			.957	-3	O-32(13-0-21)	0.6
1931	*StL-N	35	67	10	19	4	0	1	5	10	7	.284	.392	.388	780	106	1	1			.871	-4	O-20(7-0-13)	-0.4
1932	StL-N	80	201	35	46	10	1	3	29	34	31	.229	.340	.333	674	80	-5	2			.975	-5	O-62(13-0-49)/3-1	-1.3
Total	10	767	2415	467	726	133	51	50	340	331	310	.301	.395	.460	855	123	90	33	22		.963	-10	O-623L/3-14,2-7,S-4	3.0

■ **RICK BLADT** Bladt, Richard Alan b: 12/9/46, Santa Cruz, Cal. BR/TR, 6'1", 160 lbs. Deb: 6/15/69

YEAR	TM/L	G	AB	R	H	2B	3B	HR	RBI	BB	SO	AVG	OBP	SLG	OPS	OPS+	BR+	SB	CS	SBR	FA	FR	G/POS	TPR
1969	Chi-N	10	13	1	2	0	0	0	1	0	5	.154	.154	.154	308	-12	-2	0	0	0	1.000	0	/O-7(2-5-1)	-0.2
1975	NY-A	52	117	13	26	3	1	1	11	11	8	.222	.295	.291	585	67	-5	6	2	1	.973	-2	O-51(0-51-0)	-0.8
Total	2	62	130	14	28	3	1	1	12	11	13	.215	.282	.277	559	58	-7	6	2	1	.976	-2	/O-58(2-56-1)	-1.0

■ **RAE BLAEMIRE** Blaemire, Rae Bertrum b: 2/8/11, Gary, Ind. d: 12/23/75, Champaign, Ill. BR/TR, 6', 178 lbs. Deb: 9/13/41

YEAR	TM/L	G	AB	R	H	2B	3B	HR	RBI	BB	SO	AVG	OBP	SLG	OPS	OPS+	BR+	SB	CS	SBR	FA	FR	G/POS	TPR
1941	NY-N	2	5	0	2	0	0	0	0	0	0	.400	.400	.400	800	123	0	0			1.000	-0	/C-2	0.0

■ **FOOTSIE BLAIR** Blair, Clarence Vick b: 7/13/1900, Enterprise, Okla. d: 7/1/82, Texarkana, Tex. BL/TR, 6'1", 180 lbs. Deb: 4/28/29

YEAR	TM/L	G	AB	R	H	2B	3B	HR	RBI	BB	SO	AVG	OBP	SLG	OPS	OPS+	BR+	SB	CS	SBR	FA	FR	G/POS	TPR
1929	*Chi-N	26	72	10	23	5	0	1	8	3	4	.319	.347	.431	777	91	-1	1			.897	1	/3-8,1-7,2-2	0.0
1930	Chi-N	134	578	97	158	24	12	6	59	20	58	.273	.306	.388	693	66	-33	9			.958	8	*2-115,3-13	-1.8
1931	Chi-N	86	240	31	62	19	4	3	29	14	26	.258	.302	.408	710	88	-5	1			.956	-6	2-44,1-23/3-1	-0.9
Total	3	246	890	138	243	48	16	10	96	37	88	.273	.308	.397	705	73	-39	11			.958	4	2-161/1-30,3-22	-2.7

■ **BUDDY BLAIR** Blair, Louis Nathan b: 9/10/10, Columbia, Miss. d: 6/7/96, Monroe, La. BL/TR, 6', 186 lbs. Deb: 4/14/42

YEAR	TM/L	G	AB	R	H	2B	3B	HR	RBI	BB	SO	AVG	OBP	SLG	OPS	OPS+	BR+	SB	CS	SBR	FA	FR	G/POS	TPR
1942	Phi-A	137	484	48	135	26	8	5	66	30	30	.279	.325	.397	722	103	0	1	6	-2	.931	-7	*3-126	-0.4

■ **PAUL BLAIR** Blair, Paul L D b: 2/1/44, Cushing, Okla. BR/TR (BB 1971 (part)), 6', 171 lbs. Deb: 9/9/64 Career OF: (31-LF 1801-CF 58-RF)

YEAR	TM/L	G	AB	R	H	2B	3B	HR	RBI	BB	SO	AVG	OBP	SLG	OPS	OPS+	BR+	SB	CS	SBR	FA	FR	G/POS	TPR
1964	Bal-A	8	1	0	0	0	0	0	0	0	1	.000	.000	.000	0	-99	-0	0	1	-0	1.000	-2	/O-6(0-6-0)	-0.3
1965	Bal-A	119	364	49	85	19	2	5	25	32	52	.234	.303	.338	640	80	-9	8	5	0	.992	3	*O-116(0-116-0)	-1.1
1966	*Bal-A	133	303	35	84	20	2	6	33	15	36	.277	.311	.416	727	109	2	5	6	-1	.990	-11	*O-127(2-125-0)	-1.3
1967	Bal-A	151	552	72	162	27	**12**	11	64	50	68	.293	.357	.446	803	137	25	8	6	-0	.985	21	*O-146(0-146-0)	4.5
1968	Bal-A	141	421	48	89	22	1	7	38	37	60	.211	.278	.318	597	80	-10	4	2	0	.993	0	*O-132(0-132-0)/3-1	-1.5
1969	*Bal-A★	150	625	102	178	32	5	26	76	40	72	.285	.330	.477	807	122	15	20	6	2	.988	25	*O-150(0-150-0)	4.0
1970	*Bal-A	133	480	79	128	24	2	18	65	56	93	.267	.347	.438	784	114	9	24	11	1	.990	19	*O-128(0-128-0)/3-1	2.7
1971	*Bal-A	141	516	75	135	24	8	10	44	32	94	.262	.306	.397	703	99	-3	14	11	-1	.991	2	*O-138(0-138-0)	-0.5
1972	Bal-A	142	477	47	111	20	8	8	49	25	78	.233	.271	.358	629	84	-11	7	8	-1	.991	9	*O-139(0-139-0)	-0.7
1973	*Bal-A★	146	500	73	140	25	3	10	64	43	72	.280	.337	.402	739	108	5	18	8	1	.990	7	*O-144(0-144-0)/D-1	1.0
1974	*Bal-A	151	552	77	144	27	4	17	62	43	59	.261	.317	.417	733	113	8	27	9	3	.985	7	*O-151(0-151-0)	1.5
1975	Bal-A	140	440	51	96	13	4	5	31	25	82	.218	.260	.300	560	62	-23	17	11	-0	.991	-2	*O-138C/1-1,D-1	-2.9
1976	Bal-A	145	375	29	74	16	0	3	16	22	49	.197	.246	.264	510	52	-23	15	6	1	.979	-8	*O-139(0-139-0)/D-1	-3.4
1977	*NY-A	83	164	20	43	4	3	4	25	9	16	.262	.309	.396	705	91	-2	3	2	-0	.969	-13	O-79(6-42-33)/D-1	-1.6
1978	*NY-A	75	125	10	22	5	0	2	13	9	17	.176	.231	.264	495	40	-10	1	1	-0	.989	-15	O-64C/2-5,S-4,3-3	-2.7

YEAR	TM/L	G	AB	R	H	2B	3B	HR	RBI	BB	SO	AVG	OBP	SLG	OPS	OPS+	BR+	SB	CS	SBR	FA	FR	G/POS	TPR
1979	NY-A	2	5	0	1	0	0	0	0	0	1	.200	.200	.200	400	8	-1	0	0	0	1.000	0	/O-2(0-1-1)	0.0
	Cin-N	75	140	7	21	4	1	2	15	11	27	.150	.212	.236	448	22	-15	0	0	0	.992	-10	O-67(16-56-2)	-2.7
1980	NY-A	12	2	2	0	0	0	0	0	0	0	.000	.000	.000	0	-99	-1	0	0	0	1.000	-4	O-12(6-1-6)	-0.5
Total	17	1947	6042	776	1513	282	55	134	620	449	877	.250	.305	.382	687	96	-44	171	93	5	.988	29	*O-1878C/2-5,3-5,SD1	-5.5
■ WALTER BLAIR	Blair, Walter Allen "Heavy" b: 10/13/1883, Landrus, Pa. d: 8/20/48, Lewisburg, Pa. BR/TR, 6', 185 lbs. Deb: 9/17/07 M																							
1907	NY-A	7	22	1	4	0	0	0	1	2		.182	.250	.182	432	35	-2	0			.922	1	/C-7	0.1
1908	NY-A	76	211	9	40	5	1	1	13	11		.190	.237	.237	474	53	-11	4			.956	-14	C-60/O-9(2-0-7),1-3	-2.3
1909	NY-A	42	110	5	23	2	2	0	11	7		.209	.269	.264	533	68	-4	2			.964	-8	C-42	-1.0
1910	NY-A	6	22	2	5	0	1	0	2	0		.227	.227	.318	545	67	-1	0			.970	-2	/C-6	-0.3
1911	NY-A	85	222	18	43	9	2	0	26	16		.194	.257	.252	510	40	-18	2			.970	4	C-84/1-1	-0.8
1914	Buf-F	128	378	22	92	11	2	0	33	32	64	.243	.304	.283	587	59	-27	6			.984	5	*C-128	-1.2
1915	Buf-F	98	290	23	65	15	3	2	20	18	32	.224	.274	.317	591	65	-19	4			**.981**	5	C-97,M	-0.7
Total	7	442	1255	80	272	42	11	3	106	86	96	.217	.272	.275	547	56	-81	18			.974	-9	C-424/O-9(2-0-7),1-4	-6.2
■ HARRY BLAKE	Blake, Harry Cooper b: 6/16/1874, Portsmouth, Ohio d: 10/14/19, Chicago, Ill. BR/TR, 5'7", 165 lbs. Deb: 7/7/1894 Career OF: (12-LF 132-CF 373-RF)																							
1894	Cle-N	73	296	51	78	15	4	1	51	30	22	.264	.335	.351	687	63	-19	1			.932	2	O-73(0-4-69)	-1.5
1895	*Cle-N	85	318	50	88	10	1	3	45	31	33	.277	.343	.343	686	73	-13	11			.898	-2	O-84(0-0-84)	-1.6
1896	*Cle-N	104	383	66	92	12	5	1	43	46	30	.240	.322	.305	627	62	-21	10			.944	2	*O-103(0-12-92)/S-1	-2.1
1897	Cle-N	32	117	17	30	3	1	1	15	12		.256	.331	.325	656	70	-5	5			.989	4	O-32(2-25-5)	-0.3
1898	Cle-N	136	474	65	116	18	7	0	58	69		.245	.342	.312	654	89	-5	12			.952	7	*O-136(1-22-114)/1-2	-0.5
1899	StL-N	97	292	50	70	9	4	2	41	43		.240	.341	.318	660	79	-7	16			.979	-2	O-87C/2-4,S-1,1C	-1.2
Total	6	527	1880	299	474	67	22	8	253	231	85	.252	.336	.324	660	73	-70	55			.948	12	O-515R/2-4,1-3,SC	-7.2
■ CASEY BLAKE	Blake, William Casey b: 8/23/73, Des Moines, Iowa BR/TR, 6'2", 195 lbs. Deb: 8/14/99																							
1999	Tor-A	14	39	6	10	2	0	1	1	2	7	.256	.293	.385	677	70	-2	0	0	0	1.000	4	3-14	0.2
2000	Min-A	7	16	1	3	2	0	0	1	3	7	.188	.350	.313	663	66	-1	0	0	0	1.000	-1	/3-5,1-1,D-1	-0.2
Total	2	21	55	7	13	4	0	1	2	5	14	.236	.311	.364	675	69	-3	0	0	0	1.000	3	/3-19,D-1,1-1	0.0
■ LINC BLAKELY	Blakely, Lincoln Howard b: 2/12/12, Oakland, Cal. d: 9/28/76, Oakland, Cal. BR/TR, 6', 180 lbs. Deb: 4/29/34																							
1934	Cin-N	34	102	11	23	1	1	0	10	5	14	.225	.269	.255	523	42	-8	1			.987	3	O-28(6-22-0)	-0.6
■ BOB BLAKISTON	Blakiston, Robert J. (b: Robert J. Blackstone) b: 10/2/1855, San Francisco, Cal. d: 12/25/18, San Francisco, Cal 5'8.5", 180 lbs. Deb: 5/2/1882 Career OF: (2-LF 66-CF 36-RF)																							
1882	Phi-a	72	281	40	64	4	1	0	20	9		.228	.252	.249	501	62	-12				.855	0	O-38(0-4-34),3-34/2-1	-1.1
1883	Phi-a	44	167	26	41	3	3	0	26	9		.246	.284	.299	583	81	-4				.857	-4	O-37(2-35-0)/1-6,3-5	-0.8
1884	Phi-a	32	128	21	33	6	0	0		11		.258	.336	.305	640	104	1				.902	2	O-28C/3-2,1-1,2S	0.2
	Ind-a	6	18	0	4	1	0	0		1		.222	.263	.278	541	79	-0				.884	-1	/1-5,O-1(0-0-1)	-0.1
	Yr	38	146	21	37	7	0	0		12		.253	.327	.301	629	101	0				.902	1	O-29C/1-6,3-2,2S	0.1
Total	3	154	594	87	142	14	4	0	46	30		.239	.280	.276	556	77	-16				.872	-2	O-104C/3-41,1-12,2S	-1.8
■ JOHNNY BLANCHARD	Blanchard, John Edwin b: 2/26/33, Minneapolis, Minn. BL/TR, 6'1", 198 lbs. Deb: 9/25/55 Career OF: (54-LF 0-CF 115-RF)																							
1955	NY-A	1	3	0	0	0	0	0	0	1	0	.000	.250	.000	250	-29	-1	0	0	0	1.000	0	/C-1	0.0
1959	NY-A	49	59	6	10	1	0	2	4	7	12	.169	.258	.288	546	51	-4	0	0	0	.963	-2	C-12/O-8(1-0-7),1-1	-0.6
1960	*NY-A	53	99	8	24	3	1	4	14	6	17	.242	.292	.414	707	94	-1	0	0	0	.988	10	C-28	0.9
1961	*NY-A	93	243	38	74	10	1	21	54	27	28	.305	.383	.613	996	170	23	1	0	0	.990	-2	C-48,O-15(8-0-7)	2.3
1962	*NY-A	93	246	33	57	7	0	13	39	28	32	.232	.313	.419	731	98	-1	0	0	0	.987	-7	O-47R,C-15/1-2	-1.1
1963	*NY-A	76	218	22	49	4	0	16	45	26	30	.225	.307	.463	771	114	3	0	0	0	.987	-9	O-64(22-0-42)	-0.9
1964	*NY-A	77	161	18	41	8	0	7	28	24	24	.255	.351	.435	786	115	4	1	0	0	.984	-3	C-25,O-14(6-0-8)/1-3	0.1
1965	NY-A	12	34	1	5	1	0	1	3	7	3	.147	.293	.265	557	60	-2	0	0	0	.961	-1	C-12	-0.2
	KC-A	52	120	10	24	2	0	2	11	8	16	.200	.256	.267	522	49	-8	0	0	0	1.000	-10	O-20(1-0-19),C-14	-2.0
	Yr	64	154	11	29	3	0	3	14	15	19	.188	.265	.266	531	52	-10	0	0	0	.971	-11	C-26,O-20(1-0-19)	-2.2
	Mil-N	10	10	1	1	0	0	1	2	2	1	.100	.250	.400	650	79	-0	0	0	0	.000	-0	/O-1(1-0-0)	-0.1
Total	8	516	1193	137	285	36	2	67	200	136	163	.239	.320	.441	761	109	13	2	0	0	.987	-25	O-169R,C-155/1-6	-1.6
■ DAMASO BLANCO	Blanco, Damaso (Caripe) b: 11/12/41, Curiepe, Venez. BR/TR, 5'10", 165 lbs. Deb: 5/26/72																							
1972	SF-N	39	20	5	7	1	0	0	2	4	3	.350	.458	.400	858	144	1	2	1	0	.889	6	3-19/S-8,2-3	0.8
1973	SF-N	28	12	4	0	0	0	0	0	1	2	.000	.077	.000	77	-74	-3	0	0	0	1.000	2	/3-7,S-5,2-3	-0.1
1974	SF-N	5	1	0	0	0	0	0	0	0	1	.000	.000	.000	0	-96	-0	1	0	0	.000	0	H	0.0
Total	3	72	33	9	7	1	0	0	2	5	6	.212	.316	.242	558	58	-2	3	1	0	.929	8	/3-26,S-13,2-6	0.7
■ HENRY BLANCO	Blanco, Henry Ramon b: 8/29/71, Caracas, Venez. BR/TR, 5'11", 170 lbs. Deb: 7/25/97 Career OF: (1-LF 0-CF 0-RF)																							
1997	LA-N	3	5	1	2	0	0	1	1	0	1	.400	.400	1.000	1400	273	1	0	0	0	1.000	-1	/1-1,3-1	0.1
1999	Col-N	88	263	30	61	12	3	6	28	34	38	.232	.322	.369	691	58	-16	1	1	-0	.992	18	C-86/O-1(1-0-0)	0.6
2000	Mil-N	93	284	29	67	24	0	7	31	36	60	.236	.322	.394	716	81	-9	0	3	-1	.991	12	C-88	0.7
Total	3	184	552	60	130	36	3	14	60	70	99	.236	.323	.388	710	70	-24	1	4	-1	.992	30	C-174/O-1L,3-1,1-1	1.4
■ OSSIE BLANCO	Blanco, Oswaldo Carlos (Diaz) b: 9/8/45, Caracas, Venez. BR/TR, 6', 185 lbs. Deb: 5/26/70																							
1970	Chi-A	34	66	4	13	0	0	0	8	3	14	.197	.232	.197	429	19	-7	0	1	-0	.993	-1	1-22/O-1(1-0-0)	-1.0
1974	Cle-A	18	36	1	7	0	0	0	2	7	4	.194	.326	.194	520	53	-2	0	3	-1	.992	-1	1-16/D-1	-0.5
Total	2	52	102	5	20	0	0	0	10	10	18	.196	.268	.196	464	31	-9	0	4	-1	.993	-2	/1-38,D-1,O-1(1-0-0)	-1.5
■ COONIE BLANK	Blank, Frank Ignatz b: 10/18/1892, St.Louis, Mo. d: 12/8/61, St.Louis, Mo. BR/TR, 5'11", 165 lbs. Deb: 8/15/09																							
1909	StL-N	1	2	0	0	0	0	0	0	0		.000	.000	.000	0	-99	-0	0			1.000	-0	/C-1	-0.1
■ CLIFF BLANKENSHIP	Blankenship, Clifford Douglas b: 4/10/1880, Columbus, Ga. d: 4/26/56, Oakland, Cal. BR/TR, 5'10.5", 165 lbs. Deb: 4/17/05																							
1905	Cin-N	19	56	8	11	1	1	0	7	4		.196	.250	.250	500	44	-4	1			.960	-2	1-15	-0.7
1907	Was-A	37	102	4	23	2	0	0	6	3		.225	.248	.245	493	62	-5	3			.991	0	C-22/1-9	-0.3
1909	Was-A	39	60	4	15	1	0	0	9	0		.250	.250	.267	517	66	-3	2			.907	-9	C-17/O-4(1-1-2)	-1.2
Total	3	95	218	16	49	4	1	0	22	7		.225	.249	.252	501	58	-11	6			.964	-11	/C-39,1-24,O-4(1-1-2)	-2.2
■ LANCE BLANKENSHIP	Blankenship, Lance Robert b: 12/6/63, Portland, Ore. BR/TR, 6', 185 lbs. Deb: 9/4/88 Career OF: (71-LF 66-CF 71-RF)																							
1988	Oak-A	10	3	1	0	0	0	0	0	0	1	.000	.000	.000	0	-99	-1	0	1	-0	1.000	0	/2-4,D-4	-0.1
1989	*Oak-A	58	125	22	29	5	1	1	4	8	31	.232	.278	.312	590	68	-5	5	1	1	1.000	3	O-25R,2-24,D-10	-0.2
1990	*Oak-A	86	136	18	26	3	0	0	10	20	23	.191	.295	.213	508	46	-9	3	1	0	.947	-2	3-28,O-28R,2-20,/1D	-1.1
1991	Oak-A	90	185	33	46	8	0	3	21	23	42	.249	.341	.341	682	95	-1	12	3	2	.983	8	2-45,O-28L,3-14,/D	0.9
1992	*Oak-A	123	349	59	84	24	1	3	34	82	57	.241	.394	.341	735	113	11	21	7	2	.992	-3	2-78,O-51L/1-7,D-3	1.1
1993	Oak-A	94	252	43	48	8	1	2	23	67	64	.190	.364	.254	618	74	-6	13	5	1	.994	4	O-66C,2-19/1-6,SD	0.0
Total	6	461	1050	176	233	48	3	9	92	200	218	.222	.352	.299	651	86	-10	54	18	6	.987	10	O-198L,2-190/3D1S	0.6
■ LARVELL BLANKS	Blanks, Larvell b: 1/28/50, Del Rio, Tex. BR/TR, 5'8", 167 lbs. Deb: 7/19/72																							
1972	Atl-N	33	85	10	28	5	0	1	7	7	12	.329	.380	.424	804	117	2	0	0	0	1.000	6	2-18/S-4,3-2	1.0
1973	Atl-N	17	18	1	4	0	0	0	0	1	3	.222	.263	.222	485	33	-2	0	0	0	.000	-3	/3-3,2-2,S-2	-0.4
1974	Atl-N	3	8	0	2	0	0	0	1	0	0	.250	.250	.250	500	38	-1	0	0	0	.889	-0	/S-2	-0.1
1975	Atl-N	141	471	49	110	13	3	3	38	38	43	.234	.294	.293	587	61	-25	4	3	-0	.960	-12	*S-129,2-12	-2.2
1976	Cle-A	104	328	45	92	8	7	5	41	30	31	.280	.341	.393	734	116	6	1	2	-0	.977	-20	S-56,2-46/3-2,D-3	-0.6
1977	Cle-A	105	322	43	92	10	4	6	38	19	37	.286	.327	.398	725	100	-1	3	0	1	.960	-25	S-66,3-18,2-12,/D-6	-1.9
1978	Cle-A	70	193	19	49	10	0	2	20	10	16	.254	.291	.337	627	77	-6	0	0	0	.926	-10	S-43,2-17/3-3,D-1	-1.1
1979	Tex-A	68	120	13	24	5	0	1	15	11	9	.200	.267	.267	534	45	-9	0	0	0	.972	-10	S-49,2-16/D-1	-1.5
1980	Atl-N	88	221	23	45	6	0	2	12	16	27	.204	.257	.258	515	43	-17	1	2	-0	.947	7	S-56,3-43/2-1	-0.8
Total	9	629	1766	203	446	57	14	20	172	132	178	.253	.306	.335	640	78	-51	9	7	-0	.957	-66	S-407,2-124/3-71,D	-7.6

YEAR	TM/L	G	AB	R	H	2B	3B	HR	RBI	BB	SO	AVG	OBP	SLG	OPS	OPS+	BR+	SB	CS	SBR	FA	FR	G/POS	TPR
■ DON BLASINGAME	Blasingame, Don Lee b: 3/16/32, Corinth, Miss. BL/TR, 5'10", 165 lbs. Deb: 9/20/55																							
1955	StL-N	5	16	4	6	1	0	0	0	6	0	.375	.545	.438	983	165	2	1	1	-0	.955	2	/2-3,S-2	0.4
1956	StL-N	150	587	94	153	22	7	0	27	72	52	.261	.344	.322	666	81	-14	8	8	-1	.986	22	2-98,S-49/3-2	1.9
1957	StL-N	154	650	108	176	25	7	8	58	71	49	.271	.343	.368	711	89	-8	21	9	1	.984	26	*2-154	3.1
1958	StL-N★	143	547	71	150	19	10	2	36	57	47	.274	.344	.356	700	83	-12	20	5	3	.964	-1	*2-137	-0.1
1959	StL-N	150	615	90	178	26	7	1	24	67	42	.289	.361	.359	720	87	-9	15	15	-2	.979	21	*2-150	2.1
1960	SF-N	136	523	72	123	12	8	2	31	49	53	.235	.303	.300	603	70	-21	14	2	2	.979	-13	*2-133	-2.3
1961	SF-N	3	1	1	0	0	0	0	0	2	1	.000	.667	.000	667	100	0	0	0	0	.000	0	H	0.0
	*Cin-N	123	450	59	100	18	4	1	21	39	38	.222	.287	.287	574	52	-30	4	3	-0	.972	-19	*2-116	-4.0
	Yr	126	451	60	100	18	4	1	21	41	39	.222	.289	.286	576	53	-30	4	3	-0	.972	-19	*2-116	-4.0
1962	Cin-N	141	494	77	139	9	7	2	35	63	44	.281	.365	.340	705	88	-6	4	3	-0	.976	-10	*2-137	-0.4
1963	Cin-N	18	31	4	5	2	0	0	0	7	5	.161	.316	.226	542	57	-1	0	1	-0	.974	0	2-11/3-2	-0.1
	Was-A	69	254	29	65	10	2	2	12	24	18	.256	.320	.335	655	84	-5	3	2	-0	.991	1	2-64	0.2
1964	Was-A	143	506	56	135	17	2	1	34	40	44	.267	.321	.314	635	78	-14	8	5	0	.977	-30	*2-135	-3.6
1965	Was-A	129	403	47	90	8	8	1	18	35	45	.223	.289	.290	579	66	-18	5	4	-0	.984	1	*2-110	-1.0
1966	Was-A	68	200	18	43	9	0	1	11	18	21	.215	.280	.275	555	61	-10	2	1	0	.984	-1	2-58/S-1	-0.7
	KC-A	12	19	1	3	0	0	0	1	2	3	.158	.238	.158	396	17	-2	0	1	-0	1.000	-1	/2-4	-0.3
	Yr	80	219	19	46	9	0	1	12	20	24	.210	.276	.265	541	57	-12	2	2	-0	.985	-2	2-62/S-1	-1.0
Total	12	1444	5296	731	1366	178	62	21	308	552	462	.258	.330	.327	657	78	-149	105	60	2	.979	-3	*2-1310/S-52,3-4	-4.8
■ JOHNNY BLATNIK	Blatnik, John Louis b: 3/10/21, Bridgeport, Ohio BR/TR, 6', 195 lbs. Deb: 4/21/48																							
1948	Phi-N	121	415	56	108	27	8	6	45	31	77	.260	.315	.407	722	96	-4	3			.946	-1	*O-105(105-0-0)	-1.2
1949	Phi-N	6	8	3	1	0	0	0	0	4	1	.125	.417	.125	542	53	-0	0			1.000	-0	/O-2(0-0-2)	-0.1
1950	Phi-N	4	4	0	1	0	0	0	0	2	3	.250	.500	.250	750	106	0	0			1.000	-0	/O-1(1-0-0)	0.0
	StL-N	7	20	0	3	0	0	0	1	3	2	.150	.261	.150	411	11	-3	0			.875	-2	/O-7(2-0-7)	-0.5
	Yr	11	24	0	4	0	0	0	1	5	5	.167	.310	.167	477	29	-2	0			.900	-2	/O-8(3-0-7)	-0.5
Total	3	138	447	59	113	27	8	6	46	40	83	.253	.317	.389	706	91	-6	3			.945	-3	O-115(108-0-9)	-1.8
■ BUDDY BLATTNER	Blattner, Robert Garnett b: 2/8/20, St.Louis, Mo. BR/TR, 6'0.5", 180 lbs. Deb: 4/18/42																							
1942	StL-N	19	23	3	1	0	0	0	1	3	6	.043	.185	.043	229	-29	-4	0			.900	-0	S-13/2-3	-0.4
1946	NY-N	126	420	63	107	18	6	11	49	56	52	.255	.351	.405	755	113	8	12			.976	1	*2-114/1-1	1.5
1947	NY-N	55	153	28	40	9	2	0	13	21	19	.261	.351	.346	697	85	-3	4			.947	-3	2-34,3-11	-0.4
1948	NY-N	8	20	3	4	1	0	0	0	3	2	.200	.304	.250	554	51	-1	2			1.000	2	/2-7	0.1
1949	Phi-N	64	97	15	24	6	0	5	21	19	17	.247	.371	.464	835	126	4	0			.981	-10	2-15,3-12/S-1	-0.6
Total	5	272	713	112	176	34	8	16	84	102	96	.247	.347	.384	731	102	4	18			.971	-11	2-173/3-23,S-14,1-1	0.2
■ JEFF BLAUSER	Blauser, Jeffrey Michael b: 11/8/65, Los Gatos, Cal. BR/TR, 6', 170 lbs. Deb: 7/5/87 Career OF: (1-LF 3-CF 0-RF)																							
1987	Atl-N	51	165	11	40	6	3	2	15	18	34	.242	.328	.352	679	76	-5	7	3	0	.962	10	S-50	1.0
1988	Atl-N	18	67	7	16	3	1	2	7	2	11	.239	.271	.403	674	87	-1	0	1	-0	.967	3	/2-9,S-8	0.2
1989	Atl-N	142	456	63	123	24	2	12	46	38	101	.270	.327	.410	737	107	4	5	2	0	.929	-17	3-78,2-39,S-30,/O-2C	-1.1
1990	Atl-N	115	386	46	104	24	3	8	39	35	70	.269	.338	.409	747	99	-0	3	5	-1	.961	-3	S-93,2-14/3-9,O-1C	0.3
1991	*Atl-N	129	352	49	91	14	3	11	54	54	59	.259	.360	.409	769	109	6	5	6	-1	.948	-36	S-85,2-32,3-18	-2.7
1992	*Atl-N	123	343	61	90	19	3	14	46	46	82	.262	.356	.458	814	122	10	5	5	-1	.968	-47	*S-106,2-21/3-1	-3.3
1993	*Atl-N★	161	597	110	182	29	2	15	73	85	109	.305	.405	.436	841	124	24	16	6	1	.970	-23	*S-161	1.6
1994	Atl-N	96	380	56	98	21	4	6	45	38	64	.258	.333	.382	715	84	-9	1	3	-1	.970	3	S-96	0.2
1995	*Atl-N	115	431	60	91	16	2	12	31	57	107	.211	.320	.341	661	72	-17	8	5	0	.970	-1	*S-115	-0.7
1996	*Atl-N	83	265	48	65	14	1	10	35	40	54	.245	.357	.419	776	98	0	6	0	1	.926	-22	S-79	-1.3
1997	*Atl-N★	151	519	90	160	31	4	17	70	70	101	.308	.411	.482	892	130	26	5	1	1	.973	-29	*S-149/D-1	1.0
1998	*Chi-N	119	361	49	79	11	3	4	26	60	93	.219	.343	.299	642	68	-15	2	2	-0	.965	-22	*S-106	-2.8
1999	Chi-N	104	200	41	48	5	2	9	26	26	52	.240	.350	.420	770	95	-1	2	2	-0	.961	-14	2-25,S-22,3-18,/O-1L	-1.3
Total	13	1407	4522	691	1187	217	33	122	513	569	937	.262	.356	.406	762	101	21	65	41	-0	.964	-196	*S-1100,2-140,3/OD	-8.9
■ MARV BLAYLOCK	Blaylock, Marvin Edward b: 9/30/29, Ft.Smith, Ark. d: 10/23/93, Conway, Ark. BL/TL, 6'1.5", 175 lbs. Deb: 9/26/50																							
1950	NY-N	1	1	0	0	0	0	0	0	0	0	.000	.000	.000	0	-99	-0	0			.000	0	H	0.0
1955	Phi-N	113	259	30	54	7	7	3	24	31	43	.208	.296	.324	620	66	-13	6	1	1	.991	3	1-77/O-6(4-0-2)	-1.2
1956	Phi-N	136	460	61	117	14	8	10	50	50	86	.254	.330	.385	715	93	-4	5	1	1	.992	-5	*1-124/O-1(0-0-2)	-1.6
1957	Phi-N	37	26	5	4	0	0	2	4	3	8	.154	.313	.385	697	89	-0	0	0	0	1.000	0	1-12/O-1(0-0-1)	0.0
Total	4	287	746	96	175	21	15	15	78	84	137	.235	.317	.363	680	83	-18	11	2		.992	-2	1-213/O-8(4-0-5)	-2.8
■ CURT BLEFARY	Blefary, Curtis Le Roy b: 7/5/43, Brooklyn, N.Y. BL/TR, 6'2", 195 lbs. Deb: 4/14/65 Career OF: (323-LF 0-CF 232-RF)																							
1965	Bal-A	144	462	72	120	23	4	22	70	88	73	.260	.382	.470	851	138	25	4	2	0	.979	2	*O-136(63-0-73)	2.0
1966	*Bal-A	131	419	73	107	14	3	23	64	73	56	.255	.373	.468	841	142	25	1	4	-1	.976	-3	*O-109(109-0-0),1-20	1.5
1967	Bal-A	155	554	69	134	19	5	22	81	73	94	.242	.339	.413	752	122	16	4	4	-1	.968	13	*O-103(86-0-19),1-52	2.2
1968	Bal-A	137	451	50	90	8	1	15	39	65	66	.200	.306	.322	627	90	-4	6	3	0	.962	-9	O-92L,C-40,1-12	-2.0
1969	Hou-N	155	542	66	137	26	7	12	67	77	79	.253	.350	.393	743	110	8	8	7	-1	.987	6	*1-152/O-1(1-0-0)	0.1
1970	NY-A	99	269	34	57	6	0	9	37	43	37	.212	.327	.335	662	87	-4	1	3	-1	.972	-11	O-79(0-0-79)/1-6	-2.0
1971	NY-A	21	36	4	7	1	0	1	2	3	5	.194	.256	.306	562	62	-2	0	0	0	.875	-1	/O-6(0-0-6),1-4	-0.3
	*Oak-A	50	101	15	22	2	0	5	12	15	15	.218	.325	.386	711	103	0	0	1	-0	.975	-5	C-14,O-14L/3-5,2-2	-0.5
	Yr	71	137	19	29	3	0	6	14	18	20	.212	.308	.365	673	93	-1	0	1	-0	.958	-5	O-20R,C-14/3-5,12	-0.8
1972	Oak-A	8	11	1	5	2	0	0	1	0	1	.455	.455	.636	1091	234	2	0	0	0	.000	-0	/1-1,2-1,O-1(1-0-0)	0.1
	SD-N	74	102	10	20	3	0	3	9	19	18	.196	.322	.314	636	88	-1	0	0	0	.982	-8	C-12/1-6,3-3,O-3R	-1.0
Total	8	974	2947	394	699	104	20	112	382	456	444	.237	.345	.400	745	115	65	24	24	-3	.972	-15	O-544L,1-253/C-66,32	0.1
■ IKE BLESSITT	Blessitt, Isaiah b: 9/30/49, Detroit, Mich. BR/TR, 5'11", 185 lbs. Deb: 9/7/72																							
1972	Det-A	4	5	0	0	0	0	0	0	0	2	.000	.000	.000	0	-97	-1	0	0	0	1.000	-0	/O-1(1-0-1)	-0.2
■ NED BLIGH	Bligh, Edwin Forrest b: 6/30/1864, Brooklyn, N.Y. d: 4/18/1892, Brooklyn, N.Y. BR/TR, 5'11", 172 lbs. Deb: 6/26/1886																							
1886	Bal-a	3	9	0	0	0	0	0	0	1		.000	.100	.000	100	-69	-2	0			.833	-2	/C-3	-0.3
1888	Cin-a	3	5	0	0	0	0	0	0	0		.000	.000	.000	0	-95	-1	0			1.000	-1	/C-2,O-1(0-0-1)	-0.2
1889	Col-a	28	93	6	13	1	1	0	5	4	14	.140	.200	.172	372	7	-11	2			.927	-3	C-28	-1.0
1890	Col-a	8	29	2	6	2	0	0	5	2		.207	.258	.276	534	62	-1	0			.933	2	/C-8	0.1
	*Lou-a	24	73	9	15	0	0	1	9	9		.205	.293	.247	539	60	-3	1			.921	-0	C-24	-0.2
	Yr	32	102	11	21	2	0	1	14	11		.206	.283	.255	538	61	-5	1			.925	1	C-32	-0.1
Total	4	66	209	17	34	3	1	1	19	16	14	.163	.232	.201	433	28	-19	3			.923	-5	/C-65,O-1(0-0-1)	-1.6
■ ELMER BLISS	Bliss, Elmer Ward b: 3/9/1875, Penfield, Pa. d: 3/18/62, Bradford, Pa. BL/TR, 6', 180 lbs. Deb: 9/28/03																							
1903	NY-A	1	3	0	0	0	0	0	0	0		.000	.000	.000	0	-94	-1	0			.000	-0	/P-1	0.0
1904	NY-A	1	1	0	0	0	0	0	0	0		.000	.000	.000	0	-96	-0	0			.000	-0	/O-1(0-0-1)	-0.1
Total	2	2	4	0	0	0	0	0	0	0		.000	.000	.000	0	-94	-1	0			—	-1	/O-1(0-0-1),P-1	-0.1
■ FRANK BLISS	Bliss, Frank Eugene b: 12/10/1852, Chicago, Ill. d: 1/8/29, Nashville, Tenn. Deb: 6/20/1878																							
1878	Mil-N	2	8	1	1	0	0	0	0	0	0	.125	.125	.125	250	-17	-1				1.000	-0	/3-1,C-1	-0.1
■ JACK BLISS	Bliss, John Joseph Albert b: 1/9/1882, Vancouver, Wash. d: 10/23/68, Temple City, Cal. BR/TR, 5'9", 185 lbs. Deb: 5/10/08																							
1908	StL-N	44	136	9	29	4	0	1	5	8		.213	.267	.265	532	73	-4	3			.992	5	C-43	0.5
1909	StL-N	35	113	12	25	2	1	1	8	12		.221	.307	.283	590	89	-1	2			.951	1	C-32	0.3
1910	StL-N	16	33	2	2	0	0	0	3	4	8	.061	.162	.061	223	-36	-6	0			.980	-1	C-13	-0.7
1911	StL-N	97	258	36	59	6	4	1	27	42	25	.229	.341	.295	636	81	-5	5			.952	-9	C-84/S-1	-0.8
1912	StL-N	49	114	11	28	3	1	0	18	19	14	.246	.372	.289	662	84	-1	3			.973	-6	C-41	-0.4
Total	5	241	654	70	143	15	6	3	61	85	47	.219	.318	.274	591	76	-18	13			.966	-10	C-213/S-1	-1.1

YEAR	TM/L	G	AB	R	H	2B	3B	HR	RBI	BB	SO	AVG	OBP	SLG	OPS	OPS+	BR+	SB	CS	SBR	FA	FR	G/POS	TPR
■ **BRUNO BLOCK**	Block, James John (b: James John Blochowicz) b: 3/13/1885, Wisconsin Rapids, Wis. d: 8/6/37, S.Milwaukee, Wis. BR/TR, 5'9", 185 lbs. Deb: 8/5/07																							
1907	Was-A	24	57	3	8	2	1	0	2	2		.140	.169	.211	380	23	-5	0			.949	-6	C-21	-1.0
1910	Chi-A	55	152	12	32	1	1	0	9	13		.211	.273	.230	503	60	-7	3			.964	1	C-47	-0.2
1911	Chi-A	39	115	11	35	6	1	1	18	6		.304	.339	.400	739	109	1	0			.972	-3	C-38	0.1
1912	Chi-A	46	136	8	35	5	6	0	26	7		.257	.294	.382	676	96	-2	1			.980	2	C-46	0.4
1914	Chi-F	45	106	8	21	4	1	0	14	11	17	.198	.274	.255	528	47	-10	1			.966	0	C-34	-0.7
Total	5	209	566	42	131	18	10	1	69	39	17	.231	.281	.304	585	74	-22	5			.969	-5	C-186	-1.4
■ **CY BLOCK**	Block, Seymour b: 5/4/19, Brooklyn, N.Y. BR/TR, 6', 180 lbs. Deb: 9/7/42																							
1942	Chi-N	9	33	6	12	1	1	0	4	3	3	.364	.417	.455	871	161	3	2			.917	-2	/3-8,2-1	0.1
1945	*Chi-N	2	7	1	1	0	0	0	1	0	0	.143	.143	.143	286	-21	-1	0			1.000	1	/2-1,3-1	0.0
1946	Chi-N	6	13	2	3	0	0	0	0	4	0	.231	.412	.231	643	86	0	0			1.000	1	/3-4	0.1
Total	3	17	53	9	16	1	1	0	5	7	3	.302	.383	.358	742	118	1	2			.947	-0	/3-13,2-2	0.2
■ **TERRY BLOCKER**	Blocker, Terry Fennell b: 8/18/59, Columbia, S.C. BL/TL, 6'2", 195 lbs. Deb: 4/11/85																							
1985	NY-N	18	15	1	1	0	0	0	0	1	2	.067	.125	.067	192	-46	-3	0	0	0	1.000	-1	/O-5(3-1-1)	-0.4
1988	Atl-N	66	198	13	42	4	2	2	10	10	20	.212	.250	.283	533	50	-13	1	1	-0	.994	4	O-61(0-61-0)	-1.0
1989	Atl-N	26	31	1	7	1	0	0	1	1	5	.226	.250	.258	508	44	-2	1	0	0	1.000	-2	/O-8(2-2-4),P-1	-0.4
Total	3	110	244	15	50	5	2	2	11	12	27	.205	.242	.266	509	44	-18	2	1	0	.994	1	/O-74(5-64-5),P-1	-1.8
■ **WES BLOGG**	Blogg, Wesley Collins b: 1855, Norfolk, Va. d: 3/10/1897, Baltimore, Md. Deb: 6/20/1883																							
1883	Pit-a	9	34	0	5	0	0	0		0		.147	.147	.147	294	-5	-4				.881	-1	/C-6,O-3(0-0-3)	-0.4
■ **RON BLOMBERG**	Blomberg, Ronald Mark "Boomer" b: 8/23/48, Atlanta, Ga. BL/TR, 6'1", 205 lbs. Deb: 9/10/69 Career OF: (4-LF 0-CF 75-RF)																							
1969	NY-A	4	6	0	3	0	0	0	0	1	0	.500	.571	.500	1071	210	1	0	0	0	1.000	-0	/O-2(2-0-0)	0.1
1971	NY-A	64	199	30	64	6	2	7	31	14	23	.322	.366	.477	844	146	11	2	4	-1	.970	-5	O-57(0-0-57)	0.3
1972	NY-A	107	299	36	80	22	1	14	49	38	26	.268	.356	.488	844	155	20	0	2	-1	.985	-8	1-95	0.5
1973	NY-A	100	301	45	99	13	1	12	57	34	25	.329	.397	.498	895	156	22	2	0	0	.980	1	D-55,1-41	1.9
1974	NY-A	90	264	39	82	11	2	10	48	29	33	.311	.383	.481	864	150	17	2	1	0	1.000	0	D-58,O-19(2-0-17)	1.5
1975	NY-A	34	106	18	27	8	2	4	17	13	10	.255	.336	.481	817	131	4	0	0	0	1.000	0	D-27/O-1(0-0-1)	0.3
1976	NY-A	1	2	0	0	0	0	0	0	0	0	.000	.000	.000	0	-99	-0	0	0	0	.000	0	/D-1	-0.1
1978	Chi-A	61	156	16	36	7	0	5	22	11	17	.231	.281	.372	653	81	-4	0	0	0	.986	-1	D-36/1-7	-0.7
Total	8	461	1333	184	391	67	8	52	224	140	134	.293	.363	.473	835	142	71	6	7	-1	.983	-14	D-177,1-143/O-79R	3.8
■ **JOE BLONG**	Blong, Joseph Myles b: 9/17/1853, St.Louis, Mo. d: 9/16/1892, St.Louis, Mo. BR/TR, Deb: 5/4/1875																							
1875	RS-n	16	68	3	10	2	0	0	5	0	7	.147	.147	.176	324	13	-5	1	0	0	.927	3	P-15/O-4(2-2-0)	-0.1
1876	StL-N	62	266	30	62	7	4	0	30	2	9	.233	.241	.292	532	81	-5				.895	1	*O-62(0-0-62)/P-1	-0.3
1877	StL-N	58	218	17	47	8	3	0	13	4	22	.216	.230	.280	510	63	-8				.835	-3	*O-40(13-4-23),P-25	-0.7
Total	2	120	484	47	109	15	7	0	43	6	31	.225	.236	.286	522	72	-13				.867	-2	O-102(13-4-85)/P-26	-1.0
■ **JIMMY BLOODWORTH**	Bloodworth, James Henry b: 7/26/17, Tallahassee, Fla. BR/TR, 5'11", 180 lbs. Deb: 9/14/37																							
1937	Was-A	15	50	3	11	2	1	0	8	5	8	.220	.291	.300	591	51	-4	0	1	-0	.946	-1	2-14	-0.4
1939	Was-A	83	318	34	92	24	1	4	40	10	26	.289	.313	.409	722	90	-6	3	1	0	.972	14	2-73/O-5(0-0-5)	1.1
1940	Was-A	119	469	47	115	17	8	11	70	16	71	.245	.272	.386	658	73	-21	3	1	0	.978	13	2-96,1-17/3-6	-0.3
1941	Was-A	142	506	59	124	24	3	7	66	41	58	.245	.303	.346	649	75	-20	1	1	-0	.971	**35**	*2-132/3-6,S-1	2.3
1942	Det-A	137	533	62	129	23	1	13	57	35	63	.242	.295	.362	657	78	-17	2	8	-2	.972	10	*2-134/S-2	0.0
1943	Det-A	129	474	41	114	23	4	6	52	29	59	.241	.289	.344	632	79	-14	4	7	-2	.972	17	*2-129	0.9
1946	Det-A	76	249	25	61	8	1	5	36	12	26	.245	.285	.345	631	71	-10	3	3	-0	.974	-1	2-71	-0.8
1947	Pit-N	88	316	27	79	9	0	7	48	16	39	.250	.290	.345	635	66	-16	1			.979	-14	2-87	-2.5
1949	Cin-N	134	452	40	118	27	1	9	59	27	36	.261	.304	.385	689	83	-12	1			.981	-3	2-92,1-23/3-8	-1.1
1950	Cin-N	4	14	1	3	1	0	0	1	2	0	.214	.313	.286	598	58	-1	0			1.000	-3	/2-4	-0.4
	*Phi-N	54	96	6	22	2	0	0	13	6	12	.229	.275	.250	525	40	-8	0			1.000	-2	2-27/1-7,3-2	-0.9
	Yr	58	110	7	25	3	0	0	14	8	12	.227	.280	.255	534	42	-9	0			1.000	-5	2-31/1-7,3-2	-1.3
1951	Phi-N	21	42	2	6	0	0	0	1	3	9	.143	.200	.143	343	-6	-6	1	0	0	1.000	-1	/2-8,1-6	-0.7
Total	11	1002	3519	347	874	160	20	62	451	202	407	.248	.292	.358	650	74	-135	19	22		.975	64	2-867/1-53,3-22,OS	-2.8
■ **BUD BLOOMFIELD**	Bloomfield, Clyde Stalcup b: 1/5/36, Oklahoma City, Okla. BR/TR, 5'11.5", 175 lbs. Deb: 9/25/63																							
1963	StL-N	1	0	0	0	0	0	0	0	0	0	—	—	—	—	—	0	0	0	0	.000	0	/3-1	0.0
1964	Min-A	7	7	1	1	0	0	0	0	0	0	.143	.143	.143	286	-20	-1	0	0	0	1.000	1	/2-3,S-2	0.0
Total	2	8	7	1	1	0	0	0	0	0	0	.143	.143	.143	286	-20	-1	0	0	0	1.000	1	/2-3,S-2,3-1	0.0
■ **GREG BLOSSER**	Blosser, Gregory Brent b: 6/26/71, Manatee, Fla. BL/TL, 6'3", 200 lbs. Deb: 9/5/93																							
1993	Bos-A	17	28	1	2	1	0	0	1	2	7	.071	.133	.107	240	-33	-5	1	0	0	1.000	-1	/O-9(9-0-0),D-1	-0.6
1994	Bos-A	5	11	2	1	0	0	0	1	4	4	.091	.333	.091	424	16	-1	0	0	0	.727	-0	/O-3(1-0-2),D-1	-0.2
Total	2	22	39	3	3	1	0	0	2	6	11	.077	.200	.103	303	-16	-7	1	0	0	.870	-1	/O-12(10-0-2),D-2	-0.8
■ **JACK BLOTT**	Blott, John Leonard b: 8/24/02, Girard, Ohio d: 6/11/64, Ann Arbor, Mich. BR/TR, 6', 210 lbs. Deb: 7/30/24																							
1924	Cin-N	2	1	0	0	0	0	0	0	0	0	.000	.000	.000	0	-99	-0	0	0	0	1.000	-0	/C-1	0.0
■ **MIKE BLOWERS**	Blowers, Michael Roy b: 4/24/65, Wurzburg, W.Germany BR/TR, 6'2", 210 lbs. Deb: 9/1/89 Career OF: (16-LF 0-CF 6-RF)																							
1989	NY-A	13	38	2	10	0	0	0	3	3	13	.263	.317	.263	580	66	-2	0	0	0	.852	-3	3-13	-0.4
1990	NY-A	48	144	16	27	4	0	5	21	12	50	.188	.255	.319	574	59	-8	1	0	0	.899	-8	3-45/D-2	-1.7
1991	NY-A	15	35	3	7	0	0	1	1	4	3	.200	.282	.286	568	57	-2	0	0	0	.870	-3	3-14	-0.6
1992	Sea-A	31	73	7	14	3	0	1	2	6	20	.192	.253	.274	527	47	-5	0	0	0	.984	6	3-29/1-3	0.0
1993	Sea-A	127	379	55	106	23	3	15	57	44	98	.280	.358	.475	833	120	10	1	5	-2	.951	12	*3-117/O-2L,C-1,1D	2.1
1994	Sea-A	85	270	37	78	13	0	9	49	25	60	.289	.351	.437	788	100	-0	2	2	-0	.939	10	3-48,1-20/O-9L,D-9	0.7
1995	*Sea-A	134	439	59	113	24	1	23	96	53	128	.257	.337	.474	811	107	4	2	1	0	.947	-13	*3-126/1-7,O-5(2-0-3)	-0.8
1996	LA-N	92	317	31	84	19	2	6	38	37	77	.265	.344	.394	738	102	1	0	0	0	.951	-20	3-90/1-6,S-1	-1.8
1997	*Sea-A	68	150	22	44	5	0	5	20	21	33	.293	.380	.427	807	111	3	0	0	0	.990	-0	1-49,3-10/O-6L,D-1	0.0
1998	Oak-A	129	409	56	97	24	2	11	71	39	116	.237	.305	.386	691	80	-12	1	0	0	.927	-8	*3-120/1-8,D-2	-1.9
1999	Sea-A	19	46	2	11	1	0	2	7	4	12	.239	.300	.391	691	76	-2	0	0	0	1.000	0	1-14/3-4,D-1	-0.2
Total	11	761	2300	290	591	116	8	78	365	248	610	.257	.331	.416	747	97	-13	7	8	-1	.938	-27	3-616,1-108/ODSC	-4.6
■ **BERT BLUE**	Blue, Bird Wayne b: 12/9/1877, Bettsville, Ohio d: 9/2/29, Detroit, Mich. BR/TR, 6'3", 200 lbs. Deb: 6/15/08																							
1908	StL-A	11	24	2	9	1	2	0	1	3		.375	.444	.583	1028	232	3	0			.942	1	/C-8	0.5
	Phi-A	6	18	2	3	0	0	0	1	0		.167	.167	.167	333	8	-2	0			1.000	1	/C-6	0.0
	Yr	17	42	4	12	1	2	0	2	3		.286	.333	.405	738	136	2	0			.967	2	C-14	0.5
■ **LU BLUE**	Blue, Luzerne Atwell b: 3/5/1897, Washington, D.C. d: 7/28/58, Alexandria, Va. BB/TL, 5'10", 165 lbs. Deb: 4/14/21																							
1921	Det-A	153	585	103	180	33	11	5	75	103	47	.308	.416	.427	843	117	19	13	17	-3	.990	-7	*1-152	-0.1
1922	Det-A	145	584	131	175	31	9	6	45	82	48	.300	.392	.414	807	114	15	8	5	0	.991	0	*1-144	0.5
1923	Det-A	129	504	100	143	27	7	1	46	96	40	.284	.402	.371	773	106	10	10	11	-2	.992	5	*1-129	0.4
1924	Det-A	108	395	81	123	26	7	2	53	64	26	.311	.413	.428	840	119	14	9	4	1	.986	3	*1-108	1.0
1925	Det-A	150	532	91	163	18	9	3	94	83	29	.306	.403	.391	794	104	7	19	5	2	.988	0	*1-148	-0.1
1926	Det-A	128	429	92	123	24	14	1	52	90	18	.287	.413	.415	828	115	13	13	7	0	.985	-5	*1-109/O-1(0-1-0)	0.1
1927	Det-A	112	365	71	95	17	9	1	42	71	28	.260	.384	.364	748	94	-1	13	7	0	.984	-2	*1-104	-0.8
1928	StL-A	154	549	116	154	32	11	14	80	105	43	.281	.400	.455	855	120	19	12	7	0	.989	2	*1-154	1.1
1929	StL-A	151	573	111	168	40	10	6	61	126	32	.293	.422	.429	852	115	19	12	6	1	.994	-3	*1-151	0.6
1930	StL-A	117	425	85	100	27	5	4	42	81	44	.235	.363	.351	713	79	-12	12	7	0	.987	0	*1-111	-1.7
1931	Chi-A	155	589	119	179	23	15	1	62	127	60	.304	.430	.399	829	126	31	13	3	2	.990	-3	*1-155	1.5
1932	Chi-A	112	373	51	93	21	2	0	43	64	21	.249	.364	.316	680	83	-6	17	6	2	.986	9	*1-105	-0.5

YEAR	TM/L	G	AB	R	H	2B	3B	HR	RBI	BB	SO	AVG	OBP	SLG	OPS	OPS+	BR+	SB	CS	SBR	FA	FR	G/POS	TPR
1933	Bro-N	1	1	0	0	0	0	0	0	0	0	.000	.000	.000	0	-99	-0	0			1.000	-0	/1-1	0.0
Total	13	1615	5904	1151	1696	319	109	44	695	1092	436	.287	.402	.401	803	109	127	151	85		.989	1	*1-1571/O-1(0-1-0)	2.0
■ OSSIE BLUEGE Bluege, Oswald Louis b: 10/24/1900, Chicago, Ill. d: 10/14/85, Edina, Minn. BR/TR, 5'11", 162 lbs. Deb: 4/24/22 FMC Career OF: (5-LF 0-CF 0-RF)																								
1922	Was-A	19	61	5	12	1	0	0	2	7	7	.197	.300	.213	513	37	-5	1	0	0	.925	-3	3-17/S-2	-0.7
1923	Was-A	109	379	48	93	15	7	2	42	48	53	.245	.343	.338	680	84	-8	5	3	0	.936	4	*3-106/2-4	0.2
1924	*Was-A	117	402	59	113	15	4	2	49	39	36	.281	.358	.353	711	86	-7	7	5	-0	.943	-12	*3-102,2-10/S-4	-1.2
1925	*Was-A	145	522	77	150	27	4	4	79	59	56	.287	.362	.377	739	89	-8	16	15	-2	.953	1	*3-144/S-4	0.1
1926	Was-A	139	487	69	132	19	8	3	65	70	46	.271	.368	.361	730	93	-3	12	9	-1	.952	-19	*3-134/S-8	-1.3
1927	Was-A	146	503	71	138	21	10	1	66	57	47	.274	.354	.362	716	87	-9	15	5	2	.961	15	*3-146	1.6
1928	Was-A	146	518	78	154	33	7	2	75	46	27	.297	.364	.400	763	101	1	18	6	2	.960	12	*3-144/2-1	2.3
1929	Was-A	64	220	35	65	6	0	5	31	19	15	.295	.354	.391	745	91	-3	6	4	-0	.967	2	3-35,2-14,S-10	0.3
1930	Was-A	134	476	64	138	27	7	3	69	51	40	.290	.368	.395	763	93	-4	15	8	1	.964	-1	*3-134	0.4
1931	Was-A	152	570	82	155	25	7	8	98	50	39	.272	.336	.382	718	88	-10	16	10	0	**.960**	-5	*3-152/S-1	-0.9
1932	Was-A	149	507	64	131	22	4	5	64	83	41	.258	.367	.347	714	87	-7	9	7	-0	.970	6	*3-149	0.4
1933	*Was-A	140	501	63	131	14	0	6	71	55	34	.261	.338	.325	663	77	-15	6	7	-1	.965	-8	*3-138	-1.9
1934	Was-A	99	285	39	70	9	2	0	11	23	15	.246	.306	.291	598	57	-18	2	1	0	.950	8	3-41,S-30/2-5,O-5L	-0.6
1935	Was-A★	100	320	44	84	14	3	0	34	37	21	.262	.341	.325	666	75	-11	2	2	-0	.967	1	S-58,3-25/2-4	-0.5
1936	Was-A	90	319	43	92	12	1	1	55	38	16	.288	.375	.342	716	83	-7	5	3	0	.993	0	2-52,S-23,3-15	-0.1
1937	Was-A	42	127	12	36	4	2	1	13	13	9	.283	.355	.370	725	87	-2	1	1	-0	.952	2	S-28/1-2,3-2	0.2
1938	Was-A	58	184	25	48	12	1	0	21	21	11	.261	.340	.337	677	75	-7	3	1	0	.990	1	2-38,S-10/1-1,3-1	-0.3
1939	Was-A	18	59	5	9	0	0	0	3	7	2	.153	.242	.153	395	3	-9	1	0	0	.989	1	1-11/2-2,S-2,3-2	-0.8
Total	18	1867	6440	883	1751	276	67	43	848	723	515	.272	.352	.356	707	85	-130	140	87	0	.957	4	*3-1487,S-180,2/1O	-2.8
■ OTTO BLUEGE Bluege, Otto Adam "Squeaky" b: 7/20/09, Chicago, Ill. d: 6/28/77, Chicago, Ill. BR/TR, 5'10", 154 lbs. Deb: 4/12/32 F																								
1932	Cin-N	1	0	1	0	0	0	0	0	0	0	—	—	—	—	—	0	0			.000	0	R	0.0
1933	Cin-N	108	291	17	62	6	2	0	18	26	29	.213	.278	.247	525	52	-18	0			.937	-9	S-95,2-10/3-1	-2.1
Total	2	109	291	18	62	6	2	0	18	26	29	.213	.278	.247	525	52	-18	0			.937	-9	/S-95,2-10,3-1	-2.1
■ RED BLUHM Bluhm, Harvey Fred b: 6/27/1894, Cleveland, Ohio d: 5/7/52, Flint, Mich. BR/TR, 5'11", 165 lbs. Deb: 7/3/18																								
1918	Bos-A	1	1	0	0	0	0	0	0	0	0	.000	.000	.000	0	-99	-0	0			.000	0	H	0.0
■ GEOFF BLUM Blum, Geoffrey E. b: 4/26/73, Redwood City, Cal. BB/TR (BL 2000 (part)), 6'3", 193 lbs. Deb: 8/9/99																								
1999	Mon-N	45	133	21	32	7	2	8	18	17	25	.241	.327	.504	830	109	1	1	0	0	.928	-15	S-42/2-2	-1.0
2000	Mon-N	124	343	40	97	20	2	11	45	26	60	.283	.339	.449	788	96	-3	1	4	-1	.952	1	3-55,S-44,2-13,1-11	-0.1
Total	2	169	476	61	129	27	4	19	63	43	85	.271	.335	.464	800	99	-2	2	4	-1	.953	-15	/S-86,3-55,2-15,1	-1.1
■ CHET BOAK Boak, Chester Robert b: 6/19/35, New Castle, Pa. d: 11/28/83, Emporium, Pa. BR/TR, 6', 180 lbs. Deb: 9/18/60																								
1960	KC-A	5	13	1	2	0	0	0	1	0	2	.154	.214	.154	368	1	-2	0	0	0	.957	1	/2-5	-0.1
1961	Was-A	5	7	0	0	0	0	0	0	1	1	.000	.125	.000	125	-64	-2	1	0	0	1.000	-1	/2-1	-0.2
Total	2	10	20	1	2	0	0	0	1	1	3	.100	.182	.100	282	-22	-3	1	0	0	.962	0	/2-6	-0.3
■ FREDERICK BOARDMAN Boardman, Frederick Deb: 8/29/1874																								
1874	Bal-n	1	4	0	1	0	0	0	0	0	0	.250	.250	.250	500	61	-0	0	0	0	.000	-0	/O-1(0-0-1)	0.0
■ RANDY BOBB Bobb, Mark Randall b: 1/1/48, Los Angeles, Cal. d: 6/13/82, Carnelian Bay, Cal BR/TR, 6'1", 185 lbs. Deb: 8/15/68																								
1968	Chi-N	7	8	0	1	0	0	0	0	1	2	.125	.222	.125	347	6	-1	0	0	0	1.000	0	/C-7	-0.1
1969	Chi-N	3	2	0	0	0	0	0	0	0	1	.000	.000	.000	0	-89	-0	0	0	0	1.000	1	/C-2	0.0
Total	2	10	10	0	1	0	0	0	0	1	3	.100	.182	.100	282	-14	-1	0	0	0	1.000	1	/C-9	-0.1
■ HIRAM BOCACHICA Bocachica, Hiram (Colon) b: 3/4/76, Ponce, P.R. BR/TR, 5'11", 165 lbs. Deb: 9/13/2000																								
2000	LA-N	8	10	2	3	0	0	0	0	0	2	.300	.300	.300	600	55	-1	0	0	0	1.000	3	/2-2	0.2
■ JOHN BOCCABELLA Boccabella, John Dominic b: 6/29/41, San Francisco, Cal BR/TR, 6'1", 200 lbs. Deb: 9/2/63 Career OF: (41-LF 0-CF 5-RF)																								
1963	Chi-N	24	74	7	14	4	1	1	5	6	21	.189	.250	.311	561	57	-4	0	1	-0	.996	-1	1-24	-0.7
1964	Chi-N	9	23	4	9	2	1	0	6	0	3	.391	.391	.565	957	159	2	0	0	0	1.000	-1	/1-5,O-2(2-0-0)	0.1
1965	Chi-N	6	12	2	4	0	0	2	4	1	2	.333	.385	.833	1218	227	2	0	0	0	1.000	-0	/1-2,O-1(1-0-0)	0.2
1966	Chi-N	75	206	22	47	9	0	6	25	14	39	.228	.277	.359	636	74	-7	0	1	-0	.981	1	O-33(33-0-0),1-30/C-5	-1.0
1967	Chi-N	25	35	0	6	1	1	0	8	3	7	.171	.256	.257	514	45	-2	0	0	0	1.000	-1	/O-9(4-0-5),1-3,C-1	-0.4
1968	Chi-N	7	14	0	1	0	0	0	1	2	2	.071	.188	.071	259	-19	-2	0	0	0	1.000	-1	/C-4,O-1(1-0-0)	-0.3
1969	Mon-N	40	86	4	9	2	0	1	6	6	30	.105	.172	.163	335	-6	-12	1	0	0	1.000	1	C-32	-1.1
1970	Mon-N	61	145	18	39	3	1	5	17	11	24	.269	.321	.407	727	94	-2	0	1	-0	.993	10	1-33,C-24/3-1	0.6
1971	Mon-N	74	177	15	39	11	0	3	15	14	26	.220	.281	.333	615	73	-6	0	1	-0	.979	-1	C-37,1-37/3-2	-0.9
1972	Mon-N	83	207	14	47	8	1	1	10	9	29	.227	.263	.290	553	56	-12	1	2	-0	.983	8	C-73/1-7,3-1	-0.3
1973	Mon-N	118	403	25	94	13	0	7	46	26	57	.233	.281	.318	599	63	-20	1	1	-0	.980	1	*C-117/1-1	-1.5
1974	SF-N	29	80	6	11	3	0	0	5	4	6	.138	.179	.175	354	-1	-11	0	0	0	.991	-2	C-26	-1.3
Total	12	551	1462	117	320	56	5	26	148	96	246	.219	.269	.317	587	62	-75	3	7	-2	.984	14	C-319,1-142/O-46L,3	-6.6
■ MILT BOCEK Bocek, Milton Frank b: 7/16/12, Chicago, Ill. BR/TR, 6'1", 185 lbs. Deb: 9/3/33																								
1933	Chi-A	11	22	3	8	1	0	1	3	4	6	.364	.462	.545	1007	173	3	0	0	0	1.000	-2	/O-6(3-1-2)	0.0
1934	Chi-A	19	38	3	8	1	0	0	3	5	5	.211	.302	.237	539	39	-3	0	0	0	1.000	2	O-10(9-1-0)	-0.1
Total	2	30	60	6	16	2	0	1	6	9	11	.267	.362	.350	712	86	-1	0	0	0	1.000	1	/O-16(12-2-2)	-0.1
■ BRUCE BOCHTE Bochte, Bruce Anton b: 11/12/50, Pasadena, Cal. BL/TL, 6'3", 200 lbs. Deb: 7/19/74 Career OF: (372-LF 52-CF 22-RF)																								
1974	Cal-A	57	196	24	53	4	1	5	26	18	23	.270	.335	.378	712	111	3	6	3	0	.985	-4	O-39(32-5-3),1-24	-0.5
1975	Cal-A	107	375	41	107	19	3	3	48	45	43	.285	.365	.376	741	118	10	3	4	-1	.987	-7	*1-105/D-1	-0.6
1976	Cal-A	146	466	53	120	17	1	2	49	64	53	.258	.350	.311	661	101	3	4	5	-1	.988	-2	O-86L,1-59/D-1	-1.0
1977	Cal-A	25	100	12	29	4	0	2	8	7	4	.290	.336	.390	726	101	0	3	2	-0	1.000	2	O-24(0-24-0)/D-1	0.2
	Cle-A	112	392	52	119	19	1	5	43	40	38	.304	.368	.395	763	112	7	3	2	-0	.966	5	O-76(74-3-1),1-36/D-1	0.7
	Yr	137	492	64	148	23	1	7	51	47	42	.301	.362	.394	756	110	7	6	4	-0	.974	7	*O-100L,1-36/D-2	0.9
1978	Sea-A	140	486	58	128	25	3	11	51	60	47	.263	.346	.395	741	108	6	3	4	-1	.984	-4	O-91L,D-43/1-1	-0.4
1979	Sea-A★	150	554	81	175	38	6	16	100	67	64	.316	.392	.493	884	134	28	2	2	-0	.991	5	*1-147	2.2
1980	Sea-A	148	520	62	156	34	4	13	78	72	81	.300	.385	.456	841	128	22	2	3	-1	.996	6	*1-133,D-11	1.8
1981	Sea-A	99	335	39	87	16	0	6	30	47	53	.260	.354	.361	715	102	2	1	3	-1	.995	-5	1-82,O-14(14-0-0)/D-1	-0.9
1982	Sea-A	144	509	58	151	21	0	12	70	67	71	.297	.382	.409	790	114	12	8	5	0	.988	-5	O-99L,1-34,D-12	0.0
1984	Oak-A	148	469	58	124	23	0	5	52	52	59	.264	.338	.345	683	96	-2	2	5	-1	.993	-13	*1-144/D-2	-2.4
1985	Oak-A	137	424	48	125	17	1	14	60	49	58	.295	.368	.439	807	129	18	3	1	0	.990	-9	*1-128	0.2
1986	Oak-A	125	407	57	104	13	1	6	43	65	68	.256	.358	.337	695	98	1	3	2	-0	.991	2	*1-115/D-1	-0.4
Total	12	1538	5233	643	1478	250	21	100	658	653	662	.282	.363	.396	759	114	111	43	41	-5	.992	-30	*1-1008,O-429L/D-74	-1.1
■ BRUCE BOCHY Bochy, Bruce Douglas b: 4/16/55, Landes De Bussac, France BR/TR, 6'4", 210 lbs. Deb: 7/19/78 MC																								
1978	Hou-N	54	154	8	41	8	0	3	15	11	35	.266	.315	.377	692	100	-0	0	0	0	.974	3	C-53	0.4
1979	Hou-N	56	129	11	28	4	0	1	6	13	25	.217	.294	.271	565	59	-7	0	0	0	.970	-1	C-55	-0.7
1980	*Hou-N	22	22	0	4	1	0	0	0	5	7	.182	.357	.227	584	72	-0	0	0	0	1.000	-2	C-10/1-1	-0.3
1982	NY-N	17	49	4	15	4	0	2	8	4	6	.306	.358	.510	869	141	3	0	0	0	.961	4	C-16/1-1	0.7
1983	SD-N	23	42	2	9	1	1	0	3	0	9	.214	.214	.286	500	39	-4	0	0	0	1.000	2	C-11	-0.2
1984	*SD-N	37	92	10	21	5	1	4	15	3	21	.228	.253	.435	687	90	-2	0	1	-0	.988	5	C-36	0.4
1985	SD-N	48	112	16	30	2	0	6	13	6	30	.268	.305	.446	752	109	1	0	0	0	.988	1	C-46	0.3
1986	SD-N	63	127	16	32	9	0	8	22	14	23	.252	.326	.512	838	130	5	1	0	0	.991	3	C-48	0.9
1987	SD-N	38	75	8	12	3	0	2	11	11	21	.160	.267	.280	547	47	-6	0	1	-0	.962	-4	C-23	-0.9
Total	9	358	802	75	192	37	2	26	93	67	177	.239	.300	.388	687	92	-11	1	2	-0	.979	9	C-298/1-2	0.6

YEAR	TM/L	G	AB	R	H	2B	3B	HR	RBI	BB	SO	AVG	OBP	SLG	OPS	OPS+	BR+	SB	CS	SBR	FA	FR	G/POS	TPR
■ EDDIE BOCKMAN	Bockman, Joseph Edward b: 7/26/20, Santa Ana, Cal. BR/TR, 5′9″, 175 lbs. Deb: 9/11/46 Career OF: (1-LF 0-CF 0-RF)																							
1946	NY-A	4	12	2	1	1	0	0	0	1	4	.083	.154	.167	321	-10	-2	0	0	0	.933	1	/3-4	0.0
1947	Cle-A	46	66	8	17	2	2	1	14	5	17	.258	.310	.394	704	97	-1	0	0	0	.946	9	3-12/2-4,S-1,O-1L	0.8
1948	Pit-N	70	176	23	42	7	1	4	23	17	35	.239	.309	.358	667	79	-5	2			.962	8	3-51/2-1	0.2
1949	Pit-N	79	220	21	49	6	1	6	19	23	31	.223	.296	.341	637	69	-10	3			.959	6	3-68/2-5	-0.4
Total	4	199	474	54	109	16	4	11	56	46	87	.230	.299	.350	650	74	-18	5	0		.958	24	3-135/2-10,O-1L,S-1	0.6
■ PING BODIE	Bodie, Frank Stephan (b: Francesco Stephano Pezzolo) b: 10/8/1887, San Francisco, Cal. d: 12/17/61, San Francisco, Cal BR/TR, 5′8″, 195 lbs. Deb: 4/22/11 Career OF: (293-LF 625-CF 77-RF)																							
1911	Chi-A	145	551	75	159	27	13	4	97	49		.289	.348	.407	754	114	9	14			.969	7	*O-128(0-107-21),2-16	0.7
1912	Chi-A	138	472	58	139	24	7	5	72	43		.294	.358	.407	765	123	13	12			.969	-12	*O-130(8-72-50)	-0.7
1913	Chi-A	127	406	39	107	14	8	8	48	35	57	.264	.325	.397	722	112	4	5			.968	-5	*O-119(43-76-0)	-0.8
1914	Chi-A	107	327	21	75	9	5	3	29	21	35	.229	.278	.315	593	79	-9	12	11	-1	.959	-2	O-95(2-92-1)	-2.1
1917	Phi-A	148	557	51	162	28	11	7	74	53	40	.291	.356	.418	774	138	24	13			.963	5	*O-145(145-0-0)/1-1	2.4
1918	NY-A	91	324	36	83	12	6	3	46	27	24	.256	.319	.358	677	102	-0	6			.971	4	O-90(90-0-0)	0.0
1919	NY-A	134	475	45	132	27	8	6	59	36	46	.278	.334	.406	740	107	3	15			.959	-8	*O-134(0-129-5)	-1.5
1920	NY-A	129	471	63	139	26	12	7	79	40	30	.295	.350	.446	796	106	3	6	14	-4	.968	-10	*O-129(0-129-0)	-1.9
1921	NY-A	31	87	5	15	2	2	0	12	8	8	.172	.242	.241	483	23	-10	0	1	-0	.944	-6	O-25(5-20-0)	-1.7
Total	9	1050	3670	393	1011	169	72	43	516	312	240	.275	.335	.396	731	110	36	83	26		.965	-27	O-995C/2-16,1-1	-5.6
■ TONY BOECKEL	Boeckel, Norman Doxie b: 8/25/1892, Los Angeles, Cal. d: 2/16/24, Torrey Pines, Cal. BR/TR, 5′10.5″, 175 lbs. Deb: 7/23/17																							
1917	Pit-N	64	219	16	58	11	1	0	23	8	31	.265	.297	.324	621	88	-3	6			.935	-4	3-62	-0.7
1919	Pit-N	45	152	18	38	9	2	0	16	18	20	.250	.333	.336	669	98	0	11			.930	-8	3-45	-0.7
	Bos-N	95	365	42	91	11	5	1	26	35	13	.249	.317	.315	632	94	-2	10			.960	-4	3-93	-0.4
	Yr	140	517	60	129	20	7	1	42	53	33	.250	.322	.321	643	95	-2	21			.951	-12	*3-138	-1.1
1920	Bos-N	153	582	70	156	28	5	3	62	38	50	.268	.314	.349	663	94	-5	18	15	-1	.936	-7	*3-149/S-3,2-1	-0.9
1921	Bos-N	153	592	93	185	20	13	10	84	52	41	.313	.370	.441	811	120	17	20	15	-1	.933	-12	*3-153	1.4
1922	Bos-N	119	402	61	116	19	6	6	47	35	32	.289	.349	.410	759	99	-1	14	8	0	.952	-11	*3-106	-0.4
1923	Bos-N	148	568	72	169	32	4	7	79	51	31	.298	.357	.405	762	105	4	11	8	-0	.939	-10	*3-147/S-1	0.3
Total	6	777	2880	372	813	130	36	27	337	237	218	.282	.339	.381	720	102	10	90	46		.941	-55	3-755/S-4,2-1	-1.4
■ LEN BOEHMER	Boehmer, Leonard Joseph Stephen b: 6/28/41, Flinthill, Mo. BR/TR, 6′1″, 192 lbs. Deb: 6/18/67																							
1967	Cin-N	2	3	0	0	0	0	0	0	0	0	.000	.000	.000	0	-90	-1	0	0	0	1.000	-0	/2-1	-0.1
1969	NY-A	45	108	5	19	4	0	0	7	8	10	.176	.233	.213	446	26	-11	0	1	-0	.995	1	1-21/3-8,2-1,S-1	-1.2
1971	NY-A	3	5	0	0	0	0	0	0	0	0	.000	.000	.000	0	-99	-1	0	0	0	1.000	-0	/3-1	-0.2
Total	3	50	116	5	19	4	0	0	7	8	10	.164	.218	.198	416	18	-13	0	1	-0	.933	1	/1-21,3-9,2-2,S-1	-1.5
■ TIM BOGAR	Bogar, Timothy Paul b: 10/28/66, Indianapolis, Ind. BR/TR, 6′2″, 198 lbs. Deb: 4/21/93 Career OF: (2-LF 0-CF 0-RF)																							
1993	NY-N	78	205	19	50	13	0	3	25	14	29	.244	.302	.351	653	75	-7	0	1	-0	.972	15	S-66/3-7,2-6	1.2
1994	NY-N	50	52	5	8	0	0	2	5	4	11	.154	.214	.269	484	25	-6	1	0	0	.909	8	3-22,1-14/S-7,2O	0.2
1995	NY-N	78	145	17	42	7	0	1	21	9	25	.290	.331	.359	690	85	-3	1	0	0	.971	1	S-27,3-25,1-10,/2O	-0.1
1996	NY-N	91	89	17	19	4	0	0	6	8	20	.213	.293	.258	551	49	-6	1	3	-1	1.000	8	1-32,3-25,S-19,/2-8	0.1
1997	Hou-N	97	241	30	60	14	4	4	30	24	42	.249	.325	.390	715	89	-4	4	1	1	.985	24	S-80,3-14/1-1	2.5
1998	Hou-N	79	156	12	24	4	1	1	8	9	36	.154	.210	.212	421	11	-20	2	1	0	.989	18	S-55,2-11,3-11,/D-1	0.0
1999	*Hou-N	106	309	44	74	16	2	4	31	38	52	.239	.330	.343	674	72	-13	3	5	-1	.977	27	S-90,3-12/2-1	1.8
2000	Hou-N	110	304	32	63	9	2	7	33	35	56	.207	.295	.319	614	52	-22	1	1	-0	.971	7	S-95/2-2,P-2,3-1	-0.8
Total	8	689	1501	176	340	67	9	22	159	141	271	.227	.300	.327	627	63	-82	13	12	-1	.978	108	S-439,3-117/12POD	4.9
■ TERRY BOGENER	Bogener, Terry Wayne b: 9/28/55, Hannibal, Mo. BL/TL, 6′, 193 lbs. Deb: 6/14/82																							
1982	Tex-A	24	60	6	13	2	1	1	4	4	8	.217	.288	.333	621	74	-2	2	0	0	1.000	-4	O-16(4-10-2)/D-4	-0.6
■ WADE BOGGS	Boggs, Wade Anthony b: 6/15/58, Omaha, Neb. BL/TR, 6′2″, 197 lbs. Deb: 4/10/82 Career OF: (1-LF 0-CF 0-RF)																							
1982	Bos-A	104	338	51	118	14	1	5	44	35	21	.349	.410	.441	851	126	13	1	0	0	.994	18	1-49,3-44/O-1L,D-3	2.8
1983	Bos-A	153	582	100	210	44	7	5	74	92	36	**.361**	**.449**	.486	935	147	42	3	3	-0	.947	8	*3-153	4.6
1984	Bos-A	158	625	109	203	31	4	6	55	89	44	.325	.409	.416	825	123	24	3	2	-0	.959	21	*3-156/D-2	4.2
1985	Bos-A★	161	653	107	**240**	42	3	8	78	96	61	**.368**	**.452**	.478	929	149	49	2	1	0	.965	8	*3-161	5.3
1986	*Bos-A★	149	580	107	207	47	2	8	71	**105**	44	**.357**	**.455**	.486	942	156	51	0	4	-1	.953	-1	*3-149	4.5
1987	Bos-A★	147	551	108	200	40	6	24	89	105	48	**.363**	**.467**	.588	**1055**	**173**	**63**	1	3	-1	.965	3	*3-145/1-1,D-1	**5.8**
1988	*Bos-A★	155	584	**128**	214	**45**	6	5	58	**125**	34	**.366**	**.480**	.490	**970**	165	**60**	2	3	-1	.971	-5	*3-151/D-3	5.4
1989	Bos-A★	156	621	**113**	205	**51**	7	3	54	107	51	.330	**.434**	.449	883	141	39	2	6	-2	.958	-4	*3-152/D-3	3.4
1990	*Bos-A★	155	619	89	187	44	5	6	63	87	68	.302	.389	.418	807	120	19	0	0	0	.946	-22	*3-152/D-3	-0.3
1991	Bos-A★	144	546	93	181	42	2	8	51	89	32	.332	.425	.460	885	138	32	1	2	-0	.968	1	*3-140	3.3
1992	Bos-A★	143	514	62	133	22	4	7	50	74	31	.259	.356	.358	714	94	-2	1	3	-1	.952	-1	*3-117,D-21	-0.4
1993	NY-A★	143	560	83	169	26	1	2	59	74	49	.302	.383	.363	746	105	7	0	1	-0	**.970**	20	*3-134/D-8	2.6
1994	NY-A★	97	366	61	125	19	1	11	55	61	29	.342	.437	.489	926	144	27	2	1	0	.962	13	3-93/1-4	3.7
1995	*NY-A★	126	460	76	149	22	4	5	63	74	50	.324	.418	.422	839	120	18	1	1	-0	**.981**	-6	*3-117/1-9	1.1
1996	*NY-A★	132	501	80	156	29	2	2	41	67	32	.311	.393	.389	782	99	2	1	2	-0	.974	-6	*3-123/D-4	-0.3
1997	*NY-A	104	353	55	103	23	1	4	28	48	38	.292	.377	.397	773	103	3	0	1	-0	.978	3	3-76,D-19/P-1	0.4
1998	TB-A	123	435	51	122	23	4	7	52	46	54	.280	.349	.400	749	93	-4	3	2	-0	.973	-3	3-78,D-33	-0.8
1999	TB-A	90	292	40	88	14	1	2	29	38	23	.301	.382	.377	759	94	-1	1	0	0	.942	-8	3-74/1-4,P-1,D-8	-0.9
Total	18	2440	9180	1513	3010	578	61	118	1014	1412	745	.328	.419	.443	861	130	441	24	35	-7	.962	38	*3-2215,D-108/1PO	44.4
■ CHARLIE BOHN	Bohn, Charles b: 1857, Cleveland, Ohio d: 8/1/03, Cleveland, Ohio BR/TR, 5′9″, 165 lbs. Deb: 6/20/1882																							
1882	Lou-a	4	13	0	2	0	0	0	0			.154	.154	.154	308	4	-1				.667	1	/O-2(0-2-0),P-2	0.0
■ SAM BOHNE	Bohne, Samuel Arthur (b: Samuel Arthur Cohen) b: 10/22/1896, San Francisco, Cal d: 5/23/77, Palo Alto, Cal. BR/TR, 5′8.5″, 175 lbs. Deb: 9/9/16 Career OF: (1-LF 0-CF 4-RF)																							
1916	StL-N	14	38	3	9	0	0	0	0	4	6	.237	.310	.237	546	69	-1	3			.870	-4	S-14	-0.5
1921	Cin-N	153	613	98	175	28	16	3	44	54	38	.285	.347	.398	745	101	1	26	22	-2	.973	8	*2-102,3-53	1.4
1922	Cin-N	112	383	53	105	14	5	3	51	39	18	.274	.344	.360	705	83	-9	13	8	0	.958	11	2-85,S-20	0.6
1923	Cin-N	139	539	77	136	18	10	3	47	48	37	.252	.316	.340	655	74	-20	16	19	-3	.975	5	2-96,3-35/S-9,1-1	-1.2
1924	Cin-N	100	349	42	89	15	9	4	46	18	24	.255	.293	.384	677	81	-10	9	6	-0	.941	-9	2-48,S-40,3-12	-1.3
1925	Cin-N	73	214	24	55	9	1	2	24	14	14	.257	.303	.336	639	65	-12	6	4	-0	.933	-8	S-49,2-10/O-4R,13	-1.4
1926	Cin-N	25	54	8	11	0	2	0	5	4	8	.204	.259	.278	536	46	-4	1			.931	-3	S-20	-0.5
	Bro-N	47	125	4	25	3	2	1	11	12	9	.200	.270	.280	550	49	-9	1			.965	11	2-31,3-15	0.3
	Yr	72	179	12	36	3	4	1	16	16	17	.201	.267	.279	546	48	-13	2			.965	8	2-31,S-20,3-15	-0.2
Total	7	663	2315	309	605	87	45	16	228	193	154	.261	.321	.359	679	81	-63	75	59		.966	11	2-372,S-152,3/O1	-2.6
■ BRUCE BOISCLAIR	Boisclair, Bruce Armand b: 12/9/52, Putnam, Conn. BL/TL, 6′2″, 190 lbs. Deb: 9/11/74																							
1974	NY-N	7	12	0	3	1	0	0	1	1	4	.250	.308	.333	641	81	-0	0	0	0	.923	1	/O-5(2-3-0)	0.1
1976	NY-N	110	286	42	82	13	3	2	13	28	55	.287	.350	.374	724	112	5	9	5	0	.981	-6	O-87(35-39-20)	-0.4
1977	NY-N	127	307	41	90	21	1	4	44	31	57	.293	.360	.407	767	110	5	6	4	-0	.959	-9	O-91(30-9-55)/1-9	-0.8
1978	NY-N	107	214	24	48	7	1	4	15	23	43	.224	.300	.322	622	77	-7	3	3	-0	.983	-5	O-69(12-2-58)/1-1	-1.6
1979	NY-N	59	98	7	18	5	1	0	4	3	24	.184	.216	.255	471	29	-10	0	2	-1	1.000	-2	O-24(8-0-17)/1-1	-1.4
Total	5	410	917	114	241	47	6	10	77	86	183	.263	.327	.360	687	94	-7	18	14	-1	.975	-21	O-276(87-53-150)/1-11	-4.1
■ BOB BOKEN	Boken, Robert Anthony b: 2/23/08, Maryville, Ill. d: 10/6/88, Las Vegas, Nev. BR/TR, 6′2″, 165 lbs. Deb: 4/25/33																							
1933	Was-A	55	133	19	37	5	2	3	26	9	16	.278	.324	.414	737	95	-1	0	0	0	.969	-2	2-31,3-19,S-10	-0.1
1934	Was-A	11	27	5	6	1	1	0	6	3	1	.222	.300	.333	633	66	-1	2	0	0	.864	1	/3-6,2-1	0.0
	Chi-A	81	297	30	70	9	1	3	40	15	32	.236	.275	.303	578	47	-24	2	1	0	.929	-10	2-57,S-22	-2.7
	Yr	92	324	35	76	10	2	3	46	18	33	.235	.277	.306	583	49	-25	4	1	1	.929	-9	2-58,S-22/3-6	-2.7
Total	2	147	457	54	113	15	4	6	72	27	49	.247	.291	.337	628	62	-26	4	1	1	.941	-11	/2-89,S-32,3-25	-2.8

YEAR	TM/L	G	AB	R	H	2B	3B	HR	RBI	BB	SO	AVG	OBP	SLG	OPS	OPS+	BR+	SB	CS	SBR	FA	FR	G/POS	TPR
■ BOLAND	Boland Deb: 9/4/1875																							
1875	Atl-n	1	4	0	0	0	0	0	0	0	0	.000	.000	.000	0	-99	-1	0	0	0	.750	-0	/3-1	-0.1
■ ED BOLAND	Boland, Edward John b: 4/18/08, Long Island City, N.Y. d: 2/5/93, Clearwater, Fla. BL/TL, 5'10", 165 lbs. Deb: 9/18/34																							
1934	Phi-N	8	30	2	9	1	1	0	5	0	2	.300	.300	.400	700	76	-1	1			.778	-2	/O-7(0-0-7)	-0.3
1935	Phi-N	30	47	5	10	0	0	0	4	4	6	.213	.275	.213	487	30	-4	1			.833	-3	O-10(2-2-6)	-0.7
1944	Was-A	19	59	4	16	4	0	0	14	0	6	.271	.271	.339	610	77	-2	0	0	0	.889	-1	O-14(0-0-14)	-0.4
Total	3	57	136	11	35	5	1	0	23	4	14	.257	.279	.309	587	59	-8	2	0		.852	-5	/O-31(2-2-27)	-1.4
■ CHARLIE BOLD	Bold, Charles Dickens "Dutch" b: 10/27/1894, Karlskrona, Sweden d: 7/29/78, Chelsea, Mass. BR/TR, 6'2", 185 lbs. Deb: 8/24/14																							
1914	StL-A	2	1	0	0	0	0	0	0	0	1	.000	.000	.000	0	-99	-0	0			.500	-0	/1-1	-0.1
■ CARL BOLES	Boles, Carl Theodore b: 10/31/34, Center Point, Ark. BR/TR, 5'11", 185 lbs. Deb: 8/2/62																							
1962	SF-N	19	24	4	9	0	0	0	1	0	6	.375	.375	.375	750	104	0	0	0	0	.833	-1	/O-7(7-0-0)	-0.1
■ JOE BOLEY	Boley, John Peter (b: John Peter Bolinsky) b: 7/19/1896, Mahanoy City, Pa. d: 12/30/62, Mahanoy City, Pa. BR/TR, 5'11", 170 lbs. Deb: 4/12/27																							
1927	Phi-A	118	370	49	115	18	8	1	52	26	14	.311	.361	.411	772	95	-3	8	5	0	.951	-11	*S-114	-0.2
1928	Phi-A	132	425	49	112	20	3	0	49	32	11	.264	.317	.325	641	67	-20	5	1	1	.949	-17	*S-132	-2.2
1929	*Phi-A	91	303	36	76	17	6	2	47	24	16	.251	.310	.366	676	71	-14	1	0	0	.963	-10	S-88/3-1	-1.3
1930	*Phi-A	121	420	41	116	22	2	4	55	32	26	.276	.335	.367	701	74	-16	0	0	0	**.970**	-7	*S-120	-1.0
1931	*Phi-A	67	224	26	51	9	3	0	20	15	13	.228	.282	.295	577	49	-17	1	1	-0	.954	-13	S-62/2-1	-2.4
1932	Phi-A	10	34	2	7	2	0	0	4	1	4	.206	.229	.265	493	26	-4	0	1	-0	.897	-7	S-10	-1.0
	Cle-A	1	4	0	1	0	0	0	0	0	0	.250	.250	.250	500	28	-0	0	0	0	.000	0	/S-1	0.0
	Yr	11	38	2	8	2	0	0	4	1	4	.211	.231	.263	494	27	-4	0	1	-0	.897	-7	S-11	-1.0
Total	6	540	1780	203	478	88	22	7	227	130	84	.269	.323	.354	677	72	-74	15	8	1	.957	-64	S-527/2-1,3-1	-8.1
■ JIM BOLGER	Bolger, James Cyril "Dutch" b: 2/23/32, Cincinnati, Ohio BR/TR, 6'2", 180 lbs. Deb: 6/24/50																							
1950	Cin-N	2	1	0	0	0	0	0	0	0	0	.000	.000	.000	0	-99	-0	0			.000	-1	/O-2(2-0-0)	-0.1
1951	Cin-N	2	0	1	0	0	0	0	0	0	0	—	—	—	—	—	0	1	0	0	1.000	0	R	0.0
1954	Cin-N	5	3	1	1	0	0	0	0	0	1	.333	.333	.333	667	72	-0	0	0	0	.000	-1	/O-2(0-2-0)	-0.1
1955	Chi-N	64	160	19	33	5	4	0	7	9	17	.206	.257	.287	545	45	-13	2	2	-0	.955	-3	O-51(3-49-0)	-1.8
1957	Chi-N	112	273	28	75	4	1	5	29	10	36	.275	.308	.352	659	78	-9	0	1	-0	.987	2	O-63(24-28-17)/3-3	-1.0
1958	Chi-N	84	120	15	27	4	1	1	11	9	20	.225	.285	.300	585	56	-8	0	1	-0	.940	-6	O-37(28-6-5)	-1.5
1959	Cle-A	8	7	0	0	0	0	0	0	1	1	.000	.125	.000	125	-65	-2	0	0	0	.000	0	H	-0.2
	Phi-N	35	48	1	4	1	0	0	1	3	8	.083	.137	.104	241	-34	-9	0	0	0	.938	-1	/O-9(7-1-1)	-1.0
Total	7	312	612	65	140	14	6	6	48	32	83	.229	.274	.301	574	54	-40	3	4		.966	-9	O-164(64-86-23)/3-3	-5.7
■ FRANK BOLICK	Bolick, Frank Charles b: 6/28/66, Ashland, Pa. BB/TR, 5'10", 180 lbs. Deb: 4/5/93 Career OF: (0-LF 0-CF 1-RF)																							
1993	Mon-N	95	213	25	45	13	0	4	24	23	37	.211	.300	.329	629	65	-10	1	0	0	.992	3	1-51,3-24	-1.1
1998	Ana-A	21	45	3	7	2	0	1	2	11	8	.156	.321	.267	588	55	-3	0	0	0	1.000	-0	/3-7,1-1,O-1R,D-9	-0.3
Total	2	116	258	28	52	15	0	5	26	34	45	.202	.304	.318	622	64	-13	1	0	0	.992	2	/1-52,3-31,D-9,O-1R	-1.4
■ FRANK BOLLING	Bolling, Frank Elmore b: 11/16/31, Mobile, Ala. BR/TR, 6'1", 175 lbs. Deb: 4/13/54 F																							
1954	Det-A	117	368	46	87	15	2	6	38	36	51	.236	.304	.337	641	77	-12	3	5	-1	.974	-29	*2-113	-3.6
1956	Det-A	102	366	53	103	21	7	7	45	42	51	.281	.359	.434	793	108	4	6	2	1	.978	-15	*2-102	-0.3
1957	Det-A	146	576	72	149	27	6	15	40	57	64	.259	.328	.405	732	96	-3	4	9	-2	.980	-3	*2-146	0.3
1958	Det-A	154	610	91	164	25	4	14	75	54	54	.269	.332	.392	724	92	-6	6	4	-0	**.985**	8	*2-154	1.3
1959	Det-A	127	459	56	122	18	3	13	55	45	37	.266	.341	.403	744	98	-1	2	2	-0	.987	-1	*2-126	0.8
1960	Det-A	139	536	64	136	20	4	9	59	40	48	.254	.308	.356	664	77	-17	7	4	0	.978	-5	*2-138	-1.2
1961	Mil-N★	148	585	86	153	16	4	15	56	57	62	.262	.330	.379	710	93	-6	7	3	0	**.988**	1	*2-148	0.8
1962	Mil-N★	122	406	45	110	17	4	9	43	35	45	.271	.335	.399	734	99	-1	2	2	-0	**.989**	-9	*2-119	0.0
1963	Mil-N	142	542	73	132	18	2	5	43	41	47	.244	.300	.312	612	77	-15	2	1	0	.981	-5	*2-141	-0.9
1964	Mil-N	120	352	35	70	11	1	5	34	21	44	.199	.248	.278	526	48	-24	0	1	-0	**.985**	-9	*2-117	-2.7
1965	Mil-N	148	535	55	141	26	3	7	50	24	41	.264	.295	.363	658	84	-12	0	4	-1	.976	-16	*2-147	-1.8
1966	Atl-N	75	227	16	48	7	0	1	18	10	14	.211	.248	.256	503	40	-18	1	1	-0	.983	-15	2-67	-3.1
Total	12	1540	5562	692	1415	221	40	106	556	462	558	.254	.315	.366	681	85	-113	40	38	-5	.982	-98	*2-1518	-10.4
■ JACK BOLLING	Bolling, John Edward b: 2/20/17, Mobile, Ala. d: 4/13/98, Panama City, Fla. BL/TL, 5'11", 168 lbs. Deb: 6/10/39																							
1939	Phi-N	69	211	27	61	11	0	3	13	11	10	.289	.324	.384	708	92	-3	6			.982	2	1-48	-0.5
1944	Bro-N	56	131	21	46	14	1	1	25	14	4	.351	.418	.496	914	159	10	0			.991	1	1-27	1.0
Total	2	125	342	48	107	25	1	4	38	25	14	.313	.361	.427	788	118	8	6			.985	3	/1-75	0.5
■ MILT BOLLING	Bolling, Milton Joseph b: 8/9/30, Mississippi City, Miss. BR/TR, 6'1", 180 lbs. Deb: 9/10/52 F																							
1952	Bos-A	11	36	4	8	1	0	1	3	3	5	.222	.282	.333	615	66	-2	0	1	-0	.984	6	S-11	0.4
1953	Bos-A	109	323	30	85	12	1	5	28	23	41	.263	.318	.353	671	77	-11	1	4	-1	.956	5	*S-109	0.1
1954	Bos-A	113	370	42	92	20	3	6	36	47	55	.249	.340	.368	707	84	-7	2	4	-1	.946	15	*S-107/3-5	1.6
1955	Bos-A	6	5	0	1	0	0	0	0	0	1	.200	.200	.200	400	7	-1	0	0	0	.800	0	/S-2	-0.1
1956	Bos-A	45	118	19	25	3	2	3	8	18	20	.212	.321	.347	669	68	-5	0	1	-0	.947	-8	S-26,3-11/2-1	-1.2
1957	Bos-A	1	1	0	0	0	0	0	0	0	0	.000	.000	.000	0	-95	-0	0	0	0	.000	0	H	0.0
	Was-A	91	277	29	63	12	1	4	19	18	59	.227	.279	.321	601	64	-14	2	2	-0	.982	8	2-53,S-37/3-1	-0.1
	Yr	92	278	29	63	12	1	4	19	18	59	.227	.279	.320	599	64	-14	2	2	-0	.982	8	2-53,S-37/3-1	-0.1
1958	Det-A	24	31	3	6	2	0	0	0	5	7	.194	.306	.258	564	53	-2	0	0	0	.946	2	S-13/2-1,3-1	0.1
Total	7	400	1161	127	280	50	7	19	94	114	188	.241	.314	.345	660	74	-42	5	12	-3	.952	28	S-305/2-55,3-18	0.8
■ DON BOLLWEG	Bollweg, Donald Raymond b: 2/12/21, Wheaton, Ill. d: 5/26/96, Wheaton, Ill. BL/TL, 6'1", 190 lbs. Deb: 9/28/50																							
1950	StL-N	4	11	1	2	0	0	0	1	1	1	.182	.250	.182	432	15	-1	0			1.000	-1	/1-4	-0.2
1951	StL-N	6	9	1	1	1	0	0	2	0	1	.111	.111	.222	333	-13	-1	0	0	0	.941	-1	/1-2	-0.2
1953	*NY-A	70	155	24	46	6	4	6	24	21	31	.297	.384	.503	887	143	9	1	0	0	.983	-4	1-43	0.4
1954	Phi-A	103	268	35	60	15	3	5	24	35	33	.224	.320	.358	678	85	-5	1	0	0	.978	2	1-71	-0.8
1955	KC-A	12	9	1	1	0	0	0	2	3	2	.111	.333	.111	444	23	-1	0	0	0	1.000	-0	/1-3	-0.1
Total	5	195	452	62	110	22	7	11	53	60	68	.243	.337	.396	733	100	0	2	0		.980	-3	1-123	-0.9
■ CECIL BOLTON	Bolton, Cecil Glenford "Glenn" b: 2/13/04, Booneville, Miss. d: 8/25/93, Jackson, Miss. BL/TR, 6'4", 195 lbs. Deb: 9/21/28																							
1928	Cle-A	4	13	1	2	0	2	0	0	2	2	.154	.267	.462	728	87	-0	0	0	0	.955	-1	/1-4	-0.1
■ CLIFF BOLTON	Bolton, William Clifton b: 4/10/07, High Point, N.C. d: 4/21/79, Lexington, N.C. BL/TR, 5'9", 160 lbs. Deb: 4/20/31																							
1931	Was-A	23	43	3	11	1	1	0	6	1	5	.256	.273	.326	598	56	-3	0	0	0	.947	-6	C-13	-0.7
1933	*Was-A	33	39	4	16	1	1	0	6	6	3	.410	.500	.487	987	164	4	0	0	0	.889	-2	/C-9,O-1(0-0-1)	0.3
1934	Was-A	42	148	12	40	9	1	1	17	11	9	.270	.321	.365	686	80	-5	2	0	0	.981	-3	C-39	-0.5
1935	Was-A	110	375	47	114	18	11	2	55	58	13	.304	.399	.427	825	117	11	0	1	-0	.971	-23	*C-106	-0.5
1936	Was-A	86	289	41	84	18	4	2	51	25	12	.291	.349	.401	751	90	-5	1	2	-0	.979	-3	C-83	-0.3
1937	Det-A	27	57	6	15	2	0	1	7	8	6	.263	.354	.351	705	76	-2	0	0	0	.982	0	C-13	-0.1
1941	Was-A	14	11	0	0	0	0	0	1	1	2	.000	.083	.000	83	-80	-3	0	0	0	1.000	0	/C-3	-0.3
Total	7	335	962	113	280	49	18	6	143	110	50	.291	.366	.398	764	98	-2	3	3	-0	.974	-36	C-266/O-1(0-0-1)	-2.1
■ TOMMY BOND	Bond, Thomas Henry b: 4/2/1856, Granard, Ireland d: 1/24/41, Boston, Mass. BR/TR, 5'7.5", 160 lbs. Deb: 5/5/1874 MU NA OF: (0-LF 0-CF 29-RF) Career OF: (0-LF 3-CF 60-RF)																							
1874	Atl-n	55	245	25	54	10	1	0	20	1	5	.220	.224	.269	493	65	-7	0	0	0	.841	8	*P-55	0.0
1875	Har-n	72	289	32	77	11	3	0	33	0	5	.266	.266	.325	592	99	-1	5	1	1	.905	8	P-40,O-29R/1-4,2-3	0.4
1876	Har-N	45	182	18	50	8	0	0	21	0	4	.275	.275	.319	593	90	-3				.887	5	P-45	0.0
1877	Bos-N	61	259	32	59	4	3	0	30	1	15	.228	.231	.266	497	54	-13				.937	3	*P-58/O-3(0-0-3)	-0.1
1878	Bos-N	59	236	22	50	4	1	0	23	0	9	.212	.212	.237	449	44	-14				.941	1	*P-59/O-2(0-0-2)	-0.1

YEAR	TM/L	G	AB	R	H	2B	3B	HR	RBI	BB	SO	AVG	OBP	SLG	OPS	OPS+	BR+	SB	CS	SBR	FA	FR	G/POS	TPR
1879	Bos-N	65	257	35	62	3	1	0	21	6	8	.241	.259	.261	519	70	-8				**.957**	5	*P-64/O-5(0-1-4),1-1	-0.2
1880	Bos-N	76	282	27	62	4	1	0	24	8	14	.220	.241	.241	483	66	-9				.940	13	*P-63,O-26R/3-1,1-1	0.1
1881	Bos-N	3	10	0	2	0	0	0	0	0	0	.200	.200	.200	400	27	-1				1.000	1	/P-3	0.0
1882	Wor-N	8	30	1	4	0	0	0	2	2	3	.133	.188	.133	321	5	-3				.714	-3	/O-8(0-1-7),P-2,M	-0.5
1884	Bos-U	37	162	21	48	8	0	0		4		.296	.313	.346	659	101	-4				.863	1	P-23,O-17(0-0-17)/3-1	-0.3
	Ind-a	7	23	0	3	1	1	0		0		.130	.130	.261	391	25	-2				.700	-2	/P-5,O-2(0-1-1)	-0.1
Total	2 n	127	534	57	131	21	4	0	53	1	10	.245	.247	.300	546	84	-8	5	1	1	.867	17	/P-95,O-29R,1-4,2-3	0.4
Total	8	361	1441	156	340	32	7	0	121	21	53	.236	.247	.268	515	66	-58				.927	24	P-322/O-63R,3-2,1-2	-1.2
■ WALT BOND	Bond, Walter Franklin b: 10/19/37, Denmark, Tenn. d: 9/14/67, Houston, Tex. BL/TR, 6'7", 228 lbs. Deb: 4/19/60 Career OF: (57-LF 13-CF 104-RF)																							
1960	Cle-A	40	131	19	29	2	1	5	18	13	14	.221	.306	.366	673	84	-3	4	1	1	1.000	2	O-36(5-11-20)	-0.2
1961	Cle-A	38	52	7	9	1	1	2	7	6	10	.173	.271	.346	617	65	-3	1	0	0	1.000	-1	O-12(0-1-11)	-0.4
1962	Cle-A	12	50	10	19	3	0	6	17	4	9	.380	.426	.800	1226	228	9	1	0	0	1.000	-0	O-12(3-0-10)	0.8
1964	Hou-N	148	543	63	138	16	7	20	85	38	90	.254	.312	.420	732	110	6	2	2	-0	.989	-8	1-76,O-71(28-1-42)	-1.1
1965	Hou-N	117	407	46	107	17	2	7	47	42	51	.263	.339	.366	705	106	4	2	1	0	.983	-5	1-74,O-38(18-0-21)	-0.8
1967	Min-A	10	16	4	5	1	0	1	5	3	1	.313	.421	.563	984	174	2	0	0	0	.875	0	/O-3(3-0-0)	0.2
Total	6	365	1199	149	307	40	11	41	179	106	175	.256	.325	.410	736	110	14	10	4	1	.974	-11	O-172R,1-150	-1.5
■ BARRY BONDS	Bonds, Barry Lamar b: 7/24/64, Riverside, Cal. BL/TL, 6'1", 190 lbs. Deb: 5/30/86 F Career OF: (1942-LF 171-CF 1-RF)																							
1986	Pit-N	113	413	72	92	26	3	16	48	65	102	.223	.331	.416	748	102	2	36	7	5	.983	15	*O-110(0-110-0)	2.2
1987	Pit-N	150	551	99	144	34	9	25	59	54	88	.261	.331	.492	822	114	9	32	10	4	.986	20	*O-145(101-46-1)	2.7
1988	Pit-N	144	538	97	152	30	5	24	58	72	82	.283	.369	.491	860	147	33	17	11	-0	.980	5	*O-136(135-3-0)	3.5
1989	Pit-N	159	580	96	144	34	6	19	58	93	93	.248	.353	.426	779	126	21	32	10	4	.984	20	*O-156(156-0-0)	4.1
1990	*Pit-N★	151	519	104	156	32	3	33	114	93	83	.301	.410	**.565**	**974**	**172**	**53**	52	13	7	.983	15	*O-150(149-2-0)	**7.1**
1991	*Pit-N	153	510	95	149	28	5	25	116	107	73	.292	**.419**	.514	**932**	**163**	**47**	43	13	5	.991	14	*O-150(150-4-0)	**6.3**
1992	*Pit-N★	140	473	**109**	147	36	5	34	103	**127**	69	.311	**.461**	**.624**	**1085**	**207**	**73**	39	8	6	.991	11	*O-139(139-0-0)	**8.9**
1993	SF-N★	159	539	129	181	38	4	**46**	**123**	126	79	.336	**.463**	**.677**	**1140**	**207**	**87**	29	12	2	.984	5	*O-157(157-0-0)	**8.7**
1994	SF-N★	112	391	89	122	18	1	37	81	**74**	43	.312	.429	.647	1076	184	50	29	9	3	.986	8	*O-112(112-0-0)	5.6
1995	SF-N★	144	506	109	149	30	7	33	104	**120**	83	.294	**.434**	.577	**1011**	169	**56**	31	10	3	.980	15	*O-143(143-0-0)	**6.7**
1996	SF-N★	158	517	122	159	27	3	42	129	**151**	76	.308	.465	.615	1080	189	75	40	7	6	.980	10	*O-152(149-6-0)	**8.3**
1997	*SF-N★	159	532	123	155	26	5	40	101	**145**	87	.291	.450	.585	1034	173	64	37	8	5	.984	8	*O-159(159-0-0)	7.0
1998	SF-N★	156	552	120	167	44	7	37	122	130	92	.303	.442	.609	1051	184	73	28	12	2	.984	9	*O-155(155-0-0)	**7.5**
1999	SF-N	102	355	91	93	20	2	34	83	73	62	.262	.392	.617	1009	162	34	15	2	3	.984	4	O-96(96-0-0)/D-4	3.5
2000	*SF-N†	143	480	129	147	28	4	49	106	**117**	77	.306	.445	.688	1132	**194**	**73**	11	3	1	.989	10	*O-141(141-0-0)	**7.3**
Total	15	2143	7456	1584	2157	451	69	494	1405	1547	1189	.289	.415	.567	982	167	749	471	135	56	.985	169	*O-2101L/D-4	89.4
■ BOBBY BONDS	Bonds, Bobby Lee b: 3/15/46, Riverside, Cal. BR/TR, 6'1", 190 lbs. Deb: 6/25/68 FC Career OF: (65-LF 285-CF 1472-RF)																							
1968	SF-N	81	307	55	78	10	5	9	35	38	84	.254	.338	.407	745	123	9	16	7	1	.978	-3	O-80(0-35-62)	0.3
1969	SF-N	158	622	**120**	161	25	6	32	90	81	187	.259	.353	.473	826	132	26	45	4	**9**	.978	-0	*O-155(0-77-99)	2.9
1970	SF-N	157	663	134	200	36	10	26	78	77	189	.302	.376	.504	880	135	32	48	10	**7**	.969	7	*O-157(1-32-141)	3.7
1971	*SF-N★	155	619	110	178	32	4	33	102	62	137	.288	.357	.512	869	146	35	26	8	3	**.994**	3	*O-154(0-33-133)	3.5
1972	SF-N	153	626	118	162	29	5	26	80	60	137	.259	.329	.446	774	116	12	44	6	**8**	.978	11	*O-153(0-12-143)	2.4
1973	SF-N★	160	643	**131**	182	34	4	39	96	87	148	.283	.372	.530	902	141	36	43	17	4	.970	9	*O-158(0-2-158)	4.1
1974	SF-N	150	567	97	145	22	8	21	71	95	134	.256	.366	.434	800	118	15	41	11	5	.966	7	*O-148(0-8-141)	2.0
1975	NY-A★	145	529	93	143	26	3	32	85	89	137	.270	.378	.512	891	152	37	30	17	1	.987	7	*O-129(1-44-90),D-12	3.8
1976	Cal-A	99	378	48	100	10	3	10	54	41	90	.265	.341	.386	727	120	10	30	15	1	.977	5	O-98(0-0-98)/D-1	1.2
1977	Cal-A	158	592	103	156	23	9	37	115	74	141	.264	.347	.520	868	138	30	41	18	3	.986	5	*O-140(0-0-140),D-18	2.9
1978	Chi-A	26	90	8	25	4	0	2	8	10	10	.278	.350	.389	739	107	1	6	2	1	.956	1	O-22(0-0-22)/D-3	0.1
	Tex-A	130	475	85	126	15	4	29	82	69	110	.265	.361	.497	858	139	24	37	20	1	.970	5	*O-111(0-0-111),D-18	2.4
	Yr	156	565	93	151	19	4	31	90	79	120	.267	.359	.480	839	133	25	43	22	2	.968	5	*O-133(0-0-133),D-21	2.5
1979	Cle-A	146	538	93	148	24	1	25	85	74	135	.275	.371	.463	834	123	18	34	23	-1	.979	11	*O-116(0-0-116),D-29	2.1
1980	StL-N	86	231	37	47	5	3	5	24	33	74	.203	.308	.316	624	72	-8	15	5	2	.967	-5	O-70(63-0-15)	-1.5
1981	Chi-N	45	163	26	35	7	1	6	19	24	44	.215	.323	.380	703	95	-1	5	6	-1	.982	-0	O-45(0-42-3)	-0.3
Total	14	1849	7043	1258	1886	302	66	332	1024	914	1757	.268	.356	.471	827	129	277	461	169	42	.977	61	*O-1736R/D-81	29.6
■ GEORGE BONE	Bone, George Drummond b: 8/28/1876, New Haven, Conn. d: 5/26/18, West Haven, Conn. BB/TR, 5'7", 152 lbs. Deb: 9/18/01																							
1901	Mil-A	12	43	6	13	2	0	0	6	4		.302	.362	.349	711	103	0	0			.869	-2	S-12	-0.1
■ NINO BONGIOVANNI	Bongiovanni, Anthony Thomas b: 12/21/11, New Orleans, La. BL/TL, 5'10", 175 lbs. Deb: 4/23/38																							
1938	Cin-N	2	7	0	2	1	0	0	0	0	0	.286	.286	.429	714	97	-0	0			1.000	0	/O-2(2-0-0)	0.0
1939	*Cin-N	66	159	17	41	6	0	0	16	9	8	.258	.298	.296	593	60	-9	0			.989	1	O-39(6-1-32)	-1.0
Total	2	68	166	17	43	7	0	0	16	9	8	.259	.297	.301	598	61	-9	0			.990	1	/O-41(8-1-32)	-1.0
■ JUAN BONILLA	Bonilla, Juan Guillermo b: 2/12/55, Santurce, P.R. BR/TR, 5'9", 170 lbs. Deb: 4/9/81																							
1981	SD-N	99	369	30	107	13	2	1	25	25	23	.290	.338	.344	683	101	0	4	9	-2	.976	-11	2-97	-0.8
1982	SD-N	45	182	21	51	6	2	0	8	11	15	.280	.325	.335	660	90	-3	0	1	-0	.975	-8	2-45	-0.9
1983	SD-N	152	556	55	132	17	4	4	45	50	40	.237	.304	.304	608	71	-21	3	0	1	.986	-15	*2-149	-2.9
1985	NY-A	8	16	0	2	1	0	0	2	0	3	.125	.125	.188	313	-16	-3	0	0	0	.955	1	/2-7	-0.1
1986	Bal-A	102	284	33	69	10	1	1	18	25	21	.243	.311	.296	607	67	-12	0	0	0	.981	-9	2-70,3-33/D-2	-1.9
1987	NY-A	23	55	6	14	3	0	1	3	5	6	.255	.317	.364	680	81	-2	0	0	0	.965	1	2-22/3-1,D-1	0.0
Total	6	429	1462	145	375	50	9	7	101	116	108	.256	.315	.317	632	79	-40	7	10	-2	.980	-41	2-390/3-34,D-3	-6.6
■ BOBBY BONILLA	Bonilla, Roberto Martin Antonio b: 2/23/63, Bronx, N.Y. BB/TR, 6'3", 240 lbs. Deb: 4/9/86 Career OF: (202-LF 10-CF 692-RF)																							
1986	Chi-A	75	234	27	63	10	2	2	26	33	49	.269	.362	.355	717	93	-1	4	1	1	.989	-1	O-43(39-4-4),1-30	-0.5
	Pit-N	63	192	28	46	6	2	1	17	29	39	.240	.342	.307	650	79	-5	4	4	-1	.974	-7	O-51(37-6-24)/1-4,3-4	-1.5
1987	Pit-N	141	466	58	140	33	3	15	77	39	64	.300	.357	.481	838	119	12	3	5	-1	.932	-20	3-89,O-46R/1-6	-1.2
1988	Pit-N★	159	584	87	160	32	7	24	100	85	82	.274	.370	.476	846	143	34	3	5	-1	.935	-1	*3-159	3.4
1989	Pit-N★	163	616	96	173	37	10	24	86	76	93	.281	.361	.490	851	146	36	8	8	-1	.929	6	*3-156/1-8,O-1(0-0-1)	4.3
1990	*Pit-N★	160	625	112	175	39	7	32	120	45	103	.280	.329	.518	848	135	26	4	3	-0	.961	-2	*O-149R,3-14/1-3	2.0
1991	*Pit-N★	157	577	102	174	**44**	6	18	100	90	67	.302	.398	.492	890	151	41	2	4	-1	.989	3	*O-104R,3-67/1-4	4.1
1992	NY-N	128	438	62	109	23	0	19	70	66	73	.249	.349	.432	780	121	13	4	3	-0	.992	7	*O-121(0-0-121)/1-6	1.7
1993	NY-N★	139	502	81	133	21	3	34	87	72	96	.265	.357	.522	879	133	23	3	3	-0	.969	-2	O-85(0-0-85),3-52/1-6	1.6
1994	NY-N	108	403	60	117	24	1	20	67	55	101	.290	.376	.504	879	128	17	1	3	-1	.942	3	*3-107	1.9
1995	NY-N★	80	317	49	103	25	4	18	53	31	48	.325	.387	.599	986	160	27	0	3	-1	.882	-8	3-46,O-31L,1-10	1.6
	Bal-A	61	237	47	79	12	4	10	46	23	31	.333	.395	.544	939	139	13	0	2	-1	.971	1	O-39(1-0-38),3-24	1.1
1996	*Bal-A	159	595	107	171	27	5	28	116	75	85	.287	.372	.491	863	116	15	1	3	-1	.975	-2	*O-108R,D-44/1-9,3	0.3
1997	*Fla-N	153	562	77	167	39	3	17	96	73	94	.297	.383	.468	851	127	23	6	6	-1	.938	-17	*3-149/1-2,D-3	0.6
1998	Fla-N	28	97	11	27	5	0	4	15	12	22	.278	.358	.454	811	118	2	0	1	-0	.922	-5	3-26	-0.2
	LA-N	72	236	28	56	6	1	7	30	29	37	.237	.321	.360	681	84	-6	1	1	-0	.912	-11	3-59,O-12(12-0-0)	-1.6
	Yr	100	333	39	83	11	1	11	45	41	59	.249	.332	.387	719	94	-3	1	2	-0	.915	-15	3-85,O-12(12-0-0)	-1.8
1999	*NY-N	60	119	12	19	5	0	4	18	19	16	.160	.281	.303	583	49	-10	0	1	-0	.974	-1	O-25(2-0-23)/1-4,D-3	-1.2
2000	*Atl-N	114	239	23	61	13	3	5	28	37	51	.255	.357	.397	755	91	-3	0	0	0	.927	-12	O-64(63-0-1)/3-1,D-1	-1.6
Total	15	2020	7039	1067	1973	401	61	282	1152	889	1151	.280	.363	.475	838	126	259	44	56	-10	.931	-69	3-957,O-879R/1-92,D	14.8
■ LUTHER BONIN	Bonin, Ernest Luther "Bonnie" b: 1/13/1888, Greenhill, Ind. d: 1/3/65, Sycamore, Ohio BL/TR, 5'9.5", 178 lbs. Deb: 4/13/13																							
1913	StL-A	1	1	0	0	0	0	0	0	0	0	.000	.000	.000	0	-99	-0	0			.000	0	H	0.0
1914	Buf-F	20	76	6	14	4	1	0	4	7	11	.184	.253	.263	516	40	-8	3			.970	1	O-20(0-0-20)	-0.9
Total	2	21	77	6	14	4	1	0	4	7	11	.182	.250	.260	510	38	-8	3			.970	1	/O-20(0-0-20)	-0.9
■ BARRY BONNELL	Bonnell, Robert Barry b: 10/27/53, Clermont County, O. BR/TR, 6'3", 200 lbs. Deb: 5/4/77 Career OF: (395-LF 344-CF 214-RF)																							
1977	Atl-N	100	360	41	108	11	0	1	45	37	32	.300	.368	.339	707	81	-7	7	5	-0	.989	8	O-75(2-63-10),3-32	-0.1

YEAR	TM/L	G	AB	R	H	2B	3B	HR	RBI	BB	SO	AVG	OBP	SLG	OPS	OPS+	BR+	SB	CS	SBR	FA	FR	G/POS	TPR
1978	Atl-N	117	304	36	73	11	3	1	16	20	30	.240	.287	.306	593	59	-16	12	6	1	.984	-9	*O-105(53-55-11),3-15	-2.9
1979	Atl-N	127	375	47	97	20	3	12	45	26	55	.259	.312	.424	736	92	-5	8	7	-1	.983	-15	*O-124(77-74-0)/3-1	-2.4
1980	Tor-A	130	463	55	124	22	4	13	56	37	59	.268	.325	.417	742	97	-2	3	4	-1	.973	6	*O-122(5-57-61)/D-3	-0.1
1981	Tor-A	66	227	21	50	7	4	4	28	12	25	.220	.262	.339	602	68	-10	4	3	-0	.975	2	O-66(9-18-41)	-1.1
1982	Tor-A	140	437	59	128	26	3	6	49	32	51	.293	.345	.407	753	97	-1	14	2	2	.979	-18	*O-125L/3-9,D-6	-2.1
1983	Tor-A	121	377	49	120	21	3	10	54	33	52	.318	.373	.469	843	123	12	10	7	-0	.986	-13	*O-117L/3-4,D-1	-0.5
1984	Sea-A	110	363	42	96	15	4	8	48	25	51	.264	.315	.394	709	96	-2	5	2	0	.994	-11	O-94L,3-10/1-5,D-8	-1.7
1985	Sea-A	48	111	9	27	8	0	1	10	6	19	.243	.282	.342	624	70	-5	1	2	-0	.976	-1	O-22(9-0-13)/1-5,D-2	-0.7
1986	Sea-A	17	51	4	10	2	0	0	4	1	13	.196	.212	.235	447	21	-6	0	1	-0	.941	1	/O-9(9-0-0),1-8,D-2	-0.6
Total	10	976	3068	363	833	143	24	56	355	229	387	.272	.325	.389	713	89	-43	64	39	0	.982	-51	O-859L/3-71,D-22,1	-12.2
■ **FRANK BONNER**	Bonner, Frank J b: 8/20/1869, Lowell, Mass. d: 12/31/05, Kansas City, Mo. BR/TR, 5'7.5", 169 lbs. Deb: 4/26/1894																							
1894	*Bal-N	33	118	27	38	10	2	0	24	17	5	.322	.412	.441	852	101	0	12			.904	-15	2-27/O-4L,3-2,S-1	-1.0
1895	Bal-N	11	42	9	14	1	1	0	7	5	1	.333	.404	.405	809	106	1	4			.742	-5	3-11	-0.4
	StL-N	15	59	3	8	0	1	1	8	1	8	.136	.164	.220	384	-1	-9	2			.656	-5	3-10/O-5(0-0-5),C-1	-1.2
	Yr	26	101	12	22	1	2	1	15	6	9	.218	.269	.297	566	46	-9	6			.698	-10	3-21/O-5(0-0-5),C-1	-1.6
1896	Bro-N	9	34	8	6	2	0	0	5	2	8	.176	.263	.235	498	34	-3	1			.915	-1	/2-9	-0.3
1899	Was-N	85	347	41	95	20	4	2	44	18		.274	.313	.372	685	88	-7	6			.940	2	2-85	-0.1
1902	Cle-A	34	132	14	37	6	0	0	14	5		.280	.312	.326	637	80	-4	1			.907	-10	2-34	-1.3
	Phi-A	11	44	2	8	0	0	0	3	0		.182	.200	.182	382	6	-6	0			.937	-1	2-11	-0.7
	Yr	45	176	16	45	6	0	0	17	5		.256	.284	.290	574	61	-9	1			.915	-12	2-45	-2.0
1903	Bos-N	48	173	11	38	5	0	1	10	7		.220	.262	.266	528	53	-11	2			.957	-4	2-24,S-22	-1.3
Total	6	246	949	115	244	44	8	4	115	55	22	.257	.305	.333	638	73	-38	28			.931	-40	2-190/S-23,3-23,OC	-6.3
■ **BOBBY BONNER**	Bonner, Robert Averill b: 8/12/56, Uvalde, Tex. BR/TR, 6', 185 lbs. Deb: 9/12/80																							
1980	Bal-A	4	4	1	0	0	0	0	1	0	0	.000	.000	.000	0	-99	-1	0	0	0	.889	1	/S-3	0.0
1981	Bal-A	10	27	6	8	2	0	0	2	1	4	.296	.321	.370	692	99	-0	1	0	0	.976	1	/S-9	0.2
1982	Bal-A	41	77	8	13	3	1	0	5	3	12	.169	.200	.234	434	19	-9	0	0	0	.959	-5	S-38/2-3	-1.2
1983	Bal-A	6	0	0	0	0	0	0	0	0	0	—	—	—	—	—	0	0	0	0	1.000	-0	/2-5,D-1	0.0
Total	4	61	108	15	21	5	1	0	8	4	16	.194	.223	.259	482	34	-10	1	0	0	.960	-4	/S-50,2-8,D-1	-1.0
■ **ZEKE BONURA**	Bonura, Henry John b: 9/20/08, New Orleans, La. d: 3/9/87, New Orleans, La. BR/TR, 6', 210 lbs. Deb: 4/17/34																							
1934	Chi-A	127	510	86	154	35	4	27	110	64	31	.302	.380	.545	925	132	22	0	2	-1	**.996**	5	*1-127	1.3
1935	Chi-A	138	550	107	162	34	4	21	92	57	28	.295	.364	.485	849	115	11	4	0	1	.994	2	*1-138	0.1
1936	Chi-A	148	587	120	194	39	7	12	138	94	29	.330	.426	.482	908	119	21	4	2	0	**.996**	12	*1-146	1.7
1937	Chi-A	116	447	79	154	41	2	19	100	49	24	.345	.412	.573	984	146	30	5	1	1	.989	-2	*1-115	1.7
1938	Was-A	137	540	72	156	27	3	22	114	44	29	.289	.346	.472	818	111	6	2	2	-0	**.993**	3	*1-129	-0.3
1939	NY-N	123	455	75	146	26	6	11	85	46	22	.321	.388	.477	865	130	20	1			.992	5	*1-122	1.3
1940	Was-A	79	311	41	85	16	3	3	45	40	13	.273	.358	.373	731	96	-1	2	0	0	.982	-4	1-79	-1.2
	Chi-N	49	182	20	48	14	0	4	20	10	4	.264	.302	.407	709	96	-2	1			.991	5	1-44	-0.1
Total	7	917	3582	600	1099	232	29	119	704	404	180	.307	.380	.487	867	121	107	19	7		.992	27	1-900	4.5
■ **EVERETT BOOE**	Booe, Everett Little b: 9/28/1891, Mocksville, N.C. d: 5/21/69, Kenedy, Tex. BL/TR, 5'8.5", 165 lbs. Deb: 4/13/13 Career OF: (28-LF 22-CF 35-RF)																							
1913	Pit-N	29	80	9	16	0	2	0	2	6	9	.200	.256	.250	506	47	-6	2			1.000	-1	O-22(1-21-0)	-0.8
1914	Ind-F	20	31	5	7	1	0	0	6	7	6	.226	.368	.258	626	65	-2	4			.778	-2	/O-5(4-1-0),S-3	-0.3
	Buf-F	76	241	29	54	9	2	0	14	21	50	.224	.289	.278	567	54	-19	8			.959	-4	O-58R/S-8,3-2,2-1	-2.6
	Yr	96	272	34	61	10	2	0	20	28	56	.224	.299	.276	575	55	-21	12			.944	-5	O-63R,S-11/3-2,2-1	-2.9
Total	2	125	352	43	77	10	4	0	22	34	65	.219	.289	.270	559	54	-26	14			.959	-6	/O-85R,S-11,3-2,2-1	-3.7
■ **BUDDY BOOKER**	Booker, Richard Lee b: 5/28/42, Lynchburg, Va. BL/TR, 5'10", 170 lbs. Deb: 6/4/66																							
1966	Cle-A	18	28	6	6	1	0	2	5	2	6	.214	.267	.464	731	105	0	0	0	0	.964	-5	C-12	-0.5
1968	Chi-A	5	5	0	0	0	0	0	0	1	2	.000	.167	.000	167	-46	-1	0	0	0	1.000	-1	/C-3	-0.2
Total	2	23	33	6	6	1	0	2	5	3	8	.182	.250	.394	644	83	-1	0	0	0	.967	-6	/C-15	-0.7
■ **ROD BOOKER**	Booker, Roderick Stewart b: 9/4/58, Los Angeles, Cal. BL/TR, 6', 175 lbs. Deb: 4/29/87																							
1987	StL-N	44	47	9	13	1	1	0	8	7	7	.277	.370	.340	711	88	-1	2	0	0	.960	3	2-18/3-4,S-1	0.3
1988	StL-N	18	35	6	12	3	0	0	3	4	3	.343	.410	.429	839	140	2	2	2	-0	.889	-3	3-13/2-1	-0.1
1989	StL-N	10	8	1	2	0	0	0	0	0	1	.250	.250	.250	500	42	-1	0	0	0	.867	2	/2-5,3-1	0.2
1990	Phi-N	73	131	19	29	5	2	0	10	15	26	.221	.301	.290	591	64	-6	3	1	0	.976	-6	S-27,2-23,3-10	-1.0
1991	Phi-N	28	53	3	12	1	0	0	7	1	7	.226	.241	.245	486	37	-4	0	0	0	1.000	-2	S-20/3-3	-0.6
Total	5	173	274	38	68	10	3	0	28	27	44	.248	.316	.307	622	72	-10	7	3	0	.985	-5	/S-48,2-47,3-31	-1.2
■ **AL BOOL**	Bool, Albert J. b: 8/24/1897, Lincoln, Neb. d: 9/27/81, Lincoln, Neb. BR/TR, 5'11", 180 lbs. Deb: 9/29/28																							
1928	Was-A	2	7	0	1	0	0	0	1	0	0	.143	.143	.143	286	-25	-1	0	0	0	1.000	0	/C-2	-0.1
1930	Pit-N	78	216	30	56	12	4	7	46	25	29	.259	.336	.449	785	87	-5	0			.967	-1	C-65	-0.1
1931	Bos-N	49	85	5	16	1	0	0	6	9	13	.188	.266	.200	466	28	-8	0			.989	-2	C-37	-0.9
Total	3	129	308	35	73	13	4	7	53	34	42	.237	.313	.373	686	71	-15	0	0		.973	-2	C-104	-1.1
■ **AARON BOONE**	Boone, Aaron John b: 3/9/73, LaMesa, Cal. BR/TR, 6'2", 190 lbs. Deb: 6/20/97 F																							
1997	Cin-N	16	49	5	12	1	0	0	5	2	5	.245	.275	.265	540	42	-4	1	0	0	.917	-0	3-13/2-1	-0.4
1998	Cin-N	58	181	24	51	13	2	2	28	15	36	.282	.353	.409	762	99	-0	6	1	1	.950	-1	3-52/2-1,S-1	0.1
1999	Cin-N	139	472	56	132	26	5	14	72	30	79	.280	.333	.445	778	92	-7	17	6	2	.958	-1	*3-136/S-6	-0.4
2000	Cin-N	84	291	44	83	18	0	12	43	24	52	.285	.360	.471	831	103	1	6	1	1	.964	5	3-84/S-2	0.7
Total	4	297	993	129	278	58	7	28	148	71	172	.280	.342	.437	779	94	-9	30	8	4	.956	3	3-285/S-9,2-2	-0.0
■ **BRET BOONE**	Boone, Bret Robert b: 4/6/69, ElCajon, Cal. BR/TR, 5'10", 180 lbs. Deb: 8/19/92 F																							
1992	Sea-A	33	129	15	25	4	0	4	15	4	34	.194	.224	.318	542	50	-9	1	1	-0	.965	-0	2-32/3-6	-0.9
1993	Sea-A	76	271	31	68	12	2	12	38	17	52	.251	.305	.443	748	97	-2	2	3	-1	.991	-9	2-74/D-1	-0.8
1994	Cin-N	108	381	59	122	25	2	12	68	24	74	.320	.373	.491	864	124	13	3	4	-1	.974	-17	*2-106/3-2	0.0
1995	*Cin-N	138	513	63	137	34	2	15	68	41	84	.267	.329	.429	757	98	-2	5	1	1	**.994**	-16	*2-138	-1.0
1996	Cin-N	142	520	56	121	21	3	12	69	31	100	.233	.280	.354	634	65	-27	3	2	-0	**.991**	4	*2-141	-1.6
1997	Cin-N	139	443	40	99	25	1	7	46	45	101	.223	.301	.332	633	65	-23	5	5	-1	**.997**	-3	*2-136	-2.0
1998	Cin-N☆	157	583	76	155	38	1	24	95	48	104	.266	.326	.458	784	102	1	6	4	-0	.988	-5	*2-156	0.3
1999	*Atl-N	152	608	102	153	38	1	20	63	47	112	.252	.311	.416	727	82	-19	14	9	-0	.982	-3	*2-151	-1.3
2000	SD-N	127	463	61	116	18	2	19	74	50	97	.251	.330	.421	751	94	-5	8	4	0	.977	1	*2-126	0.2
Total	9	1072	3911	503	996	215	14	125	536	307	758	.255	.315	.413	728	88	-73	47	33	-1	.986	-48	*2-1060/3-8,D-1	-7.1
■ **IKE BOONE**	Boone, Isaac Morgan b: 2/17/1897, Samantha, Ala. d: 8/1/58, Northport, Ala. BL/TR, 6', 195 lbs. Deb: 4/22/22 F																							
1922	NY-N	2	2	0	1	0	0	0	0	0	1	.500	.500	.500	1000	157	0	0	0	0	.000	0	H	0.0
1923	Bos-A	5	15	1	4	0	1	0	2	1	0	.267	.313	.400	713	86	-0	0	1	-0	.929	0	/O-4(0-4-0)	-0.1
1924	Bos-A	128	487	72	164	31	4	13	98	54	32	.337	.404	.497	901	131	22	2	2	-0	.976	-7	*O-124(0-0-124)	0.5
1925	Bos-A	133	476	79	157	34	5	9	68	60	19	.330	.406	.479	885	124	18	1	4	-1	.941	-7	*O-118(0-0-118)	0.0
1927	Chi-A	29	53	10	12	4	0	1	11	3	4	.226	.268	.358	626	63	-3	0	0	0	1.000	-2	O-11(1-0-10)	-0.6
1930	Bro-N	40	101	13	30	9	1	3	13	14	8	.297	.383	.495	878	111	2	0			.960	-2	O-27(27-0-0)	-0.1
1931	Bro-N	6	5	0	1	0	0	0	0	1	1	.200	.333	.200	533	47	-0	0			.000	0	H	0.0
1932	Bro-N	13	21	2	3	1	0	0	2	5	2	.143	.308	.190	498	38	-2	0			1.000	-1	/O-8(2-0-6)	-0.3
Total	8	356	1160	177	372	79	11	26	194	138	67	.321	.394	.475	869	121	37	3	7		.960	-18	O-292(30-4-258)	-0.6
■ **LUTE BOONE**	Boone, Lute Joseph "Danny" b: 5/6/1890, Pittsburgh, Pa. d: 7/29/82, Pittsburgh, Pa. BR/TR, 5'9", 160 lbs. Deb: 9/9/13 Career OF: (0-LF 0-CF 1-RF)																							
1913	NY-A	6	12	3	4	0	0	0	1	3	1	.333	.467	.333	800	134	1	0			.857	-1	/S-4	0.0
1914	NY-A	106	370	34	82	8	2	0	21	31	41	.222	.285	.254	539	63	-17	10	18	-4	.960	23	2-90/3-9,O-1(0-0-1)	0.4
1915	NY-A	130	431	44	88	12	2	5	43	41	53	.204	.285	.276	562	68	-17	14	17	-3	.965	**21**	*2-115,S-11/3-4	0.4

YEAR	TM/L	G	AB	R	H	2B	3B	HR	RBI	BB	SO	AVG	OBP	SLG	OPS	OPS+	BR+	SB	CS	SBR	FA	FR	G/POS	TPR
1916	NY-A	46	124	14	23	4	0	1	8	8	10	.185	.252	.242	494	47	-8	7			.973	7	3-25,S-12/2-8	0.1
1918	Pit-N	27	91	7	18	3	0	0	3	8	6	.198	.263	.231	493	49	-5	1			.921	-0	S-26/2-1	-0.5
Total	5	315	1028	102	215	27	4	6	76	91	111	.209	.282	.261	543	63	-46	32	35		.964	50	2-214/S-53,3-38,O-1R	0.4

■ **RAY BOONE** Boone, Raymond Otis "Ike" b: 7/27/23, San Diego, Cal. BR/TR, 6'1", 188 lbs. Deb: 9/3/48 F

YEAR	TM/L	G	AB	R	H	2B	3B	HR	RBI	BB	SO	AVG	OBP	SLG	OPS	OPS+	BR+	SB	CS	SBR	FA	FR	G/POS	TPR
1948	*Cle-A	6	5	0	2	1	0	0	1	0	1	.400	.400	.600	1000	168	0	0	0	0	.889	1	/S-4	0.2
1949	Cle-A	86	258	39	65	4	4	4	26	38	17	.252	.352	.345	697	87	-5	0	2	-1	.947	2	S-76	0.1
1950	Cle-A	109	365	53	110	14	6	7	58	56	27	.301	.397	.430	827	116	10	4	3	-0	.945	-9	*S-102	0.6
1951	Cle-A	151	544	65	127	14	1	12	51	48	36	.233	.302	.329	631	75	-20	5	3	0	.957	-7	*S-151	-1.8
1952	Cle-A	103	316	57	83	8	2	7	45	53	33	.263	.372	.367	739	113	7	0	1	-0	.941	-10	S-96/3-2,2-1	0.3
1953	Cle-A	34	112	21	27	1	2	4	21	24	21	.241	.375	.393	768	110	2	1	2	-0	.952	-1	S-31	0.4
	Det-A	101	385	73	120	16	6	22	93	48	47	.312	.395	.556	951	156	30	2	1	0	.958	1	3-97/S-3	3.0
	Yr	135	497	94	147	17	8	26	114	72	68	.296	.390	.519	909	146	32	3	3	-0	.958	0	3-97,S-34	3.4
1954	Det-A★	148	543	76	160	19	7	20	85	71	53	.295	.378	.466	844	133	24	4	2	0	.964	2	*3-148/S-1	2.6
1955	Det-A	135	500	61	142	22	7	20	**116**	50	49	.284	.350	.476	826	123	14	1	1	-0	.953	-5	*3-126	0.8
1956	Det-A★	131	481	77	148	14	6	25	81	77	46	.308	.406	.518	924	142	30	0	0	0	.959	-7	*3-130	2.3
1957	Det-A	129	462	48	126	25	3	12	65	57	47	.273	.356	.418	774	108	6	1	1	-0	.990	-10	*1-117/3-4	-1.2
1958	Det-A	39	114	16	27	4	1	6	20	14	13	.237	.326	.447	773	103	0	0	2	-1	.988	-1	1-32	-0.3
	Chi-A	77	246	25	60	12	1	7	41	18	33	.244	.298	.386	684	89	-4	1	1	-0	.986	-2	1-63	-1.1
	Yr	116	360	41	87	16	2	13	61	32	46	.242	.307	.406	713	93	-4	1	3	-1	.986	-3	1-95	-1.4
1959	Chi-A	9	21	3	5	0	0	1	5	7	5	.238	.429	.381	810	126	1	1	0	0	.955	0	/1-6	0.1
	KC-A	61	132	19	36	6	0	2	12	27	17	.273	.396	.364	760	108	3	1	0	0	.983	1	1-38/3-3	0.2
	Yr	70	153	22	41	6	0	3	17	34	22	.268	.401	.366	767	111	4	2	0	0	.980	1	1-44/3-3	0.3
	Mil-N	13	15	3	3	0	0	1	2	4	2	.200	.368	.400	768	114	0	0	0	0	1.000	-0	/1-3	0.0
1960	Mil-N	7	12	3	3	1	0	0	4	5	1	.250	.471	.333	804	135	1	0	0	0	1.000	0	/1-4	0.1
	Bos-A	34	78	6	16	1	0	1	11	11	15	.205	.303	.256	560	51	-5	0	0	0	.994	-0	1-22	-0.6
Total	13	1373	4589	645	1260	162	46	151	737	608	463	.275	.363	.429	791	115	95	21	19	-2	.958	-46	3-510,S-464,1-285,/2	5.7

■ **BOB BOONE** Boone, Robert Raymond b: 11/19/47, San Diego, Cal. BR/TR, 6'2", 202 lbs. Deb: 9/10/72 FMC Career OF: (1-LF 0-CF 0-RF)

YEAR	TM/L	G	AB	R	H	2B	3B	HR	RBI	BB	SO	AVG	OBP	SLG	OPS	OPS+	BR+	SB	CS	SBR	FA	FR	G/POS	TPR
1972	Phi-N	16	51	4	14	1	0	1	4	5	7	.275	.339	.353	692	95	-0	1	0	0	.936	-6	C-14	-0.6
1973	Phi-N	145	521	42	136	20	2	10	61	41	36	.261	.315	.365	680	86	-10	3	4	-1	.990	6	*C-145	0.2
1974	Phi-N	146	488	41	118	24	3	3	52	35	29	.242	.298	.322	620	70	-19	3	1	0	.976	-7	*C-146	-2.0
1975	Phi-N	97	289	28	71	14	2	2	20	32	14	.246	.323	.329	652	78	-8	1	3	-1	.990	1	C-92/3-3	-0.5
1976	*Phi-N★	121	361	40	98	18	2	4	54	45	44	.271	.354	.366	719	101	2	2	5	-1	.993	-9	*C-108/1-4	-0.5
1977	*Phi-N	132	440	55	125	26	4	11	66	42	54	.284	.349	.436	786	105	3	5	5	-1	.989	3	*C-131/3-2	1.1
1978	*Phi-N★	132	435	48	123	18	4	12	62	46	37	.283	.353	.425	778	115	9	2	5	-1	**.991**	-9	*C-129/1-3,O-1(1-0-0)	0.4
1979	Phi-N★	119	398	38	114	21	3	9	58	49	33	.286	.367	.422	790	111	7	1	4	-1	.988	-12	*C-117/3-2	-0.1
1980	*Phi-N	141	480	34	110	23	1	9	55	48	41	.229	.301	.338	638	74	-17	3	4	-1	.979	5	*C-138	-0.7
1981	*Phi-N	76	227	19	48	7	0	4	24	22	16	.211	.281	.295	576	61	-11	2	2	-0	.985	-2	C-75	-1.2
1982	*Cal-A	143	472	42	121	17	0	7	58	39	34	.256	.313	.337	650	79	-14	0	2	-1	.989	7	*C-143	-0.1
1983	Cal-A★	142	468	46	120	18	0	9	52	24	42	.256	.293	.353	645	77	-15	4	3	-0	.980	4	*C-142	-0.5
1984	Cal-A	139	450	33	91	16	1	3	32	25	45	.202	.244	.262	506	40	-36	3	3	-0	.984	7	*C-137	-2.4
1985	Cal-A	150	460	37	114	17	0	5	55	37	35	.248	.308	.317	625	72	-17	1	2	-0	.987	5	*C-147	-0.6
1986	*Cal-A	144	442	48	98	12	2	7	49	43	30	.222	.291	.305	596	63	-22	1	0	0	.988	12	*C-144	-0.4
1987	Cal-A	128	389	42	94	18	0	3	33	35	36	.242	.306	.311	617	66	-18	0	2	-1	.983	0	*C-127/D-1	-1.3
1988	Cal-A	122	352	38	104	17	0	5	39	29	26	.295	.352	.386	739	110	5	2	2	-0	.986	-6	*C-121	0.5
1989	KC-A	131	405	33	111	13	2	1	43	49	37	.274	.355	.323	679	93	-2	3	2	-0	.991	4	*C-129	1.0
1990	KC-A	40	117	11	28	3	0	0	9	17	12	.239	.336	.265	601	71	-4	1	1	-0	.985	2	C-40	0.0
Total	19	2264	7245	679	1838	303	26	105	826	663	608	.254	.318	.346	664	82	-169	38	50	-9	.986	6	*C-2225/1-7,3-7,DO	-7.7

■ **BOOTH** Booth Deb: 5/1/1875

YEAR	TM/L	G	AB	R	H	2B	3B	HR	RBI	BB	SO	AVG	OBP	SLG	OPS	OPS+	BR+	SB	CS	SBR	FA	FR	G/POS	TPR
1875	NH-n	1	2	0	0	0	0	0	0	0	1	.000	.000	.000	0	-99	-0	0	0	0	.500	-0	/S-1	-0.1

■ **AMOS BOOTH** Booth, Amos Smith "Darling" b: 9/14/1853, Cincinnati, O. d: 7/1/21, Miamisburg, Ohio BR/TR, 5'9", 159 lbs. Deb: 4/25/1876 Career OF: (1-LF 0-CF 3-RF)

YEAR	TM/L	G	AB	R	H	2B	3B	HR	RBI	BB	SO	AVG	OBP	SLG	OPS	OPS+	BR+	SB	CS	SBR	FA	FR	G/POS	TPR
1876	Cin-N	63	281	31	71	3	0	0	14	9	11	.253	.285	.272	557	101	3				.760	-18	3-24,C-24,S-22,/OP	-1.1
1877	Cin-N	44	157	16	27	2	1	0	13	12	10	.172	.231	.197	428	41	-9				.853	-5	S-13,C-12,P-12,2/3O	-0.9
1880	Cin-N	1	2	0	0	0	0	0	0	0	0	.000	.000	.000	0	-99	-0				.000	0	/3-1	0.0
1882	Bal-a	1	3	0	0	0	0	0		0		.000	.000	.000	0	-99	-1				1.000	0	/3-1	-0.1
	Lou-a	1	4	0	0	0	0	0		0		.000	.000	.000	0	-99	-1				1.000	-1	/2-1	-0.1
	Yr	2	7	0	0	0	0	0		0		.000	.000	.000	0	-99	-1				1.000	-1	/3-1,2-1	-0.2
Total	4	110	447	47	98	5	1	0	27	21	21	.219	.259	.240	499	73	-8				.746	-24	/C-36,S-35,3-29,P2O	-2.2

■ **EDDIE BOOTH** Booth, Edward H. b: Brooklyn, N.Y. Deb: 4/26/1872

YEAR	TM/L	G	AB	R	H	2B	3B	HR	RBI	BB	SO	AVG	OBP	SLG	OPS	OPS+	BR+	SB	CS	SBR	FA	FR	G/POS	TPR
1872	Man-n	24	117	25	38	4	2	0	12	0	1	.325	.325	.393	718	127	4	0	0	0	.764	1	2-20/O-4(0-3-1)	0.3
	Atl-n	15	62	11	19	4	0	0	8	0	0	.306	.306	.371	677	92	-2	0	2	-1	.792	1	O-14(6-0-8)/2-1	0.0
	Yr	39	179	36	57	8	2	0	20	0	1	.318	.318	.385	704	112	2	0	2	-1	.769	2	2-21,O-18(6-3-9)	0.3
1873	Res-n	18	72	11	21	3	2	0	4	0	2	.292	.292	.389	681	109	1	0	0	0	.848	-3	O-17(15-0-2)/2-1	-0.1
	Atl-n	16	69	8	14	3	1	0	8	3	0	.203	.236	.275	511	58	-3	0	1	-0	.788	1	O-16(0-4-12)	-0.1
	Yr	34	141	19	35	6	3	0	12	3	2	.248	.264	.333	597	84	-1	0	1	-0	.818	-2	O-33(15-4-14)/2-1	-0.2
1874	Atl-n	44	185	24	47	4	3	1	16	3	3	.254	.266	.324	590	100	2	0	0	0	.809	-9	*O-44(44-0-0)/2-1	-0.5
1875	Mut-n	68	281	33	56	3	4	0	18	0	2	.199	.199	.238	438	49	-15	4	3	-0	.827	-1	*O-63(3-1-60)/2-8	-1.0
1876	NY-N	57	230	17	49	2	1	0	7	2	4	.213	.222	.232	454	59	-8				.764	-5	*O-53(0-2-51)/2-5,P-1	-1.1
Total	4 n	185	786	112	195	21	12	1	66	6	8	.248	.254	.309	563	82	-12	4	6	-1	.820	-10	O-158(68-8-83)/2-31	-1.4

■ **JOSH BOOTY** Booty, Joshua Gibson b: 4/29/75, Starkville, Miss. BR/TR, 6'3", 210 lbs. Deb: 9/24/96

YEAR	TM/L	G	AB	R	H	2B	3B	HR	RBI	BB	SO	AVG	OBP	SLG	OPS	OPS+	BR+	SB	CS	SBR	FA	FR	G/POS	TPR
1996	Fla-N	2	2	1	1	0	0	0	0	0	0	.500	.500	.500	1000	170	0	0	0	0	.000	0	/3-1	0.0
1997	Fla-N	4	5	2	3	0	0	0	1	1	1	.600	.667	.600	1267	246	1	0	0	0	.857	1	/3-4	0.2
1998	Fla-N	7	19	0	3	1	0	0	3	3	8	.158	.273	.211	483	31	-2	0	0	0	.833	-0	/3-7	-0.2
Total	3	13	26	3	7	1	0	0	4	4	9	.269	.367	.308	674	84	-0	0	0	0	.840	1	/3-12	0.0

■ **FRENCHY BORDAGARAY** Bordagaray, Stanley George b: 1/3/10, Coalinga, Cal. d: 4/13/2000, Ventura, Cal. BR/TR, 5'7.5", 175 lbs. Deb: 4/17/34
Career OF: (111-LF 170-CF 171-RF)

YEAR	TM/L	G	AB	R	H	2B	3B	HR	RBI	BB	SO	AVG	OBP	SLG	OPS	OPS+	BR+	SB	CS	SBR	FA	FR	G/POS	TPR
1934	Chi-A	29	87	12	28	3	1	0	2	3	8	.322	.344	.379	724	84	-2	1	2	-0	.938	-1	O-17(2-1-14)	-0.4
1935	Bro-N	120	422	69	119	19	6	1	39	17	29	.282	.319	.363	682	85	-9	18			.980	1	*O-105(17-61-27)	-1.2
1936	Bro-N	125	372	63	117	21	3	4	31	17	42	.315	.346	.419	766	104	2	12			.991	0	O-92C,2-11/3-6	-0.1
1937	StL-N	96	300	43	88	11	4	1	37	15	25	.293	.331	.367	698	88	-5	11			.942	-9	3-50,O-28(3-7-15)	-1.4
1938	StL-N	81	156	19	44	5	1	0	21	8	9	.282	.325	.327	652	76	-5	2			.959	0	O-29(6-14-9)/3-4	-0.6
1939	*Cin-N	63	122	19	24	5	1	0	12	9	10	.197	.252	.254	506	36	-11	3			1.000	-6	O-43(21-3-19)/2-2	-1.9
1941	*NY-A	36	73	10	19	1	0	0	4	6	8	.260	.325	.274	599	61	-4	1	0	0	.967	-3	O-19(6-0-13)	-0.7
1942	Bro-N	48	58	11	14	2	0	0	5	3	3	.241	.279	.276	555	62	-3	2			1.000	-4	O-17(0-10-7)	-0.7
1943	Bro-N	89	268	47	81	18	2	0	19	30	15	.302	.379	.384	763	120	8	6			.989	-15	O-53(28-6-20),3-25	-1.0
1944	Bro-N	130	501	85	141	26	4	6	51	36	22	.281	.331	.385	716	103	1	3			.945	-20	3-98,O-25(5-15-8)	-2.0
1945	Bro-N	113	273	32	70	9	6	2	49	29	15	.256	.328	.355	683	91	-4	7			.886	-11	3-57,O-22(9-7-6)	-1.5
Total	11	930	2632	410	745	120	28	14	270	173	186	.283	.331	.366	697	91	-32	66	2		.982	-66	O-450R,3-240/2-13	-11.5

■ **PAT BORDERS** Borders, Patrick Lance b: 5/14/63, Columbus, Ohio BR/TR, 6'2", 200 lbs. Deb: 4/6/88

YEAR	TM/L	G	AB	R	H	2B	3B	HR	RBI	BB	SO	AVG	OBP	SLG	OPS	OPS+	BR+	SB	CS	SBR	FA	FR	G/POS	TPR
1988	Tor-A	56	154	15	42	6	3	5	21	3	24	.273	.287	.448	735	102	-0	0	0	0	.973	2	C-43/2-1,3-1,D-7	0.4
1989	*Tor-A	94	241	22	62	11	1	3	29	11	45	.257	.292	.349	641	81	-6	2	1	0	.980	0	C-68,D-18	-0.4
1990	Tor-A	125	346	36	99	24	2	15	49	18	57	.286	.321	.497	819	123	9	0	1	-0	.993	0	*C-115/D-1	1.5
1991	*Tor-A	105	291	22	71	17	0	5	36	11	45	.244	.274	.354	628	70	-12	0	0	0	.993	13	*C-102	0.5
1992	*Tor-A	138	480	47	116	26	2	13	53	33	75	.242	.293	.385	679	85	-11	1	1	-0	.991	5	*C-137	0.2

YEAR	TM/L	G	AB	R	H	2B	3B	HR	RBI	BB	SO	AVG	OBP	SLG	OPS	OPS+	BR+	SB	CS	SBR	FA	FR	G/POS	TPR
1993	*Tor-A	138	488	38	124	30	0	9	55	20	66	.254	.286	.371	657	75	-19	2	2	-0	.986	5	*C-138	-0.6
1994	Tor-A	85	295	24	73	13	1	3	26	15	50	.247	.284	.329	613	57	-19	1	1	-0	.988	7	C-85	-0.6
1995	KC-A	52	143	14	33	8	1	4	13	7	22	.231	.267	.385	651	66	-8	0	0	0	1.000	-2	C-45/D-3	-0.7
	Hou-N	11	35	1	4	0	0	0	0	2	7	.114	.162	.114	276	-27	-6	0	0	0	.987	1	C-11	-0.5
1996	StL-N	26	69	3	22	3	0	0	4	1	14	.319	.329	.362	691	83	-2	0	1	-0	.984	3	C-17/1-1	0.2
	Cal-A	19	57	6	13	3	0	2	8	3	11	.228	.267	.386	653	62	-3	0	1	-0	.984	4	C-19	0.1
	Chi-A	31	94	6	26	1	0	3	6	5	18	.277	.313	.383	696	79	-3	0	0	0	.982	-1	C-30/D-1	-0.3
	Yr	50	151	12	39	4	0	5	14	8	29	.258	.296	.384	680	72	-7	0	1	-0	.983	2	C-49/D-1	-0.2
1997	Cle-A	55	159	17	47	7	1	4	15	9	27	.296	.341	.428	769	96	-1	0	2	-1	1.000	6	C-53	0.7
1998	Cle-A	54	160	12	38	6	0	0	6	10	40	.237	.291	.275	566	47	-12	0	2	-1	.974	-1	C-53/3-1	-1.1
1999	Cle-A	6	20	2	6	0	1	0	3	0	3	.300	.300	.400	700	73	-1	0	1	-0	.943	-1	/C-5	-0.2
	Tor-A	6	14	1	3	0	0	1	3	1	2	.214	.267	.429	695	72	-1	0	0	0	1.000	-0	/C-3,3-1,D-3	-0.1
	Yr	12	34	3	9	0	1	1	6	1	5	.265	.286	.412	697	73	-1	0	1	-0	.955	-2	/C-8,D-3,3-1	-0.3
Total	12	1001	3046	266	779	155	12	67	327	149	506	.256	.293	.380	673	79	-96	6	13	-3	.988	39	C-924/D-33,3-3,12	-0.9

■ MIKE BORDICK Bordick, Michael Todd b: 7/21/65, Marquette, Mich. BR/TR, 5'11", 175 lbs. Deb: 4/11/90

YEAR	TM/L	G	AB	R	H	2B	3B	HR	RBI	BB	SO	AVG	OBP	SLG	OPS	OPS+	BR+	SB	CS	SBR	FA	FR	G/POS	TPR
1990	*Oak-A	25	14	0	1	0	0	0	0	1	4	.071	.133	.071	205	-43	-3	0	0	0	1.000	-0	3-10/S-9,2-7	-0.3
1991	Oak-A	90	235	21	56	5	1	0	21	14	37	.238	.290	.268	558	59	-13	3	4	-1	.972	-4	S-84/2-5,3-1	-1.1
1992	*Oak-A	154	504	62	151	19	4	3	48	40	59	.300	.362	.371	733	111	9	12	6	1	.987	8	2-95,S-70	2.5
1993	Oak-A	159	546	60	136	21	2	3	48	60	58	.249	.335	.311	647	80	-14	10	10	-1	.982	-16	*S-159/2-1	-1.7
1994	Oak-A	114	391	38	99	18	4	2	37	38	44	.253	.324	.335	659	77	-13	7	2	1	.974	-2	*S-112/2-4	-0.4
1995	Oak-A	126	428	46	113	13	0	8	44	35	48	.264	.327	.350	677	81	-12	11	3	1	.983	7	*S-126/D-1	0.6
1996	Oak-A	155	525	46	126	18	4	5	54	52	59	.240	.310	.318	628	60	-31	5	6	-1	.979	12	*S-155	-0.7
1997	*Bal-A	153	509	55	120	19	1	7	46	33	66	.236	.285	.318	603	59	-31	0	2	-1	.980	-1	*S-153	-1.9
1998	Bal-A	151	465	59	121	29	1	13	51	39	65	.260	.331	.411	741	93	-5	6	7	-1	.990	21	*S-150	2.5
1999	Bal-A	160	631	93	175	35	7	10	77	54	102	.277	.339	.403	742	92	-8	14	4	2	**.989**	30	*S-159	3.4
2000	Bal-A★	100	391	70	116	22	1	16	59	34	71	.297	.354	.481	835	112	7	6	5	-0	.979	-17	*S-100	-0.2
	*NY-N	56	192	18	50	8	0	4	21	15	28	.260	.321	.365	685	75	-7	3	1	0	.968	-13	S-56	-1.4
Total	11	1443	4831	568	1264	207	25	71	506	415	641	.262	.327	.359	686	83	-121	77	50	-1	.981	26	*S-1333,2-112/3-11,D	1.3

■ GLENN BORGMANN Borgmann, Glenn Dennis b: 5/25/50, Paterson, N.J. BR/TR, 6'4", 210 lbs. Deb: 7/1/72

YEAR	TM/L	G	AB	R	H	2B	3B	HR	RBI	BB	SO	AVG	OBP	SLG	OPS	OPS+	BR+	SB	CS	SBR	FA	FR	G/POS	TPR
1972	Min-A	56	175	11	41	4	0	3	14	25	25	.234	.330	.309	639	86	-2	0	0	0	.965	-1	C-56	-0.1
1973	Min-A	12	34	7	9	2	0	0	9	6	10	.265	.375	.324	699	95	0	0	0	0	1.000	-2	C-12	-0.2
1974	Min-A	128	345	33	87	8	1	3	45	39	44	.252	.330	.307	637	82	-7	2	1	0	**.997**	-2	*C-128	-0.3
1975	Min-A	125	352	34	73	15	2	2	33	47	59	.207	.304	.278	583	65	-15	0	1	-0	.989	-2	*C-125	-1.3
1976	Min-A	24	65	10	16	3	0	1	6	19	7	.246	.417	.338	755	120	3	1	1	-0	.976	2	C-24	0.6
1977	Min-A	17	43	12	11	1	0	2	7	11	9	.256	.407	.419	826	128	2	0	0	0	1.000	2	C-17	0.4
1978	Min-A	49	123	16	26	4	1	3	15	18	17	.211	.312	.333	645	80	-3	0	0	0	.990	5	C-46/D-1	0.4
1979	Min-A	31	70	4	14	3	0	0	8	12	11	.200	.317	.243	560	52	-4	1	0	0	.993	7	C-31	0.4
1980	Chi-A	32	87	10	19	2	0	2	14	14	9	.218	.327	.310	637	76	-3	0	0	0	1.000	2	C-32	0.0
Total	9	474	1294	137	296	42	4	16	151	191	191	.229	.329	.304	634	79	-30	4	3	-0	.989	10	C-471/D-1	-0.1

■ BOB BORKOWSKI Borkowski, Robert Vilarian b: 1/27/26, Dayton, Ohio BR/TR, 6', 182 lbs. Deb: 4/22/50 Career OF: (59-LF 107-CF 153-RF)

YEAR	TM/L	G	AB	R	H	2B	3B	HR	RBI	BB	SO	AVG	OBP	SLG	OPS	OPS+	BR+	SB	CS	SBR	FA	FR	G/POS	TPR
1950	Chi-N	85	256	27	70	7	4	4	29	16	30	.273	.319	.379	698	84	-6	1			.975	1	O-65(7-29-30)/1-1	-0.8
1951	Chi-N	58	89	9	14	1	0	0	10	3	16	.157	.185	.169	353	-4	-13	0	0	0	.933	-4	O-25(7-9-9)	-1.8
1952	Cin-N	126	377	42	95	11	4	4	24	26	53	.252	.300	.334	634	76	-13	1	3	-1	.991	-6	*O-103(15-64-26)/1-5	-2.4
1953	Cin-N	94	249	32	67	11	1	7	29	21	41	.269	.328	.406	734	89	-4	0	1	-0	.982	-7	O-67(3-3-61)/1-2	-1.3
1954	Cin-N	73	162	13	43	12	1	1	19	8	18	.265	.304	.370	674	73	-7	0	2	-1	1.000	0	O-36(13-0-23)/1-3	-0.9
1955	Cin-N	25	18	1	3	1	0	0	1	1	2	.167	.211	.222	433	14	-2	0	0	0	1.000	-4	O-11(11-0-0)/1-1	-0.6
	Bro-N	9	19	2	2	0	0	0	0	1	6	.105	.150	.105	255	-30	-4	0	0	0	1.000	-3	/O-9(3-2-4)	-0.6
	Yr	34	37	3	5	1	0	0	1	2	8	.135	.179	.162	342	-8	-6	0	0	0	1.000	-6	O-20(14-2-4)/1-1	-1.2
Total	6	470	1170	126	294	43	10	16	112	76	166	.251	.299	.346	645	71	-48	2	6		.982	-22	O-316R/1-12	-8.4

■ RED BOROM Borom, Edward Jones b: 10/30/16, Spartanburg, S.C. BL/TR, 5'10", 175 lbs. Deb: 4/23/44

YEAR	TM/L	G	AB	R	H	2B	3B	HR	RBI	BB	SO	AVG	OBP	SLG	OPS	OPS+	BR+	SB	CS	SBR	FA	FR	G/POS	TPR
1944	Det-A	7	14	1	1	0	0	0	1	2	2	.071	.188	.071	259	-23	-2	0	0	0	.950	1	/2-4,S-1	-0.1
1945	*Det-A	55	130	19	35	4	0	0	9	7	8	.269	.307	.300	607	72	-5	4	2	0	.966	5	2-28/3-4,S-2	0.2
Total	2	62	144	20	36	4	0	0	10	9	10	.250	.294	.278	572	62	-7	4	2	0	.964	6	/2-32,3-4,S-3	0.1

■ STEVE BOROS Boros, Stephen b: 9/3/36, Flint, Mich. BR/TR, 6', 185 lbs. Deb: 6/19/57 MC Career OF: (0-LF 0-CF 11-RF)

YEAR	TM/L	G	AB	R	H	2B	3B	HR	RBI	BB	SO	AVG	OBP	SLG	OPS	OPS+	BR+	SB	CS	SBR	FA	FR	G/POS	TPR
1957	Det-A	24	41	4	6	1	0	0	2	1	8	.146	.167	.171	337	-7	-6	0	0	0	.906	3	/3-9,S-5	-0.3
1958	Det-A	6	2	0	0	0	0	0	0	0	0	.000	.000	.000	0	-93	-1	0	0	0	1.000	0	/2-1	0.0
1961	Det-A	116	396	51	107	18	2	5	62	68	42	.270	.388	.364	751	99	3	4	2	0	.953	-21	*3-116	-1.8
1962	Det-A	116	356	46	81	14	1	16	47	53	62	.228	.333	.407	740	95	-2	3	1	0	.931	-15	*3-105/2-6	-1.7
1963	Chi-N	41	90	9	19	5	1	3	7	12	19	.211	.304	.389	693	93	-1	0	2	-1	.975	-3	1-14,O-11(0-0-11)	-0.6
1964	Cin-N	117	370	31	95	12	3	2	31	47	43	.257	.344	.322	665	86	-5	4	1	1	.961	4	*3-114	-0.2
1965	Cin-N	2	0	0	0	0	0	0	0	0	0	—	—	—	—	—	0	0	0	0	1.000	0	/3-2	0.0
Total	7	422	1255	141	308	50	7	26	149	181	174	.245	.346	.359	705	90	-12	11	6	0	.948	-31	3-346/1-14,O-11R,2S	-4.6

■ BABE BORTON Borton, William Baker b: 8/14/1888, Marion, Ill. d: 7/29/54, Berkeley, Cal. BL/TL, 6', 178 lbs. Deb: 9/2/12

YEAR	TM/L	G	AB	R	H	2B	3B	HR	RBI	BB	SO	AVG	OBP	SLG	OPS	OPS+	BR+	SB	CS	SBR	FA	FR	G/POS	TPR
1912	Chi-A	31	105	15	39	3	1	0	17	8		.371	.416	.419	835	143	6	1			.997	0	1-30	0.6
1913	Chi-A	28	80	9	22	5	0	0	13	23	5	.275	.442	.338	780	130	5	1			.991	-2	1-26	0.3
	NY-A	33	108	8	14	2	0	0	11	18	19	.130	.260	.148	408	20	-10	1			.978	4	1-33	-0.8
	Yr	61	188	17	36	7	0	0	24	41	24	.191	.342	.229	571	68	-5	2			.984	3	1-59	-0.5
1915	StL-F	159	549	**97**	157	20	14	3	83	**92**	64	.286	.395	.390	785	115	8	17			.993	-10	*1-159	-0.6
1916	StL-A	66	98	10	22	1	2	1	12	19	13	.224	.350	.306	657	102	1	1			.991	-1	1-22	-0.1
Total	4	317	940	139	254	31	17	4	136	160	101	.270	.381	.352	734	108	9	21			.991	-8	1-270	-0.6

■ DON BOSCH Bosch, Donald John b: 7/15/42, San Francisco, Cal BB/TR, 5'10", 160 lbs. Deb: 9/19/66

YEAR	TM/L	G	AB	R	H	2B	3B	HR	RBI	BB	SO	AVG	OBP	SLG	OPS	OPS+	BR+	SB	CS	SBR	FA	FR	G/POS	TPR
1966	Pit-N	3	2	0	0	0	0	0	0	0	0	.000	.000	.000	0	-99	-1	0	0	0	.000	-0	/O-1(0-1-0)	-0.1
1967	NY-N	44	93	7	13	0	1	0	2	5	24	.140	.184	.161	345	-0	-12	3	1	0	1.000	-4	O-39(0-39-0)	-1.8
1968	NY-N	50	111	14	19	1	0	3	7	9	33	.171	.233	.261	495	48	-7	0	2	-1	.974	2	O-33(4-30-0)	-0.8
1969	Mon-N	49	112	13	20	5	0	1	4	8	20	.179	.233	.250	483	35	-10	1	0	0	.964	-3	O-32(2-29-1)	-1.4
Total	4	146	318	34	52	6	1	4	13	22	77	.164	.218	.226	444	28	-29	4	3	-0	.979	-5	O-105(6-99-1)	-4.1

■ RICK BOSETTI Bosetti, Richard Alan b: 8/5/53, Redding, Cal. BR/TR, 5'11", 185 lbs. Deb: 9/9/76

YEAR	TM/L	G	AB	R	H	2B	3B	HR	RBI	BB	SO	AVG	OBP	SLG	OPS	OPS+	BR+	SB	CS	SBR	FA	FR	G/POS	TPR
1976	Phi-N	13	18	6	5	1	0	0	0	1	3	.278	.316	.333	649	82	-0	3	0	1	1.000	-0	/O-6(1-4-1)	0.0
1977	StL-N	41	69	12	16	0	0	0	3	6	11	.232	.303	.232	535	47	-5	4	4	-1	1.000	-4	O-35(27-7-3)	-1.0
1978	Tor-A	136	568	61	147	25	5	5	42	30	65	.259	.300	.347	646	80	-16	6	10	-2	.986	25	*O-135(0-135-0)	0.6
1979	Tor-A	162	619	59	161	35	2	8	65	22	70	.260	.289	.362	651	73	-24	13	12	-1	.974	17	*O-162(0-162-0)	-0.9
1980	Tor-A	53	188	24	40	7	1	4	18	15	29	.213	.278	.324	603	62	-10	4	6	-1	.985	-1	O-51(0-51-0)	-1.3
1981	Tor-A	25	47	5	11	2	0	0	4	2	6	.234	.265	.277	542	53	-3	0	2	-1	1.000	-2	O-19(5-13-2)/D-1	-0.6
	*Oak-A	9	19	4	2	0	0	0	1	3	3	.105	.227	.105	333	-2	-2	0	0	0	1.000	-0	/O-5(0-4-1),D-2	-0.3
	Yr	34	66	9	13	2	0	0	5	5	9	.197	.254	.227	481	38	-5	0	2	-1	1.000	-2	O-24(5-17-3)/D-3	-0.9
1982	Oak-A	6	15	1	3	0	0	0	0	0	1	.200	.200	.200	400	11	-2	0	0	0	1.000	1	/O-6(0-6-0)	-0.1
Total	7	445	1543	172	385	70	8	17	133	79	188	.250	.290	.338	628	71	-62	30	34	-5	.982	37	O-419(33-382-7)/D-3	-3.6

■ THAD BOSLEY Bosley, Thaddis b: 9/17/56, Oceanside, Cal. BL/TL, 6'3", 175 lbs. Deb: 6/29/77 C Career OF: (267-LF 122-CF 108-RF)

YEAR	TM/L	G	AB	R	H	2B	3B	HR	RBI	BB	SO	AVG	OBP	SLG	OPS	OPS+	BR+	SB	CS	SBR	FA	FR	G/POS	TPR
1977	Cal-A	58	212	19	63	10	2	0	19	16	32	.297	.349	.363	713	98	-0	5	4	-0	.963	1	O-55(20-35-1)	-0.1
1978	Chi-A	66	219	25	59	5	1	2	13	13	32	.269	.310	.329	639	79	-6	12	11	-1	.975	0	O-64(15-39-14)	-0.9
1979	Chi-A	36	77	13	24	1	1	1	8	9	14	.312	.384	.390	773	109	1	4	1	1	.967	1	O-28(22-1-5)/D-1	0.2
1980	Chi-A	70	147	12	33	2	0	2	14	10	27	.224	.274	.279	553	52	-10	3	2	-0	.958	-7	O-52(32-18-4)	-1.8

YEAR	TM/L	G	AB	R	H	2B	3B	HR	RBI	BB	SO	AVG	OBP	SLG	OPS	OPS+	BR+	SB	CS	SBR	FA	FR	G/POS	TPR
1981	*Mil-A	42	105	11	24	2	0	0	3	6	13	.229	.270	.248	518	53	-6	2	1	0	.966	-6	O-37(7-8-22)/D-1	-1.4
1982	Sea-A	22	46	3	8	1	0	0	2	4	8	.174	.240	.196	436	21	-5	3	1	0	1.000	-5	O-19(15-3-2)	-1.1
1983	Chi-N	43	72	12	21	4	1	2	12	10	12	.292	.378	.458	836	125	3	1	1	-0	1.000	-1	O-20(16-1-3)	0.0
1984	*Chi-N	55	98	17	29	2	2	2	14	13	22	.296	.378	.418	797	113	2	5	1	1	.976	-4	O-33(11-2-21)	-0.2
1985	Chi-N	108	180	25	59	6	3	7	27	20	29	.328	.395	.511	906	137	9	5	1	1	.988	-7	O-55(46-7-8)	0.2
1986	Chi-N	87	120	15	33	4	1	1	9	18	24	.275	.370	.350	720	92	-1	3	0	1	.969	-10	O-41(32-2-8)	-1.1
1987	KC-A	80	140	13	39	6	1	1	16	9	26	.279	.322	.357	679	78	-4	0	0	0	.966	-6	O-28(13-1-14),D-13	-1.1
1988	KC-A	15	21	1	4	0	0	0	2	2	6	.190	.261	.190	451	28	-2	0	0	0	1.000	-2	/O-6(1-4-1),D-4	-0.4
	Cal-A	35	75	9	21	5	0	0	7	6	12	.280	.333	.347	680	93	-1	1	1	-0	.965	-1	O-26(24-0-2)/D-2	-0.2
	Yr	50	96	10	25	5	0	0	9	8	18	.260	.317	.313	630	78	-3	1	1	-0	.967	-3	O-32(25-4-3)/D-6	-0.6
1989	Tex-A	37	40	5	9	2	0	1	9	3	11	.225	.279	.350	629	75	-1	2	0	0	1.000	0	/O-8(6-0-2),D-5	-0.1
1990	Tex-A	30	29	3	4	0	0	1	3	4	7	.138	.242	.241	484	36	-3	1	0	0	1.000	-3	/O-9(7-1-1),D-4	-0.5
Total	14	784	1581	183	430	50	12	20	158	143	275	.272	.333	.357	689	89	-23	47	24	2	.972	-48	O-481L/D-30	-8.5

■ HARLEY BOSS Boss, Elmer Harley “Lefty” b: 11/19/08, Hodge, La. d: 5/15/64, Nashville, Tenn. BL/TL, 5'11.5", 185 lbs. Deb: 7/19/28

YEAR	TM/L	G	AB	R	H	2B	3B	HR	RBI	BB	SO	AVG	OBP	SLG	OPS	OPS+	BR+	SB	CS	SBR	FA	FR	G/POS	TPR
1928	Was-A	12	12	1	3	0	0	0	2	3	1	.250	.400	.250	650	75	-0	0	0	0	.970	-1	/1-5	-0.1
1929	Was-A	28	66	9	18	2	1	0	6	2	6	.273	.294	.333	627	61	-4	0	0	0	.977	0	1-18	-0.4
1930	Was-A	3	3	0	0	0	0	0	0	0	0	.000	.000	.000	0	-99	-1	0	0	0	1.000	-0	/1-1	-0.1
1933	Cle-A	112	438	54	118	17	7	1	53	25	27	.269	.310	.347	657	71	-19	2	5	-1	.994	6	*1-110	-2.3
Total	4	155	519	64	139	19	8	1	61	30	34	.268	.309	.341	650	69	-24	2	5	-1	.992	5	1-134	-2.9

■ HENRY BOSTICK Bostick, Henry Landers (b: Henry Lipschitz) b: 1/12/1895, Boston, Mass. d: 9/16/68, Denver, Colo. BR/TR, Deb: 5/18/15

YEAR	TM/L	G	AB	R	H	2B	3B	HR	RBI	BB	SO	AVG	OBP	SLG	OPS	OPS+	BR+	SB	CS	SBR	FA	FR	G/POS	TPR
1915	Phi-A	2	7	0	0	0	0	0	2	1	1	.000	.125	.000	125	-65	-1	0			1.000	-1	/3-2	-0.3

■ LYMAN BOSTOCK Bostock, Lyman Wesley b: 11/22/50, Birmingham, Ala. d: 9/23/78, Gary, Ind. BL/TR, 6'1", 180 lbs. Deb: 4/8/75

YEAR	TM/L	G	AB	R	H	2B	3B	HR	RBI	BB	SO	AVG	OBP	SLG	OPS	OPS+	BR+	SB	CS	SBR	FA	FR	G/POS	TPR
1975	Min-A	98	369	52	104	21	5	0	29	28	42	.282	.332	.366	698	96	-2	2	3	-1	.985	-3	O-92(12-28-55)/D-1	-1.0
1976	Min-A	128	474	75	153	21	9	4	60	33	37	.323	.368	.430	798	131	18	12	6	1	.988	6	*O-124(0-121-3)	2.2
1977	Min-A	153	593	104	199	36	12	14	90	51	59	.336	.394	.508	901	146	38	16	7	1	.989	4	*O-149(60-90-3)	3.8
1978	Cal-A	147	568	74	168	24	4	5	71	59	36	.296	.364	.379	743	113	11	15	12	-1	.989	11	*O-146(0-58-90)/D-1	1.6
Total	4	526	2004	305	624	102	30	23	250	171	174	.311	.368	.427	795	124	65	45	28	0	.988	18	O-511(72-297-151)/D-2	6.6

■ DARYL BOSTON Boston, Daryl Lamont b: 1/4/63, Cincinnati, Ohio BL/TL, 6'3", 203 lbs. Deb: 5/13/84 Career OF: (276-LF 499-CF 94-RF)

YEAR	TM/L	G	AB	R	H	2B	3B	HR	RBI	BB	SO	AVG	OBP	SLG	OPS	OPS+	BR+	SB	CS	SBR	FA	FR	G/POS	TPR
1984	Chi-A	35	83	8	14	3	1	0	3	4	20	.169	.207	.229	436	20	-9	6	0	1	.910	-6	O-34(0-30-5)/D-1	-1.4
1985	Chi-A	95	232	20	53	13	1	3	15	14	44	.228	.272	.332	604	62	-12	8	6	-0	.989	-6	O-93(0-90-4)/D-2	-1.9
1986	Chi-A	56	199	29	53	11	3	5	22	21	33	.266	.336	.427	763	103	1	9	5	0	.969	5	O-53(0-53-0)/D-1	0.5
1987	Chi-A	103	337	51	87	21	2	10	29	25	68	.258	.309	.421	731	89	-6	12	6	1	.991	-0	O-92(51-45-0)/D-5	-0.7
1988	Chi-A	105	281	37	61	12	2	15	31	21	44	.217	.272	.434	706	95	-3	9	3	1	.951	-3	O-85(44-43-1)/D-5	-0.7
1989	Chi-A	101	218	34	55	3	4	5	23	24	31	.252	.326	.372	698	99	-0	7	2	1	.971	-7	O-75(57-2-21)/D-9	-0.8
1990	Chi-A	5	1	0	0	0	0	0	0	0	0	.000	.000	.000	0	-99	-0	1	0	0	.000	-0	/O-1(0-0-1),D-3	0.0
	NY-N	115	366	65	100	21	2	12	45	28	50	.273	.328	.440	768	110	4	18	7	2	.986	-5	*O-109(1-108-0)	0.0
1991	NY-N	137	255	40	70	16	4	4	21	30	42	.275	.351	.416	767	116	5	15	8	1	.981	-17	*O-115(9-74-37)	-1.2
1992	NY-N	130	289	37	72	14	2	11	35	38	60	.249	.342	.426	768	118	7	12	6	1	.993	-6	O-95(66-16-14)	0.0
1993	Col-N	124	291	46	76	15	1	14	40	26	57	.261	.326	.464	790	93	-3	1	6	-2	.985	-6	O-79(41-31-9)	-1.2
1994	NY-A	52	77	11	14	2	0	4	14	6	20	.182	.250	.364	614	58	-5	0	1	-0	1.000	-4	O-16(7-7-2)/D-9	-0.9
Total	11	1058	2629	378	655	131	22	83	278	237	469	.249	.313	.410	724	95	-22	98	50	4	.977	-54	O-847C/D-35	-8.3

■ KEN BOSWELL Boswell, Kenneth George b: 2/23/46, Austin, Tex. BL/TR, 6', 172 lbs. Deb: 9/18/67

YEAR	TM/L	G	AB	R	H	2B	3B	HR	RBI	BB	SO	AVG	OBP	SLG	OPS	OPS+	BR+	SB	CS	SBR	FA	FR	G/POS	TPR
1967	NY-N	11	40	2	9	3	0	1	4	1	5	.225	.244	.375	619	76	-1	0	0	0	.971	2	/2-6,3-4	0.1
1968	NY-N	75	284	37	74	7	2	4	11	16	27	.261	.302	.342	644	93	-3	7	2	1	.965	-1	2-69	0.3
1969	*NY-N	102	362	48	101	14	7	3	32	36	47	.279	.348	.381	729	102	1	7	3	0	.959	-15	2-96	-0.8
1970	NY-N	105	351	32	89	13	2	5	44	41	32	.254	.335	.345	680	82	-8	5	4	-0	.996	-15	*2-101	-1.7
1971	NY-N	116	392	46	107	20	1	5	40	36	31	.273	.337	.367	705	101	1	5	2	0	.973	-29	*2-109	-2.3
1972	NY-N	100	355	35	75	9	1	9	33	32	35	.211	.276	.318	595	70	-14	2	2	-0	.990	-31	2-94	-4.4
1973	*NY-N	76	110	12	25	2	1	2	14	12	11	.227	.303	.318	621	74	-4	0	0	0	.973	0	3-17/2-3	-0.4
1974	NY-N	96	222	19	48	6	1	2	15	18	19	.216	.278	.279	557	57	-13	0	1	-0	1.000	7	2-28,3-20/O-7(2-0-5)	-0.5
1975	Hou-N	86	178	16	43	8	2	0	21	30	12	.242	.354	.309	663	92	-1	0	3	-1	.991	-10	2-31,3-23	-1.0
1976	Hou-N	91	126	12	33	8	1	0	18	8	8	.262	.306	.341	647	92	-2	1	0	0	.933	-5	3-16/2-3,O-1(1-0-0)	-0.7
1977	Hou-N	72	97	7	21	1	1	0	12	10	12	.216	.290	.247	537	50	-7	0	0	0	1.000	-3	2-26/3-2	-0.9
Total	11	930	2517	266	625	91	19	31	244	240	239	.248	.316	.337	652	85	-51	27	17	-0	.979	-100	2-566/3-82,O-8(3-0-5)	-12.3

■ JOHN BOTTARINI Bottarini, John Charles b: 9/14/08, Crockett, Cal. d: 10/8/76, Jemez Springs, N.Mex. BR/TR, 6', 190 lbs. Deb: 4/22/37

YEAR	TM/L	G	AB	R	H	2B	3B	HR	RBI	BB	SO	AVG	OBP	SLG	OPS	OPS+	BR+	SB	CS	SBR	FA	FR	G/POS	TPR
1937	Chi-N	26	40	3	11	3	0	1	7	5	10	.275	.370	.425	795	111	1	0			1.000	1	C-18/O-1(1-0-0)	0.2

■ JIM BOTTOMLEY Bottomley, James Leroy “Sunny Jim” b: 4/23/1900, Oglesby, Ill. d: 12/11/59, St.Louis, Mo. BL/TL, 6', 180 lbs. Deb: 8/18/22 MCH

YEAR	TM/L	G	AB	R	H	2B	3B	HR	RBI	BB	SO	AVG	OBP	SLG	OPS	OPS+	BR+	SB	CS	SBR	FA	FR	G/POS	TPR
1922	StL-N	37	151	29	49	8	5	5	35	6	13	.325	.358	.543	902	136	7	3	1	0	.986	-3	1-34	0.2
1923	StL-N	134	523	79	194	34	14	8	94	45	44	.371	.425	.535	960	155	42	4	6	-1	.986	-12	*1-130	1.8
1924	StL-N	137	528	87	167	31	12	14	111	35	35	.316	.362	.500	862	131	21	5	4	-0	.982	-12	*1-133/2-1	0.0
1925	StL-N	153	619	92	**227**	**44**	12	21	128	47	36	.367	.413	.578	992	147	43	3	4	-1	.987	-4	*1-153	2.6
1926	*StL-N	154	603	98	180	**40**	14	19	**120**	58	52	.299	.364	.506	870	127	21	4			.989	-15	*1-154	-0.4
1927	StL-N	152	574	95	174	31	15	19	124	74	49	.303	.387	.509	896	134	28	8			.989	-11	*1-152	0.6
1928	*StL-N	149	576	123	187	42	**20**	**31**	**136**	71	54	.325	.402	.628	1030	163	50	10			.987	-14	*1-148	2.6
1929	StL-N	146	560	108	176	31	12	29	137	70	54	.314	.391	.568	959	133	28	3			.991	-6	*1-145	1.1
1930	*StL-N	131	487	92	148	33	7	15	97	44	36	.304	.368	.493	860	102	1	5			.990	-14	*1-124	-1.8
1931	*StL-N	108	382	73	133	34	5	9	75	34	24	.348	.403	.534	937	144	23	3			.987	-3	1-93	1.1
1932	StL-N	91	311	45	92	16	3	11	48	25	32	.296	.350	.473	823	115	7	2			.986	-3	1-74	-0.3
1933	Cin-N	145	549	57	137	23	9	13	83	42	28	.250	.311	.395	706	102	1	3			.991	-9	*1-145	-2.3
1934	Cin-N	142	556	72	158	31	11	11	78	33	40	.284	.324	.439	763	105	2	1			.989	-4	*1-139	-1.4
1935	Cin-N	107	399	44	103	21	1	1	49	18	24	.258	.294	.323	617	68	-18	3			.992	-3	1-97	-3.0
1936	StL-A	140	544	72	162	39	11	12	95	44	55	.298	.354	.476	830	100	-2	0	0	0	.992	-10	*1-140	-2.2
1937	StL-A	65	109	11	26	7	0	1	12	18	15	.239	.346	.330	677	71	-5	1	0	0	.995	1	1-24,M	-0.5
Total	16	1991	7471	1177	2313	465	151	219	1422	664	591	.310	.369	.500	869	124	248	58	15		.988	-120	*1-1885/2-1	-1.9

■ ED BOUCHEE Bouchee, Edward Francis b: 3/7/33, Livingston, Mont. BL/TR, 6'1", 205 lbs. Deb: 9/19/56

YEAR	TM/L	G	AB	R	H	2B	3B	HR	RBI	BB	SO	AVG	OBP	SLG	OPS	OPS+	BR+	SB	CS	SBR	FA	FR	G/POS	TPR
1956	Phi-N	9	22	0	6	2	0	0	1	5	6	.273	.407	.364	771	112	1	0	0	0	1.000	-0	/1-6	0.0
1957	Phi-N	154	574	78	168	35	8	17	76	84	91	.293	.396	.470	866	136	32	1	0	0	.988	4	*1-154	2.7
1958	Phi-N	89	334	55	86	19	5	9	39	51	74	.257	.356	.425	781	107	4	1	0	0	.993	0	1-89	-0.1
1959	Phi-N	136	499	75	142	29	4	15	74	70	74	.285	.378	.449	827	117	14	0	4	-1	.986	-0	*1-134	0.4
1960	Phi-N	22	65	1	17	4	0	0	8	9	11	.262	.360	.323	683	89	-1	0	0	0	.994	1	1-22	-0.1
	Chi-N	98	299	33	71	11	1	5	44	45	51	.237	.341	.331	672	86	-5	2	0	0	.991	-0	1-80	-0.9
	Yr	120	364	34	88	15	1	5	52	54	62	.242	.344	.330	674	86	-5	2	0	0	.992	1	*1-102	-1.0
1961	Chi-N	112	319	49	79	12	3	12	38	58	77	.248	.372	.417	789	108	5	1	4	-1	.983	1	*1-107	-0.1
1962	NY-N	50	87	7	14	2	0	3	10	18	17	.161	.305	.287	592	59	-5	0	0	0	.976	4	1-19	-0.2
Total	7	670	2199	298	583	114	21	61	290	340	401	.265	.370	.419	790	112	46	5	8	-2	.988	9	1-611	1.7

■ AL BOUCHER Boucher, Alexander Francis “Bo” b: 11/13/1881, Franklin, Mass. d: 6/23/74, Torrance, Cal. BR/TR, 5'8.5", 156 lbs. Deb: 4/16/14

YEAR	TM/L	G	AB	R	H	2B	3B	HR	RBI	BB	SO	AVG	OBP	SLG	OPS	OPS+	BR+	SB	CS	SBR	FA	FR	G/POS	TPR
1914	StL-F	147	516	62	119	26	4	2	49	52	88	.231	.304	.308	612	64	-34	13			.916	-4	*3-147	-3.5

■ MEDRIC BOUCHER Boucher, Medric Charles Francis b: 3/12/1886, St.Louis, Mo. d: 3/12/74, Martinez, Cal. BR/TR, 5'10", 165 lbs. Deb: 5/20/14

YEAR	TM/L	G	AB	R	H	2B	3B	HR	RBI	BB	SO	AVG	OBP	SLG	OPS	OPS+	BR+	SB	CS	SBR	FA	FR	G/POS	TPR
1914	Bal-F	16	16	2	5	1	1	0	2	1	1	.313	.353	.500	853	127	0	0			.950	0	/C-7,1-1,O-1(0-0-1)	0.1
	Pit-F	1	1	0	0	0	0	0	0	0	0	.000	.000	.000	0	-99	-0	0			.000	0	H	0.0
	Yr	17	17	2	5	1	1	0	2	1	1	.294	.333	.471	804	114	-0	0			.950	0	/C-7,1-1,O-1(0-0-1)	0.1

YEAR	TM/L	G	AB	R	H	2B	3B	HR	RBI	BB	SO	AVG	OBP	SLG	OPS	OPS+	BR+	SB	CS	SBR	FA	FR	G/POS	TPR
■ **LOU BOUDREAU** Boudreau, Louis b: 7/17/17, Harvey, Ill. BR/TR, 5'11", 185 lbs. Deb: 9/9/38 MH																								
1938	Cle-A	1	1	0	0	0	0	0	0	1	0	.000	.500	.000	500	36	0	0	0	0	.000	0	/3-1	0.0
1939	Cle-A	53	225	42	58	15	4	0	19	28	24	.258	.340	.360	700	82	-6	2	1	0	.953	8	S-53	0.6
1940	Cle-A★	155	627	97	185	46	10	9	101	73	39	.295	.370	.443	814	113	13	6	3	0	**.968**	12	*S-155	3.4
1941	Cle-A★	148	579	95	149	**45**	8	10	56	85	57	.257	.355	.415	770	108	7	9	4	1	**.966**	13	*S-147	3.1
1942	Cle-A★	147	506	57	143	18	10	2	58	75	39	.283	.379	.370	749	118	15	7	16	-4	**.965**	-0	*S-146,M	2.2
1943	Cle-A☆	152	539	69	154	32	7	3	67	90	31	.286	.388	.388	776	135	27	4	7	-2	**.970**	**28**	*S-152/C-1,M	**6.9**
1944	Cle-A☆	150	584	91	191	**45**	5	3	67	73	39	**.327**	.406	.437	843	146	37	11	3	1	**.978**	26	*S-149/C-1,M	**7.8**
1945	Cle-A†	97	345	50	106	24	1	3	48	35	20	.307	.374	.409	783	133	14	0	4	-1	.983	1	S-97,M	2.3
1946	Cle-A	140	515	51	151	30	6	6	62	40	14	.293	.345	.410	755	118	11	6	7	-1	**.970**	16	*S-139,M	3.6
1947	Cle-A★	150	538	79	165	**45**	3	4	67	67	10	.307	.388	.424	811	129	22	1	0	0	**.982**	17	*S-148,M	4.9
1948	*Cle-A★	152	560	116	199	34	6	18	106	98	9	.355	.453	.534	987	166	56	3	2	-0	**.975**	8	*S-151/C-1,M	**7.0**
1949	Cle-A	134	475	53	135	20	3	4	60	70	10	.284	.381	.364	745	100	2	0	1	-0	.982	5	S-88,3-38/1-6,2M	1.1
1950	Cle-A	81	260	23	70	13	2	1	29	31	5	.269	.349	.346	695	81	-7	1	2	-0	.986	0	S-61/1-8,2-2,3-2,M	-0.3
1951	Bos-A	82	273	37	73	18	1	5	47	30	12	.267	.353	.396	748	93	-2	1	0	0	.951	-1	S-52,3-15/1-2	0.0
1952	Bos-A	4	2	1	0	0	0	0	2	0	0	.000	.000	.000	0	-93	-1	0	0	0	1.000	-0	/S-1,3-1,M	-0.1
Total	15	1646	6029	861	1779	385	66	68	789	796	309	.295	.380	.415	795	121	189	51	50	-6	.973	134	*S-1539/3-57,1-16,2C	42.5
■ **CHRIS BOURJOS** Bourjos, Christopher b: 10/16/55, Chicago, Ill. BR/TR, 6', 185 lbs. Deb: 8/31/80																								
1980	SF-N	13	22	4	5	1	0	1	2	2	7	.227	.292	.409	701	96	-0	0	0	0	1.000	-1	/O-6(2-0-4)	-0.2
■ **RAFAEL BOURNIGAL** Bournigal, Rafael Antonio (Pelletier) b: 5/12/66, Azua, D.R. BR/TR, 5'11", 165 lbs. Deb: 9/1/92 Career OF: (1-LF 0-CF 0-RF)																								
1992	LA-N	10	20	1	3	1	0	0	0	1	2	.150	.227	.200	427	22	-2	0	0	0	.967	2	/S-9	0.1
1993	LA-N	8	18	0	9	1	0	0	3	0	2	.500	.500	.556	1056	193	2	0	0	0	1.000	1	/2-4,S-4	0.3
1994	LA-N	40	116	2	26	3	1	0	11	9	5	.224	.291	.267	559	50	-8	0	0	0	.981	0	S-40	-0.5
1996	Oak-A	88	252	33	61	14	2	0	18	16	19	.242	.290	.313	603	54	-18	4	3	-0	.993	4	2-64,S-23	-0.9
1997	Oak-A	79	222	29	62	9	0	1	20	16	19	.279	.339	.333	672	78	-7	2	1	0	.980	2	S-74/2-7	0.1
1998	Oak-A	85	209	23	47	11	0	1	19	10	11	.225	.267	.292	559	46	-17	6	1	1	1.000	4	2-48,S-38/D-1	-0.8
1999	Sea-A	55	95	16	26	5	0	2	14	7	6	.274	.324	.389	713	83	-3	0	0	0	.987	2	S-28,2-17/3-8,OD	0.2
Total	7	365	932	104	234	44	3	4	85	59	64	.251	.303	.318	620	62	-52	12	5	1	.986	16	S-216,2-140/3-8,DO	-1.5
■ **PAT BOURQUE** Bourque, Patrick Daniel b: 3/23/47, Worcester, Mass. BL/TL, 6', 210 lbs. Deb: 9/6/71																								
1971	Chi-N	14	37	3	7	0	1	1	3	3	9	.189	.250	.324	574	54	-2	0	0	0	.957	2	1-11	-0.1
1972	Chi-N	11	27	3	7	1	0	0	5	2	2	.259	.310	.296	607	66	-1	0	0	0	1.000	1	/1-7	-0.1
1973	Chi-N	57	139	11	29	6	0	7	20	16	21	.209	.299	.403	702	86	-3	1	1	-0	.986	5	1-38	0.0
	*Oak-A	23	42	8	8	4	1	2	9	15	10	.190	.404	.476	880	155	4	0	0	0	1.000	-1	D-15/1-5	0.3
1974	Oak-A	73	96	6	22	4	0	1	16	15	20	.229	.333	.302	635	90	-1	0	2	-1	.988	-1	1-39/D-8	-0.4
	Min-A	23	64	5	14	2	0	1	8	7	11	.219	.296	.297	593	69	-2	0	0	0	.987	3	1-21	-0.1
	Yr	96	160	11	36	6	0	2	24	22	31	.225	.319	.300	619	82	-3	0	2	-1	.988	2	1-60/D-8	-0.5
Total	4	201	405	36	87	17	2	12	61	58	73	.215	.316	.356	672	87	-6	1	3	-1	.985	11	1-121/D-23	-0.4
■ **LARRY BOWA** Bowa, Lawrence Robert b: 12/6/45, Sacramento, Cal. BB/TR, 5'10", 155 lbs. Deb: 4/7/70 MC																								
1970	Phi-N	145	547	50	137	17	6	0	34	21	48	.250	.278	.303	582	57	-34	24	13	1	.979	-21	*S-143/2-1	-3.8
1971	Phi-N	159	650	74	162	18	5	0	25	36	61	.249	.294	.292	586	66	-28	28	11	2	**.987**	10	*S-157	0.4
1972	Phi-N	152	579	67	145	11	**13**	1	31	32	51	.250	.292	.320	612	72	-21	17	9	1	**.987**	5	*S-150	0.2
1973	Phi-N	122	446	42	94	11	3	0	23	24	31	.211	.253	.249	502	38	-37	10	6	0	.979	-0	*S-122	-2.4
1974	Phi-N★	162	669	97	184	19	10	1	36	23	52	.275	.300	.338	638	75	-23	39	11	5	**.984**	-16	*S-162	-1.6
1975	Phi-N★	136	583	79	178	18	9	2	38	24	32	.305	.335	.377	712	94	-6	24	6	3	.962	-12	*S-135	0.2
1976	*Phi-N★	156	624	71	155	15	9	0	49	32	31	.248	.285	.301	586	65	-29	30	8	4	.975	-14	*S-156	-2.2
1977	*Phi-N	154	624	93	175	19	3	4	41	32	32	.280	.316	.340	655	73	-24	32	3	6	.983	1	*S-154	0.0
1978	*Phi-N★	156	654	78	192	31	5	3	43	24	40	.294	.320	.370	690	91	-9	27	5	4	**.986**	2	*S-156	1.5
1979	Phi-N★	147	539	74	130	17	11	0	31	61	32	.241	.319	.314	633	71	-20	20	9	1	**.991**	-12	*S-146	-1.6
1980	*Phi-N	147	540	57	144	16	4	2	39	24	28	.267	.302	.322	624	70	-21	21	6	3	.975	-13	*S-147	-1.7
1981	*Phi-N	103	360	34	102	14	3	0	31	26	17	.283	.332	.339	670	87	-6	16	7	1	.975	-10	*S-102	-0.4
1982	Chi-N	142	499	50	123	15	7	0	29	39	38	.246	.302	.305	607	68	-20	8	3	1	.973	-30	*S-140	-3.7
1983	Chi-N	147	499	73	133	20	5	2	43	35	30	.267	.315	.339	653	77	-15	7	3	0	**.984**	15	*S-145	1.6
1984	*Chi-N	133	391	33	87	14	2	0	17	28	24	.223	.274	.269	543	49	-26	10	4	1	.974	7	*S-132	-0.6
1985	Chi-N	72	195	13	48	6	4	0	13	11	20	.246	.286	.318	604	62	-10	5	1	1	.970	12	S-66	0.9
	NY-N	14	19	2	2	1	0	0	2	2	2	.105	.190	.158	348	-2	-3	0	0	0	.882	1	/S-9,2-4	-0.2
	Yr	86	214	15	50	7	4	0	15	13	22	.234	.278	.304	581	57	-12	5	1	1	.965	12	S-75/2-4	0.7
Total	16	2247	8418	987	2191	262	99	15	525	474	569	.260	.301	.320	621	71	-331	318	105	33	.980	-75	*S-2222/2-5	-13.4
■ **BENNY BOWCOCK** Bowcock, Benjamin James b: 10/28/1879, Fall River, Mass. d: 6/16/61, Taunton, Mass BR/TR, 5'7", 150 lbs. Deb: 9/18/03																								
1903	StL-A	14	50	7	16	3	1	1	10	3		.320	.358	.480	838	154	3	1			.885	-7	2-14	-0.4
■ **TIM BOWDEN** Bowden, David Timon b: 8/15/1891, McDonough, Ga. d: 10/25/49, Emory, Ga. BL/TR, 5'10", 175 lbs. Deb: 9/17/14																								
1914	StL-A	7	9	0	2	0	0	0	0	1	6	.222	.300	.222	522	60	-0	0			1.000	-1	/O-4(0-1-3)	-0.2
■ **CHICK BOWEN** Bowen, Emmons Joseph b: 7/26/1897, New Haven, Conn. d: 8/9/48, New Haven, Conn. BR/TR, 5'7", 165 lbs. Deb: 9/15/19																								
1919	NY-N	3	5	0	1	0	0	0	1	1	2	.200	.333	.200	533	63	-0	0			1.000	-0	/O-2(0-1-1)	-0.1
■ **SAM BOWEN** Bowen, Samuel Thomas b: 9/18/52, Brunswick, Ga. BR/TR, 5'9", 170 lbs. Deb: 8/25/77																								
1977	Bos-A	3	2	0	0	0	0	0	0	0	2	.000	.000	.000	0	-90	-1	0	0	0	1.000	-1	/O-3(2-1-0)	-0.1
1978	Bos-A	6	7	3	1	0	0	1	1	1	2	.143	.250	.571	821	112	0	0	0	0	1.000	-2	/O-4(1-3-0)	-0.2
1980	Bos-A	7	13	0	2	0	0	0	0	2	3	.154	.267	.154	421	17	-1	1	0	0	1.000	1	/O-6(1-4-1)	0.0
Total	3	16	22	3	3	0	0	1	1	3	7	.136	.240	.273	513	38	-2	1	0	0	1.000	-1	/O-13(4-8-1)	-0.3
■ **SAM BOWENS** Bowens, Samuel Edward b: 3/23/39, Wilmington, N.C. BR/TR, 6'1.5", 195 lbs. Deb: 9/7/63																								
1963	Bal-A	15	48	8	16	3	1	1	9	4	5	.333	.385	.500	885	151	3	1	1	-0	.952	-1	O-13(0-0-13)	0.1
1964	Bal-A	139	501	58	132	25	2	22	71	42	99	.263	.325	.453	779	114	9	4	3	-0	.981	-0	*O-135(32-0-120)	-0.1
1965	Bal-A	84	203	16	33	4	1	7	20	10	41	.163	.202	.296	497	39	-17	7	1	1	.982	-2	O-68(11-0-58)	-2.3
1966	Bal-A	89	243	26	51	9	1	6	20	17	52	.210	.275	.329	605	74	-8	9	3	1	.960	-0	O-68(32-4-41)	-1.2
1967	Bal-A	62	120	13	22	2	1	5	12	11	43	.183	.258	.342	599	76	-4	3	4	-1	.977	-2	O-32(16-0-16)	-0.9
1968	Was-A	57	115	14	22	4	0	4	7	11	39	.191	.262	.330	592	81	-3	0	0	0	.957	-1	O-27(11-3-14)	-0.6
1969	Was-A	33	57	6	11	1	0	0	4	5	14	.193	.258	.211	469	34	-5	1	1	-0	.971	-5	O-30(6-3-22)	-1.2
Total	7	479	1287	141	287	48	6	45	143	100	293	.223	.284	.375	659	87	-25	25	13	1	.974	-12	O-373(108-10-284)	-6.2
■ **FRANK BOWERMAN** Bowerman, Frank Eugene "Mike" b: 12/5/1868, Romeo, Mich. d: 11/30/48, Romeo, Mich. BR/TR, 6'2", 190 lbs. Deb: 8/24/1895 M Career OF: (0-LF 1-CF 0-RF)																								
1895	Bal-N	1	1	0	0	0	0	0	0	0	0	.000	.000	.000	0	-97	-0	0			1.000	0	/C-1	0.0
1896	Bal-N	4	16	0	2	0	0	0	4	1	0	.125	.176	.125	301	-20	-3	0			.900	0	/C-3,1-1	-0.2
1897	*Bal-N	38	130	16	41	5	0	1	21	1		.315	.331	.377	708	87	-3	3			.948	3	C-36	0.3
1898	Bal-N	5	16	5	7	1	0	0	4	2		.438	.526	.500	1026	191	2	1			.950	-0	/C-4	0.2
	Pit-N	69	241	17	66	6	3	0	29	7		.274	.297	.324	621	79	-7	4			.946	5	C-59/1-9	0.3
	Yr	74	257	22	73	7	3	0	30	9		.284	.313	.335	648	87	-5	5			.946	5	C-63/1-9	0.5
1899	Pit-N	110	427	51	111	16	10	3	53	12		.260	.288	.365	654	79	-14	10			.947	13	C-80,1-28	0.6
1900	NY-N	80	270	25	65	5	3	1	42	6		.241	.268	.293	560	57	-16	10			.929	14	C-75/S-2	0.5
1901	NY-N	59	191	20	38	5	3	0	14	7		.199	.235	.257	492	44	-14	3			.950	13	C-46/2-3,S-3,3-3,1	0.4
1902	NY-N	109	373	38	93	14	6	0	27	13		.249	.276	.319	596	84	-8	12			.954	5	C-100/1-3	0.6
1903	NY-N	64	210	22	58	6	2	1	31	6		.276	.306	.338	644	80	-6	5			.977	0	C-55/1-4,O-1(0-1-0)	0.0
1904	NY-N	93	289	38	67	11	4	2	27	16		.232	.288	.318	607	84	-6	7			.977	3	C-79/1-9,2-2,P-1	0.5

YEAR	TM/L	G	AB	R	H	2B	3B	HR	RBI	BB	SO	AVG	OBP	SLG	OPS	OPS+	BR+	SB	CS	SBR	FA	FR	G/POS	TPR
1905	NY-N	98	297	37	80	8	1	3	41	12		.269	.322	.333	655	93	-3	6			.982	-3	C-72,1-17/2-1	0.0
1906	NY-N	103	285	23	65	7	3	1	42	15		.228	.274	.284	558	72	-10	5			.984	4	C-67,1-20	-0.1
1907	NY-N	96	311	31	81	8	2	0	32	17		.260	.309	.299	608	88	-4	11			.990	-5	C-62,1-29	-0.4
1908	Bos-N	86	254	16	58	8	1	1	25	13		.228	.274	.280	554	78	-7	4			.971	-3	C-63,1-11	-0.5
1909	Bos-N	33	99	6	21	2	0	0	4	2		.212	.228	.232	460	41	-7	0			.928	1	C-27,M	-0.4
Total	15	1048	3410	345	853	102	38	13	393	130	0	.250	.287	.314	601	77	-105	81			.963	51	C-829,1-132/2-6,S3PO	1.8

■ **BRENT BOWERS** Bowers, Brent Raymond b: 5/2/71, Bridgeview, Ill. BL/TR, 6'3", 200 lbs. Deb: 8/16/96

YEAR	TM/L	G	AB	R	H	2B	3B	HR	RBI	BB	SO	AVG	OBP	SLG	OPS	OPS+	BR+	SB	CS	SBR	FA	FR	G/POS	TPR
1996	Bal-A	21	39	6	12	2	0	0	3	0	7	.308	.308	.359	667	68	-2	0	0	0	1.000	-3	O-21(21-0-0)	-0.4

■ **BILLY BOWERS** Bowers, Grover Bill b: 3/25/22, Parkin, Ark. d: 9/17/96, Wynne, Ark. BL/TR, 5'9.5", 176 lbs. Deb: 4/24/49

YEAR	TM/L	G	AB	R	H	2B	3B	HR	RBI	BB	SO	AVG	OBP	SLG	OPS	OPS+	BR+	SB	CS	SBR	FA	FR	G/POS	TPR
1949	Chi-A	26	78	5	15	2	1	0	6	4	5	.192	.232	.244	475	27	-9	1	1	-0	.980	0	O-20(3-10-8)	-0.9

■ **STEW BOWERS** Bowers, Stewart Cole "Doc" b: 2/26/15, New Freedom, Pa. BB/TR, 6', 170 lbs. Deb: 8/5/35

YEAR	TM/L	G	AB	R	H	2B	3B	HR	RBI	BB	SO	AVG	OBP	SLG	OPS	OPS+	BR+	SB	CS	SBR	FA	FR	G/POS	TPR
1935	Bos-A	11	5	1	1	0	0	0	0	1	2	.200	.333	.200	533	38	-0	0	0	0	.875	0	P-10	0.0
1936	Bos-A	6	0	1	0	0	0	0	0	0	0	—	—	—	—	—	0	0	0	0	.000	-0	/P-5	0.0
1937	Bos-A	1	0	1	0	0	0	0	0	0	0	—	—	—	—	—	0	0	0	0	.000	0	R	0.0
Total	3	18	5	3	1	0	0	0	0	1	2	.200	.333	.200	533	38	-0	0	0	0	.875	-0	/P-15	0.0

■ **FRANK BOWES** Bowes, Frank M. b: 1865, Bath, N.Y. d: 1/21/1895, New York, N.Y. TR, 5'9", 160 lbs. Deb: 4/17/1890

YEAR	TM/L	G	AB	R	H	2B	3B	HR	RBI	BB	SO	AVG	OBP	SLG	OPS	OPS+	BR+	SB	CS	SBR	FA	FR	G/POS	TPR
1890	Bro-a	61	232	28	51	5	2	0	24	7		.220	.246	.259	504	50	-15	11			.813	-9	C-25,O-19R,3-13,/1S	-2.0

■ **JIM BOWIE** Bowie, James R. b: 2/17/65, Tokyo, Japan BL/TL, 6', 205 lbs. Deb: 8/3/94

YEAR	TM/L	G	AB	R	H	2B	3B	HR	RBI	BB	SO	AVG	OBP	SLG	OPS	OPS+	BR+	SB	CS	SBR	FA	FR	G/POS	TPR
1994	Oak-A	6	14	0	3	0	0	0	0	0	2	.214	.214	.214	429	12	-2	0	0	0	1.000	0	/1-6	-0.2

■ **WELDON BOWLIN** Bowlin, Lois Weldon "Hoss" b: 12/10/40, Paragould, Ark. BR/TR, 5'9", 155 lbs. Deb: 9/16/67

YEAR	TM/L	G	AB	R	H	2B	3B	HR	RBI	BB	SO	AVG	OBP	SLG	OPS	OPS+	BR+	SB	CS	SBR	FA	FR	G/POS	TPR
1967	KC-A	2	5	0	1	0	0	0	0	0	0	.200	.200	.200	400	19	-1	0	0	0	1.000	0	/3-2	0.0

■ **STEVE BOWLING** Bowling, Stephen Shaddon b: 6/26/52, Tulsa, Okla. BR/TR, 6', 185 lbs. Deb: 9/7/76

YEAR	TM/L	G	AB	R	H	2B	3B	HR	RBI	BB	SO	AVG	OBP	SLG	OPS	OPS+	BR+	SB	CS	SBR	FA	FR	G/POS	TPR
1976	Mil-A	14	42	4	7	2	0	0	2	2	5	.167	.205	.214	419	23	-4	0	0	0	.975	1	O-13(0-13-0)/D-1	-0.3
1977	Tor-A	89	194	19	40	8	1	1	13	37	42	.206	.333	.273	607	67	-8	2	3	-1	.987	-0	O-87(20-24-47)	-1.1
Total	2	103	236	23	47	10	1	1	15	39	47	.199	.313	.263	575	60	-12	2	3	-1	.985	1	O-100(20-37-47)/D-1	-1.4

■ **ELMER BOWMAN** Bowman, Elmari Wilhelm "Big Bow" b: 3/19/1897, Proctor, Vt. d: 12/17/85, Los Angeles, Cal. BR/TR, 6'0.5", 193 lbs. Deb: 8/3/20

YEAR	TM/L	G	AB	R	H	2B	3B	HR	RBI	BB	SO	AVG	OBP	SLG	OPS	OPS+	BR+	SB	CS	SBR	FA	FR	G/POS	TPR
1920	Was-A	2	1	1	0	0	0	0	0	1	0	.000	.500	.000	500	42	0	0	0	0	.000	0	H	0.0

■ **ERNIE BOWMAN** Bowman, Ernest Ferrell b: 7/28/35, Johnson City, Tenn. BR/TR, 5'10", 160 lbs. Deb: 4/12/61

YEAR	TM/L	G	AB	R	H	2B	3B	HR	RBI	BB	SO	AVG	OBP	SLG	OPS	OPS+	BR+	SB	CS	SBR	FA	FR	G/POS	TPR
1961	SF-N	38	38	10	8	0	2	0	2	1	8	.211	.231	.316	547	45	-3	2	0	0	.885	3	2-13,S-12/3-7	0.1
1962	*SF-N	46	42	9	8	1	0	1	4	1	10	.190	.227	.286	513	37	-4	0	1	-0	1.000	3	2-17,3-11,S-10	-0.1
1963	SF-N	81	125	10	23	3	0	0	4	0	15	.184	.184	.208	392	13	-14	1	2	-0	.952	4	S-40,2-26,3-12	-0.9
Total	3	165	205	29	39	4	2	1	10	2	33	.190	.202	.244	446	24	-21	3	3	-0	.950	9	/S-62,2-56,3-30	-0.9

■ **JOE BOWMAN** Bowman, Joseph Emil b: 6/17/10, Kansas City, Kan. d: 11/22/90, Kansas City, Mo. BL/TR, 6'2", 190 lbs. Deb: 4/18/32

YEAR	TM/L	G	AB	R	H	2B	3B	HR	RBI	BB	SO	AVG	OBP	SLG	OPS	OPS+	BR+	SB	CS	SBR	FA	FR	G/POS	TPR
1932	Phi-A	7	1	0	1	0	0	0	0	0	0	1.000	1.000	1.000	2000	405	0	0	0	0	.875	1	/P-7	0.0
1934	NY-N	31	29	4	5	0	1	0	4	2	3	.172	.226	.241	467	26	-3	0			1.000	-0	P-30	0.0
1935	Phi-N	49	67	6	13	1	1	1	7	4	7	.194	.239	.284	523	36	-6	1			.947	-1	P-33/O-1(0-0-1)	0.0
1936	Phi-N	44	77	9	15	1	0	0	6	6	14	.195	.253	.208	461	23	-8	0			.886	-2	P-40	0.0
1937	Pit-N	35	47	3	10	1	0	0	4	5	9	.213	.288	.234	523	43	-4	0			1.000	0	P-30	0.0
1938	Pit-N	18	21	5	7	0	1	0	1	1	3	.333	.364	.429	792	116	0	0			.909	-1	P-17	0.0
1939	Pit-N	70	96	9	33	8	1	0	18	5	9	.344	.382	.448	830	124	3	0			**1.000**	0	P-37	0.0
1940	Pit-N	57	90	11	22	5	1	1	14	14	14	.244	.352	.356	708	96	-0	0			.981	0	P-32	0.0
1941	Pit-N	22	31	4	8	1	0	0	1	1	2	.258	.281	.290	572	61	-2	0			1.000	-0	P-18	0.0
1944	Bos-A	59	100	7	20	5	2	0	16	5	19	.200	.238	.290	528	51	-7	1	0	0	.935	-2	P-26	0.0
1945	Bos-A	9	9	0	2	0	0	0	1	1	1	.222	.300	.222	522	51	-1	0	0	0	1.000	-0	/P-3	0.0
	Cin-N	29	71	4	5	2	1	0	3	2	9	.070	.096	.127	223	-39	-13	1			.927	-2	P-25	0.0
Total	11	430	639	62	141	24	8	2	75	46	90	.221	.275	.293	568	55	-39	3	0		.958	-8	P-298/O-1(0-0-1)	0.0

■ **BOB BOWMAN** Bowman, Robert Leroy b: 5/10/31, Laytonville, Cal. BR/TR, 6'1", 195 lbs. Deb: 4/16/55

YEAR	TM/L	G	AB	R	H	2B	3B	HR	RBI	BB	SO	AVG	OBP	SLG	OPS	OPS+	BR+	SB	CS	SBR	FA	FR	G/POS	TPR
1955	Phi-N	3	3	0	0	0	0	0	0	0	0	.000	.000	.000	0	-99	-1	0	0	0	1.000	-0	/O-2(1-0-1)	-0.1
1956	Phi-N	6	16	2	3	0	1	1	2	0	6	.188	.188	.500	688	78	-1	0	0	0	.833	-1	/O-5(0-1-4)	-0.2
1957	Phi-N	99	237	31	63	8	2	6	23	27	50	.266	.356	.392	748	104	2	0	0	0	.929	-2	O-81(3-0-79)	-0.2
1958	Phi-N	91	184	31	53	11	2	8	24	16	30	.288	.345	.500	845	122	5	0	1	-0	.988	-6	O-57(20-1-37)	-0.3
1959	Phi-N	57	79	7	10	0	0	2	5	5	23	.127	.179	.203	381	1	-11	0	0	0	1.000	-1	O-20(11-2-7)/P-5	-1.2
Total	5	256	519	71	129	19	5	17	54	48	109	.249	.319	.403	722	93	-5	0	1	-0	.955	-10	O-165(35-4-128)/P-5	-2.0

■ **BILL BOWMAN** Bowman, William George b: 1869, Chicago, Ill. d: 4/6/18, Arlington Heights, Ill. 5'11", 180 lbs. Deb: 6/18/1891

YEAR	TM/L	G	AB	R	H	2B	3B	HR	RBI	BB	SO	AVG	OBP	SLG	OPS	OPS+	BR+	SB	CS	SBR	FA	FR	G/POS	TPR
1891	Chi-N	15	45	2	4	1	0	0	5	5	9	.089	.196	.111	307	-10	-6	0			.915	-5	C-15	-0.9

■ **RED BOWSER** Bowser, James Harvey b: 9/20/1881, Freeport, Pa. d: 5/22/43, Moundsville, W.Va. Deb: 9/13/10

YEAR	TM/L	G	AB	R	H	2B	3B	HR	RBI	BB	SO	AVG	OBP	SLG	OPS	OPS+	BR+	SB	CS	SBR	FA	FR	G/POS	TPR
1910	Chi-A	1	2	0	0	0	0	0	0	0		.000	.000	.000	0	-99	-0	0			.000	0	/O-1	-0.1

■ **FRANK BOYD** Boyd, Frank Jay b: 4/2/1868, West Middletown, Pa d: 12/16/37, Oil City, Pa. BR/TR, Deb: 5/18/1893

YEAR	TM/L	G	AB	R	H	2B	3B	HR	RBI	BB	SO	AVG	OBP	SLG	OPS	OPS+	BR+	SB	CS	SBR	FA	FR	G/POS	TPR
1893	Cle-N	2	5	3	1	1	0	0	3	1	0	.200	.333	.400	733	89	-0	0			1.000	-0	/C-2	0.0

■ **JAKE BOYD** Boyd, Jacob Henry b: 1/19/1874, Martinsburg, W.Va. d: 8/12/32, Gettysburg, Pa. TL, 160 lbs. Deb: 9/20/1894 Career OF: (4-LF 0-CF 20-RF)

YEAR	TM/L	G	AB	R	H	2B	3B	HR	RBI	BB	SO	AVG	OBP	SLG	OPS	OPS+	BR+	SB	CS	SBR	FA	FR	G/POS	TPR
1894	Was-N	6	21	1	3	0	0	0	1	1	4	.143	.182	.143	325	-22	-4	2			.833	1	/O-3(1-0-2),P-3	-0.2
1895	Was-N	52	159	29	43	5	1	1	16	20	28	.270	.376	.333	710	85	-2	2			.786	-14	O-21R,P-15,2-10,/S3	-1.4
1896	Was-N	4	13	1	1	0	0	0	1	1	1	.077	.200	.077	277	-25	-2	0			.909	0	/P-4	0.0
Total	3	62	193	31	47	5	1	1	18	22	33	.244	.345	.295	641	66	-9	4			.794	-12	/O-24R,P-22,2-10,S3	-1.6

■ **BOB BOYD** Boyd, Robert Richard "The Rope" b: 10/1/25, Potts Camp, Miss. BL/TL, 5'10", 170 lbs. Deb: 9/8/51

YEAR	TM/L	G	AB	R	H	2B	3B	HR	RBI	BB	SO	AVG	OBP	SLG	OPS	OPS+	BR+	SB	CS	SBR	FA	FR	G/POS	TPR
1951	Chi-A	12	18	3	3	0	1	0	4	3	3	.167	.286	.278	563	54	-1	0	0	0	1.000	-1	/1-6	-0.2
1953	Chi-A	55	165	20	49	6	2	3	23	13	11	.297	.352	.412	764	103	1	1	4	-1	1.000	-2	1-29,O-16(15-0-1)	-0.5
1954	Chi-A	29	56	10	10	3	0	0	5	4	3	.179	.233	.232	465	27	-6	2	0	0	.955	-1	O-13(13-0-0),1-12	-0.8
1956	Bal-A	70	225	28	70	8	3	2	11	30	14	.311	.395	.400	795	119	7	0	5	-2	.990	-7	1-60/O-8(3-0-5)	-0.5
1957	Bal-A	141	485	73	154	16	8	4	34	55	31	.318	.389	.408	798	126	19	2	4	-1	.991	-3	*1-132/O-1(1-0-0)	0.7
1958	Bal-A	125	401	58	124	21	5	7	36	25	24	.309	.353	.439	792	123	12	1	1	-0	.994	-2	1-99	0.4
1959	Bal-A	128	415	42	110	20	2	3	41	29	14	.265	.315	.345	659	83	-10	3	1	0	.985	-9	*1-109	-2.5
1960	Bal-A	71	82	9	26	5	2	0	9	6	5	.317	.364	.427	790	114	2	0	0	0	1.000	-0	1-17	0.1
1961	KC-A	26	48	7	11	2	0	0	9	1	2	.229	.245	.271	516	37	-4	0	2	-1	1.000	-1	/1-8	-0.7
	Mil-N	36	41	3	10	0	0	0	3	1	7	.244	.262	.244	506	38	-4	0	0	0	1.000	1	/1-3	-0.2
Total	9	693	1936	253	567	81	23	19	175	167	114	.293	.351	.388	739	105	15	9	17	-4	.991	-24	1-475/O-38(32-0-6)	-4.2

■ **BILL BOYD** Boyd, William J. b: 12/22/1852, New York, N.Y. d: 9/30/12, Jamaica, N.Y. Deb: 4/22/1872 MU Career OF: (0-LF 0-CF 57-RF)

YEAR	TM/L	G	AB	R	H	2B	3B	HR	RBI	BB	SO	AVG	OBP	SLG	OPS	OPS+	BR+	SB	CS	SBR	FA	FR	G/POS	TPR
1872	Mut-n	35	165	26	44	6	1	1	32	6	7	.267	.292	.333	626	98	1	4	2	0	.730	-11	*3-34/O-1(0-0-1)	-0.7
1873	Atl-n	50	228	31	63	5	4	1	31	2	2	.276	.283	.346	629	96	1	1	1	-0	.716	1	*O-43(0-0-43)/3-8	0.3
1874	Har-n	26	117	22	41	8	4	0	19	1	2	.350	.356	.487	843	160	7	1	0	0	.664	-8	3-25/O-1(0-0-1)	-0.1
1875	Atl-n	36	151	14	44	11	0	1	10	1	0	.291	.296	.384	680	154	9	0	0	0	.774	-5	2-15,O-12R/3-9,1PSM	0.3
Total	4 n	147	661	93	192	30	9	3	92	10	11	.290	.301	.377	678	120	18	6	3	0	.704	-23	/3-76,O-57R,2-15,1SP	-0.2

■ **CLETE BOYER** Boyer, Cletis Leroy b: 2/9/37, Cassville, Mo. BR/TR, 6', 182 lbs. Deb: 6/5/55 FC

YEAR	TM/L	G	AB	R	H	2B	3B	HR	RBI	BB	SO	AVG	OBP	SLG	OPS	OPS+	BR+	SB	CS	SBR	FA	FR	G/POS	TPR
1955	KC-A	47	79	3	19	1	0	0	6	3	17	.241	.268	.253	521	40	-7	0	0	0	.963	6	S-12,3-11,2-10	0.0
1956	KC-A	67	129	15	28	3	1	1	4	11	24	.217	.284	.279	563	49	-10	1	1	-0	.971	18	2-51/3-7	1.0

YEAR	TM/L	G	AB	R	H	2B	3B	HR	RBI	BB	SO	AVG	OBP	SLG	OPS	OPS+	BR+	SB	CS	SBR	FA	FR	G/POS	TPR
1957	KC-A	10	0	0	0	0	0	0	0	0	0	—	—	—	—	—	0	0	0	0	.000	0	/2-1,3-1	0.0
1959	NY-A	47	114	4	20	2	0	0	3	6	23	.175	.217	.193	410	14	-13	1	0	0	.990	6	S-26,3-16	-0.6
1960	*NY-A	124	393	54	95	20	1	14	46	23	85	.242	.289	.405	693	90	-7	2	3	-1	.967	28	3-99,S-33	2.1
1961	*NY-A	148	504	61	113	19	5	11	55	63	83	.224	.313	.347	660	80	-14	1	3	-1	.967	**30**	*3-141,S-12/O-1R	1.5
1962	*NY-A	158	566	85	154	24	1	18	68	51	106	.272	.335	.413	749	104	2	3	2	-0	.964	**36**	*3-157	3.7
1963	*NY-A	152	557	59	140	20	3	12	54	33	91	.251	.296	.363	658	84	-13	4	2	0	.954	22	*3-141/S-9,2-1	1.1
1964	*NY-A	147	510	43	111	10	5	8	52	36	93	.218	.271	.304	574	59	-29	6	1	1	.968	19	*3-123,S-21	-0.8
1965	NY-A	148	514	69	129	23	6	18	58	39	79	.251	.306	.424	730	106	3	4	1	1	.968	**26**	*3-147/S-2	3.0
1966	NY-A	144	500	59	120	22	4	14	57	46	48	.240	.307	.384	691	101	-0	6	0	1	.966	20	3-85,S-59	2.7
1967	Atl-N	154	572	63	140	18	3	26	96	39	81	.245	.295	.423	718	105	1	6	3	0	**.970**	5	*3-150/S-6	0.7
1968	Atl-N	71	273	19	62	7	2	4	17	16	32	.227	.275	.311	586	75	-8	2	0	0	.981	-0	3-69	-1.0
1969	*Atl-N	144	496	57	124	16	1	14	57	55	87	.250	.330	.371	701	96	-3	3	7	-2	**.965**	3	*3-141	-0.2
1970	Atl-N	134	475	44	117	14	1	16	62	41	71	.246	.308	.381	689	79	-15	2	5	-1	.954	12	*3-126/S-5	-0.4
1971	Atl-N	30	98	10	24	1	0	6	19	8	11	.245	.302	.439	741	101	-0	0	0	0	.961	3	3-25/S-1	0.2
Total	16	1725	5780	645	1396	200	33	162	654	470	931	.242	.301	.372	673	87	-112	41	28	-1	.965	233	*3-1439,S-186/2-63,O	13.0
■ KEN BOYER Boyer, Kenton Lloyd b: 5/20/31, Liberty, Mo. d: 9/7/82, St.Louis, Mo. BR/TR, 6'2", 200 lbs. Deb: 4/12/55 FMC Career OF: (0-LF 111-CF 0-RF)																								
1955	StL-N	147	530	78	140	27	2	18	62	37	67	.264	.313	.425	738	94	-6	22	17	-1	.952	4	*3-139,S-18	-0.2
1956	StL-N★	150	595	91	182	30	2	26	98	38	65	.306	.349	.494	843	123	18	8	3	1	.961	9	*3-149	2.8
1957	StL-N	142	544	79	144	18	3	19	62	44	77	.265	.321	.414	734	94	-5	12	8	-0	**.996**	4	*O-105(0-105-0),3-41	-0.6
1958	StL-N	150	570	101	175	21	9	23	90	49	53	.307	.365	.496	861	121	17	11	6	0	.962	23	*3-144/O-6(0-6-0),S-1	3.9
1959	StL-N★	149	563	86	174	18	5	28	94	67	77	.309	.384	.508	892	127	23	12	6	1	.956	14	*3-143,S-12	3.6
1960	StL-N★	151	552	95	168	26	10	32	97	56	77	.304	.373	.562	934	139	29	8	7	-1	.959	13	*3-146	4.2
1961	StL-N★	153	589	109	194	26	11	24	95	68	91	.329	.400	.533	933	132	28	6	3	0	.951	13	*3-153	4.0
1962	StL-N★	160	611	92	178	27	5	24	98	75	104	.291	.370	.470	839	113	12	12	7	0	.956	4	*3-160	1.5
1963	StL-N★	159	617	86	176	28	2	24	111	70	90	.285	.360	.454	814	121	18	1	0	0	.925	-13	*3-159	0.5
1964	*StL-N★	162	628	100	185	30	10	24	**119**	70	85	.295	.367	.489	856	128	24	3	5	-1	.951	3	*3-162	2.6
1965	StL-N	144	535	71	139	18	2	13	75	57	73	.260	.332	.374	706	90	-6	2	7	-2	**.968**	-11	*3-143	-2.1
1966	NY-N	136	496	62	132	28	2	14	61	30	64	.266	.308	.415	723	101	-0	4	3	-0	.951	11	*3-130/1-2	1.0
1967	NY-N	56	166	17	39	7	2	3	13	26	22	.235	.339	.355	694	100	1	2	1	0	.949	-2	3-44/1-8	-0.2
	Chi-A	57	180	17	47	5	1	4	21	7	25	.261	.289	.367	655	96	-2	0	2	-1	.957	1	3-33,1-18	-0.2
1968	Chi-A	10	24	0	3	0	0	0	0	1	6	.125	.160	.125	285	-13	-3	0	0	0	.900	-1	/3-5,1-1	-0.5
	LA-N	83	221	20	60	7	2	6	41	16	34	.271	.324	.403	726	127	6	2	2	-0	.922	-4	3-34,1-32	0.1
1969	LA-N	25	34	0	7	2	0	0	4	2	7	.206	.250	.265	515	48	-2	0	0	0	.971	-0	/1-4	-0.3
Total	15	2034	7455	1104	2143	318	68	282	1141	713	1017	.287	.351	.462	813	115	151	105	77	-4	.952	69	*3-1785,O-111C/1-65,S	20.1
■ DOE BOYLAND Boyland, Dorian Scott b: 1/6/55, Chicago, Ill. BL/TL, 6'4", 200 lbs. Deb: 9/4/78																								
1978	Pit-N	6	8	1	2	0	0	0	1	0	1	.250	.250	.250	500	38	-1	0	0	0	1.000	-0	/1-1	-0.1
1979	Pit-N	4	3	0	0	0	0	0	0	0	2	.000	.000	.000	0	-96	-1	0	0	0	.000	0	/H	-0.1
1981	Pit-N	11	8	0	0	0	0	0	0	1	3	.000	.111	.000	111	-64	-2	0	0	0	.000	0	/H	-0.2
Total	3	21	19	1	2	0	0	0	1	1	6	.105	.150	.105	255	-26	-3	0	0	0	1.000	-0	/1-1	-0.4
■ EDDIE BOYLE Boyle, Edward J. b: 5/8/1874, Cincinnati, Ohio d: 2/9/41, Cincinnati, Ohio BR/TR, 6'3", 200 lbs. Deb: 4/17/1896 F																								
1896	Lou-N	3	9	0	0	0	0	0	0	2	2	.000	.182	.000	182	-52	-2	0			.938	1	/C-3	-0.1
	Pit-N	2	5	0	0	0	0	0	0	0	1	.000	.000	.000	0	-99	-1	0			.833	-0	/C-2	-0.1
	Yr	5	14	0	0	0	0	0	0	2	3	.000	.125	.000	125	-68	-3	0			.909	0	/C-5	-0.2
■ HENRY BOYLE Boyle, Henry J. "Handsome Henry" b: 9/20/1860, Philadelphia, Pa. d: 5/25/32, Philadelphia, Pa. TR, Deb: 7/9/1884 Career OF: (54-LF 18-CF 13-RF)																								
1884	StL-U	65	262	41	68	10	3	4		9		.260	.284	.366	651	93	-10				.885	5	O-43L,P-19/3-4,S21	-0.2
1885	StL-N	72	258	24	52	9	1	1	21	13	38	.202	.240	.256	496	64	-9				.907	-4	P-42,O-31L/2-2	-0.7
1886	StL-N	30	108	8	27	2	2	1	13	5	19	.250	.283	.333	617	93	-1	0			.852	1	P-25/O-6(0-5-1)	0.0
1887	Ind-N	41	150	17	36	9	1	2	13	9	18	.240	.250	.312	562	57	-8	2			.912	-5	P-38/O-4(2-1-1)	-0.2
1888	Ind-N	37	125	13	18	2	0	1	6	6	31	.144	.189	.184	373	19	-11	1			.933	3	P-37/1-1	0.0
1889	Ind-N	46	155	17	38	10	0	1	17	9	23	.245	.291	.329	620	72	-6	4			.958	-5	P-46/3-1	0.0
Total	6	291	1058	120	239	42	7	10	70	51	129	.226	.258	.301	559	69	-46	7			.912	-5	P-207/O-84L,3-5,21S	-1.1
■ JIM BOYLE Boyle, James John b: 1/19/04, Cincinnati, Ohio d: 12/24/58, Cincinnati, Ohio BR/TR, 6', 180 lbs. Deb: 6/20/26 F																								
1926	NY-N	1	0	0	0	0	0	0	0	0	0	—	—	—	—	—	0	0			.000	0	/C-1	0.0
■ JACK BOYLE Boyle, John Anthony "Honest Jack" b: 3/22/1866, Cincinnati, Ohio d: 1/7/13, Cincinnati, Ohio BR/TR, 6'4", 190 lbs. Deb: 10/8/1886 F Career OF: (6-LF 2-CF 7-RF)																								
1886	Cin-a	1	5	0	1	0	0	0	0	0		.200	.200	.200	400	25	-0	0			.769	-0	/C-1	0.0
1887	*StL-a	88	370	48	86	3	1	2	41	20		.232	.237	.220	457	25	-37	7			**.897**	-11	C-86/O-2R,1-2,3-1	-3.3
1888	*StL-a	71	257	33	62	8	1	1	23	13		.241	.286	.292	578	77	-8	11			**.932**	14	C-70/O-1(0-1-0)	1.1
1889	StL-a	99	347	54	85	11	5	3	42	21	42	.245	.301	.331	633	71	-15	5			.947	5	C-80,3-12/O-5L,12	-0.3
1890	Chi-P	100	369	56	96	9	5	1	49	44	29	.260	.347	.320	667	76	-13	11			.940	-4	C-50,3-30,S-16,/1O	-1.0
1891	StL-a	121	434	76	122	18	8	5	79	44	35	.281	.363	.394	757	102	-2	18			.936	-15	C-91,S-25/3-7,O21	-0.7
1892	NY-N	120	436	52	80	8	8	0	32	36	41	.183	.252	.239	491	49	-27	10			.922	14	C-79,1-40/O-2L,S-2	-0.6
1893	Phi-N	116	504	105	144	29	9	4	81	41	30	.286	.351	.403	754	100	-1	22			.988	6	*1-112/C-6,2-2	0.4
1894	Phi-N	117	510	103	152	23	10	4	89	46	27	.298	.360	.406	765	86	-11	23			.982	1	*1-117/3-1,2-1	-0.8
1895	Phi-N	133	565	90	143	17	4	0	67	35	23	.253	.302	.297	600	55	-38	13			.973	-6	*1-133	-3.6
1896	Phi-N	40	145	17	43	4	1	1	28	6	7	.297	.346	.359	705	87	-3	3			.920	-7	C-28,1-12	-0.6
1897	Phi-N	75	288	37	73	9	1	2	36	19		.253	.306	.313	619	65	-14	3			.962	-9	C-50,1-24	-1.6
1898	Phi-N	6	22	0	2	0	1	0	3	1		.091	.130	.182	312	-11	-3	0			.919	-0	/1-4,C-3	-0.3
Total	13	1087	4252	671	1089	139	54	23	570	326	234	.256	.315	.327	642	72	-172	126			.929	-12	C-544,1-458/3-51,SO2	-11.3
■ JACK BOYLE Boyle, John Bellew b: 7/9/1889, Morris, Ill. d: 4/3/71, Ft.Lauderdale, Fla. BL/TR, 5'11.5", 165 lbs. Deb: 6/28/12																								
1912	Phi-N	15	25	4	7	1	0	0	2	1	5	.280	.308	.320	628	67	-1	0			.905	5	/3-6,S-2	0.4
■ BUZZ BOYLE Boyle, Ralph Francis b: 2/9/08, Cincinnati, Ohio d: 11/12/78, Cincinnati, Ohio BL/TL, 5'11.5", 170 lbs. Deb: 9/11/29 F																								
1929	Bos-N	17	57	8	15	2	1	1	2	6	11	.263	.333	.386	719	81	-2	2			1.000	-0	O-17(17-0-0)	-0.3
1930	Bos-N	1	1	0	0	0	0	0	0	0	1	.000	.000	.000	0	-99	-0	0			.000	-1	/O-1(0-1-0)	-0.1
1933	Bro-N	93	338	38	101	13	4	0	31	16	24	.299	.331	.361	691	102	0	7			.975	-6	O-90(45-34-10)	-1.0
1934	Bro-N	128	472	88	144	26	10	7	48	51	44	.305	.376	.447	823	126	18	8			.970	11	*O-121(18-19-86)	2.1
1935	Bro-N	127	475	51	129	17	9	4	44	43	45	.272	.332	.371	703	90	-6	7			.963	3	*O-124(0-17-107)	-1.0
Total	5	366	1343	185	389	58	24	12	125	116	125	.290	.347	.395	743	105	10	24			.970	6	O-353(80-71-203)	-0.3
■ GIBBY BRACK Brack, Gilbert Herman b: 3/29/08, Chicago, Ill. d: 1/20/60, Greenville, Tex. BR/TR, 5'9", 170 lbs. Deb: 4/23/37																								
1937	Bro-N	112	372	60	102	27	9	5	38	44	93	.274	.351	.435	786	111	5	9			.969	1	*O-101(37-44-21)	0.2
1938	Bro-N	40	56	10	12	2	1	1	6	4	14	.214	.267	.339	606	64	-3	1			1.000	2	O-13(7-0-6)	-0.1
	Phi-N	72	282	40	81	20	4	4	28	18	30	.287	.332	.429	761	111	3	2			.964	-2	O-68(12-38-24)	-0.2
	Yr	112	338	50	93	22	5	5	34	22	44	.275	.321	.414	736	102	-0	3			.969	-0	O-81(19-38-30)	-0.3
1939	Phi-N	91	270	40	78	21	4	6	41	26	49	.289	.351	.463	814	121	7	1			.959	-4	O-48(2-6-40),1-19	-0.2
Total	3	315	980	150	273	70	18	16	113	92	186	.279	.341	.436	777	111	13	13			.967	-4	O-230(58-88-91)/1-19	-0.3
■ BUDDY BRADFORD Bradford, Charles William b: 7/25/44, Mobile, Ala. BR/TR, 5'11", 191 lbs. Deb: 9/9/66 Career OF: (107-LF 267-CF 259-RF)																								
1966	Chi-A	14	28	3	4	0	0	0	0	2	6	.143	.200	.143	343	0	-4	0	0	0	.833	-3	/O-9(5-0-4)	-0.7
1967	Chi-A	24	20	6	2	1	0	0	1	1	7	.100	.143	.150	293	-14	-3	1	0	0	.900	-4	O-14(6-1-8)	-0.8
1968	Chi-A	103	281	32	61	11	0	5	24	23	67	.217	.281	.310	591	78	-7	8	4	0	.965	-12	O-99(35-25-58)	-2.7
1969	Chi-A	93	273	36	70	8	2	11	27	34	75	.256	.347	.421	769	109	3	5	2	0	.961	-13	O-88(0-48-59)	-1.3
1970	Chi-A	32	91	8	17	3	0	2	8	10	30	.187	.267	.286	553	51	-6	1	2	-0	.979	-4	O-27(2-20-9)	-1.2
	Cle-A	75	163	25	32	6	1	7	23	21	43	.196	.292	.374	666	79	-5	0	1	-0	.984	-4	O-64(1-58-5)/3-1	-1.1

YEAR	TM/L	G	AB	R	H	2B	3B	HR	RBI	BB	SO	AVG	OBP	SLG	OPS	OPS+	BR+	SB	CS	SBR	FA	FR	G/POS	TPR
	Yr	107	254	33	49	9	1	9	31	31	73	.193	.283	.343	626	69	-11	1	3	-1	.982	-8	O-91(3-78-14)/3-1	-2.3
1971	Cle-A	20	38	4	6	2	1	0	3	6	10	.158	.273	.263	536	48	-3	0	0	0	.930	-0	O-18(0-18-0)	-0.3
	Cin-N	79	100	17	20	3	0	2	12	14	23	.200	.316	.290	606	74	-3	4	2	0	.986	-13	O-66(36-26-5)	-1.8
1972	Chi-A	35	48	13	13	2	0	2	8	4	13	.271	.340	.438	777	127	2	3	2	-0	1.000	-5	O-28(3-22-3)	-0.5
1973	Chi-A	53	168	24	40	3	1	8	15	17	43	.238	.316	.411	726	100	-0	4	5	-1	.992	4	O-51(1-48-2)	0.2
1974	Chi-A	39	96	16	32	2	0	5	10	13	11	.333	.418	.510	929	162	8	1	2	-0	.980	-3	O-32(10-0-24)/D-1	0.3
1975	Chi-A	25	58	8	9	3	1	2	15	8	22	.155	.290	.345	635	78	-2	3	2	-0	.966	-2	O-18(3-0-15)/D-4	-0.4
	StL-N	50	81	12	22	1	0	4	15	12	24	.272	.366	.432	798	117	2	0	2	-1	.935	-1	O-25(3-1-21)	-0.1
1976	Chi-A	55	160	20	35	5	2	4	14	19	37	.219	.309	.350	659	92	-1	6	0	1	.978	-3	O-48(2-0-46)/D-3	-0.6
Total	11	697	1605	224	363	50	8	52	175	184	411	.226	.313	.364	678	91	-19	36	24	-0	.971	-64	O-587C/D-8,3-1	-11.0

■ VIC BRADFORD

Bradford, Henry Victor b: 3/5/15, Brownsville, Tenn. d: 6/10/94, Paris, Ky. BR/TR, 6′2″, 190 lbs. Deb: 5/1/43

YEAR	TM/L	G	AB	R	H	2B	3B	HR	RBI	BB	SO	AVG	OBP	SLG	OPS	OPS+	BR+	SB	CS	SBR	FA	FR	G/POS	TPR
1943	NY-N	6	5	1	1	0	0	0	1	1	1	.200	.333	.200	533	55	-0	0			1.000	0	/O-1(1-0-0)	0.0

■ AL BRADLEY

Bradley, Al 5′10″, 185 lbs. Deb: 5/21/1884

YEAR	TM/L	G	AB	R	H	2B	3B	HR	RBI	BB	SO	AVG	OBP	SLG	OPS	OPS+	BR+	SB	CS	SBR	FA	FR	G/POS	TPR
1884	Was-U	1	3	0	0	0	0	0		2		.000	.400	.000	400	32	-0				1.000	0	/O-1(0-1-0)	0.0

■ GEORGE BRADLEY

Bradley, George Washington "Grin" b: 7/13/1852, Reading, Pa. d: 10/2/31, Philadelphia, Pa. BR/TR, 5′10.5″, 175 lbs. Deb: 5/4/1875 Career OF: (11-LF 19-CF 16-RF)

YEAR	TM/L	G	AB	R	H	2B	3B	HR	RBI	BB	SO	AVG	OBP	SLG	OPS	OPS+	BR+	SB	CS	SBR	FA	FR	G/POS	TPR
1875	StL-n	60	254	28	62	7	3	0	24	1	19	.244	.247	.295	542	96	1	3	3	-0	.896	-2	*P-60/S-2,2-1,O-1L	-0.5
1876	StL-N	64	268	29	66	7	6	0	28	3	12	.246	.257	.321	578	97	-0				.919	1	*P-64	0.0
1877	Chi-N	55	214	31	52	7	3	0	12	6	19	.243	.264	.304	567	70	-8				**.950**	-2	*P-50,3-16/1-3,O-1R	-0.3
1879	Tro-N	63	251	36	62	9	5	0	23	1	20	.247	.250	.323	573	93	-1				.867	7	P-54/3-5,1-3,O-1R,S	0.2
1880	Pro-N	82	309	32	70	7	6	0	23	5	38	.227	.239	.288	527	80	-6				.858	19	*3-57,P-28/O-7R,1-2	1.5
1881	Det-N	1	4	0	0	0	0	0	0	0	0	.000	.000	.000	0	-96	-1				.667	-1	/S-1	-0.2
	Cle-N	60	241	21	60	10	1	2	18	4	25	.249	.261	.324	585	88	-3				.865	-9	3-48/P-6,S-6,O-1L	-0.9
	Yr	61	245	21	60	10	1	2	18	4	25	.245	.257	.318	575	84	-4				.865	-10	3-48/S-7,P-6,O-1L	-1.1
1882	Cle-N	30	115	16	21	5	0	0	6	4	16	.183	.210	.226	436	41	-7				.897	3	P-18/O-9(5-4-0),1-6	-0.4
1883	Cle-N	4	16	0	5	0	1	0	1	0	1	.313	.313	.438	750	126	0				.792	-0	/S-4	0.0
	Phi-a	76	312	47	73	8	5	1	36	8		.234	.253	.301	554	71	-11				.779	3	3-44,P-26,O-11C,/1	-0.3
1884	Cin-U	58	226	31	43	4	7	0		7		.190	.215	.270	485	43	-23				.912	-0	P-41,O-16R/S-5,1-2	-0.9
1886	Phi-a	13	48	1	4	0	1	0	1	1		.083	.102	.125	227	-29	-7	2			.849	1	S-13	-0.5
1888	Bal-a	1	3	0	0	0	0	0	0	0		.000	.000	.000	0	-99	-1	0			.600	-1	/S-1	-0.1
Total	10	507	2007	244	456	57	35	3	148	39	131	.227	.242	.295	538	72	-68	2	0		.896	22	P-287,3-170/O-46C,S1	-1.9

■ GEORGE BRADLEY

Bradley, George Washington b: 4/1/14, Greenwood, Ark. d: 10/19/82, Lawrenceburg, Tenn BR/TR, 6′1.5″, 185 lbs. Deb: 4/28/46

YEAR	TM/L	G	AB	R	H	2B	3B	HR	RBI	BB	SO	AVG	OBP	SLG	OPS	OPS+	BR+	SB	CS	SBR	FA	FR	G/POS	TPR
1946	StL-A	4	12	2	2	1	0	0	3	0	1	.167	.167	.250	417	15	-1	0	0	0	1.000	-1	/O-3(0-3-0)	-0.2

■ HUGH BRADLEY

Bradley, Hugh Frederick "Corns" b: 5/23/1885, Grafton, Mass. d: 1/26/49, Worcester, Mass. BR/TR, 5′10″, 175 lbs. Deb: 4/25/10 Career OF: (0-LF 0-CF 23-RF)

YEAR	TM/L	G	AB	R	H	2B	3B	HR	RBI	BB	SO	AVG	OBP	SLG	OPS	OPS+	BR+	SB	CS	SBR	FA	FR	G/POS	TPR
1910	Bos-A	32	83	8	14	6	2	0	7	5		.169	.216	.289	505	57	-5	2			.995	-2	1-21/C-3,O-1(0-0-1)	-0.8
1911	Bos-A	12	41	9	13	2	0	1	4	2		.317	.364	.439	803	125	1	1			.993	1	1-12	0.2
1912	Bos-A	40	137	16	26	11	1	1	19	15		.190	.275	.307	581	63	-7	3			.989	0	1-40	-0.8
1914	Pit-F	118	427	41	131	20	6	0	61	27	27	.307	.359	.382	741	103	-4	7			.990	-0	*1-118	-0.8
1915	Pit-F	26	66	3	18	4	1	0	6	4	5	.273	.314	.364	678	91	-2	2			.952	-3	O-15(0-0-15)	-0.6
	Bro-F	37	126	7	31	3	2	0	18	4	9	.246	.269	.302	571	61	-9	6			.996	2	1-26/O-7(0-0-7),C-1	-0.8
	New-F	12	33	0	5	0	0	0	2	2	3	.152	.243	.152	395	13	-4	2			.986	-2	/1-8	-0.7
	Yr	75	225	10	54	7	3	0	26	10	17	.240	.278	.298	576	63	-15	10			.994	-2	1-34,O-22(0-0-22)/C-1	-2.1
Total	5	277	913	84	238	46	12	2	117	59	44	.261	.314	.344	658	84	-30	23			.991	-3	1-225/O-23R,C-4	-4.3

■ JACK BRADLEY

Bradley, John Thomas b: 9/20/1893, Denver, Colo. d: 3/18/69, Tulsa, Okla. BR/TR, 5′11″, 175 lbs. Deb: 6/18/16

YEAR	TM/L	G	AB	R	H	2B	3B	HR	RBI	BB	SO	AVG	OBP	SLG	OPS	OPS+	BR+	SB	CS	SBR	FA	FR	G/POS	TPR
1916	Cle-A	2	3	0	0	0	0	0	0	0	1	.000	.000	.000	0	-94	-1	0			1.000	-0	/C-1	-0.1

■ MARK BRADLEY

Bradley, Mark Allen b: 12/3/56, Elizabethtown, Ky. BR/TR, 6′1″, 180 lbs. Deb: 9/3/81

YEAR	TM/L	G	AB	R	H	2B	3B	HR	RBI	BB	SO	AVG	OBP	SLG	OPS	OPS+	BR+	SB	CS	SBR	FA	FR	G/POS	TPR
1981	LA-N	9	6	2	1	1	0	0	0	0	1	.167	.167	.333	500	41	-1	0	0	0	1.000	-1	/O-6(1-0-5)	-0.2
1982	LA-N	8	3	1	1	0	0	0	0	0	0	.333	.333	.333	667	89	-0	0	0	0	1.000	-1	/O-3(1-0-2)	-0.1
1983	NY-N	73	104	10	21	4	0	3	5	11	35	.202	.278	.327	605	68	-5	4	2	0	1.000	-5	O-35(14-7-16)	-1.1
Total	3	90	113	13	23	5	0	3	5	11	36	.204	.274	.327	602	67	-5	4	2	0	1.000	-7	/O-44(16-7-23)	-1.4

■ MILTON BRADLEY

Bradley, Milton Obelle b: 4/15/78, Harbor City, Fla. BB/TR, 6′, 180 lbs. Deb: 7/19/2000

YEAR	TM/L	G	AB	R	H	2B	3B	HR	RBI	BB	SO	AVG	OBP	SLG	OPS	OPS+	BR+	SB	CS	SBR	FA	FR	G/POS	TPR
2000	Mon-N	42	154	20	34	8	1	2	15	14	32	.221	.290	.325	615	54	-11	2	1	0	.979	3	O-40(0-40-0)	-0.7

■ PHIL BRADLEY

Bradley, Philip Poole b: 3/11/59, Bloomington, Ind. BR/TR, 6′, 185 lbs. Deb: 9/2/83 Career OF: (856-LF 145-CF 31-RF)

YEAR	TM/L	G	AB	R	H	2B	3B	HR	RBI	BB	SO	AVG	OBP	SLG	OPS	OPS+	BR+	SB	CS	SBR	FA	FR	G/POS	TPR
1983	Sea-A	23	67	8	18	2	0	0	5	8	5	.269	.347	.299	645	77	-2	3	1	0	.974	-6	O-21(0-27-0)/D-1	-0.7
1984	Sea-A	124	322	49	97	12	4	0	24	34	61	.301	.373	.363	737	106	4	21	8	2	.992	-11	*O-117(48-68-14)/D-3	-0.7
1985	Sea-A★	159	641	100	192	33	8	26	88	55	129	.300	.366	.498	863	133	29	22	9	2	.986	6	*O-159(126-28-10)	2.9
1986	Sea-A	143	526	88	163	27	4	12	50	77	134	.310	.406	.445	851	130	25	21	12	0	.996	1	*O-140(138-5-0)	2.0
1987	Sea-A	158	603	101	179	38	10	14	67	84	119	.297	.390	.463	853	119	19	40	10	5	.983	1	*O-158(158-0-0)	1.7
1988	Phi-N	154	569	77	150	30	5	11	56	54	106	.264	.344	.392	736	109	7	11	9	-1	.990	9	*O-153(153-3-1)	1.1
1989	Bal-A	144	545	83	151	23	10	11	55	70	103	.277	.367	.417	783	124	19	20	6	2	.990	-2	*O-140(140-0-0)/D-2	1.5
1990	Bal-A	72	289	39	78	9	1	4	26	30	35	.270	.353	.349	702	100	1	10	4	1	.987	2	O-70(70-0-0)/D-2	0.2
	Chi-A	45	133	20	30	5	1	0	5	20	26	.226	.344	.278	622	78	-3	7	3	0	.973	-4	O-38(23-14-6)/D-7	-0.8
	Yr	117	422	59	108	14	2	4	31	50	61	.256	.350	.327	677	93	-2	17	7	1	.982	-2	*O-108(93-14-6)/D-9	-0.6
Total	8	1022	3695	565	1058	179	43	78	376	432	718	.286	.371	.421	792	118	99	155	62	12	.988	-3	O-996L/D-15	7.2

■ SCOTT BRADLEY

Bradley, Scott William b: 3/22/60, Glen Ridge, N.J. BL/TR, 5′11″, 185 lbs. Deb: 9/9/84

YEAR	TM/L	G	AB	R	H	2B	3B	HR	RBI	BB	SO	AVG	OBP	SLG	OPS	OPS+	BR+	SB	CS	SBR	FA	FR	G/POS	TPR
1984	NY-A	9	21	3	6	1	0	0	2	1	1	.286	.318	.333	652	84	-0	0	0	0	1.000	-1	/O-5(5-0-0),C-3	-0.1
1985	NY-A	19	49	4	8	2	1	0	1	1	5	.163	.196	.245	441	20	-5	0	0	0	.923	-1	/C-3,D-9	-0.6
1986	Chi-A	9	21	3	6	0	0	0	0	1	0	.286	.375	.286	661	81	-0	0	2	-1	.000	-0	/O-1(1-0-0),D-6	-0.2
	Sea-A	68	199	17	60	8	3	5	28	12	7	.302	.347	.447	795	113	3	1	0	0	.990	-13	C-59/D-3	-0.7
	Yr	77	220	20	66	8	3	5	28	13	7	.300	.350	.432	782	110	3	1	2	-0	.990	-14	C-59/D-9,O-1(1-0-0)	-0.9
1987	Sea-A	102	342	34	95	15	1	5	43	15	18	.278	.314	.371	685	77	-11	0	1	-0	.983	-6	C-82/3-8,O-2R,D-6	-1.4
1988	Sea-A	103	335	45	86	17	1	4	33	17	16	.257	.297	.349	646	77	-11	1	1	-0	.991	4	C-85/O-4R,3-3,1D	-0.2
1989	Sea-A	103	270	21	74	16	0	3	37	21	23	.274	.329	.367	695	93	-3	1	1	-0	.993	3	C-70/1-2,O-1L,D-6	0.4
1990	Sea-A	101	233	11	52	9	0	1	28	15	20	.223	.270	.275	545	52	-15	0	1	-0	.995	1	C-63/3-5,1-1,D-6	-1.2
1991	Sea-A	83	172	10	35	7	0	0	11	19	19	.203	.283	.244	527	47	-12	0	0	0	.993	-5	C-65/3-4,1-1,D-2	-1.4
1992	Sea-A	2	1	0	0	0	0	0	0	1	1	.000	.500	.000	500	51	0	0	0	0	1.000	1	/C-1	0.1
	Cin-N	5	5	1	2	0	0	0	1	1	0	.400	.500	.400	900	154	0	0	0	0	1.000	-1	/C-2	0.0
Total	9	604	1648	149	424	75	6	18	184	104	110	.257	.306	.343	649	76	-54	3	6	-1	.990	-19	C-433/D-42,3-20,O1	-5.3

■ BILL BRADLEY

Bradley, William Joseph b: 2/13/1878, Cleveland, Ohio d: 3/11/54, Cleveland, Ohio BR/TR, 6′, 185 lbs. Deb: 8/26/1899 M

YEAR	TM/L	G	AB	R	H	2B	3B	HR	RBI	BB	SO	AVG	OBP	SLG	OPS	OPS+	BR+	SB	CS	SBR	FA	FR	G/POS	TPR
1899	Chi-N	35	129	26	40	6	1	2	18	12		.310	.378	.419	796	121	4	4			.884	-3	3-30/S-5	0.2
1900	Chi-N	122	444	63	125	21	8	5	49	27		.282	.330	.399	728	104	1	14			.882	17	*3-106,1-15	1.8
1901	Cle-A	133	516	95	151	28	13	1	55	26		.293	.336	.403	739	109	5	15			**.930**	10	*3-133/P-1	1.7
1902	Cle-A	137	550	104	187	39	12	11	77	27		.340	.375	.515	890	151	35	11			.923	12	*3-137	4.7
1903	Cle-A	136	536	101	168	36	22	6	68	25		.313	.348	.496	844	154	33	21			.924	12	*3-136	4.8
1904	Cle-A	154	609	94	183	32	8	6	83	26		.300	.334	.409	743	136	23	23			**.955**	9	*3-154	3.9
1905	Cle-A	146	541	63	145	34	6	0	51	27		.268	.321	.353	674	112	7	22			**.945**	13	*3-146,M	2.6
1906	Cle-A	82	302	32	83	16	2	2	25	18		.275	.324	.361	685	116	5	13			.966	4	3-82	1.2
1907	Cle-A	139	498	48	111	20	1	0	34	35		.223	.286	.267	553	76	-13	20			**.938**	5	*3-139	-0.5
1908	Cle-A	148	548	70	133	24	7	1	46	29		.243	.297	.318	614	99	-1	18			.939	-31	*3-118,S-30	-3.2
1909	Cle-A	95	334	30	62	6	3	0	22	19		.186	.236	.222	458	43	-22	8			.957	-11	3-87/1-3,2-3	-3.5

YEAR	TM/L	G	AB	R	H	2B	3B	HR	RBI	BB	SO	AVG	OBP	SLG	OPS	OPS+	BR+	SB	CS	SBR	FA	FR	G/POS	TPR
1910	Cle-A	61	214	12	42	3	0	0	12	10		.196	.236	.210	446	39	-15	6			.956	-1	3-61	-1.6
1914	Bro-F	7	6	1	3	1	0	0	3	0	0	.500	.500	.667	1167	218	1	0			.000	0	HM	0.1
1915	KC-F	66	203	15	38	9	1	0	9	9	18	.187	.225	.241	467	33	-22	6			.949	-6	3-61	-3.0
Total	14	1461	5430	754	1471	275	84	34	552	290	18	.271	.317	.371	688	108	42	181			.933	28	*3-1390/S-35,1-18,2P	9.2
■ DALLAS BRADSHAW Bradshaw, Dallas Carl "Windy" b: 11/23/1895, Wolf Creek, Ill. d: 12/11/39, Herrin, Ill. BL/TR, 5'7", 145 lbs. Deb: 6/5/17																								
1917	Phi-A	2	4	0	0	0	0	0	0	0	1	.000	.000	.000	0	-99	-1	0			1.000	1	/2-1	0.0
■ GEORGE BRADSHAW Bradshaw, George Thomas b: 9/12/24, Salisbury, N.C. d: 11/4/94, Hendersonville, N.C. BR/TR, 6'2", 185 lbs. Deb: 8/10/52																								
1952	Was-A	10	23	3	5	2	0	0	6	1	2	.217	.280	.304	584	65	-1	0	0	0	.917	-3	/C-9	-0.4
■ TERRY BRADSHAW Bradshaw, Terry Leon b: 2/3/69, Franklin, Va. BL/TR, 6', 180 lbs. Deb: 5/4/95																								
1995	StL-N	19	44	6	10	1	1	0	2	2	10	.227	.261	.295	556	46	-3	1	2	-0	.952	1	O-10(6-3-1)	-0.3
1996	StL-N	15	21	4	7	1	0	0	3	3	2	.333	.417	.381	798	113	1	0	1	-0	1.000	-2	/O-7(4-3-1)	-0.2
Total	2	34	65	10	17	2	1	0	5	5	12	.262	.314	.323	637	69	-3	1	3	-1	.960	-2	/O-17(10-6-2)	-0.5
■ BRADY Brady Deb: 9/25/1875																								
1875	Chi-n	1	4	1	1	0	1	0	0	0	0	.250	.250	.750	1000	231	1	0	0	0	.625	1	/O-1(0-1-0)	0.1
■ BRIAN BRADY Brady, Brian Phelan b: 7/11/62, Elmhurst, N.Y. BL/TL, 5'11", 185 lbs. Deb: 4/16/89																								
1989	Cal-A	2	2	0	1	1	0	0	1	0	1	.500	.500	1.000	1500	319	1	0	0	0	.000	-0	/O-1(0-0-1)	0.0
■ CLIFF BRADY Brady, Clifford Francis b: 3/6/1897, St.Louis, Mo. d: 9/25/74, Belleville, Ill. BR/TR, 5'5.5", 140 lbs. Deb: 8/8/20																								
1920	Bos-A	53	180	16	41	5	1	0	12	13	12	.228	.284	.267	550	48	-13	0	1	-0	.974	17	2-53	0.4
■ BOB BRADY Brady, Robert Jay b: 11/8/22, Lewistown, Pa. d: 4/22/96, Manchester, Conn. BL/TR, 6'1", 175 lbs. Deb: 8/24/46																								
1946	Bos-N	3	5	0	1	0	0	0	0	1	1	.200	.333	.200	533	52	-0	0			.857	0	/C-1	0.0
1947	Bos-N	1	1	0	0	0	0	0	0	0	0	.000	.000	.000	0	-99	-0	0			.000	0	H	0.0
Total	2	4	6	0	1	0	0	0	0	1	1	.167	.286	.167	452	29	-1	0			.857	0	/C-1	0.0
■ STEVE BRADY Brady, Stephen A. b: 7/14/1851, Worcester, Mass. d: 11/1/17, Hartford, Conn. 5'9.5", 165 lbs. Deb: 7/23/1874 NA OF: (1-LF 6-CF 7-RF) Career OF: (0-LF 0-CF 354-RF)																								
1874	Har-n	27	118	19	37	5	1	0	14	2	10	.314	.325	.373	698	117	2	1	2	-0	.662	-10	3-16,O-11(0-5-6)/S-1	-0.7
1875	Was-n	21	91	7	13	0	0	0	3	0	4	.143	.143	.143	286	-0	-9	5	0	1	.815	-6	2-18/O-2L,C-1,1-1	-1.3
	Har-n	1	4	0	0	0	0	0	0	0	1	.000	.000	.000	0	-95	-1	0	0	0	1.000	1	/O-1(0-1-0)	0.0
	Yr	22	95	7	13	0	0	0	3	0	5	.137	.137	.137	274	-5	-9	5	0	1	.815	-5	2-18/O-3L,C-1,1-1	-1.3
1883	NY-a	97	432	69	117	12	6	0		11		.271	.289	.326	615	94	-4				.961	3	*1-81,O-16(0-0-16)	-0.7
1884	*NY-a	112	485	102	122	11	3	1		21		.252	.283	.293	575	90	-5				.918	2	*O-110R/1-5,2-1	-0.4
1885	NY-a	108	434	60	128	14	5	3	58	25		.295	.342	.371	713	136	19				.879	-6	*O-105R/1-4,2-2,3-1	1.2
1886	NY-a	124	466	56	112	8	5	0	39	35		.240	.298	.279	577	85	-7	16			.830	-5	*O-123(0-0-123)/1-1	-1.1
Total	2 n	49	213	26	50	5	1	0	17	2	15	.235	.242	.268	509	68	-8	6	2	1	.703	-16	/2-18,3-16,O-14R,1CS	-2.0
Total	4	441	1817	287	479	45	19	4	97	92		.264	.302	.316	618	100	4	16			.875	-6	O-354R/1-91,2-3,3-1	-1.0
■ DOUG BRADY Brady, Stephen Douglas b: 11/23/69, Jacksonville, Ill. BB/TR, 5'11", 165 lbs. Deb: 9/5/95																								
1995	Chi-A	12	21	4	4	1	0	0	3	2	4	.190	.261	.238	499	32	-2	0	1	-0	1.000	6	/2-6,D-3	0.3
■ BOBBY BRAGAN Bragan, Robert Randall "Nig" b: 10/30/17, Birmingham, Ala. BR/TR, 5'10.5", 175 lbs. Deb: 4/16/40 MC																								
1940	Phi-N	132	474	36	105	14	1	7	44	28	34	.222	.265	.300	565	58	-28	2			.936	1	*S-132/3-2	-1.8
1941	Phi-N	154	557	37	140	19	3	4	69	26	29	.251	.285	.318	603	72	-22	7			.944	-7	*S-154/2-3,3-1	-1.8
1942	Phi-N	109	335	17	73	12	2	2	15	20	21	.218	.264	.284	548	63	-16	0			.939	9	S-78,C-22/2-4,3-3	0.0
1943	Bro-N	74	220	17	58	7	2	2	24	15	16	.264	.311	.341	652	88	-4	0			.973	4	C-57,3-12	0.4
1944	Bro-N	94	266	26	71	8	4	0	17	13	14	.267	.304	.327	631	79	-8	2			.954	-0	S-51,C-35/3-6,2-1	-0.3
1947	*Bro-N	25	36	3	7	2	0	0	3	7	3	.194	.326	.250	576	53	-2	1			1.000	4	C-21	0.2
1948	Bro-N	9	12	0	2	0	0	0	0	1	0	.167	.231	.167	397	9	-2	0			1.000	-0	/C-5	-0.2
Total	7	597	1900	136	456	62	12	15	172	110	117	.240	.282	.309	591	69	-81	12			.941	10	S-415,C-140/3-24,2	-3.5
■ DARREN BRAGG Bragg, Darren William b: 9/7/69, Waterbury, Conn. BL/TR, 5'9", 180 lbs. Deb: 4/12/94 Career OF: (154-LF 225-CF 257-RF)																								
1994	Sea-A	8	19	4	3	1	0	0	2	2	5	.158	.238	.211	449	17	-2	0	0	0	1.000	-1	/O-3(3-0-0),D-3	-0.3
1995	Sea-A	52	145	20	34	5	1	3	12	18	37	.234	.335	.345	680	77	-5	9	0	2	.989	4	O-47(32-0-17)/D-2	0.0
1996	Sea-A	69	195	36	53	12	1	7	25	33	35	.272	.383	.451	834	110	4	8	5	0	.992	1	O-63(48-5-16)	0.3
	Bos-A	58	222	38	56	14	1	3	22	36	39	.252	.362	.365	726	83	-5	6	4	-0	.986	-5	O-58(7-47-29)	-1.0
	Yr	127	417	74	109	26	2	10	47	69	74	.261	.371	.405	777	95	-1	14	9	-0	.989	-4	*O-121(55-52-45)	-0.7
1997	Bos-A	153	513	65	132	35	2	9	57	61	102	.257	.340	.386	726	87	-9	10	6	0	.987	6	*O-150(1-118-41)/3-1	-0.4
1998	*Bos-A	129	409	51	114	29	3	8	57	42	99	.279	.354	.423	777	99	-0	5	3	0	**.996**	-6	*O-124(7-12-112)/D-4	-1.1
1999	StL-N	93	273	38	71	12	1	6	26	44	67	.260	.369	.377	746	89	-3	3	0	1	.982	-5	O-88(22-43-33)	-0.8
2000	Col-N	71	149	16	33	7	1	3	21	17	41	.221	.301	.342	643	48	-12	4	1	1	1.000	-5	O-43(34-0-9)	-1.6
Total	7	633	1925	268	496	115	10	39	222	253	425	.258	.350	.389	738	87	-32	45	19	3	.989	-11	O-576R/D-9,3-1	-4.9
■ GLENN BRAGGS Braggs, Glenn Erick b: 10/17/62, San Bernardino, Cal BR/TR, 6'3", 210 lbs. Deb: 7/18/86																								
1986	Mil-A	58	215	19	51	8	2	4	18	11	47	.237	.278	.349	626	67	-10	1	1	-0	.910	1	O-56(51-3-5)/D-2	-1.1
1987	Mil-A	132	505	67	136	28	7	13	77	47	96	.269	.336	.430	766	98	-1	12	5	1	.972	14	*O-123(0-0-123)/D-8	0.7
1988	Mil-A	72	272	30	71	14	0	10	42	14	60	.261	.309	.423	732	102	0	6	4	-0	.978	4	O-54(0-0-54),D-18	0.2
1989	Mil-A	144	514	77	127	12	3	15	66	42	111	.247	.309	.370	679	91	-6	17	5	2	.972	-0	*O-132(127-0-9)/D-13	-0.9
1990	Mil-A	37	113	17	28	5	0	3	13	12	21	.248	.336	.372	708	98	-0	5	3	0	.965	2	O-32(13-0-20)/D-2	0.1
	*Cin-N	72	201	22	60	9	1	6	28	26	43	.299	.387	.443	830	122	7	3	4	-1	.968	6	O-60(26-0-35)	1.0
1991	Cin-N	85	250	36	65	10	0	11	39	23	46	.260	.327	.432	759	108	2	11	3	1	.966	-2	O-74(55-0-27)	-0.1
1992	Cin-N	92	266	40	63	16	3	8	38	36	48	.237	.332	.410	742	106	2	3	1	0	.946	-9	O-79(56-0-29)	-0.9
Total	7	692	2336	308	601	102	16	70	321	211	472	.257	.325	.405	730	98	-6	58	26	4	.963	16	O-610(328-3-302)/D-43	-1.0
■ DAVE BRAIN Brain, David Leonard b: 1/24/1879, Hereford, England d: 5/25/59, Los Angeles, Cal. BR/TR, 5'10", 170 lbs. Deb: 4/24/01 Career OF: (26-LF 15-CF 5-RF)																								
1901	Chi-A	5	20	2	7	1	0	0	5	1		.350	.381	.400	781	120	1	0			.909	1	/2-5	0.1
1903	StL-N	119	464	44	107	8	15	1	60	25		.231	.270	.319	589	70	-20	21			.908	10	S-72,3-46	-0.6
1904	StL-N	127	488	57	130	24	12	7	72	17		.266	.291	.408	699	120	8	18			.927	3	S-59,3-30,O-19C,2/1	1.4
1905	StL-N	44	158	11	36	4	5	1	17	8		.228	.269	.335	605	82	-4	4			.910	-9	S-29/3-6,O-6(0-4-2)	-1.3
	Pit-N	85	307	31	79	17	6	3	46	15		.257	.296	.381	677	99	-2	8			.923	6	3-78/S-4	0.6
	Yr	129	465	42	115	21	11	4	63	23		.247	.287	.366	653	93	-6	12			.929	-3	3-84,S-33/O-6(0-4-2)	-0.7
1906	Bos-N	139	525	43	131	19	5	5	45	29		.250	.293	.333	626	98	-3	11			.917	26	*3-139	2.9
1907	Bos-N	133	509	60	142	24	9	**10**	56	29		.279	.324	.420	745	134	17	10			.916	25	*3-130/O-3(3-0-0)	5.0
1908	Cin-N	16	55	4	6	0	0	0	1	8		.109	.222	.109	331	7	-5	0			.947	-1	O-16(16-0-0)	-0.8
	NY-N	11	17	2	3	0	0	0	1	2		.176	.263	.176	440	39	-1	1			.867	-3	/2-3,O-3R,3-2,S-1	-0.4
	Yr	27	72	6	9	0	0	0	2	10		.125	.232	.125	357	14	-7	1			.947	-3	O-19L/2-3,3-2,S-1	-1.2
Total	7	679	2543	254	641	97	52	27	303	134		.252	.292	.363	655	101	-10	73			.913	58	3-431,S-165/O-47L,21	6.9
■ ASA BRAINARD Brainard, Asa "Count" b: 1841, Albany, N.Y. d: 12/29/1888, Denver, Colo. TR, 5'8.5", 150 lbs. Deb: 5/5/1871																								
1871	Oly-n	30	134	24	30	4	0	0	21	7	2	.224	.262	.254	516	52	-7	4	0	1	.852	-3	*P-30	0.0
1872	Oly-n	9	43	8	16	3	0	0	6	0	0	.372	.372	.442	814	157	3	0	0	0	.625	0	/P-9	0.0
	Man-n	6	25	2	5	0	0	0	0	1	0	.200	.231	.200	431	36	-2	0	0	0	.682	-3	/2-4,P-2,O-1(0-0-1)	-0.3
	Yr	15	68	10	21	3	0	0	6	1	0	.309	.319	.353	672	112	1	0	0	0	.667	-3	P-11/2-4,O-1(0-0-1)	-0.3
1873	Bal-n	16	69	18	18	1	0	0	8	0	2	.261	.261	.275	536	60	-3	0	0	0	.800	-2	P-14/O-2(0-0-2),2-1	-0.1
1874	Bal-n	47	196	19	47	3	0	0	8	2	3	.240	.247	.255	503	62	-8	0	3	-1	.820	-7	P-30,2-21/O-2(1-1-0)	-0.7
Total	4 n	108	467	71	116	11	0	0	43	10	7	.248	.264	.272	536	66	-17	4	3	-0	.810	-15	/P-85,2-26,O-5(1-1-3)	-1.1

YEAR	TM/L	G	AB	R	H	2B	3B	HR	RBI	BB	SO	AVG	OBP	SLG	OPS	OPS+	BR+	SB	CS	SBR	FA	FR	G/POS	TPR
■ FRED BRAINERD	Brainerd, Frederick F. b: 2/17/1892, Champaign, Ill. d: 4/17/59, Galveston, Tex. BR/TR, 6', 176 lbs. Deb: 10/6/14 Career OF: (0-LF 1-CF 0-RF)																							
1914	NY-N	2	5	1	1	0	0	0	0	1	0	.200	.333	.200	533	62	-0	0			.923	1	/2-2	0.1
1915	NY-N	91	249	31	50	7	2	1	21	21	44	.201	.266	.257	523	62	-11	6	7	-1	.988	7	1-43,3-15/S-9,2O	-0.7
1916	NY-N	2	7	0	0	0	0	0	0	0	0	.000	.000	.000	0	-99	-2	0			.625	-1	/3-2	-0.3
Total	3	95	261	32	51	7	2	1	21	22	44	.195	.261	.249	510	58	-13	6	7		.857	7	/1-43,3-17,S-9,2O	-0.9
■ ART BRAMHALL	Bramhall, Arthur Washington b: 2/22/09, Oak Park, Ill. d: 9/4/85, Madison, Wis. BR/TR, 5'11", 170 lbs. Deb: 4/18/35																							
1935	Phi-N	2	1	0	0	0	0	0	0	0	0	.000	.000	.000	0	-91	-0	0			1.000	1	/S-1,3-1	0.0
■ AL BRANCATO	Brancato, Albert "Bronk" b: 5/29/19, Philadelphia, Pa. BR/TR, 5'9.5", 188 lbs. Deb: 9/7/39																							
1939	Phi-A	21	68	12	14	5	0	1	8	8	4	.206	.299	.324	622	60	-4	1	0	0	.939	-1	3-20/S-1	-0.4
1940	Phi-A	107	298	42	57	11	2	1	23	28	36	.191	.265	.252	517	36	-29	3	1	0	.949	0	S-80,3-25	-2.2
1941	Phi-A	144	530	60	124	20	9	2	49	59	49	.234	.311	.317	628	68	-24	1	5	-2	.915	-19	*S-139/3-7	-3.4
1945	Phi-A	10	34	3	4	1	0	0	0	1	3	.118	.143	.147	290	-16	-5	0	0	0	.959	-1	S-10	-0.6
Total	4	282	930	117	199	37	11	4	80	96	92	.214	.290	.290	580	54	-62	5	6	-1	.927	-21	S-230/3-52	-6.6
■ RON BRAND	Brand, Ronald George b: 1/13/40, Los Angeles, Cal. BR/TR, 5'8", 170 lbs. Deb: 5/26/63																							
1963	Pit-N	46	66	8	19	2	0	1	7	10	11	.288	.390	.364	753	118	2	0	0	0	.968	9	C-33/2-2,3-2	1.2
1965	Hou-N	117	391	27	92	6	3	2	37	19	34	.235	.281	.281	563	63	-19	10	5	0	.988	-7	*C-102/3-6,O-5(5-0-0)	-2.2
1966	Hou-N	56	123	12	30	2	0	0	10	9	13	.244	.306	.260	566	64	-6	0	2	-1	.986	-5	C-25/2-9,O-3L,3-1	-1.1
1967	Hou-N	84	215	22	52	8	1	0	18	23	17	.242	.321	.288	609	78	-5	4	0	1	.998	-3	C-67/2-1,O-1(1-0-0)	-0.5
1968	Hou-N	43	81	7	13	2	0	0	4	9	11	.160	.261	.185	446	36	-6	1	1	-0	1.000	3	C-29/3-1,O-1(0-0-1)	-0.2
1969	Mon-N	103	287	19	74	12	0	0	20	30	19	.258	.330	.300	630	77	-8	2	3	-1	.985	-8	C-84/O-2(1-1-0)	-1.3
1970	Mon-N	72	126	10	30	2	3	0	9	9	16	.238	.289	.302	590	59	-7	2	1	0	.952	-7	S-19,3-12/C-9,O2	-1.3
1971	Mon-N	47	56	3	12	0	0	0	1	3	5	.214	.254	.214	469	34	-5	1	1	-0	.957	3	S-22/3-4,O-4L,C2	-0.1
Total	8	568	1345	108	322	34	7	3	106	112	126	.239	.305	.282	586	68	-54	20	13	-0	.988	-16	C-350/S-41,3-26,O2	-5.5
■ JACKIE BRANDT	Brandt, John George b: 4/28/34, Omaha, Neb. BR/TR, 5'11", 170 lbs. Deb: 4/21/56 Career OF: (354-LF 651-CF 237-RF)																							
1956	StL-N	27	42	9	12	3	0	1	3	4	5	.286	.362	.429	790	111	1	0	1	-0	1.000	-3	O-26(3-3-20)	-0.4
	NY-N	98	351	45	105	16	8	11	47	17	31	.299	.332	.484	816	116	7	3	4	-1	.989	-6	O-96(86-3-26)	-0.4
	Yr	125	393	54	117	19	8	12	50	21	36	.298	.335	.478	813	116	8	3	5	-1	.990	-9	*O-122(89-6-46)	-0.8
1958	SF-N	18	52	7	13	1	0	0	3	6	5	.250	.328	.269	597	62	-3	1	0	0	1.000	-0	O-14(11-1-3)	-0.3
1959	SF-N	137	429	63	116	16	5	12	57	35	69	.270	.325	.415	740	98	-2	11	4	1	.984	-7	*O-116L,3-18/1-3,2	-1.3
1960	Bal-A	145	511	73	130	24	6	15	65	47	69	.254	.321	.413	734	98	-2	5	3	0	.983	-10	*O-142C/3-2,1-1	-1.9
1961	Bal-A★	139	516	93	153	18	5	16	72	62	51	.297	.373	.444	817	122	16	10	2	2	.974	-16	*O-136(21-120-34)/3-1	-0.4
1962	Bal-A	143	505	76	129	29	5	19	75	55	64	.255	.333	.446	779	115	9	9	3	1	.976	9	*O-138(0-109-30)/3-2	1.4
1963	Bal-A	142	451	49	112	15	5	15	61	34	85	.248	.301	.404	705	99	-2	4	5	-1	.986	-7	*O-134(30-92-39)/3-1	-1.6
1964	Bal-A	137	523	66	127	25	1	13	47	45	104	.243	.306	.369	676	87	-9	1	4	-1	.981	16	*O-134(10-131-0)	0.1
1965	Bal-A	96	243	35	59	17	0	8	24	21	40	.243	.303	.412	715	99	-1	1	2	-0	.961	-6	O-84(39-37-22)	-1.1
1966	Phi-N	82	164	16	41	6	1	1	15	17	36	.250	.320	.317	638	78	-4	0	2	-1	.988	-12	O-71(17-49-6)	-2.0
1967	Phi-N	16	19	1	2	1	0	0	1	0	6	.105	.105	.158	263	-25	-3	0	0	0	1.000	-1	/O-3(3-0-0)	-0.4
	Hou-N	41	89	7	21	4	1	1	15	8	9	.236	.299	.337	636	85	-2	0	0	0	.991	-2	1-14/O-6(6-0-0),3-1	-0.6
	Yr	57	108	8	23	5	1	1	16	8	15	.213	.267	.306	573	65	-5	0	0	0	.991	-3	1-14/O-9(9-0-0),3-1	-1.0
Total	11	1221	3895	540	1020	175	37	112	485	351	574	.262	.325	.412	737	102	5	45	30	-1	.980	-46	*O-1100C/3-25,1-18,2	-8.9
■ OTIS BRANNAN	Brannan, Otis Owen b: 3/13/1899, Greenbrier, Ark. d: 6/6/67, Little Rock, Ark. BL/TR, 5'9", 160 lbs. Deb: 4/11/28																							
1928	StL-A	135	483	68	118	18	3	10	66	60	19	.244	.333	.356	689	79	-15	3	9	-2	.964	-8	*2-135	-2.1
1929	StL-A	23	51	4	15	1	0	1	8	4	4	.294	.345	.373	718	82	-1	0	0	0	.975	-1	2-19	-0.2
Total	2	158	534	72	133	19	3	11	74	64	23	.249	.334	.358	692	79	-16	3	9	-2	.966	-9	2-154	-2.3
■ MIKE BRANNOCK	Brannock, Michael J. b: 1853, Guelph, Ont., Canada 5'8", 162 lbs. Deb: 10/21/1871																							
1871	Chi-n	3	14	2	1	0	0	0	0	0	0	.071	.071	.071	143	-53	-3	0	0	0	.500	-2	/3-3	-0.4
1875	Chi-n	2	9	2	1	0	0	0	0	0	0	.111	.111	.111	222	-22	-1	2	0	0	.500	-2	/3-2	-0.2
Total	2 n	5	23	4	2	0	0	0	0	0	0	.087	.087	.087	174	-43	-4	2	0	0	.500	-4	/3-5	-0.6
■ DUD BRANOM	Branom, Edgar Dudley b: 11/30/1897, Sulphur Springs, Tex. d: 2/4/80, Sun City, Ariz. BL/TL, 6'1", 190 lbs. Deb: 4/12/27																							
1927	Phi-A	30	94	8	22	1	0	0	13	2	5	.234	.250	.245	495	27	-10	2	1	0	.973	-0	1-26	-1.1
■ KITTY BRANSFIELD	Bransfield, William Edward b: 1/7/1875, Worcester, Mass. d: 5/1/47, Worcester, Mass. BR/TR, 5'11", 207 lbs. Deb: 8/22/1898 U																							
1898	Bos-N	5	9	2	2	0	1	0	1	0		.222	.222	.444	667	85	-0	0			.889	-1	/C-4,1-1	-0.1
1901	Pit-N	139	566	92	167	26	16	0	91	29		.295	.335	.398	733	109	5	23			.981	-10	*1-139	-0.8
1902	Pit-N	102	413	49	126	21	8	0	69	17		.305	.336	.395	730	121	9	23			.984	-6	*1-101	0.0
1903	*Pit-N	127	505	69	134	23	7	2	57	33		.265	.314	.350	665	87	-10	13			.981	6	*1-127	-0.6
1904	Pit-N	139	520	47	116	17	9	0	60	22		.223	.259	.290	549	68	-21	11			.981	-3	*1-139	-2.8
1905	Phi-N	151	580	55	150	23	9	3	76	27		.259	.294	.345	639	93	-7	27			.985	-1	*1-151	-1.1
1906	Phi-N	140	524	47	144	28	5	1	60	16		.275	.300	.353	653	104	-1	12			.980	-2	*1-139	-0.5
1907	Phi-N	94	348	25	81	15	2	0	38	14		.233	.262	.287	550	73	-12	8			.978	-3	1-92	-1.9
1908	Phi-N	144	527	53	160	25	7	3	71	23		.304	.335	.395	730	128	15	30			.986	-1	*1-143	1.3
1909	Phi-N	140	527	47	154	27	6	1	59	18		.292	.319	.372	691	114	6	17			**.989**	7	*1-138	1.1
1910	Phi-N	123	427	39	102	17	4	3	52	20	34	.239	.275	.319	593	71	-18	10			.982	-4	*1-110	-2.6
1911	Phi-N	23	43	4	11	1	1	0	3	0	5	.256	.256	.326	581	61	-2	1			.987	0	/1-8	-0.3
	Chi-N	3	10	0	4	2	0	0	0	2	2	.400	.500	.600	1100	207	2	0			1.000	-0	/1-3	0.1
	Yr	26	53	4	15	3	1	0	3	2	7	.283	.309	.377	686	91	-1	1			.991	-0	1-11	-0.2
Total	12	1330	4999	529	1351	225	75	13	637	221	41	.270	.304	.353	657	97	-34	175			.983	-18	*1-1291/C-4	-8.2
■ JEFF BRANSON	Branson, Jeffery Glenn b: 1/26/67, Waynesboro, Miss. BL/TR, 6', 180 lbs. Deb: 4/12/92																							
1992	Cin-N	72	115	12	34	7	1	0	15	5	16	.296	.325	.374	699	95	-1	0	1	-0	.946	2	2-33/3-8,S-1	0.1
1993	Cin-N	125	381	40	92	15	1	3	22	19	73	.241	.278	.310	587	57	-23	4	1	1	.978	5	S-59,2-45,3-14,/1-1	-1.2
1994	Cin-N	58	109	18	31	4	1	6	16	5	16	.284	.316	.505	820	110	1	0	0	0	.980	-4	2-19,3-18/S-8,1-2	-0.2
1995	*Cin-N	122	331	43	86	18	2	12	45	44	69	.260	.350	.435	785	106	3	2	1	0	.971	**22**	3-98,S-32/2-6,1-1	2.6
1996	Cin-N	129	311	34	76	16	4	9	37	31	67	.244	.315	.408	723	89	-6	2	0	0	.932	2	3-64,S-38,2-31	-0.1
1997	Cin-N	65	98	9	15	3	1	1	5	7	23	.153	.210	.235	444	16	-12	1	0	0	.971	3	3-27,2-14,S-11	-0.8
	*Cle-A	29	72	5	19	4	0	2	7	7	17	.264	.338	.403	740	89	-1	0	2	-1	.986	4	2-19/3-6,S-2,D-1	0.3
1998	*Cle-A	63	100	6	20	4	1	1	9	3	21	.200	.223	.290	513	31	-10	0	0	0	.960	-0	2-31,3-20/1-3,S-2	-0.9
2000	LA-N	18	17	3	4	1	0	0	0	1	6	.235	.278	.294	572	47	-1	0	0	0	1.000	3	/S-7,2-3,3-3	0.1
Total	8	681	1534	170	377	72	11	34	156	122	308	.246	.303	.374	677	78	-51	9	5	0	.957	36	3-258,2-201,S/1D	-0.1
■ MARSHALL BRANT	Brant, Marshall Lee b: 9/17/55, Garberville, Cal. BR/TR, 6'5", 185 lbs. Deb: 10/1/80																							
1980	NY-A	3	6	0	0	0	0	0	0	0	3	.000	.000	.000	0	-99	-2	0	0	0	1.000	0	/1-2,D-1	-0.1
1983	Oak-A	5	14	2	2	0	0	0	2	0	3	.143	.143	.143	286	-22	-2	0	0	0	.905	-1	/1-3,D-1	-0.4
Total	2	8	20	2	2	0	0	0	2	0	6	.100	.100	.100	200	-47	-4	0	0	0	.935	-1	/1-5,D-2	-0.5
■ MICKEY BRANTLEY	Brantley, Michael Charles b: 6/17/61, Catskill, N.Y. BR/TR, 5'10", 180 lbs. Deb: 8/9/86 C Career OF: (137-LF 125-CF 50-RF)																							
1986	Sea-A	27	102	12	20	3	2	3	7	10	21	.196	.268	.353	621	67	-5	1	1	-0	.983	0	O-25(1-25-0)	-0.5
1987	Sea-A	92	351	52	106	23	2	14	54	24	44	.302	.347	.499	845	115	7	13	4	1	.982	-6	O-82(6-51-35)/D-8	0.0
1988	Sea-A	149	577	76	152	25	4	15	56	26	64	.263	.298	.399	696	89	-10	18	7	2	.982	-5	*O-147(118-49-4)/D-2	-1.7
1989	Sea-A	34	108	14	17	5	0	0	8	7	7	.157	.209	.204	412	16	-12	2	2	-0	1.000	1	O-23(12-0-11)/D-7	-1.2
Total	4	302	1138	154	295	56	8	32	125	67	136	.259	.302	.407	708	89	-20	34	14	3	.984	-9	O-277L/D-17	-3.4
■ RUSSELL BRANYAN	Branyan, Russell Oles b: 12/19/75, Warner Robins, Ga. BL/TR, 6'3", 195 lbs. Deb: 9/26/98 Career OF: (18-LF 0-CF 15-RF)																							
1998	Cle-A	1	4	0	0	0	0	0	0	0	2	.000	.000	.000	0	-97	-1	0	0	0	1.000	-1	/3-1	-0.2
1999	Cle-A	11	38	4	8	2	0	1	6	3	19	.211	.286	.342	628	57	-3	0	0	0	.960	2	/3-8,D-3	-0.1

YEAR	TM/L	G	AB	R	H	2B	3B	HR	RBI	BB	SO	AVG	OBP	SLG	OPS	OPS+	BR+	SB	CS	SBR	FA	FR	G/POS	TPR
2000	Cle-A	67	193	32	46	7	2	16	38	22	76	.238	.329	.544	873	113	3	0	0	0	.968	0	O-33L,D-23/3-1	0.0
Total	3	79	235	36	54	9	2	17	44	25	97	.230	.317	.502	819	100	-1	0	0	0	.929	2	/O-33L,D-26,3-10	-0.3
■ ROY BRASHEAR	Brashear, Roy Parks b: 1/3/1874, Ashtabula, Ohio d: 4/20/51, Los Angeles, Cal. BR/TR, 5′11″, 205 lbs. Deb: 4/25/02 F Career OF: (1-LF 7-CF 8-RF)																							
1902	StL-N	110	388	36	107	8	2	1	40	32		.276	.333	.314	647	104	2	9			.980	-9	1-67,2-21,O-16R,/S	-0.9
1903	Phi-N	20	75	9	17	3	0	0	4	6		.227	.284	.267	551	59	-4	2			.918	-4	2-18/1-2	-0.8
Total	2	130	463	45	124	11	2	1	44	38		.268	.325	.307	631	96	-2	11			.978	-13	/1-69,2-39,O-16R,S	-1.7
■ JOE BRATCHER	Bratcher, Joseph Warlick "Goobers" b: 7/22/1898, Grand Saline, Tex d: 10/13/77, Fort Worth, Tex. BL/TR, 5′8.5″, 140 lbs. Deb: 8/26/24																							
1924	StL-N	4	1	1	0	0	0	0	0	0	0	.000	.000	.000	0	-99	-0	0	0	0	.000	-1	/O-1(0-1-0)	-0.1
■ FRED BRATSCHI	Bratschi, Frederick Oscar "Fritz" b: 1/16/1892, Alliance, Ohio d: 1/10/62, Massillon, Ohio BR/TR, 5′10″, 170 lbs. Deb: 7/24/21																							
1921	Chi-A	16	28	0	8	1	0	0	3	0	2	.286	.286	.321	607	55	-2	0	0	0	1.000	1	/O-5(1-0-4)	-0.1
1926	Bos-A	72	167	12	46	10	1	0	19	14	15	.275	.335	.347	682	81	-5	0	1	-0	.949	-7	O-37(29-0-8)	-1.4
1927	Bos-A	1	1	0	0	0	0	0	0	0	0	.000	.000	.000	0	-99	-0	0	0	0	.000	0	H	0.0
Total	3	89	196	12	54	11	1	0	22	14	17	.276	.327	.342	669	76	-7	0	1	-0	.956	-6	/O-42(30-0-12)	-1.5
■ STEVE BRAUN	Braun, Stephen Russell b: 5/8/48, Trenton, N.J. BL/TR, 5′10″, 180 lbs. Deb: 4/6/71 C Career OF: (465-LF 0-CF 35-RF)																							
1971	Min-A	128	343	51	87	12	2	5	35	48	50	.254	.354	.344	698	95	-0	8	3	1	.933	-13	3-73,2-28,S-10,/O-2L	-1.1
1972	Min-A	121	402	40	116	21	0	2	50	45	38	.289	.363	.356	719	109	6	4	5	-1	.970	-12	3-74,2-20,S-11,/O-9L	-0.7
1973	Min-A	115	361	46	102	28	5	6	42	74	48	.283	.409	.438	846	133	19	4	3	-0	.941	-11	*3-102/O-6(6-0-0)	0.7
1974	Min-A	129	453	53	127	12	1	8	40	56	51	.280	.362	.364	726	106	5	4	4	-1	.964	2	*O-108(108-0-0),3-17	0.1
1975	Min-A	136	453	70	137	18	3	11	45	66	55	.302	.392	.428	821	130	20	0	2	-1	.971	-2	*O-106L/1-9,3-2,2D	1.0
1976	Min-A	122	417	73	120	12	3	3	61	67	43	.288	.388	.353	740	115	11	12	4	1	.971	-3	D-71,O-32L,3-16	0.6
1977	Sea-A	139	451	51	106	19	1	5	31	80	59	.235	.353	.315	668	84	-7	8	3	1	.975	5	*O-100L,D-32/3-1	-0.6
1978	Sea-A	32	74	11	17	4	0	3	15	9	5	.230	.313	.405	719	101	0	1	0	0	1.000	-1	D-14/O-4(2-0-2)	-0.1
	*KC-A	64	137	16	36	10	1	0	14	28	16	.263	.388	.350	738	106	2	3	2	-0	.964	-5	O-33(33-0-0),3-11	-0.4
	Yr	96	211	27	53	14	1	3	29	37	21	.251	.363	.370	733	105	3	4	2	0	.967	-6	O-37L,D-14,3-11	-0.5
1979	KC-A	58	116	15	31	2	0	4	10	22	11	.267	.384	.388	772	107	2	0	0	0	1.000	1	O-18(18-0-0),D-11/3-2	0.2
1980	KC-A	14	23	0	1	0	0	0	1	2	2	.043	.120	.043	163	-53	-5	0	0	0	1.000	-2	/O-5(3-0-2),D-1	-0.7
	Tor-A	37	55	4	15	2	0	1	9	8	5	.273	.365	.364	729	96	-0	0	0	0	1.000	0	D-13/3-1	0.0
	Yr	51	78	4	16	2	0	1	10	10	7	.205	.295	.269	565	54	-5	0	0	0	1.000	-2	D-14/O-5(3-0-2),3-1	-0.7
1981	StL-N	44	46	9	9	2	1	0	2	15	7	.196	.393	.283	676	92	0	1	0	0	1.000	-1	O-12(6-0-6)/3-1	0.0
1982	*StL-N	58	62	6	17	4	0	0	4	11	10	.274	.384	.339	722	103	1	0	0	0	1.000	-5	/O-8(6-0-2),3-5	-0.4
1983	StL-N	78	92	8	25	2	1	3	7	21	7	.272	.407	.413	820	128	4	0	1	-0	1.000	-5	O-22(18-0-5)/3-4	-0.2
1984	StL-N	86	98	6	27	3	1	0	16	17	17	.276	.383	.327	709	104	1	0	0	0	1.000	-5	O-19(12-0-7)/3-1	-0.4
1985	*StL-N	64	67	7	16	4	0	1	6	10	9	.239	.346	.343	689	94	-0	0	0	0	1.000	-2	O-14(7-0-7)	-0.2
Total	15	1425	3650	466	989	155	19	52	388	579	433	.271	.373	.367	740	108	61	45	27	0	.973	-57	O-498L,3-310,D/2S1	-2.2
■ ANGEL BRAVO	Bravo, Angel Alfonso (Urdaneta) b: 8/4/42, Maracaibo, Venez. BL/TL, 5′8″, 150 lbs. Deb: 6/6/69																							
1969	Chi-A	27	90	10	26	4	2	1	3	3	5	.289	.319	.411	730	98	-0	2	0	0	.978	-4	O-25(2-24-3)	-0.5
1970	*Cin-N	65	65	10	18	1	1	0	3	9	13	.277	.365	.323	688	86	-1	0	1	-0	.947	-5	O-22(5-12-5)	-0.7
1971	Cin-N	5	5	0	1	0	0	0	0	0	1	.200	.200	.200	400	14	-1	0	0	0	.000	0	H	-0.1
	SD-N	52	58	6	9	2	0	0	6	8	12	.155	.269	.190	458	34	-5	0	1	-0	.833	-3	/O-9(5-3-1)	-0.9
	Yr	57	63	6	10	2	0	0	6	8	13	.159	.264	.190	454	33	-5	0	1	-0	.833	-3	/O-9(5-3-1)	-1.0
Total	3	149	218	26	54	7	3	1	12	20	31	.248	.317	.321	638	77	-7	2	2	-0	.957	-12	/O-56(12-39-9)	-2.2
■ BUSTER BRAY	Bray, Clarence Wilbur b: 4/1/13, Birmingham, Ala. d: 9/4/82, Evansville, Ind. BL/TL, 6′, 170 lbs. Deb: 4/18/41																							
1941	Bos-N	4	11	2	1	1	0	0	1	1	2	.091	.167	.182	348	-2	-2	0			1.000	-0	/O-3(0-3-0)	-0.2
■ FRANK BRAZILL	Brazill, Frank Leo b: 8/11/1899, Spangler, Pa. d: 11/3/76, Oakland, Cal. BL/TR, 5′11.5″, 175 lbs. Deb: 4/13/21																							
1921	Phi-A	66	177	17	48	3	1	0	19	23	21	.271	.361	.299	661	70	-7	2	4	-1	.984	-1	1-36/3-9	-1.0
1922	Phi-A	6	13	0	1	0	0	0	1	0	1	.077	.077	.077	154	-58	-3	0	0	0	.750	-2	/3-2	-0.5
Total	2	72	190	17	49	3	1	0	20	23	22	.258	.344	.284	628	62	-10	2	4	-1	.892	-3	/1-36,3-11	-1.5
■ SID BREAM	Bream, Sidney Eugene b: 8/3/60, Carlisle, Pa. BL/TL, 6′4″, 220 lbs. Deb: 9/1/83																							
1983	LA-N	15	11	0	2	0	0	0	2	2	2	.182	.308	.182	490	39	-1	0	0	0	1.000	-0	/1-4	-0.1
1984	LA-N	27	49	2	9	3	0	0	6	6	9	.184	.273	.245	518	47	-3	1	0	0	1.000	2	1-14	-0.2
1985	LA-N	24	53	4	7	0	0	3	6	7	10	.132	.233	.302	535	50	-4	0	0	0	.994	2	1-16	-0.3
	Pit-N	26	95	14	27	7	0	3	15	11	14	.284	.358	.453	811	127	3	0	2	-1	.992	2	1-25	0.3
	Yr	50	148	18	34	7	0	6	21	18	24	.230	.313	.399	712	100	-0	0	2	-1	.993	4	1-41	0.0
1986	Pit-N	154	522	73	140	37	5	16	77	60	73	.268	.345	.450	795	115	10	13	7	0	.989	23	*1-153/O-2(2-0-0)	2.5
1987	Pit-N	149	516	64	142	25	3	13	65	49	69	.275	.338	.411	749	97	-3	9	8	-1	.988	11	*1-144	-0.1
1988	Pit-N	148	462	50	122	37	0	10	65	47	64	.264	.333	.409	742	114	8	9	9	-1	.995	21	*1-138	2.0
1989	Pit-N	19	36	3	8	3	0	0	4	12	10	.222	.417	.306	722	113	2	0	4	-1	.992	-0	1-13	-0.1
1990	*Pit-N	147	389	39	105	23	2	15	67	48	65	.270	.353	.455	808	125	13	8	4	0	.993	10	*1-142	1.6
1991	*Atl-N	91	265	32	67	12	0	11	45	25	31	.253	.317	.423	740	100	-0	0	3	-1	.996	-0	1-85	-0.7
1992	*Atl-N	125	372	30	97	25	1	10	61	46	51	.261	.344	.414	758	107	4	6	0	1	.989	-3	*1-120	-0.5
1993	*Atl-N	117	277	33	72	14	1	9	35	31	43	.260	.334	.415	750	98	-1	4	2	0	.996	5	1-90	-0.2
1994	Hou-N	46	61	7	21	5	0	0	7	9	9	.344	.429	.426	855	131	3	0	1	-0	.986	2	1-10	0.4
Total	12	1088	3108	351	819	191	12	90	455	353	450	.264	.340	.420	759	107	32	50	40	-3	.992	74	1-954/O-2(2-0-0)	4.6
■ JIM BREAZEALE	Breazeale, James Leo b: 10/3/49, Houston, Tex. BL/TR, 6′2″, 210 lbs. Deb: 9/13/69																							
1969	Atl-N	2	1	1	0	0	0	0	0	2	0	.000	.667	.000	667	101	0	0	0	0	.833	-0	/1-1	0.0
1971	Atl-N	10	21	1	4	0	0	1	3	0	3	.190	.190	.333	524	43	-2	0	0	0	1.000	-0	/1-4	-0.2
1972	Atl-N	52	85	10	21	2	0	5	17	6	12	.247	.297	.447	744	100	-0	0	1	-0	1.000	-2	1-16/3-1	-0.4
1978	Chi-A	25	72	8	15	3	0	3	13	8	10	.208	.287	.375	663	84	-2	0	0	0	.992	-3	1-19/D-4	-0.6
Total	4	89	179	20	40	5	0	9	33	16	25	.223	.287	.402	689	88	-3	0	1	-0	.993	-5	/1-40,D-4,3-1	-1.2
■ BRENT BREDE	Brede, Brent David b: 9/13/71, Belleville, Ill. BL/TL, 6′4″, 190 lbs. Deb: 9/8/96 Career OF: (29-LF 0-CF 86-RF)																							
1996	Min-A	10	20	2	6	0	1	0	2	1	5	.300	.333	.400	733	83	-1	0	0	0	1.000	0	/O-7(0-0-7)	0.0
1997	Min-A	61	190	25	52	11	1	3	21	21	38	.274	.349	.389	739	91	-2	7	2	1	.957	-6	O-42(3-0-40),1-15/D-1	-1.0
1998	Ari-N	98	212	23	48	9	3	2	17	24	43	.226	.311	.325	636	68	-10	1	0	0	.964	-8	O-58R,1-12/D-1	-2.0
Total	3	169	422	50	106	20	5	5	40	46	86	.251	.329	.358	687	79	-12	8	2	1	.964	-14	O-107R/1-27,D-2	-3.0
■ DANNY BREEDEN	Breeden, Danny Richard b: 6/27/42, Albany, Ga. BR/TR, 5′11.5″, 185 lbs. Deb: 7/24/69 F																							
1969	Cin-N	3	8	0	1	0	0	0	1	0	3	.125	.125	.125	250	-28	-1	0	0	0	.941	0	/C-3	-0.1
1971	Chi-N	25	65	3	10	1	0	0	4	9	18	.154	.267	.169	436	23	-6	0	0	0	.975	4	C-25	-0.1
Total	2	28	73	3	11	1	0	0	5	9	21	.151	.253	.164	417	18	-8	0	0	0	.972	5	/C-28	-0.2
■ HAL BREEDEN	Breeden, Harold Noel b: 6/28/44, Albany, Ga. BR/TL, 6′2″, 200 lbs. Deb: 4/7/71 F																							
1971	Chi-N	23	36	1	5	1	0	1	2	2	7	.139	.184	.250	434	19	-4	0	0	0	.982	1	/1-8	-0.3
1972	Mon-N	42	87	6	20	2	0	3	10	7	15	.230	.287	.356	644	80	-2	0	0	0	.994	-1	1-26/O-1(1-0-0)	-0.5
1973	Mon-N	105	258	36	71	10	6	15	43	29	45	.275	.353	.535	888	138	12	0	1	-0	.991	3	1-66	1.1
1974	Mon-N	79	190	14	47	13	0	2	20	24	35	.247	.332	.347	679	85	-3	0	1	-0	.987	1	1-56	-0.7
1975	Mon-N	24	37	4	5	2	0	0	1	7	5	.135	.273	.189	462	29	-3	0	0	0	.989	-0	1-12	-0.5
Total	5	273	608	61	148	28	6	21	76	69	107	.243	.323	.413	735	99	-1	0	2	-1	.990	4	1-168/O-1(1-0-0)	-0.9
■ MARV BREEDING	Breeding, Marvin Eugene b: 3/8/34, Decatur, Ala. BR/TR, 6′, 175 lbs. Deb: 4/19/60																							
1960	Bal-A	152	551	69	147	25	2	3	43	35	80	.267	.314	.336	650	77	-18	10	4	1	.977	5	*2-152	-0.1
1961	Bal-A	90	244	32	51	8	0	1	16	14	33	.209	.252	.254	506	37	-22	5	2	0	.970	7	2-80	-0.9
1962	Bal-A	95	240	27	59	10	1	2	18	8	41	.246	.273	.321	594	63	-13	2	2	-0	.977	21	2-73/S-1,3-1	1.2

YEAR	TM/L	G	AB	R	H	2B	3B	HR	RBI	BB	SO	AVG	OBP	SLG	OPS	OPS+	BR+	SB	CS	SBR	FA	FR	G/POS	TPR
1963	Was-A	58	197	20	54	7	2	1	14	7	21	.274	.299	.345	644	80	-5	1	1	-0	.914	-9	3-29,2-22/S-2	-1.3
	LA-N	20	36	6	6	0	0	0	1	2	5	.167	.211	.167	377	11	-4	1	0	0	.972	-4	2-17/S-1,3-1	-0.8
Total	4	415	1268	154	317	50	5	7	92	66	180	.250	.289	.314	603	65	-62	19	9	1	.975	20	2-344/3-31,S-4	-1.9

■ HERB BREMER Bremer, Herbert Frederick b: 10/26/13, Chicago, Ill. d: 11/28/79, Columbus, Ga. BR/TR, 6', 195 lbs. Deb: 9/16/37

YEAR	TM/L	G	AB	R	H	2B	3B	HR	RBI	BB	SO	AVG	OBP	SLG	OPS	OPS+	BR+	SB	CS	SBR	FA	FR	G/POS	TPR
1937	StL-N	11	33	2	7	1	0	0	3	2	4	.212	.257	.242	500	36	-3	0			.979	-0	C-10	-0.3
1938	StL-N	50	151	14	33	5	1	2	14	9	36	.219	.262	.305	567	53	-10	1			.977	3	C-50	-0.4
1939	StL-N	9	9	0	1	0	0	0	1	0	2	.111	.111	.111	222	-38	-2	0			1.000	1	/C-8	-0.1
Total	3	70	193	16	41	6	1	2	18	11	42	.212	.255	.285	540	45	-15	1			.979	3	/C-68	-0.8

■ SAM BRENEGAN Brenegan, Olaf Selmar b: 9/1/1890, Galesville, Wis. d: 4/20/56, Galesville, Wis. BL/TR, 6'2", 185 lbs. Deb: 4/24/14

YEAR	TM/L	G	AB	R	H	2B	3B	HR	RBI	BB	SO	AVG	OBP	SLG	OPS	OPS+	BR+	SB	CS	SBR	FA	FR	G/POS	TPR
1914	Pit-N	1	0	0	0	0	0	0	0	0	0	—	—	—	—	—	0	0			.000	-0	/C-1	0.0

■ BOB BRENLY Brenly, Robert Earl b: 2/25/54, Coshocton, Ohio BR/TR, 6'2", 210 lbs. Deb: 8/14/81 C Career OF: (3-LF 0-CF 3-RF)

YEAR	TM/L	G	AB	R	H	2B	3B	HR	RBI	BB	SO	AVG	OBP	SLG	OPS	OPS+	BR+	SB	CS	SBR	FA	FR	G/POS	TPR
1981	SF-N	19	45	5	15	2	1	1	4	6	4	.333	.423	.489	912	161	4	0	1	-0	.964	-4	C-14/3-3,O-1(1-0-0)	0.0
1982	SF-N	65	180	26	51	4	1	4	15	18	26	.283	.352	.383	735	106	2	6	2	1	.961	0	C-61/3-1	0.5
1983	SF-N	104	281	36	63	12	2	7	34	37	48	.224	.319	.356	675	89	-4	10	7	-0	.983	1	C-90,1-10/O-2(1-0-1)	0.0
1984	SF-N★	145	506	74	147	28	0	20	80	48	52	.291	.355	.464	820	133	21	6	9	-2	.986	-18	*C-127,1-22/O-3R	0.6
1985	SF-N	133	440	41	97	16	1	19	56	57	62	.220	.313	.391	704	100	-0	1	4	-1	.984	-7	*C-110,3-17,1-10	-0.4
1986	SF-N	149	472	60	116	26	0	16	62	74	97	.246	.352	.403	754	113	10	10	6	0	**.995**	-7	*C-101,3-45,1-19	0.5
1987	*SF-N	123	375	55	100	19	1	18	51	47	85	.267	.353	.467	820	121	11	10	7	-0	.988	9	*C-108/1-6,3-2	2.4
1988	SF-N	73	206	13	39	7	0	5	22	20	40	.189	.268	.296	564	64	-10	1	2	-0	.984	-4	C-69	-1.1
1989	Tor-A	48	88	9	15	3	1	1	6	10	17	.170	.255	.261	516	47	-6	1	0	0	.975	2	D-28,C-13/1-5	-0.5
	SF-N	12	22	2	4	2	0	0	3	1	7	.182	.217	.273	490	40	-2	0	0	0	1.000	0	C-12	-0.1
Total	9	871	2615	321	647	119	7	91	333	318	438	.247	.333	.403	736	107	25	45	38	-3	.984	-26	C-705/1-72,3-68,DO	1.9

■ JIM BRENNAN Brennan, Jack (b: John Gottlieb Dorn) b: 1862, St.Louis, Mo. Deb: 4/20/1884 Career OF: (13-LF 9-CF 15-RF)

YEAR	TM/L	G	AB	R	H	2B	3B	HR	RBI	BB	SO	AVG	OBP	SLG	OPS	OPS+	BR+	SB	CS	SBR	FA	FR	G/POS	TPR
1884	StL-U	56	231	38	50	6	1	0		12		.216	.255	.251	506	52	-20				.891	-2	C-33,O-16L/3-7,S-1	-1.7
1885	StL-N	3	10	0	1	0	0	0	1	1	1	.100	.182	.100	282	-7	-1				.750	-1	/O-2(2-0-0),3-1	-0.2
1888	KC-a	34	118	5	20	2	0	0	6	3		.169	.203	.186	390	24	-10	3			.884	-3	C-25/O-5(2-1-2),3-5	-1.0
1889	Phi-a	31	113	12	25	4	0	0	15	10	15	.221	.285	.257	541	55	-6	1			.818	-4	C-13/O-7C,2-7,3-4	-0.8
1890	Cle-P	59	233	32	59	3	7	0	26	13	29	.253	.304	.326	630	74	-8	8			.845	-4	C-42,3-14/O-6(2-0-4)	-0.7
Total	5	183	705	87	155	15	8	0	48	39	45	.220	.267	.264	530	55	-46	12			.869	-15	C-113/O-36R,3-31,2S	-4.4

■ BILL BRENZEL Brenzel, William Richard b: 3/3/10, Oakland, Cal. d: 6/12/79, Oakland, Cal. BR/TR, 5'10", 173 lbs. Deb: 4/13/32

YEAR	TM/L	G	AB	R	H	2B	3B	HR	RBI	BB	SO	AVG	OBP	SLG	OPS	OPS+	BR+	SB	CS	SBR	FA	FR	G/POS	TPR
1932	Pit-N	9	24	0	1	1	0	0	2	0	4	.042	.042	.083	125	-69	-6	0			1.000	2	/C-9	-0.3
1934	Cle-A	15	51	4	11	3	0	0	3	2	1	.216	.245	.275	520	33	-5	0	0	0	1.000	3	C-15	-0.2
1935	Cle-A	52	142	12	31	5	1	0	14	6	10	.218	.250	.268	518	33	-14	2	2	-0	.975	-7	C-51	-1.8
Total	3	76	217	16	43	9	1	0	19	8	15	.198	.227	.249	476	23	-25	2	2		.985	-2	/C-75	-2.3

■ ROGER BRESNAHAN Bresnahan, Roger Philip "The Duke Of Tralee" b: 6/11/1879, Toledo, Ohio d: 12/4/44, Toledo, Ohio BR/TR, 5'9", 200 lbs. Deb: 8/27/1897 MCH Career OF: (19-LF 221-CF 41-RF)

YEAR	TM/L	G	AB	R	H	2B	3B	HR	RBI	BB	SO	AVG	OBP	SLG	OPS	OPS+	BR+	SB	CS	SBR	FA	FR	G/POS	TPR
1897	Was-N	6	16	1	6	0	0	0	3	1		.375	.412	.375	787	109	0	0			1.000	-1	/P-6,O-1(0-1-0)	0.0
1900	Chi-N	2	2	0	0	0	0	0	0	0		.000	.000	.000	0	-99	-1	0			.000	-0	/C-1	-0.1
1901	Bal-A	86	295	40	79	9	9	1	32	23		.268	.323	.369	692	88	-5	10			.919	-19	C-69/O-8L,3-4,P2	-1.6
1902	Bal-A	65	235	30	64	8	6	4	34	21		.272	.337	.409	746	102	0	12			.880	-7	3-30,C-22,O-15C	-0.5
	NY-N	51	178	16	51	9	3	1	22	16		.287	.352	.388	740	129	6	6			.946	-0	O-27R,C-16/1-4,S3	0.7
1903	NY-N	113	406	87	142	30	8	4	55	61		.350	.443	.493	936	160	34	34			.965	0	O-84C,1-13,C-11,/3	2.9
1904	NY-N	109	402	81	114	22	7	5	33	58		.284	.381	.410	791	138	20	13			.954	0	O-93C,1-10/S-4,23	1.6
1905	*NY-N	104	331	58	100	18	3	0	46	50		.302	.411	.375	785	132	16	11			.970	-1	C-87/O-8(0-2-4)	2.4
1906	NY-N	124	405	69	114	22	4	0	43	81		.281	**.419**	.356	775	139	25	25			.974	5	C-82,O-40(0-39-3)	3.9
1907	NY-N	110	328	57	83	9	7	4	38	61		.253	.380	.360	740	128	13	15			.986	-7	C-95/1-6,O-2C,3-1	1.8
1908	NY-N	140	449	70	127	25	3	1	54	**83**		.283	.401	.359	760	136	23	14			.985	-18	*C-139	2.2
1909	StL-N	72	234	27	57	4	1	0	23	46		.244	.370	.269	639	105	5	11			.960	-6	C-59/2-9,3-1,M	0.4
1910	StL-N	88	234	35	65	15	3	0	27	55	17	.278	.419	.368	787	135	14	13			.961	-9	C-77/O-2(1-1-0),P-1,M	1.2
1911	StL-N	81	227	22	63	17	8	3	41	45	19	.278	.404	.463	866	146	15	4			.968	-2	C-77/2-2,M	2.0
1912	StL-N	48	108	8	36	7	2	1	15	14	9	.333	.419	.463	882	145	7	4			.974	7	C-28,M	1.6
1913	Chi-N	69	162	20	37	5	2	1	21	21	11	.228	.324	.302	627	79	-4	7			.963	-5	C-58	-0.5
1914	Chi-N	101	248	42	69	10	4	0	24	49	20	.278	.401	.351	752	125	11	14			.978	-3	C-85,2-14/O-1(0-1-0)	1.5
1915	Chi-N	77	221	19	45	8	1	1	19	29	23	.204	.296	.262	558	70	-7	19	3	3	.982	3	C-68,M	0.5
Total	17	1446	4481	682	1252	218	71	26	530	714	99	.279	.386	.377	764	126	173	212	3		.971	-63	C-974,O-281C/312PS	20.0

■ RUBE BRESSLER Bressler, Raymond Bloom b: 10/23/1894, Coder, Pa. d: 11/7/66, Cincinnati, Ohio BR/TL, 6', 187 lbs. Deb: 4/24/14 Career OF: (732-LF 8-CF 99-RF)

YEAR	TM/L	G	AB	R	H	2B	3B	HR	RBI	BB	SO	AVG	OBP	SLG	OPS	OPS+	BR+	SB	CS	SBR	FA	FR	G/POS	TPR
1914	Phi-A	29	51	6	11	1	1	0	4	6	7	.216	.310	.275	585	79	-1	0			.941	-2	P-29	0.0
1915	Phi-A	33	55	9	8	0	1	1	4	9	13	.145	.277	.236	513	56	-3	0			.900	0	P-32	0.0
1916	Phi-A	4	5	1	1	0	1	0	1	0	0	.200	.200	.600	800	147	0	0			1.000	-0	/P-4	0.0
1917	Cin-N	3	5	0	1	0	0	0	0	0	2	.200	.200	.200	400	24	-0	0			1.000	-0	/P-2	0.0
1918	Cin-N	23	62	10	17	5	0	0	6	5	4	.274	.328	.355	683	110	1	0			.982	2	P-17/O-3(3-0-1)	-0.1
1919	Cin-N	61	165	22	34	3	4	2	17	23	15	.206	.311	.309	620	89	-2	2			.965	1	O-48(41-0-7),P-13	-0.4
1920	Cin-N	21	30	4	8	1	0	0	3	1	4	.267	.290	.300	590	71	-1	1	0	0	1.000	-1	P-10/O-3(0-1-2),1-2	-0.2
1921	Cin-N	109	323	41	99	18	6	1	54	39	20	.307	.385	.409	793	115	9	5	5	-1	.953	-6	O-85(9-0-76)/1-6	-0.5
1922	Cin-N	52	53	7	14	0	2	0	8	4	4	.264	.316	.340	655	70	-2	1	0	0	1.000	-2	/1-3,O-2(1-0-1)	-0.4
1923	Cin-N	54	119	25	33	3	1	0	18	20	4	.277	.399	.319	718	93	0	3	1	0	.983	-3	1-22/O-6(3-0-3)	-0.3
1924	Cin-N	115	383	41	133	14	13	4	49	22	20	.347	.389	.483	872	134	18	9	10	-2	.990	4	1-50,O-49(45-0-4)	1.4
1925	Cin-N	97	319	43	111	17	6	4	61	40	16	.348	.424	.476	900	133	17	9	5	0	.982	-3	1-52,O-38(36-0-2)	0.8
1926	Cin-N	86	297	58	106	15	9	1	51	37	20	.357	.433	.478	911	149	22	3			.970	-4	O-80(80-0-0)/1-4	1.2
1927	Cin-N	124	467	43	136	14	8	3	77	32	22	.291	.338	.375	713	94	-4	4			.972	7	*O-120(120-0-0)	-0.7
1928	Bro-N	145	501	78	148	29	13	4	70	80	33	.295	.398	.429	827	118	16	2			**.985**	-6	*O-137(137-0-0)	-0.1
1929	Bro-N	136	456	72	145	22	8	9	77	67	27	.318	.406	.461	867	117	14	4			.954	3	*O-122(122-0-0)	0.7
1930	Bro-N	109	335	53	100	12	8	3	52	51	19	.299	.394	.409	803	96	-0	4			.995	6	O-90(90-0-0)/1-7	-0.1
1931	Bro-N	67	153	22	43	4	5	0	26	11	10	.281	.329	.373	702	89	-2	0			.982	-4	O-35(23-7-3)/1-1	-0.8
1932	Phi-N	27	83	9	19	6	1	0	6	2	5	.229	.247	.325	572	47	-6	0			1.000	3	O-18(18-0-0)	-0.4
	StL-N	10	19	0	3	0	0	0	2	0	1	.158	.158	.158	316	-14	-3	0			1.000	-0	/O-4(4-0-0)	-0.3
	Yr	37	102	9	22	6	1	0	8	2	6	.216	.231	.294	525	37	-9	0			1.000	3	O-22(22-0-0)	-0.7
Total	19	1305	3881	544	1170	164	87	32	586	449	246	.301	.378	.413	791	110	71	47	21		.971	-4	O-840L,1-147,P-107	-0.3

■ EDDIE BRESSOUD Bressoud, Edward Francis b: 5/2/32, Los Angeles, Cal. BR/TR, 6'1", 175 lbs. Deb: 6/14/56 Career OF: (1-LF 0-CF 0-RF)

YEAR	TM/L	G	AB	R	H	2B	3B	HR	RBI	BB	SO	AVG	OBP	SLG	OPS	OPS+	BR+	SB	CS	SBR	FA	FR	G/POS	TPR
1956	NY-N	49	163	15	37	4	2	0	9	12	20	.227	.284	.276	560	52	-11	1	0	0	.950	-9	S-48	-1.7
1957	NY-N	49	127	11	34	2	2	5	10	4	19	.268	.301	.433	734	94	-1	0	1	-0	.940	1	S-33,3-12	0.2
1958	SF-N	66	137	19	36	5	3	0	8	14	22	.263	.331	.343	674	81	-4	0	1	-0	.966	-2	2-57/3-6,S-4	-0.3
1959	SF-N	104	315	36	79	17	2	9	26	28	55	.251	.312	.403	715	91	-5	0	0	0	.974	-6	S-92/1-1,2-1,3-1	-0.4
1960	SF-N	116	386	37	87	19	6	9	43	35	72	.225	.293	.376	669	87	-8	1	2	-0	.960	6	*S-115	0.7
1961	SF-N	59	114	14	24	6	0	3	11	11	23	.211	.280	.342	622	66	-6	1	0	0	.964	-9	S-34/3-3,2-1	-1.3
1962	Bos-A	153	599	79	166	40	9	14	68	46	118	.277	.331	.444	775	103	2	2	3	-1	.965	25	*S-153	3.8
1963	Bos-A	140	497	61	129	23	6	20	60	52	93	.260	.332	.451	783	113	9	1	1	-0	.962	-9	*S-137	1.2
1964	Bos-A☆	158	566	86	166	41	3	15	55	72	99	.293	.374	.456	830	123	19	1	1	-0	.972	-14	*S-158	2.0
1965	Bos-A	107	296	29	67	11	1	8	25	29	77	.226	.298	.351	649	79	-8	0	1	-0	.963	-5	S-86/3-2,O-1(1-0-0)	-0.7
1966	NY-N	133	405	48	91	15	5	10	49	47	107	.225	.307	.360	667	87	-7	2	2	-0	.960	8	S-94,3-32/1-9,2-7	0.8
1967	*StL-N	52	67	8	9	1	1	1	1	9	18	.134	.237	.224	461	33	-6	0	0	0	.929	-4	S-48/3-1	-0.9
Total	12	1186	3672	443	925	184	40	94	365	359	723	.252	.321	.401	721	96	-26	9	13	-3	.963	-19	*S-1002/2-66,3-57,1O	3.4

■ JIM BRETON
Breton, John Frederick b: 7/15/1891, Chicago, Ill. d: 5/30/73, Beloit, Wis. BR/TR, 5'10.5", 178 lbs. Deb: 8/25/13

YEAR	TM/L	G	AB	R	H	2B	3B	HR	RBI	BB	SO	AVG	OBP	SLG	OPS	OPS+	BR+	SB	CS	SBR	FA	FR	G/POS	TPR
1913	Chi-A	12	30	1	5	1	1	0	2	1	5	.167	.194	.267	460	35	-3	0			.938	3	/S-7,3-3	0.0
1914	Chi-A	81	231	21	49	7	2	0	24	24	42	.212	.292	.260	552	67	-9	9	6	-0	.910	3	3-79	-0.5
1915	Chi-A	16	36	3	5	1	0	0	1	5	9	.139	.262	.167	429	27	-3	2	1	0	.882	-2	3-14/2-1,S-1	-0.5
Total	3	109	297	25	59	9	3	0	27	30	56	.199	.279	.249	528	59	-15	11	7		.906	4	/3-96,S-8,2-1	-1.0

■ GEORGE BRETT
Brett, George Howard b: 5/15/53, Glen Dale, W.Va. BL/TR, 6', 200 lbs. Deb: 8/2/73 FH Career OF: (22-LF 0-CF 14-RF)

YEAR	TM/L	G	AB	R	H	2B	3B	HR	RBI	BB	SO	AVG	OBP	SLG	OPS	OPS+	BR+	SB	CS	SBR	FA	FR	G/POS	TPR
1973	KC-A	13	40	2	5	2	0	0	0	0	5	.125	.125	.175	300	-15	-6	0	0	0	.974	3	3-13	-0.3
1974	KC-A	133	457	49	129	21	5	2	47	21	38	.282	.314	.363	677	89	-7	8	5	0	.948	-9	*3-132/S-1	-1.8
1975	KC-A	159	634	84	**195**	35	**13**	11	89	46	49	.308	.356	.456	812	125	19	13	10	-1	.949	-6	*3-159/S-1	1.2
1976	*KC-A★	159	645	94	**215**	34	**14**	7	67	49	36	**.333**	.381	.462	843	145	35	21	11	1	.948	3	*3-157/S-4	4.1
1977	*KC-A★	139	564	105	176	32	13	22	88	55	24	.312	.375	.532	907	143	33	14	12	-1	.957	17	*3-135/S-1,D-3	4.5
1978	*KC-A★	128	510	79	150	**45**	8	9	62	39	35	.294	.345	.467	812	123	14	23	7	3	.961	5	*3-128/S-1	2.1
1979	KC-A★	154	645	119	**212**	42	**20**	23	107	51	36	.329	.378	.563	941	147	40	17	10	0	.944	13	*3-149/1-8,D-1	4.9
1980	*KC-A†	117	449	87	175	33	9	24	118	58	22	**.390**	**.461**	**.664**	**1124**	**203**	**64**	15	6	1	.955	4	*3-112/1-1	**6.5**
1981	*KC-A★	89	347	42	109	27	7	6	43	27	23	.314	.365	.484	849	144	19	14	6	1	.946	-9	3-88	0.9
1982	KC-A★	144	552	101	166	32	9	21	82	71	51	.301	.381	.505	887	141	32	6	1	1	.959	-6	*3-134,O-12(12-0-0)	2.4
1983	KC-A★	123	464	90	144	38	2	25	93	57	39	.310	.387	**.563**	**949**	157	36	0	1	-0	.919	-25	*3-102,1-14,O-13R,/D	0.8
1984	*KC-A★	104	377	42	107	21	3	13	69	38	37	.284	.349	.459	808	121	10	0	2	-1	.949	-4	*3-101	0.4
1985	*KC-A★	155	550	108	184	38	5	30	112	103	49	.335	.442	**.585**	**1028**	**178**	**63**	9	1	2	.967	12	*3-152/D-1	7.1
1986	KC-A†	124	441	70	128	28	4	16	73	80	45	.290	.404	.481	885	137	25	1	2	-0	.952	-2	*3-115/S-2,D-7	2.0
1987	KC-A	115	427	71	124	18	2	22	78	72	47	.290	.394	.496	890	131	21	6	3	0	.993	-5	1-83,D-21,3-11	1.0
1988	KC-A★	157	589	90	180	42	3	24	103	82	51	.306	.393	.509	903	149	40	14	3	2	.992	-9	*1-124,D-33/S-1	2.3
1989	KC-A	124	457	67	129	26	3	12	80	59	47	.282	.368	.431	799	125	16	14	4	2	.998	4	*1-104,D-17/O-2L	1.3
1990	KC-A	142	544	82	179	**45**	7	14	87	56	63	**.329**	.392	.515	906	154	39	9	2	1	.993	-1	*1-102,D-32/O-9R,3	3.0
1991	KC-A	131	505	77	129	40	2	10	61	58	75	.255	.332	.402	734	102	1	2	0	0	.989	-1	*D-118,1-10	-0.4
1992	KC-A	152	592	55	169	35	5	7	61	35	69	.285	.332	.397	729	101	-0	8	6	-0	.987	0	*D-132,1-15/3-3	-0.6
1993	KC-A	145	560	69	149	31	3	19	75	39	67	.266	.317	.434	751	94	-6	7	5	-0	.000	0	*D-140	-1.4
Total	21	2707	10349	1583	3154	665	137	317	1595	1096	908	.305	.373	.487	861	135	489	201	97	10	.951	-17	*3-1692,D-506,1/OS	40.0

■ TONY BREWER
Brewer, Anthony Bruce b: 11/25/57, Coushatta, La. BR/TR, 5'11", 190 lbs. Deb: 8/1/84 F

YEAR	TM/L	G	AB	R	H	2B	3B	HR	RBI	BB	SO	AVG	OBP	SLG	OPS	OPS+	BR+	SB	CS	SBR	FA	FR	G/POS	TPR
1984	LA-N	24	37	3	4	1	0	1	4	4	9	.108	.195	.216	411	16	-4	1	0	0	1.000	-2	O-10(8-0-2)	-0.6

■ MIKE BREWER
Brewer, Michael Quinn b: 10/24/59, Shreveport, La. BR/TR, 6'5", 190 lbs. Deb: 6/11/86 F

YEAR	TM/L	G	AB	R	H	2B	3B	HR	RBI	BB	SO	AVG	OBP	SLG	OPS	OPS+	BR+	SB	CS	SBR	FA	FR	G/POS	TPR
1986	KC-A	12	18	0	3	1	0	0	0	2	6	.167	.250	.222	472	29	-2	0	1	-0	1.000	-2	/O-9(0-0-9),D-1	-0.4

■ ROD BREWER
Brewer, Rodney Lee b: 2/24/66, Eustis, Fla. BL/TL, 6'3", 210 lbs. Deb: 9/5/90 Career OF: (19-LF 0-CF 22-RF)

YEAR	TM/L	G	AB	R	H	2B	3B	HR	RBI	BB	SO	AVG	OBP	SLG	OPS	OPS+	BR+	SB	CS	SBR	FA	FR	G/POS	TPR
1990	StL-N	14	25	4	6	1	0	0	2	0	4	.240	.240	.280	520	42	-2	0	0	0	.981	1	/1-9	-0.1
1991	StL-N	19	13	0	1	0	0	0	1	0	5	.077	.077	.077	154	-56	-3	0	0	0	1.000	-0	1-15/O-3(0-0-3)	-0.3
1992	StL-N	29	103	11	31	6	0	0	10	8	12	.301	.357	.359	716	107	1	0	1	-0	1.000	1	1-27/O-4(4-0-0)	0.0
1993	StL-N	110	147	15	42	8	0	2	20	17	26	.286	.364	.381	745	102	1	1	0	0	.960	-6	O-33R,1-32/P-1	-0.6
Total	4	172	288	30	80	15	0	2	33	25	47	.278	.340	.351	690	92	-3	1	1	-0	.995	-4	/1-83,O-40R,P-1	-1.0

■ CHARLIE BREWSTER
Brewster, Charles Lawrence b: 12/27/16, Marthaville, La. BR/TR, 5'8.5", 175 lbs. Deb: 5/2/43

YEAR	TM/L	G	AB	R	H	2B	3B	HR	RBI	BB	SO	AVG	OBP	SLG	OPS	OPS+	BR+	SB	CS	SBR	FA	FR	G/POS	TPR
1943	Cin-N	7	8	0	1	0	0	0	0	0	1	.125	.125	.125	250	-28	-1	0			1.000	-0	/2-2	-0.1
	Phi-N	49	159	13	35	2	0	0	12	10	19	.220	.275	.233	508	49	-10	1			.901	-20	S-46	-3.0
	Yr	56	167	13	36	2	0	0	12	10	20	.216	.268	.228	496	45	-12	1			.901	-20	S-46/2-2	-3.1
1944	Chi-N	10	44	4	11	2	0	0	2	5	7	.250	.327	.295	622	76	-1	0			.903	0	S-10	0.0
1946	Cle-A	3	2	0	0	0	0	0	0	1	1	.000	.333	.000	333	-1	-0	0	0	0	1.000	0	/S-1	0.0
Total	3	69	213	17	47	4	0	0	14	16	28	.221	.281	.239	521	52	-13	1	0		.902	-20	/S-57,2-2	-3.1

■ FRITZ BRICKELL
Brickell, Fritz Darrell b: 3/19/35, Wichita, Kan. d: 10/15/65, Wichita, Kan. BR/TR, 5'5.5", 157 lbs. Deb: 4/30/58 F

YEAR	TM/L	G	AB	R	H	2B	3B	HR	RBI	BB	SO	AVG	OBP	SLG	OPS	OPS+	BR+	SB	CS	SBR	FA	FR	G/POS	TPR
1958	NY-A	2	0	0	0	0	0	0	0	0	0	—	—	—	—	—	0	0	0	0	1.000	0	/2-2	0.0
1959	NY-A	18	39	4	10	1	0	1	4	1	10	.256	.275	.359	634	75	-1	0	0	0	.925	0	S-15/2-3	0.0
1961	LA-A	21	49	3	6	0	0	0	3	6	9	.122	.218	.122	341	-6	-7	0	0	0	.901	0	S-17	-0.6
Total	3	41	88	7	16	1	0	1	7	7	19	.182	.242	.227	469	26	-9	0	0	0	.911	0	/S-32,2-5	-0.6

■ FRED BRICKELL
Brickell, George Frederick b: 11/9/06, Saffordville, Kan. d: 4/8/61, Wichita, Kan. BL/TR, 5'7", 160 lbs. Deb: 8/19/26 F

YEAR	TM/L	G	AB	R	H	2B	3B	HR	RBI	BB	SO	AVG	OBP	SLG	OPS	OPS+	BR+	SB	CS	SBR	FA	FR	G/POS	TPR
1926	Pit-N	24	55	11	19	3	1	0	4	3	6	.345	.400	.436	836	119	2	0			.920	-0	O-14(14-0-0)	0.1
1927	*Pit-N	32	21	6	6	1	0	1	4	1	0	.286	.318	.476	794	103	-0	0			1.000	-1	/O-3(1-0-2)	0.0
1928	Pit-N	81	202	34	65	4	4	3	41	20	18	.322	.383	.426	809	107	2	5			.958	1	O-50(44-0-8)	0.0
1929	Pit-N	60	118	13	37	4	2	0	17	7	12	.314	.352	.381	733	80	-4	3			1.000	0	O-27(14-0-13)	-0.5
1930	Pit-N	68	219	36	65	9	3	1	14	15	20	.297	.342	.379	721	74	-9	3			.951	-4	O-61(11-50-0)	-1.4
	Phi-N	53	240	33	59	12	6	0	17	13	21	.246	.290	.346	636	49	-20	1			.963	5	O-53(0-53-0)	-1.6
	Yr	121	459	69	124	21	9	1	31	28	41	.270	.315	.362	677	61	-29	4			.958	0	*O-114(11-103-0)	-3.0
1931	Phi-N	130	514	77	130	14	5	1	31	42	39	.253	.316	.305	621	63	-26	5			.978	4	*O-122(0-122-0)	-2.5
1932	Phi-N	45	66	9	22	6	1	0	2	4	5	.333	.389	.455	843	112	1	2			.935	-0	O-12(1-11-0)	0.1
1933	Phi-N	8	13	2	4	1	1	0	1	1	0	.308	.357	.538	896	136	1	0			1.000	1	/O-4(4-0-0)	0.1
Total	8	501	1448	221	407	54	23	6	131	106	121	.281	.335	.363	697	75	-52	19			.967	5	O-346(89-236-23)	-5.7

■ GEORGE BRICKLEY
Brickley, George Vincent b: 7/19/1894, Everett, Mass. d: 2/23/47, Everett, Mass. BR/TR, 5'9", 180 lbs. Deb: 9/26/13

YEAR	TM/L	G	AB	R	H	2B	3B	HR	RBI	BB	SO	AVG	OBP	SLG	OPS	OPS+	BR+	SB	CS	SBR	FA	FR	G/POS	TPR
1913	Phi-A	5	12	0	2	0	1	0	0	0	4	.167	.231	.333	564	66	-1	0			1.000	-1	/O-4(0-0-4)	-0.2

■ JIM BRIDEWESER
Brideweser, James Ehrenfeld b: 2/13/27, Lancaster, Ohio d: 8/25/89, ElToro, Cal. BR/TR, 6', 165 lbs. Deb: 9/29/51

YEAR	TM/L	G	AB	R	H	2B	3B	HR	RBI	BB	SO	AVG	OBP	SLG	OPS	OPS+	BR+	SB	CS	SBR	FA	FR	G/POS	TPR
1951	NY-A	2	8	1	3	0	0	0	0	0	1	.375	.375	.375	750	107	0	0	0	0	.818	0	/S-2	0.0
1952	NY-A	42	38	12	10	0	0	0	2	3	5	.263	.317	.263	580	67	-2	0	0	0	.935	2	S-22/2-4,3-1	0.1
1953	NY-A	7	3	3	3	0	1	0	3	1	0	1.000	1.000	1.667	2667	631	2	0	0	0	.833	0	/S-3	0.3
1954	Bal-A	73	204	18	54	7	2	0	12	15	27	.265	.318	.319	637	81	-6	1	1	-0	.944	-12	S-48,2-19	-1.4
1955	Chi-A	34	58	6	12	3	2	0	4	3	7	.207	.246	.328	573	52	-4	0	0	0	.949	6	S-26/3-3,2-2	0.3
1956	Chi-A	10	11	0	2	1	0	0	1	0	3	.182	.250	.273	523	37	-1	0	0	0	.938	0	S-10	-0.1
	Det-A	70	156	23	34	4	0	0	10	20	19	.218	.307	.244	550	47	-12	3	1	0	.987	14	S-32,2-31/3-4	0.5
	Yr	80	167	23	36	5	0	0	11	20	22	.216	.303	.246	549	46	-13	3	1	0	.979	14	S-42,2-31/3-4	0.4
1957	Bal-A	91	142	16	38	7	1	1	18	21	16	.268	.362	.352	714	102	1	2	0	0	.943	5	S-74/3-3,2-1	1.0
Total	7	329	620	79	156	22	6	1	50	63	78	.252	.323	.311	634	75	-20	6	2	1	.946	15	S-217/2-57,3-11	0.7

■ ROCKY BRIDGES
Bridges, Everett Lamar b: 8/7/27, Refugio, Tex. BR/TR, 5'8", 175 lbs. Deb: 4/17/51 C

YEAR	TM/L	G	AB	R	H	2B	3B	HR	RBI	BB	SO	AVG	OBP	SLG	OPS	OPS+	BR+	SB	CS	SBR	FA	FR	G/POS	TPR
1951	Bro-N	63	134	13	34	7	0	1	15	10	10	.254	.306	.328	634	69	-6	0	0	0	.871	3	3-40,2-10/S-9	-0.2
1952	Bro-N	51	56	9	11	3	0	0	2	7	9	.196	.286	.250	536	49	-4	0	1	-0	.986	12	2-24,S-13/3-6	0.8
1953	Cin-N	122	432	52	98	13	2	1	21	37	42	.227	.288	.273	561	47	-33	6	3	0	.976	11	*2-115/S-6,3-3	-1.3
1954	Cin-N	53	52	4	12	1	0	0	2	7	7	.231	.322	.250	572	50	-4	0	1	-0	1.000	11	S-20,2-19,3-13	0.8
1955	Cin-N	95	168	20	48	4	0	1	18	15	19	.286	.344	.327	672	75	-5	1	1	-0	.965	7	3-59,S-26/2-9	0.2
1956	Cin-N	71	19	9	4	0	0	0	1	4	3	.211	.348	.211	558	52	-1	1	2	-0	.966	8	3-51/2-8,S-7,O-1L	0.7
1957	Cin-N	5	1	1	0	0	0	0	0	1	1	.000	.500	.000	500	46	0	0	0	0	1.000	-1	/2-2,S-1,3-1	-0.1
	Was-A	120	391	40	89	17	2	3	47	40	32	.228	.303	.304	607	67	-17	0	2	-1	.971	**29**	*S-108,2-14/3-1	2.1
1958	Was-A☆	116	377	38	99	14	3	5	28	27	32	.263	.317	.355	672	86	-7	0	3	-1	.976	3	*S-112/2-3,3-3	0.5
1959	Det-A	116	381	38	102	16	3	3	35	30	35	.268	.323	.349	672	80	-10	1	2	-0	.952	-6	*S-110/2-5	-0.7
1960	Det-A	10	5	0	1	0	0	0	0	0	0	.200	.200	.200	400	8	-1	0	0	0	1.000	3	/3-7,S-3	0.2
	Cle-A	10	27	1	9	0	0	0	3	1	2	.333	.357	.333	690	91	-0	0	0	0	1.000	3	/S-7,3-3	0.3
	Yr	20	32	1	10	0	0	0	3	1	2	.313	.333	.313	646	76	-1	0	0	0	1.000	6	3-10,S-10	0.5
	StL-N	3	0	0	0	0	0	0	0	0	0	—	—	—	—	—	0	0	0	0	1.000	1	/2-3	0.1

YEAR	TM/L	G	AB	R	H	2B	3B	HR	RBI	BB	SO	AVG	OBP	SLG	OPS	OPS+	BR+	SB	CS	SBR	FA	FR	G/POS	TPR
1961	LA-A	84	229	20	55	5	1	2	15	26	37	.240	.320	.297	617	59	-13	1	0	0	.988	10	2-58,S-25/3-4	0.3
Total	11	919	2272	245	562	80	11	16	187	205	229	.247	.312	.313	625	67	-101	10	15	-3	.968	95	S-447,2-270,3-191,/O	3.7
■ AL BRIDWELL Bridwell, Albert Henry b: 1/4/1884, Friendship, Ohio d: 1/23/69, Portsmouth, Ohio BL/TR, 5'9", 170 lbs. Deb: 4/16/05																								
1905	Cin-N	82	254	17	64	3	1	0	17	19		.252	.309	.272	581	66	-10	8			.944	0	3-43,O-18R/2-7,S1	-1.0
1906	Bos-N	120	459	41	104	9	1	0	22	44		.227	.297	.251	548	73	-13	6			.930	17	*S-119/O-1(0-0-1)	0.9
1907	Bos-N	140	509	49	111	8	2	0	26	61		.218	.309	.242	551	73	-13	17			**.942**	7	*S-140	-0.2
1908	NY-N	147	467	53	133	14	1	0	46	52		.285	.364	.319	683	113	9	20			.933	11	*S-147	2.8
1909	NY-N	145	476	59	140	11	5	0	55	67		.294	.386	.338	724	123	16	32			.940	2	*S-145	2.5
1910	NY-N	142	492	74	136	15	7	0	48	73	23	.276	.374	.335	710	107	7	14			.946	6	*S-141	1.9
1911	NY-N	76	263	28	71	10	1	0	31	33	10	.270	.358	.316	673	86	-4	8			.917	6	S-76	0.7
	Bos-N	51	182	29	53	5	0	0	10	33	8	.291	.403	.319	721	95	1	2			.950	-11	S-51	-0.6
	Yr	127	445	57	124	15	1	0	41	66	18	.279	.377	.317	694	90	-3	10			.929	-5	*S-127	0.1
1912	Bos-N	31	106	6	25	5	1	0	14	5	5	.236	.270	.302	572	55	-7	2			.936	-5	S-31	-1.0
1913	Chi-N	136	405	35	97	6	6	1	37	74	28	.240	.358	.291	650	87	-4	12			.948	2	*S-136	0.8
1914	StL-F	117	381	46	90	6	5	1	33	71	18	.236	.359	.286	645	73	-17	9			.944	-11	*S-103,2-11	-2.2
1915	StL-F	65	175	20	40	3	2	0	9	25	6	.229	.328	.269	597	65	-10	6			.952	1	2-42,3-15/1-1	-0.8
Total	11	1252	4169	457	1064	95	32	2	348	557	98	.255	.347	.295	642	89	-44	136			.939	24	*S-1094/2-60,3-58,O1	3.8
■ BUNNY BRIEF Brief, Anthony Vincent (b: Anthony John Grzeszkowski) b: 7/3/1892, Remus, Mich. d: 2/10/63, Milwaukee, Wis. BR/TR, 6', 185 lbs. Deb: 9/22/12																								
1912	StL-A	15	42	9	13	3	0	0	5	6		.310	.408	.381	789	131	2	2			.826	-1	/O-9(9-0-0),1-4	0.1
1913	StL-A	85	258	24	56	11	6	1	26	21	46	.217	.284	.318	602	78	-8	3			.986	-1	1-62/O-8(8-0-0)	-1.2
1915	Chi-A	48	154	13	33	6	2	2	17	16	28	.214	.305	.318	623	84	-3	8	6	-0	.986	-2	1-46	-0.7
1917	Pit-N	36	115	15	25	5	1	2	11	15	21	.217	.318	.330	649	96	-0	4			.988	2	1-34	0.0
Total	4	184	569	61	127	25	9	5	59	58	95	.223	.306	.325	631	87	-9	17	6		.987	-2	1-146/O-17(17-0-0)	-1.8
■ CHARLIE BRIGGS Briggs, Charles R. b: 1861, Batavia, Ill. 5'7", 170 lbs. Deb: 5/2/1884																								
1884	CP-U	49	182	29	31	8	2	1		11		.170	.218	.253	470	42	-18				.814	-5	O-37(3-28-6),2-12/S-2	-2.1
■ DAN BRIGGS Briggs, Dan Lee b: 11/18/52, Scotia, Cal. BL/TL, 6', 180 lbs. Deb: 9/10/75 Career OF: (41-LF 63-CF 30-RF)																								
1975	Cal-A	13	31	3	7	1	0	1	3	2	6	.226	.273	.355	628	82	-1	0	2	-1	.953	-1	/1-6,O-5(5-0-0),D-2	-0.3
1976	Cal-A	77	248	19	53	13	2	1	14	13	47	.214	.256	.294	550	65	-12	0	3	-1	.993	-0	1-44,O-40(2-32-9)/D-1	-1.8
1977	Cal-A	59	74	6	12	2	0	1	4	8	14	.162	.244	.230	474	31	-7	0	0	0	.993	0	1-45,O-13(0-12-1)	-0.8
1978	Cle-A	15	49	4	8	0	1	1	1	4	9	.163	.226	.265	492	38	-4	0	0	0	1.000	2	O-15(0-0-15)	-0.3
1979	SD-N	104	227	34	47	4	3	8	30	18	45	.207	.280	.357	637	77	-8	2	1	0	.986	-1	1-50,O-44(25-16-3)	-1.2
1981	Mon-N	9	11	0	1	0	0	0	0	0	3	.091	.091	.091	182	-48	-2	0	1	-0	1.000	-1	/1-3,O-3(1-2-1)	-0.4
1982	Chi-N	48	48	1	6	0	0	0	1	0	9	.125	.143	.125	268	-24	-8	0	0	0	.875	-2	O-10(8-1-1)/1-4	-1.0
Total	7	325	688	67	134	20	6	12	53	45	133	.195	.251	.294	545	56	-41	2	7	-2	.989	-2	1-152,O-130C/D-3	-5.8
■ GRANT BRIGGS Briggs, Grant b: 3/16/1865, Pittsburgh, Pa. d: 5/31/28, Pittsburgh, Pa. 5'11", 170 lbs. Deb: 4/17/1890 Career OF: (6-LF 26-CF 9-RF)																								
1890	Syr-a	86	316	44	57	6	5	0	21	16		.180	.222	.231	453	37	-25	7			.928	-4	C-46,O-33C/3-5,S-4	-2.3
1891	Lou-a	1	4	0	1	0	0	0	0	0	0	.250	.250	.250	500	44	-0	0			1.000	-0	/C-1	0.0
1892	StL-N	22	55	2	4	1	0	0	1	5	14	.073	.164	.091	255	-24	-8	2			.902	-11	C-15/O-8(2-1-5)	-1.7
1895	Lou-N	1	3	0	0	0	0	0	0	0	1	.000	.000	.000	0	-99	-1	0			1.000	-1	/C-1	-0.2
Total	4	110	378	46	62	7	5	0	22	21	15	.164	.212	.209	421	27	-34	9			.925	-15	/C-63,O-41C,3-5,S-4	-4.2
■ JOHNNY BRIGGS Briggs, John Edward b: 3/10/44, Paterson, N.J. BL/TL, 6'1", 195 lbs. Deb: 4/17/64 Career OF: (698-LF 294-CF 78-RF)																								
1964	Phi-N	61	66	16	17	2	0	1	6	9	12	.258	.347	.333	680	94	-0	1	1	-0	.957	-2	O-19(9-9-1)/1-1	-0.3
1965	Phi-N	93	229	47	54	9	4	4	23	42	44	.236	.354	.362	717	104	3	3	2	-0	.982	-3	O-66(4-62-0)	-0.3
1966	Phi-N	81	255	43	72	13	5	10	23	41	55	.282	.382	.490	872	140	15	3	2	-0	.977	-4	O-69(2-68-0)	0.9
1967	Phi-N	106	332	47	77	12	4	9	30	41	72	.232	.316	.373	690	96	-2	3	5	-1	.979	-2	O-94(31-65-1)	-0.8
1968	Phi-N	110	338	36	86	13	1	7	31	58	72	.254	.365	.361	726	119	10	8	5	0	.968	-3	O-65(10-34-21),1-36	0.2
1969	Phi-N	124	361	51	86	20	3	12	46	64	78	.238	.353	.410	763	116	9	9	6	-0	.971	0	*O-108(76-32-12)/1-2	0.4
1970	Phi-N	110	341	43	92	15	7	9	47	39	65	.270	.345	.434	779	110	5	5	4	-0	.980	6	O-95(79-11-15)	0.5
1971	Phi-N	10	22	3	4	1	0	0	3	6	2	.182	.357	.227	584	69	-1	0	0	0	.846	-1	/O-8(8-0-0)	-0.2
	Mil-A	125	375	51	99	11	1	21	59	71	79	.264	.383	.467	849	141	22	1	2	-0	.958	1	O-65(55-0-11),1-60	1.5
1972	Mil-A	135	418	58	111	14	1	21	65	54	67	.266	.351	.455	805	141	21	1	2	-0	.980	-2	*O-106(98-12-0),1-28	1.2
1973	Mil-A	142	488	78	120	20	7	18	57	87	83	.246	.362	.426	788	124	17	15	9	0	.968	7	*O-137(137-0-0)/D-1	1.7
1974	Mil-A	154	554	72	140	30	8	17	73	71	102	.253	.338	.428	765	120	14	9	7	-0	.973	5	*O-149(148-1-0)/D-2	1.0
1975	Mil-A	28	74	12	22	1	0	3	5	20	13	.297	.447	.432	879	149	6	0	2	-1	.962	2	O-21(21-0-0)/D-1	0.7
	Min-A	87	264	44	61	9	2	7	39	60	41	.231	.373	.360	733	106	5	6	2	1	.983	7	1-49,O-35L/D-2	0.7
	Yr	115	338	56	83	10	2	10	44	80	54	.246	.390	.376	766	116	11	6	4	-0	.983	9	O-56L,1-49/D-3	1.4
Total	12	1366	4117	601	1041	170	43	139	507	663	785	.253	.357	.416	773	121	123	64	49	-3	.973	12	*O-1037L,1-176/D-6	7.2
■ HARRY BRIGHT Bright, Harry James b: 9/22/29, Kansas City, Mo. d: 3/13/2000, Sacramento, Cal. BR/TR, 6', 190 lbs. Deb: 8/7/58																								
1958	Pit-N	15	24	4	6	1	0	1	3	1	6	.250	.280	.417	697	84	-1	0	0	0	1.000	0	/3-7	0.0
1959	Pit-N	40	48	4	12	1	0	3	8	5	10	.250	.321	.458	779	105	0	0	0	0	1.000	-2	/O-4(3-0-1),3-3,2-1	-0.2
1960	Pit-N	4	4	0	0	0	0	0	0	0	2	.000	.000	.000	0	-99	-1	0	0	0	.000	0	H	-0.1
1961	Was-A	72	183	20	44	6	0	4	21	19	23	.240	.312	.339	651	75	-7	0	2	-1	.928	7	3-40/C-8,2-1	0.0
1962	Was-A	113	392	55	107	15	4	17	67	26	51	.273	.321	.462	783	109	3	2	1	0	.989	-1	1-99/C-3,3-1	-0.4
1963	Cin-N	1	1	0	0	0	0	0	0	0	1	.000	.000	.000	0	-97	-0	0	0	0	1.000	-0	/1-1	0.0
	*NY-A	60	157	15	37	7	0	7	23	13	31	.236	.298	.414	712	98	-1	0	0	0	.985	-5	1-35,3-12	-0.7
1964	NY-A	4	5	0	1	0	0	0	0	1	1	.200	.333	.200	533	52	-0	0	0	0	1.000	-0	/1-2	-0.1
1965	Chi-N	27	25	1	7	1	0	0	4	0	8	.280	.280	.320	600	67	-1	0	0	0	.000	0	H	-0.1
Total	8	336	839	99	214	31	4	32	126	65	133	.255	.311	.416	727	96	-7	2	3	-1	.988	-1	1-137/3-63,C-11,O2	-1.6
■ GREG BRILEY Briley, Gregory "Peewee" b: 5/24/65, Greenville, N.C. BL/TR, 5'8", 165 lbs. Deb: 6/27/88 Career OF: (303-LF 18-CF 163-RF)																								
1988	Sea-A	13	36	6	9	2	0	1	4	5	6	.250	.341	.389	730	100	0	0	1	-0	.929	-2	O-11(11-0-0)	-0.3
1989	Sea-A	115	394	52	105	22	4	13	52	39	82	.266	.340	.442	782	115	8	11	5	1	.958	-5	*O-105L,2-10/D-2	0.1
1990	Sea-A	125	337	40	83	18	2	5	29	37	48	.246	.323	.356	679	89	-5	16	4	2	.989	-4	*O-107(43-0-67)/D-4	-1.0
1991	Sea-A	139	381	39	99	17	3	2	26	27	51	.260	.309	.336	645	78	-11	23	11	1	.980	-17	*O-125L/2-1,3-1,D-2	-3.0
1992	Sea-A	86	200	18	55	10	0	5	12	4	31	.275	.293	.400	693	92	-3	9	2	1	.967	-9	O-42L,D-12/2-4,3-4	-1.2
1993	Fla-N	120	170	17	33	6	0	3	12	12	42	.194	.251	.282	534	40	-14	6	2	1	.986	-12	O-67(32-1-36)	-2.7
Total	6	598	1518	172	384	75	9	29	135	124	260	.253	.313	.372	684	88	-26	65	25	6	.975	-48	O-457L/D-20,2-15,3	-8.1
■ BILL BRINKER Brinker, William Hutchinson "Dode" b: 8/30/1883, Warrensburg, Mo. d: 2/5/65, Arcadia, Cal. BB/TR, 6'1", 190 lbs. Deb: 4/24/12																								
1912	Phi-N	9	18	1	4	1	0	0	2	2	3	.222	.300	.278	578	55	-1	0			.778	-1	/3-2,O-2(1-1-0)	-0.2
■ CHUCK BRINKMAN Brinkman, Charles Ernest b: 9/16/44, Cincinnati, O. BR/TR, 6'1", 185 lbs. Deb: 7/10/69 F																								
1969	Chi-A	14	15	2	1	0	0	0	0	1	5	.067	.125	.067	192	-43	-3	0	0	0	1.000	1	C-14	-0.2
1970	Chi-A	9	20	4	5	1	0	0	0	3	3	.250	.348	.300	648	77	-1	0	0	0	.974	1	/C-9	0.1
1971	Chi-A	15	20	0	4	0	0	0	1	3	5	.200	.304	.200	504	44	-1	0	0	0	1.000	2	C-14	0.1
1972	Chi-A	35	52	1	7	0	0	0	0	4	7	.135	.196	.135	331	-0	-6	0	0	0	.985	7	C-33	0.2
1973	Chi-A	63	139	13	26	6	0	1	10	11	37	.187	.252	.252	503	41	-11	0	0	0	.987	10	C-63	0.1
1974	Chi-A	8	14	1	2	0	0	0	0	1	3	.143	.200	.143	343	-0	-2	0	0	0	1.000	-1	/C-8	-0.3
	Pit-N	4	7	1	1	0	0	0	1	0	0	.143	.143	.143	286	-21	-1	0	0	0	1.000	-0	/C-4	-0.2
Total	6	148	267	22	46	7	0	1	12	23	60	.172	.241	.210	450	28	-25	0	0	0	.988	20	C-145	-0.2
■ ED BRINKMAN Brinkman, Edwin Albert b: 12/8/41, Cincinnati, O. BR/TR, 6', 170 lbs. Deb: 9/6/61 FC																								
1961	Was-A	4	11	0	1	0	0	0	0	1	1	.091	.167	.091	258	-30	-2	0	0	0	.889	0	/3-3	-0.2
1962	Was-A	54	133	8	22	7	1	0	4	11	28	.165	.229	.233	462	25	-14	1	0	0	.942	2	S-38,3-10	-1.0
1963	Was-A	145	514	44	117	20	3	7	45	31	86	.228	.277	.319	596	67	-23	5	3	0	.950	7	*S-143	-0.4

YEAR	TM/L	G	AB	R	H	2B	3B	HR	RBI	BB	SO	AVG	OBP	SLG	OPS	OPS+	BR+	SB	CS	SBR	FA	FR	G/POS	TPR
1964	Was-A	132	447	54	100	20	3	8	34	26	99	.224	.273	.336	608	68	-20	2	2	-0	.969	-3	*S-125	-1.3
1965	Was-A	154	444	35	82	13	2	5	35	38	82	.185	.252	.257	509	46	-32	1	2	-0	.964	4	*S-150	-1.8
1966	Was-A	158	582	42	133	18	9	7	48	29	105	.229	.265	.326	592	70	-24	7	9	-2	.965	12	*S-158	0.0
1967	Was-A	109	320	21	60	9	2	1	18	24	58	.188	.253	.237	490	47	-21	1	3	-1	**.979**	14	*S-109	0.0
1968	Was-A	77	193	12	36	3	0	0	6	19	31	.187	.259	.202	462	43	-13	0	0	0	.967	3	S-74/2-2,O-1(1-0-0)	-0.6
1969	Was-A	151	576	71	153	18	5	2	43	50	42	.266	.330	.325	654	88	-9	2	2	-0	.976	15	*S-150	2.5
1970	Was-A	158	625	63	164	17	2	1	40	60	41	.262	.332	.301	633	79	-16	8	9	-1	.974	31	*S-157	3.4
1971	Det-A	159	527	40	120	18	2	1	37	44	54	.228	.296	.275	571	60	-27	1	4	-1	.980	12	*S-159	0.3
1972	*Det-A	156	516	42	105	19	1	6	49	38	51	.203	.262	.279	541	59	-26	0	0	0	**.990**	2	*S-156	-0.6
1973	Det-A★	162	515	55	122	16	4	7	40	34	79	.237	.285	.324	610	67	-23	0	1	-0	.968	-13	*S-162	-1.8
1974	Det-A	153	502	55	111	15	3	14	54	29	71	.221	.268	.347	614	73	-19	2	0	0	.972	13	*S-151/3-2	1.3
1975	StL-N	28	75	6	18	4	0	1	6	7	10	.240	.313	.333	647	77	-2	0	0	0	.948	0	S-24	0.0
	Tex-A	1	2	0	0	0	0	0	0	0	1	.000	.000	.000	0	-99	-1	0	0	0	1.000	-0	/3-1	-0.1
	NY-A	44	63	2	11	4	1	0	2	3	6	.175	.224	.270	494	40	-5	0	0	0	.933	-3	S-39/2-3,3-3	-0.6
	Yr	45	65	2	11	4	1	0	2	3	7	.169	.217	.262	479	35	-6	0	0	0	.933	-3	S-39/3-4,2-3	-0.7
Total	15	1845	6045	550	1355	201	38	60	461	444	845	.224	.282	.300	581	65	-275	30	35	-6	.970	94	*S-1795/3-19,2-5,O	-0.9

■ LEON BRINKOPF

Brinkopf, Leon Clarence b: 10/20/26, Cape Girardeau, Mo d: 7/2/98, Cape Girardeau, Mo BR/TR, 5′11.5″, 185 lbs. Deb: 4/18/52

YEAR	TM/L	G	AB	R	H	2B	3B	HR	RBI	BB	SO	AVG	OBP	SLG	OPS	OPS+	BR+	SB	CS	SBR	FA	FR	G/POS	TPR
1952	Chi-N	9	22	1	4	0	0	0	2	4	5	.182	.308	.182	490	38	-2	0	0	0	.955	-2	/S-6	-0.4

■ FATTY BRIODY

Briody, Charles F. "Alderman" b: 8/13/1858, Lansingburg, N.Y. d: 6/22/03, Chicago, Ill. TR, 5′8.5″, 190 lbs. Deb: 6/16/1880 Career OF: (0-LF 2-CF 2-RF)

YEAR	TM/L	G	AB	R	H	2B	3B	HR	RBI	BB	SO	AVG	OBP	SLG	OPS	OPS+	BR+	SB	CS	SBR	FA	FR	G/POS	TPR
1880	Tro-N	1	4	0	0	0	0	0	0	0	0	.000	.000	.000	0	-95	-1				.700	-1	/C-1	-0.2
1882	Cle-N	53	194	30	50	13	0	0	13	9	13	.258	.291	.325	615	100	0				.902	2	C-53	0.6
1883	Cle-N	40	145	23	34	5	1	0	10	3	13	.234	.250	.283	533	62	-6				.900	4	C-33/2-4,1-2,3-1	0.0
1884	Cle-N	43	148	17	25	6	0	1	12	6	19	.169	.201	.230	431	34	-11				.922	10	C-42/O-1(0-0-1)	0.2
	Cin-U	22	89	11	30	2	2	0		1		.337	.344	.404	749	117	-1				.943	17	C-22	1.5
1885	StL-N	62	215	14	42	9	0	1	17	12	23	.195	.238	.251	489	62	-8				.893	-9	C-60/O-1C,3-1,2-1	-1.2
1886	KC-N	56	215	14	51	10	3	0	29	3	35	.237	.248	.312	559	65	-10	0			.919	2	C-54/O-2(0-1-1),1-1	-0.3
1887	Det-N	33	137	24	38	6	1	1	26	9	10	.277	.283	.313	595	63	-7	6			.907	6	C-33	0.2
1888	KC-a	13	48	1	10	1	0	0	8	1		.208	.224	.229	454	43	-3	0			.896	-4	C-13	-0.5
Total	8	323	1195	134	280	52	7	3	115	44	113	.234	.257	.292	548	68	-46	6			.910	25	C-311/2-5,O-4C,13	0.3

■ GEORGE BRISTOW

Bristow, George T. b: 5/1870, Paw Paw, Ill. TR, Deb: 4/15/1899

YEAR	TM/L	G	AB	R	H	2B	3B	HR	RBI	BB	SO	AVG	OBP	SLG	OPS	OPS+	BR+	SB	CS	SBR	FA	FR	G/POS	TPR
1899	Cle-N	3	8	0	1	1	0	0	0	0		.125	.222	.250	472	32	-1	0			1.000	0	/O-3(1-0-2)	-0.1

■ BERNARDO BRITO

Brito, Bernardo b: 12/4/63, San Cristobal, D.R. BR/TR, 6′1″, 190 lbs. Deb: 9/15/92

YEAR	TM/L	G	AB	R	H	2B	3B	HR	RBI	BB	SO	AVG	OBP	SLG	OPS	OPS+	BR+	SB	CS	SBR	FA	FR	G/POS	TPR
1992	Min-A	8	14	1	2	1	0	0	2	0	4	.143	.143	.214	357	-1	-2	0	1	-0	.750	-1	/O-3(3-0-0),D-1	-0.3
1993	Min-A	27	54	8	13	2	0	4	9	1	20	.241	.255	.500	755	97	-1	0	0	0	1.000	-1	O-10(10-0-0)/D-7	-0.2
1995	Min-A	5	5	1	1	0	0	1	1	0	3	.200	.333	.800	1133	183	1	0	0	0	.000	0	/D-3	0.0
Total	3	40	73	10	16	3	0	5	12	1	27	.219	.240	.466	706	85	-2	0	1	-0	.941	-2	/O-13(13-0-0),D-11	-0.5

■ JORGE BRITO

Brito, Jorge Manuel (Uceta) b: 6/22/66, Moncion, D.R. BR/TR, 6′1″, 190 lbs. Deb: 4/30/95

YEAR	TM/L	G	AB	R	H	2B	3B	HR	RBI	BB	SO	AVG	OBP	SLG	OPS	OPS+	BR+	SB	CS	SBR	FA	FR	G/POS	TPR
1995	Col-N	18	51	5	11	3	0	0	7	2	17	.216	.259	.275	534	32	-5	1	0	0	.991	5	C-18	0.1
1996	Col-N	8	14	1	1	0	0	0	0	1	8	.071	.235	.071	307	-12	-2	0	0	0	1.000	4	/C-8	0.2
Total	2	26	65	6	12	3	0	0	7	3	25	.185	.254	.231	484	23	-7	1	0	0	.994	8	/C-26	0.3

■ TILSON BRITO

Brito, Tilson Manuel (Jiminez) b: 5/28/72, Santo Domingo, D.R. BR/TR, 6′, 175 lbs. Deb: 4/1/96

YEAR	TM/L	G	AB	R	H	2B	3B	HR	RBI	BB	SO	AVG	OBP	SLG	OPS	OPS+	BR+	SB	CS	SBR	FA	FR	G/POS	TPR
1996	Tor-A	26	80	10	19	7	0	1	7	10	18	.237	.344	.363	707	79	-2	1	1	-0	.956	-1	2-18/S-5,D-2	-0.2
1997	Tor-A	49	126	9	28	3	0	0	8	9	28	.222	.285	.246	531	40	-11	1	0	0	.989	1	2-25,3-17/S-8	-0.7
	Oak-A	17	46	8	13	2	1	2	6	1	10	.283	.298	.500	798	105	0	0	0	0	.920	3	3-10/S-6,2-2	0.3
	Yr	66	172	17	41	5	1	2	14	10	38	.238	.288	.314	602	57	-11	1	0	0	.961	4	2-27,3-27,S-14	-0.4
Total	2	92	252	27	60	12	1	3	21	20	56	.238	.307	.329	636	64	-13	2	1	0	.974	4	/2-45,3-27,S-19,D-2	-0.6

■ GUS BRITTAIN

Brittain, August Schuster b: 11/29/09, Wilmington, N.C. d: 2/16/74, Wilmington, N.C. BR/TR, 5′10″, 192 lbs. Deb: 7/22/37

YEAR	TM/L	G	AB	R	H	2B	3B	HR	RBI	BB	SO	AVG	OBP	SLG	OPS	OPS+	BR+	SB	CS	SBR	FA	FR	G/POS	TPR
1937	Cin-N	3	6	0	1	0	0	0	0	0	3	.167	.167	.167	333	-10	-1	0			1.000	-0	/C-1	-0.1

■ GIL BRITTON

Britton, Stephen Gilbert b: 9/21/1891, Parsons, Kan. d: 6/20/83, Parsons, Kan. BR/TR, 5′10″, 160 lbs. Deb: 9/20/13

YEAR	TM/L	G	AB	R	H	2B	3B	HR	RBI	BB	SO	AVG	OBP	SLG	OPS	OPS+	BR+	SB	CS	SBR	FA	FR	G/POS	TPR
1913	Pit-N	3	12	0	0	0	0	0	0	0	2	.000	.000	.000	0	-99	-3	0			.824	-1	/S-3	-0.4

■ GREG BROCK

Brock, Gregory Allen b: 6/14/57, McMinnville, Ore. BL/TR, 6′3″, 205 lbs. Deb: 9/1/82

YEAR	TM/L	G	AB	R	H	2B	3B	HR	RBI	BB	SO	AVG	OBP	SLG	OPS	OPS+	BR+	SB	CS	SBR	FA	FR	G/POS	TPR
1982	LA-N	18	17	1	2	1	0	0	1	1	5	.118	.167	.176	343	-4	-2	0	0	0	1.000	-0	/1-3	-0.3
1983	*LA-N	146	455	64	102	14	2	20	66	83	81	.224	.345	.396	741	105	5	5	1	1	.991	5	*1-140	0.2
1984	LA-N	88	271	33	61	6	0	14	34	39	37	.225	.323	.402	725	104	1	8	0	2	.995	7	1-83	0.6
1985	*LA-N	129	438	64	110	19	0	21	66	54	72	.251	.333	.438	772	118	10	4	2	0	.994	2	*1-122	0.5
1986	LA-N	115	325	33	76	13	0	16	52	37	60	.234	.312	.422	734	108	2	2	5	-1	.996	12	1-99	0.8
1987	Mil-A	141	532	81	159	29	3	13	85	57	63	.299	.373	.438	811	111	10	5	4	-0	.993	4	*1-141	0.4
1988	Mil-A	115	364	53	77	16	1	6	50	63	48	.212	.333	.310	643	81	-8	6	2	1	.993	9	*1-114/D-1	-0.6
1989	Mil-A	107	373	40	99	16	0	12	52	43	49	.265	.346	.405	751	112	6	6	1	1	.995	-5	*1-100/D-7	-0.5
1990	Mil-A	123	367	42	91	23	0	7	50	43	45	.248	.330	.368	698	96	-2	4	2	0	.995	-4	*1-115	-1.4
1991	Mil-A	31	60	9	17	4	0	1	6	14	9	.283	.419	.400	819	131	3	1	1	-0	1.000	-1	1-25	0.1
Total	10	1013	3202	420	794	141	6	110	462	434	469	.248	.340	.399	739	105	25	41	18	3	.994	29	1-942/D-8	-0.2

■ JOHN BROCK

Brock, John Roy b: 10/16/1896, Hamilton, Ill. d: 10/27/51, Clayton, Mo. BR/TR, 5′6.5″, 165 lbs. Deb: 8/10/17

YEAR	TM/L	G	AB	R	H	2B	3B	HR	RBI	BB	SO	AVG	OBP	SLG	OPS	OPS+	BR+	SB	CS	SBR	FA	FR	G/POS	TPR
1917	StL-N	7	15	4	6	1	0	0	2	0	2	.400	.400	.467	867	170	1	2			.944	-1	/C-4	0.1
1918	StL-N	27	52	9	11	2	0	0	4	3	10	.212	.255	.250	505	56	-3	5			.951	-2	C-18/O-1(0-0-1)	-0.4
Total	2	34	67	13	17	3	0	0	6	3	12	.254	.286	.299	584	81	-2	7			.949	-2	/C-22,O-1(0-0-1)	-0.3

■ LOU BROCK

Brock, Louis Clark b: 6/18/39, ElDorado, Ark. BL/TL (BR 1976 (1 GAME)), 5′11.5″, 170 lbs. Deb: 9/10/61 H

YEAR	TM/L	G	AB	R	H	2B	3B	HR	RBI	BB	SO	AVG	OBP	SLG	OPS	OPS+	BR+	SB	CS	SBR	FA	FR	G/POS	TPR
1961	Chi-N	4	11	1	1	0	0	0	0	1	3	.091	.167	.091	258	-29	-2	0	0	0	.750	-1	/O-3(0-3-0)	-0.3
1962	Chi-N	123	434	73	114	24	7	9	35	35	96	.263	.322	.412	734	92	-5	16	7	1	.965	2	*O-106(0-106-0)	-0.6
1963	Chi-N	148	547	79	141	19	11	9	37	31	122	.258	.302	.382	684	91	-7	24	12	1	.973	13	*O-140(0-0-140)	-0.3
1964	Chi-N	52	215	30	54	9	2	2	14	13	40	.251	.300	.340	640	77	-7	10	3	1	.959	2	O-52(0-2-51)	-0.7
	*StL-N	103	419	81	146	21	9	12	44	27	87	.348	.391	.527	918	143	24	33	15	2	.949	6	*O-102(99-2-4)	2.7
	Yr	155	634	111	200	30	11	14	58	40	127	.315	.360	.464	824	121	18	43	18	3	.953	8	*O-154(99-4-55)	2.0
1965	StL-N	155	631	107	182	35	8	16	69	45	116	.288	.345	.445	791	110	9	63	27	4	.959	8	*O-153(150-2-7)	1.3
1966	StL-N	156	643	94	183	24	12	15	46	31	134	.285	.321	.429	750	106	4	**74**	18	**10**	.936	3	*O-154(122-0-34)	0.8
1967	*StL-N★	159	689	**113**	206	32	12	21	76	24	109	.299	.328	.472	800	128	22	**52**	18	**5**	.956	7	*O-157(157-0-0)	2.6
1968	*StL-N	159	660	92	184	**46**	**14**	6	51	46	124	.279	.329	.418	747	125	18	**62**	12	**9**	.952	6	*O-156(156-0-0)	2.8
1969	StL-N	157	655	97	195	33	10	12	47	50	115	.298	.349	.434	783	118	14	**53**	14	7	.949	5	*O-157(157-0-0)	1.7
1970	StL-N	155	664	114	202	29	5	13	57	60	99	.304	.363	.422	784	107	7	51	15	6	.962	3	*O-152(149-0-3)	0.6
1971	StL-N★	157	640	**126**	200	37	7	7	61	76	107	.313	.386	.425	811	125	23	**64**	19	**7**	.951	-1	*O-157(156-0-1)	2.1
1972	StL-N☆	153	621	81	193	26	8	3	42	47	93	.311	.360	.393	753	115	13	**63**	18	8	.952	-4	*O-149(149-0-0)	0.8
1973	StL-N	160	650	110	193	29	8	7	63	71	112	.297	.366	.398	765	112	12	**70**	20	8	.963	1	*O-159(159-0-0)	1.2
1974	StL-N★	153	635	105	194	25	7	3	48	61	88	.306	.368	.381	749	111	10	**118**	33	**14**	.967	2	*O-152(152-0-0)	1.8
1975	StL-N★	136	528	78	163	27	6	3	47	38	64	.309	.359	.400	758	106	5	56	16	7	.966	1	*O-128(128-0-0)	0.4
1976	StL-N	133	498	73	150	24	5	4	67	35	75	.301	.348	.394	742	109	6	56	19	6	.983	0	*O-123(123-0-0)	0.4
1977	StL-N	141	489	69	133	22	6	2	46	30	74	.272	.317	.354	670	81	-13	35	24	-1	.954	-11	*O-130(130-0-0)	-3.1
1978	StL-N	92	298	31	66	9	0	0	12	17	29	.221	.263	.252	515	45	-22	17	5	2	.975	-6	O-79(79-0-0)	-3.1
1979	StL-N★	120	405	56	123	15	4	5	38	23	43	.304	.346	.398	743	101	1	21	12	0	.958	-3	O-98(98-0-0)	-0.6
Total	19	2616	10332	1610	3023	486	141	149	900	761	1730	.293	.344	.410	754	109	111	938	307	99	.959	32	*O-2507(2164-115-240)	10.5

YEAR	TM/L	G	AB	R	H	2B	3B	HR	RBI	BB	SO	AVG	OBP	SLG	OPS	OPS+	BR+	SB	CS	SBR	FA	FR	G/POS	TPR
■ **TARRIK BROCK**	Brock, Tarrik Jumaan b: 12/25/73, Goleta, Cal. BL/TL, 6′3″, 170 lbs. Deb: 3/29/2000																							
2000	Chi-N	13	12	1	2	0	0	0	0	4	4	.167	.375	.167	542	45	-1	1	1	-0	.889	-3	O-10(9-2-0)	-0.3
■ **MATT BRODERICK**	Broderick, Matthew Thomas b: 12/1/1877, Lattimer, Pa. d: 2/26/40, Freeland, Pa. BR/TR, 5′6.5″, 135 lbs. Deb: 5/1/03																							
1903	Bro-N	2	2	0	0	0	0	0	0	0		.000	.000	.000	0	-99	-1	0			1.000	0	/2-1	0.0
■ **STEVE BRODIE**	Brodie, Walter Scott b: 9/11/1868, Warrenton, Va. d: 10/30/35, Baltimore, Md. BL/TR, 5′11″, 180 lbs. Deb: 4/21/1890 Career OF: (17-LF 1243-CF 168-RF)																							
1890	Bos-N	132	514	77	152	19	9	0	67	66	20	.296	.387	.368	755	111	9	29			**.953**	3	*O-132(2-19-114)	0.9
1891	Bos-N	133	523	84	136	13	6	2	78	63	39	.260	.351	.319	670	85	-10	25			.951	10	*O-133(1-102-31)	-0.3
1892	StL-N	154	602	85	153	10	9	4	60	52	31	.254	.318	.321	638	98	-1	28			.943	8	*O-137C,2-16/3-2	-0.1
1893	StL-N	107	469	71	149	16	8	2	79	33	16	.318	.376	.399	775	106	4	41			.951	9	*O-107(0-102-5)	0.5
	Bal-N	25	97	18	35	7	2	0	19	12	2	.361	.446	.474	921	142	6	8			.963	-3	O-25(2-24-0)	0.1
	Yr	132	566	89	184	23	10	2	98	45	18	.325	.389	.412	800	112	10	49			.953	6	*O-132(2-126-5)	0.6
1894	*Bal-N	129	573	134	210	25	11	3	113	18	8	.366	.399	.464	863	103	2	42			.950	-6	*O-129(0-129-0)	-1.0
1895	*Bal-N	131	528	85	184	27	10	2	134	26	15	.348	.394	.449	843	114	10	35			.965	5	*O-131(0-131-0)	0.5
1896	*Bal-N	132	516	98	153	19	11	2	87	36	17	.297	.363	.388	751	96	-2	25			.972	11	*O-132(0-132-0)	0.0
1897	Pit-N	100	370	47	108	7	12	2	53	25		.292	.348	.392	740	99	-1	11			**.983**	-0	*O-100(0-100-0)	-0.6
1898	Pit-N	42	156	15	41	5	0	0	21	6		.263	.303	.295	598	73	-6	3			.958	3	O-42(0-42-0)	-0.5
	Bal-N	23	98	12	30	3	2	0	19	5		.306	.346	.378	724	105	0	3			.923	3	O-23(0-23-0)	0.1
	Yr	65	254	27	71	8	2	0	40	11		.280	.320	.327	646	86	-5	6			.946	6	O-65(0-65-0)	-0.4
1899	Bal-N	137	531	82	164	26	1	3	87	31		.309	.373	.379	751	101	1	19			**.979**	1	*O-137(0-136-1)	-0.6
1901	Bal-A	83	306	41	95	6	6	2	41	25		.310	.378	.389	766	108	4	9			.963	-3	O-83(11-72-0)	-0.3
1902	NY-N	110	420	37	118	8	2	3	42	22		.281	.326	.331	657	104	1	11			.953	8	*O-110(0-110-0)	0.4
Total	12	1438	5703	886	1728	191	89	25	900	420	148	.303	.365	.381	745	102	18	289			.959	49	*O-1421C/2-16,3-2	-0.9
■ **RICO BROGNA**	Brogna, Rico Joseph b: 4/18/70, Turners Falls, Mass. BL/TL, 6′2″, 200 lbs. Deb: 8/8/92																							
1992	Det-A	9	26	3	5	1	0	1	3	3	5	.192	.276	.346	622	73	-1	0	0	0	.982	1	/1-8,D-2	-0.1
1994	NY-N	39	131	16	46	11	2	7	20	6	29	.351	.380	.626	1006	158	10	1	0	0	.997	2	1-35	0.9
1995	NY-N	134	495	72	143	27	2	22	76	39	111	.289	.343	.485	828	119	12	0	0	0	**.998**	5	*1-131	0.6
1996	NY-N	55	188	18	48	10	1	7	30	19	50	.255	.324	.431	755	101	0	0	0	0	.996	-2	1-52	-0.6
1997	Phi-N	148	543	68	137	36	1	20	81	33	116	.252	.295	.433	728	88	-12	12	3	2	.994	10	*1-145	-1.4
1998	Phi-N	153	565	77	150	36	3	20	104	49	125	.265	.324	.446	770	99	-2	7	7	-1	.996	16	*1-151	-0.1
1999	Phi-N	157	619	90	172	29	4	24	102	54	132	.278	.338	.454	792	95	-6	8	5	0	.995	10	*1-157	-0.9
2000	Phi-N	38	129	12	32	14	0	1	13	7	28	.248	.297	.380	677	68	-7	1	0	0	.996	-1	1-34	-1.0
	Bos-A	43	56	8	11	3	0	1	8	3	13	.196	.237	.304	541	34	-6	0	0	0	.983	0	1-37/D-2	-0.6
Total	8	776	2752	364	744	167	13	103	437	213	609	.270	.324	.453	777	99	-10	29	15	1	.995	40	1-750/D-4	-3.2
■ **JACK BROHAMER**	Brohamer, John Anthony b: 2/26/50, Maywood, Cal. BL/TR (BB 1972 (part)), 5′10″, 165 lbs. Deb: 4/18/72																							
1972	Cle-A	136	527	49	123	13	2	5	35	27	46	.233	.272	.294	566	66	-22	3	2	-0	.977	6	*2-132/3-1	-0.9
1973	Cle-A	102	300	29	66	12	1	4	29	32	23	.220	.295	.307	602	69	-12	0	2	-1	.971	17	2-97	0.9
1974	Cle-A	101	315	33	85	11	1	2	30	26	22	.270	.331	.330	662	92	-3	2	1	0	.987	-4	2-99	-0.1
1975	Cle-A	69	217	15	53	5	0	6	16	14	14	.244	.290	.350	640	80	-6	2	2	-0	.976	4	2-66	0.1
1976	Chi-A	119	354	33	89	12	2	7	40	44	28	.251	.339	.356	695	103	2	1	3	-1	.984	18	*2-117/3-1	2.8
1977	Chi-A	59	152	26	39	10	3	2	20	21	8	.257	.351	.401	752	105	1	0	0	0	.923	2	3-38,2-18/D-1	0.4
1978	Bos-A	81	244	34	57	14	1	1	25	25	13	.234	.305	.311	616	67	-10	1	3	-1	.974	-3	3-30,D-25,2-23	-1.5
1979	Bos-A	64	192	25	51	7	1	1	11	15	15	.266	.319	.328	647	71	-8	0	3	-1	.982	-0	2-36,3-22	-0.7
1980	Bos-A	21	57	5	18	2	0	1	6	4	3	.316	.361	.404	764	104	0	0	0	0	.900	-1	3-13/2-4,D-3	-0.1
	Cle-A	53	142	13	32	5	1	1	15	14	6	.225	.295	.296	591	62	-7	0	1	-0	.979	-4	2-47/D-1	-0.9
	Yr	74	199	18	50	7	1	2	21	18	9	.251	.313	.327	640	74	-7	0	1	-0	.981	-5	2-51,3-13/D-4	-1.0
Total	9	805	2500	262	613	91	12	30	227	222	178	.245	.309	.327	636	79	-65	9	17	-4	.979	33	2-639,3-105/D-30	0.0
■ **HERMAN BRONKIE**	Bronkie, Herman Charles "Dutch" b: 3/31/1885, S.Manchester, Conn d: 5/27/68, Somers, Conn. BR/TR, 5′9″, 165 lbs. Deb: 9/20/10																							
1910	Cle-A	5	10	1	2	0	0	0	0	1		.200	.273	.200	473	48	-1	1			.625	-1	/3-3,S-1	-0.2
1911	Cle-A	2	6	0	1	0	0	0	0	0		.167	.167	.167	333	-7	-1	0			1.000	-1	/3-2	-0.2
1912	Cle-A	6	16	1	0	0	0	0	0	1		.000	.059	.000	59	-80	-4	0			.917	2	/3-6	-0.1
1914	Chi-N	1	1	1	1	1	0	0	1	0	0	1.000	1.000	2.000	3000	786	1	0			.000	-0	/3-1	0.0
1918	StL-N	18	68	7	15	3	0	1	7	2	4	.221	.243	.309	552	70	-3	0			.984	-1	3-18	-0.3
1919	StL-A	67	196	23	50	6	4	0	14	23	23	.255	.336	.327	663	84	-4	2			.939	4	3-34,2-16/1-2	0.1
1922	StL-A	23	64	7	18	4	1	0	2	6	7	.281	.343	.375	718	84	-1	0	2	-1	.917	-0	3-18	-0.2
Total	7	122	361	40	87	14	5	1	24	33	34	.241	.306	.316	622	74	-12	3	2		.931	2	/3-82,2-16,1-2,S-1	-0.9
■ **TOM BROOKENS**	Brookens, Thomas Dale b: 8/10/53, Chambersburg, Pa. BR/TR, 5′10″, 170 lbs. Deb: 7/10/79 Career OF: (0-LF 2-CF 6-RF)																							
1979	Det-A	60	190	23	50	5	2	4	21	11	40	.263	.310	.374	684	81	-5	10	3	1	.945	12	3-42,2-19/D-1	0.7
1980	Det-A	151	509	64	140	25	9	10	66	32	71	.275	.319	.418	738	98	-2	13	11	-1	.931	4	*3-138/2-9,S-1,D-1	-0.1
1981	Det-A	71	239	19	58	10	1	4	25	14	43	.243	.290	.343	633	79	-7	5	3	0	.952	-4	3-71	-1.3
1982	Det-A	140	398	40	92	15	3	9	58	27	63	.231	.280	.352	632	72	-16	5	9	-2	.939	10	*3-113,2-26/S-9,O-1C	-0.8
1983	Det-A	138	332	50	71	13	3	6	32	29	46	.214	.281	.325	606	68	-15	10	4	1	.928	5	*3-103,S-30,2-10,/D	-0.8
1984	*Det-A	113	224	32	55	11	4	5	26	19	33	.246	.307	.397	705	94	-2	6	6	-1	.969	20	3-68,S-28,2-26,/D-1	1.9
1985	Det-A	156	485	54	115	34	6	7	47	27	78	.237	.277	.375	653	77	-16	14	5	1	.943	3	*3-151/S-8,2-3,CD	-1.4
1986	Det-A	98	281	42	76	11	2	3	25	20	42	.270	.321	.356	677	84	-6	11	8	-0	.955	2	3-35,2-31,S-14,D/O	-0.3
1987	*Det-A	143	444	59	107	15	3	13	59	33	63	.241	.296	.376	673	80	-13	7	4	0	.954	2	*3-122,S-16,2-11	-1.0
1988	Det-A	136	441	62	107	23	5	5	38	44	74	.243	.316	.351	667	90	-6	4	4	-1	.952	-3	*3-136/S-3,2-1	-0.9
1989	NY-A	66	168	14	38	6	0	4	14	11	27	.226	.274	.333	607	71	-7	1	3	-1	.926	-4	3-51/S-7,2-5,O-3R,D	-1.2
1990	Cle-A	64	154	18	41	7	2	1	20	14	25	.266	.327	.357	685	92	-2	0	0	0	.923	4	3-35,2-21/S-3,1D	0.3
Total	12	1336	3865	477	950	175	40	71	431	281	605	.246	.299	.367	666	83	-96	86	60	-2	.943	49	*3-1065,2-162,S/DO1C	-4.9
■ **HARRY BROOKS**	Brooks, Harry Frank b: 11/30/1865, Philadelphia, Pa. d: 12/5/45, Philadelphia, Pa. Deb: 7/24/1886																							
1886	NY-a	1	1	0	0	0	0	0	0	0		.000	.000	.000	0	-99	-0	0			.500	-1	/O-1(0-1-0),P-1	0.0
■ **HUBIE BROOKS**	Brooks, Hubert b: 9/24/56, Los Angeles, Cal. BR/TR, 6′, 200 lbs. Deb: 9/4/80 Career OF: (7-LF 0-CF 576-RF)																							
1980	NY-N	24	81	8	25	2	1	1	10	5	9	.309	.364	.395	759	115	2	1	1	-0	.966	-1	3-23	0.0
1981	NY-N	98	358	34	110	21	2	4	38	23	65	.307	.351	.411	761	117	7	9	5	0	.924	-2	3-93/O-3(1-0-2),S-1	0.4
1982	NY-N	126	457	40	114	21	2	2	40	28	76	.249	.300	.317	617	73	-16	6	3	0	.931	-8	*3-126	-2.7
1983	NY-N	150	586	53	147	18	4	5	58	24	96	.251	.285	.321	606	68	-26	6	4	-0	.950	3	*3-145/2-7	-2.6
1984	NY-N	153	561	61	159	23	2	16	73	48	79	.283	.342	.417	759	114	10	6	5	-0	.929	-18	*3-129,S-26	-0.8
1985	Mon-N	156	605	67	163	34	7	13	100	34	79	.269	.314	.413	727	108	4	6	9	-2	.958	-34	*S-155	-1.6
1986	Mon-N★	80	306	50	104	18	5	14	58	25	60	.340	.393	.569	962	164	25	4	2	0	.958	-14	S-80	2.1
1987	Mon-N★	112	430	57	113	22	3	14	72	24	72	.263	.303	.426	729	88	-8	4	3	-0	.953	-26	*S-109	-2.4
1988	Mon-N	151	588	61	164	35	2	20	90	35	108	.279	.321	.447	768	113	8	7	3	0	.968	-2	*O-149(0-0-149)	0.3
1989	Mon-N	148	542	56	145	30	1	14	70	39	108	.268	.321	.404	725	105	2	6	11	-3	.964	-2	*O-140(0-0-140)	-0.7
1990	LA-N	153	568	74	151	28	1	20	91	33	108	.266	.313	.424	737	104	1	2	5	-1	.964	-3	*O-150(0-0-151)	-0.8
1991	NY-N	103	357	48	85	11	1	16	50	44	62	.238	.327	.409	736	106	3	3	1	0	.972	-1	*O-100(0-0-100)	-0.1
1992	Cal-A	82	306	28	66	13	0	8	36	12	46	.216	.248	.337	584	62	-16	3	3	-0	.986	-0	D-70/1-6	-2.0
1993	KC-A	75	168	14	48	12	0	1	24	11	27	.286	.333	.375	708	85	-3	0	1	-0	.966	-3	O-40(6-0-34)/1-3,D-9	-0.8
1994	KC-A	34	61	5	14	2	0	1	14	2	10	.230	.254	.311	565	43	-5	1	0	0	1.000	-0	D-19/1-4	-0.6
Total	15	1645	5974	656	1608	290	31	149	824	387	1005	.269	.318	.403	721	100	-13	64	56	-6	.966	-112	O-582R,3-516,S/D12	-12.3
■ **JERRY BROOKS**	Brooks, Jerome Edward b: 3/23/67, Syracuse, N.Y. BR/TR, 6′, 195 lbs. Deb: 9/6/93																							
1993	LA-N	9	9	2	2	1	0	1	1	0	2	.222	.222	.667	889	135	0	0	0	0	.000	-1	/O-2(0-0-2)	-0.1
1996	Fla-N	8	5	2	2	0	1	0	3	1	1	.400	.571	.800	1371	266	1	0	0	0	1.000	-1	/O-2(0-0-2),1-1	0.1
Total	2	17	14	4	4	1	1	1	4	1	3	.286	.375	.714	1089	191	2	0	0	0	1.000	-1	/O-4(0-0-4),1-1	0.0

YEAR	TM/L	G	AB	R	H	2B	3B	HR	RBI	BB	SO	AVG	OBP	SLG	OPS	OPS+	BR+	SB	CS	SBR	FA	FR	G/POS	TPR
■ **MANDY BROOKS**	Brooks, Jonathan Joseph (b: Jonathan Joseph Brozek) b: 8/18/1897, Milwaukee, Wis. d: 6/17/62, Kirkwood, Mo. BR/TR, 5'9", 165 lbs. Deb: 5/30/25																							
1925	Chi-N	90	349	55	98	25	7	14	72	19	28	.281	.322	.513	835	108	2	10	3	1	.977	5	O-89(0-89-0)	0.4
1926	Chi-N	26	48	7	9	1	0	1	6	5	5	.188	.278	.271	549	48	-4	0			1.000	-2	O-18(4-5-9)	-0.7
Total	2	116	397	62	107	26	7	15	78	24	33	.270	.316	.484	800	101	-2	10	3		.979	2	O-107(4-94-9)	-0.3
■ **BOBBY BROOKS**	Brooks, Robert b: 11/1/45, Los Angeles, Cal. d: 10/11/94, Harbor City, Cal. BR/TR, 5'8.5", 165 lbs. Deb: 9/1/69																							
1969	Oak-A	29	79	13	19	5	0	3	10	20	24	.241	.400	.418	818	135	5	0	2	-1	1.000	0	O-21(16-0-5)	0.3
1970	Oak-A	7	18	2	6	1	0	2	5	1	7	.333	.368	.722	1091	201	2	0	1	-0	1.000	-1	/O-5(4-0-2)	0.0
1972	Oak-A	15	39	4	7	0	0	0	5	8	8	.179	.319	.179	499	54	-2	0	1	-0	.930	2	O-11(0-11-0)	0.0
1973	Cal-A	4	7	0	1	0	0	0	0	0	3	.143	.143	.143	286	-21	-1	0	0	0	.000	-0	/O-1(1-0-0)	-0.2
Total	4	55	143	19	33	6	0	5	20	29	42	.231	.364	.378	742	116	4	0	4	-1	.964	1	/O-38(21-11-7)	0.1
■ **SCOTT BROSIUS**	Brosius, Scott David b: 8/15/66, Hillsboro, Ore. BR/TR, 6'1", 185 lbs. Deb: 8/7/91 Career OF: (37-LF 66-CF 74-RF)																							
1991	Oak-A	36	68	9	16	5	0	2	4	3	11	.235	.268	.397	665	86	-2	3	1	0	1.000	-1	2-18,O-13R/3-7,D-1	-0.2
1992	Oak-A	38	87	13	19	2	0	4	13	3	13	.218	.261	.379	640	82	-3	3	0	1	1.000	-8	O-20R,3-12/1-3,SD	-1.1
1993	Oak-A	70	213	26	53	10	1	6	25	14	37	.249	.298	.390	688	89	-4	6	0	1	.991	-2	O-46C,1-11,3-10,/SD	-0.5
1994	Oak-A	96	324	31	77	14	1	14	49	24	57	.238	.294	.417	711	88	-7	2	6	-2	.946	-4	3-93/O-7(2-2-4),1-1	-1.2
1995	Oak-A	123	389	69	102	19	2	17	46	41	67	.262	.345	.452	797	111	6	4	2	0	.918	-9	3-60,O-49C,1-18,/2SD	-0.4
1996	Oak-A	114	428	73	130	25	0	22	71	59	85	.304	.397	.516	913	131	21	7	2	1	.969	15	*3-109,1-10/O-4L	3.4
1997	Oak-A	129	479	59	97	20	1	11	41	34	102	.203	.261	.317	578	51	-35	9	4	1	.977	11	*3-107,S-30,O-22R	-2.1
1998	*NY-A★	152	530	86	159	34	0	19	98	52	97	.300	.373	.472	845	123	18	11	8	-0	.948	10	*3-150/1-3,O-1(0-0-1)	2.7
1999	*NY-A	133	473	64	117	26	1	17	71	39	74	.247	.313	.414	727	84	-12	9	3	1	**.962**	1	*3-132/D-1	-0.8
2000	*NY-A	135	470	57	108	20	0	16	64	45	73	.230	.300	.374	674	71	-22	0	3	-1	.968	-4	*3-134/1-2,O-2L,D-1	-2.4
Total	10	1026	3461	487	878	175	6	128	482	314	616	.254	.323	.419	742	93	-39	54	29	2	.959	9	3-814,O-164R/1S2D	-2.6
■ **SIG BROSKIE**	Broskie, Sigmund Theodore "Chops" b: 3/23/11, Iselin, Pa. d: 5/17/75, Canton, Ohio BR/TR, 5'11.5", 200 lbs. Deb: 9/11/40																							
1940	Bos-N	11	22	1	6	1	0	0	4	1	2	.273	.304	.318	623	76	-1	0			.935	0	C-11	0.0
■ **TONY BROTTEM**	Brottem, Anton Christian b: 4/30/1892, Halstad, Minn. d: 8/5/29, Chicago, Ill. BR/TR, 6'0.5", 176 lbs. Deb: 4/17/16																							
1916	StL-N	26	33	3	6	1	0	0	4	3	10	.182	.250	.212	462	43	-2	1			.950	-1	C-15/O-2(0-1-1)	-0.3
1918	StL-N	2	4	0	0	0	0	0	0	1	0	.000	.200	.000	200	-39	-1	0			1.000	1	/1-2	0.0
1921	Was-A	4	7	1	1	0	0	0	0	2	1	.143	.333	.143	476	26	-1	0	0	0	1.000	1	/C-4	0.1
	Pit-N	30	91	6	22	2	0	0	9	3	11	.242	.266	.264	530	40	-8	0	1	-0	.983	-2	C-29	-0.9
Total	3	62	135	10	29	3	0	0	13	9	22	.215	.264	.237	501	38	-11	1	1		.977	-1	/C-48,1-2,O-2(0-1-1)	-1.1
■ **CAL BROUGHTON**	Broughton, Cecil Calvert b: 12/28/1860, Magnolia, Wis. d: 3/15/39, Evansville, Wis. BR/TR, Deb: 5/2/1883																							
1883	Cle-N	4	10	2	2	0	0	0	1	2	2	.200	.333	.200	533	68	-0				.950	-0	/C-4	0.0
	Bal-a	9	32	1	6	0	0	0		1		.188	.212	.188	400	29	-2				.825	-2	/C-8,O-1(0-0-1)	-0.3
1884	Mil-U	11	39	5	12	5	0	0		0		.308	.308	.436	744	227	5				.937	-1	/C-7,O-5(1-4-0)	0.4
1885	StL-a	4	17	1	1	0	0	0		0		.059	.059	.059	118	-60	-3				.889	-1	/C-4	-0.4
	NY-a	11	41	1	6	1	0	0		1		.146	.167	.171	337	7	-4				.860	-2	C-11	-0.4
	Yr	15	58	2	7	1	0	0		1		.121	.136	.138	274	-14	-7				.867	-3	C-15	-0.8
1888	Det-N	1	4	0	0	0	0	0	0	0	0	.000	.000	.000	0	-99	-1				1.000	1	/C-1	0.0
Total	4	40	143	10	27	6	0	0	3	4	2	.189	.211	.231	442	44	-6				.887	-5	/C-35,O-6(1-4-1)	-0.7
■ **MARK BROUHARD**	Brouhard, Mark Steven b: 5/22/56, Burbank, Cal. BR/TR, 6'1", 210 lbs. Deb: 4/12/80 Career OF: (114-LF 0-CF 110-RF)																							
1980	Mil-A	45	125	17	29	6	0	5	16	7	24	.232	.278	.400	678	86	-3	1	0	0	.964	0	D-21,O-12(4-0-8),1-10	-0.4
1981	Mil-A	60	186	19	51	6	3	2	20	7	41	.274	.308	.371	679	100	-1	1	1	-0	.990	1	O-51(7-0-46)/D-7	-0.2
1982	*Mil-A	40	108	16	29	4	1	4	10	9	17	.269	.336	.435	771	117	2	0	3	-1	.986	2	O-30(7-0-23)/D-7	0.2
1983	Mil-A	56	185	25	51	10	1	7	23	9	39	.276	.316	.454	770	118	4	0	4	-1	.991	2	O-42(38-0-8),D-11	0.2
1984	Mil-A	66	197	20	47	7	0	6	22	16	36	.239	.302	.365	668	87	-4	0	3	-1	.983	4	O-52(48-0-4)/D-8	-0.3
1985	Mil-A	37	108	11	28	7	2	1	13	5	26	.259	.298	.389	687	87	-2	0	0	0	.964	-3	O-29(10-0-21)/D-1	-0.6
Total	6	304	909	108	235	40	7	25	104	53	183	.259	.307	.400	707	99	-3	2	11	-3	.983	7	O-216L/D-55,1-10	-1.1
■ **ART BROUTHERS**	Brouthers, Arthur H. b: 11/25/1882, Montgomery, Ala. d: 9/28/59, Charleston, S.C. TR, 6'1", Deb: 4/14/06																							
1906	Phi-A	37	144	18	30	5	1	0	14	5		.208	.240	.257	497	54	-8	4			.900	-5	3-35/2-1	-1.3
■ **DAN BROUTHERS**	Brouthers, Dennis Joseph "Big Dan" b: 5/8/1858, Sylvan Lake, N.Y. d: 8/2/32, E.Orange, N.J. BL/TL (BR 1882 (1 GAME)), 6'2", 207 lbs. Deb: 6/23/1879 H Career OF: (33-LF 0-CF 2-RF)																							
1879	Tro-N	39	168	17	46	12	1	4	17	1	18	.274	.278	.429	707	138	7				.926	-5	1-37/P-3	0.1
1880	Tro-N	3	12	0	2	0	0	0	1	1	0	.167	.231	.167	397	35	-1				.893	-1	/1-3	-0.2
1881	Buf-N	65	270	60	86	18	9	**8**	45	18	22	.319	.361	**.541**	902	182	25				.797	-5	O-35(33-0-2),1-30	1.5
1882	Buf-N	84	351	71	**129**	23	11	6	63	21	7	**.368**	**.403**	**.547**	**950**	**198**	**37**				**.974**	1	*1-84	2.8
1883	Buf-N	98	425	85	**159**	41	**17**	3	**97**	16	17	**.374**	**.397**	**.572**	**969**	**186**	**42**				.961	2	*1-97/3-1,P-1	3.0
1884	Buf-N	94	398	82	130	22	15	14	79	33	20	.327	.378	**.563**	**941**	**186**	38				.964	0	*1-93/3-1	2.6
1885	Buf-N	98	407	87	146	32	11	7	59	34	10	.359	.408	**.543**	**951**	199	43				.975	-0	*1-98	3.1
1886	Det-N	121	489	139	181	**40**	15	**11**	72	66	16	.370	.445	**.581**	**1026**	**204**	**62**	21			.968	-8	*1-121	3.8
1887	*Det-N	123	571	**153**	**240**	**36**	20	12	101	71	9	.420	**.426**	.562	**988**	**167**	**46**	34			.969	-4	*1-123	2.6
1888	Det-N	129	522	**118**	160	**33**	11	9	66	68	13	.307	.399	.464	862	174	**47**	34			.971	-2	*1-129	3.2
1889	Bos-N	126	485	105	181	26	9	7	118	66	6	**.373**	.462	.507	969	161	42	22			.974	1	*1-126	2.7
1890	Bos-P	123	460	117	152	36	9	1	97	99	17	.330	**.466**	.454	921	137	30	28			.963	2	*1-123	1.6
1891	Bos-a	130	486	117	170	26	19	5	109	87	20	**.350**	**.471**	**.512**	**983**	**184**	**59**	31			.978	-7	*1-130	3.4
1892	Bro-N	152	588	121	**197**	30	20	5	**124**	84	30	**.335**	.432	.480	**911**	**182**	**63**	31			.982	12	*1-152	**6.7**
1893	Bro-N	77	282	57	95	21	11	2	59	52	10	.337	.450	.511	961	163	28	9			.986	3	1-77	2.5
1894	*Bal-N	123	525	137	182	39	23	9	128	67	9	.347	.425	.560	985	130	24	38			.976	-2	*1-123	1.7
1895	Bal-N	5	23	2	6	2	0	0	5	1	1	.261	.292	.348	639	63	-1	0			1.000	0	/1-5	-0.1
	Lou-N	24	97	13	30	10	1	2	15	11	2	.309	.380	.495	874	133	5	1			.953	-2	1-24	0.2
	Yr	29	120	15	36	12	1	2	20	12	3	.300	.364	.467	830	119	3	1			.960	-2	1-29	0.1
1896	Phi-N	57	218	42	75	13	3	1	41	44	11	.344	.462	.445	907	141	16	7			.983	-3	1-57	1.1
1904	NY-N	2	5	0	0	0	0	0	0	0	0	.000	.000	.000	0	-96	-1	0			1.000	-0	/1-1	-0.2
Total	19	1673	6782	1523	2367	460	205	106	1296	840	238	.349	.423	.519	942	169	611	256			.971	-16	*1-1633/O-35L,P-4,3	42.1
■ **JOE BROVIA**	Brovia, Joseph John "Ox" b: 2/18/22, Davenport, Cal. d: 8/15/94, Santa Cruz, Cal. BL/TR, 6'3", 195 lbs. Deb: 7/3/55																							
1955	Cin-N	21	18	0	2	0	0	0	4	1	6	.111	.158	.111	269	-25	-3	0	0	0	.000	0	H	-0.3
■ **FRANK BROWER**	Brower, Frank Willard "Turkeyfoot" b: 3/26/1893, Gainesville, Va. d: 11/20/60, Baltimore, Md. BL/TR, 6'2", 180 lbs. Deb: 8/14/20 Career OF: (4-LF 0-CF 190-RF)																							
1920	Was-A	36	119	21	37	7	2	1	13	9	11	.311	.374	.429	803	115	3	1	1	-0	.900	-0	O-20(1-0-19)/1-9,3-1	0.1
1921	Was-A	83	203	31	53	12	3	1	35	18	7	.261	.330	.365	695	81	-6	1	1	-0	.917	3	O-46(0-0-46)/1-4	-0.6
1922	Was-A	139	471	61	138	20	6	9	71	52	25	.293	.375	.418	793	112	9	8	6	-0	.978	-4	*O-121(0-0-121)/1-7	-0.5
1923	Cle-A	126	397	77	113	25	8	16	66	62	32	.285	.392	.509	901	136	21	6	5	-0	.988	-3	*1-112/O-4(1-0-3)	1.0
1924	Cle-A	66	107	16	30	10	1	3	20	27	9	.280	.434	.477	910	133	6	1	1	-0	.990	-1	1-26/P-4,O-3(2-0-1)	0.3
Total	5	450	1297	206	371	74	20	30	205	168	84	.286	.379	.443	822	117	33	17	14	-1	.952	-4	O-194R,1-158/P-4,3	0.3
■ **LOUIS BROWER**	Brower, Louis Lester b: 7/1/1900, Cincinnati, Ohio d: 3/4/94, Tyler, Tex. BR/TR, 5'10", 155 lbs. Deb: 6/13/31																							
1931	Det-A	21	62	3	10	1	0	0	6	8	5	.161	.278	.177	455	21	-7	1	0	0	.886	-7	S-20/2-2	-1.2
■ **BOB BROWER**	Brower, Robert Richard b: 1/10/60, Jamaica, N.Y. BR/TR, 5'11", 185 lbs. Deb: 9/3/86																							
1986	Tex-A	21	9	3	1	1	0	0	0	0	3	.111	.111	.222	333	-12	-1	1	2	-0	1.000	-5	O-17(16-1-1)/D-1	-0.7
1987	Tex-A	127	303	63	79	10	3	14	46	36	66	.261	.339	.452	791	107	3	15	9	0	.964	-13	*O-106(45-67-6)/D-7	-1.2
1988	Tex-A	82	201	29	45	7	0	1	11	27	38	.224	.316	.274	589	65	-9	10	5	0	.972	-7	O-59(26-33-4),D-13	-1.7

YEAR	TM/L	G	AB	R	H	2B	3B	HR	RBI	BB	SO	AVG	OBP	SLG	OPS	OPS+	BR+	SB	CS	SBR	FA	FR	G/POS	TPR
1989	NY-A	26	69	9	16	3	0	2	3	6	11	.232	.293	.362	656	85	-2	3	1	0	.970	2	O-25(1-9-15)/D-1	0.1
Total	4	256	582	104	141	21	3	17	60	69	118	.242	.323	.376	699	89	-9	29	17	0	.968	-24	O-207(88-110-26)/D-22	-3.5
■ ADRIAN BROWN Brown, Adrian Demond b: 2/7/74, McComb, Miss. BB/TR, 6′, 175 lbs. Deb: 5/16/97																								
1997	Pit-N	48	147	17	28	6	0	1	10	13	18	.190	.274	.252	526	38	-13	8	4	0	.987	2	O-38(0-35-3)	-1.1
1998	Pit-N	41	152	20	43	4	1	0	5	9	18	.283	.323	.322	645	70	-6	4	0	1	.977	3	O-38(3-34-1)	-0.3
1999	Pit-N	116	226	34	61	5	2	4	17	33	39	.270	.365	.363	728	85	-4	5	3	0	.966	-16	O-96(4-29-66)	-2.1
2000	Pit-N	104	308	64	97	18	3	4	28	29	34	.315	.374	.432	806	104	2	13	1	3	.976	-6	O-92(7-71-15)	-0.1
Total	4	309	833	135	229	33	6	9	60	84	109	.275	.345	.361	706	81	-21	30	8	4	.976	-18	O-264(14-169-85)	-3.6
■ BRANT BROWN Brown, Brant Michael b: 6/22/71, Porterville, Cal. BL/TL, 6′3″, 220 lbs. Deb: 6/15/96 Career OF: (107-LF 93-CF 69-RF)																								
1996	Chi-N	29	69	11	21	1	0	5	9	2	17	.304	.333	.536	870	122	2	3	3	-0	1.000	3	1-18	0.3
1997	Chi-N	46	137	15	32	7	1	5	15	7	28	.234	.286	.409	694	77	-5	2	1	0	1.000	-0	O-27(27-0-0),1-12	-0.7
1998	*Chi-N	124	347	56	101	17	7	14	48	30	95	.291	.349	.501	851	116	8	4	5	-1	.963	-11	*O-102(48-69-0)/1-7	-0.5
1999	Pit-N	130	341	49	79	20	3	16	58	22	114	.232	.286	.449	735	82	-11	3	4	-1	.981	-1	O-82(0-23-59)/1-7,D-6	-1.5
2000	Fla-N	41	73	4	14	6	0	2	6	3	33	.192	.224	.356	580	46	-7	1	0	0	.923	-2	O-13(8-0-5)/1-5	-0.9
	Chi-N	54	89	7	14	1	0	3	10	10	29	.157	.250	.270	520	32	-10	2	1	0	1.000	-2	O-28(24-1-5)/1-7	-1.2
	Yr	95	162	11	28	7	0	5	16	13	62	.173	.239	.309	547	38	-16	3	1	0	.981	-4	O-41(32-1-10),1-12	-2.1
Total	5	424	1056	142	261	52	11	45	146	74	316	.247	.303	.445	748	89	-23	15	14	-2	.975	-14	O-252L/1-56,D-6	-4.5
■ CURTIS BROWN Brown, Curtis b: 9/14/45, Sacramento, Cal. BR/TR, 5′11″, 180 lbs. Deb: 5/27/73 F																								
1973	Mon-N	1	4	0	0	0	0	0	0	0	0	.000	.000	.000	0	-97	-1	0	0	0	1.000	0	/O-1(1-0-0)	-0.1
■ DARRELL BROWN Brown, Darrell Wayne b: 10/29/55, Oklahoma City, Okla BB/TR, 6′, 184 lbs. Deb: 4/11/81																								
1981	Det-A	16	4	4	1	0	0	0	0	0	1	.250	.250	.250	500	43	-0	1	0	0	1.000	-2	/O-6(1-2-3),D-4	-0.3
1982	Oak-A	8	18	2	6	0	1	0	3	1	2	.333	.368	.444	813	128	1	1	0	0	1.000	-1	/O-7(1-0-6),D-1	-0.1
1983	Min-A	91	309	40	84	6	2	0	22	10	28	.272	.297	.304	601	64	-15	3	3	-0	.995	-4	O-81(5-76-0)/D-3	-2.0
1984	Min-A	95	260	36	71	9	3	1	19	14	16	.273	.310	.342	653	77	-8	4	1	1	.993	4	O-55(19-35-0),D-13	-0.5
Total	4	210	591	82	162	15	6	1	44	25	47	.274	.305	.325	630	71	-23	9	4	1	.994	-3	O-149(26-113-9)/D-21	-2.9
■ DELOS BROWN Brown, Delos Hight b: 10/4/1892, Anna, Ill. d: 12/21/64, Carbondale, Ill. BR/TR, 5′9″, 160 lbs. Deb: 6/12/14																								
1914	Chi-A	1	1	0	0	0	0	0	0	0	1	.000	.000	.000	0	-99	-0	0			.000	0	H	0.0
■ DEE BROWN Brown, Dermal Bram b: 3/27/78, Bronx, N.Y. BL/TR, 5′11″, 210 lbs. Deb: 9/14/98																								
1998	KC-A	5	3	2	0	0	0	0	0	0	1	.000	.000	.000	0	-97	-1	0	0	0	1.000	-1	/O-2(0-0-2),D-3	-0.1
1999	KC-A	12	25	1	2	0	0	0	0	2	7	.080	.148	.080	228	-39	-5	0	0	0	.929	2	/O-3(3-0-0),D-2	-0.3
2000	KC-A	15	25	4	4	1	0	0	4	3	9	.160	.250	.200	450	16	-3	0	0	0	1.000	0	/O-5(5-0-0)	-0.3
Total	3	32	53	7	6	1	0	0	4	5	17	.113	.190	.132	322	-16	-9	0	0	0	.963	1	/O-10(8-0-2),D-5	-0.7
■ DRUMMOND BROWN Brown, Drummond Nicol b: 1/31/1885, Los Angeles, Cal. d: 1/27/27, Parkville, Mo. BR/TR, 6′, 180 lbs. Deb: 4/25/13																								
1913	Bos-N	15	34	3	11	1	0	1	2	2	9	.324	.361	.441	802	126	1	0			.960	-4	C-12	-0.2
1914	KC-F	31	58	4	11	3	0	0	5	7	6	.190	.277	.241	518	44	-5	1			.954	5	C-23/1-2	0.1
1915	KC-F	77	227	13	55	10	1	1	26	12	23	.242	.289	.308	598	71	-13	3			.961	-2	C-65/1-1	-1.0
Total	3	123	319	20	77	14	1	2	33	21	38	.241	.294	.310	605	72	-17	4			.960	-2	C-100/1-3	-1.1
■ ED BROWN Brown, Edward P. b: Chicago, Ill. TR, 178 lbs. Deb: 8/19/1882 Career OF: (4-LF 0-CF 13-RF)																								
1882	StL-a	17	60	4	11	0	0	0		4		.183	.234	.183	418	41	-4				.808	-2	O-15(2-0-13)/2-2,P-1	-0.5
1884	Tol-a	42	153	13	27	3	0	0		2		.176	.187	.196	383	24	-13				.815	-8	3-40/O-2L,C-1,P-1	-1.8
Total	2	59	213	17	38	3	0	0		6		.178	.201	.192	393	29	-16				.815	-11	/3-40,O-17R,P-2,2C	-2.3
■ EDDIE BROWN Brown, Edward William "Glass Arm Eddie" b: 7/17/1891, Milligan, Neb. d: 9/10/56, Vallejo, Cal. BR/TR, 6′3″, 190 lbs. Deb: 9/26/20																								
1920	NY-N	3	8	1	1	1	0	0	0	0	3	.125	.125	.250	375	6	-1	0	0	0	1.000	0	/O-2(0-2-0)	-0.1
1921	NY-N	70	128	16	36	6	2	0	12	4	11	.281	.324	.359	683	80	-4	1	0	0	.956	-3	O-30(2-26-2)	-0.8
1924	Bro-N	114	455	56	140	30	4	5	78	26	15	.308	.345	.424	769	108	5	3	5	-1	.975	2	*O-114(0-114-0)	0.1
1925	Bro-N	153	618	88	189	39	11	5	99	22	18	.306	.332	.429	761	95	-6	3	4	-1	.972	8	*O-153(0-153-0)	-0.5
1926	Bos-N	153	612	71	**201**	31	8	2	84	23	20	.328	.355	.415	770	117	13	5			.965	8	*O-153(73-80-0)	1.1
1927	Bos-N	155	558	64	171	35	6	2	75	28	20	.306	.340	.401	741	106	3	11			.980	2	*O-150(150-0-0)/1-1	-0.6
1928	Bos-N	142	523	45	140	28	2	2	59	24	22	.268	.305	.340	645	72	-22	6			.960	-4	*O-129(80-50-1)/1-1	-3.4
Total	7	790	2902	341	878	170	33	16	407	127	109	.303	.334	.400	735	99	-12	29	9		.970	12	O-731(305-425-3)/1-2	-4.2
■ RANDY BROWN Brown, Edwin Randolph b: 8/29/44, Leesburg, Fla. BL/TR, 5′7″, 170 lbs. Deb: 9/11/69																								
1969	Cal-A	13	25	3	4	1	0	0	0	6	1	.160	.323	.200	523	52	-1	0	0	0	1.000	-1	C-10/O-1(0-1-0)	-0.2
1970	Cal-A	5	4	0	0	0	0	0	0	0	0	.000	.000	.000	0	-99	-1	0	0	0	1.000	-0	/C-5	-0.1
Total	2	18	29	3	4	1	0	0	0	6	1	.138	.286	.172	458	32	-2	0	0	0	1.000	-1	/C-15,O-1(0-1-0)	-0.3
■ EMIL BROWN Brown, Emil Quincy b: 12/29/74, Chicago, Ill. BR/TR, 6′2″, 195 lbs. Deb: 4/3/97																								
1997	Pit-N	66	95	16	17	2	1	2	6	10	32	.179	.304	.284	588	54	-6	5	1	1	.948	-4	O-42(30-8-4)	-0.9
1998	Pit-N	13	39	2	10	1	0	0	3	1	11	.256	.293	.282	575	51	-3	0	0	0	1.000	2	O-10(9-1-1)	-0.1
1999	Pit-N	6	14	0	2	1	0	0	0	0	3	.143	.143	.214	357	-11	-2	0	0	0	1.000	-1	/O-6(6-0-0)	-0.3
2000	Pit-N	50	119	13	26	5	0	3	16	11	34	.218	.301	.336	637	61	-7	3	1	0	1.000	-4	O-38(14-12-18)	-1.1
Total	4	135	267	31	55	9	1	5	25	22	80	.206	.293	.303	597	54	-18	8	2	1	.979	-6	/O-96(59-21-23)	-2.4
■ FRED BROWN Brown, Fred Herbert b: 4/12/1879, Ossipee, N.H. d: 2/3/55, Somersworth, N.H. BR/TR, 5′10.5″, 190 lbs. Deb: 5/4/01																								
1901	Bos-N	7	14	1	2	0	0	0	2	0		.143	.143	.143	286	-16	-2	0			1.000	0	/O-5(3-0-2)	-0.2
1902	Bos-N	2	6	1	2	1	0	0	0	0		.333	.333	.500	833	155	0	0			1.000	0	/O-2(0-0-2)	0.0
Total	2	9	20	2	4	1	0	0	2	0		.200	.200	.250	450	30	-2	0			1.000	0	/O-7(3-0-4)	-0.2
■ IKE BROWN Brown, Isaac b: 4/13/42, Memphis, Tenn. BR/TR, 6′1″, 205 lbs. Deb: 6/17/69 Career OF: (44-LF 0-CF 7-RF)																								
1969	Det-A	70	170	24	39	4	3	5	12	26	43	.229	.338	.376	715	96	-1	2	3	-1	.962	-6	2-45,3-12/O-3R,S-1	-0.5
1970	Det-A	56	94	17	27	5	0	4	15	13	26	.287	.380	.468	848	132	4	0	0	0	.935	-3	2-23/O-4(3-0-1),3-1	0.2
1971	Det-A	59	110	20	28	1	0	8	19	19	25	.255	.364	.482	846	133	5	0	1	-0	1.000	-1	1-17/O-9L,2-8,3S	0.2
1972	*Det-A	51	84	12	21	3	0	2	10	17	23	.250	.376	.357	733	115	2	1	2	-0	1.000	3	O-22L,1-13/2-3,S3	0.4
1973	Det-A	42	76	12	22	2	1	1	9	15	13	.289	.407	.382	788	115	2	0	1	-0	.983	-2	1-21,O-12L/3-2,D-2	-0.1
1974	Det-A	2	2	0	0	0	0	0	0	0	0	.000	.000	.000	0	-97	-0	0	0	0	1.000	0	/3-2	0.0
Total	6	280	536	85	137	15	4	20	65	90	130	.256	.366	.410	776	115	13	3	7	-2	.956	-9	/2-79,1-51,O-50L,3SD	0.2
■ JIM BROWN Brown, James Donaldson "Don" or "Moose" b: 3/31/1897, Laurel, Md. BR/TR, 6′, 178 lbs. Deb: 9/13/15																								
1915	StL-N	1	2	0	1	0	0	0	0	2	1	.500	.750	.500	1250	281	1	0			1.000	-0	/O-1(0-1-0)	0.1
1916	Phi-A	14	42	6	10	2	1	1	5	4	9	.238	.304	.405	709	119	1	0			.895	-1	O-12(0-6-6)	-0.1
Total	2	15	44	6	11	2	1	1	5	6	10	.250	.340	.409	749	131	2	0			.900	-2	/O-13(0-7-6)	0.0
■ JIMMY BROWN Brown, James Roberson b: 4/25/10, Jamesville, N.C. d: 12/29/77, Bath, N.C. BB/TR, 5′8.5″, 165 lbs. Deb: 4/23/37 C																								
1937	StL-N	138	525	86	145	20	9	2	53	27	29	.276	.313	.360	673	81	-14	10			.964	-14	*2-112,S-25/3-1	-2.0
1938	StL-N	108	382	50	115	12	6	0	38	27	9	.301	.350	.364	714	91	-4	7			.968	1	2-49,S-30,3-24	0.3
1939	StL-N	147	645	88	192	31	8	3	51	32	18	.298	.335	.384	719	87	-11	4			.957	-5	*S-104,2-50	-0.6
1940	StL-N	107	454	56	127	17	4	0	30	24	15	.280	.317	.335	652	76	-15	9			.977	-22	2-48,3-41,S-28	-3.1
1941	StL-N	132	549	81	168	28	9	3	56	45	22	.306	.363	.406	769	109	7	2			.965	3	*3-123,2-11	1.5
1942	*StL-N★	145	606	75	155	28	4	1	71	52	11	.256	.315	.320	635	80	-15	4			.970	-12	2-82,3-66,S-12	-2.1
1943	StL-N	34	110	6	20	4	2	0	8	6	1	.182	.224	.255	479	37	-9	0			.978	2	2-19/3-9,S-6	-0.6
1946	Pit-N	79	241	23	58	6	0	0	12	18	5	.241	.293	.266	559	58	-13	3			.960	-2	S-30,2-21/3-9	-1.3
Total	8	890	3512	465	980	146	42	9	319	231	110	.279	.326	.352	678	84	-74	39			.968	-50	2-392,3-273,S-235	-7.9

YEAR	TM/L	G	AB	R	H	2B	3B	HR	RBI	BB	SO	AVG	OBP	SLG	OPS	OPS+	BR+	SB	CS	SBR	FA	FR	G/POS	TPR
■ **JIM BROWN**	Brown, James W. H. b: 12/12/1860, Clinton Co., Pa. d: 4/6/08, Williamsport, Pa. Deb: 4/17/1884																							
1884	Alt-U	21	88	12	22	2	2	1		1		.250	.258	.352	611	82	-5				.615	-3	O-14(2-4-8),P-11	-0.6
	NY-N	1	3	0	0	0	0	0	0	0	1	.000	.000	.000	0	-98	-1				.333	-0	/P-1	0.0
	StP-U	6	16	5	5	4	0	0		1		.313	.353	.563	915	320	4				.706	0	/P-6,1-1,O-1(0-0-1)	0.1
1886	Phi-a	1	3	0	0	0	0	0	0	0		.000	.000	.000	0	-99	-1	0			1.000	-0	/P-1	0.0
Total	2	29	110	17	27	6	2	1	0	2	1	.245	.259	.364	623	92	-2	0			.741	-4	/P-19,O-15(2-4-9),1-1	-0.5
■ **JARVIS BROWN**	Brown, Jarvis Ardel b: 3/26/67, Waukegan, Ill. BR/TR, 5'7", 170 lbs. Deb: 7/2/91																							
1991	*Min-A	38	37	10	8	0	0	0	0	2	8	.216	.256	.216	473	31	-3	7	1	1	.955	-11	O-32(3-11-19)/D-4	-1.3
1992	Min-A	35	15	8	1	0	0	0	0	2	4	.067	.222	.067	289	-15	-2	2	2	-0	.952	-10	O-31(4-9-18)/D-2	-1.3
1993	SD-N	47	133	21	31	9	2	0	8	15	26	.233	.338	.331	668	78	-4	3	3	-0	.982	2	O-43(5-40-0)	-0.2
1994	Atl-N	17	15	3	2	1	0	1	1	0	2	.133	.133	.400	533	31	-2	0	0	0	1.000	-2	/O-9(3-4-2)	-0.3
1995	Bal-A	18	27	2	4	1	0	0	1	7	9	.148	.324	.185	509	36	-2	1	1	-0	1.000	-5	O-17(0-13-5)	-0.7
Total	5	155	227	44	46	11	2	1	10	26	49	.203	.304	.282	586	57	-13	13	7	0	.978	-26	O-132(15-77-44)/D-6	-3.8
■ **JAKE BROWN**	Brown, Jerald Ray b: 3/22/48, Sumrall, Miss. d: 12/18/81, Houston, Tex. BR/TR, 6'2", 200 lbs. Deb: 5/17/75																							
1975	SF-N	41	43	6	9	3	0	0	4	5	13	.209	.292	.279	571	57	-2	0	0	0	.857	-3	O-14(9-1-4)	-0.6
■ **CHRIS BROWN**	Brown, John Christopher b: 8/15/61, Jackson, Miss. BR/TR, 6'2", 210 lbs. Deb: 9/3/84																							
1984	SF-N	23	84	6	24	7	0	1	11	9	19	.286	.362	.405	766	119	2	2	1	0	.900	-2	3-23	0.0
1985	SF-N	131	432	50	117	20	3	16	61	38	78	.271	.345	.442	787	125	14	2	3	-1	**.971**	5	*3-120	1.7
1986	SF-N★	116	416	57	132	16	3	7	49	33	43	.317	.380	.421	801	127	16	13	9	-0	.933	-14	*3-111/S-2	-0.1
1987	SF-N	38	132	17	32	6	0	6	17	9	16	.242	.306	.424	730	95	-1	1	3	-1	.905	-2	3-37/S-1	-0.5
	SD-N	44	155	17	36	3	0	6	23	11	30	.232	.296	.368	664	77	-5	3	1	0	.942	-4	3-43	-0.9
	Yr	82	287	34	68	9	0	12	40	20	46	.237	.300	.394	694	86	-7	4	4	-1	.923	-6	3-80/S-1	-1.4
1988	SD-N	80	247	14	58	6	0	2	19	19	49	.235	.297	.283	581	69	-10	0	0	0	.949	5	3-72	-0.5
1989	Det-A	17	57	3	11	3	0	0	4	1	17	.193	.207	.246	453	28	-6	0	0	0	.909	-1	3-17	-0.7
Total	6	449	1523	164	410	61	6	38	184	120	252	.269	.335	.392	727	105	10	21	17	-1	.943	-13	3-423/S-3	-1.0
■ **LINDSAY BROWN**	Brown, John Lindsay "Red" b: 7/22/11, Mason, Tex. d: 1/1/67, San Antonio, Tex. BR/TR, 5'10", 160 lbs. Deb: 7/13/37																							
1937	Bro-N	48	115	16	31	3	1	0	6	3	17	.270	.288	.313	601	62	-6	1			.937	6	S-45	0.3
■ **JOE BROWN**	Brown, Joseph E. b: 4/4/1859, Warren, Pa. d: 6/28/1888, Warren, Pa. 5'10", 162 lbs. Deb: 8/16/1884 Career OF: (0-LF 1-CF 9-RF)																							
1884	Chi-N	15	61	6	13	1	0	0	3	0	15	.213	.213	.230	443	36	-5				.750	-3	/O-9R,P-7,1-1,C-1	-0.5
1885	Bal-a	5	19	2	3	0	0	0	0	0		.158	.158	.158	316	-0	-2				1.000	0	/P-4,2-1	0.0
Total	2	20	80	8	16	1	0	0	3	0	15	.200	.200	.213	413	28	-7				.895	-3	/P-11,O-9R,2-1,C1	-0.5
■ **KEVIN BROWN**	Brown, Kevin Lee b: 4/21/73, Valparaiso, Ind. BR/TR, 6'2", 200 lbs. Deb: 9/12/96																							
1996	Tex-A	3	4	1	0	0	0	0	1	2	2	.000	.429	.000	429	20	-0	0	0	0	1.000	1	/C-2,D-1	0.1
1997	Tex-A	4	5	1	2	0	0	1	1	0	0	.400	.400	1.000	1400	237	1	0	0	0	.900	0	/C-4	0.1
1998	Tor-A	52	110	17	29	7	1	2	15	9	31	.264	.331	.400	731	89	-2	0	0	0	.993	7	C-52	0.7
1999	Tor-A	2	9	1	4	2	0	0	1	0	3	.444	.444	.667	1111	176	1	0	0	0	1.000	-1	/C-2	0.0
2000	Mil-N	5	17	3	4	3	0	0	1	1	5	.235	.278	.412	690	72	-1	0	0	0	.957	-2	/C-5	-0.2
Total	5	66	145	23	39	12	1	3	19	12	41	.269	.338	.428	765	96	-1	0	0	0	.988	6	/C-65,D-1	0.7
■ **LARRY BROWN**	Brown, Larry Leslie b: 3/1/40, Shinnston, W.Va. BR/TR, 5'11", 165 lbs. Deb: 7/6/63 F																							
1963	Cle-A	74	247	28	63	6	0	5	18	22	27	.255	.319	.340	659	85	-5	4	3	-0	.938	-8	S-46,2-27	-0.8
1964	Cle-A	115	335	33	77	12	1	12	40	24	55	.230	.285	.379	664	84	-8	1	2	-0	.981	11	*2-103/S-4	1.1
1965	Cle-A	124	438	52	111	22	2	8	40	38	62	.253	.316	.368	683	93	-4	5	7	-1	.977	3	S-95,2-26	0.8
1966	Cle-A	105	340	29	78	12	0	3	17	36	58	.229	.309	.291	600	73	-11	0	1	-0	.961	-4	S-90,2-10	-0.7
1967	Cle-A	152	485	38	110	16	2	7	37	53	62	.227	.311	.311	622	84	-9	4	4	-1	.967	1	*S-150	0.5
1968	Cle-A	154	495	43	116	18	3	6	35	43	46	.234	.302	.319	621	90	-6	1	1	-0	.966	-14	*S-154	-0.9
1969	Cle-A	132	469	48	112	10	2	4	24	44	43	.239	.305	.294	600	66	-21	5	3	0	.959	-17	*S-101,3-29/2-5	-2.6
1970	Cle-A	72	155	17	40	5	2	0	15	20	14	.258	.343	.316	659	79	-4	1	0	0	.950	-2	S-27,3-17,2-16	-0.3
1971	Cle-A	13	50	4	11	1	0	0	5	3	3	.220	.278	.240	518	44	-4	0	0	0	.980	-6	S-13	-0.9
	Oak-A	70	189	14	37	2	1	1	9	7	19	.196	.228	.233	461	31	-17	1	2	-0	.959	4	S-31,2-23,3-10	-1.1
	Yr	83	239	18	48	3	1	1	14	10	22	.201	.239	.234	473	35	-21	1	2	-0	.965	-2	S-44,2-23,3-10	-2.0
1972	Oak-A	47	142	11	26	2	0	0	4	13	8	.183	.252	.197	449	37	-11	0	0	0	.974	-8	2-46/3-1	-1.9
1973	*Bal-A	17	28	4	7	0	0	1	5	5	4	.250	.364	.357	721	104	0	0	0	0	.880	-2	3-15/2-1	-0.2
1974	Tex-A	54	76	10	15	2	0	0	5	9	13	.197	.282	.224	506	48	-5	0	0	0	.931	8	3-47/2-8,S-1	0.3
Total	12	1129	3449	331	803	108	13	47	254	317	414	.233	.301	.313	614	76	-103	22	23	-3	.964	-34	S-712,2-265,3-119	-6.7
■ **LEON BROWN**	Brown, Leon b: 11/16/49, Sacramento, Cal. BR/TR, 6', 185 lbs. Deb: 5/19/76 F																							
1976	NY-N	64	70	11	15	3	0	0	2	4	4	.214	.257	.257	514	49	-5	2	4	-1	1.000	-18	O-43(39-28-6)	-2.6
■ **LEW BROWN**	Brown, Lewis J. "Blower" b: 2/1/1858, Leominster, Mass. d: 1/15/1889, Boston, Mass. BR/TR, 5'10.5", 185 lbs. Deb: 6/17/1876 Career OF: (0-LF 1-CF 23-RF)																							
1876	Bos-N	45	198	23	41	6	6	2	21	3	22	.207	.222	.333	556	82	-4				.856	-2	C-45/O-1(0-1-1)	-0.4
1877	Bos-N	58	221	27	56	12	8	1	31	6	33	.253	.273	.394	667	104	0				.897	15	*C-55/1-4	1.5
1878	Pro-N	58	243	44	74	21	6	1	43	7	37	.305	.324	.453	777	153	13				.880	3	*C-45,1-15/O-1R,P-1	1.5
1879	Pro-N	53	229	23	59	13	4	2	38	4	24	.258	.270	.376	646	112	3				.847	-4	C-48/O-6(0-0-6)	0.0
	Chi-N	6	21	2	6	1	0	0	3	1	4	.286	.318	.333	652	109	0				.974	0	/1-6	0.0
	Yr	59	250	25	65	14	4	2	41	5	28	.260	.275	.372	647	112	3				.847	-4	C-48/O-6(0-0-6),1-6	0.0
1881	Det-N	27	108	16	26	3	1	3	14	3	16	.241	.261	.370	632	93	-1				.959	-1	1-27	-0.3
	Pro-N	18	75	9	18	3	1	0	10	4	13	.240	.278	.307	585	85	-1				.833	-4	O-13(0-0-13)/1-5	-0.5
	Yr	45	183	25	44	6	2	3	24	7	29	.240	.268	.344	613	90	-2				.960	-4	1-32,O-13(0-0-13)	-0.8
1883	Bos-N	14	54	5	13	4	1	0	9	3	6	.241	.281	.352	633	89	-1				.943	-2	1-14	-0.3
	Lou-a	14	60	6	11	2	1	0		1		.183	.197	.250	447	46	-3				.891	-2	1-14/C-1	-0.6
1884	Bos-U	85	325	50	75	18	3	1		13		.231	.260	.314	574	74	-20				.914	13	C-54,1-33/O-2R,P-1	-0.5
Total	7	378	1534	205	379	83	31	10	169	45	155	.247	.269	.362	631	99	-13				.884	17	C-248,1-118/O-23R,P	0.4
■ **MARTY BROWN**	Brown, Marty Leo b: 1/23/63, Lawton, Okla. BR/TR, 6'1", 190 lbs. Deb: 9/4/88																							
1988	Cin-N	10	16	0	3	1	0	0	2	1	2	.188	.235	.250	485	38	-1	0	1	-0	1.000	1	/3-8	-0.1
1989	Cin-N	16	30	2	5	1	0	0	4	4	9	.167	.265	.200	465	34	-3	0	0	0	.913	2	3-11	-0.1
1990	Bal-A	9	15	1	3	0	0	0	0	1	7	.200	.250	.200	450	28	-1	0	0	0	1.000	0	/2-3,3-2,D-4	-0.1
Total	3	35	61	3	11	2	0	0	6	6	18	.180	.254	.213	467	34	-5	0	1	-0	.943	3	/3-21,D-4,2-3	-0.3
■ **MIKE BROWN**	Brown, Michael Charles b: 12/29/59, San Francisco, Cal. BR/TR, 6'2", 195 lbs. Deb: 7/21/83																							
1983	Cal-A	31	104	12	24	5	1	3	9	7	20	.231	.279	.385	664	81	-3	1	0	0	.949	-2	O-31(18-3-11)	-0.6
1984	Cal-A	62	148	19	42	8	3	7	22	13	23	.284	.342	.520	862	136	7	0	2	-1	.968	-6	O-44(2-0-43)/D-3	-0.1
1985	Cal-A	60	153	23	41	9	1	4	20	7	21	.268	.304	.418	723	96	-1	0	1	-0	1.000	-3	O-48(1-1-46)/D-7	-0.6
	Pit-N	57	205	29	68	18	2	5	33	22	27	.332	.396	.512	909	154	15	2	2	-0	.938	-2	O-56(0-0-56)	0.9
1986	Pit-N	87	243	18	53	7	0	4	26	27	32	.218	.296	.296	593	62	-12	2	3	-1	.973	-4	O-71(0-0-71)	-2.1
1988	Cal-A	18	50	4	11	2	0	0	3	1	12	.220	.235	.260	495	40	-4	0	0	0	.946	-1	O-18(18-0-2)	-0.5
Total	5	315	903	105	239	49	7	23	113	77	135	.265	.323	.411	734	102	1	5	8	-2	.964	-17	O-268(39-4-229)/D-10	-3.0
■ **OLIVER BROWN**	Brown, Oliver S. b: 1849, Brooklyn, N.Y. d: 9/23/32, Brooklyn, N.Y. Deb: 8/1/1872																							
1872	Atl-n	4	15	0	2	0	0	0	0	0	1	.133	.133	.133	267	-15	-2	0	0	0	.889	0	/O-4(0-0-4)	-0.1
1875	Atl-n	3	10	0	0	0	0	0	0	0	0	.000	.000	.000	0	-99	-2	0	0	0	.833	-1	/1-2,O-2(0-1-1)	-0.2
Total	2 n	7	25	0	2	0	0	0	0	0	1	.080	.080	.080	160	-46	-4	0	0	0	.846	-0	/O-6(0-1-5),1-2	-0.3
■ **OLLIE BROWN**	Brown, Ollie Lee "Downtown" b: 2/11/44, Tuscaloosa, Ala. BR/TR, 6'3", 200 lbs. Deb: 9/10/65 F Career OF: (75-LF 39-CF 910-RF)																							
1965	SF-N	6	10	0	2	1	0	0	0	0	2	.200	.200	.300	500	38	-1	0	0	0	1.000	-1	/O-4(0-0-4)	-0.2

YEAR	TM/L	G	AB	R	H	2B	3B	HR	RBI	BB	SO	AVG	OBP	SLG	OPS	OPS+	BR+	SB	CS	SBR	FA	FR	G/POS	TPR
1966	SF-N	115	348	32	81	7	1	7	33	33	66	.233	.303	.319	622	71	-13	2	5	-1	.978	-7	*O-114(1-16-107)	-2.9
1967	SF-N	120	412	44	110	12	1	13	53	25	65	.267	.315	.396	711	104	1	0	2	-1	.985	-6	*O-115(0-10-111)	-1.4
1968	SF-N	40	95	7	22	4	0	0	11	3	23	.232	.270	.274	544	64	-4	1	0	0	1.000	-7	O-35(3-3-30)	-1.5
1969	SD-N	151	568	76	150	18	3	20	61	44	97	.264	.320	.412	732	108	4	10	6	0	.976	7	*O-148(0-0-148)	0.3
1970	SD-N	139	534	79	156	34	1	23	89	34	78	.292	.335	.489	823	123	14	5	3	0	.964	7	*O-137(0-0-137)	1.3
1971	SD-N	145	484	36	132	16	0	9	55	52	74	.273	.347	.362	709	108	6	3	3	-0	.982	5	*O-134(0-1-134)	0.4
1972	SD-N	23	70	3	12	2	0	0	3	5	9	.171	.227	.200	427	24	-7	0	0	0	1.000	1	O-17(0-0-17)	-0.8
	Oak-A	20	54	5	13	1	0	1	4	6	14	.241	.317	.315	631	93	-0	1	1	-0	1.000	-2	O-16(0-9-9)	-0.3
	Mil-A	66	179	21	50	8	0	3	25	17	24	.279	.345	.374	719	116	4	0	2	-1	.992	7	O-56(0-0-56)/3-1	0.8
	Yr	86	233	26	63	9	0	4	29	23	38	.270	.339	.361	699	111	3	1	3	-1	.994	5	O-72(0-9-65)/3-1	0.5
1973	Mil-A	97	296	28	83	10	1	7	32	33	53	.280	.356	.392	748	113	6	4	1	1	1.000	-1	D-82/O-4(0-0-4)	0.3
1974	Hou-N	27	69	8	15	1	0	3	6	4	15	.217	.260	.362	623	76	-3	0	0	0	1.000	-1	O-20(0-0-20)	-0.4
	Phi-N	43	99	11	24	5	2	4	13	6	20	.242	.286	.455	740	101	-1	0	1	-0	.921	-5	O-33(24-0-9)	-0.8
	Yr	70	168	19	39	6	2	7	19	10	35	.232	.275	.417	692	91	-3	0	1	-0	.961	-6	O-53(24-0-29)	-1.2
1975	Phi-N	84	145	19	44	12	0	6	26	15	29	.303	.369	.510	879	137	7	1	1	-0	1.000	-14	O-63(23-0-48)	-1.0
1976	*Phi-N	92	209	30	53	10	1	5	30	33	33	.254	.355	.383	738	106	2	2	1	0	.949	-6	O-75(9-0-69)	-0.7
1977	*Phi-N	53	70	5	17	3	1	1	13	4	14	.243	.284	.357	641	68	-3	1	1	-0	1.000	-4	O-21(15-0-7)	-0.8
Total	13	1221	3642	404	964	144	11	102	454	314	616	.265	.326	.394	720	103	12	30	27	-3	.977	-29	O-992R/D-82,3-1	-7.7

■ OSCAR BROWN

Brown, Oscar Lee b: 2/8/46, Long Beach, Cal. BR/TR, 6', 175 lbs. Deb: 9/3/69 F

YEAR	TM/L	G	AB	R	H	2B	3B	HR	RBI	BB	SO	AVG	OBP	SLG	OPS	OPS+	BR+	SB	CS	SBR	FA	FR	G/POS	TPR
1969	Atl-N	7	4	2	1	0	0	0	0	0	1	.250	.250	.250	500	40	-0	0	0	0	1.000	-1	/O-3(0-2-1)	-0.1
1970	Atl-N	28	47	6	18	2	1	1	7	7	7	.383	.473	.532	1005	159	4	0	2	-1	.960	-5	O-25(8-12-5)	-0.2
1971	Atl-N	27	43	4	9	4	0	0	5	3	8	.209	.261	.302	563	56	-3	0	0	0	1.000	-2	O-15(6-7-3)	-0.5
1972	Atl-N	76	164	19	37	5	1	3	16	4	29	.226	.244	.323	567	55	-10	0	2	-1	.899	-4	O-59(28-3-28)	-1.7
1973	Atl-N	22	58	3	12	3	0	0	0	3	10	.207	.246	.259	505	37	-5	0	0	0	1.000	2	O-13(5-3-5)	-0.4
Total	5	160	316	34	77	14	2	4	28	17	55	.244	.284	.339	623	68	-13	0	4	-1	.939	-10	O-115(47-27-42)	-2.9

■ DICK BROWN

Brown, Richard Ernest b: 1/17/35, Shinnston, W.Va. d: 4/17/70, Baltimore, Md. BR/TR, 6'3", 190 lbs. Deb: 6/20/57 F

YEAR	TM/L	G	AB	R	H	2B	3B	HR	RBI	BB	SO	AVG	OBP	SLG	OPS	OPS+	BR+	SB	CS	SBR	FA	FR	G/POS	TPR
1957	Cle-A	34	114	10	30	4	0	4	22	4	23	.263	.288	.404	692	88	-2	1	1	-0	.986	1	C-33	0.0
1958	Cle-A	68	173	20	41	5	0	7	20	14	27	.237	.305	.387	693	91	-2	1	0	0	.987	6	C-62	0.6
1959	Cle-A	48	141	15	31	7	0	5	16	11	39	.220	.290	.376	666	85	-3	0	0	0	.996	4	C-48	0.3
1960	Chi-A	16	43	4	7	0	0	3	5	3	11	.163	.217	.372	589	57	-3	0	0	0	.986	3	C-14	0.1
1961	Det-A	93	308	32	82	12	2	16	45	22	57	.266	.315	.474	789	105	1	0	2	-1	.990	-1	C-91	0.4
1962	Det-A	134	431	40	104	12	0	12	40	21	66	.241	.280	.353	632	67	-21	0	1	-0	.994	3	*C-132	-1.3
1963	Bal-A	59	171	13	42	7	0	2	13	15	35	.246	.310	.322	632	80	-4	1	0	0	.986	6	C-58	0.4
1964	Bal-A	88	230	24	59	6	0	8	32	12	45	.257	.296	.387	683	89	-4	2	0	0	.988	4	C-84	0.3
1965	Bal-A	96	255	17	59	9	1	5	30	17	53	.231	.282	.333	615	73	-9	2	2	-0	.983	10	C-92	0.4
Total	9	636	1866	175	455	62	3	62	223	119	356	.244	.293	.380	673	83	-49	7	6	-1	.989	35	C-614	1.2

■ ROBERT BROWN

Brown, Robert Deb: 7/29/1874

YEAR	TM/L	G	AB	R	H	2B	3B	HR	RBI	BB	SO	AVG	OBP	SLG	OPS	OPS+	BR+	SB	CS	SBR	FA	FR	G/POS	TPR
1874	Bal-n	2	9	0	0	0	0	0	0	0	0	.000	.000	.000	0	-99	-2	0	0	0	.727	-1	/S-2	-0.2

■ BOBBY BROWN

Brown, Robert William "Doc" b: 10/25/24, Seattle, Wash. BL/TR, 6'1", 180 lbs. Deb: 9/22/46

YEAR	TM/L	G	AB	R	H	2B	3B	HR	RBI	BB	SO	AVG	OBP	SLG	OPS	OPS+	BR+	SB	CS	SBR	FA	FR	G/POS	TPR
1946	NY-A	7	24	1	8	1	0	0	1	4	0	.333	.429	.375	804	124	1	0	0	0	1.000	-4	/S-5,3-2	-0.2
1947	*NY-A	69	150	21	45	6	1	1	18	21	9	.300	.390	.373	763	114	4	0	2	-1	.932	-11	3-27,S-11/O-3(0-2-1)	-0.8
1948	NY-A	113	363	62	109	19	5	3	48	48	16	.300	.383	.405	788	111	6	0	1	-0	.946	-18	3-41,S-26,2-17,/O-4L	-1.0
1949	*NY-A	104	343	61	97	14	4	6	61	38	18	.283	.359	.399	759	101	-0	4	3	-0	.949	-4	3-86/O-3(1-0-2)	-0.4
1950	*NY-A	95	277	33	74	4	2	4	37	39	18	.267	.360	.339	699	82	-7	3	1	0	.958	-4	3-82	-0.9
1951	*NY-A	103	313	44	84	15	2	6	51	47	18	.268	.369	.387	756	108	5	1	1	-0	.955	-5	3-90	0.0
1952	NY-A	29	89	6	22	2	0	1	14	9	6	.247	.323	.303	627	80	-2	1	1	-0	.894	3	3-24	0.0
1954	NY-A	28	60	5	13	1	0	1	7	8	3	.217	.309	.283	592	65	-3	0	1	-0	1.000	-0	3-17	-0.4
Total	8	548	1619	233	452	62	14	22	237	214	88	.279	.367	.376	742	100	4	9	10	-2	.948	-43	3-369/S-42,2-17,O	-3.7

■ BOBBY BROWN

Brown, Rogers Lee b: 5/24/54, Norfolk, Va. BB/TR (BL 1979), 6'1", 205 lbs. Deb: 4/5/79

YEAR	TM/L	G	AB	R	H	2B	3B	HR	RBI	BB	SO	AVG	OBP	SLG	OPS	OPS+	BR+	SB	CS	SBR	FA	FR	G/POS	TPR
1979	Tor-A	4	10	1	0	0	0	0	0	2	1	.000	.167	.000	167	-50	-2	0	0	0	1.000	-0	/O-4(2-0-2)	-0.2
	NY-A	30	68	7	17	3	1	0	3	2	17	.250	.271	.324	595	61	-4	2	1	0	.949	-3	O-27(7-20-0)/D-1	-0.7
	Yr	34	78	8	17	3	1	0	3	4	18	.218	.256	.282	538	46	-6	2	1	0	.955	-3	O-31(9-20-2)/D-1	-0.9
1980	*NY-A	137	412	65	107	12	5	14	47	29	82	.260	.308	.415	723	98	-2	27	8	3	.972	-1	*O-131(28-81-25)/D-1	-0.3
1981	*NY-A	31	62	5	14	1	0	0	6	5	15	.226	.284	.242	526	53	-4	4	2	0	.949	-2	O-29(6-11-14)/D-2	-0.6
1982	Sea-A	79	245	29	59	7	1	4	17	17	32	.241	.290	.327	617	67	-11	28	6	4	.968	3	O-68(51-14-4)/D-3	-0.6
1983	SD-N	57	225	40	60	5	3	5	22	23	38	.267	.335	.382	717	102	0	27	9	3	.963	-1	O-54(52-0-4)	-0.1
1984	*SD-N	85	171	28	43	7	2	3	29	11	33	.251	.297	.368	665	86	-4	16	4	2	.971	-2	O-53(27-13-16)	-0.5
1985	SD-N	79	84	8	13	3	0	0	6	5	20	.155	.202	.190	393	11	-10	6	4	-0	1.000	-7	O-28(9-9-12)	-1.8
Total	7	502	1277	183	313	38	12	26	130	94	238	.245	.297	.355	652	80	-36	110	34	12	.968	-13	O-394(182-148-77)/D-7	-4.8

■ ROOSEVELT BROWN

Brown, Roosevelt Lawayne b: 8/3/75, Vicksburg, Miss. BL/TR, 5'11", 195 lbs. Deb: 5/18/99

YEAR	TM/L	G	AB	R	H	2B	3B	HR	RBI	BB	SO	AVG	OBP	SLG	OPS	OPS+	BR+	SB	CS	SBR	FA	FR	G/POS	TPR
1999	Chi-N	33	64	6	14	6	1	1	10	2	14	.219	.242	.391	633	58	-4	1	0	0	.955	-3	O-18(13-5-1)	-0.7
2000	Chi-N	45	91	11	32	8	0	3	14	4	22	.352	.385	.538	924	133	4	0	1	-0	1.000	-4	O-28(18-9-3)	0.0
Total	2	78	155	17	46	14	1	4	24	6	36	.297	.327	.477	805	102	-0	1	1	-0	.984	-7	/O-46(31-14-4)	-0.7

■ SAM BROWN

Brown, Samuel Wakefield b: 5/21/1878, Webster, Pa. d: 11/8/31, Mount Pleasant, Pa. BR/TR, Deb: 4/21/06 Career OF: (6-LF 4-CF 1-RF)

YEAR	TM/L	G	AB	R	H	2B	3B	HR	RBI	BB	SO	AVG	OBP	SLG	OPS	OPS+	BR+	SB	CS	SBR	FA	FR	G/POS	TPR
1906	Bos-N	71	231	12	48	6	1	0	20	13		.208	.262	.242	505	59	-11	4			.970	-1	C-35,O-13L,3-12,/12	-0.9
1907	Bos-N	70	208	17	40	6	0	0	14	12		.192	.250	.221	471	48	-12	0			.970	7	C-63/1-2	0.1
Total	2	141	439	29	88	12	1	0	34	25		.200	.256	.232	489	54	-23	4			.970	7	/C-98,O-13L,3-12,12	-0.8

■ TOMMY BROWN

Brown, Thomas Michael "Buckshot" b: 12/6/27, Brooklyn, N.Y. BR/TR, 6'1", 170 lbs. Deb: 8/3/44 Career OF: (87-LF 0-CF 6-RF)

YEAR	TM/L	G	AB	R	H	2B	3B	HR	RBI	BB	SO	AVG	OBP	SLG	OPS	OPS+	BR+	SB	CS	SBR	FA	FR	G/POS	TPR
1944	Bro-N	46	146	17	24	4	0	0	8	8	17	.164	.208	.192	400	13	-17	0			.925	-9	S-46	-2.4
1945	Bro-N	57	196	13	48	3	4	2	19	6	16	.245	.267	.332	599	66	-10	3			.918	-4	S-55/O-1(0-0-1)	-1.0
1947	Bro-N	15	34	3	8	1	0	0	2	1	6	.235	.257	.265	522	37	-3	0			1.000	2	/3-6,O-3(3-0-0),S-1	-0.1
1948	Bro-N	54	145	18	35	4	0	2	20	7	17	.241	.281	.310	591	58	-9	1			.936	-1	3-43/1-1	-1.0
1949	*Bro-N	41	89	14	27	2	0	3	18	6	8	.303	.347	.427	774	102	0	0			.931	-2	O-27(27-0-0)	-0.3
1950	Bro-N	48	86	15	25	2	1	8	20	11	9	.291	.378	.616	994	153	6	0			.917	0	O-16(16-0-0)	0.5
1951	Bro-N	11	25	2	4	2	0	0	1	2	4	.160	.222	.240	462	24	-3	0	0	0	.909	0	/O-5(5-0-0)	-0.3
	Phi-N	78	196	24	43	2	1	10	32	15	21	.219	.278	.393	671	80	-6	1	2	-0	.966	-12	O-32L,2-14,1-12,/3	-2.0
	Yr	89	221	26	47	4	1	10	33	17	25	.213	.272	.376	648	73	-9	1	2	-0	.957	-11	O-37L,2-14,1-12,/3	-2.3
1952	Phi-N	18	25	2	4	1	0	1	2	4	3	.160	.276	.320	596	65	-1	0	0	0	1.000	-1	/1-3,O-3(3-0-0)	-0.2
	Chi-N	61	200	24	64	11	0	3	24	12	24	.320	.358	.420	778	114	4	1	2	-0	.911	-19	S-39,2-10/1-5	-1.4
	Yr	79	225	26	68	12	0	4	26	16	27	.302	.349	.409	757	109	2	1	2	-0	.911	-20	S-39,2-10/1-8,O-3L	-1.6
1953	Chi-N	65	138	19	27	7	1	2	13	13	17	.196	.279	.304	584	51	-10	1	0	0	.903	-6	S-25/O-6(1-0-5)	-1.4
Total	9	494	1280	151	309	39	7	31	159	85	142	.241	.292	.355	647	74	-48	7	4		.916	-52	S-166/O-93L,3-50,21	-9.6

■ TOM BROWN

Brown, Thomas Tarlton b: 9/21/1860, Liverpool, England d: 10/25/27, Washington, D.C. BL/TR, 5'10", 168 lbs. Deb: 7/6/1882 MU Career OF: (96-LF 1098-CF 593-RF)

YEAR	TM/L	G	AB	R	H	2B	3B	HR	RBI	BB	SO	AVG	OBP	SLG	OPS	OPS+	BR+	SB	CS	SBR	FA	FR	G/POS	TPR
1882	Bal-a	45	181	30	55	5	2	1	23	6		.304	.326	.370	696	146	9				.728	-0	O-45(0-0-45)/P-2	0.8
1883	Col-a	97	420	69	115	12	7	5	32	20		.274	.307	.371	678	127	14				.808	-1	*O-96(0-0-96)/P-3	1.1
1884	Col-a	107	451	93	123	9	11	5	32	24		.273	.315	.375	690	135	19				.847	-6	*O-107(0-0-107)/P-4	1.1
1885	Pit-a	108	437	81	134	16	12	4	68	34		.307	.366	.426	792	152	26				.828	-3	*O-108(0-0-108)/P-2	2.0
1886	Pit-a	115	460	106	131	11	11	1	51	56		.285	.365	.363	728	129	17	30			.837	6	*O-115(1-1-115)/P-1	1.9
1887	Pit-N	47	203	30	58	3	4	0	6	11	40	.286	.289	.302	591	69	-8	12			.870	5	O-47(0-47-0)	-0.4
	Ind-N	36	148	20	33	3	0	2	9	8	25	.223	.228	.243	471	32	-13	13			.813	-2	O-36(0-17-19)	-1.3
	Yr	83	351	50	91	6	4	2	15	19	65	.259	.263	.277	541	53	-20	25			.851	3	O-83(0-64-19)	-1.7

YEAR	TM/L	G	AB	R	H	2B	3B	HR	RBI	BB	SO	AVG	OBP	SLG	OPS	OPS+	BR+	SB	CS	SBR	FA	FR	G/POS	TPR
1888	Bos-N	107	420	62	104	10	7	9	49	30	68	.248	.299	.369	668	110	5	46			.896	-3	*O-107(6-2-99)	0.0
1889	Bos-N	90	362	93	84	10	5	2	24	59	56	.232	.341	.304	645	76	-11	63			.901	3	O-90(88-0-2)	-0.9
1890	Bos-P	128	543	146	149	23	14	4	61	86	84	.274	.377	.390	767	98	-1	79			.911	4	*O-128(0-128-0)	-0.1
1891	Bos-a	137	589	**177**	**189**	30	**21**	5	72	70	96	.321	.397	.469	865	150	37	**106**			.878	-10	*O-137(0-137-0)	1.9
1892	Lou-N	153	660	105	150	16	8	2	45	47	94	.227	.284	.285	569	78	-17	78			.919	19	*O-153(0-153-0)	-0.8
1893	Lou-N	122	529	104	127	15	7	5	54	56	63	.240	.319	.323	642	77	-17	**66**			.929	27	*O-122(0-122-0)	0.2
1894	Lou-N	130	541	123	137	22	14	9	57	60	74	.253	.331	.396	727	80	-18	66			.912	2	*O-130(0-130-0)	-1.9
1895	StL-N	84	355	73	78	11	4	1	31	48	44	.220	.316	.282	598	56	-23	34			.951	9	O-84(1-83-0)	-1.6
	Was-N	34	134	25	32	8	3	2	16	18	16	.239	.329	.388	717	86	-3	8			.909	-7	O-34(0-34-0)	-1.0
	Yr	118	489	98	110	19	7	3	47	66	60	.225	.320	.311	630	64	-26	42			.942	2	*O-118(1-117-0)	-2.6
1896	Was-N	116	435	87	128	17	6	2	59	58	49	.294	.385	.375	759	101	3	28			.928	-5	*O-116(0-114-2)	-0.8
1897	Was-N	116	469	91	137	17	2	5	45	52		.292	.364	.369	733	94	-3	25			.928	1	*O-115(0-115-0)/M	-0.8
1898	Was-N	16	55	8	9	1	0	0	2	5		.164	.233	.182	415	19	-6	3			.925	0	O-15(0-15-0)/M	-0.6
Total	17	1788	7392	1523	1973	239	138	64	736	748	709	.267	.336	.361	697	101	11	657			.890	39	*O-1785C/P-12	-1.2

■ TOM BROWN
Brown, Thomas William b: 12/12/40, Laureldale, Pa. BB/TL, 6'1", 190 lbs. Deb: 4/8/63

YEAR	TM/L	G	AB	R	H	2B	3B	HR	RBI	BB	SO	AVG	OBP	SLG	OPS	OPS+	BR+	SB	CS	SBR	FA	FR	G/POS	TPR
1963	Was-A	61	116	8	17	4	0	1	4	11	45	.147	.227	.207	433	23	-12	2	1	0	1.000	-2	O-16(10-5-1),1-14	-1.6

■ WILLARD BROWN
Brown, Willard "Big Bill" or "California"
b: 1866, San Francisco, Cal. d: 12/20/1897, San Francisco, Cal BR/TR, 6'2", 190 lbs. Deb: 5/10/1887 Career OF: (2-LF 5-CF 13-RF)

YEAR	TM/L	G	AB	R	H	2B	3B	HR	RBI	BB	SO	AVG	OBP	SLG	OPS	OPS+	BR+	SB	CS	SBR	FA	FR	G/POS	TPR
1887	NY-N	49	180	17	47	3	2	0	25	10	15	.261	.273	.259	532	51	-11	10			.914	-0	C-46/3-3,O-2(0-0-2)	-0.6
1888	*NY-N	20	59	4	16	1	0	0	6	1	8	.271	.283	.288	571	84	-1	1			.893	3	C-20	0.3
1889	*NY-N	40	139	16	36	10	0	1	29	9	9	.259	.318	.353	670	87	-3	6			.846	-5	C-37/O-3(0-3-0)	-0.5
1890	NY-P	60	230	47	64	8	4	4	43	13	13	.278	.320	.400	720	84	-7	5			.900	-5	C-34,O-13R/1-9,32	-0.8
1891	Phi-N	115	441	62	107	20	4	0	50	34	35	.243	.303	.306	609	75	-14	7			**.989**	5	*1-97,C-19/O-2(0-2-0)	-1.5
1893	Bal-N	7	32	5	4	3	0	0	5	1	3	.125	.152	.219	370	-2	-5	0			.985	-0	/1-7	-0.4
	Lou-N	111	461	80	140	23	7	1	85	50	32	.304	.373	.390	764	112	9	9			.989	-2	*1-111/C-1	0.6
	Yr	118	493	85	144	26	7	1	90	51	35	.292	.360	.379	739	104	4	9			**.988**	-2	*1-118/C-1	0.2
1894	Lou-N	13	48	5	10	2	0	0	9	5	7	.208	.283	.250	533	31	-5	1			.977	4	1-13	-0.1
	StL-N	3	9	0	1	0	0	0	0	0	2	.111	.111	.111	222	-46	-2	0			1.000	0	/1-3	-0.1
	Yr	16	57	5	11	2	0	0	9	5	9	.193	.258	.228	486	19	-7	1			.982	4	1-16	-0.2
Total	7	418	1599	236	425	70	17	6	252	123	124	.266	.319	.338	657	82	-39	39			.987	-0	1-240,C-157/O-20R,32	-3.1

■ WILLARD BROWN
Brown, Willard Jessie b: 6/26/15, Shreveport, La. d: 8/8/96, Houston, Tex. BR/TR, 5'11.5", 200 lbs. Deb: 7/19/47

YEAR	TM/L	G	AB	R	H	2B	3B	HR	RBI	BB	SO	AVG	OBP	SLG	OPS	OPS+	BR+	SB	CS	SBR	FA	FR	G/POS	TPR
1947	StL-A	21	67	4	12	3	0	1	6	0	7	.179	.179	.269	448	23	-7	2	2	-0	1.000	0	O-18(0-1-17)	-0.8

■ GATES BROWN
Brown, William James b: 5/2/39, Crestline, O. BL/TR, 5'11", 220 lbs. Deb: 6/19/63 C Career OF: (421-LF 0-CF 7-RF)

YEAR	TM/L	G	AB	R	H	2B	3B	HR	RBI	BB	SO	AVG	OBP	SLG	OPS	OPS+	BR+	SB	CS	SBR	FA	FR	G/POS	TPR
1963	Det-A	55	82	16	22	3	1	2	14	8	13	.268	.341	.402	743	104	1	2	1	0	1.000	4	O-16(16-0-0)	0.4
1964	Det-A	123	426	65	116	22	6	15	54	31	53	.272	.328	.458	785	114	7	11	4	1	.981	8	*O-106(106-0-0)	1.1
1965	Det-A	96	227	33	58	14	2	10	43	17	33	.256	.307	.467	774	115	4	6	0	1	.973	2	O-56(49-0-7)	0.5
1966	Det-A	88	169	27	45	5	1	7	27	18	19	.266	.344	.432	776	119	4	3	0	1	.980	-3	O-43(43-0-0)	0.0
1967	Det-A	51	91	17	17	1	1	2	9	13	15	.187	.288	.286	574	68	-3	0	0	0	1.000	-2	O-20(20-0-0)	-0.6
1968	*Det-A	67	92	15	34	7	2	6	15	12	4	.370	.442	.685	1127	231	14	0	0	0	1.000	-1	O-17(17-0-0)/1-1	1.4
1969	Det-A	60	93	13	19	1	2	1	6	5	17	.204	.253	.290	543	49	-6	0	0	0	.906	1	O-14(14-0-0)	-0.7
1970	Det-A	81	124	18	28	3	0	3	24	20	14	.226	.338	.323	661	82	-2	0	0	0	.950	-1	O-26(26-0-0)	-0.5
1971	Det-A	82	195	37	66	2	3	11	29	21	17	.338	.408	.549	957	163	16	4	2	0	.986	-6	O-56(56-0-0)	0.8
1972	*Det-A	103	252	33	58	5	0	10	31	26	28	.230	.307	.369	676	97	-1	3	0	1	.977	2	O-72(72-0-0)	-0.2
1973	Det-A	125	377	48	89	11	1	12	50	52	41	.236	.330	.366	696	90	-4	1	1	-0	1.000	-1	*D-119/O-2(2-0-0)	-0.8
1974	Det-A	73	99	7	24	2	0	4	17	10	15	.242	.312	.384	696	96	-1	0	0	0	.000	0	D-13	-0.1
1975	Det-A	47	35	1	6	2	0	1	3	9	6	.171	.356	.314	670	87	-0	0	0	0	.000	0	H	-0.1
Total	13	1051	2262	330	582	78	19	84	322	242	275	.257	.333	.420	753	109	28	30	8	4	.977	3	O-428L,D-132/1-1	1.2

■ BILL BROWN
Brown, William Verna "Verna" b: 7/8/1893, Coleman, Tex. d: 5/13/65, Lubbock, Tex. BL/TL, 5'8", 185 lbs. Deb: 8/15/12

YEAR	TM/L	G	AB	R	H	2B	3B	HR	RBI	BB	SO	AVG	OBP	SLG	OPS	OPS+	BR+	SB	CS	SBR	FA	FR	G/POS	TPR
1912	StL-A	9	20	0	4	0	0	0	1	0		.200	.200	.200	400	15	-2	0			.909	-2	/O-7(6-1-0)	-0.4

■ BYRON BROWNE
Browne, Byron Ellis b: 12/27/42, St.Joseph, Mo. BR/TR, 6'2", 200 lbs. Deb: 9/9/65

YEAR	TM/L	G	AB	R	H	2B	3B	HR	RBI	BB	SO	AVG	OBP	SLG	OPS	OPS+	BR+	SB	CS	SBR	FA	FR	G/POS	TPR
1965	Chi-N	4	6	0	0	0	0	0	0	0	2	.000	.000	.000	0	-98	-2	0	0	0	.667	-1	/O-4(4-0-0)	-0.3
1966	Chi-N	120	419	46	102	15	7	16	51	40	143	.243	.317	.427	744	103	2	3	3	-0	.967	-4	*O-114(67-42-10)	-0.9
1967	Chi-N	10	19	3	3	2	0	0	2	4	5	.158	.304	.263	568	61	-1	1	1	-0	1.000	-1	/O-8(0-2-6)	-0.2
1968	Hou-N	10	13	0	3	0	0	0	1	4	6	.231	.412	.231	643	99	0	0	0	0	1.000	2	/O-2(0-0-2)	0.2
1969	StL-N	22	53	9	12	0	1	1	7	11	14	.226	.359	.321	680	92	-0	0	0	0	1.000	3	O-16(5-5-8)	0.2
1970	Phi-N	104	270	29	67	17	2	10	36	33	72	.248	.330	.437	767	107	2	1	2	-0	.975	-2	O-88(6-23-61)	-0.4
1971	Phi-N	58	68	5	14	3	0	3	5	8	23	.206	.289	.382	672	89	-1	0	0	0	1.000	-8	O-30(17-4-10)	-1.1
1972	Phi-N	21	21	2	4	0	0	0	0	1	8	.190	.227	.190	418	19	-2	0	0	0	1.000	-3	/O-9(0-3-6)	-0.6
Total	8	349	869	94	205	37	10	30	102	101	273	.236	.319	.405	724	98	-2	5	6	-1	.973	-16	O-271(99-79-103)	-3.1

■ EARL BROWNE
Browne, Earl James "Snitz" b: 3/5/11, Louisville, Ky. d: 1/12/93, Whittier, Cal. BL/TL, 6', 175 lbs. Deb: 9/12/35

YEAR	TM/L	G	AB	R	H	2B	3B	HR	RBI	BB	SO	AVG	OBP	SLG	OPS	OPS+	BR+	SB	CS	SBR	FA	FR	G/POS	TPR
1935	Pit-N	9	32	6	8	2	0	0	6	2	8	.250	.294	.313	607	61	-2	0			1.000	0	/1-9	-0.2
1936	Pit-N	8	23	7	7	1	2	0	3	1	4	.304	.333	.522	855	124	1	0			1.000	0	/O-4(4-0-0),1-1	0.1
1937	Phi-N	105	332	42	97	19	3	6	52	21	41	.292	.342	.422	763	98	-1	4			.980	1	O-54(8-5-43),1-23	-0.5
1938	Phi-N	21	74	4	19	4	0	0	8	5	11	.257	.304	.311	615	71	-3	0			.978	-0	1-16/O-2(2-0-0)	-0.5
Total	4	143	461	59	131	26	5	6	69	29	64	.284	.332	.401	733	93	-5	4			.983	1	/O-60(14-5-43),1-49	-1.1

■ GEORGE BROWNE
Browne, George Edward b: 1/12/1876, Richmond, Va. d: 12/9/20, Hyde Park, N.Y. BL/TR, 5'10.5", 160 lbs. Deb: 9/27/01

YEAR	TM/L	G	AB	R	H	2B	3B	HR	RBI	BB	SO	AVG	OBP	SLG	OPS	OPS+	BR+	SB	CS	SBR	FA	FR	G/POS	TPR
1901	Phi-N	8	26	2	5	1	0	0	4	1		.192	.250	.231	481	39	-2	2			1.000	-1	/O-8(6-1-1)	-0.4
1902	Phi-N	70	281	41	73	7	1	0	26	16		.260	.304	.292	596	84	-5	11			.910	8	O-70(70-0-0)	-0.2
	NY-N	53	216	30	69	9	5	0	14	9		.319	.355	.407	763	136	8	13			.895	-0	O-53(51-0-2)	0.5
	Yr	123	497	71	142	16	6	0	40	25		.286	.326	.342	668	107	3	24			.904	7	*O-123(121-0-2)	0.3
1903	NY-N	141	591	105	185	20	3	3	45	43		.313	.364	.372	736	106	4	27			.918	-4	*O-141(1-0-140)	-0.6
1904	NY-N	150	596	**99**	169	16	5	4	39	39		.284	.332	.347	679	105	3	24			.925	-5	*O-149(0-0-149)	-0.9
1905	*NY-N	127	536	95	157	16	14	4	43	20		.293	.321	.397	718	111	5	26			.915	-9	*O-127(0-0-127)	-1.0
1906	NY-N	122	477	61	126	10	4	0	38	27		.264	.304	.302	605	87	-8	32			.934	-5	*O-121(0-0-121)	-2.0
1907	NY-N	127	458	54	119	11	10	5	37	31		.260	.308	.360	668	106	2	15			.941	-9	*O-121(0-0-121)	-1.5
1908	Bos-N	138	536	61	122	10	6	1	34	36		.228	.276	.274	550	77	-14	17			.950	4	*O-138(12-17-109)	-2.0
1909	Chi-N	12	39	7	8	0	1	0	1	5		.205	.295	.256	552	70	-1	3			.944	-2	O-12(0-11-1)	-0.4
	Was-A	103	393	40	107	15	5	1	16	17		.272	.308	.344	651	111	3	13			.935	-2	*O-101(63-4-34)	-0.5
1910	Was-A	7	22	1	4	0	0	0	0	1		.182	.217	.182	399	26	-2	0			.667	-2	/O-5(5-0-0)	-0.4
	Chi-A	30	112	17	27	4	1	0	4	12		.241	.315	.295	609	95	-0	5			.952	-4	O-29(0-20-9)	-0.6
	Yr	37	134	18	31	4	1	0	4	13		.231	.299	.276	575	84	-2	5			.917	-5	O-34(5-20-9)	-1.0
1911	Bro-N	8	12	1	4	0	0	0	2	1	1	.333	.385	.333	718	106	0	2			1.000	-0	/O-2(0-0-2)	0.0
1912	Phi-N	6	5	0	1	0	0	0	0	1	0	.200	.333	.200	533	45	-0	0			.000	0	H	0.0
Total	12	1102	4300	614	1176	119	55	18	303	259	1	.273	.318	.339	657	100	-7	190			.927	-31	*O-1077(208-53-816)	-10.0

■ JERRY BROWNE
Browne, Jerome Austin b: 2/13/66, Christiansted, V.I. BB/TR, 5'10", 170 lbs. Deb: 9/6/86 Career OF: (98-LF 67-CF 25-RF)

YEAR	TM/L	G	AB	R	H	2B	3B	HR	RBI	BB	SO	AVG	OBP	SLG	OPS	OPS+	BR+	SB	CS	SBR	FA	FR	G/POS	TPR
1986	Tex-A	12	24	6	10	2	0	0	3	1	4	.417	.440	.500	940	151	2	0	2	-1	.923	-1	/2-8	0.0
1987	Tex-A	132	454	63	123	16	6	1	38	61	50	.271	.360	.339	699	87	-7	27	17	-0	.980	-17	*2-130/D-1	-1.6
1988	Tex-A	73	214	26	49	9	2	1	17	25	32	.229	.310	.304	613	71	-8	7	5	-0	.958	-25	2-70/D-1	-3.2
1989	Cle-A	153	598	83	179	31	4	5	45	68	64	.299	.372	.390	761	113	12	14	6	1	.979	-48	*2-151/D-2	-3.2
1990	Cle-A	140	513	92	137	26	5	6	50	72	46	.267	.359	.372	732	105	6	12	7	0	.985	-21	*2-139	-1.1
1991	Cle-A	107	290	28	66	5	2	1	29	27	29	.228	.296	.269	565	57	-16	2	4	-1	.964	-10	2-47,O-17L,3-15,/D	-2.7
1992	*Oak-A	111	324	43	93	12	2	3	40	40	40	.287	.372	.364	736	113	7	3	3	-0	.965	-11	3-58,O-43C,2-19,/SD	-0.5

YEAR	TM/L	G	AB	R	H	2B	3B	HR	RBI	BB	SO	AVG	OBP	SLG	OPS	OPS+	BR+	SB	CS	SBR	FA	FR	G/POS	TPR
1993	Oak-A	76	260	27	65	13	0	2	19	22	17	.250	.309	.323	632	74	-9	4	0	1	.985	-4	O-56L,3-13/2-3,1-2	-1.3
1994	Fla-N	101	329	42	97	17	4	3	30	52	23	.295	.394	.398	792	104	4	3	0	1	.931	-7	3-62,O-30L,2-15	-0.2
1995	Fla-N	77	184	21	47	4	0	1	17	25	20	.255	.348	.293	641	71	-7	1	1	-0	.959	6	O-29L,2-27/3-7	-0.1
Total	10	982	3190	431	866	135	25	23	288	393	325	.271	.354	.351	705	94	-16	73	45	0	.977	-138	2-609,O-175L,3/D1S	-13.9

■ **PIDGE BROWNE** Browne, Prentice Almont b: 3/21/29, Peekskill, N.Y. d: 6/3/97, Houston, Tex. BL/TL, 6'1", 190 lbs. Deb: 4/13/62

YEAR	TM/L	G	AB	R	H	2B	3B	HR	RBI	BB	SO	AVG	OBP	SLG	OPS	OPS+	BR+	SB	CS	SBR	FA	FR	G/POS	TPR
1962	Hou-N	65	100	8	21	4	2	1	10	13	9	.210	.301	.320	621	72	-4	0	0	0	.983	1	1-26	-0.4

■ **PETE BROWNING** Browning, Louis Rogers "The Gladiator" b: 6/17/1861, Louisville, Ky. d: 9/10/05, Louisville, Ky. BR/TR, 6', 180 lbs. Deb: 5/2/1882 Career OF: (477-LF 490-CF 35-RF)

YEAR	TM/L	G	AB	R	H	2B	3B	HR	RBI	BB	SO	AVG	OBP	SLG	OPS	OPS+	BR+	SB	CS	SBR	FA	FR	G/POS	TPR
1882	Lou-a	69	288	67	109	17	3	5		26		**.378**	**.430**	**.510**	**940**	**229**	**40**				.890	12	2-42,S-18,3-13	**4.8**
1883	Lou-a	84	358	95	121	15	9	4		23		.338	.378	.464	842	183	34				.861	-8	O-48L,S-26,3-10,/21	2.3
1884	Lou-a	103	447	101	150	33	8	4	47	13		.336	.357	.472	829	176	36				.806	-9	3-52,O-24C,1-23,/2P	2.2
1885	Lou-a	112	481	98	**174**	34	10	9	73	25		**.362**	**.393**	.530	**923**	190	**47**				.900	5	*O-112(0-112-0)	**4.3**
1886	Lou-a	112	467	86	159	29	6	2	68	30		.340	.389	.441	830	151	26	26			.791	-10	*O-112(31-82-0)	1.0
1887	Lou-a	134	602	137	**275**	35	16	4	118	55		.457	.464	.547	1011	178	58	103			.868	-3	*O-134(0-134-0)	4.0
1888	Lou-a	99	383	58	120	22	8	3	72	37		.313	.380	.436	816	164	28	36			.888	-1	*O-99(20-79-0)	2.2
1889	Lou-a	83	324	39	83	19	5	2	32	34	30	.256	.327	.364	691	98	-1	21			.882	-3	O-83(83-0-0)	-0.5
1890	Cle-P	118	493	112	184	**40**	8	5	93	75	36	**.373**	.459	.517	976	**175**	**58**	35			.893	4	*O-118(118-0-0)	**4.6**
1891	Pit-N	50	203	35	59	14	1	4	28	27	31	.291	.377	.429	805	138	10	4			.904	5	O-50(48-0-2)	1.2
	Cin-N	55	216	29	74	10	3	0	33	24	23	.343	.413	.417	830	141	12	12			.924	-1	O-55(54-1-0)	0.9
	Yr	105	419	64	133	24	4	4	61	51	54	.317	.395	.422	818	139	22	16			.913	5	*O-105(102-1-2)	2.1
1892	Lou-N	21	77	10	19	4	0	0	4	12	7	.247	.348	.299	647	104	1	5			.911	-1	O-21(21-0-0)	-0.2
	Cin-N	83	307	47	93	12	5	3	52	40	26	.303	.383	.404	787	140	16	8			.917	-2	O-82(23-46-16)/1-2	0.7
	Yr	104	384	57	112	16	5	3	56	52	33	.292	.376	.383	759	133	17	13			.916	-3	*O-103(44-46-16)/1-2	0.5
1893	Lou-N	57	220	38	78	11	3	1	37	44	15	.355	.466	.445	912	155	22	8			.881	-3	O-57(44-0-13)	1.1
1894	StL-N	2	7	1	1	0	0	0	0	0	0	.143	.143	.143	286	-31	-1	0			1.000	-1	/O-2(0-2-0)	-0.2
	Bro-N	1	2	1	2	0	0	0	2	1	0	1.000	1.000	1.000	2000	412	1	0			1.000	-0	/O-1(0-0-1)	0.1
	Yr	3	9	2	3	0	0	0	2	1	0	.333	.400	.333	733	80	-0	0			1.000	-1	/O-3(0-2-1)	-0.1
Total	13	1183	4875	954	1701	295	85	46	659	466	168	.349	.403	.467	869	164	386	258			.883	-16	O-998C/3-75,2-49,S1P	28.5

■ **BILL BRUBAKER** Brubaker, Wilbur Lee b: 11/7/10, Cleveland, Ohio d: 4/2/78, Laguna Hills, Cal. BR/TR, 6'2", 185 lbs. Deb: 9/8/32 F Career OF: (1-LF 0-CF 0-RF)

YEAR	TM/L	G	AB	R	H	2B	3B	HR	RBI	BB	SO	AVG	OBP	SLG	OPS	OPS+	BR+	SB	CS	SBR	FA	FR	G/POS	TPR
1932	Pit-N	7	24	3	10	3	0	0	4	3	4	.417	.481	.542	1023	178	3	1			.909	-0	/3-7	0.3
1933	Pit-N	2	2	0	0	0	0	0	0	0	0	.000	.000	.000	0	-99	-1	0			1.000	0	/3-1	0.0
1934	Pit-N	3	6	0	2	1	0	0	1	1	0	.333	.429	.500	929	144	0	0			1.000	1	/3-3	0.1
1935	Pit-N	11	11	1	0	0	0	0	0	2	5	.000	.154	.000	154	-53	-2	0			.889	-0	/3-5	-0.3
1936	Pit-N	145	554	77	160	27	4	6	102	50	96	.289	.352	.384	736	96	-2	5			.940	-15	*3-145	-1.2
1937	Pit-N	120	413	57	105	20	4	6	48	47	51	.254	.335	.366	700	90	-5	2			.952	2	*3-115/S-3,1-1	0.1
1938	Pit-N	45	112	18	33	5	0	3	19	9	14	.295	.347	.420	767	109	1	2			.875	-1	3-18/1-9,S-3,O-1L	0.0
1939	Pit-N	100	345	41	80	23	1	7	43	29	51	.232	.297	.365	662	78	-11	3			.950	10	2-65,3-32/S-1	0.4
1940	Pit-N	38	78	8	15	3	1	0	7	8	16	.192	.267	.256	524	45	-6	0			.955	6	3-19/S-8,1-4	0.0
1943	Bos-N	13	19	3	8	3	0	0	1	2	2	.421	.476	.579	1055	207	3	0			.778	-1	/3-5,1-3	0.2
Total	10	479	1564	208	413	85	10	22	225	151	239	.264	.333	.373	706	90	-20	13			.938	2	3-350/2-65,1-17,SO	-0.4

■ **LOU BRUCE** Bruce, Louis R. b: 1/16/1877, St.Regis, N.Y. d: 2/9/68, Ilion, N.Y. BL/TR, 5'5", 145 lbs. Deb: 6/22/04

YEAR	TM/L	G	AB	R	H	2B	3B	HR	RBI	BB	SO	AVG	OBP	SLG	OPS	OPS+	BR+	SB	CS	SBR	FA	FR	G/POS	TPR
1904	Phi-A	30	101	9	27	3	0	0	8	5		.267	.302	.297	599	85	-2	2			.969	-2	O-25L/P-2,2-1,3-1	-0.6

■ **EARLE BRUCKER** Brucker, Earle Francis Jr. b: 8/29/25, Los Angeles, Cal. BL/TR, 6'2", 210 lbs. Deb: 10/2/48 F

YEAR	TM/L	G	AB	R	H	2B	3B	HR	RBI	BB	SO	AVG	OBP	SLG	OPS	OPS+	BR+	SB	CS	SBR	FA	FR	G/POS	TPR
1948	Phi-A	2	6	0	1	1	0	0	0	1	1	.167	.286	.333	619	64	-0	0	0	0	1.000	-0	/C-2	-0.1

■ **EARLE BRUCKER** Brucker, Earle Francis Sr. b: 5/6/01, Albany, N.Y. d: 5/8/81, San Diego, Cal. BR/TR, 5'11", 175 lbs. Deb: 4/19/37 FMC

YEAR	TM/L	G	AB	R	H	2B	3B	HR	RBI	BB	SO	AVG	OBP	SLG	OPS	OPS+	BR+	SB	CS	SBR	FA	FR	G/POS	TPR
1937	Phi-A	102	317	40	82	16	5	6	37	48	30	.259	.356	.397	754	91	-4	1	2	-0	.971	-6	C-92	-0.5
1938	Phi-A	53	171	26	64	21	1	3	35	19	16	.374	.437	.561	998	152	14	1	1	-0	.986	-2	C-44/1-1	1.3
1939	Phi-A	62	172	18	50	15	1	3	31	24	16	.291	.381	.442	823	112	3	0	1	-0	1.000	-5	C-47	0.1
1940	Phi-A	23	46	3	9	1	1	0	2	6	3	.196	.288	.261	549	44	-4	0	0	0	.966	2	C-13	-0.2
1943	Phi-A	1	1	0	0	0	0	0	0	0	0	.000	.000	.000	0	-99	-0	0	0	0	.000	0	H	0.0
Total	5	241	707	87	205	53	8	12	105	97	65	.290	.376	.438	815	108	9	2	4	-1	.980	-11	C-196/1-1	0.7

■ **J. T. BRUETT** Bruett, Joseph Timothy b: 10/8/67, Milwaukee, Wis. BL/TL, 5'11", 175 lbs. Deb: 6/3/92

YEAR	TM/L	G	AB	R	H	2B	3B	HR	RBI	BB	SO	AVG	OBP	SLG	OPS	OPS+	BR+	SB	CS	SBR	FA	FR	G/POS	TPR
1992	Min-A	56	76	7	19	4	0	0	2	6	12	.250	.313	.303	616	71	-3	6	3	0	.979	-12	O-45(5-20-22)/D-3	-1.5
1993	Min-A	17	20	2	5	2	0	0	1	1	4	.250	.318	.350	668	79	-1	0	0	0	.857	-4	O-13(2-4-8)	-0.5
Total	2	73	96	9	24	6	0	0	3	7	16	.250	.314	.313	627	73	-3	6	3	0	.952	-16	/O-58(7-24-30),D-3	-2.0

■ **FRANK BRUGGY** Bruggy, Frank Leo b: 5/4/1891, Elizabeth, N.J. d: 4/5/59, Elizabeth, N.J. BR/TR, 5'11", 195 lbs. Deb: 4/13/21

YEAR	TM/L	G	AB	R	H	2B	3B	HR	RBI	BB	SO	AVG	OBP	SLG	OPS	OPS+	BR+	SB	CS	SBR	FA	FR	G/POS	TPR
1921	Phi-N	96	277	28	86	11	2	5	28	23	37	.310	.370	.419	788	100	1	6	2	1	.953	-9	C-86/1-2	-0.2
1922	Phi-A	53	111	10	31	7	0	0	9	6	11	.279	.322	.342	664	71	-5	1	2	-0	.925	-2	C-31	-0.5
1923	Phi-A	54	105	4	22	3	0	1	6	4	9	.210	.245	.267	512	34	-10	1	1	-0	.950	0	C-34/1-5	-0.9
1924	Phi-A	50	113	9	30	6	0	0	8	8	15	.265	.314	.319	633	63	-6	4	0	1	.928	-8	C-44	-1.0
1925	Cin-N	6	14	2	3	0	0	0	1	2	0	.214	.313	.214	527	38	-1	0	0	0	.870	-0	/C-6	-0.1
Total	5	259	620	53	172	27	2	6	52	43	72	.277	.329	.356	686	76	-22	12	5	1	.941	-18	C-201/1-7	-2.7

■ **JACOB BRUMFIELD** Brumfield, Jacob Donnell b: 5/27/65, Bogalusa, La. BR/TR, 6', 185 lbs. Deb: 4/6/92 Career OF: (94-LF 329-CF 67-RF)

YEAR	TM/L	G	AB	R	H	2B	3B	HR	RBI	BB	SO	AVG	OBP	SLG	OPS	OPS+	BR+	SB	CS	SBR	FA	FR	G/POS	TPR
1992	Cin-N	24	30	6	4	0	0	0	2	2	4	.133	.212	.133	345	-0	-4	6	0	1	1.000	-2	O-16(7-8-1)	-0.5
1993	Cin-N	103	272	40	73	17	3	6	23	21	47	.268	.323	.419	742	97	-2	20	8	2	.978	-5	O-96(24-68-5)/2-4	-0.5
1994	Cin-N	68	122	36	38	10	2	4	11	15	18	.311	.387	.525	911	136	7	6	3	0	.987	-3	O-43(14-24-6)	0.3
1995	Pit-N	116	402	64	109	23	2	4	26	37	71	.271	.340	.368	708	85	-8	22	12	1	.969	7	*O-104(0-104-0)	0.1
1996	Pit-N	29	80	11	20	9	0	2	8	5	17	.250	.294	.438	732	87	-2	3	1	0	.946	-2	O-22(0-22-0)	-0.3
	Tor-A	90	308	52	79	19	2	12	52	24	58	.256	.318	.448	767	91	-5	12	3	2	.982	-3	O-83(18-39-37)/D-5	-0.8
1997	Tor-A	58	174	22	36	5	1	2	20	14	31	.207	.270	.282	551	44	-14	4	4	-1	1.000	2	O-47(14-24-10)/D-4	-1.3
1999	LA-N	18	17	4	5	0	1	0	1	0	5	.294	.294	.412	706	81	-1	0	0	0	1.000	-2	O-11(7-4-0)	-0.3
	Tor-A	62	170	25	40	8	3	2	19	19	39	.235	.312	.353	665	68	-8	1	2	-0	.978	4	O-53(10-36-8)/D-6	-0.5
Total	7	568	1575	260	404	91	14	32	162	137	290	.257	.321	.393	714	84	-37	74	33	5	.979	-6	O-475C/D-15,2-4	-3.8

■ **MIKE BRUMLEY** Brumley, Anthony Michael b: 4/9/63, Oklahoma City, Okla. BB/TR, 5'10", 165 lbs. Deb: 6/16/87 F

YEAR	TM/L	G	AB	R	H	2B	3B	HR	RBI	BB	SO	AVG	OBP	SLG	OPS	OPS+	BR+	SB	CS	SBR	FA	FR	G/POS	TPR
1987	Chi-N	39	104	8	21	2	2	1	9	10	30	.202	.278	.288	567	49	-8	7	1	1	.965	4	S-34/2-1	0.1
1989	Det-A	92	212	33	42	5	2	1	11	14	45	.198	.251	.255	506	44	-16	8	4	0	.980	-8	S-42,2-24,3-11,/OD	-2.1
1990	Sea-A	62	147	19	33	5	4	0	7	10	22	.224	.274	.313	587	63	-7	2	0	0	.983	-1	S-47/2-6,3-3,O-2L,D	-0.5
1991	Bos-A	63	118	16	25	5	0	0	5	10	22	.212	.273	.254	528	45	-9	2	0	0	.950	15	S-31,3-17/2-7,OD	0.8
1992	Bos-A	2	1	0	0	0	0	0	0	0	0	.000	.000	.000	0	-94	-0	0	0	0	.000	0	/H	0.0
1993	Hou-N	8	10	1	3	0	0	0	2	1	3	.300	.364	.300	664	83	-0	0	1	-0	.000	-1	/3-1,S-1,O-1(1-0-1)	-0.2
1994	Oak-A	11	25	0	6	0	0	0	2	1	8	.240	.269	.240	509	36	-2	0	0	0	.929	-3	/2-4,3-4,O-3L,S-1	-0.5
1995	Hou-N	18	18	1	1	0	0	1	2	0	6	.056	.056	.222	278	-33	-4	1	0	0	1.000	-1	/S-3,O-3L,1-1,3-1	-0.4
Total	8	295	635	78	131	17	8	3	38	46	136	.206	.262	.272	535	47	-46	20	6	2	.972	5	S-159/2-42,3-37,OD1	-2.8

■ **MIKE BRUMLEY** Brumley, Tony Mike b: 7/10/38, Granite, Okla. BL/TR, 5'10", 195 lbs. Deb: 4/18/64 F

YEAR	TM/L	G	AB	R	H	2B	3B	HR	RBI	BB	SO	AVG	OBP	SLG	OPS	OPS+	BR+	SB	CS	SBR	FA	FR	G/POS	TPR
1964	Was-A	136	426	36	104	19	2	2	35	40	54	.244	.310	.312	623	74	-14	1	1	-0	.991	-13	*C-132	-2.2
1965	Was-A	79	216	15	45	4	0	3	15	20	28	.208	.282	.269	550	58	-12	1	1	-0	.990	2	C-66	-0.8
1966	Was-A	9	18	1	2	1	0	0	0	0	2	.111	.111	.167	278	-22	-3	0	0	0	1.000	-1	/C-7	-0.4
Total	3	224	660	52	151	24	2	5	50	60	89	.229	.296	.294	590	67	-29	2	2	-0	.991	-12	C-205	-3.4

■ **GLENN BRUMMER** Brummer, Glenn Edward b: 11/23/54, Olney, Ill. BR/TR, 6', 200 lbs. Deb: 5/25/81

YEAR	TM/L	G	AB	R	H	2B	3B	HR	RBI	BB	SO	AVG	OBP	SLG	OPS	OPS+	BR+	SB	CS	SBR	FA	FR	G/POS	TPR
1981	StL-N	21	30	2	6	1	0	0	2	1	2	.200	.226	.233	459	30	-3	0	0	0	1.000	2	C-19	-0.1

YEAR	TM/L	G	AB	R	H	2B	3B	HR	RBI	BB	SO	AVG	OBP	SLG	OPS	OPS+	BR+	SB	CS	SBR	FA	FR	G/POS	TPR
1982	*StL-N	35	64	4	15	4	0	0	8	0	12	.234	.234	.297	531	47	-5	2	0	0	.970	3	C-32	-0.1
1983	StL-N	45	87	7	24	7	0	0	9	10	11	.276	.351	.356	707	96	-0	1	3	-1	.978	0	C-41	0.0
1984	StL-N	28	58	3	12	0	0	1	3	3	7	.207	.246	.259	505	43	-4	0	0	0	.973	4	C-26	0.0
1985	Tex-A	49	108	7	30	4	0	0	5	11	22	.278	.355	.315	670	84	-2	1	5	-2	.989	-4	C-47/O-1(0-0-1),D-1	-0.6
Total	5	178	347	23	87	16	0	1	27	25	54	.251	.305	.305	610	70	-14	4	8	-2	.981	5	C-165/D-1,O-1(0-0-1)	-0.8

■ TOM BRUNANSKY

Brunansky, Thomas Andrew b: 8/20/60, Covina, Cal. BR/TR, 6′4″, 211 lbs. Deb: 4/9/81 Career OF: (88-LF 81-CF 1569-RF)

YEAR	TM/L	G	AB	R	H	2B	3B	HR	RBI	BB	SO	AVG	OBP	SLG	OPS	OPS+	BR+	SB	CS	SBR	FA	FR	G/POS	TPR
1981	Cal-A	11	33	7	5	0	0	3	6	8	10	.152	.317	.424	741	112	1	1	0	0	.938	3	O-11(11-0-0)	0.3
1982	Min-A	127	463	77	126	30	1	20	46	71	101	.272	.378	.471	849	128	19	1	2	-0	.986	13	*O-127(3-38-97)	2.6
1983	Min-A	151	542	70	123	24	5	28	82	61	95	.227	.310	.445	754	101	-0	2	5	-1	.985	18	*O-146(0-38-119)/D-4	1.0
1984	Min-A	155	567	75	144	21	0	32	85	57	94	.254	.322	.460	782	109	6	4	5	-1	.984	5	*O-153(0-0-153)/D-1	0.1
1985	Min-A★	157	567	71	137	28	4	27	90	71	86	.242	.326	.448	774	103	2	5	3	0	.984	5	*O-155(0-1-155)	-0.1
1986	Min-A	157	593	69	152	28	1	23	75	53	98	.256	.318	.423	742	97	-3	12	4	1	.982	8	*O-152(0-1-152)/D-2	-0.3
1987	*Min-A	155	532	83	138	22	2	32	85	74	104	.259	.354	.489	843	116	13	11	11	-1	.990	-2	*O-138(58-0-107),D-17	0.1
1988	Min-A	14	49	5	9	1	0	1	6	7	11	.184	.286	.265	551	54	-3	1	2	-0	.864	-2	O-13(1-0-12)/D-1	-0.6
	StL-N	143	523	69	128	22	4	22	79	79	82	.245	.348	.428	776	121	15	16	6	1	**.996**	4	*O-143(1-0-143)	1.7
1989	StL-N	158	556	67	133	29	3	20	85	59	107	.239	.314	.410	724	102	1	5	9	-2	.977	4	*O-155(0-1-155)/1-1	-0.2
1990	StL-N	19	57	5	9	3	0	1	2	12	10	.158	.314	.263	577	60	-3	0	0	0	.950	1	O-17(0-0-17)	-0.3
	*Bos-A	129	461	61	123	24	5	15	71	54	105	.267	.347	.438	786	113	8	5	10	-2	.982	10	*O-121(0-1-121)/D-7	1.2
1991	Bos-A	142	459	54	105	24	1	16	70	49	72	.229	.307	.390	697	87	-8	1	2	-0	.989	3	*O-137(0-1-136)/D-1	-1.0
1992	Bos-A	138	458	47	122	31	3	15	74	66	96	.266	.359	.445	804	116	10	2	5	-1	.980	3	O-92R,1-28,D-17	0.7
1993	Mil-A	80	224	20	41	7	3	6	29	25	59	.183	.265	.321	586	58	-14	3	4	-1	.987	1	O-71(0-0-71)/D-6	-1.7
1994	Mil-A	16	28	2	6	2	0	0	0	1	9	.214	.241	.286	527	34	-3	0	0	0	1.000	-3	/O-6(0-0-6),1-2,D-2	-0.5
	Bos-A	48	177	22	42	10	1	10	34	23	48	.237	.325	.475	800	98	-1	0	2	-1	.989	-3	O-42(14-0-33)/1-5,D-3	-0.6
	Yr	64	205	24	48	12	1	10	34	24	57	.234	.314	.449	763	90	-4	0	2	-1	.989	-5	O-48(14-0-39)/1-7,D-5	-1.1
Total	14	1800	6289	804	1543	306	33	271	919	770	1187	.245	.331	.434	764	105	40	69	70	-9	.984	65	*O-1679R/D-61,1-36	2.4

■ ARLO BRUNSBERG

Brunsberg, Arlo Adolph b: 8/15/40, Fertile, Minn. BL/TR, 6′, 195 lbs. Deb: 9/23/66

YEAR	TM/L	G	AB	R	H	2B	3B	HR	RBI	BB	SO	AVG	OBP	SLG	OPS	OPS+	BR+	SB	CS	SBR	FA	FR	G/POS	TPR
1966	Det-A	2	3	1	1	1	0	0	0	0	0	.333	.500	.667	1167	227	1	0	0	0	1.000	-1	/C-2	0.0

■ BOB BRUSH

Brush, Robert b: 3/8/1875, Osage, Iowa d: 4/2/44, San Bernardino, Cal. Deb: 4/20/07

YEAR	TM/L	G	AB	R	H	2B	3B	HR	RBI	BB	SO	AVG	OBP	SLG	OPS	OPS+	BR+	SB	CS	SBR	FA	FR	G/POS	TPR
1907	Bos-N	2	2	0	0	0	0	0	0	0		.000	.000	.000	0	-99	-0	0			1.000	-0	/1-1	-0.1

■ BILL BRUTON

Bruton, William Haron b: 11/9/25, Panola, Ala. d: 12/5/95, Marshallton, Del. BL/TR, 6′0.5″, 169 lbs. Deb: 4/13/53

YEAR	TM/L	G	AB	R	H	2B	3B	HR	RBI	BB	SO	AVG	OBP	SLG	OPS	OPS+	BR+	SB	CS	SBR	FA	FR	G/POS	TPR
1953	Mil-N	151	613	82	153	18	14	1	41	44	100	.250	.306	.330	636	70	-27	**26**	11	2	.979	8	*O-150(0-150-0)	-2.4
1954	Mil-N	142	567	89	161	20	7	4	30	40	78	.284	.336	.365	701	88	-10	**34**	13	**3**	.981	1	*O-141(0-141-0)	-1.3
1955	Mil-N	149	636	106	175	30	12	9	47	43	72	.275	.325	.403	728	97	-4	**25**	11	2	.968	15	*O-149(0-149-0)	0.5
1956	Mil-N	147	525	73	143	23	**15**	8	56	26	63	.272	.308	.419	727	99	-3	8	6	-0	.969	3	*O-145(0-145-0)	-0.7
1957	Mil-N	79	306	41	85	16	9	5	30	19	35	.278	.322	.438	760	110	3	11	4	1	.981	1	O-79(0-79-0)	0.1
1958	*Mil-N	100	325	47	91	11	3	3	28	27	37	.280	.339	.360	699	93	-3	4	1	1	.977	-7	O-96(0-96-0)	-1.3
1959	Mil-N	133	478	72	138	22	6	6	41	35	54	.289	.339	.397	736	104	2	13	5	1	.991	4	*O-133(0-133-0)	0.1
1960	Mil-N	151	629	**112**	180	27	**13**	12	54	41	97	.286	.332	.428	760	115	11	22	13	0	.986	4	*O-149(0-149-0)	0.8
1961	Det-A	160	596	99	153	15	5	17	63	61	66	.257	.329	.384	713	87	-11	22	6	3	.988	12	*O-155(0-155-0)	-0.1
1962	Det-A	147	561	90	156	27	5	16	74	55	67	.278	.348	.430	777	104	3	14	7	1	.983	19	*O-145(0-145-0)	1.9
1963	Det-A	145	524	84	134	21	8	8	48	59	70	.256	.331	.372	703	93	-4	14	7	1	.991	10	*O-138(0-138-0)	0.3
1964	Det-A	106	296	42	82	11	5	5	33	32	54	.277	.348	.399	746	105	3	14	5	1	.987	-1	O-81(10-70-1)	0.1
Total	12	1610	6056	937	1651	241	102	94	545	482	793	.273	.329	.393	722	96	-40	207	89	14	.981	68	*O-1561(10-1550-1)	-2.0

■ ED BRUYETTE

Bruyette, Edward T. b: 8/31/1874, Manawa, Wis. d: 8/5/40, Peshastin, Wash. BL/TR, 5′10″, 170 lbs. Deb: 8/6/01

YEAR	TM/L	G	AB	R	H	2B	3B	HR	RBI	BB	SO	AVG	OBP	SLG	OPS	OPS+	BR+	SB	CS	SBR	FA	FR	G/POS	TPR
1901	Mil-A	26	82	7	15	3	0	0	4	12		.183	.295	.220	514	46	-5	1			.778	-6	O-21C/2-3,S-1,3-1	-1.1

■ BILLY BRYAN

Bryan, William Ronald b: 12/4/38, Morgan, Ga. BL/TR, 6′4″, 200 lbs. Deb: 9/12/61

YEAR	TM/L	G	AB	R	H	2B	3B	HR	RBI	BB	SO	AVG	OBP	SLG	OPS	OPS+	BR+	SB	CS	SBR	FA	FR	G/POS	TPR
1961	KC-A	9	19	2	3	0	0	1	2	2	7	.158	.238	.316	554	46	-2	0	0	0	1.000	-2	/C-4	-0.3
1962	KC-A	25	74	5	11	2	1	2	7	5	32	.149	.203	.284	486	28	-8	0	0	0	.976	-3	C-22	-0.9
1963	KC-A	24	65	11	11	1	1	3	7	9	22	.169	.270	.354	624	69	-3	0	0	0	.981	5	C-24	0.3
1964	KC-A	93	220	19	53	9	2	13	36	16	69	.241	.292	.477	770	107	1	0	0	0	.991	-9	C-65	-0.6
1965	KC-A	108	325	36	82	11	5	14	51	29	87	.252	.317	.446	764	116	6	0	0	0	.984	-6	C-95	0.5
1966	KC-A	32	76	0	10	4	0	0	7	6	17	.132	.195	.184	379	10	-9	0	0	0	.965	-1	C-21/1-3	-1.0
	NY-A	27	69	5	15	2	0	4	5	5	19	.217	.270	.420	691	99	-0	0	0	0	.988	-0	C-14/1-3	0.0
	Yr	59	145	5	25	6	0	4	12	11	36	.172	.231	.297	527	52	-9	0	0	0	.975	-2	C-35/1-6	-1.0
1967	NY-A	16	12	1	2	0	0	1	2	5	3	.167	.412	.417	828	151	1	0	0	0	1.000	1	/C-1	0.2
1968	Was-A	40	108	7	22	3	0	3	8	14	27	.204	.301	.315	616	90	-1	0	1	-0	.983	-4	C-28	-0.4
Total	8	374	968	86	209	32	9	41	125	91	283	.216	.285	.395	680	91	-14	0	1	-0	.984	-18	C-274/1-6	-2.2

■ DEREK BRYANT

Bryant, Derek Roszell b: 10/9/51, Lexington, Ky. BR/TR, 5′11″, 185 lbs. Deb: 4/24/79

YEAR	TM/L	G	AB	R	H	2B	3B	HR	RBI	BB	SO	AVG	OBP	SLG	OPS	OPS+	BR+	SB	CS	SBR	FA	FR	G/POS	TPR
1979	Oak-A	39	106	8	19	2	1	0	13	10	10	.179	.250	.217	467	29	-11	0	0	0	1.000	-2	O-33(25-0-10)/D-2	-1.4

■ DON BRYANT

Bryant, Donald Ray b: 7/13/41, Jasper, Fla. BR/TR, 6′5″, 200 lbs. Deb: 7/17/66 C

YEAR	TM/L	G	AB	R	H	2B	3B	HR	RBI	BB	SO	AVG	OBP	SLG	OPS	OPS+	BR+	SB	CS	SBR	FA	FR	G/POS	TPR
1966	Chi-N	13	26	2	8	2	0	0	4	1	4	.308	.357	.385	742	105	0	1	0	0	.978	0	C-10	0.1
1969	Hou-N	31	59	2	11	1	0	1	6	4	13	.186	.250	.254	504	42	-5	0	0	0	.993	3	C-28	-0.1
1970	Hou-N	15	24	2	5	0	0	0	3	1	8	.208	.240	.208	448	22	-3	0	0	0	.957	-0	C-13	-0.3
Total	3	59	109	6	24	3	0	1	13	6	25	.220	.274	.275	549	53	-7	1	0	0	.983	3	/C-51	-0.3

■ GEORGE BRYANT

Bryant, George F. b: 2/10/1857, Bridgeport, Conn. d: 6/12/07, Boston, Mass. Deb: 8/6/1885

YEAR	TM/L	G	AB	R	H	2B	3B	HR	RBI	BB	SO	AVG	OBP	SLG	OPS	OPS+	BR+	SB	CS	SBR	FA	FR	G/POS	TPR
1885	Det-N	1	4	0	0	0	0	0	1	0	2	.000	.000	.000	0	-99	-1				1.000	-1	/2-1	-0.2

■ RALPH BRYANT

Bryant, Ralph Wendell b: 5/20/61, Fort Gaines, Ga. BL/TR, 6′2″, 200 lbs. Deb: 9/8/85

YEAR	TM/L	G	AB	R	H	2B	3B	HR	RBI	BB	SO	AVG	OBP	SLG	OPS	OPS+	BR+	SB	CS	SBR	FA	FR	G/POS	TPR
1985	LA-N	6	6	0	2	0	0	0	1	0	2	.333	.333	.333	667	90	-0	0	0	0	.000	-1	/O-3(2-0-1)	-0.1
1986	LA-N	27	75	15	19	4	2	6	13	5	25	.253	.309	.600	909	156	5	0	1	-0	.953	-1	O-26(0-0-26)	0.3
1987	LA-N	46	69	7	17	2	1	2	10	10	24	.246	.350	.391	741	99	0	2	1	0	.917	-3	O-19(8-0-12)	-0.4
Total	3	79	150	22	38	6	3	8	24	15	51	.253	.329	.493	823	125	5	2	2	-0	.940	-5	/O-48(10-0-39)	-0.2

■ STEVE BRYE

Brye, Stephen Robert b: 2/4/49, Alameda, Cal. BR/TR, 6′, 190 lbs. Deb: 9/3/70 Career OF: (204-LF 339-CF 102-RF)

YEAR	TM/L	G	AB	R	H	2B	3B	HR	RBI	BB	SO	AVG	OBP	SLG	OPS	OPS+	BR+	SB	CS	SBR	FA	FR	G/POS	TPR
1970	Min-A	9	11	1	2	1	0	0	2	2	4	.182	.308	.273	580	60	-1	0	0	0	1.000	-2	/O-6(6-0-1)	-0.2
1971	Min-A	28	107	10	24	1	0	3	11	7	15	.224	.272	.318	590	65	-5	3	1	0	.966	1	O-28(25-7-0)	-0.6
1972	Min-A	100	253	18	61	9	3	0	12	17	38	.241	.292	.300	592	73	-8	3	1	0	.994	2	O-93(74-20-2)	-1.0
1973	Min-A	92	278	39	73	9	5	6	33	35	43	.263	.345	.396	741	104	2	3	5	-1	.986	1	O-87(12-72-4)/D-1	0.0
1974	Min-A	135	488	52	138	32	1	2	41	22	59	.283	.320	.365	685	94	-4	1	3	-1	**.997**	1	*O-129(0-128-1)	-0.8
1975	Min-A	86	246	41	62	13	1	9	34	21	37	.252	.316	.423	739	106	1	2	1	0	.983	-3	O-72(19-5-48)/D-6	-0.5
1976	Min-A	87	258	33	68	11	0	2	23	13	31	.264	.299	.329	628	82	-6	1	2	-0	.987	-13	O-78(11-57-17)/D-3	-2.3
1977	Mil-A	94	241	27	60	14	3	7	28	16	39	.249	.298	.419	718	93	-3	1	0	0	1.000	-1	O-83(29-43-17)/D-6	-0.5
1978	Pit-N	66	115	16	27	7	0	1	9	11	10	.235	.307	.322	629	73	-4	2	1	0	.983	-6	O-47(28-7-12)	-1.2
Total	9	697	1997	237	515	97	13	30	193	144	276	.258	.311	.365	676	90	-28	16	14	-1	.991	-19	O-623C/D-16	-7.1

■ HAL BUBSER

Bubser, Harold Fred b: 9/28/1895, Chicago, Ill. d: 6/22/59, Melrose Park, Ill BR/TR, 5′11″, 170 lbs. Deb: 4/15/22

YEAR	TM/L	G	AB	R	H	2B	3B	HR	RBI	BB	SO	AVG	OBP	SLG	OPS	OPS+	BR+	SB	CS	SBR	FA	FR	G/POS	TPR
1922	Chi-A	3	3	0	0	0	0	0	0	0	2	.000	.000	.000	0	-99	-1	0	0	0	.000	0	H	-0.1

■ JOHNNY BUCHA

Bucha, John George b: 1/22/25, Allentown, Pa. d: 4/28/96, Bethlehem, Pa. BR/TR, 5′11″,190 lbs. Deb: 5/2/48

YEAR	TM/L	G	AB	R	H	2B	3B	HR	RBI	BB	SO	AVG	OBP	SLG	OPS	OPS+	BR+	SB	CS	SBR	FA	FR	G/POS	TPR
1948	StL-N	2	1	0	0	0	0	0	0	1	0	.000	.500	.000	500	43	0	0			1.000	-0	/C-1	0.0
1950	StL-N	22	36	1	5	1	0	0	1	4	7	.139	.225	.167	392	5	-5	0			.959	0	C-17	-0.4
1953	Det-A	60	158	17	35	9	0	1	14	20	14	.222	.309	.297	606	65	-8	1	1	-0	.984	-4	C-56	-0.9
Total	3	84	195	18	40	10	0	1	15	25	21	.205	.295	.272	567	53	-12	1	1		.980	-4	/C-74	-1.3

YEAR	TM/L	G	AB	R	H	2B	3B	HR	RBI	BB	SO	AVG	OBP	SLG	OPS	OPS+	BR+	SB	CS	SBR	FA	FR	G/POS	TPR
■ **BRIAN BUCHANAN** Buchanan, Brian James b: 7/21/73, Miami, Fla. BR/TR, 6′4″, 230 lbs. Deb: 5/19/2000																								
2000	Min-A	30	82	10	19	3	0	1	8	8	22	.232	.308	.305	613	53	-6	0	2	-1	1.000	-3	O-25(2-0-24)D-2	-1.0
■ **JERRY BUCHEK** Buchek, Gerald Peter b: 5/9/42, St.Louis, Mo. BR/TR, 5′11″, 185 lbs. Deb: 6/30/61																								
1961	StL-N	31	90	6	12	2	0	0	9	0	28	.133	.152	.156	308	-16	-15	0	0	0	.912	-6	S-31	-1.9
1963	StL-N	3	4	0	1	0	0	0	0	0	2	.250	.250	.250	500	41	-0	0	0	0	1.000	0	/S-1	0.0
1964	*StL-N	35	30	7	6	0	2	0	1	3	11	.200	.273	.333	606	64	-1	0	0	0	.929	7	S-20/2-9,3-1	0.6
1965	StL-N	55	166	17	41	8	3	3	21	13	46	.247	.302	.386	687	84	-3	1	0	0	.994	10	2-33,S-18/3-1	1.1
1966	StL-N	100	284	23	67	10	4	4	25	23	71	.236	.293	.342	635	75	-9	0	5	-2	.974	-13	2-49,S-48/3-4	-1.8
1967	NY-N	124	411	35	97	11	2	14	41	26	101	.236	.285	.375	659	89	-7	3	5	-1	.977	4	2-95,3-17/S-9	0.4
1968	NY-N	73	192	8	35	4	0	1	11	10	53	.182	.234	.219	453	36	-15	1	1	-0	.935	-1	3-37,2-12/O-9(9-0-0)	-1.8
Total	7	421	1177	96	259	35	11	22	108	75	312	.220	.271	.325	595	67	-51	5	11	-3	.978	2	2-198,S-127/3-60,O	-3.4
■ **JIM BUCHER** Bucher, James Quinter b: 3/11/11, Manassas, Va. BL/TR, 5′11″, 170 lbs. Deb: 4/18/34 Career OF: (32-LF 1-CF 40-RF)																								
1934	Bro-N	47	84	12	19	5	2	0	8	4	7	.226	.261	.333	595	61	-5	1			.920	-1	2-20/3-6	-0.5
1935	Bro-N	123	473	72	143	22	1	7	58	10	33	.302	.317	.397	714	93	-6	4			.950	-11	2-41,3-39,O-37L	-1.5
1936	Bro-N	110	370	49	93	12	8	2	41	29	27	.251	.306	.343	649	74	-14	5			.910	-8	3-39,2-32,O-30R	-2.0
1937	Bro-N	125	380	44	96	11	2	4	37	20	18	.253	.295	.324	619	67	-18	5			.951	-14	2-49,3-43/O-6(4-1-1)	-2.7
1938	StL-N	17	57	7	13	3	1	0	7	2	2	.228	.254	.316	570	53	-4	0			.955	-4	2-14/3-1	-0.7
1944	Bos-A	80	277	39	76	9	2	4	31	19	13	.274	.326	.365	690	98	-1	3	3	-0	.958	-9	3-44,2-21	-0.9
1945	Bos-A	52	151	19	34	4	3	0	11	7	13	.225	.264	.291	556	60	-8	1	3	-1	.940	-2	3-32/2-2	-1.1
Total	7	554	1792	242	474	66	19	17	193	91	113	.265	.302	.351	653	78	-55	19	6		.939	-48	3-204,2-179/O-73R	-9.4
■ **KEVIN BUCKLEY** Buckley, Kevin John b: 1/16/59, Quincy, Mass. BR/TR, 6′1″, 200 lbs. Deb: 9/4/84																								
1984	Tex-A	5	7	1	2	1	0	0	0	2	4	.286	.444	.429	873	138	0	0	0	0	.000	0	/D-3	0.0
■ **DICK BUCKLEY** Buckley, Richard D. b: 9/21/1858, Troy, N.Y. d: 12/12/29, Pittsburgh, Pa. BR/TR, 5′10″, 195 lbs. Deb: 4/20/1888 Career OF: (1-LF 0-CF 1-RF)																								
1888	Ind-N	71	260	28	71	9	3	5	22	6	24	.273	.289	.388	678	112	3	4			.898	-21	C-51,3-22/O-1R,1-1	-1.3
1889	Ind-N	68	260	35	67	11	0	8	41	15	32	.258	.301	.392	693	91	-4	5			.877	-21	C-55,3-12/O-1L,1-1	-1.8
1890	NY-N	70	266	39	68	11	0	2	26	23	35	.256	.324	.320	644	88	-4	3			.931	9	C-62/3-8	0.9
1891	NY-N	75	253	23	55	9	1	4	31	11	30	.217	.258	.308	567	67	-11	3			.958	19	C-74/3-1	1.2
1892	StL-N	121	410	43	93	17	4	5	52	22	34	.227	.275	.324	599	85	-9	7			.937	-5	*C-119/1-2	-0.3
1893	StL-N	9	23	2	4	1	0	0	1	0	0	.174	.174	.217	391	4	-3	0			.914	1	/C-9	-0.1
1894	StL-N	29	89	5	16	1	2	1	3	6	3	.180	.240	.270	509	23	-12	1			.936	2	C-27/1-1	-0.6
	Phi-N	43	160	18	47	7	3	1	26	6	13	.294	.327	.394	721	75	-7	0			.966	3	C-42/1-1	-0.1
	Yr	72	249	23	63	8	5	2	29	12	16	.253	.295	.349	645	56	-19	1			.954	4	C-69/1-2	-0.7
1895	Phi-N	38	112	20	28	6	1	0	14	9	17	.250	.333	.321	655	69	-5	2			.919	6	C-38	0.3
Total	8	524	1833	213	449	72	14	26	216	98	188	.245	.291	.342	633	81	-53	25			.931	-7	C-477/3-43,1-6,O-2L	-1.8
■ **BILL BUCKNER** Buckner, William Joseph b: 12/14/49, Vallejo, Cal. BL/TL, 6′, 185 lbs. Deb: 9/21/69 C Career OF: (493-LF 0-CF 168-RF)																								
1969	LA-N	1	1	0	0	0	0	0	0	0	0	.000	.000	.000	0	-99	-0	0	0	0	.000	0	H	0.0
1970	LA-N	28	68	6	13	3	1	0	4	3	7	.191	.225	.265	490	32	-7	0	1	-0	1.000	1	O-20(19-0-1)/1-1	-0.7
1971	LA-N	108	358	37	99	15	1	5	41	11	18	.277	.307	.366	673	96	-3	4	1	1	.994	2	O-86(6-0-81),1-11	-0.6
1972	LA-N	105	383	47	122	14	3	5	37	17	13	.319	.349	.410	759	118	8	10	3	1	.992	-3	O-61(19-0-52),1-35	0.0
1973	LA-N	140	575	68	158	20	0	8	46	17	34	.275	.299	.351	650	83	-15	12	2	2	.998	-3	1-93,O-48(35-0-13)	-2.8
1974	*LA-N	145	580	83	182	30	3	7	58	30	24	.314	.352	.412	764	118	12	31	13	2	.976	-3	*O-137(134-0-4)/1-6	0.3
1975	LA-N	92	288	30	70	11	2	6	31	17	15	.243	.290	.358	648	82	-8	8	3	1	.986	2	O-72(72-0-0)	-1.0
1976	LA-N	154	642	76	193	28	4	7	60	26	26	.301	.329	.389	718	105	2	28	9	3	.985	7	*O-153(149-0-5)/1-1	0.3
1977	Chi-N	122	426	40	121	27	0	11	60	21	23	.284	.319	.425	744	88	-7	7	5	-0	.990	-0	1-99	-1.4
1978	Chi-N	117	446	47	144	26	1	5	74	18	17	.323	.349	.419	768	102	1	7	5	-0	.995	8	*1-105	0.2
1979	Chi-N	149	591	72	168	34	7	14	66	30	28	.284	.321	.437	758	96	-4	9	4	1	.995	18	*1-140	0.5
1980	Chi-N	145	578	69	187	41	3	10	68	30	18	**.324**	.357	.457	814	117	12	1	2	-0	.993	8	1-94,O-50(42-0-12)	1.3
1981	Chi-N★	106	421	45	131	**35**	3	10	75	26	16	.311	.353	.480	832	129	15	5	2	0	.984	1	*1-105	1.0
1982	Chi-N	161	657	93	201	34	5	15	105	36	26	.306	.347	.441	788	116	13	15	5	2	.993	16	*1-161	2.0
1983	Chi-N	153	626	79	175	**38**	6	16	66	25	30	.280	.313	.436	749	101	-1	12	4	1	.992	21	*1-144,O-15(15-0-0)	1.2
1984	Chi-N	21	43	3	9	0	0	0	2	1	1	.209	.244	.209	454	26	-4	0	0	0	1.000	2	/1-7,O-2(2-0-0)	-0.3
	Bos-A	114	439	51	122	21	2	11	67	24	38	.278	.323	.410	733	97	-2	2	2	-0	.986	5	*1-113	-0.5
1985	Bos-A	162	673	89	201	46	3	16	110	30	36	.299	.330	.447	778	106	4	18	4	3	.992	25	*1-162	2.2
1986	*Bos-A	153	629	73	168	39	2	18	102	40	25	.267	.315	.421	736	98	-3	6	4	-0	.989	20	*1-138,D-15	0.7
1987	Bos-A	75	286	23	78	6	1	2	42	13	19	.273	.304	.322	626	65	-14	1	3	-1	.991	3	1-74	-1.6
	Cal-A	57	183	16	56	12	1	3	32	9	7	.306	.339	.432	770	106	1	1	0	0	1.000	-0	D-39/1-5	0.0
	Yr	132	469	39	134	18	2	5	74	22	26	.286	.318	.365	682	80	-13	2	3	-1	.992	3	1-79,D-39	-1.6
1988	Cal-A	19	43	1	9	0	0	0	9	4	0	.209	.277	.209	486	39	-3	2	0	0	1.000	0	D-11/1-1	-0.3
	KC-A	89	242	18	62	14	0	3	34	13	19	.256	.294	.351	645	79	-7	3	1	0	.994	-0	D-42,1-21	-1.0
	Yr	108	285	19	71	14	0	3	43	17	19	.249	.291	.330	621	73	-10	5	1	1	.964	0	D-53,1-22	-1.3
1989	KC-A	79	176	7	38	4	1	1	16	6	11	.216	.242	.267	509	43	-13	1	0	0	.985	-0	1-24,D-19	-1.6
1990	Bos-A	22	43	4	8	0	0	1	3	3	2	.186	.239	.256	495	37	-4	0	0	0	1.000	-0	1-15	-0.5
Total	22	2517	9397	1077	2715	498	49	174	1208	450	453	.289	.324	.408	732	99	-28	183	73	15	.992	127	*1-1555,O-644L,D-126	-2.6
■ **MARK BUDASKA** Budaska, Mark David b: 12/27/52, Sharon, Pa. BB/TL, 6′, 180 lbs. Deb: 6/6/78																								
1978	Oak-A	4	4	0	1	1	0	0	0	1	2	.250	.400	.500	900	160	0	0	0	0	.500	-1	/O-2(1-0-1)	-0.1
1981	Oak-A	9	32	3	5	1	0	0	2	4	10	.156	.250	.188	438	29	-3	0	1	-0	.000	0	/D-9	-0.4
Total	2	13	36	3	6	2	0	0	2	5	12	.167	.268	.222	491	44	-2	0	1	-0	.500	-1	/D-9,O-2(1-0-1)	-0.5
■ **BUDD** Budd b: Cleveland, Ohio Deb: 9/10/1890																								
1890	Cle-P	1	4	0	0	0	0	0	0	0	3	.000	.000	.000	0	-99	-1	0			1.000	-0	/O-1(1-0-0)	-0.1
■ **DON BUDDIN** Buddin, Donald Thomas b: 5/5/34, Turbeville, S.C. BR/TR, 5′11″, 178 lbs. Deb: 4/17/56																								
1956	Bos-A	114	377	49	90	24	0	5	37	65	62	.239	.357	.342	699	76	-12	2	0	0	.953	14	*S-113	1.2
1958	Bos-A	136	497	74	118	25	2	12	43	82	106	.237	.350	.368	718	92	-4	0	4	-1	.958	15	*S-136	2.2
1959	Bos-A	151	485	75	117	24	1	10	53	92	99	.241	.368	.357	724	95	0	6	1	1	.949	-17	*S-150	-0.3
1960	Bos-A	124	428	62	105	21	5	6	36	62	59	.245	.342	.360	702	87	-7	4	2	0	.951	-5	*S-124	-0.1
1961	Bos-A	115	339	58	89	22	3	6	42	72	45	.263	.395	.398	793	110	8	2	1	0	.956	-1	*S-109	1.6
1962	Hou-N	40	80	10	13	4	1	2	10	17	17	.162	.316	.313	629	75	-3	0	0	0	.952	3	S-27/3-9	0.2
	Det-A	31	83	14	19	3	0	0	4	20	16	.229	.385	.265	650	76	-2	1	0	0	.978	-2	S-19/2-5,3-2	-0.2
Total	6	711	2289	342	551	123	12	41	225	410	404	.241	.360	.359	719	90	-18	15	8	1	.954	7	S-678/3-11,2-5	4.6
■ **STEVE BUECHELE** Buechele, Steven Bernard b: 9/26/61, Lancaster, Cal. BR/TR, 6′2″, 190 lbs. Deb: 7/19/85 Career OF: (3-LF 0-CF 0-RF)																								
1985	Tex-A	69	219	22	48	6	3	6	21	14	38	.219	.272	.356	629	70	-10	3	2	-0	.969	6	3-69/2-1	-0.4
1986	Tex-A	153	461	54	112	19	2	18	54	35	98	.243	.303	.410	713	90	-7	5	8	-2	.968	19	*3-137,2-33/O-2L	0.9
1987	Tex-A	136	363	45	86	20	0	13	50	28	66	.237	.293	.399	693	81	-11	2	2	-0	.964	3	*3-123,2-18/O-2L	-0.9
1988	Tex-A	155	503	68	126	21	4	16	58	65	79	.250	.342	.404	746	105	4	2	4	-1	.962	8	*3-153/2-2	1.2
1989	Tex-A	155	486	60	114	22	2	16	59	36	107	.235	.294	.387	681	89	-8	1	3	-1	.969	15	*3-145,2-18/S-1,D-1	0.7
1990	Tex-A	91	251	30	54	10	0	7	30	27	63	.215	.296	.339	635	77	-8	1	0	0	.966	6	3-88/2-4	-0.1
1991	Tex-A	121	416	58	111	17	2	18	66	39	69	.267	.337	.447	784	117	9	0	4	-1	**.991**	20	*3-111,2-13/S-4	2.8
	*Pit-N	31	114	16	28	5	1	4	19	10	28	.246	.317	.412	730	105	1	0	1	-0	.956	3	3-31	0.3
1992	Pit-N	80	285	27	71	14	1	8	43	34	61	.249	.333	.389	723	105	2	0	2	-1	.957	6	3-80	0.8
	Chi-N	65	239	25	66	9	3	1	21	18	44	.276	.340	.351	691	94	-2	1	1	-0	.960	-2	3-63/2-2	-0.4
	Yr	145	524	52	137	23	4	9	64	52	105	.261	.336	.372	708	100	1	1	3	-1	.958	4	*3-143/2-2	0.4
1993	Chi-N	133	460	53	125	27	2	15	65	48	87	.272	.347	.437	784	110	6	1	1	-0	**.975**	1	*3-129/1-6	0.8
1994	Chi-N	104	339	33	82	11	1	14	52	39	80	.242	.327	.404	731	91	-5	1	0	0	.974	-10	3-99/1-6,2-1	-1.4

YEAR	TM/L	G	AB	R	H	2B	3B	HR	RBI	BB	SO	AVG	OBP	SLG	OPS	OPS+	BR+	SB	CS	SBR	FA	FR	G/POS	TPR
1995	Chi-N	32	106	10	20	2	0	1	9	11	19	.189	.265	.236	501	34	-10	0	0	0	.942	0	3-32	-0.9
	Tex-A	9	24	0	3	0	0	0	0	4	3	.125	.250	.125	375	1	-3	0	0	0	1.000	-0	/3-9	-0.3
Total	11	1334	4266	501	1046	183	21	137	547	408	842	.245	.317	.394	712	94	-41	17	28	-6	.968	75	*3-1269/2-92,1SOD	3.1

■ **CHARLIE BUELOW** Buelow, Charles John b: 1/12/1877, Dubuque, Iowa d: 5/4/51, Dubuque, Iowa BR/TR, Deb: 6/1/01

YEAR	TM/L	G	AB	R	H	2B	3B	HR	RBI	BB	SO	AVG	OBP	SLG	OPS	OPS+	BR+	SB	CS	SBR	FA	FR	G/POS	TPR
1901	NY-N	22	72	3	8	4	0	0	4	2		.111	.147	.167	313	-10	-10	0			.853	3	3-17/2-2	-0.7

■ **FRITZ BUELOW** Buelow, Frederick William Alexander b: 2/13/1876, Berlin, Germany d: 12/27/33, Detroit, Mich. BR/TR, 5′10.5″, 170 lbs. Deb: 9/28/1899 Career OF: (3-LF 0-CF 8-RF)

YEAR	TM/L	G	AB	R	H	2B	3B	HR	RBI	BB	SO	AVG	OBP	SLG	OPS	OPS+	BR+	SB	CS	SBR	FA	FR	G/POS	TPR
1899	StL-N	7	15	4	7	0	2	0	2	2		.467	.556	.733	1289	246	3	0			1.000	-2	/C-4,O-2(2-0-0)	0.1
1900	StL-N	6	17	2	4	0	0	0	3	0		.235	.235	.235	471	30	-2	0			.864	-1	/C-4,O-1(1-0-0)	-0.2
1901	Det-A	70	231	28	52	5	5	2	29	11		.225	.269	.316	585	59	-13	2			.967	5	C-69	-0.2
1902	Det-A	66	224	23	50	5	2	2	29	9		.223	.256	.290	547	50	-15	3			.927	0	C-63/1-2	-0.9
1903	Det-A	63	192	24	41	3	6	1	13	6		.214	.249	.307	556	68	-8	4			.961	1	C-60/1-2	-0.1
1904	Det-A	42	136	6	15	1	1	0	5	8		.110	.160	.132	292	-7	-16	2			.975	1	C-42	-1.3
	Cle-A	42	119	11	21	4	1	0	5	11		.176	.252	.227	479	52	-6	2			.979	1	C-42	-0.2
	Yr	84	255	17	36	5	2	0	10	19		.141	.204	.176	380	21	-22	4			.977	1	C-84	-1.5
1905	Cle-A	75	239	11	41	4	1	1	18	6		.172	.198	.209	408	29	-19	7			.960	-7	C-60/O-8R,1-3,3-2	-2.3
1906	Cle-A	34	86	7	14	2	0	0	7	9		.163	.250	.186	436	38	-6	0			.938	3	C-33/1-1	-0.1
1907	StL-A	26	75	9	11	1	0	0	1	7		.147	.220	.160	380	21	-6	0			.983	1	C-25	-0.4
Total	9	431	1334	125	256	25	18	6	112	69		.192	.238	.251	489	46	-89	20			.960	1	C-402/O-11R,1-8,3-2	-5.6

■ **ART BUES** Bues, Arthur Frederick b: 3/3/1888, Milwaukee, Wis. d: 11/7/54, Whitefish Bay, Wis. BR/TR, 5′11″, 184 lbs. Deb: 4/17/13

YEAR	TM/L	G	AB	R	H	2B	3B	HR	RBI	BB	SO	AVG	OBP	SLG	OPS	OPS+	BR+	SB	CS	SBR	FA	FR	G/POS	TPR
1913	Bos-N	2	1	0	0	0	0	0	0	0	1	.000	.000	.000	0	-98	-0	0			.000	0	/2-1,3-1	0.0
1914	Chi-N	14	45	3	10	1	1	0	4	5	6	.222	.300	.289	589	76	-1	1			.968	-2	3-12	-0.4
Total	2	16	46	3	10	1	1	0	4	5	7	.217	.294	.283	577	72	-2	1			.968	-2	/3-13,2-1	-0.4

■ **CHARLIE BUFFINTON** Buffinton, Charles G. b: 6/14/1861, Fall River, Mass. d: 9/23/07, Fall River, Mass. BR/TR, 6′1″, 180 lbs. Deb: 5/17/1882 M Career OF: (16-LF 47-CF 78-RF)

YEAR	TM/L	G	AB	R	H	2B	3B	HR	RBI	BB	SO	AVG	OBP	SLG	OPS	OPS+	BR+	SB	CS	SBR	FA	FR	G/POS	TPR
1882	Bos-N	15	50	5	13	1	0	0	4	2	3	.260	.288	.280	568	83	-1				.615	-1	/O-7(0-0-7),P-5,1-4	-0.2
1883	Bos-N	86	341	28	81	8	3	1	26	6	24	.238	.251	.287	538	62	-16				.756	-7	O-51R,P-43/1-2	-1.4
1884	Bos-N	87	352	48	94	18	3	1	39	16	12	.267	.299	.344	643	102	1				.946	-1	P-67,O-13C,1-11	-0.5
1885	Bos-N	82	338	26	81	12	3	1	33	3	26	.240	.246	.302	548	79	-8				.912	0	P-51,O-18C,1-15	-1.0
1886	Bos-N	44	176	27	51	4	1	1	30	6	12	.290	.313	.341	654	103	1	3			.968	-6	1-19,P-18/O-9(0-1-8)	-0.6
1887	Phi-N	66	280	34	83	12	1	1	46	11	3	.296	.299	.331	630	71	-11	8			.931	2	P-40,O-22(7-7-8),1-10	-0.9
1888	Phi-N	46	160	14	29	4	1	0	12	7	5	.181	.216	.219	434	37	-11	1			.939	9	P-46/O-1(1-0-0)	0.0
1889	Phi-N	47	154	16	32	2	0	0	21	9	5	.208	.256	.221	477	31	-14	0			.916	1	P-47/O-1(1-0-0)	0.0
1890	Phi-P	42	150	24	41	3	2	1	24	9	3	.273	.319	.340	659	74	-6	1			.864	0	P-36/O-5(1-2-2),1-3,M	-0.1
1891	Bos-a	58	181	16	34	2	1	1	16	19	15	.188	.269	.227	495	43	-13	0			.934	3	P-48,O-10(5-0-6)/1-4	-0.5
1892	Bal-N	13	43	7	15	1	1	0	4	3	6	.349	.391	.419	810	141	2	1			.892	2	P-13	0.0
Total	11	586	2225	245	554	67	16	7	255	91	114	.249	.276	.299	576	72	-77	14			.916	2	P-414,O-137R/1-68	-5.2

■ **DAMON BUFORD** Buford, Damon Jackson b: 6/12/70, Baltimore, Md. BR/TR, 5′10″, 170 lbs. Deb: 5/4/93 F Career OF: (52-LF 486-CF 61-RF)

YEAR	TM/L	G	AB	R	H	2B	3B	HR	RBI	BB	SO	AVG	OBP	SLG	OPS	OPS+	BR+	SB	CS	SBR	FA	FR	G/POS	TPR
1993	Bal-A	53	79	18	18	5	0	2	9	9	19	.228	.315	.367	682	79	-2	2	2	-0	.984	-1	O-30(5-24-1),D-17	-0.4
1994	Bal-A	4	2	2	1	0	0	0	0	0	1	.500	.500	.500	1000	151	0	0	0	0	.000	-0	/O-1(1-0-0),D-1	0.0
1995	Bal-A	24	32	6	2	0	0	0	2	6	7	.063	.211	.063	273	-24	-6	3	1	0	1.000	-2	O-24(0-15-9)	-0.8
	NY-N	44	136	24	32	5	0	4	12	19	28	.235	.350	.360	710	91	-1	7	7	-1	.972	-1	O-39(25-16-0)	-0.4
1996	*Tex-A	90	145	30	41	9	0	6	20	15	34	.283	.350	.469	819	99	-0	8	5	0	1.000	-15	O-80(14-25-44)	-1.5
1997	Tex-A	122	366	49	82	18	0	8	39	30	83	.224	.288	.339	627	60	-22	18	7	2	.990	5	*O-117(0-117-0)/D-3	-1.4
1998	*Bos-A	86	216	37	61	14	4	10	42	22	43	.282	.351	.523	875	121	6	5	5	-1	1.000	-4	O-67C,D-15/2-1,3-1	0.2
1999	*Bos-A	91	297	39	72	15	2	6	38	21	74	.242	.297	.367	664	66	-16	9	2	1	.985	2	O-84(5-82-0)/D-5	-1.1
2000	Chi-N	150	495	64	124	18	3	15	48	47	118	.251	.325	.390	715	82	-14	4	6	-1	.986	2	*O-148(2-140-7)	-1.2
Total	8	664	1768	269	433	84	9	51	210	169	407	.245	.318	.389	707	79	-55	56	35	0	.989	-15	O-590C/D-41,3-1,2-1	-6.6

■ **DON BUFORD** Buford, Donald Alvin b: 2/2/37, Linden, Tex. BB/TR, 5′8″, 165 lbs. Deb: 9/14/63 FC Career OF: (512-LF 41-CF 7-RF)

YEAR	TM/L	G	AB	R	H	2B	3B	HR	RBI	BB	SO	AVG	OBP	SLG	OPS	OPS+	BR+	SB	CS	SBR	FA	FR	G/POS	TPR
1963	Chi-A	12	42	9	12	1	2	0	5	5	7	.286	.362	.405	766	116	1	1	0	0	.955	-5	/3-9,2-2	-0.4
1964	Chi-A	135	442	62	116	14	6	4	30	46	62	.262	.339	.348	687	94	-3	12	7	0	.968	-16	2-92,3-37	-1.2
1965	Chi-A	155	586	93	166	22	5	10	47	67	76	.283	.361	.389	750	120	17	17	7	1	.981	3	*2-139,3-41	3.4
1966	Chi-A	163	607	85	148	26	7	8	52	69	71	.244	.324	.349	673	100	1	51	22	4	.939	1	*3-133,2-37,O-11L	0.8
1967	Chi-A	156	535	61	129	10	9	4	32	65	51	.241	.324	.316	640	93	-3	34	21	0	.948	4	*3-121,2-51/O-1L	0.5
1968	Bal-A	130	426	65	120	13	4	15	46	57	46	.282	.372	.437	808	144	24	27	12	2	1.000	-6	O-65C,2-58/3-2	2.3
1969	*Bal-A	144	554	99	161	31	3	11	64	96	62	.291	.400	.417	817	128	24	19	18	-2	.983	-4	*O-128L,2-10/3-6	1.2
1970	*Bal-A	144	504	99	137	15	2	17	66	109	55	.272	.409	.411	820	125	23	16	8	1	.987	6	*O-130L/2-3,3-3	2.2
1971	*Bal-A★	122	449	**99**	130	19	4	19	54	89	62	.290	.415	.477	891	153	35	15	7	1	.987	3	*O-115(114-0-1)	3.4
1972	Bal-A	125	408	46	84	6	2	5	22	69	83	.206	.326	.267	594	76	-9	8	3	1	.989	-1	*O-105(104-0-1)	-1.8
Total	10	1286	4553	718	1203	157	44	93	418	672	575	.264	.364	.379	743	115	110	200	105	7	.988	-15	O-555L,2-392,3-352	10.4

■ **JAY BUHNER** Buhner, Jay Campbell b: 8/13/64, Louisville, Ky. BR/TR, 6′3″, 205 lbs. Deb: 9/11/87 Career OF: (7-LF 30-CF 1354-RF)

YEAR	TM/L	G	AB	R	H	2B	3B	HR	RBI	BB	SO	AVG	OBP	SLG	OPS	OPS+	BR+	SB	CS	SBR	FA	FR	G/POS	TPR
1987	NY-A	7	22	0	5	2	0	0	1	1	6	.227	.261	.318	579	53	-2	0	0	0	1.000	0	/O-7(2-3-2)	-0.2
1988	NY-A	25	69	8	13	0	0	3	13	3	25	.188	.253	.319	572	60	-4	0	0	0	.964	1	O-22(3-16-3)	-0.4
	Sea-A	60	192	28	43	13	1	10	25	25	68	.224	.323	.458	781	111	3	1	1	-0	.993	9	O-59(1-2-55)	1.0
	Yr	85	261	36	56	13	1	13	38	28	93	.215	.305	.421	727	98	-1	1	1	-0	.985	10	O-81(4-18-58)	0.6
1989	Sea-A	58	204	27	56	15	1	9	33	19	55	.275	.342	.490	832	128	7	1	4	-1	.966	1	O-57(0-2-56)	0.5
1990	Sea-A	51	163	16	45	12	0	7	33	17	50	.276	.359	.479	837	131	7	2	2	-0	.966	-4	O-40(0-1-39),D-10	0.1
1991	Sea-A	137	406	64	99	14	4	27	77	53	117	.244	.340	.498	837	128	15	0	1	-0	.981	6	*O-131(1-3-131)	1.7
1992	Sea-A	152	543	69	132	16	3	25	79	71	146	.243	.337	.422	759	111	8	0	6	-2	.994	11	*O-150(0-2-150)	1.2
1993	Sea-A	158	563	91	153	28	3	27	98	100	144	.272	.383	.476	859	128	24	2	5	-1	.978	-2	*O-148(0-0-148),D-10	1.1
1994	Sea-A	101	358	74	100	23	4	21	68	66	63	.279	.399	.542	941	137	21	0	1	-0	.990	6	O-96(0-1-95)/D-4	1.9
1995	*Sea-A	126	470	86	123	23	0	40	121	60	120	.262	.347	.566	912	131	19	0	1	-0	.989	-3	*O-120(0-0-120)/D-4	0.9
1996	Sea-A★	150	564	107	153	29	0	44	138	84	159	.271	.374	.557	931	131	26	0	1	-0	.989	-0	*O-142(0-0-142)/D-8	1.7
1997	*Sea-A	157	540	104	131	18	2	40	109	119	175	.243	.384	.506	890	131	27	0	0	0	**.997**	4	*O-154(0-0-154)/D-2	2.1
1998	Sea-A	72	244	33	59	7	1	15	45	38	71	.242	.346	.463	809	108	3	0	0	0	.985	2	O-70(0-0-70)/D-1	0.1
1999	Sea-A	87	266	37	59	11	0	14	38	69	100	.222	.391	.421	812	110	7	0	0	0	.993	-4	O-85(0-0-85)/1-1	-0.2
2000	*Sea-A	112	364	50	92	20	0	26	82	59	98	.253	.363	.522	885	124	13	0	2	-1	1.000	-3	*O-104(0-0-104)/D-1	0.4
Total	14	1453	4968	794	1263	231	19	308	960	784	1397	.254	.362	.494	856	124	173	6	24	-7	.988	22	*O-1385R/D-40,1-1	11.9

■ **HARRY BUKER** Buker, Henry L. "Happy" b: 1859, Chicago, Ill. d: 8/10/1899, Chicago, Ill. 140 lbs. Deb: 6/11/1884

YEAR	TM/L	G	AB	R	H	2B	3B	HR	RBI	BB	SO	AVG	OBP	SLG	OPS	OPS+	BR+	SB	CS	SBR	FA	FR	G/POS	TPR
1884	Det-N	30	111	5	15	1	0	0	3	4	15	.135	.165	.144	309	-2	-12				.867	1	S-19,O-11(0-0-11)	-1.0

■ **GEORGE BULLARD** Bullard, George Donald "Curly" b: 10/24/28, Lynn, Mass. BR/TR, 5′9.5″, 165 lbs. Deb: 9/17/54

YEAR	TM/L	G	AB	R	H	2B	3B	HR	RBI	BB	SO	AVG	OBP	SLG	OPS	OPS+	BR+	SB	CS	SBR	FA	FR	G/POS	TPR
1954	Det-A	4	1	0	0	0	0	0	0	0	0	.000	.000	.000	0	-99	-0	0	0	0	.800	1	/S-1	0.1

■ **SIM BULLAS** Bullas, Simeon Edward b: 4/10/1861, Cleveland, Ohio d: 1/14/08, Cleveland, Ohio 5′7.5″, 150 lbs. Deb: 5/2/1884

YEAR	TM/L	G	AB	R	H	2B	3B	HR	RBI	BB	SO	AVG	OBP	SLG	OPS	OPS+	BR+	SB	CS	SBR	FA	FR	G/POS	TPR
1884	Tol-a	13	45	4	4	0	1	0		1		.089	.109	.133	242	-21	-6				.909	-6	C-12/O-2(2-0-0)	-1.0

■ **SCOTT BULLETT** Bullett, Scott Douglas b: 12/25/68, Martinsburg, W.Va. BB/TL, 6′2″, 200 lbs. Deb: 9/3/91

YEAR	TM/L	G	AB	R	H	2B	3B	HR	RBI	BB	SO	AVG	OBP	SLG	OPS	OPS+	BR+	SB	CS	SBR	FA	FR	G/POS	TPR
1991	Pit-N	11	4	2	0	0	0	0	0	0	3	.000	.200	.000	200	-40	-1	1	1	-0	1.000	-1	/O-3(1-1-1)	-0.2
1993	Pit-N	23	55	2	11	0	2	0	4	3	15	.200	.241	.273	514	37	-5	3	2	-0	1.000	-2	O-19(0-18-1)	-0.7
1995	Chi-N	104	150	19	41	5	7	3	22	12	30	.273	.331	.460	791	108	1	8	3	1	.968	-11	O-64(54-12-0)	-1.0
1996	Chi-N	109	165	26	35	5	0	3	16	10	54	.212	.257	.297	554	44	-13	7	3	0	.986	-8	O-58(28-11-22)	-2.1
Total	4	247	374	49	87	10	9	6	42	25	102	.233	.284	.356	640	68	-18	19	9	1	.983	-22	O-144(83-42-24)	-4.0

YEAR	TM/L	G	AB	R	H	2B	3B	HR	RBI	BB	SO	AVG	OBP	SLG	OPS	OPS+	BR+	SB	CS	SBR	FA	FR	G/POS	TPR
■ **BUD BULLING**	Bulling, Terry Charles "Terry" b: 12/15/52, Lynwood, Cal. BR/TR, 6'1", 200 lbs. Deb: 7/3/77																							
1977	Min-A	15	32	2	5	1	0	0	5	5	5	.156	.270	.188	458	28	-3	0	0	0	.952	-0	C-10/D-3	-0.3
1981	Sea-A	62	154	15	38	3	0	2	15	21	20	.247	.341	.305	646	84	-2	0	0	0	.977	-3	C-62	-0.3
1982	Sea-A	56	154	17	34	7	0	1	8	19	16	.221	.306	.286	592	62	-8	2	1	0	.991	7	C-56	0.2
1983	Sea-A	5	5	0	0	0	0	0	0	0	0	.000	.000	.000	0	-96	-1	0	0	0	1.000	1	/C-5	0.0
Total	4	138	345	34	77	11	0	3	28	45	41	.223	.315	.281	596	66	-14	2	1	0	.983	6	C-133/D-3	-0.4
■ **ERIC BULLOCK**	Bullock, Eric Gerald b: 2/16/60, Los Angeles, Cal. BL/TL, 5'11", 185 lbs. Deb: 8/26/85 Career OF: (19-LF 1-CF 10-RF)																							
1985	Hou-N	18	25	3	7	2	0	0	2	1	3	.280	.308	.360	668	89	-0	0	1	-0	.750	-2	/O-7(4-0-3)	-0.3
1986	Hou-N	6	21	0	1	0	0	0	1	0	3	.048	.048	.048	95	-76	-5	2	0	0	.875	-1	/O-6(6-0-0)	-0.6
1988	Min-A	16	17	3	5	0	0	0	3	3	1	.294	.400	.294	694	95	0	1	0	0	.875	-1	/O-4(3-0-2),D-2	-0.1
1989	Phi-N	6	4	1	0	0	0	0	0	0	2	.000	.000	.000	0	-99	-1	0	0	0	1.000	-1	/O-3(0-1-2)	-0.2
1990	Mon-N	4	2	0	1	0	0	0	0	0	0	.500	.500	.500	1000	183	0	0	0	0	.000	0	/H	0.0
1991	Mon-N	73	72	6	16	4	0	1	6	9	13	.222	.309	.319	628	78	-2	6	1	1	1.000	-1	/O-9(6-0-3),1-3	-0.2
1992	Mon-N	8	5	0	0	0	0	0	0	0	1	.000	.000	.000	0	-99	-1	0	0	0	.000	0	/H	-0.2
Total	7	131	146	13	30	6	0	1	12	13	23	.205	.270	.267	538	52	-9	9	2	1	.892	-5	/O-29L,1-3,D-2	-1.6
■ **AL BUMBRY**	Bumbry, Alonza Benjamin (b: Alonza Benjamin Bumbrey) b: 4/21/47, Fredericksburg, Va. BL/TR, 5'8", 175 lbs. Deb: 9/5/72 C Career OF: (382-LF 928-CF 31-RF)																							
1972	Bal-A	9	11	5	4	0	1	0	0	0	0	.364	.364	.545	909	164	1	1	1	-0	1.000	0	/O-2(2-0-0)	0.1
1973	*Bal-A	110	356	73	120	15	**11**	7	34	34	49	.337	.399	.500	899	153	25	23	10	2	.978	-10	O-86(62-1-29)/D-7	1.2
1974	*Bal-A	94	270	35	63	10	3	1	19	21	46	.233	.291	.304	595	74	-9	12	4	1	.953	-1	O-67(67-0-0)/D-7	-1.3
1975	Bal-A	114	349	47	94	19	4	2	32	32	81	.269	.338	.364	702	105	2	16	3	2	1.000	-2	D-48,O-39(35-3-1)/3-1	0.0
1976	Bal-A	133	450	71	113	15	7	9	36	43	76	.251	.318	.376	693	109	5	42	10	6	.989	-12	*O-116(82-57-0),D-10	-0.7
1977	Bal-A	133	518	74	164	31	3	4	41	45	88	.317	.373	.411	785	121	16	19	8	1	.991	-10	*O-130(52-112-0)	0.5
1978	Bal-A	33	114	21	27	5	2	2	6	17	15	.237	.346	.368	714	108	2	5	3	0	.985	-2	O-28(16-17-0)	-0.1
1979	*Bal-A	148	569	80	162	29	1	7	49	43	74	.285	.338	.376	714	96	-3	37	12	4	.982	-3	*O-146(5-146-0)	-0.3
1980	Bal-A★	160	645	118	205	29	9	9	53	78	75	.318	.394	.433	826	128	27	44	11	6	.990	15	*O-160(1-160-0)	4.6
1981	Bal-A	101	392	61	107	18	2	1	27	51	51	.273	.360	.337	696	102	3	22	15	-0	.992	4	*O-100(0-100-0)	0.5
1982	Bal-A	150	562	77	147	20	4	5	40	44	77	.262	.315	.338	653	80	-15	10	5	0	.986	8	*O-147(3-146-0)/D-1	-0.8
1983	*Bal-A	124	378	63	104	14	4	3	31	31	33	.275	.330	.357	687	91	-4	12	5	1	.988	-11	*O-104(17-99-0),D-11	-1.7
1984	Bal-A	119	344	47	93	12	1	3	24	25	35	.270	.320	.337	657	84	-7	9	5	0	.988	-6	O-99(28-82-0)/D-9	-1.5
1985	SD-N	68	95	6	19	3	0	1	10	7	9	.200	.255	.263	518	46	-7	2	0	0	.939	-2	O-17(12-5-1)	-0.9
Total	14	1496	5053	778	1422	220	52	54	402	471	709	.281	.345	.378	723	104	34	254	92	24	.986	-31	*O-1241C/D-93,3-1	-0.4
■ **JOSH BUNCE**	Bunce, Joshua b: 5/10/1847, Brooklyn, N.Y. d: 4/28/12, Brooklyn, N.Y. Deb: 8/27/1877																							
1877	Har-N	1	4	0	0	0	0	0	0	0	0	.000	.000	.000	0	-99	-1				1.000	-0	/O-1(1-0-0)	-0.1
■ **NELSON BURBRINK**	Burbrink, Nelson Edward b: 12/28/21, Cincinnati, Ohio BR/TR, 5'10", 195 lbs. Deb: 6/5/55																							
1955	StL-N	58	170	11	47	8	1	0	15	14	13	.276	.335	.335	670	79	-5	1	1	-0	.979	-1	C-55	-0.3
■ **AL BURCH**	Burch, Albert William b: 10/7/1883, Albany, N.Y. d: 10/5/26, Brooklyn, N.Y. BL/TR, 5'8.5", 160 lbs. Deb: 6/19/06 Career OF: (115-LF 324-CF 123-RF)																							
1906	StL-N	91	335	40	89	5	1	0	11	37		.266	.339	.287	625	99	1	15			.934	1	O-91(0-58-33)	-0.3
1907	StL-N	48	154	18	35	3	1	0	5	17		.227	.304	.260	564	79	-3	7			.922	0	O-48(0-48-0)	-0.6
	Bro-N	40	120	12	35	2	2	0	12	11		.292	.351	.342	693	127	4	5			.890	2	O-36(27-5-5)/2-1	0.4
	Yr	88	274	30	70	5	3	0	17	28		.255	.325	.296	620	100	0	12			.908	2	O-84(27-53-5)/2-1	-0.2
1908	Bro-N	123	456	45	111	8	4	2	18	33		.243	.294	.292	586	91	-5	15			.971	13	*O-116(47-44-28)	0.2
1909	Bro-N	152	601	80	163	20	6	1	30	51		.271	.329	.329	659	108	5	38			.955	6	*O-151(41-102-9)/1-1	0.4
1910	Bro-N	103	352	41	83	8	3	1	20	22	30	.236	.281	.284	565	67	-16	13			.957	-1	O-70(0-26-45),1-13	-2.1
1911	Bro-N	54	167	18	38	2	3	0	7	15	22	.228	.291	.275	567	61	-9	3			.972	2	O-43(0-41-3)/2-3	-1.0
Total	6	611	2185	254	554	48	20	4	103	186	52	.254	.312	.299	612	91	-22	96			.950	22	O-555C/1-14,2-4	-3.0
■ **ERNIE BURCH**	Burch, Earnest W. b: 1856, DeKalb Co., Ill. BL, Deb: 8/15/1884																							
1884	Cle-N	32	124	9	26	4	0	0	7	5	24	.210	.240	.242	482	50	-7				.899	4	O-32(23-0-9)	-0.3
1886	Bro-a	113	456	78	119	22	6	2	72	39		.261	.321	.349	669	109	4	16			.884	-13	*O-113(113-0-0)	-1.0
1887	Bro-a	49	217	47	84	4	4	2	26	29		.387	.395	.388	784	118	6	15			.899	1	O-49(49-0-0)	0.4
Total	3	194	797	134	229	30	10	4	105	73	24	.287	.328	.341	669	101	3	31			.891	-8	O-194(185-0-9)	-0.9
■ **BOB BURDA**	Burda, Edward Robert b: 7/16/38, St.Louis, Mo. BL/TL, 5'11", 180 lbs. Deb: 8/25/62																							
1962	StL-N	7	14	0	1	0	0	0	0	3	1	.071	.235	.071	307	-12	-2	1	0	0	.917	-0	/O-6(1-0-5)	-0.3
1965	SF-N	31	27	0	3	0	0	0	5	5	6	.111	.250	.111	361	6	-3	0	0	0	.969	-1	1-11/O-1(1-0-0)	-0.4
1966	SF-N	37	43	3	7	3	0	0	2	2	5	.163	.200	.233	433	19	-5	0	0	0	1.000	-1	/1-7,O-4(3-0-1)	-0.6
1969	SF-N	97	161	20	37	8	0	6	27	21	12	.230	.319	.391	710	100	-0	0	1	-0	.995	-1	1-45,O-19(5-0-15)	-0.4
1970	SF-N	28	23	1	6	0	0	0	3	5	2	.261	.414	.261	675	86	-0	0	0	0	.933	-1	/1-8,O-1(1-0-0)	-0.1
	Mil-A	78	222	19	55	9	0	4	20	16	17	.248	.307	.342	649	78	-7	1	0	0	.987	-7	O-64(0-0-64)/1-7	-1.8
1971	StL-N	65	71	6	21	0	0	1	12	10	11	.296	.390	.338	728	104	1	0	0	0	1.000	0	1-13/O-1(0-0-1)	0.0
1972	Bos-A	45	73	4	12	1	0	2	9	8	11	.164	.247	.260	507	48	-5	0	0	0	.992	-0	1-15/O-1(1-0-0)	-0.7
Total	7	388	634	53	142	21	0	13	78	70	65	.224	.306	.319	625	74	-21	2	1	0	.992	-11	1-106/O-97(12-0-86)	-4.3
■ **JACK BURDOCK**	Burdock, John Joseph "Black Jack" b: 4/1852, Brooklyn, N.Y. d: 11/27/31, Brooklyn, N.Y. BR/TR, 5'9.5", 158 lbs. Deb: 5/2/1872 MU NA OF: (2-LF 1-CF 0-RF)																							
1872	Atl-n	37	174	26	46	3	0	0	15	1	1	.264	.269	.282	550	59	-11	0	1	-0	.738	-4	*S-36/C-4,2-2	-1.1
1873	Atl-n	55	245	56	62	7	1	2	36	7	4	.253	.274	.314	588	83	-2	3	1	0	.816	1	*2-55/C-2	-0.3
1874	Mut-n	61	273	45	75	11	4	1	26	1	5	.275	.277	.355	633	98	-1	4	1	1	**.820**	8	*3-60/O-3(2-1-0)	0.4
1875	Har-n	74	350	72	103	12	5	0	35	3	13	.294	.300	.357	657	121	6	20	11	1	**.895**	-4	*2-73/3-2,C-1	-0.2
1876	Har-N	69	322	66	80	9	1	0	23	13	16	.248	.289	.294	583	87	-5				.895	1	*2-69/3-1	-0.1
1877	Har-N	58	277	35	72	6	0	0	9	2	16	.260	.265	.282	547	81	-5				**.903**	7	*2-55/3-3	0.4
1878	Bos-N	60	246	37	64	12	6	0	25	3	17	.260	.269	.358	627	97	-2				**.918**	**21**	*2-60	2.1
1879	Bos-N	84	359	64	86	10	3	0	36	9	28	.240	.258	.284	542	77	-9				.911	10	*2-84	0.4
1880	Bos-N	86	356	58	90	17	4	2	35	8	26	.253	.269	.340	609	108	3				**.923**	12	*2-86	1.8
1881	Bos-N	73	282	36	67	12	4	1	24	7	18	.238	.256	.319	575	84	-5				.911	-11	*2-72/S-1	-1.2
1882	Bos-N	83	319	36	76	6	7	0	27	9	24	.238	.259	.301	560	79	-7				**.932**	3	*2-83	-0.1
1883	Bos-N	96	400	80	132	27	8	5	88	14	35	.330	.353	.475	828	145	21				.921	-1	*2-96/M	2.0
1884	Bos-N	87	361	65	97	14	4	6	49	15	52	.269	.298	.380	677	112	5				**.922**	1	*2-87/3-1	0.8
1885	Bos-N	45	169	18	24	5	0	0	7	8	18	.142	.181	.172	352	15	-15				.917	-5	2-45	-1.7
1886	Bos-N	59	221	26	48	6	1	0	25	11	27	.217	.254	.253	508	57	-11	3			.904	-8	2-59	-1.6
1887	Bos-N	65	255	36	79	6	0	0	29	18	22	.310	.320	.283	603	69	-9	19			.882	-19	2-65	-2.2
1888	Bos-N	22	79	5	16	0	0	0	4	2	5	.203	.232	.203	434	39	-5	1			.903	0	2-22	-0.4
	Bro-a	70	246	15	30	1	2	1	8	8		.122	.166	.154	320	3	-26	9			.904	2	2-70	-2.1
1891	Bro-N	3	12	1	1	0	0	0	1	1	1	.083	.154	.083	237	-31	-2	0			1.000	-1	/2-3	-0.2
Total	4 n	227	1042	199	286	33	10	3	112	12	23	.274	.283	.334	617	94	-8	27	14	1	.858	0	2-130/3-62,S-36,CO	-1.2
Total	14	960	3904	578	962	131	40	15	390	128	305	.246	.270	.310	580	83	-73	32			.912	13	2-956/3-5,S-1	-2.1
■ **JOE BURG**	Burg, Joseph Peter b: 6/4/1882, Chicago, Ill. d: 4/28/69, Joliet, Ill. BR/TR, 5'10", 150 lbs. Deb: 9/26/10																							
1910	Bos-N	13	46	7	15	0	1	0	10	7	12	.326	.415	.370	785	124	2	5			.867	3	3-12/S-1	0.5
■ **SMOKY BURGESS**	Burgess, Forrest Harrill b: 2/6/27, Caroleen, N.C. d: 9/15/91, Asheville, N.C. BL/TR, 5'8", 187 lbs. Deb: 4/19/49																							
1949	Chi-N	46	56	4	15	0	0	1	12	4	4	.268	.317	.321	638	73	-2	0			1.000	1	/C-8	-0.1
1951	Chi-N	94	219	21	55	4	2	2	20	21	12	.251	.317	.315	632	69	-9	2	0	0	.980	-3	C-64	-0.9
1952	Phi-N	110	371	49	110	27	2	6	56	49	21	.296	.380	.429	809	125	14	3	1	0	.978	-6	*C-104	1.5
1953	Phi-N	102	312	31	91	17	5	4	36	37	17	.292	.370	.417	787	105	3	3	2	-0	**.993**	-8	C-95	0.0
1954	Phi-N★	108	345	41	127	27	5	4	46	42	11	.368	.437	.510	947	146	25	1	5	-2	.975	-8	C-91	1.9

YEAR	TM/L	G	AB	R	H	2B	3B	HR	RBI	BB	SO	AVG	OBP	SLG	OPS	OPS+	BR+	SB	CS	SBR	FA	FR	G/POS	TPR
1955	Phi-N	7	21	4	4	2	0	1	1	3	1	.190	.292	.429	720	90	-0	0	0	0	1.000	0	/C-6	0.1
	Cin-N★	116	421	67	129	15	3	20	77	47	35	.306	.377	.499	876	123	14	1	1	-0	.986	-9	*C-107	1.0
	Yr	123	442	71	133	17	3	21	78	50	36	.301	.373	.495	869	122	14	1	1	-0	.987	-9	*C-113	1.1
1956	Cin-N	90	229	28	63	10	0	12	39	26	18	.275	.349	.476	825	112	4	0	1	-0	1.000	-2	C-55	0.4
1957	Cin-N	90	205	29	58	14	1	14	39	24	16	.283	.358	.566	924	134	9	0	0	0	.988	-5	C-45	0.7
1958	Cin-N	99	251	28	71	12	1	6	31	22	20	.283	.343	.410	753	93	-2	0	0	0	.988	4	C-58	0.5
1959	Pit-N★	114	377	41	112	28	5	11	59	31	16	.297	.354	.485	839	122	11	0	0	0	.984	-17	*C-101	-0.1
1960	*Pit-N★	110	337	33	99	15	2	7	39	35	13	.294	.360	.412	773	110	5	0	1	-0	**.994**	1	C-89	1.1
1961	Pit-N★	100	323	37	98	17	3	12	52	30	16	.303	.366	.486	852	123	11	1	0	0	**.991**	-14	C-92	0.2
1962	Pit-N	103	360	38	118	19	2	13	61	31	19	.328	.381	.500	881	134	17	0	1	-0	.988	-11	*C-101	1.0
1963	Pit-N	91	264	20	74	10	1	6	37	24	14	.280	.343	.394	736	111	4	0	1	-0	.990	-11	C-72	-0.5
1964	Pit-N☆	68	171	9	42	3	1	2	17	13	14	.246	.303	.310	613	73	-6	2	1	0	.992	-8	C-44	-1.2
	Chi-A	7	5	1	1	0	0	1	1	2	0	.200	.429	.800	1229	239	1	0	0	0	.000	0	H	0.1
1965	Chi-A	80	77	2	22	4	0	2	24	11	7	.286	.375	.416	791	132	4	0	0	0	1.000	-0	/C-5	0.4
1966	Chi-A	79	67	0	21	5	0	0	15	11	8	.313	.418	.388	806	143	4	0	0	0	1.000	-0	/C-2	0.5
1967	Chi-A	77	60	2	8	1	0	2	11	14	8	.133	.307	.250	557	69	-2	0	0	0	.000	0	H	-0.2
Total	18	1691	4471	485	1318	230	33	126	673	477	270	.295	.364	.446	810	116	105	13	14		.988	-96	*C-1139	6.4
■ TOM BURGESS Burgess, Thomas Roland "Tim" b: 9/1/27, London, Ont., Can. BL/TL, 6', 180 lbs. Deb: 4/17/54 C																								
1954	StL-N	17	21	2	1	1	0	0	1	3	9	.048	.167	.095	262	-29	-4	0	0	0	.750	-1	/O-4(0-0-4)	-0.6
1962	LA-A	87	143	17	28	7	1	2	13	36	20	.196	.358	.301	658	82	-2	2	0	0	.997	-3	1-35/O-2(2-0-0)	-0.6
Total	2	104	164	19	29	8	1	2	14	39	29	.177	.335	.274	609	67	-6	2	0	0	.857	-4	/1-35,O-6(2-0-4)	-1.2
■ BILL BURGO Burgo, William Ross b: 11/5/19, Johnstown, Pa. d: 10/19/88, Morgan City, La. BR/TR, 5'8", 185 lbs. Deb: 9/22/43																								
1943	Phi-A	17	70	12	26	4	2	1	9	4	1	.371	.421	.529	950	178	7	0	2	-1	.979	2	O-17(17-0-0)	0.7
1944	Phi-A	27	88	6	21	2	0	1	3	7	3	.239	.316	.295	612	76	-3	1	3	-1	.955	2	O-22(14-0-8)	-0.2
Total	2	44	158	18	47	6	2	2	12	11	4	.297	.362	.399	761	121	4	1	5	-2	.965	4	/O-39(31-0-8)	0.5
■ BILL BURICH Burich, William Max b: 5/29/18, Calumet, Mich. BR/TR, 6', 180 lbs. Deb: 4/15/42																								
1942	Phi-N	25	80	3	23	1	0	0	7	6	13	.287	.337	.300	637	92	-1	2			.917	-5	S-19/3-3	-0.5
1946	Phi-N	2	1	1	0	0	0	0	0	0	0	.000	.000	.000	0	-99	-0	0			.000	0	/3-1	0.0
Total	2	27	81	4	23	1	0	0	7	6	13	.284	.333	.296	630	89	-1	2			1.000	-5	/S-19,3-4	-0.5
■ MACK BURK Burk, Mack Edwin b: 4/21/35, Nacogdoches, Tex. BR/TR, 6'4", 180 lbs. Deb: 5/25/56																								
1956	Phi-N	15	1	3	1	0	0	0	0	0	0	1.000	1.000	1.000	2000	449	0	0	0	0	1.000	0	/C-1	0.1
1958	Phi-N	1	1	0	0	0	0	0	0	0	1	.000	.000	.000	0	-99	-0	0	0	0	.000	0	H	0.0
Total	2	16	2	3	1	0	0	0	0	0	1	.500	.500	.500	1000	171	0	0	0	0	1.000	0	/C-1	0.1
■ CHRIS BURKAM Burkam, Chauncey De Pew b: 10/13/1892, Benton Harbor, Mich. d: 5/9/64, Kalamazoo, Mich. BL/TR, 5'11", 175 lbs. Deb: 6/24/15																								
1915	StL-A	1	1	0	0	0	0	0	0	0	1	.000	.000	.000	0	-99	-0	0			.000	0	H	0.0
■ DAN BURKE Burke, Daniel L. b: 10/25/1868, Abington, Mass. d: 3/20/33, Taunton, Mass. BR/TR, 5'10", 190 lbs. Deb: 4/18/1890 Career OF: (0-LF 19-CF 10-RF)																								
1890	Roc-a	32	102	14	22	1	0	0	9	17		.216	.333	.225	559	70	-3	2			.944	-5	O-29(0-19-10)/C-4,1-2	-0.7
	Syr-a	9	20	1	0	0	0	0	0	5		.000	.231	.000	231	-35	-3	0			.900	3	/C-9	0.0
	Yr	41	122	15	22	1	0	0	9	22		.180	.315	.189	504	53	-5	2			.944	-2	O-29C,C-13/1-2	-0.7
1892	Bos-N	1	1	0	0	0	0	0	0	0	2	.000	.000	.000	0	-92	-1	0			.900	1	/C-1	0.0
Total	2	42	126	15	22	1	0	0	9	22	2	.175	.307	.183	489	48	-6	2			.892	-2	/O-29C,C-14,1-2	-0.7
■ EDDIE BURKE Burke, Edward D. b: 10/6/1866, Northumberland, Pa. d: 11/26/07, Utica, N.Y. BL/TR, 5'6", 161 lbs. Deb: 4/19/1890 Career OF: (611-LF 172-CF 9-RF)																								
1890	Phi-N	100	430	85	113	16	11	4	50	49	40	.263	.349	.379	728	109	5	38			.904	4	*O-96(0-96-0)/2-4	0.5
	Pit-N	31	124	17	26	5	2	1	7	14	9	.210	.295	.306	601	85	-2	6			.911	1	O-31(0-31-0)	-0.2
	Yr	131	554	102	139	21	13	5	57	63	49	.251	.337	.363	700	105	4	44			.906	4	*O-127(0-127-0)/2-4	0.3
1891	Mil-a	35	144	31	34	9	0	2	21	12	19	.236	.337	.340	678	78	-5	7			.918	3	O-35(0-35-0)	-0.3
1892	Cin-N	15	41	6	6	1	0	0	4	9	4	.146	.300	.171	471	44	-2	2			1.000	-3	O-14(3-5-6)/3-1	-0.6
	NY-N	89	363	81	94	10	5	6	41	46	37	.259	.350	.364	714	118	9	42			.857	3	2-59,O-30(30-0-0)	0.6
	Yr	104	404	87	100	11	5	6	45	55	41	.248	.345	.344	689	110	6	44			.857	-5	2-59,O-44(33-5-6)/3-1	0.0
1893	NY-N	135	537	122	150	23	10	9	80	51	32	.279	.369	.410	778	106	5	54			.912	2	*O-135(135-0-0)	-0.4
1894	*NY-N	138	574	124	176	23	11	4	77	39	35	.307	.361	.406	767	85	-14	36			.934	-4	*O-138(138-0-0)	-2.4
1895	NY-N	39	167	38	43	6	2	1	12	7	9	.257	.299	.335	635	65	-9	14			.914	2	O-39(39-0-0)	-0.9
	Cin-N	56	228	52	61	8	6	1	25	22	14	.268	.343	.368	711	80	-7	19			.899	2	O-56(56-0-1)	-0.8
	Yr	95	395	90	104	14	8	2	37	29	23	.263	.325	.354	679	74	-16	33			.905	4	O-95(95-0-1)	-1.7
1896	Cin-N	122	521	120	177	24	9	1	52	41	29	.340	.392	.426	818	108	6	53			.935	3	*O-122(116-5-1)	-0.2
1897	Cin-N	95	387	71	103	17	1	1	41	29		.266	.327	.323	650	67	-18	22			.940	7	*O-95(94-0-1)	-1.7
Total	8	855	3516	747	983	142	57	30	410	319	228	.280	.352	.378	730	94	-34	293			.922	14	O-791L/2-63,3-1	-6.4
■ FRANK BURKE Burke, Frank Aloysius b: 2/16/1880, Carbon Co., Pa. d: 9/17/46, Los Angeles, Cal. TR, Deb: 9/14/06																								
1906	NY-N	8	9	2	3	1	0	0	1	1		.333	.400	.667	1067	227	1	1			.667	-2	/O-4(0-3-1)	0.0
1907	Bos-N	43	129	6	23	0	1	0	8	11		.178	.243	.194	437	37	-9	3			.955	-4	O-36(32-4-1)	-1.7
Total	2	51	138	8	26	1	2	0	9	12		.188	.253	.225	478	50	-8	4			.942	-5	/O-40(32-7-2)	-1.7
■ GLENN BURKE Burke, Glenn Lawrence b: 11/16/52, Oakland, Cal. d: 5/30/95, San Leandro, Cal. BR/TR, 6', 195 lbs. Deb: 4/9/76 Career OF: (49-LF 135-CF 22-RF)																								
1976	LA-N	25	46	9	11	2	0	0	5	3	8	.239	.300	.283	583	67	-2	3	2	-0	.971	-3	O-20(5-15-0)	-0.6
1977	*LA-N	83	169	16	43	8	0	1	13	5	22	.254	.280	.320	600	61	-9	13	5	1	.971	-15	O-74(5-64-6)	-2.5
1978	LA-N	16	19	2	4	0	0	0	2	0	4	.211	.211	.211	421	18	-2	1	0	0	1.000	-5	O-15(4-11-0)	-0.7
	Oak-A	78	200	19	47	6	1	1	14	10	26	.235	.271	.290	561	61	-11	15	8	1	.987	-4	O-67C/1-1,D-2	-1.6
1979	Oak-A	23	89	4	19	2	1	0	4	4	10	.213	.247	.258	506	39	-8	3	1	0	1.000	1	O-23(22-0-2)	-0.8
Total	4	225	523	50	124	18	2	2	38	22	70	.237	.271	.291	561	56	-32	35	16	2	.983	-26	O-199C/D-2,1-1	-6.2
■ JIMMY BURKE Burke, James Timothy "Sunset Jimmy" b: 10/12/1874, St.Louis, Mo. d: 3/26/42, St.Louis, Mo. BR/TR, 5'7", 160 lbs. Deb: 10/6/1898 MC																								
1898	Cle-N	13	38	1	4	1	0	0	1	2		.105	.150	.132	282	-19	-6	1			.853	-4	3-13	-1.0
1899	StL-N	2	6	1	2	0	0	0	0	1		.333	.429	.333	762	108	0	1			.923	1	/2-2	0.1
1901	Mil-A	64	233	24	48	8	0	0	26	17		.206	.266	.240	506	43	-17	6			.860	-7	3-64	-2.1
	Chi-A	42	148	20	39	5	0	0	21	12		.264	.327	.297	624	76	-4	11			.867	-2	S-31,3-11	-0.4
	Yr	106	381	44	87	13	0	0	47	29		.228	.290	.262	552	56	-22	17			.859	-9	3-75,S-31	-2.5
	Pit-N	14	51	4	10	0	0	0	4	4		.196	.268	.196	464	35	-4	0			.877	3	3-14	-0.1
1902	Pit-N	60	203	24	60	12	2	0	26	17		.296	.359	.374	733	122	5	9			.895	-5	2-27,O-18R/3-9,S-4	0.1
1903	StL-N	115	431	55	123	13	3	0	42	23		.285	.326	.329	656	90	-6	28			.911	6	3-93,2-15/O-5(4-0-1)	0.3
1904	StL-N	118	406	37	92	10	3	0	37	15		.227	.271	.266	537	69	-15	17			.897	-7	*3-118	-2.0
1905	StL-N	122	431	34	97	9	5	1	30	21		.225	.275	.276	552	67	-18	15			.924	3	*3-122,M	-1.2
Total	7	550	1947	200	475	58	13	1	187	112		.244	.295	.289	584	73	-64	87			.899	-12	3-444/2-44,S-35,O	-6.3
■ JOHN BURKE Burke, John Patrick b: 1/27/1877, Hazleton, Pa. d: 8/4/50, Jersey City, N.J. BR/TR, Deb: 6/27/02																								
1902	NY-N	4	13	0	2	0	0	0	0	0		.154	.154	.154	308	-5	-2	0			1.000	-0	/P-2,O-2(0-0-2)	-0.1
■ JOE BURKE Burke, Joseph A. b: Cincinnati, Ohio 5'7", 160 lbs. Deb: 9/26/1890																								
1890	StL-a	2	6	3	4	0	0	0	2	1		.667	.750	.667	1417	278	2	0			.750	-0	/3-2	0.1
1891	Cin-a	1	4	0	1	0	0	0	0	0	2	.250	.250	.250	500	40	-0	0			1.000	1	/2-1	0.1
Total	2	3	10	3	5	0	0	0	3	1	2	.500	.583	.500	1083	192	1	0			.750	1	/3-2,2-1	0.2
■ LEO BURKE Burke, Leo Patrick b: 5/6/34, Hagerstown, Md. BR/TR, 5'10", 190 lbs. Deb: 9/7/58 Career OF: (7-LF 1-CF 37-RF)																								
1958	Bal-A	7	11	4	5	1	0	1	4	1	2	.455	.500	.818	1318	271	2	0	0	0	1.000	-2	/O-3(1-1-1),3-1	0.1
1959	Bal-A	5	10	0	2	0	0	0	1	0	5	.200	.273	.200	473	33	-1	0	0	0	1.000	-2	/2-2,3-2	-0.3

YEAR	TM/L	G	AB	R	H	2B	3B	HR	RBI	BB	SO	AVG	OBP	SLG	OPS	OPS+	BR+	SB	CS	SBR	FA	FR	G/POS	TPR
1961	LA-A	6	5	0	0	0	0	0	0	0	1	.000	.000	.000	0	-90	-1	0	0	0	.000	0	H	-0.1
1962	LA-A	19	64	8	17	1	0	4	14	5	11	.266	.329	.469	797	115	1	0	0	0	.958	-1	O-12(4-0-8)/3-4,S-1	-0.1
1963	StL-N	30	49	6	10	2	1	1	5	4	12	.204	.264	.347	611	68	-2	0	0	0	1.000	-2	O-11(2-0-9)/3-5	-0.5
	Chi-N	27	49	4	9	0	0	2	7	4	13	.184	.245	.306	551	55	-3	0	1	-0	.925	3	2-10/1-4	0.0
	Yr	57	98	10	19	2	1	3	12	8	25	.194	.255	.327	581	61	-5	0	1	-0	1.000	1	O-11R,2-10/3-5,1-4	-0.5
1964	Chi-N	59	103	11	27	3	1	1	14	7	31	.262	.315	.340	655	81	-2	0	0	0	1.000	-2	O-18R/2-5,3-4,1C	-0.5
1965	Chi-N	12	10	0	2	0	0	0	0	0	4	.200	.200	.200	400	13	-1	0	0	0	1.000	-0	/C-2,O-1(0-0-1)	-0.1
Total	7	165	301	33	72	7	2	9	45	21	79	.239	.295	.365	661	81	-7	0	1	-0	.985	-6	/O-45R,2-17,3-16,1CS	-1.5
■ LES BURKE Burke, Leslie Kingston "Buck" b: 12/18/02, Lynn, Mass. d: 5/6/75, Danvers, Mass. BL/TR, 5'9", 168 lbs. Deb: 5/2/23																								
1923	Det-A	7	10	2	1	0	0	0	2	0	1	.100	.100	.100	200	-48	-2	0	0	0	.500	-1	/3-2,2-1	-0.3
1924	Det-A	72	241	30	61	10	4	0	17	22	20	.253	.321	.328	649	69	-11	2	4	-1	.957	-6	2-58/S-6	-1.6
1925	Det-A	77	180	32	52	6	3	0	24	17	8	.289	.357	.356	712	82	-4	4	1	1	.962	2	2-52	-0.1
1926	Det-A	38	75	9	17	1	0	0	4	7	3	.227	.301	.240	541	42	-6	1	2	-0	.942	4	2-15/3-7,S-1	-0.2
Total	4	194	506	73	131	17	7	0	47	46	32	.259	.327	.320	647	67	-24	7	7	-1	.958	-1	2-126/3-9,S-7	-2.2
■ MIKE BURKE Burke, Michael E. b: Cincinnati, Ohio d: 6/9/1889, Albany, N.Y. BR/TR, 6', 190 lbs. Deb: 5/1/1879																								
1879	Cin-N	28	117	13	26	3	0	0	8	2	5	.222	.235	.248	483	63	-4				.786	-8	S-19/O-5(0-1-4),3-5	-1.0
■ PAT BURKE Burke, Patrick Edward b: 5/13/01, St.Louis, Mo. d: 7/7/65, St.Louis, Mo. BR/TR, 5'10.5", 170 lbs. Deb: 9/23/24																								
1924	StL-A	1	3	0	0	0	0	0	1	0	0	.000	.000	.000	0	-94	-1	0	0	0	.000	0	/3-1	-0.1
■ JESSE BURKETT Burkett, Jesse Cail "Crab" b: 12/4/1868, Wheeling, W.Va. d: 5/27/53, Worcester, Mass. BL/TL, 5'8", 155 lbs. Deb: 4/22/1890 CH Career OF: (1936-LF 7-CF 115-RF)																								
1890	NY-N	101	401	67	124	23	13	4	60	33	52	.309	.366	.461	827	140	19	14			.824	3	O-90(11-2-77),P-21	1.4
1891	Cle-N	40	167	29	45	7	4	0	13	23	19	.269	.358	.359	717	105	1	1			.892	-3	O-40(6-2-35)	-0.2
1892	*Cle-N	145	608	119	167	15	14	6	66	67	59	.275	.348	.375	723	114	10	36			.904	3	*O-145(145-0-0)	-0.1
1893	Cle-N	125	511	145	178	25	15	6	82	98	23	.348	.459	.491	951	144	35	39			.849	-8	*O-125(125-0-0)	1.3
1894	Cle-N	125	523	138	187	27	14	8	94	84	27	.358	.447	.509	956	125	23	28			.915	-4	*O-125(125-0-0)/P-1	0.6
1895	*Cle-N	132	555	153	**225**	22	13	5	83	74	32	**.405**	.482	.519	1001	149	44	41			.884	-3	*O-132(131-0-1)	2.3
1896	*Cle-N	133	586	**160**	**240**	27	16	6	72	49	19	**.410**	.461	.541	1002	155	46	34			.926	-2	*O-133(133-0-0)	2.7
1897	Cle-N	127	517	129	198	28	7	2	60	76		.383	.468	.476	944	142	35	28			.949	-2	*O-127(127-1-0)	1.9
1898	Cle-N	150	624	114	213	18	9	0	42	69		.341	.415	.399	814	135	32	19			.938	-8	*O-150(148-1-1)	1.0
1899	StL-N	141	558	116	221	21	8	7	71	67		.396	.463	.500	963	160	48	25			.938	-3	*O-140(139-0-1)/2-1	2.9
1900	StL-N	141	559	88	203	11	15	7	68	62		.363	.429	.474	904	150	40	32			.934	4	*O-141(140-1-0)	2.8
1901	StL-N	142	601	**142**	**226**	20	15	10	75	59		**.376**	**.440**	.509	949	**184**	**66**	27			.923	-1	*O-142(142-0-0)	5.5
1902	StL-A	138	553	97	169	29	9	5	52	71		.306	.390	.418	807	126	22	23			.924	6	*O-137L/P-1,S-1,3-1	1.8
1903	StL-A	132	515	73	151	20	7	3	40	52		.293	.361	.377	738	125	17	17			.941	-4	*O-132(132-0-0)	0.6
1904	StL-A	147	575	72	156	15	10	2	27	78		.271	.363	.343	706	132	25	12			.942	5	*O-147(147-0-0)	2.4
1905	Bos-A	148	573	78	147	12	13	4	47	67		.257	.339	.344	682	115	11	13			.929	-2	*O-148(148-0-0)	0.1
Total	16	2067	8426	1720	2850	320	182	75	952	1029	231	.338	.415	.446	861	140	475	389			.917	-19	*O-2054L/P-23,3-1,S2	27.0
■ MORGAN BURKHART Burkhart, Morgan b: 1/29/72, St.Louis, Mo. BB/TL, 5'11", 225 lbs. Deb: 6/27/2000																								
2000	Bos-A	25	73	16	21	3	0	4	18	17	25	.288	.447	.493	940	132	5	0	0	0	.964	-1	D-19/1-5,O-1(1-0-0)	0.2
■ ELLIS BURKS Burks, Ellis Rena b: 9/11/64, Vicksburg, Miss. BR/TR, 6'2", 205 lbs. Deb: 4/30/87 Career OF: (263-LF 1062-CF 358-RF)																								
1987	Bos-A	133	558	94	152	30	2	20	59	41	98	.272	.324	.441	765	98	-3	27	6	4	.988	14	*O-132(0-132-0)/D-1	1.4
1988	*Bos-A	144	540	93	159	37	5	18	92	62	89	.294	.370	.481	852	131	23	25	9	2	.977	12	*O-142(0-142-0)/D-2	3.5
1989	Bos-A	97	399	73	121	19	6	12	61	36	52	.303	.368	.471	839	127	14	21	5	3	.977	7	O-95(0-96-0)/D-1	2.3
1990	*Bos-A†	152	588	89	174	33	8	21	89	48	82	.296	.350	.486	836	126	19	9	11	-2	.994	2	*O-143(0-143-0)/D-6	1.8
1991	Bos-A	130	474	56	119	33	3	14	56	39	81	.251	.316	.422	738	97	-2	6	11	-3	.993	-3	*O-126(0-126-0)/D-2	-0.9
1992	Bos-A	66	235	35	60	8	3	8	30	25	48	.255	.330	.417	747	101	0	5	2	0	.984	-7	O-63(0-63-0)/D-1	-0.7
1993	*Chi-A	146	499	75	137	24	4	17	74	60	97	.275	.357	.441	798	116	11	6	9	-2	.982	0	*O-146(0-21-132)	0.3
1994	Col-N	42	149	33	48	8	3	13	24	16	39	.322	.388	.678	1066	147	10	3	1	0	.964	-2	O-39(0-39-0)	0.8
1995	*Col-N	103	278	41	74	10	6	14	49	39	72	.266	.361	.496	857	96	-1	7	3	0	.970	-4	O-80(23-65-1)	-0.5
1996	Col-N★	156	613	**142**	211	45	8	40	128	61	114	.344	.409	**.639**	1048	138	34	32	6	5	.983	2	*O-152(129-32-0)	3.6
1997	Col-N	119	424	91	123	19	2	32	82	47	75	.290	.365	.571	936	114	9	7	2	1	.982	-18	*O-112(66-89-0)	-1.0
1998	Col-N	100	357	54	102	22	5	16	54	39	80	.286	.359	.510	869	103	2	3	7	-2	.975	-11	O-98(45-78-0)	-1.1
	SF-N	42	147	22	45	6	1	5	22	19	31	.306	.396	.463	859	133	8	8	1	1	.989	-2	O-41(0-36-10)	0.7
	Yr	142	504	76	147	28	6	21	76	58	111	.292	.370	.496	866	110	8	11	8	-0	.979	-13	*O-139(45-114-10)	-0.4
1999	SF-N	120	390	73	110	19	0	31	96	69	86	.282	.398	.569	967	152	32	7	5	-0	.991	2	*O-107(0-0-107)/D-3	2.7
2000	*SF-N	122	393	74	135	21	5	24	96	56	49	.344	.427	.606	1032	168	42	5	1	1	.982	3	*O-108(0-0-108)/D-2	3.7
Total	14	1672	6044	1045	1770	334	61	285	1012	657	1093	.293	.366	.510	876	122	196	171	79	10	.983	-6	*O-1584C/D-18	16.6
■ RICK BURLESON Burleson, Richard Paul "Rooster" b: 4/29/51, Lynwood, Cal. BR/TR, 5'10", 165 lbs. Deb: 5/4/74 C																								
1974	Bos-A	114	384	36	109	22	0	4	44	21	34	.284	.324	.372	697	93	-3	3	3	-0	.957	-5	S-88,2-31/3-2	0.3
1975	*Bos-A	158	580	66	146	25	1	6	62	45	44	.252	.309	.329	638	74	-20	8	5	0	.963	-1	*S-158	-0.1
1976	Bos-A	152	540	75	157	27	1	7	42	60	37	.291	.367	.383	750	107	6	14	9	-0	.957	-7	*S-152	1.9
1977	Bos-A★	154	663	80	194	36	7	3	52	47	69	.293	.341	.382	723	87	-11	13	12	-1	.970	12	*S-154	1.6
1978	Bos-A†	145	626	75	155	32	5	5	49	40	71	.248	.297	.339	636	71	-24	8	8	-1	.981	19	*S-144	1.0
1979	Bos-A★	153	627	93	174	32	5	5	60	35	54	.278	.319	.368	687	80	-17	9	5	0	**.980**	22	*S-153	2.0
1980	Bos-A	155	644	89	179	29	2	8	51	62	51	.278	.343	.366	710	90	-8	12	13	-2	.974	26	*S-155	3.2
1981	Cal-A★	109	430	53	126	17	1	5	33	42	38	.293	.360	.372	732	111	7	4	6	-1	.979	21	*S-109	4.0
1982	Cal-A	11	45	4	7	1	0	0	2	6	3	.156	.255	.178	433	21	-5	0	0	0	.986	7	S-11	0.4
1983	Cal-A	33	119	22	34	7	0	0	11	12	12	.286	.351	.345	696	93	-1	0	2	-1	.969	-0	S-31	0.1
1984	Cal-A	7	4	2	0	0	0	0	0	0	2	.000	.000	.000	0	-99	-1	0	0	0	.000	0	/H	-0.1
1986	*Cal-A	93	271	35	77	14	0	5	29	33	32	.284	.364	.391	755	107	3	1	3	-1	.984	-7	D-38,S-37/2-6,3-4	-0.2
1987	Bal-A	62	206	26	43	14	1	2	14	17	30	.209	.279	.316	594	59	-12	0	2	-1	.977	-1	2-55/D-7	-1.1
Total	13	1346	5139	656	1401	256	23	50	449	420	477	.273	.331	.361	692	87	-85	72	68	-8	.971	86	*S-1192/2-92,D-45,3	13.0
■ HERCULES BURNETT Burnett, Hercules H. b: 8/13/1865, Louisville, Ky. d: 10/4/36, Louisville, Ky. BR, 177 lbs. Deb: 6/26/1888																								
1888	Lou-a	1	4	1	0	0	0	0	0	1		.000	.200	.000	200	-34	-1	1			.667	-0	/O-1(0-0-1)	-0.1
1895	Lou-N	5	17	6	7	0	1	2	3	2	2	.412	.474	.882	1356	261	4	2			.769	-0	/O-4(0-4-0),1-1	0.3
Total	2	6	21	7	7	0	1	2	3	3	2	.333	.417	.714	1131	211	3	3			.750	-1	/O-5(0-4-1),1-1	0.2
■ JOHNNY BURNETT Burnett, John Henderson b: 11/1/04, Bartow, Fla. d: 8/13/59, Tampa, Fla. BL/TR, 5'11", 175 lbs. Deb: 5/7/27																								
1927	Cle-A	17	8	5	0	0	0	0	0	0	3	.000	.000	.000	0	-99	-2	1	0	0	.833	2	/2-2	0.0
1928	Cle-A	3	10	3	5	0	0	0	1	0	1	.500	.500	.500	1000	162	1	0	0	0	.867	0	/S-2	0.1
1929	Cle-A	19	33	2	5	1	0	0	2	1	2	.152	.200	.182	382	-1	-5	0	0	0	.923	6	S-10/2-8	0.1
1930	Cle-A	54	170	28	53	13	0	0	20	17	8	.312	.378	.388	766	91	-2	2	2	-0	.973	-5	3-27,S-19	-0.3
1931	Cle-A	111	427	85	128	25	5	1	52	39	25	.300	.360	.389	749	92	-5	5	2	0	.938	-15	S-63,2-35,3-21,/O-1R	-1.2
1932	Cle-A	129	512	81	152	23	5	4	53	46	27	.297	.359	.385	744	87	-9	2	5	-1	.946	-22	*S-103,2-26	-2.2
1933	Cle-A	83	261	39	71	11	2	1	29	23	14	.272	.333	.341	674	76	-9	3	2	-0	.938	-5	S-41,2-17,3-12	-0.9
1934	Cle-A	72	208	28	61	11	2	3	30	18	11	.293	.352	.409	761	94	-2	1	1	-0	.981	-8	3-42/S-9,2-3,O-2L	-0.7
1935	StL-A	70	206	17	46	10	1	0	26	19	16	.223	.289	.282	570	46	-17	1	0	0	.939	-6	3-31,S-18,2-12	-1.8
Total	9	558	1835	288	521	94	15	9	213	163	107	.284	.345	.366	712	81	-49	15	12	-1	.935	-53	S-265,3-133,2-103,/O	-6.9
■ JACK BURNETT Burnett, John P. b: 12/2/1889, Missouri d: 9/8/29, Taft, Cal. Deb: 7/2/07																								
1907	StL-N	59	206	18	49	8	4	0	12	15		.238	.296	.316	611	95	-2	5			.955	-4	O-59(0-59-0)	-1.0
■ JEROMY BURNITZ Burnitz, Jeromy Neal b: 4/15/69, Westminster, Cal. BL/TR, 6', 190 lbs. Deb: 6/21/93																								
1993	NY-N	86	263	49	64	10	6	13	38	38	66	.243	.341	.475	816	117	6	3	6	-1	.977	2	O-79(0-20-61)	0.4

YEAR	TM/L	G	AB	R	H	2B	3B	HR	RBI	BB	SO	AVG	OBP	SLG	OPS	OPS+	BR+	SB	CS	SBR	FA	FR	G/POS	TPR
1994	NY-N	45	143	26	34	4	0	3	15	23	45	.238	.347	.329	676	78	-4	1	1	-0	.970	-5	O-42(0-0-42)	-1.1
1995	Cle-A	9	7	4	4	1	0	0	0	0	0	.571	.571	.714	1286	229	1	0	0	0	1.000	-1	/O-6(5-1-0),D-2	0.1
1996	Cle-A	71	128	30	36	10	0	7	26	25	31	.281	.406	.523	930	133	7	2	1	0	1.000	-4	O-30(10-6-14),D-15	0.2
	Mil-A	23	72	8	17	4	0	2	14	8	16	.236	.329	.375	704	75	-3	2	0	0	.975	-2	O-22(0-8-14)	-0.4
	Yr	94	200	38	53	14	0	9	40	33	47	.265	.380	.470	850	113	4	4	1	1	.988	-6	O-52(10-14-28),D-15	-0.2
1997	Mil-A	153	494	85	139	37	8	27	85	75	111	.281	.382	.553	934	139	28	20	13	-0	.975	-4	*O-149(5-26-124)	1.7
1998	Mil-N	161	609	92	160	28	1	38	125	70	158	.263	.343	.499	842	118	14	7	4	0	.972	7	*O-161(0-1-161)	1.2
1999	Mil-N★	130	467	87	126	33	2	33	103	91	124	.270	.406	.561	967	143	33	7	3	0	.982	7	*O-127(0-0-127)/D-3	3.1
2000	Mil-N	161	564	91	131	29	2	31	98	99	121	.232	.360	.456	816	106	6	6	4	-0	.979	6	*O-158(0-0-158)/D-1	0.4
Total	8	839	2747	472	711	156	19	154	504	429	672	.259	.368	.498	866	121	90	48	32	-1	.977	8	O-774(20-62-701)/D-21	5.6

■ C.B. BURNS Burns, Charles Birmingham b: 5/15/1879, Bay View, Md. d: 6/6/68, Havre De Grace, Md BR/TR, 6', 175 lbs. Deb: 8/19/02

YEAR	TM/L	G	AB	R	H	2B	3B	HR	RBI	BB	SO	AVG	OBP	SLG	OPS	OPS+	BR+	SB	CS	SBR	FA	FR	G/POS	TPR
1902	Bal-A	1	1	0	1	0	0	0	0	0		1.000	1.000	1.000	2000	436	0	0			.000	0	H	0.0

■ ED BURNS Burns, Edward James b: 10/31/1888, San Francisco, Cal d: 6/1/42, Monterey, Cal. BR/TR, 5'6", 165 lbs. Deb: 6/25/12

YEAR	TM/L	G	AB	R	H	2B	3B	HR	RBI	BB	SO	AVG	OBP	SLG	OPS	OPS+	BR+	SB	CS	SBR	FA	FR	G/POS	TPR
1912	StL-N	1	1	0	0	0	0	0	1	0	0	.000	.000	.000	0	-99	-0	0			.000	0	/C-1	0.0
1913	Phi-N	17	30	3	6	3	0	0	3	6	3	.200	.351	.300	651	83	-0	2			.980	-4	C-15	-0.4
1914	Phi-N	70	139	8	36	3	4	0	16	20	12	.259	.352	.338	690	99	0	5			.947	-2	C-55	0.2
1915	*Phi-N	67	174	11	42	5	0	0	16	20	12	.241	.327	.270	597	81	-3	1			.981	-6	C-62	-0.5
1916	Phi-N	78	219	14	51	8	1	0	14	16	18	.233	.294	.279	573	74	-6	3			.981	-12	C-75/S-1,O-1(0-1-0)	-1.4
1917	Phi-N	20	49	2	10	1	0	0	6	1	5	.204	.220	.224	444	35	-4	2			.971	-1	C-15	-0.4
1918	Phi-N	68	184	10	38	1	1	0	9	20	9	.207	.288	.223	511	53	-10	1			.981	-4	C-68	-1.0
Total	7	321	796	48	183	21	6	0	65	83	59	.230	.308	.271	579	73	-23	14			.974	-29	C-291/O-1(0-1-0),S-1	-3.5

■ GEORGE BURNS Burns, George Henry "Tioga George" b: 1/31/1893, Niles, Ohio d: 1/7/78, Kirkland, Wash. BR/TR, 6'1.5", 180 lbs. Deb: 4/14/14

YEAR	TM/L	G	AB	R	H	2B	3B	HR	RBI	BB	SO	AVG	OBP	SLG	OPS	OPS+	BR+	SB	CS	SBR	FA	FR	G/POS	TPR
1914	Det-A	137	478	55	139	22	5	5	57	32	56	.291	.351	.389	740	119	10	23	13	1	.982	-5	*1-137	0.2
1915	Det-A	105	392	49	99	18	3	5	50	22	51	.253	.301	.352	653	91	-6	9	3	1	.986	-4	*1-104	-1.2
1916	Det-A	135	479	60	137	22	6	4	73	22	30	.286	.327	.382	709	109	3	12			.985	-10	*1-124	-1.1
1917	Det-A	119	407	42	92	14	10	1	40	15	33	.226	.264	.317	581	77	-13	3			.990	-4	*1-104	-2.2
1918	Phi-A	130	505	61	**178**	22	9	6	70	23	25	.352	.390	.467	857	157	32	8			.983	6	*1-128/O-2(1-0-1)	3.8
1919	Phi-A	126	470	63	139	29	9	8	57	19	18	.296	.339	.447	786	118	9	15			.980	2	1-86,O-34(0-0-34)	0.8
1920	Phi-A	22	60	1	14	3	0	1	7	6	7	.233	.313	.333	647	71	-3	4	0	1	.958	1	O-13(0-0-13)	-0.2
	*Cle-A	44	56	7	15	4	1	0	13	4	3	.268	.339	.375	714	86	-1	1	0	0	.979	1	1-12/O-1(0-0-1)	0.0
	Yr	66	116	8	29	7	1	1	20	10	10	.250	.326	.353	679	78	-4	5	0	1	.958	1	O-14(0-0-14),1-12	-0.2
1921	Cle-A	84	244	52	88	21	4	0	49	13	19	.361	.398	.480	877	121	7	3	1	0	.990	2	1-73	0.5
1922	Bos-A	147	558	71	171	32	5	12	73	20	28	.306	.341	.446	787	104	1	8	2	1	.987	-1	*1-140	-0.7
1923	Bos-A	146	551	91	181	47	5	7	82	45	33	.328	.386	.470	856	124	18	9	7	-0	.990	-1	*1-146	0.7
1924	Cle-A	129	462	64	143	37	5	4	68	29	27	.310	.370	.437	807	106	4	14	5	1	.987	8	*1-127	0.5
1925	Cle-A	127	488	69	164	41	4	6	79	24	24	.336	.371	.473	844	112	7	16	11	-0	.989	-1	*1-126	-0.2
1926	Cle-A	151	603	97	**216**	**64**	3	4	114	28	33	.358	.394	.494	889	130	24	13	7	0	.988	1	*1-151	1.5
1927	Cle-A	140	549	84	175	51	2	3	78	42	27	.319	.375	.435	810	109	7	13	11	-1	.990	3	*1-139	0.0
1928	Cle-A	82	209	29	52	12	1	5	30	17	11	.249	.323	.388	711	85	-5	2	3	-1	.984	2	1-53	-0.6
	NY-A	4	4	1	2	0	0	0	0	0	1	.500	.500	.500	1000	169	0	0	0	0	1.000	-0	/1-2	0.0
	Yr	86	213	30	54	12	1	5	30	17	12	.254	.326	.390	716	87	-4	2	3	-1	.985	2	1-55	-0.6
1929	NY-A	9	9	0	0	0	0	0	0	0	4	.000	.000	.000	0	-99	-3	0	0	0	.000	0	H	-0.3
	*Phi-A	29	49	5	13	5	0	1	11	2	3	.265	.294	.429	723	81	-2	1	0	0	1.000	-0	1-19	-0.2
	Yr	38	58	5	13	5	0	1	11	2	7	.224	.250	.362	612	55	-4	1	0	0	1.000	-0	1-19	-0.5
Total	16	1866	6573	901	2018	444	72	72	951	363	433	.307	.354	.429	783	112	92	154	63		.987	0	*1-1671/O-50(1-0-49)	1.3

■ GEORGE BURNS Burns, George Joseph b: 11/24/1889, Utica, N.Y. d: 8/15/66, Gloversville, N.Y. BR/TR, 5'7", 160 lbs. Deb: 10/3/11 C Career OF: (1262-LF 186-CF 406-RF)

YEAR	TM/L	G	AB	R	H	2B	3B	HR	RBI	BB	SO	AVG	OBP	SLG	OPS	OPS+	BR+	SB	CS	SBR	FA	FR	G/POS	TPR
1911	NY-N	6	17	2	1	0	0	0	0	1	0	.059	.111	.059	170	-50	-3	0			1.000	-2	/O-6(1-4-1)	-0.5
1912	NY-N	29	51	11	15	4	0	0	3	8	8	.294	.400	.373	773	109	1	7			1.000	-4	O-23(13-5-5)	-0.4
1913	*NY-N	150	605	81	173	37	4	2	54	58	74	.286	.352	.370	723	106	5	40			.963	7	*O-150(119-0-32)	0.5
1914	NY-N	154	561	**100**	170	35	10	3	60	89	53	.303	.403	.417	820	149	**38**	**62**			.950	8	*O-154(102-0-54)	4.1
1915	NY-N	155	622	83	169	27	14	3	51	56	57	.272	.333	.375	707	121	15	27	20	-1	.960	-6	*O-155(140-0-15)	0.1
1916	NY-N	155	623	**105**	174	24	8	5	41	63	47	.279	.346	.368	714	126	20	37	26	-1	.962	3	*O-155(155-0-0)	1.7
1917	*NY-N	152	597	**103**	180	25	13	5	45	**75**	55	.302	.380	.412	792	148	35	40			.974	5	*O-152(152-0-0)	3.7
1918	NY-N	119	465	80	135	22	6	4	51	43	37	.290	.354	.389	743	129	16	40			.965	9	*O-119(119-0-0)	2.2
1919	NY-N	139	534	**86**	162	30	9	2	46	**82**	37	.303	**.396**	.404	801	142	31	**40**			**.990**	1	*O-139(139-0-0)	2.8
1920	NY-N	154	631	**115**	181	35	9	6	46	**76**	48	.287	.365	.399	765	121	19	22	22	-3	.983	1	*O-154(154-1-0)	1.1
1921	*NY-N	149	605	111	181	28	9	4	61	**80**	24	.299	.386	.395	781	107	9	19	20	-3	.972	3	*O-149(90-59-0)/3-1	0.0
1922	Cin-N	156	631	104	180	20	10	1	53	78	38	.285	.366	.353	719	88	-9	30	23	-1	.976	6	*O-156(0-109-47)	-1.2
1923	Cin-N	154	614	99	168	27	13	3	45	**101**	46	.274	.376	.375	751	101	4	12	14	-2	.960	-1	*O-154(0-3-151)	-1.2
1924	Cin-N	93	336	43	86	19	2	2	33	29	21	.256	.315	.342	657	77	-11	3	6	-1	.963	1	O-90(12-1-79)	-1.8
1925	Phi-N	88	349	65	102	29	1	1	22	33	20	.292	.353	.390	743	82	-9	4	8	-2	.990	0	O-88(66-4-22)	-1.6
Total	15	1853	7241	1188	2077	362	108	41	611	872	565	.287	.366	.384	749	115	162	383	139		.970	32	*O-1844L/3-1	9.5

■ JIM BURNS Burns, James M. b: Quincy, Ill. 5'7", 168 lbs. Deb: 9/25/1888 Career OF: (15-LF 139-CF 16-RF)

YEAR	TM/L	G	AB	R	H	2B	3B	HR	RBI	BB	SO	AVG	OBP	SLG	OPS	OPS+	BR+	SB	CS	SBR	FA	FR	G/POS	TPR
1888	KC-a	15	66	13	20	0	0	0	4	1		.303	.343	.303	646	101	0	6			.853	2	O-15(15-0-0)	0.1
1889	KC-a	134	579	103	176	23	11	5	97	20	68	.304	.335	.408	743	105	0	56			.913	-7	*O-134(0-134-0)/3-1	-1.0
1891	Was-a	20	82	15	26	6	0	0	10	6	10	.317	.378	.390	768	126	3	2			.771	-4	O-20(0-5-16)/S-1	-0.1
Total	3	169	727	131	222	29	11	5	111	27	78	.305	.341	.396	737	107	3	64			.897	-9	O-169C/S-1,3-1	-1.0

■ JACK BURNS Burns, John Irving "Slug" b: 8/31/07, Cambridge, Mass. d: 4/18/75, Brighton, Mass. BL/TL, 5'10.5", 175 lbs. Deb: 9/17/30 C

YEAR	TM/L	G	AB	R	H	2B	3B	HR	RBI	BB	SO	AVG	OBP	SLG	OPS	OPS+	BR+	SB	CS	SBR	FA	FR	G/POS	TPR
1930	StL-A	8	30	5	9	3	0	0	2	5	5	.300	.400	.400	800	100	0	0	0	0	1.000	1	/1-8	0.0
1931	StL-A	144	570	75	148	27	7	4	70	42	58	.260	.312	.353	664	72	-24	19	12	-0	.993	18	*1-143	-1.8
1932	StL-A	150	617	111	188	33	8	11	70	61	43	.305	.368	.438	806	102	2	17	11	-0	.992	4	*1-150	-0.8
1933	StL-A	144	556	89	160	43	4	7	71	56	51	.288	.353	.417	770	97	-3	11	11	-1	.992	3	*1-143	-1.4
1934	StL-A	154	612	86	157	28	8	13	73	62	47	.257	.327	.392	719	78	-21	9	3	1	.992	-0	*1-154	-3.3
1935	StL-A	143	549	77	157	28	1	5	67	68	49	.286	.366	.368	734	86	-10	3	2	-0	.992	-8	*1-141	-2.9
1936	StL-A	9	14	2	3	1	0	0	1	3	1	.214	.353	.286	639	58	-1	0	0	0	1.000	0	/1-2	-0.1
	Det-A	138	558	96	158	36	3	4	63	79	45	.283	.375	.380	755	87	-10	4	8	-2	.994	1	*1-138	-2.2
	Yr	147	572	98	161	37	3	4	64	82	46	.281	.374	.378	752	86	-11	4	8	-2	.994	1	*1-140	-2.3
Total	7	890	3506	541	980	199	31	44	417	376	299	.280	.351	.392	742	87	-66	63	47	-3	.992	19	1-879	-12.5

■ JACK BURNS Burns, John Joseph b: 5/13/1880, Avoca, Pa. d: 6/24/57, Waterford, Conn. BR/TR, 5'10", 160 lbs. Deb: 9/11/03

YEAR	TM/L	G	AB	R	H	2B	3B	HR	RBI	BB	SO	AVG	OBP	SLG	OPS	OPS+	BR+	SB	CS	SBR	FA	FR	G/POS	TPR
1903	Det-A	11	37	2	10	0	0	0	3	1		.270	.325	.270	595	82	-1	0			.981	1	2-11	0.0
1904	Det-A	4	16	3	2	0	0	0	1	1		.125	.176	.125	301	-4	-2	1			.952	-1	/2-4	-0.4
Total	2	15	53	5	12	0	0	0	4	2		.226	.281	.226	507	57	-3	1			.973	-1	/2-15	-0.4

■ JOE BURNS Burns, Joseph Francis b: 3/26/1889, Ipswich, Mass. d: 7/12/87, Beverly, Mass. BL/TL, 5'11", 170 lbs. Deb: 6/19/10

YEAR	TM/L	G	AB	R	H	2B	3B	HR	RBI	BB	SO	AVG	OBP	SLG	OPS	OPS+	BR+	SB	CS	SBR	FA	FR	G/POS	TPR
1910	Cin-N	1	1	0	1	0	0	0	0	0	0	1.000	1.000	1.000	2000	506	0	1			.000	0	H	0.1
1913	Det-A	4	13	0	5	0	0	0	1	2	4	.385	.500	.385	885	162	1	0			1.000	-1	/O-4(4-0-0)	0.1
Total	2	5	14	0	6	0	0	0	1	2	4	.429	.529	.429	958	184	2	1			1.000	-1	/O-4(4-0-0)	0.2

■ JOE BURNS Burns, Joseph Francis b: 2/25/1900, Trenton, N.J. d: 1/7/86, Trenton, N.J. BR/TR, 6', 175 lbs. Deb: 4/18/24

YEAR	TM/L	G	AB	R	H	2B	3B	HR	RBI	BB	SO	AVG	OBP	SLG	OPS	OPS+	BR+	SB	CS	SBR	FA	FR	G/POS	TPR
1924	Chi-A	8	19	1	2	0	0	0	0	0	2	.105	.105	.105	211	-47	-4	0	0	0	.933	-2	/C-6	-0.6

■ JOE BURNS Burns, Joseph James b: 6/17/16, Bryn Mawr, Pa. d: 6/24/74, Bryn Mawr, Pa. BR/TR, 5'10.5", 175 lbs. Deb: 4/24/43 Career OF: (1-LF 1-CF 21-RF)

YEAR	TM/L	G	AB	R	H	2B	3B	HR	RBI	BB	SO	AVG	OBP	SLG	OPS	OPS+	BR+	SB	CS	SBR	FA	FR	G/POS	TPR
1943	Bos-N	52	135	12	28	3	0	1	5	8	25	.207	.262	.252	514	49	-9	2			.933	-1	3-34/O-4(1-1-2)	-1.0
1944	Phi-A	28	75	5	18	2	0	1	8	4	8	.240	.278	.307	585	68	-3	0	1	-0	.919	-8	3-17/2-9	-1.2

YEAR	TM/L	G	AB	R	H	2B	3B	HR	RBI	BB	SO	AVG	OBP	SLG	OPS	OPS+	BR+	SB	CS	SBR	FA	FR	G/POS	TPR
1945	Phi-A	31	90	7	23	1	1	0	3	4	17	.256	.287	.289	576	68	-4	0	1	-0	1.000	-4	O-19(0-0-19)/3-5,1-1	-1.0
Total	3	111	300	24	69	6	1	2	16	16	50	.230	.274	.277	550	60	-16	2	2		.920	-12	/3-56,O-23R,2-9,1-1	-3.2
■ PAT BURNS Burns, Patrick Deb: 8/11/1884																								
1884	Bal-a	6	25	3	5	2	1	0		3		.200	.286	.360	646	105	0				.953	-1	/1-6	-0.1
	Bal-U	1	4	0	2	0	0	0		0		.500	.500	.500	1000	185	0				.917	-0	/1-1	0.0
Total	1	7	29	3	7	2	1	0		3		.241	.313	.379	692	117	0				.947	-1	/1-7	-0.1
■ DICK BURNS Burns, Richard Simon b: 12/26/1863, Holyoke, Mass. d: 11/16/37, Holyoke, Mass. BL/TL, 5'7", 140 lbs. Deb: 5/3/1883 Career OF: (7-LF 48-CF 30-RF)																								
1883	Det-N	37	140	11	26	7	1	0	5	2	22	.186	.197	.250	447	36	-10				.758	-6	O-24(1-1-23),P-17	-1.0
1884	Cin-U	79	350	84	107	17	**12**	4		5		.306	.315	.457	773	122	-2				.827	-3	O-44(6-33-7),P-40/S-2	-0.5
1885	StL-N	14	54	2	12	2	1	0	4	3	8	.222	.263	.296	559	86	-1				.682	-3	O-14(0-14-0)/P-1	-0.5
Total	3	130	544	97	145	26	14	4	9	10	30	.267	.280	.388	668	98	-13				.785	-12	/O-82C,P-58,S-2	-2.0
■ TOM BURNS Burns, Thomas Everett b: 3/30/1857, Honesdale, Pa. d: 3/19/02, Jersey City, N.J. BR/TR, 5'7", 152 lbs. Deb: 5/1/1880 MU																								
1880	Chi-N	85	333	47	103	17	3	0	43	12	23	.309	.333	.378	712	133	10				.864	-24	*S-79/3-9,C-2,P-1	-1.0
1881	Chi-N	84	342	41	95	20	3	4	42	14	22	.278	.306	.389	695	112	4				.870	-5	*S-80/3-3,2-3	0.2
1882	Chi-N	84	355	55	88	23	6	0	48	15	28	.248	.278	.346	625	95	-3				.911	0	2-43,S-41	0.0
1883	Chi-N	97	405	69	119	37	7	2	67	13	31	.294	.316	.435	750	116	6				.872	-1	*S-79,2-19/O-1(1-0-0)	0.7
1884	Chi-N	83	343	54	84	14	2	7	44	13	50	.245	.272	.359	631	89	-5				.838	-2	*S-80/3-3	-0.4
1885	*Chi-N	111	445	82	121	23	9	7	71	16	48	.272	.297	.411	708	112	3				.844	-2	*S-111/2-1	0.4
1886	*Chi-N	112	445	64	123	18	10	3	65	14	40	.276	.298	.382	680	92	-7	15			.890	13	*3-112	0.8
1887	Chi-N	115	458	57	146	20	10	3	60	34	32	.319	.320	.380	700	83	-12	32			.872	21	*3-107/O-8(6-2-0)	0.9
1888	Chi-N	134	483	60	115	12	6	3	70	26	49	.238	.281	.306	588	81	-11	34			.905	17	*3-134	0.9
1889	Chi-N	136	525	64	127	27	6	4	66	32	57	.242	.288	.339	627	71	-22	18			.880	3	*3-136	-1.5
1890	Chi-N	139	538	86	149	17	6	5	86	57	45	.277	.348	.359	707	102	1	44			.898	2	*3-139	0.5
1891	Chi-N	59	243	36	55	8	1	1	17	21	21	.226	.288	.280	568	66	-11	18			.892	-2	3-53/S-4,O-2(2-0-0)	-1.0
1892	Pit-N	12	39	7	8	0	0	0	4	3	8	.205	.262	.205	467	41	-3	1			.690	-5	/3-8,O-3(1-0-2),M	-0.8
Total	13	1251	4954	722	1333	236	69	39	683	270	454	.269	.303	.364	667	95	-48	162			.886	16	3-704,S-474/2-66,OCP	-0.3
■ OYSTER BURNS Burns, Thomas P. b: 9/6/1864, Philadelphia, Pa. d: 11/11/28, Brooklyn, N.Y. BL/TR, 5'8", 183 lbs. Deb: 8/18/1884 Career OF: (100-LF 15-CF 781-RF)																								
1884	Wil-U	2	7	0	1	0	1	0		1		.143	.250	.429	679	99	-0				.778	-0	/S-2	0.0
	Bal-a	35	131	34	39	2	6	6	23	7		.298	.348	.542	890	179	11				.826	-5	O-24R,2-10/P-2,3-1	0.5
1885	Bal-a	78	321	47	74	11	6	5	37	16		.231	.280	.349	629	99	-0				.908	-0	O-45R,P-15,S-10,/321	0.0
1887	Bal-a	140	614	122	251	33	**19**	9	99	63		.409	.414	.519	933	169	53	58			.841	-19	*S-98,3-42/P-3,2-1	3.0
1888	Bal-a	79	325	54	97	18	9	4	42	24		.298	.349	.446	795	158	20	23			.855	-5	O-56L,S-23/P-5,32	1.3
	Bro-a	52	204	40	58	9	6	2	25	14		.284	.339	.417	756	142	9	21			.851	-13	S-36,O-14(0-14-0)/2-3	-0.3
	Yr	131	529	94	155	27	15	6	67	38		.293	.345	.435	780	152	30	44			.847	-18	O-70L,S-59/P-5,23	1.0
1889	*Bro-a	131	504	105	153	19	13	5	100	68	26	.304	.391	.423	813	131	22	32			.920	-8	*O-113(0-0-113),S-19	1.1
1890	*Bro-N	119	472	102	134	22	12	**13**	**128**	51	42	.284	.359	.464	823	139	21	21			.941	-3	*O-116(0-0-116)/3-3	1.5
1891	Bro-N	123	470	75	134	24	13	4	83	53	30	.285	.358	.417	775	126	15	21			.922	2	*O-113R/S-6,3-5	1.4
1892	Bro-N	141	542	88	171	27	18	4	96	65	42	.315	.395	.454	849	162	42	33			.937	-13	*O-129R/3-7,S-5	2.1
1893	Bro-N	109	415	68	112	22	8	7	60	36	16	.270	.334	.412	746	103	0	14			.932	-1	*O-108(0-1-108)/S-1	-0.5
1894	Bro-N	126	509	106	180	32	14	5	107	44	18	.354	.408	.501	909	127	23	30			.949	-4	*O-126(0-0-126)	1.0
1895	Bro-N	20	76	7	14	0	1	0	7	8	2	.184	.271	.211	481	27	-8	0			.918	1	O-19(19-0-0)	-0.7
	NY-N	33	114	21	35	5	3	1	25	14	6	.307	.388	.430	817	113	3	10			.870	-5	O-32(32-0-0)/1-1	-0.4
	Yr	53	190	28	49	5	4	1	32	22	8	.258	.341	.342	683	80	-5	10			.893	-3	O-51(51-0-0)/1-1	-1.1
Total	11	1188	4704	869	1453	224	129	65	832	464	182	.309	.368	.445	814	135	211	263			.920	-74	O-895R,S-200/3P21	10.0
■ ALEX BURR Burr, Alexander Thomson b: 11/1/1893, Chicago, Ill. d: 10/12/18, Cazaux, France BR/TR, 6'3.5", 190 lbs. Deb: 4/21/14																								
1914	NY-A	1	0	0	0	0	0	0	0	0	0	—	—	—	—	—	0	0			.000	-1	/O-1(0-1-0)	-0.1
■ BUSTER BURRELL Burrell, Frank Andrew b: 12/22/1866, Weymouth, Mass. d: 5/8/62, Weymouth, Mass. BR/TR, 5'10", 165 lbs. Deb: 8/1/1891																								
1891	NY-N	15	53	1	5	0	0	0	1	3	12	.094	.158	.094	252	-27	-8	2			.856	-5	C-15/O-1(0-1-0)	-1.2
1895	Bro-N	12	28	7	4	0	0	1	5	4	3	.143	.250	.250	500	32	-3	0			.838	-2	C-12	-0.3
1896	Bro-N	62	206	19	62	11	3	0	23	15	13	.301	.348	.383	732	98	-0	1			.928	-9	C-60	-0.3
1897	Bro-N	33	103	15	25	2	0	2	18	10		.243	.310	.320	630	70	-4	1			.884	-4	C-27/1-4	-0.5
Total	4	122	390	42	96	13	3	3	47	32	28	.246	.305	.318	623	70	-16	4			.896	-19	C-114/1-4,O-1(0-1-0)	-2.3
■ PAT BURRELL Burrell, Patrick B. b: 10/10/76, Eureka Springs, Ark. BR/TR, 6'4", 230 lbs. Deb: 5/24/2000																								
2000	Phi-N	111	408	57	106	27	1	18	79	63	139	.260	.360	.463	823	104	3	0	0	0	.988	-4	1-58,O-48(48-0-0)/D-4	-0.7
■ LARRY BURRIGHT Burright, Larry Allen "Possum" b: 7/10/37, Roseville, Ill. BR/TR, 5'11", 170 lbs. Deb: 4/12/62																								
1962	LA-N	115	249	35	51	6	5	4	30	21	67	.205	.267	.317	584	60	-15	4	3	-0	.962	14	*2-109/S-1	0.5
1963	NY-N	41	100	9	22	2	1	0	3	8	25	.220	.291	.260	551	59	-5	1	0	0	.946	12	S-19,2-15/3-1	1.0
1964	NY-N	3	7	0	0	0	0	0	0	0	0	.000	.000	.000	0	-99	-2	0	0	0	1.000	4	/2-3	0.3
Total	3	159	356	44	73	8	6	4	33	29	92	.205	.269	.295	564	56	-22	5	3	0	.964	30	2-127/S-20,3-1	1.8
■ PAUL BURRIS Burris, Paul Robert b: 7/21/23, Hickory, N.C. BR/TR, 6', 190 lbs. Deb: 10/2/48																								
1948	Bos-N	2	4	0	2	0	0	0	0	0	0	.500	.500	.500	1000	174	0	0			1.000	1	/C-2	0.1
1950	Bos-N	10	23	1	4	1	0	0	3	1	2	.174	.208	.217	426	13	-3	0			1.000	1	/C-8	-0.1
1952	Bos-N	55	168	14	37	4	0	2	21	7	19	.220	.256	.280	535	50	-12	0	0	0	1.000	-4	C-50	-1.4
1953	Mil-N	2	1	0	0	0	0	0	0	0	0	.000	.000	.000	0	-99	-0	0	0	0	1.000	-0	/C-2	0.0
Total	4	69	196	15	43	5	0	2	24	8	21	.219	.254	.276	529	47	-14	0	0		1.000	-2	/C-62	-1.4
■ HENRY BURROUGHS Burroughs, Henry S. b: 1845, New Jersey d: 3/31/1878, Newark, N.J. 5'8", 147 lbs. Deb: 5/5/1871																								
1871	Oly-n	12	63	11	15	2	3	1	14	1	1	.238	.250	.413	663	91	-0	0	0	0	.706	-2	/O-8(4-0-4),3-5,2-1	-0.2
1872	Oly-n	2	7	1	1	0	0	0	0	1	0	.143	.250	.143	393	25	-1	0	0	0	.625	0	/O-2(0-2-0)	0.0
Total	2 n	14	70	12	16	2	3	1	14	2	1	.229	.250	.386	636	85	-1	0	0	0	.680	-2	/O-10(4-2-4),3-5,2-1	-0.2
■ JEFF BURROUGHS Burroughs, Jeffrey Alan b: 3/7/51, Long Beach, Cal. BR/TR, 6'1", 200 lbs. Deb: 7/20/70 Career OF: (445-LF 0-CF 845-RF)																								
1970	Was-A	6	12	1	2	0	0	0	1	2	5	.167	.286	.167	452	29	-1	0	0	0	1.000	-0	/O-3(0-0-3)	-0.1
1971	Was-A	59	181	20	42	9	0	5	25	22	55	.232	.319	.365	683	99	-0	1	0	0	.966	-5	O-50(34-0-23)	-0.8
1972	Tex-A	22	65	4	12	1	0	1	3	5	22	.185	.243	.246	489	48	-4	0	2	-1	.935	-1	O-19(17-0-2)/1-1	-0.8
1973	Tex-A	151	526	71	147	17	1	30	85	67	88	.279	.362	.487	849	143	29	0	0	0	.975	13	*O-148R/1-3,D-1	3.4
1974	Tex-A★	152	554	84	167	33	2	25	**118**	91	104	.301	.405	.504	908	164	48	2	3	-1	.972	-8	*O-150R/1-2,D-1	3.2
1975	Tex-A	152	585	81	132	20	0	29	94	79	155	.226	.319	.409	727	105	3	4	4	-1	.966	-8	*O-148(0-0-148)/D-3	-1.4
1976	Tex-A	158	604	71	143	22	2	18	86	69	93	.237	.317	.369	686	98	-1	0	0	0	.987	-2	*O-155(0-0-155)/D-3	-1.2
1977	Atl-N	154	579	91	157	19	1	41	114	86	126	.271	.365	.520	885	120	17	4	1	1	.974	-4	*O-154(0-0-154)	0.5
1978	Atl-N☆	153	488	72	147	30	6	23	77	**117**	92	.301	**.436**	.529	965	151	39	1	2	-0	.975	-0	*O-146(146-0-0)	3.3
1979	Atl-N	116	397	49	89	14	1	11	47	73	75	.224	.349	.348	696	84	-6	2	2	-0	.963	-1	*O-110(110-0-0)	-1.3
1980	Atl-N	99	278	35	73	14	0	13	51	35	57	.263	.349	.453	802	118	7	1	1	-0	.977	-4	O-73(73-0-0)	0.0
1981	Sea-A	89	319	32	81	13	1	10	41	41	64	.254	.339	.395	734	107	3	0	1	-0	.985	-9	O-87(1-0-86)/D-1	-1.1
1982	Oak-A	113	285	42	79	13	2	16	48	45	61	.277	.376	.505	881	146	18	1	3	-1	.981	-5	D-48,O-34(17-0-18)	1.0
1983	Oak-A	121	401	43	108	15	1	10	56	47	79	.269	.346	.387	733	108	5	0	2	-1	.000	0	*D-114	0.1
1984	Oak-A	58	71	5	15	1	0	2	8	18	23	.211	.371	.310	681	97	1	0	0	0	1.000	-2	D-23/O-4(4-0-0)	-0.2
1985	*Tor-A	86	191	19	49	9	3	6	28	34	36	.257	.369	.429	798	115	5	0	1	-0	.000	0	D-75	0.2
Total	16	1689	5536	720	1443	230	20	240	882	831	1135	.261	.359	.439	798	120	161	16	22	-4	.974	-36	*O-1281R,D-269/1-6	4.8
■ DICK BURRUS Burrus, Maurice Lennon b: 1/29/1898, Hatteras, N.C. d: 2/2/72, Elizabeth City, N.C BL/TL, 5'11", 175 lbs. Deb: 6/23/19																								
1919	Phi-A	70	194	17	50	3	4	0	8	9	25	.258	.294	.314	609	70	-8	2			.986	-4	1-38,O-10(0-2-8)	-1.4
1920	Phi-A	71	135	11	25	8	0	0	10	5	7	.185	.225	.244	470	24	-15	0	3	-1	.989	-2	1-31/O-2(0-0-2)	-1.8

YEAR	TM/L	G	AB	R	H	2B	3B	HR	RBI	BB	SO	AVG	OBP	SLG	OPS	OPS+	BR+	SB	CS	SBR	FA	FR	G/POS	TPR
1925	Bos-N	152	588	82	200	41	4	5	87	51	29	.340	.396	.449	845	126	24	8	9	-1	**.990**	1	*1-151	1.3
1926	Bos-N	131	486	59	131	21	1	3	61	37	16	.270	.324	.335	659	85	-10	4			.991	12	*1-128	-0.6
1927	Bos-N	72	220	22	70	8	3	0	32	17	10	.318	.370	.382	752	110	3	3			.972	1	1-61	0.1
1928	Bos-N	64	137	15	37	6	0	3	13	19	8	.270	.367	.380	747	101	1	1			.977	-2	1-32	-0.4
Total	6	560	1760	206	513	87	12	11	211	138	95	.291	.347	.373	720	97	-4	18	12		.986	7	1-441/O-12(0-2-10)	-2.8

■ **FRANK BURT** Burt, Frank J. b: Camden, N.J. Deb: 5/2/1882

YEAR	TM/L	G	AB	R	H	2B	3B	HR	RBI	BB	SO	AVG	OBP	SLG	OPS	OPS+	BR+	SB	CS	SBR	FA	FR	G/POS	TPR
1882	Bal-a	10	36	2	4	2	1	0		1		.111	.135	.222	357	20	-3				.815	-1	O-10(10-0-0)	-0.3

■ **ELLIS BURTON** Burton, Ellis Narrington b: 8/12/36, Los Angeles, Cal. BB/TR, 5'11", 165 lbs. Deb: 9/18/58

YEAR	TM/L	G	AB	R	H	2B	3B	HR	RBI	BB	SO	AVG	OBP	SLG	OPS	OPS+	BR+	SB	CS	SBR	FA	FR	G/POS	TPR
1958	StL-N	8	30	5	7	0	1	2	4	3	8	.233	.324	.500	824	110	0	0	1	-0	1.000	-0	/O-7(5-0-2)	-0.1
1960	StL-N	29	28	5	6	1	0	0	2	4	14	.214	.313	.250	563	52	-2	0	2	-1	1.000	-7	O-23(14-5-4)	-1.1
1963	Cle-A	26	31	6	6	3	0	1	1	4	4	.194	.286	.387	673	87	-1	0	0	0	1.000	-4	O-16(9-0-7)	-0.5
	Chi-N	93	322	45	74	16	1	12	41	36	59	.230	.315	.398	712	98	-0	6	3	0	.975	-9	O-90(1-76-21)	-1.3
1964	Chi-N	42	105	12	20	3	2	2	7	17	22	.190	.303	.314	618	71	-4	4	0	1	.981	-4	O-29(1-21-11)	-0.9
1965	Chi-N	17	40	6	7	1	0	0	4	1	10	.175	.195	.200	395	11	-5	1	0	0	1.000	-0	O-12(2-10-0)	-0.5
Total	5	215	556	79	120	24	4	17	59	65	117	.216	.304	.365	669	85	-11	11	6	0	.981	-24	O-177(32-112-45)	-4.4

■ **JIM BUSBY** Busby, James Franklin b: 1/8/27, Kenedy, Tex. d: 7/8/96, Augusta, Ga. BR/TR, 6'1", 175 lbs. Deb: 4/23/50 C Career OF: (12-LF 1267-CF 3-RF)

YEAR	TM/L	G	AB	R	H	2B	3B	HR	RBI	BB	SO	AVG	OBP	SLG	OPS	OPS+	BR+	SB	CS	SBR	FA	FR	G/POS	TPR
1950	Chi-A	18	48	5	10	0	0	0	4	1	5	.208	.224	.208	433	12	-6	0	2	-1	.964	-1	O-12(0-12-1)	-0.8
1951	Chi-A★	143	477	59	135	15	2	5	68	40	46	.283	.344	.354	698	91	-6	26	11	2	.982	3	*O-139(0-139-0)	-0.5
1952	Chi-A	16	39	5	5	0	0	0	0	2	7	.128	.171	.128	299	-16	-6	0	2	-1	1.000	-0	O-16(0-16-0)	-0.8
	Was-A	129	512	58	125	24	4	2	47	22	48	.244	.281	.318	599	69	-23	5	6	-1	.993	14	*O-128(0-128-0)	-1.5
	Yr	145	551	63	130	24	4	2	47	24	55	.236	.273	.305	578	62	-29	5	8	-2	.994	13	*O-144(0-144-0)	-2.3
1953	Was-A	150	586	68	183	28	7	6	82	38	45	.312	.358	.415	773	111	8	13	6	1	.988	**19**	*O-150(0-150-0)	2.0
1954	Was-A	155	628	83	187	22	7	7	80	43	56	.298	.346	.389	734	107	4	17	2	**3**	.988	12	*O-155(0-155-0)	1.2
1955	Was-A	47	191	23	44	6	2	6	14	13	22	.230	.279	.377	656	79	-7	5	0	1	.993	2	O-47(0-47-0)	-0.6
	Chi-A	99	337	38	82	13	4	1	27	25	37	.243	.296	.315	610	62	-18	7	3	0	.984	2	O-99(0-99-0)	-2.0
	Yr	146	528	61	126	19	6	7	41	38	59	.239	.290	.337	627	68	-25	12	3	2	.987	5	*O-146(0-146-0)	-2.6
1956	Cle-A	135	494	72	116	17	3	12	50	43	47	.235	.301	.354	656	71	-22	8	3	1	.989	5	*O-133(0-133-0)	-2.2
1957	Cle-A	30	74	9	14	2	1	2	4	1	8	.189	.200	.324	524	41	-6	0	1	-0	.978	-3	O-26(2-25-0)	-1.1
	Bal-A	86	288	31	72	10	1	3	19	23	36	.250	.305	.323	628	77	-10	6	3	0	.984	10	O-85(0-85-0)	-0.3
	Yr	116	362	40	86	12	2	5	23	24	44	.238	.285	.323	608	69	-16	6	4	-0	.983	6	*O-111(2-110-0)	-1.4
1958	Bal-A	113	215	32	51	7	2	3	19	24	37	.237	.322	.330	653	84	-4	6	4	-0	**.995**	-9	*O-103(0-103-0)/3-1	-1.6
1959	Bos-A	61	102	16	23	8	0	1	5	5	18	.225	.269	.333	602	61	-6	0	1	-0	.980	-6	O-34(8-25-1)	-1.3
1960	Bos-A	1	0	0	0	0	0	0	0	0	0	—	—	—	—	—	0	0	0	0	.000	-0	/O-1(1-0-0)	0.0
	Bal-A	79	159	25	41	7	1	0	12	20	14	.258	.341	.314	655	79	-4	2	3	-1	.985	-5	O-71(0-71-0)	-1.2
	Yr	80	159	25	41	7	1	0	12	20	14	.258	.341	.314	655	79	-4	2	3	-1	.985	-6	O-72(1-71-0)	-1.2
1961	Bal-A	75	89	15	23	3	1	0	6	8	10	.258	.320	.315	634	73	-3	2	0	0	.987	-16	O-71(0-71-0)	-2.0
1962	Hou-N	15	11	2	2	0	0	0	1	2	3	.182	.308	.182	490	38	-1	0	1	-0	1.000	-4	O-10(1-8-1)/C-1	-0.5
Total	13	1352	4250	541	1113	162	35	48	438	310	439	.262	.316	.350	666	82	-110	97	48	5	.988	22	*O-1280C/C-1,3-1	-13.2

■ **PAUL BUSBY** Busby, Paul Miller "Red" b: 8/25/18, Waynesboro, Miss. BL/TR, 6'1", 175 lbs. Deb: 9/14/41

YEAR	TM/L	G	AB	R	H	2B	3B	HR	RBI	BB	SO	AVG	OBP	SLG	OPS	OPS+	BR+	SB	CS	SBR	FA	FR	G/POS	TPR
1941	Phi-N	10	16	3	5	0	0	0	2	0	1	.313	.313	.313	625	79	-0	0			1.000	-1	/O-3(0-2-1)	-0.1
1943	Phi-N	26	40	13	10	1	0	0	5	2	1	.250	.286	.275	561	65	-2	2			1.000	0	O-10(2-0-8)	-0.2
Total	2	36	56	16	15	1	0	0	7	2	2	.268	.293	.286	579	69	-2	2			1.000	-1	/O-13(2-2-9)	-0.3

■ **ED BUSCH** Busch, Edgar John b: 11/16/17, Lebanon, Ill. d: 1/17/87, St.Clair Co., Ill. BR/TR, 5'10", 175 lbs. Deb: 9/30/43

YEAR	TM/L	G	AB	R	H	2B	3B	HR	RBI	BB	SO	AVG	OBP	SLG	OPS	OPS+	BR+	SB	CS	SBR	FA	FR	G/POS	TPR
1943	Phi-A	4	17	2	5	0	0	0	0	1	2	.294	.368	.294	663	95	-0	0	1	-0	.941	-3	/S-4	-0.3
1944	Phi-A	140	484	41	131	11	3	0	40	29	17	.271	.313	.306	619	78	-14	5	3	0	.940	-30	*S-111,2-27/3-4	-3.5
1945	Phi-A	126	416	37	104	10	3	0	35	32	9	.250	.305	.288	594	73	-14	2	3	-1	.952	1	*S-116/2-2,3-2,1-1	-0.6
Total	3	270	917	80	240	21	6	0	75	62	28	.262	.311	.298	608	76	-28	7	7	-1	.946	-32	S-231/2-29,3-6,1-1	-4.4

■ **MIKE BUSCH** Busch, Michael Anthony b: 7/7/68, Davenport, Iowa BR/TR, 6'5", 249 lbs. Deb: 8/30/95

YEAR	TM/L	G	AB	R	H	2B	3B	HR	RBI	BB	SO	AVG	OBP	SLG	OPS	OPS+	BR+	SB	CS	SBR	FA	FR	G/POS	TPR
1995	LA-N	13	17	3	4	0	0	3	6	0	7	.235	.235	.765	1000	165	1	0	0	0	.875	-1	3-10/1-2	0.1
1996	LA-N	38	83	8	18	4	0	4	17	5	33	.217	.261	.410	671	80	-3	0	0	0	.932	-4	3-23/1-1	-0.6
Total	2	51	100	11	22	4	0	7	23	5	40	.220	.257	.470	727	94	-2	0	0	0	.923	-4	/3-33,1-3	-0.5

■ **HOMER BUSH** Bush, Homer Giles b: 11/12/72, East St.Louis, Ill. BR/TR, 5'11", 180 lbs. Deb: 8/16/97

YEAR	TM/L	G	AB	R	H	2B	3B	HR	RBI	BB	SO	AVG	OBP	SLG	OPS	OPS+	BR+	SB	CS	SBR	FA	FR	G/POS	TPR
1997	NY-A	10	11	2	4	0	0	0	3	0	0	.364	.364	.364	727	91	-0	0	0	0	.913	4	/2-8,D-1	0.3
1998	*NY-A	45	71	17	27	3	0	1	5	5	19	.380	.421	.465	886	135	4	6	3	0	.971	6	2-24,D-12/3-3,S-2	0.9
1999	Tor-A	128	485	69	155	26	4	5	55	21	82	.320	.355	.421	776	96	-3	32	8	4	.984	8	*2-109,S-18	1.4
2000	Tor-A	76	297	38	64	8	0	1	18	18	60	.215	.272	.253	524	34	-30	9	4	1	.986	15	2-75	-1.0
Total	4	259	864	126	250	37	4	7	81	44	161	.289	.332	.366	698	77	-29	47	15	5	.983	32	2-216/S-20,D-13,3-3	1.6

■ **DONIE BUSH** Bush, Owen Joseph b: 10/8/1887, Indianapolis, Ind. d: 3/28/72, Indianapolis, Ind. BB/TR, 5'6", 140 lbs. Deb: 9/18/08 M

YEAR	TM/L	G	AB	R	H	2B	3B	HR	RBI	BB	SO	AVG	OBP	SLG	OPS	OPS+	BR+	SB	CS	SBR	FA	FR	G/POS	TPR
1908	Det-A	20	68	13	20	1	1	0	4	7		.294	.360	.338	698	122	2	2			.938	-4	S-20	-0.1
1909	*Det-A	157	532	114	145	18	2	0	33	**88**		.273	.380	.314	694	114	14	53			.925	4	*S-157	2.6
1910	Det-A	142	496	90	130	13	4	3	34	**78**		.262	.365	.323	687	108	8	49			**.940**	9	*S-141/3-1	2.4
1911	Det-A	150	561	126	130	18	5	1	36	**98**		.232	.349	.287	636	74	-16	40			.925	17	*S-150	1.1
1912	Det-A	144	511	107	118	14	8	2	38	**117**		.231	.377	.301	679	98	6	35			.929	29	*S-144	4.4
1913	Det-A	153	597	98	150	19	10	1	40	80	32	.251	.344	.322	665	96	-1	44			.938	2	*S-153	1.3
1914	Det-A	157	596	97	150	18	4	0	32	**112**	54	.252	.373	.295	668	98	4	35	26	-1	.944	**34**	*S-157	5.1
1915	Det-A	155	561	99	128	12	8	1	44	118	44	.228	.364	.283	648	89	-2	35	27	-2	.937	9	*S-155	1.7
1916	Det-A	145	550	73	124	5	9	0	34	75	42	.225	.319	.267	587	74	-16	19			.954	-15	*S-144	-2.3
1917	Det-A	147	581	**112**	163	18	3	0	24	80	40	.281	.370	.322	691	111	11	34			.932	-18	*S-147	0.4
1918	Det-A	128	500	74	117	10	3	0	22	79	31	.234	.340	.266	606	86	-5	9			.931	-20	*S-128	-1.8
1919	Det-A	129	509	82	124	11	6	0	26	75	36	.244	.343	.289	632	80	-11	22			.943	-12	*S-129	-1.4
1920	Det-A	141	506	85	133	18	5	1	33	73	32	.263	.357	.324	681	83	-9	15	7	1	.938	-17	*S-140	-1.5
1921	Det-A	104	402	72	113	6	5	0	27	45	23	.281	.355	.321	676	74	-14	8	11	-2	.949	-5	S-81,2-23	-1.1
	Was-A	23	84	15	18	1	0	0	2	12	4	.214	.313	.226	539	41	-7	2	2	-0	.932	-4	S-21	-0.9
	Yr	127	486	87	131	7	5	0	29	57	27	.270	.347	.305	652	69	-21	10	13	-2	.946	-10	*S-102,2-23	-2.0
1922	Was-A	41	134	17	32	4	1	0	7	21	7	.239	.342	.284	626	68	-6	1	1	-0	.957	-2	3-37/2-1	-0.5
1923	Was-A	10	22	6	9	0	0	0	0	0	1	.409	.409	.409	818	122	1	1	1	-0	.813	-2	/3-5,2-2,M	-0.1
Total	16	1946	7210	1280	1804	186	74	9	436	1158	346	.250	.356	.300	656	91	-41	404	75		.936	5	*S-1867/3-43,2-26	9.3

■ **RANDY BUSH** Bush, Robert Randall b: 10/5/58, Dover, Del. BL/TL, 6'1", 186 lbs. Deb: 5/1/82 Career OF: (184-LF 1-CF 371-RF)

YEAR	TM/L	G	AB	R	H	2B	3B	HR	RBI	BB	SO	AVG	OBP	SLG	OPS	OPS+	BR+	SB	CS	SBR	FA	FR	G/POS	TPR
1982	Min-A	55	119	13	29	6	1	4	13	8	28	.244	.308	.412	719	93	-1	0	0	0	1.000	-1	D-26/O-6(6-0-0)	-0.3
1983	Min-A	124	373	43	93	24	3	11	56	34	51	.249	.324	.418	742	99	-1	0	1	-0	1.000	1	*D-103/1-3	-0.4
1984	Min-A	113	311	46	69	17	1	11	43	31	60	.222	.301	.389	690	85	-7	1	2	-0	1.000	-0	D-89/1-2	-1.0
1985	Min-A	97	234	26	56	13	3	10	35	24	30	.239	.323	.449	772	103	1	3	0	1	.969	-6	O-41(39-0-4),D-28/1-1	-0.6
1986	Min-A	130	357	50	96	19	7	7	45	39	63	.269	.348	.420	768	105	3	5	3	0	.977	-7	*O-102L/1-3,D-6	-0.8
1987	*Min-A	122	293	46	74	10	2	11	46	43	49	.253	.354	.413	767	99	0	10	3	1	.982	-8	O-75(2-0-72)/1-9,D-9	-1.0
1988	Min-A	136	394	51	103	20	3	14	51	58	49	.261	.369	.434	803	120	12	8	6	-0	.979	-6	*O-109R/1-6,D-7	0.3
1989	Min-A	141	391	60	103	17	4	14	54	48	73	.263	.348	.435	783	112	6	5	8	-2	.986	-9	*O-109R,1-25/D-5	-0.8
1990	Min-A	73	181	17	44	8	0	6	18	21	27	.243	.341	.387	728	97	-0	0	3	-1	1.000	-2	O-32(2-0-32),D-29/1-6	-0.6
1991	*Min-A	93	165	21	50	10	1	6	23	24	25	.303	.401	.485	886	137	9	0	2	-1	1.000	-5	O-38R,1-12,D-10	0.2
1992	Min-A	100	182	14	39	8	1	2	22	11	37	.214	.267	.302	569	57	-11	1	1	-0	1.000	-3	O-24(3-0-21),D-24/1-8	-1.5
1993	Min-A	35	45	1	7	2	0	0	3	7	13	.156	.269	.200	469	28	-4	0	0	0	1.000	-1	/1-4,O-1(0-0-1),D-5	-0.5
Total	12	1219	3045	388	763	154	26	96	409	348	505	.251	.337	.413	750	101	8	33	29	-3	.983	-48	O-537R,D-341/1-79	-7.0

YEAR	TM/L	G	AB	R	H	2B	3B	HR	RBI	BB	SO	AVG	OBP	SLG	OPS	OPS+	BR+	SB	CS	SBR	FA	FR	G/POS	TPR
■ **DOC BUSHONG**	Bushong, Albert John b: 9/15/1856, Philadelphia, Pa. d: 8/19/08, Brooklyn, N.Y. BR/TR, 5'11", 165 lbs. Deb: 7/19/1875 Career OF: (0-LF 3-CF 3-RF)																							
1875	Atl-n	1	5	0	3	0	1	0	0	0	0	.600	.600	1.000	1600	511	2	0	0	0	.800	-0	/C-1	0.1
1876	Phi-N	5	21	4	1	0	0	0	1	0	0	.048	.048	.048	95	-69	-4				.769	-1	/C-5	-0.4
1880	Wor-N	41	146	13	25	3	0	0	19	1	16	.171	.177	.192	369	23	-12				.918	16	C-40/O-1(0-0-1),3-1	0.6
1881	Wor-N	76	275	35	64	7	4	0	21	21	23	.233	.287	.287	574	77	-7				.918	11	*C-76	0.5
1882	Wor-N	69	253	20	40	4	1	1	15	5	17	.158	.174	.194	368	18	-23				.897	-3	*C-69	-1.8
1883	Cle-N	63	215	15	37	5	0	0	9	7	19	.172	.198	.195	394	21	-20				.909	15	C-63	0.1
1884	Cle-N	62	203	24	48	6	1	0	10	17	11	.236	.295	.276	571	78	-5				.886	0	C-62/O-1(0-1-0)	0.1
1885	*StL-a	85	300	42	80	13	5	0	21	11		.267	.297	.343	640	97	-2				.932	14	*C-85/3-1	1.7
1886	*StL-a	107	386	56	86	8	0	1	31	31		.223	.281	.251	532	64	-16	12			**.942**	16	*C-106/1-1	0.8
1887	*StL-a	53	212	35	62	4	0	0	26	11		.292	.299	.274	573	55	-13	14			.927	7	C-52/O-2(0-0-2),3-2	-0.2
1888	Bro-a	69	253	23	53	5	1	0	16	5		.209	.231	.237	468	50	-14	9			.915	-7	C-69	-1.4
1889	*Bro-a	25	84	15	13	1	0	0	8	9	7	.155	.237	.167	403	16	-9	2			.894	-1	C-25	-0.7
1890	*Bro-N	16	55	5	13	2	0	0	7	6	4	.236	.311	.273	584	70	-2	2			.913	-1	C-15/O-2(0-2-0)	-0.2
Total	12	671	2403	287	522	58	12	2	184	124	97	.217	.254	.250	505	55	-126	39	0		.916	65	C-667/O-6C,3-4,1-1	-0.9
■ **JOE BUSKEY**	Buskey, Joseph Henry "Jazzbow" b: 12/18/02, Cumberland, Md. d: 4/11/49, Cumberland, Md. BR/TR, 5'10", 175 lbs. Deb: 4/19/26																							
1926	Phi-N	5	8	1	0	0	0	0	0	1	1	.000	.111	.000	111	-65	-2	0			.810	-0	/S-5	-0.2
■ **MIKE BUSKEY**	Buskey, Michael Thomas b: 1/13/49, San Francisco, Cal. BR/TR, 5'11", 160 lbs. Deb: 9/2/77																							
1977	Phi-N	6	7	1	2	0	1	0	1	0	1	.286	.375	.571	946	143	0	0	0	0	.882	2	/S-6	0.2
■ **RAY BUSSE**	Busse, Raymond Edward b: 9/25/48, Daytona Beach, Fla. BR/TR, 6'4", 175 lbs. Deb: 7/24/71																							
1971	Hou-N	10	34	2	5	3	0	0	4	2	9	.147	.194	.235	430	22	-4	0	0	0	.929	-2	/S-5,3-3	-0.6
1973	StL-N	24	70	6	10	4	2	2	5	5	21	.143	.200	.343	543	48	-5	0	1	-0	.898	-2	S-23	-0.6
	Hou-N	15	17	1	1	0	0	0	0	1	12	.059	.111	.059	170	-52	-3	0	0	0	1.000	1	/S-5,3-3	-0.2
	Yr	39	87	7	11	4	2	2	5	6	33	.126	.183	.287	470	28	-9	0	1	-0	.906	-1	S-28/3-3	-0.8
1974	Hou-N	19	34	3	7	1	0	0	0	3	12	.206	.270	.235	506	44	-3	0	0	0	.864	-0	/3-8	-0.3
Total	3	68	155	12	23	8	2	2	9	11	54	.148	.205	.265	469	31	-15	0	1	-0	.908	-3	/S-33,3-14	-1.7
■ **HANK BUTCHER**	Butcher, Henry Joseph b: 7/12/1886, Chicago, Ill. d: 12/28/79, Hazel Crest, Ill. BR/TR, 5'10", 180 lbs. Deb: 7/8/11																							
1911	Cle-A	38	133	22	32	7	3	1	11	11		.241	.303	.361	664	84	-3	9			.984	0	O-34(24-4-6)	-0.5
1912	Cle-A	26	82	9	16	4	1	1	10	6		.195	.250	.305	555	57	-5	1			.920	1	O-21(20-0-0)	-0.5
Total	2	64	215	31	48	11	4	2	21	17		.223	.283	.340	623	74	-8	10			.956	2	/O-55(44-4-6)	-1.0
■ **SAL BUTERA**	Butera, Salvatore Philip b: 9/25/52, Richmond Hill, N.Y BR/TR, 6', 190 lbs. Deb: 4/10/80 C																							
1980	Min-A	34	85	4	23	1	0	0	2	3	6	.271	.303	.282	586	57	-5	0	0	0	.950	-1	C-32/D-2	-0.5
1981	Min-A	62	167	13	40	7	1	0	18	22	14	.240	.328	.293	621	75	-5	0	0	0	.970	5	C-59/1-1,D-1	0.2
1982	Min-A	54	126	9	32	2	0	0	8	17	12	.254	.347	.270	617	70	-4	0	0	0	.988	6	C-53	0.3
1983	Det-A	4	5	1	1	0	0	0	0	0	0	.200	.200	.200	400	11	-1	0	0	0	.929	1	/C-4	0.1
1984	Mon-N	3	3	0	0	0	0	0	0	1	0	.000	.250	.000	250	-26	-0	0	0	0	1.000	1	/C-2	0.0
1985	Mon-N	67	120	11	24	1	0	3	12	13	12	.200	.284	.283	567	63	-6	0	0	0	.984	0	C-66/P-1	-0.4
1986	Cin-N	56	113	14	27	6	1	2	16	21	10	.239	.358	.363	721	95	-0	0	0	0	.979	1	C-53/P-1	0.3
1987	Cin-N	5	11	1	2	0	0	1	2	1	6	.182	.250	.455	705	78	-0	0	0	0	.920	1	/C-5	0.1
	*Min-A	51	111	7	19	5	0	1	12	7	16	.171	.220	.243	464	22	-12	0	0	0	.983	1	C-51	-1.0
1988	Tor-A	23	60	3	14	2	1	1	6	1	9	.233	.246	.350	596	65	-3	0	0	0	.991	3	C-23	0.1
Total	9	359	801	63	182	24	3	8	76	86	85	.227	.304	.295	599	65	-37	0	0	0	.978	17	C-348/D-3,P-2,1-1	-0.8
■ **ED BUTKA**	Butka, Edward Luke "Babe" b: 1/7/16, Canonsburg, Pa. BR/TR, 6'3", 193 lbs. Deb: 9/26/43																							
1943	Was-A	3	9	0	3	1	0	0	1	0	3	.333	.333	.444	778	132	0	0	0	0	1.000	1	/1-3	0.1
1944	Was-A	15	41	1	8	1	0	0	1	2	11	.195	.233	.220	452	31	-4	0	0	0	.972	0	1-14	-0.5
Total	2	18	50	1	11	2	0	0	2	2	14	.220	.250	.260	510	48	-3	0	0	0	.977	1	/1-17	-0.4
■ **ART BUTLER**	Butler, Arthur Edward (b: Arthur Edward Bouthillier) b: 12/19/1887, Fall River, Mass. d: 10/7/84, Fall River, Mass. BR/TR, 5'9", 160 lbs. Deb: 4/14/11 Career OF: (2-LF 10-CF 6-RF)																							
1911	Bos-N	27	68	11	12	2	0	0	2	6	6	.176	.263	.206	469	30	-6	0			.930	-3	3-14/2-4,S-1	-0.9
1912	Pit-N	43	154	19	42	4	2	1	17	15	13	.273	.337	.344	681	88	-2	2			.960	-22	2-43	-2.4
1913	Pit-N	82	214	40	60	9	3	0	20	32	14	.280	.379	.350	729	114	5	9			.919	-12	2-28,S-26/3-2,O-2R	-0.4
1914	StL-N	86	274	29	55	12	3	1	24	39	23	.201	.311	.277	589	76	-7	14			.927	-19	S-83/O-1(0-1-0)	-2.2
1915	StL-N	130	469	73	119	12	5	1	31	47	34	.254	.323	.307	630	91	-4	26	14	1	.916	-35	*S-125/2-2	-3.4
1916	StL-N	86	110	9	23	5	0	0	7	7	12	.209	.256	.255	511	57	-6	3			.882	-6	O-15C/2-8,S-1,3-1	-1.4
Total	6	454	1289	181	311	44	13	3	101	146	102	.241	.323	.303	626	85	-20	54	14		.919	-98	S-236/2-85,O-18C,3	-10.7
■ **BRETT BUTLER**	Butler, Brett Morgan b: 6/15/57, Los Angeles, Cal. BL/TL, 5'10", 160 lbs. Deb: 8/20/81 Career OF: (181-LF 1986-CF 10-RF)																							
1981	Atl-N	40	126	17	32	2	3	0	4	19	17	.254	.352	.317	669	89	-1	9	1	2	.987	-2	O-37(25-11-5)	-0.3
1982	*Atl-N	89	240	35	52	2	0	0	7	25	35	.217	.291	.225	516	44	-17	21	8	2	1.000	-10	O-77(0-77-0)	-2.7
1983	Atl-N	151	549	84	154	21	**13**	5	37	54	56	.281	.347	.393	741	98	-1	39	23	1	.987	6	*O-143(109-38-4)	0.1
1984	Cle-A	159	602	108	162	25	9	3	49	86	62	.269	.364	.355	720	98	2	52	22	4	.991	15	*O-156(0-155-1)	1.9
1985	Cle-A	152	591	106	184	28	14	5	50	63	42	.311	.379	.431	810	122	19	47	20	3	**.998**	22	*O-150(0-150-0)/D-1	4.2
1986	Cle-A	161	587	92	163	17	**14**	4	51	70	65	.278	.359	.375	733	102	3	32	15	2	.993	9	*O-159(0-159-0)	1.2
1987	Cle-A	137	522	91	154	25	8	9	41	91	55	.295	.401	.425	826	119	18	33	16	2	.990	15	*O-136(0-136-0)	3.1
1988	SF-N	157	568	**109**	163	27	9	6	43	97	64	.287	.395	.398	793	134	29	43	20	2	.988	6	*O-155(0-156-0)	3.9
1989	*SF-N	154	594	100	168	22	4	4	36	59	69	.283	.351	.354	704	105	5	31	16	1	.986	14	*O-152(0-152-0)	2.0
1990	SF-N	160	622	108	**192**	20	9	3	44	90	62	.309	.401	.384	785	122	23	51	19	5	.986	7	*O-159(0-159-0)	3.4
1991	LA-N★	161	615	**112**	182	13	5	2	38	**108**	79	.296	.402	.343	745	114	18	38	28	-1	**1.000**	12	*O-161(0-161-0)	2.8
1992	LA-N	157	553	86	171	14	11	3	39	95	67	.309	.413	.391	804	131	28	41	21	2	.995	2	*O-155(0-155-0)	3.2
1993	LA-N	156	607	80	181	21	10	1	42	86	69	.298	.390	.371	760	111	14	39	19	2	**1.000**	3	*O-155(0-155-0)	2.0
1994	LA-N	111	417	79	131	13	**9**	8	33	68	52	.314	.413	.446	859	133	23	27	8	3	.993	5	*O-111(0-111-0)	3.1
1995	NY-N	90	367	54	114	13	7	1	25	43	42	.311	.383	.392	775	108	6	21	7	2	.995	6	O-90(0-90-0)	1.5
	*LA-N	39	146	24	40	5	2	0	13	24	9	.274	.376	.336	712	98	1	11	1	2	.987	-1	O-38(0-38-0)	0.2
	Yr	129	513	78	154	18	**9**	1	38	67	51	.300	.381	.376	757	106	7	32	8	4	.993	4	*O-128(0-128-0)	1.7
1996	LA-N	34	131	22	35	1	1	0	8	9	22	.267	.319	.290	609	67	-6	8	3	1	.987	1	O-34(0-34-0)	-0.4
1997	LA-N	105	343	52	97	8	3	0	18	42	40	.283	.363	.324	686	88	-4	15	10	-0	1.000	0	O-91(47-49-0)/D-1	-0.5
Total	17	2213	8180	1359	2375	277	131	54	578	1129	907	.290	.379	.376	755	110	159	558	257	33	.992	110	*O-2159C/D-2	28.7
■ **FRANK BUTLER**	Butler, Frank Dean "Stuffy" or "Goldbrick" b: 7/18/1860, Savannah, Ga. d: 7/10/45, Jacksonville, Fla BL/TL, Deb: 7/30/1895																							
1895	NY-N	5	22	5	6	1	0	0	2	1	1	.273	.304	.318	623	62	-1	0			1.000	-1	/O-5(4-0-1)	-0.2
■ **KID BUTLER**	Butler, Frank Edward b: 5/1861, Boston, Mass. d: 4/9/21, S.Boston, Mass. 5'6", 140 lbs. Deb: 5/20/1884																							
1884	Bos-U	71	255	36	43	15	0	0		12		.169	.206	.227	433	32	-29				.810	-6	O-53L,2-12/S-6,3-2	-3.1
■ **JOHN BUTLER**	Butler, John Albert (a.k.a. Frederick King In 1901) b: 7/26/1879, Boston, Mass. d: 2/2/50, Boston, Mass. BR/TR, 5'7", 170 lbs. Deb: 9/28/01																							
1901	Mil-A	1	3	0	0	0	0	0	0	1		.000	.250	.000	250	-28	-0	0			1.000	-1	/C-1	-0.1
1904	StL-N	12	37	0	6	1	0	0	1	4		.162	.262	.189	451	42	-2	0			.968	-2	C-12	-0.4
1906	Bro-N	1	0	0	0	0	0	0	0	0		—	—	—	—	—	0	0			1.000	0	/C-1	0.0
1907	Bro-N	30	79	6	10	1	0	0	2	9		.127	.216	.139	355	12	-8	0			.946	-5	C-28/O-1(1-0-0)	-1.1
Total	4	44	119	6	16	2	0	0	3	14		.134	.231	.151	383	21	-11	0			.953	-8	/C-42,O-1(1-0-0)	-1.6
■ **JOHNNY BUTLER**	Butler, John Stephen "Trolley Line" b: 3/20/1893, Fall River, Kan. d: 4/29/67, Seal Beach, Cal. BR/TR, 6', 175 lbs. Deb: 4/18/26 C																							
1926	Bro-N	147	501	54	135	27	5	1	68	54	44	.269	.346	.349	696	89	-6	6			.949	-7	*S-102,3-42/2-8	0.0
1927	Bro-N	149	521	39	124	13	6	2	57	34	33	.238	.292	.298	590	58	-31	9			.959	-2	S-90,3-60	-1.9
1928	Chi-N	62	174	17	47	7	0	0	16	19	7	.270	.352	.310	662	75	-5	2			.950	10	3-59/S-2	0.8

YEAR	TM/L	G	AB	R	H	2B	3B	HR	RBI	BB	SO	AVG	OBP	SLG	OPS	OPS+	BR+	SB	CS	SBR	FA	FR	G/POS	TPR
1929	StL-N	17	55	5	9	1	1	0	5	4	5	.164	.220	.218	439	9	-8	0			.964	1	/3-9,S-8	-0.5
Total	4	375	1251	115	315	48	12	3	146	111	89	.252	.320	.317	636	70	-51	17			.954	2	S-202,3-170/2-8	-1.6
■ **RICH BUTLER**	Butler, Richard Dwight b: 5/1/73, Toronto, Ont., Canada BL/TR, 6'1", 180 lbs. Deb: 9/6/97 F																							
1997	Tor-A	7	14	3	4	1	0	0	2	2	3	.286	.375	.357	732	92	-0	0	1	-0	1.000	-0	/O-3(3-0-0),D-1	-0.1
1998	TB-A	72	217	25	49	3	3	7	20	15	37	.226	.282	.364	646	65	-11	4	2	0	1.000	1	O-61(39-0-22)	-1.1
1999	TB-A	7	20	2	3	1	0	0	0	2	4	.150	.227	.200	427	10	-3	0	0	0	1.000	-1	/O-6(2-0-4)	-0.4
Total	3	86	251	30	56	5	3	7	22	19	44	.223	.283	.351	634	62	-14	4	3	-0	1.000	0	/O-70(44-0-26),D-1	-1.6
■ **DICK BUTLER**	Butler, Richard H. b: Brooklyn, N.Y. Deb: 6/16/1897																							
1897	Lou-N	10	38	3	7	0	0	0	2	0		.184	.184	.184	368	-3	-6	1			.818	-2	C-10	-0.6
1899	Was-N	12	36	4	10	0	1	0	1	2		.278	.316	.333	649	79	-1	1			.892	-3	C-11	-0.3
Total	2	22	74	7	17	0	1	0	3	2		.230	.250	.257	507	37	-7	2			.852	-6	/C-21	-0.9
■ **ROB BUTLER**	Butler, Robert Frank John b: 4/10/70, E.York, Ont., Can. BL/TL, 5'11", 185 lbs. Deb: 6/12/93 F																							
1993	*Tor-A	17	48	8	13	4	0	0	2	7	12	.271	.375	.354	729	97	0	2	2	-0	.970	-0	O-16(15-1-0)	-0.1
1994	Tor-A	41	74	13	13	0	1	0	5	7	8	.176	.256	.203	459	20	-9	0	1	-0	.977	-5	O-31(17-13-2)/D-1	-1.4
1997	Phi-N	43	89	10	26	9	1	0	13	5	8	.292	.330	.416	746	94	-1	1	0	0	1.000	-0	O-25(4-14-8)	-0.1
1999	Tor-A	8	7	1	1	0	0	0	1	0	0	.143	.250	.143	393	4	-1	0	0	0	1.000	-1	/O-2(2-0-0),D-3	-0.2
Total	4	109	218	32	53	13	2	0	21	19	28	.243	.313	.321	634	66	-11	3	3	-0	.982	-6	/O-74(38-28-10),D-4	-1.8
■ **BILL BUTLER**	Butler, William J. b: 1861, New Orleans, La. Deb: 6/29/1884																							
1884	Ind-a	9	31	7	7	3	2	0		1		.226	.250	.452	702	128	1				.700	-2	/O-9(1-1-7)	-0.1
■ **KID BUTLER**	Butler, Willis Everett b: 8/9/1887, Franklin, Pa. d: 2/22/64, Richmond, Cal. BR/TR, 5'11", 155 lbs. Deb: 4/30/07																							
1907	StL-A	20	59	4	13	2	0	0	6	2		.220	.246	.254	500	60	-3	1			.940	-1	2-11/3-5,S-1	-0.4
■ **FRANK BUTTERY**	Buttery, Frank b: 5/13/1851, Silvermine, Conn. d: 12/16/02, Silvermine, Conn. Deb: 4/26/1872																							
1872	Man-n	18	93	19	24	0	0	0	8	0	2	.258	.258	.258	516	63	-3	0	0	0	.800	-1	/P-8,O-8(0-0-8),3-5	-0.2
■ **JOE BUZAS**	Buzas, Joseph John b: 10/2/19, Alpha, N.J. BR/TR, 6'1", 180 lbs. Deb: 4/17/45																							
1945	NY-A	30	65	8	17	2	1	0	6	2	5	.262	.284	.323	607	73	-2	2	0	0	.898	-3	S-12	-0.4
■ **BURLEY BYERS**	Byers, Burley (b: Christopher A. Bayer) b: 12/19/1875, Louisville, Ky. d: 5/30/33, Louisville, Ky. 175 lbs. Deb: 6/17/1899																							
1899	Lou-N	1	3	0	0	0	0	0	0	0		.000	.000	.000	0	-99	-1	0			.600	-1	/S-1	-0.2
■ **BILL BYERS**	Byers, James William b: 10/3/1877, Bridgeton, Ind. d: 9/8/48, Baltimore, Md. BR/TR, 5'7", 210 lbs. Deb: 4/15/04																							
1904	StL-N	19	60	3	13	0	0	0	4	1		.217	.230	.217	446	40	-4	0			.971	-1	C-16/1-1	-0.4
■ **RANDY BYERS**	Byers, Randell Parker b: 10/2/64, Bridgeton, N.J. BL/TR, 6'2", 180 lbs. Deb: 9/7/87																							
1987	SD-N	10	16	1	5	1	0	0	1	1	5	.313	.353	.375	728	96	-0	1	0	0	1.000	-0	/O-5(5-0-0)	0.0
1988	SD-N	11	10	0	2	1	0	0	0	0	5	.200	.200	.300	500	42	-1	0	0	0	.000	-1	/O-2(1-0-1)	-0.2
Total	2	21	26	1	7	2	0	0	1	1	10	.269	.296	.346	642	77	-1	1	0	0	1.000	-1	/O-7(6-0-1)	-0.2
■ **JIM BYRD**	Byrd, James Edward b: 10/3/68, Wewahitchka, Fla. BR/TR, 6'1", 185 lbs. Deb: 5/31/93																							
1993	Bos-A	2	0	0	0	0	0	0	0	0	0	—	—	—	—	—	0	0	0	0	.000	0	/R	0.0
■ **SAMMY BYRD**	Byrd, Samuel Dewey "Babe Ruth's Legs" b: 10/15/07, Bremen, Ga. d: 5/11/81, Mesa, Ariz. BR/TR, 5'10.5", 175 lbs. Deb: 5/11/29																							
1929	NY-A	62	170	32	53	12	0	5	28	28	18	.312	.409	.471	880	135	10	1	4	-1	.950	-0	O-54(6-16-32)	0.5
1930	NY-A	92	218	46	62	12	2	6	31	30	18	.284	.371	.440	811	110	4	5	1	1	.992	-12	O-85(47-12-26)	-1.0
1931	NY-A	115	248	51	67	18	2	3	32	29	26	.270	.349	.395	744	101	0	5	0	1	.974	-13	O-88(26-34-34)	-1.3
1932	*NY-A	105	209	49	62	12	1	8	30	30	20	.297	.385	.478	863	129	9	1	2	-0	.964	-18	O-91(11-70-11)	-1.0
1933	NY-A	85	107	26	30	6	1	2	11	15	12	.280	.369	.411	780	113	2	0	1	-0	.987	-16	O-71(23-15-35)	-1.5
1934	NY-A	106	191	32	47	8	0	3	23	18	22	.246	.318	.335	653	73	-8	1	2	-0	**.988**	-13	*O-104(34-13-59)	-2.3
1935	Cin-N	121	416	51	109	25	4	9	52	37	51	.262	.322	.406	729	97	-2	4			.970	3	*O-115(39-76-0)	-0.3
1936	Cin-N	59	141	17	35	8	0	2	13	11	11	.248	.303	.348	650	80	-4	0			.989	-1	O-37(15-22-0)	-0.6
Total	8	745	1700	304	465	101	10	38	220	198	178	.274	.350	.412	762	104	11	17	10		.975	-71	O-645(201-258-197)	-7.5
■ **BOBBY BYRNE**	Byrne, Robert Matthew b: 12/31/1884, St.Louis, Mo. d: 12/31/64, Wayne, Pa. BR/TR, 5'7.5", 145 lbs. Deb: 4/11/07																							
1907	StL-N	149	559	55	143	11	5	0	29	35		.256	.307	.293	600	91	-6	21			.920	22	*3-148/S-1	2.2
1908	StL-N	127	439	27	84	7	1	0	14	23		.191	.238	.212	450	46	-27	16			.925	9	*3-122/S-4	-1.7
1909	StL-N	105	421	61	90	13	6	1	33	46		.214	.302	.280	582	86	-6	21			.922	17	*3-105	1.5
	*Pit-N	46	168	31	43	6	2	0	7	32		.256	.387	.315	703	109	4	8			.987	6	3-46	1.2
	Yr	151	589	92	133	19	8	1	40	78		.226	.327	.290	618	93	-2	29			.939	23	*3-151	2.7
1910	Pit-N	148	602	101	**178**	**43**	12	2	52	66	27	.296	.366	.417	783	121	15	36			.929	-7	*3-148	1.3
1911	Pit-N	153	598	96	155	24	17	2	52	67	41	.259	.342	.366	708	94	-4	23			.930	-3	*3-152	-0.3
1912	Pit-N	130	528	99	152	31	11	3	35	54	40	.288	.358	.405	764	110	7	20			**.948**	-23	*3-130	-1.2
1913	Pit-N	113	448	54	121	22	0	1	47	29	28	.270	.322	.326	647	89	-6	10			.940	-9	*3-110	-1.3
	Phi-N	19	58	9	13	1	0	1	4	5	3	.224	.308	.293	601	69	-2	2			.963	3	3-15	0.1
	Yr	132	506	63	134	23	0	2	51	34	31	.265	.320	.322	642	86	-9	12			.943	-7	*3-125	-1.2
1914	Phi-N	126	467	61	127	12	1	0	26	45	44	.272	.339	.302	640	85	-7	9			.934	-3	*2-101,3-22	-0.8
1915	*Phi-N	105	387	50	81	6	4	0	21	39	28	.209	.290	.245	536	62	-16	4	12	-3	**.969**	-7	*3-105	-2.7
1916	Phi-N	48	141	22	33	10	1	0	9	14	7	.234	.308	.319	627	89	-2	6			.933	3	3-40	0.3
1917	Phi-N	13	14	1	5	0	0	0	0	1	2	.357	.400	.357	757	128	0	0			1.000	-1	/3-4	-0.1
	Chi-A	1	1	0	0	0	0	0	0	0	0	.000	.000	.000	0	-98	-0	0			1.000	0	/2-1	0.0
Total	11	1283	4831	667	1225	186	60	10	329	456	220	.254	.324	.323	647	91	-50	176	12		.934	6	*3-1147,2-102/S-5	-1.5
■ **ERIC BYRNES**	Byrnes, Eric James b: 2/16/76, Redwood City, Cal. BR/TR, 6'2", 200 lbs. Deb: 8/22/2000																							
2000	Oak-A	10	10	5	3	0	0	0	0	0	1	.300	.364	.300	664	73	-0	2	1	0	1.000	-1	/O-4(1-0-3),D-2	-0.1
■ **JIM BYRNES**	Byrnes, James Joseph b: 1/5/1880, San Francisco, Cal. d: 7/31/41, San Francisco, Cal BR/TR, 5'9", 150 lbs. Deb: 4/19/06																							
1906	Phi-A	10	23	2	4	0	1	0	0	0		.174	.174	.261	435	34	-2	0			.889	-0	/C-9	-0.1
■ **MILT BYRNES**	Byrnes, Milton John "Skippy" b: 11/15/16, St.Louis, Mo. d: 2/1/79, St.Louis, Mo. BL/TL, 5'10.5", 170 lbs. Deb: 4/21/43																							
1943	StL-A	129	429	58	120	28	7	4	50	53	49	.280	.362	.406	767	122	12	1	4	-1	**.997**	8	*O-114(23-66-26)	1.5
1944	*StL-A	128	407	63	120	20	4	4	45	68	50	.295	.396	.393	789	119	13	1	7	-2	.976	-6	*O-122(41-52-36)	-0.1
1945	StL-A	133	442	53	110	29	4	8	59	78	84	.249	.363	.387	750	112	8	1	3	-1	.988	5	*O-125(31-56-47)/1-2	0.7
Total	3	390	1278	174	350	77	15	16	154	199	183	.274	.373	.395	768	117	33	3	14	-4	.987	8	O-361(95-174-109)/1-2	2.1
■ **PUTSY CABALLERO**	Caballero, Ralph Joseph b: 11/5/27, New Orleans, La. BR/TR, 5'11", 175 lbs. Deb: 9/14/44																							
1944	Phi-N	4	4	0	0	0	0	0	0	0	0	.000	.000	.000	0	-99	-1	0			.889	2	/3-2	0.1
1945	Phi-N	9	1	1	0	0	0	0	1	0	0	.000	.000	.000	0	-99	-0	0			.857	2	/3-5	0.1
1947	Phi-N	2	7	2	1	0	0	0	0	1	0	.143	.250	.143	393	7	-1	0			1.000	-0	/2-2,3-1	-0.1
1948	Phi-N	113	351	33	86	12	1	0	19	24	18	.245	.293	.285	578	58	-20	7			.962	6	3-79,2-23	-1.4
1949	Phi-N	29	68	8	19	3	0	0	3	0	3	.279	.279	.324	603	63	-4	0			.981	4	2-21/S-1	0.1
1950	*Phi-N	46	24	12	4	0	0	0	0	2	2	.167	.231	.167	397	7	-3	1			.950	6	/2-5,3-4,S-2	0.3
1951	Phi-N	84	161	15	30	3	2	1	11	12	7	.186	.243	.248	491	33	-15	1	2	-0	.985	9	2-54/3-3,S-1	-0.4
1952	Phi-N	35	42	10	10	3	0	0	6	2	3	.238	.273	.310	582	62	-2	1	0	0	.857	2	/S-8,2-7,3-7	0.1
Total	8	322	658	81	150	21	3	1	40	41	34	.228	.273	.274	547	49	-47	10	2		.968	31	2-112,3-101/S-12	-1.2
■ **ENOS CABELL**	Cabell, Enos Milton b: 10/8/49, Fort Riley, Kan. BR/TR, 6'5", 185 lbs. Deb: 9/17/72 Career OF: (42-LF 1-CF 72-RF)																							
1972	Bal-A	3	5	0	0	0	0	0	1	0	0	.000	.000	.000	0	-97	-1	0	0	0	1.000	-0	/1-1	-0.2
1973	Bal-A	32	47	12	10	2	0	1	3	3	7	.213	.260	.319	579	63	-2	1	3	-1	.991	-1	1-23/3-1	-0.6

YEAR	TM/L	G	AB	R	H	2B	3B	HR	RBI	BB	SO	AVG	OBP	SLG	OPS	OPS+	BR+	SB	CS	SBR	FA	FR	G/POS	TPR
1974	*Bal-A	80	174	24	42	4	2	3	17	7	20	.241	.271	.339	610	77	-6	5	3	0	.995	2	1-28,O-22R,3-19,/2D	-0.6
1975	Hou-N	117	348	43	92	17	6	2	43	18	53	.264	.306	.365	671	92	-5	12	3	2	.973	-0	O-67L,1-25,3-22	-0.8
1976	Hou-N	144	586	85	160	13	7	2	43	29	79	.273	.310	.329	639	89	-10	35	8	5	.958	-9	*3-143/1-3	-1.5
1977	Hou-N	150	625	101	176	36	7	16	68	27	55	.282	.315	.438	753	109	5	42	22	2	.948	-6	*3-144/1-8,S-1	-0.2
1978	Hou-N	162	660	92	195	31	8	7	71	22	80	.295	.323	.398	722	109	5	33	15	2	.958	-16	*3-153,1-14/S-1	-1.3
1979	Hou-N	155	603	60	164	30	5	6	67	21	68	.272	.300	.368	668	86	-13	37	18	2	.957	-23	*3-132,1-51	-4.1
1980	*Hou-N	152	604	69	167	23	8	2	55	26	84	.276	.307	.351	658	90	-10	21	13	0	.927	-20	*3-150/1-1	-3.4
1981	SF-N	96	396	41	101	20	1	2	36	10	47	.255	.275	.326	601	71	-16	6	7	-1	.987	-1	1-69,3-22	-2.5
1982	Det-A	125	464	45	121	17	3	2	37	15	48	.261	.285	.323	609	67	-21	15	6	1	.992	-8	1-83,3-59/O-3(1-0-2)	-3.3
1983	Det-A	121	392	62	122	23	5	5	46	16	41	.311	.340	.434	774	114	7	4	8	-2	.997	7	*1-106/3-4,S-1,D-8	0.6
1984	Hou-N	127	436	52	135	17	3	8	44	21	47	.310	.343	.417	760	121	11	8	11	-2	.993	-1	*1-112	0.2
1985	Hou-N	60	143	20	35	8	1	2	14	16	15	.245	.321	.357	677	92	-2	3	1	0	.994	-1	1-49	-0.5
	*LA-N	57	192	20	56	11	0	0	22	14	21	.292	.340	.349	689	96	-1	6	2	1	.920	-2	3-32,1-21/O-4(1-0-3)	-0.4
	Yr	117	335	40	91	19	1	2	36	30	36	.272	.332	.352	684	94	-3	9	3	1	.993	-3	1-70,3-32/O-4(1-0-3)	-0.9
1986	LA-N	107	277	27	71	11	0	2	29	14	26	.256	.297	.318	615	75	-10	10	4	1	.987	0	1-61,O-16(2-1-13)/3-7	-1.3
Total	15	1688	5952	753	1647	263	56	60	596	259	691	.277	.309	.370	679	93	-70	238	124	9	.944	-77	3-888,1-655,O/DS2	-19.9

■ **ALEX CABRERA** Cabrera, Alexander Alberto b: 12/24/71, Caripito, Venez. BR/TR, 6′2″, 220 lbs. Deb: 6/26/2000

YEAR	TM/L	G	AB	R	H	2B	3B	HR	RBI	BB	SO	AVG	OBP	SLG	OPS	OPS+	BR+	SB	CS	SBR	FA	FR	G/POS	TPR
2000	Ari-N	31	80	10	21	2	1	5	14	4	21	.262	.306	.500	806	98	-1	0	0	0	1.000	0	1-15,O-12(1-0-11)	-0.2

■ **AL CABRERA** Cabrera, Alfredo A. b: 5/11/1881, Canary Islands d: 64, Batabano, Cuba TR, Deb: 5/16/13

YEAR	TM/L	G	AB	R	H	2B	3B	HR	RBI	BB	SO	AVG	OBP	SLG	OPS	OPS+	BR+	SB	CS	SBR	FA	FR	G/POS	TPR
1913	StL-N	1	2	0	0	0	0	0	0	0	0	.000	.000	.000	0	-99	-1	0			.000	0	/S-1	-0.1

■ **FRANCISCO CABRERA** Cabrera, Francisco (Paulino) b: 10/10/66, Santo Domingo, D.R. BR/TR, 6′4″, 193 lbs. Deb: 7/24/89

YEAR	TM/L	G	AB	R	H	2B	3B	HR	RBI	BB	SO	AVG	OBP	SLG	OPS	OPS+	BR+	SB	CS	SBR	FA	FR	G/POS	TPR
1989	Tor-A	3	12	1	2	1	0	0	0	1	3	.167	.231	.250	481	36	-1	0	0	0	.000	0	/D-3	-0.1
	Atl-N	4	14	0	3	2	0	0	0	0	3	.214	.214	.357	571	59	-1	0	0	0	1.000	-1	/1-2,C-1	-0.2
1990	Atl-N	63	137	14	38	5	1	7	25	5	21	.277	.303	.482	785	106	1	1	0	0	.990	-2	1-48/C-3	-0.3
1991	*Atl-N	44	95	7	23	6	0	4	23	6	20	.242	.287	.432	719	94	-1	1	1	-0	.987	-3	C-17,1-14	-0.4
1992	*Atl-N	12	10	2	3	0	0	2	3	1	1	.300	.364	.900	1264	233	2	0	0	0	.000	0	/C-1	0.2
1993	*Atl-N	70	83	8	20	3	0	4	11	8	21	.241	.308	.422	729	92	-1	0	0	0	1.000	2	1-12/C-2	0.0
Total	5	196	351	32	89	17	1	17	62	21	69	.254	.296	.453	749	99	-2	2	1	0	.989	-3	/1-76,C-24,D-3	-0.8

■ **JOLBERT CABRERA** Cabrera, Jolbert Alexis b: 12/8/72, Cartagena, Colombia BR/TR, 6′, 177 lbs. Deb: 4/12/98 Career OF: (28-LF 38-CF 29-RF)

YEAR	TM/L	G	AB	R	H	2B	3B	HR	RBI	BB	SO	AVG	OBP	SLG	OPS	OPS+	BR+	SB	CS	SBR	FA	FR	G/POS	TPR
1998	Cle-A	1	2	0	0	0	0	0	0	0	1	.000	.000	.000	0	-97	-1	0	0	0	1.000	1	/S-1	0.0
1999	Cle-A	30	37	6	7	1	0	0	0	1	8	.189	.231	.216	447	14	-5	3	0	1	.957	-3	O-16(4-12-0)/2-6	-0.7
2000	Cle-A	100	175	27	44	3	1	2	15	8	15	.251	.292	.314	606	52	-13	6	4	-0	.989	-8	O-74R,2-19/S-8,D-2	-2.0
Total	3	131	214	33	51	4	1	2	15	9	24	.238	.279	.294	573	44	-18	9	4	1	.983	-11	/O-90C,2-25,S-9,D-2	-2.7

■ **ORLANDO CABRERA** Cabrera, Orlando Luis b: 11/2/74, Cartagena, Colombia BR/TR, 5′11″, 165 lbs. Deb: 9/3/97

YEAR	TM/L	G	AB	R	H	2B	3B	HR	RBI	BB	SO	AVG	OBP	SLG	OPS	OPS+	BR+	SB	CS	SBR	FA	FR	G/POS	TPR
1997	Mon-N	16	18	4	4	0	0	0	2	1	3	.222	.263	.222	485	29	-2	1	2	-0	.875	3	/S-6,2-4	0.1
1998	Mon-N	79	261	44	73	16	5	3	22	18	27	.280	.326	.414	740	94	-2	6	2	1	.984	-3	S-52,2-28	0.1
1999	Mon-N	104	382	48	97	23	5	8	39	18	38	.254	.293	.403	696	76	-15	2	2	-0	.979	6	*S-102	-0.1
2000	Mon-N	125	422	47	100	25	1	13	55	25	28	.237	.281	.393	675	67	-22	4	4	-1	.981	13	*S-124/2-1	-0.1
Total	4	324	1083	143	274	64	11	24	118	62	96	.253	.296	.399	695	76	-42	13	10	-1	.980	19	S-284/2-33	0.0

■ **CRAIG CACEK** Cacek, Craig Thomas b: 9/10/54, Hollywood, Cal. BR/TR, 6′1″, 200 lbs. Deb: 6/18/77

YEAR	TM/L	G	AB	R	H	2B	3B	HR	RBI	BB	SO	AVG	OBP	SLG	OPS	OPS+	BR+	SB	CS	SBR	FA	FR	G/POS	TPR
1977	Hou-N	7	20	0	1	0	0	0	1	1	3	.050	.095	.050	145	-66	-5	0	0	0	.981	-1	/1-6	-0.6

■ **EDGAR CACERES** Caceres, Edgar F. b: 6/6/64, Barquisimeto, Venez BB/TR, 6′1″, 170 lbs. Deb: 6/8/95

YEAR	TM/L	G	AB	R	H	2B	3B	HR	RBI	BB	SO	AVG	OBP	SLG	OPS	OPS+	BR+	SB	CS	SBR	FA	FR	G/POS	TPR
1995	KC-A	55	117	13	28	6	2	1	17	8	15	.239	.294	.350	644	66	-6	2	2	-0	.992	1	2-36/S-8,1-6,3-3,D	-0.4

■ **CHARLIE CADY** Cady, Charles B. b: 12/1865, Chicago, Ill. d: 6/7/09, Kankakee, Ill. 5′11″, 180 lbs. Deb: 9/5/1883 Career OF: (0-LF 2-CF 2-RF)

YEAR	TM/L	G	AB	R	H	2B	3B	HR	RBI	BB	SO	AVG	OBP	SLG	OPS	OPS+	BR+	SB	CS	SBR	FA	FR	G/POS	TPR
1883	Cle-N	3	11	0	0	0	0	0	0	1	5	.000	.083	.000	83	-73	-2				1.000	-1	/O-2(0-0-2),P-1	-0.2
1884	CP-U	6	20	4	2	1	1	0		1		.100	.143	.250	393	17	-3				.909	-0	/P-4,O-2(0-2-0)	-0.1
	KC-U	2	3	0	0	0	0	0		0		.000	.000	.000	0	-99	-1				.600	-2	/C-1,2-1	-0.2
	Yr	8	23	4	2	1	1	0		1		.087	.125	.217	342	2	-4				.909	-2	/P-4,O-2C,C-1,2-1	-0.3
Total	2	11	34	4	2	1	1	0	0	2	5	.059	.111	.147	258	-23	-6				.917	-3	/P-5,O-4C,2-1,C-1	-0.5

■ **HICK CADY** Cady, Forrest Leroy (b: Forrest Leroy Bergland) b: 1/26/1886, Bishop Hill, Ill. d: 3/3/46, Cedar Rapids, Iowa BR/TR, 6′2″, 179 lbs. Deb: 4/26/12

YEAR	TM/L	G	AB	R	H	2B	3B	HR	RBI	BB	SO	AVG	OBP	SLG	OPS	OPS+	BR+	SB	CS	SBR	FA	FR	G/POS	TPR
1912	*Bos-A	47	135	19	35	13	2	0	9	10		.259	.324	.385	710	98	-1	0			.990	11	C-43/1-4	1.3
1913	Bos-A	40	96	10	24	5	2	0	6	5	14	.250	.294	.344	638	84	-2	1			.992	8	C-39	0.9
1914	Bos-A	61	159	14	41	6	1	0	8	12	22	.258	.310	.308	618	86	-3	2	1	0	.971	-3	C-58	-0.1
1915	*Bos-A	78	205	25	57	10	2	0	17	19	25	.278	.342	.346	689	109	2	0	2	-1	.980	-2	C-77	0.6
1916	*Bos-A	78	162	5	31	6	3	0	13	15	16	.191	.264	.265	529	59	-8	0			.967	-13	C-63/1-3	-2.0
1917	Bos-A	17	46	4	7	1	1	0	2	1	6	.152	.170	.217	388	18	-5	0			.959	1	C-14	-0.3
1919	Phi-N	34	98	6	21	6	0	1	19	4	8	.214	.252	.306	559	63	-4	1			.984	-7	C-29	-1.0
Total	7	355	901	83	216	47	11	1	74	66	91	.240	.297	.320	616	82	-21	4	3		.979	-4	C-323/1-7	-0.6

■ **TOM CAFEGO** Cafego, Thomas b: 8/21/11, Whipple, W.Va. d: 10/29/61, Detroit, Mich. BL/TR, 5′10″, 160 lbs. Deb: 9/3/37

YEAR	TM/L	G	AB	R	H	2B	3B	HR	RBI	BB	SO	AVG	OBP	SLG	OPS	OPS+	BR+	SB	CS	SBR	FA	FR	G/POS	TPR
1937	StL-A	4	4	1	0	0	0	0	0	0	1	.000	.000	.000	0	-99	-1	0	0	0	.500	-1	/O-1(1-0-0)	-0.2

■ **JOE CAFFIE** Caffie, Joseph Clifford "Rabbit" b: 2/14/31, Ramer, Ala. BL/TR, 5′10.5″, 180 lbs. Deb: 9/13/56

YEAR	TM/L	G	AB	R	H	2B	3B	HR	RBI	BB	SO	AVG	OBP	SLG	OPS	OPS+	BR+	SB	CS	SBR	FA	FR	G/POS	TPR
1956	Cle-A	12	38	7	13	0	0	0	1	4	8	.342	.432	.342	774	104	1	3	2	-0	1.000	1	O-10(10-0-0)	0.1
1957	Cle-A	32	89	14	24	2	1	3	10	4	11	.270	.301	.416	717	95	-1	0	1	-0	.976	-0	O-19(3-0-18)	-0.2
Total	2	44	127	21	37	2	1	3	11	8	19	.291	.343	.394	737	99	-0	3	3	-0	.984	1	/O-29(13-0-18)	-0.1

■ **BEN CAFFYN** Caffyn, Benjamin Thomas b: 2/10/1880, Peoria, Ill. d: 11/22/42, Peoria, Ill. BL/TL, 5′10″, 175 lbs. Deb: 8/21/06

YEAR	TM/L	G	AB	R	H	2B	3B	HR	RBI	BB	SO	AVG	OBP	SLG	OPS	OPS+	BR+	SB	CS	SBR	FA	FR	G/POS	TPR
1906	Cle-A	30	103	16	20	4	0	0	3	12		.194	.291	.233	524	65	-4	2			.909	-4	O-29(28-1-0)	-1.1

■ **WAYNE CAGE** Cage, Wayne Levell b: 11/23/51, Monroe, La. BL/TL, 6′4″, 205 lbs. Deb: 4/22/78

YEAR	TM/L	G	AB	R	H	2B	3B	HR	RBI	BB	SO	AVG	OBP	SLG	OPS	OPS+	BR+	SB	CS	SBR	FA	FR	G/POS	TPR
1978	Cle-A	36	98	11	24	6	1	4	13	9	28	.245	.308	.449	757	112	1	1	2	-0	.988	1	D-20,1-11	0.1
1979	Cle-A	29	56	6	13	2	0	1	6	5	16	.232	.295	.321	617	66	-3	0	2	-1	1.000	1	/1-7,D-9	-0.3
Total	2	65	154	17	37	8	1	5	19	14	44	.240	.304	.403	706	94	-2	1	4	-1	.992	2	/D-29,1-18	-0.2

■ **JOHN CAHILL** Cahill, John Patrick Parnell "Patsy" b: 4/30/1865, San Francisco, Cal d: 10/31/01, Pleasanton, Cal. BR/TR, 5′7.5″, 168 lbs. Deb: 5/31/1884 Career OF: (56-LF 4-CF 176-RF)

YEAR	TM/L	G	AB	R	H	2B	3B	HR	RBI	BB	SO	AVG	OBP	SLG	OPS	OPS+	BR+	SB	CS	SBR	FA	FR	G/POS	TPR
1884	Col-a	59	210	28	46	3	3	0		6		.219	.248	.262	510	72	-6				.843	-0	O-56(56-0-0)/S-5,P-2	-0.6
1886	StL-N	125	463	43	92	17	6	1	32	9	79	.199	.214	.268	482	49	-28	16			.866	2	*O-124R/P-2,S-1,3-1	-2.5
1887	Ind-N	68	272	22	63	4	3	0	26	9	5	.232	.234	.243	478	34	-23	34			.826	-6	O-56R/3-9,P-6,S-1	-2.4
Total	3	252	945	93	201	24	12	1	58	24	84	.213	.227	.260	487	49	-56	50			.851	-5	O-236R/3-10,P-10,S	-5.5

■ **TOM CAHILL** Cahill, Thomas H. b: 10/1868, Fall River, Mass. d: 12/25/1894, Scranton, Pa. 5′7″, 150 lbs. Deb: 4/9/1891

YEAR	TM/L	G	AB	R	H	2B	3B	HR	RBI	BB	SO	AVG	OBP	SLG	OPS	OPS+	BR+	SB	CS	SBR	FA	FR	G/POS	TPR
1891	Lou-a	119	430	68	109	17	7	3	44	41	51	.253	.327	.347	674	94	-4	38			.930	-4	C-55,S-49,O-12L,/23	-0.2

■ **BOB CAIN** Cain, Robert Max "Sugar" b: 10/16/24, Longford, Kan. d: 4/8/97, Cleveland, Ohio BL/TL, 6′, 165 lbs. Deb: 9/18/49

YEAR	TM/L	G	AB	R	H	2B	3B	HR	RBI	BB	SO	AVG	OBP	SLG	OPS	OPS+	BR+	SB	CS	SBR	FA	FR	G/POS	TPR
1949	Chi-A	6	3	0	0	0	0	0	0	0	1	.000	.000	.000	0	-99	-1	0	0	0	1.000	-0	/P-6	0.0
1950	Chi-A	35	61	7	12	2	0	0	2	3	15	.197	.234	.230	464	20	-7	0	0	0	.974	0	P-34	0.0
1951	Chi-A	4	9	1	3	1	0	0	0	0	3	.333	.333	.444	778	111	0	0	0	0	1.000	-0	/P-4	0.0
	Det-A	35	53	9	13	3	0	0	9	6	9	.245	.322	.302	624	69	-2	0	0	0	.972	0	P-35	0.0
	Yr	39	62	10	16	4	0	0	9	6	12	.258	.324	.323	646	75	-2	0	0	0	.975	-0	P-39	0.0
1952	StL-A	35	58	7	8	0	1	0	1	4	14	.138	.194	.172	366	2	-8	0	0	0	.966	-2	P-29	0.0
1953	StL-A	34	30	3	6	2	0	0	2	1	3	.200	.226	.267	492	32	-3	0	0	0	1.000	-2	P-32	0.0

YEAR	TM/L	G	AB	R	H	2B	3B	HR	RBI	BB	SO	AVG	OBP	SLG	OPS	OPS+	BR+	SB	CS	SBR	FA	FR	G/POS	TPR
1954	Chi-A	1	0	1	0	0	0	0	0	0	0	—	—	—	—	—	0	0	0	0	.000	0	R	0.0
Total	6	150	214	28	42	8	1	0	14	14	45	.196	.246	.243	489	31	-21	0	0	0	.975	-4	P-140	0.0
■ MIGUEL CAIRO	Cairo, Miguel Jesus b: 5/4/74, Anaco, Venez. BR/TR, 6', 160 lbs. Deb: 4/17/96																							
1996	Tor-A	9	27	5	6	2	0	0	1	2	9	.222	.300	.296	596	52	-2	0	0	0	1.000	0	/2-9	-0.1
1997	Chi-N	16	29	7	7	1	0	0	1	2	3	.241	.313	.276	588	54	-2	0	0	0	1.000	1	/2-9,S-2	-0.1
1998	TB-A	150	515	49	138	26	5	5	46	24	44	.268	.308	.367	675	73	-20	19	8	1	.978	19	*2-148/D-2	0.6
1999	TB-A	120	465	61	137	15	5	3	36	24	46	.295	.339	.368	706	79	-14	22	7	2	.986	22	*2-117/D-2	1.5
2000	TB-A	119	375	49	98	18	2	1	34	29	34	.261	.318	.328	646	64	-20	28	7	4	.983	1	*2-108/C-1,D-2	-0.9
Total	5	414	1411	171	386	62	12	9	118	81	136	.274	.321	.354	674	72	-58	69	22	7	.983	43	2-391/D-6,S-2,C-1	1.0
■ GEORGE CAITHAMER	Caithamer, George Theodore "Sidee" b: 7/22/10, Chicago, Ill. d: 6/1/54, Chicago, Ill. BR/TR, 5'10", 168 lbs. Deb: 9/17/34																							
1934	Chi-A	5	19	1	6	1	0	0	3	1	5	.316	.350	.368	718	83	-0	0	0	0	.958	-1	/C-5	-0.1
■ IVAN CALDERON	Calderon, Ivan (Perez) b: 3/19/62, Fajardo, P.R. BR/TR, 6'1", 220 lbs. Deb: 8/10/84 Career OF: (378-LF 11-CF 383-RF)																							
1984	Sea-A	11	24	2	5	1	0	1	1	2	5	.208	.269	.375	644	77	-1	1	0	0	1.000	-1	O-11(4-6-1)	-0.1
1985	Sea-A	67	210	37	60	16	4	8	28	19	45	.286	.351	.514	865	132	9	4	2	0	.981	1	O-53(33-1-22)/1-2,D-3	0.8
1986	Sea-A	37	131	13	31	5	0	2	13	6	33	.237	.275	.321	596	61	-7	3	1	0	.937	-1	O-32(2-2-31)	-0.9
	Chi-A	13	33	3	10	2	1	0	2	3	6	.303	.361	.424	785	109	0	0	0	0	.900	-0	/O-5(5-0-0),D-6	0.0
	Yr	50	164	16	41	7	1	2	15	9	39	.250	.293	.341	635	71	-7	3	1	0	.932	-1	O-37(7-2-31)/D-6	-0.9
1987	Chi-A	144	542	93	159	38	2	28	83	60	109	.293	.365	.526	891	129	22	10	5	0	.984	5	*O-139(6-0-135)/D-3	1.9
1988	Chi-A	73	264	40	56	14	0	14	35	34	66	.212	.302	.424	726	101	-0	4	4	-1	.954	2	O-67(4-0-63)/D-3	-0.1
1989	Chi-A	157	622	83	178	34	9	14	87	43	94	.286	.335	.437	773	119	14	7	1	1	.978	0	*O-103R,D-36,1-26	0.9
1990	Chi-A	158	607	85	166	44	2	14	74	51	79	.273	.331	.422	753	111	8	32	16	1	.975	4	*O-130L,D-27/1-2	0.8
1991	Mon-N★	134	470	69	141	22	3	19	75	53	64	.300	.375	.481	855	141	26	31	16	1	.974	5	*O-122(122-0-0)/1-4	2.8
1992	Mon-N	48	170	19	45	14	2	3	24	14	22	.265	.324	.424	748	111	2	1	2	-0	.988	0	O-46(46-0-0)	0.1
1993	Bos-A	73	213	25	47	8	2	1	19	21	28	.221	.294	.291	585	54	-13	4	2	0	1.000	-1	O-47(9-2-39),D-19	-1.7
	Chi-A	9	26	1	3	2	0	0	3	0	5	.115	.115	.192	308	-19	-4	0	0	0	.000	0	/D-6	-0.5
	Yr	82	239	26	50	10	2	1	22	21	33	.209	.276	.280	556	47	-18	4	2	0	1.000	-1	O-47(9-2-39),D-25	-2.2
Total	10	924	3312	470	901	200	25	104	444	306	556	.272	.336	.442	778	113	56	97	49	4	.976	15	O-755R,D-103/1-34	4.0
■ SAM CALDERONE	Calderone, Samuel Francis b: 2/6/26, Beverly, N.J. BR/TR, 5'10.5", 185 lbs. Deb: 4/19/50																							
1950	NY-N	34	67	9	20	1	0	1	12	2	5	.299	.319	.358	677	77	-2	0			.972	-4	C-33	-0.5
1953	NY-N	35	45	4	10	2	0	0	8	1	4	.222	.239	.267	506	31	-5	0	0	0	.966	-1	C-31	-0.4
1954	Mil-N	22	29	3	11	2	0	0	5	4	4	.379	.455	.448	903	146	2	0	0	0	1.000	3	C-16	0.5
Total	3	91	141	16	41	5	0	1	25	7	13	.291	.324	.348	672	76	-5	0	0		.978	-2	/C-80	-0.4
■ BRUCE CALDWELL	Caldwell, Bruce b: 2/8/06, Ashton, R.I. d: 2/15/59, West Haven, Conn. BR/TR, 6', 195 lbs. Deb: 6/30/28																							
1928	Cle-A	18	27	2	6	1	1	0	3	2	2	.222	.300	.333	633	66	-1	1	0	0	1.000	-2	O-10(0-0-10)/1-1	-0.3
1932	Bro-N	7	11	2	1	0	0	0	2	2	2	.091	.231	.091	322	-10	-2	0			.875	-1	/1-6	-0.3
Total	2	25	38	4	7	1	1	0	5	4	4	.184	.279	.263	542	44	-3	1	0		.900	-3	/O-10(0-0-10),1-7	-0.6
■ RAY CALDWELL	Caldwell, Raymond Benjamin "Rube" or "Sum" b: 4/26/1888, Corydon, Pa. d: 8/17/67, Salamanca, N.Y. BL/TR, 6'2", 190 lbs. Deb: 9/9/10 Career OF: (9-LF 18-CF 15-RF)																							
1910	NY-A	6	6	0	0	0	0	0	0	0		.000	.000	.000	0	-95	-1	0			1.000	-0	/P-6	0.0
1911	NY-A	59	147	14	40	4	1	0	17	11		.272	.323	.313	636	73	-5	5			.953	-2	P-41,O-11(5-0-5)	-0.1
1912	NY-A	44	76	18	18	1	2	0	6	5		.237	.284	.303	587	64	-4	4			.938	1	P-30/O-1	0.0
1913	NY-A	59	97	10	28	3	2	0	11	3	15	.289	.310	.361	671	96	-1	3			**1.000**	-1	P-27/O-3(0-1-2)	-0.1
1914	NY-A	59	113	9	22	4	0	0	10	7	24	.195	.248	.230	478	44	-8	2	1	0	.967	-4	P-31/1-6	-0.3
1915	NY-A	72	144	27	35	4	1	4	20	9	32	.243	.288	.368	656	96	-2	4	3	-0	**.988**	-3	P-36	0.0
1916	NY-A	45	93	6	19	2	0	0	4	2	17	.204	.221	.226	447	34	-8	1			.960	-1	P-21/O-2	0.0
1917	NY-A	63	124	12	32	6	1	2	12	16	16	.258	.343	.371	714	117	3	2			.973	-3	P-32/O-8(0-5-3)	-0.2
1918	NY-A	65	151	14	44	10	0	1	18	13	23	.291	.352	.377	729	117	3	2			.977	-2	P-24,O-19(2-12-5)	0.1
1919	Bos-A	33	48	5	13	1	1	0	4	0	9	.271	.271	.333	604	73	-2	0			.950	-2	P-18/O-2(2-0-0)	-0.1
	Cle-A	6	23	4	8	4	0	0	2	0	4	.348	.348	.522	870	134	1	0			.900	-1	/P-6	0.0
	Yr	39	71	9	21	5	1	0	6	0	13	.296	.296	.394	690	97	-1	0			.933	-3	P-24/O-2(2-0-0)	-0.1
1920	*Cle-A	41	89	17	19	3	0	0	7	10	13	.213	.300	.247	547	45	-7	0	2	-1	.917	-3	P-34	0.0
1921	Cle-A	38	53	2	11	4	0	1	3	2	5	.208	.236	.340	576	45	-5	0	0	0	.930	-0	P-37	0.0
Total	12	590	1164	138	289	46	8	8	114	78	158	.248	.297	.322	619	78	-36	23	6		.960	-21	P-343/O-46C,1-6	-0.7
■ JACK CALHOUN	Calhoun, John Charles "Red" b: 12/14/1879, Pittsburgh, Pa. d: 2/27/47, Cincinnati, Ohio BR/TR, 6', 185 lbs. Deb: 6/27/02																							
1902	StL-N	20	64	3	10	2	1	0	8	8		.156	.260	.219	479	50	-4	1			.972	-2	3-12/1-5,O-1(0-0-1)	-0.6
■ BILL CALHOUN	Calhoun, William Davitte "Mary" b: 6/23/1890, Rockmart, Ga. d: 1/28/55, Sandersville, Ga. BL/TL, 6', 180 lbs. Deb: 4/24/13																							
1913	Bos-N	6	13	0	1	0	0	0	0	0	3	.077	.077	.077	154	-55	-3	0			.970	-0	/1-3	-0.3
■ MARTY CALLAGHAN	Callaghan, Martin Francis b: 6/9/1900, Norwood, Mass. d: 6/23/75, Norfolk, Mass. BL/TL, 5'10", 157 lbs. Deb: 4/13/22																							
1922	Chi-N	74	175	31	45	7	4	0	20	17	17	.257	.326	.343	669	71	-7	2	3	-1	.946	-9	O-53(12-10-31)	-1.9
1923	Chi-N	61	129	18	29	1	3	0	14	8	18	.225	.275	.279	554	47	-10	2	5	-1	.969	-4	O-38(19-0-19)	-1.7
1928	Cin-N	81	238	29	69	11	4	0	24	27	10	.290	.362	.370	732	93	-2	5			.980	-4	O-69(48-22-1)	-1.0
1930	Cin-N	79	225	28	62	9	2	0	16	19	25	.276	.335	.333	668	66	-12	1			.986	3	O-54(16-38-0)	-1.1
Total	4	295	767	106	205	28	13	0	74	71	70	.267	.332	.338	669	72	-31	10	8		.973	-14	O-214(95-70-51)	-5.7
■ DAVE CALLAHAN	Callahan, David Joseph b: 7/20/1888, Ottawa, Ill. d: 10/28/69, Ottawa, Ill. BL/TR, 5'10", 165 lbs. Deb: 9/14/10																							
1910	Cle-A	13	44	6	8	1	0	0	2	4		.182	.265	.205	470	47	-3	5			1.000	0	O-12(12-0-0)	-0.3
1911	Cle-A	6	16	1	4	0	1	0	0	1		.250	.294	.375	669	85	-0	0			.875	0	/O-4(0-4-0)	0.0
Total	2	19	60	7	12	1	1	0	2	5		.200	.273	.250	523	58	-3	5			.972	1	/O-16(12-4-0)	-0.3
■ ED CALLAHAN	Callahan, Edward Joseph b: 12/11/1857, Boston, Mass. d: 2/5/47, New York, N.Y. Deb: 7/19/1884																							
1884	StL-U	1	3	0	0	0	0	0		0		.000	.000	.000	0	-97	-1				1.000	0	/O-1(1-0-0)	0.0
	KC-U	3	11	0	4	0	0	0		0		.364	.364	.364	727	139	0				.800	1	/S-3	0.1
	Bos-U	4	13	2	5	0	0	0		1		.385	.429	.385	813	151	1				.750	-1	/O-4(1-0-3)	0.0
	Yr	8	27	2	9	0	0	0		1		.333	.357	.333	690	117	-0				.778	0	/O-5(2-0-3),S-3	0.1
■ NIXEY CALLAHAN	Callahan, James Joseph b: 3/18/1874, Fitchburg, Mass. d: 10/4/34, Boston, Mass. BR/TR, 5'10.5", 180 lbs. Deb: 5/12/1894 M Career OF: (401-LF 30-CF 59-RF)																							
1894	Phi-N	9	21	4	5	0	0	0	0	0	7	.238	.238	.238	476	15	-3	0			.923	1	/P-9	0.0
1897	Chi-N	94	360	60	105	18	6	3	47	10		.292	.320	.400	720	86	-9	12			.918	5	2-30,P-23,O-21L,S/3	-0.3
1898	Chi-N	43	164	27	43	7	5	0	22	4		.262	.280	.366	646	85	-4	3			.947	-2	P-31/O-9R,S-1,21	-0.4
1899	Chi-N	47	150	21	39	4	3	0	18	8		.260	.306	.327	633	76	-5	9			.904	3	P-35/O-9C,S-2,2-1	-0.3
1900	Chi-N	32	115	16	27	3	2	0	9	6		.235	.273	.296	568	59	-7	5			.975	6	P-32	0.0
1901	Chi-A	45	118	15	39	7	3	1	19	10		.331	.383	.466	849	138	6	10			.944	4	P-27/3-6,2-2	0.0
1902	Chi-A	70	218	27	51	7	2	0	13	6		.234	.261	.284	545	53	-14	4			.941	2	P-35,O-23(6-3-15)/S-1	-0.9
1903	Chi-A	118	439	47	128	26	5	2	56	20		.292	.324	.387	711	118	9	24			.895	-6	*3-102/O-8L,P-3,M	0.5
1904	Chi-A	132	482	66	126	23	2	0	54	39		.261	.318	.317	635	105	4	29			.977	-17	*O-104L,2-28,M	-2.1
1905	Chi-A	96	345	50	94	18	6	1	43	29		.272	.336	.368	704	128	11	26			.956	-8	O-93(71-1-21)	-0.2
1911	Chi-A	120	466	64	131	13	5	3	60	15		.281	.306	.350	656	86	-11	45			.963	-9	*O-114(93-10-11)	-2.5
1912	Chi-A	111	408	45	111	9	7	1	52	12		.272	.298	.336	634	84	-10	19			.939	-16	*O-107(107-0-0),M	-3.1
1913	Chi-A	6	9	0	2	0	0	0	1	0	2	.222	.222	.222	444	30	-1	0			1.000	-0	/O-1(1-0-0),M	-0.1
Total	13	923	3295	442	901	135	46	11	394	159	9	.273	.311	.352	663	94	-34	186			.953	-36	O-489L,P-195,3/2S1	-9.4

YEAR	TM/L	G	AB	R	H	2B	3B	HR	RBI	BB	SO	AVG	OBP	SLG	OPS	OPS+	BR+	SB	CS	SBR	FA	FR	G/POS	TPR
■ JIM CALLAHAN	Callahan, James Timothy "Red" (b: James Timothy Callaghan) b: 1/12/1879, Allegheny Co., Pa. d: 3/9/68, Carnegie, Pa. BR/TR, 5'9", 145 lbs. Deb: 5/25/02																							
1902	NY-N	1	4	0	0	0	0	0	0	1		.000	.200	.000	200	-38	-1	0			.000	-0	/O-1(0-0-1)	-0.1
■ LEO CALLAHAN	Callahan, Leo David b: 8/9/1890, Jamaica Plain, Mass d: 5/2/82, Erie, Pa. BL/TL, 5'8", 142 lbs. Deb: 4/9/13																							
1913	Bro-N	33	41	6	7	3	1	0	3	4	5	.171	.244	.293	537	52	-3	0			.857	-2	/O-8(2-4-2)	-0.5
1919	Phi-N	81	235	26	54	14	4	1	9	29	19	.230	.317	.336	653	90	-2	5			.950	1	O-58(12-9-38)	-0.5
Total	2	114	276	32	61	17	5	1	12	33	24	.221	.306	.330	636	84	-5	5			.941	-1	/O-66(14-13-40)	-1.0
■ PAT CALLAHAN	Callahan, Patrick Henry b: 10/15/1866, Cleveland, Ohio d: 2/4/40, Louisville, Ky. Deb: 5/1/1884																							
1884	Ind-a	61	258	38	67	8	5	2	8			.260	.282	.353	635	109	2				.812	-7	3-61	-0.3
■ WESLEY CALLAHAN	Callahan, Wesley Leroy b: 7/3/1888, Lyons, Ind. d: 9/13/53, Dayton, Ohio BR/TR, 5'7.5", 155 lbs. Deb: 9/7/13																							
1913	StL-N	7	14	0	4	0	0	0	1	2	2	.286	.375	.286	661	91	-0	1			.920	1	/S-6	0.1
■ FRANK CALLAWAY	Callaway, Frank Burnett b: 2/26/1898, Knoxville, Tenn. d: 8/21/87, Knoxville, Tenn. BR/TR, 6', 170 lbs. Deb: 9/17/21																							
1921	Phi-A	14	50	7	12	1	1	0	4	2	11	.240	.283	.300	583	49	-4	1	0	0	.878	-5	S-14	-0.6
1922	Phi-A	29	48	5	13	0	2	0	4	0	13	.271	.271	.354	625	60	-3	0	0	0	.880	1	2-11/3-5,S-4	-0.1
Total	2	43	98	12	25	1	3	0	8	2	24	.255	.277	.327	604	54	-7	1	0	0	.889	-4	/S-18,2-11,3-5	-0.7
■ JOHNNY CALLISON	Callison, John Wesley b: 3/12/39, Qualls, Okla. BL/TR, 5'10", 175 lbs. Deb: 9/9/58 Career OF: (189-LF 26-CF 1586-RF)																							
1958	Chi-A	18	64	10	19	4	2	1	12	6	14	.297	.357	.469	826	128	2	1	0	0	.976	3	O-18(18-0-0)	0.4
1959	Chi-A	49	104	12	18	3	0	3	12	13	20	.173	.271	.288	560	54	-7	0	1	-0	.983	-3	O-41(41-0-0)	-1.2
1960	Phi-N	99	288	36	75	11	5	9	30	45	70	.260	.360	.427	787	114	7	0	4	-1	.989	1	O-86(32-16-47)	0.3
1961	Phi-N	138	455	74	121	20	11	9	47	69	76	.266	.366	.418	784	109	7	10	4	1	.967	5	*O-124(90-1-35)	0.5
1962	Phi-N★	157	603	107	181	26	**10**	23	83	54	96	.300	.363	.491	854	131	25	10	3	1	.980	23	*O-152(3-5-151)	3.8
1963	Phi-N	157	626	96	178	36	11	26	78	50	111	.284	.339	.502	841	140	31	8	3	1	.994	23	*O-157(2-1-156)	4.6
1964	Phi-N★	162	654	101	179	30	10	31	104	36	95	.274	.318	.492	810	126	20	6	3	0	.988	19	*O-162(2-0-162)	2.9
1965	Phi-N☆	160	619	93	162	25	**16**	32	101	57	117	.262	.330	.509	839	135	26	6	5	-0	.982	19	*O-159(0-0-159)	3.5
1966	Phi-N	155	612	93	169	**40**	7	11	55	56	83	.276	.340	.418	758	109	8	8	8	-1	.990	6	*O-154(0-0-154)	0.1
1967	Phi-N	149	556	62	145	30	5	14	64	55	63	.261	.331	.408	739	109	7	6	12	-3	.977	9	*O-147(0-0-147)	0.3
1968	Phi-N	121	398	46	97	18	4	14	40	42	70	.244	.321	.415	735	119	9	4	3	-0	**1.000**	2	*O-109(0-0-109)	0.4
1969	Phi-N	134	495	66	131	29	5	16	64	49	73	.265	.335	.440	775	119	11	2	1	0	.990	16	*O-129(0-0-129)	2.0
1970	Chi-N	147	477	65	126	23	2	19	68	60	63	.264	.350	.440	790	98	-1	7	2	1	.973	-0	*O-144(0-3-143)	-0.7
1971	Chi-N	103	290	27	61	12	1	8	38	36	55	.210	.302	.341	643	71	-10	2	1	0	.982	-3	O-89(1-0-88)	-1.9
1972	NY-A	92	275	28	71	10	0	9	34	18	34	.258	.304	.393	696	110	2	3	0	1	.992	-3	O-74(0-0-74)	-0.4
1973	NY-A	45	136	10	24	4	0	1	10	4	24	.176	.200	.228	428	21	-14	1	1	-0	.960	-2	O-32(0-0-32),D-10	-1.9
Total	16	1886	6652	926	1757	321	89	226	840	650	1064	.264	.333	.441	774	114	123	74	51	-2	.984	113	*O-1777R/D-10	12.7
■ JACK CALVO	Calvo, Jacinto (Gonzalez) (Born Jacinto Del Calvo) b: 6/11/1894, Havana, Cuba d: 6/15/65, Miami, Fla. BL/TL, 5'10", 156 lbs. Deb: 5/9/13																							
1913	Was-A	17	33	5	8	0	0	1	2	1	4	.242	.265	.333	598	73	-1	0			.900	-2	O-13(5-0-7)	-0.4
1920	Was-A	17	23	5	1	0	1	0	2	2	2	.043	.120	.130	250	-35	-5	0	0	0	1.000	-4	O-10(6-1-3)	-0.8
Total	2	34	56	10	9	0	1	1	4	3	6	.161	.203	.250	453	27	-6	0	0		.938	-6	/O-23(11-1-10)	-1.2
■ HANK CAMELLI	Camelli, Henry Richard b: 12/12/14, Gloucester, Mass. d: 7/14/96, Wellesley, Mass. BR/TR, 5'11", 190 lbs. Deb: 10/3/43																							
1943	Pit-N	1	3	1	0	0	0	0	0	1	0	.000	.250	.000	250	-24	-0	0			1.000	0	/C-1	0.0
1944	Pit-N	63	125	14	37	5	1	1	10	18	12	.296	.385	.376	761	110	2	0			.959	4	C-61	0.9
1945	Pit-N	1	2	0	0	0	0	0	0	1	0	.000	.333	.000	333	-3	-0	0			1.000	-0	/C-1	0.0
1946	Pit-N	42	96	8	20	2	2	0	5	8	9	.208	.269	.271	540	52	-6	0			.971	4	C-39	-0.1
1947	Bos-N	52	150	10	29	8	1	1	11	18	18	.193	.280	.280	560	50	-11	0			.977	6	C-51	-0.2
Total	5	159	376	33	86	15	4	2	26	46	39	.229	.313	.306	619	70	-15	0			.970	14	C-153	0.6
■ JACK CAMERON	Cameron, John William "Happy Jack" b: 9/1884, Nova Scotia, Can. d: 8/17/51, Boston, Mass. Deb: 9/13/06																							
1906	Bos-N	18	61	3	11	0	0	0	4	2		.180	.206	.180	387	21	-6	0			.852	-1	O-16(15-0-1)/P-2	-0.8
■ MIKE CAMERON	Cameron, Michael Terrance b: 1/8/73, LaGrange, Ga. BR/TR, 6'1", 170 lbs. Deb: 8/27/95																							
1995	Chi-A	28	38	4	7	2	0	1	2	3	15	.184	.244	.316	560	46	-3	0	0	0	1.000	-4	O-28(0-3-26)	-0.7
1996	Chi-A	11	11	1	1	0	0	0	0	1	3	.091	.167	.091	258	-34	-2	0	1	-0	1.000	-3	/O-8(2-4-5),D-2	-0.6
1997	Chi-A	116	379	63	98	18	3	14	55	55	105	.259	.360	.433	793	110	7	23	2	4	.985	5	*O-112(0-102-37)/D-4	1.5
1998	Chi-A	141	396	53	83	16	5	8	43	37	101	.210	.287	.336	623	63	-22	27	11	2	.988	-3	*O-138(0-136-2)	-2.1
1999	Cin-N	146	542	93	139	34	9	21	66	80	145	.256	.358	.469	827	104	3	38	12	4	.979	13	*O-146(0-146-0)	2.1
2000	*Sea-A	155	543	96	145	28	4	19	78	78	133	.267	.368	.438	807	106	6	24	7	3	.985	6	*O-155(0-155-1)	1.5
Total	6	597	1909	310	473	98	21	63	244	254	502	.248	.344	.420	764	96	-11	112	33	13	.985	14	O-587(2-546-71)/D-6	1.7
■ DOLPH CAMILLI	Camilli, Adolph Louis b: 4/23/07, San Francisco, Cal d: 10/21/97, San Mateo, Cal. BL/TL, 5'10", 185 lbs. Deb: 9/9/33 F																							
1933	Chi-N	16	58	8	13	2	1	2	7	4	11	.224	.274	.397	671	90	-1	3			.994	2	1-16	-0.1
1934	Chi-N	32	120	17	33	8	0	4	19	5	25	.275	.315	.442	757	102	-0	1			.988	2	1-32	-0.1
	Phi-N	102	378	52	100	20	3	12	68	48	69	.265	.350	.429	779	95	-2	3			.985	-4	*1-102	-1.5
	Yr	134	498	69	133	28	3	16	87	53	94	.267	.342	.432	774	96	-2	4			.986	-2	*1-134	-1.6
1935	Phi-N	156	602	88	157	23	5	25	83	65	113	.261	.336	.440	776	97	-3	9			.987	-1	*1-156	-1.9
1936	Phi-N	151	530	106	167	29	13	28	102	116	84	.315	.441	.577	1018	156	46	5			.988	-10	*1-150	2.1
1937	Phi-N	131	475	101	161	23	7	27	80	90	82	.339	**.446**	.587	1034	165	46	6			**.994**	4	*1-131	3.7
1938	Bro-N	146	509	106	128	25	11	24	100	**119**	101	.251	.393	.485	879	137	29	6			.995	-1	*1-145	1.4
1939	Bro-N★	157	565	105	164	30	12	26	104	**110**	107	.290	.409	.524	933	144	38	1			.990	10	*1-157	3.2
1940	Bro-N	142	512	92	147	29	13	23	96	89	83	.287	.397	.529	926	145	32	9			.992	-4	*1-140	1.6
1941	*Bro-N†	149	529	92	151	29	6	**34**	**120**	104	115	.285	.407	.556	962	162	**45**	3			.989	3	*1-148	3.4
1942	Bro-N	150	524	89	132	23	7	26	109	97	85	.252	.372	.471	843	144	30	10			.992	-1	*1-150	1.7
1943	Bro-N	95	353	56	87	15	6	6	43	65	48	.246	.365	.374	739	113	8	2			.992	-1	1-95	0.3
1945	Bos-A	63	198	24	42	5	2	2	19	35	38	.212	.330	.288	618	78	-4	2	0	0	.991	2	1-54	-0.5
Total	12	1490	5353	936	1482	261	86	239	950	947	961	.277	.388	.492	880	134	263	60	0		.990	1	*1-1476	13.3
■ DOUG CAMILLI	Camilli, Douglas Joseph b: 9/22/36, Philadelphia, Pa. BR/TR, 5'11", 195 lbs. Deb: 9/25/60 FC																							
1960	LA-N	6	24	4	8	2	0	1	3	1	4	.333	.385	.542	926	141	1	0	0	0	.980	0	/C-6	0.2
1961	LA-N	13	30	3	4	0	0	3	4	1	9	.133	.161	.433	595	47	-2	0	0	0	.986	2	C-12	0.0
1962	LA-N	45	88	16	25	5	2	4	22	12	21	.284	.370	.523	893	145	6	0	0	0	.983	-5	C-39	0.1
1963	LA-N	49	117	9	19	1	1	3	10	11	22	.162	.234	.265	499	47	-8	0	0	0	.977	8	C-47	0.2
1964	LA-N	50	123	1	22	3	0	0	10	8	19	.179	.229	.203	432	25	-12	0	0	0	.990	8	C-46	-0.2
1965	Was-A	75	193	13	37	6	1	3	18	16	34	.192	.257	.280	537	53	-12	0	0	0	.980	1	C-59	-0.9
1966	Was-A	44	107	5	22	4	0	2	8	3	19	.206	.234	.299	533	53	-7	0	0	0	.990	4	C-39	-0.1
1967	Was-A	30	82	5	15	1	0	2	5	4	16	.183	.221	.268	489	46	-6	0	0	0	.993	0	C-24	-0.5
1969	Was-A	1	3	0	1	0	0	0	0	0	2	.333	.333	.333	667	92	-0	0	0	0	1.000	-0	/C-1	0.0
Total	9	313	767	56	153	22	4	18	80	56	146	.199	.257	.309	566	61	-40	0	0	0	.984	19	C-273	-1.2
■ LOU CAMILLI	Camilli, Louis Steven b: 9/24/46, ElPaso, Tex. BB/TR, 5'10", 170 lbs. Deb: 8/9/69																							
1969	Cle-A	13	14	0	0	0	0	0	0	0	3	.000	.000	.000	0	-97	-4	0	0	0	1.000	3	3-13	0.0
1970	Cle-A	16	15	0	0	0	0	0	0	2	2	.000	.118	.000	118	-62	-3	0	0	0	1.000	-1	/S-3,2-2,3-1	-0.4
1971	Cle-A	39	81	5	16	2	0	0	0	8	10	.198	.270	.222	492	37	-6	0	0	0	.938	1	S-23,2-16	-0.4
1972	Cle-A	39	41	2	6	2	0	0	3	3	8	.146	.205	.195	400	19	-4	0	0	0	1.000	-2	/S-8,2-2	-0.6
Total	4	107	151	7	22	4	0	0	3	13	23	.146	.213	.172	386	11	-17	0	0	0	.951	2	/S-34,2-20,3-14	-1.4
■ KEN CAMINITI	Caminiti, Kenneth Gene b: 4/21/63, Hanford, Cal. BB/TR, 6', 200 lbs. Deb: 7/16/87																							
1987	Hou-N	63	203	10	50	7	1	3	23	12	44	.246	.288	.335	623	67	-10	0	0	0	.949	3	3-61	-0.7

YEAR	TM/L	G	AB	R	H	2B	3B	HR	RBI	BB	SO	AVG	OBP	SLG	OPS	OPS+	BR+	SB	CS	SBR	FA	FR	G/POS	TPR
1988	Hou-N	30	83	5	15	2	0	1	7	5	18	.181	.227	.241	468	36	-7	0	0	0	.948	-0	3-28	-0.8
1989	Hou-N	161	585	71	149	31	3	10	72	51	93	.255	.318	.369	687	99	-1	4	1	1	.954	13	*3-160	1.4
1990	Hou-N	153	541	52	131	20	2	4	51	48	97	.242	.304	.309	613	71	-21	9	4	1	.945	-11	*3-149	-3.2
1991	Hou-N	152	574	65	145	30	3	13	80	46	85	.253	.314	.383	697	101	-1	4	5	-1	.948	8	*3-152	0.7
1992	Hou-N	135	506	68	149	31	2	13	62	44	68	.294	.352	.441	793	129	18	10	4	1	.966	-9	*3-129	1.1
1993	Hou-N	143	543	75	142	31	0	13	75	49	88	.262	.323	.390	713	93	-6	8	5	0	.942	5	*3-143	0.0
1994	Hou-N★	111	406	63	115	28	2	18	75	43	71	.283	.355	.495	850	125	14	4	3	-0	.969	2	*3-108	1.6
1995	SD-N	143	526	74	159	33	0	26	94	69	94	.302	.384	.513	898	139	30	12	5	1	.936	10	*3-143	4.0
1996	*SD-N★	146	546	109	178	37	2	40	130	78	99	.326	.414	.621	1035	179	62	11	5	1	.954	12	*3-145	7.3
1997	SD-N★	137	486	92	141	28	0	26	90	80	118	.290	.394	.508	902	145	33	11	2	2	.941	14	*3-133	4.8
1998	*SD-N	131	452	87	114	29	0	29	82	71	108	.252	.359	.509	867	135	23	6	2	1	.931	-12	*3-126	1.2
1999	*Hou-N	78	273	45	78	11	1	13	56	46	58	.286	.394	.476	871	121	10	6	2	1	.932	2	3-75	1.2
2000	Hou-N	59	208	42	63	13	0	15	45	42	37	.303	.422	.582	1004	142	14	3	0	1	.915	-12	3-58	0.3
Total	14	1642	5932	858	1629	331	16	224	942	684	1078	.275	.352	.449	801	119	159	88	38	6	.946	24	*3-1610	18.9

■ HOWIE CAMP Camp, Howard Lee "Red" b: 7/1/1893, Munford, Ala. d: 5/8/60, Eastaboga, Ala. BL/TR, 5'9", 169 lbs. Deb: 9/19/17

YEAR	TM/L	G	AB	R	H	2B	3B	HR	RBI	BB	SO	AVG	OBP	SLG	OPS	OPS+	BR+	SB	CS	SBR	FA	FR	G/POS	TPR
1917	NY-A	5	21	3	6	1	0	0	0	1	2	.286	.318	.333	652	98	-0	0			.857	1	/O-5(0-4-1)	0.0

■ LEW CAMP Camp, Llewellyn Robert b: 2/22/1868, Columbus, Ohio d: 10/1/48, Omaha, Neb. BL/TR, 6', 175 lbs. Deb: 8/26/1892 F Career OF: (0-LF 13-CF 1-RF)

YEAR	TM/L	G	AB	R	H	2B	3B	HR	RBI	BB	SO	AVG	OBP	SLG	OPS	OPS+	BR+	SB	CS	SBR	FA	FR	G/POS	TPR
1892	StL-N	42	145	19	30	3	1	2	13	17	27	.207	.294	.283	577	79	-3	12			.780	-16	3-39/O-3(0-2-1)	-1.8
1893	Chi-N	38	156	37	41	7	7	2	17	19	19	.263	.347	.436	782	109	1	30			.847	-10	3-16,O-11C/2-9,S-3	-0.7
1894	Chi-N	8	33	1	6	2	0	0	1	1	6	.182	.206	.242	448	7	-5	0			.830	-3	/2-8	-0.6
Total	3	88	334	57	77	12	8	4	31	37	52	.231	.311	.350	661	85	-7	42			.801	-28	/3-55,2-17,O-14C,S	-3.1

■ ROY CAMPANELLA Campanella, Roy b: 11/19/21, Philadelphia, Pa. d: 6/26/93, Woodland Hills, Cal. BR/TR, 5'8", 200 lbs. Deb: 4/20/48 H

YEAR	TM/L	G	AB	R	H	2B	3B	HR	RBI	BB	SO	AVG	OBP	SLG	OPS	OPS+	BR+	SB	CS	SBR	FA	FR	G/POS	TPR
1948	Bro-N	83	279	32	72	11	3	9	45	36	45	.258	.345	.416	761	102	1	3			.981	10	C-78	1.5
1949	*Bro-N★	130	436	65	125	22	2	22	82	67	36	.287	.385	.498	883	130	19	3			.985	5	*C-127	3.0
1950	Bro-N★	126	437	70	123	19	3	31	89	55	51	.281	.364	.551	916	134	21	1			.985	-4	*C-123	2.2
1951	Bro-N★	143	505	90	164	33	1	33	108	53	51	.325	.393	.590	983	158	40	1	2	-0	.986	9	*C-140	5.4
1952	*Bro-N★	128	468	73	126	18	1	22	97	57	59	.269	.352	.453	805	120	13	8	4	0	**.994**	-7	*C-122	1.4
1953	*Bro-N★	144	519	103	162	26	3	41	**142**	67	58	.312	.395	.611	1006	154	40	4	2	0	.989	3	*C-140	4.8
1954	Bro-N★	111	397	43	82	14	3	19	51	42	49	.207	.286	.401	686	74	-16	1	4	-1	.989	-3	*C-111	-1.5
1955	*Bro-N†	123	446	81	142	20	1	32	107	56	41	.318	.402	.583	985	153	34	2	3	-1	.992	1	*C-121	4.0
1956	*Bro-N★	124	388	39	85	6	1	20	73	66	61	.219	.334	.394	728	88	-6	1	0	0	.985	3	*C-121	0.4
1957	Bro-N	103	330	31	80	9	0	13	62	34	50	.242	.321	.388	709	81	-8	1	0	0	**.993**	16	*C-100	1.3
Total	10	1215	4205	627	1161	178	18	242	856	533	501	.276	.362	.500	861	123	137	25	15		.988	33	*C-1183	22.5

■ BERT CAMPANERIS Campaneris, Dagoberto (Blanco) "Campy" (b: Dagoberto Campaneria (Blanco))
b: 3/9/42, Pueblo Nuevo, Cuba BR/TR, 5'10", 160 lbs. Deb: 7/23/64 Career OF: (68-LF 2-CF 1-RF)

YEAR	TM/L	G	AB	R	H	2B	3B	HR	RBI	BB	SO	AVG	OBP	SLG	OPS	OPS+	BR+	SB	CS	SBR	FA	FR	G/POS	TPR
1964	KC-A	67	269	27	69	14	3	4	22	15	41	.257	.306	.375	681	86	-5	10	2	2	.981	-6	S-38,O-27(27-0-0)/3-6	-0.9
1965	KC-A	144	578	67	156	23	**12**	6	42	41	71	.270	.328	.382	710	103	2	**51**	19	**5**	.938	-14	*S-109,O-39L/PC123	-0.1
1966	KC-A	142	573	82	153	29	10	5	42	25	72	.267	.303	.379	682	98	-3	**52**	10	**8**	.971	-17	*S-138	0.0
1967	KC-A	147	601	85	149	29	6	3	32	36	82	.248	.298	.331	629	89	-9	**55**	16	**7**	.954	-19	*S-145	-1.0
1968	Oak-A★	159	642	87	**177**	25	9	4	38	50	69	.276	.332	.361	693	116	11	**62**	22	**6**	.956	1	*S-155/O-3(3-0-0)	3.6
1969	Oak-A	135	547	71	142	15	2	2	25	30	62	.260	.303	.305	608	74	-20	62	8	**11**	.967	-5	*S-125	0.1
1970	Oak-A	147	603	97	168	28	4	22	64	36	73	.279	.323	.448	771	115	9	**42**	10	6	.973	-10	*S-143	2.4
1971	*Oak-A	134	569	80	143	18	4	5	47	29	64	.251	.290	.323	613	75	-20	34	7	5	.960	-5	*S-133	-0.4
1972	*Oak-A☆	149	625	85	150	25	2	8	32	32	88	.240	.279	.325	604	84	-15	**52**	14	**7**	.977	7	*S-148	1.9
1973	*Oak-A★	151	601	89	150	17	6	4	46	50	79	.250	.311	.318	629	82	-14	34	10	4	.969	-7	*S-149	0.0
1974	*Oak-A★	134	527	77	153	18	8	2	41	47	81	.290	.348	.366	715	113	9	34	15	2	.966	-9	*S-133/D-1	1.9
1975	*Oak-A★	137	509	69	135	15	3	4	46	50	71	.265	.339	.330	669	92	-4	24	12	1	.962	-31	*S-137	-1.8
1976	Oak-A	149	536	67	137	14	1	1	52	63	80	.256	.337	.291	628	89	-5	54	12	**8**	.969	-6	*S-149	1.5
1977	Tex-A★	150	552	77	140	19	7	5	46	47	86	.254	.317	.341	657	78	-16	27	20	-1	.968	18	*S-149	1.6
1978	Tex-A	98	269	30	50	5	3	1	17	20	36	.186	.247	.238	485	37	-22	22	4	3	.954	4	S-89/D-4	-0.7
1979	Tex-A	8	9	2	1	0	0	0	0	1	3	.111	.200	.111	311	-14	-1	1	0	0	.962	4	/S-8	0.3
	*Cal-A	85	239	27	56	4	4	0	15	19	32	.234	.296	.285	581	59	-13	12	4	1	.957	4	S-82/D-1	0.0
	Yr	93	248	29	57	4	4	0	15	20	35	.230	.293	.278	571	57	-15	13	4	1	.957	7	S-90/D-1	0.3
1980	Cal-A	77	210	32	53	8	1	2	18	14	33	.252	.302	.329	631	75	-7	10	5	0	.957	-5	S-64/2-1,D-2	-0.6
1981	Cal-A	55	82	11	21	2	1	1	10	5	10	.256	.299	.341	640	84	-2	5	2	0	.900	-2	3-45/S-3,2-2	-0.4
1983	NY-A	60	143	19	46	5	0	0	11	8	9	.322	.358	.357	714	101	0	6	7	-1	.964	-3	2-32,3-24	-0.2
Total	19	2328	8684	1181	2249	313	86	79	646	618	1142	.259	.313	.342	655	89	-125	649	199	73	.964	-102	*S-2097/3-76,O2D1CP	7.2

■ AL CAMPANIS Campanis, Alexander Sebastian (b: Alessandro Campani)
b: 11/2/16, Kos, Dodecanese Islands d: 6/21/98, Fullerton, Cal. BB/TR, 6', 185 lbs. Deb: 9/23/43 F

YEAR	TM/L	G	AB	R	H	2B	3B	HR	RBI	BB	SO	AVG	OBP	SLG	OPS	OPS+	BR+	SB	CS	SBR	FA	FR	G/POS	TPR
1943	Bro-N	7	20	3	2	0	0	0	0	4	5	.100	.250	.100	350	3	-2	0			1.000	4	/2-7	0.2

■ JIM CAMPANIS Campanis, James Alexander b: 2/9/44, New York, N.Y. BR/TR, 6', 195 lbs. Deb: 9/20/66 F

YEAR	TM/L	G	AB	R	H	2B	3B	HR	RBI	BB	SO	AVG	OBP	SLG	OPS	OPS+	BR+	SB	CS	SBR	FA	FR	G/POS	TPR
1966	LA-N	1	1	0	0	0	0	0	0	0	0	.000	.000	.000	0	-99	-0	0	0	0	1.000	0	/C-1	0.0
1967	LA-N	41	62	3	10	1	0	2	2	9	14	.161	.268	.274	542	60	-3	0	0	0	.990	-0	C-23	-0.3
1968	LA-N	4	11	0	1	0	0	0	0	1	2	.091	.167	.091	258	-23	-2	0	0	0	.960	1	/C-4	0.0
1969	KC-A	30	83	4	13	5	0	0	5	5	19	.157	.205	.217	421	18	-9	0	0	0	.982	3	C-26	-0.6
1970	KC-A	31	54	6	7	0	0	2	2	4	14	.130	.203	.241	444	22	-6	0	0	0	.986	1	C-13/O-1(0-0-1)	-0.5
1973	Pit-N	6	6	0	1	0	0	0	0	0	0	.167	.167	.167	333	-8	-1	0	0	0	.000	0	H	-0.1
Total	6	113	217	13	32	6	0	4	9	19	49	.147	.219	.230	450	27	-21	0	0	0	.983	5	/C-67,O-1(0-0-1)	-1.5

■ COUNT CAMPAU Campau, Charles Columbus b: 10/17/1863, Detroit, Mich.
d: 4/3/38, New Orleans, La. BL/TR, 5'11", 160 lbs. Deb: 7/7/1888 M Career OF: (41-LF 2-CF 103-RF)

YEAR	TM/L	G	AB	R	H	2B	3B	HR	RBI	BB	SO	AVG	OBP	SLG	OPS	OPS+	BR+	SB	CS	SBR	FA	FR	G/POS	TPR
1888	Det-N	70	251	28	51	5	3	1	18	19	36	.203	.259	.259	518	66	-9	27			.933	-4	O-70(0-0-70)	-1.4
1890	StL-a	75	314	68	101	9	12	**9**	75	26		.322	.374	.513	886	141	12	36			.934	3	O-74L/3-1,1-1,M	1.3
1894	Was-N	2	7	1	1	0	0	0	0	1	4	.143	.250	.143	393	-3	-1	0			1.000	-0	/O-2(2-0-0)	-0.1
Total	3	147	572	97	153	14	15	10	93	46	40	.267	.322	.397	719	109	2	63			.934	-1	O-146R/1-1,3-1	-0.2

■ VIN CAMPBELL Campbell, Arthur Vincent b: 1/30/1888, St.Louis, Mo. d: 11/16/69, Towson, Md. BL/TR, 6', 185 lbs. Deb: 6/6/08

YEAR	TM/L	G	AB	R	H	2B	3B	HR	RBI	BB	SO	AVG	OBP	SLG	OPS	OPS+	BR+	SB	CS	SBR	FA	FR	G/POS	TPR
1908	Chi-N	1	1	0	0	0	0	0	0	0		.000	.000	.000	0	-96	-0	0			.000	0	H	0.0
1910	Pit-N	97	282	42	92	9	5	4	21	26	23	.326	.391	.436	827	133	12	17			.895	-4	O-74(38-17-18)	0.4
1911	Pit-N	42	93	12	29	3	1	0	10	8	7	.312	.366	.366	732	101	0	6			.923	-3	O-21(9-1-11)	-0.3
1912	Bos-N	145	624	102	185	32	9	3	48	32	44	.296	.334	.391	725	96	-5	19			.938	1	*O-144(0-144-0)	-1.4
1914	Ind-F	134	544	92	173	23	11	7	44	37	47	.318	.368	.439	807	108	-1	26			.925	-5	*O-132(1-94-37)	-1.6
1915	New-F	127	525	78	163	18	10	1	44	29	35	.310	.352	.389	741	115	2	24			.947	-5	*O-126(0-12-115)	-1.1
Total	6	546	2069	326	642	85	36	15	167	132	156	.310	.357	.408	765	109	7	92			.929	-16	O-497(48-268-181)	-4.0

■ BRUCE CAMPBELL Campbell, Bruce Douglas b: 10/20/09, Chicago, Ill. d: 6/17/95, Ft.Myers Beach, Fla. BL/TR, 6'1", 185 lbs. Deb: 9/12/30

YEAR	TM/L	G	AB	R	H	2B	3B	HR	RBI	BB	SO	AVG	OBP	SLG	OPS	OPS+	BR+	SB	CS	SBR	FA	FR	G/POS	TPR
1930	Chi-A	5	10	4	5	1	1	0	5	1	2	.500	.545	.800	1345	245	2	0	0	0	1.000	-0	/O-4(4-0-0)	0.2
1931	Chi-A	4	17	4	7	2	0	2	5	0	4	.412	.444	.882	1327	256	4	0	0	0	.900	-0	/O-4(4-0-0)	0.3
1932	Chi-A	7	18	3	4	1	0	0	2	0	2	.222	.222	.278	500	31	-2	0	1	-0	1.000	-1	/O-4(3-0-1)	-0.3
	StL-A	139	593	83	169	35	11	14	85	40	102	.285	.336	.452	788	97	-5	7	5	-0	.935	6	*O-139(0-0-139)	-0.7
	Yr	146	611	86	173	36	11	14	87	40	104	.283	.333	.447	780	95	-6	7	6	-1	.935	5	*O-143(3-0-140)	-1.0
1933	StL-A	148	567	87	157	38	8	16	106	69	77	.277	.357	.457	814	108	5	10	4	1	.950	-1	*O-144(0-0-144)	-0.3
1934	StL-A	138	481	62	134	25	6	9	74	51	64	.279	.350	.412	762	88	-9	5	4	-0	.935	3	*O-123(0-0-123)	-1.2
1935	Cle-A	80	308	56	100	26	3	7	54	31	33	.325	.390	.497	887	126	11	2	1	0	.992	-5	O-75(0-0-75)	0.1
1936	Cle-A	76	172	35	64	15	2	6	30	19	17	.372	.440	.587	1028	150	14	2	1	0	.960	-4	O-47(0-0-47)	0.6
1937	Cle-A	134	448	82	135	42	11	4	61	67	49	.301	.392	.471	863	116	12	4	5	-1	.978	-2	*O-123(0-0-123)	0.2

YEAR	TM/L	G	AB	R	H	2B	3B	HR	RBI	BB	SO	AVG	OBP	SLG	OPS	OPS+	BR+	SB	CS	SBR	FA	FR	G/POS	TPR
1938	Cle-A	133	511	90	148	27	12	12	72	53	57	.290	.360	.460	820	106	3	11	7	-0	.967	-0	*O-122(0-0-122)	-0.4
1939	Cle-A	130	450	84	129	23	13	8	72	67	48	.287	.383	.449	832	116	12	7	6	-1	.942	-3	*O-115(0-0-115)	0.1
1940	*Det-A	103	297	56	84	15	5	8	44	45	28	.283	.381	.448	829	104	2	2	7	-2	.959	-2	O-74(0-0-74)	-0.6
1941	Det-A	141	512	72	141	28	10	15	93	68	67	.275	.364	.457	821	105	4	3	3	-0	.976	-8	*O-133(0-0-133)	-1.2
1942	Was-A	122	378	41	105	17	5	5	63	37	34	.278	.344	.389	733	107	3	0	6	-2	.955	-1	O-87(20-0-68)	-0.5
Total	13	1360	4762	759	1382	295	87	106	766	548	584	.290	.367	.455	822	108	57	53	50	-6	.956	-19	*O-1194(31-0-1164)	-3.7
■ SOUP CAMPBELL	Campbell, Clarence b: 3/7/15, Sparta, Va. d: 2/16/2000, Sparta, Va. BL/TR, 6'1", 188 lbs. Deb: 4/21/40																							
1940	Cle-A	35	62	8	14	1	0	0	2	7	12	.226	.304	.242	546	45	-5	0	0	0	1.000	-2	O-16(8-5-4)	-0.7
1941	Cle-A	104	328	36	82	10	4	3	35	31	21	.250	.317	.332	649	75	-12	1	9	-3	.981	2	O-78(20-59-0)	-1.5
Total	2	139	390	44	96	11	4	3	37	38	33	.246	.315	.318	633	70	-17	1	9	-3	.984	0	/O-94(28-64-4)	-2.2
■ DAVE CAMPBELL	Campbell, David Wilson b: 1/14/42, Manistee, Mich. BR/TR, 6', 185 lbs. Deb: 9/17/67																							
1967	Det-A	2	2	0	0	0	0	0	0	0	1	.000	.000	.000	0	-97	-0	0	0	0	.500	-0	/1-1	-0.1
1968	Det-A	9	8	1	1	0	0	1	2	1	3	.125	.222	.500	722	111	0	0	0	0	1.000	0	/2-5	0.1
1969	Det-A	32	39	4	4	1	0	0	2	4	15	.103	.205	.128	333	-5	-5	0	1	-0	.967	-2	1-13/2-5,3-1	-0.8
1970	SD-N	154	581	71	127	28	2	12	40	40	115	.219	.270	.336	606	64	-32	18	6	2	.974	12	*2-153	-0.8
1971	SD-N	108	365	38	83	14	2	7	29	37	75	.227	.299	.334	633	85	-8	9	6	-0	.968	-2	2-69,3-40/S-4,1O	-0.6
1972	SD-N	33	100	6	24	5	0	0	3	11	12	.240	.315	.290	605	79	-3	0	4	-1	.988	4	3-31/2-1	0.0
1973	SD-N	33	98	2	22	3	0	0	8	7	15	.224	.276	.255	531	52	-6	1	1	-0	.979	-1	2-27/1-3,3-2	-0.6
	StL-N	13	21	1	0	0	0	0	1	1	6	.000	.045	.000	45	-87	-5	0	0	0	.933	-3	/2-6	-0.8
	Hou-N	9	15	1	4	2	0	0	2	0	4	.267	.267	.400	667	83	-0	0	0	0	1.000	2	/3-5,1-2,O-1(1-0-0)	0.1
	Yr	55	134	4	26	5	0	0	11	8	25	.194	.239	.231	471	33	-12	1	1	-0	.975	-2	2-33/3-7,1-5,O-1L	-1.3
1974	Hou-N	35	23	4	2	1	0	0	2	1	8	.087	.125	.130	255	-30	-4	1	0	0	.895	6	/2-9,1-6,3-2,O-1L	0.2
Total	8	428	1252	128	267	54	4	20	89	102	254	.213	.274	.311	584	64	-64	29	18	0	.971	16	2-275/3-81,1-27,OS	-3.3
■ JIM CAMPBELL	Campbell, James Robert b: 6/24/37, Palo Alto, Cal. BR/TR, 6', 190 lbs. Deb: 7/17/62																							
1962	Hou-N	27	86	6	19	4	0	3	6	6	23	.221	.272	.372	644	77	-3	0	0	0	.970	6	C-25	0.4
1963	Hou-N	55	158	9	35	3	0	4	19	10	40	.222	.268	.316	584	72	-6	0	0	0	.979	-2	C-42	-0.6
Total	2	82	244	15	54	7	0	7	25	16	63	.221	.269	.336	605	74	-9	0	0	0	.975	4	/C-67	-0.2
■ JIM CAMPBELL	Campbell, James Robert b: 1/10/43, Hartsville, S.C. BL/TR, 6', 205 lbs. Deb: 4/11/70																							
1970	StL-N	13	13	0	3	0	0	0	1	0	3	.231	.231	.231	462	24	-1	0	0	0	.000	0	H	-0.1
■ JOE CAMPBELL	Campbell, Joseph Earl b: 3/10/44, Louisville, Ky. BR/TR, 6'1", 175 lbs. Deb: 5/3/67																							
1967	Chi-N	1	3	0	0	0	0	0	0	0	3	.000	.000	.000	0	-96	-1	0	0	0	.000	-0	/O-1(0-0-1)	-0.1
■ HUTCH CAMPBELL	Campbell, Marc Thaddeus b: 11/29/1884, Punxsutawney, Pa. d: 2/13/46, New Bethlehem, Pa. BB/TR, 5'9", 155 lbs. Deb: 9/30/07																							
1907	Pit-N	2	4	0	1	0	0	0	1	1		.250	.400	.250	650	102	0	0			.889	0	/S-2	0.0
■ MAT CAMPBELL	Campbell, Mathew b: 8/1/1850, Ireland d: 1/12/26, Scotch Plains, N.J. Deb: 4/28/1873 F																							
1873	Res-n	21	83	9	12	0	0	0	3	3	6	.145	.174	.145	319	-5	-10	1	0	0	.927	-2	1-18/S-3,O-1(0-0-1)	-0.8
■ PAUL CAMPBELL	Campbell, Paul McLaughlin b: 9/1/17, Paw Creek, N.C. BL/TL, 5'10", 185 lbs. Deb: 4/15/41																							
1941	Bos-A	1	0	0	0	0	0	0	0	0	0	—	—	—	—	—	0	0	0	0	.000	0	R	0.0
1942	Bos-A	26	15	4	1	0	0	0	0	1	5	.067	.125	.067	192	-44	-3	1	0	0	1.000	-2	/O-4(0-4-0)	-0.5
1946	*Bos-A	28	26	3	3	1	0	0	0	2	7	.115	.179	.154	332	-6	-4	0	0	0	1.000	-0	/1-5	-0.4
1948	Det-A	59	83	15	22	1	1	1	11	1	10	.265	.274	.337	611	60	-5	0	0	0	.969	3	1-27	-0.2
1949	Det-A	87	255	38	71	15	4	3	30	24	32	.278	.343	.404	747	97	-2	3	3	-0	.988	-3	1-74	-0.7
1950	Det-A	3	1	1	0	0	0	0	0	0	0	.000	.000	.000	0	-97	-0	0	0	0	.000	0	H	0.0
Total	6	204	380	61	97	17	5	4	41	28	54	.255	.308	.358	666	76	-14	4	3	-0	.984	-2	1-106/O-4(0-4-0)	-1.8
■ RON CAMPBELL	Campbell, Ronald Thomas b: 4/5/40, Chattanooga, Tenn. BR/TR, 6'1", 180 lbs. Deb: 9/1/64																							
1964	Chi-N	26	92	7	25	6	1	1	10	1	21	.272	.280	.391	671	83	-2	0	1	-0	.941	14	2-26	1.3
1965	Chi-N	2	2	0	0	0	0	0	0	0	0	.000	.000	.000	0	-98	-1	0	0	0	.000	0	H	-0.1
1966	Chi-N	24	60	4	13	1	0	0	4	6	5	.217	.288	.233	521	46	-4	1	1	-0	.980	4	S-11/3-7	0.1
Total	3	52	154	11	38	7	1	1	14	7	26	.247	.280	.325	604	67	-7	1	2	-0	.941	18	/2-26,S-11,3-7	1.3
■ SAM CAMPBELL	Campbell, Samuel b: Philadelphia, Pa. Deb: 10/11/1890																							
1890	Phi-a	2	5	0	0	0	0	0	0	1		.000	.167	.000	167	-51	-1	0			.833	-2	/2-2	-0.3
■ GILLY CAMPBELL	Campbell, William Gilthorpe b: 2/13/08, Kansas City, Kan. d: 2/21/73, Los Angeles, Cal. BL/TR, 5'7.5", 182 lbs. Deb: 4/25/33																							
1933	Chi-N	46	89	11	25	3	1	1	10	7	4	.281	.347	.371	718	105	1	0			.949	-2	C-20	0.0
1935	Cin-N	88	218	26	56	7	0	3	30	42	7	.257	.379	.330	710	95	1	3			.986	0	C-66/1-5,O-1(1-0-0)	0.4
1936	Cin-N	89	235	28	63	13	1	1	40	43	14	.268	.384	.345	728	104	4	2			.984	6	C-71/1-1	1.3
1937	Cin-N	18	40	3	11	2	0	0	2	5	1	.275	.356	.325	681	90	-0	0			.967	-1	C-17	0.0
1938	Bro-N	54	126	10	31	5	0	0	11	19	9	.246	.354	.286	639	76	-3	0			.958	-0	C-44	-0.1
Total	5	295	708	78	186	30	2	5	93	116	35	.263	.371	.332	703	96	2	5			.975	4	C-218/1-6,O-1(1-0-0)	1.6
■ FRANK CAMPOS	Campos, Francisco Jose (Lopez) b: 5/11/24, Havana, Cuba BL/TL, 5'11", 180 lbs. Deb: 9/11/51																							
1951	Was-A	8	26	4	11	3	1	0	3	0	1	.423	.423	.615	1038	182	3	0	0	0	1.000	-2	/O-7(0-0-7)	0.1
1952	Was-A	53	112	9	29	6	1	0	8	1	13	.259	.278	.330	609	71	-5	0	0	0	.978	-2	O-23(13-1-10)	-0.8
1953	Was-A	10	9	0	1	0	0	0	2	1	0	.111	.200	.111	311	-14	-1	0	0	0	.000	0	H	-0.1
Total	3	71	147	13	41	9	2	0	13	2	14	.279	.298	.367	665	86	-4	0	0	0	.981	-4	/O-30(13-1-17)	-0.8
■ SIL CAMPUSANO	Campusano, Silvestre (Diaz) b: 12/31/65, Santo Domingo, D.R. BR/TR, 6', 175 lbs. Deb: 4/4/88																							
1988	Tor-A	73	142	14	31	10	2	2	12	9	33	.218	.284	.359	643	78	-4	0	0	0	.934	-10	O-69(15-35-19)/D-2	-1.5
1990	Phi-N	66	85	10	18	1	1	2	9	6	16	.212	.272	.318	589	62	-5	1	0	0	.976	-13	O-47(16-25-7)	-1.9
1991	Phi-N	15	35	2	4	0	0	1	2	1	10	.114	.139	.200	339	-6	-5	0	0	0	1.000	-1	O-15(1-15-0)	-0.6
Total	3	154	262	26	53	11	3	5	23	16	59	.202	.261	.324	586	62	-14	1	0	0	.953	-24	O-131(32-75-26)/D-2	-4.0
■ GEORGE CANALE	Canale, George Anthony b: 8/11/65, Memphis, Tenn. BL/TR, 6'1", 190 lbs. Deb: 9/3/89																							
1989	Mil-A	13	26	5	5	1	0	1	3	2	3	.192	.250	.346	596	67	-1	0	1	-0	.989	-0	1-11	-0.3
1990	Mil-A	10	13	4	1	1	0	0	0	2	6	.077	.200	.154	354	0	-2	0	1	-0	1.000	1	/1-6,D-3	-0.1
1991	Mil-A	21	34	6	6	2	0	3	10	8	6	.176	.333	.500	833	130	1	0	0	0	.983	3	1-19	0.3
Total	3	44	73	15	12	4	0	4	13	12	15	.164	.282	.384	666	85	-2	0	2	-1	.988	3	/1-36,D-3	-0.1
■ WILLIE CANATE	Canate, Emisael William (Librada) b: 12/11/71, Maracaibo, Venez. BR/TR, 6', 170 lbs. Deb: 4/16/93																							
1993	*Tor-A	38	47	12	10	0	0	1	3	6	15	.213	.315	.277	591	60	-2	1	1	-0	1.000	-4	O-31(17-6-9)/D-1	-0.7
■ JIM CANAVAN	Canavan, James Edward b: 11/26/1866, New Bedford, Mass. d: 5/27/49, New Bedford, Mass. BR/TR, 5'8", 160 lbs. Deb: 4/8/1891 Career OF: (105-LF 10-CF 106-RF)																							
1891	Cin-a	101	426	74	97	13	14	7	66	27	44	.228	.282	.373	655	80	-15	21			.860	-11	*S-101	-2.0
	Mil-a	35	142	33	38	2	4	3	21	16	10	.268	.342	.401	743	94	-2	7			.864	-2	2-24,S-11	-0.3
	Yr	136	568	107	135	15	18	10	87	43	54	.238	.297	.380	677	84	-17	28			.860	-13	*S-112,2-24	-2.3
1892	Chi-N	118	439	48	73	10	11	0	32	48	48	.166	.248	.239	488	47	-28	33			.923	-2	*2-112/O-4(1-3-0),S-2	-2.4
1893	Cin-N	121	461	65	104	13	7	5	64	51	20	.226	.305	.317	622	64	-25	31			.931	-1	*O-117L/2-5,3-1	-2.9
1894	Cin-N	103	364	81	100	16	10	13	74	64	25	.275	.383	.481	864	103	0	13			.897	-2	*O-97R/S-3,3-2,21	-0.5
1897	Bro-N	63	240	25	52	9	3	2	34	26		.217	.299	.304	603	63	-13	9			.909	-21	2-63	-2.7
Total	5	541	2072	326	464	63	49	30	291	232	147	.224	.305	.345	650	74	-84	114			.917	-40	O-218R,2-205,S/31	-10.8
■ ROBINSON CANCEL	Cancel, Robinson Castro b: 5/4/76, Lajas, P.R. BR/TR, 6', 195 lbs. Deb: 9/3/99																							
1999	Mil-N	15	44	5	8	2	0	0	5	2	12	.182	.234	.227	461	18	-6	0	0	0	.980	4	C-15	0.0

YEAR	TM/L	G	AB	R	H	2B	3B	HR	RBI	BB	SO	AVG	OBP	SLG	OPS	OPS+	BR+	SB	CS	SBR	FA	FR	G/POS	TPR
■ **CASEY CANDAELE** Candaele, Casey Todd b: 1/12/61, Lompoc, Cal. BB/TR, 5′9″, 165 lbs. Deb: 6/5/86 Career OF: (86-LF 78-CF 38-RF)																								
1986	Mon-N	30	104	9	24	4	1	0	6	5	15	.231	.266	.288	555	53	-7	3	5	-1	.983	-2	2-24/3-4	-0.8
1987	Mon-N	138	449	62	122	23	4	1	23	38	28	.272	.331	.347	679	78	-14	7	10	-2	.985	-1	2-68,O-67C,S-25,/1	-1.3
1988	Mon-N	36	116	9	20	5	1	0	4	10	11	.172	.238	.233	471	34	-10	1	0	0	.988	1	2-35	-0.8
	Hou-N	21	31	2	5	3	0	0	1	1	6	.161	.188	.258	446	28	-3	0	1	-0	1.000	1	2-10/O-5(0-3-2),3-1	-0.3
	Yr	57	147	11	25	8	1	0	5	11	17	.170	.228	.238	466	33	-13	1	1	-0	.990	2	2-45/O-5(0-3-2),3-1	-1.1
1990	Hou-N	130	262	30	75	8	6	3	22	31	42	.286	.364	.397	761	112	5	7	5	-0	1.000	-14	O-58L,2-49,S-13,/3	-0.9
1991	Hou-N	151	461	44	121	20	7	4	50	40	49	.262	.321	.362	684	97	-2	9	3	1	.982	5	*2-109,O-26L,3-11	0.7
1992	Hou-N	135	320	19	68	12	1	1	18	24	36	.213	.274	.266	539	56	-19	7	1	1	.968	-5	S-65,3-29,O-21L,/2	-2.0
1993	Hou-N	75	121	18	29	8	0	1	7	10	14	.240	.298	.331	628	70	-5	2	3	-1	1.000	-6	2-19,O-17C,S-14,/3	-1.1
1996	*Cle-A	24	44	8	11	2	0	1	4	1	9	.250	.267	.364	630	58	-3	0	0	0	1.000	7	2-11/3-3,S-1	0.4
1997	Cle-A	14	26	5	8	1	0	0	4	1	1	.308	.333	.346	679	75	-1	1	0	0	1.000	5	/2-9,3-1,D-1	0.4
Total	9	754	1934	206	483	86	20	11	139	161	211	.250	.309	.332	641	78	-57	37	28	-2	.987	-8	2-343,O-194L,S/3D1	-5.7
■ **JOHN CANGELOSI** Cangelosi, John Anthony b: 3/10/63, Brooklyn, N.Y. BB/TL, 5′8″, 160 lbs. Deb: 6/3/85 Career OF: (265-LF 317-CF 70-RF)																								
1985	Chi-A	5	2	2	0	0	0	0	0	0	1	.000	.333	.000	333	1	-0	0	0	0	1.000	-2	/O-3(0-4-0),D-2	-0.2
1986	Chi-A	137	438	65	103	16	3	2	32	71	61	.235	.351	.299	650	77	-12	50	17	5	.969	-5	*O-129(29-98-5)/D-3	-1.4
1987	Pit-N	104	182	44	50	8	3	4	18	46	33	.275	.429	.418	846	125	9	21	6	3	.962	-4	O-47(27-16-8)	0.7
1988	Pit-N	75	118	18	30	4	1	0	8	17	16	.254	.353	.305	658	92	-1	9	4	1	.963	-2	O-24(11-12-3)/P-1	-0.2
1989	Pit-N	112	160	18	35	4	2	0	9	35	20	.219	.369	.269	637	88	-0	11	8	-0	.973	-6	O-46(12-24-10)	-0.8
1990	Pit-N	58	76	13	15	2	0	0	1	11	12	.197	.307	.224	531	50	-5	7	2	1	1.000	-1	O-12(3-9-0)	-0.5
1992	Tex-A	73	85	12	16	2	0	1	6	18	16	.188	.330	.247	577	66	-3	6	5	-0	.964	-13	O-65(36-24-10)/D-6	-1.8
1994	NY-N	62	111	14	28	4	0	0	4	19	20	.252	.371	.288	660	76	-3	5	1	1	1.000	-6	O-50(24-13-19)	-0.9
1995	Hou-N	90	201	46	64	5	2	2	18	48	42	.318	.458	.393	852	137	15	21	5	3	.950	-3	O-59(26-32-1)/P-1	1.4
1996	Hou-N	108	262	49	69	11	4	1	16	44	41	.263	.379	.347	727	101	3	17	9	1	.975	-4	O-78(53-29-0)	-0.1
1997	*Fla-N	103	192	28	47	8	0	1	12	19	33	.245	.322	.302	625	68	-9	5	1	1	1.000	-6	O-58(34-23-6)/P-1	-1.4
1998	Fla-N	104	171	19	43	8	0	1	10	30	23	.251	.366	.316	682	86	-2	2	3	-1	.969	-9	O-45(9-33-8)/D-1	-1.1
1999	Col-N	7	6	0	1	1	0	0	0	0	4	.167	.167	.333	500	18	-1	0	0	0	1.000	-0	/O-1(1-0-0)	-0.1
Total	13	1038	2004	328	501	73	15	12	134	358	322	.250	.372	.319	691	90	-8	154	61	13	.972	-59	O-617C/D-12,P-3	-6.4
■ **JAY CANIZARO** Canizaro, Jason Kyle b: 7/4/73, Beaumont, Tex. BR/TR, 5′9″, 170 lbs. Deb: 4/28/96																								
1996	SF-N	43	120	11	24	4	1	2	8	9	38	.200	.262	.300	562	50	-9	0	2	-1	.972	0	2-35/S-7	-0.8
1999	SF-N	12	18	5	8	2	0	1	9	1	2	.444	.474	.722	1196	212	3	1	0	0	1.000	-1	/2-4	0.2
2000	Min-A	102	346	43	93	21	1	7	40	24	57	.269	.318	.396	714	75	-13	4	2	0	.982	-29	2-90/D-2	-3.6
Total	3	157	484	59	125	27	2	10	57	34	97	.258	.310	.384	694	74	-19	5	4	-0	.979	-31	2-129/S-7,D-2	-4.2
■ **RIP CANNELL** Cannell, Virgin Wirt b: 1/23/1880, S.Bridgton, Maine d: 8/26/48, Bridgton, Maine BL/TR, 5′10.5″, 180 lbs. Deb: 4/14/04																								
1904	Bos-N	100	346	32	81	5	1	0	18	23		.234	.286	.254	540	70	-12	10			.897	-11	O-93(15-10-69)	-2.9
1905	Bos-N	154	567	52	140	14	4	0	36	51		.247	.311	.286	597	80	-13	17			.935	-8	*O-154(3-149-3)	-3.0
Total	2	254	913	84	221	19	5	0	54	74		.242	.302	.274	576	76	-25	27			.923	-19	O-247(18-159-72)	-5.9
■ **CHRIS CANNIZZARO** Cannizzaro, Christopher John b: 5/3/38, Oakland, Cal. BR/TR, 6′, 190 lbs. Deb: 4/17/60 C																								
1960	StL-N	7	9	0	2	0	0	0	1	1	3	.222	.300	.222	522	42	-1	0	0	0	1.000	1	/C-6	0.1
1961	StL-N	6	2	0	1	0	0	0	0	0	0	.500	.500	.500	1000	151	0	0	0	0	1.000	1	/C-5	0.1
1962	NY-N	59	133	9	32	2	1	0	9	19	26	.241	.340	.271	611	65	-6	1	1	-0	.973	2	C-56/O-1(0-0-1)	-0.2
1963	NY-N	16	33	4	8	1	0	0	4	1	8	.242	.265	.273	537	54	-2	0	0	0	1.000	-1	C-15	-0.2
1964	NY-N	60	164	11	51	10	0	0	10	14	28	.311	.369	.372	741	112	3	0	5	-2	.988	2	C-53	0.6
1965	NY-N	114	251	17	46	8	2	0	7	28	60	.183	.270	.231	502	44	-18	0	2	-1	.977	12	*C-112	-0.3
1968	Pit-N	25	58	5	14	2	2	1	7	9	13	.241	.343	.397	740	123	2	0	0	0	.976	-0	C-25	0.3
1969	SD-N☆	134	418	23	92	14	3	4	33	42	81	.220	.291	.297	588	68	-18	0	1	-0	.988	-14	*C-132	-2.7
1970	SD-N	111	341	27	95	13	3	5	42	48	49	.279	.369	.378	748	105	4	2	7	-2	.980	-16	*C-110	-0.9
1971	SD-N	21	63	2	12	1	0	1	8	11	10	.190	.320	.254	574	69	-2	0	0	0	.992	-2	C-19	-0.3
	Chi-N	71	197	18	42	8	1	5	23	28	24	.213	.314	.340	654	74	-6	0	0	0	.983	-11	C-70	-1.5
	Yr	92	260	20	54	9	1	6	31	39	34	.208	.316	.319	635	73	-8	0	0	0	.985	-12	C-89	-1.8
1972	LA-N	73	200	14	48	6	0	2	18	31	38	.240	.342	.300	642	86	-3	0	1	-0	.983	-8	C-72	-0.8
1973	LA-N	17	21	0	4	0	0	0	3	3	3	.190	.292	.190	482	38	-2	0	0	0	1.000	-0	C-13	-0.2
1974	SD-N	26	60	2	11	1	0	0	4	6	11	.183	.258	.200	458	31	-5	0	0	0	.979	5	C-26	0.0
Total	13	740	1950	132	458	66	12	18	169	241	354	.235	.321	.309	630	77	-54	3	17	-5	.983	-28	C-714/O-1(0-0-1)	-6.0
■ **JOE CANNON** Cannon, Joseph Jerome b: 7/13/53, Camp Lejeune, N.C. BL/TR, 6′3″, 193 lbs. Deb: 9/22/77																								
1977	Hou-N	9	17	3	2	2	0	0	1	0	5	.118	.118	.235	353	-9	-3	1	1	-0	1.000	0	/O-3(3-0-0)	-0.3
1978	Hou-N	8	18	1	4	0	0	0	1	0	1	.222	.222	.222	444	26	-2	0	1	-0	.778	-1	/O-5(3-2-0)	-0.4
1979	Tor-A	61	142	14	30	1	1	1	5	1	34	.211	.217	.254	470	26	-15	12	2	2	1.000	-4	O-50(17-0-40)	-1.8
1980	Tor-A	70	50	16	4	0	0	0	4	0	14	.080	.098	.080	178	-48	-10	2	2	-0	.968	-10	O-33(18-16-0)/D-1	-2.1
Total	4	148	227	34	40	3	1	1	11	1	54	.176	.183	.211	395	7	-29	15	6	1	.977	-15	/O-91(41-18-40),D-1	-4.6
■ **JOSE CANSECO** Canseco, Jose (Capas) b: 7/2/64, Havana, Cuba BR/TR, 6′4″, 240 lbs. Deb: 9/2/85 F Career OF: (356-LF 1-CF 677-RF)																								
1985	Oak-A	29	96	16	29	3	0	5	13	4	31	.302	.330	.490	820	130	4	1	1	-0	.951	-0	O-26(13-1-16)	0.2
1986	Oak-A☆	157	600	85	144	29	1	33	117	65	175	.240	.322	.457	779	118	14	15	7	1	.958	-3	*O-155(124-0-46)/D-1	0.4
1987	Oak-A	159	630	81	162	35	3	31	113	50	157	.257	.314	.470	784	111	8	15	3	2	.975	11	*O-130(130-0-0),D-30	1.4
1988	*Oak-A★	158	610	120	187	34	0	**42**	**124**	78	128	.307	.394	**.569**	963	**172**	59	40	16	3	.978	8	*O-144(0-0-144),D-13	**6.4**
1989	*Oak-A†	65	227	40	61	9	1	17	57	23	69	.269	.341	.542	883	151	14	6	3	0	.976	4	O-56(0-0-56)/D-5	1.6
1990	*Oak-A★	131	481	83	132	14	2	37	101	72	158	.274	.375	.543	917	160	38	19	10	1	.995	5	O-88(0-0-88),D-43	4.0
1991	Oak-A	154	572	115	152	32	1	**44**	122	78	152	.266	.363	.556	919	159	45	26	6	4	.965	-3	*O-131(0-0-131),D-24	4.1
1992	Oak-A†	97	366	66	90	11	0	22	72	48	104	.246	.338	.456	794	127	13	5	7	-1	.988	4	O-77(0-0-77),D-20	1.3
	Tex-A	22	73	8	17	4	0	4	15	15	24	.233	.385	.452	837	139	4	1	0	0	.970	1	O-13(0-0-13)/D-8	0.5
	Yr	119	439	74	107	15	0	26	87	63	128	.244	.346	.456	802	129	17	6	7	-1	.985	5	O-90(0-0-90),D-28	1.8
1993	Tex-A	60	231	30	59	14	1	10	46	16	62	.255	.312	.455	767	107	1	6	6	-1	.970	1	O-49(0-0-49)/P-1	-0.1
1994	Tex-A	111	429	88	121	19	2	31	90	69	114	.282	.388	.552	940	139	25	15	8	1	.000	0	*D-111	1.8
1995	*Bos-A	102	396	64	121	25	1	24	81	42	93	.306	.382	.556	938	136	20	4	0	1	1.000	-0	*D-101/O-1(0-0-1)	1.4
1996	Bos-A	96	360	68	104	22	1	28	82	63	82	.289	.403	.589	992	144	25	3	1	0	1.000	-1	D-84,O-11(10-0-2)	1.7
1997	Oak-A	108	388	56	91	19	0	23	74	51	122	.235	.328	.461	789	105	2	8	2	1	.938	-4	D-56,O-44(19-0-27)	-0.6
1998	Tor-A	151	583	98	138	26	0	46	107	65	159	.237	.320	.518	838	112	8	29	17	0	.960	-4	D-78,O-73(50-0-26)	-0.2
1999	TB-A†	113	430	75	120	18	1	34	95	58	135	.279	.374	.563	937	133	21	3	0	1	1.000	-0	*D-109/O-6(6-0-0)	1.4
2000	TB-A	61	218	31	56	15	0	9	30	41	65	.257	.384	.450	834	111	5	2	0	0	.000	0	D-60	0.1
	*NY-A	37	111	16	27	3	0	6	19	23	37	.243	.373	.432	806	105	1	0	0	0	.818	-1	D-26/O-5(4-0-1)	-0.1
	Yr	98	329	47	83	18	0	15	49	64	102	.252	.380	.444	824	109	6	2	0	0	.879	-1	D-86/O-5(4-0-1)	0.0
Total	16	1811	6801	1140	1811	332	14	446	1358	861	1867	.266	.356	.516	872	133	308	198	87	13	.971	18	*O-1009R,D-769/P-1	25.3
■ **OZZIE CANSECO** Canseco, Osvaldo (Capas) b: 7/2/64, Havana, Cuba BR/TR, 6′2″, 220 lbs. Deb: 7/18/90 F																								
1990	Oak-A	9	19	1	2	1	0	0	1	1	10	.105	.150	.158	308	-14	-3	0	0	0	1.000	-0	/O-2(1-0-1),D-4	-0.3
1992	StL-N	9	29	7	8	5	0	0	3	7	4	.276	.417	.448	865	150	2	0	0	0	.889	-2	/O-8(7-0-1)	0.0
1993	StL-N	6	17	0	3	0	0	0	0	1	3	.176	.222	.176	399	8	-2	0	0	0	.500	-2	/O-5(5-0-0)	-0.5
Total	3	24	65	8	13	6	0	0	4	9	17	.200	.297	.292	590	67	-3	0	0	0	.857	-4	/O-15(13-0-2),D-4	-0.8
■ **BART CANTZ** Cantz, Bartholomew L. b: 1/29/1860, Philadelphia, Pa. d: 2/12/43, Philadelphia, Pa. Deb: 7/25/1888																								
1888	Bal-a	37	126	7	21	2	1	0	9	2		.167	.180	.198	378	22	-11	0			.904	-9	C-33/O-4(1-0-3)	-1.6
1889	Bal-a	20	69	6	12	2	0	0	8	4	14	.174	.219	.203	422	20	-7	2			.860	-7	C-18/O-2(0-1-1)	-1.1
1890	Phi-a	5	22	1	1	0	0	0	1	0		.045	.045	.045	91	-74	-5	0			.893	-3	/C-5	-0.6
Total	3	62	217	14	34	4	1	0	18	6	14	.157	.179	.184	364	11	-23	2			.890	-19	/C-56,O-6(1-1-4)	-3.3

YEAR	TM/L	G	AB	R	H	2B	3B	HR	RBI	BB	SO	AVG	OBP	SLG	OPS	OPS+	BR+	SB	CS	SBR	FA	FR	G/POS	TPR
■ **NICK CAPRA**	Capra, Nick Lee b: 3/8/58, Denver, Colo. BR/TR, 5′8″, 165 lbs. Deb: 9/6/82																							
1982	Tex-A	13	15	2	4	0	0	1	1	3	4	.267	.421	.467	888	151	1	2	1	0	1.000	1	/O-9(4-1-4)	0.2
1983	Tex-A	8	2	2	0	0	0	0	0	0	0	.000	.000	.000	0	-99	-1	0	0	0	.000	-2	/O-4(1-1-2)	-0.2
1985	Tex-A	8	8	1	1	0	0	0	0	0	0	.125	.125	.125	250	-31	-1	0	0	0	1.000	-1	/O-8(1-3-4)	-0.3
1988	KC-A	14	29	3	4	1	0	0	0	2	3	.138	.194	.172	366	3	-4	1	0	0	1.000	-2	O-11(2-7-2)/D-1	-0.6
1991	Tex-A	2	0	1	0	0	0	0	0	1	0	—	1.000	—	1000	205	0	0	0	0	1.000	-0	/O-2(1-1-0)	0.0
Total	5	45	54	9	9	1	0	1	1	6	7	.167	.262	.241	503	41	-4	3	1	0	1.000	-5	/O-34(9-13-12),D-1	-0.9
■ **PAT CAPRI**	Capri, Patrick Nicholas b: 11/27/18, New York, N.Y. d: 6/14/89, New York, N.Y. BR/TR, 6′0.5″, 170 lbs. Deb: 7/16/44																							
1944	Bos-N	7	1	1	0	0	0	0	0	0	1	.000	.000	.000	0	-96	-0	0			1.000	1	/2-1	0.1
■ **RALPH CAPRON**	Capron, Ralph Earl b: 6/16/1889, Minneapolis, Minn d: 9/19/80, Los Angeles, Cal. BL/TR, 5′11.5″, 165 lbs. Deb: 4/25/12																							
1912	Pit-N	1	0	0	0	0	0	0	0	0	0	—	—	—	—	—	0	0			.000	0	R	0.0
1913	Phi-N	2	1	1	0	0	0	0	0	0	0	.000	.000	.000	0	-96	-0	0			.000	-1	/O-1(1-0-0)	-0.1
Total	2	3	1	1	0	0	0	0	0	0	0	.000	.000	.000	0	-96	-0	0			—	-1	/O-1(1-0-0)	-0.1
■ **RAMON CARABALLO**	Caraballo, Ramon (Sanchez) b: 5/23/69, Rio San Juan, D.R. BB/TR, 5′7″, 150 lbs. Deb: 9/9/93																							
1993	Atl-N	6	0	0	0	0	0	0	0	0	0	—	—	—	—	—	0	0	0	0	1.000	2	/2-5	0.2
1995	StL-N	34	99	10	20	4	1	2	3	6	33	.202	.269	.323	592	55	-7	3	2	-0	.956	-1	2-24	-0.7
Total	2	40	99	10	20	4	1	2	3	6	33	.202	.269	.323	592	55	-7	3	2	-0	.958	1	/2-29	-0.5
■ **JOHN CARBINE**	Carbine, John C. b: 10/12/1855, Syracuse, N.Y. d: 9/11/15, Chicago, Ill. 6′, 187 lbs. Deb: 5/8/1875																							
1875	Wes-n	10	36	0	3	0	0	0	2	0	1	.083	.083	.083	167	-40	-5	0	0	0	.950	1	1-10	-0.4
1876	Lou-N	7	25	3	4	0	0	0	1	0	0	.160	.160	.160	320	6	-3				.878	-0	/1-6,O-1(0-0-1)	-0.3
■ **BERNIE CARBO**	Carbo, Bernardo b: 8/5/47, Detroit, Mich. BL/TR, 6′, 175 lbs. Deb: 9/2/69 Career OF: (299-LF 0-CF 406-RF)																							
1969	Cin-N	4	3	0	0	0	0	0	0	0	2	.000	.000	.000	0	-95	-1	0	0	0	.000	0	H	-0.1
1970	*Cin-N	125	365	54	113	19	3	21	63	94	77	.310	.456	.551	1006	168	40	10	4	1	.979	0	*O-119(118-0-1)	3.4
1971	Cin-N	106	310	33	68	20	1	5	20	54	56	.219	.339	.339	678	94	-1	2	1	0	.982	2	O-90(90-0-0)	-0.4
1972	Cin-N	19	21	2	3	0	0	0	0	6	3	.143	.357	.143	500	50	-1	0	0	0	1.000	0	/O-4(0-0-4)	-0.1
	StL-N	99	302	42	78	13	1	7	34	57	56	.258	.385	.377	762	119	10	0	1	-0	.967	8	O-92(0-0-92)/3-1	1.4
	Yr	118	323	44	81	13	1	7	34	63	59	.251	.383	.362	745	115	9	0	1	-0	.969	8	O-96(0-0-96)/3-1	1.3
1973	StL-N	111	308	42	88	18	0	8	40	58	52	.286	.401	.422	823	128	14	2	0	0	.978	3	O-94(2-0-93)	1.3
1974	Bos-A	117	338	40	84	20	0	12	61	58	90	.249	.365	.414	779	116	8	4	3	-0	.994	-1	O-87(33-0-56),D-15	0.3
1975	*Bos-A	107	319	64	82	21	3	15	50	83	69	.257	.412	.483	895	140	20	2	4	-1	.976	-1	O-85(38-0-47),D-13	1.4
1976	Bos-A	17	55	5	13	4	0	2	6	8	17	.236	.333	.418	752	106	0	1	0	0	1.000	-0	D-15/O-1(1-0-0)	0.0
	Mil-A	69	183	20	43	7	0	3	15	33	55	.235	.352	.322	674	100	1	1	2	-0	1.000	4	O-33(4-0-29),D-24	0.2
	Yr	86	238	25	56	11	0	5	21	41	72	.235	.348	.345	692	102	2	2	2	-0	1.000	3	D-39,O-34(5-0-29)	0.2
1977	Bos-A	86	228	36	66	6	1	15	34	47	72	.289	.411	.522	933	136	13	1	2	-0	.951	2	O-67(8-0-59)/D-7	1.1
1978	Bos-A	17	46	7	12	3	0	1	6	8	8	.261	.370	.391	762	103	0	1	1	-0	1.000	1	/O-9(1-0-8),D-8	0.1
	Cle-A	60	174	21	50	8	0	4	16	20	31	.287	.364	.402	766	117	4	1	0	0	1.000	-2	D-49/O-4(0-0-4)	0.2
	Yr	77	220	28	62	11	0	5	22	28	39	.282	.365	.400	765	113	5	2	1	0	.950	-0	D-57,O-13(1-0-12)	0.3
1979	StL-N	52	64	6	18	1	0	3	12	10	22	.281	.378	.438	816	121	2	1	0	0	1.000	-5	O-17(4-0-13)	-0.4
1980	StL-N	14	11	0	2	0	0	0	0	1	0	.182	.250	.182	432	22	-1	0	0	0	.000	0	H	-0.2
	Pit-N	7	6	0	2	0	0	0	1	1	1	.333	.429	.333	762	114	0	0	0	0	.000	0	/H	0.0
	Yr	21	17	0	4	0	0	0	1	2	1	.235	.316	.235	551	55	-1	0	0	0	.000	0	-0,-0	-0.2
Total	12	1010	2733	372	722	140	9	96	358	538	611	.264	.389	.427	816	125	111	26	18	-1	.978	12	O-702R,D-131/3-1	8.2
■ **JOSE CARDENAL**	Cardenal, Jose Rosario Domec (b: Jose Rosario Domec (Cardenal)) b: 10/7/43, Matanzas, Cuba BR/TR, 5′10″, 150 lbs. Deb: 4/14/63 C Career OF: (427-LF 847-CF 549-RF)																							
1963	SF-N	9	5	1	1	0	0	0	2	1	1	.200	.333	.200	533	58	-0	0	1	-0	.000	-1	/O-2(0-1-1)	-0.2
1964	SF-N	20	15	3	0	0	0	0	0	2	3	.000	.118	.000	118	-62	-3	2	0	0	.909	-3	O-16(8-2-6)	-0.6
1965	Cal-A	134	512	58	128	23	2	11	57	27	72	.250	.290	.367	657	87	-10	37	17	2	.964	10	*O-129C/3-2,2-1	-0.1
1966	Cal-A	154	561	67	155	15	3	16	48	34	69	.276	.322	.399	721	109	5	24	11	1	.992	12	*O-146(7-140-0)	1.5
1967	Cal-A	108	381	40	90	13	5	6	27	15	63	.236	.269	.344	613	83	-9	10	5	0	.986	0	*O-101(27-70-17)	-1.4
1968	Cle-A	157	583	78	150	21	7	7	44	39	74	.257	.306	.353	659	101	-0	40	18	3	.974	13	*O-153(0-153-0)	1.2
1969	Cle-A	146	557	75	143	26	3	11	45	49	58	.257	.317	.373	690	89	-8	36	6	6	.982	11	*O-142(1-141-0)/3-5	0.5
1970	StL-N	148	552	73	162	32	6	10	74	45	70	.293	.348	.428	775	104	3	26	9	3	.969	-0	*O-134(0-133-1)	0.2
1971	StL-N	89	301	37	73	12	4	7	48	29	35	.243	.309	.379	688	90	-4	12	3	2	.969	7	O-83(0-8-78)	0.1
	Mil-A	53	198	20	51	10	0	3	32	13	20	.258	.307	.354	660	88	-4	9	5	0	.979	7	O-52(0-45-7)	0.2
1972	Chi-N	143	533	96	155	24	6	17	70	55	58	.291	.358	.454	812	117	12	25	14	1	.971	-9	*O-137(8-16-125)	-0.3
1973	Chi-N	145	522	80	158	33	2	11	68	58	62	.303	.378	.437	815	116	13	19	7	2	.980	-3	*O-142(1-2-142)	0.4
1974	Chi-N	143	542	75	159	35	3	13	72	56	67	.293	.361	.441	802	118	13	23	9	2	.965	8	*O-137(32-1-108)	1.6
1975	Chi-N	154	574	85	182	30	2	9	68	77	50	.317	.402	.423	825	124	21	34	12	3	.976	12	*O-151(137-0-18)	2.8
1976	Chi-N	136	521	64	156	25	2	8	47	32	39	.299	.341	.401	742	101	1	23	14	0	.981	7	*O-128(127-0-2)	0.0
1977	Chi-N	100	226	33	54	12	1	3	18	28	30	.239	.325	.341	666	71	-9	5	4	-0	.989	-6	O-62(54-6-2)/2-1,S-1	-1.8
1978	*Phi-N	87	201	27	50	12	0	4	33	23	16	.249	.326	.368	694	93	-2	2	3	-1	.990	-9	1-50,O-13(10-0-4)	-1.5
1979	Phi-N	29	48	4	10	3	0	0	9	8	8	.208	.321	.271	592	61	-2	1	0	0	1.000	-3	O-12(9-0-6)/1-1	-0.6
	NY-N	11	37	8	11	4	0	2	4	6	3	.297	.409	.568	977	170	4	1	0	0	1.000	-1	/O-9(0-0-9),1-2	0.2
	Yr	40	85	12	21	7	0	2	13	14	11	.247	.360	.400	760	106	1	2	0	0	1.000	-4	O-21(9-0-15)/1-3	-0.4
1980	NY-N	26	42	4	7	1	0	0	4	6	4	.167	.271	.190	461	32	-4	0	1	-0	1.000	0	/O-6(2-0-4),1-5	-0.4
	*KC-A	25	53	8	18	2	0	0	5	5	5	.340	.397	.377	774	112	1	0	0	0	.970	-3	O-23(4-0-19)	-0.2
Total	18	2017	6964	936	1913	333	46	138	775	608	807	.275	.335	.395	730	102	18	329	139	24	.976	48	*O-1778C/1-58,3-7,2S	1.6
■ **LEO CARDENAS**	Cardenas, Leonardo Lazaro (Alfonso) "Chico" b: 12/17/38, Matanzas, Cuba BR/TR, 5′10″, 163 lbs. Deb: 7/25/60																							
1960	Cin-N	48	142	13	33	2	4	1	12	6	32	.232	.264	.324	587	59	-8	0	0	0	.958	7	S-47	0.2
1961	*Cin-N	74	198	23	61	18	1	5	24	15	39	.308	.357	.485	842	119	5	1	0	0	.973	-5	S-63	0.5
1962	Cin-N	153	589	77	173	31	4	10	60	39	99	.294	.343	.411	754	98	-2	2	5	-1	.972	-7	*S-149	0.3
1963	Cin-N	158	565	42	133	22	4	7	48	23	101	.235	.270	.326	596	69	-23	3	5	-1	**.972**	-3	*S-157	-1.5
1964	Cin-N★	163	597	61	150	32	2	9	69	41	110	.251	.302	.357	658	82	-14	4	4	-1	.960	-10	*S-163	-1.1
1965	Cin-N★	156	557	65	160	25	11	11	57	60	100	.287	.358	.431	788	113	11	1	4	-1	.975	-1	*S-155	2.3
1966	Cin-N★	160	568	59	145	25	4	20	81	45	87	.255	.311	.419	730	93	-6	9	4	1	**.980**	-15	*S-160	-0.6
1967	Cin-N	108	379	30	97	14	3	2	21	34	77	.256	.320	.325	645	76	-10	4	5	-1	.971	-10	*S-108	-1.3
1968	Cin-N★	137	452	45	106	13	2	7	41	36	83	.235	.294	.319	612	79	-11	2	1	0	.955	-23	*S-136	-2.6
1969	*Min-A	160	578	67	162	24	4	10	70	66	96	.280	.358	.388	746	106	6	5	6	-1	.965	**34**	*S-160	5.9
1970	*Min-A	160	588	67	145	34	4	11	65	42	101	.247	.301	.374	675	84	-14	2	5	-1	.978	3	*S-160	0.7
1971	Min-A☆	153	554	59	146	25	4	18	75	51	69	.264	.327	.421	747	107	4	3	3	-0	**.985**	-0	*S-153	2.3
1972	Cal-A	150	551	25	123	11	2	6	42	35	73	.223	.272	.283	555	69	-22	1	2	-0	.970	3	*S-150	-0.1
1973	Cle-A	72	195	9	42	4	0	0	12	13	42	.215	.264	.236	500	41	-15	1	4	-1	.964	-8	S-67/3-5	-1.9
1974	Tex-A	34	92	5	25	3	0	0	7	2	14	.272	.287	.304	592	72	-3	1	0	0	1.000	2	3-21,S-10/D-4	-0.1
1975	Tex-A	55	102	15	24	2	0	1	5	14	12	.235	.328	.284	612	75	-3	0	0	0	.956	11	3-43/S-5,2-3	0.8
Total	16	1941	6707	662	1725	285	49	118	689	522	1135	.257	.313	.367	681	88	-105	39	48	-8	.971	-22	*S-1843/3-69,D-4,2	3.8
■ **JAVIER CARDONA**	Cardona, Javier Peterson b: 9/15/75, Santurce, P.R. BR/TR, 6′1″, 185 lbs. Deb: 5/31/2000																							
2000	Det-A	26	40	1	7	1	0	1	2	0	9	.175	.195	.275	470	18	-5	0	0	0	.973	1	C-26	-0.3
■ **ROD CAREW**	Carew, Rodney Cline b: 10/1/45, Gatun, C.Z. BL/TR, 6′, 182 lbs. Deb: 4/11/67 CH Career OF: (1-LF 0-CF 0-RF)																							
1967	Min-A★	137	514	66	150	22	7	8	51	37	91	.292	.342	.409	750	112	8	5	9	-2	.976	-10	*2-134	0.8
1968	Min-A★	127	461	46	126	27	2	1	42	26	71	.273	.314	.347	661	95	-3	12	4	1	.968	-14	*2-117/S-4	-0.6
1969	*Min-A★	123	458	79	152	30	4	8	56	37	72	**.332**	.386	.467	853	135	21	19	8	1	.970	-17	*2-118	1.3
1970	*Min-A†	51	191	27	70	12	3	4	28	11	28	.366	.407	.524	930	153	13	4	6	-1	.961	-11	2-45/1-1	0.4

YEAR	TM/L	G	AB	R	H	2B	3B	HR	RBI	BB	SO	AVG	OBP	SLG	OPS	OPS+	BR+	SB	CS	SBR	FA	FR	G/POS	TPR
1971	Min-A★	147	577	88	177	16	10	2	48	45	81	.307	.358	.380	737	106	5	6	7	-1	.976	-25	*2-142/3-2	-1.3
1972	Min-A★	142	535	61	170	21	6	0	51	43	60	**.318**	.371	.379	750	118	13	12	6	1	.978	-0	*2-139	2.5
1973	Min-A★	149	580	98	**203**	30	**11**	6	62	62	55	**.350**	.415	.471	885	143	35	41	16	3	.984	7	*2-147	**5.5**
1974	Min-A★	153	599	86	**218**	30	5	3	55	74	49	**.364**	**.435**	.446	880	149	41	38	16	3	.960	9	*2-148	**6.4**
1975	Min-A★	143	535	89	192	24	4	14	80	64	40	**.359**	**.428**	.497	926	159	43	35	9	5	.973	4	*2-123,1-14/D-2	5.8
1976	Min-A★	156	605	97	200	29	12	9	90	67	52	.331	.398	.463	861	149	38	49	22	3	.989	-2	*1-152/2-7	2.8
1977	Min-A★	155	616•	**128**	**239**	38	**16**	14	100	69	55	**.388**	**.452**	.570	**1022**	**179**	**69**	23	13	1	.994	6	*1-151/2-4,D-1	**6.4**
1978	Min-A★	152	564	85	188	26	10	5	70	78	62	**.333**	**.415**	.441	857	138	32	27	7	3	.989	1	*1-148/2-4,O-1(1-0-0)	2.8
1979	*Cal-A†	110	409	78	130	15	3	3	44	73	46	.318	.421	.391	812	125	19	18	8	1	.988	-7	*1-103/D-6	0.6
1980	Cal-A★	144	540	74	179	34	7	3	59	59	38	.331	.398	.437	835	132	25	23	15	-0	.994	-4	*1-103,D-32	1.3
1981	Cal-A★	93	364	57	111	17	1	2	21	45	45	.305	.381	.374	755	118	10	16	9	0	.995	-1	1-90/D-2	0.4
1982	*Cal-A†	138	523	88	167	25	5	3	44	67	49	.319	.399	.403	802	121	18	10	17	-4	.992	1	*1-134	0.7
1983	Cal-A★	129	472	66	160	24	2	2	44	57	48	.339	.411	.411	822	128	21	6	7	-1	.994	-9	1-89,D-24/2-2	0.5
1984	Cal-A★	93	329	42	97	8	1	3	31	40	39	.295	.371	.353	724	102	3	4	3	-0	.981	-4	1-83/D-1	-0.7
1985	Cal-A	127	443	69	124	17	3	2	39	64	47	.280	.372	.345	717	99	2	5	5	-1	.994	-8	*1-116	-1.4
Total	19	2469	9315	1424	3053	445	112	92	1015	1018	1028	.328	.395	.429	825	131	412	353	187	12	.991	-85	*1-1184,*2-1130/DS3O	34.2
■ ANDY CAREY	Carey, Andrew Arthur (b: Andrew Arthur Hexem) b: 10/18/31, Oakland, Cal. BR/TR, 6'1", 195 lbs. Deb: 5/2/52 Career OF: (1-LF 0-CF 0-RF)																							
1952	NY-A	16	40	6	6	0	0	0	1	3	10	.150	.209	.150	359	1	-5	0	0	0	.889	-1	3-14/S-1	-0.6
1953	NY-A	51	81	14	26	5	0	4	8	9	12	.321	.389	.531	920	152	6	2	1	0	.988	8	3-40/S-2,2-1	1.4
1954	NY-A	122	411	60	124	14	6	8	65	43	38	.302	.377	.423	801	123	14	5	5	-1	.967	17	*3-120	3.0
1955	*NY-A	135	510	73	131	19	**11**	7	47	44	51	.257	.317	.378	696	88	-10	3	3	-0	.954	14	*3-135	0.3
1956	*NY-A	132	422	54	100	18	2	7	50	45	53	.237	.313	.339	652	75	-16	9	6	-0	.947	-3	*3-131	-1.9
1957	*NY-A	85	247	30	63	6	5	6	33	15	42	.255	.311	.393	704	92	-3	2	2	-0	.977	3	3-81	0.0
1958	*NY-A	102	315	39	90	19	4	12	45	34	43	.286	.366	.486	852	137	16	1	2	-0	.961	10	3-99	2.6
1959	NY-A	41	101	11	26	1	0	3	9	7	17	.257	.306	.356	662	84	-2	1	1	-0	.916	2	3-34	-0.1
1960	NY-A	4	3	1	1	0	0	0	1	0	1	.333	.333	.333	667	86	-0	0	0	0	1.000	-1	/3-2,O-1(1-0-0)	-0.1
	KC-A	102	343	30	80	14	4	12	53	26	52	.233	.289	.402	692	84	-9	0	0	0	.975	-0	3-91	-0.9
	Yr	106	346	31	81	14	4	12	54	26	53	.234	.290	.402	691	85	-9	0	0	0	.975	-1	3-93/O-1(1-0-0)	-1.0
1961	KC-A	39	123	20	30	6	2	3	11	15	23	.244	.336	.398	734	94	-1	0	0	0	.944	-1	3-39	-0.3
	Chi-A	56	143	21	38	12	3	0	14	11	24	.266	.327	.392	719	93	-2	0	1	-0	.961	-5	3-54	-0.7
	Yr	95	266	41	68	18	5	3	25	26	47	.256	.331	.395	726	93	-3	0	1	-0	.953	-6	3-93	-1.0
1962	LA-N	53	111	12	26	5	1	2	13	16	23	.234	.336	.351	687	90	-1	0	0	0	.932	1	3-42	0.0
Total	11	938	2850	371	741	119	38	64	350	268	389	.260	.329	.396	725	97	-15	23	21	-2	.958	45	3-882/S-3,O-1L,2-1	2.7
■ SCOOPS CAREY	Carey, George C. b: 12/4/1870, Pittsburgh, Pa. d: 12/17/16, E.Liverpool, Ohio BR/TR, 175 lbs. Deb: 4/26/1895 Career OF: (0-LF 1-CF 0-RF)																							
1895	*Bal-N	123	490	59	128	21	6	1	75	27	32	.261	.305	.335	640	63	-28	2			**.987**	-6	*1-123/O-1C,S-1,3-1	-2.9
1898	Lou-N	8	32	1	6	1	1	0	1	1		.188	.212	.281	493	42	-3	0			.961	0	/1-8	-0.2
1902	Was-A	120	452	46	142	35	11	0	60	20		.314	.350	.440	790	117	9	3			**.989**	4	*1-120	1.0
1903	Was-A	48	183	8	37	3	2	0	23	4		.202	.223	.240	464	38	-14	0			.977	-3	1-47	-1.8
Total	4	299	1157	114	313	60	20	1	159	52	32	.271	.308	.360	667	80	-35	5			.986	-6	1-298/3-1,S-1,O-1C	-3.9
■ MAX CAREY	Carey, Max George "Scoops" (b: Maximilian Carnarius) b: 1/11/1890, Terre Haute, Ind. d: 5/30/76, Miami, Fla. BB/TR, 5'11.5", 170 lbs. Deb: 10/3/10 MCH																							
1910	Pit-N	2	6	2	3	0	1	0	2	2	1	.500	.625	.833	1458	307	2	0			1.000	2	/O-2(2-0-0)	0.3
1911	Pit-N	129	427	77	110	15	10	5	43	44	75	.258	.337	.375	712	95	-3	27			.975	7	*O-122(46-76-0)	-0.4
1912	Pit-N	150	587	114	177	23	8	5	66	61	79	.302	.372	.394	766	111	10	45			.968	8	*O-150(145-6-0)	1.1
1913	Pit-N	154	620	**99**	172	23	10	5	49	55	67	.277	.339	.371	710	107	6	**61**			.961	15	*O-154(144-11-0)	1.3
1914	Pit-N	156	593	76	144	25	**17**	1	31	59	56	.243	.313	.347	661	101	-0	38			.966	11	*O-154(154-0-0)	0.4
1915	Pit-N	140	564	76	143	26	5	3	27	57	58	.254	.326	.333	660	101	2	**36**	17	2	.982	13	*O-139(139-0-0)	1.1
1916	Pit-N	154	599	90	158	23	11	7	42	59	58	.264	.337	.374	711	117	13	**63**	19	**7**	.983	**30**	*O-154(21-134-0)	4.4
1917	Pit-N	155	588	82	174	21	12	1	51	58	38	.296	.369	.378	746	125	19	**46**			.979	25	*O-153(0-153-0)	3.7
1918	Pit-N	126	468	70	128	14	6	3	48	**62**	25	.274	.363	.348	712	113	10	**58**			.958	19	*O-126(0-126-0)	2.2
1919	Pit-N	66	244	41	75	10	2	0	9	25	24	.307	.376	.365	741	119	7	18			.947	2	O-63(0-63-0)	0.4
1920	Pit-N	130	485	74	140	18	4	1	35	59	31	.289	.369	.348	718	104	5	**52**	10	**8**	.967	1	*O-129(0-129-0)	0.4
1921	Pit-N	140	521	85	161	34	4	7	56	70	30	.309	.395	.430	825	115	14	37	12	4	.957	16	*O-139(0-139-0)	2.7
1922	Pit-N	155	629	140	207	28	12	10	70	**80**	26	.329	.408	.459	868	122	23	**51**	2	**11**	.969	19	*O-155(3-152-0)	4.2
1923	Pit-N	153	610	120	188	32	**19**	6	63	73	28	.308	.388	.452	841	119	18	**51**	8	**8**	.962	20	*O-153(0-153-0)	3.7
1924	Pit-N	149	599	113	178	30	9	8	55	58	17	.297	.366	.417	783	108	7	**49**	13	**6**	.965	9	*O-149(0-149-0)	1.6
1925	*Pit-N	133	542	109	186	39	13	5	44	66	19	.343	.418	.491	909	123	21	**46**	11	**6**	.950	9	*O-130(0-130-0)	2.8
1926	Pit-N	86	324	46	72	14	5	0	28	30	14	.222	.288	.296	584	55	-21	10			.943	4	O-82(0-82-0)	-2.0
	Bro-N	27	100	18	26	3	1	0	7	8	5	.260	.315	.310	625	70	-4	0			.933	-1	O-27(0-27-0)	-0.7
	Yr	113	424	64	98	17	6	0	35	38	19	.231	.294	.300	594	58	-25	10			.941	3	*O-109(0-109-0)	-2.7
1927	Bro-N	144	538	70	143	30	10	1	54	64	18	.266	.345	.364	709	90	-7	32			.970	6	*O-141(0-39-108)	-1.1
1928	Bro-N	108	296	41	73	11	0	2	19	47	24	.247	.354	.304	658	74	-9	18			.986	-12	O-95(1-75-35)	-2.6
1929	Bro-N	19	23	2	7	0	0	0	1	3	2	.304	.407	.304	712	81	-0	0			1.000	-1	/O-4(0-2-2)	-0.1
Total	20	2476	9363	1545	2665	419	159	70	800	1040	695	.285	.361	.386	747	107	111	738	92		.966	197	*O-2421(655-1646-145)	23.4
■ PAUL CAREY	Carey, Paul Stephan b: 1/8/68, Boston, Mass. BL/TR, 6'4", 215 lbs. Deb: 5/25/93																							
1993	Bal-A	18	47	1	10	1	0	0	3	5	14	.213	.288	.234	523	41	-4	0	0	0	.970	-2	/1-9,D-5	-0.6
■ ROGER CAREY	Carey, Roger J. Deb: 7/9/1887																							
1887	NY-N	1	4	0	0	0	0	0	2	0	1	.000	.000	.000	0	-99	-1	0			.800	1	/2-1	0.0
■ TOM CAREY	Carey, Thomas Francis Aloysius "Scoops" b: 10/11/06, Hoboken, N.J. d: 2/21/70, Rochester, N.Y. BR/TR, 5'8.5", 170 lbs. Deb: 7/19/35 C																							
1935	StL-A	76	296	29	86	18	4	0	42	13	11	.291	.320	.378	699	77	-11	0	2	-1	.961	-1	2-76	-0.7
1936	StL-A	134	488	58	133	27	6	1	57	27	25	.273	.315	.359	673	64	-28	2	1	0	.967	-1	*2-128/S-1	-1.8
1937	StL-A	130	487	54	134	24	1	1	40	21	26	.275	.306	.335	641	61	-29	1	2	-0	.983	2	2-87,S-44/3-1	-1.8
1939	Bos-A	54	161	17	39	6	2	0	20	3	9	.242	.265	.304	569	44	-14	0	0	0	1.000	6	2-35,S-10	-0.6
1940	Bos-A	43	62	4	20	4	0	0	7	2	1	.323	.344	.387	731	86	-1	0	0	0	.953	5	S-20/2-4,3-4	0.4
1941	Bos-A	25	21	7	4	0	0	0	2	0	2	.190	.190	.190	381	1	-3	0	0	0	1.000	4	/2-9,S-8,3-1	0.1
1942	Bos-A	1	1	0	1	0	0	0	1	0	0	1.000	1.000	1.000	2000	448	0	0	0	0	1.000	-0	/2-1	0.0
1946	Bos-A	3	5	0	1	0	0	0	0	0	1	.200	.200	.200	400	11	-1	0	0	0	.900	1	/2-3	0.1
Total	8	466	1521	169	418	79	13	2	169	66	75	.275	.308	.348	655	63	-87	3	5	-1	.973	17	2-343/S-83,3-6	-4.3
■ TOM CAREY	Carey, Thomas John (b: J. J. Norton) b: 1849, Brooklyn, N.Y. d: 2/13/1899, Los Angeles, Cal. BR/TR, 5'8", 145 lbs. Deb: 5/4/1871 M																							
1871	Kek-n	19	87	16	20	2	0	0	10	2	1	.230	.247	.253	500	43	-6	5	0	1	.857	0	2-19	-0.4
1872	Bal-n	42	198	42	57	7	0	2	27	0	2	.288	.288	.354	641	92	-3	4	1	1	.815	-12	2-29/S-9,3-3,O-3R,1	-1.1
1873	Bal-n	56	290	76	97	19	3	1	55	1	2	.334	.337	.431	768	127	9	1	3	-1	.845	-2	*2-54/3-4,S-3,M	0.2
1874	Mut-n	64	287	56	82	10	3	1	38	2	4	.286	.291	.352	643	102	-0	3	0	1	.776	-17	*S-51,2-13,M	-1.5
1875	Har-n	86	382	63	101	6	2	0	38	1	3	.264	.266	.291	557	89	-5	13	3	2	.844	-13	*S-86/2-1	-1.6
1876	Har-N	68	292	51	78	7	0	0	26	3	4	.267	.277	.294	572	84	-6				.882	-1	*S-68	-0.4
1877	Har-N	60	274	38	70	3	2	1	20	0	9	.255	.255	.292	547	81	-5				.826	-6	*S-60	-0.7
1878	Pro-N	61	253	33	60	10	3	0	24	0	14	.237	.237	.300	538	76	-7				.874	1	*S-61	-0.3
1879	Cle-N	80	335	30	80	14	1	0	32	5	20	.239	.250	.287	537	77	-8				.864	-3	*S-80	-0.7
Total	5 n	267	1244	253	357	44	8	4	168	6	12	.287	.290	.345	635	98	-5	26	7	3	.814	-44	S-149,2-116/3-7,O1	-4.4
Total	4	269	1154	152	288	34	6	1	102	8	47	.250	.255	.293	548	79	-25				.862	-9	S-269	-2.1
■ BOBBY CARGO	Cargo, Robert J. b: 10/1868, Pittsburgh, Pa. d: 4/27/04, Atlanta, Ga. BR/TR, Deb: 10/6/1892																							
1892	Pit-N	2	4	0	1	0	0	0	0	0	0	.250	.250	.250	500	51	-0	0			.636	1	/S-2	0.0

YEAR	TM/L	G	AB	R	H	2B	3B	HR	RBI	BB	SO	AVG	OBP	SLG	OPS	OPS+	BR+	SB	CS	SBR	FA	FR	G/POS	TPR
■ FRED CARISCH Carisch, Frederick Behlmer b: 11/14/1881, Fountain City, Wis. d: 4/19/77, San Gabriel, Cal. BR/TR, 5'10.5", 174 lbs. Deb: 8/31/03 C																								
1903	Pit-N	5	18	4	6	4	0	1	5	0		.333	.333	.722	1056	192	2	0			.969	1	/C-4	0.3
1904	Pit-N	37	125	9	31	3	1	0	8	9		.248	.299	.288	587	79	-3	3			.984	2	C-22,1-14	0.1
1905	Pit-N	32	107	7	22	0	3	0	8	2		.206	.227	.262	489	44	-8	1			.973	2	C-30	-0.3
1906	Pit-N	4	12	0	1	0	0	0	0	1		.083	.154	.083	237	-25	-2	1			.909	-0	/C-4	-0.2
1912	Cle-A	24	69	4	19	3	1	0	5	1		.275	.286	.348	634	78	-2	3			.952	6	C-23	0.6
1913	Cle-A	82	222	11	48	4	2	0	26	21	19	.216	.287	.252	539	56	-12	6			.971	13	C-79	0.8
1914	Cle-A	40	102	8	22	3	2	0	5	12	18	.216	.298	.284	583	72	-3	2	2	-0	.962	0	C-38	-0.1
1923	Det-A	2	0	0	0	0	0	0	0	0	0	—	—	—	—	—	0	0	0	0	1.000	-0	/C-2	0.0
Total	8	226	655	43	149	17	9	1	57	46	37	.227	.280	.285	566	66	-28	16	2		.968	24	C-202/1-14	1.2
■ FRED CARL Carl, Frederick E. b: 9/8/1858, Baltimore, Md. d: 5/4/19, Washington, D.C. BL/TL, 5'6", 158 lbs. Deb: 7/25/1889																								
1889	Lou-a	25	99	13	20	2	2	0	13	16	22	.202	.313	.263	576	66	-4	0			.735	0	O-18(2-4-12)/2-6,3-1	-0.3
■ LEW CARL Carl, Lewis Adolph b: 1836, Baltimore, Md. d: 5/19/1885, Newark, N.J. Deb: 9/9/1874																								
1874	Bal-n	1	3	0	0	0	0	0	0	0	0	.000	.000	.000	0	-99	-1	0	0	0	.250	-1	/C-1	-0.1
■ JIM CARLETON Carleton, James b: 1849, New York 5'8", 155 lbs. Deb: 5/4/1871																								
1871	Cle-n	29	127	31	32	8	1	0	18	8	3	.252	.296	.331	627	85	-1	2	1	0	.898	-3	*1-29	-0.2
1872	Cle-n	7	38	8	12	1	0	0	4	1	0	.316	.333	.342	675	114	1	1	0	0	.956	2	/1-7	0.2
Total	2 n	36	165	39	44	9	1	0	22	9	3	.267	.305	.333	638	91	-0	3	1	0	.908	-1	/1-36	0.0
■ JIM CARLIN Carlin, James Arthur b: 2/23/18, Wylam, Ala. BR/TR, 5'11", 165 lbs. Deb: 7/26/41																								
1941	Phi-N	16	21	2	3	1	0	1	2	3	4	.143	.250	.333	583	66	-1	0			1.000	-5	/O-9(0-4-5),3-2	-0.7
■ WALTER CARLISLE Carlisle, Walter G. "Rosy" b: 7/6/1883, Yorkshire, England d: 5/27/45, Los Angeles, Cal. BB/TR, 5'9", 154 lbs. Deb: 5/8/08																								
1908	Bos-A	3	10	0	1	0	0	0	0	1		.100	.182	.100	282	-8	-1	1			1.000	1	/O-3(3-0-0)	-0.1
■ SWEDE CARLSTROM Carlstrom, Albin Oscar b: 10/26/1886, Elizabeth, N.J. d: 4/28/35, Elizabeth, N.J. BR/TR, 6', 167 lbs. Deb: 9/13/11																								
1911	Bos-A	2	6	0	1	0	0	0	0	0		.167	.167	.167	333	-7	-1	0			1.000	0	/S-2	0.0
■ CLEO CARLYLE Carlyle, Hiram Cleo b: 9/7/02, Fairburn, Ga. d: 11/12/67, Los Angeles, Cal. BL/TR, 6', 170 lbs. Deb: 5/16/27 F																								
1927	Bos-A	95	278	31	65	12	8	1	28	36	40	.234	.324	.345	669	75	-10	4	4	-1	.965	-7	O-83(30-3-50)	-2.2
■ ROY CARLYLE Carlyle, Roy Edward "Dizzy" b: 12/10/1900, Buford, Ga. d: 11/22/56, Norcross, Ga. BL/TR, 6'2.5", 195 lbs. Deb: 4/16/25 F																								
1925	Was-A	1	1	0	0	0	0	0	0	0	1	.000	.000	.000	0	-99	-0	0	0	0	.000	0	H	0.0
	Bos-A	93	276	36	90	20	3	7	49	16	28	.326	.365	.496	862	117	6	1	1	-0	.909	-6	O-67(43-0-24)	-0.5
	Yr	94	277	36	90	20	3	7	49	16	29	.325	.364	.495	859	116	5	1	1	-0	.909	-6	O-67(43-0-24)	-0.5
1926	Bos-A	45	165	22	47	6	2	2	16	4	18	.285	.310	.382	692	82	-5	0	0	0	.904	-4	O-38(0-0-38)	-1.1
	NY-A	35	62	3	20	5	1	0	11	4	9	.323	.373	.435	809	112	1	0	0	0	.941	-3	O-15(0-0-15)	-0.3
	Yr	80	227	25	67	11	3	2	27	8	27	.295	.328	.396	724	91	-4	0	0	0	.911	-7	O-53(0-0-53)	-1.4
Total	2	174	504	61	157	31	6	9	76	24	56	.312	.348	.450	798	105	1	1	1	-0	.910	-12	O-120(43-0-77)	-1.9
■ GEORGE CARMAN Carman, George Wartman b: 3/29/1866, Philadelphia, Pa. d: 6/16/29, Lancaster, Pa. Deb: 9/4/1890																								
1890	Phi-a	28	97	9	17	2	0	0	7	8		.175	.245	.196	441	30	-8	5			.767	-9	S-15,O-10R/2-2,3-1	-1.5
■ DUKE CARMEL Carmel, Leon James b: 4/23/37, New York, N.Y. BL/TL, 6'3", 202 lbs. Deb: 9/10/59																								
1959	StL-N	10	23	2	3	1	0	0	3	1	6	.130	.167	.174	341	-9	-4	0	1	-0	1.000	-3	O-10(2-8-3)	-0.7
1960	StL-N	4	3	0	0	0	0	0	0	1	1	.000	.250	.000	250	-23	-0	1	1	-0	1.000	0	/1-2,O-1(0-0-1)	0.0
1963	StL-N	57	44	9	10	1	0	1	2	9	11	.227	.358	.318	677	88	-0	0	0	0	.974	-7	O-38(26-6-8)/1-1	-0.8
	NY-N	47	149	11	35	5	3	3	18	16	37	.235	.309	.369	678	93	-1	2	2	-0	.980	-1	O-21(0-21-0),1-18	-0.4
	Yr	104	193	20	45	6	3	4	20	25	48	.233	.321	.358	679	90	-2	2	2	-0	.977	-7	O-59(26-27-8),1-19	-1.2
1965	NY-A	6	8	0	0	0	0	0	0	0	5	.000	.000	.000	0	-99	-2	0	0	0	1.000	0	/1-2	-0.2
Total	4	124	227	22	48	7	3	4	23	27	60	.211	.295	.322	617	73	-8	3	4	-1	.981	-10	/O-70(28-35-12),1-23	-2.1
■ EDDIE CARNETT Carnett, Edwin Elliott "Lefty" b: 10/21/16, Springfield, Mo. BL/TL, 6', 185 lbs. Deb: 4/19/41 Career OF: (70-LF 26-CF 13-RF)																								
1941	Bos-N	2	0	0	0	0	0	0	0	0	0	—	—	—	—	—	0	0			.000	0	/P-2	0.0
1944	Chi-A	126	457	51	126	18	8	1	60	26	35	.276	.322	.357	678	95	-4	5	2	0	.949	-8	O-88L,1-25/P-2	-1.8
1945	Cle-A	30	73	5	16	7	0	0	7	2	9	.219	.250	.315	565	66	-4	0	1	-0	.971	-0	O-16(8-1-7)/P-2	-0.5
Total	3	158	530	56	142	25	8	1	67	28	44	.268	.312	.351	663	91	-7	5	3		.952	-8	O-104L/1-25,P-6	-2.3
■ JOHN CARNEY Carney, John Joseph "Handsome Jack" b: 11/10/1866, Salem, Mass. d: 10/19/25, Litchfield, N.H. BR/TR, 5'10.5", 175 lbs. Deb: 4/24/1889																								
1889	Was-N	69	273	25	63	7	0	1	29	14	14	.231	.271	.267	538	54	-17	12			.957	-7	1-53,O-16(1-0-15)	-2.5
1890	Buf-P	28	107	11	29	3	0	0	13	7	14	.271	.333	.299	632	76	-3	2			.972	-2	1-24/O-4(1-0-3)	-0.6
	Cle-P	25	89	15	31	5	3	0	21	14	5	.348	.442	.472	914	157	8	6			.857	-3	O-19(0-0-19)/1-6	0.3
	Yr	53	196	26	60	8	3	0	34	21	19	.306	.385	.378	762	113	5	8			.969	-6	1-30,O-23(1-0-22)	-0.3
1891	Cin-a	99	367	47	102	10	8	3	43	35	18	.278	.346	.373	719	97	-3	15			.974	1	1-99	-1.0
	Mil-a	31	110	22	33	5	2	3	23	13	8	.300	.389	.464	853	120	2	5			.986	4	1-31	0.2
	Yr	130	477	69	135	15	10	6	66	48	26	.283	.356	.394	750	103	-1	20			.977	5	*1-130	-0.8
Total	3	252	946	120	258	30	13	7	129	83	59	.273	.338	.354	693	92	-12	40			.971	-8	1-213/O-39(2-0-37)	-3.6
■ PAT CARNEY Carney, Patrick Joseph "Doc" b: 8/7/1876, Holyoke, Mass. d: 1/9/53, Worcester, Mass. BL/TL, 6', 200 lbs. Deb: 9/20/01 Career OF: (8-LF 9-CF 298-RF)																								
1901	Bos-N	13	55	6	16	2	1	0	6	3		.291	.339	.364	703	95	-0	0			.933	-3	O-13(0-0-13)	-0.4
1902	Bos-N	137	522	75	141	17	4	2	65	42		.270	.339	.330	668	105	4	27			.930	-9	*O-137(3-0-135)/P-2	-1.1
1903	Bos-N	110	392	37	94	12	4	1	49	28		.240	.297	.298	596	73	-14	10			.953	-6	O-92(3-0-90),P-10/1-1	-2.2
1904	Bos-N	78	279	24	57	5	2	0	11	12		.204	.240	.237	476	49	-17	6			.953	-2	O-71(2-9-60)/P-4,1-1	-2.3
Total	4	338	1248	142	308	36	11	3	131	85		.247	.304	.300	605	82	-27	43			.942	-20	O-313R/P-16,1-2	-6.0
■ BILL CARNEY Carney, William John b: 3/25/1874, St.Paul, Minn. d: 7/31/38, Hopkins, Minn. BB/TR, 5'10", Deb: 8/22/04																								
1904	Chi-N	2	7	0	0	0	0	0	0	1		.000	.125	.000	125	-60	-1	0			1.000	0	/O-2(0-0-2)	-0.2
■ BUBBA CARPENTER Carpenter, Charles Sydney b: 7/23/68, Dallas, Tex. BL/TL, 6'1", 195 lbs. Deb: 5/13/2000																								
2000	Col-N	15	27	4	6	0	0	3	5	4	13	.222	.323	.556	878	91	-0	0	0	0	1.000	-2	/O-6(5-0-1),D-2	-0.2
■ HICK CARPENTER Carpenter, Warren William b: 8/16/1855, Grafton, Mass. d: 4/18/37, San Diego, Cal. BR/TL, 5'11", 186 lbs. Deb: 5/1/1879 Career OF: (0-LF 0-CF 12-RF)																								
1879	Syr-N	65	261	30	53	6	0	0	20	2	15	.203	.209	.226	435	49	-13				.948	-4	1-34,3-18,O-11R,/2	-1.6
1880	Cin-N	77	300	32	72	6	4	0	23	2	15	.240	.245	.287	532	80	-6				.853	-1	*3-67/1-9,S-1	-0.5
1881	Wor-N	83	347	40	75	12	2	2	31	3	19	.216	.223	.280	502	54	-19				.848	3	*3-83	-1.2
1882	Cin-a	80	351	78	**120**	15	5	1	67	10		.342	.360	.422	782	154	18				**.835**	-1	*3-80	1.7
1883	Cin-a	95	435	99	130	18	4	3	40	19		.299	.328	.379	708	120	9				.870	-6	*3-95	0.4
1884	Cin-a	108	474	80	121	16	2	4	60	6		.255	.271	.323	593	89	-7				.881	-9	*3-108/O-1(0-0-1)	-1.3
1885	Cin-a	112	473	89	131	12	8	2	61	9		.277	.295	.349	644	101	-1				.860	-6	*3-112	-0.5
1886	Cin-a	111	458	67	101	8	5	2	61	18		.221	.262	.273	535	66	-19	8			.841	-6	*3-111	-2.0
1887	Cin-a	127	517	70	143	12	6	1	50	19		.277	.282	.303	585	62	-27	44			.846	-13	*3-127	-3.0
1888	Cin-a	136	551	68	147	14	5	3	67	5		.267	.280	.327	607	89	-9	59			.866	-12	*3-136	-1.7
1889	Cin-a	123	486	67	127	23	6	0	63	18	41	.261	.293	.333	627	76	-17	47			.835	-25	*3-121/1-2	-3.5
1892	StL-N	1	3	0	1	0	0	0	0	1	1	.333	.500	.333	833	161	0	0			.714	0	/3-1	0.0
Total	12	1118	4656	720	1221	142	47	18	543	112	91	.262	.281	.322	603	86	-90	158			.853	-80	*3-1059/1-45,O2S	-13.2
■ CHARLIE CARR Carr, Charles Carbitt b: 12/27/1876, Coatesville, Pa. d: 11/25/32, Memphis, Tenn. BR/TR, 6'2", 195 lbs. Deb: 9/15/1898																								
1898	Was-N	20	73	6	14	2	0	0	4	2		.192	.213	.219	433	24	-7	2			.950	-2	1-20	-0.9
1901	Phi-A	2	8	0	1	0	0	0	0	0		.125	.125	.125	250	-29	-1	0			.926	0	/1-2	-0.1
1903	Det-A	135	548	59	154	23	11	2	79	10		.281	.296	.374	671	103	0	10			.982	12	*1-135	1.1

YEAR	TM/L	G	AB	R	H	2B	3B	HR	RBI	BB	SO	AVG	OBP	SLG	OPS	OPS+	BR+	SB	CS	SBR	FA	FR	G/POS	TPR
1904	Det-A	92	360	29	77	13	3	0	40	14		.214	.245	.267	512	64	-15	6			.983	16	1-92	-0.1
	Cle-A	32	120	9	27	5	1	0	7	4		.225	.250	.283	533	69	-4	0			.973	-0	1-32	-0.6
	Yr	124	480	38	104	18	4	0	47	18		.217	.246	.271	517	65	-19	6			.980	16	*1-124	-0.7
1905	Cle-A	89	306	29	72	12	4	1	31	13		.235	.266	.310	577	82	-7	12			.991	-2	1-87	-1.2
1906	Cin-N	22	94	9	18	2	3	0	10	2		.191	.216	.277	493	51	-6	0			.983	1	1-22	-0.6
1914	Ind-F	115	441	44	129	11	10	3	69	26	47	.293	.333	.383	717	86	-15	19			**.991**	1	*1-115	-1.8
Total	7	507	1950	185	492	68	32	6	240	71	47	.252	.280	.329	610	81	-55	49			.984	26	1-505	-4.2
■ **CHUCK CARR**	Carr, Charles Lee Glenn b: 8/10/67, San Bernardino, Cal. BB/TR, 5'10", 165 lbs. Deb: 4/28/90																							
1990	NY-N	4	2	0	0	0	0	0	0	0	2	.000	.000	.000	0	-99	-1	1	0	0	.000	-0	/O-1(1-0-0)	-0.1
1991	NY-N	12	11	1	2	0	0	0	1	0	2	.182	.182	.182	364	3	-1	1	0	0	1.000	-2	/O-9(0-9-0)	-0.3
1992	StL-N	22	64	8	14	3	0	0	3	9	6	.219	.315	.266	581	68	-2	10	2	2	1.000	-1	O-19(5-9-6)	-0.2
1993	Fla-N	142	551	75	147	19	2	4	41	49	74	.267	.329	.330	659	73	-20	**58**	22	5	.985	16	*O-139(0-139-0)	0.2
1994	Fla-N	106	433	61	114	19	2	2	30	22	71	.263	.307	.330	637	64	-22	32	8	4	.980	10	*O-104(0-104-0)	-0.7
1995	Fla-N	105	308	54	70	20	0	2	20	46	49	.227	.331	.312	643	71	-12	25	11	2	.987	5	*O-103(0-103-0)	-0.5
1996	Mil-A	27	106	18	29	6	1	1	11	6	21	.274	.313	.377	690	71	-5	5	4	-0	1.000	5	O-27(0-27-0)	0.0
1997	Mil-A	26	46	3	6	3	0	0	0	2	11	.130	.184	.196	379	-1	-7	1	0	0	1.000	-5	O-23(0-23-0)/D-1	-1.1
	*Hou-N	63	192	34	53	11	2	4	17	15	37	.276	.335	.417	752	99	-1	11	5	1	.966	-1	O-59(1-58-0)	0.0
Total	8	507	1713	254	435	81	7	13	123	149	273	.254	.318	.332	650	70	-71	144	52	13	.984	26	O-484(7-472-6)/D-1	-2.7
■ **LEW CARR**	Carr, Lewis Smith b: 8/15/1872, Union Springs, N.Y d: 6/15/54, Moravia, N.Y. BR/TR, 6'2", 200 lbs. Deb: 7/4/01																							
1901	Pit-N	9	28	2	7	1	1	0	4	2		.250	.344	.357	701	100	0	0			.886	-5	/S-9,3-1	-0.5
■ **CHICO CARRASQUEL**	Carrasquel, Alfonso (Colon) b: 1/23/28, Caracas, Venez. BR/TR, 6', 170 lbs. Deb: 4/18/50																							
1950	Chi-A	141	524	72	148	21	5	4	46	66	46	.282	.368	.365	733	91	-6	0	2	-1	.961	11	*S-141	1.2
1951	Chi-A★	147	538	41	142	22	4	2	58	46	39	.264	.325	.331	656	79	-15	14	4	2	**.975**	13	*S-147	0.8
1952	Chi-A	100	359	36	89	7	4	1	42	33	27	.248	.315	.298	613	71	-14	2	2	-0	.964	-16	S-99	-2.5
1953	Chi-A★	149	552	72	154	30	4	2	47	38	47	.279	.330	.359	689	83	-13	5	3	0	**.976**	3	*S-149	0.3
1954	Chi-A★	155	620	106	158	28	3	12	62	85	67	.255	.349	.368	717	93	-4	7	6	-1	**.975**	11	*S-155	2.0
1955	Chi-A★	145	523	83	134	11	2	11	52	61	59	.256	.338	.348	686	83	-12	1	1	-0	.973	0	*S-144	0.0
1956	Cle-A	141	474	60	115	15	1	7	48	52	61	.243	.325	.323	648	70	-20	0	4	-1	.967	-25	*S-141/3-1	-3.5
1957	Cle-A	125	392	37	108	14	1	8	57	41	53	.276	.356	.378	734	102	2	0	2	-1	.960	-5	*S-122	0.6
1958	Cle-A	49	156	14	40	6	0	2	21	14	12	.256	.318	.333	651	81	-4	0	0	0	.931	-19	S-32,3-14	-2.2
	KC-A	59	160	19	34	5	1	2	13	21	15	.213	.304	.294	598	64	-8	0	1	-0	.976	-6	3-32,S-22	-1.3
	Yr	108	316	33	74	11	1	4	34	35	27	.234	.311	.313	624	72	-12	0	1	-0	.947	-25	S-54,3-46	-3.5
1959	Bal-A	114	346	28	77	13	0	4	28	34	41	.223	.294	.295	589	64	-17	2	3	-1	.970	-14	S-89,2-22/3-2,1-1	-2.4
Total	10	1325	4644	568	1199	172	25	55	474	491	467	.258	.334	.342	676	82	-111	31	28	-3	.969	-47	*S-1241/3-49,2-22,1	-7.0
■ **CAM CARREON**	Carreon, Camilo b: 8/6/37, Colton, Cal. d: 9/2/87, Tucson, Ariz. BR/TR, 6', 198 lbs. Deb: 9/27/59 F																							
1959	Chi-A	1	1	0	0	0	0	0	0	0	0	.000	.000	.000	0	-99	-0	0	0	0	1.000	0	/C-1	0.0
1960	Chi-A	8	17	2	4	0	0	0	2	1	3	.235	.278	.235	513	41	-1	0	0	0	1.000	0	/C-7	-0.1
1961	Chi-A	78	229	32	62	5	1	4	27	21	24	.271	.332	.354	686	85	-5	0	1	-0	.995	9	C-71	0.7
1962	Chi-A	106	313	31	80	19	1	4	37	33	37	.256	.329	.361	690	86	-6	1	1	-0	.995	8	C-93	0.6
1963	Chi-A	101	270	28	74	10	1	2	35	23	32	.274	.333	.341	674	91	-3	1	1	-0	.987	0	C-92	0.1
1964	Chi-A	37	95	12	26	5	0	0	4	7	13	.274	.330	.326	656	86	-2	0	0	0	.987	-4	C-34	-0.5
1965	Cle-A	19	52	6	12	2	1	1	7	9	6	.231	.344	.365	710	101	0	1	1	-0	1.000	0	C-19	0.1
1966	Bal-A	4	9	2	2	2	0	0	2	3	2	.222	.417	.444	861	150	1	0	0	0	1.000	0	/C-3	0.1
Total	8	354	986	113	260	43	4	11	114	97	117	.264	.331	.349	680	87	-16	3	4	-1	.993	14	C-320	1.0
■ **MARK CARREON**	Carreon, Mark Steven b: 7/19/63, Chicago, Ill. BR/TL, 6', 195 lbs. Deb: 9/8/87 F Career OF: (175-LF 68-CF 151-RF)																							
1987	NY-N	9	12	0	3	0	0	0	1	1	1	.250	.308	.250	558	53	-1	0	1	-0	.800	-1	/O-5(5-0-0)	-0.2
1988	NY-N	7	9	5	5	2	0	1	1	2	1	.556	.636	1.111	1747	413	4	0	0	0	1.000	-1	/O-4(4-0-0)	0.3
1989	NY-N	68	133	20	41	6	0	6	16	12	17	.308	.370	.489	859	151	8	2	3	-1	.983	-3	O-39(18-0-21)	0.4
1990	NY-N	82	188	30	47	12	0	10	26	15	29	.250	.312	.473	786	113	3	1	0	0	1.000	-8	O-60(16-36-13)	-0.6
1991	NY-N	106	254	18	66	6	0	4	21	12	26	.260	.299	.331	629	77	-8	2	1	0	.971	-12	O-77(43-22-22)	-2.2
1992	Det-A	101	336	34	78	11	1	10	41	22	57	.232	.281	.360	641	78	-11	3	1	0	.979	2	O-83(64-1-19),D-13	-1.2
1993	SF-N	78	150	22	49	9	1	7	33	13	16	.327	.384	.540	924	149	10	1	0	0	.943	-7	O-41(9-5-30)/1-3	0.2
1994	SF-N	51	100	8	27	4	0	3	20	7	20	.270	.330	.400	730	94	-1	0	0	0	.978	-5	O-33(10-0-24)	-0.7
1995	SF-N	117	396	53	119	24	0	17	65	23	37	.301	.345	.490	835	121	11	0	1	-0	.993	-10	1-81,O-22(3-0-19)	-0.8
1996	SF-N	81	292	40	76	22	3	9	51	22	33	.260	.319	.449	767	104	1	2	3	-1	.986	-6	1-73/O-5(3-0-2)	-1.3
	Cle-A	38	142	16	46	12	0	2	14	11	9	.324	.385	.451	835	111	3	1	1	-0	.994	-2	1-34/O-5(0-4-1),D-2	-0.2
Total	10	738	2012	246	557	108	5	69	289	140	246	.277	.330	.438	768	108	18	12	11	-1	.974	-53	O-374L,1-191/D-15	-6.3
■ **BILL CARRIGAN**	Carrigan, William Francis "Rough" b: 10/22/1883, Lewiston, Me. d: 7/8/69, Lewiston, Me. BR/TR, 5'9", 175 lbs. Deb: 7/7/06 M																							
1906	Bos-A	37	109	5	23	0	0	0	10	5		.211	.252	.211	463	45	-7	3			.940	-2	C-35	-0.6
1908	Bos-A	57	149	13	35	5	2	0	14	3		.235	.255	.295	550	77	-4	1			.955	6	C-47/1-3	0.7
1909	Bos-A	94	280	25	83	13	2	1	36	17		.296	.341	.368	709	121	6	2			.972	1	C-77/1-8	1.7
1910	Bos-A	114	342	36	85	11	1	3	53	23		.249	.307	.313	620	92	-3	10			.962	-21	*C-110	-1.6
1911	Bos-A	72	232	29	67	6	1	1	30	26		.289	.373	.336	709	99	1	5			.972	-1	C-62/1-6	0.5
1912	*Bos-A	87	266	34	70	7	1	0	24	38		.263	.359	.297	656	84	-4	7			**.970**	-12	C-87	-0.8
1913	Bos-A	87	256	17	62	15	5	0	28	27	26	.242	.319	.340	659	91	-3	6			.979	-8	C-82,M	-0.4
1914	Bos-A	82	178	18	45	5	1	1	22	40	18	.253	.395	.309	704	112	5	1	2	-0	**.984**	3	C-78,M	1.5
1915	*Bos-A	46	95	10	19	3	0	0	7	16	12	.200	.321	.232	553	68	-3	0			.975	8	C-44,M	0.9
1916	*Bos-A	33	63	7	17	2	1	0	11	11	3	.270	.378	.333	712	113	2	2			1.000	6	C-27,M	1.0
Total	10	709	1970	194	506	67	14	6	235	206	59	.257	.334	.314	648	94	-10	37	2		.971	-18	C-649/1-17	2.9
■ **MATIAS CARRILLO**	Carrillo, Matias (Garcia) b: 2/24/63, Los Mochis, Mexico BL/TL, 5'11", 190 lbs. Deb: 5/23/91																							
1991	Mil-A	3	0	0	0	0	0	0	0	0	0	—	—	—	—	—	0	0	0	0	.000	-1	/O-3(3-0-0)	-0.1
1993	Fla-N	24	55	4	14	6	0	0	3	1	7	.255	.281	.364	644	67	-3	0	0	0	1.000	-3	O-16(4-5-9)	-0.6
1994	Fla-N	80	136	13	34	7	0	0	9	9	31	.250	.297	.301	598	55	-9	3	3	-0	.982	-7	O-49(20-8-25)	-1.7
Total	3	107	191	17	48	13	0	0	12	10	38	.251	.292	.319	611	58	-11	3	3	-0	.987	-12	/O-68(27-13-34)	-2.4
■ **DIXIE CARROLL**	Carroll, Dorsey Lee b: 5/9/1891, Paducah, Ky. d: 10/13/84, Jacksonville, Fla BL/TR, 5'11", 165 lbs. Deb: 9/12/19																							
1919	Bos-N	15	49	10	13	3	1	0	7	7	1	.265	.379	.367	747	130	2	5			.921	2	O-13(6-8-1)	0.3
■ **CHICK CARROLL**	Carroll, Edward b: 1868, Arkansas d: 7/13/08, Chicago, Ill. Deb: 4/17/1884																							
1884	Was-U	4	16	1	4	0	0	0		0		.250	.250	.250	500	54	-1				.500	-1	/O-4(4-0-0)	-0.2
■ **FRED CARROLL**	Carroll, Frederick Herbert b: 7/2/1864, Sacramento, Cal. d: 11/7/04, San Rafael, Cal. BR/TR, 5'11", 185 lbs. Deb: 5/1/1884 Career OF: (144-LF 67-CF 108-RF)																							
1884	Col-a	69	252	46	70	13	5	6		13		.278	.326	.440	766	161	17				.944	16	C-54,O-15(12-2-1)	3.3
1885	Pit-a	71	280	45	75	13	8	0	30	7		.268	.298	.371	669	112	3				.926	4	C-60,O-12(10-2-0)	1.1
1886	Pit-a	122	486	92	140	28	11	5	64	52		.288	.362	.422	783	146	26	20			.921	11	C-70,O-27L,1-25,/S	3.5
1887	Pit-N	102	457	71	174	24	15	6	54	36	21	.381	.383	.499	882	152	30	23			.833	-12	O-46C,C-40,1-17,/S	1.6
1888	Pit-N	97	366	62	91	14	5	2	48	32	31	.249	.326	.331	657	119	10	18			.897	-11	C-54,O-38L/1-5,3-1	0.2
1889	Pit-N	91	318	80	105	21	11	2	51	85	26	.330	**.486**	.484	**970**	**190**	**49**	19			.930	-13	C-43,O-41L/1-7,3-1	3.2
1890	Pit-P	111	416	95	124	20	7	2	71	75	22	.298	.418	.394	813	128	24	35			.856	-17	C-56,O-49(42-6-1)/1-7	0.8
1891	Pit-N	91	353	55	77	13	4	4	48	48	36	.218	.315	.312	627	85	-6	22			.915	6	O-91(2-0-89)	-0.1
Total	8	754	2928	546	856	146	66	27	366	348	136	.292	.370	.408	778	137	153	137			.913	-15	C-377,O-319L/1-61,3S	13.6
■ **SCRAPPY CARROLL**	Carroll, John E. b: 8/27/1860, Buffalo, N.Y. d: 11/14/42, Buffalo, N.Y. BR, 5'7.5", Deb: 9/27/1884 Career OF: (21-LF 6-CF 48-RF)																							
1884	StP-U	9	31	3	3	1	0	0		2		.097	.152	.129	281	-26	-5				.824	3	/O-8(0-0-8),3-2	-0.2
1885	Buf-N	13	40	1	3	0	0	0	1	2	8	.075	.119	.075	194	-35	-6				.917	1	O-13(7-6-0)	-0.5

YEAR	TM/L	G	AB	R	H	2B	3B	HR	RBI	BB	SO	AVG	OBP	SLG	OPS	OPS+	BR+	SB	CS	SBR	FA	FR	G/POS	TPR
1887	Cle-a	57	231	30	58	5	1	0	19	15		.251	.264	.231	495	40	-17	19			.843	-5	O-54(14-0-40)/3-3,2-1	-1.9
Total	3	79	302	34	64	6	1	0	20	19	8	.212	.232	.199	431	26	-28	19			.853	-2	/O-75R,3-5,2-1	-2.6

■ PAT CARROLL
Carroll, Patrick b: 3/1853, Philadelphia, Pa. d: 2/14/16, Philadelphia, Pa. Deb: 5/10/1884

YEAR	TM/L	G	AB	R	H	2B	3B	HR	RBI	BB	SO	AVG	OBP	SLG	OPS	OPS+	BR+	SB	CS	SBR	FA	FR	G/POS	TPR
1884	Alt-U	11	49	4	13	1	0	0		1		.265	.280	.286	566	71	-3				.920	-4	/C-8,O-3(0-0-3)	-0.5
	Phi-U	5	19	1	3	1	0	0		0		.158	.158	.211	368	12	-3				.839	3	/C-5	0.0
	Yr	16	68	5	16	2	0	0		1		.235	.246	.265	511	56	-6				.877	-1	C-13/O-3(0-0-3)	-0.5

■ DOC CARROLL
Carroll, Ralph Arthur "Red" b: 12/28/1891, Worcester, Mass. d: 6/27/83, Worcester, Mass. BR/TR, 6', 170 lbs. Deb: 6/27/16

YEAR	TM/L	G	AB	R	H	2B	3B	HR	RBI	BB	SO	AVG	OBP	SLG	OPS	OPS+	BR+	SB	CS	SBR	FA	FR	G/POS	TPR
1916	Phi-A	10	22	1	2	0	0	0	0	1	8	.091	.167	.091	258	-24	-3	0			.942	0	C-10	-0.3

■ CLIFF CARROLL
Carroll, Samuel Clifford b: 10/18/1859, Clay Grove, Iowa d: 6/12/23, Portland, Ore. BB/TR, 5'8", 163 lbs. Deb: 8/3/1882

YEAR	TM/L	G	AB	R	H	2B	3B	HR	RBI	BB	SO	AVG	OBP	SLG	OPS	OPS+	BR+	SB	CS	SBR	FA	FR	G/POS	TPR
1882	Pro-N	10	41	4	5	0	0	0	2	0	4	.122	.122	.122	244	-21	-5				1.000	1	O-10(2-0-8)	-0.4
1883	Pro-N	58	238	37	63	12	3	1	20	4	28	.265	.277	.353	630	87	-4				.902	5	O-58(56-1-1)	-0.1
1884	*Pro-N	113	452	90	118	16	4	3	54	29	39	.261	.306	.334	640	103	2				.904	2	*O-113(113-0-0)	0.1
1885	Pro-N	104	426	62	99	12	3	1	40	29	29	.232	.281	.282	563	85	-6				.886	4	*O-104(104-0-0)	-0.5
1886	Was-N	111	433	73	99	11	6	2	22	44	26	.229	.300	.296	595	87	-5	31			.862	-1	*O-111(109-1-1)	-0.8
1887	Was-N	103	437	79	121	17	4	4	37	17	30	.277	.291	.336	627	78	-12	40			.902	1	*O-103(102-1-0)	-1.2
1888	Pit-N	5	20	1	0	0	0	0	0	0	8	.000	.000	.000	0	-99	-5	2			.667	-1	/O-5(1-0-4)	-0.6
1890	Chi-N	136	582	134	166	16	6	7	65	53	34	.285	.352	.369	721	106	4	34			.936	15	*O-136(112-0-24)	1.3
1891	Chi-N	130	515	87	132	20	8	7	80	50	42	.256	.340	.367	707	106	4	31			.915	-5	*O-130(0-1-130)	-0.2
1892	StL-N	101	407	82	111	14	8	4	49	47	22	.273	.363	.376	739	130	17	30			.901	4	*O-101(99-0-3)	1.0
1893	Bos-N	120	438	80	98	7	5	2	54	88	28	.224	.360	.276	636	65	-20	29			.917	2	*O-120(33-0-89)	-2.2
Total	11	991	3989	729	1012	125	47	31	423	361	290	.254	.320	.329	649	92	-31	197			.905	25	O-991(731-4-260)	-3.6

■ TOM CARROLL
Carroll, Thomas Edward b: 9/17/36, Jamaica, N.Y. BR/TR, 6'3", 186 lbs. Deb: 5/7/55

YEAR	TM/L	G	AB	R	H	2B	3B	HR	RBI	BB	SO	AVG	OBP	SLG	OPS	OPS+	BR+	SB	CS	SBR	FA	FR	G/POS	TPR
1955	*NY-A	14	6	3	2	0	0	0	0	0	2	.333	.333	.333	667	81	-0	0	0	0	.875	2	/S-4	0.2
1956	NY-A	36	17	11	6	0	0	0	0	1	3	.353	.389	.353	742	100	0	1	0	0	.857	5	3-11/S-1	0.5
1959	KC-A	14	7	1	1	0	0	0	1	0	1	.143	.143	.143	286	-21	-1	0	0	0	1.000	4	/S-9,3-3	0.3
Total	3	64	30	15	9	0	0	0	1	1	6	.300	.323	.300	623	69	-1	1	0	0	.813	11	/3-14,S-14	1.0

■ KID CARSEY
Carsey, Wilfred b: 10/22/1870, New York, N.Y. d: 3/29/60, Miami, Fla. BL/TR, 5'7", 168 lbs. Deb: 4/8/1891 Career OF: (0-LF 6-CF 11-RF)

YEAR	TM/L	G	AB	R	H	2B	3B	HR	RBI	BB	SO	AVG	OBP	SLG	OPS	OPS+	BR+	SB	CS	SBR	FA	FR	G/POS	TPR
1891	Was-a	61	187	25	28	5	2	0	15	19	38	.150	.236	.198	433	25	-18	2			.922	5	P-54/O-7(0-4-3),S-2	-0.2
1892	Phi-N	44	131	8	20	2	1	1	10	9	24	.153	.207	.206	413	25	-12	1			.888	2	P-43/O-2(0-2-0)	-0.1
1893	Phi-N	39	145	12	27	1	1	0	10	5	14	.186	.229	.207	436	16	-18	2			.925	2	P-39	0.0
1894	Phi-N	37	129	31	36	2	2	0	18	17	12	.279	.367	.326	693	70	-6	3			.939	2	P-37	0.0
1895	Phi-N	44	141	24	41	2	0	0	20	15	12	.291	.363	.305	668	73	-5	2			.878	-1	P-44	0.0
1896	Phi-N	27	81	13	18	2	2	0	7	11	12	.222	.315	.296	612	62	-4	1			.908	1	P-27	0.0
1897	Phi-N	4	13	1	3	0	0	0	1	0		.231	.231	.231	462	23	-1	0			1.000	-0	/P-4	0.0
	StL-N	13	43	2	13	2	2	0	5	1		.302	.318	.442	760	102	-0	1			.917	1	P-12	0.0
	Yr	17	56	3	16	2	2	0	6	1		.286	.298	.393	691	83	-2	1			.930	1	P-16	0.0
1898	StL-N	38	105	8	21	0	1	1	10	10		.200	.270	.248	517	47	-7	3			.935	-6	P-20,2-10/O-8(0-0-8)	-1.0
1899	Cle-N	11	36	5	10	0	0	0	4	3		.278	.333	.278	611	74	-1	0			.879	3	P-10/S-1	0.1
	Was-N	4	11	1	0	0	0	0	0	0		.000	.000	.000	0	-99	-3	0			.923	1	/P-4	0.0
	NY-N	5	18	2	6	1	0	0	1	2		.333	.400	.389	789	121	1	2			.667	-1	/3-3,S-2	0.0
	Yr	20	65	8	16	1	0	0	5	5		.246	.300	.262	562	57	-4	2			.891	3	P-14/S-3,3-3	0.1
1901	Bro-N	2	2	0	0	0	0	0	0	0		.000	.000	.000	0	-97	-0	0			1.000	-0	/P-2	0.0
Total	10	329	1042	132	223	17	11	2	101	92	112	.214	.282	.257	539	47	-75	17			.911	7	P-296/O-17R,2-10,S3	-1.2

■ KIT CARSON
Carson, Walter Lloyd b: 11/15/12, Colton, Cal. d: 6/21/83, Long Beach, Cal. BL/TL, 6', 180 lbs. Deb: 7/21/34

YEAR	TM/L	G	AB	R	H	2B	3B	HR	RBI	BB	SO	AVG	OBP	SLG	OPS	OPS+	BR+	SB	CS	SBR	FA	FR	G/POS	TPR
1934	Cle-A	5	18	4	5	2	1	0	1	2	3	.278	.350	.500	850	115	0	0	0	0	1.000	-1	/O-4(0-0-4)	-0.1
1935	Cle-A	16	22	1	5	2	0	0	1	2	6	.227	.292	.318	610	57	-1	0	1	-0	1.000	-0	/O-4(0-0-4)	-0.2
Total	2	21	40	5	10	4	1	0	2	4	9	.250	.318	.400	718	83	-1	0	1	-0	1.000	-2	/O-8(0-0-8)	-0.3

■ FRANK CARSWELL
Carswell, Frank Willis "Tex" or "Wheels" b: 11/6/19, Palestine, Tex. d: 10/16/98, Houston, Tex. BR/TR, 6', 195 lbs. Deb: 4/17/53

YEAR	TM/L	G	AB	R	H	2B	3B	HR	RBI	BB	SO	AVG	OBP	SLG	OPS	OPS+	BR+	SB	CS	SBR	FA	FR	G/POS	TPR
1953	Det-A	16	15	2	4	0	0	0	2	3	1	.267	.389	.267	656	81	-0	0	0	0	1.000	-1	/O-3(3-0-0)	-0.1

■ GARY CARTER
Carter, Gary Edmund b: 4/8/54, Culver City, Cal. BR/TR, 6'2", 215 lbs. Deb: 9/16/74 Career OF: (5-LF 0-CF 132-RF)

YEAR	TM/L	G	AB	R	H	2B	3B	HR	RBI	BB	SO	AVG	OBP	SLG	OPS	OPS+	BR+	SB	CS	SBR	FA	FR	G/POS	TPR
1974	Mon-N	9	27	5	11	0	1	1	6	1	2	.407	.429	.593	1021	174	3	2	0	0	1.000	-1	/C-6,O-2(0-0-2)	0.2
1975	Mon-N★	144	503	58	136	20	1	17	68	72	83	.270	.363	.416	778	111	8	5	2	0	.974	-16	O-92(0-0-92),C-66/3-1	-0.8
1976	Mon-N	91	311	31	68	8	1	6	38	30	43	.219	.289	.309	598	67	-13	0	2	-1	.994	3	C-60,O-36(2-0-34)	-1.1
1977	Mon-N	154	522	86	148	29	2	31	84	58	103	.284	.361	.525	886	138	27	5	5	-1	.990	3	*C-146/O-1(1-0-0)	3.5
1978	Mon-N	157	533	76	136	27	1	20	72	62	70	.255	.338	.422	760	113	9	10	6	0	.989	10	*C-152/1-1	2.6
1979	Mon-N★	141	505	74	143	26	5	22	75	40	62	.283	.342	.485	827	124	15	3	2	-0	.989	13	*C-138	3.5
1980	Mon-N★	154	549	76	145	25	5	29	101	58	78	.264	.336	.486	822	127	18	3	2	-0	**.993**	14	*C-149	4.0
1981	*Mon-N★	100	374	48	94	20	2	16	68	35	35	.251	.317	.444	761	113	5	1	5	-2	.993	2	*C-100/1-1	1.1
1982	Mon-N★	154	557	91	163	32	1	29	97	78	64	.293	.385	.510	895	146	35	2	5	-1	.991	14	*C-153	5.6
1983	Mon-N★	145	541	63	146	37	3	17	79	51	57	.270	.341	.444	784	116	11	1	1	-0	**.995**	10	*C-144/1-1	2.8
1984	Mon-N★	159	596	75	175	32	1	27	**106**	64	57	.294	.368	.487	854	145	35	2	2	-0	.993	-5	*C-143,1-25	3.5
1985	NY-N†	149	555	83	156	17	1	32	100	69	46	.281	.367	.488	855	141	30	1	1	-0	.992	5	*C-143/1-6,O-1(0-0-1)	4.2
1986	*NY-N★	132	490	81	125	14	2	24	105	62	63	.255	.346	.439	785	118	12	1	0	0	.991	6	*C-122/1-9,O-4L,3-1	2.4
1987	NY-N★	139	523	55	123	18	2	20	83	42	73	.235	.293	.392	685	84	-14	0	0	0	.991	-0	*C-135/1-4,O-1(0-0-1)	-0.8
1988	*NY-N★	130	455	39	110	16	2	11	46	34	52	.242	.304	.358	663	94	-4	0	2	-1	.990	-3	*C-119,1-10/3-1	-0.1
1989	NY-N	50	153	14	28	8	0	2	15	12	15	.183	.242	.275	517	50	-10	0	0	0	.980	-2	C-47/1-1	-1.0
1990	SF-N	92	244	24	62	10	0	9	27	25	31	.254	.326	.406	732	104	1	1	1	-0	.992	-3	C-80/1-3	0.1
1991	LA-N	101	248	22	61	14	0	6	26	22	26	.246	.325	.375	700	98	-0	2	2	-0	.988	3	C-68,1-10	0.6
1992	Mon-N	95	285	24	62	18	1	5	29	33	37	.218	.303	.340	643	83	-6	0	4	-1	.989	1	C-85/1-5	-0.2
Total	19	2296	7971	1025	2092	371	31	324	1225	848	997	.262	.338	.439	777	116	160	39	42	-6	.991	54	*C-2056,O-137R/1-76,3	30.1

■ HOWIE CARTER
Carter, John Howard b: 10/13/04, New York, N.Y. d: 7/24/91, New York, N.Y. BR/TR, 5'10", 154 lbs. Deb: 6/21/26

YEAR	TM/L	G	AB	R	H	2B	3B	HR	RBI	BB	SO	AVG	OBP	SLG	OPS	OPS+	BR+	SB	CS	SBR	FA	FR	G/POS	TPR
1926	Cin-N	5	1	0	0	0	0	0	0	0	0	.000	.000	.000	0	-99	-0	0			1.000	0	/2-3,S-1	0.0

■ JOE CARTER
Carter, Joseph Chris b: 3/7/60, Oklahoma City, Okla. BR/TR, 6'3", 215 lbs. Deb: 7/30/83 Career OF: (775-LF 432-CF 624-RF)

YEAR	TM/L	G	AB	R	H	2B	3B	HR	RBI	BB	SO	AVG	OBP	SLG	OPS	OPS+	BR+	SB	CS	SBR	FA	FR	G/POS	TPR
1983	Chi-N	23	51	6	9	1	1	0	1	0	21	.176	.176	.235	412	13	-6	1	0	0	1.000	-2	O-16(14-2-1)	-0.8
1984	Cle-A	66	244	32	67	6	1	13	41	11	48	.275	.309	.467	776	109	2	2	4	-1	.956	1	O-59(48-14-0)/1-7	0.0
1985	Cle-A	143	489	64	128	27	0	15	59	25	74	.262	.300	.409	709	93	-6	24	6	3	.983	-1	*O-135L,1-11/2-1,3D	-1.0
1986	Cle-A	162	663	108	200	36	9	29	**121**	32	95	.302	.339	.514	853	130	25	29	7	4	.976	-6	*O-104(45-9-78),1-70	1.4
1987	Cle-A	149	588	83	155	27	2	32	106	27	105	.264	.306	.480	786	103	1	31	6	5	.983	-8	1-84,O-62L/D-5	-0.9
1988	Cle-A	157	621	85	168	36	6	27	98	35	82	.271	.317	.478	795	116	11	27	5	4	.985	14	*O-156(0-155-0)	2.8
1989	Cle-A	162	651	84	158	32	4	35	105	39	112	.243	.294	.465	759	109	4	13	5	1	.978	-1	*O-146C,1-11/D-8	0.1
1990	SD-N	162	634	79	147	27	1	24	115	48	93	.232	.293	.391	684	86	-14	22	6	3	.988	9	*O-150(51-112-0),1-14	-0.6
1991	*Tor-A★	162	638	89	174	42	3	33	108	49	112	.273	.334	.503	837	124	18	20	9	1	.974	3	*O-151(57-0-100),D-11	1.7
1992	*Tor-A★	158	622	97	164	30	7	34	119	36	109	.264	.315	.498	814	119	13	12	5	1	.971	6	*O-129R,D-24/1-4	1.4
1993	*Tor-A★	155	603	92	153	33	5	33	121	47	113	.254	.317	.489	806	113	8	8	3	1	.974	1	*O-151(55-0-96)/D-3	0.2
1994	Tor-A★	111	435	70	118	25	2	27	103	33	64	.271	.326	.524	850	114	7	11	0	2	.991	0	*O-110(0-0-110)/D-1	0.3
1995	Tor-A	139	558	70	141	23	0	25	76	37	87	.253	.303	.428	731	88	-12	12	1	2	.975	3	*O-128L/1-7,D-5	-1.0
1996	Tor-A★	157	625	84	158	35	7	30	107	44	106	.253	.309	.475	784	95	-8	7	6	-1	.961	-12	*O-115L,1-41,D-15	-2.6
1997	Tor-A	157	612	76	143	30	4	21	102	40	105	.234	.288	.399	687	76	-23	8	2	1	.972	-0	D-65,O-51L,1-42	-3.0
1998	Bal-A	85	283	36	70	15	1	11	34	18	48	.247	.297	.424	721	86	-7	3	1	0	.962	2	O-50(3-0-47),D-32/1-1	-0.8
	SF-N	41	105	15	31	7	0	7	29	6	13	.295	.333	.562	895	138	5	1	0	0	1.000	-4	O-17(4-0-14),1-16	-0.1
Total	16	2189	8422	1170	2184	432	53	396	1445	527	1387	.259	.310	.464	774	104	20	231	66	28	.977	3	*O-1730L,1-308,D/32	-2.9

■ BLACKIE CARTER
Carter, Otis Leonard b: 9/30/02, Langley, S.C. d: 9/10/76, Greenville, S.C. BR/TR, 5'10", 175 lbs. Deb: 10/3/25

YEAR	TM/L	G	AB	R	H	2B	3B	HR	RBI	BB	SO	AVG	OBP	SLG	OPS	OPS+	BR+	SB	CS	SBR	FA	FR	G/POS	TPR
1925	NY-N	1	4	0	0	0	0	0	0	0	1	.000	.000	.000	0	-99	-1	0	0	0	1.000	1	/O-1(1-0-0)	-0.1
1926	NY-N	5	17	4	4	1	0	1	1	1	0	.235	.278	.471	748	100	-0	0			.917	0	/O-4(3-0-1)	0.0
Total	2	6	21	4	4	1	0	1	1	1	1	.190	.227	.381	608	61	-1	0	0		.929	1	/O-5(4-0-1)	-0.1

■ STEVE CARTER
Carter, Steven Jerome b: 12/3/64, Charlottesville, Va. BL/TR, 6'4", 201 lbs. Deb: 4/16/89

YEAR	TM/L	G	AB	R	H	2B	3B	HR	RBI	BB	SO	AVG	OBP	SLG	OPS	OPS+	BR+	SB	CS	SBR	FA	FR	G/POS	TPR
1989	Pit-N	9	16	2	2	1	0	1	3	2	5	.125	.222	.375	597	70	-1	0	0	0	1.000	-1	/O-5(0-0-5)	-0.2
1990	Pit-N	5	5	0	1	0	0	0	0	0	1	.200	.200	.200	400	11	-1	0	0	0	1.000	-1	/O-3(1-2-1)	-0.2
Total	2	14	21	2	3	1	0	1	3	2	6	.143	.217	.333	551	56	-1	0	0	0	1.000	-2	/O-8(1-2-6)	-0.4

■ ED CARTWRIGHT
Cartwright, Edward Charles "Jumbo" b: 10/6/1859, Johnstown, Pa. d: 9/3/33, St.Petersburg, Fla BR/TR, 5'10", 220 lbs. Deb: 7/10/1890

YEAR	TM/L	G	AB	R	H	2B	3B	HR	RBI	BB	SO	AVG	OBP	SLG	OPS	OPS+	BR+	SB	CS	SBR	FA	FR	G/POS	TPR
1890	StL-a	75	300	70	90	12	4	8	60	29		.300	.367	.447	814	123	6	26			.976	-1	1-75	-0.2
1894	Was-N	132	507	88	149	35	13	12	106	57	43	.294	.374	.485	859	109	6	31			.973	-2	*1-132	0.3
1895	Was-N	122	472	95	156	34	17	3	90	54	41	.331	.400	.494	894	131	22	50			.984	14	*1-122	2.8
1896	Was-N	133	499	76	138	15	10	1	62	54	44	.277	.350	.353	702	85	-10	28			.978	-0	*1-133	-0.9
1897	Was-N	33	124	19	29	4	0	0	15	8		.234	.286	.266	552	46	-10	9			.963	2	1-33	-0.6
Total	5	495	1902	348	562	100	44	24	333	202	128	.295	.368	.432	800	106	15	144			.977	13	1-495	1.4

■ RICO CARTY
Carty, Ricardo Adolfo Jacobo (b: Ricardo Adolfo Jacobo (Carty))
b: 9/1/39, San Pedro De Macoris, D.R. BR/TR, 6'3", 200 lbs. Deb: 9/15/63 Career OF: (789-LF 1-CF 18-RF)

YEAR	TM/L	G	AB	R	H	2B	3B	HR	RBI	BB	SO	AVG	OBP	SLG	OPS	OPS+	BR+	SB	CS	SBR	FA	FR	G/POS	TPR
1963	Mil-N	2	2	0	0	0	0	0	0	0	2	.000	.000	.000	0	-99	-1	0	0	0	.000	0	H	-0.1
1964	Mil-N	133	455	72	150	28	4	22	88	43	78	.330	.391	.554	945	162	37	1	2	-0	.978	1	*O-121(118-1-2)	3.2
1965	Mil-N	83	271	37	84	18	1	10	35	17	44	.310	.357	.494	852	136	12	1	4	-1	.958	1	O-73(73-0-0)	0.9
1966	Atl-N	151	521	73	170	25	2	15	76	60	74	.326	.396	.468	864	137	28	4	6	-1	.971	5	*O-126L,C-17/1-2,3	2.7
1967	Atl-N	134	444	41	113	16	2	15	64	49	70	.255	.330	.401	731	110	6	4	3	-0	.959	4	*O-112(97-0-15)/1-9	0.2
1969	*Atl-N	104	304	47	104	15	0	16	58	32	28	.342	.405	.549	954	164	26	0	2	-1	.952	-3	O-79(79-0-0)	1.8
1970	Atl-N★	136	478	84	175	23	3	25	101	77	46	**.366**	**.456**	.584	1040	167	48	1	2	-0	.974	3	*O-133(133-0-0)	4.1
1972	Atl-N	86	271	31	75	12	2	6	29	44	33	.277	.378	.402	780	111	6	0	0	0	.979	-1	O-78(78-0-0)	0.0
1973	Tex-A	86	306	24	71	12	0	3	33	36	39	.232	.315	.301	616	77	-9	2	0	0	1.000	-2	O-53(53-0-0),D-31	-1.4
	Chi-N	22	70	4	15	0	0	1	8	6	10	.214	.276	.257	533	45	-5	0	0	0	.947	-0	O-19(19-0-0)	-0.7
	Oak-A	7	8	1	2	1	0	1	1	2	1	.250	.400	.750	1150	230	1	0	0	0	.000	0	/D-2	0.1
1974	Cle-A	33	91	6	33	5	0	1	16	5	9	.363	.396	.451	846	144	5	0	0	0	.985	-2	D-14/1-8	0.3
1975	Cle-A	118	383	57	118	19	1	18	64	45	31	.308	.384	.504	888	149	25	2	2	-0	.990	-1	D-72,1-26,O-12L	1.9
1976	Cle-A	152	552	67	171	34	0	13	83	67	45	.310	.384	.442	827	143	31	1	1	-0	1.000	-2	*D-137,1-12/O-1L	2.6
1977	Cle-A	127	461	50	129	23	1	15	80	56	51	.280	.358	.432	790	118	12	1	2	-0	1.000	1	*D-123/1-2	0.8
1978	Tor-A	104	387	51	110	16	0	20	68	36	41	.284	.345	.481	826	127	13	1	1	-0	.000	0	*D-101	1.0
	Oak-A	41	141	19	39	5	1	11	31	21	16	.277	.370	.560	931	167	12	0	0	0	.000	0	D-41	1.1
	Yr	145	528	70	149	21	1	31	99	57	57	.282	.352	.502	854	138	25	1	1	-0	.896	0	*D-142	2.1
1979	Tor-A	132	461	48	118	26	0	12	55	46	45	.256	.325	.390	715	91	-6	3	1	0	.000	0	*D-129	-0.9
Total	15	1651	5606	712	1677	278	17	204	890	642	663	.299	.372	.464	836	132	241	21	26	-4	.970	3	O-807L,D-650/1-59,C3	17.6

■ MIKE CARUSO
Caruso, Michael John b: 5/27/77, Queens, N.Y. BB/TR, 6'1", 172 lbs. Deb: 3/31/98

YEAR	TM/L	G	AB	R	H	2B	3B	HR	RBI	BB	SO	AVG	OBP	SLG	OPS	OPS+	BR+	SB	CS	SBR	FA	FR	G/POS	TPR
1998	Chi-A	133	523	81	160	17	6	5	55	14	38	.306	.333	.390	723	90	-8	22	6	3	.944	-11	*S-131	-0.5
1999	Chi-A	136	529	60	132	11	4	2	35	20	36	.250	.281	.297	578	47	-42	12	14	-2	.957	-28	*S-132/D-2	-5.7
Total	2	269	1052	141	292	28	10	7	90	34	74	.278	.307	.343	650	68	-50	34	20	0	.950	-39	S-263/D-2	-6.2

■ BOB CARUTHERS
Caruthers, Robert Lee "Parisian Bob" b: 1/5/1864, Memphis, Tenn.
d: 8/5/11, Peoria, Ill. BL/TR, 5'7", 138 lbs. Deb: 9/7/1884 MU Career OF: (58-LF 30-CF 280-RF)

YEAR	TM/L	G	AB	R	H	2B	3B	HR	RBI	BB	SO	AVG	OBP	SLG	OPS	OPS+	BR+	SB	CS	SBR	FA	FR	G/POS	TPR
1884	StL-a	23	82	15	22	2	0	2		4		.268	.302	.366	668	113	1				.750	-6	O-16(0-0-16),P-13	-0.4
1885	*StL-a	60	222	37	50	10	2	1	12	20		.225	.289	.302	591	83	-4				.902	-0	P-53/O-7(6-0-1)	-0.1
1886	*StL-a	87	317	91	106	21	14	4	61	64		.334	.448	.527	974	196	37	26			.897	-6	P-44,O-43(1-0-42)/2-2	1.2
1887	*StL-a	98	430	102	196	23	11	8	73	66		.456	.463	.547	1010	164	32	49			.903	9	O-54(3-2-50),P-39/1-7	1.6
1888	Bro-a	94	335	58	77	10	5	5	53	45		.230	.328	.334	662	113	6	23			.899	1	O-51(4-16-31),P-44	0.2
1889	*Bro-a	59	172	45	43	8	3	2	31	44	17	.250	.408	.366	775	121	7	9			.968	0	P-56/O-3(0-1-2),1-2	-0.2
1890	*Bro-N	71	238	46	63	7	4	1	29	47	18	.265	.397	.340	737	115	7	13			.860	-4	O-39(37-1-1),P-37	-0.4
1891	Bro-N	56	171	24	48	5	3	2	23	25	13	.281	.372	.380	753	120	5	4			.940	-3	P-38,O-17(1-2-14)/2-1	-0.2
1892	StL-N	143	513	76	142	16	8	3	69	86	29	.277	.386	.357	742	131	24	24			.892	-11	*O-122R,P-16/2-6,1M	0.5
1893	Chi-N	1	3	0	0	0	0	0	0	0	1	.000	.000	.000	0	-99	-1	0			1.000	-0	/O-1(0-1-0)	-0.1
	Cin-N	13	48	14	14	2	0	1	8	16	1	.292	.477	.396	873	130	3	4			.857	-1	O-13(0-0-13)	0.1
	Yr	14	51	14	14	2	0	1	8	16	2	.275	.456	.373	828	119	3	4			.862	-1	O-14(0-1-13)	0.0
Total	10	705	2531	508	761	104	50	29	359	417	79	.301	.391	.400	791	134	118	152			.875	-22	O-366R,P-340/1-13,2	2.2

■ PAUL CASANOVA
Casanova, Paulino (Ortiz) b: 12/21/41, Colon, Matanzas, Cuba BR/TR, 6'4", 200 lbs. Deb: 9/18/65

YEAR	TM/L	G	AB	R	H	2B	3B	HR	RBI	BB	SO	AVG	OBP	SLG	OPS	OPS+	BR+	SB	CS	SBR	FA	FR	G/POS	TPR
1965	Was-A	5	13	2	4	1	0	0	1	1	3	.308	.357	.385	742	112	0	0	0	0	.938	-2	/C-4	-0.2
1966	Was-A	122	429	45	109	16	5	13	44	14	78	.254	.279	.406	685	95	-4	1	2	-0	.981	-10	*C-119	-1.0
1967	Was-A☆	141	528	47	131	19	1	9	53	17	65	.248	.274	.339	613	84	-13	1	1	-0	.984	-5	*C-137	-1.2
1968	Was-A	96	322	19	63	6	0	4	25	7	52	.196	.213	.252	464	42	-23	0	1	-0	.989	-9	C-92	-3.3
1969	Was-A	124	379	26	82	9	2	4	37	18	52	.216	.257	.282	540	54	-24	0	0	0	.992	-6	*C-122	-2.7
1970	Was-A	104	328	25	75	17	3	6	30	10	47	.229	.254	.354	607	69	-15	0	0	0	.988	-1	*C-100	-1.3
1971	Was-A	94	311	19	63	9	1	5	26	14	52	.203	.239	.286	525	51	-21	0	3	-1	.985	-4	C-83	-2.5
1972	Atl-N	49	136	8	28	3	0	2	10	4	28	.206	.229	.272	501	38	-11	0	1	-0	.975	-6	C-43	-1.7
1973	Atl-N	82	236	18	51	7	0	7	18	11	36	.216	.254	.335	589	58	-14	0	2	-1	.977	6	C-78	-0.6
1974	Atl-N	42	104	5	21	0	0	0	8	5	17	.202	.239	.202	440	23	-11	0	0	0	.986	-1	C-33	-1.0
Total	10	859	2786	214	627	87	12	50	252	101	430	.225	.254	.319	573	64	-136	2	10	-3	.985	-38	C-811	-15.5

■ RAUL CASANOVA
Casanova, Raul b: 8/23/72, Humacao, P.R. BB/TR, 6', 192 lbs. Deb: 5/24/96

YEAR	TM/L	G	AB	R	H	2B	3B	HR	RBI	BB	SO	AVG	OBP	SLG	OPS	OPS+	BR+	SB	CS	SBR	FA	FR	G/POS	TPR
1996	Det-A	25	85	6	16	1	0	4	9	6	18	.188	.242	.341	583	45	-7	0	0	0	.978	-4	C-22/D-3	-0.9
1997	Det-A	101	304	27	74	10	1	5	24	26	48	.243	.309	.332	642	68	-14	1	1	-0	.985	2	C-92/D-1	-0.7
1998	Det-A	16	42	4	6	2	0	1	3	5	10	.143	.250	.262	512	33	-4	0	0	0	.967	1	C-14	-0.2
2000	Mil-N	86	231	20	57	13	3	6	36	26	48	.247	.333	.407	740	87	-5	1	2	-0	.990	-4	C-72/D-3	-0.5
Total	4	228	662	57	153	26	4	16	72	63	124	.231	.306	.355	661	70	-30	2	3	-1	.984	-5	C-200/D-7	-2.3

■ GEORGE CASE
Case, George Washington b: 11/11/15, Trenton, N.J. d: 1/23/89, Trenton, N.J. BR/TR, 6', 183 lbs. Deb: 9/8/37 C

YEAR	TM/L	G	AB	R	H	2B	3B	HR	RBI	BB	SO	AVG	OBP	SLG	OPS	OPS+	BR+	SB	CS	SBR	FA	FR	G/POS	TPR
1937	Was-A	22	90	14	26	6	2	0	11	3	5	.289	.312	.400	712	82	-3	2	1	0	.945	-0	O-22(8-1-14)	-0.4
1938	Was-A	107	433	69	132	27	3	2	40	39	28	.305	.362	.395	757	96	-2	11	6	0	.964	-4	*O-101(0-19-82)	-1.1
1939	Was-A☆	128	530	103	160	20	7	2	35	56	36	.302	.369	.377	746	98	0	**51**	17	**5**	.955	3	*O-123(7-79-38)	0.3
1940	Was-A	154	656	109	192	29	5	5	56	52	39	.293	.349	.375	724	94	-5	**35**	10	**4**	.970	1	*O-154(0-118-36)	-0.5
1941	Was-A	153	649	95	176	32	8	2	53	51	37	.271	.325	.354	680	84	-16	**33**	9	**4**	.975	15	*O-151(115-0-36)	-0.5
1942	Was-A	125	513	101	164	26	2	5	43	44	30	.320	.377	.407	784	122	15	**44**	6	**8**	.951	-2	*O-120(86-0-34)	1.4
1943	Was-A★	141	613	**102**	180	36	5	1	52	41	27	.294	.341	.374	715	113	9	**61**	14	**9**	.985	1	*O-140(18-0-122)	1.0
1944	Was-A†	119	464	63	116	14	2	2	32	49	22	.250	.326	.302	627	83	-9	49	18	4	.970	6	*O-114(83-7-28)	-0.6
1945	Was-A†	123	504	72	148	19	5	1	31	49	27	.294	.360	.357	717	118	12	30	16	1	.979	13	*O-123(87-15-27)	2.0
1946	Cle-A	118	484	46	109	23	4	1	22	34	38	.225	.280	.295	576	65	-24	**28**	11	**2**	.983	-4	*O-118(118-0-0)	-3.7
1947	Was-A	36	80	11	12	1	0	0	2	8	8	.150	.227	.162	390	10	-10	5	1	1	.963	0	O-21(12-4-5)	-1.0
Total	11	1226	5016	785	1415	233	43	21	377	426	297	.282	.341	.358	699	95	-34	349	109	39	.970	30	*O-1187(534-243-422)	-3.1

■ DENNIS CASEY
Casey, Dennis Patrick b: 3/30/1858, Binghamton, N.Y. d: 1/19/09, Binghamton, N.Y. BL/TR, 5'9", 164 lbs. Deb: 8/18/1884 F

YEAR	TM/L	G	AB	R	H	2B	3B	HR	RBI	BB	SO	AVG	OBP	SLG	OPS	OPS+	BR+	SB	CS	SBR	FA	FR	G/POS	TPR
1884	Wil-U	2	8	1	2	1	0	0		0		.250	.250	.375	625	85	-0				1.000	-0	/O-2(0-2-0)	0.0
	Bal-a	37	149	20	37	7	4	3		5		.248	.273	.409	682	115	2				.898	-1	O-37(0-37-0)	0.0
1885	Bal-a	63	264	50	76	10	5	3	29	21		.288	.347	.398	745	137	12				.821	-5	O-63(0-63-0)	0.4
Total	2	102	421	71	115	18	9	6	29	26		.273	.320	.401	721	128	13				.847	-6	O-102(0-102-0)	0.4

YEAR	TM/L	G	AB	R	H	2B	3B	HR	RBI	BB	SO	AVG	OBP	SLG	OPS	OPS+	BR+	SB	CS	SBR	FA	FR	G/POS	TPR
■ **DOC CASEY**	Casey, James Patrick b: 3/15/1870, Lawrence, Mass. d: 12/31/36, Detroit, Mich. BB/TR, 5′6″, 157 lbs. Deb: 9/14/1898																							
1898	Was-N	28	112	13	31	2	0	0	15	3		.277	.302	.295	596	71	-4	15			.893	-3	3-22/S-4,C-3	-0.6
1899	Was-N	9	34	3	4	2	0	0	2	2		.118	.167	.176	343	-6	-5	1			.853	-1	/3-9	-0.5
	Bro-N	134	525	75	141	14	8	1	43	25		.269	.313	.331	644	75	-19	27			.892	-19	*3-134	-3.3
	Yr	143	559	78	145	16	8	1	45	27		.259	.304	.322	626	70	-24	28			.889	-20	*3-143	-3.8
1900	Bro-N	1	3	0	1	0	0	0	1	0		.333	.500	.333	833	125	0	0			1.000	-0	/3-1	0.0
1901	Det-A	128	540	105	153	16	9	2	46	32		.283	.335	.357	692	88	-9	34			.887	5	*3-127	0.0
1902	Det-A	132	520	69	142	18	7	3	55	44		.273	.338	.352	690	90	-7	22			.904	2	*3-132	-0.1
1903	Chi-N	112	435	56	126	8	3	1	40	19		.290	.324	.329	653	89	-7	11			.915	-19	*3-112	-2.2
1904	Chi-N	136	548	71	147	20	4	1	43	18		.268	.300	.325	625	93	-6	21			.911	-10	*3-134/C-2	-1.3
1905	Chi-N	144	526	66	122	21	10	1	56	41		.232	.295	.316	611	79	-14	22			**.949**	-9	*3-142/S-1	-2.0
1906	Bro-N	149	571	71	133	17	8	0	34	52		.233	.306	.291	597	93	-4	22			.919	-17	*3-149	-1.9
1907	Bro-N	141	527	55	122	19	3	0	19	34		.231	.282	.279	561	82	-12	16			.955	-6	*3-138	-1.6
Total	10	1114	4341	584	1122	137	52	9	354	270		.258	.310	.320	630	85	-85	191			.915	-77	*3-1100/C-5,S-5	-13.5
■ **JOE CASEY**	Casey, Joseph Felix b: 8/15/1887, Boston, Mass. d: 6/2/66, Melrose, Mass. BR/TR, 5′9″, 180 lbs. Deb: 10/1/09																							
1909	Det-A	3	5	1	0	0	0	0	0	1		.000	.167	.000	167	-45	-1	0			1.000	2	/C-3	0.1
1910	Det-A	23	62	3	12	3	0	0	2	2		.194	.231	.242	473	45	-4	1			.964	5	C-22	0.4
1911	Det-A	15	33	2	5	0	0	0	3	3		.152	.222	.152	374	5	-4	0			.956	-3	C-12/O-3(0-3-0)	-0.6
1918	Was-A	9	17	3	4	0	0	0	2	2	2	.235	.316	.235	551	68	-1	0			1.000	2	/C-8	0.2
Total	4	50	117	9	21	3	0	0	7	8	2	.179	.238	.205	443	32	-10	1			.970	6	/C-45,O-3(0-3-0)	0.1
■ **BOB CASEY**	Casey, Orrin Robinson b: 1/26/1859, Adolphustown, Ontario, Canada d: 11/28/36, Syracuse, N.Y. 5′11″, 190 lbs. Deb: 7/17/1882																							
1882	Det-N	9	39	5	9	2	1	1	7	0	15	.231	.231	.410	641	101	-0				.667	-5	/3-8,2-1	-0.4
■ **SEAN CASEY**	Casey, Sean Thomas b: 7/2/74, Willingboro, N.J. BL/TR, 6′4″, 215 lbs. Deb: 9/12/97																							
1997	Cle-A	6	10	1	2	0	0	0	1	1	2	.200	.333	.200	533	42	-1	0	0	0	1.000	-0	/1-1,D-3	-0.1
1998	Cin-N	96	302	44	82	21	1	7	52	43	45	.272	.368	.417	785	105	3	1	1	-0	.994	-8	1-86	-1.2
1999	Cin-N★	151	594	103	197	42	3	25	99	61	88	.332	.402	.539	941	131	29	0	2	-1	.995	-16	*1-148/D-1	-0.1
2000	Cin-N	133	480	69	151	33	2	20	85	52	80	.315	.390	.517	906	121	16	1	0	0	.995	-9	*1-129	-0.4
Total	4	386	1386	217	432	96	6	52	237	157	215	.312	.390	.502	892	122	48	2	3	-1	.995	-32	1-364/D-4	-1.8
■ **DAVE CASH**	Cash, David b: 6/11/48, Utica, N.Y. BR/TR, 5′11″, 175 lbs. Deb: 9/13/69 C																							
1969	Pit-N	18	61	8	17	3	1	0	4	9	9	.279	.371	.361	732	108	1	2	0	0	.990	5	2-17	0.8
1970	*Pit-N	64	210	30	66	7	6	1	28	17	25	.314	.368	.419	787	113	4	5	2	0	.974	6	2-55	1.3
1971	*Pit-N	123	478	79	138	17	4	2	34	46	33	.289	.351	.354	705	101	1	13	5	1	.987	6	*2-105,3-24/S-3	1.6
1972	*Pit-N	99	425	58	120	22	4	3	30	22	31	.282	.318	.374	692	98	-2	9	9	-1	.992	28	2-97	3.3
1973	Pit-N	116	436	59	118	21	2	2	31	38	36	.271	.329	.342	671	88	-7	2	5	-1	.979	6	2-92,3-17	0.3
1974	Phi-N★	162	687	89	206	26	11	2	58	46	33	.300	.352	.378	730	100	1	20	8	2	.977	**29**	*2-162	4.3
1975	Phi-N★	162	699	111	**213**	40	3	4	57	56	34	.305	.360	.388	747	103	4	13	6	1	.981	9	*2-162	2.5
1976	*Phi-N★	160	666	92	189	14	**12**	1	56	54	13	.284	.339	.345	685	92	-6	10	12	-2	**.988**	-2	*2-158	0.1
1977	Mon-N	153	650	91	188	42	7	0	43	52	33	.289	.344	.375	719	96	-4	21	12	0	.986	-11	*2-153	-0.6
1978	Mon-N	159	658	66	166	26	3	3	43	37	29	.252	.292	.315	607	70	-27	12	6	1	**.986**	-30	*2-159	-5.1
1979	Mon-N	76	187	24	60	11	1	2	19	12	12	.321	.362	.422	784	114	4	7	4	0	.971	-6	2-47	0.0
1980	SD-N	130	397	25	90	14	2	1	23	35	21	.227	.289	.280	569	63	-20	6	5	-0	.987	4	*2-123	-1.1
Total	12	1422	5554	732	1571	243	56	21	426	424	309	.283	.336	.358	694	93	-51	120	74	1	.984	43	*2-1330/3-41,S-3	7.4
■ **NORM CASH**	Cash, Norman Dalton b: 11/10/34, Justiceburg, Tex. d: 10/12/86, Beaver Island, Mich. BL/TL, 6′, 190 lbs. Deb: 6/18/58 Career OF: (4-LF 0-CF 7-RF)																							
1958	Chi-A	13	8	2	2	0	0	0	0	0	1	.250	.250	.250	500	39	-1	0	0	0	1.000	-1	/O-4(1-0-3)	-0.2
1959	*Chi-A	58	104	16	25	0	1	4	16	18	9	.240	.378	.375	753	109	2	1	1	-0	.984	-1	1-31	0.0
1960	Det-A	121	353	64	101	16	3	18	63	65	58	.286	.406	.501	907	140	22	4	2	0	.991	-2	1-99/O-4(3-0-1)	1.5
1961	Det-A★	159	535	119	**193**	22	8	41	132	124	85	**.361**	**.488**	.662	**1150**	198	82	11	5	1	.992	5	*1-157	7.5
1962	Det-A	148	507	94	123	16	2	39	89	104	82	.243	.385	.513	897	134	27	6	3	0	.992	7	*1-146/O-3(0-0-3)	2.5
1963	Det-A	147	493	67	133	19	1	26	79	89	76	.270	.388	.471	858	135	26	2	3	-1	.994	2	*1-142	1.9
1964	Det-A	144	479	63	123	15	5	23	83	70	66	.257	.355	.453	808	121	15	2	1	0	**.997**	4	*1-137	1.1
1965	Det-A	142	467	79	124	23	1	30	82	77	62	.266	.374	.512	886	147	30	6	6	-1	.992	5	*1-139	2.8
1966	Det-A★	160	603	98	168	18	3	32	93	66	91	.279	.354	.478	831	133	26	2	1	0	.988	4	*1-158	2.1
1967	Det-A	152	488	64	118	16	5	22	72	81	100	.242	.354	.430	785	127	18	3	2	-0	**.995**	9	*1-146	2.1
1968	*Det-A	127	411	50	108	15	1	25	63	39	70	.263	.331	.487	818	141	19	1	1	-0	.992	9	*1-117	2.4
1969	Det-A	142	483	81	135	15	4	22	74	63	80	.280	.370	.464	833	126	17	2	1	0	.994	6	*1-134	1.4
1970	Det-A	130	370	58	96	18	2	15	53	72	58	.259	.387	.441	828	127	16	0	1	-0	.989	2	*1-114	0.9
1971	Det-A★	135	452	72	128	10	3	32	91	59	86	.283	.375	.531	905	148	28	1	0	0	.992	-0	*1-131	2.0
1972	*Det-A★	137	440	51	114	16	0	22	61	50	64	.259	.340	.445	786	128	15	0	2	-1	.993	-0	*1-134	0.4
1973	Det-A	121	363	51	95	19	0	19	40	47	73	.262	.359	.471	830	124	12	1	0	0	.991	2	*1-114/D-3	0.6
1974	Det-A	53	149	17	34	3	2	7	12	19	30	.228	.327	.416	744	109	2	1	1	-0	.985	-1	1-44	-0.2
Total	17	2089	6705	1046	1820	241	41	377	1103	1043	1091	.271	.377	.488	865	138	356	43	30	-1	.992	50	*1-1943/O-11R,D-3	28.8
■ **RON CASH**	Cash, Ronald Forrest b: 11/20/49, Atlanta, Ga. BR/TR, 6′, 180 lbs. Deb: 9/4/73																							
1973	Det-A	14	39	8	16	1	1	0	6	5	5	.410	.477	.487	964	161	3	0	0	0	.900	-2	/O-7(7-0-0),3-6	0.1
1974	Det-A	20	62	6	14	2	0	0	5	0	11	.226	.226	.258	484	38	-5	0	1	-0	.979	-1	1-15/3-4	-0.8
Total	2	34	101	14	30	3	1	0	11	5	16	.297	.330	.347	677	89	-2	0	1	-0	.950	-3	/1-15,3-10,O-7(7-0-0)	-0.7
■ **CARLOS CASIMIRO**	Casimiro, Carlos Rafael b: 11/8/76, San Pedro De Macoris, D.R. BR/TR, 5′11″, 179 lbs. Deb: 7/31/2000																							
2000	Bal-A	2	8	0	1	1	0	0	3	0	2	.125	.125	.250	375	-9	-1	0	0	0	.000	0	/D-2	-0.1
■ **ED CASKIN**	Caskin, Edward James b: 12/30/1851, Danvers, Mass. d: 10/9/24, Danvers, Mass. BR/TR, 5′9.5″, 165 lbs. Deb: 5/1/1879																							
1879	Tro-N	70	304	32	78	13	2	0	21	2	14	.257	.261	.313	574	95	-1				.902	6	S-42,C-22/2-6	0.7
1880	Tro-N	82	333	36	75	5	4	0	28	7	24	.225	.241	.264	505	68	-11				.885	7	*S-82/C-2	-0.1
1881	Tro-N	63	234	33	53	7	1	0	21	13	29	.226	.267	.265	532	65	-9				.906	1	*S-63	-0.6
1883	NY-N	95	383	47	91	11	2	1	40	14	25	.238	.264	.285	549	68	-14				.855	-5	*S-81,2-13/C-1	-1.4
1884	NY-N	100	351	49	81	11	1	1	40	34	55	.231	.299	.276	575	80	-7				.883	5	*S-96/C-6	0.1
1885	StL-N	71	262	31	47	3	0	0	12	12	22	.179	.215	.191	406	34	-18				.884	-4	3-69/C-2,S-1	-1.9
1886	NY-N	1	4	1	2	0	0	0	1	0	1	.500	.500	.500	1000	203	0	0			1.000	-1	/S-1	0.0
Total	7	482	1871	229	427	50	10	2	163	82	170	.228	.261	.269	529	70	-61	0			.883	8	S-366/3-69,C-33,2	-3.2
■ **HARRY CASSADY**	Cassady, Harry Delbert (b: Harry Delbert Cassaday) b: 7/20/1880, Bellflower, Ill. d: 4/19/69, Fresno, Cal. BL/TL, 5′8″, 145 lbs. Deb: 8/8/04																							
1904	Pit-N	12	44	8	9	0	0	0	3	2		.205	.239	.205	444	36	-3	2			.867	-1	O-12(0-0-12)	-0.5
1905	Was-A	10	30	1	4	0	0	0	1	0		.133	.133	.133	267	-16	-4	0			1.000	0	/O-9(0-0-9)	-0.4
Total	2	22	74	9	13	0	0	0	4	2		.176	.197	.176	373	17	-7	2			.933	-1	/O-21(0-0-21)	-0.9
■ **JOHN CASSIDY**	Cassidy, John P. b: 1857, Brooklyn, N.Y. d: 7/2/1891, Brooklyn, N.Y. BR/TL, 5′8″, 168 lbs. Deb: 4/24/1875 Career OF: (1-LF 147-CF 411-RF)																							
1875	Atl-n	41	166	14	29	3	2	1	6	0	4	.175	.175	.235	410	47	-7	0	0	0	.782	-8	P-30,O-12R,1-10,/2	-0.9
	NH-n	6	22	3	3	1	0	0	1	0	1	.136	.136	.182	318	11	-2	0	1	-0	.988	1	/1-6	-0.1
	Yr	47	188	17	32	4	2	1	7	0	5	.170	.170	.229	399	43	-9	0	1	-0	.782	-8	P-30,1-16,O-12R,/2	-1.0
1876	Har-N	12	48	6	13	2	0	0	8	1	0	.271	.292	.319	611	95	-0				1.000	1	/O-8(0-0-8),1-4	0.0
1877	Har-N	60	251	43	95	10	5	0	27	3	3	.378	.386	.458	844	184	24				.722	-5	*O-58(0-1-57)/P-2	1.7
1878	Chi-N	60	256	33	68	7	1	0	29	9	11	.266	.291	.301	591	89	-3				.810	8	*O-60(0-0-60)/C-1	0.5
1879	Tro-N	9	37	4	7	1	0	0	1	2	4	.189	.231	.216	447	52	-2				.889	-2	/O-8(0-3-5),1-2	-0.3
1880	Tro-N	83	352	40	89	14	8	0	29	12	34	.253	.277	.338	616	102	0				.880	-2	*O-82(0-47-35)/2-1	-0.3
1881	Tro-N	85	370	57	82	13	3	1	11	18	21	.222	.258	.281	539	66	-14				.872	-9	*O-84(0-84-0)/S-1	-2.6

YEAR	TM/L	G	AB	R	H	2B	3B	HR	RBI	BB	SO	AVG	OBP	SLG	OPS	OPS+	BR+	SB	CS	SBR	FA	FR	G/POS	TPR
1882	Tro-N	29	121	14	21	3	1	0	9	3	16	.174	.194	.215	408	32	-9				.778	-9	O-16(0-12-4),3-13	-1.7
1883	Pro-N	89	366	46	87	16	5	0	42	9	38	.238	.256	.309	565	69	-14				.864	1	*O-88(1-0-87)/2-1,1-1	-1.2
1884	Bro-a	106	433	57	109	11	6	2		19		.252	.286	.319	605	96	-2				.847	-8	*O-101R/3-4,S-1	-1.0
1885	Bro-a	54	221	36	47	6	2	1	28	8		.213	.250	.271	521	64	-9				.852	-7	O-54(0-0-54)	-1.5
Total	10	587	2455	336	618	83	31	4	184	84	127	.252	.278	.316	594	89	-29				.845	-31	O-559R/3-17,1-7,S2PC	-6.4
■ JOE CASSIDY	Cassidy, Joseph Phillip b: 2/8/1883, Chester, Pa. d: 3/25/06, Chester, Pa. BR/TR, Deb: 4/18/04 Career OF: (1-LF 20-CF 11-RF)																							
1904	Was-A	152	581	63	140	12	**19**	1	33	15		.241	.265	.332	597	90	-9	17			.937	12	S-99,O-32C,3-23	0.7
1905	Was-A	151	576	67	124	16	4	1	43	25		.215	.250	.262	513	65	-23	23			.934	**34**	*S-151	1.7
Total	2	303	1157	130	264	28	23	2	76	40		.228	.258	.297	555	78	-32	40			.935	46	S-250/O-32C,3-23	2.4
■ PETE CASSIDY	Cassidy, Peter Francis b: 4/8/1873, Wilmington, Del. d: 7/9/29, Wilmington, Del. BR/TR, 5'10", 165 lbs. Deb: 4/18/1896																							
1896	Lou-N	49	184	16	39	1	1	0	12	7	7	.212	.256	.228	485	29	-19	5			.973	-7	1-38,S-11	-2.2
1899	Bro-N	6	20	2	3	1	0	0	4	1		.150	.261	.200	461	26	-2	1			1.000	-4	/3-3,S-2	-0.5
	Was-N	46	178	21	56	13	0	3	32	9		.315	.365	.438	803	121	5	5			.970	-2	1-37/3-6,S-3	0.3
	Yr	52	198	23	59	14	0	3	36	10		.298	.353	.414	768	111	3	6			.970	-5	1-37/3-9,S-5	-0.2
Total	2	101	382	39	98	15	1	3	48	17	7	.257	.307	.325	632	72	-16	11			.972	-13	/1-75,S-16,3-9	-2.4
■ JACK CASSINI	Cassini, Jack Dempsey "Gabby" or "Scat" b: 10/26/19, Dearborn, Mich. BR/TR, 5'10", 175 lbs. Deb: 4/19/49																							
1949	Pit-N	8	0	3	0	0	0	0	0	0	0	—	—	—	—	—	0	0			.000	0	R	0.0
■ PEDRO CASTELLANO	Castellano, Pedro Orlando (Arrieta) b: 3/11/70, Lara, Venez. BR/TR, 6'1", 175 lbs. Deb: 5/30/93 Career OF: (1-LF 0-CF 0-RF)																							
1993	Col-N	34	71	12	13	2	0	3	7	8	16	.183	.266	.338	604	52	-5	1	1	-0	.909	-1	3-13,1-10/S-5,2-4	-0.6
1995	Col-N	4	5	0	0	0	0	0	0	2	3	.000	.286	.000	286	-13	-1	0	0	0	1.000	-1	/3-3	-0.2
1996	Col-N	13	17	1	2	0	0	0	2	3	6	.118	.286	.118	403	9	-2	0	0	0	1.000	1	/2-3,3-1,O-1(1-0-0)	-0.1
Total	3	51	93	13	15	2	0	3	9	13	25	.161	.271	.280	551	40	-8	1	1	-0	.917	-2	/3-17,1-10,2-7,SO	-0.9
■ JIM CASTIGLIA	Castiglia, James Vincent b: 9/30/18, Passaic, N.J. BL/TR, 5'11", 200 lbs. Deb: 4/14/42																							
1942	Phi-A	16	18	2	7	0	0	0	2	1	3	.389	.421	.389	810	129	1	0	0	0	.875	-1	/C-3	0.0
■ PETE CASTIGLIONE	Castiglione, Peter Paul b: 2/13/21, Greenwich, Conn. BR/TR, 5'11", 175 lbs. Deb: 9/10/47 Career OF: (1-LF 0-CF 2-RF)																							
1947	Pit-N	13	50	6	14	0	0	0	1	2	5	.280	.308	.280	588	55	-3	0			.970	1	S-13	-0.1
1948	Pit-N	4	2	0	0	0	0	0	0	0	0	.000	.000	.000	0	-98	-1	1			1.000	0	/S-1	0.0
1949	Pit-N	118	448	57	120	20	2	6	43	20	43	.268	.299	.362	661	74	-17	2			.957	-1	3-98,S-17/O-2(0-0-2)	-1.8
1950	Pit-N	94	263	29	67	10	3	3	22	23	23	.255	.317	.350	667	73	-10	1			.970	-17	3-35,S-29/2-9,1-3	-2.6
1951	Pit-N	132	482	62	126	19	4	7	42	34	28	.261	.311	.361	672	78	-15	2	2	-0	.957	4	3-99,S-28	-1.0
1952	Pit-N	67	214	27	57	9	1	4	18	17	8	.266	.323	.374	697	90	-3	3	3	-0	.951	6	3-57/1-1,O-1(1-0-0)	0.2
1953	Pit-N	45	159	14	33	2	1	4	21	5	14	.208	.236	.308	545	41	-14	1	1	-0	.978	4	3-43	-1.1
	StL-N	67	52	9	9	2	0	0	3	2	5	.173	.204	.212	415	9	-7	0	0	0	.967	8	3-51/2-9,S-3	0.1
	Yr	112	211	23	42	4	1	4	24	7	19	.199	.228	.284	513	33	-21	1	1	-0	.976	12	3-94/2-9,S-3	-1.0
1954	StL-N	5	0	1	0	0	0	0	0	0	0	—	—	—	—	—	0	0	0	0	1.000	0	/3-5	0.0
Total	8	545	1670	205	426	62	11	24	150	103	126	.255	.300	.349	648	71	-70	10	6		.960	4	3-388/S-91,2-18,1O	-6.3
■ VINNY CASTILLA	Castilla, Vinicio (Soria) b: 7/4/67, Oaxaca, Mexico BR/TR, 6'1", 185 lbs. Deb: 9/1/91																							
1991	Atl-N	12	5	1	1	0	0	0	0	0	2	.200	.200	.200	400	12	-1	0	0	0	1.000	1	S-12	0.1
1992	Atl-N	9	16	1	4	1	0	0	1	1	4	.250	.333	.313	646	79	-0	0	0	0	.875	0	/3-4,S-4	0.0
1993	Col-N	105	337	36	86	9	7	9	30	13	45	.255	.287	.404	690	71	-14	2	5	-1	.975	8	*S-104	0.1
1994	Col-N	52	130	16	43	11	1	3	18	7	23	.331	.365	.500	865	105	1	2	1	0	.984	0	S-18,2-14/3-9,1-2	0.3
1995	*Col-N★	139	527	82	163	34	2	32	90	30	87	.309	.351	.564	915	106	4	2	8	-2	.958	-7	*3-137/S-5	-0.4
1996	Col-N	160	629	97	191	34	0	40	113	35	88	.304	.345	.548	894	106	5	7	2	1	.960	28	*3-160	3.3
1997	Col-N	159	612	94	186	25	2	40	113	44	108	.304	.358	.547	906	108	7	2	4	-1	.954	5	*3-157	1.2
1998	Col-N★	162	645	108	206	28	4	46	144	40	89	.319	.365	.589	954	120	18	5	9	-2	.970	-2	*3-162/S-1	1.5
1999	Col-N	158	615	83	169	24	1	33	102	53	75	.275	.333	.478	811	80	-18	2	3	-1	.954	2	*3-157	-1.5
2000	TB-A	85	331	22	73	9	1	6	42	14	41	.221	.259	.308	567	43	-29	1	2	-0	.967	10	3-83	-1.8
Total	10	1041	3847	540	1122	175	18	209	653	237	562	.292	.338	.509	847	96	-27	23	34	-7	.960	45	3-869,S-144/2-14,1	2.8
■ ALBERTO CASTILLO	Castillo, Alberto Terrero b: 2/10/70, San Juan De La Maguana, D.R. BR/TR, 6', 185 lbs. Deb: 5/28/95																							
1995	NY-N	13	29	2	3	0	0	0	0	3	9	.103	.212	.103	316	-14	-5	1	0	0	.974	4	C-12	0.0
1996	NY-N	6	11	1	4	0	0	0	0	0	4	.364	.364	.364	727	97	-0	0	0	0	1.000	1	/C-6	0.1
1997	NY-N	35	59	3	12	1	0	0	7	9	16	.203	.309	.220	529	43	-5	0	1	-0	.987	7	C-34	0.2
1998	NY-N	38	83	13	17	4	0	2	7	9	17	.205	.290	.325	616	63	-5	0	2	-1	.990	7	C-35/D-1	0.3
1999	StL-N	93	255	21	67	8	0	4	31	24	48	.263	.331	.341	672	70	-11	0	0	0	.991	2	C-91	-0.4
2000	Tor-A	66	185	14	39	7	0	1	16	21	36	.211	.291	.265	556	42	-16	0	0	0	.993	12	C-66	-0.1
Total	6	251	622	54	142	20	0	7	61	66	130	.228	.306	.294	601	55	-42	1	3	-1	.990	32	C-244/D-1	0.1
■ TONY CASTILLO	Castillo, Anthony b: 6/14/57, San Jose, Cal. BR/TR, 6'4", 190 lbs. Deb: 9/22/78																							
1978	SD-N	5	8	0	1	0	0	0	1	0	2	.125	.125	.125	250	-33	-1	0	0	0	.950	1	/C-5	0.0
■ BRAULIO CASTILLO	Castillo, Braulio Robinson Medrano (b: Braulio Robinson Medrano (Castillo)) b: 5/13/68, Elias Pina, D.R. BR/TR, 6', 160 lbs. Deb: 8/18/91																							
1991	Phi-N	28	52	3	9	3	0	0	2	1	15	.173	.189	.231	419	18	-6	1	1	-0	.977	-2	O-26(0-24-2)	-0.8
1992	Phi-N	28	76	12	15	3	1	2	7	4	15	.197	.237	.342	580	62	-4	1	0	0	.956	-2	O-24(2-6-16)	-0.7
Total	2	56	128	15	24	6	1	2	9	5	30	.188	.218	.297	515	44	-10	2	1	0	.966	-4	/O-50(2-30-18)	-1.5
■ MANNY CASTILLO	Castillo, Esteban Manuel Antonio (Cabrera) b: 4/1/57, Santo Domingo, D.R. BB/TR, 5'9", 160 lbs. Deb: 9/1/80																							
1980	KC-A	7	10	1	2	0	0	0	0	0	0	.200	.200	.200	400	10	-1	0	0	0	1.000	2	/3-3,2-1,D-2	0.0
1982	Sea-A	138	506	49	130	29	1	3	49	22	35	.257	.291	.336	627	70	-21	2	8	-2	.938	-24	*3-130/2-9	-5.0
1983	Sea-A	91	203	13	42	6	3	0	24	7	20	.207	.237	.266	503	37	-17	1	1	-0	.971	8	3-55,1-11/2-5,PD	-1.1
Total	3	236	719	63	174	35	4	3	73	29	55	.242	.274	.314	589	59	-40	3	9	-2	.949	-15	3-188/2-15,1-11,DP	-6.1
■ JUAN CASTILLO	Castillo, Juan (Bryas) b: 1/25/62, San Pedro De Macoris, D.R. BB/TR (BR 1988-89), 5'11", 162 lbs. Deb: 4/12/86 Career OF: (1-LF 0-CF 1-RF)																							
1986	Mil-A	26	54	6	9	0	1	0	5	5	12	.167	.250	.204	454	24	-6	1	1	-0	1.000	5	2-17/S-4,3-2,O-1R,D	0.0
1987	Mil-A	116	321	44	72	11	4	3	28	33	76	.224	.303	.312	614	62	-17	15	7	1	.973	-6	2-97,S-13/3-7	-1.6
1988	Mil-A	54	90	10	20	0	0	0	2	3	14	.222	.247	.222	470	32	-8	2	0	0	.932	7	2-18,3-17,S-13,/OD	0.0
1989	Mil-A	3	4	0	0	0	0	0	3	0	2	.000	.000	.000	0	-99	-1	0	0	0	1.000	1	/2-3	0.0
Total	4	199	469	60	101	11	5	3	38	41	104	.215	.284	.279	563	51	-32	18	8	1	.972	6	2-135/S-30,3-26,DO	-1.6
■ LUIS CASTILLO	Castillo, Luis Antonio (Donato) b: 9/12/75, San Pedro De Macoris, D.R. BB/TR, 5'11", 145 lbs. Deb: 8/8/96																							
1996	Fla-N	41	164	26	43	2	1	1	8	14	46	.262	.320	.305	625	68	-7	17	4	2	.986	1	2-41	-0.2
1997	Fla-N	75	263	27	63	8	0	0	8	27	53	.240	.310	.270	580	56	-16	16	10	0	.971	-7	2-70	-2.0
1998	Fla-N	44	153	21	31	3	2	1	10	22	33	.203	.307	.268	575	56	-9	3	0	1	.970	-2	2-44	-0.9
1999	Fla-N	128	487	76	147	23	4	0	28	67	85	.302	.386	.366	752	97	1	50	17	5	.976	-11	*2-126	0.1
2000	Fla-N	136	539	101	180	17	3	2	17	78	86	.334	.418	.388	806	111	14	**62**	22	6	.983	-9	*2-136	1.7
Total	5	424	1606	251	464	53	10	4	71	208	303	.289	.371	.342	713	89	-18	148	53	14	.978	-29	2-417	-1.3
■ MARTY CASTILLO	Castillo, Martin Horace b: 1/16/57, Long Beach, Cal. BR/TR, 6'1", 190 lbs. Deb: 8/19/81 Career OF: (1-LF 0-CF 0-RF)																							
1981	Det-A	6	8	1	1	0	0	0	0	0	2	.125	.125	.125	250	-27	-1	0	0	0	1.000	2	/3-4,C-1,O-1(1-0-0)	0.1
1982	Det-A	1	0	0	0	0	0	0	0	0	0	—	—	—	—	—	0	0	0	0	1.000	-0	/C-1	0.0
1983	Det-A	67	119	10	23	4	0	2	10	7	22	.193	.238	.277	515	42	-9	2	0	0	.990	4	3-58,C-10	-0.6
1984	*Det-A	70	141	16	33	5	2	4	17	10	33	.234	.285	.383	668	83	-3	1	0	0	.970	2	C-36,3-33/D-1	0.0
1985	Det-A	57	84	4	10	2	0	2	5	2	19	.119	.140	.214	354	-5	-12	0	2	-1	.977	7	C-32,3-25	-0.5
Total	5	201	352	31	67	11	2	8	32	19	76	.190	.232	.301	533	46	-26	3	2	-0	.978	15	3-120/C-80,D-1,O-1L	-1.0

YEAR	TM/L	G	AB	R	H	2B	3B	HR	RBI	BB	SO	AVG	OBP	SLG	OPS	OPS+	BR+	SB	CS	SBR	FA	FR	G/POS	TPR
■ CARMEN CASTILLO	Castillo, Monte Carmelo b: 6/8/58, San Pedro De Macoris, D.R. BR/TR, 6′1″, 190 lbs. Deb: 7/17/82																							
1982	Cle-A	47	120	11	25	4	0	2	11	6	17	.208	.258	.292	549	51	-8	0	0	0	.978	-3	O-43(19-8-20)/D-2	-1.2
1983	Cle-A	23	36	9	10	2	1	1	3	4	6	.278	.366	.472	838	124	1	1	1	-0	.929	-1	O-19(0-0-19)/D-1	-0.1
1984	Cle-A	87	211	36	55	9	2	10	36	21	32	.261	.333	.464	798	116	4	1	3	-1	.933	-6	O-70(0-0-70)/D-2	-0.5
1985	Cle-A	67	184	27	45	5	1	11	25	11	40	.245	.298	.462	760	105	1	3	0	1	.953	-2	O-51(0-0-51)/D-9	-0.3
1986	Cle-A	85	205	34	57	9	0	8	32	9	48	.278	.312	.439	751	103	0	2	1	0	.939	-2	O-37(0-0-37),D-35	-0.4
1987	Cle-A	89	220	27	55	17	0	11	31	16	52	.250	.301	.477	778	101	-0	1	1	-0	1.000	-1	D-43,O-23(1-0-22)	-0.4
1988	Cle-A	66	176	12	48	8	0	4	14	5	31	.273	.297	.386	683	87	-3	6	2	1	.933	-6	O-45(30-0-16)/D-9	-1.0
1989	Min-A	94	218	23	56	13	3	8	33	15	40	.257	.308	.454	762	105	1	1	2	-0	.976	-3	O-67(7-0-61),D-16	-0.5
1990	Min-A	64	137	11	30	4	0	0	12	3	23	.219	.241	.248	489	35	-12	0	1	-0	.923	-5	D-35,O-21(2-0-21)	-1.9
1991	Min-A	9	12	0	2	0	1	0	0	0	2	.167	.231	.333	564	52	-1	0	0	0	1.000	-1	/O-4(1-0-3),D-2	-0.2
Total	10	631	1519	190	383	71	8	55	197	90	291	.252	.300	.418	718	93	-17	15	11	-1	.953	-30	O-380(60-8-320),D-154	-6.5
■ JOHN CASTINO	Castino, John Anthony b: 10/23/54, Evanston, Ill. BR/TR, 5′11″, 175 lbs. Deb: 4/6/79																							
1979	Min-A	148	393	49	112	13	8	5	52	27	72	.285	.333	.397	729	92	-4	5	2	0	.963	18	*3-143/S-5	1.2
1980	Min-A	150	546	67	165	17	7	13	64	29	67	.302	.337	.430	768	101	0	7	5	-0	.961	**28**	*3-138,S-18	2.7
1981	Min-A	101	381	41	102	13	**9**	6	36	18	52	.268	.303	.396	699	94	-4	4	5	-1	**.975**	11	3-98/2-4	0.6
1982	Min-A	117	410	48	99	12	6	6	37	36	51	.241	.306	.344	650	76	-13	2	5	-1	.995	4	2-96,3-21/O-6L,D-1	-0.6
1983	Min-A	142	563	83	156	30	4	11	57	62	54	.277	.350	.403	753	103	3	4	2	0	.990	7	*2-132/3-8,D-1	1.7
1984	Min-A	8	27	5	12	1	0	0	3	5	2	.444	.531	.481	1013	174	3	0	0	0	1.000	-1	/3-8	0.2
Total	6	666	2320	293	646	86	34	41	249	177	298	.278	.331	.398	729	95	-15	22	19	-2	.967	67	3-416,2-232/S-23,OD	5.8
■ VINCE CASTINO	Castino, Vincent Charles b: 10/11/17, Willisville, Ill. d: 3/6/67, Sacramento, Cal. BR/TR, 5′9″, 175 lbs. Deb: 6/24/43																							
1943	Chi-A	33	101	14	23	1	0	2	16	12	11	.228	.310	.297	607	78	-3	0	0	0	.971	-9	C-30	-1.1
1944	Chi-A	29	78	8	18	5	0	0	3	10	13	.231	.326	.295	621	79	-2	0	1	-0	.990	1	C-26	0.0
1945	Chi-A	26	36	2	8	1	0	0	4	3	7	.222	.282	.250	532	56	-2	0	0	0	.951	-2	C-25	-0.4
Total	3	88	215	24	49	7	0	2	23	25	31	.228	.311	.288	600	75	-7	0	1	-0	.976	-11	/C-81	-1.5
■ DON CASTLE	Castle, Donald Hardy b: 2/1/50, Kokomo, Ind. BL/TL, 6′1″, 205 lbs. Deb: 9/11/73																							
1973	Tex-A	4	13	0	4	1	0	0	2	1	3	.308	.357	.385	742	114	0	0	0	0	.000	0	/D-3	0.0
■ JOHN CASTLE	Castle, John Francis b: 6/1/1883, Honey Brook, Pa. d: 4/13/29, Philadelphia, Pa. 5′10.5″, Deb: 4/30/10																							
1910	Phi-N	3	4	1	1	0	0	0	0	0	0	.250	.250	.250	500	44	-0	1			.000	-1	/O-2(1-1-0)	-0.1
■ FOSTER CASTLEMAN	Castleman, Foster Ephraim b: 1/1/31, Nashville, Tenn. BR/TR, 6′, 175 lbs. Deb: 8/4/54 Career OF: (1-LF 0-CF 0-RF)																							
1954	NY-N	13	12	0	3	0	0	0	1	0	3	.250	.308	.250	558	47	-1	0	0	0	.000	0	/3-2	-0.1
1955	NY-N	15	28	3	6	1	0	2	4	2	4	.214	.267	.464	731	89	-1	0	0	0	1.000	-3	/2-6,3-1	-0.3
1956	NY-N	124	385	33	87	16	3	14	45	15	50	.226	.259	.392	651	72	-16	2	1	0	.947	7	*3-107/S-2,2-1	-1.0
1957	NY-N	18	37	7	6	2	0	1	1	2	8	.162	.205	.297	502	33	-4	0	0	0	.867	-2	/3-7,2-1,S-1	-0.6
1958	Bal-A	98	200	15	34	5	0	3	14	16	34	.170	.242	.240	482	35	-18	2	0	0	.964	-19	S-91/2-4,3-4,O-1L	-3.3
Total	5	268	662	58	136	24	3	20	65	35	99	.205	.252	.341	593	60	-39	4	1	1	.944	-17	3-121/S-94,2-12,O-1L	-5.3
■ JUAN CASTRO	Castro, Juan Gabriel b: 6/20/72, Los Mochis, Mex. BR/TR, 5′10″, 165 lbs. Deb: 9/2/95 Career OF: (1-LF 0-CF 0-RF)																							
1995	LA-N	11	4	0	1	0	0	0	0	1	1	.250	.400	.250	650	84	-0	0	0	0	1.000	2	/3-7,S-4	0.2
1996	*LA-N	70	132	16	26	5	3	0	5	10	27	.197	.254	.280	534	44	-11	1	0	0	.982	-4	S-30,3-23/2-9,O-1L	-1.2
1997	LA-N	40	75	3	11	3	1	0	4	7	20	.147	.220	.213	433	15	-10	0	0	0	1.000	3	S-22,2-14/3-3	-0.5
1998	LA-N	89	220	25	43	7	0	2	14	15	37	.195	.247	.255	501	34	-21	0	0	0	.954	14	S-47,2-38,3-12	-0.4
1999	LA-N	2	1	0	0	0	0	0	0	0	1	.000	.000	.000	0	-99	-0	0	0	0	1.000	1	/2-1,S-1	0.1
2000	Cin-N	82	224	20	54	12	2	4	23	14	33	.241	.286	.366	652	61	-14	0	2	-1	.994	7	S-57,2-21/3-7	-0.3
Total	6	294	656	64	135	27	6	6	46	47	119	.206	.259	.293	552	44	-56	1	2	-0	.980	24	S-161/2-83,3-52,O-1L	-2.1
■ LUIS CASTRO	Castro, Luis Manuel "Jud" b: 1877, Colombia d: Venezuela BR/TR, 5′7″, Deb: 4/23/02																							
1902	Phi-A	42	143	18	35	8	1	1	15	4		.245	.265	.336	601	63	-7	2			.918	-15	2-36/O-3(0-2-1),S-1	-2.1
■ RAMON CASTRO	Castro, Ramon A. b: 3/1/76, Vega Baja, P.R. BR/TR, 6′3″, 225 lbs. Deb: 8/27/99																							
1999	Fla-N	24	67	4	12	4	0	2	4	10	14	.179	.286	.328	614	58	-4	0	0	0	.992	-3	C-24	-0.6
2000	Fla-N	50	138	10	33	4	0	2	14	16	36	.239	.323	.312	634	65	-7	0	0	0	.980	-3	C-50	-0.7
Total	2	74	205	14	45	8	0	4	18	26	50	.220	.310	.317	627	62	-12	0	0	0	.984	-6	/C-74	-1.3
■ FRANK CATALANOTTO	Catalanotto, Frank John b: 4/27/74, Smithtown, N.Y. BL/TR, 6′, 170 lbs. Deb: 9/3/97 Career OF: (0-LF 0-CF 1-RF)																							
1997	Det-A	13	26	2	8	2	0	0	3	3	7	.308	.379	.385	764	101	0	0	0	0	1.000	-1	/2-6,D-3	0.0
1998	Det-A	89	213	23	60	13	2	6	25	12	39	.282	.332	.446	778	99	-1	3	2	-0	.974	-1	2-31,D-23,1-18,/3-3	-0.3
1999	Det-A	100	286	41	79	19	0	11	35	15	49	.276	.332	.458	790	100	-1	3	4	-1	1.000	-17	1-32,2-32,3-21,/D-9	-1.8
2000	Tex-A	103	282	55	82	13	2	10	42	33	36	.291	.377	.457	834	106	3	6	2	1	.966	-9	2-49,D-20,1-17,/O-1R	-0.5
Total	4	305	807	121	229	47	4	27	105	63	131	.284	.350	.452	802	102	2	12	8	-0	.969	-27	2-118/1-67,D-55,3O	-2.6
■ DANNY CATER	Cater, Danny Anderson b: 2/25/40, Austin, Tex. BR/TR, 5′11.5″, 180 lbs. Deb: 4/14/64 Career OF: (293-LF 2-CF 16-RF)																							
1964	Phi-N	60	152	13	45	9	1	1	13	7	15	.296	.327	.388	715	102	0	1	0	0	.981	-1	O-39(36-1-2)/1-7,3-1	-0.2
1965	Chi-A	142	514	74	139	18	4	14	55	33	65	.270	.318	.403	721	110	5	3	3	-0	.978	-9	*O-127L,3-11/1-3	-1.2
1966	Chi-A	21	60	3	11	1	1	0	4	0	10	.183	.197	.233	430	25	-6	3	1	0	.909	-3	O-18(16-0-3)	-1.1
	KC-A	116	425	47	124	16	3	7	52	28	37	.292	.337	.393	730	113	6	1	4	-1	.994	-5	1-53,3-42,O-22L	-0.5
	Yr	137	485	50	135	17	4	7	56	28	47	.278	.320	.373	694	102	1	4	5	-1	.994	-8	1-53,3-42,O-40L	-1.6
1967	KC-A	142	529	55	143	17	4	4	46	34	56	.270	.319	.340	659	98	-2	4	5	-1	.916	-15	3-56,O-55L,1-44	-2.5
1968	Oak-A	147	504	53	146	28	3	6	62	35	43	.290	.338	.393	731	127	15	8	7	-1	**.995**	-4	*1-121,O-20L/2-1	0.3
1969	Oak-A	152	584	64	153	24	2	10	76	28	40	.262	.298	.361	659	87	-12	1	4	-1	.992	6	*1-132,O-20L/2-4	-1.9
1970	NY-A	155	582	64	175	26	5	6	76	34	44	.301	.341	.393	735	108	5	4	2	0	.992	-4	*1-131,3-42/O-7R	-0.8
1971	NY-A	121	428	39	118	16	5	4	50	19	25	.276	.310	.364	674	96	-4	0	3	-1	.995	8	1-78,3-52	-0.2
1972	Bos-A	92	317	32	75	17	1	8	39	15	33	.237	.275	.372	648	87	-6	0	1	-0	.993	6	1-90	-0.8
1973	Bos-A	63	195	30	61	12	0	1	24	10	22	.313	.350	.390	739	102	0	0	0	0	.997	1	1-37,3-21/D-3	-0.1
1974	Bos-A	56	126	14	31	5	0	5	20	10	13	.246	.312	.405	716	98	-1	1	0	0	1.000	1	1-23,D-14	-0.1
1975	StL-N	22	35	3	8	2	0	0	2	1	3	.229	.250	.286	536	47	-3	0	0	0	.981	0	1-12	-0.3
Total	12	1289	4451	491	1229	191	29	66	519	254	406	.276	.318	.377	695	102	-0	26	30	-5	.994	-20	1-731,O-308L,3/D2	-9.4
■ ELI CATES	Cates, Eli Eldo b: 1/26/1877, Greens Fork, Ind. d: 5/29/64, Anderson, Ind. BR/TR, 5′9.5″, 175 lbs. Deb: 4/20/08																							
1908	Was-A	40	59	5	11	1	1	0	3	6		.186	.273	.237	510	72	-2	0			.907	-0	P-19/2-3	-0.1
■ TED CATHER	Cather, Theodore Physick b: 5/20/1889, Chester, Pa. d: 4/9/45, Elkton, Md. BR/TR, 5′10.5″, 178 lbs. Deb: 9/23/12 Career OF: (91-LF 17-CF 65-RF)																							
1912	StL-N	5	19	4	8	1	1	0	2	0	4	.421	.421	.579	1000	176	2	1			.944	2	/O-5(0-4-1)	0.3
1913	StL-N	67	183	16	39	8	4	0	12	9	24	.213	.250	.301	551	58	-11	7			.915	-7	O-57(14-1-42)/P-1,1-1	-2.1
1914	StL-N	39	99	11	27	7	0	0	13	3	15	.273	.294	.343	638	90	-2	4			.981	0	O-28(23-5-0)	-0.3
	*Bos-N	50	145	19	43	11	2	0	27	7	28	.297	.338	.400	738	120	3	7			.953	-9	O-48(23-7-20)	-0.8
	Yr	89	244	30	70	18	2	0	40	10	43	.287	.320	.377	697	108	1	11			.966	-9	O-76(46-12-20)	-1.1
1915	Bos-N	40	102	10	21	3	1	2	18	15	19	.206	.319	.314	633	96	-0	2	4	-1	.902	-7	O-32(31-0-2)	-1.1
Total	4	201	548	60	138	30	8	2	72	34	90	.252	.300	.347	647	91	-7	21	4		.938	-21	O-170L/1-1,P-1	-4.0
■ HOWDY CATON	Caton, James Howard "Buster" b: 7/16/1896, Zanesville, Ohio d: 1/8/48, Zanesville, Ohio BR/TR, 5′6″, 165 lbs. Deb: 9/17/17																							
1917	Pit-N	14	57	6	12	1	2	0	4	6	7	.211	.286	.298	584	77	-1	0			.895	-2	S-14	-0.3
1918	Pit-N	80	303	37	71	5	7	0	17	32	16	.234	.312	.297	609	83	-5	12			.928	-7	S-79	-0.8
1919	Pit-N	39	102	13	18	1	2	0	5	12	10	.176	.263	.225	489	46	-6	2			.927	-11	S-17,3-14/O-1(0-1-0)	-1.8
1920	Pit-N	98	352	29	83	11	5	0	27	33	19	.236	.305	.295	600	71	-12	4	9	-2	.929	-22	S-96	-3.3
Total	4	231	814	85	184	18	16	0	53	83	52	.226	.301	.287	588	72	-26	18	9		.926	-43	S-206/3-14,O-1(0-1-0)	-6.2

■ **TOM CATTERSON** Catterson, Thomas Henry b: 8/25/1884, Warwick, R.I. d: 2/5/20, Portland, Maine BL/TL, 5'10", 170 lbs. Deb: 9/19/08

YEAR	TM/L	G	AB	R	H	2B	3B	HR	RBI	BB	SO	AVG	OBP	SLG	OPS	OPS+	BR+	SB	CS	SBR	FA	FR	G/POS	TPR
1908	Bro-N	19	68	5	13	1	1	1	2	5		.191	.257	.279	536	74	-2	0			.976	0	O-18(18-0-0)	-0.3
1909	Bro-N	9	18	0	4	0	0	0	1	3		.222	.333	.222	556	75	-0	0			.833	-2	/O-6(0-6-0)	-0.3
Total	2	28	86	5	17	1	1	1	3	8		.198	.274	.267	541	75	-2	0			.957	-2	/O-24(18-6-0)	-0.6

■ **JAKE CAULFIELD** Caulfield, John Joseph b: 11/23/17, Los Angeles, Cal. d: 12/16/86, San Francisco, Cal BR/TR, 5'11", 170 lbs. Deb: 4/24/46

YEAR	TM/L	G	AB	R	H	2B	3B	HR	RBI	BB	SO	AVG	OBP	SLG	OPS	OPS+	BR+	SB	CS	SBR	FA	FR	G/POS	TPR
1946	Phi-A	44	94	13	26	8	0	0	10	4	11	.277	.306	.362	668	87	-2	0	0	0	.929	-6	S-31/3-1	-0.7

■ **WAYNE CAUSEY** Causey, James Wayne b: 12/26/36, Ruston, La. BL/TR, 5'10.5", 175 lbs. Deb: 6/5/55

YEAR	TM/L	G	AB	R	H	2B	3B	HR	RBI	BB	SO	AVG	OBP	SLG	OPS	OPS+	BR+	SB	CS	SBR	FA	FR	G/POS	TPR
1955	Bal-A	68	175	14	34	2	1	1	9	17	25	.194	.269	.234	504	39	-15	0	1	-0	.912	-8	3-55/2-7,S-1	-2.4
1956	Bal-A	53	88	7	15	0	1	1	4	8	23	.170	.240	.227	467	26	-10	0	0	0	.980	2	3-30/2-7	-0.7
1957	Bal-A	14	10	2	2	0	0	0	1	5	2	.200	.500	.200	700	105	1	0	0	0	.960	3	/2-6,3-5	0.4
1961	KC-A	104	312	37	86	14	1	8	49	37	28	.276	.352	.404	756	100	0	0	0	0	.955	20	3-88,S-11/2-9	2.1
1962	KC-A	117	305	40	77	14	1	4	38	41	30	.252	.345	.344	689	82	-7	2	0	0	.953	2	S-51,3-26/2-9	0.0
1963	KC-A	139	554	72	155	32	4	8	44	56	54	.280	.346	.395	741	101	2	4	2	0	.978	5	*S-135/3-2	2.0
1964	KC-A	157	604	82	170	31	4	8	49	88	65	.281	.379	.386	765	110	12	0	1	-0	.967	-1	*S-131,2-17/3-9	2.4
1965	KC-A	144	513	48	134	17	8	3	34	61	48	.261	.342	.343	685	97	-1	1	3	-1	.972	-19	S-62,2-45,3-35	-1.3
1966	KC-A	28	79	1	18	0	0	0	5	7	6	.228	.291	.228	519	53	-5	1	0	0	.871	-6	3-15,S-10	-1.0
	Chi-A	78	164	23	40	8	2	0	13	24	13	.244	.340	.317	657	97	0	2	0	0	.980	-16	2-60/S-1,3-1	-1.2
	Yr	106	243	24	58	8	2	0	18	31	19	.239	.325	.288	613	83	-5	3	0	1	.980	-21	2-60,3-16,S-11	-2.2
1967	Chi-A	124	292	21	66	10	3	1	28	32	35	.226	.305	.291	596	80	-7	2	5	-1	.978	-8	2-96/S-2	-1.1
1968	Chi-A	59	100	8	18	2	0	0	7	14	7	.180	.287	.200	487	49	-6	0	0	0	.971	-13	2-41	-1.9
	Cal-A	4	11	0	0	0	0	0	0	0	1	.000	.000	.000	0	-99	-3	0	0	0	1.000	1	/2-4	-0.2
	Yr	63	111	8	18	2	0	0	7	14	8	.162	.262	.180	442	36	-8	0	0	0	.975	-13	2-45	-2.1
	Atl-N	16	37	2	4	0	1	1	4	0	9	.108	.108	.243	351	3	-4	0	0	0	1.000	-4	/2-6,S-2,3-2	-1.0
Total	11	1105	3244	357	819	130	26	35	285	390	341	.252	.335	.341	676	89	-41	12	12	-2	.969	-42	S-406,2-307,3-268	-3.9

■ **JOHN CAVANAUGH** Cavanaugh, John J. b: 6/5/1900, Scranton, Pa. d: 1/14/61, New Brunswick, N.J BR/TR, 5'9", 158 lbs. Deb: 7/7/19

YEAR	TM/L	G	AB	R	H	2B	3B	HR	RBI	BB	SO	AVG	OBP	SLG	OPS	OPS+	BR+	SB	CS	SBR	FA	FR	G/POS	TPR
1919	Phi-N	1	1	0	0	0	0	0	0	0	1	.000	.000	.000	0	-93	-0	0			.000	0	/3-1	0.0

■ **PHIL CAVARRETTA** Cavarretta, Philip Joseph b: 7/19/16, Chicago, Ill. BL/TL, 5'11.5", 175 lbs. Deb: 9/16/34 MC Career OF: (148-LF 234-CF 172-RF)

YEAR	TM/L	G	AB	R	H	2B	3B	HR	RBI	BB	SO	AVG	OBP	SLG	OPS	OPS+	BR+	SB	CS	SBR	FA	FR	G/POS	TPR
1934	Chi-N	7	21	5	8	0	1	1	6	2	3	.381	.435	.619	1054	182	2	1			1.000	1	/1-5	0.3
1935	*Chi-N	146	589	85	162	28	12	8	82	39	61	.275	.322	.404	726	93	-6	4			.986	2	*1-145	-1.8
1936	Chi-N	124	458	55	125	18	1	9	56	17	36	.273	.306	.376	682	81	-13	8			.987	-2	*1-115	-2.6
1937	Chi-N	106	329	43	94	18	7	5	56	32	35	.286	.349	.429	778	106	3	7			.972	-1	O-55(7-47-1),1-43	-0.4
1938	*Chi-N	92	268	29	64	11	4	1	28	14	27	.239	.287	.321	608	65	-13	4			.962	-7	O-52(7-8-37),1-28	-2.5
1939	Chi-N	22	55	4	15	3	1	0	0	4	3	.273	.322	.364	686	82	-1	2			.991	-1	1-13/O-1(0-0-1)	-0.4
1940	Chi-N	65	193	34	54	11	4	2	22	31	18	.280	.388	.409	797	122	7	3			.991	-1	1-52	0.1
1941	Chi-N	107	346	46	99	18	4	6	40	53	28	.286	.384	.413	797	129	15	2			.992	-8	O-66(8-53-6),1-33	0.2
1942	Chi-N	136	482	59	130	28	4	3	54	71	42	.270	.365	.363	728	118	13	7			.989	6	O-70(4-67-0),1-61	1.2
1943	Chi-N	143	530	93	154	27	9	8	73	75	42	.291	.382	.421	802	134	24	3			.987	-11	*1-134/O-7(0-7-0)	0.7
1944	Chi-N★	152	614	106	**197**	35	15	5	82	67	42	.321	.390	.451	841	137	31	4			.992	-7	*1-139,O-13(0-13-0)	1.6
1945	*Chi-N†	132	498	94	177	34	10	6	97	81	34	**.355**	**.449**	.500	949	167	49	5			.993	-1	*1-120,O-11(11-0-0)	4.0
1946	Chi-N★	139	510	89	150	28	10	8	78	88	54	.294	.401	.435	836	140	30	2			.967	1	O-86(7-13-78),1-51	2.7
1947	Chi-N★	127	459	56	144	22	5	2	63	58	35	.314	.391	.397	787	114	11	2			.977	-0	*O-100(69-26-8),1-24	0.4
1948	Chi-N	111	334	41	93	16	5	3	40	35	29	.278	.349	.383	732	102	1	4			.998	1	1-41,O-40(30-0-10)	-0.2
1949	Chi-N	105	360	46	106	22	4	8	49	45	31	.294	.374	.444	819	122	12	2			.993	9	1-70,O-25(3-0-21)	1.7
1950	Chi-N	82	256	49	70	11	1	10	31	40	31	.273	.376	.441	817	115	6	1			.986	-1	1-67/O-3(0-0-3)	0.4
1951	Chi-N	89	206	24	64	7	1	6	28	27	28	.311	.393	.442	835	122	7	0	0	0	.994	4	1-53,M	0.9
1952	Chi-N	41	63	7	15	1	1	1	8	9	3	.238	.333	.333	667	84	-1	0	0	0	.991	1	1-13,M	-0.1
1953	Chi-N	27	21	3	6	3	0	0	3	6	3	.286	.444	.429	873	126	1	0	0	0	.000	0	HM	0.1
1954	Chi-A	71	158	21	50	6	0	3	24	26	12	.316	.419	.411	831	124	7	4	0	1	.993	-4	1-44/O-9(2-0-7)	0.1
1955	Chi-A	6	4	1	0	0	0	0	0	0	1	.000	.000	.000	0	-97	-1	0	0	0	1.000	-0	/1-3	-0.1
Total	22	2030	6754	990	1977	347	99	95	920	820	598	.293	.372	.416	788	118	183	65	0		.990	-21	*1-1254,O-538C	6.3

■ **IKE CAVENEY** Caveney, James Christopher b: 12/10/1894, San Francisco, Cal d: 7/6/49, San Francisco, Cal BR/TR, 5'9", 168 lbs. Deb: 4/12/22

YEAR	TM/L	G	AB	R	H	2B	3B	HR	RBI	BB	SO	AVG	OBP	SLG	OPS	OPS+	BR+	SB	CS	SBR	FA	FR	G/POS	TPR
1922	Cin-N	118	394	41	94	12	9	3	54	29	33	.239	.301	.338	638	66	-21	6	6	-1	.934	-6	*S-118	-1.4
1923	Cin-N	138	488	58	135	21	9	4	63	26	41	.277	.315	.381	696	84	-12	5	4	-0	.942	-1	*S-138	0.2
1924	Cin-N	95	337	36	92	19	1	4	32	14	21	.273	.310	.371	681	83	-9	2	3	-1	.924	3	S-90/2-5	0.3
1925	Cin-N	115	358	38	89	9	5	2	47	28	31	.249	.303	.318	622	60	-21	2	0	0	.941	9	*S-111	-0.1
Total	4	466	1577	173	410	61	24	13	196	97	126	.260	.307	.354	661	74	-63	15	13	-1	.936	5	S-457/2-5	-1.0

■ **ANDUJAR CEDENO** Cedeno, Andujar (Donastorg) b: 8/21/69, LaRomana, D.R. d: 10/28/2000, Santo Domingo, D.R. BR/TR, 6'1", 168 lbs. Deb: 9/2/90 F

YEAR	TM/L	G	AB	R	H	2B	3B	HR	RBI	BB	SO	AVG	OBP	SLG	OPS	OPS+	BR+	SB	CS	SBR	FA	FR	G/POS	TPR
1990	Hou-N	7	8	0	0	0	0	0	0	0	5	.000	.000	.000	0	-99	-2	0	0	0	.833	-0	/S-3	-0.3
1991	Hou-N	67	251	27	61	13	2	9	36	9	74	.243	.272	.418	690	97	-3	4	3	-0	.930	-14	S-66	-1.2
1992	Hou-N	71	220	15	38	13	2	2	13	14	71	.173	.232	.277	509	46	-16	2	0	1	.959	-2	S-70	-1.4
1993	Hou-N	149	505	69	143	24	4	11	56	48	97	.283	.349	.412	761	107	5	9	7	-0	.955	-25	*S-149/3-1	-0.9
1994	Hou-N	98	342	38	90	26	0	9	49	29	79	.263	.335	.418	753	100	-0	1	1	-0	.947	1	S-95	0.8
1995	SD-N	120	390	42	82	16	2	6	31	28	92	.210	.272	.308	580	54	-26	5	3	0	.965	-7	*S-116/3-1	-2.4
1996	SD-N	49	154	10	36	2	1	3	18	9	32	.234	.280	.318	599	61	-9	3	2	-0	.946	4	S-47/3-2	-0.2
	Det-A	52	179	19	35	4	2	7	20	4	37	.196	.213	.358	571	41	-17	2	1	0	.948	-1	S-51/3-1	-1.3
	Hou-N	3	2	1	1	0	0	0	0	2	1	.500	.500	.500	1000	50	0	0	0	0	1.000	3	/S-2,3-1	0.3
Total	7	616	2051	221	485	98	13	47	223	143	488	.236	.293	.366	659	78	-69	26	17	-0	.952	-43	S-599/3-6	-6.6

■ **CESAR CEDENO** Cedeno, Cesar (Encarnacion) b: 2/25/51, Santo Domingo, D.R. BR/TR, 6'2", 195 lbs. Deb: 6/20/70 Career OF: (138-LF 1457-CF 144-RF)

YEAR	TM/L	G	AB	R	H	2B	3B	HR	RBI	BB	SO	AVG	OBP	SLG	OPS	OPS+	BR+	SB	CS	SBR	FA	FR	G/POS	TPR
1970	Hou-N	90	355	46	110	21	4	7	42	15	57	.310	.341	.451	792	115	6	17	4	2	.968	3	O-90(0-75-17)	0.8
1971	Hou-N	161	611	85	161	**40**	6	10	81	25	102	.264	.296	.398	693	97	-5	20	9	1	.989	-2	*O-157(11-125-30)/1-2	-1.1
1972	Hou-N★	139	559	103	179	**39**	8	22	82	56	62	.320	.387	.537	924	163	45	55	21	5	.981	11	*O-137(0-137-0)	**6.0**
1973	Hou-N★	139	525	86	168	35	2	25	70	41	79	.320	.377	.537	914	151	34	56	15	7	.981	15	*O-136(0-136-0)	5.4
1974	Hou-N★	160	610	95	164	29	5	26	102	64	103	.269	.342	.461	803	129	21	57	17	7	.993	21	*O-157(0-157-0)	4.5
1975	Hou-N	131	500	93	144	31	3	13	63	62	52	.288	.374	.440	814	135	24	50	17	5	.982	4	*O-131(0-131-0)	3.1
1976	Hou-N★	150	575	89	171	26	5	18	83	55	51	.297	.360	.454	814	143	30	58	15	8	.980	10	*O-146(0-146-0)	4.5
1977	Hou-N	141	530	92	148	36	8	14	71	47	50	.279	.350	.457	807	126	18	61	14	9	**.997**	12	*O-137(0-137-0)	3.7
1978	Hou-N	50	192	31	54	8	2	7	23	15	24	.281	.333	.453	786	127	6	23	2	4	.987	8	O-50(0-50-0)	1.9
1979	Hou-N	132	470	57	123	27	4	6	54	64	52	.262	.354	.374	728	105	5	30	13	2	.981	-5	1-91,O-40(0-40-0)	-0.4
1980	*Hou-N	137	499	71	154	32	8	10	73	66	72	.309	.390	.465	855	150	34	48	15	5	.977	8	*O-136(0-136-0)	4.7
1981	*Hou-N	82	306	42	83	19	0	5	34	24	31	.271	.326	.382	709	106	2	12	7	0	.991	-1	1-46,O-34(0-34-0)	-0.3
1982	Cin-N	138	492	52	142	35	1	8	57	41	41	.289	.348	.413	761	110	7	16	11	-0	.990	4	*O-131(0-131-0)/1-1	0.9
1983	Cin-N	98	332	40	77	16	0	9	39	33	53	.232	.307	.361	669	82	-8	13	9	-0	.993	2	O-73(0-1-73),1-17	-1.2
1984	Cin-N	110	380	59	105	24	2	10	47	25	54	.276	.323	.429	752	105	2	19	3	3	.980	-2	O-77(52-14-19),1-44	-0.2
1985	Cin-N	83	220	24	53	12	0	3	30	19	35	.241	.310	.336	646	77	-7	9	5	0	.990	-1	O-53(46-4-4),1-34	-1.0
	*StL-N	28	76	14	33	4	1	6	19	5	7	.434	.469	.750	1219	238	13	5	1	1	.993	-4	1-23/O-2(1-0-1)	0.9
	Yr	111	296	38	86	16	1	9	49	24	42	.291	.350	.443	792	116	6	14	6	1	.993	-4	1-57,O-55(47-4-5)	-0.1
1986	LA-N	37	78	5	18	2	1	0	6	7	13	.231	.294	.282	576	64	-4	1	1	-0	.944	-4	O-31(28-3-0)	-0.9
Total	17	2006	7310	1084	2087	436	60	199	976	664	938	.285	.350	.443	793	124	224	550	179	58	.985	79	*O-1718C,1-258	31.3

■ **DOMINGO CEDENO** Cedeno, Domingo Antonio (Donastorg) b: 11/4/68, LaRomana, D.R. BB/TR, 6'1", 170 lbs. Deb: 5/19/93 F Career OF: (1-LF 0-CF 0-RF)

YEAR	TM/L	G	AB	R	H	2B	3B	HR	RBI	BB	SO	AVG	OBP	SLG	OPS	OPS+	BR+	SB	CS	SBR	FA	FR	G/POS	TPR
1993	Tor-A	15	46	5	8	0	0	0	7	1	10	.174	.191	.174	365	-1	-6	1	0	0	.973	-3	S-10/2-5	-0.8
1994	Tor-A	47	97	14	19	2	3	0	10	10	31	.196	.271	.278	549	42	-8	1	2	-0	.935	-3	2-28/S-8,3-6,O-1L	-1.0
1995	Tor-A	51	161	18	38	6	1	4	14	10	35	.236	.289	.360	649	68	-8	0	1	-0	.980	4	S-30,2-20/3-1	-0.1
1996	Tor-A	77	282	44	79	10	2	2	17	15	60	.280	.321	.351	672	70	-13	5	3	0	.969	-2	2-62/3-6,S-5	-1.0

YEAR	TM/L	G	AB	R	H	2B	3B	HR	RBI	BB	SO	AVG	OBP	SLG	OPS	OPS+	BR+	SB	CS	SBR	FA	FR	G/POS	TPR
	Chi-A	12	19	2	3	2	0	0	3	0	4	.158	.158	.263	421	4	-3	1	0	0	.000	-1	/2-2,S-2,D-1	-0.3
	Yr	89	301	46	82	12	2	2	20	15	64	.272	.311	.346	657	66	-15	6	3	0	.969	-3	2-64/S-7,3-6,D-1	-1.3
1997	Tex-A	113	365	49	103	19	6	4	36	27	77	.282	.335	.400	735	86	-7	3	3	-0	.960	-12	2-65,S-43/3-3,D-2	-1.4
1998	Tex-A	61	141	19	37	9	1	2	21	10	32	.262	.311	.383	694	76	-5	2	1	0	.963	-2	S-35,D-14/2-7	-0.5
1999	Sea-A	21	42	4	9	2	0	2	8	5	9	.214	.313	.405	717	83	-1	1	1	-0	.941	-0	S-20/2-1,3-1	0.0
	Phi-N	32	66	5	10	4	0	1	5	5	22	.152	.211	.258	469	17	-9	0	1	-0	.982	-3	S-19/2-1	-1.0
Total	7	429	1219	160	306	54	13	15	121	83	280	.251	.303	.354	656	67	-60	14	12	-1	.964	-22	2-191,S-172/D-17,3O	-6.1

■ ROGER CEDENO

Cedeno, Roger Leandro b: 8/16/74, Valencia, Venez. BB/TR, 6′1″, 165 lbs. Deb: 6/20/95 Career OF: (133-LF 197-CF 167-RF)

YEAR	TM/L	G	AB	R	H	2B	3B	HR	RBI	BB	SO	AVG	OBP	SLG	OPS	OPS+	BR+	SB	CS	SBR	FA	FR	G/POS	TPR
1995	LA-N	40	42	4	10	2	0	0	3	3	10	.238	.289	.286	575	57	-3	1	0	0	.977	-5	O-36(19-13-5)	-0.8
1996	LA-N	86	211	26	52	11	1	2	18	24	47	.246	.326	.336	663	82	-5	5	1	1	.983	-5	O-71(20-50-4)	-0.9
1997	LA-N	80	194	31	53	10	2	3	17	25	44	.273	.365	.392	757	106	2	9	1	2	.987	2	O-71(13-55-4)	0.6
1998	LA-N	105	240	33	58	11	1	2	17	27	57	.242	.318	.321	639	73	-9	8	2	1	.978	-11	O-77(45-29-10)	-2.0
1999	*NY-N	155	453	90	142	23	4	4	36	60	100	.313	.397	.408	806	108	8	66	17	9	.989	-5	*O-149(13-21-127)/2-1	0.6
2000	Hou-N	74	259	54	73	2	5	6	26	43	47	.282	.384	.398	782	93	-2	25	11	2	.978	-1	O-67(23-29-17)	-0.2
Total	6	540	1399	238	388	59	13	17	117	182	305	.277	.363	.375	738	94	-8	114	32	14	.984	-24	O-471C/2-1	-2.7

■ ORLANDO CEPEDA

Cepeda, Orlando Manuel (Penne) "Baby Bull" or "Cha Cha"
b: 9/17/37, Ponce, P.R. BR/TR, 6′2″, 210 lbs. Deb: 4/15/58 CH Career OF: (214-LF 0-CF 18-RF)

YEAR	TM/L	G	AB	R	H	2B	3B	HR	RBI	BB	SO	AVG	OBP	SLG	OPS	OPS+	BR+	SB	CS	SBR	FA	FR	G/POS	TPR
1958	SF-N	148	603	88	188	**38**	4	25	96	29	84	.312	.346	.512	859	126	20	15	11	-1	.989	-3	*1-147	0.9
1959	SF-N★	151	605	92	192	35	4	27	105	33	100	.317	.358	.522	880	134	27	23	9	2	.984	-8	*1-122,O-44L/3-4	1.3
1960	SF-N★	151	569	81	169	36	3	24	96	34	91	.297	.345	.497	843	135	25	15	6	1	.983	0	O-91(91-0-0),1-63	1.8
1961	SF-N★	152	585	105	182	28	4	**46**	**142**	39	91	.311	.363	.609	972	158	45	12	8	-0	.997	-3	1-81,O-80(64-0-17)	3.3
1962	*SF-N★	162	625	105	191	26	1	35	114	37	97	.306	.350	.518	869	132	26	10	4	1	.991	-8	*1-160/O-2(1-0-1)	0.9
1963	SF-N☆	156	579	100	183	33	4	34	97	37	70	.316	.367	.563	930	166	47	8	3	1	.985	-8	*1-150/O-3(3-0-0)	3.2
1964	SF-N★	142	529	75	161	27	2	31	97	43	83	.304	.366	.539	904	148	33	9	4	1	.986	-4	*1-139/O-1(1-0-0)	2.2
1965	SF-N	33	34	1	6	1	0	1	5	3	9	.176	.243	.294	537	49	-2	0	0	0	1.000	-0	/1-4,O-2(2-0-0)	-0.3
1966	SF-N	19	49	5	14	2	0	3	15	4	11	.286	.352	.510	862	132	2	0	1	-0	.778	-3	/O-8(8-0-0),1-6	-0.2
	StL-N	123	452	65	137	24	0	17	58	34	68	.303	.369	.469	838	130	19	9	8	-1	.989	-6	*1-120	0.4
	Yr	142	501	70	151	26	0	20	73	38	79	.301	.367	.473	840	130	21	9	9	-1	.990	-9	*1-126/O-8(8-0-0)	0.2
1967	*StL-N★	151	563	91	183	37	0	25	**111**	62	75	.325	.403	.524	927	166	49	11	2	2	.993	-0	*1-151	4.3
1968	*StL-N	157	600	71	149	26	2	16	73	43	96	.248	.308	.378	687	107	4	8	6	-0	.988	-5	*1-154	-1.3
1969	*Atl-N	154	573	74	147	28	2	22	88	55	76	.257	.327	.428	755	109	6	12	5	1	.994	3	*1-153	-0.3
1970	Atl-N	148	567	87	173	33	0	34	111	47	75	.305	.368	.543	911	133	25	6	5	-0	.992	3	*1-148	1.6
1971	Atl-N	71	250	31	69	10	1	14	44	22	29	.276	.335	.492	827	124	7	3	6	-1	.992	2	1-63	0.3
1972	Atl-N	28	84	6	25	3	0	4	9	7	17	.298	.352	.476	828	122	2	0	0	0	1.000	1	1-22	0.2
	Oak-A	3	3	0	0	0	0	0	0	0	0	.000	.000	.000	0	-99	-1	0	0	0	.000	0	H	-0.1
1973	Bos-A	142	550	51	159	25	0	20	86	50	81	.289	.352	.444	795	116	11	0	2	-1	.000	0	*D-142	0.7
1974	KC-A	33	107	3	23	5	0	1	18	9	16	.215	.282	.290	572	61	-5	1	0	0	.000	0	D-26	-0.6
Total	17	2124	7927	1131	2351	417	27	379	1365	588	1169	.297	.353	.499	852	133	340	142	80	3	.990	-39	*1-1683,O-231L,D/3	18.3

■ ED CERMAK

Cermak, Edward Hugo b: 3/10/1882, Cleveland, Ohio d: 11/22/11, Cleveland, Ohio BR/TR, 5′11″, 170 lbs. Deb: 9/9/01

YEAR	TM/L	G	AB	R	H	2B	3B	HR	RBI	BB	SO	AVG	OBP	SLG	OPS	OPS+	BR+	SB	CS	SBR	FA	FR	G/POS	TPR
1901	Cle-A	1	4	0	0	0	0	0	0	0		.000	.000	.000	0	-99	-1	0			1.000	1	/O-1(0-0-1)	0.0

■ RICK CERONE

Cerone, Richard Aldo b: 5/19/54, Newark, N.J. BR/TR, 5′11″, 192 lbs. Deb: 8/17/75 Career OF: (0-LF 0-CF 1-RF)

YEAR	TM/L	G	AB	R	H	2B	3B	HR	RBI	BB	SO	AVG	OBP	SLG	OPS	OPS+	BR+	SB	CS	SBR	FA	FR	G/POS	TPR
1975	Cle-A	7	12	1	3	1	0	0	0	1	0	.250	.308	.333	641	81	-0	0	0	0	1.000	-1	/C-7	-0.1
1976	Cle-A	7	16	1	2	0	0	0	1	0	2	.125	.125	.125	250	-27	-3	0	0	0	.963	0	/C-6,D-1	-0.2
1977	Tor-A	31	100	7	20	4	0	1	10	6	12	.200	.245	.270	515	40	-8	0	0	0	.994	-2	C-31	-0.9
1978	Tor-A	88	282	25	63	8	2	3	20	23	32	.223	.284	.298	582	63	-14	0	3	-1	.992	-0	C-84/D-2	-1.2
1979	Tor-A	136	469	47	112	27	4	7	61	37	40	.239	.296	.358	654	75	-17	1	4	-1	.980	-8	*C-136	-2.0
1980	*NY-A	147	519	70	144	30	4	14	85	32	56	.277	.327	.432	758	108	4	1	3	-1	.990	6	*C-147	1.6
1981	*NY-A	71	234	23	57	13	2	2	21	12	24	.244	.280	.342	622	80	-7	0	2	-1	.992	-6	C-69	-1.0
1982	NY-A	89	300	29	68	10	0	5	28	19	27	.227	.275	.310	585	61	-16	0	2	-1	.989	-8	C-89	-2.1
1983	NY-A	80	246	18	54	7	0	2	22	15	29	.220	.267	.272	540	51	-16	0	0	0	.991	-0	C-78/3-1	-1.4
1984	NY-A	38	120	8	25	3	0	2	13	9	15	.208	.269	.283	553	55	-7	1	0	0	.996	3	C-38	-0.2
1985	Atl-N	96	282	15	61	9	0	3	25	29	25	.216	.292	.280	572	57	-16	0	3	-1	.986	-8	C-91	-2.2
1986	Mil-A	68	216	22	56	14	0	4	18	15	28	.259	.310	.380	690	84	-5	1	1	-0	.991	7	C-68	0.5
1987	NY-A	113	284	28	69	12	1	4	23	30	46	.243	.324	.335	658	76	-9	0	1	-0	**.998**	4	*C-111/P-2,1-2	-0.1
1988	Bos-A	84	264	31	71	13	1	3	27	20	32	.269	.328	.360	687	89	-4	0	0	0	**1.000**	-5	C-83/D-1	-0.4
1989	Bos-A	102	296	28	72	16	1	4	48	34	40	.243	.325	.345	670	84	-6	0	0	0	.984	3	C-97/O-1(0-0-1),D-1	0.2
1990	NY-A	49	139	12	42	6	0	2	11	5	13	.302	.326	.388	715	99	-1	0	0	0	.995	-3	C-35/2-1,D-6	-0.2
1991	NY-N	90	227	18	62	13	0	2	16	30	24	.273	.360	.357	717	103	2	1	1	-0	.987	-2	C-81	0.4
1992	Mon-N	33	63	10	17	4	0	1	7	3	5	.270	.313	.381	694	97	-0	1	2	-0	1.000	1	C-28	0.1
Total	18	1329	4069	393	998	190	15	59	436	320	450	.245	.304	.343	647	78	-123	6	22	-6	.990	-19	*C-1279/D-11,1P2O3	-9.2

■ BOB CERV

Cerv, Robert Henry b: 5/5/26, Weston, Neb. BR/TR, 6′, 202 lbs. Deb: 8/1/51

YEAR	TM/L	G	AB	R	H	2B	3B	HR	RBI	BB	SO	AVG	OBP	SLG	OPS	OPS+	BR+	SB	CS	SBR	FA	FR	G/POS	TPR
1951	NY-A	12	28	4	6	1	0	0	2	4	6	.214	.313	.250	563	55	-2	0	0	0	.875	-1	/O-9(0-0-9)	-0.3
1952	NY-A	36	87	11	21	3	2	1	8	9	22	.241	.313	.356	669	91	-1	0	1	-0	1.000	-2	O-27(15-12-0)	-0.5
1953	NY-A	8	6	0	0	0	0	0	0	1	1	.000	.143	.000	143	-61	-1	0	0	0	.000	0	H	-0.1
1954	NY-A	56	100	14	26	6	0	5	13	11	17	.260	.333	.470	803	122	3	0	2	-1	.897	-5	O-24(24-0-0)	-0.4
1955	*NY-A	55	85	17	29	4	2	3	22	7	16	.341	.411	.541	952	157	7	4	0	1	1.000	-4	O-20(13-7-1)	0.3
1956	*NY-A	54	115	16	35	5	6	3	25	18	13	.304	.398	.530	929	148	8	0	1	-0	.984	-4	O-44(29-15-1)	0.2
1957	KC-A	124	345	35	94	14	2	11	44	20	57	.272	.314	.420	734	97	-2	1	1	-0	.964	-7	O-89(40-35-22)	-1.4
1958	KC-A★	141	515	93	157	20	7	38	104	50	82	.305	.372	.592	964	158	39	3	3	-0	.985	20	*O-136(136-0-0)	5.1
1959	KC-A	125	463	61	132	22	4	20	87	35	87	.285	.339	.479	819	120	11	3	2	-0	.980	6	*O-119(119-0-0)	1.0
1960	KC-A	23	78	14	20	1	1	6	12	10	17	.256	.341	.526	867	130	3	0	0	0	.977	3	O-21(21-0-0)	0.4
	*NY-A	87	216	32	54	11	1	8	28	30	36	.250	.349	.421	771	114	4	0	0	0	.982	4	O-51(50-1-1)/1-3	0.5
	Yr	110	294	46	74	12	2	14	40	40	53	.252	.347	.449	796	119	7	0	0	0	.980	6	O-72(71-1-1)/1-3	0.9
1961	LA-A	18	57	3	9	3	0	2	6	1	8	.158	.172	.316	488	25	-6	0	0	0	.944	-2	O-15(15-0-0)	-1.0
	NY-A	57	118	17	32	5	1	6	20	12	17	.271	.344	.483	827	125	4	1	0	0	.983	1	O-30(28-2-0)/1-3	0.4
	Yr	75	175	20	41	8	1	8	26	13	25	.234	.291	.429	720	91	-3	1	0	0	.974	-1	O-45(43-2-0)/1-3	-0.6
1962	NY-A	14	17	1	2	1	0	0	0	2	3	.118	.250	.176	426	18	-2	0	0	0	1.000	-0	/O-3(1-0-2)	-0.3
	Hou-N	19	31	2	7	0	0	2	3	2	10	.226	.273	.419	692	89	-1	0	0	0	.833	-0	/O-6(6-0-0)	-0.1
Total	12	829	2261	320	624	96	26	105	374	212	392	.276	.343	.481	823	122	63	12	10	-1	.976	8	O-594(497-72-36)/1-6	3.8

■ RON CEY

Cey, Ronald Charles b: 2/15/48, Tacoma, Wash. BR/TR, 5′10″, 185 lbs. Deb: 9/3/71

YEAR	TM/L	G	AB	R	H	2B	3B	HR	RBI	BB	SO	AVG	OBP	SLG	OPS	OPS+	BR+	SB	CS	SBR	FA	FR	G/POS	TPR
1971	LA-N	2	2	0	0	0	0	0	0	0	2	.000	.000	.000	0	-99	-1	0	0	0	.000	0	H	-0.1
1972	LA-N	11	37	3	10	1	0	1	3	7	10	.270	.400	.378	778	125	2	0	0	0	.900	-2	3-11	-0.1
1973	LA-N	152	507	60	124	18	4	15	80	74	77	.245	.343	.385	728	106	5	1	1	-0	.961	16	*3-146	2.1
1974	*LA-N★	159	577	88	151	20	2	18	97	76	68	.262	.355	.397	751	115	12	1	1	-0	.959	17	*3-158	2.9
1975	LA-N★	158	566	72	160	29	2	25	101	78	74	.283	.376	.473	850	141	31	5	2	0	.960	-4	*3-158	2.8
1976	LA-N★	145	502	69	139	18	3	23	80	89	74	.277	.389	.462	851	144	31	0	4	-1	.965	11	*3-144	4.2
1977	*LA-N★	153	564	77	136	22	3	30	110	93	106	.241	.351	.450	801	114	11	3	4	-1	.964	17	*3-153	2.5
1978	*LA-N★	159	555	84	150	32	0	23	84	96	96	.270	.384	.452	837	134	28	2	5	-1	.966	5	*3-158	3.0
1979	LA-N★	150	487	77	137	20	1	28	81	86	85	.281	.391	.499	890	143	31	3	3	-0	**.977**	-1	*3-150	2.8
1980	LA-N	157	551	81	140	25	0	28	77	69	92	.254	.342	.452	794	122	16	2	2	-0	.972	7	*3-157	2.1
1981	*LA-N	85	312	42	90	15	2	13	50	40	55	.288	.375	.474	849	145	18	0	2	-1	.941	7	3-84	2.5
1982	LA-N	150	556	62	141	23	1	24	79	57	99	.254	.327	.428	755	113	8	3	2	-0	.963	11	*3-149	1.8
1983	Chi-N	159	581	73	160	33	1	24	90	62	85	.275	.350	.460	810	117	13	0	0	0	.955	-21	*3-157	-1.0
1984	*Chi-N	146	505	71	121	27	0	25	97	61	108	.240	.329	.442	770	105	3	3	2	-0	**.967**	-20	*3-144	-2.0
1985	Chi-N	145	500	64	116	18	2	22	63	58	106	.232	.317	.408	725	91	-6	1	1	-0	.943	-7	*3-140	-1.6

YEAR	TM/L	G	AB	R	H	2B	3B	HR	RBI	BB	SO	AVG	OBP	SLG	OPS	OPS+	BR+	SB	CS	SBR	FA	FR	G/POS	TPR
1986	Chi-N	97	256	42	70	21	0	13	36	44	66	.273	.386	.508	894	134	13	0	0	0	.952	-6	3-77	0.6
1987	Oak-A	45	104	12	23	6	0	4	11	22	32	.221	.362	.394	756	108	2	0	0	0	.982	-1	D-30/1-7,3-3	0.0
Total	17	2073	7162	977	1868	328	21	316	1139	1012	1235	.261	.357	.445	802	121	218	24	29	-5	.961	30	*3-1989/D-30,1-7	22.5
■ ELIO CHACON	Chacon, Elio (Rodriguez) b: 10/26/36, Caracas, Venez. d: 4/24/92, Caracas, Venez. BR/TR, 5′9″, 160 lbs. Deb: 4/20/60 Career OF: (3-LF 0-CF 7-RF)																							
1960	Cin-N	49	116	14	21	1	0	0	7	14	23	.181	.275	.190	464	29	-11	7	1	1	.980	5	2-43/O-2(0-0-2)	-0.2
1961	*Cin-N	61	132	26	35	4	2	2	5	21	22	.265	.374	.371	745	97	0	1	4	-1	.989	0	2-42/O-7(3-0-5)	0.2
1962	NY-N	118	368	49	87	10	3	2	27	76	64	.236	.369	.296	665	80	-7	12	7	0	.961	-3	*S-110/2-2,3-1	0.0
Total	3	228	616	89	143	15	5	4	39	111	109	.232	.353	.292	645	74	-18	20	12	0	.985	3	S-110/2-87,O-9R,3-1	0.0
■ CHET CHADBOURNE	Chadbourne, Chester James "Pop" b: 10/28/1884, Parkman, Me. d: 6/21/43, Los Angeles, Cal. BL/TR, 5′9″, 170 lbs. Deb: 9/17/06 Career OF: (161-LF 174-CF 0-RF)																							
1906	Bos-A	11	43	7	13	1	0	0	3	3		.302	.348	.326	673	111	1	1			.926	3	2-11/S-1	0.4
1907	Bos-A	10	38	0	11	0	0	0	1	7		.289	.400	.289	689	121	1	1			1.000	-0	O-10(10-0-0)	0.1
1914	KC-F	147	581	92	161	22	8	1	37	69	49	.277	.359	.348	706	97	-10	42			.965	9	*O-146(146-0-0)	-0.8
1915	KC-F	152	587	75	133	16	9	1	35	62	29	.227	.307	.290	596	71	-31	29			**.979**	1	*O-152(5-147-0)	-4.5
1918	Bos-N	27	104	9	27	2	1	0	6	5	5	.260	.300	.298	598	86	-2	5			.925	-3	O-27(0-27-0)	-0.7
Total	5	347	1353	183	345	41	18	2	82	146	83	.255	.333	.316	649	86	-41	78			.969	10	O-335C/2-11,S-1	-5.5
■ DAVE CHALK	Chalk, David Lee b: 8/30/50, Del Rio, Tex. BR/TR, 5′10″, 175 lbs. Deb: 9/4/73																							
1973	Cal-A	24	69	14	16	2	0	0	6	9	13	.232	.329	.261	590	74	-2	0	0	0	.962	2	S-22	0.2
1974	Cal-A★	133	465	44	117	9	3	5	31	30	57	.252	.307	.316	623	84	-9	10	10	-1	.938	-2	S-99,3-38	-0.1
1975	Cal-A☆	149	513	59	140	24	2	3	56	66	49	.273	.358	.345	703	107	7	6	9	-2	.976	6	*3-149	1.1
1976	Cal-A	142	438	39	95	14	1	0	33	49	62	.217	.310	.253	563	71	-14	0	0	0	.971	5	*S-102,3-49	0.2
1977	Cal-A	149	519	58	144	27	2	3	45	52	69	.277	.349	.355	703	96	-1	12	8	-0	.948	-3	*3-141/2-7,S-4	-0.5
1978	Cal-A	135	470	42	119	12	0	1	34	38	34	.253	.318	.285	604	74	-15	5	8	-2	.955	-20	S-97,2-29,3-22,/D-1	-2.7
1979	Tex-A	9	8	0	2	0	0	0	0	0	0	.250	.250	.250	500	36	-1	0	0	0	1.000	0	/S-3,2-1,D-2	-0.1
	Oak-A	66	212	15	47	6	0	2	13	29	14	.222	.318	.278	596	66	-9	2	1	0	.988	-18	2-37,S-16,3-16	-2.3
	Yr	75	220	15	49	6	0	2	13	29	14	.223	.316	.277	593	65	-10	2	1	0	.988	-18	2-38,S-19,3-16,/D-2	-2.4
1980	*KC-A	69	167	19	42	10	1	1	20	18	27	.251	.332	.341	673	84	-3	1	1	-0	.964	-3	3-33,2-17/S-1,D-6	-0.6
1981	KC-A	27	49	2	11	3	0	0	5	4	2	.224	.283	.286	569	65	-2	0	1	-0	.955	-2	3-14,2-10/S-1	-0.4
Total	9	903	2910	292	733	107	9	15	243	295	327	.252	.328	.310	638	85	-51	36	38	-5	.962	-34	3-462,S-345,2-101,/D	-5.2
■ JOE CHAMBERLAIN	Chamberlain, Joseph Jeremiah b: 5/10/10, San Francisco, Cal d: 1/28/83, San Francisco, Cal. BR/TR, 6′1″, 175 lbs. Deb: 4/17/34																							
1934	Chi-A	43	141	13	34	5	1	2	17	6	38	.241	.272	.333	605	54	-10	1	1	-0	.896	-6	S-26,3-14/2-1	-1.3
■ WES CHAMBERLAIN	Chamberlain, Wesley Polk b: 4/13/66, Chicago, Ill. BR/TR, 6′2″, 210 lbs. Deb: 8/31/90																							
1990	Phi-N	18	46	9	13	3	0	2	4	1	9	.283	.298	.478	776	110	0	4	0	1	.958	-1	O-10(10-0-2)	0.0
1991	Phi-N	101	383	51	92	16	3	13	50	31	73	.240	.300	.399	700	96	-3	9	4	1	.985	5	O-98(95-0-3)	-0.1
1992	Phi-N	76	275	26	71	18	0	9	41	10	55	.258	.287	.422	709	99	-2	4	0	1	.971	-1	O-73(28-0-48)	-0.4
1993	*Phi-N	96	284	34	80	20	2	12	45	17	51	.282	.325	.493	817	117	6	2	1	0	.993	5	O-76(0-0-76)	0.7
1994	Phi-N	24	69	7	19	5	0	2	6	3	12	.275	.306	.435	740	88	-1	0	0	0	1.000	1	O-18(0-0-18)	-0.1
	Bos-A	51	164	13	42	9	1	4	20	12	38	.256	.307	.396	703	76	-6	0	2	-1	1.000	4	O-34(0-0-34),D-12	-0.5
1995	Bos-A	19	42	4	5	1	0	1	1	3	11	.119	.178	.214	392	1	-6	1	0	0	.955	0	O-12(0-0-12)/D-5	-0.6
Total	6	385	1263	144	322	72	6	43	167	77	249	.255	.300	.424	723	95	-12	20	7	2	.984	12	O-321(133-0-193)/D-17	-1.0
■ AL CHAMBERS	Chambers, Albert Eugene b: 3/24/61, Harrisburg, Pa. BL/TL, 6′4″, 217 lbs. Deb: 7/23/83																							
1983	Sea-A	31	67	11	14	3	0	1	7	18	20	.209	.376	.299	675	85	-1	0	1	-0	1.000	-1	D-22/O-3(3-0-0)	-0.2
1984	Sea-A	22	49	4	11	1	0	1	4	3	12	.224	.269	.306	575	60	-3	2	1	0	.947	-2	O-13(13-0-0)/D-1	-0.5
1985	Sea-A	4	4	0	0	0	0	0	0	0	2	.000	.000	.000	0	-99	-1	0	0	0	.000	0	/H	-0.1
Total	3	57	120	15	25	4	0	2	11	21	34	.208	.326	.292	618	71	-4	2	2	-0	.955	-3	/D-23,O-16(16-0-0)	-0.8
■ CHRIS CHAMBLISS	Chambliss, Carroll Christopher b: 12/26/48, Dayton, O. BL/TR, 6′1″, 215 lbs. Deb: 5/28/71 C																							
1971	Cle-A	111	415	49	114	20	4	9	48	40	83	.275	.341	.407	749	102	1	2	0	0	.992	-5	*1-108	-1.3
1972	Cle-A	121	466	51	136	27	2	6	44	26	63	.292	.329	.397	726	112	6	3	4	-1	.993	-6	*1-119	-1.2
1973	Cle-A	155	572	70	156	30	2	11	53	58	76	.273	.343	.390	733	104	3	4	8	-2	.991	7	*1-154	-0.4
1974	Cle-A	17	67	8	22	4	0	0	7	5	5	.328	.375	.388	763	121	2	0	1	-0	.982	-2	1-17	-0.2
	NY-A	110	400	38	97	16	3	6	43	23	43	.243	.284	.343	626	81	-11	0	0	0	.992	7	*1-106	-1.3
	Yr	127	467	46	119	20	3	6	50	28	48	.255	.297	.349	646	87	-9	0	1	-0	.990	5	*1-123	-1.5
1975	NY-A	150	562	66	171	38	4	9	72	29	50	.304	.340	.434	774	119	12	0	1	-0	.991	3	*1-147	0.3
1976	*NY-A★	156	641	79	188	32	6	17	96	27	80	.293	.325	.441	766	124	16	1	0	0	.994	-2	*1-155/D-1	0.2
1977	*NY-A	157	600	90	172	32	6	17	90	45	73	.287	.338	.445	783	113	10	4	0	1	.989	-5	*1-157	-0.4
1978	*NY-A	162	625	81	171	26	3	12	90	41	60	.274	.323	.382	706	100	-1	2	1	0	**.997**	4	*1-155/D-7	-0.6
1979	NY-A	149	554	61	155	27	3	18	63	34	53	.280	.327	.437	764	106	4	3	2	-0	.995	0	*1-134,D-16	-0.5
1980	Atl-N	158	602	83	170	37	2	18	72	49	73	.282	.340	.440	781	113	9	7	3	0	.993	-2	*1-158	-0.2
1981	Atl-N	107	404	44	110	25	2	8	51	44	41	.272	.345	.403	749	109	5	4	1	1	.997	7	*1-107	0.7
1982	*Atl-N	157	534	57	144	25	2	20	86	57	57	.270	.340	.436	776	111	8	7	3	0	.993	14	*1-151	1.4
1983	Atl-N	131	447	59	125	24	3	20	78	63	68	.280	.369	.481	850	124	15	2	7	-2	.996	0	*1-126	0.6
1984	Atl-N	135	389	47	100	14	0	9	44	58	54	.257	.355	.362	717	95	-1	1	2	-0	.993	2	*1-109	-0.6
1985	Atl-N	101	170	16	40	7	0	3	21	18	22	.235	.309	.329	638	74	-6	0	0	0	.997	2	1-39	-0.6
1986	Atl-N	97	122	13	38	8	0	2	14	15	24	.311	.387	.426	813	117	3	0	2	-1	.993	-2	1-20	0.0
1988	NY-A	1	1	0	0	0	0	0	0	0	1	.000	.000	.000	0	-99	-0	0	0	0	.000	0	/H	0.0
Total	17	2175	7571	912	2109	392	42	185	972	632	926	.279	.336	.415	751	108	77	40	35	-3	.993	25	*1-1962/D-24	-4.1
■ MIKE CHAMPION	Champion, Robert Michael b: 2/10/55, Montgomery, Ala. BR/TR, 6′, 185 lbs. Deb: 9/14/76																							
1976	SD-N	11	38	4	9	2	0	1	2	1	3	.237	.256	.368	625	82	-1	0	0	0	.940	-4	2-11	-0.5
1977	SD-N	150	507	35	116	14	6	1	43	27	85	.229	.271	.286	557	55	-33	3	3	-0	.974	-26	*2-149	-5.4
1978	SD-N	32	53	3	12	0	2	0	4	5	13	.226	.293	.302	595	72	-2	0	0	0	.932	2	2-20/3-4	0.1
Total	3	193	598	42	137	16	8	2	49	33	101	.229	.272	.293	564	58	-36	3	3	-0	.968	-28	2-180/3-4	-5.8
■ FRANK CHANCE	Chance, Frank Leroy "Husk" or "The Peerless Leader" b: 9/9/1877, Fresno, Cal. d: 9/15/24, Los Angeles, Cal. BR/TR, 6′, 190 lbs. Deb: 4/29/1898 MH Career OF: (6-LF 2-CF 65-RF)																							
1898	Chi-N	53	147	32	41	4	3	1	14	7		.279	.338	.367	705	102	0	7			.950	-5	C-33,O-17(1-1-15)/1-3	-0.4
1899	Chi-N	64	192	37	55	6	2	1	22	15		.286	.351	.354	705	96	-1	10			.950	-2	C-57/O-1(1-0-0),1-1	0.2
1900	Chi-N	56	149	26	44	9	3	0	13	15		.295	.413	.396	809	129	8	8			.932	-1	C-51/1-1	1.0
1901	Chi-N	69	241	38	67	12	4	0	36	29		.278	.376	.361	737	119	8	27			.932	-5	O-51(4-1-46),C-13/1-6	0.1
1902	Chi-N	76	242	40	70	9	4	1	31	37		.289	.401	.372	773	143	15	29			.969	-3	1-38,C-30/O-4(0-0-4)	1.4
1903	Chi-N	125	441	83	144	24	10	2	81	78		.327	.439	.440	878	155	37	**67**			.972	-3	*1-121/C-2	3.0
1904	Chi-N	124	451	89	140	16	10	6	49	36		.310	.382	.430	812	150	27	42			.990	12	*1-123/C-1	3.8
1905	Chi-N	118	392	92	124	16	12	2	70	78		.316	**.450**	.434	883	157	34	38			.990	2	*1-115,M	3.5
1906	*Chi-N	136	474	**103**	151	24	10	3	71	70		.319	.419	.430	849	156	34	**57**			.989	-1	*1-136,M	3.4
1907	*Chi-N	111	382	58	112	19	2	1	49	51		.293	.395	.361	756	129	16	35			**.992**	7	*1-109,M	2.3
1908	*Chi-N	129	452	65	123	27	4	2	55	37		.272	.338	.363	701	119	10	27			.989	4	*1-126,M	1.3
1909	Chi-N	93	324	53	88	16	4	0	46	30		.272	.341	.346	686	110	4	29			.994	-2	1-92,M	0.1
1910	*Chi-N	88	295	54	88	12	8	0	36	37	15	.298	.395	.393	788	131	13	16			.996	-2	1-87,M	1.0
1911	Chi-N	31	88	23	21	6	3	1	17	25	13	.239	.432	.409	841	136	6	9			.990	-2	1-29,M	0.3
1912	Chi-N	2	5	2	1	0	0	0	0	3	0	.200	.500	.200	700	96	0	1			1.000	-0	/1-2,M	0.0
1913	NY-A	12	24	3	5	0	0	0	6	8	1	.208	.406	.208	615	81	0	1			1.000	1	/1-7,M	0.0
1914	NY-A	1	0	0	0	0	0	0	0	0	0	—	—	—	—	—	0	0			1.000	-0	/1-1,M	0.0
Total	17	1288	4299	798	1274	200	79	20	596	556	29	.296	.394	.394	788	135	210	403			.987	0	1-997,C-187/O-73R	21.0

YEAR	TM/L	G	AB	R	H	2B	3B	HR	RBI	BB	SO	AVG	OBP	SLG	OPS	OPS+	BR+	SB	CS	SBR	FA	FR	G/POS	TPR
■ BOB CHANCE	Chance, Robert b: 9/10/40, Statesboro, Ga. BL/TR, 6'2", 219 lbs. Deb: 9/4/63																							
1963	Cle-A	16	52	5	15	4	0	2	7	1	10	.288	.302	.481	783	116	1	0	1	-0	.909	-2	O-14(0-0-14)	-0.2
1964	Cle-A	120	390	45	109	16	1	14	75	40	101	.279	.351	.433	784	118	9	3	3	-0	.988	-12	1-81,O-31(1-0-30)	-1.0
1965	Was-A	72	199	20	51	9	0	4	14	18	44	.256	.318	.362	680	94	-2	0	1	-0	.988	-2	1-48/O-3(0-0-3)	-0.7
1966	Was-A	37	57	1	10	3	0	1	8	2	23	.175	.203	.281	484	38	-5	0	0	0	.974	-2	1-13	-0.7
1967	Was-A	27	42	5	9	2	0	3	7	7	13	.214	.340	.476	816	144	2	0	0	0	1.000	-0	1-10	0.2
1969	Cal-A	5	7	0	1	0	0	0	1	0	4	.143	.143	.143	286	-21	-1	0	0	0	.909	-0	/1-1	-0.2
Total	6	277	747	76	195	34	1	24	112	68	195	.261	.326	.406	732	106	5	3	5	-1	.987	-18	1-153/O-48(1-0-47)	-2.6
■ DARREL CHANEY	Chaney, Darrel Lee b: 3/9/48, Hammond, Ind. BB/TR (BL 1973 (part), 74-75), 6'1", 190 lbs. Deb: 4/11/69																							
1969	Cin-N	93	209	21	40	5	2	0	15	24	75	.191	.278	.234	512	43	-15	1	0	0	.947	-12	S-91	-2.1
1970	*Cin-N	57	95	7	22	3	0	1	4	3	26	.232	.263	.295	557	49	-7	1	1	-0	.941	5	S-30,2-18/3-3	0.0
1971	Cin-N	10	24	2	3	0	0	0	1	1	3	.125	.160	.125	285	-19	-4	0	1	-0	1.000	-1	/S-7,2-1,3-1	-0.4
1972	*Cin-N	83	196	29	49	7	2	2	19	29	28	.250	.347	.337	683	101	1	1	3	-1	.963	-7	S-64,2-12,3-10	-0.1
1973	*Cin-N	105	227	27	41	7	1	0	14	26	50	.181	.268	.220	488	39	-19	4	3	-0	.964	12	S-75,2-14,3-12	0.1
1974	Cin-N	117	135	27	27	6	1	2	16	26	33	.200	.329	.304	633	79	-3	1	2	-0	.952	17	3-81,2-38,S-12	1.5
1975	*Cin-N	71	160	18	35	6	0	2	26	14	38	.219	.282	.294	575	59	-9	3	0	1	.961	17	S-34,2-23,3-13	1.2
1976	Atl-N	153	496	42	125	20	8	1	50	54	92	.252	.327	.331	657	82	-11	5	7	-1	.950	-0	*S-151/2-1,3-1	0.5
1977	Atl-N	74	209	22	42	7	2	3	15	17	44	.201	.261	.297	558	44	-16	0	0	0	.979	4	S-41,2-24	-0.7
1978	Atl-N	89	245	27	55	9	1	3	20	25	48	.224	.296	.306	602	62	-12	1	0	0	.976	-6	S-77/3-8,2-1	-1.1
1979	Atl-N	63	117	15	19	5	0	0	10	19	34	.162	.279	.205	485	32	-11	2	1	0	.945	-3	S-39/2-5,3-4,C-1	-1.1
Total	11	915	2113	237	458	75	17	14	190	238	471	.217	.297	.288	585	61	-106	19	18	-2	.959	26	S-621,2-137,3-133,/C	-2.2
■ LES CHANNELL	Channell, Lester Clark "Goat" or "Gint" b: 3/3/1886, Crestline, Ohio d: 5/8/54, Denver, Colo. BL/TL, 6', 180 lbs. Deb: 5/11/10																							
1910	NY-A	6	19	3	6	0	0	0	3	2		.316	.381	.316	697	112	0	2			1.000	-1	/O-6(6-0-0)	-0.1
1914	NY-A	1	1	0	1	1	0	0	0	0	0	1.000	1.000	2.000	3000	803	1	0			.000	0	H	0.1
Total	2	7	20	3	7	1	0	0	3	2	<u>0</u>	.350	.409	.400	809	145	1	2			1.000	-1	/O-6(6-0-0)	0.0
■ CHARLIE CHANT	Chant, Charles Joseph b: 8/7/51, Bell, Cal. BR/TR, 6', 190 lbs. Deb: 9/12/75																							
1975	Oak-A	5	5	1	0	0	0	0	0	0	0	.000	.000	.000	0	-99	-1	0	0	0	1.000	-2	/O-5(3-0-2),D-1	-0.3
1976	StL-N	15	14	0	2	0	0	0	0	0	4	.143	.143	.143	286	-19	-2	0	0	0	1.000	-2	O-14(7-2-5)	-0.5
Total	2	20	19	1	2	0	0	0	0	0	4	.105	.105	.105	211	-40	-3	0	0	0	1.000	-4	/O-19(10-2-7),D-1	-0.8
■ ED CHAPLIN	Chaplin, Bert Edgar (b: Bert Edgar Chapman) b: 9/25/1893, Pelzer, S.C. d: 8/15/78, Sanford, Fla. BL/TR, 5'7", 158 lbs. Deb: 9/4/20																							
1920	Bos-A	4	5	2	1	1	0	0	1	4	1	.200	.556	.400	956	163	1	0	0	0	.900	-1	/C-2	0.1
1921	Bos-A	3	2	0	0	0	0	0	0	0	1	.000	.000	.000	0	-99	-1	0	0	0	1.000	0	/C-1	0.0
1922	Bos-A	28	69	8	13	1	1	0	6	9	9	.188	.282	.232	514	35	-6	2	1	0	.960	-3	C-21	-0.8
Total	3	35	76	10	14	2	1	0	7	13	11	.184	.303	.237	540	43	-6	2	1	0	.953	-3	/C-24	-0.7
■ CALVIN CHAPMAN	Chapman, Calvin Louis b: 12/20/10, Courtland, Miss. d: 4/1/83, Batesville, Miss. BL/TR, 5'9", 160 lbs. Deb: 9/10/35 Career OF: (21-LF 1-CF 9-RF)																							
1935	Cin-N	15	53	6	18	1	0	0	3	4	5	.340	.386	.358	744	105	1	2			.949	-3	S-12/2-4	-0.1
1936	Cin-N	96	219	35	54	7	3	1	22	16	19	.247	.301	.320	620	72	-9	5			.961	-14	O-31(21-1-9),2-23/3-1	-2.3
Total	2	111	272	41	72	8	3	1	25	20	24	.265	.317	.327	645	78	-8	7			.968	-16	/O-31L,2-27,S-12,3	-2.4
■ GLENN CHAPMAN	Chapman, Glenn Justice "Pete" b: 1/21/06, Cambridge City, Ind. d: 11/5/88, Richmond, Ind. BR/TR, 5'11.5", 170 lbs. Deb: 4/18/34																							
1934	Bro-N	67	93	19	26	5	1	1	10	7	19	.280	.330	.387	717	96	-1	1			1.000	-7	O-40(27-0-14),2-14	-0.8
■ HARRY CHAPMAN	Chapman, Harry E. b: 10/26/1887, Severance, Kan. d: 10/21/18, Nevada, Mo. BR/TR, 5'11", 160 lbs. Deb: 10/6/12 Career OF: (0-LF 1-CF 0-RF)																							
1912	Chi-N	1	4	1	1	0	1	0	1	0	0	.250	.250	.750	1000	169	0	1			1.000	1	/C-1	0.1
1913	Cin-N	2	2	0	1	0	0	0	0	0	1	.500	.500	.500	1000	187	0	0			.000	0	H	0.0
1914	StL-F	64	181	16	38	2	1	0	14	13	27	.210	.270	.232	502	36	-19	2			.973	-4	C-51/1-1,2-1,O-1C	-1.9
1915	StL-F	62	186	19	37	6	3	1	29	22	24	.199	.284	.280	563	56	-14	4			.989	8	C-53	-0.1
1916	StL-A	18	31	2	3	0	0	0	0	2	5	.097	.152	.097	248	-27	-5	0			.981	2	C-14	-0.2
Total	5	147	404	38	80	8	5	1	44	37	57	.198	.269	.250	519	43	-36	7			.982	7	C-119/O-1C,2-1,1-1	-2.1
■ JACK CHAPMAN	Chapman, John Curtis "Death To Flying Things" b: 5/8/1843, Brooklyn, N.Y. d: 6/10/16, Brooklyn, N.Y. TR, 5'11", 170 lbs. Deb: 5/5/1874 M																							
1874	Atl-n	53	242	32	64	10	2	0	24	4	11	.264	.276	.322	599	103	3	2	1	0	.741	2	*O-53(0-1-52)/1-1	0.7
1875	StL-n	43	195	28	44	5	3	0	30	1	7	.226	.230	.282	512	84	-2	4	1	1	.733	-3	O-43(0-0-43)/1-1	-0.1
1876	Lou-N	17	68	4	16	1	0	0	5	1	3	.235	.250	.254	504	58	-3				.750	-4	O-17(5-1-11)/3-1,M	-0.6
Total	2 n	96	437	60	108	15	5	0	54	5	18	.247	.256	.304	560	95	2	6	2	1	.738	-1	/O-96(0-1-95),1-2	0.6
■ JOHN CHAPMAN	Chapman, John Joseph b: 10/15/1899, Centralia, Pa. d: 11/3/53, Philadelphia, Pa. BR/TR, 5'10.5", 175 lbs. Deb: 6/28/24																							
1924	Phi-A	19	71	7	20	4	1	0	7	4	8	.282	.329	.366	695	78	-2	0	0	0	.958	-10	S-19	-1.0
■ KELVIN CHAPMAN	Chapman, Kelvin Keith b: 6/2/56, Willits, Cal. BR/TR, 5'11", 173 lbs. Deb: 4/5/79																							
1979	NY-N	35	80	7	12	1	2	0	4	5	15	.150	.200	.213	413	13	-10	0	0	0	.980	-4	2-22/3-1	-1.3
1984	NY-N	75	197	27	57	13	0	3	23	19	30	.289	.358	.401	759	115	4	8	7	-1	.979	1	2-57/3-3	0.7
1985	NY-N	62	144	16	25	3	0	0	7	9	15	.174	.232	.194	427	21	-15	5	4	-0	.970	-6	2-48/3-1	-2.1
Total	3	172	421	50	94	17	2	3	34	33	60	.223	.286	.295	581	64	-21	13	11	-1	.976	-9	2-127/3-5	-2.7
■ RAY CHAPMAN	Chapman, Raymond Johnson b: 1/15/1891, Beaver Dam, Ky. d: 8/17/20, New York, N.Y. BR/TR, 5'10", 170 lbs. Deb: 8/30/12 Career OF: (0-LF 1-CF 0-RF)																							
1912	Cle-A	31	109	29	34	6	3	0	19	10		.312	.375	.422	797	124	3	10			.904	-10	S-31	-0.5
1913	Cle-A	141	508	78	131	19	7	3	39	46	51	.258	.322	.341	662	91	-6	29			.936	-9	*S-138/O-1	-0.5
1914	Cle-A	106	375	59	103	16	10	2	42	48	48	.275	.358	.387	745	119	9	24	9	2	.913	-15	S-72,2-33	0.2
1915	Cle-A	154	570	101	154	14	17	3	67	70	82	.270	.353	.370	723	114	10	36	15	3	.944	9	*S-154	3.4
1916	Cle-A	109	346	50	80	10	5	0	27	50	46	.231	.330	.289	619	81	-7	21	14	-0	.935	13	S-52,3-36,2-16	1.2
1917	Cle-A	156	563	98	170	28	13	2	36	61	65	.302	.370	.409	779	128	18	52			.938	**24**	*S-156	5.8
1918	Cle-A	128	446	**84**	119	19	8	1	32	**84**	46	.267	.390	.352	742	113	11	30			.936	6	*S-128/O-1(0-1-0)	2.8
1919	Cle-A	115	433	75	130	23	10	3	53	31	38	.300	.351	.420	772	109	4	18			.944	-0	*S-115	1.3
1920	Cle-A	111	435	97	132	27	8	3	49	52	38	.303	.380	.423	803	109	6	13	9	-0	.959	12	*S-111	2.5
Total	9	1051	3785	671	1053	162	81	17	364	452	<u>414</u>	.278	.358	.377	735	110	49	233	<u>47</u>		.939	30	S-957/2-49,3-36,O-2C	16.2
■ SAM CHAPMAN	Chapman, Samuel Blake b: 4/11/16, Tiburon, Cal. BR/TR, 6'1", 190 lbs. Deb: 5/16/38 Career OF: (242-LF 1068-CF 8-RF)																							
1938	Phi-A	114	406	60	105	17	7	17	63	55	94	.259	.353	.461	813	105	2	3	4	-1	.952	-2	*O-110(103-8-0)	-0.6
1939	Phi-A	140	498	74	134	24	6	15	64	51	62	.269	.338	.432	770	98	-3	11	4	1	.955	4	*O-117(0-117-0),1-19	-0.2
1940	Phi-A	134	508	88	140	26	3	23	75	46	96	.276	.337	.474	811	110	6	2	6	-2	.963	4	*O-129(0-129-0)	0.5
1941	Phi-A	143	552	97	178	29	9	25	106	47	49	.322	.378	.543	921	145	33	6	9	-2	.967	14	*O-141(0-140-1)	4.0
1945	Phi-A	9	30	3	6	2	0	0	1	2	4	.200	.250	.267	517	50	-2	0	0	0	1.000	-1	/O-8(0-8-0)	-0.3
1946	Phi-A★	146	545	77	142	22	5	20	67	54	66	.261	.327	.429	757	111	6	1	3	-1	.970	10	*O-145(89-59-0)	0.8
1947	Phi-A	149	551	84	139	18	5	14	83	65	70	.252	.331	.379	710	95	-4	3	4	-1	.987	12	*O-146(12-134-0)	0.2
1948	Phi-A	123	445	58	115	18	6	13	70	55	50	.258	.341	.413	755	100	-1	6	1	1	.982	7	*O-118(0-118-0)	0.3
1949	Phi-A	154	589	89	164	24	4	24	108	80	68	.278	.367	.455	822	121	16	3	4	-1	.979	11	*O-154(0-154-0)	2.1
1950	Phi-A	144	553	93	139	20	6	23	95	68	79	.251	.338	.434	772	98	-4	3	3	-0	.978	10	*O-140(0-140-0)	0.2
1951	Phi-A	18	65	7	11	1	0	0	5	12	12	.169	.299	.185	483	32	-6	0	0	0	.957	-1	O-17(0-17-0)	-0.7
	Cle-A	94	246	24	56	9	1	6	36	27	32	.228	.304	.346	650	80	-8	3	0	1	.985	-18	O-84(38-44-7)/1-1	-2.8
	Yr	112	311	31	67	10	1	6	41	39	44	.215	.303	.312	615	69	-13	3	0	1	.978	-19	*O-101(38-61-7)/1-1	-3.5
Total	11	1368	4988	754	1329	210	52	180	773	562	682	.266	.342	.438	780	107	34	41	38	-4	.972	53	*O-1309C/1-20	3.5
■ BEN CHAPMAN	Chapman, William Benjamin b: 12/25/08, Nashville, Tenn. d: 7/7/93, Hoover, Ala. BR/TR, 6', 190 lbs. Deb: 4/15/30 MC Career OF: (404-LF 583-CF 541-RF)																							
1930	NY-A	138	513	74	162	31	10	10	81	43	58	.316	.371	.474	845	118	13	14	6	1	.912	-6	3-91,2-45	1.4
1931	NY-A	149	600	120	189	28	11	17	122	75	77	.315	.396	.483	879	138	34	**61**	23	**5**	.963	8	*O-137(90-0-50),2-11	3.7
1932	*NY-A	151	581	101	174	41	15	10	107	71	55	.299	.381	.473	854	126	23	**38**	18	2	.949	-3	*O-150(81-0-86)	1.3

YEAR	TM/L	G	AB	R	H	2B	3B	HR	RBI	BB	SO	AVG	OBP	SLG	OPS	OPS+	BR+	SB	CS	SBR	FA	FR	G/POS	TPR
1933	NY-A★	147	565	112	176	36	4	9	98	72	45	.312	.393	.437	830	127	24	**27**	18	-0	.975	11	*O-147(76-0-77)	2.5
1934	NY-A★	149	588	82	181	21	**13**	5	86	67	68	.308	.381	.413	795	113	12	26	16	0	.967	8	*O-149(41-87-23)	1.4
1935	NY-A★	140	553	118	160	38	8	8	74	61	39	.289	.361	.430	791	110	8	17	10	0	.964	17	*O-138(0-138-0)	2.0
1936	NY-A	36	139	19	37	14	3	1	21	15	20	.266	.338	.432	769	92	-2	1	2	-0	.965	2	O-36(0-36-0)	-0.1
	Was-A★	97	401	91	133	36	7	4	60	69	18	.332	.431	.486	917	133	24	19	7	2	.959	4	O-97(0-97-0)	2.4
	Yr	133	540	110	170	50	10	5	81	84	38	.315	.408	.472	880	123	21	20	9	1	.961	7	*O-133(0-133-0)	2.3
1937	Was-A	35	130	23	34	7	1	0	12	26	7	.262	.385	.331	715	86	-2	8	0	2	.957	-1	O-32(0-32-0)	-0.2
	Bos-A	113	423	76	130	23	11	7	57	57	35	.307	.391	.463	854	110	7	27	12	2	.985	9	*O-112(2-10-100)/S-1	1.0
	Yr	148	553	99	164	30	12	7	69	83	42	.297	.389	.432	822	105	6	**35**	12	**4**	.978	7	*O-144(2-42-100)/S-1	0.8
1938	Bos-A	127	480	92	163	40	8	6	80	65	33	.340	.418	.494	912	122	18	13	6	1	.966	6	*O-126(1-0-125)/3-1	1.5
1939	Cle-A	149	545	101	158	31	9	6	82	87	30	.290	.390	.413	802	109	10	18	6	2	.971	-4	*O-146(2-137-9)	0.4
1940	Cle-A	143	548	82	157	40	6	4	50	78	45	.286	.377	.403	781	105	7	13	7	0	.964	2	*O-140(62-18-62)	0.1
1941	Was-A	28	110	9	28	6	0	1	10	10	6	.255	.317	.336	653	76	-4	2	2	-0	.983	1	O-26(26-0-0)	-0.5
	Chi-A	57	190	26	43	9	1	2	19	19	14	.226	.297	.316	612	63	-10	2	2	-0	.992	1	O-49(21-22-7)	-1.1
	Yr	85	300	35	71	15	1	3	29	29	20	.237	.304	.323	627	68	-14	4	4	-1	.989	2	O-75(47-22-7)	-1.6
1944	Bro-N	20	38	11	14	4	0	0	11	5	4	.368	.442	.474	916	161	3	1			.900	-2	P-11	0.0
1945	Bro-N	13	22	2	3	0	0	0	3	2	1	.136	.208	.136	345	-3	-3	0			.938	1	P-10	0.0
	Phi-N	24	51	4	16	2	0	0	4	2	1	.314	.340	.353	693	95	-0	0			.933	-3	O-10(2-6-2)/3-4,P-3,M	-0.4
	Yr	37	73	6	19	2	0	0	7	4	2	.260	.299	.288	586	65	-3	0			.941	-3	P-13,O-10(2-6-2)/3-4	-0.4
1946	Phi-N	1	1	1	0	0	0	0	0	0	0	.000	.000	.000	0	-99	-0	0			.000	0	/P-1,M	0.0
Total	15	1717	6478	1144	1958	407	107	90	977	824	556	.302	.383	.440	823	115	161	287	135		.967	50	*O-1495C/3-96,2PS	15.4

■ FRED CHAPMAN

Chapman, William Fred "Chappie" b: 7/17/16, Liberty, S.C. d: 3/27/97, Kannapolis, N.C. BR/TR, 6'1", 185 lbs. Deb: 9/15/39

YEAR	TM/L	G	AB	R	H	2B	3B	HR	RBI	BB	SO	AVG	OBP	SLG	OPS	OPS+	BR+	SB	CS	SBR	FA	FR	G/POS	TPR
1939	Phi-A	15	49	5	14	1	1	0	1	1	3	.286	.300	.347	647	66	-3	1	0	0	.899	-4	S-15	-0.5
1940	Phi-A	26	69	6	11	1	0	0	4	6	10	.159	.227	.174	401	6	-10	1	1	-0	.862	-5	S-25	-1.3
1941	Phi-A	35	69	1	11	1	0	0	4	4	15	.159	.205	.174	379	1	-10	1	2	-0	.917	-2	S-28/3-2,2-1	-1.1
Total	3	76	187	12	36	3	1	0	9	11	28	.193	.237	.219	457	20	-22	3	3	-0	.889	-11	/S-68,3-2,2-1	-2.9

■ HARRY CHAPPAS

Chappas, Harry Perry b: 10/26/57, Mt.Rainier, Md. BB/TR, 5'3", 150 lbs. Deb: 9/7/78

YEAR	TM/L	G	AB	R	H	2B	3B	HR	RBI	BB	SO	AVG	OBP	SLG	OPS	OPS+	BR+	SB	CS	SBR	FA	FR	G/POS	TPR
1978	Chi-A	20	75	11	20	1	0	0	6	6	11	.267	.329	.280	609	72	-3	1	2	-0	1.000	0	S-20	-0.1
1979	Chi-A	26	59	9	17	1	0	1	4	5	5	.288	.354	.356	710	92	-0	1	1	-0	.929	3	S-23	0.4
1980	Chi-A	26	50	6	8	2	0	0	2	4	10	.160	.236	.200	436	21	-5	0	2	-1	.981	-1	S-19/2-1,D-2	-0.6
Total	3	72	184	26	45	4	0	1	12	15	26	.245	.312	.283	594	65	-8	2	5	-1	.967	1	/S-62,D-2,2-1	-0.3

■ LARRY CHAPPELL

Chappell, La Verne Ashford b: 2/19/1890, McClusky, Ill. d: 11/8/18, San Francisco, Cal. BL/TR, 6', 186 lbs. Deb: 7/18/13

YEAR	TM/L	G	AB	R	H	2B	3B	HR	RBI	BB	SO	AVG	OBP	SLG	OPS	OPS+	BR+	SB	CS	SBR	FA	FR	G/POS	TPR
1913	Chi-A	60	208	20	48	8	1	0	15	18	22	.231	.295	.279	574	69	-8	7			.952	-1	O-59(52-7-0)	-1.3
1914	Chi-A	21	39	3	9	0	0	0	1	4	11	.231	.302	.231	533	61	-2	0			.929	-2	/O-9(7-0-2)	-0.4
1915	Chi-A	1	1	0	0	0	0	0	0	0	0	.000	.000	.000	0	-97	-0	0			.000	0	H	0.0
1916	Cle-A	3	2	0	0	0	0	0	0	1	0	.000	.333	.000	333	1	-0	1			.000	0	H	0.0
	Bos-N	20	53	4	12	1	1	0	9	2	8	.226	.268	.283	551	72	-2	1			.957	-2	O-14(12-0-2)	-0.5
1917	Bos-N	4	2	0	0	0	0	0	1	0	1	.000	.000	.000	0	-99	-0	0			.000	-1	/O-1(0-1-0)	-0.1
Total	5	109	305	27	69	9	2	0	26	25	42	.226	.289	.269	558	66	-13	9			.951	-5	/O-83(71-8-4)	-2.3

■ JOE CHARBONEAU

Charboneau, Joseph b: 6/17/55, Belvidere, Ill. BR/TR, 6'2", 205 lbs. Deb: 4/11/80

YEAR	TM/L	G	AB	R	H	2B	3B	HR	RBI	BB	SO	AVG	OBP	SLG	OPS	OPS+	BR+	SB	CS	SBR	FA	FR	G/POS	TPR
1980	Cle-A	131	453	76	131	17	2	23	87	49	70	.289	.362	.488	850	130	18	2	4	-1	.963	1	O-67(67-0-1),D-57	1.4
1981	Cle-A	48	138	14	29	7	1	4	18	7	22	.210	.248	.362	611	75	-5	1	0	0	.963	-2	O-27(24-0-5),D-14	-0.9
1982	Cle-A	22	56	7	12	2	1	2	9	5	7	.214	.290	.393	683	86	-1	0	0	0	.955	-3	O-18(9-0-8)/D-1	-0.5
Total	3	201	647	97	172	26	4	29	114	61	99	.266	.333	.453	786	115	12	3	4	-1	.962	-4	O-112(100-0-14)/D-72	0.0

■ ED CHARLES

Charles, Edwin Douglas b: 4/29/33, Daytona Beach, Fla. BR/TR, 5'10", 170 lbs. Deb: 4/11/62

YEAR	TM/L	G	AB	R	H	2B	3B	HR	RBI	BB	SO	AVG	OBP	SLG	OPS	OPS+	BR+	SB	CS	SBR	FA	FR	G/POS	TPR
1962	KC-A	147	535	81	154	24	7	17	74	54	70	.288	.358	.454	812	111	9	20	4	3	.964	4	*3-140/2-2	1.6
1963	KC-A	158	603	82	161	28	2	15	79	58	79	.267	.336	.395	731	99	-0	15	8	1	.949	-8	*3-158	-0.9
1964	KC-A	150	557	69	134	25	2	16	63	64	92	.241	.323	.379	702	92	-6	12	7	0	.954	-15	*3-147	-2.2
1965	KC-A	134	480	55	129	19	7	8	56	44	72	.269	.335	.387	723	106	4	13	4	1	.971	-1	*3-128/2-1,S-1	0.4
1966	KC-A	118	385	52	110	18	8	9	42	30	53	.286	.337	.444	782	127	12	12	5	1	.963	-6	*3-104/1-1,O-1(1-0-0)	0.8
1967	KC-A	19	61	5	15	1	0	0	5	12	13	.246	.378	.262	641	95	0	1	0	0	.966	-0	3-18	0.1
	NY-N	101	323	32	77	13	2	3	31	24	58	.238	.305	.319	624	80	-8	4	1	1	.944	9	3-89	0.1
1968	NY-N	117	369	41	102	11	1	15	53	28	57	.276	.331	.434	764	127	12	5	4	-0	.954	1	*3-106/1-2	1.3
1969	*NY-N	61	169	21	35	8	1	3	18	18	31	.207	.287	.320	607	68	-7	4	2	0	.946	-0	3-52	-0.8
Total	8	1005	3482	438	917	147	30	86	421	332	525	.263	.332	.397	729	103	16	86	35	7	.957	-15	3-942/1-3,2-3,OS	0.4

■ FRANK CHARLES

Charles, Franklin Scott b: 2/23/69, Fontana, Cal. BR/TR, 6'4", 210 lbs. Deb: 9/5/2000

YEAR	TM/L	G	AB	R	H	2B	3B	HR	RBI	BB	SO	AVG	OBP	SLG	OPS	OPS+	BR+	SB	CS	SBR	FA	FR	G/POS	TPR
2000	Hou-N	4	7	1	3	1	0	0	2	0	2	.429	.429	.571	1000	142	0	0	0	0	1.000	1	/C-1	0.1

■ CHAPPY CHARLES

Charles, Raymond (b: Charles Shuh Achenbach)
b: 3/25/1881, Phillipsburg, N.J. d: 8/4/59, Bethlehem, Pa. BR/TR, 5'11", 175 lbs. Deb: 4/15/08

YEAR	TM/L	G	AB	R	H	2B	3B	HR	RBI	BB	SO	AVG	OBP	SLG	OPS	OPS+	BR+	SB	CS	SBR	FA	FR	G/POS	TPR
1908	StL-N	121	454	39	93	14	3	1	17	19		.205	.238	.256	494	61	-21	15			.921	-12	2-65,S-31,3-23	-3.7
1909	StL-N	99	339	33	80	7	3	0	29	31		.236	.309	.274	584	87	-5	7			.918	-2	2-71,S-26/3-2	-0.5
	Cin-N	13	43	3	11	2	0	0	5	4		.256	.319	.302	621	94	-0	2			.932	-3	2-10/S-3	-0.3
	Yr	112	382	36	91	9	3	0	34	35		.238	.310	.277	588	87	-5	9			.920	-4	2-81,S-29/3-2	-0.8
1910	Cin-N	4	15	1	2	0	1	0	0	0	1	.133	.133	.267	400	17	-2	0			.818	-2	/S-4	-0.3
Total	3	237	851	76	186	23	7	1	51	54	1	.219	.270	.266	536	72	-28	24			.920	-18	2-146/S-64,3-25	-4.8

■ MIKE CHARTAK

Chartak, Michael George "Shotgun" b: 4/28/16, Brooklyn, N.Y. d: 7/25/67, Cedar Rapids, Ia. BL/TL, 6'2", 180 lbs. Deb: 9/13/40

YEAR	TM/L	G	AB	R	H	2B	3B	HR	RBI	BB	SO	AVG	OBP	SLG	OPS	OPS+	BR+	SB	CS	SBR	FA	FR	G/POS	TPR
1940	NY-A	11	15	2	2	1	0	0	3	5	5	.133	.350	.200	550	49	-1	0	0	0	1.000	-1	/O-3(0-0-3)	-0.2
1942	NY-A	5	5	0	0	0	0	0	0	0	0	.000	.000	.000	0	-99	-1	0	0	0	.000	0	H	-0.1
	Was-A	24	92	11	20	4	2	1	8	14	16	.217	.321	.337	658	86	-2	0	1	-0	.926	-0	O-24(0-0-24)	-0.4
	StL-A	73	237	37	59	11	2	9	43	40	27	.249	.362	.426	788	119	7	3	3	-0	.974	7	O-64(0-0-64)	1.0
	Yr	102	334	48	79	15	4	10	51	54	43	.237	.346	.395	741	107	4	3	4	-1	.962	7	O-88(0-0-88)	0.5
1943	StL-A	108	344	38	88	16	2	10	37	39	55	.256	.333	.401	734	112	5	1	3	-1	.970	-4	O-77(0-0-77),1-18	-0.6
1944	*StL-A	35	72	8	17	2	1	1	7	6	9	.236	.304	.333	637	77	-2	0	0	0	1.000	3	1-12/O-7(4-0-3)	-0.3
Total	4	256	765	96	186	34	7	21	98	104	112	.243	.337	.388	725	105	5	4	7	-2	.967	3	O-175(4-0-171)/1-30	-0.6

■ HAL CHASE

Chase, Harold Homer "Prince Hal" b: 2/13/1883, Los Gatos, Cal.
d: 5/18/47, Colusa, Cal. BR/TL (BL 1909 (1 GAME)), 6', 175 lbs. Deb: 4/14/05 M Career OF: (23-LF 26-CF 1-RF)

YEAR	TM/L	G	AB	R	H	2B	3B	HR	RBI	BB	SO	AVG	OBP	SLG	OPS	OPS+	BR+	SB	CS	SBR	FA	FR	G/POS	TPR
1905	NY-A	128	465	60	116	16	6	3	49	15		.249	.277	.329	606	83	-10	22			.976	-9	*1-124/S-2,2-1	-2.4
1906	NY-A	151	597	84	193	23	10	0	76	13		.323	.341	.395	736	118	10	28			.980	-3	*1-150/2-1	0.6
1907	NY-A	125	498	72	143	23	3	2	68	19		.287	.315	.357	672	106	2	32			.973	0	*1-121/O-4(4-0-0)	-0.1
1908	NY-A	106	405	50	104	11	3	1	36	15		.257	.285	.306	591	91	-5	27			.980	-4	1-98/2-3,O-3L,3P	-1.2
1909	NY-A	118	474	60	134	17	3	4	63	20		.283	.317	.357	674	112	5	25			.978	-2	*1-118/S-1	0.1
1910	NY-A	130	524	67	152	20	5	3	73	16		.290	.312	.365	677	106	1	40			.981	-4	*1-130,M	-0.6
1911	NY-A	133	527	82	166	32	7	3	62	21		.315	.342	.419	762	105	1	36			.974	-2	*1-124/O-7C,2-2,M	-0.4
1912	NY-A	131	522	61	143	21	9	4	58	17		.274	.299	.372	671	86	-12	33			.979	-2	*1-122/2-7	-1.7
1913	NY-A	39	146	15	31	2	4	0	9	11	13	.212	.268	.281	548	60	-8	5			.982	-5	1-29/2-5,O-5(0-5-0)	-1.5
	Chi-A	102	384	49	110	11	10	2	39	16	41	.286	.320	.383	703	107	1	9			.976	1	*1-102	-0.1
	Yr	141	530	64	141	13	14	2	48	27	54	.266	.305	.355	660	94	-7	14			.977	-4	*1-131/2-5,O-5(0-5-0)	-1.6
1914	Chi-A	58	206	27	55	10	5	0	20	23	19	.267	.343	.364	708	114	4	9	4	1	.981	2	1-58	0.5
	Buf-F	75	291	43	101	19	9	3	48	6	31	.347	.365	.505	870	133	7	10			.980	-1	1-73	0.5
1915	Buf-F	145	567	85	165	31	10	**17**	89	20	50	.291	.316	.471	787	118	10	23			.983	0	*1-143/O-1(0-0-1)	-0.3
1916	Cin-N	142	542	66	**184**	29	12	4	82	19	48	**.339**	.363	.459	822	**155**	**32**	22	11	1	.986	-7	1-98,O-25L,2-16	2.5
1917	Cin-N	152	602	71	167	28	15	4	86	15	49	.277	.296	.394	690	115	7	21			.983	-3	*1-151	0.1
1918	Cin-N	74	259	30	78	12	6	2	38	13	15	.301	.339	.417	756	133	9	5			.980	-2	1-67/O-2(2-0-0)	0.6

YEAR	TM/L	G	AB	R	H	2B	3B	HR	RBI	BB	SO	AVG	OBP	SLG	OPS	OPS+	BR+	SB	CS	SBR	FA	FR	G/POS	TPR
1919	NY-N	110	408	58	116	17	7	5	45	17	40	.284	.318	.397	715	115	6	16			.984	-1	*1-107	0.2
Total	15	1919	7417	980	2158	322	124	57	941	276	306	.291	.319	.391	710	110	53	363	15		.980	-42	*1-1815/O-47C,2SP3	-3.2
■ BUSTER CHATHAM Chatham, Charles L b: 12/25/01, West, Tex. d: 12/15/75, Waco, Tex. BR/TR, 5′5″, 150 lbs. Deb: 6/1/30																								
1930	Bos-N	112	404	48	108	20	11	5	56	37	41	.267	.332	.408	740	80	-13	8			.920	-14	3-92,S-17	-1.8
1931	Bos-N	17	44	4	10	1	0	1	3	6	6	.227	.320	.318	638	75	-1	0			.762	-6	/S-6,3-6	-0.7
Total	2	129	448	52	118	21	11	6	59	43	47	.263	.331	.400	730	80	-15	8			.924	-20	/3-98,S-23	-2.5
■ JIM CHATTERTON Chatterton, James M. b: 10/14/1864, Brooklyn, N.Y. d: 12/15/44, Tewksbury, Mass. Deb: 6/7/1884																								
1884	KC-U	4	15	4	2	1	0	0		2		.133	.235	.200	435	38	-2				1.000	0	/O-2(0-2-0),1-2,P-1	-0.1
■ OSSIE CHAVARRIA Chavarria, Osvaldo (Quijano) b: 8/5/40, Colon, Panama BR/TR, 5′11″, 155 lbs. Deb: 4/14/66 Career OF: (21-LF 0-CF 8-RF)																								
1966	KC-A	86	191	26	46	10	0	2	10	18	43	.241	.306	.325	631	84	-4	3	2	-0	.939	-5	O-26L,S-23,2-14,/13	-0.8
1967	KC-A	38	59	2	6	2	0	0	4	7	16	.102	.209	.136	345	4	-7	1	0	0	1.000	2	2-17/3-7,O-3L,S-2	-0.4
Total	2	124	250	28	52	12	0	2	14	25	59	.208	.283	.280	563	65	-11	4	2	0	.990	-2	/2-31,O-29L,S-25,31	-1.2
■ ERIC CHAVEZ Chavez, Eric Cesar b: 12/7/77, Los Angeles, Cal. BL/TR, 6′1″, 195 lbs. Deb: 9/8/98																								
1998	Oak-A	16	45	6	14	4	1	0	6	3	5	.311	.354	.444	799	109	1	1	1	-0	1.000	2	3-13	0.2
1999	Oak-A	115	356	47	88	21	2	13	50	46	56	.247	.333	.427	760	96	-2	1	1	-0	.961	-8	*3-105/S-2,D-3	-0.9
2000	*Oak-A	153	501	89	139	23	4	26	86	62	94	.277	.358	.495	853	116	12	2	2	-0	.951	-5	*3-146/S-2	0.7
Total	3	284	902	142	241	48	7	39	142	111	155	.267	.348	.466	814	108	10	4	4	-1	.957	-12	3-264/S-4,D-3	0.0
■ RAUL CHAVEZ Chavez, Raul Alexander b: 3/18/73, Valencia, Venez. BR/TR, 5′11″, 175 lbs. Deb: 8/30/96																								
1996	Mon-N	4	5	1	1	0	0	0	0	1	1	.200	.333	.200	533	44	-0	1	0	0	1.000	1	/C-3	0.1
1997	Mon-N	13	26	0	7	0	0	0	2	0	5	.269	.269	.269	538	42	-2	1	0	0	1.000	1	C-13	0.0
1998	Sea-A	1	1	0	0	0	0	0	0	0	0	.000	.000	.000	0	-99	-0	0	0	0	1.000	0	/C-1	0.0
2000	Hou-N	14	43	3	11	2	0	1	5	3	6	.256	.304	.372	676	66	-2	0	0	0	.986	-2	C-14	-0.4
Total	4	32	75	4	19	2	0	1	7	4	12	.253	.291	.320	611	55	-5	2	0	0	.993	-0	/C-31	-0.3
■ HARRY CHEEK Cheek, Harry G. b: 1879, Sedalia, Mo. d: 6/25/56, Paramas, N.J. TR, Deb: 5/12/10																								
1910	Phi-N	2	4	1	2	1	0	0	0	0	0	.500	.500	.750	1250	255	1	0			1.000	-1	/C-2	0.0
■ PAUL CHERVINKO Chervinko, Paul b: 7/28/10, Trauger, Pa. d: 6/3/76, Danville, Ill. BR/TR, 5′8″, 185 lbs. Deb: 5/30/37																								
1937	Bro-N	30	48	1	7	0	1	0	2	3	16	.146	.196	.188	384	5	-6	0			1.000	0	C-26	-0.5
1938	Bro-N	12	27	0	4	0	0	0	3	2	0	.148	.207	.148	355	-1	-4	0			.974	0	C-12	-0.3
Total	2	42	75	1	11	0	1	0	5	5	16	.147	.200	.173	373	3	-10	0			.990	1	/C-38	-0.8
■ CUPID CHILDS Childs, Clarence Algernon b: 8/14/1867, Calvert Co., Md. d: 11/8/12, Baltimore, Md. BL/TR, 5′8″, 185 lbs. Deb: 4/23/1888																								
1888	Phi-N	2	4	0	0	0	0	0	0	0	0	.000	.000	.000	0	-95	-1	0			.857	0	/2-2	-0.1
1890	Syr-a	126	493	109	170	**33**	14	2	89	72		.345	.434	.481	915	189	**60**	56			.928	12	*2-125/S-1	**6.6**
1891	Cle-N	141	551	120	155	21	12	2	83	97	32	.281	.395	.374	769	119	17	39			.910	-12	*2-141	0.9
1892	*Cle-N	145	558	**136**	177	14	11	3	53	117	20	.317	**.443**	.398	841	149	40	26			.938	-6	*2-145	3.7
1893	Cle-N	124	485	145	158	19	10	3	65	120	12	.326	.463	.425	888	129	27	23			.926	10	*2-123	3.4
1894	Cle-N	118	479	143	169	21	12	2	52	107	11	.353	.475	.459	935	121	23	17			.916	-3	*2-118	2.0
1895	*Cle-N	120	466	96	134	15	4	4	90	74	24	.288	.392	.363	755	90	-5	20			.921	11	*2-120	0.9
1896	*Cle-N	132	498	106	177	24	9	1	106	100	18	.355	.467	.446	913	133	30	25			.942	**42**	*2-132	6.5
1897	Cle-N	114	444	105	150	15	9	1	61	74		.338	.435	.419	854	119	16	25			.944	17	*2-114	3.2
1898	Cle-N	110	413	90	119	9	4	1	31	69		.288	.395	.337	732	112	10	9			.931	9	*2-110	2.2
1899	StL-N	125	464	73	123	11	11	1	48	74		.265	.369	.343	711	93	-2	11			.934	-12	*2-125	-0.7
1900	Chi-N	137	531	67	128	14	5	0	44	57		.241	.323	.286	609	71	-19	15			.935	16	*2-137	0.3
1901	Chi-N	63	236	24	61	9	0	0	21	30		.258	.359	.297	656	95	0	3			.939	10	2-63	1.1
Total	13	1457	5622	1214	1721	205	101	20	743	991	117	.306	.416	.389	805	119	197	269			.930	94	*2-1455/S-1	30.0
■ PETE CHILDS Childs, Peter Pierre b: 11/15/1871, Philadelphia, Pa. d: 2/15/22, Philadelphia, Pa. TR, Deb: 4/24/01																								
1901	StL-N	29	79	12	21	1	0	0	8	14		.266	.389	.278	668	100	1	0			.907	-7	2-19/O-2(1-1-0),S-1	-0.5
	Chi-N	60	210	23	48	5	1	0	14	26		.229	.319	.262	581	72	-6	4			.958	12	2-60	0.6
	Yr	89	289	35	69	6	1	0	22	40		.239	.339	.266	606	80	-5	4			.947	5	2-79/O-2(1-1-0),S-1	0.1
1902	Phi-N	123	403	25	78	5	0	0	25	34		.194	.256	.206	462	43	-26	6			.945	-9	*2-123	-3.6
Total	2	212	692	60	147	11	1	0	47	74		.212	.292	.231	523	59	-31	10			.946	-3	2-202/O-2(1-1-0),S-1	-3.5
■ PEARCE CHILES Chiles, Pearce Nuget "What's The Use" b: 5/28/1867, Deepwater, Mo. BR/TR, 5′11″, 185 lbs. Deb: 4/18/1899 Career OF: (13-LF 2-CF 34-RF)																								
1899	Phi-N	97	338	57	108	28	7	2	76	16		.320	.352	.462	814	127	10	6			.944	-15	O-46R,1-25,2-16	-0.6
1900	Phi-N	33	111	13	24	6	2	1	23	6		.216	.256	.333	590	63	-6	4			.987	-3	1-16,2-12/O-3(0-0-3)	-0.8
Total	2	130	449	70	132	34	9	3	99	22		.294	.328	.430	758	111	4	10			.947	-18	/O-49R,1-41,2-28	-1.4
■ RICH CHILES Chiles, Richard Francis b: 11/22/49, Sacramento, Cal. BL/TL, 5′11″, 170 lbs. Deb: 4/20/71																								
1971	Hou-N	67	119	12	27	5	1	2	15	6	20	.227	.270	.336	606	73	-5	0	1	-0	1.000	-3	O-27(25-0-2)	-1.0
1972	Hou-N	9	11	0	3	1	0	0	2	1	1	.273	.333	.364	697	100	0	0	0	0	1.000	0	/O-2(2-0-0)	0.0
1973	NY-N	8	25	2	3	2	0	0	1	0	2	.120	.120	.200	320	-13	-4	0	0	0	1.000	2	/O-8(0-8-0)	-0.2
1976	Hou-N	5	4	1	2	1	0	0	0	0	0	.500	.500	.750	1250	276	1	0	0	0	1.000	-0	/O-1(1-0-0)	0.1
1977	Min-A	108	261	31	69	16	1	3	36	23	17	.264	.329	.368	696	91	-3	0	1	-0	.946	-2	D-61,O-22(1-0-21)	-0.8
1978	Min-A	87	198	22	53	12	0	1	22	20	25	.268	.341	.343	684	91	-2	1	2	-0	.965	-2	O-61(58-0-3)/D-8	-0.6
Total	6	284	618	68	157	37	2	6	76	50	65	.254	.315	.350	665	85	-13	1	4	-1	.972	-5	O-121(87-8-26)/D-69	-2.5
■ DINO CHIOZZA Chiozza, Dino Joseph "Dynamo" b: 6/30/12, Memphis, Tenn. d: 4/23/72, Memphis, Tenn. BL/TR, 6′, 170 lbs. Deb: 7/14/35 F																								
1935	Phi-N	2	0	1	0	0	0	0	0	0	0	—	—	—	—	—	0	0			1.000	-0	/S-2	0.0
■ LOU CHIOZZA Chiozza, Louis Peo b: 5/17/10, Tallulah, La. d: 2/28/71, Memphis, Tenn. BL/TR, 6′, 172 lbs. Deb: 4/17/34 F Career OF: (22-LF 107-CF 5-RF)																								
1934	Phi-N	134	484	66	147	28	5	0	44	34	35	.304	.357	.382	739	86	-8	9			.938	-24	2-85,3-26,O-17L	-2.6
1935	Phi-N	124	472	71	134	26	6	3	47	33	44	.284	.333	.383	717	84	-10	5			.947	3	*2-120/3-2	0.0
1936	Phi-N	144	572	83	170	32	6	1	48	37	39	.297	.346	.379	726	87	-10	17			.972	1	O-90C,2-33,3-26	-0.9
1937	*NY-N	117	439	49	102	11	2	4	29	20	30	.232	.266	.294	560	51	-30	6			.939	2	3-93,O-12(0-12-0)/2-2	-2.5
1938	NY-N	57	179	15	42	7	2	3	17	12	7	.235	.283	.346	629	72	-7	5			.944	-8	2-34,O-16(5-10-0)/3-1	-1.4
1939	NY-N	40	142	19	38	3	1	3	12	9	10	.268	.311	.366	677	81	-4	3			.915	-3	3-30/S-8	-0.5
Total	6	616	2288	303	633	107	22	14	197	145	165	.277	.324	.361	685	78	-70	45			.943	-30	2-274,3-178,O-135C,/S	-7.9
■ WALT CHIPPLE Chipple, Walter John (b: Walter John Chlipala) b: 9/26/18, Utica, N.Y. d: 6/8/88, Tonawanda, N.Y. BR/TR, 6′0.5″, 168 lbs. Deb: 4/17/45																								
1945	Was-A	18	44	4	6	0	0	0	5	5	6	.136	.224	.136	361	6	-5	0	1	-0	.978	3	O-13(1-11-1)	-0.3
■ TOM CHISM Chism, Thomas Raymond b: 5/9/55, Chester, Pa. BL/TL, 6′1″, 195 lbs. Deb: 9/13/79																								
1979	Bal-A	6	3	0	0	0	0	0	0	0	0	.000	.000	.000	0	-99	-1	0	0	0	1.000	-0	/1-4	-0.1
■ HARRY CHITI Chiti, Harry b: 11/16/32, Kincaid, Ill. BR/TR, 6′3″, 225 lbs. Deb: 9/27/50																								
1950	Chi-N	3	6	0	2	0	0	0	0	0	0	.333	.333	.333	667	77	-0	0			1.000	-1	/C-1	-0.1
1951	Chi-N	9	31	1	11	2	0	0	5	2	2	.355	.394	.419	813	117	1	0	0	0	.913	0	/C-8	0.1
1952	Chi-N	32	113	14	31	5	0	5	13	5	8	.274	.305	.451	756	106	0	0	1	-0	.984	6	C-32	0.7
1955	Chi-N	113	338	24	78	6	1	11	41	25	68	.231	.286	.352	638	68	-16	0	0	0	.984	1	*C-113	-1.0
1956	Chi-N	72	203	17	43	6	4	4	18	19	35	.212	.283	.340	622	68	-10	0	0	0	.981	2	C-67	-0.4
1958	KC-A	103	295	32	79	11	3	9	44	18	48	.268	.316	.417	733	98	-1	3	2	-0	.987	3	C-83	0.6
1959	KC-A	55	162	20	44	11	1	5	25	17	26	.272	.344	.444	789	113	3	0	1	-0	.988	2	C-47	0.7
1960	KC-A	58	190	16	42	7	0	5	28	17	33	.221	.288	.337	625	68	-9	1	0	0	.983	-1	C-52	-0.7
	Det-A	37	104	9	17	0	0	2	5	10	12	.163	.237	.221	458	24	-11	0	3	-1	.984	1	C-36	-1.0
	Yr	95	294	25	59	7	0	7	33	27	45	.201	.270	.296	566	52	-20	1	3	-1	.984	1	C-88	-1.7

YEAR	TM/L	G	AB	R	H	2B	3B	HR	RBI	BB	SO	AVG	OBP	SLG	OPS	OPS+	BR+	SB	CS	SBR	FA	FR	G/POS	TPR
1961	Det-A	5	12	0	1	0	0	0	0	1	2	.083	.154	.083	237	-34	-2	0	0	0	1.000	1	/C-5	-0.1
1962	NY-N	15	41	2	8	1	0	0	0	1	8	.195	.233	.220	452	22	-4	0	0	0	.971	-1	C-14	-0.5
Total	10	502	1495	135	356	49	9	41	179	115	242	.238	.296	.365	661	77	-50	4	7		.983	13	C-458	-1.7

■ FELIX CHOUINARD Chouinard, Felix George b: 10/5/1887, Chicago, Ill. d: 4/28/55, Hines, Ill. BR/TR, 5'7", 150 lbs. Deb: 9/11/10

YEAR	TM/L	G	AB	R	H	2B	3B	HR	RBI	BB	SO	AVG	OBP	SLG	OPS	OPS+	BR+	SB	CS	SBR	FA	FR	G/POS	TPR
1910	Chi-A	24	82	6	16	3	2	0	9	8		.195	.275	.280	555	77	-2	4			.962	4	O-23(0-23-0)/2-1	0.1
1911	Chi-A	14	17	3	3	0	0	0	0	0		.176	.176	.176	353	-2	-2	0			.857	1	/2-4,O-4(0-3-1)	-0.1
1914	Pit-F	9	30	2	9	1	0	1	3	0	4	.300	.300	.433	733	99	-1	1			.917	-0	/2-4,O-3(2-1-0),S-1	-0.1
	Bro-F	32	79	7	20	1	2	0	8	4	13	.253	.289	.316	606	65	-5	3			.929	-1	O-20(5-14-2)	-0.7
	Bal-F	5	9	3	4	0	0	0	1	0	1	.444	.444	.444	889	138	0	0			1.000	-0	/O-2(1-1-0)	0.0
	Yr	46	118	12	33	2	2	1	12	4	18	.280	.303	.356	659	79	-5	4			.941	-1	O-25(8-16-2)/2-4,S-1	-0.8
1915	Bro-F	4	4	1	2	0	0	0	2	0	0	.500	.500	.500	1000	183	0	0			1.000	-1	/O-2(1-1-0)	0.0
Total	4	88	221	22	54	5	4	1	23	12	18	.244	.286	.317	603	75	-10	8			.948	4	/O-54(9-43-3),2-9,S-1	-0.8

■ HARRY CHOZEN Chozen, Harry b: 9/27/15, Winnebago, Minn. d: 9/16/94, Houston, Tex. BR/TR, 5'9.5", 190 lbs. Deb: 9/21/37

YEAR	TM/L	G	AB	R	H	2B	3B	HR	RBI	BB	SO	AVG	OBP	SLG	OPS	OPS+	BR+	SB	CS	SBR	FA	FR	G/POS	TPR
1937	Cin-N	1	4	0	1	0	0	0	0	0	0	.250	.250	.250	500	38	-0	0			.833	-0	/C-1	-0.1

■ NEIL CHRISLEY Chrisley, Barbra O'Neil b: 12/16/31, Calhoun Falls, S.C BL/TR, 6'3", 187 lbs. Deb: 4/15/57 Career OF: (76-LF 12-CF 61-RF)

YEAR	TM/L	G	AB	R	H	2B	3B	HR	RBI	BB	SO	AVG	OBP	SLG	OPS	OPS+	BR+	SB	CS	SBR	FA	FR	G/POS	TPR
1957	Was-A	26	51	6	8	2	1	0	3	7	7	.157	.259	.235	494	36	-4	0	0	0	.810	-1	O-11(4-0-7)	-0.6
1958	Was-A	105	233	19	50	7	4	5	26	16	18	.215	.265	.343	608	67	-11	1	3	-1	.992	1	O-69(38-7-25)/3-1	-1.5
1959	Det-A	65	106	7	14	3	0	6	11	12	10	.132	.227	.330	557	48	-8	0	0	0	1.000	-2	O-21(3-1-17)	-1.1
1960	Det-A	96	220	27	56	10	3	5	24	19	26	.255	.317	.395	712	89	-4	2	0	0	.981	2	O-47(31-4-12)/1-2	-0.4
1961	Mil-N	10	9	1	2	0	0	0	0	1	1	.222	.300	.222	522	44	-1	0	0	0	.000	0	H	-0.1
Total	5	302	619	60	130	22	8	16	64	55	62	.210	.277	.349	626	69	-28	3	3	-0	.975	-0	O-148L/1-2,3-1	-3.7

■ LLOYD CHRISTENBURY Christenbury, Lloyd Reid "Low" b: 10/19/1893, Mecklenburg Co., N.C. d: 12/13/44, Birmingham, Ala. BL/TR, 5'7", 165 lbs. Deb: 9/20/19 Career OF: (37-LF 7-CF 9-RF)

YEAR	TM/L	G	AB	R	H	2B	3B	HR	RBI	BB	SO	AVG	OBP	SLG	OPS	OPS+	BR+	SB	CS	SBR	FA	FR	G/POS	TPR
1919	Bos-N	7	31	5	9	1	0	0	4	2	2	.290	.333	.323	656	102	0	0			.941	1	/O-7(7-0-0)	0.1
1920	Bos-N	65	106	17	22	2	2	0	14	13	12	.208	.300	.264	564	66	-4	0	1	-0	.895	-7	O-14C/S-7,2-6,3-2	-1.2
1921	Bos-N	62	125	34	44	6	2	3	16	21	7	.352	.449	.504	953	161	12	3	4	-1	.914	-13	2-32/S-2,3-2	0.0
1922	Bos-N	71	152	22	38	5	2	1	13	18	11	.250	.337	.329	666	76	-5	2	4	-1	.946	0	O-32(30-0-2)/2-5,3-2	-0.7
Total	4	205	414	78	113	14	6	4	47	54	32	.273	.362	.365	727	101	3	5	9		.936	-18	/O-53L,2-43,S-9,3-6	-1.8

■ BRUCE CHRISTENSEN Christensen, Bruce Ray b: 2/22/48, Madison, Wis. BL/TR, 5'11", 160 lbs. Deb: 7/17/71

YEAR	TM/L	G	AB	R	H	2B	3B	HR	RBI	BB	SO	AVG	OBP	SLG	OPS	OPS+	BR+	SB	CS	SBR	FA	FR	G/POS	TPR
1971	Cal-A	29	63	4	17	1	0	0	3	6	5	.270	.333	.286	619	83	-1	0	1	-0	.988	2	S-24	0.3

■ JOHN CHRISTENSEN Christensen, John Lawrence b: 9/5/60, Downey, Cal. BR/TR, 6'3", 205 lbs. Deb: 9/13/84

YEAR	TM/L	G	AB	R	H	2B	3B	HR	RBI	BB	SO	AVG	OBP	SLG	OPS	OPS+	BR+	SB	CS	SBR	FA	FR	G/POS	TPR
1984	NY-N	5	11	2	3	2	0	0	3	1	2	.273	.333	.455	788	121	0	0	1	-0	.500	-2	/O-5(3-0-2)	-0.2
1985	NY-N	51	113	10	21	4	1	3	13	19	23	.186	.303	.319	622	76	-3	1	2	-0	.956	-6	O-38(6-2-31)	-1.2
1987	Sea-A	53	132	19	32	6	1	2	12	12	28	.242	.306	.348	654	69	-6	2	0	0	1.000	-3	O-43(2-0-41)/D-8	-0.9
1988	Min-A	23	38	5	10	4	0	0	5	3	5	.263	.349	.368	717	98	0	0	0	0	1.000	-3	O-17(0-0-17)/D-1	-0.3
Total	4	132	294	36	66	16	2	5	33	35	58	.224	.311	.344	655	77	-9	3	3	-0	.977	-13	O-103(11-2-91)/D-9	-2.6

■ MC KAY CHRISTENSEN Christensen, McKay Andrew b: 8/14/75, Upland, Cal. BL/TL, 5'11", 180 lbs. Deb: 4/6/99

YEAR	TM/L	G	AB	R	H	2B	3B	HR	RBI	BB	SO	AVG	OBP	SLG	OPS	OPS+	BR+	SB	CS	SBR	FA	FR	G/POS	TPR
1999	Chi-A	28	53	10	12	1	0	1	6	4	7	.226	.281	.302	583	49	-4	2	1	0	.943	-4	O-27(0-27-0)	-0.7
2000	*Chi-A	32	19	4	2	0	0	0	1	2	6	.105	.227	.105	333	-12	-3	1	1	-0	1.000	-10	O-29(0-29-0)	-1.2
Total	2	60	72	14	14	1	0	1	7	6	13	.194	.266	.250	516	32	-7	3	2	-0	.959	-14	/O-56(0-56-0)	-1.9

■ CUCKOO CHRISTENSEN Christensen, Walter Niels "Seacap" b: 10/24/1899, San Francisco, Cal d: 12/20/84, Menlo Park, Cal. BL/TL, 5'6.5", 156 lbs. Deb: 4/13/26

YEAR	TM/L	G	AB	R	H	2B	3B	HR	RBI	BB	SO	AVG	OBP	SLG	OPS	OPS+	BR+	SB	CS	SBR	FA	FR	G/POS	TPR
1926	Cin-N	114	329	41	115	15	7	0	41	40	18	.350	.426	.438	864	136	19	8			.978	-10	O-93(72-19-9)	0.3
1927	Cin-N	57	185	25	47	6	0	0	16	20	16	.254	.330	.286	617	68	-8	4			.957	-3	O-50(11-35-4)	-1.3
Total	2	171	514	66	162	21	7	0	57	60	34	.315	.392	.383	775	112	11	12			.970	-13	O-143(83-54-13)	-1.0

■ RYAN CHRISTENSON Christenson, Ryan Alan b: 3/28/74, Redlands, Cal. BR/TR, 5'11", 175 lbs. Deb: 4/20/98

YEAR	TM/L	G	AB	R	H	2B	3B	HR	RBI	BB	SO	AVG	OBP	SLG	OPS	OPS+	BR+	SB	CS	SBR	FA	FR	G/POS	TPR
1998	Oak-A	117	370	56	95	22	2	5	40	36	106	.257	.324	.368	692	81	-10	5	6	-1	.983	2	*O-116(1-113-4)	-0.7
1999	Oak-A	106	268	41	56	12	1	4	24	38	58	.209	.309	.306	615	60	-16	7	5	-0	.969	-8	*O-104(0-104-0)/D-1	-2.2
2000	*Oak-A	121	129	31	32	2	2	4	18	19	33	.248	.349	.388	737	88	-2	1	2	-0	.951	-31	*O-114(76-27-14)	-3.2
Total	3	344	767	128	183	36	5	13	82	93	197	.239	.323	.349	673	75	-28	13	13	-2	.973	-37	O-334(77-244-18)/D-1	-6.1

■ BOB CHRISTIAN Christian, Robert Charles b: 10/17/45, Chicago, Ill. d: 2/20/74, San Diego, Cal. BR/TR, 5'10", 180 lbs. Deb: 9/2/68

YEAR	TM/L	G	AB	R	H	2B	3B	HR	RBI	BB	SO	AVG	OBP	SLG	OPS	OPS+	BR+	SB	CS	SBR	FA	FR	G/POS	TPR
1968	Det-A	3	3	0	1	1	0	0	0	0	0	.333	.333	.667	1000	191	0	0	0	0	1.000	-0	/1-1,O-1(0-0-1)	0.0
1969	Chi-A	39	129	11	28	4	0	3	16	10	19	.217	.279	.318	596	63	-6	3	0	1	.958	0	O-38(37-0-1)	-0.8
1970	Chi-A	12	15	3	4	0	0	1	3	1	4	.267	.313	.467	779	108	0	0	0	0	1.000	-1	/O-4(4-0-0)	-0.1
Total	3	54	147	14	33	5	0	4	19	11	23	.224	.283	.340	623	70	-6	3	0	1	.959	-1	/O-43(41-0-2),1-1	-0.9

■ MARK CHRISTMAN Christman, Marquette Joseph b: 10/21/13, Maplewood, Mo. d: 10/9/76, St.Louis, Mo. BR/TR, 5'11", 180 lbs. Deb: 4/20/38

YEAR	TM/L	G	AB	R	H	2B	3B	HR	RBI	BB	SO	AVG	OBP	SLG	OPS	OPS+	BR+	SB	CS	SBR	FA	FR	G/POS	TPR
1938	Det-A	95	318	35	79	6	4	1	44	27	21	.248	.307	.302	609	50	-24	5	2	0	.983	9	3-69,S-21	-1.0
1939	Det-A	6	16	0	4	2	0	0	0	0	2	.250	.250	.375	625	54	-1	0	0	0	.900	-1	/3-5	-0.2
	StL-A	79	222	27	48	6	3	0	20	20	10	.216	.281	.270	551	41	-20	2	1	0	.960	21	S-64/2-1	0.5
	Yr	85	238	27	52	8	3	0	20	20	12	.218	.279	.277	556	42	-21	2	1	0	.960	20	S-64/3-5,2-1	0.3
1943	StL-A	98	336	31	91	11	5	2	35	19	19	.271	.318	.351	669	94	-3	0	3	-1	.991	-0	3-37,S-24,1-20,2-14	-0.3
1944	*StL-A	148	547	56	148	25	1	6	83	47	37	.271	.332	.353	684	90	-7	5	2	0	**.972**	4	*3-145/1-3	-0.1
1945	StL-A	78	289	32	80	7	4	4	34	19	19	.277	.328	.370	698	98	-1	1	0	0	.973	-3	3-77	-0.3
1946	StL-A	128	458	40	118	22	2	1	41	22	29	.258	.295	.321	616	68	-20	0	2	-1	.975	9	3-77,S-47	-0.9
1947	Was-A	110	374	27	83	15	2	1	33	32	16	.222	.287	.281	568	60	-21	4	4	-1	.978	-10	*S-106/2-1	-2.6
1948	Was-A	120	409	38	106	17	2	1	40	25	19	.259	.303	.318	621	67	-20	0	3	-1	.969	-32	*S-102/3-9,2-3	-4.6
1949	Was-A	49	112	8	24	2	0	3	18	8	7	.214	.273	.313	585	56	-8	0	0	0	.967	3	3-23/1-6,S-4,2-1	-0.5
Total	9	911	3081	294	781	113	23	19	348	219	179	.253	.306	.324	630	71	-124	17	17	-2	.975	-0	3-442,S-368/1-29,2	-10.0

■ STEVE CHRISTMAS Christmas, Stephen Randall b: 12/9/57, Orlando, Fla. BL/TR, 6', 190 lbs. Deb: 9/1/83

YEAR	TM/L	G	AB	R	H	2B	3B	HR	RBI	BB	SO	AVG	OBP	SLG	OPS	OPS+	BR+	SB	CS	SBR	FA	FR	G/POS	TPR
1983	Cin-N	9	17	0	1	0	0	0	1	1	3	.059	.111	.059	170	-50	-3	0	0	0	1.000	-0	/C-7	-0.4
1984	Chi-A	12	11	1	4	0	0	1	4	0	2	.364	.364	.727	1091	185	1	0	0	0	1.000	0	/C-1	0.1
1986	Chi-N	3	9	0	1	1	0	0	2	0	1	.111	.111	.222	333	-10	-1	0	0	0	1.000	-0	/C-1,1-1	-0.2
Total	3	24	37	1	6	2	0	1	7	1	6	.162	.184	.297	482	30	-4	0	0	0	1.000	-0	/C-9,1-1	-0.5

■ JOE CHRISTOPHER Christopher, Joseph O'Neal b: 12/13/35, Frederiksted, V.I. BR/TR, 5'10", 176 lbs. Deb: 5/26/59

YEAR	TM/L	G	AB	R	H	2B	3B	HR	RBI	BB	SO	AVG	OBP	SLG	OPS	OPS+	BR+	SB	CS	SBR	FA	FR	G/POS	TPR
1959	Pit-N	15	12	6	0	0	0	0	0	1	4	.000	.077	.000	77	-78	-3	0	0	0	1.000	-3	/O-9(0-0-9)	-0.6
1960	*Pit-N	50	56	21	13	2	0	1	3	5	8	.232	.295	.321	617	68	-2	1	0	0	1.000	-2	O-17(11-5-1)	-0.5
1961	Pit-N	76	186	25	49	7	3	0	14	18	24	.263	.328	.333	662	76	-6	6	4	-0	.978	-2	O-55(45-5-5)	-1.1
1962	NY-N	119	271	36	66	10	2	6	32	35	42	.244	.339	.362	700	87	-4	11	3	1	.972	-9	O-94(19-34-42)	-1.6
1963	NY-N	64	149	19	33	5	1	1	8	13	21	.221	.297	.289	586	68	-6	1	3	-1	.983	-5	O-45(6-0-40)	-1.5
1964	NY-N	154	543	78	163	26	8	16	76	48	92	.300	.363	.466	829	135	25	6	5	-0	.974	1	*O-145(7-10-129)	1.6
1965	NY-N	148	437	38	109	18	3	5	40	35	82	.249	.314	.339	652	87	-7	4	4	-1	.989	-3	*O-112(62-0-51)	-1.9
1966	Bos-A	12	13	1	1	0	0	0	0	2	4	.077	.200	.077	277	-15	-2	0	0	0	1.000	-1	/O-2(2-0-0)	-0.3
Total	8	638	1667	224	434	68	17	29	173	157	277	.260	.331	.374	705	96	-6	29	19	-0	.979	-24	O-479(152-54-277)	-5.9

■ LOYD CHRISTOPHER Christopher, Loyd Eugene b: 12/31/19, Richmond, Cal. d: 9/5/91, Richmond, Cal. BR/TR, 6'2", 190 lbs. Deb: 4/20/45 F

YEAR	TM/L	G	AB	R	H	2B	3B	HR	RBI	BB	SO	AVG	OBP	SLG	OPS	OPS+	BR+	SB	CS	SBR	FA	FR	G/POS	TPR
1945	Bos-A	8	14	4	4	0	0	0	4	3	2	.286	.412	.286	697	101	0	0	0	0	1.000	-1	/O-3(0-3-0)	-0.1
	Chi-N	1	0	0	0	0	0	0	0	0	0	—	—	—	—	—	0	0			.000	-0	/O-1(1-0-0)	0.0
1947	Chi-A	7	23	1	5	0	1	0	0	2	4	.217	.280	.304	584	65	-1	0	1	-0	1.000	1	/O-7(7-0-0)	-0.1
Total	2	16	37	5	9	0	1	0	4	5	6	.243	.333	.297	631	80	-1	0	1		1.000	0	/O-11(8-3-0)	-0.2

YEAR	TM/L	G	AB	R	H	2B	3B	HR	RBI	BB	SO	AVG	OBP	SLG	OPS	OPS+	BR+	SB	CS	SBR	FA	FR	G/POS	TPR
■ HI CHURCH	Church, Hiram Lincoln b: 11/23/1863, Central Square, N.Y. d: 2/23/26, Jacksonville, Fla. Deb: 8/23/1890																							
1890	Bro-a	3	9	1	1	0	0	0	0	0		.111	.111	.111	222	-36	-2	0			1.000	-1	/O-3(3-0-0)	-0.3
■ JOHN CHURRY	Churry, John b: 11/26/1900, Johnstown, Pa. d: 2/8/70, Zanesville, Ohio BR/TR, 5'9", 172 lbs. Deb: 5/24/24																							
1924	Chi-N	6	7	0	1	1	0	0	0	2	0	.143	.333	.286	619	67	-0	0	0	0	1.000	0	/C-3	0.0
1925	Chi-N	3	6	1	3	0	0	0	1	0	0	.500	.500	.500	1000	154	0	0	0	0	1.000	-0	/C-3	0.0
1926	Chi-N	2	4	0	0	0	0	0	0	1	2	.000	.200	.000	200	-42	-1	0			1.000	0	/C-1	-0.1
1927	Chi-N	1	1	0	1	0	0	0	0	0	0	1.000	1.000	1.000	2000	436	0	0			1.000	0	/C-1	0.1
Total	4	12	18	1	5	1	0	0	1	3	2	.278	.381	.333	714	89	-0	0	0		1.000	0	/C-8	0.0
■ LARRY CIAFFONE	Ciaffone, Lawrence Thomas "Symphony Larry" b: 8/17/24, Brooklyn, N.Y. d: 12/14/91, Brooklyn, N.Y. BR/TR, 5'9.5", 185 lbs. Deb: 4/17/51																							
1951	StL-N	5	5	0	0	0	0	0	0	1	2	.000	.167	.000	167	-51	-1	0	0	0	1.000	-0	/O-1(1-0-0)	-0.1
■ ARCHI CIANFROCCO	Cianfrocco, Angelo Dominic b: 10/6/66, Rome, N.Y. BR/TR, 6'5", 215 lbs. Deb: 4/8/92																							
1992	Mon-N	86	232	25	56	5	2	6	30	11	66	.241	.279	.358	636	80	-7	3	0	1	.993	1	1-56,3-19/O-5(5-0-0)	-0.9
1993	Mon-N	12	17	3	4	1	0	1	1	0	5	.235	.235	.471	706	80	-1	0	0	0	1.000	-0	1-11	-0.1
	SD-N	84	279	27	68	10	2	11	47	17	64	.244	.294	.412	707	85	-7	2	0	0	.932	-5	3-64,1-31	-1.3
	Yr	96	296	30	72	11	2	12	48	17	69	.243	.291	.416	707	85	-7	2	0	0	.932	-6	3-64,1-42	-1.4
1994	SD-N	59	146	9	32	8	0	4	13	3	39	.219	.255	.356	611	59	-9	2	0	0	.920	2	3-37,1-16/S-1	-0.7
1995	SD-N	51	118	22	31	7	0	5	31	11	28	.263	.336	.449	785	109	1	0	2	-1	1.000	-2	1-30,S-15/O-7R,23	-0.1
1996	*SD-N	79	192	21	54	13	3	2	32	8	56	.281	.317	.411	728	96	-2	1	0	0	1.000	-8	1-33,3-11,S-10,/O2C	-1.1
1997	SD-N	89	220	25	54	12	0	4	26	25	80	.245	.331	.355	685	86	-4	7	1	1	.983	10	1-39,3-38,2-12,/SO	0.6
1998	SD-N	40	72	4	9	3	0	1	5	5	22	.125	.192	.208	401	6	-10	1	0	0	1.000	1	1-19,3-13/2-3,O-3R	-1.0
Total	7	500	1276	136	308	59	7	34	185	80	360	.241	.294	.379	673	81	-38	16	3	2	.994	-1	1-235,3-185/S-31,O2C	-4.6
■ DARRYL CIAS	Cias, Darryl Richard b: 4/23/57, New York, N.Y. BR/TR, 5'11", 190 lbs. Deb: 4/27/83																							
1983	Oak-A	19	18	1	6	1	0	0	1	2	4	.333	.400	.389	789	126	1	1	0	0	.967	-0	C-19	0.1
■ JOE CICERO	Cicero, Joseph Francis "Dode" b: 11/18/10, Atlantic City, N.J d: 3/30/83, Clearwater, Fla. BR/TR, 5'8", 167 lbs. Deb: 9/20/29																							
1929	Bos-A	10	32	6	10	2	2	0	4	0	2	.313	.313	.500	813	108	0	0	0	0	1.000	-1	/O-7(1-6-0)	-0.1
1930	Bos-A	18	30	5	5	1	2	0	4	1	5	.167	.194	.333	527	32	-3	0	0	0	.000	-2	/O-5(1-0-4),3-2	-0.5
1945	Phi-A	12	19	3	3	0	0	0	0	1	6	.158	.238	.158	396	16	-2	0	0	0	1.000	-2	/O-7(1-0-6)	-0.5
Total	3	40	81	14	18	3	4	0	8	2	13	.222	.250	.358	608	60	-5	0	0	0	1.000	-4	/O-19(3-6-10),3-2	-1.1
■ TED CIESLAK	Cieslak, Thaddeus Walter b: 11/22/12, Milwaukee, Wis. d: 5/9/93, Milwaukee, Wis. BR/TR, 5'10", 175 lbs. Deb: 4/18/44																							
1944	Phi-N	85	220	18	54	10	0	2	11	21	17	.245	.314	.318	632	81	-5	1			.877	-15	3-48/O-5(5-0-0)	-2.1
■ AL CIHOCKI	Cihocki, Albert Joseph b: 5/7/24, Nanticoke, Pa. BR/TR, 5'11", 185 lbs. Deb: 4/17/45																							
1945	Cle-A	92	283	21	60	9	3	0	24	11	48	.212	.241	.265	507	49	-19	2	1	0	.946	1	S-41,3-29,2-23	-1.5
■ ED CIHOCKI	Cihocki, Edward Joseph "Cy" b: 5/9/07, Wilmington, Del. d: 11/9/87, Newark, Del. BR/TR, 5'8", 163 lbs. Deb: 5/29/32																							
1932	Phi-A	1	1	0	0	0	0	0	0	0	0	.000	.000	.000	0	-97	-0	0	0	0	.000	0	H	0.0
1933	Phi-A	33	97	6	14	2	3	0	9	7	16	.144	.202	.227	429	13	-12	0	0	0	.904	-2	S-28/2-1,3-1	-1.2
Total	2	34	98	6	14	2	3	0	9	7	16	.143	.200	.224	424	12	-13	0	0	0	.904	-2	/S-28,3-1,2-1	-1.2
■ GINO CIMOLI	Cimoli, Gino Nicholas (b: Gino Anichletto Cimoli) b: 12/18/29, San Francisco, Cal. BR/TR, 6'2", 200 lbs. Deb: 4/19/56																							
1956	*Bro-N	73	36	3	4	1	0	0	4	1	8	.111	.135	.139	274	-24	-6	1	0	0	.946	-18	O-62(52-8-3)	-2.6
1957	Bro-N★	142	532	88	156	22	5	10	57	39	86	.293	.346	.410	756	93	-4	3	1	0	.979	-3	*O-138(81-24-51)	-1.4
1958	LA-N	109	325	35	80	6	3	9	27	18	49	.246	.292	.366	658	71	-14	3	3	-0	.974	-8	*O-104(34-68-12)	-2.7
1959	StL-N	143	519	61	145	40	7	8	72	37	83	.279	.330	.430	759	94	-4	7	0	2	.979	5	*O-141(43-45-55)	-0.5
1960	*Pit-N	101	307	36	82	14	4	0	28	32	43	.267	.338	.339	677	85	-5	1	0	0	.964	-7	O-91(27-58-17)	-1.7
1961	Pit-N	21	67	4	20	3	1	0	6	2	13	.299	.319	.373	692	83	-2	0	0	0	.971	-0	O-19(14-5-0)	-0.3
	Mil-N	37	117	12	23	5	0	3	4	11	15	.197	.266	.316	582	57	-7	1	0	0	.985	-3	O-31(0-30-1)	-1.1
	Yr	58	184	16	43	8	1	3	10	13	28	.234	.284	.337	621	67	-9	1	0	0	.980	-3	O-50(14-35-1)	-1.4
1962	KC-A	152	550	67	151	20	**15**	10	71	40	89	.275	.326	.420	746	95	-5	2	1	0	.968	-9	*O-147(5-10-138)	-2.3
1963	KC-A	145	529	56	139	19	11	4	48	39	72	.263	.316	.363	679	85	-10	3	1	0	.985	2	*O-136(2-13-130)	-1.8
1964	KC-A	4	9	1	0	0	0	0	0	0	1	.000	.000	.000	0	-97	-2	0	0	0	1.000	-0	/O-4(1-0-3)	-0.3
	Bal-A	38	58	6	8	3	2	0	3	2	13	.138	.167	.259	425	16	-7	0	0	0	.893	-9	O-35(11-2-23)	-1.8
	Yr	42	67	7	8	3	2	0	3	2	14	.119	.145	.224	369	1	-9	0	0	0	.912	-9	O-39(12-2-26)	-2.1
1965	Cal-A	4	5	1	0	0	0	0	1	0	2	.000	.000	.000	0	-99	-1	0	0	0	1.000	0	/O-1(0-0-1)	-0.1
Total	10	969	3054	370	808	133	48	44	321	221	474	.265	.317	.383	700	84	-69	21	6	3	.974	-50	O-909(270-263-434)	-16.6
■ FRANK CIPRIANI	Cipriani, Frank Dominick b: 4/14/41, Buffalo, N.Y. BR/TR, 6', 180 lbs. Deb: 9/8/61																							
1961	KC-A	13	36	2	9	0	0	0	2	2	4	.250	.289	.250	539	45	-3	0	0	0	1.000	-1	O-11(0-0-11)	-0.4
■ JEFF CIRILLO	Cirillo, Jeffrey Howard b: 9/23/69, Pasadena, Cal. BR/TR, 6'2", 190 lbs. Deb: 5/11/94																							
1994	Mil-A	39	126	17	30	9	0	3	12	11	16	.238	.309	.381	690	73	-5	0	1	-0	.965	-1	3-37/2-1	-0.6
1995	Mil-A	125	328	57	91	19	4	9	39	47	42	.277	.375	.442	817	106	3	7	2	1	.938	15	*3-108,2-25/1-3,S-2	1.9
1996	Mil-A	158	566	101	184	46	5	15	83	58	69	.325	.395	.504	898	120	18	4	9	-2	.950	-11	*3-154/1-2,2-1,D-3	0.6
1997	Mil-A★	154	580	74	167	46	2	10	82	60	74	.288	.369	.426	794	106	6	4	3	-0	.963	18	*3-150/D-2	2.4
1998	Mil-N	156	604	97	194	31	1	14	68	79	88	.321	.403	.445	849	123	23	10	4	1	.976	24	*3-149/1-6	4.7
1999	Mil-N	157	607	98	198	35	1	15	88	75	83	.326	.405	.461	866	120	21	7	4	0	.967	16	*3-155	3.5
2000	Col-N★	157	598	111	195	53	2	11	115	67	72	.326	.399	.477	876	94	-3	3	4	-1	.964	7	*3-155	0.4
Total	7	946	3409	555	1059	239	15	77	487	397	444	.311	.389	.457	847	110	63	35	27	-2	.962	68	3-908/2-27,1-11,DS	12.9
■ GEORGE CISAR	Cisar, George Joseph b: 8/25/12, Chicago, Ill. BR/TR, 6', 175 lbs. Deb: 9/9/37																							
1937	Bro-N	20	29	8	6	0	0	0	4	2	6	.207	.258	.207	465	27	-3	3			1.000	-3	O-13(9-0-4)	-0.6
■ BILL CISSELL	Cissell, Chalmer William b: 1/3/04, Perryville, Mo. d: 3/15/49, Chicago, Ill. BR/TR, 5'11", 170 lbs. Deb: 4/11/28																							
1928	Chi-A	125	443	66	115	22	3	1	60	29	41	.260	.307	.330	636	68	-21	18	6	2	.938	-2	*S-123	-0.7
1929	Chi-A	152	618	83	173	27	12	5	62	28	53	.280	.312	.387	699	80	-20	25	17	-0	.937	-3	*S-152	-0.7
1930	Chi-A	141	562	82	152	28	9	2	48	28	32	.270	.307	.363	670	72	-25	16	9	0	.948	-11	*2-107,3-24,S-10	-2.7
1931	Chi-A	109	409	42	90	13	5	1	46	16	26	.220	.256	.284	540	44	-34	18	6	2	.944	-10	S-83,2-23/3-1	-3.3
1932	Chi-A	12	43	7	11	1	1	1	5	1	0	.256	.273	.395	668	76	-2	0	0	0	.928	0	S-12	-0.1
	Cle-A	131	541	78	173	35	6	6	93	28	25	.320	.354	.440	794	98	-2	18	15	-1	.964	11	*2-129/S-6	1.5
	Yr	143	584	85	184	36	7	7	98	29	25	.315	.349	.437	785	97	-4	18	15	-1	.964	11	*2-129,S-18	1.4
1933	Cle-A	112	409	53	94	21	3	6	33	31	29	.230	.284	.340	624	62	-23	6	6	-1	.947	-7	2-62,S-46/3-1	-2.3
1934	Bos-A	102	416	71	111	13	4	4	44	28	23	.267	.315	.346	661	66	-22	11	4	1	.959	-4	2-96/S-7,3-2	-1.7
1937	Phi-A	34	117	15	31	7	0	1	14	17	10	.265	.358	.350	709	81	-3	0	0	0	.962	3	2-33	0.2
1938	NY-N	38	149	19	40	6	0	2	18	6	11	.268	.297	.349	646	76	-5	1			.977	9	2-33/3-6	0.6
Total	9	956	3707	516	990	173	43	29	423	212	250	.267	.308	.360	669	73	-157	113	63		.958	-14	2-483,S-439/3-34	-9.2
■ MOOSE CLABAUGH	Clabaugh, John William b: 11/13/01, Albany, Mo. d: 7/11/84, Tucson, Ariz. BL/TR, 6', 185 lbs. Deb: 8/30/26																							
1926	Bro-N	11	14	2	1	1	0	0	1	0	1	.071	.133	.143	276	-26	-3	0			.600	-1	/O-2(2-0-0)	-0.3
■ BOBBY CLACK	Clack, Robert S. "Gentlemanly Bob" (b: Robert S. Clark) b: 6/1850, England d: 10/22/33, Danvers, Mass. BR/TR, 5'9", 153 lbs. Deb: 5/13/1874																							
1874	Atl-n	33	135	22	23	1	0	0	13	4	2	.170	.194	.178	372	23	-10	0	0	0	.779	-1	O-31(1-30-0)/1-2	-0.8
1875	Atl-n	17	59	1	6	0	0	0	1	0	3	.102	.102	.102	203	-33	-7	0	0	0	.867	3	O-17(0-16-1)/1-1	-0.4
1876	Cin-N	32	123	10	19	0	1	0	5	5	12	.154	.195	.178	373	29	-7				.736	0	O-17R/2-8,1-5,3P	-0.6
Total	2 n	50	194	23	29	1	0	0	14	4	5	.149	.167	.155	321	7	-17	0	0	0	.811	2	/O-48(1-46-1),1-3	-1.2
■ DANNY CLAIRE	Claire, David Matthew b: 11/17/1897, Ludington, Mich. d: 1/7/56, Las Vegas, Nev. BR/TR, 5'8", 164 lbs. Deb: 9/17/20																							
1920	Det-A	3	7	1	1	0	0	0	0	0	0	.143	.143	.143	286	-25	-1	0	0	0	.800	-0	/S-3	-0.2

YEAR	TM/L	G	AB	R	H	2B	3B	HR	RBI	BB	SO	AVG	OBP	SLG	OPS	OPS+	BR+	SB	CS	SBR	FA	FR	G/POS	TPR
■ AL CLANCY	Clancy, Albert Harrison b: 8/14/1888, Santa Fe, N.Mex. d: 10/17/51, Las Cruces, N.Mex. BR/TR, 5'10.5", 175 lbs. Deb: 6/20/11																							
1911	StL-A	3	5	0	0	0	0	0	0	0	3	.000	.167	.000	167	-54	-1	0			.800	0	/3-2	-0.1
■ BUD CLANCY	Clancy, John William b: 9/15/1900, Odell, Ill. d: 9/26/68, Ottumwa, Iowa BL/TL, 6', 170 lbs. Deb: 8/29/24																							
1924	Chi-A	13	35	5	9	1	0	0	6	3	2	.257	.316	.286	602	58	-2	3	2	-0	.947	-2	/1-8	-0.4
1925	Chi-A	4	3	0	0	0	0	0	0	1	0	.000	.250	.000	250	-34	-1	0	0	0	.000	0	H	-0.1
1926	Chi-A	12	38	3	13	2	2	0	7	1	1	.342	.375	.500	875	132	2	0	0	0	.991	0	1-10	0.1
1927	Chi-A	130	464	46	139	21	2	3	53	24	24	.300	.337	.373	710	86	-10	4	3	-0	.991	0	*1-123	-1.7
1928	Chi-A	130	487	64	132	19	11	2	37	42	25	.271	.331	.368	699	85	-11	6	9	-2	.991	5	*1-128	-1.6
1929	Chi-A	92	290	36	82	14	6	3	45	16	19	.283	.320	.403	724	86	-7	3	1	0	.991	2	1-74	-0.8
1930	Chi-A	68	234	28	57	8	3	3	27	12	18	.244	.286	.342	628	61	-14	3	1	0	.995	-3	1-60	-2.0
1932	Bro-N	53	196	14	60	4	2	0	16	6	13	.306	.327	.347	674	83	-5	0			.996	3	1-53	-0.7
1934	Phi-N	20	49	8	12	0	0	1	7	6	4	.245	.339	.306	645	65	-2	0			1.000	-1	1-10	-0.4
Total	9	522	1796	204	504	69	26	12	198	111	106	.281	.325	.368	693	82	-50	19	16		.992	4	1-466	-7.6
■ BILL CLANCY	Clancy, William Edward b: 4/12/1879, Redfield, N.Y. d: 2/10/48, Oriskany, N.Y. BR/TR, 6'2", 180 lbs. Deb: 4/14/05																							
1905	Pit-N	56	227	23	52	11	3	2	34	4		.229	.246	.330	576	69	-10	3			.983	-4	1-52/O-4(0-0-4)	-1.5
■ UKE CLANTON	Clanton, Eucal "Cat" b: 2/19/1898, Powell, Mo. d: 2/24/60, Antlers, Okla. BL/TL, 5'8", 165 lbs. Deb: 9/21/22																							
1922	Cle-A	1	1	0	0	0	0	0	0	0	1	.000	.000	.000	0	-99	-0	0	0	0	.500	-0	/1-1	-0.1
■ CHRIS CLAPINSKI	Clapinski, Christopher Alan b: 8/20/71, Buffalo, N.Y. BB/TR, 6', 175 lbs. Deb: 7/17/99																							
1999	Fla-N	36	56	6	13	1	2	0	2	9	12	.232	.348	.321	670	75	-2	1	0	0	.882	-0	/3-9,S-6,O-3L,2D	-0.2
2000	Fla-N	34	49	12	15	4	1	1	7	5	7	.306	.370	.490	860	121	2	0	0	0	.933	3	2-14/3-3,O-3L,S-1	0.5
Total	2	70	105	18	28	5	3	1	9	14	19	.267	.358	.400	758	97	-0	1	0	0	.935	3	/2-16,3-12,S-7,OD	0.3
■ AARON CLAPP	Clapp, Aaron Bronson b: 7/1856, Ithaca, N.Y. d: 1/13/14, Sayre, Pa. TR, 5'8", 175 lbs. Deb: 5/1/1879 F																							
1879	Tro-N	36	146	24	39	9	3	0	18	6	10	.267	.296	.370	666	126	5				.935	-4	1-25,O-11(7-1-3)	-0.1
■ JOHN CLAPP	Clapp, John Edgar b: 7/17/1851, Ithaca, N.Y. d: 12/18/04, Ithaca, N.Y. BR/TR, 5'7", 194 lbs. Deb: 4/26/1872 FM NA OF: (0-LF 3-CF 14-RF) Career OF: (62-LF 19-CF 21-RF)																							
1872	Man-n	19	97	28	28	6	1	1	10	1	0	.289	.296	.402	698	119	3	2	1	0	.856	-1	C-19/S-2,1-1,O-1C,M	0.1
1873	Ath-n	45	204	36	62	10	2	1	28	2	2	.304	.311	.387	698	99	-2	4	5	-1	**.908**	3	*C-43/S-6,2-1,O-1C	0.0
1874	Ath-n	39	165	46	48	7	4	3	19	1	1	.291	.295	.436	732	121	3	2	0	0	.861	7	C-27,O-15(0-1-14)/S-1	0.8
1875	Ath-n	60	292	65	77	8	7	0	39	7	1	.264	.281	.339	620	103	-1	9	5	0	.874	18	*C-60	1.5
1876	StL-N	64	306	60	91	4	2	0	29	8	2	.297	.324	.332	656	125	9				.874	9	*C-61/O-4(0-1-3),2-1	1.7
1877	StL-N	60	255	47	81	6	6	0	34	8	6	.318	.338	.388	727	135	11				.887	-6	*C-53,O-10(2-0-9)/1-1	0.5
1878	Ind-N	63	263	42	80	10	2	0	29	13	8	.304	.337	.357	694	148	15				.890	-7	*O-44L,1-12/C-9,S2M	0.5
1879	Buf-N	70	292	47	77	12	5	1	36	11	11	.264	.290	.349	640	107	2				.906	-9	*C-63/O-7(0-0-7),M	-0.5
1880	Cin-N	80	323	33	91	16	4	1	20	21	10	.282	.326	.365	691	135	12				.897	17	*C-73,O-10(1-9-0),M	3.0
1881	Cle-N	68	261	47	66	12	2	0	25	**35**	6	.253	.341	.314	655	113	6				.890	-5	C-48,O-21(15-6-0),M	0.2
1883	NY-N	20	73	6	13	0	0	0	5	5	4	.178	.231	.178	409	27	-6				.895	5	C-16/O-5(0-3-2),M	0.0
Total	4 n	163	758	175	215	31	14	5	96	11	4	.284	.294	.381	675	107	3	17	11	-0	.878	27	C-149/O-17R,S-9,21	2.4
Total	7	425	1773	282	499	60	21	2	178	101	47	.281	.322	.344	665	122	49				.892	4	C-323,O-101L/1-13,S2	5.4
■ DENNY CLARE	Clare, Dennis J. b: 1/1853, Brooklyn, N.Y. d: 11/26/28, Brooklyn, N.Y. Deb: 9/14/1872																							
1872	Atl-n	2	7	1	1	0	0	0	0	0	0	.143	.143	.143	286	-10	-1	0	0	0	.857	-3	/2-2,S-1	-0.3
■ DOUG CLAREY	Clarey, Douglas William b: 4/20/54, Los Angeles, Cal. BR/TR, 6', 180 lbs. Deb: 4/20/76																							
1976	StL-N	9	4	2	1	0	0	1	2	0	1	.250	.250	1.000	1250	240	1	0	0	0	1.000	0	/2-7	0.1
■ ALLIE CLARK	Clark, Alfred Aloysius b: 6/16/23, S.Amboy, N.J. BR/TR, 5'11", 185 lbs. Deb: 8/5/47 Career OF: (62-LF 3-CF 178-RF)																							
1947	*NY-A	24	67	9	25	5	0	1	14	5	2	.373	.417	.493	909	154	5	0	0	0	1.000	0	O-16(6-0-10)	0.4
1948	*Cle-A	81	271	43	84	5	2	9	38	23	13	.310	.364	.443	807	117	6	0	2	-1	.982	-6	O-65(21-0-44)/3-5,1-1	-0.4
1949	Cle-A	35	74	8	13	4	0	1	9	4	7	.176	.218	.270	488	29	-8	0	0	0	1.000	-4	O-17(1-0-16)/1-1	-1.3
1950	Cle-A	59	163	19	35	6	1	6	21	11	10	.215	.264	.374	639	64	-10	0	1	-0	.987	-3	O-41(25-0-17)	-1.5
1951	Cle-A	3	10	3	3	2	0	1	3	1	2	.300	.364	.800	1164	221	1	0	0	0	1.000	-1	/O-3(0-0-3)	0.1
	Phi-A	56	161	20	40	10	1	4	22	15	7	.248	.320	.398	718	91	-2	2	0	0	.984	-1	O-32(1-1-30),3-10	-0.4
	Yr	59	171	23	43	12	1	5	25	16	9	.251	.323	.421	744	98	-1	2	0	0	.985	-1	O-35(1-1-33),3-10	-0.3
1952	Phi-A	71	186	23	51	12	0	7	29	10	19	.274	.315	.452	766	105	0	0	2	-1	.988	-3	O-48(7-2-39)/1-2	-0.5
1953	Phi-A	20	74	6	15	4	0	3	13	3	5	.203	.234	.378	612	61	-4	0	0	0	1.000	-0	O-19(0-0-19)	-0.6
	Chi-A	9	15	0	1	0	0	0	0	0	5	.067	.067	.067	133	-62	-3	0	0	0	1.000	-0	/1-1,O-1(1-0-0)	-0.4
	Yr	29	89	6	16	4	0	3	13	3	10	.180	.207	.326	532	40	-8	0	0	0	1.000	-1	O-20(1-0-19)/1-1	-1.0
Total	7	358	1021	131	267	48	4	32	149	72	70	.262	.312	.410	722	92	-16	2	5	-1	.988	-19	O-242R/3-15,1-5	-4.6
■ DAD CLARK	Clark, Alfred Robert "Fred" b: 7/16/1873, San Francisco, Cal. d: 7/26/56, Ogden, Utah BL/TL, 5'11", 170 lbs. Deb: 7/3/02																							
1902	Chi-N	12	43	1	8	1	0	0	2	4		.186	.255	.209	465	45	-3	1			.938	-1	1-12	-0.5
■ TONY CLARK	Clark, Anthony Christopher b: 6/15/72, Newton, Kan. BB/TR, 6'7", 240 lbs. Deb: 9/3/95																							
1995	Det-A	27	101	10	24	5	1	3	11	8	30	.238	.294	.396	690	78	-4	0	0	0	.985	-1	1-27	-0.6
1996	Det-A	100	376	56	94	14	0	27	72	29	127	.250	.304	.503	806	99	-3	0	1	-0	.993	-2	1-86,D-12	-1.3
1997	Det-A	159	580	105	160	28	3	32	117	93	144	.276	.379	.500	879	128	25	1	3	-1	.993	-2	*1-158/D-1	0.6
1998	Det-A	157	602	84	175	37	0	34	103	63	128	.291	.361	.522	882	125	21	3	3	-0	.991	1	*1-142,D-15	0.7
1999	Det-A	143	536	74	150	29	0	31	99	64	133	.280	.363	.507	870	120	15	2	1	0	.992	2	*1-132,D-12	0.4
2000	Det-A	60	208	32	57	14	0	13	37	24	51	.274	.349	.529	878	122	6	0	0	0	.993	4	1-58/D-1	0.4
Total	6	646	2403	361	660	127	4	140	439	281	613	.275	.353	.506	859	118	62	6	8	-1	.992	2	1-603/D-41	0.2
■ EARL CLARK	Clark, Bailey Earl b: 11/6/07, Washington, D.C. d: 1/16/38, Washington, D.C. BR/TR, 5'10", 160 lbs. Deb: 8/17/27																							
1927	Bos-N	13	44	6	12	1	0	0	3	2	4	.273	.304	.295	600	66	-2	0			1.000	-1	O-13(10-3-0)	-0.4
1928	Bos-N	28	112	18	34	9	1	0	10	4	8	.304	.339	.402	741	98	-1	0			.987	-1	O-27(0-27-0)	-0.2
1929	Bos-N	84	279	43	88	13	3	1	30	12	30	.315	.346	.394	740	86	-6	6			.978	4	O-74(4-70-1)	-0.5
1930	Bos-N	82	233	29	69	11	3	3	28	7	22	.296	.320	.408	727	77	-9	3			.977	1	O-63(1-40-22)	-1.0
1931	Bos-N	16	50	8	11	2	0	0	4	7	4	.220	.316	.260	576	58	-3	1			.970	1	O-14(14-0-0)	-0.3
1932	Bos-N	50	44	11	11	2	0	0	4	2	7	.250	.283	.295	578	58	-3	1			1.000	-2	O-16(6-3-6)	-0.5
1933	Bos-N	7	23	3	8	1	0	0	1	2	1	.348	.400	.391	791	138	1	0			1.000	-1	/O-6(3-3-0)	0.0
1934	StL-A	13	41	4	7	2	0	0	1	1	3	.171	.190	.220	410	5	-6	0	0	0	1.000	1	/O-9(2-0-7)	-0.6
Total	8	293	826	122	240	41	7	4	81	37	79	.291	.324	.372	696	78	-28	11	0		.981	2	O-222(40-146-36)	-3.5
■ BRADY CLARK	Clark, Brady William b: 4/18/73, Portland, Ore. BR/TR, 6'2", 195 lbs. Deb: 9/3/2000																							
2000	Cin-N	11	11	1	3	1	0	0	2	0	2	.273	.273	.364	636	56	-1	0	0	0	1.000	-1	/O-5(2-0-3)	-0.1
■ DANNY CLARK	Clark, Daniel Curran b: 1/18/1894, Meridian, Miss. d: 5/23/37, Meridian, Miss. BL/TR, 5'9", 167 lbs. Deb: 4/12/22 Career OF: (0-LF 0-CF 14-RF)																							
1922	Det-A	83	185	31	54	11	3	3	26	15	11	.292	.345	.432	777	105	1	1	0	0	.945	-6	2-38/O-5(0-0-5),3-1	-0.4
1924	Bos-A	104	325	36	90	23	3	2	54	51	19	.277	.378	.385	763	97	-0	4	7	-2	.943	-6	3-94	-0.2
1927	StL-N	58	72	8	17	2	2	0	13	8	7	.236	.313	.319	632	67	-3	0			.929	1	/O-9(0-0-9)	-0.3
Total	3	245	582	75	161	36	8	5	93	74	37	.277	.360	.392	752	96	-3	5	7		.943	-11	/3-95,2-38,O-14R	-0.9
■ DAVE CLARK	Clark, David Earl b: 9/3/62, Tupelo, Miss. BL/TR, 6'2", 210 lbs. Deb: 9/3/86 Career OF: (215-LF 1-CF 228-RF)																							
1986	Cle-A	18	58	10	16	1	0	3	9	7	11	.276	.354	.448	802	119	2	1	0	0	1.000	1	O-10(0-0-10)/D-7	0.2
1987	Cle-A	29	87	11	18	5	0	3	12	2	24	.207	.225	.368	593	53	-6	1	0	0	1.000	0	O-13(1-0-12),D-12	-0.6
1988	Cle-A	63	156	11	41	4	1	3	18	17	28	.263	.335	.359	694	92	-1	0	2	-1	.947	-4	D-27,O-23(10-1-15)	-0.8
1989	Cle-A	102	253	21	60	12	0	8	29	30	63	.237	.318	.379	697	94	-2	0	2	-1	.964	-5	D-55,O-21(12-0-11)	-1.0

YEAR	TM/L	G	AB	R	H	2B	3B	HR	RBI	BB	SO	AVG	OBP	SLG	OPS	OPS+	BR+	SB	CS	SBR	FA	FR	G/POS	TPR
1990	Chi-N	84	171	22	47	4	2	5	20	8	40	.275	.307	.409	717	89	-3	7	1	1	1.000	-2	O-39(39-0-0)	-0.5
1991	KC-A	11	10	1	2	0	0	0	1	1	1	.200	.273	.200	473	33	-1	0	0	0	.000	-0	/O-1(0-0-1),D-1	-0.1
1992	Pit-N	23	33	3	7	0	0	2	7	6	8	.212	.333	.394	727	106	0	0	0	0	1.000	-1	/O-8(1-0-7)	-0.1
1993	Pit-N	110	277	43	75	11	2	11	46	38	58	.271	.361	.444	805	114	6	1	0	0	.957	-11	O-91(40-0-53)	-0.7
1994	Pit-N	86	223	37	66	11	1	10	46	22	48	.296	.359	.489	848	117	5	2	2	-0	.974	2	O-57(10-0-48)	0.4
1995	Pit-N	77	196	30	55	6	0	4	24	24	38	.281	.362	.372	734	92	-1	3	3	-0	.961	-3	O-61(34-0-29)	-0.7
1996	Pit-N	92	211	28	58	12	2	8	35	31	51	.275	.368	.464	832	115	5	2	1	0	.988	-4	O-61(34-0-28)	-0.1
	*LA-N	15	15	0	3	0	0	0	1	3	2	.200	.333	.200	533	49	-1	0	0	0	.000	-0	/O-1(1-0-0)	-0.1
	Yr	107	226	28	61	12	2	8	36	34	53	.270	.365	.447	812	112	4	2	1	0	.988	-4	O-62(35-0-28)	-0.2
1997	Chi-N	102	143	19	43	8	0	5	32	19	34	.301	.390	.462	852	119	4	1	0	0	.953	0	O-25(24-0-1)/D-4	0.4
1998	*Hou-N	93	131	12	27	7	0	0	4	14	45	.206	.288	.260	547	47	-10	1	1	-0	.885	-3	O-22(9-0-13)/D-4	-1.4
Total	13	905	1964	248	518	81	8	62	284	222	451	.264	.340	.408	748	99	-3	19	12	-0	.969	-31	O-433R,D-110	-5.1

■ GLEN CLARK
Clark, Glen Ester b: 3/7/41, Austin, Tex. BB/TR, 6'1", 190 lbs. Deb: 6/3/67

YEAR	TM/L	G	AB	R	H	2B	3B	HR	RBI	BB	SO	AVG	OBP	SLG	OPS	OPS+	BR+	SB	CS	SBR	FA	FR	G/POS	TPR
1967	Atl-N	4	4	0	0	0	0	0	0	0	1	.000	.000	.000	0	-99	-1	0	0	0	.000	0	H	-0.1

■ PEP CLARK
Clark, Harry b: 3/20/1883, Union City, Ohio d: 6/8/65, Milwaukee, Wis. BR/TR, 5'7.5", 175 lbs. Deb: 9/11/03

YEAR	TM/L	G	AB	R	H	2B	3B	HR	RBI	BB	SO	AVG	OBP	SLG	OPS	OPS+	BR+	SB	CS	SBR	FA	FR	G/POS	TPR
1903	Chi-A	15	65	7	20	4	2	0	9	2		.308	.338	.431	769	135	3	5			.877	-0	3-15	0.3

■ JACK CLARK
Clark, Jack Anthony b: 11/10/55, New Brighton, Pa. BR/TR, 6'2", 205 lbs. Deb: 9/12/75 Career OF: (11-LF 23-CF 1014-RF)

YEAR	TM/L	G	AB	R	H	2B	3B	HR	RBI	BB	SO	AVG	OBP	SLG	OPS	OPS+	BR+	SB	CS	SBR	FA	FR	G/POS	TPR
1975	SF-N	8	17	3	4	0	0	0	2	1	2	.235	.278	.235	513	42	-1	1	0	0	1.000	-0	/O-3(1-2-1),3-2	-0.2
1976	SF-N	26	102	14	23	6	2	2	10	8	18	.225	.282	.382	664	85	-2	6	2	1	.987	1	O-26(5-20-8)	-0.2
1977	SF-N	136	413	64	104	17	4	13	51	49	73	.252	.334	.407	741	98	-1	12	4	1	.975	7	*O-114(0-1-113)	0.2
1978	SF-N★	156	592	90	181	46	8	25	98	50	72	.306	.363	.537	900	155	40	15	11	-1	.982	14	*O-152(0-0-152)	4.7
1979	SF-N★	143	527	84	144	25	2	26	86	63	95	.273	.352	.476	828	133	23	11	8	-0	.982	5	*O-140(0-0-140)/3-2	2.0
1980	SF-N	127	437	77	124	20	8	22	82	74	52	.284	.390	.517	907	155	33	2	5	-1	.967	10	*O-120(0-0-120)	2.8
1981	SF-N	99	385	60	103	19	2	17	53	45	45	.268	.346	.460	805	129	14	1	1	-0	.981	12	O-98(0-0-98)	2.2
1982	SF-N	157	563	90	154	30	3	27	103	90	91	.274	.375	.481	856	138	30	6	9	-2	.980	3	*O-155(0-0-155)	2.4
1983	SF-N	135	492	82	132	25	0	20	66	74	79	.268	.365	.441	806	126	18	5	3	0	.967	14	*O-133(0-0-133)/1-2	2.5
1984	SF-N	57	203	33	65	9	1	11	44	43	29	.320	.439	.537	976	179	23	1	1	-0	.990	1	O-54(0-0-55)/1-4	2.1
1985	*StL-N★	126	442	71	124	26	3	22	87	83	88	.281	.397	.502	899	151	32	1	4	-1	.988	-11	*1-121,O-12(0-0-12)	1.3
1986	StL-N	65	232	34	55	12	2	9	23	45	61	.237	.363	.422	786	117	6	1	1	-0	.995	-7	1-64	-0.5
1987	*StL-N★	131	419	93	120	23	1	35	106	**136**	139	.286	**.461**	**.597**	**1058**	**174**	52	1	2	-0	.989	-8	*1-126/O-1(0-0-1)	3.5
1988	NY-A	150	496	81	120	14	0	27	93	113	141	.242	.385	.433	818	130	24	3	2	-0	.951	-1	*D-112,O-19R,1-10	1.8
1989	SD-N	142	455	76	110	19	1	26	94	**132**	145	.242	.413	.459	873	149	36	6	2	1	.988	1	*1-131,O-12(0-0-12)	2.9
1990	SD-N	115	334	59	89	12	1	25	62	**104**	91	.266	.443	.533	976	166	36	4	3	-0	.994	-3	*1-109	2.6
1991	Bos-A	140	481	75	120	18	1	28	87	96	133	.249	.378	.466	843	126	19	0	2	-1	.000	0	*D-135	1.4
1992	Bos-A	81	257	32	54	11	0	5	33	56	87	.210	.356	.311	667	83	-4	1	1	-0	.992	-1	D-64,1-13	-0.8
Total	18	1994	6847	1118	1826	332	39	340	1180	1262	1441	.267	.383	.476	858	138	378	77	61	-4	.978	27	*O-1039R,1-580,D/3	30.7

■ JIM CLARK
Clark, James (b: James Petrosky) b: 9/21/27, Baggaley, Pa. d: 10/24/90, Santa Monica, Cal. BR/TR, 5'9", 150 lbs. Deb: 8/17/48

YEAR	TM/L	G	AB	R	H	2B	3B	HR	RBI	BB	SO	AVG	OBP	SLG	OPS	OPS+	BR+	SB	CS	SBR	FA	FR	G/POS	TPR
1948	Was-A	9	12	1	3	0	0	0	0	0	2	.250	.250	.250	500	34	-1	0	0	0	1.000	-0	/S-1,3-1	-0.1

■ JIM CLARK
Clark, James Edward b: 4/30/47, Kansas City, Kan. BR/TR, 6'1", 190 lbs. Deb: 7/16/71

YEAR	TM/L	G	AB	R	H	2B	3B	HR	RBI	BB	SO	AVG	OBP	SLG	OPS	OPS+	BR+	SB	CS	SBR	FA	FR	G/POS	TPR
1971	Cle-A	13	18	2	3	0	1	0	0	2	7	.167	.250	.278	528	45	-1	0	0	0	1.000	-0	/O-3(2-0-1),1-1	-0.1

■ JIM CLARK
Clark, James Francis b: 12/26/1887, Brooklyn, N.Y. d: 3/20/69, Beaumont, Tex. BR/TR, 5'11", 175 lbs. Deb: 9/2/11

YEAR	TM/L	G	AB	R	H	2B	3B	HR	RBI	BB	SO	AVG	OBP	SLG	OPS	OPS+	BR+	SB	CS	SBR	FA	FR	G/POS	TPR
1911	StL-N	14	18	2	3	0	1	0	3	3	4	.167	.286	.278	563	60	-1	2			1.000	-3	/O-8(1-6-1)	-0.4
1912	StL-N	2	1	0	0	0	0	0	0	0	1	.000	.000	.000	0	-99	-0	0			.000	0	H	0.0
Total	2	16	19	2	3	0	1	0	3	3	5	.158	.273	.263	536	51	-1	2			1.000	-3	/O-8(1-6-1)	-0.4

■ JERALD CLARK
Clark, Jerald Dwayne b: 8/10/63, Crockett, Tex. BR/TR, 6'4", 202 lbs. Deb: 9/19/88 F Career OF: (311-LF 11-CF 70-RF)

YEAR	TM/L	G	AB	R	H	2B	3B	HR	RBI	BB	SO	AVG	OBP	SLG	OPS	OPS+	BR+	SB	CS	SBR	FA	FR	G/POS	TPR
1988	SD-N	6	15	0	3	1	0	0	3	0	4	.200	.200	.267	467	33	-1	0	0	0	1.000	1	/O-4(4-0-0)	0.0
1989	SD-N	17	41	5	8	2	0	1	7	3	9	.195	.250	.317	567	61	-2	0	1	-0	.947	-1	O-14(10-0-4)	-0.4
1990	SD-N	53	101	12	27	4	1	5	11	5	24	.267	.302	.475	777	109	1	0	0	0	1.000	-1	1-15,O-13(5-0-9)	-0.1
1991	SD-N	118	369	26	84	16	0	10	47	31	90	.228	.298	.352	650	80	-10	2	1	0	.994	-3	O-96(85-0-13),1-16	-1.8
1992	SD-N	146	496	45	120	22	6	12	58	22	97	.242	.280	.383	663	85	-11	3	0	1	.990	12	*O-134(115-1-22),1-11	-0.3
1993	Col-N	140	478	65	135	26	6	13	67	20	60	.282	.325	.444	768	89	-8	9	6	-0	.966	2	O-96(80-0-17),1-37	-1.2
1995	Min-A	36	109	17	37	8	3	3	15	2	11	.339	.357	.550	908	132	4	3	0	1	1.000	-2	O-23L,1-11/D-3	0.3
Total	7	516	1609	170	414	79	16	44	208	83	295	.257	.302	.408	711	89	-27	17	8	1	.983	9	O-380L/1-90,D-3	-3.5

■ CAP CLARK
Clark, John Carrol b: 9/19/06, Snow Camp, N.C. d: 2/16/57, Fayetteville, N.C. BL/TR, 5'11", 180 lbs. Deb: 4/23/38

YEAR	TM/L	G	AB	R	H	2B	3B	HR	RBI	BB	SO	AVG	OBP	SLG	OPS	OPS+	BR+	SB	CS	SBR	FA	FR	G/POS	TPR
1938	Phi-N	52	74	11	19	1	1	0	4	9	10	.257	.337	.297	635	78	-2	0			.936	-3	C-29	-0.4

■ MEL CLARK
Clark, Melvin Earl b: 7/7/26, Letart, W.Va. BR/TR, 6', 180 lbs. Deb: 9/11/51

YEAR	TM/L	G	AB	R	H	2B	3B	HR	RBI	BB	SO	AVG	OBP	SLG	OPS	OPS+	BR+	SB	CS	SBR	FA	FR	G/POS	TPR
1951	Phi-N	10	31	2	10	1	0	1	3	0	3	.323	.323	.452	774	108	0	0	1	-0	1.000	-1	/O-7(1-0-6)	-0.1
1952	Phi-N	47	155	20	52	6	4	1	15	6	13	.335	.364	.445	809	125	5	2	1	0	1.000	4	O-38(12-0-27)/3-1	0.7
1953	Phi-N	60	198	31	59	10	4	0	19	11	17	.298	.338	.389	727	89	-3	1	0	0	.991	1	O-51(1-0-51)	-0.3
1954	Phi-N	83	233	26	56	9	7	1	24	17	21	.240	.292	.352	644	67	-12	0	1	-0	.961	2	O-63(21-0-42)	-1.2
1955	Phi-N	10	32	3	5	3	0	0	1	3	4	.156	.229	.250	479	27	-3	0	0	0	1.000	3	/O-8(0-0-8)	-0.1
1957	Det-A	5	7	0	0	0	0	0	1	0	3	.000	.000	.000	0	-97	-2	0	0	0	1.000	0	/O-2(2-0-0)	-0.2
Total	6	215	656	82	182	29	15	3	63	37	61	.277	.318	.381	699	85	-15	3	3	-0	.983	10	O-169(37-0-134)/3-1	-1.2

■ SPIDER CLARK
Clark, Owen F. b: 9/16/1867, Brooklyn, N.Y. d: 2/8/1892, Brooklyn, N.Y. TR, 5'10", 150 lbs. Deb: 5/2/1889 Career OF: (5-LF 4-CF 34-RF)

YEAR	TM/L	G	AB	R	H	2B	3B	HR	RBI	BB	SO	AVG	OBP	SLG	OPS	OPS+	BR+	SB	CS	SBR	FA	FR	G/POS	TPR
1889	Was-N	38	145	19	37	7	2	3	22	6	18	.255	.285	.393	678	94	-2	8			.887	6	C-14,S-13/O-9R,32	0.4
1890	Buf-P	69	260	45	69	11	1	2	25	20	16	.265	.325	.338	664	84	-5	8			.938	-4	O-34R,C-14,2/13SP	-0.6
Total	2	107	405	64	106	18	3	5	47	26	34	.262	.311	.358	669	88	-7	16			.952	2	/O-43R,C-28,2S13P	-0.2

■ PHIL CLARK
Clark, Phillip Benjamin b: 5/6/68, Crockett, Tex. BR/TR, 6', 200 lbs. Deb: 5/27/92 F Career OF: (52-LF 0-CF 50-RF)

YEAR	TM/L	G	AB	R	H	2B	3B	HR	RBI	BB	SO	AVG	OBP	SLG	OPS	OPS+	BR+	SB	CS	SBR	FA	FR	G/POS	TPR
1992	Det-A	23	54	3	22	4	0	1	5	6	9	.407	.467	.537	1004	179	6	1	0	0	.931	-1	O-13(4-0-9)/D-7	0.5
1993	SD-N	102	240	33	75	17	0	9	33	8	31	.313	.348	.496	844	121	6	2	0	0	.963	7	O-36L,1-24,C-11,/3	1.1
1994	SD-N	61	149	14	32	6	0	5	20	5	17	.215	.255	.356	610	59	-10	1	2	-0	.992	-2	1-24,O-17L/C-5,3-1	-1.4
1995	SD-N	75	97	12	21	3	0	2	7	8	18	.216	.283	.309	592	58	-6	0	2	-1	1.000	-8	O-34(14-0-21)/1-2	-1.5
1996	Bos-A	3	3	0	0	0	0	0	0	0	1	.000	.000	.000	0	-98	-1	0	0	0	1.000	0	/1-1,3-1,D-1	-0.1
Total	5	264	543	62	150	30	0	17	65	27	76	.276	.321	.425	747	97	-4	4	4	-1	.951	-3	O-100L/1-51,C-16,D3	-1.4

■ BOBBY CLARK
Clark, Robert Cale b: 6/13/55, Sacramento, Cal. BR/TR, 6', 190 lbs. Deb: 8/21/79 Career OF: (147-LF 144-CF 116-RF)

YEAR	TM/L	G	AB	R	H	2B	3B	HR	RBI	BB	SO	AVG	OBP	SLG	OPS	OPS+	BR+	SB	CS	SBR	FA	FR	G/POS	TPR
1979	*Cal-A	19	54	8	16	2	2	1	5	5	11	.296	.356	.463	819	123	2	1	1	-0	.978	2	O-19(16-3-2)	0.3
1980	Cal-A	78	261	26	60	10	1	5	23	11	42	.230	.265	.333	600	65	-13	0	1	-0	.982	8	O-77(33-46-0)	-0.7
1981	Cal-A	34	88	12	22	2	1	4	19	7	18	.250	.305	.432	737	110	1	0	0	0	1.000	0	O-34(27-8-1)	0.0
1982	*Cal-A	102	90	11	19	1	0	2	8	0	29	.211	.211	.289	500	36	-8	1	0	0	1.000	-29	*O-102(24-24-57)	-3.9
1983	Cal-A	76	212	17	49	9	1	5	21	9	45	.231	.262	.354	616	68	-10	0	0	0	1.000	-11	O-72(43-4-28)/3-1,D-2	-2.3
1984	Mil-A	58	169	17	44	7	2	2	16	16	35	.260	.328	.361	689	94	-1	1	5	-2	.981	-10	O-56(3-42-16)	-1.4
1985	Mil-A	29	93	6	21	3	0	0	8	7	19	.226	.280	.258	538	49	-6	1	1	-0	1.000	1	O-27(1-17-12)	-0.7
Total	7	396	967	97	231	34	7	19	100	55	199	.239	.282	.347	629	74	-36	4	8	-2	.990	-39	O-387L/D-2,3-1	-8.7

■ BOB CLARK
Clark, Robert H. b: 3/18/1863, Covington, Ky. d: 8/21/19, Covington, Ky. BR/TR, 5'10", 175 lbs. Deb: 4/17/1886 Career OF: (7-LF 2-CF 22-RF)

YEAR	TM/L	G	AB	R	H	2B	3B	HR	RBI	BB	SO	AVG	OBP	SLG	OPS	OPS+	BR+	SB	CS	SBR	FA	FR	G/POS	TPR
1886	Bro-a	71	269	37	58	8	2	0	26	17		.216	.262	.260	522	63	-12	14			.864	-13	C-44,O-17R,S-12	-1.8
1887	Bro-a	48	184	24	54	3	1	0	18	7		.293	.327	.294	591	64	-9	15			.871	-1	C-45/O-3(0-0-3)	-0.5
1888	Bro-a	45	150	23	36	5	3	1	20	9		.240	.292	.333	625	100	-0	11			.884	-2	C-36/O-8(1-1-6),1-1	0.1
1889	*Bro-a	53	182	32	50	5	2	0	22	26	7	.275	.368	.324	693	98	0	18			.870	7	C-53	1.0
1890	*Bro-N	43	151	24	33	3	3	0	15	15	8	.219	.306	.278	584	70	-5	10			.836	-14	C-42/O-1(0-0-1)	-1.4

YEAR	TM/L	G	AB	R	H	2B	3B	HR	RBI	BB	SO	AVG	OBP	SLG	OPS	OPS+	BR+	SB	CS	SBR	FA	FR	G/POS	TPR
1891	Cin-N	16	54	2	6	0	0	0	3	6	9	.111	.213	.111	324	-5	-7	3			.868	-5	C-16	-1.0
1893	Lou-N	12	28	3	3	1	0	0	3	5	5	.107	.242	.143	385	4	-4	0			.947	-2	C-10/O-1(0-0-1),S-1	-0.4
Total	7	288	1018	145	240	25	11	1	107	85	29	.236	.296	.280	576	71	-36	71			.867	-30	C-246/O-30R,S-13,1	-4.0
■ RON CLARK Clark, Ronald Bruce b: 1/14/43, Ft.Worth, Tex. BR/TR, 5'10", 175 lbs. Deb: 9/11/66 C																								
1966	Min-A	5	1	1	1	0	0	0	1	0	0	1.000	1.000	1.000	2000	448	0	0	0	0	.000	0	/3-1	0.0
1967	Min-A	20	60	7	10	3	1	2	11	4	9	.167	.219	.350	569	61	-3	0	0	0	.891	-1	3-16	-0.5
1968	Min-A	104	227	14	42	5	1	1	13	16	44	.185	.245	.229	474	42	-15	3	2	-0	.932	-8	3-52,S-43,2-10	-2.2
1969	Min-A	5	8	0	1	0	0	0	0	0	0	.125	.125	.125	250	-29	-1	0	0	0	1.000	-1	/3-2	-0.2
	Sea-A	57	163	9	32	5	0	0	12	13	29	.196	.260	.227	487	38	-13	1	0	0	.966	-9	S-38,3-15/2-5,1-1	-1.9
	Yr	62	171	9	33	5	0	0	12	13	29	.193	.254	.222	476	35	-15	1	0	0	.966	-10	S-38,3-17/2-5,1-1	-2.1
1971	Oak-A	2	1	0	0	0	0	0	0	1	0	.000	.500	.000	500	53	0	0	0	0	.000	0	H	0.0
1972	Oak-A	14	15	1	4	2	0	0	1	2	4	.267	.353	.400	753	130	1	0	0	0	1.000	0	2-11/3-3	0.2
	Mil-A	22	54	8	10	1	1	2	5	5	11	.185	.254	.352	606	81	-1	0	0	0	.963	5	2-11,3-10	0.5
	Yr	36	69	9	14	3	1	2	6	7	15	.203	.276	.362	639	92	-1	0	0	0	.974	6	2-22,3-13	0.7
1975	Phi-N	1	1	0	0	0	0	0	0	0	1	.000	.000	.000	0	-96	-0	0	0	0	.000	0	H	0.0
Total	7	230	530	40	100	16	3	5	43	41	98	.189	.251	.258	509	49	-34	4	2	0	.904	-13	/3-99,S-81,2-37,1-1	-4.1
■ ROY CLARK Clark, Roy Elliott "Pepper" b: 5/11/1874, New Haven, Conn. d: 11/1/25, Bridgeport, Conn. BL/TR, 5'8", 170 lbs. Deb: 4/19/02																								
1902	NY-N	22	80	4	12	1	0	0	3	1		.150	.160	.162	323	-0	-9	5			.964	-3	O-21(3-9-9)	-1.4
■ WILL CLARK Clark, William Nuschler b: 3/13/64, New Orleans, La. BL/TL, 6'1", 190 lbs. Deb: 4/8/86																								
1986	SF-N	111	408	66	117	27	2	11	41	34	76	.287	.346	.444	790	122	11	4	7	-2	.989	-2	*1-102	0.2
1987	*SF-N	150	529	89	163	29	5	35	91	49	98	.308	.372	.580	953	155	40	5	17	-5	.991	2	*1-139	2.8
1988	SF-N★	162	575	102	162	31	6	29	**109**	**100**	129	.282	.392	.508	900	163	**49**	9	1	2	.993	-3	*1-158	3.9
1989	*SF-N★	159	588	**104**	196	38	9	23	111	74	103	.333	.412	.546	958	177	59	8	3	1	.994	0	*1-158	5.1
1990	SF-N★	154	600	91	177	25	5	19	95	62	97	.295	.364	.448	812	127	22	8	2	1	.992	1	*1-153	1.3
1991	SF-N★	148	565	84	170	32	7	29	116	51	91	.301	.361	**.536**	897	154	38	4	2	0	**.997**	3	*1-144	3.2
1992	SF-N★	144	513	69	154	40	1	16	73	73	82	.300	.392	.476	867	153	37	12	7	0	.993	-0	*1-141	2.9
1993	SF-N	132	491	82	139	27	2	14	73	63	68	.283	.371	.432	803	118	14	2	2	-0	.988	-3	*1-129	-0.2
1994	Tex-A★	110	389	73	128	24	2	13	80	71	59	.329	.436	.501	938	141	27	5	1	1	.990	1	*1-107/D-1	1.7
1995	Tex-A	123	454	85	137	27	3	16	92	68	50	.302	.397	.480	878	124	18	0	1	-0	.994	-0	*1-122/D-1	0.5
1996	*Tex-A	117	436	69	124	25	1	13	72	64	67	.284	.382	.436	818	101	2	2	1	0	.996	-2	*1-117	-1.0
1997	Tex-A	110	393	56	128	29	1	12	51	49	62	.326	.404	.496	901	127	17	0	0	0	.996	-1	*1-100/D-7	0.6
1998	*Tex-A	149	554	98	169	41	1	23	102	72	97	.305	.388	.507	895	125	22	1	0	0	.989	-7	*1-134,D-15	0.1
1999	Bal-A	77	251	40	76	15	0	10	29	38	42	.303	.399	.482	881	128	12	2	2	-0	.995	2	1-63/D-4	0.6
2000	Bal-A	79	256	49	77	15	1	9	28	47	45	.301	.417	.473	890	129	13	4	2	0	.991	-1	1-72/D-6	0.5
	*StL-N	51	171	29	59	15	1	12	42	22	24	.345	.429	.655	1084	168	18	1	0	0	.992	-1	1-50	1.2
Total	15	1976	7173	1186	2176	440	47	284	1205	937	1190	.303	.388	.497	885	138	399	67	48	-2	.992	-10	*1-1889/D-34	23.4
■ WILLIE CLARK Clark, William Otis "Wee Willie" b: 8/16/1872, Pittsburgh, Pa. d: 11/13/32, Pittsburgh, Pa. BL, 6', 195 lbs. Deb: 6/20/1895																								
1895	NY-N	23	88	9	23	3	2	0	16	5	6	.261	.301	.341	642	67	-5	1			.974	1	1-23	-0.3
1896	NY-N	72	247	38	72	12	4	0	33	15	12	.291	.352	.372	724	94	-2	8			.975	-4	1-65	-0.5
1897	NY-N	116	431	63	122	17	12	1	75	37		.283	.352	.385	737	97	-1	18			.984	2	*1-107/O-7(7-0-0),3-1	0.0
1898	Pit-N	57	209	29	64	9	7	1	31	22		.306	.378	.431	808	134	9	0			.984	1	1-57	0.9
1899	Pit-N	81	300	49	85	13	10	0	44	35		.283	.377	.393	770	112	6	11			.989	1	1-79	0.6
Total	5	349	1275	188	366	54	35	2	199	114	18	.287	.359	.389	748	104	7	38			.983	0	1-331/O-7(7-0-0),3-1	0.7
■ WIN CLARK Clark, William Winfield b: 4/11/1875, Circleville, Ohio d: 4/15/59, Los Angeles, Cal. BR/TR, 5'10", 175 lbs. Deb: 7/12/1897																								
1897	Lou-N	4	16	2	3	0	0	0	2	1		.188	.235	.188	423	13	-2	1			.810	-2	/2-3,3-1	-0.3
■ ARTIE CLARKE Clarke, Arthur Franklin b: 5/6/1865, Providence, R.I. d: 11/14/49, Brookline, Mass. BR/TR, 5'8", 155 lbs. Deb: 4/19/1890 Career OF: (3-LF 2-CF 31-RF)																								
1890	NY-N	101	395	55	89	12	8	0	49	32	38	.225	.290	.296	586	71	-15	44			.908	-3	C-36,O-33R,3-16,2/S	-1.3
1891	NY-N	48	174	17	33	2	2	0	21	15	16	.190	.254	.224	478	41	-13	5			.916	-12	C-42/3-5,O-2(0-1-1)	-1.9
Total	2	149	569	72	122	14	10	0	70	47	54	.214	.279	.274	553	62	-28	49			.912	-15	/C-78,O-35R,3-21,2S	-3.2
■ FRED CLARKE Clarke, Fred Clifford "Cap" b: 10/3/1872, Winterset, Iowa d: 8/14/60, Winfield, Kan. BL/TR, 5'10.5", 165 lbs. Deb: 6/30/1894 FMCH Career OF: (2187-LF 4-CF 6-RF)																								
1894	Lou-N	76	314	55	86	11	7	7	48	26	27	.274	.337	.420	758	88	-7	26			.886	4	O-76(76-0-0)	-0.8
1895	Lou-N	132	550	96	191	21	5	4	82	34	24	.347	.396	.425	821	119	17	40			.881	11	*O-132(132-0-0)	1.3
1896	Lou-N	131	517	96	168	15	18	9	79	43	34	.325	.392	.476	868	133	25	34			.908	0	*O-131(131-0-0)	1.1
1897	Lou-N	130	526	122	205	30	13	6	67	45		.390	.461	.530	992	**167**	**54**	59			.927	6	*O-129(128-3-0),M	4.0
1898	Lou-N	149	599	116	184	23	12	3	47	48		.307	.373	.401	774	124	19	40			.940	6	*O-149(148-0-2),M	1.0
1899	Lou-N	149	606	122	206	23	9	5	70	49		.340	.404	.432	836	129	26	49			.964	1	*O-145(145-0-0)/S-3,M	1.2
1900	Pit-N	106	399	84	110	15	12	3	32	51		.276	.368	.396	764	110	6	21			.944	3	*O-104(104-0-0),M	-0.1
1901	Pit-N	129	527	118	171	24	15	6	60	51		.324	.395	.461	856	143	30	23			.970	2	*O-127L/S-1,3-1,M	2.3
1902	Pit-N	113	459	103	145	27	14	2	53	51		.316	.401	.449	850	157	32	29			.958	-1	*O-113(110-0-4),M	2.6
1903	*Pit-N	104	427	88	150	**32**	15	5	70	41		.351	.414	**.532**	**946**	**164**	34	21			.962	-8	*O-101(101-0-0)/S-2,M	1.9
1904	Pit-N	72	278	51	85	7	11	0	25	22		.306	.367	.410	777	136	12	11			.979	0	O-70(70-0-0),M	0.8
1905	Pit-N	141	525	95	157	18	15	2	51	55		.299	.368	.402	770	126	17	24			.976	4	*O-137(137-0-0),M	1.3
1906	Pit-N	118	417	69	129	14	**13**	1	39	40		.309	.371	.412	784	138	18	18			.974	6	*O-110(110-0-0),M	1.9
1907	Pit-N	148	501	97	145	18	13	2	59	68		.289	.383	.389	772	140	25	37			**.987**	6	*O-144(144-0-0),M	2.6
1908	Pit-N	151	551	83	146	18	15	2	53	65		.265	.349	.363	712	127	18	24			.973	10	*O-151(150-1-0),M	2.2
1909	*Pit-N	152	550	97	158	16	11	3	68	**80**		.287	.384	.373	756	124	18	31			**.987**	7	*O-152(152-0-0),M	1.9
1910	Pit-N	123	429	57	113	23	9	2	63	53	23	.263	.350	.373	723	105	3	12			.967	3	*O-118(118-0-0),M	-0.1
1911	Pit-N	110	392	73	127	25	13	5	49	53	27	.324	.407	.492	900	146	24	10			.970	0	*O-101(101-0-0),M	2.0
1913	Pit-N	9	13	0	1	1	0	0	0	0	0	.077	.077	.154	231	-37	-2	0			1.000	-1	/O-2(2-0-0),M	-0.3
1914	Pit-N	2	2	0	0	0	0	0	0	0	0	.000	.000	.000	0	-99	-0	0			.000	0	HM	0.0
1915	Pit-N	1	2	0	1	0	0	0	0	0	0	.500	.500	.500	1000	206	0	0			.000	-1	/O-1(1-0-0),M	0.0
Total	21	2246	8584	1622	2678	361	220	67	1015	875	135	.312	.386	.429	814	132	368	509			.952	58	*O-2193L/S-6,3-1	26.7
■ HARRY CLARKE Clarke, Harry Corson b: 1861, d: 3/3/23, Long Beach, Cal. Deb: 8/28/1889																								
1889	Was-N	1	3	0	0	0	0	0	0	0	1	.000	.000	.000	0	-99	-1	0			1.000	1	/O-1(0-0-1)	0.0
■ HENRY CLARKE Clarke, Henry Tefft b: 8/28/1875, Bellevue, Neb. d: 3/28/50, Colorado Springs, Colo. BR/TR, Deb: 6/26/1897																								
1897	Cle-N	7	25	3	7	0	0	0	3	2		.280	.333	.280	613	60	-1	0			.714	-1	/P-5,O-2(0-0-2)	-0.1
1898	Chi-N	2	4	0	1	0	0	0	0	1		.250	.400	.250	650	87	0	0			.000	-1	/O-1(0-1-0),P-1	-0.1
Total	2	9	29	3	8	0	0	0	3	3		.276	.344	.276	620	64	-1	0			.750	-2	/P-6,O-3(0-1-2)	-0.2
■ HORACE CLARKE Clarke, Horace Meredith b: 6/2/40, Frederiksted, St.Croix, V.I. BB/TR, 5'9", 178 lbs. Deb: 5/13/65																								
1965	NY-A	51	108	13	28	1	0	1	9	6	6	.259	.298	.296	595	70	-4	2	1	0	.923	3	3-17/2-7,S-1	-0.1
1966	NY-A	96	312	37	83	10	4	6	28	27	24	.266	.326	.381	708	107	3	5	3	0	.970	-19	S-63,2-16/3-4	-1.0
1967	NY-A	143	588	74	160	17	0	3	29	42	64	.272	.321	.316	637	92	-6	21	4	3	**.990**	15	*2-140	2.7
1968	NY-A	148	579	52	133	6	1	2	26	23	46	.230	.259	.254	513	58	-30	20	7	2	.984	**30**	*2-139	1.5
1969	NY-A	156	641	82	183	26	7	4	48	53	41	.285	.340	.367	707	101	1	33	13	3	.982	-4	*2-156	1.0
1970	NY-A	158	686	81	172	24	2	4	46	35	35	.251	.289	.309	598	68	-31	23	7	3	.979	-7	*2-157	-2.5
1971	NY-A	159	625	76	156	23	7	2	41	64	43	.250	.321	.318	640	87	-10	17	7	1	.981	-3	*2-156	-0.2
1972	NY-A	147	547	65	132	20	2	3	37	56	44	.241	.316	.302	618	87	-8	18	6	2	.985	6	*2-143	1.1
1973	NY-A	148	590	60	155	21	0	2	35	47	48	.263	.319	.308	628	80	-15	11	10	-1	.979	8	*2-147	0.2
1974	NY-A	24	47	3	11	1	0	0	1	4	5	.234	.294	.255	549	60	-2	1	0	0	1.000	-6	2-20/D-1	-0.7
	SD-N	42	90	5	17	1	0	0	4	8	6	.189	.255	.200	455	30	-8	0	0	0	.978	-4	2-21	-1.2
Total	10	1272	4813	548	1230	150	23	27	304	365	362	.256	.310	.313	623	82	-111	151	58	13	.983	19	*2-1102/S-64,3-21,D	0.8

■ NIG CLARKE
Clarke, Jay Justin b: 12/15/1882, Amherstburg, Ont., Canada d: 6/15/49, River Rouge, Mich BL/TR (BB 1907), 5'8", 165 lbs. Deb: 4/26/05

YEAR	TM/L	G	AB	R	H	2B	3B	HR	RBI	BB	SO	AVG	OBP	SLG	OPS	OPS+	BR+	SB	CS	SBR	FA	FR	G/POS	TPR
1905	Cle-A	5	9	2	1	1	0	0	1	1		.111	.200	.222	422	33	-1	0			1.000	-2	/C-5	-0.2
	Det-A	3	7	1	3	0	0	1	1	0		.429	.500	.857	1357	326	2	0			1.000	1	/C-2	0.3
	Cle-A	37	114	9	23	5	1	0	8	10		.202	.266	.263	529	67	-4	0			.961	-1	C-37	-0.2
	Yr	45	130	12	27	6	1	1	10	11		.208	.275	.292	567	79	-3	0			.965	-2	C-44	-0.1
1906	Cle-A	57	179	22	64	12	4	1	21	13		.358	.404	.486	890	181	16	3			.982	-1	C-54	2.2
1907	Cle-A	120	390	44	105	19	6	3	33	35		.269	.333	.372	704	123	10	3			.961	-11	*C-115	1.1
1908	Cle-A	97	290	34	70	8	6	1	27	30		.241	.315	.321	635	106	2	6			.969	-8	C-90	0.4
1909	Cle-A	55	164	15	45	4	2	0	14	9		.274	.316	.323	639	98	-1	1			.952	-3	C-44	0.1
1910	Cle-A	21	58	4	9	2	0	0	2	8		.155	.258	.190	447	40	-4	0			.974	3	C-17	0.0
1911	StL-A	82	256	22	55	10	1	0	18	26		.215	.287	.262	549	56	-15	2			.926	-5	C-73/1-4	-1.4
1919	Phi-N	26	62	4	15	3	0	0	2	4	5	.242	.299	.290	589	72	-2	1			.969	0	C-22	0.0
1920	Pit-N	3	7	0	0	0	0	0	0	2	4	.000	.222	.000	222	-32	-1	0	0	0	1.000	1	/C-3	0.0
Total	9	506	1536	157	390	64	20	6	127	138	9	.254	.318	.333	652	102	3	16	0		.960	-25	C-462/1-4	2.3

■ JOSH CLARKE
Clarke, Joshua Baldwin "Pepper" b: 3/8/1879, Winfield, Kan. d: 7/2/62, Ventura, Cal. BL/TR, 5'10", 180 lbs. Deb: 6/15/1898 F Career OF: (168-LF 6-CF 23-RF)

YEAR	TM/L	G	AB	R	H	2B	3B	HR	RBI	BB	SO	AVG	OBP	SLG	OPS	OPS+	BR+	SB	CS	SBR	FA	FR	G/POS	TPR
1898	Lou-N	6	18	0	3	0	0	0	0	1		.167	.211	.167	377	9	-2	0			.917	-1	/O-5(2-0-4)	-0.3
1905	StL-N	50	167	31	43	3	2	3	18	27		.257	.361	.353	714	117	4	8			.942	-8	O-26(2-5-19),2-16/S-4	-0.5
1908	Cle-A	131	492	70	119	8	4	1	21	76		.242	.348	.280	628	104	6	37			.963	-3	*O-131(130-1-0)	-0.4
1909	Cle-A	4	12	1	0	0	0	0	0	2		.000	.143	.000	143	-52	-2	0			.600	-2	/O-4(4-0-0)	-0.5
1911	Bos-N	32	120	16	28	7	3	1	4	29	22	.233	.387	.367	753	103	1	6			.938	4	O-30(30-0-0)	0.4
Total	5	223	809	118	193	18	9	5	43	135	22	.239	.351	.302	653	102	8	51			.949	-9	O-196L/2-16,S-4	-1.3

■ GREY CLARKE
Clarke, Richard Grey "Noisy" b: 9/26/12, Fulton, Ala. d: 11/25/93, Kannapolis, N.C. BR/TR, 5'9", 183 lbs. Deb: 4/19/44

YEAR	TM/L	G	AB	R	H	2B	3B	HR	RBI	BB	SO	AVG	OBP	SLG	OPS	OPS+	BR+	SB	CS	SBR	FA	FR	G/POS	TPR
1944	Chi-A	63	169	14	44	10	1	0	27	22	6	.260	.352	.331	684	97	0	0	4	-1	.941	1	3-45	0.0

■ SUMPTER CLARKE
Clarke, Sumpter Mills b: 10/18/1897, Savannah, Ga. d: 3/16/62, Knoxville, Tenn. BR/TR, 5'11", 170 lbs. Deb: 9/27/20 F

YEAR	TM/L	G	AB	R	H	2B	3B	HR	RBI	BB	SO	AVG	OBP	SLG	OPS	OPS+	BR+	SB	CS	SBR	FA	FR	G/POS	TPR
1920	Chi-N	1	3	0	1	0	0	0	0	0	1	.333	.333	.333	667	90	-0	0	0	0	1.000	-0	/3-1	0.0
1923	Cle-A	1	3	0	0	0	0	0	0	0	0	.000	.000	.000	0	-99	-1	0	0	0	1.000	-0	/O-1	-0.1
1924	Cle-A	35	104	17	24	6	1	0	11	6	12	.231	.273	.308	580	49	-8	0	0	0	1.000	-5	O-33(2-9-22)	-1.5
Total	3	37	110	17	25	6	1	0	11	6	13	.227	.267	.300	567	46	-9	0	0	0	1.000	-6	/O-34(2-9-22),3-1	-1.6

■ TOMMY CLARKE
Clarke, Thomas Aloysius b: 5/9/1888, New York, N.Y. d: 8/14/45, Corona, N.Y. BR/TR, 5'11", 175 lbs. Deb: 8/26/09

YEAR	TM/L	G	AB	R	H	2B	3B	HR	RBI	BB	SO	AVG	OBP	SLG	OPS	OPS+	BR+	SB	CS	SBR	FA	FR	G/POS	TPR
1909	Cin-N	18	52	8	13	3	2	0	10	6		.250	.328	.385	712	122	1	3			.965	5	C-17	0.8
1910	Cin-N	64	151	19	42	6	5	1	20	19	17	.278	.370	.404	774	131	6	1			.971	-1	C-56	1.0
1911	Cin-N	86	203	20	49	6	7	1	25	25	22	.241	.328	.355	682	94	-2	4			.970	2	C-81/1-1	0.6
1912	Cin-N	72	146	19	41	7	2	0	22	28	14	.281	.400	.356	756	111	4	9			.983	5	C-63	1.3
1913	Cin-N	114	330	29	87	11	8	1	38	39	40	.264	.345	.355	700	100	1	2			.979	-13	*C-100	-0.4
1914	Cin-N	113	313	30	82	13	7	2	25	31	30	.262	.332	.367	700	105	2	6			.973	-4	*C-106	0.7
1915	Cin-N	96	226	23	65	7	2	0	21	33	22	.288	.381	.336	717	116	6	7	3	0	.981	-4	C-72	0.9
1916	Cin-N	78	177	10	42	10	1	0	17	24	20	.237	.328	.305	633	97	0	8			.965	-10	C-51	-0.7
1917	Cin-N	58	110	11	32	3	3	1	13	11	12	.291	.361	.400	761	139	5	2			.991	-5	C-29	0.2
1918	Chi-N	1	0	0	0	0	0	0	0	0	0	—	—	—	—		0	0			.000	0	/C-1	0.0
Total	10	700	1708	169	453	66	37	6	191	216	177	.265	.351	.358	709	109	24	42	3		.975	-26	C-576/1-1	4.4

■ BOILERYARD CLARKE
Clarke, William Jones b: 10/18/1868, New York, N.Y. d: 7/29/59, Princeton, N.J. BR/TR, 5'11.5", 170 lbs. Deb: 5/1/1893

YEAR	TM/L	G	AB	R	H	2B	3B	HR	RBI	BB	SO	AVG	OBP	SLG	OPS	OPS+	BR+	SB	CS	SBR	FA	FR	G/POS	TPR
1893	Bal-N	49	183	23	32	1	3	1	24	19	14	.175	.274	.230	504	34	-18	2			.909	-3	C-38,1-11	-1.4
1894	Bal-N	28	100	18	24	8	0	1	19	16	14	.240	.361	.350	711	69	-5	2			.903	-3	C-23/1-5	-0.4
1895	*Bal-N	67	241	38	70	15	3	0	35	13	18	.290	.350	.378	727	85	-6	8			.938	6	C-60/1-6	0.5
1896	Bal-N	80	300	48	89	14	7	2	71	14	12	.297	.345	.410	755	97	-2	7			.948	-11	C-67,1-14	-0.6
1897	*Bal-N	64	241	32	65	7	1	1	38	9		.270	.320	.320	640	69	-11	5			.939	-15	C-59/1-4	-1.7
1898	Bal-N	82	285	26	69	5	2	0	27	4		.242	.289	.274	563	60	-15	2			.962	3	C-70,1-10	-0.5
1899	Bos-N	60	223	25	50	3	2	2	32	10		.224	.270	.283	553	47	-17	2			.940	-1	C-60	-1.1
1900	Bos-N	81	270	35	85	5	2	1	30	9		.315	.344	.359	703	84	-6	0			.928	7	C-67/1-8	0.6
1901	Was-A	110	422	58	118	15	5	3	54	23		.280	.335	.360	695	94	-3	7			.952	-9	*C-107/1-3	-0.1
1902	Was-A	87	291	31	78	15	0	6	40	23		.268	.330	.381	712	96	-2	1			**.972**	-3	C-87	0.4
1903	Was-A	126	465	35	111	14	6	2	38	15		.239	.273	.308	581	72	-16	12			.981	-11	1-88,C-37	-2.6
1904	Was-A	85	275	23	58	8	1	0	17	17		.211	.269	.247	517	65	-10	5			.977	0	C-52,1-29	-0.6
1905	NY-N	31	50	2	9	0	0	1	4	4		.180	.241	.240	481	42	-4	1			.973	-1	1-15,C-12	-0.4
Total	13	950	3346	394	858	110	32	20	429	176	58	.256	.310	.326	637	75	-114	54			.947	-39	C-739,1-193	-7.9

■ STU CLARKE
Clarke, William Stuart b: 1/24/06, San Francisco, Cal d: 8/26/85, Hayward, Cal. BR/TR, 5'8.5", 160 lbs. Deb: 7/17/29

YEAR	TM/L	G	AB	R	H	2B	3B	HR	RBI	BB	SO	AVG	OBP	SLG	OPS	OPS+	BR+	SB	CS	SBR	FA	FR	G/POS	TPR
1929	Pit-N	57	178	20	47	5	7	2	21	19	21	.264	.338	.404	743	81	-5	3			.919	-8	S-41,3-15/2-1	-0.8
1930	Pit-N	4	9	2	4	0	1	0	2	1	0	.444	.500	.667	1167	178	1	0			1.000	-1	/2-2	0.0
Total	2	61	187	22	51	5	8	2	23	20	21	.273	.346	.417	763	86	-4	3			1.000	-9	/S-41,3-15,2-3	-0.8

■ BUZZ CLARKSON
Clarkson, James Buster b: 3/13/15, Hopkins, S.C. d: 1/18/89, Jeannette, Pa. BR/TR, 5'11", 210 lbs. Deb: 4/30/52

YEAR	TM/L	G	AB	R	H	2B	3B	HR	RBI	BB	SO	AVG	OBP	SLG	OPS	OPS+	BR+	SB	CS	SBR	FA	FR	G/POS	TPR
1952	Bos-N	14	25	3	5	0	0	0	1	3	3	.200	.286	.200	486	38	-2	0	0	0	.938	-2	/S-6,3-2	-0.4

■ ELLIS CLARY
Clary, Ellis "Cat" b: 9/11/16, Valdosta, Ga. d: 6/2/2000, Valdosta, Ga. BR/TR, 5'8", 160 lbs. Deb: 6/7/42 C

YEAR	TM/L	G	AB	R	H	2B	3B	HR	RBI	BB	SO	AVG	OBP	SLG	OPS	OPS+	BR+	SB	CS	SBR	FA	FR	G/POS	TPR
1942	Was-A	76	240	34	66	9	0	0	16	45	25	.275	.394	.313	706	101	3	2	0	0	.969	-17	2-69/3-2	-0.9
1943	Was-A	73	254	36	65	19	1	0	19	44	31	.256	.370	.339	709	112	6	8	4	0	.945	-8	3-68/S-1	-0.1
	StL-A	23	69	15	19	2	0	0	5	11	6	.275	.375	.304	679	98	0	1	2	-0	.972	-1	3-14/2-3	-0.1
	Yr	96	323	51	84	21	1	0	24	55	37	.260	.371	.331	702	109	6	9	6	-0	.949	-9	3-82/2-3,S-1	-0.2
1944	*StL-A	25	49	6	13	1	1	0	4	12	9	.265	.410	.327	736	106	1	1	0	0	1.000	-1	3-11/2-6	0.0
1945	StL-A	26	38	6	8	1	0	1	2	2	3	.211	.250	.316	566	61	-2	0	2	-1	.947	3	3-16/2-3	0.0
Total	4	223	650	97	171	32	2	1	46	114	74	.263	.376	.323	699	103	8	12	8	-0	.953	-25	3-111/2-81,S-1	-1.1

■ DAIN CLAY
Clay, Dain Elmer "Sniffy" or "Ding-A-Ling" b: 7/10/19, Hicksville, Ohio d: 8/28/94, Chula Vista, Cal. BR/TR, 5'10.5", 160 lbs. Deb: 6/12/43

YEAR	TM/L	G	AB	R	H	2B	3B	HR	RBI	BB	SO	AVG	OBP	SLG	OPS	OPS+	BR+	SB	CS	SBR	FA	FR	G/POS	TPR
1943	Cin-N	49	93	19	25	2	4	0	9	8	14	.269	.333	.376	710	106	1	1			.936	-9	O-33(1-29-3)	-1.0
1944	Cin-N	110	356	51	89	15	0	0	17	17	18	.250	.290	.292	582	67	-16	8			.993	-2	O-98(5-93-0)	-2.1
1945	Cin-N	153	656	81	184	29	2	1	50	37	58	.280	.321	.335	656	84	-14	19			.989	6	*O-152(0-152-0)	-1.3
1946	Cin-N	121	435	52	99	17	0	2	22	53	40	.228	.318	.280	599	73	-14	11			**.988**	7	*O-120(11-107-2)	-1.1
Total	4	433	1540	203	397	63	6	3	98	115	130	.258	.314	.312	626	79	-44	39			.987	3	O-403(17-381-5)	-5.5

■ BILL CLAY
Clay, Frederick C. b: 11/23/1874, Baltimore, Md. d: 10/12/17, York, Pa. TL, 175 lbs. Deb: 8/8/02

YEAR	TM/L	G	AB	R	H	2B	3B	HR	RBI	BB	SO	AVG	OBP	SLG	OPS	OPS+	BR+	SB	CS	SBR	FA	FR	G/POS	TPR
1902	Phi-N	3	8	1	2	0	0	0	1	0		.250	.250	.250	500	54	-0	0			.750	-1	/O-3(3-0-0)	-0.2

■ ROYCE CLAYTON
Clayton, Royce Spencer b: 1/2/70, Burbank, Cal. BR/TR, 6', 183 lbs. Deb: 9/20/91

YEAR	TM/L	G	AB	R	H	2B	3B	HR	RBI	BB	SO	AVG	OBP	SLG	OPS	OPS+	BR+	SB	CS	SBR	FA	FR	G/POS	TPR
1991	SF-N	9	26	0	3	1	0	0	2	1	6	.115	.148	.154	302	-15	-4	0	0	0	.880	-6	/S-8	-1.0
1992	SF-N	98	321	31	72	7	4	4	24	26	63	.224	.282	.308	591	71	-13	8	4	0	.973	-9	S-94/3-1	-1.5
1993	SF-N	153	549	54	155	21	5	6	70	38	91	.282	.334	.372	706	91	-6	11	10	-1	.963	1	*S-153	0.6
1994	SF-N	108	385	38	91	14	6	3	30	30	74	.236	.297	.327	624	66	-20	23	3	4	.973	7	*S-108	0.0
1995	SF-N	138	509	56	124	29	3	5	58	38	109	.244	.300	.342	642	71	-22	24	9	2	.969	4	*S-136	-0.4
1996	*StL-N	129	491	64	136	20	4	6	35	33	89	.277	.324	.371	694	83	-12	33	15	2	.972	1	*S-113	0.0
1997	StL-N★	154	576	75	153	39	5	9	61	33	109	.266	.309	.398	706	84	-15	30	10	3	.973	7	*S-153	0.8
1998	StL-N	90	355	59	83	19	1	4	29	40	51	.234	.315	.327	642	70	-15	19	6	2	.970	0	S-89	-0.5
	*Tex-A	52	186	30	53	12	1	5	24	13	32	.285	.335	.441	776	96	-1	5	5	-1	.972	-4	S-52	-0.1
1999	*Tex-A	133	465	69	134	21	5	14	52	39	100	.288	.348	.445	794	96	-3	8	6	-0	.961	-3	*S-133	0.5
2000	Tex-A	148	513	70	124	21	5	14	54	42	92	.242	.303	.384	687	70	-24	11	7	-0	.977	-6	*S-148	-1.6
Total	10	1212	4376	546	1128	204	39	70	439	333	816	.258	.314	.370	684	80	-135	172	75	12	.970	-7	*S-1187/3-1	-3.2

■ CHET CLEMENS Clemens, Chester Spurgeon b: 5/10/17, San Fernando, Cal. BR/TR, 6', 175 lbs. Deb: 9/13/39

YEAR	TM/L	G	AB	R	H	2B	3B	HR	RBI	BB	SO	AVG	OBP	SLG	OPS	OPS+	BR+	SB	CS	SBR	FA	FR	G/POS	TPR
1939	Bos-N	9	23	2	5	0	0	0	1	1	3	.217	.250	.217	467	29	-2	1			.867	-1	/O-7(7-0-0)	-0.4
1944	Bos-N	19	17	7	3	1	1	0	2	2	2	.176	.263	.353	616	69	-1	0			1.000	-2	/O-7(7-0-0)	-0.3
Total	2	28	40	9	8	1	1	0	3	3	5	.200	.256	.275	531	46	-3	1			.905	-3	/O-14(14-0-0)	-0.7

■ CLEM CLEMENS Clemens, Clement Lambert "Count" (b: Clement Lambert Ulatowski)
b: 11/21/1886, Chicago, Ill. d: 11/2/67, St.Petersburg, Fla. BR/TR, 5'11", 176 lbs. Deb: 5/15/14

YEAR	TM/L	G	AB	R	H	2B	3B	HR	RBI	BB	SO	AVG	OBP	SLG	OPS	OPS+	BR+	SB	CS	SBR	FA	FR	G/POS	TPR
1914	Chi-F	13	27	4	4	0	0	0	2	3	0	.148	.233	.148	381	6	-4	0			.950	-1	/C-8	-0.5
1915	Chi-F	11	22	3	3	1	0	0	3	1	0	.136	.174	.182	356	0	-3	0			1.000	-1	/C-9,2-2	-0.4
1916	Chi-N	10	15	0	0	0	0	0	0	1	6	.000	.063	.000	63	-72	-3	0			.941	1	/C-9	-0.2
Total	3	34	64	7	7	1	0	0	5	5	6	.109	.174	.125	299	-15	-10	0			.962	-1	/C-26,2-2	-1.1

■ DOUG CLEMENS Clemens, Douglas Horace b: 6/9/39, Leesport, Pa. BL/TR, 6', 180 lbs. Deb: 10/2/60

YEAR	TM/L	G	AB	R	H	2B	3B	HR	RBI	BB	SO	AVG	OBP	SLG	OPS	OPS+	BR+	SB	CS	SBR	FA	FR	G/POS	TPR
1960	StL-N	1	0	0	0	0	0	0	0	0	0	—	—	—	—	—	0	0	0	0	1.000	0	/O-1(0-0-1)	0.0
1961	StL-N	6	12	1	2	1	0	0	0	3	1	.167	.333	.250	583	53	-1	0	0	0	.667	-1	/O-3(2-0-2)	-0.2
1962	StL-N	48	93	12	22	1	1	1	12	17	19	.237	.355	.301	656	71	-3	0	0	0	.974	-6	O-34(7-1-27)	-1.1
1963	StL-N	5	6	1	1	0	0	1	2	1	2	.167	.286	.667	952	151	0	0	0	0	1.000	0	/O-3(2-0-1)	0.1
1964	StL-N	33	78	8	16	4	3	1	9	6	16	.205	.271	.372	642	73	-3	0	0	0	.970	0	O-22(17-0-5)	-0.4
	Chi-N	54	140	23	39	10	2	2	12	18	22	.279	.365	.421	786	116	3	0	0	0	.923	0	O-40(1-2-38)	0.2
	Yr	87	218	31	55	14	5	3	21	24	38	.252	.332	.404	736	100	0	0	0	0	.937	1	O-62(18-2-43)	-0.2
1965	Chi-N	128	340	36	75	11	0	4	26	38	53	.221	.303	.288	591	66	-15	5	8	-2	.981	-6	*O-105(44-13-49)	-2.9
1966	Phi-N	79	121	10	31	1	0	1	15	16	25	.256	.353	.289	642	81	-2	1	0	0	1.000	-1	O-28(24-2-3)/1-1	-0.4
1967	Phi-N	69	73	2	13	5	0	0	4	8	15	.178	.268	.247	515	48	-5	0	0	0	1.000	-3	O-10(9-0-1)	-0.8
1968	Phi-N	29	57	6	12	1	1	2	8	7	13	.211	.297	.368	665	99	-0	0	0	0	1.000	-1	O-17(3-0-15)	-0.2
Total	9	452	920	99	211	34	7	12	88	114	166	.229	.319	.321	640	78	-25	6	8	-1	.969	-16	O-263(109-18-142)/1-1	-5.7

■ BOB CLEMENS Clemens, Robert Baxter b: 8/9/1886, Odessa, Mo. d: 4/5/64, Marshall, Mo. BR/TR, 5'9", 163 lbs. Deb: 9/17/14

YEAR	TM/L	G	AB	R	H	2B	3B	HR	RBI	BB	SO	AVG	OBP	SLG	OPS	OPS+	BR+	SB	CS	SBR	FA	FR	G/POS	TPR
1914	StL-A	7	13	1	3	0	1	0	3	2	1	.231	.375	.385	760	134	1	0	2	-1	.750	-1	/O-5(2-1-2)	-0.1

■ WALLY CLEMENT Clement, Wallace Oakes b: 7/21/1881, Auburn, Me. d: 11/1/53, Coral Gables, Fla. BL/TR, 5'11", 175 lbs. Deb: 8/17/08

YEAR	TM/L	G	AB	R	H	2B	3B	HR	RBI	BB	SO	AVG	OBP	SLG	OPS	OPS+	BR+	SB	CS	SBR	FA	FR	G/POS	TPR
1908	Phi-N	16	36	0	8	3	0	0	1	0		.222	.222	.306	528	66	-2	2			1.000	4	/O-8(8-0-0)	0.2
1909	Phi-N	3	3	0	0	0	0	0	0	0		.000	.000	.000	0	-99	-1	0			.000	0	H	-0.1
	Bro-N	92	340	35	88	8	4	0	17	18		.259	.296	.306	602	90	-5	11			.965	4	O-88(84-0-4)	-0.7
	Yr	95	343	35	88	8	4	0	17	18		.257	.294	.303	597	88	-6	11			.965	4	O-88(84-0-4)	-0.8
Total	2	111	379	35	96	11	4	0	18	18		.253	.287	.303	591	86	-7	13			.970	7	/O-96(92-0-4)	-0.6

■ EDGARD CLEMENTE Clemente, Edgard Alexis (Velazquez) (b: Edgard Alexis Velazquez) b: 12/15/75, Santurce, P.R. BR/TR, 5'11", 188 lbs. Deb: 9/10/98

YEAR	TM/L	G	AB	R	H	2B	3B	HR	RBI	BB	SO	AVG	OBP	SLG	OPS	OPS+	BR+	SB	CS	SBR	FA	FR	G/POS	TPR
1998	Col-N	11	17	2	6	0	1	0	2	2	8	.353	.421	.471	892	110	0	0	0	0	.857	-2	/O-7(0-1-6)	-0.2
1999	Col-N	57	162	24	41	10	2	8	25	7	46	.253	.284	.488	772	71	-7	0	0	0	.972	-1	O-49(2-45-4)	-0.8
2000	Ana-A	46	78	4	17	2	0	0	5	0	27	.218	.228	.244	471	19	-9	0	1	-0	1.000	-5	O-32(15-5-12),D-11	-1.5
Total	3	114	257	30	64	12	3	8	32	9	81	.249	.277	.412	690	60	-16	0	1	-0	.974	-8	/O-88(17-51-22),D-11	-2.5

■ ROBERTO CLEMENTE Clemente, Roberto (Walker) "Bob" b: 8/18/34, Carolina, P.R.
d: 12/31/72, San Juan, P.R. BR/TR, 5'11", 175 lbs. Deb: 4/17/55 H Career OF: (27-LF 63-CF 2302-RF)

YEAR	TM/L	G	AB	R	H	2B	3B	HR	RBI	BB	SO	AVG	OBP	SLG	OPS	OPS+	BR+	SB	CS	SBR	FA	FR	G/POS	TPR
1955	Pit-N	124	474	48	121	23	11	5	47	18	60	.255	.285	.382	667	76	-17	2	5	-1	.978	12	*O-118(1-10-111)	-1.2
1956	Pit-N	147	543	66	169	30	7	7	60	13	58	.311	.332	.431	763	105	3	6	6	-1	.957	2	*O-139R/2-2,3-1	-0.2
1957	Pit-N	111	451	42	114	17	7	4	30	23	45	.253	.289	.348	637	72	-18	0	4	-1	.979	13	*O-109(0-14-97)	-1.1
1958	Pit-N	140	519	69	150	24	10	6	50	31	41	.289	.329	.408	738	96	-4	8	2	1	.982	25	*O-135(0-0-135)	1.8
1959	Pit-N	105	432	60	128	17	7	4	50	15	51	.296	.324	.396	720	91	-6	2	3	-1	.948	9	*O-104(0-0-104)	-0.1
1960	*Pit-N★	144	570	89	179	22	6	16	94	39	72	.314	.360	.458	818	121	16	4	5	-1	.971	3	*O-142(0-0-142)	1.4
1961	Pit-N★	146	572	100	201	30	10	23	89	35	59	**.351**	.392	.559	951	148	38	4	1	1	.969	14	*O-144(0-1-144)	4.2
1962	Pit-N★	144	538	95	168	28	9	10	74	35	73	.312	.355	.454	809	115	11	6	4	-0	.973	13	*O-142(0-0-142)	1.4
1963	Pit-N★	152	600	77	192	23	8	17	76	31	64	.320	.357	.470	827	135	26	12	2	2	.958	-3	*O-151(0-8-143)	1.6
1964	Pit-N★	155	622	95	**211**	40	7	12	87	51	87	**.339**	.391	.484	875	145	37	5	2	0	.968	11	*O-154(0-0-154)	3.9
1965	Pit-N★	152	589	91	194	21	14	10	65	43	78	**.329**	.380	.463	843	136	28	8	0	2	.968	9	*O-145(0-5-143)	3.0
1966	Pit-N★	154	638	105	202	31	11	29	119	46	109	.317	.363	.536	899	146	38	7	5	-0	.965	15	*O-154(0-1-154)	4.3
1967	Pit-N★	147	585	103	**209**	26	10	23	110	41	103	**.357**	.402	.554	956	170	52	9	1	2	.970	9	*O-145(0-2-144)	5.5
1968	Pit-N	132	502	74	146	18	12	18	57	51	77	.291	.357	.482	839	152	31	2	3	-1	.984	12	*O-131(0-0-131)	3.7
1969	Pit-N★	138	507	87	175	20	**12**	19	91	56	73	.345	.413	.544	958	170	47	4	1	1	.980	7	*O-135(0-0-135)	4.9
1970	*Pit-N★	108	412	65	145	22	10	14	60	38	66	.352	.409	.556	965	159	34	3	0	1	.966	7	*O-104(0-0-104)	3.5
1971	*Pit-N★	132	522	82	178	29	8	13	86	26	65	.341	.372	.502	874	146	29	1	2	-0	.993	10	*O-124(0-0-124)	3.5
1972	*Pit-N†	102	378	68	118	19	7	10	60	29	49	.312	.361	.479	840	140	18	0	0	0	1.000	6	O-94(0-0-94)	2.1
Total	18	2433	9454	1416	3000	440	166	240	1305	621	1230	.317	.362	.475	837	130	363	83	46	2	.973	175	*O-2370R/2-2,3-1	42.2

■ ED CLEMENTS Clements, Edward b: Philadelphia, Pa. Deb: 6/24/1890

YEAR	TM/L	G	AB	R	H	2B	3B	HR	RBI	BB	SO	AVG	OBP	SLG	OPS	OPS+	BR+	SB	CS	SBR	FA	FR	G/POS	TPR
1890	Pit-N	1	1	0	0	0	0	0	0	0	0	.000	.000	.000	0	-99	-0	0			.400	-0	/S-1	-0.1

■ JACK CLEMENTS Clements, John J. b: 7/24/1864, Philadelphia, Pa. d: 5/23/41, Norristown, Pa. BL/TL, 5'8.5", 204 lbs. Deb: 4/22/1884 M Career OF: (8-LF 7-CF 26-RF)

YEAR	TM/L	G	AB	R	H	2B	3B	HR	RBI	BB	SO	AVG	OBP	SLG	OPS	OPS+	BR+	SB	CS	SBR	FA	FR	G/POS	TPR
1884	Phi-U	41	177	37	50	13	2	3		9		.282	.317	.429	747	134	2				.764	1	O-22(5-0-17),C-20/S-1	0.4
	Phi-N	9	30	3	7	0	0	0	0	4	8	.233	.324	.233	557	82	-0				.827	1	/C-9	0.1
1885	Phi-N	52	188	14	36	11	3	1	14	2	30	.191	.200	.298	498	61	-8				.891	-8	C-41,O-11(2-7-2)	-1.2
1886	Phi-N	54	185	15	38	5	1	0	11	7	34	.205	.234	.243	478	45	-12	4			.930	12	C-47/O-7(1-0-6)	0.3
1887	Phi-N	66	255	48	78	13	7	1	47	9	24	.306	.317	.402	719	93	-3	7			.940	9	C-59/3-4,S-3	0.9
1888	Phi-N	86	326	26	80	8	4	1	32	10	36	.245	.276	.304	580	81	-7	3			.927	-1	C-85/O-1(0-0-1)	-0.1
1889	Phi-N	78	310	51	88	17	1	4	35	29	21	.284	.347	.384	731	96	-3	3			.916	-7	C-78	-0.2
1890	Phi-N	97	381	64	120	23	8	7	74	45	30	.315	.392	.472	864	148	22	10			.944	3	C-91/1-5,M	2.8
1891	Phi-N	107	423	58	131	29	4	4	75	43	19	.310	.380	.426	806	131	16	3			.927	-5	*C-107/1-2	1.9
1892	Phi-N	109	402	50	106	25	6	8	76	43	40	.264	.339	.415	755	128	13	7			.950	5	*C-109	2.6
1893	Phi-N	94	376	64	107	20	3	17	80	39	29	.285	.360	.489	849	125	11	3			.942	-12	*C-92/1-1	0.6
1894	Phi-N	48	171	26	60	6	5	3	36	26	9	.351	.461	.497	958	134	12	6			.940	0	C-48	1.2
1895	Phi-N	88	322	64	127	27	2	13	75	22	7	.394	.446	.612	1058	170	32	3			.969	-10	*C-88	2.4
1896	Phi-N	57	184	35	66	5	7	5	45	17	14	.359	.427	.543	971	157	15	2			.966	-4	C-53	1.3
1897	Phi-N	55	185	18	44	4	2	6	36	12		.238	.305	.378	684	82	-5	3			.962	-2	C-49	-0.3
1898	StL-N	99	335	39	86	19	5	3	41	21		.257	.314	.370	684	94	-4	1			**.971**	-6	C-86	-0.2
1899	Cle-N	4	12	1	3	0	0	0	0	0		.250	.308	.250	558	58	-1	0			.938	0	/C-4	0.0
1900	Bos-N	16	42	6	13	1	0	1	10	3		.310	.370	.405	774	101	0	0			.948	1	C-10	0.2
Total	17	1160	4304	619	1240	226	60	77	687	341	301	.288	.348	.421	769	116	80	55			.937	-24	*C-1076/O-41R,1-8,3S	12.7

■ VERNE CLEMONS Clemons, Verne James "Stinger" or "Tubby" b: 9/8/1891, Clemons, Iowa d: 5/5/59, Bay Pines, Fla. BR/TR, 5'9.5", 190 lbs. Deb: 4/22/16

YEAR	TM/L	G	AB	R	H	2B	3B	HR	RBI	BB	SO	AVG	OBP	SLG	OPS	OPS+	BR+	SB	CS	SBR	FA	FR	G/POS	TPR
1916	StL-A	4	7	0	1	1	0	0	0	0	1	.143	.143	.286	429	30	-1	0			.889	0	/C-2	0.0
1919	StL-N	88	239	14	63	13	2	2	22	26	13	.264	.336	.360	696	116	5	4			.982	2	C-75	1.5
1920	StL-N	112	338	17	95	10	6	1	36	30	12	.281	.340	.355	695	103	2	1	1	-0	.977	-6	*C-103	0.4
1921	StL-N	117	341	29	109	16	2	2	48	33	17	.320	.380	.396	776	108	5	0	0	0	.985	-4	*C-107	0.7
1922	StL-N	71	160	9	41	4	0	0	15	18	5	.256	.331	.281	613	62	-8	1	0	0	.996	3	C-63	-0.2
1923	StL-N	57	130	6	37	9	1	0	13	10	11	.285	.345	.369	714	90	-2	0	0	0	.981	5	C-41	0.5
1924	StL-N	25	56	3	18	3	0	0	6	2	3	.321	.345	.375	720	94	-0	0	0	0	.983	-2	C-17	-0.1
Total	7	474	1271	78	364	56	11	5	140	119	62	.286	.348	.360	708	99	1	6	1		.983	-2	C-408	2.8

■ DONN CLENDENON Clendenon, Donn Alvin b: 7/15/35, Neosho, Mo. BR/TR, 6'3.5", 210 lbs. Deb: 9/22/61 Career OF: (27-LF 2-CF 10-RF)

YEAR	TM/L	G	AB	R	H	2B	3B	HR	RBI	BB	SO	AVG	OBP	SLG	OPS	OPS+	BR+	SB	CS	SBR	FA	FR	G/POS	TPR
1961	Pit-N	9	35	7	11	1	1	0	2	5	10	.314	.400	.400	800	113	1	0	0	0	1.000	1	/O-8(1-0-7)	0.1
1962	Pit-N	80	222	39	67	8	5	7	28	26	58	.302	.378	.477	855	128	9	16	4	2	.990	-1	1-52,O-19(16-1-2)	0.6
1963	Pit-N	154	563	65	155	28	7	15	57	39	136	.275	.328	.430	758	116	10	22	13	0	.991	7	*1-151	0.9

YEAR	TM/L	G	AB	R	H	2B	3B	HR	RBI	BB	SO	AVG	OBP	SLG	OPS	OPS+	BR+	SB	CS	SBR	FA	FR	G/POS	TPR
1964	Pit-N	133	457	53	129	23	8	12	64	26	96	.282	.324	.446	770	115	8	12	8	-0	.989	-1	*1-119	0.0
1965	Pit-N	162	612	89	184	32	14	14	96	48	128	.301	.356	.467	824	129	23	9	9	-1	.984	2	*1-158/3-1	1.5
1966	Pit-N	155	571	80	171	22	10	28	98	52	142	.299	.360	.520	880	141	31	8	7	-1	.985	-1	*1-152	2.0
1967	Pit-N	131	478	46	119	15	2	13	56	34	107	.249	.300	.370	670	90	-7	4	4	-1	.988	4	*1-123	-1.1
1968	Pit-N	158	584	63	150	20	6	17	87	47	163	.257	.313	.399	712	114	9	10	3	1	.990	10	*1-155	1.2
1969	Mon-N	38	129	14	31	6	1	4	14	6	32	.240	.274	.395	669	85	-3	0	2	-1	.987	4	1-24,O-11(9-1-1)	-0.3
	*NY-N	72	202	31	51	5	0	12	37	19	62	.252	.323	.455	778	113	3	3	2	-0	.984	-4	1-58/O-1(1-0-0)	-0.5
	Yr	110	331	45	82	11	1	16	51	25	94	.248	.304	.432	736	103	-0	3	4	-1	.985	-0	1-82,O-12(10-1-1)	-0.8
1970	NY-N	121	396	65	114	18	3	22	97	39	91	.288	.353	.515	868	129	15	4	1	1	.991	-2	*1-100	0.5
1971	NY-N	88	263	29	65	10	0	11	37	21	78	.247	.305	.411	716	103	0	1	2	-0	.985	-2	1-72	-0.8
1972	StL-N	61	136	13	26	4	0	4	9	17	37	.191	.281	.309	590	68	-6	1	2	-0	.986	3	1-36	-0.6
Total	12	1362	4648	594	1273	192	57	159	682	379	1140	.274	.331	.442	774	117	94	90	57	-0	.988	20	*1-1200/O-39L,3-1	3.5

■ ELMER CLEVELAND Cleveland, Elmer Ellsworth b: 9/15/1862, Washington, D.C. d: 10/8/13, Zimmerman, Pa. BR/TR, Deb: 8/29/1884

YEAR	TM/L	G	AB	R	H	2B	3B	HR	RBI	BB	SO	AVG	OBP	SLG	OPS	OPS+	BR+	SB	CS	SBR	FA	FR	G/POS	TPR
1884	Cin-U	29	115	24	37	9	2	0		4		.322	.345	.435	779	125	0				.843	2	3-29	0.2
1888	NY-N	9	34	6	8	0	2	2	5	3	1	.235	.297	.529	827	161	2	1			.667	-7	/3-9	-0.4
	Pit-N	30	108	10	24	2	1	2	11	5	23	.222	.270	.315	584	93	-1	3			.831	-9	3-30	-0.9
	Yr	39	142	16	32	2	3	4	16	8	24	.225	.276	.366	643	110	2	4			.806	-15	3-39	-1.3
1891	Col-a	12	41	12	7	0	0	0	4	12	9	.171	.370	.171	541	59	-1	4			.843	3	3-12	0.2
Total	3	80	298	52	76	11	5	4	20	24	33	.255	.317	.366	683	110	1	8			.830	-10	/3-80	-0.9

■ STAN CLIBURN Cliburn, Stanley Gene b: 12/19/56, Jackson, Miss. BR/TR, 6', 195 lbs. Deb: 5/6/80 F

YEAR	TM/L	G	AB	R	H	2B	3B	HR	RBI	BB	SO	AVG	OBP	SLG	OPS	OPS+	BR+	SB	CS	SBR	FA	FR	G/POS	TPR
1980	Cal-A	54	56	7	10	2	0	2	6	3	9	.179	.220	.321	542	48	-4	0	0	0	.971	5	C-54	0.2

■ HARLOND CLIFT Clift, Harlond Benton "Darkie" b: 8/12/12, ElReno, Okla. d: 4/27/92, Yakima, Wash. BR/TR, 5'11", 180 lbs. Deb: 4/17/34

YEAR	TM/L	G	AB	R	H	2B	3B	HR	RBI	BB	SO	AVG	OBP	SLG	OPS	OPS+	BR+	SB	CS	SBR	FA	FR	G/POS	TPR
1934	StL-A	147	572	104	149	30	10	14	56	84	100	.260	.357	.421	778	92	-7	7	2	1	.929	-16	*3-141	-1.6
1935	StL-A	137	475	101	140	26	4	11	69	83	39	.295	.406	.436	842	113	12	0	3	-1	.934	-6	*3-127/2-6	0.8
1936	StL-A	152	576	145	174	40	11	20	73	115	68	.302	.424	.514	938	127	27	12	4	1	.951	3	*3-152	3.2
1937	StL-A☆	155	571	103	175	36	7	29	118	98	80	.306	.413	.546	960	139	35	8	5	0	.947	**41**	*3-155	**7.3**
1938	StL-A	149	534	119	155	25	7	34	118	118	67	.290	.423	.554	977	143	38	10	5	0	**.962**	14	*3-149	5.1
1939	StL-A	151	526	90	142	25	2	15	84	**111**	55	.270	.402	.411	813	106	9	4	3	-0	.953	12	*3-149	2.4
1940	StL-A	150	523	92	143	29	5	20	87	104	62	.273	.396	.463	859	119	18	9	8	-1	**.959**	4	*3-147	2.4
1941	StL-A	154	584	108	149	33	9	17	84	113	93	.255	.376	.430	806	109	9	6	4	-0	.959	1	*3-154	1.5
1942	StL-A	143	541	108	148	39	4	7	55	106	48	.274	.394	.399	794	122	20	6	4	-0	.941	-1	*3-141/S-1	2.4
1943	StL-A	105	379	43	88	11	3	3	25	54	37	.232	.329	.301	630	83	-7	5	4	-0	.950	19	*3-104	1.4
	Was-A	8	30	4	9	0	0	0	4	5	3	.300	.417	.300	717	115	1	0	0	0	.968	-1	/3-8	0.1
	Yr	113	409	47	97	11	3	3	29	59	40	.237	.336	.301	637	85	-6	5	4	-0	.951	18	*3-112	1.5
1944	Was-A	12	44	4	7	3	0	0	3	3	3	.159	.213	.227	440	27	-4	0	0	0	.842	-3	3-12	-0.7
1945	Was-A	119	375	49	79	12	0	8	53	76	58	.211	.349	.307	656	99	3	2	1	0	.934	-4	*3-111	0.1
Total	12	1582	5730	1070	1558	309	62	178	829	1070	713	.272	.390	.441	831	115	154	69	43	0	.948	63	*3-1550/2-6,S-1	24.4

■ FLEA CLIFTON Clifton, Herman Earl b: 12/12/09, Cincinnati, Ohio d: 12/22/97, Cincinnati, Ohio BR/TR, 5'10", 160 lbs. Deb: 4/29/34

YEAR	TM/L	G	AB	R	H	2B	3B	HR	RBI	BB	SO	AVG	OBP	SLG	OPS	OPS+	BR+	SB	CS	SBR	FA	FR	G/POS	TPR
1934	Det-A	16	16	3	1	0	0	0	1	1	2	.063	.118	.063	180	-52	-4	0	0	0	1.000	2	/3-4,2-1	-0.2
1935	*Det-A	43	110	15	28	5	0	0	9	5	13	.255	.293	.300	593	56	-7	2	1	0	.934	-1	3-21/2-5,S-4	-0.7
1936	Det-A	13	26	5	5	1	0	0	1	4	3	.192	.300	.231	531	33	-3	0	1	-0	.926	-0	/S-6,3-2,2-1	-0.3
1937	Det-A	15	43	4	5	1	0	0	2	7	10	.116	.240	.140	380	-2	-7	3	0	1	.958	-0	/3-7,S-4,2-3	-0.5
Total	4	87	195	27	39	7	0	0	13	17	28	.200	.268	.236	504	30	-20	5	2	0	.937	-0	/3-34,S-14,2-10	-1.7

■ MONK CLINE Cline, John P. b: 3/3/1858, Louisville, Ky. d: 9/23/16, Louisville, Ky. BL/TL, 5'4", 150 lbs. Deb: 7/4/1882 Career OF: (61-LF 119-CF 41-RF)

YEAR	TM/L	G	AB	R	H	2B	3B	HR	RBI	BB	SO	AVG	OBP	SLG	OPS	OPS+	BR+	SB	CS	SBR	FA	FR	G/POS	TPR
1882	Bal-a	44	172	18	38	6	2	0		3		.221	.234	.279	513	79	-3				.825	6	O-39C/S-8,2-2,3-1	0.2
1884	Lou-a	94	396	91	115	16	7	2	39	27		.290	.342	.381	723	142	19				.875	6	*O-90(8-81-3)/S-6	2.0
1885	Lou-a	2	9	0	2	1	0	0	2	0		.222	.222	.333	556	74	-0				1.000	-1	/O-1(1-0-0),3-1	-0.1
1888	KC-a	73	293	45	69	13	2	0	19	20		.235	.289	.294	582	82	-7	29			.883	5	O-70(32-0-38)/2-3,3-1	-0.2
1891	Lou-a	19	70	11	21	3	1	0	11	16	2	.300	.430	.371	802	131	4	2			.929	-2	O-19(19-0-0)	0.1
Total	5	232	940	165	245	39	12	2	71	66	2	.261	.313	.334	647	110	13	31			.868	14	O-219C/S-14,2-5,3-3	2.0

■ TY CLINE Cline, Tyrone Alexander b: 6/15/39, Hampton, S.C. BL/TL, 6'0.5", 170 lbs. Deb: 9/14/60 Career OF: (112-LF 402-CF 44-RF)

YEAR	TM/L	G	AB	R	H	2B	3B	HR	RBI	BB	SO	AVG	OBP	SLG	OPS	OPS+	BR+	SB	CS	SBR	FA	FR	G/POS	TPR
1960	Cle-A	7	26	2	8	1	1	0	2	0	4	.308	.308	.423	731	99	-0	0	0	0	1.000	2	/O-6(0-6-0)	0.1
1961	Cle-A	12	43	9	9	2	1	0	1	6	1	.209	.333	.302	636	73	-1	1	0	0	1.000	-2	O-12(0-12-0)	-0.4
1962	Cle-A	118	375	53	93	15	5	2	28	28	50	.248	.309	.331	639	74	-13	5	4	-0	.992	3	*O-107(0-107-0)	-1.4
1963	Mil-N	72	174	17	41	2	1	0	10	10	31	.236	.285	.259	544	58	-9	2	1	0	.992	-0	O-62(0-62-0)	-1.2
1964	Mil-N	101	116	22	35	4	2	1	13	8	22	.302	.362	.397	759	113	2	0	1	-0	.982	-10	O-54(3-49-2)/1-6	-1.0
1965	Mil-N	123	220	27	42	5	3	0	10	16	50	.191	.246	.241	487	37	-18	2	2	-0	.969	-6	O-86(17-58-12)/1-5	-2.9
1966	Chi-N	7	17	3	6	0	0	0	2	0	2	.353	.353	.353	706	96	-0	1	0	0	1.000	-1	/O-5(0-5-0)	-0.1
	Atl-N	42	71	12	18	0	0	0	6	3	11	.254	.303	.254	556	56	-4	2	1	0	1.000	-5	O-19(7-5-10)/1-6	-1.0
	Yr	49	88	15	24	0	0	0	8	3	13	.273	.312	.273	585	63	-4	3	1	0	1.000	-6	O-24(7-10-10)/1-6	-1.1
1967	Atl-N	10	8	0	0	0	0	0	0	0	3	.000	.111	.000	111	-66	-2	0	0	0	1.000	-0	/O-1(1-0-0)	-0.2
	SF-N	64	122	18	33	5	5	0	4	9	13	.270	.326	.393	719	106	1	2	1	0	1.000	-6	O-37(17-21-3)	-0.7
	Yr	74	130	18	33	5	5	0	4	9	16	.254	.312	.369	681	96	-1	2	1	0	1.000	-6	O-38(18-21-3)	-0.9
1968	SF-N	116	291	37	65	6	3	1	28	11	26	.223	.254	.275	529	59	-15	0	2	-1	.971	-4	O-70(48-13-10),1-24	-2.8
1969	Mon-N	101	209	26	50	5	3	2	12	32	22	.239	.346	.321	666	87	-2	4	3	-0	.988	-0	O-41(7-35-0),1-17	-0.5
1970	Mon-N	2	2	0	1	0	0	0	0	0	0	.500	.500	.500	1000	169	0	0	0	0	.000	0	H	0.0
	*Cin-N	48	63	13	17	7	1	0	8	12	11	.270	.387	.413	799	114	2	1	2	-0	.966	-2	O-20(6-8-6)/1-2	-0.1
	Yr	50	65	13	18	7	1	0	8	12	11	.277	.390	.415	805	115	2	1	2	-0	.966	-2	O-20(6-8-6)/1-2	-0.1
1971	Cin-N	69	97	12	19	1	0	0	1	18	16	.196	.333	.206	540	57	-5	2	2	-0	1.000	-5	O-28(6-21-1)/1-2	-1.1
Total	12	892	1834	251	437	53	25	6	125	153	262	.238	.304	.304	609	72	-65	22	19	-2	.986	-38	O-548C/1-62	-13.3

■ GENE CLINES Clines, Eugene Anthony b: 10/6/46, San Pablo, Cal. BR/TR, 5'9", 170 lbs. Deb: 6/28/70 C Career OF: (302-LF 210-CF 132-RF)

YEAR	TM/L	G	AB	R	H	2B	3B	HR	RBI	BB	SO	AVG	OBP	SLG	OPS	OPS+	BR+	SB	CS	SBR	FA	FR	G/POS	TPR
1970	Pit-N	31	37	4	15	2	0	0	3	2	5	.405	.436	.459	895	143	2	2	1	0	1.000	-2	/O-7(2-2-3)	0.0
1971	*Pit-N	97	273	52	84	12	4	1	24	22	36	.308	.366	.392	758	115	6	15	6	1	.981	2	O-74(20-43-13)	0.7
1972	*Pit-N	107	311	52	104	15	6	0	17	16	47	.334	.371	.421	792	127	11	12	6	1	.958	-9	O-83(38-17-39)	-0.1
1973	Pit-N	110	304	42	80	11	3	1	23	26	36	.263	.327	.329	656	84	-6	8	7	-1	.968	-2	O-77(7-45-25)	-1.1
1974	*Pit-N	107	276	29	62	5	1	0	14	30	40	.225	.310	.250	560	60	-14	14	2	2	.989	2	O-78(19-51-11)	-1.2
1975	NY-N	82	203	25	46	6	3	0	10	11	21	.227	.270	.286	555	57	-12	4	4	-1	.982	-4	O-60(35-34-2)	-2.0
1976	Tex-A	116	446	52	123	12	3	0	38	16	52	.276	.307	.316	623	81	-11	11	9	-1	.987	3	*O-103(96-5-4),D-10	-1.7
1977	Chi-N	101	239	27	70	12	2	3	41	25	25	.293	.362	.397	760	93	-2	1	2	-0	.986	-8	O-63(50-3-11)	-1.2
1978	Chi-N	109	229	31	59	10	2	0	17	21	28	.258	.323	.319	641	71	-8	4	3	-0	.978	-7	O-66(35-10-24)	-1.9
1979	Chi-N	10	10	0	2	0	0	0	0	0	1	.200	.200	.200	400	9	-1	0	0	0	.000	0	/H	-0.2
Total	10	870	2328	314	645	85	24	5	187	169	291	.277	.331	.341	672	88	-35	71	40	2	.979	-24	O-611L/D-10	-8.7

■ BILLY CLINGMAN Clingman, William Frederick b: 11/21/1869, Cincinnati, Ohio d: 5/14/58, Cincinnati, Ohio BB/TR, 5'11", 150 lbs. Deb: 9/9/1890

YEAR	TM/L	G	AB	R	H	2B	3B	HR	RBI	BB	SO	AVG	OBP	SLG	OPS	OPS+	BR+	SB	CS	SBR	FA	FR	G/POS	TPR
1890	Cin-N	7	27	2	7	1	0	0	5	1	0	.259	.286	.296	582	70	-1	0			.892	-1	/S-6,2-1	-0.2
1891	Cin-a	1	5	0	1	1	0	0	0	0	0	.200	.200	.400	600	65	-0	0			.667	-1	/2-1	-0.1
1895	Pit-N	107	386	69	99	16	4	0	45	41	43	.256	.331	.319	650	72	-15	19			.888	14	*3-107	0.1
1896	Lou-N	121	423	57	99	10	2	2	37	57	51	.234	.329	.281	611	64	-20	19			.925	24	*3-121	0.5
1897	Lou-N	115	403	61	92	14	7	2	47	37		.228	.301	.313	614	64	-21	14			**.947**	**31**	*3-115	1.0
1898	Lou-N	154	538	65	138	12	6	0	50	51		.257	.327	.301	628	81	-12	15			.914	15	3-79,S-74/O-1C,2-1	0.8
1899	Lou-N	110	369	68	97	15	5	2	45	46		.263	.349	.347	696	91	-4	13			.913	-3	*S-110	0.0
1900	Chi-N	47	159	15	33	6	0	0	11	17		.208	.292	.245	537	51	-10	6			.872	-12	S-47	-1.9
1901	Was-A	137	480	66	116	10	7	2	55	42		.242	.308	.304	612	71	-18	10			**.932**	18	*S-137	0.4

YEAR	TM/L	G	AB	R	H	2B	3B	HR	RBI	BB	SO	AVG	OBP	SLG	OPS	OPS+	BR+	SB	CS	SBR	FA	FR	G/POS	TPR
1903	Cle-A	21	64	10	18	1	1	0	7	11		.281	.387	.328	715	118	2	2			.932	-0	2-11/S-7,3-3	0.2
Total	10	820	2854	413	700	86	32	8	302	303	94	.245	.323	.306	629	74	-98	98			.919	84	3-425,S-381/2-14,O	0.8

■ JIM CLINTON

Clinton, James Lawrence "Big Jim" b: 8/10/1850, New York, N.Y. d: 9/3/21, Brooklyn, N.Y. BR/TR, 5'8.5", 174 lbs. Deb: 5/18/1872 U NA OF: (0-LF 9-CF 10-RF) Career OF: (150-LF 196-CF 18-RF)

YEAR	TM/L	G	AB	R	H	2B	3B	HR	RBI	BB	SO	AVG	OBP	SLG	OPS	OPS+	BR+	SB	CS	SBR	FA	FR	G/POS	TPR
1872	Eck-n	25	97	12	25	3	1	0	6	0	2	.258	.258	.309	567	87	0	0	1	-0	.792	-6	O-11C,3-10/2-3,CS	-0.5
1873	Res-n	9	38	5	9	1	0	0	4	0	0	.237	.237	.263	500	52	-2	0	0	0	.697	-1	/3-9	-0.2
1874	Atl-n	2	11	3	2	1	0	0	2	0	2	.182	.182	.273	455	49	-0	0	0	0	.444	-2	/2-1,O-1(0-1-0)	-0.2
1875	Atl-n	22	81	3	10	0	0	0	0	0	0	.123	.123	.123	247	-16	-8	0	0	0	.830	3	P-17/O-7R,1-5,2-1	0.0
1876	Lou-N	16	65	8	22	2	0	0	0	0	0	.338	.338	.369	708	115	0				.783	1	O-14(0-0-14)/1-1,P-1	0.1
1882	Wor-N	26	98	9	16	2	0	0	3	7	13	.163	.219	.184	403	30	-7				.734	-4	O-26(21-1-4)	-1.1
1883	Bal-a	94	399	69	125	16	8	0		27		.313	.357	.393	750	137	16				.842	5	*O-92(92-0-0)/2-2	1.7
1884	Bal-a	104	437	82	118	12	6	4		29		.270	.334	.352	686	119	10				.807	-1	*O-104(37-67-0)/2-1	0.5
1885	Cin-a	105	408	48	97	5	5	0	34	15		.238	.277	.275	551	73	-12				.877	-0	*O-105(0-105-0)	-1.5
1886	Bal-a	23	83	8	15	1	0	0	6	4		.181	.227	.193	420	33	-6	3			.894	-0	O-23(0-23-0)	-0.7
Total	4 n	58	227	23	46	5	1	0	12	0	4	.203	.203	.233	436	45	-10	0	1	-0	.699	-6	/3-19,O-19R,P12SC	-0.9
Total	6	368	1490	224	393	38	19	4	43	82	13	.264	.311	.323	634	101	0	3			.838	0	O-364C/2-3,P-1,1-1	-1.0

■ LOU CLINTON

Clinton, Luciean Louis b: 10/13/37, Ponca City, Okla. d: 12/6/97, Wichita, Kan. BR/TR, 6'1", 185 lbs. Deb: 4/22/60

YEAR	TM/L	G	AB	R	H	2B	3B	HR	RBI	BB	SO	AVG	OBP	SLG	OPS	OPS+	BR+	SB	CS	SBR	FA	FR	G/POS	TPR
1960	Bos-A	96	298	37	68	17	5	6	37	20	66	.228	.283	.379	663	75	-11	4	3	-0	.966	2	O-89(0-0-89)	-1.3
1961	Bos-A	17	51	4	13	2	1	0	3	2	10	.255	.283	.333	616	63	-3	0	0	0	1.000	3	O-13(0-0-13)	-0.1
1962	Bos-A	114	398	63	117	24	10	18	75	34	79	.294	.351	.540	891	132	16	2	1	0	.979	1	*O-103(0-0-103)	1.1
1963	Bos-A	148	560	71	130	23	7	22	77	49	118	.232	.295	.416	711	94	-6	0	0	0	.982	11	*O-146(0-0-146)	-0.5
1964	Bos-A	37	120	15	31	4	3	3	6	9	33	.258	.310	.417	727	95	-1	1	0	0	1.000	5	O-35(0-0-35)	0.2
	LA-A	91	306	30	76	18	0	9	38	31	40	.248	.320	.395	715	108	3	3	0	1	.985	3	O-86(0-0-86)	0.1
	Yr	128	426	45	107	22	3	12	44	40	73	.251	.317	.401	718	104	2	4	0	1	.990	7	*O-121(0-0-121)	0.3
1965	Cal-A	89	222	29	54	12	3	1	8	23	37	.243	.317	.338	655	88	-3	2	3	-1	.983	-2	O-73(1-0-72)	-1.0
	KC-A	1	1	0	0	0	0	0	0	0	0	.000	.000	.000	0	-99	-0	0	0	0	.000	-0	/O-1(0-0-1)	-0.1
	Cle-A	12	34	2	6	1	0	1	2	3	7	.176	.243	.294	537	51	-2	0	0	0	.941	-0	/O-9(9-1-1)	-0.3
	Yr	102	257	31	60	13	3	2	10	26	44	.233	.306	.331	637	83	-6	2	3	-1	.977	-2	O-83(10-1-74)	-1.4
1966	NY-A	80	159	18	35	10	2	5	21	16	27	.220	.291	.403	694	101	-0	0	0	0	.976	-6	O-63(5-1-57)	-1.0
1967	NY-A	6	4	1	2	1	0	0	2	1	1	.500	.600	.750	1350	308	1	0	0	0	.000	-0	/O-1(1-0-0)	0.1
Total	8	691	2153	270	532	112	31	65	269	188	418	.247	.310	.418	728	99	-6	12	7	0	.980	15	O-619(16-2-603)	-2.8

■ ED CLOUGH

Clough, Edgar George "Big Ed" or "Spec" b: 10/28/06, Wiconisco, Pa. d: 1/30/44, Harrisburg, Pa. BL/TL, 6', 188 lbs. Deb: 8/28/24

YEAR	TM/L	G	AB	R	H	2B	3B	HR	RBI	BB	SO	AVG	OBP	SLG	OPS	OPS+	BR+	SB	CS	SBR	FA	FR	G/POS	TPR
1924	StL-N	7	14	0	1	0	0	0	1	0	3	.071	.071	.071	143	-63	-3	0	0	0	1.000	0	/O-6(5-0-1)	-0.3
1925	StL-N	3	4	0	1	0	0	0	0	0	0	.250	.250	.250	500	28	-0	0	0	0	1.000	-0	/P-3	0.0
1926	StL-N	1	1	0	0	0	0	0	0	0	0	.000	.000	.000	0	-96	-0	0			.000	-0	/P-1	0.0
Total	3	11	19	0	2	0	0	0	1	0	3	.105	.105	.105	211	-44	-4	0	0		1.000	0	/O-6(5-0-1),P-4	-0.3

■ DANNY CLYBURN

Clyburn, Danny b: 4/6/74, Lancaster, S.C. BR/TR, 6'3", 220 lbs. Deb: 9/15/97

YEAR	TM/L	G	AB	R	H	2B	3B	HR	RBI	BB	SO	AVG	OBP	SLG	OPS	OPS+	BR+	SB	CS	SBR	FA	FR	G/POS	TPR
1997	Bal-A	2	3	0	0	0	0	0	0	0	2	.000	.000	.000	0	-99	-1	0	0	0	.000	-0	/O-1(1-0-0)	-0.1
1998	Bal-A	11	25	6	7	0	0	1	3	1	10	.280	.308	.400	708	83	-1	0	0	0	1.000	-2	/O-8(5-0-5),D-1	-0.3
1999	TB-A	28	81	8	16	4	0	3	5	7	21	.198	.270	.358	628	58	-5	0	0	0	1.000	1	O-24(14-0-10)/D-4	-0.5
Total	3	41	109	14	23	4	0	4	8	8	33	.211	.271	.358	629	59	-7	0	0	0	1.000	-1	/O-33(20-0-15),D-5	-0.9

■ OTIS CLYMER

Clymer, Otis Edgar b: 1/27/1876, Pine Grove, Pa. d: 2/27/26, St.Paul, Minn. BB/TR, 5'11", 180 lbs. Deb: 4/14/05 Career OF: (33-LF 33-CF 262-RF)

YEAR	TM/L	G	AB	R	H	2B	3B	HR	RBI	BB	SO	AVG	OBP	SLG	OPS	OPS+	BR+	SB	CS	SBR	FA	FR	G/POS	TPR
1905	Pit-N	96	365	74	108	11	5	0	23	19		.296	.332	.353	686	102	0	23			.986	-2	O-89(4-0-85)/1-1	-0.6
1906	Pit-N	11	45	7	11	0	1	0	1	3		.244	.292	.289	581	78	-1	1			.900	-1	O-11(0-0-11)	-0.3
1907	Pit-N	22	66	8	15	2	0	0	4	5		.227	.311	.258	568	77	-1	4			.923	-3	O-15(0-0-15)/1-1	-0.5
	Was-A	57	206	30	65	5	5	1	16	18		.316	.382	.403	784	163	15	18			.912	-4	O-51(27-1-24)/1-1	0.9
1908	Was-A	110	368	32	93	11	4	1	35	20		.253	.291	.313	604	105	1	19			.933	-8	O-82(1-0-81),2-13/3-2	-1.1
1909	Was-A	45	138	11	27	5	2	0	6	17		.196	.284	.261	545	76	-3	7			.922	-4	O-41(0-1-40)	-1.1
1913	Chi-N	30	105	16	24	5	1	0	7	14	18	.229	.319	.295	615	76	-3	9			.933	-2	O-26(0-24-2)	-0.7
	Bos-N	14	37	4	12	3	1	0	6	3	3	.324	.375	.459	834	135	2	2			.880	-2	O-11(1-7-4)	-0.1
	Yr	44	142	20	36	8	2	0	13	17	21	.254	.333	.338	671	91	-1	11			.918	-4	O-37(1-31-6)	-0.8
Total	6	385	1330	182	355	42	19	2	98	99	21	.267	.322	.332	653	106	9	83			.939	-25	O-326R/2-13,1-3,3-2	-3.5

■ BILL CLYMER

Clymer, William Johnston "Derby Day Bill" b: 12/18/1873, Philadelphia, Pa. d: 12/26/36, Philadelphia, Pa. Deb: 6/26/1891 C

YEAR	TM/L	G	AB	R	H	2B	3B	HR	RBI	BB	SO	AVG	OBP	SLG	OPS	OPS+	BR+	SB	CS	SBR	FA	FR	G/POS	TPR
1891	Phi-a	3	11	0	0	0	0	0	0	1	2	.000	.154	.000	154	-55	-2	1			.867	-2	/S-3	-0.3

■ PETE COACHMAN

Coachman, Bobby Dean b: 11/11/61, Cottonwood, Ala. BR/TR, 5'9", 175 lbs. Deb: 8/18/90

YEAR	TM/L	G	AB	R	H	2B	3B	HR	RBI	BB	SO	AVG	OBP	SLG	OPS	OPS+	BR+	SB	CS	SBR	FA	FR	G/POS	TPR
1990	Cal-A	16	45	3	14	3	0	0	5	1	7	.311	.354	.378	732	107	0	0	1	-0	.958	1	/3-9,2-2,D-2	0.1

■ GIL COAN

Coan, Gilbert Fitzgerald b: 5/18/22, Monroe, N.C. BL/TR, 6', 180 lbs. Deb: 4/27/46

YEAR	TM/L	G	AB	R	H	2B	3B	HR	RBI	BB	SO	AVG	OBP	SLG	OPS	OPS+	BR+	SB	CS	SBR	FA	FR	G/POS	TPR
1946	Was-A	59	134	17	28	3	2	3	9	7	37	.209	.269	.328	597	70	-6	2	2	-0	.969	-2	O-29(27-0-2)	-1.1
1947	Was-A	11	42	5	21	3	2	0	3	5	6	.500	.553	.667	1220	245	8	2	1	0	1.000	1	O-11(0-0-11)	0.9
1948	Was-A	138	513	56	119	13	9	7	60	41	78	.232	.298	.333	631	70	-24	23	9	2	.970	12	*O-131(131-0-0)	-2.0
1949	Was-A	111	358	36	78	7	8	3	25	29	58	.218	.278	.307	586	56	-24	9	6	-0	.975	2	O-97(68-29-0)	-2.8
1950	Was-A	104	366	58	111	17	4	7	50	28	46	.303	.359	.429	788	106	2	10	5	0	.970	-3	O-98(95-3-1)	-0.6
1951	Was-A	135	538	85	163	25	7	9	62	39	62	.303	.357	.426	782	113	9	8	5	0	.965	**22**	*O-132(132-0-0)	2.0
1952	Was-A	107	332	50	68	11	6	5	20	32	35	.205	.277	.319	596	68	-15	9	4	1	.984	0	O-86(86-0-0)	-2.2
1953	Was-A	68	168	28	33	1	4	2	17	22	23	.196	.301	.286	586	60	-9	7	0	**2**	1.000	4	O-46(45-1-0)	-0.7
1954	Bal-A	94	265	29	74	11	1	2	20	16	17	.279	.323	.351	674	91	-4	9	4	1	.968	-4	O-67(36-32-0)	-1.1
1955	Bal-A	61	130	18	31	7	1	1	11	13	15	.238	.313	.331	643	79	-4	4	2	0	.983	-4	O-43(42-0-1)	-1.0
	Chi-A	17	17	0	3	0	0	0	1	0	5	.176	.176	.176	353	-5	-2	0	0	0	1.000	-1	/O-3(1-0-2)	-0.3
	Yr	78	147	18	34	7	1	1	12	13	20	.231	.298	.313	611	68	-7	4	2	0	.984	-5	O-46(43-0-3)	-1.3
	NY-N	9	13	0	2	0	0	0	0	0	1	.154	.154	.154	308	-18	-2	0	0	0	1.000	-2	/O-6(1-2-4)	-0.5
1956	NY-N	4	1	2	0	0	0	0	0	0	1	.000	.000	.000	0	-99	-0	0	0	0	.000	0	H	0.0
Total	11	918	2877	384	731	98	44	39	278	232	384	.254	.316	.359	675	84	-72	83	38	5	.973	24	O-749(664-67-21)	-9.4

■ JOE COBB

Cobb, Joseph Stanley (b: Joseph Stanley Serafin) b: 1/24/1895, Hudson, Pa. d: 12/24/47, Allentown, Pa. BR/TR, 5'9", 170 lbs. Deb: 4/25/18

YEAR	TM/L	G	AB	R	H	2B	3B	HR	RBI	BB	SO	AVG	OBP	SLG	OPS	OPS+	BR+	SB	CS	SBR	FA	FR	G/POS	TPR
1918	Det-A	1	0	0	0	0	0	0	0	1	0	—	1.000	—	1000	210	0	0			.000	0	H	0.0

■ TY COBB

Cobb, Tyrus Raymond "The Georgia Peach" b: 12/18/1886, Narrows, Ga. d: 7/17/61, Atlanta, Ga. BL/TR, 6'1", 175 lbs. Deb: 8/30/05 MH Career OF: (35-LF 2194-CF 706-RF)

YEAR	TM/L	G	AB	R	H	2B	3B	HR	RBI	BB	SO	AVG	OBP	SLG	OPS	OPS+	BR+	SB	CS	SBR	FA	FR	G/POS	TPR
1905	Det-A	41	150	19	36	6	0	1	15	10		.240	.287	.300	588	86	-3	2			.958	2	O-41(2-39-0)	-0.3
1906	Det-A	98	358	45	113	15	5	1	34	19		.316	.355	.394	749	131	12	23			.961	6	O-96(18-55-24)	1.5
1907	*Det-A	150	605	97	**212**	28	14	5	**119**	24		**.350**	.380	**.468**	**848**	**164**	**40**	**49**			.961	11	*O-150(0-0-150)	4.9
1908	*Det-A	150	581	88	**188**	**36**	**20**	4	**108**	34		**.324**	.367	**.475**	**842**	**166**	**40**	39			.944	4	*O-150(0-0-150)	4.2
1909	*Det-A	156	573	**116**	**216**	33	10	**9**	**107**	48		**.377**	**.431**	**.517**	**947**	**190**	**58**	**76**			.946	3	*O-156(0-0-156)	6.0
1910	Det-A	140	506	**106**	194	35	13	8	91	64		**.383**	**.456**	**.551**	**1008**	**202**	60	65			.958	9	*O-137(0-111-26)	6.8
1911	Det-A	146	591	**147**	**248**	**47**	**24**	8	**127**	44		**.420**	.467	**.621**	**1088**	**193**	**71**	**83**			.957	11	*O-146(0-146-0)	**6.8**
1912	Det-A	140	553	120	**226**	30	23	7	83	43		**.409**	.456	**.584**	**1040**	**203**	**72**	61			.940	1	*O-140(0-140-0)	6.1
1913	Det-A	122	428	70	167	18	16	4	67	58	31	**.390**	**.467**	.535	1002	**196**	53	51			.947	2	*O-118(0-116-2)/2-1	4.9
1914	Det-A	98	345	69	127	22	11	2	57	57	22	**.368**	.466	**.513**	979	188	40	35	17	2	.949	-10	O-96(0-96-0)	2.7
1915	Det-A	156	563	**144**	**208**	31	13	3	99	118	43	**.369**	**.486**	.487	**973**	**182**	**65**	**96**	38	**8**	.951	-3	*O-156(0-156-0)	6.1
1916	Det-A	145	542	**113**	201	31	10	5	68	78	39	.371	.452	.493	944	177	53	**68**	24	**7**	.953	-2	*O-143(0-143-0)/1-1	5.2
1917	Det-A	152	588	107	**225**	**44**	**24**	6	102	61	34	**.383**	**.444**	**.570**	**1014**	**210**	**75**	**55**			.973	13	*O-152(0-123-29)	**8.3**
1918	Det-A	111	421	83	161	19	**14**	3	64	41	21	**.382**	**.440**	.515	**955**	**196**	**48**	34			.975	2	O-95C,1-13/P-2,23	4.7
1919	Det-A	124	497	92	**191**	36	13	1	70	38	22	**.384**	.429	.515	944	168	44	28			.973	-2	*O-123(0-123-0)	3.4
1920	Det-A	112	428	86	143	28	8	2	63	58	28	.334	.416	.451	867	133	22	15	10	-0	.966	-7	*O-112(0-112-0)	0.6

YEAR	TM/L	G	AB	R	H	2B	3B	HR	RBI	BB	SO	AVG	OBP	SLG	OPS	OPS+	BR+	SB	CS	SBR	FA	FR	G/POS	TPR
1921	Det-A	128	507	124	197	37	16	12	101	56	19	.389	.452	.596	1048	167	52	22	15	-0	.970	13	*O-121(0-121-0),M	5.4
1922	Det-A	137	526	99	211	42	16	4	99	55	24	.401	.462	.565	1026	172	57	9	13	-3	.980	4	*O-134(0-133-1),M	4.9
1923	Det-A	145	556	103	189	40	7	6	88	66	14	.340	.413	.469	882	135	29	9	10	-2	.969	4	*O-141(0-141-0),M	2.5
1924	Det-A	155	625	115	211	38	10	4	79	85	18	.338	.418	.450	867	126	27	23	14	0	**.986**	5	*O-155(0-155-0),M	2.3
1925	Det-A	121	415	97	157	31	12	12	102	65	12	.378	.468	.598	**1066**	**171**	47	13	9	-0	.948	-2	*O-105(0-101-4)/P-1,M	3.6
1926	Det-A	79	233	48	79	18	5	4	62	26	2	.339	.408	.511	918	137	12	9	4	1	.950	-5	O-55(15-39-1),M	0.5
1927	Phi-A	134	490	104	175	32	7	5	93	67	12	.357	.440	.482	921	131	26	22	16	-1	.969	-5	*O-127(0-52-75)	1.1
1928	Phi-A	95	353	54	114	27	4	1	40	34	16	.323	.389	.431	819	112	7	5	8	-2	.964	-1	O-85(0-0-85)	-0.2
Total	24	3035	11434	2246	4189	724	295	117	1938	1249	357	.366	.433	.512	945	167	1006	892	178		.961	54	*O-2934C/1-14,P-3,23	92.0

■ DAVE COBLE Coble, David Lamar b: 12/24/12, Monroe, N.C. d: 10/15/71, Orlando, Fla. BR/TR, 6'1", 183 lbs. Deb: 5/1/39

YEAR	TM/L	G	AB	R	H	2B	3B	HR	RBI	BB	SO	AVG	OBP	SLG	OPS	OPS+	BR+	SB	CS	SBR	FA	FR	G/POS	TPR
1939	Phi-N	15	25	2	7	1	0	0	0	0	3	.280	.280	.320	600	63	-1	0			.938	-1	C-13	-0.2

■ GEORGE COCHRAN Cochran, George Leslie b: 2/12/1889, Rusk, Tex. d: 5/21/60, Harbor City, Cal. TR, Deb: 7/29/18

YEAR	TM/L	G	AB	R	H	2B	3B	HR	RBI	BB	SO	AVG	OBP	SLG	OPS	OPS+	BR+	SB	CS	SBR	FA	FR	G/POS	TPR
1918	Bos-A	24	60	7	7	0	0	0	3	10	6	.117	.264	.117	381	15	-6	3			.960	-4	3-22/S-1	-1.0

■ DAVE COCHRANE Cochrane, David Carter b: 1/31/63, Riverside, Cal. BB/TR, 6'2", 180 lbs. Deb: 9/2/86 Career OF: (42-LF 0-CF 12-RF)

YEAR	TM/L	G	AB	R	H	2B	3B	HR	RBI	BB	SO	AVG	OBP	SLG	OPS	OPS+	BR+	SB	CS	SBR	FA	FR	G/POS	TPR
1986	Chi-A	19	62	4	12	2	0	1	2	5	22	.194	.254	.274	528	42	-5	0	0	0	.872	-3	3-18/S-1	-0.8
1989	Sea-A	54	102	13	24	4	1	3	7	14	27	.235	.333	.382	716	98	-0	0	2	-1	.905	-13	S-30/1-9,3-9,2OC	-1.4
1990	Sea-A	15	20	0	3	0	0	0	0	0	8	.150	.150	.150	300	-16	-3	0	0	0	1.000	0	/S-5,1-3,3-3,C-1	-0.3
1991	Sea-A	65	178	16	44	13	0	2	22	9	38	.247	.287	.354	641	76	-6	0	1	-0	.969	-14	O-26L,C-19,3-13,/1D	-2.1
1992	Sea-A	65	152	10	38	5	0	2	12	12	34	.250	.309	.322	631	77	-5	1	0	0	.879	-8	O-25L,C-21,3/1SD2	-1.3
Total	5	218	514	43	121	24	1	8	43	40	129	.235	.294	.333	627	73	-19	1	3	-1	.925	-38	/O-54L,3-53,CS12D	-5.9

■ MICKEY COCHRANE Cochrane, Gordon Stanley b: 4/6/03, Bridgewater, Mass. d: 6/28/62, Lake Forest, Ill. BL/TR, 5'10.5", 180 lbs. Deb: 4/14/25 MCH

YEAR	TM/L	G	AB	R	H	2B	3B	HR	RBI	BB	SO	AVG	OBP	SLG	OPS	OPS+	BR+	SB	CS	SBR	FA	FR	G/POS	TPR
1925	Phi-A	134	420	69	139	21	5	6	55	44	19	.331	.397	.448	845	107	5	7	4	0	.984	-10	*C-133	0.3
1926	Phi-A	120	370	50	101	8	9	8	47	56	15	.273	.369	.408	777	97	-1	5	2	0	.975	12	*C-115	1.8
1927	Phi-A	126	432	80	146	20	6	12	80	50	7	.338	.409	.495	904	127	17	9	6	-0	.986	3	*C-123	2.7
1928	Phi-A	131	468	92	137	26	12	10	57	76	25	.293	.395	.464	859	122	16	7	7	-1	.966	2	*C-130	2.5
1929	*Phi-A	135	514	113	170	37	8	7	95	69	8	.331	.412	.475	887	123	20	7	6	-1	.983	8	*C-135	3.4
1930	*Phi-A	130	487	110	174	42	5	10	85	55	18	.357	.424	.526	949	133	26	5	0	1	**.993**	6	*C-130	3.7
1931	*Phi-A	122	459	87	160	31	6	17	89	56	21	.349	.423	.553	976	146	31	2	3	-1	.986	10	*C-117	4.3
1932	Phi-A	139	518	118	152	35	4	23	112	100	22	.293	.412	.510	921	132	27	0	1	-0	**.993**	10	*C-137/O-1(1-0-0)	4.1
1933	Phi-A	130	429	104	138	30	4	15	60	106	22	.322	**.459**	.515	974	156	41	8	6	-0	.989	-7	*C-128	3.8
1934	*Det-A★	129	437	74	140	32	1	2	76	78	26	.320	.428	.412	840	117	16	8	4	0	.988	-4	*C-124,M	1.8
1935	*Det-A☆	115	411	93	131	33	3	5	47	96	15	.319	.452	.450	902	139	30	5	5	-1	.989	-5	*C-110,M	2.9
1936	Det-A	44	126	24	34	8	0	2	17	46	15	.270	.465	.381	846	111	5	1	1	-0	.983	-9	C-42,M	-0.1
1937	Det-A	27	98	27	30	10	1	2	12	25	4	.306	.452	.490	941	134	6	0	1	-0	1.000	-2	C-27,M	0.6
Total	13	1482	5169	1041	1652	333	64	119	832	857	217	.320	.419	.478	897	127	239	64	46	-2	.985	14	*C-1451/O-1(1-0-0)	31.8

■ JIM COCKMAN Cockman, James b: 4/26/1873, Guelph, Ont., Can. d: 9/28/47, Guelph, Ont., Can. BR/TR, 5'6", 145 lbs. Deb: 9/28/05

YEAR	TM/L	G	AB	R	H	2B	3B	HR	RBI	BB	SO	AVG	OBP	SLG	OPS	OPS+	BR+	SB	CS	SBR	FA	FR	G/POS	TPR
1905	NY-A	13	38	5	4	0	0	0	2	4		.105	.190	.105	296	-5	-4	2			.875	-2	3-13	-0.7

■ ALAN COCKRELL Cockrell, Atlee Alan b: 12/5/62, Kansas City, Kan. BR/TR, 6'2", 210 lbs. Deb: 9/7/96

YEAR	TM/L	G	AB	R	H	2B	3B	HR	RBI	BB	SO	AVG	OBP	SLG	OPS	OPS+	BR+	SB	CS	SBR	FA	FR	G/POS	TPR
1996	Col-N	9	8	0	2	1	0	0	2	0	4	.250	.250	.375	625	50	-1	0	0	0	.000	-0	/O-1(0-0-1)	-0.1

■ JACK COFFEY Coffey, John Francis b: 1/28/1887, New York, N.Y. d: 2/14/66, Bronx, N.Y. BR/TR, 5'11", 178 lbs. Deb: 6/23/09

YEAR	TM/L	G	AB	R	H	2B	3B	HR	RBI	BB	SO	AVG	OBP	SLG	OPS	OPS+	BR+	SB	CS	SBR	FA	FR	G/POS	TPR
1909	Bos-N	73	257	21	48	4	4	0	20	11		.187	.229	.233	462	41	-18	2			.896	-12	S-73	-3.1
1918	Det-A	22	67	7	14	0	2	0	4	8	6	.209	.303	.269	571	75	-2	2			.957	0	2-22	-0.1
	Bos-A	15	44	5	7	1	0	1	2	3	2	.159	.213	.250	463	40	-3	2			.955	2	3-14/2-1	-0.1
	Yr	37	111	12	21	1	2	1	6	11	8	.189	.268	.261	530	62	-5	4			.959	2	2-23,3-14	-0.2
Total	2	110	368	33	69	5	6	1	26	22	8	.188	.241	.242	483	48	-23	6			.896	-9	/S-73,2-23,3-14	-3.3

■ IVANON COFFIE Coffie, Ivanon Angelino b: 5/16/77, Curacao, Netherlands Antilles BL/TR, 6'1", 190 lbs. Deb: 7/15/2000

YEAR	TM/L	G	AB	R	H	2B	3B	HR	RBI	BB	SO	AVG	OBP	SLG	OPS	OPS+	BR+	SB	CS	SBR	FA	FR	G/POS	TPR
2000	Bal-A	23	60	6	13	4	1	0	6	5	11	.217	.288	.317	605	55	-4	1	0	0	.971	-0	3-15/S-4,D-1	-0.3

■ FRANK COGGINS Coggins, Franklin b: 5/22/44, Griffin, Ga. BB/TR, 6'2", 187 lbs. Deb: 9/10/67

YEAR	TM/L	G	AB	R	H	2B	3B	HR	RBI	BB	SO	AVG	OBP	SLG	OPS	OPS+	BR+	SB	CS	SBR	FA	FR	G/POS	TPR
1967	Was-A	19	75	9	23	3	0	1	8	2	17	.307	.325	.387	711	114	1	1	0	0	.964	3	2-19	0.7
1968	Was-A	62	171	15	30	6	1	0	7	9	33	.175	.217	.222	439	34	-14	1	1	-0	.953	4	2-52	-0.7
1972	Chi-N	6	1	1	0	0	0	0	0	1	0	.000	.500	.000	500	48	0	0	0	0	.000	0	H	0.0
Total	3	87	247	25	53	9	1	1	15	12	50	.215	.251	.271	522	59	-13	2	1	0	.957	7	/2-71	0.0

■ RICH COGGINS Coggins, Richard Allen b: 12/7/50, Indianapolis, Ind. BL/TL, 5'8", 170 lbs. Deb: 8/29/72 Career OF: (20-LF 106-CF 203-RF)

YEAR	TM/L	G	AB	R	H	2B	3B	HR	RBI	BB	SO	AVG	OBP	SLG	OPS	OPS+	BR+	SB	CS	SBR	FA	FR	G/POS	TPR
1972	Bal-A	16	39	5	13	4	0	0	1	1	6	.333	.350	.436	786	129	1	0	2	-1	1.000	2	O-13(0-9-6)	0.3
1973	*Bal-A	110	389	54	124	19	9	7	41	28	24	.319	.365	.468	832	134	16	17	9	1	.987	-3	*O-101(0-39-76)/D-1	1.0
1974	*Bal-A	113	411	53	100	13	3	4	32	29	31	.243	.301	.319	620	81	-10	26	6	4	.984	-7	*O-105(2-30-87)	-2.0
1975	Mon-N	13	37	1	10	3	1	0	4	1	7	.270	.289	.405	695	87	-1	0	0	0	1.000	-1	O-10(9-0-2)	-0.3
	NY-A	51	107	7	24	1	0	1	6	7	16	.224	.272	.262	534	52	-7	3	3	-0	.970	-3	O-36(3-25-8)/D-9	-1.1
1976	NY-A	7	4	1	1	0	0	0	1	0	1	.250	.250	.250	500	47	-0	1	0	0	1.000	-0	/O-2(0-1-1)	0.0
	Chi-A	32	96	4	15	2	0	0	5	6	15	.156	.206	.177	383	13	-10	3	1	0	1.000	-4	O-26(6-2-23)/D-1	-1.7
	Yr	39	100	5	16	2	0	0	6	6	16	.160	.208	.180	388	14	-11	4	1	1	1.000	-4	O-28(6-3-24)/D-1	-1.7
Total	5	342	1083	125	287	42	13	12	90	72	100	.265	.314	.361	675	93	-11	50	21	4	.986	-17	O-293R/D-11	-3.8

■ ED COGSWELL Cogswell, Edward b: 2/25/1854, England d: 7/27/1888, Fitchburg, Mass. BR/TR, 5'8", 150 lbs. Deb: 7/11/1879

YEAR	TM/L	G	AB	R	H	2B	3B	HR	RBI	BB	SO	AVG	OBP	SLG	OPS	OPS+	BR+	SB	CS	SBR	FA	FR	G/POS	TPR
1879	Bos-N	49	236	51	76	8	1	1	18	8	5	.322	.344	.377	721	135	8				.967	1	1-49	0.6
1880	Tro-N	47	209	41	63	7	3	0	13	11	10	.301	.336	.364	700	130	6				.961	1	1-47	0.5
1882	Wor-N	13	51	10	7	1	0	0	1	6	6	.137	.228	.157	385	26	-4				.937	-1	1-13	-0.6
Total	3	109	496	102	146	16	4	1	32	25	21	.294	.328	.349	677	121	11				.960	1	1-109	0.5

■ ALTA COHEN Cohen, Alta Albert "Schoolboy" b: 12/25/08, New York, N.Y. BL/TL, 5'10.5", 170 lbs. Deb: 4/15/31

YEAR	TM/L	G	AB	R	H	2B	3B	HR	RBI	BB	SO	AVG	OBP	SLG	OPS	OPS+	BR+	SB	CS	SBR	FA	FR	G/POS	TPR
1931	Bro-N	1	3	1	2	0	0	0	0	0	0	.667	.667	.667	1333	261	1	0			1.000	1	/O-1(0-0-1)	0.2
1932	Bro-N	9	32	1	5	1	0	0	1	3	7	.156	.229	.188	416	14	-4	0			.850	1	/O-8(5-3-0)	-0.4
1933	Phi-N	19	32	6	6	1	0	0	1	6	4	.188	.316	.219	535	49	-2	0			1.000	-0	/O-7(7-0-0)	-0.2
Total	3	29	67	8	13	2	0	0	2	9	11	.194	.289	.224	513	42	-5	0			.925	2	/O-16(12-3-1)	-0.4

■ ANDY COHEN Cohen, Andrew Howard b: 10/25/04, Baltimore, Md. d: 10/29/88, ElPaso, Tex. BR/TR, 5'8", 155 lbs. Deb: 6/6/26 FMC

YEAR	TM/L	G	AB	R	H	2B	3B	HR	RBI	BB	SO	AVG	OBP	SLG	OPS	OPS+	BR+	SB	CS	SBR	FA	FR	G/POS	TPR
1926	NY-N	32	35	4	9	0	1	0	8	1	2	.257	.278	.314	592	60	-2	0			.792	2	2-10,S-10/3-2	0.0
1928	NY-N	129	504	64	138	24	7	9	59	31	17	.274	.318	.403	721	87	-11	3			.969	3	*2-126/S-3,3-1	-0.4
1929	NY-N	101	347	40	102	12	2	5	47	11	15	.294	.319	.383	703	73	-15	3			.964	12	2-94/S-1,3-1	-0.1
Total	3	262	886	108	249	36	10	14	114	43	34	.281	.317	.392	709	81	-28	6			.964	16	2-230/S-14,3-4	-0.5

■ JIMMIE COKER Coker, Jimmie Goodwin b: 3/28/36, Holly Hill, S.C. d: 10/29/91, Throckmorton, Tex. BR/TR, 5'11", 195 lbs. Deb: 9/11/58

YEAR	TM/L	G	AB	R	H	2B	3B	HR	RBI	BB	SO	AVG	OBP	SLG	OPS	OPS+	BR+	SB	CS	SBR	FA	FR	G/POS	TPR
1958	Phi-N	2	6	0	1	0	0	0	0	0	0	.167	.167	.167	333	-12	-1	0	0	0	1.000	0	/C-2	-0.1
1960	Phi-N	81	252	18	54	5	3	6	34	23	45	.214	.290	.329	620	69	-11	0	3	-1	.982	2	C-76	-0.6
1961	Phi-N	11	25	3	10	1	0	1	4	7	4	.400	.531	.560	1091	193	4	1	0	0	.984	0	C-11	0.5
1962	Phi-N	5	3	0	0	0	0	0	1	1	2	.000	.250	.000	250	-27	-1	0	0	0	.000	0	H	-0.1
1963	SF-N	4	5	0	1	0	0	0	0	1	2	.200	.333	.200	533	58	-0	0	0	0	1.000	-1	/C-2	-0.1
1964	Cin-N	11	32	3	10	2	0	1	4	3	5	.313	.371	.469	840	130	1	0	0	0	1.000	2	C-11	0.4
1965	Cin-N	24	61	3	15	2	0	2	9	8	16	.246	.333	.377	710	93	-0	0	0	0	.993	5	C-19	0.6
1966	Cin-N	50	111	9	28	3	0	4	14	8	5	.252	.303	.387	690	83	-3	0	1	-0	.979	4	C-39/O-2(2-0-0)	0.3
1967	Cin-N	45	97	8	18	2	1	2	4	4	20	.186	.218	.289	506	39	-8	0	1	-0	.976	-0	C-34	-0.8
Total	9	233	592	44	137	15	4	16	70	55	99	.231	.301	.351	652	77	-18	1	5	-2	.983	13	C-194/O-2(2-0-0)	0.1

YEAR	TM/L	G	AB	R	H	2B	3B	HR	RBI	BB	SO	AVG	OBP	SLG	OPS	OPS+	BR+	SB	CS	SBR	FA	FR	G/POS	TPR
■ MIKE COLANGELO	Colangelo, Michael Gus b: 10/22/76, Teaneck, N.J. BR/TR, 6'1", 185 lbs. Deb: 6/13/99																							
1999	Ana-A	1	2	0	1	0	0	0	0	1	0	.500	.667	.500	1167	205	0	0	0	0	1.000	1	/O-1(1-0-0)	0.1
■ ROCKY COLAVITO	Colavito, Rocco Domenico b: 8/10/33, New York, N.Y. BR/TR, 6'3", 190 lbs. Deb: 9/10/55 C Career OF: (524-LF 0-CF 1285-RF)																							
1955	Cle-A	5	9	3	4	2	0	0	0	0	2	.444	.444	.667	1111	189	1	0	0	0	1.000	2	/O-2(0-0-2)	0.3
1956	Cle-A	101	322	55	89	11	4	21	65	49	46	.276	.375	.531	906	134	15	0	1	-0	.968	-1	O-98(0-0-98)	1.0
1957	Cle-A	134	461	66	116	26	0	25	84	71	80	.252	.353	.471	823	124	15	1	6	-2	.962	12	*O-130(0-0-130)	2.1
1958	Cle-A	143	489	80	148	26	3	41	113	84	89	.303	.407	**.620**	1027	183	56	0	2	-1	.981	2	*O-129R,1-11/P-1	5.3
1959	Cle-A★	154	588	90	151	24	0	**42**	111	71	86	.257	.339	.512	851	135	26	3	3	-0	.985	12	*O-154(0-0-154)	3.2
1960	Det-A	145	555	67	138	18	1	35	87	53	80	.249	.319	.474	793	108	4	3	6	-1	.976	7	*O-144(0-0-144)	0.5
1961	Det-A★	163	583	129	169	30	2	45	140	113	75	.290	.407	.580	987	156	48	1	2	-0	.975	10	*O-161(150-0-20)	4.7
1962	Det-A★	161	601	90	164	30	2	37	112	96	68	.273	.375	.514	889	132	28	2	0	0	.992	18	*O-161(161-0-0)	3.6
1963	Det-A	160	597	91	162	29	2	22	91	84	78	.271	.362	.437	799	119	17	0	0	0	.988	7	*O-159(142-0-23)	1.5
1964	KC-A★	160	588	89	161	31	2	34	102	83	56	.274	.368	.507	875	136	30	3	1	0	.973	3	*O-159(3-0-157)	2.3
1965	Cle-A★	162	592	92	170	25	2	26	**108**	**93**	63	.287	.387	.468	855	140	34	1	1	-0	**1.000**	4	*O-162(1-0-162)	2.7
1966	Cle-A★	151	533	68	127	13	0	30	72	76	81	.238	.337	.432	768	119	14	2	1	0	.982	7	*O-146(0-0-146)	1.2
1967	Cle-A	63	191	10	46	9	0	5	21	24	31	.241	.329	.366	695	104	1	2	2	-0	.962	-4	O-50(28-0-31)	-0.7
	Chi-A	60	190	20	42	4	1	3	29	25	10	.221	.312	.300	612	85	-3	1	1	-0	.977	-7	O-58(11-0-54)	-1.5
	Yr	123	381	30	88	13	1	8	50	49	41	.231	.320	.333	654	95	-2	3	3	-0	.970	-11	*O-108(39-0-85)	-2.2
1968	LA-N	40	113	8	23	3	0	3	11	15	18	.204	.297	.310	607	89	-1	0	1	-0	1.000	-1	O-33(21-0-13)	-0.5
	NY-A	39	91	13	20	2	2	5	13	14	17	.220	.330	.451	781	139	4	0	0	0	.933	-4	O-28(6-0-22)/P-1	-0.2
Total	14	1841	6503	971	1730	283	21	374	1159	951	880	.266	.362	.489	851	132	288	19	27	-5	.980	66	*O-1774R/1-11,P-2	25.5
■ MIKE COLBERN	Colbern, Michael Malloy b: 4/19/55, Santa Monica, Cal. BR/TR, 6'3", 205 lbs. Deb: 7/18/78																							
1978	Chi-A	48	141	11	38	5	1	2	20	1	36	.270	.285	.362	646	80	-4	0	1	-0	.969	0	C-47/D-1	-0.3
1979	Chi-A	32	83	5	20	5	1	0	8	4	25	.241	.276	.325	601	61	-5	0	0	0	.971	3	C-32	-0.1
Total	2	80	224	16	58	10	2	2	28	5	61	.259	.281	.348	630	73	-9	0	1	-0	.970	3	/C-79,D-1	-0.4
■ CRAIG COLBERT	Colbert, Craig Charles b: 2/13/65, Iowa City, Iowa BR/TR, 6', 190 lbs. Deb: 4/6/92																							
1992	SF-N	49	126	10	29	5	2	1	16	9	22	.230	.281	.325	607	76	-4	1	0	0	.994	-7	C-35/3-9,2-2	-1.0
1993	SF-N	23	37	2	6	2	0	1	5	3	13	.162	.225	.297	522	40	-3	0	0	0	.982	2	C-10/2-2,3-1	-0.1
Total	2	72	163	12	35	7	2	2	21	12	35	.215	.269	.319	588	67	-8	1	0	0	.990	-5	/C-45,3-10,2-4	-1.1
■ NATE COLBERT	Colbert, Nathan b: 4/9/46, St.Louis, Mo. BR/TR, 6'2", 209 lbs. Deb: 4/14/66 Career OF: (58-LF 5-CF 3-RF)																							
1966	Hou-N	19	7	3	0	0	0	0	0	0	4	.000	.000	.000	0	-99	-2	0	0	0	.000	0	H	-0.2
1968	Hou-N	20	53	5	8	1	0	0	4	1	23	.151	.167	.170	336	1	-6	1	1	-0	.952	-1	O-11(3-5-3)/1-5	-1.0
1969	SD-N	139	483	64	123	20	9	24	66	45	123	.255	.322	.482	804	128	15	6	4	-0	.990	1	*1-134	0.6
1970	SD-N	156	572	84	148	17	6	38	86	56	150	.259	.329	.509	838	126	18	3	5	-1	.991	-8	*1-153/3-1	-0.4
1971	SD-N★	156	565	81	149	25	3	27	84	63	119	.264	.342	.462	804	135	24	5	2	0	.993	1	*1-153	1.4
1972	SD-N★	151	563	87	141	27	2	38	111	70	127	.250	.335	.508	843	147	32	15	6	1	.996	7	*1-150	3.0
1973	SD-N★	145	529	73	143	25	2	22	80	54	146	.270	.347	.450	797	130	20	9	8	-1	.992	3	*1-144	1.0
1974	SD-N	119	368	53	76	16	0	14	54	62	108	.207	.323	.364	687	96	-2	10	2	2	.988	8	1-79,O-48(48-0-0)	0.0
1975	Det-A	45	156	16	23	4	2	4	18	17	52	.147	.231	.276	507	41	-12	0	2	-1	.982	-4	1-44/D-1	-2.1
	Mon-N	38	81	10	14	4	1	4	11	5	31	.173	.230	.395	625	68	-4	0	0	0	.988	-1	1-22	-0.7
1976	Mon-N	14	40	5	8	2	0	2	6	9	16	.200	.347	.400	747	107	1	3	1	0	1.000	0	/O-7(7-0-0),1-6	0.0
	Oak-A	2	5	0	0	0	0	0	0	1	3	.000	.167	.000	167	-50	-1	0	0	0	.000	0	/D-2	-0.1
Total	10	1004	3422	481	833	141	25	173	520	383	902	.243	.324	.451	775	120	83	52	31	1	.991	5	1-890/O-66L,D-3,3-1	1.5
■ GREG COLBRUNN	Colbrunn, Gregory Joseph b: 7/26/69, Fontana, Cal. BR/TR, 6', 200 lbs. Deb: 7/9/92 Career OF: (0-LF 0-CF 6-RF)																							
1992	Mon-N	52	168	12	45	8	0	2	18	6	34	.268	.301	.351	652	85	-4	3	2	-0	.992	-1	1-47	-0.9
1993	Mon-N	70	153	15	39	9	0	4	23	6	33	.255	.287	.392	680	76	-5	4	2	0	.995	1	1-61	-0.8
1994	Fla-N	47	155	17	47	10	0	6	31	9	27	.303	.349	.484	833	111	2	1	1	-0	.988	-1	1-41	-0.2
1995	Fla-N	138	528	70	146	22	1	23	89	22	69	.277	.313	.453	766	99	-3	11	3	1	.996	-1	*1-134	-1.4
1996	Fla-N	141	511	60	146	26	2	16	69	25	76	.286	.336	.438	775	106	3	4	5	-1	.995	5	*1-134	-0.5
1997	Min-A	70	217	24	61	14	0	5	26	8	38	.281	.310	.415	724	86	-5	1	2	-0	.988	-1	1-64/D-2	-1.1
	*Atl-N	28	54	3	15	3	0	2	9	2	11	.278	.316	.444	760	94	-1	0	0	0	.984	0	1-14/D-3	-0.1
1998	Col-N	62	122	12	38	8	2	2	13	8	23	.311	.359	.459	818	93	-1	3	3	-0	.992	0	1-27/O-5(0-0-5),C-1	-0.3
	*Atl-N	28	44	6	13	3	0	1	10	2	11	.295	.367	.432	799	109	1	1	0	0	1.000	0	/1-9,O-1(0-0-1),D-3	0.1
	Yr	90	166	18	51	11	2	3	23	10	34	.307	.361	.452	813	98	-0	4	3	-0	.993	1	1-36/O-6R,D-3,C-1	-0.2
1999	*Ari-N	67	135	20	44	5	3	5	24	12	23	.326	.397	.519	916	129	6	1	1	-0	.996	-0	1-39/3-2,D-2	0.3
2000	Ari-N	116	329	48	103	22	1	15	57	43	45	.313	.408	.523	931	132	17	0	1	-0	.989	-2	1-99/3-1,D-2	0.7
Total	9	819	2416	287	697	130	9	81	369	143	390	.288	.340	.450	790	104	11	29	20	-1	.993	1	1-669/D-12,O-6R,3C	-4.2
■ ALEX COLE	Cole, Alexander b: 8/17/65, Fayetteville, N.C. BL/TL, 6', 170 lbs. Deb: 7/27/90																							
1990	Cle-A	63	227	43	68	5	4	0	13	28	38	.300	.379	.357	736	107	3	40	9	6	.961	2	O-59(0-59-0)/D-1	1.0
1991	Cle-A	122	387	58	114	17	3	0	21	58	47	.295	.388	.354	742	106	6	27	17	-0	.970	1	*O-107(8-101-0)/D-6	0.6
1992	Cle-A	41	97	11	20	1	0	0	5	10	21	.206	.287	.216	504	44	-7	9	2	1	.971	-4	O-24(18-5-2)/D-4	-1.1
	*Pit-N	64	205	33	57	3	7	0	10	18	46	.278	.336	.361	697	99	-0	7	4	0	.989	-1	O-53(0-1-52)	-0.3
1993	Col-N	126	348	50	89	9	4	0	24	43	58	.256	.341	.305	646	64	-16	30	13	2	.982	2	O-93(0-93-0)	-1.1
1994	Min-A	105	345	68	102	15	5	4	23	44	60	.296	.377	.403	780	101	2	29	8	4	.969	-0	*O-100(16-84-0)/D-1	0.5
1995	Min-A	28	79	10	27	3	2	1	14	8	15	.342	.409	.468	877	127	3	1	3	-1	.938	-3	O-23(0-23-0)/D-2	0.0
1996	Bos-A	24	72	13	16	5	1	0	7	8	11	.222	.300	.319	619	56	-5	5	3	0	.974	-3	O-24(0-24-0)	-0.7
Total	7	573	1760	286	493	58	26	5	117	217	296	.280	.361	.351	713	91	-14	148	59	12	.971	-7	O-483(42-390-54)/D-14	-1.1
■ DICK COLE	Cole, Richard Roy b: 5/6/26, Long Beach, Cal. BR/TR, 6'2", 175 lbs. Deb: 4/27/51 C																							
1951	StL-N	15	36	4	7	1	0	0	3	6	5	.194	.310	.222	532	45	-3	0	0	0	.969	5	2-14	0.2
	Pit-N	42	106	9	25	4	0	1	11	15	9	.236	.331	.302	632	69	-4	0	1	-0	.981	-2	2-34/S-8	-0.5
	Yr	57	142	13	32	5	0	1	14	21	14	.225	.325	.282	607	63	-7	0	1	-0	.978	2	2-48/S-8	-0.3
1953	Pit-N	97	235	29	64	13	1	0	23	38	26	.272	.374	.336	710	87	-3	2	2	-0	.965	-3	S-77/2-7,1-1	0.0
1954	Pit-N	138	486	40	131	22	5	1	40	41	48	.270	.326	.342	668	75	-17	0	0	0	.949	-11	S-66,3-55,2-17	-2.2
1955	Pit-N	77	239	16	54	8	3	0	21	18	22	.226	.286	.285	570	53	-16	0	0	0	.935	1	3-33,2-24,S-12	-1.3
1956	Pit-N	72	99	7	21	2	1	0	9	11	9	.212	.291	.253	543	49	-7	0	0	0	.947	-8	3-18,2-12/S-6	-1.4
1957	Mil-N	15	14	1	1	0	0	0	0	3	5	.071	.235	.071	307	-13	-2	0	0	0	.952	0	2-10/1-1,3-1	-0.2
Total	6	456	1215	106	303	50	10	2	107	132	124	.249	.324	.312	636	69	-52	2	3	-1	.961	-18	S-169,2-118,3-107,/1	-5.4
■ STU COLE	Cole, Stewart Bryan b: 2/7/66, Charlotte, N.C. BR/TR, 6'1", 175 lbs. Deb: 9/5/91																							
1991	KC-A	9	7	1	1	0	0	0	0	2	2	.143	.333	.143	476	37	-1	0	0	0	1.000	0	/2-5,S-1,D-2	0.0
■ WILLIS COLE	Cole, Willis Russell b: 1/6/1882, Milton Junction, Wis. d: 10/11/65, Madison, Wis. BR/TR, 5'8", 170 lbs. Deb: 8/22/09																							
1909	Chi-A	46	165	17	39	7	3	0	16	16		.236	.308	.315	623	101	0	3			.889	-3	O-46(0-46-0)	-0.6
1910	Chi-A	22	80	6	14	2	1	0	2	4		.175	.224	.225	449	42	-5	0			.974	1	O-22(0-22-0)	-0.7
Total	2	68	245	23	53	9	4	0	18	20		.216	.281	.286	567	82	-5	3			.912	-3	/O-68(0-68-0)	-1.3
■ CHOO CHOO COLEMAN	Coleman, Clarence b: 8/25/37, Orlando, Fla. BL/TR, 5'9", 165 lbs. Deb: 4/16/61																							
1961	Phi-N	34	47	3	6	1	0	0	4	2	8	.128	.180	.149	329	-12	-8	0	0	0	.977	-1	C-14	-0.8
1962	NY-N	55	152	24	38	7	2	6	17	11	24	.250	.305	.441	746	96	-1	2	4	-1	.995	-9	C-44	-0.9
1963	NY-N	106	247	22	44	0	0	3	9	24	49	.178	.264	.215	479	39	-19	5	5	-1	.969	3	C-91/O-1(1-0-0)	-1.4
1966	NY-N	6	16	2	3	0	0	0	0	0	4	.188	.188	.188	375	5	-2	0	0	0	.963	0	/C-5	-0.2
Total	4	201	462	51	91	8	2	9	30	37	85	.197	.267	.281	548	52	-30	7	9	-2	.977	-6	C-154/O-1(1-0-0)	-3.3

YEAR	TM/L	G	AB	R	H	2B	3B	HR	RBI	BB	SO	AVG	OBP	SLG	OPS	OPS+	BR+	SB	CS	SBR	FA	FR	G/POS	TPR
■ CURT COLEMAN	Coleman, Curtis Hancock b: 2/18/1887, Salem, Ore. d: 7/1/80, Newport, Ore. BL/TR, 5'11", 180 lbs. Deb: 4/13/12																							
1912	NY-A	12	37	8	9	4	0	0	4	7		.243	.364	.351	715	99	0	0			.865	0	3-10	0.0
■ DAVE COLEMAN	Coleman, David Lee b: 10/26/50, Dayton, Ohio BR/TR, 6'3", 195 lbs. Deb: 4/13/77																							
1977	Bos-A	11	12	1	0	0	0	0	0	1	3	.000	.077	.000	77	-69	-3	0	0	0	1.000	-3	/O-9(3-5-1)	-0.6
■ JERRY COLEMAN	Coleman, Gerald Francis b: 9/14/24, San Jose, Cal. BR/TR, 6', 170 lbs. Deb: 4/20/49 M																							
1949	*NY-A	128	447	54	123	21	5	2	42	63	44	.275	.367	.358	725	92	-4	8	6	-0	**.981**	1	*2-122/S-4	0.4
1950	*NY-A★	153	522	69	150	19	6	6	69	67	38	.287	.372	.381	753	96	-2	3	2	-0	.977	-15	*2-152/S-6	-0.8
1951	*NY-A	121	362	48	90	11	2	3	43	31	36	.249	.315	.315	630	73	-14	6	1	1	.968	3	*2-102,S-18	-0.4
1952	NY-A	11	42	6	17	2	1	0	4	5	4	.405	.468	.500	968	180	5	0	1	-0	.971	3	2-11	0.7
1953	NY-A	8	10	1	2	0	0	0	0	0	2	.200	.200	.200	400	9	-1	0	0	0	1.000	2	/2-7,S-1	0.1
1954	NY-A	107	300	39	65	7	1	3	21	26	29	.217	.279	.277	556	54	-19	3	0	1	.977	**18**	2-79,S-30/3-1	0.6
1955	*NY-A	43	96	12	22	5	0	0	8	11	11	.229	.321	.281	602	64	-5	0	2	-1	.966	-2	S-29,2-13/3-1	-0.5
1956	*NY-A	80	183	15	47	5	1	0	18	12	33	.257	.306	.295	601	61	-10	1	2	-0	.979	17	2-41,S-24,3-18	0.9
1957	*NY-A	72	157	23	42	7	2	2	12	20	21	.268	.354	.376	730	101	1	1	1	-0	.969	5	2-45,3-21/S-4	0.8
Total	9	723	2119	267	558	77	18	16	217	235	218	.263	.341	.339	680	83	-49	22	15	-0	.976	31	2-572,S-116/3-41	1.8
■ GORDY COLEMAN	Coleman, Gordon Calvin b: 7/5/34, Rockville, Md. d: 3/12/94, Cincinnati, Ohio BL/TR, 6'2", 218 lbs. Deb: 9/19/59																							
1959	Cle-A	6	15	5	8	0	1	0	2	1	2	.533	.563	.667	1229	245	3	0	0	0	.955	0	/1-3	0.3
1960	Cin-N	66	251	26	68	10	1	6	32	12	32	.271	.309	.390	700	89	-4	1	1	-0	.998	7	1-66	-0.1
1961	*Cin-N	150	520	63	149	27	4	26	87	45	67	.287	.346	.504	850	120	14	1	3	-1	.991	7	*1-150	1.1
1962	Cin-N	136	476	73	132	13	1	28	86	36	68	.277	.332	.485	817	113	7	2	3	-1	.989	-1	*1-128	-0.3
1963	Cin-N	123	365	38	90	20	2	14	59	29	51	.247	.306	.427	733	105	2	1	0	0	.987	1	*1-107	-0.3
1964	Cin-N	89	198	18	48	6	2	5	27	13	30	.242	.292	.369	661	82	-5	2	0	0	.990	4	1-49	-0.4
1965	Cin-N	108	325	39	98	19	0	14	57	24	38	.302	.351	.489	841	125	11	0	0	0	.991	-1	1-89	0.5
1966	Cin-N	91	227	20	57	7	0	5	37	16	45	.251	.300	.348	648	73	-8	2	1	0	.986	-1	1-65	-1.3
1967	Cin-N	4	7	0	0	0	0	0	0	1	0	.000	.125	.000	125	-55	-1	0	0	0	1.000	0	/1-2	-0.2
Total	9	773	2384	282	650	102	11	98	387	177	333	.273	.326	.448	774	106	18	9	8	-1	.990	16	1-659	-0.7
■ JOHN COLEMAN	Coleman, John Francis b: 3/6/1863, Saratoga Springs, N.Y d: 5/31/22, Detroit, Mich. BL/TR (BB 1887), 5'9.5", 170 lbs. Deb: 5/1/1883 Career OF: (47-LF 71-CF 393-RF)																							
1883	Phi-N	90	354	33	83	12	8	0	32	15	39	.234	.266	.314	579	83	-6				.886	10	P-65,O-31L/2-1	0.5
1884	Phi-N	43	171	16	42	7	2	0	22	8	20	.246	.279	.310	589	89	-2				.844	2	O-27(3-19-5),P-21/1-2	-0.1
	Phi-a	28	107	16	22	2	3	2		5		.206	.241	.336	578	81	-2				.743	-1	O-24(11-13-0)/P-3,1-2	-0.4
1885	Phi-a	96	398	71	119	15	11	3	70	25		.299	.345	.415	760	131	13				.844	-1	*O-93(1-17-76)/P-8	0.9
1886	Phi-a	121	492	67	121	18	16	0	65	33		.246	.296	.348	644	100	-1	28			.862	2	*O-115R/1-6,P-3,2-1	-0.1
	Pit-a	11	43	3	15	2	1	0	9	2		.349	.378	.442	820	157	3	1			.786	-2	O-11(11-0-0)	0.0
	Yr	132	535	70	136	20	17	0	74	35		.254	.302	.355	658	105	2	29			.858	-1	*O-126R/1-6,P-3,2-1	-0.1
1887	Pit-N	115	506	75	170	21	11	2	54	31	40	.336	.337	.396	733	110	7	25			.899	1	*O-115(0-2-113)/1-2	0.5
1888	Pit-N	116	438	49	101	11	4	0	26	29	52	.231	.285	.274	558	85	-6	15			.928	2	O-91(0-3-88),1-25	-0.7
1889	Phi-a	6	19	1	1	0	0	0	1	1	3	.053	.100	.053	153	-57	-4	1			.929	0	/P-5,O-1(1-0-0)	-0.1
1890	Pit-N	3	11	1	2	0	0	0	0	3	0	.182	.357	.182	539	66	-0	1			1.000	-1	/O-2(1-0-1),P-2	-0.1
Total	8	629	2539	332	676	88	56	7	279	152	154	.266	.302	.345	648	100	2	71			.873	11	O-510R,P-107/1-37,2	0.4
■ MICHAEL COLEMAN	Coleman, Michael Donnell b: 8/16/75, Nashville, Tenn. BR/TR, 5'11", 180 lbs. Deb: 9/1/97																							
1997	Bos-A	8	24	2	4	1	0	0	2	0	11	.167	.167	.208	375	-3	-4	1	0	0	.941	-0	/O-7(0-7-0)	-0.4
1999	Bos-A	2	5	1	1	0	0	0	0	1	0	.200	.333	.200	533	39	-0	0	0	0	.000	-1	/O-2(1-1-0)	-0.1
Total	2	10	29	3	5	1	0	0	2	1	11	.172	.200	.207	407	6	-4	1	0	0	.941	-1	/O-9(1-8-0)	-0.5
■ ED COLEMAN	Coleman, Parke Edward b: 12/1/01, Canby, Ore. d: 8/5/64, Oregon City, Ore. BL/TR, 6'2", 200 lbs. Deb: 4/15/32																							
1932	Phi-A	26	73	13	25	7	1	1	13	1	6	.342	.351	.507	858	115	1	1	0	0	1.000	1	O-16(0-0-16)	0.1
1933	Phi-A	102	388	48	109	26	3	6	68	19	51	.281	.318	.410	728	91	-7	0	0	0	.948	-1	O-89(1-0-88)	-1.2
1934	Phi-A	101	329	53	92	14	6	14	60	29	34	.280	.342	.486	828	116	6	0	1	-0	.980	-2	O-86(0-0-86)	-0.1
1935	Phi-A	10	13	0	1	0	0	0	0	0	3	.077	.077	.077	154	-61	-3	0	0	0	.000	-0	/O-1(0-0-1)	-0.3
	StL-A	108	397	66	114	15	9	17	71	53	41	.287	.373	.499	871	118	10	0	2	-1	.974	-3	*O-102(0-0-102)	0.0
	Yr	118	410	66	115	15	9	17	71	53	44	.280	.364	.485	850	113	7	0	2	-1	.974	-3	*O-103(0-0-103)	-0.3
1936	StL-A	92	137	13	40	5	4	2	34	15	17	.292	.366	.431	797	93	-2	0	0	0	.939	-3	O-18(0-0-18)	-0.5
Total	5	439	1337	193	381	67	23	40	246	117	152	.285	.345	.459	804	105	6	1	3	-1	.966	-8	O-312(1-0-311)	-2.0
■ RAY COLEMAN	Coleman, Raymond Leroy b: 6/4/22, Dunsmuir, Cal. BL/TR, 5'11", 170 lbs. Deb: 4/22/47																							
1947	StL-A	110	343	34	89	9	7	2	30	26	32	.259	.314	.344	658	81	-9	2	5	-1	.984	-2	O-93(21-0-73)	-1.7
1948	StL-A	17	29	2	5	0	1	0	2	2	5	.172	.226	.241	467	24	-3	1	0	0	.889	-1	/O-5(0-0-5)	-0.4
	Phi-A	68	210	32	51	6	6	0	21	31	17	.243	.340	.329	669	78	-6	4	3	-0	.978	2	O-53(0-32-21)	-0.6
	Yr	85	239	34	56	6	7	0	23	33	22	.234	.327	.318	645	72	-10	5	3	0	.972	1	O-58(0-32-26)	-1.0
1950	StL-A	117	384	54	104	25	6	8	55	32	37	.271	.330	.430	760	90	-7	7	5	-0	.985	3	O-98(27-43-28)	-0.8
1951	StL-A	91	341	41	96	16	5	5	55	24	32	.282	.329	.402	731	94	-4	3	4	-1	.975	1	O-87(47-5-42)	-0.8
	Chi-A	51	181	21	50	8	7	3	21	15	14	.276	.332	.448	779	112	2	2	3	-1	.980	-3	O-51(23-29-12)	-0.4
	Yr	142	522	62	146	24	12	8	76	39	46	.280	.330	.418	747	100	-2	5	7	-1	.977	-2	*O-138(70-34-54)	-1.2
1952	Chi-A	85	195	19	42	7	1	2	14	13	17	.215	.264	.292	557	54	-12	0	0	0	.978	-7	O-73(28-33-15)	-2.3
	StL-A	20	46	5	9	3	0	0	1	5	4	.196	.288	.261	549	52	-3	0	0	0	1.000	-2	O-16(5-5-6)	-0.6
	Yr	105	241	24	51	10	1	2	15	18	21	.212	.269	.286	556	54	-15	0	0	0	.982	-9	O-89(33-38-21)	-2.9
Total	5	559	1729	208	446	74	33	20	199	148	158	.258	.318	.374	692	84	-43	19	20	-3	.980	-9	O-476(151-147-202)	-7.6
■ BOB COLEMAN	Coleman, Robert Hunter b: 9/26/1890, Huntingburg, Ind. d: 7/16/59, Boston, Mass. BR/TR, 6'2", 190 lbs. Deb: 6/13/13 MC																							
1913	Pit-N	24	50	5	9	2	0	0	9	7	8	.180	.281	.220	501	46	-3	0			.978	-4	C-24	-0.6
1914	Pit-N	73	150	11	40	4	1	1	14	15	32	.267	.333	.327	660	101	0	3			.977	2	C-72	0.7
1916	Cle-A	19	28	3	6	2	0	0	4	7	6	.214	.371	.286	657	92	0	0			.972	-3	C-12	-0.2
Total	3	116	228	19	55	8	1	1	27	29	46	.241	.327	.298	625	87	-3	3			.976	-5	C-108	-0.1
■ VINCE COLEMAN	Coleman, Vincent Maurice b: 9/22/61, Jacksonville, Fla. BB/TR, 6', 185 lbs. Deb: 4/18/85 Career OF: (1154-LF 155-CF 25-RF)																							
1985	*StL-N	151	636	107	170	20	10	1	40	50	115	.267	.321	.335	656	84	-13	**110**	25	**15**	.979	9	*O-150(138-17-10)	0.5
1986	StL-N	154	600	94	139	13	8	0	29	60	98	.232	.304	.280	584	63	-30	**107**	14	**19**	.972	9	*O-149(131-20-0)	-0.9
1987	*StL-N	151	623	121	180	14	10	3	43	70	126	.289	.364	.358	721	90	-6	**109**	22	**16**	.970	9	*O-150(150-0-0)	1.2
1988	StL-N★	153	616	77	160	20	10	3	38	49	111	.260	.315	.339	655	87	-10	**81**	27	8	.971	5	*O-150(127-24-0)	-0.1
1989	StL-N★	145	563	94	143	21	9	2	28	50	90	.254	.317	.334	651	84	-11	**65**	10	**11**	.962	-5	*O-142(142-0-0)	-1.0
1990	StL-N	124	497	73	145	18	9	6	39	35	88	.292	.341	.400	741	103	2	**77**	17	**11**	.981	8	*O-120(118-0-2)	1.7
1991	NY-N	72	278	45	71	7	5	1	17	39	47	.255	.347	.327	674	91	-2	37	14	3	.979	0	O-70(0-70-0)	0.1
1992	NY-N	71	229	37	63	11	1	2	21	27	41	.275	.357	.358	715	104	2	24	9	2	.991	-1	O-61(42-21-0)	0.2
1993	NY-N	92	373	64	104	14	8	2	25	21	58	.279	.317	.375	693	86	-8	38	13	4	.982	0	O-90(90-0-0)	-0.7
1994	KC-A	104	438	61	105	14	12	2	33	29	72	.240	.288	.340	629	59	-27	50	8	8	.962	0	O-99(99-0-0)/D-5	-2.1
1995	KC-A	75	293	39	84	13	4	4	20	27	48	.287	.349	.399	748	93	-3	26	9	3	.975	-3	O-69(57-2-13)/D-4	-0.5
	*Sea-A	40	162	27	47	10	2	1	9	10	32	.290	.335	.395	730	88	-3	16	7	1	.988	4	O-38(38-0-0)	0.1
	Yr	115	455	66	131	23	6	5	29	37	80	.288	.344	.398	742	91	-6	42	16	4	.980	1	*O-107(95-2-13)/D-4	-0.4
1996	Cin-N	33	84	10	13	1	1	1	4	9	31	.155	.237	.226	463	23	-9	12	2	2	.968	0	O-20(20-0-0)	-0.8
1997	Det-A	6	14	0	1	0	0	0	0	1	3	.071	.133	.071	205	-45	-3	0	0	0	1.000	-1	/O-3(2-1-0),D-1	-0.4
Total	13	1371	5406	849	1425	176	89	28	346	477	960	.264	.325	.345	670	83	-122	752	177	103	.974	34	*O-1311L/D-10	-2.7
■ CAD COLES	Coles, Cadwallader b: 1/17/1886, Rock Hill, S.C. d: 6/30/42, Miami, Fla. BL/TR, 6'0.5", 174 lbs. Deb: 4/16/14																							
1914	KC-F	78	194	17	49	7	3	1	25	5	30	.253	.271	.335	606	67	-13	6			.889	-7	O-39(3-31-6)/1-3	-2.4

YEAR	TM/L	G	AB	R	H	2B	3B	HR	RBI	BB	SO	AVG	OBP	SLG	OPS	OPS+	BR+	SB	CS	SBR	FA	FR	G/POS	TPR
■ **CHUCK COLES**	Coles, Charles Edward b: 6/27/31, Fredericktown, Pa d: 1/25/96, Myrtle Beach, S.C. BL/TL, 5'9", 180 lbs. Deb: 9/19/58																							
1958	Cin-N	5	11	0	2	1	0	0	2	2	6	.182	.308	.273	580	52	-1	0	0	0	1.000	1	/O-4(3-1-0)	0.0
■ **DARNELL COLES**	Coles, Darnell b: 6/2/62, San Bernardino, Cal BR/TR, 6'1", 185 lbs. Deb: 9/4/83 Career OF: (123-LF 0-CF 228-RF)																							
1983	Sea-A	27	92	9	26	7	0	1	6	7	12	.283	.333	.391	725	95	-1	0	3	-1	.941	-3	3-26	-0.5
1984	Sea-A	48	143	15	23	3	1	0	6	17	26	.161	.259	.196	455	28	-14	2	1	0	.918	-3	3-42/O-3(3-0-0),D-3	-1.8
1985	Sea-A	27	59	8	14	4	0	1	5	9	17	.237	.348	.356	704	93	-0	0	1	-0	.918	1	S-15/3-7,O-2L,D-2	0.1
1986	Det-A	142	521	67	142	30	2	20	86	45	84	.273	.337	.453	790	113	9	6	2	1	.938	-5	*3-133/S-2,O-2R,D-7	0.2
1987	Det-A	53	149	14	27	5	1	4	15	15	23	.181	.265	.309	574	54	-10	0	1	-0	.847	-5	3-36/1-9,O-8R,SD	-1.6
	Pit-N	40	119	20	27	8	0	6	24	19	20	.227	.338	.445	784	105	1	1	3	-1	1.000	-5	O-26(1-0-26),3-10/1-1	-0.6
1988	Pit-N	68	211	20	49	13	1	5	36	20	41	.232	.308	.374	682	96	-1	1	1	-0	.990	-3	O-55(0-0-55)/1-1,3-1	-0.7
	Sea-A	55	195	32	57	10	1	10	34	17	26	.292	.361	.508	869	134	9	3	2	-0	.986	-3	O-47(43-0-4)/1-1,D-7	0.4
1989	Sea-A	146	535	54	135	21	3	10	59	27	61	.252	.296	.359	655	81	-14	5	4	-0	.975	7	O-89R,3-26,1-18,D	-1.1
1990	Sea-A	37	107	9	23	5	1	2	16	4	17	.215	.250	.336	586	62	-6	0	0	0	.970	1	O-20R/3-6,1-4,D-1	-0.6
	Det-A	52	108	13	22	2	0	1	4	12	21	.204	.283	.250	533	50	-7	0	4	-1	1.000	-1	D-30,O-11(4-0-9)/3-8	-1.1
	Yr	89	215	22	45	7	1	3	20	16	38	.209	.267	.293	560	56	-13	0	4	-1	.977	-0	O-31R,D-31,3-14,/1	-1.7
1991	SF-N	11	14	1	3	0	0	0	0	0	2	.214	.214	.214	429	22	-1	0	0	0	.000	-1	/O-3(0-0-3),1-1	-0.3
1992	Cin-N	55	141	16	44	11	2	3	18	3	15	.312	.326	.482	809	123	4	1	0	0	1.000	1	3-23,1-20/O-5(3-0-2)	0.4
1993	Tor-A	64	194	26	49	9	1	4	26	16	29	.253	.322	.371	694	85	-4	1	1	-0	.957	-9	O-44L,3-16/1-1,D-1	-1.4
1994	Tor-A	48	143	15	30	6	1	4	15	10	25	.210	.266	.350	616	57	-10	0	0	0	.980	-3	O-29L,1-10/3-7,D-1	-1.3
1995	StL-N	63	138	13	31	7	0	3	16	16	20	.225	.318	.341	659	74	-5	0	0	0	.951	-6	3-22,1-18/O-1(1-0-0)	-1.2
1997	Col-N	21	22	1	7	1	0	1	2	0	6	.318	.348	.500	848	97	-0	0	0	0	1.000	-1	/3-3,O-2(2-0-0)	-0.1
Total	14	957	2891	333	709	142	14	75	368	237	445	.245	.310	.382	692	88	-51	20	23	-4	.923	-41	3-366,O-347R/1-84,DS	-11.2
■ **CHRIS COLETTA**	Coletta, Christopher Michael b: 8/2/44, Brooklyn, N.Y. BL/TL, 5'11", 190 lbs. Deb: 8/15/72																							
1972	Cal-A	14	30	5	9	1	0	1	7	1	4	.300	.323	.433	756	131	1	0	0	0	1.000	-2	/O-7(5-0-2)	-0.2
■ **ED COLGAN**	Colgan, William H. b: E.St.Louis, Ill. d: 8/8/1895, Great Falls, Mont. 180 lbs. Deb: 5/3/1884																							
1884	Pit-a	48	161	10	25	4	1	0		3		.155	.171	.193	363	18	-14				.906	2	C-44/O-4(2-0-2)	-0.8
■ **LOU COLLIER**	Collier, Louis Keith b: 8/21/73, Chicago, Ill. BR/TR, 5'10", 170 lbs. Deb: 6/28/97 Career OF: (14-LF 7-CF 1-RF)																							
1997	Pit-N	18	37	3	5	0	0	0	3	1	11	.135	.158	.135	293	-22	-7	1	0	0	1.000	3	S-18	-0.3
1998	Pit-N	110	334	30	82	13	6	2	34	31	70	.246	.321	.338	659	73	-13	2	2	-0	.960	-4	*S-107	-0.8
1999	Mil-N	74	135	18	35	9	0	2	21	14	32	.259	.329	.370	699	77	-5	3	2	-0	.948	-9	S-31,O-10L/3-7,2-4	-1.2
2000	Mil-N	14	32	9	7	1	0	1	2	6	4	.219	.342	.344	686	75	-1	0	0	0	1.000	-2	O-10(5-7-0)/C-1,3-1	-0.3
Total	4	216	538	60	129	23	6	5	60	52	117	.240	.314	.333	646	68	-25	6	4	-0	.962	-13	S-156/O-20L,3-8,2C	-2.6
■ **COLLINS**	Collins Deb: 9/12/1892																							
1892	StL-N	1	2	0	0	0	0	0	0	0	2	.000	.000	.000	0	-99	-0	0			1.000	0	/O-1(0-0-1)	0.0
■ **CHUB COLLINS**	Collins, Charles Augustine b: 10/12/1857, Dundas, Ont., Canada d: 5/20/14, Dundas, Ont., Can. BB, 5'11.5", 165 lbs. Deb: 5/1/1884																							
1884	Buf-N	45	169	24	30	6	0	0	20	14	36	.178	.240	.213	453	42	-11				.914	0	2-42/S-3	-0.8
	Ind-a	38	138	18	31	3	1	0		9		.225	.272	.261	533	77	-3				.886	-8	2-38	-0.9
1885	Det-N	14	55	8	10	0	2	0	6	0	11	.182	.182	.255	436	40	-4				.792	-8	S-14	-1.1
Total	2	97	362	50	71	9	3	0	26	23	47	.196	.244	.238	482	55	-18				.901	-16	/2-80,S-17	-2.8
■ **WILSON COLLINS**	Collins, Cyril Wilson b: 5/7/1889, Pulaski, Tenn. d: 2/28/41, Knoxville, Tenn. BR/TR, 5'9.5", 165 lbs. Deb: 5/12/13																							
1913	Bos-N	16	3	3	1	0	0	0	0	0	1	.333	.333	.333	667	89	-0	0			1.000	-4	/O-9(5-3-1)	-0.4
1914	Bos-N	27	35	5	9	0	0	0	1	2	8	.257	.297	.257	554	66	-1	0			.917	-4	O-19(9-3-7)	-0.7
Total	2	43	38	8	10	0	0	0	1	2	9	.263	.300	.263	563	68	-1	0			.926	-8	/O-28(14-6-8)	-1.1
■ **DAN COLLINS**	Collins, Daniel Thomas b: 7/12/1854, St.Louis, Mo. d: 9/21/1883, New Orleans, La. Deb: 6/8/1874																							
1874	Chi-n	3	12	1	1	1	0	0	0	0	2	.083	.083	.167	250	-22	-2	1	0	0	1.000	0	/P-2,O-2(0-0-2),S-1	-0.1
1876	Lou-N	7	28	3	4	1	0	0	9	0	2	.143	.143	.179	321	5	-3				.909	1	/O-7(0-2-5)	-0.2
■ **DAVE COLLINS**	Collins, David S b: 10/20/52, Rapid City, S.D. BB/TL, 5'11", 175 lbs. Deb: 6/7/75 C Career OF: (716-LF 204-CF 220-RF)																							
1975	Cal-A	93	319	41	85	13	4	3	29	36	55	.266	.343	.361	703	106	3	24	10	2	.988	4	O-75(74-1-0),D-12	0.4
1976	Cal-A	99	365	45	96	12	1	4	28	40	55	.263	.336	.334	670	103	2	32	19	0	.994	3	O-71(52-19-0),D-22	0.1
1977	Sea-A	120	402	46	96	9	3	5	28	33	66	.239	.301	.313	615	69	-17	25	10	2	.985	0	O-73(67-3-3),D-40	-1.9
1978	Cin-N	102	102	13	22	1	0	0	7	15	18	.216	.316	.225	542	54	-6	7	7	-1	.969	-4	O-24(3-17-4)	-1.1
1979	*Cin-N	122	396	59	126	16	4	3	35	27	48	.318	.365	.402	766	108	5	16	9	0	.976	-9	O-91(45-3-50),1-10	-0.9
1980	Cin-N	144	551	94	167	20	4	3	35	53	68	.303	.367	.370	738	106	6	79	21	10	.986	3	*O-141(18-119-6)	1.8
1981	Cin-N	95	360	63	98	18	6	3	23	41	41	.272	.356	.381	737	107	4	26	10	2	.977	1	O-94(1-0-93)	0.3
1982	NY-A	111	348	41	88	12	3	3	25	28	49	.253	.318	.330	648	80	-9	13	8	0	.992	-5	O-60R,1-52/D-1	-1.9
1983	Tor-A	118	402	55	109	12	4	1	34	43	67	.271	.345	.328	673	81	-9	31	7	4	.989	6	*O-112L/1-5,D-1	-0.3
1984	Tor-A	128	441	59	136	24	**15**	2	44	33	41	.308	.369	.444	813	119	12	60	14	8	.991	1	*O-108L/1-6,D-4	1.7
1985	Oak-A	112	379	52	95	16	4	4	29	29	37	.251	.306	.346	651	84	-8	29	8	4	.978	6	O-91(91-0-0)	-0.3
1986	Det-A	124	419	44	113	18	2	1	27	44	49	.270	.342	.329	671	84	-8	27	12	2	.995	3	O-94(76-10-11),D-24	-0.8
1987	Cin-N	57	85	19	25	5	0	0	5	11	12	.294	.388	.353	741	94	-0	9	0	2	1.000	-1	O-21(18-2-1)	0.0
1988	Cin-N	99	174	12	41	6	2	0	14	11	27	.236	.289	.293	582	65	-8	7	2	1	.965	-4	O-35(13-5-18)/1-3	-1.2
1989	Cin-N	78	106	12	25	4	0	0	7	10	17	.236	.302	.274	575	63	-5	3	1	0	1.000	2	O-16(16-0-0)	-0.3
1990	StL-N	99	58	12	13	1	0	0	3	13	10	.224	.366	.241	608	70	-2	7	1	1	1.000	-6	1-49,O-12(4-1-8)	-0.7
Total	16	1701	4907	667	1335	187	52	32	373	467	660	.272	.340	.351	691	93	-39	395	139	38	.986	3	*O-1118L,1-125,D-104	-5.1
■ **EDDIE COLLINS**	Collins, Edward Trowbridge Jr. b: 11/23/16, Lansdowne, Pa. BL/TR, 5'10", 175 lbs. Deb: 7/4/39 F																							
1939	Phi-A	32	21	6	5	1	0	0	0	0	3	.238	.238	.286	524	34	-2	1	0	0	1.000	-0	/O-6(0-0-6),2-1	-0.2
1941	Phi-A	80	219	29	53	6	3	0	12	20	24	.242	.305	.297	602	61	-12	2	1	0	.968	-0	O-50(4-9-38)	-1.4
1942	Phi-A	20	34	6	8	2	0	0	4	4	2	.235	.316	.294	610	72	-1	1	0	0	.800	-4	/O-9(1-3-6)	-0.5
Total	3	132	274	41	66	9	3	0	16	24	29	.241	.302	.296	598	61	-15	4	1	1	.959	-4	/O-65(5-12-50),2-1	-2.1
■ **EDDIE COLLINS**	Collins, Edward Trowbridge Sr. "Cocky" (a.k.a. Edward T. Sullivan In 1906) b: 5/2/1887, Millerton, N.Y. d: 3/25/51, Boston, Mass. BL/TR, 5'9", 175 lbs. Deb: 9/17/06 FMCH Career OF: (2-LF 3-CF 5-RF)																							
1906	Phi-A	6	15	2	3	0	0	0	0	0		.200	.200	.200	400	25	-1	1			.900	-0	/S-3,2-1,3-1	-0.2
1907	Phi-A	14	23	0	8	0	1	0	2	0		.348	.348	.435	783	146	1	0			.833	1	/S-6	0.2
1908	Phi-A	102	330	39	90	18	7	1	40	16		.273	.312	.379	691	116	5	8			.944	-12	2-47,S-28,O-10(2-3-5)	-0.7
1909	Phi-A	153	571	104	198	30	10	3	56	62		.347	.416	.450	866	170	47	67			**.967**	8	*2-152/S-1	**6.2**
1910	*Phi-A	153	581	81	188	16	15	3	81	49		.324	.382	.418	800	152	34	**81**			**.972**	**34**	*2-153	7.5
1911	*Phi-A	132	493	92	180	22	13	3	73	62		.365	.451	.481	932	163	45	38			.967	3	*2-132	4.9
1912	Phi-A	153	543	**137**	189	25	11	0	64	101		.348	.450	.435	885	159	48	63			.955	15	*2-153	6.4
1913	*Phi-A	148	534	**125**	184	23	13	3	73	85	37	.345	.441	.453	894	165	48	55			.965	16	*2-148	6.9
1914	*Phi-A	152	526	**122**	181	23	14	2	85	97	31	.344	**.452**	.452	904	**179**	**57**	58	30	2	**.970**	0	*2-152	6.6
1915	Chi-A	155	521	118	173	22	10	4	77	**119**	27	.332	.460	.436	896	163	48	46	30	-0	**.974**	13	*2-155	**6.6**
1916	Chi-A	155	545	87	168	14	17	0	52	86	36	.308	.405	.396	802	139	29	40	21	1	**.976**	-6	*2-155	3.0
1917	*Chi-A	156	564	91	163	18	12	0	67	89	16	.289	.389	.363	752	127	22	53			.969	-26	*2-156	-0.1
1918	Chi-A	97	330	51	91	8	2	2	30	73	13	.276	.407	.330	737	121	13	22			.974	-1	2-96	1.6
1919	*Chi-A	140	518	87	165	19	7	4	80	68	27	.319	.400	.405	805	126	20	**33**			.974	3	*2-140	2.6
1920	Chi-A	153	602	117	224	38	13	3	76	69	19	.372	.438	.493	932	146	42	20	8	2	**.976**	10	*2-153	5.4
1921	Chi-A	139	526	79	177	20	10	2	58	66	11	.337	.412	.424	836	115	15	12	10	-1	**.968**	27	*2-136	4.1
1922	Chi-A	154	598	92	194	20	12	1	69	73	16	.324	.401	.403	804	110	12	20	12	0	**.976**	-10	*2-154	0.7
1923	Chi-A	145	505	89	182	22	5	5	67	84	8	.360	.455	.453	909	141	36	**48**	29	0	.975	-4	*2-142	3.4
1924	Chi-A	152	556	108	194	27	7	6	86	89	16	.349	.441	.455	896	136	34	**42**	17	**3**	**.977**	-7	*2-150,M	3.2
1925	Chi-A	118	425	80	147	26	3	3	80	87	8	.346	.461	.442	904	137	31	19	6	2	.970	-9	*2-116,M	2.5

YEAR	TM/L	G	AB	R	H	2B	3B	HR	RBI	BB	SO	AVG	OBP	SLG	OPS	OPS+	BR+	SB	CS	SBR	FA	FR	G/POS	TPR
1926	Chi-A	106	375	66	129	32	4	1	62	62	8	.344	.441	.459	900	140	25	13	8	0	.973	-6	*2-101,M	2.1
1927	Phi-A	95	226	50	76	12	1	1	15	56	9	.336	.468	.412	880	123	12	6	2	1	.965	-7	2-56/S-1	0.6
1928	Phi-A	36	33	3	10	3	0	0	7	4	4	.303	.378	.394	772	100	0	0	0	0	.000	-2	/2-2,S-1	-0.1
1929	Phi-A	9	7	0	0	0	0	0	0	2	0	.000	.222	.000	222	-37	-1	0	0	0	.000	0	H	-0.1
1930	Phi-A	3	2	1	1	0	0	0	0	0	0	.500	.500	.500	1000	148	0	0	0	0	.000	0	H	0.0
Total	25	2826	9949	1821	3315	438	187	47	1300	1499	286	.333	.424	.429	853	142	623	745	173		.970	41	*2-2650/S-40,O-10R,3	73.3
■ HUB COLLINS	Collins, Hubert B. b: 4/15/1864, Louisville, Ky. d: 5/21/1892, Brooklyn, N.Y. BR/TR, 5′8″, 160 lbs. Deb: 9/4/1886 Career OF: (241-LF 31-CF 0-RF)																							
1886	Lou-a	27	101	12	29	3	2	0	10	5		.287	.321	.356	677	106	0	7			.885	-2	O-24L/3-2,S-1,21	-0.2
1887	Lou-a	130	598	122	201	22	8	1	66	39		.336	.338	.363	701	94	-5	71			.887	-8	*O-109L,2-10/1-8,S3	-1.3
1888	Lou-a	116	485	117	149	26	11	2	50	41		.307	.366	.419	785	154	30	62			.890	13	O-82L,2-19,S-15	3.7
	Bro-a	12	42	16	13	5	1	0	3	9		.310	.442	.476	918	195	5	9			.897	-3	2-12	0.3
	Yr	128	527	133	162	**31**	12	2	53	50		.307	.373	.423	796	158	35	71			.890	10	O-82L,2-31,S-15	**4.0**
1889	*Bro-a	138	560	139	149	18	3	2	73	80	41	.266	.365	.320	684	95	-0	65			.929	-2	*2-138	0.2
1890	*Bro-N	129	510	**148**	142	32	7	3	69	85	47	.278	.385	.386	771	124	18	85			.945	5	*2-129	2.5
1891	Bro-N	107	435	82	120	16	5	3	31	59	63	.276	.365	.356	721	111	8	32			.910	-22	2-72,O-35(32-3-0)	-1.1
1892	Bro-N	21	87	17	26	5	1	0	17	14	13	.299	.396	.379	775	140	5	4			.925	-2	O-21(21-0-0)	0.1
Total	7	680	2818	653	829	127	38	11	319	332	164	.294	.365	.369	734	115	61	335			.928	-21	2-381,O-271L/S-20,13	4.2
■ HUGH COLLINS	Collins, Hugh 150 lbs. Deb: 8/1/1887																							
1887	NY-a	1	4	0	1	0	0	0	0	0		.250	.250	.250	500	41	-0	0			.250	-1	/C-1	-0.1
■ RIPPER COLLINS	Collins, James Anthony b: 3/30/04, Altoona, Pa. d: 4/15/70, New Haven, Conn. BB/TL, 5′9″, 165 lbs. Deb: 4/18/31 C																							
1931	*StL-N	89	279	34	84	20	10	4	59	18	24	.301	.350	.487	837	118	6	1			.995	5	1-68/O-3(1-0-2)	0.5
1932	StL-N	149	549	82	153	28	8	21	91	38	67	.279	.329	.474	802	110	6	4			.999	-5	1-81,O-60(15-0-45)	-1.0
1933	StL-N	132	493	66	153	26	7	10	68	38	49	.310	.363	.452	816	125	16	7			.994	3	*1-123	0.7
1934	*StL-N	154	600	116	200	40	12	**35**	128	57	50	.333	.393	**.615**	**1008**	155	45	2			.991	8	*1-154	3.7
1935	StL-N★	150	578	109	181	36	10	23	122	65	45	.313	.385	.529	915	138	31	0			.987	1	*1-150	1.7
1936	StL-N★	103	277	48	81	15	3	13	48	48	30	.292	.399	.509	908	143	18	1			.990	-2	1-61/O-9(1-0-8)	0.9
1937	Chi-N★	115	456	77	125	16	5	16	71	32	46	.274	.329	.436	765	102	0	2			.991	1	*1-111	-0.9
1938	*Chi-N	143	490	78	131	22	8	13	61	54	48	.267	.344	.424	768	107	5	1			**.996**	10	*1-135	0.2
1941	Pit-N	49	62	5	13	2	2	0	11	6	14	.210	.279	.306	586	65	-3	0			.947	-0	1-11/O-3(0-0-3)	-0.4
Total	9	1084	3784	615	1121	205	65	135	659	356	373	.296	.360	.492	852	125	124	18			.992	19	1-894/O-75(17-0-58)	5.4
■ JIMMY COLLINS	Collins, James Joseph b: 1/16/1870, Buffalo, N.Y. d: 3/6/43, Buffalo, N.Y. BR/TR, 5′9″, 178 lbs. Deb: 4/19/1895 MH Career OF: (0-LF 7-CF 21-RF)																							
1895	Bos-N	11	38	10	8	3	0	1	8	4	4	.211	.302	.368	671	67	-2	0			.714	-2	O-10(0-0-10)	-0.4
	Lou-N	96	373	65	104	17	5	6	49	33	16	.279	.352	.399	751	100	0	12			.926	21	3-77,O-18R/2-2,S-1	1.8
	Yr	107	411	75	112	20	5	7	57	37	20	.273	.347	.397	744	96	-2	12			.926	19	3-77,O-28R/2-2,S-1	1.4
1896	Bos-N	84	304	48	90	10	9	1	46	30	12	.296	.374	.398	772	98	-1	10			.909	20	3-80/S-4	1.7
1897	*Bos-N	134	529	103	183	28	13	6	132	41		.346	.400	.482	882	125	17	14			.917	21	*3-134	3.4
1898	Bos-N	152	597	107	196	35	5	**15**	111	40		.328	.377	.479	856	138	26	12			.932	15	*3-152	4.0
1899	Bos-N	151	599	98	166	28	11	5	92	40		.277	.335	.386	721	89	-11	12			.943	21	*3-151	1.1
1900	Bos-N	142	586	104	178	25	5	6	95	34		.304	.352	.394	747	94	-6	23			.935	10	*3-141/S-1	0.6
1901	Bos-A	138	564	108	187	42	16	6	94	34		.332	.375	.495	869	142	30	19			.914	14	*3-138,M	4.2
1902	Bos-A	108	429	71	138	21	10	6	61	24		.322	.360	.459	820	123	12	18			**.954**	9	*3-107,M	2.2
1903	*Bos-A	130	540	88	160	33	17	5	72	24		.296	.329	.448	777	125	14	23			**.952**	12	*3-130,M	3.1
1904	Bos-A	156	631	85	171	33	13	3	67	27		.271	.306	.379	685	110	6	19			.945	7	*3-156,M	1.8
1905	Bos-A	131	508	66	140	26	5	4	65	37		.276	.330	.370	700	120	11	18			.923	4	*3-131,M	2.1
1906	Bos-A	37	142	17	39	8	4	1	16	4		.275	.295	.408	703	120	2	1			.911	2	3-32,M	0.6
1907	Bos-A	41	158	13	46	8	0	0	10	10		.291	.333	.342	675	116	3	4			.874	-8	3-41	-0.4
	Phi-A	99	364	38	99	21	0	0	35	24		.272	.331	.330	660	108	4	4			.904	-2	3-98	0.5
	Yr	140	522	51	145	29	0	0	45	34		.278	.332	.333	665	110	6	8			.895	-10	*3-139	0.1
1908	Phi-A	115	433	34	94	14	3	0	30	20		.217	.258	.263	521	65	-17	5			.928	-7	*3-115	-2.3
Total	14	1725	6795	1055	1999	352	116	65	983	426	32	.294	.343	.409	752	112	89	194			.929	137	*3-1683/O-28R,S-6,2	24.0
■ ZIP COLLINS	Collins, John Edgar b: 5/2/1892, Brooklyn, N.Y. d: 12/19/83, Manassas, Va. BL/TL, 5′11″, 152 lbs. Deb: 7/31/14																							
1914	Pit-N	49	182	14	44	2	0	0	15	8	10	.242	.277	.253	530	61	-9	3			.962	1	O-49(0-11-40)	-1.2
1915	Pit-N	101	354	51	104	8	5	1	23	24	38	.294	.340	.353	693	112	5	6	7	-1	.942	5	O-89(0-89-0)	0.2
	Bos-N	5	14	3	4	1	1	0	0	2	1	.286	.375	.500	875	171	1	1			1.000	0	/O-4(4-0-0)	0.2
	Yr	106	368	54	108	9	6	1	23	26	39	.293	.342	.359	700	114	6	7	7	-1	.944	5	O-93(4-89-0)	0.4
1916	Bos-N	93	268	39	56	1	6	1	18	18	42	.209	.261	.269	530	66	-11	4			.947	-6	O-78(26-27-27)	-2.4
1917	Bos-N	9	27	3	4	0	1	0	2	0	4	.148	.148	.222	370	14	-3	0			1.000	1	/O-5(1-0-4)	-0.3
1921	Phi-A	24	71	14	20	5	1	0	5	6	5	.282	.354	.380	735	87	-1	1	2	-0	.915	0	O-20(0-20-0)	-0.2
Total	5	281	916	124	232	17	14	2	63	58	100	.253	.301	.309	610	85	-18	15	9		.946	1	O-245(31-147-71)	-3.7
■ SHANO COLLINS	Collins, John Francis b: 12/4/1885, Charlestown, Mass. d: 9/10/55, Newton, Mass. BR/TR, 6′, 185 lbs. Deb: 4/21/10 FM Career OF: (133-LF 292-CF 918-RF)																							
1910	Chi-A	97	315	29	62	10	8	1	24	25		.197	.258	.289	547	74	-10	10			.949	4	O-66(19-7-40),1-28	-1.1
1911	Chi-A	106	370	48	97	16	12	4	48	20		.262	.309	.403	712	101	-1	14			.978	4	1-98/2-3,O-3(2-0-0)	0.0
1912	Chi-A	153	579	75	168	34	10	2	81	29		.290	.330	.394	723	110	5	26			.969	3	*O-105(1-17-85),1-46	0.1
1913	Chi-A	148	535	53	128	26	9	1	47	32	60	.239	.286	.327	613	80	-15	22			.949	1	*O-147(2-0-145)	-2.4
1914	Chi-A	154	598	61	164	34	9	3	65	27	49	.274	.312	.376	688	108	3	30	24	-2	.970	6	*O-154(7-45-103)	-0.3
1915	Chi-A	153	576	73	148	24	17	2	85	28	50	.257	.298	.368	666	96	-6	38	19	2	.963	2	*O-104(20-21-64),1-47	-1.0
1916	Chi-A	143	527	74	128	28	12	0	42	59	51	.243	.323	.342	664	98	-1	16			.959	8	*O-137(23-2-112)/1-4	-0.1
1917	*Chi-A	82	252	38	59	13	3	1	14	10	27	.234	.269	.321	590	78	-8	14			.992	-2	O-73(9-0-64)	-1.4
1918	Chi-A	103	365	30	100	18	11	1	56	17	19	.274	.310	.392	702	111	2	7			.973	14	O-93(16-34-42)/1-5	1.2
1919	*Chi-A	63	179	21	50	6	3	1	16	7	11	.279	.317	.363	681	90	-3	3			.957	1	O-46(2-7-37)/1-8	-0.5
1920	Chi-A	133	495	70	150	21	10	1	63	23	24	.303	.339	.392	731	93	-6	12	9	-1	.988	-9	*1-116,O-13(2-1-10)	-1.8
1921	Bos-A	141	542	63	155	29	12	4	69	18	38	.286	.314	.406	720	85	-15	15	8	1	.966	4	*O-139(1-44-94)/1-3	-1.9
1922	Bos-A	135	472	33	128	24	7	1	52	7	30	.271	.289	.358	647	68	-23	7	9	-2	.951	-7	*O-117(11-45-63)/1-1	-3.9
1923	Bos-A	97	342	41	79	10	5	0	18	11	29	.231	.265	.289	555	46	-28	7	8	-1	.953	-2	O-89(0-57-32)	-3.5
1924	Bos-A	89	240	37	70	17	5	0	28	18	17	.292	.349	.404	753	94	-3	4	6	-1	.957	-10	O-56(18-11-27),1-12	-1.7
1925	Bos-A	2	3	1	1	0	0	0	1	0	0	.333	.333	.333	667	70	-0	0	0	0	.000	-1	/O-1(0-1-0)	-0.1
Total	16	1799	6390	747	1687	310	133	22	709	331	405	.264	.306	.364	671	90	-109	225	83		.962	16	*O-1343R,1-368/2-3	-18.4
■ JOE COLLINS	Collins, Joseph Edward (b: Joseph Edward Kollonige) b: 12/3/22, Scranton, Pa. d: 8/30/89, Union, N.J. BL/TL, 6′, 185 lbs. Deb: 9/25/48																							
1948	NY-A	5	5	0	1	1	0	0	2	0	1	.200	.200	.400	600	58	-0	0	0	0	.000	0	H	0.0
1949	NY-A	7	10	2	1	0	0	0	4	6	2	.100	.438	.100	538	46	-0	0	0	0	.920	-1	/1-5	-0.2
1950	*NY-A	108	205	47	48	8	3	8	28	31	34	.234	.335	.420	754	95	-2	5	0	1	.987	0	1-99/O-2(0-0-2)	-0.3
1951	*NY-A	125	262	52	75	8	5	9	48	34	23	.286	.368	.458	826	127	10	9	7	-0	.987	4	*1-114,O-15(0-0-15)	1.0
1952	*NY-A	122	428	69	120	16	8	18	59	55	47	.280	.364	.481	845	142	23	4	2	0	.990	-3	*1-119	1.7
1953	*NY-A	127	387	72	104	11	2	17	44	59	36	.269	.365	.439	805	121	12	2	6	-2	.989	1	*1-113/O-4(0-0-4)	0.5
1954	NY-A	130	343	67	93	20	2	12	46	51	37	.271	.365	.446	812	126	12	2	2	-0	.992	1	*1-117	0.8
1955	*NY-A	105	278	40	65	9	1	13	45	44	32	.234	.343	.414	756	104	2	0	2	-1	.998	5	1-73,O-27(0-0-27)	0.2
1956	*NY-A	100	262	38	59	5	3	7	43	34	33	.225	.316	.347	664	78	-9	3	1	0	.990	2	O-51(25-7-24),1-43	-1.0
1957	*NY-A	79	149	17	30	1	0	2	10	24	18	.201	.312	.248	560	56	-8	2	1	0	.987	-3	1-32,O-15(2-2-11)	-1.3
Total	10	908	2329	404	596	79	24	86	329	338	263	.256	.351	.421	772	112	38	27	21	-1	.990	7	1-715,O-114(27-9-83)	1.4
■ KEVIN COLLINS	Collins, Kevin Michael "Casey" b: 8/4/46, Springfield, Mass. BL/TR, 6′2″, 190 lbs. Deb: 9/1/65																							
1965	NY-N	11	23	3	4	1	0	0	0	1	9	.174	.208	.217	426	21	-2	0	1	-0	1.000	-1	/3-7,S-3	-0.5
1967	NY-N	4	10	1	1	0	0	0	0	0	3	.100	.100	.100	200	-43	-2	1	0	0	1.000	-0	/2-2	-0.2

YEAR	TM/L	G	AB	R	H	2B	3B	HR	RBI	BB	SO	AVG	OBP	SLG	OPS	OPS+	BR+	SB	CS	SBR	FA	FR	G/POS	TPR
1968	NY-N	58	154	12	31	5	2	1	13	7	37	.201	.236	.279	515	54	-9	0	1	-0	.955	-7	3-40/2-6,S-1	-1.8
1969	NY-N	16	40	1	6	3	0	1	2	3	10	.150	.209	.300	509	40	-3	0	0	0	.925	3	3-14	-0.1
	Mon-N	52	96	5	23	5	1	2	12	8	16	.240	.298	.375	673	87	-2	0	0	0	1.000	-7	2-20,3-16	-0.9
	Yr	68	136	6	29	8	1	3	14	11	26	.213	.272	.353	625	73	-5	0	0	0	.917	-4	3-30,2-20	-1.0
1970	Det-A	25	24	2	5	1	0	1	3	1	10	.208	.240	.375	615	67	-1	0	0	0	1.000	0	/1-1	-0.1
1971	Det-A	35	41	6	11	2	1	1	4	0	12	.268	.268	.439	707	94	-1	0	0	0	1.000	1	/3-4,O-2(1-0-1),2-1	0.0
Total	6	201	388	30	81	17	4	6	34	20	97	.209	.248	.320	567	62	-20	1	2	-0	.944	-11	/3-81,2-29,S-4,O1	-3.6

■ ORTH COLLINS Collins, Orth Stein "Buck" b: 4/27/1880, Lafayette, Ind. d: 12/13/49, Ft.Lauderdale, Fla BL/TR, 6′, 150 lbs. Deb: 6/1/04

YEAR	TM/L	G	AB	R	H	2B	3B	HR	RBI	BB	SO	AVG	OBP	SLG	OPS	OPS+	BR+	SB	CS	SBR	FA	FR	G/POS	TPR
1904	NY-A	5	17	3	6	1	1	0	1	1		.353	.389	.529	918	180	1	0			1.000	2	/O-5(0-5-1)	0.4
1909	Was-A	8	7	0	0	0	0	0	0	0		.000	.000	.000	0	-99	-2	0			1.000	-1	/O-2(0-1-1),P-1	-0.2
Total	2	13	24	3	6	1	1	0	1	1		.250	.280	.375	655	104	-0	0			1.000	1	/O-7(0-6-2),P-1	0.2

■ RIP COLLINS Collins, Robert Joseph b: 9/18/09, Pittsburgh, Pa. d: 4/19/69, Pittsburgh, Pa. BR/TR, 5′11″, 176 lbs. Deb: 4/28/40

YEAR	TM/L	G	AB	R	H	2B	3B	HR	RBI	BB	SO	AVG	OBP	SLG	OPS	OPS+	BR+	SB	CS	SBR	FA	FR	G/POS	TPR
1940	Chi-N	47	120	11	25	3	0	1	14	14	18	.208	.296	.258	555	55	-7	4			.951	-3	C-42	-0.8
1944	NY-A	3	3	0	1	0	0	0	0	1	0	.333	.500	.333	833	136	0	0	0	0	1.000	0	/C-3	0.1
Total	2	50	123	11	26	3	0	1	14	15	18	.211	.302	.260	562	58	-7	4	0		.953	-2	/C-45	-0.7

■ PAT COLLINS Collins, Tharon Leslie b: 9/13/1896, Sweet Sprgs., Mo. d: 5/20/60, Kansas City, Kan. BR/TR, 5′9″, 178 lbs. Deb: 9/5/19

YEAR	TM/L	G	AB	R	H	2B	3B	HR	RBI	BB	SO	AVG	OBP	SLG	OPS	OPS+	BR+	SB	CS	SBR	FA	FR	G/POS	TPR
1919	StL-A	11	21	2	3	1	0	0	1	4	2	.143	.280	.190	470	32	-2	0			.929	-1	/C-5	-0.2
1920	StL-A	23	28	5	6	1	0	0	6	3	5	.214	.290	.250	540	43	-2	0	0	0	1.000	-2	/C-7	-0.4
1921	StL-A	58	111	9	27	3	0	1	10	16	17	.243	.339	.297	636	60	-6	1	0	0	.961	-1	C-31	-0.5
1922	StL-A	63	127	14	39	6	0	8	23	21	21	.307	.405	.543	949	140	8	0	1	-0	.980	6	C-28/1-5	1.4
1923	StL-A	85	181	9	32	8	0	3	30	15	45	.177	.240	.271	511	32	-18	0	0	0	.980	-1	C-47	-1.6
1924	StL-A	32	54	9	17	2	0	1	11	11	14	.315	.431	.407	838	110	1	0	1	-0	.969	-1	C-20	0.1
1926	*NY-A	102	290	41	83	11	3	7	35	73	57	.286	.433	.417	850	124	15	3	2	-0	.971	2	*C-100	2.2
1927	*NY-A	92	251	38	69	9	3	7	36	54	24	.275	.407	.418	825	118	9	0	1	-0	.976	-7	C-89	0.7
1928	*NY-A	70	136	18	30	5	0	6	14	35	16	.221	.380	.390	770	106	2	0	0	0	.977	-5	C-70	0.1
1929	Bos-N	7	5	1	0	0	0	0	2	3	1	.000	.375	.000	375	2	-1	0			1.000	1	/C-6	0.1
Total	10	543	1204	146	306	46	6	33	168	235	202	.254	.378	.385	762	99	6	4	5		.974	-7	C-403/1-5	1.9

■ BILL COLLINS Collins, William J. b: 1863, Dublin, Ireland d: 6/8/1893, New York, N.Y. BR, Deb: 10/5/1889

YEAR	TM/L	G	AB	R	H	2B	3B	HR	RBI	BB	SO	AVG	OBP	SLG	OPS	OPS+	BR+	SB	CS	SBR	FA	FR	G/POS	TPR
1889	Phi-a	1	4	0	1	0	0	0	1	1	0	.250	.400	.250	650	88	0	1			.800	-1	/C-1	0.0
1890	Phi-a	1	1	0	0	0	0	0	0	0		.000	.000	.000	0	-99	-0	0			.500	-0	/S-1	0.0
1891	Cle-N	2	3	0	0	0	0	0	0	0	0	.000	.000	.000	0	-96	-1	0			.000	1	/O-1(0-0-1),C-1	0.1
Total	3	4	8	0	1	0	0	0	1	1	0	.125	.222	.125	347	1	-1	1			.867	0	/C-2,O-1(0-0-1),S-1	0.1

■ BILL COLLINS Collins, William Shirley b: 3/27/1882, Chesterton, Ind. d: 6/26/61, San Bernardino, Cal. BB/TR, 6′, 170 lbs. Deb: 4/14/10

YEAR	TM/L	G	AB	R	H	2B	3B	HR	RBI	BB	SO	AVG	OBP	SLG	OPS	OPS+	BR+	SB	CS	SBR	FA	FR	G/POS	TPR
1910	Bos-N	151	584	67	141	6	7	3	40	43	48	.241	.308	.291	599	72	-21	36			**.977**	13	*O-151(129-10-13)	-1.8
1911	Bos-N	17	44	8	6	1	1	0	8	1	8	.136	.156	.205	360	0	-6	4			1.000	0	O-13(3-8-2)/3-1	-0.6
	Chi-N	7	3	2	1	1	0	0	0	1	0	.333	.500	.667	1167	225	1	0			1.000	-2	/O-4(2-2-0)	-0.1
	Yr	24	47	10	7	2	1	0	8	2	8	.149	.184	.234	418	16	-5	4			1.000	-2	O-17(5-10-2)/3-1	-0.7
1913	Bro-N	32	95	8	18	1	0	0	4	8	11	.189	.267	.200	467	33	-8	2			.921	-3	O-27(13-15-0)	-1.4
1914	Buf-F	21	47	6	7	2	2	0	2	1	8	.149	.167	.277	443	19	-6	0			.864	-1	O-15(2-1-13)	-0.8
Total	4	228	773	91	173	11	10	3	54	54	75	.224	.287	.276	563	60	-40	42			.966	7	O-210(149-36-28)/3-1	-4.7

■ BILL COLLVER Collver, William J. b: 3/21/1867, Clyde, Ohio d: 3/24/1888, Detroit, Mich. Deb: 7/4/1885

YEAR	TM/L	G	AB	R	H	2B	3B	HR	RBI	BB	SO	AVG	OBP	SLG	OPS	OPS+	BR+	SB	CS	SBR	FA	FR	G/POS	TPR
1885	Bos-N	1	4	0	0	0	0	0	0	0	1	.000	.000	.000	0	-99	-1				.000	-0	/O-1(0-0-1)	-0.1

■ FRANK COLMAN Colman, Frank Lloyd b: 3/2/18, London, Ont., Canada d: 2/19/83, London, Ont., Can. BL/TL, 5′11″, 188 lbs. Deb: 9/12/42

YEAR	TM/L	G	AB	R	H	2B	3B	HR	RBI	BB	SO	AVG	OBP	SLG	OPS	OPS+	BR+	SB	CS	SBR	FA	FR	G/POS	TPR
1942	Pit-N	10	37	2	5	0	0	1	2	2	2	.135	.179	.216	396	15	-4	0			1.000	1	/O-8(0-0-8)	-0.4
1943	Pit-N	32	59	9	16	2	2	0	4	8	7	.271	.358	.373	731	108	1	0			1.000	0	O-11(0-0-11)	0.0
1944	Pit-N	99	226	30	61	9	5	6	53	25	27	.270	.345	.434	779	113	4	0			.964	-3	O-53(3-0-50)/1-6	-0.2
1945	Pit-N	77	153	18	32	11	1	4	30	9	16	.209	.253	.373	626	70	-7	0			.993	-1	1-22,O-12(6-0-5)	-1.0
1946	Pit-N	26	53	3	9	3	0	1	6	2	7	.170	.214	.283	497	39	-4	0			1.000	0	/O-8(4-0-4),1-2	-0.5
	NY-A	5	15	2	4	0	0	1	5	1	1	.267	.313	.467	779	114	0	0	0	0	1.000	-0	/O-5(0-0-5)	0.0
1947	NY-A	22	28	2	3	0	0	2	6	2	6	.107	.167	.321	488	34	-3	0	0	0	1.000	-1	/O-6(6-0-0)	-0.4
Total	6	271	571	66	130	25	8	15	106	49	66	.228	.291	.378	669	85	-14	0	0		.980	-4	O-103(19-0-83)/1-30	-2.5

■ CRIS COLON Colon, Cristobal b: 1/3/69, LaGuaira, Venez. BB/TR, 6′2″, 180 lbs. Deb: 9/18/92

YEAR	TM/L	G	AB	R	H	2B	3B	HR	RBI	BB	SO	AVG	OBP	SLG	OPS	OPS+	BR+	SB	CS	SBR	FA	FR	G/POS	TPR
1992	Tex-A	14	36	5	6	0	0	0	1	1	8	.167	.189	.167	356	0	-5	0	0	0	.946	3	S-14	-0.1

■ BOB COLUCCIO Coluccio, Robert Pasquali b: 10/2/51, Centralia, Wash. BR/TR, 5′11″, 183 lbs. Deb: 4/15/73 Career OF: (46-LF 150-CF 161-RF)

YEAR	TM/L	G	AB	R	H	2B	3B	HR	RBI	BB	SO	AVG	OBP	SLG	OPS	OPS+	BR+	SB	CS	SBR	FA	FR	G/POS	TPR
1973	Mil-A	124	438	65	98	21	8	15	58	54	92	.224	.313	.411	724	105	2	13	6	1	.992	10	*O-108(18-14-79),D-11	0.6
1974	Mil-A	138	394	42	88	13	4	6	31	43	61	.223	.305	.322	627	81	-9	15	9	0	.989	0	*O-131(4-103-34)/D-2	-1.3
1975	Mil-A	22	62	8	12	0	1	1	5	11	11	.194	.324	.274	599	70	-2	1	4	-1	1.000	1	O-22(0-22-0)	-0.3
	Chi-A	61	161	22	33	4	2	4	13	13	34	.205	.269	.329	598	67	-7	4	0	1	.980	-5	O-59(14-3-44)/D-1	-1.4
	Yr	83	223	30	45	4	3	5	18	24	45	.202	.285	.314	599	68	-9	5	4	-0	.987	-5	O-81(14-25-44)/D-1	-1.7
1977	Chi-A	20	37	4	10	0	0	0	7	6	2	.270	.372	.270	642	79	-1	0	2	-1	1.000	-2	O-19(9-8-3)	-0.4
1978	StL-N	5	3	0	0	0	0	0	0	1	2	.000	.250	.000	250	-25	-0	0	0	0	1.000	-1	/O-2(1-0-1)	-0.1
Total	5	370	1095	141	241	38	15	26	114	128	202	.220	.306	.353	660	87	-18	33	21	-0	.990	2	O-341R/D-14	-2.9

■ EARLE COMBS Combs, Earle Bryan "The Kentucky Colonel" b: 5/14/1899, Pebworth, Ky. d: 7/21/76, Richmond, Ky. BL/TR, 6′, 185 lbs. Deb: 4/16/24 CH

YEAR	TM/L	G	AB	R	H	2B	3B	HR	RBI	BB	SO	AVG	OBP	SLG	OPS	OPS+	BR+	SB	CS	SBR	FA	FR	G/POS	TPR
1924	NY-A	24	35	10	14	5	0	0	2	4	2	.400	.462	.543	1004	159	3	0	1	-0	1.000	-3	O-11(5-3-3)	-0.1
1925	NY-A	150	593	117	203	36	13	3	61	65	43	.342	.411	.462	873	123	22	12	13	-2	.979	4	*O-150(12-138-0)	1.6
1926	*NY-A	145	606	113	181	31	12	8	55	47	23	.299	.352	.429	781	105	2	8	6	-0	.970	1	*O-145(0-145-0)	-0.4
1927	*NY-A	152	648	137	**231**	36	**23**	6	64	62	31	.356	.414	.511	925	143	41	15	6	1	.968	2	*O-152(0-152-0)	3.5
1928	*NY-A	149	626	118	194	33	**21**	7	56	77	33	.310	.387	.463	850	127	25	10	8	-1	.980	8	*O-149(0-149-0)	2.5
1929	NY-A	142	586	119	202	33	15	3	65	69	32	.345	.414	.468	881	135	33	11	7	-0	.966	-4	*O-141(0-141-0)	2.2
1930	NY-A	137	532	129	183	30	**22**	7	82	74	26	.344	.424	.523	947	145	39	16	10	0	.969	-4	*O-135(60-45-30)	2.3
1931	NY-A	138	563	120	179	31	13	5	58	68	34	.318	.394	.446	840	128	24	11	3	1	.974	-0	*O-129(0-129-0)	2.0
1932	*NY-A	144	591	143	190	32	10	9	65	81	16	.321	.405	.455	860	129	28	3	9	-2	.967	-7	*O-139(42-115-1)	1.2
1933	NY-A	122	417	86	125	22	16	5	64	47	19	.300	.372	.465	837	128	17	6	4	-0	.975	-4	*O-104(23-80-2)	0.9
1934	NY-A	63	251	47	80	13	5	2	25	40	9	.319	.412	.434	847	127	12	3	1	0	.993	-2	O-62(12-51-0)	0.7
1935	NY-A	89	298	47	84	7	4	3	35	36	10	.282	.359	.362	722	92	-3	1	3	-1	.993	-4	O-70(57-13-1)	-1.1
Total	12	1455	5746	1186	1866	309	154	58	632	670	278	.325	.397	.462	859	127	243	96	71	-4	.974	-14	*O-1387(211-1161-37)	15.3

■ MERL COMBS Combs, Merrill Russell b: 12/11/19, Los Angeles, Cal. d: 7/8/81, Riverside, Cal. BL/TR, 6′, 172 lbs. Deb: 9/12/47 C

YEAR	TM/L	G	AB	R	H	2B	3B	HR	RBI	BB	SO	AVG	OBP	SLG	OPS	OPS+	BR+	SB	CS	SBR	FA	FR	G/POS	TPR
1947	Bos-A	17	68	8	15	1	0	1	6	9	9	.221	.329	.279	609	65	-3	0	0	0	1.000	4	3-17	0.1
1949	Bos-A	14	24	5	5	1	0	0	1	9	0	.208	.424	.250	674	75	-0	0	0	0	.923	-0	/3-9,S-1	-0.1
1950	Bos-A	1	0	0	0	0	0	0	0	1	0	—	1.000	—	1000	158	0	0	0	0	.000	0	H	0.0
	Was-A	37	102	19	25	1	0	0	6	22	16	.245	.379	.255	634	68	-4	0	0	0	.966	-1	S-30	-0.2
	Yr	38	102	19	25	1	0	0	6	23	16	.245	.384	.255	639	69	-3	0	0	0	.966	-1	S-30	-0.2
1951	Cle-A	19	28	2	5	2	0	0	2	2	3	.179	.233	.250	483	32	-3	0	0	0	.960	5	S-16	0.2
1952	Cle-A	52	139	11	23	1	1	1	10	14	15	.165	.242	.209	450	28	-14	0	1	-0	.972	9	S-49/2-3	-0.3
Total	5	140	361	45	73	6	1	2	25	57	43	.202	.314	.241	555	52	-23	0	1	-0	.968	17	/S-96,3-26,2-3	-0.3

■ WAYNE COMER Comer, Harry Wayne b: 2/3/44, Shenandoah, Va. BR/TR, 5′10″, 175 lbs. Deb: 9/17/67 Career OF: (80-LF 117-CF 70-RF)

YEAR	TM/L	G	AB	R	H	2B	3B	HR	RBI	BB	SO	AVG	OBP	SLG	OPS	OPS+	BR+	SB	CS	SBR	FA	FR	G/POS	TPR
1967	Det-A	4	3	0	1	0	0	0	0	0	0	.333	.333	.333	667	95	-0	0	0	0	.000	-0	/O-1(0-1-0)	0.0
1968	*Det-A	48	48	8	6	0	1	1	3	2	7	.125	.160	.229	389	16	-5	0	0	0	1.000	-5	O-27(26-0-1)/C-1	-1.2
1969	Sea-A	147	481	88	118	18	1	15	54	82	79	.245	.356	.380	737	108	7	18	7	2	.980	3	*O-139C/C-1,3-1	0.7
1970	Mil-A	13	17	1	1	0	0	0	1	0	3	.059	.059	.059	118	-67	-4	0	0	0	1.000	-1	/O-5(1-2-2)	-0.5

YEAR	TM/L	G	AB	R	H	2B	3B	HR	RBI	BB	SO	AVG	OBP	SLG	OPS	OPS+	BR+	SB	CS	SBR	FA	FR	G/POS	TPR
	Was-A	77	129	21	30	4	0	0	8	22	16	.233	.349	.264	612	75	-3	4	1	1	.960	-10	O-58(18-21-20)/3-1	-1.5
	Yr	90	146	22	31	4	0	0	9	22	19	.212	.320	.240	559	59	-7	4	1	1	.962	-11	O-63(19-23-22)/3-1	-2.0
1972	Det-A	27	9	1	1	0	0	0	1	0	1	.111	.111	.111	222	-33	-1	0	1	-0	1.000	-5	O-17(15-1-1)	-0.8
Total	5	316	687	119	157	22	2	16	67	106	106	.229	.333	.336	670	90	-7	22	9	2	.978	-18	O-247C/3-2,C-2	-3.3

■ CHARLIE COMISKEY

Comiskey, Charles Albert "Commy" or "The Old Roman" b: 8/15/1859, Chicago, Ill. d: 10/26/31, Eagle River, Wis. BR/TR, 6', 180 lbs. Deb: 5/2/1882 MH Career OF: (3-LF 3-CF 11-RF)

YEAR	TM/L	G	AB	R	H	2B	3B	HR	RBI	BB	SO	AVG	OBP	SLG	OPS	OPS+	BR+	SB	CS	SBR	FA	FR	G/POS	TPR
1882	StL-a	78	329	58	80	9	5	1	45	4		.243	.252	.310	562	85	-6				.967	-1	*1-77/P-2	-1.2
1883	StL-a	96	401	87	118	17	9	2	64	11		.294	.313	.397	710	120	7				.963	-2	*1-96/O-1(1-0-0),M	-0.3
1884	StL-a	108	460	76	109	17	6	2	84	5		.237	.253	.313	566	81	-11				.969	2	*1-108/2-1,P-1,M	-1.7
1885	*StL-a	83	340	68	87	15	7	2	44	14		.256	.293	.359	652	101	-1				.969	1	*1-83,M	-0.7
1886	*StL-a	131	578	95	147	15	9	3	76	10		.254	.267	.327	594	82	-15	41			.975	4	*1-122/2-9,O-2R,M	-2.0
1887	*StL-a	125	565	139	207	22	5	4	103	27		.366	.374	.416	790	109	3	117			.976	3	*1-116/2-9,O-3R,M	-0.3
1888	*StL-a	137	576	102	157	22	5	6	83	12		.273	.292	.359	652	98	-5	72			.970	-6	*1-133/O-5R,2-3,M	-2.1
1889	StL-a	137	587	105	168	28	10	3	102	19	19	.286	.312	.383	695	86	-15	65			.970	-1	*1-134/O-3R,2-3,PM	-2.4
1890	Chi-P	88	377	53	92	11	3	0	59	14	17	.244	.277	.289	566	49	-28	34			.965	-2	1-88,M	-3.2
1891	StL-a	139	572	84	148	16	2	2	88	33	25	.259	.307	.304	611	65	-29	38			.979	3	*1-139/O-2(2-0-0),M	-3.4
1892	Cin-N	141	551	61	125	14	6	3	71	32	16	.227	.274	.290	565	72	-20	30			.984	1	*1-141,M	-1.8
1893	Cin-N	64	259	38	57	12	1	0	26	11	2	.220	.257	.274	531	40	-23	9			.979	-6	1-64,M	-2.4
1894	Cin-N	63	228	26	61	9	0	0	38	5	5	.268	.295	.307	602	44	-21	10			.973	-3	1-62/O-1(0-0-1),M	-1.9
Total	13	1390	5823	992	1556	207	68	28	883	197	84	.267	.293	.337	631	81	-164	416			.973	-7	*1-1363/2-25,O-17R,P	-23.4

■ JIM COMMAND

Command, James Dalton "Igor" b: 10/15/28, Grand Rapids, Mich BL/TR, 6'2", 200 lbs. Deb: 6/20/54

YEAR	TM/L	G	AB	R	H	2B	3B	HR	RBI	BB	SO	AVG	OBP	SLG	OPS	OPS+	BR+	SB	CS	SBR	FA	FR	G/POS	TPR
1954	Phi-N	9	18	1	4	1	0	1	6	2	4	.222	.300	.444	744	91	-0	0	0	0	.929	-0	/3-6	0.0
1955	Phi-N	5	5	0	0	0	0	0	0	0	0	.000	.000	.000	0	-99	-1	0	0	0	.000	0	H	-0.1
Total	2	14	23	1	4	1	0	1	6	2	4	.174	.240	.348	588	52	-2	0	0	0	.929	-0	/3-6	-0.1

■ ADAM COMOROSKY

Comorosky, Adam Anthony b: 12/9/05, Swoyersville, Pa. d: 3/2/51, Swoyersville, Pa. BR/TR, 5'10", 167 lbs. Deb: 9/13/26

YEAR	TM/L	G	AB	R	H	2B	3B	HR	RBI	BB	SO	AVG	OBP	SLG	OPS	OPS+	BR+	SB	CS	SBR	FA	FR	G/POS	TPR
1926	Pit-N	8	15	2	4	1	1	0	0	1	2	.267	.313	.467	779	102	-0	1			1.000	-1	/O-6(6-0-0)	-0.2
1927	Pit-N	18	61	5	14	1	0	0	4	3	1	.230	.266	.246	512	35	-5	0			.978	2	O-16(15-1-0)	-0.5
1928	Pit-N	51	176	22	52	6	3	2	34	15	6	.295	.354	.398	752	92	-2	1			.968	-1	O-49(38-9-5)	-0.6
1929	Pit-N	127	473	86	152	26	11	6	97	40	22	.321	.377	.461	838	104	3	19			.963	0	*O-121(121-0-0)	-0.6
1930	Pit-N	152	597	112	187	47	**23**	12	119	51	33	.313	.371	.529	900	114	12	14			.969	1	*O-152(130-30-0)	0.2
1931	Pit-N	99	350	37	85	12	1	1	48	34	28	.243	.310	.291	601	63	-17	11			.978	3	O-90(89-0-1)	-2.0
1932	Pit-N	108	370	54	106	18	4	4	46	25	20	.286	.337	.389	726	96	-2	7			.981	7	O-92(74-18-0)	0.1
1933	Pit-N	64	162	18	46	8	1	1	15	4	9	.284	.301	.364	665	89	-3	2			1.000	-1	O-30(30-0-0)	-0.5
1934	Cin-N	127	446	46	115	12	6	0	40	34	23	.258	.315	.312	626	70	-18	1			.970	1	*O-122(47-9-66)	-2.4
1935	Cin-N	59	137	22	34	3	1	2	14	7	14	.248	.290	.328	618	68	-6	1			.953	-2	O-40(25-10-5)	-1.0
Total	10	813	2787	404	795	134	51	28	417	214	158	.285	.339	.400	739	91	-39	57			.972	9	O-718(575-77-77)	-7.5

■ PETE COMPTON

Compton, Anna Sebastian "Bash" b: 9/28/1889, San Marcos, Tex. d: 2/3/78, Kansas City, Mo. BL/TL, 5'11", 170 lbs. Deb: 9/6/11

YEAR	TM/L	G	AB	R	H	2B	3B	HR	RBI	BB	SO	AVG	OBP	SLG	OPS	OPS+	BR+	SB	CS	SBR	FA	FR	G/POS	TPR
1911	StL-A	28	107	9	29	4	0	0	5	8		.271	.322	.308	630	79	-3	2			.917	1	O-28(0-0-28)	-0.3
1912	StL-A	103	268	26	75	6	4	2	30	22		.280	.339	.354	694	102	1	11			.925	1	O-72(50-0-22)	-0.2
1913	StL-A	63	100	14	18	5	2	2	17	13	13	.180	.274	.330	604	79	-3	2			.862	-4	O-21(8-5-8)	-0.9
1915	StL-F	2	8	0	2	0	0	0	3	0	0	.250	.250	.250	500	39	-1	0			1.000	-1	/O-2(0-2-0)	-0.2
	Bos-N	35	116	10	28	7	1	1	12	8	11	.241	.290	.345	635	96	-1	4	1	1	.971	0	O-31(0-20-11)	-0.2
1916	Bos-N	34	98	13	20	2	0	0	8	7	7	.204	.264	.224	489	53	-5	5			.939	-2	O-30(3-26-1)	-1.1
	Pit-N	5	16	1	1	0	0	0	0	2	5	.063	.211	.063	273	-14	-2	0			.917	0	/O-5(0-0-5)	-0.3
	Yr	39	114	14	21	2	0	0	8	9	12	.184	.256	.202	458	43	-7	5			.936	-2	O-35(3-26-6)	-1.4
1918	NY-N	21	60	5	13	0	1	0	5	5	4	.217	.277	.250	527	62	-3	2			.971	-1	O-19(12-2-5)	-0.5
Total	6	291	773	78	186	24	8	5	80	65	40	.241	.303	.312	615	83	-17	26	1		.933	-6	O-208(73-55-80)	-3.7

■ MIKE COMPTON

Compton, Michael Lynn b: 8/15/44, Stamford, Tex. BR/TR, 5'10", 180 lbs. Deb: 4/17/70

YEAR	TM/L	G	AB	R	H	2B	3B	HR	RBI	BB	SO	AVG	OBP	SLG	OPS	OPS+	BR+	SB	CS	SBR	FA	FR	G/POS	TPR
1970	Phi-N	47	110	8	18	0	1	1	7	9	22	.164	.240	.209	449	22	-12	0	0	0	.986	8	C-40	-0.3

■ CLINT CONATSER

Conatser, Clinton Astor "Connie" (b: Astor Clinton Conatser) b: 7/24/21, Los Angeles, Cal. BR/TR, 5'11", 182 lbs. Deb: 4/21/48

YEAR	TM/L	G	AB	R	H	2B	3B	HR	RBI	BB	SO	AVG	OBP	SLG	OPS	OPS+	BR+	SB	CS	SBR	FA	FR	G/POS	TPR
1948	*Bos-N	90	224	30	62	9	3	3	23	32	27	.277	.370	.384	754	106	3	0			.974	-9	O-76(24-52-0)	-0.8
1949	Bos-N	53	152	10	40	6	0	3	16	14	19	.263	.325	.362	687	89	-3	0			.951	0	O-44(15-13-16)	-0.4
Total	2	143	376	40	102	15	3	6	39	46	46	.271	.352	.375	727	99	0	0			.965	-8	O-120(39-65-16)	-1.2

■ DAVE CONCEPCION

Concepcion, David Ismael (Benitez) b: 6/17/48, Aragua, Venez. BR/TR, 6'1", 180 lbs. Deb: 4/6/70 Career OF: (0-LF 8-CF 0-RF)

YEAR	TM/L	G	AB	R	H	2B	3B	HR	RBI	BB	SO	AVG	OBP	SLG	OPS	OPS+	BR+	SB	CS	SBR	FA	FR	G/POS	TPR
1970	*Cin-N	101	265	38	69	6	3	1	19	23	45	.260	.326	.317	643	73	-10	10	2	2	.945	-8	S-93/2-3	-0.6
1971	Cin-N	130	327	24	67	4	4	1	20	18	51	.205	.246	.251	497	42	-25	9	3	1	.974	-4	*S-112,2-10/3-7,O-5C	-1.8
1972	*Cin-N	119	378	40	79	13	2	2	29	32	65	.209	.274	.270	544	58	-21	13	6	1	.969	3	*S-114/3-9,2-1	-0.5
1973	Cin-N†	89	328	39	94	18	3	8	46	21	55	.287	.331	.433	764	116	6	22	5	3	.974	2	S-88/O-2(0-2-0)	2.2
1974	Cin-N	160	594	70	167	25	1	14	82	44	79	.281	.337	.397	734	106	4	41	6	7	.963	9	*S-160/O-1(0-1-0)	3.9
1975	*Cin-N★	140	507	62	139	23	1	5	49	39	51	.274	.328	.353	682	88	-9	33	6	5	.977	8	*S-130/3-6	2.1
1976	*Cin-N★	152	576	74	162	28	7	9	69	49	68	.281	.339	.401	740	107	5	21	10	1	.968	17	*S-150	4.2
1977	Cin-N★	156	572	59	155	26	3	8	64	46	77	.271	.325	.369	694	84	-13	29	7	4	**.986**	8	*S-156	1.6
1978	Cin-N★	153	565	75	170	33	4	6	67	51	83	.301	.360	.405	765	113	10	23	10	2	.969	-5	*S-152	2.4
1979	*Cin-N†	149	590	91	166	25	3	16	84	64	73	.281	.352	.415	767	108	7	19	7	2	.967	13	*S-148	3.8
1980	Cin-N★	156	622	72	162	31	8	5	77	37	107	.260	.303	.360	663	84	-14	12	2	2	.978	-13	*S-155/2-1	-0.9
1981	Cin-N★	106	421	57	129	28	0	5	67	37	61	.306	.364	.409	772	117	10	4	5	-1	.960	4	*S-106	2.5
1982	Cin-N★	147	572	48	164	25	4	5	53	45	61	.287	.339	.371	709	96	-2	13	6	1	.977	13	*S-145/1-1,3-1	2.7
1983	Cin-N	143	528	54	123	22	0	1	47	56	81	.233	.307	.280	587	61	-26	14	9	-0	.979	-22	*S-139/3-6,1-1	-3.5
1984	Cin-N	154	531	46	130	26	1	4	58	52	72	.245	.312	.320	632	75	-17	22	6	3	.978	-35	*S-104,3-54/1-6	-4.2
1985	Cin-N	155	560	59	141	19	2	7	48	50	67	.252	.316	.330	647	77	-16	16	12	-1	.962	-32	*S-151/3-5	-3.5
1986	Cin-N	90	311	42	81	13	2	3	30	26	43	.260	.318	.344	662	79	-9	13	2	2	.965	-2	S-60,1-12,2-10,3-10	-0.3
1987	Cin-N	104	279	32	89	15	0	1	33	28	24	.319	.381	.384	765	99	1	4	3	-0	.992	0	2-59,1-26,3-13,/S-2	0.3
1988	Cin-N	84	197	11	39	9	0	0	8	18	23	.198	.265	.244	509	45	-14	3	2	-0	.994	1	2-46,1-16,S-13,/3P	-1.3
Total	19	2488	8723	993	2326	389	48	101	950	736	1186	.267	.325	.357	682	88	-133	321	109	32	.971	-44	*S-2178,2-130,3/1OP	9.1

■ ONIX CONCEPCION

Concepcion, Onix Cardona (Cardona) b: 10/5/57, Dorado, P.R. BR/TR, 5'6", 180 lbs. Deb: 8/30/80

YEAR	TM/L	G	AB	R	H	2B	3B	HR	RBI	BB	SO	AVG	OBP	SLG	OPS	OPS+	BR+	SB	CS	SBR	FA	FR	G/POS	TPR
1980	*KC-A	12	15	1	2	0	0	0	2	0	1	.133	.133	.133	267	-26	-3	0	0	0	.833	1	/S-6	-0.2
1981	KC-A	2	0	0	0	0	0	0	0	0	0	—	—	—	—	—	0	0	0	0	.000	0	/S-1	0.0
1982	KC-A	74	205	17	48	9	1	0	15	5	18	.234	.256	.288	544	49	-14	2	1	0	.948	-2	S-46,2-24/D-1	-1.1
1983	KC-A	80	219	22	53	11	3	0	20	12	12	.242	.284	.320	604	66	-10	10	3	1	.913	1	3-31,2-28,S-21,/D-1	-0.6
1984	*KC-A	90	287	36	81	9	2	1	23	14	33	.282	.322	.338	660	82	-7	9	6	-0	.972	3	S-85/2-6,3-1	0.6
1985	*KC-A	131	314	32	64	5	1	2	20	16	29	.204	.256	.245	501	38	-27	4	4	-1	.959	5	*S-128/2-2	-1.0
1987	Pit-N	1	1	0	1	0	0	0	0	0	0	1.000	1.000	1.000	2000	429	0	0	0	0	.000	0	/H	0.0
Total	7	390	1041	108	249	34	7	3	80	47	93	.239	.279	.294	573	58	-60	25	14	1	.960	8	S-287/2-60,3-32,D-2	-2.3

■ RAMON CONDE

Conde, Ramon Luis (Roman) "Wito" b: 12/29/34, Juana Diaz, P.R. BR/TR, 5'8", 172 lbs. Deb: 7/17/62

YEAR	TM/L	G	AB	R	H	2B	3B	HR	RBI	BB	SO	AVG	OBP	SLG	OPS	OPS+	BR+	SB	CS	SBR	FA	FR	G/POS	TPR
1962	Chi-A	14	16	0	0	0	0	0	1	3	3	.000	.158	.000	158	-54	-4	0	0	0	.889	-1	/3-7	-0.4

■ FRED CONE

Cone, Joseph Frederick b: 5/1848, Rockford, Ill. d: 4/13/09, Chicago, Ill. 5'9.5", 171 lbs. Deb: 5/5/1871

YEAR	TM/L	G	AB	R	H	2B	3B	HR	RBI	BB	SO	AVG	OBP	SLG	OPS	OPS+	BR+	SB	CS	SBR	FA	FR	G/POS	TPR
1871	Bos-n	19	77	17	20	3	1	0	16	8	2	.260	.329	.325	654	86	-1	12	1	2	.854	-0	O-18(18-0-1)	0.1

■ BUNK CONGALTON

Congalton, William Millar b: 1/24/1875, Guelph, Ont., Can. d: 8/16/37, Cleveland, Ohio BL/TL, 5'11", 190 lbs. Deb: 4/18/02

YEAR	TM/L	G	AB	R	H	2B	3B	HR	RBI	BB	SO	AVG	OBP	SLG	OPS	OPS+	BR+	SB	CS	SBR	FA	FR	G/POS	TPR
1902	Chi-N	47	188	16	45	3	0	1	27	7		.239	.267	.271	538	68	-7	4			.988	0	O-47(0-5-43)	-1.0
1905	Cle-A	12	47	4	17	0	0	0	5	2		.362	.388	.362	749	136	2	3			.923	-1	O-12(0-0-12)	0.0
1906	Cle-A	117	419	51	134	13	5	3	50	24		.320	.361	.396	757	139	18	12			.957	-9	*O-114(21-1-93)	0.4

YEAR	TM/L	G	AB	R	H	2B	3B	HR	RBI	BB	SO	AVG	OBP	SLG	OPS	OPS+	BR+	SB	CS	SBR	FA	FR	G/POS	TPR
1907	Cle-A	9	22	2	4	0	0	0	2	4		.182	.308	.182	490	56	-1	0			1.000	0	/O-6(0-0-6)	-0.1
	Bos-A	124	496	44	142	11	8	2	47	20		.286	.318	.353	671	115	7	13			.969	-3	*O-123(0-0-123)	-0.2
	Yr	133	518	46	146	11	8	2	49	24		.282	.317	.346	663	112	6	13			.971	-2	*O-129(0-0-129)	-0.3
Total	4	309	1172	117	342	27	13	6	131	57		.292	.328	.352	680	116	18	32			.967	-13	O-302(21-6-277)	-0.9

■ TONY CONIGLIARO Conigliaro, Anthony Richard b: 1/7/45, Revere, Mass. d: 2/24/90, Salem, Mass. BR/TR, 6'3", 185 lbs. Deb: 4/16/64 F

YEAR	TM/L	G	AB	R	H	2B	3B	HR	RBI	BB	SO	AVG	OBP	SLG	OPS	OPS+	BR+	SB	CS	SBR	FA	FR	G/POS	TPR
1964	Bos-A	111	404	69	117	21	2	24	52	35	78	.290	.354	.530	883	135	18	2	4	-1	.973	3	*O-106(81-25-2)	1.5
1965	Bos-A	138	521	82	140	21	5	**32**	82	51	116	.269	.340	.512	852	131	20	4	2	0	.976	14	*O-137(0-2-135)	2.5
1966	Bos-A	150	558	77	148	26	7	28	93	52	112	.265	.333	.487	821	120	14	0	2	-1	.973	-0	*O-146(0-0-146)	0.3
1967	Bos-A★	95	349	59	100	11	5	20	67	27	58	.287	.346	.519	865	141	17	4	6	-1	.983	3	O-95(0-0-95)	1.4
1969	Bos-A	141	506	57	129	21	3	20	82	48	111	.255	.324	.427	751	103	1	2	4	-1	.981	-8	*O-137(0-0-137)	-1.5
1970	Bos-A	146	560	89	149	20	1	36	116	43	93	.266	.327	.498	826	116	11	4	2	0	.977	3	*O-146(0-0-146)	0.6
1971	Cal-A	74	266	23	59	18	0	4	15	23	52	.222	.286	.335	621	81	-7	3	3	-0	.994	6	O-72(0-0-72)	-0.6
1975	Bos-A	21	57	8	7	1	0	2	9	8	9	.123	.231	.246	476	32	-5	1	0	0	.000	0	D-15	-0.6
Total	8	876	3221	464	849	139	23	166	516	287	629	.264	.330	.476	806	118	69	20	23	-4	.979	21	O-839(81-27-733)/D-15	3.6

■ BILLY CONIGLIARO Conigliaro, William Michael b: 8/15/47, Revere, Mass. BR/TR, 6', 190 lbs. Deb: 4/11/69 F

YEAR	TM/L	G	AB	R	H	2B	3B	HR	RBI	BB	SO	AVG	OBP	SLG	OPS	OPS+	BR+	SB	CS	SBR	FA	FR	G/POS	TPR
1969	Bos-A	32	80	14	23	6	2	4	7	9	23	.287	.367	.563	929	149	5	1	1	-0	.926	-7	O-24(3-18-6)	-0.3
1970	Bos-A	114	398	59	108	16	3	18	58	35	73	.271	.341	.462	803	112	6	3	7	-2	.968	0	*O-108(77-25-20)	-0.1
1971	Bos-A	101	351	42	92	26	1	11	33	25	68	.262	.311	.436	747	102	0	3	2	-0	.983	4	*O-100(1-79-20)	0.2
1972	Mil-A	52	191	22	44	6	2	7	16	8	54	.230	.261	.393	654	95	-2	1	0	0	.992	6	O-50(2-6-45)	0.1
1973	*Oak-A	48	110	5	22	2	2	0	14	9	26	.200	.261	.255	515	48	-8	1	0	0	1.000	-2	O-40(21-18-3)/2-1	-1.1
Total	5	347	1130	142	289	56	10	40	128	86	244	.256	.313	.429	742	103	1	9	10	-2	.980	2	O-322(104-146-94)/2-1	-1.2

■ JEFF CONINE Conine, Jeffrey Guy b: 6/27/66, Tacoma, Wash. BR/TR, 6'1", 220 lbs. Deb: 9/16/90 Career OF: (577-LF 0-CF 50-RF)

YEAR	TM/L	G	AB	R	H	2B	3B	HR	RBI	BB	SO	AVG	OBP	SLG	OPS	OPS+	BR+	SB	CS	SBR	FA	FR	G/POS	TPR
1990	KC-A	9	20	3	5	2	0	0	2	2	5	.250	.318	.350	668	88	-0	0	0	0	.977	0	/1-9	-0.1
1992	KC-A	28	91	10	23	5	2	0	9	8	23	.253	.313	.352	665	84	-2	0	0	0	1.000	-2	O-23(22-0-1)/1-4	-0.5
1993	Fla-N	162	595	75	174	24	3	12	79	52	135	.292	.354	.403	758	97	-2	2	2	-0	.992	2	*O-147(147-0-0),1-43	-0.6
1994	Fla-N☆	115	451	60	144	27	6	18	82	40	92	.319	.376	.525	902	128	18	1	2	-0	.974	5	O-97(97-0-0),1-46	1.7
1995	Fla-N★	133	483	72	146	26	2	25	105	66	94	.302	.387	.520	907	136	26	2	0	0	.976	6	*O-118(118-0-0),1-14	2.6
1996	Fla-N	157	597	84	175	32	2	26	95	62	121	.293	.363	.484	848	125	21	1	4	-1	.975	5	*O-128(128-0-0),1-48	1.7
1997	*Fla-N	151	405	46	98	13	1	17	61	57	89	.242	.338	.405	743	98	-1	2	0	0	.992	10	*1-145/O-1(1-0-0)	-0.1
1998	KC-A	93	309	30	79	26	0	8	43	26	68	.256	.318	.417	735	87	-6	3	0	1	.993	-5	O-80L,1-12/D-3	-1.4
1999	Bal-A	139	444	54	129	31	1	13	75	30	40	.291	.340	.453	792	104	2	0	3	-1	.993	-5	1-99,D-22,O-13L,/3	-1.3
2000	Bal-A	119	409	53	116	20	2	13	46	36	53	.284	.345	.438	782	99	-1	4	3	-0	.932	2	3-44,1-39,D-20,O-19R	-0.3
Total	10	1106	3804	487	1089	206	19	132	597	379	720	.286	.354	.455	809	110	55	15	14	-2	.981	18	O-626L,1-459/3-48,D	1.7

■ JOCKO CONLAN Conlan, John Bertrand b: 12/6/1899, Chicago, Ill. d: 4/16/89, Scottsdale, Ariz. BL/TL, 5'7.5", 165 lbs. Deb: 7/6/34 UH

YEAR	TM/L	G	AB	R	H	2B	3B	HR	RBI	BB	SO	AVG	OBP	SLG	OPS	OPS+	BR+	SB	CS	SBR	FA	FR	G/POS	TPR
1934	Chi-A	63	225	35	56	11	3	0	16	19	7	.249	.310	.324	635	62	-13	2	2	-0	.955	-3	O-54(0-54-4)	-1.7
1935	Chi-A	65	140	20	40	7	1	0	15	14	6	.286	.355	.350	705	81	-4	3	3	-0	.961	-3	O-37(0-21-16)	-0.8
Total	2	128	365	55	96	18	4	0	31	33	13	.263	.327	.334	662	69	-16	5	5	-1	.957	-6	/O-91(0-75-20)	-2.5

■ JOCKO CONLON Conlon, Arthur Joseph b: 12/10/1897, Woburn, Mass. d: 8/5/87, Falmouth, Mass. BR/TR, 5'7", 145 lbs. Deb: 4/17/23

YEAR	TM/L	G	AB	R	H	2B	3B	HR	RBI	BB	SO	AVG	OBP	SLG	OPS	OPS+	BR+	SB	CS	SBR	FA	FR	G/POS	TPR
1923	Bos-N	59	147	23	32	3	0	0	17	11	11	.218	.299	.238	537	45	-11	0	3	-1	.955	1	2-36/S-6,3-4	-0.9

■ BERT CONN Conn, Albert Thomas b: 9/22/1879, Philadelphia, Pa. d: 11/2/44, Philadelphia, Pa. TR, 6', 178 lbs. Deb: 9/16/1898

YEAR	TM/L	G	AB	R	H	2B	3B	HR	RBI	BB	SO	AVG	OBP	SLG	OPS	OPS+	BR+	SB	CS	SBR	FA	FR	G/POS	TPR
1898	Phi-N	1	3	1	1	0	1	0	1	0		.333	.333	1.000	1333	291	1	0			1.000	-0	/P-1	0.0
1900	Phi-N	6	9	4	3	1	0	0	1	0		.333	.333	.444	778	115	0	0			.667	-1	/P-4	0.0
1901	Phi-N	5	18	2	4	1	0	0	0	0		.222	.263	.278	541	56	-1	0			.880	-1	/2-5	-0.2
Total	3	12	30	7	8	2	1	0	2	0		.267	.290	.400	690	95	-0	0			.714	-2	/2-5,P-5	-0.2

■ FRITZIE CONNALLY Connally, Fritzie Lee b: 5/19/58, Bryan, Tex. BR/TR, 6'3", 210 lbs. Deb: 9/9/83

YEAR	TM/L	G	AB	R	H	2B	3B	HR	RBI	BB	SO	AVG	OBP	SLG	OPS	OPS+	BR+	SB	CS	SBR	FA	FR	G/POS	TPR
1983	Chi-N	8	10	0	1	0	0	0	0	0	5	.100	.100	.100	200	-42	-2	0	0	0	1.000	0	/3-3	-0.2
1985	Bal-A	50	112	16	26	4	0	3	15	19	21	.232	.348	.348	697	94	-0	0	0	0	.976	-3	3-46/1-2,D-1	-0.4
Total	2	58	122	16	27	4	0	3	15	19	26	.221	.331	.328	659	83	-2	0	0	0	.977	-3	/3-49,1-2,D-1	-0.6

■ BRUCE CONNATSER Connatser, Broadus Milburn b: 9/19/02, Sevierville, Tenn d: 1/27/71, Terre Haute, Ind. BR/TR, 5'11.5", 170 lbs. Deb: 9/15/31

YEAR	TM/L	G	AB	R	H	2B	3B	HR	RBI	BB	SO	AVG	OBP	SLG	OPS	OPS+	BR+	SB	CS	SBR	FA	FR	G/POS	TPR
1931	Cle-A	12	49	5	14	3	0	0	4	2	3	.286	.327	.347	674	73	-2	0	0	0	1.000	1	1-12	-0.2
1932	Cle-A	23	60	8	14	3	1	0	4	4	8	.233	.281	.317	598	51	-4	1	0	0	1.000	0	1-14	-0.5
Total	2	35	109	13	28	6	1	0	8	6	11	.257	.302	.330	632	61	-6	1	0	0	1.000	2	/1-26	-0.7

■ FRANK CONNAUGHTON Connaughton, Frank Henry b: 1/1/1869, Clinton, Mass. d: 12/1/42, Boston, Mass. BR/TR, 5'9", 165 lbs. Deb: 5/28/1894 Career OF: (32-LF 2-CF 0-RF)

YEAR	TM/L	G	AB	R	H	2B	3B	HR	RBI	BB	SO	AVG	OBP	SLG	OPS	OPS+	BR+	SB	CS	SBR	FA	FR	G/POS	TPR
1894	Bos-N	46	171	42	59	9	2	2	33	16	8	.345	.407	.456	864	100	-0	3			.892	-3	S-33/C-7,O-4(2-2-0)	-0.1
1896	NY-N	88	315	53	82	3	2	2	43	25	7	.260	.319	.302	620	66	-15	22			.892	3	S-54,O-30(30-0-0)	-1.0
1906	Bos-N	12	44	3	9	0	0	0	1	3		.205	.271	.205	475	50	-2	1			.918	-3	S-11/2-1	-0.5
Total	3	146	530	98	150	12	4	4	77	44	15	.283	.344	.343	687	78	-18	26			.894	-3	/S-98,O-34L,C-7,2-1	-1.6

■ GENE CONNELL Connell, Eugene Joseph b: 5/10/06, Hazleton, Pa. d: 8/31/37, Waverly, N.Y. BR/TR, 6'0.5", 180 lbs. Deb: 7/4/31 F

YEAR	TM/L	G	AB	R	H	2B	3B	HR	RBI	BB	SO	AVG	OBP	SLG	OPS	OPS+	BR+	SB	CS	SBR	FA	FR	G/POS	TPR
1931	Phi-N	6	12	1	3	0	0	0	0	0	3	.250	.250	.250	500	32	-1	0			1.000	-1	/C-6	-0.1

■ JOE CONNELL Connell, Joseph Bernard b: 1/16/02, Bethlehem, Pa. d: 9/21/77, Trexlertown, Pa. BL/TL, 5'8", 165 lbs. Deb: 6/15/26 F

YEAR	TM/L	G	AB	R	H	2B	3B	HR	RBI	BB	SO	AVG	OBP	SLG	OPS	OPS+	BR+	SB	CS	SBR	FA	FR	G/POS	TPR
1926	NY-N	2	1	1	0	0	0	0	0	0	0	.000	.000	.000	0	-99	-0	0			.000	0	H	0.0

■ PETE CONNELL Connell, Peter J. b: Brooklyn, N.Y. Deb: 9/3/1886

YEAR	TM/L	G	AB	R	H	2B	3B	HR	RBI	BB	SO	AVG	OBP	SLG	OPS	OPS+	BR+	SB	CS	SBR	FA	FR	G/POS	TPR
1886	NY-a	1	5	0	0	0	0	0	0	0		.000	.000	.000	0	-99	-1	0			.667	-1	/3-1	-0.2

■ TERRY CONNELL Connell, Terence G. b: 6/17/1855, Philadelphia, Pa. d: 3/25/24, Philadelphia, Pa. Deb: 6/20/1874

YEAR	TM/L	G	AB	R	H	2B	3B	HR	RBI	BB	SO	AVG	OBP	SLG	OPS	OPS+	BR+	SB	CS	SBR	FA	FR	G/POS	TPR
1874	Chi-n	1	4	0	0	0	0	0	0	0	0	.000	.000	.000	0	-99	-1	0	0	0	.429	-1	/C-1	-0.1

■ TOM CONNELLY Connelly, Thomas Martin b: 10/20/1897, Chicago, Ill. d: 2/18/41, Hines, Ill. BL/TR, 5'11.5", 165 lbs. Deb: 9/24/20

YEAR	TM/L	G	AB	R	H	2B	3B	HR	RBI	BB	SO	AVG	OBP	SLG	OPS	OPS+	BR+	SB	CS	SBR	FA	FR	G/POS	TPR
1920	NY-A	1	1	0	0	0	0	0	0	0	0	.000	.000	.000	0	-97	-0	0	0	0	.000	0	H	0.0
1921	NY-A	4	5	0	1	0	0	0	0	1	0	.200	.333	.200	533	38	-0	0	0	0	1.000	0	/O-3(0-1-2)	0.0
Total	2	5	6	0	1	0	0	0	0	1	0	.167	.286	.167	452	18	-1	0	0	0	1.000	0	/O-3(0-1-2)	0.0

■ ED CONNOLLY Connolly, Edward Joseph Sr. b: 7/17/08, Brooklyn, N.Y. d: 11/12/63, Pittsfield, Mass. BR/TR, 5'8.5", 180 lbs. Deb: 9/20/29 F

YEAR	TM/L	G	AB	R	H	2B	3B	HR	RBI	BB	SO	AVG	OBP	SLG	OPS	OPS+	BR+	SB	CS	SBR	FA	FR	G/POS	TPR
1929	Bos-A	5	8	0	0	0	0	0	0	0	2	.000	.000	.000	0	-99	-2	0	0	0	.889	-1	/C-5	-0.3
1930	Bos-A	27	48	1	9	2	0	0	7	4	3	.188	.250	.229	479	23	-6	0	0	0	1.000	-1	C-26	-0.5
1931	Bos-A	42	93	3	7	1	0	0	3	5	18	.075	.131	.086	217	-44	-20	0	0	0	.981	-1	C-41	-1.8
1932	Bos-A	75	222	9	50	8	4	0	21	20	27	.225	.289	.297	587	54	-15	0	1	-0	.957	4	C-75	-0.7
Total	4	149	371	13	66	11	4	0	31	29	50	.178	.239	.229	469	23	-43	0	1	-0	.966	1	C-147	-3.3

■ RED CONNOLLY Connolly, John M. b: 1863, New York, N.Y. d: 3/2/1896, New York, N.Y. BB, Deb: 7/1/1886

YEAR	TM/L	G	AB	R	H	2B	3B	HR	RBI	BB	SO	AVG	OBP	SLG	OPS	OPS+	BR+	SB	CS	SBR	FA	FR	G/POS	TPR
1886	StL-N	2	7	0	0	0	0	0	0	0	3	.000	.000	.000	0	-99	-2	0			.000	-1	/O-2(0-2-0)	-0.2

■ JOE CONNOLLY Connolly, Joseph Aloysius b: 2/12/1886, N.Smithfield, R.I. d: 9/1/43, N.Smithfield, R.I. BL/TR, 5'7.5", 165 lbs. Deb: 4/10/13

YEAR	TM/L	G	AB	R	H	2B	3B	HR	RBI	BB	SO	AVG	OBP	SLG	OPS	OPS+	BR+	SB	CS	SBR	FA	FR	G/POS	TPR
1913	Bos-N	126	427	79	120	18	11	5	57	66	47	.281	.379	.410	788	123	14	18			.954	-8	*O-124(124-0-0)	0.1
1914	*Bos-N	120	399	64	122	28	10	9	65	49	36	.306	.393	.494	886	164	32	12			.974	-5	*O-118(115-0-5)	2.3
1915	Bos-N	104	305	48	91	14	8	0	23	39	35	.298	.387	.397	784	144	18	13	12	-1	.971	-4	O-93(81-3-9)	1.0
1916	Bos-N	62	110	11	25	5	2	0	12	14	13	.227	.320	.309	629	98	0	5			.980	-1	O-31(14-4-12)	-0.2
Total	4	412	1241	202	358	65	31	14	157	168	131	.288	.380	.425	805	139	63	48	12		.967	-17	O-366(334-7-26)	3.2

YEAR	TM/L	G	AB	R	H	2B	3B	HR	RBI	BB	SO	AVG	OBP	SLG	OPS	OPS+	BR+	SB	CS	SBR	FA	FR	G/POS	TPR
■ **JOE CONNOLLY** Connolly, Joseph George "Coaster Joe" b: 6/4/1896, San Francisco, Cal d: 3/30/60, San Francisco, Cal BR/TR, 6', 170 lbs. Deb: 10/1/21																								
1921	NY-N	2	4	0	0	0	0	0	0	1	1	.000	.200	.000	200	-42	-1	0	0	0	1.000	-0	/O-1(1-0-0)	-0.1
1922	Cle-A	12	45	6	11	2	1	0	6	5	8	.244	.320	.333	653	70	-2	1	0	0	.972	2	O-12(0-12-0)	-0.1
1923	Cle-A	52	109	25	33	10	1	3	25	13	7	.303	.377	.495	872	129	4	1	2	-0	.957	-10	O-39(2-3-34)	-0.8
1924	Bos-A	14	10	1	1	0	0	0	1	2	2	.100	.250	.100	350	-7	-2	0	0	0	1.000	-1	/O-3(0-0-3)	-0.2
Total	4	80	168	32	45	12	2	3	32	21	18	.268	.349	.417	766	100	-0	2	2	-0	.966	-9	/O-55(3-15-37)	-1.2
■ **BUD CONNOLLY** Connolly, Mervin Thomas "Mike" b: 5/25/01, San Francisco, Cal d: 6/12/64, Berkeley, Cal. BR/TR, 5'8", 154 lbs. Deb: 5/3/25																								
1925	Bos-A	43	107	12	28	7	1	0	21	23	9	.262	.392	.346	738	88	-1	0	3	-1	.950	-11	S-34/3-2	-0.9
■ **TOM CONNOLLY** Connolly, Thomas Francis "Blackie" or "Ham" b: 12/30/1892, Boston, Mass. d: 5/14/66, Boston, Mass. BL/TR, 5'11", 175 lbs. Deb: 5/12/15																								
1915	Was-A	50	141	14	26	3	2	0	7	14	19	.184	.268	.234	502	49	-9	5	4	-0	.970	-7	3-24,O-19(11-0-8)/S-4	-1.7
■ **NED CONNOR** Connor, Edward b: 1850, New York 5'9", 156 lbs. Deb: 5/18/1871																								
1871	Tro-n	7	33	6	7	0	0	0	2	0	0	.212	.212	.212	424	22	-3	0	0	0	.878	-0	/1-4,O-3(0-0-3)	-0.2
■ **JIM CONNOR** Connor, James Matthew (b: James Matthew O'Connor) b: 5/11/1863, Port Jervis, N.Y. d: 9/3/50, Providence, R.I. BR/TR, 5'10.5", 179 lbs. Deb: 7/11/1892																								
1892	Chi-N	9	34	0	2	0	0	0	0	1	7	.059	.111	.059	170	-48	-6	0			.917	-6	/2-9	-1.1
1897	Chi-N	77	285	40	83	10	5	3	38	24		.291	.355	.393	748	94	-3	10			.936	22	2-76	1.9
1898	Chi-N	138	505	51	114	9	9	0	67	42		.226	.289	.279	568	63	-24	11			.946	-3	*2-138	-2.0
1899	Chi-N	69	234	26	48	7	1	0	24	18		.205	.265	.244	508	41	-19	6			.942	4	2-44,3-25	-1.1
Total	4	293	1058	117	247	26	15	3	129	85	7	.233	.296	.295	591	64	-52	27			.942	18	2-267/3-25	-2.3
■ **JOE CONNOR** Connor, Joseph Francis b: 12/8/1874, Waterbury, Conn. d: 11/8/57, Waterbury, Conn. BR/TR, 6'2", 185 lbs. Deb: 9/9/1895 F Career OF: (0-LF 1-CF 4-RF)																								
1895	StL-N	2	7	0	0	0	0	0	0	0	2	.000	.000	.000	0	-99	-2	0			1.000	1	/3-2	-0.1
1900	Bos-N	7	19	2	4	0	0	0	4	2		.211	.286	.211	496	34	-2	1			.971	2	/C-7	0.1
1901	Mil-A	38	102	10	28	3	1	1	9	6		.275	.321	.353	674	91	-1	4			.949	0	C-30/2-1,3-1,O-1C	0.1
	Cle-A	37	121	13	17	3	1	0	6	7		.140	.200	.182	382	7	-15	2			.942	-0	C-32/O-4(0-0-4),S-1	-1.2
	Yr	75	223	23	45	6	2	1	15	13		.202	.255	.260	515	45	-16	6			.946	-0	C-62/O-5R,2-1,3S	-1.1
1905	NY-A	8	22	4	5	1	0	0	2	3		.227	.320	.273	593	79	-0	1			.978	2	/C-6,1-2	0.3
Total	4	92	271	29	54	7	2	1	22	18	2	.199	.257	.251	508	43	-21	8			.952	5	/C-75,O-5R,3-3,1S2	-0.8
■ **ROGER CONNOR** Connor, Roger b: 7/1/1857, Waterbury, Conn. d: 1/4/31, Waterbury, Conn. BL/TL, 6'3", 220 lbs. Deb: 5/1/1880 FMH																								
1880	Tro-N	83	340	53	113	18	8	3	47	13	21	.332	.357	.459	816	166	22				.821	-11	*3-83	1.4
1881	Tro-N	85	367	55	107	17	6	2	31	15	20	.292	.319	.387	706	115	6				.950	2	*1-85	0.3
1882	Tro-N	81	349	65	115	22	**18**	4	42	13	20	.330	.354	.530	884	188	34				.951	3	1-43,O-24C,3-14	2.9
1883	NY-N	98	409	80	146	28	15	1	50	25	16	.357	.394	.506	900	173	36				.958	3	*1-98	2.5
1884	NY-N	116	477	98	151	28	4	4	82	38	32	.317	.367	.417	784	143	23				.860	3	2-67,O-37C,3-12	2.4
1885	NY-N	110	455	102	**169**	23	15	1	65	51	8	**.371**	**.435**	.495	929	**203**	**53**				.975	5	*1-110	**4.4**
1886	NY-N	118	485	105	172	29	**20**	7	71	41	15	.355	.405	.540	945	183	48	17			.973	10	*1-118	4.2
1887	NY-N	127	546	113	209	26	22	17	104	75	50	.383	.392	.541	933	164	43	43			**.993**	5	*1-127	3.0
1888	*NY-N	134	481	98	140	15	17	14	71	**73**	44	.291	.389	.480	869	**178**	45	27			.982	1	*1-133/2-1	3.3
1889	*NY-N	131	496	117	157	32	17	13	**130**	93	46	.317	.426	**.528**	955	166	46	21			.977	-8	*1-131/3-1	2.2
1890	NY-P	123	484	133	169	24	15	**14**	103	88	32	.349	.450	**.548**	**998**	152	36	22			**.985**	11	*1-123	2.8
1891	NY-N	129	479	112	139	29	13	7	94	83	39	.290	.399	.449	848	153	35	27			.983	1	*1-129	2.2
1892	Phi-N	155	564	123	166	**37**	11	12	73	116	39	.294	.420	.463	883	167	51	22			**.985**	-6	*1-155	4.1
1893	NY-N	135	511	111	156	25	8	11	105	91	26	.305	.413	.450	863	129	23	24			.974	2	*1-135/3-1	2.0
1894	NY-N	22	82	10	24	7	0	1	14	8	0	.293	.356	.415	770	86	-2	2			.976	2	1-21/O-1(0-0-1)	0.0
	StL-N	99	380	83	122	28	25	7	79	51	17	.321	.410	.582	991	137	21	17			.974	5	*1-99	1.9
	Yr	121	462	93	146	35	25	8	93	59	17	.316	.400	.552	952	128	19	19			.974	7	*1-120/O-1(0-0-1)	1.9
1895	StL-N	104	401	78	131	29	9	8	78	63	10	.327	.422	.504	926	140	25	9			.986	4	*1-104	2.3
1896	StL-N	126	483	71	137	21	9	11	72	52	14	.284	.356	.433	788	112	7	10			**.988**	13	*1-126,M	1.6
1897	StL-N	22	83	13	19	3	1	1	12	13		.229	.333	.325	659	76	-3	3			.984	-0	1-22	-0.2
Total	18	1998	7872	1620	2542	441	233	138	1323	1002	449	.323	.397	.486	883	154	550	244			.978	45	*1-1759,3-111/2-68,O	43.3
■ **JERRY CONNORS** Connors, Jeremiah b: Cleveland, Ohio Deb: 7/11/1892																								
1892	Phi-N	1	3	0	0	0	0	0	0	0	1	.000	.000	.000	0	-99	-1	0			.000	-0	/O-1(0-0-1)	-0.1
■ **JOE CONNORS** Connors, Joseph P. b: Paterson, N.J. Deb: 5/3/1884																								
1884	Alt-U	3	11	0	1	0	0	0		0		.091	.091	.091	182	-44	-2				1.000	-0	/P-1,3-1,O-1(0-1-0)	-0.2
	KC-U	3	11	2	1	0	0	0		1		.091	.167	.091	258	-23	-2				1.000	0	/O-2(0-0-2),P-2	0.0
	Yr	6	22	2	2	0	0	0		1		.091	.130	.091	221	-34	-4				.750	0	/P-3,O-3(0-1-2),3-1	-0.2
■ **CHUCK CONNORS** Connors, Kevin Joseph Aloysius b: 4/10/21, Brooklyn, N.Y. d: 11/10/92, Los Angeles, Cal. BL/TL, 6'5", 190 lbs. Deb: 5/1/49																								
1949	Bro-N	1	1	0	0	0	0	0	0	0	0	.000	.000	.000	0	-96	-0	0			.000	0	H	0.0
1951	Chi-N	66	201	16	48	5	1	2	18	12	25	.239	.282	.303	585	56	-12	4	0	1	.984	-1	1-57	-1.5
Total	2	67	202	16	48	5	1	2	18	12	25	.238	.280	.302	582	56	-13	4	0		.984	-1	/1-57	-1.5
■ **MERV CONNORS** Connors, Mervyn James b: 1/23/14, Berkeley, Cal. BR/TR, 6'2", 192 lbs. Deb: 9/4/37																								
1937	Chi-A	28	103	12	24	4	1	2	12	14	19	.233	.325	.350	674	70	-5	2	1	0	.926	-3	3-28	-0.7
1938	Chi-A	24	62	14	22	4	0	6	13	9	17	.355	.437	.710	1146	178	7	0	0	0	.979	0	1-16	0.5
Total	2	52	165	26	46	8	1	8	25	23	36	.279	.367	.485	852	111	2	2	1	0	.926	-3	/3-28,1-16	-0.2
■ **BEN CONROY** Conroy, Bernard Patrick b: 3/14/1871, Philadelphia, Pa. d: 11/25/37, Philadelphia, Pa. 160 lbs. Deb: 4/21/1890																								
1890	Phi-a	117	404	45	69	13	1	0	21	45		.171	.262	.208	470	39	-30	17			.893	-6	S-74,2-42/O-1(0-1-0)	-2.9
■ **WID CONROY** Conroy, William Edward b: 4/5/1877, Camden, N.J. d: 12/6/59, Mt.Holly, N.J. BR/TR, 5'9", 158 lbs. Deb: 4/25/01 C Career OF: (224-LF 76-CF 10-RF)																								
1901	Mil-A	131	503	74	129	20	6	5	64	36		.256	.316	.350	666	89	-7	21			.922	19	*S-118,3-12	1.5
1902	Pit-N	99	365	55	89	10	6	1	47	24		.244	.299	.312	612	86	-6	10			.925	8	S-95/O-3(2-0-1)	0.5
1903	NY-A	126	503	74	137	23	12	1	45	32		.272	.322	.372	694	101	-1	33			.919	3	*3-123/S-4	0.7
1904	NY-A	140	489	58	119	18	12	1	52	43		.243	.314	.335	649	100	1	30			.944	4	*3-110,S-27/O-3C	1.0
1905	NY-A	101	385	55	105	19	11	2	25	32		.273	.329	.395	723	116	6	25			.928	7	3-48,O-25L,S-17,1/2	1.5
1906	NY-A	148	567	67	139	17	10	4	54	47		.245	.303	.332	635	89	-7	32			.968	-1	O-97C,S-49/3-2	-1.3
1907	NY-A	140	530	58	124	12	11	3	51	30		.234	.279	.315	594	83	-11	41			.955	10	*O-100(100-0-0),S-38	-0.7
1908	NY-A	141	531	44	126	22	3	1	39	14		.237	.258	.296	554	79	-14	23			.939	13	*3-119,2-12,O-10L	0.2
1909	Was-A	139	488	44	119	13	4	1	20	37		.244	.298	.293	592	91	-5	24			.938	-0	*3-120,2-13/O-5C,S	-0.3
1910	Was-A	103	351	36	89	11	3	1	27	30		.254	.314	.311	625	100	0	11			.961	2	3-46,O-46(44-0-2)/2-5	0.1
1911	Was-A	106	349	40	81	11	4	2	28	20		.232	.282	.304	585	64	-17	12			.930	6	3-85,O-15(14-0-1)/2-1	-1.0
Total	11	1374	5061	605	1257	176	82	22	452	345		.248	.301	.329	629	91	-59	262			.934	71	3-665,S-349,O/21	2.2
■ **BILL CONROY** Conroy, William Frederick "Pep" b: 1/9/1899, Chicago, Ill. d: 1/23/70, Chicago, Ill. BR/TR, 5'8.5", 160 lbs. Deb: 4/18/23																								
1923	Was-A	18	60	6	8	2	2	0	2	4	9	.133	.188	.233	421	11	-8	0	0	0	.926	-2	3-10/1-6,O-1(0-1-0)	-1.0
■ **BILL CONROY** Conroy, William Gordon b: 2/26/15, Bloomington, Ill. d: 11/13/97, Citrus Heights, Cal. BR/TR, 6', 185 lbs. Deb: 9/21/35																								
1935	Phi-A	1	4	0	1	1	0	0	0	1	0	.250	.400	.500	900	133	0	0	0	0	1.000	1	/C-1	0.1
1936	Phi-A	1	2	0	1	0	0	0	0	0	0	.500	.500	.500	1000	151	0	0	0	0	1.000	-0	/C-1	0.0
1937	Phi-A	26	60	4	12	1	1	0	3	7	9	.200	.284	.250	534	36	-6	1	0	0	1.000	-1	C-18/1-1	-0.6
1942	Bos-A	83	250	22	50	4	2	4	20	40	47	.200	.315	.280	595	66	-11	2	0	0	.971	1	C-83	-0.5
1943	Bos-A	39	89	13	16	5	0	1	6	18	19	.180	.336	.270	606	77	-2	0	0	0	.969	2	C-38	0.2
1944	Bos-A	19	47	6	10	2	0	0	4	11	9	.213	.362	.255	617	79	-1	0	0	0	.972	-0	C-19	0.0
Total	6	169	452	45	90	13	3	5	33	77	85	.199	.322	.274	596	66	-18	3	0	1	.974	1	C-160/1-1	-0.8

YEAR	TM/L	G	AB	R	H	2B	3B	HR	RBI	BB	SO	AVG	OBP	SLG	OPS	OPS+	BR+	SB	CS	SBR	FA	FR	G/POS	TPR
■ **BILLY CONSOLO** Consolo, William Angelo b: 8/18/34, Cleveland, Ohio BR/TR, 5′11″, 180 lbs. Deb: 4/20/53 C																								
1953	Bos-A	47	65	9	14	2	1	1	6	2	23	.215	.239	.323	562	48	-5	1	2	-0	.808	10	3-16,2-11	0.5
1954	Bos-A	91	242	23	55	7	1	1	11	33	69	.227	.325	.277	602	59	-12	2	1	0	.953	-3	S-50,3-18,2-12	-1.1
1955	Bos-A	8	18	4	4	0	0	0	0	5	4	.222	.391	.222	614	63	-1	0	0	0	.889	-3	/2-4	-0.3
1956	Bos-A	48	11	13	2	0	0	0	1	3	5	.182	.357	.182	539	41	-1	0	0	0	.920	8	2-25	0.7
1957	Bos-A	68	196	26	53	6	1	4	19	23	48	.270	.347	.372	719	91	-2	1	3	-1	.933	12	S-42,2-16/3-2	1.4
1958	Bos-A	46	72	13	9	2	1	0	5	6	14	.125	.192	.181	373	3	-10	0	0	0	.925	7	2-13,S-11/3-1	-0.1
1959	Bos-A	10	14	3	3	1	0	0	0	2	5	.214	.313	.286	598	63	-1	0	0	0	.818	-2	/S-2	-0.2
	Was-A	79	202	25	43	5	3	0	10	36	54	.213	.332	.267	599	67	-8	1	0	0	.952	10	S-75/2-4	0.8
	Yr	89	216	28	46	6	3	0	10	38	59	.213	.331	.269	599	66	-9	1	0	0	.948	9	S-77/2-4	0.6
1960	Was-A	100	174	23	36	4	2	3	15	25	29	.207	.310	.305	615	68	-8	1	1	-0	.938	-1	S-82,2-12/3-2	-0.5
1961	Min-A	11	5	1	0	0	0	0	0	0	1	.000	.000	.000	0	-95	-1	0	0	0	1.000	0	/2-3,S-3,3-1	-0.1
1962	Phi-N	13	5	3	2	0	0	0	0	0	1	.400	.400	.400	800	119	0	0	0	0	.000	0	/3-1	0.0
	LA-A	28	20	4	2	0	0	0	0	3	11	.100	.217	.100	317	-12	-3	2	0	0	.917	3	3-20/S-4,2-1	0.0
	KC-A	54	154	11	37	4	2	0	16	23	33	.240	.339	.292	631	68	-6	1	3	-1	.950	-1	S-48	-0.5
	Yr	82	174	15	39	4	2	0	16	26	44	.224	.325	.270	595	61	-9	3	3	-0	.944	2	S-52,3-20/2-1	-0.5
Total	10	603	1178	158	260	31	11	9	83	161	297	.221	.316	.289	605	63	-57	9	10	-2	.945	41	S-317,2-101/3-61	0.6
■ **JASON CONTI** Conti, Stanley Jason b: 1/27/75, Pittsburgh, Pa. BL/TR, 5′11″, 180 lbs. Deb: 6/29/2000																								
2000	Ari-N	47	91	11	21	4	3	1	15	7	30	.231	.293	.374	667	66	-5	3	0	1	.983	-1	O-35(2-4-33)	-0.6
■ **CHARLIE CONWAY** Conway, Charles Connell b: 4/28/1886, Youngstown, Ohio d: 9/12/68, Youngstown, Ohio BR/TR, Deb: 4/15/11																								
1911	Was-A	2	3	0	1	0	1	0	0	0		.333	.333	1.000	1333	272	1	0			.000	-1	/O-2	0.0
■ **JACK CONWAY** Conway, Jack Clements b: 7/30/19, Bryan, Tex. d: 6/11/93, Waco, Tex. BR/TR, 5′11.5″, 175 lbs. Deb: 9/9/41																								
1941	Cle-A	2	2	0	1	0	0	0	1	0	0	.500	.500	.500	1000	174	0	0	0	0	1.000	1	/S-2	0.1
1946	Cle-A	68	258	24	58	6	2	0	18	20	36	.225	.281	.264	544	56	-15	2	2	-0	.955	-7	2-50,S-14/3-3	-2.0
1947	Cle-A	34	50	3	9	2	0	0	5	3	8	.180	.226	.220	446	25	-5	0	0	0	.877	0	S-24/2-5,3-1	-0.5
1948	NY-N	24	49	8	12	2	1	1	3	5	10	.245	.315	.388	703	89	-1	0			.985	6	2-13/S-6,3-3	0.6
Total	4	128	359	35	80	10	3	1	27	28	54	.223	.279	.276	555	57	-21	2	2		.962	0	/2-68,S-46,3-7	-1.8
■ **OWEN CONWAY** Conway, Owen Sylvester b: 10/23/1890, New York, N.Y. d: 3/12/42, Philadelphia, Pa. TR, Deb: 6/21/15																								
1915	Phi-A	4	15	2	1	0	0	0	0	0	3	.067	.067	.067	133	-62	-3	0			.750	1	/3-4	-0.2
■ **PETE CONWAY** Conway, Peter J. b: 10/30/1866, Burmont, Pa. d: 1/13/03, Clifton Heights, Pa. BR/TR, 5′10.5″, 162 lbs. Deb: 8/10/1885 F Career OF: (14-LF 20-CF 10-RF)																								
1885	Buf-N	29	90	7	10	5	0	1	7	5	28	.111	.158	.200	358	15	-8				.889	-1	P-27/O-2R,S-1,1-1	-0.2
1886	KC-N	51	194	22	47	8	2	1	18	5	34	.242	.261	.320	581	71	-7	3			.857	-1	O-31(3-20-8),P-23	-0.4
	Det-N	12	43	10	8	1	0	2	3	1	8	.186	.205	.349	553	64	-2	0			.846	-1	P-11/O-1(1-0-0)	0.0
	Yr	63	237	32	55	9	2	3	21	6	42	.232	.251	.325	576	70	-9	3			.826	-1	P-34,O-32(4-20-8)	-0.4
1887	*Det-N	24	97	16	24	5	1	1	7	2	9	.247	.247	.337	584	59	-6	0			**.979**	2	P-17/O-8(8-0-0)	-0.2
1888	Det-N	45	167	28	46	4	2	3	23	8	25	.275	.320	.377	697	122	4	1			.938	2	P-45/O-1(1-0-0)	0.0
1889	Pit-N	3	10	2	1	0	0	1	2	1	3	.100	.182	.400	582	67	-1	1			.875	-0	/P-3,O-1(1-0-0)	0.0
Total	5	164	601	85	136	23	5	9	60	22	107	.226	.255	.324	579	74	-20	5			.907	2	P-126/O-44C,1-1,S-1	-0.8
■ **RIP CONWAY** Conway, Richard Daniel b: 4/18/1896, White Bear Lake, Minn. d: 12/3/71, St.Paul, Minn. BL/TR, 5′6″, 160 lbs. Deb: 4/16/18																								
1918	Bos-N	14	24	4	4	0	0	0	2	2	4	.167	.231	.167	397	23	-2	1			.810	-4	/2-5,3-1	-0.7
■ **BILL CONWAY** Conway, William F. b: 11/28/1861, Lowell, Mass. d: 12/28/43, Somerville, Mass. BR/TR, 5′8″, 170 lbs. Deb: 7/28/1884 F																								
1884	Phi-N	1	4	0	0	0	0	0	0	0	1	.000	.000	.000	0	-99	-1				1.000	0	/C-1	-0.1
1886	Bal-a	7	14	4	2	0	0	0	3	7		.143	.429	.143	571	84	0	0			.925	-3	/C-7	-0.2
Total	2	8	18	4	2	0	0	0	3	7	1	.111	.360	.111	471	52	-0	0			.936	-3	/C-8	-0.3
■ **ED CONWELL** Conwell, Edward James "Irish" b: 1/29/1890, Chicago, Ill. d: 5/1/26, Chicago, Ill. BR/TR, 5′11″, 155 lbs. Deb: 9/22/11																								
1911	StL-N	1	1	0	0	0	0	0	0	0	1	.000	.000	.000	0	-99	-0	0			.000	-0	/3-1	-0.1
■ **HERB CONYERS** Conyers, Herbert Leroy b: 1/8/21, Cowgill, Mo. d: 9/16/64, Cleveland, Ohio BL/TR, 6′4″, 205 lbs. Deb: 4/18/50																								
1950	Cle-A	7	9	2	3	0	0	1	1	1	2	.333	.400	.667	1067	175	1	1	0	0	1.000	-0	/1-1	0.1
■ **DALE COOGAN** Coogan, Dale Roger b: 8/14/30, Los Angeles, Cal. d: 3/8/89, Mission Viejo, Cal. BL/TL, 6′1″, 190 lbs. Deb: 4/22/50																								
1950	Pit-N	53	129	19	31	6	1	1	13	17	24	.240	.338	.326	663	73	-5	0			.980	2	1-32	-0.3
■ **DAN COOGAN** Coogan, Daniel George b: 2/16/1875, Philadelphia, Pa. d: 10/28/42, Philadelphia, Pa. 128 lbs. Deb: 4/25/1895																								
1895	Was-N	26	77	9	17	2	1	0	7	13	6	.221	.333	.273	606	58	-4	1			.746	-11	S-18/C-5,O-2L,3-1	-1.2
■ **JIM COOK** Cook, James Fitchie b: 11/10/1879, Dundee, Ill. d: 6/17/49, St.Louis, Mo. BR/TR, 5′9″, 163 lbs. Deb: 7/2/03																								
1903	Chi-N	8	26	3	4	1	0	0	2	2		.154	.241	.192	434	25	-3	1			1.000	-2	/O-5(0-5-0),2-2,1-1	-0.4
■ **DOC COOK** Cook, Luther Almus b: 6/24/1886, Whitt, Tex. d: 6/30/73, Lawrenceburg, Tenn. BL/TR, 6′, 170 lbs. Deb: 8/7/13																								
1913	NY-A	20	72	9	19	2	1	0	1	10	4	.264	.369	.319	688	101	1	1			.939	1	O-20(0-13-7)	0.0
1914	NY-A	132	470	59	133	11	3	1	40	44	60	.283	.356	.326	681	105	4	26	32	-5	.949	-5	*O-127(1-10-115)	-1.5
1915	NY-A	132	476	70	129	16	5	2	33	62	43	.271	.364	.338	703	111	8	29	18	0	.959	1	*O-131(0-0-131)	0.2
1916	NY-A	4	10	0	1	0	0	0	1	0	2	.100	.100	.100	200	-39	-2	0			1.000	-1	/O-3(0-0-3)	-0.3
Total	4	288	1028	138	282	29	9	3	75	116	109	.274	.359	.329	687	106	11	56	50		.953	-4	O-281(1-23-256)	-1.6
■ **PAUL COOK** Cook, Paul b: 5/5/1863, Caledonia, N.Y. d: 5/25/05, Rochester, N.Y. BR/TR, Deb: 9/13/1884 Career OF: (2-LF 2-CF 10-RF)																								
1884	Phi-N	3	12	0	1	0	0	0	0	0	2	.083	.083	.083	167	-50	-2				.818	-2	/C-3	-0.3
1886	Lou-a	66	262	28	54	5	2	0	14	10		.206	.235	.240	476	46	-17	6			.945	-9	1-43,C-21/O-2(1-0-1)	-2.5
1887	Lou-a	61	234	34	66	4	2	0	17	11		.282	.294	.283	577	60	-12	15			.916	-10	C-55/1-6	-1.4
1888	Lou-a	57	185	20	34	2	0	0	13	5		.184	.222	.195	416	35	-13	9			.901	-14	C-53/O-4(1-0-3),S-1	-2.1
1889	Lou-a	81	286	34	65	10	1	0	15	15	48	.227	.287	.269	556	60	-15	11			.925	5	C-74/O-7R,S-1,1-1	-0.3
1890	Bro-P	58	218	32	55	3	3	0	31	14	18	.252	.303	.294	597	56	-14	7			.890	-0	C-36,1-21/O-1(0-0-1)	-1.1
1891	Lou-a	45	153	21	35	3	1	0	23	11	17	.229	.285	.261	546	57	-9	4			.909	-9	C-35,1-10	-1.4
	StL-a	7	25	3	5	0	0	0	1	1	2	.200	.259	.200	459	28	-2	0			.921	3	/C-7	0.1
	Yr	52	178	24	40	3	1	0	24	12	19	.225	.281	.253	534	53	-11	4			.912	-6	C-42,1-10	-1.3
Total	7	378	1375	172	315	27	9	0	114	67	87	.229	.270	.256	526	52	-84	52			.906	-35	C-284/1-81,O-14R,S	-9.0
■ **CLIFF COOK** Cook, Raymond Clifford b: 8/20/36, Dallas, Tex. BR/TR, 6′, 188 lbs. Deb: 9/9/59 Career OF: (11-LF 2-CF 12-RF)																								
1959	Cin-N	9	21	3	8	2	1	0	5	2	8	.381	.435	.571	1006	161	2	1	0	0	.909	1	/3-9	0.3
1960	Cin-N	54	149	9	31	7	0	3	13	8	51	.208	.248	.315	564	52	-10	0	0	0	.954	4	3-47/O-4(3-1-0)	-0.7
1961	Cin-N	4	5	0	0	0	0	0	0	0	4	.000	.000	.000	0	-99	-1	0	0	0	1.000	0	/3-1	-0.1
1962	Cin-N	6	5	0	0	0	0	0	0	0	2	.000	.000	.000	0	-97	-1	0	0	0	1.000	-0	/3-4	-0.2
	NY-N	40	112	12	26	6	1	2	9	4	34	.232	.277	.357	634	68	-5	1	0	0	.875	-8	3-16,O-10(0-0-10)	-1.4
	Yr	46	117	12	26	6	1	2	9	4	36	.222	.266	.342	608	61	-7	1	0	0	.878	-8	3-20,O-10(0-0-10)	-1.6
1963	NY-N	50	106	9	15	2	1	2	8	12	37	.142	.229	.236	465	34	-9	0	1	-0	1.000	4	O-21(8-1-2)/3-9,1-5	-0.7
Total	5	163	398	33	80	17	3	7	35	26	136	.201	.255	.312	567	54	-25	2	1	0	.937	0	/3-86,O-35R,1-5	-2.8
■ **DUSTY COOKE** Cooke, Allen Lindsey b: 6/23/07, Swepsonville, N.C d: 11/21/87, Raleigh, N.C. BL/TR, 6′1″, 205 lbs. Deb: 4/15/30 MC																								
1930	NY-A	92	216	43	55	12	3	6	29	32	61	.255	.353	.421	775	100	0	4	6	-1	.978	-6	O-73(21-28-24)	-0.9
1931	NY-A	27	39	10	13	1	0	1	6	8	11	.333	.447	.436	883	141	3	4	1	1	1.000	-1	O-11(7-0-6)	0.2
1932	NY-A	3	0	1	0	0	0	0	0	1	0	—	1.000	—	1000	191	0	0	0	0	.000	0	H	0.0
1933	Bos-A	119	454	86	133	35	10	5	54	67	71	.293	.386	.447	833	121	15	7	5	-0	.956	-18	*O-118(47-70-30)	-0.8
1934	Bos-A	74	168	34	41	8	5	1	26	36	25	.244	.377	.369	746	87	-2	7	2	1	.976	-4	O-44(9-14-21)	-0.7
1935	Bos-A	100	294	51	90	18	6	3	34	46	24	.306	.400	.439	839	109	5	6	8	-1	.972	-6	O-82(7-35-44)	-0.5

YEAR	TM/L	G	AB	R	H	2B	3B	HR	RBI	BB	SO	AVG	OBP	SLG	OPS	OPS+	BR+	SB	CS	SBR	FA	FR	G/POS	TPR
1936	Bos-A	111	341	58	93	20	3	6	47	72	48	.273	.401	.402	803	93	-2	4	3	-0	.972	2	O-91(24-1-67)	-0.5
1938	Cin-N	82	233	41	64	15	1	2	33	28	36	.275	.355	.373	728	103	2	0			.963	3	O-51(46-0-7)	0.2
Total	8	608	1745	324	489	109	28	24	229	290	276	.280	.384	.416	800	106	22	32	25		.969	-30	O-470(161-148-199)	-3.0
■ FRED COOKE Cooke, Frederick B. b: Paulding, Ohio Deb: 7/30/1897																								
1897	Cle-N	5	17	2	5	2	0	0	3	3		.294	.400	.412	812	109	0	0			.857	1	/O-5(0-0-5)	0.1
■ BRENT COOKSON Cookson, Brent Adam b: 9/7/69, Van Nuys, Cal. BR/TR, 5'11", 200 lbs. Deb: 8/12/95																								
1995	KC-A	22	35	2	5	1	0	0	5	2	7	.143	.189	.171	361	-5	-5	1	0	0	1.000	-2	O-12(10-0-2)/D-2	-0.7
1999	LA-N	3	5	0	1	0	0	0	0	0	1	.200	.200	.200	400	2	-1	0	0	0	1.000	-0	/O-3(2-0-1)	-0.1
Total	2	25	40	2	6	1	0	0	5	2	8	.150	.190	.175	365	-4	-6	1	0	0	1.000	-3	/O-15(12-0-3),D-2	-0.8
■ SCOTT COOLBAUGH Coolbaugh, Scott Robert b: 6/13/66, Binghamton, N.Y. BR/TR, 5'11", 185 lbs. Deb: 9/2/89																								
1989	Tex-A	25	51	7	14	1	0	2	7	4	12	.275	.327	.412	739	105	0	0	0	0	.958	5	3-23/D-2	0.5
1990	Tex-A	67	180	21	36	6	0	2	13	15	47	.200	.265	.267	532	49	-12	1	0	0	.941	7	3-66	-0.5
1991	SD-N	60	180	12	39	8	1	2	15	19	45	.217	.295	.306	601	67	-8	0	3	-1	.952	4	3-54	-0.5
1994	StL-N	15	21	4	4	0	0	2	6	1	4	.190	.227	.476	703	79	-1	0	0	0	1.000	0	/1-4,3-4	-0.1
Total	4	167	432	44	93	15	1	8	41	39	108	.215	.283	.310	593	65	-20	1	3	-1	.949	16	3-147/1-4,D-2	-0.6
■ DUFF COOLEY Cooley, Duff Gordon "Dick" b: 3/29/1873, Leavenworth, Kan. d: 8/9/37, Dallas, Tex. BL/TR, 5'11", 158 lbs. Deb: 7/27/1893 Career OF: (549-LF 479-CF 69-RF)																								
1893	StL-N	29	107	20	37	2	3	0	21	8	9	.346	.391	.421	812	115	2	8			.947	-9	O-15(0-0-15),C-10/S-5	-0.5
1894	StL-N	54	206	35	61	3	1	1	21	12	16	.296	.335	.335	670	62	-13	7			.833	-11	O-39R,3-13/S-1,1-1	-2.0
1895	StL-N	133	567	108	194	9	20	7	75	37	29	.342	.386	.466	851	120	16	27			.934	11	*O-125L/3-5,S-3,C-1	1.3
1896	StL-N	40	166	29	51	5	3	0	13	7	3	.307	.335	.373	709	90	-3	12			.959	-1	O-40(40-0-0)	-0.6
	Phi-N	64	287	63	88	6	4	2	22	18	16	.307	.348	.376	724	92	-4	18			.901	-5	O-64(22-40-2)	-1.1
	Yr	104	453	92	139	11	7	2	35	25	19	.307	.343	.375	718	91	-6	30			.923	-5	*O-104(62-40-2)	-1.7
1897	Phi-N	133	566	124	186	14	13	4	40	51		.329	.386	.420	807	116	14	31			.960	7	*O-131(0-108-23)/1-2	1.1
1898	Phi-N	149	629	123	196	24	12	4	55	48		.312	.364	.407	771	126	21	17			.943	4	*O-149(0-149-0)	1.3
1899	Phi-N	94	406	75	112	15	8	1	31	29		.276	.330	.360	690	92	-5	15			.971	-5	1-79,O-14(0-14-0)/2-1	-1.0
1900	Pit-N	66	249	30	50	8	1	0	22	14		.201	.243	.241	484	34	-23	9			.989	-5	1-66	-2.6
1901	Bos-N	63	240	27	62	13	3	0	27	14		.258	.302	.338	639	78	-7	5			.943	2	O-53(29-24-0),1-10	-0.8
1902	Bos-N	135	548	73	162	26	8	0	58	34		.296	.339	.372	711	118	11	27			.952	-6	*O-127(94-33-0)/1-7	-0.2
1903	Bos-N	138	553	76	160	26	10	1	70	44		.289	.342	.378	720	109	6	27			.952	-5	*O-126(124-3-0),1-13	-0.6
1904	Bos-N	122	467	41	127	18	7	5	70	24		.272	.312	.373	684	115	7	14			.976	-7	*O-116(116-0-0)/1-6	-0.8
1905	Det-A	97	377	25	93	11	9	1	32	26		.247	.297	.332	629	99	-1	7			.959	7	O-96(0-96-0)	0.2
Total	13	1317	5368	849	1579	180	102	26	557	366	73	.294	.342	.380	722	104	22	224			.945	-22	*O-1095L,1-184/3CS2	-6.3
■ CECIL COOMBS Coombs, Cecil Lysander b: 3/18/1888, Moweaqua, Ill. d: 11/25/75, Fort Worth, Tex. BR/TR, 5'9", 160 lbs. Deb: 8/7/14																								
1914	Chi-A	7	23	1	4	1	0	0	1	1	7	.174	.208	.217	426	28	-2	0	1	-0	1.000	1	/O-7(0-7-0)	-0.2
■ JACK COOMBS Coombs, John Wesley "Colby Jack" b: 11/18/1882, LeGrand, Iowa d: 4/15/57, Palestine, Tex. BB/TR, 6', 185 lbs. Deb: 7/5/06 MC Career OF: (1-LF 16-CF 46-RF)																								
1906	Phi-A	24	67	9	16	2	0	0	3	1		.239	.261	.269	530	64	-3	2			.967	-0	P-23	0.0
1907	Phi-A	24	48	4	8	0	0	1	4	0		.167	.167	.229	396	25	-4	1			.979	0	P-23	0.0
1908	Phi-A	78	220	24	56	9	5	1	23	9		.255	.287	.355	642	101	-0	6			.990	6	O-47R,P-26/1-1	0.4
1909	Phi-A	37	83	4	14	4	0	0	10	4		.169	.216	.217	433	36	-6	1			.973	-0	P-30	0.0
1910	*Phi-A	46	132	20	29	3	0	0	9	7		.220	.270	.242	512	61	-6	3			**.990**	-5	P-45	0.0
1911	*Phi-A	52	141	31	45	6	1	2	23	8		.319	.356	.418	774	118	3	5			.913	-3	P-47	0.0
1912	Phi-A	56	110	10	28	2	0	0	13	14		.255	.344	.273	617	80	-2	1			**1.000**	-1	P-40	0.0
1913	Phi-A	2	3	1	1	1	0	0	0	0	2	.333	.333	.667	1000	195	0	0			.500	-0	/P-2	0.0
1914	Phi-A	5	11	0	3	1	0	0	2	1	1	.273	.333	.364	697	114	0	0	1	-0	1.000	-1	/P-2,O-2(0-2-0)	0.0
1915	Bro-N	29	75	8	21	1	1	0	5	2	17	.280	.299	.320	619	86	-1	0	1	-0	.980	-4	P-29	0.0
1916	*Bro-N	27	61	2	11	2	0	0	3	2	10	.180	.206	.213	419	28	-5	0			**1.000**	-6	P-27	0.0
1917	Bro-N	32	44	4	10	0	1	0	2	4	9	.227	.292	.273	564	72	-1	1			.971	-3	P-31	0.0
1918	Bro-N	46	113	6	19	3	2	0	3	7	5	.168	.223	.230	453	38	-8	1			.962	-7	P-27,O-13(0-3-11)	-0.8
1920	Det-A	2	2	0	0	0	0	0	0	0	0	.000	.000	.000	0	-99	-1	0	0	0	1.000	-0	/P-2	0.0
Total	14	460	1110	123	261	34	10	4	100	59	44	.235	.278	.295	573	74	-35	21	2		.966	-24	P-354/O-62R,1-1	-0.4
■ RON COOMER Coomer, Ronald Bryan b: 11/18/66, Crest Hill, Ill. BR/TR, 5'11", 195 lbs. Deb: 8/1/95																								
1995	Min-A	37	101	15	26	3	1	5	19	9	11	.257	.324	.455	780	100	-0	0	1	-0	.993	1	1-22,3-13/O-1R,D-4	-0.1
1996	Min-A	95	233	34	69	12	1	12	41	17	24	.296	.344	.511	855	110	3	3	0	1	.993	1	1-57,O-23R/3-9,D-3	0.0
1997	Min-A	140	523	63	156	30	2	13	85	22	91	.298	.327	.438	764	96	-4	4	3	-0	.966	-2	*3-119/1-9,O-7R,D-7	-0.6
1998	Min-A	137	529	54	146	22	1	15	72	18	72	.276	.300	.406	706	80	-16	2	2	-0	.972	-5	3-75,1-54,D-13,/O-3R	-2.5
1999	Min-A★	127	467	53	123	25	1	16	65	30	69	.263	.309	.424	733	82	-14	2	1	0	.996	4	1-71,3-57/O-1R,D-7	-1.5
2000	Min-A	140	544	64	147	29	1	16	82	36	50	.270	.320	.415	736	80	-17	2	0	0	.995	-0	*1-124/3-5,D-9	-2.6
Total	6	676	2397	283	667	121	7	77	364	132	317	.278	.318	.431	749	88	-49	13	7	0	.996	-2	1-337,3-278/D-43,O	-7.3
■ WILLIAM COON Coon, William K. b: 3/21/1855, Pennsylvania d: 8/30/15, Burlington, N.J. Deb: 9/4/1875																								
1875	Ath-n	4	12	1	2	0	0	0	1	0	0	.167	.167	.167	333	15	-1	1	0	0	.810	-0	/C-4,O-1(0-0-1)	-0.1
1876	Phi-N	54	222	30	50	5	1	0	22	2	4	.225	.234	.259	493	65	-8				.761	-15	O-29R,C-18/3-4,2P	-2.0
■ JIMMY COONEY Cooney, James Edward "Scoops" b: 8/24/1894, Cranston, R.I. d: 8/7/91, Warwick, R.I. BR/TR, 5'11", 160 lbs. Deb: 9/22/17 F Career OF: (1-LF 0-CF 0-RF)																								
1917	Bos-A	11	36	4	8	1	0	0	3	6	2	.222	.333	.250	583	79	-1	0			1.000	5	2-10/S-1	0.5
1919	NY-N	5	14	3	3	0	0	0	1	0	0	.214	.214	.214	429	29	-1	0			1.000	-1	/S-4,2-1	-0.2
1924	StL-N	110	383	44	113	20	8	1	57	20	20	.295	.330	.397	727	96	-3	12	10	-1	.969	1	S-99/3-7,2-1	0.8
1925	StL-N	54	187	27	51	11	2	0	18	4	5	.273	.292	.353	645	62	-11	1	3	-1	.976	-11	S-37,2-15/O-1(1-0-0)	-1.7
1926	Chi-N	141	513	52	129	18	5	1	47	23	10	.251	.288	.312	599	61	-29	11			**.972**	19	*S-141	0.6
1927	Chi-N	33	132	16	32	2	0	0	6	8	7	.242	.286	.258	543	46	-10	1			.973	-2	S-33	-0.8
	Phi-N	76	259	33	70	12	1	0	15	13	9	.270	.305	.324	629	68	-12	4			.980	17	S-74	1.2
	Yr	109	391	49	102	14	1	0	21	21	16	.261	.299	.302	600	61	-22	5			**.978**	15	*S-107	0.4
1928	Bos-N	18	51	2	7	0	0	0	3	2	5	.137	.170	.137	307	-20	-9	1			.982	2	S-11/2-4	-0.6
Total	7	448	1575	181	413	64	16	2	150	76	58	.262	.298	.327	625	67	-75	30	13		.974	30	S-400/2-31,3-7,O-1L	-0.2
■ JIMMY COONEY Cooney, James Joseph b: 7/9/1865, Cranston, R.I. d: 7/1/03, Cranston, R.I. BB/TR, 5'9", 155 lbs. Deb: 4/19/1890 F																								
1890	Chi-N	135	574	114	156	19	10	4	52	73	23	.272	.360	.361	721	106	5	45			**.936**	1	*S-135/C-1	0.8
1891	Chi-N	118	465	84	114	15	3	0	42	48	17	.245	.318	.290	609	78	-12	21			**.917**	8	*S-118	0.0
1892	Chi-N	65	238	18	41	1	0	0	20	23	5	.172	.248	.176	425	29	-20	10			.912	-8	S-65	-2.3
	Was-N	6	25	5	4	0	1	0	4	4	3	.160	.276	.240	516	58	-1	1			.862	-3	/S-6	-0.4
	Yr	71	263	23	45	1	1	0	24	27	8	.171	.251	.183	433	31	-21	11			.908	-11	S-71	-2.7
Total	3	324	1302	221	315	35	14	4	118	148	48	.242	.324	.300	623	82	-29	77			.923	-2	S-324/C-1	-1.9
■ JOHNNY COONEY Cooney, John Walter b: 3/18/01, Cranston, R.I. d: 7/8/86, Sarasota, Fla. BR/TL, 5'10", 165 lbs. Deb: 4/19/21 FMC Career OF: (37-LF 633-CF 133-RF)																								
1921	Bos-N	8	5	0	1	0	0	0	0	0	1	.200	.200	.200	400	7	-1	0	0	0	1.000	0	/P-8	0.0
1922	Bos-N	4	8	0	0	0	0	0	0	0	1	.000	.000	.000	0	-99	-2	0	0	0	1.000	0	/P-4	0.0
1923	Bos-N	42	66	7	25	1	0	0	3	4	2	.379	.414	.394	808	119	2	0	1	-0	1.000	0	P-23,O-11(2-8-1)/1-1	0.2
1924	Bos-N	55	130	10	33	2	1	0	4	9	5	.254	.302	.285	587	61	-7	0	4	-1	.962	0	P-34,O-16(0-15-1)/1-1	-0.3
1925	Bos-N	54	103	17	33	7	0	0	13	3	6	.320	.346	.388	734	96	-1	1	0	0	.949	0	P-31/1-3,O-1(1-0-0)	-0.1
1926	Bos-N	64	126	17	38	3	2	0	18	13	7	.302	.367	.357	724	105	1	6			.996	5	1-31,P-19/O-1(0-0-1)	0.3
1927	Bos-N	10	1	3	0	0	0	0	0	0	0	.000	.000	.000	0	-99	-0	0			.000	0	H	0.0
1928	Bos-N	33	41	2	7	0	0	0	2	4	3	.171	.244	.171	415	11	-5	0			1.000	2	P-24/1-3,O-2(0-1-1)	-0.2
1929	Bos-N	41	72	10	23	4	1	0	6	3	3	.319	.355	.403	758	91	-1	1			1.000	2	O-16(4-10-2),P-14	-0.1
1930	Bos-N	4	3	0	0	0	0	0	0	0	0	.000	.000	.000	0	-99	-1	0			1.000	1	/P-2	0.0

YEAR	TM/L	G	AB	R	H	2B	3B	HR	RBI	BB	SO	AVG	OBP	SLG	OPS	OPS+	BR+	SB	CS	SBR	FA	FR	G/POS	TPR
1935	Bro-N	10	29	3	9	0	1	0	1	3	2	.310	.375	.379	754	106	0	0			1.000	-1	O-10(0-10-0)	-0.1
1936	Bro-N	130	507	71	143	17	5	0	30	24	15	.282	.315	.335	650	74	-18	3			**.994**	8	*O-130(0-130-0)	-1.4
1937	Bro-N	120	430	61	126	18	5	0	37	22	10	.293	.327	.358	685	85	-9	5			.976	6	*O-111(5-104-3)/1-2	-0.6
1938	Bos-N	120	432	45	117	25	5	0	17	22	12	.271	.308	.352	660	90	-7	2			.982	-10	*O-110(17-15-84),1-13	-2.4
1939	Bos-N	118	368	39	101	8	1	2	27	21	8	.274	.317	.318	635	77	-12	2			.992	-6	*O-116(0-112-5)/1-2	-2.1
1940	Bos-N	108	365	40	116	14	3	0	21	25	9	.318	.363	.373	736	109	5	4			.992	-1	O-99(0-98-1)/1-7	0.1
1941	Bos-N	123	442	52	141	25	2	0	29	27	15	.319	.358	.385	743	114	8	3			**.996**	4	*O-111(0-111-0)/1-4	0.9
1942	Bos-N	74	198	23	41	6	0	0	7	23	5	.207	.290	.237	527	56	-10	2			.984	-14	O-54(5-16-34),1-23	-3.1
1943	Bro-N	37	34	7	7	0	0	0	2	4	3	.206	.289	.206	495	44	-2	1			1.000	-0	/1-3,O-2(0-2-0)	-0.3
1944	Bro-N	7	4	0	3	0	0	0	1	0	0	.750	.750	.750	1500	329	1	0			1.000	-0	/O-2(1-1-0)	0.1
	NY-A	10	8	1	1	0	0	0	1	1	0	.125	.222	.125	347	1	-1	0	0	0	1.000	-0	/O-2(2-0-0)	-0.1
Total	20	1172	3372	408	965	130	26	2	219	208	107	.286	.329	.342	671	87	-61	30	5		.988	-6	O-794C,P-159/1-93	-9.2

■ PHIL COONEY

Cooney, Philip Clarence (b: Philip Clarence Cohen) b: 9/14/1882, New York, N.Y. d: 10/6/57, New York, N.Y. BL/TR, 5'8", 155 lbs. Deb: 9/27/05

YEAR	TM/L	G	AB	R	H	2B	3B	HR	RBI	BB	SO	AVG	OBP	SLG	OPS	OPS+	BR+	SB	CS	SBR	FA	FR	G/POS	TPR
1905	NY-A	1	3	0	0	0	0	0	0	0		.000	.000	.000	0	-90	-1	0			1.000	-0	/3-1	-0.1

■ BILL COONEY

Cooney, William A. "Cush" b: 4/7/1883, Boston, Mass. d: 11/6/28, Roxbury, Mass. TR, Deb: 9/22/09 Career OF: (0-LF 0-CF 2-RF)

YEAR	TM/L	G	AB	R	H	2B	3B	HR	RBI	BB	SO	AVG	OBP	SLG	OPS	OPS+	BR+	SB	CS	SBR	FA	FR	G/POS	TPR
1909	Bos-N	5	10	0	3	0	0	0	0	0		.300	.300	.300	600	82	-0	0			.500	-0	/P-3,2-1,S-1	0.0
1910	Bos-N	8	12	2	3	0	0	0	1	2	0	.250	.357	.250	607	74	-0	0			.000	-1	/O-2(0-0-2)	-0.1
Total	2	13	22	2	6	0	0	0	1	2	0	.273	.333	.273	606	78	-1	0			.500	-1	/P-3,O-2R,S-1,2-1	-0.1

■ CECIL COOPER

Cooper, Cecil Celester b: 12/20/49, Brenham, Tex. BL/TL, 6'2", 190 lbs. Deb: 9/8/71

YEAR	TM/L	G	AB	R	H	2B	3B	HR	RBI	BB	SO	AVG	OBP	SLG	OPS	OPS+	BR+	SB	CS	SBR	FA	FR	G/POS	TPR
1971	Bos-A	14	42	9	13	4	1	0	3	5	4	.310	.396	.452	848	130	2	1	0	0	.988	-2	1-11	-0.1
1972	Bos-A	12	17	0	4	1	0	0	2	2	5	.235	.316	.294	610	78	-0	0	0	0	1.000	-1	/1-3	-0.1
1973	Bos-A	30	101	12	24	2	0	3	11	7	12	.238	.287	.347	634	73	-4	1	2	-0	.984	-0	1-29	-0.7
1974	Bos-A	121	414	55	114	24	1	8	43	32	74	.275	.329	.396	725	101	0	2	5	-1	.983	-1	1-74,D-41	-0.9
1975	*Bos-A	106	305	49	95	17	6	14	44	19	33	.311	.358	.544	902	140	15	1	4	-1	.995	2	D-54,1-35	1.2
1976	Bos-A	123	451	66	127	22	6	15	78	16	62	.282	.308	.457	764	109	3	7	1	1	.994	-1	1-66,D-53	-0.4
1977	Mil-A	160	643	86	193	31	7	20	78	28	110	.300	.329	.463	793	113	10	13	8	0	.992	5	*1-148,D-10	0.5
1978	Mil-A	107	407	60	127	23	2	13	54	32	72	.312	.362	.474	836	133	17	3	4	-1	.988	2	1-84,D-19	1.3
1979	Mil-A★	150	590	83	182	**44**	1	24	106	56	77	.308	.368	.508	877	134	27	15	3	2	.993	-8	*1-135,D-15	1.2
1980	Mil-A★	153	622	96	219	33	4	25	**122**	39	42	.352	.392	.539	931	157	47	17	6	2	**.997**	4	*1-142,D-11	4.3
1981	*Mil-A	106	416	70	133	**35**	1	12	60	28	30	.320	.367	.495	862	154	27	5	4	-0	.992	-0	*1-101/D-5	2.1
1982	*Mil-A★	155	654	104	205	38	3	32	121	32	53	.313	.345	.528	873	145	36	2	3	-1	.997	-1	*1-154/D-1	2.4
1983	Mil-A★	160	661	106	203	37	3	30	**126**	37	63	.307	.345	.508	853	142	35	2	1	0	.993	-10	*1-158/D-2	1.5
1984	Mil-A	148	603	63	166	28	3	11	67	27	59	.275	.309	.386	695	95	-6	8	2	1	.991	3	*1-122,D-26	-1.0
1985	Mil-A★	154	631	82	185	39	8	16	99	30	77	.293	.327	.456	784	112	9	10	3	1	.986	-2	*1-123,D-30	0.0
1986	Mil-A	134	542	46	140	24	1	12	75	41	87	.258	.312	.373	684	83	-13	1	2	-0	.988	-4	1-90,D-44	-2.5
1987	Mil-A	63	250	25	62	13	0	6	36	17	51	.248	.296	.372	668	74	-10	1	1	-0	.000	0	D-62	-1.1
Total	17	1896	7349	1012	2192	415	47	241	1125	448	911	.298	.340	.466	806	121	195	89	49	2	.992	-13	*1-1475,D-373	7.7

■ CLAUDE COOPER

Cooper, Claude William b: 4/1/1892, Troup, Tex. d: 1/21/74, Plainview, Tex. BL/TL, 5'9", 158 lbs. Deb: 4/14/13

YEAR	TM/L	G	AB	R	H	2B	3B	HR	RBI	BB	SO	AVG	OBP	SLG	OPS	OPS+	BR+	SB	CS	SBR	FA	FR	G/POS	TPR
1913	*NY-N	27	30	11	9	4	0	0	4	4	6	.300	.382	.433	816	132	1	3			.895	-5	O-15(6-10-0)	-0.4
1914	Bro-F	113	399	56	96	14	11	2	25	26	60	.241	.294	.346	640	74	-22	25			.926	-1	*O-101(45-21-38)	-2.9
1915	Bro-F	153	527	75	155	26	12	2	63	77	78	.294	.388	.400	789	123	11	31			.958	18	*O-121(112-7-2),1-32	2.5
1916	Phi-N	56	104	9	20	2	0	0	11	7	15	.192	.250	.212	462	41	-7	1			.945	-3	O-29(15-13-1)/1-1	-1.3
1917	Phi-N	24	29	5	3	1	0	0	1	5	4	.103	.235	.138	373	15	-3	0			.923	-4	O-12(9-3-2)	-0.9
Total	5	373	1089	156	283	47	23	4	104	119	163	.260	.338	.356	694	95	-19	60			.943	5	O-278(187-54-43)/1-33	-3.0

■ GARY COOPER

Cooper, Gary Clifton b: 8/13/64, Lynwood, Cal. BR/TR, 6'1", 200 lbs. Deb: 9/15/91

YEAR	TM/L	G	AB	R	H	2B	3B	HR	RBI	BB	SO	AVG	OBP	SLG	OPS	OPS+	BR+	SB	CS	SBR	FA	FR	G/POS	TPR
1991	Hou-N	9	16	1	4	1	0	0	2	3	6	.250	.368	.313	681	99	0	0	0	0	.833	-2	/3-4	-0.2

■ GARY COOPER

Cooper, Gary Nathaniel b: 12/22/56, Savannah, Ga. BB/TR, 6'3", 175 lbs. Deb: 8/25/80

YEAR	TM/L	G	AB	R	H	2B	3B	HR	RBI	BB	SO	AVG	OBP	SLG	OPS	OPS+	BR+	SB	CS	SBR	FA	FR	G/POS	TPR
1980	Atl-N	21	2	3	0	0	0	0	0	0	1	.000	.000	.000	0	-97	-1	2	1	0	1.000	-4	O-13(11-2-0)	-0.4

■ PAT COOPER

Cooper, Orge Patterson b: 11/26/17, Albemarle, N.C. d: 3/15/93, Charlotte, N.C. BR/TR, 6'3", 180 lbs. Deb: 5/11/46

YEAR	TM/L	G	AB	R	H	2B	3B	HR	RBI	BB	SO	AVG	OBP	SLG	OPS	OPS+	BR+	SB	CS	SBR	FA	FR	G/POS	TPR
1946	Phi-A	1	0	0	0	0	0	0	0	0	0	—	—	—	—	—	0	0	0	0	.000	-0	/P-1	0.0
1947	Phi-A	13	16	0	4	2	0	0	3	0	5	.250	.250	.375	625	71	-1	0	0	0	1.000	-0	/1-1	-0.1
Total	2	14	16	0	4	2	0	0	3	0	5	.250	.250	.375	625	71	-1	0	0	0	1.000	-0	/1-1,P-1	-0.1

■ SCOTT COOPER

Cooper, Scott Kendrick b: 10/13/67, St.Louis, Mo. BL/TR, 6'3", 205 lbs. Deb: 9/5/90

YEAR	TM/L	G	AB	R	H	2B	3B	HR	RBI	BB	SO	AVG	OBP	SLG	OPS	OPS+	BR+	SB	CS	SBR	FA	FR	G/POS	TPR
1990	Bos-A	2	1	0	0	0	0	0	0	0	1	.000	.000	.000	0	-96	-0	0	0	0	.000	0	/H	0.0
1991	Bos-A	14	35	6	16	4	2	0	7	2	2	.457	.486	.686	1172	210	5	0	0	0	.933	2	3-13	0.7
1992	Bos-A	123	337	34	93	21	0	5	33	37	33	.276	.348	.383	730	98	-0	1	1	-0	.990	8	1-62,3-47/2-1,SD	0.4
1993	Bos-A★	156	526	67	147	29	3	9	63	58	81	.279	.357	.397	754	96	-2	5	2	0	.937	-17	*3-154/1-2,S-1	-1.7
1994	Bos-A★	104	369	49	104	16	4	13	53	30	65	.282	.338	.453	790	97	-2	0	3	-1	.944	8	*3-104	0.4
1995	StL-N	118	374	29	86	18	2	3	40	49	85	.230	.324	.313	637	69	-16	0	3	-1	.945	9	*3-110	-0.7
1997	KC-A	75	159	12	32	6	1	3	15	17	32	.201	.287	.308	595	54	-11	1	1	-0	1.000	-4	3-39/1-8,D-5	-1.4
Total	7	592	1801	197	478	94	12	33	211	193	299	.265	.340	.386	726	89	-26	7	10	-2	.948	7	3-467/1-72,D-7,S2	-2.3

■ WALKER COOPER

Cooper, William Walker "Walk" b: 1/8/15, Atherton, Mo. d: 4/11/91, Scottsdale, Ariz. BR/TR, 6'3", 210 lbs. Deb: 9/25/40 FC

YEAR	TM/L	G	AB	R	H	2B	3B	HR	RBI	BB	SO	AVG	OBP	SLG	OPS	OPS+	BR+	SB	CS	SBR	FA	FR	G/POS	TPR
1940	StL-N	6	19	3	6	1	0	0	2	2	2	.316	.381	.368	749	102	0	1			1.000	-0	/C-6	0.0
1941	StL-N	68	200	19	49	9	1	1	20	13	14	.245	.291	.315	606	66	-9	1			.966	4	C-63	-0.2
1942	*StL-N★	125	438	58	123	32	7	7	65	29	29	.281	.327	.434	761	113	6	4			.972	3	*C-115	1.7
1943	*StL-N★	122	449	52	143	30	4	9	81	19	19	.318	.349	.463	812	128	14	1			.975	-3	*C-112	1.9
1944	*StL-N★	112	397	56	126	25	5	13	72	20	19	.317	.352	.504	855	136	17	4			.980	4	C-97	2.7
1945	StL-N	4	18	3	7	0	0	0	1	0	1	.389	.389	.389	778	114	0	0			.966	1	/C-4	0.2
1946	NY-N★	87	280	29	75	10	1	8	46	17	12	.268	.310	.396	706	99	-2	0			.972	-12	C-73	-1.1
1947	NY-N★	140	515	79	157	24	8	35	122	24	43	.305	.339	.586	926	141	25	2			.979	-9	*C-132	2.3
1948	NY-N★	91	290	40	77	12	0	16	54	28	29	.266	.332	.472	805	115	5	1			.979	-13	C-79	-0.3
1949	NY-N	42	147	14	31	4	2	4	21	7	8	.211	.261	.347	608	62	-8	0			.982	-2	C-40	-0.9
	Cin-N☆	82	307	34	86	9	2	16	62	21	24	.280	.330	.479	809	113	4	0			.978	-3	C-77	0.6
	Yr	124	454	48	117	13	4	20	83	28	32	.258	.308	.436	744	97	-4	0			.979	-5	*C-117	-0.3
1950	Cin-N	15	47	3	9	3	0	0	4	0	5	.191	.191	.255	447	16	-6	0			.972	1	C-13	-0.4
	Bos-N☆	102	337	52	111	19	3	14	60	30	26	.329	.389	.528	917	148	23	1			.973	-5	C-88	2.2
	Yr	117	384	55	120	22	3	14	64	30	31	.313	.367	.495	862	132	16	1			.973	-4	*C-101	1.8
1951	Bos-N	109	342	42	107	14	1	18	59	28	18	.313	.367	.518	884	145	20	1	1	-0	.981	-2	C-90	2.3
1952	Bos-N	102	349	33	82	12	1	10	55	22	32	.235	.282	.361	643	80	-11	1	0	0	.983	-4	C-89	-1.0
1953	Mil-N	53	137	12	30	6	0	3	16	12	15	.219	.287	.328	615	64	-7	1	0	0	.983	-5	C-35	-1.0
1954	Pit-N	14	15	0	3	2	0	0	1	2	1	.200	.294	.333	627	64	-1	0	0	0	1.000	-0	/C-2	-0.1
	Chi-N	57	158	21	49	10	2	7	32	21	23	.310	.398	.532	929	138	9	0	0	0	.978	-2	C-48	0.9
	Yr	71	173	21	52	12	2	7	33	23	24	.301	.389	.514	903	132	8	0	0	0	.978	-2	C-50	0.8
1955	Chi-N	54	111	11	31	8	1	7	15	6	19	.279	.322	.559	881	128	4	0	0	0	.961	-11	C-31	-0.6
1956	StL-N	40	68	5	18	5	1	2	14	3	8	.265	.296	.456	752	98	-0	0	0	0	.984	-3	C-16	-0.3
1957	StL-N	48	78	7	21	5	1	3	10	5	10	.269	.313	.474	788	106	0	0	0	-0	.957	-2	C-13	-0.1
Total	18	1473	4702	573	1341	240	40	173	812	309	357	.285	.332	.464	796	116	83	18	1		.977	-63	*C-1223	8.8

■ TRACE COQUILLETTE

Coquillette, Trace Robert b: 6/4/74, Carmichael, Cal. BR/TR, 6', 185 lbs. Deb: 9/7/99

YEAR	TM/L	G	AB	R	H	2B	3B	HR	RBI	BB	SO	AVG	OBP	SLG	OPS	OPS+	BR+	SB	CS	SBR	FA	FR	G/POS	TPR
1999	Mon-N	17	49	2	13	3	0	0	4	4	7	.265	.333	.327	660	70	-2	1	0	0	.944	-1	3-11/2-6	-0.2
2000	Mon-N	34	59	6	12	4	0	1	8	7	19	.203	.288	.322	610	53	-4	0	0	0	.958	-5	3-19/2-8,O-2(2-0-1)	-0.8
Total	2	51	108	8	25	7	0	1	12	11	26	.231	.308	.324	632	60	-6	1	0	0	.952	-5	/3-30,2-14,O-2(2-0-1)	-1.0

YEAR	TM/L	G	AB	R	H	2B	3B	HR	RBI	BB	SO	AVG	OBP	SLG	OPS	OPS+	BR+	SB	CS	SBR	FA	FR	G/POS	TPR
■ ALEX CORA	Cora, Jose Alexander b: 10/18/75, Caguas, P.R. BL/TR, 6', 180 lbs. Deb: 6/7/98 F																							
1998	LA-N	29	33	1	4	0	1	0	0	2	8	.121	.194	.182	376	-0	-5	0	0	0	.956	6	S-21/2-4	0.1
1999	LA-N	11	30	2	5	1	0	0	3	0	4	.167	.194	.200	394	-0	-5	0	0	0	1.000	0	/S-8,2-3	-0.4
2000	LA-N	109	353	39	84	18	6	4	32	26	53	.238	.303	.357	660	69	-17	4	1	1	.972	3	*S-101/2-8	-0.5
Total	3	149	416	42	93	19	7	4	35	28	65	.224	.287	.332	619	59	-27	4	1	1	.971	9	S-130/2-15	-0.8
■ JOEY CORA	Cora, Jose Manuel (Amaro) b: 5/14/65, Caguas, P.R. BB/TR, 5'8", 152 lbs. Deb: 4/6/87 F																							
1987	SD-N	77	241	23	57	7	2	0	13	28	26	.237	.319	.282	601	63	-12	15	11	-1	.975	-2	2-66/S-6	-1.1
1989	SD-N	12	19	5	6	1	0	0	1	1	0	.316	.350	.368	718	105	0	1	0	0	.960	2	/S-7,3-2,2-1	0.2
1990	SD-N	51	100	12	27	3	0	0	2	6	9	.270	.311	.300	611	68	-4	8	3	1	.833	-3	S-21,2-15/C-1	-0.6
1991	Chi-A	100	228	37	55	2	3	0	18	20	21	.241	.316	.276	593	67	-9	11	6	0	.970	-9	2-80/S-5,D-2	-1.7
1992	Chi-A	68	122	27	30	7	1	0	9	22	13	.246	.378	.320	698	99	1	10	3	1	.984	5	2-28,D-18/S-6,3-5	0.8
1993	*Chi-A	153	579	95	155	15	13	2	51	67	63	.268	.353	.349	702	91	-5	20	8	2	.974	-16	*2-151/3-3	-1.2
1994	Chi-A	90	312	55	86	13	4	2	30	38	32	.276	.358	.362	720	88	-4	8	4	0	.978	-13	2-84/D-1	-1.2
1995	*Sea-A	120	427	64	127	19	2	3	39	37	31	.297	.362	.372	734	91	-5	18	7	2	.955	-27	*2-112/S-1,D-1	-2.3
1996	Sea-A	144	530	90	154	37	6	6	45	35	32	.291	.343	.417	760	91	-8	5	5	-1	.979	-20	*2-140/3-1	-2.0
1997	*Sea-A★	149	574	105	172	40	4	11	54	53	49	.300	.364	.441	805	110	9	6	7	-1	.973	-17	*2-142	-0.2
1998	Sea-A	131	519	95	147	23	6	6	26	62	50	.283	.364	.385	749	95	-2	13	5	1	.962	-37	*2-130	-3.0
	*Cle-A	24	83	16	19	4	0	0	6	11	9	.229	.326	.277	603	57	-5	2	1	0	.986	-12	2-21	-1.5
	Yr	155	602	111	166	27	6	6	32	73	59	.276	.359	.370	729	90	-7	15	6	1	.965	-49	*2-151	-4.5
Total	11	1119	3734	624	1035	171	41	30	294	380	335	.277	.351	.369	720	90	-44	117	60	5	.971	-150	2-970/S-46,D-22,3C	-13.8
■ GENE CORBETT	Corbett, Eugene Louis b: 10/25/13, Winona, Minn. BL/TR, 6'1.5", 190 lbs. Deb: 9/19/36																							
1936	Phi-N	6	21	1	3	0	0	0	2	2	3	.143	.217	.143	360	-1	-3	0			1.000	-1	/1-6	-0.4
1937	Phi-N	7	12	4	4	2	0	0	1	0	0	.333	.333	.500	833	114	0	0			.800	-1	/3-3,2-1	-0.1
1938	Phi-N	24	75	7	6	1	0	2	7	6	11	.080	.148	.173	321	-12	-12	0			.995	-1	1-22	-1.5
Total	3	37	108	12	13	3	0	2	10	8	14	.120	.181	.204	385	5	-15	0			.996	-2	/1-28,3-3,2-1	-2.0
■ CLAUDE CORBITT	Corbitt, Claude Elliott b: 7/21/15, Sunbury, N.C. d: 5/1/78, Cincinnati, Ohio BR/TR, 5'10", 170 lbs. Deb: 9/23/45																							
1945	Bro-N	2	4	1	2	0	0	0	0	1	0	.500	.600	.500	1100	209	1	0			1.000	0	/3-2	0.1
1946	Cin-N	82	274	25	68	10	1	1	16	23	13	.248	.309	.303	612	77	-8	3			.947	-13	S-77	-1.8
1948	Cin-N	87	258	24	66	11	0	0	18	14	16	.256	.297	.298	595	64	-13	4			.973	-8	2-52,3-16,S-11	-1.8
1949	Cin-N	44	94	10	17	1	0	0	3	9	1	.181	.252	.191	444	20	-10	1			.984	-6	S-18,2-17/3-1	-1.5
Total	4	215	630	60	153	22	1	1	37	47	30	.243	.297	.286	583	63	-31	8			.956	-26	S-106/2-69,3-19	-5.0
■ ART CORCORAN	Corcoran, Arthur Andrew "Bunny" b: 11/23/1894, Roxbury, Mass. d: 7/27/58, Chelsea, Mass. TR, Deb: 9/9/15																							
1915	Phi-A	1	4	0	0	0	0	0	0	0	2	.000	.000	.000	0	-99	-1	0			1.000	-0	/3-1	-0.1
■ JOHN CORCORAN	Corcoran, John A. b: 1873, Cincinnati, Ohio d: 11/2/01, Cincinnati, Ohio TL, Deb: 9/17/1895																							
1895	Pit-N	6	20	0	3	0	0	0	1	0	2	.150	.150	.150	300	-24	-4	0			.895	-1	/S-4,3-2	-0.4
■ JACK CORCORAN	Corcoran, John H. b: 1860, Lowell, Mass. Deb: 5/1/1884																							
1884	Bro-a	52	185	17	39	4	3	0		8		.211	.251	.265	516	68	-6				.873	-9	C-38/O-9L,2-4,SP	-1.1
■ LARRY CORCORAN	Corcoran, Lawrence J. b: 8/10/1859, Brooklyn, N.Y. d: 10/14/1891, Newark, N.J. BL/TR (TB 1884 (part)), 120 lbs. Deb: 5/1/1880 F Career OF: (9-LF 10-CF 21-RF)																							
1880	Chi-N	72	286	41	66	11	1	0	25	10	33	.231	.257	.276	533	76	-7				.957	3	*P-63/O-8(0-5-3),S-8	-0.3
1881	Chi-N	47	189	25	42	8	0	0	9	5	22	.222	.242	.265	507	57	-9				.893	-1	P-45/S-2,O-1(1-0-0)	0.0
1882	Chi-N	40	169	23	35	10	2	1	24	6	18	.207	.234	.308	542	69	-6				.919	1	P-39/3-1	0.0
1883	Chi-N	68	263	40	55	12	7	0	25	6	62	.209	.227	.308	535	56	-14				.906	-3	P-56,O-13L/S-3,2-1	-0.6
1884	Chi-N	64	251	43	61	3	4	1	19	10	33	.243	.272	.299	571	73	-8				.882	7	P-60/O-4(0-0-4),S-2	0.0
1885	Chi-N	7	22	6	6	1	0	0	4	6	1	.273	.429	.318	747	127	1				.905	0	/P-7,S-1	0.0
	NY-N	3	14	3	5	0	0	0	2	0	1	.357	.357	.357	714	133	0				1.000	0	/P-3	0.0
	Yr	10	36	9	11	1	0	0	6	6	2	.306	.405	.333	738	129	1				.935	1	P-10/S-1	0.0
1886	NY-N	1	4	0	0	0	0	0	0	0	2	.000	.000	.000	0	-99	-1	0			.000	-1	/O-1(0-0-1)	-0.1
	Was-N	21	81	9	15	2	1	0	3	7	14	.185	.250	.235	485	51	-4	3			.619	-3	O-11(0-0-11)/S-9,P-2	-0.6
	Yr	22	85	9	15	2	1	0	3	7	16	.176	.239	.224	463	44	-5	3			.591	-3	O-12(0-0-12)/S-9,P-2	-0.7
1887	Ind-N	3	12	2	4	0	0	0	0	2	1	.333	.333	.200	533	53	-1	2			1.000	-0	/O-2(0-1-1),P-2	0.0
Total	8	326	1291	192	289	47	15	2	111	52	187	.224	.253	.287	540	67	-50	5			.910	3	P-277/O-40R,S-25,23	-1.6
■ MICKEY CORCORAN	Corcoran, Michael Joseph b: 8/26/1882, Buffalo, N.Y. d: 12/9/50, Buffalo, N.Y. BR/TR, 5'8", 165 lbs. Deb: 9/15/10																							
1910	Cin-N	14	46	3	10	3	0	0	7	5	9	.217	.308	.283	590	76	-1	0			.911	-1	2-14	-0.2
■ TOMMY CORCORAN	Corcoran, Thomas William "Corky" b: 1/4/1869, New Haven, Conn. d: 6/25/60, Plainfield, Conn. BR/TR, 5'9", 164 lbs. Deb: 4/19/1890 U																							
1890	Pit-P	123	503	80	117	14	13	1	61	38	45	.233	.289	.318	607	68	-23	43			.884	4	*S-123	-1.2
1891	Phi-a	133	511	84	130	11	15	7	71	29	56	.254	.307	.376	683	95	-6	30			**.911**	12	*S-133	0.8
1892	Bro-N	151	613	77	145	11	6	1	74	34	51	.237	.281	.279	560	72	-21	39			**.925**	-2	*S-151	-1.4
1893	Bro-N	115	459	61	126	11	10	2	58	27	12	.275	.318	.355	673	82	-13	14			.907	14	*S-115	0.6
1894	Bro-N	129	576	123	173	21	20	5	92	25	17	.300	.329	.432	762	89	-13	33			.904	-4	*S-129	-0.8
1895	Bro-N	128	540	83	145	17	10	2	69	23	11	.269	.302	.348	650	73	-22	17			.925	20	*S-128	0.4
1896	Bro-N	132	532	63	154	15	7	3	73	15	13	.289	.310	.361	671	81	-16	16			.926	24	*S-132	1.2
1897	Cin-N	109	445	76	128	30	5	3	57	13		.288	.311	.398	709	81	-15	15			.913	6	S-63,2-47	-0.3
1898	Cin-N	153	619	80	155	28	15	2	87	26		.250	.283	.354	637	77	-22	19			.932	14	*S-153	0.0
1899	Cin-N	138	540	93	150	11	8	0	81	29		.278	.317	.328	645	76	-19	32			.930	5	*S-124,2-14	-0.6
1900	Cin-N	127	523	64	128	21	9	1	54	22		.245	.278	.325	603	68	-24	27			.921	-5	*S-124/2-5	-2.1
1901	Cin-N	31	115	14	24	3	3	0	15	11		.209	.278	.287	565	68	-5	6			.919	4	S-30	0.1
1902	Cin-N	138	538	54	136	18	4	0	54	11		.253	.268	.301	569	69	-21	20			.926	-14	*S-137/2-1	-3.2
1903	Cin-N	115	459	61	113	18	7	2	73	12		.246	.267	.329	596	63	-24	12			.943	6	*S-115	-1.4
1904	Cin-N	150	578	55	133	17	9	2	74	19		.230	.257	.301	558	66	-24	19			**.936**	2	*S-150	-1.8
1905	Cin-N	151	605	70	150	21	11	2	85	23		.248	.277	.329	606	72	-22	28			**.952**	20	*S-151	0.3
1906	Cin-N	117	430	29	89	13	1	1	33	19		.207	.242	.249	491	51	-25	8			.941	8	*S-117	-1.5
1907	NY-N	62	226	21	60	9	2	0	24	7		.265	.288	.323	611	88	-4	9			.939	-5	2-62	-1.0
Total	18	2202	8812	1188	2256	289	155	34	1135	383	205	.256	.290	.336	625	74	-318	387			.924	108	*S-2075,2-129	-11.9
■ TIM CORCORAN	Corcoran, Timothy Michael b: 3/19/53, Glendale, Cal. BL/TL, 5'11", 175 lbs. Deb: 5/18/77 Career OF: (20-LF 8-CF 147-RF)																							
1977	Det-A	55	103	13	29	3	0	3	15	6	9	.282	.321	.398	719	90	-1	0	1	-0	1.000	-0	O-18(4-6-8)/D-3	-0.3
1978	Det-A	116	324	37	86	13	1	1	27	24	27	.265	.326	.321	647	80	-8	3	2	-0	.985	-6	*O-109(0-2-107)/D-1	-2.0
1979	Det-A	18	22	4	5	1	0	0	6	4	2	.227	.346	.273	619	67	-1	1	1	-0	1.000	-1	/O-9(3-0-6),1-5,D-2	-0.2
1980	Det-A	84	153	20	44	7	1	3	18	22	10	.288	.381	.405	786	113	3	0	2	-1	.985	-2	1-48,O-18(7-0-11)/D-5	-0.1
1981	Min-A	22	51	4	9	3	0	0	4	6	7	.176	.263	.235	498	42	-4	0	0	0	1.000	1	1-16/D-3	-0.4
1983	Phi-N	3	0	0	0	0	0	0	0	0	0	—	—	—	—	—	0	0	0	0	1.000	-0	/1-3	0.0
1984	Phi-N	102	208	30	71	13	1	5	36	37	27	.341	.443	.486	929	158	18	0	1	-0	.997	-4	1-51,O-17(4-0-13)	1.1
1985	Phi-N	103	182	11	39	6	1	0	22	29	20	.214	.322	.258	581	63	-8	0	0	0	.993	-2	1-59/O-3(2-0-2)	-1.4
1986	NY-N	6	7	1	0	0	0	0	0	2	0	.000	.222	.000	222	-34	-1	0	0	0	1.000	0	/1-1	-0.1
Total	9	509	1050	120	283	46	4	12	128	130	102	.270	.354	.355	709	96	-2	4	7	-2	.993	-15	1-183,O-174R/D-14	-3.4
■ WIL CORDERO	Cordero, Wilfredo (Nieva) b: 10/3/71, Mayaguez, P.R. BR/TR, 6'2", 190 lbs. Deb: 7/24/92 Career OF: (319-LF 0-CF 8-RF)																							
1992	Mon-N	45	126	17	38	4	1	2	8	9	31	.302	.353	.397	750	113	2	0	0	0	.949	-6	S-35/2-9	-0.1
1993	Mon-N	138	475	56	118	32	2	10	58	34	60	.248	.308	.387	696	81	-13	12	3	2	.941	-16	*S-134/3-2	-1.6
1994	Mon-N★	110	415	65	122	30	3	15	63	41	62	.294	.366	.489	855	119	12	16	3	2	.952	-9	*S-109	1.4
1995	Mon-N	131	514	64	147	35	2	10	49	36	88	.286	.343	.420	764	97	-2	9	5	0	.960	-22	*S-105,O-26(26-0-0)	-1.6
1996	Bos-A	59	198	29	57	14	0	3	37	11	31	.288	.332	.404	736	83	-5	2	1	0	.949	3	2-37,D-13/1-1	-0.1

YEAR	TM/L	G	AB	R	H	2B	3B	HR	RBI	BB	SO	AVG	OBP	SLG	OPS	OPS+	BR+	SB	CS	SBR	FA	FR	G/POS	TPR
1997	Bos-A	140	570	82	160	26	3	18	72	31	122	.281	.322	.432	754	93	-7	1	3	-1	.992	0	*O-137L/2-1,D-2	-1.1
1998	Chi-A	96	341	58	91	18	2	13	49	22	66	.267	.317	.446	763	98	-2	2	1	0	.992	1	1-83,O-11(4-0-8)	-0.9
1999	*Cle-A	54	194	35	58	15	0	8	32	15	37	.299	.367	.500	867	113	4	2	0	0	.981	-2	O-29(29-0-0),D-26	0.0
2000	Pit-N	89	348	46	98	24	3	16	51	25	58	.282	.337	.506	843	110	4	1	2	-0	.983	-5	O-85(85-0-0)/D-1	-0.4
	Cle-A	38	148	18	39	11	2	0	17	7	18	.264	.310	.365	675	68	-7	0	0	0	1.000	3	O-38(38-0-0)	-0.5
Total	9	900	3329	470	928	209	18	95	436	231	573	.279	.334	.438	772	98	-15	45	18	4	.950	-51	S-383,O-326L/12D3	-4.9

■ MARTY CORDOVA Cordova, Martin Keevin b: 7/10/69, Las Vegas, Nev. BR/TR, 6', 200 lbs. Deb: 4/26/95 Career OF: (522-LF 11-CF 43-RF)

YEAR	TM/L	G	AB	R	H	2B	3B	HR	RBI	BB	SO	AVG	OBP	SLG	OPS	OPS+	BR+	SB	CS	SBR	FA	FR	G/POS	TPR
1995	Min-A	137	512	81	142	27	4	24	84	52	111	.277	.355	.486	842	116	11	20	7	2	.986	19	*O-137(132-11-0)	2.6
1996	Min-A	145	569	97	176	46	1	16	111	53	96	.309	.376	.478	854	112	11	11	5	1	.991	13	*O-145(145-0-0)	1.8
1997	Min-A	103	378	44	93	18	4	15	51	30	92	.246	.307	.434	740	89	-7	5	3	0	.991	12	*O-101(101-0-0)/D-2	0.1
1998	Min-A	119	438	52	111	20	2	10	69	50	103	.253	.337	.377	713	84	-10	3	6	-1	.978	8	*O-115(115-0-0)/D-4	-0.7
1999	Min-A	124	425	62	121	28	3	14	70	48	96	.285	.369	.464	833	107	5	13	4	1	.927	-6	D-88,O-29(6-0-25)	-0.6
2000	Tor-A	62	200	23	49	7	0	4	18	18	35	.245	.317	.340	657	66	-10	3	2	-0	.982	-5	O-41(23-0-18),D-15	-1.6
Total	6	690	2522	359	692	146	14	83	403	251	533	.274	.349	.442	791	100	0	55	27	3	.985	40	O-568L,D-109	1.6

■ FRED COREY Corey, Frederick Harrison b: 1857, S.Kingston, R.I. d: 11/27/12, Providence, R.I. BR/TR, Deb: 5/1/1878 Career OF: (8-LF 29-CF 46-RF)

YEAR	TM/L	G	AB	R	H	2B	3B	HR	RBI	BB	SO	AVG	OBP	SLG	OPS	OPS+	BR+	SB	CS	SBR	FA	FR	G/POS	TPR
1878	Pro-N	7	21	3	3	0	0	0	1	0	2	.143	.143	.143	286	-6	-2				1.000	0	/P-5,2-2,1-1	-0.1
1880	Wor-N	41	138	11	24	8	1	0	6	4	27	.174	.197	.246	444	45	-8				.759	-11	O-29R,P-25/S-3,31	-1.2
1881	Wor-N	51	203	22	45	8	4	0	10	5	10	.222	.240	.300	541	65	-8				.827	2	O-25(1-0-24),P-23/S-7	-0.2
1882	Wor-N	64	255	33	63	7	12	0	29	5	31	.247	.262	.369	630	97	-1				.847	-13	S-26,P-21,O-15C,/31	-1.3
1883	Phi-a	71	298	45	77	16	2	1	40	12		.258	.287	.336	623	91	-4				.799	-2	3-34,P-18,O-14C,/2SC	-0.5
1884	Phi-a	104	439	64	121	17	16	5		17		.276	.306	.421	727	127	11				**.887**	13	*3-104	2.3
1885	Phi-a	94	384	61	94	14	8	1	38	17		.245	.282	.331	613	88	-6				.872	8	*3-92/S-1,P-1	0.3
Total	7	432	1738	239	427	70	43	7	124	60	70	.246	.273	.348	620	93	-19				.863	-4	3-237/P-93,OS21C	-0.7

■ MARK COREY Corey, Mark Mundell b: 11/3/55, Tucumcari, N.Mex. BR/TR, 6'2", 200 lbs. Deb: 9/1/79

YEAR	TM/L	G	AB	R	H	2B	3B	HR	RBI	BB	SO	AVG	OBP	SLG	OPS	OPS+	BR+	SB	CS	SBR	FA	FR	G/POS	TPR
1979	Bal-A	13	13	1	2	0	0	0	1	0	4	.154	.154	.154	308	-17	-2	1	0	0	1.000	-3	O-11(0-0-11)/D-1	-0.5
1980	Bal-A	36	36	7	10	2	0	1	2	5	7	.278	.366	.417	783	115	1	0	1	-0	1.000	-10	O-34(15-0-19)	-1.0
1981	Bal-A	10	8	2	0	0	0	0	0	2	2	.000	.200	.000	200	-38	-1	0	0	0	1.000	-2	/O-9(7-0-2)	-0.4
Total	3	59	57	10	12	2	0	1	3	7	13	.211	.297	.298	595	65	-3	1	1	-0	1.000	-15	/O-54(22-0-32),D-1	-1.9

■ CHUCK CORGAN Corgan, Charles Howard b: 12/4/02, Wagoner, Okla. d: 6/13/28, Wagoner, Okla. BB/TR, 5'11", 180 lbs. Deb: 9/19/25

YEAR	TM/L	G	AB	R	H	2B	3B	HR	RBI	BB	SO	AVG	OBP	SLG	OPS	OPS+	BR+	SB	CS	SBR	FA	FR	G/POS	TPR
1925	Bro-N	14	47	4	8	1	1	0	0	3	9	.170	.220	.234	454	16	-6	0	0	0	.908	4	S-14	-0.1
1927	Bro-N	19	57	3	15	1	0	0	1	4	4	.263	.311	.281	592	59	-3	0			.969	-1	2-13/S-3	-0.3
Total	2	33	104	7	23	2	1	0	1	7	13	.221	.270	.260	530	40	-9	0	0		.900	3	/S-17,2-13	-0.4

■ ROY CORHAN Corhan, Roy George "Irish" b: 10/21/1887, Indianapolis, Ind. d: 11/24/58, San Francisco, Cal BR/TR, 5'9.5", 165 lbs. Deb: 4/20/11

YEAR	TM/L	G	AB	R	H	2B	3B	HR	RBI	BB	SO	AVG	OBP	SLG	OPS	OPS+	BR+	SB	CS	SBR	FA	FR	G/POS	TPR
1911	Chi-A	43	131	14	28	6	2	0	8	15		.214	.304	.290	594	68	-5	2			.924	11	S-43	0.8
1916	StL-N	92	295	30	62	6	3	0	18	20	31	.210	.265	.251	516	59	-14	15			.917	1	S-84	-0.8
Total	2	135	426	44	90	12	5	0	26	35	31	.211	.277	.263	540	62	-19	17			.920	12	S-127	0.0

■ POP CORKHILL Corkhill, John Stewart b: 4/11/1858, Parkesburg, Pa. d: 4/3/21, Pennsauken, N.J. BL/TR, 5'10", 180 lbs. Deb: 5/1/1883 Career OF: (6-LF 615-CF 420-RF)

YEAR	TM/L	G	AB	R	H	2B	3B	HR	RBI	BB	SO	AVG	OBP	SLG	OPS	OPS+	BR+	SB	CS	SBR	FA	FR	G/POS	TPR
1883	Cin-a	88	375	53	81	10	8	2	46	3		.216	.222	.301	524	63	-16				**.930**	1	*O-85R/S-2,2-2,1-2	-1.4
1884	Cin-a	110	452	85	124	13	11	4	70	6		.274	.290	.378	668	111	4				**.934**	10	*O-92R,S-11/1-6,3P	1.1
1885	Cin-a	112	440	64	111	10	8	1	53	7		.252	.275	.318	594	85	-8				.938	17	*O-110R/P-8,1-3	0.7
1886	Cin-a	129	540	81	143	9	7	5	97	23		.265	.302	.335	637	96	-4	24			.919	-0	*O-112R,3-12/1-7,SP	-0.5
1887	Cin-a	128	555	79	182	19	11	5	97	14		.328	.333	.414	747	105	1	30			**.952**	15	*O-128(0-121-7)/P-5	1.0
1888	Cin-a	118	490	68	133	11	9	1	74	15		.271	.299	.337	635	98	-3	27			.958	7	*O-116C/P-2,1-1,2-1	-0.1
	Bro-a	19	71	17	27	4	3	1	19	4		.380	.429	.563	992	217	9	3			.980	2	O-19(0-19-0)	0.9
	Yr	137	561	85	160	15	12	2	93	19		.285	.316	.365	681	113	6	30			.961	8	*O-135C/P-2,1-1,2-1	0.8
1889	*Bro-a	138	537	91	134	21	9	8	78	42	24	.250	.308	.367	674	91	-8	22			**.949**	12	*O-138C/S-1,1-1	0.0
1890	Bro-N	51	204	23	46	4	2	1	21	15	11	.225	.279	.279	558	62	-10	6			.977	4	O-48(0-48-0)/1-6	-0.7
1891	Phi-a	83	349	50	73	7	7	0	31	26	15	.209	.268	.269	537	54	-22	12			.956	7	O-83(0-73-10)	-1.6
	Cin-N	1	4	0	0	0	0	0	0	0	1	.000	.000	.000	0	-99	-1	0			1.000	1	/O-1(0-1-0)	0.0
	Pit-N	41	145	16	33	1	1	3	20	7	10	.228	.268	.310	578	70	-6	7			.935	2	O-41(1-40-0)	-0.5
	Yr	42	149	16	33	1	1	3	20	7	11	.221	.261	.302	563	65	-7	7			.939	3	O-42(1-41-0)	-0.5
1892	Pit-N	68	256	23	47	1	4	0	25	12	19	.184	.229	.219	448	35	-20	6			.953	7	O-68(1-48-19)	-1.6
Total	10	1086	4418	650	1134	110	80	31	631	174	80	.257	.288	.337	625	87	-85	137			.947	83	*O-1041C/1-26,PS32	-2.7

■ PAT CORRALES Corrales, Patrick b: 3/20/41, Los Angeles, Cal. BR/TR, 6', 195 lbs. Deb: 8/2/64 MC

YEAR	TM/L	G	AB	R	H	2B	3B	HR	RBI	BB	SO	AVG	OBP	SLG	OPS	OPS+	BR+	SB	CS	SBR	FA	FR	G/POS	TPR
1964	Phi-N	2	1	1	0	0	0	0	0	1	0	.000	.500	.000	500	55	0	0	0	0	.000	0	H	0.0
1965	Phi-N	63	174	16	39	8	1	2	15	25	42	.224	.325	.316	641	83	-3	0	0	0	.982	-3	C-62	-0.4
1966	StL-N	28	72	5	13	2	0	0	3	2	17	.181	.224	.208	432	21	-8	1	0	0	.975	9	C-27	0.3
1968	Cin-N	20	56	3	15	4	0	0	6	6	16	.268	.349	.339	688	101	0	0	0	0	.991	0	C-20	0.1
1969	Cin-N	29	72	10	19	5	0	1	5	8	17	.264	.346	.375	721	97	-0	0	1	-0	.986	3	C-29	0.4
1970	*Cin-N	43	106	9	25	5	1	1	10	8	22	.236	.289	.330	620	65	-5	0	0	0	.983	4	C-42	0.0
1971	Cin-N	40	94	6	17	2	0	0	6	6	17	.181	.230	.202	432	24	-9	0	0	0	.980	1	C-39	-0.8
1972	Cin-N	2	1	0	0	0	0	0	0	2	0	.000	.667	.000	667	110	0	0	0	0	1.000	1	/C-2	0.2
	SD-N	44	119	6	23	0	0	0	6	11	26	.193	.267	.193	460	35	-10	0	0	0	.993	4	C-43	-0.5
	Yr	46	120	6	23	0	0	0	6	13	26	.192	.276	.192	468	38	-9	0	0	0	.993	5	C-45	-0.3
1973	SD-N	29	72	7	15	2	1	0	3	6	10	.208	.278	.264	542	55	-4	0	0	0	.986	-1	C-28	-0.5
Total	9	300	767	63	166	28	3	4	54	75	167	.216	.292	.276	569	61	-39	1	1	-0	.984	18	C-292	-1.2

■ ROD CORREIA Correia, Ronald Douglas b: 9/13/67, Providence, R.I. BR/TR, 5'11", 180 lbs. Deb: 6/20/93

YEAR	TM/L	G	AB	R	H	2B	3B	HR	RBI	BB	SO	AVG	OBP	SLG	OPS	OPS+	BR+	SB	CS	SBR	FA	FR	G/POS	TPR
1993	Cal-A	64	128	12	34	5	0	0	9	6	20	.266	.319	.305	624	66	-6	2	4	-1	.981	18	S-40,2-11/3-3,D-6	1.3
1994	Cal-A	6	17	4	4	1	0	0	0	0	0	.235	.316	.294	610	58	-1	0	0	0	1.000	-2	/2-5,S-1	-0.2
1995	Cal-A	14	21	3	5	1	1	0	3	0	5	.238	.238	.381	619	58	-1	0	0	0	.850	3	/S-7,2-3,3-2,D-1	0.2
Total	3	84	166	19	43	7	1	0	12	6	25	.259	.309	.313	622	65	-8	2	4	-1	.968	19	/S-48,2-19,D-7,3-5	1.3

■ VIC CORRELL Correll, Victor Crosby b: 2/5/46, Washington, D.C. BR/TR, 5'10", 185 lbs. Deb: 10/4/72

YEAR	TM/L	G	AB	R	H	2B	3B	HR	RBI	BB	SO	AVG	OBP	SLG	OPS	OPS+	BR+	SB	CS	SBR	FA	FR	G/POS	TPR
1972	Bos-A	1	4	1	2	0	0	0	1	0	1	.500	.500	.500	1000	188	0	0	0	0	1.000	1	/C-1	0.1
1974	Atl-N	73	202	20	48	15	1	4	29	21	38	.238	.322	.381	703	92	-2	0	0	0	.988	6	C-59	0.6
1975	Atl-N	103	325	37	70	12	1	11	39	42	66	.215	.307	.360	667	82	-8	0	2	-1	.973	-2	C-97	-0.7
1976	Atl-N	69	200	26	45	6	2	5	16	21	37	.225	.302	.350	652	80	-5	0	1	-0	.981	3	C-65	0.0
1977	Atl-N	54	144	16	30	7	0	7	16	22	33	.208	.317	.403	720	82	-4	2	3	-1	.973	2	C-49	0.0
1978	Cin-N	52	105	9	25	7	0	1	6	8	17	.238	.292	.333	625	74	-4	0	2	-1	.980	1	C-52	-0.2
1979	Cin-N	48	133	14	31	12	0	1	15	14	26	.233	.311	.346	657	78	-4	0	0	0	.992	7	C-47	0.5
1980	Cin-N	10	19	1	8	1	0	0	3	0	2	.421	.421	.474	895	149	1	0	0	0	.919	-0	C-10	0.1
Total	8	410	1132	124	259	60	4	29	125	128	220	.229	.312	.366	677	83	-26	2	8	-2	.979	18	C-380	0.4

■ PHIL CORRIDAN Corridan, Philip Deb: 7/16/1884

YEAR	TM/L	G	AB	R	H	2B	3B	HR	RBI	BB	SO	AVG	OBP	SLG	OPS	OPS+	BR+	SB	CS	SBR	FA	FR	G/POS	TPR
1884	CP-U	2	7	1	1	0	0	0		0		.143	.143	.143	286	-13	-1				.800	-1	/2-2,O-1(1-0-0)	-0.2

■ JOHN CORRIDEN Corriden, John Michael Jr. b: 10/6/18, Logansport, Ind. BB/TR, 5'6", 160 lbs. Deb: 4/20/46 F

YEAR	TM/L	G	AB	R	H	2B	3B	HR	RBI	BB	SO	AVG	OBP	SLG	OPS	OPS+	BR+	SB	CS	SBR	FA	FR	G/POS	TPR
1946	Bro-N	1	0	1	0	0	0	0	0	0	0	—	—	—	—	—	0	0			.000	0	R	0.0

■ RED CORRIDEN Corriden, John Michael Sr. b: 9/4/1887, Logansport, Ind. d: 9/28/59, Indianapolis, Ind BR/TR, 5'9", 165 lbs. Deb: 9/8/10 FMC Career OF: (0-LF 1-CF 0-RF)

YEAR	TM/L	G	AB	R	H	2B	3B	HR	RBI	BB	SO	AVG	OBP	SLG	OPS	OPS+	BR+	SB	CS	SBR	FA	FR	G/POS	TPR
1910	StL-A	26	84	19	13	3	0	1	4	13		.155	.297	.226	523	68	-2	5			.902	4	S-14,3-12	0.3
1912	Det-A	38	138	22	28	6	0	0	5	15		.203	.286	.246	532	54	-8	4			.929	-4	3-25/2-7,S-3	-1.1
1913	Chi-N	46	97	13	17	3	0	2	9	10	14	.175	.252	.268	520	49	-7	4			.907	-1	S-37/2-2,3-1	-0.7
1914	Chi-N	107	318	42	73	9	5	3	29	35	33	.230	.323	.318	641	91	-3	13			.894	-33	S-91/3-8,2-3	-3.2

YEAR	TM/L	G	AB	R	H	2B	3B	HR	RBI	BB	SO	AVG	OBP	SLG	OPS	OPS+	BR+	SB	CS	SBR	FA	FR	G/POS	TPR
1915	Chi-N	6	3	1	0	0	0	0	0	2	1	.000	.571	.000	571	79	1	0			.667	-1	/3-1,O-1(0-1-0)	0.0
Total	5	223	640	97	131	21	5	6	47	75	48	.205	.304	.281	585	74	-19	26			.896	-35	S-145/3-47,2-12,O-1C	-4.7
■ JESS CORTAZZO Cortazzo, John Francis b: 9/26/04, Wilmerding, Pa. d: 3/4/63, Pittsburgh, Pa. BR/TR, 5'3.5", 142 lbs. Deb: 9/1/23																								
1923	Chi-A	1	1	0	0	0	0	0	0	0	0	.000	.000	.000	0	-99	-0	0	0	0	.000	0	H	0.0
■ JOE COSCARART Coscarart, Joseph Marvin b: 11/18/09, Escondido, Cal. d: 4/5/93, Sequim, Wash. BR/TR, 6', 185 lbs. Deb: 4/26/35 F																								
1935	Bos-N	86	284	30	67	11	2	1	29	16	28	.236	.277	.299	576	59	-16	2			.962	-4	3-41,S-27,2-15	-1.6
1936	Bos-N	104	367	28	90	11	2	2	44	19	37	.245	.292	.302	594	64	-19	0			.935	2	3-97/S-6,2-1	-1.3
Total	2	190	651	58	157	22	4	3	73	35	65	.241	.285	.301	586	62	-35	2			.943	-3	3-138/S-33,2-16	-2.9
■ PETE COSCARART Coscarart, Peter Joseph b: 6/16/13, Escondido, Cal. BR/TR, 5'11.5", 175 lbs. Deb: 4/26/38 F Career OF: (0-LF 0-CF 1-RF)																								
1938	Bro-N	32	79	10	12	3	0	0	6	9	18	.152	.256	.190	445	24	-8	0			.955	1	2-27	-0.5
1939	Bro-N	115	419	59	116	22	2	4	43	46	56	.277	.354	.368	721	91	-4	10			.960	-8	*2-107/3-4,S-2	-0.5
1940	Bro-N★	143	506	55	120	24	4	9	58	53	59	.237	.311	.354	664	78	-15	5			.958	-32	*2-140	-3.8
1941	*Bro-N	43	62	13	8	1	0	0	5	7	12	.129	.217	.145	363	3	-8	1			.948	5	2-19/S-1	-0.2
1942	Pit-N	133	487	57	111	12	4	3	29	38	56	.228	.288	.287	575	67	-20	2			.952	-18	*S-108,2-25	-3.2
1943	Pit-N	133	491	57	119	19	6	0	48	46	48	.242	.307	.305	613	75	-15	4			.961	-6	2-85,S-47/3-1	-1.4
1944	Pit-N	139	554	89	146	30	4	4	42	41	57	.264	.315	.354	669	85	-12	10			.967	-7	*2-136/S-4,O-1(0-0-1)	-1.2
1945	Pit-N	123	392	59	95	17	2	8	38	55	55	.242	.341	.357	699	91	-4	2			.978	21	*2-122/S-1	2.3
1946	Pit-N	3	2	0	1	1	0	0	0	0	0	.500	.500	1.000	1500	312	1	0			.000	0	/S-1	0.1
Total	9	864	2992	399	728	129	22	28	269	295	361	.243	.314	.329	644	78	-86	34			.963	-43	2-661,S-164/3-5,O-1R	-8.4
■ RAY COSEY Cosey, Donald Ray b: 2/15/56, San Rafael, Cal. BL/TL, 5'10", 185 lbs. Deb: 4/14/80																								
1980	Oak-A	9	9	0	1	0	0	0	0	0	0	.111	.111	.111	222	-42	-2	0	0	0	.000	0	/H	-0.2
■ DAN COSTELLO Costello, Daniel Francis "Dashing Dan" b: 9/9/1891, Jessup, Pa. d: 3/26/36, Pittsburgh, Pa. BL/TR, 6'0.5", 185 lbs. Deb: 7/2/13																								
1913	NY-A	2	2	1	1	0	0	0	0	0	0	.500	.500	.500	1000	192	0	0			.000	0	H	0.0
1914	Pit-N	21	64	7	19	1	0	0	5	8	16	.297	.375	.313	688	110	1	2			.970	-1	O-20(0-0-20)	-0.1
1915	Pit-N	71	125	16	27	4	1	0	11	7	23	.216	.258	.264	522	59	-6	7	1	1	.893	-6	O-22(5-12-5)/1-1	-1.3
1916	Pit-N	60	159	11	38	1	3	0	8	6	23	.239	.267	.283	550	68	-6	3			.976	-2	O-41(33-1-7)	-1.2
Total	4	154	350	35	85	6	4	0	24	21	62	.243	.286	.283	569	73	-11	12	1		.959	-9	/O-83(38-13-32),1-1	-2.6
■ TIM COSTO Costo, Timothy Roger b: 2/16/69, Melrose Park, Ill. BR/TR, 6'5", 220 lbs. Deb: 9/18/92 Career OF: (11-LF 0-CF 16-RF)																								
1992	Cin-N	12	36	3	8	2	0	0	2	5	6	.222	.317	.278	595	68	-1	0	0	0	1.000	0	1-12	-0.2
1993	Cin-N	31	98	13	22	5	0	3	12	4	17	.224	.255	.367	622	64	-5	0	0	0	.980	0	O-26(11-0-16)/1-2,3-2	-0.6
Total	2	43	134	16	30	7	0	3	14	9	23	.224	.273	.343	616	66	-7	0	0	0	1.000	1	/O-26R,1-14,3-2	-0.8
■ HENRY COTE Cote, Henry Joseph b: 2/19/1864, Troy, N.Y. d: 4/28/40, Troy, N.Y. 5'9.5", 165 lbs. Deb: 9/16/1894																								
1894	Lou-N	10	31	7	9	2	2	0	3	5	6	.290	.389	.484	873	117	1	2			.918	5	C-10	0.5
1895	Lou-N	10	33	10	10	0	0	0	5	3	3	.303	.361	.303	664	77	-1	2			.872	-3	C-10	-0.3
Total	2	20	64	17	19	2	2	0	8	8	9	.297	.375	.391	766	97	0	4			.900	2	/C-20	0.2
■ PETE COTE Cote, Warren Peter b: 8/30/02, Cambridge, Mass. d: 10/17/87, Middleton, Mass. BR/TR, 5'6", 148 lbs. Deb: 6/18/26																								
1926	NY-N	2	1	0	0	0	0	0	0	0	0	.000	.000	.000	0	-99	-0	0			.000	0	H	0.0
■ ED COTTER Cotter, Edward Christopher b: 7/4/04, Hartford, Conn. d: 6/14/59, Hartford, Conn. BR/TR, 6', 185 lbs. Deb: 6/12/26																								
1926	Phi-N	17	26	3	8	0	1	0	1	1	4	.308	.333	.385	718	88	-0	1			.833	0	/3-8,S-5	0.0
■ HOOKS COTTER Cotter, Harvey Louis b: 5/22/1900, Holden, Mo. d: 8/6/55, Los Angeles, Cal. BL/TL, 5'10", 160 lbs. Deb: 4/15/22																								
1922	Chi-N	1	1	0	1	1	0	0	0	0	0	1.000	1.000	2.000	3000	644	1	0	0	0	.000	0	H	0.1
1924	Chi-N	98	310	39	81	16	4	4	33	36	31	.261	.338	.377	716	91	-4	3	5	-1	.989	4	1-90	-0.7
Total	2	99	311	39	82	17	4	4	33	36	31	.264	.340	.383	723	92	-3	3	5	-1	.989	4	/1-90	-0.6
■ DICK COTTER Cotter, Richard Raphael b: 10/12/1889, Manchester, N.H. d: 4/4/45, Brooklyn, N.Y. BR/TR, 5'11", 172 lbs. Deb: 8/17/11																								
1911	Phi-N	20	46	2	13	0	0	0	5	5	7	.283	.353	.283	636	78	-1	1			.975	-2	C-17	-0.2
1912	Chi-N	26	54	6	15	0	2	0	10	6	13	.278	.361	.352	713	96	-0	1			.954	-3	C-24	-0.2
Total	2	46	100	8	28	0	2	0	15	11	20	.280	.357	.320	677	87	-1	2			.964	-5	/C-41	-0.4
■ TOM COTTER Cotter, Thomas B. b: 9/30/1866, Waltham, Mass. d: 11/22/06, Brookline, Mass. BR/TR, 5'10.5", 149 lbs. Deb: 9/3/1891																								
1891	Bos-a	6	12	1	3	0	0	0	4	1	2	.250	.308	.250	558	61	-1	0			.938	-1	/C-5,O-1(0-0-1)	-0.1
■ CHUCK COTTIER Cottier, Charles Keith b: 1/8/36, Delta, Colo. BR/TR, 5'10.5", 175 lbs. Deb: 4/17/59 MC																								
1959	Mil-N	10	24	1	3	1	0	0	1	3	7	.125	.222	.167	389	6	-3	0	0	0	.976	1	2-10	-0.2
1960	Mil-N	95	229	29	52	8	0	3	19	14	21	.227	.278	.301	579	63	-12	1	0	0	.968	17	2-92	1.0
1961	Det-A	10	7	2	2	0	0	0	1	1	1	.286	.375	.286	661	77	-0	0	0	0	.889	2	/S-8,2-2	0.1
	Was-A	101	337	37	79	14	4	2	34	30	51	.234	.299	.318	616	66	-16	9	1	2	.982	15	*2-100	0.9
	Yr	111	344	39	81	14	4	2	35	31	52	.235	.301	.317	617	66	-17	9	1	2	.982	17	*2-102/S-8	1.0
1962	Was-A	136	443	50	107	14	6	6	40	44	57	.242	.313	.341	654	76	-15	14	8	0	.981	21	*2-134	1.7
1963	Was-A	113	337	30	69	16	4	5	21	24	63	.205	.258	.320	578	61	-18	2	1	0	.963	11	2-85,S-24/3-1	0.1
1964	Was-A	73	137	16	23	6	2	3	10	19	33	.168	.269	.307	576	60	-7	2	0	0	.982	14	2-53/3-3,S-2	1.0
1965	Was-A	7	1	1	0	0	0	0	0	0	0	.000	.000	.000	0	-99	-0	0	0	0	.000	0	H	0.0
1968	Cal-A	33	67	2	13	4	1	0	1	2	15	.194	.217	.284	501	53	-4	0	0	0	.963	2	3-27/2-4	-0.3
1969	Cal-A	2	2	0	0	0	0	0	0	0	0	.000	.000	.000	0	-99	-1	0	0	0	1.000	-0	/2-2	-0.1
Total	9	580	1584	168	348	63	17	19	127	137	248	.220	.284	.317	601	65	-76	28	10	3	.976	81	2-482/S-34,3-31	4.2
■ HENRY COTTO Cotto, Henry b: 1/5/61, New York, N.Y. BR/TR, 6'2", 178 lbs. Deb: 4/5/84 Career OF: (322-LF 355-CF 133-RF)																								
1984	*Chi-N	105	146	24	40	5	0	0	8	10	23	.274	.325	.308	633	72	-5	9	3	1	.984	-12	O-88(47-34-10)	-1.8
1985	NY-A	34	56	4	17	1	0	1	6	3	12	.304	.339	.375	714	98	-0	1	1	-0	.977	-7	O-30(14-20-1)	-0.8
1986	NY-A	35	80	11	17	3	0	1	6	2	17	.213	.232	.287	519	41	-7	3	0	1	1.000	-2	O-29(11-19-0)/D-1	-0.8
1987	NY-A	68	149	21	35	10	0	5	20	6	35	.235	.269	.403	672	76	-6	4	2	0	.989	-8	O-57(15-41-2)	-1.3
1988	Sea-A	133	386	50	100	18	1	8	33	23	53	.259	.304	.373	677	85	-8	27	3	5	.992	-5	*O-120(0-120-0)/D-2	-0.9
1989	Sea-A	100	295	44	78	11	2	9	33	12	44	.264	.300	.407	707	94	-3	10	4	1	.988	-7	O-90(57-30-14)/D-2	-1.1
1990	Sea-A	127	355	40	92	14	3	4	33	22	52	.259	.310	.349	659	83	-8	21	3	4	.990	-9	*O-118(41-18-67)/D-3	-1.6
1991	Sea-A	66	177	35	54	6	2	6	23	10	27	.305	.349	.463	812	123	5	16	3	2	.981	-5	O-56(38-19-8)/D-6	0.1
1992	Sea-A	108	294	42	76	11	1	5	27	14	49	.259	.294	.354	648	80	-8	23	2	4	1.000	-10	O-92(63-30-6)/D-3	-1.6
1993	Sea-A	54	105	10	20	1	0	2	7	2	22	.190	.213	.257	470	25	-11	5	4	-0	.983	-3	O-34(23-9-4),D-15	-1.6
	Fla-N	54	135	15	40	7	0	3	14	3	18	.296	.317	.415	731	89	-2	11	1	2	.977	-4	O-46(13-15-21)	-0.5
Total	10	884	2178	296	569	87	9	44	210	107	352	.261	.301	.370	671	83	-53	130	26	20	.989	-70	O-760C/D-32	-11.9
■ DENNIS COUGHLIN Coughlin, Dennis F. Deb: 4/27/1872																								
1872	Nat-n	8	37	5	12	1	0	0	7	0	0	.324	.324	.351	676	92	-1	0	0	0	.941	1	/O-5C,1-1,2-1,S-1	0.0
■ ED COUGHLIN Coughlin, Edward E. b: 8/5/1861, Hartford, Conn. d: 12/25/52, Hartford, Conn. Deb: 5/15/1884																								
1884	Buf-N	1	4	0	1	0	0	0	1	0	2	.250	.250	.250	500	56	-0				.750	0	/O-1(0-0-1),P-1	0.0
■ BILL COUGHLIN Coughlin, William Paul "Scranton Bill" b: 7/12/1878, Scranton, Pa. d: 5/7/43, Scranton, Pa. BR/TR, 5'9", 140 lbs. Deb: 8/9/1899																								
1899	Was-N	6	24	2	3	0	1	0	3	1		.125	.160	.208	368	1	-3	1			.818	-1	/3-6	-0.4
1901	Was-A	137	506	75	139	17	13	6	68	25		.275	.317	.395	712	98	-3	16			.922	0	*3-137	0.1
1902	Was-A	123	469	84	141	27	4	6	71	26		.301	.348	.414	762	110	5	29			.926	12	3-66,S-31,2-26	1.9
1903	Was-A	125	473	56	116	18	3	1	31	9		.245	.267	.302	569	69	-18	30			.952	4	*3-119/S-4,2-2	-1.1
1904	Was-A	65	265	28	73	15	4	0	17	9		.275	.307	.362	669	113	3	10			.939	2	3-64	0.8
	Det-A	56	206	22	47	6	0	0	17	5		.228	.257	.257	514	65	-8	1			.929	-3	3-56	-1.1

YEAR	TM/L	G	AB	R	H	2B	3B	HR	RBI	BB	SO	AVG	OBP	SLG	OPS	OPS+	BR+	SB	CS	SBR	FA	FR	G/POS	TPR
	Yr	121	471	50	120	21	4	0	34	14		.255	.285	.316	601	92	-5	11			.935	-1	*3-120	-0.3
1905	Det-A	137	489	48	123	20	6	0	44	34		.252	.309	.317	626	98	-1	16			.914	-9	*3-136	-0.7
1906	Det-A	147	498	54	117	15	5	2	60	36		.235	.293	.297	590	83	-10	31			.940	-11	*3-147	-1.8
1907	*Det-A	134	519	80	126	10	2	0	46	35		.243	.301	.270	570	79	-11	15			.930	-9	*3-133	-1.9
1908	*Det-A	119	405	32	87	5	1	0	23	23		.215	.269	.232	501	61	-17	10			.941	-16	*3-119	-3.4
Total	9	1049	3854	481	972	133	39	15	380	203		.252	.299	.319	617	86	-63	159			.931	-32	3-983/S-35,2-28	-7.6
■ MARLAN COUGHTRY	Coughtry, James Marlan b: 9/11/34, Hollywood, Cal. BL/TR, 6'1", 170 lbs. Deb: 9/2/60																							
1960	Bos-A	15	19	3	3	0	0	0	0	5	8	.158	.333	.158	491	36	-1	0	0	0	.909	1	2-13/3-1	0.0
1962	LA-A	11	22	0	4	0	0	0	2	0	6	.182	.182	.182	364	-2	-3	0	0	0	.867	3	/3-5,2-2	0.0
	KC-A	6	11	1	2	0	0	0	1	4	3	.182	.400	.182	582	60	-0	0	0	0	.917	1	/3-3	0.1
	Cle-A	3	2	1	1	0	0	0	1	1	1	.500	.667	.500	1167	226	1	0	0	0	.000	0	H	0.1
	Yr	20	35	2	7	0	0	0	4	5	10	.200	.300	.200	500	38	-3	0	0	0	.889	4	/3-8,2-2	0.2
Total	2	35	54	5	10	0	0	0	4	10	18	.185	.313	.185	498	37	-4	0	0	0	.915	6	/2-15,3-9	0.2
■ BOB COULSON	Coulson, Robert Jackson b: 6/17/1887, Courtney, Pa. d: 9/11/53, Washington, Pa. BR/TR, 5'10.5", 175 lbs. Deb: 8/4/08																							
1908	Cin-N	8	18	3	6	1	1	0	1	3		.333	.429	.500	929	202	2	0			1.000	1	/O-6(4-1-1)	0.3
1910	Bro-N	25	89	14	22	3	4	1	13	6	14	.247	.302	.404	707	109	0	9			.922	0	O-25(0-0-25)	0.0
1911	Bro-N	146	521	52	122	23	7	0	50	42	78	.234	.301	.305	606	73	-19	32			.968	1	*O-145(0-2-144)	-2.6
1914	Pit-F	18	64	7	13	1	0	0	3	7	10	.203	.282	.219	500	38	-6	2			.931	-2	O-18(11-0-7)	-1.0
Total	4	197	692	76	163	28	12	1	67	58	102	.236	.303	.315	618	77	-23	43			.960	0	O-194(15-3-177)	-3.3
■ CHIP COULTER	Coulter, Thomas Lee b: 6/5/45, Steubenville, O. BB/TR, 5'10", 172 lbs. Deb: 9/18/69																							
1969	StL-N	6	19	3	6	1	1	0	4	2	6	.316	.381	.474	855	138	1	0	1	-0	.960	-0	/2-6	0.1
■ CRAIG COUNSELL	Counsell, Craig John b: 8/21/70, South Bend, Ind. BL/TR, 6', 180 lbs. Deb: 9/17/95																							
1995	Col-N	3	1	0	0	0	0	0	0	1	0	.000	.500	.000	500	36	-0	0	0	0	1.000	0	/S-3	0.0
1997	Col-N	1	0	0	0	0	0	0	0	0	0	—	—	—	—	—	0	0	0	0	.000	0	/R	0.0
	*Fla-N	51	164	20	49	9	2	1	16	18	17	.299	.378	.396	775	108	3	1	1	-0	.989	18	2-51	2.2
	Yr	52	164	20	49	9	2	1	16	18	17	.299	.378	.396	775	107	2	1	1	-0	.989	18	2-51	2.2
1998	Fla-N	107	335	43	84	19	5	4	40	51	47	.251	.356	.373	730	97	-0	3	0	1	.991	9	*2-104	1.5
1999	Fla-N	37	66	4	10	1	0	0	2	5	10	.152	.211	.167	378	-3	-10	0	0	0	.980	-2	2-12	-1.1
	LA-N	50	108	20	28	6	0	0	9	9	14	.259	.316	.315	631	64	-6	1	0	0	.993	8	2-38/S-2	0.3
	Yr	87	174	24	38	7	0	0	11	14	24	.218	.277	.259	535	39	-16	1	0	0	.989	6	2-50/S-2	-0.8
2000	Ari-N	67	152	23	48	8	1	2	11	20	18	.316	.402	.421	823	108	3	3	3	-0	.974	2	2-25,3-23/S-6	0.5
Total	5	316	826	110	219	43	8	7	78	104	106	.265	.354	.362	716	89	-11	8	4	0	.989	36	2-230/3-23,S-11	3.4
■ CLINT COURTNEY	Courtney, Clinton Dawson "Scrap Iron" b: 3/16/27, Hall Summit, La. d: 6/16/75, Rochester, N.Y. BL/TR, 5'8", 180 lbs. Deb: 9/29/51 C																							
1951	NY-A	1	2	0	0	0	0	0	0	0	1	.000	.333	.000	333	-5	-0	0	0	0	.800	0	/C-1	0.0
1952	StL-A	119	413	38	118	24	3	5	50	39	26	.286	.349	.395	743	104	2	0	2	-1	**.996**	3	*C-113	1.1
1953	StL-A	106	355	28	89	12	2	4	19	25	20	.251	.302	.330	631	69	-16	0	1	-0	.980	-5	*C-103	-1.6
1954	Bal-A	122	397	25	107	18	3	4	37	30	7	.270	.326	.360	686	95	-4	2	1	0	.990	-3	*C-111	-0.1
1955	Chi-A	19	37	7	14	3	0	1	10	7	0	.378	.477	.541	1018	168	4	0	0	0	1.000	-1	C-17	0.3
	Was-A	75	238	26	71	8	4	2	30	19	9	.298	.353	.391	743	105	2	0	0	0	.983	-14	C-67	-0.9
	Yr	94	275	33	85	11	4	3	40	26	9	.309	.371	.411	782	114	6	0	0	0	.985	-15	C-84	-0.6
1956	Was-A	101	283	31	85	20	3	5	44	20	10	.300	.365	.445	811	113	5	0	5	-2	.979	-15	C-76	-0.8
1957	Was-A	91	232	23	62	14	1	6	27	16	11	.267	.346	.414	760	108	3	0	0	0	.994	-1	C-59	0.5
1958	Was-A	134	450	46	113	18	0	8	62	48	23	.251	.335	.344	680	89	-6	1	5	-2	.991	-3	*C-128	-0.4
1959	Was-A	72	189	19	44	4	1	2	18	20	19	.233	.310	.296	606	68	-8	0	1	-0	.987	-13	C-53	-1.9
1960	Bal-A	83	154	14	35	3	0	1	12	30	14	.227	.380	.266	646	79	-2	0	1	-0	.975	4	C-58	0.4
1961	KC-A	1	1	0	0	0	0	0	0	0	0	.000	.000	.000	0	-98	-0	0	0	0	.000	0	H	0.0
	Bal-A	22	45	3	12	2	0	0	4	10	3	.267	.400	.311	711	96	0	0	0	0	1.000	1	C-16	0.2
	Yr	23	46	3	12	2	0	0	4	10	3	.261	.393	.304	697	92	0	0	0	0	1.000	1	C-16	0.2
Total	11	946	2796	260	750	126	17	38	313	264	143	.268	.341	.366	708	94	-21	3	16	-5	.987	-45	C-802	-3.2
■ ERNIE COURTNEY	Courtney, Edward Ernest b: 1/20/1875, Des Moines, Iowa d: 2/29/20, Buffalo, N.Y. BL/TR, 5'8", 168 lbs. Deb: 4/17/02 Career OF: (40-LF 1-CF 6-RF)																							
1902	Bos-N	48	165	23	36	3	0	0	17	13		.218	.291	.236	528	62	-7	3			.974	-1	O-39(36-1-3)/S-3	-1.0
	Bal-A	1	4	3	2	0	1	0	1	1		.500	.600	1.000	1600	324	1	0			1.000	0	/3-1	0.1
1903	NY-A	25	79	7	21	3	3	1	8	7		.266	.341	.418	759	119	2	1			.916	-2	S-19/2-4,1-1	0.1
	Det-A	23	74	7	17	0	0	0	6	5		.230	.305	.230	535	64	-3	1			.938	-4	3-13/S-9	-0.6
	Yr	48	153	14	38	3	3	1	14	12		.248	.324	.327	650	94	-1	2			.921	-6	S-28,3-13/2-4,1-1	-0.5
1905	Phi-N	155	601	77	165	14	7	2	77	47		.275	.334	.331	665	102	2	17			.923	-17	*3-155	-1.1
1906	Phi-N	116	398	53	94	12	2	0	42	45		.236	.315	.276	592	84	-6	6			.923	-11	3-96,1-13/O-3R,S-1	-1.7
1907	Phi-N	130	440	42	107	17	4	2	43	55		.243	.335	.314	649	105	4	6			.907	-8	3-75,1-48/O-4L,2S	-0.3
1908	Phi-N	60	160	14	29	3	0	0	6	15		.181	.260	.200	460	46	-9	1			.915	-7	3-22,1-13/2-5,S-2	-1.8
Total	6	558	1921	226	471	52	17	5	200	188		.245	.321	.298	618	91	-15	35			.920	-49	3-362/1-75,O-46L,S2	-6.3
■ DEE COUSINEAU	Cousineau, Edward Thomas b: 12/16/1898, Watertown, Mass. d: 7/14/51, Watertown, Mass. BR/TR, 6', 170 lbs. Deb: 10/6/23																							
1923	Bos-N	1	2	1	2	0	0	0	2	0	0	1.000	1.000	1.000	2000	447	1	0	0	0	.000	0	/C-1	0.1
1924	Bos-N	3	2	0	0	0	0	0	0	0	0	.000	.000	.000	0	-99	-1	0	0	0	.500	-1	/C-3	-0.1
1925	Bos-N	1	0	0	0	0	0	0	0	0	0	—	—	—	—	—	0	0	0	0	.000	0	/C-1	0.0
Total	3	5	4	1	2	0	0	0	2	0	0	.500	.500	.500	1000	174	0	0	0	0	.500	-1	/C-5	0.0
■ JACK COVENEY	Coveney, John Patrick b: 6/10/1880, S.Natick, Mass. d: 3/28/61, Wayland, Mass. BR/TR, 5'9", 175 lbs. Deb: 9/19/03																							
1903	StL-N	4	14	0	2	0	0	0	0	0		.143	.143	.143	286	-19	-2	0			.923	1	/C-4	-0.1
■ SAM COVINGTON	Covington, Clarence Calvert b: 11/18/1894, Denison, Tenn. d: 1/4/63, Denison, Tex. BL/TR, 6'1", 190 lbs. Deb: 8/25/13 F																							
1913	StL-A	20	60	3	9	0	1	0	4	4	6	.150	.203	.183	386	14	-7	3			.994	3	1-16	-0.4
1917	Bos-N	17	66	8	13	2	0	1	10	5	5	.197	.264	.273	537	69	-2	1			.994	0	1-17	-0.3
1918	Bos-N	3	3	0	1	0	0	0	0	0	0	.333	.333	.333	667	108	0	0			.000	0	H	0.0
Total	3	40	129	11	23	2	1	1	14	9	11	.178	.237	.233	470	43	-9	4			.994	3	/1-33	-0.7
■ WES COVINGTON	Covington, John Wesley b: 3/27/32, Laurinburg, N.C. BL/TR, 6'1", 205 lbs. Deb: 4/19/56																							
1956	Mil-N	75	138	17	39	4	0	2	16	16	20	.283	.361	.355	716	100	0	1	0	0	.979	-3	O-35(34-0-1)	-0.5
1957	*Mil-N	96	328	51	93	4	8	21	65	29	44	.284	.345	.537	882	143	18	4	1	1	.981	0	O-89(89-0-0)	1.4
1958	*Mil-N	90	294	43	97	12	1	24	74	20	35	.330	.382	.622	1005	175	30	0	0	0	.953	-4	O-82(82-0-0)	2.1
1959	Mil-N	103	373	38	104	17	3	7	45	26	41	.279	.331	.397	728	101	-0	0	1	-0	.962	-3	O-94(94-0-0)	-0.9
1960	Mil-N	95	281	25	70	16	1	10	35	15	37	.249	.290	.420	709	99	-2	1	2	-0	.964	-5	O-72(72-0-0)	-1.2
1961	Mil-N	9	21	3	4	1	0	0	0	2	4	.190	.261	.238	499	36	-2	0	0	0	1.000	-1	/O-5(5-0-0)	-0.4
	Chi-A	22	59	5	17	1	0	4	15	4	5	.288	.333	.508	842	123	2	0	0	0	.900	-1	O-14(11-0-3)	0.0
	KC-A	17	44	3	7	0	0	1	6	4	7	.159	.260	.227	487	31	-4	0	0	0	1.000	-2	O-12(11-0-1)	-0.7
	Yr	39	103	8	24	1	0	5	21	8	12	.233	.301	.388	689	83	-3	0	0	0	.941	-3	O-26(22-0-4)	-0.7
	Phi-N	57	165	23	50	9	0	7	26	15	17	.303	.361	.485	846	124	5	0	0	0	.950	-5	O-45(10-0-36)	-0.2
1962	Phi-N	116	304	36	86	12	1	9	44	19	44	.283	.329	.418	747	102	0	0	0	0	.944	-7	O-88(88-0-0)	-1.1
1963	Phi-N	119	353	46	107	24	1	17	64	26	56	.303	.354	.521	876	150	22	1	0	0	.937	-8	*O-101(101-0-0)	1.0
1964	Phi-N	129	339	37	95	18	0	13	58	38	50	.280	.358	.448	806	127	13	0	0	0	.972	-9	*O-99(97-1-2)	-0.1
1965	Phi-N	101	235	27	58	10	1	15	45	26	47	.247	.324	.489	814	128	8	0	0	0	.968	-2	O-64(64-0-0)	0.4
1966	Chi-N	9	11	0	1	0	0	0	0	1	2	.091	.167	.091	258	-26	-2	0	0	0	1.000	0	/O-1(1-0-0)	-0.2
	*LA-N	37	33	1	4	0	1	1	6	6	5	.121	.293	.273	565	63	-1	0	0	0	1.000	-0	/O-2(2-0-0)	-0.2
	Yr	46	44	1	5	0	1	1	6	7	7	.114	.264	.227	491	41	-3	0	0	0	1.000	-0	/O-3(3-0-0)	-0.4
Total	11	1075	2978	355	832	128	17	131	499	247	414	.279	.339	.466	805	123	87	7	4	0	.961	-49	O-803(761-1-43)	-0.6

YEAR	TM/L	G	AB	R	H	2B	3B	HR	RBI	BB	SO	AVG	OBP	SLG	OPS	OPS+	BR+	SB	CS	SBR	FA	FR	G/POS	TPR
■ BILLY COWAN	Cowan, Billy Rolland b: 8/28/38, Calhoun City, Miss. BR/TR, 6', 170 lbs. Deb: 9/9/63 Career OF: (78-LF 210-CF 41-RF)																							
1963	Chi-N	14	36	1	9	1	1	1	2	0	11	.250	.250	.417	667	84	-1	0	1	-0	.917	-2	O-10(1-7-2)	-0.3
1964	Chi-N	139	497	52	120	16	4	19	50	18	128	.241	.269	.404	674	83	-12	12	3	2	.968	-3	*O-134(0-134-0)	-1.8
1965	NY-N	82	156	16	28	8	2	3	9	4	45	.179	.205	.314	519	45	-12	3	2	-0	1.000	-8	O-61(2-59-0)/2-2,S-1	-2.2
	Mil-N	19	27	4	5	1	0	0	0	0	9	.185	.185	.222	407	14	-3	0	0	0	1.000	-2	O-10(7-3-0)	-0.5
	Yr	101	183	20	33	9	2	3	9	4	54	.180	.202	.301	503	41	-15	3	2	-0	1.000	-10	O-71(9-62-0)/2-2,S-1	-2.7
1967	Phi-N	34	59	11	9	0	0	3	6	4	14	.153	.206	.305	511	44	-4	1	0	0	1.000	-4	O-20(16-0-4)/2-1,3-1	-1.0
1969	NY-A	32	48	5	8	0	0	1	3	3	9	.167	.216	.229	445	25	-5	0	0	0	1.000	-2	O-14(8-4-2)	-0.7
	Cal-A	28	56	10	17	1	0	4	10	3	9	.304	.350	.536	886	152	3	0	0	0	1.000	-0	O-13(3-2-8)/1-6	0.3
	Yr	60	104	15	25	1	0	5	13	6	18	.240	.288	.394	683	93	-1	0	0	0	1.000	-2	O-27(11-6-10)/1-6	-0.4
1970	Cal-A	68	134	20	37	9	1	5	25	11	29	.276	.336	.470	806	124	4	0	1	-0	.929	-6	O-27(3-1-23),1-14/3-2	-0.4
1971	Cal-A	74	174	12	48	8	0	4	20	7	41	.276	.304	.391	695	103	-0	1	1	-0	1.000	-2	O-40(38-0-2)/1-5	-0.5
1972	Cal-A	3	3	0	0	0	0	0	0	0	2	.000	.000	.000	0	-99	-1	0	0	0	.000	0	H	-0.1
Total	8	493	1190	131	281	44	8	40	125	50	297	.236	.269	.387	657	83	-31	17	8	1	.977	-28	O-329C/1-25,3-3,2S	-7.2
■ AL COWENS	Cowens, Alfred Edward b: 10/25/51, Los Angeles, Cal. BR/TR, 6'2", 200 lbs. Deb: 4/6/74 Career OF: (34-LF 195-CF 1288-RF)																							
1974	KC-A	110	269	28	65	7	1	1	25	23	38	.242	.304	.286	590	67	-11	5	0	1	.988	-9	*O-102R/3-2,D-4	-2.4
1975	KC-A	120	328	44	91	13	8	4	42	28	36	.277	.342	.402	744	107	3	12	7	-0	.978	-10	*O-113(22-35-65)/D-2	-1.1
1976	*KC-A	152	581	71	154	23	6	3	59	26	50	.265	.300	.341	641	87	-11	23	16	-1	.986	5	*O-148(0-12-142)/D-1	-1.4
1977	*KC-A	162	606	98	189	32	14	23	112	41	64	.312	.363	.525	888	138	30	16	12	-1	.982	3	*O-159(0-26-141)/D-1	2.4
1978	*KC-A	132	485	63	133	24	8	5	63	31	54	.274	.326	.388	713	97	-2	14	6	1	.990	2	*O-127R/3-5,D-2	-0.5
1979	KC-A	136	516	69	152	18	7	9	73	40	44	.295	.349	.409	758	102	1	10	8	-1	.986	-0	*O-134(0-1-134)/D-1	-0.6
1980	Cal-A	34	119	11	27	5	0	1	17	12	21	.227	.303	.294	597	66	-5	1	2	-0	1.000	1	O-30(3-10-19)/D-1	-0.6
	Det-A	108	403	58	113	15	3	5	42	37	40	.280	.342	.370	712	93	-3	5	6	-1	.986	2	*O-107(0-0-107)/D-1	-0.8
	Yr	142	522	69	140	20	3	6	59	49	61	.268	.333	.352	686	87	-8	6	8	-1	.989	3	*O-137(3-10-126)/D-2	-1.4
1981	Det-A	85	253	27	66	11	4	1	18	22	36	.261	.322	.348	670	90	-3	3	3	-0	.994	-6	O-83(0-65-18)	-1.2
1982	Sea-A	146	560	72	151	39	8	20	78	46	81	.270	.326	.475	801	114	9	11	7	-0	.987	7	*O-145(0-0-145)/D-1	0.8
1983	Sea-A	110	356	39	73	19	2	7	35	23	38	.205	.257	.329	586	58	-21	10	2	2	.985	2	O-70(2-4-65),D-34	-2.3
1984	Sea-A	139	524	60	145	34	2	15	78	27	83	.277	.315	.435	750	106	3	9	5	0	.987	-2	*O-130(0-2-130)/D-7	-0.6
1985	Sea-A	122	452	59	120	32	5	14	69	30	56	.265	.313	.451	764	105	2	0	0	0	.967	2	*O-110(0-0-110)/D-5	-0.2
1986	Sea-A	28	82	5	15	4	0	0	6	3	18	.183	.212	.232	443	20	-9	1	0	0	.971	-0	O-19(1-0-18)/D-1	-1.0
Total	13	1584	5534	704	1494	276	68	108	717	389	659	.270	.322	.403	725	98	-17	120	74	1	.985	-5	*O-1477R/D-61,3-7	-9.5
■ DICK COX	Cox, Elmer Joseph b: 9/30/1897, Pasadena, Cal. d: 6/1/66, Morro Bay, Cal. BR/TR, 5'7.5", 158 lbs. Deb: 4/16/25																							
1925	Bro-N	122	434	68	143	23	10	7	64	37	29	.329	.382	.477	859	121	14	4	3	-0	.968	-4	*O-111(3-0-108)	0.0
1926	Bro-N	124	398	53	118	17	4	1	45	46	20	.296	.375	.367	742	102	3	6			.964	-8	*O-117(0-1-116)	-1.4
Total	2	246	832	121	261	40	14	8	109	83	49	.314	.379	.424	803	112	17	10	3		.966	-12	O-228(3-1-224)	-1.4
■ FRANK COX	Cox, Francis Bernard "Runt" b: 8/29/1857, Waltham, Mass. d: 6/24/28, Hartford, Conn. 5'6", Deb: 8/13/1884																							
1884	Det-N	27	102	6	13	3	1	0	4	2	36	.127	.144	.176	321	0	-11				.812	-4	S-27	-1.3
■ JIM COX	Cox, James Charles b: 5/28/50, Bloomington, Ill. BR/TR, 5'11", 175 lbs. Deb: 7/19/73																							
1973	Mon-N	9	15	1	2	1	0	0	0	1	4	.133	.188	.200	388	7	-2	0	0	0	.950	-1	/2-7	-0.2
1974	Mon-N	77	236	29	52	9	1	2	26	23	36	.220	.292	.292	585	61	-12	2	3	-1	.968	15	2-72	0.6
1975	Mon-N	11	27	1	7	1	0	1	5	1	2	.259	.286	.407	693	87	-1	1	0	0	1.000	0	/2-8	0.0
1976	Mon-N	13	29	2	5	0	1	0	2	2	2	.172	.226	.241	467	31	-3	0	0	0	.958	1	2-11	-0.1
Total	4	110	307	33	66	11	2	3	33	27	44	.215	.281	.293	574	58	-17	3	3	-0	.969	16	/2-98	0.3
■ STEVE COX	Cox, Charles Steven b: 10/31/74, Delano, Cal. BL/TL, 6'4", 225 lbs. Deb: 9/19/99 Career OF: (28-LF 0-CF 30-RF)																							
1999	TB-A	6	19	0	4	1	0	0	0	0	2	.211	.211	.263	474	20	-2	0	0	0	1.000	-1	/1-4,O-2(2-0-0)	-0.3
2000	TB-A	116	318	44	90	19	1	11	35	46	47	.283	.380	.453	833	110	6	1	2	-0	.948	-2	O-56R,1-24,D-17	-0.1
Total	2	122	337	44	94	20	1	11	35	46	49	.279	.372	.442	814	106	4	1	2	-0	.949	-2	/O-58R,1-28,D-17	-0.4
■ DARRON COX	Cox, James Darron b: 11/21/67, Oklahoma City, Okla. BR/TR, 6'1", 205 lbs. Deb: 4/6/99																							
1999	Mon-N	15	25	2	6	1	0	1	2	0	5	.240	.296	.400	696	76	-1	0	0	0	.963	1	C-14	0.1
■ JEFF COX	Cox, Jeffrey Lindon b: 11/9/55, Los Angeles, Cal. BR/TR, 5'11", 170 lbs. Deb: 7/1/80																							
1980	Oak-A	59	169	20	36	3	0	0	9	14	23	.213	.273	.231	504	43	-13	8	5	0	.979	-16	2-58	-2.6
1981	Oak-A	2	0	0	0	0	0	0	0	0	0	—	—	—	—	—	0	0	0	0	1.000	0	/2-1	0.0
Total	2	61	169	20	36	3	0	0	9	14	23	.213	.273	.231	504	43	-13	8	5	0	.979	-16	/2-59	-2.6
■ LARRY COX	Cox, Larry Eugene b: 9/11/47, Bluffton, Ohio d: 2/17/90, Bellefontaine, Ohio BR/TR, 5'11", 190 lbs. Deb: 4/18/73 C																							
1973	Phi-N	1	0	0	0	0	0	0	0	0	0	—	—	—	—	—	0	0	0	0	1.000	-0	/C-1	0.0
1974	Phi-N	30	53	5	9	2	0	0	4	4	9	.170	.241	.208	449	25	-5	0	0	0	.990	2	C-29	-0.4
1975	Phi-N	11	5	0	1	0	0	0	1	1	0	.200	.333	.200	533	49	-0	1	0	0	1.000	-0	C-10	0.0
1977	Sea-A	35	93	6	23	6	0	2	6	10	12	.247	.320	.376	697	90	-1	1	1	-0	.970	-1	C-35	-0.1
1978	Chi-N	59	121	10	34	5	0	2	18	12	16	.281	.346	.372	718	90	-1	0	0	0	.967	2	C-58	0.2
1979	Sea-A	100	293	32	63	11	3	4	36	22	39	.215	.270	.314	584	56	-18	2	1	0	.981	-2	C-99	-1.6
1980	Sea-A	105	243	18	49	6	2	4	20	19	36	.202	.260	.292	552	50	-17	1	2	-0	**.993**	12	*C-104	-0.2
1981	Tex-A	5	13	0	3	1	0	0	0	0	4	.231	.231	.308	538	57	-1	0	0	0	1.000	2	/C-5	0.3
1982	Chi-N	2	4	1	0	0	0	0	0	2	1	.000	.333	.000	333	1	-0	0	0	0	1.000	1	/C-2	0.1
Total	9	348	825	72	182	31	5	12	85	70	117	.221	.282	.314	596	61	-44	5	4	-0	.983	15	C-343	-1.7
■ BOBBY COX	Cox, Robert Joseph b: 5/21/41, Tulsa, Okla. BR/TR, 5'11", 180 lbs. Deb: 4/14/68 MC																							
1968	NY-A	135	437	33	100	15	1	7	41	41	85	.229	.302	.316	618	90	-5	3	2	-0	.957	-5	*3-132	-1.2
1969	NY-A	85	191	17	41	7	1	2	17	34	41	.215	.336	.293	629	80	-4	0	1	-0	.935	11	3-56/2-6	0.7
Total	2	220	628	50	141	22	2	9	58	75	126	.225	.313	.309	622	87	-9	3	3	-0	.950	6	3-188/2-6	-0.5
■ BILLY COX	Cox, William Richard b: 8/29/19, Newport, Pa. d: 3/30/78, Harrisburg, Pa. BR/TR, 5'10", 150 lbs. Deb: 9/20/41																							
1941	Pit-N	10	37	4	10	3	1	0	2	3	2	.270	.325	.405	730	105	0	1			.943	2	S-10	0.3
1946	Pit-N	121	411	32	119	22	6	2	36	26	15	.290	.333	.387	720	101	-0	4			.935	-16	*S-114	-1.0
1947	Pit-N	132	529	75	145	30	7	15	54	29	28	.274	.313	.442	755	96	-5	5			.968	-13	*S-129	-1.0
1948	Bro-N	88	237	36	59	13	2	3	15	38	19	.249	.353	.359	711	90	-2	3			.958	-4	3-70/S-6,2-1	-0.7
1949	*Bro-N	100	390	48	91	18	2	8	40	30	18	.233	.290	.351	641	68	-18	5			.964	9	*3-100	-1.0
1950	Bro-N	119	451	62	116	17	2	8	44	35	24	.257	.311	.357	668	74	-17	6			**.957**	12	*3-107,2-13/S-9	-0.5
1951	Bro-N	142	455	62	127	25	4	9	51	37	30	.279	.336	.411	747	98	-2	5	5	-1	.967	-8	*3-139/S-1	-1.1
1952	*Bro-N	116	455	56	118	12	3	6	34	25	32	.259	.301	.338	639	76	-15	10	12	-2	.970	-9	*3-100,S-10/2-9	-2.6
1953	*Bro-N	100	327	44	95	18	1	10	44	37	21	.291	.363	.443	806	106	3	2	2	-0	.974	-2	3-89/S-6,2-1	0.1
1954	Bro-N	77	226	26	53	9	2	2	17	21	13	.235	.300	.319	618	59	-13	0	0	0	.961	2	3-58,2-11/S-8	-1.0
1955	Bal-A	53	194	25	41	7	2	3	14	17	16	.211	.275	.314	589	63	-11	1	2	-0	.969	-9	3-37,2-18/S-6	-2.0
Total	11	1058	3712	470	974	174	32	66	351	298	218	.262	.318	.380	698	85	-81	42	21		.965	-36	3-700,S-299/2-53	-10.5
■ TED COX	Cox, William Ted b: 1/24/55, Oklahoma City, Okla BR/TR, 6'3", 195 lbs. Deb: 9/18/77 Career OF: (49-LF 0-CF 5-RF)																							
1977	Bos-A	13	58	11	21	3	1	1	6	3	6	.362	.393	.500	893	127	2	0	0	0	.000	0	D-13	0.2
1978	Cle-A	82	227	14	53	7	0	1	19	16	30	.233	.287	.278	564	60	-12	0	1	-0	.980	-5	O-38L,3-20,D-12,/1S	-2.0
1979	Cle-A	78	189	17	40	6	0	4	22	14	27	.212	.273	.307	580	56	-12	3	4	-1	.964	1	3-52,O-16L/2-4,D-1	-1.2
1980	Sea-A	83	247	17	60	9	0	2	23	19	25	.243	.297	.304	601	64	-12	0	0	0	.945	-2	3-80	-1.5
1981	Tor-A	16	50	6	15	4	0	2	9	5	10	.300	.364	.500	864	138	2	0	1	-0	.897	-4	3-14/1-1,D-1	-0.3
Total	5	272	771	65	189	29	1	10	79	57	98	.245	.300	.324	624	71	-31	3	6	-1	.947	-10	3-166/O-54L,D-27,12S	-4.8
■ TOOTS COYNE	Coyne, Martin Albert b: 10/20/1894, St.Louis, Mo. d: 9/18/39, St.Louis, Mo. TR, Deb: 9/28/14																							
1914	Phi-A	1	2	0	0	0	0	0	0	0	2	.000	.000	.000	0	-99	-0	0			1.000	-0	/3-1	-0.1

■ **ESTEL CRABTREE** Crabtree, Estel Crayton "Crabby" b: 8/19/03, Crabtree, Ohio d: 1/4/67, Logan, Ohio BL/TR, 6', 168 lbs. Deb: 4/18/29 C Career OF: (57-LF 156-CF 125-RF)

YEAR	TM/L	G	AB	R	H	2B	3B	HR	RBI	BB	SO	AVG	OBP	SLG	OPS	OPS+	BR+	SB	CS	SBR	FA	FR	G/POS	TPR
1929	Cin-N	1	1	0	0	0	0	0	0	0	0	.000	.000	.000	0	-99	-0	0			.000	0	H	0.0
1931	Cin-N	117	443	70	119	12	12	4	37	23	33	.269	.309	.377	686	89	-8	3			.974	10	*O-101R/3-4,1-2	-0.4
1932	Cin-N	108	402	38	110	14	9	2	35	23	26	.274	.316	.368	684	86	-8	2			.990	9	O-95(14-73-9)	-0.2
1933	StL-N	23	34	6	9	3	0	0	3	2	3	.265	.306	.353	658	83	-1	1			.947	-0	/O-7(0-4-3)	-0.1
1941	StL-N	77	167	27	57	6	3	5	28	26	24	.341	.439	.503	942	154	13	1			1.000	-8	O-50(17-16-19)/3-1	0.3
1942	StL-N	10	9	1	3	2	0	0	2	1	3	.333	.400	.556	956	166	1	0			.000	0	H	0.1
1943	Cin-N	95	254	25	70	12	0	2	26	25	17	.276	.345	.346	692	101	1	1			.939	-5	O-65(2-44-17)	-0.7
1944	Cin-N	58	98	7	28	4	1	0	11	13	3	.286	.369	.347	716	106	1	0			1.000	-4	O-19(15-3-1)/1-2	-0.4
Total	8	489	1408	174	396	53	25	13	142	113	109	.281	.339	.382	721	100	-1	8			.976	1	O-337C/3-5,1-4	-1.4

■ **RICKEY CRADLE** Cradle, Rickey Nelson b: 6/20/73, Norfolk, Va. BR/TR, 6'2", 180 lbs. Deb: 7/1/98

YEAR	TM/L	G	AB	R	H	2B	3B	HR	RBI	BB	SO	AVG	OBP	SLG	OPS	OPS+	BR+	SB	CS	SBR	FA	FR	G/POS	TPR
1998	Sea-A	5	7	0	1	0	0	0	2	1	5	.143	.250	.143	393	6	-1	1	0	0	1.000	-1	/O-4(1-2-1)	-0.2

■ **HARRY CRAFT** Craft, Harry Francis "Wildfire" b: 4/19/15, Ellisville, Miss. d: 8/3/95, Conroe, Tex. BR/TR, 6'1", 185 lbs. Deb: 9/19/37 MC

YEAR	TM/L	G	AB	R	H	2B	3B	HR	RBI	BB	SO	AVG	OBP	SLG	OPS	OPS+	BR+	SB	CS	SBR	FA	FR	G/POS	TPR
1937	Cin-N	10	42	7	13	2	1	0	4	1	3	.310	.326	.405	730	102	-0	0			1.000	0	O-10(0-10-0)	0.0
1938	Cin-N	151	612	70	165	28	9	15	83	29	46	.270	.305	.418	723	100	-3	3			.983	16	*O-151(0-151-0)	0.9
1939	*Cin-N	134	502	58	129	20	7	13	67	27	54	.257	.299	.402	701	86	-11	5			.981	3	*O-134(0-134-0)	-1.2
1940	*Cin-N	115	422	47	103	18	5	6	48	17	46	.244	.277	.353	630	72	-17	2			**.997**	6	*O-109(0-106-3)/1-2	-1.4
1941	Cin-N	119	413	48	103	15	2	10	59	33	43	.249	.308	.368	676	90	-7	4			.983	2	*O-115(0-115-0)	-0.8
1942	Cin-N	37	113	7	20	2	1	0	6	3	11	.177	.205	.212	418	22	-11	0			.987	1	O-33(0-33-0)	-1.2
Total	6	566	2104	237	533	85	25	44	267	110	203	.253	.294	.380	674	85	-49	14			.986	28	O-552(0-549-3)/1-2	-3.7

■ **ROD CRAIG** Craig, Rodney Paul b: 1/12/58, Los Angeles, Cal. BB/TR, 6'1", 195 lbs. Deb: 9/11/79

YEAR	TM/L	G	AB	R	H	2B	3B	HR	RBI	BB	SO	AVG	OBP	SLG	OPS	OPS+	BR+	SB	CS	SBR	FA	FR	G/POS	TPR
1979	Sea-A	16	52	9	20	8	1	0	6	1	5	.385	.396	.577	973	156	4	1	1	-0	.923	-2	O-15(0-0-16)	0.1
1980	Sea-A	70	240	30	57	15	1	3	20	17	35	.237	.293	.346	639	74	-9	3	6	-1	.987	-2	O-63(3-58-2)	-1.3
1982	Cle-A	49	65	7	15	2	0	0	1	4	6	.231	.275	.262	537	49	-5	3	1	0	.966	-4	O-22(11-4-7)/D-4	-0.9
1986	Chi-A	10	10	3	2	0	0	0	0	2	2	.200	.333	.200	533	48	-1	0	0	0	.000	-1	/O-2(1-0-1)	-0.1
Total	4	145	367	49	94	25	2	3	27	24	48	.256	.305	.360	665	80	-10	7	8	-1	.977	-9	O-102(15-62-26)/D-4	-2.2

■ **DOC CRAMER** Cramer, Roger Maxwell "Flit" b: 7/22/05, Beach Haven, N.J. d: 9/9/90, Manahawkin, N.J. BL/TR, 6'2", 185 lbs. Deb: 9/18/29 C Career OF: (25-LF 2031-CF 87-RF)

YEAR	TM/L	G	AB	R	H	2B	3B	HR	RBI	BB	SO	AVG	OBP	SLG	OPS	OPS+	BR+	SB	CS	SBR	FA	FR	G/POS	TPR
1929	Phi-A	2	6	0	0	0	0	0	0	0	2	.000	.000	.000	0	-97	-2	0	0	0	1.000	1	/O-1(1-0-0)	-0.1
1930	Phi-A	30	82	12	19	1	1	0	6	2	8	.232	.250	.268	518	30	-9	0	0	0	.927	-2	O-21(6-13-2)/S-1	-1.1
1931	*Phi-A	65	223	37	58	8	2	2	20	11	15	.260	.301	.341	642	64	-12	2	1	0	.979	1	O-55(2-47-6)	-1.2
1932	Phi-A	92	384	73	129	27	6	3	46	17	27	.336	.367	.461	828	109	5	3	1	0	.976	8	O-86(0-45-42)	0.9
1933	Phi-A	152	661	109	195	27	8	8	75	36	24	.295	.331	.396	728	91	-10	5	4	-0	.971	5	*O-152(0-152-0)	-0.9
1934	Phi-A	153	649	99	202	29	9	6	46	40	35	.311	.353	.411	765	100	-1	1	5	-2	.985	5	*O-152(0-152-0)	-0.1
1935	Phi-A★	149	644	96	214	37	4	3	70	37	34	.332	.373	.416	789	105	4	6	7	-1	.975	4	*O-149(0-149-0)	0.3
1936	Bos-A	154	643	99	188	31	7	0	41	49	20	.292	.347	.362	710	71	-29	4	6	-1	.975	16	*O-154(0-154-0)	-1.5
1937	Bos-A☆	133	560	90	171	22	11	0	51	35	14	.305	.351	.384	735	82	-15	8	6	-0	.969	6	*O-133(0-133-0)	-1.2
1938	Bos-A★	148	658	116	198	36	8	0	71	51	19	.301	.354	.380	734	80	-20	4	9	-2	.986	9	*O-148(0-148-0)/P-1	-1.6
1939	Bos-A★	137	589	110	183	30	6	0	56	36	17	.311	.352	.382	734	85	-13	3	3	-0	.984	2	*O-135(0-135-0)	-1.5
1940	Bos-A☆	150	661	94	**200**	27	12	1	51	36	29	.303	.340	.384	724	84	-16	3	5	-1	.969	-5	*O-149(16-96-37)	-2.6
1941	Was-A	154	660	93	180	25	6	2	66	37	15	.273	.317	.338	655	77	-23	4	1	1	.984	-7	*O-152(0-152-0)	-3.2
1942	Det-A	151	630	71	166	26	4	0	43	43	18	.263	.314	.317	631	72	-23	4	4	-1	.981	-0	*O-150(0-150-0)	-2.9
1943	Det-A	140	606	79	182	18	4	1	43	31	13	.300	.335	.348	684	93	-6	4	3	-0	.989	1	*O-138(0-138-0)	-0.9
1944	Det-A	143	578	69	169	20	9	2	42	37	21	.292	.337	.369	706	96	-3	6	5	-0	.980	-8	*O-141(0-141-0)	-1.6
1945	*Det-A	141	541	62	149	22	8	6	58	36	21	.275	.324	.379	703	97	-3	2	9	-3	**.991**	-8	*O-140(0-140-0)	-1.9
1946	Det-A	68	204	26	60	8	2	1	26	15	8	.294	.342	.368	710	93	-2	3	0	1	1.000	-6	O-50(0-50-0)	-0.9
1947	Det-A	73	157	21	42	2	2	2	30	20	5	.268	.350	.344	694	91	-2	0	4	-1	.965	-2	O-35(0-35-0)	-0.6
1948	Det-A	4	4	1	0	0	0	0	1	3	0	.000	.429	.000	429	19	-0	0	0	0	1.000	-0	/O-1(0-1-0)	0.0
Total	20	2239	9140	1357	2705	396	109	37	842	572	345	.296	.340	.375	715	87	-177	62	73	-12	.979	19	*O-2142C/P-1,S-1	-22.6

■ **DICK CRAMER** Cramer, William B. b: Brooklyn, N.Y. d: 8/12/1885, Camden, N.J. Deb: 5/12/1883

YEAR	TM/L	G	AB	R	H	2B	3B	HR	RBI	BB	SO	AVG	OBP	SLG	OPS	OPS+	BR+	SB	CS	SBR	FA	FR	G/POS	TPR
1883	NY-N	2	6	0	0	0	0	0	0	1	5	.000	.143	.000	143	-52	-1				.000	-1	/O-2(0-1-1)	-0.2

■ **DEL CRANDALL** Crandall, Delmar Wesley b: 3/5/30, Ontario, Cal. BR/TR, 6'1", 195 lbs. Deb: 6/17/49 MC Career OF: (1-LF 0-CF 9-RF)

YEAR	TM/L	G	AB	R	H	2B	3B	HR	RBI	BB	SO	AVG	OBP	SLG	OPS	OPS+	BR+	SB	CS	SBR	FA	FR	G/POS	TPR
1949	Bos-N	67	228	21	60	10	1	4	34	9	18	.263	.291	.368	660	80	-7	2			.982	7	C-63	0.3
1950	Bos-N	79	255	21	56	11	0	4	37	13	24	.220	.257	.310	567	52	-19	0			.967	3	C-75/1-1	-1.2
1953	Mil-N†	116	382	55	104	13	1	15	51	33	47	.272	.330	.429	759	102	1	2	1	0	.986	15	*C-108	2.0
1954	Mil-N☆	138	463	60	112	18	2	21	64	40	56	.242	.306	.425	732	94	-6	0	3	-1	.989	14	*C-136	1.3
1955	Mil-N★	133	440	61	104	15	2	26	62	40	56	.236	.303	.457	760	103	0	2	1	0	.985	-2	*C-131	0.5
1956	Mil-N†	112	311	37	74	14	2	16	48	35	30	.238	.317	.450	767	110	3	1	2	-0	**.996**	3	*C-109	1.1
1957	*Mil-N	118	383	45	97	11	2	15	46	30	38	.253	.309	.410	719	98	-2	1	2	-0	.987	-8	*C-102/O-9(1-0-9),1-1	-0.6
1958	*Mil-N★	131	427	50	116	23	1	18	63	48	38	.272	.351	.457	807	122	13	4	1	1	**.990**	6	*C-124	2.6
1959	Mil-N★	150	518	65	133	19	2	21	72	46	48	.257	.321	.423	744	105	2	5	1	1	**.994**	6	*C-146	1.7
1960	Mil-N★	142	537	81	158	14	1	19	77	34	36	.294	.341	.430	771	118	12	4	6	-1	.988	-15	*C-141	0.3
1961	Mil-N	15	30	3	6	3	0	0	1	1	0	.200	.226	.300	526	40	-3	0	0	0	1.000	-2	/C-5	-0.4
1962	Mil-N★	107	350	35	104	12	3	8	45	27	24	.297	.351	.417	768	108	4	3	4	-1	**.994**	-4	C-90/1-5	0.4
1963	Mil-N	86	259	18	52	4	0	3	28	18	22	.201	.253	.251	504	46	-18	1	4	-1	.991	5	C-75/1-7	-1.2
1964	SF-N	69	195	12	45	8	1	3	11	22	21	.231	.309	.328	637	78	-5	0	3	-1	.993	13	C-65	0.9
1965	Pit-N	60	140	11	30	2	0	2	10	14	10	.214	.290	.271	562	59	-7	1	0	0	.996	5	C-60	-0.1
1966	Cle-A	50	108	10	25	2	0	4	8	14	9	.231	.320	.361	681	95	-1	0	0	0	.991	15	C-49	1.7
Total	16	1573	5026	585	1276	179	18	179	657	424	477	.254	.315	.404	718	97	-32	26	28		.989	61	*C-1479/1-14,O-9R	9.3

■ **DOC CRANDALL** Crandall, James Otis b: 10/8/1887, Wadena, Ind. d: 8/17/51, Bell, Cal. BR/TR, 5'10.5", 180 lbs. Deb: 4/24/08

YEAR	TM/L	G	AB	R	H	2B	3B	HR	RBI	BB	SO	AVG	OBP	SLG	OPS	OPS+	BR+	SB	CS	SBR	FA	FR	G/POS	TPR
1908	NY-N	34	72	8	16	4	0	2	6	4		.222	.273	.361	634	97	-0	0			.985	-2	P-32/2-1	0.0
1909	NY-N	30	41	4	10	0	1	1	1	1		.244	.262	.366	628	93	-1	0			.941	2	P-30	0.0
1910	NY-N	45	73	10	25	2	4	1	13	5	7	.342	.385	.521	905	163	5	0			.984	-2	P-42/S-1	0.0
1911	*NY-N	61	113	12	27	1	4	2	21	8	16	.239	.295	.372	667	83	-3	2			.958	-0	P-41/S-6,2-3	-0.2
1912	*NY-N	50	80	9	25	6	2	0	19	6	7	.313	.360	.438	798	114	1	0			.957	0	P-37/2-2,1-1	0.0
1913	*NY-N	31	25	4	7	2	1	0	2	1	5	.280	.308	.440	748	111	0	0			1.000	1	P-24/2-2	0.0
	StL-N	2	2	0	0	0	0	0	0	0	2	.000	.000	.000	0	-99	-1	0			.000	0	H	-0.1
	*NY-N	15	22	3	8	2	0	0	2	2	3	.364	.417	.455	871	148	1	0			1.000	1	P-11	0.0
	Yr	48	49	7	15	4	1	0	4	3	10	.306	.346	.429	775	120	1	0			1.000	2	P-35/2-2	-0.1
1914	StL-F	118	278	40	86	16	5	2	41	58	32	.309	.429	.424	853	126	9	3			.926	-18	2-63,P-27/S-1,O-1C	-0.9
1915	StL-F	84	141	18	40	2	2	1	19	27	15	.284	.406	.348	753	107	1	4			.958	1	P-51	0.0
1916	StL-A	16	12	0	1	0	0	0	0	2	4	.083	.214	.083	298	-11	-2	0			.000	-0	/P-2	0.0
1918	Bos-N	14	28	1	8	0	0	0	2	4	3	.286	.375	.286	661	107	0	0			1.000	0	/P-5,O-3(0-0-2)	0.0
Total	10	500	887	109	253	35	19	9	126	118	94	.285	.372	.398	770	114	13	9			.962	-18	P-302/2-71,S-8,O1	-1.2

■ **ED CRANE** Crane, Edward Nicholas "Cannon-Ball" b: 5/27/1862, Boston, Mass. d: 9/20/1896, Rochester, N.Y. BR/TR, 5'10.5", 204 lbs. Deb: 4/17/1884 Career OF: (37-LF 13-CF 95-RF)

YEAR	TM/L	G	AB	R	H	2B	3B	HR	RBI	BB	SO	AVG	OBP	SLG	OPS	OPS+	BR+	SB	CS	SBR	FA	FR	G/POS	TPR
1884	Bos-U	101	428	83	122	23	6	12		14		.285	.308	.451	759	129	2				.826	-5	O-57R,C-42/1-5,P-4	-0.2
1885	Pro-N	1	2	0	0	0	0	0	0	1	1	.000	.333	.000	333	15	-0				.500	0	/O-1(1-0-0)	0.0
	Buf-N	13	51	5	14	0	1	2	9	3	8	.275	.315	.431	746	135	2				.769	-3	O-13(10-3-0)	-0.1
	Yr	14	53	5	14	0	1	2	9	4	9	.264	.316	.415	731	131	2				.750	-2	O-14(11-3-0)	-0.1
1886	Was-N	80	292	20	50	11	3	0	20	13	54	.171	.207	.229	436	34	-22	8			.866	3	O-68(8-9-51),P-10/C-4	-1.6
1888	*NY-N	12	37	3	6	2	0	1	2	3	11	.162	.225	.297	522	66	-1	1			.867	1	P-12	0.0

YEAR	TM/L	G	AB	R	H	2B	3B	HR	RBI	BB	SO	AVG	OBP	SLG	OPS	OPS+	BR+	SB	CS	SBR	FA	FR	G/POS	TPR
1889	*NY-N	29	103	16	21	1	0	2	11	13	21	.204	.293	.272	565	58	-6	6			.762	-4	P-29/1-1	0.0
1890	NY-P	43	146	27	46	5	4	0	16	10	26	.315	.363	.404	767	96	-1	5			.846	-3	P-43	0.0
1891	Cin-a	34	110	13	17	0	0	1	7	8	28	.155	.212	.182	394	12	-13	4			.822	-2	P-32/O-3(0-1-2)	-0.1
	Cin-N	15	46	3	5	0	0	0	2	3	12	.109	.163	.109	272	-20	-7	3			.906	0	P-15	0.0
1892	NY-N	48	163	20	40	1	1	0	14	11	30	.245	.297	.264	561	71	-6	2			.821	-1	P-47/O-1(0-0-1)	-0.1
1893	NY-N	12	26	8	12	1	0	0	3	7	0	.462	.576	.500	1076	186	4	0			.889	-1	P-10/1-1,O-1(0-0-1)	0.0
	Bro-N	3	5	1	2	1	0	0	0	0	0	.400	.400	.600	1000	172	0	0			.500	-1	/P-2,O-1(0-0-1)	0.0
	Yr	15	31	9	14	2	0	0	3	7	0	.452	.553	.516	1069	186	5	0			.850	-2	P-12/O-2(0-0-2),1-1	0.0
Total	9	391	1409	199	335	45	15	18	84	86	191	.238	.283	.329	612	80	-48	29			.842	-15	P-204,O-145R/C-46,1	-2.1

■ FRED CRANE

Crane, Frederic William Hotchkiss b: 11/4/1840, Old Saybrook, Conn. d: 4/27/25, Brooklyn, N.Y. Deb: 5/26/1873 Career OF: (0-LF 0-CF 1-RF)

YEAR	TM/L	G	AB	R	H	2B	3B	HR	RBI	BB	SO	AVG	OBP	SLG	OPS	OPS+	BR+	SB	CS	SBR	FA	FR	G/POS	TPR
1873	Res-n	1	4	0	1	0	0	0	1	0	0	.250	.250	.250	500	53	-0	0	0	0	.667	-1	/2-1	-0.1
1875	Atl-n	21	81	7	17	1	0	0	4	0	4	.210	.210	.222	432	58	-3	0	0	0	.953	1	1-20/S-1,O-1(0-0-1)	-0.1
Total	2 n	22	85	7	18	1	0	0	5	0	4	.212	.212	.224	435	57	-3	0	0	0	.953	1	/1-20,O-1R,S-1,2-1	-0.2

■ SAM CRANE

Crane, Samuel Byren "Lucky" or "Red" b: 9/13/1894, Harrisburg, Pa.
d: 11/12/55, Philadelphia, Pa. BR/TR, 5'11.5", 154 lbs. Deb: 10/2/14 Career OF: (0-LF 0-CF 4-RF)

YEAR	TM/L	G	AB	R	H	2B	3B	HR	RBI	BB	SO	AVG	OBP	SLG	OPS	OPS+	BR+	SB	CS	SBR	FA	FR	G/POS	TPR
1914	Phi-A	2	6	0	0	0	0	0	0	2	3	.000	.250	.000	250	-25	-1	0			.929	1	/S-2	0.0
1915	Phi-A	8	23	3	2	2	0	0	1	0	4	.087	.087	.174	261	-23	-4	0			.900	2	/S-6,2-1	-0.1
1916	Phi-A	2	4	1	1	0	0	0	0	2	1	.250	.500	.250	750	132	0	0			1.000	-0	/S-2	0.0
1917	Was-A	32	95	6	17	2	0	0	4	4	14	.179	.212	.200	412	26	-9	0			.889	-4	S-32	-1.3
1920	Cin-N	54	144	20	31	4	0	0	9	7	9	.215	.261	.243	504	46	-10	5	4	-0	.945	-9	S-25,3-10/2-4,O-3R	-1.9
1921	Cin-N	73	215	20	50	10	2	0	16	14	14	.233	.292	.298	590	59	-13	2	5	-1	.953	-17	S-63/3-2,O-1(0-0-1)	-2.4
1922	Bro-N	3	8	1	2	1	0	0	0	0	1	.250	.333	.375	708	83	-0	0	0	0	.875	2	/S-3	0.2
Total	7	174	495	51	103	19	2	0	30	29	46	.208	.262	.255	516	46	-35	7	9		.931	-25	S-133/3-12,2-5,O-4R	-5.5

■ SAM CRANE

Crane, Samuel Newhall b: 1/2/1854, Springfield, Mass. d: 6/26/25, New York, N.Y. BR/TR, Deb: 5/1/1880 M Career OF: (1-LF 2-CF 5-RF)

YEAR	TM/L	G	AB	R	H	2B	3B	HR	RBI	BB	SO	AVG	OBP	SLG	OPS	OPS+	BR+	SB	CS	SBR	FA	FR	G/POS	TPR
1880	Buf-N	10	31	4	4	0	0	0	2	1	8	.129	.156	.129	285	-2	-3				.866	-2	2-10/O-1(0-1-0),M	-0.5
1883	NY-a	96	349	57	82	8	5	0		13		.235	.262	.287	549	73	-11				.859	-10	*2-96/O-1(0-1-0)	-1.5
1884	Cin-U	80	309	56	72	9	3	1		11		.233	.259	.291	551	62	-23				.858	-9	*2-80,M	-2.6
1885	Det-N	68	245	23	47	4	6	1	20	13	45	.192	.233	.269	502	62	-10				.908	-4	2-68	-1.1
1886	Det-N	47	185	24	26	2	2	1	12	8	34	.141	.176	.189	365	11	-20	8			.903	1	2-38/S-8,O-4(1-0-3)	-1.6
	StL-N	39	116	10	20	3	1	0	7	13	27	.172	.256	.216	471	48	-7	6			.897	-11	2-39	-1.4
	Yr	86	301	34	46	5	3	1	19	21	61	.153	.208	.199	407	25	-27	14			.900	-10	2-77/S-8,O-4(1-0-3)	-3.0
1887	Was-N	7	31	6	10	1	1	0	1	1	6	.323	.323	.400	723	105	0	5			.865	-1	/S-7	0.0
1890	NY-N	2	6	0	0	0	0	0	0	0	1	.000	.000	.000	0	-99	-2	1			.778	-1	/1-1,O-1(0-0-1)	-0.2
	Pit-N	22	82	3	16	3	0	0	3	0	5	.195	.205	.232	437	31	-7	5			.880	3	2-15/S-7,O-1(0-0-1)	-0.3
	NY-N	2	6	0	0	0	0	0	0	0	1	.000	.000	.000	0	-99	-2	0			1.000	1	/2-2	-0.1
	Yr	26	94	3	16	3	0	0	3	0	7	.170	.179	.202	381	12	-10	6			.883	3	2-17/S-7,O-2R,1-1	-0.6
Total	7	373	1360	183	277	30	18	3	45	60	127	.204	.237	.258	496	53	-84	25			.878	-32	2-348/S-22,O-8R,1-1	-9.3

■ GAVVY CRAVATH

Cravath, Clifford Carlton "Cactus" b: 3/23/1881, Escondido, Cal.
d: 5/23/63, Laguna Beach, Cal. BR/TR, 5'10.5", 186 lbs. Deb: 4/18/08 MC Career OF: (108-LF 40-CF 947-RF)

YEAR	TM/L	G	AB	R	H	2B	3B	HR	RBI	BB	SO	AVG	OBP	SLG	OPS	OPS+	BR+	SB	CS	SBR	FA	FR	G/POS	TPR
1908	Bos-A	94	277	43	71	10	11	1	34	38		.256	.354	.383	737	136	12	6			.925	-2	O-77(62-0-15)/1-5	0.7
1909	Chi-A	19	50	7	9	0	0	1	8	19		.180	.406	.240	646	109	2	3			.944	-2	O-18(0-18-0)	-0.1
	Was-A	4	6	0	0	0	0	0	1	1		.000	.143	.000	143	-57	-1	0			1.000	1	/O-1(0-0-1)	-0.1
	Yr	23	56	7	9	0	0	1	9	20		.161	.382	.214	596	93	1	3			.947	-2	O-19(0-18-1)	-0.2
1912	Phi-N	130	436	63	124	30	9	11	70	47	77	.284	.358	.470	828	118	9	15			.966	5	*O-113(30-14-73)	0.8
1913	Phi-N	147	525	78	**179**	34	14	**19**	**128**	55	63	.341	.407	**.568**	**974**	**169**	**46**	10			.958	-4	*O-141(3-7-133)	3.6
1914	Phi-N	149	499	76	149	27	8	**19**	100	83	72	.299	.402	.499	**901**	**157**	36	14			.930	3	*O-143(1-0-142)	3.4
1915	*Phi-N	150	522	**89**	149	31	7	**24**	**115**	**86**	77	.285	**.393**	**.510**	**902**	**170**	**46**	11	9	-1	.946	9	*O-149(0-0-149)	**5.0**
1916	Phi-N	137	448	70	127	21	8	11	70	64	89	.283	**.379**	.440	819	146	26	9			.966	-3	*O-130(0-0-130)	1.8
1917	Phi-N	140	503	70	141	29	16	**12**	83	70	57	.280	.369	.473	842	151	31	6			.946	-3	*O-139(0-0-139)	2.2
1918	Phi-N	121	426	43	99	27	5	**8**	54	54	46	.232	.320	.376	696	105	3	7			.931	-4	*O-118(7-0-110)	-0.8
1919	Phi-N	83	214	34	73	18	5	**12**	45	35	21	.341	.438	.640	1078	207	28	8			.914	-5	O-56(2-1-53),M	2.3
1920	Phi-N	46	45	2	13	5	0	1	11	9	12	.289	.407	.467	874	144	3	0	0	0	.667	-2	/O-5(3-0-2),M	0.1
Total	11	1220	3951	575	1134	232	83	119	719	561	514	.287	.380	.478	858	149	241	89	9		.944	-6	*O-1090R/1-5	18.9

■ BILL CRAVER

Craver, William H. b: 6/1844, Troy, N.Y. d: 6/17/01, Troy, N.Y. BR/TR, 5'9", 160 lbs. Deb: 5/9/1871 M

YEAR	TM/L	G	AB	R	H	2B	3B	HR	RBI	BB	SO	AVG	OBP	SLG	OPS	OPS+	BR+	SB	CS	SBR	FA	FR	G/POS	TPR
1871	Tro-n	27	118	26	38	8	1	0	26	3	0	.322	.339	.407	746	112	2	6	3	0	.870	7	2-18/S-4,C-3,1OM	0.5
1872	Bal-n	35	179	55	50	3	2	0	23	5	2	.279	.299	.318	617	86	-4	7	1	1	.873	7	C-27/O-4R,2-2,3M	0.3
1873	Bal-n	41	196	45	57	9	2	0	28	2	3	.291	.298	.357	655	94	-1	2	3	-1	.917	5	C-22,S-15/O-7C,1-3	0.2
1874	Phi-n	55	265	68	91	19	11	0	56	4	2	.343	.353	.498	851	164	17	11	3	1	.807	6	*2-54/C-5,1-1	1.6
1875	Cen-n	14	65	8	18	4	2	0	5	2	4	.277	.299	.400	699	153	4	1	0	0	.773	4	/S-9,3-4,1-1,M	0.6
	Ath-n	54	260	71	83	11	11	2	40	4	5	.319	.330	.469	799	157	13	8	4	0	.856	-6	*2-54/C-2,3-1	0.3
	Yr	68	325	79	101	15	**13**	2	45	6	9	.311	.323	.455	779	156	16	9	4	1	.856	-2	2-54/S-9,3-5,C-2,1	0.9
1876	NY-N	56	248	24	55	4	0	0	22	2	7	.222	.230	.240	470	65	-7				.814	-21	2-42,C-11/S-6,M	-2.3
1877	Lou-N	57	238	33	63	5	2	0	29	5	11	.265	.280	.303	582	71	-9				.904	-1	*S-57	-0.7
Total	5 n	226	1083	273	337	54	29	2	178	20	16	.311	.324	.420	744	129	31	35	14	3	.834	22	2-128/C-59,S-28,O31	3.5
Total	2	113	486	57	118	9	2	0	51	7	18	.243	.255	.271	525	69	-16				.897	-22	/S-63,2-42,C-11	-3.0

■ PAT CRAWFORD

Crawford, Clifford Rankin b: 1/28/02, Society Hill, S.C. d: 1/25/94, Morehead City, N.C BL/TR, 5'11", 170 lbs. Deb: 4/18/29

YEAR	TM/L	G	AB	R	H	2B	3B	HR	RBI	BB	SO	AVG	OBP	SLG	OPS	OPS+	BR+	SB	CS	SBR	FA	FR	G/POS	TPR
1929	NY-N	65	57	13	17	3	0	3	24	11	5	.298	.412	.509	921	127	3	1			1.000	-0	/1-7,3-1	0.2
1930	NY-N	25	76	11	21	3	2	3	17	7	2	.276	.345	.487	832	100	-0	0			.966	-4	2-18/1-1	-0.3
	Cin-N	76	224	24	65	7	1	3	26	23	10	.290	.359	.371	729	81	-6	2			.969	-8	2-54,1-13	-1.3
	Yr	101	300	35	86	10	3	6	43	30	12	.287	.355	.400	755	86	-6	2			.968	-12	2-72,1-14	-1.6
1933	StL-N	91	224	24	60	8	2	0	21	14	9	.268	.317	.321	638	78	-6	1			.986	3	1-29,2-15/3-7	-0.6
1934	*StL-N	61	70	3	19	2	0	0	16	5	3	.271	.320	.300	620	63	-3	0			.900	2	/3-9,2-4	-0.1
Total	4	318	651	75	182	23	5	9	104	60	29	.280	.344	.372	716	85	-13	4			.969	-8	/2-91,1-50,3-17	-2.1

■ FORREST CRAWFORD

Crawford, Forrest A. b: 5/10/1881, Rockdale, Tex. d: 3/29/08, Austin, Tex. BL/TR, Deb: 7/30/06

YEAR	TM/L	G	AB	R	H	2B	3B	HR	RBI	BB	SO	AVG	OBP	SLG	OPS	OPS+	BR+	SB	CS	SBR	FA	FR	G/POS	TPR
1906	StL-N	45	145	8	30	3	1	0	11	7		.207	.248	.241	490	55	-8	1			.927	-10	S-39/3-6	-1.8
1907	StL-N	7	22	0	5	0	0	0	3	2		.227	.292	.227	519	65	-1	0			.912	-1	/S-7	-0.2
Total	2	52	167	8	35	3	1	0	14	9		.210	.254	.240	494	56	-9	1			.924	-11	/S-46,3-6	-2.0

■ GEORGE CRAWFORD

Crawford, George Deb: 10/8/1890

YEAR	TM/L	G	AB	R	H	2B	3B	HR	RBI	BB	SO	AVG	OBP	SLG	OPS	OPS+	BR+	SB	CS	SBR	FA	FR	G/POS	TPR
1890	Phi-a	5	17	1	2	0	0	0	3	0		.118	.118	.118	235	-31	-3	1			1.000	1	/O-4(0-0-4),S-1	-0.2

■ GLENN CRAWFORD

Crawford, Glenn Martin "Shorty" b: 12/2/13, North Branch, Mich.
d: 1/2/72, Saginaw, Mich. BL/TR, 5'9", 165 lbs. Deb: 4/22/45 Career OF: (7-LF 0-CF 32-RF)

YEAR	TM/L	G	AB	R	H	2B	3B	HR	RBI	BB	SO	AVG	OBP	SLG	OPS	OPS+	BR+	SB	CS	SBR	FA	FR	G/POS	TPR
1945	StL-N	4	3	0	0	0	0	0	0	1	0	.000	.250	.000	250	-26	-0	0			.000	-1	/O-1(1-0-0)	-0.1
	Phi-N	82	302	41	89	13	2	2	24	36	15	.295	.372	.371	743	110	5	5			.976	-2	O-38R,S-34,2-14	0.4
	Yr	86	305	41	89	13	2	2	24	37	15	.292	.370	.367	737	108	4	5			.976	-2	O-39R,S-34,2-14	0.3
1946	Phi-N	1	1	0	0	0	0	0	0	0	0	.000	.000	.000	0	-99	-0	0			.000	0	H	0.0
Total	2	87	306	41	89	13	2	2	24	37	15	.291	.369	.366	735	108	4	5			—	-2	/O-39R,S-34,2-14	0.3

■ KEN CRAWFORD

Crawford, Kenneth Daniel b: 10/31/1894, South Bend, Ind. d: 11/11/76, Pittsburgh, Pa. BL/TR, 5'9", 145 lbs. Deb: 9/6/15

YEAR	TM/L	G	AB	R	H	2B	3B	HR	RBI	BB	SO	AVG	OBP	SLG	OPS	OPS+	BR+	SB	CS	SBR	FA	FR	G/POS	TPR
1915	Bal-F	23	82	4	20	2	1	0	7	1	18	.244	.253	.293	546	52	-7	0			.978	-2	1-14/O-4(1-0-3)	-1.0

■ JAKE CRAWFORD

Crawford, Rufus b: 3/20/28, Campbell, Mo. BR/TR, 6'1.5", 185 lbs. Deb: 9/7/52

YEAR	TM/L	G	AB	R	H	2B	3B	HR	RBI	BB	SO	AVG	OBP	SLG	OPS	OPS+	BR+	SB	CS	SBR	FA	FR	G/POS	TPR
1952	StL-A	7	11	1	2	1	0	0	0	1	5	.182	.250	.273	523	44	-1	1	0	0	1.000	-0	/O-3(0-2-1)	-0.1

■ SAM CRAWFORD Crawford, Samuel Earl "Wahoo Sam" b: 4/18/1880, Wahoo, Neb. d: 6/15/68, Hollywood, Cal. BL/TL, 6', 190 lbs. Deb: 9/10/1899 H Career OF: (134-LF 479-CF 1687-RF)

YEAR	TM/L	G	AB	R	H	2B	3B	HR	RBI	BB	SO	AVG	OBP	SLG	OPS	OPS+	BR+	SB	CS	SBR	FA	FR	G/POS	TPR
1899	Cin-N	31	127	25	39	3	7	1	20	2		.307	.318	.465	782	111	1	6			.970	2	O-31(9-22-0)	0.1
1900	Cin-N	101	389	68	101	15	15	7	59	28		.260	.314	.429	744	107	2	14			.948	12	*O-95(70-12-12)	0.5
1901	Cin-N	131	515	91	170	20	16	**16**	104	37		.330	.378	.524	903	172	44	13			.923	3	*O-127(1-0-126)	4.0
1902	Cin-N	140	555	92	185	18	**22**	3	78	47		.333	.386	.461	848	147	30	16			.932	4	*O-140(7-0-133)	2.8
1903	Det-A	137	550	88	184	23	**25**	4	89	25		.335	.366	.489	855	159	38	18			.960	4	*O-137(45-0-92)	3.5
1904	Det-A	150	562	49	143	22	16	2	73	44		.254	.309	.361	670	115	9	20			.973	4	*O-150(1-0-149)	0.7
1905	Det-A	154	575	73	171	38	10	6	75	50		.297	.357	.430	786	148	30	22			**.988**	12	*O-103(0-0-103),1-51	4.0
1906	Det-A	145	563	65	166	25	16	2	72	38		.295	.341	.407	747	130	18	24			.984	1	*O-116(0-2-116),1-32	1.5
1907	*Det-A	144	582	**102**	188	34	17	4	81	37		.323	.366	.460	826	157	35	18			.965	9	*O-144(0-144-0)/1-2	4.0
1908	*Det-A	152	591	102	184	33	16	**7**	80	37		.311	.355	.457	812	157	34	15			.970	-8	*O-134(0-134-0),1-17	2.2
1909	*Det-A	156	589	83	185	**35**	14	6	97	47		.314	.366	.452	817	151	32	30			.965	-7	*O-139(0-139-0),1-18	2.1
1910	Det-A	154	588	83	170	26	**19**	5	**120**	37		.289	.332	.423	756	128	16	20			.963	-11	*O-153(0-26-127)/1-1	-0.1
1911	Det-A	146	574	109	217	36	14	7	115	61		.378	.438	.526	964	160	46	37			.975	-12	*O-146(0-0-146)	2.6
1912	Det-A	149	581	81	189	30	21	4	109	42		.325	.373	.470	843	145	31	41			.984	-17	*O-149(0-0-149)	0.6
1913	Det-A	153	609	78	193	32	**23**	9	83	52	28	.317	.371	.489	860	154	37	13			.964	-10	*O-140(0-0-140),1-13	2.0
1914	Det-A	157	582	74	183	22	**26**	8	**104**	69	31	.314	.388	.483	871	157	39	25	16	-0	.977	-8	*O-157(0-0-157)	2.5
1915	Det-A	156	612	81	183	31	**19**	4	**112**	66	29	.299	.367	.431	799	132	22	24	14	0	.974	-14	*O-156(0-0-156)	0.1
1916	Det-A	100	322	41	92	11	13	0	42	37	10	.286	.359	.401	760	124	9	10			.978	-10	O-79(1-0-78)/1-2	-0.6
1917	Det-A	61	104	6	18	4	0	2	12	4	6	.173	.204	.269	473	44	-7	0			.988	-3	1-15/O-3(0-0-3)	-1.2
Total	19	2517	9570	1391	2961	458	309	97	1525	760	104	.309	.362	.452	814	143	467	366	30		.965	-48	*O-2299R,1-151	31.3

■ WILLIE CRAWFORD Crawford, Willie Murphy b: 9/7/46, Los Angeles, Cal. BL/TL, 6'1", 205 lbs. Deb: 9/16/64 Career OF: (323-LF 40-CF 653-RF)

YEAR	TM/L	G	AB	R	H	2B	3B	HR	RBI	BB	SO	AVG	OBP	SLG	OPS	OPS+	BR+	SB	CS	SBR	FA	FR	G/POS	TPR
1964	LA-N	10	16	3	5	1	0	0	0	1	7	.313	.353	.375	728	113	0	1	1	-0	1.000	0	/O-4(1-0-3)	0.0
1965	*LA-N	52	27	10	4	0	0	0	0	2	8	.148	.207	.148	355	2	-3	2	0	0	1.000	-2	/O-8(2-1-5)	-0.5
1966	LA-N	6	0	1	0	0	0	0	0	0	0	—	—	—		—	0	0	0	0	.000	0	R	0.0
1967	LA-N	4	4	0	1	0	0	0	0	1	3	.250	.400	.250	650	98	0	0	0	0	.000	-1	/O-1(0-0-1)	-0.1
1968	LA-N	61	175	25	44	12	1	4	14	20	64	.251	.335	.400	735	130	6	1	3	-1	.966	3	O-48(45-1-4)	0.7
1969	LA-N	129	389	64	96	17	5	11	41	49	85	.247	.331	.401	732	112	6	4	5	-1	.973	-4	*O-113(56-22-38)	-0.4
1970	LA-N	109	299	48	70	8	6	8	40	33	88	.234	.314	.381	696	89	-5	4	4	-1	.960	-1	O-94(34-4-64)	-1.1
1971	LA-N	114	342	64	96	16	6	9	40	28	49	.281	.337	.442	778	126	11	5	2	0	.981	-7	O-97(63-5-35)	-0.1
1972	LA-N	96	243	28	61	7	3	8	27	35	55	.251	.350	.403	753	116	6	4	2	0	.983	-8	O-74(51-0-28)	-0.6
1973	LA-N	145	457	75	135	26	2	14	66	78	91	.295	.399	.453	852	142	28	12	5	1	.978	1	*O-138(11-5-125)	2.4
1974	*LA-N	139	468	73	138	23	4	11	61	64	88	.295	.380	.432	811	132	21	7	8	-1	.966	-7	*O-133(0-2-132)	0.6
1975	LA-N	124	373	46	98	15	2	9	46	49	43	.263	.348	.386	734	108	4	5	5	-1	.990	-5	*O-113(25-0-93)	-0.7
1976	StL-N	120	392	49	119	17	5	9	50	37	53	.304	.365	.441	806	127	14	2	1	0	.982	-1	*O-107(3-0-105)	0.8
1977	Hou-N	42	114	14	29	3	0	2	18	16	10	.254	.346	.333	679	91	-1	0	0	0	.959	-2	O-30(30-0-0)	-0.4
	Oak-A	59	136	7	25	7	1	1	16	18	20	.184	.279	.272	551	52	-9	0	0	0	.978	2	O-22(2-0-20),D-18	-0.8
Total	14	1210	3435	507	921	152	35	86	419	431	664	.268	.351	.408	759	117	78	47	36	-2	.975	-30	O-982R/D-18	-0.2

■ GEORGE CREAMER Creamer, George W. (b: George W. Triebel) b: 1855, Philadelphia, Pa. d: 6/27/1886, Philadelphia, Pa. BR/TR, 6'2", Deb: 5/1/1878 M Career OF: (0-LF 17-CF 5-RF)

YEAR	TM/L	G	AB	R	H	2B	3B	HR	RBI	BB	SO	AVG	OBP	SLG	OPS	OPS+	BR+	SB	CS	SBR	FA	FR	G/POS	TPR
1878	Mil-N	50	193	30	41	7	3	0	15	5	15	.212	.232	.280	512	63	-8				.839	-5	2-28,O-17(0-16-4)/3-6	-1.1
1879	Syr-N	15	60	3	13	2	0	0	3	1	2	.217	.230	.250	480	65	-2				.825	-10	2-10/S-3,O-2(0-1-1)	-1.0
1880	Wor-N	85	306	40	61	6	3	0	27	4	21	.199	.210	.239	448	47	-17				.883	-7	*2-85	-1.9
1881	Wor-N	80	309	42	64	9	2	0	25	11	27	.207	.234	.249	484	49	-18				.904	-9	*2-80	-2.2
1882	Wor-N	81	286	27	65	16	6	1	29	14	24	.227	.263	.336	599	88	-4				.907	11	*2-81	1.0
1883	Pit-a	91	369	54	94	7	9	0		20		.255	.293	.322	616	102	2				.897	8	*2-91	1.2
1884	Pit-a	98	339	38	62	8	5	0		16		.183	.224	.236	460	51	-18				**.937**	16	*2-98,M	0.2
Total	7	500	1862	234	400	55	28	1	99	71	89	.215	.244	.276	520	67	-64				.901	6	2-473/O-19C,3-6,S-3	-3.8

■ JOE CREDE Crede, Joseph b: 4/26/78, Jefferson City, Mo. BR/TR, 6'3", 195 lbs. Deb: 9/12/2000

YEAR	TM/L	G	AB	R	H	2B	3B	HR	RBI	BB	SO	AVG	OBP	SLG	OPS	OPS+	BR+	SB	CS	SBR	FA	FR	G/POS	TPR
2000	Chi-A	7	14	2	5	1	0	0	3	0	3	.357	.357	.429	786	97	-0	0	0	0	.933	2	/3-6,D-1	0.2

■ BIRDIE CREE Cree, William Franklin b: 10/23/1882, Khedive, Pa. d: 11/8/42, Sunbury, Pa. BR/TR, 5'6", 150 lbs. Deb: 9/17/08 Career OF: (389-LF 258-CF 44-RF)

YEAR	TM/L	G	AB	R	H	2B	3B	HR	RBI	BB	SO	AVG	OBP	SLG	OPS	OPS+	BR+	SB	CS	SBR	FA	FR	G/POS	TPR
1908	NY-A	21	78	5	21	0	2	0	4	7		.269	.345	.321	665	115	2	1			1.000	1	O-21(0-21-0)	0.1
1909	NY-A	104	343	48	90	6	3	2	27	30		.262	.338	.315	653	105	3	10			.949	-7	O-79C/S-6,2-4,3-1	-0.8
1910	NY-A	134	467	58	134	19	16	4	73	40		.287	.353	.422	775	135	18	28			.955	-13	*O-134(49-85-0)	-0.1
1911	NY-A	137	520	90	181	30	22	4	88	56		.348	.415	.513	928	149	33	48			.964	0	*O-132L/S-4,2-2	2.7
1912	NY-A	50	190	25	63	11	6	0	22	20		.332	.409	.453	862	138	10	12			.948	5	O-50(50-0-0)	1.2
1913	NY-A	145	534	51	145	25	6	1	63	50	51	.272	.338	.346	685	100	0	22			**.988**	-4	*O-144(144-0-0)	-1.1
1914	NY-A	77	275	45	85	18	5	0	40	30	24	.309	.389	.411	800	141	14	4	9	-2	.976	7	O-76(0-76-0)	1.5
1915	NY-A	74	196	23	42	8	2	0	15	36	22	.214	.353	.276	628	88	-1	7	8	-1	.945	-3	O-53(0-37-16)	-0.9
Total	8	742	2603	345	761	117	62	11	332	269	97	.292	.368	.398	766	124	79	132	17		.965	-13	O-689L/S-10,2-6,3-1	2.6

■ CONNIE CREEDEN Creeden, Cornelius Stephen b: 7/21/15, Danvers, Mass. d: 11/30/69, Santa Ana, Cal. BL/TL, 6'1", 200 lbs. Deb: 4/28/43

YEAR	TM/L	G	AB	R	H	2B	3B	HR	RBI	BB	SO	AVG	OBP	SLG	OPS	OPS+	BR+	SB	CS	SBR	FA	FR	G/POS	TPR
1943	Bos-N	5	4	0	1	0	0	0	1	1	0	.250	.400	.250	650	91	0	0			.000	0	H	0.0

■ PAT CREEDEN Creeden, Patrick Francis "Whoops" b: 5/23/06, Newburyport, Mass. d: 4/20/92, Brockton, Mass. BL/TR, 5'8", 175 lbs. Deb: 4/14/31

YEAR	TM/L	G	AB	R	H	2B	3B	HR	RBI	BB	SO	AVG	OBP	SLG	OPS	OPS+	BR+	SB	CS	SBR	FA	FR	G/POS	TPR
1931	Bos-A	5	8	0	0	0	0	0	0	1	3	.000	.111	.000	111	-73	-2	0	0	0	.846	0	/2-2	-0.2

■ MARTY CREEGAN Creegan, Martin b: San Francisco, Cal. 161 lbs. Deb: 4/17/1884

YEAR	TM/L	G	AB	R	H	2B	3B	HR	RBI	BB	SO	AVG	OBP	SLG	OPS	OPS+	BR+	SB	CS	SBR	FA	FR	G/POS	TPR
1884	Was-U	9	33	4	5	0	0	0		1		.152	.176	.152	328	0	-5				.667	-1	/O-6C,C-3,3-2,1-1	-0.5

■ GUS CREELY Creely, August L. b: 6/6/1870, Florissant, Mo. d: 4/22/34, St.Louis, Mo. 5'6", 150 lbs. Deb: 10/9/1890

YEAR	TM/L	G	AB	R	H	2B	3B	HR	RBI	BB	SO	AVG	OBP	SLG	OPS	OPS+	BR+	SB	CS	SBR	FA	FR	G/POS	TPR
1890	StL-a	4	15	0	0	0	0	0	0	0		.000	.000	.000	0	-88	-4	1			.769	-3	/S-4	-0.6

■ PETE CREGAN Cregan, Peter James "Peekskill Pete" b: 4/13/1875, Kingston, N.Y. d: 5/18/45, New York, N.Y. BR/TR, 5'7.5", 150 lbs. Deb: 9/8/1899

YEAR	TM/L	G	AB	R	H	2B	3B	HR	RBI	BB	SO	AVG	OBP	SLG	OPS	OPS+	BR+	SB	CS	SBR	FA	FR	G/POS	TPR
1899	NY-N	1	2	0	0	0	0	0	0	0		.000	.000	.000	0	-99	-1	0			1.000	-0	/O-1(0-0-1)	-0.1
1903	Cin-N	6	19	0	2	0	0	0	0	1		.105	.190	.105	296	-13	-3	0			.769	-1	/O-6(5-0-1)	-0.4
Total	2	7	21	0	2	0	0	0	0	1		.095	.174	.095	269	-21	-3	0			.786	-2	/O-7(5-0-2)	-0.5

■ BERNIE CREGER Creger, Bernard Odell b: 3/21/27, Wytheville, Va. d: 11/30/97, Lynchburg, Va. BR/TR, 6', 175 lbs. Deb: 4/29/47

YEAR	TM/L	G	AB	R	H	2B	3B	HR	RBI	BB	SO	AVG	OBP	SLG	OPS	OPS+	BR+	SB	CS	SBR	FA	FR	G/POS	TPR
1947	StL-N	15	16	3	3	1	0	0	0	1	3	.188	.235	.250	485	28	-2	1			.828	-3	S-13	-0.5

■ CREEPY CRESPI Crespi, Frank Angelo Joseph b: 2/16/18, St.Louis, Mo. d: 3/1/90, Florissant, Mo. BR/TR, 5'8.5", 175 lbs. Deb: 9/14/38

YEAR	TM/L	G	AB	R	H	2B	3B	HR	RBI	BB	SO	AVG	OBP	SLG	OPS	OPS+	BR+	SB	CS	SBR	FA	FR	G/POS	TPR
1938	StL-N	7	19	2	5	2	0	0	1	2	7	.263	.333	.368	702	88	-0	0			.813	-2	/S-7	-0.2
1939	StL-N	15	29	3	5	1	0	0	6	3	6	.172	.250	.207	457	23	-3	0			.962	-0	/2-6,S-4	-0.3
1940	StL-N	3	11	2	3	1	0	0	0	1	2	.273	.333	.364	697	87	-0	1			1.000	-1	/3-2,S-1	-0.1
1941	StL-N	146	560	85	156	24	2	4	46	57	58	.279	.355	.350	705	93	-4	3			.962	0	*2-145	0.6
1942	*StL-N	93	292	33	71	4	2	0	35	27	29	.243	.309	.271	580	65	-12	4			.967	-5	2-83/S-5	-1.2
Total	5	264	911	125	240	32	4	4	88	90	102	.263	.336	.321	657	82	-19	8			.963	-7	2-234/S-17,3-2	-1.2

■ FELIPE CRESPO Crespo, Felipe Javier (Clausio) b: 3/5/73, Rio Piedras, P.R. BB/TR, 5'11", 195 lbs. Deb: 4/28/96 Career OF: (37-LF 1-CF 33-RF)

YEAR	TM/L	G	AB	R	H	2B	3B	HR	RBI	BB	SO	AVG	OBP	SLG	OPS	OPS+	BR+	SB	CS	SBR	FA	FR	G/POS	TPR
1996	Tor-A	22	49	6	9	4	0	0	4	12	13	.184	.375	.265	640	66	-2	1	0	0	.982	3	2-10/3-6,1-2	0.2
1997	Tor-A	12	28	3	8	0	1	1	5	2	4	.286	.333	.464	798	105	0	0	0	0	.933	-1	/3-7,2-1,D-2	-0.1
1998	Tor-A	66	130	11	34	8	1	1	15	15	27	.262	.347	.362	708	84	-3	4	3	-0	1.000	-7	O-42R/2-8,3-2,1D	-1.0
2000	*SF-N	89	131	17	38	6	1	4	29	10	23	.290	.359	.443	801	108	2	3	2	-0	.962	-10	O-26L,1-11/2-7,D-1	-0.9
Total	4	189	338	37	89	18	3	6	53	39	67	.263	.355	.388	742	92	-3	8	5	0	.988	-15	/O-68L,2-26,3-15,1D	-1.8

YEAR	TM/L	G	AB	R	H	2B	3B	HR	RBI	BB	SO	AVG	OBP	SLG	OPS	OPS+	BR+	SB	CS	SBR	FA	FR	G/POS	TPR
■ **LOU CRIGER**	Criger, Louis b: 2/3/1872, Elkhart, Ind. d: 5/14/34, Tucson, Ariz. BR/TR, 5'10", 165 lbs. Deb: 9/21/1896 Career OF: (1-LF 0-CF 0-RF)																							
1896	Cle-N	2	5	0	0	0	0	0	0	1	0	.000	.167	.000	167	-51	-1	1			1.000	1	/C-1	0.0
1897	Cle-N	39	138	15	31	4	1	0	22	23		.225	.340	.268	608	58	-8	5			.937	-1	C-37/1-2	-0.5
1898	Cle-N	84	287	43	80	13	4	1	32	40		.279	.377	.362	739	113	7	2			.957	15	C-82	2.7
1899	StL-N	77	258	39	66	4	5	2	44	28		.256	.333	.333	667	81	-6	14			.949	2	C-75	0.2
1900	StL-N	80	288	31	78	8	6	2	38	4		.271	.286	.361	647	78	-10	5			.953	6	C-75/3-1	0.3
1901	Bos-A	76	268	26	62	6	3	0	24	11		.231	.270	.276	546	52	-17	7			.967	22	C-68/1-8	1.0
1902	Bos-A	83	266	32	68	16	6	0	28	27		.256	.324	.361	685	87	-5	7			.965	14	C-80/O-1(1-0-0)	1.6
1903	*Bos-A	96	317	41	61	7	10	3	31	26		.192	.256	.306	562	65	-14	5			.979	23	C-96	1.9
1904	Bos-A	98	299	34	63	10	5	2	34	27		.211	.283	.298	580	79	-7	1			.981	19	C-95	2.4
1905	Bos-A	109	313	33	62	6	7	1	36	54		.198	.322	.272	593	88	-2	5			.972	5	*C-109	1.5
1906	Bos-A	7	17	0	3	1	0	0	1	1		.176	.222	.235	458	43	-1	1			.981	5	/C-6	0.4
1907	Bos-A	75	226	12	41	4	0	0	14	19		.181	.251	.199	450	44	-14	2			.978	-0	C-75	-0.7
1908	Bos-A	84	237	12	45	4	2	0	25	13		.190	.232	.224	456	47	-14	1			.980	13	C-84	0.8
1909	StL-A	74	212	15	36	1	1	0	9	25		.170	.261	.184	444	44	-13	2			.986	8	C-73	0.3
1910	NY-A	27	69	3	13	2	0	0	4	10		.188	.291	.217	509	56	-3	0			.993	-1	C-27	-0.3
1912	StL-A	1	2	1	0	0	0	0	0	0		.000	.000	.000	0	-99	-1	0			1.000	1	/C-1	0.0
Total	16	1012	3202	337	709	86	50	11	342	309	0	.221	.295	.290	584	72	-107	58			.971	130	C-984/1-10,O-1L,3-1	11.6
■ **DAVE CRIPE**	Cripe, David Gordon b: 4/7/51, Ramona, Cal. BR/TR, 6', 180 lbs. Deb: 9/10/78																							
1978	KC-A	7	13	1	2	0	0	0	1	0	2	.154	.154	.154	308	-13	-2	0	0	0	1.000	-2	/3-5	-0.4
■ **DAVE CRISCIONE**	Criscione, David Gerald b: 9/2/51, Dunkirk, N.Y. BR/TR, 5'8", 185 lbs. Deb: 7/17/77																							
1977	Bal-A	7	9	1	3	0	0	1	1	0	1	.333	.333	.667	1000	176	1	0	0	0	1.000	-1	/C-7	0.0
■ **TONY CRISCOLA**	Criscola, Anthony Paul b: 7/9/15, Walla Walla, Wash. BL/TR, 5'11.5", 180 lbs. Deb: 4/15/42																							
1942	StL-A	91	158	17	47	9	2	1	13	8	13	.297	.331	.399	730	103	0	2	2	-0	.955	-14	O-52(37-13-2)	-1.6
1943	StL-A	29	52	4	8	0	0	0	1	8	7	.154	.267	.154	421	24	-5	0	0	0	.960	-2	O-13(10-2-1)	-0.8
1944	Cin-N	64	157	14	36	3	2	0	14	14	12	.229	.297	.274	570	64	-7	0			.977	2	O-35(3-0-32)	-0.8
Total	3	184	367	35	91	12	4	1	28	30	32	.248	.307	.311	617	75	-12	2	2		.966	-15	O-100(50-15-35)	-3.2
■ **PAT CRISHAM**	Crisham, Patrick J. b: 6/4/1877, Amesbury, Mass. d: 6/12/15, Syracuse, N.Y. 6', 168 lbs. Deb: 5/5/1899																							
1899	Bal-N	53	172	23	50	5	3	0	20	4		.291	.311	.355	665	78	-6	4			.979	-5	1-26,C-22	-0.8
■ **JOE CRISP**	Crisp, Joseph Shelby b: 7/8/1889, Higginsville, Mo. d: 2/5/39, Kansas City, Mo. BR/TR, 6'4", 200 lbs. Deb: 9/2/10																							
1910	StL-A	1	1	0	0	0	0	0	0	0		.000	.000	.000	0	-99	-0	0			1.000	-0	/C-1	0.0
1911	StL-A	1	1	0	1	0	0	0	0	0		1.000	1.000	1.000	2000	477	0	0			.000	0	/H	0.0
Total	2	2	2	0	1	0	0	0	0	0		.500	.500	.500	1000	206	0	0			1.000	-0	/C-1	0.0
■ **DODE CRISS**	Criss, Dode b: 3/12/1885, Sherman, Miss. d: 9/8/55, Sherman, Miss. BL/TR, 6'2", 200 lbs. Deb: 4/20/08 Career OF: (0-LF 0-CF 11-RF)																							
1908	StL-A	64	82	15	28	6	0	0	14	9		.341	.407	.415	821	166	6	1			.933	-1	O-11(0-0-11)/P-9,1-1	0.5
1909	StL-A	35	48	2	14	6	1	0	7	0		.292	.306	.458	764	152	2	0			1.000	-1	P-11	0.0
1910	StL-A	70	91	11	21	4	2	1	11	11		.231	.320	.352	672	118	2	2			.983	-1	1-11/P-6	0.0
1911	StL-A	58	83	10	21	3	1	2	15	11		.253	.347	.386	733	109	1	0			.956	-2	1-14/P-4	-0.1
Total	4	227	304	38	84	19	4	3	47	31		.276	.349	.395	744	133	11	3			.964	-5	/P-30,1-26,O-11R	0.4
■ **CHES CRIST**	Crist, Chester Arthur "Squak" b: 2/10/1882, Cozaddale, Ohio d: 1/7/57, Cincinnati, Ohio BR/TR, 5'11", 165 lbs. Deb: 5/18/06																							
1906	Phi-N	6	11	1	0	0	0	0	0	0		.000	.083	.000	83	-74	-2	0			.800	-3	/C-6	-0.6
■ **HUGHIE CRITZ**	Critz, Hugh Melville b: 9/17/1900, Starkville, Miss. d: 1/10/80, Greenwood, Miss. BR/TR, 5'8", 147 lbs. Deb: 5/31/24																							
1924	Cin-N	102	413	67	133	15	14	3	35	19	18	.322	.352	.448	800	115	7	19	11	0	.956	3	2-96/S-1	1.3
1925	Cin-N	144	541	74	150	14	8	2	51	34	17	.277	.321	.344	665	72	-23	13	13	-2	.970	22	*2-144	0.1
1926	Cin-N	155	607	96	164	24	14	3	79	39	25	.270	.316	.371	687	87	-12	7			**.981**	**24**	*2-155	1.6
1927	Cin-N	113	396	50	110	10	8	4	49	16	18	.278	.306	.374	680	84	-10	7			.969	-2	*2-113	-0.9
1928	Cin-N	153	641	95	190	21	11	5	52	37	24	.296	.335	.387	722	90	-11	18			.971	-17	*2-153	-2.3
1929	Cin-N	107	425	55	105	17	9	1	50	27	21	.247	.292	.336	629	58	-29	9			**.974**	4	*2-106/S-1	-2.0
1930	Cin-N	28	104	15	24	3	2	0	11	6	6	.231	.273	.298	571	40	-10	1			.987	-3	2-28	-1.1
	NY-N	124	558	93	148	17	11	4	50	24	26	.265	.296	.357	652	58	-39	7			.972	5	*2-124	-2.7
	Yr	152	662	108	172	20	13	4	61	30	32	.260	.292	.347	639	55	-49	8			**.974**	2	*2-152	-3.8
1931	NY-N	66	238	33	69	7	2	4	17	8	17	.290	.313	.387	700	89	-4	4			.984	0	2-54	0.0
1932	NY-N	151	659	90	182	32	7	2	50	34	27	.276	.313	.355	668	81	-18	3			.974	1	*2-151	-0.7
1933	*NY-N	133	558	68	137	18	5	2	33	23	24	.246	.279	.306	586	68	-23	4			**.982**	**47**	*2-133	3.3
1934	NY-N	137	571	77	138	17	1	6	40	19	24	.242	.269	.306	575	55	-37	3			**.978**	**25**	*2-137	-0.3
1935	NY-N	65	219	19	41	0	3	2	14	3	10	.187	.198	.242	440	18	-25	2			.966	3	2-59	-1.9
Total	12	1478	5930	832	1591	195	95	38	531	289	257	.268	.303	.352	656	74	-234	97	24		.974	111	*2-1453/S-2	-5.6
■ **DAVEY CROCKETT**	Crockett, Daniel Solomon b: 10/5/1875, Roanoke, Va. d: 2/23/61, Charlottesville, Va. BL/TR, 6'1", 175 lbs. Deb: 7/11/01																							
1901	Det-A	28	102	10	29	2	2	0	14	6		.284	.336	.343	680	85	-2	1			.968	-0	1-27	-0.3
■ **ART CROFT**	Croft, Arthur F. b: 1/23/1855, St.Louis, Mo. d: 3/16/1884, St.Louis, Mo. Deb: 5/4/1875 Career OF: (34-LF 1-CF 1-RF)																							
1875	RS-n	19	75	5	15	3	0	0	2	0	2	.200	.200	.240	440	58	-3	5	1	1	.800	-4	O-19(10-7-2)	-0.5
1877	StL-N	54	220	23	51	5	2	0	27	1	15	.232	.235	.273	508	63	-9				.971	-3	1-28,O-25(25-1-1)/2-1	-1.3
1878	Ind-N	60	222	22	35	6	0	0	16	5	23	.158	.176	.185	361	22	-17				.963	-1	*1-51/O-9(9-0-0)	-2.0
Total	2	114	442	45	86	11	2	0	43	6	38	.195	.205	.229	434	43	-26				.965	-4	/1-79,O-34L,2-1	-3.3
■ **HARRY CROFT**	Croft, Henry T. b: 8/1/1875, Chicago, Ill. d: 12/11/33, Oak Park, Ill. Deb: 5/19/1899																							
1899	Lou-N	2	2	0	0	0	0	0	0	0		.000	.000	.000	0	-99	-1	0			.000	0	/H	0.0
	Phi-N	2	7	0	1	0	0	0	0	1		.143	.250	.143	393	9	-1	0			1.000	-1	/2-2	-0.1
	Yr	4	9	0	1	0	0	0	0	1		.111	.200	.111	311	-14	-1	0			1.000	-1	/2-2	-0.1
1901	Chi-N	3	12	1	4	0	0	0	4	0		.333	.333	.333	667	97	-0	0			1.000	2	/O-3(0-0-3)	0.2
Total	2	7	21	1	5	0	0	0	4	1		.238	.273	.238	511	47	-1	0			1.000	2	/O-3(0-0-3),2-2	0.1
■ **FRED CROLIUS**	Crolius, Fred Joseph b: 12/16/1876, Jersey City, N.J. d: 8/25/60, Ormond Beach, Fla. Deb: 4/19/01																							
1901	Bos-N	49	200	22	48	4	1	1	13	9		.240	.306	.285	591	66	-8	6			.850	-8	O-49(0-3-46)	-1.8
1902	Pit-N	9	38	4	10	2	1	0	7	0		.263	.263	.368	632	91	-1	0			1.000	-1	/O-9(0-0-9)	-0.2
Total	2	58	238	26	58	6	2	1	20	9		.244	.300	.298	598	69	-9	6			.868	-8	/O-58(0-3-55)	-2.0
■ **WARREN CROMARTIE**	Cromartie, Warren Livingston b: 9/29/53, Miami Beach, Fla. BL/TL, 6', 192 lbs. Deb: 9/6/74 Career OF: (487-LF 1-CF 296-RF)																							
1974	Mon-N	8	17	2	3	0	0	0	0	3	3	.176	.300	.176	476	34	-1	1	0	0	1.000	-1	/O-6(6-0-0)	-0.2
1976	Mon-N	33	81	8	17	1	0	0	2	1	5	.210	.220	.222	442	25	-8	1	2	-0	.943	-2	O-20(5-0-16)	-1.2
1977	Mon-N	155	620	64	175	41	7	5	50	33	40	.282	.323	.395	718	94	-6	10	3	1	.976	12	*O-155(153-0-4)	0.0
1978	Mon-N	159	607	77	180	32	6	10	56	33	60	.297	.340	.418	758	112	9	8	8	-1	.978	25	*O-158(157-0-1)/1-4	2.6
1979	Mon-N	158	659	84	181	46	5	8	46	38	78	.275	.315	.396	711	94	-7	8	7	-1	.976	20	*O-158(158-0-0)	0.5
1980	Mon-N	162	597	74	172	33	5	14	70	51	64	.288	.346	.430	777	115	12	8	8	-1	.991	-4	*1-158/O-2(2-0-0)	-0.4
1981	*Mon-N	99	358	41	109	19	2	6	42	39	27	.304	.373	.419	792	123	11	2	3	-1	.992	-1	1-62,O-38(0-0-38)	0.4
1982	Mon-N	144	497	59	126	24	3	14	62	69	60	.254	.348	.398	746	106	5	3	0	1	.979	11	*O-136(2-0-135)/1-9	1.0
1983	Mon-N	120	360	37	100	26	2	3	43	43	48	.278	.356	.386	743	106	4	8	3	1	.973	12	*O-101(0-0-101)/1-1	1.3
1991	KC-A	69	131	13	41	7	2	1	20	15	18	.313	.384	.420	803	122	4	1	3	-1	.996	-4	1-29/O-6(4-1-1),D-1	-0.3
Total	10	1107	3927	459	1104	229	32	61	391	325	403	.281	.339	.402	741	105	22	50	37	-2	.977	68	O-780L,1-263/D-1	3.7
■ **D.T. CROMER**	Cromer, David Thomas b: 3/19/71, Lake City, S.C. BL/TL, 6'2", 190 lbs. Deb: 4/5/2000 F																							
2000	Cin-N	35	47	7	16	4	0	2	8	1	14	.340	.367	.553	921	123	2	0	0	0	.964	-1	1-13	0.0

YEAR	TM/L	G	AB	R	H	2B	3B	HR	RBI	BB	SO	AVG	OBP	SLG	OPS	OPS+	BR+	SB	CS	SBR	FA	FR	G/POS	TPR
■ **TRIPP CROMER**	Cromer, Roy Bunyan b: 11/21/67, Lake City, S.C. BR/TR, 6'2", 165 lbs. Deb: 9/7/93 F																							
1993	StL-N	10	23	1	2	0	0	0	0	1	6	.087	.125	.087	212	-43	-5	0	0	0	.912	1	/S-9	-0.3
1994	StL-N	2	0	1	0	0	0	0	0	0	0	—	—	—	—	—	0	0	0	0	.000	-1	/S-2	-0.1
1995	StL-N	105	345	36	78	19	0	5	18	14	66	.226	.264	.325	589	54	-23	0	0	0	.960	2	S-95,2-11	-1.4
1997	LA-N	28	86	8	25	3	0	4	20	6	16	.291	.337	.465	802	116	2	0	1	-0	.968	-3	2-17,S-10/3-1	0.0
1998	LA-N	6	6	1	1	0	0	1	1	0	2	.167	.167	.667	833	113	0	0	0	0	.000	0	/H	0.0
1999	LA-N	33	52	5	10	0	0	2	8	5	10	.192	.263	.308	571	46	-4	0	0	0	1.000	6	/2-9,S-9,3-2,O-2L,1	0.2
2000	Hou-N	9	8	2	1	0	0	0	0	1	1	.125	.222	.125	347	-9	-1	0	0	0	.500	-1	/3-2,2-1,S-1	-0.2
Total	7	193	520	54	117	22	0	12	47	27	101	.225	.269	.337	605	59	-32	0	1	-0	.959	4	S-126/2-38,3-5,O1	-1.8
■ **NED CROMPTON**	Crompton, Edward b: 2/12/1889, Liverpool, England d: 9/28/50, Aspinwall, Pa. BL/TL, 5'10.5", 175 lbs. Deb: 9/13/09																							
1909	StL-A	17	63	7	10	2	1	0	2	7		.159	.254	.222	476	54	-3	1			.909	1	O-17(17-0-0)	-0.4
1910	Cin-N	1	2	0	0	0	0	0	0	0	2	.000	.000	.000	0	-99	-1	0			.000	-1	/O-1(0-1-0)	-0.1
Total	2	18	65	7	10	2	1	0	2	7	2	.154	.247	.215	462	49	-4	1			.909	1	/O-18(17-1-0)	-0.5
■ **HERB CROMPTON**	Crompton, Herbert Bryan "Workhorse" b: 11/7/11, Taylor Ridge, Ill. d: 8/5/63, Moline, Ill. BR/TR, 6', 185 lbs. Deb: 4/26/37																							
1937	Was-A	2	3	0	1	0	0	0	0	0	0	.333	.333	.333	667	72	-0	0	0	0	1.000	0	/C-2	0.0
1945	NY-A	36	99	6	19	3	0	0	12	2	7	.192	.208	.222	430	24	-10	0	0	0	.984	1	C-33	-0.8
Total	2	38	102	6	20	3	0	0	12	2	7	.196	.212	.225	437	25	-10	0	0	0	.984	1	/C-35	-0.8
■ **CHRIS CRON**	Cron, Christopher John b: 3/31/64, Albuquerque, N.Mex. BR/TR, 6'2", 200 lbs. Deb: 8/15/91																							
1991	Cal-A	6	15	0	2	0	0	0	0	2	5	.133	.235	.133	369	5	-2	0	0	0	1.000	2	/1-5,D-1	-0.1
1992	Chi-A	6	10	0	0	0	0	0	0	0	4	.000	.000	.000	0	-99	-3	0	0	0	.923	-1	/1-5,O-1(1-0-0)	-0.3
Total	2	12	25	0	2	0	0	0	0	2	9	.080	.148	.080	228	-35	-5	0	0	0	.980	1	/1-10,O-1(1-0-0),D-1	-0.4
■ **DAN CRONIN**	Cronin, Daniel T. b: 4/1/1857, S.Boston, Mass. d: 11/30/1885, Boston, Mass. 5'8", 170 lbs. Deb: 7/9/1884																							
1884	CP-U	1	4	1	1	0	0	0		0		.250	.250	.250	500	52	-0				.200	-2	/2-1	-0.2
	StL-U	1	5	0	0	0	0	0		0		.000	.000	.000	0	-97	-1				.000	-1	/O-1(1-0-0)	-0.2
	Yr	2	9	1	1	0	0	0		0		.111	.111	.111	222	-32	-2				.000	-3	/2-1,O-1(1-0-0)	-0.4
■ **JIM CRONIN**	Cronin, James John b: 8/7/05, Richmond, Cal. d: 6/10/83, Concord, Cal. BB/TR, 5'10.5", 150 lbs. Deb: 7/4/29																							
1929	Phi-A	25	56	7	13	2	1	0	4	5	7	.232	.295	.304	599	52	-4	0	0	0	.966	5	2-10/S-9,3-4	0.2
■ **JOE CRONIN**	Cronin, Joseph Edward b: 10/12/06, San Francisco, Cal d: 9/7/84, Barnstable, Mass. BR/TR, 5'11.5", 180 lbs. Deb: 4/29/26 MH Career OF: (1-LF 0-CF 0-RF)																							
1926	Pit-N	38	83	9	22	2	2	0	11	6	15	.265	.315	.337	652	72	-3	0			.977	6	2-27/S-7	0.3
1927	Pit-N	12	22	2	5	1	0	0	3	2	3	.227	.292	.273	564	48	-2	0			1.000	-4	/2-7,S-4,1-1	-0.5
1928	Was-A	63	227	23	55	10	4	0	25	22	27	.242	.309	.322	631	66	-11	4	0	1	.953	8	S-63	0.4
1929	Was-A	145	494	72	139	29	8	8	61	85	37	.281	.388	.421	809	107	8	5	9	-2	.923	6	*S-143/2-1	2.6
1930	Was-A	154	587	127	203	41	9	13	126	72	36	.346	.422	.513	934	135	33	17	10	0	.960	26	*S-154	6.8
1931	Was-A	156	611	103	187	44	13	12	126	81	52	.306	.391	.480	870	127	25	10	9	-1	.950	13	*S-155	4.4
1932	Was-A	143	557	95	177	43	**18**	6	116	66	45	.318	.393	.492	885	129	25	7	5	-0	**.959**	6	*S-141	3.8
1933	*Was-A★	152	602	89	186	**45**	11	5	118	87	49	.309	.398	.445	843	124	23	5	4	-0	**.960**	10	*S-152,M	4.1
1934	Was-A★	127	504	68	143	30	9	7	101	53	28	.284	.353	.421	774	103	1	8	0	2	.951	18	*S-127,M	2.9
1935	Bos-A★	144	556	70	164	37	14	9	95	63	40	.295	.370	.460	830	106	5	3	3	-0	.949	-13	*S-139/1-2,M	0.1
1936	Bos-A	81	295	36	83	22	4	2	43	32	21	.281	.354	.403	757	82	-9	1	3	-1	.930	-2	S-60,3-21,M	-0.6
1937	Bos-A★	148	570	102	175	40	4	18	110	84	73	.307	.402	.486	887	118	17	5	3	0	.958	-13	*S-148,M	1.4
1938	Bos-A★	143	530	98	172	**51**	5	17	94	91	60	.325	.428	.536	964	134	29	7	5	-0	.954	7	*S-142,M	4.2
1939	Bos-A★	143	520	97	160	33	3	19	107	87	48	.308	.407	.492	899	124	20	6	6	-1	.959	6	*S-142,M	3.3
1940	Bos-A	149	548	104	156	35	6	24	111	83	65	.285	.380	.502	882	122	18	7	5	-0	.948	2	*S-146/3-2,M	2.8
1941	Bos-A★	143	518	98	161	38	8	16	95	82	55	.311	.406	.508	914	137	29	1	4	-1	.958	-8	*S-119,3-22/O-1L,M	2.7
1942	Bos-A	45	79	7	24	3	0	4	24	15	21	.304	.415	.494	909	150	6	0	1	-0	.865	-1	3-11/1-5,S-1,M	0.5
1943	Bos-A	59	77	8	24	4	0	5	29	11	4	.312	.398	.558	956	176	7	0	0	0	.968	0	3-10,M	0.8
1944	Bos-A	76	191	24	46	7	0	5	28	34	19	.241	.358	.356	714	106	3	1	4	-1	.981	-2	1-49,M	-0.3
1945	Bos-A	3	8	1	3	0	0	0	1	3	2	.375	.545	.375	920	165	1	0	0	0	1.000	1	/3-3,M	0.2
Total	20	2124	7579	1233	2285	515	118	170	1424	1059	700	.301	.390	.468	857	119	225	87	71		.951	68	*S-1843/3-69,1-57,2O	39.9
■ **BILL CRONIN**	Cronin, William Patrick "Crungy" b: 12/26/02, W.Newton, Mass. d: 10/26/66, Newton, Mass. BR/TR, 5'9", 167 lbs. Deb: 7/4/28																							
1928	Bos-N	3	2	1	0	0	0	0	0	1	0	.000	.333	.000	333	-6	-0	0			1.000	-0	/C-3	0.0
1929	Bos-N	6	9	0	1	0	0	0	0	0	0	.111	.111	.111	222	-47	-2	0			1.000	1	/C-6	-0.1
1930	Bos-N	66	178	19	45	9	1	0	17	4	8	.253	.277	.315	592	44	-16	0			.983	7	C-64	-0.5
1931	Bos-N	51	107	8	22	6	1	0	10	7	5	.206	.267	.280	548	49	-8	0			.941	1	C-50	-0.5
Total	4	126	296	28	68	15	2	0	27	12	13	.230	.269	.294	563	43	-26	0			.968	9	C-123	-1.1
■ **TOM CROOKE**	Crooke, Thomas Aloysius b: 7/26/1884, Washington, D.C. d: 4/5/29, Quantico, Va. BR/TR, 6', 180 lbs. Deb: 9/29/09																							
1909	Was-A	3	7	2	2	1	0	0	2	2		.286	.444	.429	873	184	1	1			.969	-1	/1-3	0.0
1910	Was-A	8	21	1	4	1	0	0	1	1		.190	.227	.238	465	48	-1	0			1.000	-0	/1-5	-0.2
Total	2	11	28	3	6	2	0	0	3	3		.214	.290	.286	576	85	-0	1			.988	-1	/1-8	-0.2
■ **JACK CROOKS**	Crooks, John Charles b: 11/9/1865, St.Paul, Minn. d: 2/2/18, St.Louis, Mo. BR/TR, 5'10", 170 lbs. Deb: 9/26/1889 M																							
1889	Col-a	12	43	13	14	2	3	0	7	10	4	.326	.463	.512	975	187	6	10			.987	5	2-12	0.9
1890	Col-a	135	485	86	107	5	4	1	62	96		.221	.357	.254	611	86	-1	57			.937	-4	*2-134/3-1,O-1(1-0-0)	0.1
1891	Col-a	138	519	110	127	19	13	0	46	103	47	.245	.379	.331	710	110	13	50			**.957**	20	*2-138	3.2
1892	StL-N	128	445	82	95	7	4	7	38	**136**	52	.213	.400	.294	694	116	20	23			.929	-7	*2-101,3-25/O-2R,M	1.6
1893	StL-N	128	448	93	106	10	9	1	48	**121**	37	.237	.408	.306	714	91	2	31			.908	4	*3-123/S-4,C-1	0.7
1895	Was-N	118	412	81	117	19	8	6	58	70	39	.284	.398	.413	811	111	9	36			**.956**	15	*2-118	2.3
1896	Was-N	25	84	20	24	3	0	3	20	16	8	.286	.406	.429	835	120	3	2			.916	-3	2-20/3-4	0.1
	Lou-N	39	122	19	29	5	1	2	15	20	8	.238	.354	.344	698	88	-1	8			.925	5	2-39	0.4
	Yr	64	206	39	53	8	1	5	35	36	16	.257	.376	.379	754	101	2	10			.922	2	2-59/3-4	0.5
1898	StL-N	72	225	33	52	4	2	1	20	40		.231	.359	.280	639	82	-3	3			.959	7	2-66/3-3,S-2,O-1L	0.6
Total	8	795	2783	537	671	74	44	21	314	612	195	.241	.386	.322	708	102	47	220			.946	41	2-628,3-156/S-6,OC	9.9
■ **ED CROSBY**	Crosby, Edward Carlton b: 5/26/49, Long Beach, Cal. BL/TR, 6'2", 180 lbs. Deb: 7/12/70																							
1970	StL-N	38	95	9	24	4	1	0	6	7	5	.253	.311	.316	626	67	-4	0	0	0	.954	-1	S-35/3-3,2-2	-0.2
1972	StL-N	101	276	27	60	9	1	0	19	18	27	.217	.270	.257	528	51	-18	1	1	-0	.979	-6	S-43,2-38,3-14	-1.9
1973	StL-N	22	39	4	5	2	1	0	1	4	4	.128	.209	.231	440	22	-4	0	0	0	.938	-3	/S-7,2-5,3-4	-0.7
	*Cin-N	36	51	4	11	1	1	0	5	7	12	.216	.333	.275	608	74	-1	0	1	-0	.953	5	S-29/2-5	0.5
	Yr	58	90	8	16	3	2	0	6	11	16	.178	.282	.256	537	52	-6	0	1	-0	.950	2	S-36,2-10/3-4	-0.2
1974	Cle-A	37	86	11	18	3	0	0	6	6	12	.209	.261	.244	505	46	-6	0	1	-0	.926	-10	3-18,S-13/2-3	-1.6
1975	Cle-A	61	128	12	30	3	0	0	7	13	14	.234	.305	.258	563	60	-6	0	4	-1	.974	4	S-30,2-19,3-13	0.0
1976	Cle-A	2	2	0	1	0	0	0	0	0	0	.500	.500	.500	1000	195	0	0	0	0	1.000	1	/3-1,D-1	0.1
Total	6	297	677	67	149	22	4	0	44	55	74	.220	.284	.264	548	55	-40	1	7	-2	.964	-11	S-157/2-72,3-53,D-1	-3.8
■ **FRANKIE CROSETTI**	Crosetti, Frank Peter Joseph "Crow" b: 10/4/10, San Francisco, Cal. BR/TR, 5'10", 165 lbs. Deb: 4/12/32 C																							
1932	*NY-A	116	398	47	96	20	9	5	57	51	51	.241	.335	.374	709	88	-7	3	2	-0	.937	-5	S-84,3-33/2-1	-0.5
1933	NY-A	136	451	71	114	20	5	9	60	55	40	.253	.337	.379	716	95	-3	4	1	1	.936	-8	*S-133	-0.1
1934	NY-A	138	554	85	147	22	10	11	67	61	58	.265	.344	.401	744	98	-2	5	6	-1	.945	-10	*S-119,3-23/2-1	-0.3
1935	NY-A	87	305	49	78	17	6	8	50	41	27	.256	.351	.430	781	107	3	3	1	0	.963	-7	S-87	0.2
1936	*NY-A★	151	632	137	182	35	7	15	78	90	83	.288	.387	.437	824	107	8	18	7	2	.948	-8	*S-151	1.1
1937	*NY-A	149	611	127	143	29	5	11	49	86	105	.234	.340	.352	692	74	-24	13	7	0	.948	2	*S-147	-0.9
1938	*NY-A	157	631	113	166	35	3	9	55	106	97	.263	.382	.371	752	90	-6	**27**	12	2	.948	18	*S-157	2.2
1939	*NY-A☆	152	656	109	153	25	5	10	56	65	81	.233	.315	.332	647	67	-33	11	7	-0	**.968**	8	*S-152	-1.3

YEAR	TM/L	G	AB	R	H	2B	3B	HR	RBI	BB	SO	AVG	OBP	SLG	OPS	OPS+	BR+	SB	CS	SBR	FA	FR	G/POS	TPR
1940	NY-A	145	546	84	106	23	4	4	31	72	77	.194	.299	.273	572	52	-38	14	8	0	.954	-14	*S-145	-4.0
1941	NY-A	50	148	13	33	2	2	1	22	18	14	.223	.320	.284	603	62	-8	0	2	-1	.944	10	S-32,3-13	0.4
1942	*NY-A	74	285	50	69	5	5	4	23	31	31	.242	.335	.337	672	91	-3	1	1	-0	.951	-3	3-62/S-8,2-2	-0.2
1943	*NY-A	95	348	36	81	8	1	2	20	36	47	.233	.317	.279	596	74	-10	4	4	-1	.946	3	S-90	0.0
1944	NY-A	55	197	20	47	4	2	5	30	11	21	.239	.299	.355	654	84	-5	3	0	1	.960	-9	S-55	-0.9
1945	NY-A	130	441	57	105	12	0	4	48	59	65	.238	.341	.293	634	81	-8	7	1	1	.946	-8	*S-126	-0.5
1946	NY-A	28	59	4	17	3	0	0	3	8	2	.288	.382	.339	721	101	1	0	3	-1	.940	7	S-24	0.8
1947	NY-A	3	1	0	0	0	0	0	0	0	0	.000	.000	.000	0	-99	-0	0	0	0	.000	0	/2-1,S-1	0.0
1948	NY-A	17	14	4	4	0	1	0	0	2	0	.286	.375	.429	804	115	0	0	0	0	1.000	0	/2-6,S-5	0.1
Total	17	1683	6277	1006	1541	260	65	98	649	792	799	.245	.341	.354	695	84	-136	113	62	3	.949	-24	*S-1516,3-131/2-11	-3.9
■ AMOS CROSS	Cross, Amos C. b: 1861, Czechoslovakia d: 7/16/1888, Cleveland, Ohio Deb: 4/22/1885 F Career OF: (1-LF 0-CF 1-RF)																							
1885	Lou-a	35	130	11	37	2	1	0	14	0		.285	.290	.315	605	91	-2				.936	-1	C-35	0.0
1886	Lou-a	74	283	51	78	14	6	1	42	44		.276	.375	.378	753	129	10	13			.910	-16	C-51,1-20/S-2,O-1L	-0.3
1887	Lou-a	8	29	0	4	0	0	0	0	1		.138	.138	.107	245	-31	-5	0			.808	-4	/C-5,1-2,O-1(0-0-1)	-0.8
Total	3	117	442	62	119	16	7	1	56	45		.269	.338	.342	681	108	4	13			.916	-22	/C-91,1-22,O-2L,S-2	-1.1
■ CLARENCE CROSS	Cross, Clarence (b: Clarence Crause) b: 3/4/1856, St.Louis, Mo. d: 6/23/31, Seattle, Wash. Deb: 5/5/1884																							
1884	Alt-U	2	7	1	4	1	0	0		2		.571	.667	.714	1381	314	2				.500	-2	/3-2	0.0
	Phi-U	2	9	0	2	0	0	0		0		.222	.222	.222	444	38	-1				.545	-2	/S-2	-0.2
	KC-U	25	93	13	20	1	0	0		6		.215	.263	.226	488	57	-7				.836	3	S-24/3-1	-0.3
	Yr	29	109	14	26	2	0	0		8		.239	.291	.257	547	76	-6				.813	-1	S-26/3-3	-0.5
1887	NY-a	16	57	9	13	2	1	0	5	2		.228	.267	.273	539	53	-3	0			.833	-3	S-13/3-4	-0.5
Total	2	45	166	23	39	4	1	0	5	10		.235	.282	.262	545	67	-10	0			.818	-4	/S-39,3-7	-1.0
■ FRANK CROSS	Cross, Frank Atwell "Mickey" b: 1/20/1873, Cleveland, Ohio d: 11/2/32, Geauga Lake, Ohio TR, 5'9", 161 lbs. Deb: 5/20/01 F																							
1901	Cle-A	1	5	0	3	0	0	0	0	0		.600	.600	.600	1200	243	1	0			.000	-0	/O-1(0-0-1)	0.0
■ JEFF CROSS	Cross, Joffre James b: 8/28/18, Tulsa, Okla. d: 7/23/97, Huntsville, Tex. BR/TR, 5'11", 160 lbs. Deb: 9/27/42																							
1942	StL-N	1	4	0	1	0	0	0	1	0	0	.250	.250	.250	500	43	-0	0			1.000	-1	/S-1	-0.1
1946	StL-N	49	69	17	15	3	0	0	6	10	8	.217	.316	.261	577	62	-3	4			.970	6	S-17/2-8,3-1	0.3
1947	StL-N	51	49	4	5	1	0	0	3	10	6	.102	.254	.122	377	3	-7	0			.947	5	3-15,S-14/2-2	-0.1
1948	StL-N	2	0	0	0	0	0	0	0	0	0	—	—	—	—	—	0	0			.000	0	R	0.0
	Chi-N	16	20	1	2	0	0	0	0	0	4	.100	.100	.100	200	-48	-4	0			.786	-4	/S-9,2-1	-0.8
	Yr	18	20	1	2	0	0	0	0	0	4	.100	.100	.100	200	-47	-4	0			.786	-4	/S-9,2-1	-0.8
Total	4	119	142	22	23	4	0	0	10	20	18	.162	.265	.190	456	26	-14	4			.932	7	/S-41,3-16,2-11	-0.7
■ LAVE CROSS	Cross, Lafayette Napoleon b: 5/12/1866, Milwaukee, Wis. d: 9/6/27, Toledo, Ohio BR/TR, 5'8.5", 155 lbs. Deb: 4/23/1887 FM Career OF: (13-LF 34-CF 72-RF)																							
1887	Lou-a	54	218	32	69	8	3	0	26	15		.317	.320	.335	655	81	-5	15			.916	-3	C-44,O-10(3-1-6)	-0.4
1888	Lou-a	47	181	20	41	3	0	0	15	2		.227	.239	.243	482	56	-9	10			.929	1	C-37,O-12(2-0-10)/S-2	-0.5
1889	Phi-a	55	199	22	44	8	2	0	23	14	9	.221	.272	.281	554	58	-11	11			.934	19	C-55	1.1
1890	Phi-P	63	245	42	73	7	8	3	47	12	6	.298	.331	.429	759	100	-2	5			.885	2	C-49,O-15(0-5-10)	0.3
1891	Phi-a	110	402	66	121	20	14	5	52	38	23	.301	.366	.458	823	135	16	14			.971	-4	O-43R,C-43,3-24,/S2	1.3
1892	Phi-N	140	541	84	149	15	10	4	69	39	16	.275	.328	.362	690	109	5	18			.921	-2	3-65,C-39,O-25C,2/S	0.5
1893	Phi-N	96	415	81	124	17	6	4	78	26	7	.299	.342	.398	739	96	-4	18			.974	16	C-40,3-30,O-10C,S/1	1.3
1894	Phi-N	122	542	128	210	35	10	7	132	31	7	.387	.424	.528	951	131	27	23			.916	24	*3-103,C-16/S-7,2-1	4.1
1895	Phi-N	125	535	95	145	26	9	2	101	35	8	.271	.319	.364	684	76	-21	21			**.940**	34	*3-125	1.2
1896	Phi-N	106	406	63	104	23	5	1	73	32	14	.256	.312	.345	657	74	-16	8			.937	13	3-61,S-37/2-6,OC	0.0
1897	Phi-N	88	344	37	89	17	5	3	51	10		.259	.282	.363	645	71	-16	10			.912	2	3-47,2-38/O-2R,S-1	-1.0
1898	StL-N	151	602	71	191	28	8	3	79	28		.317	.348	.405	753	113	7	14			**.945**	18	*3-149/S-2	2.6
1899	Cle-N	38	154	15	44	5	0	1	20	8		.286	.325	.338	663	88	-2	2			.955	4	3-38,M	0.2
	StL-N	103	403	61	122	14	5	4	64	17		.303	.333	.392	725	96	-4	11			.960	29	*3-103	2.4
	Yr	141	557	76	166	19	5	5	84	25		.298	.330	.377	707	94	-6	13			**.959**	33	*3-141	2.6
1900	StL-N	16	61	6	18	1	0	0	6	1		.295	.306	.311	618	71	-2	1			.962	1	3-16	-0.1
	*Bro-N	117	461	73	135	14	6	4	67	25		.293	.332	.375	707	90	-8	20			.943	3	*3-117	-0.3
	Yr	133	522	79	153	15	6	4	73	26		.293	.329	.368	697	88	-10	21			**.945**	4	*3-133	-0.4
1901	Phi-A	100	424	82	139	28	12	2	73	19		.328	.358	.465	823	121	10	23			.919	5	*3-100	1.7
1902	Phi-A	137	559	90	191	39	8	0	108	27		.342	.374	.440	814	120	14	25			.942	7	*3-137	2.3
1903	Phi-A	137	559	60	163	22	4	2	90	10		.292	.304	.356	660	93	-6	14			.950	-3	*3-136/1-1	-0.6
1904	Phi-A	155	607	73	176	31	10	1	71	13		.290	.310	.379	689	112	6	10			.936	-10	*3-155	0.1
1905	*Phi-A	147	587	69	156	29	5	0	77	26		.266	.299	.332	631	98	-2	8			.928	-9	*3-147	-0.8
1906	Was-A	130	494	55	130	14	6	1	46	28		.263	.303	.322	625	100	-1	19			**.952**	-3	*3-130	-0.1
1907	Was-A	41	161	13	32	8	0	0	10	10		.199	.246	.248	494	62	-7	3			.978	7	3-41	0.1
Total	21	2278	9100	1338	2666	412	136	47	1378	466	90	.293	.329	.383	711	100	-29	303			.938	150	*3-1724,C-324,O/S21	15.4
■ MONTE CROSS	Cross, Montford Montgomery b: 8/31/1869, Philadelphia, Pa. d: 6/21/34, Philadelphia, Pa. BR/TR, 5'8.5", 148 lbs. Deb: 9/27/1892 U																							
1892	Bal-N	15	50	5	8	0	0	0	2	4	10	.160	.222	.160	382	16	-5	2			.864	-3	S-15	-0.7
1894	Pit-N	13	43	14	19	1	5	2	13	5	4	.442	.520	.837	1357	225	9	6			.924	2	S-13	0.8
1895	Pit-N	109	397	67	101	14	13	3	54	38	38	.254	.324	.378	702	85	-9	39			.884	-11	*S-108/2-1	-1.1
1896	StL-N	125	427	66	104	10	6	6	52	58	48	.244	.342	.337	679	83	-9	40			.892	-12	*S-125	-1.2
1897	StL-N	132	465	60	133	17	11	4	55	62		.286	.378	.396	774	107	6	38			.918	29	*S-132	3.5
1898	Phi-N	149	525	68	135	25	5	1	50	55		.257	.337	.330	666	95	-2	20			.907	15	*S-149	1.9
1899	Phi-N	154	557	85	143	25	6	3	65	56		.257	.335	.339	675	88	-8	26			.909	2	*S-154	0.2
1900	Phi-N	131	466	59	94	11	3	3	62	51		.202	.289	.258	546	52	-30	19			.928	-3	*S-131	-2.4
1901	Phi-N	139	483	49	95	14	1	1	44	52		.197	.281	.236	518	50	-29	24			.924	-16	*S-139	-4.1
1902	Phi-A	137	497	72	115	22	2	3	59	32		.231	.289	.302	590	61	-26	17			.927	11	*S-137	-1.0
1903	Phi-A	137	470	44	116	21	2	3	45	49		.247	.326	.319	645	90	-4	31			.940	8	*S-137/2-1	0.8
1904	Phi-A	153	503	33	95	23	4	1	38	46		.189	.266	.256	523	62	-20	19			.937	-16	*S-153	-3.5
1905	*Phi-A	79	252	28	67	17	2	0	24	19		.266	.332	.349	681	114	4	8			.929	-4	S-77/2-2	0.3
1906	Phi-A	134	445	32	89	23	3	1	40	50		.200	.291	.272	563	74	-12	22			.938	4	*S-134	-0.4
1907	Phi-A	77	248	37	51	9	5	0	18	39		.206	.316	.282	598	89	-2	17			.954	12	S-74	1.4
Total	15	1684	5828	719	1365	232	68	31	621	616	100	.234	.316	.313	629	80	-138	328			.920	18	*S-1678/2-4	-5.5
■ FRANK CROSSIN	Crossin, Frank Patrick b: 6/15/1891, Avondale, Pa. d: 12/6/65, Kingston, Pa. BR/TR, 5'10", 160 lbs. Deb: 9/24/12																							
1912	StL-A	8	22	2	5	0	0	0	2	1		.227	.261	.227	488	41	-2	1			.920	-5	/C-8	-0.6
1913	StL-A	4	4	1	1	0	0	0	0	1	1	.250	.500	.250	750	124	0	0			.857	-1	/C-2	0.0
1914	StL-A	43	90	5	11	1	1	0	5	10	10	.122	.225	.156	381	15	-9	3			.934	-1	C-41	-0.8
Total	3	55	116	8	17	1	1	0	7	12	11	.147	.244	.172	417	25	-10	4			.930	-6	/C-51	-1.4
■ JOE CROTTY	Crotty, Joseph P. b: 12/24/1860, Cincinnati, O. d: 6/22/26, Minneapolis, Minn BR/TR, Deb: 5/4/1882																							
1882	Lou-a	5	20	1	2	0	0	0		0		.100	.100	.100	200	-34	-3				.882	-0	/C-5	-0.2
	StL-a	8	28	2	4	1	0	0		3		.143	.226	.179	404	37	-2				.882	-1	/C-7,O-1(0-1-0)	-0.2
	Yr	13	48	3	6	1	0	0		3		.125	.176	.146	322	10	-4				.882	-2	C-12/O-1(0-1-0)	-0.4
1884	Cin-U	21	84	11	22	4	2	1		1		.262	.271	.393	663	92	-4				.896	-7	C-21	-0.8
1885	Lou-a	39	129	14	20	2	0	0	7	3		.155	.193	.171	363	15	-12				.931	1	C-38/1-1	-0.7
1886	NY-a	14	47	6	8	0	1	0	2	4		.170	.250	.213	463	48	-3	3			.933	-3	C-14	-0.4
Total	4	87	308	34	56	7	3	1	9	11		.182	.220	.234	454	42	-23	3			.915	-10	/C-85,1-1,O-1(0-1-0)	-2.3
■ JACK CROUCH	Crouch, Jack Albert "Roxy" b: 10/12/03, Salisbury, N.C. d: 8/25/72, Leesburg, Fla. BR/TR, 5'9", 165 lbs. Deb: 9/18/30																							
1930	StL-A	6	14	1	2	1	0	0	1	1	3	.143	.200	.214	414	5	-2	0	0	0	1.000	1	/C-5	-0.1
1931	StL-A	8	12	0	0	0	0	0	1	0	4	.000	.000	.000	0	-97	-3	0	0	0	.895	1	/C-7	-0.3

YEAR	TM/L	G	AB	R	H	2B	3B	HR	RBI	BB	SO	AVG	OBP	SLG	OPS	OPS+	BR+	SB	CS	SBR	FA	FR	G/POS	TPR
1933	StL-A	19	30	1	5	0	0	1	5	2	6	.167	.219	.267	485	26	-3	0	0	0	1.000	-1	/C-9	-0.3
	Cin-N	10	16	5	2	0	0	0	1	0	0	.125	.222	.125	347	1	-2	1			1.000	2	/C-6	0.0
Total	3	43	72	7	9	1	0	1	8	3	13	.125	.182	.181	362	-3	-11	1	0		.976	3	/C-27	-0.7

■ FRANK CROUCHER Croucher, Frank Donald "Dingle" b: 7/23/14, San Antonio, Tex. d: 5/21/80, Houston, Tex. BR/TR, 5'11", 165 lbs. Deb: 4/18/39

YEAR	TM/L	G	AB	R	H	2B	3B	HR	RBI	BB	SO	AVG	OBP	SLG	OPS	OPS+	BR+	SB	CS	SBR	FA	FR	G/POS	TPR
1939	Det-A	97	324	38	87	15	0	5	40	16	42	.269	.303	.361	664	64	-18	2	2	-0	.934	-8	S-93/2-3	-1.8
1940	*Det-A	37	57	3	6	0	0	0	2	4	5	.105	.164	.105	269	-26	-11	0	0	0	.936	-2	S-26/2-7,3-1	-1.1
1941	Det-A	136	489	51	124	21	4	2	39	33	72	.254	.305	.325	630	61	-28	2	0	0	.935	-3	*S-136	-2.0
1942	Was-A	26	65	2	18	1	1	0	5	3	9	.277	.309	.323	632	79	-2	0	0	0	.950	5	2-18	0.4
Total	4	296	935	94	235	37	5	7	86	56	128	.251	.296	.324	620	58	-58	4	2	0	.934	-8	S-255/2-28,3-1	-4.5

■ BUCK CROUSE Crouse, Clyde Elsworth b: 1/6/1897, Anderson, Ind. d: 10/23/83, Muncie, Ind. BL/TR, 5'8", 158 lbs. Deb: 8/1/23

YEAR	TM/L	G	AB	R	H	2B	3B	HR	RBI	BB	SO	AVG	OBP	SLG	OPS	OPS+	BR+	SB	CS	SBR	FA	FR	G/POS	TPR
1923	Chi-A	23	70	6	18	2	1	1	7	3	4	.257	.297	.357	654	73	-3	0	0	0	.955	-2	C-22	-0.4
1924	Chi-A	94	305	30	79	10	1	1	44	23	12	.259	.319	.308	627	64	-16	3	2	-0	.945	1	C-90	-0.9
1925	Chi-A	54	131	18	46	7	0	2	25	12	4	.351	.410	.450	860	125	5	1	2	-0	.952	-2	C-48	0.4
1926	Chi-A	49	135	10	32	4	1	0	17	14	7	.237	.309	.281	590	57	-8	0	0	0	.985	3	C-45	-0.3
1927	Chi-A	85	222	22	53	11	0	0	20	21	10	.239	.307	.288	596	57	-14	4	1	1	.972	7	C-81	-0.2
1928	Chi-A	78	218	17	55	5	2	2	20	19	14	.252	.315	.321	636	68	-10	3	4	-1	.959	-1	C-76	-0.7
1929	Chi-A	45	107	11	29	7	0	2	12	5	7	.271	.316	.393	708	82	-3	2	0	0	.979	6	C-40	0.5
1930	Chi-A	42	118	14	30	8	1	0	15	17	10	.254	.348	.339	687	78	-4	1	1	-0	.979	7	C-38	0.5
Total	8	470	1306	128	342	54	6	8	160	114	68	.262	.326	.331	657	72	-53	14	10	-0	.964	18	C-440	-1.1

■ DON CROW Crow, Donald Le Roy b: 8/18/58, Yakima, Wash. BR/TR, 6'4", 200 lbs. Deb: 7/25/82

YEAR	TM/L	G	AB	R	H	2B	3B	HR	RBI	BB	SO	AVG	OBP	SLG	OPS	OPS+	BR+	SB	CS	SBR	FA	FR	G/POS	TPR
1982	LA-N	4	4	0	0	0	0	0	0	0	3	.000	.000	.000	0	-99	-1	0	0	0	1.000	1	/C-4	0.0

■ GEORGE CROWE Crowe, George Daniel "Big George" b: 3/22/21, Whiteland, Ind. BL/TL, 6'2", 212 lbs. Deb: 4/16/52

YEAR	TM/L	G	AB	R	H	2B	3B	HR	RBI	BB	SO	AVG	OBP	SLG	OPS	OPS+	BR+	SB	CS	SBR	FA	FR	G/POS	TPR
1952	Bos-N	73	217	25	56	13	1	4	20	18	25	.258	.329	.382	712	100	-0	0	1	-0	.985	2	1-55	-0.1
1953	Mil-N	47	42	6	12	2	0	2	6	2	7	.286	.333	.476	810	115	1	0	0	0	1.000	0	/1-9	0.1
1955	Mil-N	104	303	41	85	12	4	15	55	45	44	.281	.375	.495	870	135	16	1	0	0	.989	2	1-79	1.3
1956	Cin-N	77	144	22	36	2	1	10	23	11	28	.250	.312	.486	798	104	0	0	0	0	.988	2	1-32	0.1
1957	Cin-N	133	494	71	134	20	1	31	92	32	62	.271	.317	.504	821	108	5	1	1	-0	.989	-2	*1-120	-0.4
1958	Cin-N☆	111	345	31	95	12	5	7	61	41	51	.275	.352	.400	752	94	-2	1	0	0	.992	-3	1-93/2-1	-1.0
1959	StL-N	77	103	14	31	6	0	8	29	5	12	.301	.333	.592	926	132	4	0	0	0	1.000	2	1-14	0.6
1960	StL-N	73	72	5	17	3	0	4	13	5	16	.236	.286	.444	730	89	-1	0	0	0	1.000	0	/1-5	-0.1
1961	StL-N	7	7	0	1	0	0	0	0	0	1	.143	.143	.143	286	-22	-1	0	0	0	.000	0	H	-0.1
Total	9	702	1727	215	467	70	12	81	299	159	246	.270	.335	.466	801	109	21	3	2	-0	.990	4	1-407/2-1	0.4

■ ED CROWLEY Crowley, Edgar Jewel b: 8/20/06, Watkinsville, Ga. d: 4/14/70, Birmingham, Ala. BR/TR, 6'1", 180 lbs. Deb: 6/21/28

YEAR	TM/L	G	AB	R	H	2B	3B	HR	RBI	BB	SO	AVG	OBP	SLG	OPS	OPS+	BR+	SB	CS	SBR	FA	FR	G/POS	TPR
1928	Was-A	2	1	0	0	0	0	0	0	0	0	.000	.000	.000	0	-99	-0	0	0	0	.000	-0	/3-2	-0.1

■ JOHN CROWLEY Crowley, John A. b: 1/12/1862, Lawrence, Mass. d: 9/23/1896, Lawrence, Mass. 5'10", 164 lbs. Deb: 5/1/1884

YEAR	TM/L	G	AB	R	H	2B	3B	HR	RBI	BB	SO	AVG	OBP	SLG	OPS	OPS+	BR+	SB	CS	SBR	FA	FR	G/POS	TPR
1884	Phi-N	48	168	26	41	7	3	0	19	15	21	.244	.306	.321	627	102	1				.832	-23	C-48	-1.6

■ TERRY CROWLEY Crowley, Terrence Michael b: 2/16/47, Staten Island, N.Y. BL/TL, 6', 180 lbs. Deb: 9/4/69 C Career OF: (20-LF 0-CF 122-RF)

YEAR	TM/L	G	AB	R	H	2B	3B	HR	RBI	BB	SO	AVG	OBP	SLG	OPS	OPS+	BR+	SB	CS	SBR	FA	FR	G/POS	TPR
1969	Bal-A	7	18	2	6	0	0	0	3	1	4	.333	.368	.333	702	97	-0	0	0	0	1.000	0	/1-3,O-2(2-0-0)	0.0
1970	*Bal-A	83	152	25	39	5	0	5	20	35	26	.257	.396	.388	784	116	5	2	0	0	.973	-5	O-27(6-0-22),1-23	-0.2
1971	Bal-A	18	23	2	4	0	0	0	1	3	4	.174	.269	.174	443	28	-2	0	0	0	1.000	-2	/O-6(1-0-5),1-2	-0.5
1972	Bal-A	97	247	30	57	10	0	11	29	32	26	.231	.321	.405	726	112	4	0	0	0	.990	-7	O-68(3-0-65),1-15	-0.8
1973	*Bal-A	54	131	16	27	4	0	3	15	16	14	.206	.297	.305	603	71	-5	0	0	0	.867	-1	D-23,O-10(2-0-8)/1-7	-0.7
1974	Cin-N	84	125	11	30	12	0	1	20	10	16	.240	.301	.360	661	86	-3	1	0	0	1.000	-2	O-22(1-0-21)/1-7	-0.6
1975	*Cin-N	66	71	8	19	6	0	1	11	7	6	.268	.333	.394	728	100	-0	0	0	0	1.000	1	/1-4,O-4(3-0-1)	0.1
1976	Atl-N	7	6	0	0	0	0	0	1	0	0	.000	.000	.000	0	-94	-1	0	0	0	.000	0	H	-0.2
	Bal-A	33	61	5	15	1	0	0	5	7	11	.246	.333	.262	596	81	-1	0	0	0	1.000	1	D-17/1-1	-0.1
1977	Bal-A	18	22	3	8	1	0	1	9	1	3	.364	.391	.545	937	162	2	0	0	0	1.000	-0	/1-1,D-2	0.2
1978	Bal-A	62	95	9	24	2	0	0	12	8	12	.253	.317	.274	591	72	-3	0	0	0	1.000	0	D-17/O-2(2-0-0),1-1	-0.4
1979	*Bal-A	61	63	8	20	5	1	1	8	14	13	.317	.449	.476	925	155	6	0	0	0	1.000	-0	D-15/1-2	0.5
1980	Bal-A	92	233	33	67	8	0	12	50	29	21	.288	.366	.476	843	130	10	0	0	0	1.000	1	D-65/1-3	0.9
1981	Bal-A	68	134	12	33	6	0	4	25	29	12	.246	.380	.381	761	120	5	0	0	0	1.000	0	D-42/1-4	0.3
1982	Bal-A	65	93	8	22	2	0	3	17	21	9	.237	.377	.355	732	103	1	0	0	0	.988	0	D-14,1-10	0.1
1983	Mon-N	50	44	2	8	0	0	0	3	9	4	.182	.333	.182	515	47	-3	0	0	0	1.000	-1	/1-4	-0.4
Total	15	865	1518	174	379	62	1	42	229	222	181	.250	.348	.375	723	104	13	3	0	1	.980	-13	D-195,O-141R/1-87	-1.8

■ BILL CROWLEY Crowley, William Michael b: 4/8/1857, Philadelphia, Pa. d: 7/14/1891, Gloucester, N.J. BR/TR, 5'7.5", 159 lbs. Deb: 4/26/1875 Career OF: (82-LF 150-CF 254-RF)

YEAR	TM/L	G	AB	R	H	2B	3B	HR	RBI	BB	SO	AVG	OBP	SLG	OPS	OPS+	BR+	SB	CS	SBR	FA	FR	G/POS	TPR
1875	Phi-n	9	37	4	3	0	0	0	3	1	0	.081	.105	.081	186	-33	-5	0	0	0	.800	-0	/3-4,O-4(0-4-0),1-1	-0.5
1877	Lou-N	61	238	30	67	9	3	1	23	4	13	.282	.293	.357	651	88	-5				.849	9	*O-58C/S-2,C-2,32	0.2
1879	Buf-N	60	261	41	75	9	5	0	30	6	14	.287	.303	.360	664	115	4				.809	-1	O-43R,C-10/1-7,2-3	0.3
1880	Buf-N	85	354	57	95	16	4	0	20	19	23	.268	.306	.336	642	115	6				.824	1	*O-74(8-21-48),C-22	0.6
1881	Bos-N	72	279	33	71	12	0	0	31	14	15	.254	.290	.297	588	89	-3				.880	-1	*O-72(0-47-26)	-0.6
1883	Phi-a	23	96	16	24	4	3	0	16	3		.250	.273	.354	627	92	-1				.810	-2	O-22(0-21-1)/1-1	-0.4
	Cle-N	11	41	3	12	5	0	0	5	1	7	.293	.310	.415	724	119	1				.923	-3	O-11(0-0-11)	-0.2
1884	Bos-N	108	407	50	110	14	6	6	61	33	74	.270	.325	.378	703	121	10				.870	-5	*O-108(0-2-107)	0.4
1885	Buf-N	92	344	29	83	14	1	1	36	21	32	.241	.285	.297	581	85	-6				.874	-4	*O-92(71-1-20)	-1.1
Total	7	512	2020	259	537	83	22	8	222	101	178	.266	.301	.341	641	103	6				.853	-6	O-480R/C-34,1-8,2S3	-0.8

■ WALTON CRUISE Cruise, Walton Edwin b: 5/6/1890, Childersburg, Ala. d: 1/9/75, Sylacauga, Ala. BL/TR, 6', 175 lbs. Deb: 4/14/14 Career OF: (317-LF 153-CF 205-RF)

YEAR	TM/L	G	AB	R	H	2B	3B	HR	RBI	BB	SO	AVG	OBP	SLG	OPS	OPS+	BR+	SB	CS	SBR	FA	FR	G/POS	TPR
1914	StL-N	95	256	20	58	9	3	4	28	25	42	.227	.303	.332	635	90	-3	3			.976	-3	O-81(43-38-0)	-1.1
1916	StL-N	3	3	0	2	0	0	0	0	1	0	.667	.750	.667	1417	339	1	0			1.000	-1	/O-2(1-1-0)	0.0
1917	StL-N	153	529	70	156	20	10	5	59	38	73	.295	.343	.399	742	131	18	16			.965	-14	*O-152(49-85-26)	-0.5
1918	StL-N	70	240	34	65	5	4	6	39	30	26	.271	.359	.400	759	136	11	2			.964	-7	O-65(48-0-17)	0.0
1919	StL-N	9	21	0	2	1	0	0	0	1	6	.095	.136	.143	279	-17	-3	0			.833	-2	/O-5(0-4-1),1-2	-0.6
	Bos-N	73	241	23	52	7	0	1	21	17	29	.216	.267	.257	525	61	-11	8			.978	-5	O-66(31-23-14)	-2.3
	Yr	82	262	23	54	8	0	1	21	18	35	.206	.257	.248	505	55	-14	8			.971	-7	O-71(31-27-15)/1-2	-2.9
1920	Bos-N	91	288	40	80	7	5	1	21	31	26	.278	.352	.347	699	106	3	5	3	0	.950	-7	O-82(0-0-82)	-0.9
1921	Bos-N	108	344	47	119	16	7	8	55	48	24	.346	.429	.503	932	154	29	10	8	-1	.963	-6	*O-102(100-2-0)/1-2	1.5
1922	Bos-N	104	352	51	98	15	10	4	46	44	20	.278	.360	.412	772	103	2	4	4	-1	.948	-0	*O-100(37-0-64)/1-2	-0.6
1923	Bos-N	21	38	4	8	2	0	0	0	3	2	.211	.268	.263	531	42	-3	1	0	0	.952	-0	/O-9(8-0-1)	-0.4
1924	Bos-N	9	9	4	4	1	0	1	3	0	2	.444	.444	.889	1333	260	2	0	0	0	.000	0	H	0.2
Total	10	736	2321	293	644	83	39	30	272	238	250	.277	.348	.386	733	114	45	49	15		.962	-45	O-664L/1-6	-4.7

■ GENE CRUMLING Crumling, Eugene Leon b: 4/5/22, Wrightsville, Pa. BR/TR, 6', 180 lbs. Deb: 9/11/45

YEAR	TM/L	G	AB	R	H	2B	3B	HR	RBI	BB	SO	AVG	OBP	SLG	OPS	OPS+	BR+	SB	CS	SBR	FA	FR	G/POS	TPR
1945	StL-N	6	12	0	1	0	0	0	1	0	1	.083	.083	.083	167	-52	-2	0			1.000	2	/C-6	-0.1

■ BUDDY CRUMP Crump, Arthur Elliott b: 11/29/01, Norfolk, Va. d: 9/7/76, Raleigh, N.C. BL/TL, 5'10", 156 lbs. Deb: 9/28/24

YEAR	TM/L	G	AB	R	H	2B	3B	HR	RBI	BB	SO	AVG	OBP	SLG	OPS	OPS+	BR+	SB	CS	SBR	FA	FR	G/POS	TPR
1924	NY-N	1	4	0	0	0	0	0	1	0	1	.000	.000	.000	0	-99	-1	0	0	0	.500	-1	/O-1(0-1-0)	-0.2

■ PRESS CRUTHERS Cruthers, Charles Preston b: 9/8/1890, Marshallton, Del. d: 12/27/76, Kenosha, Wis. BR/TR, 5'9", 152 lbs. Deb: 9/29/13

YEAR	TM/L	G	AB	R	H	2B	3B	HR	RBI	BB	SO	AVG	OBP	SLG	OPS	OPS+	BR+	SB	CS	SBR	FA	FR	G/POS	TPR
1913	Phi-A	3	12	0	3	1	0	0	0	0	0	.250	.250	.333	583	72	-1	0			.923	-3	/2-3	-0.3
1914	Phi-A	4	15	1	3	0	1	0	0	0	4	.200	.200	.333	533	63	-1	0	1	-0	1.000	2	/2-4	0.0
Total	2	7	27	1	6	1	1	0	0	0	4	.222	.222	.333	556	67	-1	0	1		.973	-1	/2-7	-0.3

YEAR	TM/L	G	AB	R	H	2B	3B	HR	RBI	BB	SO	AVG	OBP	SLG	OPS	OPS+	BR+	SB	CS	SBR	FA	FR	G/POS	TPR
■ TOMMY CRUZ	Cruz, Cirilo (Dilan) b: 2/15/51, Arroyo, P.R. BL/TL, 5'9", 165 lbs. Deb: 9/4/73 F																							
1973	StL-N	3	0	1	0	0	0	0	0	0	0	—	—	—	—	—	0	0	0	0	.000	-0	/O-1(1-0-0)	0.0
1977	Chi-A	4	2	1	0	0	0	0	0	0	0	.000	.000	.000	0	-99	-1	0	0	0	1.000	-1	/O-2(2-0-0)	-0.1
Total	2	7	2	2	0	0	0	0	0	0	0	.000	.000	.000	0	-99	-1	0	0	0	1.000	-1	/O-3(3-0-0)	-0.1
■ DEIVI CRUZ	Cruz, Deivi (Garcia) b: 11/6/75, Bani, D.R. BR/TR, 5'11", 160 lbs. Deb: 4/1/97																							
1997	Det-A	147	436	35	105	26	0	2	40	14	55	.241	.264	.314	579	51	-32	3	6	-1	.979	7	*S-147	-1.4
1998	Det-A	135	454	52	118	22	3	5	45	13	55	.260	.285	.355	640	65	-24	3	4	-1	.983	19	*S-135	0.6
1999	Det-A	155	518	64	147	35	0	13	58	12	57	.284	.305	.427	732	85	-13	1	4	-1	.983	21	*S-155	1.7
2000	Det-A	156	583	68	176	46	5	10	82	13	43	.302	.322	.449	771	95	-6	1	4	-1	.982	4	*S-156	0.9
Total	4	593	1991	219	546	129	8	30	225	52	210	.274	.296	.392	689	76	-75	8	18	-5	.982	52	S-593	1.8
■ FAUSTO CRUZ	Cruz, Fausto (Santiago) b: 5/1/72, Monte Cristi, D.R. BR/TR, 5'10", 165 lbs. Deb: 4/10/94																							
1994	Oak-A	17	28	2	3	0	0	0	0	4	6	.107	.219	.107	326	-14	-5	0	0	0	.960	3	S-10/3-4,2-1	-0.1
1995	Oak-A	8	23	0	5	0	0	0	5	3	5	.217	.308	.217	525	42	-2	1	1	-0	.971	-1	/S-8	-0.2
1996	Det-A	14	38	5	9	2	0	0	0	1	11	.237	.256	.289	546	38	-4	0	0	0	.906	-0	/2-8,S-4,D-1	-0.3
Total	3	39	89	7	17	2	0	0	5	8	22	.191	.258	.213	471	24	-10	1	1	-0	.934	2	/S-22,2-9,3-4,D-1	-0.6
■ HECTOR CRUZ	Cruz, Hector Louis (Dilan) "Heity" b: 4/2/53, Arroyo, P.R. BR/TR, 5'11", 170 lbs. Deb: 8/11/73 F Career OF: (109-LF 59-CF 177-RF)																							
1973	StL-N	11	11	1	0	0	0	0	0	1	3	.000	.083	.000	83	-75	-3	0	0	0	1.000	-1	/O-5(1-4-0)	-0.4
1975	StL-N	23	48	7	7	2	2	0	6	2	4	.146	.180	.271	451	23	-5	0	0	0	.800	-1	3-12/O-6(4-0-2)	-0.7
1976	StL-N	151	526	54	120	17	1	13	71	42	119	.228	.288	.338	626	77	-17	1	0	0	.934	-21	*3-148	-4.2
1977	StL-N	118	339	50	80	19	2	6	42	46	56	.236	.329	.357	686	85	-6	4	3	-0	.964	-9	*O-106(27-0-85)/3-2	-2.0
1978	Chi-N	30	76	8	18	5	0	2	9	3	6	.237	.266	.382	647	70	-3	0	0	0	1.000	0	O-14(1-14-0)/3-7	-0.3
	SF-N	79	197	19	44	8	1	6	24	21	39	.223	.301	.365	667	89	-3	0	2	-1	.978	-5	O-53(31-17-14),3-14	-1.1
	Yr	109	273	27	62	13	1	8	33	24	45	.227	.292	.370	662	83	-7	0	2	-1	.983	-5	O-67(32-31-14),3-21	-1.4
1979	SF-N	16	25	2	3	0	0	0	1	3	7	.120	.214	.120	334	-7	-4	0	0	0	1.000	-2	/O-6(5-0-1),3-2	-0.6
	*Cin-N	74	182	24	44	10	2	4	27	31	39	.242	.352	.385	737	100	1	0	1	-0	.984	-7	O-69(13-23-49)	-0.9
	Yr	90	207	26	47	10	2	4	28	34	46	.227	.336	.353	689	89	-3	0	1	-0	.985	-9	O-75(18-23-50)/3-2	-1.5
1980	Cin-N	52	75	5	16	4	1	1	5	8	16	.213	.289	.333	622	73	-3	0	0	0	.955	-4	O-29(15-1-15)	-0.8
1981	Chi-N	53	109	15	25	5	0	7	15	17	24	.229	.333	.468	801	120	3	2	2	-0	.925	-6	3-18,O-16(8-0-10)	-0.4
1982	Chi-N	17	19	1	4	1	0	0	0	2	4	.211	.286	.263	549	53	-1	0	0	0	1.000	-2	/O-4(4-0-1)	-0.3
Total	9	624	1607	186	361	71	9	39	200	176	317	.225	.303	.353	656	81	-42	7	8	-1	.975	-57	O-308R,3-203	-11.7
■ HENRY CRUZ	Cruz, Henry (Acosta) b: 2/27/52, Christiansted, V.I. BL/TL, 6', 175 lbs. Deb: 4/18/75																							
1975	LA-N	53	94	8	25	3	1	0	5	7	6	.266	.317	.319	636	80	-3	1	1	-0	.960	-11	O-41(17-23-4)	-1.5
1976	LA-N	49	88	8	16	2	1	4	14	9	11	.182	.258	.364	621	76	-3	0	2	-1	.976	-3	O-23(5-5-17)	-0.9
1977	Chi-A	16	21	3	6	0	0	2	5	1	3	.286	.318	.571	890	137	1	0	0	0	.833	-3	/O-9(1-2-6)	-0.2
1978	Chi-A	53	77	13	17	2	1	2	10	8	11	.221	.302	.351	653	82	-2	0	1	-0	1.000	-5	O-40(10-24-6)/D-1	-0.7
Total	4	171	280	32	64	7	3	8	34	25	31	.229	.294	.361	655	84	-7	1	4	-1	.974	-22	O-113(33-54-33)/D-1	-3.3
■ JACOB CRUZ	Cruz, Jacob b: 1/28/73, Oxnard, Cal. BL/TL, 6', 175 lbs. Deb: 7/18/96																							
1996	SF-N	33	77	10	18	3	0	3	10	12	24	.234	.352	.390	741	99	0	0	1	-0	.977	0	O-23(6-0-17)	-0.1
1997	SF-N	16	25	3	4	1	0	0	3	3	4	.160	.250	.200	450	20	-3	0	0	0	.933	-1	O-11(2-0-10)	-0.4
1998	SF-N	3	3	0	0	0	0	0	0	0	2	.000	.000	.000	0	-99	-1	0	0	0	.000	0	/H	-0.1
	Cle-A	1	1	0	0	0	0	0	0	0	1	.000	.000	.000	0	-97	-0	0	0	0	.000	0	/H	0.0
1999	Cle-A	32	88	14	29	5	1	3	17	5	13	.330	.372	.511	884	117	2	0	2	-1	1.000	-3	O-24(11-15-2)/D-3	-0.1
2000	Cle-A	11	29	3	7	3	0	0	5	5	4	.241	.371	.345	716	81	-1	1	0	0	1.000	0	/O-9(1-8-0),D-2	0.0
Total	5	96	223	30	58	12	1	6	35	25	48	.260	.345	.404	749	93	-2	1	3	-1	.984	-3	/O-67(20-23-29),D-5	-0.7
■ JOSE CRUZ	Cruz, Jose (Dilan) b: 8/8/47, Arroyo, P.R. BL/TL, 6', 175 lbs. Deb: 9/19/70 FC Career OF: (1411-LF 284-CF 474-RF)																							
1970	StL-N	6	17	2	6	1	0	0	1	4	0	.353	.500	.412	912	144	2	0	0	0	1.000	2	/O-4(1-0-3)	0.3
1971	StL-N	83	292	46	80	13	2	9	27	49	35	.274	.380	.425	805	123	10	6	3	0	.975	2	O-83(1-82-0)	1.1
1972	StL-N	117	332	33	78	14	4	2	23	36	54	.235	.312	.319	631	81	-8	9	3	1	.979	4	*O-102(10-87-7)	-0.7
1973	StL-N	132	406	51	92	22	5	10	57	51	66	.227	.314	.379	694	92	-5	10	4	1	.979	0	*O-118(1-85-37)	-0.8
1974	StL-N	107	161	24	42	4	3	5	20	20	27	.261	.343	.416	759	112	3	4	2	0	.975	-6	O-53(21-8-24)/1-1	-0.5
1975	Hou-N	120	315	44	81	15	2	9	49	52	44	.257	.364	.403	767	121	10	6	3	0	.980	4	O-94(27-2-65)	1.0
1976	Hou-N	133	439	49	133	21	5	4	61	53	46	.303	.378	.401	779	133	20	28	11	2	.972	10	*O-125(85-13-27)	2.7
1977	Hou-N	157	579	87	173	31	10	17	87	69	67	.299	.373	.475	848	138	31	44	23	2	.973	4	*O-155(0-6-155)	2.8
1978	Hou-N	153	565	79	178	34	9	10	83	57	57	.315	.378	.460	838	144	32	37	9	5	.975	3	*O-152(0-0-152)/1-2	3.4
1979	Hou-N	157	558	73	161	33	7	9	72	72	66	.289	.370	.421	791	122	18	36	14	3	.959	9	*O-156(156-0-0)	2.4
1980	*Hou-N☆	160	612	79	185	29	7	11	91	60	66	.302	.365	.426	791	130	24	36	11	4	.969	15	*O-158(158-0-0)	3.8
1981	*Hou-N	107	409	53	109	16	5	13	55	35	49	.267	.324	.425	750	117	8	5	7	-1	.984	9	*O-105(105-0-0)	1.1
1982	Hou-N	155	570	62	157	27	2	9	68	60	67	.275	.345	.377	723	110	8	21	11	1	.964	14	*O-155(155-0-0)	1.7
1983	Hou-N	160	594	85	**189**	28	8	14	92	65	86	.318	.386	.463	849	143	35	30	16	1	.979	8	*O-160(160-0-0)	3.8
1984	Hou-N	160	600	96	187	28	13	12	95	73	68	.312	.386	.462	848	148	39	22	8	2	.976	13	*O-160(160-0-0)	4.8
1985	Hou-N★	141	544	69	163	34	4	9	79	43	74	.300	.351	.426	777	120	14	16	5	2	.971	10	*O-137(136-1-0)	2.1
1986	*Hou-N	141	479	48	133	22	4	10	72	55	86	.278	.352	.403	755	111	7	3	4	-1	.984	6	*O-134(134-0-0)	0.7
1987	Hou-N	126	365	47	88	17	4	11	38	36	65	.241	.309	.400	709	90	-6	4	1	1	.984	6	O-97(97-0-0)	-0.4
1988	NY-A	38	80	9	16	2	0	1	7	8	8	.200	.273	.262	535	51	-5	0	1	-0	.889	-2	D-12/O-8(4-0-4)	-0.8
Total	19	2353	7917	1036	2251	391	94	165	1077	898	1031	.284	.358	.420	778	122	236	317	136	22	.974	111	*O-2156L/D-12,1-3	28.5
■ JOSE CRUZ	Cruz, Jose L. b: 4/19/74, Arroyo, P.R. BB/TR, 6', 190 lbs. Deb: 5/31/97 F																							
1997	Sea-A	49	183	28	49	12	1	12	34	13	45	.268	.316	.541	857	119	4	1	0	0	.966	-2	O-49(49-0-0)	0.1
	Tor-A	55	212	31	49	7	0	14	34	28	72	.231	.321	.462	783	101	-0	6	2	1	.981	0	O-55(51-4-0)	-0.1
	Yr	104	395	59	98	19	1	26	68	41	117	.248	.319	.499	818	109	4	7	2	1	.974	-2	*O-104(100-4-0)	0.0
1998	Tor-A	105	352	55	89	14	3	11	42	57	99	.253	.357	.403	760	97	-1	11	4	1	.984	2	*O-105(6-103-0)	0.3
1999	Tor-A	106	349	63	84	19	3	14	45	64	91	.241	.358	.433	791	99	0	14	4	2	.990	10	*O-106(9-97-0)	1.2
2000	Tor-A	162	603	91	146	32	5	31	76	71	129	.242	.324	.466	790	96	-6	15	5	2	.993	7	*O-162(0-162-0)	0.5
Total	4	477	1699	268	417	84	12	82	231	233	436	.245	.337	.454	791	100	-2	47	15	5	.987	18	O-477(115-366-0)	2.0
■ JULIO CRUZ	Cruz, Julio Luis b: 12/2/54, Brooklyn, N.Y. BB/TR, 5'9", 165 lbs. Deb: 7/4/77																							
1977	Sea-A	60	199	25	51	3	1	1	7	24	29	.256	.336	.296	633	75	-6	15	6	1	.983	2	2-54/D-1	0.0
1978	Sea-A	147	550	77	129	14	1	1	25	69	66	.235	.321	.269	590	68	-21	59	10	**9**	**.987**	8	*2-141/S-5,D-1	0.4
1979	Sea-A	107	414	70	112	16	2	1	29	62	61	.271	.366	.326	692	87	-5	49	9	8	.979	17	*2-107	2.4
1980	Sea-A	119	422	66	88	9	3	2	16	59	49	.209	.307	.258	565	56	-24	45	7	7	.983	1	*2-115/D-3	-1.0
1981	Sea-A	94	352	57	90	12	3	2	24	39	40	.256	.335	.324	659	87	-5	43	8	**7**	.982	8	2-92/S-1	1.6
1982	Sea-A	154	549	83	133	22	5	8	49	57	71	.242	.317	.344	661	79	-15	46	13	6	.987	4	*2-151/S-2,3-1,D-2	0.3
1983	Sea-A	61	181	24	46	10	1	2	12	20	22	.254	.335	.354	689	86	-3	33	6	5	.984	7	2-60/D-1	1.2
	*Chi-A	99	334	47	84	9	4	1	40	29	44	.251	.315	.311	626	71	-13	24	6	3	.983	10	2-97	0.6
	Yr	160	515	71	130	19	5	3	52	49	66	.252	.322	.326	648	76	-16	57	12	8	.983	17	*2-157/D-1	1.8
1984	Chi-A	143	415	42	92	14	4	5	43	45	58	.222	.298	.311	609	66	-19	14	6	1	.976	22	*2-141	1.2
1985	Chi-A	91	234	28	46	2	3	0	15	32	40	.197	.299	.231	529	46	-17	8	5	0	.982	13	2-87/D-2	0.0
1986	Chi-A	81	209	38	45	2	0	0	19	42	28	.215	.347	.225	571	58	-10	7	2	1	.985	2	2-78/D-3	-0.4
Total	10	1156	3859	557	916	113	27	23	279	478	508	.237	.324	.299	622	71	-138	343	78	48	.983	93	*2-1123/D-13,S-8,3	6.3
■ IVAN CRUZ	Cruz, Luis Ivan b: 5/3/68, Fajardo, P.R. BL/TL, 6'3", 210 lbs. Deb: 7/18/97																							
1997	NY-A	11	20	0	5	1	0	0	3	2	4	.250	.318	.300	618	63	-1	0	0	0	1.000	-0	/1-3,O-1(1-0-0),D-4	-0.1
1999	Pit-N	5	10	3	4	0	0	1	2	0	2	.400	.400	.700	1100	171	1	0	0	0	1.000	-0	/1-1,O-1(0-0-1)	0.1
2000	Pit-N	8	11	0	1	0	0	0	0	0	8	.091	.091	.091	182	-55	-3	0	0	0	1.000	-0	/1-1	-0.3
Total	3	24	41	3	10	1	0	1	5	2	14	.244	.279	.341	621	59	-3	0	0	0	1.000	-1	/1-5,D-4,O-2(1-0-1)	-0.3

YEAR	TM/L	G	AB	R	H	2B	3B	HR	RBI	BB	SO	AVG	OBP	SLG	OPS	OPS+	BR+	SB	CS	SBR	FA	FR	G/POS	TPR
■ TODD CRUZ	Cruz, Todd Ruben b: 11/23/55, Highland Park, Mich BR/TR, 6', 175 lbs. Deb: 9/4/78 Career OF: (1-LF 0-CF 0-RF)																							
1978	Phi-N	3	4	0	2	0	0	0	2	0	0	.500	.500	.500	1000	178	0	0	1	-0	1.000	2	/S-2	0.2
1979	KC-A	55	118	9	24	7	0	2	15	3	19	.203	.230	.314	543	44	-9	0	1	-0	.974	4	S-48/3-9	-0.3
1980	Cal-A	18	40	5	11	3	0	1	5	5	8	.275	.356	.425	781	116	1	0	0	0	.860	-6	S-12/3-4,2-1,O-1L	-0.4
	Chi-A	90	293	23	68	11	1	2	18	9	54	.232	.260	.297	557	52	-19	2	1	0	.956	5	S-90	-0.5
	Yr	108	333	28	79	14	1	3	23	14	62	.237	.272	.312	585	60	-18	2	1	0	.948	-1	*S-102/3-4,2-1,O-1L	-0.9
1982	Sea-A	136	492	44	113	20	2	16	57	12	95	.230	.248	.376	624	67	-24	2	10	-3	.963	19	*S-136	0.7
1983	Sea-A	65	216	21	41	4	2	7	21	7	56	.190	.222	.324	546	46	-16	1	3	-1	.964	21	S-63	1.0
	*Bal-A	81	221	16	46	9	1	3	27	15	52	.208	.262	.299	560	55	-14	3	4	-1	.942	5	3-79/2-2	-1.1
	Yr	146	437	37	87	13	3	10	48	22	108	.199	.242	.311	554	51	-30	4	7	-2	.942	25	3-79,S-63/2-2	-0.1
1984	Bal-A	96	142	15	31	4	0	3	9	8	33	.218	.265	.310	575	60	-8	1	4	-1	.955	11	3-89/P-1,D-1	0.1
Total	6	544	1526	133	336	58	6	34	154	59	317	.220	.253	.333	585	59	-89	9	24	-6	.960	60	S-351,3-181/2-3,DPO	-0.3
■ MIKE CUBBAGE	Cubbage, Michael Lee b: 7/21/50, Charlottesville, Va. BL/TR, 6', 180 lbs. Deb: 4/7/74 MC																							
1974	Tex-A	9	15	0	0	0	0	0	0	0	4	.000	.000	.000	0	-99	-4	0	0	0	1.000	2	/3-3,2-2	-0.2
1975	Tex-A	58	143	12	32	6	0	4	21	18	14	.224	.311	.350	660	87	-2	0	0	0	.962	2	2-37/3-3,D-2	0.1
1976	Tex-A	14	32	2	7	0	0	0	0	7	7	.219	.359	.219	578	70	-1	0	0	0	1.000	-0	/2-5,3-1,D-6	-0.1
	Min-A	104	342	40	89	19	5	3	49	42	37	.260	.346	.371	718	108	4	1	1	-0	.940	2	3-99/2-2,D-2	0.6
	Yr	118	374	42	96	19	5	3	49	49	44	.257	.347	.358	706	105	3	1	1	-0	.940	2	*3-100/D-8,2-7	0.5
1977	Min-A	129	417	60	110	16	5	9	55	37	49	.264	.324	.391	715	95	-3	1	4	-1	.952	9	*3-126/D-1	0.3
1978	Min-A	125	394	40	111	12	7	7	57	40	44	.282	.349	.401	750	108	5	3	1	0	.971	2	*3-115/2-5	0.5
1979	Min-A	94	243	26	67	10	1	2	23	39	26	.276	.376	.350	726	94	-1	1	8	-3	.928	-12	3-63,D-21/1-1,2-1	-1.7
1980	Min-A	103	285	29	70	9	0	8	42	23	37	.246	.304	.361	666	76	-9	0	1	-0	.996	7	1-72,3-32/2-1,D-1	-0.6
1981	NY-N	67	80	9	17	2	2	1	4	9	15	.213	.292	.325	617	76	-3	0	0	0	.963	1	3-12	-0.2
Total	8	703	1951	218	503	74	20	34	251	215	233	.258	.333	.369	702	94	-14	6	15	-4	.952	12	3-454/1-73,2-53,D	-1.3
■ AL CUCCINELLO	Cuccinello, Alfred Edward b: 11/26/14, Long Island City, N.Y. BR/TR, 5'10", 165 lbs. Deb: 5/17/35 F																							
1935	NY-N	54	165	27	41	7	1	4	20	1	20	.248	.262	.376	638	70	-7	0			.951	6	2-48/3-2	0.1
■ TONY CUCCINELLO	Cuccinello, Anthony Francis "Cooch" or "Chick" b: 11/8/07, Long Island City, N.Y. d: 9/21/95, Tampa, Fla. BR/TR, 5'7", 160 lbs. Deb: 4/15/30 FC																							
1930	Cin-N	125	443	64	138	22	5	10	78	47	44	.312	.380	.451	832	105	5	5			.920	-19	*3-109,2-15/S-4	-0.6
1931	Cin-N	154	575	67	181	39	11	2	93	54	28	.315	.374	.431	805	123	19	1			.969	5	*2-154	3.3
1932	Bro-N	154	597	76	168	32	6	12	77	46	47	.281	.337	.415	752	103	7	5			.973	19	*2-154	3.1
1933	Bro-N★	134	485	58	122	31	4	9	65	44	40	.252	.316	.388	704	105	2	4			.977	-19	*2-120,3-14	-0.9
1934	Bro-N	140	528	59	138	32	2	14	94	49	45	.261	.325	.409	734	100	-1	0			.974	12	*2-101,3-43	1.8
1935	Bro-N	102	360	49	105	20	3	8	53	40	35	.292	.366	.431	796	116	9	3			.977	6	2-64,3-36	1.8
1936	Bos-N	150	565	68	174	26	3	7	86	58	49	.308	.374	.402	776	116	14	1			.971	22	*2-150	4.4
1937	Bos-N	152	575	77	156	36	4	11	80	61	40	.271	.341	.405	746	112	9	2			.967	-10	*2-151	0.9
1938	Bos-N☆	147	555	62	147	25	2	9	76	52	32	.265	.331	.366	697	102	1	4			.974	-26	*2-147	-1.5
1939	Bos-N	81	310	42	95	17	1	2	40	26	26	.306	.360	.387	747	109	4	5			.970	-4	2-80	0.6
1940	Bos-N	34	126	14	34	9	0	0	19	8	9	.270	.319	.341	660	87	-2	1			.978	1	3-33	0.0
	NY-N	88	307	26	64	9	2	5	36	16	42	.208	.248	.300	547	50	-21	1			.987	5	2-47,3-37	-1.3
	Yr	122	433	40	98	18	2	5	55	24	51	.226	.269	.312	580	60	-24	2			.971	6	3-70,2-47	-1.3
1942	Bos-N	40	104	8	21	3	0	1	8	9	11	.202	.265	.260	525	55	-6	1			.907	-4	3-20,2-14	-0.9
1943	Bos-N	13	19	0	0	0	0	0	2	3	1	.000	.136	.000	136	-60	-4	0			.929	0	/3-4,2-2,S-1	-0.4
	Chi-A	34	103	5	28	5	0	2	11	13	13	.272	.353	.379	732	114	2	3	1	0	.965	-2	3-30	0.1
1944	Chi-A	38	130	5	34	3	0	0	17	8	16	.262	.304	.285	589	70	-5	0	0	0	.959	-2	3-30/2-6	-0.7
1945	Chi-A†	118	402	50	124	25	3	2	49	45	19	.308	.379	.400	780	130	16	6	2	1	.936	-5	*3-112	1.3
Total	15	1704	6184	730	1729	334	46	94	884	579	497	.280	.343	.394	737	105	44	42	3		.973	-18	*2-1205,3-468/S-5	11.0
■ JIM CUDWORTH	Cudworth, James Alaric "Cuddy" b: 8/22/1858, Fairhaven, Mass. d: 12/21/43, Middleboro, Mass. BR/TR, 6', 165 lbs. Deb: 7/27/1884																							
1884	KC-U	32	116	7	17	3	1	0		2		.147	.161	.190	351	7	-17				.963	2	1-19,O-12(0-12-0)/P-2	-1.3
■ MANUEL CUETO	Cueto, Manuel "Potato" b: 2/8/1892, Guanajay, Cuba d: 6/29/42, Regla, Cuba BR/TR, 5'5", 157 lbs. Deb: 6/25/14 Career OF: (51-LF 6-CF 22-RF)																							
1914	StL-F	19	43	2	4	0	0	0	2	5	7	.093	.188	.093	281	-21	-8	0			.941	-1	3-10/S-5,2-2	-0.9
1917	Cin-N	56	140	10	28	3	0	1	11	16	17	.200	.287	.243	529	66	-5	4			.963	-1	O-38(32-4-3)/2-6,C-5	-0.8
1918	Cin-N	47	108	14	32	5	1	0	14	19	5	.296	.406	.361	767	137	6	4			.929	-14	O-19L,2-10/S-9,C-6	-0.8
1919	Cin-N	29	88	10	22	2	0	0	4	10	4	.250	.340	.273	613	88	-1	5			.982	4	O-25(7-0-18)/3-1	0.2
Total	4	151	379	36	86	10	1	1	31	50	33	.227	.323	.266	590	80	-8	13			.964	-13	/O-82L,2-18,S-14,C3	-2.3
■ JOHN CUFF	Cuff, John Patrick b: 6/1864, Union City, N.J. d: 12/5/16, Hoboken, N.J. Deb: 9/11/1884																							
1884	Bal-U	3	11	1	1	1	0	0		1		.091	.167	.182	348	5	-2				.920	0	/C-3	-0.1
■ LEON CULBERSON	Culberson, Delbert Leon "Lee" b: 8/6/19, Halls, Ga. d: 9/17/89, Rome, Ga. BR/TR, 5'11", 180 lbs. Deb: 5/16/43																							
1943	Bos-A	81	312	36	85	16	6	3	34	31	35	.272	.338	.391	729	111	4	14	0	3	.978	6	O-79(28-51-0)	1.0
1944	Bos-A	75	282	41	67	11	5	2	21	20	20	.238	.288	.333	621	78	-9	6	4	-0	.979	-3	O-72(0-72-0)	-1.4
1945	Bos-A	97	331	26	91	21	6	6	45	20	37	.275	.316	.429	745	113	4	4	3	-0	.967	5	O-91(1-89-1)	0.6
1946	*Bos-A	59	179	34	56	10	1	3	18	16	19	.313	.369	.430	799	116	4	3	2	-0	.967	-7	O-49(6-18-26)/3-4	-0.5
1947	Bos-A	47	84	10	20	1	0	0	11	12	10	.238	.354	.250	604	65	-3	1	1	-0	.974	-4	O-25(5-4-16)/3-4	-0.9
1948	Was-A	12	29	1	5	0	0	0	2	8	5	.172	.351	.172	524	43	-2	0	0	0	1.000	-3	O-11(0-11-0)	-0.5
Total	6	371	1217	148	324	59	18	14	131	107	126	.266	.327	.379	706	100	-3	28	10	3	.974	-6	O-327(40-245-43)/3-8	-1.7
■ JOHN CULLEN	Cullen, John J. b: Marysville, Cal. Deb: 8/18/1884																							
1884	Wil-U	9	31	2	6	0	0	0		1		.194	.219	.194	412	25	-4				.750	-1	/O-6(4-0-2),S-3	-0.5
■ TIM CULLEN	Cullen, Timothy Leo b: 2/16/42, San Francisco, Cal. BR/TR, 6'1", 185 lbs. Deb: 8/8/66																							
1966	Was-A	18	34	8	8	1	0	0	0	2	8	.235	.278	.265	542	57	-2	0	0	0	.889	-1	/3-8,2-5	0.0
1967	Was-A	124	402	35	95	7	0	2	31	40	47	.236	.307	.269	576	74	-12	4	5	-1	.951	15	S-69,2-46,3-15,/O-1R	1.2
1968	Chi-A	72	155	16	31	7	0	2	13	15	23	.200	.275	.284	559	69	-6	0	0	0	.966	6	2-71	0.5
	Was-A	47	114	8	31	4	2	1	16	7	12	.272	.325	.368	694	113	2	0	0	0	.968	-1	S-33,2-16/3-3	0.4
	Yr	119	269	24	62	11	2	3	29	22	35	.230	.296	.320	616	87	-4	0	0	0	.965	5	2-87,S-33/3-3	0.9
1969	Was-A	119	249	22	52	7	0	1	15	14	27	.209	.257	.249	506	44	-19	1	1	-0	.981	12	*2-105/S-9,3-1	-0.2
1970	Was-A	123	262	22	56	10	2	1	18	31	38	.214	.304	.279	583	65	-12	3	2	-0	**.994**	27	*2-112/S-6	2.0
1971	Was-A	125	403	34	77	13	4	2	26	33	47	.191	.252	.258	510	47	-28	2	0	0	.997	21	2-78,S-62	0.3
1972	*Oak-A	72	142	10	37	8	1	0	15	5	17	.261	.286	.331	617	88	-3	0	1	-0	.952	-1	2-65/3-4,S-1	-0.1
Total	7	700	1761	155	387	57	9	9	134	147	219	.220	.283	.278	561	65	-80	10	9	-1	.979	80	2-498,S-180/3-31,O	4.1
■ ROY CULLENBINE	Cullenbine, Roy Joseph b: 10/18/13, Nashville, Tenn. d: 5/28/91, Mt.Clemens, Mich. BB/TR, 6'1", 190 lbs. Deb: 4/19/38 Career OF: (236-LF 12-CF 600-RF)																							
1938	Det-A	25	67	12	19	1	3	0	9	12	9	.284	.392	.388	780	91	-1	2	0	0	1.000	-0	O-17(17-0-0)	-0.1
1939	Det-A	75	179	31	43	9	2	6	23	34	29	.240	.362	.413	775	91	-2	0	1	-0	.902	-5	O-46(24-4-19)/1-2	-0.9
1940	Bro-N	22	61	8	11	1	0	1	9	23	11	.180	.405	.246	651	78	-0	2			1.000	1	O-19(0-0-19)	-0.1
	StL-A	86	257	41	59	11	2	7	31	50	34	.230	.359	.370	729	87	-4	0	1	-0	.975	-2	O-57(11-0-49)/1-6	-1.0
1941	StL-A★	149	501	82	159	29	9	9	98	121	43	.317	.452	.465	917	138	35	6	4	-0	.964	1	*O-120(108-7-5),1-22	2.6
1942	StL-A	38	109	15	21	7	1	2	14	30	20	.193	.367	.330	697	95	0	0	1	-0	.930	1	O-27(27-0-0)/1-5	-0.1
	Was-A	64	241	30	69	19	0	2	35	44	18	.286	.396	.390	787	123	9	1	2	-0	.966	8	O-35(35-0-0),3-28	1.6
	*NY-A	21	77	16	28	7	0	2	17	18	2	.364	.484	.532	1017	190	10	0	1	-0	.980	2	O-19(0-0-19)/1-1	1.1
	Yr	123	427	61	118	33	1	6	66	92	40	.276	.405	.400	805	127	20	1	4	-1	.959	11	O-81L,3-28/1-6	2.6
1943	Cle-A	138	488	66	141	24	4	8	56	96	58	.289	.407	.404	811	146	33	3	4	-1	.981	3	*O-121(0-0-121),1-13	2.8
1944	Cle-A☆	154	571	98	162	34	5	16	80	87	49	.284	.380	.445	825	141	31	4	4	-1	.967	-2	*O-151(0-1-150)	2.0
1945	Cle-A	8	13	3	1	1	0	0	0	11	0	.077	.500	.154	654	97	1	0	0	0	1.000	-2	/O-4(0-0-4),3-3	-0.1

YEAR	TM/L	G	AB	R	H	2B	3B	HR	RBI	BB	SO	AVG	OBP	SLG	OPS	OPS+	BR+	SB	CS	SBR	FA	FR	G/POS	TPR
	*Det-A	146	523	80	145	27	5	18	93	102	36	.277	.398	.451	849	137	28	2	0	0	.980	13	*O-146(2-0-145)	3.3
	Yr	154	536	83	146	28	5	18	93	**113**	36	.272	.402	.444	846	137	29	2	0	0	.980	11	*O-150(2-0-149)/3-3	3.2
1946	Det-A	113	328	63	110	21	0	15	56	88	39	.335	.477	.537	1014	172	37	3	0	1	.965	1	O-81(12-0-69),1-21	3.6
1947	Det-A	142	464	82	104	18	1	24	78	137	51	.224	.401	.422	823	125	21	3	2	-0	.989	16	*1-138	3.3
Total	10	1181	3879	627	1072	209	32	110	599	853	399	.276	.408	.432	840	132	200	26	20		.969	34	O-843R,1-208/3-31	18.0
■ DICK CULLER	Culler, Richard Broadus b: 1/15/15, High Point, N.C. d: 6/16/64, Chapel Hill, N.C. BR/TR, 5'9.5", 155 lbs. Deb: 9/19/36																							
1936	Phi-A	9	38	3	9	0	0	0	1	1	3	.237	.256	.237	493	23	-5	0	0	0	.946	-3	/2-7,S-2	-0.7
1943	Chi-A	53	148	9	32	5	1	0	11	16	11	.216	.297	.264	560	65	-6	4	5	-1	.950	11	3-26,2-19/S-3	0.5
1944	Bos-N	8	28	2	2	0	0	0	0	4	2	.071	.188	.071	259	-24	-5	0			.904	2	/S-8	-0.2
1945	Bos-N	136	527	87	138	12	1	2	30	50	35	.262	.328	.300	628	75	-17	7			.954	-8	*S-126/3-6	-1.5
1946	Bos-N	134	482	70	123	15	3	0	33	62	18	.255	.342	.299	641	82	-9	7			.948	-8	*S-132	-1.0
1947	Bos-N	77	214	20	53	5	1	0	19	19	15	.248	.309	.280	589	59	-12	1			.967	3	S-77	-0.5
1948	Chi-N	48	89	4	15	2	0	0	5	13	3	.169	.275	.191	466	29	-9	0			.968	16	S-43/2-2	0.9
1949	NY-N	7	1	0	0	0	0	0	0	1	0	.000	.500	.000	500	45	0	0			.889	2	/S-7	0.2
Total	8	472	1527	195	372	39	6	2	99	166	87	.244	.320	.281	601	68	-62	19	5		.954	14	S-398/3-32,2-28	-2.3
■ NICK CULLOP	Cullop, Henry Nicholas "Tomato Face" (b: Heinrich Nicholas Kolop) b: 10/16/1900, St.Louis, Mo. d: 12/8/78, Westerville, Ohio BR/TR, 6', 200 lbs. Deb: 4/14/26 Career OF: (90-LF 24-CF 12-RF)																							
1926	NY-A	2	2	0	1	0	0	0	0	0	1	.500	.500	.500	1000	164	0	0	0	0	.000	0	H	0.0
1927	Was-A	15	23	2	5	2	0	0	1	1	6	.217	.250	.304	554	44	-2	0	0	0	1.000	-1	/O-5(2-0-3),1-1	-0.3
	Cle-A	32	68	9	16	2	3	1	8	9	19	.235	.333	.397	730	88	-1	0	4	-1	.982	3	O-20(0-13-7)/P-1	-0.1
	Yr	47	91	11	21	4	3	1	9	10	25	.231	.314	.374	687	78	-3	0	4	-1	.984	2	O-25(2-13-10)/1-1,P-1	-0.4
1929	Bro-N	13	41	7	8	2	2	1	5	8	7	.195	.327	.415	741	84	-1	0			1.000	-1	O-11(5-6-2)/1-1	-0.2
1930	Cin-N	7	22	2	4	0	0	1	5	1	9	.182	.217	.318	536	29	-3	0			1.000	0	/O-5(0-5-0)	-0.2
1931	Cin-N	104	334	29	88	23	7	8	48	21	86	.263	.309	.446	755	107	1	1			.968	0	O-83(83-0-0)	-0.3
Total	5	173	490	49	122	29	12	11	67	40	128	.249	.308	.424	733	96	-5	1	4		.975	2	O-124L/1-2,P-1	-1.1
■ WIL CULMER	Culmer, Wilfred Hillard b: 11/11/58, Nassau, Bahamas BR/TR, 6'4", 210 lbs. Deb: 4/12/83																							
1983	Cle-A	7	19	0	2	0	0	0	1	0	4	.105	.105	.105	211	-40	-4	0	1	-0	1.000	-1	/O-4(0-0-4),D-2	-0.5
■ BENNY CULP	Culp, Benjamin Baldy b: 1/19/14, Philadelphia, Pa. BR/TR, 5'9", 175 lbs. Deb: 9/17/42 C																							
1942	Phi-N	1	0	0	0	0	0	0	0	0	0	—	—	—	—	—	0	0			.500	-0	/C-1	0.0
1943	Phi-N	10	24	4	5	1	0	0	2	3	3	.208	.296	.250	546	61	-1	0			.958	-3	C-10	-0.3
1944	Phi-N	4	2	1	0	0	0	0	0	0	0	.000	.000	.000	0	-99	-1	0			1.000	0	/C-1	0.0
Total	3	15	26	5	5	1	0	0	2	3	3	.192	.276	.231	507	49	-2	0			.926	-3	/C-12	-0.3
■ JACK CUMMINGS	Cummings, John William b: 4/1/04, Pittsburgh, Pa. d: 10/5/62, W.Mifflin, Pa. BR/TR, 6', 195 lbs. Deb: 9/11/26																							
1926	NY-N	7	16	3	5	3	0	0	4	4	2	.313	.450	.500	950	157	2	0			.958	0	/C-6	0.2
1927	NY-N	43	80	8	29	6	1	2	14	5	10	.363	.407	.538	944	151	6	0			.974	-5	C-34	0.2
1928	NY-N	33	27	4	9	2	0	2	9	3	4	.333	.400	.630	1030	165	2	0			.833	0	/C-4	0.2
1929	NY-N	3	3	0	1	0	0	0	0	0	0	.333	.333	.333	667	66	-0	0			1.000	-0	/C-1	0.0
	Bos-N	3	6	0	1	0	0	0	1	0	2	.167	.167	.167	333	-18	-1	0			.667	-1	/C-3	-0.2
	Yr	6	9	0	2	0	0	0	1	0	2	.222	.222	.222	444	11	-1	0			.714	-1	/C-4	-0.2
Total	4	89	132	15	45	11	1	4	28	12	18	.341	.400	.530	930	145	8	0			.947	-6	/C-48	0.4
■ MIDRE CUMMINGS	Cummings, Midre Almeric b: 10/14/71, St.Croix, V.I. BL/TR, 6', 196 lbs. Deb: 9/10/93																							
1993	Pit-N	13	36	5	4	1	0	0	3	4	9	.111	.200	.139	339	-7	-5	0	0	0	1.000	-1	O-11(5-5-1)	-0.7
1994	Pit-N	24	86	11	21	4	0	1	12	4	18	.244	.286	.326	611	58	-5	0	0	0	.962	0	O-24(18-5-4)	-0.6
1995	Pit-N	59	152	13	37	7	1	2	15	13	30	.243	.303	.342	645	68	-7	1	0	0	.988	-0	O-41(8-20-14)	-0.7
1996	Pit-N	24	85	11	19	3	1	3	7	0	16	.224	.224	.388	612	56	-6	0	0	0	.980	1	O-21(0-11-10)	-0.5
1997	Pit-N	52	106	11	20	6	2	3	8	8	26	.189	.252	.368	620	59	-7	0	0	0	1.000	-1	O-25(14-0-11)	-0.8
	Phi-N	63	208	24	63	16	4	1	23	23	30	.303	.372	.433	805	110	3	2	3	-1	.991	2	O-54(0-53-2)	0.5
	Yr	115	314	35	83	22	6	4	31	31	56	.264	.332	.411	743	93	-4	2	3	-1	.993	1	O-79(14-53-13)	-0.3
1998	*Bos-A	67	120	20	34	8	0	5	15	17	19	.283	.381	.475	856	118	4	3	3	-0	.941	-4	D-29,O-17(0-0-17)	-0.3
1999	Min-A	16	38	1	10	0	0	1	9	3	7	.263	.317	.342	659	66	-2	2	0	0	1.000	-2	/O-5(1-0-5),D-5	-0.3
2000	Min-A	77	181	28	50	10	0	4	22	11	25	.276	.328	.398	726	78	-6	0	0	0	1.000	-0	O-40(7-0-33),D-15	-0.8
	Bos-A	21	25	1	7	0	0	0	2	6	3	.280	.419	.280	699	79	-0	0	0	0	1.000	-0	/O-4(0-1-3),D-1	-0.1
	Yr	98	206	29	57	10	0	4	24	17	28	.277	.341	.383	724	79	-6	0	0	0	1.000	-1	O-44(7-1-36),D-16	-0.9
Total	8	416	1037	125	265	55	8	20	116	89	183	.256	.319	.382	700	80	-31	8	6	-0	.987	-5	O-242(53-95-100)/D-50	-4.3
■ GEORGE CUNNINGHAM	Cunningham, George Harold b: 7/13/1894, Sturgeon Lake, Minn. d: 3/10/72, Chattanooga, Tenn. BR/TR, 5'11", 185 lbs. Deb: 4/14/16																							
1916	Det-A	35	41	7	11	2	2	0	3	8	12	.268	.388	.415	802	136	2	0			.948	1	P-35	0.0
1917	Det-A	44	34	5	6	0	0	1	3	3	13	.176	.243	.265	508	55	-2	0			.922	0	P-44	0.0
1918	Det-A	56	112	11	25	4	1	0	2	16	34	.223	.320	.277	597	84	-2	2			.923	-6	P-27,O-20(0-2-18)	-0.8
1919	Det-A	26	23	4	5	0	0	0	5	9	8	.217	.438	.217	655	89	1	0			.857	0	P-17	0.0
1921	Det-A	1	0	0	0	0	0	0	0	0	0	—	—	—	—	—	0	0	0	0	1.000	-0	/O-1(0-0-1)	0.0
Total	5	162	210	27	47	6	3	1	13	36	67	.224	.337	.295	633	91	-1	2	0		.923	-4	P-123/O-21(0-2-19)	-0.8
■ JOE CUNNINGHAM	Cunningham, Joseph Robert b: 8/27/31, Paterson, N.J. BL/TL, 6'1", 190 lbs. Deb: 6/30/54 C																							
1954	StL-N	85	310	40	88	11	3	11	50	43	40	.284	.375	.445	820	112	6	1	1	-0	.989	2	1-85	0.3
1956	StL-N	4	3	1	0	0	0	0	0	1	1	.000	.250	.000	250	-25	-1	0	0	0	1.000	-0	/1-1	-0.1
1957	StL-N	122	261	50	83	15	0	9	52	56	29	.318	.447	.479	926	146	20	3	3	-0	1.000	-3	1-57,O-46(0-0-46)	1.4
1958	StL-N	131	337	61	105	20	3	12	57	82	23	.312	.450	.496	946	144	26	4	4	-1	.997	-6	1-67,O-66(24-0-42)	1.5
1959	StL-N★	144	458	65	158	28	6	7	60	88	47	.345	**.456**	.478	934	140	32	2	6	-2	.972	-7	*O-121(20-0-109),1-35	1.7
1960	StL-N	139	492	68	138	28	3	6	39	59	59	.280	.364	.386	751	97	0	1	7	-2	.950	-7	*O-116(1-0-116),1-15	-1.5
1961	StL-N	113	322	60	92	11	2	7	40	53	32	.286	.404	.398	802	104	4	1	0	0	.964	-9	O-86(1-1-85),1-10	-1.0
1962	Chi-A	149	526	91	155	32	7	8	70	101	59	.295	.415	.428	843	128	26	3	3	-0	**.994**	-6	*1-143/O-5(0-0-5)	1.0
1963	Chi-A	67	210	32	60	12	1	1	31	33	23	.286	.393	.367	759	116	6	1	0	0	.989	-7	1-58	-0.4
1964	Chi-A	40	108	13	27	7	0	0	10	14	15	.250	.352	.315	667	90	-1	0	1	-0	.996	-1	1-33	-0.4
	Was-A	49	126	15	27	4	0	0	7	23	13	.214	.344	.246	590	68	-4	0	1	-0	.997	-4	1-41	-1.2
	Yr	89	234	28	54	11	0	0	17	37	28	.231	.348	.278	626	78	-5	0	2	-1	.997	-5	1-74	-1.6
1965	Was-A	95	201	29	46	9	1	3	20	46	27	.229	.375	.328	703	103	3	0	1	-0	.986	-4	1-59	-0.5
1966	Was-A	3	8	0	1	0	0	0	0	0	1	.125	.125	.125	250	-28	-1	0	0	0	1.000	1	/1-3	0.0
Total	12	1141	3362	525	980	177	26	64	436	599	369	.291	.406	.417	823	119	117	16	27	-6	.993	-51	1-607,O-440(46-1-403)	0.8
■ RAY CUNNINGHAM	Cunningham, Raymond Lee b: 1/17/05, Mesquite, Tex. BR/TR, 5'7.5", 150 lbs. Deb: 9/16/31																							
1931	StL-N	3	4	0	0	0	0	0	1	0	0	.000	.000	.000	0	-96	-1	0			1.000	1	/3-3	0.0
1932	StL-N	11	22	4	4	1	0	0	0	3	4	.182	.280	.227	507	37	-2	0			1.000	3	/3-8,2-2	0.1
Total	2	14	26	4	4	1	0	0	1	3	4	.154	.241	.192	434	18	-3	0			1.000	4	/3-11,2-2	0.1
■ BILL CUNNINGHAM	Cunningham, William Aloysius b: 7/30/1895, San Francisco, Cal. d: 9/26/53, Colusa, Cal. BR/TR, 5'8", 155 lbs. Deb: 7/14/21 C Career OF: (108-LF 159-CF 1-RF)																							
1921	NY-N	40	76	10	21	2	1	1	12	3	3	.276	.313	.368	681	79	-2	0	1	-0	1.000	-4	O-20(1-18-1)	-0.7
1922	*NY-N	85	229	37	75	15	2	2	33	7	9	.328	.350	.437	787	101	-0	4	5	-1	.988	-4	O-71(2-68-0)/3-1	-0.7
1923	*NY-N	79	203	22	55	7	1	5	27	10	9	.271	.305	.389	694	83	-6	5	2	0	.992	-7	O-68(10-58-0)/2-4	-1.4
1924	Bos-N	114	437	44	119	15	8	1	40	32	27	.272	.326	.350	676	85	-9	8	5	0	.970	6	*O-109(95-15-0)	-1.1
Total	4	318	945	113	270	39	12	9	112	52	48	.286	.326	.381	707	88	-17	17	13	-1	.982	-8	O-268C/2-4,3-1	-3.9
■ BILL CUNNINGHAM	Cunningham, William John b: 6/9/1888, Schenectady, N.Y. d: 2/21/46, Schenectady, N.Y. BR/TR, 5'9", 170 lbs. Deb: 9/12/10																							
1910	Was-A	21	74	3	22	5	1	0	14	12		.297	.402	.392	794	156	5	4			.957	-5	2-21	0.1
1911	Was-A	94	331	34	63	10	5	3	37	19		.190	.239	.278	517	45	-26	10			.932	-13	2-93	-3.7

YEAR	TM/L	G	AB	R	H	2B	3B	HR	RBI	BB	SO	AVG	OBP	SLG	OPS	OPS+	BR+	SB	CS	SBR	FA	FR	G/POS	TPR
1912	Was-A	8	27	5	5	1	0	1	8	3		.185	.267	.333	600	71	-1	2			.962	-3	/2-7,S-1	-0.4
Total	3	123	432	42	90	16	6	4	59	34		.208	.271	.301	572	64	-21	16			.938	-20	2-121/S-1	-4.0
■ **DOC CURLEY** Curley, Walter James b: 3/12/1874, Upton, Mass. d: 9/23/20, Worcester, Mass. BR/TR, Deb: 9/12/1899																								
1899	Chi-N	10	37	7	4	0	1	0	2	3		.108	.233	.162	395	9	-5	0			.907	-6	2-10	-0.9
■ **PETE CURREN** Curren, Peter b: Baltimore, Md. 175 lbs. Deb: 9/12/1876																								
1876	Phi-N	3	12	5	4	1	0	0	2	0	0	.333	.333	.417	750	150	1				.588	-1	/C-2,O-1(0-0-1)	0.0
■ **PERRY CURRIN** Currin, Perry Gilmore b: 9/27/28, Washington, D.C. BL/TR, 6', 175 lbs. Deb: 6/29/47																								
1947	StL-A	3	2	0	0	0	0	0	0	1	0	.000	.333	.000	333	-3	-0	0	0	0	1.000	1	/S-1	0.1
■ **TONY CURRY** Curry, George Anthony b: 12/22/38, Nassau, Bahamas BL/TL, 5'11", 185 lbs. Deb: 4/12/60																								
1960	Phi-N	95	245	26	64	14	2	6	34	16	53	.261	.309	.408	717	94	-2	0	2	-1	.925	-8	O-64(51-3-14)	-1.4
1961	Phi-N	15	36	3	7	2	0	0	3	1	8	.194	.216	.250	466	24	-4	0	0	0	.833	-0	/O-8(8-0-0)	-0.5
1966	Cle-A	19	16	4	2	0	0	0	3	3	8	.125	.263	.125	388	16	-2	0	0	0	.000	0	H	-0.2
Total	3	129	297	33	73	16	2	6	40	20	69	.246	.296	.374	669	82	-8	0	2	-1	.915	-8	/O-72(59-3-14)	-2.1
■ **JIM CURRY** Curry, James L. b: 3/10/1893, Camden, N.J. d: 8/2/38, Grenloch, N.J. BR/TR, 5'11", 160 lbs. Deb: 10/2/09																								
1909	Phi-A	1	4	1	1	0	0	0	0	0		.250	.250	.250	500	57	-0	0			1.000	-1	/2-1	-0.1
1911	NY-A	4	11	3	2	0	0	0	0	1		.182	.250	.182	432	20	-1	0			.773	-1	/2-4	-0.3
1918	Det-A	5	20	1	5	1	0	0	0	0	0	.250	.286	.300	586	80	-1	0			.952	-3	/2-5	-0.4
Total	3	10	35	5	8	1	0	0	0	1	0	.229	.270	.257	527	56	-2	0			.867	-5	/2-10	-0.8
■ **CHAD CURTIS** Curtis, Chad David b: 11/6/68, Marion, Ind. BR/TR, 5'10", 175 lbs. Deb: 4/8/92 Career OF: (375-LF 670-CF 113-RF)																								
1992	Cal-A	139	441	59	114	16	2	10	46	51	71	.259	.343	.372	715	100	1	43	18	3	.978	-3	*O-135(48-35-62)/D-1	-0.2
1993	Cal-A	152	583	94	166	25	3	6	59	70	89	.285	.365	.369	734	95	-2	48	24	2	.980	17	*O-151(0-151-0)/2-3	1.8
1994	Cal-A	114	453	67	116	23	4	11	50	37	69	.256	.319	.397	717	82	-13	25	11	2	.988	15	*O-114(0-114-0)	0.5
1995	Det-A	144	586	96	157	29	3	21	67	70	93	.268	.353	.435	788	104	4	27	15	1	.992	2	*O-144(0-144-0)	0.8
1996	Det-A	104	400	65	105	20	1	10	37	53	73	.262	.350	.393	743	88	-7	16	10	0	.965	-7	*O-104(48-80-0)	-1.3
	*LA-N	43	104	20	22	5	0	2	9	17	15	.212	.322	.317	640	75	-3	2	1	0	.985	-3	O-40(0-40-0)	-0.6
1997	Cle-A	22	29	8	6	1	0	3	5	7	10	.207	.361	.552	913	129	1	0	0	0	1.000	-5	O-19(3-12-4)	-0.3
	*NY-A	93	320	51	93	21	1	12	50	36	49	.291	.371	.475	846	120	10	12	6	1	.978	-5	O-92(53-43-5)	0.3
	Yr	115	349	59	99	22	1	15	55	43	59	.284	.370	.481	852	120	11	12	6	1	.980	-10	*O-111(56-55-9)	0.0
1998	*NY-A	151	456	79	111	21	1	10	56	75	80	.243	.359	.360	718	91	-3	21	5	3	.984	2	*O-148(100-45-9)/D-2	-0.1
1999	*NY-A	96	195	37	51	6	0	5	24	43	35	.262	.402	.369	772	100	2	8	4	0	.990	-11	O-81(72-6-3),D-14	-1.0
2000	Tex-A	108	335	48	91	25	1	8	48	37	71	.272	.346	.424	770	91	-5	3	3	-0	.965	-4	O-80(51-0-30),D-16	-1.2
Total	9	1166	3902	624	1032	192	16	98	451	496	655	.264	.353	.397	750	96	-16	205	97	11	.981	-2	*O-1108C/D-33,2-3	-1.3
■ **ERVIN CURTIS** Curtis, Ervin Duane b: 12/27/1861, Coldwater, Mich. d: 2/14/45, N.Adams, Mass. BL/TL, 5'8.5", 157 lbs. Deb: 7/15/1891																								
1891	Cin-N	27	108	11	29	3	3	1	13	9	19	.269	.331	.380	710	106	1	3			.862	-0	O-27(0-24-3)	-0.1
	Was-a	29	103	17	26	3	2	0	12	13	16	.252	.347	.320	668	96	-0	2			.797	-1	O-29(0-20-9)	-0.2
Total	1	56	211	28	55	6	5	1	25	22	35	.261	.339	.351	690	101	0	5			.829	-2	/O-56(0-44-12)	-0.3
■ **GENE CURTIS** Curtis, Eugene Holmes "Eude" b: 5/5/1883, Bethany, W.Va. d: 1/1/19, Steubenville, Ohio BR/TR, 6'3", 220 lbs. Deb: 9/21/03																								
1903	Pit-N	5	19	2	8	1	0	0	3	1		.421	.450	.474	924	158	1	0			.833	-0	/O-5(5-0-0)	0.1
■ **FRED CURTIS** Curtis, Frederick Marion b: 10/30/1880, Beaver Lake, Mich. d: 4/5/39, Minneapolis, Minn. BR/TR, 6'1", Deb: 7/24/05																								
1905	NY-A	2	9	0	2	1	0	0	2	1		.222	.300	.333	633	90	-0	1			1.000	-0	/1-2	0.0
■ **HARRY CURTIS** Curtis, Harry Albert b: 2/19/1883, Portland, Maine d: 8/1/51, Evanston, Ill. TR, 5'10.5", 170 lbs. Deb: 8/28/07																								
1907	NY-N	6	9	2	2	0	0	0	1	2		.222	.364	.222	586	81	-0	2			.909	0	/C-6	0.0
■ **GUY CURTRIGHT** Curtright, Guy Paxton b: 10/18/12, Holliday, Mo. d: 8/23/97, Sun City Center, Fla. BR/TR, 5'11", 200 lbs. Deb: 4/21/43																								
1943	Chi-A	138	488	67	142	20	7	3	48	69	60	.291	.382	.379	761	123	16	13	12	-1	.972	-2	*O-128(128-0-0)	0.6
1944	Chi-A	72	198	22	50	8	2	2	23	23	21	.253	.330	.343	674	94	-1	4	3	-0	.948	1	O-51(35-0-17)	-0.3
1945	Chi-A	98	324	51	91	15	7	4	32	39	29	.281	.358	.407	766	125	10	3	4	-1	.986	1	O-84(26-46-13)	0.7
1946	Chi-A	23	55	7	11	2	0	0	5	11	14	.200	.333	.236	570	63	-2	0	1	-0	1.000	1	O-15(2-2-11)	-0.3
Total	4	331	1065	147	294	45	16	9	108	142	124	.276	.363	.374	737	115	23	20	20	-3	.973	2	O-278(191-48-41)	0.7
■ **TONY CUSICK** Cusick, Andrew Daniel "Andy" b: 12/1857, Fall River, Mass. d: 8/6/29, Chicago, Ill. BR/TR, 5'9.5", 190 lbs. Deb: 8/21/1884 Career OF: (2-LF 2-CF 3-RF)																								
1884	Wil-U	11	34	0	5	0	0	0		1		.147	.171	.147	318	-3	-5				.871	-0	/C-6,S-3,O-3L,23	-0.4
	Phi-N	9	29	2	4	0	0	0	1	0	3	.138	.138	.138	276	-14	-4				.930	4	/C-9	0.1
1885	Phi-N	39	141	12	25	1	0	0	5	1	24	.177	.183	.184	367	19	-12				.808	-3	C-38/O-1(0-1-0)	-1.2
1886	Phi-N	29	104	10	23	5	1	0	4	3	14	.221	.243	.288	531	61	-5	1			.891	-6	C-25/O-3(1-0-2),1-1	-0.8
1887	Phi-N	7	27	3	10	1	0	0	5	3	1	.370	.393	.333	726	98	0	0			.643	-3	/C-4,1-3,2-1	-0.3
Total	4	95	335	27	67	7	1	0	15	8	42	.200	.214	.220	434	35	-26	1			.844	-8	/C-82,O-7R,1-4,S23	-2.6
■ **JACK CUSICK** Cusick, John Peter b: 6/12/28, Weehawken, N.J. d: 11/17/89, Edgewood, N.J. BR/TR, 6', 170 lbs. Deb: 4/24/51																								
1951	Chi-N	65	164	16	29	3	2	2	16	17	29	.177	.254	.256	510	37	-15	2	1	0	.953	-2	S-56	-1.4
1952	Bos-N	49	78	5	13	1	0	0	6	6	9	.167	.226	.179	406	14	-9	0	1	-0	.969	-2	S-28/3-3	-1.1
Total	2	114	242	21	42	4	2	2	22	23	38	.174	.245	.231	477	30	-24	2	2	-0	.958	-4	/S-84,3-3	-2.5
■ **NED CUTHBERT** Cuthbert, Edgar Edward b: 6/20/1845, Philadelphia, Pa. d: 2/6/05, St.Louis, Mo. BR/TR, 5'6", 140 lbs. Deb: 5/20/1871 MU NA OF: (245-LF 4-CF 0-RF)																								
1871	Ath-n	28	150	47	37	7	5	3	30	10	2	.247	.294	.420	714	103	1	16	2	3	.890	4	*O-27(27-0-0)/C-1	0.5
1872	Ath-n	47	260	83	88	10	0	1	47	6	10	.338	.353	.388	742	127	8	14	4	2	.858	-3	*O-47(47-0-0)	0.6
1873	Phi-n	51	278	78	77	5	3	2	33	2	4	.277	.282	.338	620	80	-7	**13**	2	**2**	.848	-6	*O-51(51-0-0)	-0.7
1874	Chi-n	58	295	65	79	6	1	2	24	5	5	.268	.280	.315	595	90	-3	8	0	2	.806	-0	*O-55(55-2-0)/C-4	0.0
1875	StL-n	68	319	68	78	9	2	0	17	3	8	.245	.252	.285	537	95	0	18	1	4	.860	-13	*O-67(65-2-0)/C-3,2-1	-0.6
1876	StL-N	63	290	46	70	10	1	0	25	7	4	.241	.266	.290	555	90	-2				.843	-8	*O-63(63-0-0)	-1.3
1877	Cin-N	12	56	6	10	5	0	0	2	1	2	.179	.193	.268	461	49	-3				.830	4	O-12(12-0-0)	0.0
1882	StL-a	60	233	28	52	16	5	0		17		.223	.276	.335	611	101	0				.896	-4	*O-60(60-0-0),M	-0.5
1883	StL-a	21	71	3	12	1	0	0	3	4		.169	.213	.183	396	27	-6				.794	-1	O-20(18-1-1)/1-1	-0.6
1884	Bal-U	44	168	29	34	5	0	0		10		.202	.247	.232	479	42	-17				.750	-5	O-44(0-44-0)	-2.1
Total	5 n	252	1302	341	359	37	11	8	151	26	29	.276	.290	.339	629	98	-2	69	9	12	.846	-18	O-247L/C-8,2-1	-0.2
Total	5	200	818	112	178	37	6	0	30	39	6	.218	.255	.280	535	73	-27				.833	-14	O-199(153-45-1)/1-1	-4.5
■ **GEORGE CUTSHAW** Cutshaw, George William "Clancy" b: 7/29/1886, Wilmington, Ill. d: 8/22/73, San Diego, Cal. BR/TR, 5'9", 160 lbs. Deb: 4/25/12																								
1912	Bro-N	102	357	41	100	14	4	0	28	31	16	.280	.341	.342	683	91	-4	16			.958	8	2-91/3-5,S-1	0.5
1913	Bro-N	147	592	72	158	23	13	7	80	39	22	.267	.315	.385	701	97	-4	39			.957	18	*2-147	1.7
1914	Bro-N	153	583	69	150	22	12	2	78	30	32	.257	.297	.346	644	89	-9	34			.959	28	*2-153	2.2
1915	Bro-N	154	566	68	139	18	9	0	62	34	35	.246	.293	.309	602	81	-13	28	23	-2	**.971**	17	*2-154	0.5
1916	*Bro-N	154	581	58	151	21	4	2	63	25	32	.260	.292	.320	612	85	-11	27	20	-1	.958	8	*2-154	-0.1
1917	Bro-N	135	487	42	126	17	7	4	49	21	26	.259	.292	.347	639	93	-5	22			.963	-9	*2-134	-1.4
1918	Pit-N	126	463	56	132	16	10	5	68	27	18	.285	.326	.395	721	116	7	25			.964	-3	*2-126	0.7
1919	Pit-N	139	512	49	124	15	8	3	51	30	22	.242	.287	.320	607	79	-13	36			**.980**	-11	*2-139	-2.4
1920	Pit-N	131	488	56	123	16	8	0	47	23	10	.252	.287	.318	605	71	-18	17	14	-1	.968	1	*2-129	-1.8
1921	Pit-N	98	350	46	119	18	4	0	53	11	11	.340	.362	.414	776	102	1	14	5	1	.951	-15	2-84	-1.0
1922	Det-A	132	499	57	133	14	8	2	61	20	13	.267	.300	.339	639	68	-24	11	5	1	.972	9	*2-132	-1.1
1923	Det-A	45	143	15	32	1	2	0	13	9	5	.224	.279	.259	538	43	-12	2	1	0	.988	12	2-43/3-2	0.1
Total	12	1516	5621	629	1487	195	89	25	653	300	242	.265	.305	.344	649	86	-106	271	68		.965	61	*2-1486/3-7,S-1	-2.1

■ KIKI CUYLER Cuyler, Hazen Shirley b: 8/30/1898, Harrisville, Mich. d: 2/11/50, Ann Arbor, Mich. BR/TR, 5'10.5", 180 lbs. Deb: 9/29/21 CH

YEAR	TM/L	G	AB	R	H	2B	3B	HR	RBI	BB	SO	AVG	OBP	SLG	OPS	OPS+	BR+	SB	CS	SBR	FA	FR	G/POS	TPR
1921	Pit-N	1	3	0	0	0	0	0	0	0	1	.000	.000	.000	0	-97	-1	0	0	0	1.000	-0	/O-1(0-0-1)	-0.1
1922	Pit-N	1	0	0	0	0	0	0	0	0	0	—	—	—	—	—	0	0	0	0	.000	0	R	0.0
1923	Pit-N	11	40	4	10	1	1	0	2	5	3	.250	.348	.325	673	77	-1	2	3	-1	.931	-1	O-11(10-3-0)	-0.3
1924	Pit-N	117	466	94	165	27	16	9	85	30	62	.354	.402	.539	940	147	30	32	11	3	.943	5	*O-114(78-4-35)	2.9
1925	*Pit-N	153	617	**144**	220	43	**26**	18	102	58	56	.357	.423	.598	1021	148	44	41	13	4	.967	7	*O-153(0-25-129)	4.0
1926	Pit-N	157	614	**113**	197	31	15	8	92	50	66	.321	.380	.459	840	119	16	**35**			.968	13	*O-157(62-79-18)	2.0
1927	Pit-N	85	285	60	88	13	7	3	31	37	36	.309	.394	.435	829	114	7	20			.980	2	O-73(12-49-13)	0.4
1928	Chi-N	133	499	92	142	25	9	17	79	51	61	.285	.359	.473	832	117	12	**37**			.982	6	*O-127(13-7-108)	0.7
1929	*Chi-N	139	509	111	183	29	7	15	102	66	56	.360	.438	.532	970	139	33	**43**			.974	-0	*O-129(16-8-114)	2.1
1930	Chi-N	156	642	155	228	50	17	13	134	72	49	.355	.428	.547	975	133	36	**37**			.980	12	*O-156(29-0-131)	3.1
1931	Chi-N	154	613	110	202	37	12	9	88	72	54	.330	.404	.473	877	133	30	13			.970	-4	*O-153(0-66-84)	1.9
1932	*Chi-N	110	446	58	130	19	9	10	77	29	43	.291	.340	.442	782	109	5	9			.969	-7	*O-109(0-49-60)	-0.7
1933	Chi-N	70	262	37	83	13	3	5	35	21	29	.317	.376	.447	823	135	12	4			.978	-7	O-69(35-15-19)	0.2
1934	Chi-N★	142	559	80	189	**42**	8	6	69	31	62	.338	.377	.474	851	129	22	15			.971	0	*O-142(0-136-6)	1.8
1935	Chi-N	45	157	22	42	5	1	4	18	10	16	.268	.331	.389	720	92	-2	3			.981	-1	O-42(0-41-2)	-0.3
	Cin-N	62	223	36	56	8	3	2	22	27	18	.251	.337	.341	678	85	-4	5			.985	-3	O-57(5-49-3)	-0.8
	Yr	107	380	58	98	13	4	6	40	37	34	.258	.335	.361	695	88	-6	8			.983	-3	O-99(5-90-5)	-1.1
1936	Cin-N	144	567	96	185	29	11	7	74	47	67	.326	.380	.453	833	132	25	16			.974	-4	*O-140(22-105-14)	1.6
1937	Cin-N	117	406	48	110	12	4	0	32	36	50	.271	.333	.320	654	82	-9	10			.973	-8	*O-106(41-47-16)	-2.1
1938	Bro-N	82	253	45	69	10	8	2	23	34	23	.273	.363	.399	763	107	3	6			.993	0	O-68(8-17-43)	0.0
Total	18	1879	7161	1305	2299	394	157	128	1065	676	752	.321	.386	.474	860	125	259	328	27		.972	12	*O-1807(331-700-796)	16.4

■ MILT CUYLER Cuyler, Milton b: 10/7/68, Macon, Ga. BB/TR, 5'10", 185 lbs. Deb: 9/6/90

YEAR	TM/L	G	AB	R	H	2B	3B	HR	RBI	BB	SO	AVG	OBP	SLG	OPS	OPS+	BR+	SB	CS	SBR	FA	FR	G/POS	TPR
1990	Det-A	19	51	8	13	3	1	0	8	5	10	.255	.321	.353	674	88	-1	1	2	-0	.976	0	O-17(0-17-1)	-0.1
1991	Det-A	154	475	77	122	15	7	3	33	52	92	.257	.336	.337	673	86	-8	41	10	6	.986	8	*O-151(1-150-0)	0.4
1992	Det-A	89	291	39	70	11	1	3	28	10	62	.241	.275	.316	592	65	-14	8	5	0	.983	-0	O-89(0-88-1)	-1.5
1993	Det-A	82	249	46	53	11	7	0	19	19	53	.213	.277	.313	590	59	-15	13	2	2	.968	1	O-80(0-80-0)	-1.1
1994	Det-A	48	116	20	28	3	1	1	11	13	21	.241	.323	.310	633	64	-6	5	3	0	.975	-9	O-45(13-29-8)	-1.4
1995	Det-A	41	88	15	18	1	4	0	5	8	16	.205	.271	.307	578	50	-7	2	1	0	.929	-4	O-36(34-1-1)/D-2	-1.1
1996	Bos-A	50	110	19	22	1	2	2	12	13	19	.200	.302	.300	602	52	-8	7	3	0	.972	-3	O-45(0-30-22)/D-2	-1.0
1998	Tex-A	7	6	3	3	2	0	1	3	1	0	.500	.571	1.333	1905	360	2	0	0	0	1.000	-1	/O-3(0-3-0),D-3	0.2
Total	8	490	1386	227	329	47	23	10	119	121	273	.237	.306	.326	632	71	-56	77	26	8	.977	-7	O-466(48-398-33)/D-7	-5.6

■ AL CYPERT Cypert, Alfred Boyd "Cy" b: 8/8/1889, Little Rock, Ark. d: 1/9/73, Washington, D.C. BR/TR, 5'10.5", 150 lbs. Deb: 6/27/14

YEAR	TM/L	G	AB	R	H	2B	3B	HR	RBI	BB	SO	AVG	OBP	SLG	OPS	OPS+	BR+	SB	CS	SBR	FA	FR	G/POS	TPR
1914	Cle-A	1	1	0	0	0	0	0	0	0	1	.000	.000	.000	0	-96	-0	0			.000	0	/3-1	0.0

■ PAUL DADE Dade, Lonnie Paul b: 12/7/51, Seattle, Wash. BR/TR, 6', 195 lbs. Deb: 9/12/75 Career OF: (62-LF 41-CF 142-RF)

YEAR	TM/L	G	AB	R	H	2B	3B	HR	RBI	BB	SO	AVG	OBP	SLG	OPS	OPS+	BR+	SB	CS	SBR	FA	FR	G/POS	TPR
1975	Cal-A	11	30	5	6	4	0	0	1	6	7	.200	.333	.333	667	96	-0	0	0	0	1.000	1	/O-3(1-0-2),3-1,D-7	0.0
1976	Cal-A	13	9	2	1	0	0	0	1	3	3	.111	.333	.111	444	36	-1	0	0	0	.750	0	/O-4L,2-2,3-1,D-1	0.0
1977	Cle-A	134	461	65	134	15	3	3	45	32	58	.291	.339	.356	695	93	-4	16	8	1	.989	-7	O-99R,3-26/2-1,D-7	-1.5
1978	Cle-A	93	307	37	78	12	1	3	20	34	45	.254	.332	.329	661	88	-4	12	9	-1	.962	2	O-81(1-7-75)/D-9	-0.7
1979	Cle-A	44	170	22	48	4	1	3	18	12	22	.282	.330	.371	700	88	-3	12	6	1	.962	2	O-37(20-0-17)/3-2,D-4	-0.2
	SD-N	76	283	38	78	19	2	1	19	14	48	.276	.314	.367	682	91	-4	13	5	1	.949	6	3-70/O-4(1-3-0)	0.1
1980	SD-N	68	53	17	10	0	0	0	3	12	10	.189	.338	.189	527	54	-3	4	5	-1	.846	1	3-21/O-8(4-3-1),2-1	-0.2
Total	6	439	1313	186	355	54	7	10	107	113	193	.270	.331	.345	676	89	-19	57	33	1	.970	4	O-236R,3-121/D-28,2	-2.5

■ ANGELO DAGRES Dagres, Angelo George "Junior" b: 8/22/34, Newburyport, Mass. BL/TL, 5'11", 175 lbs. Deb: 9/11/55

YEAR	TM/L	G	AB	R	H	2B	3B	HR	RBI	BB	SO	AVG	OBP	SLG	OPS	OPS+	BR+	SB	CS	SBR	FA	FR	G/POS	TPR
1955	Bal-A	8	15	5	4	0	0	0	3	1	2	.267	.313	.267	579	61	-1	0	0	0	.818	-1	/O-5(1-0-4)	-0.2

■ BILL DAHLEN Dahlen, William Frederick "Bad Bill" b: 1/5/1870, Nelliston, N.Y. d: 12/5/50, Brooklyn, N.Y. BR/TR, 5'9", 180 lbs. Deb: 4/22/1891 M Career OF: (36-LF 11-CF 11-RF)

YEAR	TM/L	G	AB	R	H	2B	3B	HR	RBI	BB	SO	AVG	OBP	SLG	OPS	OPS+	BR+	SB	CS	SBR	FA	FR	G/POS	TPR
1891	Chi-N	135	549	114	143	18	13	9	76	67	60	.260	.348	.390	738	115	11	21			.887	9	3-84,O-37L,S-15	1.8
1892	Chi-N	143	581	114	170	23	19	5	58	45	56	.293	.349	.423	772	132	20	60			.909	25	S-72,3-68/O-2C,2-1	4.5
1893	Chi-N	116	485	113	146	28	15	5	64	58	30	.301	.381	.452	833	123	15	31			.892	3	*S-88,O-17C,2-10,/3	1.9
1894	Chi-N	122	507	150	182	32	14	15	108	76	33	.359	.445	.566	1011	135	29	42			.900	**35**	S-67,3-55	**5.1**
1895	Chi-N	129	516	106	131	19	10	7	62	61	51	.254	.344	.370	714	79	-17	38			.904	36	*S-129/O-1(0-1-0)	2.0
1896	Chi-N	125	474	137	167	30	19	9	74	64	36	.352	.438	.553	990	154	37	51			.915	25	*S-125	5.6
1897	Chi-N	75	276	67	80	18	8	6	40	43		.290	.399	.478	877	126	11	15			.930	28	S-75	3.6
1898	Chi-N	142	521	96	151	35	8	1	79	58		.290	.385	.393	779	123	18	27			.921	26	*S-142	**4.7**
1899	Bro-N	121	428	87	121	22	7	4	76	67		.283	.398	.395	793	115	12	29			.941	17	*S-110,3-11	3.2
1900	*Bro-N	133	483	87	125	16	11	1	69	73		.259	.364	.344	708	90	-4	31			.938	20	*S-133	2.0
1901	Bro-N	131	511	69	136	17	9	4	82	30		.266	.313	.358	671	92	-6	23			.929	14	*S-129/2-2	1.2
1902	Bro-N	138	527	67	139	25	8	2	74	43		.264	.329	.353	682	110	6	20			.916	-6	*S-138	0.4
1903	Bro-N	138	474	71	124	17	9	1	64	82		.262	.373	.342	715	107	8	34			**.948**	18	*S-138	2.9
1904	NY-N	145	523	70	140	26	2	2	**80**	44		.268	.326	.337	662	100	0	47			.930	28	*S-145	3.4
1905	*NY-N	148	520	67	126	20	4	7	81	62		.242	.337	.337	673	99	1	37			.948	20	*S-147/O-1(1-0-0)	2.6
1906	NY-N	143	471	63	113	18	3	1	49	76		.240	.357	.297	655	102	5	16			.938	0	*S-143	1.1
1907	NY-N	143	464	40	96	20	1	0	34	51		.207	.291	.254	545	69	-16	11			.941	7	*S-143	-0.4
1908	Bos-N	144	524	50	125	23	2	3	48	35		.239	.296	.307	604	94	-4	10			.952	**38**	*S-144	4.4
1909	Bos-N	69	197	22	46	6	1	2	16	29		.234	.332	.305	636	93	-1	4			.908	9	S-49/2-6,3-2	1.1
1910	Bro-N	3	2	0	0	0	0	0	0	0	0	.000	.000	.000	0	-99	-1	0			.000	0	HM	-0.1
1911	Bro-N	1	3	0	0	0	0	0	0	0	3	.000	.000	.000	0	-99	-1	0			1.000	2	/S-1,M	0.1
Total	21	2444	9036	1590	2461	413	163	84	1234	1064	269	.272	.358	.382	740	109	123	547			.927	352	*S-2133,3-223/O-58L,2	51.1

■ BABE DAHLGREN Dahlgren, Ellsworth Tenney b: 6/15/12, San Francisco, Cal. d: 9/4/96, Arcadia, Cal. BR/TR, 6', 190 lbs. Deb: 4/16/35 C

YEAR	TM/L	G	AB	R	H	2B	3B	HR	RBI	BB	SO	AVG	OBP	SLG	OPS	OPS+	BR+	SB	CS	SBR	FA	FR	G/POS	TPR
1935	Bos-A	149	525	77	138	27	7	9	63	56	67	.263	.337	.392	730	83	-14	6	5	-0	.988	-7	*1-149	-3.4
1936	Bos-A	16	57	6	16	3	1	1	7	7	1	.281	.359	.421	780	87	-1	2	1	0	.980	-1	1-16	-0.3
1937	NY-A	1	1	0	0	0	0	0	0	0	0	.000	.000	.000	0	-99	-0	0	0	0	.000	0	H	0.0
1938	NY-A	27	43	8	8	1	0	0	1	1	7	.186	.205	.209	414	4	-6	0	0	0	.826	-1	/3-8,1-6	-0.7
1939	*NY-A	144	531	71	125	18	6	15	89	57	54	.235	.312	.377	689	76	-20	2	3	-1	.991	-7	*1-144	-3.9
1940	NY-A	155	568	51	150	24	4	12	73	46	54	.264	.325	.384	709	86	-12	1	1	-0	.990	-10	*1-155	-3.6
1941	Bos-N	44	166	20	39	8	1	7	30	16	13	.235	.306	.422	728	108	1	0			.993	2	1-39/3-5	0.0
	Chi-N	99	359	50	101	20	1	16	59	43	39	.281	.360	.476	836	139	18	2			.991	-8	1-98	0.0
	Yr	143	525	70	140	28	2	23	89	59	52	.267	.343	.459	802	129	19	2			.992	-6	*1-137/3-5	0.0
1942	Chi-N	17	56	4	12	1	0	0	6	4	2	.214	.267	.232	499	48	-4	0			.986	1	1-14	-0.5
	StL-A	2	2	0	0	0	0	0	0	0	0	.000	.000	.000	0	-99	-1	0	0	0	.000	0	H	-0.1
	Bro-N	17	19	2	1	0	0	0	0	4	5	.053	.217	.053	270	-19	-3	0			1.000	1	1-10	-0.3
1943	Phi-N★	136	508	55	146	19	2	5	56	50	39	.287	.354	.362	716	111	8	2			.988	-23	1-73,3-35,S-25,/C-1	-1.8
1944	Pit-N	158	599	67	173	28	7	12	101	47	56	.289	.347	.419	766	110	7	2			.987	8	*1-158	0.7
1945	Pit-N	144	531	57	133	24	8	5	75	51	51	.250	.318	.354	673	84	-12	1			**.996**	1	*1-144	-1.9
1946	StL-A	28	80	2	14	1	0	0	9	8	13	.175	.250	.188	438	22	-8	0	1	-0	.981	1	1-24	-0.9
Total	12	1137	4045	470	1056	174	37	82	569	390	401	.261	.329	.383	713	92	-48	18	11		.990	-44	*1-1030/3-48,S-25,C	-16.7

■ JOHN DAILEY Dailey, John G. b: Brooklyn, N.Y. Deb: 7/12/1875

YEAR	TM/L	G	AB	R	H	2B	3B	HR	RBI	BB	SO	AVG	OBP	SLG	OPS	OPS+	BR+	SB	CS	SBR	FA	FR	G/POS	TPR
1875	Was-n	27	110	16	20	5	4	0	13	0	1	.182	.182	.300	482	67	-3	3	2	-0	.810	-3	S-20/3-5,2-2	-0.6
	Atl-n	2	8	3	1	0	0	0	0	0	1	.125	.125	.125	250	-15	-1	0	0	0	1.000	-4	/O-2(0-0-2),1-1,S-1	-0.4
	Yr	29	118	19	21	5	4	0	13	0	2	.178	.178	.288	466	62	-4	3	2	-0	.797	-7	S-21/3-5,2-2,O-2R,1	-1.0

■ VINCE DAILEY Dailey, Vincent Perry b: 12/25/1864, Osceola, Pa. d: 11/14/19, Hornell, N.Y. 6', 200 lbs. Deb: 4/21/1890

YEAR	TM/L	G	AB	R	H	2B	3B	HR	RBI	BB	SO	AVG	OBP	SLG	OPS	OPS+	BR+	SB	CS	SBR	FA	FR	G/POS	TPR
1890	Cle-N	64	246	41	71	5	7	0	32	33	23	.289	.373	.366	739	118	7	17			.859	1	O-64(0-0-64)/P-2	0.6

YEAR	TM/L	G	AB	R	H	2B	3B	HR	RBI	BB	SO	AVG	OBP	SLG	OPS	OPS+	BR+	SB	CS	SBR	FA	FR	G/POS	TPR
■ CON DAILY	Daily, Cornelius F. b: 9/11/1864, Blackstone, Mass. d: 6/14/28, Brooklyn, N.Y. BL, 6′, 192 lbs. Deb: 6/9/1884 F Career OF: (8-LF 9-CF 28-RF)																							
1884	Phi-U	2	8	0	0	0	0	0		0		.000	.000	.000	0	-99	-2				.857	-1	/C-2	-0.3
1885	Pro-N	60	223	20	58	6	1	0	19	12	20	.260	.298	.296	594	95	-1				.876	-0	C-48/1-7,O-6(1-3-2)	0.2
1886	Bos-N	50	180	25	43	4	2	0	21	19	29	.239	.312	.283	595	85	-2	2			.911	-11	C-49/O-1(1-0-0)	-0.8
1887	Bos-N	36	129	12	28	5	0	0	13	9	8	.217	.229	.200	429	20	-13	7			.889	-2	C-36	-1.1
1888	Ind-N	57	202	14	44	6	1	0	14	10	28	.218	.255	.257	512	62	-8	15			.893	-1	C-42/O-5R,3-5,12	-0.6
1889	Ind-N	62	219	35	55	6	2	0	26	28	21	.251	.347	.297	643	79	-5	14			.887	-12	C-51/O-6C,1-6,3-1	-1.1
1890	Bro-P	46	168	20	42	6	3	0	35	15	14	.250	.315	.321	637	66	-9	6			.879	-7	C-40/1-6,O-1(0-0-1)	-1.0
1891	Bro-N	60	206	25	66	10	1	0	30	15	13	.320	.378	.379	756	121	6	7			.925	-0	C-55/O-3R,S-2,1-1	0.9
1892	Bro-N	80	278	38	65	10	1	0	28	38	21	.234	.328	.277	605	87	-3	18			.943	-2	C-68,O-13(2-3-8)	0.1
1893	Bro-N	61	215	33	57	4	2	1	32	20	12	.265	.342	.316	658	79	-6	13			.935	-1	C-51/O-9(2-0-7)	-0.2
1894	Bro-N	67	234	40	60	14	7	0	32	31	22	.256	.351	.376	727	81	-7	8			.930	-3	C-60/1-7	-0.3
1895	Bro-N	40	142	17	30	3	2	1	11	10	18	.211	.268	.282	550	46	-11	3			.956	-3	C-39/O-1(1-0-0)	-0.9
1896	Chi-N	9	27	1	2	0	0	0	1	1	2	.074	.107	.074	181	-50	-6	1			.969	-2	/C-9	-0.6
Total	13	630	2231	280	550	74	22	2	262	208	208	.247	.314	.299	613	76	-67	94			.912	-43	C-550/O-45R,1-32,3S2	-5.7
■ ED DAILY	Daily, Edward M. b: 9/7/1862, Providence, R.I. d: 10/21/1891, Washington, D.C. BR/TR, 5′10.5″, 174 lbs. Deb: 5/4/1885 F Career OF: (153-LF 33-CF 311-RF)																							
1885	Phi-N	50	184	22	38	8	2	1	13	0	25	.207	.207	.288	495	60	-8				.891	-4	P-50	0.0
1886	Phi-N	79	309	40	70	17	1	4	50	7	34	.227	.244	.327	571	72	-11	23			.827	5	O-56(13-11-32),P-27	-0.5
1887	Phi-N	26	109	18	33	11	1	1	17	3	9	.303	.303	.434	737	97	-1	8			.659	-6	O-22(1-20-1)/P-6	-0.7
	Was-N	78	325	39	92	6	10	2	36	14	27	.283	.285	.354	639	81	-8	26			.855	-5	O-77(0-0-77)/P-1	-1.2
	Yr	104	434	57	125	17	11	3	53	17	36	.288	.290	.374	664	85	-9	34			.812	-11	O-99(1-20-78)/P-7	-1.9
1888	Was-N	110	453	56	102	8	4	7	39	7	42	.225	.239	.307	545	77	-12	44			.912	4	*O-100R/P-9,1-1	-0.8
1889	Col-a	136	578	105	148	22	8	3	70	38	65	.256	.303	.337	640	87	-10	60			.854	-3	*O-136(136-0-0)/P-2	-1.5
1890	Bro-a	91	394	68	94	15	7	1	39	24		.239	.284	.320	604	81	-11	49			.892	6	O-64(0-0-64),P-27	-0.4
	NY-N	4	15	1	2	1	0	0	1	0	4	.133	.133	.200	333	-3	-2	0			.500	0	/O-3(1-0-2),P-2	-0.1
	*Lou-a	23	80	24	20	0	2	0	9	13		.250	.355	.300	655	95	0	13			.925	1	P-12,O-11(0-2-9)	-0.1
1891	Lou-a	22	64	10	16	2	0	0	8	8	6	.250	.342	.281	624	80	-1	4			.884	0	P-15/O-7(2-0-5)	0.0
	Was-a	21	79	13	18	2	0	0	6	11	10	.228	.322	.253	575	68	-3	8			.719	-4	O-21(0-0-21)	-0.6
	Yr	43	143	23	34	4	0	0	14	19	16	.238	.331	.266	597	73	-4	12			.750	-3	O-28(2-0-26),P-15	-0.6
Total	7	640	2590	396	633	92	35	19	288	125	222	.244	.276	.325	601	80	-68	235			.857	-6	O-497R,P-151/1-1	-5.9
■ GEORGE DAISEY	Daisey, George K. b: Altoona, Pa. 5′11″, 190 lbs. Deb: 5/31/1884																							
1884	Alt-U	1	4	0	0	0	0	0		0		.000	.000	.000	0	-99	-1				.000	-1	/O-1(1-0-0)	-0.2
■ PETE DALENA	Dalena, Peter Martin b: 6/26/60, Fresno, Cal. BL/TR, 5′11″, 200 lbs. Deb: 7/7/89																							
1989	Cle-A	5	7	0	1	1	0	0	0	0	3	.143	.143	.286	429	18	-1	0	0	0	.000	0	/D-1	-0.1
■ MARK DALESANDRO	Dalesandro, Mark Anthony b: 5/14/68, Chicago, Ill. BR/TR, 6′, 185 lbs. Deb: 6/6/94																							
1994	Cal-A	19	25	5	5	1	0	1	2	2	4	.200	.259	.360	619	57	-2	0	0	0	1.000	-3	C-11/3-5,O-2(2-0-0)	-0.4
1995	Cal-A	11	10	1	1	1	0	0	0	0	2	.100	.100	.200	300	-25	-2	0	0	0	1.000	0	/C-8,O-1(1-0-0),D-1	-0.2
1998	Tor-A	32	67	8	20	5	0	2	14	1	6	.299	.309	.463	772	97	-1	0	0	0	.986	-5	C-18/3-8,1-2,O-1R	-0.5
1999	Tor-A	16	27	3	5	0	0	0	1	0	2	.185	.214	.185	399	3	-4	1	0	0	1.000	-0	/C-8,3-2,D-5	-0.4
Total	4	78	129	17	31	7	0	3	17	3	14	.240	.263	.364	627	60	-8	1	0	0	.992	-8	/C-45,3-15,D-6,O1	-1.5
■ JOHN DALEY	Daley, John Francis b: 5/25/1887, Pittsburgh, Pa. d: 8/31/88, Mansfield, Ohio BR/TR, 5′7.5″, 155 lbs. Deb: 7/19/12																							
1912	StL-A	18	52	7	9	0	0	1	3	9		.173	.317	.231	548	60	-2	4			.833	-4	S-17	-0.6
■ JUD DALEY	Daley, Judson Lawrence b: 3/14/1884, S.Coventry, Conn. d: 1/26/67, Gadsden, Ala. BL/TR, 5′8″, 172 lbs. Deb: 9/19/11																							
1911	Bro-N	19	65	8	15	2	1	0	7	2	8	.231	.286	.292	578	65	-3	2			.952	2	O-16(16-0-0)	-0.2
1912	Bro-N	61	199	22	51	9	1	1	13	24	17	.256	.342	.327	669	87	-3	2			.947	2	O-55(24-24-7)	-0.5
Total	2	80	264	30	66	11	2	1	20	26	25	.250	.329	.318	647	82	-6	4			.949	3	/O-71(40-24-7)	-0.7
■ PETE DALEY	Daley, Peter Harvey b: 1/14/30, Grass Valley, Cal. BR/TR, 6′, 195 lbs. Deb: 5/3/55																							
1955	Bos-A	17	50	4	11	2	1	0	5	3	6	.220	.264	.300	564	47	-4	0	0	0	1.000	3	C-14	0.0
1956	Bos-A	59	187	22	50	11	3	5	29	18	30	.267	.338	.439	777	92	-2	1	0	0	.992	-10	C-57	-0.9
1957	Bos-A	78	191	17	43	10	0	3	25	16	31	.225	.288	.325	613	64	-10	0	0	0	**1.000**	-2	C-77	-0.9
1958	Bos-A	27	56	10	18	2	1	2	8	7	11	.321	.397	.500	897	136	3	0	0	0	.990	2	C-27	0.6
1959	Bos-A	65	169	9	38	7	0	1	11	13	31	.225	.280	.284	564	53	-11	1	1	-0	.996	2	C-58	-0.6
1960	KC-A	73	228	19	60	10	2	5	25	16	41	.263	.311	.390	702	88	-4	0	0	0	.990	-5	C-61/O-1(1-0-0)	-0.6
1961	Was-A	72	203	12	39	7	1	2	17	14	37	.192	.244	.266	510	37	-18	0	1	-0	.988	7	C-72	-0.9
Total	7	391	1084	93	259	49	8	18	120	87	187	.239	.297	.349	646	71	-46	2	2	-0	.993	-2	C-366/O-1(1-0-0)	-3.3
■ TOM DALEY	Daley, Thomas Francis "Pete" b: 11/13/1884, DuBois, Pa. d: 12/2/34, Los Angeles, Cal. BL/TR, 5′5″, 168 lbs. Deb: 8/29/08																							
1908	Cin-N	14	46	5	5	0	0	0	1	3		.109	.196	.109	305	-2	-5	1			1.000	-0	O-13(0-0-13)	-0.7
1913	Phi-A	62	141	13	36	2	1	0	11	13	28	.255	.327	.284	611	81	-3	4			.963	-1	O-39(0-38-0)	-0.7
1914	Phi-A	28	86	17	22	1	3	0	7	12	14	.256	.347	.337	684	110	1	4	7	-2	1.000	2	O-24(14-10-0)	0.0
	NY-A	69	191	36	48	6	4	0	9	38	13	.251	.378	.325	703	112	5	8	8	-1	.958	6	O-58(28-29-0)	0.7
	Yr	97	277	53	70	7	7	0	16	50	27	.253	.369	.329	697	111	6	12	15	-3	.969	7	O-82(42-39-0)	0.7
1915	NY-A	10	8	2	2	0	0	0	1	2	2	.250	.400	.250	650	95	0	1			1.000	-0	/O-2(1-0-1)	0.0
Total	4	183	472	73	113	9	8	0	29	68	57	.239	.341	.292	634	92	-2	18	15		.970	6	O-136(43-77-14)	-0.7
■ DOM DALLESSANDRO	Dallessandro, Nicholas Dominic "Dim Dom" b: 10/3/13, Reading, Pa. d: 4/29/88, Indianapolis, Ind. BL/TL, 5′6″, 168 lbs. Deb: 4/24/37																							
1937	Bos-A	68	147	18	34	7	1	0	11	27	16	.231	.351	.293	643	61	-8	2	1	0	.965	-5	O-35(30-1-4)	-1.3
1940	Chi-N	107	287	33	77	19	6	1	36	34	13	.268	.348	.387	735	104	2	4			.969	-3	O-74(74-0-0)	-0.5
1941	Chi-N	140	486	73	132	36	2	6	85	68	37	.272	.362	.391	753	116	12	3			.987	-2	*O-131(69-62-0)	0.5
1942	Chi-N	96	264	30	69	12	4	4	43	36	18	.261	.350	.383	733	119	7	4			.986	-2	O-66(31-32-4)	0.3
1943	Chi-N	87	176	13	39	8	3	1	31	40	14	.222	.369	.318	687	101	2	1			.967	-4	O-45(31-14-0)	-0.4
1944	Chi-N	117	381	53	116	19	4	8	74	61	29	.304	.400	.438	839	137	21	1			.982	-2	*O-106(91-16-0)	1.3
1946	Chi-N	65	89	4	20	2	2	1	9	23	12	.225	.384	.326	710	104	2	1			.971	-3	O-20(16-0-4)	-0.2
1947	Chi-N	66	115	18	33	7	1	1	14	21	11	.287	.397	.391	788	115	3	0			1.000	-2	O-28(28-0-0)	0.0
Total	8	746	1945	242	520	110	23	22	303	310	150	.267	.369	.381	750	112	40	16	1		.980	-22	O-505(370-125-12)	-0.3
■ ABNER DALRYMPLE	Dalrymple, Abner Frank b: 9/9/1857, Warren, Ill. d: 1/25/39, Warren, Ill. BL/TR, 5′10.5″, 175 lbs. Deb: 5/1/1878																							
1878	Mil-N	61	271	52	96	10	4	0	15	6	29	**.354**	.368	.421	789	149	13				.832	7	*O-61(61-0-0)	1.5
1879	Chi-N	71	333	47	97	25	1	0	23	4	29	.291	.300	.372	672	113	4				.728	-13	*O-71(66-1-4)	-1.3
1880	Chi-N	86	382	**91**	**126**	25	12	0	36	3	18	.330	.335	.458	793	157	20				.859	4	*O-86(86-0-0)	1.8
1881	Chi-N	82	362	72	117	22	4	1	37	15	22	.323	.350	.414	764	133	13				.835	-7	*O-82(82-0-0)	0.1
1882	Chi-N	84	397	96	117	25	11	1	36	14	18	.295	.319	.421	739	129	12				.877	0	*O-84(84-0-0)	0.9
1883	Chi-N	80	363	78	108	24	4	2	37	11	29	.298	.318	.402	720	108	2				.826	-1	*O-80(80-0-0)	-0.1
1884	Chi-N	111	521	111	161	18	9	22	69	14	39	.309	.327	.505	832	146	24				.882	1	*O-111(111-0-0)	2.0
1885	*Chi-N	113	492	109	135	27	12	**11**	61	46	42	.274	.336	.445	782	133	16				.879	-0	*O-113(112-1-0)	1.1
1886	*Chi-N	82	331	62	77	7	12	3	26	33	44	.233	.302	.353	656	86	-7	16			.952	4	O-82(82-0-0)	-0.5
1887	Pit-N	92	403	45	121	18	5	2	31	45	43	.300	.311	.307	618	77	-9	29			.900	4	*O-92(92-0-0)	-0.6
1888	Pit-N	57	227	19	50	9	2	0	14	6	28	.220	.247	.278	524	72	-7	7			.909	-2	O-57(56-0-1)	-1.1
1891	Mil-a	32	135	31	42	7	5	1	22	7	18	.311	.345	.459	804	108	-0	6			.909	-1	O-32(32-0-0)	-0.1
Total	12	951	4217	813	1247	217	81	43	407	204	359	.296	.323	.410	732	120	80	58			.863	-4	O-951(944-2-5)	3.7
■ CLAY DALRYMPLE	Dalrymple, Clayton Errol b: 12/3/36, Chico, Cal. BL/TR, 6′, 199 lbs. Deb: 4/24/60																							
1960	Phi-N	82	158	11	43	6	2	4	21	15	21	.272	.347	.411	758	106	2	0	0	0	.966	-5	C-48	-0.2
1961	Phi-N	129	378	23	83	11	1	5	42	30	30	.220	.284	.294	578	54	-25	0	2	-1	.978	0	*C-122	-2.0

YEAR	TM/L	G	AB	R	H	2B	3B	HR	RBI	BB	SO	AVG	OBP	SLG	OPS	OPS+	BR+	SB	CS	SBR	FA	FR	G/POS	TPR
1962	Phi-N	123	370	40	102	13	3	11	54	70	32	.276	.396	.416	813	122	15	1	3	-1	.987	-12	*C-119	0.8
1963	Phi-N	142	452	40	114	15	3	10	40	45	55	.252	.327	.365	692	100	1	0	2	-1	.981	1	*C-142	0.8
1964	Phi-N	127	382	36	91	16	3	6	46	39	40	.238	.309	.343	652	84	-8	0	1	-0	.991	3	*C-124	0.1
1965	Phi-N	103	301	14	64	5	5	4	23	34	37	.213	.293	.302	595	69	-12	0	1	-0	.993	18	*C-102	1.0
1966	Phi-N	114	331	30	81	13	3	4	39	60	57	.245	.365	.338	704	97	1	0	0	0	.993	-4	*C-110	0.2
1967	Phi-N	101	268	12	46	7	1	3	21	36	49	.172	.272	.239	511	47	-18	1	2	-0	.994	20	C-97	0.7
1968	Phi-N	85	241	19	50	9	1	3	26	22	57	.207	.277	.290	567	70	-9	1	2	-0	.990	-3	C-80	-1.0
1969	*Bal-A	37	80	8	19	1	1	3	6	13	8	.237	.344	.387	732	103	1	0	0	0	1.000	2	C-30	0.3
1970	Bal-A	13	32	4	7	1	0	1	3	7	4	.219	.359	.344	703	94	-0	0	0	0	1.000	6	C-11	0.6
1971	Bal-A	23	49	6	10	1	0	1	6	16	13	.204	.409	.286	695	101	1	0	0	0	.971	2	C-18	0.4
Total	12	1079	3042	243	710	98	23	55	327	387	403	.233	.324	.335	659	85	-51	3	13	-4	.987	27	*C-1003	1.7

■ BILL DALRYMPLE Dalrymple, William Dunn b: 2/7/1891, Baltimore, Md. d: 7/14/67, San Diego, Cal. TR, Deb: 7/6/15

YEAR	TM/L	G	AB	R	H	2B	3B	HR	RBI	BB	SO	AVG	OBP	SLG	OPS	OPS+	BR+	SB	CS	SBR	FA	FR	G/POS	TPR
1915	StL-A	3	2	0	0	0	0	0	0	0	0	.000	.000	.000	0	-99	-0	0			1.000	0	/3-1	0.0

■ JACK DALTON Dalton, Talbot Percy b: 7/3/1885, Henderson, Tenn. BR/TR, 5'10.5", 187 lbs. Deb: 6/20/10

YEAR	TM/L	G	AB	R	H	2B	3B	HR	RBI	BB	SO	AVG	OBP	SLG	OPS	OPS+	BR+	SB	CS	SBR	FA	FR	G/POS	TPR
1910	Bro-N	77	273	33	62	9	4	1	21	26	30	.227	.304	.300	604	79	-7	5			.966	3	O-72(0-0-72)	-0.8
1914	Bro-N	128	442	65	141	13	8	1	45	53	39	.319	.396	.391	787	131	19	19			.965	-3	*O-116(5-109-2)	0.8
1915	Buf-F	132	437	68	128	17	3	2	46	50	38	.293	.368	.359	727	103	-3	28			.966	-5	*O-119(10-60-52)	-1.6
1916	Det-A	8	11	1	2	0	0	0	0	0	5	.182	.182	.182	364	9	-1	0			1.000	-1	/O-4(1-0-3)	-0.3
Total	4	345	1163	167	333	39	15	4	112	129	112	.286	.362	.356	718	107	7	52			.966	-7	O-311(16-169-129)	-1.9

■ BERT DALY Daly, Albert Joseph b: 4/8/1881, Bayonne, N.J. d: 9/3/52, Bayonne, N.J. BR/TR, 5'9", 170 lbs. Deb: 8/7/03

YEAR	TM/L	G	AB	R	H	2B	3B	HR	RBI	BB	SO	AVG	OBP	SLG	OPS	OPS+	BR+	SB	CS	SBR	FA	FR	G/POS	TPR
1903	Phi-A	10	21	2	4	0	2	0	4	1		.190	.227	.381	608	76	-1	0			.700	-4	/2-4,3-3,S-1	-0.5

■ SUN DALY Daly, James J. b: 1/6/1865, Port Henry, N.Y. d: 4/30/38, Albany, N.Y. BL, Deb: 9/30/1892

YEAR	TM/L	G	AB	R	H	2B	3B	HR	RBI	BB	SO	AVG	OBP	SLG	OPS	OPS+	BR+	SB	CS	SBR	FA	FR	G/POS	TPR
1892	Bal-N	13	48	5	12	0	2	0	7	1	4	.250	.265	.333	599	79	-2	0			.923	0	O-13(10-3-0)	-0.2

■ JOE DALY Daly, Joseph John b: 9/21/1868, Conshohocken, Pa. d: 3/21/43, Philadelphia, Pa. TR, 5'8", 157 lbs. Deb: 9/19/1890 F

YEAR	TM/L	G	AB	R	H	2B	3B	HR	RBI	BB	SO	AVG	OBP	SLG	OPS	OPS+	BR+	SB	CS	SBR	FA	FR	G/POS	TPR
1890	Phi-a	21	75	8	21	4	1	0	7	3		.280	.308	.360	668	97	-1	1			.900	-6	O-14(3-8-3)/C-9	-0.6
1891	Cle-N	1	3	0	0	0	0	0	0	0	2	.000	.000	.000	0	-96	-1	0			1.000	0	/O-1(0-0-1)	-0.1
1892	Bos-N	1	0	0	0	0	0	0	0	0	0	—	—	—	—	—	0	0			1.000	0	/C-1	0.0
Total	3	23	78	8	21	4	1	0	7	3	2	.269	.296	.346	642	90	-1	1			.909	-6	/O-15(3-8-4),C-10	-0.7

■ TOM DALY Daly, Thomas Daniel b: 12/12/1891, St.John, N.B., Can. d: 11/7/46, Medford, Mass. BR/TR, 5'11.5", 171 lbs. Deb: 9/23/13 C Career OF: (14-LF 0-CF 11-RF)

YEAR	TM/L	G	AB	R	H	2B	3B	HR	RBI	BB	SO	AVG	OBP	SLG	OPS	OPS+	BR+	SB	CS	SBR	FA	FR	G/POS	TPR
1913	Chi-A	1	3	0	0	0	0	0	0	0	0	.000	.000	.000	0	-99	-1	0			1.000	1	/C-1	0.0
1914	Chi-A	62	133	13	31	2	0	0	8	7	13	.233	.271	.248	520	57	-7	3	4	-1	.909	-10	O-23L/3-5,C-4,1-2	-2.1
1915	Chi-A	29	47	5	9	1	0	0	3	5	9	.191	.269	.213	482	43	-3	0			.958	-3	C-19/1-1	-0.5
1916	Cle-A	31	73	3	16	1	1	0	8	1	2	.219	.230	.260	490	45	-5	0			.982	-2	C-25/O-1(0-0-1)	-0.6
1918	Chi-N	1	1	0	0	0	0	0	0	0	0	.000	.000	.000	0	-98	-0	0			.667	-0	/C-1	0.0
1919	Chi-N	25	50	4	11	0	1	0	1	2	5	.220	.250	.260	510	53	-3	0			.956	-2	C-18	-0.5
1920	Chi-N	44	90	12	28	6	0	0	13	2	6	.311	.333	.378	711	102	0	1	1	-0	.981	-3	C-29	-0.2
1921	Chi-N	51	143	12	34	7	1	0	22	8	8	.238	.278	.301	579	53	-10	1	2	-0	.973	4	C-47	-0.3
Total	8	244	540	49	129	17	3	0	55	25	43	.239	.274	.281	555	59	-29	5	7		.972	-15	C-144/O-24L,3-5,1-3	-4.2

■ TOM DALY Daly, Thomas Peter "Tido" b: 2/7/1866, Philadelphia, Pa. d: 10/29/38, Brooklyn, N.Y. BB/TR, 5'7", 170 lbs. Deb: 4/30/1887 F Career OF: (9-LF 17-CF 29-RF)

YEAR	TM/L	G	AB	R	H	2B	3B	HR	RBI	BB	SO	AVG	OBP	SLG	OPS	OPS+	BR+	SB	CS	SBR	FA	FR	G/POS	TPR
1887	Chi-N	74	278	45	75	10	4	2	17	22	25	.270	.270	.301	571	52	-18	29			**.935**	33	C-64/O-8C,S-2,21	1.7
1888	Chi-N	65	219	34	42	2	6	0	29	10	26	.192	.230	.256	486	51	-12	10			.939	20	C-62/O-4(0-1-3)	1.3
1889	Was-N	71	250	39	75	13	5	1	40	38	28	.300	.394	.404	798	131	12	18			.917	3	C-57/1-8,2-4,O-3R,S	1.7
1890	*Bro-N	82	292	55	71	9	4	5	43	32	43	.243	.326	.353	679	97	-1	20			.953	7	C-69,1-12/O-1(0-0-1)	0.9
1891	Bro-N	58	200	29	50	11	5	2	27	21	34	.250	.327	.385	712	108	2	7			.881	-6	C-26,1-15,S-11,/O-7R	-0.3
1892	Bro-N	124	446	76	114	15	6	4	51	64	62	.256	.355	.343	698	116	11	34			.897	-11	3-57,O-30C,C-27,2	0.2
1893	Bro-N	126	470	94	136	21	14	8	70	76	65	.289	.388	.445	833	127	20	32			.915	-18	2-82,3-45	0.5
1894	Bro-N	124	496	135	168	22	10	8	82	77	42	.339	.433	.472	904	127	27	51			.909	-17	*2-124	1.2
1895	Bro-N	121	460	90	129	17	8	2	68	52	52	.280	.357	.365	722	94	-2	28			.931	-17	*2-121	-1.0
1896	Bro-N	67	224	43	63	13	6	3	29	33	25	.281	.385	.433	819	122	8	19			.909	-2	2-66/C-1	0.8
1898	Bro-N	23	73	11	24	3	1	0	11	14		.329	.443	.397	840	142	5	6			.993	3	2-23	0.8
1899	Bro-N	141	498	95	156	24	9	5	88	69		.313	.409	.428	837	127	21	43			.929	15	*2-141	3.8
1900	*Bro-N	97	343	72	107	17	3	4	55	46		.312	.403	.414	817	118	10	27			.921	-8	2-93/1-3,O-2(1-0-1)	0.6
1901	Bro-N	133	520	88	164	**38**	10	3	90	42		.315	.371	.444	815	132	21	31			.944	11	*2-133	3.2
1902	Chi-A	137	489	57	110	22	3	1	54	55		.225	.303	.288	592	68	-20	19			.957	-15	*2-137	-3.3
1903	Chi-A	43	150	20	31	11	0	0	19	20		.207	.304	.280	584	80	-3	6			.948	-13	2-43	-1.7
	Cin-N	80	307	42	90	14	9	1	38	16		.293	.332	.407	739	99	-2	5			.937	-10	2-79	-1.1
Total	16	1566	5715	1025	1605	262	103	49	811	687	402	.281	.361	.386	747	107	78	385			.931	-24	*2-1058,C-306,3/O1S	9.3

■ BILL DAM Dam, Elbridge Rust b: 4/4/1885, Cambridge, Mass. d: 6/22/30, Quincy, Mass. Deb: 8/23/09

YEAR	TM/L	G	AB	R	H	2B	3B	HR	RBI	BB	SO	AVG	OBP	SLG	OPS	OPS+	BR+	SB	CS	SBR	FA	FR	G/POS	TPR
1909	Bos-N	1	2	1	1	1	0	0	0	1		.500	.667	1.000	1667	398	1	0			1.000	-0	/O-1(1-0-0)	0.0

■ JACK DAMASKA Damaska, Jack Lloyd b: 8/21/37, Beaver Falls, Pa. BR/TR, 5'11", 168 lbs. Deb: 7/3/63

YEAR	TM/L	G	AB	R	H	2B	3B	HR	RBI	BB	SO	AVG	OBP	SLG	OPS	OPS+	BR+	SB	CS	SBR	FA	FR	G/POS	TPR
1963	StL-N	5	5	1	1	0	0	0	1	0	4	.200	.200	.200	400	14	-1	0	0	0	.000	-0	/2-1,O-1(1-0-0)	-0.1

■ JOHNNY DAMON Damon, Johnny David b: 11/5/73, Fort Riley, Kan. BL/TL, 6', 175 lbs. Deb: 8/12/95 Career OF: (261-LF 405-CF 141-RF)

YEAR	TM/L	G	AB	R	H	2B	3B	HR	RBI	BB	SO	AVG	OBP	SLG	OPS	OPS+	BR+	SB	CS	SBR	FA	FR	G/POS	TPR
1995	KC-A	47	188	32	53	11	5	3	23	12	22	.282	.328	.441	770	97	-1	7	0	2	.991	-2	O-47(0-44-4)	-0.2
1996	KC-A	145	517	61	140	22	5	6	50	31	64	.271	.316	.368	683	72	-22	25	5	4	.983	2	*O-144(0-89-63)/D-1	-1.7
1997	KC-A	146	472	70	130	12	8	8	48	42	70	.275	.338	.386	724	86	-9	16	10	0	.988	-3	*O-136(48-65-47)/D-5	-1.4
1998	KC-A	161	642	104	178	30	10	18	66	58	84	.277	.341	.439	780	98	-2	26	12	2	.990	1	*O-158(14-130-24)	0.1
1999	KC-A	145	583	101	179	39	9	14	77	67	50	.307	.381	.477	858	115	14	36	6	6	.987	5	*O-140(132-8-3)/D-4	1.8
2000	KC-A	159	655	**136**	214	42	10	16	88	65	60	.327	.388	.495	883	120	21	**46**	9	7	.986	8	*O-133(67-69-0),D-25	3.0
Total	6	803	3057	504	894	156	47	65	352	275	350	.292	.354	.438	792	100	0	156	42	20	.987	10	O-758C/D-35	1.6

■ HARRY DAMRAU Damrau, Harry Robert (Also Known As Arthur Lee Whitehorn)
b: 9/11/1890, Newburgh, N.Y. d: 8/21/57, Staten Island, N.Y BR/TR, 5'10", 178 lbs. Deb: 9/17/15

YEAR	TM/L	G	AB	R	H	2B	3B	HR	RBI	BB	SO	AVG	OBP	SLG	OPS	OPS+	BR+	SB	CS	SBR	FA	FR	G/POS	TPR
1915	Phi-A	16	56	4	11	1	0	0	3	5	17	.196	.262	.214	477	44	-4	1	1	-0	.870	-4	3-16	-0.8

■ JAKE DANIEL Daniel, Handley Jacob b: 4/22/11, Roanoke, Ala. d: 4/23/96, LaGrange, Ga. BL/TL, 5'11", 175 lbs. Deb: 7/24/37

YEAR	TM/L	G	AB	R	H	2B	3B	HR	RBI	BB	SO	AVG	OBP	SLG	OPS	OPS+	BR+	SB	CS	SBR	FA	FR	G/POS	TPR
1937	Bro-N	12	27	3	5	1	0	0	3	3	4	.185	.267	.222	489	34	-2	0			1.000	-0	/1-7	-0.3

■ BERT DANIELS Daniels, Bernard Elmer b: 10/31/1882, Danville, Ill. d: 6/6/58, Cedar Grove, N.J. BR/TR, 5'10", 170 lbs. Deb: 6/25/10 Career OF: (190-LF 118-CF 190-RF)

YEAR	TM/L	G	AB	R	H	2B	3B	HR	RBI	BB	SO	AVG	OBP	SLG	OPS	OPS+	BR+	SB	CS	SBR	FA	FR	G/POS	TPR
1910	NY-A	95	356	68	90	13	8	1	17	41		.253	.356	.343	699	112	7	41			.957	3	O-85(79-6-0)/3-6,1-4	0.6
1911	NY-A	131	462	74	132	16	9	2	31	48		.286	.375	.372	747	102	3	40			.941	1	*O-120(8-86-26)	-0.4
1912	NY-A	135	496	72	136	25	11	2	41	51		.274	.363	.381	744	106	5	37			.945	5	*O-131(92-0-39)	0.4
1913	NY-A	94	320	52	69	13	5	0	22	44	36	.216	.343	.287	630	85	-4	27			.966	1	O-87(0-0-87)	-0.8
1914	Cin-N	71	269	29	59	9	7	0	19	19	40	.219	.276	.305	581	70	-10	14			.974	0	O-71(11-26-38)	-1.6
Total	5	526	1903	295	486	76	40	5	130	203	76	.255	.349	.345	695	98	-0	159			.953	10	O-494L/3-6,1-4	-1.8

■ TONY DANIELS Daniels, Frederick Clinton b: 12/28/24, Gastonia, N.C. BR/TR, 5'9.5", 185 lbs. Deb: 6/12/45

YEAR	TM/L	G	AB	R	H	2B	3B	HR	RBI	BB	SO	AVG	OBP	SLG	OPS	OPS+	BR+	SB	CS	SBR	FA	FR	G/POS	TPR
1945	Phi-N	76	230	15	46	3	2	0	10	12	22	.200	.249	.230	479	35	-20	1			.955	7	2-75/3-1	-0.9

■ JACK DANIELS Daniels, Harold Jack "Sour Mash Jack" b: 12/21/27, Chester, Pa. BL/TL, 5'10", 165 lbs. Deb: 4/18/52

YEAR	TM/L	G	AB	R	H	2B	3B	HR	RBI	BB	SO	AVG	OBP	SLG	OPS	OPS+	BR+	SB	CS	SBR	FA	FR	G/POS	TPR
1952	Bos-N	106	219	31	41	5	1	2	14	28	30	.187	.288	.247	535	51	-14	3	3	-0	.977	-9	O-87(13-0-75)	-2.7

■ KAL DANIELS Daniels, Kalvoski b: 8/20/63, Vienna, Ga. BL/TR, 5'11", 195 lbs. Deb: 4/9/86

YEAR	TM/L	G	AB	R	H	2B	3B	HR	RBI	BB	SO	AVG	OBP	SLG	OPS	OPS+	BR+	SB	CS	SBR	FA	FR	G/POS	TPR
1986	Cin-N	74	181	34	58	10	4	6	23	22	30	.320	.400	.519	919	145	11	15	2	3	.967	-0	O-47(47-0-0)	1.2

YEAR	TM/L	G	AB	R	H	2B	3B	HR	RBI	BB	SO	AVG	OBP	SLG	OPS	OPS+	BR+	SB	CS	SBR	FA	FR	G/POS	TPR
1987	Cin-N	108	368	73	123	24	1	26	64	60	62	.334	.429	.617	1046	166	36	26	8	3	.968	3	O-94(94-0-0)	3.7
1988	Cin-N	140	495	95	144	29	1	18	64	87	94	.291	**.400**	.463	863	141	30	27	6	4	.982	4	*O-137(138-0-0)	3.5
1989	Cin-N	44	133	26	29	11	0	2	9	36	28	.218	.392	.346	738	109	3	6	4	-0	1.000	2	O-38(38-0-0)	0.5
	LA-N	11	38	7	13	2	0	2	8	7	5	.342	.444	.553	997	187	5	3	0	1	1.000	0	O-11(11-0-0)	0.5
	Yr	55	171	33	42	13	0	4	17	43	33	.246	.403	.392	795	125	8	9	4	1	1.000	2	O-49(49-0-0)	1.0
1990	LA-N	130	450	81	133	23	1	27	94	68	104	.296	.392	.531	923	156	35	4	3	-0	.987	2	*O-127(127-0-0)	3.3
1991	LA-N	137	461	54	115	15	1	17	73	63	116	.249	.341	.397	738	109	6	6	1	1	.979	1	*O-132(132-0-0)	0.4
1992	LA-N	35	104	9	24	5	0	2	8	10	30	.231	.304	.337	641	83	-2	0	0	0	.964	-2	O-21(21-0-0)/1-8	-0.6
	Chi-N	48	108	12	27	6	0	4	17	12	24	.250	.331	.417	747	108	1	0	2	-1	1.000	-2	O-28(28-0-0)	-0.2
	Yr	83	212	21	51	11	0	6	25	22	54	.241	.318	.377	695	95	-1	0	2	-1	.984	-4	O-49(49-0-0)/1-8	-0.8
Total	7	727	2338	391	666	125	8	104	360	365	493	.285	.385	.479	863	137	125	87	26	10	.980	8	O-635(636-0-0)/1-8	12.3

■ LAW DANIELS

Daniels, Lawrence Long b: 7/14/1862, Newton, Mass. d: 1/7/29, Waltham, Mass. BR/TR, 5'10", 170 lbs. Deb: 4/25/1887 Career OF: (24-LF 14-CF 7-RF)

YEAR	TM/L	G	AB	R	H	2B	3B	HR	RBI	BB	SO	AVG	OBP	SLG	OPS	OPS+	BR+	SB	CS	SBR	FA	FR	G/POS	TPR
1887	Bal-a	48	173	23	49	5	1	0	32	8		.283	.287	.291	578	65	-7	7			.845	-8	C-26,O-15L/1-4,2S3	-1.1
1888	KC-a	61	218	32	45	2	0	2	28	14		.206	.264	.243	507	59	-10	20			.855	-2	O-30L,C-29/3-2,S-1	-1.0
Total	2	109	391	55	94	7	1	2	60	22		.240	.274	.264	538	61	-17	27			.859	-10	/C-55,O-45L,1-4,3S2	-2.1

■ BUCK DANNER

Danner, Henry Frederick b: 6/8/1891, Dedham, Mass. d: 9/19/49, Dedham, Mass. BR/TR, 5'11", 140 lbs. Deb: 9/17/15

YEAR	TM/L	G	AB	R	H	2B	3B	HR	RBI	BB	SO	AVG	OBP	SLG	OPS	OPS+	BR+	SB	CS	SBR	FA	FR	G/POS	TPR
1915	Phi-A	3	12	1	3	0	0	0	0	0	1	.250	.250	.250	500	51	-1	1			.750	-3	/S-3	-0.4

■ HARRY DANNING

Danning, Harry "Harry The Horse" b: 9/6/11, Los Angeles, Cal. BR/TR, 6'1", 190 lbs. Deb: 7/30/33 F

YEAR	TM/L	G	AB	R	H	2B	3B	HR	RBI	BB	SO	AVG	OBP	SLG	OPS	OPS+	BR+	SB	CS	SBR	FA	FR	G/POS	TPR
1933	NY-N	3	2	0	0	0	0	0	0	1	0	.000	.333	.000	333	2	-0	0			1.000	0	/C-1	0.0
1934	NY-N	53	97	8	32	7	0	1	7	1	9	.330	.337	.433	770	107	1	1			.989	-0	C-37	0.2
1935	NY-N	65	152	16	37	11	1	2	20	9	16	.243	.286	.368	654	76	-6	0			.978	3	C-44	-0.1
1936	*NY-N	32	69	3	11	2	2	0	4	1	5	.159	.183	.246	429	15	-8	0			.988	2	C-24	-0.6
1937	*NY-N	93	292	30	84	12	4	8	51	18	20	.288	.331	.438	770	106	2	0			.982	-5	C-86	0.2
1938	NY-N☆	120	448	59	137	26	3	9	60	23	40	.306	.345	.438	783	113	7	1			.984	-8	*C-114	0.6
1939	NY-N☆	135	520	79	163	28	5	16	74	35	42	.313	.359	.479	838	122	15	4			.991	7	*C-132	3.0
1940	NY-N★	140	524	65	157	34	4	13	91	35	31	.300	.349	.454	803	119	12	3			.980	7	*C-131	2.8
1941	NY-N★	130	459	58	112	22	4	7	56	30	25	.244	.292	.355	647	80	-13	1			.993	7	*C-116/1-1	0.1
1942	NY-N	119	408	45	114	20	3	1	34	34	29	.279	.335	.350	685	100	0	3			.979	-5	*C-116	0.3
Total	10	890	2971	363	847	162	26	57	397	187	217	.285	.330	.415	745	104	9	13			.985	8	C-801/1-1	6.5

■ IKE DANNING

Danning, Ike b: 1/20/05, Los Angeles, Cal. d: 3/30/83, Santa Monica, Cal BR/TR, 5'10", 160 lbs. Deb: 9/21/28 F

YEAR	TM/L	G	AB	R	H	2B	3B	HR	RBI	BB	SO	AVG	OBP	SLG	OPS	OPS+	BR+	SB	CS	SBR	FA	FR	G/POS	TPR
1928	StL-A	2	6	0	3	0	0	0	1	1	2	.500	.571	.500	1071	178	1	0	0	0	.917	1	/C-2	0.1

■ FATS DANTONIO

Dantonio, John James b: 12/31/18, New Orleans, La. d: 5/28/93, New Orleans, La. BR/TR, 5'8", 165 lbs. Deb: 9/18/44

YEAR	TM/L	G	AB	R	H	2B	3B	HR	RBI	BB	SO	AVG	OBP	SLG	OPS	OPS+	BR+	SB	CS	SBR	FA	FR	G/POS	TPR
1944	Bro-N	3	7	0	1	0	0	0	0	0	1	.143	.143	.143	286	-20	-1	0			.846	0	/C-3	-0.1
1945	Bro-N	47	128	12	32	6	1	0	12	11	6	.250	.309	.313	622	74	-5	3			.929	-5	C-45	-0.8
Total	2	50	135	12	33	6	1	0	12	11	7	.244	.301	.304	605	69	-6	3			.923	-5	/C-48	-0.9

■ BABE DANZIG

Danzig, Harold P. b: 4/30/1887, Binghamton, N.Y. d: 7/14/31, San Francisco, Cal. BR/TR, 6'2", 205 lbs. Deb: 4/12/09

YEAR	TM/L	G	AB	R	H	2B	3B	HR	RBI	BB	SO	AVG	OBP	SLG	OPS	OPS+	BR+	SB	CS	SBR	FA	FR	G/POS	TPR
1909	Bos-A	6	13	0	2	0	0	0	0	2		.154	.313	.154	466	47	-1	0			.960	-1	/1-3	-0.2

■ CLIFF DAPPER

Dapper, Clifford Roland b: 1/2/20, Los Angeles, Cal. BR/TR, 6'2", 190 lbs. Deb: 4/19/42

YEAR	TM/L	G	AB	R	H	2B	3B	HR	RBI	BB	SO	AVG	OBP	SLG	OPS	OPS+	BR+	SB	CS	SBR	FA	FR	G/POS	TPR
1942	Bro-N	8	17	2	8	1	0	1	9	2	2	.471	.526	.706	1232	255	3	0			1.000	-0	/C-8	0.4

■ CLIFF DARINGER

Daringer, Clifford Clarence "Shanty" b: 4/10/1885, Hayden, Ind. d: 12/26/71, Sacramento, Cal. BL/TR, 5'7.5", 155 lbs. Deb: 4/20/14 F

YEAR	TM/L	G	AB	R	H	2B	3B	HR	RBI	BB	SO	AVG	OBP	SLG	OPS	OPS+	BR+	SB	CS	SBR	FA	FR	G/POS	TPR
1914	KC-F	64	160	12	42	2	1	0	16	11	7	.262	.322	.287	609	70	-9	9			.944	6	S-24,3-19,2-14	-0.1

■ ROLLA DARINGER

Daringer, Rolla Harrison b: 11/15/1888, N.Vernon, Ind. d: 5/23/74, Seymour, Ind. BL/TR, 5'10", 155 lbs. Deb: 9/19/14 F

YEAR	TM/L	G	AB	R	H	2B	3B	HR	RBI	BB	SO	AVG	OBP	SLG	OPS	OPS+	BR+	SB	CS	SBR	FA	FR	G/POS	TPR
1914	StL-N	2	4	1	2	1	0	0	0	1	2	.500	.600	.750	1350	304	1	0			.667	-1	/S-1	0.0
1915	StL-N	10	23	3	2	0	0	0	0	9	5	.087	.344	.087	431	33	-1	0	1	-0	.947	-3	S-10	-0.4
Total	2	12	27	4	4	1	0	0	0	10	7	.148	.378	.185	564	72	-0	0	1		.927	-4	/S-11	-0.4

■ ALVIN DARK

Dark, Alvin Ralph "Blackie" b: 1/7/22, Comanche, Okla. BR/TR, 5'11", 185 lbs. Deb: 7/14/46 MC Career OF: (39-LF 0-CF 4-RF)

YEAR	TM/L	G	AB	R	H	2B	3B	HR	RBI	BB	SO	AVG	OBP	SLG	OPS	OPS+	BR+	SB	CS	SBR	FA	FR	G/POS	TPR
1946	Bos-N	15	13	0	3	3	0	0	1	0	3	.231	.231	.462	692	93	-0	0			.905	2	S-12/O-1(1-0-0)	0.2
1948	*Bos-N	137	543	85	175	39	6	3	48	24	36	.322	.353	.433	786	114	9	4			.963	-12	*S-133	0.5
1949	Bos-N	130	529	74	146	23	5	3	53	31	43	.276	.317	.355	673	85	-12	5			.961	-4	*S-125/3-4	-0.8
1950	NY-N	154	587	79	164	36	5	16	67	39	60	.279	.331	.440	770	100	-1	9			.962	-15	*S-154	-0.6
1951	*NY-N★	156	646	114	196	**41**	7	14	69	42	39	.303	.352	.454	805	114	11	12	7	0	.944	1	*S-156	2.2
1952	NY-N☆	151	589	92	177	29	3	14	73	47	39	.301	.357	.431	788	117	13	6	6	-1	.965	3	*S-150	2.5
1953	NY-N	155	647	126	194	41	6	23	88	28	34	.300	.335	.488	823	109	7	7	2	1	.967	8	*S-110,2-26,O/3P	2.5
1954	*NY-N★	154	644	98	189	26	6	20	70	27	40	.293	.327	.446	773	98	-3	5	3	0	.956	4	*S-154	1.3
1955	NY-N	115	475	77	134	20	3	9	45	22	32	.282	.321	.394	714	88	-9	2	1	0	.962	-14	*S-115	-1.2
1956	NY-N	48	206	19	52	12	0	2	17	8	13	.252	.284	.340	624	67	-10	0	0	0	.961	-5	S-48	-1.1
	StL-N	100	413	54	118	14	7	4	37	21	33	.286	.323	.383	706	89	-7	3	1	0	.959	-2	S-99	0.0
	Yr	148	619	73	170	26	7	6	54	29	46	.275	.310	.368	679	82	-16	3	1	0	.960	-7	*S-147	-1.1
1957	StL-N	140	583	80	169	25	8	4	64	29	56	.290	.328	.381	709	88	-10	3	4	-1	.965	6	*S-139/3-1	0.7
1958	StL-N	18	64	7	19	0	0	1	5	2	6	.297	.318	.344	662	72	-2	0	0	0	.943	-3	/S-8,3-8	-0.5
	Chi-N	114	464	54	137	16	4	3	43	29	23	.295	.343	.366	710	89	-7	1	1	-0	.949	-3	*3-111	-1.0
	Yr	132	528	61	156	16	4	4	48	31	29	.295	.340	.364	704	87	-9	1	1	-0	.948	-6	*3-119/S-8	-1.5
1959	Chi-N	136	477	60	126	22	9	6	45	55	50	.264	.344	.386	730	95	-3	1	1	-0	.948	-2	*3-131/1-4,S-1	-0.5
1960	Phi-N	55	198	29	48	5	1	3	14	19	14	.242	.315	.323	638	75	-6	1	1	-0	.953	-8	3-53/1-1	-1.5
	Mil-N	50	141	16	42	6	2	1	18	7	13	.298	.336	.390	726	106	1	0	0	0	.960	-1	O-25L,1-10/3-4,2-3	-0.2
	Yr	105	339	45	90	11	3	4	32	26	27	.265	.323	.351	674	88	-6	1	1	-0	.954	-8	3-57,O-25L,1-11,/2	-1.7
Total	14	1828	7219	1064	2089	358	72	126	757	430	534	.289	.334	.411	745	98	-29	59	27		.960	-43	*S-1404,3-320/O21P	2.5

■ DELL DARLING

Darling, Conrad b: 12/21/1861, Erie, Pa. d: 11/20/04, Erie, Pa. BR/TR, 5'8", 170 lbs. Deb: 7/3/1883 Career OF: (0-LF 0-CF 27-RF)

YEAR	TM/L	G	AB	R	H	2B	3B	HR	RBI	BB	SO	AVG	OBP	SLG	OPS	OPS+	BR+	SB	CS	SBR	FA	FR	G/POS	TPR
1883	Buf-N	6	18	1	3	0	0	0	1	2	5	.167	.250	.167	417	29	-1				.875	-2	/C-6	-0.3
1887	Chi-N	38	163	28	67	7	4	3	20	22	18	.411	.411	.489	900	132	6	19			.786	2	O-20(0-0-20),C-20	0.8
1888	Chi-N	20	75	12	16	3	1	2	7	3	12	.213	.253	.360	613	87	-1	0			.932	3	C-20	0.3
1889	Chi-N	36	120	14	23	1	1	0	7	25	22	.192	.331	.217	548	52	-7	5			.960	4	C-36	0.0
1890	Chi-P	58	221	45	57	12	4	2	39	29	28	.258	.352	.376	727	91	-3	5			.957	-9	1-29,S-15/C-9,O23	-1.1
1891	StL-a	17	53	9	7	1	3	0	9	10	11	.132	.270	.264	534	46	-4	0			.894	2	C-17/2-2,S-1	0.0
Total	6	175	650	109	173	24	13	7	83	91	96	.266	.340	.354	694	87	-11	29			.923	-0	C-108/1-29,O-27R,S23	-0.3

■ MIKE DARR

Darr, Michael Curtis b: 3/21/76, Corona, Cal. BL/TR, 6'3", 205 lbs. Deb: 5/23/99

YEAR	TM/L	G	AB	R	H	2B	3B	HR	RBI	BB	SO	AVG	OBP	SLG	OPS	OPS+	BR+	SB	CS	SBR	FA	FR	G/POS	TPR
1999	SD-N	25	48	6	13	1	0	2	3	5	18	.271	.340	.417	756	98	-0	2	1	0	1.000	-4	O-22(0-3-21)	-0.4
2000	SD-N	58	205	21	55	14	4	1	30	23	45	.268	.342	.390	732	90	-3	9	1	2	1.000	-0	O-57(8-19-47)	-0.3
Total	2	83	253	27	68	15	4	3	33	28	63	.269	.342	.395	737	91	-3	11	2	2	1.000	-4	/O-79(8-22-68)	-0.7

■ JACK DARRAGH

Darragh, James S. b: 7/17/1866, Ebensburg, Pa. d: 8/12/39, Rochester, Pa. 6'2.5", 180 lbs. Deb: 5/13/1891

YEAR	TM/L	G	AB	R	H	2B	3B	HR	RBI	BB	SO	AVG	OBP	SLG	OPS	OPS+	BR+	SB	CS	SBR	FA	FR	G/POS	TPR
1891	Lou-a	1	2	0	1	0	0	0	0	0	0	.500	.500	.500	1000	189	0	0			1.000	0	/1-1	0.0

■ BOBBY DARWIN

Darwin, Arthur Bobby Lee b: 2/16/43, Los Angeles, Cal. BR/TR, 6'2", 200 lbs. Deb: 9/30/62 Career OF: (37-LF 87-CF 417-RF)

YEAR	TM/L	G	AB	R	H	2B	3B	HR	RBI	BB	SO	AVG	OBP	SLG	OPS	OPS+	BR+	SB	CS	SBR	FA	FR	G/POS	TPR
1962	LA-A	1	1	0	0	0	0	0	0	0	1	.000	.000	.000	0	-99	-0	0	0	0	.000	-0	/P-1	0.0
1969	LA-N	6	0	1	0	0	0	0	0	0	0	—	—	—	—	—	0	0	0	0	.000	-0	/P-3	0.0
1971	LA-N	11	20	2	5	1	0	1	4	2	9	.250	.318	.450	768	123	1	0	0	0	1.000	0	/O-4(0-0-4)	0.0
1972	Min-A	145	513	48	137	20	2	22	80	38	145	.267	.327	.442	770	122	13	2	3	-1	.980	-1	*O-142(9-86-47)	0.7
1973	Min-A	145	560	69	141	20	2	18	90	46	137	.252	.312	.391	703	93	-6	5	2	0	.980	2	*O-140(0-0-140)/D-1	-1.1
1974	Min-A	152	575	67	152	13	7	25	94	37	127	.264	.324	.442	766	115	10	1	3	-1	.970	-2	*O-142(0-0-142)	-0.1

YEAR	TM/L	G	AB	R	H	2B	3B	HR	RBI	BB	SO	AVG	OBP	SLG	OPS	OPS+	BR+	SB	CS	SBR	FA	FR	G/POS	TPR
1975	Min-A	48	169	26	37	6	0	5	18	18	44	.219	.309	.343	652	83	-4	2	0	0	.969	-4	O-27(0-0-27),D-19	-0.9
	Mil-A	55	186	19	46	6	2	8	23	11	54	.247	.300	.430	730	104	0	4	1	1	.978	1	O-43(25-0-20)/D-9	-0.1
	Yr	103	355	45	83	12	2	13	41	29	98	.234	.304	.389	693	94	-4	6	1	1	.975	-3	O-70(25-0-47),D-28	-1.0
1976	Mil-A	25	73	6	18	3	1	1	5	6	16	.247	.321	.356	677	100	0	0	0	0	.977	-1	O-21(0-1-21)/D-1	-0.2
	Bos-A	43	106	9	19	5	2	3	13	2	35	.179	.216	.349	565	57	-6	1	0	0	.964	-2	O-17(3-0-14),D-16	-0.9
	Yr	68	179	15	37	8	3	4	18	8	51	.207	.260	.352	612	73	-7	1	0	0	.972	-3	O-38(3-1-35),D-17	-1.1
1977	Bos-A	4	9	1	2	1	0	0	1	0	4	.222	.222	.333	556	44	-1	0	0	0	.500	-0	/O-1(0-0-1),D-2	-0.1
	Chi-N	11	12	2	2	1	0	0	0	0	5	.167	.167	.250	417	9	-2	0	0	0	.000	-0	/O-1(0-0-1)	-0.2
Total	9	646	2224	250	559	76	16	83	328	160	577	.251	.312	.412	724	103	5	15	9	0	.976	-8	O-538R/D-48,P-4	-2.9
■ DOUG DASCENZO Dascenzo, Douglas Craig b: 6/30/64, Cleveland, Ohio BB/TL, 5′8″, 160 lbs. Deb: 9/2/88 Career OF: (146-LF 270-CF 101-RF)																								
1988	Chi-N	26	75	9	16	3	0	0	4	9	4	.213	.298	.253	551	57	-4	6	1	1	1.000	2	O-20(0-20-0)	-0.1
1989	Chi-N	47	139	20	23	1	0	1	12	13	13	.165	.237	.194	431	23	-14	6	3	0	1.000	-2	O-45(8-37-1)	-1.7
1990	Chi-N	113	241	27	61	9	5	1	26	21	18	.253	.316	.344	660	76	-8	15	6	1	1.000	-18	*O-107(65-38-22)/P-1	-2.7
1991	Chi-N	118	239	40	61	11	0	1	18	24	26	.255	.328	.314	642	78	-6	14	7	1	.985	-19	O-86(32-59-16)/P-3	-2.7
1992	Chi-N	139	376	37	96	13	4	0	20	27	32	.255	.305	.311	616	73	-13	6	8	-1	.978	-17	*O-122(25-80-28)	-3.6
1993	Tex-A	76	146	20	29	5	1	2	10	8	22	.199	.240	.288	528	43	-12	2	0	0	.990	-12	O-68(16-35-25)/D-2	-2.4
1996	SD-N	21	9	3	1	0	0	0	0	1	2	.111	.200	.111	311	-16	-2	0	1	-0	1.000	-3	O-10(0-1-9)	-0.5
Total	7	540	1225	156	287	42	10	5	90	103	117	.234	.295	.297	592	64	-58	49	26	2	.990	-69	O-458C/P-4,D-2	-13.7
■ WALLY DASHIELL Dashiell, John Wallace b: 5/9/02, Jewett, Tex. d: 5/20/72, Pensacola, Fla. BR/TR, 5′9.5″, 170 lbs. Deb: 4/20/24																								
1924	Chi-A	1	2	0	0	0	0	0	0	0	0	.000	.000	.000	0	-99	-1	0	0	0	.667	-1	/S-1	-0.1
■ JEFF DATZ Datz, Jeffrey William b: 11/28/59, Camden, N.J. BR/TR, 6′4″, 220 lbs. Deb: 9/5/89																								
1989	Det-A	7	10	0	2	0	0	0	0	1	1	.200	.333	.200	533	55	-0	0	0	0	1.000	0	/C-6,D-1	0.0
■ BRIAN DAUBACH Daubach, Brian Michael b: 2/11/72, Belleville, Ill. BL/TR, 6′1″, 201 lbs. Deb: 9/10/98 Career OF: (9-LF 0-CF 1-RF)																								
1998	Fla-N	10	15	0	3	1	0	0	3	1	5	.200	.294	.267	561	51	-1	0	0	0	1.000	-0	/1-4	-0.2
1999	*Bos-A	110	381	61	112	33	3	21	73	36	92	.294	.360	.562	921	126	14	0	1	-0	.983	-1	1-61,D-48/O-2L,3-1	0.5
2000	Bos-A	142	495	55	123	32	2	21	76	44	130	.248	.317	.448	766	87	-11	1	1	-0	.996	2	1-83,D-41/O-8L,3-1	-1.7
Total	3	262	891	116	238	66	5	42	152	81	227	.267	.335	.494	829	103	2	1	2	-0	.991	1	1-148/D-89,O-10L,3	-1.4
■ HARRY DAUBERT Daubert, Harry "Jake" b: 6/19/1892, Columbus, Ohio d: 1/8/44, Detroit, Mich. BR/TR, 6′, 160 lbs. Deb: 9/4/15																								
1915	Pit-N	1	1	0	0	0	0	0	0	0	1	.000	.000	.000	0	-99	-0	0			.000	0	H	0.0
■ JAKE DAUBERT Daubert, Jacob Ellsworth b: 4/7/1884, Shamokin, Pa. d: 10/9/24, Cincinnati, Ohio BL/TL, 5′10.5″, 160 lbs. Deb: 4/14/10																								
1910	Bro-N	144	552	67	146	15	15	8	50	47	53	.264	.328	.389	717	112	7	23			.989	-3	*1-144	0.1
1911	Bro-N	149	573	89	176	17	8	5	45	51	56	.307	.366	.391	757	117	13	32			.989	2	*1-149	1.0
1912	Bro-N	145	559	81	172	19	16	3	66	48	45	.308	.369	.415	784	119	14	29			**.993**	0	*1-143	1.1
1913	Bro-N	139	508	76	178	17	7	2	52	44	40	**.350**	.405	.423	829	133	23	25			.991	3	*1-139	2.3
1914	Bro-N	126	474	89	156	17	7	6	45	30	34	**.329**	.375	.432	808	137	20	25			.993	-6	*1-126	1.2
1915	Bro-N	150	544	62	164	21	8	2	47	57	48	.301	.369	.381	749	125	17	11	13	-2	.993	9	*1-150	2.2
1916	*Bro-N	127	478	75	151	16	7	3	33	38	39	.316	.371	.397	769	132	19	21	7	2	**.993**	4	*1-126	2.4
1917	Bro-N	125	468	59	122	4	4	2	30	51	30	.261	.341	.299	640	94	-1	11			.991	6	*1-125	0.2
1918	Bro-N	108	396	50	122	12	**15**	2	47	27	18	.308	.360	.429	789	141	18	10			.991	0	*1-105	1.8
1919	*Cin-N	140	537	79	148	10	12	2	44	35	23	.276	.322	.350	672	105	3	11			.989	-2	*1-140	-0.3
1920	Cin-N	142	553	97	168	28	13	4	48	47	29	.304	.362	.423	785	127	19	11	13	-2	.990	-9	*1-140	0.5
1921	Cin-N	136	516	69	158	18	12	2	64	24	16	.306	.341	.399	740	100	-1	12	6	1	.993	2	*1-136	-0.7
1922	Cin-N	156	610	114	205	15	**22**	12	66	56	21	.336	.395	.492	886	130	27	14	17	-3	**.994**	-0	*1-156	1.3
1923	Cin-N	125	500	63	146	27	10	2	54	40	20	.292	.349	.398	747	99	-1	11	12	-2	.993	6	*1-121	-0.4
1924	Cin-N	102	405	47	114	14	9	1	31	28	17	.281	.331	.368	699	88	-7	5	10	-2	.990	7	*1-102	-0.9
Total	15	2014	7673	1117	2326	250	165	56	722	623	489	.303	.360	.401	760	117	171	251	78		.991	19	*1-2002	11.8
■ RICH DAUER Dauer, Richard Fremont b: 7/27/52, San Bernardino, Cal. BR/TR, 6′, 180 lbs. Deb: 9/11/76 C																								
1976	Bal-A	11	39	0	4	0	0	0	3	1	3	.103	.146	.103	249	-28	-6	0	0	0	1.000	-3	2-10	-0.9
1977	Bal-A	96	304	38	74	15	1	5	25	20	28	.243	.294	.349	643	79	-9	1	0	0	.982	6	2-83/3-9,D-2	0.1
1978	Bal-A	133	459	57	121	23	0	6	46	26	22	.264	.303	.353	656	89	-7	0	4	-1	.998	3	2-87,3-52/D-1	-0.2
1979	*Bal-A	142	479	63	123	20	0	9	61	36	36	.257	.310	.355	665	82	-12	0	1	-0	.979	-5	*2-103,3-44	-1.3
1980	Bal-A	152	557	71	158	32	0	2	63	46	19	.284	.342	.352	693	91	-6	3	2	-0	.991	-4	*2-137,3-35	-0.3
1981	Bal-A	96	369	41	97	27	0	4	38	27	18	.263	.318	.369	687	98	-1	0	0	0	**.989**	-14	2-94/3-4	-1.1
1982	Bal-A	158	558	75	156	24	2	8	57	50	34	.280	.340	.373	713	96	-2	0	1	-0	.987	-36	*2-123,3-61	-3.4
1983	*Bal-A	140	459	49	108	19	0	5	41	47	29	.235	.309	.309	618	72	-17	1	1	-0	.988	-29	*2-131,3-17	-3.9
1984	Bal-A	127	397	29	101	26	0	2	24	24	23	.254	.297	.335	632	76	-13	1	3	-1	.980	-19	*2-123/3-3	-2.6
1985	Bal-A	85	208	25	42	7	0	2	14	20	7	.202	.275	.264	540	50	-14	0	1	-0	.990	5	2-73,3-17/1-1	-0.7
Total	10	1140	3829	448	984	193	3	43	372	297	219	.257	.313	.343	655	83	-89	6	13	-3	.987	-96	2-964,3-242/D-3,1-1	-14.3
■ DOC DAUGHERTY Daugherty, Harold Ray b: 10/12/27, Paris, Pa. BR/TR, 6′, 180 lbs. Deb: 4/22/51																								
1951	Det-A	1	1	0	0	0	0	0	0	0	1	.000	.000	.000	0	-99	-0	0	0	0	.000	0	H	0.0
■ JACK DAUGHERTY Daugherty, John Michael b: 7/3/60, Hialeah, Fla. BB/TL, 6′, 195 lbs. Deb: 9/1/87 Career OF: (104-LF 1-CF 25-RF)																								
1987	Mon-N	11	10	1	1	1	0	0	1	0	3	.100	.100	.200	300	-22	-2	0	0	0	1.000	0	/1-1	-0.2
1989	Tex-A	52	106	15	32	4	2	1	10	11	21	.302	.373	.406	779	117	3	2	1	0	1.000	1	1-23/O-5(4-0-1),D-8	0.2
1990	Tex-A	125	310	36	93	20	2	6	47	22	49	.300	.350	.435	786	118	7	0	0	0	.982	-3	O-42L,1-30,D-21	0.1
1991	Tex-A	58	144	8	28	3	2	1	11	16	23	.194	.275	.264	539	51	-10	1	0	0	.981	-4	O-37(34-0-3),1-11/D-1	-1.5
1992	Tex-A	59	127	13	26	9	0	0	9	16	21	.205	.299	.276	574	64	-6	2	1	0	.939	-4	O-26L,D-13/1-8	-1.1
1993	Hou-N	4	3	0	1	0	0	0	0	0	0	.333	.333	.333	667	82	-0	0	0	0	.000	-0	/1-1,O-1(0-0-1)	0.0
	Cin-N	46	59	7	13	2	0	2	9	11	15	.220	.343	.356	699	87	-1	0	0	0	.917	-4	O-16(11-0-5)/1-2	-0.5
	Yr	50	62	7	14	2	0	2	9	11	15	.226	.342	.355	697	87	-1	0	0	0	.923	-4	O-17(11-0-6)/1-3	-0.5
Total	6	355	759	80	194	39	6	10	87	76	132	.256	.327	.362	689	92	-8	5	2	0	.969	-15	O-127L/1-76,D-43	-3.0
■ BOB DAUGHTERS Daughters, Robert Francis "Red" b: 8/5/14, Cincinnati, Ohio d: 8/22/88, Southbury, Conn. BR/TR, 6′2″, 185 lbs. Deb: 4/24/37																								
1937	Bos-A	1	0	1	0	0	0	0	0	0	0	—	—	—	—	—	0	0	0	0	.000	0	R	0.0
■ DARREN DAULTON Daulton, Darren Arthur b: 1/3/62, Arkansas City, Kan. BL/TR, 6′2″, 190 lbs. Deb: 9/25/83 Career OF: (6-LF 0-CF 73-RF)																								
1983	Phi-N	2	3	1	1	0	0	0	0	1	1	.333	.500	.333	833	137	0	0	0	0	1.000	-0	/C-2	0.0
1985	Phi-N	36	103	14	21	3	1	4	11	16	37	.204	.311	.369	680	87	-2	3	0	1	.994	0	C-28	0.1
1986	Phi-N	49	138	18	31	4	0	8	21	38	41	.225	.395	.428	823	123	6	2	3	-1	.985	-4	C-48	0.3
1987	Phi-N	53	129	10	25	6	0	3	13	16	37	.194	.283	.310	593	55	-8	0	0	0	.991	1	C-40/1-1	-0.6
1988	Phi-N	58	144	13	30	6	0	1	12	17	26	.208	.292	.271	563	61	-7	2	1	0	.977	-6	C-44/1-1	-1.1
1989	Phi-N	131	368	29	74	12	2	8	44	52	58	.201	.303	.310	613	76	-11	2	1	0	.984	-11	*C-126	-1.6
1990	Phi-N	143	459	62	123	30	1	12	57	72	72	.268	.370	.416	786	116	12	7	1	1	.989	-9	*C-139	1.3
1991	Phi-N	89	285	36	56	12	0	12	42	41	66	.196	.302	.365	667	88	-5	5	0	1	.985	-17	C-88	-1.6
1992	Phi-N★	145	485	80	131	32	5	27	**109**	88	103	.270	.389	.524	912	157	38	11	2	2	.987	-14	*C-141	3.6
1993	*Phi-N★	147	510	90	131	35	4	24	105	117	111	.257	.397	.482	880	136	30	5	0	1	.991	-9	*C-146	3.1
1994	Phi-N	69	257	43	77	17	1	15	56	33	43	.300	.381	.549	930	136	13	4	1	1	.994	7	C-68	2.4
1995	Phi-N★	98	342	44	85	19	3	9	55	55	52	.249	.361	.401	761	100	1	3	0	1	.994	-8	C-95	0.0
1996	Phi-N	5	12	3	2	0	0	0	0	7	5	.167	.500	.167	667	85	1	0	0	0	1.000	-1	/O-5(5-0-0)	0.0
1997	Phi-N	84	269	46	71	13	6	11	42	54	57	.264	.389	.480	868	126	12	4	0	1	.979	5	O-70(0-0-70)/1-3,D-6	1.3
	*Fla-N	52	126	22	33	8	2	3	21	22	17	.262	.376	.429	804	115	3	2	1	0	.984	-4	1-39/O-3(1-0-3),D-1	-0.4
	Yr	136	395	68	104	21	8	14	63	76	74	.263	.385	.463	848	123	15	6	1	1	.979	1	O-73(1-0-73),1-42/D-7	0.9
Total	14	1161	3630	511	891	197	25	137	588	629	726	.245	.360	.427	787	114	83	50	10	8	.989	-69	C-965/O-78R,1-44,D	6.8

YEAR	TM/L	G	AB	R	H	2B	3B	HR	RBI	BB	SO	AVG	OBP	SLG	OPS	OPS+	BR+	SB	CS	SBR	FA	FR	G/POS	TPR
■ YO-YO DAVALILLO Davalillo, Pompeyo Antonio (Romero) b: 6/30/31, Caracas, Venez. BR/TR, 5'3", 140 lbs. Deb: 8/1/53 F																								
1953	Was-A	19	58	10	17	1	0	0	2	1	7	.293	.305	.310	615	68	-3	1	0	0	.935	2	S-17	0.0
■ VIC DAVALILLO Davalillo, Victor Jose (Romero) b: 7/31/36, Cabimas, Venez. BL/TL, 5'7", 155 lbs. Deb: 4/9/63 F Career OF: (131-LF 752-CF 196-RF)																								
1963	Cle-A	90	370	44	108	18	5	7	36	16	41	.292	.323	.424	747	108	3	3	3	-0	.988	17	O-89(0-89-0)	1.8
1964	Cle-A	150	577	64	156	26	2	6	51	34	77	.270	.312	.354	666	85	-12	21	11	1	.986	16	*O-143(0-143-0)	0.1
1965	Cle-A★	142	505	67	152	19	1	5	40	35	50	.301	.346	.372	719	103	2	26	7	3	.988	15	*O-134(0-134-0)	1.8
1966	Cle-A	121	344	42	86	6	4	3	19	24	37	.250	.299	.317	616	77	-10	8	6	-0	.986	0	*O-108(0-108-0)	-1.4
1967	Cle-A	139	359	47	103	17	5	2	22	10	30	.287	.308	.379	687	101	-1	6	7	-1	.986	-8	*O-125(1-125-0)	-1.4
1968	Cle-A	51	180	15	43	2	3	2	13	3	19	.239	.255	.317	572	74	-6	8	6	-0	.967	2	O-49(3-2-48)	-0.9
	Cal-A	93	339	34	101	15	4	1	18	15	34	.298	.328	.375	702	117	6	17	10	0	.995	6	O-86(0-70-17)	1.0
	Yr	144	519	49	144	17	7	3	31	18	53	.277	.303	.355	658	102	-1	25	16	-0	.987	8	*O-135(3-72-65)	0.1
1969	Cal-A	33	71	10	11	1	1	0	1	6	5	.155	.231	.197	428	22	-7	3	0	1	1.000	-2	O-22(0-2-20)/1-3	-1.0
	StL-N	63	98	15	26	3	0	2	10	7	8	.265	.314	.357	671	87	-2	1	1	-0	1.000	-2	O-23(2-10-11)/P-2	-0.4
1970	StL-N	111	183	29	57	14	3	1	33	13	19	.311	.357	.437	794	109	2	4	1	1	.972	-8	O-54(12-33-13)	-0.7
1971	*Pit-N	99	295	48	84	14	6	1	33	11	31	.285	.315	.383	698	97	-2	10	2	2	.983	-2	O-61(11-20-31),1-16	-0.6
1972	*Pit-N	117	368	59	117	19	2	4	28	26	44	.318	.368	.413	781	124	11	14	1	3	.979	-1	O-97(64-7-26)/1-8	0.9
1973	Pit-N	59	83	9	15	1	0	1	3	2	7	.181	.200	.229	429	19	-9	0	2	-1	.977	-0	1-10,O-10(7-0-3)	-1.1
	*Oak-A	38	64	5	12	1	0	0	4	3	4	.188	.224	.203	427	22	-7	0	0	0	.967	2	O-19(8-1-10)/1-8,D-2	-0.9
1974	Oak-A	17	23	0	4	0	0	0	1	2	2	.174	.240	.174	414	22	-2	0	0	0	1.000	-2	/O-6(2-2-2),D-4	-0.5
1977	*LA-N	24	48	3	15	2	0	0	4	0	6	.313	.313	.354	667	79	-1	0	0	0	1.000	-3	O-12(2-4-8)	-0.5
1978	*LA-N	75	77	15	24	1	1	1	11	3	7	.312	.338	.390	727	103	0	2	1	0	1.000	-6	O-25(16-2-7)/1-1	-0.7
1979	LA-N	29	27	2	7	1	0	0	2	2	0	.259	.310	.296	607	67	-1	2	0	1	1.000	-1	/O-3(3-0-0)	-0.2
1980	LA-N	7	6	1	1	0	0	0	0	0	1	.167	.167	.167	333	-7	-1	0	0	0	1.000	-0	/1-1	-0.1
Total	16	1458	4017	509	1122	160	37	36	329	212	422	.279	.317	.364	682	94	-36	125	58	7	.986	19	*O-1066C/1-47,D-6,P	-4.8
■ JEFF DaVANON DaVanon, Jeffrey Graham b: 12/8/73, San Diego, Cal. BB/TR, 6', 180 lbs. Deb: 9/7/99 F																								
1999	Ana-A	7	20	4	4	0	1	1	4	2	7	.200	.273	.450	723	81	-1	0	1	-0	1.000	-1	/O-5(3-0-2),D-2	-0.2
■ JERRY DaVANON DaVanon, Frank Gerald b: 8/21/45, Oceanside, Cal. BR/TR, 5'11", 175 lbs. Deb: 4/11/69 F																								
1969	SD-N	24	59	4	8	1	0	0	3	3	12	.136	.177	.153	330	-7	-8	0	3	-1	.932	0	2-15/S-7	-0.9
	StL-N	16	40	7	12	3	0	1	7	6	8	.300	.391	.450	841	135	2	0	0	0	.958	1	S-16	0.4
	Yr	40	99	11	20	4	0	1	10	9	20	.202	.269	.273	541	53	-6	0	3	-1	.959	1	S-23,2-15	-0.5
1970	StL-N	11	18	2	2	1	0	0	0	2	5	.111	.200	.167	367	-1	-3	0	0	0	1.000	3	/3-5,2-3	0.0
1971	Bal-A	38	81	14	19	5	0	0	4	12	20	.235	.340	.296	637	82	-1	0	0	0	.970	-3	2-20,S-11/3-3,1-1	-0.3
1973	Cal-A	41	49	6	12	3	0	0	2	3	9	.245	.288	.306	595	73	-2	1	2	-0	.927	5	S-14,2-12/3-7	0.4
1974	StL-N	30	40	4	6	1	0	0	4	4	5	.150	.261	.175	436	24	-4	0	1	-0	.840	-2	S-14/3-8,2-7,O-1R	-0.6
1975	Hou-N	32	97	15	27	4	2	1	10	16	7	.278	.386	.392	778	125	4	2	0	1	.944	2	S-21/2-9,3-3	1.0
1976	Hou-N	61	107	19	31	3	3	1	20	21	12	.290	.411	.402	813	144	7	0	2	-1	.980	3	2-17,S-17/3-9	1.3
1977	StL-N	9	8	2	0	0	0	0	0	1	2	.000	.111	.000	111	-68	-2	0	0	0	.923	1	/2-5	0.0
Total	8	262	499	73	117	21	5	3	50	68	80	.234	.332	.315	647	86	-7	3	8	-2	.936	11	S-100/2-88,3-35,O1	1.3
■ JIM DAVENPORT Davenport, James Houston b: 8/17/33, Siluria, Ala. BR/TR, 5'11", 175 lbs. Deb: 4/15/58 MC Career OF: (0-LF 0-CF 1-RF)																								
1958	SF-N	134	434	70	111	22	3	12	41	33	64	.256	.319	.403	722	92	-6	1	3	-1	.960	-4	*3-130/S-5	-1.1
1959	SF-N	123	469	65	121	16	3	6	38	28	65	.258	.303	.343	646	73	-18	0	1	-0	**.978**	-3	*3-121/S-1	-2.2
1960	SF-N	112	363	43	91	15	3	6	38	26	58	.251	.308	.358	666	87	-7	0	2	-1	**.961**	-1	*3-103/S-7	-0.9
1961	SF-N	137	436	64	121	28	4	12	65	45	65	.278	.348	.443	790	112	7	4	3	-0	**.965**	8	*3-132	1.4
1962	*SF-N★	144	485	83	144	25	5	14	58	45	76	.297	.359	.456	815	119	13	2	5	-1	.952	4	*3-141	1.5
1963	SF-N	147	460	40	116	19	3	4	36	32	87	.252	.301	.333	633	83	-10	5	2	0	.962	1	*3-127,2-22/S-1	-0.8
1964	SF-N	116	297	24	70	10	6	2	26	29	46	.236	.304	.330	634	77	-9	2	0	0	.979	-3	S-64,3-41,2-30	-0.6
1965	SF-N	106	271	29	68	14	3	4	31	21	47	.251	.307	.369	676	87	-5	0	0	0	.949	-21	3-39,S-37,2-26	-2.3
1966	SF-N	111	305	42	76	6	2	9	30	22	40	.249	.302	.370	672	83	-7	1	1	-0	.961	-18	S-58,3-36,2-21,/1-2	-2.1
1967	SF-N	124	295	42	81	10	3	5	30	39	50	.275	.367	.380	747	116	7	1	4	-1	1.000	1	3-64,S-28,2-12	1.0
1968	SF-N	113	272	27	61	1	1	1	17	26	32	.224	.292	.246	538	63	-12	0	3	-2	.960	-7	3-82,S-17/2-1	-2.2
1969	SF-N	112	303	20	73	10	1	2	42	29	37	.241	.307	.300	608	72	-11	0	1	-0	.967	1	*3-104/1-1,S-1,O-1R	-1.1
1970	SF-N	22	37	3	9	1	0	0	4	7	6	.243	.364	.270	634	73	-1	0	0	0	1.000	-3	3-10	-0.4
Total	13	1501	4427	552	1142	177	37	77	456	382	673	.258	.320	.367	687	90	-58	16	25	-5	.964	-43	*3-1130,S-219,2/1O	-9.8
■ ANDRE DAVID David, Andre Anter b: 5/18/58, Hollywood, Cal. BL/TL, 6', 170 lbs. Deb: 6/29/84																								
1984	Min-A	33	48	5	12	2	0	1	5	7	11	.250	.357	.354	711	93	-0	0	0	0	1.000	-3	O-14(10-0-4)/D-2	-0.4
1986	Min-A	5	5	0	1	0	0	0	0	0	2	.200	.333	.200	533	48	-0	0	0	0	.000	0	/D-1	0.0
Total	2	38	53	5	13	2	0	1	5	7	13	.245	.355	.340	694	89	-1	0	0	0	1.000	-3	/O-14(10-0-4),D-3	-0.4
■ CLAUDE DAVIDSON Davidson, Claude Boucher "Davey" b: 10/13/1896, Boston, Mass. d: 4/18/56, Weymouth, Mass. BL/TR, 5'11", 155 lbs. Deb: 4/25/18																								
1918	Phi-A	31	81	4	15	1	0	0	4	5	9	.185	.233	.198	430	29	-7	0			.943	-7	2-15/O-8(1-0-7),3-1	-1.6
1919	Was-A	2	7	1	3	0	0	0	0	1	1	.429	.500	.429	929	163	1	0			1.000	-0	/3-2	0.1
Total	2	33	88	5	18	1	0	0	4	6	10	.205	.255	.216	471	41	-6	0			1.000	-7	/2-15,O-8(1-0-7),3-3	-1.5
■ CLEATUS DAVIDSON Davidson, Cleatus La Von b: 11/1/76, Bartow, Fla. BB/TR, 5'10", 170 lbs. Deb: 5/30/99																								
1999	Min-A	12	22	3	3	0	0	0	3	0	4	.136	.136	.136	273	-29	-4	2	0	0	.973	7	/2-6,S-4	0.3
■ HOMER DAVIDSON Davidson, Homer Hurd "Divvy" b: 10/14/1884, Cleveland, Ohio d: 7/26/48, Detroit, Mich. BR/TR, 5'10.5", 155 lbs. Deb: 4/25/08																								
1908	Cle-A	9	4	2	0	0	0	0	0	0		.000	.000	.000	0	-99	-1	1			1.000	2	/C-5,O-1(0-0-1)	0.1
■ MARK DAVIDSON Davidson, John Mark b: 2/15/61, Knoxville, Tenn. BR/TR, 6'2", 190 lbs. Deb: 6/20/86 Career OF: (125-LF 37-CF 198-RF)																								
1986	Min-A	36	68	5	8	3	0	0	2	6	22	.118	.189	.162	351	-3	-10	2	3	-1	.980	-4	O-31(20-5-7)/D-3	-1.5
1987	*Min-A	102	150	32	40	4	1	1	14	13	26	.267	.325	.327	652	71	-6	9	2	1	1.000	-14	O-86(36-20-33)/D-9	-1.9
1988	Min-A	100	106	22	23	7	0	1	10	10	20	.217	.291	.311	602	67	-5	3	3	-0	.955	-16	O-91(4-4-84)/3-1,D-3	-2.3
1989	Hou-N	33	65	7	13	2	1	1	5	7	14	.200	.278	.308	585	70	-3	1	0	0	1.000	-3	O-23(7-3-15)	-0.6
1990	Hou-N	57	130	12	38	5	1	1	11	10	18	.292	.343	.369	712	99	-0	0	3	-1	.981	-2	O-51(26-1-27)	-0.4
1991	Hou-N	85	142	10	27	6	0	2	15	12	28	.190	.263	.275	537	54	-9	0	0	0	1.000	-11	O-63(32-4-32)	-2.2
Total	6	413	661	88	149	27	3	6	57	58	128	.225	.291	.303	593	64	-32	15	11	-1	.983	-49	O-345R/D-15,3-1	-8.9
■ BILL DAVIDSON Davidson, William Simpson b: 5/10/1884, Lafayette, Ind. d: 5/23/54, Lincoln, Neb. BR/TR, 5'10", 170 lbs. Deb: 9/29/09																								
1909	Chi-N	2	7	2	1	0	0	0	0	1		.143	.250	.143	393	22	-1	1			1.000	-0	/O-2(1-1-0)	-0.1
1910	Bro-N	136	509	48	121	13	7	0	34	24	54	.238	.277	.291	568	68	-22	27			.961	-7	*O-131(0-127-4)	-3.7
1911	Bro-N	87	292	33	68	3	4	1	26	16	21	.233	.275	.281	556	58	-17	18			.956	-5	O-74(0-74-0)	-2.8
Total	3	225	808	83	190	16	11	1	60	41	75	.235	.276	.286	562	64	-40	46			.959	-12	O-207(1-202-4)	-6.6
■ CHICK DAVIES Davies, Lloyd Garrison b: 3/6/1892, Peabody, Mass. d: 9/5/73, Middletown, Conn. BL/TL, 5'8", 145 lbs. Deb: 7/11/14																								
1914	Phi-A	19	46	6	11	3	1	0	5	5	13	.239	.314	.348	662	103	0	1			.926	0	O-10(9-0-1)/P-1	0.0
1915	Phi-A	56	132	13	24	5	3	0	11	14	31	.182	.270	.265	535	62	-6	2	4	-1	.973	4	O-32(7-21-4)/P-4	-0.6
1925	NY-N	4	6	1	0	0	0	0	0	0	1	.000	.000	.000	0	-99	-2	0	0	0	1.000	0	/P-2,O-1(0-0-1)	-0.1
1926	NY-N	38	18	4	4	0	0	0	1	3	5	.222	.333	.222	556	53	-1	0			.938	1	P-38	0.0
Total	4	117	202	24	39	8	4	0	17	22	50	.193	.279	.272	551	65	-9	3	4		.938	6	/P-45,O-43(16-21-6)	-0.7
■ LEFTY DAVIS Davis, Alphonzo De Ford b: 2/4/1875, Nashville, Tenn. d: 2/4/19, Collins, N.Y. BL/TL, 5'10", 170 lbs. Deb: 4/18/01 Career OF: (107-LF 72-CF 162-RF)																								
1901	Bro-N	25	91	11	19	2	0	0	7	10		.209	.287	.231	518	50	-6	4			.822	-5	O-24(12-2-10)/2-1	-1.2
	Pit-N	87	335	87	105	8	11	2	33	56		.313	.415	.421	836	138	19	22			.975	7	O-86(0-0-86)	2.2
	Yr	112	426	98	124	10	11	2	40	66		.291	.389	.380	769	120	13	26			.942	2	*O-110(12-2-96)/2-1	1.0
1902	Pit-N	59	232	52	65	7	3	0	20	35		.280	.377	.336	713	116	6	19			.945	-2	O-59(0-0-59)	0.1
1903	NY-A	104	372	54	88	10	0	0	25	43		.237	.319	.263	582	72	-11	11			.906	-7	*O-102(95-1-6)/S-1	-2.5

YEAR	TM/L	G	AB	R	H	2B	3B	HR	RBI	BB	SO	AVG	OBP	SLG	OPS	OPS+	BR+	SB	CS	SBR	FA	FR	G/POS	TPR
1907	Cin-N	73	266	28	61	5	5	1	25	23		.229	.293	.297	590	82	-6	9			.972	5	O-70(0-69-1)	-0.5
Total	4	348	1296	232	338	32	19	3	110	167		.261	.348	.322	670	98	3	65			.939	-2	O-341R/S-1,2-1	-1.9
■ ALVIN DAVIS Davis, Alvin Glenn b: 9/9/60, Riverside, Cal. BL/TR, 6'1", 195 lbs. Deb: 4/11/84																								
1984	Sea-A★	152	567	80	161	34	3	27	116	97	78	.284	.395	.497	892	147	39	5	4	-0	.992	-4	*1-147/D-7	2.5
1985	Sea-A	155	578	78	166	33	1	18	78	90	71	.287	.385	.441	826	125	22	1	2	-0	.992	-5	*1-154	0.7
1986	Sea-A	135	479	66	130	18	1	18	72	76	68	.271	.375	.426	800	116	13	0	3	-1	.986	1	*1-101,D-32	0.5
1987	Sea-A	157	580	86	171	37	2	29	100	72	84	.295	.375	.516	890	126	22	0	0	0	.994	-7	*1-157	0.5
1988	Sea-A	140	478	67	141	24	1	18	69	95	53	.295	.416	.462	878	139	29	1	1	-0	.994	-6	*1-115,D-25	1.5
1989	Sea-A	142	498	84	152	30	1	21	95	101	49	.305	.428	.496	924	155	41	0	1	-0	.992	-3	*1-125,D-14	2.8
1990	Sea-A	140	494	63	140	21	0	17	68	85	68	.283	.393	.429	822	128	22	0	2	-1	.994	-1	D-87,1-52	1.3
1991	Sea-A	145	462	39	102	15	1	12	69	56	78	.221	.305	.335	641	77	-14	0	3	-1	1.000	-1	*D-126,1-14	-2.1
1992	Cal-A	40	104	5	26	8	0	0	16	13	9	.250	.333	.327	660	85	-2	0	0	0	.995	-1	1-22/D-9	-0.4
Total	9	1206	4240	568	1189	220	10	160	683	685	558	.280	.384	.450	834	127	173	7	16	-4	.992	-26	1-887,D-300	7.3
■ BILL DAVIS Davis, Arthur Willard b: 6/6/42, Graceville, Minn. BL/TL, 6'7", 215 lbs. Deb: 9/16/65																								
1965	Cle-A	10	10	0	3	1	0	0	0	0	1	.300	.300	.400	700	96	-0	0	0	0	.000	0	H	0.0
1966	Cle-A	23	38	2	6	1	0	1	4	6	9	.158	.273	.263	536	55	-2	0	0	0	.981	0	/1-9	-0.3
1969	SD-N	31	57	1	10	1	0	0	1	8	18	.175	.288	.193	481	39	-4	0	0	0	.992	-1	1-14	-0.7
Total	3	64	105	3	19	3	0	1	5	14	28	.181	.283	.238	521	50	-7	0	0	0	.988	-1	/1-23	-1.0
■ BROCK DAVIS Davis, Bryshear Barnett b: 10/19/43, Oakland, Cal. BL/TL, 5'10", 168 lbs. Deb: 4/9/63																								
1963	Hou-N	34	55	7	11	2	0	1	2	4	10	.200	.254	.291	545	60	-3	0	0	0	.864	-2	O-14(5-6-3)	-0.5
1964	Hou-N	1	3	0	0	0	0	0	0	1	1	.000	.250	.000	250	-24	-0	0	0	0	1.000	0	/O-1(1-0-0)	0.0
1966	Hou-N	10	27	2	4	1	0	0	1	5	4	.148	.281	.185	466	35	-2	1	0	0	1.000	-0	/O-7(0-7-0)	-0.2
1970	Chi-N	6	3	0	0	0	0	0	0	0	1	.000	.000	.000	0	-89	-1	0	0	0	.000	-0	/O-1(0-1-0)	-0.1
1971	Chi-N	106	301	22	77	7	5	0	28	35	34	.256	.337	.312	650	74	-9	0	6	-2	.982	4	O-93(3-85-5)	-1.0
1972	Mil-A	85	154	17	49	2	0	0	12	12	23	.318	.367	.331	699	111	2	6	4	-0	.970	-5	O-43(19-19-5)	-0.4
Total	6	242	543	48	141	12	5	1	43	57	73	.260	.332	.306	638	79	-13	7	10	-2	.973	-3	O-159(28-118-13)	-2.2
■ CHILI DAVIS Davis, Charles Theodore b: 1/17/60, Kingston, Jamaica BB/TR, 6'3", 210 lbs. Deb: 4/10/81 Career OF: (231-LF 538-CF 481-RF)																								
1981	SF-N	8	15	1	2	0	0	0	0	1	2	.133	.188	.133	321	-8	-2	2	0	0	1.000	-1	/O-6(1-2-3)	-0.3
1982	SF-N	154	641	86	167	27	6	19	76	45	115	.261	.311	.410	721	100	-1	24	13	1	.972	18	*O-153(13-142-1)	1.6
1983	SF-N	137	486	54	113	21	2	11	59	55	108	.233	.311	.352	662	86	-10	10	12	-2	.976	13	*O-133(0-121-12)	0.0
1984	SF-N★	137	499	87	157	21	6	21	81	42	74	.315	.369	.507	876	149	31	12	8	-0	.971	8	*O-123(1-67-57)	3.6
1985	SF-N	136	481	53	130	25	2	13	56	62	74	.270	.354	.412	765	119	13	15	7	1	.980	13	*O-126(0-36-91)	2.2
1986	SF-N★	153	526	71	146	28	3	13	70	84	96	.278	.378	.416	794	125	20	16	13	-1	.972	-2	*O-148(0-53-117)	1.2
1987	*SF-N	149	500	80	125	22	1	24	76	72	109	.250	.347	.442	789	113	9	16	9	0	.975	-13	*O-135(18-114-36)	-0.6
1988	Cal-A	158	600	81	161	29	3	21	93	56	118	.268	.331	.432	762	115	11	9	10	-2	.942	-4	*O-153(0-3-154)/D-3	0.1
1989	Cal-A	154	560	81	152	24	1	22	90	61	109	.271	.343	.436	779	120	14	3	0	1	.979	-4	*O-147(147-0-0)/D-6	0.6
1990	Cal-A	113	412	58	109	17	1	12	58	61	89	.265	.359	.398	757	114	9	1	2	-0	.965	-3	D-60,O-52(46-0-7)	0.3
1991	*Min-A	153	534	84	148	34	1	29	93	95	117	.277	.387	.507	895	139	30	5	6	-1	1.000	-0	*D-150/O-2(2-0-0)	2.4
1992	Min-A	138	444	63	128	27	2	12	66	73	76	.288	.392	.439	831	128	19	4	5	-1	1.000	-1	*D-125/O-4(1-0-3),1-1	1.4
1993	Cal-A	153	573	74	139	32	0	27	112	71	135	.243	.327	.440	767	101	-0	4	1	1	.000	-0	*D-150/P-1	-0.8
1994	Cal-A★	108	392	72	122	18	1	26	84	69	84	.311	.416	.561	977	147	29	3	2	-0	1.000	0	*D-106/O-2(2-0-0)	2.1
1995	Cal-A	119	424	81	135	23	0	20	86	89	79	.318	.437	.514	951	148	34	3	3	-0	.000	0	*D-119	2.5
1996	Cal-A	145	530	73	155	24	0	28	95	86	99	.292	.391	.496	887	122	19	5	2	0	.000	0	*D-143	1.0
1997	KC-A	140	477	71	133	20	0	30	90	85	96	.279	.389	.509	898	129	22	6	3	0	.000	0	*D-133	1.4
1998	*NY-A	35	103	11	30	7	0	3	9	14	18	.291	.376	.447	823	117	3	0	1	-0	.000	0	D-34	0.1
1999	*NY-A	146	476	59	128	25	1	19	78	73	100	.269	.368	.445	814	108	6	4	1	1	.000	0	*D-141	-0.5
Total	19	2436	8673	1240	2380	424	30	350	1372	1194	1698	.274	.363	.451	814	120	256	142	98	-3	.971	24	*O-1184C,D-1170/P-1,1	18.7
■ DOUG DAVIS Davis, Douglas Raymond b: 9/24/62, Bloomsburg, Pa. BR/TR, 6', 180 lbs. Deb: 7/8/88																								
1988	Cal-A	6	12	1	0	0	0	0	0	0	3	.000	.077	.000	77	-79	-3	0	0	0	1.000	-3	/C-3,3-3	-0.6
1992	Tex-A	1	1	0	1	0	0	0	0	0	0	1.000	1.000	1.000	2000	479	0	0	0	0	.000	0	/C-1	0.0
Total	2	7	13	1	1	0	0	0	0	0	3	.077	.143	.077	220	-38	-2	0	0	0	1.000	-3	/C-4,3-3	-0.6
■ ERIC DAVIS Davis, Eric Keith b: 5/29/62, Los Angeles, Cal. BR/TR, 6'3", 185 lbs. Deb: 5/19/84 Career OF: (353-LF 845-CF 256-RF)																								
1984	Cin-N	57	174	33	39	10	1	10	30	24	48	.224	.322	.466	787	114	3	10	2	2	.992	1	O-51(2-46-10)	0.5
1985	Cin-N	56	122	26	30	3	3	8	18	7	39	.246	.287	.516	803	114	2	16	3	2	.987	-6	O-47(24-28-5)	-0.3
1986	Cin-N	132	415	97	115	15	3	27	71	68	100	.277	.380	.523	903	140	23	80	11	14	.975	-9	*O-121(72-71-16)	2.6
1987	Cin-N★	129	474	120	139	23	4	37	100	84	134	.293	.401	.593	994	152	36	50	6	9	.990	28	*O-128(4-124-0)	**7.0**
1988	Cin-N	135	472	81	129	18	3	26	93	65	124	.273	.365	.489	854	138	23	35	3	7	.981	-0	*O-130(0-125-5)	3.1
1989	Cin-N★	131	462	74	130	14	2	34	101	68	116	.281	.375	.541	916	154	32	21	7	2	.984	2	*O-125(4-118-3)	3.7
1990	*Cin-N	127	453	84	118	26	2	24	86	60	100	.260	.350	.486	835	122	13	21	3	4	.993	7	*O-122(56-66-0)	2.2
1991	Cin-N	89	285	39	67	10	0	11	33	48	92	.235	.355	.386	741	104	3	14	2	2	.985	6	O-81(7-77-0)	1.1
1992	LA-N	76	267	21	61	8	1	5	32	36	71	.228	.327	.322	649	86	-4	19	1	4	.961	-5	O-74(69-5-4)	-0.8
1993	LA-N	108	376	57	88	17	0	14	53	41	88	.234	.311	.391	702	92	-5	33	5	6	.991	9	*O-103(101-3-0)	0.7
	Det-A	23	75	14	19	1	1	6	15	14	18	.253	.371	.533	904	141	4	2	2	-0	.981	1	O-18(0-18-0)/D-5	0.5
1994	Det-A	37	120	19	22	4	0	3	13	18	45	.183	.290	.292	582	50	-9	5	0	1	.989	-1	O-35(0-35-0)	-0.8
1996	Cin-N	129	415	81	119	20	0	26	83	70	121	.287	.397	.523	920	140	25	23	9	2	.989	2	*O-126(14-115-0)/1-1	2.9
1997	*Bal-A	42	158	29	48	11	0	8	25	14	47	.304	.364	.525	889	132	7	6	0	1	.975	-4	O-30(0-0-30),D-12	0.2
1998	Bal-A	131	452	81	148	29	1	28	89	44	108	.327	.393	.582	975	151	34	7	6	-1	.992	-5	O-72(0-11-64),D-53	2.1
1999	StL-N	58	191	27	49	9	2	5	30	30	49	.257	.360	.403	764	92	-2	5	4	-0	1.000	1	O-51(0-3-50)/D-2	-0.4
2000	*StL-N	92	254	38	77	14	0	6	40	36	60	.303	.392	.429	821	107	4	1	1	-0	.968	-3	O-69(0-0-69)/D-4	-0.2
Total	16	1552	5165	921	1398	232	23	278	912	727	1360	.271	.364	.486	850	126	191	348	65	54	.985	24	*O-1383C/D-76,1-1	24.1
■ GEORGE DAVIS Davis, George Stacey b: 8/23/1870, Cohoes, N.Y. d: 10/17/40, Philadelphia, Pa. BB/TR, 5'9", 180 lbs. Deb: 4/19/1890 MH Career OF: (12-LF 243-CF 48-RF)																								
1890	Cle-N	136	526	98	139	22	9	6	73	53	34	.264	.336	.375	711	109	6	22			.946	12	*O-133C/2-2,S-1	1.2
1891	Cle-N	136	570	115	165	35	12	3	89	53	29	.289	.354	.409	763	117	11	42			.931	14	*O-116C,3-22/P-3	1.8
1892	*Cle-N	144	597	95	144	27	12	5	82	58	51	.241	.312	.352	663	97	-4	36			.914	-10	3-79,O-44R,S-20,/2	-1.3
1893	NY-N	133	549	112	195	22	27	11	119	42	20	.355	.410	.554	964	155	40	37			.884	0	*3-133/S-1	3.4
1894	*NY-N	124	486	125	171	27	19	9	93	67	10	.352	.434	.541	976	135	29	42			.908	2	*3-124	2.5
1895	NY-N	110	430	108	146	36	9	5	101	55	12	.340	.417	.500	917	139	26	48			.881	15	3-80,1-14,2-10,/OM	3.3
1896	NY-N	124	494	98	158	25	12	5	99	50	24	.320	.387	.449	836	123	17	48			.917	11	3-74,S-45/O-3L,1-3	2.7
1897	NY-N	131	521	112	184	31	10	10	**136**	43		.353	.410	.509	918	146	34	65			.926	24	*S-130	5.4
1898	NY-N	121	486	80	149	20	5	2	86	32		.307	.351	.381	731	113	8	26			.933	**35**	*S-121	4.4
1899	NY-N	109	419	69	141	22	5	1	57	38		.337	.394	.420	814	128	17	35			**.946**	**49**	*S-109	**6.3**
1900	NY-N	114	426	69	136	20	4	3	61	35		.319	.376	.406	782	121	13	29			**.944**	29	*S-114,M	4.3
1901	NY-N	130	491	69	148	26	7	7	65	40		.301	.356	.426	782	131	19	27			.939	23	*S-113,3-17,M	4.5
1902	Chi-A	132	485	76	145	27	7	3	93	65		.299	.386	.402	788	124	19	31			**.951**	-2	*S-129/1-3	2.0
1903	NY-N	4	15	2	4	0	0	0	1	1		.267	.313	.267	579	63	-1	0			.870	-2	/S-4	-0.2
1904	Chi-A	152	563	75	142	27	15	1	69	43		.252	.311	.359	670	116	10	32			.937	17	*S-152	3.5
1905	Chi-A	151	550	74	153	29	1	1	55	60		.278	.353	.340	693	125	18	31			**.948**	17	*S-151	**4.3**
1906	*Chi-A	133	484	63	134	26	6	0	80	41		.277	.338	.355	694	120	12	27			.946	10	*S-129/2-1	2.8
1907	Chi-A	132	466	59	111	16	2	1	52	47		.238	.313	.288	601	95	-1	15			.949	8	*S-132	1.2
1908	Chi-A	128	419	41	91	14	1	0	26	41		.217	.298	.255	553	81	-7	22			.960	4	2-95,S-23/1-4	-0.2
1909	Chi-A	28	68	5	9	1	0	0	2	10		.132	.253	.147	400	28	-5	4			.986	1	1-17/2-2	-0.5
Total	20	2372	9045	1545	2665	453	163	73	1439	874	180	.295	.362	.405	767	121	258	619			.940	256	*S-1374,3-529,O2/1P	51.4

YEAR	TM/L	G	AB	R	H	2B	3B	HR	RBI	BB	SO	AVG	OBP	SLG	OPS	OPS+	BR+	SB	CS	SBR	FA	FR	G/POS	TPR
■ KIDDO DAVIS		Davis, George Willis b: 2/12/02, Bridgeport, Conn. d: 3/4/83, Bridgeport, Conn. BR/TR, 5'11", 178 lbs. Deb: 6/15/26																						
1926	NY-A	1	0	0	0	0	0	0	0	0	0	—	—	—	—	—	0	0	0	0	.000	-0	/O-1(0-0-1)	0.0
1932	Phi-N	137	576	100	178	39	6	5	57	44	56	.309	.359	.424	783	98	-1	16			.975	14	*O-133(1-132-0)	1.0
1933	*NY-N	126	434	61	112	20	4	7	37	25	30	.258	.298	.371	669	92	-6	10			.988	-10	*O-120(0-120-0)	-1.9
1934	StL-N	16	33	6	10	3	0	1	4	3	1	.303	.361	.485	846	117	1	1			.960	1	/O-9(0-9-0)	0.1
	Phi-N	100	393	50	115	25	5	3	48	27	28	.293	.338	.405	743	86	-7	1			.991	17	*O-100(0-100-0)	0.7
	Yr	116	426	56	125	28	5	4	52	30	29	.293	.340	.411	751	89	-6	2			.988	18	*O-109(0-109-0)	0.8
1935	NY-N	47	91	16	24	7	1	2	6	10	4	.264	.343	.429	772	108	1	2			.977	-1	O-21(2-2-17)	-0.1
1936	*NY-N	47	67	6	16	1	0	0	5	6	5	.239	.301	.254	555	51	-4	0			1.000	-1	O-22(6-11-6)	-0.6
1937	NY-N	56	76	20	20	10	0	0	9	10	7	.263	.356	.395	751	103	0	1			.932	-10	O-37(11-25-0)	-1.0
	Cin-N	40	136	19	35	6	0	1	5	16	6	.257	.340	.324	663	85	-2	1			.959	2	O-35(9-26-0)	-0.2
	Yr	96	212	39	55	16	0	1	14	26	13	.259	.346	.349	695	90	-2	2			.951	-8	O-72(20-51-0)	-1.2
1938	Cin-N	5	18	3	5	1	0	0	0	1	4	.278	.316	.333	649	81	-0	0			1.000	-1	/O-5(2-0-5)	-0.2
Total	8	575	1824	281	515	112	16	19	171	142	141	.282	.336	.393	728	92	-18	32	0		.980	10	O-483(31-425-29)	-2.2
■ GERRY DAVIS		Davis, Gerald Edward b: 12/25/58, Trenton, N.J. BR/TR, 6', 185 lbs. Deb: 9/20/83																						
1983	SD-N	5	15	3	5	2	0	0	1	3	4	.333	.444	.467	911	158	1	1	0	0	1.000	1	/O-5(0-0-5)	0.2
1985	SD-N	44	58	10	17	3	1	0	2	5	7	.293	.349	.379	729	105	0	0	0	0	.952	-4	O-23(7-1-14)	-0.4
Total	2	49	73	13	22	5	1	0	3	8	11	.301	.370	.397	768	117	2	1	0	0	.967	-3	/O-28(7-1-19)	-0.2
■ GLENN DAVIS		Davis, Glenn Earle b: 3/28/61, Jacksonville, Fla. BR/TR, 6'3", 210 lbs. Deb: 9/2/84 Career OF: (0-LF 0-CF 9-RF)																						
1984	Hou-N	18	61	6	13	5	0	2	8	4	12	.213	.262	.393	655	88	-1	0	0	0	.988	2	1-16	0.0
1985	Hou-N	100	350	51	95	11	0	20	64	27	68	.271	.336	.474	810	128	12	0	0	0	.985	-2	1-89/O-9(0-0-9)	0.4
1986	*Hou-N★	158	574	91	152	32	3	31	101	64	72	.265	.348	.493	841	133	24	3	1	0	.992	2	*1-156	1.7
1987	Hou-N	151	578	70	145	35	2	27	93	47	84	.251	.313	.458	771	105	2	4	1	1	.991	3	*1-151	-0.4
1988	Hou-N	152	561	78	152	26	0	30	99	53	77	.271	.346	.478	823	140	27	4	3	-0	**.996**	0	*1-151	1.7
1989	Hou-N★	158	581	87	156	26	1	34	89	69	123	.269	.353	.492	845	144	33	4	2	0	.992	3	*1-156	2.6
1990	Hou-N	93	327	44	82	15	4	22	64	46	54	.251	.357	.523	880	143	19	8	3	1	.995	-3	1-91	1.0
1991	Bal-A	49	176	29	40	9	1	10	28	16	29	.227	.310	.460	770	115	3	4	0	1	.976	4	1-36,D-12	0.5
1992	Bal-A	106	398	46	110	15	2	13	48	37	65	.276	.341	.422	763	110	5	1	0	0	1.000	-0	*D-103/1-2	0.1
1993	Bal-A	30	113	8	20	3	0	1	9	7	29	.177	.231	.230	461	24	-12	0	1	-0	.990	-2	1-22/D-7	-1.6
Total	10	1015	3719	510	965	177	13	190	603	370	613	.259	.335	.467	803	124	111	28	11	2	.991	6	1-870,D-122/O-9R	6.0
■ HARRY DAVIS		Davis, Harry Albert "Stinky" b: 5/7/08, Shreveport, La. d: 3/3/97, Shreveport, La. BL/TL, 5'10.5", 160 lbs. Deb: 4/13/32																						
1932	Det-A	141	590	92	159	32	13	4	74	60	53	.269	.339	.388	727	84	-14	12	7	0	.989	-5	*1-141	-3.0
1933	Det-A	66	173	24	37	8	2	0	14	22	8	.214	.303	.283	586	55	-11	2	3	-1	.978	-5	1-44	-1.9
1937	StL-A	120	450	89	124	25	3	3	35	71	26	.276	.374	.364	739	86	-7	7	6	-1	.991	-4	*1-112/O-1(0-0-1)	-2.1
Total	3	327	1213	205	320	65	18	7	123	153	87	.264	.347	.364	712	81	-32	21	16	-1	.988	-14	1-297/O-1(0-0-1)	-7.0
■ HARRY DAVIS		Davis, Harry H (b: Harry Davis) "Jasper" b: 7/19/1873, Philadelphia, Pa. d: 8/11/47, Philadelphia, Pa. BR/TR, 5'10", 180 lbs. Deb: 9/21/1895 M Career OF: (50-LF 19-CF 11-RF)																						
1895	NY-N	7	24	1	7	0	1	0	6	2	0	.292	.346	.375	721	88	-0	1			.957	0	/1-7	0.0
1896	NY-N	64	233	43	64	11	10	2	50	31	20	.275	.372	.433	805	115	5	16			.883	-4	O-40(39-1-0),1-23	-0.2
	Pit-N	44	168	24	32	5	6	0	23	13	21	.190	.257	.292	548	46	-14	9			.966	0	1-35,O-10(9-0-1)/S-1	-1.2
	Yr	108	401	67	96	16	16	2	73	44	41	.239	.325	.374	699	87	-8	25			.973	-4	1-58,O-50(48-1-1)/S-1	-1.4
1897	Pit-N	111	429	70	131	10	**28**	2	63	26		.305	.359	.473	832	123	13	21			.965	-12	1-64,3-32,O-14R,/S	0.0
1898	Pit-N	58	222	31	65	9	13	1	24	12		.293	.332	.464	796	130	7	7			.980	-2	1-53/O-6(0-6-0)	0.4
	Lou-N	37	138	18	30	5	2	1	16	7		.217	.255	.304	560	61	-7	6			.967	0	1-34/2-2,O-1(0-0-1)	-0.7
	Was-N	1	3	0	0	0	0	0	0	0		.000	.000	.000	0	-99	-1	0			.875	-0	/1-1	-0.1
	Yr	96	363	49	95	14	15	2	40	19		.262	.300	.399	700	102	-1	13			.974	-2	1-88/O-7(0-6-1),2-2	-0.4
1899	Was-N	18	64	3	12	2	3	0	8	8		.188	.288	.313	600	65	-3	2			.988	-1	1-18	-0.4
1901	Phi-A	117	496	92	152	28	10	8	76	23		.306	.340	.452	791	113	7	21			.976	8	*1-117	1.1
1902	Phi-A	133	561	89	172	**43**	8	6	92	30		.307	.343	.444	787	112	7	28			.984	7	*1-128/O-5(0-5-0)	1.1
1903	Phi-A	106	420	77	125	28	7	6	55	24		.298	.343	.440	783	128	14	24			.972	-1	*1-104/O-2(2-0-0)	1.1
1904	Phi-A	102	404	54	125	21	11	**10**	62	23		.309	.350	.490	840	156	24	12			.983	-1	*1-102	2.3
1905	*Phi-A	150	607	**93**	173	**47**	6	**8**	**83**	43		.285	.334	.422	756	137	23	36			.985	1	*1-150	2.3
1906	Phi-A	145	551	94	161	42	7	**12**	**96**	49		.292	.355	.459	815	150	30	23			.975	-0	*1-145	3.0
1907	Phi-A	149	582	84	155	**35**	8	**8**	87	42		.266	.318	.395	713	124	14	20			.977	4	*1-149	1.7
1908	Phi-A	147	513	65	127	23	9	5	62	61		.248	.332	.357	689	116	10	20			.986	1	*1-147	0.9
1909	Phi-A	149	530	73	142	22	11	4	75	51		.268	.338	.374	711	122	13	20			.988	-5	*1-149	0.6
1910	*Phi-A	139	492	61	122	19	4	1	41	53		.248	.332	.309	641	102	3	17			.986	-4	*1-139	-0.5
1911	*Phi-A	57	183	27	36	9	1	1	22	24		.197	.297	.273	570	60	-9	2			.977	2	1-53	-0.9
1912	Cle-A	2	5	0	0	0	0	0	0	0		.000	.000	.000	0	-97	-1	0			.941	0	/1-2,M	-0.1
1913	Phi-A	7	17	2	6	2	0	0	4	1	4	.353	.389	.471	859	155	1	0			1.000	1	/1-6	0.2
1914	Phi-A	5	7	0	3	0	0	0	2	1	0	.429	.556	.429	984	204	1	0	2	-1	1.000	-0	/1-1	0.0
1915	Phi-A	5	3	0	1	0	0	0	4	0	0	.333	.333	.333	667	103	-0	0			.000	0	/1-1	0.0
1916	Phi-A	1	0	0	0	0	0	0	0	1	0	—	1.000	—	1000	213	0	0			.000	0	H	0.0
1917	Phi-A	1	1	0	0	0	0	0	0	0	0	.000	.000	.000	0	-99	-0	0			.000	0	H	0.0
Total	22	1755	6653	1001	1841	361	145	75	951	525	45	.277	.335	.408	743	119	136	285	2		.980	-7	*1-1628/O-78L,32S	10.6
■ TOMMY DAVIS		Davis, Herman Thomas b: 3/21/39, Brooklyn, N.Y. BR/TR, 6'2", 205 lbs. Deb: 9/22/59 C Career OF: (1101-LF 122-CF 56-RF)																						
1959	LA-N	1	1	0	0	0	0	0	0	0	1	.000	.000	.000	0	-93	-0	0	0	0	.000	0	H	0.0
1960	LA-N	110	352	43	97	18	1	11	44	13	35	.276	.305	.426	731	92	-5	6	2	1	.975	-0	O-87(24-55-10)/3-5	-0.9
1961	LA-N	132	460	60	128	13	2	15	58	32	53	.278	.328	.413	741	87	-8	10	4	1	.973	-12	O-86(44-39-30),3-59	-2.4
1962	LA-N★	163	665	120	**230**	27	9	27	**153**	33	65	**.346**	.379	.535	914	151	45	18	6	2	.961	1	*O-146(134-13-5),3-39	3.9
1963	*LA-N★	146	556	69	181	19	3	16	88	29	59	**.326**	.363	.457	820	144	30	15	10	-0	.969	-7	*O-129(120-14-3),3-40	1.8
1964	LA-N	152	592	70	163	20	5	14	86	29	68	.275	.314	.397	711	106	3	11	8	-0	.982	14	*O-148(148-0-0)	0.8
1965	LA-N	17	60	3	15	1	1	0	9	2	4	.250	.274	.300	574	66	-3	2	1	0	1.000	0	O-16(16-0-0)	-0.4
1966	*LA-N	100	313	27	98	11	1	3	27	16	36	.313	.347	.383	730	111	4	3	3	-0	.972	-2	O-79(79-0-0)/3-2	-0.3
1967	NY-N	154	577	72	174	32	0	16	73	31	71	.302	.345	.440	785	125	17	9	3	1	.975	-2	*O-149(149-0-0)/1-1	0.8
1968	Chi-A	132	456	30	122	5	3	8	50	16	48	.268	.292	.344	637	91	-6	4	2	0	.962	-4	*O-116(115-0-4)/1-6	-1.9
1969	Sea-A	123	454	52	123	29	1	6	80	30	46	.271	.322	.379	701	97	-3	19	4	3	.967	-7	*O-112(112-0-0)/1-1	-1.4
	Hou-N	24	79	2	19	3	0	1	9	8	9	.241	.318	.316	635	80	-2	1	1	-0	1.000	0	O-21(20-1-0)	-0.4
1970	Hou-N	57	213	24	60	12	2	3	30	7	25	.282	.305	.399	704	91	-4	8	3	1	.949	-1	O-53(53-0-0)	-0.7
	Oak-A	66	200	17	58	9	1	1	27	8	18	.290	.321	.360	681	91	-3	2	4	-1	.963	-7	O-45(43-0-2)/1-8	-1.4
	Chi-N	11	42	4	11	2	0	2	8	1	8	.262	.279	.452	731	83	-1	0	1	-0	.938	-1	O-10(10-0-0)	-0.2
1971	*Oak-A	79	219	26	71	8	1	3	42	15	19	.324	.368	.411	778	123	6	7	1	1	.989	2	1-35,O-16L/2-3,3-2	0.7
1972	Chi-N	15	26	3	7	1	0	0	6	2	3	.269	.321	.308	629	72	-1	0	1	-0	1.000	-0	/1-3,O-2(1-0-1)	-0.2
	Bal-A	26	82	9	21	3	0	0	6	6	18	.256	.307	.293	600	77	-2	2	0	1	1.000	0	O-18(17-0-1)/1-3	-0.3
1973	*Bal-A	137	552	53	169	20	3	7	89	30	56	.306	.343	.391	734	107	5	11	3	1	.971	-0	*D-127/1-4	0.2
1974	*Bal-A	158	626	67	181	20	1	11	84	34	49	.289	.329	.377	706	106	4	6	2	1	.000	0	*D-155	0.0
1975	Bal-A	116	460	43	130	14	1	6	57	23	52	.283	.317	.357	673	96	-3	2	0	0	.000	0	*D-111	-0.6
1976	Cal-A	72	219	16	58	5	0	3	26	15	18	.265	.315	.329	644	95	-2	0	1	-0	1.000	-0	D-54/1-1	-0.4
	KC-A	8	19	1	5	0	0	0	0	1	0	.263	.300	.263	563	65	-1	0	0	0	.000	0	/D-3	-0.1
	Yr	80	238	17	63	5	0	3	26	16	18	.265	.314	.324	637	92	-3	0	1	-0	1.000	-0	D-57/1-1	-0.5
Total	18	1999	7223	811	2121	272	35	153	1052	381	754	.294	.332	.405	736	109	71	136	59	9	.970	-27	*O-1233L,D-450,3/12	-3.4
■ IKE DAVIS		Davis, Isaac Marion b: 6/14/1895, Pueblo, Col. d: 4/2/84, Tucson, Ariz. BR/TR, 5'7", 140 lbs. Deb: 4/23/19																						
1919	Was-A	8	14	0	0	0	0	0	0	0	6	.000	.000	.000	0	-99	-4	0			.857	-2	/S-4	-0.6
1924	Chi-A	10	33	5	8	1	1	0	4	2	5	.242	.286	.333	619	61	-2	0	0	0	.940	1	S-10	0.0

YEAR	TM/L	G	AB	R	H	2B	3B	HR	RBI	BB	SO	AVG	OBP	SLG	OPS	OPS+	BR+	SB	CS	SBR	FA	FR	G/POS	TPR
1925	Chi-A	146	562	105	135	31	9	0	61	71	58	.240	.333	.327	660	72	-23	19	14	-1	.937	8	*S-144	0.0
Total	3	164	609	110	143	32	10	0	65	73	69	.235	.324	.320	644	68	-29	19	14		.936	8	S-158	-0.6
■ **IRA DAVIS**	Davis, J. Ira "Slats" b: 7/8/1870, Philadelphia, Pa. d: 12/21/42, Brooklyn, N.Y. 162 lbs. Deb: 4/22/1899																							
1899	NY-N	6	17	3	4	1	1	0	2	0		.235	.235	.412	647	79	-1	1			.750	-0	/S-3,1-2	-0.1
■ **JACKE DAVIS**	Davis, Jacke Sylvesta b: 3/5/36, Carthage, Tex. BR/TR, 5'11", 160 lbs. Deb: 4/19/62																							
1962	Phi-N	48	75	9	16	0	1	1	6	4	20	.213	.253	.280	533	44	-6	1	0	0	.926	-6	O-26(16-5-7)	-1.2
■ **JUMBO DAVIS**	Davis, James J. b: 9/5/1861, New York, N.Y. d: 2/14/21, St.Louis, Mo. BL/TR, 5'11", 195 lbs. Deb: 7/27/1884 U																							
1884	KC-U	7	29	3	6	0	0	0		0		.207	.207	.207	414	30	-3				.633	-2	/3-7	-0.4
1886	Bal-a	60	216	23	42	5	2	1	20	11		.194	.240	.250	490	55	-11	12			.848	5	3-60	-0.5
1887	Bal-a	130	513	81	178	23	**19**	8	109	28		.347	.353	.485	838	141	25	49			.826	4	3-87,S-43	2.5
1888	KC-a	121	491	70	131	22	8	3	61	20		.267	.304	.363	666	106	1	42			.843	30	*3-113/S-8	3.0
1889	KC-a	62	241	40	64	4	3	0	30	17	35	.266	.319	.307	626	74	-9	25			.803	-0	3-62	-0.7
	StL-a	2	4	1	0	0	0	0	0	1	1	.000	.200	.000	200	-36	-1	0			1.000	-0	/S-1,O-1(1-0-0)	-0.1
	Yr	64	245	41	64	4	3	0	30	18	36	.261	.317	.302	619	72	-9	25			.803	-1	3-62/S-1,O-1(1-0-0)	-0.8
1890	StL-a	21	71	8	18	3	1	0	13	9		.254	.338	.324	661	83	-2	5			.731	-1	3-21	-0.2
	Bro-a	38	142	33	43	9	2	2	28	15		.303	.385	.437	822	147	8	10			.845	-5	3-38	0.4
	Yr	59	213	41	61	12	3	2	41	24		.286	.369	.399	768	123	6	15			.800	-6	3-59	0.2
1891	Was-a	12	44	7	14	3	2	0	9	7	5	.318	.412	.477	889	162	4	8			.820	-2	3-12	0.2
Total	7	453	1751	266	496	69	37	14	270	108	41	.283	.322	.379	701	107	13	151			.824	28	3-400/S-52,O-1(1-0-0)	4.2
■ **JODY DAVIS**	Davis, Jody Richard b: 11/12/56, Gainesville, Ga. BR/TR, 6'3", 210 lbs. Deb: 4/21/81																							
1981	Chi-N	56	180	14	46	5	1	4	21	21	28	.256	.337	.361	698	94	-1	0	1	-0	.972	-1	C-56	0.0
1982	Chi-N	130	418	41	109	20	2	12	52	36	92	.261	.321	.404	725	99	-1	0	1	-0	.984	8	*C-129	1.2
1983	Chi-N	151	510	56	138	31	2	24	84	33	93	.271	.317	.480	798	113	7	0	2	-1	.984	-14	*C-150	-0.1
1984	*Chi-N★	150	523	55	134	25	2	19	94	47	99	.256	.319	.421	739	97	-2	5	6	-1	.984	4	*C-146	0.7
1985	Chi-N	142	482	47	112	30	0	17	58	48	83	.232	.302	.400	702	85	-10	1	0	0	.990	-1	*C-138	-0.4
1986	Chi-N★	148	528	61	132	27	2	21	74	41	110	.250	.304	.428	732	92	-7	0	1	-0	.992	4	*C-145/1-1	0.3
1987	Chi-N	125	428	57	106	12	2	19	51	52	91	.248	.332	.418	750	93	-4	1	2	-0	.989	-3	*C-123	-0.2
1988	Chi-N	88	249	19	57	9	0	6	33	29	51	.229	.312	.337	649	83	-5	0	3	-1	.995	-4	C-74	-0.7
	Atl-N	2	8	2	2	0	0	1	3	0	1	.250	.250	.625	875	137	0	0	0	0	1.000	1	/C-2	0.1
	Yr	90	257	21	59	9	0	7	36	29	52	.230	.310	.346	656	84	-5	0	3	-1	.995	-4	C-76	-0.6
1989	Atl-N	78	231	12	39	5	0	4	19	23	61	.169	.247	.242	489	39	-18	0	0	0	.985	-9	C-72/1-2	-2.5
1990	Atl-N	12	28	0	2	0	0	0	1	3	3	.071	.161	.071	233	-32	-5	0	0	0	1.000	1	/1-6,C-4	-0.4
Total	10	1082	3585	364	877	164	11	127	490	333	712	.245	.310	.403	713	91	-46	7	16	-4	.987	-15	*C-1039/1-9	-2.0
■ **JOHN DAVIS**	Davis, John Humphrey "Red" b: 7/15/15, Laurel Run, Pa. BR/TR, 5'11", 172 lbs. Deb: 9/9/41																							
1941	NY-N	21	70	8	15	3	0	0	5	8	12	.214	.295	.257	552	55	-4	0			.970	1	3-21	-0.2
■ **CRASH DAVIS**	Davis, Lawrence Columbus b: 7/14/19, Canon, Ga. BR/TR, 6', 173 lbs. Deb: 6/15/40																							
1940	Phi-A	23	67	4	18	1	1	0	9	3	10	.269	.310	.313	623	63	-4	1	0	0	.963	4	2-19/S-1	0.1
1941	Phi-A	39	105	8	23	3	0	0	8	11	16	.219	.293	.248	541	45	-8	0	0	0	.952	2	2-20,1-12	-0.5
1942	Phi-A	86	272	31	61	8	1	2	26	21	30	.224	.282	.283	565	60	-15	1	0	0	.965	-6	2-57,S-26/1-3	-1.6
Total	3	148	444	43	102	12	2	2	43	35	56	.230	.289	.279	568	57	-26	2	0	0	.961	0	/2-96,S-27,1-15	-2.0
■ **MARK DAVIS**	Davis, Mark Anthony b: 11/25/64, San Diego, Cal. BR/TR, 6', 180 lbs. Deb: 7/2/91 F																							
1991	Cal-A	3	2	0	0	0	0	0	0	0	0	.000	.000	.000	0	-99	-1	0	0	0	.500	-1	/O-3(0-0-3)	-0.2
■ **BEN DAVIS**	Davis, Mark Christopher b: 3/10/77, Chester, Pa. BB/TR, 6'4", 195 lbs. Deb: 9/25/98																							
1998	SD-N	1	1	0	0	0	0	0	0	0	0	.000	.000	.000	0	-99	-0	0	0	0	1.000	0	/C-1	0.0
1999	SD-N	76	266	29	65	14	1	5	30	25	70	.244	.309	.361	670	75	-11	2	1	0	.986	-4	C-74	-1.0
2000	SD-N	43	130	12	29	6	0	3	14	14	35	.223	.299	.338	637	64	-7	1	1	-0	.996	0	C-38/D-1	-0.5
Total	3	120	397	41	94	20	1	8	44	39	105	.237	.305	.353	658	71	-18	3	2	-0	.990	-4	C-113/D-1	-1.5
■ **MIKE DAVIS**	Davis, Michael Dwayne b: 6/11/59, San Diego, Cal. BL/TL, 6'3", 185 lbs. Deb: 4/10/80 F Career OF: (33-LF 128-CF 728-RF)																							
1980	Oak-A	51	95	11	20	2	1	1	8	7	14	.211	.265	.284	549	54	-6	2	1	0	1.000	1	O-18(5-0-13)/1-7,D-6	-0.6
1981	*Oak-A	17	20	0	1	1	0	0	0	2	4	.050	.136	.100	236	-33	-3	0	0	0	1.000	-0	/O-2(2-0-0),1-1,D-3	-0.4
1982	Oak-A	23	75	12	30	4	0	1	10	2	8	.400	.416	.493	909	155	5	3	2	-0	.946	-1	O-13(8-3-5)/1-7	0.4
1983	Oak-A	128	443	61	122	24	4	8	62	27	74	.275	.324	.402	726	105	2	32	15	2	.974	9	*O-121(0-21-110)/D-3	0.8
1984	Oak-A	134	382	47	88	18	3	9	46	31	66	.230	.290	.364	654	85	-8	14	9	-0	.961	-1	*O-127(1-16-121)/D-4	-1.5
1985	Oak-A	154	547	92	157	34	1	24	82	50	99	.287	.349	.484	833	135	25	24	10	2	.979	2	*O-151(0-31-138)	2.2
1986	Oak-A	142	489	77	131	28	3	19	55	34	91	.268	.317	.454	771	115	9	27	4	5	.973	2	*O-139(0-34-120)	0.9
1987	Oak-A	139	494	69	131	32	1	22	72	42	94	.265	.324	.468	792	114	9	19	7	2	.942	-7	*O-124(0-0-124),D-14	-0.3
1988	*LA-N	108	281	29	55	11	2	2	17	25	59	.196	.261	.270	532	55	-17	7	3	0	.961	-9	O-76(1-23-63)	-2.9
1989	LA-N	67	173	21	43	7	1	5	19	16	28	.249	.312	.387	699	101	-0	6	5	-0	.987	-3	O-48(16-0-34)	-0.6
Total	10	963	2999	419	778	161	16	91	371	236	537	.259	.316	.415	730	105	16	134	56	10	.968	-8	O-819R/D-30,1-15	-2.0
■ **ODIE DAVIS**	Davis, Odie Ernest b: 8/13/55, San Antonio, Tex. BR/TR, 6'1", 178 lbs. Deb: 9/3/80																							
1980	Tex-A	17	8	0	1	0	0	0	0	0	2	.125	.125	.125	250	-32	-1	0	0	0	.880	5	S-13/3-1	0.3
■ **OTIS DAVIS**	Davis, Otis Allen "Scat" b: 9/24/20, Charleston, Ark. BL/TL, 6', 160 lbs. Deb: 4/22/46																							
1946	Bro-N	1	0	1	0	0	0	0	0	0	0	—	—	—	—	—	0	0			1.000	0	R	0.0
■ **DICK DAVIS**	Davis, Richard Earl b: 9/25/53, Long Beach, Cal. BR/TR, 6'3", 195 lbs. Deb: 7/12/77																							
1977	Mil-A	22	51	7	14	2	0	0	6	1	8	.275	.288	.314	602	64	-3	0	0	0	1.000	-2	O-12(12-0-0)/D-6	-0.5
1978	Mil-A	69	218	28	54	10	1	5	26	7	23	.248	.278	.372	649	81	-6	2	5	-1	1.000	-1	D-34,O-28(18-4-8)	-1.1
1979	Mil-A	91	335	51	89	13	1	12	41	16	46	.266	.299	.418	717	91	-5	3	3	-0	.973	-0	D-53,O-35(32-0-3)	-0.9
1980	Mil-A	106	365	50	99	26	2	4	30	11	43	.271	.298	.386	684	89	-7	5	3	0	.971	-2	D-63,O-38(13-0-27)	-1.2
1981	*Phi-N	45	96	12	32	6	1	2	19	8	13	.333	.390	.479	870	139	5	1	2	-0	.974	-4	O-32(1-0-31)	-0.1
1982	Phi-N	28	68	5	19	3	1	2	7	2	9	.279	.300	.441	741	103	-0	1	0	0	1.000	-0	O-16(0-0-16)	-0.1
	Tor-A	3	7	0	2	0	0	0	2	0	1	.286	.286	.286	571	53	-0	0	0	0	1.000	0	/O-1(1-0-0),D-1	-0.1
	Pit-N	39	77	7	14	2	1	2	10	5	9	.182	.232	.312	543	49	-5	1	0	0	.971	-4	O-28(1-0-27)	-1.1
Total	6	403	1217	160	323	62	7	27	141	50	152	.265	.298	.394	692	89	-22	13	13	-2	.981	-14	O-190(78-4-112),D-157	-5.1
■ **BRANDY DAVIS**	Davis, Robert Brandon b: 9/10/28, Newark, Del. BR/TR, 6', 170 lbs. Deb: 4/15/52 C																							
1952	Pit-N	55	95	14	17	1	1	0	1	11	28	.179	.264	.211	475	32	-9	9	2	1	.932	-3	O-29(9-9-12)	-1.1
1953	Pit-N	12	39	5	8	2	0	0	2	0	3	.205	.205	.256	462	20	-5	0	2	-1	.955	0	/O-9(9-0-0)	-0.6
Total	2	67	134	19	25	3	1	0	3	11	31	.187	.248	.224	472	29	-13	9	4	1	.938	-3	/O-38(18-9-12)	-1.7
■ **BOB DAVIS**	Davis, Robert John Eugene b: 3/1/52, Pryor, Okla. BR/TR, 6', 180 lbs. Deb: 4/6/73																							
1973	SD-N	5	11	1	1	0	0	0	0	0	5	.091	.091	.091	182	-54	-2	0	0	0	.941	2	/C-5	0.0
1975	SD-N	43	128	6	30	3	2	0	7	11	31	.234	.310	.289	599	71	-5	0	0	0	.986	3	C-43	0.0
1976	SD-N	51	83	7	17	0	1	0	5	5	13	.205	.250	.229	479	40	-7	0	0	0	.965	4	C-47	-0.2
1977	SD-N	48	94	9	17	2	0	1	10	5	24	.181	.238	.234	472	30	-9	0	0	0	.975	-1	C-46	-1.0
1978	SD-N	19	40	3	8	1	0	0	2	1	5	.200	.220	.225	445	26	-4	0	1	-0	.960	-2	C-16	-0.6
1979	Tor-A	32	89	6	11	2	0	1	8	6	15	.124	.188	.180	367	-0	-13	0	0	0	.984	-2	C-32	-1.3
1980	Tor-A	91	218	18	47	11	0	4	19	12	25	.216	.260	.321	581	56	-14	0	0	0	.983	-2	C-89	-1.3
1981	Cal-A	1	2	0	0	0	0	0	0	0	0	.000	.000	.000	0	-99	-1	0	0	0	1.000	-0	/C-1	-0.1
Total	8	290	665	50	131	19	3	6	51	40	118	.197	.250	.262	512	42	-54	0	1	-0	.978	1	C-279	-4.5

YEAR	TM/L	G	AB	R	H	2B	3B	HR	RBI	BB	SO	AVG	OBP	SLG	OPS	OPS+	BR+	SB	CS	SBR	FA	FR	G/POS	TPR
■ **RON DAVIS**	Davis, Ronald Everette b: 10/21/41, Roanoke Rapids, N.C d: 9/5/92, Houston, Tex. BR/TR, 6', 180 lbs. Deb: 8/1/62																							
1962	Hou-N	6	14	1	3	0	0	0	1	1	7	.214	.267	.214	481	33	-1	1	0	0	1.000	-1	/O-5(0-5-0)	-0.2
1966	Hou-N	48	194	21	48	10	1	2	19	13	26	.247	.308	.340	648	86	-4	2	2	-0	.982	6	O-48(0-48-0)	0.0
1967	Hou-N	94	285	31	73	19	1	7	38	17	48	.256	.303	.404	706	104	1	5	3	0	.976	-0	O-80(63-11-8)	-0.4
1968	Hou-N	52	217	22	46	10	1	1	12	13	48	.212	.269	.281	550	67	-9	0	4	-1	.971	6	O-52(0-52-0)	-0.7
	*StL-N	33	79	11	14	4	2	0	5	5	17	.177	.226	.278	505	51	-5	1	0	0	.979	0	O-25(2-10-14)	-0.6
	Yr	85	296	33	60	14	3	1	17	18	65	.203	.258	.280	538	63	-14	1	4	-1	.973	6	O-77(2-62-14)	-1.3
1969	Pit-N	62	64	10	15	1	1	0	4	7	14	.234	.310	.281	591	68	-3	0	0	0	.933	-13	O-51(22-12-20)	-1.7
Total	5	295	853	96	199	44	6	10	79	56	160	.233	.288	.334	622	82	-21	9	9	-1	.974	-2	O-261(87-138-42)	-3.6
■ **RUSS DAVIS**	Davis, Russell Stuart b: 9/13/69, Birmingham, Ala. BR/TR, 6', 170 lbs. Deb: 7/6/94																							
1994	NY-A	4	14	0	2	0	0	0	1	0	4	.143	.143	.143	286	-27	-3	0	0	0	1.000	0	/3-4	-0.2
1995	*NY-A	40	98	14	27	5	2	2	12	10	26	.276	.349	.429	777	102	0	0	0	0	.968	3	3-34/1-2,D-4	0.3
1996	Sea-A	51	167	24	39	9	0	5	18	17	50	.234	.312	.377	689	73	-7	2	0	0	.933	-8	3-51	-1.3
1997	Sea-A	119	420	57	114	29	1	20	63	27	100	.271	.318	.488	807	108	3	6	2	1	.939	3	*3-117/D-1	0.7
1998	Sea-A	141	502	68	130	30	1	20	82	34	134	.259	.310	.442	752	93	-7	4	3	-0	.906	-1	*3-137/O-3(3-0-0)	-0.7
1999	Sea-A	124	432	55	106	17	1	21	59	32	111	.245	.305	.435	740	88	-9	3	3	-0	.959	-15	*3-124/S-2	-2.2
2000	*SF-N	80	180	27	47	5	0	9	24	9	29	.261	.304	.439	743	91	-3	0	3	-1	.933	-8	3-43/1-6,D-3	-1.2
Total	7	559	1813	245	465	95	5	77	259	129	454	.256	.311	.442	753	93	-26	15	11	-1	.935	-26	3-510/D-8,1-8,OS	-4.6
■ **STEVE DAVIS**	Davis, Steven Michael b: 12/30/53, Oakland, Cal. BR/TR, 6'1", 200 lbs. Deb: 9/23/79																							
1979	Chi-N	3	4	0	0	0	0	0	1	0	0	.000	.000	.000	0	-91	-1	0	0	0	1.000	0	/2-2,3-1	-0.1
■ **TOMMY DAVIS**	Davis, Thomas James b: 5/21/73, Mobile, Ala. BR/TR, 6'1", 195 lbs. Deb: 5/14/99																							
1999	Bal-A	5	6	0	1	0	0	0	0	0	2	.167	.167	.167	333	-15	-1	0	0	0	.909	0	/C-4,1-1	-0.1
■ **TOD DAVIS**	Davis, Thomas Oscar b: 7/24/24, Los Angeles, Cal. d: 12/31/78, W.Covina, Cal. BR/TR, 6'2", 190 lbs. Deb: 4/27/49																							
1949	Phi-A	31	75	7	20	0	1	1	6	9	16	.267	.345	.333	679	83	-2	0	0	0	.912	-1	S-14,3-12/2-1	-0.2
1951	Phi-A	11	15	0	1	0	0	0	0	1	3	.067	.125	.067	192	-46	-3	0	0	0	1.000	-0	/2-2,3-1	-0.3
Total	2	42	90	7	21	0	1	1	6	10	19	.233	.310	.289	599	61	-5	0	0	0	.966	-1	/S-14,3-13,2-3	-0.5
■ **TRENCH DAVIS**	Davis, Trench Neal b: 9/12/60, Baltimore, Md. BL/TL, 6'3", 171 lbs. Deb: 6/4/85																							
1985	Pit-N	2	7	1	1	0	0	0	0	0	0	.143	.143	.143	286	-20	-1	1	0	0	.667	-1	/O-2(0-2-0)	-0.2
1986	Pit-N	15	23	2	3	0	0	0	1	0	4	.130	.130	.130	261	-27	-4	0	0	0	.917	-0	/O-7(0-7-0)	-0.5
1987	Atl-N	6	3	0	0	0	0	0	0	0	1	.000	.000	.000	0	-95	-1	0	0	0	.000	0	/H	-0.1
Total	3	23	33	3	4	0	0	0	1	0	5	.121	.121	.121	242	-32	-6	1	0	0	.867	-1	/O-9(0-9-0)	-0.8
■ **SPUD DAVIS**	Davis, Virgil Lawrence b: 12/20/04, Birmingham, Ala. d: 8/14/84, Birmingham, Ala. BR/TR, 6'1", 197 lbs. Deb: 4/30/28 MC																							
1928	StL-N	2	5	1	1	0	0	0	1	1	0	.200	.333	.200	533	42	-0	0			.750	-1	/C-2	-0.1
	Phi-N	67	163	16	46	2	0	3	18	15	11	.282	.343	.350	692	79	-5	0			.980	3	C-49	0.1
	Yr	69	168	17	47	2	0	3	19	16	11	.280	.342	.345	688	78	-5	0			.971	2	C-51	0.0
1929	Phi-N	98	263	31	90	18	0	7	48	19	17	.342	.391	.490	881	110	4	1			.961	-12	C-89	-0.3
1930	Phi-N	106	329	41	103	16	1	14	65	17	20	.313	.349	.495	844	94	-4	1			.986	-2	C-96	0.0
1931	Phi-N	120	393	30	128	32	1	4	51	36	28	.326	.382	.443	825	112	8	0			.994	1	*C-114	1.5
1932	Phi-N	125	402	44	135	23	5	14	70	40	39	.336	.399	.522	921	130	18	1			.987	-3	*C-120	2.1
1933	Phi-N	141	495	51	173	28	3	9	65	32	24	.349	.395	.473	867	130	20	2			.983	-11	*C-132	1.8
1934	*StL-N	107	347	45	104	22	4	9	65	34	27	.300	.366	.464	830	113	7	0			.988	1	C-94	1.3
1935	StL-N	102	315	28	100	24	2	1	60	33	30	.317	.386	.416	802	111	6	0			**.992**	-5	C-81/1-5	0.5
1936	StL-N	112	363	24	99	26	2	4	59	35	34	.273	.342	.388	730	97	-2	0			.985	-13	*C-103/3-2	-0.9
1937	Cin-N	76	209	19	56	10	1	3	33	23	15	.268	.341	.368	709	97	-1	0			.980	12	C-59	1.4
1938	Cin-N	12	36	3	6	1	0	0	1	5	6	.167	.286	.194	480	35	-3	0			.962	0	C-11	-0.2
	Phi-N	70	215	11	53	7	0	2	23	14	14	.247	.293	.307	600	67	-10	1			.980	-12	C-63	-1.8
	Yr	82	251	14	59	8	0	2	24	19	20	.235	.292	.291	582	62	-13	1			.977	-12	C-74	-2.0
1939	Phi-N	87	202	10	62	8	1	0	23	24	20	.307	.383	.356	740	103	2	0			**1.000**	-2	C-85	0.4
1940	Pit-N	99	285	23	93	14	1	5	39	35	20	.326	.404	.435	839	132	14	0			.967	-6	C-87	1.3
1941	Pit-N	57	107	3	27	4	1	0	6	11	11	.252	.322	.308	630	78	-3	0			1.000	-2	C-49	-0.3
1944	Pit-N	54	93	6	28	7	0	2	14	10	8	.301	.369	.441	810	122	3	0			.966	-1	C-35	0.3
1945	Pit-N	23	33	2	8	2	0	0	6	2	2	.242	.306	.303	609	67	-1	0			.968	-0	C-13	-0.1
Total	16	1458	4255	388	1312	244	22	77	647	386	326	.308	.369	.430	799	108	52	6			.984	-55	*C-1282/1-5,3-2	7.0
■ **BUTCH DAVIS**	Davis, Wallace McArthur b: 6/19/58, Martin Co., N.C. BR/TR, 6', 190 lbs. Deb: 8/23/83																							
1983	KC-A	33	122	13	42	2	6	2	18	4	19	.344	.365	.508	873	137	6	4	3	-0	.977	2	O-33(33-0-0)	0.6
1984	KC-A	41	116	11	17	3	0	2	12	10	19	.147	.214	.224	438	21	-12	4	3	-0	.959	-1	O-35(34-1-1)/D-2	-1.5
1987	Pit-N	7	7	3	1	1	0	0	0	1	3	.143	.250	.286	536	41	-1	0	0	0	1.000	0	/O-1(1-0-0)	0.0
1988	Bal-A	13	25	2	6	1	0	0	0	0	8	.240	.240	.280	520	46	-2	1	0	0	1.000	-0	O-10(2-0-8)/D-1	-0.2
1989	Bal-A	5	6	1	1	1	0	0	0	0	3	.167	.167	.333	500	39	-1	0	0	0	1.000	-1	/O-3(2-0-1),D-1	-0.1
1991	LA-N	1	1	0	0	0	0	0	0	0	0	.000	.000	.000	0	-99	-0	0	0	0	.000	0	/H	0.0
1993	Tex-A	62	159	24	39	10	4	3	20	5	28	.245	.273	.415	688	85	-4	3	1	0	.960	-2	O-44(23-10-17),D-11	-0.7
1994	Tex-A	4	17	2	4	3	0	0	0	0	3	.235	.235	.412	647	63	-1	1	0	0	1.000	1	/O-4(0-0-4)	0.0
Total	8	166	453	56	110	21	10	7	50	20	83	.243	.276	.380	656	78	-15	13	7	0	.969	-1	O-130(95-11-31)/D-15	-1.9
■ **WILLIE DAVIS**	Davis, William Henry b: 4/15/40, Mineral Springs, Ark. BL/TL, 6'2.5", 181 lbs. Deb: 9/8/60 Career OF: (10-LF 2237-CF 81-RF)																							
1960	LA-N	22	88	12	28	6	1	2	10	4	12	.318	.348	.477	825	116	2	3	5	-1	.981	1	O-22(0-22-0)	0.1
1961	LA-N	128	339	56	86	19	6	12	45	27	46	.254	.318	.451	769	93	-4	12	5	1	.983	-3	*O-114(0-114-0)	-0.8
1962	LA-N	157	600	103	171	18	**10**	21	85	42	72	.285	.338	.453	791	117	13	32	7	5	.963	13	*O-156(1-155-0)	2.5
1963	*LA-N	156	515	60	126	19	8	9	60	25	61	.245	.284	.365	649	92	-7	25	11	2	.978	14	*O-153(0-153-0)	0.5
1964	LA-N	157	613	91	180	23	7	12	77	22	59	.294	.319	.413	732	112	8	42	13	5	.983	25	*O-155(0-155-0)	3.4
1965	*LA-N	142	558	52	133	24	3	10	57	14	81	.238	.266	.346	612	76	-20	25	9	2	.967	9	*O-141(0-141-0)	-1.4
1966	*LA-N	153	624	74	177	31	6	11	61	15	68	.284	.305	.405	710	104	0	21	10	1	.970	9	*O-152(0-152-0)	0.7
1967	LA-N	143	569	65	146	27	9	6	41	29	65	.257	.296	.367	663	97	-4	20	6	2	.971	3	*O-138(0-138-0)	-0.3
1968	LA-N	160	643	86	161	24	10	7	31	31	88	.250	.286	.351	637	98	-4	36	10	4	.973	5	*O-158(0-158-0)	0.0
1969	LA-N	129	498	66	155	23	8	11	59	33	39	.311	.359	.456	815	136	22	24	10	2	.979	5	*O-125(0-125-0)	2.6
1970	LA-N	146	593	92	181	23	**16**	8	93	29	54	.305	.339	.438	777	111	7	38	14	3	.992	15	*O-143(0-139-4)	2.2
1971	LA-N★	158	641	84	198	33	10	10	74	23	47	.309	.333	.438	771	124	17	20	8	2	.981	12	*O-157(0-157-0)	2.7
1972	LA-N	149	615	81	178	22	7	19	79	27	61	.289	.320	.441	761	117	11	20	3	3	.987	11	*O-146(0-146-0)	2.3
1973	LA-N★	152	599	82	171	29	9	16	77	29	62	.285	.324	.444	768	116	10	17	5	2	.980	4	*O-146(0-146-0)	1.2
1974	Mon-N	153	611	86	180	27	9	12	89	27	69	.295	.328	.427	755	104	1	25	7	3	.969	6	*O-151(0-151-0)	0.7
1975	Tex-A	42	169	16	42	8	2	5	17	4	25	.249	.270	.408	678	90	-3	13	5	1	.990	-1	O-42(0-42-0)	-0.4
	StL-N	98	350	41	102	19	6	6	50	14	27	.291	.326	.431	758	105	1	10	1	2	.970	2	O-89(8-15-71)	0.1
1976	SD-N	141	493	61	132	18	10	5	46	19	34	.268	.298	.375	673	98	-4	14	2	2	.992	8	*O-128(0-128-0)	0.3
1979	*Cal-A	43	56	9	14	2	1	0	2	4	7	.250	.300	.321	621	70	-2	1	0	0	1.000	-1	/O-7(1-0-6),D-6	-0.3
Total	18	2429	9174	1217	2561	395	138	182	1053	418	977	.279	.314	.412	726	106	44	398	131	42	.978	137	*O-2323C/D-6	16.1
■ **TRAVIS DAWKINS**	Dawkins, Travis Sentell b: 5/12/79, Newberry, S.C. BR/TR, 6'1", 180 lbs. Deb: 9/3/99																							
1999	Cin-N	7	7	1	1	0	0	0	0	0	4	.143	.250	.143	393	3	-1	0	0	0	1.000	-0	/S-7	-0.1
2000	Cin-N	14	41	5	9	2	0	0	3	2	7	.220	.256	.268	524	31	-4	0	0	0	.965	4	S-14	0.0
Total	2	21	48	6	10	2	0	0	3	2	11	.208	.255	.250	505	27	-5	0	0	0	.968	3	/S-21	-0.1
■ **ANDRE DAWSON**	Dawson, Andre Nolan b: 7/10/54, Miami, Fla. BR/TR, 6'3", 195 lbs. Deb: 9/11/76 Career OF: (39-LF 1027-CF 1284-RF)																							
1976	Mon-N	24	85	9	20	4	1	0	7	5	13	.235	.278	.306	584	63	-4	1	2	-0	.969	2	O-24(8-14-2)	-0.4
1977	Mon-N	139	525	64	148	26	9	19	65	34	93	.282	.328	.474	802	116	9	21	7	2	.989	7	*O-136(13-129-3)	1.7

YEAR	TM/L	G	AB	R	H	2B	3B	HR	RBI	BB	SO	AVG	OBP	SLG	OPS	OPS+	BR+	SB	CS	SBR	FA	FR	G/POS	TPR
1978	Mon-N	157	609	84	154	24	8	25	72	30	128	.253	.301	.442	743	106	2	28	11	2	.988	21	*O-153(0-153-0)	2.5
1979	Mon-N	155	639	90	176	24	12	25	92	27	115	.275	.311	.468	779	111	6	35	10	4	.988	6	*O-153(0-153-0)	1.5
1980	Mon-N	151	577	96	178	41	7	17	87	44	69	.308	.364	.492	856	137	27	34	9	4	.986	20	*O-147(0-147-0)	5.2
1981	*Mon-N★	103	394	71	119	21	3	24	64	35	50	.302	.369	.553	923	157	28	26	4	4	.980	18	*O-103(0-103-0)	5.1
1982	Mon-N★	148	608	107	183	37	7	23	83	34	96	.301	.346	.498	845	131	23	39	10	5	.982	21	*O-147(0-147-0)	4.9
1983	Mon-N★	159	633	104	**189**	36	10	32	113	38	81	.299	.347	.539	886	143	33	25	11	2	.980	14	*O-157(0-157-0)	4.9
1984	Mon-N	138	533	73	132	23	6	17	86	41	80	.248	.304	.409	713	103	0	13	5	1	.975	16	*O-134(0-0-134)	1.0
1985	Mon-N	139	529	65	135	27	2	23	91	29	92	.255	.299	.444	743	112	5	13	4	1	.973	-4	*O-131(0-24-123)	-0.4
1986	Mon-N	130	496	65	141	32	2	20	78	37	79	.284	.341	.478	819	125	15	18	12	-0	.986	-0	*O-127(0-0-127)	0.8
1987	Chi-N★	153	621	90	178	24	2	**49**	**137**	32	103	.287	.329	.568	897	127	21	11	3	1	.986	6	*O-152(0-0-152)	2.0
1988	Chi-N★	157	591	78	179	31	8	24	79	37	73	.303	.348	.504	852	136	25	12	4	1	.989	1	*O-147(0-0-147)	2.5
1989	*Chi-N★	118	416	62	105	18	6	21	77	35	62	.252	.312	.476	788	114	6	8	5	0	.987	5	*O-112(0-0-112)	0.8
1990	Chi-N★	147	529	72	164	28	5	27	100	42	65	.310	.363	.535	898	134	23	16	2	3	.981	-0	*O-139(0-0-140)	2.2
1991	Chi-N★	149	563	69	153	21	4	31	104	22	80	.272	.305	.488	794	114	8	4	5	-1	.988	-1	*O-137(0-0-138)	0.1
1992	Chi-N	143	542	60	150	27	2	22	90	30	70	.277	.319	.456	775	114	8	6	2	1	.992	-1	*O-139(0-0-139)	0.4
1993	Bos-A	121	461	44	126	29	1	13	67	17	49	.273	.318	.425	743	92	-6	2	1	0	1.000	0	D-97,O-20(0-0-20)	-1.2
1994	Bos-A	75	292	34	70	18	0	16	48	9	53	.240	.272	.466	738	82	-9	2	2	-0	.000	0	D-74	-1.3
1995	Fla-N	79	226	30	58	10	3	8	37	9	45	.257	.309	.434	742	93	-3	0	0	0	.908	-6	O-59(12-0-47)	-1.1
1996	Fla-N	42	58	6	16	2	0	2	14	2	13	.276	.311	.414	725	92	-1	0	0	0	.833	-1	/O-6(6-0-0)	-0.2
Total	21	2627	9927	1373	2774	503	98	438	1591	589	1509	.279	.327	.482	809	119	217	314	109	31	.983	123	*O-2323R,D-171	31.0

■ BOOTS DAY
Day, Charles Frederick b: 8/31/47, Ilion, N.Y. BL/TL, 5'9", 160 lbs. Deb: 6/15/69

YEAR	TM/L	G	AB	R	H	2B	3B	HR	RBI	BB	SO	AVG	OBP	SLG	OPS	OPS+	BR+	SB	CS	SBR	FA	FR	G/POS	TPR
1969	StL-N	11	6	1	0	0	0	0	0	1	1	.000	.143	.000	143	-57	-1	0	0	0	.000	-0	/O-1(0-1-0)	-0.2
1970	Chi-N	11	8	2	2	0	0	0	0	0	3	.250	.250	.250	500	31	-1	0	0	0	.875	-1	/O-7(0-7-0)	-0.2
	Mon-N	41	108	14	29	4	0	0	5	6	18	.269	.307	.306	613	65	-5	3	2	-0	.987	1	O-35(5-30-0)	-0.5
	Yr	52	116	16	31	4	0	0	5	6	21	.267	.303	.302	605	61	-6	3	2	-0	.976	-0	O-42(5-37-0)	-0.7
1971	Mon-N	127	371	53	105	10	2	4	33	33	39	.283	.343	.353	696	97	-1	9	4	1	.982	4	*O-120(3-118-0)	0.1
1972	Mon-N	128	386	32	90	7	4	0	30	29	44	.233	.288	.272	560	59	-20	3	6	-1	.979	-5	*O-117(0-103-15)	-3.2
1973	Mon-N	101	207	36	57	7	0	4	28	21	28	.275	.342	.367	709	93	-2	0	3	-1	1.000	-9	O-51(12-45-6)	-1.4
1974	Mon-N	52	65	8	12	0	0	0	2	5	8	.185	.243	.185	427	20	-7	0	0	0	1.000	-2	O-16(14-0-2)	-1.0
Total	6	471	1151	146	295	28	6	8	98	95	141	.256	.314	.312	626	75	-37	15	15	-2	.983	-13	O-347(34-304-23)	-6.4

■ BRIAN DAYETT
Dayett, Brian Kelly b: 1/22/57, New London, Conn. BR/TR, 5'10", 180 lbs. Deb: 9/11/83

YEAR	TM/L	G	AB	R	H	2B	3B	HR	RBI	BB	SO	AVG	OBP	SLG	OPS	OPS+	BR+	SB	CS	SBR	FA	FR	G/POS	TPR
1983	NY-A	11	29	3	6	0	1	0	5	2	4	.207	.258	.276	534	49	-2	0	0	0	1.000	1	/O-9(9-0-0)	-0.1
1984	NY-A	64	127	14	31	8	0	4	23	9	14	.244	.299	.402	701	96	-1	0	0	0	.988	-9	O-62(55-0-10)/D-1	-1.1
1985	Chi-N	22	26	1	6	0	0	1	4	0	6	.231	.259	.346	605	61	-1	0	0	0	1.000	-2	O-10(11-0-0)	-0.4
1986	Chi-N	24	67	7	18	4	0	4	11	6	10	.269	.329	.507	836	118	1	0	1	-0	1.000	-4	O-24(15-1-12)	-0.3
1987	Chi-N	97	177	20	49	14	1	5	25	20	37	.277	.350	.452	802	106	2	0	0	0	1.000	-13	O-78(68-0-12)	-1.3
Total	5	218	426	45	110	26	2	14	68	37	71	.258	.320	.427	748	99	-1	0	1	-0	.995	-26	O-183(158-1-34)/D-1	-3.2

■ CHARLIE DEAL
Deal, Charles Albert b: 10/30/1891, Wilkinsburg, Pa. d: 9/16/79, Covina, Cal. BR/TR, 6', 160 lbs. Deb: 7/19/12

YEAR	TM/L	G	AB	R	H	2B	3B	HR	RBI	BB	SO	AVG	OBP	SLG	OPS	OPS+	BR+	SB	CS	SBR	FA	FR	G/POS	TPR
1912	Det-A	42	142	13	32	4	2	0	11	9		.225	.272	.282	553	60	-8	4			.942	10	3-41	0.4
1913	Det-A	16	50	3	11	0	2	0	3	1	7	.220	.235	.300	535	57	-3	2			.862	2	3-15	-0.1
	Bos-N	10	36	6	11	1	0	0	3	2	1	.306	.359	.333	692	96	-0	1			.935	-6	2-10	-0.6
1914	*Bos-N	79	257	17	54	13	2	0	23	20	23	.210	.270	.276	546	63	-12	4			.948	-5	3-74/S-1	-1.7
1915	StL-F	65	223	21	72	12	4	1	27	12	16	.323	.357	.426	783	114	1	10			.951	5	3-65	0.8
1916	StL-A	23	74	7	10	1	0	0	10	6	8	.135	.200	.149	349	5	-9	4			.970	-2	3-22/2-1	-1.1
	Chi-N	2	8	2	2	1	0	0	3	0	0	.250	.250	.375	625	82	-0	0			1.000	2	/3-2	0.2
1917	Chi-N	135	449	46	114	11	3	0	47	19	18	.254	.284	.292	576	71	-15	10			.957	7	*3-130	-0.6
1918	*Chi-N	119	414	43	99	9	3	2	34	21	13	.239	.279	.290	569	72	-14	11			.942	-2	*3-118	-1.5
1919	Chi-N	116	405	37	117	23	5	2	52	12	12	.289	.316	.385	701	110	3	11			**.973**	7	*3-116	1.5
1920	Chi-N	129	450	48	108	10	5	3	39	20	14	.240	.285	.304	589	68	-19	5	8	-2	**.973**	10	*3-128	-0.8
1921	Chi-N	115	422	52	122	19	8	3	66	13	9	.289	.310	.393	704	85	-10	3	5	-1	**.973**	14	*3-112	1.0
Total	10	851	2930	295	752	104	34	11	318	135	121	.257	.293	.327	620	79	-85	65	13		.958	41	3-823/2-11,S-1	-2.5

■ LINDSAY DEAL
Deal, Fred Lindsay b: 9/3/11, Lenoir, N.C. d: 4/18/79, Little Rock, Ark. BL/TR, 6', 175 lbs. Deb: 9/13/39

YEAR	TM/L	G	AB	R	H	2B	3B	HR	RBI	BB	SO	AVG	OBP	SLG	OPS	OPS+	BR+	SB	CS	SBR	FA	FR	G/POS	TPR
1939	Bro-N	4	7	0	0	0	0	0	0	0	2	.000	.000	.000	0	-97	-2	0			1.000	0	/O-1(0-1-0)	-0.2

■ SNAKE DEAL
Deal, John Wesley b: 1/21/1879, Lancaster, Pa. d: 5/9/44, Harrisburg, Pa. BR/TR, 6', 164 lbs. Deb: 7/9/06

YEAR	TM/L	G	AB	R	H	2B	3B	HR	RBI	BB	SO	AVG	OBP	SLG	OPS	OPS+	BR+	SB	CS	SBR	FA	FR	G/POS	TPR
1906	Cin-N	65	231	13	48	4	3	0	21	6		.208	.228	.251	479	47	-15	15			.985	2	1-65	-1.5

■ PAT DEALY
Dealy, Patrick E. b: Burlington, Vt. d: 12/16/24, Buffalo, N.Y. BR/TR, 5'8", 145 lbs. Deb: 9/30/1884

YEAR	TM/L	G	AB	R	H	2B	3B	HR	RBI	BB	SO	AVG	OBP	SLG	OPS	OPS+	BR+	SB	CS	SBR	FA	FR	G/POS	TPR
1884	StP-U	5	15	2	2	0	0	0		0		.133	.133	.133	267	-35	-3				.871	3	/C-4,O-1(0-0-1)	0.0
1885	Bos-N	35	130	18	29	4	1	1	9	2	14	.223	.235	.292	527	72	-4				.903	0	C-29/3-3,O-2L,S1	-0.1
1886	Bos-N	15	46	9	15	1	1	0	3	4	4	.326	.380	.391	771	140	2	5			.929	-2	C-14/O-1(1-0-0)	0.2
1887	Was-N	58	220	33	63	8	2	1	18	8	8	.286	.293	.330	623	77	-6	36			.931	-7	C-28,S-23/O-5L,3-5	-0.9
1890	Syr-a	18	66	9	12	1	0	0	4	5		.182	.250	.197	447	36	-5	4			.900	-6	C-10/3-6,O-2(0-1-1)	-0.9
Total	5	131	477	71	121	14	4	2	34	19	26	.254	.275	.301	576	74	-16	45			.914	-12	/C-85,S-25,3-14,O1	-1.7

■ CHUBBY DEAN
Dean, Alfred Lovill b: 8/24/16, Mt.Airy, N.C. d: 12/21/70, Riverside, Cal. BL/TL, 5'11", 181 lbs. Deb: 4/14/36

YEAR	TM/L	G	AB	R	H	2B	3B	HR	RBI	BB	SO	AVG	OBP	SLG	OPS	OPS+	BR+	SB	CS	SBR	FA	FR	G/POS	TPR
1936	Phi-A	111	342	41	98	21	3	1	48	24	24	.287	.337	.374	711	77	-13	3	2	-0	.989	-1	1-77	-1.9
1937	Phi-A	104	309	36	81	14	4	2	31	42	10	.262	.350	.353	703	79	-9	2	1	0	.991	-2	1-78/P-2	-1.8
1938	Phi-A	16	20	3	6	2	0	0	1	1	4	.300	.333	.400	733	85	-1	0	0	0	1.000	1	/P-6	0.0
1939	Phi-A	80	77	12	27	4	0	0	19	8	4	.351	.412	.403	814	111	2	0	0	0	.935	1	P-54	0.0
1940	Phi-A	67	90	6	26	2	0	0	6	16	9	.289	.396	.311	707	88	-1	0	0	0	.976	1	P-30/1-1	0.0
1941	Phi-A	27	37	0	9	2	0	0	9	4	3	.243	.317	.297	614	65	-2	0	0	0	1.000	0	P-18/1-1	0.0
	Cle-A	17	25	2	4	1	0	0	2	3	2	.160	.250	.200	450	21	-3	0	0	0	1.000	1	/P-8	0.0
	Yr	44	62	2	13	3	0	0	11	7	5	.210	.290	.258	548	48	-5	0	0	0	1.000	1	P-26/1-1	0.0
1942	Cle-A	70	101	4	27	1	0	0	7	11	7	.267	.339	.277	617	79	-2	0	0	0	.939	-3	P-27	0.0
1943	Cle-A	41	46	2	9	0	0	0	5	6	2	.196	.288	.196	484	45	-3	0	0	0	.929	-1	P-17	0.0
Total	8	533	1047	106	287	47	7	3	128	115	65	.274	.347	.341	688	79	-31	5	3	0	.964	-5	P-162,1-157	-3.7

■ TOMMY DEAN
Dean, Tommy Douglas b: 8/30/45, Iuka, Miss. BR/TR, 6', 165 lbs. Deb: 9/17/67

YEAR	TM/L	G	AB	R	H	2B	3B	HR	RBI	BB	SO	AVG	OBP	SLG	OPS	OPS+	BR+	SB	CS	SBR	FA	FR	G/POS	TPR
1967	LA-N	12	28	1	4	1	0	0	2	0	9	.143	.143	.179	321	-9	-4	0	0	0	.981	6	S-12	0.3
1969	SD-N	101	273	14	48	9	2	2	9	27	54	.176	.252	.245	498	42	-21	0	3	-1	.978	4	S-97/2-2	-0.9
1970	SD-N	61	158	18	35	5	1	2	13	11	29	.222	.272	.304	576	56	-10	2	0	0	.974	6	S-55	0.2
1971	SD-N	41	70	2	8	0	0	0	1	4	13	.114	.162	.114	276	-22	-11	1	0	0	.969	6	S-28,3-11/2-1	-0.3
Total	4	215	529	35	95	15	3	4	25	42	105	.180	.241	.242	483	36	-47	3	3	-0	.976	23	S-192/3-11,2-3	-0.7

■ HARRY DEANE
Deane, John Henry b: 5/6/1846, Trenton, N.J. d: 5/31/25, Indianapolis, Ind. 5'7", 150 lbs. Deb: 7/20/1871 M

YEAR	TM/L	G	AB	R	H	2B	3B	HR	RBI	BB	SO	AVG	OBP	SLG	OPS	OPS+	BR+	SB	CS	SBR	FA	FR	G/POS	TPR
1871	Kek-n	6	22	3	4	0	1	0	2	2	0	.182	.250	.273	523	49	-1	0	0	0	1.000	2	/O-6(6-0-0),M	0.0
1874	Bal-n	47	203	29	50	8	1	0	13	4	3	.246	.261	.296	556	79	-4	2	1	0	.818	-4	*O-46(0-46-0)/2-2,S-1	-0.7
Total	2 n	53	225	32	54	8	2	0	15	6	3	.240	.260	.293	553	75	-6	2	1	0	.850	-3	/O-52(6-46-0),2-2,S-1	-0.7

■ BUDDY DEAR
Dear, Paul Stanford b: 12/1/05, Norfolk, Va. d: 8/29/89, Radford, Va. BR/TR, 5'8", 143 lbs. Deb: 9/9/27

YEAR	TM/L	G	AB	R	H	2B	3B	HR	RBI	BB	SO	AVG	OBP	SLG	OPS	OPS+	BR+	SB	CS	SBR	FA	FR	G/POS	TPR
1927	Was-A	2	1	1	0	0	0	0	0	0	0	.000	.000	.000	0	-99	-0	0	0	0	.000	0	/2-1	0.0

■ CHARLIE DeARMOND
DeArmond, Charles Hommer "Hummer" b: 2/13/1877, Okeana, Ohio d: 12/17/33, Morning Sun, Ohio BR/TR, 5'10", 165 lbs. Deb: 9/19/03

YEAR	TM/L	G	AB	R	H	2B	3B	HR	RBI	BB	SO	AVG	OBP	SLG	OPS	OPS+	BR+	SB	CS	SBR	FA	FR	G/POS	TPR
1903	Cin-N	11	39	10	11	2	1	0	7	3		.282	.349	.385	733	98	-0	1			.878	-1	3-11	-0.1

■ JOHN DEASLEY
Deasley, John b: 1/1861, Philadelphia, Pa. d: 12/25/10, Philadelphia, Pa. Deb: 6/17/1884 F

YEAR	TM/L	G	AB	R	H	2B	3B	HR	RBI	BB	SO	AVG	OBP	SLG	OPS	OPS+	BR+	SB	CS	SBR	FA	FR	G/POS	TPR
1884	Was-U	31	134	20	29	1	1	0		3		.216	.234	.239	472	45	-13				.836	0	S-31	-1.0

YEAR	TM/L	G	AB	R	H	2B	3B	HR	RBI	BB	SO	AVG	OBP	SLG	OPS	OPS+	BR+	SB	CS	SBR	FA	FR	G/POS	TPR
	KC-U	13	40	3	7	2	0	0			2	.175	.214	.225	439	38	-4				.833	-0	S-13	-0.3
	Yr	44	174	23	36	3	1	0			5	.207	.229	.236	465	44	-17				.835	0	S-44	-1.3
■ PAT DEASLEY Deasley, Thomas H. b: 11/17/1857, Ireland d: 4/1/43, Philadelphia, Pa. BR/TR, 5'8.5", 154 lbs. Deb: 5/18/1881 F Career OF: (3-LF 13-CF 28-RF)																								
1881	Bos-N	43	147	13	35	5	2	0	8	5	10	.238	.263	.299	562	80	-3				.914	-4	C-28/O-7R,S-7,1-2	-0.6
1882	Bos-N	67	264	36	70	8	0	0	29	7	22	.265	.284	.295	580	86	-4				**.958**	2	*C-56,O-14R/S-1	0.2
1883	StL-a	58	206	27	53	2	1	0	15	6		.257	.278	.277	555	75	-6				**.930**	8	C-56/O-2(0-2-0)	0.6
1884	StL-a	75	254	27	52	5	4	0		7		.205	.235	.256	491	58	-12				.919	14	*C-75/O-2(1-1-0),1-1	0.7
1885	NY-N	54	207	22	53	5	1	0	24	9	20	.256	.287	.290	577	88	-3				.935	7	C-54/O-2(0-2-0),S-1	0.9
1886	NY-N	41	143	18	38	6	1	0	17	4	12	.266	.286	.322	607	84	-3	2			.925	7	C-30,O-15(1-6-8)	0.5
1887	NY-N	30	127	12	46	5	0	0	23	9	7	.362	.367	.356	723	107	2	3			.867	-13	C-24/3-7,S-1	-0.8
1888	Was-N	34	127	6	20	1	0	0	4	2	18	.157	.171	.165	336	8	-13	2			.922	8	C-31/O-1R,S-1,2-1	-0.2
Total	8	402	1475	161	367	37	9	0	120	49	89	.249	.271	.282	552	74	-42	7			.927	28	C-354/O-43R,S-11,312	1.3
■ HANK DeBERRY DeBerry, John Herman b: 12/29/1894, Savannah, Tenn. d: 9/10/51, Savannah, Tenn. BR/TR, 5'11", 195 lbs. Deb: 9/12/16																								
1916	Cle-A	15	33	7	9	4	0	0	4	6	9	.273	.385	.394	779	126	1	0			1.000	-3	C-14	-0.1
1917	Cle-A	25	33	3	9	2	0	0	1	2	7	.273	.333	.333	667	96	-0	0			.968	1	/C-9	0.1
1922	Bro-N	85	259	29	78	10	1	3	35	20	9	.301	.354	.382	736	91	-3	4	1	1	.971	-2	C-81	0.0
1923	Bro-N	78	235	21	67	11	6	1	48	20	12	.285	.346	.396	742	98	-1	2	1	0	.971	8	C-60	1.1
1924	Bro-N	77	218	20	53	10	3	3	26	20	21	.243	.307	.358	665	80	-6	0	1	-0	.993	23	C-63	2.0
1925	Bro-N	67	193	26	50	8	1	2	24	16	8	.259	.322	.342	664	72	-8	2	2	-0	.981	19	C-55	1.3
1926	Bro-N	48	115	6	33	11	0	0	13	8	5	.287	.333	.383	716	94	-1	0			.976	8	C-37	0.9
1927	Bro-N	68	201	15	47	3	2	1	21	17	8	.234	.294	.284	577	55	-13	1			.988	23	C-67	1.4
1928	Bro-N	82	258	19	65	8	2	0	23	18	15	.252	.301	.298	599	58	-16	3			.977	18	C-80	0.7
1929	Bro-N	68	210	13	55	11	1	1	25	17	15	.262	.317	.338	655	64	-12	1			.991	6	C-68	-0.1
1930	Bro-N	35	95	11	28	3	0	0	14	4	10	.295	.323	.326	650	58	-6	0			.978	12	C-35	0.7
Total	11	648	1850	170	494	81	16	11	234	148	119	.267	.323	.346	669	76	-65	13	5		.982	113	C-569	8.0
■ ADAM DEBUS Debus, Adam Joseph b: 10/7/1892, Chicago, Ill. d: 5/13/77, Chicago, Ill. BR/TR, 5'10.5", 150 lbs. Deb: 7/14/17																								
1917	Pit-N	38	131	9	30	5	4	0	7	7	14	.229	.279	.328	607	83	-3	2			.898	-6	S-21,3-18	-0.8
■ DOUG DeCINCES DeCinces, Douglas Vernon b: 8/29/50, Burbank, Cal. BR/TR, 6'2", 194 lbs. Deb: 9/9/73 Career OF: (1-LF 0-CF 0-RF)																								
1973	Bal-A	10	18	2	2	0	0	0	3	1	5	.111	.158	.111	269	-23	-3	0	0	0	.895	3	/3-8,2-2,S-1	0.0
1974	Bal-A	1	1	0	0	0	0	0	0	1	0	.000	.500	.000	500	55	0	0	0	0	1.000	0	/3-1	0.0
1975	Bal-A	61	167	20	42	6	3	4	23	13	32	.251	.309	.395	705	105	0	0	1	-0	.947	3	3-34,S-13,2-11,/1-2	0.5
1976	Bal-A	129	440	36	103	17	2	11	42	29	68	.234	.285	.357	641	93	-6	8	4	0	.941	-1	*3-109,2-17,1-11,/SD	-0.7
1977	Bal-A	150	522	63	135	28	3	19	69	64	86	.259	.342	.433	775	117	12	8	8	-1	.958	10	*3-148/1-1,2-1,D-1	1.9
1978	Bal-A	142	511	72	146	37	1	28	80	46	81	.286	.347	.526	873	152	32	7	7	-1	.975	10	*3-130,2-12	4.1
1979	*Bal-A	120	422	67	97	27	1	16	61	54	68	.230	.322	.412	734	100	-0	5	3	0	.964	-3	*3-120	-0.5
1980	Bal-A	145	489	64	122	23	2	16	64	49	83	.249	.322	.403	724	98	-2	11	6	0	.960	25	*3-142/1-1	2.1
1981	Bal-A	100	346	49	91	23	2	13	55	41	32	.263	.343	.454	797	128	12	0	3	-1	.942	-2	*3-100/1-1,O-1(1-0-0)	0.8
1982	*Cal-A	153	575	94	173	42	5	30	97	66	80	.301	.374	.548	922	149	38	7	5	-0	.961	21	*3-153/S-2	5.5
1983	Cal-A★	95	370	49	104	19	3	18	65	32	56	.281	.338	.495	833	127	13	2	0	0	.955	9	3-84,D-10	2.0
1984	Cal-A	146	547	77	147	23	3	20	82	53	79	.269	.333	.431	765	111	7	4	1	1	.964	-6	*3-140/D-5	0.0
1985	Cal-A	120	427	50	104	22	1	20	78	47	71	.244	.321	.440	762	107	3	1	4	-1	.958	-10	*3-111/D-3	-0.9
1986	*Cal-A	140	512	69	131	20	3	26	96	52	74	.256	.327	.459	786	112	8	2	2	-0	.965	-8	*3-132/S-1,D-3	-0.3
1987	Cal-A	133	453	65	106	23	0	16	63	70	87	.234	.339	.391	730	96	-1	3	4	-1	.948	-3	*3-128/1-4,S-1,D-1	-0.7
	StL-N	4	9	1	2	2	0	0	1	0	2	.222	.222	.444	667	70	-0	0	0	0	.833	1	/3-3	0.1
Total	15	1649	5809	778	1505	312	29	237	879	618	904	.259	.333	.445	778	116	114	58	48	-4	.958	49	*3-1543/2-43,D1SO	13.9
■ HARRY DECKER Decker, Earle Harry b: 9/3/1854, Lockport, Ill. BR/TR, 5'11", 180 lbs. Deb: 8/23/1884 Career OF: (12-LF 4-CF 8-RF)																								
1884	Ind-a	4	15	1	4	1	0	0		1		.267	.313	.333	646	114	0				.870	-3	/C-4	-0.3
	KC-U	23	75	8	10	2	0	0		5		.133	.188	.160	348	7	-11				.813	2	O-16(6-4-6),C-11	-0.7
1886	Det-N	14	54	2	12	1	0	0	5	2	9	.222	.250	.241	491	48	-3	0			.871	4	C-14/O-1(1-0-0)	0.2
	Was-N	7	23	0	5	1	1	0	2	1	5	.217	.250	.348	598	85	-0	0			.946	1	/C-4,3-2,S-1	0.1
	Yr	21	77	2	17	2	1	0	7	3	14	.221	.250	.273	523	59	-4	0			.886	5	C-18/3-2,O-1L,S-1	0.3
1889	Phi-N	11	30	4	3	0	0	0	2	2	5	.100	.156	.100	256	-25	-5	1			.857	-1	/2-7,C-3,O-1(1-0-0)	-0.5
1890	Phi-N	5	19	5	7	1	0	0	2	4	1	.368	.478	.421	899	159	2	4			.938	-1	/1-2,O-2(2-0-0),C-1	0.0
	Pit-N	92	354	52	97	14	3	5	38	26	36	.274	.324	.373	697	116	7	8			.909	-26	C-70,1-16/O-4L,2S	-1.3
	Yr	97	373	57	104	15	3	5	40	30	37	.279	.333	.375	708	119	9	12			.909	-27	C-71,1-18/O-6L,2S	-1.3
Total	4	156	570	72	138	20	4	5	49	41	56	.242	.293	.318	611	87	-10	13			.903	-25	C-107/O-24L,1-18,2S3	-2.5
■ FRANK DECKER Decker, Frank b: 2/26/1856, St.Louis, Mo. d: 2/5/40, St.Louis, Mo. BR/TR, Deb: 6/25/1879 Career OF: (0-LF 0-CF 1-RF)																								
1879	Syr-N	3	10	0	1	0	0	0	0	0	3	.100	.100	.100	200	-38	-1				.714	-2	/C-2,O-1(0-0-1),1-1	-0.3
1882	StL-a	2	8	0	2	0	0	0	1	0		.250	.250	.250	500	66	-0				.813	-0	/2-2	0.0
Total	2	5	18	0	3	0	0	0	1	0	3	.167	.167	.167	333	12	-2				.813	-2	/2-2,C-2,1-1,O-1R	-0.3
■ GEORGE DECKER Decker, George A "Gentleman George" b: 6/1/1869, York, Pa. d: 6/7/09, Patton, Cal. BL/TL, 6'1", 180 lbs. Deb: 7/11/1892 Career OF: (189-LF 34-CF 111-RF)																								
1892	Chi-N	78	291	32	66	6	7	1	28	20	49	.227	.277	.306	582	75	-10	9			.876	-12	O-62(0-0-62),2-16	-2.2
1893	Chi-N	81	328	57	89	9	8	2	48	24	22	.271	.325	.366	691	85	-8	22			.878	-9	O-33L,1-27,2-20,/S	-1.5
1894	Chi-N	93	393	76	122	17	7	8	93	24	20	.310	.358	.450	808	89	-9	23			.974	-7	1-49,O-29C/3-8,2S	-1.4
1895	Chi-N	73	297	51	82	9	7	2	41	17	22	.276	.324	.374	698	75	-12	11			.910	-8	O-57L,1-11/3-3,S2	-1.9
1896	Chi-N	107	421	68	118	23	11	5	61	23	14	.280	.318	.423	740	91	-8	20			.928	-3	O-71(67-3-1),1-36	-1.5
1897	Chi-N	111	428	72	124	12	7	5	63	24		.290	.333	.386	719	86	-10	11			.925	-3	O-75(74-0-1),1-38/2-1	-1.7
1898	StL-N	76	286	26	74	10	0	1	45	20		.259	.314	.304	618	76	-9	4			.980	-7	1-75	-1.6
	Lou-N	42	148	27	44	4	3	0	19	9		.297	.342	.365	707	104	1	9			.993	-1	1-32/O-6(0-0-6)	-0.1
	Yr	118	434	53	118	14	3	1	64	29		.272	.323	.325	648	85	-9	13			**.984**	-9	*1-107/O-6(0-0-6)	-1.7
1899	Lou-N	39	138	14	37	8	1	1	18	12		.268	.336	.362	698	91	-2	3			.968	-3	1-39	-0.4
	Was-N	4	9	0	0	0	0	0	0	0		.000	.000	.000	0	-99	-2	0			.955	-1	/1-2,O-1(0-0-1)	-0.3
	Yr	43	147	14	37	8	1	1	18	12		.252	.317	.340	657	80	-4	3			.968	-3	1-41/O-1(0-0-1)	-0.7
Total	8	704	2739	423	756	98	51	25	416	173	127	.276	.324	.376	700	84	-70	112			.900	-53	O-334L,1-309/2-40,3S	-12.6
■ STEVE DECKER Decker, Steven Michael b: 10/25/65, Rock Island, Ill. BR/TR, 6'3", 205 lbs. Deb: 9/18/90																								
1990	SF-N	15	54	5	16	2	0	3	8	1	10	.296	.309	.500	809	123	1	0	0	0	.989	2	C-15	0.4
1991	SF-N	79	233	11	48	7	1	5	24	16	44	.206	.266	.309	575	63	-12	0	1	-0	.984	-3	C-78	-1.1
1992	SF-N	15	43	3	7	1	0	0	1	6	7	.163	.280	.186	466	36	-3	0	0	0	1.000	2	C-15	0.0
1993	Fla-N	8	15	0	0	0	0	0	1	3	3	.000	.167	.000	167	-48	-3	0	0	0	.968	1	/C-5	-0.2
1995	Fla-N	51	133	12	30	2	1	3	13	19	22	.226	.322	.323	646	71	-5	1	0	0	.985	5	C-46/1-2	0.3
1996	SF-N	57	122	16	28	1	0	1	12	15	26	.230	.314	.262	576	56	-7	0	0	0	1.000	2	C-30/1-3,3-2	-0.4
	Col-N	10	25	8	8	2	0	1	8	3	3	.320	.393	.520	913	112	0	1	0	0	1.000	2	C-10	0.3
	Yr	67	147	24	36	3	0	2	20	18	29	.245	.327	.306	633	68	-6	1	0	0	1.000	4	C-40/1-3,3-2	-0.1
1999	Ana-A	28	63	5	15	6	0	0	5	13	9	.238	.377	.333	710	84	-1	0	0	0	.987	-2	C-17/1-6,D-3	-0.2
Total	7	263	688	60	152	21	2	13	72	76	124	.221	.303	.314	617	68	-30	2	1	0	.988	11	C-216/1-11,D-3,3-2	-0.9
■ ARTIE DEDE Dede, Arthur Richard b: 7/12/1895, Brooklyn, N.Y. d: 9/6/71, Keene, N.H. BR/TR, 5'9", 155 lbs. Deb: 10/4/16																								
1916	Bro-N	1	1	0	0	0	0	0	0	0	0	.000	.000	.000	0	-97	-0	0			1.000	-0	/C-1	-0.1
■ ROD DEDEAUX Dedeaux, Raoul Martial b: 2/17/15, New Orleans, La. BR/TR, 5'11", 160 lbs. Deb: 9/28/35																								
1935	Bro-N	2	4	0	1	0	0	0	1	0	0	.250	.250	.250	500	36	-0	0			.857	0	/S-2	0.0

YEAR	TM/L	G	AB	R	H	2B	3B	HR	RBI	BB	SO	AVG	OBP	SLG	OPS	OPS+	BR+	SB	CS	SBR	FA	FR	G/POS	TPR
■ **JIM DEE** Dee, James D. b: Buffalo, N.Y. Deb: 7/30/1884																								
1884	Pit-a	12	40	0	5	0	0	0		1		.125	.146	.125	271	-11	-5				.860	1	S-12	-0.3
■ **SHORTY DEE** Dee, Maurice Leo b: 10/4/1889, Halifax, N.S., Can. d: 8/12/71, Jamaica Plain, Mass. BR/TR, 5'6", 155 lbs. Deb: 9/14/15																								
1915	StL-A	1	3	1	0	0	0	0	0	1	0	.000	.250	.000	250	-26	-0	0	1	-0	.500	-1	/S-1	-0.3
■ **ROB DEER** Deer, Robert George b: 9/29/60, Orange, Cal. BR/TR, 6'3", 210 lbs. Deb: 9/4/84 Career OF: (186-LF 5-CF 871-RF)																								
1984	SF-N	13	24	5	4	0	0	3	3	7	10	.167	.375	.542	917	160	2	1	1	-0	.905	0	/O-9(9-0-0)	0.2
1985	SF-N	78	162	22	30	5	1	8	20	23	71	.185	.286	.377	663	88	-3	0	1	-0	.982	-4	O-37(21-0-17),1-10	-1.0
1986	Mil-A	134	466	75	108	17	3	33	86	72	179	.232	.338	.494	832	119	12	5	2	0	.974	8	*O-131(1-0-131)/1-4	1.2
1987	Mil-A	134	474	71	113	15	2	28	80	86	186	.238	.361	.456	817	112	9	12	4	1	.974	8	*O-123L,1-12/D-4	1.2
1988	Mil-A	135	492	71	124	24	0	23	85	51	153	.252	.331	.441	772	113	8	9	5	0	.990	7	*O-133(54-2-79)/D-1	1.2
1989	Mil-A	130	466	72	98	18	2	26	65	60	158	.210	.306	.425	731	105	2	4	8	-2	.972	5	*O-125(2-1-123)/D-5	0.1
1990	Mil-A	134	440	57	92	15	1	27	69	64	147	.209	.315	.432	747	108	4	2	3	-1	.970	9	*O-117R,1-21/D-1	0.8
1991	Det-A	134	448	64	80	14	2	25	64	89	175	.179	.315	.386	701	91	-5	1	3	-1	.978	11	*O-132(0-0-132)/D-2	0.1
1992	Det-A	110	393	66	97	20	1	32	64	51	131	.247	.338	.547	885	143	21	4	2	0	.983	5	*O-106(0-0-106)/D-2	2.3
1993	Det-A	90	323	48	70	11	0	14	39	38	120	.217	.305	.381	686	84	-8	3	2	-0	.975	5	O-86(0-2-84)/D-4	-0.8
	Bos-A	38	143	18	28	6	1	7	16	20	49	.196	.303	.399	702	82	-4	2	0	0	.970	5	O-36(0-0-36)/D-2	-0.1
	Yr	128	466	66	98	17	1	21	55	58	169	.210	.304	.386	691	83	-12	5	2	0	.973	9	*O-122(0-2-120)/D-6	-0.9
1996	SD-N	25	50	9	9	3	0	4	9	14	30	.180	.359	.480	839	126	2	0	0	0	1.000	-2	O-18(1-0-17)	0.0
Total	11	1155	3881	578	853	148	13	230	600	575	1409	.220	.325	.442	768	108	41	43	31	-1	.977	56	*O-1053R/1-47,D-21	5.2
■ **CHARLIE DEES** Dees, Charles Henry b: 6/24/35, Birmingham, Ala. BL/TL, 6'1", 173 lbs. Deb: 5/26/63																								
1963	LA-A	60	202	23	62	11	1	3	27	11	31	.307	.367	.416	782	126	7	3	3	-0	.986	-2	1-56	0.1
1964	LA-A	26	26	3	2	1	0	0	1	1	4	.077	.143	.115	258	-30	-5	1	2	-0	.981	0	1-12	-0.6
1965	Cal-A	12	32	1	5	0	0	0	1	1	8	.156	.182	.156	338	-3	-4	1	2	-0	.986	-1	/1-8	-0.7
Total	3	98	260	27	69	12	1	3	29	13	43	.265	.323	.354	677	95	-2	5	7	-1	.986	-3	/1-76	-1.2
■ **TONY DeFATE** DeFate, Clyde Herbert b: 2/22/1895, Kansas City, Mo. d: 9/3/63, New Orleans, La. BR/TR, 5'8.5", 158 lbs. Deb: 4/18/17																								
1917	StL-N	14	14	0	2	0	0	0	1	4	5	.143	.333	.143	476	50	-1	0			1.000	-1	/3-5,2-1	-0.1
	Det-A	3	2	1	0	0	0	0	0	0	1	.000	.000	.000	0	-99	-0	0			1.000	-0	/2-1	-0.1
Total	1	17	16	1	2	0	0	0	1	4	6	.125	.300	.125	425	33	-1	0			1.000	-1	/3-5,2-2	-0.2
■ **ARTURO DeFREITAS** DeFreitas, Arturo Marcelino (Simon) b: 4/26/53, San Pedro De Macoris, D.R. BR/TR, 6'2", 195 lbs. Deb: 9/7/78																								
1978	Cin-N	9	19	1	4	1	0	1	2	1	4	.211	.250	.421	671	84	-1	0	0	0	1.000	0	/1-6	-0.1
1979	Cin-N	23	34	2	7	2	0	0	4	0	16	.206	.206	.265	471	27	-3	0	0	0	.974	-1	/1-6,O-1(0-0-1)	-0.5
Total	2	32	53	3	11	3	0	1	6	1	20	.208	.222	.321	543	47	-4	0	0	0	.988	-1	/1-12,O-1(0-0-1)	-0.6
■ **RUBE DeGROFF** DeGroff, Edward Arthur b: 9/2/1879, Hyde Park, N.Y. d: 12/17/55, Poughkeepsie, N.Y. BL, 5'11", Deb: 9/22/05																								
1905	StL-N	15	56	3	14	2	1	0	5	5		.250	.311	.321	633	91	-1	1			.909	0	O-15(0-8-7)	-0.1
1906	StL-N	1	4	1	0	0	0	0	0	0		.000	.000	.000	0	-99	-1	0			.000	-0	/O-1(0-0-1)	-0.2
Total	2	16	60	4	14	2	1	0	5	5		.233	.292	.300	592	80	-2	1			.909	-0	/O-16(0-8-8)	-0.3
■ **KORY DeHAAN** DeHaan, Korwin Jay b: 7/16/76, Pella, Iowa BL/TR, 6'2", 187 lbs. Deb: 4/25/2000																								
2000	SD-N	90	103	19	21	7	0	2	13	5	39	.204	.241	.330	571	45	-9	4	2	0	1.000	-12	O-60(10-4-49)/D-1	-2.1
■ **HERMAN DEHLMAN** Dehlman, Herman J. "Dutch" b: 1852, Brooklyn, N.Y. d: 3/13/1885, Wilkes-Barre, Pa. Deb: 5/2/1872																								
1872	Atl-n	37	165	30	36	3	1	0	14	3	1	.218	.232	.248	481	41	-14	4	2	0	.928	-1	*1-37	-1.0
1873	Atl-n	54	221	50	52	4	1	0	17	9	7	.235	.265	.262	528	64	-7	5	0	1	.929	-4	*1-54/S-1	-0.6
1874	Atl-n	53	218	40	49	3	1	0	18	7	5	.225	.249	.248	497	68	-5	2	0	0	.944	-1	*1-53	-0.3
1875	StL-n	67	254	42	57	12	2	0	14	**11**	21	.224	.257	.287	544	98	2	23	9	2	**.955**	1	*1-67/O-2(0-0-2)	0.5
1876	StL-N	64	254	40	45	6	0	0	9	9	10	.177	.213	.208	421	43	-13				.958	0	*1-64	-1.4
1877	StL-N	32	119	24	22	4	0	0	11	7	21	.185	.230	.218	449	44	-7				.931	-3	1-31/O-1(1-0-0)	-1.1
Total	4 n	211	858	162	194	22	5	0	63	30	34	.226	.252	.263	516	68	-24	34	11	4	.941	-5	1-211/O-2(0-0-2),S-1	-1.4
Total	2	96	373	64	67	10	0	0	20	16	31	.180	.218	.212	430	43	-20				.950	-3	/1-95,O-1(1-0-0)	-2.5
■ **JIM DEIDEL** Deidel, James Lawrence b: 6/6/49, Denver, Col. BR/TR, 6'2", 195 lbs. Deb: 5/31/74																								
1974	NY-A	2	2	0	0	0	0	0	0	0	0	.000	.000	.000	0	-99	-1	0	0	0	1.000	1	/C-2	0.1
■ **PEP DEININGER** Deininger, Otto Charles b: 10/10/1877, Wasseralfingen, Germany d: 9/25/50, Boston, Mass. BL/TL, 5'8.5", 180 lbs. Deb: 4/26/02																								
1902	Bos-A	2	6	0	2	1	1	0	0	0		.333	.333	.833	1167	210	1	0			1.000	-1	/P-2	0.0
1908	Phi-N	1	0	0	0	0	0	0	0	0		—	—	—	—	—	0	0			.000	-1	/O-1(0-1-0)	-0.1
1909	Phi-N	55	169	22	44	9	0	0	16	11		.260	.309	.314	623	93	-2	5			.989	-2	O-45(1-38-6)/2-1	-0.7
Total	3	58	175	22	46	10	1	0	16	11		.263	.310	.331	642	97	-1	5			.989	-3	/O-46(1-39-6),P-2,2-1	-0.8
■ **PAT DEISEL** Deisel, Edward b: 4/29/1876, Ripley, Ohio d: 4/17/48, Cincinnati, Ohio BR/TR, 5'5 ", 145 lbs. Deb: 8/21/02																								
1902	Bro-N	1	3	0	2	0	0	0	1	1		.667	.800	.667	1467	351	1	0			1.000	0	/C-1	0.1
1903	Cin-N	2	0	0	0	0	0	0	0	1		—	1.000	—	1000	174	0	0			.000	0	/C-1	0.0
Total	2	3	3	0	2	0	0	0	1	2		.667	.833	.667	1500	352	2	0			1.000	0	/C-2	0.1
■ **BILL DEITRICK** Deitrick, William Alexander b: 4/20/02, Hanover Co., Va. d: 5/6/46, Bethesda, Md. BR/TR, 5'10", 160 lbs. Deb: 9/19/27																								
1927	Phi-N	5	6	1	1	0	0	0	0	0	0	.167	.167	.167	333	-10	-1	0			.750	-1	/S-5	-0.2
1928	Phi-N	52	100	13	20	6	0	0	7	17	10	.200	.322	.260	582	52	-7	1			1.000	-2	O-21(17-1-3)/S-8	-0.9
Total	2	57	106	14	21	6	0	0	7	17	10	.198	.315	.255	569	49	-8	1			.895	-3	/O-21(17-1-3),S-13	-1.1
■ **MIKE DEJAN** Dejan, Michael Dan b: 1/13/15, Cleveland, Ohio d: 2/2/53, W.Los Angeles, Cal. BL/TL, 6'1", 185 lbs. Deb: 7/13/40																								
1940	Cin-N	12	16	1	3	0	1	0	2	3	3	.188	.316	.313	628	73	-1	0			1.000	-0	/O-2(2-0-0)	-0.1
■ **IVAN DeJESUS** DeJesus, Ivan (Alvarez) b: 1/9/53, Santurce, P.R. BR/TR, 5'11", 175 lbs. Deb: 9/13/74																								
1974	LA-N	3	3	1	1	0	0	0	0	0	2	.333	.333	.333	667	91	-0	0	0	0	1.000	-1	/S-2	-0.1
1975	LA-N	63	87	10	16	2	1	0	2	11	15	.184	.276	.230	505	43	-7	1	2	-0	.974	7	S-63	0.3
1976	LA-N	22	41	4	7	2	1	0	2	4	9	.171	.244	.268	513	46	-3	0	1	-0	.950	5	S-13/3-7	0.3
1977	Chi-N	155	624	91	166	31	7	3	40	56	90	.266	.330	.353	683	75	-20	24	12	1	.962	**36**	*S-154	3.3
1978	Chi-N	160	619	**104**	172	24	7	3	35	74	78	.278	.357	.354	711	88	-7	41	12	5	.967	13	*S-160	2.9
1979	Chi-N	160	636	92	180	26	10	5	52	59	82	.283	.346	.379	725	89	-8	24	20	-2	.959	1	*S-160	0.8
1980	Chi-N	157	618	78	160	26	3	3	33	60	81	.259	.328	.325	654	77	-17	44	16	4	.969	8	*S-156	1.2
1981	Chi-N	106	403	49	78	8	4	0	13	46	61	.194	.276	.233	509	44	-29	21	9	1	.959	10	*S-106	-0.7
1982	Phi-N	161	536	53	128	21	5	3	59	54	70	.239	.311	.313	624	73	-18	14	4	2	.973	-8	*S-154/3-7	-0.8
1983	*Phi-N	158	497	60	126	15	7	4	45	53	77	.254	.325	.336	661	85	-10	11	4	1	.966	-14	*S-158	-0.7
1984	Phi-N	144	435	40	112	15	3	0	35	43	76	.257	.327	.306	633	77	-12	12	5	1	.951	-21	*S-141	-2.0
1985	*StL-N	59	72	11	16	5	0	0	7	4	16	.222	.263	.292	555	55	-4	2	2	-0	1.000	2	3-20,S-13	-0.2
1986	NY-A	7	4	1	0	0	0	0	0	1	1	.000	.200	.000	200	-40	-1	0	0	0	.900	0	/S-7	-0.1
1987	SF-N	9	10	0	2	0	0	0	1	0	2	.200	.200	.200	400	7	-1	0	1	-0	.840	2	/S-9	0.1
1988	Det-A	7	17	1	3	0	0	0	0	1	4	.176	.222	.176	399	14	-2	0	0	0	.893	1	/S-7	-0.1
Total	15	1371	4602	595	1167	175	48	21	324	466	664	.254	.324	.326	651	76	-139	194	88	12	.963	41	*S-1303/3-34	4.2
■ **MARK DeJOHN** DeJohn, Mark Stephen b: 9/18/53, Middletown, Conn. BB/TR, 5'11", 170 lbs. Deb: 4/28/82 C																								
1982	Det-A	24	21	1	4	2	0	0	1	4	4	.190	.320	.286	606	68	-1	1	0	0	.978	6	S-20/3-4,2-1	0.6
■ **BILL DeKONING** DeKoning, William Callahan b: 12/19/18, Brooklyn, N.Y. d: 7/26/79, Palm Harbor, Fla. BR/TR, 5'11", 185 lbs. Deb: 5/27/45																								
1945	NY-N	3	1	0	0	0	0	0	0	0	1	.000	.000	.000	0	-99	-0	0			1.000	-0	/C-2	0.0

■ TOMAS DeLA ROSA
DeLa Rosa, Tomas b: 1/28/78, LaVictoria, D.R. BR/TR, 5'10", 165 lbs. Deb: 7/17/2000

YEAR	TM/L	G	AB	R	H	2B	3B	HR	RBI	BB	SO	AVG	OBP	SLG	OPS	OPS+	BR+	SB	CS	SBR	FA	FR	G/POS	TPR
2000	Mon-N	32	66	7	19	3	1	2	9	7	11	.288	.365	.455	819	104	0	2	1	0	.980	5	S-29	0.6

■ ED DELAHANTY
Delahanty, Edward James "Big Ed" b: 10/30/1867, Cleveland, Ohio
d: 7/2/03, Niagara Falls, Ont., Canada BR/TR, 6'1", 170 lbs. Deb: 5/22/1888 FH Career OF: (1056-LF 250-CF 40-RF)

YEAR	TM/L	G	AB	R	H	2B	3B	HR	RBI	BB	SO	AVG	OBP	SLG	OPS	OPS+	BR+	SB	CS	SBR	FA	FR	G/POS	TPR
1888	Phi-N	74	290	40	66	12	2	1	31	12	26	.228	.261	.293	554	73	-9	38			.872	-10	2-56,O-17(10-1-6)	-1.7
1889	Phi-N	56	246	37	72	13	3	0	27	14	17	.293	.333	.370	703	89	-5	19			.956	-13	O-31(30-0-1),2-24/S-1	-1.5
1890	Cle-P	115	517	107	153	26	13	3	64	24	30	.296	.337	.414	751	109	6	25			.830	-7	S-76,2-20,O-18C,/31	0.1
1891	Phi-N	128	543	92	132	19	9	5	86	33	50	.243	.296	.339	635	83	-14	25			.909	1	*O-99C,1-27/2-3	-1.6
1892	Phi-N	123	477	79	146	30	**21**	6	91	31	32	.306	.360	**.495**	855	158	30	29			.944	10	*O-121(1-120-0)/3-4	3.0
1893	Phi-N	132	595	145	219	35	18	**19**	**146**	47	20	.368	.423	**.583**	1007	167	**53**	37			.948	31	*O-117L,2-15/1-6	**6.0**
1894	Phi-N	116	495	148	200	39	19	4	133	60	16	.404	.475	.584	1059	158	50	21			.927	17	*O-90L,1-12/3-9,S2	4.5
1895	Phi-N	116	480	149	194	**49**	10	11	106	86	31	.404	**.500**	.617	**1117**	**186**	**66**	46			.944	-0	*O-103L/S-9,2-6,3-1	4.6
1896	Phi-N	123	499	131	198	**44**	17	**13**	**126**	62	22	.397	.472	**.631**	**1103**	**192**	**67**	37			.952	14	*O-99L,1-22/2-1	5.9
1897	Phi-N	129	530	109	200	40	15	5	96	60		.377	.444	.538	981	163	49	26			.970	9	*O-129(128-0-1)/1-1	3.9
1898	Phi-N	144	548	115	183	36	9	4	92	77		.334	.426	.454	880	159	**46**	**58**			.964	6	*O-144(144-0-0)	3.5
1899	Phi-N	146	581	135	**238**	**55**	9	9	**137**	55		**.410**	.464	**.582**	**1046**	**193**	**74**	30			.969	0	*O-143(143-0-0)	5.4
1900	Phi-N	131	539	82	174	32	10	2	109	41		.323	.378	.430	809	124	17	16			.981	-3	*1-130	1.2
1901	Phi-N	139	542	106	192	**38**	16	8	108	65		.354	.427	.528	**955**	173	51	29			.949	-4	O-84(82-1-1),1-58	3.9
1902	Was-A	123	473	103	178	**43**	14	10	93	62		**.376**	**.453**	**.590**	**1043**	**186**	**56**	16			.961	2	*O-111(111-0-0),1-13	4.8
1903	Was-A	42	156	22	52	11	1	1	21	12		.333	.388	.436	824	144	9	3			.962	2	O-40(20-0-20)/1-1	0.9
Total	16	1837	7511	1600	2597	522	186	101	1466	741	244	.346	.411	.505	916	152	544	455			.951	56	*O-1346L,1-271,2/S3	42.9

■ FRANK DELAHANTY
Delahanty, Frank George "Pudgie" b: 1/29/1883, Cleveland, Ohio
d: 7/22/66, Cleveland, Ohio BR/TR, 5'9", 160 lbs. Deb: 8/23/05 F Career OF: (236-LF 1-CF 29-RF)

YEAR	TM/L	G	AB	R	H	2B	3B	HR	RBI	BB	SO	AVG	OBP	SLG	OPS	OPS+	BR+	SB	CS	SBR	FA	FR	G/POS	TPR
1905	NY-A	9	27	0	6	1	0	0	2	1		.222	.250	.259	509	55	-1	0			.932	-1	/1-5,O-3(3-0-0)	-0.3
1906	NY-A	92	307	37	73	11	8	2	41	16		.238	.282	.345	627	87	-5	11			.954	3	O-86(86-0-0)	-0.7
1907	Cle-A	15	52	3	9	0	1	0	4	4		.173	.232	.212	444	41	-3	2			.917	-0	O-15(9-0-6)	-0.5
1908	NY-A	37	125	12	32	1	2	0	10	10		.256	.316	.296	612	98	-0	9			.957	-1	O-36(36-0-0)	-0.3
1914	Buf-F	79	274	29	55	4	7	2	27	23	19	.201	.265	.288	553	50	-24	21			.976	-6	O-78(78-0-0)	-3.5
	Pit-F	41	159	25	38	4	4	1	7	11	11	.239	.297	.333	630	72	-9	7			.984	-3	O-36(13-1-23)/2-4	-1.5
	Yr	120	433	54	93	8	11	3	34	34	30	.215	.277	.305	581	58	-33	28			.979	-8	*O-114(91-1-23)/2-4	-5.0
1915	Pit-F	14	42	3	10	1	0	0	3	1	0	.238	.256	.262	518	46	-4	0			1.000	1	O-11(11-0-0)	-0.4
Total	6	287	986	109	223	22	22	5	94	66	30	.226	.280	.308	588	70	-47	50			.964	-7	O-265L/1-5,2-4	-7.2

■ JIM DELAHANTY
Delahanty, James Christopher b: 6/20/1879, Cleveland, Ohio
d: 10/17/53, Cleveland, Ohio BR/TR, 5'10.5", 170 lbs. Deb: 4/19/01 F Career OF: (173-LF 1-CF 12-RF)

YEAR	TM/L	G	AB	R	H	2B	3B	HR	RBI	BB	SO	AVG	OBP	SLG	OPS	OPS+	BR+	SB	CS	SBR	FA	FR	G/POS	TPR
1901	Chi-N	17	63	4	12	2	0	0	4	3		.190	.239	.222	461	35	-5	5			.877	-1	3-17/2-1	-0.6
1902	NY-N	7	26	3	6	1	0	0	3	1		.231	.259	.269	528	64	-1	0			.917	-1	/O-7(0-0-7)	-0.2
1904	Bos-N	142	499	56	142	27	8	3	60	27		.285	.333	.389	721	127	15	16			.888	1	*3-113,2-18/O-9L,P	1.9
1905	Bos-N	125	461	50	119	11	8	5	55	28		.258	.315	.349	664	100	-1	12			.962	-7	*O-124(123-0-1)/P-1	-1.6
1906	Cin-N	115	379	63	106	21	4	1	39	45		.280	.371	.364	735	124	12	21			.903	-19	*3-105/S-5,O-2(2-0-0)	-0.5
1907	StL-A	33	95	8	21	3	0	0	6	5		.221	.275	.253	527	68	-3	6			.889	-1	3-21/O-4(0-0-4),2-2	-0.4
	Was-A	108	404	44	118	18	7	2	54	36		.292	.367	.386	753	152	25	18			.941	-12	2-68,3-27/O-9L,1-4	1.5
	Yr	141	499	52	139	21	7	2	60	41		.279	.350	.361	711	135	21	24			.942	-13	2-70,3-48,O-13L,/1	1.1
1908	Was-A	83	287	33	91	11	4	1	30	24		.317	.376	.394	770	164	20	16			.963	3	2-80	2.7
1909	Was-A	90	302	18	67	13	5	1	21	23		.222	.290	.308	598	93	-3	4			.956	-3	2-85	-0.5
	*Det-A	46	150	29	38	10	1	0	20	17		.253	.364	.333	697	115	4	9			.943	-7	2-46	-0.3
	Yr	136	452	47	105	23	6	1	41	40		.232	.316	.316	632	101	2	13			.951	-10	*2-131	-0.8
1910	Det-A	106	378	67	111	16	2	3	45	43		.294	.379	.370	749	126	13	15			.940	-15	*2-106	-0.1
1911	Det-A	144	542	83	184	30	14	3	94	56		.339	.411	.463	874	137	27	15			.978	-10	1-71,2-59,3-13	1.7
1912	Det-A	79	266	34	76	14	1	0	41	42		.286	.397	.346	743	117	9	9			.930	-5	2-44,O-33(33-0-0)	0.3
1914	Bro-F	74	214	28	62	13	5	0	15	25	21	.290	.372	.397	769	110	0	4			.957	-19	2-55/1-5	-1.8
1915	Bro-F	17	25	0	6	1	0	0	2	3	3	.240	.345	.280	625	77	-1	1			.857	-1	/2-4	-0.2
Total	13	1186	4091	520	1159	191	59	19	489	378	24	.283	.357	.373	730	122	111	151			.946	-97	2-568,3-296,O/1SP	1.9

■ JOE DELAHANTY
Delahanty, Joseph Nicholas b: 10/18/1875, Cleveland, Ohio d: 1/9/36, Cleveland, Ohio BR/TR, 5'9", 168 lbs. Deb: 9/30/07 F

YEAR	TM/L	G	AB	R	H	2B	3B	HR	RBI	BB	SO	AVG	OBP	SLG	OPS	OPS+	BR+	SB	CS	SBR	FA	FR	G/POS	TPR
1907	StL-N	7	22	3	7	0	0	1	2	0		.318	.318	.455	773	147	1	3			.933	-1	/O-7(7-0-0)	0.0
1908	StL-N	140	499	37	127	14	11	1	44	32		.255	.309	.333	641	110	5	11			.977	-5	*O-138(138-0-0)	-0.9
1909	StL-N	123	411	28	88	16	4	2	54	42		.214	.292	.287	579	85	-7	10			.985	-16	O-63(14-45-7),2-48	-2.9
Total	3	270	932	68	222	30	15	4	100	74		.238	.301	.315	617	100	-1	24			.978	-21	O-208(159-45-7)/2-48	-3.8

■ TOM DELAHANTY
Delahanty, Thomas James b: 3/9/1872, Cleveland, Ohio d: 1/10/51, Sanford, Fla. BL/TR, 5'8", 175 lbs. Deb: 9/29/1894 F

YEAR	TM/L	G	AB	R	H	2B	3B	HR	RBI	BB	SO	AVG	OBP	SLG	OPS	OPS+	BR+	SB	CS	SBR	FA	FR	G/POS	TPR
1894	Phi-N	1	4	0	1	0	0	0	0	0	1	.250	.250	.250	500	21	-1	0			.875	0	/2-1	0.0
1896	Cle-N	16	56	11	13	4	0	0	4	8	4	.232	.338	.304	642	66	-3	4			.823	-1	3-16	-0.3
	Pit-N	1	3	1	1	0	0	0	0	0	0	.333	.333	.333	667	79	-0	0			.750	-0	/S-1	0.0
	Yr	17	59	12	14	4	0	0	4	8	4	.237	.338	.305	643	67	-3	4			.823	-2	3-16/S-1	-0.3
1897	Lou-N	1	4	1	1	1	0	0	2	0		.250	.250	.500	750	99	-0	0			.333	-2	/2-1	-0.2
Total	3	19	67	13	16	5	0	0	6	8	5	.239	.329	.313	642	66	-3	4			.727	-4	/3-16,2-2,S-1	-0.5

■ MIKE de la HOZ
DeLa Hoz, Miguel Angel (Piloto) b: 10/2/38, Havana, Cuba BR/TR, 5'11", 175 lbs. Deb: 7/22/60 Career OF: (2-LF 0-CF 0-RF)

YEAR	TM/L	G	AB	R	H	2B	3B	HR	RBI	BB	SO	AVG	OBP	SLG	OPS	OPS+	BR+	SB	CS	SBR	FA	FR	G/POS	TPR
1960	Cle-A	49	160	20	41	6	2	6	23	9	12	.256	.300	.431	731	98	-1	0	0	0	.950	-15	S-38/3-8	-1.3
1961	Cle-A	61	173	20	45	10	0	3	23	7	10	.260	.297	.370	667	79	-6	0	0	0	.969	3	2-17,S-17,3-16	0.0
1962	Cle-A	12	12	0	1	0	0	0	0	0	3	.083	.083	.083	167	-57	-3	0	0	0	1.000	-0	/2-2	-0.3
1963	Cle-A	67	150	15	40	10	0	5	25	9	29	.267	.313	.433	746	107	1	0	0	0	.962	4	2-34/3-6,S-2,O-2L	0.8
1964	Mil-N	78	189	25	55	7	1	4	12	14	22	.291	.346	.402	748	109	2	1	1	-0	.968	-4	2-25,3-25/S-8	0.1
1965	Mil-N	81	176	15	45	3	2	2	11	8	21	.256	.296	.330	625	75	-6	0	1	-0	.963	-10	S-41,3-22,2-10,/1-1	-1.5
1966	Atl-N	71	110	11	24	3	0	2	7	5	18	.218	.252	.300	552	52	-7	0	1	-0	.950	-2	3-30/2-8,S-1	-1.0
1967	Atl-N	74	143	10	29	3	0	3	14	4	14	.203	.224	.287	511	46	-10	1	0	0	1.000	-4	2-23,3-22/S-1	-1.5
1969	Cin-N	1	1	0	0	0	0	0	0	0	1	.000	.000	.000	0	-95	-0	0	0	0	.000	0	H	0.0
Total	9	494	1114	116	280	42	5	25	115	56	130	.251	.292	.365	657	82	-29	2	3	-1	.936	-28	3-129,2-119,S/O1	-4.7

■ BILL DeLANCEY
DeLancey, William Pinkney b: 11/28/11, Greensboro, N.C. d: 11/28/46, Phoenix, Ariz. BL/TR, 5'11.5", 185 lbs. Deb: 9/11/32

YEAR	TM/L	G	AB	R	H	2B	3B	HR	RBI	BB	SO	AVG	OBP	SLG	OPS	OPS+	BR+	SB	CS	SBR	FA	FR	G/POS	TPR
1932	StL-N	8	26	1	5	0	2	0	2	2	1	.192	.250	.346	596	57	-2	0			.930	1	/C-8	-0.1
1934	*StL-N	93	253	41	80	18	3	13	40	41	37	.316	.414	.565	979	150	18	1			.980	5	C-77	2.6
1935	StL-N	103	301	37	84	14	5	6	41	42	34	.279	.369	.419	788	107	4	0			.971	-2	C-83	0.7
1940	StL-N	15	18	0	4	0	0	0	2	0	2	.222	.222	.222	444	22	-2	0			.929	1	C-12	-0.1
Total	4	219	598	79	173	32	10	19	85	85	74	.289	.380	.472	851	121	19	1			.972	4	C-180	3.1

■ BILL DELANEY
Delaney, William L. b: 3/4/1863, Cincinnati, O. d: 3/1/42, Canton, Ohio BR/TR, Deb: 8/21/1890

YEAR	TM/L	G	AB	R	H	2B	3B	HR	RBI	BB	SO	AVG	OBP	SLG	OPS	OPS+	BR+	SB	CS	SBR	FA	FR	G/POS	TPR
1890	Cle-N	36	116	16	22	1	1	1	7	21	19	.190	.314	.241	555	64	-5	5			.926	-10	2-36	-1.2

■ JESUS de la ROSA
DeLa Rosa, Jesus (b: Jesus De Los Santos (De La Rosa)) b: 8/5/53, Santo Domingo, D.R. BR/TR, 6'1", 153 lbs. Deb: 8/2/75

YEAR	TM/L	G	AB	R	H	2B	3B	HR	RBI	BB	SO	AVG	OBP	SLG	OPS	OPS+	BR+	SB	CS	SBR	FA	FR	G/POS	TPR
1975	Hou-N	3	3	1	1	1	0	0	0	0	0	.333	.333	.667	1000	186	0	0	0	0	.000	0	H	0.0

■ ALEX DELGADO
Delgado, Alexander b: 1/11/71, Palmerejo, Venez. BR/TR, 6', 160 lbs. Deb: 4/4/96

YEAR	TM/L	G	AB	R	H	2B	3B	HR	RBI	BB	SO	AVG	OBP	SLG	OPS	OPS+	BR+	SB	CS	SBR	FA	FR	G/POS	TPR
1996	Bos-A	26	20	5	5	0	0	0	1	3	3	.250	.348	.250	598	54	-1	0	0	0	.889	-2	C-14/O-6L,3-4,12	-0.3

■ CARLOS DELGADO
Delgado, Carlos Juan (Hernandez) b: 6/25/72, Mayaguez, P.R. BL/TR, 6'3", 220 lbs. Deb: 10/1/93 Career OF: (58-LF 0-CF 0-RF)

YEAR	TM/L	G	AB	R	H	2B	3B	HR	RBI	BB	SO	AVG	OBP	SLG	OPS	OPS+	BR+	SB	CS	SBR	FA	FR	G/POS	TPR
1993	Tor-A	2	1	0	0	0	0	0	0	1	0	.000	.500	.000	500	47	0	0	0	0	1.000	0	/C-1,D-1	0.0
1994	Tor-A	43	130	17	28	2	0	9	24	25	46	.215	.354	.438	793	103	1	1	1	-0	.966	-4	O-41(41-0-0)/C-1	-0.4
1995	Tor-A	37	91	7	15	3	0	3	11	6	26	.165	.216	.297	513	32	-9	0	0	0	1.000	1	O-17(17-0-0)/1-4,D-7	-0.9

YEAR	TM/L	G	AB	R	H	2B	3B	HR	RBI	BB	SO	AVG	OBP	SLG	OPS	OPS+	BR+	SB	CS	SBR	FA	FR	G/POS	TPR
1996	Tor-A	138	488	68	132	28	2	25	92	58	139	.270	.359	.490	848	112	9	0	0	0	.983	-2	*D-108,1-27	-0.2
1997	Tor-A	153	519	79	136	42	3	30	91	64	133	.262	.352	.528	880	125	18	0	3	-1	.988	-4	*1-119,D-32	0.0
1998	Tor-A	142	530	94	155	43	1	38	115	73	139	.292	.389	.592	982	150	39	3	0	1	.992	-3	*1-141/D-1	2.1
1999	Tor-A	152	573	113	156	39	0	44	134	86	141	.272	.381	.571	952	136	31	1	1	-0	.990	-3	*1-147/D-5	1.3
2000	Tor-A★	162	569	115	196	**57**	1	41	137	123	104	.344	.472	.664	1137	181	**77**	0	1	-0	.991	-9	*1-162	4.7
Total	8	829	2901	493	818	214	7	190	604	436	728	.282	.387	.557	944	137	165	5	6	-1	.990	-25	1-600,D-154/O-58L,C	6.6

■ PUCHY DELGADO

Delgado, Luis Felipe (Robles) b: 2/2/54, Hatillo, P.R. BB/TL, 5'11", 170 lbs. Deb: 9/6/77

YEAR	TM/L	G	AB	R	H	2B	3B	HR	RBI	BB	SO	AVG	OBP	SLG	OPS	OPS+	BR+	SB	CS	SBR	FA	FR	G/POS	TPR
1977	Sea-A	13	22	4	4	0	0	0	2	1	8	.182	.217	.182	399	10	-3	0	0	0	1.000	-2	O-13(1-2-10)	-0.5

■ WILSON DELGADO

Delgado, Wilson (Duran) b: 7/15/75, San Cristobal, D.R. BB/TR, 5'11", 165 lbs. Deb: 9/24/96

YEAR	TM/L	G	AB	R	H	2B	3B	HR	RBI	BB	SO	AVG	OBP	SLG	OPS	OPS+	BR+	SB	CS	SBR	FA	FR	G/POS	TPR
1996	SF-N	6	22	3	8	0	0	0	2	1	5	.364	.440	.364	804	120	1	1	0	0	.960	-2	/S-6	-0.1
1997	SF-N	8	7	1	1	1	0	0	0	0	2	.143	.143	.286	429	9	-1	0	0	0	1.000	0	/2-3,S-1	-0.1
1998	SF-N	10	12	1	2	1	0	0	1	1	3	.167	.231	.250	481	28	-1	0	0	0	1.000	0	/S-6	-0.1
1999	SF-N	35	71	7	18	2	1	0	3	5	9	.254	.312	.310	622	62	-4	1	0	0	.932	-2	S-20,2-15	-0.5
2000	NY-A	31	45	6	11	1	0	1	4	5	9	.244	.320	.333	653	67	-2	1	0	0	.950	2	2-14,S-11/3-5	0.0
	KC-A	33	83	15	22	1	0	0	7	6	17	.265	.315	.277	592	51	-6	1	1	-0	1.000	14	2-19,S-12/3-3	0.9
	Yr	64	128	21	33	2	0	1	11	11	26	.258	.317	.297	613	57	-8	2	1	0	.986	16	2-33,S-23/3-8	0.9
Total	5	123	240	33	62	6	1	1	17	18	45	.258	.318	.304	622	61	-14	4	1	1	.960	12	/S-56,2-51,3-8	0.1

■ BOBBY Del GRECO

Del Greco, Robert George b: 4/7/33, Pittsburgh, Pa. BR/TR, 5'11", 190 lbs. Deb: 4/16/52 Career OF: (74-LF 588-CF 16-RF)

YEAR	TM/L	G	AB	R	H	2B	3B	HR	RBI	BB	SO	AVG	OBP	SLG	OPS	OPS+	BR+	SB	CS	SBR	FA	FR	G/POS	TPR
1952	Pit-N	99	341	34	74	14	2	1	20	38	70	.217	.301	.279	580	60	-18	6	5	-0	.977	6	O-93(1-88-4)	-1.6
1956	Pit-N	14	20	4	4	0	0	2	3	3	3	.200	.304	.500	804	114	0	0	0	0	1.000	-2	/O-7(0-7-0),3-3	-0.2
	StL-N	102	270	29	58	16	2	5	18	32	50	.215	.312	.344	656	76	-9	1	1	-0	.987	-9	O-99(0-99-0)	-2.2
	Yr	116	290	33	62	16	2	7	21	35	53	.214	.311	.355	666	79	-8	1	1	-0	.987	-10	*O-106(0-106-0)/3-3	-2.4
1957	Chi-N	20	40	2	8	2	0	0	3	10	17	.200	.360	.250	610	69	-1	1	0	0	.967	-2	O-16(0-16-0)	-0.3
	NY-A	8	7	3	3	0	0	0	0	2	2	.429	.556	.429	984	175	1	1	0	0	1.000	-2	/O-6(0-6-0)	-0.1
1958	NY-A	12	5	1	1	0	0	0	0	1	1	.200	.333	.200	533	52	-0	0	1	-0	1.000	-4	O-12(11-1-0)	-0.5
1960	Phi-N	100	300	48	71	16	4	10	26	54	64	.237	.355	.417	772	110	5	1	5	-2	.970	12	O-89(0-87-2)	1.2
1961	Phi-N	41	112	14	29	5	0	2	11	12	17	.259	.346	.357	704	88	-2	0	0	0	1.000	1	O-32(1-31-0)/2-1,3-1	-0.2
	KC-A	74	239	34	55	14	1	5	21	30	31	.230	.319	.360	678	79	-7	1	0	0	.983	5	O-73(0-73-0)	-0.4
1962	KC-A	132	338	61	86	21	1	9	38	49	62	.254	.370	.402	772	103	3	4	1	1	.984	0	*O-124(33-95-4)	0.0
1963	KC-A	121	306	40	65	7	1	8	29	40	52	.212	.313	.320	634	74	-10	1	2	-0	.981	-6	*O-110(24-85-6)/3-2	-2.1
1965	Phi-N	8	4	1	0	0	0	0	0	0	3	.000	.000	.000	0	-99	-1	0	0	0	.000	-1	/O-4(4-0-0)	-0.2
Total	9	731	1982	271	454	95	11	42	169	271	372	.229	.331	.352	683	84	-38	16	15	-2	.981	-2	O-665C/3-6,2-1	-6.6

■ JUAN DELIS

Delis, Juan Francisco b: 2/27/28, Santiago De Cuba, Cuba BR/TR, 5'11", 170 lbs. Deb: 4/16/55

YEAR	TM/L	G	AB	R	H	2B	3B	HR	RBI	BB	SO	AVG	OBP	SLG	OPS	OPS+	BR+	SB	CS	SBR	FA	FR	G/POS	TPR
1955	Was-A	54	132	12	25	3	1	0	11	3	15	.189	.219	.227	446	21	-15	1	2	-0	.918	-2	3-24/O-8(2-0-6),2-1	-1.8

■ EDDIE DELKER

Delker, Edward Alberts b: 4/17/06, Palo Alto, Pa. d: 5/14/97, Pottsville, Pa. BR/TR, 5'10.5", 170 lbs. Deb: 4/28/29

YEAR	TM/L	G	AB	R	H	2B	3B	HR	RBI	BB	SO	AVG	OBP	SLG	OPS	OPS+	BR+	SB	CS	SBR	FA	FR	G/POS	TPR
1929	StL-N	22	40	5	6	0	1	0	3	2	12	.150	.227	.200	427	7	-6	0			.750	-2	/S-9,2-7,3-3	-0.7
1931	StL-N	1	2	0	1	1	0	0	2	0	0	.500	.500	1.000	1500	283	0	0			1.000	-0	/3-1	0.0
1932	StL-N	20	42	1	5	4	0	0	2	8	7	.119	.260	.214	474	28	-4	0			1.000	4	2-10/3-5,S-4	0.1
	Phi-N	30	62	7	10	1	1	1	7	6	14	.161	.235	.258	493	29	-6	0			.925	-2	2-27	-0.7
	Yr	50	104	8	15	5	1	1	9	14	21	.144	.246	.240	486	29	-10	0			.946	3	2-37/3-5,S-4	-0.6
1933	Phi-N	25	41	6	7	3	1	0	1	0	12	.171	.171	.293	463	27	-4	0			.968	6	2-17/3-4	0.3
Total	4	98	187	19	29	9	3	1	15	16	45	.155	.229	.251	481	26	-20	0			.952	6	/2-61,3-13,S-13	-1.0

■ JASON DELLAERO

Dellaero, Jason Christopher b: 12/17/76, Mount Kisco, N.Y. BB/TR, 6'2", 195 lbs. Deb: 9/7/99

YEAR	TM/L	G	AB	R	H	2B	3B	HR	RBI	BB	SO	AVG	OBP	SLG	OPS	OPS+	BR+	SB	CS	SBR	FA	FR	G/POS	TPR
1999	Chi-A	11	33	1	3	0	0	0	2	1	13	.091	.118	.091	209	-46	-7	0	0	0	.917	1	S-11	-0.5

■ DAVID DELLUCCI

Dellucci, David Michael b: 10/31/73, Baton Rouge, La. BL/TL, 5'10", 180 lbs. Deb: 6/3/97

YEAR	TM/L	G	AB	R	H	2B	3B	HR	RBI	BB	SO	AVG	OBP	SLG	OPS	OPS+	BR+	SB	CS	SBR	FA	FR	G/POS	TPR
1997	Bal-A	17	27	3	6	1	0	1	3	4	7	.222	.344	.370	714	89	-0	0	0	0	1.000	1	/O-9(3-0-6),D-5	0.0
1998	Ari-N	124	416	43	108	19	**12**	5	51	33	103	.260	.319	.399	718	87	-8	3	5	-1	.987	1	*O-117(95-19-15)	-1.1
1999	Ari-N	63	109	27	43	7	1	1	15	11	24	.394	.463	.505	968	144	8	2	0	1	1.000	-5	O-31(13-4-19)/D-1	0.2
2000	Ari-N	34	50	2	15	3	0	0	2	4	9	.300	.352	.360	712	80	-1	0	2	-1	1.000	-2	O-12(1-0-11)	-0.4
Total	4	238	602	75	172	30	13	7	71	52	143	.286	.349	.414	763	98	-2	5	7	-1	.990	-5	O-169(112-23-51)/D-6	-1.3

■ BERT DELMAS

Delmas, Albert Charles b: 5/20/11, San Francisco, Cal d: 12/4/79, Huntington Beach, Cal. BL/TR, 5'11", 165 lbs. Deb: 9/10/33

YEAR	TM/L	G	AB	R	H	2B	3B	HR	RBI	BB	SO	AVG	OBP	SLG	OPS	OPS+	BR+	SB	CS	SBR	FA	FR	G/POS	TPR
1933	Bro-N	12	28	4	7	0	0	0	0	1	7	.250	.276	.250	526	53	-2	0			.912	-3	2-10	-0.5

■ LUIS de los SANTOS

DeLos Santos, Luis Manuel (Martinez) b: 12/29/66, San Cristobal, D.R. BR/TR, 6'5", 205 lbs. Deb: 9/7/88 Career OF: (3-LF 0-CF 0-RF)

YEAR	TM/L	G	AB	R	H	2B	3B	HR	RBI	BB	SO	AVG	OBP	SLG	OPS	OPS+	BR+	SB	CS	SBR	FA	FR	G/POS	TPR
1988	KC-A	11	22	1	2	1	1	0	1	4	4	.091	.231	.227	458	29	-2	0	0	0	1.000	-0	/1-5,D-3	-0.3
1989	KC-A	28	87	6	22	3	1	0	6	5	14	.253	.293	.310	604	71	-3	0	0	0	.986	0	1-27	-0.5
1991	Det-A	16	30	1	5	2	0	0	0	2	4	.167	.219	.233	452	25	-3	0	0	0	1.000	-0	/O-3L,1-2,3-2,D-9	-0.4
Total	3	55	139	8	29	6	2	0	7	11	22	.209	.267	.281	547	53	-9	0	0	0	.988	-1	/1-34,D-12,O-3L,3-2	-1.2

■ GARTON Del SAVIO

Del Savio, Garton Orville b: 11/26/13, New York, N.Y. BR/TR, 5'9.5", 165 lbs. Deb: 4/24/43

YEAR	TM/L	G	AB	R	H	2B	3B	HR	RBI	BB	SO	AVG	OBP	SLG	OPS	OPS+	BR+	SB	CS	SBR	FA	FR	G/POS	TPR
1943	Phi-N	4	11	0	1	0	0	0	1	1	0	.091	.167	.091	258	-26	-2	0			.857	0	/S-4	-0.1

■ JIM DELSING

Delsing, James Henry b: 11/13/25, Rudolph, Wis. BL/TR, 5'10", 175 lbs. Deb: 4/21/48

YEAR	TM/L	G	AB	R	H	2B	3B	HR	RBI	BB	SO	AVG	OBP	SLG	OPS	OPS+	BR+	SB	CS	SBR	FA	FR	G/POS	TPR
1948	Chi-A	20	63	5	12	0	0	0	5	5	12	.190	.261	.190	451	22	-7	0	0	0	1.000	-1	O-15(0-15-0)	-0.9
1949	NY-A	9	20	5	7	1	0	1	3	1	2	.350	.381	.550	931	145	1	0	0	0	1.000	-2	/O-5(0-5-0)	0.0
1950	NY-A	12	10	2	4	0	0	0	2	2	0	.400	.500	.400	900	137	1	0	0	0	.000	0	H	0.1
	StL-A	69	209	25	55	5	2	0	15	20	23	.263	.328	.306	634	61	-12	1	4	-1	.994	2	O-53(0-53-0)	-1.2
	Yr	81	219	27	59	5	2	0	17	22	23	.269	.336	.311	647	65	-11	1	4	-1	.994	2	O-53(0-53-0)	-1.1
1951	StL-A	131	449	59	112	20	2	8	45	56	39	.249	.338	.356	694	85	-9	2	9	-3	.983	9	*O-124(4-118-4)	-0.6
1952	StL-A	93	298	34	76	13	6	1	34	25	29	.255	.323	.349	672	85	-6	3	3	-0	.986	-1	O-85(34-44-10)	-1.1
	Det-A	33	113	14	31	2	1	3	15	11	8	.274	.344	.389	733	103	0	1	0	0	.958	-0	O-32(32-0-0)	-0.2
	Yr	126	411	48	107	15	7	4	49	36	37	.260	.329	.360	689	90	-6	4	3	-0	.979	-1	*O-117(66-44-10)	-1.3
1953	Det-A	138	479	77	138	26	6	11	62	66	39	.288	.380	.436	816	121	15	1	3	-1	.992	-2	*O-133(0-133-0)	0.7
1954	Det-A	122	371	39	92	24	2	6	38	49	38	.248	.337	.372	709	96	-2	4	4	-1	**.996**	-0	*O-108(90-5-16)	-0.9
1955	Det-A	114	356	49	85	15	2	10	60	48	40	.239	.331	.376	707	92	-4	2	0	1	.995	-5	*O-101(98-3-0)	-1.5
1956	Det-A	10	12	0	0	0	0	0	0	3	3	.000	.250	.000	250	-29	-2	0	0	0	1.000	-1	/O-3(3-0-0)	-0.3
	Chi-A	55	41	11	5	3	0	0	2	10	13	.122	.294	.195	489	31	-4	1	0	0	.957	-8	O-29(13-7-9)	-1.2
	Yr	65	53	11	5	3	0	0	2	13	16	.094	.284	.151	435	17	-6	1	0	0	.962	-8	O-32(16-7-9)	-1.5
1960	KC-A	16	40	2	10	3	0	1	5	3	5	.250	.302	.325	627	69	-2	0	0	0	1.000	1	O-10(10-0-0)	-0.1
Total	10	822	2461	322	627	112	21	40	286	299	251	.255	.340	.366	706	91	-30	15	23	-5	.989	-8	O-698(284-383-39)	-7.2

■ JOE DeMAESTRI

DeMaestri, Joseph Paul "Oats" b: 12/9/28, San Francisco, Cal. BR/TR, 6', 174 lbs. Deb: 4/19/51

YEAR	TM/L	G	AB	R	H	2B	3B	HR	RBI	BB	SO	AVG	OBP	SLG	OPS	OPS+	BR+	SB	CS	SBR	FA	FR	G/POS	TPR
1951	Chi-A	56	74	8	15	0	2	1	3	5	11	.203	.253	.297	550	49	-5	0	4	-1	.959	6	S-27,2-11/3-8	0.0
1952	StL-A	81	186	13	42	9	1	1	18	8	25	.226	.258	.301	559	54	-12	0	1	-0	.939	2	S-77/2-1,3-1	-0.7
1953	Phi-A	111	420	53	107	17	3	6	35	24	39	.255	.297	.352	649	72	-17	0	1	-0	.964	-16	*S-108	-2.5
1954	Phi-A	146	539	49	124	16	3	8	40	20	63	.230	.262	.315	577	57	-33	1	4	-1	.965	-6	*S-142/2-1,3-1	-3.0
1955	KC-A	123	457	42	114	14	1	6	37	20	47	.249	.285	.324	609	63	-25	3	5	-1	.964	-12	*S-122	-2.8
1956	KC-A	133	434	41	101	16	1	6	39	25	73	.233	.279	.316	595	57	-28	3	3	-0	.964	6	*S-132/2-2	-1.2
1957	KC-A☆	135	461	44	113	14	6	9	33	22	82	.245	.282	.360	643	73	-18	6	1	1	**.980**	-7	*S-134	-1.4
1958	KC-A	139	442	32	97	11	1	6	38	16	84	.219	.248	.290	538	47	-32	1	0	0	**.980**	11	*S-137	-1.1
1959	KC-A	118	352	31	86	16	5	6	34	28	65	.244	.307	.369	677	83	-8	1	0	0	.957	5	*S-115	0.5
1960	*NY-A	49	35	8	8	1	0	0	2	0	9	.229	.229	.257	486	33	-3	0	0	0	.952	7	2-19,S-17	0.4
1961	NY-A	30	41	1	6	0	0	0	2	0	13	.146	.146	.146	293	-23	-7	0	0	0	.981	7	S-18/2-5,3-4	0.1
Total	11	1121	3441	322	813	114	23	49	281	168	511	.236	.275	.325	601	62	-190	15	19	-3	.967	4	*S-1029/2-39,3-14	-11.7

YEAR	TM/L	G	AB	R	H	2B	3B	HR	RBI	BB	SO	AVG	OBP	SLG	OPS	OPS+	BR+	SB	CS	SBR	FA	FR	G/POS	TPR
■ FRANK DEMAREE	Demaree, Joseph Franklin (b: Joseph Franklin Dimaria) b: 6/10/10, Winters, Cal. d: 8/30/58, Los Angeles, Cal. BR/TR, 5'11.5", 185 lbs. Deb: 7/22/32																							
1932	*Chi-N	23	56	4	14	3	0	0	6	2	7	.250	.288	.304	592	60	-3	0			1.000	-1	O-17(4-9-4)	-0.5
1933	Chi-N	134	515	68	140	24	6	6	51	22	42	.272	.304	.377	681	94	-5	4			.965	0	*O-133(10-123-0)	-0.9
1935	*Chi-N	107	385	60	125	19	4	2	66	26	23	.325	.369	.410	779	108	5	6			.973	-2	O-98(0-69-29)	0.0
1936	Chi-N★	154	605	93	212	34	3	16	96	49	30	.350	.400	.496	896	137	31	4			.968	-2	*O-154(36-0-118)	2.0
1937	Chi-N★	154	615	104	199	36	6	17	115	57	31	.324	.382	.485	866	129	24	6			.980	2	*O-154(0-0-154)	1.6
1938	*Chi-N	129	476	63	130	15	7	8	62	45	34	.273	.341	.384	725	96	-2	1			.972	-8	*O-125(9-0-119)	-1.8
1939	NY-N	150	560	68	170	27	2	11	79	66	40	.304	.381	.418	799	114	12	2			.986	-1	*O-150(1-116-36)	0.7
1940	NY-N	121	460	68	139	18	6	7	61	45	39	.302	.364	.413	777	113	9	5			.980	-6	*O-119(9-74-37)	-0.2
1941	NY-N	16	35	3	6	0	0	0	1	4	1	.171	.256	.171	428	22	-4	0			1.000	-0	O-10(1-8-1)	-0.4
	Bos-N	48	113	20	26	5	2	2	15	12	5	.230	.304	.363	667	91	-2	2			1.000	-4	O-28(9-7-12)	-0.7
	Yr	64	148	23	32	5	2	2	16	16	6	.216	.293	.318	610	74	-5	2			1.000	-5	O-38(10-15-13)	-1.1
1942	Bos-N	64	187	18	42	5	0	3	24	17	10	.225	.289	.299	589	74	-6	2			1.000	4	O-49(27-0-22)	-0.6
1943	*StL-N	39	86	5	25	2	0	0	9	8	4	.291	.351	.314	665	89	-1	1			1.000	-3	O-23(12-0-12)	-0.6
1944	StL-A	16	51	4	13	2	0	0	6	6	3	.255	.333	.294	627	76	-1	0	0	0	.969	-1	O-16(15-0-1)	-0.3
Total	12	1155	4144	578	1241	190	36	72	591	359	269	.299	.357	.415	772	110	57	33	0		.978	-22	*O-1076(133-406-545)	-1.7
■ BILLY DeMARS	DeMars, William Lester "Kid" b: 8/26/25, Brooklyn, N.Y. BR/TR, 5'10", 160 lbs. Deb: 5/18/48 C																							
1948	Phi-A	18	29	3	5	0	0	0	1	5	3	.172	.294	.172	467	26	-3	0	0	0	.927	4	/S-9,2-1,3-1	0.1
1950	StL-A	61	178	25	44	5	1	0	13	22	13	.247	.330	.287	617	57	-11	0	1	-0	.933	-7	S-54/3-5	-1.5
1951	StL-A	1	4	1	1	0	0	0	0	1	0	.250	.400	.250	650	76	-0	0	0	0	1.000	-0	/S-1	0.0
Total	3	80	211	29	50	5	1	0	14	28	16	.237	.326	.270	597	53	-14	0	1	-0	.933	-4	/S-64,3-6,2-1	-1.4
■ JOHN DeMERIT	DeMerit, John Stephen "Thumper" b: 1/8/36, West Bend, Wis. BR/TR, 6'1.5", 195 lbs. Deb: 6/18/57																							
1957	*Mil-N	33	34	8	5	0	0	0	1	0	8	.147	.147	.147	294	-22	-6	1	0	0	1.000	-3	O-13(2-11-0)	-0.9
1958	Mil-N	3	3	1	2	0	0	0	0	0	0	.667	.667	.667	1333	278	1	0	0	0	1.000	-1	/O-2(0-1-1)	0.0
1959	Mil-N	11	5	4	1	0	0	0	0	1	2	.200	.333	.200	533	51	-0	0	0	0	1.000	-0	/O-4(3-1-0)	-0.1
1961	Mil-N	32	74	5	12	3	0	2	5	5	19	.162	.225	.284	509	36	-7	0	0	0	1.000	0	O-21(2-5-15)	-0.8
1962	NY-N	14	16	3	3	0	0	1	1	2	4	.188	.278	.375	653	72	-1	0	0	0	1.000	-3	/O-9(3-2-4)	-0.4
Total	5	93	132	21	23	3	0	3	7	8	33	.174	.227	.265	492	32	-13	1	0	0	1.000	-6	/O-49(10-20-20)	-2.2
■ DON DEMETER	Demeter, Donald Lee b: 6/25/35, Oklahoma City, Okla BR/TR, 6'4", 190 lbs. Deb: 9/18/56 Career OF: (143-LF 592-CF 92-RF)																							
1956	Bro-N	3	3	1	1	0	0	1	1	0	1	.333	.333	1.333	1667	297	1	0	0	0	1.000	-0	/O-1(0-1-0)	0.0
1958	LA-N	43	106	11	20	2	0	5	8	5	32	.189	.225	.349	574	48	-8	2	3	-1	1.000	-4	O-39(11-25-4)	-1.5
1959	*LA-N	139	371	55	95	11	1	18	70	16	87	.256	.298	.437	734	86	-8	5	6	-1	.983	-6	*O-124(0-124-0)	-2.0
1960	LA-N	64	168	23	46	7	1	9	29	8	34	.274	.311	.488	799	108	1	0	1	-0	.989	-8	O-62(0-61-1)	-1.0
1961	LA-N	15	29	3	5	0	0	1	2	3	6	.172	.250	.276	526	36	-3	0	0	0	.950	-1	O-14(0-3-12)	-0.4
	Phi-N	106	382	54	98	18	4	20	68	19	74	.257	.300	.482	782	105	1	2	1	0	.995	6	O-79(23-44-17),1-22	0.3
	Yr	121	411	57	103	18	4	21	70	22	80	.251	.297	.467	764	99	-2	2	1	0	.990	5	O-93(23-47-29),1-22	-0.1
1962	Phi-N	153	550	85	169	24	3	29	107	41	93	.307	.366	.520	886	139	29	2	7	-2	.937	-13	*3-105,O-63C/1-1	1.1
1963	Phi-N	154	515	63	133	20	2	22	83	31	93	.258	.308	.433	741	112	7	1	4	-1	**1.000**	-7	*O-119C,3-43,1-26	-0.7
1964	Det-A	134	441	57	113	22	1	22	80	17	85	.256	.292	.460	752	104	1	4	1	1	1.000	-2	O-88(24-52-13),1-23	-0.6
1965	Det-A	122	389	50	108	16	4	16	58	23	65	.278	.328	.463	790	121	9	4	2	0	.988	-2	O-82(1-56-25),1-34	0.3
1966	Det-A	32	99	12	21	5	0	5	12	3	19	.212	.235	.414	649	81	-3	1	0	0	.985	5	O-27(4-20-3)/1-4	0.1
	Bos-A	73	226	31	66	13	1	9	29	5	42	.292	.310	.478	788	111	3	1	0	0	.982	-2	O-57(0-55-3)/1-2	0.0
	Yr	105	325	43	87	18	1	14	41	8	61	.268	.287	.458	746	102	0	2	0	0	.984	3	O-84(4-75-6)/1-6	0.1
1967	Bos-A	20	43	7	12	5	0	1	4	3	11	.279	.326	.465	791	122	1	0	0	0	1.000	-1	O-12(3-1-9)/3-1	0.0
	Cle-A	51	121	15	25	4	0	5	12	6	16	.207	.256	.364	619	80	-3	0	0	0	.985	-2	O-35(13-28-1)/3-1	-0.7
	Yr	71	164	22	37	9	0	6	16	9	27	.226	.274	.390	665	92	-2	0	0	0	.988	-3	O-47(16-29-10)/3-2	-0.7
Total	11	1109	3443	467	912	147	17	163	563	180	658	.265	.309	.459	769	108	27	22	25	-4	.990	-37	O-802C,3-150,1-112	-5.1
■ STEVE DEMETER	Demeter, Stephen b: 1/27/35, Homer City, Pa. BR/TR, 5'9.5", 185 lbs. Deb: 7/29/59 C																							
1959	Det-A	11	18	1	2	1	0	0	1	0	1	.111	.111	.167	278	-24	-3	0	0	0	.909	1	/3-4	-0.2
1960	Cle-A	4	5	0	0	0	0	0	0	0	1	.000	.000	.000	0	-99	-1	0	0	0	1.000	0	/3-3	-0.1
Total	2	15	23	1	2	1	0	0	1	0	2	.087	.087	.130	217	-40	-4	0	0	0	.933	1	/3-7	-0.3
■ RAY DEMMITT	Demmitt, Charles Raymond b: 2/2/1884, Illiopolis, Ill. d: 2/19/56, Glen Ellyn, Ill. BL/TR, 5'8", 170 lbs. Deb: 4/12/09																							
1909	NY-A	123	427	68	105	12	12	4	30	55		.246	.340	.358	698	120	11	16			.908	5	*O-109(0-70-39)	1.2
1910	StL-A	10	23	4	4	1	0	0	2	3		.174	.296	.217	514	65	-1	0			1.000	1	/O-8(0-0-8)	0.0
1914	Det-A	1	0	0	0	0	0	0	0	0	0	—	—	—	—	—	0	0			.000	0	R	0.0
	Chi-A	146	515	63	133	13	12	2	46	61	48	.258	.344	.342	685	108	6	12	20	-4	.953	-5	*O-142(127-4-12)	-1.1
	Yr	147	515	63	133	13	12	2	46	61	48	.258	.344	.342	685	108	6	12	20	-4	.953	-5	*O-142(127-4-12)	-1.1
1915	Chi-A	9	6	0	0	0	0	0	0	1	2	.000	.143	.000	143	-55	-1	0			1.000	-1	/O-3(1-0-2)	-0.2
1917	StL-A	14	53	6	15	1	2	0	7	0	8	.283	.296	.377	674	109	0	1			1.000	-3	O-14(0-0-14)	-0.4
1918	StL-A	116	405	45	114	23	5	1	61	38	35	.281	.346	.370	716	120	9	10			.951	7	*O-114(0-0-114)	1.2
1919	StL-A	79	202	19	48	11	2	1	19	14	27	.238	.290	.327	617	71	-8	3			.868	-7	O-49(0-0-49)	-1.9
Total	7	498	1631	205	419	61	33	8	165	172	120	.257	.334	.349	684	108	16	42	20		.934	-3	O-439(128-74-238)	-1.2
■ GENE DeMONTREVILLE	DeMontreville, Eugene Napoleon b: 3/26/1874, St.Paul, Minn. d: 2/18/35, Memphis, Tenn. BR/TR, 5'8", 165 lbs. Deb: 8/20/1894 F Career OF: (0-LF 1-CF 0-RF)																							
1894	Pit-N	2	8	0	2	0	0	0	0	1	4	.250	.333	.250	583	43	-1	0			.889	-1	/S-2	-0.1
1895	Was-N	12	46	7	10	1	3	0	9	3	4	.217	.265	.370	635	63	-3	5			.929	4	S-12	0.1
1896	Was-N	133	533	94	183	24	5	8	77	29	27	.343	.381	.452	833	119	13	28			.890	16	*S-133	3.0
1897	Was-N	133	566	92	193	27	8	3	93	21		.341	.366	.433	799	111	7	30			.886	10	*S-99,2-33	2.0
1898	Bal-N	151	567	93	186	19	2	0	86	52		.328	.394	.369	763	117	14	49			.944	0	*2-123,S-28	2.0
1899	Chi-N	82	310	43	87	6	3	0	40	17		.281	.328	.319	648	80	-8	26			.902	9	S-82	0.5
	Bal-N	60	240	40	67	13	4	1	36	10		.279	.313	.379	693	85	-6	21			.961	9	2-60	0.5
	Yr	142	550	83	154	19	7	1	76	27		.280	.322	.345	667	82	-14	47			.902	18	S-82,2-60	1.0
1900	Bro-N	69	234	34	57	8	1	0	28	10		.244	.283	.286	570	54	-15	21			.952	0	2-48,S-12/3-7,O1	-1.1
1901	Bos-N	140	577	83	173	14	4	5	72	17		.300	.321	.364	685	90	-9	25			**.954**	5	*2-120,3-20	-0.2
1902	Bos-N	124	481	51	125	16	5	0	53	12		.260	.278	.314	592	82	-12	23			.940	-17	*2-112,S-10	-2.9
1903	Was-A	12	44	0	12	2	0	0	3	0		.273	.273	.318	591	75	-1	0			.931	-4	2-11/S-1	-0.6
1904	StL-A	4	9	0	1	0	0	0	0	2		.111	.273	.111	384	25	-1	0			1.000	-1	/2-3	-0.1
Total	11	922	3615	537	1096	130	35	17	497	174	35	.303	.340	.373	712	97	-20	228			.948	31	2-510,S-379/3-27,1O	3.1
■ LEE DeMONTREVILLE	DeMontreville, Leon b: 9/23/1875, Washington Co., Minn. d: 3/22/62, Pelham Manor, N.Y. BR/TR, 5'7", 140 lbs. Deb: 7/10/03 F																							
1903	StL-N	26	70	8	17	3	1	0	7	8		.243	.338	.314	652	89	-1	3			.901	-3	S-15/2-4,O-1(0-0-1)	-0.3
■ RICK DEMPSEY	Dempsey, John Rikard b: 9/13/49, Fayetteville, Tenn. BR/TR (BB 1982 (part)), 6', 190 lbs. Deb: 9/23/69 C Career OF: (6-LF 0-CF 17-RF)																							
1969	Min-A	5	6	1	3	1	0	0	0	1	0	.500	.571	.667	1238	240	1	0	0	0	.833	-1	/C-3	0.0
1970	Min-A	5	7	1	0	0	0	0	0	1	1	.000	.125	.000	125	-62	-2	0	0	0	.923	0	/C-3	-0.2
1971	Min-A	6	13	2	4	1	0	0	0	1	1	.308	.357	.385	742	107	0	0	0	0	.944	2	/C-6	0.2
1972	Min-A	25	40	0	8	1	0	0	0	6	8	.200	.304	.225	529	56	-2	0	0	0	.986	-1	C-23	-0.3
1973	NY-A	6	11	0	2	0	0	0	0	1	3	.182	.250	.182	432	24	-1	0	0	0	.818	-2	/C-5	-0.3
1974	NY-A	43	109	12	26	3	0	2	12	8	7	.239	.291	.321	612	77	-3	1	0	0	.978	4	C-31/O-2(1-0-1),D-1	0.2
1975	NY-A	71	145	18	38	8	0	1	11	21	15	.262	.355	.338	693	98	0	0	0	0	.977	3	C-19,D-18/O-8R,3-1	0.3
1976	NY-A	21	42	1	5	0	0	0	2	5	4	.119	.213	.119	332	-1	-5	0	0	0	1.000	2	/C-9,O-4(0-0-4)	-0.3
	Bal-A	59	174	11	37	2	0	0	10	13	17	.213	.275	.224	499	50	-11	1	1	-0	.987	5	C-58/O-3(1-0-2)	-0.4
	Yr	80	216	12	42	2	0	0	12	18	21	.194	.263	.204	466	40	-16	1	1	-0	.988	7	C-67/O-7(1-0-6)	-0.7
1977	Bal-A	91	270	27	61	7	4	3	34	34	34	.226	.317	.315	632	78	-8	2	3	-1	.977	-2	C-91	-0.7

YEAR	TM/L	G	AB	R	H	2B	3B	HR	RBI	BB	SO	AVG	OBP	SLG	OPS	OPS+	BR+	SB	CS	SBR	FA	FR	G/POS	TPR
1978	Bal-A	136	441	41	114	25	0	6	32	48	54	.259	.331	.356	687	99	0	7	3	0	.985	-5	*C-135	0.2
1979	*Bal-A	124	368	48	88	23	0	6	41	38	37	.239	.310	.351	661	81	-10	0	1	-0	.990	19	*C-124	1.3
1980	Bal-A	119	362	51	95	26	3	9	40	36	45	.262	.334	.425	760	108	4	3	1	0	.987	9	*C-112/O-6L,1-2,D-1	1.7
1981	Bal-A	92	251	24	54	10	1	6	15	32	36	.215	.306	.335	641	85	-5	0	1	-0	**.998**	3	C-90/D-1	0.2
1982	Bal-A	125	344	35	88	15	1	5	36	46	37	.256	.344	.349	692	91	-3	0	3	-1	.991	0	*C-124/D-1	0.1
1983	*Bal-A	128	347	33	80	16	2	4	32	40	54	.231	.315	.323	638	78	-10	1	1	-0	**.997**	21	*C-128	1.5
1984	Bal-A	109	330	37	76	11	0	11	34	40	58	.230	.315	.364	679	89	-5	1	2	-0	.992	-4	*C-108	-0.5
1985	Bal-A	132	362	54	92	19	0	12	52	50	87	.254	.346	.406	752	108	5	0	1	-0	.987	-11	*C-131	-0.1
1986	Bal-A	122	327	42	68	15	1	13	29	45	78	.208	.309	.379	689	87	-6	1	0	0	.990	5	*C-121	0.4
1987	Cle-A	60	141	16	25	10	0	1	9	23	29	.177	.297	.270	566	51	-10	0	0	0	.984	1	C-59	-0.6
1988	*LA-N	77	167	25	42	13	0	7	30	25	44	.251	.349	.455	804	133	7	1	0	0	.989	5	C-74	1.7
1989	LA-N	79	151	16	27	7	0	4	16	30	37	.179	.319	.305	623	80	-3	1	0	0	.984	3	C-62	0.3
1990	LA-N	62	128	13	25	5	0	2	15	23	29	.195	.318	.281	599	68	-5	1	0	0	.992	0	C-53	-0.3
1991	Mil-A	61	147	15	34	5	0	4	21	23	20	.231	.335	.347	682	91	-1	0	2	-1	.993	4	C-56/P-2,1-1	0.5
1992	Bal-A	8	9	2	1	0	0	0	0	2	1	.111	.273	.111	384	11	-1	0	0	0	1.000	-1	/C-8	-0.2
Total	24	1766	4692	525	1093	223	12	96	471	592	736	.233	.321	.347	668	88	-72	20	19	-2	.988	59	*C-1633/O-23R,D1P3	4.7
■ TOD DENNEHEY Dennehey, Thomas Francis b: 5/12/1899, Philadelphia, Pa. d: 8/8/77, Philadelphia, Pa. BL/TL, 5'10", 180 lbs. Deb: 4/21/23																								
1923	Phi-N	9	24	4	7	2	0	0	2	1	3	.292	.320	.375	695	74	-1	0	0	0	1.000	-1	/O-9(7-0-2)	-0.2
■ OTTO DENNING Denning, Otto George "Dutch" b: 12/28/12, Hays, Kan. d: 5/25/92, Chicago, Ill. BR/TR, 6', 180 lbs. Deb: 4/15/42																								
1942	Cle-A	92	214	15	45	14	0	1	19	18	14	.210	.275	.290	564	62	-11	0	0	0	**.992**	-2	C-78/O-2(2-0-0)	-1.0
1943	Cle-A	37	129	8	31	6	0	0	13	5	1	.240	.269	.287	555	67	-6	3	1	0	.966	-3	1-34	-1.2
Total	2	129	343	23	76	20	0	1	32	23	15	.222	.272	.289	561	64	-17	3	1	0	**.99**	-6	/C-78,1-34,O-2(2-0-0)	-2.2
■ JERRY DENNY Denny, Jeremiah Dennis (b: Jeremiah Dennis Eldridge) b: 3/16/1859, New York, N.Y. d: 8/16/27, Houston, Tex. BR/TR, 5'11.5", 180 lbs. Deb: 5/2/1881 Career OF: (1-LF 2-CF 7-RF)																								
1881	Pro-N	85	320	38	77	16	2	1	24	5	44	.241	.252	.313	565	78	-8				.840	6	*3-85	0.0
1882	Pro-N	84	329	54	81	10	9	2	42	4	46	.246	.255	.350	605	92	-3				.861	13	*3-84	1.0
1883	Pro-N	98	393	73	108	26	8	8	55	9	48	.275	.291	.443	734	116	6				**.876**	10	*3-98	1.6
1884	*Pro-N	110	439	57	109	22	9	6	59	14	58	.248	.272	.380	652	105	2				.874	-2	*3-99/1-9,2-3,C-1	0.1
1885	Pro-N	83	318	40	71	14	4	3	24	12	53	.223	.252	.321	572	87	-5				.869	-0	*3-83	-0.3
1886	StL-N	119	475	58	122	24	6	9	62	14	68	.257	.278	.389	668	108	4	16			.895	23	*3-117/S-3	2.6
1887	Ind-N	122	523	86	178	34	12	11	97	13	22	.340	.344	.502	846	137	23	29			.889	23	*3-116/S-4,O-1R,2-1	4.0
1888	Ind-N	126	524	92	137	27	7	12	63	9	79	.261	.277	.408	685	114	6	32			.894	25	*3-96,S-25/2-5,OP	3.2
1889	Ind-N	133	578	96	163	24	0	18	112	27	63	.282	.314	.417	731	101	-2	22			**.913**	12	*3-123/2-7,S-5	1.1
1890	NY-N	114	437	50	93	18	7	3	42	28	62	.213	.270	.307	576	68	-19	11			.889	5	*3-106/S-7,2-1	-1.1
1891	NY-N	4	16	0	4	1	0	0	1	0	3	.250	.250	.313	563	66	-1	2			.700	-3	/3-4	-0.4
	Cle-N	36	138	17	31	5	0	0	21	12	23	.225	.291	.261	552	59	-7	3			.884	-3	3-29/O-7(1-1-6)	-0.9
	Phi-N	19	73	5	21	1	1	0	11	4	6	.288	.325	.329	653	88	-1	1			.977	-1	1-12/3-7	-0.3
	Yr	59	227	22	56	7	1	0	33	16	32	.247	.299	.286	586	69	-9	6			.876	-8	3-40,1-12/O-7(1-1-6)	-1.6
1893	Lou-N	44	175	22	43	5	4	1	22	9	15	.246	.283	.337	620	70	-8	4			.920	1	S-42/3-2	-0.4
1894	Lou-N	60	221	26	61	11	7	0	32	13	12	.276	.325	.389	714	77	-9	10			.874	3	3-60	-0.4
Total	13	1237	4959	714	1299	238	76	74	667	173	602	.262	.287	.384	671	98	-22	130			.882	109	*3-1109/S-86,12OPC	9.8
■ DREW DENSON Denson, Andrew b: 11/16/65, Cincinnati, Ohio BB/TR, 6'5", 210 lbs. Deb: 9/13/89																								
1989	Atl-N	12	36	1	9	1	0	0	5	3	9	.250	.308	.278	585	67	-1	1	0	0	.988	2	1-12	0.0
1993	Chi-A	4	5	0	1	0	0	0	0	0	2	.200	.200	.200	400	8	-1	0	0	0	.800	-0	/1-3	-0.1
Total	2	16	41	1	10	1	0	0	5	3	11	.244	.295	.268	564	60	-2	1	0	0	.977	2	/1-15	-0.1
■ BUCKY DENT Dent, Russell Earl (b: Russell Earl O'Dey) b: 11/25/51, Savannah, Ga. BR/TR, 5'11", 181 lbs. Deb: 6/1/73 MC																								
1973	Chi-A	40	117	17	29	2	0	0	10	10	18	.248	.313	.265	577	62	-6	2	3	-1	.963	5	S-36/2-3,3-1	0.3
1974	Chi-A	154	496	55	136	15	3	5	45	28	48	.274	.317	.347	664	89	-7	3	4	-1	.972	9	*S-154	2.0
1975	Chi-A★	157	602	52	159	29	4	3	58	36	48	.264	.306	.341	646	81	-15	2	4	-1	**.981**	27	*S-157	3.0
1976	Chi-A	158	562	44	138	18	4	2	52	43	45	.246	.301	.302	604	77	-16	3	5	-1	.976	-6	*S-158	-0.4
1977	*NY-A	158	477	54	118	18	4	8	49	39	28	.247	.306	.352	658	80	-14	1	1	-0	.974	-11	*S-158	-0.9
1978	*NY-A	123	379	40	92	11	1	5	40	23	24	.243	.290	.317	606	72	-14	3	1	0	.981	-8	*S-123	-1.0
1979	NY-A	141	431	47	99	14	2	2	32	37	30	.230	.292	.285	577	58	-25	0	0	0	.977	32	*S-141	2.1
1980	*NY-A★	141	489	57	128	26	2	5	52	48	37	.262	.330	.354	684	89	-7	0	3	-1	**.982**	13	*S-141	2.0
1981	NY-A★	73	227	20	54	11	0	7	27	19	17	.238	.302	.379	681	97	-1	0	1	-0	.970	-2	S-73	0.4
1982	NY-A	59	160	11	27	1	1	0	9	8	11	.169	.208	.188	396	10	-20	0	0	0	.962	17	S-58	0.2
	Tex-A	46	146	16	32	9	0	1	14	13	10	.219	.283	.301	584	64	-7	0	0	0	.980	-2	S-45	-0.5
	Yr	105	306	27	59	10	1	1	23	21	21	.193	.245	.242	486	35	-27	0	0	0	.970	15	*S-103	-0.3
1983	Tex-A	131	417	36	99	15	2	2	34	23	31	.237	.279	.297	576	60	-23	3	7	-2	**.979**	-8	*S-129/D-1	-2.0
1984	KC-A	11	9	2	3	0	0	0	1	1	2	.333	.400	.333	733	105	0	0	0	0	1.000	-1	/S-9,3-2	0.0
Total	12	1392	4512	451	1114	169	23	40	423	328	349	.247	.300	.321	621	74	-155	17	29	-6	.976	66	*S-1382/3-3,2-3,D-1	5.2
■ SAM DENTE Dente, Samuel Joseph "Blackie" b: 4/26/22, Harrison, N.J. BR/TR, 5'11", 175 lbs. Deb: 7/10/47																								
1947	Bos-A	46	168	14	39	4	2	0	11	19	15	.232	.310	.280	590	60	-9	0	1	-0	.939	-3	3-46	-1.3
1948	StL-A	98	267	26	72	11	2	0	22	22	8	.270	.328	.326	653	72	-11	1	3	-1	.958	-2	S-76/3-6	-0.9
1949	Was-A	153	590	48	161	24	4	1	53	31	24	.273	.309	.332	641	71	-26	4	4	-1	.957	-9	*S-153	-2.6
1950	Was-A	155	603	56	144	20	5	2	59	39	19	.239	.286	.299	585	52	-45	1	1	-0	.952	1	*S-128,2-29	-3.2
1951	Was-A	88	273	21	65	8	1	0	29	25	10	.238	.302	.275	577	58	-16	3	0	1	.962	3	S-65,2-10/3-5	-0.8
1952	Chi-A	62	145	12	32	0	1	0	11	5	8	.221	.257	.234	491	37	-12	0	0	0	.942	2	S-27,3-18/2-6,O1	-0.9
1953	Chi-A	2	0	0	0	0	0	0	0	0	0	—	—	—	—	—	0	0	0	0	.000	0	/S-1	0.0
1954	*Cle-A	68	169	18	45	7	1	1	19	14	4	.266	.322	.337	660	79	-5	0	0	0	.971	-3	S-60/2-7	-0.4
1955	Cle-A	73	105	10	27	4	0	0	10	12	8	.257	.333	.295	629	68	-4	0	0	0	.976	7	S-53,3-13/2-4	0.5
Total	9	745	2320	205	585	78	16	4	214	167	96	.252	.303	.305	608	62	-127	9	9	-1	.958	-5	S-563/3-88,2-56,O1	-9.6
■ MIKE DePANGHER DePangher, Michael Anthony b: 9/11/1858, Marysville, Cal. d: 7/7/15, San Francisco, Cal BL, 5'8", 190 lbs. Deb: 8/8/1884																								
1884	Phi-N	4	10	0	2	0	0	0	0	1	3	.200	.273	.200	473	54	-0				.920	1	/C-4	0.0
■ TONY DePHILLIPS DePhillips, Anthony Andrew b: 9/20/12, New York, N.Y. d: 5/5/94, Port Jefferson, N.Y. BR/TR, 6'2", 185 lbs. Deb: 4/25/43																								
1943	Cin-N	35	20	0	2	1	0	0	2	1	5	.100	.143	.150	293	-16	-3	0			.981	5	C-35	0.3
■ GENE DERBY Derby, Eugene A. b: 2/3/1860, Fitchburg, Mass. d: 9/13/17, Waterbury, Conn. 5'7", 160 lbs. Deb: 9/3/1885																								
1885	Bal-a	10	31	4	4	0	0	0	2	1		.129	.182	.129	311	-1	-3				.952	1	/C-9,O-1(1-0-0)	-0.2
■ BOB DERNIER Dernier, Robert Eugene b: 1/5/57, Kansas City, Mo. BR/TR, 6', 165 lbs. Deb: 9/7/80																								
1980	Phi-N	10	7	5	4	0	0	0	1	1	0	.571	.625	.571	1196	224	1	3	0	1	1.000	0	/O-3(0-3-0)	0.2
1981	Phi-N	10	4	0	3	0	0	0	0	0	0	.750	.750	.750	1500	313	1	2	1	0	1.000	-2	/O-5(0-5-0)	-0.1
1982	Phi-N	122	370	56	92	10	2	4	21	36	69	.249	.317	.319	636	77	-11	42	12	5	.981	-0	*O-119(0-70-62)	-1.0
1983	*Phi-N	122	221	41	51	10	0	1	15	18	21	.231	.289	.290	578	61	-11	35	7	5	.988	-11	*O-107(12-68-31)	-2.0
1984	*Chi-N	143	536	94	149	26	5	3	32	63	60	.278	.356	.362	718	94	-3	45	17	4	.986	5	*O-140(1-139-0)	0.5
1985	Chi-N	121	469	63	119	20	3	1	21	40	44	.254	.316	.316	632	70	-18	31	8	4	.972	9	*O-116(0-116-0)	-0.6
1986	Chi-N	108	324	32	73	14	1	4	18	22	41	.225	.275	.312	586	57	-19	27	2	5	.987	1	*O-105(0-105-0)	-1.4
1987	Chi-N	93	199	38	63	4	4	8	21	19	19	.317	.379	.497	876	125	7	16	7	1	.989	-12	O-71(0-72-0)	-0.4
1988	Phi-N	68	166	19	48	3	1	1	10	9	19	.289	.330	.337	667	90	-2	13	6	1	.980	-4	O-54(0-53-1)	-0.6
1989	Phi-N	107	187	26	32	5	0	1	13	14	28	.171	.229	.214	443	27	-18	4	3	-0	.970	-13	O-74(28-29-20)	-3.4
Total	10	904	2483	374	634	92	16	23	152	222	301	.255	.318	.333	652	77	-72	218	63	26	.982	-26	O-794(41-660-114)	-8.8

YEAR	TM/L	G	AB	R	H	2B	3B	HR	RBI	BB	SO	AVG	OBP	SLG	OPS	OPS+	BR+	SB	CS	SBR	FA	FR	G/POS	TPR
■ **MARK DeROSA**	DeRosa, Mark Thomas b: 2/26/75, Passaic, N.J. BR/TR, 6'1", 185 lbs. Deb: 9/2/98																							
1998	Atl-N	5	3	2	1	0	0	0	0	0	1	.333	.333	.333	667	76	-0	0	0	0	1.000	-0	/S-4	0.0
1999	Atl-N	7	8	0	0	0	0	0	0	0	2	.000	.000	.000	0	-99	-2	0	0	0	1.000	0	/S-2	-0.2
2000	Atl-N	22	13	9	4	1	0	0	3	2	1	.308	.400	.385	785	101	0	0	0	0	1.000	3	S-10	0.3
Total	3	34	24	11	5	1	0	0	3	2	4	.208	.269	.250	519	33	-2	0	0	0	1.000	3	/S-16	0.1
■ **CLAUD DERRICK**	Derrick, Claud Lester "Deek" b: 6/11/1886, Burton, Ga. d: 7/15/74, Clayton, Ga. BR/TR, 6', 175 lbs. Deb: 9/8/10																							
1910	Phi-A	2	1	0	0	0	0	0	0	0		.000	.000	.000	0	-99	-0	0			.500	-0	/S-1	-0.1
1911	Phi-A	36	100	14	23	1	2	0	5	7		.230	.294	.280	574	61	-5	7			.960	1	2-21/S-6,1-3,3-2	-0.4
1912	Phi-A	21	58	7	14	0	1	0	7	5		.241	.313	.276	588	71	-2	1			.884	1	S-18	0.0
1913	NY-A	23	65	7	19	1	0	1	7	5	8	.292	.352	.354	706	106	1	2			.874	0	S-17/3-4,2-1	0.2
1914	Cin-N	3	6	2	2	1	0	0	1	0	0	.333	.333	.500	833	142	0	1			.889	0	/S-2	0.1
	Chi-N	28	96	5	21	3	1	0	13	5	13	.219	.257	.271	528	57	-5	2			.895	3	/S-28	-0.1
	Yr	31	102	7	23	4	1	0	14	5	13	.225	.262	.284	546	62	-5	3			.894	3	S-30	0.0
Total	5	113	326	35	79	6	4	1	33	22	21	.242	.298	.294	593	72	-12	13			.892	4	/S-72,2-22,3-6,1-3	-0.3
■ **MIKE DERRICK**	Derrick, James Michael b: 9/19/43, Columbia, S.C. BL/TR, 6', 190 lbs. Deb: 4/9/70																							
1970	Bos-A	24	33	3	7	1	0	0	5	0	11	.212	.212	.242	455	23	-3	0	1	-0	1.000	0	/O-2(2-0-0),1-1	-0.4
■ **RUSS DERRY**	Derry, Alva Russell b: 10/7/16, Princeton, Mo. BL/TR, 6'1", 180 lbs. Deb: 7/4/44																							
1944	NY-A	38	114	14	29	3	0	4	14	20	19	.254	.366	.386	752	111	2	1	0	0	.949	-1	O-28(16-0-12)	-0.1
1945	NY-A	78	253	37	57	6	2	13	45	31	49	.225	.312	.419	731	107	1	1	0	0	.978	0	O-68(10-44-15)	-0.1
1946	Phi-A	69	184	17	38	8	5	0	14	27	54	.207	.311	.304	616	73	-6	0	0	0	.985	4	O-50(45-2-5)	-0.6
1949	StL-N	2	2	0	0	0	0	0	0	0	2	.000	.000	.000	0	-96	-1	0			.000	0	H	-0.1
Total	4	187	553	68	124	17	7	17	73	78	124	.224	.322	.373	695	95	-3	2	0		.976	3	O-146(71-46-32)	-0.9
■ **JOE DeSA**	DeSa, Joseph b: 7/27/59, Honolulu, Hawaii d: 12/20/86, San Juan, P.R. BL/TL, 5'11", 170 lbs. Deb: 9/6/80																							
1980	StL-N	7	11	0	3	0	0	0	0	0	2	.273	.273	.273	545	51	-1	0	0	0	1.000	-0	/1-1,O-1(0-0-1)	-0.1
1985	Chi-A	28	44	5	8	2	0	2	7	3	6	.182	.234	.364	598	58	-3	0	0	0	1.000	1	/1-9,O-1(1-0-0),D-4	-0.2
Total	2	35	55	5	11	2	0	2	7	3	8	.200	.241	.345	587	57	-3	0	0	0	1.000	1	/1-10,D-4,O-2(1-0-1)	-0.3
■ **GENE DESAUTELS**	Desautels, Eugene Abraham "Red" b: 6/13/07, Worcester, Mass. d: 11/5/94, Flint, Mich. BR/TR, 5'11", 170 lbs. Deb: 6/22/30																							
1930	Det-A	42	126	13	24	4	2	0	9	7	9	.190	.239	.254	493	25	-15	2	0	0	.996	9	C-42	-0.3
1931	Det-A	3	11	1	1	0	0	0	1	0	1	.091	.091	.091	182	-50	-2	0	0	0	1.000	-1	/C-3	-0.3
1932	Det-A	28	72	8	17	2	0	0	2	13	11	.236	.360	.264	624	62	-3	0	0	0	.984	4	C-24	0.2
1933	Det-A	30	42	5	6	1	0	0	4	4	6	.143	.234	.167	401	8	-6	0	0	0	.976	2	C-30	-0.2
1937	Bos-A	96	305	33	74	10	3	0	27	36	26	.243	.325	.295	620	55	-20	1	2	-0	**.993**	4	C-94	-1.1
1938	Bos-A	108	333	47	97	16	2	2	48	57	31	.291	.396	.369	766	89	-4	1	1	-0	.985	6	*C-108	0.8
1939	Bos-A	76	226	26	55	14	0	0	21	33	13	.243	.340	.305	645	64	-12	3	1	0	.994	10	C-73	0.2
1940	Bos-A	71	222	19	50	7	1	0	17	32	13	.225	.328	.266	594	54	-14	0	1	-0	.992	-3	C-70	-1.3
1941	Cle-A	66	189	20	38	5	1	1	17	14	12	.201	.260	.254	514	38	-17	1	0	0	.997	6	C-66	-0.7
1942	Cle-A	62	162	14	40	5	0	0	9	12	13	.247	.303	.278	581	68	-7	1	0	0	.975	-8	C-61	-1.2
1943	Cle-A	68	185	14	38	6	1	0	19	11	16	.205	.250	.249	499	49	-12	2	0	0	.982	2	C-66	-0.8
1945	Cle-A	10	9	1	1	0	0	0	0	1	1	.111	.200	.111	311	-9	-1	0	0	0	1.000	0	C-10	-0.1
1946	Phi-A	52	130	10	28	3	1	0	13	12	16	.215	.282	.254	536	51	-8	1	1	-0	.989	2	C-52	-0.5
Total	13	712	2012	211	469	73	11	3	187	232	168	.233	.315	.285	600	57	-122	12	6	1	.989	31	C-699	-5.3
■ **DELINO DeSHIELDS**	DeShields, Delino Lamont b: 1/15/69, Seaford, Del. BL/TR, 6'1", 170 lbs. Deb: 4/9/90 Career OF: (39-LF 2-CF 0-RF)																							
1990	Mon-N	129	499	69	144	28	6	4	45	66	96	.289	.376	.393	769	116	13	42	22	2	.981	-8	*2-128	1.0
1991	Mon-N	151	563	83	134	15	4	10	51	95	151	.238	.350	.332	682	94	-1	56	23	4	.962	-22	*2-148	-1.5
1992	Mon-N	135	530	82	155	19	8	7	56	54	108	.292	.361	.398	759	116	12	46	15	5	.976	-22	*2-134	-0.2
1993	Mon-N	123	481	75	142	17	7	2	29	72	64	.295	.390	.372	762	101	4	43	10	6	.983	-1	*2-123	1.5
1994	LA-N	89	320	51	80	11	3	2	33	54	53	.250	.358	.322	680	85	-5	27	7	3	.986	6	2-88,S-10	0.9
1995	*LA-N	127	425	66	109	18	3	8	37	63	83	.256	.354	.369	723	100	1	39	14	4	.980	1	*2-113	1.1
1996	*LA-N	154	581	75	130	12	8	5	41	53	124	.224	.290	.298	588	60	-34	48	11	7	.975	-18	*2-154	-3.7
1997	StL-N	150	572	92	169	26	**14**	11	58	55	72	.295	.360	.448	808	111	9	55	14	7	.972	-9	*2-147	1.4
1998	StL-N	117	420	74	122	21	8	7	44	56	61	.290	.374	.429	803	111	8	26	10	2	.983	-21	*2-111/1-1	-0.5
1999	Bal-A	96	330	46	87	11	2	6	34	37	52	.264	.340	.364	703	83	-8	11	8	-0	.977	-18	2-93	-2.0
2000	Bal-A	151	561	84	166	43	5	10	86	69	82	.296	.374	.444	818	109	9	37	10	5	.975	-19	2-96,O-41L,D-10	-0.2
Total	11	1422	5282	797	1438	221	68	72	514	674	946	.272	.357	.381	737	100	9	430	144	44	.977	-131	*2-1335/O-41L,DS1	-2.2
■ **ORESTES DESTRADE**	Destrade, Orestes (Cucuas) b: 5/8/62, Santiago De Cuba, Cuba BB/TR, 6'4", 210 lbs. Deb: 9/11/87																							
1987	NY-A	9	19	5	5	0	0	0	1	5	5	.263	.417	.263	680	87	-0	0	0	0	1.000	-0	/1-3,D-2	0.0
1988	Pit-N	36	47	2	7	1	0	1	3	5	17	.149	.231	.234	465	34	-4	0	0	0	1.000	-1	/1-8	-0.6
1993	Fla-N	153	569	61	145	20	3	20	87	58	130	.255	.327	.406	733	90	-8	0	2	-1	.987	-7	*1-152	-3.0
1994	Fla-N	39	130	12	27	4	0	5	15	19	32	.208	.318	.354	672	73	-5	1	0	0	.983	-3	1-37	-1.1
Total	4	237	765	80	184	25	3	26	106	87	184	.241	.322	.383	705	84	-17	1	2	-0	.987	-11	1-200/D-2	-4.7
■ **BOB DETHERAGE**	Detherage, Robert Wayne b: 9/20/54, Springfield, Mo. BR/TR, 6', 180 lbs. Deb: 4/11/80																							
1980	KC-A	20	26	2	8	2	0	1	7	1	4	.308	.333	.500	833	124	1	1	1	-0	1.000	-7	O-20(12-0-11)	-0.7
■ **GEORGE DeTORE**	DeTore, George Francis b: 11/11/06, Utica, N.Y. d: 2/7/91, Utica, N.Y. BR/TR, 5'8", 170 lbs. Deb: 9/14/30 C																							
1930	Cle-A	3	12	0	2	1	0	0	2	0	2	.167	.167	.250	417	4	-2	0	0	0	.750	-2	/3-3	-0.3
1931	Cle-A	30	56	3	15	6	0	0	7	8	2	.268	.359	.375	734	88	-1	0	2	-1	.958	4	3-13,S-10/2-3	0.3
Total	2	33	68	3	17	7	0	0	9	8	4	.250	.329	.353	682	74	-3	0	2	-1	.929	2	/3-16,S-10,2-3	0.0
■ **DUCKY DETWEILER**	Detweiler, Robert Sterling b: 2/15/19, Trumbauersville, Pa. BR/TR, 5'11", 178 lbs. Deb: 9/12/42																							
1942	Bos-N	12	44	3	14	2	1	0	5	2	7	.318	.348	.409	757	123	1	0			.929	-4	3-12	-0.3
1946	Bos-N	1	1	0	0	0	0	0	0	0	0	.000	.000	.000	0	-99	-0	0			.000	0	H	0.0
Total	2	13	45	3	14	2	1	0	5	2	7	.311	.340	.400	740	118	1	0			.929	-4	/3-12	-0.3
■ **CESAR DEVAREZ**	Devarez, Cesar Salvatore (Santana) b: 9/22/69, San Francisco De Macoris, D.R. BR/TR, 5'10", 175 lbs. Deb: 6/2/95																							
1995	Bal-A	6	4	0	0	0	0	0	0	0	0	.000	.000	.000	0	-99	-1	0	0	0	1.000	1	/C-6	0.0
1996	Bal-A	10	18	3	2	0	1	0	0	1	3	.111	.158	.222	380	-5	-3	0	0	0	1.000	1	C-10	-0.2
Total	2	16	22	3	2	0	1	0	0	1	3	.091	.130	.182	312	-22	-4	0	0	0	1.000	2	/C-16	-0.2
■ **MIKE DEVEREAUX**	Devereaux, Michael b: 4/10/63, Casper, Wyo. BR/TR, 6', 195 lbs. Deb: 9/2/87 Career OF: (81-LF 774-CF 226-RF)																							
1987	LA-N	19	54	7	12	3	0	0	4	3	10	.222	.263	.278	541	45	-4	3	1	0	1.000	-2	O-18(11-2-5)	-0.6
1988	LA-N	30	43	4	5	1	0	0	2	2	10	.116	.156	.140	295	-15	-6	0	1	-0	1.000	-5	O-26(0-17-8)	-1.3
1989	Bal-A	122	391	55	104	14	3	8	46	36	60	.266	.331	.379	710	103	1	22	11	1	.983	-4	*O-112(4-80-35)/D-5	-0.3
1990	Bal-A	108	367	48	88	18	1	12	49	28	48	.240	.294	.392	686	93	-5	13	12	-1	.983	6	*O-104(0-104-0)/D-3	-0.1
1991	Bal-A	149	608	82	158	27	10	19	59	47	115	.260	.315	.431	746	109	5	16	9	0	.993	12	*O-149(1-148-0)	1.6
1992	Bal-A	156	653	76	180	29	11	24	107	44	94	.276	.325	.464	789	116	11	10	8	-1	.989	5	*O-155(0-155-0)	1.5
1993	Bal-A	131	527	72	132	31	3	14	75	43	99	.250	.308	.400	709	85	-12	3	3	-0	.988	2	*O-130(0-130-0)	-0.9
1994	Bal-A	85	301	35	61	8	2	9	33	22	72	.203	.259	.332	591	49	-24	1	2	-0	.995	0	O-84(0-84-0)/D-1	-2.2
1995	Chi-A	92	333	48	102	21	1	10	55	25	51	.306	.355	.465	820	117	7	6	6	-1	.985	3	O-90(0-9-87)	0.6
	*Atl-N	29	55	7	14	3	0	1	8	2	11	.255	.281	.364	644	66	-3	2	0	0	1.000	-2	O-27(14-9-4)	-0.4
1996	*Bal-A	127	323	49	74	11	2	8	34	34	53	.229	.306	.350	656	66	-17	8	2	1	.983	-19	*O-112(45-30-62),D-10	-3.5
1997	Tex-A	29	72	8	15	3	0	0	7	7	10	.208	.278	.250	528	37	-7	1	0	0	1.000	-6	O-28(5-3-24)	-1.2
1998	LA-N	9	13	0	4	1	0	0	1	3	2	.308	.438	.385	822	126	1	0	1	-0	1.000	1	/O-5(1-3-1)	0.1
Total	12	1086	3740	491	949	170	33	105	480	296	635	.254	.311	.401	712	91	-51	85	56	-1	.988	-8	*O-1040C/D-19	-6.7

YEAR	TM/L	G	AB	R	H	2B	3B	HR	RBI	BB	SO	AVG	OBP	SLG	OPS	OPS+	BR+	SB	CS	SBR	FA	FR	G/POS	TPR
■ **JIM DEVINE**	Devine, Walter James b: 10/5/1858, Brooklyn, N.Y. d: 1/11/05, Syracuse, N.Y. TL, Deb: 5/9/1883																							
1883	Bal-a	2	9	4	2	0	0	0		0		.222	.222	.222	444	42	-1				.500	-1	/P-2,O-1(0-0-1)	0.0
1886	NY-N	1	3	0	0	0	0	0	0	0	1	.000	.000	.000	0	-99	-1	0			.000	-0	/O-1(0-0-1)	-0.1
Total	2	3	12	4	2	0	0	0	0	0	1	.167	.167	.167	333	6	-1	0			—	-1	/O-2(0-0-2),P-2	-0.1
■ **MICKEY DEVINE**	Devine, William Patrick b: 5/9/1892, Albany, N.Y. d: 10/1/37, Albany, N.Y. BR/TR, 5′10″, 165 lbs. Deb: 8/2/18																							
1918	Phi-N	4	8	0	1	1	0	0	0	0	1	.125	.125	.250	375	13	-1	0			.909	0	/C-3	-0.1
1920	Bos-A	8	12	1	2	0	0	0	0	1	2	.167	.231	.167	397	7	-2	1	0	0	.955	1	/C-5	-0.1
1925	NY-N	21	33	6	9	3	0	0	4	2	3	.273	.314	.364	678	76	-1	0	0	0	.933	2	C-11/3-1	0.1
Total	3	33	53	7	12	4	0	0	4	3	6	.226	.268	.302	570	51	-4	1	0		.936	2	/C-19,3-1	-0.1
■ **BERNIE DeVIVEIROS**	DeViveiros, Bernard John b: 4/19/01, Oakland, Cal. d: 7/5/94, Oakland, Cal. BR/TR, 5′7″, 160 lbs. Deb: 9/13/24																							
1924	Chi-A	1	1	0	0	0	0	0	0	0	0	.000	.000	.000	0	-99	-0	0	0	0	.333	-1	/S-1	-0.1
1927	Det-A	24	22	4	5	1	0	0	2	2	8	.227	.292	.273	564	46	-2	1	0	0	.913	0	S-14/3-1	-0.1
Total	2	25	23	4	5	1	0	0	2	2	8	.217	.280	.261	541	40	-2	1	0	0	.846	-1	/S-15,3-1	-0.2
■ **ART DEVLIN**	Devlin, Arthur McArthur b: 10/16/1879, Washington, D.C. d: 9/18/48, Jersey City, N.J. BR/TR, 6′, 175 lbs. Deb: 4/14/04 C Career OF: (1-LF 0-CF 0-RF)																							
1904	NY-N	130	474	81	133	16	8	1	66	62		.281	.371	.354	725	119	13	33			.907	7	*3-130	2.5
1905	*NY-N	153	525	74	129	14	7	2	61	66		.246	.344	.310	655	94	-1	**59**			.932	5	*3-153	0.8
1906	NY-N	148	498	76	149	23	8	2	65	74		.299	.396	.390	786	142	27	54			.944	**28**	*3-148	6.4
1907	NY-N	143	491	61	136	16	2	1	54	63		.277	.376	.324	700	116	13	38			.940	0	*3-140/S-3	1.9
1908	NY-N	157	534	59	135	18	4	2	45	62		.253	.346	.313	659	106	6	19			**.947**	13	*3-157	2.7
1909	NY-N	143	491	61	130	19	8	0	56	65		.265	.362	.336	698	115	11	26			.934	18	*3-143	3.6
1910	NY-N	147	493	71	128	17	5	2	67	62	32	.260	.353	.327	679	98	1	28			.933	5	*3-147	1.0
1911	NY-N	95	260	42	71	16	2	0	25	42	19	.273	.386	.350	736	103	3	9			.944	2	3-79/1-6,2-6,S-6	0.7
1912	Bos-N	124	436	59	126	18	8	0	54	51	37	.289	.367	.367	734	99	1	11			.992	0	1-69,S-26,3-26,/O-1L	0.1
1913	Bos-N	73	210	19	48	7	5	0	12	29	17	.229	.328	.310	637	81	-4	8			.973	9	3-69	0.6
Total	10	1313	4412	603	1185	164	57	10	505	576	105	.269	.364	.338	702	109	69	285			.938	87	*3-1192/1-75,S-35,2O	20.3
■ **JIM DEVLIN**	Devlin, James Alexander b: 1849, Philadelphia, Pa. d: 10/10/1883, Philadelphia, Pa. BR/TR, 5′11″, 175 lbs. Deb: 4/21/1873 NA OF: (0-LF 3-CF 19-RF)																							
1873	Phi-n	23	99	18	24	4	4	0	10	2	4	.242	.257	.364	621	79	-3	0	0	0	.938	-3	1-12/3-6,S-5,O-1R	-0.4
1874	Chi-n	45	203	26	58	5	0	0	26	2	9	.286	.293	.310	603	93	-2	2	1	0	.930	-3	1-24,O-17(0-0-17)/3-5	-0.3
1875	Chi-n	69	318	60	92	17	6	0	40	4	4	.289	.298	.381	679	133	10	6	1	1	.934	-0	1-42,P-28/O-4(0-3-1)	0.6
1876	Lou-N	68	299	38	94	14	1	0	28	1	11	.314	.318	.369	687	109	0				.941	2	*P-68/1-1	0.0
1877	Lou-N	61	268	38	72	6	3	1	27	7	27	.269	.287	.325	612	78	-8				.933	2	*P-61	0.0
Total	3 n	137	620	104	174	26	10	0	76	8	17	.281	.290	.355	645	110	5	8	2	1	.933	-6	/1-78,P-28,O-22R,3S	-0.1
Total	2	129	567	76	166	20	4	1	55	8	38	.293	.303	.348	651	94	-8				.937	4	P-129/1-1	0.0
■ **JIM DEVLIN**	Devlin, James Raymond b: 8/25/22, Plains, Pa. BL/TR, 5′11.5″, 165 lbs. Deb: 4/27/44																							
1944	Cle-A	1	1	0	0	0	0	0	0	0	0	.000	.000	.000	0	-99	-0	0	0	0	1.000	0	/C-1	0.0
■ **REX DeVOGT**	DeVogt, Rex Eugene b: 1/4/1888, Clare, Mich. d: 11/9/35, Alma, Mich. BR/TR, 5′9″, 170 lbs. Deb: 4/17/13																							
1913	Bos-N	3	6	0	0	0	0	0	0	0	3	.000	.000	.000	0	-98	-2	0			.941	1	/C-3	0.0
■ **JOSH DEVORE**	Devore, Joshua D. b: 11/13/1887, Murray City, Ohio d: 10/6/54, Chillicothe, Ohio BL/TL, 5′6″, 160 lbs. Deb: 9/25/08																							
1908	NY-N	5	6	1	1	0	0	0	2	1		.167	.286	.167	452	43	-0	1			1.000	-1	/O-2(0-0-2)	-0.1
1909	NY-N	22	28	6	4	1	0	0	1	2		.143	.250	.179	429	33	-2	3			.824	-4	O-12(3-10-1)	-0.7
1910	NY-N	133	490	92	149	11	10	2	27	46	67	.304	.371	.380	750	119	12	43			.929	-12	*O-130(106-2-22)	-0.7
1911	*NY-N	149	565	96	158	19	10	3	50	81	69	.280	.376	.365	740	104	6	61			.934	1	*O-149(104-0-48)	0.0
1912	*NY-N	106	327	66	90	14	6	2	37	51	43	.275	.381	.373	754	104	3	27			.918	-8	O-96(76-1-19)	-0.9
1913	NY-N	16	21	4	4	0	1	0	1	3	4	.190	.320	.286	606	73	-1	6			1.000	-2	/O-8(1-5-2)	-0.3
	Cin-N	66	217	30	58	6	4	3	14	12	21	.267	.309	.373	682	95	-2	17			.920	-3	O-57(0-57-1)	-1.0
	Phi-N	23	39	9	11	1	0	0	5	4	7	.282	.364	.308	671	89	-0	0			.889	-3	O-14(8-6-0)	-0.4
	Yr	105	277	43	73	7	5	3	20	19	32	.264	.318	.357	675	92	-3	23			.919	-9	O-79(9-68-3)	-1.7
1914	Phi-N	30	53	5	16	2	0	0	7	4	5	.302	.351	.340	690	99	-0	0			.947	2	/O-9(7-2-0)	0.2
	*Bos-N	51	128	22	29	4	0	1	5	18	14	.227	.327	.281	608	82	-2	2			.915	-8	O-42(23-20-0)	-1.4
	Yr	81	181	27	45	6	0	1	12	22	19	.249	.333	.298	632	87	-2	2			.923	-6	O-51(30-22-0)	-1.2
Total	7	601	1874	331	520	58	31	11	149	222	230	.277	.361	.359	720	103	13	160			.925	-38	O-519(328-103-95)	-5.3
■ **AL DeVORMER**	DeVormer, Albert E. b: 8/19/1891, Grand Rapids, Mich d: 8/29/66, Grand Rapids, Mich BR/TR, 6′0.5″, 175 lbs. Deb: 8/4/18																							
1918	Chi-A	8	19	2	5	2	0	0	0	0	4	.263	.263	.368	632	90	-0	1			1.000	-2	/C-6,O-1(0-0-1)	-0.2
1921	*NY-A	22	49	6	17	4	0	0	7	2	4	.347	.373	.429	801	102	0	2	0	0	.950	-1	C-17	0.1
1922	NY-A	24	59	8	12	4	1	0	11	1	6	.203	.217	.305	522	34	-6	0	0	0	.968	-1	C-17/1-1	-0.6
1923	Bos-A	74	209	20	54	7	3	0	18	6	21	.258	.282	.321	603	58	-13	3	0	1	.979	0	C-55/1-2	-0.8
1927	NY-N	68	141	14	35	3	1	2	21	11	11	.248	.312	.326	638	71	-6	1			.953	-4	C-54/1-3	-0.8
Total	5	196	477	50	123	20	5	2	57	20	46	.258	.292	.333	625	65	-25	7	0		.967	-7	C-149/1-6,O-1(0-0-1)	-2.3
■ **WALT DeVOY**	DeVoy, Walter Joseph b: 3/14/1886, St.Louis, Mo. d: 12/17/53, St.Louis, Mo. BR/TR, 5′11″, 165 lbs. Deb: 9/13/09																							
1909	StL-A	19	69	7	17	3	1	0	8	3		.246	.278	.319	597	95	-1	4			.944	-2	O-16(0-0-16)/1-3	-0.3
■ **JEFF DeWILLIS**	DeWillis, Jeffrey Allen b: 4/13/65, Houston, Tex. BR/TR, 6′2″, 170 lbs. Deb: 4/19/87																							
1987	Tor-A	13	25	2	3	1	0	1	2	2	12	.120	.185	.280	465	21	-3	0	0	0	.964	2	C-13	-0.1
■ **CHARLIE DEXTER**	Dexter, Charles Dana b: 6/15/1876, Evansville, Ind. d: 6/9/34, Cedar Rapids, Iowa BR/TR, 5′7″, 155 lbs. Deb: 4/17/1896 Career OF: (8-LF 159-CF 236-RF)																							
1896	Lou-N	107	402	65	112	18	7	3	37	17	34	.279	.318	.381	698	87	-9	21			.903	-3	C-55,O-47(0-46-1)	-0.9
1897	Lou-N	76	257	43	72	12	5	2	46	21		.280	.342	.389	731	96	-2	12			.907	-5	O-32R,C-23,3-14,/S	-0.5
1898	Lou-N	112	421	76	132	13	5	1	66	26		.314	.363	.375	739	114	7	44			.958	-1	O-95(0-0-95)/2-8,C-7	0.3
1899	Lou-N	81	298	47	76	7	1	1	34	21		.255	.315	.295	610	68	-13	21			.943	2	O-72(1-0-71)/S-6	-1.3
1900	Chi-N	40	125	7	25	5	0	2	20	2		.200	.213	.288	501	39	-11	2			.943	8	C-22,O-13(0-0-13)/2-1	-0.2
1901	Chi-N	116	460	46	123	9	5	1	66	16		.267	.302	.315	617	82	-11	22			.982	3	1-54,3-25,O-21R,2/C	-0.9
1902	Chi-N	71	273	31	62	13	0	2	26	19		.227	.290	.297	586	83	-5	13			.846	-12	3-41,1-22,O-10(1-4-5)	-1.8
	Bos-N	48	183	33	47	3	0	1	18	16		.257	.323	.290	613	88	-2	16			.901	-4	S-22,2-19/O-7C,3-1	-0.5
	Yr	119	456	64	109	16	0	3	44	35		.239	.303	.294	597	85	-7	29			.847	-16	3-42,1-22,S-22,2O	-2.3
1903	Bos-N	123	457	82	102	15	1	3	34	61		.223	.323	.280	603	75	-12	32			.941	-10	*O-106C/S-9,C-6	-2.5
Total	8	774	2876	430	751	95	24	16	347	198	34	.261	.318	.328	646	85	-57	183			.942	-22	O-403R,C-116/312S	-8.3
■ **ALEX DIAZ**	Diaz, Alexis b: 10/5/68, Brooklyn, N.Y. BB/TR, 5′11″, 180 lbs. Deb: 7/25/92 Career OF: (56-LF 169-CF 66-RF)																							
1992	Mil-A	22	9	5	1	0	0	0	1	0	0	.111	.111	.111	222	-38	-2	3	2	-0	1.000	-4	O-11(2-10-0)/D-2	-0.6
1993	Mil-A	32	69	9	22	2	0	0	1	0	12	.319	.319	.348	667	80	-2	5	3	0	.979	-4	O-28(4-12-13)/D-1	-0.6
1994	Mil-A	79	187	17	47	5	7	1	17	10	19	.251	.289	.369	658	65	-10	5	5	-1	.993	-9	O-73(0-58-20)/2-2,D-1	-1.8
1995	*Sea-A	103	270	44	67	14	0	3	27	13	27	.248	.288	.333	621	60	-16	18	8	1	.987	-7	O-88(17-69-4)	-2.1
1996	Sea-A	38	79	11	19	2	0	1	5	2	8	.241	.277	.304	581	47	-6	6	3	0	.982	-1	O-28(19-5-5)/D-1	-0.7
1997	Tex-A	28	90	8	20	4	0	2	12	5	13	.222	.271	.333	604	54	-6	1	1	-0	.980	1	O-23(3-0-20)/1-1,2-1	-0.6
1998	SF-N	34	62	5	8	2	0	0	5	0	15	.129	.129	.161	290	-26	-11	1	1	-0	1.000	-2	O-21(4-15-3)	-1.4
1999	Hou-N	30	50	3	11	2	0	1	7	3	13	.220	.264	.320	584	48	-4	2	2	-0	.900	-1	/O-8(7-0-1)	-0.5
Total	8	366	816	102	195	31	7	8	75	33	107	.239	.273	.324	596	53	-57	41	25	0	.986	-27	O-280C/D-5,2-3,1-1	-8.3
■ **BO DIAZ**	Diaz, Baudilio Jose (Seijas) b: 3/23/53, Cua, Venezuela d: 11/23/90, Caracas, Venez. BR/TR, 5′11″, 190 lbs. Deb: 9/6/77																							
1977	Bos-A	2	1	0	0	0	0	0	0	0	1	.000	.000	.000	0	-90	-0	0	0	0	1.000	1	/C-2	0.0
1978	Cle-A	44	127	12	30	4	0	2	11	4	17	.236	.260	.315	575	61	-7	0	0	0	.971	-1	C-44	-0.6
1979	Cle-A	15	32	0	5	2	0	0	1	2	6	.156	.206	.219	425	15	-4	0	0	0	.958	4	C-15	0.0
1980	Cle-A	76	207	15	47	11	2	3	32	7	27	.227	.252	.343	595	61	-12	1	0	0	.989	3	C-75	-0.6

YEAR	TM/L	G	AB	R	H	2B	3B	HR	RBI	BB	SO	AVG	OBP	SLG	OPS	OPS+	BR+	SB	CS	SBR	FA	FR	G/POS	TPR
1981	Cle-A★	63	182	25	57	19	0	7	38	13	23	.313	.362	.533	895	157	13	2	2	-0	.975	-3	C-51/D-3	1.1
1982	Phi-N	144	525	69	151	29	1	18	85	36	87	.288	.337	.450	786	116	10	3	6	-1	.989	-9	*C-144	0.6
1983	*Phi-N	136	471	49	111	17	0	15	64	38	57	.236	.295	.367	663	84	-11	1	4	-1	.986	14	*C-134	0.7
1984	Phi-N	27	75	5	16	4	0	1	9	5	13	.213	.262	.307	569	58	-4	0	0	0	.992	-0	C-23	-0.4
1985	Phi-N	26	76	9	16	5	1	2	16	6	7	.211	.268	.382	650	78	-3	0	0	0	.972	2	C-24	0.0
	Cin-N	51	161	12	42	8	0	3	15	15	18	.261	.328	.366	694	89	-2	0	0	0	.988	9	C-51	0.9
	Yr	77	237	21	58	13	1	5	31	21	25	.245	.309	.371	680	86	-5	0	0	0	.983	11	C-75	0.9
1986	Cin-N	134	474	50	129	21	0	10	56	40	52	.272	.329	.380	709	91	-6	1	1	-0	.984	-6	*C-134	-0.7
1987	Cin-N★	140	496	49	134	28	1	15	82	19	73	.270	.304	.421	725	86	-11	1	0	0	.992	-6	*C-137	-1.1
1988	Cin-N	92	315	26	69	9	0	10	35	7	41	.219	.238	.343	581	63	-16	0	2	-1	.990	-3	C-88	-1.6
1989	Cin-N	43	132	6	27	5	0	1	8	6	7	.205	.239	.265	504	43	-10	0	2	-1	.984	-0	C-43	-0.9
Total	13	993	3274	327	834	162	5	87	452	198	429	.255	.300	.387	687	87	-63	9	17	-4	.986	3	C-965/D-3	-2.6

■ CARLOS DIAZ Diaz, Carlos Francisco b: 12/24/64, Elizabeth, N.J. BR/TR, 6'3", 195 lbs. Deb: 5/8/90

YEAR	TM/L	G	AB	R	H	2B	3B	HR	RBI	BB	SO	AVG	OBP	SLG	OPS	OPS+	BR+	SB	CS	SBR	FA	FR	G/POS	TPR
1990	Tor-A	9	3	1	1	0	0	0	0	0	2	.333	.333	.333	667	85	-0	0	0	0	1.000	2	/C-9	0.2

■ EDDY DIAZ Diaz, Eddy Javier b: 9/29/71, Barquisimeto, Venez. BR/TR, 5'10", 160 lbs. Deb: 4/17/97

YEAR	TM/L	G	AB	R	H	2B	3B	HR	RBI	BB	SO	AVG	OBP	SLG	OPS	OPS+	BR+	SB	CS	SBR	FA	FR	G/POS	TPR
1997	Mil-A	16	50	4	11	2	1	0	7	1	5	.220	.235	.300	535	38	-5	0	0	0	1.000	2	2-14/3-1,S-1	-0.2

■ EDGAR DIAZ Diaz, Edgar (Serrano) b: 2/8/64, Santurce, P.R. BR/TR, 6', 155 lbs. Deb: 9/16/86

YEAR	TM/L	G	AB	R	H	2B	3B	HR	RBI	BB	SO	AVG	OBP	SLG	OPS	OPS+	BR+	SB	CS	SBR	FA	FR	G/POS	TPR
1986	Mil-A	5	13	0	3	0	0	0	0	1	3	.231	.286	.231	516	41	-1	0	0	0	.875	-1	/S-5	-0.1
1990	Mil-A	86	218	27	59	2	2	0	14	21	32	.271	.338	.298	636	80	-5	3	2	-0	.950	-1	S-65,2-15/3-7,D-1	-0.1
Total	2	91	231	27	62	2	2	0	14	22	35	.268	.335	.294	629	78	-6	3	2	-0	.946	-1	/S-70,2-15,3-7,D-1	-0.2

■ EDWIN DIAZ Diaz, Edwin (Rosario) b: 1/15/75, Bayamon, P.R. BR/TR, 5'11", 172 lbs. Deb: 3/31/98

YEAR	TM/L	G	AB	R	H	2B	3B	HR	RBI	BB	SO	AVG	OBP	SLG	OPS	OPS+	BR+	SB	CS	SBR	FA	FR	G/POS	TPR
1998	Ari-N	3	7	0	0	0	0	0	0	0	2	.000	.000	.000	0	-99	-2	0	0	0	.938	2	/2-3	0.0
1999	Ari-N	4	5	2	2	2	0	0	1	3	1	.400	.625	.800	1425	256	2	0	0	0	1.000	0	/2-2,S-2	0.2
Total	2	7	12	2	2	2	0	0	1	3	3	.167	.333	.333	667	73	-0	0	0	0	.947	2	/2-5,S-2	0.2

■ EINAR DIAZ Diaz, Einar Antonio b: 12/28/72, Chiriqui, Panama BR/TR, 5'10", 165 lbs. Deb: 9/9/96

YEAR	TM/L	G	AB	R	H	2B	3B	HR	RBI	BB	SO	AVG	OBP	SLG	OPS	OPS+	BR+	SB	CS	SBR	FA	FR	G/POS	TPR
1996	Cle-A	4	1	0	0	0	0	0	0	0	0	.000	.000	.000	0	-99	-0	0	0	0	1.000	1	/C-4	0.0
1997	Cle-A	5	7	1	1	1	0	0	1	0	2	.143	.143	.286	429	8	-1	0	0	0	.955	2	/C-5	0.1
1998	*Cle-A	17	48	8	11	1	0	2	9	3	2	.229	.302	.375	677	72	-2	0	0	0	.973	3	C-17	0.1
1999	*Cle-A	119	392	43	110	21	1	3	32	23	41	.281	.329	.362	691	73	-16	11	4	1	.988	8	*C-119	0.0
2000	Cle-A	75	250	29	68	14	2	4	25	11	29	.272	.323	.392	715	78	-9	4	2	0	.994	20	C-74/3-1	1.5
Total	5	220	698	81	190	37	3	9	67	37	74	.272	.323	.372	695	74	-28	15	6	1	.989	34	C-219/3-1	1.7

■ MARIO DIAZ Diaz, Mario Rafael (Torres) b: 1/10/62, Humacao, P.R. BR/TR, 5'10", 160 lbs. Deb: 9/12/87

YEAR	TM/L	G	AB	R	H	2B	3B	HR	RBI	BB	SO	AVG	OBP	SLG	OPS	OPS+	BR+	SB	CS	SBR	FA	FR	G/POS	TPR
1987	Sea-A	11	23	4	7	0	1	0	3	0	4	.304	.304	.391	696	79	-1	0	0	0	.972	4	S-10	0.3
1988	Sea-A	28	72	6	22	5	0	0	9	3	5	.306	.333	.375	708	94	-1	0	0	0	.985	-4	S-21/2-4,1-1,3-1	-0.4
1989	Sea-A	52	74	9	10	0	0	1	7	7	7	.135	.210	.176	386	9	-9	0	0	0	.930	-9	S-37,2-14/3-3	-1.7
1990	NY-N	16	22	0	3	1	0	0	1	0	3	.136	.136	.182	318	-13	-3	0	0	0	.958	2	S-10/2-1	-0.2
1991	Tex-A	96	182	24	48	7	0	1	22	15	18	.264	.320	.319	638	79	-5	0	1	-0	.962	-2	S-65,2-20/3-8,D-1	-0.4
1992	Tex-A	19	31	2	7	1	0	0	1	1	2	.226	.250	.258	508	44	-2	0	1	-0	.975	1	S-16/2-3,3-1	-0.1
1993	Tex-A	71	205	24	56	10	1	2	24	8	13	.273	.304	.361	665	81	-6	1	0	0	.986	-4	S-57,3-12/1-1	-0.6
1994	Fla-N	32	77	10	25	4	2	0	11	6	6	.325	.381	.429	810	107	1	0	0	0	.964	-0	3-11/2-7,S-7	0.1
1995	Fla-N	49	87	5	20	3	0	1	6	1	12	.230	.239	.299	537	41	-8	0	0	0	.944	-2	/2-9,S-5,3-3	-0.9
Total	9	374	773	84	198	31	4	5	84	41	70	.256	.295	.326	621	69	-33	1	2	-0	.972	-15	S-228/2-58,3-39,1D	-3.9

■ MIKE DIAZ Diaz, Michael Anthony b: 4/15/60, San Francisco, Cal. BR/TR, 6'2", 195 lbs. Deb: 9/15/83 Career OF: (73-LF 0-CF 20-RF)

YEAR	TM/L	G	AB	R	H	2B	3B	HR	RBI	BB	SO	AVG	OBP	SLG	OPS	OPS+	BR+	SB	CS	SBR	FA	FR	G/POS	TPR
1983	Chi-N	6	7	2	2	1	0	0	1	0	0	.286	.286	.429	714	91	-0	0	0	0	1.000	-0	/C-3	-0.1
1986	Pit-N	97	209	22	56	9	0	12	36	19	43	.268	.335	.483	818	120	5	0	1	-0	.966	-5	O-38L,1-20/3-5,C-1	-0.3
1987	Pit-N	103	241	28	58	8	2	16	48	31	42	.241	.335	.490	824	114	4	1	0	0	.960	-6	O-37L,1-32/C-8	-0.4
1988	Pit-N	47	74	6	17	3	0	0	5	16	13	.230	.367	.270	637	87	-0	0	0	0	1.000	-5	O-19(9-0-9)/1-6,C-1	-0.6
	Chi-A	40	152	12	36	6	0	3	12	5	30	.237	.266	.336	601	67	-7	0	1	-0	.987	-2	1-39/D-1	-1.2
Total	4	293	683	70	169	27	2	31	102	71	128	.247	.324	.429	753	103	2	1	2	-0	.988	-18	/1-97,O-94L,C-13,3D	-2.6

■ PAUL DICKEN Dicken, Paul Franklin b: 10/2/43, DeLand, Fla. BR/TR, 6'5", 195 lbs. Deb: 6/7/64

YEAR	TM/L	G	AB	R	H	2B	3B	HR	RBI	BB	SO	AVG	OBP	SLG	OPS	OPS+	BR+	SB	CS	SBR	FA	FR	G/POS	TPR
1964	Cle-A	11	11	0	0	0	0	0	0	0	5	.000	.000	.000	0	-99	-3	0	0	0	.000	0	H	-0.3
1966	Cle-A	2	2	0	0	0	0	0	0	0	1	.000	.000	.000	0	-99	-1	0	0	0	.000	0	H	-0.1
Total	2	13	13	0	0	0	0	0	0	0	6	.000	.000	.000	0	-99	-3	0	0	0	.000	0	-0,-0	-0.4

■ BUTTERCUP DICKERSON Dickerson, Lewis Pessano b: 10/11/1858, Tyaskin, Md. d: 7/23/20, Baltimore, Md. BL/TR, 5'6", 140 lbs. Deb: 7/15/1878 Career OF: (216-LF 117-CF 64-RF)

YEAR	TM/L	G	AB	R	H	2B	3B	HR	RBI	BB	SO	AVG	OBP	SLG	OPS	OPS+	BR+	SB	CS	SBR	FA	FR	G/POS	TPR
1878	Cin-N	29	123	17	38	5	1	0	9	0	7	.309	.309	.366	675	134	4				.877	-1	O-29(10-19-0)	0.1
1879	Cin-N	81	350	73	102	18	**14**	2	57	3	27	.291	.297	.440	737	147	17				.801	-4	*O-81(81-0-0)	0.7
1880	Tro-N	30	119	15	23	2	2	0	10	2	3	.193	.207	.244	450	49	-6				.903	6	O-30(0-29-1)/S-1	-0.1
	Wor-N	31	133	22	39	8	6	0	20	1	2	.293	.299	.444	742	136	4				.852	-2	O-31(0-31-0)	0.1
	Yr	61	252	37	62	10	8	0	30	3	5	.246	.255	.349	604	96	-2				.883	4	O-61(0-60-1)/S-1	0.0
1881	Wor-N	80	367	48	116	18	6	1	31	8	8	.316	.331	.406	737	123	9				.892	10	*O-80(79-0-1)	1.2
1883	Pit-a	85	354	62	88	15	1	0		18		.249	.285	.297	582	91	-2				.798	0	*O-78R/S-8,2-2	-0.3
1884	StL-U	46	211	49	77	15	1	0		8		.365	.388	.445	834	147	6				.895	5	O-42(42-0-0)/3-4	0.9
	Bal-a	13	56	9	12	2	1	0		4		.214	.290	.286	576	85	-1				.941	-2	O-12(0-0-12)/3-1	-0.3
	Lou-a	8	28	6	4	0	2	1		3		.143	.226	.393	619	103	0				.813	-1	/O-8(1-5-3)	0.0
	Yr	21	84	15	16	2	3	1		7		.190	.269	.321	590	91	-1				.879	-3	O-20(1-5-15)/3-1	-0.3
1885	Buf-N	5	21	1	1	1	0	0	0	1	4	.048	.091	.095	186	-38	-3				1.000	1	/O-5(2-3-0)	-0.3
Total	7	408	1762	302	500	84	34	4	127	48	51	.284	.304	.377	680	118	29				.854	12	O-396L/S-9,3-5,2-2	2.0

■ GEORGE DICKEY Dickey, George Willard "Skeets" b: 7/10/15, Kensett, Ark. d: 6/16/76, DeWitt, Ark. BB/TR, 6'2", 180 lbs. Deb: 9/21/35 F

YEAR	TM/L	G	AB	R	H	2B	3B	HR	RBI	BB	SO	AVG	OBP	SLG	OPS	OPS+	BR+	SB	CS	SBR	FA	FR	G/POS	TPR
1935	Bos-A	5	11	1	0	0	0	0	1	1	3	.000	.083	.000	83	-72	-3	0	0	0	1.000	-1	/C-4	-0.4
1936	Bos-A	10	23	0	1	1	0	0	0	2	3	.043	.120	.087	207	-46	-5	0	0	0	.912	0	C-10	-0.4
1941	Chi-A	32	55	6	11	1	0	2	8	5	7	.200	.267	.327	594	57	-4	0	0	0	1.000	1	C-17	-0.2
1942	Chi-A	59	116	6	27	3	0	1	17	9	11	.233	.288	.284	572	63	-6	0	0	0	.918	-4	C-29	-0.8
1946	Chi-A	37	78	8	15	1	0	0	1	12	13	.192	.300	.205	505	45	-5	0	2	-1	1.000	2	C-30	-0.3
1947	Chi-A	83	211	15	47	6	0	1	27	34	25	.223	.331	.265	596	69	-8	4	2	0	.985	2	C-80	-0.2
Total	6	226	494	36	101	12	0	4	54	63	62	.204	.294	.253	547	53	-31	4	4	-1	.974	-0	C-170	-2.3

■ BILL DICKEY Dickey, William Malcolm b: 6/6/07, Bastrop, La. d: 11/12/93, Little Rock, Ark. BL/TR, 6'1.5", 185 lbs. Deb: 8/15/28 FMCH

YEAR	TM/L	G	AB	R	H	2B	3B	HR	RBI	BB	SO	AVG	OBP	SLG	OPS	OPS+	BR+	SB	CS	SBR	FA	FR	G/POS	TPR
1928	NY-A	10	15	1	3	1	1	0	2	0	2	.200	.200	.400	600	56	-1	0	0	0	1.000	-1	/C-6	-0.2
1929	NY-A	130	447	60	145	30	6	10	65	14	16	.324	.346	.485	832	120	10	4	3	-0	.979	1	*C-127	1.8
1930	NY-A	109	366	55	124	25	7	5	65	21	14	.339	.375	.486	861	122	11	7	1	1	.977	-12	*C-101	0.7
1931	NY-A	130	477	65	156	17	10	6	78	39	20	.327	.378	.442	820	122	15	2	1	0	**.996**	4	*C-125	2.5
1932	*NY-A	108	423	66	131	20	4	15	84	34	13	.310	.361	.482	843	123	13	2	4	-1	.987	-2	*C-108	1.5
1933	NY-A☆	130	478	58	152	24	8	14	97	47	14	.318	.381	.490	871	138	25	3	4	-1	.993	0	*C-127	3.1
1934	NY-A★	104	395	56	127	24	4	12	72	38	18	.322	.384	.494	878	134	19	0	3	-1	.986	-2	*C-104	2.1
1935	NY-A	120	448	54	125	26	6	14	81	35	11	.279	.339	.458	797	111	5	1	1	-0	**.995**	-2	*C-118	1.0
1936	*NY-A★	112	423	99	153	26	8	22	107	46	16	.362	.428	.617	1045	161	39	0	2	-1	.976	0	*C-107	3.9
1937	*NY-A★	140	530	87	176	35	2	29	133	73	22	.332	.417	.570	987	145	37	3	2	-0	.991	12	*C-137	5.2
1938	*NY-A★	132	454	84	142	27	4	27	115	75	22	.313	.412	.568	981	144	31	3	0	1	.987	4	*C-126	3.8
1939	*NY-A★	128	480	98	145	23	3	24	105	77	37	.302	.403	.512	915	135	26	5	0	1	**.989**	8	*C-126	3.9
1940	NY-A★	106	372	45	92	11	1	9	54	48	32	.247	.336	.355	691	83	-9	0	3	-1	.994	-1	*C-102	-0.4
1941	*NY-A★	109	348	35	99	15	5	7	71	45	17	.284	.371	.417	788	110	5	2	1	0	**.994**	1	*C-104	1.2

YEAR	TM/L	G	AB	R	H	2B	3B	HR	RBI	BB	SO	AVG	OBP	SLG	OPS	OPS+	BR+	SB	CS	SBR	FA	FR	G/POS	TPR
1942	*NY-A†	82	268	28	79	13	1	2	37	26	11	.295	.359	.373	732	108	3	2	2	-0	.976	3	C-80	1.1
1943	*NY-A☆	85	242	29	85	18	2	4	33	41	12	.351	.445	.492	937	173	24	2	1	0	.994	-1	C-71	2.9
1946	NY-A★	54	134	10	35	8	0	2	10	19	12	.261	.357	.366	723	101	1	0	1	-0	.987	10	C-39,M	1.3
Total	17	1789	6300	930	1969	343	72	202	1209	678	289	.313	.382	.486	868	128	254	36	29	-2	.988	24	*C-1708	35.4

■ JOHNNY DICKSHOT Dickshot, John Oscar "Ugly" (b: John Oscar Dicksus)
b: 1/24/10, Waukegan, Ill. d: 11/4/97, Waukegan, Ill. BR/TR, 6', 195 lbs. Deb: 4/16/36

YEAR	TM/L	G	AB	R	H	2B	3B	HR	RBI	BB	SO	AVG	OBP	SLG	OPS	OPS+	BR+	SB	CS	SBR	FA	FR	G/POS	TPR
1936	Pit-N	9	9	2	2	0	0	0	1	1	2	.222	.300	.222	522	42	-1	0			.000	-1	/O-1(0-1-0)	-0.1
1937	Pit-N	82	264	42	67	8	4	3	33	26	36	.254	.323	.348	672	82	-6	0			.950	-2	O-64(58-0-6)	-1.2
1938	Pit-N	29	35	3	8	0	0	0	4	8	5	.229	.372	.229	601	68	-1	3			1.000	-1	O-10(5-0-5)	-0.3
1939	NY-N	10	34	3	8	0	0	0	5	5	3	.235	.333	.235	569	55	-2	0			1.000	-1	O-10(0-0-10)	-0.3
1944	Chi-A	62	162	18	41	8	5	0	15	13	10	.253	.313	.364	677	94	-2	2	0	0	.974	-3	O-40(35-0-5)	-0.6
1945	Chi-A	130	486	74	147	19	10	4	58	48	41	.302	.366	.407	774	128	17	18	3	**3**	.971	1	*O-124(124-0-0)	1.4
Total	6	322	990	142	273	35	19	7	116	101	97	.276	.345	.371	715	104	5	23	3		.968	-7	O-249(222-1-26)	-1.1

■ BOB DIDIER Didier, Robert Daniel b: 2/16/49, Hattiesburg, Miss. BB/TR, 6', 190 lbs. Deb: 4/7/69 C

YEAR	TM/L	G	AB	R	H	2B	3B	HR	RBI	BB	SO	AVG	OBP	SLG	OPS	OPS+	BR+	SB	CS	SBR	FA	FR	G/POS	TPR
1969	*Atl-N	114	352	30	90	16	1	0	32	34	39	.256	.321	.307	628	76	-10	1	3	-1	.994	-2	*C-114	-0.9
1970	Atl-N	57	168	9	25	2	1	0	7	12	11	.149	.210	.173	383	3	-23	1	0	0	.988	1	C-57	-2.0
1971	Atl-N	51	155	9	34	4	1	0	5	6	17	.219	.248	.258	507	41	-12	0	0	0	1.000	3	C-50	-0.7
1972	Atl-N	13	40	5	12	2	1	0	5	2	4	.300	.349	.400	749	103	0	0	0	0	1.000	2	C-11	0.3
1973	Det-A	7	22	3	10	1	0	0	1	3	0	.455	.520	.500	1020	177	2	0	0	0	1.000	2	/C-7	0.5
1974	Bos-A	5	14	0	1	0	0	0	1	2	1	.071	.188	.071	259	-22	-2	0	0	0	.968	1	/C-5	-0.1
Total	6	247	751	56	172	25	4	0	51	59	72	.229	.287	.273	560	55	-45	2	3	-1	.994	6	C-244	-2.9

■ ERNIE DIEHL Diehl, Ernest Guy b: 10/2/1877, Cincinnati, Ohio d: 11/6/58, Miami, Fla. BR/TR, 6'1", 190 lbs. Deb: 5/31/03

YEAR	TM/L	G	AB	R	H	2B	3B	HR	RBI	BB	SO	AVG	OBP	SLG	OPS	OPS+	BR+	SB	CS	SBR	FA	FR	G/POS	TPR
1903	Pit-N	1	3	0	1	0	0	0	0	0		.333	.333	.333	667	87	-0	0			.000	-1	/O-1(1-0-0)	-0.1
1904	Pit-N	12	37	6	6	0	0	0	4	6		.162	.311	.162	473	46	-2	3			1.000	1	/O-7(2-0-5),S-4	-0.1
1906	Bos-N	3	11	1	5	0	1	0	0	0		.455	.455	.636	1091	247	2	0			1.000	0	/O-2(2-0-0),S-1	0.2
1909	Bos-N	1	4	1	2	1	0	0	0	0		.500	.500	.750	1250	275	1	0			.800	1	/O-1(1-0-0)	0.1
Total	4	17	55	8	14	1	1	0	4	6		.255	.349	.309	658	101	0	3			.944	2	/O-11(6-0-5),S-5	0.1

■ CHUCK DIERING Diering, Charles Edward Allen b: 2/5/23, St.Louis, Mo. BR/TR, 5'10", 165 lbs. Deb: 4/15/47 Career OF: (60-LF 527-CF 47-RF)

YEAR	TM/L	G	AB	R	H	2B	3B	HR	RBI	BB	SO	AVG	OBP	SLG	OPS	OPS+	BR+	SB	CS	SBR	FA	FR	G/POS	TPR
1947	StL-N	105	74	22	16	3	1	2	11	19	22	.216	.383	.365	748	95	0	3			1.000	-22	O-75(13-31-31)	-2.2
1948	StL-N	7	7	2	0	0	0	0	0	2	2	.000	.222	.000	222	-33	-1	1			1.000	-1	/O-5(5-0-0)	-0.2
1949	StL-N	131	369	60	97	21	8	3	38	35	49	.263	.328	.388	716	87	-7	1			.987	-2	*O-124(0-123-1)	-1.1
1950	StL-N	89	204	34	51	12	0	3	18	35	38	.250	.360	.353	713	84	-4	1			.989	-1	O-81(0-78-3)	-0.6
1951	StL-N	64	85	9	22	5	1	0	8	6	15	.259	.308	.341	649	74	-3	0	1	-0	1.000	-8	O-44(6-33-5)	-1.2
1952	NY-N	41	23	2	4	1	1	0	2	4	3	.174	.296	.304	601	66	-1	0	2	-1	1.000	-10	O-36(27-4-5)	-1.2
1954	Bal-A	128	418	35	108	14	1	2	29	56	57	.258	.351	.311	662	89	-4	3	7	-2	.983	13	*O-119(0-119-0)	0.1
1955	Bal-A	137	371	38	95	16	2	3	31	57	45	.256	.355	.334	689	93	-2	5	8	-2	.976	3	*O-107C,3-34,S-12	-0.4
1956	Bal-A	50	97	15	18	4	0	1	4	23	19	.186	.342	.258	599	65	-4	2	5	-1	1.000	-4	O-40(7-34-2)/3-2	-1.1
Total	9	752	1648	217	411	76	14	14	141	237	250	.249	.346	.338	684	86	-27	16	23		.987	-31	O-631C/3-36,S-12	-7.9

■ DICK DIETZ Dietz, Richard Allen b: 9/18/41, Crawfordsville, Ind. BR/TR, 6'1", 195 lbs. Deb: 6/18/66

YEAR	TM/L	G	AB	R	H	2B	3B	HR	RBI	BB	SO	AVG	OBP	SLG	OPS	OPS+	BR+	SB	CS	SBR	FA	FR	G/POS	TPR
1966	SF-N	13	23	1	1	0	0	0	0	0	9	.043	.083	.043	127	-62	-5	0	0	0	1.000	-1	/C-6	-0.6
1967	SF-N	56	120	10	27	3	0	4	19	25	44	.225	.363	.350	713	106	2	0	1	-0	.983	0	C-43	0.4
1968	SF-N	98	301	21	82	14	2	6	38	34	68	.272	.348	.392	740	122	9	1	1	-0	.976	-8	C-90	0.6
1969	SF-N	79	244	28	56	8	1	11	35	53	53	.230	.373	.406	779	120	8	0	0	0	.973	-5	C-73	0.7
1970	SF-N★	148	493	82	148	36	2	22	107	109	106	.300	.430	.515	945	154	42	0	1	-0	.984	-18	*C-139	3.0
1971	*SF-N	142	453	58	114	19	0	19	72	97	86	.252	.388	.419	808	131	22	1	3	-1	.982	-12	*C-135	1.7
1972	LA-N	27	56	4	9	1	0	1	6	14	11	.161	.329	.232	561	63	-2	2	0	0	1.000	3	C-22	0.2
1973	Atl-N	83	139	22	41	8	1	3	24	49	25	.295	.479	.432	910	143	12	0	0	0	.989	1	1-36,C-20	1.2
Total	8	646	1829	226	478	89	6	66	301	381	402	.261	.392	.425	817	130	88	4	6	-1	.980	-39	C-528/1-36	7.2

■ ROY DIETZEL Dietzel, Leroy Louis b: 1/9/31, Baltimore, Md. BR/TR, 6', 190 lbs. Deb: 9/2/54

YEAR	TM/L	G	AB	R	H	2B	3B	HR	RBI	BB	SO	AVG	OBP	SLG	OPS	OPS+	BR+	SB	CS	SBR	FA	FR	G/POS	TPR
1954	Was-A	9	21	1	5	0	0	0	1	5	4	.238	.385	.238	623	78	-0	0	0	0	.960	-2	/2-7,3-2	-0.2

■ JAY DIFANI Difani, Clarence Joseph b: 12/21/23, Crystal City, Mo. BR/TR, 6', 170 lbs. Deb: 4/23/48

YEAR	TM/L	G	AB	R	H	2B	3B	HR	RBI	BB	SO	AVG	OBP	SLG	OPS	OPS+	BR+	SB	CS	SBR	FA	FR	G/POS	TPR
1948	Was-A	2	2	0	0	0	0	0	0	0	2	.000	.000	.000	0	-99	-1	0	0	0	.000	0	H	-0.1
1949	Was-A	2	1	0	1	1	0	0	0	0	0	1.000	1.000	2.000	3000	699	1	0	0	0	1.000	0	/2-1	0.1
Total	2	4	3	0	1	1	0	0	0	0	2	.333	.333	.667	1000	166	0	0	0	0	1.000	0	/2-1	0.0

■ MIKE DIFELICE Difelice, Michael William b: 5/28/69, Philadelphia, Pa. BR/TR, 6'2", 205 lbs. Deb: 9/1/96

YEAR	TM/L	G	AB	R	H	2B	3B	HR	RBI	BB	SO	AVG	OBP	SLG	OPS	OPS+	BR+	SB	CS	SBR	FA	FR	G/POS	TPR
1996	StL-N	4	7	0	2	1	0	0	2	0	1	.286	.286	.429	714	86	-0	0	0	0	1.000	1	/C-4	0.1
1997	StL-N	93	260	16	62	10	1	4	30	19	61	.238	.298	.331	629	65	-13	1	1	-0	.991	22	C-91/1-1	1.2
1998	TB-A	84	248	17	57	12	3	3	23	15	56	.230	.277	.339	615	58	-16	0	0	0	.993	14	C-84	0.3
1999	TB-A	51	179	21	55	11	0	6	27	8	23	.307	.347	.469	817	105	1	0	0	0	.987	7	C-51	1.0
2000	TB-A	60	204	23	49	13	1	6	19	12	40	.240	.282	.402	684	71	-10	0	0	0	.980	7	C-59	0.1
Total	5	292	898	77	225	47	5	19	101	54	181	.251	.298	.378	676	73	-38	1	1	-0	.988	50	C-289/1-1	2.7

■ STEVE DIGNAN Dignan, Stephen E. b: 4/16/1859, Boston, Mass. d: 7/11/1881, Boston, Mass. Deb: 6/1/1880

YEAR	TM/L	G	AB	R	H	2B	3B	HR	RBI	BB	SO	AVG	OBP	SLG	OPS	OPS+	BR+	SB	CS	SBR	FA	FR	G/POS	TPR
1880	Bos-N	8	34	4	11	1	0	0	4	0	3	.324	.324	.353	676	133	1				.684	0	/O-8(1-0-7)	0.1
	Wor-N	3	10	1	3	0	1	0	2	0	1	.300	.300	.500	800	153	0				.750	-1	/O-3(0-3-0)	-0.1
	Yr	11	44	5	14	1	1	0	6	0	4	.318	.318	.386	705	137	2				.696	-1	O-11(1-3-7)	0.0

■ DON DILLARD Dillard, David Donald b: 1/8/37, Greenville, S.C. BL/TR, 6'1", 200 lbs. Deb: 4/24/59

YEAR	TM/L	G	AB	R	H	2B	3B	HR	RBI	BB	SO	AVG	OBP	SLG	OPS	OPS+	BR+	SB	CS	SBR	FA	FR	G/POS	TPR
1959	Cle-A	10	10	0	4	0	0	0	1	0	2	.400	.400	.400	800	125	0	0	0	0	.000	0	H	0.0
1960	Cle-A	6	7	0	1	0	0	0	0	1	3	.143	.250	.143	393	9	-1	0	0	0	.000	-0	/O-1(0-0-1)	-0.1
1961	Cle-A	74	147	27	40	5	0	7	17	15	28	.272	.340	.449	788	112	2	0	0	0	1.000	-4	O-39(14-24-1)	-0.3
1962	Cle-A	95	174	22	40	5	1	5	14	11	25	.230	.276	.356	632	71	-8	0	1	-0	.965	-10	O-50(28-20-4)	-2.0
1963	Mil-N	67	119	9	28	6	4	1	12	5	21	.235	.272	.378	650	86	-2	0	2	-1	.951	-0	O-30(24-5-1)	-0.5
1965	Mil-N	20	19	1	3	0	0	1	3	0	6	.158	.158	.316	474	30	-2	0	0	0	.000	-0	/O-1(1-0-0)	-0.2
Total	6	272	476	59	116	16	5	14	47	32	85	.244	.293	.387	679	86	-10	0	3	-1	.976	-15	O-121(67-49-7)	-3.1

■ PAT DILLARD Dillard, Robert Lee b: 6/12/1873, Chattanooga, Tenn d: 7/22/07, Denver, Colo. BL/TR, 6', 180 lbs. Deb: 4/21/00

YEAR	TM/L	G	AB	R	H	2B	3B	HR	RBI	BB	SO	AVG	OBP	SLG	OPS	OPS+	BR+	SB	CS	SBR	FA	FR	G/POS	TPR
1900	StL-N	57	183	24	42	5	2	0	12	13		.230	.284	.279	563	56	-11	7			.942	-4	O-26(0-20-6),3-21/S-3	-1.5

■ STEVE DILLARD Dillard, Stephen Bradley b: 2/8/51, Memphis, Tenn. BR/TR, 6'1", 180 lbs. Deb: 9/28/75

YEAR	TM/L	G	AB	R	H	2B	3B	HR	RBI	BB	SO	AVG	OBP	SLG	OPS	OPS+	BR+	SB	CS	SBR	FA	FR	G/POS	TPR
1975	Bos-A	1	5	2	2	0	0	0	0	0	0	.400	.400	.400	800	117	0	1	0	0	1.000	1	/2-1	0.1
1976	Bos-A	57	167	22	46	14	0	1	15	17	20	.275	.342	.377	720	99	-0	6	4	-0	.918	-4	3-18,2-17,S-12,/D-7	-0.2
1977	Bos-A	66	141	22	34	7	0	1	13	7	13	.241	.277	.312	589	54	-9	4	3	-0	.967	8	2-45/S-9,D-6	0.1
1978	Det-A	56	130	21	29	5	2	0	7	6	11	.223	.257	.292	550	53	-8	1	2	-0	.958	17	2-41/D-4	1.0
1979	Chi-N	89	166	31	47	6	1	5	24	17	24	.283	.353	.422	775	101	0	1	0	0	.988	9	2-60/3-9	1.2
1980	Chi-N	100	244	31	55	8	1	4	27	20	54	.225	.287	.316	602	63	-12	2	2	-0	.908	2	3-51,2-38/S-2	-0.9
1981	Chi-N	53	119	18	26	7	1	2	11	8	20	.218	.268	.345	612	70	-5	0	0	0	.974	3	2-32/3-7,S-2	-0.1
1982	Chi-A	16	41	1	7	3	1	0	5	1	5	.171	.190	.293	483	30	-4	0	1	-0	.959	3	2-16	-0.1
Total	8	438	1013	148	246	50	6	13	102	76	147	.243	.297	.343	640	73	-37	15	12	-1	.973	37	2-250/3-85,S-25,D	1.1

■ PICKLES DILLHOEFER Dillhoefer, William Martin b: 10/13/1894, Cleveland, Ohio d: 2/23/22, St.Louis, Mo. BR/TR, 5'7", 154 lbs. Deb: 4/16/17

YEAR	TM/L	G	AB	R	H	2B	3B	HR	RBI	BB	SO	AVG	OBP	SLG	OPS	OPS+	BR+	SB	CS	SBR	FA	FR	G/POS	TPR
1917	Chi-N	42	95	3	12	1	1	0	8	2	9	.126	.144	.158	302	-7	-12	1			.985	8	C-37	-0.2
1918	Phi-N	8	11	0	1	0	0	0	0	1	1	.091	.167	.091	258	-19	-2	2			.923	-1	/C-6	-0.2
1919	StL-N	45	108	11	23	3	2	0	12	8	6	.213	.267	.278	545	68	-4	5			.967	-5	C-39	-0.7

YEAR	TM/L	G	AB	R	H	2B	3B	HR	RBI	BB	SO	AVG	OBP	SLG	OPS	OPS+	BR+	SB	CS	SBR	FA	FR	G/POS	TPR
1920	StL-N	76	224	26	59	8	3	0	13	13	7	.263	.304	.326	630	84	-5	2	1	0	.953	-0	C-74	0.0
1921	StL-N	76	162	19	39	4	4	0	15	11	7	.241	.289	.315	604	61	-9	2	1	0	.953	2	C-69	-0.4
Total	5	247	600	59	134	16	10	0	48	35	30	.223	.266	.283	549	58	-32	12	2		.961	4	C-225	-1.5
■ BOB DILLINGER	Dillinger, Robert Bernard "Duke" b: 9/17/18, Glendale, Cal. BR/TR, 5'11.5", 170 lbs. Deb: 4/16/46																							
1946	StL-A	83	225	33	63	6	3	0	11	19	32	.280	.341	.333	675	85	-4	8	1	1	.922	-3	3-54/S-1	-0.6
1947	StL-A	137	571	70	168	23	6	3	37	56	38	.294	.361	.371	733	102	2	**34**	13	**3**	.958	2	*3-137	0.7
1948	StL-A	153	644	110	**207**	34	10	2	44	65	34	.321	.385	.415	799	110	9	**28**	11	**2**	.955	-16	*3-153	-0.4
1949	StL-A★	137	544	68	176	22	13	1	51	51	40	.324	.385	.417	802	108	6	**20**	14	-1	.938	-25	*3-133	-2.0
1950	Phi-A	84	356	55	110	21	9	3	41	31	20	.309	.366	.444	810	109	4	5	3	0	.957	-2	3-84	0.1
	Pit-N	58	222	23	64	8	2	1	9	13	22	.288	.328	.356	684	77	-7	4			.957	2	3-51	-0.6
1951	Pit-N	12	43	3	10	3	0	0	0	1	0	.233	.250	.302	552	47	-3	2	0	0	.963	-2	3-10	-0.5
	Chi-A	89	299	39	90	6	4	0	20	15	17	.301	.337	.348	684	87	-6	5	5	-1	.930	-6	3-70	-1.2
Total	6	753	2904	401	888	123	47	10	213	251	203	.306	.363	.391	754	100	1	106	47		.948	-50	3-692/S-1	-4.5
■ POP DILLON	Dillon, Frank Edward b: 10/17/1873, Normal, Ill. d: 9/12/31, Pasadena, Cal. BL/TR, 6'1", 185 lbs. Deb: 9/8/1899																							
1899	Pit-N	30	121	21	31	5	0	0	20	5		.256	.286	.298	583	60	-7	5			.988	1	1-30	-0.5
1900	Pit-N	5	18	3	2	1	0	0	1	0		.111	.111	.167	278	-24	-3	0			.981	1	/1-5	-0.2
1901	Det-A	74	281	40	81	14	6	1	42	15		.288	.324	.391	716	94	-3	14			.979	3	1-74	-0.2
1902	Det-A	66	243	21	50	6	3	0	22	16		.206	.255	.255	510	41	-19	2			.976	5	1-66	-1.5
	Bal-A	2	7	1	2	0	1	0	0	2		.286	.444	.571	1016	173	1	0			.960	0	/1-2	0.1
	Yr	68	250	22	52	6	4	0	22	18		.208	.261	.264	525	45	-19	2			.975	6	1-68	-1.4
1904	Bro-N	135	511	60	132	18	6	0	31	40		.258	.313	.317	630	97	-1	13			.982	3	*1-134	-0.1
Total	5	312	1181	146	298	44	16	1	116	78		.252	.299	.319	618	79	-33	34			.980	14	1-311	-2.4
■ JOHN DILLON	Dillon, John Deb: 5/8/1875 F																							
1875	RS-n	1	1	0	0	0	0	0	0	0	0	.000	.000	.000	0	-99	-0	0	0	0	.000	0	/S-1	0.0
■ PACKY DILLON	Dillon, Packard Andrew b: St.Louis, Mo. d: 1/8/1890, Guelph, Ont., Canada Deb: 5/4/1875 F																							
1875	RS-n	3	13	1	3	1	0	0	1	0	0	.231	.231	.308	538	94	0	0	0	0	.923	-2	/C-3	-0.2
■ MIGUEL DILONE	Dilone, Miguel Angel (Reyes) b: 11/1/54, Santiago, D.R. BB/TR, 6', 160 lbs. Deb: 9/2/74 Career OF: (380-LF 103-CF 75-RF)																							
1974	Pit-N	12	2	3	0	0	0	0	0	1	0	.000	.333	.000	333	-1	-0	2	0	0	1.000	-1	/O-2(0-1-1)	-0.1
1975	Pit-N	18	6	8	0	0	0	0	0	0	1	.000	.000	.000	0	-99	-2	2	2	-0	1.000	-0	/O-2(0-2-0)	-0.2
1976	Pit-N	16	17	7	4	0	0	0	0	0	0	.235	.235	.235	471	34	-1	5	1	1	1.000	1	/O-3(1-2-0)	0.0
1977	Pit-N	29	44	5	6	0	0	0	0	2	3	.136	.174	.136	310	-15	-7	12	0	3	1.000	-3	O-17(9-7-2)	-0.7
1978	Oak-A	135	258	34	59	8	0	1	14	23	30	.229	.294	.271	566	63	-12	50	23	3	.985	-7	O-99L,D-11/3-3	-2.0
1979	Oak-A	30	91	15	17	1	2	1	6	6	7	.187	.237	.275	512	40	-8	6	5	-0	.959	-2	O-25(5-0-20)	-1.1
	Chi-N	43	36	14	11	0	0	0	1	2	5	.306	.342	.306	648	71	-1	15	5	2	1.000	-5	O-22(4-18-0)	-0.5
1980	Cle-A	132	528	82	180	30	9	0	40	28	45	.341	.376	.432	808	120	15	61	18	7	.973	-0	*O-118(90-23-13),D-11	1.6
1981	Cle-A	72	269	33	78	5	5	0	19	18	28	.290	.334	.346	680	98	-1	29	10	3	.971	6	O-56(56-0-0),D-11	0.5
1982	Cle-A	104	379	50	89	12	3	3	25	25	36	.235	.286	.306	592	63	-19	33	5	6	.964	-3	O-97(96-1-0)/D-1	-2.1
1983	Cle-A	32	68	15	13	3	1	0	7	10	5	.191	.295	.265	560	53	-4	5	1	1	1.000	1	O-19(19-0-0)	-0.3
	Chi-A	4	3	1	0	0	0	0	0	0	0	.000	.000	.000	0	-96	-1	1	0	0	1.000	-1	/O-2(0-2-0),D-2	-0.1
	Yr	36	71	16	13	3	1	0	7	10	5	.183	.284	.254	537	47	-5	6	1	1	1.000	0	O-21(19-2-0)/D-2	-0.4
	Pit-N	7	0	1	0	0	0	0	0	0	0	—	—	—	—	—	0	2	0	0	.000	0	/R	0.0
1984	Mon-N	88	169	28	47	8	2	1	10	17	18	.278	.348	.367	714	106	1	27	2	5	.987	1	O-41(41-0-0)	0.7
1985	Mon-N	51	84	10	16	0	2	0	6	6	11	.190	.244	.238	483	38	-7	7	3	0	.974	-2	O-22(8-13-2)	-1.0
	SD-N	27	46	8	10	0	1	0	1	4	8	.217	.280	.261	541	53	-3	10	3	1	.917	-2	O-14(4-9-1)	-0.4
	Yr	78	130	18	26	0	3	0	7	10	19	.200	.257	.246	503	43	-10	17	6	2	.952	-4	O-36(12-22-3)	-1.4
Total	12	800	2000	314	530	67	25	6	129	142	197	.265	.316	.333	648	81	-50	267	78	31	.975	-16	O-539L/D-36,3-3	-5.7
■ DOM DiMAGGIO	DiMaggio, Dominic Paul "The Little Professor" b: 2/12/17, San Francisco, Cal. BR/TR, 5'9", 168 lbs. Deb: 4/16/40 F																							
1940	Bos-A	108	418	81	126	32	6	8	46	41	46	.301	.367	.464	831	109	6	7	6	-1	.977	10	O-94(11-59-26)	1.1
1941	Bos-A★	144	584	117	165	37	6	8	58	90	57	.283	.385	.408	792	107	9	13	6	1	.964	6	*O-144(0-144-0)	1.2
1942	Bos-A☆	151	622	110	178	36	8	14	48	70	52	.286	.364	.437	801	121	17	16	10	0	.987	17	*O-151(0-151-0)	3.0
1946	*Bos-A★	142	534	85	169	24	7	7	73	66	58	.316	.393	.427	820	122	17	10	6	0	.985	7	*O-142(0-142-0)	2.2
1947	Bos-A	136	513	75	145	21	5	8	71	74	62	.283	.376	.390	766	105	6	10	6	0	.977	19	*O-134(0-134-0)	2.2
1948	Bos-A	155	648	127	185	40	4	9	87	101	58	.285	.383	.401	785	104	5	10	2	2	.981	16	*O-155(0-155-0)	1.8
1949	Bos-A★	145	605	126	186	34	5	8	60	96	55	.307	.404	.420	824	110	11	9	7	-0	.977	14	*O-144(0-144-0)	2.0
1950	Bos-A★	141	588	**131**	193	30	**11**	7	70	82	68	.328	.414	.452	866	111	12	**15**	4	**2**	.983	9	*O-140(0-140-0)	1.7
1951	Bos-A★	146	639	**113**	189	34	4	12	72	73	53	.296	.370	.418	788	103	3	4	7	-2	.973	3	*O-146(0-146-0)	0.0
1952	Bos-A★	128	486	81	143	20	1	6	33	57	61	.294	.371	.377	747	100	2	6	8	-1	.975	0	*O-123(0-123-0)	-0.3
1953	Bos-A	3	3	0	1	0	0	0	0	0	1	.333	.333	.333	667	76	-0	0	0	0	.000	0	H	0.0
Total	11	1399	5640	1046	1680	308	57	87	618	750	571	.298	.383	.419	802	109	87	100	62	0	.978	101	*O-1373(11-1338-26)	14.9
■ JOE DiMAGGIO	DiMaggio, Joseph Paul "Joltin' Joe" or "The Yankee Clipper" b: 11/25/14, Martinez, Cal. d: 3/8/99, Hollywood, Fla. BR/TR, 6'2", 193 lbs. Deb: 5/3/36 FCH Career OF: (66-LF 1638-CF 18-RF)																							
1936	*NY-A★	138	637	132	206	44	**15**	29	125	24	39	.323	.352	.576	928	130	24	4	0	1	.978	15	*O-138(66-55-18)	2.9
1937	*NY-A★	151	621	**151**	215	35	15	**46**	167	64	37	.346	.412	**.673**	1085	168	60	3	0	1	.962	11	*O-150(0-150-0)	6.2
1938	*NY-A★	145	599	129	194	32	13	32	140	59	21	.324	.386	.581	967	140	33	6	1	1	.963	4	*O-145(0-145-0)	3.1
1939	*NY-A★	120	462	108	176	32	6	30	126	52	20	**.381**	.448	.671	1119	**185**	58	3	0	1	.986	8	*O-117(0-117-0)	**5.8**
1940	NY-A★	132	508	93	179	28	9	31	133	61	30	**.352**	.425	.626	1051	**176**	**56**	1	2	-0	.978	1	*O-130(0-130-0)	**4.9**
1941	*NY-A★	139	541	122	193	43	11	30	**125**	76	13	.357	.440	.643	1083	186	66	4	2	0	.978	10	*O-139(0-139-0)	6.9
1942	*NY-A★	154	610	123	186	29	13	21	114	68	36	.305	.376	.498	875	148	37	4	2	0	.981	2	*O-154(0-154-0)	3.6
1946	NY-A☆	132	503	81	146	20	8	25	95	59	24	.290	.367	.511	878	142	27	1	0	0	.982	4	*O-131(0-131-0)	2.8
1947	*NY-A★	141	534	97	168	31	10	20	97	64	32	.315	.391	.522	913	154	38	3	0	1	**.997**	-13	*O-139(0-139-0)	2.2
1948	NY-A★	153	594	110	190	26	11	**39**	**155**	67	30	.320	.396	.598	994	164	50	1	1	-0	.972	4	*O-152(0-152-0)	4.7
1949	*NY-A★	76	272	58	94	14	6	14	67	55	18	.346	.459	.596	1055	178	32	0	1	-0	.985	-1	O-76(0-76-0)	2.7
1950	*NY-A★	139	525	114	158	33	10	32	122	80	33	.301	.394	**.585**	979	152	39	0	0	0	.976	1	*O-137(0-137-0)/1-1	3.3
1951	*NY-A☆	116	415	72	109	22	4	12	71	61	36	.263	.365	.422	787	117	10	0	0	0	.990	4	*O-113(0-113-0)	1.1
Total	13	1736	6821	1390	2214	389	131	361	1537	790	369	.325	.398	.579	977	156	529	30	9	3	.978	51	*O-1721C/1-1	50.2
■ VINCE DiMAGGIO	DiMaggio, Vincent Paul b: 9/6/12, Martinez, Cal. d: 10/3/86, N.Hollywood, Cal. BR/TR, 5'11", 183 lbs. Deb: 4/19/37 F Career OF: (4-LF 1070-CF 7-RF)																							
1937	Bos-N	132	493	56	126	18	4	13	69	39	111	.256	.311	.387	699	98	-3	8			.982	16	*O-130(0-129-1)	0.9
1938	Bos-N	150	540	71	123	28	3	14	61	65	134	.228	.313	.369	682	96	-3	11			.973	13	*O-149(0-149-0)/2-1	0.6
1939	Cin-N	8	14	1	1	1	0	0	2	2	10	.071	.188	.143	330	-10	-2	0			1.000	-0	/O-7(3-3-1)	-0.2
1940	Cin-N	2	4	2	1	0	0	0	0	1	0	.250	.400	.250	650	82	-0	0			1.000	0	/O-1(0-0-1)	0.0
	Pit-N	110	356	59	103	26	0	19	54	37	83	.289	.364	.522	887	143	20	11			.979	-2	*O-108(1-103-4)	1.6
	Yr	112	360	61	104	26	0	19	54	38	83	.289	.365	.519	884	142	20	11			.979	-2	*O-109(1-103-5)	1.6
1941	Pit-N	151	528	73	141	27	5	21	100	68	100	.267	.354	.456	810	128	19	10			.976	7	*O-151(0-151-0)	2.2
1942	Pit-N	143	496	57	118	22	3	15	75	52	87	.238	.311	.385	697	101	-1	10			.978	**20**	*O-138(0-138-0)	1.7
1943	Pit-N★	157	580	64	144	41	2	15	88	70	126	.248	.329	.403	733	107	5	11			.985	15	*O-156(0-156-0)/S-1	1.6
1944	Pit-N★	109	342	41	82	20	4	9	50	33	83	.240	.307	.401	707	94	-4	6			.984	-6	*O-101(0-101-0)/3-1	-1.2
1945	Phi-N	127	452	64	116	25	3	19	84	43	91	.257	.321	.451	773	117	7	12			.994	10	*O-121(0-121-0)	1.4
1946	Phi-N	6	19	1	4	1	0	0	1	0	7	.211	.211	.263	474	35	-2	0			1.000	-1	/O-6(0-6-0)	-0.3
	NY-N	15	25	2	0	0	0	0	0	2	5	.000	.074	.000	74	-78	-6	0			.967	-1	O-13(0-13-0)	-0.8
	Yr	21	44	3	4	1	0	0	1	2	12	.091	.130	.114	244	-31	-8	0			.975	-2	O-19(0-19-0)	-1.1
Total	10	1110	3849	491	959	209	24	125	584	412	837	.249	.324	.413	737	108	30	79			.981	70	*O-1081C/3-1,S-1,2	7.5

YEAR	TM/L	G	AB	R	H	2B	3B	HR	RBI	BB	SO	AVG	OBP	SLG	OPS	OPS+	BR+	SB	CS	SBR	FA	FR	G/POS	TPR
■ **MIKE DIMMEL** Dimmel, Michael Wayne b: 10/16/54, Albert Lea, Minn. BR/TR, 6', 180 lbs. Deb: 9/2/77																								
1977	Bal-A	25	5	8	0	0	0	0	0	0	1	.000	.000	.000	0	-99	-1	1	0	0	1.000	-6	O-23(0-1-22)	-0.7
1978	Bal-A	8	0	2	0	0	0	0	0	0	0	—	—	—	—	—	0	0	1	-0	.667	-3	/O-7(1-1-5)	-0.3
1979	StL-N	6	3	1	1	0	0	0	0	0	0	.333	.333	.333	667	82	-0	0	1	-0	1.000	-2	/O-5(5-1-0)	-0.2
Total	3	39	8	11	1	0	0	0	0	0	1	.125	.125	.125	250	-33	-1	1	2	-0	.952	-11	/O-35(6-3-27)	-1.2
■ **KERRY DINEEN** Dineen, Kerry Michael b: 7/1/52, Englewood, N.J. BL/TL, 5'11", 165 lbs. Deb: 6/14/75																								
1975	NY-A	7	22	3	8	1	0	0	1	2	1	.364	.417	.409	826	136	1	0	0	0	1.000	0	/O-7(0-7-0)	0.1
1976	NY-A	4	7	0	2	0	0	0	1	1	2	.286	.375	.286	661	96	0	1	1	-0	.900	-0	/O-4(0-2-2)	-0.1
1978	Phi-N	5	8	0	2	1	0	0	0	1	0	.250	.333	.375	708	97	-0	0	0	0	1.000	-0	/O-1(1-0-0)	0.0
Total	3	16	37	3	12	2	0	0	2	4	3	.324	.390	.378	769	120	1	1	1	-0	.967	-0	/O-12(1-9-2)	0.0
■ **VANCE DINGES** Dinges, Vance George b: 5/29/15, Elizabeth, N.J. d: 10/4/90, Harrisonburg, Va. BL/TL, 6'2", 175 lbs. Deb: 4/17/45																								
1945	Phi-N	109	397	46	114	15	4	1	36	35	17	.287	.346	.353	699	97	-1	5			.986	-1	O-65(16-18-33),1-42	-0.7
1946	Phi-N	50	104	7	32	5	1	1	10	9	12	.308	.363	.404	767	121	3	2			.985	-0	1-26/O-1(1-0-0)	0.2
Total	2	159	501	53	146	20	5	2	46	44	29	.291	.350	.363	713	102	2	7			.986	-1	/1-68,O-66(17-18-33)	-0.5
■ **BOB DiPIETRO** DiPietro, Robert Louis Paul b: 9/1/27, San Francisco, Cal BR/TR, 5'11", 185 lbs. Deb: 9/23/51																								
1951	Bos-A	4	11	0	1	0	0	0	0	1	1	.091	.167	.091	258	-26	-2	0	0	0	.833	0	/O-3(0-0-3)	-0.2
■ **GARY DiSARCINA** DiSarcina, Gary Thomas b: 11/19/67, Malden, Mass. BR/TR, 6'1", 178 lbs. Deb: 9/23/89																								
1989	Cal-A	2	0	0	0	0	0	0	0	0	0	—	—	—	—	—	0	0	0	0	.000	0	/S-1	0.0
1990	Cal-A	18	57	8	8	1	1	0	0	3	10	.140	.183	.193	376	5	-7	1	0	0	.940	2	S-14/2-3	-0.4
1991	Cal-A	18	57	5	12	2	0	0	3	3	4	.211	.274	.246	520	45	-4	0	0	0	.915	-1	S-10/2-7,3-2	-0.4
1992	Cal-A	157	518	48	128	19	0	3	42	20	50	.247	.284	.301	586	64	-25	9	7	-0	.967	12	*S-157	-0.2
1993	Cal-A	126	416	44	99	20	1	3	45	15	38	.238	.275	.313	587	56	-26	5	7	-1	.975	-13	*S-126	-2.9
1994	Cal-A	112	389	53	101	14	2	3	33	18	28	.260	.296	.329	625	60	-23	3	7	-2	.983	8	*S-110	-0.7
1995	Cal-A★	99	362	61	111	28	6	5	41	20	25	.307	.346	.459	805	108	4	7	4	0	.986	-4	S-98	0.7
1996	Cal-A	150	536	62	137	26	4	5	48	21	36	.256	.286	.347	633	59	-34	2	1	0	.971	5	*S-150	-1.5
1997	Ana-A	154	549	52	135	28	2	4	47	17	29	.246	.274	.326	600	56	-36	7	8	-1	.977	-9	*S-153	-3.2
1998	Ana-A	157	551	73	158	39	3	3	56	21	51	.287	.322	.385	707	82	-14	11	7	-0	.980	-6	*S-157	-0.7
1999	Ana-A	81	271	32	62	7	1	1	29	15	32	.229	.274	.273	547	41	-24	2	2	-0	.963	0	S-81	-1.6
2000	Ana-A	12	38	6	15	2	0	1	11	1	3	.395	.425	.526	951	138	2	0	1	-0	.934	7	S-12	0.8
Total	12	1086	3744	444	966	186	20	28	355	154	306	.258	.294	.341	635	66	-189	47	44	-5	.973	-0	*S-1069/2-10,3-2	-10.1
■ **BENNY DISTEFANO** Distefano, Benito James b: 1/23/62, Brooklyn, N.Y. BL/TL, 6'1", 195 lbs. Deb: 5/18/84 Career OF: (14-LF 0-CF 32-RF)																								
1984	Pit-N	45	78	10	13	1	2	3	9	5	13	.167	.226	.346	572	59	-5	0	1	-0	.946	1	O-20(7-0-15),1-17	-0.5
1986	Pit-N	31	39	3	7	1	0	1	5	1	5	.179	.200	.282	482	31	-4	0	0	0	1.000	-1	/O-9(0-0-9),1-1	-0.5
1988	Pit-N	16	29	6	10	3	1	1	6	3	4	.345	.406	.621	1027	194	3	0	0	0	1.000	-0	/1-5,O-2(0-0-2)	0.3
1989	Pit-N	96	154	12	38	8	0	2	15	17	30	.247	.333	.338	671	96	-0	1	0	0	.981	-3	1-48/C-3,O-1(0-0-1)	-0.6
1992	Hou-N	52	60	4	14	0	2	0	7	5	14	.233	.303	.300	603	75	-2	0	0	0	1.000	-0	O-12(7-0-5)/1-6	-0.3
Total	5	240	360	35	82	13	5	7	42	31	66	.228	.298	.350	648	85	-7	1	1	-0	.985	-3	/1-77,O-44R,C-3	-1.6
■ **DUTCH DISTEL** Distel, George Adam b: 4/15/1896, Madison, Ind. d: 2/12/67, Madison, Ind. BR/TR, 5'9", 165 lbs. Deb: 6/21/18																								
1918	StL-N	8	17	3	3	1	1	0	1	2	3	.176	.263	.353	616	90	-0	0			.900	-2	/2-5,S-2,O-1(0-0-1)	-0.2
■ **JACK DITTMER** Dittmer, John Douglas b: 1/10/28, Elkader, Iowa BL/TR, 6'1", 175 lbs. Deb: 6/17/52																								
1952	Bos-N	93	326	26	63	7	2	7	41	26	26	.193	.255	.291	546	53	-21	1	0	0	.982	6	2-90	-1.1
1953	Mil-N	138	504	54	134	22	1	9	63	18	35	.266	.293	.367	660	75	-20	1	0	0	.965	-29	*2-138	-3.7
1954	Mil-N	66	192	22	47	8	0	6	20	19	17	.245	.322	.380	703	88	-4	0	1	-0	.977	-3	2-55	-0.4
1955	Mil-N	38	72	4	9	1	1	1	4	4	15	.125	.171	.208	379	0	-11	0	0	0	.977	-2	2-28	-1.1
1956	Mil-N	44	102	8	25	4	0	1	6	8	8	.245	.300	.314	614	69	-4	0	0	0	.979	3	2-42	0.0
1957	Det-A	16	22	3	5	1	0	0	2	2	1	.227	.292	.273	564	54	-1	0	0	0	1.000	-1	/3-3,2-1	-0.3
Total	6	395	1218	117	283	43	4	24	136	77	102	.232	.281	.333	614	66	-61	2	1	0	.974	-26	2-354/3-3	-6.6
■ **MOXIE DIVIS** Divis, Edward George b: 1/16/1894, Cleveland, Ohio d: 12/19/55, Lakewood, Ohio Deb: 8/4/16																								
1916	Phi-A	3	6	0	1	0	0	0	1	0	2	.167	.167	.167	333	0	-1	0			1.000	1	/O-1(1-0-0)	0.0
■ **LEO DIXON** Dixon, Leo Moses b: 9/4/1894, Chicago, Ill. d: 4/11/84, Chicago, Ill. BR/TR, 5'11", 170 lbs. Deb: 4/14/25																								
1925	StL-A	76	205	27	46	11	1	1	19	24	42	.224	.318	.302	620	55	-14	3	2	-0	.981	9	C-75	-0.1
1926	StL-A	33	89	7	17	3	1	0	8	11	14	.191	.294	.247	541	40	-8	1	4	-1	.977	4	C-33	-0.3
1927	StL-A	36	103	6	20	3	1	0	12	7	6	.194	.245	.243	488	26	-11	0	1	-0	.937	3	C-35	-0.6
1929	Cin-N	14	30	0	5	2	0	0	2	3	7	.167	.242	.233	476	19	-4	0			1.000	4	C-14	0.1
Total	4	159	427	40	88	19	3	1	41	45	69	.206	.291	.272	562	43	-37	4	7		.971	21	C-157	-0.9
■ **WALT DOANE** Doane, Walter Rudolph b: 3/12/1887, Bellevue, Idaho d: 10/19/35, W.Brandywine Township, Pa. BL/TR, 6', 165 lbs. Deb: 9/20/09																								
1909	Cle-A	4	9	1	1	0	0	0	0	1		.111	.200	.111	311	-1	-1	0			.778	1	/O-2(2-0-0),P-1	0.0
1910	Cle-A	6	7	0	2	1	0	0	2	1		.286	.375	.429	804	150	0	0			.750	-1	/P-6	0.0
Total	2	10	16	1	3	1	0	0	2	2		.188	.278	.250	528	64	-1	0			.800	-0	/P-7,O-2(2-0-0)	0.0
■ **DAN DOBBEK** Dobbek, Daniel John b: 12/6/34, Ontonagon, Mich. BL/TR, 6', 195 lbs. Deb: 9/9/59																								
1959	Was-A	16	60	8	15	1	2	1	5	5	13	.250	.308	.383	691	89	-1	0	0	0	1.000	1	O-16(0-0-16)	-0.1
1960	Was-A	110	248	32	54	8	2	10	30	35	41	.218	.317	.387	704	90	-4	4	3	-0	.973	-8	O-78(12-58-17)	-1.5
1961	Min-A	72	125	12	21	3	1	4	14	13	18	.168	.257	.304	561	47	-10	1	2	-0	.985	-9	O-48(32-10-13)	-2.0
Total	3	198	433	52	90	12	5	15	49	53	72	.208	.299	.363	661	77	-14	5	5	-1	.980	-16	O-142(44-68-46)	-3.6
■ **JOHN DOBBS** Dobbs, John Gordon b: 6/3/1875, Chattanooga, Tenn. d: 9/9/34, Charlotte, N.C. BL/TR, 5'9.5", 170 lbs. Deb: 4/20/01 Career OF: (65-LF 494-CF 3-RF)																								
1901	Cin-N	109	435	71	119	17	4	2	27	36		.274	.338	.345	682	105	4	19			.948	-7	*O-100(0-100-0)/3-8	-0.7
1902	Cin-N	63	256	39	76	7	3	1	16	19		.297	.348	.359	707	108	2	7			.963	8	O-63(63-0-0)	0.6
	Chi-N	59	235	31	71	8	2	0	35	18		.302	.352	.353	705	121	6	3			.977	1	O-59(0-59-0)	0.4
	Yr	122	491	70	147	15	5	1	51	37		.299	.350	.356	706	114	8	10			.970	9	*O-122(63-59-0)	1.0
1903	Chi-N	16	61	8	14	1	1	0	4	7		.230	.329	.279	607	76	-2	0			1.000	1	O-16(0-16-0)	-0.2
	Bro-N	111	414	61	98	15	7	2	59	48		.237	.323	.321	645	86	-6	23			.966	4	*O-110(0-110-0)	-0.8
	Yr	127	475	69	112	16	8	2	63	55		.236	.324	.316	640	85	-8	23			.970	4	*O-126(0-126-0)	-1.0
1904	Bro-N	101	363	36	90	16	2	0	30	28		.248	.304	.303	607	90	-4	11			.936	0	O-92(2-86-3)/2-2,S-2	-0.9
1905	Bro-N	123	460	59	117	21	4	2	36	31		.254	.304	.330	635	96	-3	15			.938	-6	*O-123(0-123-0)	-1.6
Total	5	582	2224	305	585	85	23	7	207	187		.263	.325	.331	656	98	-3	78			.954	0	O-563C/3-8,S-2,2-2	-3.2
■ **LARRY DOBY** Doby, Lawrence Eugene b: 12/13/23, Camden, S.C. BL/TR, 6'1", 182 lbs. Deb: 7/5/47 MCH Career OF: (20-LF 1329-CF 101-RF)																								
1947	Cle-A	29	32	3	5	1	0	0	2	1	11	.156	.182	.188	369	3	-4	0	0	0	1.000	-1	/2-4,1-1,S-1	-0.5
1948	*Cle-A	121	439	83	132	23	9	14	66	54	77	.301	.384	.490	873	135	21	9	9	-1	.955	3	*O-114(0-68-46)	1.9
1949	Cle-A★	147	547	106	153	25	3	24	85	91	90	.280	.389	.468	857	129	23	10	9	-1	.976	-7	*O-147(0-117-39)	1.0
1950	Cle-A★	142	503	110	164	25	5	25	102	98	71	.326	**.442**	.545	**986**	**156**	**46**	8	6	-0	.987	-6	*O-140(0-140-0)	3.3
1951	Cle-A★	134	447	84	132	27	5	20	69	101	81	.295	.428	.512	941	**163**	43	4	1	1	.977	-1	*O-132(0-132-0)	3.8
1952	Cle-A★	140	519	**104**	143	26	8	**32**	104	90	111	.276	.383	**.541**	924	**166**	45	5	2	0	.986	11	*O-136(0-136-0)	**5.3**
1953	Cle-A★	149	513	92	135	18	5	29	102	96	121	.263	.385	.487	873	138	29	3	2	-0	.984	-7	*O-146(0-146-0)	1.5
1954	*Cle-A★	153	577	94	157	18	4	**32**	**126**	85	94	.272	.368	.484	852	130	23	3	1	0	.995	6	*O-153(0-153-0)	2.3
1955	Cle-A☆	131	491	91	143	17	5	26	75	61	100	.291	.372	.505	877	129	19	2	0	0	.994	3	*O-129(0-129-0)	1.6
1956	Chi-A	140	504	89	135	22	3	24	102	102	105	.268	.395	.466	861	125	20	0	1	-0	.987	6	*O-137(0-137-0)	1.9
1957	Chi-A	119	416	57	120	27	2	14	79	56	79	.288	.376	.464	839	127	16	2	3	-1	.985	-4	*O-110(0-110-0)	0.7
1958	Cle-A	89	247	41	70	10	1	13	45	26	49	.283	.352	.490	842	132	10	0	2	-1	1.000	1	O-68(8-59-1)	0.8
1959	Det-A	18	55	5	12	3	1	0	4	8	9	.218	.317	.309	627	69	-2	0	0	0	.960	-1	O-16(11-0-5)	-0.4

YEAR	TM/L	G	AB	R	H	2B	3B	HR	RBI	BB	SO	AVG	OBP	SLG	OPS	OPS+	BR+	SB	CS	SBR	FA	FR	G/POS	TPR
	Chi-A	21	58	1	14	1	1	0	9	2	13	.241	.267	.293	560	54	-4	1	0	0	.955	-1	O-12(1-2-10)/1-2	-0.5
	Yr	39	113	6	26	4	2	0	13	10	22	.230	.293	.301	594	62	-6	1	0	0	.957	-1	O-28(12-2-15)/1-2	-0.9
Total	13	1533	5348	960	1515	243	52	253	970	871	1011	.283	.387	.490	877	137	285	47	36	-2	.983	3	*O-1440C/2-4,1-3,S	22.7

■ ONA DODD

Dodd, Ona Melvin. b: 10/14/1886, Springtown, Tex. d: 12/17/56, Carter, Okla. BR/TR, 5'8", 150 lbs. Deb: 7/26/12

YEAR	TM/L	G	AB	R	H	2B	3B	HR	RBI	BB	SO	AVG	OBP	SLG	OPS	OPS+	BR+	SB	CS	SBR	FA	FR	G/POS	TPR
1912	Pit-N	5	9	0	0	0	0	0	1	1	3	.000	.100	.000	100	-73	-2				1.000	0	/3-4,2-1	-0.2

■ TOM DODD

Dodd, Thomas Marion b: 8/15/58, Portland, Ore. BR/TR, 6', 190 lbs. Deb: 7/25/86

YEAR	TM/L	G	AB	R	H	2B	3B	HR	RBI	BB	SO	AVG	OBP	SLG	OPS	OPS+	BR+	SB	CS	SBR	FA	FR	G/POS	TPR
1986	Bal-A	8	13	1	3	0	0	1	2	2	2	.231	.375	.462	837	128	1	0	0	0	.000	-0	/3-1,D-6	0.0

■ JOHN DODGE

Dodge, John Lewis b: 4/27/1889, Bolivar, Tenn. d: 6/19/16, Mobile, Ala. BR/TR, 5'11.5", 165 lbs. Deb: 8/29/12

YEAR	TM/L	G	AB	R	H	2B	3B	HR	RBI	BB	SO	AVG	OBP	SLG	OPS	OPS+	BR+	SB	CS	SBR	FA	FR	G/POS	TPR
1912	Phi-N	30	92	3	11	1	0	0	3	4	11	.120	.156	.130	287	-20	-15	2			1.000	8	3-23/2-5,S-1	-0.7
1913	Phi-N	3	3	0	1	0	0	0	0	2	0	.333	.600	.333	933	164	1	0			1.000	-1	/S-3	0.0
	Cin-N	94	323	35	78	8	8	4	45	10	34	.241	.269	.353	622	77	-11	11			.908	1	3-91	-0.8
	Yr	97	326	35	79	8	8	4	45	12	34	.242	.274	.353	626	78	-10	11			.908	1	3-91/S-3	-0.8
Total	2	127	418	38	90	9	8	4	48	16	45	.215	.248	.304	552	55	-26	13			.926	8	3-114/2-5,S-4	-1.5

■ PAT DODSON

Dodson, Patrick Neal b: 10/11/59, Santa Monica, Cal. BL/TL, 6'4", 210 lbs. Deb: 9/5/86

YEAR	TM/L	G	AB	R	H	2B	3B	HR	RBI	BB	SO	AVG	OBP	SLG	OPS	OPS+	BR+	SB	CS	SBR	FA	FR	G/POS	TPR
1986	Bos-A	9	12	3	5	2	0	1	3	3	3	.417	.533	.833	1367	264	3	0	0	0	1.000	-1	/1-7	0.2
1987	Bos-A	26	42	4	7	3	0	2	6	8	13	.167	.300	.381	681	77	-1	0	0	0	1.000	-1	1-21/D-1	-0.3
1988	Bos-A	17	45	5	8	3	1	1	1	6	17	.178	.275	.356	630	72	-2	0	0	0	1.000	2	1-17	-0.1
Total	3	52	99	12	20	8	1	4	10	17	33	.202	.319	.424	743	97	-0	0	0	0	1.000	0	/1-45,D-1	-0.2

■ BOBBY DOERR

Doerr, Robert Pershing b: 4/7/18, Los Angeles, Cal. BR/TR, 5'11", 175 lbs. Deb: 4/20/37 CH

YEAR	TM/L	G	AB	R	H	2B	3B	HR	RBI	BB	SO	AVG	OBP	SLG	OPS	OPS+	BR+	SB	CS	SBR	FA	FR	G/POS	TPR
1937	Bos-A	55	147	22	33	5	1	2	14	18	25	.224	.313	.313	626	56	-10	2	4	-1	.973	4	2-47	-0.4
1938	Bos-A	145	509	70	147	26	7	5	80	59	39	.289	.363	.397	760	86	-11	5	10	-2	.968	6	*2-145	0.2
1939	Bos-A	127	525	75	167	28	2	12	73	38	32	.318	.365	.448	813	103	2	1	10	-3	.976	**27**	*2-126	3.1
1940	Bos-A	151	595	87	173	37	10	22	105	57	53	.291	.353	.497	850	113	10	10	5	0	.977	18	*2-151	3.6
1941	Bos-A★	132	500	74	141	28	4	16	93	43	43	.282	.339	.450	789	105	2	1	3	-1	.971	-6	*2-132	0.3
1942	Bos-A☆	144	545	71	158	35	5	15	102	67	55	.290	.369	.455	824	127	19	4	4	-1	**.975**	11	*2-142	3.9
1943	Bos-A★	155	604	78	163	32	3	16	75	62	59	.270	.339	.412	751	117	12	8	8	-1	**.990**	15	*2-155	3.6
1944	Bos-A★	125	468	95	152	30	10	15	81	58	31	.325	.399	**.528**	927	166	39	5	2	0	.976	4	*2-125	5.2
1946	*Bos-A★	151	583	95	158	34	9	18	116	66	67	.271	.346	.453	799	115	11	5	6	-1	**.986**	**27**	*2-151	4.7
1947	Bos-A★	146	561	79	145	23	10	17	95	59	47	.258	.329	.426	755	101	-0	3	3	-0	.981	**24**	*2-146	3.2
1948	Bos-A★	140	527	94	150	23	6	27	111	83	49	.285	.386	.505	891	129	21	3	2	-0	.993	9	*2-138	3.6
1949	Bos-A	139	541	91	167	30	9	18	109	75	33	.309	.393	.497	890	126	19	2	2	-0	.980	**28**	*2-139	5.2
1950	Bos-A★	149	586	103	172	29	**11**	27	120	67	42	.294	.367	.519	886	114	9	3	4	-1	**.988**	9	*2-149	2.4
1951	Bos-A★	106	402	60	116	21	2	13	73	57	33	.289	.378	.448	826	112	7	2	1	0	.981	6	*2-106	1.9
Total	14	1865	7093	1094	2042	381	89	223	1247	809	608	.288	.362	.461	823	114	130	54	64	-11	.980	181	*2-1852	40.5

■ JOHN DOHERTY

Doherty, John Michael b: 8/22/51, Woburn, Mass. BL/TL, 5'11", 185 lbs. Deb: 6/1/74

YEAR	TM/L	G	AB	R	H	2B	3B	HR	RBI	BB	SO	AVG	OBP	SLG	OPS	OPS+	BR+	SB	CS	SBR	FA	FR	G/POS	TPR
1974	Cal-A	74	223	20	57	14	1	3	15	8	13	.256	.281	.368	649	91	-4	2	1	0	.991	-1	1-70/D-2	-0.9
1975	Cal-A	30	94	7	19	3	0	1	12	8	12	.202	.265	.266	531	54	-6	1	1	-0	.983	-1	1-26/D-1	-0.9
Total	2	104	317	27	76	17	1	4	27	16	25	.240	.276	.338	614	80	-9	3	2	-0	.989	-2	/1-96,D-3	-1.8

■ COZY DOLAN

Dolan, Albert J. (b: James Alberts) b: 12/23/1889, Chicago, Ill. d: 12/10/58, Chicago, Ill. BR/TR, 5'10", 160 lbs. Deb: 8/15/09 C Career OF: (126-LF 48-CF 33-RF)

YEAR	TM/L	G	AB	R	H	2B	3B	HR	RBI	BB	SO	AVG	OBP	SLG	OPS	OPS+	BR+	SB	CS	SBR	FA	FR	G/POS	TPR
1909	Cin-N	3	6	2	1	0	0	0	0	2		.167	.375	.167	542	69	-0	0			.750	-1	/3-3	-0.1
1911	NY-A	19	69	19	21	1	2	0	6	8		.304	.385	.377	761	106	1	12			.947	-1	3-19	0.0
1912	NY-A	18	60	15	12	1	3	0	11	5		.200	.273	.317	589	64	-3	5			.768	-5	3-17	-0.8
	Phi-N	11	50	8	14	2	2	0	7	1	10	.280	.294	.400	694	83	-1	3			.872	-1	3-11	-0.2
1913	Phi-N	55	126	15	33	4	0	0	8	1	21	.262	.273	.294	567	59	-7	9			.905	-7	O-12L,S-10/2-9,31	-1.4
	Pit-N	35	133	22	27	5	2	0	9	15	14	.203	.289	.271	559	63	-6	14			.937	-1	3-35	-0.7
	Yr	90	259	37	60	9	2	0	17	16	35	.232	.282	.282	563	61	-13	23			.932	-9	3-39,O-12L,S-10,/21	-2.1
1914	StL-N	126	421	76	101	16	3	4	32	55	74	.240	.335	.321	655	96	-0	42			.955	-8	O-96(90-1-5),3-27	-1.3
1915	StL-N	111	322	53	90	14	9	2	38	34	37	.280	.356	.398	753	127	11	17	11	-0	.929	-11	O-98(28-47-24)	-0.6
1922	NY-N	1	0	0	0	0	0	0	0	0	0	—	—	—	—	—	0	0	0	0	.000	0	R	0.0
Total	7	379	1187	210	299	43	21	6	111	121	156	.252	.328	.339	666	95	-6	102	11		.940	-34	O-206L,3-116/S-10,21	-5.1

■ JOE DOLAN

Dolan, Joseph b: 2/24/1873, Baltimore, Md. d: 3/24/38, Omaha, Neb. TR, 5'10", 155 lbs. Deb: 8/11/1896

YEAR	TM/L	G	AB	R	H	2B	3B	HR	RBI	BB	SO	AVG	OBP	SLG	OPS	OPS+	BR+	SB	CS	SBR	FA	FR	G/POS	TPR
1896	Lou-N	44	165	14	35	2	1	3	18	9	12	.212	.253	.291	544	45	-14	6			.940	10	S-44	-0.1
1897	Lou-N	36	133	10	28	2	2	0	7	8		.211	.271	.256	526	41	-11	6			.849	-3	S-18,2-18	-1.1
1899	Phi-N	61	222	27	57	6	3	1	30	11		.257	.298	.324	622	73	-9	3			.915	-11	2-61	-1.6
1900	Phi-N	74	257	39	51	7	3	1	27	16		.198	.259	.261	520	44	-20	10			.931	3	3-31,2-29,S-12	-1.4
1901	Phi-N	10	37	0	3	0	0	0	2	2		.081	.128	.081	209	-38	-6	0			.973	-3	2-10	-0.9
	Phi-A	98	338	50	73	21	2	1	38	26		.216	.282	.299	581	58	-19	3			.881	16	S-61,3-35/2-1,O-1R	-0.1
Total	5	323	1152	140	247	38	11	6	122	72	12	.214	.270	.282	552	51	-79	28			.902	11	S-135,2-119/3-66,O	-5.2

■ BIDDY DOLAN

Dolan, Leon Mark b: 7/9/1881, Onalaska, Wis. d: 7/15/50, Indianapolis, Ind BR/TR, 6', Deb: 4/16/14

YEAR	TM/L	G	AB	R	H	2B	3B	HR	RBI	BB	SO	AVG	OBP	SLG	OPS	OPS+	BR+	SB	CS	SBR	FA	FR	G/POS	TPR
1914	Ind-F	32	103	13	23	4	2	1	15	12	13	.223	.316	.330	646	69	-6	5			.979	1	1-31	-0.6

■ COZY DOLAN

Dolan, Patrick Henry b: 12/3/1872, Cambridge, Mass. d: 3/29/07, Louisville, Ky. BL/TL, 5'10", 160 lbs. Deb: 4/26/1895 Career OF: (8-LF 207-CF 509-RF)

YEAR	TM/L	G	AB	R	H	2B	3B	HR	RBI	BB	SO	AVG	OBP	SLG	OPS	OPS+	BR+	SB	CS	SBR	FA	FR	G/POS	TPR
1895	Bos-N	26	83	12	20	4	1	0	7	6	7	.241	.300	.313	613	54	-6	3			.949	3	P-25/O-1(0-1-0)	-0.1
1896	Bos-N	6	14	4	2	0	0	0	0	0	1	.143	.143	.143	286	-23	-3	0			.765	-0	/P-6	0.0
1900	Chi-N	13	48	5	13	1	0	0	2	2		.271	.300	.292	592	66	-2	2			.826	-2	O-13(0-0-13)	-0.4
1901	Chi-N	43	171	29	45	1	2	0	16	7		.263	.296	.292	588	74	-6	3			.878	2	O-41(0-0-41)	-0.6
	Bro-N	66	253	33	66	11	1	0	29	17		.261	.313	.312	625	79	-7	7			.967	-2	O-64(2-57-5)	-1.1
	Yr	109	424	62	111	12	3	0	45	24		.262	.306	.304	610	77	-12	10			.931	0	*O-105(2-57-46)	-1.7
1902	Bro-N	141	592	72	166	16	7	1	54	33		.280	.324	.336	660	103	1	24			.936	-9	*O-141(1-140-0)	-1.5
1903	Chi-A	27	104	16	27	5	1	0	7	6		.260	.313	.327	639	96	-0	5			.971	2	1-19/O-4(2-2-0)	0.1
	Cin-N	93	385	64	111	20	3	0	58	28		.288	.340	.356	696	88	-6	11			.937	-7	O-93(0-0-93)	-1.7
1904	Cin-N	129	465	88	132	8	10	6	51	39		.284	.342	.383	725	113	7	19			.939	-4	*O-102(0-7-95),1-24	-0.2
1905	Cin-N	22	77	7	18	2	1	0	4	7		.234	.306	.286	592	69	-3	2			.965	-4	1-13/O-9(1-0-8)	-0.7
	Bos-N	112	433	44	119	11	7	3	48	27		.275	.322	.353	675	103	1	21			.946	4	*O-111R/P-2,1-2	0.0
	Yr	134	510	51	137	13	8	3	52	34		.269	.319	.343	662	97	-2	23			.931	0	*O-120R,1-15/P-2	-0.7
1906	Bos-N	152	549	54	136	20	4	0	39	55		.248	.318	.299	617	95	-2	17			.928	-2	*O-144R/2-7,P-2,1-1	-1.1
Total	9	830	3174	428	855	99	37	10	315	227	8	.269	.322	.333	656	94	-25	114			.931	-18	O-723R/1-59,P-35,2	-7.3

■ TOM DOLAN

Dolan, Thomas J. b: 1/10/1859, New York, N.Y. d: 1/16/13, St.Louis, Mo. BR/TR, Deb: 9/30/1879 Career OF: (24-LF 22-CF 5-RF)

YEAR	TM/L	G	AB	R	H	2B	3B	HR	RBI	BB	SO	AVG	OBP	SLG	OPS	OPS+	BR+	SB	CS	SBR	FA	FR	G/POS	TPR
1879	Chi-N	1	4	0	0	0	0	0	0	0	2	.000	.000	.000	0	-94	-1				1.000	1	/C-1	0.0
1882	Buf-N	22	89	12	14	0	1	0	8	2	11	.157	.176	.180	356	14	-8				.941	-8	C-18/O-4(1-2-1),3-2	-1.4
1883	StL-a	81	295	32	63	9	2	1	18	9		.214	.237	.268	505	59	-14				.957	13	C-42,O-40L/P-1	0.1
1884	StL-a	35	137	19	36	6	2	0		6		.263	.299	.336	634	103	0				.873	-6	C-34/O-2(1-0-1)	-0.3
	StL-U	19	69	9	13	3	0	0		4		.188	.233	.232	465	40	-7				.897	11	C-14/3-3,O-2(0-1-1)	0.4
1885	StL-N	3	9	1	2	0	0	0	0	2	1	.222	.364	.222	586	99	0				.810	-1	/C-3	0.0
1886	StL-N	15	44	8	11	3	0	0	1	7	9	.250	.353	.318	671	113	1	2			.928	6	C-15	0.8
	Bal-a	38	125	13	19	3	2	0	12	8		.152	.203	.208	411	30	-10	8			.918	-6	C-35/O-3(3-0-0)	-1.2
1888	StL-a	11	36	1	7	1	0	0	1	1		.194	.216	.222	438	37	-3	1			.914	-0	C-11	-0.2
Total	7	225	808	95	165	25	7	1	40	39	23	.204	.242	.256	498	57	-41	11			.916	8	C-173/O-51L,3-5,P-1	-1.8

■ LESTER DOLE

Dole, Lester Carrington b: 7/8/1855, Meriden, Conn. d: 12/10/18, Concord, N.H. 5'11", Deb: 5/27/1875

YEAR	TM/L	G	AB	R	H	2B	3B	HR	RBI	BB	SO	AVG	OBP	SLG	OPS	OPS+	BR+	SB	CS	SBR	FA	FR	G/POS	TPR
1875	NH-n	1	4	1	2	0	0	0	0	0	0	.500	.500	.500	1000	285	1	0	0	0	.750	0	/O-1(0-1-0)	0.1

YEAR	TM/L	G	AB	R	H	2B	3B	HR	RBI	BB	SO	AVG	OBP	SLG	OPS	OPS+	BR+	SB	CS	SBR	FA	FR	G/POS	TPR
■ FRANK DOLJACK	Doljack, Frank Joseph "Dolie" b: 10/5/07, Cleveland, Ohio d: 1/23/48, Cleveland, Ohio BR/TR, 5'11", 175 lbs. Deb: 9/4/30																							
1930	Det-A	20	74	10	19	5	1	3	17	2	11	.257	.286	.473	759	87	-2	0	1	-0	.930	0	O-20(0-4-16)	-0.3
1931	Det-A	63	187	20	52	13	3	4	20	15	17	.278	.335	.444	779	100	-1	3	2	-0	.925	3	O-54(3-44-8)	0.0
1932	Det-A	8	26	5	10	1	0	1	7	2	2	.385	.429	.538	967	143	2	1	0	0	1.000	-2	/O-6(6-0-0)	0.0
1933	Det-A	42	147	18	42	5	2	0	22	14	13	.286	.348	.347	695	83	-3	2	6	-2	.941	2	O-37(32-0-5)	-0.5
1934	*Det-A	56	120	15	28	7	1	1	19	13	15	.233	.313	.333	647	67	-6	2	1	0	.943	-3	O-30(6-12-12)/1-3	-0.9
1943	Cle-A	3	7	0	0	0	0	0	0	1	2	.000	.125	.000	125	-66	-1	0	0	0	1.000	-1	/O-2(1-0-1)	-0.2
Total	6	192	561	68	151	31	7	9	85	47	60	.269	.329	.398	726	87	-12	8	10	-2	.934	-0	O-149(48-60-42)/1-3	-1.9
■ ART DOLL	Doll, Arthur James "Moose" b: 5/7/13, Chicago, Ill. d: 4/28/78, Calumet City, Ill. BR/TR, 6'1", 190 lbs. Deb: 9/21/35																							
1935	Bos-N	3	10	0	1	0	0	0	0	0	1	.100	.100	.100	200	-50	-2	0			.867	0	/C-3	-0.2
1936	Bos-N	1	2	0	0	0	0	0	0	0	2	.000	.000	.000	0	-99	-1	0			1.000	-0	/P-1	0.0
1938	Bos-N	3	1	0	1	0	0	0	0	0	0	1.000	1.000	1.000	2000	501	1	0			1.000	0	/P-3	0.0
Total	3	7	13	0	2	0	0	0	0	0	3	.154	.154	.154	308	-18	-2	0			1.000	0	/P-4,C-3	-0.2
■ SHE DONAHUE	Donahue, Charles Michael b: 6/29/1877, Oswego, N.Y. d: 8/28/47, New York, N.Y. BR/TR, 5'9", Deb: 4/29/04																							
1904	StL-N	4	15	1	4	0	0	0	2	0		.267	.267	.267	533	68	-1	3			.846	-3	/2-3,S-1	-0.4
	Phi-N	58	200	21	43	4	0	0	14	3		.215	.227	.235	462	44	-13	7			.857	-17	S-29,3-24/1-3,2-2	-3.1
	Yr	62	215	22	47	4	0	0	16	3		.219	.229	.237	467	46	-14	10			.852	-20	S-30,3-24/2-5,1-3	-3.5
■ JIM DONAHUE	Donahue, James Augustus b: 1/8/1862, Lockport, Ill. d: 4/19/35, Lockport, Ill. BR/TR, 6', 175 lbs. Deb: 4/19/1886 Career OF: (38-LF 28-CF 6-RF)																							
1886	NY-a	49	186	14	37	0	0	0	9	10		.199	.251	.199	450	44	-11	1			.803	-2	O-32(12-21-1),C-19	-1.1
1887	NY-a	60	241	33	83	4	1	1	29	21		.344	.350	.323	673	92	-1	6			.890	-8	C-51/O-5R,1-4,32	-0.4
1888	KC-a	88	337	29	79	11	3	1	28	21		.234	.281	.294	575	79	-9	12			.902	-11	C-67,O-18L/3-5,2-1	-1.3
1889	KC-a	67	252	30	59	5	4	0	32	21	20	.234	.293	.286	579	61	-13	12			.887	-8	C-46,O-14L,3-10	-1.5
1891	Col-a	77	280	27	61	4	3	0	35	31	18	.218	.298	.254	552	62	-13	2			.942	3	C-75/O-1(0-0-1),1-1	-0.3
Total	5	341	1296	133	319	24	11	2	133	104	38	.246	.295	.275	570	69	-47	33			.911	-25	C-258/O-70L,3-16,12	-4.6
■ JIGGS DONAHUE	Donahue, John Augustus b: 7/13/1879, Springfield, Ohio d: 7/19/13, Columbus, Ohio BL/TL, 6'1", 178 lbs. Deb: 9/10/00 F																							
1900	Pit-N	3	10	1	2	0	1	0	3	0		.200	.200	.400	600	63	-1	1			.889	-1	/C-2,O-1(0-0-1)	-0.2
1901	Pit-N	2	0	0	0	0	0	0	0	0		—	—	—	—	—	0	0			.000	-1	/C-1,O-1(1-0-0)	-0.1
	Mil-A	37	107	10	34	5	4	0	16	10		.318	.387	.439	826	135	5	4			.933	-2	C-19,1-13	0.5
1902	StL-A	30	89	11	21	1	1	1	7	12		.236	.327	.303	630	76	-2	2			.956	-1	C-23/1-5	-0.1
1904	Chi-A	102	367	46	91	9	7	1	48	25		.248	.298	.319	617	99	-1	18			.979	7	*1-101	0.5
1905	Chi-A	149	533	71	153	22	4	1	76	44		.287	.346	.349	695	126	16	32			**.988**	8	*1-149	2.3
1906	*Chi-A	154	556	70	143	17	7	1	57	48		.257	.320	.318	638	103	2	36			**.988**	9	*1-154	0.9
1907	Chi-A	157	609	75	158	16	4	0	68	28		.259	.295	.299	594	93	-6	27			**.994**	21	*1-157	1.3
1908	Chi-A	93	304	22	62	8	2	0	22	25		.204	.271	.243	515	69	-10	14			.994	5	1-83	-0.8
1909	Chi-A	2	4	0	0	0	0	0	2	1		.000	.200	.000	200	-38	-1	0			1.000	-0	/1-2	-0.1
	Was-A	84	283	13	67	12	1	0	28	22		.237	.294	.286	580	87	-4	9			.984	-4	1-81	-1.1
	Yr	86	287	13	67	12	1	0	30	23		.233	.293	.282	575	86	-5	9			.984	-4	1-83	-1.2
Total	9	813	2862	319	731	90	31	4	327	215		.255	.311	.313	624	99	-0	143			.987	40	1-745/C-45,O-2(1-0-1)	3.1
■ JOHN DONAHUE	Donahue, John Frederick "Jiggs" b: 4/19/1894, Roxbury, Mass. d: 10/3/49, Boston, Mass. BB/TR, 5'8", 170 lbs. Deb: 9/25/23																							
1923	Bos-A	10	36	5	10	4	0	0	1	4	5	.278	.350	.389	739	94	-0	0	1	-0	1.000	3	/O-9(0-0-9)	0.2
■ PAT DONAHUE	Donahue, Patrick William b: 11/8/1884, Springfield, Ohio d: 1/31/66, Springfield, Ohio BR/TR, 6', 175 lbs. Deb: 5/29/08 F																							
1908	Bos-A	35	86	8	17	2	0	1	6	9		.198	.289	.256	544	75	-2	0			.959	0	C-32/1-3	0.1
1909	Bos-A	65	177	14	42	4	1	2	25	17		.237	.308	.305	613	92	-2	2			.982	-3	C-58	0.1
1910	Bos-A	2	4	0	0	0	0	0	0	0		.000	.000	.000	0	-98	-1	0			1.000	0	/C-1	-0.1
	Phi-A	14	34	2	5	0	0	0	4	3		.147	.237	.147	384	21	-3	1			1.000	3	C-13	0.2
	Cle-A	2	6	0	1	0	0	0	0	0		.167	.167	.167	333	4	-1	0			1.000	-1	/C-2,1-1	-0.1
	Phi-A	1	1	0	0	0	0	0	0	0		.000	.000	.000	0	-99	-0	0			1.000	1	/C-1	0.0
	Yr	19	45	2	6	0	0	0	4	3		.133	.204	.133	337	6	-5	1			1.000	3	C-17/1-1	0.0
Total	3	119	308	24	65	6	1	3	35	29		.211	.287	.266	554	75	-8	3			.978	1	C-107/1-4	0.2
■ TIM DONAHUE	Donahue, Timothy Cornelius "Bridget" b: 6/8/1870, Raynham, Mass. d: 6/12/02, Taunton, Mass. BL/TR, 5'11", 180 lbs. Deb: 7/28/1891																							
1891	Bos-a	4	7	0	0	0	0	0	0	0	5	.000	.000	.000	0	-99	-2	0			.833	-1	/C-4	-0.3
1895	Chi-N	63	219	29	59	9	1	2	36	20	25	.269	.339	.347	686	73	-9	5			.915	-2	C-63	-0.5
1896	Chi-N	57	188	27	41	10	1	0	20	11	15	.218	.276	.282	558	45	-15	11			.934	5	C-57	-0.5
1897	Chi-N	58	188	28	45	7	3	0	21	9		.239	.281	.309	590	54	-13	3			.947	7	C-55/S-2,1-1	-0.1
1898	Chi-N	122	396	52	87	12	3	0	39	49		.220	.318	.265	583	68	-15	17			.962	6	*C-122	0.2
1899	Chi-N	92	278	39	69	9	3	0	29	34		.248	.345	.302	647	80	-6	10			.951	4	C-91/1-1	0.5
1900	Chi-N	67	216	21	51	10	1	0	17	19		.236	.313	.292	604	70	-8	8			.928	-7	C-66/2-1	-0.9
1902	Was-A	3	8	0	2	0	0	0	1	0		.250	.250	.250	500	39	-1	0			1.000	0	/C-3	0.0
Total	8	466	1500	196	354	57	12	2	163	142	45	.236	.314	.294	608	66	-70	54			.943	11	C-461/1-2,S-2,2-1	-1.6
■ JOHN DONALDSON	Donaldson, John David b: 5/5/43, Charlotte, N.C. BL/TR, 5'11", 165 lbs. Deb: 8/26/66																							
1966	KC-A	15	30	4	4	0	0	0	1	3	4	.133	.212	.133	345	2	-4	1	0	0	1.000	-2	/2-9	-0.6
1967	KC-A	105	377	27	104	16	5	0	28	37	39	.276	.344	.345	689	107	4	6	3	0	.982	-18	*2-101/S-1	-0.5
1968	Oak-A	127	363	37	80	9	2	2	27	45	44	.220	.310	.273	582	82	-7	5	5	-1	.971	-4	2-98/3-5,S-1	-0.4
1969	Oak-A	12	13	1	1	0	0	0	0	2	4	.077	.200	.077	277	-21	-2	0	0	0	.857	0	/2-1	-0.2
	Sea-A	95	338	22	79	8	3	1	19	36	36	.234	.307	.284	592	67	-14	6	1	1	.974	-1	2-90/3-2,S-1	-0.8
	Yr	107	351	23	80	8	3	1	19	38	40	.228	.303	.276	580	64	-16	6	1	1	.972	-0	2-91/3-2,S-1	-1.0
1970	Oak-A	41	89	4	22	2	1	1	11	9	6	.247	.316	.326	642	80	-2	1	0	0	.986	-3	2-21/S-6,3-1	-0.3
1974	Oak-A	10	15	1	2	0	0	0	0	0	0	.133	.133	.133	267	-25	-2	0	0	0	.962	1	/2-7,3-3	-0.1
Total	6	405	1225	96	292	35	11	4	86	132	133	.238	.314	.295	609	81	-28	19	9	1	.976	-26	2-327/3-11,S-9	-2.9
■ LEN DONDERO	Dondero, Leonard Peter "Mike" b: 9/12/03, Newark, Cal. d: 1/1/99, Fremont, Cal. BR/TR, 5'11", 178 lbs. Deb: 4/21/29																							
1929	StL-A	19	31	2	6	0	0	1	8	0	4	.194	.194	.290	484	22	-4	0	0	0	.857	-3	3-10/2-5	-0.6
■ MIKE DONLIN	Donlin, Michael Joseph "Turkey Mike" b: 5/30/1878, Peoria, Ill. d: 9/24/33, Hollywood, Cal. BL/TL, 5'9", 170 lbs. Deb: 7/19/1899 Career OF: (286-LF 341-CF 243-RF)																							
1899	StL-N	66	266	49	86	9	6	6	27	17		.323	.366	.470	836	126	8	20			.873	-7	O-51C,1-13/S-3,P-3	-0.3
1900	StL-N	78	276	40	90	8	6	10	48	14		.326	.361	.507	868	139	13	14			.922	-4	O-47(2-35-10),1-21	0.6
1901	Bal-A	121	476	107	162	23	13	5	67	53		.340	.409	.475	883	138	25	33			.918	9	O-74(73-1-0),1-47	2.6
1902	Cin-N	34	143	30	41	5	4	0	9	9		.287	.333	.378	711	109	1	9			.877	-1	O-32(30-0-2)/P-1,S-1	-0.2
1903	Cin-N	126	496	110	174	25	18	7	67	56		.351	.420	.516	936	150	31	26			.900	-2	*O-118(70-0-48)/1-7	2.2
1904	Cin-N	60	236	42	84	11	7	1	38	18		.356	.406	.475	881	158	16	21			.872	-3	O-53(52-0-1)/1-6	1.0
	NY-N	42	132	17	37	7	3	2	14	10		.280	.340	.424	765	130	4	1			.918	-7	O-37(23-11-3)	-0.4
	Yr	102	368	59	121	18	10	3	52	28		.329	.382	.457	839	148	20	22			.886	-9	O-90(75-11-4)/1-6	0.6
1905	*NY-N	150	606	**124**	216	31	16	7	80	56		.356	.413	.495	908	166	49	33			.934	-12	*O-150(4-147-0)	3.1
1906	NY-N	37	121	15	38	5	1	1	14	11		.314	.371	.397	768	136	5	9			.929	-6	O-29(0-29-0)/1-1	-0.3
1908	NY-N	155	593	71	198	26	13	6	106	23		.334	.364	.452	816	153	32	30			.977	0	*O-155(29-0-127)	2.9
1911	NY-N	12	12	3	4	0	0	1	1	0	1	.333	.333	.583	917	150	1	2			1.000	-1	/O-3(0-2-1)	-0.1
	Bos-N	56	222	33	70	16	1	2	34	22	17	.315	.377	.423	800	115	4	7			.912	-3	O-56(0-56-0)	-0.3
	Yr	68	234	36	74	16	1	3	35	22	18	.316	.375	.432	807	117	5	9			.913	-4	O-59(0-58-1)	-0.4
1912	Pit-N	77	244	27	77	9	8	2	35	20	16	.316	.370	.443	812	124	7	8			.982	-2	O-62(2-10-51)	0.2
1914	NY-N	35	31	1	5	1	1	1	3	3	5	.161	.235	.355	590	77	-1	0			.000	0	H	-0.1
Total	12	1049	3854	669	1282	176	97	51	543	312	39	.333	.386	.468	854	142	195	213			.924	-37	O-867C/1-95,P-4,S-4	10.9

YEAR	TM/L	G	AB	R	H	2B	3B	HR	RBI	BB	SO	AVG	OBP	SLG	OPS	OPS+	BR+	SB	CS	SBR	FA	FR	G/POS	TPR
■ JIM DONNELLY Donnelly, James B. b: 7/19/1865, New Haven, Conn. d: 3/5/15, New Haven, Conn. BR/TR, 5'10.5", 155 lbs. Deb: 8/11/1884 Career OF: (2-LF 2-CF 2-RF)																								
1884	Ind-a	40	134	22	34	2	2	0		5		.254	.301	.299	599	99	0				.850	-5	3-24/S-8,O-6L,2-2	-0.4
1885	Det-N	56	211	24	49	4	3	1	22	10	29	.232	.267	.294	561	81	-4				.850	-3	3-56	-0.6
1886	KC-N	113	438	51	88	11	3	0	38	36	57	.201	.262	.240	501	50	-26	16			.845	0	*3-113	-2.2
1887	Was-N	117	441	51	101	9	6	1	46	16	26	.229	.234	.256	491	38	-35	42			.867	16	*3-115/S-2	-1.4
1888	Was-N	122	428	43	86	9	4	0	23	20	16	.201	.242	.241	482	57	-20	44			.875	-5	*3-117/S-5	-2.2
1889	Was-N	4	13	3	2	0	0	0	0	2	0	.154	.267	.154	421	20	-1	1			.667	-2	/3-4	-0.2
1890	StL-a	11	42	11	14	0	0	0	3	8		.333	.451	.333	784	115	1	5			.795	-3	3-11	-0.1
1891	Col-a	17	54	6	13	0	0	0	9	13	5	.241	.388	.241	629	85	0	7			.855	3	3-17	0.3
1896	Bal-N	106	396	70	130	14	10	0	71	34	11	.328	.387	.414	801	110	6	38			.884	-2	*3-106	0.5
1897	Pit-N	44	161	22	31	4	0	0	14	16		.193	.270	.217	487	31	-16	14			.920	1	3-44	-1.2
	NY-N	23	85	19	16	3	0	0	11	9		.188	.266	.224	489	31	-8	6			.869	-6	3-23	-1.2
	Yr	67	246	41	47	7	0	0	25	25		.191	.268	.220	488	31	-24	20			.905	-5	3-67	-2.4
1898	StL-N	1	1	0	1	0	0	0	0	0		1.000	1.000	1.000	2000	463	0	0			.500	0	/3-1	0.0
Total	11	654	2404	322	565	56	28	2	237	169	144	.235	.285	.279	565	65	-103	173			.865	-4	3-631/S-15,O-6L,2-2	-8.7
■ JIM DONNELLY Donnelly, James J. 5'10.5", 155 lbs. Deb: 7/11/1884																								
1884	KC-U	6	23	2	3	1	0	0		1		.130	.167	.174	341	4	-3				.536	-4	/3-5,C-1	-0.6
■ JOHN DONNELLY Donnelly, John b: Elizabeth, N.J. Deb: 4/14/1873 F Career OF: (0-LF 6-CF 3-RF)																								
1873	Was-n	30	137	15	35	1	0	0	20	1	0	.255	.261	.263	524	58	-6	0	0	0	.783	1	S-13,2-12/O-6C,3-1	-0.5
1874	Phi-n	6	22	2	5	0	0	0	2	0	0	.227	.227	.227	455	45	-1	0	0	0	.667	-3	/O-3(0-0-3),S-2,2-1	-0.3
Total	2 n	36	159	17	40	1	0	0	22	1	0	.252	.256	.258	514	56	-8	0	0	0	.763	-2	/S-15,2-13,O-9C,3-1	-0.8
■ PETE DONNELLY Donnelly, Peter J. b: 10/8/1849, Philadelphia, Pa. d: 10/1/1890, Jersey City, N.J. Deb: 5/13/1871 F																								
1871	Kek-n	9	34	7	7	1	1	0	3	1	2	.206	.229	.294	523	48	-2	0	0	0	.714	-5	/O-9(2-1-6),3-2	-0.5
■ CHRIS DONNELS Donnels, Chris Barton b: 4/21/66, Los Angeles, Cal. BL/TR, 6', 185 lbs. Deb: 5/7/91 Career OF: (6-LF 0-CF 0-RF)																								
1991	NY-N	37	89	7	20	2	0	0	5	14	19	.225	.330	.247	577	65	-4	1	1	-0	1.000	3	1-15,3-11	-0.2
1992	NY-N	45	121	8	21	4	0	0	6	17	25	.174	.275	.207	482	39	-9	1	0	0	.941	4	3-29,2-12	-0.6
1993	Hou-N	88	179	18	46	14	2	2	24	19	33	.257	.328	.391	719	95	-1	2	0	0	.898	-0	3-31,1-23/2-1	-0.2
1994	Hou-N	54	86	12	23	5	0	3	5	13	18	.267	.364	.430	794	112	2	1	0	0	1.000	1	3-14/1-4,2-4	0.2
1995	Hou-N	19	30	4	9	0	0	0	2	3	6	.300	.364	.300	664	83	-1	0	0	0	.818	-2	/3-9,2-1	-0.2
	Bos-A	40	91	13	23	2	2	2	11	9	18	.253	.320	.385	705	80	-3	0	0	0	.927	1	3-27/1-8,2-3	-0.2
2000	LA-N	27	34	8	10	3	0	4	9	6	7	.294	.400	.735	1135	187	4	0	0	0	1.000	-2	/O-6L,1-4,3-2,2-1	0.2
Total	6	310	630	70	152	30	4	11	62	81	126	.241	.328	.354	682	85	-12	5	1	1	.929	4	3-123/1-54,2-22,O-6L	-1.0
■ JOE DONOHUE Donohue, Joseph F. b: 1869, Syracuse, N.Y. Deb: 8/24/1891																								
1891	Phi-N	6	22	2	7	1	0	0	2	1	3	.318	.375	.364	739	113	0	0			1.000	-0	/O-4(0-4-0),S-2	0.0
■ TOM DONOHUE Donohue, Thomas James b: 11/15/52, Mineola, N.Y. BR/TR, 6', 185 lbs. Deb: 4/6/79																								
1979	Cal-A	38	107	13	24	3	1	3	14	3	29	.224	.259	.355	614	66	-5	2	0	0	.981	-3	C-38	-0.6
1980	Cal-A	84	218	18	41	4	1	2	14	7	63	.188	.217	.243	460	26	-22	5	1	1	.986	-10	C-84	-2.8
Total	2	122	325	31	65	7	2	5	28	10	92	.200	.231	.280	511	40	-28	7	1	1	.985	-12	C-122	-3.4
■ FRED DONOVAN Donovan, Frederick Maurice b: 7/4/1864, New Hampshire d: 3/7/16, Bloomington, Ill. BR/TR, Deb: 6/23/1895																								
1895	Cle-N	3	12	1	1	0	0	0	1	1	2	.083	.154	.083	237	-36	-2	0			.938	-0	/C-3	-0.2
■ JERRY DONOVAN Donovan, Jeremiah Francis b: 9/3/1876, Lock Haven, Pa. d: 6/27/38, St.Petersburg, Fla. BR/TR, Deb: 4/12/06 F																								
1906	Phi-N	61	166	11	33	4	0	0	15	6		.199	.236	.223	459	43	-11	2			.955	-4	C-53/S-1,O-1(1-0-0)	-1.2
■ MIKE DONOVAN Donovan, Michael Berchman b: 10/18/1881, Brooklyn, N.Y. d: 2/3/38, New York, N.Y. BR/TR, 5'8", 155 lbs. Deb: 5/29/04																								
1904	Cle-A	2	2	0	0	0	0	0	0	0		.000	.000	.000	0	-99	-0	0			.000	0	/S-1	-0.1
1908	NY-A	5	19	2	5	1	0	0	2	0		.263	.263	.316	579	87	-0	0			1.000	1	/3-5	0.1
Total	2	7	21	2	5	1	0	0	2	0		.238	.238	.286	524	69	-1	0			1.000	1	/3-5,S-1	0.0
■ PATSY DONOVAN Donovan, Patrick Joseph b: 3/16/1865, County Cork, Ireland d: 12/25/53, Lawrence, Mass. BL/TL, 5'11.5", 175 lbs. Deb: 4/19/1890 M																								
1890	Bos-N	32	140	17	36	0	0	0	9	8	17	.257	.307	.257	564	60	-7	10			.891	-5	O-32(0-32-0)	-1.2
	*Bro-N	28	105	17	23	5	1	0	8	5	5	.219	.268	.286	554	61	-5	3			1.000	2	O-28(1-24-3)	-0.4
	Yr	60	245	34	59	5	1	0	17	13	22	.241	.290	.269	559	61	-13	13			.952	-3	O-60(1-56-3)	-1.6
1891	Lou-a	105	439	73	141	10	3	2	53	30	18	.321	.375	.371	747	115	9	27			.912	5	*O-105(105-0-0)	0.9
	Was-a	17	70	9	14	1	0	0	3	4	5	.200	.243	.214	458	33	-6	1			.857	-2	O-17(0-13-4)	-0.8
	Yr	122	509	82	155	11	3	2	56	34	23	.305	.358	.350	707	104	3	28			.907	2	*O-122(105-13-4)	0.1
1892	Was-N	40	163	29	39	3	3	0	12	11	13	.239	.295	.294	590	81	-4	16			.844	1	O-40(14-0-26)	-0.5
	Pit-N	90	388	77	114	15	3	2	26	20	16	.294	.333	.363	697	110	4	40			.872	-3	O-90(1-1-90)	-0.4
	Yr	130	551	106	153	18	6	2	38	31	29	.278	.322	.343	665	102	-0	56			.862	-2	*O-130(15-1-116)	-0.9
1893	Pit-N	113	499	114	158	5	8	2	56	42	8	.317	.373	.371	744	100	1	46			.937	-1	*O-112(0-0-112)	-0.5
1894	Pit-N	133	577	147	175	21	10	4	76	36	12	.303	.350	.395	745	80	-20	41			.933	9	*O-133(0-0-133)	-1.3
1895	Pit-N	126	522	115	162	18	6	1	58	48	19	.310	.377	.374	751	99	2	36			.961	-5	*O-126(0-1-125)	-0.8
1896	Pit-N	131	573	113	183	20	5	3	59	35	18	.319	.370	.387	757	104	4	48			.954	7	*O-131(0-0-131)	0.4
1897	Pit-N	120	479	82	154	16	7	0	57	25		.322	.360	.384	744	100	0	34			.949	1	*O-120(0-0-120),M	-0.4
1898	Pit-N	147	610	112	184	16	9	0	37	34		.302	.346	.357	703	104	2	41			.928	0	*O-147(0-0-147)	-0.4
1899	Pit-N	122	536	82	156	11	7	1	56	17		.291	.319	.343	662	82	-14	26			.942	-12	*O-122(0-1-121),M	-2.9
1900	StL-N	126	503	78	159	11	1	0	61	38		.316	.368	.342	710	97	-1	**45**			.951	-5	*O-124(0-0-124)	-1.1
1901	StL-N	130	531	92	161	23	5	1	73	27		.303	.344	.371	715	113	9	28			.979	4	*O-129(0-0-129),M	0.6
1902	StL-N	126	502	70	158	12	4	0	35	28		.315	.363	.355	718	127	16	34			.959	10	*O-126(0-0-126),M	2.1
1903	StL-N	105	410	63	134	15	3	0	39	25		.327	.370	.378	748	117	9	25			.952	-1	*O-105(0-0-105),M	0.4
1904	Was-A	125	436	30	100	6	0	0	19	24		.229	.271	.243	514	64	-17	17			.963	9	*O-122(0-2-120),M	-1.5
1906	Bro-N	7	21	1	5	0	0	0	0	0		.238	.238	.238	476	53	-1	0			1.000	-1	/O-6(0-0-6),M	-0.2
1907	Bro-N	1	1	0	0	0	0	0	0	0		.000	.000	.000	0	-99	-0	0			1.000	0	/O-1(0-0-1),M	0.0
Total	17	1824	7505	1321	2256	208	75	16	737	457	131	.301	.348	.355	702	98	-20	518			.941	14	*O-1816(121-74-1623)	-8.0
■ TOM DONOVAN Donovan, Thomas Joseph b: 1/1/1873, West Troy, N.Y. d: 3/25/33, Watervliet, N.Y. BR/TR, 6'2", 168 lbs. Deb: 9/10/01 F																								
1901	Cle-A	18	71	9	18	3	1	0	5	0		.254	.254	.324	577	62	-4	1			.862	-1	O-18(0-0-18)/P-1	-0.5
■ BILL DONOVAN Donovan, William Edward "Wild Bill" b: 10/13/1876, Lawrence, Mass. d: 12/9/23, Forsyth, N.Y. BR/TR, 5'11", 190 lbs. Deb: 4/22/1898 MC Career OF: (17-LF 8-CF 12-RF)																								
1898	Was-N	39	103	11	17	2	2	2	8	4		.165	.211	.282	493	41	-8	2			.933	1	O-20R,P-17/S-1,2-1	-0.5
1899	Bro-N	5	13	2	3	1	0	0	0	0		.231	.231	.308	538	46	-1	0			.857	-0	/P-5	0.0
1900	Bro-N	5	13	0	0	0	0	0	2	0		.000	.000	.000	0	-94	-3	0			1.000	1	/P-5	0.0
1901	Bro-N	46	135	16	23	3	0	2	13	8		.170	.217	.237	454	31	-12	1			.927	-1	P-45	0.0
1902	Bro-N	48	161	16	28	3	2	1	16	9		.174	.227	.236	463	43	-11	7			.948	2	P-35/1-8,O-4L,2-1	-0.3
1903	Det-A	40	124	11	30	3	2	0	12	4		.242	.266	.298	564	71	-4	3			.938	-2	P-35/S-2,2-1,O-1C	0.1
1904	Det-A	46	140	12	38	2	1	1	6	3		.271	.287	.321	608	95	-1	2			.967	-3	P-34/1-8,O-1(4-0-0)	-0.4
1905	Det-A	44	130	16	25	4	0	0	5	12		.192	.266	.223	489	55	-6	8			.933	-0	P-34/O-8(5-0-0),2-2	0.1
1906	Det-A	28	91	5	11	0	1	0	0	1		.121	.130	.143	273	-14	-12	6			.961	-1	P-25/2-3,O-1(0-1-0)	-0.2
1907	*Det-A	37	109	20	29	7	2	0	19	6		.266	.304	.367	671	110	1	4			.945	-6	P-32	0.0
1908	*Det-A	30	82	5	13	1	0	0	2	10		.159	.250	.171	421	36	-5	2			.917	-6	P-29	0.0
1909	*Det-A	22	45	6	9	0	0	0	1	2		.200	.250	.200	450	41	-3	0			.974	-2	P-21	0.0
1910	Det-A	26	69	6	10	1	0	0	2	5		.145	.203	.159	362	13	-7	0			.955	-6	P-26	0.0
1911	Det-A	24	60	11	12	3	1	1	6	11		.200	.324	.333	657	79	-2	1			.935	-5	P-20	0.0
1912	Det-A	6	13	3	1	0	0	0	0	1		.077	.143	.077	220	-38	-2	0			1.000	-2	/P-3,1-2,O-2(0-0-2)	-0.3

YEAR	TM/L	G	AB	R	H	2B	3B	HR	RBI	BB	SO	AVG	OBP	SLG	OPS	OPS+	BR+	SB	CS	SBR	FA	FR	G/POS	TPR
1915	NY-A	10	12	1	1	0	0	0	0	1	6	.083	.154	.083	237	-29	-2	0			1.000	-1	/P-9,M	0.0
1916	NY-A	1	0	0	0	0	0	0	0	0	0	—	—	—	—	—	0	0			.000	-0	/P-1,M	0.0
1918	Det-A	2	2	1	1	0	0	0	1	0	0	.500	.500	.500	1000	210	0	0			1.000	-0	/P-2	0.0
Total	18	459	1302	142	251	30	11	7	93	77	6	.193	.241	.249	490	49	-80	36			.944	-30	P-378/O-37L,1-18,2S	-1.5

■ RED DOOIN

Dooin, Charles Sebastian b: 6/12/1879, Cincinnati, Ohio d: 5/14/52, Rochester, N.Y. BR/TR, 5'9.5", 165 lbs. Deb: 4/18/02 M Career OF: (11-LF 3-CF 2-RF)

YEAR	TM/L	G	AB	R	H	2B	3B	HR	RBI	BB	SO	AVG	OBP	SLG	OPS	OPS+	BR+	SB	CS	SBR	FA	FR	G/POS	TPR
1902	Phi-N	94	333	20	77	7	3	0	35	10		.231	.262	.270	533	64	-14	8			.950	5	C-84/O-6(6-0-0)	-0.2
1903	Phi-N	62	188	18	41	5	1	0	14	8		.218	.254	.255	509	47	-13	9			.940	-4	C-51/1-1,O-1(0-0-1)	-1.2
1904	Phi-N	108	355	41	86	11	4	6	36	8		.242	.261	.346	607	90	-6	15			.938	7	C-96/1-4,O-3C,3-1	1.1
1905	Phi-N	113	380	45	95	13	5	0	36	10		.250	.269	.311	580	75	-13	12			.965	8	*C-107/3-1	0.6
1906	Phi-N	113	351	25	86	19	1	0	32	13		.245	.274	.305	579	80	-9	15			.948	-10	*C-107	-1.0
1907	Phi-N	101	313	18	66	8	4	0	14	15		.211	.252	.262	513	62	-14	10			.959	2	C-94/2-1,O-1(1-0-0)	-0.3
1908	Phi-N	133	435	28	108	17	4	0	41	17		.248	.283	.306	589	85	-8	20			.966	12	*C-132	2.0
1909	Phi-N	141	468	42	105	14	1	2	38	21		.224	.264	.271	535	66	-20	14			.958	4	*C-140	-0.2
1910	Phi-N	103	331	30	80	13	4	0	30	22	17	.242	.289	.305	594	71	-13	10			.956	-4	C-91/O-3(1-1-1),M	-0.8
1911	Phi-N	74	247	18	81	15	1	1	16	14	12	.328	.366	.409	775	115	4	6			.967	5	C-74,M	1.5
1912	Phi-N	69	184	20	43	9	0	0	22	5	12	.234	.262	.283	544	46	-14	8			.958	0	C-58,M	-0.9
1913	Phi-N	55	129	6	33	4	1	0	13	3	9	.256	.273	.302	575	62	-7	1			.962	3	C-50,M	-0.1
1914	Phi-N	53	118	10	21	2	0	1	8	4	14	.178	.205	.220	425	25	-11	4			.967	-0	C-40/O-2(2-0-0),M	-0.9
1915	Cin-N	10	31	2	10	0	0	0	0	2	5	.323	.364	.323	686	106	0	1			.915	-4	C-10	-0.3
	NY-N	46	124	9	27	2	2	0	9	3	15	.218	.236	.266	502	55	-7	0	2	-1	.964	0	C-46	-0.5
	Yr	56	155	11	37	2	2	0	9	5	20	.239	.262	.277	540	66	-7	1	2	-0	.956	-3	C-56	-0.8
1916	NY-N	15	17	1	2	0	0	0	0	0	3	.118	.118	.118	235	-29	-3	0			.972	0	C-15	-0.2
Total	15	1290	4004	333	961	139	31	10	344	155	87	.240	.272	.298	570	72	-147	133	2		.957	25	*C-1195/O-16L,1-5,32	-1.4

■ MICKEY DOOLAN

Doolan, Michael Joseph "Doc" (b: Michael Joseph Doolittle)
b: 5/7/1880, Ashland, Pa. d: 11/1/51, Orlando, Fla. BR/TR, 5'10.5", 170 lbs. Deb: 4/14/05 C

YEAR	TM/L	G	AB	R	H	2B	3B	HR	RBI	BB	SO	AVG	OBP	SLG	OPS	OPS+	BR+	SB	CS	SBR	FA	FR	G/POS	TPR
1905	Phi-N	136	492	53	125	27	11	1	48	24		.254	.292	.360	651	97	-4	17			.935	-9	*S-135	-0.9
1906	Phi-N	154	535	41	123	19	7	1	55	27		.230	.270	.297	567	77	-16	16			.930	6	*S-154	-0.6
1907	Phi-N	145	509	33	104	19	7	1	47	25		.204	.243	.275	518	63	-23	18			.929	14	*S-145	-0.5
1908	Phi-N	129	445	29	104	25	4	2	49	17		.234	.267	.321	588	85	-9	5			.939	0	*S-129	-0.5
1909	Phi-N	147	493	39	108	12	10	1	35	37		.219	.276	.290	566	75	-15	10			.939	**25**	*S-147	1.6
1910	Phi-N	148	536	58	141	31	6	2	57	35	56	.263	.315	.354	670	92	-7	16			**.948**	21	*S-148	2.0
1911	Phi-N	146	512	51	122	23	6	1	49	44	65	.238	.301	.313	614	71	-21	14			.936	20	*S-145	1.0
1912	Phi-N	146	532	47	137	26	6	1	62	34	59	.258	.305	.335	639	70	-23	6			.950	8	*S-146	-0.4
1913	Phi-N	151	518	32	113	12	6	1	43	29	68	.218	.262	.270	533	50	-34	17			.941	17	*S-148/2-3	-0.7
1914	Bal-F	145	486	58	119	23	6	1	53	40	47	.245	.311	.323	634	71	-27	30			**.949**	**29**	*S-145	1.3
1915	Bal-F	119	404	41	75	13	7	2	21	24	39	.186	.238	.267	506	41	-39	10			.946	32	*S-119	0.2
	Chi-F	24	86	9	23	1	1	0	9	2	7	.267	.292	.302	594	72	-5	5			.914	1	S-24	-0.2
	Yr	143	490	50	98	14	8	2	30	26	46	.200	.248	.273	521	46	-44	15			.941	**33**	*S-143	0.0
1916	Chi-N	28	70	4	15	2	1	0	5	8	7	.214	.295	.271	566	67	-2	0			.918	3	S-24	0.2
	NY-N	18	51	4	12	3	1	1	3	2	4	.235	.264	.392	656	106	0	1			.975	2	S-16/2-2	0.3
	Yr	46	121	8	27	5	2	1	8	10	11	.223	.282	.322	605	82	-3	1			.939	4	S-40/2-2	0.5
1918	Bro-N	92	308	14	55	8	2	0	18	22	24	.179	.233	.218	451	38	-23	8			**.968**	10	2-91	-1.3
Total	13	1728	5977	513	1376	244	81	15	554	370	376	.230	.279	.306	585	71	-247	173			.940	178	*S-1625/2-96	1.5

■ HARRY DOOMS

Dooms, Henry E. "Jack" b: 1/30/1867, St.Louis, Mo. d: 12/14/1899, St.Louis, Mo. Deb: 8/7/1892

YEAR	TM/L	G	AB	R	H	2B	3B	HR	RBI	BB	SO	AVG	OBP	SLG	OPS	OPS+	BR+	SB	CS	SBR	FA	FR	G/POS	TPR
1892	Lou-N	1	4	0	0	0	0	0	0	1	3	.000	.200	.000	200	-42	-1	0			.000	-1	/O-1(0-0-1)	-0.1

■ TOM DORAN

Doran, Thomas J. "Long Tom" b: 12/2/1880, Westchester Co., N.Y. d: 6/22/10, New York, N.Y. BL/TR, 5'11", 152 lbs. Deb: 4/19/04

YEAR	TM/L	G	AB	R	H	2B	3B	HR	RBI	BB	SO	AVG	OBP	SLG	OPS	OPS+	BR+	SB	CS	SBR	FA	FR	G/POS	TPR
1904	Bos-A	12	32	1	4	0	1	0	0	4		.125	.243	.188	431	35	-2	1			.898	-5	C-11	-0.7
1905	Bos-A	3	3	0	0	0	0	0	0	0		.000	.000	.000	0	-99	-1	0			1.000	0	/C-1	0.0
	Det-A	34	94	8	15	3	0	0	4	8		.160	.248	.191	439	40	-6	2			.963	-5	C-32	-0.9
	Yr	37	97	8	15	3	0	0	4	8		.155	.241	.186	426	35	-7	2			.964	-5	C-33	-0.9
1906	Bos-A	2	3	1	0	0	0	0	0	0		.000	.000	.000	0	-99	-1	0			1.000	-0	/C-2	-0.1
Total	3	51	132	10	19	3	1	0	4	12		.144	.236	.182	418	33	-10	3			.950	-10	/C-46	-1.7

■ BILL DORAN

Doran, William Donald b: 5/28/58, Cincinnati, Ohio BB/TR, 5'11", 175 lbs. Deb: 9/6/82

YEAR	TM/L	G	AB	R	H	2B	3B	HR	RBI	BB	SO	AVG	OBP	SLG	OPS	OPS+	BR+	SB	CS	SBR	FA	FR	G/POS	TPR
1982	Hou-N	26	97	11	27	3	0	0	6	4	11	.278	.307	.309	616	79	-3	5	0	1	.975	-3	2-26	-0.4
1983	Hou-N	154	535	70	145	12	7	8	39	86	67	.271	.372	.364	736	112	11	12	12	-2	.979	5	*2-153	2.4
1984	Hou-N	147	548	92	143	18	11	4	41	66	69	.261	.343	.356	698	104	4	21	12	0	.986	6	*2-139,S-13	1.9
1985	Hou-N	148	578	84	166	31	6	14	59	71	69	.287	.365	.434	799	126	21	23	15	-0	.980	7	*2-147	3.7
1986	*Hou-N	145	550	92	152	29	3	6	37	81	57	.276	.371	.373	744	109	9	42	19	3	.974	-42	*2-144	-2.3
1987	Hou-N	162	625	82	177	23	3	16	79	82	64	.283	.369	.406	775	109	10	31	11	3	**.992**	-16	*2-162/S-3	0.6
1988	Hou-N	132	480	66	119	18	1	7	53	65	60	.248	.339	.333	672	97	0	17	4	2	**.987**	-3	*2-130	0.3
1989	Hou-N	142	507	65	111	25	2	8	58	59	63	.219	.303	.323	626	82	-12	22	3	4	.980	-27	*2-138	-3.4
1990	Hou-N	109	344	49	99	21	2	6	32	71	53	.288	.410	.413	822	131	18	18	9	1	.989	-11	2-99	1.1
	Cin-N	17	59	10	22	8	0	1	5	8	5	.373	.448	.559	1007	168	6	5	0	1	.985	1	2-12/3-4	0.8
	Yr	126	403	59	121	29	2	7	37	79	58	.300	.415	.434	849	137	24	23	9	2	.988	-10	*2-111/3-4	1.9
1991	Cin-N	111	361	51	101	12	2	6	35	46	39	.280	.361	.374	735	103	3	5	4	-0	.981	-14	2-88/O-6(6-0-0),1-4	-1.0
1992	Cin-N	132	387	48	91	16	2	8	47	64	40	.235	.344	.349	693	94	-1	7	4	0	.988	-9	*2-104,1-25	-1.0
1993	Mil-A	28	60	7	13	4	0	0	6	6	3	.217	.288	.283	571	55	-4	1	0	0	.964	-5	2-17/1-4	-0.8
Total	12	1453	5131	727	1366	220	39	84	497	709	600	.266	.356	.373	730	107	63	209	93	13	.983	-112	*2-1359/1-33,S-16,O3	1.9

■ BILL DORAN

Doran, William James b: 6/14/1898, San Francisco, Cal. d: 3/9/78, Santa Monica, Cal. BL/TR, 5'11.5", 175 lbs. Deb: 6/23/22

YEAR	TM/L	G	AB	R	H	2B	3B	HR	RBI	BB	SO	AVG	OBP	SLG	OPS	OPS+	BR+	SB	CS	SBR	FA	FR	G/POS	TPR
1922	Cle-A	3	2	0	1	0	0	0	0	1	0	.500	.667	.500	1167	206	0	0	0	0	.000	0	/3-2	0.0

■ JERRY DORGAN

Dorgan, Jeremiah F. b: 1856, Meriden, Conn. d: 6/10/1891, New Haven, Conn. BL/TR, 165 lbs. Deb: 7/8/1880 F Career OF: (1-LF 2-CF 96-RF)

YEAR	TM/L	G	AB	R	H	2B	3B	HR	RBI	BB	SO	AVG	OBP	SLG	OPS	OPS+	BR+	SB	CS	SBR	FA	FR	G/POS	TPR
1880	Wor-N	10	35	2	7	1	0	0	1	0	1	.200	.200	.229	429	41	-2				.750	-3	/O-9(0-0-9),C-1	-0.5
1882	Phi-a	44	181	25	51	9	1	0	24	4		.282	.297	.343	640	103	-0				.880	-1	C-25,O-22(1-1-20)/3-1	0.1
1884	Ind-a	34	141	22	42	6	1	0		2		.298	.317	.355	672	122	3				.793	-2	O-29(0-0-29)/C-5	0.1
	Bro-a	4	13	2	4	0	0	0		0		.308	.308	.308	615	101	-0				.921	2	/C-4	0.2
	Yr	38	154	24	46	6	1	0		2		.299	.316	.351	667	120	3				.793	-0	O-29(0-0-29)/C-9	0.3
1885	Det-N	39	161	23	46	6	2	0	24	8	10	.286	.320	.348	667	115	3				.857	-3	O-39(0-1-38)	-0.1
Total	4	131	531	74	150	22	4	0	49	14	11	.282	.303	.339	642	107	3				.817	-7	/O-99R,C-35,3-1	-0.2

■ MIKE DORGAN

Dorgan, Michael Cornelius b: 10/2/1853, Middletown, Conn.
d: 4/26/09, Hartford, Conn. BR/TR, 5'9", 180 lbs. Deb: 5/8/1877 FM Career OF: (29-LF 17-CF 556-RF)

YEAR	TM/L	G	AB	R	H	2B	3B	HR	RBI	BB	SO	AVG	OBP	SLG	OPS	OPS+	BR+	SB	CS	SBR	FA	FR	G/POS	TPR
1877	StL-N	60	266	45	82	9	7	0	23	9	13	.308	.331	.395	726	135	11				.824	-8	*O-50R,C-12/3-2,S2	0.2
1879	Syr-N	59	270	38	72	11	5	1	17	4	13	.267	.277	.356	633	120	7				.954	-5	1-21,O-16R,3/SCP2	0.1
1880	Pro-N	79	321	45	79	10	1	0	31	10	18	.246	.269	.283	552	90	-3				.858	2	*O-77R/3-2,P-1,M	-0.1
1881	Wor-N	51	220	36	61	5	0	0	18	8	4	.277	.303	.300	603	85	-4				.953	1	1-26,O-23R/S-2,M	-0.4
	Det-N	8	34	5	8	1	0	0	5	1	0	.235	.257	.265	522	62	-1				1.000	-0	/O-5(0-4-1),3-2,1-1	-0.2
	Yr	59	254	41	69	6	0	0	23	9	4	.272	.297	.295	592	82	-5				.897	0	O-28R,1-27/S-2,3-2	-0.6
1883	NY-N	64	261	32	61	11	3	0	27	2	23	.234	.240	.299	538	63	-11				.847	-5	O-59(0-9-51)/C-6,P-1	-1.5
1884	NY-N	83	341	61	94	11	6	1	48	13	27	.276	.302	.352	654	103	0				.851	1	O-64R,P-14/C-6,2-3	0.1
1885	NY-N	89	347	60	113	17	8	0	46	11	24	.326	.346	.421	767	149	18				.905	-2	*O-88(0-0-88)/1-1	1.4
1886	NY-N	118	442	61	129	19	4	2	79	29	37	.292	.335	.367	702	112	6	9			.888	-8	*O-116(6-1-110)/1-3	-0.3
1887	NY-N	71	298	41	88	10	0	0	34	15	20	.295	.302	.293	596	69	-11	22			.870	-1	O-69(1-0-68)/1-2	-1.1
1890	Syr-a	33	139	19	30	8	0	0	18	16		.216	.301	.273	575	77	-3	8			.900	-2	O-33(0-0-33)	-0.5
Total	10	715	2939	443	817	112	34	4	346	118	179	.278	.303	.340	643	102	9	39			.867	-30	O-600R/1-54,CP3S2	-2.3

■ RED DORMAN Dorman, Charles Dwight "Curlie" b: 10/3/05, Jacksonville, Ill. d: 12/7/74, Anaheim, Cal. BR/TR, 5'10.5", 180 lbs. Deb: 8/21/28

YEAR	TM/L	G	AB	R	H	2B	3B	HR	RBI	BB	SO	AVG	OBP	SLG	OPS	OPS+	BR+	SB	CS	SBR	FA	FR	G/POS	TPR
1928	Cle-A	25	77	12	28	6	0	0	11	9	6	.364	.430	.442	872	128	4	1	0	0	.915	-3	O-24(5-19-0)	0.0

■ CHARLIE DORMAN Dorman, Charles William "Slats" b: 4/23/1898, San Francisco, Cal d: 11/15/28, San Francisco, Cal BR/TR, 6'2", 185 lbs. Deb: 5/14/23

YEAR	TM/L	G	AB	R	H	2B	3B	HR	RBI	BB	SO	AVG	OBP	SLG	OPS	OPS+	BR+	SB	CS	SBR	FA	FR	G/POS	TPR
1923	Chi-A	1	2	0	1	0	0	0	0	0	0	.500	.500	.500	1000	166	0	0	0	0	1.000	-0	/C-1	0.0

■ BRIAN DORSETT Dorsett, Brian Richard b: 4/9/61, Terre Haute, Ind. BR/TR, 6'3", 220 lbs. Deb: 9/8/87

YEAR	TM/L	G	AB	R	H	2B	3B	HR	RBI	BB	SO	AVG	OBP	SLG	OPS	OPS+	BR+	SB	CS	SBR	FA	FR	G/POS	TPR
1987	Cle-A	5	11	2	3	0	0	1	3	0	3	.273	.333	.545	879	127	0	0	0	0	1.000	-2	/C-4	-0.1
1988	Cal-A	7	11	0	1	0	0	0	2	1	5	.091	.167	.091	258	-26	-2	0	0	0	1.000	1	/C-7	-0.1
1989	NY-A	8	22	3	8	1	0	0	4	1	3	.364	.391	.409	800	127	1	0	0	0	1.000	-0	/C-8	0.1
1990	NY-A	14	35	2	5	2	0	0	0	2	4	.143	.189	.200	389	9	-4	0	0	0	1.000	-1	/C-9,D-5	-0.5
1991	SD-N	11	12	0	1	0	0	0	1	0	3	.083	.083	.083	167	-51	-2	0	0	0	1.000	0	/1-2	-0.2
1993	Cin-N	25	63	7	16	4	0	2	12	3	14	.254	.288	.413	701	85	-2	0	0	0	1.000	2	C-18/1-3	0.1
1994	Cin-N	76	216	21	53	8	0	5	26	21	33	.245	.315	.352	667	74	-8	0	0	0	.991	-1	C-73/1-1	-0.5
1996	Chi-N	17	41	3	5	0	0	1	3	4	8	.122	.200	.195	395	5	-6	0	0	0	1.000	1	C-15	-0.4
Total	8	163	411	38	92	15	0	9	51	32	73	.224	.283	.326	609	62	-23	0	0	0	.995	-0	C-134/1-6,D-5	-1.6

■ JERRY DORSEY Dorsey, Jeremiah b: 1885, Oakland, Cal. BL/TL, 5'11", 175 lbs. Deb: 9/23/11

YEAR	TM/L	G	AB	R	H	2B	3B	HR	RBI	BB	SO	AVG	OBP	SLG	OPS	OPS+	BR+	SB	CS	SBR	FA	FR	G/POS	TPR
1911	Pit-N	2	6	0	0	0	0	0	0	0	1	.000	.000	.000	0	-96	-2	0			1.000	0	/O-1(0-1-0)	-0.1

■ JERRY DORSEY Dorsey, Michael Jeremiah b: 1854, Canada d: 11/3/38, Auburn, N.Y. BL, Deb: 7/9/1884

YEAR	TM/L	G	AB	R	H	2B	3B	HR	RBI	BB	SO	AVG	OBP	SLG	OPS	OPS+	BR+	SB	CS	SBR	FA	FR	G/POS	TPR
1884	Bal-U	1	3	0	0	0	0	0		0		.000	.000	.000	0	-91	-1				.000	-0	/O-1(0-0-1),P-1	-0.1

■ HERM DOSCHER Doscher, John Henry Sr. b: 12/20/1852, New York, N.Y. d: 3/20/34, Buffalo, N.Y. BR/TR, 5'10", 182 lbs. Deb: 9/4/1872 FU

YEAR	TM/L	G	AB	R	H	2B	3B	HR	RBI	BB	SO	AVG	OBP	SLG	OPS	OPS+	BR+	SB	CS	SBR	FA	FR	G/POS	TPR
1872	Atl-n	6	25	4	9	0	0	0	5	0	1	.360	.360	.360	720	104	-0	0	0	0	.769	1	/O-6(0-0-6)	0.0
1873	Atl-n	1	6	1	1	0	0	0	1	0	0	.167	.167	.167	333	-1	-1	0	0	0	.500	-0	/O-1(0-1-0)	-0.1
1875	Was-n	22	81	5	15	4	0	0	5	0	6	.185	.185	.235	420	46	-4	1	0	0	.752	1	3-22	-0.3
1879	Tro-N	47	191	16	42	8	0	0	18	2	10	.220	.228	.262	490	65	-6				.806	-4	3-47	-0.8
	Chi-N	3	11	1	2	0	0	0	1	0	3	.182	.182	.182	364	19	-1				.700	-1	/3-3	-0.2
	Yr	50	202	17	44	8	0	0	19	2	13	.218	.225	.257	483	62	-7				.800	-5	3-50	-1.0
1881	Cle-N	5	19	2	4	0	0	0	0	0	2	.211	.211	.211	421	35	-1				.895	-0	/3-5	-0.1
1882	Cle-N	25	104	7	25	2	0	0	10	0	11	.240	.240	.260	500	62	-4				.857	-2	3-22/O-2(2-0-0),S-1	-0.5
Total	3 n	29	112	10	25	4	0	0	11	0	7	.223	.223	.259	482	60	-5	1	0	0	.733	1	/3-22,O-7(0-1-6)	-0.4
Total	3	80	325	26	73	10	0	0	29	2	26	.225	.229	.255	485	61	-13				.823	-7	/3-77,O-2(2-0-0),S-1	-1.6

■ DAVID DOSTER Doster, David Eric b: 10/8/70, Ft.Wayne, Ind. BR/TR, 5'10", 185 lbs. Deb: 6/16/96

YEAR	TM/L	G	AB	R	H	2B	3B	HR	RBI	BB	SO	AVG	OBP	SLG	OPS	OPS+	BR+	SB	CS	SBR	FA	FR	G/POS	TPR
1996	Phi-N	39	105	14	28	8	0	1	8	7	21	.267	.313	.371	684	79	-3	0	0	0	.973	-1	2-24/3-1	-0.3
1999	Phi-N	99	97	9	19	2	0	3	10	12	23	.196	.284	.309	594	49	-8	1	0	0	.993	19	2-77/3-6,S-5	1.2
Total	2	138	202	23	47	10	0	4	18	19	44	.233	.299	.342	640	64	-11	1	0	0	.984	18	2-101/3-7,S-5	0.9

■ DUTCH DOTTERER Dotterer, Henry John b: 11/11/31, Syracuse, N.Y. d: 10/9/99, Syracuse, N.Y. BR/TR, 6', 209 lbs. Deb: 9/25/57

YEAR	TM/L	G	AB	R	H	2B	3B	HR	RBI	BB	SO	AVG	OBP	SLG	OPS	OPS+	BR+	SB	CS	SBR	FA	FR	G/POS	TPR
1957	Cin-N	4	12	0	1	0	0	0	2	1	2	.083	.154	.083	237	-32	-2	0	0	0	1.000	-1	/C-4	-0.3
1958	Cin-N	11	28	1	7	1	0	1	2	2	4	.250	.300	.393	693	77	-1	0	0	0	.981	4	/C-8	0.3
1959	Cin-N	52	161	21	43	7	0	2	17	16	23	.267	.333	.348	681	79	-4	0	0	0	.992	-0	C-51	-0.2
1960	Cin-N	33	79	4	18	5	0	2	11	13	10	.228	.337	.367	704	91	-1	0	1	-0	.979	1	C-31	0.1
1961	Was-A	7	19	1	5	2	0	0	1	3	5	.263	.364	.368	732	98	0	0	0	0	1.000	2	/C-7	0.2
Total	5	107	299	27	74	15	0	5	33	35	44	.247	.326	.348	674	79	-8	0	1	-0	.988	7	C-101	0.1

■ CHARLIE DOUGHERTY Dougherty, Charles William b: 2/7/1862, Darlington, Wis. d: 2/18/25, Milwaukee, Wis. Deb: 4/17/1884

YEAR	TM/L	G	AB	R	H	2B	3B	HR	RBI	BB	SO	AVG	OBP	SLG	OPS	OPS+	BR+	SB	CS	SBR	FA	FR	G/POS	TPR
1884	Alt-U	23	85	6	22	5	0	0		2		.259	.276	.318	594	78	-5				.854	0	2-16/O-8(2-2-4),S-1	-0.3

■ PATSY DOUGHERTY Dougherty, Patrick Henry b: 10/27/1876, Andover, N.Y. d: 4/30/40, Bolivar, N.Y. BL/TR, 6'2", 190 lbs. Deb: 4/19/02

YEAR	TM/L	G	AB	R	H	2B	3B	HR	RBI	BB	SO	AVG	OBP	SLG	OPS	OPS+	BR+	SB	CS	SBR	FA	FR	G/POS	TPR
1902	Bos-A	108	438	77	150	12	6	0	34	42		.342	.407	.397	805	120	14	20			.899	-9	*O-102(102-0-0)/3-1	-0.1
1903	*Bos-A	139	590	**107**	**195**	19	12	4	59	33		.331	.372	.424	796	131	22	35			.952	4	*O-139(139-0-0)	1.8
1904	Bos-A	49	195	33	53	5	4	0	4	25		.272	.355	.338	693	113	4	10			.925	0	O-49(49-0-0)	0.1
	NY-A	106	452	80	128	13	10	6	22	19		.283	.316	.396	712	119	9	11			.925	-8	*O-106(106-0-0)	-0.7
	Yr	155	647	**113**	181	18	14	6	26	44		.280	.329	.379	707	117	12	21			.925	-8	*O-155(155-0-0)	-0.6
1905	NY-A	116	418	56	110	9	6	3	29	28		.263	.319	.335	654	96	-2	17			.898	-6	*O-108(108-0-0)/3-1	-1.5
1906	NY-A	12	52	3	10	2	0	0	4	0		.192	.192	.231	423	29	-4	0			1.000	2	O-12(12-0-0)	-0.3
	*Chi-A	75	253	30	59	9	4	1	27	19		.233	.295	.312	607	92	-2	11			.985	-1	O-74(74-0-0)	-0.8
	Yr	87	305	33	69	11	4	1	31	19		.226	.278	.298	577	81	-7	11			.987	1	O-86(86-0-0)	-1.1
1907	Chi-A	148	533	69	144	17	2	1	59	36		.270	.322	.315	637	107	4	33			.946	-7	*O-148(148-0-0)	-1.2
1908	Chi-A	138	482	68	134	11	6	0	45	58		.278	.367	.326	693	128	18	**47**			.947	-15	*O-128(128-0-0)	-0.5
1909	Chi-A	139	491	71	140	23	13	1	55	51		.285	.359	.391	751	143	25	36			.942	-16	*O-138(138-0-0)	0.1
1910	Chi-A	127	443	45	110	8	6	1	43	41		.248	.318	.300	618	98	-1	22			.923	-13	*O-121(121-0-0)	-2.3
1911	Chi-A	76	211	39	61	10	9	0	32	26		.289	.380	.422	802	128	8	19			.933	-6	O-56(56-0-0)	0.0
Total	10	1233	4558	678	1294	138	78	17	413	378		.284	.346	.360	705	117	95	261			.935	-75	*O-1181(1181-0-0)/3-2	-5.4

■ JOHN DOUGLAS Douglas, John Franklin b: 9/14/17, Thayer, W.Va. d: 2/11/84, Miami, Fla. BL/TL, 6'2.5", 195 lbs. Deb: 4/21/45

YEAR	TM/L	G	AB	R	H	2B	3B	HR	RBI	BB	SO	AVG	OBP	SLG	OPS	OPS+	BR+	SB	CS	SBR	FA	FR	G/POS	TPR
1945	Bro-N	5	9	0	0	0	0	0	0	2	4	.000	.182	.000	182	-47	-2	0			.971	-1	/1-4	-0.3

■ ASTYANAX DOUGLASS Douglass, Astyanax Saunders b: 9/19/1899, Covington, Tex. d: 1/26/75, ElPaso, Tex. BL/TR, 6'1", 190 lbs. Deb: 7/30/21

YEAR	TM/L	G	AB	R	H	2B	3B	HR	RBI	BB	SO	AVG	OBP	SLG	OPS	OPS+	BR+	SB	CS	SBR	FA	FR	G/POS	TPR
1921	Cin-N	4	7	1	1	0	0	0	0	0	1	.143	.143	.143	286	-25	-1	0	0	0	1.000	0	/C-4	-0.1
1925	Cin-N	7	17	1	3	0	0	0	1	1	3	.176	.222	.176	399	3	-2	0	0	0	.889	-1	/C-7	-0.3
Total	2	11	24	2	4	0	0	0	1	1	4	.167	.200	.167	367	-4	-4	0	0	0	.926	-0	/C-11	-0.4

■ KLONDIKE DOUGLASS Douglass, William Bingham b: 5/10/1872, Boston, Pa. d: 12/13/53, Bend, Ore. BL/TR, 6', 200 lbs. Deb: 4/23/1896 Career OF: (68-LF 9-CF 55-RF)

YEAR	TM/L	G	AB	R	H	2B	3B	HR	RBI	BB	SO	AVG	OBP	SLG	OPS	OPS+	BR+	SB	CS	SBR	FA	FR	G/POS	TPR
1896	StL-N	81	296	42	78	6	4	1	28	35	15	.264	.351	.321	672	81	-7	18			.894	-7	O-74(29-5-41)/C-6,S-2	-1.5
1897	StL-N	126	519	77	170	15	3	6	50	52		.328	.402	.403	805	115	14	12			.948	-11	C-61,O-44L,1-17,/3S	0.5
1898	Phi-N	146	582	105	150	26	4	2	48	55		.258	.333	.326	660	93	-4	18			.976	2	*1-146	-0.2
1899	Phi-N	77	275	26	70	6	6	0	27	10		.255	.296	.320	616	71	-11	7			.970	-5	C-66/3-4,1-4,O-1C	-0.9
1900	Phi-N	50	160	23	48	9	4	0	25	13		.300	.360	.406	766	112	3	7			.934	-3	C-47/3-2	0.3
1901	Phi-N	51	173	14	56	6	1	0	23	11		.324	.371	.370	741	113	3	10			.979	2	C-41/1-6,O-2(1-1-0)	0.8
1902	Phi-N	109	408	37	95	12	3	0	37	23		.233	.274	.277	551	70	-15	6			.986	-8	1-69,C-29,O-10L	-2.3
1903	Phi-N	105	377	43	96	5	4	1	36	28		.255	.308	.297	605	75	-12	6			.985	-1	1-97	-1.4
1904	Phi-N	3	10	1	3	0	0	0	1	0		.300	.364	.300	664	109	0	0			.970	-0	/1-3	0.0
Total	9	748	2800	368	766	85	29	10	275	227	15	.274	.337	.335	672	91	-28	84			.981	-32	1-342,C-250,O/3S	-4.7

■ TAYLOR DOUTHIT Douthit, Taylor Lee b: 4/22/01, Little Rock, Ark. d: 5/28/86, Fremont, Cal. BR/TR, 5'11.5", 175 lbs. Deb: 9/14/23

YEAR	TM/L	G	AB	R	H	2B	3B	HR	RBI	BB	SO	AVG	OBP	SLG	OPS	OPS+	BR+	SB	CS	SBR	FA	FR	G/POS	TPR
1923	StL-N	9	27	3	5	0	2	0	0	0	4	.185	.185	.333	519	35	-3	1	0	0	1.000	-0	/O-7(3-0-4)	-0.3
1924	StL-N	53	173	24	48	13	1	0	13	16	19	.277	.349	.364	713	93	-1	4	3	-0	.976	2	O-50(9-22-19)	-0.2
1925	StL-N	30	73	13	20	3	1	1	8	2	6	.274	.312	.384	695	75	-3	0	0	0	.981	-1	O-21(4-16-1)	-0.4
1926	*StL-N	139	530	96	163	20	4	3	52	55	46	.308	.375	.377	752	99	1	23			.958	18	*O-138(1-137-0)	1.3
1927	StL-N	130	488	81	128	29	6	5	50	52	45	.262	.336	.377	713	88	-8	6			.964	8	*O-125(1-122-1)	-0.6
1928	*StL-N	154	648	111	191	35	3	3	43	84	36	.295	.384	.372	756	97	1	11			.984	24	*O-154(0-154-0)	1.8
1929	StL-N	150	613	128	206	42	7	9	62	79	49	.336	.416	.471	888	118	20	8			.974	4	*O-150(0-150-0)	1.6
1930	*StL-N	154	664	109	201	41	10	7	93	60	38	.303	.364	.426	790	87	-13	4			.964	8	*O-154(0-154-0)	-1.0
1931	StL-N	36	133	21	44	11	2	1	21	11	9	.331	.386	.466	852	123	4	1			.972	0	O-36(0-35-1)	0.4
	Cin-N	95	374	42	98	9	1	0	24	42	24	.262	.340	.291	631	76	-11	4			.983	5	O-95(0-95-0)	-0.9
	Yr	131	507	63	142	20	3	1	45	53	33	.280	.352	.337	689	89	-6	5			.980	5	*O-131(0-130-1)	-0.5
1932	Cin-N	96	333	28	81	12	1	0	25	31	29	.243	.311	.285	597	64	-16	3			.985	1	O-88(2-86-0)	-1.7
1933	Cin-N	1	0	1	0	0	0	0	0	0	0	—	—	—	—	—	0	0			.000	0	R	0.0

YEAR	TM/L	G	AB	R	H	2B	3B	HR	RBI	BB	SO	AVG	OBP	SLG	OPS	OPS+	BR+	SB	CS	SBR	FA	FR	G/POS	TPR
	Chi-N	27	71	8	16	5	0	0	5	11	7	.225	.329	.296	625	80	-1	2			.930	-0	O-18(5-13-0)	-0.2
	Yr	28	71	9	16	5	0	0	5	11	7	.225	.329	.296	625	80	-1	2			.930	-0	O-18(5-13-0)	-0.2
Total	11	1074	4127	665	1201	220	38	29	396	443	312	.291	.364	.384	748	93	-30	67	3		.972	69	*O-1036(25-984-26)	-0.2

■ CLARENCE DOW Dow, Clarence G. b: 10/2/1854, Charlestown, Mass. d: 3/11/1893, West Somerville, Mass. Deb: 9/22/1884

YEAR	TM/L	G	AB	R	H	2B	3B	HR	RBI	BB	SO	AVG	OBP	SLG	OPS	OPS+	BR+	SB	CS	SBR	FA	FR	G/POS	TPR
1884	Bos-U	1	6	1	2	0	0	0		0		.333	.333	.333	667	104	-0				.333	-1	/O-1(0-0-1)	-0.1

■ JOHN DOWD Dowd, John Leo (b: John Leo O'Dowd) b: 1/3/1891, Weymouth, Mass. d: 1/31/81, Ft.Lauderdale, Fla BR/TR, 5'8", 170 lbs. Deb: 7/3/12

YEAR	TM/L	G	AB	R	H	2B	3B	HR	RBI	BB	SO	AVG	OBP	SLG	OPS	OPS+	BR+	SB	CS	SBR	FA	FR	G/POS	TPR
1912	NY-A	10	31	1	6	1	0	0	0	6		.194	.342	.226	568	60	-1	0			.840	-3	S-10	-0.4

■ SNOOKS DOWD Dowd, Raymond Bernard b: 12/20/1897, Springfield, Mass. d: 4/4/62, Northampton, Mass. BR/TR, 5'8", 163 lbs. Deb: 4/27/19 Career OF: (0-LF 1-CF 0-RF)

YEAR	TM/L	G	AB	R	H	2B	3B	HR	RBI	BB	SO	AVG	OBP	SLG	OPS	OPS+	BR+	SB	CS	SBR	FA	FR	G/POS	TPR
1919	Det-A	1	0	0	0	0	0	0	0	0	0	—	—	—	—	—	0	0			.000	0	R	0.0
	Phi-A	13	18	4	3	0	0	0	6	0	5	.167	.167	.167	333	-6	-3	2			.800	1	/2-3,S-2,3-1,O-1C	-0.2
	Yr	14	18	4	3	0	0	0	6	0	5	.167	.167	.167	333	-6	-3	2			.800	1	/2-3,S-2,3-1,O-1C	-0.2
1926	Bro-N	2	8	0	0	0	0	0	0	0	0	.000	.000	.000	0	-99	-2	0			1.000	-2	/2-2	-0.5
Total	2	16	26	4	3	0	0	0	6	0	5	.115	.115	.115	231	-36	-5	2			.875	-1	/2-5,S-2,O-1C,3-1	-0.7

■ TOMMY DOWD Dowd, Thomas Jefferson "Buttermilk Tommy" b: 4/20/1869, Holyoke, Mass. d: 7/2/33, Holyoke, Mass. BR/TR, 5'8", 173 lbs. Deb: 4/8/1891 M Career OF: (284-LF 331-CF 350-RF)

YEAR	TM/L	G	AB	R	H	2B	3B	HR	RBI	BB	SO	AVG	OBP	SLG	OPS	OPS+	BR+	SB	CS	SBR	FA	FR	G/POS	TPR
1891	Bos-a	4	11	1	1	0	0	0	0	0	1	.091	.091	.091	182	-49	-2	0			.000	-2	/O-4(0-0-4)	-0.3
	Was-a	112	464	66	120	9	10	1	44	19	44	.259	.291	.328	618	81	-13	39			.885	-17	*2-107/O-5(5-0-0)	-2.3
	Yr	116	475	67	121	9	10	1	44	19	45	.255	.286	.322	608	77	-16	39			.885	-19	*2-107/O-9(5-0-4)	-2.6
1892	Was-N	144	584	94	142	9	10	1	50	34	49	.243	.286	.298	584	79	-16	49			.891	-33	2-98,O-23R,3-18,/S	-4.2
1893	StL-N	132	581	114	164	18	7	1	54	49	23	.282	.340	.343	683	81	-16	59			.944	3	*O-132(64-5-63)/2-1	-1.8
1894	StL-N	123	524	92	142	16	8	4	62	54	33	.271	.341	.355	696	68	-28	31			.930	-7	*O-117R/2-7,3-1	-3.3
1895	StL-N	130	508	95	164	19	17	7	74	31	31	.323	.365	.469	834	116	10	32			.928	-7	*O-116R,3-17/2-2	-0.3
1896	StL-N	126	521	93	138	17	11	5	46	42	19	.265	.322	.369	691	85	-12	40			.920	-13	2-78,O-48(0-48-0),M	-2.1
1897	StL-N	35	145	25	38	9	1	0	9	6		.262	.291	.338	629	67	-7	11			.915	-7	O-30(0-30-0)/2-5,M	-1.4
	Phi-N	91	391	68	114	14	4	0	43	19		.292	.324	.348	672	80	-12	30			.919	-6	O-73(0-23-50),2-19	-1.8
	Yr	126	536	93	152	23	5	0	52	25		.284	.316	.345	661	76	-19	41			.918	-12	*O-103(0-53-50),2-24	-3.2
1898	StL-N	139	586	70	143	17	7	0	32	30		.244	.287	.297	584	66	-27	16			.920	-17	*O-129(9-42-82),2-11	-4.9
1899	Cle-N	147	605	81	168	17	6	2	35	48		.278	.333	.336	668	90	-7	28			.954	-2	*O-147(0-147-0)	-1.8
1901	Bos-A	138	594	104	159	18	7	3	52	38		.268	.315	.337	652	82	-14	33			.937	1	*O-137L/1-2,3-1	-1.9
Total	10	1321	5514	903	1493	163	88	24	501	370	200	.271	.319	.345	664	82	-145	368			.933	-105	O-961R,2-328/3-37,S1	-26.1

■ KEN DOWELL Dowell, Kenneth Allen b: 1/19/61, Sacramento, Cal. BR/TR, 5'9", 160 lbs. Deb: 6/24/87

YEAR	TM/L	G	AB	R	H	2B	3B	HR	RBI	BB	SO	AVG	OBP	SLG	OPS	OPS+	BR+	SB	CS	SBR	FA	FR	G/POS	TPR
1987	Phi-N	15	39	4	5	0	0	0	1	2	5	.128	.171	.128	299	-19	-7	0	0	0	1.000	0	S-15	-0.5

■ JOE DOWIE Dowie, Joseph E. b: 7/15/1865, New Orleans, La. d: 3/4/17, New Orleans, La. 5'8", 150 lbs. Deb: 7/10/1889

YEAR	TM/L	G	AB	R	H	2B	3B	HR	RBI	BB	SO	AVG	OBP	SLG	OPS	OPS+	BR+	SB	CS	SBR	FA	FR	G/POS	TPR
1889	Bal-a	20	75	12	17	5	0	0	8	2	10	.227	.266	.293	559	58	-4	5			.947	0	O-20(0-0-20)	-0.4

■ RED DOWNEY Downey, Alexander Cummings b: 2/6/1889, Aurora, Ind. d: 7/10/49, Detroit, Mich. BL/TL, 5'11", 174 lbs. Deb: 9/14/09

YEAR	TM/L	G	AB	R	H	2B	3B	HR	RBI	BB	SO	AVG	OBP	SLG	OPS	OPS+	BR+	SB	CS	SBR	FA	FR	G/POS	TPR
1909	Bro-N	19	78	7	20	1	0	0	8	2		.256	.275	.269	544	71	-3	4			1.000	-1	O-19(0-3-16)	-0.6

■ TOM DOWNEY Downey, Thomas Edward b: 1/1/1884, Lewiston, Me. d: 8/3/61, Passaic, N.J. BR/TR, 5'10", 178 lbs. Deb: 5/7/09 Career OF: (0-LF 0-CF 1-RF)

YEAR	TM/L	G	AB	R	H	2B	3B	HR	RBI	BB	SO	AVG	OBP	SLG	OPS	OPS+	BR+	SB	CS	SBR	FA	FR	G/POS	TPR
1909	Cin-N	119	416	39	96	9	6	1	32	32		.231	.287	.288	576	79	-10	16			.909	-6	*S-119/C-1	-1.4
1910	Cin-N	111	378	43	102	9	3	2	32	34	28	.270	.335	.325	660	97	-1	12			.879	-7	S-68,3-41	-0.5
1911	Cin-N	111	360	50	94	16	7	0	36	44	38	.261	.345	.344	689	97	-1	10			.906	-12	S-93/2-6,3-5,1-2,O	-0.6
1912	Phi-N	54	171	27	50	6	3	1	23	21	20	.292	.370	.380	750	99	-0	3			.893	-3	3-46/S-3	-0.1
	Chi-N	13	22	4	4	0	2	0	4	1	5	.182	.217	.364	581	58	-1	0			.792	1	/S-5,3-3,2-1	0.0
	Yr	67	193	31	54	6	5	1	27	22	25	.280	.353	.378	732	95	-1	3			.892	-2	3-49/S-8,2-1	-0.1
1914	Buf-F	151	541	69	118	20	3	2	42	40	55	.218	.273	.277	550	49	-47	35			**.962**	13	*2-129,S-16/3-5	-3.3
1915	Buf-F	92	282	24	56	9	1	1	19	26	26	.199	.269	.248	517	45	-25	11			.930	2	2-48,3-35/S-2,1-1	-2.3
Total	6	651	2170	256	520	69	25	7	188	198	172	.240	.306	.304	610	74	-86	87			.901	-12	S-306,2-184,3/1OC	-8.2

■ BRIAN DOWNING Downing, Brian Jay b: 10/9/50, Los Angeles, Cal. BR/TR, 5'10", 194 lbs. Deb: 5/31/73 Career OF: (737-LF 0-CF 41-RF)

YEAR	TM/L	G	AB	R	H	2B	3B	HR	RBI	BB	SO	AVG	OBP	SLG	OPS	OPS+	BR+	SB	CS	SBR	FA	FR	G/POS	TPR
1973	Chi-A	34	73	5	13	1	0	2	4	10	17	.178	.277	.274	551	54	-4	0	0	0	1.000	0	O-13L,C-11/3-8,D-1	-0.4
1974	Chi-A	108	293	41	66	12	1	10	39	51	72	.225	.344	.375	719	104	3	0	1	-0	.994	-7	C-63,O-39(5-0-34)/D-9	-0.3
1975	Chi-A	138	420	58	101	12	1	7	41	76	75	.240	.361	.324	685	93	-1	13	4	1	.990	2	*C-137/D-1	1.0
1976	Chi-A	104	317	38	81	14	0	3	30	40	55	.256	.341	.328	669	96	-1	7	3	0	.988	-12	C-93,D-11	-0.9
1977	Chi-A	69	169	28	48	4	2	4	25	34	21	.284	.410	.402	812	123	7	1	2	-0	.983	3	C-61/O-3(2-0-1),D-2	1.2
1978	Cal-A	133	412	42	105	15	0	7	46	52	47	.255	.347	.342	689	98	1	3	2	-0	.993	-7	*C-128/D-2	0.0
1979	*Cal-A★	148	509	87	166	27	3	12	75	77	57	.326	.420	.462	881	142	34	3	3	-0	.985	-21	*C-129,D-18	1.7
1980	Cal-A	30	93	5	27	6	0	2	25	12	12	.290	.371	.419	791	119	3	0	2	-1	1.000	-4	C-16,D-13	-0.1
1981	Cal-A	93	317	47	79	14	0	9	41	46	35	.249	.351	.379	730	110	5	1	1	-0	.990	-9	O-56(56-0-0),C-37/D-5	-0.4
1982	*Cal-A	158	623	109	175	37	2	28	84	86	58	.281	.373	.482	854	132	29	2	1	0	**1.000**	2	*O-158(158-0-0)	2.3
1983	Cal-A	113	403	68	99	15	1	19	53	62	59	.246	.353	.429	782	115	9	1	2	-0	.994	-0	O-84(84-0-0),D-26	0.4
1984	Cal-A	156	539	65	148	28	2	23	91	70	66	.275	.365	.462	827	128	21	0	4	-1	**1.000**	1	*O-131(131-0-0),D-21	1.5
1985	Cal-A	150	520	80	137	23	1	20	85	78	61	.263	.373	.427	800	119	16	5	3	0	.992	2	*O-121(121-0-0),D-25	1.2
1986	*Cal-A	152	513	90	137	27	4	20	95	90	84	.267	.394	.452	846	131	26	4	4	-1	.989	1	*O-138(138-0-0),D-10	2.0
1987	Cal-A	155	567	110	154	29	3	29	77	**106**	85	.272	.401	.487	888	139	36	5	5	-1	1.000	-3	*D-118,O-34(34-0-0)	2.6
1988	Cal-A	135	484	80	117	18	2	25	64	81	63	.242	.366	.442	808	129	21	3	4	-1	.000	0	*D-132	1.6
1989	Cal-A	142	544	59	154	25	2	14	59	56	87	.283	.356	.414	770	118	14	0	2	-1	.000	0	*D-141	0.9
1990	Cal-A	96	330	47	90	18	2	14	51	50	45	.273	.378	.467	845	138	18	0	0	0	.000	0	D-87	1.5
1991	Tex-A	123	407	76	113	17	2	17	49	58	70	.278	.378	.455	833	132	19	1	1	-0	.000	0	*D-109	1.5
1992	Tex-A	107	320	53	89	18	0	10	39	62	58	.278	.408	.428	836	139	20	1	0	0	.000	0	D-93	1.8
Total	20	2344	7853	1188	2099	360	28	275	1073	1197	1127	.267	.373	.425	798	122	276	50	44	-4	.995	-51	D-824,O-777L,C-675,/3	19.1

■ RED DOWNS Downs, Jerome Willis b: 8/22/1883, Neola, Iowa d: 10/19/39, Council Bluffs, Ia BR/TR, 5'11", 155 lbs. Deb: 5/2/07 Career OF: (12-LF 8-CF 0-RF)

YEAR	TM/L	G	AB	R	H	2B	3B	HR	RBI	BB	SO	AVG	OBP	SLG	OPS	OPS+	BR+	SB	CS	SBR	FA	FR	G/POS	TPR
1907	Det-A	105	374	28	82	13	5	1	42	13		.219	.249	.289	538	69	-14	3			.930	-24	2-80,O-20L/S-1,3-1	-4.4
1908	*Det-A	84	289	28	64	10	3	1	35	5		.221	.237	.287	524	67	-11	2			.925	1	2-82/3-1	-1.1
1912	Bro-N	9	32	2	8	3	0	0	3	1	5	.250	.273	.344	616	71	-1	3			.881	-1	/2-9	-0.3
	Chi-N	43	95	9	25	4	3	1	14	9	17	.263	.327	.400	727	99	-0	5			.907	2	2-16/S-9,3-5	0.2
	Yr	52	127	11	33	7	3	1	17	10	22	.260	.314	.386	700	92	-2	8			.896	0	2-25/S-9,3-5	-0.1
Total	3	241	790	67	179	30	11	3	94	28	22	.227	.256	.304	560	72	-27	13			.924	-23	2-187/O-20L,S-10,3	-5.6

■ TOM DOWSE Dowse, Thomas Joseph b: 8/12/1866, Ireland d: 12/14/46, Riverside, Cal. BR/TR, 5'11", 175 lbs. Deb: 4/21/1890 Career OF: (12-LF 3-CF 25-RF)

YEAR	TM/L	G	AB	R	H	2B	3B	HR	RBI	BB	SO	AVG	OBP	SLG	OPS	OPS+	BR+	SB	CS	SBR	FA	FR	G/POS	TPR
1890	Cle-N	40	159	20	33	2	1	0	9	12	22	.208	.267	.233	500	47	-11	3			.870	-3	O-26R,1-10/C-3,P-1	-1.3
1891	Col-a	55	201	24	45	7	0	0	22	13	22	.224	.278	.259	536	57	-11	2			.919	-6	C-51/O-5(2-0-3)	-1.2
1892	Lou-N	41	145	10	21	2	0	0	7	2	15	.145	.173	.159	332	1	-17	1			.918	2	C-29,1-11/O-3R,2-1	-1.2
	Cin-N	1	4	0	0	0	0	0	0	0	0	.000	.000	.000	0	-99	-1	0			1.000	-1	/C-1	-0.2
	Phi-N	16	54	3	10	0	0	0	6	2	4	.185	.228	.185	413	25	-5	0			.973	-1	C-15	-0.4
	Was-N	7	27	5	7	1	0	0	2	0	3	.259	.259	.296	556	70	-1	0			.800	0	/O-4(4-0-0),C-3	-0.1
	Yr	65	230	18	38	3	0	0	15	4	22	.165	.193	.178	372	13	-24	2			.931	1	C-48,1-11/O-7L,2-1	-1.9
Total	3	160	590	62	116	12	1	0	46	29	66	.197	.243	.220	463	38	-46	7			.921	-8	C-102/O-38R,1-21,2P	-4.4

■ BRIAN DOYLE Doyle, Brian Reed b: 1/26/55, Glasgow, Ky. BL/TR, 5'10", 160 lbs. Deb: 4/30/78 F

YEAR	TM/L	G	AB	R	H	2B	3B	HR	RBI	BB	SO	AVG	OBP	SLG	OPS	OPS+	BR+	SB	CS	SBR	FA	FR	G/POS	TPR
1978	*NY-A	39	52	6	10	0	0	0	0	0	3	.192	.192	.192	385	9	-6	0	3	-1	.989	13	2-29/S-7,3-5	0.7
1979	NY-A	20	32	2	4	2	0	0	5	3	1	.125	.200	.188	388	5	-4	0	0	0	.944	1	2-13/3-6	-0.3
1980	NY-A	34	75	8	13	1	0	1	5	6	7	.173	.235	.227	461	27	-7	1	1	-0	.953	5	2-20,S-12/3-2	-0.1
1981	Oak-A	17	40	2	5	0	0	0	3	1	2	.125	.146	.125	271	-22	-6	0	1	-0	1.000	1	2-17	-0.5
Total	4	110	199	18	32	3	0	1	13	10	13	.161	.201	.191	392	10	-24	1	5	-2	.977	20	/2-79,S-19,3-13	-0.2

YEAR	TM/L	G	AB	R	H	2B	3B	HR	RBI	BB	SO	AVG	OBP	SLG	OPS	OPS+	BR+	SB	CS	SBR	FA	FR	G/POS	TPR
■ **CONNY DOYLE**	Doyle, Cornelius J. b: 1862, Ireland d: 7/29/21, ElPaso, Tex. 5'10", 185 lbs. Deb: 6/23/1883																							
1883	Phi-N	16	68	3	15	3	2	0	3	0	15	.221	.221	.324	544	69	-2				.788	-1	O-16(16-0-0)	-0.4
1884	Pit-a	15	58	8	17	3	2	0		2		.293	.317	.414	730	138	2				.818	-1	O-14(14-0-0)/S-1	0.1
Total	2	31	126	11	32	6	4	0	3	2	15	.254	.266	.365	631	101	-0				.800	-3	/O-30(30-0-0),S-1	-0.3
■ **DANNY DOYLE**	Doyle, Howard James b: 1/24/17, McLoud, Okla. BB/TR, 6'1", 195 lbs. Deb: 9/14/43																							
1943	Bos-A	13	43	2	9	1	0	0	6	7	9	.209	.320	.233	553	62	-2	0	1	-0	.964	-2	C-13	-0.4
■ **JIM DOYLE**	Doyle, James Francis b: 12/25/1881, Detroit, Mich. d: 2/1/12, Syracuse, N.Y. BR/TR, 5'10", 168 lbs. Deb: 5/4/10																							
1910	Cin-N	7	13	1	2	2	0	0	1	0	2	.154	.154	.308	462	36	-1	0			.875	-1	/3-3,O-1(0-1-0)	-0.3
1911	Chi-N	130	472	69	133	23	12	5	62	40	54	.282	.340	.413	754	110	5	19			.922	10	*3-127	1.8
Total	2	137	485	70	135	25	12	5	63	40	56	.278	.336	.410	746	109	4	19			.921	8	3-130/O-1(0-1-0)	1.5
■ **JEFF DOYLE**	Doyle, Jeffrey Donald b: 10/2/56, Havre, Mont. BB/TR, 5'9", 160 lbs. Deb: 9/13/83																							
1983	StL-N	13	37	4	11	1	2	0	2	1	3	.297	.316	.432	748	105	0	0	0	0	.966	1	2-12	0.2
■ **JACK DOYLE**	Doyle, John Joseph "Dirty Jack" b: 10/25/1869, Killorglin, Ireland d: 12/31/58, Holyoke, Mass. BR/TR, 5'9", 155 lbs. Deb: 8/27/1889 MU Career OF: (13-LF 45-CF 76-RF)																							
1889	Col-a	11	36	6	10	1	1	0	3	6	6	.278	.381	.361	742	118	1	9			.897	-3	/C-7,O-3(0-0-3),2-2	-0.1
1890	Col-a	77	298	47	80	17	7	2	44	13		.268	.299	.393	692	111	2	27			.887	-6	C-38,S-25/O-9C,23	0.0
1891	Cle-N	69	250	43	69	14	4	0	43	26	44	.276	.351	.364	715	104	1	24			.897	-3	C-29,O-21R,3-20,/S	0.0
1892	Cle-N	24	88	17	26	4	1	1	14	6	10	.295	.340	.398	738	118	2	5			.875	-1	O-12R/C-9,1-1,S-1	0.1
	NY-N	90	366	61	109	22	1	5	55	18	30	.298	.336	.404	740	126	10	42			.864	-18	2-31,C-26,O-17C,3/S	-0.5
	Yr	114	454	78	135	26	2	6	69	24	40	.297	.337	.403	740	124	11	47			.890	-18	C-35,2-31,O-29R,3/S1	-0.4
1893	NY-N	82	318	56	102	17	5	1	51	27	12	.321	.383	.415	798	112	5	40			.919	3	C-48,O-29C/S-4,31	0.9
1894	*NY-N	107	427	94	157	30	8	3	102	37	3	.368	.422	.496	918	122	15	43			.965	-1	*1-101/C-6	1.1
1895	NY-N	82	319	52	100	21	3	1	66	24	12	.313	.365	.408	773	102	1	35			.968	-2	1-58,2-13/3-6,CM	0.0
1896	*Bal-N	118	487	116	165	29	4	1	101	42	15	.339	.400	.421	821	115	11	73			.974	-11	*1-118/2-1	0.0
1897	*Bal-N	114	460	91	163	29	4	2	87	29		.354	.394	.448	842	122	14	62			.979	4	*1-114	1.5
1898	Was-N	43	177	26	54	2	2	2	26	7		.305	.335	.373	708	103	0	9			.963	-2	1-38/2-5,M	-0.2
	NY-N	82	297	42	84	15	3	1	43	12		.283	.317	.364	681	98	-2	14			.860	0	O-38R,1-24,S-15,/3C	-0.3
	Yr	125	474	68	138	17	5	3	69	19		.291	.324	.367	691	100	-2	23			.970	-2	1-62,O-38R,S-15,/23C	-0.5
1899	NY-N	119	452	56	135	16	7	3	77	33		.299	.352	.385	737	106	3	35			.976	6	*1-114/C-5	0.9
1900	NY-N	133	505	69	135	24	1	1	66	34		.267	.317	.325	642	81	-13	34			.971	6	*1-133	-0.6
1901	Chi-N	75	285	21	66	9	2	0	39	7		.232	.263	.277	540	59	-15	8			.973	7	1-75	-0.9
1902	NY-N	51	193	22	58	13	0	0	18	11		.301	.341	.368	709	120	4	12			.991	5	1-51	0.9
	Was-A	78	312	52	77	15	2	1	20	29		.247	.311	.317	628	74	-11	6			.929	-11	2-68/1-7,O-4R,C-2	-2.1
1903	Bro-N	139	524	84	164	27	6	0	91	54		.313	.383	.387	770	123	17	34			.981	2	*1-139	1.6
1904	Bro-N	8	22	2	5	1	0	0	2	6		.227	.414	.273	687	116	1	1			1.000	1	/1-8	0.2
	Phi-N	66	236	20	52	10	3	1	22	19		.220	.281	.301	582	83	-5	4			.977	4	1-65/2-1	-0.3
	Yr	74	258	22	57	11	3	1	24	25		.221	.295	.298	593	86	-4	5			.980	5	1-73/2-1	-0.1
1905	NY-A	1	3	0	0	0	0	0	0	0		.000	.000	.000	0	-90	-1	0			.833	-1	/1-1	-0.1
Total	17	1569	6055	977	1811	316	64	25	970	440	132	.299	.351	.385	736	106	43	517			.975	-18	*1-1048,C-176,O2/S3	2.1
■ **JOE DOYLE**	Doyle, Joseph K. b: Cincinnati, Ohio Deb: 4/20/1872																							
1872	Nat-n	9	41	6	12	1	0	0	9	0	0	.293	.293	.317	610	75	-2	0	0	0	.667	-4	/S-8,2-1	-0.4
■ **LARRY DOYLE**	Doyle, Lawrence Joseph "Laughing Larry" b: 7/31/1886, Caseyville, Ill. d: 3/1/74, Saranac Lake, N.Y. BL/TR, 5'10", 165 lbs. Deb: 7/22/07																							
1907	NY-N	69	227	16	59	3	0	0	16	20		.260	.320	.273	593	83	-4	3			.917	-22	2-69	-2.9
1908	NY-N	104	377	65	116	16	9	0	33	22		.308	.354	.398	752	134	13	17			.935	-10	*2-102	0.5
1909	NY-N	147	570	86	**172**	27	11	6	49	45		.302	.360	.419	779	140	25	31			.940	-18	*2-144	0.9
1910	NY-N	151	575	97	164	21	14	8	69	71	26	.285	.369	.412	781	128	20	39			.930	-17	*2-151	0.5
1911	*NY-N	143	526	102	163	25	**25**	13	77	71	39	.310	.397	.527	924	153	36	38			.944	-24	*2-141	1.4
1912	*NY-N	143	558	98	184	33	8	10	90	56	20	.330	.393	.471	864	132	24	36			.948	-8	*2-143	1.8
1913	*NY-N	132	482	67	135	25	6	5	73	59	29	.280	.364	.388	752	114	10	38			.955	-13	*2-130	0.0
1914	NY-N	145	539	87	140	19	8	5	63	58	25	.260	.343	.353	695	111	8	17			.959	-19	*2-145	-0.9
1915	NY-N	150	591	86	**189**	**40**	10	4	70	32	28	**.320**	.358	.442	799	150	33	22	18	-1	.947	-8	*2-147	2.8
1916	NY-N	113	441	55	118	24	10	2	47	27	23	.268	.316	.381	697	120	9	17			.960	16	*2-113	3.0
	Chi-N	9	38	6	15	5	1	1	7	1	1	.395	.410	.658	1068	203	4	2			.982	5	/2-9	1.0
	Yr	122	479	61	133	29	11	3	54	28	24	.278	.323	.403	726	127	14	19			.962	20	*2-122	4.0
1917	Chi-N	135	476	48	121	19	5	6	61	48	28	.254	.323	.353	675	99	0	5			.952	-2	*2-128	0.0
1918	NY-N	75	257	38	67	7	4	3	36	37	10	.261	.354	.354	708	118	7	10			.969	-12	2-73	-0.4
1919	NY-N	113	381	61	110	14	10	7	52	31	17	.289	.350	.433	783	136	16	12			.956	2	*2-100	2.2
1920	NY-N	137	471	48	134	21	2	4	50	47	28	.285	.352	.363	715	107	5	11	9	-1	.967	-26	*2-133	-2.1
Total	14	1766	6509	960	1887	299	123	74	793	625	274	.290	.357	.408	765	126	207	298	27		.949	-156	*2-1728	7.8
■ **DENNY DOYLE**	Doyle, Robert Dennis b: 1/17/44, Glasgow, Ky. BL/TR, 5'9", 175 lbs. Deb: 4/7/70 F																							
1970	Phi-N	112	413	43	86	10	7	2	16	33	64	.208	.267	.281	548	48	-31	6	5	-0	.978	-16	*2-103	-4.2
1971	Phi-N	95	342	34	79	12	1	3	24	19	31	.231	.281	.298	580	64	-16	4	2	0	.967	4	2-91	-0.7
1972	Phi-N	123	442	33	110	14	2	1	26	31	33	.249	.298	.296	594	68	-18	6	7	-1	.982	-9	*2-119	-2.3
1973	Phi-N	116	370	45	101	9	3	3	26	31	32	.273	.329	.338	667	83	-8	1	3	-1	.974	9	*2-114	0.7
1974	Cal-A	147	511	47	133	19	2	1	34	25	49	.260	.296	.311	607	79	-14	6	7	-1	.983	16	*2-146/S-2	1.1
1975	Cal-A	8	15	0	1	0	0	0	0	1	1	.067	.125	.067	192	-48	-3	0	0	0	.926	2	/2-6,3-1	-0.1
	*Bos-A	89	310	50	96	21	2	4	36	14	11	.310	.342	.429	771	107	2	5	7	-1	.974	-31	2-84/3-6,S-2	-2.5
	Yr	97	325	50	97	21	2	4	36	15	12	.298	.331	.412	744	102	0	5	7	-1	.970	-29	2-90/3-7,S-2	-2.6
1976	Bos-A	117	432	51	108	15	5	0	26	22	39	.250	.286	.308	594	66	-18	8	5	0	.977	-25	*2-112	-3.9
1977	Bos-A	137	455	54	109	13	6	2	49	29	50	.240	.291	.308	599	57	-27	2	4	-1	.979	-10	*2-137	-3.0
Total	8	944	3290	357	823	113	28	16	237	205	310	.250	.296	.316	612	70	-133	38	40	-6	.977	-61	2-912/3-7,S-4	-14.9
■ **D. J. DOZIER**	Dozier, William Henry b: 9/21/65, Norfolk, Va. BR/TR, 6', 202 lbs. Deb: 5/6/92																							
1992	NY-N	25	47	4	9	2	0	0	2	4	19	.191	.269	.234	503	44	-3	4	0	1	.971	0	O-17(17-0-0)	-0.3
■ **DELOS DRAKE**	Drake, Delos Daniel b: 12/3/1886, Girard, Ohio d: 10/3/65, Findlay, Ohio BR/TL, 5'11.5", 170 lbs. Deb: 4/30/11 Career OF: (150-LF 103-CF 49-RF)																							
1911	Det-A	95	315	37	88	9	9	1	36	17		.279	.324	.375	699	90	-5	20			.942	-10	O-83(74-5-5)/1-2	-1.9
1914	StL-F	138	514	51	129	18	8	3	42	31	57	.251	.295	.335	630	68	-31	17			.957	-1	*O-116(69-36-11),1-18	-4.1
1915	StL-F	102	343	32	91	23	4	1	41	23	27	.265	.313	.364	678	86	-12	6			.974	-5	O-97(7-62-33)/1-1	-2.4
Total	3	335	1172	120	308	50	21	5	119	71	84	.263	.308	.354	662	79	-48	43			.959	-16	O-296L/1-21	-8.4
■ **LARRY DRAKE**	Drake, Larry Francis b: 5/4/21, McKinney, Tex. d: 7/14/85, Houston, Tex. BL/TR, 6'1.5", 195 lbs. Deb: 7/20/45																							
1945	Phi-A	1	2	0	0	0	0	0	0	0	2	.000	.000	.000	0	-99	-1	0	0	0	1.000	-0	/O-1(1-0-0)	-0.1
1948	Was-A	4	7	0	2	0	0	0	1	1	3	.286	.375	.286	661	79	-0	0	0	0	1.000	-0	/O-2(0-0-2)	0.0
Total	2	5	9	0	2	0	0	0	1	1	5	.222	.300	.222	522	44	-1	0	0	0	1.000	-0	/O-3(1-0-2)	-0.1
■ **LYMAN DRAKE**	Drake, Lyman Daniel b: 2/9/1852, Berea, Ohio d: 2/6/32, Muskegon, Mich. 6', Deb: 6/29/1884																							
1884	Was-a	2	7	0	2	1	0	0	2	0		.286	.286	.429	714	147	0				.000	-1	/O-2(0-0-2)	-0.1
■ **SAMMY DRAKE**	Drake, Samuel Harrison b: 10/7/34, Little Rock, Ark. BB/TR, 5'11", 175 lbs. Deb: 4/17/60 F																							
1960	Chi-N	15	15	5	1	0	0	0	0	1	4	.067	.125	.067	192	-46	-3	0	0	0	1.000	-1	/3-6,2-2	-0.4
1961	Chi-N	13	5	1	0	0	0	0	0	1	1	.000	.167	.000	167	-50	-1	0	0	0	1.000	-0	/O-1(0-0-1)	-0.1
1962	NY-N	25	52	2	10	0	0	0	7	6	12	.192	.276	.192	468	28	-5	0	0	0	.977	-2	2-10/3-6	-0.7
Total	3	53	72	8	11	0	0	0	7	8	17	.153	.237	.153	390	8	-9	0	0	0	.978	-3	/2-12,3-12,O-1(0-0-1)	-1.2

YEAR	TM/L	G	AB	R	H	2B	3B	HR	RBI	BB	SO	AVG	OBP	SLG	OPS	OPS+	BR+	SB	CS	SBR	FA	FR	G/POS	TPR
■ **SOLLY DRAKE** Drake, Solomon Louis b: 10/23/30, Little Rock, Ark. BB/TR, 6', 170 lbs. Deb: 4/17/56 F																								
1956	Chi-N	65	215	29	55	9	1	2	15	23	35	.256	.331	.335	665	81	-5	9	5	0	.993	2	O-53(0-53-0)	-0.5
1959	LA-N	9	8	2	2	0	0	0	0	1	3	.250	.333	.250	583	54	-0	1	0	0	.667	-1	/O-4(0-0-4)	-0.2
	Phi-N	67	62	10	9	1	0	0	3	8	15	.145	.243	.161	404	10	-8	5	5	-1	1.000	-10	O-37(22-11-9)	-1.9
	Yr	76	70	12	11	1	0	0	3	9	18	.157	.253	.171	425	15	-8	6	5	-0	.974	-11	O-41(22-11-13)	-2.1
Total	2	141	285	41	66	10	1	2	18	32	53	.232	.311	.295	606	64	-14	15	10	-0	.989	-9	/O-94(22-64-13)	-2.6
■ **KELLY DRANSFELDT** Dransfeldt, Kelly Daniel b: 4/16/75, Joliet, Ill. BR/TR, 6'2", 195 lbs. Deb: 5/1/99																								
1999	Tex-A	16	53	3	10	1	0	1	5	3	12	.189	.232	.264	496	25	-6	0	0	0	.966	3	S-16	-0.1
2000	Tex-A	16	26	2	3	2	0	0	2	1	14	.115	.148	.192	340	-14	-5	0	0	0	1.000	5	S-14/2-2	0.1
Total	2	32	79	5	13	3	0	1	7	4	26	.165	.205	.241	445	12	-11	0	0	0	.977	8	/S-30,2-2	0.0
■ **JAKE DRAUBY** Drauby, Jacob C. b: 1865, Harrisburg, Pa. 5'10", 163 lbs. Deb: 10/3/1892																								
1892	Was-N	10	34	3	7	0	1	0	3	2	12	.206	.250	.265	515	57	-2	0			.763	-2	3-10	-0.3
■ **BILL DREESEN** Dreesen, William Richard b: 7/26/04, New York, N.Y. d: 11/9/71, Mt.Vernon, N.Y. BL/TR, 5'7.5", 160 lbs. Deb: 5/1/31																								
1931	Bos-N	48	180	38	40	10	4	1	10	23	23	.222	.310	.339	649	77	-6	1			.910	-8	3-47	-1.2
■ **BILL DRESCHER** Drescher, William Clayton "Dutch" b: 5/23/21, Congers, N.Y. d: 5/15/68, Haverstraw, N.Y. BL/TR, 6'2", 190 lbs. Deb: 4/19/44																								
1944	NY-A	4	7	0	1	0	0	0	0	0	0	.143	.143	.143	286	-18	-1	0	0	0	.875	0	/C-1	-0.1
1945	NY-A	48	126	10	34	3	1	0	15	8	5	.270	.313	.310	623	77	-4	0	2	-1	.991	-8	C-33	-1.1
1946	NY-A	5	6	0	2	1	0	0	1	0	0	.333	.333	.500	833	129	0	0	0	0	1.000	1	/C-3	0.1
Total	3	57	139	10	37	4	1	0	16	8	5	.266	.306	.309	615	75	-4	0	2	-1	.985	-7	/C-37	-1.1
■ **CHUCK DRESSEN** Dressen, Charles Walter b: 9/20/1898, Decatur, Ill. d: 8/10/66, Detroit, Mich. BR/TR, 5'5.5", 146 lbs. Deb: 4/17/25 MC Career OF: (4-LF 0-CF 1-RF)																								
1925	Cin-N	76	215	35	59	8	2	3	19	12	4	.274	.319	.372	691	78	-7	5	3	0	.951	2	3-47/2-5,O-4(3-0-1)	-0.3
1926	Cin-N	127	474	76	126	27	11	4	48	49	31	.266	.338	.395	733	99	-1	0			.966	17	*3-123/S-1,O-1(1-0-0)	2.3
1927	Cin-N	144	548	78	160	36	10	2	55	71	32	.292	.376	.405	781	113	12	7			**.967**	12	*3-142/S-2	3.2
1928	Cin-N	135	498	72	145	26	3	1	59	43	22	.291	.355	.361	716	89	-7	10			.938	-2	*3-135	0.0
1929	Cin-N	110	401	49	98	22	3	1	36	41	21	.244	.321	.322	642	63	-23	8			.932	-20	3-98/2-8	-3.4
1930	Cin-N	33	19	0	4	0	0	0	1	1	3	.211	.250	.211	461	14	-3	0			1.000	3	3-10/2-3	0.0
1931	Cin-N	5	15	0	1	0	0	0	0	1	1	.067	.125	.067	192	-50	-3	0			.846	-0	/3-4	-0.3
1933	NY-N	16	45	3	10	4	0	0	3	1	4	.222	.239	.311	550	57	-3	0			.972	0	3-16	-0.2
Total	8	646	2215	313	603	123	29	11	221	219	118	.272	.343	.369	711	89	-35	30	3		.953	12	3-575/2-16,O-5L,S-3	1.3
■ **LEE DRESSEN** Dressen, Lee August b: 7/23/1889, Ellinwood, Kan. d: 6/30/31, Diller, Neb. BL/TL, 6', 165 lbs. Deb: 4/21/14																								
1914	StL-N	46	103	16	24	2	1	0	7	11	20	.233	.307	.272	579	73	-3	2			.982	-1	1-38	-0.6
1918	Det-A	31	107	10	19	1	2	0	3	21	10	.178	.323	.224	547	68	-3	2			.988	-3	1-30	-0.8
Total	2	77	210	26	43	3	3	0	10	32	30	.205	.316	.248	563	71	-6	4			.985	-5	/1-68	-1.4
■ **CAMERON DREW** Drew, Cameron Steward b: 2/12/64, Boston, Mass. BL/TR, 6'5", 230 lbs. Deb: 9/9/88																								
1988	Hou-N	7	16	1	3	0	1	0	1	0	1	.188	.188	.313	500	43	-1	0	0	0	1.000	0	/O-5(3-0-2)	-0.1
■ **DAVE DREW** Drew, David Deb: 5/14/1884																								
1884	Phi-U	2	9	1	4	0	0	0		0		.444	.444	.444	889	184	1				.000	-0	/P-1,2-1,S-1	0.1
	Was-U	13	53	8	16	1	2	0		1		.302	.315	.396	711	118	-0				.806	1	/S-8,1-5,O-1(0-1-0)	0.0
	Yr	15	62	9	20	1	2	0		1		.323	.333	.403	737	127	0				.813	1	/S-9,1-5,P-1,2-1,O	0.1
■ **J.D. DREW** Drew, David Jonathan b: 11/20/75, Tallahassee, Fla. BL/TR, 6'1", 190 lbs. Deb: 9/8/98 F																								
1998	StL-N	14	36	9	15	3	1	5	13	4	10	.417	.475	.972	1447	271	9	0	0	0	1.000	-0	O-11(6-2-5)	0.8
1999	StL-N	104	368	72	89	16	6	13	39	50	77	.242	.342	.424	766	92	-5	19	3	3	.972	9	O-98(1-97-0)	0.8
2000	*StL-N	135	407	73	120	17	2	18	57	67	99	.295	.402	.479	881	121	15	17	9	1	.966	-5	*O-127(24-26-98)	0.6
Total	3	253	811	154	224	36	9	36	109	121	186	.276	.378	.476	854	114	19	36	12	4	.970	4	O-236(31-125-103)	2.2
■ **FRANK DREWS** Drews, Frank John b: 5/25/16, Buffalo, N.Y. d: 4/22/72, Buffalo, N.Y. BR/TR, 5'10", 175 lbs. Deb: 8/13/44																								
1944	Bos-N	46	141	14	29	9	1	0	10	25	14	.206	.329	.284	613	71	-5	0			.959	1	2-46	-0.1
1945	Bos-N	49	147	13	30	4	1	0	19	16	18	.204	.282	.245	527	47	-10	0			.976	5	2-48	-0.3
Total	2	95	288	27	59	13	2	0	29	41	32	.205	.306	.264	570	59	-15	0			.967	5	/2-94	-0.4
■ **DAN DRIESSEN** Driessen, Daniel b: 7/29/51, Hilton Head Island, S.C. BL/TR, 5'11", 190 lbs. Deb: 6/9/73 Career OF: (30-LF 0-CF 23-RF)																								
1973	*Cin-N	102	366	49	110	15	2	4	47	24	37	.301	.347	.385	732	108	4	8	3	1	.946	-10	3-87,1-35/O-1(0-0-1)	-0.7
1974	Cin-N	150	470	63	132	23	6	7	56	48	62	.281	.349	.400	749	111	6	10	5	0	.915	-21	*3-126,1-47/O-3R	-1.7
1975	*Cin-N	88	210	38	59	8	1	7	38	35	30	.281	.389	.429	817	124	8	10	3	1	.986	-5	1-41,O-29(10-0-19)	0.0
1976	*Cin-N	98	219	32	54	11	1	7	44	43	32	.247	.370	.402	772	116	6	14	1	3	.997	-3	1-40,O-20(20-0-0)	0.2
1977	Cin-N	151	536	75	161	31	4	17	91	64	85	.300	.378	.468	846	123	19	31	13	2	.994	-3	*1-148	0.8
1978	Cin-N	153	524	68	131	23	3	16	70	75	79	.250	.348	.397	745	108	7	28	9	3	**.996**	3	*1-151	0.4
1979	*Cin-N	150	515	72	129	24	3	18	75	62	77	.250	.334	.414	748	102	2	11	5	1	.993	-3	*1-143	-1.0
1980	Cin-N	154	524	81	139	36	1	14	74	**93**	68	.265	.382	.418	800	123	20	19	6	2	.995	-4	*1-151	0.9
1981	Cin-N	82	233	35	55	14	0	7	33	40	31	.236	.353	.386	739	108	3	2	4	-1	.995	-5	1-74	-0.8
1982	Cin-N	149	516	64	139	25	1	17	57	82	62	.269	.372	.421	792	119	15	11	6	0	**.998**	-7	*1-144	0.0
1983	Cin-N	122	386	57	107	17	1	12	57	75	51	.277	.395	.420	814	121	14	6	4	-0	**.996**	-2	*1-112	0.5
1984	Cin-N	81	218	27	61	13	0	7	28	37	25	.280	.384	.436	820	124	8	2	1	0	.991	-4	1-70	0.1
	Mon-N	51	169	20	43	11	0	9	32	17	15	.254	.323	.479	802	128	6	0	1	-0	.995	-2	1-45	0.1
	Yr	132	387	47	104	24	0	16	60	54	40	.269	.358	.455	813	126	14	2	2	-0	.992	-5	*1-115	0.2
1985	Mon-N	91	312	31	78	18	0	6	25	33	29	.250	.326	.365	691	99	-1	2	2	-0	.997	3	1-88	-0.4
	SF-N	54	181	22	42	8	0	3	22	17	22	.232	.302	.326	627	79	-5	0	0	0	.998	-2	1-49	-1.0
	Yr	145	493	53	120	26	0	9	47	50	51	.243	.317	.351	668	92	-6	2	2	-0	.997	1	*1-137	-1.4
1986	SF-N	15	16	2	3	2	0	0	0	4	4	.188	.350	.313	663	89	-0	0	0	0	1.000	1	/1-4	0.0
	Hou-N	17	24	5	7	1	0	1	3	5	2	.292	.414	.458	872	144	2	0	0	0	1.000	-0	1-12	0.1
	Yr	32	40	7	10	3	0	1	3	9	6	.250	.388	.400	788	122	2	0	0	0	1.000	0	1-16	0.1
1987	*StL-N	24	60	5	14	2	0	1	11	7	8	.233	.313	.317	630	66	-3	0	0	0	.993	-0	1-21	-0.4
Total	15	1732	5479	746	1464	282	23	153	763	761	719	.267	.359	.411	770	113	109	154	63	12	.995	-64	*1-1375,3-213/O-53L	-2.9
■ **LEW DRILL** Drill, Lewis L b: 5/9/1877, Browerville, Minn. d: 7/4/69, St.Paul, Minn. BR/TR, 5'6", 186 lbs. Deb: 4/23/02 Career OF: (1-LF 3-CF 18-RF)																								
1902	Was-A	38	123	21	34	7	2	1	16	16		.276	.369	.390	759	110	2	0			.919	-11	C-28/2-4,O-4R,3-1	-0.6
	Bal-A	2	8	2	2	0	0	0	0	0		.250	.250	.250	500	37	-1	0			1.000	1	/C-1,1-1	0.0
	Was-A	33	98	12	24	3	2	0	13	10		.245	.327	.316	644	78	-3	5			.926	-4	C-25/O-4(0-0-4),2-1	-0.4
	Yr	73	229	35	60	10	4	1	29	26		.262	.347	.354	701	94	-1	5			.924	-15	C-54/O-8R,2-5,31	-1.0
1903	Was-A	51	154	11	39	9	3	0	23	15		.253	.331	.351	682	103	1	4			.966	-4	C-47/1-3	0.2
1904	Was-A	46	142	17	38	7	2	1	11	21		.268	.385	.366	751	140	8	3			.934	-7	C-29,O-14(0-3-11)	0.4
	Det-A	51	160	7	39	6	1	0	13	20		.244	.335	.294	629	103	1	2			.950	-7	C-49/1-2	0.0
	Yr	97	302	24	77	13	3	1	24	41		.255	.359	.328	687	121	10	5			.944	-14	C-78,O-14(0-3-11)/1-2	0.4
1905	Det-A	72	211	17	55	9	0	0	24	32		.261	.366	.303	669	112	5	7			.970	-2	C-71	1.1
Total	4	293	896	87	231	41	10	2	100	114		.258	.353	.333	686	108	14	21			.953	-34	C-250/O-22R,1-6,23	0.7
■ **JIM DRISCOLL** Driscoll, James Bernard b: 5/14/44, Medford, Mass. BL/TR, 5'11", 175 lbs. Deb: 6/17/70																								
1970	Oak-A	21	52	2	10	0	0	1	2	2	15	.192	.236	.250	486	35	-5	0	0	0	.967	-3	/2-7,S-7	-0.6
1972	Tex-A	15	18	0	0	0	0	0	0	2	3	.000	.100	.000	100	-72	-4	0	0	0	.900	1	/2-4,3-2	-0.3
Total	2	36	70	2	10	0	0	1	2	4	18	.143	.200	.186	386	9	-8	0	0	0	.950	-1	/2-11,S-7,3-2	-0.9
■ **DENNIS DRISCOLL** Driscoll, Dennis F. d: 2/21/01, Providence, R.I. Deb: 7/25/1885																								
1885	Buf-N	7	19	2	3	0	0	0	0	2	5	.158	.238	.158	396	29	-1				.719	-5	/2-7	-0.6

YEAR	TM/L	G	AB	R	H	2B	3B	HR	RBI	BB	SO	AVG	OBP	SLG	OPS	OPS+	BR+	SB	CS	SBR	FA	FR	G/POS	TPR
■ DENNY DRISCOLL Driscoll, John F. b: 11/19/1855, Lowell, Mass. d: 7/11/1886, Lowell, Mass. BL/TL, 5'10.5", 160 lbs. Deb: 7/1/1880 Career OF: (1-LF 17-CF 2-RF)																								
1880	Buf-N	18	65	1	10	1	0	0	4	1	7	.154	.167	.169	336	14	-6				.895	-2	O-14(0-14-0)/P-6	-0.6
1882	Pit-a	23	80	12	11	2	0	1		3		.138	.169	.200	369	25	-6				.885	-4	P-23	0.0
1883	Pit-a	41	148	19	27	2	1	0		4		.182	.204	.209	413	35	-10				.890	4	P-41/O-4(0-2-2),3-1	-0.2
1884	Lou-a	13	48	5	9	1	0	0	1	2		.188	.220	.208	428	42	-3				.816	2	P-13/O-2(1-1-0)	-0.1
Total	4	95	341	37	57	6	1	1	5	10	7	.167	.191	.199	390	30	-24				.872	0	/P-83,O-20C,3-1	-0.9
■ PADDY DRISCOLL Driscoll, John Leo b: 1/11/1895, Evanston, Ill. d: 6/28/68, Chicago, Ill. BR/TR, 5'8.5", 155 lbs. Deb: 6/12/17																								
1917	Chi-N	13	28	2	3	1	0	0	3	2	6	.107	.167	.143	310	-4	-3	2			.882	2	/2-8,3-2,S-1	-0.1
■ MIKE DRISSEL Drissel, Michael F. b: 12/19/1864, St.Louis, Mo. d: 2/26/13, St.Louis, Mo. BR/TR, 5'11", Deb: 9/5/1885																								
1885	StL-a	6	20	0	1	0	0	0	0	0		.050	.050	.050	100	-65	-4				.971	-0	/C-6	-0.3
■ WALT DROPO Dropo, Walter "Moose" b: 1/30/23, Moosup, Conn. BR/TR, 6'5", 220 lbs. Deb: 4/19/49																								
1949	Bos-A	11	41	3	6	2	0	0	1	3	7	.146	.205	.195	400	6	-6	0	0	0	1.000	-1	1-11	-0.7
1950	Bos-A★	136	559	101	180	28	8	34	**144**	45	75	.322	.378	.583	961	130	22	0	0	0	.988	-4	*1-134	1.2
1951	Bos-A	99	360	37	86	14	0	11	57	38	52	.239	.312	.369	681	76	-13	0	0	0	.987	-1	1-93	-1.6
1952	Bos-A	37	132	13	35	7	1	6	27	11	22	.265	.331	.470	801	112	2	0	0	0	.994	-1	1-35	-0.1
	Det-A	115	459	56	128	17	3	23	70	26	63	.279	.320	.479	800	120	9	2	2	-0	.989	-1	*1-115	0.4
	Yr	152	591	69	163	24	4	29	97	37	85	.276	.323	.477	800	118	10	2	2	-0	.990	-2	*1-150	0.3
1953	Det-A	152	606	61	150	30	3	13	96	29	69	.248	.289	.371	660	78	-21	2	0	0	.990	12	*1-150	-1.8
1954	Det-A	107	320	27	90	14	2	4	44	24	41	.281	.331	.375	706	95	-3	0	1	-0	.996	1	1-95	-0.8
1955	Chi-A	141	453	55	127	15	2	19	79	42	71	.280	.344	.448	792	109	4	0	1	-0	.995	-5	*1-140	-0.9
1956	Chi-A	125	361	42	96	13	1	8	52	37	51	.266	.339	.374	713	87	-7	1	0	0	**.993**	-3	*1-117	-1.5
1957	Chi-A	93	223	24	57	2	0	13	49	16	40	.256	.305	.439	745	101	-1	0	1	-0	.987	2	1-69	-0.2
1958	Chi-A	28	52	3	10	1	0	2	8	5	11	.192	.276	.327	603	67	-2	0	0	0	1.000	1	1-16	-0.3
	Cin-N	63	162	18	47	7	2	7	31	12	31	.290	.343	.488	831	111	2	0	0	0	1.000	1	1-43	0.1
1959	Cin-N	26	39	4	4	1	0	1	2	4	7	.103	.205	.205	410	9	-5	0	0	0	1.000	2	1-23	-0.4
	Bal-A	62	151	17	42	9	0	6	21	12	20	.278	.331	.457	788	117	3	0	0	0	.990	-2	1-54/3-2	-0.1
1960	Bal-A	79	179	16	48	8	0	4	21	20	19	.268	.345	.380	725	97	-1	0	1	-0	.993	-1	1-67/3-1	-0.4
1961	Bal-A	14	27	1	7	0	0	1	2	4	3	.259	.355	.370	725	97	-0	0	0	0	1.000	1	1-12	0.0
Total	13	1288	4124	478	1113	168	22	152	704	328	582	.270	.327	.432	759	100	-16	5	6	-1	.992	-1	*1-1174/3-3	-7.1
■ KEITH DRUMRIGHT Drumright, Keith Alan b: 10/21/54, Springfield, Mo. BL/TR, 5'10", 170 lbs. Deb: 9/1/78																								
1978	Hou-N	17	55	5	9	0	0	0	2	3	4	.164	.207	.164	371	5	-7	0	1	-0	.944	-1	2-17	-0.8
1981	*Oak-A	31	86	8	25	1	1	0	11	4	4	.291	.322	.326	648	91	-1	0	0	0	.989	-5	2-19/D-5	-0.6
Total	2	48	141	13	34	1	1	0	13	7	8	.241	.277	.262	539	58	-8	0	1	-0	.969	-6	/2-36,D-5	-1.4
■ JEAN DUBUC Dubuc, Jean Joseph Octave Arthur "Chauncey" b: 9/15/1888, St.Johnsbury, Vt. d: 8/28/58, Fort Myers, Fla. BR/TR, 5'10.5", 185 lbs. Deb: 6/25/08 C																								
1908	Cin-N	15	29	2	4	1	0	0	2	0		.138	.138	.172	310	-1	-3	0			.943	1	P-15	0.0
1909	Cin-N	19	18	1	3	0	0	0	0	2		.167	.250	.167	417	30	-1	0			.844	0	P-19	0.0
1912	Det-A	40	108	16	29	6	2	1	9	3		.269	.295	.389	684	98	-1	0			.972	4	P-37/O-2(0-0-2)	0.0
1913	Det-A	68	135	17	36	5	3	2	11	2	17	.267	.277	.393	670	97	-2	1			.953	6	P-36/O-3(1-0-2)	-0.2
1914	Det-A	71	124	9	28	8	1	1	11	7	11	.226	.273	.331	603	79	-4	1			.942	3	P-36	0.0
1915	Det-A	60	112	7	23	2	1	0	14	8	15	.205	.258	.241	499	47	-7	0			.969	1	P-39	0.0
1916	Det-A	52	78	3	20	0	2	0	7	7	12	.256	.318	.308	625	85	-1	0			.952	4	P-36	0.0
1918	*Bos-A	5	6	0	1	0	0	0	0	1	2	.167	.286	.167	452	37	-0	0			1.000	-0	/P-2	0.0
1919	NY-N	37	42	2	6	1	1	0	2	0	6	.143	.143	.214	357	7	-5	0			.964	2	P-36	0.0
Total	9	367	652	57	150	23	10	4	56	30	63	.230	.266	.314	580	72	-25	2			.952	21	P-256/O-5(1-0-4)	-0.2
■ ROB DUCEY Ducey, Robert Thomas b: 5/24/65, Toronto, Ont., Can. BL/TR, 6'2", 180 lbs. Deb: 5/1/87 Career OF: (227-LF 85-CF 155-RF)																								
1987	Tor-A	34	48	12	9	1	0	1	6	8	10	.188	.304	.271	574	53	-3	2	0	0	1.000	-7	O-28(17-11-3)/D-1	-1.0
1988	Tor-A	27	54	15	17	4	1	0	6	5	7	.315	.373	.426	799	123	2	1	0	0	1.000	-6	O-26(1-25-0)/D-1	-0.4
1989	Tor-A	41	76	5	16	4	0	0	7	9	25	.211	.294	.263	557	59	-4	2	1	0	1.000	-2	O-35(16-2-18)/D-1	-0.6
1990	Tor-A	19	53	7	16	5	0	0	7	7	15	.302	.393	.396	790	119	2	1	1	-0	1.000	-0	O-19(19-0-0)	0.1
1991	*Tor-A	39	68	8	16	2	2	1	4	6	26	.235	.297	.368	665	80	-2	2	0	0	.892	-4	O-24(18-1-6)/D-2	-0.5
1992	Tor-A	23	21	3	1	1	0	0	0	0	10	.048	.048	.095	143	-58	-4	0	1	-0	1.000	-3	O-13(3-2-8)/D-4	-0.8
	Cal-A	31	59	4	14	3	0	0	2	5	12	.237	.297	.288	585	64	-3	2	3	-1	.944	-1	O-20(17-1-2)/D-1	-0.5
	Yr	54	80	7	15	4	0	0	2	5	22	.188	.235	.237	473	32	-7	2	4	-1	.957	-4	O-33(20-3-10)/D-5	-1.3
1993	Tex-A	27	85	15	24	6	3	2	9	10	17	.282	.358	.494	852	132	4	2	3	-1	1.000	-2	O-26(1-14-13)	0.1
1994	Tex-A	11	29	1	5	1	0	0	1	2	1	.172	.226	.207	433	13	-4	0	0	0	.882	-2	O-10(0-0-10)	-0.6
1997	*Sea-A	76	143	25	41	15	2	5	10	6	31	.287	.315	.524	840	115	2	3	3	-0	.986	-14	O-69(43-12-19)	-1.2
1998	Sea-A	97	217	30	52	18	2	5	23	23	61	.240	.337	.410	747	93	-2	4	3	-0	.970	-8	O-83(23-6-61)	-1.2
1999	Phi-N	104	188	29	49	10	2	8	33	38	57	.261	.385	.463	848	110	4	2	1	0	1.000	-4	O-58(39-9-11)/D-2	-0.1
2000	Phi-N	70	106	16	20	3	1	6	20	20	36	.189	.317	.406	723	80	-4	1	0	0	.921	-2	O-26(24-1-1)/D-5	-0.5
	Tor-A	5	13	2	2	1	0	0	1	2	2	.154	.267	.231	497	27	-1	0	0	0	.889	0	/O-3(2-0-1)	-0.1
	Phi-N	42	46	8	10	1	0	0	5	9	11	.217	.345	.239	585	51	-3	0	0	0	1.000	-1	/O-7(4-1-2)	-0.4
Total	12	646	1206	180	292	75	13	28	134	150	321	.242	.331	.396	726	90	-17	22	16	-1	.975	-53	O-447L/D-17	-7.7
■ JOHN DUDRA Dudra, John Joseph b: 5/27/16, Assumption, Ill. d: 10/24/65, Pana, Ill. BR/TR, 5'11.5", 175 lbs. Deb: 9/7/41																								
1941	Bos-N	14	25	3	9	3	1	0	3	3	4	.360	.429	.560	989	185	3	0			.933	0	/2-5,3-5,1-1,S-1	0.3
■ PAT DUFF Duff, Patrick Henry b: 5/6/1875, Providence, R.I. d: 9/11/25, Providence, R.I. TR, Deb: 4/16/06																								
1906	Was-A	1	1	0	0	0	0	0	0	0		.000	.000	.000	0	-99	-0	0			.000	0	H	0.0
■ CHARLIE DUFFEE Duffee, Charles Edward "Home Run" b: 1/27/1866, Mobile, Ala. d: 12/24/1894, Mobile, Ala. BR/TR, Deb: 4/17/1889 Career OF: (152-LF 257-CF 48-RF)																								
1889	StL-a	137	509	93	124	15	11	16	86	60	81	.244	.327	.411	738	97	-6	21			.936	18	*O-132C/3-5,2-2	0.6
1890	StL-a	98	378	68	104	11	7	3	54	37		.275	.344	.365	710	96	-4	20			.951	10	O-66(1-65-0),3-33/S-1	0.4
1891	Col-a	137	552	86	166	28	4	10	90	42	36	.301	.353	.420	774	129	19	41			.927	11	*O-128L/3-7,S-2	2.2
1892	Was-N	132	492	64	122	12	11	6	51	36	33	.248	.302	.354	656	101	-1	28			.913	19	*O-125L/3-6,1-4	0.8
1893	Cin-N	4	12	3	2	1	0	0	0	5	0	.167	.412	.250	662	76	-0	0			.400	-2	/O-4(4-0-0)	-0.2
Total	5	508	1943	314	518	67	33	35	281	180	150	.267	.332	.389	721	106	7	110			.927	56	O-455C/3-51,1-4,S2	3.8
■ ED DUFFY Duffy, Edward Charles b: 1844, Ireland d: 6/21/1889, Brooklyn, N.Y. TR, 5'7.5", 152 lbs. Deb: 5/8/1871																								
1871	Chi-n	26	121	30	28	5	0	0	15	3	2	.231	.250	.273	523	45	-10	11	4	1	.750	-3	*S-26/3-1	-0.8
■ FRANK DUFFY Duffy, Frank Thomas b: 10/14/46, Oakland, Cal. BR/TR, 6'1", 180 lbs. Deb: 9/4/70																								
1970	Cin-N	6	11	1	2	2	0	0	0	1	2	.182	.250	.364	614	62	-1	1	0	0	1.000	1	/S-5	0.1
1971	Cin-N	13	16	0	3	1	0	0	1	1	2	.188	.235	.250	485	38	-1	0	0	0	.944	5	S-10	0.4
	*SF-N	21	28	4	5	0	0	0	2	0	10	.179	.179	.179	357	1	-4	0	0	0	.968	5	/S-6,2-1,3-1	0.2
	Yr	34	44	4	8	1	0	0	3	1	12	.182	.200	.205	405	15	-5	0	0	0	.955	10	S-16/2-1,3-1	0.6
1972	Cle-A	130	385	23	92	16	4	3	27	31	54	.239	.297	.325	622	82	-8	6	2	1	.977	3	*S-126	1.0
1973	Cle-A	116	361	34	95	16	4	8	50	25	41	.263	.314	.396	711	97	-2	6	6	-1	**.986**	12	*S-115	2.3
1974	Cle-A	158	549	62	128	18	0	8	48	30	64	.233	.273	.310	583	68	-23	7	8	-1	.980	-8	*S-158	-1.5
1975	Cle-A	146	482	44	117	22	2	1	47	27	60	.243	.286	.303	589	66	-22	10	10	-1	.977	14	*S-145	0.8
1976	Cle-A	133	392	38	83	11	2	2	30	29	50	.212	.270	.265	535	58	-21	10	0	2	**.983**	11	*S-132	0.6
1977	Cle-A	122	334	30	67	13	2	4	31	21	47	.201	.248	.287	535	47	-25	8	3	1	.967	3	*S-121	-1.1
1978	Bos-A	64	104	12	27	5	0	0	4	6	11	.260	.306	.308	614	66	-5	1	1	-0	.960	6	3-22,S-21,2-12,/D-6	0.4
1979	Bos-A	6	3	0	0	0	0	0	0	0	1	.000	.000	.000	0	-95	-1	0	0	0	1.000	1	/2-3,1-1	0.0
Total	10	915	2665	248	619	104	14	26	240	171	342	.232	.281	.311	592	69	-112	49	30	0	.977	53	S-839/3-23,2-16,D1	3.2

■ HUGH DUFFY
Duffy, Hugh b: 11/26/1866, Cranston, R.I. d: 10/19/54, Boston, Mass. BR/TR, 5'7", 168 lbs. Deb: 6/23/1888 MCH Career OF: (574-LF 677-CF 437-RF)

YEAR	TM/L	G	AB	R	H	2B	3B	HR	RBI	BB	SO	AVG	OBP	SLG	OPS	OPS+	BR+	SB	CS	SBR	FA	FR	G/POS	TPR
1888	Chi-N	71	298	60	84	10	4	7	41	9	32	.282	.305	.413	718	119	5	13			.910	5	O-67(3-0-64)/S-3,3-1	0.9
1889	Chi-N	136	584	144	172	21	7	12	89	46	30	.295	.348	.416	764	108	4	52			.894	-15	*O-126(0-0-126),S-10	-1.1
1890	Chi-P	138	596	**161**	**191**	36	16	7	82	59	20	.320	.384	.470	853	122	16	78			.917	13	*O-137(0-17-120)	2.2
1891	Bos-a	127	536	134	180	20	8	9	**110**	61	29	.336	.408	.453	861	149	34	85			.917	0	*O-124R/3-3,S-1	2.8
1892	*Bos-N	147	612	125	184	28	12	5	81	60	37	.301	.364	.410	774	123	15	51			.942	-9	*O-146(0-146-0)/3-2	-0.4
1893	Bos-N	131	560	147	203	23	7	6	118	50	13	**.363**	.416	.461	876	123	17	44			.953	-2	*O-131(0-128-3)	0.5
1894	Bos-N	125	539	160	**237**	**51**	16	**18**	145	66	15	**.440**	.502	.694	**1196**	172	62	48			.927	4	*O-124(4-121-0)/S-2	4.4
1895	Bos-N	131	533	112	188	30	6	9	100	65	17	.353	.428	.482	910	125	19	42			.946	7	*O-131(0-131-0)	1.4
1896	Bos-N	131	527	97	158	16	8	5	113	52	19	.300	.365	.389	754	93	-6	39			.957	0	*O-120L/2-9,S-2	-1.4
1897	*Bos-N	134	550	130	187	25	10	**11**	129	52		.340	.403	.482	885	125	19	41			.975	-1	*O-129L/2-6,S-2	0.6
1898	Bos-N	152	568	97	169	13	3	8	108	59		.298	.365	.373	738	106	4	29			.956	2	*O-152L/3-1,1-1,C-1	-0.6
1899	Bos-N	147	588	103	164	29	7	5	102	39		.279	.327	.378	705	85	-14	26			.970	-4	*O-147(138-8-1)	-2.9
1900	Bos-N	55	181	27	55	5	4	2	31	16		.304	.360	.409	769	100	-1	11			.957	-1	O-49(44-5-0)/2-1	-0.5
1901	Mil-A	79	285	40	86	15	9	2	45	16		.302	.341	.439	780	121	7	12			.967	-6	O-77(12-65-0),M	-0.2
1904	Phi-N	18	46	10	13	1	1	0	5	13		.283	.441	.348	789	150	4	3			.850	-3	O-14(8-6-0),M	0.0
1905	Phi-N	15	40	7	12	2	1	0	3	1		.300	.317	.400	717	117	1	0			.909	1	/O-8(0-3-5),M	0.1
1906	Phi-N	1	1	0	0	0	0	0	0	0		.000	.000	.000	0	-99	-0	0			.000	0	HM	0.0
Total	17	1738	7044	1554	2283	325	119	106	1302	664	212	.324	.385	.449	834	121	187	574			.943	-9	*O-1682C/S-20,23C1	5.8

■ JOE DUGAN
Dugan, Joseph Anthony "Jumping Joe" b: 5/12/1897, Mahanoy City, Pa. d: 7/7/82, Norwood, Mass. BR/TR, 5'11", 160 lbs. Deb: 7/5/17

YEAR	TM/L	G	AB	R	H	2B	3B	HR	RBI	BB	SO	AVG	OBP	SLG	OPS	OPS+	BR+	SB	CS	SBR	FA	FR	G/POS	TPR
1917	Phi-A	43	134	9	26	8	0	0	16	3	16	.194	.229	.254	482	48	-9	0			.917	1	S-39/2-2	-0.7
1918	Phi-A	121	411	26	80	11	3	3	34	16	55	.195	.230	.258	488	47	-28	4			.930	17	S-86,2-34	-0.5
1919	Phi-A	104	387	25	105	17	2	1	30	11	30	.271	.300	.333	634	77	-13	9			.929	1	S-98/2-4,3-2	-0.5
1920	Phi-A	123	491	65	158	40	5	3	60	19	51	.322	.351	.442	793	108	4	5	8	-2	.948	-1	3-60,S-32,2-31	0.6
1921	Phi-A	119	461	54	136	22	6	10	58	28	45	.295	.342	.434	776	96	-4	5	1	1	.953	-25	*3-119	-2.0
1922	Bos-A	84	341	45	98	22	3	3	38	9	28	.287	.308	.396	704	83	-10	2	3	-1	.943	-9	3-64,S-21	-1.3
	*NY-A	60	252	44	72	9	1	3	25	13	21	.286	.331	.365	696	79	-8	1	0	0	.967	-10	3-60	-1.3
	Yr	144	593	89	170	31	4	6	63	22	49	.287	.318	.383	701	81	-17	3	3	-0	.954	-19	*3-124,S-21	-2.6
1923	*NY-A	146	644	111	182	30	7	7	67	25	41	.283	.311	.384	695	81	-20	4	2	0	**.974**	-11	*3-146	-2.2
1924	NY-A	148	610	105	184	31	7	3	56	31	33	.302	.341	.390	731	88	-12	1	2	-0	.962	-15	*3-148/2-2	-1.7
1925	NY-A	102	404	50	118	19	4	0	31	19	20	.292	.330	.359	689	76	-15	2	4	-1	.970	7	3-96	-0.3
1926	*NY-A	123	434	39	125	19	5	1	64	25	16	.288	.328	.362	690	81	-13	2	4	-1	.955	-16	*3-122	-2.1
1927	*NY-A	112	387	44	104	24	3	2	43	27	37	.269	.321	.362	683	79	-12	1	4	-1	.938	-19	*3-111	-2.5
1928	*NY-A	94	312	33	86	15	0	6	34	16	15	.276	.317	.381	699	85	-7	1	0	0	.952	-18	3-91/2-1	-1.9
1929	Bos-N	60	125	14	38	10	0	0	15	8	8	.304	.346	.384	730	84	-3	0			.918	-9	3-24/S-5,2-2,O-2L	-1.0
1931	Det-A	8	17	1	4	0	0	0	0	0	3	.235	.235	.235	471	23	-2	0	0	0	.900	-1	/3-5	-0.2
Total	14	1447	5410	665	1516	277	46	42	571	250	419	.280	.317	.372	689	82	-152	37	28		.957	-107	*3-1048,S-281/2-76,O	-17.6

■ BILL DUGAN
Dugan, William H. b: 1864, New York, N.Y. d: 7/24/21, New York, N.Y. Deb: 8/5/1884 F

YEAR	TM/L	G	AB	R	H	2B	3B	HR	RBI	BB	SO	AVG	OBP	SLG	OPS	OPS+	BR+	SB	CS	SBR	FA	FR	G/POS	TPR
1884	Ric-a	9	28	4	3	1	0	0		0		.107	.138	.143	281	-8	-3				.889	-3	/C-9	-0.5
	KC-U	3	6	0	0	0	0	0		0		.000	.000	.000	0	-99	-2				.400	-1	/O-3(1-2-0)	-0.3
Total	1	12	34	4	3	1	0	0		0		.088	.114	.118	232	-26	-5				.889	-4	/C-9,O-3(1-2-0)	-0.8

■ GUS DUGAS
Dugas, Augustin Joseph b: 3/24/07, St.Jean De Matha, Que., Canada d: 4/14/97, Colchester, Conn. BL/TL, 5'9", 165 lbs. Deb: 9/17/30

YEAR	TM/L	G	AB	R	H	2B	3B	HR	RBI	BB	SO	AVG	OBP	SLG	OPS	OPS+	BR+	SB	CS	SBR	FA	FR	G/POS	TPR
1930	Pit-N	9	31	8	9	2	0	0	1	7	4	.290	.421	.355	776	90	-0	0			.864	-1	/O-9(0-0-9)	-0.2
1932	Pit-N	55	97	13	23	3	3	3	12	7	11	.237	.288	.423	711	90	-2	0			.952	-3	O-20(6-1-13)	-0.5
1933	Phi-N	37	71	4	12	3	0	0	9	1	9	.169	.181	.211	392	10	-8	0			.984	-0	1-11/O-1(0-1-0)	-1.0
1934	Was-A	24	19	2	1	1	0	0	1	3	3	.053	.182	.105	287	-25	-4	0	0	0	1.000	-0	/O-2(0-1-1)	-0.4
Total	4	125	218	27	45	9	3	3	23	18	27	.206	.267	.317	583	54	-14	0	0		.926	-4	/O-32(6-3-23),1-11	-2.1

■ DAN DUGDALE
Dugdale, Daniel Edward b: 10/28/1864, Peoria, Ill. d: 3/9/34, Seattle, Wash. 5'8", 180 lbs. Deb: 5/20/1886

YEAR	TM/L	G	AB	R	H	2B	3B	HR	RBI	BB	SO	AVG	OBP	SLG	OPS	OPS+	BR+	SB	CS	SBR	FA	FR	G/POS	TPR
1886	KC-N	12	40	4	7	0	0	0	2	2	13	.175	.214	.175	389	18	-4	1			.884	-2	/C-7,O-6(0-1-5)	-0.5
1894	Was-N	38	134	19	32	4	2	0	16	13	14	.239	.306	.299	605	48	-11	7			.874	-5	C-33/3-3,O-2(2-0-0)	-1.1
Total	2	50	174	23	39	4	2	0	18	15	27	.224	.286	.270	556	42	-15	8			.877	-7	/C-40,O-8(2-1-5),3-3	-1.6

■ OSCAR DUGEY
Dugey, Oscar Joseph "Jake" b: 10/25/1887, Palestine, Tex. d: 1/1/66, Dallas, Tex. BR/TR, 5'8", 160 lbs. Deb: 9/13/13 C Career OF: (1-LF 2-CF 16-RF)

YEAR	TM/L	G	AB	R	H	2B	3B	HR	RBI	BB	SO	AVG	OBP	SLG	OPS	OPS+	BR+	SB	CS	SBR	FA	FR	G/POS	TPR
1913	Bos-N	5	8	1	2	0	0	0	0	1	1	.250	.333	.250	583	67	-0	0			.500	-1	/3-2,2-1,S-1	-0.1
1914	Bos-N	58	109	17	21	2	0	1	10	10	15	.193	.267	.239	505	51	-6	10			.933	-2	O-16(0-0-16),2-16/3-1	-1.0
1915	*Phi-N	42	39	4	6	1	0	0	0	7	5	.154	.283	.179	462	41	-3	2	1	0	.941	3	2-14	0.1
1916	Phi-N	41	50	9	11	3	0	0	1	9	8	.220	.339	.280	619	88	-0	3			.967	3	2-12	0.3
1917	Phi-N	44	72	12	14	4	1	0	9	4	9	.194	.237	.278	515	55	-4	2			.871	0	2-15/O-4(1-2-0)	-0.4
1920	Bos-N	5	0	2	0	0	0	0	0	0	0	—	—	—	—	—	0	0	0	0	.000	0	R	0.0
Total	6	195	278	45	54	10	1	1	20	31	38	.194	.277	.248	526	58	-13	17	1		.915	3	/2-58,O-20R,3-3,S-1	-1.1

■ JIM DUGGAN
Duggan, James Elmer "Mer" b: 6/1/1885, Whiteland, Ind. d: 12/5/51, Indianapolis, Ind. BL/TL, 5'10", 165 lbs. Deb: 6/29/11

YEAR	TM/L	G	AB	R	H	2B	3B	HR	RBI	BB	SO	AVG	OBP	SLG	OPS	OPS+	BR+	SB	CS	SBR	FA	FR	G/POS	TPR
1911	StL-A	1	4	1	0	0	0	0	1	1		.000	.200	.000	200	-44	-1	0			1.000	0	/1-1	-0.1

■ TOM DUNBAR
Dunbar, Thomas Jerome b: 11/24/59, Graniteville, S.C. BL/TL, 6'2", 192 lbs. Deb: 9/7/83

YEAR	TM/L	G	AB	R	H	2B	3B	HR	RBI	BB	SO	AVG	OBP	SLG	OPS	OPS+	BR+	SB	CS	SBR	FA	FR	G/POS	TPR
1983	Tex-A	12	24	3	6	0	0	0	3	5	7	.250	.379	.250	629	79	-0	3	1	0	.875	-3	/O-9(2-0-7),D-1	-0.3
1984	Tex-A	34	97	9	25	2	0	2	10	6	16	.258	.301	.340	641	75	-3	1	0	0	.939	-3	O-20(9-0-11)/D-6	-0.7
1985	Tex-A	45	104	7	21	4	0	1	5	12	9	.202	.291	.269	560	54	-6	0	3	-1	.933	-3	D-18,O-14(12-0-3)	-1.2
Total	3	91	225	19	52	6	0	3	18	23	32	.231	.305	.298	603	66	-10	4	4	-1	.929	-9	/O-43(23-0-21),D-25	-2.2

■ DAVE DUNCAN
Duncan, David Edwin b: 9/26/45, Dallas, Tex. BR/TR, 6'2", 200 lbs. Deb: 5/6/64 C

YEAR	TM/L	G	AB	R	H	2B	3B	HR	RBI	BB	SO	AVG	OBP	SLG	OPS	OPS+	BR+	SB	CS	SBR	FA	FR	G/POS	TPR
1964	KC-A	25	53	2	9	0	1	1	5	2	20	.170	.200	.264	464	27	-5	0	0	0	.981	3	C-22	-0.1
1967	KC-A	34	101	9	19	4	0	5	11	4	50	.188	.219	.376	595	75	-4	0	1	-0	.979	-6	C-32	-1.0
1968	Oak-A	82	246	15	47	4	0	7	28	25	68	.191	.268	.293	561	73	-8	1	2	-0	.987	0	C-79	-0.5
1969	Oak-A	58	127	11	16	3	0	3	22	19	41	.126	.240	.220	460	31	-12	0	0	0	.982	-12	C-56	-2.3
1970	Oak-A	86	232	21	60	7	0	10	29	22	38	.259	.323	.418	741	107	1	0	0	0	.978	3	C-73	0.8
1971	*Oak-A☆	103	363	39	92	13	1	15	40	28	77	.253	.309	.419	727	106	2	1	1	-0	.984	3	*C-102	1.0
1972	*Oak-A	121	403	39	88	13	0	19	59	34	68	.218	.287	.392	679	106	1	0	2	-1	.993	2	*C-113	0.9
1973	Cle-A	95	344	43	80	11	1	17	43	35	86	.233	.309	.419	728	101	-0	3	3	-0	.988	-1	C-86/D-9	0.3
1974	Cle-A	136	425	45	85	10	1	16	46	42	91	.200	.275	.341	616	77	-13	0	4	-1	.976	-8	*C-134/1-3,D-1	-1.8
1975	Bal-A	96	307	30	63	7	0	12	41	16	82	.205	.247	.345	592	70	-14	0	0	0	.982	-7	C-95	-1.7
1976	Bal-A	93	284	20	58	7	0	4	17	25	56	.204	.271	.271	542	63	-13	0	0	0	.985	-11	C-93	-2.2
Total	11	929	2885	274	617	79	4	109	341	252	677	.214	.280	.357	638	85	-65	5	13	-3	.984	-32	C-885/D-10,1-3	-6.6

■ JIM DUNCAN
Duncan, James William b: 7/1/1871, Saltsburg, Pa. d: 10/16/01, Foxburg, Pa. BR/TR, 5'8", 140 lbs. Deb: 7/18/1899

YEAR	TM/L	G	AB	R	H	2B	3B	HR	RBI	BB	SO	AVG	OBP	SLG	OPS	OPS+	BR+	SB	CS	SBR	FA	FR	G/POS	TPR
1899	Was-N	15	47	5	11	2	0	0	5	4		.234	.294	.277	571	57	-3	1			.940	-1	C-14	-0.2
	Cle-N	31	105	9	24	2	3	2	9	4		.229	.257	.362	619	74	-4	0			.971	-4	1-17,C-14	-0.7
	Yr	46	152	14	35	4	3	2	14	8		.230	.269	.336	604	69	-7	1			.904	-5	C-28,1-17	-0.9

■ PAT DUNCAN
Duncan, Louis Baird b: 10/6/1893, Coalton, Ohio d: 7/17/60, Columbus, Ohio BR/TR, 5'9", 170 lbs. Deb: 7/16/15

YEAR	TM/L	G	AB	R	H	2B	3B	HR	RBI	BB	SO	AVG	OBP	SLG	OPS	OPS+	BR+	SB	CS	SBR	FA	FR	G/POS	TPR
1915	Pit-N	3	5	0	1	0	0	0	0	0	1	.200	.200	.200	400	22	-0	0			1.000	-0	/O-1(0-1-0)	-0.1
1919	*Cin-N	31	90	9	22	3	3	2	17	8	7	.244	.306	.411	717	118	2	2			.982	-1	O-27(27-0-0)	0.0
1920	Cin-N	154	576	75	170	16	11	2	83	42	42	.295	.350	.372	722	109	7	18	18	-2	.964	5	*O-154(154-0-0)	0.3
1921	Cin-N	145	532	57	164	27	10	2	60	44	33	.308	.367	.408	775	110	8	7	18	-5	.971	9	*O-145(129-16-1)	0.1
1922	Cin-N	151	607	94	199	44	12	8	94	40	31	.328	.370	.479	850	120	16	12	28	-7	.971	4	*O-151(151-0-0)	0.0
1923	Cin-N	147	566	92	185	26	8	7	83	30	27	.327	.363	.438	801	113	9	15	13	-1	**.993**	-1	*O-146(144-3-0)	-0.4

YEAR	TM/L	G	AB	R	H	2B	3B	HR	RBI	BB	SO	AVG	OBP	SLG	OPS	OPS+	BR+	SB	CS	SBR	FA	FR	G/POS	TPR
1924	Cin-N	96	319	34	86	21	6	2	37	20	23	.270	.313	.392	705	89	-6	1	7	-2	.927	-14	O-83(82-0-1)	-2.8
Total	7	727	2695	361	827	137	50	23	374	184	164	.307	.355	.420	775	110	37	55	84		.970	1	O-707(687-20-2)	-2.9

■ MARIANO DUNCAN
Duncan, Mariano (Nalasco) b: 3/13/63, San Pedro De Macoris, D.R. BR/TR (BB 1985-87), 6', 185 lbs. Deb: 4/9/85 Career OF: (88-LF 2-CF 6-RF)

YEAR	TM/L	G	AB	R	H	2B	3B	HR	RBI	BB	SO	AVG	OBP	SLG	OPS	OPS+	BR+	SB	CS	SBR	FA	FR	G/POS	TPR
1985	*LA-N	142	562	74	137	24	6	6	39	38	113	.244	.295	.340	635	79	-16	38	8	6	.954	-8	*S-123,2-19	-0.5
1986	LA-N	109	407	47	93	7	0	8	30	30	78	.229	.285	.305	589	67	-19	48	13	6	.951	-2	*S-106	-0.3
1987	LA-N	76	261	31	56	8	1	6	18	17	62	.215	.268	.322	590	57	-17	11	1	2	.930	-1	S-67/2-7,O-2(1-0-1)	-0.9
1989	LA-N	49	84	9	21	5	1	0	8	0	15	.250	.267	.333	601	72	-3	3	3	-0	.943	-0	S-16/2-8,O-7(4-0-4)	-0.3
	Cin-N	45	174	23	43	10	1	3	13	8	36	.247	.292	.368	660	85	-4	6	2	1	.955	-7	S-44/2-5	-0.8
	Yr	94	258	32	64	15	2	3	21	8	51	.248	.284	.357	641	81	-7	9	5	0	.952	-8	S-60,2-13/O-7(4-0-4)	-1.1
1990	*Cin-N	125	435	67	133	22	**11**	10	55	24	67	.306	.348	.476	824	119	10	13	7	0	.973	1	*2-115,S-12/O-1L	1.5
1991	Cin-N	100	333	46	86	7	4	12	40	12	57	.258	.290	.411	702	92	-5	5	4	-0	.974	-6	2-62,S-32/O-7(6-2-0)	-0.8
1992	Phi-N	142	574	71	153	40	3	8	50	17	108	.267	.294	.389	682	92	-8	23	3	4	.976	-23	O-65L,2-52,S-42,/3	-2.7
1993	*Phi-N	124	496	68	140	26	4	11	73	12	88	.282	.305	.417	722	92	-7	6	5	-0	.969	-28	2-65,S-59	-2.8
1994	Phi-N★	88	347	49	93	22	1	8	48	17	72	.268	.310	.406	716	83	-9	10	2	2	.972	-17	2-37,3-28,S-19,/1-6	-2.1
1995	Phi-N	52	196	20	56	12	1	3	23	0	43	.286	.289	.403	692	80	-6	1	2	-0	.957	5	2-24,S-14,1-12,/3-1	0.0
	*Cin-N	29	69	16	20	2	1	3	13	5	19	.290	.338	.478	816	113	1	0	1	-0	.963	-3	/2-7,1-6,S-6,O-3L	-0.2
	Yr	81	265	36	76	14	2	6	36	5	62	.287	.303	.423	725	88	-5	1	3	-1	.958	2	2-31,S-20,1-18,/O3	-0.2
1996	*NY-A	109	400	62	136	34	3	8	56	9	77	.340	.356	.500	856	113	7	4	3	-0	.975	-25	*2-104/3-3,O-3L,D-2	-1.2
1997	NY-A	50	172	16	42	8	0	1	13	6	39	.244	.270	.308	578	51	-12	2	1	0	.976	-8	2-41/O-6(6-0-0),D-2	-1.8
	Tor-A	39	167	20	38	6	0	0	12	6	39	.228	.267	.263	531	39	-15	4	2	0	.984	1	2-39	-1.1
	Yr	89	339	36	80	14	0	1	25	12	78	.236	.268	.286	554	45	-27	6	3	0	.980	-7	2-80/O-6(6-0-0),D-2	-2.9
Total	12	1279	4677	619	1247	233	37	87	491	201	913	.267	.302	.388	690	86	-102	174	57	18	.972	-121	2-585,S-540/O31D	-14.0

■ TAYLOR DUNCAN
Duncan, Taylor McDowell b: 5/12/53, Memphis, Tenn. BR/TR, 6', 170 lbs. Deb: 9/15/77

YEAR	TM/L	G	AB	R	H	2B	3B	HR	RBI	BB	SO	AVG	OBP	SLG	OPS	OPS+	BR+	SB	CS	SBR	FA	FR	G/POS	TPR
1977	StL-N	8	12	2	4	0	0	1	2	2	1	.333	.429	.583	1012	172	1	0	0	0	1.000	-2	/3-5	-0.1
1978	Oak-A	104	319	25	82	15	2	2	37	19	38	.257	.299	.335	634	82	-8	1	2	-0	.953	-21	3-84,2-11/S-1,D-7	-3.2
Total	2	112	331	27	86	15	2	3	39	21	39	.260	.304	.344	648	86	-7	1	2	-0	.953	-23	/3-89,2-11,D-7,S-1	-3.3

■ VERN DUNCAN
Duncan, Vernon Van Duke b: 1/6/1890, Clayton, N.C. d: 6/1/54, Daytona Beach, Fla BL/TR, 5'9", 155 lbs. Deb: 9/11/13 Career OF: (97-LF 165-CF 13-RF)

YEAR	TM/L	G	AB	R	H	2B	3B	HR	RBI	BB	SO	AVG	OBP	SLG	OPS	OPS+	BR+	SB	CS	SBR	FA	FR	G/POS	TPR
1913	Phi-N	8	12	3	5	1	0	0	1	0	3	.417	.417	.500	917	155	1	0			1.000	-0	/O-3(1-0-2)	0.1
1914	Bal-F	157	557	99	160	20	8	2	53	67	55	.287	.375	.363	737	98	-7	13			.914	-3	*O-148C/3-8,2-1	-2.0
1915	Bal-F	146	531	68	142	18	4	2	43	54	40	.267	.337	.328	665	85	-17	19			.965	-0	*O-124C,3-21/2-1	-2.6
Total	3	311	1100	170	307	39	12	4	97	121	98	.279	.357	.347	705	93	-23	32			.939	-3	O-275C/3-29,2-2	-4.5

■ GUS DUNDON
Dundon, Augustus Joseph b: 7/10/1874, Columbus, Ohio d: 9/1/40, Pittsburgh, Pa. BR/TR, 5'10", 165 lbs. Deb: 4/14/04

YEAR	TM/L	G	AB	R	H	2B	3B	HR	RBI	BB	SO	AVG	OBP	SLG	OPS	OPS+	BR+	SB	CS	SBR	FA	FR	G/POS	TPR
1904	Chi-A	108	373	40	85	9	3	0	36	30		.228	.292	.268	560	81	-7	19			**.973**	-15	*2-103/3-3,S-2	-2.4
1905	Chi-A	106	364	30	70	7	3	0	22	23		.192	.248	.228	476	53	-19	14			.983	13	*2-100/S-6	-0.5
1906	Chi-A	33	96	7	13	1	0	0	4	11		.135	.224	.146	370	17	-9	4			.921	7	2-18,S-14	-0.1
Total	3	247	833	77	168	17	6	0	62	64		.202	.265	.236	502	61	-35	37			.972	6	2-221/S-22,3-3	-3.0

■ ED DUNDON
Dundon, Edward Joseph "Dummy" b: 7/10/1859, Columbus, Ohio d: 8/18/1893, Columbus, Ohio TR, Deb: 6/2/1883 Career OF: (20-LF 3-CF 2-RF)

YEAR	TM/L	G	AB	R	H	2B	3B	HR	RBI	BB	SO	AVG	OBP	SLG	OPS	OPS+	BR+	SB	CS	SBR	FA	FR	G/POS	TPR
1883	Col-a	26	93	8	15	1	0	0		3		.161	.188	.172	360	18	-8				.804	0	P-20/O-9(6-2-1),2-1	-0.2
1884	Col-a	26	86	6	12	2	2	0		5		.140	.196	.209	405	35	-6				.966	3	O-16(14-1-1),P-11/1-3	-0.2
Total	2	52	179	14	27	3	2	0		8		.151	.191	.190	381	26	-13				.866	4	/P-31,O-25L,1-3,2-1	-0.4

■ SAM DUNGAN
Dungan, Samuel Morrison b: 7/29/1866, Ferndale, Cal. d: 3/16/39, Santa Ana, Cal. BR, 5'11", 180 lbs. Deb: 4/12/1892

YEAR	TM/L	G	AB	R	H	2B	3B	HR	RBI	BB	SO	AVG	OBP	SLG	OPS	OPS+	BR+	SB	CS	SBR	FA	FR	G/POS	TPR
1892	Chi-N	113	433	46	123	19	7	0	53	35	19	.284	.346	.360	706	112	6	15			.905	-6	*O-113(37-0-76)	-0.7
1893	Chi-N	107	465	86	138	23	7	2	64	29	8	.297	.350	.389	739	98	-2	11			.920	4	*O-107(1-0-106)	-0.4
1894	Chi-N	10	39	5	9	2	0	0	3	7	1	.231	.348	.282	630	51	-3	1			1.000	0	O-10(0-0-10)	-0.2
	Lou-N	8	32	6	11	1	0	0	3	4	1	.344	.417	.375	792	99	0	2			.941	0	/O-8(0-0-8)	0.0
	Yr	18	71	11	20	3	0	0	6	11	2	.282	.378	.324	702	71	-3	3			.971	1	O-18(0-0-18)	-0.2
1900	Chi-N	6	15	1	4	0	0	0	1	1		.267	.313	.267	579	63	-1	0			.800	-1	/O-3(0-3-0)	-0.2
1901	Was-A	138	559	70	179	26	12	1	73	40		.320	.368	.415	783	118	14	9			.947	-5	*O-104(1-0-103),1-35	0.3
Total	5	382	1543	214	464	71	26	3	197	116	29	.301	.356	.386	742	107	14	38			.924	-8	O-345(39-3-303)/1-35	-1.2

■ LEE DUNHAM
Dunham, Leland Huffield b: 6/9/02, Atlanta, Ill. d: 5/11/61, Atlanta, Ill. BL/TL, 5'11", 185 lbs. Deb: 4/17/26

YEAR	TM/L	G	AB	R	H	2B	3B	HR	RBI	BB	SO	AVG	OBP	SLG	OPS	OPS+	BR+	SB	CS	SBR	FA	FR	G/POS	TPR
1926	Phi-N	5	4	0	1	0	0	0	1	0	1	.250	.250	.250	500	33	-0	0			1.000	-0	/1-2	0.0

■ FRED DUNLAP
Dunlap, Frederick C. "Sure Shot" b: 5/21/1859, Philadelphia, Pa.
d: 12/1/02, Philadelphia, Pa. BR/TR, 5'8", 165 lbs. Deb: 5/1/1880 M Career OF: (0-LF 1-CF 2-RF)

YEAR	TM/L	G	AB	R	H	2B	3B	HR	RBI	BB	SO	AVG	OBP	SLG	OPS	OPS+	BR+	SB	CS	SBR	FA	FR	G/POS	TPR
1880	Cle-N	85	373	61	103	**27**	9	4	30	7	32	.276	.289	.429	718	143	16				.911	8	*2-85	2.6
1881	Cle-N	80	351	60	114	25	4	3	24	18	24	.325	.358	.444	802	159	24				.909	6	*2-79/3-1	3.1
1882	Cle-N	84	364	68	102	19	4	0	28	23	26	.280	.323	.354	677	121	9				.900	18	*2-84,M	2.7
1883	Cle-N	93	396	81	129	34	2	4	37	22	21	.326	.361	.452	813	147	22				.911	8	*2-93/O-1(0-0-1)	2.9
1884	StL-U	101	449	**160**	**185**	39	8	**13**		29		**.412**	**.448**	**.621**	**1069**	**213**	**49**				**.926**	**31**	*2-100/O-1R,P-1,M	**7.1**
1885	StL-N	106	423	70	114	11	5	2	25	41	24	.270	.334	.333	667	124	14				**.934**	**26**	*2-106,M	4.0
1886	StL-N	71	285	53	76	15	2	3	32	28	30	.267	.332	.365	697	119	8	7			.931	16	2-71/O-1(0-1-0)	2.4
	Det-N	51	196	32	56	8	3	4	37	16	21	.286	.340	.418	758	126	6	13			.918	3	2-51	1.0
	Yr	122	481	85	132	23	5	7	69	44	51	.274	.335	.387	722	122	14	20			.926	19	*2-122/O-1(0-1-0)	3.4
1887	*Det-N	65	297	60	97	13	10	5	45	25	12	.327	.327	.441	768	108	2	15			.948	24	2-65/P-1	2.4
1888	Pit-N	82	321	41	84	12	4	1	36	16	30	.262	.303	.333	636	111	5	24			.940	12	2-82	1.9
1889	Pit-N	121	451	59	106	19	0	2	65	46	33	.235	.309	.290	599	75	-13	21			**.950**	-6	*2-121,M	-1.3
1890	Pit-N	17	64	9	11	1	1	0	3	7	6	.172	.264	.219	483	46	-4	2			.874	-3	2-17	-0.6
	NY-P	1	4	1	2	0	0	0	0	0	0	.500	.500	.500	1000	154	0	0			1.000	-1	/2-1	-0.1
1891	Was-a	8	25	4	5	1	1	0	4	5	4	.200	.355	.320	675	98	0	3			.818	-3	/2-8	-0.3
Total	12	965	3999	759	1184	224	53	41	366	283	263	.296	.340	.406	745	132	138	85			.924	137	2-963/O-3R,P-2,3-1	27.8

■ GRANT DUNLAP
Dunlap, Grant Lester "Snap" b: 12/20/23, Stockton, Cal. BR/TR, 6'2", 180 lbs. Deb: 4/21/53

YEAR	TM/L	G	AB	R	H	2B	3B	HR	RBI	BB	SO	AVG	OBP	SLG	OPS	OPS+	BR+	SB	CS	SBR	FA	FR	G/POS	TPR
1953	StL-N	16	17	2	6	0	1	1	3	0	2	.353	.353	.647	1000	154	1	0	0	0	.000	-0	/O-1(0-0-1)	0.1

■ BILL DUNLAP
Dunlap, William James b: 5/1/09, Palmer, Mass. d: 11/29/80, Reading, Pa. BR/TR, 5'11", 170 lbs. Deb: 9/2/29

YEAR	TM/L	G	AB	R	H	2B	3B	HR	RBI	BB	SO	AVG	OBP	SLG	OPS	OPS+	BR+	SB	CS	SBR	FA	FR	G/POS	TPR
1929	Bos-N	10	29	6	12	0	1	1	4	4	4	.414	.485	.586	1071	171	3	0			.889	-1	/O-9(8-0-1)	0.1
1930	Bos-N	16	29	3	2	1	0	0	0	0	6	.069	.069	.103	172	-61	-8	0			1.000	-1	/O-7(0-2-5)	-0.8
Total	2	26	58	9	14	1	1	1	4	4	10	.241	.290	.345	635	57	-4	0			.939	-2	/O-16(8-2-6)	-0.7

■ JACK DUNLEAVY
Dunleavy, John Francis b: 9/14/1879, Harrison, N.J. d: 4/11/44, S.Norwalk, Conn. TL, 5'6", 167 lbs. Deb: 5/30/03 Career OF: (24-LF 3-CF 183-RF)

YEAR	TM/L	G	AB	R	H	2B	3B	HR	RBI	BB	SO	AVG	OBP	SLG	OPS	OPS+	BR+	SB	CS	SBR	FA	FR	G/POS	TPR
1903	StL-N	61	193	23	48	3	3	0	10	13		.249	.306	.295	602	74	-6	10			.972	6	O-38(6-0-32),P-14	-0.1
1904	StL-N	51	172	23	40	7	3	1	14	16		.233	.305	.326	631	99	-0	8			.987	1	O-44(5-3-36)/P-7	-0.2
1905	StL-N	119	435	52	105	8	8	1	25	55		.241	.328	.303	631	91	-3	15			.962	2	*O-118(13-0-115)/2-1	-0.7
Total	3	231	800	98	193	18	14	2	49	84		.241	.318	.306	624	89	-9	33			.969	9	O-200R/P-21,2-1	-1.0

■ GEORGE DUNLOP
Dunlop, George Henry b: 7/19/1888, Meriden, Conn. d: 12/12/72, Meriden, Conn. BR/TR, 5'10", 170 lbs. Deb: 9/9/13

YEAR	TM/L	G	AB	R	H	2B	3B	HR	RBI	BB	SO	AVG	OBP	SLG	OPS	OPS+	BR+	SB	CS	SBR	FA	FR	G/POS	TPR
1913	Cle-A	7	17	3	4	1	0	0	0	0	5	.235	.235	.294	529	53	-1	0			.923	1	/S-4,3-3	0.0
1914	Cle-A	1	3	0	0	0	0	0	0	1	1	.000	.250	.000	250	-23	-0	0			1.000	-1	/S-1	-0.2
Total	2	8	20	3	4	1	0	0	0	1	6	.200	.238	.250	488	42	-1	0			.929	0	/S-5,3-3	-0.2

■ JACK DUNN
Dunn, John Joseph b: 10/6/1872, Meadville, Pa. d: 10/22/28, Towson, Md. BR/TR, 5'9", Deb: 5/6/1897

YEAR	TM/L	G	AB	R	H	2B	3B	HR	RBI	BB	SO	AVG	OBP	SLG	OPS	OPS+	BR+	SB	CS	SBR	FA	FR	G/POS	TPR
1897	Bro-N	36	131	20	29	4	0	0	17	4		.221	.244	.252	496	33	-13	2			.911	-1	P-25/2-4,O-3L,3S	-0.5
1898	Bro-N	51	167	21	41	0	1	0	19	7		.246	.280	.257	537	54	-10	3			.939	-1	P-41/O-4C,S-4,3-2	-0.2
1899	Bro-N	43	122	21	30	2	1	0	16	3		.246	.270	.279	549	49	-9	3			.963	3	P-41/S-1	0.0
1900	Bro-N	10	26	2	6	0	0	0	1	1		.231	.259	.231	490	34	-2	0			.960	1	P-10	0.0

YEAR	TM/L	G	AB	R	H	2B	3B	HR	RBI	BB	SO	AVG	OBP	SLG	OPS	OPS+	BR+	SB	CS	SBR	FA	FR	G/POS	TPR
	Phi-N	10	33	3	10	1	0	0	5	0		.303	.303	.333	636	76	-1	1			.920	-1	P-10	0.0
	Yr	20	59	5	16	1	0	0	6	1		.271	.283	.288	571	56	-4	1			.940	1	P-20	0.0
1901	Phi-N	2	1	1	1	0	0	0	0	1		1.000	1.000	1.000	2000	471	1	0			1.000	-0	/P-2	0.0
	Bal-A	96	362	41	90	9	4	0	36	21		.249	.301	.296	596	63	-18	10			.872	-7	3-67,S-19/P-9,2O	-2.0
1902	NY-N	100	342	26	72	11	1	0	14	20		.211	.256	.249	505	56	-18	13			.962	-9	O-43R,S-36,3-18,/P2	-2.9
1903	NY-N	78	257	35	62	15	1	0	37	15		.241	.291	.307	598	68	-11	12			.907	-7	S-27,3-25,2-19,/O-1L	-1.6
1904	NY-N	64	181	27	56	12	2	1	19	11		.309	.356	.414	770	132	6	11			.914	-8	3-28,S-10/2-9,OP	-0.1
Total	8	490	1622	197	397	54	10	1	164	83		.245	.287	.292	580	66	-74	55			.890	-30	3-143,P-142/S-98,O2	-7.3
■ JOE DUNN Dunn, Joseph Edward b: 3/11/1885, Springfield, Ohio d: 3/19/44, Springfield, Ohio BR/TR, 5'9", 160 lbs. Deb: 9/12/08																								
1908	Bro-N	20	64	3	11	3	0	0	5	0		.172	.172	.219	391	26	-6	0			.957	7	C-20	0.4
1909	Bro-N	10	25	1	4	1	0	0	2	0		.160	.192	.200	392	23	-2	0			.952	-2	/C-7	-0.4
Total	2	30	89	4	15	4	0	0	7	0		.169	.178	.213	391	25	-8	0			.956	6	/C-27	0.0
■ RON DUNN Dunn, Ronald Ray b: 1/24/50, Oklahoma City, Okla BR/TR, 5'11", 180 lbs. Deb: 9/3/74																								
1974	Chi-N	23	68	6	20	7	0	2	15	12	8	.294	.400	.485	885	141	4	0	0	0	.917	-7	2-21/3-6	-0.2
1975	Chi-N	32	44	2	7	3	0	1	6	6	17	.159	.260	.295	555	52	-3	0	0	0	.957	-1	3-11/O-2(2-0-0),2-1	-0.4
Total	2	55	112	8	27	10	0	3	21	18	25	.241	.346	.411	757	106	1	0	0	0	.918	-7	/2-22,3-17,O-2(2-0-0)	-0.6
■ STEVE DUNN Dunn, Stephen B. b: 12/21/1858, London, Ont., Can. d: 5/5/33, London, Ont., Can. BL, 5'9.5", 173 lbs. Deb: 9/27/1884																								
1884	StP-U	9	32	2	8	2	0	0		0		.250	.250	.313	563	128	0				.972	1	/1-9,3-1	0.1
■ STEVE DUNN Dunn, Steven Robert b: 4/18/70, Champaign, Ill. BL/TL, 6'4", 225 lbs. Deb: 5/3/94																								
1994	Min-A	14	35	2	8	5	0	0	4	1	12	.229	.250	.371	621	57	-2	0	0	0	.990	1	1-12	-0.2
1995	Min-A	5	6	0	0	0	0	0	0	1	3	.000	.143	.000	143	-59	-1	0	0	0	1.000	-0	/1-3	-0.2
Total	2	19	41	2	8	5	0	0	4	2	15	.195	.233	.317	550	40	-4	0	0	0	.990	1	/1-15	-0.4
■ TODD DUNN Dunn, Todd Kent b: 7/29/70, Tulsa, Okla. BR/TR, 6'5", 220 lbs. Deb: 9/8/96																								
1996	Mil-A	6	10	2	3	1	0	0	1	0	3	.300	.300	.400	700	72	-0	0	0	0	1.000	-1	/O-6(1-1-4)	-0.2
1997	Mil-A	44	118	17	27	5	0	3	9	2	39	.229	.242	.347	589	51	-9	3	0	1	.909	-4	O-27(19-2-7),D-14	-1.3
Total	2	50	128	19	30	6	0	3	10	2	42	.234	.246	.352	598	53	-9	3	0	1	.920	-5	/O-33(20-3-11),D-14	-1.5
■ SHAWON DUNSTON Dunston, Shawon Donnell b: 3/21/63, Brooklyn, N.Y. BR/TR, 6'1", 175 lbs. Deb: 4/9/85 Career OF: (77-LF 43-CF 22-RF)																								
1985	Chi-N	74	250	40	65	12	4	4	18	19	42	.260	.312	.388	700	85	-5	11	3	1	.958	13	S-73	1.8
1986	Chi-N	150	581	66	145	37	3	17	68	21	114	.250	.279	.411	691	82	-16	13	11	-1	.961	20	*S-149	2.0
1987	Chi-N	95	346	40	85	18	3	5	22	10	68	.246	.269	.358	627	62	-19	12	3	2	.969	5	S-94	-0.3
1988	Chi-N☆	155	575	69	143	23	6	9	56	16	108	.249	.272	.357	628	76	-19	30	9	3	.973	6	*S-151	0.2
1989	*Chi-N	138	471	52	131	20	6	9	60	30	86	.278	.323	.403	726	99	-1	19	11	0	.972	7	*S-138	1.7
1990	Chi-N★	146	545	73	143	22	8	17	66	15	87	.262	.286	.426	712	87	-11	25	5	4	.970	6	*S-144	0.9
1991	Chi-N	142	492	59	128	22	7	12	50	23	64	.260	.299	.407	705	92	-6	21	6	3	.968	-6	*S-142	0.1
1992	Chi-N	18	73	8	23	3	1	0	2	3	13	.315	.342	.384	726	103	0	2	3	-1	.986	-5	S-18	-0.5
1993	Chi-N	7	10	3	4	2	0	0	2	0	1	.400	.400	.600	1000	166	1	0	0	0	1.000	-1	/S-2	0.0
1994	Chi-N	88	331	38	92	19	0	11	35	16	48	.278	.315	.435	750	94	-4	3	8	-2	.966	-7	S-84	-0.6
1995	Chi-N	127	477	58	141	30	6	14	69	10	75	.296	.318	.472	790	107	3	10	5	0	.969	-12	*S-125	0.2
1996	SF-N	82	287	27	86	12	2	5	25	13	40	.300	.332	.408	740	98	-1	8	0	2	.957	-2	S-78	0.4
1997	Chi-N	114	419	57	119	18	4	9	41	8	64	.284	.302	.411	713	82	-12	29	7	4	.970	-26	*S-108/O-7(7-0-0)	-2.5
	Pit-N	18	71	14	28	4	1	5	16	0	11	.394	.394	.690	1085	174	7	3	1	0	.965	-0	S-18	0.8
	Yr	132	490	71	147	22	5	14	57	8	75	.300	.315	.451	766	96	-5	32	8	4	.969	-26	*S-126/O-7(7-0-0)	-1.7
1998	Cle-A	62	156	26	37	11	3	3	12	6	18	.237	.270	.404	674	70	-7	9	2	1	.978	-2	2-24,S-14,O-12L,/D	-0.6
	SF-N	36	51	10	9	2	0	3	8	0	10	.176	.222	.392	614	61	-3	0	2	-1	.938	-5	/S-9,O-6(0-6-0),2-1	-0.9
1999	StL-N	62	150	23	46	5	2	5	25	2	23	.307	.329	.467	796	98	-1	6	3	0	1.000	-4	O-23C/1-8,S-7,3D	-0.4
	*NY-N	42	93	12	32	6	1	0	16	0	16	.344	.358	.430	788	101	0	4	1	1	.978	-3	O-27(9-16-5)/3-1	-0.2
	Yr	104	243	35	78	11	3	5	41	2	39	.321	.340	.453	793	99	-1	10	4	1	.988	-6	O-50C/1-8,S-7,3D	-0.6
2000	*StL-N	98	216	28	54	11	2	12	43	6	47	.250	.280	.486	766	88	-5	3	1	0	.989	-11	O-58L/S-8,1-6,3D	-1.6
Total	16	1654	5594	703	1511	277	59	140	634	198	935	.270	.300	.416	715	89	-100	208	81	17	.967	-25	*S-1362,O-133L/213D	0.5
■ TODD DUNWOODY Dunwoody, Todd Franklin b: 4/11/75, Lafayette, Ind. BL/TL, 6'1", 190 lbs. Deb: 5/10/97																								
1997	Fla-N	19	50	7	13	2	2	2	7	7	21	.260	.362	.500	862	129	2	2	0	0	.929	-1	O-14(6-8-0)	0.2
1998	Fla-N	116	434	53	109	27	7	5	28	21	113	.251	.292	.380	672	79	-14	5	1	1	.989	11	*O-111(0-111-0)	-0.2
1999	Fla-N	64	186	20	41	6	3	2	20	12	41	.220	.271	.317	589	51	-14	3	4	-1	.981	-3	O-55(8-44-5)	-1.7
2000	KC-A	61	178	12	37	9	0	1	23	8	42	.208	.246	.275	521	31	-19	3	0	1	.976	-3	O-40(14-19-9),D-11	-2.1
Total	4	260	848	92	200	44	12	10	78	48	217	.236	.282	.351	634	65	-45	13	5	1	.982	4	O-220(28-182-14)/D-11	-3.8
■ DAN DURAN Duran, Daniel James b: 3/16/54, Palo Alto, Cal. BL/TL, 5'11", 190 lbs. Deb: 4/17/81																								
1981	Tex-A	13	16	1	4	0	0	0	0	1	1	.250	.294	.250	544	61	-1	0	0	0	1.000	-1	/O-7(7-0-0),1-1	-0.2
■ MIKE DURANT Durant, Michael Joseph b: 9/14/69, Columbus, Ohio BR/TR, 6'2", 200 lbs. Deb: 4/3/96																								
1996	Min-A	40	81	15	17	3	0	0	5	10	15	.210	.297	.247	544	39	-7	3	0	1	.975	9	C-37	0.3
■ ERUBIEL DURAZO Durazo, Erubiel (Cardenas) b: 1/23/74, Hermosillo, Mex. BL/TL, 6'3", 225 lbs. Deb: 7/26/99																								
1999	*Ari-N	52	155	31	51	4	2	11	30	26	43	.329	.429	.594	1022	154	13	1	1	-0	1.000	-2	1-44	0.7
2000	Ari-N	67	196	35	52	11	0	8	33	34	43	.265	.377	.444	821	105	2	1	0	0	.989	-5	1-60	-0.7
Total	2	119	351	66	103	15	2	19	63	60	86	.293	.400	.510	909	127	16	2	1	0	.994	-6	1-104	0.0
■ KID DURBIN Durbin, Blaine Alphonsus b: 9/10/1886, Lamar, Mo. d: 9/11/43, Kirkwood, Mo. BL/TL, 5'8", 155 lbs. Deb: 4/24/07																								
1907	Chi-N	11	18	2	6	0	0	0	0	1		.333	.368	.333	702	113	0	0			1.000	0	/P-5,O-5(1-0-4)	0.0
1908	Chi-N	14	28	3	7	1	0	0	0	2		.250	.323	.286	608	91	-0	0			1.000	-3	O-14(0-11-0)	-0.4
1909	Cin-N	6	5	1	1	0	0	0	0	1		.200	.333	.200	533	66	-0	0			.000	0	H	0.0
	Pit-N	1	0	0	0	0	0	0	0	0		—	—	—	—	—	0	0			.000	0	R	0.0
	Yr	7	5	1	1	0	0	0	0	1		.200	.333	.200	533	65	-0	0			.000	0	-0,-0	0.0
Total	3	32	51	6	14	1	0	0	0	4		.275	.339	.294	633	96	-0	0			1.000	-2	/O-19(1-11-4),P-5	-0.4
■ JOE DURHAM Durham, Joseph Vann "Pop" b: 7/31/31, Newport News, Va. BR/TR, 6'1", 186 lbs. Deb: 9/10/54																								
1954	Bal-A	10	40	4	9	0	0	1	3	4	7	.225	.295	.300	595	68	-2	0	0	0	.917	-1	O-10(10-1-0)	-0.3
1957	Bal-A	77	157	19	29	2	0	4	17	16	42	.185	.260	.274	534	49	-11	1	1	-0	1.000	-11	O-59(36-5-25)	-2.6
1959	StL-N	6	5	2	0	0	0	0	0	0	1	.000	.000	.000	0	-94	-1	0	0	0	1.000	0	/O-1(0-0-1)	-0.1
Total	3	93	202	25	38	2	0	5	20	20	50	.188	.261	.272	534	49	-14	1	1	-0	.979	-12	/O-70(46-6-26)	-3.0
■ LEON DURHAM Durham, Leon b: 7/31/57, Cincinnati, Ohio BL/TL, 6'2", 210 lbs. Deb: 5/27/80 Career OF: (86-LF 116-CF 219-RF)																								
1980	StL-N	96	303	42	82	15	4	8	42	18	55	.271	.314	.426	739	101	-0	8	5	0	.987	7	O-78(35-2-43)/1-8	0.3
1981	Chi-N	87	328	42	95	14	6	10	35	27	53	.290	.344	.460	804	121	8	25	11	2	.970	2	O-83(0-0-83)/1-3	0.8
1982	Chi-N☆	148	539	84	168	33	7	22	90	66	77	.312	.389	.521	910	148	35	28	14	1	.963	-3	*O-143(0-74-89)/1-1	2.9
1983	Chi-N★	100	337	58	87	18	8	12	55	66	83	.258	.384	.466	850	128	15	12	6	1	.966	-7	O-95(51-40-4)/1-6	0.6
1984	*Chi-N	137	473	86	132	30	4	23	96	69	86	.279	.372	.505	877	132	21	16	8	1	.994	6	*1-130	2.1
1985	Chi-N	153	542	58	153	32	2	21	75	64	99	.282	.358	.465	823	116	12	7	6	-1	.995	3	*1-151	0.5
1986	Chi-N	141	484	66	127	18	7	20	65	67	98	.262	.353	.452	806	112	8	8	7	-1	.995	-7	*1-141	-0.8
1987	Chi-N	131	439	70	120	22	1	27	63	51	92	.273	.349	.513	862	120	12	2	2	-0	.990	-9	*1-123	-0.5
1988	Chi-N	24	73	10	16	6	1	3	6	9	20	.219	.305	.452	757	110	1	0	1	-0	.995	1	1-20	0.0
	Cin-N	21	51	4	11	3	0	1	2	5	12	.216	.286	.333	619	74	-2	0	0	0	.993	-1	1-17	-0.4
	Yr	45	124	14	27	9	1	4	8	14	32	.218	.297	.403	700	95	-1	0	1	-0	.994	-0	1-37	-0.4
1989	StL-N	29	18	2	1	1	0	0	1	2	4	.056	.190	.111	302	-11	-3	0	1	-0	.961	1	1-18	-0.2
Total	10	1067	3587	522	992	192	40	147	530	444	679	.277	.358	.475	833	122	107	106	61	2	.994	-8	1-618,O-399R	5.3

■ **RAY DURHAM** Durham, Ray b: 11/30/71, Charlotte, N.C. BB/TR, 5'8", 170 lbs. Deb: 4/26/95

YEAR	TM/L	G	AB	R	H	2B	3B	HR	RBI	BB	SO	AVG	OBP	SLG	OPS	OPS+	BR+	SB	CS	SBR	FA	FR	G/POS	TPR
1995	Chi-A	125	471	68	121	27	6	7	51	31	83	.257	.311	.384	695	83	-12	18	5	2	.973	-29	*2-122/D-1	-3.1
1996	Chi-A	156	557	79	153	33	5	10	65	58	95	.275	.354	.406	759	96	-3	30	4	5	.984	-21	*2-150/D-3	-1.0
1997	Chi-A	155	634	106	172	27	5	11	53	61	96	.271	.341	.382	723	92	-7	33	16	2	.974	-31	*2-153/D-1	-2.8
1998	Chi-A★	158	635	126	181	35	8	19	67	73	105	.285	.364	.455	819	115	14	36	9	5	.976	-6	*2-158	2.0
1999	Chi-A	153	612	109	181	30	8	13	60	73	105	.296	.374	.435	809	105	6	34	11	4	.974	-11	*2-148/D-4	0.6
2000	*Chi-A★	151	614	121	172	35	9	17	75	75	105	.280	.365	.450	814	104	4	25	13	1	.980	-3	*2-151	0.9
Total	6	898	3523	609	980	187	41	77	371	371	589	.278	.353	.420	774	100	3	176	58	18	.977	-101	2-882/D-9	-3.4

■ **BOBBY DURNBAUGH** Durnbaugh, Robert Eugene "Scroggy" b: 1/15/33, Dayton, Ohio BR/TR, 5'8", 170 lbs. Deb: 9/22/57

YEAR	TM/L	G	AB	R	H	2B	3B	HR	RBI	BB	SO	AVG	OBP	SLG	OPS	OPS+	BR+	SB	CS	SBR	FA	FR	G/POS	TPR
1957	Cin-N	2	1	0	0	0	0	0	0	0	0	.000	.000	.000	0	-93	-0	0	0	0	.500	-0	/S-2	0.0

■ **GEORGE DURNING** Durning, George Dewey b: 5/9/1898, Philadelphia, Pa. d: 4/18/86, Tampa, Fla. BR/TR, 5'11", 175 lbs. Deb: 9/12/25

YEAR	TM/L	G	AB	R	H	2B	3B	HR	RBI	BB	SO	AVG	OBP	SLG	OPS	OPS+	BR+	SB	CS	SBR	FA	FR	G/POS	TPR
1925	Phi-N	5	14	3	5	0	0	0	1	2	1	.357	.438	.357	795	97	0	0	0	0	1.000	2	/O-4(0-0-4)	0.2

■ **LEO DUROCHER** Durocher, Leo Ernest "Lippy"
b: 7/27/05, W.Springfield, Mass. d: 10/7/91, Palm Springs, Cal. BR/TR (BB 1928-29), 5'10", 160 lbs. Deb: 10/2/25 MCH

YEAR	TM/L	G	AB	R	H	2B	3B	HR	RBI	BB	SO	AVG	OBP	SLG	OPS	OPS+	BR+	SB	CS	SBR	FA	FR	G/POS	TPR
1925	NY-A	2	1	1	0	0	0	0	0	0	0	.000	.000	.000	0	-99	-0	0	0	0	.000	0	H	0.0
1928	*NY-A	102	296	46	80	8	6	0	31	22	52	.270	.327	.338	665	77	-10	1	4	-1	.948	12	2-66,S-29	0.5
1929	NY-A	106	341	53	84	4	5	0	32	34	33	.246	.320	.287	607	62	-19	3	1	0	.958	**26**	S-93,2-12	1.6
1930	Cin-N	119	354	31	86	15	3	3	32	20	45	.243	.287	.328	615	51	-29	0			.959	10	*S-103,2-13	-0.7
1931	Cin-N	121	361	26	82	11	5	1	29	18	32	.227	.264	.294	557	53	-25	0			.965	-4	*S-120	-2.1
1932	Cin-N	143	457	43	99	22	5	1	33	36	40	.217	.275	.293	569	55	-29	3			.960	-14	*S-142	-3.3
1933	Cin-N	16	51	6	11	1	0	1	3	4	5	.216	.273	.294	567	63	-2	0			.953	6	S-16	0.4
	StL-N	123	395	45	102	18	4	2	41	26	32	.258	.306	.339	645	80	-10	3			.961	-1	*S-123	-0.2
	Yr	139	446	51	113	19	4	3	44	30	37	.253	.302	.334	636	78	-12	3			**.960**	5	*S-139	0.2
1934	*StL-N	146	500	62	130	26	5	3	70	33	40	.260	.308	.350	658	71	-20	2			.957	1	*S-146	-0.8
1935	StL-N	143	513	62	136	23	5	8	78	29	46	.265	.304	.376	681	79	-16	4			.963	9	*S-142	0.4
1936	StL-N★	136	510	57	146	22	3	1	58	29	47	.286	.327	.347	674	82	-13	3			**.971**	-11	*S-136	-1.3
1937	StL-N	135	477	46	97	11	3	1	47	38	36	.203	.262	.245	507	38	-41	6			.959	-11	*S-134	-4.2
1938	Bro-N★	141	479	41	105	18	5	1	56	47	30	.219	.293	.284	577	58	-27	3			**.966**	-5	*S-141	-2.2
1939	Bro-N	116	390	42	108	21	6	1	34	27	24	.277	.325	.369	695	83	-9	2			.957	-7	*S-113/3-1,M	-0.9
1940	Bro-N☆	62	160	10	37	9	1	1	14	12	13	.231	.285	.319	604	62	-8	1			.959	1	S-53/2-4,M	-0.4
1941	Bro-N	18	42	2	12	1	0	0	6	1	3	.286	.302	.310	612	70	-2	0			.917	-0	S-12/2-1,M	-0.1
1943	Bro-N	6	18	1	4	0	0	0	1	1	2	.222	.263	.222	485	41	-1	0			1.000	2	/S-6,M	0.2
1945	Bro-N	2	5	1	1	0	0	0	2	0	0	.200	.200	.200	400	11	-1	0			1.000	1	/2-2,M	0.0
Total	17	1637	5350	575	1320	210	56	24	567	377	480	.247	.299	.320	619	66	-261	31	5		.961	16	*S-1509/2-98,3-1	-13.1

■ **RED DURRETT** Durrett, Elmer Cable b: 2/3/21, Sherman, Tex. d: 1/17/92, Waxahachie, Tex. BL/TL, 5'10", 170 lbs. Deb: 9/14/44

YEAR	TM/L	G	AB	R	H	2B	3B	HR	RBI	BB	SO	AVG	OBP	SLG	OPS	OPS+	BR+	SB	CS	SBR	FA	FR	G/POS	TPR
1944	Bro-N	11	32	3	5	1	0	1	1	7	10	.156	.308	.281	589	68	-1	0			.933	1	/O-9(0-5-4)	0.0
1945	Bro-N	8	16	2	2	0	0	0	0	3	3	.125	.263	.125	388	10	-2	0			1.000	-1	/O-4(0-4-0)	-0.3
Total	2	19	48	5	7	1	0	1	1	10	13	.146	.293	.229	522	48	-3	0			.947	1	/O-13(0-9-4)	-0.3

■ **TRENT DURRINGTON** Durrington, Trent John b: 8/27/75, Sydney, Australia BR/TR, 5'10", 172 lbs. Deb: 8/6/99

YEAR	TM/L	G	AB	R	H	2B	3B	HR	RBI	BB	SO	AVG	OBP	SLG	OPS	OPS+	BR+	SB	CS	SBR	FA	FR	G/POS	TPR
1999	Ana-A	43	122	14	22	2	0	0	2	9	28	.180	.237	.197	433	12	-16	4	3	-0	.966	-4	2-41	-1.7
2000	Ana-A	4	3	0	0	0	0	0	0	0	0	.000	.000	.000	0	-99	-1	0	0	0	1.000	1	/2-1	0.0
Total	2	47	125	14	22	2	0	0	2	9	28	.176	.231	.192	423	10	-17	4	3	-0	.967	-3	/2-42	-1.7

■ **CEDRIC DURST** Durst, Cedric Montgomery b: 8/23/1896, Austin, Tex. d: 2/16/71, San Diego, Cal. BL/TL, 5'11", 160 lbs. Deb: 5/30/22

YEAR	TM/L	G	AB	R	H	2B	3B	HR	RBI	BB	SO	AVG	OBP	SLG	OPS	OPS+	BR+	SB	CS	SBR	FA	FR	G/POS	TPR
1922	StL-A	15	12	5	4	1	0	0	0	0	1	.333	.333	.417	750	91	-0	0	0	0	.857	-2	/O-6(1-4-1)	-0.2
1923	StL-A	45	85	11	18	2	0	5	11	8	14	.212	.280	.412	691	76	-4	0	0	0	1.000	-2	O-10(4-5-1)/1-8	-0.7
1926	StL-A	80	219	32	52	7	5	3	16	22	19	.237	.310	.356	666	70	-10	0	5	-2	.980	2	O-57(5-42-10)/1-4	-1.3
1927	*NY-A	65	129	18	32	4	3	0	25	6	7	.248	.281	.326	607	59	-8	0	3	-1	.980	-7	O-36(13-6-17)/1-2	-1.7
1928	*NY-A	74	135	18	34	2	1	2	10	7	9	.252	.289	.326	615	63	-7	1	0	0	.983	-3	O-33(13-5-15)/1-3	-1.1
1929	NY-A	92	202	32	52	3	3	4	31	15	25	.257	.309	.361	670	77	-7	3	2	-0	.987	-0	O-72(46-6-20)/1-1	-1.1
1930	NY-A	8	19	0	3	1	0	0	5	0	1	.158	.158	.211	368	-8	-3	0	0	0	1.000	-0	/O-6(6-0-0)	-0.3
	Bos-A	102	302	29	74	19	5	1	24	17	24	.245	.290	.351	641	64	-17	3	1	0	.968	-2	O-75(46-0-29)	-2.2
	Yr	110	321	29	77	20	5	1	29	17	25	.240	.282	.343	625	60	-20	3	1	0	.970	-2	O-81(52-0-29)	-2.5
Total	7	481	1103	145	269	39	17	15	122	75	100	.244	.294	.351	645	67	-57	7	11	-2	.979	-15	O-295(134-68-93)/1-18	-8.6

■ **ERV DUSAK** Dusak, Ervin Frank "Four Sack" b: 7/29/20, Chicago, Ill. d: 11/6/94, Glendale Heights, Ill. BR/TR, 6'2", 185 lbs. Deb: 9/18/41 Career OF: (105-LF 106-CF 67-RF)

YEAR	TM/L	G	AB	R	H	2B	3B	HR	RBI	BB	SO	AVG	OBP	SLG	OPS	OPS+	BR+	SB	CS	SBR	FA	FR	G/POS	TPR
1941	StL-N	6	14	1	2	0	0	0	3	2	6	.143	.250	.143	393	12	-2	1			1.000	1	/O-4(1-2-1)	0.0
1942	StL-N	12	27	4	5	3	0	0	3	3	7	.185	.267	.296	563	60	-1	0			1.000	0	/O-8(5-0-3),3-1	-0.1
1946	*StL-N	100	275	38	66	9	1	9	42	33	63	.240	.321	.378	700	94	-2	7			.993	3	O-77(72-5-0),3-11/2-2	-0.4
1947	StL-N	111	328	56	93	7	3	6	28	50	34	.284	.378	.378	756	97	0	1			.970	1	O-89(22-28-47)/3-7	-0.2
1948	StL-N	114	311	60	65	9	2	6	19	49	55	.209	.317	.309	625	66	-14	3			.992	-5	O-68C,2-29/3-9,PS	-1.9
1949	StL-N	1	0	1	0	0	0	0	0	0	0	—	—	—	—	—	0	0			.000	0	R	0.0
1950	StL-N	23	12	0	1	1	0	0	0	0	3	.083	.083	.167	250	-34	-2	0			1.000	0	P-14/O-2(0-2-0)	0.0
1951	StL-N	5	2	1	1	0	0	1	1	0	1	.500	.500	2.000	2500	537	1	0	0	0	1.000	0	/P-5	0.0
	Pit-N	21	39	6	12	3	0	1	7	3	11	.308	.357	.462	819	115	1	0	0	0	1.000	-6	O-12C/P-3,2-2,3-2	-0.5
	Yr	26	41	7	13	3	0	2	8	3	12	.317	.364	.537	900	136	2	0	0	0	1.000	-6	O-12C/P-8,2-2,3-2	-0.5
1952	Pit-N	20	27	1	6	0	0	1	3	2	8	.222	.276	.333	609	66	-1	0	0	0	.818	-2	O-11(2-4-3)	-0.3
Total	9	413	1035	168	251	32	6	24	106	142	188	.243	.334	.355	688	84	-21	12	0		.981	-6	O-271C/2-33,3-30,PS	-3.4

■ **AL DWIGHT** Dwight, Albert Ward b: 1/4/1856, New York, N.Y. d: 2/20/03, San Francisco, Cal Deb: 6/19/1884

YEAR	TM/L	G	AB	R	H	2B	3B	HR	RBI	BB	SO	AVG	OBP	SLG	OPS	OPS+	BR+	SB	CS	SBR	FA	FR	G/POS	TPR
1884	KC-U	12	43	8	10	2	0	0		2		.233	.267	.279	546	75	-2				.953	-1	C-10/O-1(0-1-0),2-1	-0.2

■ **JIM DWYER** Dwyer, James Edward "Pig Pen" b: 1/3/50, Evergreen Park, Ill. BL/TL, 5'10", 175 lbs. Deb: 6/10/73 Career OF: (250-LF 75-CF 329-RF)

YEAR	TM/L	G	AB	R	H	2B	3B	HR	RBI	BB	SO	AVG	OBP	SLG	OPS	OPS+	BR+	SB	CS	SBR	FA	FR	G/POS	TPR
1973	StL-N	28	57	7	11	1	1	0	0	1	5	.193	.207	.246	453	25	-6	0	0	0	1.000	-2	O-20(9-10-1)	-0.9
1974	StL-N	74	86	13	24	1	0	2	11	11	16	.279	.367	.360	728	105	1	0	0	0	1.000	-3	O-25(8-1-16)/1-3	-0.3
1975	StL-N	21	31	4	6	1	0	0	1	4	6	.194	.286	.226	512	42	-2	0	0	0	1.000	-1	/O-9(5-3-2)	-0.3
	Mon-N	60	175	22	50	7	1	3	20	23	30	.286	.369	.389	757	106	2	4	1	1	.959	1	O-52(46-3-3)	0.1
	Yr	81	206	26	56	8	1	3	21	27	36	.272	.356	.364	720	96	-0	4	1	1	.966	1	O-61(51-6-5)	-0.2
1976	Mon-N	50	92	7	17	3	1	0	5	11	10	.185	.272	.239	511	44	-7	0	0	0	.970	-2	O-19(15-0-5)	-1.0
	NY-N	11	13	2	2	0	0	0	0	2	1	.154	.267	.154	421	23	-1	0	0	0	1.000	-0	/O-2(0-0-2)	-0.2
	Yr	61	105	9	19	3	1	0	5	13	11	.181	.271	.229	500	42	-8	0	0	0	.972	-2	O-21(15-0-7)	-1.2
1977	StL-N	13	31	3	7	1	0	0	2	4	5	.226	.351	.258	609	68	-1	0	0	0	1.000	-2	O-12(3-0-10)	-0.4
1978	StL-N	34	65	8	14	3	0	1	4	9	3	.215	.320	.308	628	77	-2	1	0	0	.952	-4	O-22(18-0-5)	-0.7
	SF-N	73	173	22	39	9	2	5	22	28	29	.225	.333	.387	721	105	1	6	0	1	.987	1	O-36(3-26-9),1-29	0.2
	Yr	107	238	30	53	12	2	6	26	37	32	.223	.330	.366	695	97	-1	7	0	2	.979	-3	O-58(21-26-14),1-29	-0.5
1979	Bos-A	76	113	19	30	7	0	2	14	17	9	.265	.366	.381	747	96	-0	3	1	0	.981	-0	1-25,O-19(6-1-12)/D-4	-0.1
1980	Bos-A	93	260	41	74	11	1	9	38	28	23	.285	.359	.438	797	111	4	3	2	-0	.975	-3	O-65C,D-12/1-9	-0.1
1981	Bal-A	68	134	16	30	0	1	3	10	20	19	.224	.325	.306	631	83	-2	0	2	-1	.977	-11	O-59(43-2-19)/1-3,D-1	-1.6
1982	Bal-A	71	148	28	45	4	3	6	15	27	24	.304	.411	.493	905	148	11	2	0	0	.976	-8	O-49(16-0-37)/1-1,D-1	0.2
1983	*Bal-A	100	196	37	56	17	1	8	38	31	29	.286	.383	.505	888	145	13	1	1	-0	.966	-7	O-56(7-0-49),D-10/1-4	0.3
1984	Bal-A	76	161	22	41	9	1	2	21	23	24	.255	.348	.360	708	98	0	0	2	-1	.966	-4	O-52(1-0-51)/D-3	-0.7
1985	Bal-A	101	233	35	58	8	3	7	36	37	31	.249	.354	.399	753	109	4	0	3	-1	.993	-3	O-78(46-0-33)/D-3	-0.3
1986	Bal-A	94	160	18	39	13	1	8	31	23	31	.244	.346	.488	833	126	6	0	2	-1	1.000	-0	O-24(8-0-16),D-24/1-1	0.3
1987	Bal-A	92	241	54	66	7	1	15	33	37	57	.274	.373	.498	871	132	11	4	1	1	1.000	-1	D-41,O-30(3-0-29)	0.8
1988	Bal-A	35	53	3	12	0	0	0	3	12	11	.226	.369	.226	596	73	-1	0	0	0	1.000	-0	D-17/O-2(1-0-1)	-0.2
	Min-A	20	41	6	12	1	0	2	15	13	8	.293	.473	.463	936	159	4	0	0	0	.000	0	D-13	0.4

YEAR	TM/L	G	AB	R	H	2B	3B	HR	RBI	BB	SO	AVG	OBP	SLG	OPS	OPS+	BR+	SB	CS	SBR	FA	FR	G/POS	TPR
	Yr	55	94	9	24	1	0	2	18	25	19	.255	.417	.330	746	113	3	0	0	0	1.000	-0	D-30/O-2(1-0-1)	0.2
1989	Min-A	88	225	34	71	11	0	3	23	28	23	.316	.391	.404	796	117	6	2	0	0	.000	-0	D-74/O-1(0-0-1)	0.4
	Mon-N	13	10	1	3	1	0	0	2	1	1	.300	.364	.400	764	116	0	0	0	0	.000	0	H	0.0
1990	Min-A	37	63	7	12	0	0	1	5	12	7	.190	.320	.238	558	55	-3	0	0	0	1.000	-0	D-23/O-2(1-0-1)	-0.5
Total	18	1328	2761	409	719	115	17	77	349	402	402	.260	.357	.398	755	107	37	26	15	0	.979	-50	O-634R,D-226/1-75	-4.6
■ **JOHN DWYER** Dwyer, John E. Deb: 5/16/1882																								
1882	Cle-N	1	3	0	0	0	0	0	1	0	0	.000	.000	.000	0	-99	-1				.000	-1	/O-1(1-0-0),C-1	-0.2
■ **DOUBLE JOE DWYER** Dwyer, Joseph Michael b: 3/27/03, Orange, N.J. d: 10/21/92, Glen Ridge, N.J. BL/TL, 5'9", 186 lbs. Deb: 4/20/37																								
1937	Cin-N	12	11	2	3	0	0	0	1	1	0	.273	.333	.273	606	70	-0	0			.000	0	H	0.0
■ **JERRY DYBZINSKI** Dybzinski, Jerome Matthew b: 7/7/55, Cleveland, Ohio BR/TR, 6'2", 180 lbs. Deb: 4/11/80																								
1980	Cle-A	114	248	32	57	11	1	1	23	13	35	.230	.274	.294	568	55	-15	4	1	1	.971	21	S-73,2-29/3-4,D-2	1.3
1981	Cle-A	48	57	10	17	0	0	0	6	5	8	.298	.355	.298	653	91	-0	7	1	1	.970	8	S-34/2-3,3-3,D-1	1.1
1982	Cle-A	80	212	19	49	6	2	0	22	21	25	.231	.309	.278	588	63	-10	3	5	-1	.957	17	S-77/3-3	1.3
1983	*Chi-A	127	256	30	59	10	1	1	32	18	29	.230	.286	.289	575	57	-15	11	4	1	.966	1	*S-118/3-9	-0.4
1984	Chi-A	94	132	17	31	5	1	1	10	13	12	.235	.313	.311	624	70	-5	7	2	1	.974	18	S-76,3-14/2-1,D-1	1.8
1985	Pit-N	5	4	0	0	0	0	0	0	0	0	.000	.000	.000	0	-99	-1	0	0	0	.900	1	/S-5	0.0
Total	6	468	909	108	213	32	5	3	93	70	109	.234	.296	.290	586	61	-47	32	13	2	.966	67	S-383/3-33,2-33,D-4	5.1
■ **JIM DYCK** Dyck, James Robert b: 2/3/22, Omaha, Neb. d: 1/11/99, Cheney, Wash. BR/TR, 6'2", 205 lbs. Deb: 9/27/51 Career OF: (125-LF 27-CF 10-RF)																								
1951	StL-A	4	15	1	1	0	0	0	0	1	1	.067	.125	.067	192	-46	-3	0	0	0	1.000	0	/3-4	-0.3
1952	StL-A	122	402	60	108	22	3	15	64	50	68	.269	.354	.450	804	119	10	0	4	-1	.962	9	3-74,O-48(39-8-2)	1.5
1953	StL-A	112	334	38	71	15	1	9	27	38	40	.213	.299	.344	643	72	-14	3	2	-0	.981	-6	O-55(32-19-8),3-51	-2.2
1954	Cle-A	2	1	0	1	0	0	0	1	1	0	1.000	1.000	1.000	2000	441	1	0	0	0	.000	0	H	0.1
1955	Bal-A	61	197	32	55	13	1	2	22	28	21	.279	.372	.386	757	112	4	1	0	0	.989	-0	O-45(45-0-0),3-17	0.2
1956	Bal-A	11	23	3	5	2	0	0	0	10	5	.217	.455	.304	759	112	1	0	0	0	.923	-0	/O-9(9-0-0)	0.1
	Cin-N	18	11	5	1	0	0	0	0	3	5	.091	.286	.091	377	7	-1	0	0	0	1.000	0	/1-1,3-1	-0.1
Total	6	330	983	139	242	52	5	26	114	131	140	.246	.339	.389	728	98	-2	4	6	-1	.982	3	O-157L,3-147/1-1	-0.7
■ **JERMAINE DYE** Dye, Jermaine Terrell b: 1/28/74, Oakland, Cal. BR/TR, 6'4", 210 lbs. Deb: 5/17/96																								
1996	*Atl-N	98	292	32	82	16	0	12	37	8	67	.281	.307	.459	766	93	-4	1	4	-1	.950	-6	O-92(25-4-71)	-1.4
1997	KC-A	75	263	26	62	14	0	7	22	17	51	.236	.285	.369	654	67	-13	2	1	0	.966	6	O-75(1-0-75)	-1.0
1998	KC-A	60	214	24	50	5	1	5	23	11	46	.234	.274	.336	611	56	-14	2	2	-0	.987	9	O-59(0-0-59)	-0.8
1999	KC-A	158	608	96	179	44	8	27	119	58	119	.294	.357	.526	883	119	16	2	3	-1	.984	18	*O-157(0-0-157)/D-1	2.3
2000	KC-A★	157	601	107	193	41	2	33	118	69	99	.321	.394	.561	954	136	33	0	1	-0	.976	4	*O-146(0-0-146),D-10	2.6
Total	5	548	1978	285	566	120	11	84	319	163	382	.286	.343	.485	829	107	18	7	11	-2	.975	32	O-529(26-4-508)/D-11	1.7
■ **BEN DYER** Dyer, Benjamin Franklin b: 2/13/1893, Chicago, Ill. d: 8/7/59, Kenosha, Wis. BR/TR, 5'11", 170 lbs. Deb: 5/23/14 Career OF: (1-LF 0-CF 2-RF)																								
1914	NY-N	7	4	1	1	0	0	0	0	0	1	.250	.250	.250	500	50	-0	1			1.000	1	/S-6,2-1	0.1
1915	NY-N	7	19	4	4	0	1	0	0	4	3	.211	.375	.316	691	117	1	0			.889	-0	/3-6,S-1	0.1
1916	Det-A	4	14	4	4	1	0	0	1	1	1	.286	.333	.357	690	104	0	0			1.000	-2	/S-4	-0.2
1917	Det-A	30	67	6	14	5	0	0	0	2	17	.209	.232	.284	515	57	-4	3			.846	2	S-14/3-8	-0.1
1918	Det-A	13	18	1	5	0	0	0	2	0	6	.278	.278	.278	556	71	-1	0			1.000	0	/P-2,1-2,O-2L,2-1	-0.1
1919	Det-A	44	85	11	21	4	0	0	15	8	19	.247	.312	.294	606	72	-3	0			.953	6	3-23,S-11/O-1(0-0-1)	0.4
Total	6	105	207	27	49	10	1	0	18	15	47	.237	.291	.295	586	74	-7	4			.937	7	/3-37,S-36,O-3R,1P2	0.2
■ **DUFFY DYER** Dyer, Don Robert b: 8/15/45, Dayton, Ohio BR/TR, 6', 195 lbs. Deb: 9/21/68 C																								
1968	NY-N	1	3	0	1	0	0	0	0	1	1	.333	.500	.333	833	153	0	0	0	0	1.000	0	/C-1	0.1
1969	*NY-N	29	74	5	19	3	1	3	12	4	22	.257	.295	.446	741	103	-0	0	0	0	.991	-1	C-19	0.0
1970	NY-N	59	148	8	31	1	0	2	12	21	32	.209	.308	.257	564	53	-9	1	1	-0	.991	2	C-57	-0.6
1971	NY-N	59	169	13	39	7	1	2	18	14	45	.231	.293	.320	613	75	-6	1	0	0	.992	0	C-53	-0.3
1972	NY-N	94	325	33	75	17	3	8	36	28	71	.231	.302	.375	677	94	-3	0	1	-0	.993	18	C-91/O-1(0-0-1)	1.9
1973	NY-N	70	189	9	35	6	1	1	9	13	40	.185	.245	.243	488	36	-16	0	1	-0	.994	-1	C-60	-1.6
1974	NY-N	63	142	14	30	1	1	0	10	18	15	.211	.304	.232	537	53	-8	0	0	0	.982	-4	C-45	-1.1
1975	*Pit-N	48	132	8	30	5	2	3	16	6	22	.227	.266	.364	630	74	-5	0	0	0	.990	6	C-36	0.2
1976	Pit-N	69	184	12	41	8	0	3	9	29	35	.223	.338	.315	653	85	-3	0	0	0	.994	7	C-58	0.7
1977	Pit-N	94	270	27	65	11	1	3	19	54	49	.241	.373	.322	695	86	-3	6	0	1	**.996**	5	C-93	0.7
1978	Pit-N	58	175	7	37	8	1	0	13	18	32	.211	.296	.269	564	56	-10	2	1	0	.991	6	C-55	-0.2
1979	Mon-N	28	74	4	18	6	0	1	8	9	17	.243	.325	.365	690	89	-1	0	0	0	.993	7	C-27	0.6
1980	Det-A	48	108	11	20	1	0	4	11	13	34	.185	.273	.306	578	57	-6	0	0	0	.986	3	C-37,D-10	-0.3
1981	Det-A	2	0	0	0	0	0	0	0	0	0	—	—	—	—	—	0	0	0	0	.000	0	/C-2	0.0
Total	14	722	1993	151	441	74	11	30	173	228	415	.221	.307	.315	622	73	-71	10	4	1	.992	46	C-634/D-10,O-1(0-0-1)	0.1
■ **EDDIE DYER** Dyer, Edwin Hawley b: 10/11/1900, Morgan City, La. d: 4/20/64, Houston, Tex. BL/TL, 5'11.5", 168 lbs. Deb: 7/8/22 M																								
1922	StL-N	6	3	1	1	1	0	0	0	0	0	.333	.333	.667	1000	159	0	0	0	0	1.000	0	/P-2	0.0
1923	StL-N	35	45	17	12	3	0	2	5	3	5	.267	.313	.467	779	105	0	1	0	0	1.000	-1	/O-8(7-2-0),P-4	-0.1
1924	StL-N	50	76	8	18	2	3	0	8	3	8	.237	.266	.342	608	63	-4	1	0	0	.909	1	P-29/O-1(0-1-0)	-0.1
1925	StL-N	31	31	4	3	1	0	0	0	3	1	.097	.176	.129	306	-20	-6	1	1	-0	.917	0	P-27	0.0
1926	StL-N	6	2	1	1	0	0	0	0	0	0	.500	.500	.500	1000	164	0	0			1.000	0	/P-6	0.0
1927	StL-N	1	0	0	0	0	0	0	0	1	0	—	1.000	—	1000	181	0	0			.000	-0	/P-1	0.0
Total	6	129	157	31	35	7	3	2	13	10	14	.223	.269	.344	613	61	-9	3	1		.921	-0	/P-69,O-9(7-3-0)	-0.2
■ **JIMMY DYKES** Dykes, James Joseph b: 11/10/1896, Philadelphia, Pa. d: 6/15/76, Philadelphia, Pa. BR/TR, 5'9", 185 lbs. Deb: 5/6/18 MC Career OF: (2-LF 4-CF 1-RF)																								
1918	Phi-A	59	186	13	35	3	3	0	13	19	32	.188	.267	.237	504	51	-11	3			.940	10	2-56/3-1	0.0
1919	Phi-A	17	49	4	9	1	0	0	1	7	11	.184	.286	.204	490	38	-4	0			.945	6	2-16	0.2
1920	Phi-A	142	546	81	140	25	4	8	35	55	73	.256	.334	.361	695	83	-13	6	9	-2	.957	17	*2-108,3-34	0.5
1921	Phi-A	155	613	88	168	32	13	16	77	60	75	.274	.353	.447	800	102	1	6	5	-0	.954	25	*2-155	2.8
1922	Phi-A	145	501	66	138	23	7	12	68	55	98	.275	.359	.421	780	100	0	6	2	1	.945	-8	*3-141/2-5	0.2
1923	Phi-A	124	416	50	105	28	1	4	43	35	40	.252	.318	.353	671	76	-15	6	4	-0	.964	4	*2-102,S-20/3-2	-0.6
1924	Phi-A	110	410	68	128	26	6	3	50	38	60	.312	.372	.427	799	105	3	1	3	-1	.961	16	2-77,3-27/S-4	2.0
1925	Phi-A	122	465	93	150	32	11	5	55	46	49	.323	.393	.471	864	111	8	3	2	-0	.944	10	3-64,2-58/S-2	2.1
1926	Phi-A	124	429	54	123	32	5	1	44	49	34	.287	.370	.392	762	94	-3	6	2	1	.950	**26**	3-82,2-44/S-1	2.9
1927	Phi-A	121	417	61	135	33	6	3	60	44	23	.324	.394	.453	847	113	8	2	3	-1	.989	-3	1-82,3-25/S-5,O2P	0.1
1928	Phi-A	85	242	39	67	11	0	5	30	27	21	.277	.361	.384	746	93	-2	2	1	0	.982	-2	2-32,S-22,3-20,/1O	0.0
1929	*Phi-A	119	401	76	131	34	6	13	79	51	25	.327	.412	.539	950	138	23	8	3	1	.928	-11	S-60,3-48,2-12	2.1
1930	*Phi-A	125	435	69	131	28	4	6	73	74	53	.301	.414	.425	840	109	9	3	3	-0	.960	-13	*3-123/O-1(1-0-0)	0.3
1931	*Phi-A	101	355	48	97	28	2	3	46	49	47	.273	.371	.389	759	94	-2	1	2	-0	.974	-2	3-87,S-15	0.0
1932	Phi-A	153	558	71	148	29	5	7	90	77	65	.265	.358	.373	731	87	-10	8	2	1	**.980**	-5	*3-141,S-10/2-1	-0.7
1933	Chi-A★	151	554	49	144	22	6	1	68	69	37	.260	.354	.327	681	85	-9	3	7	-2	.953	-1	*3-151	-0.7
1934	Chi-A☆	127	456	52	122	17	4	7	82	64	28	.268	.363	.368	731	86	-8	1	1	-0	.944	-5	3-74,1-27,2-27,M	-1.0
1935	Chi-A	117	403	45	116	24	2	4	61	59	28	.288	.381	.387	769	97	-0	4	3	-0	.953	-5	3-98,1-16/2-3,M	-0.3
1936	Chi-A	127	435	62	116	16	3	7	60	61	36	.267	.362	.366	728	77	-15	1	3	-1	.951	-6	*3-125,M	-1.6
1937	Chi-A	30	85	10	26	5	0	1	23	9	7	.306	.372	.400	772	95	-1	0	0	0	.993	0	1-15,3-11,M	-0.1
1938	Chi-A	26	89	9	27	4	2	2	13	10	8	.303	.374	.461	834	105	1	0	0	0	.941	1	2-23/S-1,3-1,M	0.3
1939	Chi-A	2	1	0	0	0	0	0	0	0	0	.000	.000	.000	0	-97	-0	0	0	0	.667	0	/3-2,M	0.0
Total	22	2282	8046	1108	2256	453	90	108	1071	958	850	.280	.365	.399	764	96	-40	70	55		.952	56	*3-1257,2-722,1S/OP	8.5
■ **LENNY DYKSTRA** Dykstra, Leonard Kyle b: 2/10/63, Santa Ana, Cal. BL/TL, 5'10", 167 lbs. Deb: 5/3/85																								
1985	NY-N	83	236	40	60	9	3	1	19	30	24	.254	.341	.331	671	91	-2	15	2	3	.994	4	O-74(0-74-0)	0.4
1986	*NY-N	147	431	77	127	27	7	8	45	58	55	.295	.378	.445	824	130	19	31	7	4	.990	4	*O-139(1-138-0)	2.6

YEAR	TM/L	G	AB	R	H	2B	3B	HR	RBI	BB	SO	AVG	OBP	SLG	OPS	OPS+	BR+	SB	CS	SBR	FA	FR	G/POS	TPR
1987	NY-N	132	431	86	123	37	3	10	43	40	67	.285	.352	.455	806	118	10	27	7	3	.988	1	*O-118(0-118-0)	1.3
1988	*NY-N	126	429	57	116	19	3	8	33	30	43	.270	.323	.385	707	107	3	30	8	4	.996	7	*O-112(0-112-0)	1.4
1989	NY-N	56	159	27	43	12	1	3	13	23	15	.270	.370	.415	785	130	7	13	1	3	.984	2	O-51(0-51-0)	1.2
	Phi-N	90	352	39	78	20	3	4	19	37	38	.222	.297	.330	627	79	-10	17	11	-0	.991	7	O-88(0-89-0)	-0.4
	Yr	146	511	66	121	32	4	7	32	60	53	.237	.321	.356	677	95	-3	30	12	2	.988	9	*O-139(0-140-0)	0.8
1990	Phi-N★	149	590	106	**192**	35	3	9	60	89	48	.325	.420	.441	861	137	35	33	5	6	.987	20	*O-149(0-149-0)	5.9
1991	Phi-N	63	246	48	73	13	5	3	12	37	20	.297	.391	.427	818	131	11	24	4	4	.977	8	O-63(0-63-0)	2.3
1992	Phi-N	85	345	53	104	18	0	6	39	40	32	.301	.379	.406	785	123	11	30	5	5	.989	13	O-85(0-85-0)	3.0
1993	*Phi-N	161	637	**143**	**194**	44	6	19	66	**129**	64	.305	.423	.482	905	144	45	37	12	4	.979	17	*O-160(0-160-0)	6.6
1994	Phi-N†	84	315	68	86	26	5	5	24	68	44	.273	.405	.435	840	116	10	15	4	2	.984	9	O-82(0-83-0)	2.1
1995	Phi-N★	62	254	37	67	15	1	2	18	33	28	.264	.355	.354	710	87	-4	10	5	0	.987	6	O-61(9-52-0)	0.3
1996	Phi-N	40	134	21	35	6	3	3	13	26	25	.261	.389	.418	807	112	3	3	1	0	1.000	7	O-39(0-39-0)	1.0
Total	12	1278	4559	802	1298	281	43	81	404	640	503	.285	.376	.419	795	120	140	285	72	38	.987	103	*O-1221(10-1213-0)	27.7

■ JOHN DYLER
Dyler, John F. b: 6/1852, Louisville, Ky. Deb: 7/22/1882 U

YEAR	TM/L	G	AB	R	H	2B	3B	HR	RBI	BB	SO	AVG	OBP	SLG	OPS	OPS+	BR+	SB	CS	SBR	FA	FR	G/POS	TPR
1882	Lou-a	1	4	0	0	0	0	0		0		.000	.000	.000	0	-99	-1				.000	-0	/O-1(1-0-0)	-0.1

■ DON EADDY
Eaddy, Donald Johnson b: 2/16/34, Grand Rapids, Mich BR/TR, 5'11", 165 lbs. Deb: 4/24/59

YEAR	TM/L	G	AB	R	H	2B	3B	HR	RBI	BB	SO	AVG	OBP	SLG	OPS	OPS+	BR+	SB	CS	SBR	FA	FR	G/POS	TPR
1959	Chi-N	15	1	3	0	0	0	0	0	0	1	.000	.000	.000	0	-99	-0	0	0	0	.500	0	/3-1	0.0

■ TRUCK EAGAN
Eagan, Charles Eugene b: 8/10/1877, San Francisco, Cal d: 3/19/49, San Francisco, Cal BR/TR, 5'11", 190 lbs. Deb: 5/1/01

YEAR	TM/L	G	AB	R	H	2B	3B	HR	RBI	BB	SO	AVG	OBP	SLG	OPS	OPS+	BR+	SB	CS	SBR	FA	FR	G/POS	TPR
1901	Pit-N	4	12	0	1	0	0	0	2	0		.083	.083	.083	167	-50	-2	1			.923	-1	/S-3	-0.3
	Cle-A	5	18	2	3	0	1	0	2	1		.167	.211	.278	488	36	-2	0			1.000	0	/2-5,3-1	-0.1
Total	1	9	30	2	4	0	1	0	4	1		.133	.161	.200	361	2	-4	1			1.000	-1	/2-5,S-3,3-1	-0.4

■ BILL EAGAN
Eagan, William "Bad Bill" b: 6/1/1869, Camden, N.J. d: 2/13/05, Denver, Colo. Deb: 4/8/1891

YEAR	TM/L	G	AB	R	H	2B	3B	HR	RBI	BB	SO	AVG	OBP	SLG	OPS	OPS+	BR+	SB	CS	SBR	FA	FR	G/POS	TPR
1891	StL-a	82	297	49	65	11	4	4	43	44	53	.219	.326	.323	649	75	-11	21			.929	18	2-82	0.8
1893	Chi-N	6	19	3	5	0	0	0	2	5	5	.263	.417	.263	680	83	-0	4			.912	0	/2-6	0.0
1898	Pit-N	19	61	14	20	2	3	0	5	8		.328	.453	.459	912	165	6	1			.914	3	2-17	0.9
Total	3	107	377	66	90	13	7	4	50	57	58	.239	.352	.342	694	88	-5	26			.926	21	2-105	1.7

■ BILL EAGLE
Eagle, William Lycurgus b: 7/25/1877, Rockville, Md. d: 4/27/51, Churchton, Md. Deb: 8/20/1898

YEAR	TM/L	G	AB	R	H	2B	3B	HR	RBI	BB	SO	AVG	OBP	SLG	OPS	OPS+	BR+	SB	CS	SBR	FA	FR	G/POS	TPR
1898	Was-N	4	13	0	4	1	0	0	2	0		.308	.308	.385	692	98	-0	0			.750	0	/O-4(1-0-1)	0.0

■ CHARLIE EAKLE
Eakle, Charles Emory b: 9/27/1887, Maryland d: 6/15/59, Baltimore, Md. Deb: 8/20/15

YEAR	TM/L	G	AB	R	H	2B	3B	HR	RBI	BB	SO	AVG	OBP	SLG	OPS	OPS+	BR+	SB	CS	SBR	FA	FR	G/POS	TPR
1915	Bal-F	2	7	0	2	1	0	0	0	0	0	.286	.286	.429	714	97	-0	1			.600	-2	/2-2	-0.3

■ HOWARD EARL
Earl, Howard J. "Slim Jim" b: 2/27/1869, Massachusetts d: 12/22/16, North Bay, N.Y. 6'2", 180 lbs. Deb: 4/19/1890 Career OF: (0-LF 0-CF 79-RF)

YEAR	TM/L	G	AB	R	H	2B	3B	HR	RBI	BB	SO	AVG	OBP	SLG	OPS	OPS+	BR+	SB	CS	SBR	FA	FR	G/POS	TPR
1890	Chi-N	92	384	57	95	10	3	7	51	18	47	.247	.285	.344	628	80	-12	17			.861	-4	O-49R,2-39/S-4,1-3	-1.3
1891	Mil-a	31	129	21	32	5	2	1	17	5	13	.248	.281	.341	623	65	-7	3			.978	-1	O-30(0-0-30)/1-2	-0.8
Total	2	123	513	78	127	15	5	8	68	23	60	.248	.284	.343	627	76	-19	20			.904	-5	/O-79R,2-39,1-5,S-4	-2.1

■ SCOTT EARL
Earl, William Scott b: 9/18/60, Seymour, Ind. BR/TR, 5'11", 165 lbs. Deb: 9/10/84

YEAR	TM/L	G	AB	R	H	2B	3B	HR	RBI	BB	SO	AVG	OBP	SLG	OPS	OPS+	BR+	SB	CS	SBR	FA	FR	G/POS	TPR
1984	Det-A	14	35	3	4	0	1	0	1	0	9	.114	.114	.171	286	-22	-6	1	0	0	.959	1	2-14	-0.4

■ BILLY EARLE
Earle, William Moffat "The Little Globetrotter"
b: 11/10/1867, Philadelphia, Pa. d: 5/30/46, Omaha, Neb. BR/TR, 5'10.5", 170 lbs. Deb: 4/27/1889 Career OF: (3-LF 1-CF 26-RF)

YEAR	TM/L	G	AB	R	H	2B	3B	HR	RBI	BB	SO	AVG	OBP	SLG	OPS	OPS+	BR+	SB	CS	SBR	FA	FR	G/POS	TPR
1889	Cin-a	53	169	37	45	4	7	4	31	30	24	.266	.386	.444	830	132	7	26			.776	-2	O-26(2-1-23),C-23/1-5	0.6
1890	StL-a	22	73	16	17	3	1	0	12	7		.233	.317	.301	618	72	-3	6			.955	5	C-18/O-3R,S-1,32	0.3
1892	Pit-N	5	13	5	7	2	0	0	3	4	1	.538	.647	.692	1339	304	4	2			.909	-1	/C-5	0.3
1893	Pit-N	27	95	21	24	4	4	2	15	7	6	.253	.304	.442	746	99	-1	1			.959	1	C-27	0.2
1894	Lou-N	21	65	10	23	1	0	0	7	9	3	.354	.432	.369	802	102	1	2			.954	3	C-18/1-1,2-1,3-1,O	0.5
	Bro-N	14	50	13	17	6	0	0	6	6	2	.340	.421	.460	881	121	2	4			.930	-2	C-12/2-1	0.1
	Yr	35	115	23	40	7	0	0	13	15	5	.348	.427	.409	836	110	3	6			.944	2	C-30/2-2,1-1,3-1,O	0.6
Total	5	142	465	102	133	20	12	6	74	63	36	.286	.378	.419	798	114	11	41			.929	5	C-103/O-30R,1-6,23S	2.0

■ JAKE EARLY
Early, Jacob Willard b: 5/19/15, Kings Mountain, N.C. d: 5/31/85, Melbourne, Fla. BL/TR, 5'11", 168 lbs. Deb: 5/4/39

YEAR	TM/L	G	AB	R	H	2B	3B	HR	RBI	BB	SO	AVG	OBP	SLG	OPS	OPS+	BR+	SB	CS	SBR	FA	FR	G/POS	TPR
1939	Was-A	32	84	8	22	7	2	0	14	5	14	.262	.303	.393	696	83	-3	0	0	0	.963	-1	C-24	-0.2
1940	Was-A	80	206	26	53	8	4	5	14	23	22	.257	.335	.408	743	98	-1	0	1	-0	.969	5	C-56	0.7
1941	Was-A	104	355	42	102	20	7	10	54	24	38	.287	.338	.468	805	117	6	0	1	-0	.965	-11	*C-100	0.1
1942	Was-A	104	353	31	72	14	2	3	46	37	37	.204	.281	.280	562	59	-19	0	0	0	.981	-2	C-98	-1.6
1943	Was-A★	126	423	37	109	23	3	5	60	53	43	.258	.346	.362	708	111	7	5	3	0	.980	-8	*C-122	0.7
1946	Was-A	64	189	13	38	6	0	4	18	23	27	.201	.288	.296	584	67	-8	0	0	0	.960	2	C-64	-0.3
1947	StL-A	87	214	25	48	9	3	3	19	54	34	.224	.381	.336	717	98	2	0	1	-0	.989	-3	C-85	0.3
1948	Was-A	97	246	22	54	7	2	1	28	36	33	.220	.322	.276	598	62	-13	2	1	0	.991	2	C-92	-0.6
1949	Was-A	53	138	12	34	4	0	1	11	26	11	.246	.370	.297	667	79	-3	0	1	-0	.973	-4	C-53	-0.4
Total	9	747	2208	216	532	98	23	32	264	281	259	.241	.330	.350	679	89	-32	7	8	-1	.976	-19	C-694	-1.3

■ MIKE EASLER
Easler, Michael Anthony b: 11/29/50, Cleveland, Ohio BL/TR, 6'1", 196 lbs. Deb: 9/5/73 C Career OF: (479-LF 0-CF 82-RF)

YEAR	TM/L	G	AB	R	H	2B	3B	HR	RBI	BB	SO	AVG	OBP	SLG	OPS	OPS+	BR+	SB	CS	SBR	FA	FR	G/POS	TPR
1973	Hou-N	6	7	1	0	0	0	0	0	2	4	.000	.222	.000	222	-34	-1	0	0	0	.500	-1	/O-2(1-0-1)	-0.2
1974	Hou-N	15	15	0	1	0	0	0	0	0	5	.067	.067	.067	133	-65	-3	0	0	0	.000	0	H	-0.4
1975	Hou-N	5	5	0	0	0	0	0	0	0	1	.000	.000	.000	0	-99	-1	0	0	0	.000	0	H	-0.2
1976	Cal-A	21	54	6	13	1	1	0	4	2	11	.241	.268	.296	564	69	-2	1	1	-0	.000	0	D-16	-0.3
1977	Pit-N	10	18	3	8	2	0	1	5	0	1	.444	.444	.722	1167	202	2	0	0	0	1.000	-0	/O-4(1-0-3)	0.2
1979	*Pit-N	55	54	8	15	1	1	2	11	8	13	.278	.371	.444	815	116	1	0	1	-0	.000	-2	/O-4(2-0-2)	-0.1
1980	Pit-N	132	393	66	133	27	3	21	74	43	65	.338	.404	.583	986	170	36	5	9	-2	.986	-8	*O-119(91-0-42)	2.2
1981	Pit-N★	95	339	43	97	18	5	7	42	24	45	.286	.333	.431	764	112	5	4	7	-2	.980	7	O-90(72-0-25)	0.7
1982	Pit-N	142	475	52	131	27	2	15	58	40	85	.276	.340	.436	776	112	7	1	1	-0	.973	1	*O-138(137-0-3)	0.2
1983	Pit-N	115	381	44	117	17	2	10	54	22	64	.307	.350	.441	791	115	7	4	2	0	.965	-3	*O-105(105-0-0)	0.0
1984	Bos-A	156	601	87	188	31	5	27	91	58	134	.313	.377	.516	893	138	31	1	1	-0	.976	2	*D-126,1-29	2.7
1985	Bos-A	155	568	71	149	29	4	16	74	53	129	.262	.329	.412	740	97	-2	0	1	-0	.914	-2	*D-130,O-20(18-0-2)	-0.9
1986	NY-A	146	490	64	148	26	2	14	78	49	87	.302	.365	.449	814	122	15	3	2	-0	.958	-0	*D-129,O-11(8-0-3)	1.0
1987	Phi-N	33	110	7	31	4	0	1	10	6	20	.282	.319	.345	664	74	-4	0	1	-0	.981	2	O-30(30-0-0)	-0.4
	NY-A	65	167	13	47	6	0	4	21	14	32	.281	.341	.389	730	94	-1	1	0	0	1.000	-1	D-32,O-15(14-0-1)	-0.3
Total	14	1151	3677	465	1078	189	25	118	522	321	696	.293	.353	.454	807	118	88	20	26	-5	.974	-5	O-538L,D-433/1-29	4.2

■ DAMION EASLEY
Easley, Jacinto Damion b: 11/11/69, New York, N.Y. BR/TR, 5'11", 185 lbs. Deb: 8/13/92 Career OF: (0-LF 2-CF 0-RF)

YEAR	TM/L	G	AB	R	H	2B	3B	HR	RBI	BB	SO	AVG	OBP	SLG	OPS	OPS+	BR+	SB	CS	SBR	FA	FR	G/POS	TPR
1992	Cal-A	47	151	14	39	5	0	1	12	8	26	.258	.309	.311	620	74	-5	9	5	0	.970	8	3-45/S-3	0.3
1993	Cal-A	73	230	33	72	13	2	2	22	28	35	.313	.395	.413	808	114	5	6	6	-1	.978	-11	2-54,3-14/D-1	-0.3
1994	Cal-A	88	316	41	68	16	1	6	30	29	48	.215	.289	.329	619	58	-20	4	5	-1	.953	-7	3-47,2-40	-2.3
1995	Cal-A	114	357	35	77	14	2	4	35	32	47	.216	.291	.300	591	55	-24	5	2	0	.981	-8	2-88,S-25	-2.4
1996	Cal-A	28	45	4	7	1	0	2	7	6	12	.156	.255	.311	566	42	-4	0	0	0	.943	3	S-13/2-9,3-3,O-2C,D	0.0
	Det-A	21	67	10	23	1	0	2	10	4	13	.343	.389	.448	837	111	1	3	1	0	.974	-1	/2-8,S-8,3-2,D-1	0.1
	Yr	49	112	14	30	2	0	4	17	10	25	.268	.333	.393	726	83	-3	3	1	0	.951	2	S-21,2-17/3-5,DO	0.1
1997	Det-A	151	527	97	139	37	3	22	72	68	102	.264	.365	.471	836	117	14	28	13	2	.981	-13	*2-137,S-21/D-4	1.0
1998	Det-A★	153	594	84	161	38	2	27	100	39	112	.271	.333	.478	811	107	5	15	5	2	**.985**	22	*2-140,S-30/D-2	3.4
1999	Det-A	151	549	83	146	30	1	20	65	51	124	.266	.349	.434	782	99	-1	11	3	1	.989	3	*2-147,S-19	1.0
2000	Det-A	126	464	76	120	27	2	14	58	55	79	.259	.351	.416	767	96	-2	13	4	1	**.990**	15	*2-125	1.8
Total	9	952	3300	477	852	182	13	100	411	320	598	.258	.338	.412	750	94	-31	94	44	5	.985	11	2-748,S-119,3/DO	2.6

■ CARL EAST
East, Carlton William b: 8/27/1894, Marietta, Ga. d: 1/15/53, Whitesburg, Ga. BL/TR, 6'2", 178 lbs. Deb: 8/24/15

YEAR	TM/L	G	AB	R	H	2B	3B	HR	RBI	BB	SO	AVG	OBP	SLG	OPS	OPS+	BR+	SB	CS	SBR	FA	FR	G/POS	TPR
1915	StL-A	1	1	0	0	0	0	0	0	0	0	.000	.000	.000	0	-99	-0	0			.000	-0	/P-1	0.0

YEAR	TM/L	G	AB	R	H	2B	3B	HR	RBI	BB	SO	AVG	OBP	SLG	OPS	OPS+	BR+	SB	CS	SBR	FA	FR	G/POS	TPR
1924	Was-A	2	6	1	2	1	0	0	2	2	1	.333	.500	.500	1000	163	1	0	0	0	.800	-0	/O-2(0-0-2)	0.0
Total	2	3	7	1	2	1	0	0	2	2	1	.286	.444	.429	873	134	0	0	0	0	.800	-1	/O-2(0-0-2),P-1	0.0
■ HARRY EAST East, Henry H. b: 4/1863, St.Louis, Mo. Deb: 6/17/1882																								
1882	Bal-a	1	4	0	0	0	0	0		0		.000	.000	.000	0	-99	-1				.600	-0	/3-1	-0.1
■ LUKE EASTER Easter, Luscious Luke b: 8/4/15, Jonestown, Miss. d: 3/29/79, Euclid, Ohio BL/TR, 6'4.5", 240 lbs. Deb: 8/11/49 C																								
1949	Cle-A	21	45	6	10	3	0	0	2	8	6	.222	.340	.289	629	68	-2	0	1	-0	1.000	-4	O-12(0-0-12)	-0.6
1950	Cle-A	141	540	96	151	20	4	28	107	70	95	.280	.373	.487	860	123	17	0	3	-1	.991	-3	*1-128,O-13(0-0-13)	0.8
1951	Cle-A	128	486	65	131	12	5	27	103	37	71	.270	.333	.481	814	125	14	0	1	-0	.988	-7	*1-125	0.2
1952	Cle-A	127	437	63	115	10	3	31	97	44	84	.263	.337	.513	850	144	22	1	1	-0	.983	4	*1-118	2.3
1953	Cle-A	68	211	26	64	9	0	7	31	15	35	.303	.361	.445	806	120	5	0	2	-1	.981	-2	1-56	0.0
1954	Cle-A	6	6	0	1	0	0	0	0	0	2	.167	.167	.167	333	-8	-1	0	0	0	.000	0	H	-0.1
Total	6	491	1725	256	472	54	12	93	340	174	293	.274	.350	.481	830	126	56	1	8	-3	.986	-12	1-427/O-25(0-0-25)	2.6
■ HENRY EASTERDAY Easterday, Henry P. b: 9/16/1864, Philadelphia, Pa. d: 3/30/1895, Philadelphia, Pa. BR/TR, 5'6", 145 lbs. Deb: 6/23/1884																								
1884	Phi-U	28	115	12	28	5	0	0		5		.243	.275	.287	562	76	-6				.875	6	S-28	0.1
1888	KC-a	115	401	42	76	7	6	3	37	31		.190	.256	.259	516	61	-18	23			**.888**	26	*S-115	1.1
1889	Col-a	95	324	43	56	5	8	4	34	41	57	.173	.270	.275	544	58	-17	10			.890	12	S-89/2-5,3-1	-0.2
1890	Col-a	58	197	25	31	5	1	1	17	23		.157	.249	.208	457	37	-15	5			.879	6	S-58	-0.6
	Phi-a	19	68	17	10	1	0	1	3	10		.147	.256	.206	462	37	-5	4			.860	-2	S-19	-0.6
	Lou-a	7	24	2	2	0	0	0	1	2		.083	.185	.083	269	-21	-4	1			.886	1	/S-6,3-1	-0.3
	Yr	84	289	44	43	6	1	2	21	35		.149	.245	.197	443	32	-24	10			.875	5	S-83/3-1	-1.5
Total	4	322	1129	141	203	23	15	9	92	112	57	.180	.259	.251	510	54	-65	43			.884	50	S-315/2-5,3-2	-0.5
■ PAUL EASTERLING Easterling, Paul b: 9/28/05, Reidsville, Ga. d: 3/15/93, Reidsville, Ga. BR/TR, 5'11", 180 lbs. Deb: 4/11/28																								
1928	Det-A	43	114	17	37	7	1	3	12	8	24	.325	.374	.482	856	122	3	2	1	0	.921	-2	O-34(32-0-2)	-0.1
1930	Det-A	29	79	7	16	6	0	1	14	6	18	.203	.259	.316	575	44	-7	0	1	-0	1.000	-2	O-25(8-1-16)	-1.0
1938	Phi-A	4	7	1	2	0	0	0	0	1	2	.286	.375	.286	661	70	-0	0	0	0	.750	-0	/O-1(0-1-0)	0.0
Total	3	76	200	25	55	13	1	4	26	15	44	.275	.329	.410	739	88	-4	2	2	-0	.938	-4	/O-60(40-2-18)	-1.1
■ TED EASTERLY Easterly, Theodore Harrison b: 4/20/1885, Lincoln, Neb. d: 7/6/51, Clearlake Highlands, Cal. BL/TR, 5'8", 165 lbs. Deb: 4/17/09																								
1909	Cle-A	98	287	32	75	14	10	1	27	13		.261	.293	.390	684	111	2	8			.965	0	C-76	1.1
1910	Cle-A	110	363	34	111	16	6	0	55	21		.306	.344	.383	727	126	10	10			.964	-9	C-65,O-32(0-0-32)	0.7
1911	Cle-A	99	287	34	93	19	5	1	37	8		.324	.345	.436	780	116	4	6			.910	-12	O-54(0-2-52),C-22	-0.8
1912	Cle-A	65	186	17	55	4	0	2	21	7		.296	.328	.349	678	91	-3	3			.958	-4	C-51	-0.2
	Chi-A	30	55	5	20	2	0	0	14	2		.364	.386	.400	786	129	2	1			.964	-4	C-10/O-1(1-0-0)	-0.1
	Yr	95	241	22	75	6	0	2	35	9		.311	.341	.361	702	100	-1	4			.959	-8	C-61/O-1(1-0-0)	-0.3
1913	Chi-A	60	97	3	23	1	0	0	8	4	9	.237	.267	.247	515	51	-6	2			.976	2	C-19	-0.2
1914	KC-F	134	436	58	146	20	12	1	67	31	25	.335	.384	.443	827	130	11	10			.969	-18	*C-128	0.4
1915	KC-F	110	309	32	84	12	5	3	32	21	15	.272	.320	.372	692	99	-6	2			.969	4	C-88	0.6
Total	7	706	2020	215	607	88	38	8	261	107	49	.300	.338	.394	732	112	14	42			.965	-41	C-459/O-87(1-2-84)	1.5
■ ROY EASTERWOOD Easterwood, Roy Charles "Shag" b: 1/12/15, Waxahachie, Tex. d: 8/24/84, Graham, Tex. BR/TR, 6'0.5", 196 lbs. Deb: 4/21/44																								
1944	Chi-N	17	33	1	7	2	0	1	2	1	11	.212	.235	.364	599	67	-2	0			1.000	-1	C-12	-0.2
■ JOHN EASTON Easton, John David "Goose" b: 3/4/33, Trenton, N.J. BR/TR, 6'2", 185 lbs. Deb: 6/19/55																								
1955	Phi-N	1	0	0	0	0	0	0	0	0	0	—	—	—	—	—	0	0	0	0	.000	0	R	0.0
1959	Phi-N	3	3	0	0	0	0	0	0	0	3	.000	.000	.000	0	-98	-1	0	0	0	.000	0	H	-0.1
Total	2	4	3	0	0	0	0	0	0	0	3	.000	.000	.000	0	-98	-1	0	0	0		0	-0,-0	-0.1
■ EDDIE EAYRS Eayrs, Edwin b: 11/10/1890, Blackstone, Mass. d: 11/30/69, Warwick, R.I. BL/TL, 5'7", 160 lbs. Deb: 6/30/13																								
1913	Pit-N	4	6	0	1	0	0	0	0	0	1	.167	.167	.167	333	-5	-1	0			.667	-0	/P-2	0.0
1920	Bos-N	87	244	31	80	5	2	1	24	30	18	.328	.410	.377	787	133	12	4	3	-0	.950	-4	O-63(43-7-13)/P-7	0.3
1921	Bos-N	15	15	0	1	0	0	0	1	0	4	.067	.067	.067	133	-68	-4	0	0	0	.000	-0	/P-2	0.0
	Bro-N	8	6	1	1	0	0	0	1	2	0	.167	.375	.167	542	47	-0	0	0	0	.000	-1	/O-1(0-0-1)	-0.1
	Yr	23	21	1	2	0	0	0	2	2	4	.095	.174	.095	269	-27	-4	0	0	0	.000	-1	/P-2,O-1(0-0-1)	-0.1
Total	3	114	271	32	83	5	2	1	26	32	23	.306	.388	.351	738	116	7	4	3		.950	-5	/O-64(43-7-14),P-11	0.2
■ HI EBRIGHT Ebright, Hiram C. "Buck" b: 6/12/1859, Lancaster Co., Pa d: 10/24/16, Milwaukee, Wis. BR/TR, Deb: 4/24/1889																								
1889	Was-N	16	59	7	15	2	2	1	6	3	8	.254	.302	.407	708	103	0	1			.875	4	/C-9,O-4(0-0-4),S-3	0.4
■ ANGEL ECHEVARRIA Echevarria, Angel Santos b: 5/25/71, Bridgeport, Conn. BR/TR, 6'4", 215 lbs. Deb: 7/15/96																								
1996	Col-N	26	21	2	6	0	0	0	6	2	5	.286	.375	.286	661	63	-1	0	0	0	1.000	-4	O-11(4-0-7)	-0.5
1997	Col-N	15	20	4	5	2	0	0	0	2	5	.250	.318	.350	668	61	-1	0	0	0	1.000	-1	/O-7(2-2-3)	-0.2
1998	Col-N	19	29	7	11	3	0	1	9	2	3	.379	.455	.586	1041	141	2	0	0	0	1.000	-1	/1-4,O-4(3-0-1)	0.1
1999	Col-N	102	191	28	56	7	0	11	35	17	34	.293	.360	.503	863	91	-3	1	3	-1	.985	-4	O-49(20-0-31),1-10	-0.9
2000	Col-N	10	9	0	1	0	0	0	2	0	2	.111	.111	.111	222	-34	-2	0	0	0	1.000	-0	/1-2,O-1(1-0-0)	-0.2
	Mil-N	31	42	3	9	2	0	1	4	7	9	.214	.327	.333	660	69	-2	0	0	0	1.000	-1	/1-9,O-5(2-0-3)	-0.3
	Yr	41	51	3	10	2	0	1	6	7	11	.196	.293	.294	587	46	-4	0	0	0	1.000	-1	1-11/O-6(3-0-3)	-0.5
Total	5	203	312	44	88	14	0	13	56	30	58	.282	.356	.452	808	86	-7	1	3	-1	.988	-11	/O-77(32-2-45),1-25	-2.0
■ JOHNNY ECHOLS Echols, John Gresham b: 1/9/17, Atlanta, Ga. d: 11/13/72, Atlanta, Ga. BR/TR, 5'10.5", 175 lbs. Deb: 5/24/39																								
1939	StL-N	2	0	0	0	0	0	0	0	0	0	—	—	—	—	—	0	0			.000	0	R	0.0
■ OX ECKHARDT Eckhardt, Oscar George b: 12/23/01, Yorktown, Tex. d: 4/22/51, Yorktown, Tex. BL/TR, 6'1", 185 lbs. Deb: 4/16/32																								
1932	Bos-N	8	8	1	2	0	0	0	1	0	1	.250	.250	.250	500	36	-1	0			.000	0	H	-0.1
1936	Bro-N	16	44	5	8	1	0	1	6	5	2	.182	.265	.273	538	45	-3	0			1.000	1	O-10(0-0-10)	-0.3
Total	2	24	52	6	10	1	0	1	7	5	3	.192	.263	.269	532	43	-4	0			1.000	1	/O-10(0-0-10)	-0.4
■ CHARLIE EDEN Eden, Charles M. b: 1/18/1855, Lexington, Ky. d: 9/17/20, Cincinnati, Ohio BL/TL, 168 lbs. Deb: 8/17/1877 Career OF: (96-LF 32-CF 94-RF)																								
1877	Chi-N	15	55	9	12	0	1	0	5	3	6	.218	.259	.255	513	56	-3				.679	-2	O-15(0-0-15)	-0.4
1879	Cle-N	81	353	40	96	**31**	7	3	34	6	20	.272	.284	.425	709	131	12				.808	-4	*O-80(0-1-79)/1-3,C-1	0.7
1884	Pit-a	32	122	12	33	7	4	1		7		.270	.341	.418	759	148	7				.759	-4	O-31(0-31-0)/P-2	0.1
1885	Pit-a	98	405	57	103	18	6	0	38	17		.254	.298	.328	626	99	-0				.814	-16	*O-96(96-0-0)/P-4,3-2	-1.6
Total	4	226	935	118	244	56	18	4	77	33	26	.261	.296	.372	669	115	15				.793	-25	O-222L/P-6,1-3,3C	-1.2
■ MIKE EDEN Eden, Edward Michael b: 5/22/49, Fort Clayton, Canal Zone BB/TR, 5'10", 170 lbs. Deb: 8/2/76																								
1976	Atl-N	5	8	0	0	0	0	0	1	0	0	.000	.000	.000	0	-94	-2	0	0	0	1.000	1	/2-2	-0.1
1978	Chi-A	10	17	1	2	0	0	0	0	4	0	.118	.286	.118	403	17	-2	0	0	0	.905	-0	/S-5,2-4	-0.2
Total	2	15	25	1	2	0	0	0	1	4	0	.080	.207	.080	287	-16	-4	0	0	0	1.000	0	/2-6,S-5	-0.3
■ STUMP EDINGTON Edington, Jacob Frank b: 7/4/1891, Koleen, Ind. d: 11/11/69, Bastrop, La. BL/TL, 5'8", 170 lbs. Deb: 6/20/12																								
1912	Pit-N	15	53	4	16	0	2	0	12	3	1	.302	.339	.377	717	97	-0	0			1.000	1	O-14(0-0-14)	0.0
■ DAVE EDLER Edler, David Delmar b: 8/5/56, Sioux City, Iowa BR/TR, 6', 185 lbs. Deb: 9/4/80																								
1980	Sea-A	28	89	11	20	1	0	3	9	8	16	.225	.289	.337	626	70	-4	2	3	-1	.965	4	3-28	-0.1
1981	Sea-A	29	78	7	11	3	0	0	5	11	13	.141	.256	.179	435	26	-7	3	3	-0	.884	-3	3-26/S-1	-1.1
1982	Sea-A	40	104	14	29	2	2	2	18	11	13	.279	.348	.394	742	100	0	4	2	0	.922	3	3-31/O-2(1-0-1),D-2	0.2
1983	Sea-A	29	63	2	12	1	1	1	4	5	11	.190	.261	.286	547	49	-4	3	3	-0	.875	-2	3-13/1-5,O-1R,D-6	-0.7
Total	4	126	334	34	72	7	3	6	36	35	53	.216	.294	.308	602	66	-15	12	11	-1	.922	2	/3-98,D-8,1-5,OS	-1.7

■ **JIM EDMONDS** Edmonds, James Patrick b: 6/27/70, Fullerton, Cal. BL/TL, 6'1", 190 lbs. Deb: 9/9/93 Career OF: (60-LF 712-CF 34-RF)

YEAR	TM/L	G	AB	R	H	2B	3B	HR	RBI	BB	SO	AVG	OBP	SLG	OPS	OPS+	BR+	SB	CS	SBR	FA	FR	G/POS	TPR
1993	Cal-A	18	61	5	15	4	1	0	4	2	16	.246	.270	.344	614	62	-3	0	2	-1	.981	5	O-17(1-1-15)	0.1
1994	Cal-A	94	289	35	79	13	1	5	37	30	72	.273	.344	.377	721	85	-6	4	2	0	.981	0	O-77(59-5-19),1-22	-0.9
1995	Cal-A★	141	558	120	162	30	4	33	107	51	130	.290	.355	.536	891	129	22	1	4	-1	.998	19	*O-139(0-139-0)	3.9
1996	Cal-A	114	431	73	131	28	3	27	66	46	101	.304	.376	.571	947	135	22	4	0	1	.997	8	*O-111(0-111-0)/D-1	2.8
1997	Ana-A	133	502	82	146	27	0	26	80	60	80	.291	.371	.500	871	125	18	5	7	-1	.985	14	*O-115C,1-11/D-8	2.9
1998	Ana-A	154	599	115	184	42	1	25	91	57	114	.307	.368	.506	874	124	20	7	5	-0	.988	11	*O-153(0-153-0)	3.1
1999	Ana-A	55	204	34	51	17	2	5	23	28	45	.250	.341	.426	767	95	-2	5	4	-0	.992	6	O-42(0-42-0)/1-2,D-9	0.4
2000	*StL-N★	152	525	129	155	25	0	42	108	103	167	.295	.416	.583	999	148	41	10	3	1	.989	11	*O-146(0-146-0)/1-6	5.1
Total	8	861	3169	593	923	186	12	163	516	377	725	.291	.370	.512	882	124	112	36	27	-2	.990	74	O-800C/1-41,D-18	17.4

■ **BOB EDMONDSON** Edmondson, Robert E. b: 4/30/1879, Paris, Ky. d: 8/14/31, Lawrence, Kan. BR/TR, 5'11", 185 lbs. Deb: 9/15/06

YEAR	TM/L	G	AB	R	H	2B	3B	HR	RBI	BB	SO	AVG	OBP	SLG	OPS	OPS+	BR+	SB	CS	SBR	FA	FR	G/POS	TPR
1906	Was-A	3	3	1	1	0	0	0	0	0		.333	.333	.333	667	114	0	0			1.000	-0	/P-2,O-1(0-0-1)	0.0
1908	Was-A	26	80	5	15	4	1	0	2	7		.188	.261	.262	524	77	-2	0			.878	-2	O-24(1-9-14)	-0.6
Total	2	29	83	6	16	4	1	0	2	7		.193	.264	.265	529	78	-2	0			.878	-2	/O-25(1-9-15),P-2	-0.6

■ **EDDIE EDMONSON** Edmonson, Earl Edward b: 11/20/1889, Hopewell, Pa. d: 5/10/71, Leesburg, Fla. BL/TR, 6', 175 lbs. Deb: 10/4/13

YEAR	TM/L	G	AB	R	H	2B	3B	HR	RBI	BB	SO	AVG	OBP	SLG	OPS	OPS+	BR+	SB	CS	SBR	FA	FR	G/POS	TPR
1913	Cle-A	2	5	0	0	0	0	0	0	0	0	.000	.000	.000	0	-97	-1	0			1.000	-1	/1-1,O-1	-0.2

■ **BRUCE EDWARDS** Edwards, Charles Bruce "Bull" b: 7/15/23, Quincy, Ill. d: 4/25/75, Sacramento, Cal. BR/TR, 5'7", 194 lbs. Deb: 6/23/46 Career OF: (25-LF 0-CF 0-RF)

YEAR	TM/L	G	AB	R	H	2B	3B	HR	RBI	BB	SO	AVG	OBP	SLG	OPS	OPS+	BR+	SB	CS	SBR	FA	FR	G/POS	TPR
1946	Bro-N	92	292	24	78	13	5	1	25	34	20	.267	.348	.356	704	99	0	1			.982	6	C-91	1.2
1947	*Bro-N★	130	471	53	139	15	8	9	80	49	55	.295	.364	.418	782	103	3	2			.983	5	*C-128	1.5
1948	Bro-N	96	286	36	79	17	2	8	54	26	28	.276	.341	.434	774	105	1	4			.984	-8	C-48,O-21L,3-14,/1	-0.5
1949	*Bro-N	64	148	24	31	3	0	8	25	25	15	.209	.324	.392	716	87	-3	0			.990	-3	C-41/O-4(4-0-0),3-1	-0.4
1950	Bro-N	50	142	16	26	4	1	8	16	13	22	.183	.256	.394	651	67	-8	1			.980	-4	C-38/1-2	-0.9
1951	Bro-N	17	36	6	9	2	0	1	8	1	3	.250	.270	.389	659	74	-1	0	0	0	1.000	0	/C-9	-0.1
	Chi-N☆	51	141	19	33	9	2	3	17	16	14	.234	.316	.390	707	87	-3	1	2	-0	.962	-3	C-28/1-9	-0.5
	Yr	68	177	25	42	11	2	4	25	17	17	.237	.308	.390	698	85	-4	1	2	-0	.971	-3	C-37/1-9	-0.6
1952	Chi-N	50	94	7	23	2	2	1	12	8	12	.245	.304	.340	644	77	-3	0	0	0	.989	-3	C-22/2-1	-0.4
1954	Chi-N	4	3	1	0	0	0	0	1	2	2	.000	.400	.000	400	15	-0	0	0	0	.000	0	H	0.0
1955	Was-A	30	57	5	10	2	0	0	3	16	6	.175	.356	.211	567	58	-3	0	1	-0	.980	7	C-22/3-5	0.4
1956	Cin-N	7	5	0	1	0	0	0	0	0	2	.200	.200	.200	400	8	-1	0	0	0	.000	-1	/C-2,2-1,3-1	-0.1
Total	10	591	1675	191	429	67	20	39	241	190	179	.256	.335	.390	725	93	-17	9	3		.982	-3	C-429/O-25L,3-21,12	0.2

■ **DAVE EDWARDS** Edwards, David Leonard b: 2/24/54, Los Angeles, Cal. BR/TR, 6', 177 lbs. Deb: 9/11/78 F Career OF: (103-LF 113-CF 67-RF)

YEAR	TM/L	G	AB	R	H	2B	3B	HR	RBI	BB	SO	AVG	OBP	SLG	OPS	OPS+	BR+	SB	CS	SBR	FA	FR	G/POS	TPR
1978	Min-A	15	44	7	11	3	0	1	3	7	13	.250	.377	.386	764	113	1	1	1	-0	.950	1	O-15(10-8-0)	0.1
1979	Min-A	96	229	42	57	8	0	8	35	24	45	.249	.323	.389	711	88	-4	6	3	0	.983	-4	O-86(37-31-23)/D-3	-1.0
1980	Min-A	81	200	26	50	9	1	2	20	12	51	.250	.296	.335	631	68	-9	2	1	0	.932	-6	O-72(27-47-2)/D-3	-1.6
1981	SD-N	58	112	13	24	4	1	2	13	11	24	.214	.285	.321	606	77	-4	3	1	0	.970	-5	O-49(11-2-40)	-1.1
1982	SD-N	71	55	7	10	2	0	1	2	1	14	.182	.196	.273	469	32	-5	0	0	0	.944	-14	O-45(18-25-2)/1-1	-2.1
Total	5	321	640	95	152	26	2	14	73	55	147	.237	.302	.350	652	77	-21	12	6	1	.958	-28	O-267C/D-6,1-1	-5.7

■ **HANK EDWARDS** Edwards, Henry Albert b: 1/29/19, Elmwood Place, O. d: 6/22/88, Santa Ana, Cal. BL/TL, 6', 190 lbs. Deb: 9/10/41

YEAR	TM/L	G	AB	R	H	2B	3B	HR	RBI	BB	SO	AVG	OBP	SLG	OPS	OPS+	BR+	SB	CS	SBR	FA	FR	G/POS	TPR
1941	Cle-A	16	68	10	15	1	1	1	6	2	4	.221	.243	.309	552	47	-5	0	0	0	.929	-1	O-16(2-0-14)	-0.7
1942	Cle-A	13	48	6	12	2	1	0	7	5	8	.250	.321	.333	654	89	-1	2	1	0	.968	-1	O-12(0-12-0)	-0.2
1943	Cle-A	92	297	38	82	18	6	3	28	30	34	.276	.343	.407	750	127	9	4	8	-2	.983	-5	O-74(0-74-0)	0.1
1946	Cle-A	124	458	62	138	33	**16**	10	54	43	48	.301	.361	.509	870	151	28	1	3	-1	.968	1	*O-123(0-1-122)	2.6
1947	Cle-A	108	393	54	102	12	3	15	59	31	55	.260	.315	.420	735	106	1	1	3	-1	.990	-7	*O-100(39-0-67)	-1.2
1948	Cle-A	55	160	27	43	9	2	3	18	18	18	.269	.346	.406	753	102	0	1	1	-0	.987	-3	O-41(0-0-41)	-0.4
1949	Cle-A	5	15	3	4	0	0	1	1	1	2	.267	.313	.467	779	107	-0	0	0	0	1.000	-1	/O-5(0-0-5)	-0.1
	Chi-N	58	176	25	51	8	4	7	21	19	22	.290	.359	.500	859	131	7	0			.988	-4	O-51(18-0-34)	0.1
1950	Chi-N	41	110	13	40	11	1	2	21	10	13	.364	.417	.536	953	150	8	0			.976	-3	O-29(0-0-29)	0.4
1951	Bro-N	35	31	1	7	3	0	0	3	4	9	.226	.314	.323	637	70	-1	0	0	0	.000	0	H	-0.1
	Cin-N	41	127	14	40	9	1	3	20	13	17	.315	.379	.472	851	126	5	0	2	-1	.985	-3	O-34(26-0-8)	-0.1
	Yr	76	158	15	47	12	1	3	23	17	26	.297	.366	.443	809	115	3	0	2	-1	.985	-3	O-34(26-0-8)	-0.2
1952	Cin-N	74	184	24	52	7	6	6	28	19	22	.283	.350	.484	833	129	7	0	3	-1	.988	-4	O-51(33-0-18)	-0.1
	Chi-A	8	18	2	6	0	0	0	1	0	2	.333	.333	.333	667	85	-0	0	0	0	1.000	0	/O-3(3-0-0)	0.0
1953	StL-A	65	106	6	21	3	0	0	9	13	10	.198	.286	.226	512	39	-9	0	1	-0	1.000	-1	O-21(11-4-7)	-1.1
Total	11	735	2191	285	613	116	41	51	276	208	264	.280	.343	.440	783	119	49	9	22		.981	-31	O-560(132-91-345)	-0.8

■ **DOC EDWARDS** Edwards, Howard Rodney b: 12/10/36, Red Jacket, W.Va. BR/TR, 6'2", 215 lbs. Deb: 4/21/62 MC

YEAR	TM/L	G	AB	R	H	2B	3B	HR	RBI	BB	SO	AVG	OBP	SLG	OPS	OPS+	BR+	SB	CS	SBR	FA	FR	G/POS	TPR
1962	Cle-A	53	143	13	39	6	0	3	9	9	14	.273	.325	.378	702	91	-2	0	0	0	.992	9	C-39	0.8
1963	Cle-A	10	31	6	8	2	0	0	0	2	6	.258	.303	.323	626	76	-1	0	0	0	.988	5	C-10	0.4
	KC-A	71	240	16	60	12	0	6	35	11	23	.250	.289	.375	664	80	-7	0	1	-0	.987	-5	C-63	-0.9
	Yr	81	271	22	68	14	0	6	35	13	29	.251	.290	.369	659	79	-8	0	1	-0	.987	-0	C-73	-0.5
1964	KC-A	97	294	25	66	10	0	5	28	13	40	.224	.265	.310	574	57	-17	0	1	-0	.986	1	C-79/1-7	-1.4
1965	KC-A	6	20	1	3	0	0	0	0	1	2	.150	.190	.150	340	-2	-3	0	0	0	1.000	-0	/C-6	-0.3
	NY-A	45	100	3	19	3	0	1	9	13	14	.190	.289	.250	539	55	-6	1	2	-0	.986	2	C-43	-0.2
	Yr	51	120	4	22	3	0	1	9	14	16	.183	.274	.233	507	46	-8	1	2	-0	.988	2	C-49	-0.5
1970	Phi-N	35	78	5	21	0	0	0	6	4	10	.269	.313	.269	582	59	-4	0	0	0	.970	6	C-34	0.3
Total	5	317	906	69	216	33	0	15	87	53	109	.238	.287	.325	612	68	-39	1	4	-1	.986	18	C-274/1-7	-1.3

■ **JOHNNY EDWARDS** Edwards, John Alban b: 6/10/38, Columbus, Ohio BL/TR, 6'4", 220 lbs. Deb: 6/27/61

YEAR	TM/L	G	AB	R	H	2B	3B	HR	RBI	BB	SO	AVG	OBP	SLG	OPS	OPS+	BR+	SB	CS	SBR	FA	FR	G/POS	TPR
1961	*Cin-N	52	145	14	27	5	0	2	14	18	28	.186	.280	.262	543	45	-11	1	0	0	.982	-4	C-52	-1.2
1962	Cin-N	133	452	47	115	28	5	8	50	45	70	.254	.323	.392	715	88	-8	1	1	-0	.987	12	*C-130	1.1
1963	Cin-N★	148	495	46	128	19	4	11	67	45	93	.259	.325	.380	705	99	0	1	5	-2	**.995**	13	*C-148	2.0
1964	Cin-N★	126	423	47	119	23	1	7	55	34	65	.281	.336	.390	726	100	1	1	2	-0	.992	23	*C-120	3.0
1965	Cin-N☆	114	371	47	99	22	2	17	51	50	45	.267	.355	.474	830	123	12	0	0	0	.990	5	*C-110	2.3
1966	Cin-N	98	282	24	54	8	0	6	39	31	42	.191	.272	.284	555	50	-18	1	3	-1	.992	9	C-98	-0.7
1967	Cin-N	80	209	10	43	6	0	2	20	16	28	.206	.262	.263	525	46	-14	1	4	-1	.990	15	C-73	0.3
1968	*StL-N	85	230	14	55	9	1	3	29	16	20	.239	.291	.326	618	86	-4	1	1	-0	.992	2	C-54	0.0
1969	Hou-N	151	496	52	115	20	6	6	50	53	69	.232	.309	.333	641	81	-12	2	1	0	**.994**	5	*C-151	0.0
1970	Hou-N	140	458	46	101	16	4	7	49	51	63	.221	.300	.319	619	69	-20	1	0	0	**.995**	13	*C-139	-0.1
1971	Hou-N	106	317	18	74	13	4	1	23	26	38	.233	.292	.309	601	72	-12	1	1	-0	**.995**	8	*C-104	0.0
1972	Hou-N	108	332	33	89	16	2	5	40	50	39	.268	.366	.373	739	113	7	2	4	-1	.988	-8	*C-105	0.3
1973	Hou-N	79	250	24	61	10	2	5	27	19	23	.244	.303	.360	663	83	-6	1	0	0	.989	-1	C-76	-0.4
1974	Hou-N	50	117	8	26	7	1	1	10	11	12	.222	.295	.325	619	76	-4	1	1	-0	.989	5	C-32	0.3
Total	14	1470	4577	430	1106	202	32	81	524	465	635	.242	.314	.353	667	85	-91	15	23	-5	.992	97	*C-1392	6.9

■ **MARSHALL EDWARDS** Edwards, Marshall Lynn b: 8/27/52, Fort Lewis, Wash. BL/TL, 5'9", 157 lbs. Deb: 4/11/81 F

YEAR	TM/L	G	AB	R	H	2B	3B	HR	RBI	BB	SO	AVG	OBP	SLG	OPS	OPS+	BR+	SB	CS	SBR	FA	FR	G/POS	TPR
1981	*Mil-A	40	58	10	14	1	1	0	4	0	2	.241	.241	.293	534	56	-3	6	2	1	.979	-9	O-36(2-21-14)/D-1	-1.2
1982	*Mil-A	69	178	24	44	4	1	2	14	4	8	.247	.264	.315	578	62	-10	10	4	1	.984	-2	O-54(4-13-41)/D-6	-1.2
1983	Mil-A	51	74	14	22	1	1	0	5	1	9	.297	.307	.338	645	84	-2	5	5	-1	1.000	-3	O-35(12-12-13)/D-4	-0.6
Total	3	160	310	48	80	6	3	2	23	5	19	.258	.270	.316	586	66	-15	21	11	1	.987	-13	O-125(18-46-68)/D-11	-3.0

■ **MIKE EDWARDS** Edwards, Michael Lewis b: 8/27/52, Fort Lewis, Wash. BR/TR, 5'10", 154 lbs. Deb: 9/10/77 F Career OF: (0-LF 0-CF 1-RF)

YEAR	TM/L	G	AB	R	H	2B	3B	HR	RBI	BB	SO	AVG	OBP	SLG	OPS	OPS+	BR+	SB	CS	SBR	FA	FR	G/POS	TPR
1977	Pit-N	7	6	1	0	0	0	0	0	0	3	.000	.143	.000	143	-56	-1	0	2	-1	1.000	3	/2-4	0.1
1978	Oak-A	142	414	48	113	16	2	1	23	16	32	.273	.303	.329	632	82	-11	27	21	-1	.964	-28	*2-133/S-9,D-4	-3.4
1979	Oak-A	122	400	35	93	12	2	1	23	15	37	.233	.264	.280	544	49	-29	10	6	0	.962	-14	*2-113/S-3,D-2	-3.6
1980	Oak-A	46	59	10	14	0	0	0	3	1	5	.237	.250	.237	487	37	-5	1	1	-0	.971	4	2-23/O-1(0-0-1),D-5	-0.1
Total	4	317	879	94	220	28	4	2	49	32	77	.250	.281	.298	579	63	-46	38	30	-2	.964	-34	2-273/S-12,D-11,O-1R	-7.0

YEAR	TM/L	G	AB	R	H	2B	3B	HR	RBI	BB	SO	AVG	OBP	SLG	OPS	OPS+	BR+	SB	CS	SBR	FA	FR	G/POS	TPR
■ RALPH EDWARDS Edwards, Ralph Strunk b: 12/14/1882, Brewster, N.Y. d: 1/5/49, White Plains, N.Y. BR/TR, 5'9", 165 lbs. Deb: 9/17/15																								
1915	Phi-A	2	5	0	0	0	0	0	0	0	3	.000	.000	.000	0	-99	-1	0			1.000	-1	/2-1	-0.3
■ ROBERT EENHOORN Eenhoorn, Robert Franciscus b: 2/9/68, Rotterdam, Netherlands BR/TR, 6'3", 170 lbs. Deb: 4/27/94																								
1994	NY-A	3	4	1	2	1	0	0	0	0	0	.500	.500	.750	1250	225	1	0	0	0	1.000	-1	/S-3	0.0
1995	NY-A	5	14	1	2	1	0	0	2	1	3	.143	.200	.214	414	8	-2	0	0	0	1.000	-1	/2-3,S-2	-0.3
1996	NY-A	12	14	2	1	0	0	0	2	2	3	.071	.188	.071	259	-31	-3	0	0	0	1.000	2	2-10/3-2	0.0
	Cal-A	6	15	1	4	0	0	0	0	0	2	.267	.267	.267	533	35	-1	0	0	0	.875	-1	/S-4,2-2	-0.2
	Yr	18	29	3	5	0	0	0	2	2	5	.172	.226	.172	398	3	-4	0	0	0	.971	1	2-12/S-4,3-2	-0.2
1997	Ana-A	11	20	2	7	1	0	1	6	0	2	.350	.350	.550	900	130	1	0	0	0	.833	-2	/3-5,2-3,S-2	-0.1
Total	4	37	67	7	16	3	0	1	10	3	10	.239	.271	.328	600	53	-5	0	0	0	.963	-3	/2-18,S-11,3-7	-0.6
■ BEN EGAN Egan, Arthur Augustus b: 11/20/1883, Augusta, N.Y. d: 2/18/68, Sherrill, N.Y. BR/TR, 6', 195 lbs. Deb: 9/29/08 C																								
1908	Phi-A	2	6	1	1	1	0	0	0	1		.167	.286	.333	619	95	-0	0			.933	0	/C-2	0.0
1912	Phi-A	49	138	9	24	3	4	0	13	6		.174	.208	.254	462	33	-13	3			.958	4	C-46	-0.6
1914	Cle-A	29	88	7	20	2	1	0	11	3	20	.227	.277	.273	549	63	-4	0	1	-0	.975	4	C-27	0.2
1915	Cle-A	42	120	4	13	3	0	0	6	8	14	.108	.164	.133	297	-11	-16	0			.970	8	C-40	-0.6
Total	4	122	352	21	58	9	5	0	30	18	34	.165	.212	.219	431	27	-33	3	1		.966	16	C-115	-1.0
■ JIM EGAN Egan, James K. "Troy Terrier" b: 1858, Derby, Conn. d: 9/26/1884, New Haven, Conn. TL, Deb: 5/15/1882																								
1882	Tro-N	30	115	15	23	3	2	0	10	1	21	.200	.207	.261	468	51	-6				.625	-8	O-18(2-16-0),P-12/C-2	-0.9
■ DICK EGAN Egan, Richard Joseph b: 6/23/1884, Portland, Ore. d: 7/7/47, Oakland, Cal. BR/TR, 5'11", 162 lbs. Deb: 9/15/08 Career OF: (11-LF 2-CF 14-RF)																								
1908	Cin-N	18	68	8	14	3	1	0	5	2		.206	.229	.279	508	64	-3	7			.891	-3	2-18	-0.7
1909	Cin-N	127	480	59	132	14	3	2	53	37		.275	.329	.329	659	105	3	39			.950	24	*2-116,S-10	3.1
1910	Cin-N	135	474	70	116	11	5	0	46	53	38	.245	.322	.289	611	82	-10	41			.961	-11	*2-131/S-3	-2.1
1911	Cin-N	153	558	80	139	11	5	1	56	59	50	.249	.322	.292	614	75	-18	37			.949	10	*2-152	-0.5
1912	Cin-N	149	507	69	125	14	5	0	52	56	26	.247	.324	.294	618	72	-18	24			**.973**	3	*2-149	-1.3
1913	Cin-N	60	195	15	55	7	3	0	22	15	13	.282	.333	.349	682	95	-1	6			.972	-5	2-37,S-17/3-2	-0.5
1914	Bro-N	106	337	30	76	10	3	1	21	22	25	.226	.273	.282	555	64	-15	8			.914	-9	S-83,3-10/O-3C,21	-2.0
1915	Bro-N	3	3	0	0	0	0	0	0	0	0	.000	.000	.000	0	-98	-1	0			.000	0	H	-0.1
	Bos-N	83	220	20	57	9	1	0	21	28	18	.259	.343	.309	652	102	2	3	4	-1	.974	-2	O-24R,2-22,S-10,/13	-0.2
	Yr	86	223	20	57	9	1	0	21	28	18	.256	.339	.305	644	100	1	3	4	-1	.974	-2	O-24R,2-22,S-10,/13	-0.3
1916	Bos-N	83	238	23	53	8	3	0	16	19	21	.223	.280	.282	562	76	-7	2			.949	-21	2-59,S-12/3-8	-3.1
Total	9	917	3080	374	767	87	29	4	292	291	191	.249	.315	.300	615	82	-69	167	4		.956	-14	2-686,S-135/O-27R,31	-7.4
■ TOM EGAN Egan, Thomas Patrick b: 6/9/46, Los Angeles, Cal. BR/TR (BB 1974 (part), 75), 6'4", 218 lbs. Deb: 5/27/65																								
1965	Cal-A	18	38	3	10	0	1	0	1	3	12	.263	.317	.316	633	82	-1	0	0	0	1.000	-0	C-16	-0.1
1966	Cal-A	7	11	0	0	0	0	0	0	1	5	.000	.083	.000	83	-76	-2	0	0	0	1.000	2	/C-6	-0.1
1967	Cal-A	1	1	0	0	0	0	0	0	0	0	.000	.000	.000	0	-99	-0	0	0	0	1.000	0	/C-1	0.0
1968	Cal-A	16	43	2	5	1	0	1	4	2	15	.116	.156	.209	365	10	-5	0	0	0	1.000	2	C-14	-0.3
1969	Cal-A	46	120	7	17	1	0	5	16	17	41	.142	.254	.275	529	50	-8	0	1	-0	.985	6	C-46	0.0
1970	Cal-A	79	210	14	50	6	0	4	20	14	67	.238	.289	.324	613	71	-9	0	0	0	.988	-1	C-79	-0.7
1971	Chi-A	85	251	29	60	11	1	10	34	26	94	.239	.320	.410	731	102	1	1	0	0	.986	3	C-77/1-1	0.8
1972	Chi-A	50	141	8	27	3	0	2	9	4	48	.191	.224	.255	480	42	-10	0	0	0	.986	3	C-46	-0.6
1974	Cal-A	43	94	4	11	0	0	0	4	8	40	.117	.194	.117	311	-9	-13	1	0	0	.996	16	C-41	0.4
1975	Cal-A	28	70	7	16	3	1	0	3	5	14	.229	.280	.300	580	69	-3	0	0	0	.965	4	C-28	0.2
Total	10	373	979	74	196	25	3	22	91	80	336	.200	.267	.299	566	62	-51	2	1	0	.987	35	C-354/1-1	-0.4
■ ELMER EGGERT Eggert, Elmer Albert "Mose" b: 1/29/02, Rochester, N.Y. d: 4/9/71, Rochester, N.Y. BR/TR, 5'9", 160 lbs. Deb: 4/27/27																								
1927	Bos-A	5	3	0	0	0	0	0	0	1	1	.000	.250	.000	250	-31	-1	0	0	0	.000	0	/2-1	-0.1
■ DAVE EGGLER Eggler, David Daniel b: 4/30/1851, Brooklyn, N.Y. d: 4/5/02, Buffalo, N.Y. BR/TR, 5'9", 165 lbs. Deb: 5/18/1871 NA OF: (10-LF 256-CF 0-RF)																								
1871	Mut-n	33	147	37	47	7	3	0	18	4	3	.320	.338	.408	746	124	6	14	3	2	.910	6	*O-33(0-33-0)	0.9
1872	Mut-n	56	290	**94**	98	20	0	0	20	8	9	.338	.356	.407	763	143	17	**18**	5	**2**	**.922**	15	*O-56(1-55-0)	2.3
1873	Mut-n	53	268	82	90	13	4	0	34	5	2	.336	.348	.414	762	126	9	4	1	1	.862	5	*O-53(0-53-0)/3-1	1.0
1874	Phi-n	58	299	70	95	13	8	0	31	5	1	.318	.329	.415	744	132	10	5	6	-1	**.906**	9	*O-57(7-50-0)/2-2	1.3
1875	Ath-n	66	295	66	89	13	7	0	33	1	10	.302	.304	.393	697	126	6	6	5	-0	**.921**	4	*O-66(2-65-0)	0.8
1876	Phi-N	39	176	28	52	4	0	0	19	2	4	.295	.307	.322	629	111	2				.913	5	O-39(1-37-1)	0.5
1877	Chi-N	33	136	20	36	3	0	0	20	1	5	.265	.270	.287	557	67	-5				.861	3	O-33(0-33-0)	-0.4
1879	Buf-N	78	317	41	66	5	7	0	27	11	41	.208	.235	.268	503	64	-12				.919	-6	*O-78(0-78-0)	-2.0
1883	Bal-a	53	202	15	38	2	0	0	7	1		.188	.192	.198	390	25	-17				.916	1	O-53(0-53-0)	-1.6
	Buf-N	38	153	13	38	2	1	0	13	2	29	.248	.258	.275	533	61	-7				.845	-1	O-38(1-37-0)	-0.8
1884	Buf-N	63	241	25	47	3	1	0	20	6	54	.195	.215	.216	430	35	-18				.887	1	O-63(2-61-0)	-1.8
1885	Buf-N	6	24	0	2	0	0	0	0	2	4	.083	.154	.083	237	-21	-3				.938	1	/O-6(0-6-0)	-0.3
Total	5 n	266	1299	349	419	66	22	0	136	23	25	.323	.334	.407	742	131	46	47	20	3	.905	39	O-265C/2-2,3-1	6.3
Total	6	310	1249	142	279	19	9	0	106	25	137	.223	.239	.253	492	56	-60				.894	3	O-310(4-305-1)	-6.4
■ RED EHRET Ehret, Philip Sydney b: 8/31/1868, Louisville, Ky. d: 7/28/40, Cincinnati, Ohio BR/TR, 6', 175 lbs. Deb: 7/7/1888 Career OF: (11-LF 3-CF 18-RF)																								
1888	KC-a	17	63	4	12	4	0	0	4	1		.190	.203	.254	457	43	-4	1			.750	-4	O-10L/P-7,2-1,1-1	-0.7
1889	Lou-a	67	258	27	65	6	6	1	31	4	23	.252	.263	.333	597	71	-11	4			.891	-1	P-45,O-22R/S-1,32	-0.6
1890	*Lou-a	43	146	11	31	2	1	0	10	1		.212	.218	.240	457	36	-12	1			.859	-3	P-43	0.0
1891	Lou-a	26	91	9	22	2	1	0	9	5	15	.242	.281	.286	567	63	-5	3			.871	0	P-26	0.0
1892	Pit-N	40	132	12	34	2	0	0	19	7	22	.258	.295	.273	568	72	-5	1			.855	-4	P-39	0.0
1893	Pit-N	40	136	16	24	3	0	1	17	10	18	.176	.233	.221	453	21	-16	1			.893	1	P-39	0.0
1894	Pit-N	46	135	6	23	4	1	0	11	8	22	.170	.217	.215	432	4	-22	0			.859	-1	P-46	0.0
1895	StL-N	37	96	13	21	2	1	1	9	6	12	.219	.265	.292	556	44	-8	0			.848	0	P-37	0.0
1896	Cin-N	34	102	10	20	2	0	1	20	10	12	.196	.268	.245	513	33	-10	2			.923	1	P-34/1-1	0.0
1897	Cin-N	34	66	6	13	2	0	0	6	4		.197	.254	.227	481	26	-7	2			.957	-1	P-34	0.0
1898	Lou-N	13	40	3	9	3	1	0	4	1		.225	.262	.350	612	76	-1	0			.800	-1	P-12	0.0
Total	11	397	1265	117	274	32	11	4	140	57	124	.217	.252	.269	520	44	-101	15			.882	-12	P-362/O-32R,1-2,23S	-1.3
■ HACK EIBEL Eibel, Henry Hack b: 12/6/1893, Brooklyn, N.Y. d: 10/16/45, Macon, Ga. BL/TL, 5'11", 220 lbs. Deb: 6/13/12																								
1912	Cle-A	1	3	0	0	0	0	0	0	0		.000	.000	.000	0	-97	-1	0			.000	-0	/O-1(0-0-1)	-0.1
1920	Bos-A	29	43	4	8	2	0	0	6	3	6	.186	.239	.233	472	26	-5	1	1	-0	.800	-2	/O-5(3-0-2),P-3,1-1	-0.6
Total	2	30	46	4	8	2	0	0	6	3	6	.174	.224	.217	442	19	-5	1	1		.800	-2	/O-6(3-0-3),P-3,1-1	-0.7
■ IKE EICHRODT Eichrodt, Frederick George b: 1/6/03, Chicago, Ill. d: 7/14/65, Indianapolis, Ind BR/TR, 5'11.5", 167 lbs. Deb: 9/7/25																								
1925	Cle-A	15	52	4	12	3	1	0	4	2	7	.231	.259	.327	586	48	-4	0	0	0	.938	-2	O-13(0-13-0)	-0.7
1926	Cle-A	37	80	14	25	7	1	0	7	2	11	.313	.329	.425	754	95	-1	1	0	0	.976	-4	O-27(19-6-2)	-0.5
1927	Cle-A	85	267	24	59	19	2	0	25	16	25	.221	.265	.307	572	48	-21	2	3	-1	.979	1	O-81(13-64-5)	-2.3
1931	Chi-A	34	117	9	25	5	1	0	15	1	8	.214	.220	.274	494	31	-12	0	0	0	1.000	-5	O-32(0-30-3)	-1.6
Total	4	171	516	51	121	34	5	0	51	21	51	.234	.264	.320	584	52	-39	3	3	-0	.979	-9	O-153(32-113-10)	-5.1
■ JIM EISENREICH Eisenreich, James Michael b: 4/18/59, St.Cloud, Minn. BL/TL, 5'11", 195 lbs. Deb: 4/6/82 Career OF: (362-LF 166-CF 625-RF)																								
1982	Min-A	34	99	10	30	6	0	2	9	11	13	.303	.378	.424	803	117	3	0	0	0	.973	-1	O-30(0-30-0)	0.1
1983	Min-A	2	7	1	2	1	0	0	0	1	1	.286	.375	.429	804	116	0	0	0	0	1.000	1	/O-2(0-2-0)	0.1
1984	Min-A	12	32	1	7	1	0	0	3	2	4	.219	.265	.250	515	41	-3	2	0	0	1.000	-1	/O-3(0-2-1),D-6	-0.3
1987	KC-A	44	105	10	25	8	2	4	21	7	13	.238	.286	.467	752	93	-2	1	1	-0	.000	0	D-26	-0.2
1988	KC-A	82	202	26	44	8	1	1	19	6	31	.218	.240	.282	523	45	-15	9	3	1	.965	-8	O-64(30-15-21),D-13	-2.4
1989	KC-A	134	475	64	139	33	7	9	59	37	44	.293	.344	.448	792	122	13	27	8	3	.989	-11	*O-123(26-67-58),D-10	0.2

YEAR	TM/L	G	AB	R	H	2B	3B	HR	RBI	BB	SO	AVG	OBP	SLG	OPS	OPS+	BR+	SB	CS	SBR	FA	FR	G/POS	TPR
1990	KC-A	142	496	61	139	29	7	5	51	42	51	.280	.338	.397	735	106	4	12	14	-2	**.996**	-9	*O-138(70-19-78)/D-2	-1.2
1991	KC-A	135	375	47	113	22	3	2	47	20	35	.301	.338	.392	730	101	0	5	3	0	.973	-17	*O-105L,1-15/D-1	-2.0
1992	KC-A	113	353	31	95	13	3	2	28	24	36	.269	.316	.340	656	81	-9	11	6	0	.995	-2	O-88(24-1-66)/D-8	-1.4
1993	*Phi-N	153	362	51	115	17	4	7	54	26	36	.318	.365	.445	810	117	9	5	0	1	.996	-6	*O-137(1-3-133)/1-1	-0.1
1994	Phi-N	104	290	42	87	15	4	4	43	33	31	.300	.373	.421	794	104	3	6	2	1	.989	0	O-93(0-5-90)	0.0
1995	Phi-N	129	377	46	119	22	2	10	55	38	44	.316	.380	.464	844	120	11	10	0	2	**1.000**	1	*O-111(39-6-68)	1.0
1996	Phi-N	113	338	45	122	24	3	3	41	31	32	.361	.416	.476	893	133	17	11	1	2	.977	1	O-91(43-3-50)	1.6
1997	*Fla-N	120	293	36	82	19	1	2	34	30	28	.280	.349	.372	721	93	-3	0	0	0	.987	-4	O-55L,1-29/D-4	-1.0
1998	Fla-N	30	64	9	16	1	0	1	7	4	14	.250	.294	.313	607	63	-3	2	0	0	.965	-3	1-10/O-8(5-0-3)	-0.7
	LA-N	75	127	12	25	2	2	0	6	12	22	.197	.266	.244	510	38	-12	4	0	1	.971	-2	O-24(22-0-2)/1-9,D-2	-1.3
	Yr	105	191	21	41	3	2	1	13	16	36	.215	.275	.267	542	46	-15	6	0	1	.977	-4	O-32(27-0-5),1-19/D-2	-2.0
Total	15	1422	3995	492	1160	221	39	52	477	324	435	.290	.345	.404	749	103	15	105	38	10	.988	-62	*O-1072R/D-72,1-64	-7.6

■ ELAND

Eland Deb: 4/14/1873

YEAR	TM/L	G	AB	R	H	2B	3B	HR	RBI	BB	SO	AVG	OBP	SLG	OPS	OPS+	BR+	SB	CS	SBR	FA	FR	G/POS	TPR
1873	Mar-n	1	3	0	0	0	0	0	0	0	0	.000	.000	.000	0	-99	-1	0	0	0	.667	-0	/O-1(0-0-1)	-0.1

■ KID ELBERFELD

Elberfeld, Norman Arthur "The Tabasco Kid" b: 4/13/1875, Pomeroy, Ohio d: 1/13/44, Chattanooga, Tenn. BR/TR, 5'7", 158 lbs. Deb: 5/30/1898 M

YEAR	TM/L	G	AB	R	H	2B	3B	HR	RBI	BB	SO	AVG	OBP	SLG	OPS	OPS+	BR+	SB	CS	SBR	FA	FR	G/POS	TPR
1898	Phi-N	14	38	1	9	4	0	0	7	5		.237	.420	.342	762	124	2	0			.795	-5	3-14	-0.3
1899	Cin-N	41	138	23	36	4	2	0	22	15		.261	.378	.319	697	90	-1	5			.878	-4	S-24,3-18	-0.3
1901	Det-A	121	432	76	133	21	11	3	76	57		.308	.397	.428	825	123	15	23			.907	22	*S-121	3.7
1902	Det-A	130	488	70	127	17	6	1	64	55		.260	.348	.326	674	86	-7	19			.921	9	*S-130	0.6
1903	Det-A	35	132	29	45	5	3	0	19	11		.341	.412	.424	836	156	10	6			.932	6	S-34/3-1	1.7
	NY-A	90	349	49	100	18	5	0	45	22		.287	.346	.367	713	107	4	16			.914	7	S-90	1.4
	Yr	125	481	78	145	23	8	0	64	33		.301	.365	.383	747	120	13	22			.919	13	*S-124/3-1	3.1
1904	NY-A	122	445	55	117	13	5	2	46	37		.263	.337	.328	665	106	4	18			.933	15	*S-122	2.6
1905	NY-A	111	390	48	102	18	2	0	53	23		.262	.329	.318	647	95	-2	18			.908	-5	*S-108	-0.3
1906	NY-A	99	346	59	106	11	5	2	31	30		.306	.378	.384	763	126	11	19			.925	-4	S-98	1.2
1907	NY-A	120	447	61	121	17	6	0	51	36		.271	.343	.336	678	108	5	22			.930	8	*S-118	1.8
1908	NY-A	19	56	11	11	3	0	0	5	6		.196	.328	.250	578	87	-0	1			.916	-3	S-17,M	-0.3
1909	NY-A	106	379	47	90	9	5	0	26	28		.237	.314	.288	601	89	-4	23			.943	-3	S-61,3-44	-0.3
1910	Was-A	127	455	53	114	9	2	2	42	35		.251	.322	.292	614	97	-0	19			**.943**	-10	*3-113,2-10/S-3	-0.8
1911	Was-A	127	404	58	110	19	4	0	47	65		.272	.405	.339	744	110	11	24			.957	10	2-68,3-52	2.3
1914	Bro-N	30	62	7	14	1	0	0	1	2	4	.226	.304	.242	546	62	-3	0			.901	-4	S-18/2-1	-0.6
Total	14	1292	4561	647	1235	169	56	10	535	427	4	.271	.355	.339	694	105	46	213			.920	41	S-944,3-242/2-79	12.4

■ GEORGE ELDER

Elder, George Rezin b: 3/10/21, Lebanon, Ky. BL/TR, 5'11", 180 lbs. Deb: 7/22/49

YEAR	TM/L	G	AB	R	H	2B	3B	HR	RBI	BB	SO	AVG	OBP	SLG	OPS	OPS+	BR+	SB	CS	SBR	FA	FR	G/POS	TPR
1949	StL-A	41	44	9	11	3	0	0	2	4	11	.250	.313	.318	631	64	-2	0	0	0	1.000	-1	O-10(10-0-0)	-0.4

■ LEE ELIA

Elia, Lee Constantine b: 7/16/37, Philadelphia, Pa. BR/TR, 5'11", 175 lbs. Deb: 4/23/66 MC

YEAR	TM/L	G	AB	R	H	2B	3B	HR	RBI	BB	SO	AVG	OBP	SLG	OPS	OPS+	BR+	SB	CS	SBR	FA	FR	G/POS	TPR
1966	Chi-A	80	195	16	40	5	2	3	22	15	39	.205	.269	.297	566	67	-9	0	1	-0	.954	4	S-75	0.0
1968	Chi-N	15	17	1	3	0	0	0	3	0	6	.176	.222	.176	399	20	-2	0	0	0	1.000	-1	/S-2,2-1,3-1	-0.3
Total	2	95	212	17	43	5	2	3	25	15	45	.203	.265	.288	553	63	-10	0	1	-0	.954	3	/S-77,3-1,2-1	-0.3

■ PETE ELKO

Elko, Peter "Piccolo Pete" b: 6/17/18, Wilkes-Barre, Pa. d: 9/17/93, Wilkes-Barre, Pa. BR/TR, 5'11", 185 lbs. Deb: 9/17/43

YEAR	TM/L	G	AB	R	H	2B	3B	HR	RBI	BB	SO	AVG	OBP	SLG	OPS	OPS+	BR+	SB	CS	SBR	FA	FR	G/POS	TPR
1943	Chi-N	9	30	1	4	0	0	0	0	4	5	.133	.235	.133	369	8	-3	0			.852	-2	/3-9	-0.6
1944	Chi-N	7	22	2	5	1	0	0	0	0	1	.227	.227	.273	500	40	-2	0			1.000	-0	/3-6	-0.2
Total	2	16	52	3	9	1	0	0	0	4	6	.173	.232	.192	424	22	-5	0			.902	-2	/3-15	-0.8

■ ROY ELLAM

Ellam, Roy "Whitey" or "Slippery" b: 2/8/1886, W.Conshohocken, Pa. d: 10/28/48, Conshohocken, Pa. BR/TR, 5'10.5", 203 lbs. Deb: 9/18/09

YEAR	TM/L	G	AB	R	H	2B	3B	HR	RBI	BB	SO	AVG	OBP	SLG	OPS	OPS+	BR+	SB	CS	SBR	FA	FR	G/POS	TPR
1909	Cin-N	10	21	4	4	0	1	1	4	7		.190	.393	.429	821	156	2	1			.895	-1	/S-9	0.1
1918	Pit-N	26	77	9	10	1	1	0	2	17	17	.130	.302	.169	471	43	-4	2			.924	-8	S-26	-1.2
Total	2	36	98	13	14	1	2	1	6	24	17	.143	.323	.224	547	67	-3	3			.917	-10	/S-35	-1.1

■ FRANK ELLERBE

Ellerbe, Francis Rogers "Governor"
b: 12/25/1895, Marion Co., S.C. d: 7/8/88, Latta, S.C. BR/TR, 5'10.5", 165 lbs. Deb: 8/28/19 Career OF: (0-LF 0-CF 1-RF)

YEAR	TM/L	G	AB	R	H	2B	3B	HR	RBI	BB	SO	AVG	OBP	SLG	OPS	OPS+	BR+	SB	CS	SBR	FA	FR	G/POS	TPR
1919	Was-A	28	105	13	29	4	1	0	16	2	15	.276	.290	.333	623	75	-4	5			.945	-4	S-28	-0.6
1920	Was-A	101	336	38	98	14	2	0	36	19	23	.292	.331	.345	677	82	-9	5	4	-0	.934	-5	3-75,S-19/O-1(0-0-1)	-1.1
1921	Was-A	10	10	1	2	0	1	0	1	0	2	.200	.200	.400	600	52	-1	0	0	0	.000	0	H	-0.1
	StL-A	105	430	65	124	20	12	2	49	22	42	.288	.327	.405	732	81	-13	1	6	-2	.953	2	*3-105	-0.6
	Yr	115	440	66	126	20	13	2	50	22	44	.286	.325	.405	729	81	-14	1	6	-2	.953	2	*3-105	-0.7
1922	StL-A	91	342	42	84	16	3	1	33	25	36	.246	.303	.319	621	60	-20	1	1	-0	.955	16	3-91	0.1
1923	StL-A	18	49	6	9	0	0	0	1	1	5	.184	.200	.184	384	1	-7	0	1	-0	.967	-3	3-14	-0.9
1924	StL-A	21	61	7	12	3	0	0	2	2	3	.197	.222	.246	468	19	-7	0	1	-0	.953	3	3-21	-0.4
	Cle-A	46	120	7	31	1	3	1	14	1	10	.258	.270	.342	612	56	-8	0	0	0	.975	5	3-39/2-2	-0.2
	Yr	67	181	14	43	4	3	1	16	3	13	.238	.254	.309	563	44	-16	0	1	-0	.967	8	3-60/2-2	-0.6
Total	6	420	1453	179	389	58	22	4	152	72	136	.268	.306	.346	652	68	-70	12	13		.952	14	3-345/S-47,2-2,O-1R	-3.8

■ JOE ELLICK

Ellick, Joseph J. b: 4/3/1854, Cincinnati, Ohio d: 4/21/23, Kansas City, Kan. 5'10", 162 lbs. Deb: 5/13/1875 MU Career OF: (3-LF 0-CF 56-RF)

YEAR	TM/L	G	AB	R	H	2B	3B	HR	RBI	BB	SO	AVG	OBP	SLG	OPS	OPS+	BR+	SB	CS	SBR	FA	FR	G/POS	TPR
1875	RS-n	7	27	1	6	1	0	0	1	0	1	.222	.222	.259	481	74	-1	1	0	0	.471	-3	/3-5,O-2(0-2-0)	-0.3
1878	Mil-N	3	13	2	2	0	0	0	1	0	1	.154	.154	.154	308	1	-1				.769	-3	/C-2,3-1,P-1	-0.3
1880	Wor-N	5	18	1	1	0	0	0	0	1	2	.056	.105	.056	161	-40	-3				.882	0	/3-5	-0.2
1884	CP-U	92	394	71	93	11	0	0		16		.236	.266	.264	530	61	-29				.903	-2	O-57R,S-33/2-4,M	-2.7
	KC-U	2	8	0	0	0	0	0		0		.000	.000	.000	0	-99	-2				.778	-1	/2-1,O-1(0-0-1)	-0.3
	Bal-U	7	27	2	4	0	0	0		2		.148	.207	.148	355	8	-4				.714	-1	/S-6,O-1(0-0-1)	-0.4
	Yr	101	429	73	97	11	0	0		18		.226	.257	.252	509	55	-35				.894	-3	O-59(3-0-56),S-39/2-5	-3.4
Total	3	109	460	76	100	11	0	0	1	19	3	.217	.248	.241	490	50	-39				.889	-6	/O-59R,S-39,3-6,2CP	-3.9

■ LARRY ELLIOT

Elliot, Lawrence Lee b: 3/5/38, San Diego, Cal. BL/TL, 6'2", 200 lbs. Deb: 4/19/62

YEAR	TM/L	G	AB	R	H	2B	3B	HR	RBI	BB	SO	AVG	OBP	SLG	OPS	OPS+	BR+	SB	CS	SBR	FA	FR	G/POS	TPR
1962	Pit-N	8	10	2	3	0	0	1	2	0	1	.300	.300	.600	900	135	0	0	0	0	1.000	-1	/O-3(0-0-3)	0.0
1963	Pit-N	4	4	0	0	0	0	0	0	0	3	.000	.000	.000	0	-99	-1	0	0	0	.000	0	H	-0.1
1964	NY-N	80	224	27	51	8	0	9	22	28	55	.228	.322	.384	705	100	0	1	2	-0	.985	-2	O-63(4-57-4)	-0.4
1966	NY-N	65	199	24	49	14	2	5	32	17	46	.246	.306	.412	718	100	-0	0	1	-0	.912	0	O-54(25-0-31)	-0.4
Total	4	157	437	53	103	22	2	15	56	45	105	.236	.311	.398	710	99	-1	1	3	-1	.956	-2	O-120(29-57-38)	-0.9

■ ALLEN ELLIOTT

Elliott, Allen Clifford "Ace" b: 12/25/1897, St.Louis, Mo. d: 5/6/79, St.Louis, Mo. BL/TR, 6', 170 lbs. Deb: 6/14/23

YEAR	TM/L	G	AB	R	H	2B	3B	HR	RBI	BB	SO	AVG	OBP	SLG	OPS	OPS+	BR+	SB	CS	SBR	FA	FR	G/POS	TPR
1923	Chi-N	53	168	21	42	8	2	2	29	2	12	.250	.267	.357	625	63	-9	3	3	-0	.992	-2	1-52	-1.4
1924	Chi-N	10	14	0	2	0	0	0	0	0	1	.143	.143	.143	286	-23	-2	0	0	0	1.000	-1	1-10	-0.3
Total	2	63	182	21	44	8	2	2	29	2	13	.242	.258	.341	599	57	-12	3	3	-0	.992	-2	/1-62	-1.7

■ CARTER ELLIOTT

Elliott, Carter Ward b: 11/29/1893, Atchison, Kan. d: 5/21/59, Palm Springs, Cal. BL/TR, 5'11", 165 lbs. Deb: 9/10/21

YEAR	TM/L	G	AB	R	H	2B	3B	HR	RBI	BB	SO	AVG	OBP	SLG	OPS	OPS+	BR+	SB	CS	SBR	FA	FR	G/POS	TPR
1921	Chi-N	12	28	5	7	2	0	0	0	5	3	.250	.364	.321	685	83	-0	0	0	0	.964	4	S-10	0.4

■ GENE ELLIOTT

Elliott, Eugene Birminghouse b: 2/8/1889, Fayette Co., Pa. d: 1/5/76, Huntingdon, Pa. BL/TR, 5'7", 150 lbs. Deb: 4/13/11

YEAR	TM/L	G	AB	R	H	2B	3B	HR	RBI	BB	SO	AVG	OBP	SLG	OPS	OPS+	BR+	SB	CS	SBR	FA	FR	G/POS	TPR
1911	NY-A	5	13	1	1	1	0	0	1	2		.077	.200	.154	354	-1	-2	0			.000	-1	/O-2(0-0-2),3-1	-0.3

■ ROWDY ELLIOTT

Elliott, Harold B. b: 7/8/1890, Kokomo, Ind. d: 2/12/34, San Francisco, Cal. BR/TR, 5'9", 160 lbs. Deb: 9/24/10

YEAR	TM/L	G	AB	R	H	2B	3B	HR	RBI	BB	SO	AVG	OBP	SLG	OPS	OPS+	BR+	SB	CS	SBR	FA	FR	G/POS	TPR
1910	Bos-N	3	2	0	0	0	0	0	0	0	0	.000	.000	.000	0	-96	-0	0			1.000	-0	/C-1	-0.1
1916	Chi-N	23	55	5	14	3	0	0	3	3	5	.255	.293	.309	602	77	-1	1			.969	-1	C-18	-0.1
1917	Chi-N	85	223	18	56	8	5	0	28	11	11	.251	.292	.332	624	84	-4	4			.969	4	C-73	0.6
1918	Chi-N	5	10	0	0	0	0	0	0	2	1	.000	.167	.000	167	-47	-2	0			.952	0	/C-5	-0.1
1920	Bro-N	41	112	13	27	4	0	1	13	3	6	.241	.267	.304	571	62	-6	0	0	0	.964	5	C-39	0.2
Total	5	157	402	36	97	15	5	1	44	19	23	.241	.281	.311	592	73	-13	5	0		.967	7	C-136	0.5

■ **HARRY ELLIOTT** Elliott, Harry Lewis b: 12/30/23, San Francisco, Cal BR/TR, 5'9", 175 lbs. Deb: 8/1/53

YEAR	TM/L	G	AB	R	H	2B	3B	HR	RBI	BB	SO	AVG	OBP	SLG	OPS	OPS+	BR+	SB	CS	SBR	FA	FR	G/POS	TPR
1953	StL-N	24	59	6	15	6	1	1	6	3	8	.254	.302	.441	742	91	-1	0	0	0	1.000	1	O-17(15-0-2)	-0.1
1955	StL-N	68	117	9	30	4	0	1	12	11	9	.256	.326	.316	642	71	-5	0	2	-1	.978	-2	O-28(8-0-20)	-0.9
Total	2	92	176	15	45	10	1	2	18	14	17	.256	.318	.358	676	78	-6	0	2	-1	.988	-2	/O-45(23-0-22)	-1.0

■ **RANDY ELLIOTT** Elliott, Randy Lee b: 6/5/51, Oxnard, Cal. BR/TR, 6'2", 190 lbs. Deb: 9/10/72 Career OF: (53-LF 0-CF 17-RF)

YEAR	TM/L	G	AB	R	H	2B	3B	HR	RBI	BB	SO	AVG	OBP	SLG	OPS	OPS+	BR+	SB	CS	SBR	FA	FR	G/POS	TPR
1972	SD-N	14	49	5	10	3	1	0	6	2	11	.204	.235	.306	541	57	-3	0	0	0	1.000	1	O-13(0-0-13)	-0.3
1974	SD-N	13	33	5	7	1	0	1	2	7	9	.212	.350	.333	683	96	0	0	0	-0	1.000	-2	O-11(7-0-4)/1-1	-0.3
1977	SF-N	73	167	17	40	5	1	7	26	8	24	.240	.278	.407	686	82	-5	0	2	-1	.973	1	O-46(46-0-0)	-0.7
1980	Oak-A	14	39	4	5	3	0	0	1	1	13	.128	.150	.205	355	-4	-6	0	0	0	.000	0	D-11	-0.6
Total	4	114	288	31	62	12	2	8	35	18	57	.215	.264	.354	618	69	-14	0	3	-1	.982	-1	/O-70L,D-11,1-1	-1.9

■ **BOB ELLIOTT** Elliott, Robert Irving "Mr. Team" b: 11/26/16, San Francisco, Cal. d: 5/4/66, San Diego, Cal. BR/TR, 6', 185 lbs. Deb: 9/2/39 MC Career OF: (63-LF 63-CF 415-RF)

YEAR	TM/L	G	AB	R	H	2B	3B	HR	RBI	BB	SO	AVG	OBP	SLG	OPS	OPS+	BR+	SB	CS	SBR	FA	FR	G/POS	TPR
1939	Pit-N	32	129	18	43	10	3	3	19	9	4	.333	.377	.527	904	143	7	0			.978	3	O-30(0-30-0)	0.9
1940	Pit-N	148	551	88	161	34	11	5	64	45	28	.292	.348	.421	769	112	9	13			.978	2	*O-147(4-31-113)	0.2
1941	Pit-N★	141	527	74	144	24	10	3	76	64	52	.273	.353	.374	727	105	5	6			.970	2	*O-139(4-2-134)	-0.2
1942	Pit-N★	143	560	75	166	26	7	9	89	52	35	.296	.358	.416	774	123	16	2			.927	-2	*3-142/O-1(1-0-0)	2.0
1943	Pit-N	156	581	82	183	30	12	7	101	56	24	.315	.376	.444	820	132	23	4			.949	-8	*3-151/2-2,S-1	1.9
1944	Pit-N★	143	538	85	160	28	16	10	108	75	42	.297	.383	.465	848	132	24	9			.944	-1	*3-140/S-1	2.5
1945	Pit-N†	144	541	80	157	36	6	8	108	64	38	.290	.366	.423	790	115	11	5			.928	8	3-81,O-61(0-0-61)	1.6
1946	Pit-N	140	486	50	128	25	3	5	68	64	44	.263	.351	.358	709	99	1	6			.995	3	O-92(0-0-92),3-43	0.1
1947	Bos-N†	150	555	93	176	35	5	22	113	87	60	.317	.410	.517	927	148	40	3			**.956**	-2	*3-148	3.6
1948	*Bos-N★	151	540	99	153	24	5	23	100	**131**	57	.283	.423	.474	897	145	40	6			.945	-10	*3-150	2.9
1949	Bos-N	139	482	77	135	29	5	17	76	90	38	.280	.395	.467	862	138	28	0			.963	11	*3-130	3.8
1950	Bos-N	142	531	94	162	28	5	24	107	68	67	.305	.386	.512	898	143	33	2			.952	-17	*3-137	1.5
1951	Bos-N★	136	480	73	137	29	2	15	70	65	56	.285	.371	.448	819	128	19	2	0	0	.941	-8	*3-127	1.2
1952	NY-N	98	272	33	62	6	2	10	35	36	20	.228	.323	.375	698	92	-3	1	0	0	.978	-6	O-65(52-0-15),3-13	-1.3
1953	StL-A	48	160	19	40	7	1	5	29	30	18	.250	.368	.400	768	105	2	0	1	-0	.954	-2	3-45	0.0
	Chi-A	67	208	24	54	11	1	4	32	31	21	.260	.358	.380	738	96	-0	1	1	-0	.963	-11	3-58/O-2(2-0-0)	-1.1
	Yr	115	368	43	94	18	2	9	61	61	39	.255	.363	.389	751	100	1	1	2	-0	.959	-12	*3-103/O-2(2-0-0)	-1.1
Total	15	1978	7141	1064	2061	382	94	170	1195	967	604	.289	.375	.440	815	124	254	60	2		.947	-38	*3-1365,O-537R/S-2,2	19.6

■ **BEN ELLIS** Ellis, Alfred Benjamin b: 7/1870, New York, N.Y. d: 7/26/31, Schenectady, N.Y. 5'10", 165 lbs. Deb: 7/16/1896

YEAR	TM/L	G	AB	R	H	2B	3B	HR	RBI	BB	SO	AVG	OBP	SLG	OPS	OPS+	BR+	SB	CS	SBR	FA	FR	G/POS	TPR
1896	Phi-N	4	16	0	1	0	0	0	0	3	6	.063	.211	.063	273	-26	-3	0			.800	-1	/S-2,3-2	-0.3

■ **RUBE ELLIS** Ellis, George William b: 11/17/1885, Downey, Cal. d: 3/13/38, Rivera, Cal. BL/TL, 6', 170 lbs. Deb: 4/15/09

YEAR	TM/L	G	AB	R	H	2B	3B	HR	RBI	BB	SO	AVG	OBP	SLG	OPS	OPS+	BR+	SB	CS	SBR	FA	FR	G/POS	TPR
1909	StL-N	149	575	76	154	10	9	3	46	54		.268	.334	.332	666	114	9	16			.955	13	*O-145(144-0-1)	1.5
1910	StL-N	142	550	87	142	18	8	4	54	62	70	.258	.339	.342	681	102	2	25			.942	0	*O-141(141-0-0)	-0.6
1911	StL-N	155	555	69	139	20	11	2	66	66	64	.250	.332	.337	669	90	-7	9			.938	1	*O-148(148-0-0)	-1.3
1912	StL-N	109	305	47	82	18	2	4	33	34	36	.269	.342	.380	723	100	-0	6			.929	0	O-76(65-4-7)	-0.4
Total	4	555	1985	279	517	66	30	13	199	216	170	.260	.336	.344	680	101	4	56			.943	14	O-510(498-4-8)	-0.8

■ **JOHN ELLIS** Ellis, John Charles b: 8/21/48, New London, Conn. BR/TR, 6'2.5", 225 lbs. Deb: 5/17/69

YEAR	TM/L	G	AB	R	H	2B	3B	HR	RBI	BB	SO	AVG	OBP	SLG	OPS	OPS+	BR+	SB	CS	SBR	FA	FR	G/POS	TPR
1969	NY-A	22	62	2	18	4	0	1	8	1	11	.290	.313	.403	716	103	-0	0	2	-1	.978	1	C-15	0.0
1970	NY-A	78	226	24	56	12	1	7	29	18	47	.248	.309	.403	712	100	-1	0	1	-0	.992	1	1-53/3-5,C-2	-0.5
1971	NY-A	83	238	16	58	12	1	3	34	23	42	.244	.326	.340	666	95	-2	0	0	0	.990	-3	1-65/C-2	-1.0
1972	NY-A	52	136	13	40	5	1	5	25	8	22	.294	.333	.456	789	138	6	0	0	0	.965	1	C-25/1-8	0.8
1973	Cle-A	127	437	59	118	12	2	14	68	46	57	.270	.344	.403	746	108	5	0	0	0	.980	-18	C-72,D-38,1-12	-1.2
1974	Cle-A	128	477	58	136	23	6	10	64	32	53	.285	.331	.421	753	116	9	1	2	-0	.992	-8	1-69,C-42,D-21	-0.4
1975	Cle-A	92	296	22	68	11	1	7	32	14	33	.230	.269	.345	614	72	-12	0	1	-0	.976	-8	C-84/1-2,D-3	-1.6
1976	Tex-A	11	31	4	13	2	0	1	8	0	4	.419	.419	.581	1000	187	3	0	0	0	1.000	-1	/C-7,D-3	0.2
1977	Tex-A	49	119	7	28	7	0	4	15	8	26	.235	.283	.395	678	82	-3	0	0	0	1.000	-2	C-16,D-15/1-8	-0.6
1978	Tex-A	34	94	7	23	4	0	3	17	6	20	.245	.290	.383	673	88	-2	0	1	-0	.958	-2	C-22/D-7	-0.4
1979	Tex-A	111	316	33	90	12	0	12	61	15	55	.285	.321	.437	758	103	1	2	2	-0	.978	-3	D-62,1-30/C-7	-0.6
1980	Tex-A	73	182	12	43	9	1	1	23	14	23	.236	.294	.313	608	69	-8	3	0	1	.992	-2	1-39,D-20/C-3	-1.2
1981	Tex-A	23	58	2	8	3	0	1	7	5	10	.138	.219	.241	460	34	-5	0	1	-0	.993	-1	1-18/D-1	-0.7
Total	13	883	2672	259	699	116	13	69	391	190	403	.262	.315	.392	707	99	-9	6	10	-2	.989	-46	1-304,C-297,D-170,/3	-7.2

■ **ROB ELLIS** Ellis, Robert Walter b: 7/3/50, Grand Rapids, Mich. BR/TR, 5'11", 180 lbs. Deb: 6/18/71 Career OF: (10-LF 1-CF 21-RF)

YEAR	TM/L	G	AB	R	H	2B	3B	HR	RBI	BB	SO	AVG	OBP	SLG	OPS	OPS+	BR+	SB	CS	SBR	FA	FR	G/POS	TPR
1971	Mil-A	36	111	9	22	2	0	0	6	12	24	.198	.282	.216	498	43	-8	0	2	-1	.923	-7	3-19,O-15(1-1-13)	-1.8
1974	Mil-A	22	48	4	14	2	0	0	4	4	11	.292	.346	.333	679	97	-0	0	0	0	1.000	-1	O-11(4-0-8)/3-1,D-9	-0.1
1975	Mil-A	6	7	3	2	0	0	0	0	0	0	.286	.286	.286	571	62	-0	0	0	0	1.000	-2	/O-5(5-0-0),D-1	-0.2
Total	3	64	166	16	38	4	0	0	10	16	35	.229	.301	.253	554	59	-8	0	2	-1	.976	-10	/O-31R,3-20,D-10	-2.1

■ **BABE ELLISON** Ellison, Herbert Spencer "Bert" b: 11/15/1895, Rutland, Ark. d: 8/11/55, San Francisco, Cal BR/TR, 5'11", 170 lbs. Deb: 9/18/16 Career OF: (1-LF 3-CF 14-RF)

YEAR	TM/L	G	AB	R	H	2B	3B	HR	RBI	BB	SO	AVG	OBP	SLG	OPS	OPS+	BR+	SB	CS	SBR	FA	FR	G/POS	TPR
1916	Det-A	2	7	0	1	1	0	0	1	0	1	.143	.143	.143	286	-14	-1	0			1.000	-1	/3-2	-0.3
1917	Det-A	9	29	2	5	1	2	1	4	6	3	.172	.333	.448	782	139	1	0			.980	-2	/1-9	-0.1
1918	Det-A	7	23	1	6	1	0	0	2	3	1	.261	.346	.304	651	100	0	1			1.000	-0	/O-4(0-0-4),2-3	-0.1
1919	Det-A	56	134	18	29	4	0	0	11	13	24	.216	.291	.246	537	53	-8	4			.966	-7	2-25,O-10(1-1-8)/S-1	-1.6
1920	Det-A	61	155	11	34	7	2	0	21	8	26	.219	.258	.290	548	46	-12	4	1	1	.997	2	1-38/O-4(0-2-2),3-1	-1.1
Total	5	135	348	32	75	13	4	1	39	30	55	.216	.282	.284	566	58	-20	9	1		.994	-9	/1-47,2-28,O-18R,3S	-3.2

■ **VERDO ELMORE** Elmore, Verdo Wilson "Ellie" b: 12/10/1899, Gordo, Ala. d: 8/5/69, Birmingham, Ala. BL/TR, 5'11", 185 lbs. Deb: 9/11/24

YEAR	TM/L	G	AB	R	H	2B	3B	HR	RBI	BB	SO	AVG	OBP	SLG	OPS	OPS+	BR+	SB	CS	SBR	FA	FR	G/POS	TPR
1924	StL-A	7	17	2	3	3	0	0	0	1	3	.176	.222	.353	575	44	-2	0	0	0	.000	-2	/O-3(0-0-3)	-0.3

■ **ROY ELSH** Elsh, Eugene Reybold b: 3/1/1892, Penns Grove, N.J. d: 11/12/78, Philadelphia, Pa. BR/TR, 5'9", 165 lbs. Deb: 4/19/23

YEAR	TM/L	G	AB	R	H	2B	3B	HR	RBI	BB	SO	AVG	OBP	SLG	OPS	OPS+	BR+	SB	CS	SBR	FA	FR	G/POS	TPR
1923	Chi-A	81	209	28	52	7	2	0	24	16	23	.249	.305	.301	607	61	-12	16	8	1	.957	1	O-57(50-6-1)	-1.3
1924	Chi-A	60	147	21	45	9	1	0	11	10	14	.306	.350	.381	731	91	-2	6	1	1	.953	-6	O-38(2-5-31)/1-2	-0.9
1925	Chi-A	32	48	6	9	1	0	0	4	5	7	.188	.264	.208	472	22	-6	2	0	0	.964	-1	O-16(2-3-11)/1-3	-0.7
Total	3	173	404	55	106	17	3	0	39	31	44	.262	.317	.319	636	67	-20	24	9	2	.957	-6	O-111(54-14-43)/1-5	-2.9

■ **KEVIN ELSTER** Elster, Kevin Daniel b: 8/3/64, San Pedro, Cal. BR/TR, 6'2", 200 lbs. Deb: 9/2/86

YEAR	TM/L	G	AB	R	H	2B	3B	HR	RBI	BB	SO	AVG	OBP	SLG	OPS	OPS+	BR+	SB	CS	SBR	FA	FR	G/POS	TPR
1986	*NY-N	19	30	3	5	1	0	0	0	3	8	.167	.242	.200	442	24	-3	0	0	0	.962	4	S-19	0.2
1987	NY-N	5	10	1	4	2	0	0	1	0	1	.400	.400	.600	1000	169	1	0	0	0	.909	-0	/S-3	0.1
1988	*NY-N	149	406	41	87	11	1	9	37	35	47	.214	.282	.313	594	74	-14	2	0	1	.977	5	*S-148	0.1
1989	NY-N	151	458	52	106	25	2	10	55	34	77	.231	.287	.360	648	88	-8	4	3	-0	.976	7	*S-150	1.0
1990	NY-N	92	314	36	65	20	1	9	45	30	54	.207	.278	.363	641	75	-11	2	0	1	.960	15	S-92	1.1
1991	NY-N	115	348	33	84	16	2	6	36	40	53	.241	.321	.351	672	90	-4	2	3	-1	.970	11	*S-107	1.4
1992	NY-N	6	18	0	4	0	0	0	0	0	2	.222	.222	.222	444	27	-2	0	0	0	1.000	-1	/S-5	-0.2
1994	NY-A	7	20	0	0	0	0	0	0	1	6	.000	.048	.000	48	-90	-6	0	0	0	1.000	5	/S-7	-0.1
1995	NY-A	10	17	1	2	1	0	0	0	1	5	.118	.167	.176	343	-11	-3	0	0	0	1.000	1	S-10/2-1	-0.2
	Phi-N	26	53	10	11	4	1	1	9	7	14	.208	.311	.377	689	80	-2	0	0	0	.982	-0	S-19/1-4,3-2	-0.1
1996	*Tex-A	157	515	79	130	32	2	24	99	52	138	.252	.323	.462	786	91	-9	4	1	1	.981	4	*S-157	0.8
1997	Pit-N	39	138	14	31	6	2	7	25	21	39	.225	.331	.449	781	100	-0	0	2	-1	.994	2	S-39	0.4
1998	Tex-A	84	297	33	69	10	1	8	37	33	66	.232	.313	.354	667	70	-13	0	2	-1	.976	-5	S-84	-1.1
2000	LA-N	80	220	29	50	8	0	14	32	38	52	.227	.341	.455	796	103	1	0	0	0	.946	-12	S-55/3-8,1-1	-0.7
Total	13	940	2844	332	648	136	12	88	376	295	562	.228	.303	.377	680	83	-73	14	11	-1	.974	35	S-895/3-10,1-5,2-1	2.7

■ **BONES ELY** Ely, William Frederick b: 6/7/1863, N.Girard, Pa. d: 1/10/52, Berkeley, Cal. BR/TR, 6'1", 155 lbs. Deb: 6/19/1884 Career OF: (74-LF 9-CF 1-RF)

YEAR	TM/L	G	AB	R	H	2B	3B	HR	RBI	BB	SO	AVG	OBP	SLG	OPS	OPS+	BR+	SB	CS	SBR	FA	FR	G/POS	TPR
1884	Buf-N	1	4	0	0	0	0	0	0	0	2	.000	.000	.000	0	-97	-1				.000	-1	/O-1(0-0-1),P-1	-0.1
1886	Lou-a	10	32	5	5	0	0	0	6	2		.156	.206	.156	362	13	-3	1			1.000	-0	/P-6,O-5(4-1-0)	-0.2

YEAR	TM/L	G	AB	R	H	2B	3B	HR	RBI	BB	SO	AVG	OBP	SLG	OPS	OPS+	BR+	SB	CS	SBR	FA	FR	G/POS	TPR
1890	Syr-a	119	496	72	130	16	6	0	64	31		.262	.308	.319	627	95	-3	44			.915	19	O-78L,S-36/1-4,23P	1.3
1891	Bro-N	31	111	9	17	0	1	0	11	7	9	.153	.203	.171	375	9	-13	4			.870	8	S-28/3-2,2-1	-0.3
1893	StL-N	44	178	25	45	1	6	0	16	17	13	.253	.318	.326	644	71	-8	2			.905	-3	S-44	-0.7
1894	StL-N	127	510	85	156	20	12	12	89	30	34	.306	.344	.463	807	93	-9	23			.901	1	*S-126/2-1,P-1	-0.1
1895	StL-N	118	471	68	122	16	2	1	47	19	18	.259	.288	.308	596	54	-33	29			.925	7	*S-118	-1.6
1896	Pit-N	128	537	85	153	15	9	3	77	33	33	.285	.326	.363	689	85	-12	18			.918	-2	*S-128	-0.6
1897	Pit-N	133	516	63	146	20	8	2	74	25		.283	.317	.364	682	83	-14	10			.927	3	*S-133	-0.3
1898	Pit-N	148	519	49	110	14	5	2	44	24		.212	.247	.270	517	49	-36	6			**.943**	8	*S-148	-1.8
1899	Pit-N	139	526	67	146	18	6	3	72	22		.278	.313	.352	665	82	-14	8			.928	6	*S-133/2-6	-0.1
1900	*Pit-N	130	475	60	116	6	6	0	51	17		.244	.272	.282	554	53	-31	6			.935	13	*S-130	-1.1
1901	Pit-N	65	240	18	50	6	3	0	28	6		.208	.234	.258	492	41	-18	5			.916	-8	S-64/3-1	-2.4
	Phi-A	45	171	11	37	6	2	0	16	3		.216	.230	.275	505	38	-15	6			.913	1	S-45	-1.1
1902	Was-A	105	381	39	100	11	2	1	62	21		.262	.301	.310	611	69	-16	3			.923	-9	*S-105	-2.0
Total	14	1343	5167	656	1333	149	68	24	657	257	109	.258	.295	.327	622	70	-225	165			.923	42	*S-1238/O-84L,2P31	-11.1

■ **CHESTER EMERSON** Emerson, Chester Arthur "Chuck" b: 10/27/1889, Stow, Me. d: 7/2/71, Augusta, Me. BL/TR, 5'8", 165 lbs. Deb: 9/27/11

YEAR	TM/L	G	AB	R	H	2B	3B	HR	RBI	BB	SO	AVG	OBP	SLG	OPS	OPS+	BR+	SB	CS	SBR	FA	FR	G/POS	TPR
1911	Phi-A	7	18	2	4	0	0	0	0	6		.222	.417	.222	639	82	0	1			1.000	1	/O-7(0-1-6)	0.0
1912	Phi-A	1	1	0	0	0	0	0	0	0		.000	.000	.000	0	-99	-0	0			.000	0	H	0.0
Total	2	8	19	2	4	0	0	0	0	6		.211	.400	.211	611	74	-0	1			1.000	1	/O-7(0-1-6)	0.0

■ **CAL EMERY** Emery, Calvin Wayne b: 6/28/37, Centre Hall, Pa. BL/TL, 6'2", 205 lbs. Deb: 7/15/63 C

YEAR	TM/L	G	AB	R	H	2B	3B	HR	RBI	BB	SO	AVG	OBP	SLG	OPS	OPS+	BR+	SB	CS	SBR	FA	FR	G/POS	TPR
1963	Phi-N	16	19	0	3	1	0	0	0	0	2	.158	.158	.211	368	5	-2	0	0	0	1.000	-0	/1-2	-0.3

■ **SPOKE EMERY** Emery, Herrick Smith b: 12/10/1898, Bay City, Mich. d: 6/2/75, Cape Canaveral, Fla. BR/TR, 5'9", 165 lbs. Deb: 7/18/24

YEAR	TM/L	G	AB	R	H	2B	3B	HR	RBI	BB	SO	AVG	OBP	SLG	OPS	OPS+	BR+	SB	CS	SBR	FA	FR	G/POS	TPR
1924	Phi-N	5	3	3	2	0	0	0	0	0	0	.667	.667	.667	1333	230	1	0	1	-0	1.000	-0	/O-1(1-0-0)	0.0

■ **FRANK EMMER** Emmer, Frank William b: 2/17/1896, Crestline, Ohio d: 10/18/63, Homestead, Fla. BR/TR, 5'8", 150 lbs. Deb: 4/25/16 Career OF: (2-LF 0-CF 0-RF)

YEAR	TM/L	G	AB	R	H	2B	3B	HR	RBI	BB	SO	AVG	OBP	SLG	OPS	OPS+	BR+	SB	CS	SBR	FA	FR	G/POS	TPR
1916	Cin-N	42	89	8	13	3	1	0	2	7	27	.146	.208	.202	411	27	-8	1			.899	5	S-29/O-2L,2-1,3-1	-0.2
1926	Cin-N	80	224	22	44	7	6	0	18	13	30	.196	.244	.281	525	42	-19	1			.918	-7	S-79	-1.8
Total	2	122	313	30	57	10	7	0	20	20	57	.182	.234	.259	492	38	-26	2			.913	-3	S-108/O-2L,3-1,2-1	-2.0

■ **BOB EMMERICH** Emmerich, Robert George b: 8/1/1897, New York, N.Y. d: 11/22/48, Bridgeport, Conn. BR/TR, 5'3", 155 lbs. Deb: 9/22/23

YEAR	TM/L	G	AB	R	H	2B	3B	HR	RBI	BB	SO	AVG	OBP	SLG	OPS	OPS+	BR+	SB	CS	SBR	FA	FR	G/POS	TPR
1923	Bos-N	13	24	3	2	0	0	0	0	2	3	.083	.154	.083	237	-37	-5	1	1	-0	1.000	-1	/O-8(0-8-0)	-0.6

■ **ANGELO ENCARNACION** Encarnacion, Angelo Benjamin b: 4/18/73, Santo Domingo, D.R. BR/TR, 5'8", 180 lbs. Deb: 5/2/95

YEAR	TM/L	G	AB	R	H	2B	3B	HR	RBI	BB	SO	AVG	OBP	SLG	OPS	OPS+	BR+	SB	CS	SBR	FA	FR	G/POS	TPR
1995	Pit-N	58	159	18	36	7	2	2	10	13	28	.226	.285	.333	618	61	-9	1	1	-0	.979	6	C-55	0.0
1996	Pit-N	7	22	3	7	2	0	0	1	0	5	.318	.318	.409	727	88	-0	0	0	0	.951	-1	/C-7	-0.1
1997	Ana-A	11	17	2	7	1	0	1	4	0	1	.412	.412	.647	1059	171	2	2	0	0	.940	3	C-11	0.5
Total	3	76	198	23	50	10	2	3	15	13	34	.253	.299	.369	667	73	-8	3	1	0	.971	9	/C-73	0.4

■ **JUAN ENCARNACION** Encarnacion, Juan De Dios b: 3/8/76, Las Matas De Farfan, D.R. BR/TR, 6'2", 160 lbs. Deb: 9/2/97

YEAR	TM/L	G	AB	R	H	2B	3B	HR	RBI	BB	SO	AVG	OBP	SLG	OPS	OPS+	BR+	SB	CS	SBR	FA	FR	G/POS	TPR
1997	Det-A	11	33	3	7	1	1	1	5	3	12	.212	.316	.394	710	84	-1	3	1	0	1.000	-1	O-10(0-2-10)	-0.2
1998	Det-A	40	164	30	54	9	4	7	21	7	31	.329	.360	.561	921	134	8	7	4	0	.985	-4	O-39(8-13-21)/D-1	0.3
1999	Det-A	132	509	62	130	30	6	19	74	14	113	.255	.288	.450	737	85	-14	33	12	3	.968	0	*O-131(118-22-1)	-1.3
2000	Det-A	141	547	75	158	25	6	14	72	29	90	.289	.333	.433	766	95	-5	16	4	2	.987	4	*O-141(0-141-0)	0.2
Total	4	324	1253	170	349	65	17	41	172	53	246	.279	.318	.456	773	96	-12	59	21	6	.980	0	O-321(126-178-32)/D-1	-1.0

■ **BILL ENDICOTT** Endicott, William Franklin b: 9/4/18, Acorn, Mo. BL/TL, 5'11.5", 175 lbs. Deb: 4/21/46

YEAR	TM/L	G	AB	R	H	2B	3B	HR	RBI	BB	SO	AVG	OBP	SLG	OPS	OPS+	BR+	SB	CS	SBR	FA	FR	G/POS	TPR
1946	StL-N	20	20	2	4	3	0	0	3	4	4	.200	.333	.350	683	90	-0	0			1.000	-0	/O-2(2-0-0)	0.0

■ **CLYDE ENGLE** Engle, Arthur Clyde "Hack" b: 3/19/1884, Dayton, Ohio d: 12/26/39, Boston, Mass. BR/TR, 5'10", 190 lbs. Deb: 4/12/09 Career OF: (142-LF 111-CF 25-RF)

YEAR	TM/L	G	AB	R	H	2B	3B	HR	RBI	BB	SO	AVG	OBP	SLG	OPS	OPS+	BR+	SB	CS	SBR	FA	FR	G/POS	TPR
1909	NY-A	135	492	66	137	20	5	3	71	47		.278	.347	.358	705	122	13	18			.946	14	*O-134(119-16-0)	2.2
1910	NY-A	5	13	0	3	0	0	0	0	2		.231	.333	.231	564	73	-0	1			.857	-0	/O-3(3-0-0)	-0.1
	Bos-A	106	363	59	96	18	7	2	38	31		.264	.326	.369	695	115	5	12			.915	0	3-51,2-27,O-15C,/S	0.8
	Yr	111	376	59	99	18	7	2	38	33		.263	.326	.364	690	113	5	13			.915	0	3-51,2-27,O-18C,/S	0.7
1911	Bos-A	146	514	58	139	13	3	2	48	51		.270	.343	.319	662	86	-8	24			.975	-4	1-65,3-51,2-13,O-10C	-1.3
1912	*Bos-A	58	171	32	40	5	3	0	18	28		.234	.348	.298	647	81	-3	12			.977	-8	1-25,2-15,3-11,/SO	-1.1
1913	Bos-A	143	498	75	144	17	12	2	50	53	41	.289	.363	.384	747	116	10	28			.987	-7	*1-133/O-2(0-1-1)	-0.1
1914	Bos-A	59	134	14	26	2	0	0	9	14	11	.194	.275	.209	484	46	-8	4	9	-2	.976	-4	1-29/2-5,3-3,O-1	-1.8
	Buf-F	32	110	12	28	4	1	0	12	11	18	.255	.328	.309	637	73	-6	5			.889	-7	3-23/O-9(3-0-7)	-1.3
1915	Buf-F	141	501	56	131	22	8	3	71	34	43	.261	.312	.355	668	86	-17	24			.969	-3	*O-100C,2-21,3-17,/1	-2.8
1916	Cle-A	11	26	1	4	0	0	0	1	0	6	.154	.154	.154	308	-7	-3	0			.810	-2	/3-7,1-2,O-1(0-0-1)	-0.6
Total	8	836	2822	373	748	101	39	12	318	271	119	.265	.335	.341	676	97	-18	128	9		.959	-21	O-276L,1-255,3/2S	-6.1

■ **CHARLIE ENGLE** Engle, Charlie August "Cholly" b: 8/27/03, New York, N.Y. d: 10/12/83, San Antonio, Tex. BR/TR, 5'8", 145 lbs. Deb: 9/14/25

YEAR	TM/L	G	AB	R	H	2B	3B	HR	RBI	BB	SO	AVG	OBP	SLG	OPS	OPS+	BR+	SB	CS	SBR	FA	FR	G/POS	TPR
1925	Phi-A	1	0	0	0	0	0	0	0	0	0	—	—	—	—	—	0	0	0	0	.000	0	/S-1	0.0
1926	Phi-A	19	19	7	2	0	0	0	0	10	6	.105	.433	.105	539	43	-1	0	0	0	.930	2	S-16	0.2
1930	Pit-N	67	216	34	57	10	1	0	15	22	20	.264	.335	.319	654	59	-14	1			.975	-1	3-24,S-23,2-10	-0.9
Total	3	87	235	41	59	10	1	0	15	32	26	.251	.346	.302	648	59	-15	1	0		.937	2	/S-40,3-24,2-10	-0.7

■ **DAVE ENGLE** Engle, Ralph David b: 11/30/56, San Diego, Cal. BR/TR, 6'3", 216 lbs. Deb: 4/14/81 C Career OF: (17-LF 1-CF 119-RF)

YEAR	TM/L	G	AB	R	H	2B	3B	HR	RBI	BB	SO	AVG	OBP	SLG	OPS	OPS+	BR+	SB	CS	SBR	FA	FR	G/POS	TPR
1981	Min-A	82	248	29	64	14	4	5	32	13	37	.258	.298	.407	705	95	-2	0	1	-0	.980	-0	O-76(0-0-76)/3-1,D-1	-0.7
1982	Min-A	58	186	20	42	7	2	4	16	10	22	.226	.269	.349	618	67	-9	0	0	0	.985	0	O-34(2-1-32),D-20	-1.1
1983	Min-A	120	374	46	114	22	4	8	43	28	39	.305	.355	.449	804	115	8	2	1	0	.973	-19	C-73,D-29/O-4(0-0-4)	-0.9
1984	Min-A☆	109	391	56	104	20	1	4	38	26	22	.266	.312	.353	665	80	-11	0	1	-0	.981	-7	C-86,D-22	-1.5
1985	Min-A	70	172	28	44	8	2	7	25	21	28	.256	.337	.448	784	106	1	2	2	-0	.984	-0	D-38,C-17/O-3(3-0-0)	0.0
1986	Det-A	35	86	6	22	7	0	0	4	7	13	.256	.312	.337	649	77	-3	0	0	0	1.000	-1	1-23/O-4L,C-3,D-5	-0.5
1987	Mon-N	59	84	7	19	4	0	1	14	6	11	.226	.278	.310	587	54	-6	1	0	0	1.000	0	O-11L/C-6,1-2,3-1	-0.6
1988	Mon-N	34	37	4	8	3	0	0	1	5	5	.216	.310	.297	607	72	-1	0	0	0	1.000	-1	/C-9,O-4(1-0-3),3-1	-0.2
1989	Mil-A	27	65	5	14	3	0	2	8	4	13	.215	.261	.354	615	72	-3	0	0	0	.973	0	1-18/C-3,D-3	-0.4
Total	9	594	1643	201	431	88	13	31	181	120	190	.262	.314	.388	702	90	-24	5	5	-1	.979	-29	C-197,O-136R,D/13	-5.9

■ **CHARLIE ENGLISH** English, Charles Dewie b: 4/8/10, Darlington, S.C. d: 6/25/99, Pasadena, Cal. BR/TR, 5'9.5", 160 lbs. Deb: 7/23/32

YEAR	TM/L	G	AB	R	H	2B	3B	HR	RBI	BB	SO	AVG	OBP	SLG	OPS	OPS+	BR+	SB	CS	SBR	FA	FR	G/POS	TPR
1932	Chi-A	24	63	7	20	3	1	1	8	3	7	.317	.348	.444	793	111	1	0	0	0	.821	-2	3-13/S-1	-0.1
1933	Chi-A	3	9	2	4	2	0	0	1	1	1	.444	.500	.667	1167	216	2	0	0	0	.923	-1	/2-3	0.1
1936	NY-N	6	1	0	0	0	0	0	0	0	0	.000	.000	.000	0	-99	-0	0			.000	0	/2-1	0.0
1937	Cin-N	17	63	1	15	3	1	0	4	0	2	.238	.238	.317	556	52	-4	0			.958	2	3-15/2-2	-0.2
Total	4	50	136	10	39	8	2	1	13	4	10	.287	.307	.397	704	90	-2	0	0		.897	-2	/3-28,2-6,S-1	-0.2

■ **WOODY ENGLISH** English, Elwood George b: 3/2/07, Fredonia, Ohio d: 9/26/97, Newark, Ohio BR/TR, 5'10", 155 lbs. Deb: 4/26/27

YEAR	TM/L	G	AB	R	H	2B	3B	HR	RBI	BB	SO	AVG	OBP	SLG	OPS	OPS+	BR+	SB	CS	SBR	FA	FR	G/POS	TPR
1927	Chi-N	87	334	46	97	14	4	1	28	16	26	.290	.325	.365	690	84	-8	1			.940	7	S-84/3-1	0.8
1928	Chi-N	116	475	68	142	22	4	2	34	30	28	.299	.343	.375	718	89	-8	4			.946	6	*S-114/3-2	1.0
1929	*Chi-N	144	608	131	168	29	3	1	52	68	50	.276	.352	.339	691	72	-25	13			.955	15	*S-144	0.6
1930	Chi-N	156	638	152	214	36	17	14	59	100	72	.335	.430	.511	941	125	30	3			.973	-13	3-83,S-78	2.7
1931	Chi-N	156	634	117	202	38	8	2	53	68	80	.319	.391	.413	804	114	15	12			.965	1	*S-138,3-18	2.7
1932	*Chi-N	127	522	70	142	23	7	3	47	55	73	.272	.344	.360	704	90	-6	5			.957	-2	3-93,S-38	-0.2
1933	Chi-N★	105	398	54	104	19	2	3	41	53	44	.261	.348	.342	690	98	1	5			**.973**	-15	*3-103/S-1	-1.1
1934	Chi-N	109	421	65	117	26	5	3	31	48	65	.278	.353	.385	738	99	1	6			.971	-10	S-56,3-46/2-7	-0.3
1935	Chi-N	34	84	11	17	2	0	2	8	20	4	.202	.368	.298	666	81	-1	1			.868	-5	3-16,S-12	-0.5
1936	Chi-N	64	182	33	45	9	0	0	20	40	28	.247	.394	.297	691	86	-1	1			.976	1	S-42,3-17/2-1	0.4
1937	Bro-N	129	378	45	90	16	2	1	42	65	55	.238	.350	.299	649	77	-10	4			.956	-17	*S-116,2-11	-1.9

YEAR	TM/L	G	AB	R	H	2B	3B	HR	RBI	BB	SO	AVG	OBP	SLG	OPS	OPS+	BR+	SB	CS	SBR	FA	FR	G/POS	TPR
1938	Bro-N	34	72	9	18	2	0	0	7	8	11	.250	.333	.278	611	68	-3	2			.958	1	3-21/2-3,S-3	-0.1
Total	12	1261	4746	801	1356	236	52	32	422	571	536	.286	.366	.378	743	95	-14	57			.957	-31	S-826,3-400/2-22	4.1
■ **GIL ENGLISH** English, Gilbert Raymond b: 7/2/09, Glenola, N.C. d: 8/31/96, Trinity, N.C. BR/TR, 5'11", 180 lbs. Deb: 9/20/31 Career OF: (3-LF 0-CF 0-RF)																								
1931	NY-N	3	8	0	0	0	0	0	0	1	3	.000	.111	.000	111	-69	-2	0			1.000	-1	/3-3	-0.3
1932	NY-N	59	204	22	46	7	5	2	19	5	20	.225	.244	.338	582	56	-13	0			.931	4	3-39,S-23	-0.7
1936	Det-A	1	1	0	0	0	0	0	0	0	1	.000	.000	.000	0	-99	-0	0	0	0	1.000	0	/3-1	0.0
1937	Det-A	18	65	6	17	1	0	1	6	6	4	.262	.333	.323	656	65	-3	1	1	-0	.962	-8	2-12/3-6	-1.0
	Bos-N	79	269	25	78	5	2	2	37	23	27	.290	.348	.346	694	98	-0	3			.958	-7	3-71	-0.5
1938	Bos-N	53	165	17	41	6	0	2	21	15	16	.248	.315	.321	636	84	-4	1			.956	-4	3-43/O-3L,2-2,S-2	-0.6
1944	Bro-N	27	79	4	12	3	0	1	7	6	7	.152	.212	.228	440	24	-8	0			.918	-3	S-13,3-11/2-2	-1.1
Total	6	240	791	74	194	22	7	8	90	56	78	.245	.298	.321	619	72	-31	5	1		.950	-18	3-174/S-38,2-16,O-3L	-4.2
■ **DEL ENNIS** Ennis, Delmer b: 6/8/25, Philadelphia, Pa. d: 2/8/96, Huntingdon Valley, Pa. BR/TR, 6', 195 lbs. Deb: 4/28/46 Career OF: (1291-LF 1-CF 568-RF)																								
1946	Phi-N★	141	540	70	169	30	6	17	73	39	65	.313	.364	.485	849	144	28	5			.975	14	*O-138(138-0-1)	3.3
1947	Phi-N	139	541	71	149	25	6	12	81	37	51	.275	.325	.410	736	98	-4	9			.979	9	*O-135(135-0-2)	-0.4
1948	Phi-N	152	589	86	171	40	4	30	95	47	58	.290	.345	.525	869	135	25	2			.957	5	*O-151(0-0-151)	2.5
1949	Phi-N	154	610	92	184	39	11	25	110	59	61	.302	.367	.525	892	140	32	2			.966	6	*O-154(154-0-0)	2.6
1950	*Phi-N	153	595	92	185	34	8	31	**126**	56	59	.311	.372	.551	923	142	34	2			.970	-1	*O-149(14-1-140)	2.6
1951	Phi-N★	144	532	76	142	20	5	15	73	68	42	.267	.352	.408	760	105	5	4	2	0	.969	-1	*O-135(26-0-116)	-0.2
1952	Phi-N	151	592	90	171	30	10	20	107	47	65	.289	.341	.475	816	125	18	6	4	-0	.970	-1	*O-149(120-0-31)	0.7
1953	Phi-N	152	578	79	165	22	3	29	125	57	53	.285	.355	.484	839	117	13	1	3	-1	.980	4	*O-150(150-0-0)	0.7
1954	Phi-N	145	556	73	145	23	2	25	119	50	60	.261	.324	.444	768	98	-3	2	1	0	.957	3	*O-142(72-0-71)/1-1	-0.7
1955	Phi-N★	146	564	82	167	24	7	29	120	46	46	.296	.351	.518	869	129	22	4	2	0	.987	6	*O-145(143-0-3)	1.8
1956	Phi-N	153	630	80	164	23	3	26	95	33	62	.260	.300	.430	730	95	-6	7	3	0	.962	0	*O-153(153-0-0)	-1.6
1957	StL-N	136	490	61	140	24	3	24	105	37	50	.286	.337	.494	831	117	11	1	3	-1	.943	-15	*O-127(74-0-53)	-1.2
1958	StL-N	106	329	22	86	18	1	3	47	15	35	.261	.296	.350	645	67	-15	0	1	-0	.993	3	O-84(84-0-0)	-1.8
1959	Cin-N	5	12	1	4	0	0	0	1	2	2	.333	.429	.333	762	103	0	0	0	0	1.000	-0	/O-3(3-0-0)	0.0
	Chi-A	26	96	10	21	6	0	2	7	4	10	.219	.250	.344	594	62	-5	0	0	0	.909	-3	O-25(25-0-0)	-1.1
Total	14	1903	7254	985	2063	358	69	288	1284	597	719	.284	.341	.472	813	117	154	45	19		.969	28	*O-1840L/1-1	7.2
■ **RUSS ENNIS** Ennis, Russell Elwood "Hack" b: 3/10/1897, Superior, Wis. d: 1/21/49, Superior, Wis. BR/TR, 5'11.5", 160 lbs. Deb: 9/19/26																								
1926	Was-A	1	0	0	0	0	0	0	0	0	0	—	—	—	—	—	0	0	0	0	.000	0	/C-1	0.0
■ **GEORGE ENRIGHT** Enright, George Albert b: 5/9/54, New Britain, Conn. BR/TR, 5'11", 175 lbs. Deb: 8/8/76																								
1976	Chi-A	2	1	0	0	0	0	0	0	0	0	.000	.000	.000	0	-99	-0	0	0	0	1.000	1	/C-2	0.0
■ **MUTZ ENS** Ens, Anton b: 11/8/1884, St.Louis, Mo. d: 6/28/50, St.Louis, Mo. BL/TL, 6'1", 180 lbs. Deb: 9/2/12 F																								
1912	Chi-A	3	6	0	0	0	0	0	0	0		.000	.000	.000	0	-99	-2	0			.857	-1	/1-3	-0.2
■ **JEWEL ENS** Ens, Jewel Winklemeyer b: 8/24/1889, St.Louis, Mo. d: 1/17/50, Syracuse, N.Y. BR/TR, 5'10.5", 165 lbs. Deb: 4/29/22 FMC																								
1922	Pit-N	47	142	18	42	7	3	0	17	7	9	.296	.338	.387	725	85	-3	3	0	1	.951	-17	2-29/3-3,1-2,S-1	-1.7
1923	Pit-N	12	29	3	8	1	1	0	5	0	3	.276	.276	.379	655	70	-1	2	0	0	.975	-0	/1-4,3-3	-0.1
1924	Pit-N	5	10	2	3	0	0	0	0	0	3	.300	.300	.300	600	60	-1	0	0	0	1.000	-0	/1-5	-0.1
1925	Pit-N	3	5	2	1	0	0	1	2	0	1	.200	.200	.800	1000	133	0	0	0	0	1.000	-0	/1-3	0.0
Total	4	67	186	25	54	8	4	1	24	7	16	.290	.323	.392	716	83	-5	5	0	1	.990	-17	/2-29,1-14,3-6,S-1	-1.9
■ **MORGAN ENSBERG** Ensberg, Morgan P. b: 8/26/75, Redondo Beach, Cal. BR/TR, 6'2", 210 lbs. Deb: 9/20/2000																								
2000	Hou-N	4	7	0	2	0	0	0	0	0	1	.286	.286	.286	571	43	-1	0	0	0	.667	-0	/3-1	-0.1
■ **CHARLIE ENWRIGHT** Enwright, Charles Massey b: 10/6/1887, Sacramento, Cal. d: 1/19/17, Sacramento, Cal. BL/TR, 5'10", Deb: 4/19/09																								
1909	StL-N	3	7	1	1	0	0	0	1	2		.143	.333	.143	476	51	-0	0			.444	-3	/S-2	-0.4
■ **JACK ENZENROTH** Enzenroth, Clarence Herman b: 11/4/1885, Mineral Point, Wis. d: 2/21/44, Detroit, Mich. BR/TR, 5'7", 160 lbs. Deb: 5/1/14																								
1914	StL-A	3	6	0	1	0	0	0	0	2	3	.167	.444	.167	611	88	0	0	1	-0	.923	-1	/C-3	-0.1
	KC-F	26	67	7	12	4	1	0	5	5	19	.179	.236	.269	505	39	-7	0			.965	-2	C-24	-0.8
1915	KC-F	14	19	3	3	0	0	0	3	6	0	.158	.360	.158	518	50	-1	0			.973	2	/C-8	0.1
Total	2	43	92	10	16	4	1	0	8	13	22	.174	.283	.239	522	47	-8	0	1		.963	-1	/C-35	-0.8
■ **JIM EPPARD** Eppard, James Gerhard b: 4/27/60, South Bend, Ind. BL/TL, 6'2", 180 lbs. Deb: 9/8/87 Career OF: (17-LF 0-CF 1-RF)																								
1987	Cal-A	8	9	2	3	0	0	0	0	2	0	.333	.455	.333	788	118	0	0	0	0	1.000	-0	/O-1(0-0-1)	0.0
1988	Cal-A	56	113	7	32	3	1	0	14	11	15	.283	.347	.327	674	92	-1	0	0	0	.971	-0	O-17(17-0-0),D-10/1-6	-0.2
1989	Cal-A	12	12	0	3	0	0	0	2	1	4	.250	.308	.250	558	60	-1	0	0	0	1.000	-0	/1-4	-0.1
1990	Tor-A	6	5	0	1	0	0	0	0	0	2	.200	.333	.200	533	52	-0	0	0	0	.000	0	/H	0.0
Total	4	82	139	9	39	3	1	0	16	14	21	.281	.351	.317	667	90	-1	0	0	0	.972	-1	/O-18L,1-10,D-10	-0.3
■ **AUBREY EPPS** Epps, Aubrey Lee "Yo-Yo" b: 3/3/12, Memphis, Tenn. d: 11/13/84, Ackerman, Miss. BR/TR, 5'10", 170 lbs. Deb: 9/29/35																								
1935	Pit-N	1	4	1	3	0	1	0	3	0	0	.750	.750	1.250	2000	414	2	0			.750	-0	/C-1	0.1
■ **HAL EPPS** Epps, Harold Franklin b: 3/26/14, Athens, Ga. BL/TL, 6', 175 lbs. Deb: 9/9/38																								
1938	StL-N	17	50	8	15	0	0	1	3	2	4	.300	.327	.360	687	84	-1	2			.963	-0	O-10(0-10-0)	-0.2
1940	StL-N	11	15	6	3	0	0	0	1	0	3	.200	.200	.200	400	10	-2	0			.800	-1	/O-3(0-3-0)	-0.3
1943	StL-A	8	35	2	10	4	0	0	1	3	4	.286	.342	.400	742	114	1	1	1	-0	1.000	-1	/O-8(0-8-0)	-0.1
1944	StL-A	22	62	15	11	1	1	0	3	14	14	.177	.338	.226	563	59	-3	0	1	-0	.962	1	O-18(0-18-0)	-0.3
	Phi-A	67	229	27	60	8	8	0	13	18	18	.262	.316	.367	683	96	-2	2	1	0	.973	-3	O-60(0-44-16)	-0.7
	Yr	89	291	42	71	9	9	0	16	32	32	.244	.321	.337	658	88	-4	2	2	-0	.970	-2	O-78(0-62-16)	-1.0
Total	4	125	391	58	99	13	9	1	21	37	43	.253	.319	.340	660	86	-7	5	3		.968	-4	/O-99(0-83-16)	-1.6
■ **MIKE EPSTEIN** Epstein, Michael Peter "Superjew" b: 4/4/43, Bronx, N.Y. BL/TL, 6'3.5", 230 lbs. Deb: 9/16/66																								
1966	Bal-A	6	11	1	2	0	1	0	3	1	3	.182	.250	.364	614	75	-0	0	0	0	1.000	0	/1-4	0.0
1967	Bal-A	9	13	0	2	0	0	0	0	3	5	.154	.313	.154	466	42	-1	0	0	0	1.000	-0	/1-3	-0.1
	Was-A	96	284	32	65	7	4	9	29	38	74	.229	.332	.377	709	114	5	1	4	-1	.987	-2	1-80	-0.2
	Yr	105	297	32	67	7	4	9	29	41	79	.226	.331	.367	698	110	5	1	4	-1	.988	-2	1-83	-0.3
1968	Was-A	123	385	40	90	8	2	13	33	48	91	.234	.339	.366	705	117	9	1	1	-0	.987	1	*1-110	0.5
1969	Was-A	131	403	73	112	18	1	30	85	85	99	.278	.416	.551	967	178	45	2	5	-1	.990	-1	*1-118	3.5
1970	Was-A	140	430	55	110	15	3	20	56	73	117	.256	.375	.444	819	131	20	2	3	-1	.992	-3	*1-122	0.7
1971	Was-A	24	85	6	21	1	1	1	9	12	31	.247	.366	.318	684	101	1	1	0	0	.992	-1	1-24	-0.2
	*Oak-A	104	329	43	77	13	0	18	51	62	71	.234	.368	.438	806	130	15	0	3	-1	.995	-2	1-96	0.5
	Yr	128	414	49	98	14	1	19	60	74	102	.237	.368	.413	781	124	16	1	3	-1	.994	-2	*1-120	0.3
1972	*Oak-A	138	455	63	123	18	2	26	70	68	68	.270	.378	.490	868	166	38	0	1	-0	.990	-2	*1-137	2.7
1973	Tex-A	27	85	9	16	3	0	1	6	14	19	.188	.324	.259	582	69	-3	0	0	0	.991	-1	1-25	-0.6
	Cal-A	91	312	30	67	8	2	8	32	34	54	.215	.302	.330	632	84	-6	0	0	0	.993	-0	1-86	-1.4
	Yr	118	397	39	83	11	2	9	38	48	73	.209	.307	.315	622	81	-9	0	0	0	.993	-1	*1-111	-2.0
1974	Cal-A	18	62	10	10	2	0	4	6	10	13	.161	.288	.387	675	98	-0	0	0	0	.993	1	1-18	-0.1
Total	9	907	2854	362	695	93	16	130	380	448	645	.244	.360	.424	784	130	122	7	17	-4	.991	-10	1-823	5.3
■ **JOE ERAUTT** Erautt, Joseph Michael "Stubby" b: 9/1/21, Vibank, Sask., Can. d: 10/6/76, Portland, Ore. BR/TR, 5'9", 175 lbs. Deb: 5/9/50 F																								
1950	Chi-A	16	18	0	4	0	0	0	1	1	3	.222	.263	.222	485	26	-2	0	0	0	1.000	1	/C-5	-0.1
1951	Chi-A	16	25	3	4	1	0	0	0	3	2	.160	.276	.200	476	31	-2	0	0	0	.977	3	C-12	0.1
Total	2	32	43	3	8	1	0	0	1	4	5	.186	.271	.209	480	29	-4	0	0	0	.983	4	/C-17	0.0
■ **HANK ERICKSON** Erickson, Henry Nels "Popeye" b: 11/11/07, Chicago, Ill. d: 12/13/64, Louisville, Ky. BR/TR, 6'1", 185 lbs. Deb: 4/17/35																								
1935	Cin-N	37	88	9	23	3	2	1	4	6	4	.261	.323	.375	698	90	-1	0			.972	2	C-25	0.2

YEAR	TM/L	G	AB	R	H	2B	3B	HR	RBI	BB	SO	AVG	OBP	SLG	OPS	OPS+	BR+	SB	CS	SBR	FA	FR	G/POS	TPR
■ **CAL ERMER** Ermer, Calvin Coolidge b: 11/10/23, Baltimore, Md. BR/TR, 6'0.5", 175 lbs. Deb: 9/26/47 MC																								
1947	Was-A	1	3	0	0	0	0	0	0	0	0	.000	.000	.000	0	-99	-1	0	0	0	1.000	1	/2-1	0.0
■ **FRANK ERNAGA** Ernaga, Frank John b: 8/22/30, Susanville, Cal. BR/TR, 6'1", 195 lbs. Deb: 5/24/57																								
1957	Chi-N	20	35	9	11	3	2	2	7	9	14	.314	.455	.686	1140	204	6	0	0	0	.950	-0	O-10(3-0-7)	0.5
1958	Chi-N	9	8	0	1	0	0	0	0	0	2	.125	.125	.125	250	-34	-2	0	0	0	.000	0	H	-0.2
Total	2	29	43	9	12	3	2	2	7	9	16	.279	.404	.581	985	163	4	0	0	0	.950	-0	/O-10(3-0-7)	0.3
■ **DARIN ERSTAD** Erstad, Darin Charles b: 6/4/74, Jamestown, N.D. BL/TL, 6'2", 195 lbs. Deb: 6/14/96 Career OF: (260-LF 72-CF 1-RF)																								
1996	Cal-A	57	208	34	59	5	1	4	20	17	29	.284	.338	.375	713	80	-6	3	3	-0	.976	3	O-48(11-36-1)	-0.3
1997	Ana-A	139	539	99	161	34	4	16	77	51	86	.299	.364	.466	829	115	12	23	8	2	.990	-8	*1-126/O-1(0-1-0),D-9	-0.6
1998	Ana-A★	133	537	84	159	39	3	19	82	43	77	.296	.355	.486	841	115	11	20	6	2	.992	-3	O-72(70-3-0),1-70/D-2	0.2
1999	Ana-A	142	585	84	148	22	5	13	53	47	101	.253	.310	.374	684	74	-24	13	7	0	.999	13	1-78,O-69(67-2-0)/D-2	-1.9
2000	Ana-A★	157	676	121	**240**	39	6	25	100	64	82	.355	.412	.541	953	138	40	28	8	3	.992	13	*O-136L,D-20/1-3	4.6
Total	5	628	2545	422	767	139	19	77	332	222	375	.301	.360	.462	822	109	33	87	32	8	.991	17	O-326L,1-277/D-33	2.0
■ **TEX ERWIN** Erwin, Ross Emil b: 12/22/1885, Forney, Tex. d: 4/5/53, Rochester, N.Y. BL/TR, 6', 185 lbs. Deb: 8/26/07																								
1907	Det-A	4	5	0	1	0	0	0	1	1		.200	.333	.200	533	68	-0	0			.909	0	/C-4	0.0
1910	Bro-N	81	202	15	38	3	1	1	10	24	12	.188	.278	.228	505	49	-13	3			.949	-1	C-68	-0.8
1911	Bro-N	91	218	30	59	13	2	7	34	31	23	.271	.367	.445	811	132	9	5			.971	-5	C-74	1.0
1912	Bro-N	59	133	14	28	3	0	2	14	18	16	.211	.305	.278	583	62	-7	1			.949	-2	C-41	-0.5
1913	Bro-N	20	31	6	8	1	0	0	3	4	5	.258	.343	.290	633	80	-1	0			.950	-3	C-13	-0.3
1914	Bro-N	9	11	0	5	0	0	0	1	2	1	.455	.538	.455	993	192	1	1			1.000	-1	/C-4	0.1
	Cin-N	12	35	5	11	3	0	1	7	2	3	.314	.351	.486	837	144	2	0			.962	1	C-12	0.3
	Yr	21	46	5	16	3	0	1	8	4	4	.348	.400	.478	878	157	3	1			.966	-0	C-16	0.4
Total	6	276	635	70	150	23	3	11	70	82	60	.236	.326	.334	660	90	-8	10			.957	-11	C-216	-0.2
■ **NICK ESASKY** Esasky, Nicholas Andrew b: 2/24/60, Hialeah, Fla. BR/TR, 6'3", 205 lbs. Deb: 6/19/83 Career OF: (98-LF 0-CF 0-RF)																								
1983	Cin-N	85	302	41	80	10	5	12	46	27	99	.265	.331	.450	782	111	4	6	2	1	.935	-10	3-84	-0.7
1984	Cin-N	113	322	30	62	10	5	10	45	52	103	.193	.305	.348	653	79	-9	1	2	-0	.910	-8	3-82,1-25	-2.1
1985	Cin-N	125	413	61	108	21	0	21	66	41	102	.262	.334	.465	799	115	8	3	4	-1	.946	-6	3-62,O-54L,1-12	-0.3
1986	Cin-N	102	330	35	76	17	2	12	41	47	97	.230	.328	.403	731	96	-1	0	2	-1	.991	-3	1-70,O-42(42-0-0)/3-1	-1.0
1987	Cin-N	100	346	48	94	19	2	22	59	29	76	.272	.328	.529	857	117	7	0	0	0	.994	-11	1-93/3-1,O-1(1-0-0)	-1.0
1988	Cin-N	122	391	40	95	17	2	15	62	48	104	.243	.332	.412	744	108	4	7	2	1	.994	-9	*1-116	-1.2
1989	Bos-A	154	564	79	156	26	5	30	108	66	117	.277	.355	.500	855	130	22	1	2	-0	.996	4	*1-153/O-1(1-0-0)	1.5
1990	Atl-N	9	35	2	6	0	0	0	0	4	14	.171	.256	.171	428	19	-4	0	0	0	.944	-2	/1-9	-0.6
Total	8	810	2703	336	677	120	21	122	427	314	712	.250	.332	.446	778	109	32	18	14	-1	.993	-45	1-478,3-230/O-98L	-5.4
■ **NINO ESCALERA** Escalera, Saturnino Cuadrado b: 12/1/29, Santurce, P.R. BL/TR, 5'10", 165 lbs. Deb: 4/17/54																								
1954	Cin-N	73	69	15	11	1	1	0	3	7	11	.159	.237	.203	440	15	-9	1	0	0	.962	0	O-14(1-3-10)/1-8,S-1	-0.9
■ **JIM ESCHEN** Eschen, James Godrich b: 8/21/1891, Brooklyn, N.Y. d: 9/27/60, Sloatsburg, N.Y. BR/TR, 5'10.5", 160 lbs. Deb: 7/10/15 F																								
1915	Cle-A	15	42	11	10	1	0	0	2	5	9	.238	.319	.262	581	73	-1	0	1	-0	.968	1	O-10(0-10-0)	-0.1
■ **LARRY ESCHEN** Eschen, Lawrence Edward b: 9/22/20, Suffern, N.Y. BR/TR, 6', 180 lbs. Deb: 6/16/42 F																								
1942	Phi-A	12	11	0	0	0	0	0	0	4	6	.000	.267	.000	267	-22	-2	0	0	0	.824	-1	/S-7,2-1	-0.3
■ **ANGEL ESCOBAR** Escobar, Angel Rubenque (Rivas) b: 5/12/65, LaSabana, Venez. BB/TR, 6', 160 lbs. Deb: 5/17/88																								
1988	SF-N	3	3	1	1	0	0	0	0	0	0	.333	.333	.333	667	96	-0	0	0	0	1.000	0	/S-1,3-1	0.0
■ **JOSE ESCOBAR** Escobar, Jose Elias (Sanchez) b: 10/30/60, Las Flores, Venez. BR/TR, 5'10", 140 lbs. Deb: 4/13/91																								
1991	Cle-A	10	15	0	3	0	0	0	1	1	4	.200	.250	.200	450	26	-1	0	0	0	1.000	2	/S-5,2-4,3-1	0.0
■ **JIMMY ESMOND** Esmond, James Joseph b: 10/8/1889, Albany, N.Y. d: 6/26/48, Troy, N.Y. BR/TR, 5'11", 167 lbs. Deb: 4/20/11																								
1911	Cin-N	73	198	27	54	4	6	1	11	17	30	.273	.330	.369	699	99	-1	7			.918	1	S-44,3-14/2-2	0.3
1912	Cin-N	82	231	24	45	5	3	1	40	20	31	.195	.259	.255	514	42	-19	11			.930	-7	S-74	-2.1
1914	Ind-F	151	542	74	160	23	**15**	2	49	40	48	.295	.344	.404	748	93	-13	25			.919	-7	*S-151	-1.0
1915	New-F	155	569	79	147	20	10	5	62	59	54	.258	.329	.355	684	98	-11	18			.939	6	*S-155	0.6
Total	4	461	1540	204	406	52	34	9	162	136	163	.264	.324	.359	683	88	-43	61			.929	-8	S-424/3-14,2-2	-2.2
■ **JUAN ESPINO** Espino, Juan (Reyes) b: 3/16/56, Bonao, D.R. BR/TR, 6'1", 190 lbs. Deb: 6/25/82																								
1982	NY-A	3	2	0	0	0	0	0	0	0	1	.000	.000	.000	0	-99	-1	0	0	0	1.000	0	/C-3	0.0
1983	NY-A	10	23	1	6	0	0	1	3	1	5	.261	.292	.391	683	89	-0	0	0	0	1.000	-0	C-10	0.0
1985	NY-A	9	11	0	4	0	0	0	0	0	0	.364	.364	.364	727	102	0	0	0	0	1.000	1	/C-9	0.1
1986	NY-A	27	37	1	6	2	0	0	5	2	9	.162	.205	.216	421	15	-4	0	0	0	.987	3	C-27	-0.1
Total	4	49	73	2	16	2	0	1	8	3	15	.219	.250	.288	538	48	-5	0	0	0	.993	4	/C-49	0.0
■ **ALVARO ESPINOZA** Espinoza, Alvaro Alberto b: 2/19/62, Valencia, Venez. BR/TR, 6', 181 lbs. Deb: 9/14/84																								
1984	Min-A	1	0	0	0	0	0	0	0	0	0	—	—	—	—	—	0	0	0	0	.000	0	/S-1	0.0
1985	Min-A	32	57	5	15	2	0	0	9	1	9	.263	.288	.298	586	58	-3	0	1	-0	.949	7	S-31	0.5
1986	Min-A	37	42	4	9	1	0	0	1	1	10	.214	.233	.238	471	28	-4	0	1	-0	.941	6	2-19,S-18	0.3
1988	NY-A	3	3	0	0	0	0	0	0	0	0	.000	.000	.000	0	-99	-1	0	0	0	1.000	1	/2-2,S-1	0.0
1989	NY-A	146	503	51	142	23	1	0	41	14	60	.282	.303	.332	635	80	-14	3	3	-0	.970	17	*S-146	1.3
1990	NY-A	150	438	31	98	12	2	2	20	16	54	.224	.259	.274	533	49	-30	1	2	-0	.977	**21**	*S-150	0.1
1991	NY-A	148	480	51	123	23	2	5	33	16	57	.256	.283	.344	627	72	-19	4	1	1	.969	20	*S-147/3-2,P-1	1.2
1993	Cle-A	129	263	34	73	15	0	4	27	8	36	.278	.301	.380	682	82	-7	2	2	-0	.937	1	3-99,S-35/2-2	-0.4
1994	Cle-A	90	231	27	55	13	0	1	19	6	33	.238	.261	.307	568	46	-19	1	3	-1	.915	24	3-37,S-36,2-20,/1-3	0.7
1995	*Cle-A	66	143	15	36	4	0	2	17	2	16	.252	.267	.322	589	52	-10	0	2	-1	.966	9	2-22,3-22,S-19,/1D	-0.1
1996	Cle-A	59	112	12	25	4	2	4	11	6	18	.223	.281	.402	683	70	-6	1	1	-0	.947	4	3-20,1-18,S-16,/2D	-0.2
	NY-N	48	134	19	41	7	2	4	16	4	19	.306	.326	.478	804	114	2	0	2	-1	.900	-6	3-38/S-7,2-2,1-1	-0.4
1997	Sea-A	33	72	3	13	1	0	0	7	2	12	.181	.213	.194	408	7	-10	1	1	-0	.965	4	S-17,2-14/3-1	-0.4
Total	12	942	2478	252	630	105	9	22	201	76	324	.254	.281	.331	611	66	-120	13	19	-4	.971	108	S-624,3-219/2-86,1DP	2.6
■ **SAMMY ESPOSITO** Esposito, Samuel b: 12/15/31, Chicago, Ill. BR/TR, 5'9", 165 lbs. Deb: 9/28/52																								
1952	Chi-A	1	4	0	1	0	0	0	0	0	2	.250	.250	.250	500	39	-0	0	1	-0	.500	-1	/S-1	-0.2
1955	Chi-A	3	4	3	0	0	0	0	0	1	0	.000	.200	.000	200	-41	-1	0	0	0	1.000	-1	/3-2	-0.2
1956	Chi-A	81	184	30	42	8	2	3	25	41	19	.228	.374	.342	717	89	-1	1	2	-0	.962	4	3-61,S-19/2-3	0.2
1957	Chi-A	94	176	26	36	3	0	2	15	38	27	.205	.346	.256	601	66	-7	5	1	1	.960	16	3-53,S-22/2-4,O-1C	1.2
1958	Chi-A	98	81	16	20	3	0	0	3	12	6	.247	.358	.284	642	81	-2	1	1	-0	.979	11	3-63,S-22/2-2,O-1L	1.0
1959	*Chi-A	69	66	12	11	1	0	1	5	11	16	.167	.286	.227	513	43	-5	0	1	-0	.979	9	3-45,S-14/2-2	0.4
1960	Chi-A	57	77	14	14	5	0	1	11	10	20	.182	.276	.286	562	53	-5	0	0	0	.929	1	3-37,S-11/2-5	-0.4
1961	Chi-A	63	94	12	16	5	0	1	8	12	21	.170	.264	.255	519	40	-8	0	0	0	.976	12	3-28,S-20,2-11	0.5
1962	Chi-A	75	81	14	19	1	0	0	4	17	13	.235	.367	.247	614	69	-3	0	1	-0	.846	3	3-41,S-20/2-7	0.2
1963	Chi-A	1	0	0	0	0	0	0	0	0	0	—	—	—	—	—	0	0	0	0	.000	0	R	0.0
	KC-A	18	25	3	5	1	0	0	2	3	3	.200	.286	.240	526	47	-2	0	0	0	1.000	-2	/2-7,S-4,3-3	-0.3
	Yr	19	25	3	5	1	0	0	2	3	3	.200	.286	.240	526	47	-2	0	0	0	1.000	-2	/2-7,S-4,3-3	-0.3
Total	10	560	792	130	164	27	2	8	73	145	127	.207	.333	.277	609	66	-33	7	7	-1	.957	51	3-333,S-133/2-41,O	2.4
■ **CECIL ESPY** Espy, Cecil Edward b: 1/20/63, San Diego, Cal. BB/TR, 6'3", 195 lbs. Deb: 9/2/83 Career OF: (95-LF 263-CF 89-RF)																								
1983	LA-N	20	11	4	3	1	0	0	1	1	2	.273	.333	.364	697	94	-0	0	0	0	1.000	-5	O-15(0-15-0)	-0.5
1987	Tex-A	14	8	1	0	0	0	0	0	1	3	.000	.111	.000	111	-67	-2	2	0	0	1.000	-1	/O-8(5-0-3)	-0.2
1988	Tex-A	123	347	46	86	17	6	2	39	20	83	.248	.291	.349	639	76	-11	33	10	4	.972	-4	O-98L,D-12/S-3,C12	-1.3

YEAR	TM/L	G	AB	R	H	2B	3B	HR	RBI	BB	SO	AVG	OBP	SLG	OPS	OPS+	BR+	SB	CS	SBR	FA	FR	G/POS	TPR
1989	Tex-A	142	475	65	122	12	7	3	31	38	99	.257	.315	.331	645	81	-12	45	20	3	.990	-3	*O-133(3-131-1)/D-3	-1.3
1990	Tex-A	52	71	10	9	0	0	0	1	10	20	.127	.235	.127	361	4	-9	11	5	1	1.000	-7	O-39(4-28-9)/2-1,D-4	-1.6
1991	*Pit-N	43	82	7	20	4	0	1	11	5	17	.244	.287	.329	617	74	-3	4	0	1	.966	-3	O-35(2-25-11)	-0.6
1992	*Pit-N	112	194	21	50	7	3	1	20	15	40	.258	.311	.340	651	85	-4	6	3	0	.955	-20	O-82(11-18-56)	-2.7
1993	Cin-N	40	60	6	14	2	0	0	5	14	13	.233	.378	.267	645	76	-1	2	2	-0	.931	-1	O-18(18-0-1)	-0.3
Total	8	546	1248	160	304	43	16	7	108	104	277	.244	.303	.321	624	74	-42	103	40	9	.977	-43	O-428C/D-19,S-3,2C1	-8.5

■ CHUCK ESSEGIAN

Essegian, Charles Abraham b: 8/9/31, Boston, Mass. BR/TR, 5′11″, 202 lbs. Deb: 4/15/58

YEAR	TM/L	G	AB	R	H	2B	3B	HR	RBI	BB	SO	AVG	OBP	SLG	OPS	OPS+	BR+	SB	CS	SBR	FA	FR	G/POS	TPR
1958	Phi-N	39	114	15	28	5	2	5	16	12	34	.246	.317	.456	774	103	0	0	0	0	.952	1	O-30(28-2-0)	-0.1
1959	StL-N	17	39	2	7	2	1	0	5	1	13	.179	.200	.282	482	25	-4	0	0	0	1.000	-1	/O-9(9-0-0)	-0.6
	*LA-N	24	46	6	14	6	0	1	5	4	11	.304	.360	.500	860	118	1	0	0	0	1.000	-1	O-10(4-0-6)	-0.1
	Yr	41	85	8	21	8	1	1	10	5	24	.247	.289	.400	689	76	-3	0	0	0	1.000	-2	O-19(13-0-6)	-0.7
1960	LA-N	52	79	8	17	3	0	3	11	8	24	.215	.287	.367	654	73	-3	0	0	0	.968	0	O-18(13-0-5)	-0.4
1961	Bal-A	1	1	0	0	0	0	0	0	0	0	.000	.000	.000	0	-99	-0	0	0	0	.000	0	H	0.0
	KC-A	4	6	1	2	1	0	0	1	1	2	.333	.429	.500	929	145	0	0	0	0	1.000	0	/O-1(1-0-0)	0.1
	Cle-A	60	166	25	48	7	1	12	35	10	33	.289	.333	.560	894	138	8	0	0	0	.968	-2	O-49(16-19-16)	0.4
	Yr	65	173	26	50	8	1	12	36	11	35	.289	.335	.555	890	137	8	0	0	0	.969	-1	O-50(17-19-16)	0.5
1962	Cle-A	106	336	59	92	12	0	21	50	42	68	.274	.366	.497	863	134	16	0	0	0	.994	-4	O-90(88-1-1)	0.7
1963	KC-A	101	231	23	52	9	0	5	27	19	48	.225	.287	.329	616	68	-10	0	0	0	.990	-0	O-53(53-0-0)	-1.3
Total	6	404	1018	139	260	45	4	47	150	97	233	.255	.326	.446	772	106	8	0	0	0	.981	-7	O-260(212-22-28)	-1.3

■ JIM ESSIAN

Essian, James Sarkis b: 1/2/51, Detroit, Mich. BR/TR, 6′2″, 195 lbs. Deb: 9/15/73 M Career OF: (3-LF 0-CF 1-RF)

YEAR	TM/L	G	AB	R	H	2B	3B	HR	RBI	BB	SO	AVG	OBP	SLG	OPS	OPS+	BR+	SB	CS	SBR	FA	FR	G/POS	TPR
1973	Phi-N	2	3	0	0	0	0	0	0	0	1	.000	.000	.000	0	-97	-1	0	0	0	.000	0	/C-1	-0.1
1974	Phi-N	17	20	1	2	0	0	0	0	2	1	.100	.182	.100	282	-19	-3	0	0	0	.976	1	C-15/1-1,3-1	-0.2
1975	Phi-N	2	1	1	1	0	0	0	1	1	0	1.000	1.000	1.000	2000	439	1	0	0	0	1.000	0	/C-2	0.1
1976	Chi-A	78	199	20	49	7	0	0	21	23	28	.246	.327	.281	609	79	-4	2	1	0	.974	3	C-77/1-2,3-1	0.1
1977	Chi-A	114	322	50	88	18	2	10	44	52	35	.273	.376	.435	811	120	10	1	4	-1	.986	5	*C-111/3-2	1.8
1978	Oak-A	126	278	21	62	9	1	3	26	44	22	.223	.329	.295	624	81	-6	2	1	0	.981	14	*C-119/1-3,2-1,D-1	1.2
1979	Oak-A	98	313	34	76	16	0	8	40	25	29	.243	.303	.371	674	85	-7	0	1	-0	.981	9	C-70,3-10/1-4,OD	0.5
1980	Oak-A	87	285	19	66	11	0	5	29	30	18	.232	.305	.323	628	78	-9	1	3	-1	.987	6	C-68,D-11/1-1	-0.1
1981	Chi-A	27	52	6	16	3	0	0	5	4	5	.308	.357	.365	723	111	1	0	1	-0	.990	5	C-25/3-2	0.6
1982	Sea-A	48	153	14	42	8	0	3	20	11	7	.275	.327	.386	713	92	-2	2	0	1	.994	6	C-48	0.7
1983	Cle-A	48	93	11	19	4	0	2	11	16	8	.204	.321	.312	633	72	-3	0	1	-0	.989	3	C-47/3-1	0.1
1984	Oak-A	63	136	17	32	9	0	2	10	23	17	.235	.350	.346	696	100	1	1	1	-0	.985	11	C-59/3-1,D-1	1.3
Total	12	710	1855	194	453	85	3	33	207	231	171	.244	.330	.347	676	90	-22	9	13	-3	.984	63	C-642/3-18,D-16,1O2	6.0

■ BOBBY ESTALELLA

Estalella, Robert M b: 8/23/74, Hialeah, Fla. BR/TR, 6′1″, 200 lbs. Deb: 9/17/96 F

YEAR	TM/L	G	AB	R	H	2B	3B	HR	RBI	BB	SO	AVG	OBP	SLG	OPS	OPS+	BR+	SB	CS	SBR	FA	FR	G/POS	TPR
1996	Phi-N	7	17	5	6	0	0	2	4	1	6	.353	.389	.706	1095	179	2	1	0	0	1.000	-0	/C-4	0.2
1997	Phi-N	13	29	9	10	1	0	4	9	7	7	.345	.472	.793	1265	224	5	0	0	0	1.000	-4	C-11	0.2
1998	Phi-N	47	165	16	31	6	1	8	20	13	49	.188	.251	.382	633	63	-10	0	0	0	.988	-6	C-47	-1.3
1999	Phi-N	9	18	2	3	0	0	0	1	4	7	.167	.318	.167	485	27	-2	0	1	-0	.976	1	/C-7	-0.1
2000	*SF-N	106	299	45	70	22	3	14	53	57	92	.234	.360	.468	829	115	7	3	0	1	.993	9	*C-106	2.1
Total	5	182	528	77	120	29	4	28	87	82	161	.227	.334	.456	791	104	3	4	1	1	.991	-1	C-175	1.1

■ BOBBY ESTALELLA

Estalella, Roberto (Ventoza) b: 4/25/11, Cardenas, Cuba
d: 1/6/91, Hialeah, Fla. BR/TR, 5′8″, 180 lbs. Deb: 9/7/35 F Career OF: (211-LF 224-CF 55-RF)

YEAR	TM/L	G	AB	R	H	2B	3B	HR	RBI	BB	SO	AVG	OBP	SLG	OPS	OPS+	BR+	SB	CS	SBR	FA	FR	G/POS	TPR
1935	Was-A	15	51	7	16	2	0	2	10	17	7	.314	.485	.471	956	153	5	1	0	0	.895	2	3-15	0.8
1936	Was-A	13	9	2	2	0	2	0	0	4	5	.222	.462	.667	1128	186	1	0	0	0	.000	0	H	0.1
1939	Was-A	82	280	51	77	18	6	8	41	40	27	.275	.368	.468	835	121	9	2	3	-1	.964	-3	O-74(70-0-4)	0.1
1941	StL-A	46	83	7	20	6	1	0	14	18	13	.241	.376	.337	714	87	-1	0	0	0	1.000	-4	O-17(15-0-2)	-0.5
1942	Was-A	133	429	68	119	24	5	8	65	85	42	.277	.400	.413	813	130	21	5	2	0	.941	-14	3-78,O-36(17-2-17)	0.8
1943	Phi-A	117	367	43	95	14	4	11	63	52	44	.259	.352	.409	761	123	11	1	3	-1	.975	-1	O-97(95-1-1)	0.3
1944	Phi-A	140	506	54	151	17	9	7	60	59	60	.298	.374	.409	783	125	18	3	3	-0	.988	-2	*O-128(5-103-25)/1-6	1.0
1945	Phi-A	126	451	45	135	25	6	8	52	74	46	.299	.399	.435	834	142	26	1	6	-2	.988	1	*O-124(9-118-0)	2.3
1949	Phi-A	8	20	2	5	0	0	0	3	1	2	.250	.286	.250	536	44	-2	0	0	0	1.000	0	/O-6(0-0-6)	-0.2
Total	9	680	2196	279	620	106	33	44	308	350	246	.282	.383	.421	804	127	88	13	17	-3	.982	-21	O-482C/3-93,1-6	4.7

■ DUDE ESTERBROOK

Esterbrook, Thomas John b: 6/20/1857, Staten Is., N.Y.
d: 4/30/01, Middletown, N.Y. BR/TR, 5′11″, 167 lbs. Deb: 5/1/1880 M Career OF: (40-LF 24-CF 12-RF)

YEAR	TM/L	G	AB	R	H	2B	3B	HR	RBI	BB	SO	AVG	OBP	SLG	OPS	OPS+	BR+	SB	CS	SBR	FA	FR	G/POS	TPR
1880	Buf-N	64	253	20	61	12	1	0	35	0	15	.241	.241	.296	538	80	-6				.939	-3	1-47,O-15C/2-6,SC	-1.1
1882	Cle-N	45	179	13	44	4	3	0	19	5	12	.246	.266	.302	568	85	-3				.893	10	O-45(38-7-0)/1-1	0.5
1883	NY-a	97	407	55	103	9	7	0		15		.253	.280	.310	589	86	-7				.871	-4	*3-97	-0.9
1884	*NY-a	112	477	110	150	29	11	1		12		.314	.345	.428	772	154	28				.886	10	*3-112	3.5
1885	NY-N	88	359	48	92	14	5	2	44	4	28	.256	.264	.340	604	96	-2				.885	2	*3-84/O-4(1-0-3)	0.0
1886	NY-N	123	473	62	125	20	6	3	43	8	43	.264	.277	.351	627	89	-8	13			**.895**	-3	*3-123	-0.8
1887	NY-a	26	107	11	23	1	0	0	7	6		.215	.222	.178	400	13	-11	8			.950	-7	/1-9,O-7R,S-5,2-5	-1.6
1888	Ind-N	64	246	21	54	8	0	0	17	2	20	.220	.232	.252	484	53	-13	11			.976	-3	1-61/3-3	-2.2
	Lou-a	23	93	9	21	6	0	0	7	3		.226	.265	.290	556	80	-2	5			.962	0	1-23	-0.4
1889	Lou-a	11	44	8	14	3	0	0	9	5	2	.318	.400	.386	786	127	2	6			.931	-1	/1-8,O-2(0-0-2),S-1,M	0.0
1890	NY-N	45	197	29	57	14	1	0	29	10	8	.289	.333	.371	704	105	1	12			.984	0	1-45	-0.3
1891	Bro-N	3	8	1	3	0	0	0	0	0	1	.375	.444	.375	819	140	0	0			1.000	-1	/O-2(0-0-2),2-1	0.0
Total	11	701	2843	387	747	120	34	6	210	70	129	.263	.284	.334	618	94	-21	55			.884	-1	3-419,1-194/O2SC	-3.3

■ FRANK ESTRADA

Estrada, Francisco (Soto) b: 2/12/48, Navojoa, Mexico BR/TR, 5′8″, 182 lbs. Deb: 9/14/71

YEAR	TM/L	G	AB	R	H	2B	3B	HR	RBI	BB	SO	AVG	OBP	SLG	OPS	OPS+	BR+	SB	CS	SBR	FA	FR	G/POS	TPR
1971	NY-N	1	2	0	1	0	0	0	0	0	0	.500	.500	.500	1000	187	0	0	0	0	1.000	-1	/C-1	-0.1

■ ANDY ETCHEBARREN

Etchebarren, Andrew Auguste b: 6/20/43, Whittier, Cal. BR/TR, 6′1″, 197 lbs. Deb: 9/26/62 C

YEAR	TM/L	G	AB	R	H	2B	3B	HR	RBI	BB	SO	AVG	OBP	SLG	OPS	OPS+	BR+	SB	CS	SBR	FA	FR	G/POS	TPR
1962	Bal-A	2	6	0	2	0	0	0	1	0	2	.333	.333	.333	667	85	-0	0	0	0	.875	-1	/C-2	-0.1
1965	Bal-A	5	6	1	1	0	0	1	4	0	2	.167	.167	.667	833	123	0	0	0	0	1.000	3	/C-5	0.3
1966	*Bal-A☆	121	412	49	91	14	6	11	50	38	106	.221	.295	.364	659	89	-6	0	1	-0	.989	-4	*C-121	-0.4
1967	Bal-A☆	112	330	29	71	13	0	7	35	38	80	.215	.300	.318	618	83	-6	0	0	0	.989	0	*C-110	-0.1
1968	Bal-A	74	189	20	44	11	2	5	20	19	46	.233	.313	.392	704	112	3	0	0	0	.998	9	C-70	1.6
1969	*Bal-A	73	217	29	54	9	2	3	26	28	42	.249	.353	.350	703	96	-0	1	2	-0	.990	2	C-72	0.5
1970	*Bal-A	78	230	19	56	10	1	4	28	21	41	.243	.315	.348	663	82	-6	4	1	1	.984	2	C-76	-0.1
1971	*Bal-A	70	222	21	60	8	0	9	29	16	40	.270	.322	.428	750	112	3	1	4	-1	.986	2	C-70	0.7
1972	Bal-A	71	188	11	38	6	1	2	21	17	43	.202	.279	.277	555	64	-8	0	2	-1	.992	7	C-70	0.1
1973	*Bal-A	54	152	16	39	9	1	2	23	12	21	.257	.319	.368	688	94	-1	1	1	-0	.991	2	C-51	0.2
1974	*Bal-A	62	180	13	40	8	0	2	15	6	26	.222	.251	.300	551	60	-10	1	0	0	.976	6	C-60	-0.1
1975	Bal-A	8	20	0	4	1	0	0	3	0	3	.200	.200	.250	450	28	-2	0	0	0	1.000	0	/C-7	-0.1
	Cal-A	31	100	10	28	0	1	3	17	14	19	.280	.368	.390	758	123	3	1	0	0	.981	-4	C-31	0.1
	Yr	39	120	10	32	1	1	3	20	14	22	.267	.343	.367	710	108	1	1	0	0	.983	-3	C-38	0.0
1976	Cal-A	103	247	15	56	9	1	0	21	24	37	.227	.305	.271	577	74	-7	0	2	-1	.980	6	*C-102	0.1
1977	Cal-A	80	114	11	29	2	2	0	14	12	19	.254	.325	.307	632	77	-3	3	1	0	.987	1	C-80	0.0
1978	Mil-A	4	5	1	2	1	0	0	2	1	2	.400	.500	.600	1100	207	1	0	0	0	1.000	2	/C-4	0.3
Total	15	948	2618	245	615	101	17	49	309	246	529	.235	.308	.343	651	88	-40	13	14	-2	.987	32	C-931	3.0

■ BUCK ETCHISON

Etchison, Clarence Hampton b: 1/27/15, Baltimore, Md. d: 1/24/80, Cambridge, Md. BL/TL, 6′1″, 190 lbs. Deb: 9/22/43

YEAR	TM/L	G	AB	R	H	2B	3B	HR	RBI	BB	SO	AVG	OBP	SLG	OPS	OPS+	BR+	SB	CS	SBR	FA	FR	G/POS	TPR
1943	Bos-N	10	19	2	6	3	0	0	2	2	2	.316	.381	.474	855	148	1	0			.956	-1	/1-6	0.0
1944	Bos-N	109	308	30	66	16	0	8	33	33	50	.214	.292	.344	637	76	-10	1			.993	-1	1-85	-1.6
Total	2	119	327	32	72	19	0	8	35	35	52	.220	.298	.352	649	79	-9	1			.991	-2	/1-91	-1.6

YEAR	TM/L	G	AB	R	H	2B	3B	HR	RBI	BB	SO	AVG	OBP	SLG	OPS	OPS+	BR+	SB	CS	SBR	FA	FR	G/POS	TPR
■ **BOBBY ETHERIDGE**	Etheridge, Bobby Lamar "Luke" b: 11/25/42, Greenville, Miss. BR/TR, 5'9", 170 lbs. Deb: 7/16/67																							
1967	SF-N	40	115	13	26	7	2	1	15	7	12	.226	.299	.348	647	86	-2	0	0	0	.925	-1	3-37	-0.4
1969	SF-N	56	131	13	34	9	0	1	10	19	26	.260	.358	.351	709	101	1	0	0	0	.899	-2	3-39/S-1	-0.2
Total	2	96	246	26	60	16	2	2	25	26	38	.244	.331	.350	681	94	-1	0	0	0	.911	-4	/3-76,S-1	-0.6
■ **NICK ETTEN**	Etten, Nicholas Raymond Thomas b: 9/19/13, Spring Grove, Ill. d: 10/18/90, Hinsdale, Ill. BL/TL, 6'2", 198 lbs. Deb: 9/8/38																							
1938	Phi-A	22	81	6	21	6	2	0	11	9	7	.259	.333	.383	716	81	-3	1	0	0	.987	-2	1-22	-0.5
1939	Phi-A	43	155	20	39	11	2	3	29	16	11	.252	.322	.406	728	87	-4	0	0	0	.990	-3	1-41	-0.9
1941	Phi-N	151	540	78	168	27	4	14	79	82	33	.311	.405	.454	859	147	36	9			.984	-3	*1-150	2.0
1942	Phi-N	139	459	37	121	21	3	8	41	67	26	.264	.357	.375	732	120	13	3			.985	1	*1-135	0.1
1943	*NY-A	154	583	78	158	35	5	14	107	76	31	.271	.355	.420	775	126	19	3	7	-2	.989	-11	*1-154	-0.3
1944	NY-A	154	573	88	168	25	4	**22**	91	**97**	29	.293	.399	.466	865	142	34	4	2	0	.989	4	*1-154	3.1
1945	NY-A†	152	565	77	161	24	4	18	**111**	90	23	.285	.387	.437	824	133	26	2	3	-1	.989	-9	*1-152	0.8
1946	NY-A	108	323	37	75	14	1	9	49	38	35	.232	.315	.365	680	88	-5	0	1	-0	.991	-0	1-84	-0.9
1947	Phi-N	14	41	5	10	4	0	1	8	5	4	.244	.326	.415	741	99	-0	0			.990	1	1-11	0.1
Total	9	937	3320	426	921	167	25	89	526	480	199	.277	.371	.423	794	125	116	22	13		.988	-22	1-903	3.5
■ **FRED EUNICK**	Eunick, Fernandas Bowen b: 4/22/1892, Baltimore, Md. d: 12/9/59, Baltimore, Md. BR/TR, 5'6", 148 lbs. Deb: 8/29/17																							
1917	Cle-A	1	2	0	0	0	0	0	0	0	0	.000	.000	.000	0	-93	-0	0			1.000	-0	/3-1	-0.1
■ **TONY EUSEBIO**	Eusebio, Raul Antonio Bare (b: Raul Antontio Bare (Eusebio)) b: 4/27/67, San Jose De Los Llanos, D.R. BR/TR, 6'2", 180 lbs. Deb: 8/8/91																							
1991	Hou-N	10	19	4	2	1	0	0	0	6	8	.105	.320	.158	478	41	-1	0	0	0	.981	2	/C-9	0.1
1994	Hou-N	55	159	18	47	9	1	5	30	8	33	.296	.329	.459	788	108	1	0	1	-0	.993	-5	C-52	-0.1
1995	Hou-N	113	368	46	110	21	1	6	58	31	59	.299	.358	.410	769	110	5	0	2	-1	.993	-13	*C-103	-0.3
1996	Hou-N	58	152	15	41	7	2	1	19	18	20	.270	.347	.362	709	95	-1	0	1	-0	.996	-9	C-47	-0.8
1997	*Hou-N	60	164	12	45	2	0	1	18	19	27	.274	.364	.305	669	80	-4	0	1	-0	.987	-1	C-43	-0.3
1998	*Hou-N	66	182	13	46	6	1	1	36	18	31	.253	.323	.313	637	70	-7	1	0	0	.992	1	C-54	-0.3
1999	*Hou-N	103	323	31	88	15	0	4	33	40	67	.272	.353	.356	709	81	-8	0	0	0	.994	1	C-98	-0.2
2000	Hou-N	74	218	24	61	18	0	7	33	25	45	.280	.364	.459	823	100	0	0	0	0	.988	-5	C-68	-0.1
Total	8	539	1585	163	440	79	5	25	227	165	290	.278	.350	.381	731	93	-15	1	5	-2	.992	-29	C-474	-2.0
■ **FRANK EUSTACE**	Eustace, Frank John b: 11/7/1873, New York, N.Y. d: 10/16/32, Pottsville, Pa. 5'9", 160 lbs. Deb: 4/16/1896																							
1896	Lou-N	25	100	18	17	2	2	1	11	6	14	.170	.217	.260	477	26	-11	4			.841	-5	S-22/2-3	-1.3
■ **EVANS**	Evans Deb: 6/1/1875																							
1875	NH-n	1	4	1	2	0	0	0	1	0	0	.500	.500	.500	1000	285	1	0	0	0	.000	-0	/O-1(1-0-0)	0.0
■ **AL EVANS**	Evans, Alfred Hubert b: 9/28/16, Kenly, N.C. d: 4/6/79, Wilson, N.C. BR/TR, 5'11", 190 lbs. Deb: 9/13/39																							
1939	Was-A	7	21	2	7	0	0	0	1	5	2	.333	.462	.333	795	115	1	0	0	0	.964	-1	/C-6	0.1
1940	Was-A	14	25	1	8	2	0	0	7	6	7	.320	.452	.400	852	131	2	1	0	0	1.000	-1	/C-9	0.2
1941	Was-A	53	159	16	44	8	4	1	19	9	18	.277	.315	.396	712	91	-3	0	3	-1	.969	2	C-51	0.0
1942	Was-A	74	223	22	51	4	1	0	10	25	36	.229	.309	.256	565	60	-11	3	0	1	.961	-3	C-67	-1.0
1944	Was-A	14	22	5	2	0	0	0	0	2	6	.091	.167	.091	258	-27	-4	0	0	0	.933	-1	/C-8	-0.5
1945	Was-A	51	150	19	39	11	2	2	19	17	22	.260	.339	.400	739	125	4	2	1	0	.973	-6	C-41	0.1
1946	Was-A	88	272	30	69	10	4	2	30	30	28	.254	.332	.342	674	94	-2	1	2	-0	.966	-12	C-81	-1.1
1947	Was-A	99	319	17	77	8	3	2	23	28	25	.241	.303	.304	607	71	-13	2	1	0	.989	-2	C-94	-1.0
1948	Was-A	93	228	19	59	6	3	2	28	38	20	.259	.367	.338	705	91	-2	1	1	-0	.983	-3	C-85	-0.1
1949	Was-A	109	321	32	87	12	3	2	42	50	19	.271	.369	.346	715	92	-3	4	1	1	**.992**	-16	*C-107	-1.2
1950	Was-A	90	289	24	68	8	3	2	30	29	21	.235	.309	.304	614	61	-17	0	0	0	.987	-13	C-88	-2.5
1951	Bos-A	12	24	1	3	1	0	0	2	4	2	.125	.250	.167	417	13	-3	0	0	0	1.000	1	C-10	-0.2
Total	12	704	2053	188	514	70	23	13	211	243	206	.250	.332	.326	658	82	-50	14	9	-0	.979	-56	C-647	-7.2
■ **BARRY EVANS**	Evans, Barry Steven b: 11/30/56, Atlanta, Ga. BR/TR, 6'1", 180 lbs. Deb: 9/4/78																							
1978	SD-N	24	90	7	24	1	1	0	4	4	10	.267	.298	.300	598	73	-3	0	0	0	.947	1	3-24	-0.3
1979	SD-N	56	162	9	35	5	0	1	14	5	16	.216	.240	.265	505	40	-14	0	2	-1	.952	11	3-53/S-2,2-1	-0.4
1980	SD-N	73	125	11	29	3	2	1	14	17	21	.232	.324	.312	636	83	-2	1	1	-0	.983	-3	3-43,2-19/S-4,1-1	-0.5
1981	SD-N	54	93	11	30	5	0	0	7	9	9	.323	.382	.376	759	125	3	2	2	-0	.969	-4	3-24,1-10/2-6,S-2	-0.1
1982	NY-A	17	31	2	8	3	0	0	2	6	6	.258	.395	.355	750	109	1	0	0	0	1.000	1	/2-8,3-6,S-4	0.2
Total	5	224	501	40	126	17	3	2	41	41	62	.251	.309	.309	619	77	-16	3	5	-1	.960	7	3-150/2-34,S-12,1	-1.1
■ **DARRELL EVANS**	Evans, Darrell Wayne b: 5/26/47, Pasadena, Cal. BL/TR, 6'2", 205 lbs. Deb: 4/20/69 C Career OF: (84-LF 0-CF 0-RF)																							
1969	Atl-N	12	26	3	6	0	0	0	1	1	8	.231	.259	.231	490	38	-2	0	0	0	.917	-2	/3-6	-0.4
1970	Atl-N	12	44	4	14	1	1	0	9	7	5	.318	.423	.386	809	112	1	0	0	0	.941	-1	3-12	0.0
1971	Atl-N	89	260	42	63	11	1	12	38	39	54	.242	.343	.431	774	111	4	2	3	-1	.937	4	3-72/O-3(3-0-0)	0.7
1972	Atl-N	125	418	67	106	12	0	19	71	90	58	.254	.391	.419	809	119	14	4	2	0	.941	9	*3-123	2.4
1973	Atl-N★	161	595	114	167	25	8	41	104	**124**	104	.281	.407	.556	964	153	45	6	3	0	.953	8	*3-146,1-20	5.2
1974	Atl-N	160	571	99	137	21	3	25	79	**126**	88	.240	.383	.419	801	119	18	4	2	0	.955	16	*3-160	3.5
1975	Atl-N	156	567	82	138	22	2	22	73	105	106	.243	.364	.406	769	109	9	12	3	2	.938	23	*3-156/1-3	3.4
1976	Atl-N	44	139	11	24	0	0	1	10	30	33	.173	.320	.194	514	45	-9	3	0	1	.994	0	1-36/3-7	-1.1
	SF-N	92	257	42	57	9	1	10	36	42	38	.222	.331	.381	712	99	0	6	1	1	.991	9	1-83/3-5	0.4
	Yr	136	396	53	81	9	1	11	46	72	71	.205	.327	.316	643	80	-9	9	1	2	.992	9	*1-119,3-12	-0.7
1977	SF-N	144	461	64	117	18	3	17	72	69	50	.254	.355	.416	771	106	5	9	6	-0	.937	-1	O-81L,1-41,3-35	-0.1
1978	SF-N	159	547	82	133	24	2	20	78	105	64	.243	.365	.404	769	119	17	4	5	-1	.952	10	*3-155	2.4
1979	SF-N	160	562	68	142	23	2	17	70	91	80	.253	.359	.391	750	112	11	6	7	-1	.943	22	*3-159	3.1
1980	SF-N	154	556	69	147	23	0	20	78	83	65	.264	.362	.414	776	119	16	17	5	2	.946	17	*3-140,1-14	3.3
1981	SF-N	102	357	51	92	13	4	12	48	54	33	.258	.358	.417	776	122	11	2	3	-1	.953	7	3-87,1-12	1.6
1982	SF-N	141	465	64	119	20	4	16	61	77	64	.256	.364	.419	783	119	13	5	4	-0	.933	-2	3-84,1-49,S-13	0.8
1983	SF-N★	142	523	94	145	29	3	30	82	84	81	.277	.379	.516	896	151	36	6	6	-1	.993	1	*1-113,3-32/S-9	3.0
1984	*Det-A	131	401	60	93	11	1	16	63	77	70	.232	.356	.384	740	105	5	2	2	-0	.997	2	D-62,1-47,3-19	0.2
1985	Det-A	151	505	81	125	17	0	**40**	94	85	85	.248	.357	.519	876	137	26	0	4	-1	.984	11	*1-113,D-33/3-7	2.7
1986	Det-A	151	507	78	122	15	0	29	85	91	105	.241	.357	.442	799	116	13	3	2	-0	.998	11	*1-105,D-42/3-2	1.5
1987	*Det-A	150	499	90	128	20	0	34	99	100	84	.257	.383	.501	884	138	30	6	5	-0	.997	12	*1-105,D-44/3-7	3.1
1988	Det-A	144	437	48	91	9	0	22	64	84	89	.208	.337	.380	717	104	4	1	4	-1	.993	5	D-72,1-65	0.1
1989	Atl-N	107	276	31	57	6	1	11	39	41	46	.207	.309	.355	664	87	-4	0	1	-0	.985	6	1-50,3-28	-0.3
Total	21	2687	8973	1344	2223	329	36	414	1354	1605	1410	.248	.364	.431	795	119	265	98	68	-2	.946	165	*3-1442,1-856,D/OS	35.5
■ **DWIGHT EVANS**	Evans, Dwight Michael "Dewey" b: 11/3/51, Santa Monica, Cal. BR/TR, 6'2", 205 lbs. Deb: 9/16/72 C Career OF: (35-LF 32-CF 2092-RF)																							
1972	Bos-A	18	57	2	15	3	1	1	6	7	13	.263	.344	.404	747	115	1	0	0	0	1.000	1	O-17(16-0-1)	0.2
1973	Bos-A	119	282	46	63	13	1	10	32	40	52	.223	.322	.383	705	92	-3	5	0	1	.995	-6	*O-113(17-2-95)/D-2	-1.2
1974	Bos-A	133	463	60	130	19	8	10	70	38	77	.281	.338	.421	759	110	5	4	4	-1	.990	11	*O-122(1-3-120)/D-7	1.0
1975	*Bos-A	128	412	61	113	24	6	13	56	47	60	.274	.354	.456	811	118	9	3	4	-1	.987	18	*O-115(0-0-115)/D-7	2.2
1976	Bos-A	146	501	61	121	34	5	17	62	57	92	.242	.326	.431	757	107	4	6	7	-1	**.994**	9	*O-145(0-8-140)/D-1	0.6
1977	Bos-A	73	230	39	66	9	2	14	36	28	58	.287	.364	.526	890	125	8	4	2	0	.992	-2	O-63(0-14-54)/D-6	0.3
1978	Bos-A★	147	497	75	123	24	2	24	63	65	119	.247	.337	.449	786	108	5	8	5	0	.982	8	*O-142(0-3-140)/D-4	0.5
1979	Bos-A	152	489	69	134	24	1	21	58	69	76	.274	.365	.456	821	114	10	6	9	-2	.988	10	*O-149(0-0-149)	1.0
1980	Bos-A	148	463	72	123	37	5	18	60	64	98	.266	.361	.484	845	123	15	3	1	0	.982	2	*O-144(0-1-144)/D-2	1.0
1981	Bos-A★	108	412	84	122	19	4	**22**	71	**85**	85	.296	.418	.522	**940**	160	**34**	3	2	-0	.993	14	*O-108(1-0-107)	4.3
1982	Bos-A	162	609	122	178	37	7	32	98	112	125	.292	**.403**	.534	937	146	41	3	2	-0	.973	6	*O-161(0-0-161)/D-1	3.8
1983	Bos-A	126	470	74	112	19	4	22	58	70	97	.238	.339	.436	776	104	3	3	0	1	.987	7	O-99(0-0-99),D-21	0.5
1984	Bos-A	162	630	**121**	186	37	8	32	104	96	115	.295	.392	.532	**924**	146	41	3	1	0	.994	2	*O-161(0-0-161)/D-1	3.4
1985	Bos-A	159	617	110	162	29	1	29	78	**114**	105	.263	.382	.454	836	123	22	7	2	1	.990	3	*O-152(0-0-152)/D-7	1.7

YEAR	TM/L	G	AB	R	H	2B	3B	HR	RBI	BB	SO	AVG	OBP	SLG	OPS	OPS+	BR+	SB	CS	SBR	FA	FR	G/POS	TPR
1986	*Bos-A	152	529	86	137	33	2	26	97	97	117	.259	.380	.476	856	131	25	3	3	-0	.983	5	*O-149(0-0-149)/D-1	2.0
1987	Bos-A★	154	541	109	165	37	2	34	123	**106**	98	.305	.422	.569	991	155	46	4	6	-1	.982	-7	1-79,O-77(0-0-77)/D-4	2.7
1988	*Bos-A	149	559	96	164	31	7	21	111	76	99	.293	.379	.487	866	135	27	5	1	1	.987	-6	O-85(0-1-84),1-64/D-6	1.5
1989	Bos-A	146	520	82	148	27	3	20	100	99	84	.285	.402	.463	865	135	27	3	3	-0	.981	2	O-77(0-0-77),D-69	2.4
1990	*Bos-A	123	445	66	111	18	3	13	63	67	73	.249	.353	.391	744	103	3	3	4	-1	.000	0	*D-122	-0.1
1991	Bal-A	101	270	35	73	9	1	6	38	54	54	.270	.396	.378	773	120	10	2	3	-1	.984	0	O-67(0-0-67),D-21	0.7
Total	20	2606	8996	1470	2446	483	73	385	1384	1391	1697	.272	.373	.470	843	126	335	78	59	-3	.987	76	*O-2146R,D-282,1-143	28.5
■ **JOE EVANS** Evans, Joseph Patton "Doc" b: 5/15/1895, Meridian, Miss. d: 8/9/53, Gulfport, Miss. BR/TR, 5'9", 160 lbs. Deb: 7/3/15 Career OF: (172-LF 85-CF 54-RF)																								
1915	Cle-A	42	109	17	28	4	2	0	11	22	18	.257	.382	.330	712	111	2	6	1	1	.885	-0	3-30/2-2	0.4
1916	Cle-A	33	82	4	12	1	0	0	1	7	12	.146	.213	.159	372	11	-9	4			.915	4	3-28	-0.5
1917	Cle-A	132	385	36	73	4	5	2	33	42	44	.190	.271	.242	513	53	-22	12			.939	3	*3-127	-1.7
1918	Cle-A	79	243	38	64	6	7	1	22	30	29	.263	.344	.358	702	102	1	7			.932	4	3-74	0.8
1919	Cle-A	21	14	9	1	0	0	0	0	2	1	.071	.188	.071	259	-24	-2	1			.923	4	/S-6	0.1
1920	*Cle-A	56	172	32	60	9	9	0	23	15	3	.349	.404	.506	910	136	9	6	2	1	.966	-3	O-43(43-0-0)/S-6	0.5
1921	Cle-A	57	153	36	51	11	0	0	21	19	5	.333	.410	.405	816	107	3	4	1	1	.933	-1	O-47(47-0-0)	0.0
1922	Cle-A	75	145	35	39	6	2	0	22	8	4	.269	.307	.338	645	67	-7	11	2	2	.969	-7	O-49(30-17-3)	-1.4
1923	Was-A	106	372	42	98	15	3	0	38	27	18	.263	.313	.320	633	70	-16	6	4	-0	.982	-4	O-72(2-65-5),3-21/1-5	-2.2
1924	StL-A	77	209	30	53	3	3	0	19	24	12	.254	.330	.297	627	59	-12	4	4	-1	.969	2	O-49(38-1-10)	-1.4
1925	StL-A	55	159	27	50	12	0	0	20	16	6	.314	.377	.390	767	90	-2	6	2	1	1.000	-1	O-47(12-2-36)	-0.5
Total	11	733	2043	306	529	71	31	3	210	212	152	.259	.329	.328	658	79	-56	67	16		.971	0	O-307L,3-280/S-12,12	-5.9
■ **STEVE EVANS** Evans, Louis Richard b: 2/17/1885, Cleveland, Ohio d: 12/28/43, Cleveland, Ohio BL/TL, 5'10", 175 lbs. Deb: 4/16/08																								
1908	NY-N	2	2	0	1	0	0	0	0	0		.500	.500	.500	1000	209	0	0			.000	-1	/O-1(0-1-0)	0.0
1909	StL-N	143	498	67	129	17	6	2	56	66		.259	.362	.329	691	122	16	14			.947	-4	*O-141(0-0-141)/1-2	0.6
1910	StL-N	151	506	73	122	21	8	2	73	78	63	.241	.376	.326	702	109	11	10			.968	-6	*O-141(0-0-141),1-10	-0.2
1911	StL-N	154	547	74	161	24	13	5	71	46	52	.294	.369	.413	782	122	16	13			.972	-2	*O-150(0-0-150)	0.6
1912	StL-N	135	491	59	139	23	9	6	72	36	51	.283	.353	.403	756	109	6	11			.942	-0	*O-134(0-0-134)	-0.2
1913	StL-N	97	245	18	61	15	6	1	31	20	28	.249	.321	.371	692	99	-1	5			.983	-6	O-74(2-1-71)/1-1	-1.0
1914	Bro-F	145	514	93	179	41	**15**	12	96	50	49	.348	.416	**.556**	973	**165**	**38**	18			.941	-5	*O-112(36-1-76),1-27	2.8
1915	Bro-F	63	216	44	64	14	4	3	30	35	22	.296	.411	.440	851	140	10	7			.960	-2	O-61(0-0-61)/1-1	0.5
	Bal-F	88	340	50	107	20	6	1	37	28	34	.315	.379	.418	796	120	5	8			.925	-6	O-88(0-0-88)/1-4	-0.6
	Yr	151	556	94	171	**34**	10	4	67	63	56	.308	.392	.426	818	128	15	15			.940	-8	*O-149(0-0-149)/1-5	-0.1
Total	8	978	3359	478	963	175	67	32	466	359	299	.287	.374	.407	782	125	102	86			.955	-31	O-902(38-3-862)/1-45	2.5
■ **TOM EVANS** Evans, Thomas John b: 7/9/74, Kirkland, Wash. BR/TR, 6'1", 200 lbs. Deb: 9/2/97																								
1997	Tor-A	12	38	7	11	2	0	1	2	2	10	.289	.341	.421	763	97	-0	0	1	-0	.917	1	3-12	0.0
1998	Tor-A	7	10	0	0	0	0	0	0	1	2	.000	.091	.000	91	-73	-3	0	0	0	.889	-0	/3-7	-0.3
2000	Tex-A	23	54	10	15	4	0	0	5	10	13	.278	.400	.352	752	90	-0	0	3	-1	.909	4	3-21/1-1,D-1	0.3
Total	3	42	102	17	26	6	0	1	7	13	25	.255	.350	.343	694	77	-3	0	4	-1	.910	5	/3-40,D-1,1-1	0.0
■ **JAKE EVANS** Evans, Uriah L. P. "Bloody Jake" b: 9/1856, Baltimore, Md. d: 1/16/07, Baltimore, Md. TR, 5'8", 154 lbs. Deb: 5/1/1879 Career OF: (25-LF 17-CF 411-RF)																								
1879	Tro-N	72	280	30	65	9	5	0	17	5	18	.232	.246	.300	546	84	-4				.884	18	*O-72(2-7-64)	1.2
1880	Tro-N	47	180	31	46	8	1	0	22	7	15	.256	.283	.311	595	96	-1				.906	0	O-47(0-6-41)/P-1	-0.1
1881	Tro-N	83	315	35	76	11	5	0	28	14	30	.241	.274	.308	581	78	-8				.926	14	*O-83(0-0-83)	0.6
1882	Wor-N	80	334	33	71	10	4	0	25	7	22	.213	.229	.266	495	57	-16				.910	20	*O-68R,S-11/3-1,2P	0.4
1883	Cle-N	90	332	36	79	13	2	0	31	8	38	.238	.256	.289	545	66	-13				.902	6	*O-86R/S-3,3-3,2P	-0.7
1884	Cle-N	80	313	32	81	18	3	1	38	15	49	.259	.293	.345	638	97	-2				**.917**	8	*O-76R/2-4,S-2	0.5
1885	Bal-a	20	77	18	17	1	1	0	7	7		.221	.318	.260	578	85	-1				.894	2	O-20(0-0-20)	0.1
Total	7	472	1831	215	435	70	21	1	168	63	172	.238	.264	.300	565	78	-44				.907	67	O-452R/S-16,2-6,3P	2.0
■ **CARL EVERETT** Everett, Carl Edward b: 6/3/71, Tampa, Fla. BB/TR, 6', 190 lbs. Deb: 7/1/93																								
1993	Fla-N	11	19	0	2	0	0	0	0	1	9	.105	.150	.105	255	-29	-3	1	0	0	.857	-3	/O-8(0-8-0)	-0.6
1994	Fla-N	16	51	7	11	1	0	2	6	3	15	.216	.259	.353	612	56	-3	4	0	1	1.000	-0	O-16(1-8-8)	-0.3
1995	NY-N	79	289	48	75	13	1	12	54	39	67	.260	.352	.436	788	110	4	2	5	-1	.981	5	O-77(0-10-68)	0.4
1996	NY-N	101	192	29	46	8	1	1	16	21	53	.240	.327	.307	634	72	-7	6	0	1	.935	-3	O-55(8-15-37)	-1.0
1997	NY-N	142	443	58	110	28	3	14	57	32	102	.248	.309	.420	729	92	-7	17	9	1	.971	-9	*O-128(9-71-65)	-1.7
1998	*Hou-N	133	467	72	138	34	4	15	76	44	102	.296	.360	.482	842	122	15	14	12	-1	.987	13	*O-123(0-121-5)	2.7
1999	*Hou-N	123	464	86	151	33	3	25	108	50	94	.325	.404	.571	975	145	32	27	7	3	.978	1	*O-121(2-118-16)/D-2	3.5
2000	Bos-A★	137	496	82	149	32	4	34	108	52	113	.300	.376	.587	963	133	24	11	4	1	.980	3	*O-126(0-126-0)/D-5	2.7
Total	8	742	2421	382	682	149	16	103	425	242	555	.282	.355	.484	840	116	54	82	37	5	.976	6	O-654(20-477-199)/D-7	5.7
■ **BILL EVERITT** Everitt, William Lee "Wild Bill" b: 12/13/1868, Ft.Wayne, Ind. d: 1/19/38, Denver, Colo. BL/TR, 6'0.5", 185 lbs. Deb: 4/18/1895 Career OF: (31-LF 10-CF 2-RF)																								
1895	Chi-N	133	550	129	197	16	10	3	88	33	42	.358	.399	.440	839	109	7	47			.854	-8	*3-130/2-3	0.1
1896	Chi-N	132	575	130	184	16	13	2	46	41	43	.320	.367	.403	771	99	-2	46			.882	-10	*3-97,O-35(27-6-2)	-1.1
1897	Chi-N	92	379	63	119	14	7	5	39	36		.314	.373	.427	801	107	3	26			.864	-5	3-83/O-8(4-4-0)	-0.1
1898	Chi-N	149	596	102	190	15	6	0	69	53		.319	.377	.364	741	113	11	28			.974	-2	*1-149	0.8
1899	Chi-N	136	536	87	166	17	5	1	74	31		.310	.351	.366	717	99	-1	30			.971	8	*1-136	0.6
1900	Chi-N	23	91	10	24	4	0	0	17	3		.264	.287	.308	595	67	-4	2			.979	-1	1-23	-0.5
1901	Was-A	33	115	14	22	3	2	0	8	15		.191	.301	.252	553	55	-6	7			.967	-4	1-33	-1.0
Total	7	698	2842	535	902	85	43	11	341	212	85	.317	.368	.389	757	103	8	186			.973	-23	1-341,3-310/O-43L,2	-1.2
■ **JOHNNY EVERS** Evers, John Joseph "Crab" or "Trojan" b: 7/21/1881, Troy, N.Y. d: 3/28/47, Albany, N.Y. BL/TR, 5'9", 125 lbs. Deb: 9/1/02 FMCH																								
1902	Chi-N	26	90	7	20	0	0	0	2	3		.222	.263	.222	485	51	-5	1			.990	-1	2-18/S-8	-0.6
1903	Chi-N	124	464	70	136	27	7	0	52	19		.293	.325	.381	707	104	1	25			.937	-14	*2-110,S-11/3-2	-1.2
1904	Chi-N	152	532	49	141	14	7	0	47	28		.265	.307	.318	624	93	-5	26			.943	31	*2-152	2.9
1905	Chi-N	99	340	44	94	11	2	1	37	27		.276	.333	.329	663	94	-2	19			.937	3	2-99	0.1
1906	*Chi-N	154	533	65	136	17	6	1	51	36		.255	.305	.315	620	88	-8	49			.947	6	*2-153/3-1	-0.1
1907	*Chi-N	151	508	66	127	18	4	2	51	38		.250	.309	.313	622	89	-6	46			.964	**28**	*2-151	2.5
1908	*Chi-N	126	416	83	125	19	6	0	37	66		.300	.402	.375	777	143	23	36			.960	-0	*2-122/O-1(0-0-1)	2.8
1909	Chi-N	127	463	88	122	19	6	1	24	73		.263	.369	.337	705	116	12	28			.942	3	*2-126	1.7
1910	Chi-N	125	433	87	114	11	7	0	28	108	18	.263	.413	.321	734	115	16	28			.950	-4	*2-125	1.4
1911	Chi-N	46	155	29	35	4	3	0	7	34	10	.226	.372	.290	662	86	-1	6			.975	-6	2-33,3-11	-0.6
1912	Chi-N	143	478	73	163	23	11	1	63	74	18	.341	**.431**	.441	873	139	29	16			.959	6	*2-143	3.7
1913	Chi-N	136	446	81	127	20	5	3	49	50	14	.285	.361	.372	733	109	7	11			.960	**30**	*2-136,M	**3.9**
1914	*Bos-N	139	491	81	137	20	3	1	40	87	26	.279	.390	.338	728	118	16	12			**.976**	5	*2-139	2.4
1915	Bos-N	83	278	38	73	4	1	1	22	50	16	.263	.375	.295	670	109	6	7	8	-1	.959	-2	2-82	0.5
1916	Bos-N	71	241	33	52	4	1	0	15	40	19	.216	.330	.241	570	80	-4	5			.951	-18	2-71	-2.3
1917	Bos-N	24	83	5	16	0	0	0	0	13	8	.193	.302	.193	495	56	-4	1			.950	-7	2-24	-1.2
	Phi-N	56	183	20	41	5	1	1	12	30	13	.224	.333	.279	612	85	-2	8			.983	-5	2-49/3-7	-0.7
	Yr	80	266	25	57	5	1	1	12	43	21	.214	.324	.252	576	77	-5	9			.973	-12	2-73/3-7	-1.9
1922	Chi-A	1	3	0	0	0	0	0	1	2	0	.000	.400	.000	400	12	-0	0	0	0	1.000	-0	/2-1	0.0
1929	Bos-N	1	0	0	0	0	0	0	0	0	0	—	—	—	—	—	0	0			.000	-1	/2-1	-0.1
Total	18	1784	6137	919	1659	216	70	12	538	778	142	.270	.356	.334	690	106	72	324	8		.955	53	*2-1735/3-21,S-19,O	15.1
■ **JOE EVERS** Evers, Joseph Francis b: 9/10/1891, Troy, N.Y. d: 1/4/49, Albany, N.Y. BR/TR, 5'9", 135 lbs. Deb: 4/24/13 F																								
1913	NY-N	1	0	0	0	0	0	0	0	0	0	—	—	—	—	—	0	0			.000	0	R	0.0
■ **TOM EVERS** Evers, Thomas Francis b: 3/31/1852, Troy, N.Y. d: 3/23/25, Washington, D.C. TL, Deb: 5/25/1882																								
1882	Bal-a	1	4	0	0	0	0	0		0		.000	.000	.000	0	-99	-1				.500	-2	/2-1	-0.3

YEAR	TM/L	G	AB	R	H	2B	3B	HR	RBI	BB	SO	AVG	OBP	SLG	OPS	OPS+	BR+	SB	CS	SBR	FA	FR	G/POS	TPR
1884	Was-U	109	427	54	99	6	1	0		7		.232	.244	.251	495	52	-37				.869	11	*2-109	-1.9
Total	2	110	431	54	99	6	1	0		7		.230	.242	.248	490	51	-38				.866	9	2-110	-2.2

■ HOOT EVERS

Evers, Walter Arthur b: 2/8/21, St.Louis, Mo. d: 1/25/91, Houston, Tex. BR/TR, 6'2", 185 lbs. Deb: 9/16/41 C

YEAR	TM/L	G	AB	R	H	2B	3B	HR	RBI	BB	SO	AVG	OBP	SLG	OPS	OPS+	BR+	SB	CS	SBR	FA	FR	G/POS	TPR
1941	Det-A	1	4	0	0	0	0	0	0	0	2	.000	.000	.000	0	-91	-1	0	0	0	.000	-0	/O-1(0-0-1)	-0.2
1946	Det-A	81	304	42	81	8	4	4	33	34	43	.266	.344	.359	703	91	-3	7	1	1	.975	0	O-76(1-76-0)	-0.4
1947	Det-A	126	460	67	136	24	5	10	67	45	49	.296	.366	.435	801	119	11	8	7	-1	.978	8	*O-123(0-123-0)	1.5
1948	Det-A★	139	538	81	169	33	6	10	103	51	31	.314	.378	.454	831	117	12	3	4	-1	.973	2	*O-138(0-138-0)	1.0
1949	Det-A	132	432	68	131	21	6	7	72	70	38	.303	.403	.428	831	120	14	6	7	-1	.994	11	*O-123(81-42-2)	1.6
1950	Det-A★	143	526	100	170	35	**11**	21	103	71	40	.323	.408	.551	959	139	30	5	9	-2	**.997**	8	*O-139(139-3-0)	2.3
1951	Det-A	116	393	47	88	15	2	11	46	40	47	.224	.297	.356	653	76	-14	5	3	0	.976	-4	*O-108(66-45-1)	-2.4
1952	Det-A	1	1	0	1	0	0	0	0	0	0	1.000	1.000	1.000	2000	454	0	0	0	0	.000	0	H	0.0
	Bos-A	106	401	53	105	17	4	14	59	29	55	.262	.318	.429	747	99	-2	5	2	0	.974	-5	*O-105(90-12-20)	-1.4
	Yr	107	402	53	106	17	4	14	59	29	55	.264	.320	.430	750	100	-2	5	2	0	.974	-5	*O-105(90-12-20)	-1.4
1953	Bos-A	99	300	39	72	10	1	11	31	23	41	.240	.301	.390	691	81	-9	2	1	0	.988	-7	O-93(78-16-0)	-2.1
1954	Bos-A	6	8	1	0	0	0	0	0	0	2	.000	.000	.000	0	-90	-2	0	0	0	1.000	-0	/O-1(1-0-0)	-0.2
	NY-N	12	11	1	1	0	0	1	3	0	6	.091	.091	.364	455	12	-2	0	0	0	1.000	-1	/O-4(2-2-0)	-0.3
	Det-A	30	60	5	11	4	0	0	5	5	8	.183	.258	.250	508	40	-5	1	0	0	1.000	-4	O-24(17-2-6)	-1.0
1955	Bal-A	60	185	21	44	10	1	6	30	19	28	.238	.309	.400	709	96	-2	2	1	0	.991	-4	O-55(10-16-31)	-0.8
	Cle-A	39	66	10	19	7	1	2	9	3	12	.288	.319	.515	834	117	1	0	1	-0	1.000	-4	O-25(15-9-2)	-0.4
	Yr	99	251	31	63	17	2	8	39	22	40	.251	.311	.430	742	101	-1	2	2	-0	.993	-8	O-80(25-25-33)	-1.2
1956	Cle-A	3	0	1	0	0	0	0	0	1	0	—	1.000	—	1000	180	0	0	0	0	.000	0	H	0.0
	Bal-A	48	112	20	27	3	0	1	4	24	18	.241	.375	.295	670	85	-1	1	0	0	.985	-3	O-36(3-2-34)	-0.5
	Yr	51	112	21	27	3	0	1	4	25	18	.241	.380	.295	674	86	-1	1	0	0	.985	-3	O-36(3-2-34)	-0.5
Total	12	1142	3801	556	1055	187	41	98	565	415	420	.278	.353	.426	778	106	28	45	36	-3	.983	-4	*O-1051(503-486-97)	-3.3

■ GEORGE EWELL

Ewell, George W. b: 2/1851, Philadelphia, Pa. d: 10/20/10, Philadelphia, Pa. Deb: 6/26/1871

YEAR	TM/L	G	AB	R	H	2B	3B	HR	RBI	BB	SO	AVG	OBP	SLG	OPS	OPS+	BR+	SB	CS	SBR	FA	FR	G/POS	TPR
1871	Cle-n	1	3	0	0	0	0	0	0	0	0	.000	.000	.000	0	-99	-1	0	0	0	1.000	-0	/O-1(0-0-1)	-0.1

■ JOHN EWING

Ewing, John "Long Jong" b: 6/1/1863, Cincinnati, Ohio d: 4/23/1895, Denver, Colo. TR, Deb: 6/18/1883 F

YEAR	TM/L	G	AB	R	H	2B	3B	HR	RBI	BB	SO	AVG	OBP	SLG	OPS	OPS+	BR+	SB	CS	SBR	FA	FR	G/POS	TPR
1883	StL-a	1	5	0	0	0	0	0		0		.000	.000	.000	0	-95	-1				.333	-1	/O-1(0-1-0)	-0.2
1884	Cin-U	1	4	0	0	0	0	0		0		.000	.000	.000	0	-93	-1				1.000	-0	/O-1(0-0-1)	-0.1
	Was-U	1	5	1	1	0	1	0		0		.200	.200	.600	800	138	0				.500	0	/O-1(0-1-0)	0.0
	Yr	2	9	1	1	0	1	0		0		.111	.111	.333	444	29	-1				.600	0	/O-2(0-1-1)	-0.1
1888	Lou-a	21	79	6	16	1	1	0	5	1		.203	.213	.241	453	46	-5	7			.907	0	P-21	0.0
1889	Lou-a	41	134	12	23	2	0	0	6	9	30	.172	.234	.187	421	21	-14	5			.953	2	P-40/1-1	0.0
1890	NY-P	35	114	18	24	2	1	2	17	5	35	.211	.244	.298	542	41	-10	2			.949	0	P-35	0.0
1891	NY-N	33	113	10	23	1	0	0	8	3	14	.204	.224	.212	437	28	-10	4			.917	0	P-33	0.0
Total	6	133	454	47	87	6	3	2	36	18	79	.192	.226	.231	457	31	-41	18			.935	2	P-129/O-3(0-2-1),1-1	-0.3

■ REUBEN EWING

Ewing, Reuben (b: Reuben Cohen) b: 11/30/1899, Odessa, Russia d: 10/5/70, W.Hartford, Conn. BR/TR, 5'4.5", 150 lbs. Deb: 6/21/21

YEAR	TM/L	G	AB	R	H	2B	3B	HR	RBI	BB	SO	AVG	OBP	SLG	OPS	OPS+	BR+	SB	CS	SBR	FA	FR	G/POS	TPR
1921	StL-N	3	1	0	0	0	0	0	0	0	1	.000	.000	.000	0	-99	-0	0	0	0	1.000	0	/S-1	0.0

■ SAM EWING

Ewing, Samuel James b: 4/9/49, Lewisburg, Tenn. BL/TL, 6'3", 200 lbs. Deb: 9/11/73 Career OF: (15-LF 0-CF 34-RF)

YEAR	TM/L	G	AB	R	H	2B	3B	HR	RBI	BB	SO	AVG	OBP	SLG	OPS	OPS+	BR+	SB	CS	SBR	FA	FR	G/POS	TPR
1973	Chi-A	11	20	1	3	1	0	0	2	2	6	.150	.227	.200	427	20	-2	0	0	0	1.000	1	/1-4	-0.2
1976	Chi-A	19	41	3	9	2	1	0	2	2	8	.220	.256	.317	573	67	-2	0	0	0	1.000	-0	D-12/1-1	-0.2
1977	Tor-A	97	244	24	70	8	2	4	34	19	42	.287	.338	.385	724	95	-1	1	1	-0	.957	-5	O-46R,D-27/1-2	-0.9
1978	Tor-A	40	56	3	10	0	0	2	9	5	9	.179	.246	.286	532	48	-4	0	0	0	1.000	-1	/O-3(0-0-3),D-9	-0.5
Total	4	167	361	31	92	11	3	6	47	28	65	.255	.308	.352	660	81	-9	1	1	-0	.959	-5	/O-49R,D-48,1-7	-1.8

■ BUCK EWING

Ewing, William b: 10/17/1859, Hoagland, Ohio d: 10/20/06, Cincinnati, Ohio BR/TR, 5'10", 188 lbs. Deb: 9/9/1880 FMH Career OF: (9-LF 34-CF 193-RF)

YEAR	TM/L	G	AB	R	H	2B	3B	HR	RBI	BB	SO	AVG	OBP	SLG	OPS	OPS+	BR+	SB	CS	SBR	FA	FR	G/POS	TPR
1880	Tro-N	13	45	1	8	1	0	0	5	1	3	.178	.196	.200	396	33	-3				.864	-4	C-10/O-4(0-0-4)	-0.7
1881	Tro-N	67	272	40	68	14	7	0	25	7	8	.250	.269	.353	622	89	-4				.915	**25**	C-44,S-22/O-2L,3-1	2.2
1882	Tro-N	74	328	67	89	16	11	2	29	10	15	.271	.293	.405	698	127	10				.887	14	3-44,C-25/2-4,O1P	2.4
1883	NY-N	88	376	90	114	11	13	**10**	41	20	14	.303	.338	.481	820	147	21				.922	1	C-63,O-14C,2-11,/S3	2.4
1884	NY-N	94	382	90	106	15	**20**	3	41	28	22	.277	.327	.445	772	137	16				.933	4	*C-80,O-12R/S-3,3P	2.4
1885	NY-N	81	342	81	104	15	12	6	63	13	17	.304	.330	.471	800	159	21				.918	9	C-63,O-14R/3-8,S1P	3.3
1886	NY-N	73	275	59	85	11	7	4	31	16	17	.309	.347	.444	791	138	12	18			.921	3	C-50,O-23(2-18-3)/1-2	1.6
1887	NY-N	77	348	83	127	17	13	6	44	30	33	.365	.370	.497	867	146	20	26			.863	-1	3-51,2-19/C-8	1.8
1888	*NY-N	103	415	83	127	18	15	6	58	24	28	.306	.348	.465	813	159	27	53			.947	5	C-78,3-21/S-4,P-2	3.8
1889	*NY-N	99	407	91	133	23	13	4	87	37	32	.327	.383	.477	860	139	20	34			.937	16	*C-97/P-3,O-1(1-0-0)	3.7
1890	NY-P	83	352	98	119	19	15	8	72	39	12	.338	.406	.545	951	141	18	36			**.949**	14	C-81/2-1,P-1,M	3.0
1891	NY-N	14	49	8	17	2	1	0	18	5	5	.347	.407	.429	836	150	3	5			.881	-3	/2-8,C-6	0.1
1892	NY-N	105	393	58	122	10	15	8	76	38	26	.310	.371	.473	845	157	26	42			.974	8	1-73,C-30/2-2	3.3
1893	Cle-N	116	500	117	172	28	15	6	122	41	18	.344	.394	.496	890	128	17	47			.927	-1	*O-112R/2-5,1-1,C-1	0.9
1894	Cle-N	53	211	32	53	12	4	2	39	24	9	.251	.328	.374	702	66	-13	18			.912	-2	O-52(0-0-52)/2-1	-1.3
1895	Cin-N	105	434	90	138	24	13	5	94	30	22	.318	.363	.468	831	109	3	34			.976	8	*1-105,M	0.9
1896	Cin-N	69	263	41	73	14	4	1	38	29	13	.278	.349	.373	722	85	-6	41			.980	4	1-69,M	-0.2
1897	Cin-N	1	1	0	0	0	0	0	0	0		.000	.500	.000	500	36	0	0			.800	-0	/1-1,M	0.0
Total	18	1315	5393	1129	1655	250	178	71	883	392	294	.307	.351	.456	807	130	187	354			.931	101	C-636,1-253,O3/2SP	29.6

■ ART EWOLDT

Ewoldt, Arthur Lee "Sheriff" b: 1/8/1894, Paullina, Iowa d: 12/8/77, Des Moines, Iowa BR/TR, 5'10", 165 lbs. Deb: 9/17/19

YEAR	TM/L	G	AB	R	H	2B	3B	HR	RBI	BB	SO	AVG	OBP	SLG	OPS	OPS+	BR+	SB	CS	SBR	FA	FR	G/POS	TPR
1919	Phi-A	9	32	2	7	1	0	0	2	1	5	.219	.242	.250	492	38	-3	0			1.000	0	/3-9	-0.2

■ HOMER EZZELL

Ezzell, Homer Estell b: 2/28/1896, Victoria, Tex. d: 8/3/76, San Antonio, Tex. BR/TR, 5'10", 158 lbs. Deb: 4/22/23

YEAR	TM/L	G	AB	R	H	2B	3B	HR	RBI	BB	SO	AVG	OBP	SLG	OPS	OPS+	BR+	SB	CS	SBR	FA	FR	G/POS	TPR
1923	StL-A	88	279	31	68	6	0	0	14	15	20	.244	.287	.265	552	44	-23	4	3	-0	.961	8	3-73/2-8	-1.1
1924	Bos-A	90	277	35	75	8	4	0	32	14	21	.271	.311	.329	639	65	-15	12	5	1	.984	9	3-64,S-21/C-1	0.1
1925	Bos-A	58	186	40	53	6	4	0	15	19	18	.285	.351	.360	711	81	-5	9	7	-0	.916	-7	3-47/2-9	-0.9
Total	3	236	742	106	196	20	8	0	61	48	59	.264	.312	.313	625	61	-43	25	15	0	.957	10	3-184/S-21,2-17,C-1	-1.9

■ JAY FAATZ

Faatz, Jayson S. b: 10/24/1860, Weedsport, N.Y. d: 4/10/23, Syracuse, N.Y. BR/TR, 6'4", 196 lbs. Deb: 8/22/1884 M

YEAR	TM/L	G	AB	R	H	2B	3B	HR	RBI	BB	SO	AVG	OBP	SLG	OPS	OPS+	BR+	SB	CS	SBR	FA	FR	G/POS	TPR
1884	Pit-a	29	112	18	27	2	3	0		1		.241	.274	.313	586	92	-1				.963	-1	1-29	-0.4
1888	Cle-a	120	470	73	124	10	2	0	51	12		.264	.312	.294	606	97	-1	64			**.989**	2	*1-120	-0.9
1889	Cle-N	117	442	50	102	12	5	2	38	17	28	.231	.275	.294	569	60	-24	27			.981	6	*1-117	-2.6
1890	Buf-P	32	111	18	21	0	2	1	16	9	5	.189	.297	.252	549	52	-7	2			.982	-3	1-32,M	-1.0
Total	4	298	1135	159	274	24	12	3	105	39	33	.241	.293	.292	584	77	-33	93			.982	4	1-298	-4.9

■ JORGE FABREGAS

Fabregas, Jorge b: 3/13/70, Miami, Fla. BL/TR, 6'3", 205 lbs. Deb: 4/24/94

YEAR	TM/L	G	AB	R	H	2B	3B	HR	RBI	BB	SO	AVG	OBP	SLG	OPS	OPS+	BR+	SB	CS	SBR	FA	FR	G/POS	TPR
1994	Cal-A	43	127	12	36	3	0	0	16	7	18	.283	.321	.307	628	62	-7	2	1	0	.987	-2	C-41	-0.6
1995	Cal-A	73	227	24	56	10	0	1	22	17	28	.247	.299	.304	603	58	-14	0	2	-1	.986	1	C-73	-0.9
1996	Cal-A	90	254	18	73	6	0	2	26	17	27	.287	.332	.335	667	69	-12	0	1	-0	.989	10	C-89/D-1	0.2
1997	Ana-A	21	38	2	3	1	0	0	3	3	3	.079	.146	.105	252	-33	-7	0	0	0	.989	2	C-21	-0.5
	Chi-A	100	322	31	90	10	1	7	48	11	43	.280	.305	.382	687	81	-9	1	1	-0	.988	-4	C-92/1-1	-0.8
	Yr	121	360	33	93	11	1	7	51	14	46	.258	.288	.353	641	68	-17	1	1	-0	.988	-3	*C-113/1-1	-1.3
1998	Ari-N	50	151	8	30	4	0	1	15	13	26	.199	.267	.245	512	36	-14	0	0	0	.996	0	C-41	-1.1
	NY-N	20	32	3	6	0	0	1	5	1	6	.188	.212	.281	493	29	-3	0	0	0	.971	4	C-12	0.1
	Yr	70	183	11	36	4	0	2	20	14	32	.197	.258	.251	509	35	-17	0	0	0	.991	5	C-53	-1.0
1999	Fla-N	82	223	20	46	10	2	3	21	26	27	.206	.295	.309	604	56	-15	0	0	0	.989	1	C-78	-0.9
	*Atl-N	6	8	0	0	0	0	0	0	0	0	.000	.000	.000	0	-99	-2	0	0	0	1.000	2	/C-4,1-1	0.0
	Yr	88	231	20	46	10	2	3	21	26	27	.199	.286	.299	584	51	-18	0	0	0	.990	4	C-82/1-1	-0.9
2000	KC-A	43	142	13	40	4	0	3	17	8	11	.282	.320	.373	693	74	-6	1	0	0	.992	1	C-39/D-1	-0.2
Total	7	528	1524	131	380	48	3	18	173	103	189	.249	.299	.320	619	60	-90	4	5	-1	.989	16	C-490/1-2,D-2	-4.7

YEAR	TM/L	G	AB	R	H	2B	3B	HR	RBI	BB	SO	AVG	OBP	SLG	OPS	OPS+	BR+	SB	CS	SBR	FA	FR	G/POS	TPR
■ BUNNY FABRIQUE Fabrique, Albert La Verne b: 12/23/1887, Clinton, Mich. d: 1/10/60, Ann Arbor, Mich. BB/TR, 5'8.5", 150 lbs. Deb: 10/4/16																								
1916	Bro-N	2	2	0	0	0	0	0	0	0	1	.000	.000	.000	0	-97	-0	0			1.000	0	/S-2	0.0
1917	Bro-N	25	88	8	18	3	0	1	3	8	9	.205	.271	.273	544	65	-4	0			.874	-2	S-21	-0.5
Total	2	27	90	8	18	3	0	1	3	8	10	.200	.265	.267	532	62	-4	0			.878	-2	/S-23	-0.5
■ LENNY FAEDO Faedo, Lecnardo Lago b: 5/13/60, Tampa, Fla. BR/TR, 6', 170 lbs. Deb: 9/6/80																								
1980	Min-A	5	8	1	2	1	0	0	0	0	0	.250	.250	.375	625	64	-0	0	0	0	.818	-1	/S-5	-0.1
1981	Min-A	12	41	3	8	0	1	0	6	1	5	.195	.214	.244	458	30	-4	0	0	0	.971	2	S-12	-0.1
1982	Min-A	90	255	16	62	8	0	3	22	16	22	.243	.290	.310	600	63	-13	1	0	0	.967	3	S-88/D-1	-0.1
1983	Min-A	51	173	16	48	7	0	1	18	4	19	.277	.294	.335	629	70	-7	0	0	0	.954	-15	S-51	-1.7
1984	Min-A	16	52	6	13	1	0	1	6	4	3	.250	.304	.327	630	71	-2	0	0	0	.968	-5	S-15/D-1	-0.6
Total	5	174	529	42	133	17	1	5	52	25	49	.251	.286	.316	602	64	-26	1	0	0	.961	-16	S-171/D-2	-2.6
■ FRED FAGIN Fagin, Frederick H. b: Cincinnati, Ohio Deb: 6/25/1895																								
1895	StL-N	1	3	0	1	0	0	0	2	0	0	.333	.333	.333	667	73	-0	0			.636	0	/C-1	0.0
■ FRANK FAHEY Fahey, Francis Raymond b: 1/22/1896, Milford, Mass. d: 3/19/54, Boston, Mass. BB/TR, 6'1", 190 lbs. Deb: 4/25/18																								
1918	Phi-A	10	17	2	3	1	0	0	1	0	3	.176	.176	.235	412	24	-2	0			1.000	-2	/O-5(4-1-0),P-3	-0.4
■ HOWARD FAHEY Fahey, Howard Simpson "Cap" or "Kid" b: 6/24/1892, Medford, Mass. d: 10/24/71, Clearwater, Fla. BR/TR, 5'7.5", 145 lbs. Deb: 7/23/12																								
1912	Phi-A	5	8	0	0	0	0	0	0	0		.000	.000	.000	0	-99	-2	0			1.000	-1	/3-2,2-1,S-1	-0.3
■ BILL FAHEY Fahey, William Roger b: 6/14/50, Detroit, Mich. BL/TR, 6', 200 lbs. Deb: 9/26/71 C																								
1971	Was-A	2	8	0	0	0	0	0	0	0	0	.000	.000	.000	0	-99	-2	0	0	0	.909	-0	/C-2	-0.3
1972	Tex-A	39	119	8	20	2	0	1	10	12	23	.168	.250	.210	460	40	-9	4	0	1	.992	11	C-39	0.5
1974	Tex-A	6	16	1	4	0	0	0	0	0	1	.250	.250	.250	500	45	-1	0	0	0	1.000	-1	/C-6	-0.2
1975	Tex-A	21	37	3	11	1	1	0	3	1	10	.297	.316	.378	694	96	-0	0	0	0	.983	-1	C-21	-0.1
1976	Tex-A	38	80	12	20	2	0	1	9	11	6	.250	.348	.313	660	92	-0	1	0	0	.993	2	C-38	0.3
1977	Tex-A	37	68	3	15	4	0	0	5	1	8	.221	.232	.279	511	38	-6	0	0	0	1.000	-1	C-34	-0.6
1979	SD-N	73	209	14	60	8	1	3	19	21	17	.287	.352	.378	730	106	2	1	1	-0	.994	-3	C-68	0.1
1980	SD-N	93	241	18	62	4	0	1	22	21	16	.257	.317	.286	603	74	-8	2	0	0	.977	-4	C-85	-0.9
1981	Det-A	27	67	5	17	2	0	1	9	2	4	.254	.275	.328	604	71	-3	0	1	-0	.981	3	C-27	0.1
1982	Det-A	28	67	7	10	2	0	0	4	0	5	.149	.149	.179	328	-10	-10	1	0	0	1.000	5	C-28	-0.4
1983	Det-A	19	22	4	6	1	0	0	2	5	3	.273	.407	.318	726	106	0	0	0	0	1.000	1	C-18	0.1
Total	11	383	934	75	225	26	2	7	83	74	93	.241	.298	.296	594	69	-37	9	2	1	.989	11	C-366	-1.4
■ FERRIS FAIN Fain, Ferris Roy "Burrhead" b: 5/29/21, San Antonio, Tex. BL/TL, 5'11", 186 lbs. Deb: 4/15/47																								
1947	Phi-A	136	461	70	134	28	6	7	71	95	34	.291	.414	.423	837	130	23	4	5	-1	.985	1	*1-132	1.9
1948	Phi-A	145	520	81	146	27	6	7	88	113	37	.281	.412	.396	808	115	16	10	5	0	.989	9	*1-145	2.0
1949	Phi-A	150	525	81	138	21	5	3	78	136	51	.263	.415	.339	754	104	11	8	1	1	.984	4	*1-150	1.1
1950	Phi-A★	151	522	83	147	25	4	10	83	133	26	.282	.430	.402	832	116	20	8	5	0	.987	8	*1-151	2.2
1951	Phi-A★	117	425	63	146	30	3	6	57	80	20	**.344**	.451	.471	921	146	32	0	3	-1	.990	13	*1-108,O-11(1-0-10)	3.8
1952	Phi-A☆	145	538	82	176	**43**	3	2	59	105	26	**.327**	**.438**	.429	867	133	30	3	5	-1	.984	16	*1-144	4.1
1953	Chi-A★	128	446	73	114	18	2	6	52	108	28	.256	.405	.345	750	101	7	3	2	-0	.989	10	*1-127	0.9
1954	Chi-A†	65	235	30	71	10	1	5	51	40	14	.302	.406	.417	823	121	9	5	1	1	.987	-4	1-64	0.1
1955	Det-A	58	140	23	37	8	0	2	23	52	12	.264	.464	.364	828	128	10	2	1	0	.988	0	1-44	0.8
	Cle-A	56	118	9	30	3	0	0	8	42	13	.254	.453	.280	733	97	3	3	0	1	.992	3	1-51	0.5
	Yr	114	258	32	67	11	0	2	31	94	25	.260	.459	.326	785	113	13	5	1	1	.990	4	1-95	1.3
Total	9	1151	3930	595	1139	213	30	48	570	904	261	.290	.425	.396	821	120	161	46	28	0	.987	59	*1-1116/O-11(1-0-10)	17.4
■ GEORGE FAIR Fair, George T. b: 1/14/1856, Boston, Mass. d: 2/12/39, Roslindale, Mass. 5'7.5", 140 lbs. Deb: 7/29/1876																								
1876	NY-N	1	4	0	0	0	0	0	0	0	0	.000	.000	.000	0	-99	-1				.750	0	/2-1	-0.1
■ JIM FAIREY Fairey, James Burke b: 9/22/44, Orangeburg, S.C. BL/TL, 5'10", 190 lbs. Deb: 4/14/68																								
1968	LA-N	99	156	17	31	3	3	1	10	9	32	.199	.242	.276	518	60	-8	1	1	-0	.944	-8	O-63(40-2-23)	-2.1
1969	Mon-N	20	49	6	14	1	0	1	6	1	7	.286	.300	.367	667	86	-1	0	2	-1	.913	-1	O-13(1-12-0)	-0.3
1970	Mon-N	92	211	35	51	9	3	3	25	14	38	.242	.295	.355	651	74	-8	1	3	-1	.978	-8	O-59(33-30-4)	-1.9
1971	Mon-N	92	200	19	49	8	1	1	19	12	23	.245	.288	.310	598	69	-8	3	3	-0	.968	1	O-58(56-2-1)	-1.1
1972	Mon-N	86	141	9	33	7	0	1	15	10	21	.234	.285	.305	590	66	-6	1	3	-1	.932	-7	O-37(20-1-18)	-1.7
1973	LA-N	10	9	0	2	0	0	0	0	1	1	.222	.300	.222	522	49	-1	0	0	0	.000	0	H	-0.1
Total	6	399	766	86	180	28	7	7	75	47	122	.235	.281	.317	598	69	-32	6	12	-3	.957	-23	O-230(150-47-46)	-7.2
■ RON FAIRLY Fairly, Ronald Ray b: 7/12/38, Macon, Ga. BL/TL, 5'10", 181 lbs. Deb: 9/9/58 Career OF: (212-LF 120-CF 727-RF)																								
1958	LA-N	15	53	6	15	1	0	2	8	6	7	.283	.356	.415	771	100	0	0	0	0	.971	-1	O-15(4-11-1)	-0.2
1959	*LA-N	118	244	27	58	12	1	4	23	31	29	.238	.326	.344	670	73	-9	0	4	-1	.963	-10	O-88(7-23-62)	-2.3
1960	LA-N	14	37	6	4	0	3	1	3	7	12	.108	.250	.351	601	59	-2	0	0	0	1.000	-1	O-13(5-0-8)	-0.4
1961	LA-N	111	245	42	79	15	2	10	48	48	22	.322	.435	.522	958	140	16	0	0	0	.989	-6	O-71(6-15-53),1-23	0.6
1962	LA-N	147	460	80	128	15	7	14	71	75	59	.278	.383	.433	816	126	19	1	1	-0	.989	-23	*1-120,O-48(4-5-42)	-1.2
1963	*LA-N	152	490	62	133	21	0	12	77	58	69	.271	.350	.388	737	120	14	5	2	0	**.995**	-11	*1-119,O-45(16-22-10)	-0.6
1964	LA-N	150	454	62	116	19	5	10	74	65	59	.256	.351	.385	737	116	11	4	0	1	.987	-1	*1-141	0.3
1965	*LA-N	158	555	73	152	28	1	9	70	76	72	.274	.364	.377	741	117	15	2	0	0	.982	-1	*O-148(0-17-133),1-13	0.4
1966	*LA-N	117	351	53	101	20	0	14	61	52	38	.288	.383	.464	847	146	23	3	2	-0	.974	-15	O-98(0-6-95),1-25	0.2
1967	LA-N	153	486	45	107	19	0	10	55	54	51	.220	.299	.321	620	85	-10	1	4	-1	.986	-4	O-97(1-0-97),1-68	-2.5
1968	LA-N	141	441	32	103	15	1	4	43	41	61	.234	.305	.299	604	89	-6	0	2	-1	.989	0	*O-105(0-0-105),1-36	-1.7
1969	LA-N	30	64	3	14	3	2	0	8	9	6	.219	.315	.328	643	86	-1	0	0	0	.981	-1	1-12,O-10(1-0-10)	-0.4
	Mon-N	70	253	35	73	13	4	12	39	28	22	.289	.359	.514	873	142	13	1	0	0	.991	1	1-52,O-21(3-18-0)	1.0
	Yr	100	317	38	87	16	6	12	47	37	28	.274	.350	.476	827	132	13	1	0	0	.989	-0	1-64,O-31(4-18-10)	0.6
1970	Mon-N	119	385	54	111	19	0	15	61	72	64	.288	.406	.455	860	130	19	10	2	2	.995	5	*1-118/O-4(2-2-0)	1.6
1971	Mon-N	146	447	58	115	23	0	13	71	81	65	.257	.377	.396	773	119	14	1	3	-1	.992	5	*1-135,O-10(10-1-0)	0.8
1972	Mon-N	140	446	51	124	15	1	17	68	46	45	.278	.349	.430	780	118	11	3	4	-1	.985	6	O-70(0-0-70),1-68	0.8
1973	Mon-N★	142	413	70	123	13	1	17	49	86	33	.298	.422	.458	880	139	26	2	2	-0	.974	-8	*O-121(121-0-0)/1-5	1.1
1974	Mon-N	101	282	35	69	9	1	12	43	57	28	.245	.374	.411	785	113	6	2	1	0	.989	1	1-67,O-20(19-0-1)	0.2
1975	StL-N	107	229	32	69	13	2	7	37	45	22	.301	.422	.467	890	142	15	0	1	-0	.980	0	1-56,O-20(4-0-16)	1.0
1976	StL-N	73	110	13	29	4	0	0	21	23	12	.264	.391	.300	691	97	1	0	0	0	.995	3	1-27	0.2
	Oak-A	15	46	9	11	1	0	3	10	9	12	.239	.364	.457	820	145	3	0	0	0	1.000	1	1-15	0.2
1977	Tor-A★	132	458	60	128	24	2	19	64	58	58	.279	.363	.465	828	122	14	0	4	-1	.986	3	D-58,1-40,O-33R	1.0
1978	Cal-A	91	235	23	51	5	0	10	40	25	31	.217	.295	.366	661	88	-4	0	1	-0	.998	-2	1-78/D-5	-1.0
Total	21	2442	7184	931	1913	307	33	215	1044	1052	877	.266	.363	.408	771	117	189	35	33	-4	.991	-60	*1-1218,O-1037R/D-63	-0.9
■ ANTON FALCH Falch, Anton C. b: 12/4/1860, Milwaukee, Wis. d: 3/31/36, Wauwatosa, Wis. 6'6", 220 lbs. Deb: 9/30/1884																								
1884	Mil-U	5	18	0	2	0	0	0		0		.111	.111	.111	222	-60	-4				.600	-1	/O-3(3-0-0),C-2	-0.5
■ BIBB FALK Falk, Bibb August "Jockey" b: 1/27/1899, Austin, Tex. d: 6/8/89, Austin, Tex. BL/TL, 6', 175 lbs. Deb: 9/17/20 FMC																								
1920	Chi-A	7	17	1	5	1	1	0	2	0	5	.294	.294	.471	765	100	-0	0	0	0	1.000	-1	/O-4(0-0-4)	-0.1
1921	Chi-A	152	585	62	167	31	11	5	82	37	69	.285	.330	.402	732	87	-13	4	4	-1	.958	-14	*O-149(148-1-0)	-3.7
1922	Chi-A	131	483	58	144	27	1	12	79	27	55	.298	.335	.433	768	99	-2	2	6	-2	.963	-9	*O-129(126-2-1)	-2.2
1923	Chi-A	87	274	44	84	18	6	5	38	25	12	.307	.367	.471	837	121	7	5	5	-1	.951	-7	O-80(80-0-0)	-0.6
1924	Chi-A	138	526	77	185	37	8	6	99	47	21	.352	.406	.487	893	134	26	6	6	-1	.970	10	*O-134(134-0-0)	2.3
1925	Chi-A	154	602	80	181	35	9	4	99	51	25	.301	.357	.409	766	99	-2	4	5	-1	.959	-4	*O-153(153-0-0)	-1.7
1926	Chi-A	155	566	86	195	43	4	8	108	66	22	.345	.415	.477	892	137	32	9	10	-2	**.992**	8	*O-155(155-0-0)	2.5
1927	Chi-A	145	535	76	175	35	6	9	83	52	19	.327	.391	.465	856	125	19	5	7	-1	.978	18	*O-145(145-0-0)	2.4

YEAR	TM/L	G	AB	R	H	2B	3B	HR	RBI	BB	SO	AVG	OBP	SLG	OPS	OPS+	BR+	SB	CS	SBR	FA	FR	G/POS	TPR
1928	Chi-A	98	286	42	83	18	4	1	37	25	16	.290	.347	.392	739	95	-2	5	1	1	.972	2	O-78(78-0-0)	-0.5
1929	Cle-A	125	426	65	133	30	7	13	93	42	14	.312	.374	.507	881	120	12	4	4	-1	.943	-4	*O-120(61-0-61)	-0.1
1930	Cle-A	82	191	34	62	12	1	4	36	23	8	.325	.397	.461	858	113	4	2	0	0	.967	1	O-42(25-0-18)	0.2
1931	Cle-A	79	161	30	49	13	1	2	28	17	13	.304	.371	.435	806	105	1	1	1	-0	.949	-3	O-33(2-0-31)	-0.4
Total	12	1353	4652	655	1463	300	59	69	784	412	279	.314	.372	.449	821	113	83	47	49	-7	.967	-3	*O-1222(1107-3-115)	-1.9
■ **CHARLIE FALLON**	Fallon, Charles Augustus b: 3/7/1881, New York, N.Y. d: 6/10/60, Kings Park, N.Y. BR/TR, 5'6", Deb: 6/30/05																							
1905	NY-A	1	0	0	0	0	0	0	0	0		—	—	—	—	—	0	0			.000	0	R	0.0
■ **GEORGE FALLON**	Fallon, George Decatur "Flash" b: 7/8/14, Jersey City, N.J. d: 10/25/94, Lake Worth, Fla. BR/TR, 5'9", 155 lbs. Deb: 9/27/37																							
1937	Bro-N	4	8	0	2	1	0	0	0	1	0	.250	.333	.375	708	91	-0	0			.895	1	/2-4	0.1
1943	StL-N	36	78	6	18	1	0	0	5	2	9	.231	.259	.244	503	44	-6	0			.968	15	2-36	1.1
1944	*StL-N	69	141	16	28	6	0	1	9	16	11	.199	.285	.262	547	54	-8	1			.973	4	2-38,S-24/3-6	-0.2
1945	StL-N	24	55	4	13	2	1	0	7	6	6	.236	.311	.309	621	71	-2	1			.948	-2	S-20/2-4	-0.3
Total	4	133	282	26	61	10	1	1	21	25	26	.216	.285	.270	554	56	-16	2			.966	18	/2-82,S-44,3-6	0.7
■ **PETE FALSEY**	Falsey, Peter James b: 4/24/1891, New Haven, Conn. d: 5/23/76, Los Angeles, Cal. BL/TL, 5'6.5", 132 lbs. Deb: 7/16/14																							
1914	Pit-N	3	1	0	0	0	0	0	0	0	1	.000	.000	.000	0	-99	-0	0			.000	0	H	0.0
■ **RIKKERT FANEYTE**	Faneyte, Rikkert b: 5/31/69, Amsterdam, Netherlands BR/TR, 6'1", 170 lbs. Deb: 8/29/93																							
1993	SF-N	7	15	2	2	0	0	0	0	2	4	.133	.235	.133	369	2	-2	0	0	0	1.000	-1	/O-6(1-5-0)	-0.3
1994	SF-N	19	26	1	3	3	0	0	4	3	11	.115	.207	.231	438	15	-3	0	0	0	.900	-1	/O-6(0-2-4)	-0.5
1995	SF-N	46	86	7	17	4	1	0	4	11	27	.198	.289	.267	556	49	-6	1	0	0	.981	-4	O-34(3-22-11)	-1.0
1996	Tex-A	8	5	0	1	0	0	0	1	0	0	.200	.200	.200	400	1	-1	0	0	0	1.000	-1	/O-6(2-4-0),D-2	-0.1
Total	4	80	132	10	23	7	1	0	9	16	42	.174	.264	.242	506	35	-12	1	0	0	.976	-6	/O-52(6-33-15),D-2	-1.9
■ **JIM FANNING**	Fanning, William James b: 9/14/27, Chicago, Ill. BR/TR, 5'11", 180 lbs. Deb: 9/11/54 MC																							
1954	Chi-N	11	38	2	7	0	0	0	1	1	7	.184	.205	.184	389	2	-5	0	0	0	1.000	-1	C-11	-0.6
1955	Chi-N	5	10	0	0	0	0	0	0	1	2	.000	.091	.000	91	-73	-3	0	0	0	1.000	3	/C-5	0.1
1956	Chi-N	1	4	0	1	0	0	0	0	0	0	.250	.250	.250	500	36	-0	0	0	0	.800	1	/C-1	0.0
1957	Chi-N	47	89	3	16	2	0	0	4	4	17	.180	.223	.202	426	16	-11	0	0	0	.981	2	C-35	-0.7
Total	4	64	141	5	24	2	0	0	5	6	26	.170	.209	.184	394	6	-19	0	0	0	.979	5	/C-52	-1.2
■ **CARMEN FANZONE**	Fanzone, Carmen Ronald b: 8/30/43, Detroit, Mich. BR/TR, 6', 200 lbs. Deb: 7/21/70																							
1970	Bos-A	10	15	0	3	1	0	0	3	2	2	.200	.333	.267	600	63	-1	0	0	0	.750	0	/3-5	-0.1
1971	Chi-N	12	43	5	8	2	0	2	5	2	7	.186	.222	.372	594	57	-2	0	0	0	1.000	0	/O-6(5-0-1),3-3,1-2	-0.3
1972	Chi-N	86	222	26	50	11	0	8	42	35	45	.225	.338	.383	721	95	-1	2	3	-1	.923	3	3-36,1-21,2-13,/SO	0.1
1973	Chi-N	64	150	22	41	7	0	6	22	20	38	.273	.359	.440	799	112	3	1	2	-0	.922	-3	3-25,1-24/O-6(6-0-0)	-0.2
1974	Chi-N	65	158	13	30	6	0	4	22	15	27	.190	.269	.304	572	57	-9	0	1	-0	.885	-1	3-35,2-10/1-7,O-1L	-1.1
Total	5	237	588	66	132	27	0	20	94	74	119	.224	.317	.372	690	86	-11	3	6	-1	.896	-1	3-104/1-54,2-23,OS	-1.6
■ **PAUL FARIES**	Faries, Paul Tyrrell b: 2/20/65, Berkeley, Cal. BR/TR, 5'10", 165 lbs. Deb: 9/6/90																							
1990	SD-N	14	37	4	7	1	0	0	2	4	7	.189	.286	.216	502	40	-3	0	1	-0	1.000	6	/2-7,S-4,3-1	0.3
1991	SD-N	57	130	13	23	3	1	0	7	14	21	.177	.262	.215	477	35	-11	3	1	0	.988	8	2-36,3-12/S-8	-0.1
1992	SD-N	10	11	3	5	1	0	0	1	1	2	.455	.500	.545	1045	193	1	0	0	0	1.000	-2	/2-4,3-2,S-1	0.0
1993	SF-N	15	36	6	8	2	1	0	4	1	4	.222	.243	.333	577	54	-2	2	0	0	1.000	-1	/2-7,S-4,3-1	-0.3
Total	4	96	214	26	43	7	2	0	14	20	34	.201	.275	.252	528	47	-15	5	2	0	.992	11	/2-54,S-17,3-16	-0.1
■ **MONTY FARISS**	Fariss, Monty Ted b: 10/13/67, Cordell, Okla. BR/TR, 6'4", 180 lbs. Deb: 9/6/91 Career OF: (37-LF 10-CF 19-RF)																							
1991	Tex-A	19	31	6	8	1	0	1	6	7	11	.258	.395	.387	782	119	1	0	0	0	1.000	4	/O-8(8-0-0),2-4,D-4	0.5
1992	Tex-A	67	166	13	36	7	1	3	21	17	51	.217	.297	.325	623	77	-5	0	2	-1	1.000	-15	O-49L,2-17/1-1,D-4	-2.2
1993	Fla-N	18	29	3	5	2	1	0	2	5	13	.172	.294	.310	604	59	-2	0	0	0	1.000	-1	/O-8(1-0-7)	-0.3
Total	3	104	226	22	49	10	2	4	29	29	75	.217	.311	.332	643	81	-6	0	2	-1	1.000	-12	/O-65L,2-21,D-8,1-1	-2.0
■ **BOB FARLEY**	Farley, Robert Jacob b: 11/15/37, Watsontown, Pa. BL/TL, 6'2", 200 lbs. Deb: 4/15/61																							
1961	SF-N	13	20	3	2	0	0	0	1	3	5	.100	.217	.100	317	-13	-3	0	0	0	1.000	-1	/O-3(3-0-0),1-1	-0.4
1962	Chi-A	35	53	7	10	1	1	1	4	13	13	.189	.348	.302	650	77	-1	0	1	-0	.989	-1	1-14	-0.3
	Det-A	36	50	9	8	2	0	1	4	14	10	.160	.344	.260	604	63	-2	0	0	0	.857	-4	O-11(0-0-11)/1-6	-0.7
	Yr	71	103	16	18	3	1	2	8	27	23	.175	.346	.282	628	70	-3	0	1	-0	.974	-5	1-20,O-11(0-0-11)	-1.0
Total	2	84	123	19	20	3	1	2	9	30	28	.163	.327	.252	579	58	-7	0	1	-0	.975	-6	/1-21,O-14(3-0-11)	-1.4
■ **TOM FARLEY**	Farley, Thomas T. b: Chicago, Ill. Deb: 6/24/1884																							
1884	Was-a	14	52	5	11	4	0	0		1		.212	.241	.288	529	81	-1				.867	1	O-14(14-0-0)	0.0
■ **ALEX FARMER**	Farmer, Alexander Johnson b: 5/9/1880, New York, N.Y. d: 3/5/20, New York, N.Y. BR/TR, 6', 175 lbs. Deb: 9/1/08																							
1908	Bro-N	12	30	1	5	1	0	0	2	1		.167	.194	.200	394	27	-3	0			.966	-0	C-11	-0.2
■ **JACK FARMER**	Farmer, Floyd Haskell b: 7/14/1892, Granville, Tenn. d: 5/21/70, Columbia, La. BR/TR, 6', 180 lbs. Deb: 7/8/16 Career OF: (10-LF 0-CF 8-RF)																							
1916	Pit-N	55	166	10	45	6	4	0	14	7	24	.271	.309	.355	664	103	0	1			.929	-9	2-31,O-15L/S-4,3-1	-1.0
1918	Cle-A	7	9	1	2	0	0	0	1	0	3	.222	.300	.222	522	53	-0	2			.429	-2	/O-3(2-0-1)	-0.2
Total	2	62	175	11	47	6	4	0	15	7	27	.269	.308	.349	657	100	-0	3			.829	-11	/2-31,O-18L,S-4,3-1	-1.2
■ **BILL FARMER**	Farmer, William b: 12/27/1870, BR/TR, 5'11.5", 187 lbs. Deb: 5/1/1888																							
1888	Pit-N	2	4	0	0	0	0	0	0	0	1	.000	.000	.000	0	-99	-1	0			.667	0	/C-1,O-1(0-0-1)	-0.1
	Phi-a	3	12	0	2	0	0	0	1	0		.167	.167	.167	333	7	-1	0			.960	0	/C-3	-0.1
Total	1	5	16	0	2	0	0	0	1	0	1	.125	.125	.125	250	-20	-2	0			.903	1	/C-4,O-1(0-0-1)	-0.2
■ **SID FARRAR**	Farrar, Sidney Douglas b: 8/10/1859, Paris Hill, Me. d: 5/7/35, New York, N.Y. TR, 5'10", 185 lbs. Deb: 5/1/1883																							
1883	Phi-N	99	377	41	88	19	8	0	29	4	37	.233	.241	.326	568	77	-9				.965	-0	*1-99	-1.6
1884	Phi-N	111	428	62	105	16	6	1	45	9	25	.245	.261	.318	579	85	-7				.966	5	*1-111	-1.1
1885	Phi-N	111	420	49	103	20	3	3	36	28	34	.245	.292	.329	621	103	2				.975	4	*1-111	-0.4
1886	Phi-N	118	439	55	109	19	7	5	50	16	47	.248	.275	.358	632	90	-6	10			**.980**	3	*1-118	-1.3
1887	Phi-N	116	485	83	167	20	9	4	72	42	29	.344	.358	.395	753	103	2	24			.977	3	*1-116	-0.5
1888	Phi-N	131	508	53	124	24	7	1	53	31	38	.244	.304	.325	629	96	-2	21			.979	3	*1-131	-1.2
1889	Phi-N	130	477	70	128	22	2	3	58	52	36	.268	.348	.342	689	86	-10	28			.978	-5	*1-130	-2.3
1890	Phi-P	127	481	84	123	17	11	1	69	51	23	.256	.333	.343	676	79	-15	9			.973	-2	*1-127	-2.3
Total	8	943	3615	497	947	157	53	18	412	233	269	.262	.305	.342	647	90	-45	92			.974	10	1-943	-10.7
■ **DUKE FARRELL**	Farrell, Charles Andrew b: 8/31/1866, Oakdale, Mass. d: 2/15/25, Boston, Mass. BB/TR, 6'1", 208 lbs. Deb: 4/21/1888 Career OF: (48-LF 22-CF 39-RF)																							
1888	Chi-N	64	241	34	56	6	3	3	19	4	41	.232	.245	.320	564	73	-8	8			.874	-12	C-33,O-31R/1-1	-1.7
1889	Chi-N	101	407	66	101	19	7	11	75	41	21	.248	.318	.410	729	98	-3	13			.910	4	C-76,O-25(7-15-3)	0.5
1890	Chi-P	117	451	79	131	21	12	2	84	42	28	.290	.352	.404	756	98	-3	8			.929	**27**	C-90,1-22,O-10(0-2-8)	2.4
1891	Bos-a	122	473	108	143	19	13	**12**	**110**	59	48	.302	.384	.474	858	148	28	21			.918	19	3-66,C-37,O-23L,/1	**4.3**
1892	Pit-N	152	605	96	130	10	13	8	77	46	53	.215	.276	.314	590	78	-18	20			.879	-3	*3-133,O-20(11-3-6)	-1.9
1893	Was-N	124	511	84	144	13	13	4	75	47	12	.282	.348	.382	730	96	-3	11			.923	14	C-81,3-41/1-3	1.5
1894	*NY-N	116	404	50	116	20	12	5	69	38	15	.287	.353	.433	786	89	-8	9			.925	30	*C-105/3-5,1-4	2.4
1895	NY-N	90	312	38	90	16	9	1	58	38	18	.288	.371	.407	778	103	2	11			.941	4	C-62,3-24/1-2	1.0
1896	NY-N	58	191	23	54	7	3	1	37	19	7	.283	.351	.366	717	92	-2	2			.954	-7	C-34,S-13/3-7	-0.4
	Was-N	37	130	18	39	7	3	1	30	7	3	.300	.345	.423	768	102	-0	2			1.000	-1	C-18,3-14	0.1
	Yr	95	321	41	93	14	6	2	67	26	10	.290	.349	.389	738	96	-2	4			.970	-7	C-52,3-21,S-13	-0.3
1897	Was-N	78	261	41	84	9	6	0	53	17		.322	.366	.402	768	103	1	8			.945	9	C-63/1-1	1.4
1898	Was-N	99	338	47	106	12	6	1	53	34		.314	.383	.393	776	123	11	12			.929	-6	C-61,1-28	1.0
1899	Was-N	5	12	2	4	1	0	0	1	2		.333	.429	.417	845	134	1	1			1.000	-0	/C-4	0.1

YEAR	TM/L	G	AB	R	H	2B	3B	HR	RBI	BB	SO	AVG	OBP	SLG	OPS	OPS+	BR+	SB	CS	SBR	FA	FR	G/POS	TPR
	Bro-N	80	254	40	76	10	7	2	55	35		.299	.399	.417	816	121	9	6			.948	11	C-78	2.3
	Yr	85	266	42	80	11	7	2	56	37		.301	.400	.417	817	122	9	7			.949	10	C-82	2.4
1900	*Bro-N	76	273	33	75	11	5	0	39	11		.275	.310	.352	662	78	-9	3			.944	-4	C-74	-0.6
1901	Bro-N	80	284	38	84	10	6	1	31	7		.296	.320	.384	704	101	-1	7			.979	6	C-59,1-17	1.1
1902	Bro-N	74	264	14	64	5	2	0	24	12		.242	.281	.277	557	71	-9	6			.976	7	C-49,1-24	0.3
1903	*Bos-A	17	52	5	21	5	1	0	8	5		.404	.466	.538	1004	190	6	1			.960	-0	C-17	0.8
1904	Bos-A	68	198	11	42	9	2	0	15	15		.212	.281	.278	559	73	-6	1			.958	-7	C-56	-0.8
1905	Bos-A	7	21	2	6	1	0	0	2	1		.286	.318	.333	652	105	0	0			1.000	2	/C-7	0.3
Total	18	1565	5682	829	1566	211	123	52	915	480	246	.276	.337	.383	721	99	-13	150			.938	92	*C-1004,3-290,O1/S	14.1
■ DOC FARRELL	Farrell, Edward Stephen b: 12/26/01, Johnson City, N.Y. d: 12/20/66, Livingston, N.J. BR/TR, 5'8", 160 lbs. Deb: 6/15/25																							
1925	NY-N	27	56	6	12	1	0	0	4	4	6	.214	.267	.232	499	30	-6	0	1	-0	.900	1	S-13/3-7,2-1	-0.3
1926	NY-N	67	171	19	49	10	1	2	23	12	17	.287	.341	.392	732	98	-1	4			.950	-11	S-53/2-3	-0.6
1927	NY-N	42	142	13	55	10	1	3	34	12	11	.387	.442	.535	978	161	12	0			.919	-1	S-36/3-2	1.5
	Bos-N	110	424	44	124	13	2	1	58	14	21	.292	.315	.340	655	82	-12	4			.931	-5	S-57,2-40,3-18	-0.9
	Yr	152	566	57	179	23	3	4	92	26	32	.316	.348	.389	737	103	2	4			.926	-6	S-93,2-40,3-20	0.6
1928	Bos-N	134	483	36	104	14	2	3	43	26	26	.215	.263	.271	534	42	-42	3			.933	-17	*S-132/2-1	-4.4
1929	Bos-N	5	8	0	1	0	0	0	2	0	1	.125	.125	.125	250	-39	-2	0			.000	-1	/2-1,S-1	-0.2
	NY-N	63	178	18	38	6	0	0	16	9	17	.213	.251	.247	499	24	-21	2			.925	7	3-28,2-25/S-4	-1.1
	Yr	68	186	18	39	6	0	0	18	9	18	.210	.246	.242	488	22	-23	2			.925	7	3-28,2-26/S-5	-1.3
1930	StL-N	23	61	3	13	1	1	0	6	4	2	.213	.262	.262	524	26	-7	1			.944	2	S-15/2-6,1-1	-0.4
	Chi-N	46	113	21	33	6	0	1	16	9	5	.292	.344	.372	716	73	-5	0			.937	3	S-38/2-1	0.1
	Yr	69	174	24	46	7	1	1	22	13	7	.264	.316	.333	649	56	-12	1			.938	5	S-53/2-7,1-1	-0.3
1932	NY-A	26	63	4	11	1	1	0	4	2	8	.175	.212	.222	434	13	-8	0	0	0	.963	-1	2-16/S-5,1-2,3-1	-0.7
1933	NY-A	44	93	16	25	0	0	0	6	16	6	.269	.376	.269	645	78	-2	0	0	0	.947	-4	S-22,2-20	-0.4
1935	Bos-A	4	7	1	2	1	0	0	1	1	0	.286	.375	.429	804	101	0	0	0	0	.917	-1	/2-4	0.0
Total	9	591	1799	181	467	63	8	10	213	109	120	.260	.306	.320	626	66	-92	14	1		.934	-25	S-376,2-118/3-56,1	-7.4
■ JACK FARRELL	Farrell, John "Hartford Jack" b: 1/2/1856, Hartford, Conn. d: 11/15/16, Hartford, Conn. Deb: 10/27/1874																							
1874	Har-n	3	13	3	5	0	0	0	0	1	0	.385	.429	.385	813	155	1	0	0	0	1.000	0	/O-3(0-3-0)	0.1
■ JACK FARRELL	Farrell, John A. "Moose" b: 7/5/1857, Newark, N.J. d: 2/10/14, Cedar Grove, N.J. BR/TR, 5'9", 165 lbs. Deb: 5/1/1879 M Career OF: (0-LF 3-CF 0-RF)																							
1879	Syr-N	54	241	40	73	6	2	1	21	3	13	.303	.311	.357	668	135	10				.870	-15	2-54	-0.2
	Pro-N	12	51	5	13	2	0	0	5	0	0	.255	.255	.294	549	82	-1				.915	7	2-12	0.6
	Yr	66	292	45	86	8	2	1	26	3	13	.295	.302	.346	648	125	8				.879	-7	2-66	0.4
1880	Pro-N	80	339	46	92	12	5	3	36	10	6	.271	.292	.363	655	125	9				.887	-8	*2-80	0.4
1881	Pro-N	84	345	69	82	16	5	5	36	29	23	.238	.297	.357	653	106	3				.881	-5	*2-82/O-3(0-3-0),M	0.1
1882	Pro-N	84	366	67	93	21	6	2	31	16	23	.254	.285	.361	646	106	2				.875	-5	*2-84	0.1
1883	Pro-N	95	420	92	128	24	11	3	61	15	21	.305	.329	.436	764	126	12				**.924**	**25**	*2-95	**3.5**
1884	*Pro-N	111	469	70	102	13	6	1	37	35	44	.217	.272	.277	549	74	-13				.922	-4	*2-109/3-3	-1.1
1885	Pro-N	68	257	27	53	7	1	1	19	10	25	.206	.236	.253	489	60	-11				.900	-15	2-68	-2.3
1886	Phi-N	17	60	7	11	0	1	0	3	3	11	.183	.222	.217	439	34	-5	1			.825	-3	2-17	-0.6
	Was-N	47	171	24	41	11	4	2	18	15	12	.240	.301	.386	687	114	3	12			.913	-13	2-47	-0.7
	Yr	64	231	31	52	11	5	2	21	18	23	.225	.281	.342	623	92	-2	13			.888	-15	2-64	-1.3
1887	Was-N	87	359	40	95	14	9	0	41	20	12	.265	.267	.316	582	64	-16	31			.876	-8	S-48,2-40	-1.8
1888	Bal-a	103	398	72	81	19	5	4	36	26		.204	.256	.307	562	82	-8	29			.902	11	S-54,2-52	0.6
1889	Bal-a	42	157	25	33	3	0	1	26	15	15	.210	.287	.248	536	52	-10	14			.891	-6	S-42	-1.2
Total	11	884	3633	584	897	148	55	23	370	197	205	.247	.283	.333	616	94	-24	87			.899	-38	2-740,S-144/3-3,O-3C	-2.6
■ JACK FARRELL	Farrell, John J. b: 6/16/1892, Chicago, Ill. d: 3/24/18, Chicago, Ill. BB/TR, 5'8", 145 lbs. Deb: 4/16/14																							
1914	Chi-F	156	524	58	123	23	4	0	35	52	65	.235	.307	.294	601	68	-32	12			.954	0	*2-155/S-3	-3.0
1915	Chi-F	70	222	27	48	10	1	0	14	25	18	.216	.298	.270	569	64	-14	8			.941	-5	2-70/S-1	-1.9
Total	2	226	746	85	171	33	5	0	49	77	83	.229	.305	.287	592	67	-45	20			.950	-4	2-225/S-4	-4.9
■ JOHN FARRELL	Farrell, John Sebastian b: 12/4/1876, Covington, Ky. d: 5/13/21, Kansas City, Mo. BR/TR, 5'10", 160 lbs. Deb: 4/26/01 Career OF: (2-LF 72-CF 0-RF)																							
1901	Was-A	135	555	100	151	32	11	3	63	52		.272	.336	.386	721	101	1	25			.915	17	2-72,O-62(0-62-0)/3-1	1.3
1902	StL-N	138	565	68	141	13	5	0	25	43		.250	.308	.290	599	88	-7	9			.947	**34**	*2-118,S-21	2.9
1903	StL-N	130	519	83	141	25	8	1	32	48		.272	.336	.356	692	100	0	17			.927	**28**	*2-118,O-12(2-10-0)	2.7
1904	StL-N	131	509	72	130	23	3	0	20	46		.255	.320	.312	632	100	1	16			.934	16	*2-130	1.9
1905	StL-N	7	24	6	4	0	1	0	1	4		.167	.286	.250	536	62	-1	1			.892	-3	/2-7	-0.4
Total	5	541	2172	329	567	93	28	4	141	193		.261	.324	.335	659	97	-6	68			.932	92	2-445/O-74C,S-21,3	8.4
■ JOE FARRELL	Farrell, Joseph F. b: 1857, Brooklyn, N.Y. d: 4/18/1893, Brooklyn, N.Y. BR, 5'6", 160 lbs. Deb: 5/1/1882 Career OF: (1-LF 1-CF 0-RF)																							
1882	Det-N	69	283	34	70	12	2	1	24	4	20	.247	.258	.314	572	83	-6				.816	-11	3-42,2-18/S-9	-1.4
1883	Det-N	101	444	58	108	13	5	0	36	5	29	.243	.252	.295	547	69	-16				.845	13	*3-101	-0.1
1884	Det-N	110	461	59	104	10	5	3	41	14	66	.226	.248	.289	537	73	-13				.842	-7	*3-110/O-1(1-0-0)	-1.7
1886	Bal-a	73	301	36	63	8	3	1	31	12		.209	.240	.266	505	60	-14	5			.870	-15	2-45,3-27/O-1(0-1-0)	-2.4
Total	4	353	1489	187	345	43	15	5	132	35	115	.232	.249	.291	540	71	-49	5			.840	-21	3-280/2-63,S-9,O-2L	-5.6
■ KERBY FARRELL	Farrell, Major Kerby b: 9/3/13, Leapwood, Tenn. d: 12/17/75, Nashville, Tenn. BL/TL, 5'11", 172 lbs. Deb: 4/24/43 MC																							
1943	Bos-N	85	280	11	75	14	1	0	21	16	15	.268	.307	.325	632	84	-6	1			.996	2	1-69/P-5	-0.8
1945	Chi-A	103	396	44	102	11	3	0	34	24	18	.258	.300	.301	601	76	-12	4	9	-2	.989	-0	1-97	-2.2
Total	2	188	676	55	177	25	4	0	55	40	33	.262	.303	.311	614	80	-19	5	9		.992	1	1-166/P-5	-3.0
■ BILL FARRELL	Farrell, William Deb: 5/3/1882																							
1882	Phi-a	2	7	2	2	1	0	0	1	1		.286	.375	.429	804	153	0				.000	-1	/O-2(0-1-1),C-1	-0.1
1883	Bal-a	2	7	0	0	0	0	0		1		.000	.125	.000	125	-55	-1				.750	-1	/S-2	-0.2
Total	2	4	14	2	2	1	0	0	1	2		.143	.250	.214	464	51	-1				.750	-2	/S-2,O-2(0-1-1),C-1	-0.3
■ JOHN FARROW	Farrow, John Jacob b: 11/8/1853, Verplanck, N.Y d: 12/31/14, Perth Amboy, N.J. BL/TR, Deb: 4/28/1873 Career OF: (0-LF 2-CF 4-RF)																							
1873	Res-n	12	48	2	8	1	0	0	3	0	3	.167	.167	.188	354	5	-5	0	0	0	.673	-3	/C-9,O-3R,1-1,S-1	-0.6
1874	Atl-n	27	122	16	26	3	0	0	10	1	1	.213	.220	.238	457	53	-5	0	0	0	.694	-2	C-16,2-12/O-3(0-2-1)	-0.6
1884	Bro-a	16	58	7	11	2	0	0		3		.190	.230	.224	454	48	-3				.915	-1	C-16	-0.2
Total	2 n	39	170	18	34	4	0	0	13	1	4	.200	.205	.224	428	38	-10	0	0	0	.686	-5	/C-25,2-12,O-6R,S1	-1.2
■ SAL FASANO	Fasano, Salvatore Frank b: 8/10/71, Chicago, Ill. BR/TR, 6'2", 220 lbs. Deb: 4/3/96																							
1996	KC-A	51	143	20	29	2	0	6	19	14	25	.203	.283	.343	626	57	-10	1	1	-0	.984	11	C-51	0.3
1997	KC-A	13	38	4	8	2	0	1	1	1	12	.211	.231	.342	573	46	-3	0	0	0	.982	-1	C-12/D-1	-0.4
1998	KC-A	74	216	21	49	10	0	8	31	10	56	.227	.310	.384	694	77	-7	1	0	0	.996	-2	C-70/1-5,3-1	-0.5
1999	KC-A	23	60	11	14	2	0	5	16	7	17	.233	.378	.517	895	123	2	0	1	-0	1.000	7	C-23	0.9
2000	*Oak-A	52	126	21	27	6	0	7	19	14	47	.214	.308	.429	736	86	-3	0	0	0	.981	3	C-52	0.2
Total	5	213	583	77	127	22	0	27	86	46	157	.218	.306	.395	700	77	-21	2	2	-0	.989	18	C-208/1-5,3-1,D-1	0.5
■ BUCK FAUSETT	Fausett, Robert Shaw "Leaky" b: 4/8/08, Sheridan, Ark. d: 5/2/94, College Station, Tex. BL/TR, 5'10", 170 lbs. Deb: 4/18/44																							
1944	Cin-N	13	31	2	3	0	1	0	1	1	2	.097	.125	.161	286	-21	-5	0			1.000	3	/3-6,P-2	-0.1
■ JOE FAUTSCH	Fautsch, Joseph Roamon b: 2/28/1887, Minneapolis, Minn. d: 3/16/71, New Hope, Minn. BR/TR, 5'10", 162 lbs. Deb: 4/24/16																							
1916	Chi-A	1	1	0	0	0	0	0	0	0	0	.000	.000	.000	0	-99	-0	0			.000	0	H	0.0
■ ERNIE FAZIO	Fazio, Ernest Joseph b: 1/25/42, Oakland, Cal. BR/TR, 5'7", 165 lbs. Deb: 7/3/62																							
1962	Hou-N	12	12	3	1	0	0	0	1	2	5	.083	.214	.083	298	-18	-2	0	0	0	.783	0	S-10	-0.1
1963	Hou-N	102	228	31	42	10	3	2	5	27	70	.184	.273	.281	554	64	-11	4	4	-1	.972	-11	2-84/S-1,3-1	-1.8

YEAR	TM/L	G	AB	R	H	2B	3B	HR	RBI	BB	SO	AVG	OBP	SLG	OPS	OPS+	BR+	SB	CS	SBR	FA	FR	G/POS	TPR
1966	KC-A	27	34	3	7	0	1	0	2	4	10	.206	.289	.265	554	62	-2	1	0	0	1.000	2	2-10/S-4	0.1
Total	3	141	274	37	50	10	4	2	8	33	85	.182	.273	.270	543	60	-14	5	4	-0	.974	-9	/2-94,S-15,3-1	-1.8
■ **CARLOS FEBLES** Febles, Carlos Manuel b: 5/24/76, ElSeibo, D.R. BR/TR, 5'11", 170 lbs. Deb: 9/14/98																								
1998	KC-A	11	25	5	10	1	2	0	2	4	7	.400	.483	.600	1083	175	3	2	1	0	1.000	0	2-11	0.3
1999	KC-A	123	453	71	116	22	9	10	53	47	91	.256	.338	.411	749	88	-8	20	4	3	.979	1	*2-122	0.1
2000	KC-A	100	339	59	87	12	1	2	29	36	48	.257	.345	.316	661	68	-15	17	6	2	.978	-13	2-99	-2.0
Total	3	234	817	135	213	35	12	12	84	87	146	.261	.346	.377	723	82	-21	39	11	5	.979	-12	2-232	-1.6
■ **AL FEDEROFF** Federoff, Alfred "Whitey" b: 7/11/24, Bairdford, Pa. BR/TR, 5'10.5", 165 lbs. Deb: 9/27/51																								
1951	Det-A	2	4	0	0	0	0	0	0	0	0	.000	.000	.000	0	-99	-1	0	0	0	.889	1	/2-1	0.0
1952	Det-A	74	231	14	56	4	2	0	14	16	13	.242	.294	.277	571	59	-13	1	0	0	.976	0	2-70/S-7	-0.9
Total	2	76	235	14	56	4	2	0	14	16	13	.238	.290	.272	562	56	-14	1	0	0	.973	1	/2-71,S-7	-0.9
■ **DUTCH FEHRING** Fehring, William Paul "Bill" b: 5/31/12, Columbus, Ind. BB/TR, 6', 195 lbs. Deb: 6/25/34																								
1934	Chi-A	1	1	0	0	0	0	0	0	0	1	.000	.000	.000	0	-97	-0	0	0	0	1.000	0	/C-1	0.0
■ **EDDIE FEINBERG** Feinberg, Edward Isadore "Itzzy" b: 9/29/17, Philadelphia, Pa. d: 4/20/86, Hollywood, Fla. BB/TR, 5'9", 165 lbs. Deb: 9/11/38																								
1938	Phi-N	10	20	0	3	0	0	0	0	0	1	.150	.150	.150	300	-18	-3	0			.957	3	/S-4,O-2(1-0-2)	0.0
1939	Phi-N	6	18	2	4	1	0	0	0	2	0	.222	.300	.278	578	58	-1	0			.909	-4	/2-4,S-1	-0.5
Total	2	16	38	2	7	1	0	0	0	2	1	.184	.225	.211	436	20	-4	0			.957	-2	/S-5,2-4,O-2(1-0-2)	-0.5
■ **MIKE FELDER** Felder, Michael Otis b: 11/18/61, Vallejo, Cal. BB/TR, 5'8", 160 lbs. Deb: 9/11/85 Career OF: (408-LF 212-CF 169-RF)																								
1985	Mil-A	15	56	8	11	1	0	0	0	5	6	.196	.262	.214	477	33	-5	4	1	1	1.000	-0	O-14(0-14-0)	-0.5
1986	Mil-A	44	155	24	37	2	4	1	13	13	16	.239	.298	.323	620	67	-7	16	2	3	1.000	2	O-42(30-7-6)/D-1	-0.4
1987	Mil-A	108	289	48	77	5	7	2	31	28	23	.266	.331	.353	684	79	-8	34	8	5	.975	1	O-99(80-22-0)/2-1,D-3	-0.5
1988	Mil-A	50	81	14	14	1	0	0	5	0	11	.173	.183	.185	368	3	-10	8	2	1	.976	-5	O-28L,D-16/2-1	-1.6
1989	Mil-A	117	315	50	76	11	3	3	23	23	38	.241	.293	.324	617	74	-11	26	5	4	.985	-1	O-93R,D-11,2-10	-1.0
1990	Mil-A	121	237	38	65	7	2	3	27	22	17	.274	.336	.359	695	95	-1	20	9	1	.972	-12	*O-109L/2-1,3-1,D-1	-1.5
1991	SF-N	132	343	51	92	10	6	0	18	30	31	.264	.325	.328	652	87	-6	21	6	3	.985	-11	*O-107L/3-3,2-1	-1.7
1992	SF-N	145	322	44	92	13	3	4	23	21	29	.286	.333	.382	715	108	3	14	4	2	.994	-20	*O-105(53-58-11)/2-3	-1.9
1993	Sea-A	109	342	31	72	7	5	1	20	22	34	.211	.262	.269	531	43	-28	15	9	0	.987	-3	O-95(89-7-0)/3-2,D-6	-3.2
1994	Hou-N	58	117	10	28	2	2	0	13	4	12	.239	.264	.291	555	47	-9	3	0	1	.974	-6	O-32(8-6-21)	-1.5
Total	10	899	2262	318	564	59	32	14	173	168	217	.249	.303	.322	625	73	-83	161	46	19	.984	-55	O-724L/D-38,2-17,3	-13.8
■ **MARV FELDERMAN** Felderman, Marvin Wilfred "Coonie" b: 12/20/15, Bellevue, Iowa BR/TR, 6'1", 187 lbs. Deb: 4/19/42																								
1942	Chi-N	3	6	0	1	0	0	0	0	1	4	.167	.286	.167	452	35	-0	0			1.000	1	/C-2	0.0
■ **GUS FELIX** Felix, August Guenther b: 5/24/1895, Cincinnati, Ohio d: 5/12/60, Montgomery, Ala. BR/TR, 6', 180 lbs. Deb: 4/19/23 Career OF: (344-LF 196-CF 5-RF)																								
1923	Bos-N	139	506	64	138	17	2	6	44	51	65	.273	.348	.350	697	88	-7	8	13	-3	.950	0	*O-123L/2-5,3-4	-1.8
1924	Bos-N	59	204	25	43	7	1	1	10	18	16	.211	.275	.270	544	48	-15	0	3	-1	.950	5	O-51(11-38-2)	-1.4
1925	Bos-N	121	459	60	141	25	7	2	66	30	34	.307	.356	.405	762	103	2	5	5	-1	.972	10	*O-114(42-74-3)	0.5
1926	Bro-N	134	432	64	121	21	7	3	53	51	32	.280	.360	.382	742	101	2	9			.956	-2	*O-125(53-74-0)	-0.7
1927	Bro-N	130	445	43	118	21	8	0	57	39	47	.265	.327	.348	675	81	-12	6			.947	-3	*O-119(117-4-0)	-2.4
Total	5	583	2046	256	561	91	25	12	230	189	194	.274	.341	.361	701	89	-30	28	21		.957	11	O-532L/2-5,3-4	-5.8
■ **JUNIOR FELIX** Felix, Junior Francisco (Sanchez) b: 10/3/67, Laguna Salada, D.R. BB/TR, 5'11", 165 lbs. Deb: 5/3/89																								
1989	*Tor-A	110	415	62	107	14	8	9	46	33	101	.258	.317	.395	712	101	0	18	12	-0	.966	3	*O-107(0-24-86)/D-2	0.0
1990	Tor-A	127	463	73	122	23	7	15	65	45	99	.263	.331	.441	772	112	7	13	8	0	.966	2	*O-125(0-28-99)/D-1	0.5
1991	Cal-A	66	230	32	65	10	2	2	26	11	55	.283	.324	.370	693	91	-3	7	5	-0	.977	-6	O-65(0-63-2)	-1.0
1992	Cal-A	139	509	63	125	22	5	9	72	33	128	.246	.294	.361	656	82	-13	8	8	-1	.983	7	*O-128(0-125-4)/D-8	-0.9
1993	Fla-N	57	214	25	51	11	1	7	22	10	50	.238	.276	.397	673	73	-9	2	1	0	.940	-2	O-52(0-3-50)	-1.3
1994	Det-A	86	30[illegible]	54	92	25	1	13	49	26	76	.306	.376	.525	901	129	13	1	6	-2	.980	5	O-81(5-2-72)/D-2	1.1
Total	6	585	2132	309	562	105	24	55	280	158	509	.264	.320	.413	733	99	-5	49	40	-3	.972	8	O-558(5-245-313)/D-13	-1.6
■ **PEDRO FELIZ** Feliz, Pedro Julio b: 4/27/77, Azua, D.R. BR/TR, 6'1", 180 lbs. Deb: 9/5/2000																								
2000	SF-N	8	7	1	2	0	0	0	0	0	1	.286	.286	.286	571	48	-1	0	0	0	.000	-1	/3-4	-0.1
■ **JACK FELLER** Feller, Jack Leland b: 12/10/36, Adrian, Mich. BR/TR, 5'10.5", 185 lbs. Deb: 9/13/58																								
1958	Det-A	1	0	0	0	0	0	0	0	0	0	—	—	—	—	—	0	0	0	0	1.000	-0	/C-1	0.0
■ **HAPPY FELSCH** Felsch, Oscar Emil b: 8/22/1891, Milwaukee, Wis. d: 8/17/64, Milwaukee, Wis. BR/TR, 5'11", 175 lbs. Deb: 4/14/15																								
1915	Chi-A	121	427	65	106	18	11	3	53	51	59	.248	.334	.363	697	105	2	16	18	-3	.959	-3	*O-118(34-73-10)	-1.2
1916	Chi-A	146	546	73	164	24	12	7	70	31	67	.300	.341	.427	768	129	16	13			**.981**	7	*O-141(0-141-0)	1.4
1917	*Chi-A	152	575	75	177	17	10	6	102	33	52	.308	.352	.403	755	128	17	26			.985	19	*O-152(0-152-0)	2.8
1918	Chi-A	53	206	16	52	2	5	1	20	15	13	.252	.306	.325	632	90	-3	6			.957	5	O-53(0-53-0)	-0.2
1919	*Chi-A	135	502	68	138	34	11	7	86	40	35	.275	.336	.428	764	113	7	19			.968	21	*O-135(0-135-0)	2.0
1920	Chi-A	142	556	88	188	40	15	14	115	37	25	.338	.384	.540	923	143	31	8	13	-3	.981	18	*O-142(0-142-0)	3.5
Total	6	749	2812	385	825	135	64	38	446	207	251	.293	.347	.427	774	123	70	88	31		.975	67	O-741(34-696-10)	8.3
■ **JOHN FELSKE** Felske, John Frederick b: 5/30/42, Chicago, Ill. BR/TR, 6'3", 195 lbs. Deb: 7/26/68 MC																								
1968	Chi-N	4	2	0	0	0	0	0	0	0	1	.000	.000	.000	0	-94	-0	0	0	0	.833	1	/C-3	0.0
1972	Mil-A	37	80	6	11	3	0	1	5	8	23	.138	.216	.213	428	28	-7	0	0	0	.972	-2	C-23/1-8	-1.0
1973	Mil-A	13	22	1	3	0	1	0	4	1	11	.136	.174	.227	401	12	-3	0	0	0	1.000	0	/C-7,1-6	-0.3
Total	3	54	104	7	14	3	1	1	9	9	35	.135	.204	.212	415	23	-10	0	0	0	.969	-1	/C-33,1-14	-1.3
■ **FRANK FENNELLY** Fennelly, Francis John b: 2/18/1860, Fall River, Mass. d: 8/4/20, Fall River, Mass. BR/TR, 5'8", 168 lbs. Deb: 5/1/1884 Career OF: (2-LF 2-CF 0-RF)																								
1884	Was-a	62	257	52	75	17	7	2		20		.292	.343	.436	779	172	22				.863	13	S-60/2-4	3.2
	Cin-a	28	122	42	43	5	8	2		11		.352	.415	.574	989	209	14				.813	-6	S-28	0.8
	Yr	90	379	94	118	22	15	4		31		.311	.367	.480	847	186	37				.849	7	S-88/2-4	4.0
1885	Cin-a	112	454	82	124	14	17	10	**89**	38		.273	.333	.445	778	142	21				.873	-11	*S-112	1.1
1886	Cin-a	132	497	113	124	13	17	6	72	60		.249	.351	.380	732	125	15	32			.848	14	*S-132	2.9
1887	Cin-a	134	608	133	222	15	16	8	97	82		.365	.369	.401	770	112	10	74			.855	-9	*S-134	0.4
1888	Cin-a	120	448	64	88	8	7	2	56	63		.196	.297	.259	556	75	-12	43			.858	17	*S-112/2-4,O-4(2-2-0)	0.8
	Phi-a	15	47	13	11	2	2	1	12	9		.234	.357	.426	783	151	3	5			.912	-1	S-15	0.2
	Yr	135	495	77	99	10	9	3	68	72		.200	.303	.275	578	82	-9	48			.863	16	*S-127/2-4,O-4(2-2-0)	1.0
1889	Phi-a	138	513	70	132	20	5	1	64	65	78	.257	.344	.322	666	91	-4	15			.872	-20	*S-138	-1.7
1890	Bro-a	45	178	40	44	8	3	2	18	30		.247	.356	.360	715	115	4	6			.858	0	S-38/3-7	0.5
Total	7	786	3124	609	863	102	82	34	408	378	78	.276	.345	.378	723	118	73	175			.860	-4	S-769/2-8,3-7,O-4L	8.2
■ **BOBBY FENWICK** Fenwick, Robert Richard b: 12/10/46, Naha, Okinawa BR/TR, 5'9", 165 lbs. Deb: 4/26/72																								
1972	Hou-N	36	50	7	9	3	0	0	4	3	13	.180	.226	.240	466	33	-4	0	1	-0	.945	3	2-17/S-4,3-2	-0.1
1973	StL-N	5	6	0	1	0	0	0	1	0	2	.167	.167	.167	333	-7	-1	0	0	0	.750	-1	/2-3	-0.2
Total	2	41	56	7	10	3	0	0	5	3	15	.179	.220	.232	452	29	-5	0	1	-0	.932	3	/2-20,S-4,3-2	-0.3
■ **JOE FERGUSON** Ferguson, Joseph Vance b: 9/19/46, San Francisco, Cal. BR/TR, 6'2", 200 lbs. Deb: 9/12/70 C Career OF: (18-LF 1-CF 188-RF)																								
1970	LA-N	5	4	0	1	0	0	0	1	2	2	.250	.500	.250	750	112	0	0	0	0	1.000	0	/C-3	0.0
1971	LA-N	36	102	13	22	3	0	2	7	12	15	.216	.304	.304	608	77	-3	1	0	0	.983	-2	C-35	-0.3
1972	LA-N	8	24	2	7	3	0	1	5	2	4	.292	.346	.542	888	152	2	0	0	0	1.000	2	/C-7,O-2(0-0-2)	0.3
1973	LA-N	136	487	84	128	26	0	25	88	87	81	.263	.376	.470	846	139	27	1	1	-0	**.996**	-0	*C-122,O-20(5-1-14)	3.3
1974	*LA-N	111	349	54	88	14	1	16	57	75	73	.252	.384	.436	820	134	18	2	2	-0	.988	-10	C-82,O-32(0-0-32)	1.1
1975	LA-N	66	202	15	42	2	1	5	23	35	47	.208	.328	.302	630	79	-5	2	1	0	.994	-1	C-35,O-34(2-0-32)	-0.6
1976	LA-N	54	185	24	41	7	0	6	18	25	41	.222	.318	.357	674	93	-2	2	0	0	.966	-1	O-39(0-0-39),C-17	-0.4

YEAR	TM/L	G	AB	R	H	2B	3B	HR	RBI	BB	SO	AVG	OBP	SLG	OPS	OPS+	BR+	SB	CS	SBR	FA	FR	G/POS	TPR
	StL-N	71	189	22	38	8	4	4	21	32	40	.201	.320	.349	669	89	-2	4	2	0	.978	3	C-48,O-14(0-0-14)	0.3
	Yr	125	374	46	79	15	4	10	39	57	81	.211	.319	.353	672	91	-4	6	2	1	.975	2	C-65,O-53(0-0-53)	-0.1
1977	Hou-N	132	421	59	108	21	3	16	61	85	79	.257	.381	.435	816	130	20	6	2	1	.985	-10	*C-122/1-1	1.6
1978	Hou-N	51	150	20	31	5	0	7	22	37	30	.207	.367	.380	747	118	5	0	0	0	.994	-6	C-51	0.2
	*LA-N	67	198	20	47	11	0	7	28	34	41	.237	.352	.399	751	110	3	1	2	-0	.984	-10	C-62/O-3(2-0-1)	-0.5
	Yr	118	348	40	78	16	0	14	50	71	71	.224	.359	.391	749	113	8	1	2	-0	.989	-16	*C-113/O-3(2-0-1)	-0.3
1979	LA-N	122	363	54	95	14	0	20	69	70	68	.262	.384	.466	849	133	18	1	0	0	.981	-12	C-67,O-52(5-0-47)	0.7
1980	LA-N	77	172	20	41	3	2	9	29	38	46	.238	.376	.436	812	128	8	2	2	-0	.982	-3	C-66/O-1(0-0-1)	0.7
1981	LA-N	17	14	2	2	1	0	0	1	2	5	.143	.250	.214	464	34	-1	0	0	0	.000	-0	/O-1(0-0-1)	-0.2
	Cal-A	12	30	5	7	1	0	1	5	9	8	.233	.410	.367	777	125	2	0	0	0	.976	0	/C-8,O-4(3-0-1)	0.2
1982	Cal-A	36	84	10	19	2	0	3	8	12	19	.226	.323	.357	680	87	-1	0	0	0	.993	5	C-32/O-2(0-0-2)	0.5
1983	Cal-A	12	27	3	2	0	0	0	2	5	8	.074	.219	.074	293	-15	-4	0	0	0	.968	-2	/C-9,O-3(1-0-2)	-0.6
Total	14	1013	3001	407	719	121	11	122	445	562	607	.240	.361	.409	770	117	85	22	12	1	.987	-47	C-766,O-207R/1-1	6.3
■ **BOB FERGUSON**	Ferguson, Robert Vavasour b: 1/31/1845, Brooklyn, N.Y. d: 5/3/1894, Brooklyn, N.Y. BB/TR, 5'9.5", 149 lbs. Deb: 5/18/1871 MU Career OF: (0-LF 1-CF 5-RF)																							
1871	Mut-n	33	158	30	38	6	1	0	25	3	2	.241	.255	.291	546	62	-6	4	4	-1	.774	4	*3-20,2-11/C-5,PM	-0.2
1872	Atl-n	37	165	33	46	5	0	0	19	3	0	.279	.292	.309	601	72	-8	4	2	0	.809	**36**	*3-37/C-1,M	1.9
1873	Atl-n	51	228	36	59	3	5	0	25	4	9	.259	.272	.316	587	83	-2	1	2	-0	.755	**32**	*3-50/P-4,M	1.9
1874	Atl-n	56	245	34	64	4	0	0	19	2	7	.261	.267	.278	545	85	-2	5	3	0	.760	3	*3-55/C-2,P-1,M	-0.1
1875	Har-n	85	366	65	88	10	4	0	43	3	5	.240	.247	.290	536	82	-8	2	1	0	**.827**	8	*3-85/P-1,M	-0.2
1876	Har-N	69	312	48	82	8	5	0	32	2	11	.263	.269	.323	592	89	-5				.826	2	*3-69,M	-0.1
1877	Har-N	58	254	40	65	7	2	0	35	3	10	.256	.265	.299	564	86	-3				.841	17	*3-56/P-3,M	1.4
1878	Chi-N	61	259	44	91	10	2	0	39	10	12	.351	**.375**	.405	781	147	12				.881	16	*S-57/2-4,C-1,M	2.8
1879	Tro-N	30	123	18	31	5	2	0	4	4	3	.252	.276	.325	601	104	1				.808	2	3-24/2-6,M	0.4
1880	Tro-N	82	332	55	87	9	0	0	22	**24**	24	.262	.312	.289	601	100	0				.904	-3	*2-82,M	0.1
1881	Tro-N	85	339	56	96	13	5	1	35	29	12	.283	.340	.360	700	114	6				.904	-10	*2-85,M	-0.1
1882	Tro-N	81	319	44	82	15	2	0	32	23	21	.257	.307	.317	624	106	3				.914	-13	*2-79/S-2,M	-0.6
1883	Phi-N	86	329	39	85	9	2	0	27	18	21	.258	.297	.298	595	89	-2				.862	-8	*2-86/P-1,M	-0.6
1884	Pit-a	10	41	2	6	0	0	0		0		.146	.146	.146	293	-4	-5				.714	-3	/O-6(0-1-5),1-3,3-1,M	-0.8
Total	5 n	262	1162	198	295	28	10	0	131	15	23	.254	.263	.295	559	78	-25	16	12	-1	.787	82	3-247/2-11,C-8,P-7	3.3
Total	9	562	2308	346	625	76	20	1	226	113	114	.271	.305	.323	628	102	8				.895	-0	2-342,3-150/SOP1C	2.5
■ **FELIX FERMIN**	Fermin, Felix Jose (Minaya) b: 10/9/63, Mao Valverde, D.R. BR/TR, 5'11", 170 lbs. Deb: 7/8/87																							
1987	Pit-N	23	68	6	17	0	0	0	4	4	9	.250	.301	.250	551	48	-5	0	0	0	.980	1	S-23	-0.1
1988	Pit-N	43	87	9	24	0	2	0	2	8	10	.276	.357	.322	679	98	0	3	1	0	.955	-5	S-43	-0.3
1989	Cle-A	156	484	50	115	9	1	0	21	41	27	.238	.302	.260	563	59	-25	6	4	-0	.967	18	*S-153/2-2	0.4
1990	Cle-A	148	414	47	106	13	2	1	40	26	22	.256	.300	.304	604	70	-17	3	3	-0	.975	4	*S-147/2-1	-0.2
1991	Cle-A	129	424	30	111	13	2	0	31	26	27	.262	.309	.302	611	69	-17	5	4	-0	.980	1	*S-129	-0.7
1992	Cle-A	79	215	27	58	7	2	0	13	18	10	.270	.329	.321	650	84	-4	0	0	0	.971	-5	S-55,3-17/2-7,1-2	-0.6
1993	Cle-A	140	480	48	126	16	2	2	45	24	14	.262	.303	.317	620	67	-22	4	5	-1	.960	-29	*S-140	-4.0
1994	Sea-A	101	379	52	120	21	0	1	35	11	22	.317	.343	.380	723	84	-9	4	4	-1	.974	-6	S-77,2-25	-0.7
1995	*Sea-A	73	200	21	39	6	0	0	15	6	6	.195	.233	.225	458	20	-24	2	0	0	.971	13	S-46,2-29	-0.6
1996	Chi-N	11	16	4	2	1	0	0	1	2	0	.125	.222	.188	410	9	-2	0	0	0	.875	-3	/2-6,S-2	-0.5
Total	10	903	2767	294	718	86	11	4	207	166	147	.259	.307	.303	610	67	-124	27	21	-1	.971	-11	S-815/2-70,3-17,1-2	-7.3
■ **ED FERNANDES**	Fernandes, Edward Paul b: 3/11/18, Oakland, Cal. d: 11/27/68, Hayward, Cal. BB/TR, 5'9", 185 lbs. Deb: 6/9/40																							
1940	Pit-N	28	33	1	4	1	0	0	2	7	6	.121	.275	.152	427	21	-3	0			.981	0	C-27	-0.2
1946	Chi-A	14	32	4	8	2	0	0	4	8	7	.250	.400	.313	713	105	1	0	0	0	.922	-1	C-12	0.0
Total	2	42	65	5	12	3	0	0	6	15	13	.185	.338	.231	568	61	-3	0	0		.952	-0	/C-39	-0.2
■ **FRANK FERNANDEZ**	Fernandez, Frank b: 4/16/43, Staten Island, N.Y. BR/TR, 6'1", 192 lbs. Deb: 9/12/67																							
1967	NY-A	9	28	1	6	2	0	1	4	2	7	.214	.290	.393	683	104	0	1	1	-0	1.000	0	/C-7,O-2(0-0-2)	0.0
1968	NY-A	51	135	15	23	6	1	7	30	35	50	.170	.341	.385	726	124	5	1	0	0	.989	6	C-45/O-4(0-0-4)	1.4
1969	NY-A	89	229	34	51	6	1	12	29	65	68	.223	.401	.415	816	133	14	1	3	-1	.994	-8	C-65,O-14(0-0-14)	0.8
1970	Oak-A	94	252	30	54	5	0	15	44	40	76	.214	.327	.413	739	106	2	1	0	0	.993	-1	C-76/O-1(1-0-0)	0.5
1971	Oak-A	2	4	0	0	0	0	0	0	1	2	.000	.200	.000	200	-40	-1	0	0	0	1.000	2	/C-2	0.1
	Was-A	18	30	0	3	0	0	0	4	4	10	.100	.206	.100	306	-12	-4	0	0	0	1.000	-1	/O-6(3-1-2),C-1	-0.6
	Oak-A	2	5	1	1	1	0	0	1	0	1	.200	.200	.400	600	68	-0	0	0	0	1.000	-0	/C-1	-0.1
	Yr	22	39	1	4	1	0	0	5	5	13	.103	.205	.128	333	-4	-5	0	0	0	1.000	0	/O-6(3-1-2),C-4	-0.6
	Chi-N	17	41	11	7	1	0	4	4	17	15	.171	.414	.488	902	135	3	0	0	0	.980	0	C-16	0.4
1972	Chi-N	3	3	0	0	0	0	0	0	0	2	.000	.000	.000	0	-90	-1	0	0	0	1.000	-0	/C-1	-0.1
Total	6	285	727	92	145	21	2	39	116	164	231	.199	.351	.395	746	114	17	4	4	-1	.992	-2	C-214/O-27(4-1-22)	2.4
■ **NANNY FERNANDEZ**	Fernandez, Froilan b: 10/25/18, Wilmington, Cal. d: 9/19/96, Lomita, Cal. BR/TR, 5'9", 170 lbs. Deb: 4/14/42 Career OF: (56-LF 3-CF 8-RF)																							
1942	Bos-N	145	577	63	147	29	3	6	55	38	61	.255	.303	.347	650	92	-8	15			.914	6	3-98,O-44(42-3-0)	-0.1
1946	Bos-N	115	372	37	95	15	2	2	42	30	44	.255	.313	.323	635	79	-10	1			.940	-2	3-81,S-18,O-14L	-1.4
1947	Bos-N	83	209	16	43	4	0	2	21	22	20	.206	.281	.254	535	44	-17	2			.933	-13	S-62/O-8(0-0-8),3-6	-2.7
1950	Pit-N	65	198	23	51	11	0	6	27	19	17	.258	.326	.404	730	88	-4	2			.925	-3	3-52	-0.7
Total	4	408	1356	139	336	59	5	16	145	109	142	.248	.306	.334	640	80	-38	20			.925	-13	3-237/S-80,O-66L	-4.9
■ **CHICO FERNANDEZ**	Fernandez, Humberto (Perez) b: 3/2/32, Havana, Cuba BR/TR, 6', 170 lbs. Deb: 7/14/56																							
1956	Bro-N	34	66	11	15	2	0	1	9	3	10	.227	.261	.303	564	47	-5	2	3	-1	.978	7	S-25	0.3
1957	Phi-N	149	500	42	131	14	4	5	51	31	64	.262	.306	.336	642	75	-18	18	5	2	.960	-25	*S-149	-2.9
1958	Phi-N	148	522	38	120	18	5	6	51	37	48	.230	.283	.318	601	60	-31	12	6	1	.975	-12	*S-148	-3.0
1959	Phi-N	45	123	15	26	5	1	0	3	10	11	.211	.271	.268	539	43	-10	2	1	0	.958	-3	S-40/2-2	-1.0
1960	Det-A	133	435	44	105	13	3	4	35	39	50	.241	.305	.313	618	66	-20	13	4	1	.947	-4	*S-130	-1.3
1961	Det-A	133	435	41	108	15	4	3	40	36	45	.248	.306	.322	628	66	-21	8	5	0	.958	-8	*S-121/3-8	-1.9
1962	Det-A	141	503	64	125	17	2	20	59	42	69	.249	.306	.410	716	88	-10	10	3	1	.960	-27	*S-138/3-2,1-1	-2.4
1963	Det-A	15	49	3	7	1	0	0	2	6	11	.143	.236	.163	400	14	-6	0	1	-0	.947	2	S-14	-0.3
	NY-N	58	145	12	29	6	0	1	9	9	30	.200	.247	.262	509	46	-10	3	0	1	.944	-16	S-45/3-5,2-3	-2.4
Total	8	856	2778	270	666	91	19	40	259	213	338	.240	.295	.329	624	67	-130	68	28	5	.960	-86	S-810/3-15,2-5,1-1	-14.9
■ **JOSE FERNANDEZ**	Fernandez, Jose Mayobanex (Rojas) b: 11/2/74, LaVega, D.R. BR/TR, 6'2", 220 lbs. Deb: 7/3/99																							
1999	Mon-N	8	24	0	5	2	0	0	1	1	7	.208	.240	.292	532	35	-2	0	0	0	.889	-1	/3-6	-0.3
■ **CHICO FERNANDEZ**	Fernandez, Lorenzo Marto (Mosquera) b: 4/23/39, Havana, Cuba BR/TR, 5'10", 160 lbs. Deb: 4/20/68																							
1968	Bal-A	24	18	0	2	0	0	0	0	1	2	.111	.158	.111	269	-17	-3	0	0	0	.923	3	/S-7,2-4	0.0
■ **TONY FERNANDEZ**	Fernandez, Octavio Antonio (Castro) (b: Octavio Antonio Fernando (Castro)) b: 6/30/62, San Pedro De Macoris, D.R. BB/TR, 6'2", 175 lbs. Deb: 9/2/83																							
1983	Tor-A	15	34	5	9	1	1	0	2	2	2	.265	.324	.353	677	81	-1	0	1	-0	1.000	-3	S-13/D-1	-0.3
1984	Tor-A	88	233	29	63	5	3	3	19	17	15	.270	.320	.356	676	84	-5	5	7	-1	.974	3	S-73,3-10/D-1	0.3
1985	*Tor-A	161	564	71	163	31	10	2	51	43	41	.289	.342	.390	732	97	-2	13	6	1	.962	5	*S-160	2.1
1986	Tor-A★	163	687	91	213	33	9	10	65	27	52	.310	.340	.428	768	105	4	25	12	1	**.983**	3	*S-163	2.5
1987	Tor-A★	146	578	90	186	29	8	5	67	51	48	.322	.382	.426	807	112	11	32	12	3	.979	6	*S-146	3.3
1988	Tor-A	154	648	76	186	41	4	5	70	45	65	.287	.337	.386	723	101	1	15	5	2	.981	10	*S-154	2.4
1989	*Tor-A★	140	573	64	147	25	9	11	64	29	51	.257	.296	.389	685	93	-7	22	6	3	**.992**	18	*S-140	2.5
1990	Tor-A	161	635	84	175	27	**17**	4	66	71	70	.276	.355	.391	745	106	7	26	13	1	.989	9	*S-161	2.9
1991	SD-N	145	558	81	152	27	5	4	38	55	74	.272	.338	.360	698	93	-4	23	9	2	.972	3	*S-145	1.3
1992	SD-N★	155	622	84	171	32	4	4	37	56	62	.275	.339	.359	697	96	-2	20	20	-3	.983	-17	*S-154	-1.1
1993	NY-N	48	173	20	39	5	2	1	14	25	19	.225	.327	.295	621	69	-7	6	2	1	.975	7	S-48	0.5

YEAR	TM/L	G	AB	R	H	2B	3B	HR	RBI	BB	SO	AVG	OBP	SLG	OPS	OPS+	BR+	SB	CS	SBR	FA	FR	G/POS	TPR
	*Tor-A	94	353	45	108	18	9	4	50	31	26	.306	.362	.442	804	114	7	15	8	1	.985	5	S-94	2.0
1994	Cin-N	104	366	50	102	18	6	8	50	44	40	.279	.364	.426	790	106	4	12	7	0	**.991**	2	3-93/S-9,2-5	0.7
1995	*NY-A	108	384	57	94	20	2	5	45	42	40	.245	.326	.346	672	76	-13	6	6	-1	.976	-13	*S-103/2-4	-1.7
1997	*Cle-A	120	409	55	117	21	1	11	44	22	47	.286	.326	.423	749	90	-6	6	6	-1	.980	17	*2-109,S-10/D-1	1.4
1998	Tor-A	138	486	71	156	36	2	9	72	45	53	.321	.391	.459	850	120	15	13	8	0	.975	-17	2-82,3-54/D-1	0.3
1999	Tor-A★	142	485	73	159	41	0	6	75	77	62	.328	.430	.449	880	123	21	6	7	-1	.939	-12	*3-132,D-11/2-1	0.8
Total	16	2082	7788	1046	2240	410	92	92	829	682	767	.288	.350	.399	749	101	23	245	135	7	.980	27	*S-1573,3-289,2/D	19.9

■ AL FERRARA

Ferrara, Alfred John "The Bull" b: 12/22/39, Brooklyn, N.Y. BR/TR, 6'1", 203 lbs. Deb: 7/30/63

YEAR	TM/L	G	AB	R	H	2B	3B	HR	RBI	BB	SO	AVG	OBP	SLG	OPS	OPS+	BR+	SB	CS	SBR	FA	FR	G/POS	TPR
1963	LA-N	21	44	2	7	0	0	1	1	6	9	.159	.275	.227	502	50	-3	0	0	0	.950	1	O-11(7-0-4)	-0.3
1965	LA-N	41	81	5	17	2	1	1	10	9	20	.210	.297	.296	593	72	-3	0	0	0	.927	-3	O-27(10-0-19)	-0.8
1966	*LA-N	63	115	15	31	4	0	5	23	9	35	.270	.339	.435	773	123	3	0	0	0	.956	-3	O-32(4-1-27)	-0.2
1967	LA-N	122	347	41	96	16	1	16	50	33	73	.277	.345	.467	812	142	18	0	0	-0	.978	-10	O-94(27-0-71)	0.2
1968	LA-N	2	7	0	1	0	0	0	0	0	2	.143	.143	.143	286	-15	-1	0	0	0	.500	-1	/O-2(2-0-0)	-0.2
1969	SD-N	138	366	39	95	22	1	14	56	45	69	.260	.352	.440	792	125	12	0	0	0	.958	-2	O-96(95-1-0)	0.5
1970	SD-N	138	372	44	103	15	4	13	51	46	63	.277	.373	.444	817	123	13	0	0	0	.968	-8	O-96(96-0-0)	-0.1
1971	SD-N	17	17	0	2	1	0	0	2	5	5	.118	.318	.176	495	47	-1	0	0	0	1.000	-1	/O-2(2-0-0)	-0.2
	Cin-N	32	33	2	6	0	0	1	5	3	10	.182	.270	.273	543	55	-2	0	0	0	1.000	-1	/O-5(5-0-0)	-0.3
	Yr	49	50	2	8	1	0	1	7	8	15	.160	.288	.240	528	53	-3	0	0	0	1.000	-1	/O-7(7-0-0)	-0.5
Total	8	574	1382	148	358	60	7	51	198	156	286	.259	.346	.423	769	120	37	0	1	-0	.962	-28	O-365(248-2-121)	-1.4

■ MIKE FERRARO

Ferraro, Michael Dennis b: 8/18/44, Kingston, N.Y. BR/TR, 5'11", 175 lbs. Deb: 9/6/66 MC

YEAR	TM/L	G	AB	R	H	2B	3B	HR	RBI	BB	SO	AVG	OBP	SLG	OPS	OPS+	BR+	SB	CS	SBR	FA	FR	G/POS	TPR
1966	NY-A	10	28	4	5	0	0	0	0	3	3	.179	.281	.179	460	37	-2	0	0	0	.926	1	3-10	-0.1
1968	NY-A	23	87	5	14	0	1	0	1	2	17	.161	.180	.184	364	11	-9	0	0	0	.975	4	3-22	-0.6
1969	Sea-A	5	4	0	0	0	0	0	0	1	0	.000	.200	.000	200	-41	-1	0	0	0	.000	0	H	-0.1
1972	Mil-A	124	381	19	97	18	1	2	29	17	41	.255	.286	.323	609	83	-9	0	5	-2	.950	-16	*3-115/S-1	-3.1
Total	4	162	500	28	116	18	2	2	30	23	61	.232	.267	.288	555	67	-21	0	5	-2	.953	-10	3-147/S-1	-3.9

■ RICK FERRELL

Ferrell, Richard Benjamin b: 10/12/05, Durham, N.C. d: 7/27/95, Bloomfield Hills, Mich. BR/TR, 5'10", 160 lbs. Deb: 4/19/29 FCH

YEAR	TM/L	G	AB	R	H	2B	3B	HR	RBI	BB	SO	AVG	OBP	SLG	OPS	OPS+	BR+	SB	CS	SBR	FA	FR	G/POS	TPR
1929	StL-A	64	144	21	33	6	1	0	20	32	10	.229	.373	.285	658	69	-5	1	2	-0	.962	0	C-45	-0.3
1930	StL-A	101	314	43	84	18	4	1	41	46	10	.268	.363	.360	723	81	-8	1	4	-1	.983	-9	*C-101	-1.1
1931	StL-A	117	386	47	118	30	4	3	57	56	12	.306	.394	.427	821	112	8	2	3	-1	.973	4	*C-108	1.7
1932	StL-A	126	438	67	138	30	5	2	65	66	18	.315	.406	.420	826	108	8	5	5	-1	.986	-2	*C-120	1.2
1933	StL-A	22	72	8	18	2	0	1	5	12	4	.250	.357	.319	677	76	-2	2	0	0	.991	3	C-21	0.2
	Bos-A★	118	421	50	125	19	4	3	72	58	19	.297	.385	.382	767	105	5	2	2	-0	.990	5	*C-116	1.6
	Yr	140	493	58	143	21	4	4	77	70	23	.290	.381	.373	754	100	3	4	2	0	.990	8	*C-137	1.8
1934	Bos-A☆	132	437	50	130	29	4	1	48	66	20	.297	.390	.389	779	95	-1	0	0	0	**.990**	3	*C-128	0.9
1935	Bos-A☆	133	458	54	138	34	4	3	61	65	15	.301	.388	.413	801	100	2	5	8	-2	.979	13	*C-131	2.0
1936	Bos-A★	121	410	59	128	27	5	8	55	65	17	.312	.406	.461	867	108	6	0	1	-0	.987	9	*C-121	1.9
1937	Bos-A	18	65	8	20	2	0	1	4	15	4	.308	.438	.385	822	105	1	0	0	0	.990	0	C-18	0.2
	Was-A☆	86	279	31	64	6	0	1	32	50	18	.229	.348	.262	610	59	-16	1	1	-0	.987	-6	C-84	-1.5
	Yr	104	344	39	84	8	0	2	36	65	22	.244	.366	.285	651	68	-14	1	1	-0	.988	-6	*C-102	-1.3
1938	Was-A☆	135	411	55	120	24	5	1	58	75	17	.292	.401	.382	783	104	6	1	0	0	.981	-5	*C-131	0.9
1939	Was-A	87	274	32	77	13	1	0	31	41	12	.281	.377	.336	712	90	-2	1	1	-0	.976	-6	C-83	-0.3
1940	Was-A	103	326	35	89	18	2	0	28	47	15	.273	.365	.340	705	90	-3	1	1	-0	.980	-6	C-99	-0.3
1941	Was-A	21	66	8	18	5	0	0	13	15	4	.273	.407	.348	756	107	2	1	0	0	.980	-1	C-21	0.2
	StL-A	100	321	30	81	14	3	2	23	52	22	.252	.357	.333	690	81	-7	2	1	0	.995	-5	C-98	-0.6
	Yr	121	387	38	99	19	3	2	36	67	26	.256	.366	.336	702	85	-6	3	1	0	.992	-6	*C-119	-0.4
1942	StL-A	99	273	20	61	6	1	0	26	33	13	.223	.307	.253	560	57	-15	0	1	-0	.986	9	C-95	-0.1
1943	StL-A	74	209	12	50	7	0	0	20	34	14	.239	.348	.273	621	81	-3	0	0	0	.987	13	C-70	1.4
1944	Was-A☆	99	339	14	94	11	1	0	25	46	13	.277	.364	.316	679	99	2	2	1	0	.981	3	C-96	1.2
1945	Was-A†	91	286	33	76	12	1	1	38	43	13	.266	.366	.325	691	110	6	2	4	-1	.990	-2	C-83	0.8
1947	Was-A	37	99	10	30	11	0	0	12	14	7	.303	.389	.414	804	127	4	0	0	0	.994	3	C-37	0.9
Total	18	1884	6028	687	1692	324	45	28	734	931	277	.281	.378	.363	741	95	-14	29	35	-6	.984	20	*C-1806	10.9

■ WES FERRELL

Ferrell, Wesley Cheek b: 2/2/08, Greensboro, N.C. d: 12/9/76, Sarasota, Fla. BR/TR, 6'2", 195 lbs. Deb: 9/9/27 F

YEAR	TM/L	G	AB	R	H	2B	3B	HR	RBI	BB	SO	AVG	OBP	SLG	OPS	OPS+	BR+	SB	CS	SBR	FA	FR	G/POS	TPR
1927	Cle-A	1	0	0	0	0	0	0	0	0	0	—	—	—	—	—	0	0	0	0	.000	-0	/P-1	0.0
1928	Cle-A	2	4	0	1	0	1	0	0	0	0	.250	.250	.750	1000	152	0	0	0	0	1.000	0	/P-2	0.0
1929	Cle-A	47	93	12	22	5	3	1	12	6	28	.237	.283	.387	670	68	-5	1	0	0	.973	3	P-43	0.0
1930	Cle-A	53	118	19	35	8	3	0	14	12	15	.297	.362	.415	777	93	-1	0	0	0	.967	-3	P-43	0.0
1931	Cle-A	48	116	24	37	6	1	9	30	10	21	.319	.373	.621	994	149	7	0	0	0	.969	5	P-40	0.0
1932	Cle-A	55	128	14	31	5	2	2	18	6	21	.242	.276	.359	635	59	-8	0	0	0	.986	1	P-38	0.0
1933	Cle-A☆	61	140	26	38	7	0	7	26	20	22	.271	.363	.471	834	114	3	0	0	0	**1.000**	2	P-28,O-13(13-0-0)	0.1
1934	Bos-A	34	78	12	22	4	0	4	17	7	15	.282	.341	.487	828	104	0	1	0	0	.969	-2	P-26	0.0
1935	Bos-A	75	150	25	52	5	1	7	32	21	16	.347	.427	.533	960	138	9	0	0	0	.977	2	P-41	0.0
1936	Bos-A	61	135	20	36	6	1	5	24	14	10	.267	.336	.437	773	84	-4	0	0	0	.962	-3	P-39	0.0
1937	Bos-A	18	33	7	12	2	0	1	9	7	3	.364	.475	.515	990	144	3	0	0	0	.964	2	P-12	0.0
	Was-A☆	53	106	7	27	5	0	0	16	9	18	.255	.313	.302	615	58	-7	0	0	0	.975	-1	P-25	0.0
	Yr	71	139	14	39	7	0	1	25	16	21	.281	.355	.353	707	81	-4	0	0	0	.971	1	P-37	0.0
1938	Was-A	26	49	6	11	2	0	1	6	15	7	.224	.406	.327	733	92	0	0	0	0	.976	1	P-23	0.0
	NY-A	5	12	1	2	1	0	0	1	1	4	.167	.231	.250	481	20	-2	0	0	0	.917	1	/P-5	0.0
	Yr	31	61	7	13	3	0	1	7	16	11	.213	.377	.311	688	79	-1	0	0	0	.962	2	P-28	0.0
1939	NY-A	3	8	0	1	1	0	0	1	0	2	.125	.125	.250	375	-6	-1	0	0	0	1.000	0	/P-3	0.0
1940	Bro-N	2	2	0	0	0	0	0	0	0	2	.000	.000	.000	0	-94	-1	0			1.000	1	/P-1	0.0
1941	Bos-N	4	4	2	2	0	0	1	2	1	1	.500	.600	1.250	1850	430	2	0			1.000	-0	/P-4	0.0
Total	15	548	1176	175	329	57	12	38	208	129	185	.280	.351	.446	797	99	-4	2	0		.975	7	P-374/O-13(13-0-0)	0.1

■ SERGIO FERRER

Ferrer, Sergio (Marrero) b: 1/29/51, Santurce, P.R. BB/TR, 5'7", 145 lbs. Deb: 4/5/74

YEAR	TM/L	G	AB	R	H	2B	3B	HR	RBI	BB	SO	AVG	OBP	SLG	OPS	OPS+	BR+	SB	CS	SBR	FA	FR	G/POS	TPR
1974	Min-A	24	57	12	16	0	2	0	0	8	6	.281	.379	.351	730	107	1	3	2	-0	.855	-12	S-20/2-1	-0.9
1975	Min-A	32	81	14	20	3	1	0	2	3	11	.247	.282	.309	591	66	-4	3	4	-1	.924	-1	S-18,2-10/D-2	-0.3
1978	NY-N	37	33	8	7	0	1	0	1	4	7	.212	.316	.273	589	68	-1	1	0	0	.971	10	S-29/2-3,3-2	1.0
1979	NY-N	32	7	7	0	0	0	0	0	2	3	.000	.222	.000	222	-35	-1	0	2	-1	.833	6	3-12/S-5,2-4	0.4
Total	4	125	178	41	43	3	4	0	3	17	27	.242	.318	.303	622	76	-5	7	8	-1	.922	2	/S-72,2-18,3-14,D-2	0.2

■ HOBE FERRIS

Ferris, Albert Sayles b: 12/7/1877, Providence, R.I. d: 3/18/38, Detroit, Mich. BR/TR, 5'8", 162 lbs. Deb: 4/26/01

YEAR	TM/L	G	AB	R	H	2B	3B	HR	RBI	BB	SO	AVG	OBP	SLG	OPS	OPS+	BR+	SB	CS	SBR	FA	FR	G/POS	TPR
1901	Bos-A	138	523	68	131	16	15	2	63	23		.250	.290	.350	640	78	-16	13			.930	9	*2-138/S-1	-0.6
1902	Bos-A	134	499	57	122	16	14	8	63	21		.244	.276	.381	657	79	-16	11			.952	**27**	*2-134	1.1
1903	*Bos-A	141	525	69	132	19	7	9	66	25		.251	.287	.366	652	90	-7	11			.950	15	*2-139/S-2	1.0
1904	Bos-A	156	563	50	120	23	10	3	63	23		.213	.245	.306	551	70	-20	7			.962	2	*2-156	-1.9
1905	Bos-A	142	523	51	115	24	16	6	59	23		.220	.253	.361	614	93	-7	11			.960	14	*2-142	0.9
1906	Bos-A	130	495	47	121	25	13	2	44	10		.244	.262	.360	622	94	-6	8			.960	9	*2-126/3-4	0.4
1907	Bos-A	150	561	41	135	25	2	4	60	10		.241	.254	.314	568	82	-14	11			.967	13	*2-150	0.1
1908	StL-A	148	555	54	150	26	7	2	74	14		.270	.291	.353	644	108	3	6			**.952**	16	*3-148	2.5
1909	StL-A	148	556	36	120	18	5	4	58	12		.216	.232	.288	520	69	-22	11			.937	7	*3-114,2-34	-1.4
Total	9	1287	4800	473	1146	192	89	40	550	161		.239	.265	.341	606	84	-107	89			.954	111	*2-1019,3-266/S-3	2.1

■ WILLY FETZER

Fetzer, William McKinnon b: 6/24/1884, Concord, N.C. d: 5/3/59, Butner, N.C. BL/TR, 5'10.5", 180 lbs. Deb: 9/4/06

YEAR	TM/L	G	AB	R	H	2B	3B	HR	RBI	BB	SO	AVG	OBP	SLG	OPS	OPS+	BR+	SB	CS	SBR	FA	FR	G/POS	TPR
1906	Phi-A	1	1	0	0	0	0	0	0	0		.000	.000	.000	0	-97	-0	0			.000	0	H	0.0

■ CHICK FEWSTER

Fewster, Wilson Lloyd b: 11/10/1895, Baltimore, Md. d: 4/16/45, Baltimore, Md. BR/TR, 5'11", 160 lbs. Deb: 9/19/17 Career OF: (42-LF 52-CF 30-RF)

YEAR	TM/L	G	AB	R	H	2B	3B	HR	RBI	BB	SO	AVG	OBP	SLG	OPS	OPS+	BR+	SB	CS	SBR	FA	FR	G/POS	TPR
1917	NY-A	11	36	2	8	0	0	0	1	5	5	.222	.317	.222	539	64	-1	1			.919	2	2-11	0.1

YEAR	TM/L	G	AB	R	H	2B	3B	HR	RBI	BB	SO	AVG	OBP	SLG	OPS	OPS+	BR+	SB	CS	SBR	FA	FR	G/POS	TPR
1918	NY-A	5	2	1	1	0	0	0	0	0	0	.500	.500	.500	1000	197	0	0			.000	0	/2-2	0.0
1919	NY-A	81	244	38	69	9	3	1	15	34	36	.283	.386	.357	743	108	5	8			.946	8	O-41R,S-24/2-4,3-2	1.2
1920	NY-A	21	21	8	6	1	0	0	1	7	2	.286	.464	.333	798	110	1	0	1	-0	.840	0	/S-6,2-3	0.1
1921	*NY-A	66	207	44	58	19	0	1	19	28	43	.280	.382	.386	768	94	-1	4	4	-1	.974	0	O-43(7-35-1),2-15	-0.5
1922	NY-A	44	132	20	32	4	1	1	9	16	23	.242	.324	.311	635	65	-7	2	4	-1	.975	1	O-38(35-4-0)/2-2	-0.9
	Bos-A	23	83	8	24	4	1	0	9	6	10	.289	.344	.361	706	85	-2	8	3	1	.959	4	3-23	0.4
	Yr	67	215	28	56	8	2	1	18	22	33	.260	.332	.330	662	72	-8	10	7	-0	.975	5	O-38(35-4-0),3-23/2-2	-0.5
1923	Bos-A	90	284	32	67	10	1	0	15	39	35	.236	.334	.278	613	62	-14	7	14	-3	.938	-10	2-49,S-37/3-3	-2.2
1924	Cle-A	101	322	36	86	12	2	0	36	24	36	.267	.324	.317	641	65	-17	12	12	-2	.961	-22	2-94/3-5	-3.6
1925	Cle-A	93	294	39	73	16	1	1	38	36	25	.248	.330	.320	650	65	-15	6	9	-2	.939	-9	2-83,3-10/O-1(0-0-1)	-2.2
1926	Bro-N	105	337	53	82	16	3	2	24	45	49	.243	.341	.326	667	82	-7	9			.953	-15	*2-103	-1.9
1927	Bro-N	4	1	1	0	0	0	0	0	0	0	.000	.000	.000	0	-99	-0	0			.000	0	H	0.0
Total	11	644	1963	282	506	91	12	6	167	240	264	.258	.346	.326	672	77	-59	57	47		.945	-43	2-366,O-123C/S-67,3	-9.5
■ **NEIL FIALA**	Fiala, Neil Stephen b: 8/24/56, St.Louis, Mo. BL/TR, 6'1", 185 lbs. Deb: 9/3/81																							
1981	StL-N	3	3	0	0	0	0	0	0	0	1	.000	.000	.000	0	-97	-1	0	0	0	.000	0	/H	-0.1
	Cin-N	2	2	1	1	0	0	0	1	0	1	.500	.500	.500	1000	181	0	0	0	0	.000	0	/H	0.0
	Yr	5	5	1	1	0	0	0	1	0	2	.200	.200	.200	400	13	-1	0	0	0	.000	0	-0,-0	-0.1
■ **ROBERT FICK**	Fick, Robert Charles John b: 3/15/74, Torrance, Cal. BL/TR, 6'1", 189 lbs. Deb: 9/19/98																							
1998	Det-A	7	22	6	8	1	0	3	7	2	7	.364	.417	.818	1235	209	3	1	0	0	.950	-1	/C-3,1-1,D-2	0.3
1999	Det-A	15	41	6	9	0	0	3	10	7	6	.220	.333	.439	772	96	-0	1	0	0	1.000	-1	/C-4,D-8	0.0
2000	Det-A	66	163	18	41	7	2	3	22	22	39	.252	.344	.374	718	84	-4	2	1	0	.984	-4	1-34,C-16,D-12	-0.9
Total	3	88	226	30	58	8	2	9	39	31	52	.257	.349	.429	778	99	-0	4	1	1	.984	-6	/1-35,C-23,D-22	-0.6
■ **JIM FIELD**	Field, James C. b: 4/24/1863, Philadelphia, Pa. d: 5/13/53, Atlantic City, N.J 6'1", 170 lbs. Deb: 6/2/1883																							
1883	Col-a	76	295	31	75	10	6	1		7		.254	.272	.339	611	104	2				.938	-7	*1-76	-1.0
1884	Col-a	105	417	74	97	9	7	4		23		.233	.292	.317	609	107	6				.958	-4	*1-105	-0.7
1885	Pit-a	56	209	28	50	9	1	1	15	13		.239	.306	.306	612	95	-1				.965	-0	1-56	-0.5
	Bal-a	38	144	16	30	3	2	0	10	13		.208	.278	.257	535	71	-4				.963	1	1-38	-0.6
	Yr	94	353	44	80	12	3	1	25	26		.227	.295	.286	581	85	-5				.964	1	1-94	-1.1
1890	Roc-a	52	188	30	38	7	5	4	25	21		.202	.309	.356	665	104	1	8			.964	-4	1-51/P-2	-0.7
1898	Was-N	5	21	1	2	0	0	0	0	0		.095	.095	.095	190	-46	-4	1			.979	-0	/1-5	-0.4
Total	5	332	1274	180	292	38	21	10	50	77		.229	.288	.316	603	96	-0	9			.956	-15	1-331/P-2	-3.9
■ **SAM FIELD**	Field, Samuel Jay b: 10/12/1848, Philadelphia, Pa. d: 10/28/04, Sinking Spring, Pa BR/TR, 5'9.5", 182 lbs. Deb: 5/19/1875																							
1875	Cen-n	3	11	2	1	0	0	0	0	0	0	.091	.091	.091	182	-40	-1	0	0	0	.714	-1	/C-2,O-1(0-0-1)	-0.2
	Was-n	5	16	0	5	0	0	0	1	0	1	.313	.313	.313	625	122	0	1	0	0	.731	-2	/C-4,O-1(0-0-1)	-0.1
	Yr	8	27	2	6	0	0	0	1	0	1	.222	.222	.222	444	58	-1	1	0	0	.723	-3	/C-6,O-2(0-0-2)	-0.3
1876	Cin-N	4	15	2	0	0	0	0	0	1	3	.000	.067	.000	67	-89	-3				.667	-3	/C-3,2-2	-0.5
■ **CECIL FIELDER**	Fielder, Cecil Grant b: 9/21/63, Los Angeles, Cal. BR/TR, 6'3", 240 lbs. Deb: 7/20/85 Career OF: (1-LF 0-CF 0-RF)																							
1985	*Tor-A	30	74	6	23	4	0	4	16	6	16	.311	.363	.527	890	137	4	0	0	0	.979	1	1-25	0.3
1986	Tor-A	34	83	7	13	2	0	4	13	6	27	.157	.222	.325	548	46	-7	0	0	0	1.000	-1	D-22/1-7,3-2,O-1L	-0.8
1987	Tor-A	82	175	30	47	7	1	14	32	20	48	.269	.347	.560	907	132	8	0	1	-0	1.000	-1	D-55,1-16/3-2	0.4
1988	Tor-A	74	174	24	40	6	1	9	23	14	53	.230	.291	.431	722	99	-1	0	1	-0	.991	0	D-50,1-17/3-3,2-2	-0.3
1990	Det-A★	159	573	104	159	25	1	**51**	**132**	90	182	.277	.380	**.592**	972	167	50	0	1	-0	.989	3	*1-143,D-15	4.2
1991	Det-A★	162	624	102	163	25	0	**44**	**133**	78	151	.261	.349	.513	862	133	27	0	0	0	.993	-3	*1-122,D-42	1.3
1992	Det-A	155	594	80	145	22	0	35	**124**	73	151	.244	.329	.458	787	118	13	0	0	0	.991	2	*1-114,D-43	0.5
1993	Det-A★	154	573	80	153	23	0	30	117	90	125	.267	.370	.464	835	124	20	0	1	-0	.991	-2	*1-119,D-36	0.5
1994	Det-A	109	425	67	110	16	2	28	90	50	110	.259	.340	.504	843	113	7	0	0	0	.993	16	*1-102/D-7	1.2
1995	Det-A	136	494	70	120	18	1	31	82	75	116	.243	.348	.472	820	112	8	0	1	-0	.993	6	1-77,D-58	0.3
1996	Det-A	107	391	55	97	12	0	26	80	63	91	.248	.357	.478	835	109	5	2	0	0	.989	4	1-71,D-36	0.0
	*NY-A	53	200	30	52	8	0	13	37	24	48	.260	.345	.495	840	109	2	0	0	0	1.000	-1	D-43/1-9	-0.2
	Yr	160	591	85	149	20	0	39	117	87	139	.252	.353	.484	837	109	7	2	0	0	.990	3	1-80,D-79	-0.2
1997	*NY-A	98	361	40	94	15	0	13	61	51	87	.260	.363	.410	773	102	2	0	0	0	1.000	0	D-87/1-8	-0.3
1998	Ana-A	103	381	48	92	16	1	17	68	52	98	.241	.337	.423	760	95	-2	0	1	-0	.997	-2	1-72,D-31	-1.2
	Cle-A	14	35	1	5	1	0	0	0	1	13	.143	.189	.171	361	-5	-5	0	0	0	.933	0	D-10/1-3	-0.6
	Yr	117	416	49	97	17	1	17	68	53	111	.233	.326	.401	727	87	-8	0	1	-0	.995	-2	1-75,D-41	-1.8
Total	13	1470	5157	744	1313	200	7	319	1008	693	1316	.255	.348	.482	829	119	131	2	6	-2	.992	24	1-905,D-535/3-7,2O	5.3
■ **BRUCE FIELDS**	Fields, Bruce Alan b: 10/6/60, Cleveland, Ohio BL/TR, 6', 185 lbs. Deb: 9/3/86																							
1986	Det-A	16	43	4	12	1	1	0	6	1	6	.279	.295	.349	644	75	-2	1	1	-0	.962	-1	O-14(14-0-0)/D-1	-0.3
1988	Sea-A	39	67	8	18	5	0	1	5	4	11	.269	.310	.388	698	90	-1	0	1	-0	1.000	-5	O-23(14-1-8)/D-6	-0.6
1989	Sea-A	3	3	2	1	1	0	0	0	0	1	.333	.333	.667	1000	170	0	0	0	0	.000	-0	/O-1(0-0-1)	0.0
Total	3	58	113	14	31	7	1	1	11	5	18	.274	.305	.381	686	86	-2	1	2	-0	.980	-6	/O-38(28-1-9),D-7	-0.9
■ **GEORGE FIELDS**	Fields, George W. b: 7/1853, Waterbury, Conn. d: 9/22/33, Waterbury, Conn. Deb: 5/2/1872																							
1872	Man-n	18	87	16	21	3	1	0	9	0	2	.241	.241	.299	540	69	-3	0	0	0	.563	-13	3-12/O-5(1-0-4),S-1	-1.1
■ **JOCKO FIELDS**	Fields, John Joseph b: 10/20/1864, Cork, Ireland d: 10/14/50, Jersey City, N.J. BR/TR, 5'10", 160 lbs. Deb: 5/31/1887 Career OF: (160-LF 20-CF 27-RF)																							
1887	Pit-N	43	171	26	51	9	2	0	17	7	13	.298	.306	.348	654	86	-3	7			.933	1	O-27C,C-14/1-3,3P	-0.1
1888	Pit-N	45	169	22	33	7	2	1	15	8	19	.195	.232	.278	510	67	-6	9			.887	-5	O-29(23-2-4),C-14/3-3	-1.0
1889	Pit-N	75	289	41	90	22	5	2	43	29	30	.311	.376	.443	819	142	17	7			.860	-6	O-60(54-2-4),C-16	0.9
1890	Pit-P	126	526	101	148	18	20	9	86	57	52	.281	.355	.443	798	123	17	24			.879	-13	O-80L,2-30,C-15,/S	0.3
1891	Pit-N	23	75	10	18	3	0	0	5	10	13	.240	.337	.280	617	82	-1	1			.897	-3	C-15/S-8	-0.3
	Phi-N	8	30	4	7	2	1	0	5	4	2	.233	.324	.367	690	98	-0	0			.769	-4	/C-8	-0.3
	Yr	31	105	14	25	5	1	0	10	14	15	.238	.333	.305	638	87	-1	1			.857	-7	C-23/S-8	-0.6
1892	NY-N	21	66	8	18	4	2	0	5	9	10	.273	.368	.394	762	133	3	2			.917	-1	O-11(0-0-11),C-10	0.2
Total	6	341	1326	212	365	65	32	12	176	124	139	.275	.338	.397	734	114	27	50			.883	-31	O-207L/C-92,2S31P	-0.3
■ **MIKE FIGGA**	Figga, Michael Anthony b: 7/31/70, Tampa, Fla. BR/TR, 6', 200 lbs. Deb: 9/16/97																							
1997	NY-A	2	4	0	0	0	0	0	0	0	3	.000	.000	.000	0	-99	-1	0	0	0	1.000	1	/C-1,D-1	-0.1
1998	NY-A	1	4	1	1	0	0	0	0	0	1	.250	.250	.250	500	32	-0	0	0	0	1.000	-1	/C-1	-0.1
1999	NY-A	2	0	0	0	0	0	0	0	0	0	—	—	—	—	—	0	0	0	0	1.000	1	/C-2	0.1
	Bal-A	41	86	12	19	4	0	1	5	2	27	.221	.239	.302	541	38	-8	0	2	-1	.973	3	C-41	-0.4
	Yr	43	86	12	19	4	0	1	5	2	27	.221	.239	.302	541	38	-8	0	2	-1	.973	4	C-43	-0.3
Total	3	46	94	13	20	4	0	1	5	2	31	.213	.229	.287	516	32	-10	0	2	-1	.975	3	/C-45,D-1	-0.5
■ **BIEN FIGUEROA**	Figueroa, Bienvenido b: 2/7/64, Santo Domingo, D.R. BR/TR, 5'10", 170 lbs. Deb: 5/17/92																							
1992	StL-N	12	11	1	2	1	0	0	4	1	2	.182	.250	.273	523	49	-1	0	0	0	.938	1	/S-9,2-3	0.0
■ **JESUS FIGUEROA**	Figueroa, Jesus Maria (Figueroa) b: 2/20/57, Santo Domingo, D.R. BL/TL, 5'10", 160 lbs. Deb: 4/22/80																							
1980	Chi-N	115	198	20	50	5	0	1	11	14	16	.253	.308	.293	601	64	-9	2	1	0	.979	-4	O-57(22-36-1)	-1.4
■ **SAM FILE**	File, Lawrence Samuel b: 5/18/22, Chester, Pa. BR/TR, 5'11", 160 lbs. Deb: 9/10/40																							
1940	Phi-N	7	13	0	1	0	0	0	1	0	2	.077	.077	.077	154	-60	-3	0			.850	1	/S-6,3-1	-0.2
■ **STEVE FILIPOWICZ**	Filipowicz, Stephen Charles "Flip" b: 6/28/21, Donora, Pa. d: 2/21/75, Wilkes-Barre, Pa. BR/TR, 5'8", 195 lbs. Deb: 9/3/44																							
1944	NY-N	15	41	10	8	2	1	0	7	3	7	.195	.250	.293	543	52	-3	0			1.000	-1	O-10(6-4-0)/C-1	-0.5
1945	NY-N	35	112	14	23	5	0	2	16	4	13	.205	.239	.304	543	50	-8	0			.935	-6	O-31(27-2-2)	-1.6

YEAR	TM/L	G	AB	R	H	2B	3B	HR	RBI	BB	SO	AVG	OBP	SLG	OPS	OPS+	BR+	SB	CS	SBR	FA	FR	G/POS	TPR
1948	Cin-N	7	26	0	9	0	1	0	3	2	1	.346	.393	.423	816	125	1	0			1.000	-0	/O-7(7-0-0)	0.0
Total	3	57	179	24	40	7	2	2	26	9	21	.223	.265	.318	583	61	-10	0			.961	-8	/O-48(40-6-2),C-1	-2.1
■ JACK FIMPLE Fimple, John Joseph b: 2/10/59, Darby, Pa. BR/TR, 6'2", 185 lbs. Deb: 7/30/83																								
1983	*LA-N	54	148	16	37	8	1	2	22	11	39	.250	.302	.358	660	83	-4	1	0	0	.989	12	C-54	1.1
1984	LA-N	12	26	2	5	1	0	0	3	1	6	.192	.222	.231	453	28	-3	0	0	0	.983	2	C-12	-0.1
1986	LA-N	13	13	2	1	0	0	0	2	6	6	.077	.368	.077	445	32	-1	0	0	0	1.000	1	/C-7,1-1,2-1	0.0
1987	Cal-A	13	10	1	2	0	0	0	1	1	2	.200	.273	.200	473	29	-1	0	0	0	.913	1	C-13	0.0
Total	4	92	197	21	45	9	1	2	28	19	53	.228	.296	.315	611	70	-8	1	0	0	.986	15	/C-86,2-1,1-1	1.0
■ JIM FINIGAN Finigan, James Leroy b: 8/19/28, Quincy, Ill. d: 5/16/81, Quincy, Ill. BR/TR, 5'11", 175 lbs. Deb: 4/25/54																								
1954	Phi-A☆	136	487	57	147	25	6	7	51	64	66	.302	.383	.421	804	120	14	2	8	-2	.948	2	*3-136	1.4
1955	KC-A★	150	545	72	139	30	7	9	68	61	49	.255	.333	.385	719	92	-7	1	3	-1	.975	-7	2-90,3-59	-0.8
1956	KC-A	91	250	29	54	7	2	2	21	30	28	.216	.302	.284	586	55	-16	3	1	0	.969	-1	2-52,3-32	-1.3
1957	Det-A	64	174	20	47	4	2	0	17	23	18	.270	.359	.316	675	84	-3	1	1	-0	.954	4	3-59/2-3	0.1
1958	SF-N	23	25	3	5	2	0	0	1	3	5	.200	.310	.280	590	59	-1	0	0	0	.917	-2	/2-8,3-4	-0.3
1959	Bal-A	48	119	14	30	6	0	1	10	9	10	.252	.305	.328	632	75	-4	1	0	0	.959	0	3-42/2-6,S-2	-0.3
Total	6	512	1600	195	422	74	17	19	168	190	176	.264	.344	.367	711	92	-17	8	13	-3	.948	-3	3-332,2-159/S-2	-1.2
■ BOB FINLEY Finley, Robert Edward b: 11/25/15, Ennis, Tex. d: 1/2/86, W.Covina, Cal. BR/TR, 6'1", 200 lbs. Deb: 7/4/43																								
1943	Phi-N	28	81	9	21	2	0	1	7	4	10	.259	.294	.321	615	81	-2	0			.962	3	C-24	0.2
1944	Phi-N	94	281	18	70	11	1	1	21	12	25	.249	.292	.306	598	71	-11	1			.967	-2	C-74	-0.9
Total	2	122	362	27	91	13	1	2	28	16	35	.251	.292	.309	602	73	-13	1			.966	1	/C-98	-0.7
■ STEVE FINLEY Finley, Steven Allen b: 3/12/65, Paducah, Ky. BL/TL, 6'2", 180 lbs. Deb: 4/3/89 Career OF: (36-LF 1481-CF 183-RF)																								
1989	Bal-A	81	217	35	54	5	2	2	25	15	30	.249	.300	.318	618	77	-7	17	3	3	.986	-8	O-76(14-23-41)/D-3	-1.4
1990	Bal-A	142	464	46	119	16	4	3	37	32	53	.256	.307	.328	635	80	-12	22	9	2	.977	-1	*O-133(21-44-73)/D-2	-1.5
1991	Hou-N	159	596	84	170	28	10	8	54	42	65	.285	.334	.406	740	114	10	34	18	1	.985	-6	*O-153(1-124-69)	0.3
1992	Hou-N	162	607	84	177	29	13	5	55	58	63	.292	.356	.407	763	121	17	44	9	7	.993	10	*O-160(0-160-0)	3.4
1993	Hou-N	142	545	69	145	15	**13**	8	44	28	65	.266	.306	.385	691	87	-12	19	6	2	.988	9	*O-140(0-140-0)	0.1
1994	Hou-N	94	373	64	103	16	5	11	33	28	52	.276	.330	.434	764	102	0	13	7	0	.982	5	O-92(0-92-0)	0.7
1995	SD-N	139	562	104	167	23	8	10	44	59	62	.297	.367	.420	787	111	10	36	12	4	.977	5	*O-138(0-138-0)	1.9
1996	*SD-N	161	655	126	195	45	9	30	95	56	87	.298	.357	.531	888	138	34	22	8	2	.982	12	*O-160(0-160-0)	4.8
1997	SD-N★	143	560	101	146	26	5	28	92	43	92	.261	.317	.475	792	112	7	15	3	2	.989	16	*O-140(0-140-0)	2.6
1998	*SD-N	159	619	92	154	40	6	14	67	45	103	.249	.303	.401	703	90	-11	12	3	2	.981	12	*O-157(0-157-0)	0.4
1999	*Ari-N	156	590	100	156	32	10	34	103	63	94	.264	.338	.525	864	113	10	8	4	0	.995	14	*O-155(0-155-0)/D-1	2.5
2000	Ari-N★	152	539	100	151	27	5	35	96	65	87	.280	.366	.544	910	125	19	12	6	1	.992	10	*O-148(0-148-0)/D-2	3.0
Total	12	1690	6327	1005	1737	302	90	188	745	534	853	.275	.335	.440	774	109	64	254	88	25	.986	78	*O-1652C/D-8	16.8
■ BILL FINLEY Finley, William James b: 10/4/1863, New York, N.Y. d: 10/6/12, Asbury Park, N.J. 5'3", 170 lbs. Deb: 7/12/1886																								
1886	NY-N	13	44	2	8	0	0	0	5	1	8	.182	.200	.182	382	17	-4	2			.800	-3	/O-8(0-7-1),C-8	-0.6
■ NEAL FINN Finn, Cornelius Francis "Mickey" b: 1/24/04, Brooklyn, N.Y. d: 7/7/33, Allentown, Pa. BR/TR, 5'11", 168 lbs. Deb: 4/21/30																								
1930	Bro-N	87	273	42	76	13	0	3	30	26	18	.278	.350	.359	709	73	-11	3			.948	-6	2-81	-1.3
1931	Bro-N	118	413	46	113	22	2	0	45	21	42	.274	.314	.337	650	75	-14	2			.975	0	*2-112	-0.7
1932	Bro-N	65	189	22	45	5	2	0	14	11	15	.238	.284	.286	569	55	-12	2			.933	4	3-50/2-2,S-1	-0.7
1933	Phi-N	51	169	15	40	4	1	0	13	10	14	.237	.287	.272	559	54	-10	2			.964	-1	2-51	-0.8
Total	4	321	1044	125	274	44	5	3	102	68	89	.262	.314	.323	637	67	-47	9			.964	-3	2-246/3-50,S-1	-3.5
■ HAL FINNEY Finney, Harold Wilson b: 7/30/05, Lafayette, Ala. d: 12/20/91, Lafayette, Ala. BR/TR, 5'11", 170 lbs. Deb: 6/24/31 F																								
1931	Pit-N	10	26	2	8	1	0	0	2	0	1	.308	.333	.346	679	84	-1	1			1.000	-0	/C-6	0.0
1932	Pit-N	31	33	14	7	3	0	0	4	3	4	.212	.297	.303	600	63	-2	0			.971	3	C-11	0.1
1933	Pit-N	56	133	17	31	4	1	1	18	3	19	.233	.250	.301	551	57	-8	0			.993	-2	C-47	-0.8
1934	Pit-N	5	0	3	0	0	0	0	0	0	0	—	1.000	—	1000	188	0	0			.000	0	/C-1	0.0
1936	Pit-N	21	35	3	0	0	0	0	3	0	8	.000	.000	.000	0	-98	-10	0			.956	1	C-14	-0.8
Total	5	123	227	39	46	8	1	1	27	6	32	.203	.233	.260	493	37	-19	1			.983	1	/C-79	-1.5
■ LOU FINNEY Finney, Louis Klopsche b: 8/13/10, Buffalo, Ala. d: 4/22/66, Lafayette, Ala. BL/TR, 6', 180 lbs. Deb: 9/12/31 F Career OF: (113-LF 104-CF 479-RF)																								
1931	Phi-A	9	24	7	9	0	1	0	3	6	1	.375	.516	.458	974	149	2	0	0	0	1.000	1	/O-8(0-0-8)	0.3
1933	Phi-A	74	240	26	64	12	2	3	32	13	17	.267	.307	.371	678	78	-8	1	3	-1	.947	2	O-63(17-1-46)	-1.0
1934	Phi-A	92	272	32	76	11	4	1	28	14	17	.279	.315	.360	675	77	-10	4	3	-0	.943	0	O-54(12-4-40),1-15	-1.3
1935	Phi-A	109	410	45	112	11	6	0	31	18	18	.273	.307	.329	636	65	-22	7	2	1	.943	-2	O-76(5-0-72),1-18	-2.7
1936	Phi-A	151	653	100	197	26	10	1	41	47	22	.302	.351	.377	728	81	-19	7	9	-2	.990	-4	1-78,O-73(22-21-32)	-3.2
1937	Phi-A	92	379	53	95	14	9	1	20	20	16	.251	.288	.343	631	59	-25	2	5	-1	.989	-4	1-50,O-39(2-37-0)/2-1	-3.3
1938	Phi-A	122	454	61	125	21	12	10	48	39	25	.275	.333	.441	773	94	-6	5	8	-2	.990	-3	1-64,O-46(19-21-6)	-1.6
1939	Phi-A	9	22	1	3	0	0	0	1	2	0	.136	.208	.136	345	-10	-4	0	0	0	1.000	0	/O-4(0-3-1)	-0.3
	Bos-A	95	249	43	81	18	3	1	46	24	11	.325	.385	.434	818	105	2	2	5	-1	.986	-6	1-32,O-24(3-16-5)	-0.8
	Yr	104	271	44	84	18	3	1	47	26	11	.310	.370	.410	780	96	-1	2	5	-1	.986	-6	1-32,O-28(3-19-6)	-1.1
1940	Bos-A★	130	534	73	171	31	15	5	73	33	13	.320	.360	.463	822	107	5	5	2	0	.975	2	O-69(0-0-69),1-51	-0.2
1941	Bos-A	127	497	83	143	24	10	4	53	38	17	.288	.340	.400	740	93	-6	2	5	-1	.945	-3	O-92(1-0-91),1-24	-1.8
1942	Bos-A	113	397	58	113	16	7	3	61	29	11	.285	.335	.383	718	98	-2	3	3	-0	.976	2	O-95(3-1-92)/1-2	-0.6
1944	Bos-A	68	251	37	72	11	2	0	32	23	7	.287	.347	.347	693	100	0	1	0	0	.987	-5	1-59/O-2(1-0-1)	-0.8
1945	Bos-A	2	2	0	0	0	0	0	0	0	1	.000	.000	.000	0	-98	-0	0	0	0	.000	0	H	-0.1
	StL-A	57	213	24	59	8	4	2	22	21	6	.277	.345	.380	725	105	1	0	0	0	.986	-2	O-36L,1-22/3-1	-0.4
	Yr	59	215	24	59	8	4	2	22	21	7	.274	.342	.377	719	103	1	0	0	0	.986	-2	O-36L,1-22/3-1	-0.5
1946	StL-A	16	30	0	9	0	0	0	3	2	4	.300	.344	.300	644	77	-1	0	0	0	.938	0	/O-7(4-0-3)	-0.1
1947	Phi-N	4	4	0	0	0	0	0	0	0	0	.000	.000	.000	0	-99	-1	0			.000	0	H	-0.1
Total	15	1270	4631	643	1329	203	85	31	494	329	186	.287	.336	.388	723	88	-92	39	45		.961	-22	O-688R,1-415/3-1,2	-18.0
■ MIKE FIORE Fiore, Michael Gary Joseph b: 10/11/44, Brooklyn, N.Y. BL/TL, 6', 185 lbs. Deb: 9/21/68																								
1968	Bal-A	6	17	2	1	0	0	0	0	4	4	.059	.273	.059	332	5	-2	0	0	0	.943	-0	/1-5,O-1(1-0-0)	-0.3
1969	KC-A	107	339	53	93	14	1	12	35	84	63	.274	.421	.428	849	137	21	4	4	-1	.988	10	1-91,O-13(3-8-2)	2.3
1970	KC-A	25	72	6	13	2	0	0	4	13	24	.181	.306	.208	514	44	-5	1	1	-0	.986	1	1-20	-0.6
	Bos-A	41	50	5	7	0	0	0	4	8	4	.140	.259	.140	399	12	-6	0	0	0	1.000	0	1-17/O-2(1-0-1)	-0.7
	Yr	66	122	11	20	2	0	0	8	21	28	.164	.287	.180	467	30	-11	1	1	-0	.991	1	1-37/O-2(1-0-1)	-1.3
1971	Bos-A	51	62	9	11	2	0	1	6	12	14	.177	.311	.258	569	58	-3	0	3	-1	1.000	-0	1-12	-0.5
1972	StL-N	17	10	0	1	0	0	0	1	2	3	.100	.250	.100	350	3	-1	0	0	0	1.000	-1	/1-6,O-1(0-0-1)	-0.2
	SD-N	7	6	0	0	0	0	0	0	1	3	.000	.143	.000	143	-61	-1	0	0	0	.000	0	H	-0.1
	Yr	24	16	0	1	0	0	0	1	3	6	.063	.211	.063	273	-20	-2	0	0	0	1.000	-1	/1-6,O-1(0-0-1)	-0.3
Total	5	254	556	75	126	18	1	13	50	124	115	.227	.370	.333	703	97	3	5	8	-2	.988	9	1-151/O-17(5-8-4)	-0.1
■ DAN FIROVA Firova, Daniel Michael b: 10/16/56, Refugio, Tex. BR/TR, 6', 185 lbs. Deb: 9/1/81																								
1981	Sea-A	13	2	0	0	0	0	0	0	0	1	.000	.000	.000	0	-96	-0	0	0	0	1.000	1	C-13	0.0
1982	Sea-A	3	5	0	0	0	0	0	0	0	0	.000	.000	.000	0	-97	-1	0	0	0	.900	-0	/C-3	-0.1
1988	Cle-A	1	0	0	0	0	0	0	0	0	0	—	—	—	—	—	0	0	0	0	.000	0	/C-1	0.0
Total	3	17	7	0	0	0	0	0	0	0	1	.000	.000	.000	0	-97	-2	0	0	0	.944	1	/C-17	-0.1
■ WILLIAM FISCHER Fischer, William Charles b: 3/2/1891, New York, N.Y. d: 9/4/45, Richmond, Va. BL/TR, 6', 174 lbs. Deb: 6/11/13																								
1913	Bro-N	62	165	16	44	9	4	1	12	10	5	.267	.313	.388	700	97	-1	0			.974	-3	C-51	0.0
1914	Bro-N	43	105	12	27	1	2	0	8	8	12	.257	.310	.305	614	81	-2	1			.958	3	C-30	0.3
1915	Chi-F	105	292	30	96	15	4	4	50	24	19	.329	.384	.449	832	142	12	5			.972	-6	C-80	1.3
1916	Chi-N	65	179	15	35	9	2	1	14	11	8	.196	.246	.285	531	57	-9	2			.973	4	C-56	-0.1

YEAR	TM/L	G	AB	R	H	2B	3B	HR	RBI	BB	SO	AVG	OBP	SLG	OPS	OPS+	BR+	SB	CS	SBR	FA	FR	G/POS	TPR
	Pit-N	42	113	11	29	7	1	1	6	10	3	.257	.323	.363	685	109	1	1			.974	5	C-35	1.0
	Yr	107	292	26	64	16	3	2	20	21	11	.219	.276	.315	591	76	-8	3			.973	8	C-91	0.9
1917	Pit-N	95	245	25	70	9	2	3	25	27	19	.286	.359	.376	734	121	7	11			.961	-9	C-69/1-2	0.4
Total	5	412	1099	109	301	50	15	10	115	90	66	.274	.332	.374	706	107	7	20			.969	-8	C-321/1-2	2.9

■ MIKE FISCHLIN Fischlin, Michael Thomas b: 9/13/55, Sacramento, Cal. BR/TR, 6′1″, 165 lbs. Deb: 9/3/77

YEAR	TM/L	G	AB	R	H	2B	3B	HR	RBI	BB	SO	AVG	OBP	SLG	OPS	OPS+	BR+	SB	CS	SBR	FA	FR	G/POS	TPR
1977	Hou-N	13	15	0	3	0	0	0	0	0	2	.200	.200	.200	400	8	-2	0	0	0	1.000	1	S-12	0.0
1978	Hou-N	44	86	3	10	1	0	0	0	4	9	.116	.165	.128	293	-19	-14	1	0	0	.928	-4	S-41	-1.6
1980	Hou-N	1	1	0	0	0	0	0	0	0	1	.000	.000	.000	0	-99	-0	0	0	0	1.000	-0	/S-1	0.0
1981	Cle-A	22	43	3	10	1	0	0	5	3	6	.233	.283	.256	538	57	-2	3	2	-0	.955	-0	S-19/2-1	-0.1
1982	Cle-A	112	276	34	74	12	1	0	21	34	36	.268	.353	.319	671	86	-4	9	5	0	.970	-7	*S-101/3-8,2-6,C-1	-0.1
1983	Cle-A	95	225	31	47	5	2	2	23	26	32	.209	.296	.276	572	56	-13	9	2	1	.965	21	2-71,S-15/3-4,D-1	1.3
1984	Cle-A	85	133	17	30	4	2	1	14	12	20	.226	.290	.308	598	64	-6	2	2	-0	.981	18	2-55,3-17,S-15	1.4
1985	Cle-A	73	60	12	12	4	1	0	2	5	7	.200	.262	.300	562	54	-4	0	1	-0	.990	27	2-31,S-22/1-6,3D	2.3
1986	NY-A	71	102	9	21	2	0	0	3	8	29	.206	.264	.225	489	35	-9	0	1	-0	.955	7	S-42,2-27	0.0
1987	Atl-N	1	0	0	0	0	0	0	0	0	0	—	—	—	—	—	0	0	0	0	.000	0	/R	0.0
Total	10	517	941	109	207	29	6	3	68	92	142	.220	.293	.273	566	57	-54	24	13	1	.959	63	S-268,2-191/3-32,1DC	3.2

■ SAM FISHBURN Fishburn, Samuel E. b: 5/15/1893, Haverhill, Mass. d: 4/11/65, Bethlehem, Pa. BR/TR, 5′9″, 157 lbs. Deb: 9/30/19

YEAR	TM/L	G	AB	R	H	2B	3B	HR	RBI	BB	SO	AVG	OBP	SLG	OPS	OPS+	BR+	SB	CS	SBR	FA	FR	G/POS	TPR
1919	StL-N	9	6	0	2	1	0	0	2	0	0	.333	.333	.500	833	158	0	0			1.000	0	/1-1,2-1	0.1

■ JOHN FISHEL Fishel, John Alan b: 11/8/62, Fullerton, Cal. BR/TR, 5′11″, 185 lbs. Deb: 7/14/88

YEAR	TM/L	G	AB	R	H	2B	3B	HR	RBI	BB	SO	AVG	OBP	SLG	OPS	OPS+	BR+	SB	CS	SBR	FA	FR	G/POS	TPR
1988	Hou-N	19	26	1	6	0	0	1	2	3	6	.231	.310	.346	656	92	-0	0	0	0	1.000	-2	/O-6(5-0-2)	-0.3

■ GUS FISHER Fisher, August Harris b: 10/21/1885, Pottsboro, Tex. d: 4/8/72, Portland, Ore. BL/TR, 5′10″, 175 lbs. Deb: 4/18/11

YEAR	TM/L	G	AB	R	H	2B	3B	HR	RBI	BB	SO	AVG	OBP	SLG	OPS	OPS+	BR+	SB	CS	SBR	FA	FR	G/POS	TPR
1911	Cle-A	70	203	20	53	6	3	0	12	7		.261	.302	.320	623	73	-8	6			.956	8	C-58/1-1	0.4
1912	NY-A	4	10	1	1	0	0	0	0	0		.100	.100	.100	200	-40	-2	0			1.000	1	/C-4	-0.1
Total	2	74	213	21	54	6	3	0	12	7		.254	.293	.310	603	68	-10	6			.958	8	/C-62,1-1	0.3

■ CHARLES FISHER Fisher, Charles Deb: 6/15/1889

YEAR	TM/L	G	AB	R	H	2B	3B	HR	RBI	BB	SO	AVG	OBP	SLG	OPS	OPS+	BR+	SB	CS	SBR	FA	FR	G/POS	TPR
1889	Lou-a	1	2	0	1	0	0	0	0	0	0	.500	.500	.500	1000	189	0	0			.000	-1	/O-1(1-0-0)	0.0

■ CHARLES FISHER Fisher, Charles G. (b: Charles G. Fish) b: 3/10/1852, Boxford, Mass. d: 2/18/17, Eagle, Alaska BL/TR, 5′8″, 143 lbs. Deb: 6/7/1884

YEAR	TM/L	G	AB	R	H	2B	3B	HR	RBI	BB	SO	AVG	OBP	SLG	OPS	OPS+	BR+	SB	CS	SBR	FA	FR	G/POS	TPR
1884	KC-U	10	40	3	8	2	0	0		0		.200	.200	.250	450	41	-4				.711	-0	/3-9,S-1	-0.4
	CP-U	1	3	1	2	0	0	0		1		.667	.750	.667	1417	335	1				.500	-1	/3-1	0.0
	Yr	11	43	4	10	2	0	0		1		.233	.250	.279	529	68	-3				.702	-1	3-10/S-1	-0.4

■ SHOWBOAT FISHER Fisher, George Aloys b: 1/16/1899, Wesley, Iowa d: 5/15/94, St.Cloud, Minn. BL/TR, 5′10″, 170 lbs. Deb: 4/24/23

YEAR	TM/L	G	AB	R	H	2B	3B	HR	RBI	BB	SO	AVG	OBP	SLG	OPS	OPS+	BR+	SB	CS	SBR	FA	FR	G/POS	TPR
1923	Was-A	13	23	4	6	2	0	0	2	4	3	.261	.370	.348	718	95	-0	0	0	0	.750	0	/O-5(0-0-5)	0.0
1924	Was-A	15	41	7	9	1	0	0	6	6	6	.220	.319	.244	563	48	-3	2	0	0	.933	-2	O-11(0-0-11)	-0.6
1930	*StL-N	92	254	49	95	18	6	8	61	25	21	.374	.432	.587	1019	139	16	4			.962	-3	O-67(24-0-42)	0.7
1932	StL-A	18	22	2	4	0	0	0	2	2	5	.182	.250	.182	432	13	-3	0	0	0	1.000	-1	/O-5(5-0-0)	-0.4
Total	4	138	340	62	114	21	6	8	71	37	35	.335	.402	.503	905	119	10	6	0		.946	-6	/O-88(29-0-58)	-0.3

■ GEORGE FISHER Fisher, George C. b: Wilmington, Del. BL, Deb: 8/9/1884 Career OF: (0-LF 6-CF 1-RF)

YEAR	TM/L	G	AB	R	H	2B	3B	HR	RBI	BB	SO	AVG	OBP	SLG	OPS	OPS+	BR+	SB	CS	SBR	FA	FR	G/POS	TPR
1884	Cle-N	6	24	2	3	0	0	0	0	0	3	.125	.125	.125	250	-20	-3				.897	-3	/2-6,C-1	-0.5
	Wil-U	8	29	0	2	0	0	0		0		.069	.069	.069	138	-56	-6				.818	-1	/O-6(0-6-1),S-2	-0.7
Total	1	14	53	2	5	0	0	0	0	0	3	.094	.094	.094	189	-40	-10				.818	-4	/O-6C,2-6,S-2,C-1	-1.2

■ HARRY FISHER Fisher, Harry Devereux b: 1/3/26, Newbury, Ont., Can. d: 9/20/81, Waterloo, Ont., Canada BL/TR, 6′, 180 lbs. Deb: 9/16/51

YEAR	TM/L	G	AB	R	H	2B	3B	HR	RBI	BB	SO	AVG	OBP	SLG	OPS	OPS+	BR+	SB	CS	SBR	FA	FR	G/POS	TPR
1951	Pit-N	3	3	0	0	0	0	0	0	0	3	.000	.000	.000	0	-97	-1	0	0	0	.000	0	H	-0.1
1952	Pit-N	15	15	0	5	1	0	0	1	0	3	.333	.333	.400	733	100	-0	0	0	0	1.000	-1	/P-8	0.0
Total	2	18	18	0	5	1	0	0	1	0	3	.278	.278	.333	611	66	-1	0	0	0	1.000	-1	/P-8	-0.1

■ RED FISHER Fisher, John Gus b: 6/22/1887, Pittsburgh, Pa. d: 1/31/40, Louisville, Ky. BL/TR, Deb: 4/25/10

YEAR	TM/L	G	AB	R	H	2B	3B	HR	RBI	BB	SO	AVG	OBP	SLG	OPS	OPS+	BR+	SB	CS	SBR	FA	FR	G/POS	TPR
1910	StL-A	23	72	5	9	2	1	0	3	8		.125	.222	.181	403	28	-6	5			.935	-1	O-19(14-0-5)	-0.9

■ NEWT FISHER Fisher, Newton "Ike" b: 6/28/1871, Nashville, Tenn. d: 2/28/47, Norwood Park, Ill. BR/TR, 5′9.5″, 171 lbs. Deb: 5/17/1898 F

YEAR	TM/L	G	AB	R	H	2B	3B	HR	RBI	BB	SO	AVG	OBP	SLG	OPS	OPS+	BR+	SB	CS	SBR	FA	FR	G/POS	TPR
1898	Phi-N	9	26	0	3	1	0	0	0	0		.115	.148	.154	302	-14	-4	1			.844	-1	/C-8,3-1	-0.4

■ BOB FISHER Fisher, Robert Taylor b: 11/3/1886, Nashville, Tenn. d: 8/4/63, Jacksonville, Fla. BR/TR, 5′9.5″, 170 lbs. Deb: 6/3/12 F Career OF: (1-LF 0-CF 0-RF)

YEAR	TM/L	G	AB	R	H	2B	3B	HR	RBI	BB	SO	AVG	OBP	SLG	OPS	OPS+	BR+	SB	CS	SBR	FA	FR	G/POS	TPR
1912	Bro-N	82	257	27	60	10	3	0	26	14	32	.233	.273	.296	569	58	-16	7			.917	-14	S-74/2-1,3-1	-2.5
1913	Bro-N	132	474	42	124	11	10	4	54	10	43	.262	.278	.352	631	77	-16	16			.923	-19	*S-131	-2.7
1914	Chi-N	15	50	5	15	2	2	0	5	3	4	.300	.340	.420	760	126	1	2			.943	-1	S-15	0.1
1915	Chi-N	147	568	70	163	22	5	5	53	30	51	.287	.326	.370	696	110	6	9	20	-5	.933	-20	*S-145	-1.0
1916	Cin-N	61	136	9	37	4	3	0	11	8	14	.272	.313	.346	658	104	0	7			.905	-12	S-29/2-6,O-1(1-0-0)	-1.1
1918	StL-N	63	246	36	78	11	3	2	20	15	11	.317	.356	.411	767	138	11	7			.979	19	2-63	3.3
1919	StL-N	3	11	0	3	1	0	0	1	0	2	.273	.273	.364	636	96	-0	0			.900	0	/2-3	0.0
Total	7	503	1742	189	480	61	26	11	170	80	157	.276	.309	.359	668	96	-13	48	20		.925	-48	S-394/2-73,O-1L,3-1	-3.9

■ WILBUR FISHER Fisher, Wilbur McCullough b: 7/18/1894, Green Bottom, W.Va. d: 10/24/60, Welch, W.Va. BL/TR, 6′, 174 lbs. Deb: 6/13/16

YEAR	TM/L	G	AB	R	H	2B	3B	HR	RBI	BB	SO	AVG	OBP	SLG	OPS	OPS+	BR+	SB	CS	SBR	FA	FR	G/POS	TPR
1916	Pit-N	1	1	0	0	0	0	0	0	0	0	.000	.000	.000	0	-99	-0	0			.000	0	H	0.0

■ CHEROKEE FISHER Fisher, William Charles b: 12/1845, Philadelphia, Pa. d: 9/26/12, New York, N.Y. BR/TR, 5′9″, 164 lbs. Deb: 5/6/1871 NA OF: (5-LF 14-CF 66-RF) Career OF: (0-LF 7-CF 4-RF)

YEAR	TM/L	G	AB	R	H	2B	3B	HR	RBI	BB	SO	AVG	OBP	SLG	OPS	OPS+	BR+	SB	CS	SBR	FA	FR	G/POS	TPR
1871	Rok-n	25	123	24	28	3	3	1	22	3	1	.228	.246	.325	571	65	-5	1	2	-0	**.927**	4	*P-24/1-2,2-1	0.0
1872	Bal-n	46	225	39	52	10	3	1	36	2	5	.231	.238	.316	553	66	-10	0	1	-0	.761	-9	P-19,O-19R,3-18	-1.1
1873	Ath-n	51	253	50	66	4	3	1	35	4	5	.261	.272	.312	585	68	-11	1	2	-0	.743	5	*O-45R,P-13/2-3,1-1	-0.1
1874	Har-n	52	241	28	54	7	0	0	31	2	7	.224	.230	.253	484	52	-13	2	3	-1	.833	-6	P-39,O-12C/3-7,S-2	-0.7
1875	Phi-n	41	177	26	41	3	1	0	11	1	6	.232	.236	.260	496	69	-6	4	3	-0	.896	-5	P-41/O-5(4-1-0)	-0.1
1876	Cin-N	35	129	12	32	1	0	0	4	0	8	.248	.248	.256	504	80	-2				.793	-5	P-28,O-11C/S-1,1-1	-0.3
1877	Chi-N	1	4	0	0	0	0	0	0	0	2	.000	.000	.000	0	-89	-1				.667	-0	/3-1	-0.1
1878	Pro-N	1	3	0	0	0	0	0	0	0	0	.000	.000	.000	0	-99	-1				1.000	0	/P-1	0.0
Total	5 n	215	1019	167	241	27	10	3	135	12	24	.237	.245	.291	537	64	-45	8	11	-2	.862	-10	P-136/O-81R,3-25,21S	-2.0
Total	3	37	136	12	32	1	0	0	4	0	10	.235	.235	.243	478	68	-3				.803	-5	/P-29,O-11C,3-1,1S	-0.4

■ CARLTON FISK Fisk, Carlton Ernest "Pudge" b: 12/26/47, Bellows Falls, Vt. BR/TR, 6′2″, 220 lbs. Deb: 9/18/69 H Career OF: (41-LF 0-CF 0-RF)

YEAR	TM/L	G	AB	R	H	2B	3B	HR	RBI	BB	SO	AVG	OBP	SLG	OPS	OPS+	BR+	SB	CS	SBR	FA	FR	G/POS	TPR
1969	Bos-A	2	5	0	0	0	0	0	0	0	2	.000	.000	.000	0	-95	-1	0	0	0	1.000	-1	/C-1	-0.3
1971	Bos-A	14	48	7	15	2	1	2	6	1	10	.313	.327	.521	847	128	1	0	0	0	.975	-1	C-14	0.1
1972	Bos-A★	131	457	74	134	28	**9**	22	61	52	83	.293	.370	.538	909	159	33	5	2	0	.984	1	*C-131	4.5
1973	Bos-A★	135	508	65	125	21	0	26	71	37	99	.246	.310	.441	751	103	1	7	2	1	.983	6	*C-131/D-3	1.4
1974	Bos-A†	52	187	36	56	12	1	11	26	24	23	.299	.385	.551	936	156	13	5	1	1	.980	2	C-50/D-2	1.9
1975	*Bos-A	79	263	47	87	14	4	10	52	27	32	.331	.397	.529	926	147	16	4	3	-0	.979	-4	C-71/D-6	1.5
1976	Bos-A★	134	487	76	124	17	5	17	58	56	71	.255	.339	.415	754	107	4	12	5	1	.984	10	*C-133/D-1	2.2
1977	Bos-A★	152	536	106	169	26	3	26	102	75	85	.315	.408	.521	929	135	28	7	6	-1	.987	0	*C-151	3.4
1978	Bos-A★	157	571	94	162	39	5	20	88	71	83	.284	.370	.475	844	123	18	7	2	1	.980	11	*C-154/O-1(1-0-0),D-1	3.7
1979	Bos-A	91	320	49	87	23	2	10	42	10	38	.272	.307	.450	757	96	-3	3	0	1	.982	-12	D-42,C-39/O-1(1-0-0)	-1.3
1980	Bos-A★	131	478	73	138	25	3	18	62	36	62	.289	.355	.467	821	117	11	11	5	1	.983	-7	*C-115/O-5L,1-3,3D	0.9
1981	Chi-A★	96	338	44	89	12	0	7	45	38	37	.263	.358	.361	719	110	6	3	2	-0	.990	-2	C-92/1-1,3-1,O-1L	0.8
1982	Chi-A★	135	476	66	127	17	3	14	65	46	60	.267	.339	.403	742	103	2	17	2	3	.994	-1	*C-133/1-2	1.0
1983	*Chi-A	138	488	85	141	26	4	26	86	46	88	.289	.357	.518	876	133	21	9	6	-0	.991	-2	*C-133/D-2	2.5
1984	Chi-A	102	359	54	83	20	1	21	43	26	60	.231	.292	.468	760	102	-0	6	0	1	.987	-17	C-90/D-5	-1.2
1985	Chi-A★	153	543	85	129	23	1	37	107	52	81	.238	.324	.488	812	114	9	17	9	1	.989	-4	*C-130,D-28	1.1

YEAR	TM/L	G	AB	R	H	2B	3B	HR	RBI	BB	SO	AVG	OBP	SLG	OPS	OPS+	BR+	SB	CS	SBR	FA	FR	G/POS	TPR
1986	Chi-A	125	457	42	101	11	0	14	63	22	92	.221	.266	.337	603	61	-25	2	4	-1	.991	2	C-71,O-31L/D-22	-2.3
1987	Chi-A	135	454	68	116	22	1	23	71	39	72	.256	.325	.460	786	103	1	1	4	-1	.990	2	*C-122/1-9,O-2L,D-7	0.6
1988	Chi-A	76	253	37	70	8	1	19	50	37	40	.277	.380	.542	921	155	19	0	0	0	.995	-5	C-74	1.8
1989	Chi-A	103	375	47	110	25	2	13	68	36	60	.293	.360	.475	835	137	18	1	0	0	**.993**	-15	C-90,D-13	0.8
1990	Chi-A	137	452	65	129	21	0	18	65	61	73	.285	.379	.451	830	134	22	7	2	1	.994	5	*C-116,D-14	3.4
1991	Chi-A★	134	460	42	111	25	0	18	74	32	86	.241	.301	.413	714	98	-3	1	2	-0	.993	-2	*C-106,D-13,1-12	0.0
1992	Chi-A	62	188	12	43	4	1	3	21	23	38	.229	.316	.309	625	77	-5	3	0	1	.993	-6	C-54/D-2	-0.7
1993	Chi-A	25	53	2	10	0	0	1	4	2	11	.189	.232	.245	477	29	-5	0	1	-0	1.000	-4	C-25	-0.9
Total	24	2499	8756	1276	2356	421	47	376	1330	849	1386	.269	.343	.457	800	116	180	128	58	8	.988	-44	*C-2226,D-166/O13	24.9

■ WES FISLER

Fisler, Weston Dickson "Icicle" b: 7/5/1841, Camden, N.J. d: 12/25/22, Philadelphia, Pa. 5'6", 137 lbs. Deb: 5/20/1871 Career OF: (0-LF 1-CF 10-RF)

YEAR	TM/L	G	AB	R	H	2B	3B	HR	RBI	BB	SO	AVG	OBP	SLG	OPS	OPS+	BR+	SB	CS	SBR	FA	FR	G/POS	TPR
1871	Ath-n	28	147	43	41	8	2	0	16	3	2	.279	.293	.361	654	88	-2	6	3	0	**.972**	1	*1-26/2-2	0.0
1872	Ath-n	47	243	49	85	13	3	0	48	4	4	.350	.360	.428	788	141	11	3	0	1	.889	8	*2-47	1.1
1873	Ath-n	44	218	44	75	11	4	1	42	2	2	.344	.350	.445	795	125	5	2	1	0	**.855**	3	*2-36,1-10	0.4
1874	Ath-n	37	180	26	59	12	1	0	22	0	1	.328	.328	.406	733	123	3	2	0	0	.953	4	1-28/2-9,O-1(0-0-1)	0.6
1875	Ath-n	58	268	54	74	13	3	0	31	4	4	.276	.287	.347	634	107	0	1	4	-1	.958	-0	1-46,O-10(0-1-9)/2-5	0.0
1876	Phi-N	59	280	42	80	15	1	1	30	2	4	.286	.293	.360	653	117	5				.911	1	O-24C,2-21,1-14,/S	0.4
Total	5 n	214	1056	216	334	57	13	1	159	13	13	.316	.325	.398	722	118	17	14	8	0	.951	15	1-110/2-99,O-11R	2.1

■ CHARLIE FITZBERGER

Fitzberger, Charles Casper b: 2/13/04, Baltimore, Md. d: 1/25/65, Baltimore, Md. BL/TL, 6'1.5", 170 lbs. Deb: 9/11/28

YEAR	TM/L	G	AB	R	H	2B	3B	HR	RBI	BB	SO	AVG	OBP	SLG	OPS	OPS+	BR+	SB	CS	SBR	FA	FR	G/POS	TPR
1928	Bos-N	7	7	0	2	0	0	0	0	0	3	.286	.286	.286	571	52	-0	0			.000	0	H	0.0

■ DENNIS FITZGERALD

Fitzgerald, Dennis S. b: 3/1865, England d: 10/16/36, New Haven, Conn. 5'10", 160 lbs. Deb: 4/17/1890

YEAR	TM/L	G	AB	R	H	2B	3B	HR	RBI	BB	SO	AVG	OBP	SLG	OPS	OPS+	BR+	SB	CS	SBR	FA	FR	G/POS	TPR
1890	Phi-a	2	8	0	2	0	0	0	0	0		.250	.250	.250	500	48	-1	0			.667	-2	/S-2	-0.2

■ ED FITZ GERALD

Fitz Gerald, Edward Raymond b: 5/21/24, Santa Ynez, Cal. BR/TR, 6', 180 lbs. Deb: 4/19/48 C

YEAR	TM/L	G	AB	R	H	2B	3B	HR	RBI	BB	SO	AVG	OBP	SLG	OPS	OPS+	BR+	SB	CS	SBR	FA	FR	G/POS	TPR
1948	Pit-N	102	262	31	70	9	3	1	35	32	37	.267	.349	.336	685	84	-5	3			.961	-2	C-96	-0.2
1949	Pit-N	75	160	16	42	7	0	2	18	8	27	.262	.302	.344	646	71	-7	1			.974	-5	C-56	-0.9
1950	Pit-N	6	15	1	1	1	0	0	0	0	3	.067	.067	.133	200	-47	-3	0			.950	-0	/C-5	-0.3
1951	Pit-N	55	97	8	22	6	0	0	13	7	10	.227	.286	.289	574	53	-6	1	1	-0	.965	-2	C-38	-0.7
1952	Pit-N	51	73	4	17	1	0	1	7	7	15	.233	.300	.288	588	62	-4	0	2	-1	1.000	-1	C-18/3-2	-0.5
1953	Pit-N	6	17	2	2	1	0	0	1	0	2	.118	.118	.176	294	-25	-3	0	0	0	1.000	-1	/C-5	-0.4
	Was-A	88	288	23	72	13	0	3	39	19	34	.250	.299	.326	625	70	-12	2	1	0	.989	-3	C-85	-1.1
1954	Was-A	115	360	33	104	13	5	4	40	33	22	.289	.352	.386	738	108	4	0	1	-0	.973	-17	*C-107	-0.9
1955	Was-A	74	236	28	56	3	1	4	19	25	23	.237	.318	.309	628	73	-9	0	1	-0	.982	-7	C-72	-1.2
1956	Was-A	64	148	15	45	8	0	2	12	20	16	.304	.387	.399	786	108	2	0	0	0	.974	2	C-50	0.6
1957	Was-A	45	125	14	34	8	0	1	13	10	9	.272	.331	.360	691	90	-2	2	0	0	.963	-8	C-37	-0.8
1958	Was-A	58	114	7	30	3	0	0	11	8	15	.263	.311	.289	601	68	-5	0	0	0	.970	-6	C-21/1-5	-1.1
1959	Was-A	19	62	5	12	3	0	0	5	4	8	.194	.242	.242	484	34	-6	0	0	0	1.000	-1	C-16	-0.6
	Cle-A	49	129	12	35	6	1	1	4	12	14	.271	.343	.357	699	96	-1	0	0	0	.978	0	C-45	0.2
	Yr	68	191	17	47	9	1	1	9	16	22	.246	.311	.319	630	76	-6	0	0	0	.984	-0	C-61	-0.4
Total	12	807	2086	199	542	82	10	19	217	185	235	.260	.324	.336	660	80	-56	9	6		.975	-49	C-651/1-5,3-2	-7.9

■ HOWIE FITZGERALD

Fitzgerald, Howard Chumney "Lefty" b: 5/16/02, Eagle Lake, Tex. d: 2/27/59, Matthews, Tex. BL/TL, 5'11.5", 163 lbs. Deb: 9/17/22

YEAR	TM/L	G	AB	R	H	2B	3B	HR	RBI	BB	SO	AVG	OBP	SLG	OPS	OPS+	BR+	SB	CS	SBR	FA	FR	G/POS	TPR
1922	Chi-N	10	24	3	8	1	0	0	4	3	2	.333	.407	.375	782	101	0	1	0	0	.818	-2	/O-6(0-0-6)	-0.1
1924	Chi-N	7	19	1	3	0	0	0	2	0	2	.158	.158	.158	316	-15	-3	0	0	0	1.000	-2	/O-5(0-1-4)	-0.5
1926	Bos-A	31	97	11	25	2	0	0	8	5	7	.258	.294	.278	572	52	-7	1	4	-1	.882	-5	O-23(21-0-2)	-1.4
Total	3	48	140	15	36	3	0	0	14	8	11	.257	.297	.279	576	52	-10	2	4	-1	.878	-8	/O-34(21-1-12)	-2.0

■ JUSTIN FITZGERALD

Fitzgerald, Justin Howard b: 6/22/1890, San Mateo, Cal. d: 1/17/45, San Mateo, Cal. BL/TR, 5'8", 160 lbs. Deb: 6/20/11

YEAR	TM/L	G	AB	R	H	2B	3B	HR	RBI	BB	SO	AVG	OBP	SLG	OPS	OPS+	BR+	SB	CS	SBR	FA	FR	G/POS	TPR
1911	NY-A	16	37	6	10	1	0	0	6	4		.270	.341	.297	639	74	-1	4			1.000	-2	/O-9(9-0-0)	-0.3
1918	Phi-N	66	133	21	39	8	0	0	6	13	6	.293	.361	.353	714	110	2	3			.966	-14	O-59(34-2-19)	-1.5
Total	2	82	170	27	49	9	0	0	12	17	6	.288	.356	.341	698	102	1	7			.971	-15	/O-68(43-2-19)	-1.8

■ MATTY FITZGERALD

Fitzgerald, Matthew William b: 8/31/1880, Albany, N.Y. d: 9/22/49, Albany, N.Y. BR/TR, 6', 185 lbs. Deb: 9/15/06

YEAR	TM/L	G	AB	R	H	2B	3B	HR	RBI	BB	SO	AVG	OBP	SLG	OPS	OPS+	BR+	SB	CS	SBR	FA	FR	G/POS	TPR
1906	NY-N	4	6	2	4	0	0	0	2	0		.667	.667	.667	1333	309	1	1			1.000	-1	/C-3	0.1
1907	NY-N	7	15	1	2	1	0	0	1	0		.133	.133	.200	333	4	-2	0			.952	-1	/C-6	-0.3
Total	2	11	21	3	6	1	0	0	3	0		.286	.286	.333	619	91	-0	1			.967	-2	/C-9	-0.2

■ MIKE FITZGERALD

Fitzgerald, Michael Patrick b: 3/28/64, Savannah, Ga. BR/TR, 6'1", 196 lbs. Deb: 6/23/88

YEAR	TM/L	G	AB	R	H	2B	3B	HR	RBI	BB	SO	AVG	OBP	SLG	OPS	OPS+	BR+	SB	CS	SBR	FA	FR	G/POS	TPR
1988	StL-N	13	46	4	9	1	0	0	1	0	9	.196	.213	.217	430	23	-5	0	0	0	.990	-2	1-12	-0.8

■ MIKE FITZGERALD

Fitzgerald, Michael Roy b: 7/13/60, Long Beach, Cal. BR/TR, 5'11", 190 lbs. Deb: 9/13/83 Career OF: (15-LF 0-CF 15-RF)

YEAR	TM/L	G	AB	R	H	2B	3B	HR	RBI	BB	SO	AVG	OBP	SLG	OPS	OPS+	BR+	SB	CS	SBR	FA	FR	G/POS	TPR
1983	NY-N	8	20	1	2	0	0	1	2	3	6	.100	.217	.250	467	29	-2	0	0	0	.957	2	/C-8	0.1
1984	NY-N	112	360	20	87	15	1	2	33	24	71	.242	.291	.306	596	69	-15	1	0	0	**.995**	8	*C-107	-0.3
1985	Mon-N	108	295	25	61	7	1	5	34	38	55	.207	.301	.288	590	70	-11	5	3	0	.987	-6	*C-108	-1.4
1986	Mon-N	73	209	20	59	13	1	6	37	27	34	.282	.367	.440	807	123	7	3	2	-0	.993	-7	C-71	0.3
1987	Mon-N	107	287	32	69	11	0	3	36	42	54	.240	.339	.310	649	71	-11	3	4	-1	.981	-1	*C-104/1-1,2-1	-0.8
1988	Mon-N	63	155	17	42	6	1	5	23	19	22	.271	.351	.419	770	115	3	2	2	-0	.979	4	C-47/O-4(3-0-1)	1.0
1989	Mon-N	100	290	33	69	18	2	7	42	35	61	.238	.324	.386	710	101	0	3	4	-1	.984	-6	C-77/3-8,O-6(6-0-0)	-0.2
1990	Mon-N	111	313	36	76	18	1	9	41	60	60	.243	.368	.393	761	114	8	8	1	1	.990	-4	C-98/O-6(1-0-5)	1.1
1991	Mon-N	71	198	17	40	5	2	4	28	22	35	.202	.282	.308	590	67	-9	4	2	0	.994	2	C-54/1-3,O-3(0-0-3)	-0.4
1992	Cal-A	95	189	19	40	2	0	6	17	22	34	.212	.294	.317	611	71	-7	2	2	-0	.990	-15	C-74,O-11R/3-3,12D	-1.9
Total	10	848	2316	220	545	95	9	48	293	292	432	.235	.323	.346	670	87	-37	31	20	-0	.988	-21	C-748/O-30L,3-11,12D	-2.5

■ RAY FITZGERALD

Fitzgerald, Raymond Francis b: 12/5/04, Chicopee, Mass. d: 9/6/77, Westfield, Mass. BR/TR, 5'9", 168 lbs. Deb: 4/18/31

YEAR	TM/L	G	AB	R	H	2B	3B	HR	RBI	BB	SO	AVG	OBP	SLG	OPS	OPS+	BR+	SB	CS	SBR	FA	FR	G/POS	TPR
1931	Cin-N	1	1	0	0	0	0	0	0	0	0	.000	.000	.000	0	-99	-0	0			.000	0	H	0.0

■ SHAUN FITZMAURICE

Fitzmaurice, Shaun Earle b: 8/25/42, Worcester, Mass. BR/TR, 6', 180 lbs. Deb: 9/9/66

YEAR	TM/L	G	AB	R	H	2B	3B	HR	RBI	BB	SO	AVG	OBP	SLG	OPS	OPS+	BR+	SB	CS	SBR	FA	FR	G/POS	TPR
1966	NY-N	9	13	2	2	0	0	0	0	2	6	.154	.267	.154	421	21	-1	1	0	0	1.000	1	/O-5(2-3-0)	-0.1

■ ED FITZPATRICK

Fitzpatrick, Edward Henry b: 12/9/1889, Lewistown, Pa. d: 10/23/65, Bethlehem, Pa. BR/TR, 5'8", 165 lbs. Deb: 4/17/15 Career OF: (6-LF 16-CF 52-RF)

YEAR	TM/L	G	AB	R	H	2B	3B	HR	RBI	BB	SO	AVG	OBP	SLG	OPS	OPS+	BR+	SB	CS	SBR	FA	FR	G/POS	TPR
1915	Bos-N	105	303	54	67	19	3	0	24	43	36	.221	.344	.304	648	101	3	13	8	0	.967	-6	2-71,O-29(0-7-22)	-0.4
1916	Bos-N	83	216	17	46	8	0	1	18	15	26	.213	.280	.264	544	70	-7	5			.950	-12	2-46,O-28(2-3-23)	-2.3
1917	Bos-N	63	178	20	45	8	4	0	17	12	22	.253	.318	.343	661	109	2	4			.929	-13	2-22,O-19(4-6-7),3-15	-1.3
Total	3	251	697	91	158	35	7	1	59	70	84	.227	.319	.301	620	94	-2	22	8		.956	-31	2-139/O-76R,3-15	-4.0

■ TOM FITZSIMMONS

Fitzsimmons, Thomas William b: 4/6/1890, Oakland, Cal. d: 12/20/71, Oakland, Cal. BR/TR, 6'1", 190 lbs. Deb: 6/12/19

YEAR	TM/L	G	AB	R	H	2B	3B	HR	RBI	BB	SO	AVG	OBP	SLG	OPS	OPS+	BR+	SB	CS	SBR	FA	FR	G/POS	TPR
1919	Bro-N	4	4	1	0	0	0	0	0	1	2	.000	.200	.000	200	-36	-1	0			.500	-1	/3-4	-0.2

■ MAX FLACK

Flack, Max John b: 2/5/1890, Belleville, Ill. d: 7/31/75, Belleville, Ill. BL/TL, 5'7", 148 lbs. Deb: 4/16/14

YEAR	TM/L	G	AB	R	H	2B	3B	HR	RBI	BB	SO	AVG	OBP	SLG	OPS	OPS+	BR+	SB	CS	SBR	FA	FR	G/POS	TPR
1914	Chi-F	134	502	66	124	15	3	2	39	51	48	.247	.324	.301	625	75	-25	37			.973	-1	*O-133(112-0-23)	-3.3
1915	Chi-F	141	523	88	164	20	14	3	45	40	21	.314	.365	.423	787	129	11	37			.969	2	*O-138(61-0-81)	0.6
1916	Chi-N	141	465	65	120	14	3	3	20	42	43	.258	.320	.320	640	87	-6	24	19	-1	**.991**	2	*O-136(0-0-136)	-1.4
1917	Chi-N	131	447	65	111	18	7	0	21	51	34	.248	.325	.320	645	91	-3	17			.947	-3	*O-117(40-6-77)	-1.4
1918	*Chi-N	123	478	74	123	17	10	4	41	56	19	.257	.343	.360	702	111	8	17			.978	3	*O-121(0-0-121)	0.5
1919	Chi-N	116	469	71	138	20	4	6	35	34	13	.294	.346	.392	738	121	12	18			.986	-0	*O-116(0-0-116)	0.6
1920	Chi-N	135	520	85	157	30	6	4	49	52	15	.302	.373	.406	779	121	16	13	19	-4	.967	-5	*O-132(0-1-131)	-0.1
1921	Chi-N	133	572	80	172	31	4	6	37	32	15	.301	.342	.400	742	96	-4	17	11	-0	**.989**	4	*O-130(0-0-130)	-1.1
1922	Chi-N	17	54	7	12	1	0	0	6	2	4	.222	.250	.241	491	27	-6	2	1	0	.933	-2	O-15(0-0-15)	-0.9
	StL-N	66	267	46	78	12	1	2	21	31	11	.292	.368	.367	735	95	-1	3	5	-1	.968	-4	O-66(0-1-65)	-1.1
	Yr	83	321	53	90	13	1	2	27	33	15	.280	.349	.346	695	83	-7	5	6	-1	.961	-6	O-81(0-1-80)	-2.0

YEAR	TM/L	G	AB	R	H	2B	3B	HR	RBI	BB	SO	AVG	OBP	SLG	OPS	OPS+	BR+	SB	CS	SBR	FA	FR	G/POS	TPR
1923	StL-N	128	505	82	147	16	9	3	28	41	16	.291	.348	.376	724	93	-5	7	8	-1	.951	-6	*O-121(0-0-121)	-2.1
1924	StL-N	67	209	31	55	11	3	2	21	21	5	.263	.330	.373	704	90	-3	3	5	-1	.971	1	O-52(0-0-52)	-0.7
1925	StL-N	79	241	23	60	7	8	0	28	21	9	.249	.309	.344	654	65	-13	5	3	0	.991	-2	O-59(5-0-54)	-1.8
Total	12	1411	5252	783	1461	212	72	35	391	474	253	.278	.342	.366	708	99	-19	200	71		.972	-12	*O-1336(218-8-1122)	-12.2
■ WALLY FLAGER	Flager, Walter Leonard b: 11/3/21, Chicago Heights, Ill. d: 12/16/90, Keizer, Ore. BL/TR, 5′11″, 160 lbs. Deb: 4/17/45																							
1945	Cin-N	21	52	5	11	1	0	0	6	8	5	.212	.317	.231	547	55	-3	0			.933	-7	S-15	-0.9
	Phi-N	49	168	21	42	4	1	2	15	17	15	.250	.323	.321	644	82	-4	1			.946	1	S-48/2-1	0.1
	Yr	70	220	26	53	5	1	2	21	25	20	.241	.321	.300	621	75	-7	1			.943	-6	S-63/2-1	-0.8
■ IRA FLAGSTEAD	Flagstead, Ira James "Pete" b: 9/22/1893, Montague, Mich. d: 3/13/40, Olympia, Wash. BR/TR, 5′9″, 165 lbs. Deb: 7/20/17 Career OF: (56-LF 695-CF 288-RF)																							
1917	Det-A	4	4	0	0	0	0	0	0	0	1	.000	.000	.000	0	-99	-1	0			.000	-1	/O-2(0-0-2)	-0.2
1919	Det-A	97	287	43	95	22	3	5	41	35	39	.331	.416	.481	897	155	22	6			.951	2	O-83(0-0-83)	2.0
1920	Det-A	110	311	40	73	13	5	3	35	37	27	.235	.318	.338	656	76	-11	3	4	-1	.967	7	O-82(1-6-75)	-0.9
1921	Det-A	85	259	40	79	16	2	0	31	21	21	.305	.371	.382	753	93	-2	8	4	0	.903	-5	S-55,O-12L/2-8,3-1	-0.2
1922	Det-A	44	91	21	28	5	3	3	8	14	16	.308	.411	.527	939	148	7	0	1	-0	.967	-2	O-32(8-9-15)	0.3
1923	Det-A	1	1	0	0	0	0	0	0	0	0	.000	.000	.000	0	-99	-0	0	0	0	.000	0	H	0.0
	Bos-A	109	382	55	119	23	4	8	53	37	26	.312	.380	.455	835	119	10	7	10	-2	.965	19	*O-102(0-3-99)/S-1	1.8
	Yr	110	383	55	119	23	4	8	53	37	26	.311	.379	.454	833	118	10	7	10	-2	.965	19	*O-102(0-3-99)/S-1	1.8
1924	Bos-A	149	560	106	172	35	7	5	43	77	41	.307	.401	.421	823	112	13	10	13	-2	.975	-2	*O-144(0-143-1)	0.2
1925	Bos-A	148	572	84	160	38	2	6	61	63	30	.280	.356	.385	741	88	-10	5	6	-1	.976	**20**	*O-144(0-144-0).	0.2
1926	Bos-A	98	415	65	124	31	7	3	31	36	22	.299	.363	.429	792	110	5	4	6	-1	.982	9	O-98(0-98-0)	0.8
1927	Bos-A	131	466	63	133	26	8	4	69	57	25	.285	.374	.401	775	103	4	12	2	2	**.986**	11	*O-129(0-128-1)	1.0
1928	Bos-A	140	510	84	148	41	4	1	39	60	23	.290	.366	.392	758	101	2	12	9	-1	.973	5	*O-135(0-135-0)	0.1
1929	Bos-A	14	36	9	11	2	0	0	3	5	1	.306	.390	.361	751	97	0	1	3	-1	.955	-3	O-13(13-1-0)	-0.4
	Was-A	18	39	5	7	1	0	0	9	4	5	.179	.256	.205	461	20	-5	1	0	0	.971	3	O-11(1-10-0)	-0.2
	Yr	32	75	14	18	3	0	0	12	9	6	.240	.321	.280	601	57	-5	2	3	-1	.965	0	O-24(14-11-0)	-0.6
	Pit-N	26	50	8	14	2	1	0	6	4	2	.280	.333	.360	693	70	-2	1			1.000	0	/O-9(6-1-2)	-0.2
1930	Pit-N	44	156	21	39	7	4	2	21	17	9	.250	.324	.385	708	70	-8	1			.961	-3	O-40(21-15-5)	-1.2
Total	13	1218	4139	644	1202	262	50	40	450	467	288	.290	.370	.407	776	103	23	71	58		.974	59	*O-1036C/S-56,2-8,3	3.1
■ JOHN FLAHERTY	Flaherty, John Timothy b: 10/21/67, New York, N.Y. BR/TR, 6′1″, 195 lbs. Deb: 4/12/92																							
1992	Bos-A	35	66	3	13	2	0	0	2	3	7	.197	.232	.227	459	27	-6	0	0	0	.982	-3	C-34	-0.9
1993	Bos-A	13	25	3	3	2	0	0	2	2	6	.120	.214	.200	414	11	-3	0	0	0	1.000	-1	C-13	-0.4
1994	Det-A	34	40	2	6	1	0	0	4	1	11	.150	.171	.175	346	-11	-7	0	1	-0	1.000	6	C-33/D-1	-0.1
1995	Det-A	112	354	39	86	22	1	11	40	18	47	.243	.285	.404	689	77	-13	0	0	0	.982	-11	*C-112	-1.6
1996	Det-A	47	152	18	38	12	0	4	23	8	25	.250	.292	.408	700	75	-6	1	0	0	.981	-13	C-46	-1.5
	*SD-N	72	264	22	80	12	0	9	41	9	36	.303	.331	.451	782	110	3	2	3	-1	.990	-7	C-72	-0.1
1997	SD-N	129	439	38	120	21	1	9	46	33	62	.273	.324	.387	711	92	-6	4	4	-1	.987	-18	*C-124	-1.7
1998	TB-A	91	304	21	63	11	0	3	24	22	46	.207	.263	.273	536	39	-27	0	5	-2	.993	-3	C-91	-2.5
1999	TB-A	117	446	53	124	19	0	14	71	19	64	.278	.316	.415	731	84	-12	0	2	-1	.993	3	*C-115/D-1	-0.2
2000	TB-A	109	394	36	103	15	0	10	39	20	57	.261	.297	.376	673	69	-19	0	0	0	.993	1	*C-108	-1.1
Total	9	759	2484	235	636	117	2	60	292	135	361	.256	.298	.377	675	74	-97	7	15	-4	.989	-46	C-748/D-2	-10.1
■ MARTIN FLAHERTY	Flaherty, Martin J. b: 9/24/1853, Worcester, Mass d: 6/10/20, Providence, R.I. BL/TL, Deb: 8/18/1881																							
1881	Wor-N	1	2	0	0	0	0	0	0	0	2	.000	.000	.000	0	-95	-0				.000	-1	/O-1(1-1-0)	-0.2
■ PAT FLAHERTY	Flaherty, Patrick Henry b: 1/31/1866, St.Louis, Mo. d: 1/28/46, Chicago, Ill. 5′9″, 166 lbs. Deb: 7/11/1894																							
1894	Lou-N	39	149	15	43	5	3	0	15	10	7	.289	.338	.362	700	74	-6	2			.852	-4	3-39	-0.7
■ PATSY FLAHERTY	Flaherty, Patrick Joseph b: 6/29/1876, Mansfield, Pa. d: 1/23/68, Alexandria, La. BL/TL, 5′8″, 165 lbs. Deb: 9/8/1899																							
1899	Lou-N	7	24	3	5	1	1	0	6	3		.208	.296	.333	630	73	-1	0			.692	-1	/P-5,O-2(0-0-2)	0.0
1900	Pit-N	4	9	0	1	0	0	0	0	1		.111	.200	.111	311	-13	-1	0			1.000	1	/P-4	0.0
1903	Chi-A	40	102	7	14	4	0	0	5	5		.137	.178	.176	354	7	-11	4			.914	3	P-40	0.0
1904	Chi-A	5	12	1	4	1	0	0	0	4		.333	.500	.417	917	199	2	0			.880	1	/P-5	0.0
	Pit-N	36	104	9	22	3	4	2	19	8		.212	.268	.375	643	95	-1	0			.965	5	P-29/O-2(0-2-0)	0.0
1905	Pit-N	30	76	7	15	4	2	0	4	3		.197	.228	.303	530	56	-4	0			.894	2	P-27/O-2(0-1-1)	-0.1
1907	Bos-N	41	115	9	22	3	2	2	11	2		.191	.212	.304	516	62	-6	1			.907	3	P-27/O-8(6-0-2)	-0.1
1908	Bos-N	32	86	8	12	0	2	0	5	6		.140	.196	.186	382	22	-8	2			.961	2	P-31	0.0
1910	Phi-N	2	2	0	1	0	0	0	0	0	0	.500	.500	.500	1000	186	0	0			.000	-0	/P-1,O-1(0-1-0)	0.0
1911	Bos-N	38	94	9	27	3	2	2	20	8	11	.287	.343	.426	769	106	0	2			.933	-4	O-19(1-11-7)/P-4	-0.4
Total	9	235	624	53	123	19	13	6	70	40	11	.197	.247	.298	545	63	-30	9			.921	11	P-173/O-34(7-15-12)	-0.6
■ AL FLAIR	Flair, Albert Dell "Broadway" b: 7/24/16, New Orleans, La. d: 7/25/88, New Orleans, La. BL/TL, 6′4″, 195 lbs. Deb: 9/6/41																							
1941	Bos-A	10	30	3	6	2	1	0	2	1	1	.200	.226	.333	559	45	-3	1	1	-0	1.000	-0	/1-8	-0.3
■ CHARLIE FLANAGAN	Flanagan, Charles James b: 12/31/1891, Oakland, Cal. d: 1/8/30, San Francisco, Cal. BR/TR, 6′, 175 lbs. Deb: 7/9/13																							
1913	StL-A	4	3	0	0	0	0	0	0	1	0	.000	.250	.000	250	-26	-0	0			.000	-1	/3-1,O-1(1-0-0)	-0.1
■ ED FLANAGAN	Flanagan, Edward J. "Sleepy" b: 9/15/1861, Lowell, Mass. d: 11/10/26, Lowell, Mass. 6′1″, 190 lbs. Deb: 4/16/1887																							
1887	Phi-a	19	83	12	23	5	0	1	10	3		.277	.286	.350	636	77	-3	3			.948	-1	1-19	-0.5
1889	Lou-a	23	88	11	22	7	3	0	8	7	11	.250	.305	.398	703	101	-0	1			.953	-1	1-23	-0.2
Total	2	42	171	23	45	12	3	1	18	10	11	.263	.296	.375	671	89	-3	4			.951	-2	/1-42	-0.7
■ STEAMER FLANAGAN	Flanagan, James Paul b: 4/20/1881, Kingston, Pa. d: 4/21/47, Wilkes-Barre, Pa. BL/TL, 6′1″, 185 lbs. Deb: 9/25/05																							
1905	Pit-N	7	25	7	7	1	1	0	3	1		.280	.308	.400	708	108	0	3			1.000	1	/O-5(0-5-0)	0.1
■ JOHN FLANNERY	Flannery, John Michael b: 1/25/57, Long Beach, Cal. BR/TR, 6′3″, 173 lbs. Deb: 9/2/77																							
1977	Chi-A	7	2	1	0	0	0	0	0	1	1	.000	.333	.000	333	0	-0	0	0	0	1.000	1	/S-4,3-1,D-1	0.1
■ TIM FLANNERY	Flannery, Timothy Earl b: 9/29/57, Tulsa, Okla. BL/TR, 5′11″, 175 lbs. Deb: 9/3/79 C																							
1979	SD-N	22	65	2	10	0	1	0	4	4	5	.154	.225	.185	410	14	-8	0	0	0	.991	2	2-21	-0.5
1980	SD-N	95	292	15	70	12	0	0	25	18	30	.240	.284	.281	565	62	-15	2	2	-0	.988	-4	2-53,3-41	-1.9
1981	SD-N	37	67	4	17	4	1	0	6	2	4	.254	.275	.343	619	80	-2	1	0	0	.967	-1	3-15/2-7	-0.3
1982	SD-N	122	379	40	100	11	7	0	30	30	32	.264	.321	.330	651	87	-6	1	0	0	.974	-24	*2-104/3-5,S-2	-2.7
1983	SD-N	92	214	24	50	7	3	3	19	20	23	.234	.314	.336	650	83	-5	2	2	-0	.969	10	3-52,2-21/S-7	0.6
1984	*SD-N	86	128	24	35	3	3	2	10	12	17	.273	.350	.391	740	108	2	4	1	1	.944	-6	2-22,3-14,S-14	-0.2
1985	SD-N	126	384	50	108	14	3	1	40	58	39	.281	.388	.341	729	107	7	2	5	-1	.977	-19	*2-121/3-1	-0.7
1986	SD-N	134	368	48	103	11	2	3	28	54	61	.280	.379	.345	724	103	4	3	6	-1	.993	-7	*2-108,3-23/S-8	0.1
1987	SD-N	106	276	23	63	5	1	0	20	42	30	.228	.334	.254	588	61	-14	2	4	-1	.986	3	2-84/3-8,S-2	-0.8
1988	SD-N	79	170	16	45	5	4	0	19	24	32	.265	.369	.341	710	107	3	3	2	-0	.972	-4	3-51/2-2,S-1	-0.1
1989	SD-N	73	130	9	30	5	0	0	8	13	20	.231	.301	.269	570	64	-6	2	0	0	.920	2	3-33/2-1	-0.4
Total	11	972	2473	255	631	77	25	9	209	277	293	.255	.338	.317	655	86	-40	22	22	-3	.982	-47	2-544,3-243/S-34	-6.9
■ ROY FLASKAMPER	Flaskamper, Raymond Harold "Flash" b: 10/31/01, St.Louis, Mo. d: 2/3/78, San Antonio, Tex. BB/TR, 5′7″, 140 lbs. Deb: 8/16/27																							
1927	Chi-A	26	95	12	21	5	0	0	6	3	8	.221	.260	.274	534	40	-9	0	0	0	.962	0	S-25	-0.6
■ FRANK FLEET	Fleet, Frank H. b: 1848, New York, N.Y. d: 6/13/1900, New York, N.Y. Deb: 10/18/1871 Career OF: (1-LF 2-CF 1-RF)																							
1871	Mut-n	1	6	1	2	0	0	0	1	0	0	.333	.333	.333	667	101	0	0	0	0	1.000	1	/P-1	0.0
1872	Eck-n	13	53	10	13	1	0	0	5	0	1	.245	.245	.264	509	67	-1	1	0	0	.760	3	3-10/2-2,O-2(0-1-1)	0.1
1873	Res-n	22	90	11	23	2	0	0	10	1	2	.256	.264	.278	542	66	-3	0	1	-0	.864	1	/2-9,S-9,P-3,3-2,1	-0.2
1874	Atl-n	22	97	18	22	0	0	0	10	1	1	.227	.235	.227	461	55	-4	1	0	0	.759	-4	C-13,2-11/O-1(1-0-0)	-0.7

YEAR	TM/L	G	AB	R	H	2B	3B	HR	RBI	BB	SO	AVG	OBP	SLG	OPS	OPS+	BR+	SB	CS	SBR	FA	FR	G/POS	TPR
1875	StL-n	4	16	1	1	0	0	0	1	0	0	.063	.063	.063	125	-62	-2	0	0	0	.900	-0	/P-3,3-1,O-1(0-1-0)	-0.1
	Atl-n	26	111	13	25	2	0	0	9	1	1	.225	.232	.243	475	75	-2	0	0	0	.719	-8	C-11,2-10/S-9,P3	-0.9
	Yr	30	127	14	26	2	0	0	10	1	1	.205	.211	.220	431	57	-4	0	0	0	.719	-8	C-11,2-10/S-9,P3O	-1.0
Total	5 n	88	373	54	86	5	0	0	36	3	5	.231	.237	.244	481	61	-12	2	1	0	.782	-7	/2-32,C-24,S-18,3PO1	-1.8
■ ANGEL FLEITAS	Fleitas, Angel Felix Husta b: 11/10/14, Los Abreus, Cuba BR/TR, 5'9", 160 lbs. Deb: 7/5/48																							
1948	Was-A	15	13	1	1	0	0	0	1	3	5	.077	.250	.077	327	-11	-2	0	2	-1	.952	3	/S-7	0.0
■ LES FLEMING	Fleming, Leslie Harvey "Moe" b: 8/7/15, Singleton, Tex. d: 3/5/80, Cleveland, Tex. BL/TL, 5'10", 185 lbs. Deb: 4/22/39																							
1939	Det-A	8	16	0	0	0	0	0	1	0	4	.000	.000	.000	0	-93	-5	0	0	0	1.000	-0	/O-3(1-0-2)	-0.5
1941	Cle-A	2	8	0	2	1	0	0	2	0	0	.250	.250	.375	625	67	-0	0	0	0	1.000	-0	/1-2	-0.1
1942	Cle-A	156	548	71	160	27	4	14	82	106	57	.292	.412	.432	845	146	39	6	8	-1	**.993**	-9	*1-156	1.3
1945	Cle-A	42	140	18	46	10	2	3	22	11	5	.329	.382	.493	874	160	10	0	0	0	.938	-2	O-33(0-0-33)/1-5	0.6
1946	Cle-A	99	306	40	85	17	5	8	42	50	42	.278	.383	.444	827	140	17	1	0	0	.984	3	1-80/O-1(0-0-1)	1.8
1947	Cle-A	103	281	39	68	14	2	4	43	53	42	.242	.362	.349	711	101	2	0	0	0	.989	4	1-77	0.3
1949	Pit-N	24	31	0	8	0	2	0	7	6	2	.258	.395	.387	782	108	1	0			1.000	-1	/1-5	-0.1
Total	7	434	1330	168	369	69	15	29	199	226	152	.277	.386	.417	804	131	63	7	8		.990	-6	1-325/O-37(1-0-36)	3.3
■ TOM FLEMING	Fleming, Thomas Vincent "Sleuth" b: 11/20/1873, Philadelphia, Pa. d: 12/26/57, Boston, Mass. BL/TL, 5'11", 155 lbs. Deb: 9/19/1899																							
1899	NY-N	22	77	9	16	1	1	0	4	1		.208	.218	.247	465	28	-8	1			.909	-1	O-22(0-22-0)	-0.9
1902	Phi-N	5	16	2	6	0	0	0	2	1		.375	.412	.375	787	143	1	0			1.000	0	/O-5(0-0-5)	0.1
1904	Phi-N	3	6	0	0	0	0	0	0	0		.000	.000	.000	0	-99	-1	0			1.000	0	/O-1(0-0-1)	-0.1
Total	3	30	99	11	22	1	1	0	6	2		.222	.238	.253	490	39	-8	1			.920	-0	/O-28(0-22-6)	-0.9
■ ART FLETCHER	Fletcher, Arthur b: 1/5/1885, Collinsville, Ill. d: 2/6/50, Los Angeles, Cal. BR/TR, 5'10.5", 170 lbs. Deb: 4/15/09 MC																							
1909	NY-N	33	98	7	21	0	1	0	6	1		.214	.238	.235	472	46	-6	0			.893	4	S-22/2-7,3-6	-0.2
1910	NY-N	51	125	12	28	2	1	0	13	4	9	.224	.248	.256	504	47	-9	9			.895	-5	S-22,2-11,3-11	-1.4
1911	*NY-N	112	326	73	104	17	8	1	37	30	27	.319	.400	.429	829	128	13	20			.926	4	S-74,3-21,2-13	2.2
1912	*NY-N	129	419	64	118	17	9	1	57	16	29	.282	.330	.372	702	89	-7	16			.927	16	*S-126/2-2,3-1	1.7
1913	*NY-N	136	538	76	160	20	9	4	71	24	35	.297	.345	.390	735	109	6	32			.932	-7	*S-136	0.8
1914	NY-N	135	514	62	147	26	8	2	79	22	37	.286	.332	.379	711	115	8	15			.922	6	*S-135	2.5
1915	NY-N	149	562	59	143	17	7	3	74	6	36	.254	.280	.326	606	88	-10	12	18	-4	.936	**33**	*S-149	3.2
1916	NY-N	133	500	53	143	23	8	3	66	13	36	.286	.323	.382	705	122	11	15			.940	20	*S-133	4.5
1917	*NY-N	151	557	70	145	24	5	4	56	23	28	.260	.312	.343	655	104	2	12			**.956**	27	*S-151	4.4
1918	NY-N	124	468	51	123	20	2	0	47	18	26	.263	.311	.314	625	93	-4	12			**.959**	**22**	*S-124	2.9
1919	NY-N	127	488	54	135	20	5	3	54	9	28	.277	.300	.357	656	98	-3	6			.944	24	*S-127	3.3
1920	NY-N	41	171	21	44	7	2	0	24	1	15	.257	.282	.322	604	74	-6	3	2	-0	.914	-2	S-41	-0.6
	Phi-N	102	379	36	112	25	7	4	38	15	28	.296	.329	.430	759	112	5	4	6	-1	.958	12	*S-102	2.4
	Yr	143	550	57	156	32	9	4	62	16	43	.284	.315	.396	711	100	-1	7	8	-1	.945	10	*S-143	1.8
1922	Phi-N	110	396	46	111	20	5	7	53	21	14	.280	.325	.409	734	80	-12	3	2	-0	.939	7	*S-106	0.5
Total	13	1533	5541	684	1534	238	77	32	675	203	348	.277	.319	.365	684	100	-13	159	28		.939	160	*S-1448/3-39,2-33	26.2
■ DARRIN FLETCHER	Fletcher, Darrin Glen b: 10/3/66, Elmhurst, Ill. BL/TR, 6'1", 199 lbs. Deb: 9/10/89 F																							
1989	LA-N	5	8	1	4	0	0	1	2	1	0	.500	.556	.875	1431	308	2	0	0	0	1.000	0	/C-5	0.2
1990	LA-N	2	1	0	0	0	0	0	0	0	1	.000	.000	.000	0	-99	-0	0	0	0	.000	0	/C-1	0.0
	Phi-N	9	22	3	3	1	0	0	1	1	5	.136	.174	.182	356	-2	-3	0	0	0	1.000	1	/C-6	-0.2
	Yr	11	23	3	3	1	0	0	1	1	6	.130	.167	.174	341	-6	-3	0	0	0	1.000	1	/C-7	-0.2
1991	Phi-N	46	136	5	31	8	0	1	12	5	15	.228	.255	.309	564	59	-8	0	1	-0	.992	3	C-45	-0.3
1992	Mon-N	83	222	13	54	10	2	2	26	14	28	.243	.294	.333	627	78	-7	0	2	-1	.995	-0	C-69	-0.4
1993	Mon-N	133	396	33	101	20	1	9	60	34	40	.255	.323	.379	702	84	-9	0	0	0	.988	-10	*C-127	-1.2
1994	Mon-N★	94	285	28	74	18	1	10	57	25	23	.260	.326	.435	761	95	-2	0	0	0	.996	-8	C-81	-0.6
1995	Mon-N	110	350	42	100	21	1	11	45	32	23	.286	.352	.446	798	105	3	0	1	-0	.994	-3	C-98	0.5
1996	Mon-N	127	394	41	105	22	0	12	57	27	42	.266	.323	.414	737	90	-6	0	0	0	.992	-17	*C-112	-1.6
1997	Mon-N	96	310	39	86	20	1	17	55	17	35	.277	.325	.513	838	116	6	1	1	-0	.994	-3	C-83	0.8
1998	Tor-A	124	407	37	115	23	1	9	52	25	39	.283	.333	.410	744	92	-5	0	0	0	.991	6	*C-121/D-1	0.8
1999	Tor-A	115	412	48	120	26	0	18	80	26	47	.291	.342	.485	828	106	3	0	0	0	.997	-20	*C-113	-1.0
2000	Tor-A	122	416	43	133	19	1	20	58	20	45	.320	.358	.514	873	116	9	1	0	0	.994	-13	*C-117/D-2	0.3
Total	12	1066	3359	333	926	188	8	110	505	227	343	.276	.330	.435	764	97	-18	2	5	-1	.993	-64	C-978/D-3	-2.7
■ ELBIE FLETCHER	Fletcher, Elburt Preston b: 3/18/16, Milton, Mass. d: 3/9/94, Milton, Mass. BL/TL, 6', 180 lbs. Deb: 9/16/34																							
1934	Bos-N	8	4	4	2	0	0	0	0	0	2	.500	.500	.500	1000	182	0	1			.875	-0	/1-1	0.0
1935	Bos-N	39	148	12	35	7	1	1	9	7	13	.236	.271	.318	589	63	-8	1			.997	2	1-39	-0.9
1937	Bos-N	148	539	56	133	22	4	1	38	56	64	.247	.321	.308	629	79	-15	3			.993	1	*1-148	-2.9
1938	Bos-N	147	529	71	144	24	7	6	48	60	40	.272	.351	.378	729	112	9	5			.990	10	*1-146	0.6
1939	Bos-N	35	106	14	26	2	0	0	6	19	5	.245	.365	.264	629	77	-2	1			.986	-5	1-31	-1.0
	Pit-N	102	370	49	112	23	4	12	71	48	28	.303	.386	.484	869	134	18	3			.993	-4	*1-101	0.5
	Yr	137	476	63	138	25	4	12	77	67	33	.290	.381	.435	816	122	16	4			.991	-9	*1-132	-0.5
1940	Pit-N	147	510	94	139	22	7	16	104	**119**	54	.273	**.418**	.437	856	137	33	5			.993	4	*1-147	2.3
1941	Pit-N	151	521	95	150	29	13	11	74	**118**	54	.288	**.421**	.457	878	148	39	5			.991	9	*1-151	3.4
1942	Pit-N	145	506	86	146	22	5	7	57	105	60	.289	**.417**	.393	810	134	28	0			.992	12	*1-144	2.7
1943	Pit-N★	154	544	91	154	24	5	9	70	95	49	.283	.395	.395	791	124	21	1			**.996**	3	*1-154	1.7
1946	Pit-N	148	532	72	136	25	8	4	66	111	37	.256	.384	.355	739	108	10	4			.995	1	*1-147	0.7
1947	Pit-N	69	157	22	38	9	1	1	22	29	24	.242	.364	.331	695	83	-3	2			.986	-0	1-50	-0.4
1949	Bos-N	122	413	57	108	19	3	11	51	84	65	.262	.396	.402	798	121	16	1			.991	0	*1-121	1.3
Total	12	1415	4879	723	1323	228	58	79	616	851	495	.271	.384	.390	774	118	147	32			.993	33	*1-1380	8.0
■ GEORGE FLETCHER	Fletcher, George Horace Elliot b: 4/21/1845, Brooklyn, N.Y. d: 6/18/1879, Brooklyn, N.Y. Deb: 6/21/1872																							
1872	Eck-n	2	8	1	3	0	0	0	0	0	0	.375	.375	.375	750	155	1	0	0	0	.500	-1	/O-2(0-0-2)	0.0
■ FRANK FLETCHER	Fletcher, Oliver Frank b: 3/6/1891, Hildreth, Ill. d: 10/7/74, St.Petersburg, Fla. BR/TR, 5'10", 165 lbs. Deb: 7/14/14																							
1914	Phi-N	1	1	0	0	0	0	0	0	0	1	.000	.000	.000	0	-94	-0	0			.000	0	H	0.0
■ SCOTT FLETCHER	Fletcher, Scott Brian b: 7/30/58, Fort Walton Beach, Fla. BR/TR, 5'11", 173 lbs. Deb: 4/25/81																							
1981	Chi-N	19	46	6	10	4	0	0	1	2	4	.217	.250	.304	554	54	-3	0	0	0	.972	6	2-13/S-4,3-1	0.4
1982	Chi-N	11	24	4	4	0	0	0	1	4	5	.167	.286	.167	452	29	-2	1	0	0	1.000	-0	S-11	-0.2
1983	*Chi-A	114	262	42	62	16	5	3	31	29	22	.237	.317	.370	688	85	-5	5	1	1	.965	18	*S-100,2-12/3-7,D-1	2.2
1984	Chi-A	149	456	46	114	13	3	3	35	46	46	.250	.329	.311	641	75	-14	10	4	1	.973	0	*S-134,2-28/3-3	0.1
1985	Chi-A	119	301	38	77	8	1	2	31	35	47	.256	.333	.309	642	74	-10	5	5	-1	.934	-3	3-55,S-44,2-37,/D-2	-0.9
1986	Tex-A	147	530	82	159	34	5	3	50	47	59	.300	.361	.400	761	104	4	12	11	-1	.973	-6	*S-136,3-12,2-11,/D	1.1
1987	Tex-A	156	588	82	169	28	4	5	63	61	66	.287	.359	.374	733	95	-3	13	12	-1	.966	5	*S-155	1.6
1988	Tex-A	140	515	59	142	19	4	0	47	62	34	.276	.367	.328	695	94	-1	8	5	0	.983	1	*S-139	1.1
1989	Tex-A	83	314	47	75	14	1	0	22	38	41	.239	.325	.290	615	73	-10	1	0	0	.960	-18	S-81/D-1	-2.2
	Chi-A	59	232	30	63	11	1	1	21	26	19	.272	.347	.341	688	97	-0	1	1	-0	1.000	-3	2-53/S-8	-0.1
	Yr	142	546	77	138	25	2	1	43	64	60	.253	.334	.311	646	83	-10	2	1	0	.957	-21	S-89,2-53/D-1	-2.3
1990	Chi-A	151	509	54	123	18	3	4	56	45	63	.242	.307	.312	619	75	-16	1	3	-1	.988	-6	*2-151	-2.0
1991	Chi-A	90	248	14	51	10	1	1	28	17	26	.206	.265	.266	531	48	-17	0	2	-1	.992	-6	2-86/3-4	-2.2
1992	Mil-A	123	386	53	106	18	3	3	51	30	33	.275	.338	.360	698	98	-1	17	10	0	.992	10	*2-106,S-22/3-1	1.3
1993	Bos-A	121	480	81	137	31	5	5	45	37	35	.285	.343	.402	745	94	-4	16	3	2	.982	5	*2-116/S-2,3-1,D-1	0.9
1994	Bos-A	63	185	31	42	9	1	3	11	16	14	.227	.296	.335	631	59	-11	8	1	1	.996	19	2-53/D-4	1.1
1995	Det-A	67	182	19	42	10	1	1	17	19	27	.231	.314	.313	627	64	-9	1	0	0	1.000	9	2-63/S-3,1-1,D-1	0.2
Total	15	1612	5258	688	1376	243	38	34	510	514	541	.262	.334	.342	676	84	-103	99	58	1	.971	30	S-839,2-729/3-84,D1	2.4

YEAR	TM/L	G	AB	R	H	2B	3B	HR	RBI	BB	SO	AVG	OBP	SLG	OPS	OPS+	BR+	SB	CS	SBR	FA	FR	G/POS	TPR
■ **ELMER FLICK**	Flick, Elmer Harrison b: 1/11/1876, Bedford, Ohio d: 1/9/71, Bedford, Ohio BL/TR, 5'9", 168 lbs. Deb: 5/2/1898 H Career OF: (9-LF 127-CF 1320-RF)																							
1898	Phi-N	134	453	84	137	16	13	8	81	86		.302	.430	.448	878	158	40	23			.931	7	*O-133(0-0-133)	3.7
1899	Phi-N	127	485	98	166	22	11	2	98	42		.342	.407	.445	852	138	27	31			.931	9	*O-125(0-0-125)	2.6
1900	Phi-N	138	545	106	200	32	16	11	**110**	56		.367	.441	.545	986	173	**55**	35			.914	3	*O-138(0-0-138)	4.6
1901	Phi-N	138	540	112	180	32	17	8	88	52		.333	.399	.500	899	157	39	30			.962	15	*O-138(1-0-137)	4.5
1902	Phi-A	11	37	15	11	2	1	0	3	6		.297	.435	.405	840	128	2	4			.947	-0	O-11(0-0-11)	0.1
	Cle-A	110	424	70	126	19	11	2	61	47		.297	.371	.408	779	121	13	20			.929	-4	*O-110(0-0-110)	0.4
	Yr	121	461	85	137	21	12	2	64	53		.297	.377	.408	785	121	15	24			.930	-5	*O-121(0-0-121)	0.5
1903	Cle-A	140	523	81	155	23	16	2	51	51		.296	.368	.413	781	136	24	24			.955	1	*O-140(6-0-134)	1.9
1904	Cle-A	150	579	97	177	31	17	6	56	51		.306	.371	.449	820	160	40	**38**			.955	10	*O-145(0-6-139)/2-6	4.7
1905	Cle-A	132	500	72	154	29	**18**	4	64	53		**.308**	.383	**.462**	**845**	**165**	**37**	35			.939	1	*O-131(0-0-131)/2-1	3.5
1906	Cle-A	157	624	**98**	194	34	**22**	1	62	54		.311	.372	.441	813	156	40	**39**			.981	-12	*O-150(0-86-65)/2-8	2.3
1907	Cle-A	147	549	80	166	15	**18**	3	58	64		.302	.386	.412	798	153	35	41			.956	1	*O-147(1-23-122)	3.2
1908	Cle-A	9	35	4	8	1	1	0	2	3		.229	.289	.314	604	96	-0	0			1.000	-0	/O-9(0-0-9)	-0.1
1909	Cle-A	66	235	28	60	10	2	0	15	22		.255	.322	.315	637	97	-0	9			.958	-4	O-61(1-12-48)	-0.8
1910	Cle-A	24	68	5	18	2	1	1	7	10		.265	.359	.368	727	126	2	1			.955	-3	O-18(0-0-18)	-0.2
Total	13	1483	5597	950	1752	268	164	48	756	597		.313	.389	.445	834	149	353	330			.947	23	*O-1456R/2-15	30.4
■ **LEW FLICK**	Flick, Lewis Miller "Noisy" b: 2/18/15, Bristol, Tenn. d: 12/7/90, Weber City, Va. BL/TL, 5'9", 155 lbs. Deb: 9/28/43																							
1943	Phi-A	1	5	2	3	0	0	0	0	0	0	.600	.600	.600	1200	253	1	0	0	0	1.000	0	/O-1(0-0-1)	0.1
1944	Phi-A	19	35	1	4	0	0	0	2	1	2	.114	.139	.114	253	-28	-6	1	0	0	1.000	-1	/O-6(0-1-5)	-0.7
Total	2	20	40	3	7	0	0	0	2	1	2	.175	.195	.175	370	6	-5	1	0	0	1.000	-1	/O-7(0-1-6)	-0.6
■ **DON FLINN**	Flinn, Don Raphael b: 11/17/1892, Bluff Dale, Tex. d: 3/9/59, Waco, Tex. BR/TR, 6'1", 185 lbs. Deb: 9/2/17																							
1917	Pit-N	14	37	1	11	1	1	0	1	1	6	.297	.316	.378	694	109	0	1			1.000	0	O-12(7-1-4)	0.0
■ **SILVER FLINT**	Flint, Frank Sylvester b: 8/3/1855, Philadelphia, Pa. d: 1/14/1892, Chicago, Ill. BR/TR, 6', 180 lbs. Deb: 5/4/1875 M Career OF: (5-LF 4-CF 57-RF)																							
1875	RS-n	17	61	4	5	0	0	0	1	1	10	.082	.097	.082	179	-41	-8	2	0	0	.820	-2	C-16/O-2(1-0-1),3-1	-0.8
1878	Ind-N	63	254	23	57	7	0	0	18	2	15	.224	.230	.252	482	67	-7				.908	-1	*C-59/O-9(5-0-4)	-0.7
1879	Chi-N	79	324	46	92	22	6	1	41	6	44	.284	.297	.398	695	120	6				.915	3	*C-78/O-1(0-0-1),M	1.0
1880	Chi-N	74	284	30	46	10	4	0	17	5	32	.162	.176	.225	402	33	-20				**.934**	8	*C-67,O-13(0-4-10)	-0.9
1881	Chi-N	80	306	46	95	18	0	1	34	6	39	.310	.324	.379	703	115	4				.938	-8	*C-80/O-8(0-0-8),1-1	-0.1
1882	Chi-N	81	331	48	83	18	8	4	44	2	50	.251	.255	.390	645	99	-1				.935	-3	*C-81,O-10(0-0-10)	0.3
1883	Chi-N	85	332	57	88	23	4	0	32	3	69	.265	.272	.358	630	83	-8				.877	-8	*C-83,O-23(0-0-23)	-0.9
1884	Chi-N	73	279	35	57	5	2	9	45	7	57	.204	.224	.333	557	67	-11				.884	-2	C-73	-0.6
1885	*Chi-N	68	249	27	52	8	2	1	17	2	52	.209	.215	.269	484	49	-15				**.927**	13	C-68/O-1(0-0-1)	0.4
1886	*Chi-N	54	173	30	35	6	2	1	13	12	36	.202	.254	.277	532	54	-10	1			.893	15	C-54/1-3	0.8
1887	Chi-N	49	191	22	54	8	6	3	21	4	28	.283	.283	.422	705	83	-6	7			.909	3	C-47/1-2	0.1
1888	Chi-N	22	77	6	14	3	0	0	3	1	21	.182	.203	.221	423	33	-6	1			.926	-2	C-22	-0.6
1889	Chi-N	15	56	6	13	1	0	1	9	3	18	.232	.271	.304	575	58	-3	1			.903	-1	C-15	-0.3
Total	12	743	2856	376	686	129	34	21	294	53	461	.240	.253	.330	584	78	-77	10	0		.913	19	C-727/O-65R,1-6	-1.5
■ **CURT FLOOD**	Flood, Curtis Charles b: 1/18/38, Houston, Tex. d: 1/20/97, Los Angeles, Cal. BR/TR, 5'9", 165 lbs. Deb: 9/9/56 Career OF: (3-LF 1693-CF 1-RF)																							
1956	Cin-N	5	1	0	0	0	0	0	0	0	1	.000	.000	.000	0	-94	-0	0	0	0	.000	0	H	0.0
1957	Cin-N	3	3	2	1	0	0	1	1	0	0	.333	.333	1.333	1667	299	1	0	0	0	.000	-1	/3-2,2-1	0.0
1958	StL-N	121	422	50	110	17	2	10	41	31	56	.261	.317	.382	699	81	-12	2	12	-4	.978	19	*O-120(0-120-0)/3-1	-0.1
1959	StL-N	121	208	24	53	7	3	7	26	16	35	.255	.308	.418	726	86	-4	2	1	0	.967	-19	*O-106(2-103-1)/2-1	-2.6
1960	StL-N	140	396	37	94	20	1	8	38	35	54	.237	.306	.354	659	73	-14	0	3	-1	**.993**	0	*O-134(1-133-0)/3-1	-2.1
1961	StL-N	132	335	53	108	15	5	2	21	35	33	.322	.391	.415	806	104	3	6	2	1	.984	2	*O-119(0-119-0)	0.3
1962	StL-N	151	635	99	188	30	5	12	70	42	57	.296	.349	.416	765	95	-4	8	6	-0	.990	16	*O-151(0-151-0)	0.7
1963	StL-N	158	662	112	200	34	9	5	63	42	57	.302	.346	.403	749	105	5	17	12	-0	.988	20	*O-158(0-158-0)	2.1
1964	*StL-N★	162	679	97	**211**	25	3	5	46	43	53	.311	.356	.378	735	98	0	8	11	-2	.988	13	*O-162(0-162-0)	0.7
1965	StL-N	156	617	90	191	30	3	11	83	51	50	.310	.368	.421	789	111	11	9	3	1	.986	11	*O-151(0-151-0)	1.9
1966	StL-N★	160	626	64	167	21	5	10	78	26	50	.267	.300	.364	665	83	-15	14	7	1	**1.000**	10	*O-159(0-159-0)	-0.9
1967	*StL-N	134	514	68	172	24	1	5	50	37	46	.335	.382	.414	796	129	20	2	2	-0	.988	11	*O-126(0-126-0)	2.8
1968	*StL-N★	150	618	71	186	17	4	5	60	33	58	.301	.341	.366	707	114	10	11	6	0	.983	18	*O-149(0-149-0)	2.6
1969	StL-N	153	606	80	173	31	3	4	57	48	57	.285	.345	.366	711	99	-0	9	7	-0	.989	17	*O-152(0-152-0)	1.3
1971	Was-A	13	35	4	7	0	0	0	2	5	2	.200	.300	.200	500	47	-2	0	1	-0	.941	-2	O-10(0-10-0)	-0.5
Total	15	1759	6357	851	1861	271	44	85	636	444	609	.293	.344	.389	733	99	-1	88	73	-6	.987	114	*O-1697C/3-4,2-2	6.2
■ **TIM FLOOD**	Flood, Timothy A. b: 3/13/1877, Montgomery City, Mo. d: 6/15/29, St.Louis, Mo. BR/TR, 5'9", 160 lbs. Deb: 9/24/1899																							
1899	StL-N	10	31	0	9	0	0	0	3	4		.290	.371	.290	662	81	-1	1			.878	-2	2-10	-0.2
1902	Bro-N	132	476	43	104	11	4	3	51	23		.218	.268	.277	545	68	-18	8			.942	-16	*2-132/O-1(1-0-0)	-3.5
1903	Bro-N	89	309	27	77	15	2	0	32	15		.249	.291	.311	601	73	-11	14			.924	-9	2-84/S-2,O-1(0-1-0)	-1.9
Total	3	231	816	70	190	26	6	3	86	42		.233	.280	.290	571	70	-30	23			.933	-26	2-226/S-2,O-2(1-1-0)	-5.6
■ **KEVIN FLORA**	Flora, Kevin Scot b: 6/10/69, Fontana, Cal. BR/TR, 6', 180 lbs. Deb: 9/27/91																							
1991	Cal-A	3	8	1	1	0	0	0	0	1	5	.125	.222	.125	347	-1	-1	1	0	0	.846	-2	/2-3	-0.3
1995	Cal-A	2	1	1	0	0	0	0	0	0	1	.000	.000	.000	0	-99	-0	0	0	0	.000	0	/D-1	0.0
	Phi-N	24	75	12	16	3	0	2	7	4	22	.213	.253	.333	586	53	-5	1	0	0	1.000	-1	O-20(5-15-0)	-0.6
Total	2	29	84	14	17	3	0	2	7	5	28	.202	.247	.310	557	46	-7	2	0	0	1.000	-2	/O-20(5-15-0),2-3,D-1	-0.9
■ **PAUL FLORENCE**	Florence, Paul Robert "Pep" b: 4/22/1900, Chicago, Ill. d: 5/28/86, Gainesville, Fla. BB/TR, 6'1", 185 lbs. Deb: 5/22/26																							
1926	NY-N	76	188	19	43	4	3	2	14	23	12	.229	.322	.314	636	73	-7	2			.937	-9	C-76	-1.1
■ **GIL FLORES**	Flores, Gilberto (Garcia) b: 10/27/52, Ponce, P.R. BR/TR, 6', 185 lbs. Deb: 5/8/77																							
1977	Cal-A	104	342	41	95	19	4	1	26	23	39	.278	.325	.365	691	92	-4	12	10	-1	.978	-2	O-85(41-45-9)/D-8	-0.9
1978	NY-N	11	29	8	8	0	1	0	1	3	5	.276	.344	.345	689	96	0	1	0	0	.944	-1	/O-8(1-6-2)	-0.1
1979	NY-N	70	93	9	18	1	1	1	10	8	17	.194	.265	.258	523	45	-7	2	0	0	.976	-7	O-32(0-6-28)	-1.5
Total	3	185	464	58	121	20	6	2	37	34	61	.261	.314	.343	657	82	-11	15	10	-0	.976	-10	O-125(42-57-39)/D-8	-2.5
■ **DICKIE FLOWERS**	Flowers, Charles Richard b: 1850, Philadelphia, Pa. d: 10/5/1892, Philadelphia, Pa. Deb: 6/3/1871																							
1871	Tro-n	21	105	39	33	5	4	0	18	4	0	.314	.339	.438	778	120	2	8	2	1	.769	-3	*S-20/P-1,2-1	0.0
1872	Ath-n	3	15	1	4	0	0	0	4	2	2	.267	.353	.267	620	93	0	0	0	0	.643	-2	/S-3	-0.1
Total	2 n	24	120	40	37	5	4	0	22	6	2	.308	.341	.417	758	117	2	8	2	1	.757	-5	/S-23,2-1,P-1	-0.1
■ **JAKE FLOWERS**	Flowers, D'Arcy Raymond b: 3/16/02, Cambridge, Md. d: 12/27/62, Clearwater, Fla. BR/TR, 5'11.5", 170 lbs. Deb: 9/7/23 C Career OF: (0-LF 0-CF 2-RF)																							
1923	StL-N	13	32	0	3	1	0	0	2	2	7	.094	.147	.125	272	-28	-6	1	2	-0	.971	-1	/S-7,2-2,3-2	-0.6
1926	*StL-N	40	74	13	20	1	0	3	9	5	9	.270	.325	.405	730	92	-1	1			.984	1	2-11/1-3,S-1	0.0
1927	Bro-N	67	231	26	54	5	5	2	20	21	25	.234	.300	.325	625	67	-11	3			.944	-8	S-65/2-1	-1.2
1928	Bro-N	103	339	51	93	11	6	2	44	47	30	.274	.366	.360	726	92	-3	10			.971	-6	2-94/S-6	-0.6
1929	Bro-N	46	130	16	26	6	0	1	16	22	6	.200	.316	.269	585	47	-10	9			.962	-5	2-39	-1.4
1930	Bro-N	89	253	37	81	18	3	2	50	21	18	.320	.372	.439	811	96	-1	5			.949	-8	2-65/O-1(0-0-1)	-0.6
1931	Bro-N	22	31	3	7	0	0	0	1	7	4	.226	.368	.226	594	64	-1	1			1.000	1	/2-6,S-1	0.1
	*StL-N	45	137	19	34	11	1	2	19	9	6	.248	.295	.387	681	79	-4	7			.971	3	S-24,2-21/3-1	0.1
	Yr	67	168	22	41	11	1	2	20	16	10	.244	.310	.357	667	77	-5	8			.991	4	2-27,S-25/3-1	0.2
1932	StL-N	67	247	35	63	11	1	2	18	31	18	.255	.341	.332	672	79	-6	7			.980	-0	3-54/S-7,2-2	-0.4
1933	Bro-N	78	210	28	49	11	2	2	22	24	15	.233	.312	.333	645	88	-3	13			.955	-11	S-36,2-19/3-8,O-1R	-1.1
1934	Cin-N	13	9	1	3	0	0	0	0	1	1	.333	.455	.333	788	117	0	1			.000	0	H	0.0
Total	10	583	1693	229	433	75	18	16	201	190	139	.256	.333	.350	683	80	-46	58	2		.967	-34	2-260,S-147/3-65,1O	-5.7

YEAR	TM/L	G	AB	R	H	2B	3B	HR	RBI	BB	SO	AVG	OBP	SLG	OPS	OPS+	BR+	SB	CS	SBR	FA	FR	G/POS	TPR
■ CLIFF FLOYD	Floyd, Cornelius Clifford b: 12/5/72, Chicago, Ill. BL/TL, 6'4", 230 lbs. Deb: 9/18/93 Career OF: (428-LF 28-CF 25-RF)																							
1993	Mon-N	10	31	3	7	0	0	1	2	0	9	.226	.226	.323	548	43	-3	0	0	0	1.000	-0	1-10	-0.4
1994	Mon-N	100	334	43	94	19	4	4	41	24	63	.281	.335	.398	733	89	-5	10	3	1	.991	-3	1-77,O-26(17-0-9)	-1.3
1995	Mon-N	29	69	6	9	1	0	1	8	7	22	.130	.221	.188	409	9	-9	3	0	1	.987	-1	1-18/O-4(2-1-1)	-1.1
1996	Mon-N	117	227	29	55	15	4	6	26	30	52	.242	.344	.423	766	98	-0	7	1	1	.960	-13	O-85(69-16-7)/1-2	-1.4
1997	*Fla-N	61	137	23	32	9	1	6	19	24	33	.234	.356	.445	801	113	3	6	2	1	.970	0	O-38(24-9-6)/1-9	0.3
1998	Fla-N	153	588	85	166	45	3	22	90	47	112	.282	.339	.481	820	118	14	27	14	1	.974	6	*O-146(146-2-2)/D-3	1.6
1999	Fla-N	69	251	37	76	19	1	11	49	30	47	.303	.382	.518	900	132	12	5	6	-1	.952	2	O-62(62-0-0)/D-3	1.1
2000	Fla-N	121	420	75	126	30	0	22	91	50	82	.300	.385	.529	914	135	22	24	3	4	.951	1	*O-108(108-0-0)/D-1	2.3
Total	8	660	2057	301	565	138	13	73	326	212	420	.275	.349	.461	810	111	34	82	29	8	.962	-7	O-469L,1-116/D-7	1.1
■ BUBBA FLOYD	Floyd, Leslie Roe b: 6/23/17, Dallas, Tex. BR/TR, 5'11", 160 lbs. Deb: 6/16/44																							
1944	Det-A	3	9	1	4	1	0	0	0	1	0	.444	.500	.556	1056	191	1	0	0	0	1.000	-1	/S-3	0.0
■ BOBBY FLOYD	Floyd, Robert Nathan b: 10/20/43, Hawthorne, Cal. BR/TR, 6', 181 lbs. Deb: 9/18/68																							
1968	Bal-A	5	9	0	1	1	0	0	1	0	3	.111	.111	.222	333	-1	-1	0	0	0	1.000	2	/S-4	0.1
1969	Bal-A	39	84	7	17	4	0	0	1	6	17	.202	.256	.250	506	41	-7	0	0	0	.984	11	2-15,S-15/3-9	0.7
1970	Bal-A	3	2	0	0	0	0	0	0	0	2	.000	.000	.000	0	-99	-1	0	0	0	1.000	-1	/S-2,2-1	-0.1
	KC-A	14	43	5	14	4	0	0	9	4	9	.326	.383	.419	802	121	1	0	1	-0	.880	1	/S-8,3-6	0.3
	Yr	17	45	5	14	4	0	0	9	4	11	.311	.367	.400	767	111	1	0	1	-0	.882	1	S-10/3-6,2-1	0.2
1971	KC-A	31	66	8	10	3	0	0	2	7	21	.152	.233	.197	430	23	-7	0	0	0	.970	5	S-15/2-8,3-1	0.0
1972	KC-A	61	134	9	24	3	0	0	5	5	29	.179	.209	.201	410	23	-13	1	0	0	.967	-2	3-30,S-29/2-2	-1.5
1973	KC-A	51	78	10	26	3	1	0	8	4	14	.333	.366	.397	763	107	1	1	1	-0	1.000	9	2-25,S-24	1.1
1974	KC-A	10	9	1	1	0	0	0	0	2	4	.111	.273	.111	384	13	-1	0	0	0	1.000	2	/2-5,3-2,S-1	0.2
Total	7	214	425	40	93	18	1	0	26	28	99	.219	.267	.266	533	52	-27	2	2	-0	.940	27	/S-98,2-56,3-48	0.8
■ JOHN FLUHRER	Fluhrer, John Lister (a.k.a. Wm. G. Morris 1 Game In 1915) b: 1/3/1894, Adrian, Mich. d: 7/17/46, Columbus, Ohio BR/TR, 5'9", 165 lbs. Deb: 9/5/15																							
1915	Chi-N	6	6	0	2	0	0	0	0	1	0	.333	.429	.333	762	132	0	1			.500	-1	/O-2(2-0-0)	0.0
■ ED FLYNN	Flynn, Edward J. b: 1/25/1864, Chicago, Ill. BL, 5'9", 165 lbs. Deb: 5/5/1887																							
1887	Cle-a	7	28	0	6	1	0	0	4	1		.214	.214	.222	437	22	-3	3			.786	-0	/3-6,O-1(0-0-1)	-0.2
■ GEORGE FLYNN	Flynn, George A. "Dibby" b: 5/24/1871, Chicago, Ill. d: 12/28/01, Chicago, Ill. Deb: 4/17/1896																							
1896	Chi-N	29	106	15	27	1	2	0	4	11	9	.255	.336	.302	638	66	-5	12			.878	2	O-29(29-0-0)	-0.5
■ JOCKO FLYNN	Flynn, John A. b: 6/30/1864, Lawrence, Mass. d: 12/30/07, Lawrence, Mass. TR, 5'6.5", 143 lbs. Deb: 5/1/1886																							
1886	Chi-N	57	205	40	41	6	2	4	19	18	45	.200	.265	.307	572	64	-10	9			.916	-5	P-32,O-28(5-3-20)	-1.0
1887	Chi-N	1	0	0	0	0	0	0	0	0	0	—	—	—	—	—	0	0			.000	-1	/O-1(0-0-1)	-0.1
Total	2	58	205	40	41	6	2	4	19	18	45	.200	.265	.307	572	64	-10	9			.850	-6	/P-32,O-29(5-3-21)	-1.1
■ JOHN FLYNN	Flynn, John Anthony b: 9/7/1883, Providence, R.I. d: 3/23/35, Providence, R.I. BR/TR, 6'0.5", 175 lbs. Deb: 4/22/10																							
1910	Pit-N	96	332	32	91	10	2	6	52	30	47	.274	.336	.370	707	100	-1	6			.977	-3	1-93	-0.6
1911	Pit-N	33	59	5	12	0	1	0	3	9	8	.203	.309	.237	546	52	-4	0			1.000	0	1-13/O-1(0-0-1)	-0.4
1912	Was-A	20	71	9	12	4	1	0	5	7		.169	.253	.254	507	45	-5	2			.974	1	1-20	-0.4
Total	3	149	462	46	115	14	4	6	60	46	55	.249	.320	.335	655	85	-9	8			.978	-1	1-126/O-1(0-0-1)	-1.4
■ JOE FLYNN	Flynn, Joseph Nicholas b: 1/1862, Providence, R.I. d: 12/22/33, Providence, R.I. Deb: 4/18/1884																							
1884	Phi-U	52	209	38	52	9	4	4		11		.249	.286	.388	674	111	-4				.778	-15	O-43R,C-10/1-1,S-1	-1.7
	Bos-U	9	31	4	7	2	0	0		2		.226	.273	.290	563	72	-2				.864	4	/C-7,O-4(1-2-2),1-1	0.2
	Yr	61	240	42	59	11	4	4		13		.246	.285	.375	660	105	-6				.764	-11	O-47R,C-17/1-2,S-1	-1.5
■ MIKE FLYNN	Flynn, Michael J. b: 3/15/1872, County Kildare, Ireland d: 6/16/41, Los Angeles, Cal. Deb: 8/31/1891																							
1891	Bos-a	1	2	0	0	0	0	0	0	0	1	.000	.000	.000	0	-99	-1	0			1.000	1	/C-1	0.0
■ DOUG FLYNN	Flynn, Robert Douglas b: 4/18/51, Lexington, Ky. BR/TR, 5'11", 165 lbs. Deb: 4/9/75																							
1975	Cin-N	89	127	17	34	7	0	1	20	11	13	.268	.326	.346	673	85	-3	3	0	1	.962	10	3-40,2-30,S-17	1.1
1976	*Cin-N	93	219	20	62	5	2	1	20	10	24	.283	.314	.338	652	83	-5	2	0	0	.988	-4	2-55,3-23,S-20	-0.4
1977	Cin-N	36	32	0	8	1	1	0	5	0	6	.250	.250	.344	594	56	-2	0	0	0	1.000	7	3-25/2-9,S-4	0.5
	NY-N	90	282	14	54	6	1	0	14	11	23	.191	.222	.220	442	20	-32	1	3	-1	.954	-13	S-65,2-29/3-2	-4.0
	Yr	126	314	14	62	7	2	0	19	11	29	.197	.225	.232	457	24	-34	1	3	-1	.956	-6	S-69,2-38,3-27	-3.5
1978	NY-N	156	532	37	126	12	8	0	36	30	50	.237	.279	.289	568	61	-28	3	5	-1	.986	2	*2-128,S-60	-1.8
1979	NY-N	157	555	35	135	19	5	4	61	17	46	.243	.266	.317	583	61	-31	0	3	-1	.983	1	*2-148,S-20	-2.4
1980	NY-N	128	443	46	113	9	8	0	24	22	20	.255	.290	.312	602	70	-18	2	2	-0	**.991**	3	*2-128/S-3	-1.0
1981	NY-N	105	325	24	72	12	4	1	20	11	19	.222	.247	.292	539	53	-21	1	2	-0	.987	12	*2-100/S-5	-0.4
1982	Tex-A	88	270	13	57	6	2	0	19	4	14	.211	.223	.248	471	31	-26	6	2	1	.989	4	2-55,S-35	-1.6
	Mon-N	58	193	13	47	6	2	0	20	4	23	.244	.259	.295	554	54	-12	0	2	-1	.983	5	2-58	-0.5
1983	Mon-N	143	452	44	107	18	4	0	26	19	38	.237	.268	.294	562	56	-27	2	1	0	.986	7	*2-107,S-37	-1.3
1984	Mon-N	124	366	23	89	12	1	0	17	12	41	.243	.267	.281	549	57	-21	0	0	0	.979	-8	2-88,S-34	-2.4
1985	Mon-N	9	6	0	1	0	0	0	0	0	0	.167	.167	.167	333	-7	-1	0	0	0	1.000	-1	/2-6,S-1	-0.1
	Det-A	32	51	2	13	2	1	0	2	0	3	.255	.255	.333	588	60	-3	0	0	0	.984	8	2-20/S-8,3-4	0.6
Total	11	1308	3853	288	918	115	39	7	284	151	320	.238	.267	.294	561	57	-230	20	20	-3	.986	33	2-961,S-309/3-94	-13.7
■ CLIPPER FLYNN	Flynn, William b: 4/29/1849, Lansingburg, N.Y. d: 11/11/1881, Lansingburg, N.Y. TR, 5'7", 140 lbs. Deb: 5/9/1871 Career OF: (0-LF 0-CF 8-RF)																							
1871	Tro-n	29	142	43	48	6	1	0	27	4	2	.338	.356	.394	751	114	2	3	3	-0	.955	5	1-19/O-8R,2-1,3-1	0.5
1872	Oly-n	9	40	4	9	1	0	0	2	0	0	.225	.225	.250	475	48	-2	0	0	0	.900	-1	/1-9	-0.2
Total	2 n	38	182	47	57	7	1	0	29	4	2	.313	.328	.363	691	101	0	3	3	-0	.934	4	/1-28,O-8R,3-1,2-1	0.3
■ JIM FOGARTY	Fogarty, James G. b: 2/12/1864, San Francisco, Cal d: 5/20/1891, Philadelphia, Pa. BR/TR, 5'10.5", 180 lbs. Deb: 5/1/1884 FM Career OF: (0-LF 312-CF 373-RF)																							
1884	Phi-N	97	378	42	80	12	6	1	37	20	54	.212	.251	.283	534	71	-11				.915	3	*O-78C,3-14/2-4,SP	-0.9
1885	Phi-N	111	427	49	99	13	3	0	39	30	37	.232	.282	.276	559	83	-7				.941	25	*O-88C,2-10/S-8,3-5	1.4
1886	Phi-N	77	280	54	82	13	5	3	47	42	16	.293	.385	.407	792	140	15	30			.953	-3	O-60R,2-13/S-3,3P	1.0
1887	Phi-N	126	577	113	211	26	12	8	50	**82**	44	.366	.376	.410	787	112	9	102			.920	32	*O-123R/S-2,3-2,2P	3.4
1888	Phi-N	121	454	72	107	14	6	1	35	53	66	.236	.325	.300	624	95	-1	58			.930	14	*O-117R/3-5,S-1	1.2
1889	Phi-N	128	499	107	129	15	17	3	54	65	60	.259	.352	.375	727	95	-4	**99**			**.961**	19	*O-128(0-128-0)/P-4	1.0
1890	Phi-P	91	347	71	83	17	6	4	58	59	50	.239	.364	.357	721	91	-3	36			.963	8	O-91(0-23-68)/3-1,M	0.3
Total	7	751	2962	508	791	110	55	20	320	351	327	.267	.335	.343	678	97	-3	325			.940	98	O-685R/3-30,2-28,SP	7.4
■ JOE FOGARTY	Fogarty, Joseph J. b: San Francisco, Cal. Deb: 9/18/1885 F																							
1885	StL-N	2	8	1	1	0	0	0	0	0	1	.125	.125	.125	250	-20	-1				1.000	-0	/O-2(2-0-0)	-0.1
■ LEE FOHL	Fohl, Leo Alexander b: 11/28/1876, Lowell, Ohio d: 10/30/65, Cleveland, Ohio BL/TR, 5'10", 175 lbs. Deb: 8/29/02 MC																							
1902	Pit-N	1	3	0	0	0	0	0	1	0		.000	.000	.000	0	-97	-1	0			.875	0	/C-1	0.0
1903	Cin-N	4	14	3	5	1	1	0	2	0		.357	.400	.571	971	158	1	0			.955	-0	/C-4	0.1
Total	2	5	17	3	5	1	1	0	3	0		.294	.333	.471	804	120	0	0			.933	0	/C-5	0.1
■ HANK FOILES	Foiles, Henry Lee b: 6/10/29, Richmond, Va. BR/TR, 6', 195 lbs. Deb: 4/21/53																							
1953	Cin-N	5	13	1	2	0	0	0	0	1	2	.154	.214	.154	368	-2	-2	0	0	0	.909	-1	/C-3	-0.2
	Cle-A	7	7	2	1	0	0	0	0	1	1	.143	.250	.143	393	9	-1	0	0	0	.933	1	/C-7	0.0
1955	Cle-A	62	111	13	29	9	0	1	7	17	18	.261	.359	.369	729	93	-1	0	0	0	.988	14	C-41	1.5
1956	Cle-A	1	0	0	0	0	0	0	0	0	0	—	—	—	—	—	0	0	0	0	.000	0	/C-1	0.0
	Pit-N	79	222	24	47	10	2	7	25	17	56	.212	.268	.369	637	71	-10	0	1	-0	.988	-2	C-73	-0.9

YEAR	TM/L	G	AB	R	H	2B	3B	HR	RBI	BB	SO	AVG	OBP	SLG	OPS	OPS+	BR+	SB	CS	SBR	FA	FR	G/POS	TPR
1957	Pit-N★	109	281	32	76	10	4	9	36	37	53	.270	.355	.431	786	113	6	1	3	-1	.981	-6	*C-109	0.4
1958	Pit-N	104	264	31	54	10	2	8	30	45	53	.205	.323	.348	671	80	-7	0	1	-0	.990	8	*C-103	0.5
1959	Pit-N	53	80	10	18	3	0	3	4	7	16	.225	.287	.375	662	75	-3	0	0	0	1.000	9	C-51	0.7
1960	KC-A	6	7	1	4	0	0	0	1	3	2	.571	.700	.571	1271	246	2	0	0	0	.900	-0	/C-2	0.2
	Cle-A	24	68	9	19	1	0	1	6	7	5	.279	.347	.338	685	89	-1	0	0	0	.982	0	C-22	0.0
	Det-A	26	56	5	14	3	0	0	3	1	8	.250	.263	.304	567	51	-4	1	0	0	1.000	4	C-22	0.1
	Yr	56	131	15	37	4	0	1	10	11	15	.282	.338	.336	674	83	-3	1	0	0	.987	5	C-46	0.3
1961	Bal-A	43	124	18	34	6	0	6	19	12	27	.274	.338	.468	806	117	3	0	2	-1	.995	3	C-38	0.6
1962	Cin-N	43	131	17	36	6	1	7	25	13	39	.275	.340	.496	836	118	3	0	0	0	.981	1	C-41	0.6
1963	Cin-N	1	3	0	0	0	0	0	0	1	0	.000	.250	.000	250	-21	-0	1	0	0	1.000	-0	/C-1	0.0
	LA-A	41	84	8	18	1	1	4	10	8	13	.214	.290	.393	683	95	-1	0	0	0	.974	3	C-30	0.3
1964	LA-A	4	4	0	1	0	0	0	0	0	2	.250	.250	.250	500	44	-0	0	0	0	.000	0	H	0.0
Total	11	608	1455	171	353	59	10	46	166	170	295	.243	.323	.392	714	92	-17	3	7	-2	.986	35	C-544	3.8

■ CURRY FOLEY

Foley, Charles Joseph b: 1/14/1856, Milltown, Ireland d: 10/20/1898, Boston, Mass. TL, 5'10", 160 lbs. Deb: 5/13/1879 Career OF: (4-LF 28-CF 185-RF)

YEAR	TM/L	G	AB	R	H	2B	3B	HR	RBI	BB	SO	AVG	OBP	SLG	OPS	OPS+	BR+	SB	CS	SBR	FA	FR	G/POS	TPR
1879	Bos-N	35	146	16	46	3	1	0	17	3	4	.315	.329	.349	678	121	3				.857	-7	P-21,O-17(0-2-15)/1-2	-0.4
1880	Bos-N	80	332	44	97	13	2	2	31	8	14	.292	.309	.361	670	130	10				.953	-3	P-36,O-35R,1-25	0.2
1881	Buf-N	83	375	58	96	20	2	1	25	7	27	.256	.270	.328	598	88	-5				.795	-4	O-55R,1-27,P-10	-0.9
1882	Buf-N	84	341	51	104	16	4	3	49	12	26	.305	.329	.402	730	131	11				.833	0	*O-84(0-1-84)/P-1	1.0
1883	Buf-N	23	111	23	30	5	3	0	6	4	12	.270	.296	.369	665	98	-0				.885	-2	O-23(1-21-1)/P-1	-0.2
Total	5	305	1305	192	373	57	12	6	128	34	83	.286	.304	.362	666	114	19				.819	-16	O-214R/P-69,1-54	-0.3

■ MARV FOLEY

Foley, Marvis Edwin b: 8/29/53, Stanford, Ky. BL/TR, 6', 195 lbs. Deb: 9/11/78 C

YEAR	TM/L	G	AB	R	H	2B	3B	HR	RBI	BB	SO	AVG	OBP	SLG	OPS	OPS+	BR+	SB	CS	SBR	FA	FR	G/POS	TPR
1978	Chi-A	11	34	3	12	0	0	0	6	4	6	.353	.421	.353	774	119	1	0	1	-0	.938	-3	C-10	-0.2
1979	Chi-A	34	97	6	24	3	0	2	10	7	5	.247	.298	.340	638	72	-4	0	0	0	.993	-1	C-33	-0.4
1980	Chi-A	68	137	14	29	5	0	4	15	9	22	.212	.270	.336	606	65	-7	0	0	0	.991	2	C-64/1-3	-0.3
1982	Chi-A	27	36	1	4	0	0	0	1	6	4	.111	.238	.111	349	-0	-5	0	0	0	.980	1	C-15/3-2,1-1,D-1	-0.3
1984	Tex-A	63	115	13	25	2	0	6	19	15	24	.217	.313	.391	704	91	-1	0	0	0	.988	1	C-36/1-1,3-1,D-4	0.1
Total	5	203	419	37	94	10	0	12	51	41	61	.224	.298	.334	632	73	-16	0	1	-0	.986	0	C-158/D-5,1-5,3-3	-1.1

■ RAY FOLEY

Foley, Raymond Kirwin b: 6/23/06, Naugatuck, Conn. d: 3/22/80, Vero Beach, Fla. BL/TR, 5'11", 173 lbs. Deb: 7/4/28

YEAR	TM/L	G	AB	R	H	2B	3B	HR	RBI	BB	SO	AVG	OBP	SLG	OPS	OPS+	BR+	SB	CS	SBR	FA	FR	G/POS	TPR
1928	NY-N	2	1	1	0	0	0	0	0	1	1	.000	.500	.000	500	41	0	0			.000	0	H	0.0

■ TOM FOLEY

Foley, Thomas J. b: 1847, Chicago, Ill. d: 1/4/1896, LaGrange, Ill. 5'9.5", 157 lbs. Deb: 5/8/1871

YEAR	TM/L	G	AB	R	H	2B	3B	HR	RBI	BB	SO	AVG	OBP	SLG	OPS	OPS+	BR+	SB	CS	SBR	FA	FR	G/POS	TPR
1871	Chi-n	18	84	18	22	3	1	0	13	3	2	.262	.287	.321	609	67	-4	1	4	-1	.633	-5	O-16(2-9-5)/C-4,3-1	-0.7

■ TOM FOLEY

Foley, Thomas Michael b: 9/9/59, Columbus, Ga. BL/TR, 6'1", 180 lbs. Deb: 4/9/83 Career OF: (1-LF 0-CF 0-RF)

YEAR	TM/L	G	AB	R	H	2B	3B	HR	RBI	BB	SO	AVG	OBP	SLG	OPS	OPS+	BR+	SB	CS	SBR	FA	FR	G/POS	TPR
1983	Cin-N	68	98	7	20	4	1	0	9	13	17	.204	.297	.265	563	55	-6	1	0	0	.983	9	S-37/2-5	0.6
1984	Cin-N	106	277	26	70	8	3	5	27	24	36	.253	.312	.357	670	84	-6	3	2	-0	.965	1	S-83,2-10/3-1	0.2
1985	Cin-N	43	92	7	18	5	1	0	6	6	16	.196	.245	.272	517	42	-7	1	0	0	.983	3	2-18,S-15/3-1	-0.3
	Phi-N	46	158	17	42	8	0	3	17	13	18	.266	.322	.373	695	91	-2	1	3	-1	.981	-5	S-45	-0.3
	Yr	89	250	24	60	13	1	3	23	19	34	.240	.294	.336	630	73	-9	2	3	-1	.978	-3	S-60,2-18/3-1	-0.6
1986	Phi-N	39	61	8	18	2	1	0	5	10	11	.295	.394	.361	755	106	1	2	0	0	.975	0	S-24/2-1,3-1	0.3
	Mon-N	64	202	18	52	13	2	1	18	20	26	.257	.324	.356	681	88	-3	8	3	1	.965	-5	S-29,2-25,3-15	-0.4
	Yr	103	263	26	70	15	3	1	23	30	37	.266	.341	.357	699	92	-2	10	3	1	.970	-5	S-53,2-26,3-16	-0.1
1987	Mon-N	106	280	35	82	18	3	5	28	11	40	.293	.322	.432	754	95	-3	6	10	-2	.963	1	S-49,2-39/3-9	0.2
1988	Mon-N	127	377	33	100	21	3	5	43	30	49	.265	.321	.377	698	95	-2	2	7	-2	.972	3	2-89,S-32/3-9	0.3
1989	Mon-N	122	375	34	86	19	2	7	39	45	53	.229	.317	.347	663	88	-5	2	3	-1	.988	20	*2-108,3-16,S-14,/P	1.8
1990	Mon-N	73	164	11	35	2	1	0	12	12	22	.213	.267	.238	505	42	-13	0	1	-0	.987	3	S-45,2-20/3-7,1-1	-0.8
1991	Mon-N	86	168	12	35	11	1	0	15	14	30	.208	.273	.286	559	58	-9	2	0	0	.967	-2	S-43,1-31/3-6,2-2	-1.0
1992	Mon-N	72	115	7	20	3	1	0	5	8	21	.174	.234	.217	451	29	-11	3	0	1	.967	6	S-33,2-13,1-12,/3O	-0.2
1993	Pit-N	86	194	18	49	11	1	3	22	11	26	.253	.293	.366	659	75	-7	0	0	0	.993	1	2-35,1-12/3-7,S-6	-0.5
1994	Pit-N	59	123	13	29	7	0	3	15	13	18	.236	.309	.366	675	74	-5	0	0	0	.986	11	2-17,3-14/S-8,1-3	0.7
1995	Mon-N	11	24	2	5	2	0	0	2	2	4	.208	.269	.292	561	46	-2	1	0	0	1.000	-1	/1-4,2-3	-0.3
Total	13	1108	2708	248	661	134	20	32	263	232	387	.244	.305	.344	649	78	-79	32	29	-3	.972	45	S-463,2-385/3-90,1OP	0.3

■ WILL FOLEY

Foley, William Brown b: 11/15/1855, Chicago, Ill. d: 11/12/16, Chicago, Ill. BR/TR, 5'9.5", 150 lbs. Deb: 8/23/1875 Career OF: (0-LF 0-CF 25-RF)

YEAR	TM/L	G	AB	R	H	2B	3B	HR	RBI	BB	SO	AVG	OBP	SLG	OPS	OPS+	BR+	SB	CS	SBR	FA	FR	G/POS	TPR
1875	Chi-n	3	12	0	3	1	0	0	1	0	2	.250	.250	.333	583	100	-0	0	0	0	.813	1	/3-3	0.1
1876	Cin-N	58	221	19	50	3	2	0	9	0	14	.226	.226	.258	484	71	-5				.804	2	3-46,C-20	-0.1
1877	Cin-N	56	216	23	41	5	1	0	18	4	13	.190	.205	.222	427	39	-14				.836	6	*3-56	-0.5
1878	Mil-N	56	229	33	62	8	5	0	22	7	14	.271	.292	.349	642	103	0				.812	-9	*3-53/C-7	-0.6
1879	Cin-N	56	218	22	46	5	1	0	25	2	16	.211	.218	.243	461	55	-10				.820	3	3-29,O-25(0-0-25)/2-3	-0.6
1881	Det-N	5	15	0	2	0	0	0	1	2	3	.133	.235	.133	369	18	-1				.769	-1	/3-5	-0.3
1884	CP-U	19	71	15	20	1	1	0		5		.282	.329	.324	653	99	-2				.804	-3	3-19	-0.4
Total	6	250	970	112	221	22	10	0	75	20	60	.228	.243	.271	515	70	-31				.817	-2	3-208/C-27,O-25R,2	-2.5

■ TIM FOLI

Foli, Timothy John b: 12/8/50, Culver City, Cal. BR/TR, 6', 179 lbs. Deb: 9/11/70 C

YEAR	TM/L	G	AB	R	H	2B	3B	HR	RBI	BB	SO	AVG	OBP	SLG	OPS	OPS+	BR+	SB	CS	SBR	FA	FR	G/POS	TPR
1970	NY-N	5	11	0	4	0	0	0	1	0	2	.364	.364	.364	727	95	-0	0	0	0	1.000	2	/S-2,3-2	0.2
1971	NY-N	97	288	32	65	12	2	0	24	18	50	.226	.274	.281	555	58	-16	5	0	1	.964	14	2-58,3-36,S-12,/O-1C	0.3
1972	Mon-N	149	540	45	130	12	2	2	35	25	43	.241	.282	.281	563	59	-28	11	7	-0	.966	9	*S-148/2-1	-0.1
1973	Mon-N	126	458	37	110	11	0	2	36	28	40	.240	.285	.277	563	55	-28	6	3	0	.960	8	*S-123/2-2,O-1(0-1-0)	-0.4
1974	Mon-N	121	441	41	112	10	3	0	39	28	27	.254	.303	.290	593	63	-21	8	2	1	.971	19	*S-120/3-1	1.4
1975	Mon-N	152	572	64	136	25	2	1	29	36	49	.238	.285	.294	579	58	-32	13	3	2	.973	6	*S-151/2-1	-0.7
1976	Mon-N	149	546	41	144	36	1	6	54	16	33	.264	.285	.366	651	80	-15	6	5	-0	.975	7	*S-146/3-1	0.9
1977	Mon-N	13	57	2	10	5	1	0	3	0	4	.175	.175	.298	474	25	-6	0	0	0	1.000	1	S-13	-0.4
	SF-N	104	368	30	84	17	3	4	27	11	16	.228	.251	.323	574	53	-25	2	4	-1	.974	2	*S-102/2-1,3-1,O-1L	-1.4
	Yr	117	425	32	94	22	4	4	30	11	20	.221	.241	.320	561	49	-31	2	4	-1	.977	3	*S-115/2-1,3-1,O-1L	-1.8
1978	NY-N	113	413	37	106	21	1	1	27	14	30	.257	.284	.320	604	71	-17	2	5	-1	.966	-15	*S-112	-2.3
1979	NY-N	3	7	0	0	0	0	0	0	0	0	.000	.000	.000	0	-99	-2	0	0	0	1.000	1	/S-3	-0.1
	*Pit-N	133	525	70	153	23	1	1	65	28	14	.291	.338	.345	683	83	-11	6	5	-0	.978	-1	*S-132	0.2
	Yr	136	532	70	153	23	1	1	65	28	14	.288	.334	.340	674	81	-13	6	5	-0	.978	0	*S-135	0.1
1980	Pit-N	127	495	61	131	22	0	3	38	19	23	.265	.300	.327	627	74	-17	11	7	-0	**.981**	-0	*S-125	-0.5
1981	Pit-N	86	316	32	78	12	2	0	20	17	10	.247	.287	.297	585	64	-15	7	7	-1	.965	-9	S-81	-1.8
1982	*Cal-A	150	480	46	121	14	2	3	56	14	22	.252	.276	.308	585	60	-26	2	4	-1	**.985**	8	*S-139/2-8,3-2	-0.5
1983	Cal-A	88	330	29	83	10	0	2	29	5	18	.252	.265	.300	565	56	-20	2	3	-1	.975	10	S-74,3-13	-0.2
1984	NY-A	61	163	8	41	11	0	0	16	2	16	.252	.265	.319	584	63	-8	0	0	0	.950	7	S-28,2-21,3-10,/1-2	0.2
1985	Pit-N	19	37	1	7	0	0	0	2	4	2	.189	.268	.189	457	30	-3	0	0	0	.980	3	S-13	0.1
Total	16	1696	6047	576	1515	241	20	25	501	265	399	.251	.286	.309	595	64	-293	81	55	-1	.973	73	*S-1524/2-92,3-66,O1	-5.1

■ DEE FONDY

Fondy, Dee Virgil b: 10/31/24, Slaton, Tex. d: 8/19/99, Redlands, Cal. BL/TL, 6'3", 196 lbs. Deb: 4/17/51

YEAR	TM/L	G	AB	R	H	2B	3B	HR	RBI	BB	SO	AVG	OBP	SLG	OPS	OPS+	BR+	SB	CS	SBR	FA	FR	G/POS	TPR
1951	Chi-N	49	170	23	46	7	2	3	20	11	20	.271	.319	.388	707	88	-3	5	6	-1	.976	-3	1-44	-0.8
1952	Chi-N	145	554	69	166	21	9	10	67	28	60	.300	.334	.424	759	108	4	13	11	-1	.990	2	*1-143	0.0
1953	Chi-N	150	595	79	184	24	11	18	78	44	106	.309	.358	.477	835	113	11	10	7	-0	.987	4	*1-149	0.5
1954	Chi-N	141	568	77	162	30	4	9	49	35	84	.285	.328	.400	727	87	-11	20	5	3	.993	7	*1-138	-0.9
1955	Chi-N	150	574	69	152	23	8	17	65	35	87	.265	.309	.422	731	92	-8	8	9	-1	.991	1	*1-147	-1.7
1956	Chi-N	137	543	52	146	22	9	9	46	20	74	.269	.295	.392	687	84	-13	9	7	-0	.985	-3	*1-133	-2.6
1957	Chi-N	11	51	3	16	3	1	0	2	0	9	.314	.314	.412	725	94	-1	1	2	-0	.991	-1	1-11	-0.3
	Pit-N	95	323	42	101	13	2	2	35	25	59	.313	.364	.384	748	104	2	11	5	1	.982	-3	1-73	-0.4
	Yr	106	374	45	117	16	3	2	37	25	68	.313	.357	.388	745	103	2	12	7	0	.983	-4	1-84	-0.7
1958	Cin-N	89	124	23	27	1	1	1	11	5	27	.218	.248	.266	514	34	-12	7	1	1	.987	-1	1-36,O-22(7-0-15)	-1.3
Total	8	967	3502	437	1000	144	47	69	373	203	526	.286	.326	.413	739	95	-30	84	53	-0	.988	3	1-874/O-22(7-0-15)	-7.5

YEAR	TM/L	G	AB	R	H	2B	3B	HR	RBI	BB	SO	AVG	OBP	SLG	OPS	OPS+	BR+	SB	CS	SBR	FA	FR	G/POS	TPR
■ LEW FONSECA	Fonseca, Lewis Albert b: 1/21/1899, Oakland, Cal. d: 11/26/89, Ely, Iowa BR/TR, 5'10.5", 180 lbs. Deb: 4/13/21 M Career OF: (99-LF 15-CF 5-RF)																							
1921	Cin-N	82	297	38	82	10	3	1	41	8	13	.276	.304	.340	644	74	-12	2	3	-1	.961	-3	2-50,1-16,O-16L	-1.5
1922	Cin-N	81	291	55	105	20	3	4	45	14	18	.361	.390	.491	882	128	12	7	8	-1	.970	8	2-71	1.9
1923	Cin-N	65	237	33	66	11	4	3	28	9	16	.278	.310	.397	707	87	-5	4	0	1	.957	8	2-45,1-14	0.4
1924	Cin-N	20	57	5	13	2	1	0	9	4	4	.228	.279	.298	577	55	-4	1	0	0	1.000	-2	2-10/1-6	-0.6
1925	Phi-N	126	467	78	149	30	5	7	60	21	42	.319	.352	.450	802	95	-4	6	2	1	.956	-8	2-69,1-55	-1.3
1927	Cle-A	112	428	60	133	20	7	2	40	12	17	.311	.333	.404	737	90	-8	12	4	1	.973	-6	2-96,1-13	-1.0
1928	Cle-A	75	263	38	86	19	4	3	36	13	17	.327	.361	.464	825	114	5	4	2	0	1.000	5	1-56,3-15/S-4,2-1	0.7
1929	Cle-A	148	566	97	209	44	15	6	103	50	23	**.369**	.427	.532	959	140	35	19	11	0	.995	6	*1-147	2.9
1930	Cle-A	40	129	20	36	9	2	0	17	7	7	.279	.316	.380	696	73	-5	1	0	0	.980	2	1-28/3-6	-0.4
1931	Cle-A	26	108	21	40	9	1	1	14	8	7	.370	.419	.500	919	133	5	3	2	-0	.993	0	1-26	0.3
	Chi-A	121	465	65	139	26	5	2	71	32	22	.299	.348	.389	737	99	-1	4	4	-1	.974	-17	O-95L,2-21/1-2,3-1	-2.0
	Yr	147	573	86	179	35	6	3	85	40	29	.312	.361	.410	772	106	5	7	6	-1	.974	-16	O-95L,1-28,2-21,/3	-1.7
1932	Chi-A	18	37	0	5	1	0	0	6	1	7	.135	.158	.162	320	-18	-7	0	0	0	1.000	1	/O-8(5-0-3),P-1,M	-0.6
1933	Chi-A	23	59	8	12	2	0	2	15	7	6	.203	.288	.339	627	68	-3	1	0	0	1.000	2	1-12,M	-0.1
Total	12	937	3404	518	1075	203	50	31	485	186	199	.316	.355	.432	788	103	9	64	36	1	.994	-3	1-375,2-363,O/3SP	-1.3
■ CHAD FONVILLE	Fonville, Chad Everette b: 3/5/71, Jacksonville, N.C. BB/TR, 5'6", 155 lbs. Deb: 4/28/95 Career OF: (30-LF 22-CF 0-RF)																							
1995	Mon-N	14	12	2	4	0	0	0	0	0	3	.333	.333	.333	667	74	-0	0	2	-1	.000	0	/2-2	-0.1
	*LA-N	88	308	41	85	6	1	0	16	23	39	.276	.328	.302	630	74	-11	20	5	3	.971	-3	S-38,2-36,O-11L	-0.7
	Yr	102	320	43	89	6	1	0	16	23	42	.278	.328	.303	632	73	-12	20	7	2	.971	-3	2-38,S-38,O-11L	-0.8
1996	LA-N	103	201	34	41	4	1	0	13	17	31	.204	.266	.234	500	36	-18	7	2	1	.964	-3	O-35L,2-23,S-20,/3	-1.9
1997	LA-N	9	14	1	2	0	0	0	1	2	3	.143	.250	.143	393	7	-2	0	1	-0	.833	-2	/2-3	-0.4
	Chi-A	9	9	1	1	0	0	0	1	1	1	.111	.200	.111	311	-17	-2	2	0	0	1.000	0	/O-3C,2-2,S-2,D-1	-0.1
1999	Bos-A	3	2	1	0	0	0	0	0	2	0	.000	.500	.000	500	41	0	1	0	0	.900	1	/2-2	0.1
Total	4	226	546	80	133	10	2	0	31	45	77	.244	.302	.269	572	57	-33	30	10	3	.964	-7	/2-68,S-60,O-49L,3D	-3.1
■ BARRY FOOTE	Foote, Barry Clifton b: 2/16/52, Smithfield, N.C. BR/TR, 6'3", 210 lbs. Deb: 9/14/73 C																							
1973	Mon-N	6	6	0	4	0	1	0	1	0	0	.667	.667	1.000	1667	343	2	0	0	0	.000	0	H	0.2
1974	Mon-N	125	420	44	110	23	4	11	60	35	74	.262	.323	.414	737	100	-1	2	1	0	.984	9	*C-122	1.4
1975	Mon-N	118	387	25	75	16	1	7	30	17	48	.194	.230	.295	524	43	-31	0	1	-0	.985	11	*C-115	-1.6
1976	Mon-N	105	350	32	82	12	2	7	27	17	32	.234	.272	.340	612	70	-14	2	1	0	.989	7	C-96/3-2,1-1	-0.3
1977	Mon-N	15	49	4	12	3	1	2	8	4	10	.245	.302	.469	771	106	0	0	0	0	.988	0	C-13	0.1
	Phi-N	18	32	3	7	1	0	1	3	3	6	.219	.286	.344	629	65	-2	0	0	0	.980	1	C-17	-0.2
	Yr	33	81	7	19	4	1	3	11	7	16	.235	.295	.420	715	88	-2	0	0	0	.985	-0	C-30	-0.1
1978	*Phi-N	39	57	4	9	0	0	1	4	1	11	.158	.172	.211	383	6	-7	0	0	0	1.000	2	C-31	-0.5
1979	Chi-N	132	429	47	109	26	0	16	56	34	49	.254	.316	.427	743	92	-5	5	2	0	.979	-3	*C-129	-0.3
1980	Chi-N	63	202	16	48	13	1	6	28	13	18	.238	.284	.401	685	83	-5	1	1	-0	.992	1	C-55	-0.2
1981	Chi-N	9	22	0	0	0	0	0	1	3	7	.000	.120	.000	120	-61	-5	0	0	0	1.000	-1	/C-8	-0.6
	*NY-A	40	125	12	26	4	0	6	10	8	21	.208	.256	.384	640	83	-3	0	0	0	.996	9	C-34/1-1,D-4	0.7
1982	NY-A	17	48	4	7	5	0	0	2	1	11	.146	.163	.250	413	12	-6	0	0	0	.973	-4	C-17	-0.9
Total	10	687	2127	191	489	103	10	57	230	136	287	.230	.279	.368	647	75	-77	10	6	0	.985	31	C-637/D-4,1-2,3-2	-2.2
■ JIM FORAN	Foran, James H. b: 1848, New York d: 1/30/28, Los Angeles, Cal. 5'6.5", 159 lbs. Deb: 5/4/1871																							
1871	Kek-n	19	89	21	31	1	3	1	18	2	1	.348	.363	.461	823	132	3	1	0	0	.878	1	1-16/O-4(3-1-0)	0.3
■ P.J. FORBES	Forbes, Patrick Joseph b: 9/22/67, Pittsburg, Kan. BR/TR, 5'10", 160 lbs. Deb: 7/21/98																							
1998	Bal-A	9	10	0	1	0	0	0	2	0	0	.100	.100	.100	200	-48	-2	0	0	0	1.000	1	/2-7,3-1,S-1	-0.1
■ DAVY FORCE	Force, David W. "Wee Davy" or "Tom Thumb" b: 7/27/1849, New York, N.Y. d: 6/21/18, Englewood, N.J. BR/TR, 5'4", 130 lbs. Deb: 5/5/1871																							
1871	Oly-n	32	162	45	45	9	4	0	29	4	0	.278	.295	.383	678	98	1	8	0	2	**.844**	**18**	*S-31/3-1	1.2
1872	Tro-n	25	130	40	53	11	0	0	16	1	0	.408	.412	.492	905	174	11	2	2	-0	.871	4	3-16/S-9	0.9
	Bal-n	19	95	29	41	2	2	0	13	1	0	.432	.438	.495	932	178	8	3	0	1	.846	5	3-19	0.9
	Yr	44	225	69	94	13	2	0	29	2	0	.418	.423	.493	916	176	19	5	2	0	**.857**	8	3-35/S-9	1.8
1873	Bal-n	49	234	77	86	8	1	0	31	9	0	.368	.391	.410	801	139	12	1	0	0	**.820**	6	3-34,S-17/P-3	1.1
1874	Chi-n	59	294	61	92	9	0	0	26	3	1	.313	.320	.344	663	112	3	4	0	1	.802	11	*3-42,S-18/P-1	1.0
1875	Ath-n	77	386	78	120	22	5	0	49	5	5	.311	.323	.394	717	133	10	6	3	0	**.887**	10	*S-77/3-2	1.5
1876	Phi-N	60	289	48	66	6	0	0	17	5	3	.228	.246	.254	499	67	-9				.898	21	*S-60/3-2	1.1
	NY-N	1	3	0	0	0	0	0	0	0	0	.000	.000	.000	0	-99	-1				.833	0	/S-1	0.0
	Yr	61	292	48	66	6	0	0	17	5	3	.226	.243	.251	494	66	-10				.897	21	S-61/3-2	1.2
1877	StL-N	58	225	24	59	5	3	0	22	11	15	.262	.297	.311	608	97	0				**.914**	6	*S-50/3-8	0.7
1879	Buf-N	79	316	36	66	5	2	0	8	13	37	.209	.240	.237	477	57	-14				**.929**	2	*S-78/3-1	-0.9
1880	Buf-N	81	290	22	49	10	0	0	17	10	35	.169	.197	.203	400	35	-19				.939	31	2-53,S-30	1.5
1881	Buf-N	75	278	21	50	9	1	0	15	11	29	.180	.211	.219	430	36	-20				.937	24	2-51,S-21/O-3R,3-1	0.7
1882	Buf-N	73	278	39	67	10	1	1	28	12	17	.241	.272	.295	567	81	-6				**.908**	7	*S-61,3-11/2-1	0.3
1883	Buf-N	96	378	40	82	11	3	0	35	12	39	.217	.241	.262	503	52	-22				.884	-6	*S-78,3-13/2-7	-2.2
1884	Buf-N	106	403	47	83	13	3	0	36	27	41	.206	.256	.253	509	59	-19				**.898**	-3	*S-105/2-1	-1.7
1885	Buf-N	71	253	20	57	6	1	0	15	13	19	.225	.263	.257	520	66	-9				.882	-4	2-42,S-24/3-6	-1.0
1886	Was-N	68	242	26	44	5	1	0	16	17	26	.182	.236	.211	446	39	-17	9			.909	17	S-56/2-8,3-4	0.3
Total	5 n	261	1301	330	437	61	12	0	164	25	6	.336	.348	.401	750	132	44	24	5	4	.861	53	S-152,3-114/P-4	6.6
Total	10	768	2955	323	623	80	15	1	209	131	261	.211	.245	.249	494	58	-135	9			.908	96	S-564,2-163/3-46,O	-1.1
■ CURT FORD	Ford, Curtis Glenn b: 10/11/60, Jackson, Miss. BL/TR, 5'10", 150 lbs. Deb: 6/22/85 Career OF: (90-LF 7-CF 146-RF)																							
1985	StL-N	11	12	2	6	2	0	0	3	4	1	.500	.625	.667	1292	264	3	1	0	0	.750	-2	/O-4(1-0-4)	0.2
1986	StL-N	85	214	30	53	15	2	2	29	23	29	.248	.321	.364	685	89	-3	13	5	1	.975	1	O-64(24-0-40)	-0.3
1987	*StL-N	89	228	32	65	9	5	3	26	14	32	.285	.329	.408	737	92	-3	11	8	-0	.981	1	O-75(15-2-61)	-0.5
1988	StL-N	91	128	11	25	6	0	1	18	8	26	.195	.243	.266	508	45	-9	6	1	1	.965	-4	O-40(24-3-13)/1-7	-1.4
1989	Phi-N	108	142	13	31	5	1	1	13	16	33	.218	.302	.289	591	70	-5	5	3	0	1.000	-8	O-52(26-2-25)/1-1,2-1	-1.5
1990	Phi-N	22	18	0	2	0	0	0	0	1	5	.111	.158	.111	269	-25	-3	0	0	0	1.000	-1	/O-3(0-0-3)	-0.4
Total	6	406	742	88	182	37	8	7	89	66	126	.245	.309	.345	654	80	-20	36	17	2	.977	-12	O-238R/1-8,2-1	-3.9
■ DAN FORD	Ford, Darnell Glenn b: 5/19/52, Los Angeles, Cal. BR/TR, 6'1", 185 lbs. Deb: 4/12/75 Career OF: (2-LF 295-CF 783-RF)																							
1975	Min-A	130	440	72	123	21	1	15	59	30	79	.280	.333	.434	767	114	7	6	7	-1	.988	-9	*O-120(0-118-2)/D-3	-0.6
1976	Min-A	145	514	87	137	24	7	20	86	36	118	.267	.327	.457	784	125	15	17	6	2	.968	-5	*O-139(1-0-139)/D-3	0.4
1977	Min-A	144	453	66	121	25	7	11	60	41	79	.267	.341	.426	767	109	6	6	4	-0	.964	-10	*O-137(1-3-135)/D-3	-1.0
1978	Min-A	151	592	78	162	36	10	11	82	48	88	.274	.333	.424	757	109	7	7	7	-1	.977	-2	*O-149(0-145-4)/D-1	0.2
1979	*Cal-A	142	569	100	165	26	5	21	101	40	86	.290	.340	.464	804	118	13	8	5	0	.977	7	*O-141(0-29-124)	1.3
1980	Cal-A	65	226	22	63	11	0	7	26	19	45	.279	.340	.420	760	110	3	0	1	-0	.940	-2	O-45(0-0-45),D-15	-0.2
1981	Cal-A	97	375	53	104	14	1	15	48	23	71	.277	.328	.440	768	119	8	2	2	-0	.960	-2	O-97(0-0-97)	0.0
1982	Bal-A	123	421	46	99	21	3	10	43	23	71	.235	.281	.371	652	78	-14	5	2	0	.975	4	*O-119(0-0-119)/D-1	-1.5
1983	*Bal-A	103	407	63	114	30	4	9	55	29	55	.280	.333	.440	772	113	6	9	2	1	.987	1	*O-103(0-0-103)	0.3
1984	Bal-A	25	91	7	21	4	0	1	5	7	13	.231	.286	.308	593	66	-4	1	0	1	1.000	2	O-15(0-0-15)/D-8	-0.3
1985	Bal-A	28	75	4	14	2	0	1	1	7	17	.187	.256	.253	509	41	-6	0	1	-0	.000	0	D-28	-0.7
Total	11	1153	4163	598	1123	214	38	121	566	303	722	.270	.326	.427	753	109	40	61	37	0	.974	-17	*O-1065R/D-62	-2.1
■ ED FORD	Ford, Edward L. b: 1862, Richmond, Va. 5'9.5", 160 lbs. Deb: 10/9/1884																							
1884	Ric-a	2	5	0	0	0	0	0		0		.000	.000	.000	0	-99	-1				.556	1	/S-1,1-1	0.0
■ HOD FORD	Ford, Horace Hills b: 7/23/1897, New Haven, Conn. d: 1/29/77, Winchester, Mass. BR/TR, 5'10", 165 lbs. Deb: 9/8/19																							
1919	Bos-N	10	28	4	6	0	1	0	3	2	6	.214	.290	.286	576	77	-1	0			.946	3	/S-8,3-2	0.3
1920	Bos-N	88	257	16	62	12	5	1	30	18	25	.241	.296	.339	635	86	-5	3	3	-0	.972	15	2-59,S-18/1-4	1.2

YEAR	TM/L	G	AB	R	H	2B	3B	HR	RBI	BB	SO	AVG	OBP	SLG	OPS	OPS+	BR+	SB	CS	SBR	FA	FR	G/POS	TPR
1921	Bos-N	152	555	50	155	29	5	2	61	36	49	.279	.328	.360	688	87	-11	2	11	-3	**.973**	16	*2-119,S-33	0.9
1922	Bos-N	143	515	58	140	23	9	2	60	30	36	.272	.317	.363	680	78	-17	2	1	0	.953	-4	*S-115,2-28	-0.7
1923	Bos-N	111	380	27	103	16	7	2	50	31	30	.271	.326	.366	692	86	-8	1	1	-0	.970	-10	2-95,S-19	-1.3
1924	Phi-N	145	530	58	144	27	5	3	53	27	40	.272	.308	.358	667	70	-22	1	9	-3	.970	12	*2-145	-0.9
1925	Bro-N	66	216	32	59	11	0	1	15	26	15	.273	.357	.338	695	81	-5	0	3	-1	.966	-0	S-66	0.0
1926	Cin-N	57	197	14	55	6	1	0	18	14	12	.279	.336	.320	656	79	-5	1			.963	5	S-57	0.5
1927	Cin-N	115	409	45	112	16	2	1	46	33	34	.274	.331	.330	661	80	-11	0			.952	-8	*S-104,2-12	-0.7
1928	Cin-N	149	506	49	122	17	4	0	54	47	31	.241	.308	.291	599	58	-30	1			**.972**	12	*S-149	-0.2
1929	Cin-N	148	529	68	146	14	6	3	50	41	25	.276	.329	.342	671	70	-25	8			.953	8	*S-108,2-42	-0.3
1930	Cin-N	132	424	36	98	16	7	1	34	24	28	.231	.272	.309	581	42	-40	2			.974	2	S-74,2-66	-2.7
1931	Cin-N	84	175	18	40	8	1	0	13	13	13	.229	.286	.286	571	57	-10	0			.954	1	S-73/2-3,3-1	-0.6
1932	StL-N	1	2	0	0	0	0	0	0	0	0	.000	.000	.000	0	-97	-1	0			.750	0	/S-1	0.0
	Bos-N	40	95	9	26	5	2	0	6	6	9	.274	.324	.368	692	89	-1	0			.984	-3	2-20,S-16/3-2	-0.2
	Yr	41	97	9	26	5	2	0	6	6	9	.268	.317	.361	678	85	-2	0			.984	-3	2-20,S-17/3-2	-0.2
1933	Bos-N	5	15	0	1	0	0	0	1	3	1	.067	.222	.067	289	-16	-2	0			1.000	5	/S-5	0.3
Total	15	1446	4833	484	1269	200	55	16	494	351	354	.263	.316	.337	652	72	-195	21	28		.960	54	S-846,2-589/3-5,1-4	-4.4

■ TED FORD
Ford, Theodore Henry b: 2/7/47, Vineland, N.J. BR/TR, 5'10", 180 lbs. Deb: 4/7/70

YEAR	TM/L	G	AB	R	H	2B	3B	HR	RBI	BB	SO	AVG	OBP	SLG	OPS	OPS+	BR+	SB	CS	SBR	FA	FR	G/POS	TPR
1970	Cle-A	26	46	5	8	1	0	1	1	3	13	.174	.224	.261	485	32	-4	0	0	0	1.000	1	O-12(2-1-10)	-0.4
1971	Cle-A	74	196	15	38	6	0	2	14	9	34	.194	.229	.255	484	34	-17	2	2	-0	1.000	-1	O-55(12-20-29)	-2.2
1972	Tex-A	129	429	43	101	19	1	14	50	37	80	.235	.301	.382	683	107	2	4	3	-0	.977	9	*O-119(16-0-104)	0.6
1973	Cle-A	11	40	3	9	0	1	0	3	2	7	.225	.262	.275	537	50	-3	1	0	0	1.000	-4	O-10(0-6-5)	-0.7
Total	4	240	711	66	156	26	2	17	68	51	134	.219	.275	.333	608	76	-22	7	5	-0	.985	6	O-196(30-27-148)	-2.7

■ BROOK FORDYCE
Fordyce, Brook Alexander b: 5/7/70, New London, Conn. BR/TR, 6'1", 185 lbs. Deb: 4/26/95

YEAR	TM/L	G	AB	R	H	2B	3B	HR	RBI	BB	SO	AVG	OBP	SLG	OPS	OPS+	BR+	SB	CS	SBR	FA	FR	G/POS	TPR
1995	NY-N	4	2	1	1	1	0	0	0	1	0	.500	.667	1.000	1667	343	1	0	0	0	.000	0	-0,-0	0.1
1996	Cin-N	4	7	0	2	1	0	0	1	3	1	.286	.500	.429	929	147	1	0	0	0	1.000	-0	/C-4	0.1
1997	Cin-N	47	96	7	20	5	0	1	8	8	15	.208	.269	.292	561	46	-8	2	0	0	.983	1	C-30/D-1	-0.5
1998	Cin-N	57	146	8	37	9	0	3	14	11	28	.253	.306	.377	682	77	-5	0	1	-0	.978	5	C-54	0.2
1999	Chi-A	105	333	36	99	25	1	9	49	21	48	.297	.345	.459	804	102	1	2	0	0	.987	-13	*C-103	-0.6
2000	Chi-A	40	125	18	34	7	1	5	21	6	23	.272	.316	.464	780	93	-2	0	0	0	1.000	4	C-40	0.4
	Bal-A	53	177	23	57	11	0	9	28	11	27	.322	.368	.537	905	129	7	0	0	0	.988	-5	C-52	0.5
	Yr	93	302	41	91	18	1	14	49	17	50	.301	.347	.507	853	114	6	0	0	0	.993	-1	C-92	0.9
Total	6	310	886	93	250	59	2	27	121	61	142	.282	.333	.445	778	97	-4	4	1	1	.987	-8	C-283/D-1	0.2

■ FRANK FOREMAN
Foreman, Francis Isaiah "Monkey" b: 5/1/1863, Baltimore, Md. d: 11/19/57, Baltimore, Md. BL/TL, 6', 160 lbs. Deb: 5/15/1884 F

YEAR	TM/L	G	AB	R	H	2B	3B	HR	RBI	BB	SO	AVG	OBP	SLG	OPS	OPS+	BR+	SB	CS	SBR	FA	FR	G/POS	TPR
1884	CP-U	3	11	0	1	0	0	0		0		.091	.091	.091	182	-45	-2				.857	-1	/P-3,O-2(1-1-0)	-0.1
	KC-U	1	3	0	0	0	0	0		0		.000	.000	.000	0	-99	-1				.900	1	/P-1	0.0
	Yr	4	14	0	1	0	0	0		0		.071	.071	.071	143	-59	-3				.882	0	/P-4,O-2(1-1-0)	-0.1
1885	Bal-a	3	14	4	4	0	1	0	2	0		.286	.286	.429	714	125	0				.800	-1	/P-3,O-1(0-0-1)	0.0
1889	Bal-a	54	181	18	26	2	1	1	11	12	35	.144	.201	.182	383	9	-22	7			.853	-3	P-51/O-3(0-2-1)	-0.1
1890	Cin-N	25	75	13	10	1	3	1	7	10	13	.133	.253	.267	520	52	-5	0			.867	-3	P-25/O-1(0-0-1)	0.0
1891	Cin-N	1	4	0	1	1	0	0	0	0	0	.250	.250	.500	750	116	0	0			.000	-0	/O-1(1-0-0)	0.0
	Was-a	50	153	26	34	4	5	4	19	23	35	.222	.339	.392	731	114	3	6			.952	-1	P-43/O-8(0-6-2)	0.1
1892	Was-N	11	28	5	13	2	2	1	3	3	3	.464	.516	.786	1302	301	7	0			.632	-1	P-11	0.0
	Bal-N	7	23	2	4	1	1	0	1	3	3	.174	.269	.304	574	71	-1	1			.750	-0	/O-5(5-0-1),P-4	-0.1
	Yr	18	51	7	17	3	3	1	4	6	6	.333	.404	.569	972	195	6	1			.731	-1	P-15/O-5(5-0-1)	-0.1
1893	NY-N	2	3	0	0	0	0	0	0	0	0	.000	.000	.000	0	-99	-1	0			1.000	-0	/P-2	0.0
1895	Cin-N	32	94	14	29	7	0	2	11	4	14	.309	.350	.447	797	100	-0	1			.882	-3	P-32	0.0
1896	Cin-N	27	74	9	18	2	0	0	8	4	6	.243	.282	.270	552	43	-6	2			.912	-1	P-27	0.0
1901	Bos-A	1	4	0	0	0	0	0	0	0		.000	.000	.000	0	-99	-1	0			1.000	-0	/P-1	0.0
	Bal-A	24	80	12	26	2	2	0	10	3		.325	.349	.400	749	103	0	1			.887	-3	P-24	0.0
	Yr	25	84	12	26	2	2	0	10	3		.310	.333	.381	714	94	-1	1			.891	-3	P-25	0.0
1902	Bal-A	2	7	1	3	1	0	0	1	0		.429	.429	.571	1000	168	1	0			.818	1	/P-2	0.0
Total	11	243	754	104	169	23	15	9	73	62	109	.224	.291	.330	621	74	-28	18			.881	-16	P-229/O-21(7-9-6)	-0.2

■ TOM FORSTER
Forster, Thomas W. b: 5/1/1859, New York, N.Y. d: 7/17/46, New York, N.Y. BR/TR, 5'9", 153 lbs. Deb: 8/4/1882 Career OF: (5-LF 4-CF 0-RF)

YEAR	TM/L	G	AB	R	H	2B	3B	HR	RBI	BB	SO	AVG	OBP	SLG	OPS	OPS+	BR+	SB	CS	SBR	FA	FR	G/POS	TPR
1882	Det-N	21	76	5	7	0	0	0	2	5	12	.092	.148	.092	240	-21	-10				.830	-7	2-21	-1.5
1884	Pit-a	35	126	10	28	5	0	0		7		.222	.263	.262	525	73	-4				.897	6	S-28/3-6,2-1	0.3
1885	NY-a	57	213	28	47	7	2	0	18	17		.221	.281	.272	554	82	-3				.903	-12	2-52/O-5(3-2-0)	-1.2
1886	NY-a	67	251	33	49	3	2	1	20	20		.195	.263	.235	498	59	-11	9			.891	-7	2-62/O-4(2-2-0),S-1	-1.4
Total	4	180	666	76	131	15	4	1	40	49	12	.197	.256	.236	492	59	-27	9			.885	-19	2-136/S-29,O-9L,3-6	-3.8

■ ED FORSYTHE
Forsythe, Edward James b: 4/30/1887, Kingston, N.Y. d: 6/22/56, Hoboken, N.J. BR/TR, 5'10", 155 lbs. Deb: 10/2/15

YEAR	TM/L	G	AB	R	H	2B	3B	HR	RBI	BB	SO	AVG	OBP	SLG	OPS	OPS+	BR+	SB	CS	SBR	FA	FR	G/POS	TPR
1915	Bal-F	1	3	0	0	0	0	0	0	1	0	.000	.250	.000	250	-26	-1	0			.667	-0	/3-1	-0.1

■ GEORGE FOSS
Foss, George Dueward "Deeby" b: 6/13/1897, Register, Ga. d: 11/10/69, Brandon, Fla. BR/TR, 5'10.5", 170 lbs. Deb: 4/16/21

YEAR	TM/L	G	AB	R	H	2B	3B	HR	RBI	BB	SO	AVG	OBP	SLG	OPS	OPS+	BR+	SB	CS	SBR	FA	FR	G/POS	TPR
1921	Was-A	4	7	0	0	0	0	0	0	0	1	.000	.000	.000	0	-99	-2	0	0	0	.750	0	/3-1	-0.2

■ RAY FOSSE
Fosse, Raymond Earl b: 4/4/47, Marion, Ill. BR/TR, 6'2", 215 lbs. Deb: 9/8/67

YEAR	TM/L	G	AB	R	H	2B	3B	HR	RBI	BB	SO	AVG	OBP	SLG	OPS	OPS+	BR+	SB	CS	SBR	FA	FR	G/POS	TPR
1967	Cle-A	7	16	0	1	0	0	0	0	0	5	.063	.063	.063	125	-62	-3	0	0	0	1.000	5	/C-7	0.2
1968	Cle-A	1	0	0	0	0	0	0	0	0	0	—	—	—		—	0	0	0	0	1.000	-0	/C-1	0.0
1969	Cle-A	37	116	11	20	3	0	2	9	8	29	.172	.232	.250	482	34	-10	1	0	0	.977	3	C-37	-0.6
1970	Cle-A★	120	450	62	138	17	1	18	61	39	55	.307	.363	.469	832	122	13	1	5	-2	.989	6	*C-120	2.4
1971	Cle-A†	133	486	53	134	21	1	12	62	36	62	.276	.331	.397	728	97	-2	4	1	1	.988	-3	*C-126/1-4	0.1
1972	Cle-A	134	457	42	110	20	1	10	41	45	46	.241	.313	.354	667	95	-3	5	1	1	.985	6	*C-124/1-3	1.1
1973	*Oak-A	143	492	37	126	23	2	7	52	25	62	.256	.293	.354	647	86	-11	2	2	-0	.987	2	*C-141/D-2	-0.2
1974	*Oak-A	69	204	20	40	8	3	4	23	11	31	.196	.244	.324	568	66	-10	1	1	-0	.973	-1	C-68/D-1	-0.9
1975	*Oak-A	82	136	14	19	3	2	0	12	8	19	.140	.193	.191	384	9	-16	0	1	-0	.981	6	C-82/1-1,2-1	-0.9
1976	Cle-A	90	276	26	83	9	1	2	30	20	20	.301	.348	.362	710	109	3	1	2	-0	.987	1	C-85/1-3,D-1	0.7
1977	Cle-A	78	238	25	63	7	1	6	27	7	26	.265	.294	.378	673	84	-6	0	5	-2	.983	9	C-77/1-1,D-1	0.4
	Sea-A	11	34	3	12	3	0	0	5	2	2	.353	.389	.441	830	127	1	0	1	-0	.968	-3	/C-8,D-2	-0.2
	Yr	89	272	28	75	10	1	6	32	9	28	.276	.306	.386	692	90	-4	0	6	-2	.982	5	C-85/D-3,1-1	0.2
1979	Mil-A	19	52	6	12	3	1	0	2	2	6	.231	.286	.327	613	65	-3	0	0	0	1.000	-1	C-13/1-1,D-5	-0.3
Total	12	924	2957	299	758	117	13	61	324	203	363	.256	.308	.367	675	90	-45	15	19	-3	.985	28	C-889/1-13,D-12,2-1	1.8

■ POP FOSTER
Foster, Clarence Francis b: 4/8/1878, New Haven, Conn. d: 4/16/44, Princeton, N.J. BR/TR, 5'8.5", Deb: 9/13/1898 Career OF: (121-LF 0-CF 108-RF)

YEAR	TM/L	G	AB	R	H	2B	3B	HR	RBI	BB	SO	AVG	OBP	SLG	OPS	OPS+	BR+	SB	CS	SBR	FA	FR	G/POS	TPR
1898	NY-N	32	112	10	30	6	1	0	9	0		.268	.268	.339	607	76	-4	0			.967	-5	O-21(17-0-4),3-10/S-2	-1.0
1899	NY-N	84	301	48	89	9	7	3	57	20		.296	.348	.402	750	109	3	7			.949	-10	O-84(1-0-84)/S-1,3-1	-1.0
1900	NY-N	31	84	19	22	3	1	0	11	11		.262	.347	.321	669	89	-1	0			1.000	-3	O-12(1-0-11)/S-7,2-5	-0.3
1901	Was-A	103	392	65	109	16	9	6	54	41		.278	.352	.411	763	113	7	10			.925	-1	*O-102(102-0-0)/S-2	0.0
	Chi-A	12	35	4	10	2	2	1	6	4		.286	.359	.543	902	152	2	0			.909	-1	/O-9(0-0-9)	0.1
	Yr	115	427	69	119	18	11	7	60	45		.279	.353	.422	774	116	9	10			.924	-2	*O-111(102-0-9)/S-2	0.1
Total	4	262	924	146	260	36	20	10	137	76		.281	.341	.396	737	107	8	17			.938	-19	O-228L/S-12,3-11,2	-2.2

■ EDDIE FOSTER
Foster, Edward Cunningham "Kid" b: 2/13/1887, Chicago, Ill. d: 1/15/37, Washington, D.C. BR/TR, 5'6.5", 145 lbs. Deb: 4/14/10

YEAR	TM/L	G	AB	R	H	2B	3B	HR	RBI	BB	SO	AVG	OBP	SLG	OPS	OPS+	BR+	SB	CS	SBR	FA	FR	G/POS	TPR
1910	NY-A	30	83	5	11	2	0	0	1	8		.133	.217	.157	374	16	-8	2			.909	-2	S-22	-1.1
1912	Was-A	154	618	98	176	34	9	2	70	53		.285	.345	.379	724	106	4	27			.920	12	*3-154	2.0
1913	Was-A	106	409	56	101	11	5	1	41	36	31	.247	.309	.306	615	78	-11	22			.901	4	*3-105	-0.5
1914	Was-A	157	616	82	174	16	10	2	50	60	47	.282	.348	.351	699	106	5	31	18	1	.929	-18	*3-157	-0.9
1915	Was-A	154	618	75	170	25	10	0	52	48	30	.275	.329	.348	677	101	-1	20	6	2	.919	-5	3-79,2-75	-0.1

YEAR	TM/L	G	AB	R	H	2B	3B	HR	RBI	BB	SO	AVG	OBP	SLG	OPS	OPS+	BR+	SB	CS	SBR	FA	FR	G/POS	TPR
1916	Was-A	158	606	75	153	18	9	1	44	68	26	.252	.332	.317	649	96	-2	23	16	-1	.929	-16	3-84,2-72	-1.7
1917	Was-A	143	554	66	130	16	8	0	43	46	23	.235	.293	.292	586	80	-14	11			.935	-6	3-86,2-57	-1.8
1918	Was-A	129	519	70	147	13	3	0	29	41	20	.283	.339	.320	659	101	0	12			.936	2	*3-127/2-2	0.6
1919	Was-A	120	478	57	126	12	5	0	26	33	21	.264	.314	.310	623	76	-15	20			.946	7	*3-115	-0.5
1920	Bos-A	117	386	48	100	17	6	0	41	42	17	.259	.336	.334	671	82	-9	10	4	1	.957	15	3-88,2-21	0.8
1921	Bos-A	120	412	51	117	18	6	0	35	57	15	.284	.371	.357	728	89	-5	13	7	0	.943	-14	3-94,2-22	-1.1
1922	Bos-A	48	109	11	23	3	0	0	3	9	10	.211	.277	.239	516	36	-10	1	1	-0	.886	-11	3-28/S-3	-1.9
	StL-A	37	144	29	44	4	0	0	12	20	8	.306	.394	.333	727	88	-1	3	1	0	.916	-2	3-37	0.0
	Yr	85	253	40	67	7	0	0	15	29	18	.265	.345	.292	638	67	-11	4	2	0	.905	-12	3-65/S-3	-1.9
1923	StL-A	27	100	9	18	2	0	0	4	7	7	.180	.241	.200	441	16	-12	0	0	0	.961	-8	2-20/3-7	-1.9
Total	13	1500	5652	732	1490	191	71	6	451	528	255	.264	.329	.326	655	89	-80	195	53		.930	-42	*3-1161,2-269/S-25	-8.1

■ ELMER FOSTER Foster, Elmer Ellsworth b: 8/15/1861, Minneapolis, Minn. d: 7/22/46, Deephaven, Minn. BR/TL, 5'10", 178 lbs. Deb: 6/18/1884 Career OF: (25-LF 59-CF 1-RF)

YEAR	TM/L	G	AB	R	H	2B	3B	HR	RBI	BB	SO	AVG	OBP	SLG	OPS	OPS+	BR+	SB	CS	SBR	FA	FR	G/POS	TPR
1884	Phi-a	4	11	4	2	0	0	0		3		.182	.357	.182	539	76	-0				.885	-2	/C-4,O-1(0-0-1)	-0.2
	Phi-U	1	3	0	1	0	1	0		0		.333	.333	1.000	1333	313	1				.625	-1	/C-1	0.0
1886	NY-a	35	125	16	23	0	1	0	7	7		.184	.239	.200	439	40	-8	3			.853	-0	2-21,O-14(9-5-0)	-0.7
1888	NY-N	37	136	15	20	3	2	0	10	9	20	.147	.216	.199	415	33	-10	13			.852	-2	O-37(16-21-0)/3-1	-1.3
1889	NY-N	2	4	2	0	0	0	0	0	3	1	.000	.429	.000	429	25	-0	2			1.000	-0	/O-2(0-2-0)	0.0
1890	Chi-N	27	105	20	26	4	2	5	23	9	21	.248	.325	.467	791	125	2	18			.986	2	O-27(0-27-0)	0.3
1891	Chi-N	4	16	3	3	0	0	1	1	1	2	.188	.235	.375	610	77	-1	1			.875	-0	/O-4(0-4-0)	-0.1
Total	6	110	400	60	75	7	6	6	41	32	44	.188	.261	.280	541	67	-16	37			.883	-4	/O-85C,2-21,C-5,3-1	-2.0

■ GEORGE FOSTER Foster, George Arthur b: 12/1/48, Tuscaloosa, Ala. BR/TR, 6'1", 185 lbs. Deb: 9/10/69 Career OF: (1534-LF 267-CF 178-RF)

YEAR	TM/L	G	AB	R	H	2B	3B	HR	RBI	BB	SO	AVG	OBP	SLG	OPS	OPS+	BR+	SB	CS	SBR	FA	FR	G/POS	TPR
1969	SF-N	9	5	1	2	0	0	0	1	0	1	.400	.400	.400	800	127	0	0	0	0	1.000	-3	/O-8(0-0-8)	-0.3
1970	SF-N	9	19	2	6	1	1	1	4	2	5	.316	.381	.632	1013	168	2	0	0	0	1.000	-0	/O-7(6-0-1)	0.1
1971	SF-N	36	105	11	28	5	0	3	8	6	27	.267	.306	.400	706	100	-0	0	1	-0	.980	-2	O-30(24-0-7)	-0.4
	Cin-N	104	368	39	86	18	4	10	50	23	93	.234	.291	.386	677	92	-5	7	6	-1	.986	11	*O-102(1-101-1)	0.3
	Yr	140	473	50	114	23	4	13	58	29	120	.241	.295	.389	684	94	-5	7	7	-1	.985	9	*O-132(25-101-8)	-0.1
1972	*Cin-N	59	145	15	29	4	1	2	12	5	44	.200	.232	.283	515	48	-10	2	1	0	.973	-5	O-47(2-1-44)	-1.8
1973	Cin-N	17	39	6	11	3	0	4	9	4	7	.282	.349	.667	1016	185	4	0	1	-0	1.000	-3	O-13(1-11-5)	0.0
1974	Cin-N	106	276	31	73	18	0	7	41	30	52	.264	.345	.406	751	111	4	3	2	-0	.989	-16	O-98(6-45-69)	-1.5
1975	*Cin-N	134	463	71	139	24	4	23	78	40	73	.300	.360	.518	878	139	22	2	1	0	.990	5	*O-125(95-30-18)/1-1	2.2
1976	*Cin-N★	144	562	86	172	21	9	29	**121**	52	89	.306	.369	.530	899	149	34	17	3	3	**.994**	-2	*O-142(116-36-24)/1-1	2.8
1977	Cin-N★	158	615	**124**	197	31	2	**52**	**149**	61	107	.320	.386	**.631**	**1017**	165	**54**	6	4	-0	.992	16	*O-158(136-32-1)	6.2
1978	Cin-N★	158	604	97	170	26	7	**40**	**120**	70	138	.281	.363	.546	909	151	39	4	4	-1	.971	7	*O-157(154-11-0)	4.1
1979	*Cin-N★	121	440	68	133	18	3	30	98	59	105	.302	.388	.561	950	155	33	0	2	-1	.982	4	*O-116(116-0-0)	3.1
1980	Cin-N	144	528	79	144	21	5	25	93	75	99	.273	.364	.473	838	132	23	1	0	0	.997	10	*O-141(141-0-0)	2.8
1981	Cin-N★	108	414	64	122	23	2	22	90	51	75	.295	.376	.519	895	150	26	4	0	1	.991	8	*O-108(108-0-0)	3.2
1982	NY-N	151	550	64	136	23	2	13	70	50	123	.247	.312	.367	680	90	-8	1	1	-0	.974	12	*O-138(138-0-0)	-0.2
1983	NY-N	157	601	74	145	19	2	28	90	38	111	.241	.291	.419	710	95	-6	1	1	-0	.988	10	*O-153(153-0-0)	-0.3
1984	NY-N	146	553	67	149	22	1	24	86	30	122	.269	.314	.443	757	112	7	2	2	-0	.976	11	*O-141(141-0-0)	1.1
1985	NY-N	129	452	57	119	24	1	21	77	46	87	.263	.334	.460	794	123	13	0	1	-0	.976	1	*O-123(123-0-0)	0.8
1986	NY-N	72	233	28	53	6	1	13	38	21	53	.227	.291	.429	721	99	-1	1	1	-0	.962	-0	O-62(62-0-0)	-0.4
	Chi-A	15	51	2	11	0	2	1	4	3	8	.216	.259	.353	612	63	-3	0	0	0	1.000	1	O-11(11-0-0)/D-3	-0.2
Total	18	1977	7023	986	1925	307	47	348	1239	666	1419	.274	.341	.480	821	127	228	51	31	0	.984	65	*O-1880L/D-3,1-2	21.6

■ LEO FOSTER Foster, Leonard Norris b: 2/2/51, Covington, Ky. BR/TR, 5'11", 165 lbs. Deb: 7/9/71 Career OF: (0-LF 0-CF 1-RF)

YEAR	TM/L	G	AB	R	H	2B	3B	HR	RBI	BB	SO	AVG	OBP	SLG	OPS	OPS+	BR+	SB	CS	SBR	FA	FR	G/POS	TPR
1971	Atl-N	9	10	1	0	0	0	0	0	0	1	.000	.000	.000	0	-94	-2	0	0	0	.900	2	/S-3	-0.1
1973	Atl-N	3	6	1	1	1	0	0	0	0	2	.167	.167	.333	500	33	-1	0	0	0	1.000	-0	/S-1	-0.1
1974	Atl-N	72	112	16	22	2	0	1	5	9	22	.196	.256	.241	497	38	-9	1	2	-0	.977	-1	S-43,2-10/3-3,O-1R	-0.8
1976	NY-N	24	59	11	12	2	0	1	15	8	5	.203	.299	.288	587	71	-2	3	0	1	.920	1	/3-9,S-7,2-3	0.0
1977	NY-N	36	75	6	17	3	0	0	6	5	14	.227	.284	.267	551	51	-5	3	1	0	.968	-4	2-20/S-8,3-2	-0.8
Total	5	144	262	35	52	8	0	2	26	22	44	.198	.263	.252	515	44	-20	7	3	0	.964	-3	/S-62,2-33,3-14,O-1R	-1.8

■ REDDY FOSTER Foster, Oscar E. b: 8/1864, Richmond, Va. d: 12/19/08, Richmond, Va. Deb: 6/3/1896

YEAR	TM/L	G	AB	R	H	2B	3B	HR	RBI	BB	SO	AVG	OBP	SLG	OPS	OPS+	BR+	SB	CS	SBR	FA	FR	G/POS	TPR
1896	NY-N	1	1	0	0	0	0	0	0	0	0	.000	.000	.000	0	-99	-0	0			.000	0	H	0.0

■ ROY FOSTER Foster, Roy b: 7/29/45, Bixby, Okla. BR/TR, 6', 185 lbs. Deb: 4/7/70

YEAR	TM/L	G	AB	R	H	2B	3B	HR	RBI	BB	SO	AVG	OBP	SLG	OPS	OPS+	BR+	SB	CS	SBR	FA	FR	G/POS	TPR
1970	Cle-A	139	477	66	128	26	0	23	60	54	75	.268	.357	.468	825	120	13	3	3	-0	.965	-3	*O-131(114-0-17)	0.2
1971	Cle-A	125	396	51	97	21	1	18	45	35	48	.245	.316	.439	755	103	1	6	1	1	.968	-1	*O-107(46-0-64)	-0.5
1972	Cle-A	73	143	19	32	4	0	4	13	21	23	.224	.331	.336	667	96	-0	0	2	-1	.966	-6	O-45(15-0-31)	-1.0
Total	3	337	1016	136	257	51	1	45	118	110	146	.253	.338	.438	776	110	14	9	6	-0	.967	-11	O-283(175-0-112)	-1.3

■ BOB FOTHERGILL Fothergill, Robert Roy "Fats" b: 8/16/1897, Massillon, Ohio d: 3/20/38, Detroit, Mich. BR/TR, 5'10.5", 230 lbs. Deb: 4/18/22

YEAR	TM/L	G	AB	R	H	2B	3B	HR	RBI	BB	SO	AVG	OBP	SLG	OPS	OPS+	BR+	SB	CS	SBR	FA	FR	G/POS	TPR
1922	Det-A	42	152	20	49	12	4	0	29	8	9	.322	.356	.454	810	113	2	1	5	-2	.945	-7	O-38(2-10-26)	-0.8
1923	Det-A	101	241	34	76	18	2	1	49	12	19	.315	.358	.419	777	106	2	5	4	-0	.977	-8	O-68(45-20-3)	-1.0
1924	Det-A	54	166	28	50	8	3	0	15	5	13	.301	.326	.386	711	84	-4	2	3	-1	.968	-3	O-45(43-0-2)	-1.1
1925	Det-A	71	204	38	72	14	0	2	28	6	3	.353	.377	.451	828	111	3	3	2	-0	.977	-2	O-59(40-16-4)	-0.2
1926	Det-A	110	387	63	142	31	7	3	73	33	23	.367	.421	.506	927	139	22	4	12	-3	.961	-1	*O-103(76-19-9)	1.1
1927	Det-A	143	527	93	189	38	9	9	114	47	31	.359	.413	.516	929	138	29	9	15	-3	.961	-6	*O-137(137-0-0)	0.9
1928	Det-A	111	347	49	110	28	10	3	63	24	19	.317	.366	.481	848	119	9	8	3	1	.959	-3	O-90(70-0-20)	-0.1
1929	Det-A	115	277	42	98	24	9	6	62	11	11	.354	.378	.570	949	140	15	3	1	0	.967	-4	O-59(39-0-20)	0.7
1930	Det-A	55	143	14	37	9	3	2	14	6	10	.259	.289	.406	694	72	-7	1	1	-0	.947	-5	O-38(32-0-6)	-1.3
	Chi-A	52	135	10	40	9	0	0	24	4	8	.296	.326	.363	689	77	-5	0	0	0	.879	-3	O-31(8-0-22)	-0.9
	Yr	107	278	24	77	18	3	2	38	10	18	.277	.307	.385	692	75	-11	1	1	-0	.913	-8	O-69(40-0-28)	-2.2
1931	Chi-A	108	312	25	88	9	4	3	56	17	17	.282	.323	.365	689	86	-7	2	2	-0	.972	1	O-74(48-0-26)	-1.0
1932	Chi-A	116	346	36	102	24	1	7	50	27	10	.295	.348	.431	778	107	3	4	4	-1	.952	-11	O-86(53-0-34)	-1.2
1933	Bos-A	28	32	1	11	1	0	0	5	2	4	.344	.382	.375	757	102	0	0	0	0	1.000	-1	/O-4(1-0-3)	-0.1
Total	12	1106	3269	453	1064	225	52	36	582	202	177	.325	.368	.459	828	115	63	42	52	-9	.961	-53	O-832(594-65-175)	-5.0

■ JACK FOURNIER Fournier, John Frank b: 9/28/1889, AuSable, Mich. d: 9/5/73, Tacoma, Wash. BL/TR, 6', 195 lbs. Deb: 4/13/12 Career OF: (53-LF 14-CF 20-RF)

YEAR	TM/L	G	AB	R	H	2B	3B	HR	RBI	BB	SO	AVG	OBP	SLG	OPS	OPS+	BR+	SB	CS	SBR	FA	FR	G/POS	TPR
1912	Chi-A	35	73	6	14	5	2	0	2	4		.192	.262	.315	578	67	-3	1			.988	3	1-17	-0.1
1913	Chi-A	68	172	20	40	8	5	1	23	21	23	.233	.323	.355	678	99	-0	9			.990	4	1-29,O-23(11-0-12)	0.2
1914	Chi-A	109	379	44	118	14	9	6	44	31	44	.311	.368	.443	811	146	20	10	13	-2	.978	5	1-97/O-6(3-1-2)	2.1
1915	Chi-A	126	422	86	136	20	18	5	77	64	37	.322	.429	**.491**	920	170	38	21	16	-1	.986	3	1-65,O-57(38-13-6)	3.7
1916	Chi-A	105	313	36	75	13	9	3	44	36	40	.240	.328	.367	695	108	3	19			.976	-3	1-85/O-1(1-0-0)	-0.2
1917	Chi-A	1	1	0	0	0	0	0	0	0	1	.000	.000	.000	0	-98	-0	0			.000	0	H	0.0
1918	NY-A	27	100	9	35	6	1	0	12	7	7	.350	.393	.430	823	145	5	7			.976	-2	1-27	0.2
1920	StL-N	141	530	77	162	33	14	3	61	42	42	.306	.370	.438	808	136	25	26	20	-1	.983	1	*1-138	2.3
1921	StL-N	149	574	103	197	27	9	16	86	56	48	.343	.409	.505	914	144	37	20	22	-3	.987	-4	*1-149	1.9
1922	StL-N	128	404	64	119	23	9	10	61	40	21	.295	.368	.470	838	120	12	6	8	-1	.982	2	*1-109/P-1	0.5
1923	Bro-N	133	515	91	181	30	13	22	102	43	28	.351	.411	.588	999	165	47	11	4	1	.985	4	*1-133	4.1
1924	Bro-N	154	563	93	188	25	4	**27**	116	83	46	.334	.428	.536	965	162	52	7	5	-0	.985	7	*1-153	4.8
1925	Bro-N	145	545	99	191	21	16	22	130	**86**	39	.350	.446	.569	1015	162	54	4	6	-1	.989	3	*1-145	4.2
1926	Bro-N	87	243	39	69	9	2	11	48	30	16	.284	.365	.473	838	126	9	0			.986	-2	1-64	0.3
1927	Bos-N	122	374	55	106	18	2	10	53	44	16	.283	.368	.422	790	121	12	4			.989	0	*1-102	0.5
Total	15	1530	5208	822	1631	252	113	136	859	587	408	.313	.392	.483	875	143	309	145	94		.984	20	*1-1313/O-87L,P-1	24.5

■ BILL FOUSER Fouser, William C. b: 10/1855, Philadelphia, Pa. d: 3/1/19, Philadelphia, Pa. Deb: 4/22/1876

YEAR	TM/L	G	AB	R	H	2B	3B	HR	RBI	BB	SO	AVG	OBP	SLG	OPS	OPS+	BR+	SB	CS	SBR	FA	FR	G/POS	TPR
1876	Phi-N	21	89	11	12	0	1	0	2	0	0	.135	.135	.157	292	-3	-9				.827	3	2-14/O-7(0-1-6),1-1	-0.5

YEAR	TM/L	G	AB	R	H	2B	3B	HR	RBI	BB	SO	AVG	OBP	SLG	OPS	OPS+	BR+	SB	CS	SBR	FA	FR	G/POS	TPR
■ **DAVE FOUTZ**	Foutz, David Luther "Scissors" b: 9/7/1856, Carroll Co., Md. d: 3/5/1897, Waverly, Md. BR/TR, 6'2", 161 lbs. Deb: 7/29/1884 FM Career OF: (92-LF 33-CF 196-RF)																							
1884	StL-a	33	119	17	27	4	0	0		8		.227	.276	.261	536	73	-3				.940	-3	P-25,O-14(0-3-11)	-0.5
1885	*StL-a	65	238	42	59	6	4	0	34	11		.248	.281	.307	588	82	-5				.899	6	P-47,1-15/O-4(4-0-0)	-0.3
1886	*StL-a	102	414	66	116	18	9	3	59	9		.280	.297	.389	686	109	1	17			.949	4	P-59,O-34R,1-11	0.1
1887	*StL-a	102	446	79	174	26	13	4	108	23		.390	.393	.508	901	136	17	22			.899	-4	O-50R,P-40,1-15	0.4
1888	Bro-a	140	563	91	156	20	13	3	99	28		.277	.314	.375	688	121	11	35			.895	3	O-78R,1-42,P-23	0.5
1889	*Bro-a	138	553	118	152	19	8	6	113	64	23	.275	.353	.371	724	106	5	43			.979	-3	*1-134,P-12	-1.0
1890	*Bro-N	129	509	106	154	25	13	5	98	52	25	.303	.368	.432	801	133	20	42			.978	-1	*1-113,O-13C/P-5	0.7
1891	Bro-N	130	521	87	134	26	8	2	73	40	25	.257	.313	.349	662	93	-6	48			.976	-3	*1-124/P-6,S-1	-1.7
1892	Bro-N	61	220	33	41	5	3	1	26	14	14	.186	.235	.250	485	48	-14	19			.850	-2	O-29L,P-27/1-6	-1.3
1893	Bro-N	130	557	91	137	20	10	7	67	32	34	.246	.287	.355	642	74	-24	39			.913	-6	O-77L,1-54/P-6,M	-3.1
1894	Bro-N	73	297	40	90	12	9	0	52	14	13	.303	.337	.404	741	84	-8	14			.976	-3	1-73/P-1,M	-0.8
1895	Bro-N	31	115	14	34	4	1	0	21	4	2	.296	.319	.348	667	78	-4	1			.879	-5	O-20(7-2-11)/1-8,M	-0.8
1896	Bro-N	2	8	0	2	1	0	0	0	1	0	.250	.333	.375	708	92	-0	0			1.000	0	/O-1(0-0-1),1-1,M	0.0
Total	13	1136	4560	784	1276	186	91	31	750	300	136	.280	.323	.378	701	101	-10	280			.977	-14	1-596,O-320R,P-251,/S	-7.8
■ **FRANK FOUTZ**	Foutz, Frank Hayes b: 4/8/1877, Baltimore, Md. d: 12/25/61, Lima, Ohio BR/TR, 5'11", 165 lbs. Deb: 4/26/01 F																							
1901	Bal-A	20	72	13	17	4	1	2	14	8		.236	.321	.403	724	96	-1	0			.959	-0	1-20	-0.1
■ **BOOB FOWLER**	Fowler, Joseph Chester "Gink" b: 11/11/1900, Waco, Tex. d: 10/8/88, Dallas, Tex. BL/TR, 5'11.5", 180 lbs. Deb: 5/6/23																							
1923	Cin-N	11	33	9	11	0	1	1	6	1	3	.333	.353	.485	838	121	1	1	0	0	.847	-1	S-10	0.1
1924	Cin-N	59	129	20	43	6	1	0	9	5	15	.333	.358	.395	754	103	1	2	2	-0	.936	-7	S-32/2-4,3-2	-0.3
1925	Cin-N	6	5	0	2	1	0	0	2	0	1	.400	.400	.600	1000	155	0	0	0	0	.000	0	H	0.0
1926	Bos-A	2	8	1	1	0	0	0	1	0	0	.125	.125	.125	250	-36	-2	0	0	0	.800	0	/3-2	-0.1
Total	4	78	175	30	57	7	2	1	18	6	19	.326	.348	.406	754	102	0	3	2	-0	.910	-7	/S-42,3-4,2-4	-0.3
■ **ANDY FOX**	Fox, Andrew Junipero b: 1/12/71, Sacramento, Cal. BL/TR, 6'4", 205 lbs. Deb: 4/7/96 Career OF: (20-LF 9-CF 45-RF)																							
1996	*NY-A	113	189	26	37	4	0	3	13	20	28	.196	.276	.265	541	38	-18	11	3	1	.958	13	2-72,3-31/S-9,OD	-0.1
1997	*NY-A	22	31	13	7	1	0	0	1	7	9	.226	.368	.258	626	68	-1	2	1	0	1.000	8	3-11/2-5,S-2,O-2R,D	0.6
1998	Ari-N	139	502	67	139	21	6	9	44	43	97	.277	.355	.396	752	98	-1	14	7	1	.982	-25	2-60,O-48R,3-26,1	-2.5
1999	*Ari-N	99	274	34	70	12	2	6	33	33	61	.255	.354	.380	734	85	-5	4	1	1	.958	-5	S-82,3-12	-0.4
2000	Ari-N	31	86	10	18	4	0	1	10	4	16	.209	.244	.291	535	34	-9	2	1	0	.952	-1	3-20/O-6(1-1-4),1-1	-0.9
	Fla-N	69	164	19	40	4	2	3	10	18	37	.244	.330	.348	677	75	-6	8	3	1	.932	6	S-33,O-14L,3-12,/2	0.2
	Yr	100	250	29	58	8	2	4	20	22	53	.232	.302	.328	630	61	-15	10	4	1	.932	5	S-33,3-32,O-20L,/21	-0.7
Total	5	473	1246	169	311	46	10	22	111	125	248	.250	.333	.356	689	78	-40	41	16	3	.973	-5	2-139,S-126,3/O1D	-3.1
■ **CHARLIE FOX**	Fox, Charles Francis "Irish" b: 10/7/21, New York, N.Y. BR/TR, 5'11", 180 lbs. Deb: 9/24/42 MC																							
1942	NY-N	3	7	1	3	0	0	0	1	1	2	.429	.500	.429	929	172	1	0			1.000	-1	/C-3	0.0
■ **ERIC FOX**	Fox, Eric Hollis b: 8/15/63, Lemoore, Cal. BB/TL, 5'10", 180 lbs. Deb: 7/7/92																							
1992	*Oak-A	51	143	24	34	5	2	3	13	13	29	.238	.301	.364	665	90	-2	3	4	-1	.990	-5	O-43(20-19-16)/D-4	-0.9
1993	Oak-A	29	56	5	8	1	0	1	5	2	7	.143	.172	.214	387	3	-8	0	2	-1	1.000	-3	O-26(5-18-3)/D-2	-1.2
1994	Oak-A	26	44	7	9	2	0	1	1	3	8	.205	.255	.318	574	51	-3	2	0	0	1.000	-4	O-24(0-16-8)	-0.6
1995	Tex-A	10	15	2	0	0	0	0	0	3	4	.000	.167	.000	167	-51	-3	0	0	0	1.000	-1	/O-8(3-2-3),D-1	-0.4
Total	4	116	258	38	51	8	2	5	19	21	48	.198	.258	.302	560	55	-17	5	6	-1	.995	-13	O-101(28-55-30)/D-7	-3.1
■ **PETE FOX**	Fox, Ervin b: 3/8/09, Evansville, Ind. d: 7/5/66, Detroit, Mich. BR/TR, 5'11", 165 lbs. Deb: 4/12/33																							
1933	Det-A	128	535	82	154	26	13	7	57	23	38	.288	.320	.424	744	94	-7	9	6	-0	.978	1	*O-124(0-116-8)	-0.9
1934	*Det-A	128	516	101	147	31	2	2	45	49	53	.285	.351	.364	716	85	-11	25	10	2	.974	8	*O-121(0-11-110)	-0.7
1935	*Det-A	131	517	116	166	38	8	15	73	45	52	.321	.382	.513	895	134	25	14	4	2	.988	-0	*O-125(0-6-123)	1.7
1936	Det-A	73	220	46	67	12	1	4	26	34	23	.305	.405	.423	827	104	3	4	3	-1	.968	0	O-55(5-0-50)	-0.1
1937	Det-A	148	628	116	208	39	8	12	82	41	43	.331	.372	.476	848	110	8	12	8	-0	.976	-3	*O-143(11-27-106)	-0.2
1938	Det-A	155	634	91	186	35	10	7	96	31	39	.293	.328	.413	742	80	-21	16	7	1	**.994**	-2	*O-155(1-0-154)	-2.9
1939	Det-A	141	519	69	153	24	6	7	66	35	41	.295	.342	.405	746	84	-13	23	12	1	.970	9	*O-126(0-0-126)	-1.0
1940	*Det-A	93	350	49	101	17	4	5	48	21	30	.289	.329	.403	732	81	-10	7	7	-1	.967	0	O-85(2-1-82)	-1.5
1941	Bos-A	73	268	38	81	12	7	0	31	21	32	.302	.357	.399	757	98	-1	9	2	1	.977	-1	O-62(8-5-49)	-0.4
1942	Bos-A	77	256	42	67	15	5	3	42	20	28	.262	.323	.395	717	98	-1	8	7	-1	.966	-9	O-71(7-0-64)	-1.6
1943	Bos-A	127	489	54	141	24	4	2	44	34	40	.288	.337	.366	703	104	2	22	8	2	.961	-3	*O-125(3-0-122)	-0.8
1944	Bos-A☆	121	496	70	156	37	6	1	64	27	34	.315	.354	.419	773	122	13	10	5	0	.987	-1	*O-119(0-0-119)	0.4
1945	Bos-A	66	208	21	51	4	1	0	20	11	18	.245	.296	.274	570	64	-9	2	2	-0	.989	-6	O-57(0-0-57)	-2.1
Total	13	1461	5636	895	1678	314	75	65	694	392	471	.298	.347	.415	762	98	-24	158	81	6	.977	-7	*O-1368(37-166-1170)	-10.1
■ **PADDY FOX**	Fox, George B. b: 12/1/1868, Pottstown, Pa. d: 5/8/14, Philadelphia, Pa. Deb: 7/13/1891																							
1891	Lou-a	6	19	1	2	0	1	0	2	2	3	.105	.261	.211	471	36	-2	0			.929	-2	/3-6	-0.3
1899	Pit-N	13	41	4	10	0	1	1	3	3		.244	.311	.366	677	86	-1	2			.971	2	/1-9,C-3	0.1
Total	2	19	60	5	12	0	2	1	5	5	3	.200	.294	.317	611	70	-2	2			.971	-1	/1-9,3-6,C-3	-0.2
■ **NELLIE FOX**	Fox, Jacob Nelson b: 12/25/27, St.Thomas, Pa. d: 12/1/75, Baltimore, Md. BL/TR, 5'9", 150 lbs. Deb: 6/8/47 CH																							
1947	Phi-A	7	3	2	0	0	0	0	0	1	0	.000	.250	.000	250	-26	-0	0	0	0	1.000	0	/2-1	0.0
1948	Phi-A	3	13	0	2	0	0	0	0	1	0	.154	.214	.154	368	-1	-2	1	0	0	.950	-2	/2-3	-0.3
1949	Phi-A	88	247	42	63	6	2	0	21	32	9	.255	.354	.296	650	75	-8	2	2	-0	.982	-1	2-77	-0.5
1950	Chi-A	130	457	45	113	12	7	0	30	35	17	.247	.304	.304	608	58	-30	4	3	-0	.974	-0	*2-121	-2.2
1951	Chi-A★	147	604	93	189	32	12	4	55	43	11	.313	.372	.425	798	118	15	9	12	-2	.981	-3	*2-147	1.7
1952	Chi-A☆	152	648	76	**192**	25	10	0	39	34	14	.296	.334	.366	700	94	-6	5	5	-1	**.985**	8	*2-151	1.0
1953	Chi-A★	154	624	92	178	31	8	3	72	49	18	.285	.344	.375	719	91	-7	4	5	-1	.983	3	*2-154	0.7
1954	Chi-A★	155	631	111	**201**	24	8	2	47	51	12	.319	.374	.391	766	106	6	16	9	-1	**.989**	-6	*2-155	1.3
1955	Chi-A★	154	636	100	198	28	7	6	59	38	15	.311	.366	.406	772	104	4	7	9	-2	.974	**27**	*2-154	4.0
1956	Chi-A★	154	649	109	192	20	10	4	52	44	14	.296	.350	.376	726	90	-9	8	4	0	**.986**	3	*2-154	0.6
1957	Chi-A★	155	619	110	**196**	27	8	6	61	75	13	.317	.404	.415	819	124	24	5	6	-1	.986	21	*2-155	5.6
1958	Chi-A★	155	623	82	**187**	21	6	0	49	47	11	.300	.360	.353	713	99	1	5	6	-1	.985	2	*2-155	1.3
1959	*Chi-A★	156	624	84	191	34	6	2	70	71	13	.306	.383	.389	773	114	15	5	6	-1	**.988**	-3	*2-156	2.2
1960	Chi-A★	150	605	85	175	24	**10**	2	59	50	13	.289	.353	.372	725	97	-1	2	4	-1	.985	12	*2-149	2.1
1961	Chi-A★	159	606	67	152	11	5	2	51	59	12	.251	.326	.295	622	69	-25	2	3	-1	.982	-6	*2-159	-1.8
1962	Chi-A	157	621	79	166	27	7	2	54	38	12	.267	.317	.343	660	78	-19	1	2	-0	**.990**	1	*2-154	-0.5
1963	Chi-A★	137	539	54	140	19	0	2	42	24	17	.260	.300	.306	606	72	-20	0	2	-1	**.988**	-8	*2-134	-1.9
1964	Hou-N	133	442	45	117	12	6	0	28	27	13	.265	.322	.319	641	86	-8	0	2	-1	.977	-6	*2-115	-0.5
1965	Hou-N	21	41	3	11	2	0	0	1	0	2	.268	.286	.317	603	75	-1	0	0	0	1.000	-0	/3-6,1-2,2-1	-0.2
Total	19	2367	9232	1279	2663	355	112	35	790	719	216	.288	.349	.363	712	94	-73	76	80	-11	.984	42	*2-2295/3-6,1-2	12.6
■ **JACK FOX**	Fox, John Paul b: 5/21/1885, Reading, Pa. d: 6/28/63, Reading, Pa. BR/TR, 5'10", 185 lbs. Deb: 6/2/08																							
1908	Phi-A	9	30	2	6	0	0	0	0	0		.200	.200	.200	400	28	-2	2			.923	-1	/O-8(0-1-7)	-0.4
■ **BILL FOX**	Fox, William Henry b: 1/15/1872, Sturbridge, Mass. d: 5/7/46, Minneapolis, Minn. BB/TR, 5'10", 160 lbs. Deb: 8/20/1897																							
1897	Was-N	4	14	4	4	0	0	0	0	1		.286	.333	.286	619	65	-1	0			.700	0	/S-2,2-2	0.0
1901	Cin-N	43	159	9	28	2	1	0	7	4		.176	.201	.201	402	18	-17	9			.948	5	2-43	-1.1
Total	2	47	173	13	32	2	1	0	7	5		.185	.212	.208	420	22	-17	9			.944	6	/2-45,S-2	-1.1
■ **JIMMIE FOXX**	Foxx, James Emory "Beast" or "Double X" b: 10/22/07, Sudlersville, Md. d: 7/21/67, Miami, Fla. BR/TR, 6', 195 lbs. Deb: 5/1/25 CH Career OF: (12-LF 0-CF 9-RF)																							
1925	Phi-A	10	9	2	6	1	0	0	0	0	1	.667	.667	.778	1444	249	2	0	0	0	.000	0	/C-1	0.2
1926	Phi-A	26	32	8	10	2	1	0	5	1	6	.313	.333	.438	771	95	-0	1	0	0	1.000	2	C-12/O-3(0-0-3)	0.1

YEAR	TM/L	G	AB	R	H	2B	3B	HR	RBI	BB	SO	AVG	OBP	SLG	OPS	OPS+	BR+	SB	CS	SBR	FA	FR	G/POS	TPR
1927	Phi-A	61	130	23	42	6	5	3	20	14	11	.323	.393	.515	908	127	5	2	1	0	.975	-2	1-32/C-5	0.2
1928	Phi-A	118	400	85	131	29	10	13	79	60	43	.327	.416	.548	964	147	28	3	8	-2	.940	-2	3-60,1-30,C-19	2.6
1929	*Phi-A	149	517	123	183	23	9	33	118	103	70	.354	**.463**	.625	1088	171	58	9	7	-0	.995	-4	*1-142/3-8	4.2
1930	*Phi-A	153	562	127	188	33	13	37	156	93	66	.335	.429	.637	1066	159	51	7	7	-1	.990	-2	*1-153	3.4
1931	*Phi-A	139	515	93	150	32	10	30	120	73	84	.291	.380	.567	947	138	26	4	3	-0	.993	-3	*1-112,3-26/O-1L	1.3
1932	Phi-A	154	585	**151**	213	33	9	**58**	**169**	116	96	.364	.469	**.749**	**1218**	203	**90**	3	7	-2	**.994**	-5	*1-141,3-13	**6.4**
1933	Phi-A☆	149	573	125	204	37	9	**48**	**163**	96	93	**.356**	.449	**.703**	**1153**	**199**	**81**	2	2	-0	.990	6	*1-149/S-1	**6.7**
1934	Phi-A★	150	539	120	180	28	6	44	130	**111**	75	.334	.449	.653	1102	188	72	11	2	2	.993	4	*1-140/3-9	5.9
1935	Phi-A★	147	535	118	185	33	7	**36**	115	114	99	.346	.461	**.636**	**1096**	**182**	68	6	4	-0	**.997**	6	*1-121,C-26/3-2	**5.9**
1936	Bos-A★	155	585	130	198	32	8	41	143	105	119	.338	.440	.631	1071	153	48	13	4	1	.991	-1	*1-139,O-16L/3-1	3.1
1937	Bos-A★	150	569	111	162	24	6	36	127	99	96	.285	.392	.538	929	127	23	10	8	-1	**.994**	10	*1-150/C-1	1.7
1938	Bos-A★	149	565	139	197	33	9	50	**175**	**119**	76	**.349**	**.462**	**.704**	**1166**	**180**	**71**	5	4	-0	.987	6	*1-149	**5.5**
1939	Bos-A☆	124	467	130	168	31	10	**35**	105	89	72	.360	**.464**	**.694**	**1158**	185	**61**	4	3	-0	.992	7	*1-123/P-1	5.1
1940	Bos-A★	144	515	106	153	30	4	36	119	101	87	.297	.412	.581	993	148	38	4	7	-2	.990	-2	1-95,C-42/3-1	2.7
1941	Bos-A★	135	487	87	146	27	8	19	105	93	103	.300	.412	.505	917	138	29	2	5	-1	.992	7	*1-124/3-5,O-1(0-0-1)	2.1
1942	Bos-A	30	100	18	27	4	0	5	14	18	15	.270	.392	.460	852	134	5	0	0	0	.996	6	1-27	0.9
	Chi-N	70	205	25	42	8	0	3	19	22	55	.205	.282	.288	570	69	-8	1			.983	-4	1-52/C-1	-1.8
1944	Chi-N	15	20	0	1	1	0	0	2	2	5	.050	.136	.100	236	-33	-4	0			1.000	2	/3-2,C-1	-0.2
1945	Phi-N	89	224	30	60	11	1	7	38	23	39	.268	.336	.420	756	112	3	0			.988	-3	1-40,3-14/P-9	-0.1
Total	20	2317	8134	1751	2646	458	125	534	1922	1452	1311	.325	.428	.609	1038	161	748	87	72		.992	30	*1-1919,3-141,C/OPS	55.9

■ JOE FOY

Foy, Joseph Anthony b: 2/21/43, New York, N.Y. d: 10/12/89, Bronx, N.Y. BR/TR, 6', 215 lbs. Deb: 4/13/66 Career OF: (5-LF 13-CF 2-RF)

YEAR	TM/L	G	AB	R	H	2B	3B	HR	RBI	BB	SO	AVG	OBP	SLG	OPS	OPS+	BR+	SB	CS	SBR	FA	FR	G/POS	TPR
1966	Bos-A	151	554	97	145	23	8	15	63	91	80	.262	.368	.413	781	112	12	2	5	-1	.953	-1	*3-139,S-13	1.1
1967	*Bos-A	130	446	70	112	22	4	16	49	46	87	.251	.325	.426	751	111	6	8	6	-0	.921	-10	*3-118/O-1(0-0-1)	-0.5
1968	Bos-A	150	515	65	116	18	2	10	60	84	91	.225	.338	.326	665	96	0	26	8	3	.935	2	*3-147/O-3(3-0-0)	0.5
1969	KC-A	145	519	72	136	19	2	11	71	74	75	.262	.360	.370	729	104	5	37	15	3	.964	-9	*3-113,1-16,O/S2	-0.3
1970	NY-N	99	322	39	76	12	0	6	37	68	58	.236	.376	.329	705	90	-1	22	13	0	.937	-1	3-97	-0.2
1971	Was-A	41	128	12	30	8	0	0	11	27	14	.234	.368	.297	665	96	1	4	1	1	.960	4	3-37/2-3,S-1	0.5
Total	6	716	2484	355	615	102	16	58	291	390	405	.248	.354	.372	725	103	22	99	48	5	.943	-14	3-651/O-20C,S-19,12	1.1

■ JULIO FRANCO

Franco, Julio Cesar (b: Julio Cesar Robles (Franco)) b: 8/23/58, Hato Mayor, D.R. BR/TR, 6', 190 lbs. Deb: 4/23/82 Career OF: (4-LF 0-CF 1-RF)

YEAR	TM/L	G	AB	R	H	2B	3B	HR	RBI	BB	SO	AVG	OBP	SLG	OPS	OPS+	BR+	SB	CS	SBR	FA	FR	G/POS	TPR
1982	Phi-N	16	29	3	8	1	0	0	3	2	4	.276	.323	.310	633	76	-1	0	2	-1	1.000	-0	S-11/3-2	-0.1
1983	Cle-A	149	560	68	153	24	8	8	80	27	50	.273	.309	.387	696	87	-10	32	12	3	.961	-7	*S-149	0.1
1984	Cle-A	160	658	82	188	22	5	3	79	43	68	.286	.335	.348	683	88	-10	19	10	1	.955	-1	*S-159/D-1	0.7
1985	Cle-A	160	636	97	183	33	4	6	90	54	74	.288	.347	.381	728	100	1	13	9	-0	.949	-22	*S-151/2-8,D-1	-0.5
1986	Cle-A	149	599	80	183	30	5	10	74	32	66	.306	.341	.422	763	108	6	10	7	-0	.971	-5	*S-134,2-13/D-3	1.5
1987	Cle-A	128	495	86	158	24	3	8	52	57	56	.319	.393	.428	821	117	14	32	9	4	.963	-24	*S-111/2-9,D-8	0.5
1988	Cle-A	152	613	88	186	23	6	10	54	56	72	.303	.364	.409	773	113	12	25	11	2	.982	-10	*2-151/D-1	0.8
1989	Tex-A★	150	548	80	173	31	5	13	92	66	69	.316	.390	.462	852	137	28	21	3	4	.980	-6	*2-140,D-10	2.9
1990	Tex-A★	157	582	96	172	27	1	11	69	82	83	.296	.384	.402	786	120	18	31	10	3	.975	-2	*2-152/D-3	2.4
1991	Tex-A☆	146	589	108	201	27	3	15	78	65	78	**.341**	.408	.474	883	146	38	36	9	5	.979	-31	*2-146	1.6
1992	Tex-A	35	107	19	25	7	0	2	8	15	17	.234	.328	.355	683	95	-1	1	1	-0	.906	-6	D-15/2-9,O-4(4-0-1)	-0.7
1993	Tex-A	144	532	85	154	31	3	14	84	62	95	.289	.365	.438	803	119	15	9	3	1	.000	0	*D-140	0.8
1994	Chi-A	112	433	72	138	19	2	20	98	62	75	.319	.410	.510	920	138	26	8	1	1	.969	-1	D-99,1-14	1.8
1996	*Cle-A	112	432	72	139	20	1	14	76	61	82	.322	.409	.470	879	122	17	8	8	-1	.990	4	1-97,D-13	0.8
1997	Cle-A	78	289	46	82	13	1	3	25	38	75	.284	.367	.367	734	89	-3	8	5	0	.983	3	D-42,2-35/1-1	-0.1
	Mil-A	42	141	22	34	3	0	4	19	31	41	.241	.382	.348	729	91	-1	7	1	1	.992	1	D-28,1-13	-0.1
	Yr	120	430	68	116	16	1	7	44	69	116	.270	.372	.360	732	90	-4	15	6	1	.983	4	D-70,2-35,1-14	-0.2
1999	TB-A	1	1	0	0	0	0	0	0	0	1	.000	.000	.000	0	-99	-0	0	0	0	1.000	-0	/1-1	0.0
Total	16	1891	7244	1104	2177	335	47	141	981	753	1006	.301	.369	.418	787	113	149	260	101	22	.960	-107	S-715,2-663,D1/O3	12.4

■ MATT FRANCO

Franco, Matthew Neil b: 8/19/69, Santa Monica, Cal. BL/TR, 6'2", 200 lbs. Deb: 9/6/95 Career OF: (31-LF 0-CF 4-RF)

YEAR	TM/L	G	AB	R	H	2B	3B	HR	RBI	BB	SO	AVG	OBP	SLG	OPS	OPS+	BR+	SB	CS	SBR	FA	FR	G/POS	TPR
1995	Chi-N	16	17	3	5	1	0	0	1	0	4	.294	.294	.353	647	71	-1	0	0	0	1.000	-1	/2-3,1-1,3-1	-0.2
1996	NY-N	14	31	3	6	1	0	1	2	1	5	.194	.242	.323	565	50	-2	0	0	0	.824	-1	/3-8,1-2	-0.3
1997	NY-N	112	163	21	45	5	0	5	21	13	23	.276	.330	.399	728	93	-2	1	0	0	.937	2	3-39,1-13/O-1L,D-1	0.0
1998	NY-N	103	161	20	44	7	2	1	13	23	26	.273	.368	.360	728	94	-1	0	1	-0	1.000	-2	3-13,O-13L,1-11,/D	-0.4
1999	*NY-N	122	132	18	31	5	0	4	21	28	21	.235	.369	.364	732	89	-1	0	0	0	1.000	-0	1-19,O-19L,3-12,/PD	-0.2
2000	*NY-N	101	134	9	32	4	0	2	14	21	22	.239	.342	.313	655	70	-6	0	0	0	.990	-3	1-28,3-22/O-3L,2D	-1.0
Total	6	468	638	74	163	23	2	13	72	86	101	.255	.346	.359	705	85	-13	1	1	-0	.928	-6	/3-95,1-74,OD2P	-2.1

■ TITO FRANCONA

Francona, John Patsy b: 11/4/33, Aliquippa, Pa. BL/TL, 5'11", 190 lbs. Deb: 4/17/56 F Career OF: (546-LF 105-CF 299-RF)

YEAR	TM/L	G	AB	R	H	2B	3B	HR	RBI	BB	SO	AVG	OBP	SLG	OPS	OPS+	BR+	SB	CS	SBR	FA	FR	G/POS	TPR
1956	Bal-A	139	445	62	115	16	4	9	57	51	60	.258	.336	.373	709	94	-4	11	5	1	.977	-8	*O-122(1-41-97),1-21	-1.6
1957	Bal-A	97	279	35	65	8	3	7	38	29	48	.233	.312	.358	670	88	-5	7	3	0	.992	-10	O-73(28-2-55)/1-4	-1.8
1958	Chi-A	41	128	10	33	3	2	1	10	14	24	.258	.331	.336	667	86	-2	2	3	-1	1.000	-4	O-35(7-0-32)	-0.8
	Det-A	45	69	11	17	5	0	0	10	15	16	.246	.381	.319	700	88	-0	0	0	0	1.000	-3	O-18(11-0-9)/1-1	-0.5
	Yr	86	197	21	50	8	2	1	20	29	40	.254	.350	.330	680	86	-3	2	3	-1	1.000	-7	O-53(18-0-41)/1-1	-1.3
1959	Cle-A	122	399	68	145	17	2	20	79	35	42	.363	.419	.566	985	174	**40**	2	0	0	.972	-4	O-64(4-61-0),1-35	3.1
1960	Cle-A	147	544	84	159	**36**	2	17	79	67	67	.292	.375	.460	835	128	22	4	1	1	.989	5	*O-138(138-0-1),1-13	1.8
1961	Cle-A☆	155	592	87	178	30	8	16	85	56	52	.301	.365	.459	824	122	18	2	1	0	.987	4	*O-138(138-0-0),1-14	1.4
1962	Cle-A	158	621	82	169	28	5	14	70	47	74	.272	.330	.401	731	99	-2	3	2	-0	.986	2	*1-158	-1.0
1963	Cle-A	142	500	57	114	29	0	10	41	47	77	.228	.297	.346	643	80	-13	9	1	2	.986	-2	*O-122(121-0-1),1-11	-2.3
1964	Cle-A	111	270	35	67	13	2	8	24	44	46	.248	.362	.400	762	113	6	1	3	-1	.985	-12	O-69(1-1-68),1-17	-1.3
1965	StL-N	81	174	15	45	6	2	5	19	17	30	.259	.325	.402	727	95	-1	0	0	0	.972	-9	O-34(1-0-34),1-13	-1.4
1966	StL-N	83	156	14	33	4	1	4	17	7	27	.212	.250	.327	577	59	-9	0	0	0	.987	1	1-30/O-9(9-0-0)	-1.0
1967	Phi-N	27	73	7	15	1	0	0	3	7	10	.205	.275	.219	494	43	-5	0	1	-0	1.000	1	1-24/O-1(0-0-1)	-0.6
	Atl-N	82	254	28	63	5	1	6	25	20	34	.248	.305	.346	652	87	-4	1	0	0	.991	-1	1-56/O-6(5-0-1)	-0.9
	Yr	109	327	35	78	6	1	6	28	27	44	.239	.299	.318	617	77	-10	1	1	-0	.993	1	1-80/O-7(5-0-2)	-1.5
1968	Atl-N	122	346	32	99	13	1	2	47	51	45	.286	.378	.347	725	118	10	3	0	1	.978	-8	O-65(65-0-0),1-33	-0.3
1969	Atl-N	51	88	5	26	1	0	2	22	13	10	.295	.386	.375	761	114	2	0	1	-0	.957	-0	O-15(15-0-0)/1-7	0.0
	Oak-A	32	85	12	29	6	1	3	20	12	11	.341	.423	.541	964	175	9	0	0	0	.988	-2	1-19/O-1(1-0-0)	0.5
1970	Oak-A	32	33	2	8	0	0	1	6	6	6	.242	.375	.333	708	100	0	0	0	0	1.000	1	/1-6,O-1(1-0-0)	0.1
	Mil-A	52	65	4	15	3	0	0	4	6	15	.231	.296	.277	573	58	-4	1	0	0	1.000	1	1-13	-0.3
	Yr	84	98	6	23	3	0	1	10	12	21	.235	.324	.296	620	73	-3	1	0	0	1.000	2	1-19/O-1(1-0-0)	-0.2
Total	15	1719	5121	650	1395	224	34	125	656	544	694	.272	.346	.403	749	108	57	46	21	3	.984	-49	O-911L,1-475	-6.9

■ TERRY FRANCONA

Francona, Terry Jon b: 4/22/59, Aberdeen, S.D. BL/TL, 6'1", 190 lbs. Deb: 8/19/81 FMC Career OF: (104-LF 6-CF 100-RF)

YEAR	TM/L	G	AB	R	H	2B	3B	HR	RBI	BB	SO	AVG	OBP	SLG	OPS	OPS+	BR+	SB	CS	SBR	FA	FR	G/POS	TPR
1981	*Mon-N	34	95	11	26	0	1	1	8	5	6	.274	.317	.326	643	82	-2	1	0	0	1.000	1	O-26(24-0-2)/1-1	-0.2
1982	Mon-N	46	131	14	42	3	0	0	9	8	11	.321	.360	.344	703	96	-0	2	3	-1	.936	-6	O-33(30-1-3),1-16	-0.9
1983	Mon-N	120	230	21	59	11	1	3	22	6	20	.257	.275	.352	628	73	-9	0	2	-1	.978	-2	O-51(13-3-37),1-47	-1.5
1984	Mon-N	58	214	18	74	19	2	1	18	5	12	.346	.364	.467	831	138	10	0	0	0	.994	6	1-50/O-6(5-0-2)	1.3
1985	Mon-N	107	281	19	75	15	1	2	31	12	12	.267	.299	.349	648	86	-6	5	5	-1	.988	2	1-57,O-28(5-0-24)/3-1	-0.9
1986	Chi-N	86	124	13	31	3	0	2	8	6	8	.250	.290	.323	613	64	-6	0	1	-0	1.000	-7	O-30(20-2-10),1-23	-1.6
1987	Cin-N	102	207	16	47	5	0	3	12	10	12	.227	.266	.295	561	46	-16	2	0	0	.995	3	1-57/O-8(2-0-6)	-1.5
1988	Cle-A	62	212	24	66	8	0	1	12	5	18	.311	.327	.363	690	91	-3	0	0	0	.977	0	D-38/1-5,O-5(5-0-0)	-0.4
1989	Mil-A	90	233	26	54	10	1	3	23	8	20	.232	.257	.322	579	63	-12	2	1	0	.989	-2	1-46,D-23,O-16R,/P	-1.8
1990	Mil-A	3	4	1	0	0	0	0	0	0	0	.000	.000	.000	0	-99	-1	0	0	0	1.000	-0	/1-2,D-1	-0.1
Total	10	708	1731	163	474	74	6	16	143	65	119	.274	.302	.351	653	81	-46	12	12	-2	.992	-4	1-304,O-203L/D-62,P3	-7.6

■ CHARLIE FRANK

Frank, Charles b: 5/30/1870, Mobile, Ala. d: 5/24/22, Memphis, Tenn. TL, 5'10", 170 lbs. Deb: 8/18/1893 Career OF: (117-LF 0-CF 1-RF)

YEAR	TM/L	G	AB	R	H	2B	3B	HR	RBI	BB	SO	AVG	OBP	SLG	OPS	OPS+	BR+	SB	CS	SBR	FA	FR	G/POS	TPR
1893	StL-N	40	164	29	55	6	3	1	17	18	8	.335	.408	.427	834	122	5	8			.930	3	O-40(40-0-0)	0.4

YEAR	TM/L	G	AB	R	H	2B	3B	HR	RBI	BB	SO	AVG	OBP	SLG	OPS	OPS+	BR+	SB	CS	SBR	FA	FR	G/POS	TPR
1894	StL-N	80	319	52	89	12	7	4	42	44	13	.279	.372	.398	770	86	-7	14			.869	-2	O-77(77-0-1)/1-3,P-2	-1.2
Total	2	120	483	81	144	18	10	5	59	62	21	.298	.384	.408	792	97	-2	22			.889	1	O-117L/1-3,P-2	-0.8
■ FRED FRANK	Frank, Frederick b: 3/11/1874, Louisa, Ky. d: 3/27/50, Ashland, Ky. Deb: 9/27/1898																							
1898	Cle-N	17	53	3	11	1	1	0	3	4		.208	.276	.264	540	56	-3	1			.915	3	O-17(0-6-11)	-0.1
■ MIKE FRANK	Frank, Stephen Michael b: 1/14/74, Pomona, Cal. BL/TL, 6'2", 185 lbs. Deb: 6/19/98																							
1998	Cin-N	28	89	14	20	6	0	0	7	7	12	.225	.281	.292	573	51	-6	0	0	0	1.000	1	O-28(1-25-2)	-0.6
■ FRANKLIN	Franklin Deb: 9/27/1884																							
1884	Was-U	1	3	0	0	0	0	0		0		.000	.000	.000	0	-99	-1				1.000	0	/O-1(0-1-0)	-0.1
■ MICAH FRANKLIN	Franklin, Micah Ishanti b: 4/25/72, San Francisco, Cal. BB/TR, 6', 205 lbs. Deb: 5/13/97																							
1997	StL-N	17	34	6	11	0	0	2	2	3	10	.324	.378	.500	878	129	1	0	0	0	1.000	-2	O-13(4-0-9)	-0.1
■ MOE FRANKLIN	Franklin, Murray Asher b: 4/1/14, Chicago, Ill. d: 3/16/78, Harbor City, Cal. BR/TR, 6', 175 lbs. Deb: 8/12/41																							
1941	Det-A	13	10	1	3	1	0	0	0	2	2	.300	.417	.400	817	106	0	0	0	0	.750	-1	/S-4,3-1	-0.1
1942	Det-A	48	154	24	40	7	0	2	16	7	5	.260	.301	.344	645	75	-5	0	0	0	.967	-6	S-32/2-7	-0.9
Total	2	61	164	25	43	8	0	2	16	9	7	.262	.309	.348	656	77	-5	0	0	0	.961	-7	/S-36,2-7,3-1	-1.0
■ HERMAN FRANKS	Franks, Herman Louis b: 1/4/14, Price, Utah BL/TR, 5'10.5", 187 lbs. Deb: 4/27/39 MC																							
1939	StL-N	17	17	1	1	0	0	0	3	3	3	.059	.200	.059	259	-26	-3	0			.973	3	C-13	0.0
1940	Bro-N	65	131	11	24	4	0	1	14	20	6	.183	.296	.237	533	46	-9	2			.990	9	C-43	0.2
1941	*Bro-N	57	139	10	28	7	0	1	11	14	13	.201	.275	.273	548	52	-9	0			.986	2	C-54/O-1(0-0-1)	-0.4
1947	Phi-A	8	15	2	3	0	1	0	1	4	4	.200	.368	.333	702	94	0	0	0	0	1.000	-1	/C-4	-0.1
1948	Phi-A	40	98	10	22	7	1	1	14	16	11	.224	.345	.347	692	84	-2	0	0	0	.977	3	C-27	0.2
1949	NY-N	1	3	1	2	0	0	0	0	0	0	.667	.667	.667	1333	259	1	0			1.000	0	/C-1	0.1
Total	6	188	403	35	80	18	2	3	43	57	37	.199	.302	.275	578	57	-22	2	0		.985	16	C-142/O-1(0-0-1)	-0.0
■ LOU FRAZIER	Frazier, Arthur Louis b: 1/26/65, St.Louis, Mo. BB/TR, 6'2", 175 lbs. Deb: 4/8/93 Career OF: (148-LF 35-CF 7-RF)																							
1993	Mon-N	112	189	27	54	7	1	1	16	16	24	.286	.341	.349	691	82	-4	17	2	3	.986	-8	O-60(52-7-2)/1-8,2-1	-1.0
1994	Mon-N	76	140	25	38	3	1	0	14	18	23	.271	.358	.307	666	75	-4	20	4	3	1.000	-2	O-36(31-5-0)/2-6,1-1	-0.4
1995	Mon-N	35	63	6	12	2	0	0	3	8	12	.190	.301	.222	524	39	-5	4	0	1	.973	-3	O-25(10-11-5)/2-1	-0.8
	Tex-A	49	99	19	21	2	0	0	8	7	20	.212	.278	.232	510	34	-9	9	1	2	.973	-6	O-47(43-6-0)/D-2	-1.3
1996	Tex-A	30	50	5	13	2	1	0	5	8	10	.260	.373	.340	713	78	-1	4	2	0	.971	1	O-15(12-3-0),D-13/2-1	-0.1
1998	Chi-A	7	7	0	0	0	0	0	0	2	6	.000	.222	.000	222	-36	-1	4	0	1	1.000	-1	/O-3(0-3-0)	-0.1
Total	5	309	548	82	138	16	3	1	46	59	95	.252	.331	.297	629	65	-26	58	9	10	.982	-17	O-186L/D-15,2-9,1-9	-3.7
■ JOE FRAZIER	Frazier, Joseph Filmore b: 10/6/22, Liberty, N.C. BL/TR, 6', 180 lbs. Deb: 8/31/47 M																							
1947	Cle-A	9	14	1	1	1	0	0	0	1	1	.071	.133	.143	276	-24	-2	0	0	0	.857	-1	/O-5(0-0-5)	-0.4
1954	StL-N	81	88	8	26	5	2	3	18	13	17	.295	.392	.500	892	129	4	0	0	0	.938	-1	O-11(2-0-8)/1-1	0.3
1955	StL-N	58	70	12	14	1	0	4	9	6	12	.200	.273	.386	658	72	-3	0	0	0	1.000	-3	O-14(1-0-13)	-0.6
1956	StL-N	14	19	1	4	2	0	1	4	3	3	.211	.318	.474	792	109	0	0	1	-0	.800	-1	/O-3(0-0-3)	-0.1
	Cin-N	10	17	2	4	0	0	1	2	1	7	.235	.278	.412	690	77	-1	0	0	0	.000	-2	/O-4(4-0-0)	-0.2
	Yr	24	36	3	8	2	0	2	6	4	10	.222	.300	.444	744	94	-0	0	1	-0	.800	-2	/O-7(4-0-3)	-0.3
	Bal-A	45	74	7	19	6	0	1	12	11	6	.257	.360	.378	739	103	1	0	0	0	1.000	-0	O-19(0-0-19)	0.0
Total	4	217	282	31	68	15	2	10	45	35	46	.241	.331	.415	746	97	-1	0	1	-0	.961	-7	/O-56(7-0-48),1-1	-1.0
■ JOHNNY FREDERICK	Frederick, John Henry b: 1/26/02, Denver, Colo. d: 6/18/77, Tigard, Ore. BL/TL, 5'11", 165 lbs. Deb: 4/18/29																							
1929	Bro-N	148	628	127	206	**52**	6	24	75	39	34	.328	.372	.545	917	126	23	6			.975	8	*O-143(0-143-0)	2.2
1930	Bro-N	142	616	120	206	44	11	17	76	46	34	.334	.383	.524	908	118	17	1			.990	12	*O-142(0-142-0)	2.0
1931	Bro-N	146	611	81	165	34	8	17	71	31	46	.270	.312	.435	747	99	-3	2			.965	2	*O-145(0-145-0)	-0.4
1932	Bro-N	118	384	54	115	28	2	16	56	25	35	.299	.349	.508	856	130	15	1			.976	-3	O-88(1-47-39)	0.8
1933	Bro-N	147	556	65	171	22	7	7	64	36	14	.308	.355	.410	765	123	16	9			.971	-7	*O-138(10-26-102)	0.2
1934	Bro-N	104	307	51	91	20	1	4	35	33	13	.296	.370	.407	777	114	7	4			.957	-3	O-77(22-0-55)/1-1	0.0
Total	6	805	3102	498	954	200	35	85	377	210	176	.308	.357	.477	833	118	75	23			.974	9	O-733(33-503-196)/1-1	4.8
■ ED FREED	Freed, Edwin Charles b: 8/22/19, Centre Valley, Pa. BR/TR, 5'6", 165 lbs. Deb: 9/11/42																							
1942	Phi-N	13	33	3	10	3	1	0	1	4	3	.303	.378	.455	833	151	2	1			1.000	-1	O-11(3-7-1)	0.1
■ ROGER FREED	Freed, Roger Vernon b: 6/2/46, Los Angeles, Cal. d: 1/9/96, Chino, Cal. BR/TR, 6', 190 lbs. Deb: 9/18/70 Career OF: (11-LF 0-CF 156-RF)																							
1970	Bal-A	4	13	0	2	0	0	0	1	3	4	.154	.313	.154	466	32	-1	0	0	0	1.000	0	/1-3,O-1(0-0-1)	-0.1
1971	Phi-N	118	348	23	77	12	1	6	37	44	86	.221	.314	.313	627	78	-9	0	3	-1	.989	-5	*O-106(7-0-99)/C-1	-2.2
1972	Phi-N	73	129	10	29	4	0	6	18	23	39	.225	.346	.395	742	108	2	0	1	-0	.971	-2	O-46(1-0-45)	-0.2
1974	Cin-N	6	6	1	2	0	0	1	3	1	1	.333	.429	.833	1262	251	1	0	0	0	1.000	-0	/1-1	0.1
1976	Mon-N	8	15	0	3	1	0	0	1	0	3	.200	.200	.267	467	30	-1	0	0	0	1.000	-0	/1-3,O-1(0-0-1),	-0.2
1977	StL-N	49	83	10	33	2	1	5	21	11	9	.398	.468	.627	1095	194	11	0	0	0	1.000	-2	1-18/O-6(0-0-7)	0.8
1978	StL-N	52	92	3	22	6	0	2	20	8	17	.239	.300	.370	670	87	-2	1	0	0	.992	-1	1-15/O-6(3-0-3)	-0.4
1979	StL-N	34	31	2	8	2	0	2	8	5	7	.258	.361	.516	877	135	1	0	0	0	.889	0	/1-1	0.2
Total	8	344	717	49	176	27	2	22	109	95	166	.245	.337	.381	718	101	2	1	4	-1	.982	-10	O-166R/1-41,C-1	-2.0
■ BILL FREEHAN	Freehan, William Ashley b: 11/29/41, Detroit, Mich. BR/TR, 6'2", 205 lbs. Deb: 9/26/61																							
1961	Det-A	4	10	1	4	0	0	0	4	1	0	.400	.455	.400	855	127	0	0	0	0	1.000	1	/C-3	0.2
1963	Det-A	100	300	37	73	12	2	9	36	39	56	.243	.334	.387	721	98	-0	2	0	0	.995	-1	C-73,1-19	0.2
1964	Det-A☆	144	520	69	156	14	8	18	80	36	68	.300	.355	.462	816	123	16	5	1	1	.993	-2	*C-141/1-1	2.3
1965	Det-A★	130	431	45	101	15	0	10	43	39	63	.234	.308	.339	647	83	-9	4	2	0	.996	-1	*C-129	-0.5
1966	Det-A★	136	492	47	115	22	0	12	46	40	72	.234	.295	.352	647	83	-11	5	2	0	**.996**	1	*C-132/1-5	-0.4
1967	Det-A★	155	517	66	146	23	1	20	74	73	71	.282	.392	.447	839	143	31	1	2	-0	.992	-9	*C-147,1-11	3.1
1968	*Det-A★	155	540	73	142	24	2	25	84	65	64	.263	.367	.454	821	143	30	0	1	-0	.994	6	*C-138,1-21/O-1R	4.6
1969	Det-A★	143	489	61	128	16	3	16	49	53	55	.262	.344	.405	749	104	3	1	2	-0	.992	4	*C-120,1-20	1.1
1970	Det-A★	117	395	44	95	17	3	16	52	52	48	.241	.335	.420	755	106	3	0	3	-1	**.997**	-16	*C-114	-0.8
1971	Det-A★	148	516	57	143	26	4	21	71	54	48	.277	.356	.465	821	126	17	2	7	-2	.996	-12	*C-144/O-1(1-0-0)	1.1
1972	*Det-A★	111	374	51	98	18	2	10	56	48	51	.262	.355	.401	756	121	11	0	1	-0	.989	0	*C-105/1-1	1.7
1973	Det-A☆	110	380	33	89	10	1	6	29	40	30	.234	.325	.313	638	75	-11	0	0	0	**.995**	9	C-98/1-7,D-3	0.1
1974	Det-A	130	445	58	132	17	5	18	60	42	44	.297	.364	.479	842	136	20	2	0	0	.994	-8	1-65,C-63/D-1	1.0
1975	Det-A☆	120	427	42	105	17	3	14	47	32	56	.246	.308	.398	706	94	-4	2	0	0	.991	-8	*C-113/1-5	-0.7
1976	Det-A	71	237	22	64	10	1	5	27	12	27	.270	.308	.384	692	98	-1	0	0	0	.983	-2	C-61/1-2,D-3	0.0
Total	15	1774	6073	706	1591	241	35	200	758	626	753	.262	.342	.412	754	111	95	24	21	-2	.993	-38	*C-1581,1-157/D-7,O	13.0
■ JERRY FREEMAN	Freeman, Frank Ellsworth "Buck" b: 12/26/1879, Placerville, Cal. d: 9/30/52, Los Angeles, Cal. BL/TR, 6'2", 220 lbs. Deb: 4/14/08																							
1908	Was-A	154	531	45	134	15	5	1	45	36		.252	.304	.305	609	107	4	6			.975	-13	*1-154	-1.4
1909	Was-A	19	48	2	8	0	1	0	3	4		.167	.245	.208	454	46	-3	3			.956	-2	1-14/O-1(1-0-0)	-0.6
Total	2	173	579	47	142	15	6	1	48	40		.245	.299	.297	596	101	1	9			.974	-15	1-168/O-1(1-0-0)	-2.0
■ JOHN FREEMAN	Freeman, John Edward b: 1/24/01, Boston, Mass. d: 4/14/58, Washington, D.C. BR/TR, 5'8", 160 lbs. Deb: 6/17/27																							
1927	Bos-A	4	2	0	0	0	0	0	0	0	0	.000	.000	.000	0	-99	-1	0	0	0	.000	-2	/O-3(1-2-0)	-0.2
■ BUCK FREEMAN	Freeman, John Frank b: 10/30/1871, Catasauqua, Pa. d: 6/25/49, Wilkes-Barre, Pa. BL/TL, 5'9", 169 lbs. Deb: 6/27/1891 Career OF: (16-LF 7-CF 814-RF)																							
1891	Was-a	5	18	1	4	1	0	0	1	2	2	.222	.300	.278	578	69	-1	0			.769	-0	/P-5	0.0
1898	Was-N	29	107	19	39	2	3	3	21	7		.364	.424	.523	947	171	10	2			.978	1	O-29(0-0-29)	0.8
1899	Was-N	155	588	107	187	19	25	**25**	122	23		.318	.362	.563	925	154	38	21			.944	-12	*O-155(0-0-155)/P-2	1.6
1900	Bos-N	117	418	58	126	19	13	6	65	25		.301	.355	.452	808	109	3	10			.950	-11	O-91(16-3-72),1-19	-1.2
1901	Bos-A	129	490	88	166	23	15	12	114	44		.339	.400	.520	920	157	37	17			.974	-5	*1-128/2-1,O-1(0-0-1)	2.7

YEAR	TM/L	G	AB	R	H	2B	3B	HR	RBI	BB	SO	AVG	OBP	SLG	OPS	OPS+	BR+	SB	CS	SBR	FA	FR	G/POS	TPR
1902	Bos-A	138	564	75	174	38	19	11	**121**	32		.309	.352	.502	854	131	21	17			.944	-1	*O-138(0-0-138)	1.3
1903	*Bos-A	141	567	74	163	39	20	**13**	**104**	30		.287	.328	.496	823	137	23	5			.933	-6	*O-141(0-0-141)	1.1
1904	Bos-A	157	597	64	167	20	**19**	7	84	32		.280	.329	.412	741	126	17	7			.954	-6	*O-157(0-0-157)	0.5
1905	Bos-A	130	455	59	109	20	8	3	49	46		.240	.316	.338	655	106	4	8			.973	-14	1-66,O-57(0-1-56)/3-2	-1.5
1906	Bos-A	121	392	42	98	18	9	1	30	28		.250	.302	.349	651	104	1	5			.989	1	O-65(0-3-62),1-43/3-4	-0.1
1907	Bos-A	4	12	1	2	0	0	1	2	3		.167	.333	.417	750	140	1	0			1.000	0	/O-3(0-0-3)	0.0
Total	11	1126	4208	588	1235	199	131	82	713	272	2	.293	.346	.462	808	131	153	92			.950	-53	O-837R,1-256/P-7,32	5.2
■ **LA VEL FREEMAN**	Freeman, La Vel Maurice b: 2/18/63, Oakland, Cal. BL/TL, 5'9", 170 lbs. Deb: 4/7/89																							
1989	Mil-A	2	3	1	0	0	0	0	0	0	2	.000	.000	.000	0	-99	-1	0	0	0	.000	0	/D-2	-0.1
■ **GENE FREESE**	Freese, Eugene Lewis “Augie” b: 1/8/34, Wheeling, W.Va. BR/TR, 5'11", 175 lbs. Deb: 4/13/55 F																							
1955	Pit-N	134	455	69	115	21	8	14	44	34	57	.253	.310	.426	737	94	-5	5	1	1	.943	-2	3-65,2-57	-0.2
1956	Pit-N	65	207	17	43	9	0	3	14	16	45	.208	.274	.295	569	54	-13	2	1	0	.963	-7	3-47,2-26	-2.0
1957	Pit-N	114	346	44	98	18	2	6	31	17	42	.283	.321	.399	719	95	-3	9	4	1	.924	-3	3-74,2-10,O-10L	-0.5
1958	Pit-N	17	18	1	3	0	0	1	2	1	2	.167	.211	.333	544	42	-2	0	0	0	.800	1	/3-1	-0.1
	StL-N	62	191	28	49	11	1	6	16	10	32	.257	.294	.419	712	83	-5	1	1	-0	.924	-25	S-28,2-14/3-3	-2.7
	Yr	79	209	29	52	11	1	7	18	11	34	.249	.286	.411	698	80	-7	1	1	-0	.924	-24	S-28,2-14/3-4	-2.8
1959	Phi-N	132	400	60	107	14	5	23	70	43	61	.268	.346	.500	846	120	11	8	4	0	.916	-24	*3-109/2-6	-1.3
1960	Chi-A	127	455	60	124	32	6	17	79	29	65	.273	.318	.481	799	114	7	10	6	0	.946	0	*3-122	0.6
1961	*Cin-N	152	575	78	159	27	2	26	87	27	78	.277	.309	.466	775	101	-1	8	2	1	.950	-17	*3-151/2-1	-1.8
1962	Cin-N	18	42	2	6	1	0	0	1	6	8	.143	.250	.167	417	14	-5	0	0	0	1.000	-2	3-10	-0.7
1963	Cin-N	66	217	20	53	9	1	6	26	17	42	.244	.305	.378	683	93	-2	4	2	0	.930	-6	3-62/O-1(0-0-1)	-0.9
1964	Pit-N	99	289	33	65	13	2	9	40	19	45	.225	.273	.377	650	81	-8	1	2	-0	.920	-6	3-72	-1.5
1965	Pit-N	43	80	6	21	4	0	0	8	6	18	.262	.330	.313	642	82	-2	0	2	-1	.951	-1	3-19	-0.3
	Chi-A	17	32	2	9	0	1	1	4	5	9	.281	.378	.438	816	140	2	0	0	0	.824	-3	/3-8	-0.1
1966	Chi-A	48	106	8	22	2	0	3	10	8	20	.208	.270	.311	581	71	-4	2	1	0	.894	3	3-34	-0.1
	Hou-N	21	33	1	3	0	0	0	0	5	11	.091	.211	.091	301	-13	-5	1	0	0	.800	-0	/3-4,2-3,O-1(1-0-0)	-0.5
Total	12	1115	3446	429	877	161	28	115	432	243	535	.254	.307	.418	725	94	-36	51	26	2	.934	-90	3-781,2-117/S-28,O	-12.1
■ **GEORGE FREESE**	Freese, George Walter “Bud” b: 9/12/26, Wheeling, W.Va. BR/TR, 6', 190 lbs. Deb: 4/29/53 FC																							
1953	Det-A	1	1	0	0	0	0	0	0	0	0	.000	.000	.000	0	-99	-0	0	0	0	.000	0	H	0.0
1955	Pit-N	51	179	17	46	8	2	3	22	17	18	.257	.328	.374	703	87	-3	1	1	-0	.936	-8	3-50	-1.2
1961	Chi-N	9	7	0	2	0	0	0	1	1	4	.286	.375	.286	661	78	-0	0	0	0	.000	0	H	0.0
Total	3	61	187	17	48	8	2	3	23	18	22	.257	.329	.369	697	86	-4	1	1	-0	.936	-8	/3-50	-1.2
■ **JIM FREGOSI**	Fregosi, James Louis b: 4/4/42, San Francisco, Cal. BR/TR, 6'1", 190 lbs. Deb: 9/14/61 M Career OF: (8-LF 0-CF 0-RF)																							
1961	LA-A	11	27	7	6	0	0	0	3	1	4	.222	.250	.222	472	25	-3	0	0	0	.944	-0	S-11	-0.2
1962	LA-A	58	175	15	51	3	4	3	23	18	27	.291	.358	.406	763	108	2	2	1	0	.943	4	S-52	1.0
1963	LA-A	154	592	83	170	29	12	9	50	36	104	.287	.328	.422	750	115	10	2	2	-0	.964	2	*S-151	2.6
1964	LA-A★	147	505	86	140	22	9	18	72	72	87	.277	.372	.463	835	145	32	8	3	1	.966	1	*S-137	**4.6**
1965	Cal-A	161	602	66	167	19	7	15	64	54	107	.277	.341	.407	748	114	11	13	5	1	.968	6	*S-160	3.3
1966	Cal-A★	162	611	78	154	32	7	13	67	67	89	.252	.328	.391	719	109	7	17	8	1	.959	15	*S-162/1-1	3.9
1967	Cal-A★	151	590	75	171	23	6	9	56	49	77	.290	.349	.395	744	124	18	9	6	-0	.965	-7	*S-151	2.6
1968	Cal-A★	159	614	77	150	21	**13**	9	49	60	101	.244	.317	.365	681	110	7	9	4	1	.962	-14	*S-159	0.9
1969	Cal-A★	161	580	78	151	22	6	12	47	93	86	.260	.364	.381	745	114	13	9	2	1	.972	-16	*S-160	1.9
1970	Cal-A★	158	601	95	167	33	5	22	82	69	92	.278	.355	.459	814	127	22	0	2	-1	.973	4	*S-150/1-6	4.3
1971	Cal-A	107	347	31	81	15	1	5	33	39	61	.233	.320	.326	645	90	-4	2	1	0	.938	-10	S-74,1-18/O-7(7-0-0)	-0.8
1972	NY-N	101	340	31	79	15	4	5	32	38	71	.232	.311	.344	655	88	-5	0	1	-0	.935	-7	3-85/S-6,1-3	-1.3
1973	NY-N	45	124	7	29	4	1	0	11	20	25	.234	.340	.282	623	75	-3	1	2	-0	.906	-6	S-17,3-17/1-3,O-1L	-0.8
	Tex-A	45	157	25	42	6	2	6	16	12	31	.268	.324	.446	769	120	3	0	1	-0	.937	-9	3-34,1-10/S-6	-0.6
1974	Tex-A	78	230	31	60	5	0	12	34	22	41	.261	.325	.439	765	121	6	0	1	-0	1.000	-1	1-47,3-32	0.1
1975	Tex-A	77	191	25	50	5	0	7	33	20	39	.262	.335	.398	733	107	2	0	1	-0	.985	2	1-54,D-13/3-4	0.0
1976	Tex-A	58	133	17	31	7	0	2	12	23	33	.233	.346	.331	677	97	0	2	0	0	.995	-0	1-26,D-18/3-5	-0.2
1977	Tex-A	13	28	4	7	1	0	1	5	3	4	.250	.323	.393	715	93	-0	0	0	0	1.000	1	/1-5,D-3	0.0
	Pit-N	36	56	10	16	1	1	3	16	13	10	.286	.420	.500	920	142	4	2	0	0	.981	-1	1-15/3-1	0.2
1978	Pit-N	20	20	3	4	1	0	0	1	6	8	.200	.385	.250	635	77	-0	0	0	0	.667	-1	/3-5,1-2,2-1	-0.2
Total	18	1902	6523	844	1726	264	78	151	706	715	1097	.265	.340	.398	739	114	120	76	40	3	.963	-40	*S-1396,1-190,3/DO2	21.3
■ **VERN FREIBURGER**	Freiburger, Vern Donald b: 12/19/23, Detroit, Mich. d: 2/27/90, Palm Springs, Cal. BR/TL, 6'1", 170 lbs. Deb: 9/6/41																							
1941	Cle-A	2	8	0	1	0	0	0	1	0	2	.125	.125	.125	250	-35	-2	0	0	0	.947	1	/1-2	-0.1
■ **HOWARD FREIGAU**	Freigau, Howard Earl “Ty” b: 8/1/02, Dayton, Ohio d: 7/18/32, Chattanooga, Tenn BR/TR, 5'10.5", 160 lbs. Deb: 9/13/22 Career OF: (1-LF 1-CF 0-RF)																							
1922	StL-N	3	1	0	0	0	0	0	0	0	0	.000	.000	.000	0	-99	-0	0	0	0	1.000	1	/S-2,3-1	0.1
1923	StL-N	113	358	30	94	18	1	1	35	25	36	.263	.314	.327	641	71	-15	5	4	-0	.929	1	S-87,2-16/1-9,3O	-0.5
1924	StL-N	98	376	35	101	17	6	2	39	19	24	.269	.306	.362	667	80	-11	10	3	1	.958	3	3-98/S-2	-0.1
1925	StL-N	9	26	2	4	0	0	0	0	2	1	.154	.214	.154	368	-4	-4	0	0	0	.936	3	/S-7,2-1	0.0
	Chi-N	117	476	77	146	22	10	8	71	30	31	.307	.349	.445	794	100	-1	10	6	0	.913	-5	3-96,S-17/1-7	0.2
	Yr	126	502	79	150	22	10	8	71	32	32	.299	.342	.430	772	94	-5	10	6	0	.913	-1	3-96,S-24/1-7,2-1	0.2
1926	Chi-N	140	508	51	137	27	7	3	51	43	42	.270	.327	.368	695	86	-10	6			**.966**	-3	*3-135/S-2,O-1(0-1-0)	-0.5
1927	Chi-N	30	86	12	20	5	0	0	10	9	10	.233	.313	.291	603	62	-4	0			.883	1	3-30	-0.2
1928	Bro-N	17	34	6	7	2	0	0	3	1	3	.206	.229	.265	493	29	-4	0			.810	-4	3-10/S-1	-0.7
	Bos-N	52	109	11	28	8	1	1	17	9	14	.257	.319	.376	695	86	-3	1			.938	-10	S-14,2-11	-1.0
	Yr	69	143	17	35	10	1	1	20	10	17	.245	.299	.350	648	72	-6	1			.938	-13	S-15,2-11,3-10	-1.7
Total	7	579	1974	224	537	99	25	15	226	138	161	.272	.322	.370	692	82	-52	32	13		.940	-12	3-371,S-132/2-28,1O	-2.7
■ **CHARLIE FRENCH**	French, Charles Calvin b: 10/12/1883, Indianapolis, Ind. d: 3/30/62, Indianapolis, Ind. BL/TR, 5'6", 140 lbs. Deb: 5/23/09 Career OF: (0-LF 0-CF 16-RF)																							
1909	Bos-A	51	167	15	42	3	1	0	13	15		.251	.324	.281	606	90	-1	8			.921	-8	2-28,S-23	-1.0
1910	Bos-A	9	40	4	8	1	0	0	3	1		.200	.220	.225	445	38	-3	0			.889	1	/2-8	-0.3
	Chi-A	45	170	17	28	1	1	0	4	10		.165	.224	.182	406	29	-14	5			.930	-14	2-28,O-16(0-0-16)	-3.3
	Yr	54	210	21	36	2	1	0	7	11		.171	.223	.190	414	31	-17	5			.919	-14	2-36,O-16(0-0-16)	-3.6
Total	2	105	377	36	78	5	2	0	20	26		.207	.269	.231	500	58	-18	13			.920	-22	/2-64,S-23,O-16R	-4.6
■ **PAT FRENCH**	French, Frank Alexander b: 9/22/1893, Dover, N.H. d: 7/13/69, Bath, Maine BR/TR, 6'1", 180 lbs. Deb: 7/2/17																							
1917	Phi-A	3	2	0	0	0	0	0	0	0	0	.000	.000	.000	0	-99	-0	0			1.000	-0	/O-1(0-0-1)	-0.1
■ **RAY FRENCH**	French, Raymond Edward b: 1/9/1895, Alameda, Cal. d: 4/3/78, Alameda, Cal. BR/TR, 5'9.5", 158 lbs. Deb: 9/17/20																							
1920	NY-A	2	2	2	0	0	0	0	1	0	1	.000	.000	.000	0	-97	-1	0	0	0	.500	-0	/S-1	-0.1
1923	Bro-N	43	73	14	16	2	1	0	7	4	7	.219	.269	.274	543	45	-6	0	0	0	.874	4	S-30	0.1
1924	Chi-A	37	112	13	20	4	0	0	11	10	13	.179	.246	.214	460	20	-14	3	1	0	.927	-3	S-28/2-3	-1.2
Total	3	82	187	29	36	6	1	0	19	14	21	.193	.252	.235	488	28	-20	3	1	0	.897	1	/S-59,2-3	-1.2
■ **JIM FRENCH**	French, Richard James b: 8/13/41, Warren, Ohio BL/TR, 5'7", 182 lbs. Deb: 9/12/65																							
1965	Was-A	13	37	4	11	0	0	1	7	9	5	.297	.435	.378	813	135	2	1	0	0	.974	-0	C-13	0.3
1966	Was-A	10	24	0	5	1	0	0	3	4	5	.208	.321	.250	571	67	-1	0	1	-0	.979	-1	C-10	-0.2
1967	Was-A	6	16	0	1	0	0	0	1	3	4	.063	.211	.063	273	-16	-2	0	0	0	.968	-1	/C-6	-0.3
1968	Was-A	59	165	9	32	5	0	1	10	19	19	.194	.281	.242	524	62	-7	1	2	-0	.984	2	C-53	-0.4
1969	Was-A	63	158	14	29	6	3	2	13	41	15	.184	.352	.297	649	88	-1	1	0	0	.989	9	C-63	1.2
1970	Was-A	69	166	20	35	3	1	1	13	38	23	.211	.358	.259	617	76	-3	0	1	-0	.973	-6	C-62/O-1(1-0-0)	-0.8
1971	Was-A	14	41	6	6	2	0	0	4	7	7	.146	.271	.195	466	36	-3	0	2	-1	.985	-1	C-14	-0.5
Total	7	234	607	53	119	17	4	5	51	121	78	.196	.331	.262	593	74	-16	3	6	-1	.982	2	C-221/O-1(1-0-0)	-0.7

YEAR	TM/L	G	AB	R	H	2B	3B	HR	RBI	BB	SO	AVG	OBP	SLG	OPS	OPS+	BR+	SB	CS	SBR	FA	FR	G/POS	TPR
■ WALTER FRENCH	French, Walter Edward "Piggy" or "Fitz" b: 7/12/1899, Moorestown, N.J. d: 5/13/84, Mountain Home, Ark BL/TR, 5'7.5", 155 lbs. Deb: 9/15/23																							
1923	Phi-A	16	39	7	9	3	0	0	2	5	7	.231	.318	.308	626	64	-2	0	1	-0	1.000	-1	O-10(0-10-0)	-0.4
1925	Phi-A	67	100	20	37	9	0	0	14	1	9	.370	.376	.460	836	104	0	1	1	-0	.971	0	O-19(3-0-16)	-0.1
1926	Phi-A	112	397	51	121	18	7	1	36	18	24	.305	.340	.393	733	86	-9	2	3	-1	.971	3	O-99(0-1-98)	-1.4
1927	Phi-A	109	326	48	99	10	5	0	41	16	14	.304	.338	.365	703	78	-11	9	1	2	.956	0	O-94(8-5-81)	-1.4
1928	Phi-A	48	74	9	19	4	0	0	7	2	5	.257	.286	.311	597	55	-5	1	1	-0	1.000	-1	O-19(8-0-11)	-0.7
1929	*Phi-A	45	45	7	12	1	0	1	9	2	3	.267	.298	.356	653	65	-2	0	0	0	1.000	-3	O-10(6-1-3)	-0.5
Total	6	397	981	142	297	45	12	2	109	44	62	.303	.336	.379	715	81	-28	13	7	0	.968	-2	O-251(25-17-209)	-4.5
■ BILL FRENCH	French, William b: Baltimore, Md. Deb: 4/14/1873																							
1873	Mar-n	5	18	3	4	0	0	0	1	0	0	.222	.222	.222	444	42	-1	0	0	0	.905	-0	/1-2,O-2R,P-1,3-1	0.0
■ LONNY FREY	Frey, Linus Reinhard "Junior" b: 8/23/10, St.Louis, Mo. BL/TR (BB 1933-38), 5'10", 160 lbs. Deb: 8/29/33 Career OF: (7-LF 15-CF 12-RF)																							
1933	Bro-N	34	135	25	43	5	3	0	12	13	13	.319	.378	.400	778	128	5	4			.896	-14	S-34	-0.6
1934	Bro-N	125	490	77	139	24	5	8	57	52	54	.284	.358	.402	760	109	7	11			.945	13	*S-109,3-13	2.7
1935	Bro-N	131	515	88	135	35	11	11	77	66	68	.262	.352	.437	788	113	10	6			.937	-4	*S-127/2-4	1.5
1936	Bro-N	148	524	63	146	29	4	4	60	71	56	.279	.369	.372	741	99	2	7			.918	-32	*S-117,2-30/O-1C	-2.0
1937	Chi-N	78	198	33	55	9	3	1	22	33	15	.278	.381	.369	750	100	1	6			.938	-19	S-30,2-13/3-9,O-5L	-1.4
1938	Cin-N	124	501	76	133	26	6	4	36	49	50	.265	.331	.365	696	94	-4	4			.964	-8	*2-121/S-3	-0.4
1939	*Cin-N★	125	484	95	141	27	9	11	55	72	46	.291	.387	.452	840	124	18	5			.976	15	*2-124	4.1
1940	*Cin-N	150	563	102	150	23	6	8	54	80	48	.266	.361	.371	732	101	3	**22**			.977	18	*2-150	3.1
1941	Cin-N★	146	543	78	138	29	5	6	59	72	37	.254	.345	.359	704	98	-0	16			**.970**	-2	*2-145	0.7
1942	Cin-N	141	523	66	139	23	6	2	39	87	38	.266	.373	.344	717	111	11	9			.977	5	*2-140	2.6
1943	Cin-N★	144	586	78	154	20	8	2	43	76	56	.263	.347	.334	682	99	1	7			**.985**	12	*2-144	2.2
1946	Cin-N	111	333	46	82	10	3	3	24	63	31	.246	.368	.321	689	100	3	5			.963	-3	2-65,O-28(3-13-12)	0.2
1947	Chi-N	24	43	4	9	0	0	0	3	4	6	.209	.277	.209	486	32	-4	0			1.000	-2	/2-9	-0.6
	*NY-A	24	28	10	5	2	0	0	2	10	1	.179	.410	.250	660	87	0	3	0	1	.923	3	/2-8	0.4
1948	NY-A	1	0	1	0	0	0	0	0	0	0	—	—	—	—	—	0	0	0	0	.000	0	R	0.0
	NY-N	29	51	6	13	1	0	1	6	4	6	.255	.309	.333	642	73	-2	0			.920	-2	2-13	-0.3
Total	14	1535	5517	848	1482	263	69	61	549	752	525	.269	.359	.374	734	104	51	105	0		.973	-18	2-966,S-420/O-34C,3	12.2
■ HANLEY FRIAS	Frias, Hanley (Acevedo) b: 12/5/73, Villa Altagracia, D.R. BB/TR, 6', 160 lbs. Deb: 6/21/97																							
1997	Tex-A	14	26	4	5	1	0	0	1	1	4	.192	.222	.231	453	18	-3	0	0	0	1.000	-4	S-12/2-1	-0.6
1998	Ari-N	15	23	4	3	0	1	1	2	0	5	.130	.130	.348	478	20	-3	0	0	0	1.000	2	/2-3,3-2,S-2	-0.1
1999	*Ari-N	69	150	27	41	3	2	1	16	29	18	.273	.391	.340	731	87	-2	4	3	-0	.965	-10	S-53/2-8	-0.8
2000	Ari-N	75	112	18	23	5	0	2	6	17	18	.205	.310	.304	614	55	-8	2	2	-0	.938	-1	S-21,2-15/3-7	-0.7
Total	4	173	311	53	72	9	3	4	25	47	45	.232	.332	.318	651	66	-15	6	5	-0	.962	-12	/S-88,2-27,3-9	-2.2
■ PEPE FRIAS	Frias, Jesus Maria (Andujar) b: 7/14/48, San Pedro De Macoris, D.R. BR/TR (BB 1976 (part), 1977-7), 5'10", 159 lbs. Deb: 4/6/73																							
1973	Mon-N	100	225	19	52	10	1	0	22	10	24	.231	.267	.284	551	51	-15	1	3	-1	.950	17	S-46,2-44/3-6,O-1R	0.7
1974	Mon-N	75	112	12	24	4	1	0	7	7	10	.214	.261	.268	528	45	-8	1	0	0	.962	17	S-30,3-27,2-15,/O-3R	1.1
1975	Mon-N	51	64	4	8	2	0	0	4	3	13	.125	.164	.156	320	-10	-10	0	1	-0	.938	14	S-29,3-11/2-7	0.6
1976	Mon-N	76	113	7	28	5	0	0	8	4	14	.248	.274	.292	566	58	-6	1	1	-0	.957	14	2-35,S-35/3-4,O-1C	1.1
1977	Mon-N	53	70	10	18	1	0	0	5	0	10	.257	.257	.271	529	43	-6	1	0	0	.978	8	2-16,S-14/3-1	0.3
1978	Mon-N	73	15	5	4	2	1	0	5	0	3	.267	.267	.533	800	120	0	0	0	0	1.000	13	2-61/S-3	1.4
1979	Atl-N	140	475	41	123	18	4	1	44	20	36	.259	.292	.320	612	62	-24	3	2	-0	.954	0	*S-137	-1.0
1980	Tex-A	116	227	27	55	5	1	0	10	4	23	.242	.259	.273	532	47	-16	5	1	1	.947	-16	*S-106/3-7,2-2	-2.5
	LA-N	14	9	1	2	1	0	0	0	0	0	.222	.222	.333	556	54	-1	0	0	0	.933	2	S-11	0.2
1981	LA-N	25	36	6	9	1	0	0	3	1	3	.250	.289	.278	567	64	-2	0	0	0	.906	-5	S-15/2-6,3-1	-0.6
Total	9	723	1346	132	323	49	8	1	108	49	136	.240	.269	.290	560	52	-87	12	8	-0	.951	63	S-426,2-186/3-57,O	1.3
■ BERNIE FRIBERG	Friberg, Bernard Albert (b: Gustaf Bernhard Friberg) b: 8/18/1899, Manchester, N.H. d: 12/8/58, Lynn, Mass. BR/TR, 5'11", 178 lbs. Deb: 8/20/19 Career OF: (84-LF 52-CF 62-RF)																							
1919	Chi-N	8	20	0	4	1	0	0	1	0	2	.200	.200	.250	450	35	-2	0			1.000	-1	/O-7(2-5-0)	-0.3
1920	Chi-N	50	114	11	24	5	1	0	7	6	20	.211	.250	.272	522	49	-8	2	2	-0	.963	1	2-24,O-24(15-8-3)	-0.8
1922	Chi-N	97	296	51	92	8	2	0	23	37	37	.311	.391	.351	742	91	-2	8	10	-2	.972	-2	O-74R/1-6,3-5,2-3	-1.0
1923	Chi-N	146	547	91	174	27	11	12	88	45	49	.318	.372	.473	846	122	16	13	19	-4	.955	7	*3-146	2.8
1924	Chi-N	142	495	67	138	19	3	5	82	66	53	.279	.369	.360	729	95	-1	19	27	-5	.954	4	*3-142	0.6
1925	Chi-N	44	152	12	39	5	3	1	16	14	22	.257	.327	.349	676	72	-6	0	1	-0	.889	-5	3-26,O-12L/1-6,S-2	-1.1
	Phi-N	91	304	41	82	12	1	5	22	39	35	.270	.353	.365	718	77	-10	1	1	-0	.965	4	2-77,3-14/P-1,C-1	-0.3
	Yr	135	456	53	121	17	4	6	38	53	57	.265	.344	.360	704	75	-16	1	2	-0	.965	-2	2-77,3-40,O/1SPC	-1.4
1926	Phi-N	144	478	38	128	21	3	1	51	57	77	.268	.346	.331	676	79	-13	2			.976	22	*2-144	1.3
1927	Phi-N	111	335	31	78	8	2	1	28	41	49	.233	.322	.278	600	61	-17	3			.959	25	*3-103/2-5	1.4
1928	Phi-N	52	94	11	19	3	0	1	7	12	16	.202	.292	.266	558	45	-7	0			.908	1	S-31/3-5,2-3,O-3L,1	-0.4
1929	Phi-N	128	455	74	137	21	10	7	55	49	54	.301	.370	.437	808	93	-5	1			.923	-26	S-73,O-40C/2-8,1-2	-2.3
1930	Phi-N	105	331	62	113	21	1	4	42	47	35	.341	.425	.447	872	104	4	1			.953	-4	2-44,O-35L,S-12,/3	0.0
1931	Phi-N	103	353	33	92	19	5	1	26	33	25	.261	.324	.351	675	75	-12	1			.955	6	2-64,3-25/1-5,S-3	-0.1
1932	Phi-N	61	154	17	37	8	2	0	14	19	23	.240	.324	.318	642	66	-7	0			.957	-1	2-56	-0.5
1933	Bos-A	17	41	5	13	3	0	0	9	6	1	.317	.404	.390	794	112	1	0	0	0	.950	1	/2-6,3-5,S-2	0.3
Total	14	1299	4169	544	1170	181	44	38	471	471	498	.281	.356	.373	728	87	-67	51	60		.953	32	3-479,2-434,OS/1CP	-0.4
■ JIM FRIDLEY	Fridley, James Riley "Big Jim" b: 9/6/24, Philippi, W.Va. BR/TR, 6'2", 205 lbs. Deb: 4/15/52																							
1952	Cle-A	62	175	23	44	2	0	4	16	14	40	.251	.311	.331	642	84	-4	3	3	-0	.978	-5	O-54(37-0-20)	-1.3
1954	Bal-A	85	240	25	59	8	5	4	36	21	41	.246	.312	.371	683	93	-3	0	1	-0	.985	-1	O-67(64-0-3)	-0.9
1958	Cin-N	5	9	2	2	2	0	0	1	0	2	.222	.222	.444	667	67	-0	0	0	0	1.000	-1	/O-2(2-0-0)	-0.1
Total	3	152	424	50	105	12	5	8	53	35	83	.248	.310	.356	666	89	-8	3	4	-1	.982	-7	O-123(103-0-23)	-2.3
■ PAT FRIEL	Friel, Patrick Henry b: 6/11/1860, Lewisburg, W.Va. d: 1/15/24, Providence, R.I. BB, 5'11", 170 lbs. Deb: 7/13/1890 F																							
1890	Syr-a	62	261	51	65	8	2	3	21	17		.249	.302	.330	632	96	-1	34			.913	-6	O-62(13-0-49)	-0.7
1891	Phi-a	2	8	2	2	1	0	0	0	0	0	.250	.250	.375	625	78	-0	0			1.000	-1	/O-2(0-0-2)	-0.1
Total	2	64	269	53	67	9	2	3	21	17	0	.249	.301	.331	632	96	-2	34			.914	-7	/O-64(13-0-51)	-0.8
■ BILL FRIEL	Friel, William Edward b: 4/1/1876, Renovo, Pa. d: 12/24/59, St.Louis, Mo. BL/TR, 5'10", 165 lbs. Deb: 5/3/01 FUC Career OF: (6-LF 27-CF 39-RF)																							
1901	Mil-A	106	376	51	100	13	7	4	35	23		.266	.310	.370	680	92	-4	15			.866	-9	3-61,O-29C/2-9,S-6	-1.1
1902	StL-A	80	267	26	64	9	2	2	20	14		.240	.283	.311	594	65	-13	4			.921	-14	O-33R,2-25,1/3SPC	-2.5
1903	StL-A	97	351	46	80	11	8	0	25	23		.228	.279	.305	584	77	-10	4			.915	-11	2-63,3-24/O-9(0-4-6)	-2.0
Total	3	283	994	123	244	33	17	6	80	60		.245	.292	.331	623	80	-27	23			.924	-33	/2-97,3-93,O1SCP	-5.6
■ FRANK FRIEND	Friend, Frank B. (b: Frederick Freund) b: 7/5/1875, Jeffersonville, Ind. d: 11/5/33, Jeffersonville, Ind. TR, 5'10", 180 lbs. Deb: 8/2/1896																							
1896	Lou-N	2	5	1	1	0	0	0	0	1	1	.200	.333	.200	533	44	-0	0			1.000	-0	/C-2	0.0
■ OWEN FRIEND	Friend, Owen Lacey "Red" b: 3/21/27, Granite City, Ill. BR/TR, 6'1", 180 lbs. Deb: 10/2/49 C																							
1949	StL-A	2	8	1	3	0	0	0	1	0	0	.375	.375	.375	750	95	-0	0	0	0	1.000	1	/2-2	0.1
1950	StL-A	119	372	48	88	15	2	8	50	40	68	.237	.312	.352	664	67	-19	2	1	0	.961	10	2-93,3-24/S-3	-0.4
1953	Det-A	31	96	10	17	4	0	3	10	6	9	.177	.233	.313	546	47	-8	0	1	-0	.947	4	2-26	-0.2
	Cle-A	34	68	7	16	2	0	2	13	5	16	.235	.288	.353	641	74	-3	0	0	0	1.000	6	2-19/S-8,3-1	0.4
	Yr	65	164	17	33	6	0	5	23	11	25	.201	.256	.329	585	58	-10	0	1	-0	.964	10	2-45/S-8,3-1	0.2
1955	Bos-A	14	42	3	11	3	0	0	2	4	11	.262	.326	.333	659	71	-2	0	0	0	.951	2	S-14/2-1	0.1
	Chi-N	6	10	0	1	0	0	0	0	0	3	.100	.100	.100	200	-47	-2	0	0	0	1.000	-1	/3-2,S-1	-0.3
1956	Chi-N	2	2	0	0	0	0	0	0	0	2	.000	.000	.000	0	-99	-1	0	0	0	.000	0	H	-0.1
Total	5	208	598	69	136	24	2	13	76	55	109	.227	.295	.339	634	63	-34	2	2	-0	.963	23	2-141/3-27,S-26	-0.4

YEAR	TM/L	G	AB	R	H	2B	3B	HR	RBI	BB	SO	AVG	OBP	SLG	OPS	OPS+	BR+	SB	CS	SBR	FA	FR	G/POS	TPR
■ BUCK FRIERSON	Frierson, Robert Lawrence b: 7/29/17, Chicota, Tex. d: 6/26/96, Paris, Tex. BR/TR, 6'3", 195 lbs. Deb: 9/9/41																							
1941	Cle-A	5	11	2	3	1	0	0	2	1	1	.273	.333	.364	697	89	-0	0	0	0	1.000	-1	/O-3(2-0-1)	-0.1
■ PETE FRIES	Fries, Peter Martin b: 10/30/1857, Scranton, Pa. d: 7/30/37, Chicago, Ill. BL/TL, 5'8", 160 lbs. Deb: 8/10/1883																							
1883	Col-a	3	10	1	3	1	0	0	1			.300	.364	.400	764	158	1				.857	0	/P-3	0.0
1884	Ind-a	1	3	0	1	1	0	0	1			.333	.500	.667	1167	285	1				.333	0	/O-1(0-0-1)	0.1
Total	2	4	13	1	4	2	0	0	2			.308	.400	.462	862	190	1				.857	0	/P-3,O-1(0-0-1)	0.1
■ FRED FRINK	Frink, Frederick Ferdinand b: 8/25/11, Macon, Ga. d: 5/19/95, Miami Springs, Fla. BR/TR, 6'1", 180 lbs. Deb: 7/1/34																							
1934	Phi-N	2	0	0	0	0	0	0	0	0	0	—	—	—	—	—	0	0			.000	-1	/O-1(0-1-0)	-0.1
■ CHARLIE FRISBEE	Frisbee, Charles Augustus "Bunt" b: 2/2/1874, Dows, Iowa d: 11/7/54, Alden, Iowa BB/TR, 5'9", 175 lbs. Deb: 6/22/1899																							
1899	Bos-N	42	152	22	50	4	2	0	20	9		.329	.374	.382	756	98	-1	10			.875	-2	O-40(0-36-4)	-0.5
1900	NY-N	4	13	2	2	1	0	0	3	2		.154	.267	.231	497	40	-1	0			.400	-2	/O-4(0-0-4)	-0.3
Total	2	46	165	24	52	5	2	0	23	11		.315	.365	.370	735	94	-2	10			.849	-4	/O-44(0-36-8)	-0.8
■ FRANKIE FRISCH	Frisch, Frank Francis "The Fordham Flash" b: 9/9/1898, Bronx, N.Y. d: 3/12/73, Wilmington, Del. BB/TR, 5'11", 165 lbs. Deb: 6/14/19 MCH																							
1919	NY-N	54	190	21	43	3	2	2	24	4	14	.226	.242	.295	537	62	-9	15			.972	4	2-29,3-20/S-1	-0.5
1920	NY-N	110	440	57	123	10	10	4	77	20	18	.280	.311	.375	686	97	-3	34	11	4	.967	9	*3-109/S-2	1.4
1921	*NY-N	153	618	121	211	31	17	8	100	42	28	.341	.384	.485	870	128	25	**49**	13	**6**	.936	4	3-93,2-61	4.2
1922	*NY-N	132	514	101	168	16	13	5	51	47	13	.327	.387	.438	824	111	9	31	17	1	.975	13	2-85,3-53/S-1	2.7
1923	*NY-N	151	641	116	**223**	32	10	12	111	46	12	.348	.395	.485	880	133	30	29	12	2	**.973**	-8	*2-135,3-17	2.7
1924	*NY-N	145	603	**121**	198	33	15	7	69	56	24	.328	.387	.468	855	132	27	22	9	2	.972	25	*2-143,S-10/3-2	5.7
1925	NY-N	120	502	89	166	26	6	11	48	32	14	.331	.374	.472	846	119	14	21	12	0	.931	3	3-46,2-42,S-39	2.4
1926	NY-N	135	545	75	171	29	4	5	44	33	16	.314	.353	.409	762	106	4	23			.975	11	*2-127/3-7	1.8
1927	StL-N	153	617	112	208	31	11	10	78	43	10	.337	.387	.472	858	125	22	**48**			**.979**	**49**	*2-153/S-1	**7.2**
1928	*StL-N	141	547	107	164	29	9	10	86	64	17	.300	.374	.441	815	110	9	29			**.976**	3	*2-139	1.5
1929	StL-N	138	527	93	176	40	12	5	74	53	12	.334	.397	.484	881	116	14	24			.970	-4	*2-121,3-13/S-1	1.2
1930	*StL-N	133	540	121	187	46	9	10	114	55	16	.346	.407	.520	927	118	17	15			.969	**28**	*2-123,3-10	4.2
1931	*StL-N	131	518	96	161	24	4	4	82	45	13	.311	.368	.396	764	101	2	**28**			.974	16	*2-129	2.6
1932	StL-N	115	486	59	142	26	2	3	60	25	13	.292	.327	.372	699	85	-10	18			.971	16	2-75,3-37/S-4	1.3
1933	StL-N★	147	585	74	177	32	6	4	66	48	16	.303	.358	.398	757	110	9	18			.982	-3	*2-132,S-15,M	1.6
1934	*StL-N★	140	550	74	168	30	6	3	75	45	10	.305	.359	.398	757	96	-2	11			.977	5	*2-115,3-25,M	1.0
1935	StL-N☆	103	354	52	104	16	2	1	55	33	16	.294	.356	.359	714	89	-4	2			.982	-7	2-88/3-5,M	-0.6
1936	StL-N	93	303	40	83	10	0	1	26	36	10	.274	.353	.317	670	82	-6	2			.965	-13	2-60,3-22/S-1,M	-1.4
1937	StL-N	17	32	3	7	2	0	0	4	1	0	.219	.242	.281	524	41	-3	0			1.000	-1	/2-5,M	-0.4
Total	19	2311	9112	1532	2880	466	138	105	1244	728	272	.316	.369	.432	801	110	143	419	74		.974	148	*2-1762,3-459/S-75	38.6
■ EMIL FRISK	Frisk, John Emil b: 10/15/1874, Kalkaska, Mich. d: 1/27/22, Seattle, Wash. BL/TR, 6'1", 190 lbs. Deb: 9/2/1899																							
1899	Cin-N	9	25	5	7	1	0	0	2	2		.280	.357	.320	677	85	-0	0			.950	-0	/P-9	0.0
1901	Det-A	20	48	10	15	3	0	1	7	3		.313	.365	.438	803	117	1	0			.851	2	P-11/O-2(0-1-1)	0.0
1905	StL-A	124	429	58	112	11	6	3	36	42		.261	.342	.336	678	122	12	7			.923	-7	*O-115(0-0-115)	0.0
1907	StL-A	5	4	0	1	0	0	0	0	1		.250	.400	.250	650	108	0	0			.000	0	H	0.0
Total	4	158	506	73	135	15	6	4	45	48		.267	.346	.344	690	119	13	7			.918	-5	O-117(0-1-116)/P-20	0.0
■ HARRY FRITZ	Fritz, Harry Koch "Dutchman" b: 9/30/1890, Philadelphia, Pa. d: 11/4/74, Columbus, Ohio BR/TR, 5'8", 170 lbs. Deb: 9/29/13																							
1913	Phi-A	5	13	1	0	0	0	0	0	2	4	.000	.188	.000	188	-45	-2	0			.846	-1	/3-5	-0.4
1914	Chi-F	65	174	16	37	5	1	0	13	18	18	.213	.297	.253	550	54	-14	2			.912	-9	3-46/S-9,2-1	-2.3
1915	Chi-F	79	236	27	59	8	4	3	26	13	27	.250	.298	.356	654	89	-8	4			.964	-8	3-70/2-6,S-1	-1.6
Total	3	149	423	44	96	13	5	3	39	33	49	.227	.294	.303	596	70	-24	6			.941	-18	3-121/S-10,2-7	-4.3
■ LARRY FRITZ	Fritz, Lawrence Joseph b: 2/14/49, E.Chicago, Ind. BL/TL, 6'2", 225 lbs. Deb: 5/30/75																							
1975	Phi-N	1	1	0	0	0	0	0	0	0	0	.000	.000	.000	0	-96	-0	0	0	0	.000	0	H	0.0
■ DOUG FROBEL	Frobel, Douglas Steven b: 6/6/59, Ottawa, Ont., Can. BL/TR, 6'4", 196 lbs. Deb: 9/5/82																							
1982	Pit-N	16	34	5	7	2	0	2	3	1	11	.206	.229	.441	670	81	-1	1	1	-0	1.000	-1	O-12(0-0-12)	-0.3
1983	Pit-N	32	60	10	17	4	1	3	11	4	17	.283	.328	.533	861	132	2	1	1	-0	.964	-4	O-24(18-0-6)	-0.2
1984	Pit-N	126	276	33	56	9	3	12	28	24	84	.203	.272	.388	659	83	-7	7	5	-0	.956	1	*O-112(0-0-112)	-1.1
1985	Pit-N	53	109	14	22	5	0	0	7	19	24	.202	.320	.248	568	62	-5	4	3	-0	.941	-3	O-36(20-0-16)	-1.0
	Mon-N	12	23	3	3	1	0	1	4	2	6	.130	.200	.304	504	42	-2	0	0	0	.923	-0	/O-6(1-2-3)	-0.3
	Yr	65	132	17	25	6	0	1	11	21	30	.189	.301	.258	558	59	-7	4	3	-0	.938	-3	O-42(21-2-19)	-1.3
1987	Cle-A	29	40	5	4	0	0	2	5	5	13	.100	.200	.250	450	18	-5	0	0	0	1.000	-3	O-12(2-2-7)/D-5	-0.8
Total	5	268	542	70	109	21	4	20	58	55	155	.201	.277	.365	642	78	-18	13	10	-1	.957	-10	O-202(41-4-156)/D-5	-3.7
■ BEN FROELICH	Froelich, William Palmer b: 11/12/1887, Pittsburgh, Pa. d: 9/1/16, Pittsburgh, Pa. BR/TR, Deb: 7/2/09																							
1909	Phi-N	1	1	0	0	0	0	0	0	0		.000	.000	.000	0	-99	-0	0			.000	0	/C-1	0.0
■ JERRY FRY	Fry, Jerry Ray b: 2/29/56, Salinas, Cal. BR/TR, 6', 185 lbs. Deb: 9/4/78																							
1978	Mon-N	4	9	0	0	0	0	0	0	1	5	.000	.100	.000	100	-71	-2	0	0	0	1.000	1	/C-4	-0.1
■ JEFF FRYE	Frye, Jeffrey Dustin b: 8/31/66, Oakland, Cal. BR/TR, 5'9", 165 lbs. Deb: 7/9/92 Career OF: (8-LF 8-CF 18-RF)																							
1992	Tex-A	67	199	24	51	9	1	1	12	16	27	.256	.321	.327	648	85	-4	1	3	-1	.978	8	2-67	0.5
1994	Tex-A	57	205	37	67	20	3	0	18	29	23	.327	.413	.454	866	124	8	6	1	1	.983	-16	2-54/3-1,D-1	-0.4
1995	Tex-A	90	313	38	87	15	2	4	29	24	45	.278	.339	.377	716	84	-7	3	3	-0	.975	3	2-83	0.0
1996	Bos-A	105	419	74	120	27	2	4	41	54	57	.286	.374	.389	763	92	-4	18	4	3	.983	14	*2-100/O-5L,S-3,D-1	1.6
1997	Bos-A	127	404	56	126	36	2	3	51	27	44	.312	.358	.433	791	103	2	19	8	1	.991	8	2-80,3-18,O-13L,D/S1	1.4
1999	Bos-A	41	114	14	32	3	0	1	12	14	11	.281	.364	.333	698	77	-3	2	2	-0	.980	-4	2-26/3-7,S-2,D-2	-0.6
2000	Bos-A	69	239	35	69	13	0	1	13	28	38	.289	.366	.356	721	81	-6	1	3	-1	.991	-7	2-53,O-15R/3-3,D-3	-1.1
	Col-N	37	87	14	31	6	0	0	3	8	16	.356	.417	.425	842	89	-1	4	0	1	.989	2	2-27/3-1	0.3
Total	7	593	1980	292	583	129	10	14	179	200	261	.294	.365	.391	756	93	-15	54	24	3	.983	7	2-490/O-33R,3-30,DS1	1.7
■ TRAVIS FRYMAN	Fryman, David Travis b: 3/25/69, Lexington, Ky. BR/TR, 6'1", 194 lbs. Deb: 7/7/90																							
1990	Det-A	66	232	32	69	11	1	9	27	17	51	.297	.348	.470	818	126	7	3	3	-0	.915	5	3-48,S-17/D-1	1.3
1991	Det-A	149	557	65	144	36	3	21	91	40	149	.259	.312	.447	759	106	3	12	5	1	.946	-9	3-85,S-71	-0.1
1992	Det-A★	161	659	87	175	31	4	20	96	45	144	.266	.318	.416	734	104	1	8	4	0	.970	-4	*S-137,3-26	0.8
1993	Det-A★	151	607	98	182	37	5	22	97	77	128	.300	.382	.486	868	133	28	9	4	1	.953	-5	S-81,3-69/D-1	3.0
1994	Det-A★	114	464	66	122	34	5	18	85	45	128	.263	.335	.474	809	105	2	2	2	-0	.955	-5	*3-114	-0.2
1995	Det-A	144	567	79	156	21	5	15	81	63	100	.275	.351	.409	760	97	-2	4	2	0	.969	**27**	*3-144	2.4
1996	Det-A★	157	616	90	165	32	3	22	100	57	118	.268	.334	.437	771	93	-8	4	3	-0	**.979**	17	*3-128,S-29	1.2
1997	Det-A	154	595	90	163	27	3	22	102	46	113	.274	.331	.440	772	100	-1	16	3	2	**.978**	9	*3-153	1.1
1998	*Cle-A	146	557	74	160	33	2	28	96	44	125	.287	.343	.504	847	113	9	10	8	-1	.963	-9	*3-144/S-3,D-2	0.1
1999	*Cle-A	85	322	45	82	16	2	10	48	25	57	.255	.310	.410	720	78	-11	2	1	0	.969	-5	3-85	-1.4
2000	Cle-A★	155	574	93	184	38	4	22	106	73	111	.321	.398	.516	914	126	23	1	1	-0	**.978**	0	*3-154/1-1,D-1	2.2
Total	11	1482	5750	819	1602	316	37	209	929	532	1224	.279	.343	.455	799	107	54	71	36	3	.967	21	*3-1150,S-338/D-5,1	10.4
■ MIKE FUENTES	Fuentes, Michael Jay b: 7/11/58, Miami, Fla. BR/TR, 6'3", 190 lbs. Deb: 9/2/83																							
1983	Mon-N	6	4	1	1	0	0	0	0	0	2	.250	.250	.250	500	39	-0	0	0	0	.000	0	/H	-0.1
1984	Mon-N	3	4	0	1	0	0	0	0	1	2	.250	.400	.250	650	90	0	0	0	0	1.000	0	/O-1(1-0-0)	0.0
Total	2	9	8	1	2	0	0	0	0	1	4	.250	.333	.250	583	67	-0	0	0	0	1.000	0	/O-1(1-0-0)	-0.1
■ TITO FUENTES	Fuentes, Rigoberto (Peat) b: 1/4/44, Havana, Cuba BB/TR (BR 1965-67, 70 (part)), 5'11", 175 lbs. Deb: 8/18/65																							
1965	SF-N	26	72	12	15	1	0	0	1	5	14	.208	.269	.222	491	39	-6	0	1	-0	.919	-7	S-18/2-7,3-1	-1.3

YEAR	TM/L	G	AB	R	H	2B	3B	HR	RBI	BB	SO	AVG	OBP	SLG	OPS	OPS+	BR+	SB	CS	SBR	FA	FR	G/POS	TPR
1966	SF-N	133	541	63	141	21	3	9	40	9	57	.261	.277	.360	637	73	-20	6	3	0	.957	-14	S-76,2-60	-2.2
1967	SF-N	133	344	27	72	12	1	5	29	27	61	.209	.267	.294	560	61	-17	4	3	-0	.980	25	*2-130/S-5	1.7
1969	SF-N	67	183	28	54	4	3	1	14	15	25	.295	.352	.366	718	103	1	2	4	-1	.925	-6	3-36,S-30	-0.4
1970	SF-N	123	435	49	116	13	7	2	32	36	52	.267	.327	.343	670	81	-12	4	5	-1	.966	-2	2-78,S-36,3-24	-0.7
1971	*SF-N	152	630	63	172	28	6	4	52	18	46	.273	.300	.356	655	86	-13	12	2	2	.973	1	*2-152	0.0
1972	SF-N	152	572	64	151	33	6	7	53	39	56	.264	.314	.379	694	95	-5	16	5	2	.964	-21	*2-152	-1.5
1973	SF-N	160	656	78	182	25	5	6	63	45	62	.277	.331	.358	689	87	-11	12	6	1	**.993**	-5	*2-160/3-1	-0.5
1974	SF-N	108	390	33	97	15	2	0	22	22	32	.249	.294	.297	591	63	-19	7	3	0	.979	-4	*2-103	-1.7
1975	SD-N	146	565	57	158	21	3	4	43	25	51	.280	.314	.349	662	89	-10	8	8	-1	.970	4	*2-142	0.3
1976	SD-N	135	520	48	137	18	0	2	36	18	38	.263	.289	.310	599	76	-18	5	3	0	.971	2	*2-127	-0.8
1977	Det-A	151	615	83	190	19	10	5	51	38	61	.309	.351	.397	748	98	-1	4	4	-1	.970	3	*2-151/D-1	0.9
1978	Oak-A	13	43	5	6	1	0	0	2	1	6	.140	.159	.163	322	-10	-6	0	0	0	.944	-12	2-13	-1.9
Total	13	1499	5566	610	1491	211	46	45	438	298	561	.268	.309	.347	656	82	-136	80	47	1	.974	-37	*2-1275,S-165/3-62,D	-8.1
■ OLLIE FUHRMAN	Fuhrman, Alfred George b: 7/20/1896, Jordan, Minn. d: 1/11/69, Peoria, Ill. BB/TR, 5′11″, 185 lbs. Deb: 4/13/22																							
1922	Phi-A	6	6	1	2	1	0	0	0	0	0	.333	.333	.500	833	112	0	0	0	0	1.000	0	/C-4	0.0
■ DOT FULGHUM	Fulghum, James Lavoisier b: 7/4/1900, Valdosta, Ga. d: 11/11/67, Miami, Fla. BR/TR, 5′8.5″, 165 lbs. Deb: 9/15/21																							
1921	Phi-A	2	2	0	0	0	0	0	0	1	1	.000	.333	.000	333	-9	-0	0	0	0	.000	0	/S-1	0.0
■ NIG FULLER	Fuller, Charles F. b: 3/30/1879, Toledo, Ohio d: 11/12/47, Toledo, Ohio BR/TR, 5′11″, 165 lbs. Deb: 7/1/02																							
1902	Bro-N	3	9	0	0	0	0	0	1	0		.000	.000	.000	0	-99	-2	0			1.000	-1	/C-3	-0.3
■ FRANK FULLER	Fuller, Frank Edward "Rabbit" b: 1/1/1893, Detroit, Mich. d: 10/29/65, Warren, Mich. BB/TR, 5′7″, 150 lbs. Deb: 4/14/15																							
1915	Det-A	14	32	6	5	0	0	0	2	9	7	.156	.341	.156	498	47	-2	2	3	-1	.962	-6	/2-9,S-1	-0.9
1916	Det-A	20	10	2	1	0	0	0	1	1	4	.100	.182	.100	282	-15	-1	3			.846	3	/2-8,S-1	0.1
1923	Bos-A	6	21	3	5	0	0	0	0	1	1	.238	.273	.238	511	35	-2	1	1	-0	.952	2	/2-6	0.0
Total	3	40	63	11	11	0	0	0	3	11	12	.175	.297	.175	472	35	-5	6	4		.938	-1	/2-23,S-2	-0.8
■ HARRY FULLER	Fuller, Henry W. b: 12/5/1862, Cincinnati, Ohio d: 12/12/1895, Cincinnati, Ohio Deb: 4/8/1891 F																							
1891	StL-a	1	2	0	0	0	0	0	0	0	1	.000	.000	.000	0	-87	-0	0			.000	-1	/3-1	-0.1
■ JIM FULLER	Fuller, James Hardy b: 11/28/50, Bethesda, Md. BR/TR, 6′3″, 215 lbs. Deb: 9/10/73 Career OF: (30-LF 0-CF 62-RF)																							
1973	Bal-A	9	26	2	3	0	0	2	4	1	17	.115	.148	.346	494	36	-2	0	0	0	1.000	1	/O-5(0-0-5),1-2,D-1	-0.1
1974	Bal-A	64	189	17	42	11	0	7	28	8	68	.222	.265	.392	657	90	-3	1	0	0	.960	-2	O-59(4-0-56)/1-4,D-2	-0.8
1977	Hou-N	34	100	5	16	6	0	2	9	10	45	.160	.243	.280	523	44	-8	0	1	-0	.983	5	O-27(26-0-1)/1-1	-0.5
Total	3	107	315	24	61	17	0	11	41	19	130	.194	.249	.352	601	70	-14	1	1	-0	.969	4	/O-91R,1-7,D-3	-1.4
■ JOHN FULLER	Fuller, John Edward b: 1/29/50, Lynwood, Cal. BL/TL, 6′2″, 180 lbs. Deb: 5/9/74																							
1974	Atl-N	3	3	1	1	0	0	0	0	0	0	.333	.333	.333	667	83	-0	0	0	0	1.000	-0	/O-1(0-1-0)	0.0
■ VERN FULLER	Fuller, Vernon Gordon b: 3/1/44, Menomonie, Wis. BR/TR, 6′1″, 170 lbs. Deb: 9/5/64																							
1964	Cle-A	2	1	0	0	0	0	0	0	0	0	.000	.000	.000	0	-99	-0	0	0	0	.000	0	H	0.0
1966	Cle-A	16	47	7	11	2	1	2	2	7	6	.234	.357	.447	804	129	2	0	0	0	1.000	-4	2-16	-0.1
1967	Cle-A	73	206	18	46	10	0	7	21	19	55	.223	.301	.374	675	98	-1	2	3	-1	.986	0	2-64/S-2	0.4
1968	Cle-A	97	244	14	59	8	2	0	18	24	49	.242	.320	.291	611	87	-3	2	2	-0	.988	-12	2-73,3-23/S-4	-1.2
1969	Cle-A	108	254	25	60	11	1	4	22	20	53	.236	.297	.335	632	74	-9	2	1	0	.978	9	*2-102/3-7	0.5
1970	Cle-A	29	33	3	6	2	0	1	2	3	9	.182	.250	.333	583	57	-2	0	0	0	.919	3	2-16/3-4,1-1	0.1
Total	6	325	785	67	182	33	4	14	65	73	172	.232	.307	.338	644	87	-13	6	6	-1	.982	-4	2-271/3-34,S-6,1-1	-0.3
■ SHORTY FULLER	Fuller, William Benjamin b: 10/10/1867, Cincinnati, Ohio d: 4/11/04, Cincinnati, Ohio BR/TR, 5′6″, 157 lbs. Deb: 7/19/1888 F Career OF: (0-LF 0-CF 2-RF)																							
1888	Was-N	49	170	11	31	5	2	0	12	10	14	.182	.232	.235	467	52	-9	6			.845	-6	S-47/2-2	-1.3
1889	StL-a	140	517	91	117	18	6	0	51	52	56	.226	.303	.284	587	60	-29	38			**.913**	0	*S-140	-2.1
1890	StL-a	130	526	118	146	9	9	1	40	73		.278	.377	.335	712	96	-3	60			.870	-1	*S-130	0.1
1891	StL-a	135	576	105	122	14	7	2	61	67	28	.212	.298	.271	569	55	-37	42			.857	-13	*S-102,2-38	-3.9
1892	NY-N	141	508	74	116	11	4	1	48	52	24	.228	.300	.272	572	74	-15	37			.888	1	*S-141	-0.6
1893	NY-N	130	474	78	112	14	8	0	51	60	21	.236	.325	.300	624	66	-23	26			.911	11	*S-130	-0.4
1894	*NY-N	95	377	82	104	14	4	2	46	52	16	.276	.367	.350	717	74	-15	32			.881	-1	*S-91/O-2R,3-2,2-1	-0.8
1895	NY-N	126	458	82	103	11	3	0	32	64	34	.225	.323	.262	585	53	-30	15			.913	34	*S-126	0.9
1896	NY-N	18	72	10	12	0	0	0	7	14	5	.167	.310	.167	477	28	-7	4			.874	1	S-18	-0.4
Total	9	964	3678	651	863	96	43	6	348	444	198	.235	.322	.289	611	67	-166	260			.890	27	S-925/2-41,3-2,O-2R	-8.5
■ CHICK FULLIS	Fullis, Charles Philip b: 2/27/04, Girardville, Pa. d: 3/28/46, Ashland, Pa. BR/TR, 5′9″, 170 lbs. Deb: 4/13/28 Career OF: (105-LF 348-CF 10-RF)																							
1928	NY-N	11	1	5	0	0	0	0	0	1	1	.000	.500	.000	500	41	0	0			.000	0	H	0.0
1929	NY-N	86	274	67	79	11	1	7	29	30	26	.288	.365	.412	777	92	-3	7			.962	-12	O-78(33-46-1)	-1.7
1930	NY-N	13	6	2	0	0	0	0	0	0	1	.000	.000	.000	0	-99	-2	1			.000	-1	/O-2(1-1-0)	-0.3
1931	NY-N	89	302	61	99	15	2	3	28	23	13	.328	.383	.421	804	119	8	13			.988	-4	O-68(1-65-0)/2-9	0.4
1932	NY-N	96	235	35	70	14	3	1	21	11	12	.298	.332	.396	728	97	-1	1			.990	-8	O-55(36-19-0)/2-1	-1.1
1933	Phi-N	151	647	91	200	31	6	1	45	36	34	.309	.350	.380	731	96	-2	18			.977	8	*O-151(0-151-0)/3-1	0.3
1934	Phi-N	28	102	8	23	6	0	0	12	10	4	.225	.301	.284	585	51	-7	2			.956	-4	O-27(24-3-0)	-1.2
	*StL-N	69	199	21	52	9	1	0	26	14	11	.261	.310	.317	626	64	-10	4			.969	-3	O-56(8-48-0)	-1.4
	Yr	97	301	29	75	15	1	0	38	24	15	.249	.307	.306	612	59	-17	6			.966	-6	O-83(32-51-0)	-2.6
1936	StL-N	47	89	15	25	6	1	0	6	7	11	.281	.333	.371	704	90	-1	0			1.000	-1	O-26(2-15-9)	-0.3
Total	8	590	1855	305	548	92	14	12	167	132	113	.295	.347	.380	726	92	-17	46			.977	-23	O-463C/2-10,3-1	-5.3
■ BRAD FULLMER	Fullmer, Bradley Ryan b: 1/17/75, Chatsworth, Cal. BL/TR, 6′1″, 185 lbs. Deb: 9/2/97 Career OF: (2-LF 0-CF 0-RF)																							
1997	Mon-N	19	40	4	12	2	0	3	8	2	7	.300	.349	.575	924	137	2	0	0	0	.982	-0	/1-8,O-2(2-0-0)	0.1
1998	Mon-N	140	505	58	138	44	2	13	73	39	70	.273	.328	.446	773	103	1	6	6	-1	.985	-7	*1-137	-1.9
1999	Mon-N	100	347	38	96	34	2	9	47	22	35	.277	.323	.464	787	99	-2	2	3	-1	.991	-6	1-94	-1.6
2000	Tor-A	133	482	76	142	29	1	32	104	30	68	.295	.344	.558	902	122	14	3	1	0	1.000	0	*D-129/1-1	0.6
Total	4	392	1374	176	388	109	5	57	232	93	180	.282	.333	.493	826	110	14	11	10	-1	.987	-13	1-240,D-129/O-2L	-2.8
■ CHICK FULMER	Fulmer, Charles John b: 2/12/1851, Philadelphia, Pa. d: 2/15/40, Philadelphia, Pa. BR/TR, 6′, 158 lbs. Deb: 8/23/1871 FU Career OF: (0-LF 1-CF 1-RF)																							
1871	Rok-n	16	63	11	17	1	3	0	3	5	1	.270	.324	.381	704	106	1	0	0	0	.770	2	S-16/1-1	0.2
1872	Mut-n	36	166	28	51	1	1	1	14	2	3	.307	.315	.343	659	109	3	1	1	-0	.752	-1	3-22,S-14	0.0
1873	Phi-n	49	236	42	66	11	3	1	38	2	3	.280	.286	.364	650	88	-4	3	1	0	.801	19	*S-49/P-2,C-1,1-1	0.9
1874	Phi-n	57	258	49	72	3	2	0	37	2	5	.279	.285	.306	591	86	-4	0	2	-1	.793	8	S-32,3-25	0.1
1875	Phi-n	69	295	50	65	6	1	0	24	0	6	.220	.220	.247	468	60	-12	10	4	1	.835	-1	*S-53,3-17	-1.2
1876	Lou-N	66	268	28	73	9	5	1	29	1	10	.272	.276	.356	632	93	-4				.861	-3	*S-66	-0.4
1879	Buf-N	76	306	30	82	11	5	0	28	5	34	.268	.280	.337	616	100	-0				.905	17	*2-76	1.9
1880	Buf-N	11	44	3	7	0	0	0	1	2	4	.159	.196	.159	355	21	-3				.882	-2	2-11	-0.5
1882	Cin-a	79	324	54	91	13	4	0	27	10		.281	.302	.346	648	112	3				**.897**	-13	*S-79	-0.7
1883	Cin-a	92	362	52	92	13	5	5	52	12		.254	.278	.359	637	98	-2				.863	-2	*S-92	0.0
1884	Cin-a	31	114	13	20	2	1	0	8	1		.175	.183	.211	393	27	-9				.786	-10	S-29/O-2(0-1-1),3-1	-1.7
	StL-a	1	5	0	0	0	0	0		0		.000	.000	.000	0	-97	-1				.778	-1	/2-1	-0.2
	Yr	32	119	13	20	2	1	0	8	1		.168	.175	.202	377	22	-10				.786	-11	S-29/O-2C,3-1,2-1	-1.9
Total	5 n	227	1018	180	271	22	10	2	116	11	18	.266	.274	.313	587	85	-17	14	8	0	.807	26	S-164/3-64,P-2,1C	0.0
Total	6	356	1423	180	365	48	20	6	145	31	48	.257	.273	.331	604	92	-17				.867	-13	S-266/2-88,O-2C,3-1	-1.6
■ CHRIS FULMER	Fulmer, Christopher b: 7/4/1858, Tamaqua, Pa. d: 11/9/31, Tamaqua, Pa. BR/TR, 5′8″, 165 lbs. Deb: 8/4/1884 Career OF: (16-LF 24-CF 17-RF)																							
1884	Was-U	48	181	39	50	9	0	0		11		.276	.318	.326	644	99	-5				.937	0	C-34,O-16(0-7-9)/1-5	-0.2
1886	Bal-a	80	270	54	66	9	3	1	30	48		.244	.363	.311	674	115	8	29			.949	-4	C-68,O-12(6-5-1)/P-1	0.8

YEAR	TM/L	G	AB	R	H	2B	3B	HR	RBI	BB	SO	AVG	OBP	SLG	OPS	OPS+	BR+	SB	CS	SBR	FA	FR	G/POS	TPR
1887	Bal-a	56	237	52	90	11	4	0	32	36		.380	.382	.363	746	115	7	35			.913	-11	C-48/O-8(8-0-0)	-0.1
1888	Bal-a	52	166	20	31	5	1	0	10	21		.187	.286	.229	515	67	-5	10			.903	-16	C-45/O-7(2-1-4)	-1.6
1889	Bal-a	16	58	11	15	3	1	0	13	6	12	.259	.338	.345	683	93	-0	2			.938	-5	O-14(0-11-3)/C-2	-0.5
Total	5	252	912	176	252	37	9	1	85	122	12	.276	.343	.313	655	101	4	76			.929	-36	C-197/O-57C,1-5,P-1	-1.6
■ WASHINGTON FULMER Fulmer, Washington Fayette b: 6/15/1840, Philadelphia, Pa. d: 12/8/07, Philadelphia, Pa. Deb: 7/19/1875 F																								
1875	Atl-n	1	4	1	2	0	0	0	1	0	0	.500	.500	.500	1000	285	1	0	0	0	.750	0	/O-1(0-1-0)	0.1
■ DAVE FULTZ Fultz, David Lewis b: 5/29/1875, Staunton, Va. d: 10/29/59, DeLand, Fla. BR/TR, 5'11", 170 lbs. Deb: 7/1/1898 Career OF: (34-LF 510-CF 10-RF)																								
1898	Phi-N	19	55	7	10	2	2	0	5	6		.182	.262	.291	553	61	-3	1			.871	-2	O-14(8-3-3)/2-3,S-1	-0.5
1899	Phi-N	2	5	0	2	0	0	0	0	0		.400	.400	.400	800	124	0	1			.750	-1	/2-1,S-1	-0.1
	Bal-N	57	210	31	62	3	2	0	18	13		.295	.342	.329	671	80	-6	17			.940	-7	O-31L,3-20/2-2,1-1	-1.3
	Yr	59	215	31	64	3	2	0	18	13		.298	.343	.330	674	81	-6	18			.940	-7	O-31L,3-20/2-3,S1	-1.4
1901	Phi-A	132	561	95	164	17	9	0	52	32		.292	.334	.355	689	87	-10	36			.935	-6	*O-106C,2-18/S-9	-1.9
1902	Phi-A	129	506	**109**	153	20	5	1	49	62		.302	.381	.368	748	104	5	44			.961	-2	*O-114(0-114-0),2-16	-0.3
1903	NY-A	79	295	39	66	12	1	0	25	25		.224	.295	.271	567	67	-11	29			.933	-2	O-77(1-73-3)/3-2	-1.7
1904	NY-A	97	339	39	93	17	4	2	32	24		.274	.324	.366	690	113	5	17			.976	3	O-90(0-90-0)	0.4
1905	NY-A	129	422	49	98	13	3	0	42	39		.232	.308	.277	585	77	-10	44			.966	-6	*O-122(0-121-1)	-2.4
Total	7	644	2393	369	648	84	26	3	223	201		.271	.332	.331	664	89	-30	189			.952	-22	O-554C/2-40,3-22,S1	-7.8
■ MARK FUNDERBURK Funderburk, Mark Clifford b: 5/16/57, Charlotte, N.C. BR/TR, 6'4", 226 lbs. Deb: 9/4/81 Career OF: (11-LF 0-CF 0-RF)																								
1981	Min-A	8	15	2	3	1	0	0	2	2	1	.200	.294	.267	561	59	-1	0	0	0	1.000	-1	/O-6(6-0-0),D-1	-0.2
1985	Min-A	23	70	7	22	7	1	2	13	5	12	.314	.360	.529	889	132	3	0	1	-0	1.000	-1	D-15/O-5(5-0-0),1-1	0.1
Total	2	31	85	9	25	8	1	2	15	7	13	.294	.348	.482	830	120	2	0	1	-0	1.000	-2	/D-16,O-11L,1-1	-0.1
■ LIZ FUNK Funk, Elias Calvin b: 10/28/04, LaCygne, Kan. d: 1/16/68, Norman, Okla. BL/TL, 5'8.5", 160 lbs. Deb: 4/26/29																								
1929	NY-A	1	0	0	0	0	0	0	0	0	0	—	—	—	—	—	0	0	0	0	.000	0	R	0.0
1930	Det-A	140	527	74	145	26	11	4	65	29	39	.275	.319	.389	708	77	-19	12	6	1	.965	8	*O-129(0-128-1)	-1.5
1932	Chi-A	122	440	59	114	21	5	2	40	43	19	.259	.325	.343	668	78	-14	17	15	-2	.979	7	*O-120(4-115-1)	-1.1
1933	Chi-A	10	9	1	2	0	0	0	0	1	0	.222	.300	.222	522	42	-1	0	0	0	.000	-1	/O-2(1-1-0)	-0.2
Total	4	273	976	134	261	47	16	6	105	73	58	.267	.322	.367	688	77	-34	29	21	-1	.972	14	O-251(5-244-2)	-2.8
■ RAFAEL FURCAL Furcal, Rafael b: 8/24/80, Loma De Cabrera, D.R. BB/TR, 5'10", 150 lbs. Deb: 4/4/2000																								
2000	*Atl-N	131	455	87	134	20	4	4	37	73	80	.295	.395	.382	778	99	2	40	14	4	.950	-11	*S-110,2-31	0.5
■ CARL FURILLO Furillo, Carl Anthony "Skoonj" or "The Reading Rifle" b: 3/8/22, Stony Creek Mills, Pa. d: 1/21/89, Stony Creek Mills, Pa. BR/TR, 6', 190 lbs. Deb: 4/16/46																								
1946	Bro-N	117	335	29	95	18	6	3	35	31	20	.284	.346	.400	746	110	4	6			.984	9	*O-112(5-103-4)	1.1
1947	*Bro-N	124	437	61	129	24	7	8	88	34	24	.295	.347	.437	785	103	1	7			.977	2	*O-121(28-93-2)	0.0
1948	Bro-N	108	364	55	108	20	4	4	44	43	32	.297	.374	.407	781	108	5	6			.983	9	*O-104(0-96-12)	1.1
1949	*Bro-N	142	549	95	177	27	10	18	106	37	29	.322	.368	.506	875	127	19	4			.965	5	*O-142(0-0-142)	2.0
1950	Bro-N	153	620	99	189	30	6	18	106	41	40	.305	.353	.460	813	110	8	8			.971	3	*O-153(0-0-153)	0.6
1951	Bro-N	158	667	93	197	32	4	16	91	43	33	.295	.344	.427	772	104	3	8	7	-1	.986	16	*O-157(0-0-157)	1.3
1952	*Bro-N☆	134	425	52	105	18	1	8	59	31	33	.247	.304	.351	655	80	-12	1	4	-1	.988	-1	*O-131(0-0-131)	-1.8
1953	*Bro-N☆	132	479	82	165	38	6	21	92	34	32	**.344**	.393	.580	973	146	31	1	1	-0	.988	4	*O-131(0-0-131)	3.0
1954	Bro-N	150	547	56	161	23	1	19	96	49	35	.294	.358	.444	802	104	3	2	4	-1	.972	4	*O-149(3-5-145)	0.1
1955	*Bro-N	140	523	83	164	24	3	26	95	43	43	.314	.373	.520	894	130	22	4	5	-1	.981	-3	*O-140(6-1-139)	1.3
1956	*Bro-N	149	523	66	151	30	0	21	83	57	41	.289	.360	.467	826	111	9	1	1	-0	.984	-9	*O-146(9-3-143)	-0.6
1957	Bro-N	119	395	61	121	17	4	12	66	29	33	.306	.361	.461	822	108	5	0	2	-1	.988	-5	*O-107(1-0-106)	-0.4
1958	LA-N	122	411	54	119	19	3	18	83	35	28	.290	.348	.482	830	113	7	0	2	-1	.975	-8	*O-119(1-7-116)	-0.5
1959	*LA-N	50	93	8	27	4	0	0	13	7	11	.290	.340	.333	673	75	-3	0	0	0	.920	-5	O-25(0-0-25)	-0.9
1960	LA-N	8	10	1	2	0	1	0	1	0	2	.200	.200	.400	600	56	-1	0	0	0	1.000	-0	/O-2(0-0-2)	-0.1
Total	15	1806	6378	895	1910	324	56	192	1058	514	436	.299	.356	.458	814	112	104	48	26		.979	22	*O-1739(53-308-1408)	6.2
■ EDDIE FUSSELBACK Fusselback, Edward L. b: 7/17/1856, Philadelphia, Pa. d: 4/14/26, Philadelphia, Pa. 5'6", 156 lbs. Deb: 5/3/1882 Career OF: (5-LF 2-CF 13-RF)																								
1882	StL-a	35	136	13	31	2	0	0		5		.228	.255	.243	498	66	-5				.853	2	C-19,O-15(4-0-11)/P-4	0.0
1884	Bal-U	68	303	60	86	16	3	1		3		.284	.291	.366	657	89	-13				.912	19	C-54/3-6,S-5,O-4C	0.9
1885	Phi-a	5	19	2	6	1	0	0	2	0		.316	.316	.368	684	109	0				.911	1	/C-5	0.1
1888	Lou-a	1	4	0	1	0	0	0	1	0		.250	.250	.250	500	62	-0	0			1.000	0	/O-1(0-0-1)	0.0
Total	4	109	462	75	124	19	3	1	3	8		.268	.281	.329	610	84	-18	0			.901	22	/C-78,O-20R,3-6,SP	1.0
■ LES FUSSELMAN Fusselman, Lester Leroy b: 3/7/21, Pryor, Okla. d: 5/21/70, Cleveland, Ohio BR/TR, 6'1", 195 lbs. Deb: 4/16/52																								
1952	StL-N	32	63	5	10	3	0	1	3	0	9	.159	.159	.254	413	13	-8	0	0	0	.991	3	C-32	-0.4
1953	StL-N	11	8	1	2	1	0	0	0	0	0	.250	.250	.375	625	60	-0	0	0	0	1.000	2	C-11	0.1
Total	2	43	71	6	12	4	0	1	3	0	9	.169	.169	.268	437	18	-8	0	0	0	.992	5	/C-43	-0.3
■ GABE GABLER Gabler, William Louis b: 8/4/30, St.Louis, Mo. BL/TR, 6'1", 190 lbs. Deb: 9/16/58																								
1958	Chi-N	3	3	0	0	0	0	0	0	0	3	.000	.000	.000	0	-99	-1	0	0	0	.000	0	H	-0.1
■ LEN GABRIELSON Gabrielson, Leonard Gary b: 2/14/40, Oakland, Cal. BL/TR, 6'4", 210 lbs. Deb: 9/9/60 F Career OF: (269-LF 21-CF 183-RF)																								
1960	Mil-N	4	3	1	0	0	0	0	0	1	0	.000	.250	.000	250	-27	-1	0	0	0	.000	-0	/O-1(1-0-0)	-0.1
1963	Mil-N	46	120	14	26	5	0	3	15	8	23	.217	.266	.333	599	72	-4	1	1	-0	1.000	-3	O-22(18-6-1),1-16/3-3	-1.0
1964	Mil-N	24	38	0	7	2	0	0	1	1	8	.184	.205	.237	442	24	-4	1	0	0	1.000	-1	1-12/O-2(0-0-2)	-0.5
	Chi-N	89	272	22	67	11	2	5	23	19	37	.246	.298	.357	655	80	-7	9	4	1	.984	-1	O-68(1-12-58)/1-8	-1.3
	Yr	113	310	22	74	13	2	5	24	20	45	.239	.287	.342	629	74	-11	10	4	1	.984	-2	O-70(1-12-60),1-20	-1.8
1965	Chi-N	28	48	4	12	0	0	3	5	7	16	.250	.345	.438	783	116	1	0	2	-1	1.000	-3	O-14(0-2-12)/1-1	-0.3
	SF-N	88	269	36	81	6	5	4	26	26	48	.301	.367	.405	772	114	6	4	0	1	.975	1	O-77(70-0-9)/1-5	0.3
	Yr	116	317	40	93	6	5	7	31	33	64	.293	.364	.410	774	114	7	4	2	0	.977	-2	O-91(70-2-21)/1-6	0.0
1966	SF-N	94	240	27	52	7	0	4	16	21	51	.217	.280	.296	576	58	-13	0	1	-0	.948	-9	O-67(61-0-9)/1-6	-2.8
1967	Cal-A	11	12	2	1	0	0	0	2	2	4	.083	.214	.083	298	-9	-2	0	0	0	.000	-0	/O-1(1-0-0)	-0.2
	LA-N	90	238	20	62	10	3	7	29	15	41	.261	.307	.416	723	114	3	3	1	0	.980	-4	O-68(47-1-26)	-0.4
1968	LA-N	108	304	38	82	16	1	10	35	32	47	.270	.339	.428	767	140	14	1	1	-0	.976	-3	O-86(57-0-30)	0.7
1969	LA-N	83	178	13	48	5	1	1	18	12	25	.270	.316	.326	642	86	-3	1	2	-0	.981	-7	O-47(13-0-34)/1-2	-1.4
1970	LA-N	43	42	1	8	2	0	0	6	1	15	.190	.209	.238	447	20	-5	0	0	0	1.000	-0	/O-2(0-0-2),1-1	-0.5
Total	9	708	1764	178	446	64	12	37	176	145	315	.253	.311	.366	677	94	-15	20	12	0	.977	-31	O-455L/1-51,3-3	-7.5
■ LEN GABRIELSON Gabrielson, Leonard Hilbourne b: 9/8/15, Oakland, Cal. BL/TL, 6'3", 210 lbs. Deb: 4/21/39 F																								
1939	Phi-N	5	18	3	4	0	0	0	1	2	3	.222	.300	.222	522	43	-1	0			.977	2	/1-5	0.0
■ EDDIE GAEDEL Gaedel, Edward Carl (b: Edward Carl Gaedele) b: 6/8/25, Chicago, Ill. d: 6/18/61, Chicago, Ill. BR/TL, 3'7", 65 lbs. Deb: 8/19/51																								
1951	StL-A	1	0	0	0	0	0	0	0	1	0	—	1.000	—	1000	182	0	0	0	0	.000	0	H	0.0
■ GARY GAETTI Gaetti, Gary Joseph b: 8/19/58, Centralia, Ill. BR/TR, 6', 200 lbs. Deb: 9/20/81 Career OF: (13-LF 0-CF 1-RF)																								
1981	Min-A	9	26	4	5	0	0	2	3	0	6	.192	.192	.423	615	68	-1	0	0	0	1.000	1	/3-8,D-1	0.0
1982	Min-A	145	508	59	117	25	4	25	84	37	107	.230	.286	.443	729	94	-6	0	4	-1	.963	-3	*3-142/S-2,D-1	-1.2
1983	Min-A	157	584	81	143	30	3	21	78	54	121	.245	.313	.414	727	95	-5	7	1	1	.967	13	*3-154/S-3,D-1	0.7
1984	Min-A	162	588	55	154	29	4	5	65	44	81	.262	.318	.350	668	81	-15	11	5	1	.960	15	*3-154/O-8(8-0-0),S-2	-0.2
1985	Min-A	160	560	71	138	31	0	20	63	37	89	.246	.301	.409	710	87	-11	13	5	1	.962	17	*3-156/O-4L,1-1,D-1	0.4
1986	Min-A	157	596	91	171	34	1	34	108	52	108	.287	.350	.518	869	129	23	14	15	-2	.956	19	*3-156/S-2,2-1,O-1L	3.6
1987	*Min-A	154	584	95	150	36	2	31	109	37	92	.257	.304	.485	789	101	-1	10	7	-0	.973	-4	*3-150/D-2	-0.7
1988	Min-A★	133	468	66	141	29	2	28	88	36	85	.301	.358	.551	909	146	27	7	4	0	.977	-6	*3-115/S-2,D-5	2.2
1989	Min-A★	130	498	63	125	11	4	19	75	25	87	.251	.291	.404	694	88	-9	6	2	1	.973	11	*3-125/1-2,D-3	0.3

YEAR	TM/L	G	AB	R	H	2B	3B	HR	RBI	BB	SO	AVG	OBP	SLG	OPS	OPS+	BR+	SB	CS	SBR	FA	FR	G/POS	TPR
1990	Min-A	154	577	61	132	27	5	16	85	36	101	.229	.278	.376	654	76	-20	6	1	1	.959	14	*3-151/1-2,S-2	-0.5
1991	Cal-A	152	586	58	144	22	1	18	66	33	104	.246	.295	.379	674	85	-13	5	5	-1	.965	**25**	*3-152	1.1
1992	Cal-A	130	456	41	103	13	2	12	48	21	79	.226	.269	.342	611	70	-19	3	1	0	.927	13	3-67,1-44,D-17	-0.9
1993	Cal-A	20	50	3	9	2	0	0	4	5	12	.180	.255	.220	475	28	-5	1	0	0	.857	2	/3-7,1-6,D-5	-0.3
	KC-A	82	281	37	72	18	1	14	46	16	75	.256	.315	.477	792	103	0	0	3	-1	.974	5	3-72,1-18/D-1	0.4
	Yr	102	331	40	81	20	1	14	50	21	87	.245	.306	.438	744	92	-5	1	3	-1	.970	7	3-79,1-24/D-6	0.1
1994	KC-A	90	327	53	94	15	3	12	57	19	63	.287	.330	.462	792	97	-2	0	2	-1	**.982**	3	3-85/1-9	0.0
1995	KC-A	137	514	76	134	27	0	35	96	47	91	.261	.332	.518	850	115	9	3	3	-0	.954	-5	*3-123,1-11/D-6	0.4
1996	*StL-N	141	522	71	143	27	4	23	80	35	97	.274	.329	.473	802	110	6	2	2	-0	.970	-16	*3-133,1-14	-1.1
1997	StL-N	148	502	63	126	24	1	17	69	36	88	.251	.309	.404	713	86	-12	7	3	0	**.978**	4	*3-132,1-20/P-1	-0.7
1998	StL-N	91	306	39	81	23	1	11	43	31	39	.265	.342	.454	796	108	3	1	1	-0	.985	-4	3-83/1-3,P-1,2-1,O	-0.1
	*Chi-N	37	128	21	41	11	0	8	27	12	23	.320	.400	.594	994	152	10	0	0	0	.979	-0	3-36	0.9
	Yr	128	434	60	122	34	1	19	70	43	62	.281	.359	.495	855	121	13	1	1	-0	**.983**	-5	*3-119/1-3,P-1,2O	0.8
1999	Chi-N	113	280	22	57	9	1	9	46	21	51	.204	.264	.339	603	52	-21	0	1	-0	.962	4	3-81/1-8,S-1,P-1	-1.7
2000	Bos-A	5	10	0	0	0	0	0	1	0	3	.000	.000	.000	0	-96	-3	0	0	0	.000	0	/D-5	-0.3
Total	20	2507	8951	1130	2280	443	39	360	1341	634	1602	.255	.311	.434	745	97	-64	96	65	-2	.965	106	*3-2282,1-138/DOSP2	2.3

■ FABIAN GAFFKE
Gaffke, Fabian Sebastian b: 8/5/13, Milwaukee, Wis. d: 2/8/92, Milwaukee, Wis. BR/TR, 5′10″, 185 lbs. Deb: 9/9/36

YEAR	TM/L	G	AB	R	H	2B	3B	HR	RBI	BB	SO	AVG	OBP	SLG	OPS	OPS+	BR+	SB	CS	SBR	FA	FR	G/POS	TPR
1936	Bos-A	15	55	5	7	2	0	1	3	4	5	.127	.200	.218	418	3	-9	0	0	0	1.000	-1	O-15(5-0-10)	-1.0
1937	Bos-A	54	184	32	53	10	4	6	34	15	25	.288	.342	.484	825	102	-0	1	2	-0	.965	-4	O-50(16-1-33)	-0.7
1938	Bos-A	15	10	2	1	0	0	0	1	3	2	.100	.308	.100	408	6	-1	0	0	0	.000	-1	/O-2(0-0-2),C-1	-0.2
1939	Bos-A	1	1	0	0	0	0	0	1	0	0	.000	.000	.000	0	-96	-0	0	0	0	.000	0	H	0.0
1941	Cle-A	4	4	0	1	0	0	0	0	2	2	.250	.500	.250	750	109	0	0	0	0	1.000	-1	/O-2(0-2-0)	0.0
1942	Cle-A	40	67	4	11	2	0	0	3	6	13	.164	.243	.194	437	25	-7	1	0	0	1.000	-2	O-16(5-1-10)	-0.9
Total	6	129	321	43	73	14	4	7	42	30	47	.227	.297	.361	659	67	-17	2	2	-0	.979	-9	/O-85(26-4-55),C-1	-2.8

■ PHIL GAGLIANO
Gagliano, Philip Joseph b: 12/27/41, Memphis, Tenn. BR/TR, 6′1″, 185 lbs. Deb: 4/16/63 F Career OF: (34-LF 0-CF 31-RF)

YEAR	TM/L	G	AB	R	H	2B	3B	HR	RBI	BB	SO	AVG	OBP	SLG	OPS	OPS+	BR+	SB	CS	SBR	FA	FR	G/POS	TPR
1963	StL-N	10	5	1	2	0	0	0	1	1	1	.400	.500	.400	900	149	0	0	0	0	1.000	2	/2-3,3-1	0.2
1964	StL-N	40	58	5	15	4	0	1	9	3	10	.259	.295	.379	674	81	-1	0	1	-0	.918	1	2-12/O-2L,1-1,3-1	0.0
1965	StL-N	122	363	46	87	14	2	8	53	40	45	.240	.317	.355	672	81	-8	2	1	0	.960	-12	2-57,O-25R,3-19	-1.8
1966	StL-N	90	213	23	54	8	2	2	15	24	29	.254	.332	.338	670	86	-3	2	1	0	.982	-4	3-41/1-8,O-5L,2-1	-0.8
1967	*StL-N	73	217	20	48	7	0	2	21	19	26	.221	.287	.281	568	64	-10	0	0	0	.972	-13	2-27,3-25/1-4,S-2	-2.3
1968	*StL-N	53	105	13	24	4	2	0	13	7	12	.229	.283	.305	588	77	-3	0	0	0	.982	-3	2-17,3-10/O-5(4-0-1)	-0.6
1969	StL-N	62	128	7	29	2	0	1	10	14	12	.227	.303	.266	568	60	-6	0	0	0	.989	-2	2-20/1-9,3-9,O-2R	-0.8
1970	StL-N	18	32	0	6	0	0	0	2	1	3	.188	.212	.188	400	8	-4	0	1	-0	1.000	-1	/3-6,1-3,2-2	-0.6
	Chi-N	26	40	5	6	0	0	0	5	5	5	.150	.244	.150	394	7	-5	0	0	0	1.000	1	2-16/1-1,3-1	-0.4
	Yr	44	72	5	12	0	0	0	7	6	8	.167	.231	.167	397	8	-9	0	1	-0	.980	-0	2-18/3-7,1-4	-1.0
1971	Bos-A	47	68	11	22	5	0	0	13	11	5	.324	.418	.397	815	123	3	0	0	0	1.000	-5	O-11(7-0-4)/2-7,3-4	-0.2
1972	Bos-A	52	82	9	21	4	1	0	10	10	13	.256	.337	.329	666	94	-0	1	0	0	.962	2	O-12L/3-5,2-4,1-2	0.2
1973	*Cin-N	63	69	8	20	2	0	0	7	13	16	.290	.402	.319	721	108	2	0	0	0	.824	-1	/3-7,2-4,1-1,O-1L	0.0
1974	Cin-N	46	31	2	2	0	0	0	0	15	7	.065	.370	.065	434	27	-2	0	0	0	1.000	0	/2-2,1-1,3-1	-0.2
Total	12	702	1411	150	336	50	7	14	159	163	184	.238	.319	.313	632	77	-39	5	4	-0	.969	-34	2-172,3-130/O-63L,1S	-7.3

■ RALPH GAGLIANO
Gagliano, Ralph Michael b: 10/8/46, Memphis, Tenn. BL/TR, 5′11″, 170 lbs. Deb: 9/21/65 F

YEAR	TM/L	G	AB	R	H	2B	3B	HR	RBI	BB	SO	AVG	OBP	SLG	OPS	OPS+	BR+	SB	CS	SBR	FA	FR	G/POS	TPR
1965	Cle-A	1	0	0	0	0	0	0	0	0	0	—	—	—	—	—	0	0	0	0	.000	0	R	0.0

■ GREG GAGNE
Gagne, Gregory Carpenter b: 11/12/61, Fall River, Mass. BR/TR, 5′11″, 172 lbs. Deb: 6/5/83 Career OF: (0-LF 7-CF 1-RF)

YEAR	TM/L	G	AB	R	H	2B	3B	HR	RBI	BB	SO	AVG	OBP	SLG	OPS	OPS+	BR+	SB	CS	SBR	FA	FR	G/POS	TPR
1983	Min-A	10	27	2	3	1	0	0	3	0	6	.111	.111	.148	259	-28	-5	0	0	0	.923	-5	S-10	-1.0
1984	Min-A	2	1	0	0	0	0	0	0	0	0	.000	.000	.000	0	-96	-0	0	0	0	.000	0	/H	0.0
1985	Min-A	114	293	37	66	15	3	2	23	20	57	.225	.282	.317	599	60	-16	10	4	1	.968	4	*S-106/D-5	-0.2
1986	Min-A	156	472	63	118	22	6	12	54	30	108	.250	.303	.398	701	87	-9	12	10	-1	.959	-16	*S-155/2-4	-1.0
1987	*Min-A	137	437	68	116	28	7	10	40	25	84	.265	.311	.430	741	91	-7	6	6	-1	.970	17	*S-136/O-4C,2-1,D-1	2.1
1988	Min-A	149	461	70	109	20	6	14	48	27	110	.236	.289	.397	686	87	-9	15	7	1	.970	-15	*S-146/O-2C,2-1,3-1	-1.3
1989	Min-A	149	460	69	125	29	7	9	48	17	80	.272	.301	.424	725	96	-4	11	4	1	.971	-4	*S-146/O-1(0-1-0)	0.3
1990	Min-A	138	388	38	91	22	3	7	38	24	76	.235	.281	.361	642	73	-14	8	8	-1	.976	2	*S-135/O-1(0-1-0),D-2	-0.4
1991	*Min-A	139	408	52	108	23	3	8	42	26	72	.265	.314	.395	708	90	-6	11	9	-1	.984	4	*S-137/D-1	0.7
1992	Min-A	146	439	53	108	23	0	7	39	19	83	.246	.280	.346	627	72	-17	6	7	-1	.973	21	*S-141	1.3
1993	KC-A	159	540	66	151	32	3	10	57	33	93	.280	.321	.406	727	89	-9	10	12	-2	**.986**	5	*S-159	0.7
1994	KC-A	107	375	39	97	23	3	7	51	27	79	.259	.315	.392	707	78	-13	10	17	-4	.977	8	*S-106	0.0
1995	KC-A	120	430	58	110	25	4	6	49	38	60	.256	.319	.374	694	79	-14	3	5	-1	.969	7	*S-118/D-2	0.2
1996	*LA-N	128	428	48	109	13	2	10	55	50	93	.255	.335	.364	700	92	-5	4	2	0	.966	13	*S-127	1.8
1997	LA-N	144	514	49	129	20	3	9	57	31	120	.251	.299	.354	653	76	-19	2	5	-1	.971	-28	*S-143	-3.7
Total	15	1798	5673	712	1440	296	50	111	604	367	1121	.254	.304	.382	686	82	-147	108	96	-10	.972	13	*S-1765/D-11,O-8C,23	-0.5

■ ED GAGNIER
Gagnier, Edward James b: 4/16/1883, Paris, France d: 9/13/46, Detroit, Mich. BR/TR, 5′9″, 170 lbs. Deb: 4/14/14

YEAR	TM/L	G	AB	R	H	2B	3B	HR	RBI	BB	SO	AVG	OBP	SLG	OPS	OPS+	BR+	SB	CS	SBR	FA	FR	G/POS	TPR
1914	Bro-F	94	337	22	63	12	2	0	25	13	24	.187	.219	.234	454	24	-42	8			.933	-1	S-88/3-6	-3.9
1915	Bro-F	20	50	8	13	1	0	0	4	10	5	.260	.393	.280	673	92	-1	2			.930	2	S-13/2-6	0.3
	Buf-F	1	2	0	0	0	0	0	0	0	0	.000	.000	.000	0	-98	-1	0			.800	-0	/2-1	-0.1
	Yr	21	52	8	13	1	0	0	4	10	5	.250	.381	.269	650	85	-1	2			.930	2	S-13/2-7	0.2
Total	2	115	389	30	76	13	2	0	29	23	29	.195	.244	.239	483	33	-43	10			.933	2	S-101/2-7,3-6	-3.7

■ CHICK GAGNON
Gagnon, Harold Dennis b: 9/27/1897, Millbury, Mass. d: 4/30/70, Wilmington, Del. BR/TR, 5′7.5″, 158 lbs. Deb: 6/27/22

YEAR	TM/L	G	AB	R	H	2B	3B	HR	RBI	BB	SO	AVG	OBP	SLG	OPS	OPS+	BR+	SB	CS	SBR	FA	FR	G/POS	TPR
1922	Det-A	10	4	2	1	0	0	0	0	0	2	.250	.250	.250	500	32	-0	0	0	0	.000	-1	/S-1,3-1	-0.1
1924	Was-A	4	5	1	1	0	0	0	1	0	0	.200	.200	.200	400	3	-1	0	0	0	1.000	1	/S-2	0.0
Total	2	14	9	3	2	0	0	0	1	0	2	.222	.222	.222	444	16	-1	0	0	0	1.000	0	/S-3,3-1	-0.1

■ DEL GAINER
Gainer, Dellos Clinton "Sheriff" b: 11/10/1886, Montrose, W.Va. d: 1/29/47, Elkins, W.Va. BR/TR, 6′, 180 lbs. Deb: 10/2/09 Career OF: (24-LF 10-CF 1-RF)

YEAR	TM/L	G	AB	R	H	2B	3B	HR	RBI	BB	SO	AVG	OBP	SLG	OPS	OPS+	BR+	SB	CS	SBR	FA	FR	G/POS	TPR
1909	Det-A	2	5	0	1	0	0	0	0	0		.200	.200	.200	400	25	-0	0			.929	-0	/1-2	-0.1
1911	Det-A	70	248	32	75	11	4	2	25	20		.302	.366	.403	770	109	3	10			.975	-4	1-69	-0.3
1912	Det-A	52	179	28	43	5	6	0	20	18		.240	.320	.335	655	90	-2	14			.986	-3	1-50/O-1	-0.7
1913	Det-A	105	363	47	97	16	8	2	25	30	45	.267	.333	.372	705	108	3	10			.988	-5	*1-103	-0.5
1914	Det-A	1	0	0	0	0	0	0	0	0	0	—	—	—	—	—	0	0			1.000	-0	/1-1	0.0
	Bos-A	38	84	11	20	9	2	2	13	8	14	.238	.312	.464	776	133	3	2	2	-0	.981	-3	1-18,2-11/O-1(0-1-0)	0.0
	Yr	39	84	11	20	9	2	2	13	8	14	.238	.312	.464	776	133	3	2	2	-0	.982	-3	1-19,2-11/O-1(0-1-0)	0.0
1915	*Bos-A	82	200	30	59	5	8	1	29	21	31	.295	.371	.415	786	139	9	7	2	1	.988	0	1-56/O-6(0-5-1)	1.0
1916	*Bos-A	56	142	14	36	6	0	3	18	10	24	.254	.303	.359	662	98	-1	5			.997	1	1-48/2-2	-0.1
1917	Bos-A	52	172	28	53	10	2	2	19	15	21	.308	.374	.424	798	145	9	1			.989	-1	1-50	0.8
1919	Bos-A	47	118	9	28	6	2	0	13	13	15	.237	.318	.322	640	85	-2	5			.978	-3	1-21,O-18(18-0-0)	-0.7
1922	StL-N	43	97	19	26	7	4	2	23	14	6	.268	.360	.485	845	122	3	0	2	-1	.979	-1	1-26,O-10(6-4-0)	-0.1
Total	10	548	1608	218	438	75	36	14	185	149	156	.272	.342	.390	732	113	24	54	6		.985	-19	1-444/O-36L,2-13	-0.7

■ JAY GAINER
Gainer, Johnathan Keith b: 10/8/66, Panama City, Fla. BL/TL, 6′, 190 lbs. Deb: 5/14/93

YEAR	TM/L	G	AB	R	H	2B	3B	HR	RBI	BB	SO	AVG	OBP	SLG	OPS	OPS+	BR+	SB	CS	SBR	FA	FR	G/POS	TPR
1993	Col-N	23	41	4	7	0	0	3	6	4	12	.171	.244	.390	635	57	-3	1	1	-0	.982	-1	/1-7	-0.5

■ JOE GAINES
Gaines, Arnesta Joe b: 11/22/36, Bryan, Tex. BR/TR, 6′1″, 190 lbs. Deb: 6/29/60

YEAR	TM/L	G	AB	R	H	2B	3B	HR	RBI	BB	SO	AVG	OBP	SLG	OPS	OPS+	BR+	SB	CS	SBR	FA	FR	G/POS	TPR
1960	Cin-N	11	15	2	3	0	0	0	1	0	1	.200	.200	.200	400	10	-2	0	0	0	1.000	-1	/O-3(1-1-2)	-0.3
1961	Cin-N	5	3	2	0	0	0	0	0	2	1	.000	.400	.000	400	18	-0	0	0	0	.500	-1	/O-3(1-2-0)	-0.2
1962	Cin-N	64	52	12	12	3	0	1	7	8	16	.231	.333	.346	679	80	-1	0	0	0	1.000	-3	O-13(11-0-2)	-0.4
1963	Bal-A	66	126	24	36	4	1	6	20	20	39	.286	.384	.476	860	145	8	2	1	0	.945	-6	O-39(34-4-2)	0.1
1964	Bal-A	16	26	2	4	0	0	1	2	3	7	.154	.241	.269	511	42	-2	0	0	0	.846	0	/O-5(5-0-0)	-0.2
	Hou-N	89	307	37	78	9	7	7	34	27	69	.254	.318	.397	716	106	2	8	2	1	.957	-2	O-81(1-0-81)	-0.5

YEAR	TM/L	G	AB	R	H	2B	3B	HR	RBI	BB	SO	AVG	OBP	SLG	OPS	OPS+	BR+	SB	CS	SBR	FA	FR	G/POS	TPR
1965	Hou-N	100	229	21	52	8	1	6	31	18	59	.227	.292	.349	641	86	-5	4	1	1	.913	-8	O-65(26-0-39)	-1.7
1966	Hou-N	11	13	4	1	1	0	0	0	3	5	.077	.250	.154	404	17	-1	0	0	0	.500	-1	/O-3(1-0-2)	-0.3
Total	7	362	771	104	186	25	9	21	95	81	197	.241	.317	.379	696	99	-1	14	4	2	.934	-21	O-212(80-7-128)	-3.5
TY GAINEY	Gainey, Telmanch b: 12/25/60, Cheraw, S.C. BL/TR, 6'1", 190 lbs. Deb: 4/24/85																							
1985	Hou-N	13	37	5	6	0	0	0	0	2	9	.162	.244	.162	406	16	-4	0	0	0	.913	-0	/O-9(0-8-1)	-0.5
1986	Hou-N	26	50	6	15	3	1	1	6	6	19	.300	.375	.460	835	133	2	3	1	0	1.000	-3	O-19(7-14-3)	-0.1
1987	Hou-N	18	24	1	3	0	0	0	1	2	9	.125	.192	.125	317	-14	-4	1	0	0	1.000	-0	/O-6(6-0-0)	-0.4
Total	3	57	111	12	24	3	1	1	7	10	37	.216	.293	.288	581	62	-6	4	1	1	.968	-3	/O-34(13-22-4)	-1.0
AUGIE GALAN	Galan, August John b: 5/25/12, Berkeley, Cal. d: 12/28/93, Fairfield, Cal. BB/TR (BL 1943 (part), 44-49), 6', 175 lbs. Deb: 4/29/34 C Career OF: (1000-LF 335-CF 38-RF)																							
1934	Chi-N	66	192	31	50	6	2	5	22	16	15	.260	.317	.391	708	90	-3	4			.961	-9	2-43/3-3,S-1	-0.9
1935	*Chi-N	154	646	**133**	203	41	11	12	79	87	53	.314	.399	.467	866	131	31	**22**			.978	7	*O-154(154-0-0)	2.8
1936	Chi-N★	145	575	74	152	26	4	8	81	67	50	.264	.344	.365	709	89	-8	16			.987	5	*O-145(8-139-0)	-0.6
1937	Chi-N	147	611	104	154	24	10	18	78	79	48	.252	.339	.412	751	99	-1	**23**			.980	13	*O-140L/2-8,S-2	0.5
1938	*Chi-N	110	395	52	113	16	9	6	69	49	17	.286	.368	.418	785	112	8	8			.987	2	*O-103(103-0-0)	0.4
1939	Chi-N	148	549	104	167	36	8	6	71	75	26	.304	.392	.432	823	119	17	8			.970	-2	*O-145(145-0-0)	0.6
1940	Chi-N	68	209	33	48	14	2	3	22	37	23	.230	.346	.359	704	96	-0	9			.984	0	O-54(31-24-0)/2-2	-0.2
1941	Chi-N	65	120	18	25	3	0	1	13	22	10	.208	.331	.258	589	70	-4	0			.959	-5	O-31(17-11-4)	-1.0
	*Bro-N	17	27	3	7	3	0	0	4	3	1	.259	.333	.370	704	94	-0	0			1.000	-0	/O-6(0-6-0)	0.0
	Yr	82	147	21	32	6	0	1	17	25	11	.218	.331	.279	610	74	-4	0			.967	-5	O-37(17-17-4)	-1.0
1942	Bro-N	69	209	24	55	16	0	0	22	24	12	.263	.339	.340	679	97	-0	2			.990	-5	O-55C/1-4,2-3	-0.8
1943	Bro-N★	139	495	83	142	26	3	9	67	**103**	39	.287	.412	.406	818	136	28	6			.981	16	*O-124(28-97-0),1-13	4.1
1944	Bro-N★	151	547	96	174	43	9	12	93	**101**	23	.318	.426	.495	922	162	49	4			.988	-2	*O-147(126-25-2)/2-2	3.9
1945	Bro-N	152	576	114	177	36	7	9	92	114	27	.307	.423	.441	864	142	38	13			.988	-8	1-66,O-49L,3-40	2.3
1946	Bro-N	99	274	53	85	22	5	3	38	68	21	.310	.451	.460	910	157	25	8			.935	-10	O-60L,3-19,1-12	1.2
1947	Cin-N	124	392	60	123	18	2	6	61	94	19	.314	**.449**	.416	865	132	24	0			.988	-4	*O-118(118-1-1)	1.1
1948	Cin-N	54	77	18	22	3	2	2	16	26	4	.286	.471	.455	926	157	8	0			.967	-2	O-18(1-0-17)	0.6
1949	NY-N	22	17	0	1	1	0	0	2	5	3	.059	.273	.118	390	8	-2	0			1.000	-1	/1-3,O-1(0-0-1)	-0.3
	Phi-A	12	26	4	8	2	0	0	0	9	2	.308	.486	.385	870	136	2	0	0	0	1.000	-1	/O-9(7-0-2)	0.1
Total	16	1742	5937	1004	1706	336	74	100	830	979	393	.287	.390	.419	810	122	212	123	0		.981	-4	*O-1359L/1-98,32S	13.8
ANDRES GALARRAGA	Galarraga, Andres Jose (b: Andres Jose Padovani (Galarraga)) b: 6/18/61, Caracas, Venez. BR/TR, 6'3", 235 lbs. Deb: 8/23/85																							
1985	Mon-N	24	75	9	14	1	0	2	4	3	18	.187	.228	.280	508	44	-6	1	2	-0	.995	4	1-23	-0.4
1986	Mon-N	105	321	39	87	13	0	10	42	30	79	.271	.339	.405	744	105	2	6	5	-0	.995	-8	*1-102	-1.2
1987	Mon-N	147	551	72	168	40	3	13	90	41	127	.305	.364	.459	823	113	10	7	10	-2	.993	0	*1-146	-0.1
1988	Mon-N★	157	609	99	**184**	**42**	8	29	92	39	153	.302	.354	.540	894	147	34	13	4	1	.991	-4	*1-156	2.2
1989	Mon-N	152	572	76	147	30	1	23	85	48	158	.257	.329	.434	762	115	10	12	5	1	.992	-2	*1-147	-0.2
1990	Mon-N	155	579	65	148	29	0	20	87	40	169	.256	.308	.409	718	99	-2	10	1	2	.993	-5	*1-154	-1.7
1991	Mon-N	107	375	34	82	13	2	9	33	23	86	.219	.268	.336	604	70	-16	5	6	-1	.991	2	*1-105	-2.3
1992	StL-N	95	325	38	79	14	2	10	39	11	69	.243	.285	.391	676	92	-5	5	4	-0	.991	-1	1-90	-1.3
1993	Col-N★	120	470	71	174	35	4	22	98	24	73	**.370**	.408	.602	1010	143	28	2	4	-1	.990	7	*1-119	2.3
1994	Col-N	103	417	77	133	21	0	31	85	19	93	.319	.360	.592	953	123	13	8	3	1	.992	-5	*1-103	-0.1
1995	*Col-N	143	554	89	155	29	3	31	106	32	146	.280	.334	.511	845	92	-6	12	2	2	.991	6	*1-142	-1.2
1996	Col-N	159	626	119	190	39	3	**47**	**150**	40	157	.304	.362	.601	962	120	17	18	8	1	.992	-2	*1-159/3-1	0.1
1997	Col-N★	154	600	120	191	31	3	41	**140**	54	141	.318	.390	.585	975	123	21	15	8	1	.991	-2	*1-154	0.5
1998	*Atl-N★	153	555	103	169	27	1	44	121	63	146	.305	.400	.595	994	157	46	7	6	-1	.992	-8	*1-149/D-2	2.3
2000	*Atl-N★	141	494	67	149	25	1	28	100	36	126	.302	.369	.526	896	124	17	3	5	-1	.988	-9	*1-132/D-1	-0.5
Total	15	1915	7123	1078	2070	389	31	360	1272	503	1741	.291	.351	.506	856	118	164	124	73	-2	.991	-28	*1-1881/D-3,3-1	-1.6
MILT GALATZER	Galatzer, Milton b: 5/4/07, Chicago, Ill. d: 1/29/76, San Francisco, Cal BL/TL, 5'10", 168 lbs. Deb: 6/25/33 Career OF: (28-LF 31-CF 154-RF)																							
1933	Cle-A	57	160	19	38	2	1	1	17	23	21	.237	.333	.281	615	61	-8	2	3	-1	.975	-0	O-40(11-4-25)/1-5	-1.1
1934	Cle-A	49	196	29	53	10	2	0	15	21	8	.270	.344	.342	686	76	-7	3	2	-0	.980	3	O-49(3-0-46)	-0.6
1935	Cle-A	93	259	45	78	9	3	0	19	35	8	.301	.389	.359	748	93	-1	4	5	-1	.934	-8	O-81(8-18-56)	-1.3
1936	Cle-A	49	97	12	23	4	1	0	6	13	8	.237	.333	.299	632	57	-6	1	2	-0	.964	-8	O-42(6-9-27)/P-1,1-1	-1.4
1939	Cin-N	3	5	0	0	0	0	0	0	0	1	.000	.000	.000	0	-99	-1	0			1.000	0	/1-2	-0.2
Total	5	251	717	105	192	25	7	1	57	92	46	.268	.354	.326	681	75	-24	10	12		.959	-14	O-212R/1-8,P-1	-4.6
AL GALLAGHER	Gallagher, Alan Mitchell Edward George Patrick Henry b: 10/19/45, San Francisco, Cal. BR/TR, 6', 180 lbs. Deb: 4/7/70																							
1970	SF-N	109	282	31	75	15	2	4	28	30	37	.266	.337	.376	712	92	-3	2	1	0	.971	1	3-91	-0.2
1971	*SF-N	136	429	47	119	18	5	5	57	40	57	.277	.342	.378	719	105	3	2	1	0	.951	-16	*3-128	-1.4
1972	SF-N	82	233	19	52	3	1	2	18	33	39	.223	.322	.270	592	69	-8	2	1	0	.974	-4	3-69	-1.3
1973	SF-N	5	9	1	2	0	0	0	1	0	0	.222	.300	.222	522	45	-1	0	0	0	.833	-1	/3-5	-0.2
	Cal-A	110	311	16	85	6	1	0	26	35	31	.273	.349	.299	648	91	-2	1	3	-1	.961	4	3-98/2-1,S-1	0.1
Total	4	442	1264	114	333	42	9	11	130	138	164	.263	.338	.337	675	91	-11	7	6	-1	.961	-15	3-391/S-1,2-1	-3.0
SHORTY GALLAGHER	Gallagher, Charles William b: 4/30/1872, Detroit, Mich. d: 6/23/24, Detroit, Mich. Deb: 8/13/01																							
1901	Cle-A	2	4	0	0	0	0	0	0	0		.000	.000	.000	0	-99	-1	0			.667	-1	/O-2(0-0-2)	-0.2
DAVE GALLAGHER	Gallagher, David Thomas b: 9/20/60, Trenton, N.J. BR/TR, 6', 184 lbs. Deb: 4/12/87 Career OF: (166-LF 396-CF 173-RF)																							
1987	Cle-A	15	36	2	4	1	1	0	1	2	5	.111	.158	.194	352	-7	-6	2	0	0	.972	1	O-14(0-14-0)	-0.4
1988	Chi-A	101	347	59	105	15	3	5	31	29	40	.303	.356	.406	763	113	6	5	4	-0	1.000	-1	O-95(5-78-17)/D-2	0.3
1989	Chi-A	161	601	74	160	22	2	1	46	46	79	.266	.320	.314	635	82	-14	5	6	-1	.993	1	*O-160(1-138-27)/D-1	-1.6
1990	Chi-A	45	75	5	21	3	1	0	5	3	9	.280	.316	.347	663	87	-1	0	1	-0	.981	-6	O-37(14-22-1)/D-4	-0.8
	Bal-A	23	51	7	11	1	0	0	2	4	3	.216	.273	.235	508	45	-4	1	1	-0	.980	2	O-20(17-2-1)/D-2	-0.2
	Yr	68	126	12	32	4	1	0	7	7	12	.254	.299	.302	600	70	-5	1	2	-0	.980	-4	O-57(31-24-2)/D-6	-1.0
1991	Cal-A	90	270	32	79	17	0	1	30	24	43	.293	.355	.367	721	100	1	2	4	-1	1.000	1	O-87(7-61-23)/D-2	0.0
1992	NY-N	98	175	20	42	11	1	1	21	19	16	.240	.318	.331	649	85	-3	4	5	-1	.982	-8	O-76(22-13-48)	-1.4
1993	NY-N	99	201	34	55	12	2	6	28	20	18	.274	.339	.443	782	109	2	1	1	-0	1.000	-7	O-72(19-39-20)/1-9	-0.6
1994	Atl-N	89	152	27	34	5	0	2	14	22	17	.224	.326	.296	622	62	-8	0	2	-1	.989	-9	O-77(71-5-7)/1-1	-1.8
1995	Phi-N	62	157	12	50	12	0	1	12	16	20	.318	.382	.414	796	109	2	0	0	0	1.000	-4	O-55(8-21-28)	-0.3
	Cal-A	11	16	1	3	1	0	0	0	2	1	.188	.278	.250	528	39	-1	0	0	0	1.000	0	/O-6(2-3-1),D-1	-0.1
Total	9	794	2081	273	564	100	10	17	190	187	251	.271	.333	.353	686	90	-25	20	24	-4	.993	-30	O-699C/D-12,1-10	-6.9
JIM GALLAGHER	Gallagher, James E. b: Findlay, Ohio d: 3/29/1894, Scranton, Pa. Deb: 9/4/1886																							
1886	Was-N	1	5	1	1	0	0	0	0	0	2	.200	.200	.200	400	23	-0	0			.875	1	/S-1	0.0
JOHN GALLAGHER	Gallagher, John Carroll b: 2/18/1892, Pittsburgh, Pa. d: 3/30/52, Norfolk, Va. BR/TR, 5'10.5", 156 lbs. Deb: 8/20/15																							
1915	Bal-F	40	126	11	25	4	0	0	4	5	22	.198	.229	.230	459	28	-14	1			.945	-2	2-37/S-5,3-1	-1.7
JACKIE GALLAGHER	Gallagher, John Laurence b: 1/28/02, Providence, R.I. d: 9/10/84, Gladwyne, Pa. BL/TR, 5'10", 175 lbs. Deb: 8/24/23																							
1923	Cle-A	1	1	0	1	0	0	0	0	0	0	1.000	1.000	1.000	2000	428	0	0	0	0	.000	-1	/O-1(1-0-0)	0.0
JOE GALLAGHER	Gallagher, Joseph Emmett "Muscles" b: 3/7/14, Buffalo, N.Y. d: 2/25/98, Houston, Tex. BR/TR, 6'2", 210 lbs. Deb: 4/20/39																							
1939	NY-A	14	41	8	10	0	1	2	9	3	8	.244	.311	.439	750	91	-1	1	0	0	1.000	-1	O-12(0-0-12)	-0.2
	StL-A	71	266	41	75	17	2	9	40	17	42	.282	.327	.462	790	98	-2	0	1	-0	.944	2	O-67(56-0-11)	-0.4
	Yr	85	307	49	85	17	3	11	49	20	50	.277	.325	.459	785	97	-3	1	1	-0	.950	1	O-79(56-0-23)	-0.6
1940	StL-A	23	70	14	19	3	1	2	8	4	12	.271	.311	.429	739	88	-2	2	0	0	.966	-1	O-15(15-0-0)	-0.3
	Bro-N	57	110	10	29	6	1	3	16	2	14	.264	.283	.418	701	86	-2	1			.941	-2	O-20(3-0-17)	-0.6
Total	2	165	487	73	133	26	5	16	73	26	76	.273	.314	.446	760	93	-7	4	1		.950	-3	O-114(74-0-40)	-1.5

YEAR	TM/L	G	AB	R	H	2B	3B	HR	RBI	BB	SO	AVG	OBP	SLG	OPS	OPS+	BR+	SB	CS	SBR	FA	FR	G/POS	TPR
■ GIL GALLAGHER Gallagher, Lawrence Kirby b: 9/5/1896, Washington, D.C. d: 1/6/57, Washington, D.C. BB/TR, 5'8", 155 lbs. Deb: 9/13/22																								
1922	Bos-N	7	22	1	1	1	0	0	2	1	7	.045	.087	.091	178	-57	-5	0	0	0	.893	-2	/S-6	-0.6
■ BOB GALLAGHER Gallagher, Robert Collins b: 7/7/48, Newton, Mass. BL/TL, 6'3", 185 lbs. Deb: 5/17/72 F																								
1972	Bos-A	7	5	0	0	0	0	0	0	0	3	.000	.000	.000	0	-95	-1	0	0	0	.000	0	H	-0.1
1973	Hou-N	71	148	16	39	3	1	2	10	3	27	.264	.278	.338	616	70	-6	0	1	-0	1.000	-2	O-42(15-12-16)/1-1	-1.0
1974	Hou-N	102	87	13	15	2	0	0	3	12	23	.172	.280	.195	475	36	-7	1	0	0	.978	-21	O-62(5-53-4)/1-4	-3.0
1975	NY-N	33	15	5	2	1	0	0	0	1	3	.133	.188	.200	388	8	-2	0	0	0	.900	-5	O-16(10-1-5)	-0.7
Total	4	213	255	34	56	6	1	2	13	16	56	.220	.268	.275	543	52	-16	1	1	-0	.985	-27	O-120(30-66-25)/1-5	-4.8
■ WILLIAM GALLAGHER Gallagher, William Howard b: 2/4/1874, Boston, Mass. d: 3/11/50, Worcester, Mass. Deb: 8/19/1896																								
1896	Phi-N	14	49	9	15	2	0	0	6	10	0	.306	.433	.347	780	108	1	0			.894	-4	S-14	-0.2
■ BILL GALLAGHER Gallagher, William John b: Philadelphia, Pa. TL, Deb: 5/2/1883																								
1883	Bal-a	16	61	9	10	3	1	0		3		.164	.203	.246	449	43	-4				.824	-2	/O-9(1-0-8),P-7,S-4	-0.3
	Phi-N	2	8	1	0	0	0	0	0	0	4	.000	.000	.000	0	-99	-2				1.000	-0	/O-2(0-2-0)	-0.2
1884	Phi-U	3	11	1	1	0	0	0		0		.091	.091	.091	182	-48	-2				.800	0	/P-3	0.0
Total	2	21	80	11	11	3	1	0	0	3	4	.138	.169	.200	369	16	-8				.850	-2	/O-11(1-2-8),P-10,S-4	-0.5
■ STAN GALLE Galle, Stanley Joseph (b: Stanley Joseph Galazewski) b: 2/7/19, Milwaukee, Wis. BR/TR, 5'7", 165 lbs. Deb: 4/14/42																								
1942	Was-A	13	18	3	2	0	0	0	1	1	0	.111	.158	.111	269	-24	-3	0	0	0	.857	-1	/3-3	-0.3
■ MIKE GALLEGO Gallego, Michael Anthony b: 10/31/60, Whittier, Cal. BR/TR, 5'8", 160 lbs. Deb: 4/11/85 Career OF: (0-LF 0-CF 1-RF)																								
1985	Oak-A	76	77	13	16	5	1	1	9	12	14	.208	.322	.338	660	87	-1	1	1	-0	.991	12	2-42,S-21,3-12	1.2
1986	Oak-A	20	37	2	10	2	0	0	4	1	6	.270	.289	.324	614	72	-1	0	2	-1	.986	9	2-19/3-2,S-1	0.7
1987	Oak-A	72	124	18	31	6	0	2	14	12	21	.250	.321	.347	668	83	-3	0	1	-0	.968	17	2-31,3-24,S-17	1.5
1988	*Oak-A	129	277	38	58	8	0	2	20	34	53	.209	.298	.260	558	60	-14	2	3	-1	.993	4	2-83,S-42,3-16	-0.8
1989	*Oak-A	133	357	45	90	14	2	3	30	35	43	.252	.329	.328	657	89	-4	7	5	-0	.967	18	S-94,2-41/3-3,D-1	2.1
1990	*Oak-A	140	389	36	80	13	2	3	34	35	50	.206	.278	.272	551	57	-22	5	5	-1	.990	14	2-83,S-38,3-27,/OD	-0.5
1991	Oak-A	159	482	67	119	15	4	12	49	67	84	.247	.345	.369	714	103	4	6	9	-2	.989	-16	*2-135,S-55	-0.8
1992	NY-A	53	173	24	44	7	1	3	14	20	22	.254	.345	.358	704	98	0	0	1	-0	.990	1	2-40,S-14	0.3
1993	NY-A	119	403	63	114	20	1	10	54	50	65	.283	.368	.412	780	113	8	3	2	-0	.976	17	S-55,2-52,3-27,/D-1	3.0
1994	NY-A	89	306	39	73	17	1	6	41	38	46	.239	.330	.359	690	81	-8	0	1	-0	.970	20	S-72,2-26	1.6
1995	Oak-A	43	120	11	28	0	0	0	8	9	24	.233	.292	.233	526	41	-10	0	1	-0	.960	0	2-18,S-14,3-12	-0.8
1996	*StL-N	51	143	12	30	2	0	0	4	12	31	.210	.276	.224	499	34	-13	0	0	0	.985	7	2-43/3-7,S-1	-0.4
1997	StL-N	27	43	6	7	2	0	0	1	1	6	.163	.182	.209	391	2	-6	0	0	0	.962	5	2-11,S-10/3-7	-0.1
Total	13	1111	2931	374	700	111	12	42	282	326	465	.239	.322	.328	650	81	-72	24	31	-6	.986	107	2-624,S-434,3/DO	7.0
■ JIM GALLIGAN Galligan, James M. b: 1862, Easton, Pa. d: 7/17/01, New York, N.Y. 5'10", 160 lbs. Deb: 9/2/1889																								
1889	Lou-a	31	120	6	20	0	2	0	7	6	17	.167	.213	.200	413	18	-13	1			.915	2	O-31(31-0-0)	-1.0
■ CHICK GALLOWAY Galloway, Clarence Edward b: 8/4/1896, Clinton, S.C. d: 11/7/69, Clinton, S.C. BR/TR, 5'8", 160 lbs. Deb: 9/9/19																								
1919	Phi-A	17	63	2	9	0	0	0	4	1	8	.143	.156	.143	299	-16	-10	0			.969	1	S-17	-0.8
1920	Phi-A	98	298	28	60	9	3	0	18	22	22	.201	.259	.252	510	35	-28	2	2	-0	.928	4	S-84/2-4,3-3	-1.8
1921	Phi-A	131	465	42	123	28	5	3	47	29	43	.265	.310	.366	676	72	-21	12	7	0	.922	-22	*S-110,3-20/2-1	-2.8
1922	Phi-A	155	571	83	185	26	9	6	69	39	39	.324	.368	.433	801	105	4	10	19	-4	.952	1	*S-155	1.7
1923	Phi-A	134	504	64	140	18	9	2	62	37	30	.278	.327	.361	688	80	-15	12	10	-1	.944	2	*S-134	0.0
1924	Phi-A	129	464	41	128	16	4	2	48	23	23	.276	.311	.341	652	67	-23	11	12	-2	.952	2	*S-129	-0.8
1925	Phi-A	149	481	52	116	11	4	3	71	59	28	.241	.324	.299	623	55	-32	16	9	0	.954	-3	*S-148	-1.7
1926	Phi-A	133	408	37	98	13	6	0	49	31	20	.240	.295	.301	597	53	-28	8	7	-1	.935	-13	*S-133	-2.8
1927	Phi-A	77	181	25	48	10	4	0	22	18	9	.265	.332	.365	696	76	-6	1	3	-1	.946	5	S-61/3-7	0.3
1928	Det-A	53	148	17	39	5	2	1	17	15	3	.264	.331	.345	676	77	-5	7	2	1	.914	-4	S-22,3-21/1-1,O-1L	-0.4
Total	10	1076	3583	391	946	136	46	17	407	274	225	.264	.317	.342	659	69	-165	79	71		.943	-28	S-993/3-51,2-5,O1	-9.1
■ JIM GALLOWAY Galloway, James Cato "Bad News" b: 9/16/1887, Iredell, Tex. d: 5/3/50, Fort Worth, Tex. BB/TR, 6'3", 187 lbs. Deb: 8/24/12																								
1912	StL-N	21	54	4	10	2	0	0	4	5	8	.185	.254	.222	476	32	-5	2			.971	1	2-16/S-1	-0.4
■ JIM GALVIN Galvin, James Joseph b: 8/11/07, Somerville, Mass. d: 9/30/69, Marietta, Ga. BR/TR, 5'11.5", 180 lbs. Deb: 9/27/30																								
1930	Bos-A	2	2	0	0	0	0	0	0	0	0	.000	.000	.000	0	-99	-1	0	0	0	.000	0	H	-0.1
■ JOHN GALVIN Galvin, John S. b: Brooklyn, N.Y. d: 4/20/04, Brooklyn, N.Y. Deb: 5/7/1872																								
1872	Atl-n	1	4	0	0	0	0	0	0	0	0	.000	.000	.000	0	-85	-1	0	0	0	.200	-2	/2-1	-0.2
■ JOHN GAMBLE Gamble, John Robert b: 2/10/48, Reno, Nev. BR/TR, 5'10", 165 lbs. Deb: 9/7/72																								
1972	Det-A	6	3	0	0	0	0	0	0	0	0	.000	.000	.000	0	-97	-1	0	0	0	1.000	1	/S-1	0.1
1973	Det-A	7	0	1	0	0	0	0	0	0	0	—	—	—	—	—	0	0	0	0	.000	0	R	0.0
Total	2	13	3	1	0	0	0	0	0	0	0	.000	.000	.000	0	-97	-1	0	0	0	1.000	1	/S-1	0.1
■ LEE GAMBLE Gamble, Lee Jesse b: 6/28/10, Renovo, Pa. d: 10/5/94, Punxsutawney, Pa. BL/TR, 6'1", 170 lbs. Deb: 9/15/35																								
1935	Cin-N	2	4	2	2	1	0	0	2	1	0	.500	.600	.750	1350	269	1	1			1.000	-0	/O-2(2-0-0)	0.1
1938	Cin-N	53	75	13	24	3	1	0	5	0	6	.320	.320	.387	707	96	-1	0			1.000	-0	/O-9(9-0-0)	-0.1
1939	*Cin-N	72	221	24	59	7	2	0	14	9	14	.267	.296	.317	612	64	-11	5			.989	-3	O-56(55-1-0)	-1.8
1940	Cin-N	38	42	12	6	1	0	0	0	0	1	.143	.143	.167	310	-15	-6	0			1.000	0	O-10(2-0-8)	-0.7
Total	4	165	342	51	91	12	3	0	21	10	21	.266	.287	.319	606	64	-17	6			.993	-4	/O-77(68-1-8)	-2.5
■ OSCAR GAMBLE Gamble, Oscar Charles b: 12/20/49, Ramer, Ala. BL/TR, 5'11", 165 lbs. Deb: 8/27/69 Career OF: (274-LF 81-CF 469-RF)																								
1969	Chi-N	24	71	6	16	1	1	1	5	10	12	.225	.321	.310	631	69	-3	0	2	-1	.913	-2	O-24(1-23-0)	-0.6
1970	Phi-N	88	275	31	72	12	4	1	19	27	37	.262	.330	.345	675	84	-6	5	4	-0	.956	1	O-74(0-47-28)	-0.8
1971	Phi-N	92	280	24	62	11	1	6	23	21	35	.221	.278	.332	610	72	-11	5	2	0	.970	-4	O-80(54-1-26)	-2.0
1972	Phi-N	74	135	17	32	5	2	1	13	19	16	.237	.335	.326	661	86	-2	0	1	-0	1.000	-1	O-35(0-0-35)/1-1	-0.5
1973	Cle-A	113	390	56	104	11	3	20	44	34	37	.267	.330	.464	794	120	9	3	4	-1	.971	-1	D-70,O-37(2-1-35)	0.3
1974	Cle-A	135	454	74	132	16	4	19	59	48	51	.291	.365	.469	834	140	23	5	6	-1	1.000	-1	*D-115,O-13(12-0-1)	1.8
1975	Cle-A	121	348	60	91	16	3	15	45	53	39	.261	.362	.454	816	130	14	11	5	1	.987	1	O-82(81-0-1),D-29	1.1
1976	*NY-A	110	340	43	79	13	1	17	57	38	38	.232	.317	.426	743	117	7	5	3	0	.981	-0	*O-104(0-0-104)/D-1	0.2
1977	Chi-A	137	408	75	121	22	2	31	83	54	54	.297	.387	.588	975	162	35	1	2	-0	.987	-5	D-79,O-49(5-7-38)	2.5
1978	SD-N	126	375	46	103	15	3	7	47	51	45	.275	.370	.387	757	121	12	1	2	-0	.979	-0	*O-107(39-0-70)	0.7
1979	Tex-A	64	161	27	54	6	0	8	32	37	15	.335	.462	.522	984	167	17	2	1	0	1.000	1	D-37,O-21(0-0-21)	1.6
	NY-A	36	113	21	44	4	1	11	32	13	13	.389	.452	.735	1187	219	19	0	0	0	.943	0	O-27(25-2-0)/D-6	1.7
	Yr	100	274	48	98	10	1	19	64	50	28	.358	.458	.609	1068	188	36	2	1	0	.969	2	O-48(25-2-21),D-43	3.3
1980	*NY-A	78	194	40	54	10	2	14	50	28	21	.278	.381	.567	948	159	16	2	0	0	1.000	-6	O-49(36-0-14),D-20	0.8
1981	*NY-A	80	189	24	45	8	0	10	27	35	23	.238	.360	.439	799	131	8	0	2	-1	1.000	-2	O-43(16-0-27),D-33	0.3
1982	NY-A	108	316	49	86	21	2	18	57	58	47	.272	.392	.522	914	151	23	6	3	0	1.000	5	D-74,O-29(1-0-28)	2.4
1983	NY-A	74	180	26	47	10	2	7	26	25	23	.261	.361	.456	816	128	7	0	0	0	.942	-0	O-32(2-0-30),D-21	0.5
1984	NY-A	54	125	17	23	2	0	10	27	25	18	.184	.320	.440	760	112	2	1	0	0	1.000	-1	D-28,O-12(0-0-11)	0.0
1985	Chi-A	70	148	20	30	5	0	4	20	34	22	.203	.355	.318	673	83	-2	0	0	0	.000	0	D-48	-0.4
Total	17	1584	4502	656	1195	188	31	200	666	610	546	.265	.358	.454	813	127	168	47	37	-3	.977	-15	O-818R,D-561/1-1	9.6
■ DAFF GAMMONS Gammons, John Ashley b: 3/17/1876, New Bedford, Mass. d: 9/24/63, E.Greenwich, R.I. BR/TR, 5'11", 170 lbs. Deb: 4/23/01																								
1901	Bos-N	28	93	10	18	0	1	0	10	3		.194	.242	.215	457	30	-8	5			.880	-3	O-23(20-0-3)/2-2,3-1	-1.2
■ CHICK GANDIL Gandil, Arnold b: 1/19/1887, St.Paul, Minn. d: 12/13/70, Calistoga, Cal. BR/TR, 6'1.5", 190 lbs. Deb: 4/14/10																								
1910	Chi-A	77	275	21	53	7	3	2	21	24		.193	.267	.262	529	69	-10	12			.989	7	1-74/O-2(2-0-0)	-0.5

YEAR	TM/L	G	AB	R	H	2B	3B	HR	RBI	BB	SO	AVG	OBP	SLG	OPS	OPS+	BR+	SB	CS	SBR	FA	FR	G/POS	TPR
1912	Was-A	117	443	59	135	20	15	2	81	27		.305	.350	.431	781	122	11	21			**.990**	3	*1-117	1.0
1913	Was-A	148	550	61	175	25	8	1	72	36	33	.318	.363	.398	762	120	13	22			.990	8	*1-145	1.8
1914	Was-A	145	526	48	136	24	10	3	75	44	44	.259	.324	.359	683	101	-0	30	19	-0	.991	24	*1-145	2.2
1915	Was-A	136	485	53	141	20	15	2	64	29	33	.291	.340	.406	746	121	10	20	13	-0	.986	-1	*1-134	0.6
1916	Cle-A	146	533	51	138	26	9	0	72	36	48	.259	.312	.341	653	91	-7	13			**.995**	8	*1-145	-0.3
1917	*Chi-A	149	553	53	151	9	7	0	57	30	36	.273	.316	.315	631	91	-7	16			**.995**	-6	*1-149	-1.8
1918	Chi-A	114	439	49	119	18	4	0	55	27	19	.271	.319	.330	649	95	-4	9			.992	-3	*1-114	-1.0
1919	*Chi-A	115	441	54	128	24	7	1	60	20	20	.290	.325	.383	709	98	-2	10			**.997**	-4	*1-115	-1.0
Total	9	1147	4245	449	1176	173	78	11	557	273	233	.277	.327	.362	689	103	3	153	32		.992	36	*1-1138/O-2(2-0-0)	1.0
■ BOB GANDY Gandy, Robert Brinkley "String" b: 8/25/1893, Jacksonville, Fla. d: 6/19/45, Jacksonville, Fla BL/TR, 6'3", 180 lbs. Deb: 10/5/16																								
1916	Phi-N	1	2	0	0	0	0	0	0	0	1	.000	.000	.000	0	-97	-0	0			1.000	0	/O-1(0-1-0)	0.0
■ BOB GANLEY Ganley, Robert Stephen b: 4/23/1875, Lowell, Mass. d: 10/9/45, Lowell, Mass. BL/TL, 5'7", 156 lbs. Deb: 9/1/05																								
1905	Pit-N	32	127	12	40	1	2	0	7	8		.315	.356	.354	710	109	1	3			1.000	-2	O-32(0-6-27)	-0.3
1906	Pit-N	137	511	63	132	7	6	0	31	41		.258	.316	.295	611	87	-8	19			.965	-2	*O-134(0-12-122)	-1.8
1907	Was-A	154	605	73	167	10	5	1	35	54		.276	.337	.314	651	117	13	40			.940	9	*O-154(62-13-78)	1.6
1908	Was-A	150	549	61	131	19	9	1	36	45		.239	.299	.311	610	107	5	30			.964	4	*O-150(150-0-0)	-0.1
1909	Was-A	19	63	5	16	3	0	0	5	1		.254	.266	.302	567	83	-1	4			1.000	-3	O-17(11-5-1)	-0.7
	Phi-A	80	274	32	54	4	2	0	9	28		.197	.272	.226	498	56	-13	16			.980	8	O-77(0-77-0)	-1.0
	Yr	99	337	37	70	7	2	0	14	29		.208	.270	.240	511	61	-15	20			.982	4	O-94(11-82-1)	-1.7
Total	5	572	2129	246	540	44	24	2	123	177		.254	.313	.300	612	97	-3	112			.962	13	O-564(223-113-228)	-2.3
■ BILL GANNON Gannon, William G. b: 1876, New Haven, Conn. d: 4/26/27, Fort Worth, Tex. 5'9", 170 lbs. Deb: 9/9/01																								
1901	Chi-N	15	61	2	9	0	0	0	0	1		.148	.161	.148	309	-11	-8	5			1.000	-1	O-15(0-0-15)	-1.1
■ RON GANT Gant, Ronald Edwin b: 3/2/65, Victoria, Tex. BR/TR, 6', 192 lbs. Deb: 9/6/87 Career OF: (1036-LF 298-CF 3-RF)																								
1987	Atl-N	21	83	9	22	4	0	2	9	1	11	.265	.274	.386	659	69	-4	4	2	0	.972	-0	2-20	-0.3
1988	Atl-N	146	563	85	146	28	8	19	60	46	118	.259	.319	.439	757	110	6	19	10	1	.963	-1	*2-122,3-22	1.0
1989	Atl-N	75	260	26	46	8	3	9	25	20	63	.177	.238	.335	573	61	-14	9	6	-0	.887	3	3-53,O-14(2-14-0)	-1.2
1990	Atl-N	152	575	107	174	34	3	32	84	50	86	.303	.359	.539	899	136	27	33	16	2	.978	7	*O-146(38-113-3)	3.3
1991	*Atl-N	154	561	101	141	35	3	32	105	71	104	.251	.341	.496	836	125	18	34	15	2	.983	8	*O-148(0-148-0)	2.7
1992	*Atl-N★	153	544	74	141	22	6	17	80	45	101	.259	.324	.415	739	102	1	32	10	4	.986	-4	*O-147(138-23-0)	-0.3
1993	*Atl-N	157	606	113	166	27	4	36	117	67	117	.274	.348	.510	858	125	20	26	9	3	.962	-3	*O-155(155-0-0)	1.5
1995	*Cin-N★	119	410	79	113	19	4	29	88	74	108	.276	.390	.554	944	146	28	23	8	2	.985	4	*O-117(117-0-0)	3.0
1996	*StL-N	122	419	74	103	14	2	30	82	73	98	.246	.362	.504	865	126	16	13	4	1	.978	6	*O-116(116-0-0)	2.0
1997	StL-N	139	502	68	115	21	4	17	62	58	162	.229	.310	.388	699	82	-14	14	6	1	.977	7	*O-128(128-0-0)/D-1	-1.0
1998	StL-N	121	383	60	92	17	1	26	67	51	92	.240	.333	.493	826	115	7	8	0	2	.971	-2	*O-104(104-0-0)	0.5
1999	Phi-N	138	516	107	134	27	5	17	77	85	112	.260	.365	.430	796	98	-1	13	3	2	.993	10	*O-133(133-0-0)/D-2	0.7
2000	Phi-N	89	343	54	87	16	2	20	38	36	73	.254	.326	.487	813	100	-1	5	4	-0	.968	9	O-84(84-0-0)	0.5
	Ana-A	34	82	15	19	3	1	6	16	20	18	.232	.382	.512	895	123	3	1	2	-0	.977	0	O-21(21-0-0),D-12	0.2
Total	13	1620	5847	972	1499	275	46	292	910	697	1263	.256	.339	.469	808	112	93	234	95	18	.978	43	*O-1313L,2-142/3-75,D	12.6
■ JOE GANTENBEIN Gantenbein, Joseph Steven "Sep" b: 8/25/16, San Francisco, Cal d: 8/2/93, Novato, Cal. BL/TR, 5'9", 168 lbs. Deb: 4/20/39 Career OF: (1-LF 0-CF 0-RF)																								
1939	Phi-A	111	348	47	101	14	4	4	36	32	22	.290	.353	.388	741	91	-4	1	5	-2	.948	-34	2-76,3-14/S-5	-3.2
1940	Phi-A	75	197	21	47	6	2	4	23	11	21	.239	.282	.350	633	64	-11	1	0	0	.930	-8	3-45/1-6,S-3,O-1L	-1.7
Total	2	186	545	68	148	20	6	8	59	43	43	.272	.328	.374	703	82	-15	2	5	-1	.934	-42	/2-76,3-59,S-8,1O	-4.9
■ JIM GANTNER Gantner, James Elmer b: 1/5/53, Fond Du Lac, Wis. BL/TR, 6', 180 lbs. Deb: 9/3/76 C																								
1976	Mil-A	26	69	6	17	1	0	0	7	6	11	.246	.316	.261	577	71	-2	1	0	0	.982	-3	3-24/D-2	-0.6
1977	Mil-A	14	47	4	14	1	0	1	2	2	5	.298	.327	.383	710	93	-1	2	1	0	.902	1	3-14	0.1
1978	Mil-A	43	97	14	21	1	0	1	8	5	10	.216	.269	.258	527	49	-7	2	0	0	.980	5	2-21,3-15/1-1,S-1	0.0
1979	Mil-A	70	208	29	59	10	3	2	22	16	17	.284	.341	.389	730	96	-1	3	5	-1	.952	4	3-42,2-22/S-3,P-1	0.3
1980	Mil-A	132	415	47	117	21	3	4	40	30	29	.282	.332	.376	708	97	-2	11	10	-1	.938	-1	3-69,2-66/S-1	-0.1
1981	*Mil-A	107	352	35	94	14	1	2	33	29	29	.267	.328	.330	658	95	-2	3	6	-1	.984	16	*2-107	1.9
1982	*Mil-A	132	447	48	132	17	2	4	43	26	36	.295	.337	.369	706	100	-0	6	3	0	.982	9	*2-131	1.6
1983	Mil-A	161	603	85	170	23	8	11	74	38	46	.282	.331	.401	732	109	6	5	6	-1	.984	10	*2-158	2.4
1984	Mil-A	153	613	61	173	27	1	3	56	30	51	.282	.319	.344	663	87	-11	6	5	-0	.985	10	*2-153	0.7
1985	Mil-A	143	523	63	133	15	4	5	44	33	42	.254	.302	.327	629	73	-19	11	8	-0	.988	1	*2-124,3-24/S-1	-1.2
1986	Mil-A	139	497	58	136	25	1	7	38	26	50	.274	.318	.370	688	84	-11	13	7	0	.985	-12	*2-135/3-3,S-1,D-1	-1.5
1987	Mil-A	81	265	37	72	14	0	4	30	19	22	.272	.332	.370	702	84	-6	6	2	1	.984	5	2-57,3-38/D-1	0.2
1988	Mil-A	155	539	67	149	28	2	0	47	34	50	.276	.323	.336	659	84	-11	20	8	2	.986	-8	*2-154/3-1	-1.4
1989	Mil-A	116	409	51	112	18	3	0	34	21	33	.274	.325	.333	658	86	-7	20	6	2	.987	9	*2-114/D-2	0.8
1990	Mil-A	88	323	36	85	8	5	0	25	29	19	.263	.328	.319	647	82	-7	18	3	3	.982	-7	2-80/3-9	-1.0
1991	Mil-A	140	526	63	149	27	4	2	47	27	34	.283	.322	.361	683	91	-7	4	6	-1	.976	4	3-90,2-59	-0.2
1992	Mil-A	101	256	22	63	12	1	1	18	12	17	.246	.280	.313	592	67	-12	6	2	1	.994	7	2-68,3-31/1-2,D-2	-0.3
Total	17	1801	6189	726	1696	262	38	47	568	383	501	.274	.322	.351	673	88	-99	137	78	3	.985	50	*2-1449,3-360/DS1P	1.7
■ CHARLIE GANZEL Ganzel, Charles William b: 6/18/1862, Waterford, Wis. d: 4/7/14, Quincy, Mass. BR/TR, 6', 161 lbs. Deb: 9/27/1884 F Career OF: (25-LF 5-CF 71-RF)																								
1884	StP-U	7	23	2	5	0	0	0		0		.217	.217	.217	435	59	-2				.956	-2	/C-6,O-1(0-1-0)	-0.3
1885	Phi-N	34	125	15	21	3	1	0	6	4	13	.168	.194	.208	402	31	-9				.888	0	C-33/O-1(0-1-0)	-0.6
1886	Phi-N	1	3	0	0	0	0	0	0	0	1	.000	.000	.000	0	-99	-1	0			.600	-1	/C-1	-0.1
	Det-N	57	213	28	58	7	2	1	31	7	22	.272	.295	.338	633	90	-3	5			.911	3	C-45/O-7(7-0-0),1-5	0.3
	Yr	58	216	28	58	7	2	1	31	7	23	.269	.291	.333	625	87	-4	5			.903	3	C-46/O-7(7-0-0),1-5	0.2
1887	*Det-N	57	235	40	67	6	5	0	20	8	2	.285	.288	.330	619	69	-10	3			.913	9	C-51/O-4L,1-2,3-1	0.3
1888	Det-N	95	386	45	96	13	5	1	46	14	15	.249	.277	.316	593	89	-5	12			.900	-1	2-49,C-28/3-9,OS1	-0.1
1889	Bos-N	73	275	30	73	3	5	1	43	15	11	.265	.308	.324	632	72	-11	13			.927	5	C-39,O-26R/1-7,S3	-0.3
1890	Bos-N	38	163	21	44	7	3	0	24	5	6	.270	.300	.350	650	83	-5	1			.958	3	C-22,O-15R/S-3,2-1	0.1
1891	Bos-N	70	263	33	68	18	5	1	29	12	13	.259	.304	.376	680	87	-6	7			.956	4	C-59,O-13(5-1-7)	0.3
1892	*Bos-N	54	198	25	53	9	3	0	25	18	12	.268	.332	.343	675	95	-2	7			.933	-6	C-51/O-2(1-1-0),1-1	-0.3
1893	Bos-N	73	281	50	75	10	2	1	48	22	9	.267	.325	.327	652	68	-14	6			.952	-2	C-40,O-23R,1-10	-1.1
1894	Bos-N	70	266	51	74	7	6	3	56	19	6	.278	.326	.383	710	65	-16	1			.897	-5	C-59/1-7,O-3R,S2	-1.3
1895	Bos-N	81	280	38	73	2	5	1	52	25	6	.261	.324	.314	638	60	-17	1			.963	20	C-77/S-2,1-2	0.8
1896	Bos-N	47	179	28	47	2	0	1	18	9	5	.263	.305	.291	596	54	-12	2			.989	6	C-41/1-3,S-2	-0.2
1897	Bos-N	30	105	15	28	4	3	0	14	4		.267	.300	.362	662	70	-5	2			.942	2	C-27/1-2	-0.1
Total	14	787	2995	421	782	91	45	10	412	162	121	.261	.301	.330	631	73	-117	60			.935	37	C-579,O-100R/21S3	-2.6
■ BABE GANZEL Ganzel, Foster Pirie b: 5/22/01, Malden, Mass. d: 2/6/78, Jacksonville, Fla. BR/TR, 5'10.5", 172 lbs. Deb: 9/19/27 F																								
1927	Was-A	13	48	7	21	4	2	1	13	7	3	.438	.509	.667	1176	206	8	0	0	0	.944	0	O-13(4-9-0)	0.7
1928	Was-A	10	26	2	2	1	0	0	4	1	4	.077	.111	.115	226	-41	-5	0	0	0	1.000	-1	/O-7(4-2-2)	-0.7
Total	2	23	74	9	23	5	2	1	17	8	7	.311	.378	.473	851	122	2	0	0	0	.957	-1	/O-20(8-11-2)	0.0
■ JOHN GANZEL Ganzel, John Henry b: 4/7/1874, Kalamazoo, Mich. d: 1/14/59, Orlando, Fla. BR/TR, 6'0.5", 195 lbs. Deb: 4/21/1898 FM																								
1898	Pit-N	15	45	5	6	0	0	0	2	4		.133	.220	.133	353	2	-6	0			.963	-1	1-12	-0.7
1900	Chi-N	78	284	29	78	14	4	4	32	10		.275	.316	.394	710	99	-1	5			.980	-4	1-78	-0.5
1901	NY-N	138	526	42	113	13	3	2	66	20		.215	.256	.262	518	52	-32	6			**.986**	2	*1-138	-3.2
1903	NY-A	129	476	62	132	25	7	3	71	30		.277	.336	.378	714	107	4	9			**.988**	7	*1-129	0.9
1904	NY-A	130	465	50	121	16	10	6	48	24		.260	.309	.376	686	111	5	13			.988	-2	*1-118/2-9,S-1	0.1
1907	Cin-N	145	531	61	135	20	**16**	2	64	29		.254	.297	.363	660	102	-1	9			.990	1	*1-143	-0.3
1908	Cin-N	112	388	32	97	16	10	1	53	19		.250	.289	.351	639	107	1	6			**.990**	-2	*1-108,M	-0.3
Total	7	747	2715	281	682	104	50	18	336	136		.251	.298	.346	644	93	-29	48			.987	0	1-726/2-9,S-1	-4.0

YEAR	TM/L	G	AB	R	H	2B	3B	HR	RBI	BB	SO	AVG	OBP	SLG	OPS	OPS+	BR+	SB	CS	SBR	FA	FR	G/POS	TPR
■ JOE GARAGIOLA	Garagiola, Joseph Henry b: 2/12/26, St.Louis, Mo. BL/TR, 6', 190 lbs. Deb: 5/26/46																							
1946	*StL-N	74	211	21	50	4	1	3	22	23	25	.237	.312	.308	620	73	-7	0			.990	-5	C-70	-0.9
1947	StL-N	77	183	20	47	10	2	5	25	40	14	.257	.398	.415	814	111	4	0			.987	1	C-74	0.8
1948	StL-N	24	56	9	6	1	0	2	7	12	9	.107	.275	.232	508	36	-5	0			.990	2	C-23	-0.2
1949	StL-N	81	241	25	63	14	0	3	26	31	19	.261	.348	.357	705	85	-4	0			.984	7	C-80	0.7
1950	StL-N	34	88	8	28	6	1	2	20	10	7	.318	.388	.477	865	120	3	0			1.000	-3	C-30	0.1
1951	StL-N	27	72	9	14	3	2	2	9	9	7	.194	.284	.375	659	75	-3	0	0	0	1.000	-3	C-23	-0.4
	Pit-N	72	212	24	54	8	2	9	35	32	20	.255	.358	.439	796	110	3	4	1	1	.986	-9	C-61	-0.1
	Yr	99	284	33	68	11	4	11	44	41	27	.239	.339	.423	762	101	1	4	1	1	**.989**	-11	C-84	-0.5
1952	Pit-N	118	344	35	94	15	4	8	54	50	24	.273	.369	.410	779	113	7	0	1	-0	.978	-3	*C-105	1.0
1953	Pit-N	27	73	9	17	5	0	2	14	10	11	.233	.341	.384	725	89	-1	1	0	0	.989	-4	C-22	-0.3
	Chi-N	74	228	21	62	9	4	1	21	21	23	.272	.336	.360	696	80	-6	0	0	0	.988	0	C-68	-0.3
	Yr	101	301	30	79	14	4	3	35	31	34	.262	.337	.365	703	82	-7	1	0	0	.988	-4	C-90	-0.6
1954	Chi-N	63	153	16	43	5	0	5	21	28	12	.281	.405	.412	817	112	4	0	0	0	.982	-8	C-55	-0.1
	NY-N	5	11	1	3	2	0	0	1	1	2	.273	.333	.455	788	102	0	0	0	0	1.000	0	/C-3	0.0
	Yr	68	164	17	46	7	0	5	22	29	14	.280	.401	.415	816	112	4	0	0	0	.983	-8	C-58	-0.1
Total	9	676	1872	198	481	82	16	42	255	267	173	.257	.355	.385	740	96	-5	5	2		.986	-23	C-614	0.3
■ MIKE GARBARK	Garbark, Nathaniel Michael (b: Nathaniel Michael Garbach) b: 2/3/16, Houston, Tex. d: 8/31/94, Charlotte, N.C. BR/TR, 6', 200 lbs. Deb: 4/18/44 F																							
1944	NY-A	89	299	23	78	9	4	1	33	25	27	.261	.320	.328	648	82	-7	0	1	-0	.988	8	C-85	0.6
1945	NY-A	60	176	23	38	5	3	1	26	23	12	.216	.310	.295	605	73	-6	0	1	-0	.972	4	C-59	0.1
Total	2	149	475	46	116	14	7	2	59	48	39	.244	.316	.316	632	79	-12	0	2	-1	.982	12	C-144	0.7
■ BOB GARBARK	Garbark, Robert Michael (b: Robert Michael Garbach) b: 11/13/09, Houston, Tex. d: 8/15/90, Meadville, Pa. BR/TR, 5'11", 178 lbs. Deb: 9/3/34 F																							
1934	Cle-A	5	11	1	0	0	0	0	0	1	3	.000	.083	.000	83	-76	-3	0	0	0	1.000	-2	/C-5	-0.4
1935	Cle-A	6	18	4	6	1	0	0	4	5	1	.333	.478	.389	867	124	1	0	0	0	1.000	2	/C-6	0.3
1937	Chi-N	1	1	0	0	0	0	0	0	0	0	.000	.000	.000	0	-96	-0	0			.000	0	H	0.0
1938	Chi-N	23	54	2	14	0	0	0	5	1	0	.259	.273	.259	532	46	-4	0			1.000	1	C-20/1-1	-0.2
1939	Chi-N	24	21	1	3	0	0	0	0	0	3	.143	.143	.143	286	-23	-4	0			1.000	1	C-21	-0.3
1944	Phi-A	18	23	2	6	2	0	0	2	1	0	.261	.292	.348	639	83	-1	0	0	0	1.000	-0	C-15	-0.1
1945	Bos-A	68	199	21	52	6	0	0	17	18	10	.261	.329	.291	620	79	-5	0	1	-0	.993	-3	C-67	-0.5
Total	7	145	327	31	81	9	0	0	28	26	17	.248	.307	.275	582	64	-15	0	1		.996	-2	C-134/1-1	-1.2
■ BARBARO GARBEY	Garbey, Barbaro (Garbey) b: 12/4/56, Santiago De Cuba, Cuba BR/TR, 5'10", 170 lbs. Deb: 4/3/84 Career OF: (25-LF 2-CF 16-RF)																							
1984	*Det-A	110	327	45	94	17	1	5	52	17	35	.287	.327	.391	718	98	-1	6	7	-1	.989	-5	1-65,3-20,D-17,O/2	-1.2
1985	Det-A	86	237	27	61	9	1	6	29	15	37	.257	.310	.380	690	88	-4	3	2	-0	.991	-2	1-37,O-24R,D-21,/3	-0.9
1988	Tex-A	30	62	4	12	2	0	0	5	4	11	.194	.242	.226	468	31	-6	0	0	0	.900	-0	/O-8L,1-7,3-3,D-7	-0.6
Total	3	226	626	76	167	28	2	11	86	36	83	.267	.312	.371	682	88	-11	9	9	-1	.990	-8	1-109/D-45,O-42L,32	-2.7
■ ALEX GARBOWSKI	Garbowski, Alexander b: 6/25/25, Yonkers, N.Y BR/TR, 6'1", 185 lbs. Deb: 4/16/52																							
1952	Det-A	2	0	0	0	0	0	0	0	0	0	—	—	—	—	—	0	0	0	0	.000	0	R	0.0
■ KIKO GARCIA	Garcia, Alfonso Rafael b: 10/14/53, Martinez, Cal. BR/TR, 5'11", 180 lbs. Deb: 9/11/76																							
1976	Bal-A	11	32	2	7	1	1	1	4	0	4	.219	.219	.406	625	86	-1	2	1	0	1.000	1	S-11	0.1
1977	Bal-A	65	131	20	29	6	0	2	10	6	31	.221	.255	.313	568	58	-8	2	3	-1	.966	20	S-61/2-2	1.5
1978	Bal-A	79	186	17	49	6	4	0	13	7	43	.263	.290	.339	629	81	-5	7	1	1	.945	4	S-74/2-3	0.6
1979	*Bal-A	126	417	54	103	15	9	5	24	32	87	.247	.304	.362	666	82	-11	11	9	-1	.955	-18	*S-113,2-25/3-2,O-2L	-1.8
1980	Bal-A	111	311	27	62	8	0	1	27	24	57	.199	.257	.235	491	36	-27	8	4	0	.974	2	S-96,2-27/O-1(1-0-0)	-1.6
1981	*Hou-N	48	136	9	37	6	1	0	15	10	16	.272	.327	.331	657	91	-2	2	2	-0	.950	3	S-28,3-13/2-9	0.4
1982	Hou-N	34	76	5	16	5	0	1	5	3	15	.211	.241	.316	556	59	-4	1	0	0	.946	5	S-21/3-2,2-1	0.2
1983	Phi-N	84	118	22	34	7	1	2	9	9	20	.288	.344	.415	759	111	2	1	2	-0	.970	19	2-52,S-22,3-10	2.2
1984	Phi-N	57	60	6	14	2	0	0	5	4	11	.233	.281	.267	548	54	-4	0	0	0	.965	5	S-30,3-23/2-1	0.2
1985	Phi-N	4	3	0	0	0	0	0	0	0	1	.000	.000	.000	0	-97	-1	0	0	0	1.000	-1	/S-3,3-1	-0.2
Total	10	619	1470	162	351	56	16	12	112	95	285	.239	.287	.323	610	70	-61	34	22	-0	.961	39	S-459,2-120/3-51,O	1.6
■ AMAURY GARCIA	Garcia, Amaury Miguel (Paula) b: 5/20/75, Santo Domingo, D.R. BR/TR, 5'10", 160 lbs. Deb: 7/5/99																							
1999	Fla-N	10	24	6	6	0	1	2	2	3	11	.250	.333	.583	917	133	1	0	0	0	.932	4	/2-8	0.5
■ CARLOS GARCIA	Garcia, Carlos Jesus (Guerrero) b: 10/15/67, Tachira, Venez. BR/TR, 6'1", 185 lbs. Deb: 9/20/90																							
1990	Pit-N	4	4	1	2	0	0	0	0	0	2	.500	.500	.500	1000	183	0	0	0	0	1.000	1	/S-3	0.1
1991	Pit-N	12	24	2	6	0	2	0	1	1	8	.250	.280	.417	697	95	-0	0	0	0	.947	2	/S-9,3-2,2-1	0.2
1992	*Pit-N	22	39	4	8	1	0	0	4	0	9	.205	.205	.231	436	23	-4	0	0	0	.977	2	2-14/S-8	-0.1
1993	Pit-N	141	546	77	147	25	5	12	47	31	67	.269	.319	.399	718	91	-8	18	11	0	.983	-26	*2-140/S-3	-2.7
1994	Pit-N★	98	412	49	114	15	2	6	28	16	67	.277	.310	.367	677	75	-15	18	9	0	.978	8	2-98	-0.1
1995	Pit-N	104	367	41	108	24	2	6	50	25	55	.294	.343	.420	762	98	-1	8	4	0	.982	14	2-92,S-15	1.8
1996	Pit-N	101	390	66	111	18	4	6	44	23	58	.285	.331	.397	728	89	-6	16	6	1	.985	3	2-77,S-19,3-14	0.3
1997	Tor-A	103	350	29	77	18	2	3	23	15	60	.220	.256	.309	565	46	-28	11	3	1	.981	-7	2-96/S-5,3-4	-2.7
1998	Ana-A	19	35	4	5	1	0	0	0	3	11	.143	.231	.171	402	7	-5	2	0	0	.978	6	2-11/S-5,D-3	0.2
1999	SD-N	6	11	1	2	0	0	0	0	1	3	.182	.250	.182	432	13	-1	0	0	0	.778	-1	/3-4,1-1	-0.2
Total	10	610	2178	274	580	102	17	33	197	115	340	.266	.310	.374	684	79	-69	73	33	5	.982	4	2-529/S-67,3-24,D1	-3.2
■ DAMASO GARCIA	Garcia, Damaso Domingo (Sanchez) b: 2/7/55, Moca, D.R. BR/TR, 6', 170 lbs. Deb: 6/24/78																							
1978	NY-A	18	41	5	8	0	0	0	1	2	6	.195	.233	.195	428	22	-4	1	0	0	.959	2	2-16/S-3	-0.2
1979	NY-A	11	38	3	10	1	0	0	4	0	2	.263	.263	.289	553	50	-3	2	0	0	.902	-6	S-10/3-1	-0.7
1980	Tor-A	140	543	50	151	30	7	4	46	12	55	.278	.297	.381	679	81	-15	13	13	-2	.980	16	*2-138/D-1	0.7
1981	Tor-A	64	250	24	63	8	1	1	13	9	32	.252	.278	.304	582	64	-12	13	3	2	.972	-15	2-62/D-1	-2.2
1982	Tor-A	147	597	89	185	32	3	5	42	21	44	.310	.339	.399	737	93	-5	54	20	5	.980	10	*2-141/D-4	1.7
1983	Tor-A	131	525	84	161	23	6	3	38	24	34	.307	.339	.390	730	94	-4	31	17	1	.981	-16	*2-130	-1.2
1984	Tor-A★	152	633	79	180	32	5	5	46	16	46	.284	.312	.374	686	86	-13	46	12	6	.980	-14	*2-149/D-1	-1.3
1985	*Tor-A★	146	600	70	169	25	4	8	65	15	41	.282	.304	.377	680	83	-15	28	15	1	.981	-34	*2-143	-4.0
1986	Tor-A	122	424	57	119	22	0	6	46	13	32	.281	.308	.375	683	83	-10	9	6	-0	.985	-7	*2-106,D-11/1-1	-1.2
1988	Atl-N	21	60	3	7	1	0	1	4	3	10	.117	.159	.183	342	-2	-8	1	0	0	.984	-4	2-13	-1.2
1989	Mon-N	80	203	26	55	9	1	3	18	15	20	.271	.321	.369	691	96	-1	5	4	-0	.972	6	2-62/3-1	0.6
Total	11	1032	3914	490	1108	183	27	36	323	130	322	.283	.311	.371	682	84	-90	203	90	13	.980	-62	2-960/D-18,S-13,31	-9.0
■ DANNY GARCIA	Garcia, Daniel Raphael b: 4/29/54, Brooklyn, N.Y. BL/TL, 6'1", 182 lbs. Deb: 4/26/81																							
1981	KC-A	12	14	4	2	0	0	0	0	0	2	.143	.143	.143	286	-18	-2	0	0	0	1.000	-2	/O-6(1-0-5),1-2	-0.4
■ FREDDY GARCIA	Garcia, Freddy Adrian (Felix) b: 8/1/72, LaRomana, D.R. BR/TR, 6'2", 190 lbs. Deb: 5/3/95 Career OF: (28-LF 0-CF 7-RF)																							
1995	Pit-N	42	57	5	8	1	1	0	1	8	17	.140	.246	.193	439	17	-7	0	1	-0	1.000	2	O-10(10-0-0)/3-8	-0.5
1997	Pit-N	20	40	4	6	1	0	3	5	2	17	.150	.190	.400	590	49	-3	0	0	0	.842	-2	3-10/1-2	-0.5
1998	Pit-N	56	172	27	44	11	1	9	26	18	45	.256	.333	.488	822	111	2	0	2	-1	.949	5	3-47/1-4	0.6
1999	Pit-N	55	130	16	30	5	0	6	23	4	41	.231	.254	.408	661	64	-8	0	0	0	.977	-1	O-24(17-0-7)/3-9,D-2	-0.9
	Atl-N	2	2	1	1	0	0	1	1	1	1	.500	.667	2.000	2667	540	1	0	0	0	.000	-1	/1-1,O-1(1-0-0)	0.1
	Yr	57	132	17	31	5	0	7	24	5	42	.235	.263	.432	695	72	-6	0	0	0	.977	-1	O-25L/3-9,D-2,1-1	-0.8
Total	4	175	401	53	89	18	2	19	56	33	121	.222	.284	.419	703	79	-14	0	3	-1	.938	3	/3-74,O-35L,1-7,D-2	-1.2
■ GUILLERMO GARCIA	Garcia, Guillermo Antonio (Morel) b: 4/4/72, Santiago, D.R. BR/TR, 6'3", 215 lbs. Deb: 7/19/98																							
1998	Cin-N	12	36	3	7	2	0	2	4	2	13	.194	.237	.417	654	67	-2	0	0	0	.988	3	C-11	0.2
1999	Fla-N	4	4	0	1	0	0	0	0	0	2	.250	.250	.250	500	29	-0	0	0	0	1.000	-0	C-3	-0.1
Total	2	16	40	3	8	2	0	2	4	2	15	.200	.238	.400	638	63	-2	0	0	0	.988	3	/C-14	0.1

YEAR	TM/L	G	AB	R	H	2B	3B	HR	RBI	BB	SO	AVG	OBP	SLG	OPS	OPS+	BR+	SB	CS	SBR	FA	FR	G/POS	TPR
■ **KARIM GARCIA**	Garcia, Gustavo Karim b: 10/29/75, Ciudad Obregon, Mexico BL/TL, 6', 200 lbs. Deb: 9/2/95																							
1995	LA-N	13	20	1	4	0	0	0	0	0	4	.200	.200	.200	400	6	-3	0	0	0	1.000	1	/O-5(2-0-3)	-0.2
1996	LA-N	1	1	0	0	0	0	0	0	0	1	.000	.000	.000	0	-99	-0	0	0	0	.000	0	/H	0.0
1997	LA-N	15	39	5	5	0	0	1	8	6	14	.128	.244	.205	450	21	-5	0	0	0	1.000	-2	O-12(12-0-2)	-0.7
1998	Ari-N	113	333	39	74	10	8	9	43	18	78	.222	.262	.381	643	67	-17	5	4	-0	.975	0	*O-103(0-7-100)	-2.1
1999	Det-A	96	288	38	69	10	3	14	32	20	67	.240	.289	.441	730	83	-9	2	4	-1	.958	-2	O-81(35-0-55)/D-6	-1.4
2000	Det-A	8	17	1	3	0	0	0	0	0	4	.176	.176	.176	353	-10	-3	0	0	0	1.000	-1	/O-7(0-0-7),D-1	-0.4
	Bal-A	8	16	0	0	0	0	0	0	0	6	.000	.000	.000	0	-99	-5	0	0	0	1.000	-0	/O-2(2-0-0),D-4	-0.5
	Yr	16	33	1	3	0	0	0	0	0	10	.091	.091	.091	182	-55	-8	0	0	0	1.000	-2	/O-9(2-0-7),D-5	-0.9
Total	6	254	714	84	155	20	11	24	83	44	174	.217	.263	.377	639	64	-41	7	8	-1	.970	-5	O-210(51-7-167)/D-11	-5.3
■ **JESSE GARCIA**	Garcia, Jesus Jesse b: 9/24/73, Corpus Christi, Tex. BR/TR, 5'10", 155 lbs. Deb: 4/5/99																							
1999	Bal-A	17	29	6	6	0	0	2	2	2	3	.207	.258	.414	672	70	-1	0	0	0	1.000	2	/S-7,2-6,3-2,D-1	0.1
2000	Bal-A	14	17	2	1	0	0	0	0	2	2	.059	.158	.059	217	-43	-4	0	0	0	1.000	6	/2-6,S-5	0.2
Total	2	31	46	8	7	0	0	2	2	4	5	.152	.220	.283	503	28	-5	0	0	0	1.000	8	/2-12,S-12,3-2,D-1	0.3
■ **LEO GARCIA**	Garcia, Leonardo Antonio (Peralta) b: 11/6/62, Santiago, D.R. BL/TL, 5'8", 160 lbs. Deb: 4/6/87																							
1987	Cin-N	31	30	8	6	0	0	1	2	4	8	.200	.294	.300	594	55	-2	3	1	0	1.000	-2	O-14(0-13-1)	-0.4
1988	Cin-N	23	28	2	4	1	0	0	0	4	5	.143	.250	.179	429	24	-3	0	1	-0	1.000	-1	/O-9(2-4-3)	-0.5
Total	2	54	58	10	10	1	0	1	2	8	13	.172	.273	.241	514	41	-5	3	2	-0	1.000	-4	/O-23(2-17-4)	-0.9
■ **LUIS GARCIA**	Garcia, Luis Rafael b: 5/20/75, San Francisco De Macoris, D.R. BR/TR, 6', 175 lbs. Deb: 4/5/99																							
1999	Det-A	8	9	0	1	1	0	0	0	0	2	.111	.111	.222	333	-18	-2	0	0	0	1.000	-2	/S-7,2-1	-0.3
■ **PEDRO GARCIA**	Garcia, Pedro Modesto (Delfi) b: 4/17/50, Guayama, P.R. BR/TR, 5'10", 175 lbs. Deb: 4/6/73																							
1973	Mil-A	160	580	67	142	**32**	5	15	54	40	119	.245	.299	.395	694	96	-5	11	10	-1	.970	-12	*2-160	-0.7
1974	Mil-A	141	452	46	90	15	4	12	54	26	67	.199	.251	.330	580	66	-21	8	5	0	.970	-11	*2-140	-2.4
1975	Mil-A	98	302	40	68	15	2	6	38	18	59	.225	.273	.348	621	74	-11	12	6	1	.985	19	2-94/D-1	1.5
1976	Mil-A	41	106	12	23	7	1	1	9	4	23	.217	.259	.330	589	73	-4	2	2	-0	.971	-3	2-39	-0.5
	Det-A	77	227	21	45	10	2	3	20	9	40	.198	.242	.300	541	56	-13	2	3	-1	.958	-0	2-77	-1.0
	Yr	118	333	33	68	17	3	4	29	13	63	.204	.247	.309	556	61	-17	4	5	-1	.962	-3	*2-116	-1.5
1977	Tor-A	41	130	10	27	10	1	0	9	5	21	.208	.254	.300	554	50	-9	0	0	0	.971	-2	2-34/D-4	-0.9
Total	5	558	1797	196	395	89	15	37	184	102	329	.220	.270	.348	618	75	-63	35	26	-1	.971	-8	2-544/D-5	-4.0
■ **CHICO GARCIA**	Garcia, Vinicio Uzcanga b: 12/24/24, Veracruz, Mexico BR/TR, 5'8", 170 lbs. Deb: 4/24/54																							
1954	Bal-A	39	62	6	7	0	2	0	5	8	3	.113	.214	.177	392	9	-8	0	0	0	.962	8	2-24	0.1
■ **NOMAR GARCIAPARRA**	Garciaparra, Anthony Nomar b: 7/23/73, Whittier, Cal. BR/TR, 6', 165 lbs. Deb: 8/31/96																							
1996	Bos-A	24	87	11	21	2	3	4	16	4	14	.241	.275	.471	746	82	-3	5	0	1	.988	-5	S-22/2-1,D-1	-0.4
1997	Bos-A★	153	684	122	**209**	44	**11**	30	98	35	92	.306	.345	.534	878	122	20	22	9	2	.971	-0	*S-153	3.2
1998	*Bos-A	143	604	111	195	37	8	35	122	33	62	.323	.366	.584	950	139	32	12	6	1	.962	-18	*S-143	2.6
1999	*Bos-A★	135	532	103	190	42	4	27	104	51	39	**.357**	.421	.603	1025	153	42	14	3	2	.972	-11	*S-134	4.1
2000	Bos-A★	140	529	104	197	51	3	21	96	61	50	**.372**	.439	.599	1038	153	44	5	2	0	.971	-9	*S-136/D-1	4.3
Total	5	595	2436	451	812	176	29	117	436	184	257	.333	.386	.573	959	139	136	58	20	6	.969	-42	S-588/D-2,2-1	13.8
■ **AL GARDELLA**	Gardella, Alfred Stephan b: 1/11/18, New York, N.Y. BL/TL, 5'10", 172 lbs. Deb: 5/17/45 F																							
1945	NY-N	16	26	2	2	0	0	0	1	4	3	.077	.226	.077	303	-14	-4	0			.961	-1	/1-9,O-1(0-1-0)	-0.6
■ **DANNY GARDELLA**	Gardella, Daniel Lewis b: 2/26/20, New York, N.Y. BL/TL, 5'7.5", 160 lbs. Deb: 5/14/44 F																							
1944	NY-N	47	112	20	28	2	2	6	14	11	13	.250	.323	.464	787	120	2	0			.912	2	O-25(11-4-10)	0.3
1945	NY-N	121	430	54	117	10	1	18	71	46	55	.272	.349	.426	775	113	7	2			.954	-2	O-94(85-0-9),1-15	-0.1
1950	StL-N	1	1	0	0	0	0	0	0	0	0	.000	.000	.000	0	-95	-0	0			.000	0	H	0.0
Total	3	169	543	74	145	12	3	24	85	57	68	.267	.343	.433	776	114	9	2			.943	-0	O-119(96-4-19)/1-15	0.2
■ **RON GARDENHIRE**	Gardenhire, Ronald Clyde b: 10/24/57, Butzbach, W.Germany BR/TR, 6', 175 lbs. Deb: 9/1/81 C																							
1981	NY-N	27	48	2	13	1	0	0	3	5	9	.271	.340	.292	631	82	-1	2	2	-0	.969	4	S-18/2-6,3-1	0.4
1982	NY-N	141	384	29	92	17	1	3	33	23	55	.240	.283	.313	595	67	-17	5	6	-1	.956	15	*S-135/2-1,3-1	0.9
1983	NY-N	17	32	1	2	0	0	0	1	1	4	.063	.091	.063	153	-57	-7	0	0	0	1.000	0	S-15	-0.6
1984	NY-N	74	207	20	51	7	1	1	10	9	43	.246	.278	.304	582	64	-10	6	1	1	.947	-4	S-49,2-18/3-7	-0.8
1985	NY-N	26	39	5	7	2	1	0	2	8	11	.179	.319	.282	601	71	-1	0	0	0	.911	-1	S-13/2-5,3-2	-0.1
Total	5	285	710	57	165	27	3	4	49	46	122	.232	.279	.296	575	62	-36	13	9	-0	.955	15	S-230/2-30,3-11	-0.2
■ **ALEX GARDNER**	Gardner, Alexander b: 4/28/1861, Toronto, Ont., Can. d: 6/18/26, Danvers, Mass. Deb: 5/10/1884																							
1884	Was-a	1	3	0	0	0	0	0		0		.000	.000	.000	0	-99	-1				.600	-1	/C-1	-0.1
■ **ART GARDNER**	Gardner, Arthur Junior b: 9/21/52, Madden, Miss. BL/TL, 5'11", 175 lbs. Deb: 9/2/75																							
1975	Hou-N	13	31	3	6	0	0	0	2	1	8	.194	.242	.194	436	24	-3	1	0	0	1.000	-1	/O-8(3-1-4)	-0.4
1977	Hou-N	66	65	7	10	0	0	0	3	3	15	.154	.203	.154	357	-3	-9	0	0	0	1.000	-4	O-26(14-9-4)	-1.4
1978	SF-N	7	3	2	0	0	0	0	0	0	2	.000	.000	.000	0	-99	-1	0	1	-0	.000	0	H	-0.1
Total	3	86	99	12	16	0	0	0	5	4	25	.162	.210	.162	371	2	-13	1	1	-0	1.000	-4	/O-34(17-10-8)	-1.9
■ **EARLE GARDNER**	Gardner, Earle McClurkin b: 1/24/1884, Sparta, Ill. d: 3/2/43, Sparta, Ill. BR/TR, 5'11", 160 lbs. Deb: 9/18/08																							
1908	NY-A	20	75	7	16	2	0	0	4	1		.213	.234	.240	474	53	-4	0			.947	4	2-20	0.0
1909	NY-A	22	85	12	28	4	0	0	15	3		.329	.352	.376	729	129	3	4			.945	-8	2-22	-0.6
1910	NY-A	86	271	36	66	4	2	1	24	21		.244	.303	.284	587	79	-6	9			.936	5	2-70	0.0
1911	NY-A	102	357	36	94	13	2	0	39	20		.263	.312	.311	622	69	-15	14			.959	-3	*2-101	-1.6
1912	NY-A	43	160	14	45	3	1	0	26	5		.281	.303	.313	616	72	-6	11			.922	-4	2-43	-0.9
Total	5	273	948	105	249	26	5	1	108	50		.263	.305	.304	609	76	-29	38			.944	-5	2-256	-3.1
■ **GID GARDNER**	Gardner, Frank Washington b: 6/9/1859, Attleboro, Mass. d: 8/1/14, Cambridge, Mass. 165 lbs. Deb: 8/23/1879 Career OF: (16-LF 36-CF 69-RF)																							
1879	Tro-N	2	6	1	1	0	0	0	0	0	0	.167	.167	.167	333	11	-1				.429	-1	/P-2	0.0
1880	Cle-N	10	32	0	6	1	1	0	4	2	4	.188	.235	.281	517	76	-1				.850	-1	/P-9,O-1(0-1-0)	0.0
1883	Bal-a	42	161	28	44	10	3	1		18		.273	.346	.391	738	133	6				.837	-1	O-35C/2-4,3-3,P-2	0.4
1884	Bal-a	41	173	32	37	6	8	2		14		.214	.280	.376	656	108	1				.860	4	O-40(1-0-39)/1-2	0.4
	CP-U	38	149	22	38	10	2	0		10		.255	.302	.349	651	97	-5				.872	-1	O-29L/3-8,P-1,2-1	-0.6
	Bal-U	1	4	0	1	0	0	0		0		.250	.250	.250	500	47	-0				.714	-0	/S-1	0.0
	Yr	39	153	22	39	10	2	0		10		.255	.301	.346	647	96	-5				.872	-1	O-29L/3-8,P-1,2S	-0.6
1885	Bal-a	44	170	22	37	5	4	0	17	12		.218	.269	.294	563	79	-4				.891	3	2-39/O-5R,1-1,P-1	0.1
1887	Ind-N	18	75	8	23	1	0	1	8	12	11	.307	.307	.238	545	55	-3	7			1.000	-3	O-11(0-0-11)/2-7	-0.6
1888	Was-N	1	3	0	1	0	0	0	0	1	1	.333	.500	.333	833	180	0	0			.750	0	/S-1	0.1
	Phi-N	1	3	0	2	0	0	0	1	0	0	.667	.667	.667	1333	310	1	0			1.000	-1	/2-1	0.0
	Was-N	1	1	0	0	0	0	0	0	0	0	.000	.000	.000	0	-99	-0	0			1.000	-0	/2-1	-0.1
	Yr	3	7	0	3	0	0	0	1	1	1	.429	.500	.429	929	202	1	0			1.000	-1	/2-2,S-1	0.0
Total	7	199	777	113	190	33	18	4	30	69	16	.245	.298	.339	636	98	-5	7			.855	0	O-121R/2-53,P-15,31S	-0.3
■ **JEFF GARDNER**	Gardner, Jeffrey Scott b: 2/4/64, Newport Beach, Cal. BL/TR, 5'11", 165 lbs. Deb: 9/10/91																							
1991	NY-N	13	37	3	6	0	0	0	1	4	6	.162	.244	.162	406	17	-4	0	0	0	.818	-2	/S-8,2-3	-0.6
1992	SD-N	15	19	0	2	0	0	0	0	1	8	.105	.150	.105	255	-26	-3	0	0	0	1.000	4	2-11	0.1
1993	SD-N	140	404	53	106	21	7	1	24	45	69	.262	.338	.356	694	85	-8	2	6	-2	.983	-8	*2-133/3-1,S-1	-1.2
1994	Mon-N	18	32	4	7	0	1	0	1	3	5	.219	.286	.281	567	48	-2	0	0	0	.714	-5	/3-9,2-4	-0.8
Total	4	186	492	60	121	21	8	1	26	53	88	.246	.321	.327	648	73	-18	2	6	-2	.984	-11	2-151/3-10,S-9	-2.5

YEAR	TM/L	G	AB	R	H	2B	3B	HR	RBI	BB	SO	AVG	OBP	SLG	OPS	OPS+	BR+	SB	CS	SBR	FA	FR	G/POS	TPR
■ **RAY GARDNER**	Gardner, Raymond Vincent b: 10/25/01, Frederick, Md. d: 5/3/68, Frederick, Md. BR/TR, 5′8″, 145 lbs. Deb: 4/16/29																							
1929	Cle-A	82	256	28	67	3	2	1	24	29	16	.262	.337	.301	638	63	-13	10	13	-2	.952	8	S-82	0.1
1930	Cle-A	33	13	7	1	0	0	0	1	0	0	.077	.077	.077	154	-59	-3	0	1	-0	.861	8	S-22/2-5,3-1	0.4
Total	2	115	269	35	68	3	2	1	25	29	16	.253	.326	.290	615	57	-16	10	14	-3	.945	16	S-104/2-5,3-1	0.5
■ **BILLY GARDNER**	Gardner, William Frederick "Shotgun" b: 7/19/27, Waterford, Conn. BR/TR, 6′, 180 lbs. Deb: 4/22/54 MC																							
1954	NY-N	62	108	10	23	5	0	1	7	6	19	.213	.261	.287	548	42	-9	0	1	-0	.987	10	3-30,2-13/S-5	0.1
1955	NY-N	59	187	26	38	10	1	3	17	13	19	.203	.262	.316	578	52	-13	0	0	0	.940	0	S-38,3-10/2-4	-1.0
1956	Bal-A	144	515	53	119	16	2	11	50	29	53	.231	.281	.334	615	67	-27	5	5	-1	.974	-12	*2-132,S-25/3-6	-2.9
1957	Bal-A	154	644	79	169	**36**	3	6	55	53	67	.262	.326	.356	682	92	-8	10	7	-0	**.987**	6	*2-148/S-9	1.0
1958	Bal-A	151	560	32	126	28	2	3	33	34	53	.225	.273	.298	571	60	-31	2	3	-1	.985	-22	*2-151,S-13	-4.4
1959	Bal-A	140	401	34	87	13	2	6	27	38	61	.217	.286	.304	591	64	-20	2	1	0	.976	**31**	*2-139/S-1,3-1	2.0
1960	Was-A	145	592	71	152	26	5	9	56	43	76	.257	.314	.363	677	83	-14	0	4	-1	.973	-2	*2-145,S-13	-0.7
1961	Min-A	45	154	13	36	9	0	1	11	10	14	.234	.280	.312	592	55	-10	0	0	0	.973	-4	2-41/3-2	-1.1
	*NY-A	41	99	11	21	5	0	1	2	6	18	.212	.278	.293	571	56	-6	0	0	0	.952	3	3-33/2-6	-0.3
	Yr	86	253	24	57	14	0	2	13	16	32	.225	.279	.304	584	56	-16	0	0	0	.975	-1	2-47,3-35	-1.4
1962	NY-A	4	1	1	0	0	0	0	0	0	1	.000	.000	.000	0	-99	-0	0	0	0	1.000	1	/2-1,3-1	0.0
	Bos-A	53	199	22	54	9	2	0	12	10	39	.271	.310	.337	646	72	-8	0	1	-0	.963	-8	2-38/3-7,S-4	-1.3
	Yr	57	200	23	54	9	2	0	12	10	40	.270	.308	.335	643	71	-8	0	1	-0	.963	-7	2-39/3-8,S-4	-1.3
1963	Bos-A	36	84	4	16	2	1	0	1	4	19	.190	.236	.238	474	32	-8	0	0	0	.989	7	2-21/3-2	0.0
Total	10	1034	3544	356	841	159	18	41	271	246	439	.237	.293	.327	620	70	-154	19	22	-4	.978	8	2-839,S-108/3-92	-8.6
■ **LARRY GARDNER**	Gardner, William Lawrence b: 5/13/1886, Enosburg Falls, Vt d: 3/11/76, St.George, Vt. BL/TR, 5′8″, 165 lbs. Deb: 6/25/08																							
1908	Bos-A	3	10	0	3	1	0	0	1	0		.300	.300	.400	700	124	0	0			.571	-2	/3-3	-0.2
1909	Bos-A	19	37	7	11	1	2	0	5	4		.297	.381	.432	813	153	2	1			.800	-4	/3-8,S-5	-0.1
1910	Bos-A	113	413	56	117	12	10	2	36	41		.283	.354	.375	729	125	12	8			.944	-9	*2-113	0.5
1911	Bos-A	138	492	80	140	17	8	4	44	64		.285	.373	.376	749	110	8	27			.962	24	3-72,2-62	3.4
1912	*Bos-A	143	517	88	163	24	18	3	86	56		.315	.383	.449	832	131	20	25			.930	-1	*3-143	2.3
1913	Bos-A	131	473	64	133	17	10	0	63	47	34	.281	.347	.359	707	104	3	18			.943	-16	*3-130	-1.1
1914	Bos-A	155	553	50	143	23	19	3	68	35	39	.259	.303	.385	688	107	1	16	23	-5	.942	0	*3-153	0.1
1915	*Bos-A	127	430	51	111	14	6	1	55	39	24	.258	.327	.326	653	98	-1	11	12	-2	.933	-7	*3-127	-0.6
1916	*Bos-A	148	493	47	152	19	7	2	62	48	27	.308	.372	.387	759	128	17	12			.953	-14	*3-147	0.7
1917	Bos-A	146	501	53	133	23	7	1	61	54	37	.265	.341	.345	686	110	7	16			.937	-7	*3-146	0.5
1918	Phi-A	127	463	50	132	22	6	1	52	43	22	.285	.346	.365	711	113	7	9			.964	10	*3-127	2.3
1919	Cle-A	139	524	67	157	29	7	2	79	39	29	.300	.352	.393	745	103	1	7			.946	-6	*3-139	-0.1
1920	*Cle-A	154	597	72	185	31	11	3	118	53	25	.310	.367	.414	781	103	3	3	20	-6	**.976**	-2	*3-154	-0.1
1921	Cle-A	153	586	101	187	32	14	3	120	65	16	.319	.391	.437	828	109	9	3	3	-0	.950	-1	*3-152	1.6
1922	Cle-A	137	470	74	134	31	3	2	68	49	21	.285	.355	.377	732	90	-6	9	8	-1	.951	-5	*3-128	-0.5
1923	Cle-A	52	79	4	20	5	1	0	12	12	7	.253	.352	.342	693	83	-2	0	1	-0	.962	3	3-19	0.1
1924	Cle-A	38	50	3	10	0	0	0	4	5	1	.200	.273	.200	473	23	-6	0	1	-0	.875	-4	/3-8,2-6	-0.9
Total	17	1923	6688	867	1931	301	129	27	934	654	282	.289	.355	.384	739	109	76	165	68		.948	-40	*3-1656,2-181/S-5	7.9
■ **ART GARIBALDI**	Garibaldi, Arthur Edward b: 8/20/07, San Francisco, Cal d: 10/19/67, Sacramento, Cal. BR/TR, 5′8″, 165 lbs. Deb: 6/20/36																							
1936	StL-N	71	232	30	64	12	0	1	20	16	30	.276	.323	.341	663	79	-7	3			.925	-5	3-46,2-24	-0.9
■ **DEBS GARMS**	Garms, Debs C. "Tex" b: 6/26/08, Bangs, Tex. d: 12/16/84, Glen Rose, Tex. BL/TR, 5′8.5″, 165 lbs. Deb: 8/10/32 Career OF: (263-LF 73-CF 171-RF)																							
1932	StL-A	34	134	20	38	7	1	1	8	17	7	.284	.364	.373	737	86	-2	4	3	-0	.953	-1	O-33(0-32-1)	-0.4
1933	StL-A	78	189	35	60	10	2	4	24	30	21	.317	.416	.455	871	123	7	2	5	-1	.960	-2	O-47(28-17-3)	0.2
1934	StL-A	91	232	25	68	14	4	0	31	27	19	.293	.372	.388	760	89	-3	0	0	0	.942	-3	O-56(42-1-13)	-0.8
1935	StL-A	10	15	1	4	0	0	0	0	2	2	.267	.353	.267	620	59	-1	0	0	0	.800	-0	/O-2(0-0-2)	-0.1
1937	Bos-N	125	478	60	124	15	8	2	37	37	33	.259	.317	.337	653	85	-10	2			.977	-8	O-81(64-15-2),3-36	-2.0
1938	Bos-N	117	428	62	135	19	1	0	47	34	22	.315	.371	.364	736	114	9	4			.985	-7	O-63L,3-54/2-1	0.1
1939	Bos-N	132	513	68	153	24	9	2	37	39	20	.298	.350	.392	742	107	4	2			.964	-4	O-96(25-0-73),3-37	-0.4
1940	Pit-N	103	358	76	127	23	7	5	57	23	6	**.355**	.395	.500	895	147	22	3			.964	-1	3-64,O-19(8-4-8)	2.3
1941	Pit-N	83	220	25	58	9	3	3	42	22	12	.264	.331	.373	703	98	-1	0			.911	-10	3-29,O-24(23-0-1)	-1.1
1943	*StL-N	90	249	26	64	10	2	0	22	13	8	.257	.299	.313	612	74	-8	1			.980	-5	O-47R,3-23/S-1	-1.8
1944	*StL-N	73	149	17	30	3	0	0	5	13	8	.201	.265	.221	487	37	-12	0			1.000	-8	O-23(3-2-18),3-21	-2.2
1945	StL-N	74	146	23	49	7	2	0	18	31	3	.336	.452	.411	863	137	10	0			.956	-10	3-32,O-10(1-0-9)	-0.1
Total	12	1010	3111	438	910	141	39	17	328	288	161	.293	.355	.379	735	103	15	18	8		.966	-58	O-501L,3-296/S-1,2	-6.3
■ **PHIL GARNER**	Garner, Philip Mason b: 4/30/49, Jefferson City, Tenn. BR/TR, 5′10″, 177 lbs. Deb: 9/10/73 MC																							
1973	Oak-A	9	5	0	0	0	0	0	0	0	3	.000	.000	.000	0	-99	-1	0	0	0	1.000	1	/3-9	-0.1
1974	Oak-A	30	28	4	5	1	0	0	1	1	5	.179	.207	.214	421	23	-3	1	1	-0	.955	4	3-19/S-8,2-3,D-2	0.1
1975	*Oak-A	160	488	46	120	21	5	6	54	30	65	.246	.296	.346	643	83	-12	4	6	-1	.968	-16	*2-160/S-1	-1.9
1976	Oak-A★	159	555	54	145	29	12	8	74	36	71	.261	.309	.400	709	111	5	35	13	3	.975	-14	*2-159	0.6
1977	Pit-N	153	585	99	152	35	10	17	77	55	65	.260	.326	.441	767	101	-0	32	9	4	.971	1	*3-107,2-50,S-12	0.6
1978	Pit-N	154	528	66	138	25	9	10	66	66	71	.261	.349	.400	749	104	4	27	14	1	.976	10	2-81,3-81/S-4	1.9
1979	*Pit-N	150	549	76	161	32	8	11	59	55	74	.293	.361	.441	802	112	10	17	8	1	.981	6	2-83,3-78,S-14	2.1
1980	Pit-N★	151	548	62	142	27	6	5	58	46	53	.259	.319	.358	676	87	-9	32	7	5	.976	16	*2-151/S-1	2.0
1981	Pit-N★	56	181	22	46	6	2	1	20	21	21	.254	.332	.326	658	84	-3	4	6	-1	.968	-6	2-50	-0.9
	*Hou-N	31	113	13	27	3	1	0	6	15	11	.239	.328	.283	611	79	-3	6	2	1	.982	0	2-31	0.0
	Yr	87	294	35	73	9	3	1	26	36	32	.248	.330	.310	640	82	-6	10	8	-1	.973	-6	2-81	-0.9
1982	Hou-N	155	588	65	161	33	8	13	83	40	92	.274	.323	.423	747	116	10	24	13	1	.980	1	*2-136,3-18	2.0
1983	Hou-N	154	567	76	135	24	2	14	79	63	84	.238	.320	.362	681	94	-5	18	12	-0	.945	4	*3-154	-0.3
1984	Hou-N	128	374	60	104	17	6	4	45	43	63	.278	.359	.388	746	118	10	3	2	-0	.979	23	3-82,2-35	3.4
1985	Hou-N	135	463	65	124	23	10	6	51	34	72	.268	.321	.400	720	103	1	4	4	-1	.932	-9	*3-123,2-15	-1.0
1986	*Hou-N	107	313	43	83	14	3	9	41	30	45	.265	.331	.415	747	108	3	12	6	1	.896	1	3-84/2-7	0.3
1987	Hou-N	43	112	15	25	5	0	3	15	8	20	.223	.275	.348	623	66	-6	1	0	0	.976	2	3-36/2-2	-0.4
	LA-N	70	126	14	24	4	0	2	8	20	24	.190	.301	.270	571	54	-8	5	1	1	.923	6	3-46,2-12/S-2	-0.1
	Yr	113	238	29	49	9	0	5	23	28	44	.206	.289	.307	596	60	-14	6	1	1	.947	8	3-82,2-14/S-2	-0.5
1988	SF-N	15	13	0	2	0	0	0	1	1	3	.154	.214	.154	368	8	-2	0	1	-0	.000	0	/3-2	-0.2
Total	16	1860	6136	780	1594	299	82	109	738	564	842	.260	.326	.389	714	100	-9	225	105	13	.974	30	2-975,3-839/S-42,D	8.1
■ **RALPH GARR**	Garr, Ralph Allen "Road Runner" b: 12/12/45, Monroe, La. BL/TR, 5′11″, 197 lbs. Deb: 9/3/68 Career OF: (844-LF 62-CF 337-RF)																							
1968	Atl-N	11	7	3	2	0	0	0	0	1	0	.286	.375	.286	661	100	0	1	0	0	.000	0	H	0.0
1969	Atl-N	22	27	6	6	1	0	0	2	2	4	.222	.276	.259	535	50	-2	1	1	-0	.857	-1	/O-7(7-0-0)	-0.4
1970	Atl-N	37	96	18	27	3	0	0	8	5	12	.281	.317	.313	629	65	-5	5	2	0	1.000	0	O-21(1-8-12)	-0.5
1971	Atl-N	154	639	101	219	24	6	9	44	30	68	.343	.374	.441	815	122	18	30	14	2	.968	16	*O-153(153-0-0)	2.9
1972	Atl-N	134	554	87	180	22	0	12	53	25	41	.325	.361	.430	790	113	10	25	9	2	.962	-4	*O-131(70-13-59)	0.1
1973	Atl-N	148	668	94	200	32	6	11	55	22	64	.299	.324	.415	738	96	-5	35	11	4	.968	1	*O-148(21-0-127)	-0.8
1974	Atl-N★	143	606	87	**214**	24	**17**	11	54	28	52	**.353**	.384	.503	887	141	30	26	16	0	.967	-19	*O-139(107-0-80)	0.4
1975	Atl-N	151	625	74	174	26	**11**	6	31	44	50	.278	.329	.384	713	94	-6	14	9	-0	.966	6	*O-148(148-0-0)	-0.9
1976	Chi-A	136	527	63	158	22	6	4	36	17	41	.300	.324	.387	711	107	3	14	5	1	.978	-6	*O-125(35-41-57)/D-6	-0.8
1977	Chi-A	134	543	78	163	29	7	10	54	27	44	.300	.333	.435	768	108	5	12	7	0	.987	3	*O-126(125-0-1)/D-2	0.2
1978	Chi-A	118	443	67	122	18	9	3	29	24	41	.275	.314	.377	691	93	-5	7	5	-0	.959	1	*O-109(109-0-0)/D-9	-1.0
1979	Chi-A	102	307	34	86	10	2	9	39	17	19	.280	.320	.414	734	96	-2	2	4	-1	.951	-8	O-67(67-0-0),D-17	-1.4
	Cal-A	6	24	0	3	0	0	0	0	0	3	.125	.125	.125	250	-33	-4	0	0	0	.000	0	/D-6	-0.5
	Yr	108	331	34	89	10	2	9	39	17	22	.269	.307	.393	699	87	-7	2	4	-1	.951	-8	O-67(67-0-0),D-23	-1.9
1980	Cal-A	21	42	5	8	1	0	0	3	4	6	.190	.261	.214	475	33	-4	0	0	0	.750	-0	/O-2(1-0-1),D-8	-0.4
Total	13	1317	5108	717	1562	212	64	75	408	246	445	.306	.340	.416	756	106	34	172	83	9	.968	-11	*O-1176L/D-48	-3.1

YEAR	TM/L	G	AB	R	H	2B	3B	HR	RBI	BB	SO	AVG	OBP	SLG	OPS	OPS+	BR+	SB	CS	SBR	FA	FR	G/POS	TPR
■ ADRIAN GARRETT	Garrett, Henry Adrian "Pat" b: 1/3/43, Brooksville, Fla. BL/TR, 6'3", 185 lbs. Deb: 4/13/66 FC Career OF: (10-LF 0-CF 8-RF)																							
1966	Atl-N	4	3	0	0	0	0	0	0	0	2	.000	.000	.000	0	-99	-1	0	0	0	.000	-0	/O-1(0-0-1)	-0.1
1970	Chi-N	3	3	0	0	0	0	0	0	0	3	.000	.000	.000	0	-89	-1	0	0	0	.000	0	H	-0.1
1971	Oak-A	14	21	1	3	0	0	1	2	5	7	.143	.308	.286	593	70	-1	0	0	0	1.000	-0	/O-5(4-0-1)	-0.1
1972	Oak-A	14	11	0	0	0	0	0	0	1	4	.000	.083	.000	83	-78	-2	0	0	0	1.000	-1	/O-2(2-0-0)	-0.3
1973	Chi-N	36	54	7	12	0	0	3	8	4	18	.222	.276	.389	665	77	-2	1	0	0	1.000	-1	/O-7(3-0-4),C-6	-0.3
1974	Chi-N	10	8	0	0	0	0	0	0	1	1	.000	.111	.000	111	-64	-2	0	0	0	1.000	0	/C-3,1-1,O-1(1-0-0)	-0.1
1975	Chi-N	16	21	1	2	0	0	1	6	1	8	.095	.136	.238	374	2	-3	0	0	0	1.000	1	/1-4	-0.2
	Cal-A	37	107	17	28	5	0	6	18	14	28	.262	.347	.477	824	141	6	3	0	1	1.000	-0	D-23,1-10/O-2R,C-1	0.5
1976	Cal-A	29	48	4	6	3	0	0	3	5	16	.125	.208	.188	395	17	-5	0	0	0	.974	-4	C-15/1-1,D-4	-0.9
Total	8	163	276	30	51	8	0	11	37	31	87	.185	.267	.333	600	71	-11	4	0	1	.959	-5	/D-27,C-25,O-18L,1	-1.6
■ WAYNE GARRETT	Garrett, Ronald Wayne b: 12/3/47, Brooksville, Fla. BL/TR, 5'11", 183 lbs. Deb: 4/12/69 F																							
1969	*NY-N	124	400	38	87	11	3	1	39	40	75	.218	.293	.268	561	57	-22	4	2	0	.951	-13	3-72,2-47/S-9	-3.5
1970	NY-N	114	366	74	93	17	4	12	45	81	60	.254	.392	.421	813	118	12	5	1	1	.944	-19	3-70,2-45/S-1	-0.4
1971	NY-N	56	202	20	43	2	0	1	11	28	31	.213	.312	.238	549	58	-10	1	3	-1	.967	-4	3-53/2-9	-1.6
1972	NY-N	111	298	41	69	13	3	2	29	70	58	.232	.378	.315	693	101	4	3	2	-0	.960	2	3-82,2-22	0.8
1973	*NY-N	140	504	76	129	20	3	16	58	72	74	.256	.350	.403	753	110	8	6	5	-0	.942	11	*3-130/S-9,2-6	1.9
1974	NY-N	151	522	55	117	14	3	13	53	89	96	.224	.339	.337	676	91	-4	4	6	-1	.955	14	*3-144/S-9	0.9
1975	NY-N	107	274	49	73	8	3	6	34	50	45	.266	.382	.383	765	118	9	3	2	-0	.966	11	3-94/S-3,2-1	1.9
1976	NY-N	80	251	36	56	8	1	4	26	52	26	.223	.359	.311	669	97	1	7	5	-0	.948	3	3-64,2-10/S-1	0.5
	Mon-N	59	177	15	43	4	1	2	11	30	20	.243	.353	.311	663	86	-2	2	2	-0	.982	1	2-54/3-2	0.2
	Yr	139	428	51	99	12	2	6	37	82	46	.231	.356	.311	667	92	-1	9	7	-0	.949	4	3-66,2-64/S-1	0.7
1977	Mon-N	68	159	17	43	6	1	2	22	30	18	.270	.389	.358	748	105	3	2	2	-0	1.000	2	3-49/2-1	0.4
1978	Mon-N	49	69	6	12	0	0	1	2	8	10	.174	.260	.217	477	35	-6	0	0	0	.969	1	3-13	-0.6
	StL-N	33	63	11	21	4	0	1	10	11	16	.333	.432	.444	877	148	5	1	0	0	.927	-2	3-19	0.2
	Yr	82	132	17	33	4	0	2	12	19	26	.250	.344	.326	670	89	-1	1	0	0	.945	-2	3-32	-0.4
Total	10	1092	3285	438	786	107	22	61	340	561	529	.239	.352	.341	693	95	-4	38	30	-2	.956	7	3-792,2-195/S-32	0.7
■ GIL GARRIDO	Garrido, Gil Gonzalo b: 6/26/41, Panama City, Pan. BR/TR, 5'8", 160 lbs. Deb: 4/24/64																							
1964	SF-N	14	25	1	2	0	0	0	1	2	7	.080	.148	.080	228	-33	-4	1	0	0	.969	-1	S-14	-0.5
1968	Atl-N	18	53	5	11	0	0	0	2	2	2	.208	.236	.208	444	34	-4	0	0	0	.987	3	S-17	0.0
1969	*Atl-N	82	227	18	50	5	1	0	10	16	11	.220	.272	.251	523	47	-16	0	0	0	.973	-11	S-81	-2.0
1970	Atl-N	101	367	38	97	5	4	1	19	15	16	.264	.293	.308	601	58	-22	0	2	-1	.975	-1	S-80,2-26	-1.3
1971	Atl-N	79	125	8	27	3	0	0	12	15	12	.216	.300	.240	540	51	-7	0	1	-0	.961	4	S-32,3-28,2-18	0.0
1972	Atl-N	40	75	11	20	1	0	0	7	11	6	.267	.368	.280	648	79	-1	1	1	-0	.989	1	2-21,S-10/3-3	0.1
Total	6	334	872	81	207	14	5	1	51	61	54	.237	.288	.268	556	53	-55	2	4	-1	.974	-4	S-234/2-65,3-31	-3.7
■ CECIL GARRIOTT	Garriott, Virgil Cecil b: 8/15/16, Harristown, Ill. d: 2/20/90, Lake Elsinore, Cal BL/TR, 5'8", 165 lbs. Deb: 9/4/46																							
1946	Chi-N	6	5	1	0	0	0	0	0	0	2	.000	.167	.000	167	-52	-1	0			.000	0	H	-0.1
■ FORD GARRISON	Garrison, Robert Ford "Rocky" or "Snapper" b: 8/29/15, Greenville, S.C. BR/TR, 5'10.5", 180 lbs. Deb: 4/22/43 C																							
1943	Bos-A	36	129	13	36	5	1	1	11	5	14	.279	.306	.357	663	92	-2	0	1	-0	.988	-0	O-32(26-6-0)	-0.4
1944	Bos-A	13	49	5	12	3	0	0	2	6	4	.245	.327	.306	633	82	-1	0	0	0	.969	1	O-12(0-0-12)	-0.1
	Phi-A	121	449	58	121	13	2	4	37	22	40	.269	.307	.334	641	84	-10	10	4	1	.987	6	*O-119(95-0-24)	-1.1
	Yr	134	498	63	133	16	2	4	39	28	44	.267	.309	.331	640	84	-11	10	4	1	.985	7	*O-131(95-0-36)	-1.2
1945	Phi-A	6	23	3	7	1	0	1	6	4	3	.304	.407	.478	886	157	2	1	0	0	1.000	1	/O-5(5-0-0)	0.2
1946	Phi-A	9	37	1	4	0	0	0	0	0	6	.108	.108	.108	216	-40	-7	0	0	0	1.000	-2	/O-8(8-0-0)	-1.1
Total	4	185	687	80	180	22	3	6	56	37	67	.262	.302	.329	631	81	-18	11	5	1	.986	5	O-176(134-6-36)	-2.5
■ WEBSTER GARRISON	Garrison, Webster Leotis b: 8/24/65, Marrero, La. BR/TR, 5'11", 170 lbs. Deb: 8/2/96																							
1996	Oak-A	5	9	0	0	0	0	0	0	1	0	.000	.100	.000	100	-73	-2	0	0	0	.875	-1	/2-3,1-1	-0.3
■ HANK GARRITY	Garrity, Francis Joseph b: 2/4/08, Boston, Mass. d: 9/1/62, Boston, Mass. BR/TR, 6'1", 185 lbs. Deb: 7/26/31																							
1931	Chi-A	8	14	0	3	1	0	0	2	1	2	.214	.267	.286	552	48	-1	0	0	0	.941	0	/C-7	-0.1
■ STEVE GARVEY	Garvey, Steven Patrick b: 12/22/48, Tampa, Fla. BR/TR, 5'10", 192 lbs. Deb: 9/1/69 Career OF: (8-LF 0-CF 2-RF)																							
1969	LA-N	3	3	0	1	0	0	0	0	0	1	.333	.333	.333	667	94	-0	0	0	0	.000	0	H	0.0
1970	LA-N	34	93	8	25	5	0	1	6	6	17	.269	.313	.355	668	82	-2	1	1	-0	.943	6	3-27/2-1	0.3
1971	LA-N	81	225	27	51	12	1	7	26	21	33	.227	.293	.382	675	95	-2	1	2	-0	.939	19	3-79	1.7
1972	LA-N	96	294	36	79	14	2	9	30	19	36	.269	.315	.422	737	110	3	4	2	0	.902	13	3-85/1-3	1.7
1973	LA-N	114	349	37	106	17	3	8	50	11	42	.304	.331	.438	769	116	6	0	2	-1	.993	-8	1-76,O-10(8-0-2)	-0.9
1974	*LA-N★	156	642	95	200	32	3	21	111	31	66	.312	.346	.469	815	132	23	5	4	-0	.995	-13	*1-156	-0.3
1975	LA-N★	160	659	85	210	38	6	18	95	33	66	.319	.354	.476	830	135	27	11	2	2	**.995**	-10	*1-160	0.6
1976	LA-N★	162	631	85	200	37	4	13	80	50	69	.317	.368	.450	818	134	27	19	8	1	**.998**	-16	*1-162	-0.1
1977	*LA-N★	162	646	91	192	25	3	33	115	38	90	.297	.337	.498	836	121	17	9	6	-0	**.995**	-16	*1-160	-0.9
1978	*LA-N★	162	639	89	**202**	36	9	21	113	40	70	.316	.357	.499	857	138	29	10	5	0	.994	-9	*1-161	1.1
1979	LA-N★	162	648	92	204	32	1	28	110	37	59	.315	.354	.497	851	131	25	3	6	-1	.995	-2	*1-162	1.3
1980	LA-N★	163	658	78	**200**	27	1	26	106	36	67	.304	.343	.467	809	126	21	6	11	-3	.996	3	*1-162	1.2
1981	*LA-N★	110	431	63	122	23	1	10	64	25	49	.283	.324	.411	735	111	5	3	5	-1	**.999**	-6	*1-110	-1.0
1982	LA-N	162	625	66	176	35	1	16	86	20	86	.282	.305	.418	723	103	-0	5	3	0	.995	1	*1-158	-0.9
1983	SD-N	100	388	76	114	22	0	14	59	29	39	.294	.348	.459	806	126	12	4	1	1	.994	-11	*1-100	-0.4
1984	*SD-N★	161	617	72	175	27	2	8	86	24	64	.284	.312	.373	684	92	-8	1	2	-0	**1.000**	-4	*1-159	-2.4
1985	SD-N★	162	654	80	184	34	6	17	81	35	67	.281	.321	.430	750	110	6	0	0	0	.997	-8	*1-162	-1.3
1986	SD-N	155	557	58	142	22	0	21	81	23	72	.255	.286	.408	693	91	-9	1	2	-0	.994	-18	*1-148	-3.8
1987	SD-N	27	76	5	16	2	0	1	9	1	10	.211	.231	.276	507	35	-7	0	0	0	1.000	0	1-20	-0.8
Total	19	2332	8835	1143	2599	440	43	272	1308	479	1003	.294	.333	.446	779	117	172	83	62	-3	.996	-78	*1-2059,3-191/O-10L,2	-4.9
■ ROD GASPAR	Gaspar, Rodney Earl b: 4/3/46, Long Beach, Cal. BB/TR, 5'11", 165 lbs. Deb: 4/8/69																							
1969	*NY-N	118	215	26	49	6	1	1	14	25	19	.228	.314	.279	593	66	-9	7	3	0	.983	-7	O-91(22-16-64)	-1.9
1970	NY-N	11	14	4	0	0	0	0	0	1	4	.000	.067	.000	67	-80	-4	1	0	0	1.000	-1	/O-8(0-4-5)	-0.5
1971	SD-N	16	17	1	2	0	0	0	2	3	3	.118	.250	.118	368	8	-2	0	1	-0	1.000	0	/O-2(2-0-0)	-0.3
1974	SD-N	33	14	4	3	0	0	0	1	4	3	.214	.389	.214	603	75	-0	0	0	0	1.000	-2	/O-8(2-5-1),1-2	-0.3
Total	4	178	260	35	54	6	1	1	17	33	29	.208	.302	.250	552	55	-15	8	4	0	.986	-10	O-109(26-25-70)/1-2	-3.0
■ TOM GASTALL	Gastall, Thomas Everett b: 6/13/32, Fall River, Mass. d: 9/20/56, Riviera Beach, Md. BR/TR, 6'2", 187 lbs. Deb: 6/21/55																							
1955	Bal-A	20	27	4	4	1	0	0	0	3	5	.148	.233	.185	419	15	-3	0	0	0	.967	-1	C-15	-0.4
1956	Bal-A	32	56	3	11	2	0	0	4	3	8	.196	.250	.232	482	30	-6	0	0	0	1.000	1	C-20	-0.4
Total	2	52	83	7	15	3	0	0	4	6	13	.181	.244	.217	461	25	-9	0	0	0	.990	0	/C-35	-0.8
■ ED GASTFIELD	Gastfield, Edward b: 8/1/1865, Chicago, Ill. d: 12/1/1899, Chicago, Ill. BR, 5'9.5", 155 lbs. Deb: 8/13/1884																							
1884	Det-N	23	82	6	6	1	0	0	2	2	34	.073	.095	.085	181	-45	-13				.827	9	C-19/O-2(0-0-2),1-2	-0.3
1885	Det-N	1	3	0	0	0	0	0	0	0	2	.000	.000	.000	0	-99	-1				.714	-0	/C-1	-0.1
	Chi-N	1	3	0	0	0	0	0	0	0	1	.000	.000	.000	0	-88	-1				1.000	1	/C-1	0.1
	Yr	2	6	0	0	0	0	0	0	0	3	.000	.000	.000	0	-93	-1				.889	1	/C-2	0.0
Total	2	25	88	6	6	1	0	0	2	2	37	.068	.089	.080	168	-49	-14				.832	10	/C-21,1-2,O-2(0-0-2)	-0.3
■ ALEX GASTON	Gaston, Alexander Nathaniel b: 3/12/1893, New York, N.Y. d: 2/8/79, Santa Monica, Cal. BR/TR, 5'9", 170 lbs. Deb: 9/26/20 F																							
1920	NY-N	4	10	2	1	0	0	0	1	1	2	.100	.182	.100	282	-18	-1	0	0	0	.917	-1	/C-3	-0.3
1921	NY-N	20	22	1	5	1	1	0	3	1	9	.227	.261	.364	625	63	-1	0	0	0	.950	-0	C-11	-0.1
1922	NY-N	16	26	1	5	0	0	0	1	0	3	.192	.192	.192	385	-1	-4	1	0	0	1.000	0	C-13	-0.3

YEAR	TM/L	G	AB	R	H	2B	3B	HR	RBI	BB	SO	AVG	OBP	SLG	OPS	OPS+	BR+	SB	CS	SBR	FA	FR	G/POS	TPR
1923	NY-N	22	39	3	8	2	0	1	5	0	6	.205	.225	.333	558	46	-3	0	0	0	.957	-0	C-21	-0.3
1926	Bos-A	98	301	37	67	5	3	0	21	21	28	.223	.282	.259	541	43	-25	3	0	1	.981	-10	C-98	-2.7
1929	Bos-A	55	116	14	26	5	2	2	9	6	8	.224	.262	.353	616	58	-8	1	0	0	.986	-1	C-49	-0.6
Total	6	215	514	58	112	13	6	3	40	29	56	.218	.266	.284	550	45	-43	5	0	1	.979	-13	C-195	-4.3

■ CITO GASTON Gaston, Clarence Edwin b: 3/17/44, San Antonio, Tex. BR/TR, 6'4", 210 lbs. Deb: 9/14/67 MC Career OF: (92-LF 412-CF 282-RF)

YEAR	TM/L	G	AB	R	H	2B	3B	HR	RBI	BB	SO	AVG	OBP	SLG	OPS	OPS+	BR+	SB	CS	SBR	FA	FR	G/POS	TPR
1967	Atl-N	9	25	1	3	0	1	0	1	0	5	.120	.120	.200	320	-10	-4	1	0	0	.800	-1	/O-7(0-6-1)	-0.5
1969	SD-N	129	391	20	90	11	7	2	28	24	117	.230	.276	.309	586	67	-18	4	4	-1	.959	6	*O-113(0-113-0)	-1.7
1970	SD-N★	146	584	92	186	26	9	29	93	41	142	.318	.365	.543	908	146	35	4	1	1	.975	4	*O-142(1-142-0)	3.5
1971	SD-N	141	518	57	118	13	9	17	61	24	121	.228	.265	.386	651	88	-11	1	0	0	.982	-0	*O-133(6-126-1)	-1.6
1972	SD-N	111	379	30	102	14	0	7	44	22	76	.269	.313	.361	674	98	-2	0	2	-1	.977	1	O-94(18-7-73)	-0.8
1973	SD-N	133	476	51	119	18	4	16	57	20	88	.250	.282	.405	687	96	-6	0	0	0	.947	2	*O-119(1-0-118)	-1.1
1974	SD-N	106	267	19	57	11	0	6	33	16	51	.213	.261	.322	583	65	-14	0	0	0	.992	3	O-63(18-0-50)	-1.5
1975	Atl-N	64	141	17	34	4	0	6	15	17	33	.241	.323	.397	720	95	-1	1	0	0	.974	-1	O-35(2-17-17)/1-1	-0.4
1976	Atl-N	69	134	15	39	4	0	4	25	13	21	.291	.354	.410	764	109	2	1	0	0	.977	-2	O-28(25-0-3)/1-2	-0.1
1977	Atl-N	56	85	6	23	4	0	3	21	5	19	.271	.311	.424	735	85	-2	1	0	0	1.000	-0	/O-9(7-0-2),1-5	-0.2
1978	Atl-N	60	118	5	27	1	0	1	9	3	20	.229	.248	.263	511	38	-9	0	0	0	.957	-4	O-29(13-1-17)/1-4	-1.5
	Pit-N	2	2	1	1	0	0	0	0	0	0	.500	.500	.500	1000	172	0	0	0	0	.000	-0	/O-1(1-0-0)	0.0
	Yr	62	120	6	28	1	0	1	9	3	20	.233	.252	.267	519	41	-9	0	0	0	.957	-4	O-30(14-1-17)/1-4	-1.5
Total	11	1026	3120	314	799	106	30	91	387	185	693	.256	.300	.397	696	95	-30	13	7	0	.970	6	O-773C/1-12	-5.9

■ BRENT GATES Gates, Brent Robert b: 3/14/70, Grand Rapids, Mich. BB/TR, 6'1", 180 lbs. Deb: 5/5/93 Career OF: (1-LF 0-CF 0-RF)

YEAR	TM/L	G	AB	R	H	2B	3B	HR	RBI	BB	SO	AVG	OBP	SLG	OPS	OPS+	BR+	SB	CS	SBR	FA	FR	G/POS	TPR
1993	Oak-A	139	535	64	155	29	2	7	69	56	75	.290	.361	.391	752	109	8	7	3	0	.981	-3	*2-139	1.2
1994	Oak-A	64	233	29	66	11	1	2	24	21	32	.283	.345	.365	710	91	-3	3	0	1	.974	-17	2-63/1-1	-1.4
1995	Oak-A	136	524	60	133	24	4	5	56	46	84	.254	.314	.344	658	75	-19	3	3	-0	.982	11	*2-132/1-1,D-3	-0.2
1996	Oak-A	64	247	26	65	19	2	2	30	18	35	.263	.318	.381	699	77	-9	1	1	-0	.973	-2	2-63	-0.7
1997	*Sea-A	65	151	18	36	8	0	3	20	14	21	.238	.303	.351	654	71	-7	0	0	0	.934	-2	3-32,2-21/S-5,1OD	-0.8
1998	Min-A	107	333	31	83	15	0	3	42	36	46	.249	.326	.321	647	68	-15	3	3	-0	.961	-8	3-77,2-21/1-1,SD	-2.1
1999	Min-A	110	306	40	78	13	2	3	38	34	56	.255	.331	.340	671	69	-14	1	3	-1	.972	-8	3-61,2-47/1-5,SD	-2.0
Total	7	685	2329	268	616	119	11	25	279	225	349	.264	.332	.357	689	82	-58	18	13	-1	.980	-28	2-486,3-170/1-9,SDO	-6.0

■ JOE GATES Gates, Joseph Daniel b: 10/3/54, Gary, Ind. BL/TR, 5'7", 175 lbs. Deb: 9/12/78

YEAR	TM/L	G	AB	R	H	2B	3B	HR	RBI	BB	SO	AVG	OBP	SLG	OPS	OPS+	BR+	SB	CS	SBR	FA	FR	G/POS	TPR
1978	Chi-A	8	24	6	6	0	0	0	1	4	6	.250	.379	.250	629	80	-0	1	0	0	.972	-2	/2-8	-0.2
1979	Chi-A	16	16	5	1	0	1	0	1	2	3	.063	.167	.188	354	-5	-2	1	1	-0	.966	5	/2-8,3-1,D-1	0.2
Total	2	24	40	11	7	0	1	0	2	6	9	.175	.298	.225	523	46	-3	2	1	0	.969	3	/2-16,D-1,3-1	0.0

■ MIKE GATES Gates, Michael Grant b: 9/20/56, Culver City, Cal. BL/TR, 6', 165 lbs. Deb: 5/6/81

YEAR	TM/L	G	AB	R	H	2B	3B	HR	RBI	BB	SO	AVG	OBP	SLG	OPS	OPS+	BR+	SB	CS	SBR	FA	FR	G/POS	TPR
1981	Mon-N	1	2	1	1	0	1	0	1	0	1	.500	.500	1.500	2000	445	1	0	0	0	1.000	-0	/2-1	0.0
1982	Mon-N	36	121	16	28	2	3	0	8	9	19	.231	.285	.298	582	62	-6	0	0	0	1.000	-9	2-36	-1.5
Total	2	37	123	17	29	2	4	0	9	9	20	.236	.288	.317	605	68	-5	0	0	0	1.000	-10	/2-37	-1.5

■ FRANK GATINS Gatins, Frank Anthony b: 3/6/1871, Johnstown, Pa. d: 11/8/11, Johnstown, Pa. Deb: 9/21/1898

YEAR	TM/L	G	AB	R	H	2B	3B	HR	RBI	BB	SO	AVG	OBP	SLG	OPS	OPS+	BR+	SB	CS	SBR	FA	FR	G/POS	TPR
1898	Was-N	17	58	6	13	2	0	0	5	3		.224	.274	.259	533	53	-4	2			.790	-8	S-17	-1.0
1901	Bro-N	50	197	21	45	7	2	1	21	5		.228	.255	.299	554	59	-11	6			.919	-9	3-46/S-5	-1.9
Total	2	67	255	27	58	9	2	1	26	8		.227	.259	.290	550	58	-14	8			.841	-17	/3-46,S-22	-2.9

■ JIM GAUDET Gaudet, James Jennings b: 6/3/55, New Orleans, La. BR/TR, 6', 185 lbs. Deb: 9/10/78

YEAR	TM/L	G	AB	R	H	2B	3B	HR	RBI	BB	SO	AVG	OBP	SLG	OPS	OPS+	BR+	SB	CS	SBR	FA	FR	G/POS	TPR
1978	KC-A	3	8	0	0	0	0	0	0	0	3	.000	.000	.000	0	-97	-2	0	0	0	.938	1	/C-3	-0.1
1979	KC-A	3	6	0	1	0	0	0	0	0	0	.167	.167	.167	333	-10	-1	0	0	0	1.000	1	/C-3	0.0
Total	2	6	14	0	1	0	0	0	0	0	3	.071	.071	.071	143	-59	-3	0	0	0	.966	2	/C-6	-0.1

■ MIKE GAULE Gaule, Michael John b: 8/4/1869, Baltimore, Md. d: 1/24/18, Baltimore, Md. BL/TL, 6'2", Deb: 6/15/1889

YEAR	TM/L	G	AB	R	H	2B	3B	HR	RBI	BB	SO	AVG	OBP	SLG	OPS	OPS+	BR+	SB	CS	SBR	FA	FR	G/POS	TPR
1889	Lou-a	1	2	0	0	0	0	0	0	0	1	.000	.000	.000	0	-99	-1	0			.000	-1	/O-1(0-1-0)	-0.1

■ DOC GAUTREAU Gautreau, Walter Paul "Punk" b: 7/26/01, Cambridge, Mass. d: 8/23/70, Salt Lake City, Ut BR/TR, 5'4", 129 lbs. Deb: 6/22/25

YEAR	TM/L	G	AB	R	H	2B	3B	HR	RBI	BB	SO	AVG	OBP	SLG	OPS	OPS+	BR+	SB	CS	SBR	FA	FR	G/POS	TPR
1925	Phi-A	4	7	0	0	0	0	0	0	0	3	.000	.000	.000	0	-94	-2	0	0	0	.933	1	/2-4	-0.1
	Bos-N	68	279	45	73	13	3	0	23	35	13	.262	.346	.330	676	81	-7	11	7	-0	.976	-4	2-68	-0.8
1926	Bos-N	79	266	36	71	9	4	0	8	35	24	.267	.356	.331	687	94	-1	17			.942	-20	2-74	-1.8
1927	Bos-N	87	236	38	58	12	2	0	20	25	20	.246	.321	.314	634	76	-8	11			.965	-3	2-57	-0.9
1928	Bos-N	23	18	3	5	0	1	0	1	4	3	.278	.409	.389	798	116	1	1			.750	-1	/2-4,S-1	0.0
Total	4	261	806	122	207	34	10	0	52	99	63	.257	.341	.324	665	83	-17	40	7		.960	-25	2-207/S-1	-3.6

■ SID GAUTREAUX Gautreaux, Sidney Allen "Pudge" b: 5/4/12, Schriever, La. d: 4/19/80, Morgan City, La. BB/TR, 5'8", 190 lbs. Deb: 4/15/36

YEAR	TM/L	G	AB	R	H	2B	3B	HR	RBI	BB	SO	AVG	OBP	SLG	OPS	OPS+	BR+	SB	CS	SBR	FA	FR	G/POS	TPR
1936	Bro-N	75	71	8	19	3	0	0	16	9	7	.268	.358	.310	668	80	-2	0			.963	-1	C-15	-0.2
1937	Bro-N	11	10	0	1	1	0	0	2	1	1	.100	.182	.200	382	4	-1	0			.000	0	H	-0.1
Total	2	86	81	8	20	4	0	0	18	10	8	.247	.337	.296	633	71	-3	0			.963	-1	/C-15	-0.3

■ GAVERN Gavern Deb: 6/15/1874

YEAR	TM/L	G	AB	R	H	2B	3B	HR	RBI	BB	SO	AVG	OBP	SLG	OPS	OPS+	BR+	SB	CS	SBR	FA	FR	G/POS	TPR
1874	Atl-n	1	4	1	0	0	0	0	0	0	0	.000	.000	.000	0	-99	-1	0	0	0	.750	2	/2-1	0.0

■ MIKE GAZELLA Gazella, Michael b: 10/13/1896, Olyphant, Pa. d: 9/11/78, Odessa, Tex. BR/TR, 5'7.5", 165 lbs. Deb: 7/2/23

YEAR	TM/L	G	AB	R	H	2B	3B	HR	RBI	BB	SO	AVG	OBP	SLG	OPS	OPS+	BR+	SB	CS	SBR	FA	FR	G/POS	TPR
1923	NY-A	8	13	2	1	0	0	0	1	2	3	.077	.200	.077	277	-25	-2	0	0	0	1.000	-1	/S-4,2-2,3-2	-0.3
1926	*NY-A	66	168	21	39	6	0	0	20	25	24	.232	.335	.268	603	60	-9	2	2	-0	.913	-4	3-45,S-11	-1.0
1927	NY-A	54	115	17	32	8	4	0	9	23	16	.278	.403	.417	820	117	4	4	1	1	.961	-6	3-44/S-6	0.0
1928	NY-A	32	56	11	13	0	0	0	2	6	7	.232	.317	.232	550	48	-4	2	1	0	.969	-1	3-16/2-4,S-3	-0.4
Total	4	160	352	51	85	14	4	0	32	56	50	.241	.350	.304	654	73	-12	8	4	0	.940	-12	3-107/S-24,2-6	-1.7

■ DALE GEAR Gear, Dale Dudley b: 2/2/1872, Lone Elm, Kan. d: 9/23/51, Topeka, Kan. BR/TR, 5'11", 165 lbs. Deb: 8/15/1896 Career OF: (12-LF 7-CF 22-RF)

YEAR	TM/L	G	AB	R	H	2B	3B	HR	RBI	BB	SO	AVG	OBP	SLG	OPS	OPS+	BR+	SB	CS	SBR	FA	FR	G/POS	TPR
1896	Cle-N	4	15	5	6	1	1	0	3	1	1	.400	.438	.600	1038	163	1	0			.857	-1	/P-3,1-1	0.0
1897	Cle-N	7	24	3	4	1	0	0	2	3		.167	.286	.208	494	30	-2	2			.750	0	/O-6(0-6-0)	-0.2
1901	Was-A	58	199	17	47	9	2	0	20	4		.236	.251	.302	553	54	-13	2			.944	1	O-35(12-1-22),P-24	-0.9
Total	3	69	238	25	57	11	3	0	25	8	1	.239	.267	.311	578	59	-14	4			.900	0	/O-41R,P-27,1-1	-1.1

■ GARY GEARHART Gearhart, Lloyd William b: 8/10/23, New Lebanon, Ohio BR/TL, 5'11", 180 lbs. Deb: 4/18/47

YEAR	TM/L	G	AB	R	H	2B	3B	HR	RBI	BB	SO	AVG	OBP	SLG	OPS	OPS+	BR+	SB	CS	SBR	FA	FR	G/POS	TPR
1947	NY-N	73	179	26	44	9	0	6	17	17	30	.246	.315	.397	711	87	-4	1			.961	-1	O-44(17-28-0)	-0.6

■ HUCK GEARY Geary, Eugene Francis Joseph b: 1/22/17, Buffalo, N.Y. d: 1/27/81, Cuba, N.Y. BL/TR, 5'10.5", 170 lbs. Deb: 7/17/42

YEAR	TM/L	G	AB	R	H	2B	3B	HR	RBI	BB	SO	AVG	OBP	SLG	OPS	OPS+	BR+	SB	CS	SBR	FA	FR	G/POS	TPR
1942	Pit-N	9	22	3	5	0	0	0	2	2	3	.227	.292	.227	519	52	-1	0			.939	0	/S-8	-0.1
1943	Pit-N	46	166	17	25	4	0	1	13	18	6	.151	.234	.193	426	23	-16	3			.956	-6	S-46	-2.1
Total	2	55	188	20	30	4	0	1	15	20	9	.160	.240	.197	437	26	-17	3			.954	-6	/S-54	-2.2

■ ELMER GEDEON Gedeon, Elmer John b: 4/15/17, Cleveland, Ohio d: 4/20/44, St.Pol, France BR/TR, 6'4", 196 lbs. Deb: 9/18/39

YEAR	TM/L	G	AB	R	H	2B	3B	HR	RBI	BB	SO	AVG	OBP	SLG	OPS	OPS+	BR+	SB	CS	SBR	FA	FR	G/POS	TPR
1939	Was-A	5	15	1	3	0	0	0	1	2	5	.200	.294	.200	494	31	-2	0	0	0	1.000	1	/O-5(0-4-1)	-0.1

■ JOE GEDEON Gedeon, Elmer Joseph b: 12/5/1893, Sacramento, Cal. d: 5/19/41, San Francisco, Cal BR/TR, 6', 167 lbs. Deb: 5/13/13 Career OF: (14-LF 1-CF 2-RF)

YEAR	TM/L	G	AB	R	H	2B	3B	HR	RBI	BB	SO	AVG	OBP	SLG	OPS	OPS+	BR+	SB	CS	SBR	FA	FR	G/POS	TPR
1913	Was-A	29	71	3	13	1	3	0	6	1	6	.183	.205	.282	487	41	-6	3			.929	2	O-15L/3-7,2-2,SP	-0.4
1914	Was-A	4	2	0	0	0	0	0	1	0	1	.000	.333	.000	333	1	-0	0			.667	-1	/O-4(0-1-2)	-0.1
1916	NY-A	122	435	50	92	14	4	0	27	40	61	.211	.282	.262	544	62	-20	14			.955	-10	*2-122	-3.1
1917	NY-A	33	117	15	28	7	0	0	8	7	13	.239	.288	.299	587	78	-3	4			.983	4	2-31	0.1
1918	StL-A	123	441	39	94	14	3	1	41	27	29	.213	.271	.265	536	64	-20	7			**.977**	16	*2-123	-0.3
1919	StL-A	120	437	57	111	13	4	0	27	50	35	.254	.340	.302	642	79	-10	4			**.975**	-3	*2-118	-1.2
1920	StL-A	153	606	95	177	33	6	0	61	55	36	.292	.355	.366	721	89	-9	1	3	-1	.964	-26	*2-153	-3.3
Total	7	584	2109	259	515	82	20	1	171	180	181	.244	.311	.303	615	75	-69	33	3		.969	-18	2-549/O-19L,3-7,SP	-8.3

■ **RICH GEDMAN** Gedman, Richard Leo b: 9/26/59, Worcester, Mass. BL/TR, 6', 215 lbs. Deb: 9/7/80

YEAR	TM/L	G	AB	R	H	2B	3B	HR	RBI	BB	SO	AVG	OBP	SLG	OPS	OPS+	BR+	SB	CS	SBR	FA	FR	G/POS	TPR
1980	Bos-A	9	24	2	5	0	0	0	1	0	5	.208	.208	.208	417	14	-3	0	0	0	.867	-0	/C-2,D-4	-0.3
1981	Bos-A	62	205	22	59	15	0	5	26	9	31	.288	.321	.434	755	109	2	0	0	0	.990	-2	C-59	0.2
1982	Bos-A	92	289	30	72	17	2	4	26	10	37	.249	.279	.363	642	71	-12	0	1	-0	.977	-7	C-86	-1.6
1983	Bos-A	81	204	21	60	16	1	2	18	15	37	.294	.345	.412	757	100	0	0	1	-0	.980	-3	C-68	0.0
1984	Bos-A	133	449	54	121	26	4	24	72	29	72	.269	.315	.506	821	118	9	0	0	0	.977	-8	*C-125	0.7
1985	Bos-A★	144	498	66	147	30	5	18	80	50	79	.295	.363	.484	847	124	17	2	0	0	.983	4	*C-139	2.6
1986	*Bos-A★	135	462	49	119	29	0	16	65	37	61	.258	.318	.424	742	100	-1	1	0	0	.994	10	*C-134	1.5
1987	Bos-A	52	151	11	31	8	0	1	13	10	24	.205	.255	.278	533	40	-13	0	0	0	.976	-4	C-51	-1.4
1988	*Bos-A	95	299	33	69	14	0	9	39	18	49	.231	.281	.368	649	77	-10	0	0	0	.992	2	C-93/D-1	-0.2
1989	Bos-A	93	260	24	55	9	0	4	16	23	47	.212	.276	.292	568	57	-15	0	1	-0	.981	-0	C-91	-1.1
1990	Bos-A	10	15	3	3	0	0	0	0	5	6	.200	.429	.200	629	78	0	0	0	0	.970	0	/C-9	0.1
	Hou-N	40	104	4	21	7	0	1	10	15	24	.202	.303	.298	601	68	-4	0	0	0	1.000	6	C-39	0.4
1991	StL-N	46	94	7	10	1	0	3	8	4	15	.106	.143	.213	356	-1	-13	0	1	-0	.976	10	C-43	-0.2
1992	StL-N	41	105	5	23	4	0	1	8	11	22	.219	.293	.286	579	67	-5	0	0	0	.988	11	C-40	0.8
Total	13	1033	3159	331	795	176	12	88	382	236	509	.252	.307	.399	705	90	-47	3	4	-1	.984	20	C-979/D-5	1.5

■ **COUNT GEDNEY** Gedney, Alfred W. b: 5/10/1849, Brooklyn, N.Y. d: 3/26/22, Hackensack, N.J. 5'9", 140 lbs. Deb: 4/27/1872 Career OF: (189-LF 9-CF 1-RF)

YEAR	TM/L	G	AB	R	H	2B	3B	HR	RBI	BB	SO	AVG	OBP	SLG	OPS	OPS+	BR+	SB	CS	SBR	FA	FR	G/POS	TPR
1872	Tro-n	9	47	14	20	3	0	3	18	0	0	.426	.426	.681	1106	232	7	1	0	0	.933	-1	/O-9(0-9-0)	0.4
	Eck-n	18	71	4	13	1	0	0	7	0	1	.183	.183	.197	380	20	-5	2	1	0	.911	1	O-18(18-0-0)	-0.2
	Yr	27	118	18	33	4	0	3	25	0	1	.280	.280	.390	669	115	3	3	1	0	.915	0	O-27(18-9-0)	0.2
1873	Mut-n	53	224	41	60	5	5	1	25	7	5	.268	.290	.348	638	89	-3	1	0	0	.867	15	*O-53(53-0-0)	1.0
1874	Ath-n	54	222	49	61	4	1	1	34	7	11	.275	.297	.315	612	89	-4	2	2	-0	.822	-2	*O-51(51-0-0)/1-4	-0.3
1875	Mut-n	68	267	30	55	12	2	0	17	0	8	.206	.206	.266	472	60	-11	2	3	-1	.843	12	*O-67(67-0-1)/P-2	0.2
Total	4 n	202	831	138	209	25	8	5	101	14	25	.252	.264	.319	583	83	-16	8	6	-0	.853	25	O-198L/1-4,P-2	1.1

■ **BILLY GEER** Geer, William Henry Harrison (b: George Harrison Geer) b: 8/13/1849, Syracuse N.Y. d: 1/3/22, Syracuse, N.Y. TR, 5'8", 160 lbs. Deb: 10/15/1874 NA OF: (5-LF 12-CF 3-RF) Career OF: (0-LF 0-CF 1-RF)

YEAR	TM/L	G	AB	R	H	2B	3B	HR	RBI	BB	SO	AVG	OBP	SLG	OPS	OPS+	BR+	SB	CS	SBR	FA	FR	G/POS	TPR
1874	Mut-n	2	8	0	2	0	0	0	1	0	0	.250	.250	.250	500	59	-0	0	0	0	.889	2	/O-2(1-1-0)	0.1
1875	NH-n	37	164	20	40	4	1	0	9	1	4	.244	.248	.280	529	96	1	2	2	-0	.765	3	O-17C,2-13/S-6,13	0.2
1878	Cin-N	61	237	31	52	13	2	0	20	10	18	.219	.251	.291	542	86	-2				.867	-4	*S-60/2-2	-0.4
1880	Wor-N	2	6	0	0	0	0	0	0	0	0	.000	.000	.000	0	-92	-1				1.000	-1	/O-1(0-0-1),S-1	-0.2
1884	Phi-U	9	36	7	9	2	1	0		4		.250	.325	.361	686	116	-0				.772	1	/S-9	0.1
	Bro-a	107	391	68	82	15	7	0		38		.210	.281	.284	565	84	-6				.870	17	*S-107/P-2,2-2	1.3
1885	Lou-a	14	51	2	6	2	0	0	3	2		.118	.167	.157	324	3	-6				.872	2	S-14	-0.3
Total	2 n	39	172	20	42	4	1	0	10	1	4	.244	.249	.279	528	93	0	2	2	-0	.791	5	/O-19C,2-13,S-6,31	0.3
Total	4	193	721	108	149	32	10	0	23	54	18	.207	.264	.279	543	79	-15				.864	15	S-191/2-4,P-2,O-1R	0.5

■ **LOU GEHRIG** Gehrig, Henry Louis "The Iron Horse" b: 6/19/03, New York, N.Y. d: 6/2/41, Riverdale, N.Y. BL/TL, 6', 200 lbs. Deb: 6/15/23 H Career OF: (3-LF 0-CF 6-RF)

YEAR	TM/L	G	AB	R	H	2B	3B	HR	RBI	BB	SO	AVG	OBP	SLG	OPS	OPS+	BR+	SB	CS	SBR	FA	FR	G/POS	TPR
1923	NY-A	13	26	6	11	4	1	1	9	2	5	.423	.464	.769	1234	217	4	0	0	0	.933	-1	/1-9	0.3
1924	NY-A	10	12	2	6	1	0	0	5	1	3	.500	.538	.583	1122	190	2	0	0	0	1.000	-0	/1-2,O-1(0-0-1)	0.1
1925	NY-A	126	437	73	129	23	10	20	68	46	49	.295	.365	.531	896	127	15	6	3	0	.989	-9	*1-114/O-6(2-0-4)	-0.1
1926	*NY-A	155	572	135	179	47	**20**	16	112	105	73	.313	.420	.549	969	154	46	6	5	-0	.991	-8	*1-155	2.6
1927	*NY-A	155	584	149	218	**52**	18	47	**175**	109	84	.373	.474	.765	1240	224	**107**	10	8	-1	.992	-6	*1-155	8.3
1928	*NY-A	154	562	139	210	**47**	13	27	**142**	95	69	.374	**.467**	.648	1115	197	81	4	11	-3	.989	-8	*1-154	5.7
1929	NY-A	154	553	127	166	32	10	35	126	122	68	.300	.431	.584	1015	170	62	4	4	-1	.994	-5	*1-154	4.3
1930	NY-A	154	581	143	220	42	17	41	**174**	101	63	.379	.473	.721	1194	207	97	12	14	-2	.989	1	*1-153/O-1(1-0-0)	**7.6**
1931	NY-A	155	619	**163**	**211**	31	15	**46**	**184**	117	56	.341	.446	.662	1108	199	90	17	12	-0	.991	-10	*1-154/O-1(0-0-1)	5.9
1932	*NY-A	156	596	138	208	42	9	34	151	108	38	.349	.451	.621	1072	184	78	4	11	-3	.987	-6	*1-156	4.9
1933	NY-A★	152	593	**138**	198	41	12	32	139	92	42	.334	.424	.605	1030	181	69	9	13	-3	.993	-3	*1-152	4.5
1934	NY-A★	154	579	128	210	40	6	**49**	**165**	109	31	**.363**	**.465**	**.706**	**1172**	**213**	**98**	9	5	-0	.994	1	*1-153/S-1	**7.7**
1935	NY-A★	149	535	**125**	176	26	10	30	119	**132**	38	.329	**.466**	.583	1049	180	**70**	8	7	-1	.990	0	*1-149	5.1
1936	*NY-A★	155	579	**167**	205	37	7	**49**	152	**130**	46	.354	**.478**	**.696**	**1174**	**193**	**89**	3	4	-1	.994	1	*1-155	**6.5**
1937	*NY-A★	157	569	138	200	37	9	37	159	**127**	49	.351	**.473**	.643	**1116**	**177**	**72**	4	3	-0	.989	-6	*1-157	4.6
1938	*NY-A★	157	576	115	170	32	6	29	114	107	75	.295	.410	.523	932	133	30	6	1	1	.991	-1	*1-157	1.4
1939	NY-A†	8	28	2	4	0	0	0	1	5	1	.143	.273	.143	416	9	-4	0	0	0	.971	-1	/1-8	-0.5
Total	17	2164	8001	1888	2721	534	163	493	1995	1508	790	.340	.447	.632	1080	182	1007	102	101	-13	.991	-60	*1-2137/O-9R,S-1	68.9

■ **CHARLIE GEHRINGER** Gehringer, Charles Leonard "The Mechanical Man" b: 5/11/03, Fowlerville, Mich. d: 1/21/93, Bloomfield Hills, Mich. BL/TR, 5'11", 180 lbs. Deb: 9/22/24 CH

YEAR	TM/L	G	AB	R	H	2B	3B	HR	RBI	BB	SO	AVG	OBP	SLG	OPS	OPS+	BR+	SB	CS	SBR	FA	FR	G/POS	TPR
1924	Det-A	5	13	2	6	0	0	0	1	0	2	.462	.462	.462	923	141	1	1	1	-0	.967	4	/2-5	0.4
1925	Det-A	8	18	3	3	0	0	0	0	2	0	.167	.250	.167	417	7	-3	0	1	-0	1.000	4	/2-6	0.1
1926	Det-A	123	459	62	127	19	17	1	48	30	42	.277	.322	.399	721	86	-11	9	7	-0	.973	-10	*2-112/3-6	-1.7
1927	Det-A	133	508	110	161	29	11	4	61	52	31	.317	.383	.441	824	112	9	17	8	1	.965	**20**	*2-121	3.1
1928	Det-A	154	603	108	193	29	16	6	74	69	22	.320	.395	.451	846	120	19	15	9	0	.962	2	*2-154	2.4
1929	Det-A	155	634	**131**	**215**	**45**	**19**	13	106	64	19	.339	.405	.532	936	139	36	**27**	9	**3**	**.975**	-3	*2-154	3.7
1930	Det-A	154	610	144	201	47	15	16	98	69	17	.330	.404	.534	938	133	31	19	15	-1	**.979**	2	*2-154	3.3
1931	Det-A	101	383	67	119	24	5	4	53	29	15	.311	.359	.431	790	103	1	13	4	1	.979	-1	2-78/1-9	0.6
1932	Det-A	152	618	112	184	44	11	19	107	68	34	.298	.370	.497	867	118	15	9	8	-1	.967	-1	*2-152	2.1
1933	Det-A★	155	628	103	204	42	6	12	105	68	27	.325	.393	.468	862	125	23	5	4	-0	.981	7	*2-155	3.7
1934	*Det-A★	154	601	**134**	**214**	50	7	11	127	99	25	.356	.450	.517	967	149	47	11	8	-0	.981	7	*2-154	5.9
1935	*Det-A★	150	610	123	201	32	8	19	108	79	16	.330	.409	.502	911	139	36	11	4	1	**.985**	3	*2-149	4.6
1936	Det-A★	154	641	144	227	**60**	12	15	116	83	13	.354	.431	.555	987	141	43	4	1	1	**.974**	16	*2-154	6.0
1937	Det-A★	144	564	133	209	40	1	14	96	90	25	**.371**	.458	.520	978	143	41	11	4	1	**.986**	6	*2-142	5.2
1938	Det-A★	152	568	133	174	32	5	20	107	113	21	.306	.425	.486	911	121	21	14	1	3	.976	-1	*2-152	3.0
1939	Det-A	118	406	86	132	29	6	16	86	68	16	.325	.423	.544	967	135	23	4	3	-0	**.977**	1	*2-107	2.8
1940	*Det-A	139	515	108	161	33	3	10	81	101	17	.313	.428	.447	875	116	17	10	0	2	.972	-20	*2-138	0.8
1941	Det-A	127	436	65	96	19	4	3	46	95	26	.220	.363	.303	666	71	-15	1	2	-0	**.982**	-3	*2-116	-1.1
1942	Det-A	45	45	6	12	0	0	1	7	7	4	.267	.365	.333	699	90	-0	0	0	0	1.000	1	/2-3	0.1
Total	19	2323	8860	1774	2839	574	146	184	1427	1186	372	.320	.404	.480	884	123	335	181	89	9	.976	33	*2-2206/1-9,3-6	45.0

■ **PHIL GEIER** Geier, Philip Louis "Little Phil" b: 11/3/1875, Washington, D.C. d: 9/25/67, Spokane, Wash. BL/TR, 5'7", 145 lbs. Deb: 8/17/1896 Career OF: (14-LF 167-CF 98-RF)

YEAR	TM/L	G	AB	R	H	2B	3B	HR	RBI	BB	SO	AVG	OBP	SLG	OPS	OPS+	BR+	SB	CS	SBR	FA	FR	G/POS	TPR
1896	Phi-N	17	56	12	13	0	1	0	6	6	7	.232	.317	.268	585	56	-3	3			.813	-2	O-12(2-0-10)/2-3,C-2	-0.5
1897	Phi-N	92	316	51	88	6	2	1	35	56		.278	.392	.320	712	91	-0	19			.932	-7	O-45R,2-37/S-6,3-2	-0.6
1900	Cin-N	30	113	18	29	1	4	0	10	7		.257	.306	.336	642	79	-3	3			.941	1	O-27(0-9-18)/3-2	-0.3
1901	Phi-A	50	211	42	49	5	2	0	23	24		.232	.314	.275	588	61	-11	7			.934	-5	O-50(6-14-30)/S-2,3-1	-1.6
	Mil-A	11	39	4	7	1	1	0	1	5		.179	.273	.256	529	50	-3	4			1.000	-1	/O-8(0-8-0),3-3	-0.4
	Yr	61	250	46	56	6	3	0	24	29		.224	.307	.272	579	60	-13	11			.941	-6	O-58(6-22-30)/3-4,S-2	-2.0
1904	Bos-N	149	580	70	141	17	2	1	27	56		.243	.314	.284	599	88	-6	18			.933	-3	*O-137C/3-7,2-5,S-1	-1.6
Total	5	349	1315	197	327	30	12	2	102	154	7	.249	.332	.294	626	81	-26	54			.932	-16	O-279C/2-45,3-15,SC	-5.0

■ **GARY GEIGER** Geiger, Gary Merle b: 4/4/37, Sand Ridge, Ill. d: 4/24/96, Murphysboro, Ill. BL/TR, 6', 168 lbs. Deb: 4/15/58 Career OF: (117-LF 542-CF 114-RF)

YEAR	TM/L	G	AB	R	H	2B	3B	HR	RBI	BB	SO	AVG	OBP	SLG	OPS	OPS+	BR+	SB	CS	SBR	FA	FR	G/POS	TPR
1958	Cle-A	91	195	28	45	3	1	1	6	27	43	.231	.333	.272	605	70	-7	2	2	-0	.986	4	O-53(1-44-8)/3-2,P-1	-0.5
1959	Bos-A	120	335	45	82	10	4	11	48	21	55	.245	.289	.397	686	83	-9	9	3	1	.989	-10	O-95(46-61-1)	-2.3
1960	Bos-A	77	245	32	74	13	3	9	33	23	38	.302	.369	.490	859	126	9	2	2	-0	1.000	4	O-66(5-7-59)	1.0
1961	Bos-A	140	499	82	116	21	6	18	64	87	91	.232	.351	.407	758	99	1	16	4	2	.988	10	*O-137(0-137-0)	0.9
1962	Bos-A	131	466	67	116	18	4	16	54	67	66	.249	.346	.408	754	99	-0	18	11	0	.987	8	*O-129(0-129-0)	0.4
1963	Bos-A	121	399	67	105	13	5	16	44	36	63	.263	.329	.441	770	110	5	9	4	1	.984	14	O-95(2-89-4)/1-6	1.7
1964	Bos-A	5	13	3	5	0	1	0	1	2	2	.385	.467	.538	1005	170	1	0	0	0	1.000	-0	/O-4(0-1-3)	0.1
1965	Bos-A	24	45	5	9	3	0	1	2	13	10	.200	.379	.333	713	98	0	3	0	1	.970	0	O-16(5-10-1)	0.1
1966	Atl-N	78	126	23	33	5	3	4	10	21	29	.262	.372	.444	816	124	5	0	1	-0	.982	-9	O-49(5-33-15)	-0.6

YEAR	TM/L	G	AB	R	H	2B	3B	HR	RBI	BB	SO	AVG	OBP	SLG	OPS	OPS+	BR+	SB	CS	SBR	FA	FR	G/POS	TPR
1967	Atl-N	69	117	17	19	1	1	1	5	20	35	.162	.285	.214	498	45	-8	1	1	-0	.980	-6	O-38(6-26-7)	-1.6
1969	Hou-N	93	125	19	28	4	1	0	16	24	34	.224	.353	.272	625	79	-2	2	1	0	.968	-7	O-65(47-5-14)	-1.2
1970	Hou-N	5	4	0	1	0	0	0	0	0	0	.250	.250	.250	500	36	-0	0	0	0	1.000	-1	/O-2(0-0-2)	-0.1
Total	12	954	2569	388	633	91	29	77	283	341	466	.246	.339	.394	733	98	-5	62	29	3	.986	8	O-749C/1-6,3-2,P-1	-2.1

■ **BILL GEIS** Geis, William J. (b: William J. Geiss) b: 7/15/1858, Chicago, Ill. d: 9/18/24, Chicago, Ill. 5'10", 164 lbs. Deb: 5/1/1884 F

YEAR	TM/L	G	AB	R	H	2B	3B	HR	RBI	BB	SO	AVG	OBP	SLG	OPS	OPS+	BR+	SB	CS	SBR	FA	FR	G/POS	TPR
1884	Det-N	75	283	22	50	11	4	2	16	6	60	.177	.194	.265	459	46	-17				.862	-7	2-73/O-1R,1-1,P-1	-1.9

■ **EMIL GEISS** Geiss, Emil August b: 3/20/1867, Chicago, Ill. d: 10/4/11, Chicago, Ill. BR/TR, 5'11", 170 lbs. Deb: 5/18/1887 F

YEAR	TM/L	G	AB	R	H	2B	3B	HR	RBI	BB	SO	AVG	OBP	SLG	OPS	OPS+	BR+	SB	CS	SBR	FA	FR	G/POS	TPR
1887	Chi-N	3	12	0	1	0	0	0	0	0	7	.083	.083	.083	167	-47	-2	0			.571	-1	/2-1,1-1,P-1	-0.2

■ **CHARLIE GELBERT** Gelbert, Charles Magnus b: 1/26/06, Scranton, Pa. d: 1/13/67, Easton, Pa. BR/TR, 5'11", 170 lbs. Deb: 4/16/29

YEAR	TM/L	G	AB	R	H	2B	3B	HR	RBI	BB	SO	AVG	OBP	SLG	OPS	OPS+	BR+	SB	CS	SBR	FA	FR	G/POS	TPR
1929	StL-N	146	512	60	134	29	8	3	65	51	46	.262	.329	.367	696	71	-23	8			.948	7	*S-146	0.0
1930	*StL-N	139	513	92	156	39	11	3	72	43	41	.304	.360	.441	801	89	-9	6			.947	9	*S-139	1.3
1931	*StL-N	131	447	61	129	29	5	1	62	54	31	.289	.365	.383	748	97	-0	7			.959	13	*S-130	2.2
1932	StL-N	122	455	60	122	28	9	1	45	39	30	.268	.330	.376	706	87	-8	8			.945	0	*S-122	0.2
1935	StL-N	62	168	24	49	7	2	2	21	17	18	.292	.357	.393	750	97	-0	0			.978	5	3-37,S-21/2-3	0.7
1936	StL-N	93	280	33	64	15	2	3	27	25	26	.229	.292	.329	620	67	-13	2			.965	8	3-60,S-28/2-8	-0.1
1937	Cin-N	43	114	12	22	4	0	1	13	15	12	.193	.287	.254	541	51	-8	1			.968	-2	S-37/2-9,3-1	-0.7
	Det-A	20	47	4	4	2	0	0	1	4	11	.085	.157	.128	285	-27	-9	0	0	0	.934	-0	S-16	-0.8
1939	Was-A	68	188	36	48	7	5	3	29	30	11	.255	.361	.394	754	100	1	2	0	0	.970	-4	S-28,3-20/2-1	0.0
1940	Was-A	22	54	7	20	7	1	0	7	4	3	.370	.424	.537	961	157	5	0	0	0	.920	-5	S-12/P-2,2-1	0.0
	Bos-A	30	91	9	18	2	0	0	8	8	16	.198	.263	.220	482	25	-10	0	0	0	.926	5	3-29/S-1	-0.4
	Yr	52	145	16	38	9	1	0	15	12	19	.262	.323	.338	661	72	-6	0	0	0	.926	-1	3-29,S-13/P-2,2-1	-0.4
Total	9	876	2869	398	766	169	43	17	350	290	245	.267	.336	.374	709	82	-75	34	0		.951	35	S-680,3-147/2-22,P	2.4

■ **FRANK GENINS** Genins, C. Frank "Frenchy" b: 11/2/1866, St.Louis, Mo. d: 9/30/22, St.Louis, Mo. TR, Deb: 7/5/1892 Career OF: (21-LF 36-CF 13-RF)

YEAR	TM/L	G	AB	R	H	2B	3B	HR	RBI	BB	SO	AVG	OBP	SLG	OPS	OPS+	BR+	SB	CS	SBR	FA	FR	G/POS	TPR
1892	Cin-N	35	110	12	20	4	0	0	7	12	12	.182	.262	.218	480	46	-7	7			.901	4	S-17,O-14(7-7-0)/3-4	-0.3
	StL-N	15	51	5	10	1	0	0	4	1	11	.196	.212	.216	427	31	-4	3			.821	-8	S-14/O-1(0-0-1)	-1.1
	Yr	50	161	17	30	5	0	0	11	13	23	.186	.247	.217	465	42	-11	10			.868	-4	S-31,O-15(7-7-1)/3-4	-1.4
1895	Pit-N	73	252	43	63	8	0	2	24	22	14	.250	.315	.306	621	64	-13	19			.931	-8	O-29L,3-16,2-16,/S1	-1.7
1901	Cle-A	26	101	15	23	5	0	0	9	8		.228	.284	.277	562	58	-5	3			.940	1	O-26(0-26-0)	-0.5
Total	3	149	514	75	116	18	0	2	44	43	37	.226	.288	.272	560	56	-30	32			.934	-10	/O-70C,S-39,3-20,21	-3.6

■ **GEORGE GENOVESE** Genovese, George Michael b: 2/22/22, Staten Island, N.Y BL/TR, 5'6.5", 160 lbs. Deb: 4/29/50

YEAR	TM/L	G	AB	R	H	2B	3B	HR	RBI	BB	SO	AVG	OBP	SLG	OPS	OPS+	BR+	SB	CS	SBR	FA	FR	G/POS	TPR
1950	Was-A	3	1	1	0	0	0	0	0	1	0	.000	.500	.000	500	39	0	0	0	0	.000	0	H	0.0

■ **JIM GENTILE** Gentile, James Edward "Diamond Jim" b: 6/3/34, San Francisco, Cal. BL/TL, 6'4", 215 lbs. Deb: 9/10/57

YEAR	TM/L	G	AB	R	H	2B	3B	HR	RBI	BB	SO	AVG	OBP	SLG	OPS	OPS+	BR+	SB	CS	SBR	FA	FR	G/POS	TPR
1957	Bro-N	4	6	1	1	0	0	1	1	1	1	.167	.286	.667	952	133	0	0	0	0	1.000	-0	/1-2	0.0
1958	LA-N	12	30	0	4	1	0	0	4	4	6	.133	.235	.167	402	9	-4	0	0	0	.981	-1	/1-8	-0.6
1960	Bal-A★	138	384	67	112	17	0	21	98	68	72	.292	.407	.500	907	146	27	0	0	0	.993	-6	*1-124	1.5
1961	Bal-A★	148	486	96	147	25	2	46	141	96	106	.302	.428	.646	1074	189	64	1	1	-0	.989	2	*1-144	5.6
1962	Bal-A★	152	545	80	137	21	1	33	87	77	100	.251	.351	.475	827	128	21	1	0	0	.988	6	*1-150	1.8
1963	Bal-A	145	496	65	123	16	1	24	72	76	101	.248	.355	.429	784	123	17	1	0	0	**.995**	7	*1-143	1.7
1964	KC-A	136	439	71	110	10	0	28	71	84	122	.251	.376	.465	840	128	19	0	0	0	.988	-0	*1-128	1.2
1965	KC-A	38	118	14	29	5	0	10	22	9	26	.246	.305	.542	847	138	5	0	0	0	.981	-1	1-35	0.2
	Hou-N	81	227	22	55	11	0	7	31	34	72	.242	.353	.392	745	118	6	0	0	0	.993	2	1-68	0.5
1966	Hou-N	49	144	16	35	6	1	7	18	21	39	.243	.355	.444	799	129	6	0	0	0	.989	2	1-43	0.6
	Cle-A	33	47	2	6	1	0	2	4	5	18	.128	.212	.277	488	39	-4	0	0	0	.944	-0	/1-9	-0.5
Total	9	936	2922	434	759	113	6	179	549	475	663	.260	.372	.486	858	137	158	3	1	0	.990	10	1-854	12.0

■ **SAM GENTILE** Gentile, Samuel Christopher b: 10/12/16, Charlestown, Mass. d: 5/4/98, Everett, Mass. BL/TR, 5'11", 180 lbs. Deb: 4/24/43

YEAR	TM/L	G	AB	R	H	2B	3B	HR	RBI	BB	SO	AVG	OBP	SLG	OPS	OPS+	BR+	SB	CS	SBR	FA	FR	G/POS	TPR
1943	Bos-N	8	4	1	1	1	0	0	0	1	0	.250	.400	.500	900	162	0	0			.000	0	H	0.0

■ **HARVEY GENTRY** Gentry, Harvey William b: 5/27/26, Winston-Salem, N.C BL/TR, 6', 170 lbs. Deb: 4/14/54 F

YEAR	TM/L	G	AB	R	H	2B	3B	HR	RBI	BB	SO	AVG	OBP	SLG	OPS	OPS+	BR+	SB	CS	SBR	FA	FR	G/POS	TPR
1954	NY-N	5	4	0	1	0	0	0	1	1	0	.250	.400	.250	650	73	-0	0	0	0	.000	0	H	0.0

■ **ALEX GEORGE** George, Alex Thomas M. b: 9/27/38, Kansas City, Mo. BL/TR, 5'11.5", 170 lbs. Deb: 9/16/55

YEAR	TM/L	G	AB	R	H	2B	3B	HR	RBI	BB	SO	AVG	OBP	SLG	OPS	OPS+	BR+	SB	CS	SBR	FA	FR	G/POS	TPR
1955	KC-A	5	10	0	1	0	0	0	0	1	7	.100	.182	.100	282	-22	-2	0	0	0	.917	-1	/S-5	-0.3

■ **GREEK GEORGE** George, Charles Peter b: 12/25/12, Waycross, Ga. d: 8/15/99, Metairie, La. BR/TR, 6'2", 200 lbs. Deb: 6/30/35

YEAR	TM/L	G	AB	R	H	2B	3B	HR	RBI	BB	SO	AVG	OBP	SLG	OPS	OPS+	BR+	SB	CS	SBR	FA	FR	G/POS	TPR
1935	Cle-A	2	0	0	0	0	0	0	0	0	0	—	—	—	—	—	0	0	0	0	1.000	0	/C-1	0.0
1936	Cle-A	23	77	3	15	3	0	0	5	9	16	.195	.279	.234	513	28	-9	0	0	0	.994	16	C-22	0.7
1938	Bro-N	7	20	0	4	0	1	0	2	0	4	.200	.200	.300	500	35	-2	0			1.000	2	/C-7	0.0
1941	Chi-N	35	64	4	10	2	0	0	6	2	10	.156	.182	.188	369	4	-8	0			.973	2	C-18	-0.5
1945	Phi-A	51	138	8	24	4	1	0	11	17	29	.174	.265	.217	482	41	-10	0	0	0	.972	-6	C-46	-1.5
Total	5	118	299	15	53	9	2	0	24	28	59	.177	.248	.221	468	29	-29	0	0		.983	14	/C-94	-1.3

■ **BILL GEORGE** George, William M. b: 1/27/1865, Bellaire, Ohio d: 8/23/16, Wheeling, W.Va. BR/TL, 5'8", 165 lbs. Deb: 5/11/1887

YEAR	TM/L	G	AB	R	H	2B	3B	HR	RBI	BB	SO	AVG	OBP	SLG	OPS	OPS+	BR+	SB	CS	SBR	FA	FR	G/POS	TPR
1887	NY-N	13	54	6	10	0	0	0	5	1	6	.185	.185	.170	355	-1	-7	2			.854	1	P-13/O-1(0-0-1)	0.0
1888	*NY-N	9	39	7	9	1	0	1	6	0	2	.231	.231	.333	564	79	-1	1			1.000	-1	/O-6(0-0-6),P-4	-0.2
1889	NY-N	3	15	1	4	0	0	0	0	0	3	.267	.267	.267	533	49	-1	1			.875	-0	/O-3(0-1-2)	-0.1
	Col-a	5	17	1	4	0	0	0	3	1	1	.235	.278	.235	513	49	-1	1			.667	-1	/O-4(0-0-4),P-2	-0.2
Total	3	30	125	15	27	1	0	1	14	2	12	.216	.222	.242	464	36	-10	5			.860	-1	/P-19,O-14(0-1-13)	-0.5

■ **BEN GERAGHTY** Geraghty, Benjamin Raymond b: 7/19/12, Jersey City, N.J. d: 6/18/63, Jacksonville, Fla BR/TR, 5'11", 175 lbs. Deb: 4/17/36

YEAR	TM/L	G	AB	R	H	2B	3B	HR	RBI	BB	SO	AVG	OBP	SLG	OPS	OPS+	BR+	SB	CS	SBR	FA	FR	G/POS	TPR
1936	Bro-N	51	129	11	25	4	0	0	9	8	16	.194	.241	.225	466	26	-13	4			.922	-7	S-31/2-9,3-5	-1.7
1943	Bos-N	8	1	2	0	0	0	0	0	0	0	.000	.000	.000	0	-99	-0	0			1.000	1	/2-1,S-1,3-1	0.1
1944	Bos-N	11	16	3	4	0	0	0	0	1	2	.250	.294	.250	544	52	-1	0			1.000	0	/2-4,3-3	-0.1
Total	3	70	146	16	29	4	0	0	9	9	18	.199	.245	.226	471	28	-15	4			.922	-6	/S-32,2-14,3-9	-1.7

■ **CRAIG GERBER** Gerber, Craig Stuart b: 1/8/59, Chicago, Ill. BL/TR, 6', 175 lbs. Deb: 4/11/85

YEAR	TM/L	G	AB	R	H	2B	3B	HR	RBI	BB	SO	AVG	OBP	SLG	OPS	OPS+	BR+	SB	CS	SBR	FA	FR	G/POS	TPR
1985	Cal-A	65	91	8	24	1	2	0	6	2	3	.264	.280	.319	598	64	-5	0	3	-1	.970	19	S-53/3-9,2-1,D-1	1.5

■ **WALLY GERBER** Gerber, Walter "Spooks" b: 8/18/1891, Columbus, Ohio d: 6/19/51, Columbus, Ohio BR/TR, 5'10", 152 lbs. Deb: 9/23/14

YEAR	TM/L	G	AB	R	H	2B	3B	HR	RBI	BB	SO	AVG	OBP	SLG	OPS	OPS+	BR+	SB	CS	SBR	FA	FR	G/POS	TPR
1914	Pit-N	17	54	5	13	1	1	0	5	2	8	.241	.281	.296	577	75	-2	0			.921	1	S-17	0.0
1915	Pit-N	56	144	8	28	2	0	0	7	9	16	.194	.252	.208	460	40	-10	6	1	1	.930	2	3-23,S-21/2-2	-0.6
1917	StL-A	14	39	2	12	1	1	0	2	3	2	.308	.357	.385	742	131	1	1			.939	-2	S-12/2-2	0.0
1918	StL-A	56	171	10	41	4	0	0	10	19	11	.240	.316	.263	579	77	-4	2			.922	-9	S-56	-1.0
1919	StL-A	140	462	43	105	14	6	1	37	49	36	.227	.308	.290	598	67	-20	1			.940	-8	*S-140	-1.9
1920	StL-A	154	584	70	163	26	2	2	60	58	32	.279	.346	.341	687	80	-16	4	13	-4	.939	7	*S-154	-0.1
1921	StL-A	114	436	55	121	12	9	2	48	34	19	.278	.337	.360	697	73	-17	4	7	-2	.943	-3	*S-113	-0.9
1922	StL-A	153	604	81	161	22	8	1	51	52	34	.267	.326	.334	660	70	-26	6	4	-0	.944	0	*S-153	-0.9
1923	StL-A	154	605	85	170	26	3	1	62	54	50	.281	.342	.339	681	75	-21	4	6	-1	.950	6	*S-154	0.1
1924	StL-A	148	496	61	135	20	4	0	55	43	34	.272	.341	.329	670	69	-22	4	5	-1	.946	-7	*S-147	-1.3
1925	StL-A	72	246	29	67	13	1	0	19	26	15	.272	.344	.333	678	69	-11	1	2	-0	.949	5	S-71	0.1
1926	StL-A	131	411	37	111	8	0	0	42	40	29	.270	.339	.290	629	62	-21	0	2	-1	.944	3	*S-129	-0.5
1927	StL-A	142	438	44	98	13	9	0	45	35	25	.224	.284	.295	579	49	-34	3	6	-1	.946	9	*S-141/3-1	-1.1
1928	StL-A	6	18	1	5	1	0	0	0	1	3	.278	.316	.333	649	69	-1	0	0	0	.783	-2	/S-6	-0.2
	Bos-A	104	300	21	64	6	1	0	28	32	31	.213	.289	.240	529	41	-25	6	1	1	.955	34	*S-103	1.8
	Yr	110	318	22	69	7	1	0	28	33	34	.217	.291	.245	536	43	-26	6	1	1	.948	**32**	*S-109	1.6

YEAR	TM/L	G	AB	R	H	2B	3B	HR	RBI	BB	SO	AVG	OBP	SLG	OPS	OPS+	BR+	SB	CS	SBR	FA	FR	G/POS	TPR
1929	Bos-A	61	91	6	15	3	1	0	5	8	12	.165	.232	.220	452	17	-11	1	0	0	.937	14	S-30,2-22	0.5
Total	15	1522	5099	558	1309	172	46	7	476	465	357	.257	.323	.313	635	67	-240	43	47		.943	51	*S-1447/2-26,3-24	-6.0
■ **BOB GEREN** Geren, Robert Peter b: 9/22/61, San Diego, Cal. BR/TR, 6'3", 221 lbs. Deb: 5/17/88																								
1988	NY-A	10	10	0	1	0	0	0	0	2	3	.100	.250	.100	350	2	-1	0	0	0	1.000	1	C-10	0.0
1989	NY-A	65	205	26	59	5	1	9	27	12	44	.288	.330	.454	784	120	5	0	0	0	.991	0	C-60/D-2	0.9
1990	NY-A	110	277	21	59	7	0	8	31	13	73	.213	.261	.325	586	63	-14	0	0	0	.993	12	*C-107/D-1	0.3
1991	NY-A	64	128	7	28	3	0	2	12	9	31	.219	.270	.289	559	55	-8	0	1	-0	.989	9	C-63	0.2
1993	SD-N	58	145	8	31	6	0	3	6	13	28	.214	.278	.317	596	58	-9	0	0	0	.993	4	C-49/1-1,3-1	-0.2
Total	5	307	765	62	178	21	1	22	76	49	179	.233	.284	.349	633	74	-28	0	1	-0	.992	26	C-289/D-3,3-1,1-1	1.2
■ **JOE GERHARDT** Gerhardt, John Joseph "Move Up Joe" b: 2/14/1855, Washington, D.C. d: 3/11/22, Middletown, N.Y. BR/TR, 6', 160 lbs. Deb: 9/1/1873 M NA OF: (1-LF 0-CF 0-RF) Career OF: (2-LF 1-CF 0-RF)																								
1873	Was-n	13	56	6	12	3	0	0	7	0	5	.214	.214	.268	482	44	-4	0	0	0	.700	-5	S-13	-0.7
1874	Bal-n	14	61	10	19	0	1	0	6	0	0	.311	.311	.344	656	111	1	0	0	0	.750	3	S-14	0.3
1875	Mut-n	58	252	29	54	7	3	0	20	0	2	.214	.214	.266	480	62	-10	0	5	-2	.753	-1	3-47,2-13/S-1,O-1L	-1.3
1876	Lou-N	65	295	33	76	10	3	2	18	3	5	.258	.268	.336	603	85	-7				.944	5	*1-54/2-5,S-3,O3	-0.3
1877	Lou-N	59	250	41	76	6	5	1	35	5	8	.304	.318	.380	698	101	-1				.888	**20**	*2-57/O-1C,S-1,1-1	1.9
1878	Cin-N	60	259	46	77	7	2	0	28	7	14	.297	.316	.340	656	127	8				.906	5	*2-60	1.5
1879	Cin-N	79	313	22	62	12	3	1	39	3	19	.198	.206	.265	471	57	-13				.908	7	2-55,3-16/1-8,S-1	-0.4
1881	Det-N	80	297	35	72	13	6	0	36	7	31	.242	.260	.327	586	80	-7				.908	8	*2-79/3-1	0.4
1883	Lou-a	78	319	56	84	11	9	0		14		.263	.294	.354	649	116	7				.906	20	*2-78,M	2.6
1884	Lou-a	106	404	39	89	7	8	0	40	13		.220	.254	.277	531	76	-9				.920	27	*2-106	2.0
1885	NY-N	112	399	43	62	12	2	0	33	24	47	.155	.203	.195	399	30	-30				.911	11	*2-112	-1.4
1886	NY-N	123	426	44	81	11	7	0	40	22	63	.190	.230	.249	479	45	-28	8			.924	14	*2-123	-0.9
1887	NY-N	1	4	0	0	0	0	0	0	0	0	.000	.000	.000	0	-99	-1	0			1.000	0	/3-1	-0.1
	NY-a	85	331	40	92	13	2	0	27	24		.278	.280	.277	557	58	-17	15			.896	15	2-84/3-1	0.1
1890	Bro-a	99	369	34	75	10	4	2	40	30		.203	.270	.268	539	61	-18	9			.938	37	*2-99	1.9
	StL-a	37	125	15	32	0	0	1	11	9		.256	.321	.280	601	68	-5	5			.955	5	2-20,3-17,M	0.0
	Yr	136	494	49	107	10	4	3	51	39		.217	.283	.271	555	63	-24	14			**.940**	**42**	*2-119,3-17	1.9
1891	Lou-a	2	6	0	0	0	0	0	0	1	0	.000	.143	.000	143	-59	-1	0			.833	-0	/2-2	-0.1
Total	3 n	85	369	45	85	10	4	0	33	0	7	.230	.230	.279	509	67	-13	0	5	-2	.732	-2	/3-47,S-28,2-13,O-1L	-1.7
Total	12	986	3797	448	878	112	51	7	347	162	187	.231	.261	.289	550	71	-123	37			.913	173	2-880/1-63,3-38,SO	7.2
■ **KEN GERHART** Gerhart, Harold Kenneth b: 5/19/61, Charleston, S.C. BR/TR, 6', 190 lbs. Deb: 9/14/86																								
1986	Bal-A	20	69	4	16	2	0	1	7	4	18	.232	.274	.304	578	58	-4	0	1	-0	.971	-3	O-20(6-14-0)	-0.8
1987	Bal-A	92	284	41	69	10	2	14	34	17	53	.243	.288	.440	728	92	-4	9	2	1	.973	-6	O-91(53-42-0)	-1.1
1988	Bal-A	103	262	27	51	10	1	9	23	21	57	.195	.260	.344	603	69	-11	7	3	0	.975	-8	O-93(30-57-10)/D-3	-2.0
Total	3	215	615	72	136	22	3	24	64	42	128	.221	.274	.384	658	79	-20	16	6	1	.974	-16	O-204(89-113-10)/D-3	-3.9
■ **GEORGE GERKEN** Gerken, George Herbert "Pickles" b: 7/28/03, Chicago, Ill. d: 10/23/77, Arcadia, Cal. BR/TR, 5'11.5", 175 lbs. Deb: 4/19/27																								
1927	Cle-A	6	14	1	3	0	0	0	2	1	3	.214	.267	.214	481	26	-2	0	0	0	.917	0	/O-5(2-3-0)	-0.2
1928	Cle-A	38	115	16	26	7	2	0	9	12	22	.226	.305	.322	626	64	-6	3	3	-0	.940	-1	O-34(14-16-4)	-0.9
Total	2	44	129	17	29	7	2	0	11	13	25	.225	.301	.310	611	60	-8	3	3	-0	.937	-1	/O-39(16-19-4)	-1.1
■ **JOHNNY GERLACH** Gerlach, John Glenn b: 5/11/17, Shullsburg, Wis. d: 8/28/99, Madison, Wis. BR/TR, 5'9", 165 lbs. Deb: 9/3/38																								
1938	Chi-A	9	25	2	7	0	0	0	1	4	2	.280	.379	.280	659	66	-1	0	0	0	.949	1	/S-8	0.0
1939	Chi-A	3	2	0	2	0	0	0	0	0	0	1.000	1.000	1.000	2000	402	1	0	0	0	1.000	0	/3-1	0.1
Total	2	12	27	2	9	0	0	0	1	4	2	.333	.419	.333	753	89	-0	0	0	0	.949	1	/S-8,3-1	0.1
■ **DICK GERNERT** Gernert, Richard Edward b: 9/28/28, Reading, Pa. BR/TR, 6'3", 210 lbs. Deb: 4/16/52 C																								
1952	Bos-A	102	367	58	89	20	2	19	67	35	83	.243	.317	.463	780	107	2	4	1	1	.987	-1	1-99	-0.2
1953	Bos-A	139	494	73	125	15	1	21	71	88	82	.253	.371	.415	786	106	6	0	7	-2	.986	-3	*1-136	-0.7
1954	Bos-A	14	23	2	6	2	0	0	1	6	4	.261	.414	.348	762	99	0	0	0	0	1.000	-1	/1-6	-0.1
1955	Bos-A	7	20	6	4	2	0	0	1	1	5	.200	.238	.300	538	40	-2	0	0	0	.974	-0	/1-5	-0.2
1956	Bos-A	106	306	53	89	11	0	16	68	56	57	.291	.404	.484	888	119	9	1	0	0	.985	1	O-50(50-0-0),1-37	0.6
1957	Bos-A	99	316	45	75	13	3	14	58	39	62	.237	.327	.430	757	99	-1	1	1	-0	.989	-2	1-71,O-16(16-0-0)	-0.8
1958	Bos-A	122	431	59	102	19	1	20	69	59	78	.237	.331	.425	756	100	-0	2	0	0	.991	8	*1-114	0.1
1959	Bos-A	117	298	41	78	14	1	11	42	52	49	.262	.371	.426	798	113	7	1	2	-0	.995	3	1-75,O-25(21-0-7)	0.5
1960	Chi-N	52	96	8	24	3	0	0	11	10	19	.250	.321	.281	602	67	-4	1	0	0	.987	3	1-18/O-5(5-0-0)	-0.2
	Det-A	21	50	6	15	4	0	1	5	4	5	.300	.352	.440	792	110	1	0	0	0	1.000	-2	1-13/O-6(6-0-0)	-0.2
1961	Det-A	6	5	1	1	0	0	1	1	1	2	.200	.333	.800	1133	187	1	0	0	0	.000	0	H	0.1
	*Cin-N	40	63	4	19	1	0	0	7	7	9	.302	.371	.317	689	84	-1	0	0	0	.993	3	1-21	0.1
1962	Hou-N	10	24	1	5	0	0	0	1	5	7	.208	.345	.208	553	57	-1	0	0	0	1.000	-1	/1-9	-0.2
Total	11	835	2493	357	632	104	8	103	402	363	462	.254	.352	.426	778	104	17	10	11	-2	.990	9	1-604,O-102(98-0-7)	-1.2
■ **CESAR GERONIMO** Geronimo, Cesar Francisco (Zorrilla) b: 3/11/48, ElSeibo, D.R. BL/TL, 6'2", 170 lbs. Deb: 4/16/69 Career OF: (87-LF 1079-CF 225-RF)																								
1969	Hou-N	28	8	8	2	1	0	0	0	0	3	.250	.250	.375	625	74	-0	0	0	0	1.000	-3	/O-9(4-1-4)	-0.3
1970	Hou-N	47	37	5	9	0	0	0	2	2	5	.243	.300	.243	543	49	-3	0	0	0	.920	-6	O-26(12-5-10)	-0.9
1971	Hou-N	94	82	13	18	2	2	1	6	5	31	.220	.264	.329	594	69	-4	2	2	-0	.977	-16	O-64(47-3-15)	-2.2
1972	*Cin-N	120	255	32	70	9	7	4	29	24	64	.275	.344	.412	756	121	7	2	7	-2	.982	-10	*O-106(0-21-91)	-1.0
1973	*Cin-N	139	324	35	68	14	3	4	33	23	74	.210	.269	.309	577	63	-17	5	5	-1	.992	-6	*O-130(0-104-26)	-2.7
1974	Cin-N	150	474	73	133	17	8	7	54	46	96	.281	.347	.395	741	109	5	9	5	0	.987	12	*O-145(0-145-0)	1.4
1975	*Cin-N	148	501	69	129	25	5	6	53	48	97	.257	.327	.363	691	90	-7	13	5	1	.993	14	*O-148(0-148-0)	0.4
1976	*Cin-N	149	486	59	149	24	11	2	49	56	95	.307	.385	.414	799	124	17	22	5	3	.985	4	*O-146(0-146-0)	2.2
1977	Cin-N	149	492	54	131	22	4	10	52	35	89	.266	.321	.388	710	88	-9	10	4	1	.992	12	*O-147(0-147-0)	0.3
1978	Cin-N	122	296	28	67	15	1	5	27	43	67	.226	.330	.334	665	86	-5	8	3	1	.981	0	*O-115(0-116-0)	-0.5
1979	*Cin-N	123	356	38	85	17	4	4	38	37	56	.239	.314	.343	657	79	-10	1	1	-0	.993	7	*O-118(0-118-0)	-0.4
1980	Cin-N	103	145	16	37	5	0	2	9	14	24	.255	.321	.331	652	82	-3	2	1	0	1.000	-18	O-86(0-86-0)	-2.3
1981	*KC-A	59	118	14	29	0	2	2	13	11	16	.246	.310	.331	641	85	-2	6	1	1	.980	-6	O-57(5-4-50)	-1.0
1982	KC-A	53	119	14	32	6	3	4	23	8	16	.269	.315	.471	786	112	2	2	0	0	1.000	-2	O-44(10-32-3)/D-1	0.0
1983	KC-A	38	87	2	18	4	0	0	4	2	13	.207	.242	.253	495	36	-8	0	1	-0	.986	-2	O-35(9-3-26)	-1.1
Total	15	1522	3780	460	977	161	50	51	392	354	746	.258	.327	.368	695	93	-37	82	40	4	.988	-20	*O-1376C/D-1	-8.1
■ **LOU GERTENRICH** Gertenrich, Louis Wilhelm b: 5/4/1875, Chicago, Ill. d: 10/23/33, Chicago, Ill. BR/TR, 5'8", 175 lbs. Deb: 9/15/01																								
1901	Mil-A	2	3	1	1	0	0	0	0	0		.333	.333	.333	667	90	-0	0			.000	-0	/O-1(0-0-1)	0.0
1903	Pit-N	1	3	0	0	0	0	0	0	0		.000	.000	.000	0	-97	-1	0			1.000	0	/O-1(0-0-1)	-0.1
Total	2	3	6	1	1	0	0	0	0	0		.167	.167	.167	333	-6	-1	0			1.000	-0	/O-2(0-0-2)	-0.1
■ **DOC GESSLER** Gessler, Harry Homer "Brownie" b: 12/23/1880, Greensburg, Pa. d: 12/25/24, Pittsburgh, Pa. BL/TR, 5'10", 180 lbs. Deb: 4/23/03 M Career OF: (17-LF 94-CF 602-RF)																								
1903	Det-A	29	105	9	25	5	4	0	12	3		.238	.273	.362	635	92	-1	1			.974	-2	O-28(0-0-28)	-0.5
	Bro-N	49	154	20	38	8	3	0	18	17		.247	.366	.338	704	104	2	9			.984	-3	O-43(0-2-41)	-0.2
1904	Bro-N	104	341	41	99	18	4	2	28	30		.290	.355	.384	739	131	13	13			.920	2	O-88(14-72-2)/1-1,2-1	1.1
1905	Bro-N	126	431	44	125	17	4	3	46	38		.290	.366	.369	735	129	17	26			.973	2	*1-107,O-12(1-1-10)	1.7
1906	Bro-N	9	33	3	8	1	2	0	4	3		.242	.324	.394	718	134	1	3			.946	1	/1-9	0.2
	*Chi-N	34	83	8	21	3	0	0	10	12		.253	.354	.289	643	95	0	4			1.000	-1	O-21(0-19-2)/1-1	-0.2
	Yr	43	116	11	29	4	2	0	14	15		.250	.346	.319	665	104	1	7			1.000	-1	O-21(0-19-2),1-10	0.0
1908	Bos-A	128	435	55	134	13	14	3	63	51		.308	**.394**	.423	817	161	31	19			.950	-7	*O-126(0-0-126)	2.1
1909	Bos-A	111	396	57	115	24	1	0	46	31		.290	.354	.356	710	122	10	16			.933	-1	*O-109(0-0-109)	0.5
	Was-A	17	54	10	13	2	1	0	8	12		.241	.406	.315	721	134	3	4			1.000	-1	O-16(0-0-16)/1-1	0.2
	Yr	128	450	67	128	26	2	0	54	43		.284	.361	.351	712	123	13	20			.940	-2	*O-125(0-0-125)/1-1	0.7

YEAR	TM/L	G	AB	R	H	2B	3B	HR	RBI	BB	SO	AVG	OBP	SLG	OPS	OPS+	BR+	SB	CS	SBR	FA	FR	G/POS	TPR
1910	Was-A	145	487	58	126	17	12	2	50	62		.259	.361	.355	716	131	20	18			.953	-3	*O-144(0-0-144)	1.2
1911	Was-A	128	450	65	127	19	5	4	78	74		.282	.406	.373	780	120	17	29			.943	-10	*O-126(2-0-124)/1-1	0.1
Total	8	880	2969	370	831	127	50	14	363	333		.280	.370	.370	741	128	114	142			.945	-23	O-713R,1-120/2-1	6.2

■ CHARLIE GETTIG Gettig, Charles Henry b: 12/1870, Baltimore, Md. d: 4/11/35, Baltimore, Md. BR, 5'10", 172 lbs. Deb: 8/5/1896 Career OF: (3-LF 1-CF 21-RF)

YEAR	TM/L	G	AB	R	H	2B	3B	HR	RBI	BB	SO	AVG	OBP	SLG	OPS	OPS+	BR+	SB	CS	SBR	FA	FR	G/POS	TPR
1896	NY-N	6	9	3	3	1	0	0	0	0	0	.333	.333	.444	778	107	0	0			1.000	0	/P-4	0.0
1897	NY-N	22	75	8	15	6	0	0	12	6		.200	.277	.280	557	49	-6	3			.556	-8	/3-7,2-6,O-3L,SP	-1.2
1898	NY-N	64	196	30	49	6	2	0	26	15		.250	.310	.301	611	78	-6	5			.833	-10	O-21R,P-17,2/S31C	-1.4
1899	NY-N	34	97	7	24	3	0	0	9	7		.247	.305	.278	583	62	-5	4			.833	-4	P-18/3-8,2-3,1-3,O	-0.5
Total	4	126	377	48	91	16	2	0	47	28	0	.241	.302	.294	597	68	-16	12			.879	-22	/P-42,O-25R,23S1C	-3.1

■ TOM GETTINGER Gettinger, Lewis Thomas Leyton (b: Lewis Thomas Leyton Gittinger)
b: 12/11/1868, Frederick, Md. d: 7/26/43, Pensacola, Fla. BL/TL, 5'10", 180 lbs. Deb: 9/21/1889

YEAR	TM/L	G	AB	R	H	2B	3B	HR	RBI	BB	SO	AVG	OBP	SLG	OPS	OPS+	BR+	SB	CS	SBR	FA	FR	G/POS	TPR
1889	StL-a	4	16	2	7	0	0	1	2	2	1	.438	.500	.625	1125	194	2	0			.750	-1	/O-4(1-3-0)	0.0
1890	StL-a	58	227	31	54	7	5	3	30	20		.238	.302	.352	655	81	-7	8			.886	-6	O-58(58-0-0)	-1.3
1895	Lou-N	63	260	28	70	11	5	2	32	8	15	.269	.296	.373	669	77	-10	6			.910	-3	O-63(0-34-29)/P-2	-1.4
Total	3	125	503	61	131	18	10	6	64	30	16	.260	.306	.372	678	82	-15	14			.897	-10	O-125(59-37-29)/P-2	-2.7

■ JAKE GETTMAN Gettman, Jacob John b: 10/25/1876, Frank, Russia d: 10/4/56, Denver, Colo. BB/TL, 5'11", 185 lbs. Deb: 8/20/1897

YEAR	TM/L	G	AB	R	H	2B	3B	HR	RBI	BB	SO	AVG	OBP	SLG	OPS	OPS+	BR+	SB	CS	SBR	FA	FR	G/POS	TPR
1897	Was-N	36	143	28	45	7	3	3	29	7		.315	.359	.469	828	118	3	8			.981	-3	O-36(0-0-36)	-0.1
1898	Was-N	142	567	75	157	16	5	5	47	29		.277	.319	.349	668	92	-7	32			.926	2	*O-139(6-19-114)/1-3	-1.2
1899	Was-N	19	62	5	13	1	0	0	2	4		.210	.258	.226	483	33	-6	4			1.000	-1	O-16(6-10-0)/1-2	-0.8
Total	3	197	772	108	215	24	8	8	78	40		.278	.322	.361	683	92	-10	44			.941	-2	O-191(12-29-150)/1-5	-2.1

■ GUS GETZ Getz, Gustave "Gee-Gee" b: 8/3/1889, Pittsburgh, Pa. d: 5/28/69, Red Bank, N.J. BR/TR, 5'11", 165 lbs. Deb: 8/15/09

YEAR	TM/L	G	AB	R	H	2B	3B	HR	RBI	BB	SO	AVG	OBP	SLG	OPS	OPS+	BR+	SB	CS	SBR	FA	FR	G/POS	TPR
1909	Bos-N	40	148	6	33	2	0	0	9	1		.223	.228	.236	465	42	-10	2			.934	0	3-36/2-2,S-2	-1.0
1910	Bos-N	54	144	14	28	0	1	0	7	6	10	.194	.232	.208	440	27	-13	2			.915	3	3-22,2-13/O-8L,S-4	-1.1
1914	Bro-N	55	210	13	52	8	1	0	20	2	15	.248	.255	.295	550	62	-10	9			.949	12	3-55	0.4
1915	Bro-N	130	477	39	123	10	5	2	46	8	14	.258	.275	.312	587	76	-15	19	15	-1	.951	8	*3-128/S-2	-0.5
1916	*Bro-N	40	96	9	21	1	2	0	8	0	5	.219	.219	.271	490	49	-6	9			.913	-3	3-20/S-7,1-3	-0.9
1917	Cin-N	7	14	2	4	0	0	0	3	3	0	.286	.412	.286	697	121	1	0			.875	-3	/2-4,3-3	-0.2
1918	Cle-A	6	15	2	2	1	0	0	0	4	1	.133	.350	.200	550	60	-0	0			.941	-0	/3-5	-0.1
	Pit-N	7	10	0	2	0	0	0	0	0	1	.200	.200	.200	400	21	-1	0			.875	1	/3-2	0.0
Total	7	339	1114	85	265	22	9	2	93	24	46	.238	.257	.279	536	60	-56	41	15		.942	18	3-271/2-19,S-15,O1	-3.4

■ CHAPPIE GEYGAN Geygan, James Edward b: 6/3/03, Ironton, Ohio d: 3/15/66, Columbus, Ohio BR/TR, 5'11", 170 lbs. Deb: 7/16/24

YEAR	TM/L	G	AB	R	H	2B	3B	HR	RBI	BB	SO	AVG	OBP	SLG	OPS	OPS+	BR+	SB	CS	SBR	FA	FR	G/POS	TPR
1924	Bos-A	33	82	7	21	5	2	0	4	4	16	.256	.307	.366	673	73	-4	0	2	-1	.952	4	S-32	0.2
1925	Bos-A	3	11	0	2	0	0	0	0	0	2	.182	.182	.182	364	-8	-2	0	0	0	.813	-1	/S-3	-0.3
1926	Bos-A	4	10	0	3	0	0	0	0	1	1	.300	.364	.300	664	77	-0	0	0	0	.800	-1	/3-3	-0.1
Total	3	40	103	7	26	5	2	0	4	5	19	.252	.300	.340	640	65	-6	0	2	-1	.938	2	/S-35,3-3	-0.2

■ PATSY GHARRITY Gharrity, Edward Patrick b: 3/13/1892, Parnell, Iowa d: 10/10/66, Beloit, Wis. BR/TR, 5'10", 170 lbs. Deb: 5/16/16 C Career OF: (31-LF 2-CF 2-RF)

YEAR	TM/L	G	AB	R	H	2B	3B	HR	RBI	BB	SO	AVG	OBP	SLG	OPS	OPS+	BR+	SB	CS	SBR	FA	FR	G/POS	TPR
1916	Was-A	39	92	8	21	5	1	0	9	8	18	.228	.297	.304	601	81	-2	2			1.000	-3	C-16,1-16	-0.5
1917	Was-A	76	176	15	50	5	0	0	18	14	18	.284	.337	.313	649	99	-0	7			.980	1	1-46/C-5,O-1(0-0-1)	0.0
1918	Was-A	4	4	0	1	1	0	0	2	0	1	.250	.250	.500	750	129	0	0			.000	0	H	0.0
1919	Was-A	111	347	35	94	19	4	2	43	25	39	.271	.325	.366	691	95	-3	4			.969	-5	C-60,O-33(30-2-1)/1-7	-0.4
1920	Was-A	131	428	51	105	18	3	3	44	37	52	.245	.307	.322	629	69	-19	6	5	-0	.965	-3	*C-121/1-7,O-1(1-0-0)	-1.2
1921	Was-A	121	387	62	120	19	8	7	55	45	44	.310	.386	.455	841	120	12	4	3	-0	.977	-0	*C-115	1.8
1922	Was-A	96	273	40	70	16	6	5	45	36	30	.256	.351	.414	765	104	2	3	3	-0	.981	3	C-87	0.9
1923	Was-A	93	251	26	52	9	4	3	33	22	27	.207	.276	.311	587	57	-16	6	2	1	.986	1	C-35,1-33	-1.5
1929	Was-A	3	2	0	0	0	0	0	0	1	2	.000	.333	.000	333	-7	-0	0	0	0	.000	0	H	0.0
1930	Was-A	2	1	0	0	0	0	0	0	0	0	.000	.000	.000	0	-99	-0	0	0	0	1.000	-0	/1-1	0.0
Total	10	676	1961	237	513	92	26	20	249	188	231	.262	.331	.366	696	90	-28	32	13		.974	-7	C-439,1-110/O-35L	-0.9

■ JASON GIAMBI Giambi, Jason Gilbert b: 1/8/71, W.Covina, Cal. BL/TR, 6'2", 200 lbs. Deb: 5/8/95 F Career OF: (112-LF 0-CF 1-RF)

YEAR	TM/L	G	AB	R	H	2B	3B	HR	RBI	BB	SO	AVG	OBP	SLG	OPS	OPS+	BR+	SB	CS	SBR	FA	FR	G/POS	TPR
1995	Oak-A	54	176	27	45	7	0	6	25	28	31	.256	.367	.398	765	105	2	2	1	0	.960	-3	3-30,1-26/D-2	-0.2
1996	Oak-A	140	536	84	156	40	1	20	79	51	95	.291	.358	.481	839	112	9	0	1	-0	.993	2	1-45,O-45L,3-39,D	0.4
1997	Oak-A	142	519	66	152	41	2	20	81	55	89	.293	.367	.495	862	124	18	0	1	-0	.982	-2	O-68L,1-51,D-25	0.7
1998	Oak-A	153	562	92	166	28	0	27	110	81	102	.295	.389	.489	878	130	26	2	2	-0	.990	-12	*1-146/D-7	0.0
1999	Oak-A	158	575	115	181	36	1	33	123	105	106	.315	.426	.553	980	154	51	1	1	-0	.995	-14	*1-142,D-15/3-1	2.1
2000	*Oak-A★	152	510	108	170	29	1	43	137	**137**	96	.333	**.482**	.647	1129	**187**	76	2	0	0	.995	-7	*1-124,D-24	5.1
Total	6	799	2878	492	870	181	5	149	555	457	519	.302	.404	.524	928	140	183	7	6	-1	.993	-36	1-534,O-113L/D-85,3	8.1

■ JEREMY GIAMBI Giambi, Jeremy Dean b: 9/30/74, San Jose, Cal. BL/TL, 6', 185 lbs. Deb: 9/1/98 F Career OF: (20-LF 0-CF 49-RF)

YEAR	TM/L	G	AB	R	H	2B	3B	HR	RBI	BB	SO	AVG	OBP	SLG	OPS	OPS+	BR+	SB	CS	SBR	FA	FR	G/POS	TPR
1998	KC-A	18	58	6	13	4	0	2	8	11	9	.224	.348	.397	744	91	-1	0	1	-0	1.000	0	/O-9(9-0-0),D-7	-0.1
1999	KC-A	90	288	34	82	13	1	3	34	40	67	.285	.378	.368	746	89	-3	0	0	0	.991	-4	D-52,1-26/O-5(5-0-0)	-1.2
2000	*Oak-A	104	260	42	66	10	2	10	50	32	61	.254	.342	.423	765	95	-2	0	0	0	.966	-5	O-55R,D-21,1-15	-1.0
Total	3	212	606	82	161	27	3	15	92	83	137	.266	.360	.394	754	92	-6	0	1	-0	.972	-9	/D-80,O-69R,1-41	-2.3

■ RAY GIANNELLI Giannelli, Raymond John b: 2/5/66, Brooklyn, N.Y. BL/TR, 6', 195 lbs. Deb: 5/4/91

YEAR	TM/L	G	AB	R	H	2B	3B	HR	RBI	BB	SO	AVG	OBP	SLG	OPS	OPS+	BR+	SB	CS	SBR	FA	FR	G/POS	TPR
1991	Tor-A	9	24	2	4	1	0	0	0	5	9	.167	.310	.208	519	45	-2	1	0	0	.923	-2	/3-9	-0.3
1995	StL-N	9	11	0	1	0	0	0	0	3	4	.091	.286	.091	377	5	-1	0	0	0	1.000	-1	/1-2,O-2(1-0-1)	-0.2
Total	2	18	35	2	5	1	0	0	0	8	13	.143	.302	.171	474	32	-3	1	0	0	.923	-2	/3-9,O-2(1-0-1),1-2	-0.5

■ JOE GIANNINI Giannini, Joseph Francis b: 9/8/1888, San Francisco, Cal d: 9/26/42, San Francisco, Cal. BL/TR, 5'8", 155 lbs. Deb: 8/7/11

YEAR	TM/L	G	AB	R	H	2B	3B	HR	RBI	BB	SO	AVG	OBP	SLG	OPS	OPS+	BR+	SB	CS	SBR	FA	FR	G/POS	TPR
1911	Bos-A	1	2	0	1	1	0	0	0	0		.500	.500	1.000	1500	317	1	0			.500	-0	/S-1	0.0

■ JOHN GIBBONS Gibbons, John Michael b: 6/8/62, Great Falls, Mont. BR/TR, 5'11", 187 lbs. Deb: 4/11/84

YEAR	TM/L	G	AB	R	H	2B	3B	HR	RBI	BB	SO	AVG	OBP	SLG	OPS	OPS+	BR+	SB	CS	SBR	FA	FR	G/POS	TPR
1984	NY-N	10	31	1	2	0	0	0	1	3	11	.065	.171	.065	236	-32	-5	0	0	0	.983	-1	/C-9	-0.7
1986	NY-N	8	19	4	9	4	0	1	1	3	5	.474	.545	.842	1388	285	5	0	0	0	1.000	1	/C-8	0.6
Total	2	18	50	5	11	4	0	1	2	6	16	.220	.316	.360	676	90	-1	0	0	0	.990	-0	/C-17	-0.1

■ JAKE GIBBS Gibbs, Jerry Dean b: 11/7/38, Grenada, Miss. BL/TR, 6', 185 lbs. Deb: 9/11/62

YEAR	TM/L	G	AB	R	H	2B	3B	HR	RBI	BB	SO	AVG	OBP	SLG	OPS	OPS+	BR+	SB	CS	SBR	FA	FR	G/POS	TPR
1962	NY-A	2	0	2	0	0	0	0	0	0	0	—	—	—	—	—	0	0	0	0	.000	0	/3-1	0.0
1963	NY-A	4	8	1	2	0	0	0	0	0	1	.250	.250	.250	500	41	-1	0	0	0	1.000	-1	/C-1	-0.1
1964	NY-A	3	6	1	1	0	0	0	0	0	2	.167	.167	.167	333	-7	-1	0	0	0	1.000	0	/C-2	0.0
1965	NY-A	37	68	6	15	1	0	2	7	4	20	.221	.274	.324	598	70	-3	0	0	0	.991	2	C-21	0.0
1966	NY-A	62	182	19	47	6	0	3	20	19	16	.258	.328	.341	669	96	-1	5	2	0	.988	4	C-54	0.7
1967	NY-A	116	374	33	87	7	1	4	25	28	57	.233	.293	.289	582	75	-11	7	6	-1	.975	1	C-99	-0.7
1968	NY-A	124	423	31	90	12	3	3	29	27	68	.213	.270	.277	546	68	-17	9	8	-1	.991	-4	*C-121	-1.8
1969	NY-A	71	219	18	49	9	2	0	18	23	30	.224	.298	.283	581	65	-10	3	4	-1	.990	8	C-66	0.0
1970	NY-A	49	153	23	46	9	2	8	26	7	14	.301	.335	.542	878	146	8	2	0	0	.987	3	C-44	1.3
1971	NY-A	70	206	23	45	9	0	5	21	12	23	.218	.271	.335	606	76	-7	2	2	-0	.988	-5	C-51	-1.1
Total	10	538	1639	157	382	53	8	25	146	120	231	.233	.291	.321	612	81	-42	28	22	-2	.986	8	C-459/3-1	-1.7

■ STEVE GIBRALTER Gibralter, Stephan Benson b: 10/9/72, Dallas, Tex. BR/TR, 6', 185 lbs. Deb: 6/1/95

YEAR	TM/L	G	AB	R	H	2B	3B	HR	RBI	BB	SO	AVG	OBP	SLG	OPS	OPS+	BR+	SB	CS	SBR	FA	FR	G/POS	TPR
1995	Cin-N	4	3	0	1	0	0	0	0	0	0	.333	.333	.333	667	77	-0	0	0	0	1.000	-1	/O-2(0-2-0)	-0.1
1996	Cin-N	2	2	0	0	0	0	0	0	0	2	.000	.000	.000	0	-99	-1	0	0	0	.000	-1	/O-2(1-1-0)	-0.2
Total	2	6	5	0	1	0	0	0	0	0	2	.200	.200	.200	400	6	-1	0	0	0	.500	-2	/O-4(1-3-0)	-0.3

■ CHARLIE GIBSON Gibson, Charles Ellsworth "Gibby" b: 11/17/1879, Sharon, Pa. d: 11/22/54, Sharon, Pa. BR/TR, 6', 160 lbs. Deb: 9/23/05

YEAR	TM/L	G	AB	R	H	2B	3B	HR	RBI	BB	SO	AVG	OBP	SLG	OPS	OPS+	BR+	SB	CS	SBR	FA	FR	G/POS	TPR
1905	StL-A	1	3	0	0	0	0	0	0	0		.000	.000	.000	0	-99	-1	0			1.000	-0	/C-1	-0.1

YEAR	TM/L	G	AB	R	H	2B	3B	HR	RBI	BB	SO	AVG	OBP	SLG	OPS	OPS+	BR+	SB	CS	SBR	FA	FR	G/POS	TPR
■ CHARLIE GIBSON Gibson, Charles Griffin b: 11/21/1899, LaGrange, Ga. d: 12/18/90, LaGrange, Ga. BR/TR, 5'8", 160 lbs. Deb: 5/30/24																								
1924	Phi-A	12	15	1	2	0	0	0	1	2	0	.133	.235	.133	369	-3	-2	0	0	0	.870	-0	C-12	-0.2
■ DERRICK GIBSON Gibson, Derrick Lamont b: 2/5/75, Winter Haven, Fla. BR/TR, 6'2", 244 lbs. Deb: 9/8/98																								
1998	Col-N	7	21	4	9	1	0	0	2	1	4	.429	.478	.476	954	125	1	0	0	0	.929	1	/O-7(7-0-0)	0.2
1999	Col-N	10	28	2	5	1	0	2	6	0	7	.179	.207	.429	635	43	-2	0	0	0	.944	1	O-10(0-0-10)	-0.2
Total	2	17	49	6	14	2	0	2	8	1	11	.286	.327	.449	776	78	-2	0	0	0	.938	2	/O-17(7-0-10)	0.0
■ FRANK GIBSON Gibson, Frank Gilbert b: 9/27/1890, Omaha, Neb. d: 4/27/61, Austin, Tex. BB/TR (BL 1913), 6'0.5", 172 lbs. Deb: 4/22/13 Career OF: (0-LF 0-CF 1-RF)																								
1913	Det-A	23	57	8	8	1	0	0	2	3	9	.140	.197	.158	355	4	-7	2			.914	-6	C-19/O-2(0-0-1)	-1.3
1921	Bos-N	63	125	14	33	5	4	2	13	3	17	.264	.292	.416	708	90	-2	0	0	0	.979	1	C-41	0.1
1922	Bos-N	66	164	15	49	7	2	3	20	10	27	.299	.339	.421	760	99	-1	4	1	1	.981	-1	C-29,1-20	-0.1
1923	Bos-N	41	50	13	15	1	0	0	5	7	7	.300	.386	.320	706	92	-0	0	2	-1	.923	-2	C-20	-0.2
1924	Bos-N	90	229	25	71	15	6	1	30	10	23	.310	.342	.441	783	113	3	1	1	-0	.972	2	C-46,1-10/3-2	0.7
1925	Bos-N	104	316	36	88	23	5	2	50	15	28	.278	.313	.402	715	89	-6	3	3	-0	.968	-2	C-86/1-2	-0.3
1926	Bos-N	24	47	3	16	4	0	0	7	4	6	.340	.392	.426	818	132	2	0			1.000	2	C-13	0.4
1927	Bos-N	60	167	7	37	1	2	0	19	3	10	.222	.235	.251	487	33	-16	2			.965	-4	C-47	-1.7
Total	8	471	1155	121	317	57	19	8	146	55	127	.274	.310	.377	688	86	-27	12	7		.967	-10	C-301/1-32,3-2,O-2R	-2.4
■ GEORGE GIBSON Gibson, George C. "Moon" b: 7/22/1880, London, Ont., Can. d: 1/25/67, London, Ont., Can. BR/TR, 5'11.5", 190 lbs. Deb: 7/2/05 MC																								
1905	Pit-N	46	135	14	24	2	2	2	14	15		.178	.270	.267	536	59	-7	2			.966	3	C-44	0.0
1906	Pit-N	81	259	8	46	6	1	0	20	16		.178	.225	.208	434	34	-20	1			.971	-5	C-81	-2.0
1907	Pit-N	113	382	28	84	8	7	3	35	18		.220	.261	.301	562	75	-12	2			.972	-3	*C-109/1-1	-0.5
1908	Pit-N	143	486	37	111	19	4	2	45	19		.228	.260	.296	557	78	-14	4			.973	-14	*C-140	-1.6
1909	*Pit-N	150	510	42	135	25	9	2	52	44		.265	.326	.361	686	104	2	9			**.983**	2	*C-150	2.1
1910	Pit-N	143	482	53	125	22	6	3	44	47	31	.259	.333	.349	681	93	-4	7			**.984**	3	*C-143	1.4
1911	Pit-N	100	311	32	65	12	2	0	19	29	16	.209	.281	.260	541	50	-21	3			.979	0	C-98	-1.3
1912	Pit-N	95	300	23	72	14	3	2	35	20	16	.240	.290	.327	616	69	-13	0			**.990**	-1	C-94	-0.6
1913	Pit-N	48	118	6	33	4	2	0	12	10	8	.280	.341	.347	689	101	0	2			.986	-9	C-48	-0.5
1914	Pit-N	102	274	19	78	9	5	0	30	27	27	.285	.359	.354	713	117	7	4			.974	-9	*C-101	0.6
1915	Pit-N	120	351	28	88	15	6	1	30	31	25	.251	.313	.336	649	98	-1	5	2	0	.965	6	*C-118	1.7
1916	Pit-N	33	84	4	17	2	2	0	4	3	7	.202	.239	.274	512	57	-4	0			.989	7	C-29	0.6
1917	NY-N	35	82	1	14	3	0	0	5	7	2	.171	.236	.207	443	38	-6	1			.986	1	C-35	-0.3
1918	NY-N	4	2	0	1	1	0	0	0	0	0	.500	.500	1.000	1500	360	1	0			1.000	0	/C-4	0.1
Total	14	1213	3776	295	893	142	49	15	345	286	132	.236	.295	.312	607	81	-93	40	2		.977	-20	*C-1194/1-1	-0.3
■ RUSS GIBSON Gibson, John Russell b: 5/6/39, Fall River, Mass. BR/TR, 6'1", 195 lbs. Deb: 4/14/67																								
1967	*Bos-A	49	138	8	28	7	0	1	15	12	31	.203	.267	.275	542	56	-7	0	0	0	1.000	-6	C-48	-1.3
1968	Bos-A	76	231	15	52	11	1	3	20	8	38	.225	.251	.320	571	68	-9	1	2	-0	.983	1	C-74/1-1	-0.7
1969	Bos-A	85	287	21	72	9	1	3	27	15	25	.251	.290	.321	611	67	-13	1	1	-0	.979	-6	C-83	-1.6
1970	SF-N	24	69	3	16	6	0	0	6	7	12	.232	.303	.319	621	67	-3	0	0	0	.971	2	C-23	-0.1
1971	SF-N	25	57	2	11	1	1	1	7	2	13	.193	.220	.298	519	46	-4	0	0	0	.965	0	C-22	-0.4
1972	SF-N	5	12	0	2	0	1	0	3	0	4	.167	.167	.333	500	38	-1	0	0	0	1.000	-1	/C-5	-0.2
Total	6	264	794	49	181	34	4	8	78	44	123	.228	.269	.311	580	64	-38	2	3	-1	.983	-10	C-255/1-1	-4.3
■ KIRK GIBSON Gibson, Kirk Harold b: 5/28/57, Pontiac, Mich. BL/TL, 6'3", 215 lbs. Deb: 9/8/79 Career OF: (477-LF 325-CF 456-RF)																								
1979	Det-A	12	38	3	9	3	0	1	4	1	3	.237	.256	.395	651	70	-2	3	3	-0	1.000	-1	O-10(7-1-2)	-0.4
1980	Det-A	51	175	23	46	2	1	9	16	10	45	.263	.306	.440	746	100	-1	4	7	-2	.992	-2	O-49(0-49-0)/D-1	-0.5
1981	Det-A	83	290	41	95	11	3	9	40	18	64	.328	.371	.479	850	138	14	17	5	2	.973	-4	O-67(8-26-37)/D-9	0.9
1982	Det-A	69	266	34	74	16	2	8	35	25	41	.278	.342	.444	786	113	5	9	7	-0	.994	3	O-64(0-64-0)/D-4	0.7
1983	Det-A	128	401	60	91	12	9	15	51	53	96	.227	.323	.414	737	104	2	14	3	2	.975	1	D-66,O-54(29-22-4)	-0.1
1984	*Det-A	149	531	92	150	23	10	27	91	63	103	.282	.367	.516	883	142	30	29	9	3	.954	-9	*O-139(0-1-140)/D-6	1.7
1985	Det-A	154	581	96	167	37	5	29	97	71	137	.287	.370	.518	888	141	33	30	4	5	.963	-7	*O-144(0-20-127)/D-8	2.4
1986	Det-A	119	441	84	118	11	2	28	86	68	107	.268	.374	.492	866	134	22	34	6	5	.990	-9	*O-114(0-1-114)/D-4	1.2
1987	*Det-A	128	487	95	135	25	3	24	79	71	117	.277	.375	.489	863	132	24	26	7	3	.974	5	*O-121(119-2-0)/D-4	2.5
1988	*LA-N	150	542	106	157	28	1	25	76	73	120	.290	.381	.483	864	151	37	31	4	5	.964	8	*O-148(148-1-0)	4.8
1989	LA-N	71	253	35	54	8	2	9	28	35	55	.213	.314	.368	681	96	-1	12	3	2	.980	1	O-70(62-15-0)	-0.1
1990	LA-N	89	315	59	82	20	0	8	38	39	65	.260	.347	.400	747	108	4	26	2	5	.995	5	O-81(11-70-0)	1.3
1991	KC-A	132	462	81	109	17	6	16	55	69	103	.236	.343	.403	745	105	4	18	4	3	.976	-2	O-94(91-0-3),D-30	0.1
1992	Pit-N	16	56	6	11	0	0	2	5	3	12	.196	.237	.304	541	53	-4	3	1	0	1.000	1	O-13(0-0-13)	-0.3
1993	Det-A	116	403	62	105	18	6	13	62	44	87	.261	.339	.432	771	106	3	15	6	1	.987	-1	D-76,O-32(2-30-0)	-0.1
1994	Det-A	98	330	71	91	17	2	23	72	42	69	.276	.363	.548	911	130	14	4	5	-1	.988	-2	D-56,O-38(0-23-15)	0.7
1995	Det-A	70	227	37	59	12	2	9	35	33	61	.260	.361	.449	811	110	4	9	2	1	.000	-0	D-63/O-1(0-0-1)	0.1
Total	17	1635	5798	985	1553	260	54	255	870	718	1285	.268	.355	.463	818	123	188	284	78	35	.976	-17	*O-1239L,D-327	14.9
■ WHITEY GIBSON Gibson, Leighton P. b: 10/6/1868, Lancaster, Pa. d: 10/11/07, Talmage, Pa. TR, 5'9", 178 lbs. Deb: 5/2/1888																								
1888	Phi-a	1	3	0	0	0	0	0	0	0		.000	.000	.000	0	-99	-1	0			1.000	1	/C-1	0.0
■ JOE GIEBEL Giebel, Joseph Henry b: 11/30/1891, Washington, D.C. d: 3/17/81, Silver Spring, Md. BR/TR, 5'10.5", 175 lbs. Deb: 9/30/13																								
1913	Phi-A	1	3	0	1	0	0	0	0	0	1	.333	.333	.333	667	97	-0	0			1.000	-0	/C-1	0.0
■ NORM GIGON Gigon, Norman Phillip b: 5/12/38, Teaneck, N.J. BR/TR, 6', 195 lbs. Deb: 4/12/67																								
1967	Chi-N	34	70	8	12	3	1	1	6	4	14	.171	.237	.286	523	47	-5	0	0	0	.982	-3	2-12/O-4(0-0-4),3-1	-0.8
■ BENJI GIL Gil, Romar Benjamin (Aguilar) b: 10/6/72, Tijuana, Mex. BR/TR, 6'2", 180 lbs. Deb: 4/5/93																								
1993	Tex-A	22	57	3	7	0	0	0	2	5	22	.123	.194	.123	316	-13	-9	1	2	-0	.954	8	S-22	0.0
1995	Tex-A	130	415	36	91	20	3	9	46	26	147	.219	.267	.347	614	57	-27	2	4	-1	.974	16	*S-130	-0.1
1996	Tex-A	5	5	0	2	0	0	0	1	1	1	.400	.500	.400	900	125	0	0	1	-0	.923	1	/S-5	0.1
1997	Tex-A	110	317	35	71	13	2	5	31	17	96	.224	.266	.325	591	50	-23	1	2	-0	.963	**22**	*S-106/D-4	0.6
2000	Ana-A	110	301	28	72	14	1	6	23	30	59	.239	.318	.352	671	69	-14	10	6	0	.957	17	S-94/2-7,1-3,D-6	0.9
Total	5	377	1095	102	243	47	6	20	103	79	325	.222	.279	.331	609	56	-73	14	15	-2	.965	64	S-357/D-10,2-7,1-3	1.5
■ GUS GIL Gil, Tomas Gustavo (Guillen) b: 4/19/39, Caracas, Venez. BR/TR, 5'10", 180 lbs. Deb: 4/11/67																								
1967	Cle-A	51	96	11	11	4	0	0	5	9	18	.115	.198	.156	354	6	-11	0	0	0	1.000	2	2-49/1-1	-0.7
1969	Sea-A	92	221	20	49	7	0	0	17	16	28	.222	.274	.253	528	49	-15	2	0	0	.942	1	3-38,2-18,S-12	-1.3
1970	Mil-A	64	119	12	22	4	0	1	12	21	12	.185	.307	.244	551	53	-7	2	0	0	.978	3	2-38,3-14	-0.2
1971	Mil-A	14	32	3	5	1	0	0	3	10	5	.156	.357	.188	545	59	-1	1	0	0	.977	-0	/2-8,3-6	-0.1
Total	4	221	468	46	87	16	0	1	37	56	63	.186	.274	.226	501	43	-34	5	0	1	.987	7	2-113/3-58,S-12,1-1	-2.3
■ SHAWN GILBERT Gilbert, Albert Shawn b: 3/12/65, Camden, N.J. BR/TR, 5'9", 170 lbs. Deb: 6/4/97 Career OF: (9-LF 4-CF 2-RF)																								
1997	NY-N	29	22	3	3	0	0	1	1	1	8	.136	.174	.273	447	15	-3	1	0	0	.875	1	/2-8,S-6,3-3,O-1L	-0.2
1998	NY-N	3	3	1	0	0	0	0	0	0	1	.000	.000	.000	0	-99	-1	0	0	0	.000	-0	/3-1	-0.1
	StL-N	4	2	0	1	0	0	0	0	0	1	.500	.500	.500	1000	166	0	1	0	0	1.000	0	/2-2	0.1
	Yr	7	5	1	1	0	0	0	0	0	2	.200	.200	.200	400	6	-1	1	0	0	1.000	0	/2-2,3-1	0.0
2000	LA-N	15	20	5	3	1	0	1	3	2	7	.150	.227	.350	577	45	-2	0	0	0	.941	-1	O-14(8-4-2)	-0.3
Total	3	51	47	9	7	1	0	2	4	3	17	.149	.200	.298	498	27	-5	2	0	0	.941	-1	/O-15L,2-10,S-6,3-4	-0.5
■ ANDY GILBERT Gilbert, Andrew b: 7/18/14, Bradenville, Pa. d: 8/29/92, Davis, Cal. BR/TR, 6', 203 lbs. Deb: 9/14/42 C																								
1942	Bos-A	6	11	0	1	0	0	0	1	1	3	.091	.167	.091	258	-26	-2	0	0	0	1.000	-2	/O-5(0-5-0)	-0.4
1946	Bos-A	2	1	1	0	0	0	0	0	0	0	.000	.000	.000	0	-95	-0	0	0	0	.000	-1	/O-1(0-1-0)	-0.1
Total	2	8	12	1	1	0	0	0	1	1	3	.083	.154	.083	237	-31	-2	0	0	0	1.000	-2	/O-6(0-6-0)	-0.5

YEAR	TM/L	G	AB	R	H	2B	3B	HR	RBI	BB	SO	AVG	OBP	SLG	OPS	OPS+	BR+	SB	CS	SBR	FA	FR	G/POS	TPR
■ CHARLIE GILBERT Gilbert, Charles Mader b: 7/8/19, New Orleans, La. d: 8/13/83, New Orleans, La. BL/TL, 5'9", 165 lbs. Deb: 4/16/40 F																								
1940	Bro-N	57	142	23	35	9	1	2	8	8	13	.246	.287	.366	653	74	-5	0			.960	-2	O-43(0-43-0)	-0.8
1941	Chi-N	39	86	11	24	2	1	0	12	11	6	.279	.361	.326	686	98	0	1			1.000	-1	O-22(0-21-1)	-0.1
1942	Chi-N	74	179	18	33	6	3	0	7	25	24	.184	.284	.251	536	60	-9	1			.981	0	O-47(3-44-0)	-1.0
1943	Chi-N	8	20	1	3	0	0	0	0	3	3	.150	.261	.150	411	20	-2	1			1.000	-1	/O-6(3-3-0)	-0.3
1946	Chi-N	15	13	2	1	0	0	0	1	1	4	.077	.143	.077	220	-38	-2	0			1.000	0	/O-2(0-2-0)	-0.3
	Phi-N	88	260	34	63	5	2	1	17	25	18	.242	.314	.288	602	73	-9	3			1.000	6	O-69(8-16-46)	-0.5
	Yr	103	273	36	64	5	2	1	18	26	22	.234	.306	.278	584	68	-11	3			1.000	6	O-71(8-18-46)	-0.8
1947	Phi-N	83	152	20	36	5	2	2	10	13	14	.237	.301	.336	637	72	-6	1			.961	-0	O-37(18-7-12)	-0.8
Total	6	364	852	109	195	27	9	5	55	86	82	.229	.302	.299	601	70	-33	7			.982	3	O-226(32-136-59)	-3.8
■ BUDDY GILBERT Gilbert, Drew Edward b: 7/26/35, Knoxville, Tenn. BL/TR, 6'3", 195 lbs. Deb: 9/9/59																								
1959	Cin-N	7	20	4	3	0	0	2	2	3	4	.150	.261	.450	711	82	-1	0	0	0	1.000	1	/O-6(0-0-6)	0.0
■ TOOKIE GILBERT Gilbert, Harold Joseph b: 4/4/29, New Orleans, La. d: 6/23/67, New Orleans, La. BL/TR, 6'2.5", 185 lbs. Deb: 5/5/50 F																								
1950	NY-N	113	322	40	71	12	2	4	32	43	36	.220	.314	.307	622	64	-16	3			.988	1	*1-111	-1.8
1953	NY-N	70	160	12	27	3	0	3	16	22	21	.169	.269	.244	513	34	-15	1	0	0	.995	1	1-44	-1.6
Total	2	183	482	52	98	15	2	7	48	65	57	.203	.299	.286	586	54	-32	4	0		.991	2	1-155	-3.4
■ HARRY GILBERT Gilbert, Harry H. b: 7/7/1868, Pottstown, Pa. d: 12/23/09, Pottstown, Pa. Deb: 6/23/1890 F																								
1890	Pit-N	2	8	1	2	0	0	0	0	0	3	.250	.250	.250	500	52	-0	0			1.000	-1	/2-2	-0.1
■ JOHN GILBERT Gilbert, John G. b: 1/8/1864, Pottstown, Pa. d: 11/12/03, Pottstown, Pa. Deb: 6/23/1890 F																								
1890	Pit-N	2	8	0	0	0	0	0	0	0	2	.000	.000	.000	0	-99	-2	0			1.000	-0	/S-2	-0.2
■ JACK GILBERT Gilbert, John Robert "Jackrabbit" b: 9/4/1875, Rhinecliff, N.Y. d: 7/7/41, Albany, N.Y. Deb: 9/11/1898																								
1898	Was-N	2	5	0	1	0	0	0	1	1		.200	.429	.200	629	82	0	1			.500	-0	/O-2(0-1-1)	0.0
	NY-N	1	4	0	1	0	0	0	0	0		.250	.250	.250	500	45	-0	1			.500	-0	/O-1(0-0-1)	-0.1
	Yr	3	9	0	2	0	0	0	1	1		.222	.364	.222	586	70	-0	2			.500	-1	/O-3(0-1-2)	-0.1
1904	Pit-N	25	87	13	21	0	0	0	3	12		.241	.353	.241	594	82	-1	3			.857	-6	O-25(25-0-0)	-0.9
Total	2	28	96	13	23	0	0	0	4	13		.240	.354	.240	594	81	-1	5			.821	-6	/O-28(25-1-2)	-1.0
■ LARRY GILBERT Gilbert, Lawrence William b: 12/3/1891, New Orleans, La. d: 2/17/65, New Orleans, La. BL/TL, 5'9", 158 lbs. Deb: 4/14/14 F																								
1914	*Bos-N	72	224	32	60	6	1	5	25	26	34	.268	.347	.371	717	114	4	3			.979	-0	O-60(3-6-51)	0.1
1915	Bos-N	45	106	11	16	4	0	0	4	11	13	.151	.231	.189	419	29	-9	4	1	1	.941	-2	O-27(2-0-26)	-1.4
Total	2	117	330	43	76	10	1	5	29	37	47	.230	.310	.312	622	88	-5	7	1		.969	-3	/O-87(5-6-77)	-1.3
■ MARK GILBERT Gilbert, Mark David b: 8/22/56, Atlanta, Ga. BB/TR, 6', 175 lbs. Deb: 7/21/85																								
1985	Chi-A	7	22	3	6	1	0	0	3	4	5	.273	.385	.318	703	92	-0	0	0	0	1.000	-1	/O-7(2-5-1)	-0.1
■ PETE GILBERT Gilbert, Peter b: 9/6/1867, Baltic, Conn. d: 1/1/12, Springfield, Mass. TR, 5'8", 180 lbs. Deb: 9/6/1890																								
1890	Bal-a	29	100	25	28	2	1	1	18	10		.280	.363	.350	713	105	1	12			.899	-3	3-29	-0.1
1891	Bal-a	139	513	81	118	15	7	3	72	37	77	.230	.317	.304	621	77	-16	31			.862	2	*3-139	-1.0
1892	Bal-N	4	15	0	3	0	0	0	0	1	3	.200	.250	.200	450	35	-1	1			.889	1	/3-4	0.0
1894	Bro-N	6	25	1	2	0	0	0	1	1	3	.080	.148	.080	228	-47	-6	2			.938	1	/2-3,3-3	-0.4
	Lou-N	28	108	13	33	3	1	1	14	5	4	.306	.353	.380	733	82	-3	2			.742	-6	3-28	-0.6
	Yr	34	133	14	35	3	1	1	15	6	7	.263	.315	.323	638	58	-9	4			.766	-4	3-31/2-3	-1.0
Total	4	206	761	120	184	20	9	5	105	54	87	.242	.321	.311	633	76	-25	48			.851	-4	3-203/2-3	-2.1
■ WALLY GILBERT Gilbert, Walter John b: 12/19/1900, Oscoda, Mich. d: 9/7/58, Duluth, Minn. BR/TR, 6', 180 lbs. Deb: 8/18/28																								
1928	Bro-N	39	153	26	31	4	0	0	3	14	8	.203	.274	.229	503	33	-15	2			.965	-1	3-39	-1.3
1929	Bro-N	143	569	88	173	31	4	3	58	42	29	.304	.359	.388	748	87	-11	7			.956	7	*3-142	0.4
1930	Bro-N	150	623	92	183	34	5	3	67	47	33	.294	.345	.379	724	76	-24	7			.944	9	*3-150	-0.5
1931	Bro-N	145	552	60	147	25	6	0	46	39	38	.266	.322	.333	655	77	-17	3			.948	8	*3-145	-0.4
1932	Cin-N	114	420	35	90	18	2	1	40	20	23	.214	.252	.274	526	43	-34	2			.929	-6	*3-111	-3.7
Total	5	591	2317	301	624	112	17	7	214	162	131	.269	.322	.341	663	71	-101	21			.947	17	3-587	-5.5
■ BILLY GILBERT Gilbert, William Oliver b: 6/21/1876, Tullytown, Pa. d: 8/8/27, New York, N.Y. BR/TR, 5'4", 153 lbs. Deb: 4/25/01																								
1901	Mil-A	127	492	77	133	14	7	0	43	31		.270	.320	.327	647	84	-10	19			.936	-0	*2-127	-0.8
1902	Bal-A	129	445	74	109	12	3	2	38	45		.245	.327	.299	626	71	-16	38			.907	-5	*S-129	-1.6
1903	NY-N	128	413	62	104	9	0	1	40	41		.252	.348	.281	629	77	-10	37			.935	11	*2-128	0.2
1904	NY-N	146	478	57	121	13	3	1	54	46		.253	.340	.299	639	94	-1	33			.946	8	*2-146	0.8
1905	*NY-N	115	376	45	93	11	3	0	24	41		.247	.331	.293	624	84	-6	11			.947	25	*2-115	2.1
1906	NY-N	104	307	44	71	6	1	1	27	42		.231	.341	.267	608	88	-2	22			.940	23	2-98	2.3
1908	StL-N	89	276	12	59	7	0	0	10	20		.214	.274	.239	513	67	-10	6			.952	6	2-89	-0.3
1909	StL-N	12	29	4	5	0	0	0	1	4		.172	.333	.172	506	61	-1	1			.922	0	2-12	-0.1
Total	8	850	2816	375	695	72	17	5	237	270		.247	.328	.290	618	81	-56	167			.942	68	2-715,S-129	2.6
■ ROD GILBREATH Gilbreath, Rodney Joe b: 9/24/52, Laurel, Miss. BR/TR (BB 1975 (part)), 6'2", 185 lbs. Deb: 6/17/72																								
1972	Atl-N	18	38	2	9	1	0	0	1	2	10	.237	.293	.263	556	54	-2	1	1	-0	1.000	3	/2-7,3-4	0.1
1973	Atl-N	29	74	10	21	2	1	0	2	6	10	.284	.346	.338	684	84	-1	2	1	0	.960	-0	3-22	-0.2
1974	Atl-N	3	6	2	2	0	0	0	0	2	0	.333	.500	.333	833	131	0	0	0	0	1.000	0	/2-2	0.1
1975	Atl-N	90	202	24	49	3	1	2	16	24	26	.243	.326	.297	623	71	-7	5	5	-1	.980	2	2-52,3-10/S-1	-0.3
1976	Atl-N	116	383	57	96	11	8	1	32	42	36	.251	.331	.329	660	83	-8	7	7	-1	.975	7	*2-104/3-7,S-1	0.5
1977	Atl-N	128	407	47	99	15	2	8	43	45	79	.243	.322	.349	670	71	-16	3	9	-2	.978	3	*2-122/3-1	-1.0
1978	Atl-N	116	326	22	80	13	3	3	31	26	51	.245	.301	.331	632	69	-13	7	6	-1	.968	-3	3-62,2-39	-1.7
Total	7	500	1436	164	356	45	15	14	125	147	212	.248	.322	.329	651	74	-47	25	29	-5	.978	11	2-326,3-106/S-2	-2.5
■ DON GILE Gile, Donald Loren "Bear" b: 4/19/35, Modesto, Cal. BR/TR, 6'6", 220 lbs. Deb: 9/25/59																								
1959	Bos-A	3	10	1	2	1	0	0	1	0	2	.200	.273	.300	573	55	-1	0	0	0	1.000	-0	/C-3	-0.1
1960	Bos-A	29	51	6	9	1	1	1	4	1	13	.176	.192	.294	486	29	-5	0	0	0	1.000	-1	C-15,1-11	-0.6
1961	Bos-A	8	18	2	5	0	0	1	1	1	5	.278	.316	.444	760	98	-0	0	0	0	.958	-1	/1-6,C-1	-0.1
1962	Bos-A	18	41	3	2	0	0	1	3	3	15	.049	.133	.122	255	-30	-8	0	0	0	.990	-1	1-14	-0.9
Total	4	58	120	12	18	2	1	3	9	5	35	.150	.197	.258	455	21	-14	0	0	0	.982	-2	/1-31,C-19	-1.7
■ BRIAN GILES Giles, Brian Jeffrey b: 4/27/60, Manhattan, Kan. BR/TR, 6'1", 165 lbs. Deb: 9/12/81																								
1981	NY-N	9	7	0	0	0	0	0	0	0	3	.000	.000	.000	0	-99	-2	0	0	0	1.000	3	/2-2,S-2	0.2
1982	NY-N	45	138	14	29	5	0	3	10	12	29	.210	.273	.312	585	64	-7	6	1	1	.992	15	2-45/S-2	1.2
1983	NY-N	145	400	39	98	15	0	2	27	36	77	.245	.311	.298	608	70	-16	17	10	0	.980	15	*2-140,S-12	0.7
1985	Mil-A	34	58	6	10	1	0	1	1	7	16	.172	.262	.241	503	39	-5	2	1	0	.963	8	S-20,2-13/D-2	0.4
1986	Chi-A	9	11	0	3	0	0	0	1	0	2	.273	.273	.273	545	48	-1	0	0	0	1.000	4	/2-7,S-1	0.3
1990	Sea-A	45	95	15	22	6	0	4	11	15	24	.232	.336	.421	757	109	1	2	1	0	.978	7	S-37/2-2,3-1,D-1	1.1
Total	6	287	709	74	162	27	0	10	50	70	151	.228	.300	.309	609	70	-29	27	13	1	.985	52	2-209/S-74,D-3,3-1	3.9
■ BRIAN GILES Giles, Brian Stephen b: 1/21/71, ElCajon, Cal. BL/TL, 5'11", 195 lbs. Deb: 9/16/95 Career OF: (242-LF 203-CF 103-RF)																								
1995	Cle-A	6	9	6	5	0	0	1	3	0	1	.556	.556	.889	1444	265	2	0	0	0	1.000	0	/O-3(0-0-3),D-1	0.2
1996	*Cle-A	51	121	26	43	14	1	5	27	19	13	.355	.443	.612	1054	164	12	3	0	1	1.000	-1	D-21,O-16(11-0-5)	0.9
1997	*Cle-A	130	377	62	101	15	3	17	61	63	50	.268	.374	.459	833	112	8	13	3	2	.972	-7	*O-115(82-20-25)/D-9	-0.1
1998	*Cle-A	112	350	56	94	19	0	16	66	73	75	.269	.399	.460	859	119	12	10	5	0	.978	5	*O-101(95-3-6)/D-6	1.4
1999	Pit-N	141	521	109	164	33	3	39	115	95	80	.315	.423	.614	1037	159	48	6	2	1	.990	4	*O-138(8-108-25)/D-3	4.9
2000	Pit-N★	156	559	111	176	37	7	35	123	114	69	.315	.437	.594	1031	158	54	6	0	1	.982	8	*O-155(46-72-39)	5.7
Total	6	596	1937	370	583	118	14	113	395	364	288	.301	.415	.551	966	143	136	38	10	5	.982	10	O-528L/D-40	13.0

YEAR	TM/L	G	AB	R	H	2B	3B	HR	RBI	BB	SO	AVG	OBP	SLG	OPS	OPS+	BR+	SB	CS	SBR	FA	FR	G/POS	TPR
■ **GEORGE GILHAM** Gilham, George Louis b: 9/17/1899, Shamokin, Pa. d: 4/25/37, Lansdowne, Pa. BR/TR, 5′11″, 164 lbs. Deb: 9/24/20																								
1920	StL-N	1	3	0	0	0	0	0	0	0	1	.000	.000	.000	0	-99	-1	0	0	0	.750	-1	/C-1	-0.2
1921	StL-N	1	1	0	0	0	0	0	0	0	0	.000	.000	.000	0	-99	-0	0	0	0	.000	0	H	0.0
Total	2	2	4	0	0	0	0	0	0	0	1	.000	.000	.000	0	-99	-1	0	0	0	.750	-1	/C-1	-0.2
■ **FRANK GILHOOLEY** Gilhooley, Frank Patrick "Flash" b: 6/10/1892, Toledo, Ohio d: 7/11/59, Toledo, Ohio BL/TR, 5′8″, 155 lbs. Deb: 9/18/11																								
1911	StL-N	1	0	0	0	0	0	0	0	0	0	—	—	—	—	—	0	0			.000	-0	/O-1(0-0-1)	0.0
1912	StL-N	13	49	5	11	0	0	0	2	3	8	.224	.269	.224	494	37	-4	0			1.000	-2	O-11(0-11-0)	-0.7
1913	NY-A	24	85	10	29	2	1	0	14	4	9	.341	.378	.388	766	124	2	6			.977	-1	O-24(0-0-24)	0.1
1914	NY-A	1	3	0	2	0	0	0	0	1	0	.667	.750	.667	1417	327	1	0			.000	-0	/O-1(0-0-1)	0.1
1915	NY-A	1	4	0	0	0	0	0	0	0	1	.000	.000	.000	0	-99	-1	0			1.000	-0	/O-1(0-0-1)	-0.1
1916	NY-A	58	223	40	62	5	3	1	10	37	17	.278	.383	.341	724	115	6	16			.971	3	O-57(0-2-55)	0.6
1917	NY-A	54	165	14	40	6	1	0	8	30	13	.242	.362	.291	653	99	1	6			.933	-1	O-46(0-0-46)	-0.2
1918	NY-A	112	427	59	118	13	5	1	23	53	24	.276	.358	.337	695	107	5	7			.961	1	*O-111(0-4-107)	-0.1
1919	Bos-A	48	112	14	27	4	0	0	1	12	8	.241	.315	.277	591	71	-4	2			.922	-5	O-33(30-2-1)	-1.1
Total	9	312	1068	142	289	30	10	2	58	140	80	.271	.357	.323	680	102	6	37			.957	-7	O-285(30-19-236)	-1.4
■ **BERNARD GILKEY** Gilkey, Otis Bernard b: 9/24/66, St.Louis, Mo. BR/TR, 6′, 190 lbs. Deb: 9/4/90 Career OF: (969-LF 3-CF 79-RF)																								
1990	StL-N	18	64	11	19	5	2	1	3	8	5	.297	.375	.484	859	134	3	6	1	1	.961	3	O-18(18-1-0)	0.6
1991	StL-N	81	268	28	58	7	2	5	20	39	33	.216	.318	.313	632	78	-7	14	8	0	.994	9	O-74(74-0-0)	-0.1
1992	StL-N	131	384	56	116	19	4	7	43	39	52	.302	.368	.427	795	128	15	18	12	-0	.978	7	*O-111(110-0-1)	2.0
1993	StL-N	137	557	99	170	40	5	16	70	56	66	.305	.373	.481	854	129	23	15	10	-0	.969	3	*O-134(133-0-2)/1-3	2.1
1994	StL-N	105	380	52	96	22	1	6	45	39	65	.253	.338	.363	701	84	-8	15	8	1	.983	5	*O-102(102-0-0)	-0.5
1995	StL-N	121	480	73	143	33	4	17	69	42	70	.298	.361	.490	850	122	15	12	6	1	.986	10	*O-118(118-0-0)	2.1
1996	NY-N	153	571	108	181	44	3	30	117	73	125	.317	.398	.562	960	157	47	17	9	1	.982	24	*O-151(151-0-0)	6.4
1997	NY-N	145	518	85	129	31	1	18	78	70	111	.249	.345	.417	762	102	2	7	11	-2	.989	13	*O-136(136-1-0)/D-2	0.8
1998	NY-N	82	264	33	60	15	0	4	28	32	66	.227	.320	.330	650	72	-10	5	1	1	.992	4	O-77(76-1-4)	-0.7
	Ari-N	29	101	8	25	0	0	1	5	11	14	.248	.327	.277	605	61	-5	4	2	0	.981	3	O-27(27-0-0)	-0.3
	Yr	111	365	41	85	15	0	5	33	43	80	.233	.322	.315	637	69	-15	9	3	1	.989	7	*O-104(103-1-4)	-1.0
1999	*Ari-N	94	204	28	60	16	1	8	39	29	42	.294	.387	.500	887	122	7	2	2	-0	.969	-1	O-53(15-0-40)	0.4
2000	Ari-N	38	73	6	8	1	0	2	6	7	16	.110	.188	.205	393	-1	-12	0	0	0	1.000	-0	O-17(2-0-16)	-1.2
	Bos-A	36	91	11	21	5	1	1	9	10	12	.231	.327	.341	668	67	-5	0	0	0	1.000	-1	O-22(7-0-16)/D-8	-0.6
Total	11	1170	3955	598	1086	238	24	116	532	455	677	.275	.355	.435	790	111	64	115	70	1	.982	79	*O-1040L/D-10,1-3	11.0
■ **BOB GILKS** Gilks, Robert James b: 7/2/1864, Cincinnati, Ohio d: 8/21/44, Brunswick, Ga. BR/TR, 5′8″, 178 lbs. Deb: 8/25/1887 Career OF: (181-LF 56-CF 21-RF)																								
1887	Cle-a	22	86	12	29	2	0	0	13	3		.337	.352	.337	690	96	-0	5			.881	2	P-13/1-6,O-3C,2-1	0.0
1888	Cle-a	119	484	59	111	14	4	1	63	7		.229	.245	.281	526	70	-17	16			.899	-1	O-87L,3-28/S-4,P2	-1.7
1889	Cle-N	53	210	17	50	5	2	0	18	7	20	.238	.273	.281	554	56	-13	6			1.000	0	O-29C,S-13,1-10,/2	-1.2
1890	Cle-N	130	544	65	116	10	3	0	41	32	38	.213	.265	.243	507	49	-35	17			.941	1	*O-123L/P-4,S-3,2-2	-3.2
1893	Bal-N	15	64	10	17	2	0	0	7	0	3	.266	.277	.297	574	52	-5	3			.969	3	O-15(1-0-15)	-0.2
Total	5	339	1388	163	323	33	9	1	142	49	61	.233	.265	.270	535	60	-69	47			.937	5	O-257L/3-28,P-21,S12	-6.3
■ **JIM GILL** Gill, James C. b: 7/1866, d: 4/10/23, Beaver Falls, Pa. Deb: 6/27/1889																								
1889	StL-a	2	8	2	2	1	0	0	1	1	2	.250	.333	.375	708	90	-0	1			1.000	-0	/O-1(0-1-0),2-1	-0.1
■ **JOHNNY GILL** Gill, John Wesley "Patcheye" b: 3/27/05, Nashville, Tenn. d: 12/26/84, Nashville, Tenn. BL/TR, 6′2″, 190 lbs. Deb: 8/28/27																								
1927	Cle-A	21	60	8	13	3	0	1	4	7	13	.217	.319	.317	636	65	-3	1	1	-0	1.000	-2	O-17(14-3-0)	-0.6
1928	Cle-A	2	2	0	0	0	0	0	0	0	1	.000	.000	.000	0	-99	-1	0	0	0	.000	0	H	-0.1
1931	Was-A	8	30	2	8	2	1	0	5	1	6	.267	.313	.400	713	86	-1	0	1	-0	1.000	3	/O-8(0-0-8)	0.2
1934	Was-A	13	53	7	13	3	0	2	7	2	3	.245	.286	.415	701	82	-2	0	0	0	1.000	-1	O-13(2-0-11)	-0.3
1935	Chi-N	3	3	2	1	1	0	0	1	0	1	.333	.333	.667	1000	161	0	0			.000	0	H	0.0
1936	Chi-N	71	174	20	44	8	0	7	28	13	19	.253	.309	.420	728	92	-2	0			.938	-3	O-41(35-1-5)	-0.7
Total	6	118	322	39	79	17	1	10	45	23	43	.245	.306	.398	703	84	-8	1	2		.968	-2	/O-79(51-4-24)	-1.5
■ **WARREN GILL** Gill, Warren Darst "Doc" b: 12/21/1878, Ladoga, Ind. d: 11/26/52, Laguna Beach, Cal. BR/TR, 6′1″, 175 lbs. Deb: 8/26/08																								
1908	Pit-N	27	76	10	17	0	1	0	14	11		.224	.366	.250	616	97	1	3			1.000	-3	1-25	-0.2
■ **SAM GILLEN** Gillen, Samuel (b: Samuel Gilleland) b: 1/1871, Pittsburgh, Pa. d: 5/13/05, Pittsburgh, Pa. 5′8″, Deb: 8/19/1893																								
1893	Pit-N	3	6	0	0	0	0	0	0	0	1	.000	.000	.000	0	-99	-2	0			.750	-0	/S-3	-0.2
1897	Phi-N	75	270	32	70	10	3	0	27	35		.259	.353	.319	671	80	-6	2			.896	-29	S-69/3-6	-2.8
Total	2	78	276	32	70	10	3	0	27	35	1	.254	.346	.312	658	76	-8	2			.892	-30	/S-72,3-6	-3.0
■ **TOM GILLEN** Gillen, Thomas J. b: 5/18/1862, Philadelphia, Pa. d: 1/26/1889, Philadelphia, Pa. 5′8″, 160 lbs. Deb: 4/18/1884																								
1884	Phi-U	29	116	5	18	2	0	0		1		.155	.162	.172	335	2	-17				.895	-4	C-27/O-3(1-0-0)	-1.7
1886	Det-N	2	10	2	4	0	0	0	4	0	1	.400	.400	.400	800	140	0	0			.889	-2	/C-2	-0.1
Total	2	31	126	7	22	2	0	0	4	1	1	.175	.181	.190	372	14	-17	0			.895	-6	/C-29,O-3(1-0-0)	-1.8
■ **CARDEN GILLENWATER** Gillenwater, Carden Edison b: 5/13/18, Riceville, Tenn. BR/TR, 6′1″, 178 lbs. Deb: 9/22/40																								
1940	StL-N	7	25	1	4	1	0	0	5	0	2	.160	.160	.200	360	-1	-3	0			1.000	-1	/O-7(5-2-0)	-0.5
1943	Bro-N	8	17	1	3	0	0	0	2	2	3	.176	.263	.176	440	28	-2	0			1.000	-0	/O-4(2-1-1)	-0.2
1945	Bos-N	144	517	74	149	20	2	7	72	73	70	.288	.379	.375	755	110	9	13			.979	24	*O-140(0-140-0)	2.9
1946	Bos-N	99	224	30	51	10	1	1	14	39	27	.228	.342	.295	637	81	-4	3			.979	1	O-78(11-67-0)	-0.6
1948	Was-A	77	221	23	54	10	4	3	21	39	36	.244	.358	.367	724	96	-1	4	2	0	.974	-1	O-67(1-65-1)	-0.3
Total	5	335	1004	129	261	41	7	11	114	153	138	.260	.359	.348	707	96	-1	20	2		.979	23	O-296(19-275-2)	1.3
■ **JIM GILLESPIE** Gillespie, James Wheatfield b: 9/1858, Canada BL/TR, Deb: 10/1/1890																								
1890	Buf-P	1	3	0	0	0	0	0	0	0	2	.000	.000	.000	0	-99	-1	0			.250	-0	/O-1(0-0-1)	-0.1
■ **PAUL GILLESPIE** Gillespie, Paul Allen b: 9/18/20, Sugar Valley, Ga. d: 8/11/70, Anniston, Ala. BL/TR, 6′3″, 195 lbs. Deb: 9/11/42																								
1942	Chi-N	5	16	3	4	0	0	2	4	1	2	.250	.294	.625	919	172	1	0			1.000	-1	/C-4	0.0
1944	Chi-N	9	26	2	7	1	0	1	2	3	3	.269	.345	.423	768	116	1	0			.903	-1	/C-7	0.0
1945	*Chi-N	75	163	12	47	6	0	3	25	18	9	.288	.366	.380	746	110	3	2			.989	1	C-45/O-1(0-0-1)	0.6
Total	3	89	205	17	58	7	0	6	31	22	14	.283	.358	.405	763	115	4	2			.978	-1	/C-56,O-1(0-0-1)	0.6
■ **PETE GILLESPIE** Gillespie, Peter Patrick b: 11/30/1851, Carbondale, Pa. d: 5/5/10, Carbondale, Pa. BL/TR, 6′1.5″, 178 lbs. Deb: 5/1/1880																								
1880	Tro-N	82	346	50	84	20	5	2	24	17	35	.243	.278	.347	625	105	1				.905	6	*O-82(82-0-0)	0.3
1881	Tro-N	84	348	43	96	14	3	0	41	9	24	.276	.294	.333	627	92	-4				.933	4	*O-84(84-0-0)	-0.5
1882	Tro-N	74	298	46	82	5	4	2	33	9	14	.275	.296	.339	635	108	3				.827	-6	*O-74(74-0-0)	-0.4
1883	NY-N	98	411	64	129	23	12	1	62	9	27	.314	.329	.436	764	131	15				.897	7	*O-98(97-1-0)	1.6
1884	NY-N	101	413	75	109	7	4	2	44	19	35	.264	.296	.315	611	90	-5				.893	-3	*O-101(100-0-1)	-1.0
1885	NY-N	102	420	67	123	17	6	0	52	15	32	.293	.317	.362	679	121	9				**.942**	-4	*O-102(102-0-0)	0.2
1886	NY-N	97	396	65	108	13	8	0	58	16	30	.273	.301	.346	647	95	-3	17			.901	-10	*O-97(95-1-1)	-1.4
1887	NY-N	76	307	40	90	9	3	3	37	12	21	.293	.304	.346	650	84	-6	37			.946	-2	O-76(76-0-0)/3-1	-0.8
Total	8	714	2939	450	821	108	45	10	351	106	218	.279	.303	.354	657	104	11	54			.903	-8	O-714(710-2-2)/3-1	-2.0
■ **JIM GILLIAM** Gilliam, James William "Junior" b: 10/17/28, Nashville, Tenn. d: 10/8/78, Inglewood, Cal. BB/TR, 5′10.5″, 175 lbs. Deb: 4/14/53 C Career OF: (207-LF 5-CF 26-RF)																								
1953	*Bro-N	151	605	125	168	31	**17**	6	63	100	38	.278	.383	.415	798	106	8	21	14	-0	.976	3	*2-149	2.1
1954	Bro-N	146	607	107	171	28	8	13	52	76	30	.282	.364	.418	782	100	1	8	7	-1	.977	-11	*2-143/O-4(4-0-2)	0.0
1955	*Bro-N	147	538	110	134	20	8	7	40	70	37	.249	.342	.355	697	83	-12	15	15	-2	.968	-9	2-99,O-46(41-4-7)	-1.8
1956	*Bro-N☆	153	594	102	178	23	8	6	43	95	39	.300	.400	.396	795	107	10	21	9	1	.981	18	*2-102,O-56(53-0-7)	3.4
1957	Bro-N	149	617	89	154	26	4	2	37	64	31	.250	.324	.314	639	66	-27	26	10	2	**.986**	3	*2-148/O-2(2-0-0)	-1.1

YEAR	TM/L	G	AB	R	H	2B	3B	HR	RBI	BB	SO	AVG	OBP	SLG	OPS	OPS+	BR+	SB	CS	SBR	FA	FR	G/POS	TPR
1958	LA-N	147	555	81	145	25	5	2	43	78	22	.261	.352	.335	687	81	-13	18	11	0	.987	8	O-75L,3-44,2-32	-0.7
1959	*LA-N★	145	553	91	156	18	4	3	34	**96**	25	.282	.388	.345	734	91	-3	23	10	2	.958	2	*3-132/2-8,O-3(3-0-1)	0.0
1960	LA-N	151	557	96	138	20	2	5	40	96	28	.248	.361	.318	679	82	-10	12	9	-1	.960	9	*3-130,2-30	0.1
1961	LA-N	144	439	74	107	26	3	4	32	79	34	.244	.359	.344	703	81	-10	8	4	0	.956	2	3-74,2-71,O-11L	-0.3
1962	LA-N	160	588	83	159	24	1	4	43	93	35	.270	.372	.335	707	97	2	17	7	1	.981	-14	*2-113,3-90/O-1L	-0.2
1963	*LA-N	148	525	77	148	27	4	6	49	60	28	.282	.358	.383	741	122	16	19	5	2	.985	-8	*2-119,3-55	2.1
1964	LA-N	116	334	44	76	8	3	2	27	42	21	.228	.319	.287	607	78	-9	4	4	-1	.936	-20	3-86,2-25/O-2(0-0-2)	-2.9
1965	*LA-N	111	372	54	104	19	4	4	39	53	31	.280	.375	.384	760	123	13	9	5	0	.960	-13	3-80,O-22(21-0-1)/2-5	-0.1
1966	*LA-N	88	235	30	51	9	0	1	16	34	17	.217	.316	.268	584	70	-9	2	1	0	.953	-12	3-70/1-2,2-2	-2.2
Total	14	1956	7119	1163	1889	304	71	65	558	1036	416	.265	.361	.355	717	92	-41	203	111	6	.979	-43	*2-1046,3-761,O/1	-1.6

■ BARNEY GILLIGAN Gilligan, Andrew Bernard b: 1/3/1856, Cambridge, Mass. d: 4/1/34, Lynn, Mass. BR/TR, 5′6.5″, 130 lbs. Deb: 9/25/1875 Career OF: (23-LF 14-CF 7-RF)

YEAR	TM/L	G	AB	R	H	2B	3B	HR	RBI	BB	SO	AVG	OBP	SLG	OPS	OPS+	BR+	SB	CS	SBR	FA	FR	G/POS	TPR
1875	Atl-n	2	8	2	2	0	0	0	0	0	0	.250	.250	.250	500	85	-0	0	0	0	1.000	-1	/C-1,O-1(0-0-1)	-0.1
1879	Cle-N	52	205	20	35	6	2	0	11	0	13	.171	.171	.220	390	28	-15				.870	-0	C-27,O-23(21-2-0)/S-2	-1.5
1880	Cle-N	30	99	9	17	4	3	1	13	6	12	.172	.219	.303	522	77	-2				.969	4	C-23/O-4(0-4-0),S-4	0.3
1881	Pro-N	46	183	19	40	7	2	0	20	9	24	.219	.255	.279	534	69	-6				.930	-1	C-36,S-10/O-1(0-1-0)	-0.6
1882	Pro-N	56	201	32	45	7	6	0	26	4	26	.224	.239	.318	557	77	-5				.932	10	C-54/S-2	0.8
1883	Pro-N	74	263	34	52	13	3	0	24	26	32	.198	.270	.270	540	63	-11				.900	10	*C-74	0.5
1884	*Pro-N	82	294	47	72	13	2	1	38	35	41	.245	.325	.313	638	104	3				.928	17	*C-81/3-1,1-1	2.4
1885	Pro-N	71	252	23	54	7	3	0	12	23	33	.214	.280	.266	546	80	-5				.872	-3	C-65/S-5,O-1L,2-1	-0.2
1886	Was-N	81	273	23	52	9	2	0	17	39	35	.190	.292	.238	530	66	-9	6			.925	-9	C-71,O-14R/S-1,3-1	-1.1
1887	Was-N	28	95	7	23	2	0	1	6	5	18	.242	.242	.256	498	40	-7	2			.874	-4	C-26/S-3,O-1(0-1-0)	-0.8
1888	Det-N	1	5	1	1	0	0	0	0	0	1	.200	.200	.200	400	28	-0	0			.875	-0	/C-1	0.0
Total	10	521	1870	215	391	68	23	3	167	147	235	.209	.265	.273	538	70	-58	8	0		.912	24	C-458/O-44L,S-27,321	-0.2

■ GRANT GILLIS Gillis, Grant b: 1/24/01, Grove Hill, Ala. d: 2/4/81, Thomasville, Ala. BR/TR, 5′10″, 165 lbs. Deb: 9/19/27

YEAR	TM/L	G	AB	R	H	2B	3B	HR	RBI	BB	SO	AVG	OBP	SLG	OPS	OPS+	BR+	SB	CS	SBR	FA	FR	G/POS	TPR
1927	Was-A	10	36	8	8	3	1	0	2	2	0	.222	.263	.361	624	61	-2	0	0	0	1.000	-2	S-10	-0.3
1928	Was-A	24	87	13	22	5	1	0	10	4	5	.253	.309	.333	642	69	-4	0	1	-0	.910	-10	S-16/2-5,3-3	-1.3
1929	Bos-A	28	73	5	18	4	0	0	11	6	8	.247	.304	.301	605	58	-5	0	1	-0	.956	-4	2-25	-0.7
Total	3	62	196	26	48	12	2	0	23	12	13	.245	.299	.327	625	63	-11	0	2	-1	.948	-16	/2-30,S-26,3-3	-2.3

■ JIM GILMAN Gilman, James Deb: 7/10/1893

YEAR	TM/L	G	AB	R	H	2B	3B	HR	RBI	BB	SO	AVG	OBP	SLG	OPS	OPS+	BR+	SB	CS	SBR	FA	FR	G/POS	TPR
1893	Cle-N	2	7	1	2	0	0	0	1	0	2	.286	.286	.286	571	49	-1	0			.667	-1	/3-2	-0.1

■ PIT GILMAN Gilman, Pitkin Clark b: 3/14/1864, Laporte, Ohio d: 8/17/50, Elyria, Ohio BL/TL, 170 lbs. Deb: 9/18/1884

YEAR	TM/L	G	AB	R	H	2B	3B	HR	RBI	BB	SO	AVG	OBP	SLG	OPS	OPS+	BR+	SB	CS	SBR	FA	FR	G/POS	TPR
1884	Cle-N	2	10	0	1	0	0	0	0	0	3	.100	.100	.100	200	-36	-2				1.000	0	/O-2(2-0-0)	-0.1

■ GROVER GILMORE Gilmore, Ernest Grover b: 11/1/1888, Chicago, Ill. d: 11/25/19, Sioux City, Iowa BL/TL, 5′9.5″, 170 lbs. Deb: 4/18/14

YEAR	TM/L	G	AB	R	H	2B	3B	HR	RBI	BB	SO	AVG	OBP	SLG	OPS	OPS+	BR+	SB	CS	SBR	FA	FR	G/POS	TPR
1914	KC-F	139	530	91	152	25	5	1	32	37	108	.287	.337	.358	695	93	-14	23			.973	3	*O-132(0-10-122)	-1.9
1915	KC-F	119	411	53	117	22	15	1	47	26	50	.285	.347	.418	765	120	4	19			.979	7	*O-119(0-0-119)	0.4
Total	2	258	941	144	269	47	20	2	79	63	158	.286	.341	.385	726	105	-10	42			.976	10	O-251(0-10-241)	-1.5

■ JIM GILMORE Gilmore, James b: 5/1853, Baltimore, Md. d: 11/18/28, Baltimore, Md. Deb: 4/26/1875

YEAR	TM/L	G	AB	R	H	2B	3B	HR	RBI	BB	SO	AVG	OBP	SLG	OPS	OPS+	BR+	SB	CS	SBR	FA	FR	G/POS	TPR
1875	Was-n	3	12	2	3	0	0	0	0	0	3	.250	.250	.250	500	77	-0	0	0	0	.667	-1	/C-2,3-1,O-1(0-0-1)	-0.1

■ GILROY Gilroy Deb: 9/7/1874

YEAR	TM/L	G	AB	R	H	2B	3B	HR	RBI	BB	SO	AVG	OBP	SLG	OPS	OPS+	BR+	SB	CS	SBR	FA	FR	G/POS	TPR
1874	Chi-n	8	38	4	8	1	0	0	7	1	3	.211	.231	.237	468	50	-2	0	0	0	.816	-2	/C-8	-0.3
1875	Ath-n	2	6	0	1	0	0	0	0	0	0	.167	.167	.167	333	15	-1	0	0	0	.800	1	/C-1,O-1(0-0-1)	0.1
Total	2 n	10	44	4	9	1	0	0	7	1	3	.205	.222	.227	449	45	-3	0	0	0	.814	-1	/C-9,O-1(0-0-1)	-0.2

■ TINSLEY GINN Ginn, Tinsley Rucker b: 9/26/1891, Royston, Ga. d: 8/30/31, Atlanta, Ga. BL/TR, 5′9″, 180 lbs. Deb: 6/27/14

YEAR	TM/L	G	AB	R	H	2B	3B	HR	RBI	BB	SO	AVG	OBP	SLG	OPS	OPS+	BR+	SB	CS	SBR	FA	FR	G/POS	TPR
1914	Cle-A	2	1	0	0	0	0	0	0	0	0	.000	.000	.000	0	-96	-0	0			.000	0	/O-2	0.0

■ JOE GINSBERG Ginsberg, Myron Nathan b: 10/11/26, New York, N.Y. BL/TR, 5′11″, 180 lbs. Deb: 9/15/48

YEAR	TM/L	G	AB	R	H	2B	3B	HR	RBI	BB	SO	AVG	OBP	SLG	OPS	OPS+	BR+	SB	CS	SBR	FA	FR	G/POS	TPR
1948	Det-A	11	36	7	13	0	0	0	1	3	1	.361	.410	.361	771	103	0	0	0	0	.943	-2	C-11	-0.1
1950	Det-A	36	95	12	22	6	0	0	12	11	6	.232	.318	.295	612	56	-6	1	0	0	.981	-4	C-31	-0.8
1951	Det-A	102	304	44	79	10	2	8	37	43	21	.260	.355	.385	740	100	0	0	2	-1	.978	-1	C-95	0.3
1952	Det-A	113	307	29	68	13	2	6	36	51	21	.221	.338	.336	673	87	-4	1	1	-0	.984	-14	*C-101	-1.4
1953	Det-A	18	53	6	16	2	0	0	3	10	1	.302	.422	.340	761	109	1	0	0	0	.988	0	C-15	0.2
	Cle-A	46	109	10	31	4	0	0	10	14	4	.284	.371	.321	692	91	-1	0	0	0	.966	-5	C-39	-0.4
	Yr	64	162	16	47	6	0	0	13	24	5	.290	.388	.327	715	97	1	0	0	0	.974	-5	C-54	-0.2
1954	Cle-A	3	2	0	1	0	1	0	1	0	0	.500	.667	1.500	2167	473	1	0	0	0	1.000	-0	/C-1	0.1
1956	KC-A	71	195	15	48	8	1	1	12	23	17	.246	.326	.313	639	69	-8	1	1	-0	.989	-2	C-57	-0.8
	Bal-A	15	28	0	2	0	0	0	2	2	4	.071	.133	.071	205	-48	-6	0	0	0	1.000	-0	/C-8	-0.6
	Yr	86	223	15	50	8	1	1	14	25	21	.224	.302	.283	585	56	-14	1	1	-0	.990	-3	C-65	-1.4
1957	Bal-A	85	175	15	48	8	2	1	18	18	19	.274	.349	.360	709	100	0	2	1	0	.986	1	C-66	0.4
1958	Bal-A	61	109	4	23	1	0	3	16	13	14	.211	.306	.303	609	72	-4	0	0	0	.994	3	C-39	0.0
1959	Bal-A	65	166	14	30	2	0	1	14	21	13	.181	.273	.211	484	35	-14	1	0	0	.993	3	C-62	-0.9
1960	Bal-A	14	30	3	8	1	0	0	6	6	1	.267	.389	.300	689	90	-0	0	0	0	.940	0	C-14	0.1
	Chi-A	28	75	8	19	4	0	0	9	10	8	.253	.349	.307	656	80	-2	1	0	0	.993	4	C-25	0.4
	Yr	42	105	11	27	5	0	0	15	16	9	.257	.361	.305	665	83	-2	1	0	0	.976	5	C-39	0.5
1961	Chi-A	6	3	0	0	0	0	0	0	1	2	.000	.250	.000	250	-27	-1	0	0	0	1.000	0	/C-2	0.0
	Bos-A	19	24	1	6	0	0	0	5	0	2	.250	.250	.250	500	33	-2	0	0	0	1.000	-1	/C-6	-0.3
	Yr	25	27	1	6	0	0	0	5	1	4	.222	.250	.222	472	27	-3	0	0	0	1.000	-1	/C-8	-0.3
1962	NY-N	2	5	0	0	0	0	0	0	0	1	.000	.000	.000	0	-98	-1	0	0	0	1.000	1	/C-2	0.0
Total	13	695	1716	168	414	59	8	20	182	226	135	.241	.334	.320	654	79	-46	7	5	-0	.983	-17	C-574	-3.8

■ KEITH GINTER Ginter, Keith Michael b: 5/5/76, Norwalk, Cal. BR/TR, 5′10″, 190 lbs. Deb: 9/20/2000

YEAR	TM/L	G	AB	R	H	2B	3B	HR	RBI	BB	SO	AVG	OBP	SLG	OPS	OPS+	BR+	SB	CS	SBR	FA	FR	G/POS	TPR
2000	Hou-N	5	8	3	2	0	0	1	3	1	3	.250	.333	.625	958	128	0	0	0	0	1.000	1	/2-2	0.1

■ AL GIONFRIDDO Gionfriddo, Albert Francis b: 3/8/22, Dysart, Pa. BL/TL, 5′6″, 165 lbs. Deb: 9/23/44

YEAR	TM/L	G	AB	R	H	2B	3B	HR	RBI	BB	SO	AVG	OBP	SLG	OPS	OPS+	BR+	SB	CS	SBR	FA	FR	G/POS	TPR
1944	Pit-N	4	6	0	1	0	0	0	0	1	1	.167	.286	.167	452	28	-1	0			1.000	0	/O-1(0-1-0)	-0.1
1945	Pit-N	122	409	74	116	18	9	2	42	60	22	.284	.377	.386	763	108	6	12			.964	-8	*O-106(13-82-11)	-0.6
1946	Pit-N	64	102	11	26	2	2	0	10	14	5	.255	.345	.314	659	85	-2	1			.944	-5	O-33(8-13-12)	-0.8
1947	Pit-N	1	1	0	0	0	0	0	0	0	0	.000	.000	.000	0	-97	-0	0			.000	0	H	0.0
	*Bro-N	37	62	10	11	2	1	0	6	16	11	.177	.346	.242	588	57	-3	2			.938	-2	O-17(11-0-6)	-0.6
	Yr	38	63	10	11	2	1	0	6	16	11	.175	.342	.238	580	54	-4	2			.938	-2	O-17(11-0-6)	-0.6
Total	4	228	580	95	154	22	12	2	58	91	39	.266	.366	.355	721	97	0	15			.959	-15	O-157(32-96-29)	-2.1

■ TOMMY GIORDANO Giordano, Thomas Arthur "T-Bone" (b: Carmine Arthur Giordano) b: 10/9/25, Newark, N.J. BR/TR, 6′, 175 lbs. Deb: 9/11/53

YEAR	TM/L	G	AB	R	H	2B	3B	HR	RBI	BB	SO	AVG	OBP	SLG	OPS	OPS+	BR+	SB	CS	SBR	FA	FR	G/POS	TPR
1953	Phi-A	11	40	6	7	2	0	2	5	5	6	.175	.267	.375	642	69	-2	0	1	-0	.984	1	2-11	-0.1

■ ED GIOVANOLA Giovanola, Edward Thomas b: 3/4/69, Los Gatos, Cal. BL/TR, 5′10″, 170 lbs. Deb: 9/10/95

YEAR	TM/L	G	AB	R	H	2B	3B	HR	RBI	BB	SO	AVG	OBP	SLG	OPS	OPS+	BR+	SB	CS	SBR	FA	FR	G/POS	TPR
1995	Atl-N	13	14	2	1	0	0	0	0	3	5	.071	.235	.071	307	-14	-2	0	0	0	1.000	-2	/2-7,3-3,S-1	-0.4
1996	Atl-N	43	82	10	19	2	0	0	7	8	13	.232	.308	.256	564	48	-6	1	0	0	.983	-2	S-25/3-6,2-5	-0.6
1997	Atl-N	14	8	0	2	0	0	0	0	2	1	.250	.400	.250	650	73	-0	0	0	0	1.000	1	/3-8,2-1,S-1	0.1
1998	SD-N	92	139	19	32	3	3	1	9	22	22	.230	.335	.317	652	79	-4	1	2	-0	.965	18	3-37,2-36/S-1	1.4
1999	SD-N	56	58	10	11	0	1	0	3	9	8	.190	.299	.224	523	38	-5	2	0	0	.938	7	3-25,2-19/S-7,P-1	0.3
Total	5	218	301	41	65	5	4	1	19	44	49	.216	.318	.269	587	57	-18	4	2	0	.964	22	/3-79,2-68,S-35,P-1	0.8

■ CHARLES GIPSON Gipson, Charles Wells b: 12/16/72, Orange, Cal. BR/TR, 6′2″, 180 lbs. Deb: 3/31/98 Career OF: (36-LF 28-CF 57-RF)

YEAR	TM/L	G	AB	R	H	2B	3B	HR	RBI	BB	SO	AVG	OBP	SLG	OPS	OPS+	BR+	SB	CS	SBR	FA	FR	G/POS	TPR
1998	Sea-A	44	51	11	12	1	0	0	2	5	9	.235	.316	.255	571	51	-3	2	1	0	.973	-7	O-36(14-11-13)/3-4	-1.0

YEAR	TM/L	G	AB	R	H	2B	3B	HR	RBI	BB	SO	AVG	OBP	SLG	OPS	OPS+	BR+	SB	CS	SBR	FA	FR	G/POS	TPR
1999	Sea-A	55	80	16	18	5	2	0	9	6	13	.225	.287	.338	625	60	-5	3	4	-1	.960	5	O-28R,3-17/2-3,SD	-0.1
2000	*Sea-A	59	29	7	9	1	1	0	3	4	9	.310	.394	.414	808	108	0	2	3	-1	1.000	-13	O-48R/3-5,S-5,D-1	-1.2
Total	3	158	160	34	39	7	3	0	14	15	31	.244	.316	.325	641	66	-8	7	8	-1	.976	-16	O-112R/3-26,S-8,D2	-2.3
■ JOE GIRARDI	Girardi, Joseph Elliott b: 10/14/64, Peoria, Ill. BR/TR, 5'11", 195 lbs. Deb: 4/4/89																							
1989	*Chi-N	59	157	15	39	10	0	1	14	11	26	.248	.306	.331	637	76	-5	2	1	0	.981	13	C-59	1.2
1990	Chi-N	133	419	36	113	24	2	1	38	17	50	.270	.303	.344	647	72	-16	8	3	1	.985	-9	*C-133	-1.7
1991	Chi-N	21	47	3	9	2	0	0	6	6	6	.191	.283	.234	517	45	-3	0	0	0	.972	4	C-21	0.1
1992	Chi-N	91	270	19	73	3	1	1	12	19	38	.270	.321	.300	621	75	-8	0	2	-1	.991	-4	C-86	-1.0
1993	Col-N	86	310	35	90	14	5	3	31	24	41	.290	.347	.397	744	85	-6	6	6	-1	.989	-8	C-84	-1.0
1994	Col-N	93	330	47	91	9	4	4	34	21	48	.276	.323	.364	687	67	-15	3	3	-0	.992	5	C-93	-0.5
1995	*Col-N	125	462	63	121	17	2	8	55	29	76	.262	.308	.359	668	59	-26	3	3	-0	.988	-3	*C-122	-2.2
1996	*NY-A	124	422	55	124	22	3	2	45	30	55	.294	.348	.374	722	83	-10	13	4	1	.996	6	*C-120/D-2	0.4
1997	*NY-A	112	398	38	105	23	1	1	50	26	53	.264	.312	.334	646	69	-18	2	3	-1	.994	17	*C-111/D-1	0.6
1998	*NY-A	78	254	31	70	11	4	3	31	14	38	.276	.319	.386	704	85	-6	2	4	-1	.995	20	C-78	1.7
1999	*NY-A	65	209	23	50	16	1	2	27	10	26	.239	.274	.354	628	59	-13	3	1	0	.984	15	C-65	0.6
2000	Chi-N☆	106	363	47	101	15	1	6	40	32	61	.278	.342	.375	716	83	-9	1	0	0	.993	-9	*C-103	-1.1
Total	12	1093	3641	412	986	166	24	32	383	239	518	.271	.320	.356	676	73	-136	43	30	-1	.990	48	*C-1075/D-3	-2.9
■ TONY GIULIANI	Giuliani, Angelo John b: 11/24/12, St.Paul, Minn. BR/TR, 5'11", 175 lbs. Deb: 4/18/36																							
1936	StL-A	71	198	17	43	3	0	0	13	11	13	.217	.258	.232	491	21	-25	0	0	0	.966	5	C-66	-1.4
1937	StL-A	19	53	6	16	1	0	0	3	3	3	.302	.339	.321	660	67	-3	0	0	0	.986	-0	C-19	-0.2
1938	Was-A	46	115	10	25	4	0	0	15	8	3	.217	.268	.252	520	33	-12	1	0	0	1.000	-1	C-46	-0.9
1939	Was-A	54	172	20	43	6	2	0	18	4	7	.250	.267	.308	575	50	-13	0	1	-0	.979	1	C-50	-0.9
1940	Bro-N	1	1	0	0	0	0	0	0	0	1	.000	.000	.000	0	-94	-0	0			1.000	-0	/C-1	0.0
1941	Bro-N	3	2	0	0	0	0	0	0	0	0	.000	.000	.000	0	-96	-1	0			1.000	1	/C-3	0.0
1943	Was-A	49	133	5	30	4	1	0	20	12	14	.226	.290	.271	560	67	-6	0	1	-0	.962	-1	C-49	-0.5
Total	7	243	674	58	157	18	3	0	69	38	41	.233	.274	.269	542	42	-59	1	2		.976	6	C-234	-3.9
■ JIM GLADD	Gladd, James Walter b: 10/2/22, Ft.Gibson, Okla. d: 11/8/77, Long Beach, Cal. BR/TR, 6'2", 190 lbs. Deb: 9/9/46																							
1946	NY-N	4	11	0	1	0	0	0	0	1	4	.091	.167	.091	258	-26	-2	0			1.000	4	/C-4	0.2
■ DAN GLADDEN	Gladden, Clinton Daniel b: 7/7/57, San Jose, Cal. BR/TR, 5'11", 180 lbs. Deb: 9/5/83 Career OF: (798-LF 349-CF 4-RF)																							
1983	SF-N	18	63	6	14	2	0	1	9	5	11	.222	.279	.302	581	63	-3	4	3	-0	1.000	2	O-18(0-17-1)	-0.2
1984	SF-N	86	342	71	120	17	2	4	31	33	37	.351	.411	.447	859	146	22	31	16	1	.988	9	O-85(0-85-0)	3.2
1985	SF-N	142	502	64	122	15	8	7	41	40	78	.243	.308	.347	654	87	-9	32	15	2	.975	1	*O-124(14-111-1)	-0.9
1986	SF-N	102	351	55	97	16	1	4	29	39	59	.276	.357	.362	719	104	3	27	10	2	.987	12	O-89(0-90-0)	1.7
1987	*Min-A	121	438	69	109	21	2	8	38	38	72	.249	.313	.361	674	75	-15	25	9	2	.987	6	*O-111(105-8-2)/D-4	-1.1
1988	Min-A	141	576	91	155	32	6	11	62	46	74	.269	.327	.403	730	100	-0	28	8	3	.991	16	*O-140L/2-1,3-1,P-1	1.5
1989	Min-A	121	461	69	136	23	3	8	46	23	53	.295	.335	.410	745	102	1	23	7	3	.966	5	*O-117L/P-1,D-2	0.5
1990	Min-A	136	534	64	147	27	6	5	40	26	67	.275	.316	.376	693	87	-9	25	9	2	.980	12	*O-133(133-1-0)/D-2	0.0
1991	*Min-A	126	461	65	114	14	9	6	52	36	60	.247	.309	.356	665	80	-13	15	9	0	.988	1	*O-126(126-0-0)	-1.6
1992	Det-A	113	417	57	106	20	1	7	42	30	64	.254	.307	.357	665	85	-9	4	2	0	.987	0	*O-108(95-17-0)/D-2	-1.1
1993	Det-A	91	356	52	95	16	2	13	56	21	50	.267	.313	.433	746	99	-2	8	5	0	.986	8	O-86(69-18-0)/D-5	0.4
Total	11	1197	4501	663	1215	203	40	74	446	337	625	.270	.327	.382	709	94	-35	222	93	16	.984	73	*O-1137L/D-15,P-2,32	2.4
■ BUCK GLADMAN	Gladman, John H. b: 1864, Washington, D.C. Deb: 7/7/1883																							
1883	Phi-N	1	4	1	0	0	0	0	0	0	2	.000	.000	.000	0	-99	-1				1.000	-1	/3-1	-0.1
1884	Was-a	56	224	17	35	5	3	1		3		.156	.178	.219	397	33	-15				.796	-3	3-53/O-2(0-0-2),S-1	-1.6
1886	Was-N	44	152	17	21	5	3	1	15	12	30	.138	.201	.230	431	33	-12	5			.830	-6	3-44	-1.6
Total	3	101	380	35	56	10	6	2	15	15	32	.147	.186	.221	407	31	-28	5			.812	-10	/3-98,O-2(0-0-2),S-1	-3.3
■ ROLAND GLADU	Gladu, Roland Edouard b: 5/10/11, Montreal, Que., Can d: 7/26/94, Montreal, Que., Can. BL/TR, 5'8.5", 185 lbs. Deb: 4/18/44																							
1944	Bos-N	21	66	5	16	2	1	1	7	3	8	.242	.275	.348	624	72	-3	0			.891	-5	3-15/O-3(3-0-0)	-0.8
■ DOUG GLANVILLE	Glanville, Douglas Metunwa b: 8/25/70, Hackensack, N.J. BR/TR, 6'2", 170 lbs. Deb: 6/9/96																							
1996	Chi-N	49	83	10	20	5	1	1	10	3	11	.241	.267	.361	629	62	-5	2	0	0	.973	-6	O-35(19-9-8)	-1.1
1997	Chi-N	146	474	79	142	22	5	4	35	24	46	.300	.335	.392	727	87	-9	19	11	0	.989	4	*O-138(120-30-1)	-0.7
1998	Phi-N	158	678	106	189	28	7	8	49	42	89	.279	.326	.376	703	83	-17	23	6	3	.995	13	*O-158(0-158-0)	0.2
1999	Phi-N	150	628	101	204	38	6	11	73	48	82	.325	.378	.457	835	107	7	34	2	7	.980	19	*O-148(0-148-0)	3.3
2000	Phi-N	154	637	89	175	27	6	8	52	31	76	.275	.310	.374	684	71	-29	31	8	4	.990	15	*O-150(0-150-0)	-0.8
Total	5	657	2500	385	730	120	25	32	219	148	304	.292	.335	.398	734	86	-52	109	27	15	.988	45	O-629(139-495-9)	0.9
■ JACK GLASSCOCK	Glasscock, John Wesley "Pebbly Jack" b: 7/22/1859, Wheeling, W.Va. d: 2/24/47, Wheeling, W.Va. BR/TR, 5'8", 160 lbs. Deb: 5/1/1879 M Career OF: (0-LF 0-CF 1-RF)																							
1879	Cle-N	80	325	31	68	9	3	0	29	6	24	.209	.224	.255	479	58	-14				.919	-6	*2-66,3-14	-1.5
1880	Cle-N	77	296	37	72	13	3	0	27	2	21	.243	.248	.307	556	89	-3				.891	7	*S-77	0.7
1881	Cle-N	85	335	49	86	9	5	0	33	15	8	.257	.289	.313	602	94	-1				**.911**	9	*S-79/2-6	1.1
1882	Cle-N	84	358	66	104	27	9	4	46	13	9	.291	.315	.450	765	147	19				.900	**24**	*S-83/3-1	**4.0**
1883	Cle-N	96	383	67	110	19	6	0	46	13	23	.287	.311	.368	679	107	3				**.922**	17	*S-93/2-3	2.0
1884	Cle-N	72	281	45	70	4	4	1	22	25	16	.249	.310	.302	613	91	-3				.893	27	S-69/2-3,P-2	2.3
	Cin-U	38	172	48	72	9	5	2		8		.419	.444	.564	1008	189	14				.889	1	S-36/2-2	1.3
1885	StL-N	111	446	66	125	18	3	1	40	29	10	.280	.324	.341	665	123	13				**.917**	19	*S-110/2-1	3.3
1886	StL-N	121	486	96	158	29	7	3	40	38	13	.325	.374	.432	806	154	33	38			**.906**	14	*S-120/O-1(0-0-1)	4.5
1887	Ind-N	122	524	91	183	18	7	0	40	41	8	.349	.361	.360	722	105	6	62			.906	**35**	*S-122/P-1	3.7
1888	Ind-N	113	442	63	119	17	3	1	45	14	17	.269	.302	.328	630	99	-1	48			**.901**	11	*S-110/2-3,P-1	1.3
1889	Ind-N	134	582	128	**205**	40	3	7	85	31	10	.352	.390	.467	857	136	26	57			**.915**	**36**	*S-132/2-2,P-1,M	**5.6**
1890	NY-N	124	512	91	**172**	32	9	1	66	41	8	**.336**	.395	.439	834	143	27	54			.910	22	*S-124	**4.6**
1891	NY-N	97	369	46	89	12	6	0	55	36	11	.241	.317	.306	623	85	-6	29			.913	-2	*S-97	-0.5
1892	StL-N	139	566	83	151	27	5	3	72	44	19	.267	.327	.348	675	110	7	26			.916	5	*S-139,M	1.8
1893	StL-N	48	195	32	56	8	1	1	26	25	3	.287	.382	.354	736	96	-0	20			.907	-7	S-48	-0.4
	Pit-N	66	293	49	100	7	11	1	74	17	4	.341	.385	.451	836	124	9	16			.934	12	S-66	2.0
	Yr	114	488	81	156	15	12	2	100	42	7	.320	.384	.412	796	113	9	36			.923	6	*S-114	1.6
1894	Pit-N	87	335	47	94	10	7	1	65	32	4	.281	.350	.361	712	72	-15	18			.933	9	S-86	-0.1
1895	Lou-N	18	74	9	25	3	1	1	6	3	1	.338	.387	.446	833	122	3	1			.900	2	S-13/1-5	0.4
	Was-N	25	100	20	23	2	0	0	10	7	3	.230	.300	.250	550	43	-8	3			.895	6	S-25	-0.1
	Yr	43	174	29	48	5	1	1	16	10	4	.276	.337	.333	670	76	-6	4			.897	8	S-38/1-5	0.3
Total	17	1737	7074	1164	2082	313	98	27	827	440	212	.294	.337	.374	712	112	107	372			.910	242	*S-1629/2-86,31PO	36.0
■ TROY GLAUS	Glaus, Troy b: 8/3/76, Newport Beach, Cal. BR/TR, 6'5", 220 lbs. Deb: 7/31/98																							
1998	Ana-A	48	165	19	36	9	0	1	23	15	51	.218	.283	.291	574	50	-12	1	0	0	.941	2	3-48	-0.9
1999	Ana-A	154	551	85	132	29	0	29	79	71	143	.240	.333	.450	783	98	-3	5	1	1	.954	-5	*3-153/D-1	-0.5
2000	Ana-A★	159	563	120	160	37	1	**47**	102	112	163	.284	.405	.604	1009	150	44	14	11	-1	.933	7	*3-156/S-6,D-4	4.7
Total	3	361	1279	224	328	75	1	77	204	198	357	.256	.360	.497	857	115	29	20	12	0	.942	4	3-357/S-6,D-5	3.3
■ TOMMY GLAVIANO	Glaviano, Thomas Giatano "Rabbit" b: 10/26/23, Sacramento, Cal. BR/TR, 5'9", 175 lbs. Deb: 4/19/49 Career OF: (2-LF 14-CF 1-RF)																							
1949	StL-N	87	258	32	69	16	1	6	36	41	35	.267	.380	.407	787	106	4	0			.929	14	3-73/2-7	1.7
1950	StL-N	115	410	92	117	29	2	11	44	90	74	.285	.421	.446	867	122	17	6			.935	6	*3-106/2-5,S-1	2.2
1951	StL-N	54	104	20	19	4	0	1	4	26	18	.183	.356	.250	606	66	-4	3	0	1	.972	-3	O-17(2-14-1)/2-9	-0.6
1952	StL-N	80	162	30	39	5	1	3	19	27	26	.241	.366	.340	705	97	0	0	0	0	.934	4	3-52/2-1	0.4
1953	Phi-N	53	74	17	15	1	2	3	5	24	20	.203	.410	.392	802	111	2	2	0	0	.892	-2	3-14,2-12/S-1	0.1
Total	5	389	1008	191	259	55	6	24	108	208	173	.257	.395	.395	789	108	20	11	0		.931	18	3-245/2-34,O-17C,S	3.8

YEAR	TM/L	G	AB	R	H	2B	3B	HR	RBI	BB	SO	AVG	OBP	SLG	OPS	OPS+	BR+	SB	CS	SBR	FA	FR	G/POS	TPR
■ **HARRY GLEASON** Gleason, Harry Gilbert b: 3/28/1875, Camden, N.J. d: 10/21/61, Camden, N.J. BR/TR, 5'6", 160 lbs. Deb: 9/27/01 F Career OF: (8-LF 16-CF 0-RF)																								
1901	Bos-A	1	1	0	1	0	0	0	0	0		1.000	1.000	1.000	2000	464	0	1			.667	1	/3-1	0.1
1902	Bos-A	71	240	30	54	5	5	2	25	10		.225	.265	.313	577	58	-14	6			.930	-0	3-35,O-23(8-15-0)/2-4	-1.4
1903	Bos-A	6	13	3	2	1	0	0	2	0		.154	.154	.231	385	13	-1	0			.750	-1	/3-2	-0.3
1904	StL-A	46	155	10	33	7	1	0	6	4		.213	.247	.271	518	68	-6	1			.908	-3	S-20,3-20/2-5,O-1C	-0.9
1905	StL-A	150	535	45	116	11	5	1	57	34		.217	.269	.262	530	72	-17	23			.911	-15	*3-144/2-7	-3.0
Total	5	274	944	88	206	24	11	3	90	48		.218	.263	.276	540	67	-38	31			.914	-19	3-202/O-24C,S-20,2	-5.5
■ **JACK GLEASON** Gleason, John Day b: 7/14/1854, St.Louis, Mo. d: 9/4/44, St.Louis, Mo. BR/TR, 170 lbs. Deb: 10/2/1877 F Career OF: (9-LF 1-CF 6-RF)																								
1877	StL-N	1	4	0	1	0	0	0	0	0	1	.250	.250	.250	500	61	-0				.000	-0	/O-1(0-1-0)	-0.1
1882	StL-a	78	331	53	84	10	1	2		**27**		.254	.310	.308	618	105	2				.768	2	*3-73/O-6(0-0-6),2-1	0.5
1883	StL-a	9	34	2	8	0	0	0		4		.235	.316	.235	551	76	-1				.833	0	/O-9(9-0-0),3-1	-0.1
	Lou-a	84	355	69	106	11	4	2		25		.299	.345	.369	714	140	18				.795	-33	*3-83/S-1	-1.2
	Yr	93	389	71	114	11	4	2		29		.293	.342	.357	699	134	17				.798	-33	3-84/O-9(9-0-0),S-1	-1.3
1884	StL-U	92	395	90	128	30	2	4		23		.324	.361	.441	802	137	7				.768	-6	*3-92	0.2
1885	StL-N	2	7	0	1	0	0	0	0	0	1	.143	.143	.143	286	-8	-1				.857	-0	/3-2	-0.1
1886	Phi-a	77	299	39	56	8	7	1	31	16		.187	.255	.271	526	64	-13	8			.797	-6	3-77	-1.5
Total	6	343	1425	253	384	59	14	9	31	95	2	.269	.320	.349	670	112	12	8			.781	-43	3-328/O-16L,S-1,2-1	-2.3
■ **ROY GLEASON** Gleason, Roy William b: 4/9/43, Melrose Park, Ill. BB/TR, 6'5.5", 220 lbs. Deb: 9/3/63																								
1963	LA-N	8	1	3	1	1	0	0	0	0	0	1.000	1.000	2.000	3000	795	1	0	0	0	.000	0	H	0.1
■ **BILL GLEASON** Gleason, William G. "Will" b: 11/12/1858, St.Louis, Mo. d: 7/21/32, St.Louis, Mo. BR/TR, 5'8", 170 lbs. Deb: 5/2/1882 FU																								
1882	StL-a	79	347	63	100	11	6	1		6		.288	.300	.363	663	118	5				.833	9	*S-79	1.5
1883	StL-a	98	425	81	122	21	9	2	42	15		.287	.311	.393	704	119	7				.871	-2	*S-98	0.8
1884	StL-a	110	472	97	127	21	7	1		27		.269	.325	.350	674	116	8				.867	-17	*S-110/3-1	-0.5
1885	*StL-a	112	472	79	119	9	5	3	53	29		.252	.316	.311	627	94	-3				.869	-42	*S-112	-3.7
1886	*StL-a	125	524	97	141	18	5	0	61	43		.269	.333	.323	655	101	0	19			.853	-29	*S-125	-2.2
1887	*StL-a	135	639	135	213	19	1	0	76	41		.333	.342	.323	664	78	-20	23			.875	-10	*S-135	-2.1
1888	Phi-a	123	499	55	112	10	2	0	61	12		.224	.256	.253	508	63	-20	27			.858	-14	*S-121/3-1,1-1	-2.8
1889	Lou-a	16	58	6	14	2	0	0	5	4	1	.241	.302	.276	577	66	-2	1			.822	-3	S-16	-0.4
Total	8	798	3436	613	948	111	35	7	298	177	1	.276	.313	.327	640	95	-24	70			.860	-106	S-796/3-2,1-1	-9.4
■ **KID GLEASON** Gleason, William J. b: 10/26/1866, Camden, N.J. d: 1/2/33, Philadelphia, Pa. BB/TR, 5'7", 158 lbs. Deb: 4/20/1888 FMC Career OF: (14-LF 15-CF 13-RF)																								
1888	Phi-N	24	83	4	17	2	0	0	5	3	16	.205	.233	.229	461	45	-5	3			.841	-3	P-24/O-1(0-0-1)	0.0
1889	Phi-N	30	99	11	25	5	0	0	8	8	12	.253	.308	.303	611	65	-5	4			.862	-1	P-29/O-3(0-1-0),2-2	-0.1
1890	Phi-N	63	224	22	47	3	0	0	17	12	21	.210	.250	.223	473	37	-18	10			.937	-1	P-60/2-2	-0.1
1891	Phi-N	65	214	31	53	5	2	0	17	20	17	.248	.318	.290	608	75	-6	6			.896	-6	P-53/O-9(1-8-0),S-4	-0.4
1892	StL-N	66	233	35	50	4	2	3	25	34	23	.215	.315	.288	602	87	-3	7			.934	3	P-47,O-10R/2-9,1-1	-0.2
1893	StL-N	59	199	25	51	6	4	0	20	19	8	.256	.327	.327	654	74	-8	2			.907	-0	P-48,O-11(5-0-6)/S-1	-0.3
1894	StL-N	9	28	3	7	0	1	0	1	2	1	.250	.300	.321	621	50	-2	0			.885	1	/P-8,1-1	0.0
	*Bal-N	26	86	22	30	5	1	0	17	7	2	.349	.398	.430	828	95	-1	1			.900	-2	P-21/1-1	0.0
	Yr	35	114	25	37	5	2	0	18	9	3	.325	.374	.404	777	85	-3	1			.894	-0	P-29/1-2	0.0
1895	*Bal-N	112	421	90	130	14	12	0	74	33	18	.309	.366	.399	765	95	-4	19			.899	-17	2-85,3-12/P-9,O-4L	-1.4
1896	NY-N	133	541	79	162	17	5	4	89	42	13	.299	.352	.372	724	93	-5	46			.938	3	*2-130/3-3,O-1(0-1-0)	0.3
1897	NY-N	132	543	86	172	16	4	1	106	27		.317	.353	.366	719	93	-6	44			.930	2	*2-130/S-3	0.2
1898	NY-N	150	570	78	126	8	5	0	62	39		.221	.278	.253	531	54	-33	21			.938	21	*2-144/S-6	-0.6
1899	NY-N	147	580	73	154	14	5	0	59	24		.266	.295	.307	602	67	-27	29			.946	29	*2-147	0.8
1900	NY-N	111	420	60	104	11	3	1	29	17		.248	.280	.295	575	62	-22	23			.931	14	*2-111/S-1	-0.3
1901	Det-A	135	547	82	150	16	12	3	75	41		.274	.327	.364	691	87	-10	32			.925	6	*2-135	-0.3
1902	Det-A	118	441	42	109	11	4	1	38	25		.247	.292	.297	589	62	-22	17			.941	6	*2-118	-1.5
1903	Phi-N	106	412	65	117	19	6	1	49	23		.284	.326	.367	693	101	-0	12			.959	-4	*2-102/O-4(0-2-0)	-0.4
1904	Phi-N	153	587	61	161	23	6	0	42	37		.274	.319	.334	653	106	4	17			.942	1	*2-152/3-1	0.6
1905	Phi-N	155	608	95	150	17	7	1	50	45		.247	.302	.303	604	83	-12	16			.947	-8	*2-155	-1.9
1906	Phi-N	135	494	47	112	17	2	0	34	36		.227	.281	.269	550	71	-17	17			.947	-29	*2-135	-5.1
1907	Phi-N	36	126	11	18	3	0	0	6	7		.143	.200	.167	367	15	-12	3			.979	-2	2-26/1-4,S-4,O-1C	-1.6
1908	Phi-N	2	1	0	0	0	0	0	0	0		.000	.000	.000	0	-97	-0	0			1.000	0	/2-1,O-1(1-0-0)	0.0
1912	Chi-A	1	2	0	1	0	0	0	0	0		.500	.500	.500	1000	192	0	0			1.000	-0	/2-1	0.0
Total	22	1968	7459	1022	1946	216	81	15	823	501	131	.261	.311	.318	628	78	-215	329			.938	12	*2-1585,P-299/OS31	-12.3
■ **BILLY GLEASON** Gleason, William Patrick b: 9/6/1894, Chicago, Ill. d: 1/9/57, Holyoke, Mass. BR/TR, 5'6.5", 157 lbs. Deb: 9/25/16																								
1916	Pit-N	1	2	0	0	0	0	0	0	0	0	.000	.000	.000	0	-99	-0	0			1.000	-0	/2-1	-0.1
1917	Pit-N	13	42	3	7	1	0	0	0	5	5	.167	.255	.190	446	36	-3	1			.978	-5	2-13	-0.9
1921	StL-A	26	74	6	19	0	1	0	8	6	6	.257	.329	.284	613	54	-5	0	1	-0	.960	-5	2-25	-0.9
Total	3	40	118	9	26	1	1	0	8	11	11	.220	.298	.246	543	47	-8	1	1		.966	-10	/2-39	-1.9
■ **JIM GLEESON** Gleeson, James Joseph "Gee Gee" b: 3/5/12, Kansas City, Mo. d: 5/1/96, Kansas City, Mo. BB/TR, 6'1", 191 lbs. Deb: 4/25/36 C																								
1936	Cle-A	41	139	26	36	9	2	4	12	18	17	.259	.344	.439	783	91	-2	2	1	0	.958	-2	O-33(4-0-30)	-0.5
1939	Chi-N	111	332	43	74	19	6	4	45	39	46	.223	.308	.352	661	76	-11	7			.957	-4	O-91(13-12-66)	-2.0
1940	Chi-N	129	485	76	152	39	11	5	61	54	52	.313	.389	.470	859	139	26	4			.983	3	*O-123(32-82-13)	2.4
1941	Cin-N	102	301	47	70	10	0	3	34	45	30	.233	.340	.296	636	80	-6	7			.981	-8	O-84(22-15-50)	-1.9
1942	Cin-N	9	20	3	4	0	0	0	2	2	2	.200	.304	.200	504	49	-1	0			.889	-0	/O-5(0-0-5)	-0.2
Total	5	392	1277	195	336	77	19	16	154	158	147	.263	.350	.391	741	101	5	20	1		.972	-11	O-336(71-109-164)	-2.2
■ **FRANK GLEICH** Gleich, Frank Elmer "Inch" b: 3/7/1894, Columbus, Ohio d: 3/27/49, Columbus, Ohio BL/TR, 5'11", 175 lbs. Deb: 9/17/19																								
1919	NY-A	5	4	0	1	0	0	0	1	1	0	.250	.400	.250	650	84	-0	0			.000	-2	/O-4(3-1-0)	-0.2
1920	NY-A	24	41	6	5	0	0	0	3	6	10	.122	.234	.122	356	-4	-6	0	0	0	.864	-4	O-15(9-4-2)	-1.1
Total	2	29	45	6	6	0	0	0	4	7	10	.133	.250	.133	383	4	-6	0	0		.826	-7	/O-19(12-5-2)	-1.3
■ **BOB GLENALVIN** Glenalvin, Robert J. (b: Robert J. Dowling) b: 1/17/1867, Indianapolis, Ind. d: 3/24/44, Detroit, Mich. TR, 5'9", 160 lbs. Deb: 7/12/1890																								
1890	Chi-N	66	250	43	67	10	3	4	26	19	31	.268	.337	.380	717	105	1	30			.928	-14	2-66	-1.0
1893	Chi-N	16	61	11	21	3	1	0	12	7	3	.344	.412	.426	838	125	2	7			.928	-5	2-16	-0.2
Total	2	82	311	54	88	13	4	4	38	26	34	.283	.352	.389	741	109	3	37			.928	-19	/2-82	-1.2
■ **ED GLENN** Glenn, Edward C. "Mouse" b: 9/19/1860, Richmond, Va. d: 2/10/1892, Richmond, Va. BR/TR, 5'10", 160 lbs. Deb: 8/5/1884																								
1884	Ric-a	43	175	26	43	2	4	1		5		.246	.271	.320	591	93	-1				.833	5	O-43(43-0-0)	0.2
1886	Pit-a	71	277	32	53	6	5	0	26	17		.191	.241	.249	490	54	-15	19			.865	0	O-71(71-0-0)	-1.4
1888	KC-a	3	8	0	0	0	0	0	0	0		.000	.200	.000	200	-32	-1	1			.857	-0	/O-3(3-0-0)	-0.1
	Bos-N	20	65	8	10	0	2	0	3	2	8	.154	.203	.215	418	33	-5	0			.957	2	O-19(19-0-0)/3-1	-0.3
Total	3	137	525	66	106	8	11	1	29	24	8	.202	.245	.265	510	62	-22	20			.867	7	O-136(136-0-0)/3-1	-1.6
■ **ED GLENN** Glenn, Edward D. b: 10/1875, Ohio d: 12/6/11, Ludlow, Ky. BR/TR, Deb: 9/7/1898																								
1898	Was-N	1	4	0	0	0	0	0	0	0		.000	.000	.000	0	-99	-1	0			1.000	-1	/S-1	-0.2
	NY-N	2	4	1	1	0	0	0	0	3		.250	.571	.250	821	142	1	1			.750	-3	/S-2	-0.2
	Yr	3	8	1	1	0	0	0	0	3		.125	.364	.125	489	42	-0	1			.857	-3	/S-3	-0.4
1902	Chi-N	2	7	0	0	0	0	0	0	1		.000	.125	.000	125	-63	-1	0			1.000	-1	/S-2	-0.3
Total	2	5	15	1	1	0	0	0	0	4		.067	.263	.067	330	-2	-2	1			.923	-5	/S-5	-0.7
■ **HARRY GLENN** Glenn, Harry Melville "Husky" b: 6/9/1890, Shelburn, Ind. d: 10/12/18, St.Paul, Minn. BR/TR, 6'1", 200 lbs. Deb: 4/14/15																								
1915	StL-N	6	16	1	5	0	0	0	1	3	0	.313	.421	.313	734	123	1	0			.929	-1	/C-5	0.0

YEAR	TM/L	G	AB	R	H	2B	3B	HR	RBI	BB	SO	AVG	OBP	SLG	OPS	OPS+	BR+	SB	CS	SBR	FA	FR	G/POS	TPR
■ JOHN GLENN Glenn, John b: 7/10/28, Moultrie, Ga. BR/TR, 6'3", 180 lbs. Deb: 6/16/60																								
1960	StL-N	32	31	4	8	0	1	0	5	0	9	.258	.258	.323	581	53	-2	0	0	0	1.000	-7	O-28(19-5-4)	-1.0
■ JOHN GLENN Glenn, John W. b: 1849, Rochester, N.Y. d: 11/10/1888, Sandy Hill, N.Y. BR/TR, 5'8.5", 169 lbs. Deb: 5/13/1871																								
1871	Oly-n	26	120	25	37	3	2	0	21	3	1	.308	.325	.367	692	104	1	1	1	-0	.860	1	*O-26(1-0-25)	0.2
1872	Oly-n	9	39	6	6	0	0	0	3	1	0	.154	.175	.154	329	2	-4	0	1	-0	.800	3	/O-9(9-0-0)	-0.1
	Nat-n	1	4	0	2	0	0	0	0	0	0	.500	.500	.500	1000	179	0	0	0	0	.667	-0	/O-1(0-1-0)	0.0
	Yr	10	43	6	8	0	0	0	3	1	0	.186	.205	.186	391	21	-4	0	1	-0	.791	3	O-10(9-1-0)	-0.1
1873	Was-n	39	185	39	49	8	2	1	21	3	0	.265	.277	.346	623	87	-2	2	1	0	.928	-2	*1-39	-0.2
1874	Chi-n	55	237	33	67	9	0	0	32	5	4	.283	.298	.321	618	97	-1	2	2	-0	.918	2	1-37,O-19(2-1-17)	0.2
1875	Chi-n	69	308	46	75	8	0	0	27	3	6	.244	.251	.269	520	80	-6	10	2	2	.898	-2	O-44(39-7-1),1-29	-0.4
1876	Chi-N	66	288	55	84	9	2	0	32	12	6	.292	.333	.351	685	115	3				.881	-2	*O-56(56-0-0),1-15	-0.2
1877	Chi-N	50	202	31	46	6	1	0	20	8	16	.228	.257	.267	524	58	-10				.948	0	O-36(36-0-1),1-14	-1.1
Total	5 n	199	893	149	236	28	4	1	104	15	11	.264	.276	.308	584	87	-12	15	7	1	.923	2	1-105/O-99(51-9-43)	-0.3
Total	2	116	490	86	130	15	3	0	52	20	22	.265	.301	.316	617	90	-7				.904	-2	/O-92(92-0-1),1-29	-1.3
■ JOE GLENN Glenn, Joseph Charles "Gabby" (b: Joseph Charles Gurzensky) b: 11/19/08, Dickson City, Pa. d: 5/6/85, Tunkhannock, Pa. BR/TR, 5'11", 175 lbs. Deb: 9/15/32																								
1932	NY-A	6	16	0	2	0	0	0	0	1	5	.125	.222	.125	347	-8	-3	0	0	0	1.000	-2	/C-5	-0.4
1933	NY-A	5	21	1	3	0	0	0	1	0	3	.143	.143	.143	286	-26	-4	0	0	0	1.000	-2	/C-5	-0.5
1935	NY-A	17	43	7	10	4	0	0	6	4	4	.233	.298	.326	623	65	-2	0	0	0	.984	0	C-16	-0.1
1936	NY-A	44	129	21	35	7	0	1	20	20	10	.271	.373	.349	722	82	-3	1	1	-0	.970	3	C-44	0.2
1937	NY-A	25	53	6	15	2	2	0	4	10	11	.283	.397	.396	793	100	0	0	0	0	.978	4	C-24	0.4
1938	NY-A	41	123	10	32	7	2	0	25	10	14	.260	.316	.350	665	67	-6	1	0	0	.974	0	C-40	-0.4
1939	StL-A	88	286	29	78	13	1	4	29	31	40	.273	.344	.367	711	80	-8	4	4	-1	.968	-13	C-82	-1.6
1940	Bos-A	22	47	3	6	1	0	0	4	5	7	.128	.212	.149	360	-5	-7	0	0	0	.961	-0	C-19	-0.7
Total	8	248	718	77	181	34	5	5	89	81	91	.252	.330	.334	664	69	-33	6	5	-0	.972	-10	C-235	-3.1
■ ROSS GLOAD Gload, Ross P. b: 4/5/76, Brooklyn, N.Y. BL/TL, 6'2", 210 lbs. Deb: 8/30/2000																								
2000	Chi-N	18	31	4	6	0	1	1	3	3	10	.194	.265	.355	620	56	-2	0	0	0	1.000	-1	/O-8(7-0-1),1-2	-0.4
■ NORM GLOCKSON Glockson, Norman Stanley b: 6/15/1894, Blue Island, Ill. d: 8/5/55, Maywood, Ill. BR/TR, 6'2", 200 lbs. Deb: 9/16/14																								
1914	Cin-N	7	12	0	0	0	0	0	0	1	6	.000	.077	.000	77	-74	-3	0			.923	-1	/C-7	-0.3
■ AL GLOSSOP Glossop, Alban b: 7/23/15, Christopher, Ill. d: 7/2/91, Walnut Creek, Cal. BB/TR, 6', 170 lbs. Deb: 9/23/39 Career OF: (0-LF 0-CF 1-RF)																								
1939	NY-N	10	32	3	6	0	0	1	3	4	2	.188	.278	.281	559	50	-2	0			.980	0	2-10	-0.1
1940	NY-N	27	91	16	19	3	0	4	8	10	16	.209	.294	.374	668	82	-2	1			.952	0	2-24	0.0
	Bos-N	60	148	17	35	2	1	3	14	17	22	.236	.315	.324	639	81	-4	1			.938	6	2-18,3-18/S-1	0.4
	Yr	87	239	33	54	5	1	7	22	27	38	.226	.307	.343	650	82	-6	2			.947	7	2-42,3-18/S-1	0.4
1942	Phi-N	121	454	33	102	15	1	4	40	29	35	.225	.273	.289	561	68	-20	3			.961	7	*2-118/3-1	-0.5
1943	Bro-N	87	217	28	37	9	0	3	21	28	27	.171	.268	.253	522	51	-13	0			.927	-7	S-33,2-24,3-17,/O-1R	-1.9
1946	Chi-N	4	10	2	0	0	0	0	0	1	3	.000	.231	.000	231	-32	-2	0			1.000	-2	/2-2,S-2	-0.3
Total	5	309	952	99	199	29	2	15	86	89	105	.209	.280	.291	571	66	-43	5			.954	6	2-196/S-36,3-36,O-1R	-2.4
■ BILL GLYNN Glynn, William Vincent b: 7/30/25, Sussex, N.J. BL/TL, 6', 190 lbs. Deb: 9/16/49																								
1949	Phi-N	8	10	0	2	0	0	0	1	0	3	.200	.200	.200	400	8	-1	0			1.000	0	/1-1	-0.1
1952	Cle-A	44	92	15	25	5	0	2	7	5	16	.272	.309	.391	701	101	-0	1	0	-0	.973	0	1-32	-0.1
1953	Cle-A	147	411	60	100	14	2	3	30	44	65	.243	.324	.309	633	74	-14	1	3	-1	**.993**	6	*1-135/O-2(1-0-1)	-1.6
1954	*Cle-A	111	171	19	43	3	2	5	18	12	21	.251	.301	.380	681	84	-4	3	2	-0	.987	3	1-96/O-1(0-0-1)	-0.4
Total	4	310	684	94	170	22	4	10	56	61	105	.249	.315	.336	651	79	-20	5	5		.989	9	1-264/O-3(1-0-2)	-2.2
■ JOHN GOCHNAUER Gochnauer, John Peter b: 9/12/1875, Altoona, Pa. d: 9/27/29, Altoona, Pa. BR/TR, 5'9", 160 lbs. Deb: 9/29/01																								
1901	Bro-N	3	11	1	4	0	0	0	2	1		.364	.417	.364	780	124	0	1			1.000	-1	/S-3	0.0
1902	Cle-A	127	459	45	85	16	4	0	37	38		.185	.247	.237	485	36	-39	7			.933	-3	*S-127	-3.7
1903	Cle-A	134	438	48	81	16	4	0	48	48		.185	.265	.240	505	53	-24	10			.869	-21	*S-134	-4.2
Total	3	264	908	94	170	32	8	0	87	87		.187	.258	.240	498	45	-62	18			.901	-24	S-264	-7.9
■ JOHN GODAR Godar, John Michael b: 10/25/1864, Cincinnati, Ohio d: 6/23/49, Park Ridge, Ill. BR/TR, 5'9", 170 lbs. Deb: 7/8/1892																								
1892	Bal-N	5	14	2	3	0	0	0	1	2	1	.214	.353	.214	567	70	-0	1			1.000	-0	/O-5(0-0-5)	-0.1
■ DANNY GODBY Godby, Danny Ray b: 11/4/46, Logan, W.Va. BR/TR, 6', 185 lbs. Deb: 8/10/74																								
1974	StL-N	13	13	2	2	0	0	0	1	3	4	.154	.313	.154	466	34	-1	0	0	0	1.000	1	/O-4(2-0-2)	0.0
■ JOE GODDARD Goddard, Joseph Harold b: 7/23/50, Beckley, W.Va. BR/TR, 5'11", 181 lbs. Deb: 7/31/72																								
1972	SD-N	12	35	0	7	2	0	0	2	5	9	.200	.300	.257	557	64	-2	0	0	0	.973	-2	C-12	-0.4
■ JOHN GODWIN Godwin, John Henry "Bunny" b: 3/10/1877, E.Liverpool, Ohio d: 5/5/56, E.Liverpool, Ohio BR/TR, 6', 190 lbs. Deb: 8/14/05 Career OF: (5-LF 3-CF 9-RF)																								
1905	Bos-A	15	43	4	14	1	0	0	10	3		.326	.408	.349	757	139	2	3			.950	1	/O-7(5-2-0),2-5	0.3
1906	Bos-A	66	193	11	36	2	1	0	15	6		.187	.215	.207	422	32	-15	6			.907	2	3-27,S-14,O-10R,/21	-1.4
Total	2	81	236	15	50	3	1	0	25	9		.212	.253	.233	486	53	-13	9			.935	3	/3-27,O-17R,S-14,21	-1.1
■ ED GOEBEL Goebel, Edwin b: 9/1/1899, Brooklyn, N.Y. d: 8/12/59, Brooklyn, N.Y. BR/TR, 5'11", 170 lbs. Deb: 5/13/22																								
1922	Was-A	37	59	13	16	1	0	1	3	8	16	.271	.358	.339	697	87	-1	1	1	-0	1.000	-1	O-16(2-1-13)	-0.2
■ BILLY GOECKEL Goeckel, William John b: 9/3/1871, Wilkes-Barre, Pa. d: 11/1/22, Philadelphia, Pa. BR/TL, Deb: 8/10/1899																								
1899	Phi-N	37	141	17	37	3	1	0	16	1		.262	.283	.298	581	61	-8	6			.978	-3	1-36	-1.0
■ JERRY GOFF Goff, Jerry Leroy b: 4/12/64, San Rafael, Cal. BL/TR, 6'3", 207 lbs. Deb: 5/15/90																								
1990	Mon-N	52	119	14	27	1	0	3	7	21	36	.227	.343	.311	654	84	-2	0	2	-1	.963	-1	C-38/1-3,3-3	-0.2
1992	Mon-N	3	3	0	0	0	0	0	0	0	3	.000	.000	.000	0	-99	-1	0	0	0	.000	0	/H	-0.1
1993	Pit-N	14	37	5	11	2	0	2	6	8	9	.297	.422	.514	936	149	3	0	0	0	.984	-2	C-14	0.1
1994	Pit-N	8	25	0	2	0	0	0	1	0	11	.080	.080	.080	160	-57	-6	0	0	0	.950	-1	/C-7	-0.7
1995	Hou-N	12	26	2	4	2	0	1	3	4	13	.154	.267	.346	613	64	-1	0	0	0	1.000	7	C-11	0.5
1996	Hou-N	1	4	1	2	0	0	1	2	0	1	.500	.500	1.250	1750	371	1	0	0	0	1.000	0	/C-1	0.1
Total	6	90	214	22	46	5	0	7	19	33	73	.215	.320	.336	656	80	-5	0	2	-1	.974	2	/C-71,3-3,1-3	-0.3
■ CHUCK GOGGIN Goggin, Charles Francis b: 7/7/45, Pompano Beach, Fla. BB/TR, 5'11", 175 lbs. Deb: 9/8/72 Career OF: (5-LF 0-CF 1-RF)																								
1972	Pit-N	5	7	0	2	0	0	0	0	1	1	.286	.375	.286	661	92	-0	0	0	0	1.000	0	/2-1	0.0
1973	Pit-N	1	1	1	1	0	0	0	0	0	0	1.000	1.000	1.000	2000	468	0	0	0	0	1.000	-0	/C-1	0.0
	Atl-N	64	90	18	26	5	0	0	7	9	19	.289	.354	.344	698	88	-1	0	1	-0	.938	-10	2-19/O-6L,S-5,C-1	-1.1
	Yr	65	91	19	27	5	0	0	7	9	19	.297	.360	.352	712	91	-1	0	1	-0	.938	-10	2-19/O-6L,S-5,C-2	-1.1
1974	Bos-A	2	1	0	0	0	0	0	0	0	1	.000	.000	.000	0	-93	-0	0	0	0	.667	1	/2-2	0.0
Total	3	72	99	19	29	5	0	0	7	10	21	.293	.358	.343	701	90	-1	0	1	-0	.927	-9	/2-22,O-6L,S-5,C-2	-1.1
■ MIKE GOLDEN Golden, Michael Henry b: 9/11/1851, Shirley, Mass. d: 1/11/29, Rockford, Ill. BR/TR, 5'8", 168 lbs. Deb: 5/5/1875																								
1875	Wes-n	13	46	6	6	0	0	0	1	0	3	.130	.130	.130	261	-9	-5	0	0	0	.844	-1	P-13	0.0
	Chi-n	39	155	16	40	3	0	0	14	2	10	.258	.268	.277	545	89	-2	3	2	-0	.833	-1	O-27(25-0-2),P-14	0.0
	Yr	52	201	22	46	3	0	0	15	2	13	.229	.236	.244	480	66	-7	3	2	-0	.833	-1	P-27,O-27(25-0-2)	0.0
1878	Mil-N	55	214	16	44	6	3	0	20	3	35	.206	.217	.262	478	53	-11				.831	-3	O-39C,P-22/1-1	-1.1
■ JONAH GOLDMAN Goldman, Jonah John b: 8/29/06, New York, N.Y. d: 8/17/80, Palm Beach, Fla. BR/TR, 5'7", 170 lbs. Deb: 9/22/28																								
1928	Cle-A	7	21	1	5	1	0	0	2	3	0	.238	.333	.286	619	63	-1	0	0	0	.878	0	/S-7	0.0
1930	Cle-A	111	306	32	74	18	0	1	44	28	25	.242	.312	.310	622	56	-20	3	5	-1	.945	21	S-93,3-20	0.8

YEAR	TM/L	G	AB	R	H	2B	3B	HR	RBI	BB	SO	AVG	OBP	SLG	OPS	OPS+	BR+	SB	CS	SBR	FA	FR	G/POS	TPR
1931	Cle-A	30	62	0	8	1	0	0	3	4	6	.129	.182	.145	327	-12	-10	1	1	-0	.947	14	S-30	0.5
Total	3	148	389	33	87	20	0	1	49	35	31	.224	.293	.283	576	46	-31	4	6	-1	.941	35	S-130/3-20	1.3
■ GORDON GOLDSBERRY	Goldsberry, Gordon Frederick b: 8/30/27, Sacramento, Cal. d: 2/23/96, Lake Forest, Cal. BL/TL, 6', 170 lbs. Deb: 4/20/49																							
1949	Chi-A	39	145	25	36	3	2	1	13	18	9	.248	.331	.317	649	74	-5	2	0	0	.990	-1	1-38	-0.7
1950	Chi-A	82	127	19	34	8	2	2	25	26	18	.268	.392	.409	802	108	2	0	2	-1	.989	3	1-40/O-3(1-0-2)	0.4
1951	Chi-A	10	11	4	1	0	0	0	1	2	2	.091	.231	.091	322	-11	-2	0	0	0	1.000	1	/1-8	0.0
1952	StL-A	86	227	30	52	9	3	3	17	34	37	.229	.330	.335	664	83	-5	0	2	-1	.983	-3	1-72/O-2(2-0-0)	-1.1
Total	4	217	510	78	123	20	7	6	56	80	66	.241	.344	.343	687	85	-9	2	4	-1	.987	1	1-158/O-5(3-0-2)	-1.4
■ WALT GOLDSBY	Goldsby, Walton Hugh b: 12/31/1861, Louisiana d: 1/11/14, Dallas, Tex. BL, Deb: 5/28/1884																							
1884	StL-a	5	20	2	4	0	0	0	1	0		.200	.200	.200	400	30	-2				.800	-1	/O-5(1-4-0)	-0.2
	Was-a	6	24	4	9	0	0	0	3	1		.375	.400	.375	775	174	2				.909	1	/O-6(1-3-2)	0.2
	Ric-a	11	40	4	9	1	0	0	4	1		.225	.262	.250	512	69	-1				.737	-1	O-11(2-6-3)	-0.2
	Yr	22	84	10	22	1	0	0	8	2		.262	.287	.274	561	87	-1				.800	-1	O-22(4-13-5)	-0.2
1886	Was-N	6	18	0	4	1	0	0	1	2	3	.222	.300	.278	578	81	-0	0			.818	-1	/O-6(0-5-1)	-0.2
1888	Bal-a	45	165	13	39	1	1	0	14	8		.236	.288	.255	543	76	-4	17			.903	-6	O-45(45-0-0)	-1.0
Total	3	73	267	23	65	3	1	0	23	12	3	.243	.289	.262	551	80	-5	17			.858	-8	/O-73(49-18-6)	-1.4
■ FRED GOLDSMITH	Goldsmith, Fredrick Ernest b: 5/15/1852, New Haven, Conn. d: 3/28/39, Berkley, Mich. BR/TR, 6'1", 195 lbs. Deb: 10/23/1875 U Career OF: (11-LF 16-CF 6-RF)																							
1875	NH-n	1	4	0	2	0	0	0	1	0	0	.500	.500	.500	1000	285	1	0	0	0	.700	0	/2-1	0.1
1879	Tro-N	9	38	6	9	1	0	0	2	1	3	.237	.256	.263	520	77	-1				.833	0	/P-8,O-2(0-2-0),1-1	0.0
1880	Chi-N	35	142	24	37	4	2	0	15	2	15	.261	.271	.317	588	93	-1				.968	1	P-26,O-10(0-10-0)/1-4	-0.2
1881	Chi-N	42	158	24	38	3	4	0	16	6	17	.241	.268	.310	578	78	-4				.863	5	P-39/O-3(0-1-2)	0.0
1882	Chi-N	45	183	23	42	11	1	0	19	4	29	.230	.246	.301	547	71	-6				.939	-2	P-45/1-1	0.0
1883	Chi-N	60	235	38	52	12	3	1	16	4	35	.221	.234	.311	545	59	-12				.865	1	P-46,O-16(10-3-3)/1-2	-0.4
1884	Chi-N	22	81	11	11	2	0	2	6	7	26	.136	.205	.235	439	35	-6				.774	-3	P-21/O-2(1-0-1)	0.0
	Bal-a	4	14	2	2	0	0	0		2		.143	.250	.143	393	30	-1				.889	1	/P-4,1-1	0.0
Total	6	217	851	128	191	33	10	3	74	26	125	.224	.247	.297	545	68	-32				.882	4	P-189/O-33C,1-9	-0.6
■ WALLY GOLDSMITH	Goldsmith, Wallace b: 1849, Baltimore, Md. 5'7", 146 lbs. Deb: 5/4/1871																							
1871	Kek-n	19	88	8	18	1	0	0	12	4	2	.205	.239	.216	455	31	-8	0	0	0	.767	-10	S-14/3-8,C-2	-1.2
1872	Oly-n	9	41	4	10	2	0	0	5	0	0	.244	.244	.293	537	68	-1	0	0	0	.679	-1	/S-5,2-4	-0.2
1873	Mar-n	1	4	0	0	0	0	0	0	0	0	.000	.000	.000	0	-99	-1	0	0	0	.667	-0	/2-1	-0.1
1875	Wes-n	13	51	3	6	0	0	0	1	0	2	.118	.118	.118	235	-17	-6	0	0	0	.814	-1	3-13	-0.6
Total	4 n	42	184	15	34	3	0	0	18	4	4	.185	.202	.201	403	24	-16	0	0	0	.694	-13	/3-21,S-19,2-5,C-2	-2.1
■ LONNIE GOLDSTEIN	Goldstein, Leslie Elmer b: 5/13/18, Austin, Tex. BL/TL, 6'2.5", 190 lbs. Deb: 9/11/43																							
1943	Cin-N	5	5	1	1	0	0	0	0	2	1	.200	.429	.200	629	85	0	0			1.000	-0	/1-2	0.0
1946	Cin-N	6	5	1	0	0	0	0	0	1	1	.000	.167	.000	167	-53	-1	0			.000	0	H	-0.1
Total	2	11	10	2	1	0	0	0	0	3	2	.100	.308	.100	408	20	-1	0			1.000	-0	/1-2	-0.1
■ PURNAL GOLDY	Goldy, Purnal William b: 11/28/37, Camden, N.J. BR/TR, 6'5", 200 lbs. Deb: 4/12/62																							
1962	Det-A	20	70	8	16	1	1	3	12	0	12	.229	.239	.400	639	66	-4	0	0	0	.964	-0	O-15(0-0-15)	-0.5
1963	Det-A	9	8	1	2	0	0	0	0	0	4	.250	.250	.250	500	39	-1	0	0	0	.000	0	H	-0.1
Total	2	29	78	9	18	1	1	3	12	0	16	.231	.241	.385	625	64	-4	0	0	0	.964	-0	/O-15(0-0-15)	-0.6
■ STAN GOLETZ	Goletz, Stanley "Stash" b: 5/21/18, Crescent, Ohio d: 6/7/97, Temple, Tex. BL/TL, 6'3", 200 lbs. Deb: 9/9/41																							
1941	Chi-A	5	5	0	3	0	0	0	0	0	2	.600	.600	.600	1200	221	1	0	0	0	.000	0	H	0.1
■ MIKE GOLIAT	Goliat, Mike Mitchel b: 11/5/25, Yatesboro, Pa. BR/TR, 6', 180 lbs. Deb: 8/3/49																							
1949	Phi-N	55	189	24	40	6	3	3	19	20	32	.212	.290	.323	613	66	-9	0			.969	-2	2-50/1-5	-0.9
1950	*Phi-N	145	483	49	113	13	6	13	64	53	75	.234	.314	.366	680	80	-15	3			.972	-18	*2-145	-2.4
1951	Phi-N	41	138	14	31	2	1	4	15	9	18	.225	.277	.341	618	66	-7	0	1	-0	.968	-7	2-37/3-2	-1.3
	StL-A	5	11	0	2	0	0	0	1	0	1	.182	.182	.182	364	-1	-2	0	0	0	1.000	0	/2-2	-0.1
1952	StL-A	3	4	0	0	0	0	0	0	1	1	.000	.200	.000	200	-40	-1	0	0	0	1.000	1	/2-3	0.0
Total	4	249	825	87	186	21	10	20	99	83	127	.225	.300	.348	648	73	-33	3	1		.971	-26	2-237/1-5,3-2	-4.7
■ WALT GOLVIN	Golvin, Walter George b: 2/1/1894, Hershey, Neb. d: 6/11/73, Gardena, Cal. BL/TL, 6', 165 lbs. Deb: 4/15/22																							
1922	Chi-N	2	2	0	0	0	0	0	1	0	0	.000	.000	.000	0	-98	-1	0	0	0	1.000	-0	/1-2	-0.1
■ CHRIS GOMEZ	Gomez, Christopher Cory b: 6/16/71, Los Angeles, Cal. BR/TR, 6'1", 183 lbs. Deb: 7/19/93																							
1993	Det-A	46	128	11	32	7	1	0	11	9	17	.250	.304	.320	625	69	-6	2	2	-0	.963	11	S-29,2-17/D-1	0.7
1994	Det-A	84	296	32	76	19	0	8	53	33	64	.257	.337	.402	739	89	-5	5	3	0	.981	-17	S-57,2-30	-1.5
1995	Det-A	123	431	49	96	20	2	11	50	41	96	.223	.295	.355	650	68	-21	4	1	1	.973	3	S-97,2-31/D-2	-0.8
1996	Det-A	48	128	21	31	5	0	1	16	18	20	.242	.340	.305	645	65	-6	1	1	-0	.970	3	S-47	0.0
	*SD-N	89	328	32	86	16	1	3	29	39	64	.262	.351	.345	696	90	-4	2	2	-0	.967	-6	S-89	-0.3
1997	SD-N	150	522	62	132	19	2	5	54	53	114	.253	.328	.326	653	77	-17	5	8	-2	.978	-2	*S-150	-0.7
1998	*SD-N	145	449	55	120	32	3	4	39	51	87	.267	.349	.379	727	99	-0	1	3	-1	**.980**	3	*S-143	1.4
1999	SD-N	76	234	20	59	8	1	1	15	27	49	.252	.332	.308	640	69	-11	1	2	-0	.961	3	S-75	-0.3
2000	SD-N	33	54	4	12	0	0	0	3	7	5	.222	.311	.222	534	40	-5	0	0	0	.928	4	S-17/2-3	0.1
Total	8	794	2570	286	644	126	10	33	270	278	516	.251	.330	.346	676	80	-73	21	22	-3	.972	3	S-704/2-81,D-3	-1.4
■ CHILE GOMEZ	Gomez, Jose Luis (Gonzales) b: 5/23/09, Villa Union, Mex. d: 12/1/92, Nuevo Laredo, Mex. BR/TR, 5'10", 165 lbs. Deb: 7/27/35																							
1935	Phi-N	67	222	24	51	3	0	0	16	17	34	.230	.285	.243	528	39	-18	2			.948	12	S-36,2-32	-0.2
1936	Phi-N	108	332	24	77	4	1	0	28	14	32	.232	.265	.250	515	36	-29	0			.948	18	2-71,S-40	-0.5
1942	Was-A	25	73	8	14	2	2	0	6	9	7	.192	.280	.274	554	57	-4	1	0	0	.973	-1	2-23/3-1	-0.4
Total	3	200	627	56	142	9	3	0	50	40	73	.226	.274	.250	524	39	-52	3	0		.954	29	2-126/S-76,3-1	-1.1
■ LEO GOMEZ	Gomez, Leonardo (Velez) b: 3/2/66, Canovanas, P.R. BR/TR, 6', 208 lbs. Deb: 9/17/90																							
1990	Bal-A	12	39	3	9	0	0	0	1	8	7	.231	.362	.231	592	71	-1	0	0	0	.886	-2	3-12	-0.3
1991	Bal-A	118	391	40	91	17	2	16	45	40	82	.233	.307	.409	716	100	-1	1	1	-0	.972	-13	*3-105,D-10/1-3	-1.4
1992	Bal-A	137	468	62	124	24	0	17	64	63	78	.265	.362	.425	787	117	12	2	3	-1	.951	-13	*3-137	-0.2
1993	Bal-A	71	244	30	48	7	0	10	25	32	60	.197	.297	.348	646	70	-11	0	1	-0	.951	6	3-70/D-1	-0.5
1994	Bal-A	84	285	46	78	20	0	15	56	41	55	.274	.371	.502	873	116	7	0	0	0	.975	4	3-78/1-1,D-5	1.0
1995	Bal-A	53	127	16	30	5	0	4	12	18	23	.236	.340	.370	710	83	-3	0	1	-0	.978	2	3-44/1-3,D-5	-0.1
1996	Chi-N	136	362	44	86	19	0	17	56	53	94	.238	.346	.431	777	101	1	1	4	-1	**.972**	-5	*3-124/1-8,S-1	-0.5
Total	7	611	1916	241	466	92	2	79	259	255	399	.243	.340	.417	757	101	4	4	10	-3	.962	-22	3-570/D-21,1-15,S-1	-2.0
■ LUIS GOMEZ	Gomez, Luis (Sanchez) b: 8/19/51, Guadalajara, Mex. BR/TR, 5'9", 150 lbs. Deb: 4/28/74 Career OF: (0-LF 2-CF 0-RF)																							
1974	Min-A	82	168	18	35	1	0	0	3	12	16	.208	.261	.214	475	37	-13	2	3	-1	.960	20	S-74/2-2,D-1	1.3
1975	Min-A	89	72	7	10	0	0	0	5	4	12	.139	.184	.139	323	-7	-10	0	2	-1	.975	20	S-70/2-6,D-7	1.1
1976	Min-A	38	57	5	11	1	0	0	3	3	3	.193	.233	.211	444	30	-5	1	0	0	.988	7	S-24/2-8,3-4,O-1C,D	0.4
1977	Min-A	32	65	6	16	4	2	0	11	4	9	.246	.290	.369	659	79	-2	0	0	0	.983	4	2-19/S-7,3-4,O-1C,D	0.2
1978	Tor-A	153	413	39	92	7	3	0	32	34	41	.223	.282	.254	536	51	-26	2	10	-3	.976	-10	*S-153	-2.5
1979	Tor-A	59	163	11	39	7	0	0	11	6	17	.239	.266	.282	548	48	-12	1	0	0	1.000	4	3-22,2-20,S-15	-0.6
1980	Atl-N	121	278	18	53	6	0	0	24	17	27	.191	.240	.212	452	26	-27	0	4	-1	.968	12	*S-119	-0.7
1981	Atl-N	35	35	4	7	0	0	0	1	6	4	.200	.317	.200	517	48	-2	0	1	-0	.895	-3	S-21/3-9,2-3,P-1	-0.5
Total	8	609	1251	108	263	26	5	0	90	86	129	.210	.262	.239	501	40	-98	6	22	-6	.970	54	S-483/2-58,3-39,DOP	-1.3
■ PRESTON GOMEZ	Gomez, Pedro (Martinez) b: 4/20/23, Preston, Cuba BR/TR, 5'11", 170 lbs. Deb: 5/5/44 MC																							
1944	Was-A	8	7	2	2	1	0	0	2	0	4	.286	.286	.429	714	107	0	0	0	0	1.000	-1	/2-2,S-2	-0.1

YEAR	TM/L	G	AB	R	H	2B	3B	HR	RBI	BB	SO	AVG	OBP	SLG	OPS	OPS+	BR+	SB	CS	SBR	FA	FR	G/POS	TPR
■ **RANDY GOMEZ**	Gomez, Randell Scott b: 2/4/57, San Mateo, Cal. BR/TR, 5'10", 185 lbs. Deb: 8/21/84																							
1984	SF-N	14	30	0	5	1	0	0	0	8	3	.167	.342	.200	542	57	-1	0	0	0	.951	3	C-14	0.3
■ **JESSE GONDER**	Gonder, Jesse Lemar b: 1/20/36, Monticello, Ark. BL/TR, 5'10", 190 lbs. Deb: 9/23/60																							
1960	NY-A	7	7	1	2	0	0	1	3	1	1	.286	.375	.714	1089	199	1	0	0	0	1.000	1	/C-1	0.2
1961	NY-A	15	12	2	4	1	0	0	3	3	1	.333	.467	.417	883	146	1	0	0	0	.000	0	H	0.1
1962	Cin-N	4	4	0	0	0	0	0	0	0	3	.000	.000	.000	0	-97	-1	0	0	0	.000	0	H	-0.1
1963	Cin-N	31	32	5	10	2	0	3	5	1	12	.313	.333	.656	990	172	3	0	0	0	1.000	1	/C-7	0.4
	NY-N	42	126	12	38	4	0	3	15	6	25	.302	.333	.405	738	110	1	1	2	-0	.978	-14	C-31	-1.3
	Yr	73	158	17	48	6	0	6	20	7	37	.304	.333	.456	789	122	4	1	2	-0	.981	-13	C-38	-0.9
1964	NY-N	131	341	28	92	11	1	7	35	29	65	.270	.331	.370	700	99	-0	0	0	0	.979	-1	C-97	0.3
1965	NY-N	53	105	6	25	4	0	4	9	11	20	.238	.310	.390	701	100	-0	0	0	0	.992	-5	C-31	-0.4
	Mil-N	31	53	2	8	2	0	1	5	4	9	.151	.211	.245	456	28	-5	0	0	0	.989	5	C-13	0.0
	Yr	84	158	8	33	6	0	5	14	15	29	.209	.277	.342	619	75	-5	0	0	0	.991	-0	C-44	-0.4
1966	Pit-N	59	160	13	36	3	1	7	16	12	39	.225	.287	.387	675	85	-3	0	0	0	.978	-2	C-52	-0.3
1967	Pit-N	22	36	4	5	1	0	0	3	5	9	.139	.279	.167	446	30	-3	0	0	0	.971	-0	C-18	-0.3
Total	8	395	876	73	220	28	2	26	94	72	184	.251	.312	.377	689	94	-7	1	2	-0	.981	-15	C-250	-1.4
■ **DAN GONZALES**	Gonzales, Daniel David b: 9/30/53, Whittier, Cal. BL/TR, 6'1", 195 lbs. Deb: 4/7/79																							
1979	Det-A	7	18	1	4	1	0	0	2	0	2	.222	.222	.278	500	33	-2	1	0	0	1.000	-1	/O-3(0-0-3),D-1	-0.2
1980	Det-A	2	7	1	1	0	0	0	0	0	1	.143	.143	.143	286	-21	-1	0	0	0	.750	0	/O-1(1-0-0),D-1	-0.1
Total	2	9	25	2	5	1	0	0	2	0	3	.200	.200	.240	440	18	-3	1	0	0	.857	-1	/O-4(1-0-3),D-2	-0.3
■ **LARRY GONZALES**	Gonzales, Lawrence Christopher b: 3/28/67, West Covina, Cal. BR/TR, 6'3", 200 lbs. Deb: 6/13/93																							
1993	Cal-A	2	2	0	1	0	0	0	1	1	0	.500	.667	.500	1167	212	0	0	0	0	1.000	-0	/C-2	0.0
■ **RENE GONZALES**	Gonzales, Rene Adrian b: 9/3/60, Austin, Tex. BR/TR, 6'3", 201 lbs. Deb: 7/27/84 Career OF: (1-LF 0-CF 2-RF)																							
1984	Mon-N	29	30	5	7	1	0	0	2	2	5	.233	.303	.267	570	64	-1	0	0	0	.957	1	S-27	0.0
1986	Mon-N	11	26	1	3	0	0	0	0	2	7	.115	.179	.115	294	-17	-4	0	2	-1	1.000	2	/S-6,3-5	-0.3
1987	Bal-A	37	60	14	16	2	1	1	7	3	11	.267	.302	.383	685	82	-2	1	0	0	.963	6	3-29/2-6,S-1	0.4
1988	Bal-A	92	237	13	51	6	0	2	15	13	32	.215	.265	.266	531	50	-16	2	0	0	.966	15	3-80,2-14/S-2,1O	0.0
1989	Bal-A	71	166	16	36	4	0	1	11	12	30	.217	.270	.259	529	51	-11	5	3	0	.978	-1	2-54,3-17/S-1	-1.1
1990	Bal-A	67	103	13	22	3	1	1	12	12	14	.214	.296	.291	587	67	-4	1	2	-0	.994	9	2-43,3-16/S-9,O-1R	0.5
1991	*Tor-A	71	118	16	23	3	0	1	6	12	22	.195	.291	.246	537	48	-8	0	0	0	.973	10	S-36,3-26,2-11,/1-2	0.4
1992	Cal-A	104	329	47	91	17	1	7	38	41	46	.277	.364	.398	762	113	6	7	4	0	.954	5	3-53,2-42,1-13,/S-8	1.3
1993	Cal-A	118	335	34	84	17	0	2	31	49	45	.251	.348	.319	667	78	-9	5	5	-1	.956	-0	3-79,1-31/S-5,2P	-1.1
1994	Cle-A	22	23	6	8	1	1	1	5	5	3	.348	.464	.609	1073	173	3	2	0	0	.952	3	3-13/1-4,S-4,2-1	0.5
1995	Cal-A	30	18	1	6	1	0	1	3	0	4	.333	.333	.556	889	127	1	0	0	0	1.000	2	3-18/2-6,S-1,D-1	0.2
1996	*Tex-A	51	92	19	20	4	0	2	5	10	11	.217	.294	.326	620	54	-7	0	0	0	.989	6	1-23,3-15,S-10,/2O	-0.1
1997	Col-N	2	2	0	1	0	0	0	1	0	0	.500	.500	.500	1000	133	0	0	0	0	.000	0	/3-1	0.0
Total	13	705	1539	185	368	59	4	19	136	161	230	.239	.316	.320	636	75	-51	23	16	-1	.957	55	3-352,2-186,S/1ODP	0.7
■ **ALEX GONZALEZ**	Gonzalez, Alexander b: 2/15/77, Cagua, Ven. BR/TR, 6', 170 lbs. Deb: 8/25/98																							
1998	Fla-N	25	86	11	13	2	0	3	7	9	30	.151	.240	.279	519	38	-8	0	0	0	.978	-4	S-25	-1.0
1999	Fla-N★	136	560	81	155	28	8	14	59	15	113	.277	.310	.430	740	90	-11	3	5	-1	.955	-12	*S-135	-1.2
2000	Fla-N	109	385	35	77	17	4	7	42	13	77	.200	.230	.319	549	39	-38	7	1	1	.957	-3	*S-104	-2.9
Total	3	270	1031	127	245	47	12	24	108	37	220	.238	.274	.376	651	66	-57	10	6	0	.958	-18	S-264	-5.1
■ **ALEX GONZALEZ**	Gonzalez, Alexander Scott b: 4/8/73, Miami, Fla. BR/TR, 6', 180 lbs. Deb: 4/4/94																							
1994	Tor-A	15	53	7	8	3	1	0	1	4	17	.151	.224	.245	469	21	-6	3	0	1	.918	1	S-15	-0.4
1995	Tor-A	111	367	51	89	19	4	10	42	44	114	.243	.325	.398	723	88	-7	4	4	-1	.957	-29	S-97/3-9,D-3	-2.7
1996	Tor-A	147	527	64	124	30	5	14	64	45	127	.235	.302	.391	692	74	-23	16	6	1	.973	23	*S-147	1.3
1997	Tor-A	126	426	46	102	23	2	12	35	34	94	.239	.303	.387	691	78	-14	15	6	1	**.986**	0	*S-125	-0.2
1998	Tor-A	158	568	70	136	28	1	13	51	28	121	.239	.282	.361	643	66	-30	21	6	3	.976	-11	*S-158	-2.3
1999	Tor-A	38	154	22	45	13	0	2	12	16	23	.292	.370	.416	786	98	0	4	2	0	.980	12	S-37/D-1	1.4
2000	Tor-A	141	527	68	133	31	2	15	69	43	113	.252	.314	.404	718	79	-18	4	4	-1	.975	-7	*S-141	-1.2
Total	7	736	2622	328	637	147	15	66	274	214	609	.243	.306	.386	692	76	-98	67	28	5	.973	-12	S-720/3-9,D-4	-4.1
■ **TONY GONZALEZ**	Gonzalez, Andres Antonio (Gonzalez) b: 8/28/36, Central Cunagua, Cuba BL/TR, 5'9", 170 lbs. Deb: 4/12/60																							
1960	Cin-N	39	99	10	21	5	1	3	14	4	27	.212	.250	.374	624	67	-5	1	0	0	.957	-4	O-31(1-0-30)	-0.9
	Phi-N	78	241	27	72	17	5	6	33	11	47	.299	.337	.485	823	122	6	2	2	-0	.981	-1	O-67(3-61-5)	0.3
	Yr	117	340	37	93	22	6	9	47	15	74	.274	.312	.453	765	106	2	3	2	-0	.975	-4	O-98(4-61-35)	-0.6
1961	Phi-N	126	426	58	118	16	8	12	58	49	66	.277	.360	.437	796	112	8	15	5	2	.984	-1	*O-118(1-86-34)	0.3
1962	Phi-N	118	437	76	132	16	4	20	63	40	82	.302	.372	.494	867	134	21	17	8	1	**1.000**	6	*O-114(0-114-1)	2.4
1963	Phi-N	155	555	78	170	36	12	4	66	53	68	.306	.375	.436	811	134	25	13	8	0	.986	-6	*O-151(56-107-9)	1.5
1964	Phi-N	131	421	55	117	25	3	4	40	44	74	.278	.355	.380	735	108	6	0	5	-2	**.996**	1	*O-119(6-114-0)	0.2
1965	Phi-N	108	370	48	109	19	1	13	41	31	52	.295	.354	.457	811	129	14	3	4	-1	.983	-6	*O-104(53-60-2)	0.3
1966	Phi-N	132	384	53	110	20	4	6	40	26	60	.286	.337	.406	743	105	3	2	6	-2	.986	-1	*O-121(73-47-4)	-0.4
1967	Phi-N	149	508	74	172	23	9	9	59	47	58	.339	.400	.472	872	147	32	10	9	-1	**.993**	3	*O-143(105-29-16)	3.1
1968	Phi-N	121	416	45	110	13	4	3	38	40	42	.264	.339	.337	676	103	3	6	5	-0	.979	-4	*O-117(19-98-4)	-0.6
1969	SD-N	53	182	17	41	4	0	2	8	19	24	.225	.309	.280	589	69	-7	1	0	0	.975	5	O-49(40-11-3)	-0.5
	*Atl-N	89	320	51	94	15	2	10	50	27	22	.294	.358	.447	805	124	10	3	1	0	.989	2	O-82(35-49-0)	0.9
	Yr	142	502	68	135	19	2	12	58	46	46	.269	.340	.386	726	104	3	4	1	1	.983	6	*O-131(75-60-3)	0.4
1970	Atl-N	123	430	57	114	18	2	7	55	46	45	.265	.347	.365	712	86	-7	3	5	-1	.987	-3	*O-119(3-116-0)	-1.4
	Cal-A	26	92	9	28	2	0	1	12	2	11	.304	.326	.359	685	92	-1	3	2	-0	.960	-1	O-24(0-23-1)	-0.3
1971	Cal-A	111	314	32	77	9	2	3	38	28	28	.245	.313	.315	628	84	-7	0	1	-0	.987	-6	O-88(67-18-9)	-1.9
Total	12	1559	5195	690	1485	238	57	103	615	467	706	.286	.353	.413	766	114	100	79	61	-4	.987	-12	*O-1447(462-933-118)	3.0
■ **DENNY GONZALEZ**	Gonzalez, Denio Mariano (Manzueta) b: 7/22/63, Sabana Grande De Boya, D.R. BR/TR, 5'11", 185 lbs. Deb: 8/6/84 Career OF: (16-LF 0-CF 0-RF)																							
1984	Pit-N	26	82	9	15	3	1	0	4	7	21	.183	.247	.244	491	38	-7	1	1	-0	1.000	1	3-11,S-10/O-3(3-0-0)	-0.5
1985	Pit-N	35	124	11	28	4	0	4	12	13	27	.226	.299	.355	654	83	-3	2	4	-1	.894	-4	3-21,O-13(13-0-0)/2-6	-0.9
1987	Pit-N	5	7	1	0	0	0	0	0	1	2	.000	.125	.000	125	-63	-2	0	0	0	1.000	-1	/S-1	-0.2
1988	Pit-N	24	32	5	6	1	0	0	1	6	10	.188	.316	.219	535	57	-2	0	0	0	1.000	0	S-14/2-4,3-2	-0.1
1989	Cle-A	8	17	3	5	1	0	0	1	0	4	.294	.333	.353	686	92	-0	0	0	0	.000	-0	/3-1,D-6	-0.1
Total	5	98	262	29	54	9	1	4	18	27	64	.206	.283	.294	577	62	-13	3	5	-1	.925	-4	/3-35,S-25,O-16L,2D	-1.8
■ **EUSEBIO GONZALEZ**	Gonzalez, Eusebio Miguel (Lopez) "Papo" b: 7/13/1892, Havana, Cuba d: 2/14/76, Havana, Cuba BR/TR, 5'10", 165 lbs. Deb: 7/26/18																							
1918	Bos-A	3	5	2	2	0	1	0	0	1	1	.400	.571	.800	1371	319	1	0			1.000	-1	/S-2,3-1	0.1
■ **FERNANDO GONZALEZ**	Gonzalez, Jose Fernando (Quinones) b: 6/19/50, Arecibo, P.R. BR/TR, 5'10", 170 lbs. Deb: 9/15/72 Career OF: (15-LF 0-CF 1-RF)																							
1972	Pit-N	3	2	0	0	0	0	0	0	0	2	.000	.000	.000	0	-99	-1	0	0	0	.500	0	/3-1	-0.1
1973	Pit-N	37	49	5	11	0	1	1	5	1	11	.224	.255	.327	581	62	-3	0	0	0	.923	-1	/3-5	-0.4
1974	KC-A	9	21	1	3	1	0	0	2	0	4	.143	.143	.190	333	-5	-3	1	0	0	1.000	-0	/3-8,D-1	-0.3
	NY-A	51	121	11	26	5	1	1	7	7	7	.215	.258	.298	555	60	-6	0	0	0	.982	2	2-42/3-7,S-3	-0.2
	Yr	60	142	12	29	6	1	1	9	7	11	.204	.242	.282	523	50	-9	1	0	0	.982	2	2-42,3-15/S-3,D-1	-0.5
1977	Pit-N	80	181	17	50	10	0	4	27	13	21	.276	.325	.398	723	90	-3	3	3	-0	.972	-8	3-37,O-16L/2-6,S-2	-1.2
1978	Pit-N	9	21	2	4	1	0	0	0	2	2	.190	.227	.238	465	29	-2	0	0	0	.923	-4	/2-4,3-3	-0.7
	SD-N	101	320	27	80	10	2	2	29	18	32	.250	.290	.313	602	74	-12	4	4	-1	.982	0	2-94	-0.8
	Yr	110	341	29	84	11	2	2	29	19	35	.246	.286	.308	594	71	-14	4	4	-1	.981	-4	2-98/3-3	-1.5
1979	SD-N	114	323	22	70	13	3	9	34	18	34	.217	.258	.359	617	71	-15	0	0	0	.976	-14	*2-103/3-3	-2.4
Total	6	404	1038	85	244	40	7	17	104	58	114	.235	.276	.336	612	71	-43	8	7	-1	.979	-24	2-249/3-64,O-16L,SD	-6.1

■ **JOSE GONZALEZ** Gonzalez, Jose Rafael (Gutierrez) b: 11/23/64, Puerto Plata, D.R. BR/TR, 6'2", 196 lbs. Deb: 9/2/85 Career OF: (100-LF 164-CF 132-RF)

YEAR	TM/L	G	AB	R	H	2B	3B	HR	RBI	BB	SO	AVG	OBP	SLG	OPS	OPS+	BR+	SB	CS	SBR	FA	FR	G/POS	TPR
1985	LA-N	23	11	6	3	2	0	0	0	1	3	.273	.333	.455	788	122	0	1	1	-0	1.000	-6	O-18(5-6-8)	-0.6
1986	LA-N	57	93	15	20	5	1	2	6	7	29	.215	.270	.355	625	76	-3	4	3	-0	.924	-10	O-57(0-49-8)	-1.5
1987	LA-N	19	16	2	3	2	0	0	0	0	2	.188	.235	.313	548	45	-1	5	0	1	1.000	-1	O-16(8-5-3)	-0.2
1988	*LA-N	37	24	7	2	1	0	0	0	2	10	.083	.154	.125	279	-20	-4	3	0	1	.938	-8	O-24(9-9-9)	-1.2
1989	LA-N	95	261	31	70	11	2	3	18	23	53	.268	.327	.360	688	98	-1	9	3	1	.968	-0	O-87(4-55-34)	-0.1
1990	LA-N	106	99	15	23	5	3	2	8	6	27	.232	.283	.404	687	89	-2	3	1	0	1.000	-22	O-81(43-18-25)	-2.5
1991	LA-N	42	28	3	0	0	0	0	0	2	9	.000	.067	.000	67	-82	-7	0	0	0	1.000	-7	O-27(12-1-15)	-1.4
	Pit-N	16	20	2	2	0	0	1	3	0	6	.100	.100	.250	350	-5	-3	0	0	0	1.000	-1	O-14(3-6-5)	-0.5
	Yr	58	48	5	2	0	0	1	3	2	15	.042	.080	.104	184	-50	-10	0	0	0	1.000	-8	O-41(15-7-20)	-1.9
	Cle-A	33	69	10	11	2	1	1	4	11	27	.159	.284	.261	545	51	-4	8	0	2	.981	-3	O-32(5-10-17)	-0.6
1992	Cal-A	33	55	4	10	2	0	0	2	7	20	.182	.274	.218	492	39	-4	0	1	-0	1.000	-4	O-22(11-5-8)/D-1	-0.9
Total	8	461	676	95	144	30	7	9	42	60	186	.213	.279	.318	597	69	-29	33	9	4	.972	-62	O-378C/D-1	-9.5

■ **JUAN GONZALEZ** Gonzalez, Juan Alberto (Vazquez) b: 10/20/69, Arecibo, P.R. BR/TR, 6'3", 210 lbs. Deb: 9/1/89 Career OF: (366-LF 252-CF 492-RF)

YEAR	TM/L	G	AB	R	H	2B	3B	HR	RBI	BB	SO	AVG	OBP	SLG	OPS	OPS+	BR+	SB	CS	SBR	FA	FR	G/POS	TPR
1989	Tex-A	24	60	6	9	3	0	1	7	6	17	.150	.227	.250	477	34	-5	0	0	0	.964	-2	O-24(1-24-0)	-0.7
1990	Tex-A	25	90	11	26	7	1	4	12	2	18	.289	.319	.522	841	131	3	0	1	-0	1.000	-1	O-16(1-12-4)/D-9	0.1
1991	Tex-A	142	545	78	144	34	1	27	102	42	118	.264	.323	.479	802	121	13	4	4	-1	.981	-19	*O-136(92-93-8)/D-4	-0.9
1992	Tex-A	155	584	77	152	24	2	**43**	109	35	143	.260	.308	.529	837	135	23	0	1	-0	.975	5	*O-148(31-123-1)/D-4	2.5
1993	Tex-A★	140	536	105	166	33	1	**46**	118	37	99	.310	.369	**.632**	1001	170	49	4	1	1	.985	5	*O-129(129-0-0),D-10	4.7
1994	Tex-A	107	422	57	116	18	4	19	85	30	66	.275	.333	.472	805	105	2	6	4	-0	.991	7	*O-107(107-0-0)	0.5
1995	Tex-A	90	352	57	104	20	2	27	82	17	66	.295	.328	.594	922	131	13	0	0	0	1.000	0	D-83/O-5(5-0-0)	0.8
1996	*Tex-A	134	541	89	170	33	2	47	144	45	82	.314	.370	.643	1013	142	32	2	0	0	.988	-4	*O-102(0-0-102),D-32	1.9
1997	Tex-A	133	533	87	158	24	3	42	131	33	107	.296	.341	.589	930	130	20	0	0	0	.971	3	D-69,O-64(0-0-64)	1.5
1998	*Tex-A★	154	606	110	193	**50**	2	45	**157**	46	126	.318	.372	.630	1003	148	40	2	1	0	.982	0	*O-116(0-0-116),D-38	3.0
1999	*Tex-A	144	562	114	183	36	1	39	128	51	105	.326	.386	.601	987	140	33	3	3	-0	.983	-4	*O-131(0-0-131),D-16	1.8
2000	Det-A	115	461	69	133	30	2	22	67	32	84	.289	.337	.505	843	113	7	1	2	-0	.992	-1	O-66(0-0-66),D-48	-0.1
Total	12	1363	5292	860	1554	312	21	362	1142	376	1031	.294	.346	.566	912	134	231	22	17	-1	.982	-12	*O-1044R,D-313	15.1

■ **JULIO GONZALEZ** Gonzalez, Julio Cesar (Hernandez) b: 12/25/52, Caguas, P.R. BR/TR, 5'11", 165 lbs. Deb: 4/8/77

YEAR	TM/L	G	AB	R	H	2B	3B	HR	RBI	BB	SO	AVG	OBP	SLG	OPS	OPS+	BR+	SB	CS	SBR	FA	FR	G/POS	TPR
1977	Hou-N	110	383	34	94	18	3	1	27	19	45	.245	.288	.316	604	68	-18	3	3	-0	.921	-26	S-63,2-45	-3.6
1978	Hou-N	78	223	24	52	3	1	1	16	8	31	.233	.263	.269	532	53	-14	6	1	1	.983	-20	2-54,S-17/3-4	-3.2
1979	Hou-N	68	181	16	45	5	2	0	10	5	14	.249	.280	.298	579	62	-10	2	1	0	.987	1	2-32,S-21/3-9	-0.5
1980	Hou-N	40	52	5	6	1	0	0	1	1	8	.115	.132	.135	267	-28	-9	1	0	0	1.000	3	S-16,3-11/2-2	-0.5
1981	StL-N	20	22	2	7	1	0	1	3	1	3	.318	.348	.500	848	135	1	0	0	0	1.000	1	/S-5,2-4,3-2	0.2
1982	StL-N	42	87	9	21	3	2	1	7	1	24	.241	.258	.356	615	70	-4	1	1	-0	.907	-1	3-21/2-9,S-1	-0.5
1983	Det-A	12	21	0	3	1	0	0	2	1	7	.143	.182	.190	372	3	-3	0	0	0	.889	3	/S-6,2-5,3-1	0.1
Total	7	370	969	90	228	32	8	4	66	36	132	.235	.269	.297	566	59	-57	13	6	1	.976	-39	2-151,S-129/3-48	-8.0

■ **LUIS GONZALEZ** Gonzalez, Luis Emilio b: 9/3/67, Tampa, Fla. BL/TR, 6'2", 180 lbs. Deb: 9/4/90 Career OF: (1360-LF 9-CF 0-RF)

YEAR	TM/L	G	AB	R	H	2B	3B	HR	RBI	BB	SO	AVG	OBP	SLG	OPS	OPS+	BR+	SB	CS	SBR	FA	FR	G/POS	TPR
1990	Hou-N	12	21	1	4	2	0	0	0	2	5	.190	.261	.286	547	52	-1	0	0	0	1.000	2	/3-4,1-2	0.1
1991	Hou-N	137	473	51	120	28	9	13	69	40	101	.254	.322	.433	756	117	10	10	7	-0	.984	13	*O-133(133-0-0)	1.9
1992	Hou-N	122	387	40	94	19	3	10	55	24	52	.243	.291	.385	676	94	-5	7	7	-1	.993	15	*O-111(111-0-0)	0.7
1993	Hou-N	154	540	82	162	34	3	15	72	47	83	.300	.367	.457	824	124	18	20	9	1	.978	20	*O-149(149-0-0)	3.5
1994	Hou-N	112	392	57	107	29	4	8	67	49	57	.273	.358	.429	787	110	6	15	13	-1	.991	12	*O-111(111-0-0)	1.3
1995	Hou-N	56	209	35	54	10	4	6	35	18	30	.258	.326	.431	757	105	1	1	3	-1	.980	2	O-55(55-0-0)	0.0
	Chi-N	77	262	34	76	19	4	7	34	39	33	.290	.388	.473	861	128	12	5	5	-1	.978	10	O-76(74-6-0)	1.9
	Yr	133	471	69	130	29	8	13	69	57	63	.276	.361	.454	816	118	13	6	8	-1	.978	12	*O-131(129-6-0)	1.9
1996	Chi-N	146	483	70	131	30	4	15	79	61	49	.271	.358	.443	801	107	5	9	6	-0	.988	3	*O-139(139-0-0)/1-2	0.4
1997	*Hou-N	152	550	78	142	31	2	10	68	71	67	.258	.348	.376	725	93	-4	10	7	-0	.982	9	*O-146(146-0-0)/1-1	0.0
1998	Det-A	154	547	84	146	35	5	23	71	57	62	.267	.345	.475	820	110	7	12	7	0	.988	-3	*O-132(132-3-0),D-19	0.0
1999	*Ari-N★	153	614	112	**206**	45	4	26	111	66	63	.336	.406	.549	955	138	36	9	5	0	.983	10	*O-148(148-0-0)/D-4	3.9
2000	Ari-N	162	618	106	192	47	2	31	114	78	85	.311	.398	.544	942	134	33	2	4	-1	.990	9	*O-162(162-0-0)	3.3
Total	11	1437	5096	750	1434	329	44	164	775	552	687	.281	.359	.460	819	116	117	100	73	-4	.985	102	*O-1362L/D-23,1-5,3	17.0

■ **MIKE GONZALEZ** Gonzalez, Miguel Angel (Cordero) b: 9/24/1890, Havana, Cuba d: 2/19/77, Havana, Cuba BR/TR, 6'1", 200 lbs. Deb: 9/28/12 MC

YEAR	TM/L	G	AB	R	H	2B	3B	HR	RBI	BB	SO	AVG	OBP	SLG	OPS	OPS+	BR+	SB	CS	SBR	FA	FR	G/POS	TPR
1912	Bos-N	1	2	0	0	0	0	0	0	1	1	.000	.333	.000	333	-5	-0	0			.875	1	/C-1	0.1
1914	Cin-N	95	176	19	41	6	0	0	10	13	16	.233	.293	.267	560	65	-7	2			.954	10	C-83	0.8
1915	StL-N	51	97	12	22	2	2	0	10	8	9	.227	.306	.289	594	80	-2	4	2	0	.992	3	C-32/1-8	0.3
1916	StL-N	118	331	33	79	15	4	0	29	28	18	.239	.304	.308	612	89	-4	5			.981	7	C-93,1-13	1.1
1917	StL-N	106	290	28	76	8	1	1	28	22	24	.262	.316	.307	623	94	-2	12			.977	0	C-68,1-18/O-1(0-0-1)	0.4
1918	StL-N	117	349	33	88	13	4	3	20	39	30	.252	.327	.338	665	107	3	14			.978	-1	*C-100/O-5(1-1-3),1-2	1.2
1919	NY-N	58	158	18	30	6	0	0	8	20	9	.190	.293	.228	521	58	-7	3			.962	-3	C-52/1-4	-0.7
1920	NY-N	11	13	1	3	0	0	0	0	3	1	.231	.375	.231	606	77	-0	1	0	0	1.000	-1	/C-8	0.0
1921	NY-N	13	24	3	9	1	0	0	1	0	0	.375	.400	.417	817	116	1	0	0	0	.981	-0	/1-6,C-2	0.0
1924	StL-N	120	402	34	119	27	1	3	53	24	22	.296	.337	.391	728	96	-2	1	5	-2	.986	-7	*C-119	-0.3
1925	StL-N	22	71	9	22	3	0	0	4	6	2	.310	.380	.352	732	86	-1	1	2	-0	.982	4	C-22	0.4
	Chi-N	70	197	26	52	13	1	3	18	13	15	.264	.316	.386	702	77	-7	2	1	0	.989	1	C-50/1-9	-0.4
	Yr	92	268	35	74	16	1	3	22	19	17	.276	.333	.377	710	80	-8	3	3	-0	.987	5	C-72/1-9	0.0
1926	Chi-N	80	253	24	63	13	3	1	23	13	17	.249	.288	.336	624	67	-12	3			**.989**	6	C-78	-0.1
1927	Chi-N	39	108	15	26	4	1	1	15	10	8	.241	.311	.324	635	70	-5	1			.994	9	C-36	0.6
1928	Chi-N	49	158	12	43	9	2	1	21	12	7	.272	.324	.373	697	83	-4	2			.983	8	C-45	0.7
1929	*Chi-N	60	167	15	40	3	0	0	18	18	14	.240	.317	.257	575	44	-14	1			.992	6	C-60	-0.4
1931	StL-N	15	19	1	2	0	0	0	3	0	3	.105	.105	.105	211	-42	-4	0			1.000	-0	C-12	-0.4
1932	StL-N	17	14	0	2	0	0	0	3	0	2	.143	.143	.143	286	-22	-2	0			1.000	2	/C-7	-0.1
Total	17	1042	2829	283	717	123	19	13	263	231	198	.253	.314	.324	638	81	-71	52	10		.980	44	C-868/1-60,O-6(1-1-4)	3.2

■ **ORLANDO GONZALEZ** Gonzalez, Orlando Eugene b: 11/15/51, Havana, Cuba BL/TL, 6'2", 180 lbs. Deb: 6/7/76 Career OF: (6-LF 0-CF 14-RF)

YEAR	TM/L	G	AB	R	H	2B	3B	HR	RBI	BB	SO	AVG	OBP	SLG	OPS	OPS+	BR+	SB	CS	SBR	FA	FR	G/POS	TPR
1976	Cle-A	28	68	5	17	2	0	0	4	5	7	.250	.301	.279	581	72	-2	1	2	-0	.992	-2	1-15/O-7(3-0-4),D-2	-0.6
1978	*Phi-N	26	26	1	5	0	0	0	0	1	1	.192	.222	.192	415	17	-3	0	0	0	1.000	-2	O-11(1-0-10)/1-3	-0.6
1980	Oak-A	25	70	10	17	0	0	0	1	9	8	.243	.329	.243	572	64	-3	0	2	-1	.990	1	1-11/O-2(2-0-0),D-8	-0.3
Total	3	79	164	16	39	2	0	0	5	15	16	.238	.302	.250	552	59	-8	1	4	-1	.991	-3	/1-29,O-20R,D-10	-1.5

■ **PEDRO GONZALEZ** Gonzalez, Pedro (Olivares) b: 12/12/37, San Pedro De Macoris, D.R. BR/TR, 6', 176 lbs. Deb: 4/11/63 Career OF: (5-LF 0-CF 19-RF)

YEAR	TM/L	G	AB	R	H	2B	3B	HR	RBI	BB	SO	AVG	OBP	SLG	OPS	OPS+	BR+	SB	CS	SBR	FA	FR	G/POS	TPR
1963	NY-A	14	26	3	5	1	0	0	1	0	5	.192	.192	.231	423	18	-3	0	1	-0	.963	-1	/2-7	-0.4
1964	*NY-A	80	112	18	31	8	1	0	5	7	22	.277	.331	.366	697	92	-1	3	4	-1	.992	1	1-31,O-20R/3-9,2-6	-0.2
1965	NY-A	7	5	0	2	1	0	0	0	0	2	.400	.400	.600	1000	181	0	0	0	0	.000	0	H	0.1
	Cle-A	116	400	38	101	14	3	5	39	18	57	.253	.290	.340	630	78	-12	7	4	0	.980	8	*2-112/O-3(0-0-3),3-2	0.6
	Yr	123	405	38	103	15	3	5	39	18	59	.254	.291	.343	634	79	-12	7	4	0	.980	8	*2-112/O-3(0-0-3),3-2	0.7
1966	Cle-A	110	352	21	82	9	2	2	17	15	54	.233	.268	.287	555	60	-18	8	5	0	.984	11	*2-104/3-1,O-1(0-0-1)	0.1
1967	Cle-A	80	189	19	43	6	0	1	8	12	36	.228	.277	.275	552	63	-9	4	6	-1	.971	-5	2-64/1-4,3-4,S-3	-1.1
Total	5	407	1084	99	264	39	6	8	70	52	176	.244	.283	.313	596	70	-43	22	20	-2	.980	14	2-293/1-35,O-24R,3S	-0.9

■ **RAUL GONZALEZ** Gonzalez, Victor Raul b: 12/27/73, Santurce, P.R. BR/TR, 5'8", 190 lbs. Deb: 5/25/2000

YEAR	TM/L	G	AB	R	H	2B	3B	HR	RBI	BB	SO	AVG	OBP	SLG	OPS	OPS+	BR+	SB	CS	SBR	FA	FR	G/POS	TPR
2000	Chi-N	3	2	0	0	0	0	0	0	0	2	.000	.000	.000	0	-99	-1	0	0	0	.000	-1	/O-2(2-0-0)	-0.1

■ **WIKI GONZALEZ** Gonzalez, Wiklenman Vicente b: 5/17/74, Aragua, Venez. BR/TR, 5'11", 175 lbs. Deb: 8/14/99

YEAR	TM/L	G	AB	R	H	2B	3B	HR	RBI	BB	SO	AVG	OBP	SLG	OPS	OPS+	BR+	SB	CS	SBR	FA	FR	G/POS	TPR
1999	SD-N	30	83	7	21	2	1	3	12	1	8	.253	.271	.410	680	75	-4	0	0	0	.992	1	C-17	-0.2
2000	SD-N	95	284	25	66	15	1	5	30	30	31	.232	.312	.345	657	70	-13	1	2	-0	.991	4	C-87	-0.5
Total	2	125	367	32	87	17	2	8	42	31	39	.237	.303	.360	663	71	-17	1	2	-0	.991	5	C-104	-0.7

YEAR	TM/L	G	AB	R	H	2B	3B	HR	RBI	BB	SO	AVG	OBP	SLG	OPS	OPS+	BR+	SB	CS	SBR	FA	FR	G/POS	TPR
■ CHARLIE GOOCH	Gooch, Charles Furman b: 6/5/02, Smyrna, Tenn. d: 5/30/82, Lanham, Md. BR/TR, 5'9", 170 lbs. Deb: 4/18/29																							
1929	Was-A	39	57	6	16	2	1	0	5	7	8	.281	.359	.351	710	83	-1	0	1	-0	.970	-2	/1-7,3-7,S-1	-0.3
■ JOHNNY GOOCH	Gooch, John Beverley b: 11/9/1897, Smyrna, Tenn. d: 5/15/75, Nashville, Tenn. BB/TR, 5'11", 175 lbs. Deb: 9/9/21 C																							
1921	Pit-N	13	38	2	9	0	0	0	3	3	3	.237	.293	.237	530	41	-3	1	0	0	.985	3	C-13	0.1
1922	Pit-N	105	353	45	116	15	3	1	42	39	15	.329	.403	.397	800	106	5	1	1	-0	.970	-3	*C-103	0.8
1923	Pit-N	66	202	16	56	10	2	1	20	17	13	.277	.336	.361	698	82	-5	2	1	0	.975	5	C-66	0.4
1924	Pit-N	70	224	26	65	6	5	0	25	16	12	.290	.343	.362	705	88	-4	1	3	-1	.988	-6	C-69	-0.6
1925	*Pit-N	79	215	24	64	8	4	0	30	20	16	.298	.357	.372	730	81	-6	1	0	0	.968	-5	C-76	-0.6
1926	Pit-N	86	218	19	59	15	1	1	42	20	14	.271	.340	.362	703	85	-4	1			.980	-5	C-80	-0.5
1927	*Pit-N	101	291	22	75	17	2	2	48	19	21	.258	.305	.351	656	70	-12	0			.974	3	C-91	-0.4
1928	Pit-N	31	80	7	19	2	1	0	5	3	6	.237	.265	.287	553	43	-7	0			.957	4	C-31	-0.1
	Bro-N	42	101	9	32	1	2	0	12	7	9	.317	.361	.366	727	92	-1	0			.969	-2	C-38	-0.1
	Yr	73	181	16	51	3	3	0	17	10	15	.282	.319	.331	651	70	-8	0			.964	2	C-69	-0.2
1929	Bro-N	1	1	0	0	0	0	0	0	0	0	.000	.000	.000	0	-99	-0	0			.000	0	H	0.0
	Cin-N	92	287	22	86	13	5	0	34	24	10	.300	.356	.380	736	86	-6	4			.975	5	C-86	0.4
	Yr	93	288	22	86	13	5	0	34	24	10	.299	.355	.378	733	86	-6	4			.975	5	C-86	0.4
1930	Cin-N	82	276	29	67	10	3	2	30	27	15	.243	.315	.322	637	57	-19	0			.955	-5	C-79	-1.7
1933	Bos-A	37	77	6	14	1	1	0	2	11	7	.182	.284	.221	505	36	-7	0	0	0	.991	4	C-26	-0.1
Total	11	805	2363	227	662	98	29	7	293	206	141	.280	.342	.355	697	79	-69	11	5		.973	-2	C-758	-2.4
■ LEE GOOCH	Gooch, Lee Currin b: 2/23/1890, Oxford, N.C. d: 5/18/66, Raleigh, N.C. BR/TR, 6', 190 lbs. Deb: 8/17/15																							
1915	Cle-A	2	2	0	1	0	0	0	0	0	0	.500	.500	.500	1000	196	0	0			.000	0	H	0.0
1917	Phi-A	17	59	4	17	2	0	1	8	4	10	.288	.333	.373	706	117	1	0			.893	-2	O-16(0-0-16)	-0.2
Total	2	19	61	4	18	2	0	1	8	4	10	.295	.338	.377	716	120	1	0			.893	-2	/O-16(0-0-16)	-0.2
■ GENE GOOD	Good, Eugene J. b: 12/13/1882, Roxbury, Mass. d: 8/6/47, Boston, Mass. BL/TL, 5'6", 130 lbs. Deb: 4/12/06																							
1906	Bos-N	34	119	4	18	0	0	0	0	13		.151	.246	.151	398	25	-10	2			.873	-2	O-34(24-10-0)	-1.6
■ WILBUR GOOD	Good, Wilbur David "Lefty" b: 9/28/1885, Punxsutawney, Pa. d: 12/30/63, Brooksville, Fla. BL/TL, 5'6", 165 lbs. Deb: 8/18/05																							
1905	NY-A	5	8	2	3	0	0	0	0	0		.375	.375	.375	750	124	0	0			.889	0	/P-5	0.0
1908	Cle-A	46	154	23	43	1	3	1	14	13		.279	.351	.344	695	126	5	7			.845	-8	O-42(2-17-23)	-0.6
1909	Cle-A	94	318	33	68	6	5	0	17	28		.214	.296	.264	560	74	-9	13			.953	2	O-80(0-0-80)	-1.2
1910	Bos-N	23	86	15	29	5	4	0	11	6	13	.337	.394	.488	882	150	5	5			.969	5	O-23(0-22-1)	0.9
1911	Bos-N	43	165	21	44	9	3	0	15	12	22	.267	.316	.358	674	82	-4	3			.945	8	O-43(0-41-2)	0.0
	Chi-N	58	145	27	39	5	4	2	21	11	17	.269	.329	.400	729	103	0	10			.928	-5	O-40(3-34-3)	-0.7
	Yr	101	310	48	83	14	7	2	36	23	39	.268	.322	.377	700	92	-4	13			.938	3	O-83(3-75-5)	-0.7
1912	Chi-N	39	35	7	5	0	0	0	1	3	7	.143	.211	.143	353	-2	-5	3			1.000	-3	O-10(5-4-1)	-0.8
1913	Chi-N	49	91	11	23	3	2	1	12	11	16	.253	.340	.363	702	100	0	5			.974	-3	O-26(3-1-22)	-0.4
1914	Chi-N	154	580	70	158	24	7	2	43	53	74	.272	.341	.348	689	105	4	31			.930	-1	*O-154(0-0-154)	-0.6
1915	Chi-N	128	498	66	126	18	9	2	27	34	65	.253	.307	.337	645	95	-4	19	17	-2	.936	-2	*O-125(0-1-125)	-1.5
1916	Phi-N	75	136	25	34	4	3	1	15	8	13	.250	.306	.346	652	96	-1	7			.983	-5	O-46(9-1-36)	-0.8
1918	Chi-A	35	148	24	37	9	4	0	11	11	16	.250	.315	.365	680	104	0	1			.982	4	O-35(1-33-1)	0.2
Total	11	749	2364	324	609	84	44	9	187	190	243	.258	.322	.342	664	98	-7	104	17		.942	-8	O-624(23-154-448)/P-5	-5.5
■ BILL GOODENOUGH	Goodenough, William B. b: 1863, St.Louis, Mo. d: 5/24/05, St.Louis, Mo. 6'1", 170 lbs. Deb: 8/31/1893																							
1893	StL-N	10	31	4	5	1	0	0	2	3	4	.161	.297	.194	491	31	-3	2			.880	-1	O-10(0-10-0)	-0.4
■ MIKE GOODFELLOW	Goodfellow, Michael J. b: 10/3/1866, Port Jervis, N.Y. d: 2/12/20, Newark, N.J. BR/TR, 6', 180 lbs. Deb: 6/13/1887 Career OF: (11-LF 0-CF 52-RF)																							
1887	StL-a	1	4	0	0	0	0	0	0	0		.000	.000	.000	0	-90	-1	0			.800	-0	/C-1	-0.1
1888	Cle-a	68	269	24	66	7	0	0	29	11		.245	.283	.271	554	80	-6	7			.863	-3	O-62R/C-4,1-3,S-1	-0.9
Total	2	69	273	24	66	7	0	0	29	11		.242	.279	.267	546	77	-7	7			.909	-3	/O-62R,C-5,1-3,S-1	-1.0
■ IVAL GOODMAN	Goodman, Ival Richard "Goodie" b: 7/23/08, Northview, Mo. d: 11/25/84, Cincinnati, Ohio BL/TR, 5'11", 170 lbs. Deb: 4/16/35																							
1935	Cin-N	148	592	86	159	23	**18**	12	72	35	50	.269	.314	.429	743	101	-1	14			.960	8	*O-146(2-0-144)	-0.2
1936	Cin-N	136	489	81	139	15	**14**	17	71	38	53	.284	.347	.476	823	128	17	6			.972	3	*O-120(1-1-118)	1.2
1937	Cin-N	147	549	86	150	25	12	12	55	55	58	.273	.347	.428	775	115	11	10			.974	6	*O-141(7-1-133)	0.8
1938	Cin-N★	145	568	103	166	27	10	30	92	53	51	.292	.368	.533	901	149	36	3			.988	5	*O-142(0-0-142)	3.3
1939	*Cin-N★	124	470	85	152	37	16	7	84	54	32	.323	.401	.515	916	144	29	2			.981	7	*O-123(0-0-123)	2.8
1940	*Cin-N	136	519	78	134	20	6	12	63	60	54	.258	.335	.389	724	98	-1	9			.970	-5	*O-135(0-0-135)	-1.5
1941	Cin-N	42	149	14	40	5	2	1	12	16	15	.268	.343	.349	692	95	-1	1			.966	1	O-40(0-0-40)	-0.3
1942	Cin-N	87	226	21	55	18	1	0	15	24	32	.243	.319	.332	651	91	-3	0			.991	1	O-57(0-0-57)	-0.6
1943	Chi-N	80	225	31	72	10	5	3	45	24	20	.320	.390	.449	839	144	13	4			.968	-7	O-61(55-10-0)	0.3
1944	Chi-N	62	141	24	37	8	1	1	16	23	15	.262	.377	.355	732	107	2	0			1.000	-6	O-35(23-14-0)	-0.5
Total	10	1107	3928	609	1104	188	85	95	525	382	380	.281	.352	.445	797	120	104	49			.975	12	O-1000(88-26-892)	5.3
■ JAKE GOODMAN	Goodman, Jacob b: 9/14/1853, Lancaster, Pa. d: 3/9/1890, Reading, Pa. 6'1.5", Deb: 5/2/1878																							
1878	Mil-N	60	252	28	62	4	3	1	27	7	33	.246	.266	.298	564	80	-6				.944	-4	*1-60	-1.2
1882	Pit-a	10	41	5	13	2	2	0		2		.317	.349	.463	812	180	3				.962	1	1-10	0.3
Total	2	70	293	33	75	6	5	1	27	9	33	.256	.278	.321	599	92	-2				.946	-3	/1-70	-0.9
■ BILLY GOODMAN	Goodman, William Dale b: 3/22/26, Concord, N.C. d: 10/1/84, Sarasota, Fla. BL/TR, 5'11", 165 lbs. Deb: 4/19/47 C Career OF: (68-LF 0-CF 43-RF)																							
1947	Bos-A	12	11	1	2	0	0	0	1	1	2	.182	.250	.182	432	20	-1	0	0	0	1.000	0	/O-1(0-0-1)	-0.1
1948	Bos-A	127	445	65	138	27	2	1	66	74	44	.310	.414	.387	801	108	9	5	3	0	.993	-4	*1-117/2-2,3-2	0.1
1949	Bos-A★	122	443	54	132	23	3	0	56	58	21	.298	.382	.363	745	91	-4	2	0	0	**.992**	-1	*1-117	-0.9
1950	Bos-A	110	424	91	150	25	3	4	68	52	25	**.354**	.427	.455	882	115	11	2	4	-1	.991	-2	O-45L,3-27,1-21,/2S	0.4
1951	Bos-A	141	546	92	162	34	4	0	50	79	37	.297	.388	.374	761	97	0	7	4	0	.995	-2	1-62,2-44,O-38R,/3	-0.2
1952	Bos-A	138	513	79	157	27	3	4	56	48	23	.306	.370	.394	764	104	4	8	2	1	.975	**20**	*2-103,1-23/3-5,O-4L	3.1
1953	Bos-A★	128	514	73	161	33	5	2	41	57	11	.313	.384	.409	793	108	7	1	4	-1	.974	-11	*2-112,1-20	0.3
1954	Bos-A	127	489	71	148	25	4	1	36	51	15	.303	.371	.376	747	95	-2	3	3	-0	.979	1	2-72,1-27,O-13L,3	0.2
1955	Bos-A	149	599	100	176	31	2	0	52	99	44	.294	.397	.352	749	94	-0	5	5	-1	.969	-18	*2-143/1-5,O-1(0-0-1)	-0.8
1956	Bos-A	105	399	61	117	22	8	2	38	40	22	.293	.358	.404	761	90	-5	0	3	-1	.966	-11	2-95	-1.0
1957	Bos-A	18	16	1	1	1	0	0	0	2	1	.063	.167	.125	292	-18	-3	0	0	0	.000	0	H	-0.3
	Bal-A	73	263	36	81	10	3	3	33	21	18	.308	.366	.403	769	117	6	0	2	-1	.961	-10	3-54/O-9R,1-8,2S	-0.5
	Yr	91	279	37	82	11	3	3	33	23	19	.294	.354	.387	741	106	3	0	2	-1	.961	-10	3-54/O-9R,1-8,2S	-0.8
1958	Chi-A	116	425	41	127	15	5	0	40	37	21	.299	.358	.358	715	100	1	1	0	0	.954	-18	*3-111/1-3,2-1,S-1	-1.8
1959	*Chi-A	104	268	21	67	14	1	1	28	19	20	.250	.304	.321	625	73	-10	3	0	1	.950	-2	3-74/2-3	-1.2
1960	Chi-A	30	77	5	18	4	0	0	6	12	8	.234	.337	.286	623	71	-3	0	0	0	.982	3	3-20/2-7	0.1
1961	Chi-A	41	51	4	13	4	0	1	10	7	6	.255	.345	.392	737	98	-0	0	0	0	.944	-0	/3-7,1-2,2-1	0.0
1962	Hou-N	82	161	12	41	4	1	0	10	12	11	.255	.306	.292	598	66	-8	0	0	0	.972	-9	2-31,3-17/1-1	-1.5
Total	16	1623	5644	807	1691	299	44	19	591	669	329	.300	.377	.378	755	98	3	37	30	-2	.972	-63	2-624,1-406,3O/S	-4.1
■ ED GOODSON	Goodson, James Edward b: 1/25/48, Pulaski, Va. BL/TR (BB 1975 (part)), 6'3", 185 lbs. Deb: 9/5/70 Career OF: (2-LF 0-CF 0-RF)																							
1970	SF-N	7	11	1	3	0	0	0	0	0	2	.273	.273	.273	545	47	-1	0	0	0	.941	0	/1-2	-0.1
1971	SF-N	20	42	4	8	1	0	0	1	2	4	.190	.227	.214	442	26	-4	0	0	0	1.000	1	1-14	-0.5
1972	SF-N	58	150	15	42	1	1	6	30	8	12	.280	.321	.420	741	107	1	0	0	0	.991	2	1-42	0.1
1973	SF-N	102	384	37	116	20	1	12	53	15	44	.302	.332	.453	785	111	4	0	1	-0	.911	-14	3-93	-1.1
1974	SF-N	98	298	25	81	15	0	6	48	18	22	.272	.320	.383	702	91	-4	1	0	0	.997	-4	1-73/3-8	-1.3
1975	SF-N	39	121	10	25	7	0	1	8	7	14	.207	.250	.289	539	47	-9	0	1	-0	.993	2	1-16,3-13	-0.9
	Atl-N	47	76	5	16	2	0	1	8	2	8	.211	.231	.276	507	39	-6	0	0	0	.990	0	1-13/3-1	-0.8
	Yr	86	197	15	41	9	0	2	16	9	22	.208	.243	.284	527	44	-15	0	1	-0	.992	2	1-29,3-14	-1.7

YEAR	TM/L	G	AB	R	H	2B	3B	HR	RBI	BB	SO	AVG	OBP	SLG	OPS	OPS+	BR+	SB	CS	SBR	FA	FR	G/POS	TPR
1976	LA-N	83	118	8	27	4	0	3	17	8	19	.229	.278	.339	617	76	-4	0	0	0	.833	-4	3-16/1-3,O-2L,2-1	-0.9
1977	*LA-N	61	66	3	11	1	0	1	5	3	10	.167	.203	.227	430	15	-8	0	1	-0	1.000	1	1-13/3-4	-0.8
Total	8	515	1266	108	329	51	2	30	170	63	135	.260	.298	.374	673	84	-30	1	3	-1	.994	-16	1-176,3-135/O-2L,2	-6.3
■ **PEP GOODWIN**	Goodwin, Claire Vernon b: 12/19/1891, Pocatello, Idaho d: 2/15/72, Oakland, Cal. BL/TR, 5'10.5", 160 lbs. Deb: 4/16/14																							
1914	KC-F	112	374	38	88	15	6	1	32	27	23	.235	.290	.316	606	68	-24	4			.907	-13	S-67,3-40/1-1	-3.2
1915	KC-F	81	229	22	54	5	1	0	16	15	23	.236	.291	.266	558	60	-16	6			.906	-8	S-42,2-23	-2.2
Total	2	193	603	60	142	20	7	1	48	42	46	.235	.291	.297	588	65	-39	10			.907	-20	S-109/3-40,2-23,1-1	-5.4
■ **CURTIS GOODWIN**	Goodwin, Curtis La Mar b: 9/30/72, Oakland, Cal. BL/TL, 5'11", 180 lbs. Deb: 6/2/95																							
1995	Bal-A	87	289	40	76	11	3	1	24	15	53	.263	.304	.332	636	64	-15	22	4	3	.990	1	O-84(0-84-0)/D-3	-0.9
1996	Cin-N	49	136	20	31	3	0	0	5	19	34	.228	.323	.250	573	53	-9	15	6	1	.970	-5	O-42(9-28-6)	-1.2
1997	Cin-N	85	265	27	67	11	0	1	12	24	53	.253	.317	.306	623	63	-14	22	13	0	1.000	6	O-71(32-41-1)	-0.8
1998	Col-N	119	159	27	39	7	0	1	6	16	40	.245	.314	.308	622	53	-10	5	1	1	.983	-18	O-91(14-74-7)	-2.7
1999	Chi-N	89	157	15	38	6	1	0	9	13	38	.242	.300	.293	593	52	-11	2	4	-1	.983	-7	O-76(36-42-0)	-1.9
	Tor-A	2	8	0	0	0	0	0	0	0	3	.000	.000	.000	0	-99	-2	0	0	0	1.000	1	/O-2(0-2-0)	-0.1
Total	5	431	1014	129	251	38	4	3	56	87	221	.248	.309	.302	611	58	-62	66	28	5	.988	-21	O-366(91-271-14)/D-3	-7.6
■ **DANNY GOODWIN**	Goodwin, Danny Kay b: 9/2/53, St.Louis, Mo. BL/TR, 6'1", 195 lbs. Deb: 9/3/75																							
1975	Cal-A	4	10	0	1	0	0	0	0	0	5	.100	.100	.100	200	-47	-2	0	0	0	.000	0	/D-3	-0.2
1977	Cal-A	35	91	5	19	6	1	1	8	5	19	.209	.250	.330	580	59	-5	0	0	0	.000	0	D-23	-0.6
1978	Cal-A	24	58	9	16	5	0	2	10	10	13	.276	.382	.466	848	143	4	0	0	0	.000	0	D-15	0.3
1979	Min-A	58	159	22	46	8	5	5	27	11	23	.289	.335	.497	832	117	3	0	0	0	1.000	-0	D-51/1-8	0.1
1980	Min-A	55	115	12	23	5	0	1	11	17	32	.200	.303	.270	573	54	-7	0	0	0	1.000	0	D-38,1-13	-0.8
1981	Min-A	59	151	18	34	6	1	2	17	16	32	.225	.299	.318	617	73	-5	3	1	0	.992	-2	1-40/O-1(1-0-0),D-5	-1.0
1982	Oak-A	17	52	6	11	2	1	2	8	2	13	.212	.241	.404	645	77	-2	0	0	0	.000	0	D-15	-0.2
Total	7	252	636	72	150	32	8	13	81	61	137	.236	.303	.373	675	84	-15	3	1	0	.994	-2	D-150/1-61,O-1(1-0-0)	-2.4
■ **TOM GOODWIN**	Goodwin, Thomas Jones b: 7/27/68, Fresno, Cal. BL/TR, 6'1", 170 lbs. Deb: 9/1/91																							
1991	LA-N	16	7	3	1	0	0	0	0	0	0	.143	.143	.143	286	-20	-1	1	1	-0	1.000	-1	/O-5(2-4-0)	-0.2
1992	LA-N	57	73	15	17	1	1	0	3	6	10	.233	.291	.274	565	62	-4	7	3	0	1.000	-9	O-45(35-9-2)	-1.4
1993	LA-N	30	17	6	5	1	0	0	1	1	4	.294	.333	.353	686	89	-0	1	2	-0	1.000	-4	O-12(6-4-2)	-0.4
1994	KC-A	2	2	0	0	0	0	0	0	0	1	.000	.000	.000	0	-96	-1	0	0	0	1.000	-0	/O-1(0-0-1),D-1	-0.1
1995	KC-A	133	480	72	138	16	3	4	28	38	72	.287	.346	.358	704	83	-11	50	18	5	.990	-2	*O-130(37-95-1)/D-2	-0.8
1996	KC-A	143	524	80	148	14	4	1	35	39	79	.282	.335	.330	665	69	-24	66	22	7	.984	-7	*O-136(75-81-0)/D-5	-2.3
1997	KC-A	97	367	51	100	13	4	2	22	19	51	.272	.312	.346	658	70	-16	34	10	4	.996	1	O-96(0-96-0)	-0.9
	Tex-A	53	207	39	49	13	2	0	17	25	37	.237	.322	.319	641	65	-10	16	6	1	.986	4	O-51(5-49-0)	-0.5
	Yr	150	574	90	149	26	6	2	39	44	88	.260	.316	.336	652	68	-26	50	16	5	.992	5	*O-147(5-145-0)	-1.4
1998	*Tex-A	154	520	102	151	13	3	2	33	73	90	.290	.380	.338	718	85	-8	38	20	1	.992	3	*O-150(0-150-0)/D-1	-0.1
1999	*Tex-A	109	405	63	105	12	6	3	33	40	61	.259	.326	.341	667	67	-19	39	11	5	.989	1	*O-107(0-107-0)	-1.2
2000	Col-N	91	317	65	86	8	8	5	47	50	76	.271	.372	.394	767	73	-12	39	7	6	.986	2	O-88(0-88-0)	-0.2
	LA-N	56	211	29	53	3	1	1	11	18	41	.251	.310	.289	599	55	-14	16	3	2	1.000	4	O-55(10-48-0)	-0.7
	Yr	147	528	94	139	11	9	6	58	68	117	.263	.348	.352	701	67	-25	55	10	9	.992	7	*O-143(10-136-0)	-0.9
Total	10	941	3130	525	853	94	32	18	230	309	522	.273	.340	.340	681	73	-120	307	103	31	.990	-7	O-876(170-731-6)/D-9	-8.8
■ **RAY GOOLSBY**	Goolsby, Raymond Daniel "Ox" b: 9/5/19, Florala, Ala. d: 11/13/99, Apopka, Fla. BR/TR, 6'1", 185 lbs. Deb: 4/18/46																							
1946	Was-A	3	4	0	0	0	0	0	0	1	1	.000	.200	.000	200	-43	-1	0	0	0	1.000	-0	/O-1(1-0-0)	-0.1
■ **GREG GOOSSEN**	Goossen, Gregory Bryant b: 12/14/45, Los Angeles, Cal. BR/TR, 6'1.5", 210 lbs. Deb: 9/3/65																							
1965	NY-N	11	31	2	9	0	0	1	2	1	5	.290	.313	.387	700	99	-0	0	0	0	.979	-1	/C-8	-0.1
1966	NY-N	13	32	1	6	2	0	1	5	1	11	.188	.235	.344	579	60	-2	0	0	0	1.000	-4	C-11	-0.6
1967	NY-N	37	69	2	11	1	0	0	3	4	26	.159	.216	.174	390	13	-8	0	0	0	.973	-1	C-23	-0.9
1968	NY-N	38	106	4	22	7	0	0	6	10	21	.208	.288	.274	562	69	-4	0	0	0	.992	2	1-31/C-1	-0.4
1969	Sea-A	52	139	19	43	8	1	10	24	14	29	.309	.385	.597	982	174	13	1	1	-0	.993	2	1-31/O-2(2-0-0)	1.3
1970	Mil-A	21	47	3	12	3	0	1	3	10	12	.255	.407	.383	790	118	2	0	0	0	.990	-1	1-15	-0.1
	Was-A	21	36	2	8	3	0	0	1	2	8	.222	.263	.306	569	59	-2	0	0	0	1.000	-0	/O-5(5-0-0),1-2	-0.3
	Yr	42	83	5	20	6	0	1	4	12	20	.241	.351	.349	700	96	-0	0	0	0	.992	-2	1-17/O-5(5-0-0)	-0.4
Total	6	193	460	33	111	24	1	13	44	42	112	.241	.317	.383	700	99	-1	1	1	-0	.992	-5	/1-79,C-43,O-7(7-0-0)	-1.1
■ **GLEN GORBOUS**	Gorbous, Glen Edward b: 7/8/30, Drumheller, Alberta, Canada d: 6/12/90, Calgary, Alberta, Canada BL/TR, 6'2", 175 lbs. Deb: 4/11/55																							
1955	Cin-N	8	18	2	6	3	0	0	4	3	1	.333	.429	.500	929	137	1	0	0	0	.857	-0	/O-5(5-0-0)	0.1
	Phi-N	91	224	25	53	9	1	4	23	21	17	.237	.302	.339	641	71	-9	0	3	-1	.984	6	O-57(0-4-53)	-0.6
	Yr	99	242	27	59	12	1	4	27	24	18	.244	.312	.351	663	77	-8	0	3	-1	.971	6	O-62(5-4-53)	-0.5
1956	Phi-N	15	33	1	6	0	0	0	1	0	1	.182	.182	.182	364	-2	-5	0	0	0	1.000	-2	/O-8(0-0-8)	-0.7
1957	Phi-N	3	2	1	1	0	0	0	1	1	0	.500	.667	1.000	1667	351	1	0	0	0	.000	0	H	0.1
Total	3	117	277	29	66	13	1	4	29	25	19	.238	.301	.336	637	70	-12	0	3	-1	.973	4	/O-70(5-4-61)	-1.1
■ **JOE GORDON**	Gordon, Joseph Lowell "Flash" b: 2/18/15, Los Angeles, Cal. d: 4/14/78, Sacramento, Cal. BR/TR, 5'10", 180 lbs. Deb: 4/18/38 MC																							
1938	*NY-A	127	458	83	117	24	7	25	97	56	72	.255	.340	.502	843	109	3	11	3	1	.960	**24**	*2-126	3.3
1939	*NY-A★	151	567	92	161	32	5	28	111	75	57	.284	.370	.506	876	124	19	11	10	-1	.967	6	*2-151	3.0
1940	NY-A★	155	616	112	173	32	10	30	103	52	57	.281	.340	.511	851	122	17	18	8	1	.975	14	*2-155	3.9
1941	*NY-A★	156	588	104	162	26	7	24	87	72	80	.276	.358	.466	824	118	14	10	9	-1	.958	6	*2-131,1-30	2.5
1942	*NY-A★	147	538	88	173	29	4	18	103	79	95	.322	.409	.491	900	156	41	12	6	1	.966	4	*2-147	5.5
1943	*NY-A☆	152	543	82	135	28	5	17	69	98	75	.249	.365	.413	778	126	20	4	7	-2	.969	26	*2-152	5.6
1946	NY-A★	112	376	35	79	15	0	11	47	49	72	.210	.308	.338	645	79	-10	2	5	-1	.974	22	*2-108	1.6
1947	Cle-A★	155	562	89	153	27	6	29	93	62	49	.272	.346	.496	842	136	24	7	3	0	.978	-4	*2-155	2.9
1948	*Cle-A★	144	550	96	154	21	4	32	124	77	68	.280	.371	.507	879	136	26	5	2	0	.971	-7	*2-144/S-2	2.6
1949	Cle-A★	148	541	74	136	18	3	20	84	83	33	.251	.355	.407	762	103	2	5	6	-1	.980	-18	*2-145	-0.9
1950	Cle-A	119	368	59	87	12	1	19	57	56	44	.236	.340	.429	770	99	-2	4	1	1	.969	-18	*2-105	-1.2
Total	11	1566	5707	914	1530	264	52	253	975	759	702	.268	.357	.466	822	121	154	89	60	-1	.970	54	*2-1519/1-30,S-2	28.8
■ **KEITH GORDON**	Gordon, Keith Bradley b: 1/22/69, Bethesda, Md. BR/TR, 6'1", 205 lbs. Deb: 7/9/93																							
1993	Cin-N	3	6	0	1	0	0	0	0	0	2	.167	.167	.167	333	-10	-1	0	0	0	1.000	-0	/O-2(2-0-0)	-0.1
■ **MIKE GORDON**	Gordon, Michael William b: 9/11/53, Leominster, Mass. BB/TR, 6'3", 215 lbs. Deb: 4/7/77																							
1977	Chi-N	8	23	0	1	0	0	0	2	2	8	.043	.120	.043	163	-49	-5	0	0	0	.970	-3	/C-8	-0.8
1978	Chi-N	4	5	0	1	0	0	0	0	3	2	.200	.556	.200	756	106	0	0	0	0	1.000	-0	/C-4	0.0
Total	2	12	28	0	2	0	0	0	2	5	10	.071	.235	.071	307	-11	-4	0	0	0	.979	-3	/C-12	-0.8
■ **SID GORDON**	Gordon, Sidney b: 8/13/17, Brooklyn, N.Y. d: 6/17/75, New York, N.Y. BR/TR, 5'10", 185 lbs. Deb: 9/11/41 Career OF: (806-LF 6-CF 108-RF)																							
1941	NY-N	9	31	4	8	1	1	0	4	6	1	.258	.378	.355	733	105	0	0			1.000	-1	/O-9(3-6-0)	-0.1
1942	NY-N	6	19	4	6	0	1	0	2	3	2	.316	.409	.421	830	142	1	0			.913	1	/3-6	0.3
1943	NY-N	131	474	50	119	9	11	9	63	43	32	.251	.315	.373	688	98	-2	2			.941	3	3-53,1-41,O-28L,/2	-0.2
1946	NY-N	135	450	64	132	15	4	5	45	60	27	.293	.380	.378	758	115	11	1			.995	1	*O-101(101-0-0),3-30	0.4
1947	NY-N	130	437	57	119	19	8	13	57	50	21	.272	.347	.442	789	107	4	2			.971	1	*O-124(124-0-0)/3-2	-0.4
1948	NY-N☆	142	521	100	156	26	4	30	107	74	39	.299	.390	.537	927	148	34	8			**.948**	-5	*3-115,O-23(18-0-2)	2.8
1949	NY-N★	141	489	87	139	26	2	26	90	95	37	.284	.404	.505	909	142	32	1			.958	-23	*3-123,O-15R/1-1	0.8
1950	Bos-N	134	481	78	146	33	4	27	103	78	31	.304	.403	.557	960	160	42	2			.990	6	*O-123(123-0-0),3-10	3.7
1951	Bos-N	150	550	96	158	28	1	29	109	80	32	.287	.383	.500	883	146	36	2	0	0	.984	-4	*O-122(103-0-23),3-34	2.4
1952	Bos-N	144	522	69	151	22	2	25	75	77	49	.289	.384	.483	866	144	32	0	4	-1	**.996**	2	*O-142(142-0-0)/3-2	2.2
1953	Mil-N	140	464	67	127	22	4	19	75	71	40	.274	.372	.461	834	123	17	1	1	-0	.977	-1	*O-137(137-0-0)	0.8
1954	Pit-N	131	363	38	111	12	0	12	49	67	24	.306	.414	.438	852	124	16	0	0	0	.977	-6	O-73(8-0-66),3-40	0.6

YEAR	TM/L	G	AB	R	H	2B	3B	HR	RBI	BB	SO	AVG	OBP	SLG	OPS	OPS+	BR+	SB	CS	SBR	FA	FR	G/POS	TPR
1955	Pit-N	16	47	2	8	1	0	0	1	2	6	.170	.204	.191	396	6	-6	0	0	0	1.000	2	/3-8,O-4(4-0-0)	-0.5
	NY-N	66	144	19	35	6	1	7	25	25	15	.243	.355	.444	799	110	2	0	0	0	1.000	6	3-31,O-17(12-0-5)	0.7
	Yr	82	191	21	43	7	1	7	26	27	21	.225	.321	.382	703	86	-4	0	0	0	1.000	7	3-39,O-21(16-0-5)	0.2
Total	13	1475	4992	735	1415	220	43	202	805	731	356	.283	.377	.466	844	130	219	19	5		.985	-19	O-918L,3-454/1-42,2	13.5
■ GEORGE GORE	Gore, George F. "Piano Legs" b: 5/3/1857, Saccarappa, Me. d: 9/16/33, Utica, N.Y. BL/TR, 5'11", 195 lbs. Deb: 5/1/1879 M Career OF: (96-LF 1175-CF 31-RF)																							
1879	Chi-N	63	266	43	70	17	4	0	32	8	30	.263	.285	.357	642	104	1				.872	-2	O-54(0-48-6)/1-9	-0.3
1880	Chi-N	77	322	70	116	23	2	2	47	21	10	**.360**	**.399**	**.463**	**862**	**180**	**26**				.879	6	*O-74(0-73-1)/1-7	2.8
1881	Chi-N	73	309	**86**	92	18	9	1	44	27	23	.298	.354	.424	778	137	13				.874	2	*O-72(0-72-0)/3-1,1-1	1.1
1882	Chi-N	84	367	**99**	117	15	7	3	51	**29**	19	.319	.369	.422	791	146	19				.842	6	*O-84(0-84-0)	1.9
1883	Chi-N	92	392	105	131	30	9	2	52	27	13	.334	.377	.472	849	144	20				.867	11	*O-92(0-92-0)	2.4
1884	Chi-N	103	422	104	134	18	4	5	34	**61**	26	.318	.404	.415	818	146	23				.868	2	*O-103(0-103-1)	1.9
1885	*Chi-N	109	441	115	138	21	13	5	57	68	25	.313	.405	.454	858	156	27				.884	-3	*O-109(1-108-0)	1.9
1886	*Chi-N	118	444	150	135	20	12	6	63	**102**	30	.304	.434	.444	878	146	27	23			.876	-3	*O-118(0-115-3)	1.8
1887	NY-N	111	501	95	175	16	5	1	49	42	18	.349	.358	.353	711	103	4	39			.889	1	*O-111(0-111-0)	0.2
1888	*NY-N	64	254	37	56	4	4	2	17	30	31	.220	.308	.291	599	93	-1	11			.836	-9	O-64(42-21-1)	-1.2
1889	*NY-N	120	488	132	149	21	7	7	54	84	28	.305	.416	.420	836	134	26	28			.864	-8	*O-120(0-118-3)	1.2
1890	NY-P	93	399	132	127	26	8	10	55	77	23	.318	.432	.499	931	136	21	28			.877	-12	O-93(52-33-10)	0.5
1891	NY-N	130	528	103	150	22	7	2	48	74	34	.284	.379	.364	743	122	18	19			.909	-6	*O-130(1-127-3)	0.7
1892	NY-N	53	193	47	49	11	2	0	11	49	16	.254	.412	.332	744	127	10	20			.932	1	O-53(0-50-3)	0.8
	StL-N	20	73	9	15	0	1	0	4	18	6	.205	.363	.233	596	85	0	2			.844	-2	O-20(0-20-0),M	-0.3
	Yr	73	266	56	64	11	3	0	15	67	22	.241	.399	.305	703	116	10	22			.908	-0	O-73(0-70-3)	0.5
Total	14	1310	5399	1327	1654	262	94	46	618	717	332	.306	.386	.411	797	134	235	170			.876	-15	*O-1297C/1-17,3-1	15.4
■ BOB GORINSKI	Gorinski, Robert John b: 1/7/52, Latrobe, Pa. BR/TR, 6'3", 215 lbs. Deb: 4/10/77																							
1977	Min-A	54	118	14	23	4	1	3	22	5	29	.195	.228	.322	550	49	-9	1	0	0	.936	-7	O-37(30-0-7)/D-9	-1.7
■ HERB GORMAN	Gorman, Herbert Allen b: 12/18/24, San Francisco, Cal d: 4/5/53, San Diego, Cal. BL/TL, 5'11", 180 lbs. Deb: 4/19/52																							
1952	StL-N	1	1	0	0	0	0	0	0	0	0	.000	.000	.000	0	-99	-0	0	0	0	.000	0	H	0.0
■ HOWIE GORMAN	Gorman, Howard Paul "Lefty" b: 5/14/13, Pittsburgh, Pa. d: 4/29/84, Harrisburg, Pa. BL/TL, 6'2", 160 lbs. Deb: 8/7/37																							
1937	Phi-N	13	19	3	4	1	0	0	1	1	1	.211	.250	.263	513	37	-2	1			.500	-3	/O-7(0-0-7)	-0.5
1938	Phi-N	1	1	0	0	0	0	0	0	0	0	.000	.000	.000	0	-99	-0	0			.000	0	H	0.0
Total	2	14	20	3	4	1	0	0	1	1	1	.200	.238	.250	488	30	-2	1			.500	-3	/O-7(0-0-7)	-0.5
■ JACK GORMAN	Gorman, John F. "Stooping Jack" b: 1859, St.Louis, Mo. d: 9/9/1889, St.Louis, Mo. Deb: 7/1/1883 Career OF: (6-LF 1-CF 2-RF)																							
1883	StL-a	1	4	0	0	0	0	0		0		.000	.000	.000	0	-95	-1				.667	0	/O-1(1-0-0)	0.0
1884	KC-U	33	137	25	38	5	2	0		4		.277	.298	.343	641	108	-3				.954	-2	1-24/O-5(5-0-0),3-4	-0.6
	Pit-a	8	27	3	4	0	1	0		1		.148	.179	.222	401	30	-2				.750	-2	/P-3,O-3(0-1-2),3-2	-0.3
Total	2	42	168	28	42	5	3	0		5		.250	.272	.315	587	89	-5				.944	-4	/1-24,O-9L,3-6,P-3	-0.9
■ JOHNNY GORYL	Goryl, John Albert b: 10/21/33, Cumberland, R.I. BR/TR, 5'10", 175 lbs. Deb: 9/20/57 MC																							
1957	Chi-N	9	38	7	8	2	0	0	1	5	9	.211	.318	.263	581	59	-2	0	1	-0	.952	-1	/3-9	-0.4
1958	Chi-N	83	219	27	53	9	3	4	14	27	34	.242	.331	.365	696	85	-4	0	1	-0	.931	11	3-44,2-35	0.8
1959	Chi-N	25	48	1	9	3	1	1	6	5	3	.188	.264	.354	618	63	-3	1	1	-0	.973	0	2-11/3-4	-0.2
1962	Min-A	37	26	6	5	0	1	2	2	2	6	.192	.250	.500	750	93	-0	0	0	0	.923	-0	/2-4,S-1	-0.1
1963	Min-A	64	150	29	43	5	3	9	24	15	29	.287	.355	.540	895	144	9	0	0	0	.958	-9	2-34,3-11/S-7	0.3
1964	Min-A	58	114	9	16	0	2	0	1	10	25	.140	.216	.175	391	10	-14	1	0	0	.975	2	2-28,3-13	-1.0
Total	6	276	595	79	134	19	10	16	48	64	106	.225	.306	.371	677	83	-15	2	3	-1	.960	3	2-112/3-81,S-8	-0.6
■ JIM GOSGER	Gosger, James Charles b: 11/6/42, Port Huron, Mich. BL/TL, 5'11", 185 lbs. Deb: 5/4/63 Career OF: (216-LF 291-CF 83-RF)																							
1963	Bos-A	19	16	3	1	0	0	0	0	3	5	.063	.211	.063	273	-19	-3	0	0	0	.818	-0	/O-4(0-2-2)	-0.3
1965	Bos-A	81	324	45	83	15	4	9	35	29	61	.256	.321	.410	732	100	0	3	1	0	.975	9	O-81(0-61-22)	0.6
1966	Bos-A	40	126	16	32	4	0	5	17	15	20	.254	.333	.405	738	101	0	0	1	-0	.985	-1	O-32(0-29-4)	-0.3
	KC-A	88	272	34	61	14	1	5	27	37	53	.224	.322	.338	660	93	-2	5	3	0	.994	1	O-77(47-33-1)	-0.4
	Yr	128	398	50	93	18	1	10	44	52	73	.234	.325	.359	685	96	-1	5	4	-0	.991	0	*O-109(47-62-5)	-0.7
1967	KC-A	134	356	31	86	14	5	5	36	53	69	.242	.340	.351	691	108	5	5	7	-1	.981	-1	*O-113(54-30-40)	-0.3
1968	Oak-A	88	150	7	27	1	1	0	5	17	21	.180	.263	.200	463	44	-10	4	0	1	1.000	-2	O-64(39-26-4)	-1.5
1969	Sea-A	39	55	4	6	2	1	1	1	6	11	.109	.197	.236	433	21	-6	2	1	0	1.000	-3	O-26(1-24-1)	-1.0
	NY-N	10	15	0	2	2	0	0	1	1	6	.133	.188	.267	454	25	-2	0	0	0	1.000	-1	/O-5(4-1-0)	-0.3
1970	Mon-N	91	274	38	72	11	2	5	37	35	35	.263	.348	.372	721	93	-2	5	3	0	1.000	-3	O-71(21-50-4),1-19	-0.8
1971	Mon-N	51	102	7	16	2	2	0	8	9	17	.157	.232	.216	448	27	-10	1	1	-0	.952	-2	O-23(20-6-1)/1-6	-1.4
1973	NY-N	38	92	9	22	2	0	0	10	9	16	.239	.307	.261	568	60	-5	0	1	-0	1.000	-7	O-35(21-18-0)	-1.4
1974	NY-N	26	33	3	3	0	0	0	0	3	2	.091	.167	.091	258	-27	-6	0	0	0	1.000	-7	O-24(9-11-4)	-1.4
Total	10	705	1815	197	411	67	16	30	177	217	316	.226	.311	.331	642	83	-39	25	18	-1	.985	-17	O-555C/1-25	-8.5
■ GOOSE GOSLIN	Goslin, Leon Allen b: 10/16/1900, Salem, N.J. d: 5/15/71, Bridgeton, N.J. BL/TR, 5'11.5", 185 lbs. Deb: 9/16/21 H Career OF: (1949-LF 84-CF 170-RF)																							
1921	Was-A	14	50	8	13	1	1	1	6	6	5	.260	.351	.380	731	91	-1	0	0	0	1.000	0	O-14(1-0-14)	-0.2
1922	Was-A	101	358	44	116	19	7	3	53	25	26	.324	.373	.441	814	117	9	4	4	-1	.932	-4	O-92(88-0-5)	-0.3
1923	Was-A	150	600	86	180	29	**18**	9	99	40	53	.300	.347	.453	800	115	10	7	2	1	.957	7	*O-149(149-0-0)	0.6
1924	*Was-A	154	579	100	199	30	17	12	**129**	68	29	.344	.421	.516	937	145	39	15	14	-2	.960	6	*O-154(154-0-0)	3.0
1925	*Was-A	150	601	116	201	34	**20**	18	113	53	50	.334	.394	.547	941	140	33	27	8	**3**	.971	14	*O-150(140-20-0)	3.6
1926	Was-A	147	568	105	201	26	15	17	108	63	38	.354	.425	.542	967	155	45	8	8	-1	.964	19	*O-147(86-61-0)	5.1
1927	Was-A	148	581	96	194	37	15	13	120	50	28	.334	.392	.516	908	136	29	21	6	3	.955	2	*O-148(146-2-0)	2.0
1928	Was-A	135	456	80	173	36	10	17	102	48	19	**.379**	.442	.614	1056	176	50	16	3	**2**	.962	3	*O-125(125-0-2)	4.3
1929	Was-A	145	553	82	159	28	7	18	91	66	33	.288	.366	.461	827	111	8	10	3	1	.968	-4	*O-142(142-0-0)	-0.6
1930	Was-A	47	188	34	51	11	5	7	38	19	19	.271	.344	.495	839	110	2	3	2	-0	.937	-5	O-47(47-0-0)	-0.6
	StL-A	101	396	81	129	25	7	30	100	48	35	.326	.400	.652	1052	156	32	14	9	-0	.973	12	*O-101(101-0-0)	3.2
	Yr	148	584	115	180	36	12	37	138	67	54	.308	.382	.601	983	142	34	17	11	-0	.964	7	*O-148(148-0-0)	2.6
1931	StL-A	151	591	114	194	42	10	24	105	80	41	.328	.412	.555	967	147	40	9	6	-0	.960	5	*O-151(151-0-0)	3.3
1932	StL-A	150	572	88	171	28	9	17	104	92	35	.299	.398	.469	866	117	16	12	9	-1	.951	8	*O-149(148-1-0)/3-1	1.4
1933	*Was-A	132	549	97	163	35	10	10	64	42	32	.297	.348	.452	800	112	7	5	2	0	.965	8	*O-128(3-0-125)	0.7
1934	*Det-A	151	614	106	187	38	7	13	100	65	38	.305	.373	.453	826	112	10	5	4	-0	.953	2	*O-149(145-0-4)	0.3
1935	*Det-A	147	590	88	172	34	6	9	109	56	31	.292	.355	.415	770	102	1	5	4	-0	.965	0	*O-144(128-0-18)	-0.7
1936	Det-A★	147	572	122	180	33	8	24	125	85	50	.315	.403	.526	930	127	24	14	4	2	.955	-5	*O-144(144-0-0)	1.2
1937	Det-A	79	181	30	43	11	1	4	35	35	18	.238	.367	.376	743	86	-3	0	1	-0	.954	-2	O-40(39-0-1)/1-1	-0.7
1938	Was-A	38	57	6	9	3	0	2	8	8	5	.158	.262	.316	577	47	-5	0	0	0	1.000	-1	O-13(12-0-1)	-0.6
Total	18	2287	8656	1483	2735	500	173	248	1609	949	585	.316	.387	.500	887	128	349	175	89	7	.960	62	*O-2187L/1-1,3-1	25.0
■ HOWIE GOSS	Goss, Howard Wayne b: 11/1/34, Wewoka, Okla. d: 7/31/96, Reno, Nev. BR/TR, 6'4", 204 lbs. Deb: 4/10/62																							
1962	Pit-N	89	111	19	27	6	0	2	10	9	36	.243	.306	.351	657	76	-4	5	2	0	.985	-12	O-66(47-18-6)	-1.6
1963	Hou-N	133	411	37	86	18	2	9	44	31	128	.209	.265	.328	593	74	-15	4	6	-1	.993	7	*O-123(0-123-0)	-1.4
Total	2	222	522	56	113	24	2	11	54	40	164	.216	.274	.333	607	75	-18	9	8	-1	.991	-5	O-189(47-141-6)	-3.0
■ DICK GOSSETT	Gossett, John Star b: 8/21/1891, Dennison, Ohio d: 10/6/62, Massillon, Ohio BR/TR, 5'11", 185 lbs. Deb: 4/30/13																							
1913	NY-A	39	105	9	17	2	0	0	9	10	22	.162	.254	.181	435	28	-9	1			.972	-5	C-38	-1.2
1914	NY-A	10	21	3	3	0	0	0	1	5	5	.143	.333	.143	476	44	-1	0			.977	-1	C-10	-0.2
Total	2	49	126	12	20	2	0	0	10	15	27	.159	.269	.175	444	31	-10	1			.973	-6	/C-48	-1.4
■ JULIO GOTAY	Gotay, Julio Enrique (Sanchez) b: 6/9/39, Fajardo, P.R. BR/TR, 6', 180 lbs. Deb: 8/6/60																							
1960	StL-N	3	8	1	3	0	0	0	0	0	2	.375	.375	.375	750	98	-0	1	0	0	.750	-2	/S-2,3-1	-0.1

YEAR	TM/L	G	AB	R	H	2B	3B	HR	RBI	BB	SO	AVG	OBP	SLG	OPS	OPS+	BR+	SB	CS	SBR	FA	FR	G/POS	TPR
1961	StL-N	10	45	5	11	4	0	0	5	3	5	.244	.292	.333	625	59	-3	0	0	0	.804	-4	S-10	-0.6
1962	StL-N	127	369	47	94	12	1	2	27	27	47	.255	.316	.309	625	62	-19	7	3	0	.956	5	*S-120/2-8,O-2L,3-1	-0.4
1963	Pit-N	4	2	0	1	0	0	0	0	1	0	.500	.500	.500	1000	188	0	0	0	0	.667	0	/2-1	0.0
1964	Pit-N	3	2	0	1	0	0	0	0	1	0	.500	.667	.500	1167	235	1	0	0	0	.000	0	H	0.1
1965	Cal-A	40	77	6	19	4	0	1	3	4	9	.247	.284	.338	622	78	-2	0	0	0	.961	3	2-23/3-9,S-1	0.2
1966	Hou-N	4	5	0	0	0	0	0	0	0	0	.000	.000	.000	0	-99	-1	0	0	0	1.000	0	/3-1	-0.1
1967	Hou-N	77	234	30	66	10	2	2	15	15	30	.282	.331	.368	698	103	1	1	1	-0	.971	-4	2-30,S-20/3-3	0.2
1968	Hou-N	75	165	9	41	3	0	1	11	4	21	.248	.271	.285	555	68	-7	1	2	-0	.982	10	2-48/3-1	0.7
1969	Hou-N	46	81	7	21	5	0	0	9	7	13	.259	.318	.321	639	81	-2	2	1	0	.987	6	2-16/3-1	0.5
Total	10	389	988	106	257	38	3	6	70	61	127	.260	.309	.323	632	75	-32	12	7	0	.944	15	S-153,2-126/3-17,O	0.5

■ CHARLIE GOULD

Gould, Charles Harvey b: 8/21/1847, Cincinnati, Ohio d: 4/10/17, Flushing, N.Y. BR/TR, 6', 172 lbs. Deb: 5/5/1871 M

YEAR	TM/L	G	AB	R	H	2B	3B	HR	RBI	BB	SO	AVG	OBP	SLG	OPS	OPS+	BR+	SB	CS	SBR	FA	FR	G/POS	TPR
1871	Bos-n	31	151	38	43	9	2	2	32	3	1	.285	.299	.411	709	98	-1	6	2	1	.906	-3	*1-30/O-1(0-0-1)	-0.2
1872	Bos-n	45	211	40	54	9	**8**	0	33	2	3	.256	.263	.374	637	89	-4	0	0	0	.933	0	*1-44/O-2(0-0-2)	-0.2
1874	Bal-n	33	143	19	32	6	0	0	14	2	2	.224	.234	.266	500	60	-6	1	0	0	.951	1	1-32/C-1	-0.3
1875	NH-n	27	109	9	29	4	1	0	8	1	2	.266	.273	.321	594	121	3	0	1	-0	.946	-4	1-26/C-1,O-1(0-0-1),M	0.0
1876	Cin-N	61	264	27	65	7	0	0	11	6	11	.246	.269	.279	548	97	1				.939	1	*1-61/P-2,M	0.0
1877	Cin-N	24	91	5	25	2	1	0	13	5	5	.275	.313	.319	631	112	2				.922	-1	1-24/O-1(1-0-0)	0.0
Total	4 n	136	614	106	158	28	11	2	87	8	8	.257	.267	.349	615	90	-8	7	3	0	.934	-6	1-132/O-4(0-0-4),C-2	-0.7
Total	2	85	355	32	90	9	1	0	24	11	16	.254	.281	.289	570	101	3				.934	0	/1-85,P-2,O-1(1-0-0)	0.0

■ NICK GOULISH

Goulish, Nicholas Edward b: 11/13/17, Punxsutawney, Pa. d: 5/15/84, Youngstown, Ohio BL/TL, 6'1", 179 lbs. Deb: 4/19/44

YEAR	TM/L	G	AB	R	H	2B	3B	HR	RBI	BB	SO	AVG	OBP	SLG	OPS	OPS+	BR+	SB	CS	SBR	FA	FR	G/POS	TPR
1944	Phi-N	1	1	0	0	0	0	0	0	0	0	.000	.000	.000	0	-99	-0	0			.000	0	H	0.0
1945	Phi-N	13	11	4	3	0	0	0	2	1	3	.273	.333	.273	606	72	-0	0			1.000	-1	/O-2(1-0-1)	-0.1
Total	2	14	12	4	3	0	0	0	2	1	3	.250	.308	.250	558	58	-1	0			1.000	-1	/O-2(1-0-1)	-0.1

■ CLAUDE GOUZZIE

Gouzzie, Claude b: 1873, France d: 9/21/07, Denver, Colo. BR/TR, 5'9", 170 lbs. Deb: 7/22/03

YEAR	TM/L	G	AB	R	H	2B	3B	HR	RBI	BB	SO	AVG	OBP	SLG	OPS	OPS+	BR+	SB	CS	SBR	FA	FR	G/POS	TPR
1903	StL-A	1	1	0	0	0	0	0	0	0		.000	.000	.000	0	-99	-0	0			1.000	0	/2-1	0.0

■ HANK GOWDY

Gowdy, Henry Morgan b: 8/24/1889, Columbus, Ohio d: 8/1/66, Columbus, Ohio BR/TR, 6'2", 182 lbs. Deb: 9/13/10 MC

YEAR	TM/L	G	AB	R	H	2B	3B	HR	RBI	BB	SO	AVG	OBP	SLG	OPS	OPS+	BR+	SB	CS	SBR	FA	FR	G/POS	TPR
1910	NY-N	7	14	1	3	1	0	0	2	2	3	.214	.313	.286	598	75	-0	1			.943	0	/1-5	0.0
1911	NY-N	4	4	1	1	1	0	0	0	2	0	.250	.500	.500	1000	175	1	0			1.000	-0	/1-2	0.0
	Bos-N	29	97	9	28	4	2	0	16	4	19	.289	.324	.371	695	87	-2	2			.966	-1	1-26/C-1	-0.4
	Yr	33	101	10	29	5	2	0	16	6	19	.287	.333	.376	710	92	-1	2			.969	-1	1-28/C-1	-0.4
1912	Bos-N	44	96	16	26	6	1	3	10	16	13	.271	.386	.448	834	126	4	3			.926	-2	C-22/1-7	0.4
1913	Bos-N	3	5	0	3	1	0	0	2	3	2	.600	.750	.800	1550	336	2	0			1.000	-1	/C-2	0.1
1914	*Bos-N	128	366	42	89	17	6	3	46	48	40	.243	.337	.347	684	104	3	14			.968	-5	*C-115/1-9	0.7
1915	Bos-N	118	316	27	78	15	3	2	30	41	34	.247	.339	.332	671	108	4	10	4	1	.974	-1	*C-114	1.5
1916	Bos-N	118	349	32	88	14	1	1	34	24	33	.252	.311	.307	618	94	-2	8			.980	3	*C-116	1.2
1917	Bos-N	49	154	12	33	7	0	0	14	15	13	.214	.288	.260	548	73	-5	2			.969	-1	C-49	-0.2
1919	Bos-N	78	219	18	61	8	1	1	22	19	16	.279	.339	.338	677	108	3	5			.977	5	C-74/1-1	1.5
1920	Bos-N	80	214	14	52	11	2	0	18	20	15	.243	.314	.313	627	84	-4	6	1	1	.980	11	C-74	1.4
1921	Bos-N	64	164	17	49	7	2	2	17	16	11	.299	.368	.402	771	110	3	2	0	0	.981	-1	C-53	0.5
1922	Bos-N	92	221	23	70	11	1	1	27	24	13	.317	.391	.389	780	107	3	2	1	0	.971	1	C-72/1-1	0.8
1923	Bos-N	23	48	5	6	1	1	0	5	15	5	.125	.354	.188	541	48	-3	1	1	-0	.982	-2	C-15	-0.4
	*NY-N	53	122	13	40	6	3	1	18	21	9	.328	.427	.451	877	133	7	2	0	0	.986	-7	C-43	0.2
	Yr	76	170	18	46	7	4	1	23	36	14	.271	.404	.376	780	109	4	3	1	0	.985	-10	C-58	-0.2
1924	*NY-N	87	191	25	62	9	1	4	37	26	11	.325	.411	.445	856	133	10	1	0	0	.982	5	C-78	1.9
1925	NY-N	47	114	14	37	4	3	3	19	12	7	.325	.389	.491	880	128	5	0	0	0	1.000	1	C-41	0.8
1929	Bos-N	10	16	1	7	0	0	0	3	0	2	.438	.438	.438	875	122	1	0			1.000	-0	/C-9	0.0
1930	Bos-N	16	25	0	5	1	0	0	2	3	1	.200	.310	.240	550	37	-3	0			.972	1	C-15	-0.1
Total	17	1050	2735	270	738	124	27	21	322	311	247	.270	.351	.358	709	105	26	59	7		.975	5	C-893/1-51	9.9

■ BILLY GRABARKEWITZ

Grabarkewitz, Billy Cordell b: 1/18/46, Lockhart, Tex. BR/TR, 5'10", 170 lbs. Deb: 4/22/69

YEAR	TM/L	G	AB	R	H	2B	3B	HR	RBI	BB	SO	AVG	OBP	SLG	OPS	OPS+	BR+	SB	CS	SBR	FA	FR	G/POS	TPR
1969	LA-N	34	65	4	6	1	1	0	5	4	19	.092	.145	.138	283	-22	-11	1	0	0	.954	-2	S-18/3-6,2-3	-1.2
1970	LA-N★	156	529	92	153	20	8	17	84	95	149	.289	.403	.454	857	135	30	19	9	1	.959	-1	3-97,S-50,2-20	3.4
1971	LA-N	44	71	9	16	5	0	0	6	19	16	.225	.389	.296	685	102	1	1	2	-0	1.000	4	2-13,3-10/S-1	0.6
1972	LA-N	53	144	17	24	4	0	4	16	18	53	.167	.268	.278	546	57	-8	3	0	1	.902	-4	3-24,2-19/S-2	-1.1
1973	Cal-A	61	129	27	21	6	1	3	9	28	27	.163	.316	.295	611	79	-3	2	2	-0	.965	-6	2-18,3-12/S-1,OD	-0.9
	Phi-N	25	66	12	19	2	0	2	7	12	18	.288	.397	.409	807	121	2	3	1	0	.960	0	2-20/3-3,O-1(0-0-1)	0.4
1974	Phi-N	34	30	7	4	0	0	1	2	5	10	.133	.257	.233	490	36	-3	3	1	0	1.000	-1	/O-5(5-0-0),3-1	-0.3
	Chi-N	53	125	21	31	3	2	1	12	21	28	.248	.361	.328	689	90	-1	1	2	-0	.954	2	2-45/S-7,3-6	0.3
	Yr	87	155	28	35	3	2	2	14	26	38	.226	.341	.310	650	80	-3	4	3	-0	.954	2	2-45/3-7,S-7,O-5L	0.0
1975	Oak-A	6	2	0	0	0	0	0	0	0	1	.000	.000	.000	0	-99	-1	0	0	0	.833	0	/2-4,D-1	0.0
Total	7	466	1161	189	274	41	12	28	141	202	321	.236	.354	.364	718	101	8	33	17	1	.952	-8	3-159,2-142/S-79,OD	1.2

■ ROD GRABER

Graber, Rodney Blaine b: 6/20/30, Massillon, Ohio BL/TL, 5'11", 175 lbs. Deb: 9/9/58

YEAR	TM/L	G	AB	R	H	2B	3B	HR	RBI	BB	SO	AVG	OBP	SLG	OPS	OPS+	BR+	SB	CS	SBR	FA	FR	G/POS	TPR
1958	Cle-A	4	8	0	1	0	0	0	0	1	2	.125	.222	.125	347	-2	-1	0	0	0	1.000	-0	/O-2(0-2-0)	-0.1

■ JOHNNY GRABOWSKI

Grabowski, John Patrick "Nig" b: 1/7/1900, Ware, Mass. d: 5/23/46, Albany, N.Y. BR/TR, 5'10", 185 lbs. Deb: 7/11/24

YEAR	TM/L	G	AB	R	H	2B	3B	HR	RBI	BB	SO	AVG	OBP	SLG	OPS	OPS+	BR+	SB	CS	SBR	FA	FR	G/POS	TPR
1924	Chi-A	20	56	10	14	3	0	0	3	2	4	.250	.276	.304	579	51	-4	0	0	0	.972	1	C-19	-0.2
1925	Chi-A	21	46	5	14	4	1	0	10	2	4	.304	.333	.435	768	99	-0	0	1	-0	.983	0	C-21	0.0
1926	Chi-A	48	122	6	32	1	1	1	11	4	15	.262	.286	.311	597	58	-8	0	1	-0	.973	-2	C-38/1-1	-0.8
1927	*NY-A	70	195	29	54	2	4	0	25	20	15	.277	.350	.328	678	79	-5	0	0	0	.984	0	C-68	-0.1
1928	NY-A	75	202	21	48	7	1	1	21	10	21	.238	.274	.297	571	51	-14	0	0	0	.987	2	C-75	-0.8
1929	NY-A	22	59	4	12	1	0	0	2	3	6	.203	.242	.220	462	21	-7	1	0	0	.943	-0	C-22	-0.5
1931	Det-A	40	136	9	32	7	1	1	14	6	19	.235	.268	.324	591	53	-10	0	0	0	.984	2	C-39	-0.5
Total	7	296	816	84	206	25	8	3	86	47	84	.252	.295	.314	609	60	-49	1	2	-0	.979	4	C-282/1-1	-2.9

■ JOE GRACE

Grace, Joseph Laverne b: 1/5/14, Gorham, Ill. d: 9/18/69, Murphysboro, Ill. BL/TR, 6'1", 180 lbs. Deb: 9/24/38 Career OF: (129-LF 25-CF 234-RF)

YEAR	TM/L	G	AB	R	H	2B	3B	HR	RBI	BB	SO	AVG	OBP	SLG	OPS	OPS+	BR+	SB	CS	SBR	FA	FR	G/POS	TPR
1938	StL-A	12	47	7	16	1	0	0	4	2	3	.340	.367	.362	729	83	-1	0	1	-0	.933	-2	O-12(0-0-12)	-0.4
1939	StL-A	74	207	35	63	11	2	3	22	19	24	.304	.363	.420	783	98	-1	3	2	-0	.968	-4	O-53(10-22-21)	-0.6
1940	StL-A	80	229	45	59	14	2	5	25	26	23	.258	.336	.402	738	88	-4	2	2	-0	.958	-5	O-51(3-0-48),C-12	-1.1
1941	StL-A	115	362	53	112	17	4	6	60	57	31	.309	.410	.428	839	118	12	1	3	-1	.983	-2	O-88(0-0-88)/C-9	0.4
1946	StL-A	48	161	21	37	7	2	1	13	16	20	.230	.307	.317	624	71	-6	1	3	-1	.967	1	O-43(0-0-43)	-0.7
	Was-A	77	321	39	97	17	4	2	31	24	19	.302	.358	.399	757	118	7	1	4	-1	.959	4	O-74(60-0-14)	0.5
	Yr	125	482	60	134	24	6	3	44	40	39	.278	.341	.371	712	101	0	2	7	-2	.962	5	*O-117(60-0-57)	-0.2
1947	Was-A	78	234	25	58	9	4	3	17	35	15	.248	.348	.359	707	99	0	1	2	-0	.976	2	O-67(56-3-8)	-0.2
Total	6	484	1561	225	442	76	18	20	172	179	135	.283	.362	.393	755	102	8	9	17	-4	.969	-6	O-388R/C-21	-2.1

■ MARK GRACE

Grace, Mark Eugene b: 6/28/64, Winston-Salem, N.C BL/TL, 6'2", 190 lbs. Deb: 5/2/88

YEAR	TM/L	G	AB	R	H	2B	3B	HR	RBI	BB	SO	AVG	OBP	SLG	OPS	OPS+	BR+	SB	CS	SBR	FA	FR	G/POS	TPR
1988	Chi-N	134	486	65	144	23	4	7	57	60	43	.296	.374	.403	777	118	13	3	3	-0	.987	-4	*1-133	-0.1
1989	*Chi-N	142	510	74	160	28	3	13	79	80	42	.314	.407	.457	864	136	27	14	7	1	.996	13	*1-142	3.2
1990	Chi-N	157	589	72	182	32	1	9	82	59	54	.309	.377	.413	789	109	9	15	6	1	.992	27	*1-153	2.6
1991	Chi-N	160	619	87	169	28	5	8	58	70	53	.273	.350	.373	723	99	0	3	4	-1	.995	20	*1-160	0.9
1992	Chi-N	158	603	72	185	37	5	9	79	72	36	.307	.384	.430	814	127	23	6	1	1	.998	9	*1-157	2.3
1993	Chi-N★	155	594	86	193	39	4	14	98	71	32	.325	.398	.475	873	135	31	8	4	0	.997	1	*1-154	1.7
1994	Chi-N	106	403	55	120	23	3	6	44	48	41	.298	.373	.414	787	106	5	0	1	-0	.993	1	*1-103	-0.4
1995	Chi-N★	143	552	97	180	**51**	3	16	92	65	46	.326	.399	.516	915	142	34	6	2	1	.995	4	*1-143	2.4
1996	Chi-N	142	547	88	181	39	1	9	75	62	41	.331	.400	.455	855	122	19	2	3	-1	.997	3	*1-141	0.8
1997	Chi-N★	151	555	87	177	32	5	13	78	88	45	.319	.414	.465	879	127	25	2	4	-1	.995	5	*1-148	1.4

YEAR	TM/L	G	AB	R	H	2B	3B	HR	RBI	BB	SO	AVG	OBP	SLG	OPS	OPS+	BR+	SB	CS	SBR	FA	FR	G/POS	TPR
1998	*Chi-N	158	595	92	184	39	3	17	89	93	56	.309	.405	.471	876	125	25	4	7	-2	.994	4	*1-156	1.3
1999	Chi-N	161	593	107	183	44	5	16	91	83	44	.309	.395	.481	876	122	22	3	4	-1	.994	-3	*1-160	0.3
2000	Chi-N	143	510	75	143	41	1	11	82	95	28	.280	.399	.429	829	112	13	1	2	-0	**.997**	5	*1-140	0.4
Total	13	1910	7156	1057	2201	456	43	148	1004	946	561	.308	.391	.445	836	122	246	67	48	-2	.995	85	*1-1890	16.8

■ MIKE GRACE
Grace, Michael Lee b: 6/14/56, Pontiac, Mich. BR/TR, 6', 175 lbs. Deb: 4/18/78

YEAR	TM/L	G	AB	R	H	2B	3B	HR	RBI	BB	SO	AVG	OBP	SLG	OPS	OPS+	BR+	SB	CS	SBR	FA	FR	G/POS	TPR
1978	Cin-N	5	3	0	0	0	0	0	0	0	2	.000	.000	.000	0	-99	-1	0	0	0	1.000	1	/3-2	0.0

■ EARL GRACE
Grace, Robert Earl b: 2/24/07, Barlow, Ky. d: 12/22/80, Phoenix, Ariz. BL/TR, 6', 175 lbs. Deb: 4/23/29

YEAR	TM/L	G	AB	R	H	2B	3B	HR	RBI	BB	SO	AVG	OBP	SLG	OPS	OPS+	BR+	SB	CS	SBR	FA	FR	G/POS	TPR
1929	Chi-N	27	80	7	20	1	0	2	17	9	7	.250	.333	.338	671	67	-4	0			1.000	3	C-27	0.1
1931	Chi-N	7	9	2	1	0	0	0	1	4	1	.111	.385	.111	496	39	-1	0			1.000	-0	/C-2	0.0
	Pit-N	47	150	8	42	6	1	1	20	13	5	.280	.337	.353	691	87	-3	0			.974	-1	C-45	-0.1
	Yr	54	159	10	43	6	1	1	21	17	6	.270	.341	.340	681	84	-3	0			.976	-1	C-47	-0.1
1932	Pit-N	115	390	41	107	17	5	8	55	14	23	.274	.305	.405	710	91	-6	0			**.998**	-7	*C-114	-0.6
1933	Pit-N	93	291	22	84	13	1	3	44	26	23	.289	.349	.371	720	106	3	0			.980	1	C-88	0.9
1934	Pit-N	95	289	27	78	17	1	4	24	20	19	.270	.317	.377	694	83	-7	0			.982	-9	C-83/1-1	-1.0
1935	Pit-N	77	224	19	59	8	1	3	29	32	17	.263	.355	.348	704	87	-3	1			.990	3	C-69	0.3
1936	Phi-N	86	221	24	55	11	0	4	32	34	20	.249	.352	.353	705	82	-5	0			.976	-4	C-65	-0.5
1937	Phi-N	80	223	19	47	10	1	6	29	33	15	.211	.313	.345	658	73	-8	0			.990	-3	C-64	-0.7
Total	8	627	1877	169	493	83	10	31	251	185	130	.263	.331	.367	698	86	-34	1			.987	-17	C-557/1-1	-1.6

■ JOHN GRADY
Grady, John J. b: 6/18/1860, Lowell, Mass. d: 7/15/1893, Lowell, Mass. 5'7", 150 lbs. Deb: 5/10/1884

YEAR	TM/L	G	AB	R	H	2B	3B	HR	RBI	BB	SO	AVG	OBP	SLG	OPS	OPS+	BR+	SB	CS	SBR	FA	FR	G/POS	TPR
1884	Alt-U	9	36	5	11	3	0	0		2		.306	.342	.389	731	119	-0				.909	-1	/1-8,O-1(0-1-0)	-0.2

■ MIKE GRADY
Grady, Michael William b: 12/23/1869, Kennett Square, Pa d: 12/3/43, Kennett Square, Pa. BR/TR, 5'11", 190 lbs. Deb: 4/24/1894

YEAR	TM/L	G	AB	R	H	2B	3B	HR	RBI	BB	SO	AVG	OBP	SLG	OPS	OPS+	BR+	SB	CS	SBR	FA	FR	G/POS	TPR
1894	Phi-N	61	190	45	69	13	8	0	40	14	13	.363	.427	.516	942	130	9	3			.878	-12	C-45,1-11/O-2(1-0-1)	0.1
1895	Phi-N	46	123	21	40	3	1	1	23	14	8	.325	.407	.390	797	106	2	5			.926	-11	C-38/O-5L,3-1,1-1	-0.5
1896	Phi-N	72	242	49	77	20	7	1	44	16	19	.318	.382	.471	853	126	9	10			.942	-7	C-61/3-7	0.6
1897	Phi-N	4	13	1	2	0	0	0	0	1		.154	.214	.154	368	-2	-2	0			1.000	1	/C-3	-0.1
	StL-N	84	326	49	91	11	3	8	57	26		.279	.351	.405	756	101	0	7			.974	-1	1-84/O-1(0-0-1)	-0.1
	Yr	88	339	50	93	11	3	8	57	27		.274	.346	.395	741	97	-2	7			.974	-0	1-84/C-3,O-1(0-0-1)	-0.2
1898	NY-N	93	287	64	85	19	5	3	49	38		.296	.399	.429	827	142	17	20			.944	-4	C-57,O-30R/1-7,S-3	1.5
1899	NY-N	87	315	49	106	18	8	2	54	29		.337	.405	.463	868	143	19	20			.940	-12	C-44,3-35/O-4R,1-4	1.1
1900	NY-N	83	251	36	55	8	4	0	27	34		.219	.331	.283	614	74	-7	9			.932	-14	C-41,1-12,S-11,/3O2	-1.6
1901	Was-A	94	347	57	99	17	10	9	56	27		.285	.351	.470	821	128	12	14			.975	6	1-59,C-30/O-3(3-0-0)	1.8
1904	StL-N	101	323	44	101	15	11	5	43	31		.313	.376	.474	850	169	26	6			.955	-20	C-77,1-11/2-3,3-1	1.5
1905	StL-N	100	311	41	89	20	7	4	41	33		.286	.360	.434	794	141	15	15			.956	-11	C-71,1-20	1.2
1906	StL-N	97	280	33	70	11	3	3	27	48		.250	.369	.343	712	127	11	5			.983	-10	C-60,1-38	0.6
Total	11	922	3008	489	884	155	67	36	461	311	40	.294	.374	.426	800	127	111	114			.946	-94	C-527,1-247/3-51,OS2	6.1

■ FRED GRAFF
Graff, Frederick Gottleib b: 8/25/1889, Canton, Ohio d: 10/4/79, Chattanooga, Tenn. BR/TR, 5'10.5", 164 lbs. Deb: 5/14/13

YEAR	TM/L	G	AB	R	H	2B	3B	HR	RBI	BB	SO	AVG	OBP	SLG	OPS	OPS+	BR+	SB	CS	SBR	FA	FR	G/POS	TPR
1913	StL-A	4	5	1	2	1	0	0	2	3	3	.400	.625	.600	1225	266	2	0			1.000	-1	/3-4	0.1

■ LOUIS GRAFF
Graff, Louis George "Chappie" b: 7/25/1866, Philadelphia, Pa. d: 4/16/55, Bryn Mawr, Pa. TR, Deb: 6/23/1890

YEAR	TM/L	G	AB	R	H	2B	3B	HR	RBI	BB	SO	AVG	OBP	SLG	OPS	OPS+	BR+	SB	CS	SBR	FA	FR	G/POS	TPR
1890	Syr-a	1	5	0	2	1	0	0	3	0		.400	.400	.600	1000	217	1	0			.333	-2	/C-1	-0.1

■ MILT GRAFF
Graff, Milton Edward b: 12/30/30, Jefferson Center, Pa. BL/TR, 5'7.5", 158 lbs. Deb: 4/16/57 C

YEAR	TM/L	G	AB	R	H	2B	3B	HR	RBI	BB	SO	AVG	OBP	SLG	OPS	OPS+	BR+	SB	CS	SBR	FA	FR	G/POS	TPR
1957	KC-A	56	155	16	28	4	3	0	10	15	10	.181	.262	.245	507	39	-13	2	5	-1	.988	1	2-53	-1.0
1958	KC-A	5	1	0	0	0	0	0	0	0	0	.000	.000	.000	0	-98	-0	0	0	0	1.000	0	/2-1	0.0
Total	2	61	156	16	28	4	3	0	10	15	10	.179	.260	.244	504	38	-13	2	5	-1	.988	2	/2-54	-1.0

■ TONY GRAFFANINO
Graffanino, Anthony Joseph b: 6/6/72, Amityville, N.Y. BR/TR, 6'1", 175 lbs. Deb: 4/19/96

YEAR	TM/L	G	AB	R	H	2B	3B	HR	RBI	BB	SO	AVG	OBP	SLG	OPS	OPS+	BR+	SB	CS	SBR	FA	FR	G/POS	TPR
1996	Atl-N	22	46	7	8	1	1	0	2	4	13	.174	.255	.239	494	30	-5	0	0	0	.969	4	2-18	-0.1
1997	*Atl-N	104	186	33	48	9	1	8	20	26	46	.258	.352	.446	798	105	1	6	4	-0	.982	12	2-75/3-2,S-2,1-1	1.6
1998	*Atl-N	105	289	32	61	14	1	5	22	24	68	.211	.276	.318	595	56	-19	1	4	-1	.971	13	2-93/S-2,3-1	-0.4
1999	TB-A	39	130	20	41	9	4	2	19	9	22	.315	.364	.492	857	115	3	3	2	-0	.990	8	2-17,S-17/3-1	1.2
2000	TB-A	13	20	8	6	1	0	0	1	1	2	.300	.364	.350	714	82	-0	0	0	0	1.000	4	/2-6,3-3,S-1	0.3
	*Chi-A	57	148	25	40	5	1	2	16	21	25	.270	.365	.358	723	83	-3	7	4	0	.966	13	S-21,2-19,3-12,/D-3	1.1
	Yr	70	168	33	46	6	1	2	17	22	27	.274	.365	.357	722	83	-4	7	4	0	.973	17	2-25,S-22,3-15,/D-3	1.4
Total	5	340	819	125	204	39	8	17	80	85	176	.249	.325	.379	703	81	-23	17	14	-1	.976	54	2-228/S-43,3-19,D1	3.7

■ MOONLIGHT GRAHAM
Graham, Archibald Wright b: 11/9/1876, Fayetteville, N.C. d: 8/25/65, Chisholm, Minn. BL/TR, 5'10.5", 170 lbs. Deb: 6/29/05

YEAR	TM/L	G	AB	R	H	2B	3B	HR	RBI	BB	SO	AVG	OBP	SLG	OPS	OPS+	BR+	SB	CS	SBR	FA	FR	G/POS	TPR
1905	NY-N	1	0	0	0	0	0	0	0	0		—	—	—	—	—	0	0			.000	-0	/O-1(0-0-1)	0.0

■ SKINNY GRAHAM
Graham, Arthur William b: 8/12/09, Somerville, Mass. d: 7/10/67, Cambridge, Mass. BL/TR, 5'7", 162 lbs. Deb: 9/14/34

YEAR	TM/L	G	AB	R	H	2B	3B	HR	RBI	BB	SO	AVG	OBP	SLG	OPS	OPS+	BR+	SB	CS	SBR	FA	FR	G/POS	TPR
1934	Bos-A	13	47	7	11	2	1	0	3	6	13	.234	.321	.319	640	61	-3	2	2	-0	1.000	-1	O-13(0-4-9)	-0.4
1935	Bos-A	8	10	1	3	0	0	0	1	1	3	.300	.364	.300	664	69	-0	1	0	0	1.000	-1	/O-2(0-0-2)	-0.1
Total	2	21	57	8	14	2	1	0	4	7	16	.246	.328	.316	644	62	-3	3	2	-0	1.000	-2	/O-15(0-4-11)	-0.5

■ BARNEY GRAHAM
Graham, Barney b: Philadelphia, Pa. d: 12/31/1896, Mobile, Ala. Deb: 9/4/1889

YEAR	TM/L	G	AB	R	H	2B	3B	HR	RBI	BB	SO	AVG	OBP	SLG	OPS	OPS+	BR+	SB	CS	SBR	FA	FR	G/POS	TPR
1889	Phi-a	4	18	0	3	0	0	0	0	0	0	.167	.167	.167	333	-5	-2	0			.933	1	/3-4	-0.1

■ BERNIE GRAHAM
Graham, Bernard W. b: 1860, Beloit, Wis. d: 10/30/1886, Mobile, Ala. BL, Deb: 7/11/1884

YEAR	TM/L	G	AB	R	H	2B	3B	HR	RBI	BB	SO	AVG	OBP	SLG	OPS	OPS+	BR+	SB	CS	SBR	FA	FR	G/POS	TPR
1884	CP-U	1	5	2	1	0	0	0		0		.200	.200	.200	400	22	-1				1.000	-0	/O-1(1-0-0)	-0.1
	Bal-U	41	167	21	45	11	0	0		2		.269	.278	.335	613	77	-10				.814	1	O-40(0-25-15)/1-1	-0.8
	Yr	42	172	23	46	11	0	0		2		.267	.276	.331	607	76	-10				.816	1	O-41(1-25-15)/1-1	-0.9

■ BERT GRAHAM
Graham, Bert "B.G." b: 4/3/1886, Tilton, Ill. d: 6/19/71, Cottonwood, Ariz. BB/TR, 5'11.5", 187 lbs. Deb: 9/9/10

YEAR	TM/L	G	AB	R	H	2B	3B	HR	RBI	BB	SO	AVG	OBP	SLG	OPS	OPS+	BR+	SB	CS	SBR	FA	FR	G/POS	TPR
1910	StL-A	8	26	1	3	2	1	0	5	1		.115	.148	.269	417	32	-2	0			.964	1	/1-5,2-2	-0.1

■ CHARLIE GRAHAM
Graham, Charles Henry b: 4/24/1878, Santa Clara, Cal. d: 8/29/48, San Francisco, Cal BR/TR, 6', 190 lbs. Deb: 4/16/06

YEAR	TM/L	G	AB	R	H	2B	3B	HR	RBI	BB	SO	AVG	OBP	SLG	OPS	OPS+	BR+	SB	CS	SBR	FA	FR	G/POS	TPR
1906	Bos-A	30	90	10	21	1	0	1	12	10		.233	.330	.278	608	91	-0	1			.963	7	C-27	1.0

■ DAN GRAHAM
Graham, Daniel Jay b: 7/19/54, Ray, Ariz. BL/TR, 6'1", 205 lbs. Deb: 6/8/79 Career OF: (0-LF 0-CF 1-RF)

YEAR	TM/L	G	AB	R	H	2B	3B	HR	RBI	BB	SO	AVG	OBP	SLG	OPS	OPS+	BR+	SB	CS	SBR	FA	FR	G/POS	TPR
1979	Min-A	2	4	0	0	0	0	0	0	0	0	.000	.000	.000	0	-96	-1	0	0	0	.000	0	/D-1	-0.1
1980	Bal-A	86	266	32	74	7	1	15	54	14	40	.278	.314	.481	795	116	4	0	0	0	.981	0	C-73/3-9,O-1R,D-2	0.8
1981	Bal-A	55	142	7	25	3	0	2	11	13	32	.176	.245	.239	485	40	-11	0	0	0	.975	-4	C-40/3-4,D-6	-1.4
Total	3	143	412	39	99	10	1	17	65	27	72	.240	.287	.393	680	88	-7	0	0	0	.979	-4	C-113/3-13,D-9,O-1R	-0.7

■ TINY GRAHAM
Graham, Dawson Francis b: 9/9/1892, Nashville, Tenn. d: 12/29/62, Nashville, Tenn. BR/TR, 6'2", 185 lbs. Deb: 8/30/14

YEAR	TM/L	G	AB	R	H	2B	3B	HR	RBI	BB	SO	AVG	OBP	SLG	OPS	OPS+	BR+	SB	CS	SBR	FA	FR	G/POS	TPR
1914	Cin-N	25	61	5	14	1	0	0	3	3	10	.230	.266	.246	512	51	-4	1			.961	-2	1-25	-0.6

■ PEACHES GRAHAM
Graham, George Frederick b: 3/23/1877, Aledo, Ill. d: 7/25/39, Long Beach, Cal. BR/TR, 5'9", 180 lbs. Deb: 9/14/02 F Career OF: (1-LF 0-CF 4-RF)

YEAR	TM/L	G	AB	R	H	2B	3B	HR	RBI	BB	SO	AVG	OBP	SLG	OPS	OPS+	BR+	SB	CS	SBR	FA	FR	G/POS	TPR
1902	Cle-A	2	6	0	2	0	0	0	1	1		.333	.429	.333	762	118	0	0			1.000	0	/2-1	0.0
1903	Chi-N	1	2	0	0	0	0	0	0	0		.000	.000	.000	0	-99	-1	0			1.000	0	/P-1	0.0
1908	Bos-N	75	215	22	59	5	0	0	22	23		.274	.361	.298	658	112	4	4			.955	-3	C-62/2-5	0.9
1909	Bos-N	92	267	27	64	6	3	0	17	24		.240	.302	.285	587	79	-7	7			.948	-4	C-76/O-6R,S-1,3-1	-0.3
1910	Bos-N	110	291	31	82	13	2	0	21	33	15	.282	.359	.340	699	100	1	5			.966	-8	C-87/3-2,1-1,O-1R	0.2
1911	Bos-N	33	88	7	24	6	1	0	12	14	5	.273	.373	.364	736	98	0	2			.912	-5	C-26	-0.3
	Chi-N	36	71	6	17	3	0	0	8	11	8	.239	.365	.282	646	82	-1	2			.972	-5	C-28	-0.4
	Yr	69	159	13	41	9	1	0	20	25	13	.258	.369	.327	696	92	-1	4			.937	-10	C-54	-0.7
1912	Phi-N	24	59	6	17	1	0	1	4	8	5	.288	.373	.356	729	94	-0	1			.944	-2	C-19	0.0
Total	7	373	999	99	265	34	6	1	85	114	33	.265	.347	.314	661	95	-3	21			.953	-25	C-298/O-7R,2-6,31SP	0.1

YEAR	TM/L	G	AB	R	H	2B	3B	HR	RBI	BB	SO	AVG	OBP	SLG	OPS	OPS+	BR+	SB	CS	SBR	FA	FR	G/POS	TPR
■ JACK GRAHAM Graham, John Bernard b: 12/24/16, Minneapolis, Minn. d: 12/30/98, Los Alamitos, Cal. BL/TL, 6'2", 200 lbs. Deb: 4/16/46 F																								
1946	Bro-N	2	5	0	1	0	0	0	0	0	0	.200	.200	.200	400	14	-1	0			1.000	0	/1-2	-0.1
	NY-N	100	270	34	59	6	4	14	47	23	37	.219	.282	.426	708	99	-2	1			.949	-1	O-62(1-0-60)/1-7	-0.6
	Yr	102	275	34	60	6	4	14	47	23	37	.218	.281	.422	703	97	-3	1			.949	-1	O-62(1-0-60)/1-9	-0.7
1949	StL-A	137	500	71	119	22	1	24	79	61	62	.238	.326	.430	756	95	-6	0	1	-0	.984	-6	*1-136	-1.7
Total	2	239	775	105	179	28	5	38	126	84	99	.231	.310	.427	737	96	-9	1	1		.985	-7	1-145/O-62(1-0-60)	-2.4
■ LEE GRAHAM Graham, Lee Willard b: 9/22/59, Summerfield, Fla. BL/TL, 5'10", 170 lbs. Deb: 9/3/83																								
1983	Bos-A	5	6	2	0	0	0	0	1	0	0	.000	.000	.000	0	-93	-2	0	1	-0	1.000	1	/O-3(0-2-1)	-0.1
■ ROY GRAHAM Graham, Roy Vincent b: 2/22/1895, San Francisco, Cal d: 4/26/33, Manila, Philippines BR/TR, 5'10.5", 175 lbs. Deb: 5/28/22																								
1922	Chi-A	5	3	0	0	0	0	0	0	0	0	.000	.400	.000	400	12	-0	0	0	0	1.000	-0	/C-3	0.0
1923	Chi-A	36	82	3	16	2	0	0	6	9	6	.195	.290	.220	510	36	-7	0	0	0	.949	-7	C-33	-1.3
Total	2	41	85	3	16	2	0	0	6	9	6	.188	.296	.212	508	35	-8	0	0	0	.950	-7	/C-36	-1.3
■ WAYNE GRAHAM Graham, Wayne Leon b: 4/6/37, Yoakum, Tex. BR/TR, 6', 200 lbs. Deb: 4/10/63																								
1963	Phi-N	10	22	1	4	0	0	0	0	3	1	.182	.280	.182	462	36	-2	0	0	0	.857	-1	/O-6(6-0-0)	-0.3
1964	NY-N	20	33	1	3	1	0	0	0	0	5	.091	.091	.121	212	-42	-6	0	0	0	1.000	-2	3-11	-0.9
Total	2	30	55	2	7	1	0	0	0	3	6	.127	.172	.145	318	-9	-8	0	0	0	1.000	-3	/3-11,O-6(6-0-0)	-1.2
■ ALEX GRAMMAS Grammas, Alexander Peter b: 4/3/26, Birmingham, Ala. BR/TR, 6', 178 lbs. Deb: 4/13/54 MC																								
1954	StL-N	142	401	57	106	17	4	2	29	40	29	.264	.339	.342	680	77	-13	6	1	1	.966	30	*S-142/3-1	2.8
1955	StL-N	128	366	32	88	19	2	3	25	33	36	.240	.308	.328	636	69	-16	4	1	1	.968	7	*S-126	0.1
1956	StL-N	6	12	1	3	0	0	0	1	1	2	.250	.308	.250	558	52	-1	0	0	0	1.000	0	/S-5	-0.1
	Cin-N	77	140	17	34	11	0	0	16	16	18	.243	.325	.321	646	70	-6	0	1	-0	.968	4	3-58,S-12/2-5	-0.2
	Yr	83	152	18	37	11	0	0	17	17	20	.243	.324	.316	639	69	-6	0	1	-0	.968	4	3-58,S-17/2-5	-0.3
1957	Cin-N	73	99	14	30	4	0	0	8	10	6	.303	.367	.343	710	86	-1	1	3	-1	.966	2	S-42,2-20/3-9	0.2
1958	Cin-N	105	216	25	47	8	0	0	12	34	24	.218	.329	.255	584	54	-13	2	2	-0	.993	-2	S-61,3-38,2-14	-1.3
1959	StL-N	131	368	43	99	14	2	3	30	38	26	.269	.339	.342	681	77	-11	3	3	-0	.964	12	*S-130	1.1
1960	StL-N	102	196	20	48	4	1	4	17	12	15	.245	.292	.337	629	66	-9	0	1	-0	.972	20	S-46,2-38,3-13	1.4
1961	StL-N	89	170	23	36	10	1	0	21	19	21	.212	.295	.282	577	49	-12	0	1	-0	.960	17	S-65,2-18/3-3	0.9
1962	StL-N	21	18	0	2	0	0	0	1	1	6	.111	.158	.111	269	-24	-3	0	0	0	.933	1	S-16/2-2	-0.1
	Chi-N	23	60	3	14	3	0	0	3	2	7	.233	.270	.283	553	47	-4	1	1	-0	1.000	1	S-13/2-3,3-1	-0.2
	Yr	44	78	3	16	3	0	0	4	3	13	.205	.244	.244	487	29	-8	1	1	-0	.978	3	S-29/2-5,3-1	-0.3
1963	Chi-N	16	27	1	5	0	0	0	0	0	3	.185	.185	.185	370	7	-3	0	0	0	.955	-3	S-13	-0.6
Total	10	913	2073	236	512	90	10	12	163	206	193	.247	.320	.317	637	67	-92	17	14	-1	.968	88	S-671,3-123,2-100	4.0
■ JACK GRANEY Graney, John Gladstone b: 6/10/1886, St.Thomas, Ont., Can. d: 4/20/78, Louisiana, Mo. BL/TL, 5'9", 180 lbs. Deb: 4/30/08 Career OF: (1176-LF 62-CF 46-RF)																								
1908	Cle-A	2	0	0	0	0	0	0	0	0		—	—	—	—	—	0	0			.000	-0	/P-2	0.0
1910	Cle-A	116	454	62	107	13	9	1	31	37		.236	.293	.311	604	88	-7	18			.949	1	*O-114(53-43-18)	-1.4
1911	Cle-A	146	527	84	142	25	5	1	45	66		.269	.363	.342	704	96	-1	21			.927	2	*O-142(139-1-2)	-0.5
1912	Cle-A	78	264	44	64	13	2	0	20	50		.242	.367	.307	674	90	-1	9			.958	4	O-75(75-0-0)	0.0
1913	Cle-A	148	517	56	138	18	12	3	68	48	55	.267	.335	.366	701	102	1	27			.970	2	*O-148(144-0-4)	-0.4
1914	Cle-A	130	460	63	122	17	10	1	39	67	46	.265	.362	.352	714	111	8	20	18	-2	.935	5	*O-127(127-0-0)	0.6
1915	Cle-A	116	404	42	105	20	7	1	56	59	29	.260	.357	.351	708	110	6	12	15	-3	.972	5	*O-115(107-1-8)	0.4
1916	Cle-A	155	589	106	142	**41**	14	5	54	102	72	.241	.355	.384	739	115	12	10			.959	3	*O-154(154-0-0)	0.9
1917	Cle-A	146	535	87	122	29	7	3	35	**94**	49	.228	.348	.325	673	98	2	16			.959	-7	*O-145(145-0-0)	-1.4
1918	Cle-A	70	177	27	42	7	4	0	9	28	13	.237	.351	.322	673	94	-0	3			.975	-6	O-45(44-0-1)	-0.9
1919	Cle-A	128	461	79	108	22	8	1	30	**105**	39	.234	.380	.323	703	93	0	7			.961	6	*O-125(125-0-0)	0.0
1920	*Cle-A	62	152	31	45	11	1	0	13	27	21	.296	.412	.382	794	108	3	4	2	0	.941	-6	O-47(44-2-1)	-0.4
1921	Cle-A	68	107	19	32	3	0	2	18	20	9	.299	.414	.383	797	103	2	1	1	-0	.933	-9	O-32(17-11-5)	-0.9
1922	Cle-A	37	58	6	9	0	0	0	2	9	12	.155	.279	.155	435	16	-7	0	0	0	.862	-1	O-13(2-4-7)	-0.9
Total	14	1402	4705	706	1178	219	79	18	420	712	345	.250	.354	.342	696	100	17	148	36		.953	-3	*O-1282L/P-2	-4.9
■ EDDIE GRANT Grant, Edward Leslie "Harvard Eddie" b: 5/21/1883, Franklin, Mass. d: 10/5/18, Argonne Forest, France BL/TR, 5'11.5", 168 lbs. Deb: 8/4/05																								
1905	Cle-A	2	8	1	3	0	0	0	0	0		.375	.375	.375	750	136	0	0			.833	-2	/2-2	-0.2
1907	Phi-N	74	268	26	65	4	3	0	19	10		.243	.272	.280	552	74	-9	10			.916	-2	3-74	-1.0
1908	Phi-N	147	598	69	146	13	8	0	32	35		.244	.289	.293	582	83	-12	27			.930	2	*3-134,S-13	-0.7
1909	Phi-N	154	631	75	170	18	4	1	37	35		.269	.311	.315	626	94	-6	28			.957	3	*3-154	0.2
1910	Phi-N	152	579	70	155	15	5	1	67	39	54	.268	.315	.316	631	81	-14	25			.935	-10	*3-152	-2.2
1911	Cin-N	136	458	49	102	12	7	1	53	51	47	.223	.301	.286	587	67	-20	28			.953	-7	*3-122,S-11	-2.3
1912	Cin-N	96	255	37	61	6	1	2	20	18	27	.239	.292	.294	586	62	-13	11			.948	0	S-56,3-15	-0.9
1913	Cin-N	27	94	12	20	1	0	0	9	11	10	.213	.295	.223	519	49	-6	7			.929	-4	3-26	-1.0
	*NY-N	27	20	8	4	1	0	0	1	2	2	.200	.273	.250	523	49	-1	1			1.000	6	/3-5,2-3,S-1	0.5
	Yr	54	114	20	24	2	0	0	10	13	12	.211	.291	.228	519	49	-7	8			.940	2	3-31/2-3,S-1	-0.5
1914	NY-N	88	282	34	78	7	1	0	29	23	21	.277	.333	.309	642	94	-2	11			.948	-7	3-52,S-21,2-16	-0.6
1915	NY-N	87	192	18	40	2	1	0	10	9	20	.208	.248	.229	477	47	-12	5	6	-1	.970	-5	3-35/2-9,1-1,S-1	-1.9
Total	10	990	3385	399	844	79	30	5	277	233	181	.249	.300	.295	595	78	-94	153	6		.942	-26	3-769,S-103/2-30,1	-10.1
■ JIMMY GRANT Grant, James Charles b: 10/6/18, Racine, Wis. d: 7/8/70, Rochester, Minn. BL/TR, 5'8", 166 lbs. Deb: 9/8/42																								
1942	Chi-A	12	36	0	6	1	1	0	1	5	6	.167	.268	.250	518	47	-3	0	0	0	.944	1	3-10	-0.2
1943	Chi-A	58	197	23	51	9	2	4	22	18	34	.259	.321	.386	707	106	1	4	3	-0	.893	1	3-51	0.2
	Cle-A	15	22	3	3	2	0	0	1	4	7	.136	.269	.227	497	49	-1	0	0	0	.941	2	/3-5	0.0
	Yr	73	219	26	54	11	2	4	23	22	41	.247	.315	.370	685	101	-0	4	3	-0	.897	3	3-56	0.2
1944	Cle-A	61	99	12	27	4	3	1	12	11	20	.273	.357	.404	761	122	3	1	0	0	.926	-4	2-20/3-4	0.1
Total	3	146	354	38	87	16	6	5	36	38	67	.246	.322	.367	690	101	0	5	3	0	.907	-0	/3-70,2-20	0.1
■ TOM GRANT Grant, Thomas Raymond b: 5/28/57, Worcester, Mass. BL/TR, 6'2", 190 lbs. Deb: 6/17/83																								
1983	Chi-N	16	20	2	3	1	0	0	2	3	4	.150	.261	.200	461	28	-2	0	0	0	1.000	-2	O-10(5-0-5)	-0.4
■ GEORGE GRANTHAM Grantham, George Farley "Boots" b: 5/20/1900, Galena, Kan. d: 3/16/54, Kingman, Ariz. BL/TR, 5'10", 170 lbs. Deb: 9/20/22 Career OF: (19-LF 0-CF 0-RF)																								
1922	Chi-N	7	23	3	4	1	1	0	3	1	3	.174	.208	.304	513	30	-2	2	0	0	1.000	-3	/3-5	-0.4
1923	Chi-N	152	570	81	160	36	8	8	70	71	92	.281	.360	.414	774	104	4	43	28	-0	.942	1	*2-150	0.8
1924	Chi-N	127	469	85	148	19	6	12	60	55	63	.316	.390	.458	848	125	18	21	21	-3	.941	1	*2-118/3-6	2.0
1925	*Pit-N	114	359	74	117	24	6	8	52	50	29	.326	.413	.493	906	122	13	14	4	2	.989	-4	*1-102	0.4
1926	Pit-N	141	449	66	143	27	13	8	70	60	42	.318	.400	.490	890	131	21	6			.990	-2	*1-132	1.0
1927	*Pit-N	151	531	96	162	33	11	8	66	74	39	.305	.396	.454	850	119	16	9			.953	-24	*2-124,1-29	-0.6
1928	Pit-N	124	440	93	142	24	9	10	85	59	37	.323	.408	.486	894	128	19	9			.986	1	*1-119/2-1,3-1	1.2
1929	Pit-N	110	349	85	107	23	10	12	90	93	38	.307	.454	.533	987	140	26	10			.967	-5	2-76,O-19L,1-12	2.0
1930	Pit-N	146	552	120	179	34	14	18	99	81	66	.324	.413	.534	947	126	25	5			.958	-13	*2-141/1-4	1.3
1931	Pit-N	127	465	91	142	26	6	10	46	71	50	.305	.400	.452	851	130	22	5			.985	-22	1-78,2-51	-0.4
1932	Cin-N	126	493	81	144	29	6	6	39	56	40	.292	.364	.412	776	112	9	4			.959	-29	*2-115,1-10	-1.3
1933	Cin-N	87	260	32	53	14	3	4	28	38	21	.204	.310	.327	637	83	-5	4			.948	-11	2-72,1-12	-1.4
1934	NY-N	32	29	5	7	2	0	1	4	8	6	.241	.405	.414	819	123	1	0			1.000	0	/1-4,3-2	0.1
Total	13	1444	4989	912	1508	292	93	105	712	717	526	.302	.392	.461	854	121	167	132	53		.949	-109	2-848,1-502/O-19L,3	4.7
■ MICKEY GRASSO Grasso, Newton Michael b: 5/10/20, Newark, N.J. d: 10/15/75, Miami, Fla. BR/TR, 6', 195 lbs. Deb: 9/18/46																								
1946	NY-N	7	22	1	3	0	0	0	1	0	3	.136	.136	.136	273	-22	-4	0			.967	0	/C-7	-0.3
1950	Was-A	75	195	25	56	4	1	1	22	25	31	.287	.374	.333	707	86	-3	1	1	-0	.942	6	C-69	0.5
1951	Was-A	52	175	16	36	3	0	1	14	14	17	.206	.268	.240	508	39	-15	0	0	0	.967	-2	C-49	-1.5

YEAR	TM/L	G	AB	R	H	2B	3B	HR	RBI	BB	SO	AVG	OBP	SLG	OPS	OPS+	BR+	SB	CS	SBR	FA	FR	G/POS	TPR
1952	Was-A	115	361	22	78	9	0	0	27	29	36	.216	.276	.241	517	46	-26	1	0	0	.970	6	*C-114	-1.5
1953	Was-A	61	196	13	41	7	0	2	22	9	20	.209	.251	.276	527	43	-16	0	0	0	.984	1	C-59	-1.3
1954	*Cle-A	4	6	1	2	0	0	1	1	1	1	.333	.500	.833	1333	256	1	0	0	0	.833	-1	/C-4	0.1
1955	NY-N	8	2	0	0	0	0	0	0	3	0	.000	.600	.000	600	77	0	0	0	0	.900	-0	/C-8	0.0
Total	7	322	957	78	216	23	1	5	87	81	108	.226	.291	.268	558	53	-62	2	1		.964	9	C-310	-4.0
■ **LEW GRAULICH**	Graulich, Lewis b: Camden, N.J. Deb: 9/17/1891																							
1891	Phi-N	7	26	2	8	0	0	0	3	1	2	.308	.333	.308	641	85	-1	0			.640	-3	/C-4,1-3	-0.3
■ **FRANK GRAVES**	Graves, Frank M. b: 11/2/1860, Cincinnati, Ohio 6', 163 lbs. Deb: 5/10/1886																							
1886	StL-N	43	138	7	21	2	0	0	9	7	48	.152	.193	.167	360	11	-14	11			.885	4	C-41/O-3(0-3-0),P-1	-0.6
■ **JOE GRAVES**	Graves, Joseph Ebenezer b: 2/26/06, Marblehead, Mass. d: 12/22/80, Salem, Mass. BR/TR, 5'10", 160 lbs. Deb: 9/26/26 F																							
1926	Chi-N	2	5	0	0	0	0	0	0	0	1	.000	.000	.000	0	-99	-1	0			.250	-1	/3-2	-0.3
■ **SID GRAVES**	Graves, Samuel Sidney "Whitey" b: 11/30/01, Marblehead, Mass. d: 12/26/83, Biddeford, Maine BR/TR, 6', 170 lbs. Deb: 7/23/27 F																							
1927	Bos-N	7	20	5	5	1	1	0	2	0	1	.250	.250	.400	650	78	-1	1			.857	0	/O-5(0-5-0)	-0.1
■ **GARY GRAY**	Gray, Gary George b: 9/21/52, New Orleans, La. BR/TR, 6', 203 lbs. Deb: 6/23/77 Career OF: (11-LF 0-CF 0-RF)																							
1977	Tex-A	1	2	0	0	0	0	0	0	0	1	.000	.000	.000	0	-99	-1	0	0	0	.000	-0	/O-1(1-0-0)	-0.1
1978	Tex-A	17	50	4	12	1	0	2	6	1	12	.240	.255	.380	635	76	-2	1	0	0	.000	0	D-11	-0.2
1979	Tex-A	16	42	4	10	0	0	0	1	2	8	.238	.273	.238	511	40	-3	1	1	-0	.000	0	D-13	-0.4
1980	Cle-A	28	54	4	8	1	0	2	4	3	13	.148	.193	.278	471	27	-6	0	0	0	1.000	-2	/1-6,O-6(6-0-0),D-9	-0.8
1981	Sea-A	69	208	27	51	7	1	13	31	4	44	.245	.259	.476	735	104	-0	2	0	0	.993	-2	1-34,D-15/O-4(4-0-0)	-0.5
1982	Sea-A	80	269	26	69	14	2	7	29	24	59	.257	.322	.401	724	95	-2	1	1	-0	.984	-3	1-60,D-14	-0.9
Total	6	211	625	65	150	23	3	24	71	34	137	.240	.281	.402	683	86	-14	5	2	0	.988	-7	1-100/D-62,O-11L	-2.9
■ **REDDY GRAY**	Gray, James W. b: 8/7/1862, Pittsburgh, Pa. d: 1/31/38, Allegheny, Pa. TR, Deb: 10/9/1884																							
1884	Pit-a	1	2	0	1	0	0	0		0		.500	.500	.500	1000	230	0				.500	-0	/3-1	0.0
1890	Pit-P	2	9	3	2	0	0	1	3	0	2	.222	.222	.556	778	114	0	0			.813	-1	/2-2	-0.1
	Pit-N	1	3	0	0	0	0	0	0	0	1	.000	.000	.000	0	-99	-1	0			.571	-1	/S-1	-0.1
1893	Pit-N	2	9	0	4	1	0	0	2	0	1	.444	.444	.556	1000	168	1	0			.800	-3	/S-2	-0.2
Total	3	6	23	3	7	1	0	1	5	0	4	.304	.304	.478	783	119	0	0			.667	-4	/S-3,2-2,3-1	-0.4
■ **LORENZO GRAY**	Gray, Lorenzo b: 3/4/58, Mound Bayou, Miss. BR/TR, 6'1", 180 lbs. Deb: 7/8/82																							
1982	Chi-A	17	28	4	8	1	0	0	0	2	4	.286	.333	.321	655	81	-1	1	0	0	.864	-3	3-16	-0.4
1983	Chi-A	41	78	18	14	3	0	1	4	8	16	.179	.256	.256	512	40	-6	1	0	0	.940	2	3-31/D-7	-0.5
Total	2	58	106	22	22	4	0	1	4	10	20	.208	.276	.274	549	50	-7	2	0	0	.921	-1	/3-47,D-7	-0.9
■ **MILT GRAY**	Gray, Milton Marshall b: 2/21/14, Louisville, Ky. d: 6/30/69, Quincy, Fla. BR/TR, 6'1", 170 lbs. Deb: 5/27/37																							
1937	Was-A	2	6	0	0	0	0	0	0	0	1	.000	.000	.000	0	-99	-2	0	0	0	1.000	0	/C-2	-0.1
■ **PETE GRAY**	Gray, Peter J. (b: Peter Wyshner) b: 3/6/15, Nanticoke, Pa. BL/TL, 6'1", 169 lbs. Deb: 4/17/45																							
1945	StL-A	77	234	26	51	6	2	0	13	13	11	.218	.259	.261	520	49	-15	5	6	-1	.959	1	O-61(35-29-0)	-1.9
■ **DICK GRAY**	Gray, Richard Benjamin b: 7/11/31, Jefferson, Pa. BR/TR, 5'11", 165 lbs. Deb: 4/15/58 Career OF: (1-LF 0-CF 0-RF)																							
1958	LA-N	58	197	25	49	5	6	9	30	19	30	.249	.327	.472	799	105	1	1	1	-0	.929	14	3-55	1.5
1959	LA-N	21	52	8	8	1	0	2	4	6	12	.154	.241	.288	530	38	-5	0	0	0	1.000	-0	3-11	-0.5
	StL-N	36	51	9	16	1	0	1	6	6	8	.314	.386	.392	778	101	0	3	0	1	.958	-9	S-13/3-6,2-2,O-1L	-0.7
	Yr	57	103	17	24	2	0	3	10	12	20	.233	.313	.340	653	69	-4	3	0	1	.935	-9	3-17,S-13/2-2,O-1L	-1.2
1960	StL-N	9	5	1	0	0	0	0	1	2	2	.000	.286	.000	286	-13	-1	0	0	0	1.000	1	/2-4,3-1	0.1
Total	3	124	305	43	73	7	6	12	41	33	52	.239	.322	.420	741	91	-4	4	1	1	.930	6	/3-73,S-13,2-6,O-1L	0.4
■ **STAN GRAY**	Gray, Stanley Oscar b: 12/10/1888, Ladonia, Tex. d: 10/11/64, Snyder, Tex. BR/TR, 6'0.5", 184 lbs. Deb: 9/17/12																							
1912	Pit-N	6	20	4	5	0	1	0	2	0	3	.250	.250	.350	600	64	-1	0			1.000	-1	/1-4	-0.2
■ **CRAIG GREBECK**	Grebeck, Craig Allen b: 12/29/64, Johnstown, Pa. BR/TR, 5'7", 148 lbs. Deb: 4/13/90 Career OF: (4-LF 0-CF 1-RF)																							
1990	Chi-A	59	119	7	20	3	1	1	9	8	24	.168	.233	.235	468	32	-11	0	0	0	.987	8	3-35,S-16/2-6,D-1	-0.3
1991	Chi-A	107	224	37	63	16	3	6	31	38	40	.281	.388	.460	848	137	12	1	3	-1	.933	-1	3-49,2-36,S-26	1.3
1992	Chi-A	88	287	24	77	21	2	3	35	30	34	.268	.344	.387	731	106	2	0	3	-1	.980	-4	S-85/3-7,O-2(1-0-1)	0.4
1993	*Chi-A	72	190	25	43	5	0	1	12	26	26	.226	.319	.268	588	61	-10	1	2	-0	.983	14	S-46,2-16,3-14	0.7
1994	Chi-A	35	97	17	30	5	0	0	5	12	5	.309	.391	.361	752	97	0	0	0	0	.982	-3	2-14,S-14/3-7	-0.1
1995	Chi-A	53	154	19	40	12	0	1	18	21	23	.260	.360	.357	717	91	-1	0	0	0	.961	6	S-31,3-18/2-8	0.7
1996	Fla-N	50	95	8	20	1	0	1	9	4	14	.211	.250	.253	503	34	-9	0	0	0	.985	10	2-29/S-2,3-1	0.2
1997	Ana-A	63	126	12	34	9	0	1	6	18	11	.270	.361	.365	726	90	-1	0	1	-0	1.000	-1	2-26,S-20,3-15,/OD	0.0
1998	Tor-A	102	301	33	77	17	2	2	27	29	42	.256	.329	.346	675	76	-10	2	2	-0	.975	14	2-91/S-6,3-4	0.7
1999	Tor-A	34	113	18	41	7	0	0	10	15	13	.363	.446	.425	871	122	5	0	0	0	.959	-8	2-17,D-12/S-4,3-2	-0.2
2000	Tor-A	66	241	38	71	19	0	3	23	25	33	.295	.366	.411	776	95	-1	0	0	0	.968	-6	2-56/S-8	-0.3
Total	11	729	1947	238	516	115	8	19	185	226	265	.265	.347	.362	709	90	-24	4	11	-3	.981	29	2-299,S-258,3/DO	3.1
■ **SCARBOROUGH GREEN**	Green, Bertrum Scarborough b: 6/9/74, Creve Coeur, Mo. BB/TR, 5'10", 170 lbs. Deb: 8/2/97																							
1997	StL-N	20	31	5	3	0	0	0	1	2	5	.097	.152	.097	248	-34	-6	0	0	0	.952	-3	O-19(7-12-0)	-0.9
1999	Tex-A	18	13	4	4	0	0	0	0	1	2	.308	.357	.308	665	69	-1	0	1	-0	1.000	-3	/O-9(3-4-3),D-4	-0.4
2000	Tex-A	79	124	21	29	1	1	0	9	10	26	.234	.291	.258	549	39	-11	10	6	0	1.000	-4	O-65(3-41-23)/D-6	-1.4
Total	3	117	168	30	36	1	1	0	10	13	33	.214	.271	.232	503	29	-18	10	7	-0	.993	-11	/O-93(13-57-26),D-10	-2.7
■ **DAVID GREEN**	Green, David Alejandro (Casaya) b: 12/4/60, Managua, Nicaragua BR/TR, 6'3", 170 lbs. Deb: 9/4/81 Career OF: (29-LF 89-CF 147-RF)																							
1981	StL-N	21	34	6	5	1	0	0	2	6	5	.147	.275	.176	451	29	-3	0	1	-0	.970	-3	O-18(0-18-0)	-0.7
1982	*StL-N	76	166	21	47	7	1	2	23	8	29	.283	.320	.373	693	92	-2	11	3	1	.991	-8	O-68(7-46-19)	-1.0
1983	StL-N	146	422	52	120	14	10	8	69	26	76	.284	.327	.422	749	106	2	34	16	2	.970	-8	*O-136(20-19-100)	-0.8
1984	StL-N	126	452	49	121	14	4	15	65	20	105	.268	.300	.416	716	102	-1	17	9	1	.991	-5	*1-117,O-14(0-6-8)	-1.3
1985	SF-N	106	294	36	73	10	2	5	20	22	58	.248	.303	.347	650	85	-6	6	5	-0	.987	-3	1-78,O-12(1-0-11)	-1.5
1987	StL-N	14	30	4	8	2	1	1	1	2	5	.267	.313	.500	813	109	0	0	1	-0	.882	-1	O-10(1-0-9)/1-3	-0.1
Total	6	489	1398	168	374	48	18	31	180	84	278	.268	.311	.394	705	97	-9	68	35	3	.972	-27	O-258R,1-198	-5.4
■ **DANNY GREEN**	Green, Edward b: 11/6/1876, Burlington, N.J. d: 11/9/14, Camden, N.J. BL/TR, Deb: 8/17/1898																							
1898	Chi-N	47	188	26	59	4	3	4	27	7		.314	.342	.431	773	121	4	12			.970	5	O-47(8-2-37)	0.6
1899	Chi-N	117	475	90	140	12	11	6	56	35		.295	.352	.404	756	110	6	18			.947	1	*O-115(9-0-106)	0.1
1900	Chi-N	103	389	63	116	21	5	5	49	17		.298	.339	.416	755	112	5	28			.938	0	*O-102(3-60-39)	-0.1
1901	Chi-N	133	537	82	168	16	12	6	61	40		.313	.364	.421	785	132	22	31			.932	8	*O-133(0-133-0)	2.2
1902	Chi-A	129	481	77	150	16	11	0	62	53		.312	.388	.391	779	122	17	35			.942	-3	*O-129(18-2-110)	0.7
1903	Chi-A	135	499	75	154	26	7	6	62	47		.309	.375	.425	800	146	29	29			.933	2	*O-133(0-0-133)	2.6
1904	Chi-A	147	536	83	142	16	10	2	62	63		.265	.352	.343	695	125	18	28			.964	1	*O-146(0-0-146)	1.4
1905	Chi-A	112	379	56	92	13	6	0	44	53		.243	.345	.309	653	112	8	11			.914	-11	*O-107(0-7-100)	-0.8
Total	8	923	3484	552	1021	124	65	29	423	315		.293	.359	.391	750	124	109	192			.941	4	O-912(38-204-671)	6.7
■ **PUMPSIE GREEN**	Green, Elijah Jerry b: 10/27/33, Oakland, Cal. BB/TR, 6', 175 lbs. Deb: 7/21/59																							
1959	Bos-A	50	172	30	40	6	3	1	10	29	22	.233	.350	.320	670	81	-3	4	2	0	.972	4	2-45/S-1	0.4
1960	Bos-A	133	260	36	63	10	3	3	21	44	47	.242	.354	.338	693	85	-4	3	4	-1	.982	-13	2-69,S-41	-1.3
1961	Bos-A	88	219	33	57	12	3	6	27	42	32	.260	.379	.425	804	112	5	4	2	0	.940	-5	S-57/2-7	0.5
1962	Bos-A	56	91	12	21	2	1	2	11	11	18	.231	.314	.341	654	74	-3	1	0	0	.953	-9	2-18/S-5	-1.1
1963	NY-N	17	54	8	15	1	2	1	5	12	13	.278	.409	.426	835	139	3	0	2	-1	.857	-1	3-16	0.2
Total	5	344	796	119	196	31	12	13	74	138	132	.246	.360	.364	724	94	-3	12	10	-1	.975	-24	2-139,S-104/3-16	-1.3

■ **GARY GREEN** Green, Gary Allan b: 1/14/62, Pittsburgh, Pa. BR/TR, 6'3", 175 lbs. Deb: 9/14/86 F

YEAR	TM/L	G	AB	R	H	2B	3B	HR	RBI	BB	SO	AVG	OBP	SLG	OPS	OPS+	BR+	SB	CS	SBR	FA	FR	G/POS	TPR
1986	SD-N	13	33	2	7	1	0	0	2	1	11	.212	.235	.242	478	33	-3	0	0	0	1.000	5	S-13	0.3
1989	SD-N	15	27	4	7	3	0	0	0	1	1	.259	.286	.370	656	86	-1	0	1	-0	.921	4	S-11/3-1	0.3
1990	Tex-A	62	88	10	19	3	0	0	8	6	18	.216	.266	.250	516	45	-6	1	1	-0	.972	21	S-58	1.6
1991	Tex-A	8	20	0	3	1	0	0	1	1	6	.150	.190	.200	390	8	-2	0	0	0	.968	1	/S-8	-0.2
1992	Cin-N	8	12	3	4	1	0	0	0	0	2	.333	.333	.417	750	108	0	0	0	0	1.000	-1	/S-6,3-1	-0.1
Total	5	106	180	19	40	9	0	0	11	9	38	.222	.259	.272	531	49	-12	1	2	-0	.970	29	/S-96,3-2	1.9

■ **GENE GREEN** Green, Gene Leroy b: 6/26/33, Los Angeles, Cal. d: 5/23/81, St.Louis, Mo. BR/TR, 6'2", 205 lbs. Deb: 9/10/57 Career OF: (4-LF 1-CF 166-RF)

YEAR	TM/L	G	AB	R	H	2B	3B	HR	RBI	BB	SO	AVG	OBP	SLG	OPS	OPS+	BR+	SB	CS	SBR	FA	FR	G/POS	TPR
1957	StL-N	6	15	0	3	1	0	0	2	0	3	.200	.200	.267	467	23	-2	0	0	0	1.000	-1	/O-3(0-0-3)	-0.3
1958	StL-N	137	442	47	124	18	3	13	55	37	48	.281	.338	.423	761	96	-3	2	1	0	.956	9	O-75(0-1-75),C-48	0.6
1959	StL-N	30	74	8	14	6	0	1	3	5	18	.189	.241	.311	551	43	-6	0	0	0	.944	4	O-19(0-0-19),C-11	-0.3
1960	Bal-A	1	4	0	1	0	0	0	0	0	0	.250	.250	.250	500	36	-0	0	0	0	1.000	0	/O-1(0-0-1)	0.0
1961	Was-A	110	364	52	102	16	3	18	62	35	65	.280	.345	.489	834	122	10	0	2	-1	.986	-22	C-79,O-21(0-0-21)	-0.9
1962	Cle-A	66	143	16	40	4	1	11	28	8	21	.280	.318	.552	870	133	6	0	0	0	.964	-2	O-33(3-0-30)/1-2	0.2
1963	Cle-A	43	78	4	16	3	0	2	7	4	22	.205	.262	.321	582	63	-4	0	0	0	1.000	-3	O-18(1-0-17)	-0.9
	Cin-N	15	31	3	7	1	0	1	3	0	8	.226	.250	.355	605	70	-1	0	0	0	.932	-2	/C-8	-0.3
Total	7	408	1151	130	307	49	7	46	160	89	185	.267	.322	.441	763	101	-0	2	3	-1	.963	-16	O-170R,C-146/1-2	-1.9

■ **JIM GREEN** Green, James R. b: Cleveland, Ohio Deb: 7/19/1884

YEAR	TM/L	G	AB	R	H	2B	3B	HR	RBI	BB	SO	AVG	OBP	SLG	OPS	OPS+	BR+	SB	CS	SBR	FA	FR	G/POS	TPR
1884	Was-U	10	36	4	5	1	0	0		0		.139	.139	.167	306	-8	-6				.818	-0	/3-9,O-1(0-0-1)	-0.5

■ **JOE GREEN** Green, Joseph Henry (a.k.a. Joseph Henry Greene) b: 9/17/1897, Philadelphia, Pa. d: 2/4/72, Bryn Mawr, Pa. BR/TR, 6'2", 170 lbs. Deb: 7/2/24

YEAR	TM/L	G	AB	R	H	2B	3B	HR	RBI	BB	SO	AVG	OBP	SLG	OPS	OPS+	BR+	SB	CS	SBR	FA	FR	G/POS	TPR
1924	Phi-A	1	1	0	0	0	0	0	0	0	0	.000	.000	.000	0	-99	-0	0	0	0	.000	0	H	0.0

■ **LENNY GREEN** Green, Leonard Charles b: 1/6/33, Detroit, Mich. BL/TL, 5'11", 170 lbs. Deb: 8/25/57

YEAR	TM/L	G	AB	R	H	2B	3B	HR	RBI	BB	SO	AVG	OBP	SLG	OPS	OPS+	BR+	SB	CS	SBR	FA	FR	G/POS	TPR
1957	Bal-A	19	33	2	6	1	1	1	5	1	4	.182	.206	.364	570	56	-2	0	1	-0	.950	-4	O-15(3-12-2)	-0.8
1958	Bal-A	69	91	10	21	4	0	0	4	9	10	.231	.300	.275	575	63	-5	0	2	-1	.965	-11	O-53(28-30-6)	-1.8
1959	Bal-A	27	24	3	7	0	0	1	2	1	3	.292	.346	.417	763	111	0	0	0	0	1.000	-6	O-23(20-0-5)	-0.7
	Was-A	88	190	29	46	6	1	2	15	20	15	.242	.314	.316	630	74	-7	9	5	0	.979	-4	O-58(21-13-27)	-1.3
	Yr	115	214	32	53	6	1	3	17	21	18	.248	.318	.327	645	78	-6	9	5	0	.981	-11	O-81(41-13-32)	-2.0
1960	Was-A	127	330	62	97	16	7	5	33	43	25	.294	.385	.430	816	121	11	21	8	2	.991	-6	*O-100(20-92-0)	0.3
1961	Min-A	156	600	92	171	28	7	9	50	81	50	.285	.376	.400	776	102	4	17	11	-0	.978	-15	*O-153(56-141-4)	-1.7
1962	Min-A	158	619	97	168	33	3	14	63	88	36	.271	.369	.402	771	104	6	8	4	0	.995	-17	*O-156(88-146-0)	-1.7
1963	Min-A	145	280	41	67	10	1	4	27	31	21	.239	.319	.325	644	80	-7	11	5	1	.988	-25	*O-119(15-118-0)	-3.6
1964	Min-A	26	15	3	0	0	0	0	0	4	6	.000	.211	.000	211	-35	-3	0	1	-0	1.000	-2	/O-7(6-1-0)	-0.6
	LA-A	39	92	13	23	2	0	2	4	10	8	.250	.330	.337	667	96	-0	2	0	0	.977	-1	O-23(11-13-0)	-0.2
	Bal-A	14	21	0	4	0	0	0	1	7	3	.190	.393	.190	583	69	-0	1	0	0	1.000	1	/O-8(2-6-0)	0.1
	Yr	79	128	16	27	2	0	2	5	21	17	.211	.327	.273	600	72	-4	3	1	0	.985	-2	O-38(19-20-0)	-0.7
1965	Bos-A	119	373	69	103	24	6	7	24	48	43	.276	.363	.429	792	117	9	8	2	1	.980	2	O-95(12-86-0)	0.9
1966	Bos-A	85	133	18	32	6	0	1	12	15	19	.241	.327	.308	635	76	-4	0	1	-0	.978	-1	O-27(4-23-0)	-0.6
1967	Det-A	58	151	22	42	8	1	1	13	9	17	.278	.319	.364	683	99	-0	1	1	-0	.983	-4	O-44(43-2-0)	-0.7
1968	Det-A	6	4	0	1	0	0	0	0	1	0	.250	.400	.250	650	97	0	0	0	0	.000	-1	/O-2(2-0-0)	-0.1
Total	12	1136	2956	461	788	138	27	47	253	368	260	.267	.353	.379	733	99	3	78	41	3	.984	-95	O-883(331-683-44)	-12.5

■ **DICK GREEN** Green, Richard Larry b: 4/21/41, Sioux City, Iowa BR/TR, 5'10", 180 lbs. Deb: 9/9/63

YEAR	TM/L	G	AB	R	H	2B	3B	HR	RBI	BB	SO	AVG	OBP	SLG	OPS	OPS+	BR+	SB	CS	SBR	FA	FR	G/POS	TPR
1963	KC-A	13	37	5	10	2	0	1	4	2	10	.270	.325	.405	730	98	-0	0	0	0	.941	2	/S-6,2-4	0.3
1964	KC-A	130	435	48	115	14	5	11	37	27	87	.264	.312	.395	707	92	-5	3	3	-0	.990	17	*2-120	2.2
1965	KC-A	133	474	64	110	15	1	15	55	50	110	.232	.309	.363	672	92	-5	0	2	-1	.980	-7	*2-126	-0.2
1966	KC-A	140	507	58	127	24	3	9	62	27	101	.250	.298	.363	661	92	-6	6	1	1	.979	-1	*2-137/3-2	0.6
1967	KC-A	122	349	26	69	12	4	5	37	30	68	.198	.261	.298	559	67	-15	6	3	0	.946	-2	3-59,2-50/1-1,S-1	-1.5
1968	Oak-A	76	202	19	47	6	0	6	18	21	41	.233	.308	.351	660	104	1	3	1	0	.974	13	2-61/C-1,3-1	2.1
1969	Oak-A	136	483	61	133	25	6	12	64	53	94	.275	.357	.427	783	123	15	2	3	-1	**.986**	10	*2-131	3.4
1970	Oak-A	135	384	34	73	7	0	4	29	38	73	.190	.268	.240	508	43	-30	3	0	1	.978	0	*2-127/3-5,C-1	-2.2
1971	*Oak-A	144	475	58	116	14	1	12	49	51	83	.244	.321	.354	675	93	-4	1	1	-0	.986	8	*2-143/S-1	1.4
1972	*Oak-A	26	42	1	12	1	1	0	3	3	5	.286	.348	.357	705	116	1	0	1	-0	.964	2	2-26	0.4
1973	*Oak-A	133	332	33	87	17	0	3	42	21	63	.262	.310	.340	650	88	-6	0	2	-1	.988	-9	*2-133/S-1,3-1	-0.8
1974	*Oak-A	100	287	20	61	8	2	2	22	22	50	.213	.269	.275	544	61	-15	2	3	-1	.983	-5	*2-100	-1.5
Total	12	1288	4007	427	960	145	23	80	422	345	785	.240	.305	.347	652	87	-69	26	20	-1	.983	28	*2-1158/3-68,S-9,C1	4.2

■ **SHAWN GREEN** Green, Shawn David b: 11/10/72, Des Plaines, Ill. BL/TL, 6'4", 190 lbs. Deb: 9/28/93

YEAR	TM/L	G	AB	R	H	2B	3B	HR	RBI	BB	SO	AVG	OBP	SLG	OPS	OPS+	BR+	SB	CS	SBR	FA	FR	G/POS	TPR
1993	Tor-A	3	6	0	0	0	0	0	0	0	1	.000	.000	.000	0	-99	-2	0	0	0	1.000	-1	/O-2(0-0-2),D-1	-0.2
1994	Tor-A	14	33	1	3	1	0	0	1	1	8	.091	.118	.121	239	-38	-7	1	0	0	1.000	-2	O-14(10-0-5)	-0.8
1995	Tor-A	121	379	52	109	31	4	15	54	20	68	.288	.328	.509	838	115	6	1	2	-0	.973	6	*O-109(0-0-109)	0.7
1996	Tor-A	132	422	52	118	32	3	11	45	33	75	.280	.343	.448	791	98	-2	5	1	1	.992	7	*O-127(0-2-127)/D-1	0.0
1997	Tor-A	135	429	57	123	22	4	16	53	36	99	.287	.343	.469	812	109	5	14	3	2	.984	4	O-91(45-0-46),D-35	0.5
1998	Tor-A	158	630	106	175	33	4	35	100	50	142	.278	.336	.510	845	115	12	35	12	4	.979	5	*O-157(0-32-128)	1.4
1999	Tor-A★	153	614	134	190	**45**	0	42	123	66	117	.309	.386	.588	974	142	38	20	7	2	.997	9	*O-152(0-0-152)	3.7
2000	LA-N	162	610	98	164	44	4	24	99	90	121	.269	.370	.472	842	116	16	24	5	4	.980	-0	*O-161(0-1-161)	1.0
Total	8	878	3123	500	882	208	19	143	475	296	631	.282	.351	.499	850	116	67	100	30	12	.985	29	O-813(55-35-730)/D-37	6.3

■ **HANK GREENBERG** Greenberg, Henry Benjamin "Hammerin' Hank" b: 1/1/11, New York, N.Y. d: 9/4/86, Beverly Hills, Cal BR/TR, 6'3.5", 210 lbs. Deb: 9/14/30 H Career OF: (239-LF 0-CF 0-RF)

YEAR	TM/L	G	AB	R	H	2B	3B	HR	RBI	BB	SO	AVG	OBP	SLG	OPS	OPS+	BR+	SB	CS	SBR	FA	FR	G/POS	TPR
1930	Det-A	1	1	0	0	0	0	0	0	0	0	.000	.000	.000	0	-98	-0	0	0	0	.000	0	H	0.0
1933	Det-A	117	449	59	135	33	3	12	87	46	78	.301	.367	.468	835	118	11	6	2	1	.988	1	*1-117	0.1
1934	*Det-A	153	593	118	201	**63**	7	26	139	63	93	.339	.404	.600	1005	156	46	9	5	0	.990	1	*1-153	3.1
1935	*Det-A	152	619	121	203	46	16	**36**	**170**	87	91	.328	.411	.628	1039	171	63	4	3	-0	.992	6	*1-152	5.0
1936	Det-A	12	46	10	16	6	2	1	16	9	6	.348	.455	.630	1085	165	5	1	0	0	.992	1	1-12	0.4
1937	Det-A☆	154	594	137	200	49	14	40	**183**	102	101	.337	.436	.668	1105	171	64	8	3	1	.992	5	*1-154	5.0
1938	Det-A†	155	556	**144**	175	23	4	**58**	146	**119**	92	.315	.438	.683	1122	167	57	7	5	-0	.991	7	*1-155	4.4
1939	Det-A★	138	500	112	156	42	7	33	112	91	95	.312	.420	.622	1042	152	38	8	3	1	**.993**	-1	*1-136	2.3
1940	*Det-A★	148	573	129	195	**50**	8	**41**	**150**	93	75	.340	.433	**.670**	**1103**	166	55	6	3	0	.954	1	*O-148(148-0-0)	4.5
1941	Det-A	19	67	12	18	5	1	2	12	16	12	.269	.410	.463	872	118	2	1	0	0	.914	-3	O-19(19-0-0)	-0.2
1945	*Det-A†	78	270	47	84	20	2	13	60	42	40	.311	.404	.544	948	164	22	3	1	0	1.000	-6	O-72(72-0-0)	1.2
1946	Det-A	142	523	91	145	29	5	**44**	**127**	80	88	.277	.373	.604	977	160	40	5	1	1	.989	2	*1-140	3.9
1947	Pit-N	125	402	71	100	13	2	25	74	**104**	73	.249	.408	.478	885	131	21	0			.992	2	*1-119	1.8
Total	13	1394	5193	1051	1628	379	71	331	1276	852	844	.313	.412	.605	1017	157	424	58	26		.991	15	*1-1138,O-239L	31.5

■ **AL GREENE** Greene, Altar Alphonse b: 11/9/54, Detroit, Mich. BL/TR, 5'11", 190 lbs. Deb: 7/23/79

YEAR	TM/L	G	AB	R	H	2B	3B	HR	RBI	BB	SO	AVG	OBP	SLG	OPS	OPS+	BR+	SB	CS	SBR	FA	FR	G/POS	TPR
1979	Det-A	29	59	9	8	1	0	3	6	10	15	.136	.261	.305	566	50	-4	0	1	-0	1.000	0	D-15/O-6(4-0-2)	-0.5

■ **CHARLIE GREENE** Greene, Charles Patrick b: 1/23/71, Miami, Fla. BR/TR, 6'1", 170 lbs. Deb: 9/15/96

YEAR	TM/L	G	AB	R	H	2B	3B	HR	RBI	BB	SO	AVG	OBP	SLG	OPS	OPS+	BR+	SB	CS	SBR	FA	FR	G/POS	TPR
1996	NY-N	2	1	0	0	0	0	0	0	0	0	.000	.000	.000	0	-99	-0	0	0	0	1.000	-0	/C-1	0.0
1997	Bal-A	5	2	0	0	0	0	0	1	0	1	.000	.000	.000	0	-99	-1	0	0	0	1.000	0	/C-4	0.0
1998	Bal-A	13	21	1	4	1	0	0	0	0	8	.190	.190	.238	429	11	-3	0	0	0	1.000	4	C-13	0.2
1999	Mil-N	32	42	4	8	1	0	0	1	5	11	.190	.277	.214	491	27	-5	0	0	0	.991	7	C-31	0.2
2000	Tor-A	3	9	0	1	0	0	0	0	0	5	.111	.111	.111	222	-43	-2	0	0	0	1.000	-1	/C-3	-0.2
Total	5	55	75	5	13	2	0	0	2	5	25	.173	.225	.200	425	10	-10	0	0	0	.995	11	/C-52	0.2

■ **JUNE GREENE** Greene, Julius Foust b: 6/25/1899, Ramseur, N.C. d: 3/19/74, Glendora, Cal. BL/TR, 6'2.5", 185 lbs. Deb: 4/20/28

YEAR	TM/L	G	AB	R	H	2B	3B	HR	RBI	BB	SO	AVG	OBP	SLG	OPS	OPS+	BR+	SB	CS	SBR	FA	FR	G/POS	TPR
1928	Phi-N	11	6	0	3	0	0	0	0	3	1	.500	.667	.500	1167	202	1	0			1.000	0	/P-1	0.0

YEAR	TM/L	G	AB	R	H	2B	3B	HR	RBI	BB	SO	AVG	OBP	SLG	OPS	OPS+	BR+	SB	CS	SBR	FA	FR	G/POS	TPR
1929	Phi-N	21	19	1	4	1	0	0	0	2	4	.211	.286	.263	549	35	-2	0			1.000	0	/P-5	0.0
Total	2	32	25	1	7	1	0	0	0	5	5	.280	.400	.320	720	79	-1	0			1.000	1	/P-6	0.0

■ PADDY GREENE

Greene, Patrick Joseph "Patsy" (a.k.a. Patrick Foley In 1902) b: 3/20/1875, Providence, R.I. d: 10/20/34, Providence, R.I. BR/TR, 5'8", 150 lbs. Deb: 9/10/02

YEAR	TM/L	G	AB	R	H	2B	3B	HR	RBI	BB	SO	AVG	OBP	SLG	OPS	OPS+	BR+	SB	CS	SBR	FA	FR	G/POS	TPR
1902	Phi-N	19	65	6	11	1	0	0	1	2		.169	.206	.185	390	21	-6	2			.912	0	3-19	-0.6
1903	NY-A	4	13	1	4	1	0	0	0	0		.308	.308	.385	692	100	-0	0			1.000	1	/3-2,S-1	0.2
	Det-A	1	3	0	0	0	0	0	0	0		.000	.000	.000	0	-99	-1	0			.750	-0	/3-1	-0.1
	Yr	5	16	1	4	1	0	0	0	0		.250	.250	.313	563	65	-1	0			.933	1	/3-3,S-1	0.1
Total	2	24	81	7	15	2	0	0	1	2		.185	.214	.210	424	30	-7	2			.916	2	/3-22,S-1	-0.5

■ TODD GREENE

Greene, Todd Anthony b: 5/8/71, Augusta, Ga. BR/TR, 5'10", 195 lbs. Deb: 7/30/96 Career OF: (18-LF 0-CF 25-RF)

YEAR	TM/L	G	AB	R	H	2B	3B	HR	RBI	BB	SO	AVG	OBP	SLG	OPS	OPS+	BR+	SB	CS	SBR	FA	FR	G/POS	TPR
1996	Cal-A	29	79	9	15	1	0	2	9	4	11	.190	.238	.278	517	30	-9	2	0	0	1.000	1	C-26/D-1	-0.5
1997	Ana-A	34	124	24	36	6	0	9	24	7	25	.290	.328	.556	885	126	4	2	0	0	1.000	-5	C-26/D-8	0.1
1998	Ana-A	29	71	3	18	4	0	1	7	2	20	.254	.274	.352	626	61	-4	0	0	0	1.000	-3	O-12(12-0-0)/1-3,D-4	-0.7
1999	Ana-A	97	321	36	78	20	0	14	42	12	63	.243	.277	.436	713	79	-12	1	4	-1	.974	-8	D-44,O-30R,C-12	-2.3
2000	Tor-A	34	85	11	20	2	0	5	10	5	18	.235	.278	.435	713	76	-3	0	0	0	1.000	-2	D-23/C-2,O-1(1-0-0)	-0.6
Total	5	223	680	83	167	33	0	31	92	30	137	.246	.282	.431	712	79	-24	5	4	-0	.997	-17	/D-80,C-66,O-43R,1	-4.0

■ WILLIE GREENE

Greene, Willie Louis b: 9/23/71, Milledgeville, Ga. BL/TR, 5'11", 184 lbs. Deb: 9/1/92 Career OF: (26-LF 0-CF 72-RF)

YEAR	TM/L	G	AB	R	H	2B	3B	HR	RBI	BB	SO	AVG	OBP	SLG	OPS	OPS+	BR+	SB	CS	SBR	FA	FR	G/POS	TPR
1992	Cin-N	29	93	10	25	5	2	2	13	10	23	.269	.340	.430	770	114	2	0	2	-1	.948	-1	3-25	0.0
1993	Cin-N	15	50	7	8	1	1	2	5	2	19	.160	.192	.340	532	39	-5	0	0	0	.978	4	S-10/3-5	0.0
1994	Cin-N	16	37	5	8	2	0	0	3	6	14	.216	.326	.270	596	58	-2	0	0	0	.958	0	3-13/O-1(1-0-0)	-0.2
1995	Cin-N	8	19	1	2	0	0	0	0	3	7	.105	.227	.105	333	-9	-3	0	0	0	1.000	1	/3-7	-0.2
1996	Cin-N	115	287	48	70	5	5	19	63	36	88	.244	.328	.495	823	113	4	0	1	-0	.927	7	3-74,O-10L/1-2,S-1	1.1
1997	Cin-N	151	495	62	125	22	1	26	91	78	111	.253	.355	.459	814	110	7	6	0	1	.934	-6	*3-103,O-39R/1-7,S	0.1
1998	Cin-N	111	356	57	96	18	1	14	49	56	80	.270	.373	.444	817	113	8	6	3	0	.936	-6	3-76,O-28R/S-2,D-1	0.1
	Bal-A	24	40	8	6	1	0	1	5	13	10	.150	.358	.250	608	63	-2	1	0	0	.941	-2	O-14(1-0-13)/D-1	-0.4
1999	Tor-A	81	226	22	46	7	0	12	41	20	56	.204	.268	.394	662	65	-13	0	0	0	.917	-3	D-52/3-7,O-3(0-0-3)	-1.7
2000	Chi-N	105	299	34	60	15	2	10	37	36	69	.201	.291	.365	655	66	-17	4	0	1	.967	6	3-90	-0.9
Total	9	655	1902	254	446	76	12	86	307	260	477	.234	.328	.423	751	94	-20	17	6	2	.943	-0	3-400/O-95R,D-54,S1	-2.1

■ JIM GREENGRASS

Greengrass, James Raymond b: 10/24/27, Addison, N.Y. BR/TR, 6'1", 200 lbs. Deb: 9/9/52

YEAR	TM/L	G	AB	R	H	2B	3B	HR	RBI	BB	SO	AVG	OBP	SLG	OPS	OPS+	BR+	SB	CS	SBR	FA	FR	G/POS	TPR
1952	Cin-N	18	68	10	21	2	1	5	24	7	12	.309	.373	.588	962	163	5	0	0	0	.965	2	O-17(4-13-0)	0.6
1953	Cin-N	154	606	86	173	22	7	20	100	47	83	.285	.340	.444	784	102	1	6	4	-0	.983	8	*O-153(153-0-0)	-0.1
1954	Cin-N	139	542	79	152	27	4	27	95	41	81	.280	.331	.494	826	109	5	0	3	-1	.968	5	*O-137(137-0-0)	0.0
1955	Cin-N	13	39	1	4	2	0	0	1	9	9	.103	.271	.154	425	16	-5	0	0	0	1.000	2	O-11(11-0-0)	-0.3
	Phi-N	94	323	43	88	20	2	12	37	33	43	.272	.342	.458	800	112	5	0	2	-1	.988	2	O-83(5-0-79)/3-2	0.3
	Yr	107	362	44	92	22	2	12	38	42	52	.254	.333	.425	759	100	0	0	2	-1	.990	4	O-94(16-0-79)/3-2	0.0
1956	Phi-N	86	215	24	44	9	2	5	25	28	43	.205	.296	.335	631	71	-9	0	0	0	.991	-2	O-62(0-0-62)	-1.4
Total	5	504	1793	243	482	82	16	69	282	165	271	.269	.332	.448	780	102	3	6	9	-2	.980	17	O-463(310-13-141)/3-2	-0.9

■ MIKE GREENWELL

Greenwell, Michael Lewis b: 7/18/63, Louisville, Ky. BL/TR, 6', 200 lbs. Deb: 9/5/85 Career OF: (1124-LF 1-CF 47-RF)

YEAR	TM/L	G	AB	R	H	2B	3B	HR	RBI	BB	SO	AVG	OBP	SLG	OPS	OPS+	BR+	SB	CS	SBR	FA	FR	G/POS	TPR
1985	Bos-A	17	31	7	10	1	0	4	8	3	4	.323	.382	.742	1124	191	4	1	0	0	1.000	-5	O-17(16-0-3)	-0.1
1986	*Bos-A	31	35	4	11	2	0	0	4	5	7	.314	.400	.371	771	111	1	0	0	0	1.000	-1	O-15(8-0-7)/D-3	-0.1
1987	Bos-A	125	412	71	135	31	6	19	89	35	40	.328	.389	.570	959	146	27	5	4	-0	.971	1	O-91L,D-15/C-1	2.2
1988	*Bos-A★	158	590	86	192	39	8	22	119	87	38	.325	.420	.531	950	158	48	16	8	0	.981	7	*O-147(143-0-8),D-11	5.0
1989	Bos-A★	145	578	87	178	36	0	14	95	56	44	.308	.372	.443	815	121	17	13	5	1	.967	-4	*O-139(139-0-0)/D-5	0.9
1990	*Bos-A	159	610	71	181	30	6	14	73	65	43	.297	.368	.434	803	118	16	8	7	-1	.977	4	*O-159(159-0-0)	1.4
1991	Bos-A	147	544	76	163	26	6	9	83	43	35	.300	.354	.419	773	108	6	15	5	2	.989	6	*O-143(143-0-0)/D-1	0.9
1992	Bos-A	49	180	16	42	2	0	2	18	18	19	.233	.310	.278	588	62	-9	2	3	-1	1.000	1	O-41(41-0-0)/D-6	-1.0
1993	Bos-A	146	540	77	170	38	6	13	72	54	46	.315	.381	.480	861	122	17	5	4	-0	.993	3	*O-134(134-0-0),D-10	1.5
1994	Bos-A	95	327	60	88	25	1	11	45	38	26	.269	.352	.453	805	101	0	2	2	-0	.993	2	O-84(84-0-0)/D-6	0.0
1995	*Bos-A	120	481	67	143	25	4	15	76	38	35	.297	.351	.459	811	105	3	9	5	0	.972	0	*O-118(118-0-0)/D-2	0.0
1996	Bos-A	77	295	35	87	20	1	7	44	18	27	.295	.340	.441	780	93	-3	4	0	1	.973	4	O-76(75-1-1)	-0.1
Total	12	1269	4623	657	1400	275	38	130	726	460	364	.303	.371	.463	834	119	126	80	43	3	.981	18	*O-1164L/D-59,C-1	10.6

■ BILL GREENWOOD

Greenwood, William F. b: 1857, Philadelphia, Pa. d: 5/2/02, Philadelphia, Pa. BB/TL, 5'7.5", 180 lbs. Deb: 9/16/1882

YEAR	TM/L	G	AB	R	H	2B	3B	HR	RBI	BB	SO	AVG	OBP	SLG	OPS	OPS+	BR+	SB	CS	SBR	FA	FR	G/POS	TPR
1882	Phi-a	7	30	8	9	1	0	0	1	1		.300	.323	.333	656	109	0				.909	-1	/O-7(0-0-7),2-2	-0.1
1884	Bro-a	92	385	52	83	8	3	3		10		.216	.237	.275	513	66	-14				.900	-8	*2-92/S-1	-1.7
1887	Bal-a	118	549	114	184	16	6	0	65	54		.335	.336	.319	656	88	-5	71			**.928**	7	*2-117/O-1(1-0-0)	0.5
1888	Bal-a	115	409	69	78	13	1	0	29	30		.191	.256	.227	484	57	-18	46			.913	-22	2-86,S-28/O-1(0-0-1)	-3.5
1889	Col-a	118	414	62	93	7	10	3	49	58	71	.225	.327	.312	639	86	-5	37			.914	-3	*2-118	-0.3
1890	Roc-a	124	437	76	97	11	6	2	41	48		.222	.310	.288	599	83	-8	40			.921	2	*2-123/S-1	-0.1
Total	6	574	2224	381	544	56	26	8	185	201	71	.245	.298	.287	584	78	-50	194			.916	-26	2-538/S-30,O-9(1-0-8)	-5.2

■ BRIAN GREER

Greer, Brian Keith b: 5/14/59, Lynwood, Cal. BR/TR, 6'3", 210 lbs. Deb: 9/13/77

YEAR	TM/L	G	AB	R	H	2B	3B	HR	RBI	BB	SO	AVG	OBP	SLG	OPS	OPS+	BR+	SB	CS	SBR	FA	FR	G/POS	TPR
1977	SD-N	1	1	0	0	0	0	0	0	0	1	.000	.000	.000	0	-99	-0	0	0	0	.000	0	H	0.0
1979	SD-N	4	3	0	0	0	0	0	0	0	1	.000	.000	.000	0	-99	-1	0	0	0	1.000	-1	/O-4(0-4-0)	-0.2
Total	2	5	4	0	0	0	0	0	0	0	2	.000	.000	.000	0	-99	-1	0	0	0	1.000	-1	/O-4(0-4-0)	-0.2

■ ED GREER

Greer, Edward C. b: 1865, Philadelphia, Pa. d: 2/4/1890, Philadelphia, Pa. BR, Deb: 6/24/1885

YEAR	TM/L	G	AB	R	H	2B	3B	HR	RBI	BB	SO	AVG	OBP	SLG	OPS	OPS+	BR+	SB	CS	SBR	FA	FR	G/POS	TPR
1885	Bal-a	56	211	32	42	7	0	0	21	8		.199	.235	.232	468	49	-12				.908	-0	O-47(2-38-7),C-12	-1.2
1886	Bal-a	11	38	2	5	1	0	0	4	2		.132	.175	.158	333	5	-4	4			.875	-2	/O-9(9-0-0),C-2	-0.6
	Phi-a	71	264	33	51	5	3	1	20	8		.193	.223	.246	469	46	-17	12			.921	6	O-70(0-66-4)/C-1	-1.2
	Yr	82	302	35	56	6	3	1	24	10		.185	.217	.235	452	41	-21	16			.919	4	O-79(9-66-4)/C-3	-1.8
1887	Phi-a	3	11	1	2	0	0	0	0	0		.182	.182	.182	364	2	-1	2			.857	0	/O-3(0-3-0)	-0.1
	Bro-a	91	352	49	108	13	2	2	48	25		.307	.318	.324	643	78	-9	33			.921	3	O-76(76-0-0),C-16	-0.6
	Yr	94	363	50	110	13	2	2	48	25		.303	.314	.320	634	76	-11	35			.918	3	O-79(76-3-0),C-16	-0.7
Total	3	232	876	117	208	26	5	3	93	43		.237	.261	.268	529	58	-44	51			.916	6	O-205(87-107-11)/C-31	-3.7

■ RUSTY GREER

Greer, Thurman Clyde b: 1/21/69, Fort Rucker, Ala. BL/TL, 6', 190 lbs. Deb: 5/16/94 Career OF: (742-LF 49-CF 155-RF)

YEAR	TM/L	G	AB	R	H	2B	3B	HR	RBI	BB	SO	AVG	OBP	SLG	OPS	OPS+	BR+	SB	CS	SBR	FA	FR	G/POS	TPR
1994	Tex-A	80	277	36	87	16	1	10	46	46	46	.314	.415	.487	903	132	15	0	0	0	.976	-7	O-73(11-23-53)/1-9	0.5
1995	Tex-A	131	417	58	113	21	2	13	61	55	66	.271	.357	.424	782	100	1	3	1	0	.982	-15	*O-125(51-4-101)/1-3	-1.8
1996	*Tex-A	139	542	96	180	41	6	18	100	62	86	.332	.404	.530	933	127	23	9	0	2	.984	8	*O-137L/1-1,D-1	2.6
1997	Tex-A	157	601	112	193	42	3	26	87	83	87	.321	.406	.531	937	135	32	9	5	0	.965	-2	*O-153(148-19-1)/D-2	2.5
1998	*Tex-A	155	598	107	183	31	5	16	108	80	93	.306	.391	.455	846	115	15	2	4	-1	.990	3	*O-154(154-2-0)	1.2
1999	*Tex-A	147	556	107	167	41	3	20	101	96	67	.300	.408	.493	901	123	22	2	2	-0	.983	-0	*O-145(145-0-0)/D-1	1.5
2000	Tex-A	105	394	65	117	34	3	8	65	51	61	.297	.382	.459	841	108	6	4	1	1	.985	1	O-97(97-0-0)/D-2	0.3
Total	7	914	3385	581	1040	226	23	111	568	473	506	.307	.395	.486	881	120	113	29	13	2	.981	-11	O-884L/1-13,D-6	6.8

■ TOMMY GREGG

Gregg, William Thomas b: 7/29/63, Boone, N.C. BL/TL, 6'1", 190 lbs. Deb: 9/14/87

YEAR	TM/L	G	AB	R	H	2B	3B	HR	RBI	BB	SO	AVG	OBP	SLG	OPS	OPS+	BR+	SB	CS	SBR	FA	FR	G/POS	TPR
1987	Pit-N	10	8	3	2	1	0	0	0	0	2	.250	.250	.375	625	62	-0	0	0	0	1.000	-2	/O-4(1-2-2)	-0.2
1988	Pit-N	14	15	4	3	1	0	1	3	1	4	.200	.250	.467	717	103	-0	0	1	-0	1.000	-2	/O-6(5-0-1)	-0.2
	Atl-N	11	29	1	10	3	0	0	4	2	2	.345	.387	.448	835	132	1	0	0	0	1.000	2	/O-7(5-3-0)	0.3
	Yr	25	44	5	13	4	0	1	7	3	6	.295	.340	.455	795	125	1	0	1	-0	1.000	0	O-13(10-3-1)	0.1
1989	Atl-N	102	276	24	67	8	0	6	23	18	45	.243	.289	.337	626	76	-9	3	4	-1	.967	-10	O-48(7-2-41),1-37	-2.4
1990	Atl-N	124	239	18	63	13	1	5	32	20	39	.264	.323	.389	712	90	-3	4	3	-0	.987	-2	1-50,O-20(7-0-12)	-0.9
1991	*Atl-N	72	107	13	20	8	1	1	4	12	24	.187	.275	.308	583	60	-6	2	2	-0	1.000	-2	O-14(9-0-5),1-13	-0.9
1992	Atl-N	18	19	1	5	0	0	1	1	1	7	.263	.300	.421	721	96	-0	1	0	0	1.000	-1	/O-9(2-4-4)	-0.1
1993	Cin-N	10	12	1	2	0	0	0	1	0	0	.167	.167	.167	333	-10	-2	0	0	0	1.000	-1	/O-4(3-0-1)	-0.3
1995	Fla-N	72	156	20	37	5	0	6	20	16	33	.237	.316	.385	701	83	-4	3	1	0	.984	-3	O-38(6-4-30)/1-2	-0.8

YEAR	TM/L	G	AB	R	H	2B	3B	HR	RBI	BB	SO	AVG	OBP	SLG	OPS	OPS+	BR+	SB	CS	SBR	FA	FR	G/POS	TPR
1997	*Atl-N	13	19	1	5	2	0	0	0	1	2	.263	.300	.368	668	72	-1	1	1	-0	1.000	-2	/O-6(5-0-1),1-1	-0.3
Total	9	446	880	86	214	41	2	20	88	71	158	.243	.303	.363	665	81	-23	14	12	-1	.981	-22	O-156(50-15-97),1-103	-5.8
■ **ED GREMMINGER**	Gremminger, Lorenzo Edward "Battleship" b: 3/30/1874, Canton, Ohio d: 5/26/42, Canton, Ohio BR/TR, 6'1", 200 lbs. Deb: 4/21/1895																							
1895	Cle-N	20	78	10	21	1	0	0	15	5	13	.269	.313	.282	595	51	-6	0			.873	-1	3-20	-0.5
1902	Bos-N	140	522	55	134	20	12	1	65	39		.257	.314	.347	661	103	1	7			**.951**	3	*3-140	0.9
1903	Bos-N	140	511	57	135	24	9	5	56	31		.264	.313	.376	688	100	-2	12			.935	16	*3-140	1.7
1904	Det-A	83	309	18	66	13	3	1	28	14		.214	.257	.285	542	73	-10	3			.950	-16	3-83	-2.7
Total	4	383	1420	140	356	58	24	7	164	89	13	.251	.301	.340	642	92	-16	22			.940	2	3-383	-0.6
■ **BUDDY GREMP**	Gremp, Lewis Edward b: 8/5/19, Denver, Col. d: 1/30/95, Manteca, Cal. BR/TR, 6'1", 175 lbs. Deb: 9/13/40																							
1940	Bos-N	4	9	0	2	0	0	0	2	0	0	.222	.222	.222	444	24	-1	0			1.000	-0	/1-3	-0.1
1941	Bos-N	37	75	7	18	3	0	0	10	5	3	.240	.287	.280	568	63	-4	0			.977	-3	1-21/2-6,C-3	-0.9
1942	Bos-N	72	207	12	45	11	0	3	19	13	21	.217	.267	.314	581	71	-8	1			.991	1	1-62/3-1	-1.3
Total	3	113	291	19	65	14	0	3	31	18	24	.223	.271	.302	573	67	-13	1			.988	-3	/1-86,2-6,C-3,3-1	-2.3
■ **REDDY GREY**	Grey, Romer Carl (b: Romer Carl Gray) b: 4/8/1875, Zanesville, Ohio d: 11/9/34, Altadena, Cal. BL/TL, 5'11", 175 lbs. Deb: 5/28/03																							
1903	Pit-N	1	3	1	1	0	0	0	1	1		.333	.500	.333	833	135	0	0			1.000	-0	/O-1(1-0-0)	0.0
■ **BILL GREY**	Grey, William Tobin b: 4/15/1871, Philadelphia, Pa. d: 12/8/32, Philadelphia, Pa. 5'11", 175 lbs. Deb: 5/14/1890																							
1890	Phi-N	34	128	20	31	8	4	0	21	6	3	.242	.287	.367	654	88	-3	5			1.000	-11	O-10L/3-8,2-8,C1	-1.2
1891	Phi-N	23	75	11	18	0	0	0	7	3	10	.240	.296	.240	536	55	-4	3			.804	-6	C-11,O-10R/S-3,3-1	-0.8
1895	Cin-N	52	181	24	55	17	4	1	29	15	8	.304	.364	.459	822	107	1	4			.906	-4	3-27,2-16/S-5,CO	-0.1
1896	Cin-N	46	121	15	25	2	1	0	17	19	11	.207	.314	.240	554	44	-10	6			.927	1	2-12,C-11/S-8,O13	-0.6
1898	Pit-N	137	528	56	121	17	5	0	67	28		.229	.283	.280	564	63	-26	5			.879	-20	*3-137	-4.1
Total	5	292	1033	126	250	44	14	1	141	71	32	.242	.303	.315	617	72	-41	23			.879	-40	3-174/2-36,C-34,OS1	-6.8
■ **BOBBY GRICH**	Grich, Robert Anthony b: 1/15/49, Muskegon, Mich. BR/TR, 6'2", 190 lbs. Deb: 6/29/70																							
1970	Bal-A	30	95	11	20	1	3	0	8	9	21	.211	.279	.284	563	55	-6	1	1	-0	.915	2	S-20/2-9,3-1	-0.1
1971	Bal-A	7	30	7	9	0	0	1	6	5	8	.300	.400	.400	800	128	1	1	0	0	1.000	3	/S-5,2-2	0.5
1972	Bal-A★	133	460	66	128	21	3	12	50	53	96	.278	.362	.415	777	127	16	13	6	1	.950	-25	S-81,2-45,1-16,/3-8	0.4
1973	*Bal-A	162	581	82	146	29	7	12	50	107	91	.251	.374	.387	761	116	16	17	9	1	**.995**	21	*2-162	4.9
1974	*Bal-A★	160	582	92	153	29	6	19	82	90	117	.263	.380	.431	811	137	31	17	11	-0	.979	-0	*2-160	5.2
1975	Bal-A	150	524	81	136	26	4	13	57	107	88	.260	.393	.399	792	133	28	14	10	-0	.977	24	*2-150	6.2
1976	Bal-A★	144	518	93	138	31	4	13	54	86	99	.266	.374	.417	791	140	29	14	6	1	.985	-1	*2-140/3-2,D-2	4.0
1977	Cal-A	52	181	24	44	6	0	7	23	37	40	.243	.374	.392	767	114	5	6	6	-1	.983	-3	S-52	0.6
1978	Cal-A	144	487	68	122	16	2	6	42	75	83	.251	.359	.329	687	98	2	4	3	-0	.983	0	*2-144	1.0
1979	*Cal-A★	153	534	78	157	30	5	30	101	59	84	.294	.366	.537	904	145	33	1	0	0	.984	1	*2-153	4.1
1980	Cal-A★	150	498	60	135	22	2	14	62	84	108	.271	.381	.408	788	119	16	3	7	-2	.989	3	*2-146/1-3	2.5
1981	Cal-A	100	352	56	107	14	2	**22**	61	40	71	.304	.381	**.543**	924	**164**	28	2	4	-1	.983	11	*2-100	4.5
1982	*Cal-A★	145	506	74	132	28	5	19	65	82	109	.261	.372	.449	821	124	19	3	3	-0	.986	11	*2-142/D-1	3.7
1983	Cal-A	120	387	65	113	17	0	16	62	76	62	.292	.417	.460	877	142	26	2	4	-1	.969	16	*2-118/S-1	4.7
1984	Cal-A	116	363	60	93	15	1	18	58	57	70	.256	.360	.452	812	124	13	2	5	-1	.982	3	2-91,1-25,3-21	1.8
1985	Cal-A	144	479	74	116	17	3	13	53	81	77	.242	.355	.372	727	100	2	3	5	-1	**.997**	15	*2-116,1-16,3-15,/D	2.1
1986	*Cal-A	98	313	42	84	18	0	9	30	39	54	.268	.355	.412	767	109	5	1	3	-1	.980	-10	2-87,1-11/3-2	-0.3
Total	17	2008	6890	1033	1833	320	47	224	864	1087	1278	.266	.373	.424	796	125	265	104	83	-6	.984	80	*2-1765,S-159/13D	45.8
■ **TIM GRIESENBECK**	Griesenbeck, Carlos Phillipe Timothy b: 12/10/1897, San Antonio, Tex. d: 3/25/53, San Antonio, Tex. BR/TR, 5'10.5", 190 lbs. Deb: 9/11/20																							
1920	StL-N	5	3	1	1	0	0	0	0	0	0	.333	.333	.333	667	95	-0	0	0	0	1.000	0	/C-3	0.0
■ **BEN GRIEVE**	Grieve, Benjamin b: 5/4/76, Arlington, Tex. BL/TR, 6'4", 220 lbs. Deb: 9/3/97 F																							
1997	Oak-A	24	93	12	29	6	0	3	24	13	25	.312	.402	.473	875	129	4	0	0	0	1.000	-1	O-24(0-0-24)	0.2
1998	Oak-A★	155	583	94	168	41	2	18	89	85	123	.288	.387	.458	845	122	21	2	2	-0	.993	-7	*O-151(0-0-151)/D-3	0.6
1999	Oak-A	148	486	80	129	21	0	28	86	63	108	.265	.359	.481	841	117	12	4	0	1	.988	-6	*O-137(131-0-8)/D-4	0.3
2000	*Oak-A	158	594	92	166	40	1	27	104	73	130	.279	.361	.487	848	115	13	3	0	1	.988	-8	*O-144(144-0-0),D-12	0.1
Total	4	485	1756	278	492	108	3	76	303	234	386	.280	.371	.475	846	118	51	9	2	1	.990	-22	O-456(275-0-183)/D-19	1.2
■ **TOM GRIEVE**	Grieve, Thomas Alan b: 3/4/48, Pittsfield, Mass. BR/TR, 6'2", 190 lbs. Deb: 7/5/70 F Career OF: (253-LF 16-CF 135-RF)																							
1970	Was-A	47	116	12	23	5	1	3	10	14	38	.198	.290	.336	626	76	-4	0	0	0	.939	-7	O-39(15-1-24)	-1.3
1972	Tex-A	64	142	12	29	2	1	3	11	11	39	.204	.271	.296	567	72	-5	1	3	-1	.985	-4	O-49(45-3-5)	-1.3
1973	Tex-A	66	123	22	38	6	0	7	21	7	25	.309	.351	.528	880	151	8	1	0	0	1.000	-12	O-59(34-10-19)/D-1	-0.6
1974	Tex-A	84	259	30	66	10	4	9	32	20	48	.255	.313	.429	742	114	4	0	0	0	1.000	2	D-40,O-38(31-0-7)/1-1	0.3
1975	Tex-A	118	369	46	102	17	1	14	61	22	74	.276	.317	.442	759	113	5	0	2	-1	.990	-7	O-63(46-2-16),D-45	-0.6
1976	Tex-A	149	546	57	139	23	3	20	81	35	119	.255	.304	.418	722	108	3	4	1	1	.983	2	D-96,O-52(45-0-8)	0.0
1977	Tex-A	79	236	24	53	9	0	7	30	13	57	.225	.274	.352	626	68	-11	1	0	0	.976	-6	O-60(30-0-32),D-13	-1.9
1978	NY-N	54	101	5	21	3	0	2	8	9	23	.208	.273	.297	570	61	-5	0	1	-0	.979	1	O-26(2-0-24)/1-2	-0.7
1979	StL-N	9	15	1	3	1	0	0	0	4	1	.200	.368	.267	635	76	-0	0	0	0	.875	-1	/O-5(5-0-0)	-0.1
Total	9	670	1907	209	474	76	10	65	254	135	424	.249	.303	.401	704	100	-6	7	7	-1	.982	-31	O-391L,D-195/1-3	-6.2
■ **KEN GRIFFEY**	Griffey, George Kenneth Jr. "Junior" b: 11/21/69, Donora, Pa. BL/TL, 6'3", 205 lbs. Deb: 4/3/89 F Career OF: (2-LF 1626-CF 2-RF)																							
1989	Sea-A	127	455	61	120	23	0	16	61	44	83	.264	.331	.420	751	107	4	16	7	1	.969	5	*O-127(0-127-0)	0.9
1990	Sea-A★	155	597	91	179	28	7	22	80	63	81	.300	.369	.481	849	134	27	16	11	-0	.980	1	*O-151(0-151-0)/D-2	2.6
1991	Sea-A★	154	548	76	179	42	1	22	100	71	82	.327	.405	.527	932	156	42	18	6	2	.989	9	*O-152(0-152-0)/D-1	5.1
1992	Sea-A★	142	565	83	174	39	4	27	103	44	67	.308	.363	.535	898	148	34	10	5	0	.997	6	*O-137(0-137-0)/D-3	3.9
1993	Sea-A★	156	582	113	180	38	3	45	109	96	91	.309	.412	.617	1029	170	58	17	9	1	.991	2	*O-139C,D-19/1-1	**5.8**
1994	Sea-A★	111	433	94	140	24	4	**40**	90	56	73	.323	.403	.674	1078	168	43	11	3	1	.983	5	*O-103(0-103-1)/D-9	4.5
1995	*Sea-A†	72	260	52	67	7	0	17	42	52	53	.258	.381	.481	862	121	9	4	2	0	.990	10	O-70(0-70-0)/D-2	1.8
1996	Sea-A†	140	545	125	165	26	2	49	140	78	104	.303	.397	.628	1024	153	44	16	1	3	.990	16	*O-137(0-137-0)/D-5	**5.8**
1997	*Sea-A★	157	608	**125**	185	34	3	**56**	**147**	76	121	.304	.389	**.646**	1035	165	57	15	4	2	.985	14	*O-153(1-153-0)/D-4	**6.9**
1998	Sea-A★	161	633	120	180	33	3	**56**	146	76	121	.284	.367	.611	979	148	43	20	5	3	.988	15	*O-158C/1-1,D-3	5.8
1999	Sea-A★	160	606	123	173	26	3	**48**	134	91	108	.285	.385	.576	961	144	40	24	7	3	.978	6	*O-158(0-158-0)/D-6	4.7
2000	Cin-N†	145	520	100	141	22	3	40	118	94	117	.271	.392	.556	947	130	25	6	4	-0	.987	14	*O-141(0-141-0)	3.8
Total	12	1680	6352	1163	1883	342	33	438	1270	841	1101	.296	.384	.568	951	147	425	173	64	16	.986	102	*O-1626C/D-54,1-2	51.6
■ **KEN GRIFFEY**	Griffey, George Kenneth Sr. b: 4/10/50, Donora, Pa. BL/TL, 6', 200 lbs. Deb: 8/25/73 FC Career OF: (532-LF 203-CF 989-RF)																							
1973	*Cin-N	25	86	19	33	5	1	3	14	6	10	.384	.424	.570	994	182	9	4	2	0	1.000	-3	O-21(0-0-21)	0.5
1974	Cin-N	88	227	24	57	9	5	2	19	27	43	.251	.333	.361	695	96	-1	9	4	1	1.000	-1	O-70(2-0-68)	-0.5
1975	*Cin-N	132	463	95	141	15	9	4	46	67	67	.305	.394	.402	795	119	14	16	7	1	.967	-5	*O-119(0-0-119)	0.4
1976	*Cin-N★	148	562	111	189	28	9	6	74	62	65	.336	.403	.450	853	139	30	34	11	4	.979	-1	*O-144(0-0-144)	2.6
1977	Cin-N☆	154	585	117	186	35	8	12	57	69	84	.318	.390	.467	857	126	23	17	8	1	.990	9	*O-147(0-0-147)	2.5
1978	Cin-N	158	614	90	177	33	8	10	63	54	70	.288	.346	.417	763	112	9	23	5	3	.969	4	*O-154(0-13-142)	1.0
1979	Cin-N	95	380	62	120	27	4	8	32	36	39	.316	.376	.471	848	129	15	12	5	1	.984	-3	O-93(0-8-92)	0.8
1980	Cin-N★	146	544	89	160	28	10	13	85	62	77	.294	.367	.454	821	128	21	23	1	5	.978	-0	*O-138(0-2-138)	1.9
1981	Cin-N	101	396	65	123	21	6	2	34	39	42	.311	.374	.409	783	120	11	12	4	1	.989	10	O-99(0-99-0)	2.2
1982	NY-A	127	484	70	134	23	2	12	54	39	58	.277	.331	.407	738	103	2	10	4	1	.983	7	*O-125(0-26-102)	0.4
1983	NY-A	118	458	60	140	21	3	11	46	34	45	.306	.356	.437	793	121	13	6	1	1	.992	-2	*1-101/O-14C,D-2	0.6
1984	NY-A	120	399	44	109	20	1	7	56	29	32	.273	.324	.381	705	98	-1	2	2	-0	.974	-0	O-82L,1-27/D-2	-0.6
1985	NY-A	127	438	68	120	28	4	10	69	41	51	.274	.336	.425	761	109	5	7	7	-1	.970	5	*O-110L/1-1,D-7	0.4
1986	NY-A	59	198	33	60	7	0	9	26	15	24	.303	.355	.475	830	125	7	2	2	0	.971	1	O-51(50-2-1)/D-2	0.5
	Atl-N	80	292	36	90	15	3	12	32	20	43	.308	.353	.503	856	126	10	12	7	0	.986	1	O-77(77-0-0)/1-1	0.8
1987	Atl-N	122	399	65	114	24	1	14	64	46	54	.286	.361	.456	817	109	6	4	7	-2	.995	1	*O-107(107-1-0)/1-3	0.0

YEAR	TM/L	G	AB	R	H	2B	3B	HR	RBI	BB	SO	AVG	OBP	SLG	OPS	OPS+	BR+	SB	CS	SBR	FA	FR	G/POS	TPR
1988	Atl-N	69	193	21	48	5	0	2	19	17	26	.249	.310	.306	615	74	-6	1	3	-1	.969	-4	O-42(41-0-2),1-11	-1.4
	Cin-N	25	50	5	14	1	0	2	4	2	5	.280	.308	.420	728	103	0	0	0	0	.986	-0	1-10	-0.1
	Yr	94	243	26	62	6	0	4	23	19	31	.255	.309	.329	638	80	-6	1	3	-1	.969	-4	O-42(41-0-2),1-21	-1.5
1989	Cin-N	106	236	26	62	8	3	8	30	29	42	.263	.346	.424	770	115	5	4	2	0	.987	-8	O-58(58-0-1)/1-9	-0.5
1990	Cin-N	46	63	6	13	2	0	1	8	2	5	.206	.242	.286	528	43	-5	2	1	0	.979	0	/1-9,O-6(5-0-1)	-0.5
	Sea-A	21	77	13	29	2	0	3	18	10	3	.377	.448	.519	968	168	7	0	0	0	.963	-2	O-20(20-0-0)	0.5
1991	Sea-A	30	85	10	24	7	0	1	9	13	13	.282	.384	.400	784	117	2	0	0	0	1.000	-4	O-26(26-0-0)/D-1	-0.2
Total	19	2097	7229	1129	2143	364	77	152	859	719	898	.296	.361	.431	792	118	176	200	83	15	.981	4	*O-1703R,1-172/D-14	11.3

■ ALFREDO GRIFFIN

Griffin, Alfredo Claudino (b: Alfredo Claudino Baptist (Griffin)) b: 10/6/57, Santo Domingo, D.R. BB/TR, 5'11", 165 lbs. Deb: 9/4/76 C

YEAR	TM/L	G	AB	R	H	2B	3B	HR	RBI	BB	SO	AVG	OBP	SLG	OPS	OPS+	BR+	SB	CS	SBR	FA	FR	G/POS	TPR
1976	Cle-A	12	4	0	1	0	0	0	0	0	2	.250	.250	.250	500	47	-0	0	1	-0	.750	0	/S-6,D-4	0.0
1977	Cle-A	14	41	5	6	1	0	0	3	3	5	.146	.205	.171	375	4	-5	2	2	-0	.940	-1	S-13/D-1	-0.6
1978	Cle-A	5	4	1	2	1	0	0	0	2	1	.500	.667	.750	1417	301	1	0	0	0	.917	3	/S-2	0.4
1979	Tor-A	153	624	81	179	22	10	2	31	40	59	.287	.335	.364	699	87	-11	21	16	-1	.956	6	*S-153	1.0
1980	Tor-A	155	653	63	166	26	**15**	2	41	24	58	.254	.285	.349	634	70	-28	18	23	-4	.955	2	*S-155	-1.3
1981	Tor-A	101	388	30	81	19	6	0	21	17	38	.209	.244	.289	533	50	-25	8	12	-2	.937	-19	S-97/3-4,2-1	-3.9
1982	Tor-A	162	539	57	130	20	8	1	48	22	48	.241	.271	.314	584	55	-33	10	8	-1	.968	6	*S-162	-1.0
1983	Tor-A	162	528	62	132	22	9	4	47	27	44	.250	.290	.348	639	71	-21	8	11	-2	.965	-4	*S-157/2-5,D-1	-1.2
1984	Tor-A★	140	419	53	101	8	2	4	30	4	33	.241	.250	.298	548	49	-29	11	3	1	.962	-5	*S-115,2-21/D-5	-2.1
1985	Oak-A	162	614	75	166	18	7	2	64	20	50	.270	.293	.332	626	77	-21	24	9	2	.960	-15	*S-162	-1.6
1986	Oak-A	162	594	74	169	23	6	4	51	35	52	.285	.326	.364	690	95	-5	33	16	2	.966	-11	*S-162	0.3
1987	Oak-A	144	494	69	130	23	5	3	60	28	41	.263	.308	.348	656	79	-15	26	13	1	.963	0	*S-137/2-1	0.1
1988	*LA-N	95	316	39	63	8	3	1	27	24	30	.199	.260	.253	513	49	-21	7	5	-0	.965	2	S-93	-1.3
1989	LA-N	136	506	49	125	27	2	0	29	29	57	.247	.288	.308	596	72	-19	10	7	-0	.975	-8	*S-131	-1.8
1990	LA-N	141	461	38	97	11	3	1	35	29	65	.210	.260	.254	514	43	-36	6	3	0	.959	10	*S-139	-1.6
1991	LA-N	109	350	27	85	6	2	0	27	22	49	.243	.290	.271	561	60	-18	5	4	-0	.961	19	*S-109	0.9
1992	*Tor-A	63	150	21	35	7	0	0	10	9	19	.233	.277	.280	557	54	-9	3	1	0	.981	-1	S-48,2-16	-0.7
1993	*Tor-A	46	95	15	20	3	0	0	3	3	13	.211	.235	.242	477	28	-10	0	0	0	.960	4	S-20,2-11/3-6	-0.4
Total	18	1962	6780	759	1688	245	78	24	527	338	664	.249	.287	.319	606	67	-304	192	134	-5	.961	-10	*S-1861/2-55,D-11,3	-14.8

■ DOUG GRIFFIN

Griffin, Douglas Lee b: 6/4/47, South Gate, Cal. BR/TR, 6', 170 lbs. Deb: 9/11/70

YEAR	TM/L	G	AB	R	H	2B	3B	HR	RBI	BB	SO	AVG	OBP	SLG	OPS	OPS+	BR+	SB	CS	SBR	FA	FR	G/POS	TPR
1970	Cal-A	18	55	2	7	1	0	0	4	6	5	.127	.213	.145	359	1	-7	0	0	0	.964	1	2-11/3-8	-0.6
1971	Bos-A	125	483	51	118	23	2	3	27	31	45	.244	.293	.319	611	68	-20	11	5	1	.986	7	*2-124	-0.5
1972	Bos-A	129	470	43	122	12	1	2	35	45	48	.260	.327	.302	629	83	-8	9	2	1	.978	2	*2-129	0.5
1973	Bos-A	113	396	43	101	14	5	1	33	21	42	.255	.298	.323	621	71	-15	7	5	-0	.990	-14	*2-113	-2.3
1974	Bos-A	93	312	35	83	12	4	0	33	28	21	.266	.330	.330	661	85	-6	2	8	-2	.979	-13	2-91/S-1	-1.6
1975	*Bos-A	100	287	21	69	6	0	1	29	18	29	.240	.290	.272	562	55	-17	2	2	-0	.967	-10	2-99/S-1	-2.2
1976	Bos-A	49	127	14	24	2	0	0	4	9	14	.189	.248	.205	453	30	-11	2	1	0	.989	-1	2-44/D-2	-1.0
1977	Bos-A	5	6	0	0	0	0	0	0	0	0	.000	.000	.000	0	-90	-2	0	0	0	1.000	0	/2-3	-0.1
Total	8	632	2136	209	524	70	12	7	165	158	204	.245	.301	.299	600	68	-86	33	23	-1	.981	-28	2-614/3-8,D-2,S-2	-7.8

■ PUG GRIFFIN

Griffin, Francis Arthur b: 4/24/1896, Lincoln, Neb. d: 10/12/51, Colorado Springs, Colo. BR/TR, 5'11.5", 187 lbs. Deb: 7/27/17

YEAR	TM/L	G	AB	R	H	2B	3B	HR	RBI	BB	SO	AVG	OBP	SLG	OPS	OPS+	BR+	SB	CS	SBR	FA	FR	G/POS	TPR
1917	Phi-A	18	25	4	5	1	0	1	3	1	9	.200	.231	.360	591	81	-1	1			1.000	1	/1-3	0.0
1920	NY-N	5	4	0	1	0	0	0	0	1	2	.250	.400	.250	650	90	0	0	0	0	1.000	-1	/O-2(0-1-1)	-0.1
Total	2	23	29	4	6	1	0	1	3	2	11	.207	.258	.345	603	83	-1	1	0		1.000	-0	/1-3,O-2(0-1-1)	-0.1

■ IVY GRIFFIN

Griffin, Ivy Moore b: 11/16/1896, Thomasville, Ala. d: 8/25/57, Gainesville, Fla. BL/TR, 5'11", 180 lbs. Deb: 9/9/19

YEAR	TM/L	G	AB	R	H	2B	3B	HR	RBI	BB	SO	AVG	OBP	SLG	OPS	OPS+	BR+	SB	CS	SBR	FA	FR	G/POS	TPR
1919	Phi-A	17	68	5	20	2	2	0	6	3	10	.294	.333	.382	716	99	-0	0			.989	4	1-17	0.3
1920	Phi-A	129	467	46	111	15	1	0	20	17	49	.238	.281	.274	555	47	-36	3	3	-0	.990	5	*1-127/2-2	-3.3
1921	Phi-A	39	103	14	33	4	2	0	13	5	6	.320	.369	.398	767	95	-1	1	2	-0	.973	-2	1-27	-0.5
Total	3	185	638	65	164	21	5	0	39	25	65	.257	.301	.306	607	60	-36	4	5		.988	7	1-171/2-2	-3.5

■ MIKE GRIFFIN

Griffin, Michael Joseph b: 3/20/1865, Utica, N.Y. d: 4/10/08, Utica, N.Y. BL/TR, 5'7", 160 lbs. Deb: 4/16/1887 M Career OF: (7-LF 1461-CF 14-RF)

YEAR	TM/L	G	AB	R	H	2B	3B	HR	RBI	BB	SO	AVG	OBP	SLG	OPS	OPS+	BR+	SB	CS	SBR	FA	FR	G/POS	TPR
1887	Bal-a	136	587	142	215	32	13	3	94	55		.366	.375	.427	801	131	24	94			.924	-12	*O-136(1-135-0)	0.6
1888	Bal-a	137	542	103	139	21	11	0	46	55		.256	.331	.336	666	117	12	46			.938	7	*O-137(0-137-0)	1.3
1889	Bal-a	137	531	**152**	148	21	14	4	48	91	29	.279	.387	.394	781	120	17	39			.910	-10	*O-109C,S-25/2-5	0.3
1890	Phi-P	115	489	127	140	29	6	6	54	64	19	.286	.377	.407	784	107	5	30			**.954**	18	*O-115(4-100-13)	1.5
1891	Bro-N	134	521	106	139	**36**	9	3	65	57	31	.267	.340	.388	728	113	8	65			**.960**	26	*O-134(2-132-0)	2.6
1892	Bro-N	129	452	103	125	17	11	3	66	68	36	.277	.376	.383	759	134	21	49			**.986**	13	*O-127(0-126-1)/S-2	2.4
1893	Bro-N	95	362	85	103	21	7	6	59	59	23	.285	.396	.431	827	126	15	30			**.965**	9	*O-93(0-93-0)/2-2	1.5
1894	Bro-N	108	406	123	145	29	4	5	76	78	14	.357	.465	.485	950	139	33	39			.966	6	*O-107(0-107-0)	2.4
1895	Bro-N	132	524	140	174	38	7	4	65	93	30	.332	.442	.454	896	143	41	27			**.969**	14	*O-132(0-132-0)/S-1	3.8
1896	Bro-N	122	493	101	152	27	9	4	51	48	25	.308	.380	.424	804	118	14	23			.961	3	*O-122(0-122-0)	0.8
1897	Bro-N	134	534	136	169	25	11	2	56	81		.316	.416	.416	832	127	26	16			.956	5	*O-134(0-134-0)	1.9
1898	Bro-N	134	537	88	161	18	6	2	40	60		.300	.379	.367	745	114	12	15			**.974**	10	*O-134(0-134-0),M	1.2
Total	12	1513	5978	1406	1810	314	108	42	720	809	207	.303	.388	.407	795	124	229	473			.956	88	*O-1480C/S-28,2-7	20.3

■ THOMAS GRIFFIN

Griffin, Thomas William b: 1/1857, Titusville, Pa. d: 4/17/33, Rockford, Ill. Deb: 9/27/1884

YEAR	TM/L	G	AB	R	H	2B	3B	HR	RBI	BB	SO	AVG	OBP	SLG	OPS	OPS+	BR+	SB	CS	SBR	FA	FR	G/POS	TPR
1884	Mil-U	11	41	5	9	2	0	0		3		.220	.273	.268	541	119	0				.918	-2	1-11	-0.2

■ SANDY GRIFFIN

Griffin, Tobias Charles b: 10/24/1858, Fayetteville, N.Y d: 6/4/26, Syracuse, N.Y. BR/TR, 5'10", 160 lbs. Deb: 5/26/1884 M

YEAR	TM/L	G	AB	R	H	2B	3B	HR	RBI	BB	SO	AVG	OBP	SLG	OPS	OPS+	BR+	SB	CS	SBR	FA	FR	G/POS	TPR
1884	NY-N	16	62	7	11	2	0	0	6	1	19	.177	.190	.210	400	25	-5				.842	-3	O-16(0-5-11)	-0.8
1890	Roc-a	107	407	85	125	28	4	5	53	50		.307	.388	.432	821	153	28	21			.856	-19	*O-107(0-107-0)/2-1	0.5
1891	Was-a	20	69	15	19	4	2	0	10	10	3	.275	.398	.391	789	132	4	2			.939	-3	O-20(0-20-0),M	0.0
1893	StL-N	23	92	9	18	1	1	0	9	16	2	.196	.315	.228	543	45	-7	2			.906	-2	O-23(23-0-0)	-0.9
Total	4	166	630	116	173	35	7	5	78	77	24	.275	.361	.376	737	120	20	25			.873	-27	O-166(23-132-11)/2-1	-1.2

■ BERT GRIFFITH

Griffith, Bartholomew Joseph "Buck" b: 3/30/1896, St.Louis, Mo. d: 5/5/73, Bishop, Cal. BR/TR, 5'11", 185 lbs. Deb: 4/13/22

YEAR	TM/L	G	AB	R	H	2B	3B	HR	RBI	BB	SO	AVG	OBP	SLG	OPS	OPS+	BR+	SB	CS	SBR	FA	FR	G/POS	TPR
1922	Bro-N	106	325	45	100	22	8	2	35	5	11	.308	.322	.443	765	96	-3	5	7	-1	.981	-1	O-77(0-8-69)/1-6	-1.1
1923	Bro-N	79	248	23	73	8	4	2	37	13	16	.294	.332	.383	715	91	-4	1	2	-0	.949	-8	O-62(51-9-3)	-1.5
1924	Was-A	6	8	1	1	0	0	0	0	0	1	.125	.125	.125	250	-37	-2	0	0	0	1.000	0	/O-2(0-2-0)	-0.1
Total	3	191	581	69	174	30	12	4	72	18	28	.299	.324	.413	737	92	-8	6	9	-2	.968	-9	O-141(51-19-72)/1-6	-2.7

■ CLARK GRIFFITH

Griffith, Clark Calvin "The Old Fox" b: 11/20/1869, Clear Creek, Mo. d: 10/27/55, Washington, D.C. BR/TR, 5'6.5", 156 lbs. Deb: 4/11/1891 MH Career OF: (6-LF 4-CF 7-RF)

YEAR	TM/L	G	AB	R	H	2B	3B	HR	RBI	BB	SO	AVG	OBP	SLG	OPS	OPS+	BR+	SB	CS	SBR	FA	FR	G/POS	TPR
1891	StL-a	27	77	11	12	1	0	1	8	8	15	.156	.253	.208	461	28	-8	2			.930	0	P-27	0.0
	Bos-a	10	23	6	4	1	1	1	3	6	5	.174	.367	.435	801	131	1	1			.778	-1	/P-7,O-3(2-0-1)	0.0
	Yr	37	100	17	16	2	1	2	11	14	20	.160	.282	.260	542	50	-7	3			.909	-1	P-34/O-3(2-0-1)	0.0
1893	Chi-N	4	11	1	2	0	0	0	2	0	1	.182	.182	.182	364	-3	-2	0			1.000	1	/P-4	0.0
1894	Chi-N	46	142	27	33	5	4	0	15	23	9	.232	.339	.324	663	57	-10	6			.942	-3	P-36/O-7(0-3-4),S-1	-0.4
1895	Chi-N	43	144	20	46	3	0	1	27	16	9	.319	.391	.361	752	89	-2	2			.923	1	P-42/O-1(0-0-1)	0.0
1896	Chi-N	38	135	22	36	5	2	1	16	9	7	.267	.313	.356	668	73	-6	3			.917	1	P-36	0.0
1897	Chi-N	46	162	27	38	8	4	0	21	18		.235	.311	.333	644	68	-8	2			.947	2	P-41/O-2L,S-2,31	-0.1
1898	Chi-N	38	122	15	20	2	3	0	15	13		.164	.244	.230	474	36	-10	1			.952	1	P-38	0.0
1899	Chi-N	39	120	15	31	5	0	0	14	14		.258	.346	.300	646	80	-3	2			.933	6	P-38/S-1	-0.1
1900	Chi-N	30	95	16	24	4	1	1	7	8		.253	.311	.347	658	84	-2	2			.917	-1	P-30	0.0
1901	Chi-A	35	89	21	27	3	1	2	14	23		.303	.446	.427	873	147	7	0			.946	0	P-35,M	0.0
1902	Chi-A	35	92	11	20	3	0	0	8	7		.217	.273	.250	523	48	-6	0			**1.000**	-2	P-28/O-3(2-0-1),M	-0.1
1903	NY-A	25	69	5	11	4	0	1	7	11		.159	.284	.261	545	60	-3	1			.983	-3	P-25,M	0.0
1904	NY-A	16	42	2	6	2	0	0	1	4		.143	.217	.190	408	28	-3	0			.946	-1	P-16,M	0.0
1905	NY-A	26	32	2	7	1	1	0	5	3		.219	.286	.313	598	80	-1	0			.960	-2	P-25/O-1(1-0-0),M	0.0

YEAR	TM/L	G	AB	R	H	2B	3B	HR	RBI	BB	SO	AVG	OBP	SLG	OPS	OPS+	BR+	SB	CS	SBR	FA	FR	G/POS	TPR
1906	NY-A	17	18	0	2	0	0	0	1	3		.111	.238	.111	349	9	-2	0			1.000	1	P-17,M	0.0
1907	NY-A	5	2	0	0	0	0	0	0	0		.000	.000	.000	0	-93	-0	0			.800	0	/P-4,M	0.0
1909	Cin-N	1	2	0	0	0	0	0	0	0		.000	.000	.000	0	-99	-0	0			1.000	1	/P-1,M	0.0
1910	Cin-N	1	0	1	0	0	0	0	0	0	0	—	—	—	—	—	0	0			.000	0	RM	0.0
1912	Was-A	1	1	0	0	0	0	0	0	0		.000	.000	.000	0	-99	-0	0			.000	1	/P-1,2-1,M	0.0
1913	Was-A	1	1	0	1	1	0	0	1	0	0	1.000	1.000	2.000	3000	758	1	0			.000	-0	/P-1,O-1,M	0.0
1914	Was-A	1	1	0	1	1	0	0	1	0	0	1.000	1.000	2.000	3000	769	1	0	1	-0	.000	-0	/P-1,M	0.0
Total	21	485	1380	202	321	49	17	8	166	166	46	.233	.318	.310	628	69	-56	22	1		.942	1	P-453/O-18R,S-4,213	-0.7

■ **DERRELL GRIFFITH** Griffith, Robert Derrell b: 12/12/43, Anadarko, Okla. BL/TR, 6', 168 lbs. Deb: 9/26/63 Career OF: (21-LF 1-CF 26-RF)

YEAR	TM/L	G	AB	R	H	2B	3B	HR	RBI	BB	SO	AVG	OBP	SLG	OPS	OPS+	BR+	SB	CS	SBR	FA	FR	G/POS	TPR
1963	LA-N	1	2	0	0	0	0	0	0	0	0	.000	.000	.000	0	-99	-1	0	0	0	.000	0	/2-1	-0.1
1964	LA-N	78	238	27	69	16	2	4	23	5	21	.290	.307	.424	732	112	3	5	1	1	.769	-12	3-35,O-29(6-0-23)	-1.1
1965	LA-N	22	41	3	7	0	0	1	2	0	9	.171	.171	.244	415	16	-5	0	0	0	1.000	-0	O-11(10-0-1)	-0.6
1966	LA-N	23	15	3	1	0	0	0	2	2	3	.067	.176	.067	243	-32	-3	0	0	0	1.000	-2	/O-7(5-1-2)	-0.5
Total	4	124	296	33	77	16	2	5	27	7	33	.260	.280	.378	658	90	-5	5	1	1	.970	-14	/O-47R,3-35,2-1	-2.3

■ **TOMMY GRIFFITH** Griffith, Thomas Herman b: 10/26/1889, Prospect, Ohio d: 4/13/67, Cincinnati, Ohio BL/TR, 5'10", 175 lbs. Deb: 8/28/13

YEAR	TM/L	G	AB	R	H	2B	3B	HR	RBI	BB	SO	AVG	OBP	SLG	OPS	OPS+	BR+	SB	CS	SBR	FA	FR	G/POS	TPR
1913	Bos-N	37	127	16	32	4	1	1	12	9	8	.252	.301	.323	624	77	-4	1			.886	1	O-35(0-0-35)	-0.5
1914	Bos-N	16	48	3	5	0	0	0	1	2	6	.104	.140	.104	244	-27	-7	0			.931	3	O-14(1-0-14)	-0.6
1915	Cin-N	160	583	59	179	31	16	4	85	41	34	.307	.355	.436	790	136	24	6	24	-7	.952	-13	*O-160(2-0-160)	-0.5
1916	Cin-N	155	595	50	158	28	7	2	61	36	37	.266	.310	.346	656	104	2	16			.967	6	*O-155(0-0-155)	-0.1
1917	Cin-N	115	363	45	98	18	7	1	45	19	23	.270	.308	.366	674	111	4	5			.974	6	*O-100(0-0-100)	0.5
1918	Cin-N	118	427	47	113	10	4	2	48	39	30	.265	.326	.321	647	99	0	10			.969	2	*O-118(0-0-118)	-0.5
1919	Bro-N	125	484	65	136	18	4	6	57	23	32	.281	.315	.372	687	104	1	8			.954	-1	*O-125(0-0-125)	-0.7
1920	*Bro-N	93	334	41	87	9	4	2	30	15	18	.260	.292	.329	622	76	-11	3	3	-0	.972	-11	O-92(0-0-92)	-2.9
1921	Bro-N	129	455	66	142	21	6	12	71	36	13	.312	.364	.464	828	113	8	3	3	-0	.972	7	*O-124(0-0-124)	0.5
1922	Bro-N	99	329	44	104	17	8	4	49	23	10	.316	.361	.453	814	110	4	7	1	1	.952	4	O-82(0-0-82)	0.3
1923	Bro-N	131	481	70	141	21	9	8	66	50	19	.293	.361	.424	785	109	7	8	2	1	.927	-7	*O-127(0-0-127)	-0.9
1924	Bro-N	140	482	43	121	19	5	3	67	34	19	.251	.300	.330	630	71	-20	0	5	-2	.965	-11	*O-139(0-0-139)	-4.4
1925	Bro-N	7	4	2	0	0	0	0	0	3	2	.000	.429	.000	429	20	-0	1	0	0	1.000	-1	/O-2(0-0-2)	-0.1
	Chi-N	76	235	38	67	12	1	7	27	21	11	.285	.346	.434	780	97	-1	2	4	-1	.937	-3	O-60(4-4-53)	-1.0
	Yr	83	239	40	67	12	1	7	27	24	13	.280	.348	.427	775	96	-2	3	4	-1	.938	-4	O-62(4-4-55)	-1.1
Total	13	1401	4947	589	1383	208	72	52	619	351	262	.280	.328	.382	711	102	6	70	42		.956	-19	*O-1333(7-4-1326)	-10.9

■ **ART GRIGGS** Griggs, Arthur Carle b: 12/10/1883, Topeka, Kan. d: 12/19/38, Los Angeles, Cal. BR/TR, 5'11", 185 lbs. Deb: 5/2/09 Career OF: (44-LF 2-CF 50-RF)

YEAR	TM/L	G	AB	R	H	2B	3B	HR	RBI	BB	SO	AVG	OBP	SLG	OPS	OPS+	BR+	SB	CS	SBR	FA	FR	G/POS	TPR
1909	StL-A	108	364	38	102	17	5	0	43	24		.280	.330	.354	684	125	10	11			.982	-6	1-49,O-41L/2-8,S-1	0.0
1910	StL-A	123	416	28	98	22	5	2	30	25		.236	.281	.327	607	96	-3	11			.878	-1	O-49R,2-41,1-17,/S3	-0.7
1911	Cle-A	27	68	7	17	3	2	1	7	5		.250	.301	.397	698	93	-1	1			.949	-2	2-11/O-4R,3-3,1-1	-0.3
1912	Cle-A	89	273	29	83	16	7	0	39	33		.304	.381	.414	795	123	9	10			.986	1	1-71	0.8
1914	Bro-F	40	112	10	32	6	1	1	15	5	11	.286	.328	.384	712	94	-3	1			.980	-3	1-27/O-1(1-0-0)	-0.7
1915	Bro-F	27	38	4	11	1	0	1	2	3	7	.289	.372	.395	767	117	0	0			1.000	1	/1-5,O-1(0-0-1)	0.1
1918	Det-A	28	99	11	36	8	0	0	16	10	5	.364	.422	.444	866	168	8	2			.986	-3	1-25	0.5
Total	7	442	1370	127	379	73	20	5	152	105	23	.277	.332	.370	702	115	19	36			.983	-13	1-195/O-96R,2-60,3S	-0.3

■ **DENVER GRIGSBY** Grigsby, Denver Clarence b: 3/25/01, Jackson, Ky. d: 11/10/73, Sapulpa, Okla. BL/TR, 5'9", 155 lbs. Deb: 9/1/23

YEAR	TM/L	G	AB	R	H	2B	3B	HR	RBI	BB	SO	AVG	OBP	SLG	OPS	OPS+	BR+	SB	CS	SBR	FA	FR	G/POS	TPR
1923	Chi-N	24	72	8	21	5	2	0	5	7	5	.292	.363	.417	779	105	1	1	3	-1	1.000	-2	O-22(6-1-16)	-0.4
1924	Chi-N	124	411	58	123	18	2	3	48	31	47	.299	.357	.375	732	95	-2	10	19	-4	.974	3	*O-121(108-5-8)	-1.2
1925	Chi-N	51	137	20	35	5	0	0	20	19	12	.255	.346	.292	638	64	-7	1	1	-0	.966	-1	O-39(21-15-3)	-1.0
Total	3	199	620	86	179	28	4	3	73	57	64	.289	.355	.361	717	89	-8	12	23	-5	.975	0	O-182(135-21-27)	-2.6

■ **JOHN GRIM** Grim, John Helm b: 8/9/1867, Lebanon, Ky. d: 7/28/61, Indianapolis, Ind BR/TR, 6'2", 175 lbs. Deb: 9/29/1888 Career OF: (2-LF 0-CF 12-RF)

YEAR	TM/L	G	AB	R	H	2B	3B	HR	RBI	BB	SO	AVG	OBP	SLG	OPS	OPS+	BR+	SB	CS	SBR	FA	FR	G/POS	TPR
1888	Phi-N	2	7	0	1	0	0	0	0	0	0	.143	.143	.143	286	-8	-1	0			.000	-1	/O-1(0-0-1),2-1	-0.1
1890	Roc-a	50	192	30	51	6	9	2	34	7		.266	.299	.422	720	121	4	14			.851	-7	S-21,C-15/3-8,2O1P	-0.1
1891	Mil-a	29	119	14	28	5	1	1	14	2	5	.235	.248	.319	567	52	-9	1			.926	3	C-16,3-10/2-3	-0.3
1892	Lou-N	97	370	40	90	16	4	1	36	13	24	.243	.280	.316	596	87	-6	18			.940	-9	C-69,1-11,2-10,/OS3	-0.9
1893	Lou-N	99	415	68	111	19	8	3	54	12	10	.267	.303	.373	676	86	-10	15			.952	-4	*C-92/1-3,2-2,OS	-0.5
1894	Lou-N	109	412	66	123	27	7	7	71	17	15	.299	.342	.449	791	96	-4	14			.927	12	C-78,2-24/1-7,3-1	1.2
1895	Bro-N	94	333	55	93	17	5	0	44	13	9	.279	.320	.360	680	82	-9	10			.947	1	*C-92/O-1(1-0-0),1-1	0.0
1896	Bro-N	81	281	32	75	13	1	2	35	12	14	.267	.311	.342	653	76	-10	7			.939	-1	C-77/1-5	-0.3
1897	Bro-N	80	290	26	72	10	1	0	25	1		.248	.259	.290	548	47	-23	3			.947	5	C-77	-0.9
1898	Bro-N	52	178	17	50	5	1	0	11	8		.281	.323	.320	643	85	-4	1			.950	-4	C-52	-0.3
1899	Bro-N	15	47	3	13	1	0	0	7	1		.277	.320	.298	618	68	-2	0			.966	1	C-12	0.1
Total	11	708	2644	351	707	119	37	16	331	86	77	.267	.303	.359	661	82	-73	83			.943	-4	C-580/2-44,1-29,S3OP	-2.1

■ **ROY GRIMES** Grimes, Austin Roy "Bummer" b: 9/11/1893, Bergholz, Ohio d: 9/13/54, Hanover Twsp., O. BR/TR, 6'1", 176 lbs. Deb: 7/31/20 F

YEAR	TM/L	G	AB	R	H	2B	3B	HR	RBI	BB	SO	AVG	OBP	SLG	OPS	OPS+	BR+	SB	CS	SBR	FA	FR	G/POS	TPR
1920	NY-N	26	57	5	9	1	0	0	3	3	8	.158	.200	.175	375	8	-7	1	1	-0	.948	-1	2-21	-0.9

■ **ED GRIMES** Grimes, Edward Adelbert b: 9/8/05, Chicago, Ill. d: 10/5/74, Chicago, Ill. BR/TR, 5'10", 165 lbs. Deb: 4/19/31

YEAR	TM/L	G	AB	R	H	2B	3B	HR	RBI	BB	SO	AVG	OBP	SLG	OPS	OPS+	BR+	SB	CS	SBR	FA	FR	G/POS	TPR
1931	StL-A	43	57	9	15	1	2	0	5	9	3	.263	.364	.351	715	86	-1	1	0	0	.892	-2	3-22/2-4,S-3	-0.2
1932	StL-A	31	68	7	16	0	1	0	13	6	12	.235	.297	.265	562	44	-6	0	1	-0	.891	2	3-18/2-2,S-1	-0.3
Total	2	74	125	16	31	1	3	0	18	15	15	.248	.329	.304	633	63	-6	1	1	-0	.891	0	/3-40,2-6,S-4	-0.5

■ **OSCAR GRIMES** Grimes, Oscar Ray Jr. b: 4/13/15, Minerva, Ohio d: 5/19/93, Westlake, Ohio BR/TR, 5'11", 178 lbs. Deb: 9/28/38 F

YEAR	TM/L	G	AB	R	H	2B	3B	HR	RBI	BB	SO	AVG	OBP	SLG	OPS	OPS+	BR+	SB	CS	SBR	FA	FR	G/POS	TPR
1938	Cle-A	4	10	2	2	0	1	0	2	2	0	.200	.333	.400	733	85	-0	0	0	0	1.000	-1	/2-2,1-1	-0.1
1939	Cle-A	119	364	51	98	20	5	4	56	56	61	.269	.368	.385	753	96	-1	8	3	1	.968	-11	2-48,1-43,S-37,/3-3	-0.9
1940	Cle-A	11	13	3	0	0	0	0	0	0	5	.000	.000	.000	0	-99	-4	0	0	0	.958	2	/1-4,3-1	-0.2
1941	Cle-A	77	244	28	58	9	3	4	24	39	47	.238	.345	.348	693	88	-3	4	0	1	.995	-5	1-62,2-13/3-1	-1.2
1942	Cle-A	51	84	10	15	2	0	0	2	13	17	.179	.289	.202	491	42	-6	3	2	-0	.944	-3	2-24/3-8,1-1,S-1	-0.9
1943	NY-A	9	20	4	3	0	0	0	1	3	7	.150	.261	.150	411	21	-2	0	0	0	1.000	-1	/S-3,1-1	-0.3
1944	NY-A	116	387	44	108	17	8	5	46	59	57	.279	.377	.403	780	119	11	6	0	1	.945	-10	3-97,S-20	0.5
1945	NY-A†	142	480	64	127	19	7	4	45	97	73	.265	.395	.358	753	114	13	7	6	-1	.937	3	*3-141/1-1	1.8
1946	NY-A	14	39	1	8	1	0	0	4	1	7	.205	.225	.231	456	27	-4	0	1	-0	.895	0	/S-7,2-5	-0.4
	Phi-A	59	191	28	50	5	0	1	20	27	29	.262	.356	.304	660	86	-2	2	0	0	.958	-12	2-43/3-6,S-4	-1.2
	Yr	73	230	29	58	6	0	1	24	28	36	.252	.336	.291	627	76	-6	2	1	0	.957	-12	2-48,S-11/3-6	-1.6
Total	9	602	1832	235	469	73	24	18	200	297	303	.256	.363	.352	715	98	2	30	12	2	.940	-39	3-257,2-135,1-113,/S	-2.9

■ **RAY GRIMES** Grimes, Oscar Ray Sr. b: 9/11/1893, Bergholz, Ohio d: 5/25/53, Minerva, Ohio BR/TR, 5'11", 168 lbs. Deb: 9/24/20 F

YEAR	TM/L	G	AB	R	H	2B	3B	HR	RBI	BB	SO	AVG	OBP	SLG	OPS	OPS+	BR+	SB	CS	SBR	FA	FR	G/POS	TPR
1920	Bos-A	1	4	1	1	0	0	0	0	1	0	.250	.400	.250	650	78	-0	0	0	0	1.000	-0	/1-1	0.0
1921	Chi-N	147	530	91	170	38	6	6	79	70	55	.321	.406	.449	855	126	22	5	8	-2	.993	-5	*1-147	0.6
1922	Chi-N	138	509	99	180	45	12	14	99	75	33	.354	.442	.572	1014	157	45	7	7	-1	.987	-2	*1-138	3.1
1923	Chi-N	64	216	32	71	7	2	2	36	24	17	.329	.401	.407	808	114	5	5	0	1	.991	-1	1-62	0.2
1924	Chi-N	51	177	33	53	6	5	5	34	28	15	.299	.401	.475	876	132	9	4	2	0	.982	-7	1-50	-0.1
1926	Phi-N	32	101	13	30	5	0	0	15	6	13	.297	.343	.347	689	82	-2	0			.981	0	1-28	-0.4
Total	6	433	1537	269	505	101	25	27	263	204	133	.329	.413	.480	892	132	79	21	17		.989	-14	1-426	3.4

■ **CHARLIE GRIMM** Grimm, Charles John "Jolly Cholly" b: 8/28/1898, St.Louis, Mo.
d: 11/15/83, Scottsdale, Ariz. BL/TL, 5'11.5", 173 lbs. Deb: 7/30/16 MC Career OF: (3-LF 1-CF 5-RF)

YEAR	TM/L	G	AB	R	H	2B	3B	HR	RBI	BB	SO	AVG	OBP	SLG	OPS	OPS+	BR+	SB	CS	SBR	FA	FR	G/POS	TPR
1916	Phi-A	12	22	0	2	0	0	0	0	2	4	.091	.167	.091	258	-24	-3	0			.875	-2	/O-7(3-1-3)	-0.6
1918	StL-N	50	141	11	31	7	0	0	12	6	15	.220	.262	.270	531	64	-6	2			.971	-3	1-42/O-2(0-0-2),3-1	-1.1
1919	Pit-N	14	44	6	14	1	3	0	6	2	4	.318	.348	.477	825	141	2	1			.968	-3	1-13	-0.1
1920	Pit-N	148	533	38	121	13	7	2	54	30	40	.227	.273	.289	562	60	-27	7	8	-1	**.995**	4	*1-148	-3.1
1921	Pit-N	151	562	62	154	21	17	7	71	31	38	.274	.314	.409	724	88	-11	6	8	-1	.994	-6	*1-150	-2.9

YEAR	TM/L	G	AB	R	H	2B	3B	HR	RBI	BB	SO	AVG	OBP	SLG	OPS	OPS+	BR+	SB	CS	SBR	FA	FR	G/POS	TPR
1922	Pit-N	154	593	64	173	28	13	0	76	43	15	.292	.343	.383	726	86	-12	6	10	-2	.994	-4	*1-154	-2.7
1923	Pit-N	152	563	78	194	29	13	7	99	41	43	.345	.389	.480	869	125	20	6	9	-2	**.995**	2	*1-152	1.0
1924	Pit-N	151	542	53	156	25	12	2	63	37	22	.288	.336	.389	725	92	-6	3	6	-1	**.995**	-3	*1-151	-2.1
1925	Chi-N	141	519	73	159	29	5	10	76	38	25	.306	.354	.439	793	100	-1	4	3	-0	.989	0	*1-139	-0.9
1926	Chi-N	147	524	58	145	30	6	8	82	49	25	.277	.342	.403	745	99	-1	3			.988	-6	*1-147	-1.7
1927	Chi-N	147	543	68	169	29	6	2	74	45	21	.311	.367	.398	765	105	4	3			.990	3	*1-147	-0.3
1928	Chi-N	147	547	67	161	25	5	5	62	39	20	.294	.342	.386	728	91	-7	7			**.993**	-2	*1-147	-1.9
1929	*Chi-N	120	463	66	138	28	3	10	91	42	25	.298	.358	.436	794	95	-4	3			.992	0	*1-120	-1.0
1930	Chi-N	114	429	58	124	27	2	6	65	41	26	.289	.359	.403	763	83	-11	1			**.995**	1	*1-113	-1.6
1931	Chi-N	146	531	65	176	33	11	4	66	53	29	.331	.393	.458	851	126	20	1			**.993**	2	*1-144	0.8
1932	*Chi-N	149	570	66	175	42	2	7	80	35	22	.307	.349	.425	774	108	6	2			.993	10	*1-149,M	0.3
1933	Chi-N	107	384	38	95	15	2	3	37	23	15	.247	.290	.320	610	74	-13	1			**.996**	9	*1-104,M	-1.4
1934	Chi-N	75	267	24	79	8	1	5	47	16	12	.296	.338	.390	728	96	-2	1			.995	1	1-74,M	-0.7
1935	Chi-N	2	8	0	0	0	0	0	0	0	1	.000	.000	.000	0	-99	-2	0			1.000	-0	/1-2,M	-0.3
1936	Chi-N	39	132	13	33	4	0	1	16	5	8	.250	.277	.303	580	55	-8	0			1.000	5	1-35,M	-0.6
Total	20	2166	7917	908	2299	394	108	79	1077	578	410	.290	.341	.397	738	95	-62	57	44		.993	10	*1-2131/O-9R,3-1	-20.9

■ MYRON GRIMSHAW

Grimshaw, Myron Frederick b: 11/30/1875, St.Johnsville, N.Y d: 12/11/36, Canajoharie, N.Y. BB/TR, 6'1", 173 lbs. Deb: 4/25/05 Career OF: (1-LF 0-CF 22-RF)

YEAR	TM/L	G	AB	R	H	2B	3B	HR	RBI	BB	SO	AVG	OBP	SLG	OPS	OPS+	BR+	SB	CS	SBR	FA	FR	G/POS	TPR
1905	Bos-A	85	285	39	68	8	2	4	35	21		.239	.293	.323	616	94	-2	4			.980	-5	1-74	-1.0
1906	Bos-A	110	428	46	124	16	12	0	48	23		.290	.332	.383	715	124	11	5			.987	-1	*1-110	0.8
1907	Bos-A	64	181	19	37	7	2	0	33	16		.204	.273	.265	538	72	-5	6			.980	-6	1-20,O-18(1-0-22)/S-2	-1.4
Total	3	259	894	104	229	31	16	4	116	60		.256	.307	.340	647	104	3	15			.984	-12	1-204/O-18R,S-2	-1.6

■ MARQUIS GRISSOM

Grissom, Marquis Deon b: 4/17/67, Atlanta, Ga. BR/TR, 5'11", 190 lbs. Deb: 8/22/89

YEAR	TM/L	G	AB	R	H	2B	3B	HR	RBI	BB	SO	AVG	OBP	SLG	OPS	OPS+	BR+	SB	CS	SBR	FA	FR	G/POS	TPR
1989	Mon-N	26	74	16	19	2	0	1	2	12	21	.257	.360	.324	685	96	0	1	0	0	.943	-4	O-23(1-22-1)	-0.4
1990	Mon-N	98	288	42	74	14	2	3	29	27	40	.257	.321	.351	671	88	-5	22	2	4	.988	-4	O-87(18-35-40)	-0.6
1991	Mon-N	148	558	73	149	23	9	6	39	34	89	.267	.310	.373	683	93	-6	**76**	17	**11**	.984	20	*O-138(3-125-11)	2.4
1992	Mon-N	159	653	99	180	39	6	14	66	42	81	.276	.324	.418	742	110	7	**78**	13	**13**	.983	7	*O-157(0-157-0)	2.6
1993	Mon-N★	157	630	104	188	27	2	19	95	52	76	.298	.355	.438	793	106	6	53	10	**8**	.984	11	*O-157(0-157-0)	2.7
1994	Mon-N★	110	475	96	137	25	4	11	45	41	66	.288	.346	.427	774	99	-1	36	6	6	.985	16	*O-109(0-109-0)	2.2
1995	*Atl-N	139	551	80	142	23	3	12	42	47	61	.258	.319	.376	695	80	-16	29	9	3	.994	11	*O-136(0-136-0)	0.0
1996	*Atl-N	158	671	106	207	32	10	23	74	41	73	.308	.351	.489	840	112	11	28	11	2	.997	9	*O-158(0-158-0)	2.4
1997	*Cle-A	144	558	74	146	27	6	12	66	43	89	.262	.321	.396	717	83	-14	22	13	0	.992	8	*O-144(0-144-0)	-0.4
1998	Mil-N	142	542	57	147	28	1	10	60	24	78	.271	.305	.382	686	79	-17	13	8	0	.991	8	*O-137(0-137-0)	-0.8
1999	Mil-N	154	603	92	161	27	1	20	83	49	109	.267	.322	.415	737	86	-14	24	6	3	.987	6	*O-149(0-149-0)	-0.3
2000	Mil-N	146	595	67	145	18	2	14	62	39	99	.244	.290	.351	641	62	-35	20	10	1	.992	3	*O-142(0-142-0)	-2.9
Total	12	1581	6198	906	1695	285	46	145	663	451	882	.273	.325	.404	730	91	-85	402	105	52	.988	91	*O-1537(22-1471-52)	6.9

■ DICK GROAT

Groat, Richard Morrow b: 11/4/30, Wilkinsburg, Pa. BR/TR, 5'11.5", 180 lbs. Deb: 6/19/52

YEAR	TM/L	G	AB	R	H	2B	3B	HR	RBI	BB	SO	AVG	OBP	SLG	OPS	OPS+	BR+	SB	CS	SBR	FA	FR	G/POS	TPR
1952	Pit-N	95	384	38	109	6	1	1	29	19	27	.284	.319	.313	632	74	-13	2	4	-1	.952	1	S-94	-0.7
1955	Pit-N	151	521	45	139	28	2	4	51	38	26	.267	.318	.351	669	78	-16	0	2	-1	.961	15	*S-149	1.1
1956	Pit-N	142	520	40	142	19	3	0	37	35	25	.273	.319	.321	640	74	-18	0	3	-1	.954	0	*S-141/3-2	-0.7
1957	Pit-N	125	501	58	158	30	5	7	54	27	28	.315	.354	.437	791	114	10	0	1	-0	.968	-1	*S-123/3-2	1.9
1958	Pit-N	151	584	67	175	36	9	3	66	23	32	.300	.331	.408	738	97	-4	2	2	-0	.975	3	*S-149	1.2
1959	Pit-N★	147	593	74	163	22	7	5	51	32	35	.275	.314	.361	675	80	-17	0	2	-1	.964	3	*S-145	-0.3
1960	*Pit-N★	138	573	85	186	26	4	2	50	39	35	**.325**	.372	.394	766	109	8	0	2	-1	.966	11	*S-136	3.1
1961	Pit-N	148	596	71	164	25	6	6	55	40	44	.275	.322	.367	689	82	-15	0	4	-1	.957	9	*S-144/3-1	0.5
1962	Pit-N★	161	678	76	199	34	3	2	61	31	61	.294	.327	.361	689	85	-15	2	1	0	.956	14	*S-161	1.3
1963	StL-N★	158	631	85	201	**43**	11	6	73	56	58	.319	.380	.450	830	126	23	3	1	0	.964	-13	*S-158	2.5
1964	*StL-N★	161	636	70	186	35	6	1	70	44	42	.292	.338	.371	709	92	-6	2	3	-1	.949	-12	*S-160	-0.5
1965	StL-N	153	587	55	149	26	5	0	52	56	50	.254	.320	.315	635	73	-19	1	1	-0	.962	-8	*S-148/3-2	-1.6
1966	Phi-N	155	584	58	152	21	4	2	53	40	38	.260	.313	.320	633	77	-18	2	1	0	.974	11	*S-139,3-20/1-1	0.6
1967	Phi-N	10	26	3	3	0	0	0	1	4	4	.115	.233	.115	349	3	-3	0	0	0	.947	2	/S-6	0.0
	SF-N	34	70	4	12	1	1	0	4	6	7	.171	.237	.214	451	30	-6	0	0	0	.912	-8	S-24/2-1	-1.4
	Yr	44	96	7	15	1	1	0	5	10	11	.156	.236	.188	423	23	-9	0	0	0	.925	-5	S-30/2-1	-1.4
Total	14	1929	7484	829	2138	352	67	39	707	490	512	.286	.332	.366	698	89	-110	14	27	-6	.961	28	*S-1877/3-27,2-1,1	7.0

■ HEINIE GROH

Groh, Henry Knight b: 9/18/1889, Rochester, N.Y. d: 8/22/68, Cincinnati, Ohio BR/TR, 5'8", 158 lbs. Deb: 4/12/12 FM

YEAR	TM/L	G	AB	R	H	2B	3B	HR	RBI	BB	SO	AVG	OBP	SLG	OPS	OPS+	BR+	SB	CS	SBR	FA	FR	G/POS	TPR
1912	NY-N	27	48	8	13	2	1	0	3	8	7	.271	.375	.354	729	97	0	6			.887	3	2-12/S-7,3-6	0.3
1913	NY-N	4	2	0	0	0	0	0	0	0	1	.000	.000	.000	0	-99	-1	0			1.000	1	/3-2,S-1	0.0
	Cin-N	117	397	51	112	19	5	3	48	38	36	.282	.351	.378	729	109	5	24			.963	10	*2-113/S-4	1.7
	Yr	121	399	51	112	19	5	3	48	38	37	.281	.349	.376	725	107	4	24			.963	10	*2-113/S-5,3-2	1.7
1914	Cin-N	139	455	59	131	18	4	2	32	64	28	.288	.391	.358	749	120	15	24			.936	-7	*2-134/S-2	1.0
1915	Cin-N	160	587	72	170	32	9	3	50	50	33	.290	.354	.390	745	123	17	12	17	-3	.969	11	*3-131,2-29	3.1
1916	Cin-N	149	553	85	149	24	14	2	28	**84**	34	.269	.370	.374	744	132	24	13			.957	19	*3-110,2-33/S-5	**5.3**
1917	Cin-N	156	599	91	**182**	**39**	11	1	53	71	30	.304	**.385**	.411	796	150	38	15			**.966**	8	*3-154/2-2	5.5
1918	Cin-N	126	493	**86**	158	**28**	3	1	37	54	24	.320	**.395**	.396	791	144	**28**	11			**.969**	2	*3-126,M	3.7
1919	*Cin-N	122	448	79	139	17	11	5	63	56	26	.310	.392	.431	**823**	151	29	21			.971	-2	*3-121	3.4
1920	Cin-N	145	550	86	164	28	12	0	49	60	29	.298	.375	.393	768	122	18	16	19	-3	.969	-6	*3-144/S-1	1.4
1921	Cin-N	97	357	54	118	19	6	0	48	36	17	.331	.398	.417	815	122	13	22	14	-0	.950	1	3-97	1.9
1922	*NY-N	115	426	63	113	21	3	3	51	53	21	.265	.353	.350	703	81	-10	5	6	-1	**.965**	1	*3-110	-0.3
1923	*NY-N	123	465	91	135	22	5	4	48	60	22	.290	.379	.385	763	103	4	3	4	-1	**.975**	4	*3-118	1.4
1924	*NY-N	145	559	82	157	32	3	2	46	52	29	.281	.354	.360	713	94	-3	8	6	-0	**.983**	5	*3-145	1.1
1925	NY-N	25	65	7	15	4	0	0	4	6	3	.231	.296	.292	588	53	-5	0	0	0	.909	-6	3-16/2-2	-0.9
1926	NY-N	12	35	2	8	2	0	0	3	2	3	.229	.270	.286	556	50	-2	0			.950	-1	/3-7	-0.3
1927	*Pit-N	14	35	2	10	1	0	0	3	2	2	.286	.324	.314	639	67	-2	0			.958	-1	3-12	-0.2
Total	16	1676	6074	918	1774	308	87	26	566	696	345	.292	.373	.384	757	119	168	180	66		.967	41	*3-1299,2-325/S-20	28.1

■ LEW GROH

Groh, Lewis Carl "Silver" b: 10/16/1883, Rochester, N.Y. d: 10/20/60, Rochester, N.Y. BR/TR, Deb: 8/2/19 F

YEAR	TM/L	G	AB	R	H	2B	3B	HR	RBI	BB	SO	AVG	OBP	SLG	OPS	OPS+	BR+	SB	CS	SBR	FA	FR	G/POS	TPR
1919	Phi-A	2	4	0	0	0	0	0	0	0	2	.000	.000	.000	0	-99	-1	0			1.000	-0	/3-1	-0.1

■ HOWDY GROSKLOSS

Groskloss, Howard Hoffman b: 4/9/07, Pittsburgh, Pa. BR/TR, 5'9", 176 lbs. Deb: 6/23/30

YEAR	TM/L	G	AB	R	H	2B	3B	HR	RBI	BB	SO	AVG	OBP	SLG	OPS	OPS+	BR+	SB	CS	SBR	FA	FR	G/POS	TPR
1930	Pit-N	2	3	0	1	0	0	0	1	0	0	.333	.333	.333	667	62	-0	0			.000	-1	/S-1	-0.1
1931	Pit-N	53	161	13	45	7	2	0	20	11	16	.280	.326	.348	673	82	-4	1			.981	-1	2-39/S-3	-0.3
1932	Pit-N	17	20	1	2	0	0	0	0	0	3	.100	.100	.100	200	-47	-4	0			.800	-1	/S-1	-0.5
Total	3	72	184	14	48	7	2	0	21	11	19	.261	.303	.321	623	68	-8	1			.700	-3	/2-39,S-5	-0.9

■ EMIL GROSS

Gross, Emil Michael b: 3/3/1858, Chicago, Ill. d: 8/24/21, Eagle River, Wis. BR/TR, 6', 190 lbs. Deb: 8/13/1879

YEAR	TM/L	G	AB	R	H	2B	3B	HR	RBI	BB	SO	AVG	OBP	SLG	OPS	OPS+	BR+	SB	CS	SBR	FA	FR	G/POS	TPR
1879	Pro-N	30	132	31	46	9	5	0	24	4	8	.348	.368	.492	860	183	12				.897	-5	C-30	0.7
1880	Pro-N	87	347	43	90	18	3	1	34	16	15	.259	.292	.337	629	116	6				.866	-14	*C-87	-0.5
1881	Pro-N	51	182	15	50	9	4	1	24	13	11	.275	.323	.385	708	124	5				.893	-4	C-50/O-1(0-0-1)	0.3
1883	Phi-N	57	231	39	71	25	7	1	25	12	18	.307	.342	.489	831	163	18				.789	-24	C-55/O-2(1-1-0)	-0.2
1884	CP-U	23	95	13	34	6	2	4		6		.358	.396	.589	986	196	8				.860	-3	C-15/O-9(6-0-3)	0.6
Total	5	248	987	141	291	67	21	7	107	51	52	.295	.329	.427	756	146	49				.859	-50	C-237/O-12(7-1-4)	0.9

■ TURKEY GROSS

Gross, Ewell b: 2/21/1896, Mesquite, Tex. d: 1/11/36, Dallas, Tex. BR/TR, 6', 165 lbs. Deb: 4/14/25

YEAR	TM/L	G	AB	R	H	2B	3B	HR	RBI	BB	SO	AVG	OBP	SLG	OPS	OPS+	BR+	SB	CS	SBR	FA	FR	G/POS	TPR
1925	Bos-A	9	32	2	3	0	1	0	2	2	2	.094	.171	.156	328	-16	-6	0	0	0	.976	-1	/S-9	-0.5

■ GREG GROSS

Gross, Gregory Eugene b: 8/1/52, York, Pa. BL/TL, 5'11", 175 lbs. Deb: 9/5/73 Career OF: (623-LF 176-CF 524-RF)

YEAR	TM/L	G	AB	R	H	2B	3B	HR	RBI	BB	SO	AVG	OBP	SLG	OPS	OPS+	BR+	SB	CS	SBR	FA	FR	G/POS	TPR
1973	Hou-N	14	39	5	9	2	1	0	1	4	4	.231	.302	.333	636	76	-1	2	1	0	1.000	1	/O-9(4-2-3)	-0.1

YEAR	TM/L	G	AB	R	H	2B	3B	HR	RBI	BB	SO	AVG	OBP	SLG	OPS	OPS+	BR+	SB	CS	SBR	FA	FR	G/POS	TPR
1974	Hou-N	156	589	78	185	21	8	0	36	76	39	.314	.393	.377	770	121	20	12	20	-4	.994	-9	*O-151(56-0-143)	-0.2
1975	Hou-N	132	483	67	142	14	10	0	41	63	37	.294	.375	.364	740	114	11	2	2	-0	.958	5	*O-121(60-0-61)	0.9
1976	Hou-N	128	426	52	122	12	3	0	27	64	39	.286	.380	.329	708	112	10	2	6	-2	.978	3	*O-115(0-0-115)	0.5
1977	Chi-N	115	239	43	77	10	4	5	32	33	19	.322	.404	.460	865	118	7	0	1	-0	.991	-8	O-71(45-25-9)	-0.3
1978	Chi-N	124	347	34	92	12	7	1	39	33	19	.265	.329	.349	678	80	-9	3	1	0	.979	-14	*O-111(40-70-12)	-2.6
1979	Phi-N	111	174	21	58	6	3	0	15	29	5	.333	.429	.402	831	124	7	5	2	0	.978	-12	O-73(49-19-11)	-0.6
1980	*Phi-N	127	154	19	37	7	2	0	12	24	7	.240	.346	.312	658	80	-3	1	1	-0	.973	-22	O-91(58-14-26)/1-1	-2.9
1981	*Phi-N	83	102	14	23	6	1	0	7	15	5	.225	.325	.304	629	76	-3	2	2	-0	.982	-7	O-55(13-5-38)	-1.2
1982	Phi-N	119	134	14	40	4	0	0	10	19	8	.299	.386	.328	714	99	1	4	3	-0	.983	-18	O-71(50-12-19)	-1.9
1983	*Phi-N	136	245	25	74	12	3	0	29	34	16	.302	.389	.376	765	114	6	3	5	-1	.991	-28	*O-110(77-27-25)/1-1	-2.6
1984	Phi-N	112	202	19	65	9	1	0	16	24	11	.322	.396	.376	773	116	5	1	0	0	.986	-4	O-48(30-1-20),1-28	0.0
1985	Phi-N	93	169	21	44	5	2	0	14	32	9	.260	.378	.314	692	93	-0	1	0	0	1.000	-7	O-52(46-0-9)/1-8	-0.9
1986	Phi-N	87	101	11	25	5	0	0	8	21	11	.248	.382	.297	679	87	-1	1	0	0	1.000	-3	O-27(21-1-6)/1-5,P-1	-0.4
1987	Phi-N	114	133	14	38	4	1	1	12	25	12	.286	.403	.353	756	99	1	0	0	0	1.000	-12	O-50(49-0-1),1-11	-1.2
1988	Phi-N	98	133	10	27	1	0	0	5	16	3	.203	.293	.211	504	46	-9	0	0	0	1.000	-11	O-37(20-0-19),1-14	-2.3
1989	Hou-N	60	75	2	15	0	0	0	4	11	6	.200	.310	.200	510	51	-4	0	0	0	.929	-3	O-12(5-0-7)/1-6,P-1	-0.8
Total	17	1809	3745	449	1073	130	46	7	308	523	250	.287	.375	.351	727	103	40	39	44	-7	.982	-148	*O-1204L/1-74,P-2	-16.6
■ WAYNE GROSS	Gross, Wayne Dale b: 1/14/52, Riverside, Cal. BL/TR, 6′2″, 210 lbs. Deb: 8/21/76																							
1976	Oak-A	10	18	0	4	0	0	0	1	2	1	.222	.300	.222	522	57	-1	0	0	0	.966	-1	/1-3,O-2(0-0-2),D-3	-0.2
1977	Oak-A☆	146	485	66	113	21	1	22	63	86	84	.233	.354	.416	771	111	9	5	4	-0	.932	-23	*3-145/1-1	-1.7
1978	Oak-A	118	285	18	57	10	2	7	23	40	63	.200	.309	.323	632	82	-6	0	2	-1	.917	-8	*3-106,1-15	-1.7
1979	Oak-A	138	442	54	99	19	1	14	50	72	62	.224	.334	.367	700	94	-3	4	3	-0	.943	-10	*3-120,1-18/O-2L	-1.5
1980	Oak-A	113	366	45	103	20	3	14	61	44	39	.281	.360	.467	827	134	17	5	3	0	.948	-28	3-99,1-10/D-1	-1.2
1981	*Oak-A	82	243	29	50	7	1	10	31	34	28	.206	.308	.366	674	98	-0	2	1	0	.946	-9	3-73/1-2,D-1	-1.1
1982	Oak-A	129	386	43	97	14	0	9	41	53	50	.251	.345	.358	702	98	0	3	1	0	.970	-7	*3-108,1-16/D-1	-0.9
1983	Oak-A	137	339	34	79	18	0	12	44	36	52	.233	.312	.392	704	98	-1	3	5	-1	.996	-5	1-74,3-67/P-1,D-1	-1.1
1984	Bal-A	127	342	53	74	9	1	22	64	68	69	.216	.348	.442	789	119	10	1	2	-0	.937	-5	*3-117/1-3,D-1	0.3
1985	Bal-A	103	217	31	51	8	0	11	18	46	48	.235	.369	.424	793	120	7	1	1	-0	.933	-0	3-67,D-10/1-9	0.5
1986	Oak-A	3	2	0	0	0	0	0	0	1	0	.000	.333	.000	333	0	-0	0	0	0	.000	-0	/3-1	-0.1
Total	11	1106	3125	373	727	126	9	121	396	482	496	.233	.339	.395	734	106	32	24	22	-2	.941	-96	3-903,1-151/D-18,OP	-8.7
■ GEORGE GROSSART	Grossart, George Albert b: 4/11/1880, Meadville, Pa. d: 4/18/02, Pittsburgh, Pa. Deb: 6/7/01																							
1901	Bos-N	7	26	4	3	0	0	0	1	0		.115	.115	.115	231	-30	-4	0			1.000	0	/O-7(7-0-0)	-0.4
■ JERRY GROTE	Grote, Gerald Wayne b: 10/6/42, San Antonio, Tex. BR/TR, 5′10″, 190 lbs. Deb: 9/21/63 Career OF: (1-LF 0-CF 2-RF)																							
1963	Hou-N	3	5	0	1	0	0	0	1	1	3	.200	.333	.200	533	61	-0	0	0	0	1.000	-1	/C-3	-0.1
1964	Hou-N	100	298	26	54	9	3	3	24	20	75	.181	.242	.262	504	44	-22	0	2	-1	.985	2	C-98	-1.7
1966	NY-N	120	317	26	75	12	2	3	31	40	81	.237	.328	.315	643	82	-7	4	3	-0	.981	0	*C-115/3-2	-0.2
1967	NY-N	120	344	25	67	8	0	4	23	14	65	.195	.228	.253	481	38	-28	2	2	-0	.990	2	*C-119	-2.3
1968	NY-N★	124	404	29	114	18	0	3	31	44	81	.282	.357	.349	706	112	7	1	5	-2	.994	7	*C-115	2.2
1969	*NY-N	113	365	38	92	12	3	6	40	32	59	.252	.314	.351	665	84	-8	2	1	0	.991	19	*C-112	1.7
1970	NY-N	126	415	38	106	14	1	2	34	36	39	.255	.316	.308	625	68	-18	2	1	0	.991	10	*C-125	-0.3
1971	NY-N	125	403	35	109	25	0	2	35	40	47	.270	.339	.347	687	96	-1	1	4	-1	.990	5	*C-122	0.9
1972	NY-N	64	205	15	43	5	1	3	21	26	27	.210	.308	.288	595	72	-7	1	0	0	.998	3	C-59/3-3,O-1(0-0-1)	-0.1
1973	*NY-N	84	285	17	73	10	2	1	32	13	23	.256	.291	.316	607	69	-12	0	0	0	.995	9	C-81/3-2	0.0
1974	NY-N★	97	319	25	82	8	1	5	36	33	33	.257	.331	.335	666	88	-5	0	1	-0	.988	-3	C-94	-0.4
1975	NY-N	119	386	28	114	14	5	2	39	38	23	.295	.360	.373	733	109	5	0	1	-0	**.995**	6	*C-111	1.7
1976	NY-N	101	323	30	88	14	2	4	28	38	19	.272	.351	.365	716	110	5	1	2	-0	.993	12	C-95/O-2(1-0-1)	2.1
1977	NY-N	42	115	8	31	3	1	0	7	9	12	.270	.333	.313	646	78	-3	0	0	0	1.000	-2	C-28,3-11	-0.4
	*LA-N	18	27	3	7	0	0	0	4	2	5	.259	.310	.259	570	55	-2	0	1	-0	1.000	4	C-16/3-2	0.2
	Yr	60	142	11	38	3	1	0	11	11	17	.268	.329	.303	632	73	-5	0	1	-0	1.000	2	C-44,3-13	-0.2
1978	*LA-N	41	70	5	19	5	0	0	9	10	5	.271	.363	.343	705	98	0	0	0	0	.985	8	C-32/3-7	0.9
1981	KC-A	22	56	4	17	3	1	1	9	3	2	.304	.350	.446	796	129	2	1	0	0	1.000	4	C-22	0.7
	LA-N	2	2	0	0	0	0	0	0	0	1	.000	.000	.000	0	-99	-1	0	0	0	1.000	0	/C-1	0.0
Total	16	1421	4339	352	1092	160	22	39	404	399	600	.252	.318	.326	644	83	-94	15	23	-5	.991	85	*C-1348/3-27,O-3R	4.9
■ JEFF GROTEWOLD	Grotewold, Jeffrey Scott b: 12/8/65, Madera, Cal. BL/TR, 6′, 215 lbs. Deb: 4/12/92 Career OF: (2-LF 0-CF 0-RF)																							
1992	Phi-N	72	65	7	13	2	0	3	5	9	16	.200	.307	.369	676	91	-1	0	0	0	1.000	-1	/C-2,O-2(2-0-0),1-1	-0.2
1995	KC-A	15	36	4	10	1	0	1	6	9	7	.278	.422	.389	811	111	1	0	0	0	.750	-0	D-11/1-1	0.0
Total	2	87	101	11	23	3	0	4	11	18	23	.228	.350	.376	726	99	0	0	0	0	.833	-2	/D-11,1-2,O-2L,C-2	-0.2
■ JOHNNY GROTH	Groth, John Thomas b: 7/23/26, Chicago, Ill. BR/TR, 6′, 182 lbs. Deb: 9/5/46																							
1946	Det-A	4	9	1	0	0	0	0	0	0	3	.000	.000	.000	0	-94	-2	0	0	0	1.000	-1	/O-4(0-4-0)	-0.4
1947	Det-A	2	4	1	1	0	0	0	0	2	1	.250	.500	.250	750	109	0	0	0	0	1.000	1	/O-1(1-0-0)	0.1
1948	Det-A	6	17	3	8	3	0	1	5	1	1	.471	.500	.824	1324	242	3	0	0	0	.900	0	/O-4(0-4-0)	0.3
1949	Det-A	103	348	60	102	19	5	11	73	65	27	.293	.407	.471	878	132	17	3	7	-2	.966	1	O-99(0-99-0)	1.3
1950	Det-A	157	566	95	173	30	8	12	85	95	27	.306	.407	.451	858	116	16	1	5	-2	.985	-12	*O-157(0-157-0)	-0.2
1951	Det-A	118	428	41	128	29	1	3	49	31	32	.299	.349	.393	742	100	-1	1	1	-0	**.993**	-1	*O-112(0-112-0)	-0.4
1952	Det-A	141	524	56	149	22	2	4	51	51	39	.284	.348	.357	705	96	-3	2	10	-3	.986	0	*O-139(2-137-0)	-1.0
1953	StL-A	141	557	65	141	27	4	10	57	42	53	.253	.308	.370	678	81	-16	5	6	-1	.991	17	*O-141(0-141-0)	-0.7
1954	Chi-A	125	422	41	116	20	0	7	60	42	37	.275	.343	.372	715	93	-4	3	9	-2	.988	-1	*O-125(9-116-2)	-1.4
1955	Chi-A	32	77	13	26	7	0	2	11	6	13	.338	.386	.506	892	135	4	1	0	0	1.000	-0	O-26(0-26-0)	0.2
	Was-A	63	183	22	40	4	5	2	17	18	18	.219	.289	.328	616	69	-9	2	0	0	.984	-1	O-48(12-40-1)	-1.1
	Yr	95	260	35	66	11	5	4	28	24	31	.254	.317	.381	698	89	-5	3	0	1	.989	-1	O-74(12-66-1)	-0.9
1956	KC-A	95	244	22	63	13	3	5	37	30	31	.258	.339	.398	737	94	-2	1	2	-0	1.000	-7	O-84(13-56-18)	-1.3
1957	KC-A	55	59	10	15	0	0	0	2	7	6	.254	.333	.254	588	62	-3	0	0	0	.974	-13	O-50(9-3-38)	-1.7
	Det-A	38	103	11	30	10	0	0	16	6	7	.291	.336	.388	725	95	-1	0	0	0	1.000	-3	O-36(12-25-0)	-0.5
	Yr	93	162	21	45	10	0	0	18	13	13	.278	.335	.340	675	83	-4	0	0	0	.991	-16	O-86(21-28-38)	-2.2
1958	Det-A	88	146	24	41	5	2	2	11	13	19	.281	.340	.384	723	92	-1	0	1	-0	.990	-11	O-80(52-19-10)	-1.6
1959	Det-A	55	102	12	24	7	1	1	10	7	14	.235	.284	.353	637	70	-4	0	0	0	.983	-6	O-41(11-18-13)	-1.2
1960	Det-A	25	19	3	7	1	0	0	2	3	1	.368	.455	.421	876	135	1	0	1	-0	1.000	-3	/O-8(0-7-1)	-0.2
Total	15	1248	3808	480	1064	197	31	60	486	419	329	.279	.353	.395	747	99	-5	19	42	-11	.987	-40	*O-1155(121-964-83)	-9.8
■ ROY GROVER	Grover, Roy Arthur b: 1/17/1892, Snohomish, Wash. d: 2/7/78, Milwaukie, Ore. BR/TR, 5′8″, 150 lbs. Deb: 9/13/16																							
1916	Phi-A	20	77	8	21	1	2	0	7	6	10	.273	.325	.338	663	104	0	5			.952	-7	2-20	-0.7
1917	Phi-A	141	482	45	108	15	7	0	34	43	53	.224	.292	.284	576	77	-14	12			.960	5	*2-139	-0.7
1919	Phi-A	22	56	8	13	1	0	0	2	5	6	.232	.295	.250	545	53	-3	0			.915	-6	2-12/3-3	-1.0
	Was-A	24	75	6	14	0	0	0	7	6	10	.187	.256	.187	443	25	-7	2			.947	-4	2-24	-1.1
	Yr	46	131	14	27	1	0	0	9	11	16	.206	.273	.214	486	37	-11	2			.936	-10	2-36/3-3	-2.1
Total	3	207	690	67	156	17	9	0	50	60	79	.226	.292	.277	569	72	-24	19			.956	-12	2-195/3-3	-3.5
■ HARVEY GRUBB	Grubb, Harvey Harrison b: 9/18/1890, Lexington, N.C. d: 1/25/70, Corpus Christi, Tex. BR/TR, 6′, 165 lbs. Deb: 9/27/12																							
1912	Cle-A	1	0	0	0	0	0	0	0	0		—	1.000	—	1000	187	0	0			1.000	0	/3-1	0.0
■ JOHNNY GRUBB	Grubb, John Maywood b: 8/4/48, Richmond, Va. BL/TR, 6′3″, 188 lbs. Deb: 9/10/72 Career OF: (389-LF 408-CF 280-RF)																							
1972	SD-N	7	21	4	7	1	1	0	1	1	3	.333	.364	.476	840	147	1	0	1	-0	1.000	0	/O-6(0-6-0)	0.1
1973	SD-N	113	389	52	121	22	3	8	37	37	50	.311	.374	.445	819	137	19	9	3	1	.988	7	*O-102(1-102-0)/3-2	2.5
1974	SD-N★	140	444	53	127	20	4	8	42	46	47	.286	.358	.403	761	118	11	4	0	1	.976	12	*O-122(8-114-0)/3-2	2.1
1975	SD-N	144	553	72	149	36	2	4	38	59	59	.269	.345	.363	709	103	3	2	7	-2	.991	-4	*O-139(0-139-0)	-0.7
1976	SD-N	109	384	54	109	22	1	5	27	65	53	.284	.393	.385	778	132	19	1	2	-0	.974	-9	O-98L/1-9,3-3	0.4

YEAR	TM/L	G	AB	R	H	2B	3B	HR	RBI	BB	SO	AVG	OBP	SLG	OPS	OPS+	BR+	SB	CS	SBR	FA	FR	G/POS	TPR
1977	Cle-A	34	93	8	28	3	3	2	14	19	18	.301	.425	.462	887	146	7	0	3	-1	1.000	-0	O-28(27-0-1)/D-4	0.5
1978	Cle-A	113	378	54	100	16	6	14	61	59	60	.265	.367	.450	816	130	16	5	1	1	.973	5	*O-110(108-0-6)	1.7
	Tex-A	21	33	8	13	3	0	1	6	11	5	.394	.545	.576	1121	215	6	1	1	-0	1.000	-1	O-13(8-0-5)/D-3	0.5
	Yr	134	411	62	113	19	6	15	67	70	65	.275	.383	.460	843	137	22	6	2	1	.974	5	*O-123(116-0-11)/D-3	2.2
1979	Tex-A	102	289	42	79	14	0	10	37	34	44	.273	.352	.426	777	110	4	2	4	-1	.986	-8	O-82(38-29-25)/D-6	-0.7
1980	Tex-A	110	274	40	76	12	1	9	32	42	35	.277	.377	.427	804	124	10	2	3	-1	.952	-7	O-77(19-3-60)/D-8	0.0
1981	Tex-A	67	199	26	46	9	1	3	26	23	25	.231	.317	.332	649	92	-2	0	3	-1	.990	-4	O-58(2-0-56)	-1.0
1982	Tex-A	103	308	35	86	13	3	3	26	39	37	.279	.371	.370	741	110	6	0	3	-1	.965	-6	O-77(41-0-40),D-18	-0.5
1983	Det-A	57	134	20	34	5	2	4	22	28	17	.254	.390	.410	801	124	6	0	0	0	1.000	-3	O-26(2-0-24),D-18	0.1
1984	*Det-A	86	176	25	47	5	0	8	17	36	36	.267	.397	.432	829	130	9	1	0	0	1.000	-6	O-36(27-0-9),D-33	0.1
1985	Det-A	78	155	19	38	7	1	5	25	24	25	.245	.350	.400	750	106	2	0	1	-0	1.000	-3	D-33,O-18(14-0-4)	-0.3
1986	Det-A	81	210	32	70	13	1	13	51	28	28	.333	.417	.590	1007	171	21	0	1	-0	1.000	-2	D-52,O-19(10-0-10)	1.6
1987	*Det-A	59	114	9	23	6	0	2	13	15	16	.202	.295	.307	602	63	-6	0	0	0	1.000	-4	O-31L,D-16/3-1	-1.0
Total	16	1424	4154	553	1153	207	29	99	475	566	558	.278	.369	.413	782	121	132	27	33	-6	.981	-31	*O-1042C,D-191/1-9,3	5.4
■ **FRANK GRUBE**	Grube, Franklin Thomas "Hans" b: 1/7/05, Easton, Pa. d: 7/2/45, New York, N.Y. BR/TR, 5'9", 190 lbs. Deb: 5/12/31																							
1931	Chi-A	88	265	29	58	13	2	1	24	22	22	.219	.284	.294	578	55	-17	2	2	-0	.977	-10	C-81	-2.2
1932	Chi-A	93	277	36	78	16	2	0	31	33	13	.282	.362	.354	716	92	-2	6	1	1	.957	-2	C-92	0.2
1933	Chi-A	85	256	23	59	13	0	0	23	38	20	.230	.334	.281	616	67	-11	1	1	-0	.984	-7	C-83	-1.3
1934	StL-A	65	170	22	49	10	0	0	11	24	11	.288	.379	.347	727	82	-4	2	1	0	.963	-0	C-55	-0.1
1935	StL-A	3	6	3	2	1	0	0	0	0	1	.333	.333	.500	833	108	0	0	0	0	1.000	0	/C-3	0.0
	Chi-A	9	19	1	7	2	0	0	6	3	2	.368	.455	.474	928	137	1	0	0	0	.944	3	/C-9	0.4
	Yr	12	25	4	9	3	0	0	6	3	3	.360	.429	.480	909	131	1	0	0	0	.955	3	C-12	0.4
1936	Chi-A	33	93	6	15	2	1	0	11	9	15	.161	.235	.204	440	9	-14	1	0	0	.991	2	C-32	-0.9
1941	StL-A	18	39	1	6	2	0	0	1	2	4	.154	.195	.205	400	6	-5	0	0	0	.951	3	C-18	-0.2
Total	7	394	1125	121	274	59	5	1	107	131	88	.244	.326	.308	634	67	-52	12	5	1	.970	-13	C-373	-4.1
■ **KELLY GRUBER**	Gruber, Kelly Wayne b: 2/26/62, Houston, Tex. BR/TR, 6', 185 lbs. Deb: 4/20/84 Career OF: (8-LF 6-CF 25-RF)																							
1984	Tor-A	15	16	1	1	0	0	1	2	0	5	.063	.063	.250	313	-18	-3	0	0	0	.933	1	3-12/O-2(0-0-2),S-1	-0.1
1985	Tor-A	5	13	0	3	0	0	0	1	0	3	.231	.231	.231	462	26	-1	0	0	0	1.000	-1	/3-5,2-1	-0.2
1986	Tor-A	87	143	20	28	4	1	5	15	5	27	.196	.223	.343	566	50	-10	2	5	-1	.940	7	3-42,2-14,D-14,/OS	-0.5
1987	Tor-A	138	341	50	80	14	3	12	36	17	70	.235	.285	.399	684	77	-12	12	2	2	.948	8	*3-119,S-21/2-7,OD	-0.2
1988	Tor-A	158	569	75	158	33	5	16	81	38	92	.278	.331	.438	768	113	9	23	5	3	.971	25	*3-156/2-7,O-2C,SD	3.7
1989	*Tor-A☆	135	545	83	158	24	4	18	73	30	60	.290	.330	.448	778	120	12	10	5	0	.945	19	*3-119,O-16R/S-1,D	3.2
1990	Tor-A★	150	592	92	162	36	6	31	118	48	94	.274	.336	.512	848	132	23	14	2	2	.955	-3	*3-145/O-6(0-0-6),D-1	2.2
1991	*Tor-A	113	429	58	108	18	2	20	65	31	70	.252	.311	.443	754	102	0	12	7	0	.962	4	*3-111/D-2	0.5
1992	*Tor-A	120	446	42	102	16	3	11	43	26	72	.229	.277	.352	629	72	-18	7	7	-1	.949	-4	*3-120	-2.3
1993	Cal-A	18	65	10	18	3	0	3	9	2	11	.277	.309	.462	770	101	-0	0	0	0	.938	6	3-17/O-1(1-0-0),D-1	0.6
Total	10	939	3159	431	818	148	24	117	443	197	504	.259	.310	.432	742	102	-0	80	33	6	.955	64	3-846/O-38R,2-29,SD	6.9
■ **MARK GRUDZIELANEK**	Grudzielanek, Mark James b: 6/30/70, Milwaukee, Wis. BR/TR, 6'1", 185 lbs. Deb: 4/28/95																							
1995	Mon-N	78	269	27	66	12	2	1	20	14	47	.245	.300	.316	616	60	-15	8	3	1	.987	7	S-34,3-31,2-13	-0.4
1996	Mon-N★	153	657	99	201	34	4	6	49	26	83	.306	.341	.397	738	92	-8	33	7	5	.959	-11	*S-153	-0.1
1997	Mon-N	156	649	76	177	**54**	3	4	51	23	76	.273	.308	.384	692	80	-20	25	9	2	.955	-7	*S-156	-1.1
1998	Mon-N	105	396	51	109	15	1	8	41	21	50	.275	.326	.379	705	86	-8	11	5	1	.950	-16	*S-105	-1.4
	LA-N	51	193	11	51	6	0	2	21	5	23	.264	.290	.326	616	66	-10	7	0	2	.962	13	S-51	0.9
	Yr	156	589	62	160	21	1	10	62	26	73	.272	.315	.362	676	80	-18	18	5	2	.954	-3	*S-156	-0.5
1999	LA-N	123	488	72	159	23	5	7	46	31	65	.326	.378	.436	815	112	9	6	6	-1	.973	-16	*S-119	0.3
2000	LA-N	148	617	101	172	35	6	7	49	45	81	.279	.337	.389	726	87	-13	12	3	2	.976	0	*2-148/S-1	-0.3
Total	6	814	3269	437	935	179	21	35	277	165	425	.286	.331	.386	717	87	-64	102	33	11	.961	-29	S-619,2-161/3-31	-2.1
■ **SIG GRYSKA**	Gryska, Sigmund Stanley b: 11/4/14, Chicago, Ill. d: 8/27/94, Hines, Ill. BR/TR, 5'11.5", 173 lbs. Deb: 9/28/38																							
1938	StL-A	7	21	3	10	2	1	0	4	3	3	.476	.542	.667	1208	202	3	0	0	0	.912	1	/S-7	0.4
1939	StL-A	18	49	4	13	2	0	0	8	6	10	.265	.345	.306	652	66	-2	3	1	0	.873	-4	S-14	-0.5
Total	2	25	70	7	23	4	1	0	12	9	13	.329	.405	.414	819	107	1	3	1	0	.887	-4	/S-21	-0.1
■ **CREIGHTON GUBANICH**	Gubanich, Creighton Wade b: 3/27/72, Belleville, N.J. BR/TR, 6'3", 200 lbs. Deb: 4/16/99																							
1999	Bos-A	18	47	4	13	2	1	1	11	3	13	.277	.346	.426	772	93	-1	0	0	0	.979	-4	C-14/3-1,D-2	-0.4
■ **MARV GUDAT**	Gudat, Marvin John b: 8/27/05, Goliad, Tex. d: 3/1/54, Los Angeles, Cal. BL/TL, 5'11", 162 lbs. Deb: 5/21/29																							
1929	Cin-N	9	10	0	2	0	0	0	0	0	0	.200	.200	.200	400	-1	-2	0			.800	-1	/P-7	0.0
1932	*Chi-N	60	94	15	24	4	1	1	15	16	10	.255	.369	.351	720	96	0	0			.933	-6	O-14(5-1-9)/1-8,P-1	-0.7
Total	2	69	104	15	26	4	1	1	15	16	10	.250	.355	.337	692	87	-1	0			.800	-6	/O-14(5-1-9),1-8,P-8	-0.7
■ **MIKE GUERRA**	Guerra, Fermin (Romero) b: 10/11/12, Havana, Cuba d: 10/9/92, Miami Beach, Fla. BR/TR, 5'9", 162 lbs. Deb: 9/19/37																							
1937	Was-A	1	3	0	0	0	0	0	0	0	2	.000	.000	.000	0	-99	-1	0	0	0	.750	-1	/C-1	-0.1
1944	Was-A	75	210	29	59	7	2	1	29	13	14	.281	.323	.348	670	96	-2	8	2	1	.960	-5	C-58/O-1(1-0-0)	0.6
1945	Was-A	56	138	11	29	1	1	1	15	10	12	.210	.268	.254	522	57	-8	4	1	1	.990	5	C-38	0.0
1946	Was-A	41	83	3	21	2	1	0	4	5	6	.253	.295	.301	597	71	-3	1	0	0	.938	-2	C-27	-0.4
1947	Phi-A	72	209	20	45	2	2	0	18	10	15	.215	.251	.244	495	37	-18	1	2	-0	.964	3	C-62	-1.3
1948	Phi-A	53	142	18	30	4	2	1	23	18	13	.211	.300	.289	589	57	-9	2	3	-1	.973	-0	C-47	-0.7
1949	Phi-A	98	298	41	79	14	1	3	31	37	26	.265	.346	.349	695	87	-5	3	0	1	.982	-3	C-95	-0.3
1950	Phi-A	87	252	25	71	10	4	2	26	16	12	.282	.325	.377	702	81	-8	1	0	0	.990	-6	C-78	-0.9
1951	Bos-A	10	32	1	5	0	0	0	2	6	5	.156	.289	.156	446	21	-3	1	0	0	1.000	1	C-10	-0.3
	Was-A	72	214	20	43	2	1	1	20	16	18	.201	.257	.234	490	34	-20	4	4	-1	.977	-11	C-66	-2.8
	Yr	82	246	21	48	2	1	1	22	22	23	.195	.261	.224	485	32	-23	5	4	-0	.982	-11	C-76	-3.1
Total	9	565	1581	168	382	42	14	9	168	131	123	.242	.300	.303	603	65	-77	25	12	1	.975	-20	C-482/O-1(1-0-0)	-7.0
■ **JUAN GUERRERO**	Guerrero, Juan Antonio b: 2/1/67, Los Llanos, D.R. BR/TR, 5'11", 160 lbs. Deb: 4/9/92																							
1992	Hou-N	79	125	8	25	4	2	1	14	10	32	.200	.265	.288	553	59	-7	1	0	0	.980	-7	S-19,3-12/O-3L,2-2	-1.4
■ **MARIO GUERRERO**	Guerrero, Mario Miguel (Abud) b: 9/28/49, Santo Domingo, D.R. BR/TR, 5'10", 155 lbs. Deb: 4/8/73																							
1973	Bos-A	66	219	19	51	5	2	0	11	10	21	.233	.273	.274	547	51	-14	2	2	-0	.974	1	S-46,2-24	-0.8
1974	Bos-A	93	284	18	70	6	2	0	23	13	22	.246	.284	.282	566	59	-15	3	1	0	.969	-0	S-93	-0.5
1975	StL-N	64	184	17	44	9	0	0	11	10	7	.239	.286	.288	574	57	-10	0	0	0	.955	6	S-64	0.2
1976	Cal-A	83	268	24	76	12	0	1	18	7	12	.284	.309	.340	649	96	-2	0	0	0	.973	-12	2-41,S-41/D-7	-0.9
1977	Cal-A	86	244	17	69	8	2	1	28	4	16	.283	.294	.344	639	76	-8	0	0	0	.985	-2	S-31,D-19,2-12	-0.7
1978	Oak-A	143	505	27	139	18	4	3	38	15	35	.275	.304	.345	649	87	-10	0	5	-2	.958	-40	*S-142	-3.9
1979	Oak-A	46	166	12	38	5	0	0	18	6	7	.229	.256	.259	515	42	-14	0	1	-0	.952	-4	S-43	-1.4
1980	Oak-A	116	381	32	91	16	2	2	23	19	32	.239	.277	.307	584	64	-19	3	3	0	.962	-42	*S-116	-5.0
Total	8	697	2251	166	578	79	12	7	170	84	152	.257	.288	.312	600	69	-92	8	12	-2	.961	-95	S-576/2-77,D-26	-13.0
■ **PEDRO GUERRERO**	Guerrero, Pedro b: 6/29/56, San Pedro De Macoris, D.R. BR/TR, 6', 195 lbs. Deb: 9/22/78 Career OF: (216-LF 108-CF 239-RF)																							
1978	LA-N	5	8	3	5	0	1	0	1	0	0	.625	.625	.875	1500	316	2	0	0	0	1.000	0	/1-4	0.2
1979	LA-N	25	62	7	15	2	0	2	9	1	14	.242	.254	.371	625	69	-3	2	0	1	1.000	-3	O-12(4-1-9)/1-8,3-3	-0.6
1980	LA-N	75	183	27	59	9	1	7	31	12	31	.322	.364	.497	861	141	9	2	1	0	.987	-3	O-40C,2-12/3-3,1-2	0.6
1981	*LA-N★	98	347	46	104	17	2	12	48	34	57	.300	.366	.464	830	139	17	5	9	-2	.974	3	O-75(0-8-70),3-21/1-1	1.5
1982	LA-N	150	575	87	175	27	5	32	100	65	89	.304	.380	.536	915	157	43	22	5	3	.976	2	*O-137(0-44-105),3-24	4.4
1983	*LA-N★	160	584	87	174	28	6	32	103	72	110	.298	.377	.531	908	150	38	23	7	3	.934	6	*3-157/1-2	4.6
1984	LA-N	144	535	85	162	29	4	16	72	49	105	.303	.362	.462	824	132	22	9	8	-1	.917	-8	3-76,O-58R,1-16	0.8
1985	*LA-N†	137	487	99	156	22	2	33	87	83	68	.320	**.425**	**.577**	**1002**	**183**	**56**	12	4	1	.974	8	O-81L,3-44,1-12	**6.3**
1986	LA-N	31	61	7	15	3	0	5	10	2	19	.246	.281	.541	822	131	2	0	0	0	1.000	-2	O-10(10-0-0)/1-4	-0.1

YEAR	TM/L	G	AB	R	H	2B	3B	HR	RBI	BB	SO	AVG	OBP	SLG	OPS	OPS+	BR+	SB	CS	SBR	FA	FR	G/POS	TPR
1987	LA-N★	152	545	89	184	25	2	27	89	74	85	.338	.421	.539	960	156	46	9	7	-0	.971	1	*O-109(109-0-0),1-40	3.8
1988	LA-N	59	215	24	64	7	1	5	35	25	33	.298	.379	.409	788	130	9	2	1	0	.895	-13	3-45,1-15/O-2(1-0-1)	-0.5
	StL-N	44	149	16	40	7	1	5	30	21	26	.268	.366	.430	796	126	6	2	0	0	1.000	-2	1-37/O-7(7-0-0)	0.1
	Yr	103	364	40	104	14	2	10	65	46	59	.286	.373	.418	791	128	15	4	1	1	.998	-15	1-52,3-45/O-9(8-0-1)	-0.4
1989	StL-N★	162	570	60	177	**42**	1	17	117	79	84	.311	.398	.477	875	145	35	2	0	0	.990	-14	*1-160	1.1
1990	StL-N	136	498	42	140	31	1	13	80	44	70	.281	.341	.426	766	109	6	1	1	-0	.989	-10	*1-132	-1.4
1991	StL-N	115	427	41	116	12	1	8	70	37	46	.272	.331	.361	692	94	-3	4	2	0	.985	-8	*1-112	-2.0
1992	StL-N	43	146	10	32	6	1	1	16	11	25	.219	.274	.295	568	63	-7	2	2	-0	.988	-7	1-28,O-10(10-0-0)	-1.9
Total	15	1536	5392	730	1618	267	29	215	898	609	862	.300	.374	.480	854	138	278	97	47	5	.988	-49	1-573,O-541R,3-373,/2	16.9
■ VLADIMIR GUERRERO	Guerrero, Vladimir b: 2/9/76, Nizao Bani, D.R. BR/TR, 6'2", 158 lbs. Deb: 9/19/96 F																							
1996	Mon-N	9	27	2	5	0	0	1	1	0	3	.185	.185	.296	481	24	-3	0	0	0	1.000	-1	/O-8(0-1-7)	-0.4
1997	Mon-N	90	325	44	98	22	2	11	40	19	39	.302	.353	.483	836	117	7	3	4	-1	.929	4	O-85(0-1-84)	0.6
1998	Mon-N	159	623	108	202	37	7	38	109	42	95	.324	.374	.589	963	150	43	11	9	-1	.951	10	*O-157(0-0-157)	4.3
1999	Mon-N★	160	610	102	193	37	5	42	131	55	62	.316	.379	.600	979	147	41	14	7	1	.948	13	*O-160(0-0-160)	4.3
2000	Mon-N★	154	571	101	197	28	11	44	123	58	74	.345	.413	.664	1077	164	55	9	10	-2	.969	8	*O-151(0-0-151)/D-2	5.0
Total	5	572	2156	357	695	124	25	136	404	174	273	.322	.381	.592	973	147	143	37	30	-2	.952	35	O-561(0-2-559)/D-2	13.8
■ WILTON GUERRERO	Guerrero, Wilton b: 10/24/74, Don Gregorio, D.R. BB/TR (BR 1996), 5'11", 145 lbs. Deb: 9/3/96 F Career OF: (70-LF 14-CF 24-RF)																							
1996	LA-N	5	2	1	0	0	0	0	0	0	2	.000	.000	.000	0	-99	-1	0	0	0	.000	0	/H	-0.1
1997	LA-N	111	357	39	104	10	9	4	32	8	52	.291	.307	.403	710	91	-6	6	5	-0	.989	-22	2-90/S-5	-2.4
1998	LA-N	64	180	21	51	4	3	0	7	4	33	.283	.303	.339	642	73	-7	5	2	0	.968	-12	2-32,S-14/O-7(6-1-0)	-1.7
	Mon-N	52	222	29	63	10	6	2	20	10	30	.284	.315	.410	725	90	-4	3	0	1	.975	-8	2-52	-0.9
	Yr	116	402	50	114	14	9	2	27	14	63	.284	.309	.378	687	83	-11	8	2	1	.972	-21	2-84,S-14/O-7(6-1-0)	-2.6
1999	Mon-N	132	315	42	92	15	7	2	31	13	38	.292	.324	.403	727	85	-8	7	6	-1	.931	-19	2-54,O-22(22-0-0)/D-5	-2.5
2000	Mon-N	127	288	30	77	7	2	2	23	19	41	.267	.313	.326	639	61	-17	8	1	1	.967	-5	O-75L/2-1,D-6	-2.1
Total	5	491	1364	162	387	46	27	10	113	54	196	.284	.312	.379	691	80	-42	29	14	1	.971	-68	2-229,O-104L/S-19,D	-9.7
■ GIOMAR GUEVARA	Guevara, Giomar Antonio (Diaz) b: 10/23/72, Miranda, Venez. BB/TR, 5'8", 150 lbs. Deb: 9/19/97																							
1997	Sea-A	5	4	0	0	0	0	0	0	0	2	.000	.000	.000	0	-99	-1	1	0	0	.875	2	/2-2,S-1,D-2	0.1
1998	Sea-A	11	13	4	3	2	0	0	0	4	4	.231	.444	.385	829	118	1	0	0	0	1.000	2	/2-5,S-5	0.2
1999	Sea-A	10	12	2	3	2	0	0	2	0	2	.250	.250	.417	667	68	-1	0	0	0	.870	1	/S-9	0.0
Total	3	26	29	6	6	4	0	0	2	4	8	.207	.324	.345	668	74	-1	1	0	0	.900	4	/S-15,2-7,D-2	0.3
■ CARLOS GUILLEN	Guillen, Carlos Alfonso b: 9/30/75, Maracay, Venez. BB/TR, 6'1", 180 lbs. Deb: 9/6/98																							
1998	Sea-A	10	39	9	13	1	1	0	5	3	9	.333	.381	.410	791	106	0	2	0	0	1.000	2	2-10	0.3
1999	Sea-A	5	19	2	3	0	0	1	3	1	6	.158	.200	.316	516	30	-2	0	0	0	.938	1	/S-3,2-2	0.0
2000	*Sea-A	90	288	45	74	15	2	7	42	28	53	.257	.327	.396	723	84	-7	1	3	-1	.911	-14	3-68,S-23	-1.8
Total	3	105	346	56	90	16	3	8	50	32	68	.260	.326	.393	719	84	-9	3	3	-0	.946	-11	/3-68,S-26,2-12	-1.5
■ JOSE GUILLEN	Guillen, Jose Manuel b: 5/17/76, San Cristobal, D.R. BR/TR, 5'11", 165 lbs. Deb: 4/1/97																							
1997	Pit-N	143	498	58	133	20	5	14	70	17	88	.267	.302	.412	714	83	-13	1	2	-0	.963	-1	*O-136(0-4-134)	-2.0
1998	Pit-N	153	573	60	153	38	2	14	84	21	100	.267	.300	.414	714	84	-14	3	5	-1	.968	12	*O-151(0-2-149)	-1.1
1999	Pit-N	40	120	18	32	6	0	1	18	10	21	.267	.323	.342	665	69	-6	1	0	0	.952	-2	O-37(0-0-37)	-0.9
	TB-A	47	168	24	41	10	0	2	13	10	36	.244	.314	.339	653	66	-9	0	0	0	.966	0	O-47(0-0-47)	-1.0
2000	TB-A	105	316	40	80	16	5	10	41	18	65	.253	.320	.430	750	88	-6	3	1	0	.978	-1	O-99(0-1-98)	-1.0
Total	4	488	1675	200	439	90	12	41	226	76	310	.262	.308	.404	711	82	-48	8	8	-1	.967	9	O-470(0-7-465)	-6.0
■ OZZIE GUILLEN	Guillen, Oswaldo Jose (Barrios) b: 1/20/64, Oculare Del Tuy, Venezuela BL/TR, 5'11", 150 lbs. Deb: 4/9/85 Career OF: (2-LF 0-CF 0-RF)																							
1985	Chi-A	150	491	71	134	21	9	1	33	12	36	.273	.292	.358	650	74	-18	7	4	0	**.980**	12	*S-150	0.8
1986	Chi-A	159	547	58	137	19	4	2	47	12	52	.250	.268	.311	579	55	-34	8	4	0	.970	14	*S-157/D-1	-0.3
1987	Chi-A	149	560	64	156	22	7	2	51	22	52	.279	.307	.354	661	73	-22	25	8	3	.975	13	*S-149	0.9
1988	Chi-A†	156	566	58	148	16	7	0	39	25	40	.261	.295	.314	610	71	-22	25	13	1	.977	**43**	*S-156	3.3
1989	Chi-A	155	597	63	151	20	8	1	54	15	48	.253	.271	.318	589	67	-27	36	17	2	.973	14	*S-155	0.1
1990	Chi-A★	160	516	61	144	21	4	1	58	26	37	.279	.315	.341	656	85	-11	13	17	-3	.977	3	*S-159	0.2
1991	Chi-A★	154	524	52	143	20	3	3	49	11	38	.273	.288	.340	628	75	-19	21	15	-1	.970	-3	*S-149	-1.2
1992	Chi-A	12	40	5	8	4	0	0	7	1	5	.200	.220	.300	520	45	-3	1	0	0	1.000	1	S-12	-0.1
1993	*Chi-A	134	457	44	128	23	4	4	50	10	41	.280	.296	.374	670	80	-14	5	4	-0	.972	-12	*S-133	-1.5
1994	Chi-A	100	365	46	105	9	5	1	39	14	35	.288	.314	.348	662	72	-15	5	4	-0	.959	-23	S-99	-2.8
1995	Chi-A	122	415	50	103	20	3	1	41	13	25	.248	.271	.318	589	55	-28	6	7	-1	.976	-1	*S-120/D-1	-1.9
1996	Chi-A	150	499	62	131	24	8	4	45	10	27	.263	.277	.367	644	64	-28	6	5	-0	.981	-24	*S-146/O-2(2-0-0)	-3.8
1997	Chi-A	142	490	59	120	21	6	4	52	22	24	.245	.277	.337	614	62	-28	5	3	0	.974	-25	*S-139	-3.9
1998	Bal-A	12	16	2	1	0	0	0	0	1	2	.063	.118	.063	180	-52	-4	0	1	-0	.933	-1	/S-6,3-1	-0.4
	*Atl-N	83	264	35	73	15	1	1	22	24	25	.277	.339	.352	691	82	-6	1	4	-1	.977	-4	S-71/2-2,1-1,3-1	-0.6
1999	*Atl-N	92	232	21	56	16	0	1	20	15	17	.241	.287	.323	611	54	-16	4	2	0	.965	-1	S-53/3-6,2-1	-1.3
2000	TB-A	63	107	22	26	4	0	2	12	6	7	.243	.283	.336	620	56	-7	1	0	0	.948	3	S-42,3-11/1-5,2-2	-0.2
Total	16	1993	6686	773	1764	275	69	28	619	239	511	.264	.290	.338	628	69	-302	169	108	-1	.974	10	*S-1896/3-19,1-6,2OD	-12.7
■ BOBBY GUINDON	Guindon, Robert Joseph b: 9/4/43, Brookline, Mass. BL/TL, 6'2", 185 lbs. Deb: 9/19/64																							
1964	Bos-A	5	8	0	1	1	0	0	0	1	4	.125	.222	.250	472	30	-1	0	0	0	1.000	-0	/1-1,O-1(1-0-0)	-0.1
■ BEN GUINEY	Guiney, Benjamin Franklin b: 11/16/1858, Detroit, Mich. d: 12/5/30, Detroit, Mich. BB/TR, 6', 170 lbs. Deb: 9/4/1883																							
1883	Det-N	1	5	1	1	0	0	0	0	0	1	.200	.200	.200	400	23	-0				.000	-1	/O-1(0-1-0)	-0.1
1884	Det-N	2	7	0	0	0	0	0	0	0	3	.000	.000	.000	0	-99	-2				.750	-2	/C-2	-0.3
Total	2	3	12	1	1	0	0	0	0	0	4	.083	.083	.083	167	-51	-2				.750	-2	/C-2,O-1(0-1-0)	-0.4
■ BEN GUINTINI	Guintini, Benjamin John b: 1/13/19, Los Banos, Cal. d: 12/2/98, Roseville, Cal. BR/TR, 6'1.5", 190 lbs. Deb: 4/21/46																							
1946	Pit-N	2	3	0	0	0	0	0	0	0	0	.000	.000	.000	0	-98	-1	0			1.000	-0	/O-1(0-0-1)	-0.1
1950	Phi-A	3	4	0	0	0	0	0	0	0	1	.000	.000	.000	0	-99	-1	0	0	0	1.000	0	/O-1(1-0-0)	-0.1
Total	2	5	7	0	0	0	0	0	0	0	1	.000	.000	.000	0	-99	-2	0	0		1.000	0	/O-2(1-0-1)	-0.2
■ LOU GUISTO	Guisto, Louis Joseph b: 1/16/1895, Napa, Cal. d: 10/15/89, Napa, Cal. BR/TR, 5'11", 193 lbs. Deb: 9/10/16																							
1916	Cle-A	6	19	2	3	0	0	0	2	4	3	.158	.304	.158	462	37	-1	1			1.000	0	/1-6	-0.2
1917	Cle-A	73	200	9	37	4	2	0	29	25	18	.185	.282	.225	507	51	-11	3			.989	-1	1-59	-1.5
1921	Cle-A	2	2	0	1	0	0	0	1	0	1	.500	.500	.500	1000	153	0	0	0	0	1.000	0	/1-1	0.0
1922	Cle-A	35	84	7	21	10	1	0	9	2	7	.250	.276	.393	669	72	-4	0	0	0	.995	1	1-24	-0.4
1923	Cle-A	40	144	17	26	5	0	0	18	15	15	.181	.262	.215	478	27	-15	1	1	-0	.988	1	1-40	-1.6
Total	5	156	449	35	88	19	3	0	59	46	44	.196	.277	.252	528	47	-31	5	1		.990	1	1-130	-3.7
■ MIKE GULAN	Gulan, Michael Watts b: 12/18/70, Steubenville, O. BR/TR, 6'1", 192 lbs. Deb: 5/14/97																							
1997	StL-N	5	9	2	0	0	0	0	1	1	5	.000	.100	.000	100	-72	-2	0	0	0	1.000	-1	/3-3	-0.3
■ BRAD GULDEN	Gulden, Bradley Lee b: 6/10/56, New Ulm, Minn. BL/TR, 5'11", 180 lbs. Deb: 9/22/78																							
1978	LA-N	3	4	0	0	0	0	0	0	0	2	.000	.000	.000	0	-99	-1	0	0	0	1.000	1	/C-3	0.0
1979	NY-A	40	92	10	15	4	0	0	6	9	16	.163	.238	.207	444	21	-10	0	1	-0	.995	11	C-40	0.2
1980	NY-A	2	3	1	1	0	0	1	2	0	0	.333	.333	1.333	1667	340	1	0	0	0	1.000	-1	/C-2	0.0
1981	Sea-A	8	16	0	3	2	0	0	1	0	2	.188	.188	.313	500	40	-1	0	0	0	1.000	2	/C-6	0.1
1982	Mon-N	5	6	1	0	0	0	0	0	1	1	.000	.143	.000	143	-56	-1	0	0	0	1.000	1	/C-2	0.0
1984	Cin-N	107	292	31	66	8	2	4	33	33	35	.226	.309	.308	617	71	-11	2	2	-0	.975	-4	*C-100	-1.2
1986	SF-N	17	22	2	2	0	0	0	1	2	5	.091	.167	.091	258	-28	-4	0	0	0	1.000	-1	C-10	-0.5
Total	7	182	435	45	87	14	2	5	43	45	61	.200	.278	.276	554	53	-27	2	3	-1	.982	9	C-163	-1.4

■ TOM GULLEY
Gulley, Thomas Jefferson b: 12/25/1899, Garner, N.C. d: 11/24/66, St.Charles, Ark. BL/TR, 5'11", 178 lbs. Deb: 8/24/23

YEAR	TM/L	G	AB	R	H	2B	3B	HR	RBI	BB	SO	AVG	OBP	SLG	OPS	OPS+	BR+	SB	CS	SBR	FA	FR	G/POS	TPR
1923	Cle-A	2	3	1	1	1	0	0	0	0	0	.333	.333	.667	1000	159	0	0	0	0	1.000	-0	/O-1(0-1-0)	0.0
1924	Cle-A	8	20	4	3	0	1	0	1	3	2	.150	.261	.250	511	32	-2	0	0	0	.933	0	/O-5(0-2-3)	-0.2
1926	Chi-A	16	35	5	8	3	1	0	8	5	2	.229	.325	.371	696	84	-1	0	0	0	1.000	-2	O-12(0-0-12)	-0.3
Total	3	26	58	10	12	4	2	0	9	8	4	.207	.303	.345	648	69	-3	0	0	0	.971	-2	/O-18(0-3-15)	-0.5

■ TED GULLIC
Gullic, Tedd Jasper b: 1/2/07, Koshkonong, Mo. d: 1/28/2000, West Plains, Mo. BR/TR, 6'2", 175 lbs. Deb: 4/15/30 Career OF: (14-LF 16-CF 89-RF)

YEAR	TM/L	G	AB	R	H	2B	3B	HR	RBI	BB	SO	AVG	OBP	SLG	OPS	OPS+	BR+	SB	CS	SBR	FA	FR	G/POS	TPR
1930	StL-A	92	308	39	77	7	5	4	44	27	43	.250	.310	.344	655	64	-17	4	0	1	.967	3	O-82(0-0-82)/1-3	-1.9
1933	StL-A	104	304	34	74	18	3	5	35	15	38	.243	.281	.372	653	67	-15	3	1	0	.988	10	O-36C,3-33,1-14	-0.6
Total	2	196	612	73	151	25	8	9	79	42	81	.247	.296	.358	654	65	-32	7	1	1	.975	12	O-118R/3-33,1-17	-2.5

■ GLENN GULLIVER
Gulliver, Glenn James b: 10/15/54, Detroit, Mich. BL/TR, 5'11", 175 lbs. Deb: 7/17/82

YEAR	TM/L	G	AB	R	H	2B	3B	HR	RBI	BB	SO	AVG	OBP	SLG	OPS	OPS+	BR+	SB	CS	SBR	FA	FR	G/POS	TPR
1982	Bal-A	50	145	24	29	7	0	1	5	37	18	.200	.363	.269	632	77	-3	0	0	0	.970	-4	3-50	-0.7
1983	Bal-A	23	47	5	10	3	0	0	2	9	5	.213	.339	.277	616	73	-1	0	1	-0	1.000	0	3-21	-0.2
Total	2	73	192	29	39	10	0	1	7	46	23	.203	.357	.271	628	76	-4	0	1	-0	.978	-4	/3-71	-0.9

■ FRED GUNKLE
Gunkle, Frederick William b: 10/26/1857, Reading, Pa. d: 12/21/36, Long Beach, Cal. Deb: 5/17/1879

YEAR	TM/L	G	AB	R	H	2B	3B	HR	RBI	BB	SO	AVG	OBP	SLG	OPS	OPS+	BR+	SB	CS	SBR	FA	FR	G/POS	TPR
1879	Cle-N	1	3	1	0	0	0	0	0	0	1	.000	.000	.000	0	-99	-1				1.000	-2	/O-1(0-0-1),C-1	-0.3

■ HY GUNNING
Gunning, Hyland b: 8/6/1888, Maplewood, N.J. d: 3/28/75, Togus, Me. BL/TR, 6'1.5", 189 lbs. Deb: 8/8/11

YEAR	TM/L	G	AB	R	H	2B	3B	HR	RBI	BB	SO	AVG	OBP	SLG	OPS	OPS+	BR+	SB	CS	SBR	FA	FR	G/POS	TPR
1911	Bos-A	4	9	0	1	0	0	0	2	2		.111	.273	.111	384	9	-1	0			1.000	-1	/1-4	-0.2

■ TOM GUNNING
Gunning, Thomas Francis b: 3/4/1862, Newmarket, N.H. d: 3/17/31, Fall River, Mass. BR/TR, 5'10", 160 lbs. Deb: 7/26/1884 U

YEAR	TM/L	G	AB	R	H	2B	3B	HR	RBI	BB	SO	AVG	OBP	SLG	OPS	OPS+	BR+	SB	CS	SBR	FA	FR	G/POS	TPR
1884	Bos-N	12	45	4	5	1	1	0	2	1	12	.111	.130	.178	308	-4	-5				.914	-5	C-12	-0.9
1885	Bos-N	48	174	17	32	3	0	0	15	5	29	.184	.207	.201	408	34	-12				.877	-8	C-48	-1.5
1886	Bos-N	27	98	15	22	2	1	0	7	3	19	.224	.248	.265	513	58	-5	3			.892	-5	C-27	-0.7
1887	Phi-N	28	109	22	32	6	1	1	16	5	6	.294	.306	.365	672	81	-3	18			.895	6	C-28	0.5
1888	Phi-a	23	92	18	18	0	0	0	5	2		.196	.237	.196	433	40	-6	14			.894	-1	C-23	-0.5
1889	Phi-a	8	24	3	6	0	1	1	1	0	4	.250	.250	.458	708	101	-0	3			.838	-2	/C-8	-0.1
Total	6	146	542	79	115	12	4	2	46	16	70	.212	.235	.253	488	50	-32	38			.887	-15	C-146	-3.2

■ JOE GUNSON
Gunson, Joseph Brook b: 3/23/1863, Philadelphia, Pa. d: 11/15/42, Philadelphia, Pa. BR/TR, 5'6", 160 lbs. Deb: 6/14/1884 Career OF: (12-LF 13-CF 20-RF)

YEAR	TM/L	G	AB	R	H	2B	3B	HR	RBI	BB	SO	AVG	OBP	SLG	OPS	OPS+	BR+	SB	CS	SBR	FA	FR	G/POS	TPR
1884	Was-U	45	166	15	23	2	0	0		3		.139	.154	.151	304	-8	-26				.915	10	C-33,O-18(0-10-9)	-1.3
1889	KC-a	34	122	15	24	3	1	0	12	3	17	.197	.228	.238	466	31	-11	2			.862	-6	C-32/O-1(1-0-0),3-1	-1.3
1892	Bal-N	89	314	35	67	10	5	0	32	16	17	.213	.267	.277	544	63	-15	2			.921	-1	C-67,O-20L/1-2,2-1	-1.0
1893	StL-N	40	151	20	41	5	0	0	15	6	6	.272	.321	.305	626	66	-7	0			.927	3	C-35/O-5(1-0-4)	-0.1
	Cle-N	21	73	11	19	1	0	0	9	6	0	.260	.316	.274	590	54	-5	0			.942	2	C-20	-0.1
	Yr	61	224	31	60	6	0	0	24	12	6	.268	.320	.295	614	62	-12	0			.932	5	C-55/O-5(1-0-4)	-0.2
Total	4	229	826	96	174	21	6	0	68	34	40	.211	.254	.251	505	45	-65	4			.912	8	C-187/O-44R,1-2,2,3	-3.8

■ ERNIE GUST
Gust, Ernest Herman Frank "Red" b: 1/24/1888, Bay City, Mich. d: 10/26/45, Maupin, Ore. BR/TR, 6', 170 lbs. Deb: 8/17/11

YEAR	TM/L	G	AB	R	H	2B	3B	HR	RBI	BB	SO	AVG	OBP	SLG	OPS	OPS+	BR+	SB	CS	SBR	FA	FR	G/POS	TPR
1911	StL-A	3	12	0	0	0	0	0	0	0		.000	.000	.000	0	-99	-3	0			.974	-0	/1-3	-0.4

■ FRANKIE GUSTINE
Gustine, Frank William b: 2/20/20, Hoopeston, Ill. d: 4/1/91, Davenport, Iowa BR/TR, 6', 180 lbs. Deb: 9/13/39 C

YEAR	TM/L	G	AB	R	H	2B	3B	HR	RBI	BB	SO	AVG	OBP	SLG	OPS	OPS+	BR+	SB	CS	SBR	FA	FR	G/POS	TPR
1939	Pit-N	22	70	5	13	3	0	0	3	9	4	.186	.278	.229	507	38	-6	0			.896	4	3-22	-0.2
1940	Pit-N	133	524	59	147	32	7	1	55	35	39	.281	.328	.374	702	94	-5	7			.941	-8	*2-130	-0.4
1941	Pit-N	121	463	46	125	24	7	1	46	28	38	.270	.313	.359	672	89	-8	5			.954	-1	*2-104,3-15	-0.2
1942	Pit-N	115	388	34	89	11	4	2	35	29	27	.229	.286	.294	580	68	-16	5			.954	-10	*2-108/S-2,3-2,C-1	-2.0
1943	Pit-N	112	414	40	120	21	3	0	43	32	36	.290	.341	.355	696	98	-1	12			.938	-6	S-68,2-40/1-1	0.1
1944	Pit-N	127	405	42	93	18	3	2	42	33	41	.230	.288	.304	591	64	-19	8			.938	-27	*S-116,2-11/3-1	-3.9
1945	Pit-N	128	478	67	134	27	5	2	66	37	33	.280	.335	.370	705	92	-5	8			.930	-19	*S-104,2-29/C-1	-1.5
1946	Pit-N★	131	495	60	128	23	6	8	52	40	52	.259	.318	.378	696	95	-5	2			.967	8	*2-113,S-13/3-7	1.1
1947	Pit-N★	156	616	102	183	30	6	9	67	63	65	.297	.364	.409	773	102	3	5			.944	15	*3-156	1.7
1948	Pit-N★	131	449	68	120	19	2	9	42	42	62	.267	.333	.379	711	90	-6	5			.947	9	*3-118	0.3
1949	Chi-N	76	261	29	59	13	4	4	27	18	22	.226	.279	.352	631	70	-12	3			.931	1	3-55,2-16	-1.0
1950	StL-A	9	19	1	3	1	0	0	2	3	8	.158	.273	.211	483	24	-2	0	1	-0	.857	-0	/3-6	-0.3
Total	12	1261	4582	553	1214	222	47	38	480	369	427	.265	.322	.359	681	87	-82	60	1		.955	-35	2-551,3-382,S/C1	-6.3

■ BUCKY GUTH
Guth, Charles Henry b: 8/18/47, Baltimore, Md. BR/TR, 6'1", 180 lbs. Deb: 9/12/72

YEAR	TM/L	G	AB	R	H	2B	3B	HR	RBI	BB	SO	AVG	OBP	SLG	OPS	OPS+	BR+	SB	CS	SBR	FA	FR	G/POS	TPR
1972	Min-A	3	3	1	0	0	0	0	0	0	0	.000	.000	.000	0	-95	-1	0	0	0	1.000	1	/S-1	0.0

■ CESAR GUTIERREZ
Gutierrez, Cesar Dario "Cocoa" b: 1/26/43, Coro, Venez. BR/TR, 5'9", 155 lbs. Deb: 4/16/67

YEAR	TM/L	G	AB	R	H	2B	3B	HR	RBI	BB	SO	AVG	OBP	SLG	OPS	OPS+	BR+	SB	CS	SBR	FA	FR	G/POS	TPR
1967	SF-N	18	21	4	3	0	0	0	0	1	4	.143	.217	.143	360	5	-3	1	0	0	.946	3	S-15/2-1	0.1
1969	SF-N	15	23	4	5	1	0	0	0	6	2	.217	.379	.261	640	84	-0	1	0	0	.882	-0	/3-7,S-4	0.0
	Det-A	17	49	5	12	1	0	0	0	5	3	.245	.315	.265	580	61	-2	1	2	-0	.946	1	S-16	0.0
1970	Det-A	135	415	40	101	11	6	0	22	18	39	.243	.276	.299	575	58	-24	4	3	-0	.957	-18	*S-135	-2.9
1971	Det-A	38	37	8	7	0	0	0	4	0	3	.189	.211	.189	400	13	-4	0	0	0	.971	5	S-14/3-5,2-2	0.2
Total	4	223	545	61	128	13	6	0	26	30	51	.235	.279	.281	559	55	-33	7	5	-0	.955	-9	S-184/3-12,2-3	-2.6

■ JACKIE GUTIERREZ
Gutierrez, Joaquin Fernando b: 6/27/60, Cartagena, Colombia BR/TR, 5'11", 175 lbs. Deb: 9/6/83

YEAR	TM/L	G	AB	R	H	2B	3B	HR	RBI	BB	SO	AVG	OBP	SLG	OPS	OPS+	BR+	SB	CS	SBR	FA	FR	G/POS	TPR
1983	Bos-A	5	10	2	3	0	0	0	0	1	1	.300	.364	.300	664	79	-0	0	1	-0	.938	-0	/S-4	-0.1
1984	Bos-A	151	449	55	118	12	3	2	29	15	49	.263	.287	.316	603	64	-22	12	5	1	.949	-33	*S-150	-4.0
1985	Bos-A	103	275	33	60	5	2	2	21	12	37	.218	.251	.273	524	42	-22	10	2	2	.943	5	S-99	-0.7
1986	Bal-A	61	145	8	27	3	0	0	4	3	27	.186	.208	.207	415	14	-17	3	1	0	.990	7	2-53/3-6,D-1	-0.8
1987	Bal-A	3	1	0	0	0	0	0	0	0	0	.000	.000	.000	0	-99	-0	0	0	0	.000	0	/2-1,3-1	0.0
1988	Phi-N	33	77	8	19	4	0	0	9	2	9	.247	.266	.299	565	61	-4	0	0	0	.919	-2	S-22,3-13	-0.6
Total	6	356	957	106	227	24	5	4	63	33	123	.237	.263	.285	549	50	-66	25	9	2	.945	-23	S-275/2-54,3-20,D-1	-6.2

■ RICKY GUTIERREZ
Gutierrez, Ricardo b: 5/23/70, Miami, Fla. BR/TR, 6'1", 175 lbs. Deb: 4/13/93 Career OF: (3-LF 0-CF 2-RF)

YEAR	TM/L	G	AB	R	H	2B	3B	HR	RBI	BB	SO	AVG	OBP	SLG	OPS	OPS+	BR+	SB	CS	SBR	FA	FR	G/POS	TPR
1993	SD-N	133	438	76	110	10	5	5	26	50	97	.251	.335	.331	666	78	-13	4	3	-0	.971	-15	*S-117/2-6,O-5L,3-4	-1.8
1994	SD-N	90	275	27	66	11	2	1	28	32	54	.240	.324	.305	629	67	-13	2	6	-2	.925	-8	S-78/2-7	-1.6
1995	Hou-N	52	156	22	43	6	0	0	12	10	33	.276	.323	.314	637	74	-6	5	0	1	.956	-6	S-44/3-2	-0.7
1996	Hou-N	89	218	28	62	8	1	1	15	23	42	.284	.361	.344	705	94	-1	6	1	1	.953	-10	S-74/3-6,2-5	-0.5
1997	*Hou-N	102	303	33	79	14	4	3	34	21	50	.261	.315	.363	678	80	-9	5	2	0	.967	-6	S-64,3-22/2-9	-1.0
1998	*Hou-N	141	491	55	128	24	3	2	46	54	84	.261	.341	.334	675	81	-12	13	7	0	.976	9	*S-141	0.9
1999	*Hou-N	85	268	33	70	7	5	1	25	37	45	.261	.355	.336	691	77	-8	2	5	-1	.971	-5	S-80/3-1	-0.7
2000	Chi-N	125	449	73	124	19	2	11	56	66	58	.276	.377	.401	778	99	1	8	2	1	**.986**	-22	*S-121	-0.9
Total	8	817	2598	347	682	99	22	24	242	293	463	.263	.344	.345	689	82	-60	45	26	1	.967	-61	S-719/3-35,2-27,O-5L	-6.3

■ DON GUTTERIDGE
Gutteridge, Donald Joseph b: 6/19/12, Pittsburg, Kan. BR/TR, 5'10.5", 165 lbs. Deb: 9/7/36 MC

YEAR	TM/L	G	AB	R	H	2B	3B	HR	RBI	BB	SO	AVG	OBP	SLG	OPS	OPS+	BR+	SB	CS	SBR	FA	FR	G/POS	TPR
1936	StL-N	23	91	13	29	3	4	3	16	1	14	.319	.326	.538	865	130	3	3			.967	0	3-23	0.4
1937	StL-N	119	447	66	121	26	10	7	61	25	66	.271	.311	.421	731	95	-4	12			.978	2	*3-105/S-8	0.1
1938	StL-N	142	552	61	141	21	15	9	64	29	49	.255	.293	.397	689	83	-14	14			.945	0	3-73,S-68	-0.6
1939	StL-N	148	524	71	141	27	4	7	54	27	70	.269	.309	.376	685	78	-17	5			.934	-18	*3-143/S-2	-3.0
1940	StL-N	69	108	19	29	5	0	3	14	5	15	.269	.301	.398	699	86	-2	3			.877	-2	3-39	-0.3
1942	StL-A	147	616	90	157	27	11	1	50	59	54	.255	.320	.339	659	84	-13	16	13	-1	.973	3	*2-145/3-2	-0.2
1943	StL-A	132	538	77	147	35	6	1	36	50	46	.273	.335	.366	701	103	2	10	9	-1	.958	-31	*2-132	-2.5
1944	*StL-A	148	603	89	148	27	11	3	36	51	63	.245	.304	.342	646	80	-16	20	8	2	.957	-8	*2-146	-1.5
1945	StL-A	143	543	72	129	24	3	2	49	43	46	.238	.295	.304	599	70	-21	9	6	-0	.970	-20	*2-128,O-14(14-0-0)	-3.8
1946	*Bos-A	22	47	8	11	3	0	1	6	2	7	.234	.265	.362	627	70	-2	0	0	0	1.000	-1	/2-9,3-8	-0.3
1947	Bos-A	54	131	20	22	2	0	2	5	17	13	.168	.264	.229	493	35	-11	3	1	0	.938	-1	2-20,3-19	-1.2

YEAR	TM/L	G	AB	R	H	2B	3B	HR	RBI	BB	SO	AVG	OBP	SLG	OPS	OPS+	BR+	SB	CS	SBR	FA	FR	G/POS	TPR
1948	Pit-N	4	2	0	0	0	0	0	0	0	1	.000	.000	.000	0	-98	-1	0			.000	0	H	-0.1
Total	12	1151	4202	586	1075	200	64	39	391	309	444	.256	.308	.362	669	84	-97	95	37		.964	-76	2-580,3-412/S-78,O	-13.0
■ **CRISTIAN GUZMAN** Guzman, Cristian b: 3/21/78, Santo Domingo, D.R. BB/TR, 6′, 180 lbs. Deb: 4/6/99																								
1999	Min-A	131	420	47	95	12	3	1	26	22	90	.226	.270	.276	546	38	-39	9	7	-0	.959	0	*S-131	-2.7
2000	Min-A	156	631	89	156	25	**20**	8	54	46	101	.247	.300	.388	689	69	-31	28	10	3	.967	-15	*S-151/D-1	-2.8
Total	2	287	1051	136	251	37	23	9	80	68	191	.239	.288	.343	632	57	-70	37	17	2	.963	-14	S-282/D-1	-5.5
■ **EDWARDS GUZMAN** Guzman, Edwards b: 9/11/76, Bayamon, P.R. BL/TR, 5′11″, 205 lbs. Deb: 4/6/99																								
1999	SF-N	14	15	0	0	0	0	0	0	0	4	.000	.000	.000	0	-99	-5	0	0	0	1.000	2	/3-5,C-1	-0.3
■ **DOUG GWOSDZ** Gwosdz, Douglas Wayne "Eye Chart" b: 6/20/60, Houston, Tex. BR/TR, 5′11″, 185 lbs. Deb: 8/17/81																								
1981	SD-N	16	24	1	4	2	0	0	3	3	6	.167	.259	.250	509	48	-2	0	0	0	1.000	2	C-13	0.1
1982	SD-N	7	17	1	3	0	0	0	0	2	7	.176	.263	.176	440	27	-2	0	0	0	1.000	2	/C-7	0.0
1983	SD-N	39	55	7	6	1	0	1	4	7	19	.109	.210	.182	391	10	-7	0	0	0	.971	2	C-32	-0.5
1984	SD-N	7	8	0	2	0	0	0	1	2	5	.250	.400	.250	650	86	-0	0	0	0	.963	2	/C-6	0.2
Total	4	69	104	9	15	3	0	1	8	14	37	.144	.246	.202	448	27	-10	0	0	0	.981	8	/C-58	-0.2
■ **TONY GWYNN** Gwynn, Anthony Keith b: 5/9/60, Los Angeles, Cal. BL/TL, 5′11″, 199 lbs. Deb: 7/19/82 F Career OF: (49-LF 158-CF 2127-RF)																								
1982	SD-N	54	190	33	55	12	2	1	17	14	16	.289	.338	.389	728	109	2	8	3	1	.991	-6	O-52(23-28-13)	-0.5
1983	SD-N	86	304	34	94	12	2	1	37	23	21	.309	.358	.372	730	106	3	7	4	0	.994	6	O-81(26-6-54)	0.5
1984	*SD-N★	158	606	88	**213**	21	10	5	71	59	23	**.351**	.411	.444	855	140	34	33	18	1	.989	16	*O-156(0-1-156)	4.3
1985	SD-N★	154	622	90	197	29	5	6	46	45	33	.317	.365	.408	773	118	15	14	11	-1	.989	17	*O-152(0-0-152)	2.3
1986	SD-N★	160	642	**107**	**211**	33	7	14	59	52	35	.329	.382	.467	849	136	31	37	9	5	.989	20	*O-160(0-0-160)	4.8
1987	SD-N★	157	589	119	**218**	36	13	7	54	82	35	**.370**	.450	.511	961	160	**54**	56	12	8	.981	9	*O-156(0-0-156)	6.1
1988	SD-N	133	521	64	163	22	5	7	70	51	40	**.313**	.374	.415	789	128	20	26	11	2	.982	3	*O-133(0-32-102)	2.3
1989	SD-N★	158	604	82	**203**	27	7	4	62	56	30	**.336**	.393	.424	817	133	27	40	16	3	.984	11	*O-157(0-86-73)	4.1
1990	SD-N★	141	573	79	177	29	10	4	72	44	23	.309	.359	.415	775	112	9	17	8	1	.985	15	*O-141(0-0-141)	2.1
1991	SD-N★	134	530	69	168	27	11	4	62	34	19	.317	.358	.432	790	118	12	8	8	-1	.990	11	*O-134(0-0-134)	1.8
1992	SD-N★	128	520	77	165	27	3	6	41	46	16	.317	.373	.415	788	121	15	3	6	-1	.982	12	*O-127(0-0-127)	2.2
1993	SD-N★	122	489	70	175	41	3	7	59	36	19	.358	.403	.497	900	137	26	14	1	3	.981	4	*O-121(0-4-121)	2.6
1994	SD-N★	110	419	79	**165**	35	1	12	64	48	19	**.394**	.458	.568	1026	171	45	5	0	1	.985	2	*O-106(0-1-105)	4.1
1995	SD-N★	135	535	82	**197**	33	1	9	90	35	15	**.368**	.408	.484	892	139	30	17	5	2	.992	4	*O-133(0-0-133)	2.9
1996	*SD-N†	116	451	67	159	27	2	3	50	39	17	**.353**	.405	.441	847	131	21	11	4	1	.989	-5	*O-111(0-0-111)	1.1
1997	SD-N★	149	592	97	**220**	49	2	17	119	43	28	**.372**	.417	.547	964	162	52	12	5	1	.983	-5	*O-143(0-0-143)/D-3	4.0
1998	*SD-N★	127	461	65	148	35	0	16	69	35	18	.321	.370	.501	871	137	23	3	1	0	.993	-10	*O-116(0-0-116)/D-3	0.8
1999	SD-N†	111	411	59	139	27	0	10	62	29	14	.338	.385	.477	862	126	16	7	2	1	.993	-7	*O-104(0-0-104)/D-2	0.4
2000	SD-N	36	127	17	41	12	0	1	17	9	4	.323	.372	.441	813	111	2	0	1	-0	1.000	-4	O-26(0-0-26)/D-6	-0.3
Total	19	2369	9186	1378	3108	534	84	134	1121	780	425	.338	.392	.459	850	134	438	318	125	26	.987	95	*O-2309R/D-14	45.6
■ **CHRIS GWYNN** Gwynn, Christopher Karlton b: 10/13/64, Los Angeles, Cal. BL/TL, 6′, 210 lbs. Deb: 8/14/87 F Career OF: (198-LF 12-CF 87-RF)																								
1987	LA-N	17	32	2	7	1	0	0	2	1	7	.219	.242	.250	492	32	-3	0	0	0	1.000	-1	O-10(10-0-0)	-0.5
1988	LA-N	12	11	1	2	0	0	0	0	1	2	.182	.250	.182	432	27	-1	0	0	0	.000	-2	/O-4(4-0-0)	-0.3
1989	LA-N	32	68	8	16	4	1	0	7	2	9	.235	.257	.324	581	66	-3	1	0	0	1.000	-2	O-19(14-5-2)	-0.6
1990	LA-N	101	141	19	40	2	1	5	22	7	28	.284	.318	.418	736	104	0	0	1	-0	1.000	-9	O-44(32-5-8)	-1.1
1991	LA-N	94	139	18	35	5	1	5	22	10	23	.252	.307	.410	717	102	-0	1	0	0	1.000	-9	O-41(31-2-14)	-1.0
1992	KC-A	34	84	10	24	3	2	1	7	3	10	.286	.310	.405	715	96	-1	0	0	0	1.000	-2	O-19(5-0-14)/D-2	-0.3
1993	KC-A	103	287	36	86	14	4	1	25	24	34	.300	.356	.387	743	94	-2	0	1	-0	.994	0	O-83(66-0-19)/1-1,D-5	-0.5
1994	LA-N	58	71	9	19	0	0	3	13	7	7	.268	.333	.394	728	95	-1	0	2	-1	1.000	-4	O-20(19-0-1)	-0.6
1995	*LA-N	67	84	8	18	3	2	1	10	6	23	.214	.275	.333	608	65	-4	0	0	0	1.000	-1	O-17(12-0-5)/1-2	-0.6
1996	*SD-N	81	90	8	16	4	0	1	10	10	28	.178	.260	.256	516	39	-8	0	0	0	1.000	-7	O-29(5-0-24)/1-1	-1.5
Total	10	599	1007	119	263	36	11	17	118	71	171	.261	.312	.369	681	85	-23	2	4	-1	.997	-36	O-286L/D-7,1-4	-7.0
■ **DICK GYSELMAN** Gyselman, Richard Renald b: 4/6/08, San Francisco, Cal. d: 9/20/90, Seattle, Wash. BR/TR, 6′2″, 170 lbs. Deb: 4/20/33																								
1933	Bos-N	58	155	10	37	6	2	0	12	7	21	.239	.272	.303	575	70	-6	0			.926	6	3-42/2-5,S-1	0.1
1934	Bos-N	24	36	7	6	1	1	0	4	2	11	.167	.211	.250	461	25	-4	0			.739	-2	3-15/2-2	-0.5
Total	2	82	191	17	43	7	3	0	16	9	32	.225	.260	.293	553	61	-10	0			.901	4	/3-57,2-7,S-1	-0.4
■ **YAMID HAAD** Haad, Yamid Salcedo b: 9/2/77, Cartenga, Colombia BR/TR, 6′2″, 204 lbs. Deb: 7/5/99																								
1999	Pit-N	1	1	0	0	0	0	0	0	0	0	.000	.000	.000	0	-99	-0	0	0	0	.000	0	/H	0.0
■ **BERT HAAS** Haas, Berthold John b: 2/8/14, Naperville, Ill. d: 6/23/99, Tampa, Fla. BR/TR, 5′11″, 180 lbs. Deb: 9/9/37 Career OF: (11-LF 76-CF 7-RF)																								
1937	Bro-N	16	25	2	10	3	0	0	2	1	1	.400	.423	.520	943	152	2	0			1.000	-1	/O-4(0-0-4),1-3	0.1
1938	Bro-N	1	0	0	0	0	0	0	0	0	0	—	—	—	—	—	0	0			.000	0	H	0.0
1942	Cin-N	154	585	59	140	21	6	6	54	59	54	.239	.310	.326	637	86	-10	6			.925	-10	*3-146/1-6,O-2(2-0-0)	-1.7
1943	Cin-N	101	332	39	87	17	6	4	44	22	26	.262	.308	.386	693	101	-1	6			.993	9	1-44,3-23,O-18C	0.6
1946	Cin-N	140	535	57	141	24	7	3	50	33	42	.264	.310	.351	661	91	-8	22			.994	0	*1-140/3-6	-1.4
1947	Cin-N★	135	482	58	138	17	7	3	67	42	27	.286	.346	.369	715	91	-6	9			.956	-4	O-69(8-58-0),1-53	-1.4
1948	Phi-N	95	333	35	94	9	2	4	34	36	25	.282	.354	.357	711	95	-2	8			.892	-8	3-54,1-35	-1.1
1949	Phi-N	2	1	0	0	0	0	0	0	1	1	.000	.500	.000	500	47	0	0			.000	0	H	0.0
	NY-N	54	104	12	27	2	3	1	10	5	8	.260	.294	.365	659	76	-4	0			.983	-1	1-23,3-11	-0.6
	Yr	56	105	12	27	2	3	1	10	6	9	.257	.297	.362	659	76	-4	0			.983	-1	1-23,3-11	-0.6
1951	Chi-A	23	43	1	7	0	1	1	2	5	4	.163	.250	.279	529	44	-4	0	0	0	1.000	-1	/1-7,O-4(1-0-3),3-1	-0.5
Total	9	721	2440	263	644	93	32	22	263	204	188	.264	.323	.355	678	91	-32	51	0		.991	-17	1-311,3-241/O-97C	-6.0
■ **BRUNO HAAS** Haas, Bruno Philip "Boon" b: 5/5/1891, Worcester, Mass. d: 6/5/52, Sarasota, Fla. BB/TL, 5′10″, 180 lbs. Deb: 6/23/15																								
1915	Phi-A	12	18	1	1	0	0	0	0	1	7	.056	.105	.056	161	-54	-3	0			.875	1	/P-6,O-3(3-0-0)	-0.2
■ **EDDIE HAAS** Haas, George Edwin b: 5/26/35, Paducah, Ky. BL/TR, 5′11″, 178 lbs. Deb: 9/8/57 MC																								
1957	Chi-N	14	24	1	5	1	0	0	4	1	5	.208	.240	.250	490	32	-2	0	0	0	1.000	-1	/O-4(3-1-0)	-0.3
1958	Mil-N	9	14	2	5	0	0	0	1	2	1	.357	.438	.357	795	124	1	0	0	0	1.000	-0	/O-3(0-2-1)	0.0
1960	Mil-N	32	32	4	7	2	0	1	5	5	14	.219	.324	.375	699	98	-0	0	0	0	1.000	-0	/O-2(1-0-1)	-0.1
Total	3	55	70	7	17	3	0	1	10	8	20	.243	.321	.329	649	80	-2	0	0	0	1.000	-2	/O-9(4-3-2)	-0.4
■ **MULE HAAS** Haas, George William b: 10/15/03, Montclair, N.J. d: 6/30/74, New Orleans, La. BL/TR, 6′1″, 175 lbs. Deb: 8/15/25 C Career OF: (13-LF 809-CF 205-RF)																								
1925	Pit-N	4	3	1	0	0	0	0	0	0	1	.000	.000	.000	0	-94	-1	0	0	0	1.000	-1	/O-2(0-1-1)	-0.2
1928	Phi-A	91	332	41	93	21	4	6	39	23	20	.280	.331	.422	752	94	-4	2	3	-1	.974	-3	O-82(10-69-4)	-1.1
1929	*Phi-A	139	578	115	181	41	9	16	82	34	38	.313	.356	.498	854	113	9	0	4	-1	.982	2	*O-139(1-139-0)	0.3
1930	*Phi-A	132	532	91	159	33	7	2	68	43	33	.299	.352	.398	751	86	-11	2	2	-0	.976	12	*O-131(0-131-0)	-0.4
1931	*Phi-A	102	440	82	142	29	7	8	56	30	29	.323	.366	.475	841	113	7	0	0	0	.989	4	*O-102(0-102-0)	0.7
1932	Phi-A	143	558	91	170	28	5	6	65	62	49	.305	.376	.405	781	99	0	1	0	0	.987	7	*O-137(0-108-29)	0.2
1933	Chi-A	146	585	97	168	33	4	1	51	65	41	.287	.360	.362	723	96	-2	0	5	-2	.983	-5	*O-146(0-146-0)	-1.1
1934	Chi-A	106	351	54	94	16	3	2	22	47	22	.268	.354	.348	702	79	-10	1	0	0	.991	-2	O-89(0-85-4)	-1.3
1935	Chi-A	92	327	44	95	22	1	2	40	37	17	.291	.363	.382	745	90	-4	4	1	1	.989	-1	O-84(0-22-64)	-0.9
1936	Chi-A	119	408	75	116	26	2	0	46	64	29	.284	.383	.358	741	81	-10	1	1	-0	.989	-6	O-96(2-1-94)/1-7	-2.0
1937	Chi-A	54	111	8	23	3	3	0	15	16	10	.207	.313	.288	601	52	-8	1	0	0	.975	0	1-32/O-2(0-0-2)	-0.9
1938	Phi-A	40	78	7	16	2	0	0	12	12	10	.205	.311	.231	542	39	-7	0	0	0	1.000	-2	O-12(0-5-7)/1-6	-1.0
Total	12	1168	4303	706	1257	254	45	43	496	433	299	.292	.359	.402	761	93	-40	12	16	-3	.984	5	*O-1022C/1-45	-7.7
■ **EMIL HABERER** Haberer, Emil Karl b: 2/2/1878, Cincinnati, Ohio d: 10/19/51, Louisville, Ky. BR/TR, 6′1″, 204 lbs. Deb: 7/9/01																								
1901	Cin-N	6	18	2	3	0	1	0	1	3		.167	.286	.278	563	68	-1	0			.545	-2	/3-3,1-2	-0.2
1903	Cin-N	5	13	1	1	0	0	0	0	2		.077	.200	.077	277	-18	-2	0			.933	-2	/C-4	-0.4

YEAR	TM/L	G	AB	R	H	2B	3B	HR	RBI	BB	SO	AVG	OBP	SLG	OPS	OPS+	BR+	SB	CS	SBR	FA	FR	G/POS	TPR
1909	Cin-N	5	16	1	3	1	0	0	2	0		.188	.188	.250	438	36	-1	0			.895	-2	/C-4	-0.3
Total	3	16	47	4	7	1	1	0	3	5		.149	.231	.213	444	31	-4	0			.912	-6	/C-8,3-3,1-2	-0.9
■ IRV HACH	Hach, Irvin William "Major" b: 6/6/1873, Louisville, Ky. d: 8/13/36, Louisville, Ky. BR/TR, Deb: 7/1/1897																							
1897	Lou-N	16	51	5	11	2	0	0	3	5		.216	.322	.255	577	55	-3	1			.889	-2	/2-9,3-7	-0.4
■ STAN HACK	Hack, Stanley Camfield "Smiling Stan" b: 12/6/09, Sacramento, Cal d: 12/15/79, Dixon, Ill. BL/TR, 6', 170 lbs. Deb: 4/12/32 MC																							
1932	*Chi-N	72	178	32	42	5	6	2	19	17	16	.236	.306	.365	671	80	-5	5			.913	-5	3-51	-0.8
1933	Chi-N	20	60	10	21	3	1	1	2	8	3	.350	.451	.483	934	167	6	4			.983	6	3-17	1.3
1934	Chi-N	111	402	54	116	16	6	1	21	45	42	.289	.363	.366	729	98	0	11			.949	0	*3-109	0.4
1935	*Chi-N	124	427	75	133	23	9	4	64	65	17	.311	.406	.436	842	125	18	14			.942	11	*3-111/1-7	3.1
1936	Chi-N	149	561	102	167	27	4	6	78	89	39	.298	.396	.392	788	110	12	17			.950	-12	*3-140,1-11	0.4
1937	Chi-N	154	582	106	173	27	6	2	63	83	42	.297	.388	.375	762	104	7	16			.968	-9	*3-150/1-4	0.3
1938	*Chi-N★	152	609	109	195	34	11	4	67	94	39	.320	.411	.432	843	128	28	**16**			.954	7	*3-152	3.9
1939	Chi-N★	156	641	112	191	28	6	8	56	65	35	.298	.364	.398	762	103	4	**17**			.956	-7	*3-156	0.3
1940	Chi-N	149	603	101	**191**	38	6	8	40	75	24	.317	.395	.439	834	132	29	21			.954	14	*3-148/1-1	4.7
1941	Chi-N★	151	586	111	**186**	33	5	7	45	99	40	.317	.417	.427	844	143	38	10			.954	-16	*3-150/1-1	2.8
1942	Chi-N	140	553	91	166	36	3	6	39	94	40	.300	.402	.409	811	143	34	9			**.965**	-10	*3-139	3.0
1943	Chi-N★	144	533	78	154	24	4	3	35	82	27	.289	.384	.366	750	119	16	5			.960	-7	*3-136	1.1
1944	Chi-N	98	383	65	108	16	1	3	32	53	21	.282	.369	.352	722	104	4	5			.939	2	3-75,1-18	0.6
1945	*Chi-N†	150	597	110	193	29	7	2	43	99	30	.323	.420	.405	826	133	32	12			**.975**	18	*3-146/1-5	5.0
1946	Chi-N	92	323	55	92	13	4	0	26	83	32	.285	.431	.350	781	125	17	3			.968	-3	3-90	1.4
1947	Chi-N	76	240	28	65	11	2	0	12	41	19	.271	.377	.333	711	94	-0	0			.962	7	3-66	0.7
Total	16	1938	7278	1239	2193	363	81	57	642	1092	466	.301	.394	.397	791	120	238	165			.957	-4	*3-1836/1-47	28.2
■ RICH HACKER	Hacker, Richard Warren b: 10/6/47, Belleville, Ill. BB/TR (BR 1971 (part)), 6', 160 lbs. Deb: 7/2/71 C																							
1971	Mon-N	16	33	2	4	1	0	0	2	3	12	.121	.194	.152	346	-1	-4	0	0	0	.984	5	S-16	0.1
■ JIM HACKETT	Hackett, James Joseph "Sunny Jim" b: 10/1/1877, Jacksonville, Ill. d: 3/28/61, Douglas, Mich. BR/TR, 6'2", 185 lbs. Deb: 9/14/02																							
1902	StL-N	6	21	2	6	1	0	0	4	2		.286	.348	.333	681	115	0	1			.833	-1	/P-4,O-2(0-0-2)	0.0
1903	StL-N	99	351	24	80	13	8	0	36	19		.228	.272	.311	582	68	-16	2			.972	-6	1-89/P-7	-2.2
Total	2	105	372	26	86	14	8	0	40	21		.231	.276	.312	588	70	-15	3			.893	-7	/1-89,P-11,O-2(0-0-2)	-2.2
■ MERT HACKETT	Hackett, Mortimer Martin b: 11/11/1859, Cambridge, Mass. d: 2/22/38, Cambridge, Mass. BR/TR, 5'10.5", 175 lbs. Deb: 5/2/1883 F Career OF: (1-LF 9-CF 9-RF)																							
1883	Bos-N	46	179	20	42	8	6	2	24	1	48	.235	.239	.380	619	82	-4				.909	-6	C-44/O-4(0-3-1)	-0.6
1884	Bos-N	72	268	28	55	13	2	1	20	2	66	.205	.211	.280	491	53	-14				.928	12	C-71/3-1	0.3
1885	Bos-N	34	115	9	21	7	1	0	4	2	28	.183	.197	.261	457	49	-6				.901	5	C-34	0.2
1886	KC-N	62	230	18	50	8	3	3	25	4	59	.217	.231	.317	548	61	-11	1			.926	-17	C-53,O-13(0-6-7)	-2.2
1887	Ind-N	42	154	12	42	6	3	2	10	7	24	.273	.282	.361	643	80	-4	4			.938	-9	C-40/O-2(1-0-1),1-1	-0.8
Total	5	256	946	87	210	42	15	8	83	16	225	.222	.231	.318	549	65	-40	5			.921	-15	C-242/O-19C,1-1,3-1	-3.1
■ WALTER HACKETT	Hackett, Walter Henry b: 8/15/1857, Cambridge, Mass. d: 10/2/20, Cambridge, Mass. Deb: 4/17/1884 F																							
1884	Bos-U	103	415	71	101	19	0	1		7		.243	.256	.296	552	68	-28				**.855**	12	*S-103	-1.1
1885	Bos-N	35	125	8	23	3	0	0	9	3	22	.184	.203	.208	411	34	-9				.893	-12	2-20,S-15	-1.9
Total	2	138	540	79	124	22	0	1	9	10	22	.230	.244	.276	520	61	-37				.852	0	S-118/2-20	-3.0
■ KENT HADLEY	Hadley, Kent William b: 12/17/34, Pocatello, Idaho BL/TL, 6'3", 190 lbs. Deb: 9/14/58																							
1958	KC-A	3	11	1	2	0	0	0	0	0	4	.182	.182	.182	364	0	-1	0	0	0	1.000	-1	/1-2	-0.2
1959	KC-A	113	288	40	73	11	1	10	39	24	74	.253	.313	.403	716	93	-3	1	2	-0	.989	-2	1-95	-1.0
1960	NY-A	55	64	8	13	2	0	4	11	6	19	.203	.271	.422	693	90	-1	0	0	0	.991	-0	1-24	-0.2
Total	3	171	363	49	88	13	1	14	50	30	97	.242	.302	.399	701	90	-6	1	2	-0	.989	-2	1-121	-1.4
■ BILL HAEFFNER	Haeffner, William Bernhard b: 7/8/1894, Philadelphia, Pa. d: 1/27/82, Springfield, Pa. BR/TR, 5'9", 165 lbs. Deb: 6/29/15																							
1915	Phi-A	3	4	0	1	0	0	0	0	0	1	.250	.250	.250	500	51	-0	0			1.000	-1	/C-3	-0.2
1920	Pit-N	54	175	8	34	4	1	0	14	8	14	.194	.230	.229	458	31	-15	1	1	-0	.972	-3	C-52	-1.6
1928	NY-N	2	1	0	0	0	0	0	0	0	0	.000	.000	.000	0	-99	-0	0			.750	0	/C-2	0.0
Total	3	59	180	8	35	4	1	0	14	8	15	.194	.229	.228	457	30	-16	1	1		.968	-5	/C-57	-1.8
■ CHICK HAFEY	Hafey, Charles James b: 2/12/03, Berkeley, Cal. d: 7/2/73, Calistoga, Cal. BR/TR, 6', 185 lbs. Deb: 8/28/24 H																							
1924	StL-N	24	91	10	23	5	2	2	22	4	8	.253	.292	.418	709	90	-2	1	0	0	.927	-1	O-24(16-7-1)	-0.4
1925	StL-N	93	358	36	108	25	2	5	57	10	29	.302	.321	.425	745	87	-8	3	7	-2	.955	-1	O-88(25-5-58)	-1.7
1926	*StL-N	78	225	30	61	19	2	4	38	11	36	.271	.311	.427	738	93	-3	2			.974	-6	O-64(28-0-36)	-1.3
1927	StL-N	103	346	62	114	26	5	18	63	36	41	.329	.401	**.590**	990	157	27	12			.980	5	O-94(71-3-22)	2.4
1928	*StL-N	138	520	101	175	46	6	27	111	40	53	.337	.386	.604	990	152	37	8			.965	3	*O-133(117-0-16)	2.8
1929	StL-N	134	517	101	175	47	9	29	125	45	42	.338	.394	.632	1026	148	36	7			.966	3	*O-130(130-0-0)	2.6
1930	*StL-N	120	446	108	150	39	12	26	107	46	51	.336	.407	.652	1059	146	31	12			.976	-3	*O-116(116-0-0)	1.7
1931	*StL-N	122	450	94	157	35	8	16	95	39	43	**.349**	**.404**	.569	973	153	33	11			.983	-4	*O-118(118-0-0)	2.2
1932	Cin-N	83	253	34	87	19	3	2	36	22	20	.344	.403	.466	869	137	14	4			.965	-3	O-65(65-0-0)	0.8
1933	Cin-N★	144	568	77	172	34	6	7	62	40	44	.303	.351	.421	772	121	15	3			.987	8	*O-144(59-85-0)	1.9
1934	Cin-N	140	535	75	157	29	6	18	67	52	63	.293	.359	.471	830	123	17	4			.967	4	*O-140(18-122-0)	1.7
1935	Cin-N	15	59	10	20	6	1	1	9	4	5	.339	.400	.525	925	151	4	1			.912	-3	O-15(0-15-0)	0.1
1937	Cin-N	89	257	39	67	11	5	9	41	23	42	.261	.324	.447	771	113	4	2			.971	-2	O-64(20-44-0)	0.0
Total	13	1283	4625	777	1466	341	67	164	833	372	477	.317	.372	.526	898	133	205	70	7		.971	1	*O-1195(783-281-133)	12.8
■ BUD HAFEY	Hafey, Daniel Albert b: 8/6/12, Berkeley, Cal. d: 7/27/86, Sacramento, Cal. BR/TR, 6', 185 lbs. Deb: 4/21/35 F																							
1935	Chi-A	2	0	1	0	0	0	0	0	0	0	—	—	—	—	—	0	0	0	0	.000	0	R	0.0
	Pit-N	58	184	29	42	11	2	6	16	16	48	.228	.290	.408	698	83	-5	0			.970	4	O-47(1-36-10)	-0.3
1936	Pit-N	39	118	19	25	6	1	4	13	10	27	.212	.273	.381	655	73	-5	0			.932	0	O-29(0-18-10)	-0.6
1939	Cin-N	6	13	1	2	1	0	0	1	1	4	.154	.214	.231	445	19	-1	1			1.000	-0	/O-4(4-0-0)	-0.2
	Phi-N	18	51	3	9	1	0	0	3	3	12	.176	.222	.196	418	14	-6	1			1.000	1	O-13(3-1-9)/P-2	-0.6
	Yr	24	64	4	11	2	0	0	4	4	16	.172	.221	.203	424	15	-8	2			1.000	1	O-17(7-1-9)/P-2	-0.8
Total	3	123	366	53	78	19	3	10	33	30	91	.213	.273	.363	636	68	-18	2	0		.963	4	/O-93(8-55-29),P-2	-1.7
■ TOM HAFEY	Hafey, Thomas Francis "Heave-O" or "The Arm" b: 7/12/13, Berkeley, Cal. d: 10/2/96, ElCerrito, Cal. BR/TR, 6'1", 180 lbs. Deb: 7/21/39 F																							
1939	NY-N	70	256	37	62	10	1	6	26	10	44	.242	.271	.359	630	67	-13	1			.960	-0	3-70	-1.0
1944	StL-A	8	14	1	5	2	0	0	2	1	4	.357	.400	.500	900	148	1	0	0	0	1.000	-0	/O-4(3-0-1),1-1	0.1
Total	2	78	270	38	67	12	1	6	28	11	48	.248	.278	.367	644	72	-12	1	0		.960	-0	/3-70,O-4(3-0-1),1-1	-0.9
■ JOE HAGUE	Hague, Joe Clarence b: 4/25/44, Huntington, W.Va. d: 11/5/94, San Antonio, Tex. BL/TL, 6', 198 lbs. Deb: 9/19/68																							
1968	StL-N	7	17	2	4	0	0	1	1	2	2	.235	.316	.412	728	119	0	0	0	0	.800	-1	/O-3(0-0-3),1-2	-0.1
1969	StL-N	40	100	8	17	2	1	2	8	12	23	.170	.259	.270	529	48	-7	0	2	-1	.939	-0	O-17(1-0-16)/1-9	-1.0
1970	StL-N	139	451	58	122	16	4	14	68	63	87	.271	.361	.417	778	106	4	2	1	0	.994	-4	1-82,O-52(6-0-47)	-0.8
1971	StL-N	129	380	46	86	9	3	16	54	58	69	.226	.332	.392	724	100	1	0	3	-1	.996	-3	1-91,O-36(0-0-36)	-1.1
1972	StL-N	27	76	8	18	5	1	3	11	17	18	.237	.376	.447	824	135	4	0	1	-0	1.000	-0	1-22/O-3(0-0-3)	0.2
	*Cin-N	69	138	17	34	7	1	4	20	20	18	.246	.342	.399	740	116	3	1	1	-0	1.000	-2	1-22,O-19(0-0-19)	-0.1
	Yr	96	214	25	52	12	2	7	31	37	36	.243	.355	.416	770	124	7	1	2	-0	1.000	-2	1-44,O-22(0-0-22)	0.1
1973	Cin-N	19	33	2	5	2	0	0	1	5	5	.152	.263	.212	475	35	-3	1	0	0	1.000	-1	/O-5(0-0-5),1-4	-0.5
Total	6	430	1195	141	286	41	10	40	163	177	222	.239	.339	.391	730	101	3	4	8	-2	.996	-11	1-232,O-135(7-0-129)	-3.4
■ BILL HAGUE	Hague, William L. (b: William L. Haug) b: 1852, Philadelphia, Pa. BR/TR, 5'9", 164 lbs. Deb: 5/4/1875																							
1875	StL-n	62	260	24	57	2	0	0	22	2	9	.219	.225	.227	452	63	-8	3	4	-1	.781	3	*3-62/1-1	-0.6

YEAR	TM/L	G	AB	R	H	2B	3B	HR	RBI	BB	SO	AVG	OBP	SLG	OPS	OPS+	BR+	SB	CS	SBR	FA	FR	G/POS	TPR
1876	Lou-N	67	296	31	78	8	0	1	22	2	10	.264	.270	.303	573	77	-9				.754	-26	*3-67/S-1	-3.0
1877	Lou-N	59	263	38	70	7	1	1	24	7	18	.266	.285	.312	597	75	-9				.843	-19	*3-59	-2.4
1878	Pro-N	62	250	21	51	3	0	0	25	5	34	.204	.220	.216	436	44	-15				**.925**	19	*3-62	0.6
1879	Pro-N	51	209	20	47	3	1	0	21	3	19	.225	.236	.249	485	61	-8				.822	5	3-51	-0.2
Total	4	239	1018	110	246	21	2	2	92	17	81	.242	.255	.273	527	66	-41				.843	-22	3-239/S-1	-5.0

■ DON HAHN Hahn, Donald Antone b: 11/16/48, San Francisco, Cal. BR/TR, 6'1", 185 lbs. Deb: 4/8/69

YEAR	TM/L	G	AB	R	H	2B	3B	HR	RBI	BB	SO	AVG	OBP	SLG	OPS	OPS+	BR+	SB	CS	SBR	FA	FR	G/POS	TPR
1969	Mon-N	4	9	0	1	0	0	0	2	0	5	.111	.111	.111	222	-37	-2	0	0	0	1.000	0	/O-3(0-3-0)	-0.2
1970	Mon-N	82	149	22	38	8	0	0	8	27	27	.255	.376	.309	685	86	-2	4	2	0	.986	-7	O-61(42-14-9)	-1.0
1971	NY-N	98	178	16	42	5	1	1	11	21	32	.236	.320	.292	612	76	-5	2	3	-1	.973	-6	O-80(0-80-0)	-1.4
1972	NY-N	17	37	0	6	0	0	0	1	4	12	.162	.244	.162	406	18	-4	0	0	0	1.000	-2	O-10(0-1-9)	-0.7
1973	*NY-N	93	262	22	60	10	0	2	21	22	43	.229	.289	.290	579	62	-13	2	1	0	.989	-3	O-87(4-83-2)	-2.0
1974	NY-N	110	323	34	81	14	1	4	28	37	34	.251	.330	.337	667	88	-5	2	0	0	.987	-1	*O-106(0-104-2)	-0.8
1975	Phi-N	9	5	0	0	0	0	0	0	0	2	.000	.000	.000	0	-96	-1	0	0	0	1.000	-2	/O-7(1-4-2)	-0.3
	StL-N	7	8	3	1	0	0	0	0	1	1	.125	.222	.125	347	-2	-1	0	0	0	1.000	-1	/O-4(1-2-1)	-0.2
	SD-N	34	26	7	6	1	2	0	3	10	2	.231	.444	.423	868	151	3	1	0	0	1.000	-7	O-26(17-11-0)	-0.5
	Yr	50	39	10	7	1	2	0	3	11	5	.179	.360	.308	668	89	-0	1	0	0	1.000	-10	O-37(19-17-3)	-1.0
Total	7	454	997	104	235	38	4	7	74	122	158	.236	.321	.303	624	75	-30	11	6	0	.985	-29	O-384(65-302-25)	-7.1

■ DICK HAHN Hahn, Richard Frederick b: 7/24/16, Canton, Ohio d: 11/5/92, Orlando, Fla. BR/TR, 5'11", 176 lbs. Deb: 9/7/40

YEAR	TM/L	G	AB	R	H	2B	3B	HR	RBI	BB	SO	AVG	OBP	SLG	OPS	OPS+	BR+	SB	CS	SBR	FA	FR	G/POS	TPR
1940	Was-A	1	3	0	0	0	0	0	0	0	0	.000	.000	.000	0	-99	-1	0	0	0	1.000	0	/C-1	-0.1

■ ED HAHN Hahn, William Edgar b: 8/27/1875, Nevada, Ohio d: 11/29/41, Des Moines, Iowa BL/TR, 160 lbs. Deb: 8/31/05

YEAR	TM/L	G	AB	R	H	2B	3B	HR	RBI	BB	SO	AVG	OBP	SLG	OPS	OPS+	BR+	SB	CS	SBR	FA	FR	G/POS	TPR
1905	NY-A	43	160	32	51	5	0	0	11	25		.319	.426	.350	776	132	8	1			.957	2	O-43(20-10-13)	0.8
1906	NY-A	11	22	2	2	1	0	0	1	3		.091	.259	.136	396	23	-2	2			1.000	-1	/O-7(3-4-0)	-0.3
	*Chi-A	130	484	80	110	7	5	0	27	69		.227	.335	.262	597	90	-2	19			.949	-6	*O-130(55-0-75)	-1.5
	Yr	141	506	82	112	8	5	0	28	72		.221	.331	.257	588	86	-4	21			.952	-6	*O-137(58-4-75)	-1.8
1907	Chi-A	156	592	87	151	9	7	0	45	84		.255	.359	.294	653	112	14	17			**.990**	-5	*O-156(0-0-156)	0.1
1908	Chi-A	122	447	58	112	12	8	0	21	39		.251	.329	.313	642	111	7	11			.965	-11	*O-118(18-14-86)	-1.2
1909	Chi-A	76	287	30	52	6	0	1	16	31		.181	.268	.213	480	54	-14	9			.990	-7	O-76(0-0-76)	-2.8
1910	Chi-A	15	53	2	6	2	0	0	1	7		.113	.217	.151	368	16	-5	0			.933	-3	O-15(0-0-15)	-1.0
Total	6	553	2045	291	484	42	20	1	122	258		.237	.335	.278	613	97	6	59			.970	-30	O-545(96-28-421)	-5.9

■ ED HAIGH Haigh, Edward E. b: 2/7/1867, Philadelphia, Pa. d: 2/13/53, Atlantic City, N.J Deb: 8/14/1892

YEAR	TM/L	G	AB	R	H	2B	3B	HR	RBI	BB	SO	AVG	OBP	SLG	OPS	OPS+	BR+	SB	CS	SBR	FA	FR	G/POS	TPR
1892	StL-N	1	4	0	1	0	0	0	0	0	2	.250	.250	.250	500	54	-0	0			1.000	1	/O-1(1-0-0)	0.0

■ HINKEY HAINES Haines, Henry Luther b: 12/23/1898, Red Lion, Pa. d: 1/9/79, Sharon Hill, Pa. BR/TR, 5'10", 170 lbs. Deb: 4/20/23

YEAR	TM/L	G	AB	R	H	2B	3B	HR	RBI	BB	SO	AVG	OBP	SLG	OPS	OPS+	BR+	SB	CS	SBR	FA	FR	G/POS	TPR
1923	*NY-A	28	25	9	4	2	0	0	3	4	5	.160	.276	.240	516	36	-2	3	1	0	1.000	-3	O-14(2-8-4)	-0.5

■ JERRY HAIRSTON Hairston, Jerry Wayne Jr. b: 5/29/76, Naperville, Ill. BR/TR, 5'10", 172 lbs. Deb: 9/11/98 F

YEAR	TM/L	G	AB	R	H	2B	3B	HR	RBI	BB	SO	AVG	OBP	SLG	OPS	OPS+	BR+	SB	CS	SBR	FA	FR	G/POS	TPR
1998	Bal-A	6	7	2	0	0	0	0	0	0	1	.000	.000	.000	0	-99	-2	0	0	0	.750	-0	/2-4	-0.2
1999	Bal-A	50	175	26	47	12	1	4	17	11	24	.269	.323	.417	740	90	-3	9	4	1	1.000	10	2-50	0.9
2000	Bal-A	49	180	27	46	5	0	5	19	21	22	.256	.353	.367	719	85	-3	8	5	0	.981	6	2-49	0.4
Total	3	105	362	55	93	17	1	9	36	32	47	.257	.333	.384	716	84	-8	17	9	1	.987	15	2-103	1.1

■ JERRY HAIRSTON Hairston, Jerry Wayne Sr. b: 2/16/52, Birmingham, Ala. BB/TR, 5'10", 180 lbs. Deb: 7/26/73 F Career OF: (216-LF 39-CF 69-RF)

YEAR	TM/L	G	AB	R	H	2B	3B	HR	RBI	BB	SO	AVG	OBP	SLG	OPS	OPS+	BR+	SB	CS	SBR	FA	FR	G/POS	TPR
1973	Chi-A	60	210	25	57	11	1	0	23	33	30	.271	.373	.333	706	97	1	0	0	0	.944	2	O-33(33-0-0),1-19/D-8	-0.1
1974	Chi-A	45	109	8	25	7	0	0	8	13	18	.229	.311	.294	605	73	-3	0	2	-1	.926	-4	O-22(19-0-3),D-10	-1.0
1975	Chi-A	69	219	26	62	8	0	0	23	46	23	.283	.410	.320	729	107	5	1	0	0	.951	1	O-59(57-0-3)/D-8	0.3
1976	Chi-A	44	119	20	27	2	2	0	10	24	19	.227	.357	.277	634	87	-1	1	1	-0	.973	-3	O-40(1-0-39)	-0.6
1977	Chi-A	13	26	3	8	2	0	0	4	5	7	.308	.419	.385	804	121	1	0	0	0	1.000	-2	O-11(6-6-0)	-0.1
	Pit-N	51	52	5	10	2	0	2	6	6	10	.192	.276	.346	622	64	-3	0	0	0	.923	-4	O-14(6-0-8)/2-1	-0.7
1981	Chi-A	9	25	5	7	1	0	1	6	2	4	.280	.357	.440	797	131	1	0	0	0	.933	-1	/O-7(4-2-1)	0.0
1982	Chi-A	85	90	11	21	5	0	5	18	9	15	.233	.303	.456	759	105	0	0	0	0	1.000	-8	O-36(22-7-7)/D-2	-0.8
1983	*Chi-A	101	126	17	37	9	1	5	22	23	16	.294	.403	.500	903	141	8	0	1	-0	.968	-9	O-32(19-11-3)/D-4	-0.2
1984	Chi-A	115	227	41	59	13	2	5	19	41	29	.260	.375	.401	776	110	4	2	1	0	.967	-5	O-37(22-13-3),D-20	-0.2
1985	Chi-A	95	140	9	34	8	0	2	20	29	18	.243	.380	.343	723	96	1	0	0	0	1.000	-1	D-29/O-5(5-0-0)	-0.1
1986	Chi-A	101	225	32	61	15	0	5	26	26	26	.271	.349	.404	754	101	1	0	0	0	1.000	-3	D-29,1-19,O-11(9-0-2)	-0.4
1987	Chi-A	66	126	14	29	8	0	5	20	25	25	.230	.362	.413	775	102	1	0	0	0	1.000	-0	O-13(13-0-0),D-13/1-7	0.0
1988	Chi-A	2	2	0	0	0	0	0	0	0	0	.000	.000	.000	0	-99	-1	0	0	0	.000	0	/H	-0.1
1989	Chi-A	3	3	0	1	0	0	0	0	0	0	.333	.333	.333	667	91	-0	0	0	0	.000	0	/D-2	0.0
Total	14	859	1699	216	438	91	6	30	205	282	240	.258	.366	.371	737	103	15	4	5	-1	.963	-35	O-320L,D-125/1-45,2	-4.0

■ JOHNNY HAIRSTON Hairston, John Louis b: 8/27/44, Birmingham, Ala. BR/TR, 6'2", 200 lbs. Deb: 9/6/69 F

YEAR	TM/L	G	AB	R	H	2B	3B	HR	RBI	BB	SO	AVG	OBP	SLG	OPS	OPS+	BR+	SB	CS	SBR	FA	FR	G/POS	TPR
1969	Chi-N	3	4	0	1	0	0	0	0	0	2	.250	.250	.250	500	36	-0	0	0	0	1.000	-1	/C-1,O-1(1-0-0)	-0.1

■ SAMMY HAIRSTON Hairston, Samuel Harding b: 1/20/20, Crawford, Miss. d: 10/31/97, Birmingham, Ala. BR/TR, 5'10.5", 187 lbs. Deb: 7/21/51 FC

YEAR	TM/L	G	AB	R	H	2B	3B	HR	RBI	BB	SO	AVG	OBP	SLG	OPS	OPS+	BR+	SB	CS	SBR	FA	FR	G/POS	TPR
1951	Chi-A	4	5	1	2	1	0	0	1	2	0	.400	.571	.600	1171	222	1	0	0	0	1.000	-1	/C-2	0.0

■ CHET HAJDUK Hajduk, Chester b: 7/21/18, Chicago, Ill. BR/TR, 6', 195 lbs. Deb: 4/16/41

YEAR	TM/L	G	AB	R	H	2B	3B	HR	RBI	BB	SO	AVG	OBP	SLG	OPS	OPS+	BR+	SB	CS	SBR	FA	FR	G/POS	TPR
1941	Chi-A	1	1	0	0	0	0	0	0	0	0	.000	.000	.000	0	-99	-0	0	0	0	.000	0	H	0.0

■ DAVE HAJEK Hajek, David Vincent b: 10/14/67, Roseville, Cal. BR/TR, 5'10", 165 lbs. Deb: 9/15/95

YEAR	TM/L	G	AB	R	H	2B	3B	HR	RBI	BB	SO	AVG	OBP	SLG	OPS	OPS+	BR+	SB	CS	SBR	FA	FR	G/POS	TPR
1995	Hou-N	5	2	0	0	0	0	0	0	1	1	.000	.333	.000	333	-3	-0	1	0	0	.000	0	-0,-0	0.0
1996	Hou-N	8	10	3	3	1	0	0	0	2	0	.300	.417	.400	817	127	0	0	0	0	1.000	1	/3-3,2-2	0.2
Total	2	13	12	3	3	1	0	0	0	3	1	.250	.400	.333	733	104	0	1	0	0	1.000	1	/3-3,2-2	0.2

■ GEORGE HALAS Halas, George Stanley b: 2/2/1895, Chicago, Ill. d: 10/31/83, Chicago, Ill. BB/TR, 6', 164 lbs. Deb: 5/6/19

YEAR	TM/L	G	AB	R	H	2B	3B	HR	RBI	BB	SO	AVG	OBP	SLG	OPS	OPS+	BR+	SB	CS	SBR	FA	FR	G/POS	TPR
1919	NY-A	12	22	0	2	0	0	0	0	0	8	.091	.091	.091	182	-49	-4	0			1.000	-1	/O-6(0-1-5)	-0.6

■ JOHN HALDEMAN Haldeman, John Avery b: 12/2/1855, Pewee Valley, Ky. d: 9/17/1899, Louisville, Ky. BL/TR, 5'10", 175 lbs. Deb: 7/3/1877

YEAR	TM/L	G	AB	R	H	2B	3B	HR	RBI	BB	SO	AVG	OBP	SLG	OPS	OPS+	BR+	SB	CS	SBR	FA	FR	G/POS	TPR
1877	Lou-N	1	4	0	0	0	0	0	0	0	0	.000	.000	.000	0	-85	-1				.571	-1	/2-1	-0.2

■ ODELL HALE Hale, Arvel Odell "Bad News" b: 8/10/08, Hosston, La. d: 6/9/80, ElDorado, Ark. BR/TR, 5'10", 175 lbs. Deb: 8/1/31

YEAR	TM/L	G	AB	R	H	2B	3B	HR	RBI	BB	SO	AVG	OBP	SLG	OPS	OPS+	BR+	SB	CS	SBR	FA	FR	G/POS	TPR
1931	Cle-A	25	92	14	26	2	4	1	5	8	8	.283	.340	.424	764	94	-1	2	0	0	.918	-4	3-15,2-10/S-1	-0.4
1933	Cle-A	98	351	49	97	19	8	10	64	30	37	.276	.333	.462	795	104	1	2	3	-1	.954	3	2-73,3-21	0.8
1934	Cle-A	143	563	82	170	44	6	13	101	48	50	.302	.357	.471	827	110	7	8	12	-2	.956	**26**	*2-137/3-5	3.6
1935	Cle-A	150	589	80	179	37	11	16	101	52	55	.304	.361	.486	847	115	11	15	13	-1	.938	7	*3-149/2-1	2.0
1936	Cle-A	153	620	126	196	50	13	14	87	64	43	.316	.380	.506	887	116	14	8	5	0	.946	17	*3-148/2-3	3.1
1937	Cle-A	154	561	74	150	32	4	6	82	56	41	.267	.335	.371	706	77	-20	9	6	-0	.964	26	3-90,2-64	1.2
1938	Cle-A	130	496	69	138	32	2	8	69	44	39	.278	.338	.399	737	86	-12	8	1	1	.963	-13	*2-127	-1.4
1939	Cle-A	108	253	36	79	16	2	4	48	25	18	.312	.374	.439	813	111	4	4	5	-1	.966	-16	2-73/3-2	-0.8
1940	Cle-A	48	50	3	11	3	1	0	6	5	7	.220	.291	.320	611	60	-3	0	0	0	.700	-1	/3-3	-0.3
1941	Bos-A	12	24	5	5	2	0	1	1	3	4	.208	.296	.417	713	85	-1	0	0	0	.857	-3	/3-6,2-1	-0.4
	NY-N	41	102	13	20	3	0	0	9	18	13	.196	.317	.225	542	53	-6	1			.964	1	2-29	-0.3
Total	10	1062	3701	551	1071	240	51	73	573	353	315	.289	.352	.441	793	100	-5	57	45		.959	42	2-518,3-439/S-1	7.1

■ GEORGE HALE Hale, George Wagner "Ducky" b: 8/3/1894, Dexter, Kan. d: 11/1/45, Wichita, Kan. BR/TR, 5'10", 160 lbs. Deb: 8/24/14

YEAR	TM/L	G	AB	R	H	2B	3B	HR	RBI	BB	SO	AVG	OBP	SLG	OPS	OPS+	BR+	SB	CS	SBR	FA	FR	G/POS	TPR
1914	StL-A	6	11	1	2	0	0	0	0	0	3	.182	.182	.182	364	10	-1	0			.895	-0	/C-6	-0.1
1916	StL-A	4	1	0	0	0	0	0	0	0	1	.000	.500	.000	500	54	0	0			1.000	0	/C-3	0.0
1917	StL-A	38	61	4	12	2	1	0	8	10	12	.197	.310	.262	572	78	-1	0			.927	3	C-28	0.3
1918	StL-A	12	30	0	4	1	0	0	1	1	5	.133	.161	.167	328	-1	-4	0			.981	2	C-11	-0.1
Total	4	60	103	5	18	3	1	0	9	11	21	.175	.261	.223	484	49	-6	0			.940	5	/C-48	0.1

YEAR	TM/L	G	AB	R	H	2B	3B	HR	RBI	BB	SO	AVG	OBP	SLG	OPS	OPS+	BR+	SB	CS	SBR	FA	FR	G/POS	TPR
■ **JOHN HALE**	Hale, John Steven b: 8/5/53, Fresno, Cal. BL/TR, 6'2", 195 lbs. Deb: 9/8/74																							
1974	LA-N	4	4	2	4	1	0	0	2	0	0	1.000	1.000	1.250	2250	549	2	0	0	0	.000	-1	/O-3(0-0-3)	0.1
1975	LA-N	71	204	20	43	7	0	6	22	26	51	.211	.306	.333	639	81	-5	1	2	-0	.977	-7	O-68(0-35-42)	-1.6
1976	LA-N	44	91	4	14	2	1	0	8	16	14	.154	.294	.198	491	42	-6	4	1	1	.983	-4	O-37(0-11-27)	-1.2
1977	LA-N	79	108	10	26	4	1	2	11	15	28	.241	.333	.352	685	84	-2	2	1	0	.986	-16	O-73(25-13-37)	-2.0
1978	Sea-A	107	211	24	36	8	0	4	22	34	64	.171	.286	.265	551	56	-12	3	4	-1	.988	-13	O-98(27-24-47)/D-3	-2.9
1979	Sea-A	54	63	6	14	3	0	2	7	12	26	.222	.347	.365	712	91	-1	0	0	0	1.000	-11	O-42(34-0-9)/D-2	-1.2
Total	6	359	681	66	137	25	2	14	72	103	183	.201	.310	.305	615	72	-24	10	8	-1	.985	-52	O-321(86-83-165)/D-5	-8.8
■ **BOB HALE**	Hale, Robert Houston b: 11/7/33, Sarasota, Fla. BL/TL, 5'10", 195 lbs. Deb: 7/4/55																							
1955	Bal-A	67	182	13	65	7	1	0	29	5	19	.357	.378	.407	784	119	4	0	2	-1	.974	2	1-44	0.3
1956	Bal-A	85	207	18	49	10	1	1	24	11	10	.237	.279	.309	588	60	-13	0	2	-1	.975	-0	1-51	-1.6
1957	Bal-A	42	44	2	11	0	0	0	7	2	2	.250	.283	.250	533	50	-3	0	0	0	1.000	-0	/1-5	-0.4
1958	Bal-A	19	20	2	7	2	0	0	3	2	1	.350	.409	.450	859	144	1	0	0	0	1.000	1	/1-2	0.2
1959	Bal-A	40	54	2	10	3	0	0	7	2	6	.185	.214	.241	455	25	-6	0	0	0	1.000	-1	/1-8	-0.7
1960	Cle-A	70	70	2	21	7	0	0	12	3	6	.300	.329	.400	729	99	-0	0	0	0	.944	0	/1-5	0.0
1961	Cle-A	42	36	0	6	0	0	0	6	1	7	.167	.211	.167	377	2	-5	0	0	0	.000	0	H	-0.5
	NY-A	11	13	2	2	0	0	1	1	0	0	.154	.154	.385	538	41	-1	0	0	0	1.000	-0	/1-5	-0.1
	Yr	53	49	2	8	0	0	1	7	1	7	.163	.196	.224	421	12	-6	0	0	0	1.000	-0	/1-5	-0.6
Total	7	376	626	41	171	29	2	2	89	26	51	.273	.305	.335	641	76	-22	0	4	-1	.977	2	1-120	-2.8
■ **SAMMY HALE**	Hale, Samuel Douglas b: 9/10/1896, Glen Rose, Tex. d: 9/6/74, Wheeler, Tex. BR/TR, 5'8.5", 160 lbs. Deb: 4/20/20 Career OF: (4-LF 4-CF 2-RF)																							
1920	Det-A	76	116	13	34	3	3	1	14	5	15	.293	.322	.397	719	92	-2	2	0	0	.886	-3	3-16/O-4(0-4-0),2-1	-0.4
1921	Det-A	9	2	2	0	0	0	0	0	0	1	.000	.000	.000	0	-99	-1	0	1	-0	.000	0	H	-0.1
1923	Phi-A	115	434	68	125	22	8	3	51	17	31	.288	.327	.396	723	89	-9	8	3	1	.916	-19	*3-107	-2.0
1924	Phi-A	80	261	41	83	14	2	2	17	17	19	.318	.367	.410	777	99	-1	3	2	-0	.948	-8	3-55/O-5(4-0-1),S-1	-0.5
1925	Phi-A	110	391	62	135	30	11	8	63	17	27	.345	.376	.540	915	122	11	7	4	0	.919	-4	3-96/2-1	1.2
1926	Phi-A	111	327	49	92	22	9	4	43	13	36	.281	.311	.440	751	89	-7	1	4	-1	.947	-2	3-77/O-1(0-0-1)	-0.6
1927	Phi-A	131	501	77	157	24	8	5	81	32	32	.313	.358	.423	781	97	-3	11	3	1	.961	1	*3-128	0.7
1928	Phi-A	88	314	38	97	20	9	4	58	9	21	.309	.334	.468	803	106	1	2	0	0	.932	12	3-79	1.8
1929	Phi-A	101	379	51	105	14	3	1	40	12	18	.277	.303	.338	641	62	-21	6	2	1	.956	-7	3-99/2-1	-2.1
1930	StL-A	62	190	21	52	8	1	2	25	8	18	.274	.303	.358	661	65	-10	1	1	-0	.947	-3	3-47	-1.0
Total	10	883	2915	422	880	157	54	30	392	130	218	.302	.336	.424	760	93	-41	41	20	2	.939	-33	3-704/O-10L,2-3,S-1	-3.0
■ **CHIP HALE**	Hale, Walter William b: 12/2/64, San Jose, Cal. BL/TR, 5'11", 191 lbs. Deb: 8/27/89 Career OF: (0-LF 0-CF 4-RF)																							
1989	Min-A	28	67	6	14	3	0	0	4	1	6	.209	.221	.254	474	31	-6	0	0	0	.980	-3	2-16/3-9,D-2	-0.9
1990	Min-A	1	2	0	0	0	0	0	2	0	1	.000	.000	.000	0	-94	-1	0	0	0	1.000	1	/2-1	0.1
1993	Min-A	69	186	25	62	6	1	3	27	18	17	.333	.410	.425	834	124	7	2	1	0	.952	-3	2-21,3-19,D-19,/1S	0.4
1994	Min-A	67	118	13	31	9	0	1	11	16	14	.263	.356	.364	720	86	-2	0	2	-1	.964	5	3-21,D-10/1-7,2O	0.1
1995	Min-A	69	103	10	27	4	0	2	18	11	20	.262	.333	.359	693	80	-3	0	0	0	1.000	1	D-27/2-7,3-5,1-3	-0.4
1996	Min-A	85	87	8	24	5	0	1	16	10	6	.276	.351	.368	718	81	-2	0	0	0	1.000	1	2-14,D-10/1-6,3O	-0.1
1997	LA-N	14	12	0	1	0	0	0	0	2	4	.083	.214	.083	298	-20	-2	0	0	0	1.000	-0	/3-2	-0.2
Total	7	333	575	62	159	27	1	7	78	58	68	.277	.350	.363	713	88	-9	2	3	-1	.969	2	/D-68,2-64,3-59,1OS	-1.0
■ **FRED HALEY**	Haley, Frederick b: 6/18/1853, Wheeling, W.Va. TR, Deb: 6/22/1880																							
1880	Tro-N	2	7	0	0	0	0	0	0	1	2	.000	.125	.000	125	-51	-1				.750	-2	/C-2	-0.3
■ **RAY HALEY**	Haley, Raymond Timothy "Pat" b: 1/23/1891, Danbury, Iowa d: 10/8/73, Bradenton, Fla. BR/TR, 5'11", 180 lbs. Deb: 4/21/15																							
1915	Bos-A	5	7	2	1	1	0	0	0	1	0	.143	.250	.286	536	62	-0	0			1.000	0	/C-4	0.0
1916	Bos-A	1	1	0	0	0	0	0	0	0	1	.000	.000	.000	0	-99	-0	0			.000	0	H	0.0
	Phi-A	34	108	8	25	5	0	0	4	6	19	.231	.278	.278	556	70	-4	0			.982	6	C-33	0.5
	Yr	35	109	8	25	5	0	0	4	6	20	.229	.276	.275	551	69	-4	0			.982	6	C-33	0.5
1917	Phi-A	41	98	7	27	2	1	0	11	4	12	.276	.311	.316	627	93	-1	2			.947	-6	C-34	-0.5
Total	3	81	214	17	53	8	1	0	15	11	32	.248	.291	.294	585	80	-6	2			.970	1	/C-71	0.0
■ **ALBERT HALL**	Hall, Albert b: 3/7/58, Birmingham, Ala. BB/TR, 5'11", 155 lbs. Deb: 9/12/81																							
1981	Atl-N	6	2	1	0	0	0	0	0	1	1	.000	.333	.000	333	1	-0	0	0	0	.000	-1	/O-2(1-0-1)	-0.1
1982	Atl-N	5	0	1	0	0	0	0	0	0	0	—	—	—	—	—	0	0	0	0	.000	0	/R	0.0
1983	Atl-N	10	8	2	0	0	0	0	0	2	2	.000	.200	.000	200	-37	-1	1	1	-0	.750	-2	/O-4(4-1-0)	-0.3
1984	Atl-N	87	142	25	37	6	1	1	9	10	18	.261	.309	.338	647	76	-4	6	4	-0	.932	-10	O-66(48-2-17)	-1.7
1985	Atl-N	54	47	5	7	0	1	0	3	9	12	.149	.286	.191	477	34	-4	1	1	-0	.900	-4	O-13(6-6-3)	-0.8
1986	Atl-N	16	50	6	12	2	0	0	1	5	6	.240	.309	.280	589	60	-3	8	3	1	.900	0	O-14(0-0-14)	-0.3
1987	Atl-N	92	292	54	83	20	4	3	24	38	36	.284	.370	.411	781	102	2	33	10	4	.981	3	O-69(0-68-1)	0.7
1988	Atl-N	85	231	27	57	7	1	1	15	21	35	.247	.315	.299	614	73	-7	15	10	-0	.973	2	O-63(1-63-0)	-0.7
1989	Pit-N	20	33	4	6	2	1	0	1	3	5	.182	.250	.303	553	59	-2	3	0	1	.909	-3	O-12(5-1-6)	-0.5
Total	9	375	805	125	202	37	8	5	53	89	115	.251	.329	.335	664	80	-20	67	29	5	.958	-15	O-243(65-141-42)	-3.7
■ **AL HALL**	Hall, Archibald W. b: Worcester, Mass. d: 2/10/1885, Warren, Pa. Deb: 5/1/1879																							
1879	Tro-N	67	306	30	79	7	3	0	14	3	13	.258	.265	.301	566	92	-2				.842	5	*O-67(2-63-2)	0.0
1880	Cle-N	3	8	1	1	0	0	0	0	0	0	.125	.125	.125	250	-15	-1				1.000	-1	/O-3(3-0-0)	-0.2
Total	2	70	314	31	80	7	3	0	14	3	13	.255	.262	.296	558	90	-3				.843	4	/O-70(5-63-2)	-0.2
■ **CHARLIE HALL**	Hall, Charles Walter "Doc" b: 8/24/1863, Toulon, Ill. d: 6/24/21, Tacoma, Wash. Deb: 5/3/1887																							
1887	NY-a	3	14	1	3	0	0	0	0	2		.214	.214	.083	298	-16	-2	1			1.000	0	/O-3(0-3-0)	-0.1
■ **GEORGE HALL**	Hall, George William b: 3/29/1849, Stepney, England d: 6/11/23, Ridgewood, N.J. BL, 5'7", 142 lbs. Deb: 5/5/1871																							
1871	Oly-n	32	136	31	40	3	3	2	17	8	0	.294	.333	.404	738	117	4	2	1	0	.913	7	*O-32(1-31-0)	0.7
1872	Bal-n	53	250	69	84	17	6	1	37	3	1	.336	.344	.464	808	140	10	6	1	1	.836	-3	*O-52(3-51-0)/1-1	0.5
1873	Bal-n	35	168	44	58	6	3	0	30	2	0	.345	.353	.417	770	128	6	0	0	0	.840	2	*O-35(0-35-0)	0.6
1874	Bos-n	47	222	58	64	10	8	1	34	1	0	.288	.291	.419	710	118	3	2	0	0	.811	-3	*O-47(20-21-7)	0.2
1875	Ath-n	77	358	71	107	10	12	4	62	3	4	.299	.305	.427	732	136	10	8	5	0	.887	4	*O-77(74-0-3)/1-1	1.4
1876	Phi-N	60	276	51	98	7	13	**5**	45	8	4	.355	.384	.545	929	208	30				.801	-2	*O-60(59-0-1)	2.1
1877	Lou-N	61	269	53	87	15	8	0	26	12	19	.323	.352	.439	791	125	6				**.900**	-6	*O-61(61-0-0)	-0.3
Total	5 n	244	1134	273	353	46	32	8	180	17	5	.311	.321	.429	751	130	33	18	7	2	.861	7	O-243(98-138-10)/1-2	3.4
Total	2	121	545	104	185	22	21	5	71	20	23	.339	.368	.492	860	162	36				.837	-7	O-121(120-0-1)	1.8
■ **IRV HALL**	Hall, Irvin Gladstone b: 10/7/18, Alberton, Md. BR/TR, 5'10.5", 160 lbs. Deb: 4/20/43																							
1943	Phi-A	151	544	37	139	15	4	0	54	22	42	.256	.292	.298	590	73	-19	10	7	-0	.948	-11	*S-148/2-1,3-1	-2.0
1944	Phi-A	143	559	60	150	20	8	0	45	31	46	.268	.309	.333	642	85	-12	2	5	-1	.980	-5	2-97,S-40/1-4	-1.1
1945	Phi-A	151	616	62	161	17	5	0	50	35	42	.261	.307	.305	613	78	-17	3	10	-3	.978	**26**	*2-151	1.5
1946	Phi-A	63	185	19	46	6	2	0	19	9	18	.249	.287	.303	590	65	-9	1	1	-0	.973	-4	2-40/S-7	-1.1
Total	4	508	1904	178	496	58	19	0	168	97	148	.261	.302	.311	613	77	-58	16	23	-5	.977	6	2-289,S-195/1-4,3-1	-2.7
■ **JIM HALL**	Hall, James d: 1/30/1886, Brooklyn, N.Y. Deb: 5/20/1872																							
1872	Atl-n	13	57	9	18	0	1	0	6	1	0	.316	.328	.351	678	93	-1	0	0	0	.750	-3	2-13	-0.4
1874	Atl-n	2	9	0	1	0	0	0	0	0	0	.111	.111	.111	222	-32	-1	0	0	0	.857	-1	/2-2,O-1(0-0-1)	-0.2
1875	Wes-n	1	3	0	1	0	1	0	1	0	0	.333	.333	1.000	1333	327	1	0	0	0	.000	-1	/O-1(1-0-0)	0.0
Total	3 n	16	69	9	20	0	2	0	7	1	0	.290	.300	.348	648	89	-2	0	0	0	.758	-5	/2-15,O-2(1-0-1)	-0.6
■ **JIMMIE HALL**	Hall, Jimmie Randolph b: 3/17/38, Mt.Holly, N.C. BL/TR, 6', 175 lbs. Deb: 4/9/63 Career OF: (221-LF 443-CF 217-RF)																							
1963	Min-A	156	497	88	129	21	5	33	80	63	101	.260	.343	.521	864	136	23	3	3	-0	.982	-10	*O-143(87-93-16)	0.7
1964	Min-A★	149	510	61	144	20	3	25	75	44	112	.282	.341	.480	821	125	16	5	2	0	.985	13	*O-137(0-137-0)	2.7

YEAR	TM/L	G	AB	R	H	2B	3B	HR	RBI	BB	SO	AVG	OBP	SLG	OPS	OPS+	BR+	SB	CS	SBR	FA	FR	G/POS	TPR
1965	*Min-A★	148	522	81	149	25	4	20	86	51	79	.285	.350	.464	814	124	16	14	7	1	.976	-2	*O-141(6-140-6)	1.1
1966	Min-A	120	356	52	85	7	4	20	47	33	66	.239	.303	.449	753	106	2	1	2	-0	.978	-1	*O-103(69-27-12)	-0.4
1967	Cal-A	129	401	54	100	8	3	16	55	42	65	.249	.321	.404	725	117	8	4	1	1	.990	-2	*O-120(2-6-116)	-0.1
1968	Cal-A	46	126	15	27	3	0	1	8	16	19	.214	.303	.262	565	75	-3	1	0	0	.981	-4	O-39(4-2-33)	-1.1
	Cle-A	53	111	4	22	4	0	1	8	10	19	.198	.264	.261	526	61	-5	1	0	0	.983	2	O-29(20-6-4)	-0.5
	Yr	99	237	19	49	7	0	2	16	26	38	.207	.285	.262	547	68	-9	2	0	0	.982	-2	O-68(24-8-37)	-1.6
1969	Cle-A	4	10	1	0	0	0	0	0	2	3	.000	.167	.000	167	-48	-2	1	0	0	1.000	-0	/O-3(2-1-0)	-0.2
	NY-A	80	212	21	50	8	5	3	26	19	34	.236	.299	.363	662	88	-4	8	3	1	.963	-5	O-50(9-19-22)/1-7	-1.2
	Yr	84	222	22	50	8	5	3	26	21	37	.225	.292	.347	639	81	-6	9	3	1	.966	-5	O-53(11-20-22)/1-7	-1.4
	Chi-N	11	24	1	5	1	0	0	1	1	5	.208	.240	.250	490	33	-2	0	0	0	1.000	-1	/O-5(1-4-0)	-0.4
1970	Chi-N	28	32	2	3	1	0	0	1	4	12	.094	.194	.125	319	-11	-5	0	0	0	1.000	-2	/O-8(2-7-0)	-0.7
	Atl-N	39	47	7	10	2	0	2	4	2	14	.213	.245	.383	628	62	-3	0	0	0	1.000	-6	O-28(19-1-8)	-0.9
	Yr	67	79	9	13	3	0	2	5	6	26	.165	.224	.278	502	31	-8	0	0	0	1.000	-7	O-36(21-8-8)	-1.6
Total	8	963	2848	387	724	100	24	121	391	287	529	.254	.323	.434	757	112	40	38	18	2	.982	-17	O-806C/1-7	-1.0

■ JOE HALL

Hall, Joseph Geroy b: 3/6/66, Paducah, Ky. BR/TR, 6', 180 lbs. Deb: 4/5/94

YEAR	TM/L	G	AB	R	H	2B	3B	HR	RBI	BB	SO	AVG	OBP	SLG	OPS	OPS+	BR+	SB	CS	SBR	FA	FR	G/POS	TPR
1994	Chi-A	17	28	6	11	3	0	1	5	2	4	.393	.452	.607	1059	173	3	0	0	0	.917	-2	/O-9(7-0-2),D-2	0.1
1995	Det-A	7	15	2	2	0	0	0	0	2	3	.133	.235	.133	369	-1	-2	0	0	0	1.000	1	/O-5(5-0-0),D-2	-0.1
1997	Det-A	2	4	1	2	1	0	0	3	0	0	.500	.500	.750	1250	222	1	0	0	0	1.000	-0	/O-1(0-0-1)	0.0
Total	3	26	47	9	15	4	0	1	8	4	7	.319	.385	.468	853	121	2	0	0	0	.960	-1	/O-15(12-0-3),D-4	0.0

■ MEL HALL

Hall, Melvin b: 9/16/60, Lyons, N.Y. BL/TL, 6'1", 205 lbs. Deb: 9/3/81 Career OF: (716-LF 145-CF 214-RF)

YEAR	TM/L	G	AB	R	H	2B	3B	HR	RBI	BB	SO	AVG	OBP	SLG	OPS	OPS+	BR+	SB	CS	SBR	FA	FR	G/POS	TPR
1981	Chi-N	10	11	1	1	0	0	1	2	1	4	.091	.167	.364	530	45	-1	0	0	0	.000	-2	/O-3(1-2-0)	-0.3
1982	Chi-N	24	80	6	21	3	2	0	4	5	17	.262	.322	.350	672	86	-1	0	1	-0	.939	1	O-22(0-21-1)	-0.1
1983	Chi-N	112	410	60	116	23	5	17	56	42	101	.283	.354	.488	842	125	13	6	6	-1	.988	0	*O-112(5-108-0)	1.2
1984	Chi-N	48	150	25	42	11	3	4	22	12	23	.280	.333	.473	807	114	2	2	1	0	.961	-2	O-46(5-5-40)	-0.1
	Cle-A	83	257	43	66	13	1	7	30	35	55	.257	.350	.397	747	104	2	1	1	-0	.993	0	O-69(64-1-6)/D-9	-0.1
1985	Cle-A	23	66	7	21	6	0	0	12	8	12	.318	.392	.409	801	121	2	0	1	-0	1.000	-3	O-15(15-0-1)/D-5	-0.2
1986	Cle-A	140	442	68	131	29	2	18	77	33	65	.296	.348	.493	841	128	16	6	2	1	.972	-7	*O-126(123-0-14)/D-7	0.5
1987	Cle-A	142	485	57	136	21	1	18	76	20	68	.280	.310	.439	749	95	-5	5	4	-0	.989	6	*O-122(122-0-0),D-14	-0.4
1988	Cle-A	150	515	69	144	32	4	6	71	28	50	.280	.317	.392	709	95	-4	7	3	0	.967	-3	*O-141(135-7-3)/D-6	-1.1
1989	NY-A	113	361	54	94	9	0	17	58	21	37	.260	.301	.427	728	104	1	0	0	0	.993	-2	O-75(46-0-31),D-34	-0.5
1990	NY-A	113	360	41	93	23	2	12	46	6	46	.258	.274	.433	708	95	-5	0	0	0	.973	-6	D-54,O-50(36-0-15)	-1.3
1991	NY-A	141	492	67	140	23	2	19	80	26	40	.285	.324	.455	780	113	7	0	1	-0	.987	-0	*O-120(62-1-65),D-10	0.2
1992	NY-A	152	583	67	163	36	3	15	81	29	53	.280	.315	.429	744	107	3	4	2	0	.990	6	*O-136(99-0-37),D-11	0.5
1996	SF-N	25	25	3	3	0	0	0	5	1	4	.120	.154	.120	274	-28	-5	0	0	0	.000	-1	/O-4(3-0-1)	-0.6
Total	13	1276	4237	568	1171	229	25	134	620	267	575	.276	.322	.437	759	107	27	31	22	-1	.981	-13	*O-1041L,D-150	-2.3

■ DICK HALL

Hall, Richard Wallace b: 9/27/30, St.Louis, Mo. BR/TR, 6'6", 200 lbs. Deb: 4/15/52 Career OF: (43-LF 59-CF 20-RF)

YEAR	TM/L	G	AB	R	H	2B	3B	HR	RBI	BB	SO	AVG	OBP	SLG	OPS	OPS+	BR+	SB	CS	SBR	FA	FR	G/POS	TPR
1952	Pit-N	26	80	6	11	1	0	0	2	2	17	.138	.159	.150	309	-14	-12	0	1	-0	.972	0	O-14(0-12-2)/3-5	-1.3
1953	Pit-N	7	24	2	4	0	0	0	1	1	3	.167	.200	.167	367	-3	-4	1	1	-0	.978	4	/2-7	0.1
1954	Pit-N	112	310	38	74	8	4	2	27	33	46	.239	.312	.310	622	64	-16	3	0	1	.956	-2	*O-102(42-44-18)	-2.2
1955	Pit-N	21	40	3	7	1	0	1	3	6	5	.175	.283	.275	558	50	-3	0	0	0	1.000	-3	P-15/O-3(1-3-0)	-0.2
1956	Pit-N	33	29	5	10	0	0	0	1	5	7	.345	.441	.345	786	118	1	0	0	0	1.000	-1	P-19/1-1	0.0
1957	Pit-N	10	1	0	0	0	0	0	0	0	1	.000	.000	.000	0	-99	-0	0	0	0	.000	-0	/P-8	0.0
1959	Pit-N	2	2	0	0	0	0	0	0	0	0	.000	.000	.000	0	-99	-1	0	0	0	1.000	-0	/P-2	0.0
1960	KC-A	32	56	5	6	0	0	0	4	4	15	.107	.167	.107	274	-24	-10	1	0	0	.925	-1	P-29	0.0
1961	Bal-A	30	36	4	5	0	0	0	1	3	13	.139	.205	.139	344	-6	-5	0	0	0	.970	1	P-29	0.0
1962	Bal-A	44	24	3	4	1	0	0	1	4	9	.167	.286	.208	494	38	-2	0	0	0	1.000	-0	P-43	0.0
1963	Bal-A	48	28	7	13	1	0	1	4	0	8	.464	.464	.607	1071	205	4	0	0	0	1.000	1	P-47	0.0
1964	Bal-A	45	16	1	2	0	0	0	3	1	3	.125	.176	.125	301	-14	-2	0	0	0	1.000	-0	P-45	0.0
1965	Bal-A	49	15	1	5	2	0	0	4	1	4	.333	.412	.467	878	146	1	0	0	0	.923	-1	P-48	0.0
1966	Bal-A	32	12	0	2	0	0	0	2	0	5	.167	.231	.167	397	17	-1	0	0	0	1.000	0	P-32	0.0
1967	Phi-N	48	14	1	1	0	0	0	0	0	5	.071	.071	.071	143	-58	-3	0	0	0	1.000	1	P-48	0.0
1968	Phi-N	32	3	0	1	0	0	0	0	0	1	.333	.333	.333	667	101	-0	0	0	0	1.000	-0	P-32	0.0
1969	*Bal-A	39	7	1	2	0	0	0	2	1	1	.286	.375	.286	661	86	-0	1	0	0	1.000	-1	P-39	0.0
1970	*Bal-A	32	12	2	1	0	0	0	1	0	3	.083	.083	.083	167	-53	-2	0	0	0	1.000	-1	P-32	0.0
1971	*Bal-A	27	5	0	2	1	0	0	0	0	1	.400	.400	.600	1000	182	0	0	0	0	.800	-1	P-27	0.0
Total	19	669	714	79	150	15	4	4	56	61	147	.210	.274	.259	533	44	-56	6	2	1	.976	-5	P-495,O-119C/2-7,31	-3.6

■ BOB HALL

Hall, Robert Prill b: 12/20/1878, Baltimore, Md. d: 12/1/50, Wellesley, Mass. TR, 5'10", 158 lbs. Deb: 4/18/04 Career OF: (24-LF 12-CF 8-RF)

YEAR	TM/L	G	AB	R	H	2B	3B	HR	RBI	BB	SO	AVG	OBP	SLG	OPS	OPS+	BR+	SB	CS	SBR	FA	FR	G/POS	TPR
1904	Phi-N	46	163	11	26	4	0	0	17	14		.160	.226	.184	410	28	-13	5			.843	-10	3-20,S-15,1-11	-2.5
1905	NY-N	1	3	1	1	0	0	0	0	0		.333	.333	.333	667	97	-0	0			.000	-0	/O-1(0-0-1)	0.0
	Bro-N	56	203	21	48	4	1	2	15	11		.236	.279	.296	575	77	-6	8			.939	6	O-42(24-12-7)/2-7,1-3	-0.3
	Yr	57	206	22	49	4	1	2	15	11		.238	.280	.296	576	77	-6	8			.939	5	O-43(24-12-8)/2-7,1-3	-0.3
Total	2	103	369	33	75	8	1	2	32	25		.203	.256	.247	502	55	-19	13			.968	-5	/O-43L,3-20,S-15,12	-2.8

■ RUSS HALL

Hall, Robert Russell b: 9/29/1871, Shelbyville, Ky. d: 7/1/37, Los Angeles, Cal. TL, 5'10", 170 lbs. Deb: 4/15/1898

YEAR	TM/L	G	AB	R	H	2B	3B	HR	RBI	BB	SO	AVG	OBP	SLG	OPS	OPS+	BR+	SB	CS	SBR	FA	FR	G/POS	TPR
1898	StL-N	39	143	13	35	2	1	0	10	7		.245	.285	.273	557	59	-8	1			.835	-14	S-35/3-3,O-1(0-0-1)	-1.9
1901	Cle-A	1	4	2	2	0	0	0	0	0		.500	.500	.500	1000	185	0	0			.500	-1	/S-1	-0.1
Total	2	40	147	15	37	2	1	0	10	7		.252	.290	.279	569	62	-7	1			.824	-16	/S-36,3-3,O-1(0-0-1)	-2.0

■ TOBY HALL

Hall, Toby Jason b: 10/21/75, Tacoma, Wash. BR/TR, 6'3", 205 lbs. Deb: 9/15/2000

YEAR	TM/L	G	AB	R	H	2B	3B	HR	RBI	BB	SO	AVG	OBP	SLG	OPS	OPS+	BR+	SB	CS	SBR	FA	FR	G/POS	TPR
2000	TB-A	4	12	1	2	0	0	1	1	1	0	.167	.231	.417	647	60	-1	0	0	0	1.000	0	/C-4	0.0

■ BILL HALL

Hall, William Lemuel b: 7/30/28, Moultrie, Ga. d: 1/1/86, Moultrie, Ga. BL/TR, 5'11", 165 lbs. Deb: 4/18/54

YEAR	TM/L	G	AB	R	H	2B	3B	HR	RBI	BB	SO	AVG	OBP	SLG	OPS	OPS+	BR+	SB	CS	SBR	FA	FR	G/POS	TPR
1954	Pit-N	5	7	0	0	0	0	0	0	0	0	.000	.000	.000	0	-99	-2	0	0	0	1.000	-0	/C-1	-0.2
1956	Pit-N	1	3	0	0	0	0	0	0	0	1	.000	.000	.000	0	-99	-1	0	0	0	1.000	0	/C-1	0.0
1958	Pit-N	51	116	15	33	6	0	1	15	15	13	.284	.366	.362	728	96	-0	0	0	0	.982	7	C-51	0.9
Total	3	57	126	15	33	6	0	1	15	15	14	.262	.340	.333	674	81	-3	0	0	0	.983	8	/C-53	0.7

■ TOM HALLER

Haller, Thomas Frank b: 6/23/37, Lockport, Ill. BL/TR, 6'4", 195 lbs. Deb: 4/11/61 C Career OF: (2-LF 0-CF 9-RF)

YEAR	TM/L	G	AB	R	H	2B	3B	HR	RBI	BB	SO	AVG	OBP	SLG	OPS	OPS+	BR+	SB	CS	SBR	FA	FR	G/POS	TPR
1961	SF-N	30	62	5	9	1	0	2	8	9	23	.145	.264	.258	522	41	-5	0	1	-0	1.000	2	C-25	-0.3
1962	*SF-N	99	272	53	71	13	1	18	55	51	59	.261	.385	.515	900	142	17	1	4	-1	.992	-2	C-91	1.7
1963	SF-N	98	298	32	76	8	1	14	44	34	45	.255	.335	.430	765	120	8	4	6	-1	.994	-4	C-85/O-7(1-0-6)	0.6
1964	SF-N	117	388	43	98	14	3	16	48	55	51	.253	.348	.428	776	115	9	4	2	0	.989	-1	*C-113/O-3(1-0-2)	1.4
1965	SF-N	134	422	40	106	4	3	16	49	47	67	.251	.338	.389	726	101	2	0	0	0	.987	-5	*C-133	0.4
1966	SF-N☆	142	471	74	113	19	2	27	67	53	74	.240	.325	.461	785	112	7	1	3	-1	.991	-7	*C-136/1-4	0.6
1967	SF-N★	141	455	54	114	23	5	14	49	62	61	.251	.345	.415	761	118	12	0	4	-1	.997	-1	*C-136/O-1(0-0-1)	1.7
1968	LA-N★	144	474	37	135	27	5	4	53	46	76	.285	.351	.388	739	132	18	1	4	-1	.994	3	*C-139	3.0
1969	LA-N	134	445	46	117	18	3	6	39	48	58	.263	.337	.357	695	102	1	0	3	-1	.992	-9	*C-132	-0.3
1970	LA-N	112	325	47	93	16	6	10	47	32	35	.286	.354	.465	818	123	10	3	0	1	.993	-8	*C-106	0.7
1971	LA-N	84	202	23	54	5	0	5	32	25	30	.267	.354	.366	720	111	3	0	2	-1	.978	4	C-67	1.0
1972	*Det-A	59	121	7	25	5	2	2	13	15	14	.207	.294	.331	625	83	-2	0	1	-0	1.000	8	C-36	0.7
Total	12	1294	3935	461	1011	153	31	134	504	477	593	.257	.342	.414	756	114	79	14	30	-7	.992	-20	*C-1199/O-11R,1-4	11.2

■ NEWT HALLIDAY

Halliday, Newton Schurz b: 6/18/1896, Chicago, Ill. d: 4/6/18, Great Lakes, Ill. BR/TR, 6'1", 175 lbs. Deb: 8/19/16

YEAR	TM/L	G	AB	R	H	2B	3B	HR	RBI	BB	SO	AVG	OBP	SLG	OPS	OPS+	BR+	SB	CS	SBR	FA	FR	G/POS	TPR
1916	Pit-N	1	1	0	0	0	0	0	0	0	1	.000	.000	.000	0	-99	-0	0			1.000	0	/1-1	0.0

■ JOCKO HALLIGAN

Halligan, William E. b: 12/8/1868, Avon, N.Y. d: 2/13/45, Buffalo, N.Y. BL, 5'9", 166 lbs. Deb: 5/13/1890 Career OF: (2-LF 5-CF 145-RF)

YEAR	TM/L	G	AB	R	H	2B	3B	HR	RBI	BB	SO	AVG	OBP	SLG	OPS	OPS+	BR+	SB	CS	SBR	FA	FR	G/POS	TPR
1890	Buf-P	57	211	28	53	9	2	3	33	20	19	.251	.319	.355	674	87	-4	7			.824	-5	O-43(1-5-37),C-16	-0.7
1891	Cin-N	61	247	43	77	13	6	3	44	24	25	.312	.375	.449	824	139	12	5			.856	-3	O-61(0-0-61)	0.7

YEAR	TM/L	G	AB	R	H	2B	3B	HR	RBI	BB	SO	AVG	OBP	SLG	OPS	OPS+	BR+	SB	CS	SBR	FA	FR	G/POS	TPR
1892	Cin-N	26	101	14	29	4	0	2	12	12	9	.287	.363	.386	749	128	4	3			.875	-1	O-26(0-0-26)	0.1
	Bal-N	46	178	38	48	4	7	2	43	30	24	.270	.381	.404	785	134	8	8			.861	-7	O-22(1-0-21),1-19/C-5	0.0
	Yr	72	279	52	77	8	7	4	55	42	33	.276	.375	.398	772	132	12	11			.869	-8	O-48(1-0-47),1-19/C-5	0.1
Total	3	190	737	123	207	30	15	10	132	86	77	.281	.359	.403	762	121	20	23			.848	-16	O-152R/C-21,1-19	0.1
■ ED HALLINAN Hallinan, Edward S. b: 8/23/1888, San Francisco, Cal d: 8/24/40, San Francisco, Cal BR/TR, 5'9", 168 lbs. Deb: 5/13/11																								
1911	StL-A	52	169	13	35	3	1	0	14	14		.207	.268	.237	504	43	-13	4			.902	-6	S-34,2-15/3-3	-1.6
1912	StL-A	28	86	11	19	2	0	0	1	5		.221	.272	.244	516	50	-6	3			.866	-7	S-26	-1.1
Total	2	80	255	24	54	5	1	0	15	19		.212	.269	.239	508	45	-18	7			.887	-12	/S-60,2-15,3-3	-2.7
■ JIMMY HALLINAN Hallinan, James H. b: 5/27/1849, Ireland d: 10/28/1879, Chicago, Ill. BL/TL, 5'9", 172 lbs. Deb: 7/26/1871 Career OF: (13-LF 1-CF 21-RF)																								
1871	Kek-n	5	25	7	5	0	0	0	2	2	0	.200	.259	.200	459	34	-2	1	1	-0	.475	-6	/S-5	-0.6
1875	Wes-n	13	51	12	14	2	1	0	3	0	1	.275	.275	.353	627	110	0	2	2	-0	.742	-5	S-13	-0.4
	Mut-n	44	203	29	58	6	3	3	21	1	2	.286	.289	.389	678	127	5	2	2	-0	.765	-10	S-43/3-1,O-1(0-0-1)	-0.6
	Yr	57	254	41	72	8	4	3	24	1	3	.283	.286	.382	668	123	5	4	4	-1	.761	-15	S-56/3-1,O-1(0-0-1)	-1.0
1876	NY-N	54	242	45	67	7	6	2	36	2	4	.277	.285	.383	668	139	11				.764	-15	*S-50/2-4,O-2(0-0-2)	-0.2
1877	Cin-N	16	73	18	27	1	1	0	7	1	1	.370	.378	.411	789	167	6				.854	-6	2-16	0.0
	Chi-N	19	89	17	25	4	1	0	11	4	2	.281	.312	.348	660	96	-1				.800	-2	O-19(0-0-19)	-0.2
	Yr	35	162	35	52	5	2	0	18	5	3	.321	.341	.377	718	124	4				.800	-8	O-19(0-0-19),2-16	-0.2
1878	Chi-N	16	67	14	19	3	0	0	2	5	6	.284	.333	.328	662	111	1				.789	-4	O-11(11-0-0)/2-5	-0.3
	Ind-N	3	12	0	3	2	0	0	1	0	2	.250	.250	.417	667	134	0				.667	-1	/O-3(2-1-0)	0.0
	Yr	19	79	14	22	5	0	0	3	5	8	.278	.321	.342	663	114	1				.760	-5	O-14(13-1-0)/2-5	-0.3
Total	2 n	62	279	48	77	8	4	3	26	3	3	.276	.284	.366	649	114	3	5	5	-1	.728	-22	/S-61,O-1(0-0-1),3-1	-1.6
Total	3	108	483	94	141	17	8	2	57	12	15	.292	.310	.374	685	129	17				.783	-28	/S-50,O-35R,2-25	-0.7
■ BILL HALLMAN Hallman, William Harry b: 3/15/1876, Philadelphia, Pa. d: 4/23/50, Philadelphia, Pa. BL/TL, 5'8", 165 lbs. Deb: 4/25/01																								
1901	Mil-A	139	549	70	135	27	6	2	47	41		.246	.301	.328	629	78	-16	12			.905	-2	*O-139(49-15-75)	-2.3
1903	Chi-A	63	207	29	43	7	4	0	18	31		.208	.320	.280	600	85	-2	11			.953	2	O-57(51-0-6)	-0.4
1906	Pit-N	23	89	12	24	3	1	1	6	15		.270	.375	.360	735	124	3	3			.935	-1	O-23(8-15-0)	0.1
1907	Pit-N	94	302	39	67	6	2	0	15	33		.222	.305	.255	560	74	-8	21			.966	-6	O-84(14-28-45)	-2.0
Total	4	319	1147	150	269	43	13	3	86	120		.235	.311	.303	614	82	-23	47			.933	-7	O-303(122-58-126)	-4.6
■ BILL HALLMAN Hallman, William Wilson b: 3/31/1867, Pittsburgh, Pa. d: 9/11/20, Philadelphia, Pa. BR/TR, 5'8", 160 lbs. Deb: 4/23/1888 M Career OF: (3-LF 4-CF 32-RF)																								
1888	Phi-N	18	63	5	13	4	1	0	6	1	12	.206	.219	.302	520	61	-3	1			.898	-7	C-10/2-4,O-3L,S3	-0.9
1889	Phi-N	119	462	67	117	21	8	2	60	36	54	.253	.313	.346	659	77	-16	20			.895	7	*S-106,2-13/C-1	-0.4
1890	Phi-P	84	356	59	95	16	7	1	37	33	24	.267	.338	.360	697	84	-9	6			.885	-8	O-34R,C-26,2-14,3/S	-1.1
1891	Phi-a	141	587	112	166	21	13	6	69	38	56	.283	.332	.394	725	107	2	18			.930	-5	*2-141	0.2
1892	Phi-N	138	586	106	171	27	10	2	84	32	52	.292	.335	.382	717	117	10	19			.936	-23	*2-138	-0.6
1893	Phi-N	132	596	119	183	28	7	5	76	51	27	.307	.367	.403	769	105	3	22			.950	-15	*2-120,1-12	-0.5
1894	Phi-N	122	519	111	162	19	0	0	69	37	15	.312	.364	.383	747	82	-14	37			.932	-14	*2-122	-1.7
1895	Phi-N	124	539	94	169	26	5	1	91	34	20	.314	.359	.386	745	92	-7	16			.943	5	*2-122/S-3	0.3
1896	Phi-N	120	469	82	150	21	3	2	83	45	23	.320	.382	.390	772	105	5	16			.945	3	*2-120/P-1	1.1
1897	Phi-N	31	126	16	33	3	0	0	15	8		.262	.326	.286	612	64	-6	1			.958	-10	2-31	-1.3
	StL-N	80	302	32	67	7	2	0	26	24		.222	.288	.258	546	46	-23	12			.940	5	2-78/1-3,M	-1.3
	Yr	111	428	48	100	10	2	0	41	32		.234	.299	.266	566	51	-29	13			.945	-5	*2-109/1-3	-2.6
1898	Bro-N	134	509	57	124	10	7	2	63	29		.244	.291	.303	594	70	-20	9			.944	-3	*2-124,3-10	-1.6
1901	Cle-A	5	19	2	4	0	0	0	3	2		.211	.286	.211	496	41	-1	0			.815	-3	/S-5	-0.4
	Phi-N	123	445	46	82	13	5	0	38	26		.184	.236	.236	472	36	-36	13			.971	-5	2-90,3-33	-3.9
1902	Phi-N	73	254	14	63	8	4	0	35	14		.248	.287	.311	598	85	-5	9			.932	-5	3-72	-0.9
1903	Phi-N	63	198	20	42	11	2	0	17	16		.212	.271	.288	559	61	-10	2			.932	-3	2-22,3-19/1-9,OS	-1.3
Total	14	1507	6030	942	1641	235	83	21	772	426	283	.272	.326	.349	675	85	-131	201			.941	-79	*2-1139,3-145,S/OC1P	-14.3
■ JIM HALPIN Halpin, James Nathaniel b: 10/4/1863, England d: 1/4/1893, Boston, Mass. Deb: 6/15/1882																								
1882	Wor-N	2	8	0	0	0	0	0	0	0	2	.000	.000	.000	0	-98	-2				.625	-1	/3-2	-0.3
1884	Was-U	46	168	24	31	3	0	0		2		.185	.194	.202	396	21	-21				.809	-7	S-39/3-7	-2.4
1885	Det-N	15	54	3	7	2	0	0	1	1	12	.130	.145	.167	312	1	-6				.846	1	S-15	-0.4
Total	3	63	230	27	38	5	0	0	1	3	14	.165	.176	.187	363	12	-28				.821	-8	/S-54,3-9	-3.1
■ AL HALT Halt, Alva William b: 11/23/1890, Sandusky, Ohio d: 1/22/73, Sandusky, Ohio BR/TR, 6', 180 lbs. Deb: 5/29/14 Career OF: (0-LF 1-CF 0-RF)																								
1914	Bro-F	80	261	26	61	6	2	3	25	13	39	.234	.270	.307	577	57	-20	11			.890	-11	S-71/2-3,O-1(0-1-0)	-2.8
1915	Bro-F	151	524	41	131	22	7	3	64	39	79	.250	.307	.336	643	81	-21	20			.930	3	*3-111,S-40	-1.4
1918	Cle-A	26	69	9	12	2	0	0	1	9	12	.174	.269	.203	472	39	-5	4			.971	-1	3-14/2-4,S-4,1-2	-0.6
Total	3	257	854	76	204	30	9	6	90	61	130	.239	.293	.316	609	70	-47	35			.933	-9	3-125,S-115/2-7,1O	-4.8
■ SHANE HALTER Halter, Shane David b: 11/8/69, LaPlata, Md. BR/TR, 5'10", 160 lbs. Deb: 4/6/97 Career OF: (18-LF 15-CF 24-RF)																								
1997	KC-A	74	123	16	34	5	1	2	10	10	28	.276	.341	.382	723	86	-2	4	3	-0	1.000	-9	O-32R,2-18,3-12,/SD	-1.0
1998	KC-A	86	204	17	45	12	0	2	13	12	38	.221	.267	.309	576	48	-16	2	5	-1	.964	-1	S-66/O-9L,3-8,21P	-1.3
1999	NY-N	7	0	0	0	0	0	0	0	0	0	—	—	—	—	—	0	0	0	0	.000	-1	/O-2(0-1-1),S-1	-0.1
2000	Det-A	105	238	26	62	12	2	3	27	14	49	.261	.304	.366	670	71	-11	5	2	0	.937	8	3-55,1-29,S-17,2/OCP	-0.3
Total	4	272	565	59	141	29	3	7	50	36	115	.250	.299	.349	648	66	-29	11	10	-1	.966	-2	/S-89,3-75,O21DCP	-2.7
■ RALPH HAM Ham, Ralph A. b: 3/1849, Troy, N.Y. d: 2/13/05, Troy, N.Y. 5'8", 158 lbs. Deb: 5/6/1871																								
1871	Rok-n	25	113	25	28	4	0	0	12	1	7	.248	.254	.283	538	57	-6	6	2	1	.723	-5	O-19(19-0-0)/3-7,S-2	-0.6
■ CHARLIE HAMBURG Hamburg, Charles M. (b: Charles M. Hambrick) b: 11/22/1863, Louisville, Ky. d: 5/18/31, Union, N.J. 6', 175 lbs. Deb: 4/18/1890																								
1890	*Lou-a	133	485	93	132	22	2	3	77	69		.272	.370	.344	714	113	11	46			.946	-2	*O-133(133-0-0)	0.5
■ JIM HAMBY Hamby, James Sanford "Cracker" b: 7/29/1897, Wilkesboro, N.C. d: 10/21/91, Springfield, Ill. BR/TR, 6', 170 lbs. Deb: 9/20/26																								
1926	NY-N	1	3	0	0	0	0	0	0	0	0	.000	.000	.000	0	-99	-1	0			.600	-1	/C-1	-0.2
1927	NY-N	21	52	6	10	0	1	0	5	7	7	.192	.288	.231	519	40	-4	1			.904	-0	C-19	-0.3
Total	2	22	55	6	10	0	1	0	5	7	7	.182	.274	.218	492	33	-5	1			.885	-1	/C-20	-0.5
■ BOB HAMELIN Hamelin, Robert James b: 11/29/67, Elizabeth, N.J. BL/TL, 6', 235 lbs. Deb: 9/12/93																								
1993	KC-A	16	49	2	11	3	0	2	5	6	15	.224	.309	.408	717	86	-1	0	0	0	.986	-0	1-15	-0.2
1994	KC-A	101	312	64	88	25	1	24	65	56	62	.282	.393	.599	992	145	21	4	3	-0	.992	1	D-70,1-24	1.4
1995	KC-A	72	208	20	35	7	1	7	25	26	56	.168	.279	.313	592	53	-15	0	1	-0	1.000	1	D-56/1-8	-1.7
1996	KC-A	89	239	31	61	14	1	9	40	54	58	.255	.397	.435	832	110	6	5	2	0	.984	0	D-47,1-33	0.1
1997	Det-A	110	318	47	86	15	0	18	52	48	72	.270	.368	.487	855	122	10	2	1	0	1.000	-1	D-95/1-7	0.4
1998	Mil-N	109	146	15	32	6	0	7	22	16	30	.219	.301	.404	705	83	-4	0	1	-0	.992	-4	1-51/D-1	-1.1
Total	6	497	1272	179	313	70	3	67	209	206	293	.246	.356	.464	820	109	17	11	8	-0	.990	-3	D-269,1-138	-1.1
■ DARRYL HAMILTON Hamilton, Darryl Quinn b: 12/3/64, Baton Rouge, La. BL/TR, 6'1", 180 lbs. Deb: 6/3/88 Career OF: (152-LF 843-CF 249-RF)																								
1988	Mil-A	44	103	14	19	4	0	1	11	12	9	.184	.276	.252	528	49	-7	7	3	0	1.000	-1	O-37(8-6-23)/D-3	-0.8
1990	Mil-A	89	156	27	46	5	0	1	18	9	12	.295	.333	.346	679	91	-2	10	3	1	.992	-6	O-72(41-6-25)/D-9	-0.8
1991	Mil-A	122	405	64	126	15	6	1	57	33	38	.311	.363	.385	748	110	6	16	6	1	.996	-10	*O-117(25-55-49)	-0.5
1992	Mil-A	128	470	67	140	19	7	5	62	45	42	.298	.360	.400	760	115	10	41	14	4	**1.000**	1	*O-124(30-32-74)	1.2
1993	Mil-A	135	520	74	161	21	1	9	48	45	62	.310	.368	.406	774	109	8	21	13	0	.992	6	*O-129(31-49-70)/D-1	1.0
1994	Mil-A	36	141	23	37	10	1	1	13	15	17	.262	.333	.369	702	77	-5	3	0	1	1.000	-4	O-32(0-32-0)/D-4	-0.7
1995	Mil-A	112	398	54	108	20	6	5	44	47	35	.271	.353	.389	742	88	-6	11	1	2	.989	-2	*O-109(0-109-0)/D-2	-0.4
1996	*Tex-A	148	627	94	184	29	4	6	51	54	66	.293	.351	.381	733	81	-17	15	5	2	**1.000**	7	*O-147(0-147-0)	-0.7
1997	*SF-N	125	460	78	124	23	3	5	43	61	61	.270	.355	.365	720	92	-4	15	10	-0	.980	-2	*O-118(0-118-0)	-0.4
1998	SF-N	97	367	65	108	19	2	1	26	59	53	.294	.395	.365	760	108	7	9	8	-1	1.000	-2	O-96(0-96-0)	0.6

YEAR	TM/L	G	AB	R	H	2B	3B	HR	RBI	BB	SO	AVG	OBP	SLG	OPS	OPS+	BR+	SB	CS	SBR	FA	FR	G/POS	TPR
	Col-N	51	194	30	65	9	1	5	25	23	20	.335	.408	.469	877	107	3	4	1	1	.990	-1	O-48(0-48-0)	0.3
	Yr	148	561	95	173	28	3	6	51	82	73	.308	.399	.401	800	107	10	13	9	-0	.997	-3	*O-144(0-144-0)	0.9
1999	Col-N	91	337	63	102	11	3	4	24	38	21	.303	.375	.389	764	74	-12	4	5	-1	1.000	5	O-82(0-82-0)	-0.7
	*NY-N	55	168	19	57	8	1	5	21	19	18	.339	.410	.488	898	130	8	2	3	-1	1.000	-1	O-52(0-52-0)	0.6
	Yr	146	505	82	159	19	4	9	45	57	39	.315	.387	.422	808	90	-5	6	8	-1	1.000	4	*O-134(0-134-0)	-0.1
2000	*NY-N	43	105	20	29	4	1	1	6	14	20	.276	.361	.362	723	87	-2	2	0	0	1.000	-4	O-33(17-11-8)	-0.6
Total	12	1276	4451	692	1306	197	36	50	449	474	474	.293	.363	.388	751	96	-13	160	72	10	.995	-13	*O-1196C/D-19	-1.9
■ JEFF HAMILTON	Hamilton, Jeffrey Robert b: 3/19/64, Flint, Mich. BR/TR, 6'3", 207 lbs. Deb: 6/28/86																							
1986	LA-N	71	147	22	33	5	0	5	19	2	43	.224	.235	.361	595	66	-8	0	0	0	.968	11	3-66/S-2	0.3
1987	LA-N	35	83	5	18	3	0	0	1	7	22	.217	.286	.253	539	45	-6	0	1	-0	.935	9	3-31/S-1	0.2
1988	*LA-N	111	309	34	73	14	2	6	33	10	51	.236	.269	.353	622	80	-9	0	2	-1	.941	-0	*3-105/S-2,1-1	-1.1
1989	LA-N	151	548	45	134	35	1	12	56	20	71	.245	.275	.378	653	86	-12	0	0	0	.951	-6	*3-147/P-1,2-1,S-1	-1.9
1990	LA-N	7	24	1	3	0	0	0	1	0	3	.125	.125	.125	250	-32	-4	0	0	0	1.000	1	/3-7	-0.4
1991	LA-N	41	94	4	21	4	0	1	14	4	21	.223	.255	.298	553	56	-6	0	0	0	.928	0	3-33/S-1	-0.6
Total	6	416	1205	111	282	61	3	24	124	43	211	.234	.265	.349	615	74	-45	0	3	-1	.948	15	3-389/S-7,2-1,P1	-3.5
■ TOM HAMILTON	Hamilton, Thomas Ball "Ham" b: 9/29/25, Altoona, Kan. d: 11/29/73, Tyler, Tex. BL/TR, 6'4", 213 lbs. Deb: 9/4/52																							
1952	Phi-A	9	10	1	2	1	0	0	1	1	1	.200	.273	.300	573	56	-1	0	0	0	1.000	-0	/1-5	-0.1
1953	Phi-A	58	56	8	11	2	0	0	5	7	11	.196	.286	.232	518	40	-5	0	0	0	1.000	-1	/1-7,O-2(0-0-2)	-0.6
Total	2	67	66	9	13	3	0	0	6	8	12	.197	.284	.242	526	42	-5	0	0	0	1.000	-1	/1-12,O-2(0-0-2)	-0.7
■ BILLY HAMILTON	Hamilton, William Robert "Sliding Billy" b: 2/16/1866, Newark, N.J. d: 12/16/40, Worcester, Mass. BL/TR, 5'6", 165 lbs. Deb: 7/31/1888 H																							
1888	KC-a	35	129	21	34	4	4	0	11	4		.264	.307	.357	663	106	0	19			.961	-2	O-35(3-0-32)	-0.2
1889	KC-a	137	534	144	161	17	12	3	77	87	41	.301	.413	.395	808	123	19	**111**			.857	-7	*O-137(7-0-130)	1.0
1890	Phi-N	123	496	133	161	13	9	2	49	83	37	.325	.430	.399	829	139	29	**102**			.882	4	*O-123(123-0-0)	2.6
1891	Phi-N	133	527	**141**	**179**	23	7	2	60	**102**	28	**.340**	**.453**	.421	874	151	41	**111**			.907	5	*O-133(133-0-0)	3.8
1892	Phi-N	139	554	132	183	21	7	3	53	81	29	.330	.423	.410	833	152	39	57			.919	14	*O-139(138-1-0)	3.7
1893	Phi-N	82	355	110	135	22	7	5	44	63	7	.380	**.490**	.524	**1014**	**170**	40	43			.937	4	O-82(19-63-0)	3.1
1894	Phi-N	132	558	**198**	225	25	15	4	90	**128**	19	.403	**.522**	.523	1045	156	**65**	**100**			.962	5	*O-132(0-132-0)	4.6
1895	Phi-N	123	517	**166**	201	22	6	7	74	**96**	30	.389	.490	.495	985	154	49	**97**			.913	-1	*O-123(3-120-0)	3.2
1896	Bos-N	131	524	153	192	24	10	3	55	**110**	29	.366	**.478**	.468	946	141	38	83			.934	-11	*O-131(6-125-0)	1.5
1897	*Bos-N	127	507	**152**	174	17	5	3	61	**105**		.343	.461	.414	875	124	24	66			.962	-3	*O-126(0-126-0)	1.1
1898	Bos-N	110	417	110	154	16	5	3	50	87		.369	**.480**	.453	**933**	**159**	38	54			.904	-15	*O-110(0-110-0)	1.5
1899	Bos-N	84	297	63	92	7	1	1	33	72		.310	.446	.350	796	109	8	19			.952	-2	O-81(2-78-1)	0.0
1900	Bos-N	136	520	103	173	20	5	1	47	107		.333	.449	.396	845	119	19	32			.947	2	*O-136(0-136-0)	1.1
1901	Bos-N	102	348	71	100	11	2	3	38	64		.287	.404	.356	760	111	8	20			.945	1	O-99(0-98-1)	0.4
Total	14	1594	6283	1697	2164	242	95	40	742	1189	<u>220</u>	.344	.455	.432	888	139	418	914			.926	-6	*O-1587(434-989-164)	27.4
■ KEN HAMLIN	Hamlin, Kenneth Lee b: 5/18/35, Detroit, Mich. BR/TR, 5'10", 170 lbs. Deb: 6/17/57																							
1957	Pit-N	2	1	0	0	0	0	0	0	0	0	.000	.000	.000	0	-99	-0	0	0	0	1.000	0	/S-1	0.0
1959	Pit-N	3	8	1	1	0	0	0	0	2	1	.125	.300	.125	425	19	-1	0	0	0	1.000	-1	/S-3	-0.2
1960	KC-A	140	428	51	96	10	2	2	24	44	48	.224	.298	.271	569	55	-26	1	1	-0	.955	-41	*S-139	-5.8
1961	LA-A	42	91	4	19	3	0	1	5	11	9	.209	.301	.275	576	49	-6	0	1	-0	.963	13	S-39	0.8
1962	Was-A	98	292	29	74	12	0	3	22	22	22	.253	.306	.325	631	70	-12	7	7	-1	.963	-11	S-87/2-2	-1.8
1965	Was-A	117	362	45	99	21	1	4	22	33	45	.273	.336	.370	706	102	1	8	2	1	.976	-29	2-77,S-47/3-1	-2.0
1966	Was-A	66	158	13	34	7	1	1	16	13	21	.215	.275	.291	566	63	-7	1	0	0	.963	6	2-50/3-1	0.2
Total	7	468	1340	143	323	53	4	11	89	125	146	.241	.307	.311	618	71	-52	17	11	-0	.959	-63	S-316,2-129/3-2	-8.8
■ STEVE HAMMOND	Hammond, Steven Benjamin b: 5/9/57, Atlanta, Ga. BL/TR, 6'2", 190 lbs. Deb: 6/28/82 F																							
1982	KC-A	46	126	14	29	5	1	1	11	4	18	.230	.254	.310	563	54	-8	0	1	-0	1.000	3	O-37(0-0-37)/D-1	-0.8
■ JACK HAMMOND	Hammond, Walter Charles "Wobby" b: 2/26/1891, Amsterdam, N.Y. d: 3/4/42, Kenosha, Wis. BR/TR, 5'11", 170 lbs. Deb: 4/15/15																							
1915	Cle-A	35	84	9	18	2	1	0	4	1	19	.214	.224	.262	485	44	-6	0	1	-0	.957	-8	2-19	-1.5
1922	Cle-A	1	4	1	1	0	0	0	0	0	0	.250	.250	.250	500	30	-0	0	0	0	.333	-2	/2-1	-0.2
	Pit-N	9	11	3	3	0	0	0	0	1	0	.273	.333	.273	606	57	-1	0	0	0	1.000	2	/2-4	0.1
Total	2	45	99	13	22	2	1	0	4	2	19	.222	.238	.263	500	45	-7	0	1	-0	.943	-8	/2-24	-1.6
■ JEFFREY HAMMONDS	Hammonds, Jeffrey Bryan b: 3/5/71, Plainfield, N.J. BR/TR, 6', 195 lbs. Deb: 6/25/93 Career OF: (203-LF 120-CF 346-RF)																							
1993	Bal-A	33	105	10	32	8	0	3	19	2	16	.305	.318	.467	784	104	0	4	0	1	.961	1	O-23(14-0-10)/D-8	0.1
1994	Bal-A	68	250	45	74	18	2	8	31	17	39	.296	.346	.480	826	105	1	5	0	1	.962	4	O-66(9-0-58)	0.3
1995	Bal-A	57	178	18	43	9	1	4	23	9	30	.242	.282	.371	653	67	-9	4	2	0	.989	1	O-46(0-0-46)/D-5	-0.9
1996	Bal-A	71	248	38	56	10	1	9	27	23	53	.226	.302	.383	685	72	-11	3	3	-0	.980	-0	O-70(64-1-11)/D-1	-1.3
1997	*Bal-A	118	397	71	105	19	3	21	55	32	73	.264	.324	.486	810	111	5	15	1	3	.980	-3	*O-114(31-40-54)/D-4	0.2
1998	Bal-A	63	171	36	46	12	1	6	28	26	38	.269	.375	.456	831	117	5	7	2	1	.980	-6	O-53(7-24-29)/D-7	-0.1
	Cin-N	26	86	14	26	4	1	0	11	13	18	.302	.394	.372	766	102	1	1	1	-0	.985	4	O-25(0-25-0)	0.5
1999	Cin-N	123	262	43	73	13	0	17	41	27	64	.279	.348	.523	871	113	5	3	6	-1	1.000	-11	*O-106(46-21-53)	-1.0
2000	Col-N★	122	454	94	152	24	2	20	106	44	83	.335	.400	.529	928	103	3	14	7	1	.991	-2	*O-118(32-9-85)	-0.3
Total	8	681	2151	369	607	117	11	88	341	193	414	.282	.347	.470	816	101	-1	56	22	5	.982	-12	O-621R/D-25	-2.5
■ GRANNY HAMNER	Hamner, Granville Wilbur b: 4/26/27, Richmond, Va. d: 9/12/93, Philadelphia, Pa. BR/TR, 5'10", 163 lbs. Deb: 9/14/44 F																							
1944	Phi-N	21	77	6	19	1	0	0	5	3	7	.247	.275	.260	535	53	-5	0			.933	6	S-21	0.3
1945	Phi-N	14	41	3	7	2	0	0	6	1	3	.171	.190	.220	410	14	-5	0			.861	3	S-13	-0.1
1946	Phi-N	2	7	0	1	0	0	0	0	0	3	.143	.143	.143	286	-19	-1	0			.857	-1	/S-2	-0.2
1947	Phi-N	2	7	1	2	0	0	0	0	1	0	.286	.375	.286	661	81	-0	0			1.000	0	/S-2	0.0
1948	Phi-N	129	446	42	116	21	5	3	48	22	39	.260	.298	.350	648	76	-16	2			.967	-8	2-87,S-37/3-3	-1.7
1949	Phi-N	154	662	83	174	32	5	6	53	25	47	.263	.290	.353	643	74	-26	6			.961	-0	*S-154	-1.7
1950	*Phi-N	157	637	78	172	27	5	11	82	39	35	.270	.314	.380	694	83	-17	2			.944	-5	*S-157	-1.1
1951	Phi-N	150	589	61	150	23	7	9	72	29	32	.255	.290	.363	653	76	-22	10	5	0	.958	-2	*S-150	-1.4
1952	Phi-N★	151	596	74	164	30	5	17	87	27	51	.275	.307	.428	734	103	-0	7	3	0	.951	-4	*S-151	0.6
1953	Phi-N★	154	609	90	168	30	8	21	92	32	28	.276	.313	.455	768	98	-4	2	1	0	.970	-8	2-93,S-71	0.0
1954	Phi-N★	152	596	83	178	39	11	13	89	53	44	.299	.356	.466	822	112	10	1	2	-0	.978	-23	*2-152/S-1	-0.2
1955	Phi-N	104	405	57	104	12	4	5	43	41	30	.257	.327	.343	670	79	-11	0	1	-0	.960	-36	2-82,S-32	-3.9
1956	Phi-N	122	401	42	90	24	3	4	42	30	42	.224	.278	.329	608	64	-21	2	0	0	.937	-13	*S-110,2-11/P-3	-2.4
1957	Phi-N	133	502	59	114	19	5	10	62	34	42	.227	.276	.345	621	68	-24	3	1	0	.963	-39	*2-125/S-5,P-1	-5.5
1958	Phi-N	35	133	18	40	7	3	2	18	8	16	.301	.340	.444	784	107	1	0	0	0	.984	-3	3-22,2-11/S-3	-0.1
1959	Phi-N	21	64	10	19	4	0	2	6	5	5	.297	.348	.453	801	109	1	0	1	-0	.947	-7	S-15/3-1	-0.5
	Cle-A	27	67	4	11	1	1	1	3	1	8	.164	.176	.254	430	17	-8	0	0	0	.960	-2	S-10/2-7,3-5	-0.9
1962	KC-A	3	0	0	0	0	0	0	0	0	0	—	—	—	—	—	0	0	0	0	1.000	0	/P-3	0.0
Total	17	1531	5839	711	1529	272	62	104	708	351	432	.262	.304	.383	688	84	-148	35	<u>14</u>		.946	-139	S-934,2-568/3-31,P	-18.8
■ GARVIN HAMNER	Hamner, Wesley Garvin b: 3/18/24, Richmond, Va. BR/TR, 5'11", 172 lbs. Deb: 4/17/45 F																							
1945	Phi-N	32	101	12	20	3	0	0	5	7	9	.198	.250	.228	478	34	-9	2			.962	-4	2-21/S-9,3-1	-1.2
■ IKE HAMPTON	Hampton, Isaac Bernard b: 8/22/51, Camden, S.C. BB/TR (BR 1978-79), 6'1", 185 lbs. Deb: 9/12/74																							
1974	NY-N	4	4	0	0	0	0	0	1	0	1	.000	.000	.000	0	-99	-1	0	0	0	1.000	-0	/C-1	-0.1
1975	Cal-A	31	66	8	10	3	0	0	4	7	19	.152	.243	.197	440	28	-6	0	0	0	.947	-5	C-28/S-2,3-1	-1.0
1976	Cal-A	3	2	0	0	0	0	0	0	0	0	.000	.000	.000	0	-99	-1	0	0	0	1.000	1	/C-2,S-1	0.0
1977	Cal-A	52	44	5	13	1	0	3	9	2	10	.295	.340	.523	863	137	2	0	0	0	.968	1	C-47/D-2	0.3
1978	Cal-A	19	14	2	3	0	1	1	4	2	7	.214	.313	.571	884	149	1	1	0	0	.905	1	C-13/1-1,D-4	0.2
1979	Cal-A	4	5	0	2	0	0	0	0	0	1	.400	.400	.400	800	121	0	0	0	0	1.000	1	/1-2	0.1
Total	6	113	135	15	28	4	1	4	18	11	38	.207	.277	.341	618	75	-5	1	0	0	.953	-2	/C-91,D-6,1-3,S3	-0.5

■ BERT HAMRIC Hamric, Odbert Herman b: 3/1/28, Clarksburg, W.Va. d: 8/8/84, Springboro, Ohio BL/TR, 6', 165 lbs. Deb: 4/24/55

YEAR	TM/L	G	AB	R	H	2B	3B	HR	RBI	BB	SO	AVG	OBP	SLG	OPS	OPS+	BR+	SB	CS	SBR	FA	FR	G/POS	TPR
1955	Bro-N	2	1	0	0	0	0	0	0	0	1	.000	.000	.000	0	-97	-0	0	0	0	.000	0	H	0.0
1958	Bal-A	8	8	0	1	0	0	0	0	0	6	.125	.125	.125	250	-33	-1	0	0	0	.000	0	H	-0.2
Total	2	10	9	0	1	0	0	0	0	0	7	.111	.111	.111	222	-41	-2	0	0	0		0	-0,-0	-0.2

■ RAY HAMRICK Hamrick, Raymond Bernard b: 8/1/21, Nashville, Tenn. BR/TR, 5'11.5", 160 lbs. Deb: 8/14/43

YEAR	TM/L	G	AB	R	H	2B	3B	HR	RBI	BB	SO	AVG	OBP	SLG	OPS	OPS+	BR+	SB	CS	SBR	FA	FR	G/POS	TPR
1943	Phi-N	44	160	12	32	3	1	0	9	8	28	.200	.238	.231	469	37	-13	0			.960	-11	2-31,S-12	-2.4
1944	Phi-N	74	292	22	60	10	1	1	23	23	34	.205	.268	.257	525	50	-19	1			.948	20	S-74	0.7
Total	2	118	452	34	92	13	2	1	32	31	62	.204	.258	.248	506	46	-32	1			.946	9	/S-86,2-31	-1.7

■ BUDDY HANCKEN Hancken, Morris Medlock b: 8/30/14, Birmingham, Ala. BR/TR, 6'1", 175 lbs. Deb: 5/14/40 C

YEAR	TM/L	G	AB	R	H	2B	3B	HR	RBI	BB	SO	AVG	OBP	SLG	OPS	OPS+	BR+	SB	CS	SBR	FA	FR	G/POS	TPR
1940	Phi-A	1	0	0	0	0	0	0	0	0	0	—	—	—	—	—	0	0	0	0	1.000	-0	/C-1	0.0

■ FRED HANCOCK Hancock, Fred James b: 3/28/20, Allenport, Pa. d: 3/12/86, Clearwater, Fla. BR/TR, 5'8", 170 lbs. Deb: 4/26/49

YEAR	TM/L	G	AB	R	H	2B	3B	HR	RBI	BB	SO	AVG	OBP	SLG	OPS	OPS+	BR+	SB	CS	SBR	FA	FR	G/POS	TPR
1949	Chi-A	39	52	7	7	2	1	0	9	8	9	.135	.262	.212	474	27	-6	0	1	-0	.978	-3	S-27/3-3,O-1(0-0-1)	-0.8

■ GARRY HANCOCK Hancock, Ronald Garry b: 1/23/54, Tampa, Fla. BL/TL, 6', 175 lbs. Deb: 7/16/78 Career OF: (45-LF 33-CF 70-RF)

YEAR	TM/L	G	AB	R	H	2B	3B	HR	RBI	BB	SO	AVG	OBP	SLG	OPS	OPS+	BR+	SB	CS	SBR	FA	FR	G/POS	TPR
1978	Bos-A	38	80	10	18	3	0	0	4	1	12	.225	.235	.262	497	36	-7	0	0	0	1.000	-0	O-19(4-5-10),D-13	-0.8
1980	Bos-A	46	115	9	33	6	0	4	19	3	11	.287	.305	.443	749	97	-1	0	3	-1	.963	-2	O-27(6-20-1),D-12	-0.5
1981	Bos-A	26	45	4	7	3	0	0	3	2	4	.156	.191	.222	414	18	-5	0	0	0	1.000	-0	/O-8(0-5-3),D-4	-0.5
1982	Bos-A	11	14	3	0	0	0	0	0	1	1	.000	.067	.000	67	-75	-3	0	0	0	1.000	-2	/O-7(0-0-7)	-0.6
1983	Oak-A	101	256	29	70	7	3	8	30	5	13	.273	.290	.418	708	98	-2	2	0	0	.981	-9	O-67R,1-27/D-9	-1.4
1984	Oak-A	51	60	2	13	2	0	0	8	0	1	.217	.217	.250	467	31	-6	0	0	0	1.000	-5	O-18L/1-4,P-1,D-5	-1.1
Total	6	273	570	57	141	21	3	12	64	12	42	.247	.264	.358	622	71	-23	2	3	-1	.982	-19	O-146R/D-43,1-31,P	-4.9

■ MIKE HANDIBOE Handiboe, Aloysius James "Coalyard Mike" b: 7/21/1887, Washington, D.C. d: 1/31/53, Savannah, Ga. BL/TL, 5'10", 155 lbs. Deb: 9/8/11

YEAR	TM/L	G	AB	R	H	2B	3B	HR	RBI	BB	SO	AVG	OBP	SLG	OPS	OPS+	BR+	SB	CS	SBR	FA	FR	G/POS	TPR
1911	NY-A	5	15	0	1	0	0	0	0	0	2	.067	.176	.067	243	-29	-3	0			1.000	-0	/O-4(2-0-2)	-0.3

■ GENE HANDLEY Handley, Eugene Louis b: 11/25/14, Kennett, Mo. BR/TR, 5'10.5", 165 lbs. Deb: 4/16/46 F

YEAR	TM/L	G	AB	R	H	2B	3B	HR	RBI	BB	SO	AVG	OBP	SLG	OPS	OPS+	BR+	SB	CS	SBR	FA	FR	G/POS	TPR
1946	Phi-A	89	251	31	63	8	5	0	21	22	25	.251	.311	.323	634	78	-8	8	3	1	.947	-17	2-68/3-4,S-1	-2.2
1947	Phi-A	36	90	10	23	2	1	0	8	10	2	.256	.330	.300	630	74	-3	1	0	0	.973	-5	2-17,3-10/S-1	-0.8
Total	2	125	341	41	86	10	6	0	29	32	27	.252	.316	.317	633	77	-10	9	3	1	.952	-23	/2-85,3-14,S-2	-3.0

■ LEE HANDLEY Handley, Lee Elmer "Jeep" b: 7/31/13, Clarion, Iowa d: 4/8/70, Pittsburgh, Pa. BR/TR, 5'7", 160 lbs. Deb: 4/15/36 F

YEAR	TM/L	G	AB	R	H	2B	3B	HR	RBI	BB	SO	AVG	OBP	SLG	OPS	OPS+	BR+	SB	CS	SBR	FA	FR	G/POS	TPR
1936	Cin-N	24	78	10	24	1	0	2	8	7	16	.308	.365	.397	762	112	1	3			.926	-0	2-16/3-7	0.2
1937	Pit-N	127	480	59	120	21	12	3	37	37	40	.250	.305	.363	668	81	-14	5			.950	-14	*2-126/3-1	-2.0
1938	Pit-N	139	570	91	153	25	8	6	51	53	31	.268	.332	.372	704	93	-6	7			.948	9	*3-136	0.8
1939	Pit-N	101	376	43	107	14	5	1	42	32	20	.285	.341	.356	697	89	-6	**17**			.936	-10	*3-100	-1.2
1940	Pit-N	98	302	50	85	7	4	1	19	27	16	.281	.340	.341	681	89	-4	7			.925	1	3-80/2-2	-0.1
1941	Pit-N	124	459	59	132	18	4	0	33	35	22	.288	.338	.344	682	93	-4	16			.947	-1	*3-114	-0.1
1944	Pit-N	40	86	7	19	2	0	0	5	3	5	.221	.247	.244	491	37	-7	1			.947	2	2-19,3-11/S-3	-0.4
1945	Pit-N	98	312	39	93	16	2	1	32	20	16	.298	.340	.372	712	94	-3	7			.947	15	3-79	1.3
1946	Pit-N	116	416	43	99	8	7	1	28	29	20	.238	.289	.298	587	65	-19	4			.958	13	*3-102/2-3	-0.7
1947	Phi-N	101	277	17	70	10	3	0	42	24	18	.253	.312	.310	623	68	-12	1			.975	2	3-83/2-3,S-1	-1.0
Total	10	968	3356	418	902	122	45	15	297	267	204	.269	.323	.345	669	84	-73	68			.949	16	3-713,2-169/S-4	-3.2

■ HARRY HANEBRINK Hanebrink, Harry Aloysius b: 11/12/27, St.Louis, Mo. d: 9/9/96, Bridgeton, Mo. BL/TR, 6', 165 lbs. Deb: 5/3/53 Career OF: (24-LF 0-CF 10-RF)

YEAR	TM/L	G	AB	R	H	2B	3B	HR	RBI	BB	SO	AVG	OBP	SLG	OPS	OPS+	BR+	SB	CS	SBR	FA	FR	G/POS	TPR
1953	Mil-N	51	80	8	19	1	1	1	8	6	8	.237	.291	.313	603	61	-5	1	0	0	.979	4	2-21/3-1	0.0
1957	Mil-N	6	7	0	2	0	0	0	0	1	2	.286	.375	.286	661	87	-0	0	0	0	1.000	1	/3-2	0.1
1958	*Mil-N	63	133	14	25	3	0	4	10	13	9	.188	.270	.301	571	56	-9	0	1	-0	.982	-0	O-33(24-0-9)/3-7	-1.1
1959	Phi-N	57	97	10	25	3	1	1	7	2	12	.258	.273	.340	613	61	-5	0	0	0	.889	-6	2-15/3-9,O-1(0-0-1)	-1.1
Total	4	177	317	32	71	7	2	6	25	22	31	.224	.279	.315	594	60	-19	1	1	-0	.959	-2	/2-36,O-34L,3-19	-2.1

■ FRED HANEY Haney, Fred Girard "Pudge" b: 4/25/1898, Albuquerque, N.Mex d: 11/9/77, Beverly Hills, Cal. BR/TR, 5'6", 170 lbs. Deb: 4/18/22 MC Career OF: (0-LF 1-CF 0-RF)

YEAR	TM/L	G	AB	R	H	2B	3B	HR	RBI	BB	SO	AVG	OBP	SLG	OPS	OPS+	BR+	SB	CS	SBR	FA	FR	G/POS	TPR
1922	Det-A	81	213	41	75	7	4	0	25	32	14	.352	.439	.423	862	129	11	3	8	-2	.937	2	3-53,1-11/S-2	1.3
1923	Det-A	142	503	85	142	13	4	4	67	45	23	.282	.347	.348	695	85	-10	13	5	1	.955	-2	2-69,3-55,S-16	-0.5
1924	Det-A	86	256	54	79	11	1	1	30	39	13	.309	.400	.371	771	101	2	7	4	0	.933	4	3-59/S-4,2-3	1.0
1925	Det-A	114	398	84	111	15	3	0	40	66	29	.279	.384	.332	716	84	-7	11	1	2	.953	-2	*3-106	0.0
1926	Bos-A	138	462	47	102	15	7	0	52	74	28	.221	.330	.284	613	63	-23	13	6	1	.957	6	*3-137	-0.8
1927	Bos-A	47	116	23	32	4	1	3	12	25	14	.276	.404	.405	809	113	3	4	1	1	.936	-2	3-34/O-1(0-1-0)	0.3
	Chi-N	4	3	0	0	0	0	0	0	0	0	.000	.000	.000	0	-99	-1	0			.000	0	H	-0.1
1929	StL-N	10	26	4	3	1	1	0	2	1	2	.115	.179	.231	409	1	-4	0			.958	3	/3-6	-0.1
Total	7	622	1977	338	544	66	21	8	228	282	123	.275	.368	.342	710	87	-28	51	25		.949	8	3-450/2-72,S-22,1O	1.1

■ TODD HANEY Haney, Todd Michael b: 7/30/65, Waco, Tex. BR/TR, 5'9", 165 lbs. Deb: 9/9/92 Career OF: (1-LF 0-CF 0-RF)

YEAR	TM/L	G	AB	R	H	2B	3B	HR	RBI	BB	SO	AVG	OBP	SLG	OPS	OPS+	BR+	SB	CS	SBR	FA	FR	G/POS	TPR
1992	Mon-N	7	10	0	3	1	0	0	1	0	0	.300	.300	.400	700	97	-0	0	0	0	1.000	-0	/2-5	0.0
1994	Chi-N	17	37	6	6	0	0	1	2	3	3	.162	.244	.243	487	28	-4	2	1	0	.979	-0	2-11/3-3	-0.4
1995	Chi-N	25	73	11	30	8	0	2	6	7	11	.411	.463	.603	1065	182	9	0	0	0	.978	3	2-17/3-4	1.2
1996	Chi-N	49	82	11	11	1	0	0	3	7	15	.134	.202	.146	349	-6	-13	1	0	0	.978	7	2-23/3-4,S-3	-0.4
1998	NY-N	3	3	0	0	0	0	0	0	1	0	.000	.250	.000	250	-27	-1	0	0	0	.000	-1	/2-1,O-1(1-0-0)	-0.2
Total	5	101	205	28	50	10	0	3	12	18	29	.244	.308	.337	645	70	-8	3	1	0	.979	9	/2-57,3-11,S-3,O-1L	0.2

■ LARRY HANEY Haney, Wallace Larry b: 11/19/42, Charlottesville, Va BR/TR, 6'2", 195 lbs. Deb: 7/27/66 FC

YEAR	TM/L	G	AB	R	H	2B	3B	HR	RBI	BB	SO	AVG	OBP	SLG	OPS	OPS+	BR+	SB	CS	SBR	FA	FR	G/POS	TPR
1966	Bal-A	20	56	3	9	1	0	1	3	1	15	.161	.190	.232	422	21	-6	0	0	0	.985	3	C-20	-0.2
1967	Bal-A	58	164	13	44	11	0	3	20	6	28	.268	.294	.390	684	101	-0	1	0	0	.991	2	C-57	0.5
1968	Bal-A	38	89	5	21	3	1	1	5	0	19	.236	.236	.326	562	69	-4	0	0	0	.994	4	C-32	0.1
1969	Sea-A	22	59	3	15	3	0	2	7	6	12	.254	.323	.407	730	105	0	1	1	-0	.956	-2	C-20	-0.1
	Oak-A	53	86	8	13	4	0	2	12	7	19	.151	.223	.267	491	38	-7	0	0	0	.994	-0	C-53	-0.7
	Yr	75	145	11	28	7	0	4	19	13	31	.193	.264	.324	588	66	-7	1	1	-0	.979	-2	C-73	-0.8
1970	Oak-A	2	2	2	0	0	0	0	0	2	1	.000	.500	.000	500	51	0	0	0	0	1.000	0	/C-1	0.0
1972	Oak-A	5	4	0	0	0	0	0	0	0	1	.000	.000	.000	0	-99	-1	0	0	0	.800	-1	/C-4,2-1	-0.3
1973	Oak-A	2	2	0	1	0	0	0	0	0	0	.500	.500	.500	1000	192	0	0	0	0	1.000	-0	/C-2	0.0
	StL-N	2	1	0	0	0	0	0	0	0	1	.000	.000	.000	0	-99	-0	0	0	0	1.000	0	/C-2	0.0
1974	*Oak-A	76	121	12	20	4	0	2	3	3	18	.165	.185	.248	433	25	-12	1	0	0	.992	10	C-73/3-3,1-2	0.0
1975	Oak-A	47	26	3	5	0	0	1	2	1	4	.192	.222	.308	530	50	-2	0	0	0	1.000	7	C-43/3-4	0.6
1976	Oak-A	88	177	12	40	2	0	0	10	13	26	.226	.283	.237	520	56	-10	0	1	-0	.974	9	C-87	0.2
1977	Mil-A	63	127	7	29	2	0	0	10	5	30	.228	.258	.244	502	38	-11	0	0	0	.985	8	C-63	-0.1
1978	Mil-A	4	5	0	1	0	0	0	1	0	1	.200	.200	.200	400	13	-1	0	0	0	1.000	-0	/C-4	-0.1
Total	12	480	919	68	198	30	1	12	73	44	175	.215	.254	.289	543	57	-53	3	2	-0	.985	40	C-461/3-7,1-2,2-1	-0.1

■ CHARLIE HANFORD Hanford, Charles Joseph b: 6/3/1881, Tunstall, England d: 7/19/63, Trenton, N.J. BR/TR, 5'6.5", 145 lbs. Deb: 4/13/14

YEAR	TM/L	G	AB	R	H	2B	3B	HR	RBI	BB	SO	AVG	OBP	SLG	OPS	OPS+	BR+	SB	CS	SBR	FA	FR	G/POS	TPR
1914	Buf-F	155	597	83	174	28	13	12	90	32	81	.291	.332	.442	774	107	-5	37			.973	10	*O-155(0-155-0)	-0.7
1915	Chi-F	77	179	27	43	4	5	0	22	12	28	.240	.295	.318	614	77	-9	10			.971	-4	O-43(10-1-32)	-1.6
Total	2	232	776	110	217	32	18	12	112	44	109	.280	.323	.414	737	101	-14	47			.972	6	O-198(10-156-32)	-2.3

■ JAY HANKINS Hankins, Jay Nelson b: 11/7/35, St.Louis Co., Mo. BL/TR, 5'7", 170 lbs. Deb: 4/15/61

YEAR	TM/L	G	AB	R	H	2B	3B	HR	RBI	BB	SO	AVG	OBP	SLG	OPS	OPS+	BR+	SB	CS	SBR	FA	FR	G/POS	TPR
1961	KC-A	76	173	23	32	0	3	3	6	8	17	.185	.225	.272	497	32	-17	2	0	0	.970	-10	O-65(23-31-14)	-2.9
1963	KC-A	10	34	2	6	0	1	1	4	0	3	.176	.176	.324	500	35	-3	0	1	-0	.952	1	/O-9(0-9-0)	-0.3
Total	2	86	207	25	38	0	4	4	10	8	20	.184	.218	.280	498	32	-20	2	1	0	.967	-10	/O-74(23-40-14)	-3.2

YEAR	TM/L	G	AB	R	H	2B	3B	HR	RBI	BB	SO	AVG	OBP	SLG	OPS	OPS+	BR+	SB	CS	SBR	FA	FR	G/POS	TPR
■ **FRANK HANKINSON**	Hankinson, Frank Edward b: 4/29/1856, New York, N.Y. d: 4/5/11, Palisades Park, N.J BR/TR, 5′11″, 168 lbs. Deb: 5/1/1878 Career OF: (26-LF 8-CF 1-RF)																							
1878	Chi-N	58	240	38	64	8	3	1	27	5	36	.267	.282	.338	619	96	-2				.875	8	*3-57/P-1	0.8
1879	Chi-N	44	171	14	31	4	0	0	8	2	14	.181	.191	.205	395	29	-13				.933	6	P-26,O-14(10-4-0)/3-5	-0.4
1880	Cle-N	69	263	32	55	7	4	1	19	1	23	.209	.212	.278	490	66	-9				.844	-12	*3-56,O-12L/P-4	-2.0
1881	Tro-N	85	321	34	62	15	0	1	19	10	41	.193	.218	.249	467	44	-20				.907	7	*3-84/S-1	-1.0
1883	NY-N	94	337	40	74	13	6	2	30	19	38	.220	.261	.312	573	74	-10				.870	-4	*3-93/O-1(0-0-1)	-1.1
1884	NY-N	105	389	44	90	16	7	2	43	23	59	.231	.274	.324	598	85	-7				.871	-1	*3-105/O-1(0-1-0)	-0.5
1885	NY-a	94	362	43	81	12	2	2	44	12		.224	.251	.285	535	75	-9				**.906**	18	*3-94/P-1	0.9
1886	NY-a	136	522	66	126	14	5	2	63	49		.241	.306	.299	605	94	-2	10			.873	25	*3-136	2.3
1887	NY-a	127	550	79	175	29	11	1	71	38		.318	.318	.373	691	97	-2	19			.864	8	*3-127	0.7
1888	KC-a	37	155	20	27	4	1	1	20	11		.174	.229	.232	461	45	-10	2			.947	-5	2-13/S-9,O-7L,31	-1.3
Total	10	849	3310	410	785	122	39	13	344	170	211	.237	.267	.301	568	76	-84	31			.875	50	3-764/O-35L,P-32,2S1	-1.6
■ **NED HANLON**	Hanlon, Edward Hugh b: 8/22/1857, Montville, Conn. d: 4/14/37, Baltimore, Md. BL/TR, 5′9.5″, 170 lbs. Deb: 5/1/1880 MH Career OF: (119-LF 1130-CF 1-RF)																							
1880	Cle-N	73	280	30	69	10	3	0	32	11	30	.246	.275	.304	578	98	-0				.804	-3	*O-69(67-2-0)/S-4	-0.7
1881	Det-N	76	305	63	85	14	8	2	28	22	11	.279	.327	.397	724	122	7				.897	-5	*O-74(2-72-0)/S-2	-0.1
1882	Det-N	82	347	68	80	18	6	5	38	26	25	.231	.284	.360	644	105	3				.887	14	*O-82(0-82-0)/2-1	1.2
1883	Det-N	100	413	65	100	13	2	1	40	34	44	.242	.300	.291	590	84	-6				.884	2	*O-90(2-88-0),2-11	-0.6
1884	Det-N	114	450	86	119	18	6	5	39	40	52	.264	.324	.364	689	124	14				.874	13	*O-114(0-114-0)	2.1
1885	Det-N	105	424	93	128	18	8	1	29	47	18	.302	.372	.389	761	146	23				.863	4	*O-105(0-104-0)	2.2
1886	Det-N	126	494	105	116	6	6	4	60	57	39	.235	.314	.296	610	84	-8	50			.929	-4	*O-126(0-126-0)/2-1	-1.5
1887	*Det-N	118	501	79	159	13	7	4	69	30	24	.317	.320	.357	677	85	-10	69			.904	3	*O-118(1-117-0)	-0.9
1888	Det-N	109	459	64	122	6	8	5	39	15	32	.266	.295	.346	641	104	1	38			.919	-6	*O-109(0-109-0)	-0.8
1889	Pit-N	116	461	81	110	14	10	2	37	58	25	.239	.326	.325	652	91	-3	53			.919	-3	*O-116(0-116-0),M	-0.8
1890	Pit-P	118	472	106	131	16	6	1	44	80	24	.278	.389	.343	732	105	10	65			.911	-2	*O-118(0-118-0),M	0.3
1891	Pit-N	119	455	87	121	12	8	0	60	48	30	.266	.341	.327	669	97	-0	54			.881	0	*O-119(39-80-0)/S-1,M	-0.3
1892	Bal-N	11	43	3	7	1	1	0	2	3	3	.163	.217	.233	450	35	-3	0			.786	-0	O-11(8-2-1),M	-0.5
Total	13	1267	5104	930	1347	159	79	30	517	471	357	.264	.325	.340	664	102	27	329			.891	14	*O-1251C/2-13,S-7	-0.4
■ **BILL HANLON**	Hanlon, William Joseph "Big Bill" b: 6/24/1876, Los Angeles, Cal. d: 11/23/05, Los Angeles, Cal. 6′, Deb: 4/16/03																							
1903	Chi-N	8	21	4	2	0	0	0	2	6		.095	.296	.095	392	14	-2	1			.980	-0	/1-8	-0.2
■ **JOHN HANNA**	Hanna, John b: 11/3/1863, Philadelphia, Pa. d: 11/7/30, Philadelphia, Pa. Deb: 5/23/1884																							
1884	Was-a	23	76	8	5	0	0	0		6		.066	.134	.066	200	-37	-11				.874	0	C-18/O-6(1-1-4)	-0.9
	Ric-a	22	67	6	13	2	1	0		0		.194	.206	.254	460	50	-4				.924	4	C-21/S-1	0.2
	Yr	45	143	14	18	2	1	0		6		.126	.167	.154	321	6	-14				.900	4	C-39/O-6(1-1-4),S-1	-0.7
■ **TRUCK HANNAH**	Hannah, James Harrison b: 6/5/1889, Larimore, N.D. d: 4/27/82, Fountain Valley, Cal. BR/TR, 6′1″, 190 lbs. Deb: 4/15/18																							
1918	NY-A	90	250	24	55	6	0	2	21	51	25	.220	.361	.268	629	88	-1	5			.974	3	C-88	1.0
1919	NY-A	75	227	14	54	8	3	1	20	22	19	.238	.313	.313	626	76	-7	0			**.984**	-9	C-73/1-1	-1.0
1920	NY-A	79	259	24	64	11	1	2	25	24	35	.247	.313	.320	634	66	-13	2	0	0	.961	-6	C-78	-1.1
Total	3	244	736	62	173	25	4	5	66	97	79	.235	.331	.300	631	76	-21	7	0		.973	-11	C-239/1-1	-1.1
■ **PAT HANNIFAN**	Hannifan, Patrick James b: 4/20/1866, Halifax, N.S., Can. d: 11/5/08, Springfield, Mass. TL, Deb: 4/29/1897																							
1897	Bro-N	10	20	4	5	0	0	0	2	1		.250	.375	.250	625	71	-1	4			.867	2	/O-3(1-2-0),2-2	0.1
■ **JACK HANNIFIN**	Hannifin, John Joseph b: 2/25/1883, Holyoke, Mass. d: 10/27/45, Northampton, Mass. BR/TR, 5′11″, 167 lbs. Deb: 4/19/06 Career OF: (2-LF 2-CF 4-RF)																							
1906	Phi-A	1	1	0	1	0	0	0	0	0		1.000	1.000	1.000	2000	511	0	0			.000	0	H	0.0
	NY-N	10	30	4	6	0	1	0	3	2		.200	.250	.267	517	60	-1	1			.903	-1	/S-6,3-3,2-1	-0.2
1907	NY-N	56	149	16	34	7	3	1	15	15		.228	.303	.336	639	97	-1	6			.996	-4	1-29,3-10/S-9,O-2C	-0.5
1908	NY-N	1	2	0	0	0	0	0	0	0		.000	.000	.000	0	-95	-0	0			.000	-0	/O-1(0-0-1)	-0.1
	Bos-N	90	257	30	53	6	2	2	22	28		.206	.284	.268	553	78	-6	7			.930	5	3-35,2-22,S-15,/O-7L	0.0
	Yr	91	259	30	53	6	2	2	22	28		.205	.282	.266	549	77	-6	7			.930	5	3-35,2-22,S-15,/O-8R	-0.1
Total	3	158	439	50	94	13	6	3	40	45		.214	.289	.292	580	84	-8	14			.937	0	/3-48,S-30,1-29,2O	-0.8
■ **DAVE HANSEN**	Hansen, David Andrew b: 11/24/68, Long Beach, Cal. BL/TR, 6′, 195 lbs. Deb: 9/16/90																							
1990	LA-N	5	7	0	1	0	0	0	1	0	3	.143	.143	.143	286	-22	-1	0	0	0	.500	-1	/3-2	-0.2
1991	LA-N	53	56	3	15	4	0	1	5	2	12	.268	.293	.393	686	93	-1	1	0	0	1.000	2	3-21/S-1	0.1
1992	LA-N	132	341	30	73	11	0	6	22	34	49	.214	.287	.299	586	67	-15	0	2	-1	**.968**	7	*3-108	-0.9
1993	LA-N	84	105	13	38	3	0	4	30	21	13	.362	.468	.505	973	170	12	0	1	-0	.927	-1	3-18	1.1
1994	LA-N	40	44	3	15	3	0	0	5	5	5	.341	.408	.409	817	122	2	0	0	0	.857	-1	/3-7	0.1
1995	*LA-N	100	181	19	52	10	0	1	14	28	28	.287	.386	.359	745	107	3	0	0	0	.933	-6	3-58	-0.3
1996	*LA-N	80	104	7	23	1	0	0	6	11	22	.221	.296	.231	526	45	-8	0	0	0	.962	-0	3-19/1-8	-0.9
1997	Chi-N	90	151	19	47	8	2	3	21	31	32	.311	.432	.450	882	128	8	1	2	-0	.922	-9	3-51/1-4,2-1	-0.2
1999	LA-N	100	107	14	27	8	1	2	17	26	20	.252	.407	.402	809	112	3	0	0	0	.982	-1	1-20,3-13/O-2R,D-2	0.1
2000	LA-N	102	121	18	35	6	2	8	26	26	32	.289	.415	.570	985	153	10	0	1	-0	.980	0	1-16,3-16/O-3L,D-5	0.9
Total	10	786	1217	126	326	54	5	25	147	184	216	.268	.366	.382	748	105	14	2	6	-2	.948	-11	3-313/1-48,D-7,O2S	-0.2
■ **DOUG HANSEN**	Hansen, Douglas William b: 12/16/28, Los Angeles, Cal. d: 9/16/99, Orem, Utah BR/TR, 6′, 180 lbs. Deb: 9/4/51																							
1951	Cle-A	3	0	2	0	0	0	0	0	0	0	—	—	—	—	—	0	0	0	0	.000	0	R	0.0
■ **JED HANSEN**	Hansen, Jed Ramon b: 8/19/72, Tacoma, Wash. BR/TR, 6′1″, 195 lbs. Deb: 7/29/97 Career OF: (0-LF 2-CF 0-RF)																							
1997	KC-A	34	94	11	29	6	1	1	14	13	29	.309	.398	.426	824	112	2	3	2	-0	.993	-2	2-31	0.2
1998	KC-A	4	3	0	0	0	0	0	0	0	3	.000	.000	.000	0	-97	-1	0	0	0	1.000	-0	/2-2	-0.1
1999	KC-A	49	79	16	16	1	0	3	5	10	32	.203	.292	.329	621	57	-5	0	1	-0	.989	4	2-21,S-10/3-4,O1D	0.0
Total	3	87	176	27	45	7	1	4	19	23	64	.256	.345	.375	720	84	-4	3	3	-0	.991	2	/2-54,S-10,3-4,DO1	0.1
■ **BOB HANSEN**	Hansen, Robert Joseph b: 5/26/48, Boston, Mass. BL/TL, 6′, 195 lbs. Deb: 5/10/74																							
1974	Mil-A	58	88	8	26	4	1	2	9	3	16	.295	.319	.432	750	115	1	2	1	0	1.000	-0	D-18/1-3	0.1
1976	Mil-A	24	61	4	10	1	0	0	4	6	8	.164	.239	.180	419	24	-6	0	0	0	.000	-0	D-14/1-1	-0.7
Total	2	82	149	12	36	5	1	2	13	9	24	.242	.285	.329	614	78	-4	2	1	0	1.000	-0	/D-32,1-4	-0.6
■ **RON HANSEN**	Hansen, Ronald Lavern b: 4/5/38, Oxford, Neb. BR/TR, 6′3″, 200 lbs. Deb: 4/15/58 C																							
1958	Bal-A	12	19	1	0	0	0	0	1	0	7	.000	.050	.000	50	-90	-5	0	0	0	.943	-0	S-12	-0.5
1959	Bal-A	2	4	0	0	0	0	0	0	1	1	.000	.200	.000	200	-41	-1	0	0	0	.889	1	/S-2	0.0
1960	Bal-A★	153	530	72	135	22	5	22	86	69	94	.255	.343	.440	782	111	8	3	3	-0	.964	6	*S-153	2.6
1961	Bal-A	155	533	51	132	13	2	12	51	66	96	.248	.332	.347	679	85	-11	1	3	-1	.959	12	*S-149/2-7	1.4
1962	Bal-A	71	196	12	34	7	0	3	17	30	36	.173	.289	.255	545	51	-13	0	1	-0	.965	4	S-64	-0.5
1963	Chi-A	144	482	55	109	17	2	13	67	78	74	.226	.334	.351	685	94	-2	1	1	-0	.983	**27**	*S-144	3.8
1964	Chi-A	158	575	85	150	25	3	20	68	73	73	.261	.350	.419	769	116	13	1	0	0	.975	16	*S-158	4.5
1965	Chi-A	162	587	61	138	23	4	11	66	60	73	.235	.308	.344	652	91	-7	1	1	-0	.969	17	*S-161/2-1	2.5
1966	Chi-A	23	74	3	13	1	0	0	4	15	10	.176	.322	.189	511	55	-4	0	1	-0	.946	3	S-23	0.1
1967	Chi-A	157	498	35	116	20	0	8	51	64	51	.233	.320	.321	642	94	-3	0	3	-1	.964	2	*S-157	1.3
1968	Was-A	86	275	28	51	12	0	8	28	35	49	.185	.282	.316	598	84	-5	0	0	0	.963	2	S-81/3-5	0.4
	Chi-A	40	87	7	20	3	0	1	4	11	12	.230	.316	.299	615	86	-1	0	0	0	.959	6	3-29/S-7,2-2	0.6
	Yr	126	362	35	71	15	0	9	32	46	61	.196	.290	.312	602	84	-7	0	0	0	.963	7	S-88,3-34/2-2	1.0
1969	Chi-A	85	185	15	48	6	1	2	22	18	25	.259	.328	.335	664	82	-4	2	0	0	.967	-1	2-26,1-21/S-8,3-7	-0.5
1970	NY-A	59	91	13	27	4	0	4	14	19	9	.297	.423	.473	896	155	8	0	1	-0	.983	-3	S-15,3-11/2-1	0.7
1971	NY-A	61	145	6	30	3	0	2	20	9	27	.207	.253	.269	522	51	-10	0	0	0	.918	-3	3-30/2-9,S-3	-1.3
1972	KC-A	16	30	2	4	0	0	0	2	3	6	.133	.212	.133	345	4	-3	0	0	0	.944	3	/S-6,3-4,2-1	0.0
Total	15	1384	4311	446	1007	156	17	106	501	551	643	.234	.323	.351	675	92	-41	9	14	-3	.968	90	*S-1143/3-86,2-47,1	15.1

YEAR	TM/L	G	AB	R	H	2B	3B	HR	RBI	BB	SO	AVG	OBP	SLG	OPS	OPS+	BR+	SB	CS	SBR	FA	FR	G/POS	TPR
■ **DON HANSKI**	Hanski, Donald Thomas (b: Donald Thomas Hanyzewski) b: 2/27/16, LaPorte, Ind. d: 9/2/57, Worth, Ill. BL/TL, 5'11", 180 lbs. Deb: 5/6/43																							
1943	Chi-A	9	21	1	5	1	0	0	2	0	5	.238	.238	.286	524	53	-1	0	1	-0	.952	-0	/1-5,P-1	-0.2
1944	Chi-A	2	1	0	0	0	0	0	0	0	0	.000	.000	.000	0	-99	-0	0	0	0	.000	-0	/P-2	0.0
Total	2	11	22	1	5	1	0	0	2	0	5	.227	.227	.273	500	46	-2	0	1	-0	—	-1	/1-5,P-3	-0.2
■ **HARRY HANSON**	Hanson, Harry Francis b: 1/17/1896, Elgin, Ill. d: 10/5/66, Savannah, Ga. BR/TR, 5'11", Deb: 7/14/13																							
1913	NY-A	1	2	0	0	0	0	0	0	0	0	.000	.000	.000	0	-99	-0	0			1.000	-0	/C-1	-0.1
■ **CLIFF HAPPENNY**	Happenny, John Clifford b: 5/18/01, Waltham, Mass. d: 12/29/88, Coral Springs, Fla BR/TR, 5'11", 165 lbs. Deb: 7/2/23																							
1923	Chi-A	32	86	7	19	5	0	0	10	3	13	.221	.256	.279	535	41	-8	0	0	0	.947	0	2-19/S-9,3-2	-0.6
■ **BILL HARBIDGE**	Harbidge, William Arthur "Yaller Bill" b: 3/29/1855, Philadelphia, Pa. d: 3/17/24, Philadelphia, Pa. BL/TL, 162 lbs. Deb: 5/15/1875 Career OF: (13-LF 112-CF 47-RF)																							
1875	Har-n	53	208	32	50	3	3	0	26	9	3	.240	.272	.284	556	89	-3	2	4	-1	.871	-0	C-31,O-13R,2-11,/1S	-0.3
1876	Har-N	30	109	11	23	2	1	0	6	3	2	.211	.239	.255	493	59	-5				.799	1	C-24/O-6(0-2-4),1-2	-0.3
1877	Har-N	41	167	18	37	5	2	0	8	3	6	.222	.235	.275	511	68	-5				.881	-4	C-32/O-5C,2-4,3-1	-0.8
1878	Chi-N	54	240	32	71	12	0	0	37	6	13	.296	.313	.346	659	109	2				.878	-8	*C-53/O-8(4-3-1)	-0.5
1879	Chi-N	4	18	2	2	0	0	0	1	0	5	.111	.111	.111	222	-25	-2				.571	-1	/O-4(1-3-0)	-0.3
1880	Tro-N	9	27	3	10	0	1	0	2	0	3	.370	.370	.444	815	166	2				.887	0	/C-9,O-1(0-1-1)	0.2
1882	Tro-N	32	123	11	23	1	1	0	13	10	17	.187	.248	.211	460	52	-6				.836	-4	O-23(0-23-0)/1-6,C-3	-1.0
1883	Phi-N	73	280	32	62	12	3	0	21	24	20	.221	.283	.286	569	81	-4				.796	-11	O-44C,S-11/2-9,C3	-1.4
1884	Cin-U	82	341	59	95	12	5	2		25		.279	.328	.361	689	101	-9				.906	5	*O-80C/S-3,1-2	-0.6
Total	8	325	1305	168	323	44	13	2	<u>88</u>	71	<u>66</u>	.248	.287	.306	593	86	-29				.849	-22	O-171C,C-128/S213	-4.7
■ **SCOTT HARDESTY**	Hardesty, Scott Durbin b: 1/26/1870, Bellville, Ohio d: 10/29/44, Fostoria, Ohio Deb: 8/17/1899																							
1899	NY-N	22	72	4	16	0	0	0	4	1		.222	.243	.222	465	29	-7	2			.895	2	S-20/1-2	-0.3
■ **PAT HARDGROVE**	Hardgrove, William Henry b: 5/10/1895, Palmyra, Kan. d: 1/26/73, Jackson, Miss. BR/TR, 5'10", 158 lbs. Deb: 6/8/18																							
1918	Chi-A	2	2	0	0	0	0	0	0	0	0	.000	.000	.000	0	-99	-0	0			.000	0	H	-0.1
■ **LOU HARDIE**	Hardie, Louis W. b: 8/24/1864, New York, N.Y. d: 3/5/29, Oakland, Cal. BR, 5'11", 180 lbs. Deb: 5/22/1884 Career OF: (6-LF 7-CF 20-RF)																							
1884	Phi-N	3	8	0	3	2	0	0	0	0	2	.375	.375	.625	1000	219	1				.857	-3	/C-3	-0.1
1886	Chi-N	16	51	4	9	0	0	0	3	4	10	.176	.236	.176	413	24	-5	1			.964	-0	C-13/O-2(0-0-2),3-1	-0.4
1890	Bos-N	47	185	17	42	8	0	3	17	18	36	.227	.296	.319	614	73	-7	4			.886	-0	C-25,O-15L/3-7,S1	-0.5
1891	Bal-a	15	56	7	13	0	3	0	1	8	8	.232	.328	.339	667	90	-1	3			1.000	1	O-15(0-3-12)	0.0
Total	4	81	300	28	67	10	3	3	21	30	56	.223	.294	.307	601	71	-12	8			.910	-2	/C-41,O-32R,3-8,1S	-1.0
■ **BUD HARDIN**	Hardin, William Edgar b: 6/14/22, Shelby, N.C. d: 7/28/97, Rancho Santa Fe, Cal. BR/TR, 5'10", 165 lbs. Deb: 4/15/52																							
1952	Chi-N	3	7	1	1	0	0	0	0	0	0	.143	.143	.143	286	-20	-1	0	0	0	1.000	0	/S-2,2-1	-0.1
■ **LOU HARDING**	Harding, Louis Edward "Jumbo" b: 1865, San Francisco, Cal. 5'9.5", 213 lbs. Deb: 10/5/1886																							
1886	StL-a	1	3	0	1	1	0	0	1	0		.333	.333	.667	1000	201	0	0			.889	1	/C-1	0.1
■ **JASON HARDTKE**	Hardtke, Jason Robert b: 9/15/71, Milwaukee, Wis. BB/TR, 5'10", 175 lbs. Deb: 9/8/96 Career OF: (0-LF 0-CF 1-RF)																							
1996	NY-N	19	57	3	11	5	0	0	6	2	12	.193	.233	.281	514	36	-5	0	0	0	1.000	-2	2-18	-0.6
1997	NY-N	30	56	9	15	2	0	2	8	4	6	.268	.328	.411	739	95	-0	1	1	-0	.981	-6	2-21/3-1	-0.6
1998	Chi-N	18	21	2	5	0	0	0	2	2	6	.238	.304	.238	542	44	-2	0	0	0	1.000	-2	/3-7,O-1(0-0-1),D-1	-0.3
Total	3	67	134	14	31	7	0	2	16	8	24	.231	.285	.328	613	62	-7	1	1	-0	.991	-10	/2-39,3-8,D-1,O-1R	-1.5
■ **CARROLL HARDY**	Hardy, Carroll William b: 5/18/33, Sturgis, S.Dak. BR/TR, 6', 185 lbs. Deb: 4/15/58																							
1958	Cle-A	27	49	10	10	3	0	1	6	6	14	.204	.304	.327	630	75	-2	1	2	-0	1.000	1	O-17(0-16-1)	-0.2
1959	Cle-A	32	53	12	11	1	0	0	2	3	7	.208	.250	.226	476	33	-5	1	1	-0	1.000	1	O-15(1-14-0)	-0.5
1960	Cle-A	29	18	7	2	1	0	0	1	2	2	.111	.200	.167	367	0	-3	0	0	0	1.000	-4	O-17(4-9-5)	-0.7
	Bos-A	73	145	26	34	5	2	2	15	17	40	.234	.315	.338	653	74	-5	3	2	-0	.968	-6	O-59(44-8-14)	-1.4
	Yr	102	163	33	36	6	2	2	16	19	42	.221	.302	.319	621	67	-7	3	2	-0	.973	-11	O-76(48-17-19)	-2.1
1961	Bos-A	85	281	46	74	20	2	3	36	26	53	.263	.330	.381	711	87	-5	4	2	0	.961	-1	O-76(20-38-21)	-0.9
1962	Bos-A	115	362	52	78	13	5	8	36	54	68	.215	.321	.345	666	77	-11	3	7	-2	.991	1	*O-105(3-45-64)	-1.7
1963	Hou-N	15	44	5	10	3	0	0	3	3	7	.227	.277	.295	572	69	-2	1	0	0	.947	1	O-10(10-0-0)	-0.2
1964	Hou-N	46	157	13	29	1	1	2	12	8	30	.185	.234	.242	476	36	-13	0	0	0	.990	5	O-41(5-33-4)	-1.1
1967	Min-A	11	8	1	3	0	0	1	2	1	1	.375	.444	.750	1194	229	1	0	0	0	.000	-1	/O-4(1-0-3)	0.0
Total	8	433	1117	172	251	47	10	17	113	120	222	.225	.304	.330	634	72	-44	13	14	-2	.981	-5	O-344(88-163-112)	-6.7
■ **JACK HARDY**	Hardy, John Doolittle b: 6/23/1877, Cleveland, Ohio d: 10/20/21, Cleveland, Ohio BR/TR, 6', 185 lbs. Deb: 8/29/03																							
1903	Cle-A	5	19	1	3	1	0	0	1	1		.158	.200	.211	411	24	-2	1			1.000	-1	/O-5(0-0-5)	-0.3
1907	Chi-N	1	4	0	1	0	0	0	0	0		.250	.250	.250	500	53	-0	0			.909	0	/C-1	0.0
1909	Was-A	10	24	3	4	0	0	0	4	1		.167	.200	.167	367	17	-2	0			.974	-2	/C-9,2-1	-0.4
1910	Was-A	7	8	1	2	0	0	0	0	0		.250	.250	.250	500	59	-0	0			.933	1	/C-4,O-1(1-0-0)	0.0
Total	4	23	55	5	10	1	0	0	5	2		.182	.211	.200	411	28	-5	1			.953	-2	/C-14,O-6(1-0-5),2-1	-0.7
■ **SHAWN HARE**	Hare, Shawn Robert b: 3/26/67, St.Louis, Mo. BL/TL, 6'2", 190 lbs. Deb: 9/6/91 Career OF: (21-LF 0-CF 18-RF)																							
1991	Det-A	9	19	0	1	1	0	0	0	2	1	.053	.143	.105	248	-30	-3	0	0	0	1.000	0	/O-6(0-0-6),D-2	-0.4
1992	Det-A	15	26	0	3	1	0	0	5	2	4	.115	.179	.154	332	-6	-4	0	0	0	1.000	-2	/O-9(3-0-7),1-4	-0.6
1994	NY-N	22	40	7	9	1	1	0	2	4	11	.225	.295	.300	595	56	-3	0	0	0	1.000	-0	O-14(14-0-0)	-0.3
1995	Tex-A	18	24	2	6	1	0	0	2	4	6	.250	.357	.292	649	70	-1	0	0	0	1.000	-1	/O-9(4-0-5),1-1,D-3	-0.2
Total	4	64	109	9	19	4	1	0	9	12	22	.174	.256	.229	486	31	-11	0	0	0	1.000	-3	/O-38L,1-5,D-5	-1.5
■ **GARY HARGIS**	Hargis, Gary Lynn b: 11/2/56, Minneapolis, Minn. BR/TR, 5'11", 165 lbs. Deb: 9/29/79																							
1979	Pit-N	1	0	0	0	0	0	0	0	0	0	—	—	—	—	—	0	0	0	0	.000	0	/R	0.0
■ **BUBBLES HARGRAVE**	Hargrave, Eugene Franklin b: 7/15/1892, New Haven, Ind. d: 2/23/69, Cincinnati, Ohio BR/TR, 5'10.5", 174 lbs. Deb: 9/18/13 F																							
1913	Chi-N	3	3	0	1	0	0	0	1	0	0	.333	.333	.333	667	91	-0	0			1.000	0	/C-2	0.0
1914	Chi-N	23	36	3	8	2	0	0	2	0	4	.222	.222	.278	500	48	-2	2			.930	-4	C-16	-0.6
1915	Chi-N	15	19	2	3	0	1	0	2	1	5	.158	.200	.263	463	40	-1	0			1.000	-1	/C-9	-0.2
1921	Cin-N	93	263	28	76	17	8	1	38	12	15	.289	.327	.426	753	102	0	4	2	0	.973	-7	C-73	-0.2
1922	Cin-N	98	320	49	101	22	10	7	57	26	18	.316	.371	.512	883	128	12	7	4	0	.982	-9	C-87	0.9
1923	Cin-N	118	378	54	126	23	9	10	78	44	22	.333	.419	.521	941	150	28	4	5	-1	.988	3	*C-109	3.6
1924	Cin-N	98	312	42	94	19	10	3	33	30	20	.301	.370	.455	825	122	10	2	2	-0	.983	-1	C-91	1.5
1925	Cin-N	87	273	28	82	13	6	2	33	25	23	.300	.361	.414	775	100	0	4	3	-0	.979	-6	C-84	-0.1
1926	Cin-N	105	326	42	115	22	8	6	62	25	17	**.353**	.406	.525	930	153	24	2			.988	-12	C-93	1.8
1927	Cin-N	102	305	36	94	18	3	0	35	31	18	.308	.376	.387	763	108	4	0			**.988**	-10	C-92	0.1
1928	Cin-N	65	190	19	56	12	3	0	23	13	14	.295	.353	.389	742	95	-1	4			.991	2	C-57	0.4
1930	NY-A	45	108	11	30	7	0	0	12	10	9	.278	.339	.343	682	77	-4	0	0	0	.992	-5	C-34	-0.6
Total	12	852	2533	314	786	155	58	29	376	217	165	.310	.372	.452	824	119	70	29	<u>16</u>		.983	-50	C-747	6.6
■ **PINKY HARGRAVE**	Hargrave, William McKinley b: 1/31/1896, New Haven, Ind. d: 10/3/42, Ft.Wayne, Ind. BB/TR (BR 1923-26), 5'8.5", 180 lbs. Deb: 5/18/23 F																							
1923	Was-A	33	59	4	17	2	0	0	8	2	6	.288	.311	.322	634	70	-3	0	0	0	.917	-4	/3-8,C-5,O-1(1-0-0)	-0.6
1924	Was-A	24	33	3	5	1	1	0	5	1	4	.152	.176	.242	419	8	-5	0	0	0	1.000	-1	/C-8	-0.5
1925	Was-A	5	6	0	3	0	0	0	0	1	2	.500	.571	.500	1071	177	1	0	0	0	1.000	1	/C-1	0.2
	StL-A	67	225	34	64	15	2	8	43	13	13	.284	.326	.476	802	97	-3	2	0	0	.981	-6	C-62	-0.4
	Yr	72	231	34	67	15	2	8	43	14	15	.290	.333	.476	810	99	-2	2	0	0	.981	-5	C-63	-0.2
1926	StL-A	92	235	20	66	16	3	7	37	10	38	.281	.319	.464	782	98	-2	3	0	1	.977	-2	C-58	0.0
1928	Det-A	121	320	38	88	13	5	10	63	32	28	.275	.343	.441	783	103	1	4	1	1	.977	-14	C-88	-0.7

YEAR	TM/L	G	AB	R	H	2B	3B	HR	RBI	BB	SO	AVG	OBP	SLG	OPS	OPS+	BR+	SB	CS	SBR	FA	FR	G/POS	TPR
1929	Det-A	76	185	26	61	12	0	3	26	20	24	.330	.401	.443	844	117	5	2	2	-0	.973	-1	C-48	0.7
1930	Det-A	55	137	18	39	8	0	5	18	20	12	.285	.380	.453	832	108	2	2	0	0	.984	-4	C-40	0.1
	Was-A	10	31	3	6	2	2	1	7	3	1	.194	.265	.484	749	85	-1	1	0	0	1.000	1	/C-9	0.1
	Yr	65	168	21	45	10	2	6	25	23	13	.268	.359	.458	818	104	1	3	0	1	.987	-3	C-49	0.2
1931	Was-A	40	80	6	26	8	0	1	19	9	12	.325	.393	.463	856	124	3	1	0	0	.978	-2	C-25	0.2
1932	Bos-N	82	217	20	57	14	3	4	33	24	18	.263	.336	.410	746	103	1	1			.968	-4	C-73	0.1
1933	Bos-N	45	73	5	13	0	0	0	6	5	7	.178	.241	.178	419	23	-7	1			.957	1	C-25	-0.6
Total	10	650	1601	177	445	91	16	39	265	140	165	.278	.339	.428	767	98	-8	17	3		.976	-35	C-442/3-8,O-1(1-0-0)	-1.4

■ CHARLIE HARGREAVES

Hargreaves, Charles Russell b: 12/14/1896, Trenton, N.J. d: 5/9/79, Neptune, N.J. BR/TR, 6', 170 lbs. Deb: 6/27/23

YEAR	TM/L	G	AB	R	H	2B	3B	HR	RBI	BB	SO	AVG	OBP	SLG	OPS	OPS+	BR+	SB	CS	SBR	FA	FR	G/POS	TPR
1923	Bro-N	20	57	5	16	0	0	0	4	1	2	.281	.293	.281	574	54	-4	0	0	0	.921	-4	C-15	-0.6
1924	Bro-N	15	27	4	11	2	0	0	5	1	1	.407	.429	.481	910	148	2	0	1	-0	1.000	-1	/C-9	0.0
1925	Bro-N	45	83	9	23	3	1	0	13	6	1	.277	.326	.337	663	72	-3	1	1	-0	.986	2	C-18/1-2	-0.1
1926	Bro-N	85	208	14	52	13	2	2	23	19	10	.250	.316	.361	676	83	-5	1			.986	4	C-70	0.2
1927	Bro-N	46	133	9	38	3	1	0	11	14	7	.286	.362	.323	686	85	-2	1			.985	-1	C-44	0.0
1928	Bro-N	20	61	3	12	2	0	0	5	6	6	.197	.269	.230	498	32	-6	1			.979	2	C-20	-0.3
	Pit-N	79	260	15	74	8	2	1	32	12	9	.285	.319	.342	661	70	-11	1			.962	-5	C-77	-1.1
	Yr	99	321	18	86	10	2	1	37	18	15	.268	.309	.321	630	63	-17	2			.966	-3	C-97	-1.4
1929	Pit-N	102	328	33	88	12	5	1	44	16	12	.268	.306	.345	651	60	-21	1			.981	2	*C-101	-1.1
1930	Pit-N	11	31	4	7	1	0	0	2	2	1	.226	.273	.258	531	29	-4	0			1.000	6	C-11	0.2
Total	8	423	1188	96	321	44	11	4	139	77	49	.270	.318	.336	654	69	-55	6	2		.977	4	C-365/1-2	-2.8

■ MIKE HARGROVE

Hargrove, Dudley Michael b: 10/26/49, Perryton, Tex. BL/TL, 6', 195 lbs. Deb: 4/7/74 MC Career OF: (167-LF 0-CF 0-RF)

YEAR	TM/L	G	AB	R	H	2B	3B	HR	RBI	BB	SO	AVG	OBP	SLG	OPS	OPS+	BR+	SB	CS	SBR	FA	FR	G/POS	TPR
1974	Tex-A	131	415	57	134	18	6	4	66	49	42	.323	.400	.424	824	141	23	0	0	0	.987	9	1-91,D-32/O-6(6-0-0)	2.6
1975	Tex-A★	145	519	82	157	22	2	11	62	79	66	.303	.399	.416	815	132	25	4	3	-0	.964	3	O-96L,1-48,D-12	1.9
1976	Tex-A	151	541	80	155	30	1	7	58	**97**	64	.287	.401	.384	785	128	24	2	3	-1	.984	1	*1-141/D-5	1.4
1977	Tex-A	153	525	98	160	28	4	18	69	103	59	.305	.424	.476	900	143	37	2	5	-1	.993	-0	*1-152	2.5
1978	Tex-A	146	494	63	124	24	1	7	40	**107**	47	.251	.391	.346	738	109	12	2	5	-1	.987	7	*1-140/D-4	0.9
1979	SD-N	52	125	15	24	5	0	0	8	25	15	.192	.327	.232	559	59	-6	0	2	-1	.986	-2	1-37	-1.1
	Cle-A	100	338	60	110	21	4	10	56	63	40	.325	.438	.500	938	152	28	2	3	-1	.993	0	O-65(65-0-0),1-28/D-7	2.2
1980	Cle-A	160	589	86	179	22	2	11	85	111	36	.304	.421	.404	825	127	28	4	2	0	.993	-5	*1-160	1.3
1981	Cle-A	94	322	43	102	21	0	2	49	60	16	.317	**.432**	.401	832	143	22	5	4	-0	.989	6	1-88/D-4	2.3
1982	Cle-A	160	591	67	160	26	1	4	65	101	58	.271	.380	.338	718	100	5	2	2	-0	.996	11	*1-153/D-5	0.6
1983	Cle-A	134	469	57	134	21	4	3	57	78	40	.286	.393	.367	760	107	8	0	6	-2	.994	12	*1-131/D-1	1.0
1984	Cle-A	133	352	44	94	14	2	2	44	53	38	.267	.363	.335	698	93	-1	0	2	-1	.991	6	*1-124	-0.2
1985	Cle-A	107	284	31	81	14	1	1	27	39	29	.285	.372	.352	724	100	2	1	0	0	.991	5	1-85	0.2
Total	12	1666	5564	783	1614	266	28	80	686	965	550	.290	.400	.391	791	121	205	24	37	-8	.991	52	*1-1378,O-167L/D-70	15.6

■ TIM HARKNESS

Harkness, Thomas William b: 12/23/37, Lachine, Que., Can. BL/TL, 6'2", 182 lbs. Deb: 9/12/61

YEAR	TM/L	G	AB	R	H	2B	3B	HR	RBI	BB	SO	AVG	OBP	SLG	OPS	OPS+	BR+	SB	CS	SBR	FA	FR	G/POS	TPR
1961	LA-N	5	8	4	4	2	0	0	0	3	1	.500	.636	.750	1386	245	2	1	0	0	1.000	-0	/1-2	0.2
1962	LA-N	92	62	9	16	2	0	2	7	10	20	.258	.370	.387	757	110	1	1	0	0	1.000	1	1-59	0.2
1963	NY-N	123	375	35	79	12	3	10	41	36	79	.211	.292	.339	631	80	-10	4	3	-0	.986	16	*1-106	0.0
1964	NY-N	39	117	11	33	2	1	2	13	9	18	.282	.339	.368	706	101	0	1	1	-0	.993	3	1-32	0.2
Total	4	259	562	59	132	18	4	14	61	58	118	.235	.316	.356	672	90	-6	7	4	0	.989	21	1-199	0.6

■ DICK HARLEY

Harley, Richard Joseph b: 9/25/1872, Philadelphia, Pa. d: 4/3/52, Philadelphia, Pa. BL/TR, 5'10.5", 165 lbs. Deb: 6/2/1897

YEAR	TM/L	G	AB	R	H	2B	3B	HR	RBI	BB	SO	AVG	OBP	SLG	OPS	OPS+	BR+	SB	CS	SBR	FA	FR	G/POS	TPR
1897	StL-N	90	333	43	96	6	4	3	35	36		.288	.378	.357	735	97	0	23			.901	2	*O-90(1-89-0)	-0.3
1898	StL-N	142	549	74	135	6	5	0	42	34		.246	.316	.275	591	68	-22	13			.926	9	*O-141(135-5-1)	-2.4
1899	Cle-N	142	567	70	142	15	7	1	50	40		.250	.315	.307	621	76	-17	15			.924	5	*O-142(140-0-2)	-2.4
1900	Cin-N	5	21	2	9	1	0	0	5	1		.429	.455	.476	931	161	2	4			1.000	-1	/O-5(5-0-0)	0.0
1901	Cin-N	133	535	69	146	13	2	4	27	31		.273	.323	.327	651	95	-3	37			.898	-5	*O-133(133-0-0)	-1.5
1902	Det-A	125	491	59	138	9	8	2	44	36		.281	.345	.344	689	90	-6	20			.930	-2	*O-125(125-0-0)	-1.4
1903	Chi-N	104	386	72	89	9	1	0	33	45		.231	.328	.259	587	70	-13	27			.923	3	*O-103(0-0-103)	-1.3
Total	7	741	2882	389	755	59	27	10	236	223		.262	.332	.312	644	83	-58	139			.918	11	O-739(539-94-106)	-9.3

■ LARRY HARLOW

Harlow, Larry Duane b: 11/13/51, Colorado Springs, Colo. BL/TL, 6'2", 185 lbs. Deb: 9/20/75 Career OF: (39-LF 258-CF 113-RF)

YEAR	TM/L	G	AB	R	H	2B	3B	HR	RBI	BB	SO	AVG	OBP	SLG	OPS	OPS+	BR+	SB	CS	SBR	FA	FR	G/POS	TPR
1975	Bal-A	4	3	1	1	0	0	0	0	0	1	.333	.333	.333	667	95	-0	0	0	0	1.000	-2	/O-4(2-2-0)	-0.2
1977	Bal-A	46	48	4	10	0	1	0	0	5	8	.208	.283	.250	533	50	-3	6	1	1	.887	-12	O-38(0-37-1)	-1.4
1978	Bal-A	147	460	67	112	25	1	8	26	55	72	.243	.326	.354	680	97	-1	14	11	-1	.979	-5	*O-138(0-135-3)/P-1	-0.9
1979	Bal-A	38	41	5	11	1	0	0	1	7	4	.268	.375	.293	668	86	-0	1	3	-1	.970	-10	O-31(0-12-22)/D-1	-1.1
	*Cal-A	62	159	22	37	8	2	0	14	25	34	.233	.344	.308	652	80	-4	1	3	-1	.975	-2	O-58(11-33-15)	-0.8
	Yr	100	200	27	48	9	2	0	15	32	38	.240	.350	.305	655	81	-4	2	6	-2	.974	-12	O-89(11-45-37)/D-1	-1.9
1980	Cal-A	109	301	47	83	13	4	4	27	48	61	.276	.377	.385	763	112	7	3	2	-0	.976	12	O-94(5-32-59)/1-1,D-1	1.5
1981	Cal-A	43	82	13	17	1	0	0	4	16	25	.207	.337	.220	556	63	-3	1	1	-0	.981	-8	O-39(21-7-13)	-1.3
Total	6	449	1094	159	271	48	8	12	72	156	205	.248	.344	.339	683	94	-5	26	21	-2	.971	-26	O-402C/D-2,1-1,P-1	-4.2

■ BILL HARMAN

Harman, William Bell b: 1/2/19, Bridgewater, Va. BR/TR, 6'4", 200 lbs. Deb: 6/17/41

YEAR	TM/L	G	AB	R	H	2B	3B	HR	RBI	BB	SO	AVG	OBP	SLG	OPS	OPS+	BR+	SB	CS	SBR	FA	FR	G/POS	TPR
1941	Phi-N	15	14	1	1	0	0	0	0	0	3	.071	.071	.071	143	-62	-3	0			1.000	-1	/P-5,C-5	-0.2

■ CHUCK HARMON

Harmon, Charles Byron b: 4/23/24, Washington, Ind. BR/TR, 6'2", 175 lbs. Deb: 4/17/54 Career OF: (57-LF 10-CF 18-RF)

YEAR	TM/L	G	AB	R	H	2B	3B	HR	RBI	BB	SO	AVG	OBP	SLG	OPS	OPS+	BR+	SB	CS	SBR	FA	FR	G/POS	TPR
1954	Cin-N	94	286	39	68	7	3	2	25	17	27	.238	.283	.304	587	52	-20	7	3	0	.961	4	3-67/1-3	-1.6
1955	Cin-N	96	198	31	50	6	3	5	28	26	24	.253	.348	.389	737	90	-2	9	9	-1	.935	4	3-39,O-32(32-2-0)/1-4	-0.2
1956	Cin-N	13	4	2	0	0	0	0	0	0	0	.000	.000	.000	0	-94	-1	1	0	0	1.000	-2	/O-6(1-1-4),1-2	-0.3
	StL-N	20	15	2	0	0	0	0	0	2	2	.000	.118	.000	118	-65	-4	0	0	0	1.000	-4	O-11(3-4-5)/1-2,3-1	-0.8
	Yr	33	19	4	0	0	0	0	0	2	2	.000	.095	.000	95	-70	-5	1	0	0	1.000	-6	O-17(4-5-9)/1-4,3-1	-1.1
1957	StL-N	9	3	2	1	0	1	0	1	0	0	.333	.333	1.000	1333	236	1	1	0	0	1.000	-3	/O-8(0-1-7)	-0.2
	Phi-N	57	86	14	22	2	1	0	5	1	4	.256	.264	.302	567	53	-6	7	2	1	1.000	-2	O-25(21-2-2)/3-5,1-2	-0.8
	Yr	66	89	16	23	2	2	0	6	1	4	.258	.267	.326	593	60	-5	8	2	1	1.000	-5	O-33(21-3-9)/3-5,1-2	-1.0
Total	4	289	592	90	141	15	8	7	59	46	57	.238	.298	.326	624	62	-32	25	14	1	.952	-3	3-112/O-82L,1-13	-3.9

■ TERRY HARMON

Harmon, Terry Walter b: 4/12/44, Toledo, Ohio BR/TR, 6'2", 180 lbs. Deb: 7/23/67

YEAR	TM/L	G	AB	R	H	2B	3B	HR	RBI	BB	SO	AVG	OBP	SLG	OPS	OPS+	BR+	SB	CS	SBR	FA	FR	G/POS	TPR
1967	Phi-N	2	0	0	0	0	0	0	0	0	0	—	—	—	—	—	0	0	0	0	.000	0	R	0.0
1969	Phi-N	87	201	25	48	8	1	0	16	22	31	.239	.323	.289	612	74	-6	1	2	-0	.968	8	S-38,2-19/3-2	0.7
1970	Phi-N	71	129	16	32	2	4	0	7	12	22	.248	.317	.326	642	75	-5	6	3	0	.989	-3	S-35,2-14/3-2	-0.4
1971	Phi-N	79	221	27	45	4	2	0	12	20	45	.204	.282	.240	521	49	-14	3	2	-0	.986	8	2-58/S-9,3-3,1-2	-0.2
1972	Phi-N	73	218	35	62	8	2	2	13	29	28	.284	.373	.367	740	108	4	3	2	-0	.996	-1	2-50,S-15/3-5	0.7
1973	Phi-N	72	148	17	31	3	0	0	8	13	14	.209	.278	.230	508	41	-11	1	0	0	.988	2	2-43,S-19/3-1	-0.7
1974	Phi-N	27	15	5	2	0	0	0	0	3	3	.133	.278	.133	411	17	-2	0	0	0	1.000	3	/S-7,2-5	0.1
1975	Phi-N	48	72	14	13	1	2	0	5	9	13	.181	.280	.250	530	46	-5	0	0	0	.989	1	S-25/2-7,3-1	-0.2
1976	*Phi-N	42	61	12	18	4	1	0	6	3	10	.295	.328	.393	722	101	-0	3	0	1	.960	3	S-19,2-13/3-5	0.5
1977	Phi-N	46	60	13	11	1	0	2	5	6	9	.183	.269	.300	569	50	-4	0	2	-1	.982	8	2-28,S-16/3-3	0.4
Total	10	547	1125	164	262	31	12	4	72	117	175	.233	.312	.292	605	69	-44	17	11	-0	.989	29	2-237,S-183/3-22,1	0.9

■ BRIAN HARPER

Harper, Brian David b: 10/16/59, Los Angeles, Cal. BR/TR, 6'2", 195 lbs. Deb: 9/29/79 Career OF: (78-LF 0-CF 38-RF)

YEAR	TM/L	G	AB	R	H	2B	3B	HR	RBI	BB	SO	AVG	OBP	SLG	OPS	OPS+	BR+	SB	CS	SBR	FA	FR	G/POS	TPR
1979	Cal-A	1	2	0	0	0	0	0	0	0	1	.000	.000	.000	0	-99	-1	0	0	0	.000	0	/D-1	-0.1
1981	Cal-A	4	11	1	3	0	0	0	1	0	0	.273	.273	.273	545	58	-1	1	0	0	.833	-0	/O-2(1-0-1),D-1	-0.1
1982	Pit-N	20	29	4	8	1	0	2	4	1	4	.276	.300	.517	817	121	1	0	0	0	1.000	-1	/O-8(0-0-8)	-0.1
1983	Pit-N	61	131	16	29	4	1	7	20	2	15	.221	.239	.427	666	79	-4	0	0	0	1.000	-5	O-35(33-0-2)/1-1	-1.1
1984	Pit-N	46	112	4	29	4	0	2	11	5	11	.259	.303	.348	651	82	-3	0	0	0	.981	-2	O-37(34-0-4)/C-2	-0.6
1985	*StL-N	43	52	5	13	4	0	0	8	2	3	.250	.278	.327	605	69	-2	0	0	0	1.000	-4	O-13L/3-6,C-2,1-1	-0.7
1986	Det-A	19	36	2	5	1	0	0	3	3	3	.139	.205	.167	372	3	-5	0	0	0	.929	-2	O-11R/C-2,1-2,D-6	-0.7

YEAR	TM/L	G	AB	R	H	2B	3B	HR	RBI	BB	SO	AVG	OBP	SLG	OPS	OPS+	BR+	SB	CS	SBR	FA	FR	G/POS	TPR
1987	Oak-A	11	17	1	4	1	0	0	3	0	4	.235	.235	.294	529	42	-1	0	0	0	.000	-0	/O-1(1-0-0),D-7	-0.2
1988	Min-A	60	166	15	49	11	1	3	20	10	12	.295	.346	.428	774	112	3	0	3	-1	.991	-7	C-48/3-2,D-5	-0.3
1989	Min-A	126	385	43	125	24	0	8	57	13	16	.325	.356	.449	806	118	8	2	4	-1	.978	-14	*C-101,D-19/O-3R,13	-0.2
1990	Min-A	134	479	61	141	42	3	6	54	19	27	.294	.331	.432	763	105	2	3	2	-0	.985	2	*C-120,D-11/3-3,1-2	1.1
1991	*Min-A	123	441	54	137	28	1	10	69	14	22	.311	.341	.447	787	111	5	1	2	-0	.988	-6	*C-119/1-1,O-1L,D-2	0.6
1992	Min-A	140	502	58	154	25	0	9	73	26	22	.307	.350	.410	760	109	5	0	1	-0	.984	-7	*C-133/D-2	0.6
1993	Min-A	147	530	52	161	26	1	12	73	29	29	.304	.350	.425	775	107	5	1	3	-1	.988	-14	*C-134/D-7	-0.2
1994	Mil-A	64	251	23	73	15	0	4	32	9	18	.291	.323	.398	722	81	-7	0	2	-1	.981	2	D-36,C-25/O-3(1-0-3)	-0.6
1995	Oak-A	2	7	0	0	0	0	0	0	0	1	.000	.000	.000	0	-99	-2	0	0	0	1.000	-1	/C-2	-0.3
Total	16	1001	3151	339	931	186	7	63	428	133	188	.295	.333	.419	752	102	3	8	17	-4	.985	-60	C-688,O-114L/D-97,31	-2.9

■ GEORGE HARPER

Harper, George Washington b: 6/24/1892, Arlington, Ky. d: 8/18/78, Magnolia, Ark. BL/TR, 5'8", 167 lbs. Deb: 4/15/16

YEAR	TM/L	G	AB	R	H	2B	3B	HR	RBI	BB	SO	AVG	OBP	SLG	OPS	OPS+	BR+	SB	CS	SBR	FA	FR	G/POS	TPR
1916	Det-A	44	56	4	9	1	0	0	3	5	8	.161	.230	.179	408	22	-5	0			.938	-4	O-14(2-4-8)	-1.0
1917	Det-A	47	117	6	24	3	0	0	12	11	15	.205	.290	.231	521	59	-5	2			.980	-3	O-31(0-3-28)	-1.1
1918	Det-A	69	227	19	55	5	2	0	16	18	14	.242	.301	.282	583	79	-6	3			.956	-1	O-64(0-1-63)	-1.2
1922	Cin-N	128	430	67	146	22	8	2	68	35	22	.340	.397	.442	839	118	13	11	10	-1	.955	1	*O-109(1-5-103)	0.4
1923	Cin-N	61	125	14	32	4	2	3	16	11	9	.256	.316	.392	708	88	-3	0	2	-1	.967	-2	O-29(9-17-3)	-0.7
1924	Cin-N	28	74	7	20	3	0	0	3	13	5	.270	.393	.311	704	92	0	1	3	-1	.964	1	O-22(12-10-0)	-0.1
	Phi-N	109	411	68	121	26	6	16	55	38	23	.294	.361	.504	865	115	8	10	11	-2	.991	3	*O-109(0-3-107)	0.2
	Yr	137	485	75	141	29	6	16	58	51	28	.291	.366	.474	841	113	9	11	14	-2	.986	4	*O-131(12-13-107)	0.1
1925	Phi-N	132	495	86	173	35	7	18	97	28	32	.349	.391	.558	949	128	20	10	8	-1	.971	6	*O-126(36-61-33)	1.6
1926	Phi-N	56	194	32	61	6	5	7	38	16	7	.314	.367	.505	872	126	7	6			.942	-6	O-55(44-8-8)	-0.3
1927	NY-N	145	483	85	160	19	6	16	87	84	27	.331	.435	.495	930	149	37	7			.975	-2	*O-142(0-0-142)	2.4
1928	NY-N	19	57	11	13	1	0	2	7	10	4	.228	.353	.351	704	84	-1	1			.957	2	O-18(0-0-18)	0.0
	*StL-N	99	272	41	83	8	2	17	58	51	15	.305	.418	.537	955	145	19	2			.988	1	O-84(0-0-84)	1.3
	Yr	118	329	52	96	9	2	19	65	61	19	.292	.407	.505	912	135	18	3			.982	3	*O-102(0-0-102)	1.3
1929	Bos-N	136	457	65	133	25	5	10	68	69	27	.291	.389	.433	822	108	7	5			.972	-1	*O-130(119-1-10)	-0.4
Total	11	1073	3398	505	1030	158	43	91	528	389	208	.303	.380	.455	836	118	91	58	34		.970	-5	O-933(223-113-607)	1.1

■ TERRY HARPER

Harper, Terry Joe b: 8/19/55, Douglasville, Ga. BR/TR, 6'4", 195 lbs. Deb: 9/12/80

YEAR	TM/L	G	AB	R	H	2B	3B	HR	RBI	BB	SO	AVG	OBP	SLG	OPS	OPS+	BR+	SB	CS	SBR	FA	FR	G/POS	TPR
1980	Atl-N	21	54	3	10	2	1	0	3	6	5	.185	.279	.259	538	49	-4	2	1	0	.968	-2	O-18(15-1-3)	-0.6
1981	Atl-N	40	73	9	19	1	0	2	8	11	17	.260	.357	.356	713	100	0	5	1	1	.976	-2	O-27(9-0-18)	-0.2
1982	*Atl-N	48	150	16	43	3	0	2	16	14	28	.287	.352	.347	698	92	-1	7	4	0	.987	-0	O-41(29-1-16)	-0.3
1983	Atl-N	80	201	19	53	13	1	3	26	20	43	.264	.333	.383	716	91	-2	6	5	-0	.952	-1	O-60(28-2-32)	-0.7
1984	Atl-N	40	102	4	16	3	1	0	8	4	21	.157	.196	.206	402	12	-12	4	1	1	1.000	4	O-29(28-0-1)	-0.9
1985	Atl-N	138	492	58	130	15	2	17	72	44	76	.264	.328	.407	735	98	-1	9	9	-1	.978	1	*O-131(129-0-2)	-0.7
1986	Atl-N	106	265	26	68	12	0	8	30	29	39	.257	.332	.392	725	94	-2	3	6	-1	.970	-11	O-83(66-0-25)	-1.9
1987	Det-A	31	64	4	13	3	0	3	10	9	8	.203	.301	.391	692	85	-1	1	0	0	.952	-2	D-15,O-14(1-0-13)	-0.4
	Pit-N	36	66	8	19	3	0	1	7	7	11	.288	.356	.379	735	94	-0	0	1	-1	1.000	-3	O-20(10-0-11)	-0.4
Total	8	540	1467	147	371	55	5	36	180	144	248	.253	.323	.371	694	88	-23	37	28	-2	.976	-16	O-423(315-4-121)/D-15	-6.1

■ TOMMY HARPER

Harper, Tommy b: 10/14/40, Oak Grove, La. BR/TR, 5'10", 168 lbs. Deb: 4/9/62 C Career OF: (683-LF 258-CF 348-RF)

YEAR	TM/L	G	AB	R	H	2B	3B	HR	RBI	BB	SO	AVG	OBP	SLG	OPS	OPS+	BR+	SB	CS	SBR	FA	FR	G/POS	TPR
1962	Cin-N	6	23	1	4	0	0	0	1	2	6	.174	.240	.174	414	13	-3	1	0	0	.929	-1	/3-6	-0.4
1963	Cin-N	129	408	67	106	12	3	10	37	44	72	.260	.336	.377	714	102	2	12	1	2	.983	6	*O-118(1-23-94)/3-1	0.3
1964	Cin-N	102	317	42	77	5	2	4	22	39	56	.243	.328	.309	637	78	-8	24	3	4	.994	5	O-92(88-4-0)/3-2	-0.4
1965	Cin-N	159	646	**126**	166	28	3	18	64	78	127	.257	.342	.393	735	99	1	35	6	6	.983	7	*O-159L/3-2,2-1	0.5
1966	Cin-N	149	553	85	154	22	5	5	31	57	85	.278	.349	.363	713	91	-5	29	10	3	.996	-13	*O-147(73-25-95)	-2.6
1967	Cin-N	103	365	55	82	17	3	7	22	43	51	.225	.306	.345	652	77	-10	23	8	2	.995	7	*O-100(2-4-97)	-0.8
1968	Cle-A	130	235	26	51	15	2	6	26	26	56	.217	.298	.374	672	104	1	11	7	-0	.984	-16	*O-115(67-7-46)/2-2	-2.2
1969	Sea-A	148	537	78	126	10	2	9	41	95	90	.235	.351	.311	662	88	-5	**73**	18	10	.959	-15	2-59,3-59,O-26C	-0.8
1970	Mil-A★	154	604	104	179	35	4	31	82	77	107	.296	.380	.522	901	145	37	38	16	3	.943	-3	*3-128,2-22,O-13L	3.7
1971	Mil-A	152	585	79	151	26	3	14	52	65	92	.258	.333	.385	718	104	3	25	3	3	.975	-19	O-90L,3-70/2-1	-1.8
1972	Bos-A	144	556	92	141	29	2	14	49	67	104	.254	.343	.388	732	111	9	25	7	3	.985	1	*O-144(0-144-0)	1.1
1973	Bos-A	147	566	92	159	23	3	17	71	61	93	.281	.352	.422	774	111	8	**54**	14	**7**	.985	3	*O-143(139-5-0)/D-1	0.9
1974	Bos-A	118	443	66	105	15	3	5	24	46	65	.237	.313	.318	631	77	-13	28	12	2	.982	-3	O-61(61-0-0),D-51	-1.9
1975	Cal-A	89	285	40	68	10	1	3	31	38	51	.239	.332	.312	645	89	-3	19	8	1	.992	-2	D-57,1-19/O-9(2-0-7)	-0.7
	*Oak-A	34	69	11	22	4	0	2	7	5	9	.319	.373	.464	837	139	3	7	0	2	.963	-3	1-16/O-9L,3-2,D-3	0.1
	Yr	123	354	51	90	14	1	5	38	43	60	.254	.340	.342	682	99	0	26	8	3	.978	-5	D-60,1-35,O-18R,/3	-0.6
1976	Bal-A	46	77	8	18	5	0	1	7	10	16	.234	.322	.338	660	99	0	4	3	-0	1.000	-1	D-27/1-1,O-1(1-0-0)	-0.1
Total	15	1810	6269	972	1609	256	36	146	567	753	1080	.257	.340	.379	719	100	18	408	116	49	.986	-47	*O-1227L,3-270,D/21	-5.1

■ TOBY HARRAH

Harrah, Colbert Dale b: 10/26/48, Sissonville, W.Va. BR/TR, 6', 180 lbs. Deb: 9/5/69 MC Career OF: (0-LF 0-CF 1-RF)

YEAR	TM/L	G	AB	R	H	2B	3B	HR	RBI	BB	SO	AVG	OBP	SLG	OPS	OPS+	BR+	SB	CS	SBR	FA	FR	G/POS	TPR
1969	Was-A	8	1	4	0	0	0	0	0	0	0	.000	.000	.000	0	-99	-0	0	0	0	.000	0	/S-1	0.0
1971	Was-A	127	383	45	88	11	3	2	22	40	48	.230	.303	.290	592	73	-14	10	9	-1	.955	-7	*S-116/3-7	-1.0
1972	Tex-A†	116	374	47	97	14	3	1	31	34	31	.259	.321	.321	642	95	-2	16	7	1	.960	-9	*S-106	0.3
1973	Tex-A	118	461	64	120	16	1	10	50	46	49	.260	.330	.364	694	100	-0	10	3	1	.951	-13	S-76,3-52	-0.3
1974	Tex-A	161	573	79	149	23	2	21	74	50	65	.260	.322	.417	739	114	9	15	14	-2	.963	-2	*S-158/3-3	2.5
1975	Tex-A☆	151	522	81	153	24	1	20	93	98	71	.293	.406	.458	864	145	34	23	9	2	.963	14	*S-118,3-28,2-21	**6.4**
1976	Tex-A★	155	584	64	152	21	1	15	67	91	59	.260	.363	.377	740	114	13	8	5	0	.955	-0	*S-146/3-5,D-4	3.2
1977	Tex-A	159	539	90	142	25	5	27	87	**109**	73	.263	.397	.479	875	136	31	27	5	4	.963	-24	*3-159/S-1	0.8
1978	Tex-A	139	450	56	103	17	3	12	59	83	66	.229	.351	.360	711	100	3	31	8	4	.965	-8	3-91,S-49	0.2
1979	Cle-A	149	527	99	147	25	1	20	77	89	60	.279	.391	.444	835	124	21	20	9	1	.940	-49	*3-127,S-33/D-9	-2.6
1980	Cle-A	160	561	100	150	22	4	11	72	98	60	.267	.383	.380	763	109	11	17	2	3	.971	2	*3-156/S-2,D-3	1.4
1981	Cle-A	103	361	64	105	12	4	5	44	57	44	.291	.389	.388	777	126	15	12	1	2	.949	-12	*3-101/S-3,D-1	0.4
1982	Cle-A☆	162	602	100	183	29	4	25	78	84	52	.304	.400	.490	890	144	39	17	3	3	.971	-19	*3-159/2-3,S-2	2.0
1983	Cle-A	138	526	81	140	23	1	9	53	75	49	.266	.365	.365	730	98	1	16	10	0	**.971**	-11	*3-137/2-1,D-1	-1.2
1984	NY-A	88	253	40	55	9	4	1	26	42	28	.217	.333	.296	630	79	-6	3	0	1	.968	3	3-74/2-4,O-1R,D-2	-0.3
1985	Tex-A	126	396	65	107	18	1	9	44	113	60	.270	.437	.389	826	127	22	11	4	1	.989	-14	*2-122/S-2,D-1	1.6
1986	Tex-A	95	289	36	63	18	2	7	41	44	53	.218	.325	.367	692	86	-5	2	5	-1	.982	-20	2-93	-2.2
Total	17	2155	7402	1115	1954	307	40	195	918	1153	868	.264	.368	.395	763	114	172	238	94	19	.963	-167	*3-1099,S-813,2/DO	11.2

■ JOHN HARRELL

Harrell, John Robert b: 11/27/47, Long Beach, Cal. BR/TR, 6'2", 190 lbs. Deb: 10/1/69

YEAR	TM/L	G	AB	R	H	2B	3B	HR	RBI	BB	SO	AVG	OBP	SLG	OPS	OPS+	BR+	SB	CS	SBR	FA	FR	G/POS	TPR
1969	SF-N	2	6	0	3	0	0	0	2	2	1	.500	.625	.500	1125	223	1	0	0	0	1.000	-0	/C-2	0.1

■ BILLY HARRELL

Harrell, William b: 7/18/28, Norristown, Pa. BR/TR, 6'1.5", 180 lbs. Deb: 9/2/55 Career OF: (0-LF 0-CF 1-RF)

YEAR	TM/L	G	AB	R	H	2B	3B	HR	RBI	BB	SO	AVG	OBP	SLG	OPS	OPS+	BR+	SB	CS	SBR	FA	FR	G/POS	TPR
1955	Cle-A	13	19	2	8	0	0	0	1	3	3	.421	.500	.421	921	144	1	1	0	0	.926	-0	S-11	0.2
1957	Cle-A	22	57	6	15	1	1	1	5	4	7	.263	.311	.368	680	86	-1	3	1	0	.893	-4	S-14/3-6,2-1	-0.4
1958	Cle-A	101	229	36	50	4	0	7	19	15	36	.218	.272	.328	600	66	-11	12	2	2	.986	-7	3-46,S-45/2-7,O-1R	-1.3
1961	Bos-A	37	37	10	6	2	0	0	1	1	8	.162	.184	.216	400	6	-5	1	0	0	1.000	7	3-10/S-7,1-3	0.2
Total	4	173	342	54	79	7	1	8	26	23	54	.231	.283	.327	611	68	-16	17	3	3	.933	-5	/S-77,3-62,2-8,1O	-1.3

■ BUD HARRELSON

Harrelson, Derrel McKinley b: 6/6/44, Niles, Cal. BB/TR (BR 1965, 1975 (part)), 5'11", 160 lbs. Deb: 9/2/65 MC

YEAR	TM/L	G	AB	R	H	2B	3B	HR	RBI	BB	SO	AVG	OBP	SLG	OPS	OPS+	BR+	SB	CS	SBR	FA	FR	G/POS	TPR
1965	NY-N	19	37	3	4	1	1	0	0	2	11	.108	.154	.189	343	-4	-5	0	0	0	.955	4	S-18	-0.1
1966	NY-N	33	99	20	22	2	4	0	4	13	23	.222	.313	.323	636	79	-3	7	3	0	.993	5	S-29	0.5
1967	NY-N	151	540	59	137	16	4	1	28	48	64	.254	.319	.304	623	80	-13	12	13	-2	.958	7	*S-149	0.5
1968	NY-N	111	402	38	88	7	3	0	14	29	68	.219	.273	.251	524	58	-20	4	5	-1	.972	-5	*S-106	-1.9
1969	*NY-N	123	395	42	98	11	6	0	24	54	54	.248	.341	.306	648	81	-8	1	3	-1	.969	-5	*S-119	0.1
1970	NY-N★	157	564	72	137	18	8	1	42	95	74	.243	.355	.309	663	79	-13	23	4	4	.971	-28	*S-156	-1.9
1971	NY-N★	142	547	55	138	16	6	0	32	53	59	.252	.321	.303	624	79	-14	28	7	4	.978	11	*S-140	1.8
1972	NY-N	115	418	54	90	10	4	1	24	58	57	.215	.315	.266	581	68	-16	12	4	1	.970	-12	*S-115	-1.3
1973	*NY-N	106	356	35	92	12	3	0	20	48	49	.258	.348	.309	657	85	-6	5	1	1	.979	-3	*S-103	0.5

YEAR	TM/L	G	AB	R	H	2B	3B	HR	RBI	BB	SO	AVG	OBP	SLG	OPS	OPS+	BR+	SB	CS	SBR	FA	FR	G/POS	TPR
1974	NY-N	106	331	48	75	10	0	1	13	71	39	.227	.366	.266	632	80	-5	9	4	1	.968	16	S-97	2.4
1975	NY-N	34	73	5	16	2	0	0	3	12	13	.219	.329	.247	576	65	-3	0	0	0	.941	1	S-34	0.1
1976	NY-N	118	359	34	84	12	4	1	26	63	56	.234	.351	.298	649	91	-2	9	3	1	.962	-5	*S-117	0.8
1977	NY-N	107	269	25	48	6	2	1	12	27	28	.178	.256	.227	483	32	-26	5	4	-0	.984	-2	S-98	-1.9
1978	Phi-N	71	103	16	22	1	0	0	9	18	21	.214	.331	.223	554	57	-5	5	2	0	.972	15	2-43,S-15	1.2
1979	Phi-N	53	71	7	20	6	0	0	7	13	14	.282	.400	.366	766	107	1	3	3	-0	.990	6	2-25,S-17/3-9,O-1L	0.8
1980	Tex-A	87	180	26	49	6	0	1	9	29	23	.272	.373	.322	695	95	0	4	4	-1	.952	11	S-87/2-2	1.8
Total	16	1533	4744	539	1120	136	45	7	267	633	653	.236	.329	.288	617	75	-136	127	60	7	.969	16	*S-1400/2-70,3-9,O	3.4
■ **KEN HARRELSON**	Harrelson, Kenneth Smith "Hawk" b: 9/4/41, Woodruff, S.C. BR/TR, 6'2", 190 lbs. Deb: 6/9/63																							
1963	KC-A	79	226	16	52	10	1	6	23	23	58	.230	.301	.363	664	81	-6	1	1	-0	.980	-5	1-34,O-28(28-0-0)	-1.5
1964	KC-A	49	139	15	27	5	0	7	12	13	34	.194	.263	.381	644	74	-5	0	1	-0	.977	3	O-24(24-0-0),1-15	-0.5
1965	KC-A	150	483	61	115	17	3	23	66	66	112	.238	.331	.429	759	116	10	9	7	-0	.992	-4	*1-125/O-4(3-0-1)	-0.2
1966	KC-A	63	210	24	47	5	0	5	22	27	59	.224	.312	.319	631	85	-4	9	2	1	.985	2	1-58/O-3(3-0-1)	-0.4
	Was-A	71	250	25	62	8	1	7	28	26	53	.248	.321	.372	693	100	-0	4	1	1	.991	-4	1-70	-0.8
	Yr	134	460	49	109	13	1	12	50	53	112	.237	.317	.348	665	93	-4	13	3	2	.989	-2	*1-128/O-3(3-0-1)	-1.2
1967	Was-A	26	79	10	16	0	0	3	10	7	15	.203	.267	.316	584	75	-3	1	0	0	.996	0	1-23	-0.4
	KC-A	61	174	23	53	11	0	6	30	17	17	.305	.366	.471	838	151	11	8	2	1	.992	-1	1-45	0.9
	*Bos-A	23	80	9	16	4	1	3	14	5	12	.200	.247	.387	635	79	-2	1	1	-0	.929	-3	O-23(0-0-23)/1-1	-0.8
	Yr	110	333	42	85	15	1	12	54	29	44	.255	.315	.414	729	115	5	10	3	1	.993	-4	1-69,O-23(0-0-23)	-0.3
1968	Bos-A★	150	535	79	147	17	4	35	**109**	69	90	.275	.360	.518	877	153	34	2	6	-2	**1.000**	8	*O-132(0-0-132),1-19	3.4
1969	Bos-A	10	46	6	10	1	0	3	8	4	6	.217	.280	.435	715	92	-1	0	1	-0	.991	2	1-10	0.0
	Cle-A	149	519	83	115	13	4	27	84	95	96	.222	.344	.418	762	109	7	17	8	1	.985	5	*O-144(7-0-137),1-16	0.5
	Yr	159	565	89	125	14	4	30	92	99	102	.221	.339	.419	759	107	6	17	9	1	.985	6	*O-144(7-0-137),1-26	0.5
1970	Cle-A	17	39	3	11	1	0	1	1	6	4	.282	.378	.385	762	106	1	0	0	0	1.000	1	1-13	0.0
1971	Cle-A	52	161	20	32	2	0	5	14	24	21	.199	.303	.304	607	66	-7	1	0	0	.988	-1	1-40/O-7(5-0-2)	-1.2
Total	9	900	2941	374	703	94	14	131	421	382	577	.239	.328	.414	742	109	35	53	30	1	.990	2	1-469,O-365(70-0-296)	-1.0
■ **ANDY HARRINGTON**	Harrington, Andrew Matthew b: 2/12/03, Mountain View, Cal d: 1/26/79, Boise, Idaho BR/TR, 5'11", 170 lbs. Deb: 4/18/25																							
1925	Det-A	1	1	0	0	0	0	0	0	0	0	.000	.000	.000	0	-99	-0	0	0	0	.000	0	H	0.0
■ **MICKEY HARRINGTON**	Harrington, Charles Michael b: 10/8/34, Hattiesburg, Miss. BR/TR, 6'4", 205 lbs. Deb: 7/10/63																							
1963	Phi-N	1	0	0	0	0	0	0	0	0	0	—	—	—	—	—	0	0	0	0	.000	0	R	0.0
■ **JERRY HARRINGTON**	Harrington, Jeremiah Peter b: 8/12/1869, Keokuk, Iowa d: 4/16/13, Keokuk, Iowa BR/TR, 5'11", 220 lbs. Deb: 4/30/1890																							
1890	Cin-N	65	236	25	58	7	1	1	23	15	29	.246	.299	.297	596	74	-8	4			.957	5	C-65	0.3
1891	Cin-N	92	333	25	76	10	5	2	41	19	34	.228	.272	.306	578	68	-15	4			.908	-3	C-92/3-1	-0.9
1892	Cin-N	22	61	6	13	1	0	0	3	6	1	.213	.284	.230	513	56	-3	0			.989	1	C-22/1-1	-0.1
1893	Lou-N	10	36	4	4	1	0	0	6	3	9	.111	.179	.139	318	-16	-6	0			.853	-4	C-10	-0.7
Total	4	189	666	60	151	19	6	3	73	43	73	.227	.278	.287	564	64	-32	8			.932	-1	C-189/1-1,3-1	-1.4
■ **JOE HARRINGTON**	Harrington, Joseph C. b: 12/21/1869, Fall River, Mass. d: 9/13/33, Fall River, Mass. BR/TR, 5'8.5", 162 lbs. Deb: 9/10/1895																							
1895	Bos-N	18	65	21	18	0	2	2	13	7	5	.277	.356	.431	787	95	-1	3			.912	0	2-18	0.0
1896	Bos-N	54	199	26	40	5	3	1	25	19	17	.201	.274	.271	545	42	-17	2			.816	-10	3-49/S-4,2-1	-2.3
Total	2	72	264	47	58	5	5	3	38	26	22	.220	.295	.311	605	55	-18	5			.901	-10	/3-49,2-19,S-4	-2.3
■ **CANDY HARRIS**	Harris, Alonzo b: 9/17/47, Selma, Ala. BB/TR, 6', 160 lbs. Deb: 4/13/67																							
1967	Hou-N	6	1	0	0	0	0	0	0	0	1	.000	.000	.000	0	-99	-0	0	0	0	.000	0	H	0.0
■ **SPENCER HARRIS**	Harris, Anthony Spencer b: 8/12/1900, Duluth, Minn. d: 7/3/82, Minneapolis, Minn. BL/TL, 5'9", 145 lbs. Deb: 4/14/25																							
1925	Chi-A	56	92	12	26	2	0	1	13	14	13	.283	.383	.337	720	89	-1	1	3	-1	.957	-5	O-27(1-12-17)	-0.7
1926	Chi-A	80	222	36	56	11	3	2	27	20	15	.252	.317	.356	673	78	-8	8	3	1	.949	-6	O-63(7-11-48)	-1.7
1929	Was-A	6	14	1	3	1	0	0	1	0	3	.214	.214	.286	500	27	-2	1	0	0	1.000	-1	/O-4(0-4-0)	-0.2
1930	Phi-A	22	49	4	9	1	0	0	5	5	2	.184	.259	.204	463	18	-6	0	0	0	.958	0	O-13(10-1-2)	-0.6
Total	4	164	377	53	94	15	3	3	46	39	33	.249	.323	.329	652	70	-16	10	6	0	.954	-11	O-107(18-28-67)	-3.2
■ **GAIL HARRIS**	Harris, Boyd Gail b: 10/15/31, Abingdon, Va. BL/TL, 6', 195 lbs. Deb: 6/3/55																							
1955	NY-N	79	263	27	61	9	0	12	36	20	46	.232	.291	.403	694	82	-8	0	0	0	.982	0	1-75	-1.1
1956	NY-N	12	38	2	5	0	1	1	1	3	10	.132	.233	.263	496	33	-4	0	0	0	.975	0	1-11	-0.4
1957	NY-N	90	225	28	54	7	3	9	31	16	28	.240	.308	.418	725	93	-3	1	0	0	.985	-2	1-61	-0.8
1958	Det-A	134	451	63	123	18	8	20	83	36	60	.273	.332	.481	813	113	7	1	2	-0	.986	3	*1-122	0.2
1959	Det-A	114	349	39	77	4	3	9	39	29	49	.221	.292	.327	618	66	-16	0	1	-0	.992	3	1-93	-2.0
1960	Det-A	8	5	0	0	0	0	0	0	2	1	.000	.286	.000	286	-15	-1	0	0	0	1.000	0	/1-5	-0.1
Total	6	437	1331	159	320	38	15	51	190	106	194	.240	.306	.406	713	88	-24	2	3	-1	.986	4	1-367	-4.2
■ **CHARLIE HARRIS**	Harris, Charles Jenkins b: 10/21/1877, Macon, Ga. d: 3/14/63, Gainesville, Fla. BR/TR, 5'8", 200 lbs. Deb: 5/25/1899																							
1899	Bal-N	30	68	16	19	3	0	0	1	3		.279	.319	.324	643	73	-3	4			.872	-5	3-21/O-3L,2-2,S-1	-0.7
■ **DAVE HARRIS**	Harris, David Stanley "Sheriff" b: 7/14/1900, Summerfield, N.C. d: 9/18/73, Atlanta, Ga. BR/TR, 5'11", 170 lbs. Deb: 4/14/25 Career OF: (164-LF 36-CF 186-RF)																							
1925	Bos-N	92	340	49	90	8	7	5	36	27	44	.265	.321	.374	694	84	-9	6	4	-0	.962	8	O-90(87-4-0)	-0.7
1928	Bos-N	7	17	2	2	1	0	0	0	2	6	.118	.211	.176	387	2	-2	0			.833	-1	/O-6(6-0-0)	-0.4
1930	Chi-A	33	86	16	21	2	1	5	13	7	22	.244	.309	.465	774	96	-1	0	0	0	1.000	-0	O-23(23-0-0)/2-1	-0.3
	Was-A	73	205	40	65	19	8	4	44	28	35	.317	.399	.546	945	137	11	6	3	0	.983	1	O-59(19-12-28)	0.8
	Yr	106	291	56	86	21	9	9	57	35	57	.296	.373	.522	895	125	11	6	3	0	.988	1	O-82(42-12-28)/2-1	0.5
1931	Was-A	77	231	49	72	14	8	5	50	49	38	.312	.434	.506	941	146	17	7	6	-1	.950	-2	O-60(3-0-57)	1.0
1932	Was-A	81	156	26	51	7	4	6	29	19	34	.327	.400	.538	938	143	10	4	4	-1	.932	-2	O-34(7-8-20)	0.5
1933	*Was-A	82	177	33	46	9	2	5	38	25	26	.260	.358	.418	776	106	2	3	1	0	.964	-7	O-45(4-11-32)/1-6,3-2	-0.7
1934	Was-A	97	235	28	59	14	3	2	37	39	40	.251	.358	.362	719	89	-3	2	3	-1	.973	-4	O-64(15-1-49)/3-5	-0.9
Total	7	542	1447	243	406	74	33	32	247	196	245	.281	.368	.444	812	112	25	28	21		.963	-8	O-381R/3-7,1-6,2-1	-0.7
■ **DONALD HARRIS**	Harris, Donald b: 11/12/67, Waco, Tex. BR/TR, 6'1", 185 lbs. Deb: 9/4/91																							
1991	Tex-A	18	8	4	3	0	0	1	2	1	3	.375	.444	.750	1194	228	1	1	0	0	1.000	-5	O-12(2-7-5)/D-3	-0.3
1992	Tex-A	24	33	3	6	1	0	0	1	0	15	.182	.182	.212	394	10	-4	1	0	0	.974	-4	O-24(5-15-5)	-0.8
1993	Tex-A	40	76	10	15	2	0	1	8	5	18	.197	.256	.263	519	41	-6	0	1	-0	.943	-7	O-38(1-27-11)/D-3	-1.4
Total	3	82	117	17	24	3	0	2	11	6	36	.205	.250	.282	532	46	-9	2	1	0	.959	-16	/O-74(8-49-21),D-6	-2.5
■ **FRANK HARRIS**	Harris, Frank W. b: 11/2/1858, Pittsburgh, Pa. d: 11/26/39, E.Moline, Ill. BR/TR, Deb: 4/17/1884																							
1884	Alt-U	24	95	10	25	2	1	0		3		.263	.286	.305	591	78	-5				.941	-1	1-17/O-7(4-3-1)	-0.7
■ **BILLY HARRIS**	Harris, James William b: 11/24/43, Hamlet, N.C. BL/TR, 6', 175 lbs. Deb: 6/16/68																							
1968	Cle-A	38	94	10	20	5	1	0	3	8	22	.213	.275	.287	562	71	-3	2	0	0	.970	-1	2-27,3-10/S-1	-0.2
1969	KC-A	5	7	1	2	1	0	0	0	0	1	.286	.286	.429	714	97	-0	0	0	0	1.000	-0	/2-1	0.0
Total	2	43	101	11	22	6	1	0	3	8	23	.218	.275	.297	572	73	-3	2	0	0	.971	-1	/2-28,3-10,S-1	-0.2
■ **JOHN HARRIS**	Harris, John Thomas b: 9/13/54, Portland, Ore. BL/TL, 6'3", 205 lbs. Deb: 9/26/79 Career OF: (13-LF 0-CF 0-RF)																							
1979	Cal-A	1	2	0	0	0	0	0	0	0	0	.000	.000	.000	0	-99	-1	0	0	0	1.000	-0	/1-1	-0.1
1980	Cal-A	19	41	8	12	5	0	2	7	7	4	.293	.396	.561	957	163	4	0	1	-0	1.000	-0	1-10/O-3(3-0-0)	0.3
1981	Cal-A	36	77	5	19	3	0	3	9	3	11	.247	.275	.403	678	93	-1	0	0	0	.976	-4	1-11,O-10(10-0-0)/D-1	-0.6
Total	3	56	120	13	31	8	0	5	16	10	15	.258	.315	.450	765	115	2	0	1	-0	.987	-4	/1-22,O-13L,D-1	-0.4
■ **JOE HARRIS**	Harris, Joseph "Moon" b: 5/20/1891, Coulters, Pa. d: 12/10/59, Renton, Pa. BR/TR, 5'9", 170 lbs. Deb: 6/9/14 Career OF: (235-LF 0-CF 84-RF)																							
1914	NY-A	2	1	0	0	0	0	0	0	3	1	.000	.800	.000	800	143	1	0			1.000	-1	/1-1,O-1(1-0-0)	0.0
1917	Cle-A	112	369	40	112	22	4	0	65	55	32	.304	.398	.385	783	129	15	11			.985	10	1-95/O-5(0-0-5),3-2	2.5

YEAR	TM/L	G	AB	R	H	2B	3B	HR	RBI	BB	SO	AVG	OBP	SLG	OPS	OPS+	BR+	SB	CS	SBR	FA	FR	G/POS	TPR
1919	Cle-A	62	184	30	69	16	1	1	46	33	21	.375	.472	.489	962	160	17	2			.988	2	1-46/S-4	1.8
1922	Bos-A	119	408	53	129	30	9	6	54	30	15	.316	.364	.478	842	119	10	2	6	-2	.953	7	O-83(71-0-12),1-21	0.7
1923	Bos-A	142	483	82	162	28	11	13	76	52	27	.335	.406	.520	925	142	28	7	3	0	.968	-2	*O-132(132-0-0)/1-9	1.6
1924	Bos-A	133	491	82	148	36	9	3	77	81	25	.301	.406	.430	835	115	14	6	1	1	.993	6	*1-128/O-3(3-0-0)	1.2
1925	Bos-A	8	19	4	3	0	1	1	2	5	5	.158	.333	.421	754	90	-0	0	0	0	1.000	-1	/1-6	-0.2
	*Was-A	100	300	60	97	21	9	12	59	51	28	.323	.430	.573	1003	156	26	6	3	0	.989	-0	1-58,O-41(16-0-25)	1.8
	Yr	108	319	64	100	21	10	13	61	56	33	.313	.424	.564	988	152	26	6	3	0	.990	-1	1-64,O-41(16-0-25)	1.6
1926	Was-A	92	257	43	79	13	9	5	55	37	9	.307	.405	.486	891	135	14	2	3	-1	.994	-3	1-36,O-35(3-0-32)	0.5
1927	*Pit-N	129	411	57	134	27	9	5	73	48	19	.326	.402	.472	874	125	15	0			.990	2	*1-116/O-3(3-0-0)	0.9
1928	Pit-N	16	23	2	9	2	1	0	2	4	2	.391	.500	.565	1065	171	3	0			1.000	1	/1-6	0.4
	Bro-N	55	89	8	21	6	1	1	8	14	4	.236	.340	.360	699	84	-2	0			.958	-2	O-16(6-0-10)	-0.5
	Yr	71	112	10	30	8	2	1	10	18	6	.268	.374	.402	776	103	1	0			.958	-0	O-16(6-0-10)/1-6	-0.1
Total	10	970	3035	461	963	201	64	47	517	413	188	.317	.404	.472	877	131	140	36	16		.989	20	1-522,O-319L/S-4,3	10.7
■ LENNY HARRIS	Harris, Leonard Anthony b: 10/28/64, Miami, Fla. BL/TR, 5'10", 205 lbs. Deb: 9/7/88 Career OF: (124-LF 3-CF 148-RF)																							
1988	Cin-N	16	43	7	16	1	0	0	8	5	4	.372	.438	.395	833	135	2	4	1	1	1.000	1	3-10/2-6	0.4
1989	Cin-N	61	188	17	42	4	0	2	11	9	20	.223	.263	.277	539	52	-12	10	6	0	.980	1	2-32,S-17,3-16	-0.9
	LA-N	54	147	19	37	6	1	1	15	11	13	.252	.308	.327	635	83	-3	4	3	-0	1.000	-7	O-21L,2-14/3-8,S-1	-1.1
	Yr	115	335	36	79	10	1	3	26	20	33	.236	.283	.299	581	66	-15	14	9	-0	.975	-5	2-46,3-24,O-21L,S	-2.0
1990	LA-N	137	431	61	131	16	4	2	29	29	31	.304	.349	.374	723	102	1	15	10	-0	.959	-8	3-94,2-44/O-2C,S-1	-0.6
1991	LA-N	145	429	59	123	16	1	3	38	37	32	.287	.350	.350	700	100	1	12	3	2	.943	-1	*3-113,2-27,S-20,/O	0.3
1992	LA-N	135	347	28	94	11	0	0	30	24	24	.271	.320	.303	622	78	-9	19	7	2	.963	17	2-81,3-33,O-15R,S	1.1
1993	LA-N	107	160	20	38	6	1	2	11	15	15	.237	.303	.325	628	72	-6	3	1	0	.987	2	2-35,3-17/S-3,O-2R	-0.3
1994	Cin-N	66	100	13	31	3	1	0	14	5	13	.310	.343	.360	703	84	-2	7	2	1	.846	-0	3-15/1-4,O-3R,2-2	-0.2
1995	*Cin-N	101	197	32	41	8	3	2	16	14	20	.208	.261	.310	570	50	-15	10	1	2	.939	-2	3-24,1-23/O-8L,2-1	-1.7
1996	Cin-N	125	302	33	86	17	2	5	32	21	31	.285	.333	.404	737	93	-3	14	6	1	1.000	-6	O-37L,3-24,1-16,/2	-1.0
1997	Cin-N	120	238	32	65	13	1	3	28	18	18	.273	.329	.374	703	83	-6	4	3	-0	.977	-14	O-42L,2-20,3-13,1	-2.0
1998	Cin-N	57	122	12	36	8	0	0	10	8	9	.295	.344	.361	704	85	-3	1	3	-1	.929	-3	O-32(13-0-20)/P-1	-0.8
	NY-N	75	168	18	39	7	0	6	17	9	12	.232	.275	.381	656	71	-7	5	2	0	.988	-11	O-65R,3-10/2-2,1D	-2.0
	Yr	132	290	30	75	15	0	6	27	17	21	.259	.304	.372	677	77	-10	6	5	-0	.968	-14	O-97R,3-10/2-2,P1D	-2.8
1999	Col-N	91	158	15	47	12	0	0	13	6	6	.297	.323	.373	697	59	-9	1	1	-0	.924	3	2-24,O-14R/3-2,D-2	-0.6
	*Ari-N	19	29	2	11	1	0	1	7	0	1	.379	.379	.517	897	123	1	1	0	0	1.000	0	/3-5,O-2(0-0-2)	0.1
	Yr	110	187	17	58	13	0	1	20	6	7	.310	.332	.396	727	68	-9	2	1	0	.924	3	2-24,O-16R/3-7,D-2	-0.5
2000	Ari-N	36	85	9	16	1	1	1	13	3	5	.188	.216	.259	475	19	-11	5	0	1	.909	-2	3-20/O-3(0-0-3)	-1.1
	*NY-N	76	138	22	42	6	3	3	13	17	17	.304	.381	.457	837	114	3	8	1	1	.854	0	3-16,O-11L,1-10,/2D	0.4
	Yr	112	223	31	58	7	4	4	26	20	22	.260	.321	.381	702	78	-8	13	1	3	.880	-2	3-36,O-14R,1-10,/2D	-0.7
Total	13	1421	3282	399	895	136	18	31	305	231	271	.273	.323	.353	677	83	-78	123	50	10	.936	-30	3-420,2-299,O/1SDP	-10.0
■ NED HARRIS	Harris, Robert Ned b: 7/9/16, Ames, Iowa d: 12/18/76, W.Palm Beach, Fla. BL/TL, 5'11", 175 lbs. Deb: 4/20/41																							
1941	Det-A	26	61	11	13	3	1	1	4	6	13	.213	.284	.344	628	59	-4	1	0	0	1.000	-2	O-12(12-0-0)	-0.6
1942	Det-A	121	398	53	108	16	10	9	45	49	35	.271	.351	.430	781	110	5	5	4	-0	.944	-10	*O-104(0-0-104)	-1.2
1943	Det-A	114	354	43	90	14	3	6	32	47	29	.254	.343	.362	705	99	0	6	8	-1	.961	-3	O-96(4-6-86)	-1.1
1946	Det-A	1	1	0	0	0	0	0	0	0	0	.000	.000	.000	0	-94	-0	0	0	0	.000	0	H	0.0
Total	4	262	814	107	211	33	14	16	81	102	77	.259	.342	.393	736	101	1	12	12	-2	.955	-15	O-212(16-6-190)	-2.9
■ BUCKY HARRIS	Harris, Stanley Raymond b: 11/8/1896, Port Jervis, N.Y. d: 11/8/77, Bethesda, Md. BR/TR, 5'9.5", 156 lbs. Deb: 8/28/19 MH Career OF: (0-LF 0-CF 1-RF)																							
1919	Was-A	8	28	0	6	2	0	0	4	1	3	.214	.267	.286	552	56	-2	0			.925	2	/2-8	0.1
1920	Was-A	136	506	76	152	26	6	1	68	41	36	.300	.377	.381	758	104	5	16	17	-2	.958	-10	*2-134	-0.6
1921	Was-A	154	584	82	169	22	8	0	54	54	39	.289	.367	.354	722	89	-7	29	9	3	.959	12	*2-154	1.2
1922	Was-A	154	602	95	162	24	8	2	40	52	38	.269	.341	.346	687	84	-14	25	11	2	.970	**26**	*2-154	1.8
1923	Was-A	145	532	60	150	21	13	2	70	50	29	.282	.358	.382	740	100	0	23	16	-1	.961	19	*2-144/S-1	2.2
1924	*Was-A	143	544	88	146	28	9	1	58	56	41	.268	.344	.358	703	84	-13	20	10	1	.968	-13	*2-143,M	-2.0
1925	*Was-A	144	551	91	158	30	3	1	66	64	21	.287	.370	.358	728	87	-9	14	12	-1	.970	3	*2-144,M	-0.2
1926	Was-A	141	537	94	152	39	9	1	63	58	41	.283	.363	.395	757	100	0	16	11	-0	.963	-11	*2-141,M	-0.6
1927	Was-A	128	475	98	127	20	3	1	55	66	33	.267	.363	.328	691	81	-11	18	3	3	**.972**	1	*2-128,M	-0.3
1928	Was-A	99	358	34	73	11	5	0	28	27	26	.204	.264	.263	526	39	-32	5	2	0	.970	11	2-96/3-1,O-1(0-0-1),M	-1.8
1929	Det-A	7	11	3	1	0	0	0	0	2	2	.091	.231	.091	322	-14	-2	1	0	0	.900	0	/2-4,S-1,M	-0.1
1931	Det-A	4	8	1	1	1	0	0	0	1	1	.125	.222	.250	472	23	-1	0	0	0	1.000	0	/2-3,M	-0.1
Total	12	1263	4736	722	1297	224	64	9	506	472	310	.274	.352	.354	706	86	-84	167	91		.965	43	*2-1253/S-2,O-1R,3	-0.4
■ VIC HARRIS	Harris, Victor Lanier b: 3/27/50, Los Angeles, Cal. BB/TR, 6', 170 lbs. Deb: 7/21/72 Career OF: (28-LF 147-CF 32-RF)																							
1972	Tex-A	61	186	8	26	5	1	0	10	12	39	.140	.192	.177	369	11	-21	7	3	0	.960	0	2-58/S-1	-1.9
1973	Tex-A	152	555	71	138	14	7	8	44	55	81	.249	.319	.342	661	90	-7	13	12	-1	.977	2	*O-113C,3-25,2-18	-0.9
1974	Chi-N	62	200	18	39	6	3	0	11	29	26	.195	.297	.255	552	53	-12	9	3	1	.943	-17	2-56	-2.5
1975	Chi-N	51	56	6	10	0	0	0	5	6	7	.179	.258	.179	437	22	-6	0	0	0	.900	-2	O-11(9-2-0)/3-7,2-5	-0.8
1976	StL-N	97	259	21	59	12	3	1	19	16	55	.228	.275	.309	584	65	-12	1	2	-0	.945	-8	2-37,O-35C,3-12,/S	-2.0
1977	SF-N	69	165	28	43	12	0	2	14	19	36	.261	.337	.370	707	90	-2	2	1	0	.973	-10	2-27,S-11/3-9,O-3C	-1.0
1978	SF-N	53	100	8	15	4	0	1	11	11	24	.150	.234	.220	454	29	-10	0	0	0	.934	-7	S-22,2-10/O-6(4-2-1)	-1.6
1980	Mil-A	34	89	8	19	4	1	1	7	12	13	.213	.307	.315	622	73	-3	4	1	1	.967	-2	O-31(4-5-22)/3-2,2-1	-0.6
Total	8	579	1610	168	349	57	15	13	121	160	281	.217	.289	.295	584	65	-73	36	22	0	.954	-43	2-212,O-199C/3-55,S	-11.3
■ CHUCK HARRISON	Harrison, Charles William b: 4/25/41, Abilene, Tex. BR/TR, 5'10", 190 lbs. Deb: 9/15/65																							
1965	Hou-N	15	45	2	9	4	0	1	9	8	9	.200	.321	.356	676	97	-0	0	0	0	.983	0	1-12	-0.1
1966	Hou-N	119	434	52	111	23	2	9	52	37	69	.256	.317	.380	697	100	-1	2	0	0	.992	4	*1-114	-0.4
1967	Hou-N	70	177	13	43	7	3	2	26	13	30	.243	.295	.350	645	87	-3	0	0	0	.987	-0	1-59	-0.7
1969	KC-A	75	213	18	47	5	1	3	18	16	20	.221	.278	.296	574	60	-11	1	2	-0	.993	2	1-55	-1.5
1971	KC-A	49	143	9	31	4	0	2	21	11	19	.217	.273	.287	559	59	-8	0	0	0	.992	0	1-39	-1.1
Total	5	328	1012	94	241	43	6	17	126	85	147	.238	.299	.343	642	83	-23	3	2	-0	.991	5	1-279	-3.8
■ BEN HARRISON	Harrison, Leo J. BR, Deb: 9/27/01																							
1901	Was-A	1	2	0	0	0	0	0	0	1		.000	.333	.000	333	-2	-0	0			.000	-0	/O-1(1-0-0)	-0.1
■ TOM HARRISON	Harrison, Thomas James b: 1/18/45, Trail, B.C., Canada BR/TR, 6'3", 200 lbs. Deb: 5/7/65																							
1965	KC-A	2	0	0	0	0	0	0	0	0	0	—	—	—	—	—	0	0	0	0	.000	-0	/P-1	0.0
■ RIT HARRISON	Harrison, Washington Ritter b: 9/16/1849, Waterbury, Conn. d: 11/7/1888, Bridgeport, Conn. Deb: 5/20/1875																							
1875	NH-n	1	4	0	2	1	0	0	1	0	0	.500	.500	.750	1250	376	1	0	1	-0	.333	-2	/C-1,S-1	-0.1
■ SAM HARSHANEY	Harshaney, Samuel b: 4/24/10, Madison, Ill. BR/TR, 6', 180 lbs. Deb: 9/28/37																							
1937	StL-A	5	11	0	1	1	0	0	0	3	0	.091	.286	.182	468	20	-1	0	0	0	.905	1	/C-4	-0.1
1938	StL-A	11	24	2	7	0	0	0	0	3	2	.292	.370	.292	662	68	-1	0	0	0	.975	-0	C-10	-0.1
1939	StL-A	42	145	15	35	2	0	0	15	9	8	.241	.290	.255	545	40	-13	0	1	-0	.994	-2	C-36	-1.2
1940	StL-A	3	1	0	0	0	0	0	0	1	0	.000	.500	.000	500	41	0	0	0	0	.000	0	/C-2	0.0
Total	4	61	181	17	43	3	0	0	15	16	10	.238	.303	.254	557	43	-15	0	1	-0	.983	-2	/C-52	-1.4
■ JACK HARSHMAN	Harshman, John Elvin b: 7/12/27, San Diego, Cal. BL/TL, 6'2", 185 lbs. Deb: 9/16/48																							
1948	NY-N	5	8	0	2	0	0	0	1	1	3	.250	.333	.250	583	60	-0	0			1.000	0	/1-3	0.0
1950	NY-N	9	32	3	4	0	0	2	4	3	6	.125	.200	.313	513	32	-3	0			.989	0	/1-9	-0.3
1952	NY-N	3	2	0	0	0	0	0	0	0	0	.000	.000	.000	0	-99	-1	0	0	0	1.000	0	/P-2	0.0
1954	Chi-A	36	56	6	8	1	0	2	5	12	21	.143	.294	.268	562	53	-4	0	0	0	.967	-1	P-35/1-1	0.0
1955	Chi-A	32	60	6	11	1	0	2	8	9	17	.183	.290	.300	590	57	-4	0	0	0	.970	-0	P-32	0.0
1956	Chi-A	36	71	8	12	1	0	6	19	11	21	.169	.280	.437	717	86	-2	0	0	0	.886	-2	P-34	0.0

YEAR	TM/L	G	AB	R	H	2B	3B	HR	RBI	BB	SO	AVG	OBP	SLG	OPS	OPS+	BR+	SB	CS	SBR	FA	FR	G/POS	TPR
1957	Chi-A	30	45	5	10	1	0	2	5	10	17	.222	.364	.378	741	102	0	0	0	0	.947	-3	P-30	0.0
1958	Bal-A	47	82	11	16	1	0	6	14	17	22	.195	.333	.427	760	114	2	0	0	0	.980	0	P-34/O-1(0-1-0)	0.0
1959	Bal-A	15	10	3	2	0	0	1	1	2	2	.200	.333	.500	833	128	0	0	0	0	1.000	1	P-14	0.0
	Bos-A	9	7	1	1	0	0	0	2	2	2	.143	.333	.143	476	34	-1	0	0	0	1.000	-1	/P-8	0.0
	Cle-A	21	34	3	7	1	0	0	5	5	4	.206	.308	.235	543	53	-2	0	0	0	1.000	-0	P-13	0.0
	Yr	45	51	7	10	1	0	1	8	9	8	.196	.317	.275	591	65	-2	0	0	0	1.000	1	P-35	0.0
1960	Cle-A	15	17	0	3	1	0	0	1	0	4	.176	.176	.235	412	11	-2	0	0	0	1.000	-1	P-15	0.0
Total	10	258	424	46	76	7	0	21	65	72	119	.179	.298	.344	643	74	-16	0	0		.962	-5	P-217/1-13,O-1(0-1-0)	-0.3

■ BURT HART
Hart, James Burton b: 6/28/1870, Brown Co., Minn. d: 1/29/21, Sacramento, Cal. BB, 6'3", 200 lbs. Deb: 6/6/01

YEAR	TM/L	G	AB	R	H	2B	3B	HR	RBI	BB	SO	AVG	OBP	SLG	OPS	OPS+	BR+	SB	CS	SBR	FA	FR	G/POS	TPR
1901	Bal-A	58	206	33	64	3	5	0	23	20		.311	.383	.374	756	106	2	7			.976	-8	1-58	-0.6

■ HUB HART
Hart, James Henry b: 2/2/1878, Everett, Mass. d: 10/10/60, Fort Wayne, Ind. BL/TR, 5'11", 170 lbs. Deb: 7/16/05

YEAR	TM/L	G	AB	R	H	2B	3B	HR	RBI	BB	SO	AVG	OBP	SLG	OPS	OPS+	BR+	SB	CS	SBR	FA	FR	G/POS	TPR
1905	Chi-A	11	20	3	2	0	0	0	4	3		.100	.217	.100	317	2	-2	0			1.000	-2	/C-7	-0.4
1906	Chi-A	17	37	1	6	0	0	0	0	2		.162	.205	.162	367	16	-4	0			.935	-4	C-15	-0.7
1907	Chi-A	29	70	6	19	1	0	0	7	5		.271	.329	.286	615	100	0	1			.956	-5	C-25	-0.3
Total	3	57	127	10	27	1	0	0	11	10		.213	.275	.220	496	59	-5	1			.957	-11	/C-47	-1.4

■ MIKE HART
Hart, James Michael b: 12/20/51, Kalamazoo, Mich. BB/TR, 6'3", 185 lbs. Deb: 6/12/80

YEAR	TM/L	G	AB	R	H	2B	3B	HR	RBI	BB	SO	AVG	OBP	SLG	OPS	OPS+	BR+	SB	CS	SBR	FA	FR	G/POS	TPR
1980	Tex-A	5	4	1	1	0	0	0	0	1	1	.250	.400	.250	650	85	-0	0	0	0	1.000	-1	/O-2(0-2-0)	-0.1

■ JIM RAY HART
Hart, James Ray b: 10/30/41, Hookerton, N.C. BR/TR, 5'11", 185 lbs. Deb: 7/7/63 Career OF: (257-LF 0-CF 7-RF)

YEAR	TM/L	G	AB	R	H	2B	3B	HR	RBI	BB	SO	AVG	OBP	SLG	OPS	OPS+	BR+	SB	CS	SBR	FA	FR	G/POS	TPR
1963	SF-N	7	20	1	4	1	0	0	2	3	6	.200	.360	.250	610	80	-0	0	0	0	1.000	0	/3-7	0.0
1964	SF-N	153	566	71	162	15	6	31	81	47	94	.286	.345	.498	843	132	23	5	2	0	.937	4	*3-149/O-6(1-0-5)	2.8
1965	SF-N	160	591	91	177	30	6	23	96	47	75	.299	.353	.487	840	130	23	6	4	-0	.919	-13	*3-144,O-15(14-0-1)	0.9
1966	SF-N★	156	578	88	165	23	4	33	93	48	75	.285	.344	.510	855	130	22	2	5	-1	.941	-5	*3-139,O-17(16-0-1)	1.5
1967	SF-N	158	578	98	167	26	7	29	99	77	100	.289	.376	.509	885	153	40	1	1	-0	.937	-15	3-89,O-72(72-0-0)	2.3
1968	SF-N	136	480	67	124	14	3	23	78	46	74	.258	.327	.444	771	130	17	3	1	0	.925	-12	3-72,O-65(65-0-0)	0.2
1969	SF-N	95	236	27	60	9	0	3	26	28	49	.254	.346	.331	676	92	-2	0	0	0	.943	-7	O-68(68-0-0)/3-3	-1.2
1970	SF-N	76	255	30	72	12	1	8	37	30	29	.282	.365	.431	796	114	5	0	0	0	.908	-17	3-56,O-18(18-0-0)	-1.3
1971	*SF-N	31	39	5	10	0	0	2	5	6	8	.256	.356	.410	766	118	1	0	1	-0	.833	-1	/3-3,O-3(3-0-0)	0.0
1972	SF-N	24	79	10	24	5	0	5	8	6	10	.304	.360	.557	917	155	5	0	1	-0	.886	-9	3-20	-0.4
1973	SF-N	5	3	0	0	0	0	0	1	3	1	.000	.500	.000	500	48	0	0	0	0	.600	0	/3-1	0.0
	NY-A	114	339	29	86	13	2	13	52	36	45	.254	.325	.419	744	112	5	0	2	-1	.000	0	*D-106	0.1
1974	NY-A	10	19	1	1	0	0	0	0	3	7	.053	.182	.053	234	-30	-3	0	0	0	.000	0	/D-4	-0.3
Total	12	1125	3783	518	1052	148	29	170	578	380	573	.278	.348	.467	816	128	136	17	17	-2	.929	-73	3-683,O-264L,D-110	4.6

■ MIKE HART
Hart, Michael Lawrence b: 2/17/58, Milwaukee, Wis. BL/TL, 5'11", 185 lbs. Deb: 5/8/84

YEAR	TM/L	G	AB	R	H	2B	3B	HR	RBI	BB	SO	AVG	OBP	SLG	OPS	OPS+	BR+	SB	CS	SBR	FA	FR	G/POS	TPR
1984	Min-A	13	29	0	5	0	0	0	5	1	2	.172	.200	.172	372	4	-4	0	1	-0	1.000	1	O-11(8-0-3)	-0.4
1987	Bal-A	34	76	7	12	2	0	4	12	6	19	.158	.220	.342	562	47	-6	1	4	-1	1.000	-2	O-32(4-29-1)	-0.9
Total	2	47	105	7	17	2	0	4	17	7	21	.162	.214	.295	510	35	-10	1	5	-2	1.000	-1	/O-43(12-29-4)	-1.3

■ TOM HART
Hart, Thomas Henry "Bushy" b: 6/15/1869, Canaan, N.Y. d: 9/17/39, Gardner, Mass. 5'7", 160 lbs. Deb: 4/15/1891

YEAR	TM/L	G	AB	R	H	2B	3B	HR	RBI	BB	SO	AVG	OBP	SLG	OPS	OPS+	BR+	SB	CS	SBR	FA	FR	G/POS	TPR
1891	Was-a	8	24	1	3	0	0	0	2	2	1	.125	.192	.125	317	-9	-3	1			1.000	1	/C-5,O-3(0-3-0)	-0.2

■ BILL HART
Hart, William Woodrow b: 3/4/13, Wiconisco, Pa. d: 7/29/68, Lykens, Pa. BR/TR, 6', 175 lbs. Deb: 9/18/43

YEAR	TM/L	G	AB	R	H	2B	3B	HR	RBI	BB	SO	AVG	OBP	SLG	OPS	OPS+	BR+	SB	CS	SBR	FA	FR	G/POS	TPR
1943	Bro-N	8	19	0	3	0	0	0	1	1	2	.158	.200	.158	358	4	-2	0			1.000	4	/3-6,S-1	0.2
1944	Bro-N	29	90	8	16	4	2	0	4	9	7	.178	.253	.267	519	47	-6	1			.941	-8	S-25/3-2	-1.3
1945	Bro-N	58	161	27	37	6	2	3	27	14	21	.230	.291	.348	639	78	-5	7			.913	-2	3-39/S-8	-0.7
Total	3	95	270	35	56	10	4	3	32	24	30	.207	.272	.307	580	63	-14	8			.924	-6	/3-47,S-34	-1.8

■ CHUCK HARTENSTEIN
Hartenstein, Charles Oscar "Twiggy" b: 5/26/42, Seguin, Tex. BR/TR, 5'11", 165 lbs. Deb: 9/11/65 C

YEAR	TM/L	G	AB	R	H	2B	3B	HR	RBI	BB	SO	AVG	OBP	SLG	OPS	OPS+	BR+	SB	CS	SBR	FA	FR	G/POS	TPR
1965	Chi-N	1	0	0	0	0	0	0	0	0	0	—	—	—	—	—	0	0	0	0	.000	0	R	0.0
1966	Chi-N	5	0	0	0	0	0	0	0	0	0	—	—	—	—	—	0	0	0	0	1.000	0	/P-5	0.0
1967	Chi-N	45	16	0	1	0	0	0	1	0	9	.063	.063	.063	125	-61	-3	0	0	0	.950	-0	P-45	0.0
1968	Chi-N	28	2	0	0	0	0	0	0	0	0	.000	.000	.000	0	-94	-0	0	0	0	.818	-0	P-28	0.0
1969	Pit-N	56	14	0	1	0	0	0	0	1	8	.071	.133	.071	205	-42	-3	0	0	0	1.000	1	P-56	0.0
1970	Pit-N	17	1	1	0	0	0	0	0	0	0	.000	.000	.000	0	-99	-0	0	0	0	.900	1	P-17	0.0
	StL-N	6	2	0	0	0	0	0	0	1	2	.000	.333	.000	333	-3	-0	0	0	0	1.000	0	/P-6	0.0
	Yr	23	3	1	0	0	0	0	0	1	2	.000	.250	.000	250	-27	-1	0	0	0	.923	1	P-23	0.0
	Bos-A	17	2	0	0	0	0	0	0	1	2	.000	.333	.000	333	-0	-0	0	0	0	1.000	-1	P-17	0.0
1977	Tor-A	13	0	0	0	0	0	0	0	0	0	—	—	—	—	—	0	0	0	0	1.000	-0	P-13	0.0
Total	7	188	37	1	2	0	0	0	1	3	21	.054	.125	.054	179	-47	-7	0	0	0	.952	2	P-187	0.0

■ BRUCE HARTFORD
Hartford, Bruce Daniel b: 5/14/1892, Chicago, Ill. d: 5/25/75, Los Angeles, Cal. BR/TR, 6'0.5", 190 lbs. Deb: 6/3/14

YEAR	TM/L	G	AB	R	H	2B	3B	HR	RBI	BB	SO	AVG	OBP	SLG	OPS	OPS+	BR+	SB	CS	SBR	FA	FR	G/POS	TPR
1914	Cle-A	8	22	5	4	1	0	0	0	4	9	.182	.308	.227	535	59	-1	0			.913	-3	/S-8	-0.4

■ CHRIS HARTJE
Hartje, Christian Henry b: 3/25/15, San Francisco, Cal d: 6/26/46, Seattle, Wash. BR/TR, 5'10.5", 165 lbs. Deb: 9/9/39

YEAR	TM/L	G	AB	R	H	2B	3B	HR	RBI	BB	SO	AVG	OBP	SLG	OPS	OPS+	BR+	SB	CS	SBR	FA	FR	G/POS	TPR
1939	Bro-N	9	16	2	5	1	0	0	5	1	0	.313	.353	.375	728	92	-0	0			.909	-2	/C-8	-0.2

■ GROVER HARTLEY
Hartley, Grover Allen "Slick" b: 7/2/1888, Osgood, Ind. d: 10/19/64, Daytona Beach, Fla BR/TR, 5'11", 175 lbs. Deb: 5/13/11 C Career OF: (0-LF 2-CF 0-RF)

YEAR	TM/L	G	AB	R	H	2B	3B	HR	RBI	BB	SO	AVG	OBP	SLG	OPS	OPS+	BR+	SB	CS	SBR	FA	FR	G/POS	TPR
1911	NY-N	11	18	1	4	2	0	0	1	1	1	.222	.263	.333	596	64	-1	1			.962	3	C-10	0.2
1912	NY-N	25	34	3	8	2	1	0	7	0	4	.235	.257	.353	610	64	-2	2			.960	2	C-25	0.1
1913	NY-N	23	19	4	6	0	0	0	0	1	2	.316	.350	.316	666	90	-0	4			.978	2	C-21/1-1	0.2
1914	StL-F	86	212	24	61	13	2	1	25	12	26	.288	.329	.382	711	89	-7	4			.956	-9	C-32,2-13/1-9,3O	-1.4
1915	StL-F	120	394	47	108	21	6	1	50	42	21	.274	.356	.365	721	98	-5	10			.972	-7	*C-113/1-1	-0.3
1916	StL-A	89	222	19	50	8	0	0	12	30	24	.225	.325	.261	587	80	-4	4			.968	1	C-75	0.2
1917	StL-A	19	13	2	3	0	0	0	0	2	1	.231	.333	.231	564	75	-0	0			.875	1	/C-4,S-1,3-1	0.1
1924	NY-N	4	7	1	2	1	0	0	1	1	0	.286	.375	.429	804	118	0	1	0	0	1.000	-0	/C-3	0.0
1925	NY-N	46	95	9	30	1	1	0	8	8	3	.316	.375	.347	722	89	-1	2	0	0	.974	4	C-37/1-8	0.4
1926	NY-N	13	21	0	1	0	0	0	0	5	0	.048	.231	.048	278	-22	-4	0			1.000	0	C-13	-0.3
1927	Bos-A	103	244	23	67	11	0	1	31	22	14	.275	.337	.332	669	76	-8	1	0	0	.967	-13	C-86	-1.5
1929	Cle-A	24	33	2	9	0	1	0	8	2	1	.273	.314	.333	648	64	-2	0	0	0	1.000	-3	C-13	-0.4
1930	Cle-A	1	4	0	3	0	0	0	1	0	0	.750	.750	.750	1500	271	1	0	0	0	.750	-0	/C-1	0.1
1934	StL-A	5	3	0	1	1	0	0	0	1	0	.333	.500	.667	1167	183	0	0	0	0	1.000	0	/C-2	0.1
Total	14	569	1319	135	353	60	11	3	144	127	97	.268	.339	.337	675	85	-33	29	0		.968	-19	C-435/1-19,2-13,3OS	-2.5

■ CHICK HARTLEY
Hartley, Walter Scott b: 8/22/1880, Philadelphia, Pa. d: 7/18/48, Philadelphia, Pa. BR/TR, 5'8", 180 lbs. Deb: 6/4/02

YEAR	TM/L	G	AB	R	H	2B	3B	HR	RBI	BB	SO	AVG	OBP	SLG	OPS	OPS+	BR+	SB	CS	SBR	FA	FR	G/POS	TPR
1902	NY-N	1	4	0	0	0	0	0	0	0		.000	.000	.000	0	-99	-1	0			1.000	-0	/O-1(1-0-0)	-0.1

■ FRED HARTMAN
Hartman, Frederick Orrin "Dutch" b: 4/25/1868, Allegheny, Pa. d: 11/11/38, McKeesport, Pa. BR/TR, 5'8", 170 lbs. Deb: 7/26/1894

YEAR	TM/L	G	AB	R	H	2B	3B	HR	RBI	BB	SO	AVG	OBP	SLG	OPS	OPS+	BR+	SB	CS	SBR	FA	FR	G/POS	TPR
1894	Pit-N	49	182	41	58	4	7	2	20	16	11	.319	.389	.451	840	103	1	12			.876	-4	3-49	-0.1
1897	StL-N	125	519	67	158	21	8	2	67	26		.304	.350	.387	737	96	-3	18			.867	-3	*3-125	-0.4
1898	NY-N	123	475	57	129	16	11	2	88	25		.272	.313	.364	678	97	-3	11			.882	9	*3-123	0.7
1899	NY-N	51	177	25	42	3	5	1	17	12		.237	.322	.328	649	81	-4	2			.883	-3	3-51	-0.6
1901	Chi-A	120	473	77	146	23	13	3	89	25		.309	.355	.431	786	120	12	31			.894	-6	*3-119	0.9
1902	StL-N	114	416	30	90	10	3	0	52	14		.216	.251	.255	505	58	-21	14			.908	-3	*3-105/S-4,1-3	-2.3
Total	6	582	2242	297	623	77	47	10	333	118	11	.278	.326	.368	694	95	-19	88			.886	-10	3-572/S-4,1-3	-1.8

■ J C HARTMAN
Hartman, J C b: 4/15/34, Cottonton, Ala. BR/TR, 6', 175 lbs. Deb: 7/21/62

YEAR	TM/L	G	AB	R	H	2B	3B	HR	RBI	BB	SO	AVG	OBP	SLG	OPS	OPS+	BR+	SB	CS	SBR	FA	FR	G/POS	TPR
1962	Hou-N	51	148	11	33	5	0	0	5	4	16	.223	.248	.257	505	39	-13	1	1	-0	.972	7	S-48	-0.3

YEAR	TM/L	G	AB	R	H	2B	3B	HR	RBI	BB	SO	AVG	OBP	SLG	OPS	OPS+	BR+	SB	CS	SBR	FA	FR	G/POS	TPR
1963	Hou-N	39	90	2	11	1	0	0	3	2	13	.122	.151	.133	284	-19	-14	1	0	0	.950	0	S-32	-1.3
Total	2	90	238	13	44	6	0	0	8	6	29	.185	.211	.210	421	18	-27	2	1	0	.964	7	/S-80	-1.6
■ GABBY HARTNETT Hartnett, Charles Leo b: 12/20/1900, Woonsocket, R.I. d: 12/20/72, Park Ridge, Ill. BR/TR, 6'1", 195 lbs. Deb: 4/12/22 MCH																								
1922	Chi-N	31	72	4	14	1	1	0	4	6	8	.194	.256	.236	493	27	-8	1	0	0	.982	6	C-27	-0.1
1923	Chi-N	85	231	28	62	12	2	8	39	25	22	.268	.347	.442	789	107	2	4	0	1	.994	4	C-39,1-31	0.7
1924	Chi-N	111	354	56	106	17	7	16	67	39	37	.299	.377	.523	899	137	18	10	2	2	.963	-4	*C-105	2.3
1925	Chi-N	117	398	61	115	28	3	24	67	36	77	.289	.351	.555	906	126	13	1	5	-2	.958	10	*C-110	2.7
1926	Chi-N	93	284	35	78	25	3	8	41	32	37	.275	.352	.468	821	118	7	0			.978	5	C-88	1.7
1927	Chi-N	127	449	56	132	32	5	10	80	44	42	.294	.361	.454	815	117	10	2			.973	4	*C-126	2.3
1928	Chi-N	120	388	61	117	26	9	14	57	65	32	.302	.404	.523	928	143	25	3			**.989**	9	*C-118	4.0
1929	*Chi-N	25	22	2	6	2	1	1	9	5	5	.273	.407	.591	998	144	2	1			1.000	-0	/C-1	0.1
1930	Chi-N	141	508	84	172	31	3	37	122	55	62	.339	.404	.630	1034	144	35	0			**.989**	3	*C-136	4.1
1931	Chi-N	116	380	53	107	32	1	8	70	52	48	.282	.370	.434	804	113	8	3			.981	2	*C-105	1.6
1932	*Chi-N	121	406	52	110	25	3	12	52	51	59	.271	.354	.436	790	112	7	0			.982	6	*C-117/1-1	2.0
1933	Chi-N★	140	490	55	135	21	4	16	88	37	51	.276	.326	.433	759	115	9	1			.989	7	*C-140	2.6
1934	Chi-N★	130	438	58	131	21	1	22	90	37	46	.299	.358	.502	860	130	18	0			**.996**	14	*C-129	3.7
1935	*Chi-N★	116	413	67	142	32	6	13	91	41	46	.344	.404	.545	949	152	30	1			.984	15	*C-110	4.9
1936	Chi-N★	121	424	49	130	25	6	7	64	30	36	.307	.361	.443	804	113	7	0			**.991**	9	*C-114	2.2
1937	Chi-N★	110	356	47	126	21	6	12	82	43	19	.354	.424	.548	971	156	28	0			**.996**	1	*C-103	3.4
1938	*Chi-N☆	88	299	40	82	19	1	10	59	48	17	.274	.380	.445	825	123	10	1			**.995**	-4	C-83,M	1.2
1939	Chi-N	97	306	36	85	18	2	12	59	37	32	.278	.358	.467	825	118	7	0			.992	-8	C-86,M	0.5
1940	Chi-N	37	64	3	17	3	0	1	12	8	7	.266	.347	.359	707	97	-0	0			.951	1	C-22/1-1,M	0.2
1941	NY-N	64	150	20	45	5	0	5	26	12	14	.300	.356	.433	789	119	4	0			.994	-3	C-34	0.2
Total	20	1990	6432	867	1912	396	64	236	1179	703	697	.297	.370	.489	858	126	232	28	7		.984	74	*C-1793/1-33	40.3
■ PAT HARTNETT Hartnett, Patrick J. "Happy" b: 10/20/1863, Boston, Mass. d: 4/10/35, Boston, Mass. 6'1", 175 lbs. Deb: 4/18/1890																								
1890	StL-a	14	53	6	10	2	1	0	4	6		.189	.283	.264	547	54	-3	1			.954	-1	1-14	-0.5
■ GREG HARTS Harts, Gregory Rudolph b: 4/21/50, Atlanta, Ga. BL/TL, 6', 168 lbs. Deb: 9/15/73																								
1973	NY-N	3	2	0	1	0	0	0	0	0	0	.500	.500	.500	1000	181	0	0	0	0	.000	0	H	0.0
■ TOPSY HARTSEL Hartsel, Tully Frederick b: 6/26/1874, Polk, Ohio d: 10/14/44, Toledo, Ohio BL/TL, 5'5", 155 lbs. Deb: 9/14/1898																								
1898	Lou-N	22	71	11	23	0	0	0	9	11		.324	.422	.324	746	116	2	2			.931	-2	O-21(0-0-21)	-0.1
1899	Lou-N	30	75	8	18	1	1	1	7	11		.240	.345	.320	665	83	-1	1			.927	-2	O-22(7-0-15)	-0.4
1900	Cin-N	18	64	10	21	2	1	2	5	8		.328	.403	.484	887	148	4	7			.957	-5	O-18(18-0-0)	-0.2
1901	Chi-N	140	558	111	187	25	16	7	54	74		.335	.414	.475	889	164	47	41			.951	-1	*O-140(131-0-9)	3.7
1902	Phi-A	137	545	**109**	154	20	12	5	58	**87**		.283	.383	.391	774	110	10	**47**			.955	-1	*O-137(137-0-0)	0.1
1903	Phi-A	98	373	65	116	19	14	5	26	49		.311	.391	.477	868	152	25	13			.968	-6	O-96(94-2-0)	1.4
1904	Phi-A	147	534	79	135	17	12	2	25	75		.253	.347	.341	688	112	10	19			.959	-4	*O-147(122-25-0)	-0.3
1905	*Phi-A	150	538	88	148	22	8	0	28	**121**		.275	**.409**	.346	755	138	31	37			.939	-7	*O-149(134-15-0)	1.7
1906	Phi-A	144	533	96	136	21	9	1	30	**88**		.255	.363	.334	697	115	13	31			.969	0	*O-144(144-0-0)	0.5
1907	Phi-A	143	507	93	142	23	6	3	29	**106**		.280	**.405**	.367	771	143	31	20			.967	-11	*O-143(143-0-0)	1.2
1908	Phi-A	129	460	73	112	16	6	4	29	**93**		.243	.371	.330	701	120	15	15			.960	-5	*O-129(129-0-0)	0.3
1909	Phi-A	83	267	30	72	4	4	1	18	48		.270	.381	.326	707	121	9	3			.966	-4	O-74(72-0-2)	0.1
1910	*Phi-A	90	285	45	63	10	3	0	22	58		.221	.353	.277	630	99	3	11			.945	-6	O-83(83-0-0)	-0.9
1911	Phi-A	25	38	8	9	2	0	0	1	8		.237	.396	.289	685	94	0	0			.941	1	/O-9(9-0-0)	0.1
Total	14	1356	4848	826	1336	182	92	31	341	837		.276	.384	.370	754	128	199	247			.956	-53	*O-1312(1223-42-47)	7.2
■ ROY HARTSFIELD Hartsfield, Roy Thomas "Spec" b: 10/25/25, Chattahoochee, Ga. BR/TR, 5'9", 165 lbs. Deb: 4/28/50 MC																								
1950	Bos-N	107	419	62	116	15	2	7	24	27	61	.277	.322	.372	694	88	-8	7			.949	-24	2-96	-2.6
1951	Bos-N	120	450	63	122	11	2	6	31	41	73	.271	.333	.344	678	89	-7	7	2	1	.969	-5	*2-114	-0.5
1952	Bos-N	38	107	13	28	4	3	0	4	5	12	.262	.295	.355	650	82	-3	0	0	0	.950	-6	2-29	-0.7
Total	3	265	976	138	266	30	7	13	59	73	146	.273	.324	.358	682	88	-18	14	2		.959	-34	2-239	-3.8
■ CLINT HARTUNG Hartung, Clinton Clarence "Floppy" or "The Hondo Hurricane" b: 8/10/22, Hondo, Tex. BR/TR, 6'4", 215 lbs. Deb: 4/15/47 Career OF: (11-LF 0-CF 35-RF)																								
1947	NY-N	34	94	13	29	4	3	4	13	3	21	.309	.330	.543	872	127	3	0			1.000	-2	P-23/O-7(7-0-0)	-0.1
1948	NY-N	43	56	5	10	1	1	0	3	7	24	.179	.270	.232	502	37	-5	0			1.000	-0	P-36	0.0
1949	NY-N	38	63	7	12	0	0	4	7	4	21	.190	.239	.381	620	64	-4	0			.957	2	P-33	0.0
1950	NY-N	32	43	7	13	2	1	3	10	1	13	.302	.318	.605	923	136	2	0			.939	3	P-20/O-2(1-0-1),1-1	0.0
1951	*NY-N	21	44	4	9	1	0	0	2	1	9	.205	.222	.227	449	21	-5	0	0	0	1.000	-2	O-12(0-0-12)	-0.8
1952	NY-N	28	78	6	17	2	1	3	8	9	24	.218	.299	.385	683	88	-1	0	0	0	.932	-1	O-24(3-0-22)	-0.3
Total	6	196	378	42	90	10	6	14	43	25	112	.238	.285	.407	693	84	-10	0	0		.972	-2	P-112/O-45R,1-1	-1.2
■ ROY HARTZELL Hartzell, Roy Allen b: 7/6/1881, Golden, Colo. d: 11/6/61, Golden, Colo. BL/TR, 5'8.5", 155 lbs. Deb: 4/17/06 Career OF: (213-LF 32-CF 306-RF)																								
1906	StL-A	113	404	43	86	7	0	0	24	19		.213	.266	.230	496	58	-19	21			.889	-3	*3-103/S-6,2-2	-2.1
1907	StL-A	60	220	20	52	3	5	0	13	11		.236	.285	.295	581	85	-4	7			.911	0	3-38,2-12/S-2,O-2R	-0.3
1908	StL-A	115	422	41	112	5	6	2	32	19		.265	.302	.320	622	101	-0	24			.943	-6	O-82R,S-18/3-7,2-4	-1.0
1909	StL-A	152	595	64	161	12	5	0	32	29		.271	.312	.308	620	103	1	14			.940	4	O-85(0-0-85),S-65/2-1	0.4
1910	StL-A	151	542	52	118	13	5	2	30	49		.218	.290	.271	561	81	-11	18			.929	1	3-89,S-38,O-23R	-0.9
1911	NY-A	144	527	67	156	17	11	3	91	63		.296	.375	.387	763	106	5	22			.936	-12	*3-124,S-12/O-8R	-0.3
1912	NY-A	125	416	50	113	10	11	1	38	64		.272	.370	.356	726	102	2	20			.906	-0	3-56,O-56R,S-10,/2	0.2
1913	NY-A	141	490	60	127	18	1	0	38	67	40	.259	.353	.300	653	91	-3	26			.942	-0	2-81,O-31R,3-21,/S	-0.3
1914	NY-A	137	481	55	112	15	9	1	32	68	38	.233	.335	.308	643	94	-2	22	25	-4	.973	0	*O-128(91-3-34)/2-5	-1.3
1915	NY-A	119	387	39	97	11	2	3	60	57	37	.251	.351	.313	664	99	1	7	19	-5	.963	-3	*O-107L/2-5,3-2	-1.2
1916	NY-A	33	64	12	12	1	0	0	7	9	3	.188	.297	.203	500	49	-4	1			1.000	-6	O-28(11-1-16)	-1.2
Total	11	1290	4548	503	1146	112	55	12	397	455	118	.252	.327	.309	635	93	-32	182	44		.959	-26	O-550R,3-440,S-1551,2	-8.0
■ LUTHER HARVEL Harvel, Luther Raymond "Red" b: 9/30/05, Cambria, Ill. d: 4/10/86, Kansas City, Mo. BR/TR, 5'11", 180 lbs. Deb: 7/31/28																								
1928	Cle-A	40	136	12	30	6	1	0	12	4	17	.221	.264	.279	543	42	-11	1	1	-0	.948	-2	O-39(0-39-0)	-1.4
■ ZAZA HARVEY Harvey, Ervin King b: 1/5/1879, Saratoga, Cal. d: 6/3/54, Santa Monica, Cal. BL/TL, 6', 190 lbs. Deb: 5/3/00																								
1900	Chi-N	2	3	0	0	0	0	0	0	0		.000	.000	.000	0	-99	-1	0			1.000	-0	/P-1	0.0
1901	Chi-A	17	40	11	10	3	1	0	3	2		.250	.302	.375	677	89	-1	1			.930	2	P-16	0.0
	Cle-A	45	170	21	60	5	5	1	24	9		.353	.392	.459	851	141	9	15			.890	2	O-45(21-0-24)	0.8
	Yr	62	210	32	70	8	6	1	27	11		.333	.375	.443	818	131	9	16			.890	3	O-45(21-0-24),P-16	0.8
1902	Cle-A	12	46	5	16	2	0	0	5	3		.348	.388	.391	779	121	1	1			1.000	0	O-12(0-0-12)	0.1
Total	3	76	259	37	86	10	6	1	32	14		.332	.373	.429	802	127	9	17			.907	4	/O-57(21-0-36),P-17	0.9
■ ZIGGY HASBROOK Hasbrook, Robert Lyndon "Ziggy" b: 11/21/1893, Grundy Center, Ia. d: 2/9/76, Garland, Tex. BR/TR, 6'1", 180 lbs. Deb: 9/6/16																								
1916	Chi-A	9	8	1	1	0	0	0	0	1	2	.125	.222	.125	347	4	-1	0			1.000	1	/1-7	0.0
1917	Chi-A	2	1	1	0	0	0	0	0	0	0	.000	.000	.000	0	-98	-0	0			1.000	1	/2-1	0.0
Total	2	11	9	2	1	0	0	0	0	1	2	.111	.200	.111	311	-6	-1	0			1.000	1	/1-7,2-1	0.0
■ BILL HASELMAN Haselman, William Joseph b: 5/25/66, Long Branch, N.J. BR/TR, 6'3", 220 lbs. Deb: 9/3/90 Career OF: (2-LF 0-CF 4-RF)																								
1990	Tex-A	7	13	0	2	0	0	0	3	1	5	.154	.214	.154	368	5	-2	0	0	0	1.000	0	/C-1,D-3	-0.1
1992	Sea-A	8	19	1	5	0	0	0	0	0	7	.263	.263	.263	526	48	-1	0	0	0	1.000	-2	/C-5,O-2(2-0-0)	-0.3
1993	Sea-A	58	137	21	35	8	0	5	16	12	19	.255	.320	.423	743	97	-1	2	1	0	.992	-2	C-49/O-2(0-0-2),D-4	0.0
1994	Sea-A	38	83	11	16	7	1	1	8	3	11	.193	.230	.337	567	43	-7	1	0	0	.982	-1	C-33/O-2(0-0-2),D-3	-0.6
1995	*Bos-A	64	152	22	37	6	1	5	23	17	30	.243	.327	.395	722	84	-4	0	2	-1	.989	8	C-48,D-11/1-1,3-1	0.4
1996	Bos-A	77	237	33	65	13	1	8	34	19	52	.274	.331	.439	770	91	-4	4	2	0	.994	19	C-69/1-2,D-2	1.7
1997	Bos-A	67	212	22	50	15	0	6	26	15	44	.236	.293	.392	684	75	-8	0	2	-1	.983	4	C-66	-0.1

YEAR	TM/L	G	AB	R	H	2B	3B	HR	RBI	BB	SO	AVG	OBP	SLG	OPS	OPS+	BR+	SB	CS	SBR	FA	FR	G/POS	TPR
1998	Tex-A	40	105	11	33	6	0	6	17	3	17	.314	.333	.543	876	118	2	0	0	0	.995	3	C-36/D-2	0.7
1999	Det-A	48	143	13	39	8	0	4	14	10	26	.273	.320	.413	733	86	-3	2	0	0	.996	6	C-39,D-11	0.4
2000	Tex-A	62	193	23	53	18	0	6	26	15	36	.275	.330	.461	791	94	-2	0	1	-0	.989	3	C-62	0.3
Total	10	469	1294	157	335	81	3	41	167	95	247	.259	.314	.421	735	86	-30	9	8	-1	.990	38	C-408/D-36,O-6R,13	2.4
■ **DON HASENMAYER** Hasenmayer, Donald Irvin b: 4/4/27, Roslyn, Pa. BR/TR, 5'10.5", 180 lbs. Deb: 5/2/45																								
1945	Phi-N	5	18	1	2	0	0	0	1	2	1	.111	.200	.111	311	-13	-3	0			.920	3	/2-4,3-1	0.0
1946	Phi-N	6	12	0	1	1	0	0	0	0	2	.083	.083	.167	250	-31	-2	0			1.000	2	/3-3	0.0
Total	2	11	30	1	3	1	0	0	1	2	3	.100	.156	.133	290	-19	-5	0			1.000	5	/3-4,2-4	0.0
■ **MICKEY HASLIN** Haslin, Michael Joseph b: 10/31/10, Wilkes-Barre, Pa. BR/TR, 5'8", 165 lbs. Deb: 9/7/33																								
1933	Phi-N	26	89	3	21	2	0	0	9	3	5	.236	.261	.258	519	43	-6	1			.956	-4	2-26	-1.0
1934	Phi-N	72	166	28	44	8	2	1	11	16	13	.265	.330	.355	685	74	-6	1			.941	-3	3-26,2-21/S-4	-0.6
1935	Phi-N	110	407	53	108	17	3	3	52	19	25	.265	.300	.344	644	66	-19	5			.931	-3	S-87,3-11/2-9	-1.4
1936	Phi-N	16	64	6	22	1	1	0	6	3	5	.344	.373	.391	764	96	-0	0			.938	-5	2-12/3-5	-0.4
	Bos-N	36	104	14	29	1	2	2	11	5	9	.279	.312	.385	697	93	-1	0			.892	-5	3-17/2-7	-0.5
	Yr	52	168	20	51	2	3	2	17	8	14	.304	.335	.387	722	95	-1	0			.854	-10	3-22,2-19	-0.9
1937	NY-N	27	42	8	8	1	0	0	5	9	3	.190	.333	.214	548	51	-2	1			.920	6	/S-9,2-4,3-4	0.4
1938	NY-N	31	102	13	33	3	0	3	15	4	4	.324	.361	.441	802	119	2	0			.902	-2	3-15,2-13	0.2
Total	6	318	974	125	265	33	8	9	109	59	64	.272	.316	.350	666	74	-33	8			.927	-15	S-100/2-92,3-78	-3.3
■ **PETE HASNEY** Hasney, Peter James b: 5/26/1865, England d: 5/24/08, Philadelphia, Pa. Deb: 9/13/1890																								
1890	Phi-a	2	7	1	1	0	0	0	0	1		.143	.250	.143	393	16	-1	0			.000	-1	/O-2(0-0-2)	-0.2
■ **BILL HASSAMAER** Hassamaer, William Louis "Roaring Bill" b: 7/26/1864, St.Louis, Mo. d: 5/29/10, St.Louis, Mo. 6', 180 lbs. Deb: 4/19/1894 Career OF: (3-LF 0-CF 140-RF)																								
1894	Was-N	118	494	106	159	33	17	4	90	41	20	.322	.375	.482	857	109	6	16			.916	5	O-68R,3-31,2-14,/S	0.6
1895	Was-N	86	363	42	101	18	4	1	60	26	13	.278	.326	.358	685	77	-13	8			.964	-7	O-75R/1-10,S-1,3-1	-1.9
	Lou-N	23	96	7	20	2	2	0	14	3	4	.208	.232	.271	503	31	-10	0			.980	3	1-21/2-1,S-1	-0.6
	Yr	109	459	49	121	20	6	1	74	29	17	.264	.307	.340	647	68	-22	8			.964	-5	O-75R,1-31/S-2,32	-2.5
1896	Lou-N	30	106	8	26	5	0	2	14	14	7	.245	.333	.349	682	83	-2	1			.976	6	1-29	0.3
Total	3	257	1059	163	306	58	23	7	178	84	44	.289	.342	.407	749	89	-19	25			.938	7	O-143R/1-60,3-32,2S	-1.6
■ **BUDDY HASSETT** Hassett, John Aloysius b: 9/5/11, New York, N.Y. d: 8/23/97, Westwood, N.J. BL/TL, 5'11", 180 lbs. Deb: 4/14/36																								
1936	Bro-N	156	635	79	197	29	11	3	82	35	17	.310	.350	.405	755	102	1	5			.983	5	*1-156	-0.9
1937	Bro-N	137	556	71	169	31	6	1	53	20	19	.304	.334	.387	721	94	-5	13			.984	9	*1-131/O-7(1-6-1)	-0.9
1938	Bro-N	115	335	49	98	11	6	0	40	32	19	.293	.356	.361	717	95	-1	3			.945	-2	O-71(71-0-2)/1-8	-0.8
1939	Bos-N	147	590	72	182	15	3	2	60	29	14	.308	.342	.354	696	94	-5	13			.985	9	*1-123,O-23(0-0-23)	-0.9
1940	Bos-N	124	458	59	107	19	4	0	27	25	16	.234	.273	.293	566	59	-26	4			.979	7	1-98,O-13(0-0-13)	-2.9
1941	Bos-N	118	405	59	120	9	4	1	33	36	15	.296	.354	.346	699	102	2	10			.991	7	1-99	-0.1
1942	*NY-A	132	538	80	153	16	6	5	48	32	16	.284	.325	.364	689	95	-5	5	5	-1	.991	11	*1-132	-0.7
Total	7	929	3517	469	1026	130	40	12	343	209	116	.292	.333	.362	695	92	-40	53	5		.985	45	1-747,O-114(72-6-39)	-7.2
■ **RON HASSEY** Hassey, Ronald William b: 2/27/53, Tucson, Ariz. BL/TR, 6'2", 200 lbs. Deb: 4/23/78 C																								
1978	Cle-A	25	74	5	15	0	0	2	9	5	7	.203	.262	.284	546	54	-5	2	0	0	.993	5	C-24	0.2
1979	Cle-A	75	223	20	64	14	0	4	32	19	19	.287	.343	.404	747	100	0	1	0	0	.992	7	C-68/1-2,D-1	1.0
1980	Cle-A	130	390	43	124	18	4	8	65	49	51	.318	.395	.446	842	130	17	0	2	-1	.993	-7	*C-113/1-3,D-7	1.4
1981	Cle-A	61	190	8	44	4	0	1	25	17	11	.232	.301	.268	570	66	-8	0	1	-0	.991	8	C-56/1-5,D-1	0.2
1982	Cle-A	113	323	33	81	18	0	5	34	53	32	.251	.358	.353	711	97	0	3	2	-0	.993	8	*C-105/1-2,D-2	1.3
1983	Cle-A	117	341	48	92	21	0	6	42	38	35	.270	.346	.384	731	97	-1	2	2	-0	.995	-3	*C-113/D-1	0.1
1984	Cle-A	48	149	11	38	5	1	0	19	15	26	.255	.323	.302	625	73	-5	1	0	0	1.000	-1	C-44/1-1,D-1	-0.5
	Chi-N	19	33	5	11	0	0	2	5	4	6	.333	.405	.515	921	144	2	0	1	-0	1.000	-0	/C-6,1-4	0.2
1985	NY-A	92	267	31	79	16	1	13	42	28	21	.296	.369	.509	878	141	15	0	0	0	.984	-2	C-69/1-2,D-2	1.6
1986	NY-A	64	191	23	57	14	0	6	29	24	16	.298	.382	.466	848	131	9	1	1	-0	.985	-13	C-51/D-3	-0.2
	Chi-A	49	150	22	53	11	1	3	20	22	11	.353	.439	.500	939	150	11	0	0	0	1.000	1	D-34,C-11	1.2
	Yr	113	341	45	110	25	1	9	49	46	27	.323	.408	.481	889	140	20	1	1	-0	.988	-12	C-62,D-37	1.0
1987	Chi-A	49	145	15	31	9	0	3	12	17	11	.214	.305	.338	643	69	-6	0	0	0	1.000	1	C-24,D-18	-0.5
1988	*Oak-A	107	323	32	83	15	0	7	45	30	42	.257	.328	.368	696	98	-1	2	0	0	.994	-1	C-91/D-9	0.3
1989	*Oak-A	97	268	29	61	12	0	5	23	24	45	.228	.294	.328	622	78	-8	1	0	0	.991	7	C-78/1-1,D-2	0.3
1990	*Oak-A	94	254	18	54	7	0	5	22	27	29	.213	.291	.299	590	68	-11	0	0	0	.997	3	C-59,D-15/1-3	-0.5
1991	Mon-N	52	119	5	27	8	0	1	14	13	16	.227	.303	.319	622	76	-4	1	1	-0	.989	-4	C-34	-0.6
Total	14	1192	3440	348	914	172	7	71	438	385	378	.266	.343	.382	725	100	7	14	10	-0	.993	10	C-946/D-96,1-23	5.5
■ **JOE HASSLER** Hassler, Joseph Frederick b: 4/7/05, Ft.Smith, Ark. d: 9/4/71, Duncan, Okla. BR/TR, 6', 165 lbs. Deb: 5/26/28																								
1928	Phi-A	28	34	5	9	2	0	0	3	2	4	.265	.306	.324	629	64	-2	0	1	-0	.879	1	S-28	0.0
1929	Phi-A	4	4	1	0	0	0	0	0	0	2	.000	.000	.000	0	-97	-1	0	0	0	.600	-0	/S-2	-0.1
1930	StL-A	5	8	3	2	0	0	0	1	0	1	.250	.250	.250	500	26	-1	0	0	0	1.000	1	/S-3	0.1
Total	3	37	46	9	11	2	0	0	4	2	7	.239	.271	.283	553	43	-4	0	1	-0	.875	2	/S-33	0.0
■ **GENE HASSON** Hasson, Charles Eugene b: 7/20/15, Connellsville, Pa BL/TL, 6', 197 lbs. Deb: 9/9/37																								
1937	Phi-A	28	98	12	30	6	3	3	14	13	14	.306	.387	.520	908	129	4	0	0	0	1.000	-2	1-28	0.0
1938	Phi-A	19	69	10	19	6	2	1	12	12	7	.275	.383	.464	846	114	2	0	0	0	.958	-4	1-19	-0.3
Total	2	47	167	22	49	12	5	4	26	25	21	.293	.385	.497	882	123	6	0	0	0	.985	-6	/1-47	-0.3
■ **SCOTT HASTINGS** Hastings, Winfield Scott b: 8/10/1847, Hillsboro, Ohio d: 8/14/07, Sawtelle, Cal. BR/TR, 5'8", 161 lbs. Deb: 5/6/1871 M NA OF: (3-LF 44-CF 34-RF)																								
1871	Rok-n	25	118	27	30	6	4	0	20	2	4	.254	.267	.373	640	85	-2	11	2	2	.856	-1	*C-23/2-2,O-2L,1M	-0.1
1872	Cle-n	22	115	34	45	4	0	0	16	3	2	.391	.407	.426	833	165	9	5	1	1	.797	-7	C-12/O-8(0-3-5),2-6,M	0.2
	Bal-n	13	62	16	19	3	1	0	4	1	2	.306	.317	.387	705	111	0	0	1	-0	.900	4	C-12/2-2,O-1(0-1-0)	0.2
	Yr	35	177	50	64	7	1	0	20	4	4	.362	.376	.412	788	145	9	5	2	0	.851	-3	C-24/O-9(0-4-5),2-8	0.4
1873	Bal-n	30	146	41	41	4	0	0	15	4	1	.281	.300	.308	608	81	-3	4	2	0	.892	-3	C-19,O-12(0-12-0)/2-1	-0.4
1874	Har-n	52	247	60	80	11	2	0	30	4	3	.324	.335	.385	719	124	5	10	5	0	.753	-14	C-39,O-26R/2-1,S-1	-0.6
1875	Chi-n	65	287	43	73	9	0	0	30	9	14	.254	.277	.286	563	95	-1	13	11	-1	.815	3	C-46,O-29C/2-3	0.1
1876	Lou-N	67	288	36	73	6	1	0	21	5	11	.253	.271	.286	557	73	-10				.872	-7	*O-65(0-65-0)/C-5	-1.8
1877	Cin-N	20	71	7	10	1	0	0	3	3	6	.141	.176	.155	331	6	-7				.791	-9	C-20/O-1(0-1-0)	-1.4
Total	5 n	207	975	221	288	37	7	0	115	23	26	.295	.312	.348	659	108	9	43	22	2	.822	-19	C-151/O-78C,2-15,S1	-0.6
Total	2	87	359	43	83	7	1	0	24	8	17	.231	.251	.260	511	61	-17				.872	-17	/O-66(0-66-0),C-25	-3.2
■ **CHRIS HATCHER** Hatcher, Christopher Kenneth b: 1/7/69, Anaheim, Cal. BR/TR, 6'3", 220 lbs. Deb: 9/6/98																								
1998	KC-A	8	15	0	1	0	0	0	1	1	7	.067	.125	.067	192	-47	-3	0	0	0	1.000	-1	/O-5(5-0-0)	-0.4
■ **MICKEY HATCHER** Hatcher, Michael Vaughn b: 3/15/55, Cleveland, Ohio BR/TR, 6'2", 200 lbs. Deb: 8/3/79 C Career OF: (345-LF 88-CF 146-RF)																								
1979	LA-N	33	93	9	25	4	1	1	5	7	12	.269	.327	.366	692	90	-1	1	3	-1	.974	-1	O-19(1-1-18),3-17	-0.4
1980	LA-N	57	84	4	19	2	0	1	5	2	12	.226	.244	.286	530	48	-6	0	2	-1	1.000	-5	O-25(4-0-21),3-18	-1.3
1981	Min-A	99	377	36	96	23	2	3	37	15	29	.255	.287	.350	637	77	-11	3	1	0	.992	4	O-91C/1-7,3-2,D-1	-0.9
1982	Min-A	84	277	23	69	13	2	3	26	8	27	.249	.270	.343	613	65	-13	0	2	-1	.988	0	O-47L,D-29/3-5	-1.7
1983	Min-A	106	375	50	119	15	3	9	47	14	19	.317	.344	.445	789	111	5	2	0	0	.979	6	O-56R,D-39/1-7,3-1	0.7
1984	Min-A	152	576	61	174	35	5	5	69	37	34	.302	.346	.406	753	103	2	0	1	-0	.974	13	*O-100L,D-37,1-17,/3	0.8
1985	Min-A	116	444	46	125	28	0	3	49	16	23	.282	.310	.365	674	79	-13	0	0	0	.991	8	O-97(96-0-1),D-11/1-4	-1.0
1986	Min-A	115	317	40	88	13	3	3	32	19	26	.278	.318	.366	684	84	-7	2	1	0	.971	-3	O-46L,D-28,1-22,/3	-1.4
1987	LA-N	101	287	27	81	19	1	7	42	20	19	.282	.331	.429	760	102	0	2	3	-1	.929	0	3-49,1-37/O-7(1-0-6)	-0.3
1988	*LA-N	88	191	22	56	8	0	1	25	7	7	.293	.325	.351	676	97	-1	0	0	0	1.000	-2	O-29(8-0-21),1-25/3-3	-0.6
1989	LA-N	94	224	18	66	9	2	2	25	13	16	.295	.336	.379	716	106	1	1	2	-0	.961	-3	O-48L,3-16/1-5,P-1	-0.3

YEAR	TM/L	G	AB	R	H	2B	3B	HR	RBI	BB	SO	AVG	OBP	SLG	OPS	OPS+	BR+	SB	CS	SBR	FA	FR	G/POS	TPR
1990	LA-N	85	132	12	28	3	1	0	13	6	22	.212	.252	.250	502	40	-11	0	0	0	1.000	-4	1-25,3-10,O-10L	-1.7
Total	12	1130	3377	348	946	172	20	38	375	164	246	.280	.316	.377	693	89	-55	11	15	-3	.983	13	O-575L,1-149,D3/P	-8.1

■ **BILLY HATCHER** Hatcher, William Augustus b: 10/4/60, Williams, Ariz. BR/TR, 5'9", 175 lbs. Deb: 9/10/84 C Career OF: (583-LF 553-CF 87-RF)

YEAR	TM/L	G	AB	R	H	2B	3B	HR	RBI	BB	SO	AVG	OBP	SLG	OPS	OPS+	BR+	SB	CS	SBR	FA	FR	G/POS	TPR
1984	Chi-N	8	9	1	1	0	0	0	0	1	0	.111	.200	.111	311	-10	-1	2	0	0	1.000	-0	/O-4(4-0-0)	-0.1
1985	Chi-N	53	163	24	40	12	1	2	10	8	12	.245	.293	.368	661	75	-5	2	4	-1	.988	-3	O-44(16-27-3)	-1.1
1986	*Hou-N	127	419	55	108	15	4	6	36	22	52	.258	.303	.356	658	83	-10	38	14	3	.983	-5	*O-121(39-95-9)	-1.5
1987	Hou-N	141	564	96	167	28	3	11	63	42	70	.296	.354	.415	769	107	6	53	9	9	.986	10	*O-140(51-94-6)	2.1
1988	Hou-N	145	530	79	142	25	4	7	52	37	56	.268	.325	.370	695	103	2	32	13	2	.983	2	*O-142(124-25-0)	0.2
1989	Hou-N	108	395	49	90	15	3	3	44	30	53	.228	.284	.304	588	71	-15	22	6	3	.991	2	*O-104(96-11-0)	-1.4
	Pit-N	27	86	10	21	4	0	1	7	0	9	.244	.253	.326	578	67	-4	2	1	0	1.000	-4	O-20(2-10-9)	-0.9
	Yr	135	481	59	111	19	3	4	51	30	62	.231	.279	.308	586	70	-19	24	7	3	.992	-2	*O-124(98-21-9)	-2.3
1990	*Cin-N	139	504	68	139	28	5	5	25	33	42	.276	.328	.381	709	91	-6	30	10	3	**.997**	8	*O-131(76-69-0)	0.2
1991	Cin-N	138	442	45	116	25	3	4	41	26	55	.262	.314	.360	673	86	-8	11	9	-1	.981	-2	*O-121(81-54-0)	-1.4
1992	Cin-N	43	94	10	27	3	0	2	10	5	11	.287	.323	.383	706	97	-1	0	2	-1	.967	-3	O-23(23-0-0)	-0.5
	Bos-A	75	315	37	75	16	2	1	23	17	41	.238	.284	.311	595	62	-16	4	6	-1	.968	-1	O-75(63-13-0)	-2.1
1993	Bos-A	136	508	71	146	24	3	9	57	28	46	.287	.338	.400	738	92	-6	14	7	1	.993	-4	*O-130(0-129-2)/2-2	-0.8
1994	Bos-A	44	164	24	40	9	1	1	18	11	14	.244	.295	.329	625	58	-10	4	5	-1	.968	1	O-43(0-0-43)/D-1	-1.1
	Phi-N	43	134	15	33	5	1	2	13	6	14	.246	.279	.343	622	60	-8	4	1	1	1.000	-3	O-40(7-26-11)	-1.1
1995	Tex-A	6	12	2	1	1	0	0	0	1	1	.083	.154	.167	321	-16	-2	0	0	0	1.000	1	/O-5(1-0-4),D-1	-0.2
Total	12	1233	4339	586	1146	210	30	54	399	267	476	.264	.315	.364	679	85	-86	218	87	18	.986	-1	*O-1143L/D-2,2-2	-9.7

■ **FRED HATFIELD** Hatfield, Fred James b: 3/18/25, Lanett, Ala. d: 5/22/98, Tallahassee, Fla. BL/TR, 6'1", 171 lbs. Deb: 8/31/50 C

YEAR	TM/L	G	AB	R	H	2B	3B	HR	RBI	BB	SO	AVG	OBP	SLG	OPS	OPS+	BR+	SB	CS	SBR	FA	FR	G/POS	TPR
1950	Bos-A	10	12	3	3	0	0	0	2	3	1	.250	.400	.250	650	63	-0	0	0	0	1.000	3	/3-3	0.2
1951	Bos-A	80	163	23	28	4	2	2	14	22	27	.172	.274	.258	532	40	-14	1	0	0	.959	21	3-49	0.7
1952	Bos-A	19	25	6	8	1	1	1	3	4	2	.320	.433	.560	993	162	2	0	3	-1	1.000	4	3-17	0.5
	Det-A	112	441	42	104	12	2	2	25	35	52	.236	.301	.286	587	63	-21	2	2	-0	.968	14	*3-107/S-9	-0.8
	Yr	131	466	48	112	13	3	3	28	39	54	.240	.309	.300	609	69	-19	2	5	-1	**.971**	18	*3-124/S-9	-0.3
1953	Det-A	109	311	41	79	11	1	3	19	40	34	.254	.341	.325	666	81	-7	3	5	-1	.978	9	3-54,2-28/S-1	0.2
1954	Det-A	81	218	31	64	12	0	2	25	28	24	.294	.386	.376	763	112	5	4	2	0	.972	-7	2-54,3-15	0.1
1955	Det-A	122	413	51	96	15	3	8	33	61	49	.232	.338	.341	680	85	-8	3	2	-0	.975	-6	2-92,3-16,S-14	-0.6
1956	Det-A	8	12	2	3	0	0	0	2	2	1	.250	.400	.250	650	75	-0	0	0	0	1.000	-1	/2-4	-0.1
	Chi-A	106	321	46	84	9	1	7	33	37	36	.262	.352	.361	714	88	-5	1	0	0	.961	5	*3-100/S-3	-0.1
	Yr	114	333	48	87	9	1	7	35	39	37	.261	.354	.357	712	87	-5	1	0	0	.961	4	*3-100/2-4,S-3	-0.2
1957	Chi-A	69	114	14	23	3	0	0	8	15	20	.202	.321	.228	549	52	-7	1	0	0	.951	2	3-44	-0.5
1958	Cle-A	3	8	0	1	0	0	0	1	1	1	.125	.222	.125	347	-2	-1	0	0	0	1.000	1	/3-2	-0.1
	Cin-N	3	1	0	0	0	0	0	0	0	0	.000	.000	.000	0	-95	-0	0	0	0	.000	0	/2-1,3-1	0.0
Total	9	722	2039	259	493	67	10	25	165	248	247	.242	.334	.321	655	78	-57	15	14	-2	.962	43	3-408,2-179/S-27	-0.5

■ **GIL HATFIELD** Hatfield, Gilbert "Colonel" b: 1/27/1855, Hoboken, N.J. d: 5/26/21, Hoboken, N.J. TR, 5'9.5", 168 lbs. Deb: 9/24/1885 F

YEAR	TM/L	G	AB	R	H	2B	3B	HR	RBI	BB	SO	AVG	OBP	SLG	OPS	OPS+	BR+	SB	CS	SBR	FA	FR	G/POS	TPR
1885	Buf-N	11	30	1	4	0	1	0	0	0	11	.133	.133	.200	333	6	-3				.913	-0	/3-8,2-3	-0.3
1887	NY-N	2	7	2	3	1	0	0	3	0	1	.429	.429	.571	1000	184	1	0			1.000	0	/3-2	0.1
1888	*NY-N	28	105	7	19	1	0	0	9	2	18	.181	.211	.190	401	29	-8	8			.813	-1	3-14,S-13/O-1C,2-1	-0.9
1889	NY-N	32	125	21	23	2	0	1	12	9	15	.184	.250	.224	474	33	-11	9			.858	1	S-24/P-6,3-2	-0.7
1890	NY-P	71	287	32	80	13	6	2	37	17	19	.279	.328	.387	715	83	-9	12			.842	-19	3-42,S-27/P-3,O-1C	-2.1
1891	Was-a	134	500	83	128	11	8	1	48	50	39	.256	.335	.316	651	90	-5	43			.869	9	*S-105,3-27/P-4,O-3R	0.7
1893	Bro-N	34	120	24	35	3	3	2	19	17	5	.292	.388	.417	805	119	4	9			.875	-7	3-34	-0.2
1895	Lou-N	5	16	3	3	0	0	0	1	1	1	.188	.278	.188	465	23	-2	0			.889	-1	/3-3,S-2	-0.2
Total	8	317	1190	173	295	31	18	6	129	96	109	.248	.315	.319	634	79	-33	81			.850	-17	S-171,3-132/P-13,O2	-3.6

■ **JOHN HATFIELD** Hatfield, John Van Buskirk b: 7/20/1847, New Jersey d: 2/20/09, Long Island City, N.Y. 5'10", 165 lbs. Deb: 5/18/1871 FM Career OF: (83-LF 0-CF 1-RF)

YEAR	TM/L	G	AB	R	H	2B	3B	HR	RBI	BB	SO	AVG	OBP	SLG	OPS	OPS+	BR+	SB	CS	SBR	FA	FR	G/POS	TPR
1871	Mut-n	33	168	41	43	3	2	0	22	4	0	.256	.273	.298	571	70	-4	10	3	1	.853	5	*O-24(24-0-0)/2-7,3-2	0.1
1872	Mut-n	56	288	76	92	15	1	1	45	9	6	.319	.340	.389	729	132	13	12	5	1	.847	6	*2-56,M	1.1
1873	Mut-n	52	255	54	78	5	6	2	45	3	2	.306	.314	.396	710	110	3	2	0	0	.744	-8	*3-45,2-11/O-1R,M	-0.4
1874	Mut-n	63	292	47	66	12	1	0	29	7	12	.226	.244	.274	518	64	-12	4	0	1	.874	7	*O-58L/3-7,P-3,1S	-0.2
1875	Mut-n	1	4	1	2	1	0	0	1	0	0	.500	.500	.750	1250	312	1	0	0	0	1.000	0	/O-1(1-0-0)	0.1
1876	NY-N	1	4	0	1	0	0	0	1	0	0	.250	.250	.250	500	77	-0				.833	-0	/2-1	0.0
Total	5 n	205	1007	219	281	36	10	3	142	23	20	.279	.295	.344	639	97	1	28	8	3	.868	11	/O-84L,2-74,3-54,PS1	0.7

■ **SCOTT HATTEBERG** Hatteberg, Scott Allen b: 12/14/69, Salem, Ore. BL/TR, 6'1", 185 lbs. Deb: 9/8/95

YEAR	TM/L	G	AB	R	H	2B	3B	HR	RBI	BB	SO	AVG	OBP	SLG	OPS	OPS+	BR+	SB	CS	SBR	FA	FR	G/POS	TPR
1995	Bos-A	2	2	1	1	0	0	0	0	0	0	.500	.500	.500	1000	156	0	0	0	0	1.000	0	/C-2	0.0
1996	Bos-A	10	11	3	2	1	0	0	0	3	2	.182	.357	.273	630	61	-1	0	0	0	1.000	2	C-10	0.1
1997	Bos-A	114	350	46	97	23	1	10	44	40	70	.277	.355	.434	789	102	2	0	1	-0	.983	-9	*C-106/D-1	-0.1
1998	*Bos-A	112	359	46	99	23	1	12	43	43	58	.276	.361	.446	807	106	4	0	0	0	.993	9	*C-108	1.8
1999	*Bos-A	30	80	12	22	5	0	1	11	18	14	.275	.414	.375	789	100	1	0	0	0	.993	2	C-23/D-6	0.4
2000	Bos-A	92	230	21	61	15	0	8	36	38	39	.265	.369	.435	804	99	0	0	1	-0	.981	1	C-48,D-20/3-1	0.2
Total	6	360	1032	129	282	67	2	31	134	142	183	.273	.365	.432	798	102	6	0	2	-1	.988	5	C-297/D-27,3-1	2.4

■ **GRADY HATTON** Hatton, Grady Edgebert b: 10/7/22, Beaumont, Tex. BL/TR, 5'9", 175 lbs. Deb: 4/16/46 MC

YEAR	TM/L	G	AB	R	H	2B	3B	HR	RBI	BB	SO	AVG	OBP	SLG	OPS	OPS+	BR+	SB	CS	SBR	FA	FR	G/POS	TPR
1946	Cin-N	116	436	56	118	18	3	14	69	66	53	.271	.369	.422	791	129	17	6			.941	-19	*3-116/O-2(2-0-0)	-0.3
1947	Cin-N	146	524	91	147	24	8	16	77	81	50	.281	.377	.448	825	119	15	7			.938	-8	*3-136	0.6
1948	Cin-N	133	458	58	110	17	2	9	44	72	50	.240	.343	.345	688	90	-5	7			.932	4	*3-123/2-3,S-2,O-1L	-0.1
1949	Cin-N	137	537	71	141	38	5	11	69	62	48	.263	.342	.413	756	101	0	4			**.975**	-1	*3-136	-0.1
1950	Cin-N	130	438	67	114	17	1	11	54	70	39	.260	.366	.379	745	96	-1	6			.954	-3	*3-126/2-1,S-1	-0.4
1951	Cin-N	96	331	41	84	9	3	4	37	33	32	.254	.321	.335	657	76	-11	4	2	0	.972	3	3-87/O-2(2-0-0)	-0.8
1952	Cin-N☆	128	433	48	92	14	1	9	57	66	60	.212	.319	.312	631	76	-13	5	4	-0	**.990**	-17	*2-120	-2.5
1953	Cin-N	83	159	22	37	3	1	7	22	29	24	.233	.351	.396	747	94	-1	0	1	-0	.991	-11	2-35,1-10/3-5	-1.1
1954	Cin-N	1	1	0	0	0	0	0	0	0	0	.000	.000	.000	0	-97	-0	0	0	0	.000	0	H	0.0
	Chi-A	13	30	3	5	1	0	0	3	5	3	.167	.286	.200	486	34	-3	1	0	0	1.000	-1	3-10/1-3	-0.4
	Bos-A	99	302	40	85	12	3	5	33	58	25	.281	.401	.391	791	106	5	1	1	-0	.966	6	3-93/1-1,S-1	1.1
	Yr	112	332	43	90	13	3	5	36	63	28	.271	.390	.373	764	100	3	2	1	0	**.969**	5	*3-103/1-4,S-1	0.7
1955	Bos-A	126	380	48	93	11	4	4	49	76	28	.245	.371	.326	697	81	-7	0	1	-0	.976	-2	*3-111/2-1	-1.1
1956	Bos-A	5	5	0	2	0	0	0	2	0	0	.400	.400	.400	800	100	0	0	0	0	.000	0	H	0.0
	StL-N	44	73	10	18	1	2	0	7	13	7	.247	.360	.315	676	84	-1	1	0	0	.951	-4	2-13/3-1	-0.4
	Bal-A	27	61	4	9	1	0	1	3	13	6	.148	.297	.213	510	40	-5	0	0	0	1.000	-5	2-15,3-12	-0.9
1960	Chi-N	28	38	3	13	0	0	0	7	2	5	.342	.390	.342	732	104	0	0	0	0	.931	-2	/2-8	-0.1
Total	12	1312	4206	562	1068	166	33	91	533	646	430	.254	.355	.374	729	96	-9	42	9		.956	-60	3-956,2-196/1-14,OS	-6.5

■ **ARTHUR HAUGER** Hauger, John Arthur b: 11/18/1893, Delhi, Ohio d: 8/2/44, Redwood City, Cal BL/TR, 5'11", 168 lbs. Deb: 7/17/12

YEAR	TM/L	G	AB	R	H	2B	3B	HR	RBI	BB	SO	AVG	OBP	SLG	OPS	OPS+	BR+	SB	CS	SBR	FA	FR	G/POS	TPR
1912	Cle-A	15	18	0	1	0	0	0	0	1		.056	.105	.056	161	-52	-4	0			1.000	-2	/O-5(1-2-2)	-0.5

■ **ARNOLD HAUSER** Hauser, Arnold George "Peewee" or "Stub" b: 9/25/1888, Chicago, Ill. d: 5/22/66, Aurora, Ill. BR/TR, 5'6", 145 lbs. Deb: 4/21/10

YEAR	TM/L	G	AB	R	H	2B	3B	HR	RBI	BB	SO	AVG	OBP	SLG	OPS	OPS+	BR+	SB	CS	SBR	FA	FR	G/POS	TPR
1910	StL-N	119	375	37	77	7	2	2	36	49	39	.205	.312	.251	562	67	-14	15			.931	-8	*S-117/3-1	-1.9
1911	StL-N	136	515	61	124	11	8	3	46	26	67	.241	.286	.311	597	69	-23	24			.918	-15	*S-134/3-2	-2.9
1912	StL-N	133	479	73	124	14	7	1	42	39	69	.259	.319	.324	642	78	-15	26			.934	10	*S-132	0.4
1913	StL-N	22	45	3	13	0	3	0	9	2	2	.289	.347	.422	769	121	1	1			.848	-3	/S-8,2-4	-0.2
1915	Chi-F	23	54	6	11	1	0	0	4	5	7	.204	.283	.222	506	46	-5	2			.851	-3	S-16/3-6	-0.8
Total	5	433	1468	180	349	33	20	6	137	121	184	.238	.305	.300	605	72	-55	68			.924	-19	S-407/3-9,2-4	-5.4

■ **JOE HAUSER** Hauser, Joseph John "Unser Choe" b: 1/12/1899, Milwaukee, Wis. d: 7/11/97, Sheboygan, Wis. BL/TL, 5'10.5", 175 lbs. Deb: 4/18/22

YEAR	TM/L	G	AB	R	H	2B	3B	HR	RBI	BB	SO	AVG	OBP	SLG	OPS	OPS+	BR+	SB	CS	SBR	FA	FR	G/POS	TPR
1922	Phi-A	111	368	61	119	21	5	9	43	30	37	.323	.378	.481	858	119	10	1	5	-2	.986	-3	1-94	-0.1

YEAR	TM/L	G	AB	R	H	2B	3B	HR	RBI	BB	SO	AVG	OBP	SLG	OPS	OPS+	BR+	SB	CS	SBR	FA	FR	G/POS	TPR
1923	Phi-A	146	537	93	165	21	9	17	94	69	52	.307	.398	.475	873	127	22	6	6	-1	.990	-3	*1-146	0.8
1924	Phi-A	149	562	97	162	31	8	27	115	56	52	.288	.358	.516	874	123	15	7	5	-0	.993	-3	*1-146	0.2
1926	Phi-A	91	229	31	44	10	0	8	36	39	35	.192	.312	.341	653	66	-12	1	1	-0	.996	0	1-65	-1.5
1928	Phi-A	95	300	61	78	19	5	16	59	52	45	.260	.369	.517	886	127	11	4	2	0	.986	-6	1-88	0.0
1929	Cle-A	37	48	8	12	1	1	3	9	4	8	.250	.321	.500	821	104	0	0	0	0	.986	1	/1-8	0.0
Total	6	629	2044	351	580	103	28	80	356	250	229	.284	.368	.479	847	117	47	19	19	-2	.990	-14	1-547	-0.6

■ **GEORGE HAUSMANN** Hausmann, George John b: 2/11/16, St.Louis, Mo. BR/TR, 5′5″, 145 lbs. Deb: 4/18/44

YEAR	TM/L	G	AB	R	H	2B	3B	HR	RBI	BB	SO	AVG	OBP	SLG	OPS	OPS+	BR+	SB	CS	SBR	FA	FR	G/POS	TPR
1944	NY-N	131	466	70	124	20	4	1	30	40	25	.266	.324	.333	657	85	-9	3			.960	-7	*2-122	-0.9
1945	NY-N	154	623	98	174	15	8	2	45	73	46	.279	.356	.339	694	92	-4	7			.968	5	*2-154	0.9
1949	NY-N	16	47	5	6	0	1	0	3	7	6	.128	.241	.170	411	12	-6	0			.984	-0	2-13	-0.5
Total	3	301	1136	173	304	35	13	3	78	120	77	.268	.338	.329	667	86	-19	10			.965	-3	2-289	-0.5

■ **CHARLIE HAUTZ** Hautz, Charles A. b: 2/5/1852, St.Louis, Mo. d: 1/24/29, St.Louis, Mo. BR, 5′7″, 150 lbs. Deb: 5/4/1875

YEAR	TM/L	G	AB	R	H	2B	3B	HR	RBI	BB	SO	AVG	OBP	SLG	OPS	OPS+	BR+	SB	CS	SBR	FA	FR	G/POS	TPR
1875	RS-n	19	83	5	25	3	0	0	4	0	9	.301	.301	.337	639	134	3	5	1	1	.921	-1	1-19	0.2
1884	Pit-a	7	24	0	5	0	0	0		3		.208	.296	.208	505	68	-1				.980	0	/1-5,O-2(0-2-0)	-0.1

■ **ROY HAWES** Hawes, Roy Lee b: 7/5/26, Shiloh, Ill. BL/TL, 6′2″, 190 lbs. Deb: 9/23/51

YEAR	TM/L	G	AB	R	H	2B	3B	HR	RBI	BB	SO	AVG	OBP	SLG	OPS	OPS+	BR+	SB	CS	SBR	FA	FR	G/POS	TPR
1951	Was-A	3	6	0	1	0	0	0	0	0	1	.167	.167	.167	333	-10	-1	0	0	0	1.000	-0	/1-1	-0.1

■ **BILL HAWES** Hawes, William Hildreth b: 11/17/1853, Nashua, N.H. d: 6/16/40, Lowell, Mass. BR/TR, 5′10″, 155 lbs. Deb: 5/1/1879 Career OF: (23-LF 16-CF 54-RF)

YEAR	TM/L	G	AB	R	H	2B	3B	HR	RBI	BB	SO	AVG	OBP	SLG	OPS	OPS+	BR+	SB	CS	SBR	FA	FR	G/POS	TPR
1879	Bos-N	38	155	19	31	3	3	0	9	2	13	.200	.210	.258	468	52	-8				.828	-3	O-34(1-7-26)/C-5	-1.0
1884	Cin-U	79	349	80	97	7	4	4		5		.278	.288	.355	643	87	-16				.827	-7	O-58(22-9-28),1-21	-2.3
Total	2	117	504	99	128	10	7	4	9	7	13	.254	.264	.325	590	77	-24				.827	-10	/O-92R,1-21,C-5	-3.3

■ **THORNY HAWKES** Hawkes, Thorndike Proctor b: 10/15/1852, Danvers, Mass. d: 2/3/29, Danvers, Mass. BR/TR, 5′8″, 135 lbs. Deb: 5/1/1879

YEAR	TM/L	G	AB	R	H	2B	3B	HR	RBI	BB	SO	AVG	OBP	SLG	OPS	OPS+	BR+	SB	CS	SBR	FA	FR	G/POS	TPR
1879	Tro-N	64	250	24	52	6	1	0	20	4	14	.208	.220	.240	460	55	-11				.896	16	*2-64	0.7
1884	Was-a	38	151	16	42	4	2	0		4		.278	.297	.331	628	118	3				.917	3	2-38/O-2(0-2-0)	0.7
Total	2	102	401	40	94	10	3	0	20	8	14	.234	.249	.274	524	79	-7				.903	19	2-102/O-2(0-2-0)	1.4

■ **CHICKEN HAWKS** Hawks, Nelson Louis b: 2/3/1896, San Francisco, Cal. d: 5/26/73, San Rafael, Cal. BL/TL, 5′11″, 167 lbs. Deb: 4/14/21

YEAR	TM/L	G	AB	R	H	2B	3B	HR	RBI	BB	SO	AVG	OBP	SLG	OPS	OPS+	BR+	SB	CS	SBR	FA	FR	G/POS	TPR
1921	NY-A	41	73	16	21	2	3	2	15	5	12	.288	.333	.479	813	103	-0	0	1	-0	.970	-2	O-15(5-10-0)	-0.3
1925	Phi-N	105	320	52	103	15	5	5	45	32	33	.322	.387	.447	834	103	2	3	6	-1	.986	-0	1-90	-0.4
Total	2	146	393	68	124	17	8	7	60	37	45	.316	.377	.453	830	103	2	3	7	-2	.986	-2	/1-90,O-15(5-10-0)	-0.7

■ **HOWIE HAWORTH** Haworth, Homer Howard "Cully" b: 8/27/1893, Newberg, Ore. d: 1/28/53, Troutdale, Ore. BL/TR, 5′10.5″, 165 lbs. Deb: 8/14/15

YEAR	TM/L	G	AB	R	H	2B	3B	HR	RBI	BB	SO	AVG	OBP	SLG	OPS	OPS+	BR+	SB	CS	SBR	FA	FR	G/POS	TPR
1915	Cle-A	7	7	0	1	0	0	0	1	2	2	.143	.333	.143	476	42	-0	0			.917	-1	/C-5	-0.1

■ **JACK HAYDEN** Hayden, John Francis b: 10/21/1880, Bryn Mawr, Pa. d: 8/3/42, Haverford, Pa. BL/TL, 5′9″, Deb: 4/26/01

YEAR	TM/L	G	AB	R	H	2B	3B	HR	RBI	BB	SO	AVG	OBP	SLG	OPS	OPS+	BR+	SB	CS	SBR	FA	FR	G/POS	TPR
1901	Phi-A	51	211	35	56	6	4	0	17	18		.265	.323	.332	655	78	-6	4			.841	-4	O-50(30-4-16)	-1.1
1906	Bos-A	85	322	22	80	6	4	1	14	17		.248	.292	.301	594	86	-5	6			.973	-1	O-85(0-0-85)	-1.1
1908	Chi-N	11	45	3	9	2	0	0	2	1		.200	.217	.244	462	45	-3	1			1.000	-1	O-11(0-0-11)	-0.5
Total	3	147	578	60	145	14	8	1	33	36		.251	.298	.308	606	80	-14	11			.929	-5	O-146(30-4-112)	-2.7

■ **CHARLIE HAYES** Hayes, Charles Dewayne b: 5/29/65, Hattiesburg, Miss. BR/TR, 6′, 207 lbs. Deb: 9/11/88 Career OF: (4-LF 0-CF 1-RF)

YEAR	TM/L	G	AB	R	H	2B	3B	HR	RBI	BB	SO	AVG	OBP	SLG	OPS	OPS+	BR+	SB	CS	SBR	FA	FR	G/POS	TPR
1988	SF-N	7	11	0	1	0	0	0	0	0	3	.091	.091	.091	182	-50	-2	0	0	0	1.000	-1	/O-4(3-0-1),3-3	-0.3
1989	SF-N	3	5	0	1	0	0	0	0	0	1	.200	.200	.200	400	15	-1	0	0	0	1.000	-0	/3-3	-0.1
	Phi-N	84	299	26	77	15	1	8	43	11	49	.258	.284	.395	679	92	-4	3	1	0	.910	10	3-82	0.7
	Yr	87	304	26	78	15	1	8	43	11	50	.257	.283	.391	674	91	-5	3	1	0	.911	10	3-85	0.6
1990	Phi-N	152	561	56	145	20	0	10	57	28	91	.258	.296	.348	644	77	-19	4	4	-1	.957	24	*3-146/1-4,2-1	0.5
1991	Phi-N	142	460	34	106	23	1	12	53	16	75	.230	.258	.363	621	74	-18	3	3	-0	.958	7	*3-138/S-2	-1.1
1992	NY-A	142	509	52	131	19	2	18	66	28	100	.257	.300	.409	709	98	-4	3	5	-1	.963	-11	*3-139/1-4	-1.6
1993	Col-N	157	573	89	175	**45**	2	25	98	43	82	.305	.359	.522	881	114	11	11	6	0	.954	4	*3-154/S-1	1.5
1994	Col-N	113	423	46	122	23	4	10	50	36	71	.288	.348	.433	781	88	-7	3	6	-1	.944	1	*3-110	-0.7
1995	Phi-N	141	529	58	146	30	3	11	85	50	88	.276	.343	.406	749	96	-3	5	1	1	.963	-6	*3-141	-0.6
1996	Pit-N	128	459	51	114	21	2	10	62	36	78	.248	.303	.368	671	74	-18	6	0	1	.950	17	*3-124	0.1
	*NY-A	20	67	7	19	3	0	2	13	1	12	.284	.294	.418	712	77	-2	0	0	0	1.000	3	3-19	0.1
1997	*NY-A	100	353	39	91	16	0	11	53	40	66	.258	.335	.397	732	91	-5	3	2	-0	.947	3	3-98/2-5	-0.1
1998	SF-N	111	329	39	94	8	0	12	62	34	61	.286	.353	.419	772	108	4	2	1	0	.989	-2	3-46,1-45/D-2	-0.1
1999	SF-N	95	264	33	54	9	1	6	48	33	41	.205	.295	.314	610	59	-17	3	1	0	.940	-5	3-55,1-20/O-1L,D-2	-2.2
2000	Mil-N	121	370	46	93	17	0	9	46	57	84	.251	.353	.370	723	85	-8	1	1	-0	.976	-7	3-59,1-57/D-1	-1.8
Total	13	1516	5212	576	1369	249	16	144	736	413	902	.263	.319	.399	719	89	-91	47	31	-1	.954	36	*3-1317,1-130/2DOS	-5.7

■ **FRANKIE HAYES** Hayes, Franklin Witman "Blimp" b: 10/13/14, Jamesburg, N.J. d: 6/22/55, Point Pleasant, N.J. BR/TR, 6′, 185 lbs. Deb: 9/21/33

YEAR	TM/L	G	AB	R	H	2B	3B	HR	RBI	BB	SO	AVG	OBP	SLG	OPS	OPS+	BR+	SB	CS	SBR	FA	FR	G/POS	TPR
1933	Phi-A	3	5	0	0	0	0	0	0	0	2	.000	.000	.000	0	-99	-1	0	0	0	.889	0	/C-3	-0.1
1934	Phi-A	92	248	24	56	10	0	6	30	20	44	.226	.286	.339	625	63	-15	2	1	0	.955	-11	C-89	-1.9
1936	Phi-A	144	505	59	137	25	2	10	67	46	58	.271	.335	.388	723	79	-17	3	5	-1	.972	-22	*C-143	-2.8
1937	Phi-A	60	188	24	49	11	1	10	38	29	34	.261	.359	.489	849	114	3	0	0	0	.971	-4	C-56	0.2
1938	Phi-A	99	316	56	92	19	3	11	55	54	51	.291	.396	.475	871	120	11	2	3	-1	.975	-16	C-90	0.0
1939	Phi-A☆	124	431	66	122	28	5	20	83	40	55	.283	.348	.510	859	119	10	4	1	1	.978	-12	*C-114	0.5
1940	Phi-A★	136	465	73	143	23	4	16	70	61	59	.308	.389	.477	866	126	19	9	3	1	.971	-13	*C-134/1-2	1.4
1941	Phi-A★	126	439	66	123	27	4	12	63	62	56	.280	.369	.442	811	117	11	2	0	0	.983	-11	*C-123	0.8
1942	Phi-A	21	63	8	15	4	0	0	5	9	8	.238	.333	.302	635	80	-1	1	1	-0	1.000	-4	C-20	-0.5
	StL-A	56	159	14	40	6	0	2	17	28	39	.252	.364	.327	691	94	-0	0	0	0	.971	-8	C-51	-0.5
	Yr	77	222	22	55	10	0	2	22	37	47	.248	.355	.320	675	90	-2	1	1	-0	.979	-12	C-71	-1.0
1943	StL-A	88	250	16	47	7	0	5	30	37	36	.188	.295	.276	571	66	-10	1	0	0	.983	-9	C-76/1-1	-1.5
1944	Phi-A★	155	581	62	144	18	6	13	78	57	59	.248	.315	.367	682	96	-4	2	1	0	.982	3	*C-155/1-1	0.9
1945	Phi-A	32	110	12	25	2	1	3	14	18	14	.227	.336	.345	681	98	0	1	0	0	.994	2	C-32	0.4
	Cle-A†	119	385	39	91	15	6	6	43	53	52	.236	.335	.353	688	104	3	1	1	-0	.988	2	*C-119	1.2
	Yr	151	495	51	116	17	7	9	57	71	66	.234	.335	.352	687	103	3	2	1	0	.989	3	*C-151	1.6
1946	Cle-A★	51	156	11	40	12	0	3	18	21	26	.256	.345	.391	736	112	3	1	3	-1	.981	-1	C-50	0.4
	Chi-A	53	179	15	38	6	0	2	16	29	33	.212	.322	.279	601	72	-6	1	1	-0	.979	-3	C-52	-0.7
	Yr	104	335	26	78	18	0	5	34	50	59	.233	.332	.331	664	90	-4	2	4	-1	.980	-4	*C-102	-0.3
1947	Bos-A	5	13	0	2	0	0	0	1	0	1	.154	.154	.154	308	-13	-2	0	0	0	.917	1	/C-4	0.0
Total	14	1364	4493	545	1164	213	32	119	628	564	627	.259	.343	.400	744	100	1	30	20	-0	.977	-106	*C-1311/1-4	-2.2

■ **JACKIE HAYES** Hayes, John J. b: 6/27/1861, Brooklyn, N.Y. TR, Deb: 5/2/1882 Career OF: (4-LF 75-CF 24-RF)

YEAR	TM/L	G	AB	R	H	2B	3B	HR	RBI	BB	SO	AVG	OBP	SLG	OPS	OPS+	BR+	SB	CS	SBR	FA	FR	G/POS	TPR
1882	Wor-N	78	326	27	88	22	4	4	54	6	26	.270	.283	.399	682	113	4				.855	-10	*O-58C,C-15/3-5,S-1	-0.6
1883	Pit-a	85	351	41	92	23	5	3		15		.262	.292	.382	674	120	8				.911	-18	C-62,O-18C/S-5,12	-0.4
1884	Pit-a	33	124	11	28	6	1	0		4		.226	.256	.290	546	79	-3				.912	-1	C-24/1-5,O-3R,2-1	-0.2
	Bro-a	16	51	4	12	3	0	0		3		.235	.278	.294	572	86	-1				.946	6	C-14/O-2(1-1-0)	0.6
	Yr	49	175	15	40	9	1	0		7		.229	.262	.291	554	81	-4				.925	6	C-38/1-5,O-5R,2-1	0.4
1885	Bro-a	42	137	10	18	3	0	0	10	5		.131	.179	.153	333	6	-14				.900	-2	C-42	-1.2
1886	Was-N	26	89	8	17	3	0	3	9	4	23	.191	.226	.326	552	70	-3	0			.926	-4	C-14,O-12(1-4-7)/2-1	-0.6
1887	Bal-a	8	28	2	4	3	0	0	3	0		.143	.143	.250	393	9	-3	0			.250	-4	/O-4(2-0-2),3-3,C-1	-0.6
1890	Bro-P	12	42	3	8	0	0	0	5	2	4	.190	.227	.190	418	11	-5	0			.867	-3	/O-6R,S-3,C-2,2-1	-0.6
Total	7	300	1148	106	267	63	10	10	81	39	53	.233	.260	.331	591	87	-18	0			.906	-36	C-174,O-103C/1S32	-3.6

■ **MIKE HAYES** Hayes, Michael b: 1853, Cleveland, Ohio 5′7.5″, 170 lbs. Deb: 9/9/1876

YEAR	TM/L	G	AB	R	H	2B	3B	HR	RBI	BB	SO	AVG	OBP	SLG	OPS	OPS+	BR+	SB	CS	SBR	FA	FR	G/POS	TPR
1876	NY-N	5	21	1	3	0	2	0	2	0	0	.143	.143	.333	476	63	-1				.882	0	/O-5(5-0-0)	-0.1

■ JACKIE HAYES

Hayes, Minter Carney b: 7/19/06, Clanton, Ala. d: 2/9/83, Birmingham, Ala. BR/TR, 5′10.5″, 165 lbs. Deb: 8/5/27

YEAR	TM/L	G	AB	R	H	2B	3B	HR	RBI	BB	SO	AVG	OBP	SLG	OPS	OPS+	BR+	SB	CS	SBR	FA	FR	G/POS	TPR
1927	Was-A	10	29	2	7	0	0	0	2	1	2	.241	.267	.241	508	33	-3	0	0	0	.969	-1	/S-8,3-1	-0.3
1928	Was-A	60	210	30	54	7	3	0	22	5	10	.257	.274	.319	593	56	-14	3	0	1	.974	8	2-41,S-15/3-2	-0.2
1929	Was-A	123	424	52	117	20	3	2	57	24	29	.276	.316	.351	668	71	-18	4	5	-1	.945	3	3-63,2-57/S-2	-1.0
1930	Was-A	51	166	25	47	7	2	1	20	7	8	.283	.312	.367	680	71	-7	2	3	-1	.981	8	2-29/3-9,1-8	0.1
1931	Was-A	38	108	11	24	2	1	0	8	6	4	.222	.263	.259	522	38	-10	2	0	0	.962	-4	2-19/3-8,S-3	-1.1
1932	Chi-A	117	475	53	122	20	5	2	54	30	28	.257	.302	.333	635	69	-22	7	4	0	.967	1	2-97,S-10,3-10	-1.3
1933	Chi-A	138	535	65	138	23	5	2	47	55	36	.258	.331	.331	661	79	-15	2	3	-1	.981	10	*2-138	0.3
1934	Chi-A	62	226	19	58	9	1	1	31	23	20	.257	.325	.319	644	65	-12	3	2	-0	.980	-9	2-61	-1.5
1935	Chi-A	89	329	45	88	14	0	4	45	29	15	.267	.327	.347	673	72	-13	3	1	0	.966	-6	2-85	-1.3
1936	Chi-A	108	417	53	130	34	3	5	84	35	25	.312	.366	.444	810	96	-3	4	2	0	.979	**17**	2-89,S-13/3-2	1.8
1937	Chi-A	143	573	63	131	27	4	2	79	41	37	.229	.282	.300	583	47	-47	1	6	-2	.984	21	*2-143	-1.8
1938	Chi-A	62	238	40	78	21	2	1	20	24	6	.328	.389	.445	835	106	2	3	2	-0	.976	-3	2-61	0.3
1939	Chi-A	72	269	34	67	12	3	0	23	27	10	.249	.320	.316	636	62	-15	0	3	-1	.974	5	2-69	-0.6
1940	Chi-A	18	41	2	8	0	1	0	1	2	11	.195	.233	.244	476	23	-5	0	0	0	.981	-0	2-15	-0.4
Total	14	1091	4040	494	1069	196	33	20	493	309	241	.265	.318	.344	663	70	-184	34	31	-3	.976	52	2-904/3-95,S-51,1-8	-7.0

■ VON HAYES

Hayes, Von Francis b: 8/31/58, Stockton, Cal. BL/TR, 6′5″, 185 lbs. Deb: 4/14/81 Career OF: (237-LF 398-CF 555-RF)

YEAR	TM/L	G	AB	R	H	2B	3B	HR	RBI	BB	SO	AVG	OBP	SLG	OPS	OPS+	BR+	SB	CS	SBR	FA	FR	G/POS	TPR
1981	Cle-A	43	109	21	28	8	2	1	17	14	10	.257	.352	.394	746	116	3	8	1	1	.939	1	D-21,O-13(12-0-1)/3-5	0.4
1982	Cle-A	150	527	65	132	25	3	14	82	42	63	.250	.311	.389	700	91	-7	32	13	2	.981	6	*O-139R/3-5,1-4	-0.5
1983	*Phi-N	124	351	45	93	9	5	6	32	36	55	.265	.338	.370	709	97	-1	20	12	0	.972	-19	*O-103(33-39-77)	-2.5
1984	Phi-N	152	561	85	164	27	6	16	67	59	84	.292	.360	.447	807	124	17	48	13	6	.988	-8	*O-148(14-116-36)	1.3
1985	Phi-N	152	570	76	150	30	4	13	70	61	99	.263	.334	.398	733	101	1	21	8	2	.984	-6	*O-146(66-123-14)	-0.7
1986	Phi-N	158	610	**107**	186	**46**	2	19	98	74	77	.305	.381	.480	861	131	27	24	12	1	.990	2	*1-134,O-31(24-6-3)	2.1
1987	Phi-N	158	556	84	154	36	5	21	84	121	77	.277	.406	.473	879	128	27	16	7	1	.990	-13	*1-144,O-32(5-29-3)	0.5
1988	Phi-N	104	367	43	100	28	2	6	45	49	59	.272	.360	.409	768	118	9	20	9	1	.990	-1	1-85,O-16(4-12-2)/3-3	0.3
1989	Phi-N★	154	540	93	140	27	2	26	78	101	103	.259	.380	.461	841	139	30	28	7	4	.980	3	*O-128R,1-30,3-10	3.4
1990	Phi-N	129	467	70	122	14	3	17	73	87	81	.261	.382	.413	795	119	15	16	7	1	.979	5	*O-127(45-4-81)	1.7
1991	Phi-N	77	284	43	64	15	1	0	21	31	42	.225	.308	.285	593	69	-11	9	2	1	.990	11	O-72(20-49-6)	0.0
1992	Cal-A	94	307	35	69	17	1	4	29	37	54	.225	.308	.326	634	77	-9	11	6	0	.983	-1	O-85(0-0-85)/1-4,D-5	-1.3
Total	12	1495	5249	767	1402	282	36	143	696	712	804	.267	.357	.416	773	113	102	253	97	22	.983	-20	*O-1040R,1-401/D-26,3	4.7

■ BILL HAYES

Hayes, William Ernest b: 10/24/57, Cheverly, Md. BR/TR, 6′, 195 lbs. Deb: 9/30/80 C

YEAR	TM/L	G	AB	R	H	2B	3B	HR	RBI	BB	SO	AVG	OBP	SLG	OPS	OPS+	BR+	SB	CS	SBR	FA	FR	G/POS	TPR
1980	Chi-N	4	9	0	2	1	0	0	0	0	3	.222	.222	.333	556	49	-1	0	0	0	1.000	-0	/C-3	-0.1
1981	Chi-N	1	0	0	0	0	0	0	0	0	0	—	—	—	—	—	0	0	0	0	.000	0	/C-1	0.0
Total	2	5	9	0	2	1	0	0	0	0	3	.222	.222	.333	556	49	-1	0	0	0	1.000	-0	/C-4	-0.1

■ RED HAYWORTH

Hayworth, Myron Claude b: 5/14/16, High Point, N.C. BR/TR, 6′1.5″, 200 lbs. Deb: 4/21/44 F

YEAR	TM/L	G	AB	R	H	2B	3B	HR	RBI	BB	SO	AVG	OBP	SLG	OPS	OPS+	BR+	SB	CS	SBR	FA	FR	G/POS	TPR
1944	*StL-A	90	270	20	60	11	1	1	25	10	13	.222	.253	.281	534	50	-18	0	0	0	.967	1	C-87	-1.3
1945	StL-A	56	160	7	31	4	0	0	17	7	6	.194	.228	.219	446	28	-15	0	2	-1	.992	4	C-55	-0.9
Total	2	146	430	27	91	15	1	1	42	17	19	.212	.243	.258	501	42	-32	0	2	-1	.976	4	C-142	-2.2

■ RAY HAYWORTH

Hayworth, Raymond Hall b: 1/29/04, High Point, N.C. BR/TR, 6′, 180 lbs. Deb: 6/27/26 FC

YEAR	TM/L	G	AB	R	H	2B	3B	HR	RBI	BB	SO	AVG	OBP	SLG	OPS	OPS+	BR+	SB	CS	SBR	FA	FR	G/POS	TPR
1926	Det-A	12	11	1	3	0	0	0	5	1	5	.273	.333	.273	606	59	-1	0	0	0	1.000	-1	/C-8	-0.1
1929	Det-A	14	43	5	11	0	0	0	4	3	8	.256	.304	.256	560	45	-3	0	0	0	.951	0	C-14	-0.2
1930	Det-A	77	227	24	63	15	4	0	22	20	19	.278	.336	.379	715	79	-7	0	2	-1	.977	-13	C-76	-1.4
1931	Det-A	88	273	28	70	10	3	0	25	19	27	.256	.307	.315	622	62	-15	0	1	-0	.973	4	C-88	-0.6
1932	Det-A	109	338	41	99	20	2	2	44	31	22	.293	.354	.382	736	87	-6	1	1	-0	.991	3	*C-106	0.2
1933	Det-A	134	425	37	104	14	3	1	45	35	28	.245	.302	.299	601	59	-25	0	0	0	.994	2	*C-133	-1.5
1934	*Det-A	54	167	20	49	5	2	0	27	16	22	.293	.355	.347	702	82	-4	0	2	-1	.984	7	C-54	0.4
1935	Det-A	51	175	22	54	14	2	0	22	9	14	.309	.342	.411	754	98	-1	0	0	0	.996	11	C-48	1.2
1936	Det-A	81	250	31	60	10	0	1	30	39	18	.240	.347	.292	639	59	-15	0	0	0	**.988**	-4	C-81	-1.3
1937	Det-A	30	78	9	21	2	0	1	8	14	15	.269	.394	.333	727	83	-1	0	0	0	.992	6	C-28	0.5
1938	Det-A	8	19	1	4	0	0	0	5	3	4	.211	.318	.211	529	33	-2	1	0	0	.971	2	/C-7	0.1
	Bro-N	5	4	0	0	0	0	0	0	1	1	.000	.200	.000	200	-40	-1	0			1.000	0	/C-3	-0.1
1939	Bro-N	21	26	0	4	2	0	0	1	4	7	.154	.267	.231	497	34	-2	0			1.000	1	C-18	-0.1
	NY-N	5	13	1	3	0	0	0	0	0	1	.231	.231	.231	462	24	-1	0			1.000	1	/C-5	0.0
	Yr	26	39	1	7	2	0	0	1	4	8	.179	.256	.231	487	31	-4	0			1.000	2	C-23	-0.1
1942	StL-A	1	1	0	1	0	0	0	0	0	0	1.000	1.000	1.000	2000	456	0	0	0	0	.000	0	H	0.0
1944	Bro-N	7	10	1	0	0	0	0	0	2	1	.000	.167	.000	167	-51	-2	0			1.000	2	/C-6	0.0
1945	Bro-N	2	2	0	0	0	0	0	0	1	0	.000	.333	.000	333	-3	-0	0			1.000	0	/C-2	0.0
Total	15	699	2062	221	546	92	16	5	238	198	188	.265	.331	.332	663	71	-87	2	6		.987	20	C-677	-2.9

■ DRUNGO HAZEWOOD

Hazewood, Drungo La Rue b: 9/2/59, Mobile, Ala. BR/TR, 6′3″, 210 lbs. Deb: 9/19/80

YEAR	TM/L	G	AB	R	H	2B	3B	HR	RBI	BB	SO	AVG	OBP	SLG	OPS	OPS+	BR+	SB	CS	SBR	FA	FR	G/POS	TPR
1980	Bal-A	6	5	1	0	0	0	0	0	0	4	.000	.000	.000	0	-99	-1	0	0	0	1.000	-1	/O-3(0-0-3)	-0.2

■ BOB HAZLE

Hazle, Robert Sidney "Hurricane" b: 12/9/30, Laurens, S.C. d: 4/25/92, Columbia, S.C. BL/TR, 6′, 190 lbs. Deb: 9/8/55

YEAR	TM/L	G	AB	R	H	2B	3B	HR	RBI	BB	SO	AVG	OBP	SLG	OPS	OPS+	BR+	SB	CS	SBR	FA	FR	G/POS	TPR
1955	Cin-N	6	13	0	3	0	0	0	0	0	3	.231	.231	.231	462	22	-1	0	0	0	1.000	2	/O-3(3-0-0)	0.0
1957	*Mil-N	41	134	26	54	12	0	7	27	18	15	.403	.477	.649	1126	214	22	1	3	-1	.906	-5	O-40(0-0-40)	1.5
1958	Mil-N	20	56	6	10	0	0	0	5	9	4	.179	.303	.179	482	34	-5	0	0	0	1.000	-1	O-20(0-0-20)	-0.7
	Det-A	43	58	5	14	2	0	2	5	5	13	.241	.302	.379	681	80	-2	0	0	0	1.000	-2	O-12(8-0-4)	-0.4
Total	3	110	261	37	81	14	0	9	37	32	35	.310	.390	.467	857	135	14	1	3	-1	.951	-7	/O-75(11-0-64)	0.4

■ DOC HAZLETON

Hazleton, Willard Carpenter b: 8/28/1876, Strafford, Vt. d: 3/10/41, Burlington, Vt. Deb: 4/17/02

YEAR	TM/L	G	AB	R	H	2B	3B	HR	RBI	BB	SO	AVG	OBP	SLG	OPS	OPS+	BR+	SB	CS	SBR	FA	FR	G/POS	TPR
1902	StL-N	7	23	0	3	0	0	0	0	2		.130	.231	.130	361	12	-2	0			.973	0	/1-7	-0.3

■ FRAN HEALY

Healy, Francis Xavier b: 9/6/46, Holyoke, Mass. BR/TR, 6′5″, 220 lbs. Deb: 9/3/69

YEAR	TM/L	G	AB	R	H	2B	3B	HR	RBI	BB	SO	AVG	OBP	SLG	OPS	OPS+	BR+	SB	CS	SBR	FA	FR	G/POS	TPR
1969	KC-A	6	10	0	4	1	0	0	0	0	5	.400	.400	.500	900	149	1	0	0	0	1.000	0	/C-5	0.1
1971	SF-N	47	93	10	26	3	0	2	11	15	24	.280	.380	.376	756	117	3	1	0	0	.966	-2	C-22	0.2
1972	SF-N	45	99	12	15	4	0	1	8	13	24	.152	.257	.222	479	37	-8	0	1	-0	.995	7	C-43	-0.1
1973	KC-A	95	279	25	77	15	2	6	34	31	56	.276	.348	.409	757	104	2	3	4	-1	.979	-3	C-92/D-1	0.2
1974	KC-A	139	445	59	112	24	2	9	53	62	73	.252	.344	.375	720	101	2	16	8	1	.977	-7	*C-138	0.2
1975	KC-A	56	188	16	48	5	2	2	18	14	19	.255	.307	.335	642	79	-5	4	3	-0	.982	-7	C-51/D-4	-1.0
1976	KC-A	8	24	2	3	0	0	0	1	4	10	.125	.250	.125	375	12	-3	2	0	0	1.000	0	/C-6,D-1	-0.2
	NY-A	46	120	10	32	3	0	0	9	9	17	.267	.318	.292	609	80	-3	3	1	0	.983	3	C-31/D-9	0.2
	Yr	54	144	12	35	3	0	0	10	13	27	.243	.306	.264	570	68	-5	5	1	1	.987	3	C-37,D-10	0.0
1977	NY-A	27	67	10	15	5	0	0	7	6	13	.224	.288	.299	586	61	-4	1	0	0	.971	-0	C-26	-0.3
1978	NY-A	1	1	0	0	0	0	0	0	0	1	.000	.000	.000	0	-99	-0	0	0	0	.000	0	/C-1	0.0
Total	9	470	1326	144	332	60	6	20	141	154	242	.250	.329	.350	679	90	-16	30	17	1	.980	-8	C-415/D-15	-0.7

■ FRANCIS HEALY

Healy, Francis Xavier Paul b: 6/29/10, Holyoke, Mass. BR/TR, 5′9.5″, 175 lbs. Deb: 4/29/30

YEAR	TM/L	G	AB	R	H	2B	3B	HR	RBI	BB	SO	AVG	OBP	SLG	OPS	OPS+	BR+	SB	CS	SBR	FA	FR	G/POS	TPR
1930	NY-N	7	2	2	0	0	0	0	0	0	0	.000	.000	.000	0	-99	-1	0			.000	0	/C-1	-0.1
1931	NY-N	6	7	1	1	0	0	0	0	0	0	.143	.143	.143	286	-24	-1	0			1.000	0	/C-4	-0.1
1932	NY-N	14	32	5	8	2	0	0	4	2	8	.250	.294	.313	607	65	-2	0			.960	2	C-11	0.1
1934	StL-N	15	13	1	4	1	0	0	1	0	2	.308	.308	.385	692	79	-0	0			1.000	1	/C-2,3-1,O-1(0-0-1)	0.0
Total	4	42	54	9	13	3	0	0	5	2	10	.241	.268	.296	564	51	-4	0			.969	3	/C-18,O-1(0-0-1),3-1	-0.1

■ THOMAS HEALY

Healy, Thomas Fitzgerald b: 10/30/1895, Altoona, Pa. d: 1/15/74, Cleveland, Ohio BR/TR, 6′, 172 lbs. Deb: 7/13/15

YEAR	TM/L	G	AB	R	H	2B	3B	HR	RBI	BB	SO	AVG	OBP	SLG	OPS	OPS+	BR+	SB	CS	SBR	FA	FR	G/POS	TPR
1915	Phi-A	23	77	11	17	1	0	0	5	6	4	.221	.310	.234	544	65	-3	0	4	-1	.933	5	3-17/S-1	0.1
1916	Phi-A	6	23	4	6	1	1	0	2	1	2	.261	.320	.391	711	119	0	1			.947	-1	/3-6	0.0
Total	2	29	100	15	23	2	1	0	7	7	6	.230	.313	.270	583	77	-3	1	4		.936	4	/3-23,S-1	0.1

YEAR	TM/L	G	AB	R	H	2B	3B	HR	RBI	BB	SO	AVG	OBP	SLG	OPS	OPS+	BR+	SB	CS	SBR	FA	FR	G/POS	TPR
■ **CHARLIE HEARD**	Heard, Charles b: 1/30/1872, Philadelphia, Pa. d: 2/20/45, Philadelphia, Pa. BR/TR, 6'2", 190 lbs. Deb: 7/14/1890																							
1890	Pit-N	12	43	2	8	2	0	0	0	1	15	.186	.205	.233	437	31	-4	0			.600	-3	/O-6(1-0-5),P-6	-0.4
■ **ED HEARN**	Hearn, Edmund b: 9/17/1888, Ventura, Cal. d: 9/8/52, Sawtelle, Cal. BR/TR, 5'9", 160 lbs. Deb: 6/9/10																							
1910	Bos-A	2	2	0	0	0	0	0	0	0		.000	.000	.000	0	-98	-0	0			1.000	2	/S-2	0.1
■ **ED HEARN**	Hearn, Edward John b: 8/23/60, Stuart, Fla. BR/TR, 6'3", 215 lbs. Deb: 5/17/86																							
1986	NY-N	49	136	16	36	5	0	4	10	12	19	.265	.324	.390	714	99	-0	0	1	-0	.987	-6	C-45	-0.5
1987	KC-A	6	17	2	5	2	0	0	3	4	2	.294	.429	.412	840	121	1	0	0	0	1.000	-2	/C-5	-0.1
1988	KC-A	7	18	1	4	2	0	0	1	0	1	.222	.222	.333	556	53	-1	0	0	0	1.000	-0	/C-4,D-2	-0.1
Total	3	62	171	19	45	9	0	4	14	16	22	.263	.326	.386	712	97	-1	0	1	-0	.989	-8	/C-54,D-2	-0.7
■ **HUGHIE HEARNE**	Hearne, Hugh Joseph b: 4/18/1873, Troy, N.Y. d: 9/22/32, Troy, N.Y. BR/TR, 5'8", 182 lbs. Deb: 8/29/01																							
1901	Bro-N	2	5	1	2	0	0	0	3	0		.400	.400	.400	800	129	0	0			1.000	0	/C-2	0.0
1902	Bro-N	66	231	22	65	10	0	0	28	16		.281	.336	.325	661	103	1	3			.966	-10	C-65	-0.2
1903	Bro-N	26	57	8	16	3	2	0	4	3		.281	.328	.404	731	111	1	2			.960	3	C-17/1-2	0.5
Total	3	94	293	31	83	13	2	0	35	19		.283	.335	.341	677	105	2	5			.965	-6	/C-84,1-2	0.3
■ **JEFF HEARRON**	Hearron, Jeffrey Vernon b: 11/19/61, Long Beach, Cal. BR/TR, 6'1", 195 lbs. Deb: 8/25/85																							
1985	*Tor-A	4	7	0	1	0	0	0	0	0	2	.143	.143	.143	286	-21	-1	0	0	0	1.000	2	/C-4	0.0
1986	Tor-A	12	23	2	5	1	0	0	4	3	7	.217	.308	.261	569	55	-1	0	0	0	.980	1	C-12	0.0
Total	2	16	30	2	6	1	0	0	4	3	9	.200	.273	.233	506	39	-2	0	0	0	.985	2	/C-16	0.0
■ **JEFF HEATH**	Heath, John Geoffrey b: 4/1/15, Ft.William, Ont., Canada d: 12/9/75, Seattle, Wash. BL/TR, 5'11.5", 200 lbs. Deb: 9/13/36																							
1936	Cle-A	12	41	6	14	3	3	1	8	3	4	.341	.386	.634	1021	147	3	1	0	0	1.000	-3	O-12(10-2-0)	0.0
1937	Cle-A	20	61	8	14	1	4	0	8	0	9	.230	.230	.377	607	50	-5	0	1	-0	1.000	-1	O-14(2-0-12)	-0.6
1938	Cle-A	126	502	104	172	31	**18**	21	112	33	55	.343	.383	.602	985	146	32	3	1	0	.974	1	*O-122(113-0-9)	2.3
1939	Cle-A	121	431	64	126	31	7	14	69	41	64	.292	.354	.494	848	119	10	8	4	0	.964	6	*O-108(108-0-0)	1.0
1940	Cle-A	100	356	55	78	16	3	14	50	40	62	.219	.298	.399	697	81	-11	5	3	0	.971	2	O-90(90-0-0)	-1.4
1941	Cle-A★	151	585	89	199	32	**20**	24	123	50	69	.340	.396	.586	982	165	51	18	12	-0	.949	-4	*O-151(25-0-126)	3.6
1942	Cle-A	147	568	82	158	37	13	10	76	62	66	.278	.350	.442	792	130	20	9	9	-1	.980	2	*O-146(145-0-2)	1.3
1943	Cle-A★	118	424	58	116	22	6	18	79	63	58	.274	.369	.481	850	157	30	5	8	-2	.968	-4	*O-111(107-3-4)	1.9
1944	Cle-A†	60	151	20	50	5	2	5	33	18	12	.331	.402	.490	892	160	12	0	1	-0	.952	-1	O-37(31-5-1)	0.9
1945	Cle-A†	102	370	60	113	16	7	15	61	56	39	.305	.398	.508	906	169	33	3	1	0	.973	-4	*O-101(101-0-0)	2.4
1946	Was-A	48	166	23	47	12	3	4	27	36	36	.283	.411	.464	875	153	13	0	4	-1	.969	-2	O-47(47-0-0)	0.6
	StL-A	86	316	46	87	20	4	12	57	37	37	.275	.353	.478	831	124	10	0	2	-1	.962	-6	O-83(83-0-0)	-0.4
	Yr	134	482	69	134	32	7	16	84	73	73	.278	.374	.473	847	134	22	0	6	-2	.965	-9	*O-130(130-0-0)	0.2
1947	StL-A	141	491	81	123	20	7	27	85	88	87	.251	.366	.485	850	133	21	2	1	0	.987	-3	*O-140(140-0-0)	0.8
1948	Bos-N	115	364	64	116	26	5	20	76	51	46	.319	.404	.582	986	167	33	2			**.991**	-2	*O-106(99-7-0)	2.4
1949	Bos-N	36	111	17	34	7	0	9	23	15	26	.306	.389	.613	1002	174	11	0			.983	-2	O-31(26-0-5)	0.7
Total	14	1383	4937	777	1447	279	102	194	887	593	670	.293	.370	.509	879	140	263	56	47		.972	-20	*O-1299(1127-17-159)	15.5
■ **KELLY HEATH**	Heath, Kelly Mark b: 9/4/57, Plattsburgh, N.Y. BR/TR, 5'7", 155 lbs. Deb: 4/20/82																							
1982	KC-A	1	1	0	0	0	0	0	0	0	0	.000	.000	.000	0	-99	-0	0	0	0	1.000	1	/2-1	0.1
■ **MIKE HEATH**	Heath, Michael Thomas b: 2/5/55, Tampa, Fla. BR/TR, 5'11", 190 lbs. Deb: 6/3/78 Career OF: (79-LF 1-CF 142-RF)																							
1978	*NY-A	33	92	6	21	3	1	0	8	4	9	.228	.268	.283	551	56	-5	0	0	0	.970	3	C-33	-0.2
1979	Oak-A	74	258	19	66	8	0	3	27	17	18	.256	.309	.322	631	75	-9	1	0	0	.978	-1	O-46L,C-22/3-7,D-3	-1.1
1980	Oak-A	92	305	27	74	10	2	1	33	16	28	.243	.280	.298	579	63	-16	3	3	-0	.986	8	C-47,D-31/O-8(4-0-4)	-0.7
1981	*Oak-A	84	301	26	71	7	1	8	30	13	36	.236	.270	.346	615	80	-9	3	3	-0	.978	4	C-78/O-6(5-0-1)	-0.2
1982	Oak-A	101	318	43	77	18	4	3	39	27	36	.242	.301	.352	654	82	-8	8	3	1	.973	-8	C-90,O-10(9-0-2)/3-5	-1.2
1983	Oak-A	96	345	45	97	17	0	6	33	18	59	.281	.319	.383	701	98	-2	3	4	-1	.973	-10	C-80,O-24R/3-2,D-2	-1.0
1984	Oak-A	140	475	49	118	21	5	13	64	26	72	.248	.289	.396	685	94	-6	7	4	0	.986	-19	*C-108,O-45R/3-2,S	-2.2
1985	Oak-A	138	436	71	109	18	6	13	55	41	63	.250	.316	.408	724	104	2	7	7	-1	.981	-13	*C-112,O-35R,3-13	-0.9
1986	StL-N	65	190	19	39	8	1	4	25	23	36	.205	.294	.321	615	70	-8	2	3	-1	.967	-7	C-63/O-2(1-0-1)	-1.3
	Det-A	30	98	11	26	3	0	4	11	4	17	.265	.294	.418	712	92	-1	4	1	1	.987	-2	C-29/3-1	-0.2
1987	*Det-A	93	270	34	76	16	0	8	33	21	42	.281	.340	.430	770	107	3	1	5	-2	.989	2	C-67,O-24R/1-4,3S2D	0.5
1988	Det-A	86	219	24	54	7	2	5	18	18	32	.247	.307	.365	672	91	-3	1	0	0	.984	-1	C-75/O-9(0-0-9)	0.0
1989	Det-A	122	396	38	104	16	2	10	43	24	71	.263	.311	.389	700	98	-2	7	1	1	.986	0	*C-117/3-4,O-3L,D-1	0.6
1990	Det-A	122	370	46	100	18	2	7	38	19	71	.270	.313	.386	699	94	-4	7	6	-1	.980	-2	*C-117/O-3R,S-1,D-2	0.1
1991	Atl-N	49	139	4	29	3	1	1	12	7	26	.209	.252	.266	518	43	-10	0	0	0	.991	-0	C-45	-0.9
Total	14	1325	4212	462	1061	173	27	86	469	278	616	.252	.302	.367	669	87	-77	54	40	-2	.981	-46	*C-1083,O-215R/D31S2	-8.7
■ **MICKEY HEATH**	Heath, Minor Wilson b: 10/30/03, Toledo, Ohio d: 7/30/86, Dallas, Tex. BL/TL, 6', 175 lbs. Deb: 4/18/31																							
1931	Cin-N	7	26	2	7	0	0	0	3	2	5	.269	.321	.269	591	64	-1	0			1.000	-0	/1-7	-0.2
1932	Cin-N	39	134	14	27	1	3	0	15	20	23	.201	.310	.254	563	55	-8	0			.991	2	1-39	-1.0
Total	2	46	160	16	34	1	3	0	18	22	28	.213	.311	.256	568	57	-9	0			.992	2	/1-46	-1.2
■ **TOMMY HEATH**	Heath, Thomas George b: 8/18/13, Akron, Col. d: 2/26/67, Los Gatos, Cal. BR/TR, 5'10", 185 lbs. Deb: 4/23/35																							
1935	StL-A	47	93	10	22	3	0	0	9	20	13	.237	.372	.269	640	65	-4	0	0	0	.982	-2	C-37	-0.4
1937	StL-A	17	43	4	10	0	2	1	3	10	3	.233	.377	.395	773	94	-0	0	0	0	1.000	-0	C-14	0.0
1938	StL-A	70	194	22	44	13	0	2	22	35	24	.227	.345	.325	670	69	-9	0	1	-0	.986	7	C-65	0.1
Total	3	134	330	36	76	16	2	3	34	65	40	.230	.357	.318	675	71	-13	0	1	-0	.987	5	C-116	-0.3
■ **BILL HEATH**	Heath, William Chris b: 3/10/39, Yuba City, Cal. BL/TR, 5'8", 175 lbs. Deb: 10/3/65																							
1965	Chi-A	1	1	0	0	0	0	0	0	0	0	.000	.000	.000	0	-99	-0	0	0	0	.000	0	H	0.0
1966	Hou-N	55	123	12	37	6	0	0	8	9	11	.301	.353	.350	703	103	1	1	0	0	.995	-1	C-37	0.1
1967	Hou-N	9	11	0	1	0	0	0	0	4	3	.091	.333	.091	424	28	-1	0	0	0	1.000	1	/C-5	0.0
	Det-A	20	32	0	4	0	0	0	4	1	4	.125	.152	.125	277	-17	-5	0	0	0	1.000	1	/C-7	-0.3
1969	Chi-N	27	32	1	5	0	1	0	1	12	4	.156	.386	.219	605	65	-1	0	0	0	.979	0	/C-9	-0.1
Total	4	112	199	13	47	6	1	0	13	26	22	.236	.327	.276	604	73	-6	1	0	0	.993	1	/C-58	-0.3
■ **CLIFF HEATHCOTE**	Heathcote, Clifton Earl b: 1/24/1898, Glen Rock, Pa. d: 1/19/39, York, Pa. BL/TL, 5'10.5", 160 lbs. Deb: 6/4/18 Career OF: (31-LF 408-CF 728-RF)																							
1918	StL-N	88	348	37	90	12	3	4	32	20	40	.259	.301	.345	646	100	-1	12			.934	-4	O-87(3-84-0)	-1.2
1919	StL-N	114	401	53	112	13	4	1	29	20	41	.279	.315	.339	654	103	1	27			.967	-3	*O-101(1-85-17)/1-2	-1.0
1920	StL-N	133	489	55	139	18	8	3	56	25	31	.284	.320	.372	693	102	0	21	14	-0	.964	10	*O-129(0-74-57)	0.2
1921	StL-N	62	156	18	38	6	2	0	9	10	9	.244	.293	.308	601	61	-9	7	5	-0	.926	-8	O-51(1-40-10)	-1.9
1922	StL-N	34	98	11	24	5	2	0	14	9	4	.245	.315	.337	652	71	-4	0	2	-1	.950	2	O-32(0-32-0)	-0.4
	Chi-N	76	243	37	68	8	7	1	34	18	15	.280	.330	.383	712	82	-7	5	2	0	.986	-1	O-60(0-21-40)	-1.1
	Yr	110	341	48	92	13	9	1	48	27	19	.270	.325	.370	695	79	-11	5	4	-0	.971	0	O-92(0-53-40)	-1.5
1923	Chi-N	117	393	48	98	14	3	1	27	25	22	.249	.298	.308	606	60	-23	32	17	1	.980	4	*O-112(1-0-111)	-2.5
1924	Chi-N	113	392	66	121	19	7	0	30	28	28	.309	.356	.393	749	100	0	26	24	-3	.979	-2	*O-111(1-20-90)	-1.3
1925	Chi-N	109	380	57	100	14	5	5	39	39	26	.263	.343	.366	709	80	-11	15	11	-1	.970	14	O-99(3-8-88)	-0.5
1926	Chi-N	139	510	98	141	33	3	10	53	58	30	.276	.353	.412	764	104	3	18			**.985**	13	*O-133(13-13-110)	0.5
1927	Chi-N	83	228	28	67	12	4	2	25	20	16	.294	.359	.408	766	105	2	6			.987	8	O-57(0-9-49)	0.6
1928	Chi-N	67	137	26	39	8	0	3	18	17	12	.285	.364	.409	772	103	1	6			.973	-2	O-39(7-13-20)	-0.4
1929	*Chi-N	82	224	45	70	17	0	2	31	25	17	.313	.384	.415	799	98	-0	9			.985	3	O-52(1-6-45)	-0.1
1930	Chi-N	70	150	30	39	10	1	9	18	18	15	.260	.343	.520	863	104	0	4			.986	-2	O-35(0-3-32)	-0.4
1931	Cin-N	90	252	24	65	15	6	0	28	32	16	.258	.342	.365	707	96	-1	3			.989	12	O-59(0-0-59)	0.7
1932	Cin-N	8	3	3	0	0	0	0	0	0	0	.000	.000	.000	0	-99	-1	0			.000	0	H	-0.1
	Phi-N	30	39	7	11	2	0	1	5	3	3	.282	.333	.410	744	88	-1	0			.962	-0	/1-7	-0.1

YEAR	TM/L	G	AB	R	H	2B	3B	HR	RBI	BB	SO	AVG	OBP	SLG	OPS	OPS+	BR+	SB	CS	SBR	FA	FR	G/POS	TPR
	Yr	38	42	10	11	2	0	1	5	3	3	.262	.311	.381	692	78	-1	0			.962	-0	/1-7	-0.2
Total	15	1415	4443	643	1222	206	55	42	448	367	325	.275	.333	.375	708	92	-50	191	75		.971	44	*O-1157R/1-9	-9.0

■ RICHIE HEBNER

Hebner, Richard Joseph b: 11/26/47, Boston, Mass. BL/TR, 6′1″, 197 lbs. Deb: 9/23/68 C Career OF: (5-LF 0-CF 27-RF)

YEAR	TM/L	G	AB	R	H	2B	3B	HR	RBI	BB	SO	AVG	OBP	SLG	OPS	OPS+	BR+	SB	CS	SBR	FA	FR	G/POS	TPR
1968	Pit-N	2	1	0	0	0	0	0	0	0	0	.000	.000	.000	0	-99	-0	0	0	0	.000	0	H	0.0
1969	Pit-N	129	459	72	138	23	4	8	47	53	53	.301	.383	.420	803	127	18	4	1	1	.944	3	*3-124/1-1	2.2
1970	*Pit-N	120	420	60	122	24	8	11	46	42	48	.290	.365	.464	829	123	13	2	3	-1	.940	1	*3-117	1.3
1971	*Pit-N	112	388	50	105	17	8	17	67	32	68	.271	.331	.487	818	130	14	2	2	-0	.949	-8	*3-108	0.5
1972	*Pit-N	124	427	63	128	24	4	19	72	52	54	.300	.384	.508	892	155	31	0	0	0	.969	-15	*3-121	1.6
1973	Pit-N	144	509	73	138	28	1	25	74	56	60	.271	.348	.477	825	130	19	0	1	-0	.939	-14	*3-139	0.5
1974	*Pit-N	146	550	97	160	21	6	18	68	60	53	.291	.367	.449	816	132	23	0	3	-1	.937	-6	*3-141	1.6
1975	*Pit-N	128	472	65	116	16	4	15	57	43	48	.246	.322	.392	714	98	-2	0	1	-0	.946	-15	*3-126	-1.9
1976	Pit-N	132	434	60	108	21	3	8	51	47	39	.249	.328	.366	694	96	-2	1	3	-1	.953	-10	*3-126	-1.4
1977	*Phi-N	118	397	67	113	17	4	18	62	61	46	.285	.384	.484	868	125	15	7	8	-1	.991	2	*1-103,3-13/2-1	1.0
1978	*Phi-N	137	435	61	123	22	3	17	71	53	58	.283	.372	.464	837	131	19	4	7	-2	.994	-2	*1-117,3-19/2-1	0.9
1979	NY-N	136	473	54	127	25	2	10	79	59	59	.268	.359	.393	752	109	7	3	1	0	.940	-7	*3-134/1-6	-0.2
1980	Det-A	104	341	48	99	10	7	12	82	38	45	.290	.365	.466	831	123	11	0	3	-1	.998	-5	1-61,3-32/D-5	0.1
1981	Det-A	78	226	19	51	8	2	5	28	27	28	.226	.314	.345	659	87	-4	1	2	-0	.995	-3	1-61,D-11	-1.1
1982	Det-A	68	179	25	49	6	0	8	18	25	21	.274	.363	.441	804	119	5	1	1	-0	.990	2	1-40,D-20	0.4
	Pit-N	25	70	6	21	2	0	2	12	5	3	.300	.347	.414	761	109	1	4	0	1	.964	-2	O-21(0-0-21)/1-4,3-1	-0.2
1983	Pit-N	78	162	23	43	4	1	5	26	17	28	.265	.339	.395	734	100	0	8	3	1	.967	-6	3-40/1-7,O-7(2-0-5)	-0.6
1984	*Chi-N	44	81	12	27	3	0	2	8	10	15	.333	.407	.444	851	127	3	1	0	0	.963	-2	3-14/1-3,O-3(2-0-1)	0.2
1985	Chi-N	83	120	10	26	2	0	3	22	7	15	.217	.266	.308	574	54	-7	0	1	-0	.991	-0	1-12/3-7,O-1(1-0-0)	-0.9
Total	18	1908	6144	865	1694	273	57	203	890	687	741	.276	.356	.438	793	120	165	38	40	-6	.946	-85	*3-1262,1-415/DO2	4.0

■ MIKE HECHINGER

Hechinger, Michael Vincent b: 2/14/1890, Chicago, Ill. d: 8/13/67, Chicago, Ill. BR/TR, 6′, 175 lbs. Deb: 9/27/12

YEAR	TM/L	G	AB	R	H	2B	3B	HR	RBI	BB	SO	AVG	OBP	SLG	OPS	OPS+	BR+	SB	CS	SBR	FA	FR	G/POS	TPR
1912	Chi-N	2	3	0	0	0	0	0	0	2	0	.000	.400	.000	400	14	-0	0			1.000	0	/C-2	0.0
1913	Chi-N	2	2	0	0	0	0	0	0	0	0	.000	.000	.000	0	-99	-1	0			.000	0	H	-0.1
	Bro-N	9	11	1	2	1	0	0	0	0	2	.182	.182	.273	455	28	-1	0			1.000	-1	/C-4	-0.2
	Yr	11	13	1	2	1	0	0	0	0	2	.154	.154	.231	385	9	-2	0			1.000	-1	/C-4	-0.3
Total	2	13	16	1	2	1	0	0	0	2	2	.125	.222	.188	410	16	-2	0			1.000	-1	/C-6	-0.3

■ GUY HECKER

Hecker, Guy Jackson b: 4/3/1856, Youngsville, Pa. d: 12/3/38, Wooster, Ohio BR/TR, 6′, 190 lbs. Deb: 5/2/1882 MU Career OF: (44-LF 18-CF 13-RF)

YEAR	TM/L	G	AB	R	H	2B	3B	HR	RBI	BB	SO	AVG	OBP	SLG	OPS	OPS+	BR+	SB	CS	SBR	FA	FR	G/POS	TPR
1882	Lou-a	78	340	62	94	14	4	3		5		.276	.287	.368	655	126	9				.958	5	*1-66,P-13/O-2(0-2-0)	0.3
1883	Lou-a	81	332	59	90	6	6	1		12		.271	.297	.334	631	111	5				.933	4	P-53,O-23C,1-10	0.0
1884	Lou-a	78	316	53	94	14	8	4	42	10		.297	.323	.430	754	150	17				.951	6	*P-75/O-5(4-1-0)	0.0
1885	Lou-a	70	297	48	81	9	2	2	35	5		.273	.287	.337	624	97	-2				.927	3	P-53,1-17/O-3(3-0-0)	-0.3
1886	Lou-a	84	343	76	117	14	5	4	48	32		**.341**	.402	.446	848	157	22	25			.875	-6	P-49,1-22,O-17R	0.1
1887	Lou-a	91	401	89	149	21	6	4	50	31		.372	.381	.441	821	126	13	48			.954	-4	1-43,P-34,O-16L	-0.4
1888	Lou-a	56	211	32	48	9	2	0	29	11		.227	.285	.289	574	86	-3	20			.936	-4	1-30,P-26/O-1(1-0-0)	-0.9
1889	Lou-a	81	327	42	93	17	5	1	36	18	27	.284	.333	.376	709	104	1	17			.969	-0	1-65,P-19/O-1(0-0-1)	-0.5
1890	Pit-N	86	340	43	77	13	9	0	38	19	17	.226	.285	.318	603	86	-6	13			.962	1	1-69,P-14/O-7L,M	-0.8
Total	9	705	2907	504	843	117	47	19	278	143	44	.290	.324	.376	699	117	56	123			.934	5	P-336,1-322/O-75L	-2.5

■ DANNY HEEP

Heep, Daniel William b: 7/3/57, San Antonio, Tex. BL/TL, 5′11″, 185 lbs. Deb: 8/31/79 Career OF: (181-LF 26-CF 232-RF)

YEAR	TM/L	G	AB	R	H	2B	3B	HR	RBI	BB	SO	AVG	OBP	SLG	OPS	OPS+	BR+	SB	CS	SBR	FA	FR	G/POS	TPR
1979	Hou-N	14	14	0	2	0	0	0	2	1	4	.143	.200	.143	343	-5	-2	0	0	0	1.000	1	/O-2(2-0-0)	-0.1
1980	*Hou-N	33	87	6	24	8	0	0	6	8	9	.276	.344	.368	712	107	1	0	0	0	.990	-2	1-22	-0.2
1981	Hou-N	33	96	6	24	3	0	0	11	10	11	.250	.321	.281	602	76	-3	0	0	0	.990	-3	1-22/O-1(0-0-1)	-0.8
1982	Hou-N	85	198	16	47	14	1	4	22	21	31	.237	.314	.379	692	100	-0	0	2	-1	1.000	-3	O-39(1-0-39),1-16	-0.7
1983	NY-N	115	253	30	64	12	0	8	21	29	40	.253	.332	.395	727	102	1	3	3	-0	1.000	-5	O-61(11-19-31),1-14	-0.7
1984	NY-N	99	199	36	46	9	2	1	12	27	22	.231	.326	.312	638	81	-4	3	1	0	.967	1	O-48(25-0-23),1-10	-0.5
1985	NY-N	95	271	26	76	17	0	7	42	27	27	.280	.348	.421	768	117	6	2	2	-0	.977	-5	O-78(45-7-31)/1-4	-0.3
1986	*NY-N	86	195	24	55	8	2	5	33	30	31	.282	.381	.421	801	124	7	1	4	-1	.988	-2	O-56(44-0-13)	0.2
1987	LA-N	60	98	7	16	4	0	0	9	8	10	.163	.226	.204	430	16	-12	1	0	0	.962	-1	O-22(17-0-6)/1-6	-1.4
1988	*LA-N	95	149	14	36	2	0	0	11	22	13	.242	.343	.255	598	76	-3	2	0	0	1.000	-2	O-32L,1-12/P-1	-0.7
1989	Bos-A	113	320	36	96	17	0	5	49	29	26	.300	.360	.400	760	107	3	0	1	-0	.989	-12	O-75R,1-19/D-9	-1.2
1990	*Bos-A	41	69	3	12	1	1	0	8	7	14	.174	.260	.217	477	33	-6	0	0	0	1.000	-0	O-14R/1-5,P-1,D-6	-0.7
1991	Atl-N	14	12	4	5	1	0	0	3	1	4	.417	.462	.500	962	161	1	0	1	-0	1.000	-0	/1-1,O-1(1-0-0)	0.0
Total	13	883	1961	208	503	96	6	30	229	220	242	.257	.334	.357	692	95	-12	12	14	-2	.986	-34	O-429R,1-131/D-15,P	-7.1

■ BERT HEFFERNAN

Heffernan, Bertram Alexander b: 3/3/65, Centereach, N.Y. BL/TR, 5′10″, 185 lbs. Deb: 5/13/92

YEAR	TM/L	G	AB	R	H	2B	3B	HR	RBI	BB	SO	AVG	OBP	SLG	OPS	OPS+	BR+	SB	CS	SBR	FA	FR	G/POS	TPR
1992	Sea-A	8	11	0	1	1	0	0	1	0	1	.091	.091	.182	273	-25	-2	0	0	0	1.000	1	/C-5,D-1	-0.1

■ DON HEFFNER

Heffner, Donald Henry "Jeep" b: 2/8/11, Rouzerville, Pa. d: 8/1/89, Pasadena, Cal. BR/TR, 5′10″, 155 lbs. Deb: 4/17/34 MC Career OF: (0-LF 0-CF 1-RF)

YEAR	TM/L	G	AB	R	H	2B	3B	HR	RBI	BB	SO	AVG	OBP	SLG	OPS	OPS+	BR+	SB	CS	SBR	FA	FR	G/POS	TPR
1934	NY-A	72	241	29	63	8	3	0	25	25	18	.261	.331	.320	650	73	-9	1	1	-0	.971	-8	2-68	-1.3
1935	NY-A	10	36	3	11	3	1	0	8	4	1	.306	.375	.444	819	118	1	0	0	0	.980	-1	2-10	0.1
1936	NY-A	19	48	7	11	2	1	0	6	6	5	.229	.315	.313	627	57	-3	0	0	0	.971	4	/3-8,2-5,S-3	0.1
1937	NY-A	60	201	23	50	6	5	0	21	19	19	.249	.314	.328	642	62	-12	1	4	-1	.980	-8	2-38,S-13/3-3,1O	-1.6
1938	StL-A	141	473	47	116	23	3	2	69	65	53	.245	.341	.319	661	67	-23	1	1	-0	.971	-9	*2-141	-2.1
1939	StL-A	110	375	45	100	10	2	1	35	48	39	.267	.350	.312	662	69	-16	1	7	-2	.944	-4	S-73,2-32	-1.4
1940	StL-A	126	487	52	115	23	2	3	53	39	37	.236	.295	.310	606	56	-32	5	5	-1	**.977**	**19**	*2-125	-0.5
1941	StL-A	110	399	48	93	14	2	0	17	38	27	.233	.303	.278	581	53	-26	5	6	-1	.974	3	*2-105	-1.8
1942	StL-A	19	36	2	6	2	0	0	3	1	4	.167	.189	.222	411	15	-4	1	0	0	.906	1	/2-6,1-4	-0.2
1943	StL-A	18	33	2	4	1	0	0	2	2	2	.121	.171	.152	323	-5	-4	0	0	0	.974	-0	2-13/1-1	-0.5
	Phi-A	52	178	17	37	6	0	0	8	18	12	.208	.284	.242	526	55	-10	3	2	-0	.978	-10	2-47/1-1	-1.9
	Yr	70	211	19	41	7	0	0	10	20	14	.194	.267	.227	495	45	-14	3	2	-0	.978	-10	2-60/1-2	-2.4
1944	Det-A	6	19	0	4	1	0	0	1	5	1	.211	.375	.263	638	80	-0	0	0	0	.962	-1	/2-5	-0.1
Total	11	743	2526	275	610	99	19	6	248	270	218	.241	.317	.303	620	61	-139	18	26	-5	.973	-13	2-595/S-89,3-11,1O	-11.2

■ JIM HEGAN

Hegan, James Edward b: 8/3/20, Lynn, Mass. d: 6/17/84, Swampscott, Mass. BR/TR, 6′2″, 195 lbs. Deb: 9/9/41 FC

YEAR	TM/L	G	AB	R	H	2B	3B	HR	RBI	BB	SO	AVG	OBP	SLG	OPS	OPS+	BR+	SB	CS	SBR	FA	FR	G/POS	TPR
1941	Cle-A	16	47	4	15	2	0	1	5	4	7	.319	.373	.426	798	116	1	0	0	0	.973	-0	C-16	0.2
1942	Cle-A	68	170	10	33	5	0	0	11	11	31	.194	.243	.224	467	34	-15	1	3	-1	.977	8	C-66	-0.5
1946	Cle-A	88	271	29	64	11	5	0	17	17	44	.236	.284	.314	597	71	-11	1	4	-1	.991	9	C-87	0.1
1947	Cle-A☆	135	378	38	94	14	5	4	42	41	49	.249	.324	.344	668	88	-6	3	1	0	.989	7	*C-133	0.7
1948	*Cle-A	144	472	60	117	21	6	14	61	48	74	.248	.317	.407	724	94	-7	6	3	0	.990	22	*C-142	2.2
1949	Cle-A☆	152	468	54	105	19	5	8	55	49	89	.224	.298	.338	635	69	-23	1	0	0	.990	10	*C-152	-0.4
1950	Cle-A★	131	415	53	91	16	5	14	58	42	52	.219	.291	.383	674	74	-19	1	0	0	.993	24	*C-129	1.1
1951	Cle-A★	133	416	60	99	17	5	6	43	38	72	.238	.302	.346	648	79	-13	0	3	-1	.991	11	*C-129	0.3
1952	Cle-A☆	112	333	39	75	17	2	4	41	29	47	.225	.287	.324	612	75	-12	0	2	-1	.987	7	*C-107	-0.1
1953	Cle-A	112	299	37	65	10	1	9	37	25	41	.217	.280	.348	628	71	-13	1	2	-0	.976	3	*C-106	-0.7
1954	*Cle-A	139	423	56	99	12	7	11	40	34	48	.234	.291	.374	665	80	-13	0	1	-0	**.994**	13	*C-137	0.6
1955	Cle-A	116	304	30	67	5	2	9	40	34	33	.220	.299	.339	638	69	-14	0	1	-0	**.997**	7	*C-111	-0.3
1956	Cle-A	122	315	42	70	15	2	6	34	49	54	.222	.327	.340	667	75	-11	1	1	-0	.985	16	*C-118	0.9
1957	Cle-A	58	148	14	32	7	0	4	15	16	23	.216	.293	.345	637	74	-5	0	1	-0	1.000	3	C-58	-0.1
1958	Det-A	45	130	14	25	6	0	1	7	10	32	.192	.250	.262	512	38	-11	0	0	0	.996	1	C-45	-0.8
	Phi-N	25	59	5	13	6	0	0	6	4	16	.220	.270	.322	592	57	-4	0	0	0	.991	4	C-25	0.1
1959	Phi-N	25	51	1	10	1	0	0	8	3	10	.196	.241	.216	456	22	-6	0	1	-0	.990	1	C-25	-0.5
	SF-N	21	30	0	4	1	0	0	0	1	10	.133	.161	.167	328	-13	-5	0	1	-0	.975	5	C-21	0.0
	Yr	46	81	1	14	2	0	0	8	4	20	.173	.212	.198	409	10	-10	0	2	-1	.983	5	C-46	-0.5
1960	Chi-N	24	43	4	9	2	1	1	5	1	10	.209	.244	.372	617	67	-2	0	0	0	.977	2	C-22	0.1
Total	17	1666	4772	550	1087	187	46	92	525	456	742	.228	.296	.344	640	74	-190	15	24	-5	.990	149	*C-1629	2.9

YEAR	TM/L	G	AB	R	H	2B	3B	HR	RBI	BB	SO	AVG	OBP	SLG	OPS	OPS+	BR+	SB	CS	SBR	FA	FR	G/POS	TPR
■ MIKE HEGAN	Hegan, James Michael b: 7/21/42, Cleveland, Ohio BL/TL, 6'1", 190 lbs. Deb: 9/13/64 F Career OF: (57-LF 1-CF 119-RF)																							
1964	*NY-A	5	5	0	0	0	0	0	0	1	2	.000	.167	.000	167	-48	-1	0	0	0	1.000	1	/1-2	0.0
1966	NY-A	13	39	7	8	0	1	0	2	7	11	.205	.326	.256	582	73	-1	1	1	-0	.991	-0	1-13	-0.2
1967	NY-A	68	118	12	16	4	1	1	3	20	40	.136	.266	.212	478	44	-8	7	1	1	1.000	1	1-54,O-10(0-0-10)	-0.9
1969	Sea-A†	95	267	54	78	9	6	8	37	62	61	.292	.427	.461	888	151	21	6	5	-0	.955	2	O-64(2-1-61),1-19	1.9
1970	Mil-A	148	476	70	116	21	2	11	52	67	116	.244	.338	.366	704	93	-3	9	7	-0	.994	11	*1-139/O-8(2-0-6)	-0.4
1971	Mil-A	46	122	19	27	4	1	4	11	26	19	.221	.358	.369	727	107	2	1	1	-0	1.000	4	1-45	0.4
	*Oak-A	65	55	5	13	3	0	0	3	5	13	.236	.300	.291	591	69	-2	1	0	0	1.000	2	1-47/O-2(1-0-1)	-0.1
	Yr	111	177	24	40	7	1	4	14	31	32	.226	.341	.345	686	96	-0	2	1	0	1.000	6	1-92/O-2(1-0-1)	0.3
1972	*Oak-A	98	79	13	26	3	1	1	5	7	20	.329	.384	.430	814	150	5	1	0	0	1.000	2	1-64/O-3(0-0-3)	0.6
1973	Oak-A	75	71	8	13	2	0	1	5	5	17	.183	.237	.254	490	40	-6	0	0	0	.988	-3	1-56/O-3(2-0-1),D-3	-1.0
	NY-A	37	131	12	36	3	2	6	14	7	34	.275	.312	.466	777	121	3	0	0	0	.992	2	1-37	0.2
	Yr	112	202	20	49	5	2	7	19	12	51	.243	.285	.391	676	93	-3	0	0	0	.991	-1	1-93/O-3(2-0-1),D-3	-0.8
1974	NY-A	18	53	3	12	2	0	2	9	5	9	.226	.317	.377	694	101	0	1	1	-0	1.000	-0	1-17	-0.1
	Mil-A	89	190	21	45	7	1	7	32	33	34	.237	.350	.395	745	114	4	0	4	-1	.991	-2	D-37,1-17,O-17R	-0.2
	Yr	107	243	24	57	9	1	9	41	38	43	.235	.343	.391	734	111	4	1	5	-2	.996	-2	D-37,1-34,O-17R	-0.3
1975	Mil-A	93	203	19	51	11	0	5	22	31	42	.251	.350	.379	730	106	2	1	1	-0	.984	-4	O-42(33-0-9),1-27/D-5	-0.5
1976	Mil-A	80	218	30	54	4	3	5	31	25	54	.248	.328	.362	690	104	1	0	0	0	1.000	-3	D-40,O-20R,1-10	-0.4
1977	Mil-A	35	53	8	9	0	0	2	3	10	17	.170	.313	.283	596	64	-2	0	0	0	1.000	-3	/O-8(8-0-0),1-6,D-7	-0.6
Total	12	965	2080	281	504	73	18	53	229	311	489	.242	.343	.371	714	103	15	28	21	-1	.995	11	1-553,O-177R/D-92	-1.3
■ BOB HEGMAN	Hegman, Robert Hilmer b: 2/26/58, Springfield, Minn. BR/TR, 6'1", 180 lbs. Deb: 8/8/85																							
1985	KC-A	1	0	0	0	0	0	0	0	0	0	—	—	—	—	—	0	0	0	0	.000	0	/2-1	0.0
■ JACK HEIDEMANN	Heidemann, Jack Seale b: 7/11/49, Brenham, Tex. BR/TR, 6', 178 lbs. Deb: 5/2/69																							
1969	Cle-A	3	3	0	0	0	0	0	0	0	2	.000	.250	.000	250	-24	-0	0	0	0	1.000	1	/S-3	0.0
1970	Cle-A	133	445	44	94	14	2	6	37	34	88	.211	.270	.292	562	52	-29	2	4	-1	.961	-2	*S-132	-1.8
1971	Cle-A	81	240	16	50	7	0	0	9	12	46	.208	.252	.237	489	36	-20	1	3	-1	.977	-9	S-81	-2.3
1972	Cle-A	10	20	0	3	0	0	0	0	2	3	.150	.261	.150	411	24	-2	0	0	0	.964	-1	S-10	-0.3
1974	Cle-A	12	11	2	1	0	0	0	0	0	2	.091	.091	.091	182	-48	-2	0	0	0	1.000	-1	/3-6,S-4,1-1,2-1	-0.3
	StL-N	47	70	8	19	1	0	0	3	5	10	.271	.320	.286	606	71	-3	0	0	0	.967	-10	S-45/3-1	-1.1
1975	NY-N	61	145	12	31	4	2	1	16	17	28	.214	.296	.290	586	66	-7	1	0	0	.951	-12	S-44/3-4,2-1	-1.5
1976	NY-N	5	12	0	1	0	0	0	0	0	0	.083	.083	.083	167	-56	-2	0	0	0	1.000	0	/S-3,2-1	-0.2
	Mil-A	69	146	11	32	1	0	2	10	7	24	.219	.255	.267	522	54	-9	1	3	-1	.962	-7	3-40,2-24/D-1	-1.6
1977	Mil-A	5	1	1	0	0	0	0	0	1	0	.000	.500	.000	500	50	0	0	0	0	1.000	1	/2-1,D-3	0.1
Total	8	426	1093	94	231	27	4	9	75	78	203	.211	.268	.268	536	49	-73	5	10	-2	.965	-42	S-322/3-51,2-28,D1	-9.0
■ EMMET HEIDRICK	Heidrick, R. Emmet "Snags" b: 7/9/1876, Queenstown, Pa. d: 1/20/16, Clarion, Pa. BL/TR, 6', 185 lbs. Deb: 9/14/1898 Career OF: (3-LF 596-CF 150-RF)																							
1898	Cle-N	19	76	10	23	2	2	0	8	3		.303	.329	.382	711	105	0	3			.850	-1	O-19(1-12-7)	-0.1
1899	StL-N	146	591	109	194	21	14	2	82	34		.328	.368	.421	789	113	9	55			.925	4	*O-145(0-2-143)	0.5
1900	StL-N	85	339	51	102	6	8	2	45	18		.301	.338	.383	721	100	-1	22			.959	15	O-83(0-83-0)	0.8
1901	StL-N	118	502	94	170	24	12	6	67	21		.339	.366	.470	837	149	29	32			.945	1	*O-118(0-118-0)	2.3
1902	StL-A	110	447	75	129	19	10	3	56	34		.289	.339	.396	735	105	2	17			.940	2	*O-109C/P-1,S-1,3-1	-0.1
1903	StL-A	120	461	55	129	20	15	1	42	19		.280	.310	.395	705	113	6	19			.954	2	*O-119(0-119-0)/C-1	0.2
1904	StL-A	133	538	66	147	14	10	1	36	16		.273	.294	.342	636	107	3	35			.963	11	*O-130(0-130-0)	0.9
1908	StL-A	26	93	8	20	2	2	1	6	1		.215	.223	.312	535	73	-3	3			.957	-1	O-25(2-23-0)	-0.6
Total	8	757	3047	468	914	108	73	16	342	146		.300	.333	.399	732	114	46	186			.946	33	O-748C/C-1,3-1,SP	3.9
■ FRANK HEIFER	Heifer, Franklin "Heck" b: 1/18/1854, Reading, Pa. d: 8/29/1893, Reading, Pa. 5'10.5", 175 lbs. Deb: 6/4/1875																							
1875	Bos-n	11	50	11	14	0	3	0	5	0	0	.280	.280	.400	680	129	1	0	0	0	.885	-2	/1-9,O-6(4-1-1),P-2	0.0
■ CHINK HEILEMAN	Heileman, John George b: 8/10/1872, Cincinnati, Ohio d: 7/19/40, Cincinnati, Ohio BR/TR, 5'8", 155 lbs. Deb: 7/8/01																							
1901	Cin-N	5	15	1	2	1	0	0	1	0		.133	.133	.200	333	-4	-2	0			.667	-1	/3-4,2-1	-0.3
■ HARRY HEILMANN	Heilmann, Harry Edwin "Slug" b: 8/3/1894, San Francisco, Cal. d: 7/9/51, Southfield, Mich. BR/TR, 6'1", 195 lbs. Deb: 5/16/14 CH Career OF: (13-LF 62-CF 1518-RF)																							
1914	Det-A	68	182	25	41	8	1	2	18	22	29	.225	.316	.313	629	86	-3	1	8	-3	.870	-6	O-31(2-28-0),1-16/2-6	-1.5
1916	Det-A	136	451	57	127	30	11	2	73	42	40	.282	.349	.410	760	124	12	9			.952	-10	O-77(5-6-66),1-30/2-9	-0.2
1917	Det-A	150	556	57	156	22	11	5	86	41	54	.281	.333	.387	720	120	11	11			.960	-2	*O-123(0-28-95),1-27	0.2
1918	Det-A	79	286	34	79	10	6	5	39	35	10	.276	.359	.406	765	136	12	13			.957	-4	O-40(0-0-40),1-37/2-2	0.5
1919	Det-A	140	537	74	172	30	15	8	93	37	41	.320	.366	.477	843	139	25	7			.979	-10	*1-140	1.2
1920	Det-A	145	543	66	168	28	5	9	89	39	32	.309	.358	.429	787	111	7	3	7	-2	.985	-1	*1-122,O-22(0-0-22)	0.1
1921	Det-A	149	602	114	**237**	43	14	19	139	53	37	**.394**	.444	.606	1051	167	60	2	6	-2	.962	-11	*O-147(0-0-147)/1-3	3.3
1922	Det-A	118	455	92	162	27	10	21	92	58	28	.356	.432	.598	1030	172	47	8	4	0	.948	-10	*O-115(0-0-115)/1-5	2.7
1923	Det-A	144	524	121	211	44	11	18	115	74	40	**.403**	.481	.632	1113	195	74	9	7	-0	.960	2	*O-130(6-0-124),1-12	6.1
1924	Det-A	153	570	107	197	**45**	16	10	114	78	41	.346	.428	.533	961	149	42	13	5	1	.970	9	*O-147(0-0-147)/1-4	3.8
1925	Det-A	150	573	97	225	40	11	13	134	67	27	**.393**	.457	.569	1026	161	**55**	6	6	-1	.970	-3	*O-148(0-0-148)	3.6
1926	Det-A	141	502	90	184	41	8	9	103	67	19	.367	.445	.534	979	153	40	6	7	-1	.972	-2	*O-134(0-0-134)	2.6
1927	Det-A	141	505	106	201	50	9	14	120	72	16	**.398**	.475	.616	1091	179	60	11	5	1	.966	-8	*O-135(0-0-135)	4.0
1928	Det-A	151	558	83	183	38	10	14	107	57	45	.328	.390	.507	897	132	25	7	3	0	.971	1	*O-125(0-0-125),1-25	1.5
1929	Det-A	125	453	86	156	41	7	15	120	50	39	.344	.412	.565	977	148	32	5	6	-1	.966	-6	*O-114(0-0-114)/1-2	1.5
1930	Cin-N	142	459	79	153	43	6	19	91	64	50	.333	.416	.577	993	144	33	2			.955	12	*O-106(0-0-106),1-19	3.1
1932	Cin-N	15	31	3	8	2	0	0	6	0	2	.258	.258	.323	581	57	-2	0			.981	-0	/1-6	-0.3
Total	17	2147	7787	1291	2660	542	151	183	1539	856	550	.342	.410	.520	930	148	533	113	64		.962	-48	*O-1594R,1-448/2-17	32.2
■ VAL HEIM	Heim, Val Raymond b: 11/4/20, Plymouth, Wis. BL/TR, 5'11", 170 lbs. Deb: 8/31/42																							
1942	Chi-A	13	45	6	9	1	1	0	7	5	3	.200	.294	.267	561	60	-2	1	0	0	.958	-1	O-12(9-0-3)	-0.4
■ BUD HEINE	Heine, William Henry b: 9/22/1900, Elmira, N.Y. d: 9/2/76, Ft.Lauderdale, Fla BL/TR, 5'8", 145 lbs. Deb: 10/1/21																							
1921	NY-N	1	2	0	0	0	0	0	0	0	0	.000	.000	.000	0	-99	-1	0	0	0	1.000	-0	/2-1	-0.1
■ TOM HEINTZELMAN	Heintzelman, Thomas Kenneth b: 11/3/46, St.Charles, Mo. BR/TR, 6'1", 180 lbs. Deb: 8/12/73 F																							
1973	StL-N	23	29	5	9	0	0	0	0	3	3	.310	.375	.310	685	92	-0	0	0	0	1.000	1	/2-6	0.1
1974	StL-N	38	74	10	17	4	0	1	6	9	14	.230	.313	.324	638	79	-2	0	0	0	.978	0	2-28/3-2,S-1	-0.1
1977	SF-N	2	2	0	0	0	0	0	0	0	0	.000	.000	.000	0	-99	-1	0	0	0	.000	0	H	-0.1
1978	SF-N	27	35	2	8	1	0	2	6	2	5	.229	.270	.429	699	96	-0	0	0	0	1.000	2	/2-5,3-3,1-2	0.2
Total	4	90	140	17	34	5	0	3	12	14	22	.243	.312	.343	655	84	-3	0	0	0	.984	4	/2-39,3-5,1-2,S-1	0.1
■ JACK HEINZMAN	Heinzman, John Peter b: 9/27/1863, New Albany, Ind. d: 11/10/14, Louisville, Ky. BR/TR, Deb: 10/2/1886																							
1886	Lou-a	1	5	1	0	0	0	0	0	0		.000	.000	.000	0	-95	-1	0			1.000	-0	/1-1	-0.1
■ BOB HEISE	Heise, Robert Lowell b: 5/12/47, San Antonio, Tex. BR/TR, 6', 175 lbs. Deb: 9/12/67 Career OF: (1-LF 0-CF 0-RF)																							
1967	NY-N	16	62	7	20	4	0	0	3	3	1	.323	.354	.387	741	114	1	0	1	-0	.973	2	2-12/S-3,3-2	0.4
1968	NY-N	6	23	3	5	0	0	0	1	1	1	.217	.250	.217	467	41	-2	0	0	0	.929	-5	/S-6,2-1	-0.8
1969	NY-N	4	10	1	3	1	0	0	0	3	2	.300	.462	.400	862	140	1	0	0	0	1.000	-3	/S-3	-0.1
1970	SF-N	67	154	15	36	5	1	1	22	5	13	.234	.258	.299	557	49	-11	0	1	-0	.915	-1	S-33,2-28/3-2	-0.9
1971	SF-N	13	11	2	0	0	0	0	0	0	1	.000	.000	.000	0	-99	-3	0	0	0	.833	0	/S-3,3-2,2-1	-0.3
	Mil-A	68	189	10	48	7	0	0	7	7	15	.254	.281	.291	572	63	-9	1	1	-0	.961	7	S-51,3-11/2-3,O-1L	0.3
1972	Mil-A	95	271	23	72	10	1	0	12	12	14	.266	.302	.310	612	84	-6	1	1	-0	.990	-3	2-49,3-24/S-9	-0.7
1973	Mil-A	49	98	8	20	2	0	0	4	4	4	.204	.235	.224	460	31	-9	1	0	0	.956	-1	S-29/3-9,1-4,2-4,D	-0.8
1974	StL-N	3	7	0	1	0	0	0	0	0	0	.143	.143	.143	286	-20	-1	0	0	0	1.000	2	/2-3	0.1
	Cal-A	29	75	7	20	7	0	0	6	5	10	.267	.313	.360	673	99	-0	0	1	-0	1.000	2	2-17/3-6,S-3	0.2

YEAR	TM/L	G	AB	R	H	2B	3B	HR	RBI	BB	SO	AVG	OBP	SLG	OPS	OPS+	BR+	SB	CS	SBR	FA	FR	G/POS	TPR
1975	Bos-A	63	126	12	27	3	0	0	21	4	6	.214	.250	.238	488	35	-11	0	0	0	.940	11	3-45,2-14/S-4,1-1	0.1
1976	Bos-A	32	56	5	15	2	0	0	5	1	2	.268	.293	.304	597	67	-2	0	1	-0	.968	2	3-22/S-9,2-1	0.0
1977	KC-A	54	62	11	16	2	1	0	5	2	8	.258	.292	.323	615	67	-3	0	1	-0	1.000	10	2-21,S-21,3-12,/1-1	0.8
Total	11	499	1144	104	283	43	3	1	86	47	77	.247	.281	.293	574	63	-55	3	7	-2	.945	23	S-174,2-154,3/1DO	-1.7

■ AL HEIST

Heist, Alfred Michael b: 10/5/27, Brooklyn, N.Y. BR/TR, 6'2", 185 lbs. Deb: 7/17/60 C

YEAR	TM/L	G	AB	R	H	2B	3B	HR	RBI	BB	SO	AVG	OBP	SLG	OPS	OPS+	BR+	SB	CS	SBR	FA	FR	G/POS	TPR
1960	Chi-N	41	102	11	28	5	3	1	6	10	12	.275	.339	.412	751	106	1	3	1	0	.985	-2	O-33(1-32-0)	-0.2
1961	Chi-N	109	321	48	82	14	3	7	37	39	51	.255	.338	.383	721	90	-4	3	3	-0	.978	0	O-99(0-99-0)	-0.7
1962	Hou-N	27	72	4	16	1	0	0	3	3	9	.222	.263	.236	499	38	-6	0	0	0	.974	-3	O-23(0-23-0)	-1.0
Total	3	177	495	63	126	20	6	8	46	52	72	.255	.328	.368	696	86	-10	6	4	-0	.979	-4	O-155(1-154-0)	-1.9

■ HEINIE HEITMULLER

Heitmuller, William Frederick b: 5/25/1883, San Francisco, Cal d: 10/8/12, Los Angeles, Cal. BR/TR, 6'2", 215 lbs. Deb: 4/26/09

YEAR	TM/L	G	AB	R	H	2B	3B	HR	RBI	BB	SO	AVG	OBP	SLG	OPS	OPS+	BR+	SB	CS	SBR	FA	FR	G/POS	TPR
1909	Phi-A	64	210	36	60	9	8	0	15	18		.286	.351	.405	755	136	8	7			.927	-2	O-61(54-7-0)	0.4
1910	Phi-A	31	111	11	27	2	2	0	7	7		.243	.288	.297	585	84	-2	6			.981	-0	O-28(15-11-2)	-0.5
Total	2	95	321	47	87	11	10	0	22	25		.271	.330	.368	697	118	6	13			.943	-2	/O-89(69-18-2)	-0.1

■ WOODIE HELD

Held, Woodson George b: 3/25/32, Sacramento, Cal. BR/TR, 5'11", 180 lbs. Deb: 9/5/54 Career OF: (113-LF 276-CF 111-RF)

YEAR	TM/L	G	AB	R	H	2B	3B	HR	RBI	BB	SO	AVG	OBP	SLG	OPS	OPS+	BR+	SB	CS	SBR	FA	FR	G/POS	TPR
1954	NY-A	4	3	2	0	0	0	0	0	2	1	.000	.400	.000	400	17	-0	0	0	0	1.000	-1	/S-4,3-1	-0.1
1957	NY-A	1	1	0	0	0	0	0	0	0	0	.000	.000	.000	0	-99	-0	0	0	0	.000	0	H	0.0
	KC-A	92	326	48	78	14	3	20	50	37	81	.239	.322	.485	807	116	6	4	0	1	.996	17	O-92(0-92-0)	1.9
	Yr	93	327	48	78	14	3	20	50	37	81	.239	.322	.483	805	115	5	4	0	1	.996	17	O-92(0-92-0)	1.9
1958	KC-A	47	131	13	28	2	0	4	16	10	28	.214	.280	.321	600	64	-7	0	1	-0	1.000	-3	O-41(0-41-0)/3-4,S-1	-1.2
	Cle-A	67	144	12	28	4	1	3	17	15	36	.194	.288	.299	587	63	-7	1	2	-0	.966	-0	O-43(7-37-0),S-14/3-4	-0.9
	Yr	114	275	25	56	6	1	7	33	25	64	.204	.284	.309	593	64	-14	1	3	-1	.982	-4	O-84(7-78-0),S-15/3-8	-2.1
1959	Cle-A	143	525	82	132	19	3	29	71	46	118	.251	.314	.465	779	115	9	1	2	-0	.962	-9	*S-103,3-40/O-6C,2	0.7
1960	Cle-A	109	376	45	97	15	1	21	67	44	73	.258	.344	.471	814	122	11	0	1	-0	.967	9	*S-109	2.8
1961	Cle-A	146	509	67	136	23	5	23	78	69	111	.267	.358	.468	826	122	16	0	0	0	.960	-14	*S-144	1.4
1962	Cle-A	139	466	55	116	12	2	19	58	73	107	.249	.364	.406	769	110	9	5	1	1	.956	-14	*S-133/3-5,O-1(0-1-0)	0.7
1963	Cle-A	133	416	61	103	19	4	17	61	61	96	.248	.355	.435	790	121	13	2	2	-0	.982	-3	2-96,O-35L/S-5,3-3	1.6
1964	Cle-A	118	364	50	86	13	0	18	49	43	88	.236	.329	.420	749	107	4	1	0	0	.966	0	2-52,O-41C,3-30	0.6
1965	Was-A	122	332	46	82	16	2	16	54	49	74	.247	.349	.452	801	128	12	0	0	0	.963	-19	*O-106L/3-5,2-4,S-2	-1.2
1966	Bal-A	56	82	6	17	3	1	1	7	12	30	.207	.309	.305	613	78	-2	0	0	0	1.000	-4	O-10L/2-5,S-3,3-3	-0.6
1967	Bal-A	26	41	4	6	3	0	1	6	6	12	.146	.286	.293	578	72	-1	0	0	0	.974	1	/2-9,3-5,O-2(2-0-0)	0.0
	Cal-A	58	141	15	31	3	0	4	17	18	41	.220	.317	.326	643	94	-1	0	2	-1	.979	-4	3-19,O-17C,S-13,/2	-0.6
	Yr	84	182	19	37	6	0	5	23	24	53	.203	.310	.319	628	88	-2	0	2	-1	.962	-3	3-24,O-19L,S-13,2	-0.6
1968	Cal-A	33	45	4	5	1	0	0	0	5	15	.111	.231	.133	364	13	-5	0	0	0	1.000	-3	/2-5,S-5,3-5,O-3R	-0.9
	Chi-A	40	54	5	9	1	0	0	2	5	14	.167	.250	.185	435	33	-4	0	0	0	1.000	-6	O-33(9-3-23)/3-5,2-1	-1.2
	Yr	73	99	9	14	2	0	0	2	10	29	.141	.241	.162	403	24	-9	0	0	0	1.000	-9	O-36R,3-10/2-6,S-5	-2.1
1969	Chi-A	56	63	9	9	2	0	3	6	13	19	.143	.299	.317	616	69	-3	0	0	0	1.000	-3	O-18C/S-3,3-3,2-1	-0.6
Total	14	1390	4019	524	963	150	22	179	559	508	944	.240	.333	.421	755	109	49	14	11	-1	.960	-56	S-539,O-448C,2-1791,3	2.4

■ HANK HELF

Helf, Henry Hartz b: 8/26/13, Austin, Tex. d: 10/27/84, Austin, Tex. BR/TR, 6'1", 196 lbs. Deb: 5/5/38

YEAR	TM/L	G	AB	R	H	2B	3B	HR	RBI	BB	SO	AVG	OBP	SLG	OPS	OPS+	BR+	SB	CS	SBR	FA	FR	G/POS	TPR
1938	Cle-A	6	13	1	1	0	0	0	1	1	1	.077	.143	.077	220	-44	-3	0	0	0	.947	0	/C-5	-0.2
1940	Cle-A	1	1	0	0	0	0	0	0	0	0	.000	.000	.000	0	-99	-0	0	0	0	1.000	-0	/C-1	0.0
1946	StL-A	71	182	17	35	11	0	6	21	9	40	.192	.234	.352	586	59	-11	0	1	-0	.965	12	C-69	0.4
Total	3	78	196	18	36	11	0	6	22	10	41	.184	.227	.332	559	51	-14	0	1	-0	.964	12	/C-75	0.2

■ ERIC HELFAND

Helfand, Eric James b: 3/25/69, Erie, Pa. BL/TR, 6', 195 lbs. Deb: 9/4/93

YEAR	TM/L	G	AB	R	H	2B	3B	HR	RBI	BB	SO	AVG	OBP	SLG	OPS	OPS+	BR+	SB	CS	SBR	FA	FR	G/POS	TPR
1993	Oak-A	8	13	1	3	0	0	0	1	0	1	.231	.231	.231	462	26	-1	0	0	0	1.000	4	/C-5	0.2
1994	Oak-A	7	6	1	1	0	0	0	1	0	1	.167	.167	.167	333	-15	-1	0	0	0	1.000	1	/C-6	0.0
1995	Oak-A	38	86	9	14	2	1	0	7	11	25	.163	.265	.209	475	27	-9	0	0	0	.994	3	C-36	-0.4
Total	3	53	105	11	18	2	1	0	9	11	27	.171	.256	.210	466	25	-12	0	0	0	.996	8	/C-47	-0.2

■ TY HELFRICH

Helfrich, Emory Wilbur b: 10/9/1890, Pleasantville, N.J. d: 3/18/55, Pleasantville, N.J BR/TR, 5'10", 178 lbs. Deb: 6/30/15

YEAR	TM/L	G	AB	R	H	2B	3B	HR	RBI	BB	SO	AVG	OBP	SLG	OPS	OPS+	BR+	SB	CS	SBR	FA	FR	G/POS	TPR
1915	Bro-F	43	104	12	25	6	0	0	5	15	21	.240	.336	.298	634	80	-4	2			.912	-4	2-34/O-1(0-0-1)	-0.8

■ HELLINGS

Hellings b: Philadelphia, Pa. Deb: 7/19/1875

YEAR	TM/L	G	AB	R	H	2B	3B	HR	RBI	BB	SO	AVG	OBP	SLG	OPS	OPS+	BR+	SB	CS	SBR	FA	FR	G/POS	TPR
1875	Atl-n	1	4	0	1	0	0	0	0	0	0	.250	.250	.250	500	85	-0	0	0	0	.750	-0	/2-1	0.0

■ TONY HELLMAN

Hellman, Anthony J. b: 1861, Cincinnati, Ohio d: 3/29/1898, Cincinnati, Ohio Deb: 10/10/1886

YEAR	TM/L	G	AB	R	H	2B	3B	HR	RBI	BB	SO	AVG	OBP	SLG	OPS	OPS+	BR+	SB	CS	SBR	FA	FR	G/POS	TPR
1886	Bal-a	1	3	0	0	0	0	0	0	0		.000	.000	.000	0	-99	-1	0			1.000	1	/C-1	0.0

■ TOMMY HELMS

Helms, Tommy Vann b: 5/5/41, Charlotte, N.C. BR/TR, 5'10", 175 lbs. Deb: 9/23/64 MC

YEAR	TM/L	G	AB	R	H	2B	3B	HR	RBI	BB	SO	AVG	OBP	SLG	OPS	OPS+	BR+	SB	CS	SBR	FA	FR	G/POS	TPR
1964	Cin-N	2	1	0	0	0	0	0	0	0	1	.000	.000	.000	0	-97	-0	0	0	0	.000	0	H	0.0
1965	Cin-N	21	42	4	16	2	2	0	6	3	7	.381	.435	.524	959	158	3	1	0	0	.973	-2	/S-8,3-2,2-1	0.3
1966	Cin-N	138	542	72	154	23	1	9	49	24	31	.284	.317	.380	697	85	-10	3	4	-1	.961	-13	*3-113,2-20	-2.4
1967	Cin-N★	137	497	40	136	27	4	2	35	24	41	.274	.307	.356	663	80	-12	5	10	-2	.978	-9	2-88,S-46	-1.4
1968	Cin-N★	127	507	35	146	28	2	2	47	12	27	.288	.307	.363	670	94	-4	5	6	-1	.979	8	*2-127/S-2,3-1	1.6
1969	Cin-N	126	480	38	129	18	1	1	40	18	33	.269	.297	.317	613	68	-20	4	6	-1	.975	-3	*2-125/S-4	-1.7
1970	*Cin-N	150	575	42	136	21	1	1	45	21	33	.237	.263	.282	545	46	-44	2	2	-0	**.983**	1	*2-148,S-12	-3.4
1971	Cin-N	150	547	40	141	26	1	3	52	26	33	.258	.293	.325	618	76	-18	3	4	-1	**.990**	14	*2-149	0.6
1972	Hou-N	139	518	45	134	20	5	5	60	24	27	.259	.297	.346	642	84	-12	4	3	-0	.979	**27**	*2-139	2.5
1973	Hou-N	146	543	44	156	28	2	4	61	32	21	.287	.327	.368	695	93	-6	1	1	-0	.988	-1	*2-145	0.2
1974	Hou-N	137	452	32	126	21	1	5	50	23	27	.279	.315	.363	678	93	-5	5	4	-0	**.985**	-11	*2-133	-0.9
1975	Hou-N	64	135	7	28	2	0	0	14	10	8	.207	.267	.222	489	40	-11	0	0	0	.988	-0	2-42/3-3,S-1	-1.0
1976	Pit-N	62	87	10	24	5	1	1	13	10	5	.276	.357	.391	748	111	1	0	0	0	.921	2	3-22,2-11/S-1	0.4
1977	Pit-N	15	12	0	0	0	0	0	0	0	3	.000	.000	.000	0	-97	-3	0	0	0	.000	0	H	-0.4
	Bos-A	21	59	5	16	2	0	1	5	4	4	.271	.328	.356	684	77	-2	0	0	0	1.000	-2	D-13/3-2,2-1	-0.4
Total	14	1435	4997	414	1342	223	21	34	477	231	301	.269	.303	.342	645	79	-143	33	40	-7	.983	11	*2-1129,3-143/S-74,D	-6.0

■ WES HELMS

Helms, Wesley Ray b: 5/12/76, Gastonia, N.C. BR/TR, 6'4", 230 lbs. Deb: 9/5/98

YEAR	TM/L	G	AB	R	H	2B	3B	HR	RBI	BB	SO	AVG	OBP	SLG	OPS	OPS+	BR+	SB	CS	SBR	FA	FR	G/POS	TPR
1998	Atl-N	7	13	2	4	1	0	1	2	0	4	.308	.308	.615	923	135	1	0	0	0	.750	-1	/3-4	-0.1
2000	Atl-N	6	5	0	1	0	0	0	0	0	2	.200	.200	.200	400	1	-1	0	0	0	.833	1	/3-5	0.0
Total	2	13	18	2	5	1	0	1	2	0	6	.278	.278	.500	778	97	-0	0	0	0	.800	-0	/3-9	-0.1

■ TODD HELTON

Helton, Todd Lynn b: 8/20/73, Knoxville, Tenn. BL/TL, 6'2", 195 lbs. Deb: 8/2/97

YEAR	TM/L	G	AB	R	H	2B	3B	HR	RBI	BB	SO	AVG	OBP	SLG	OPS	OPS+	BR+	SB	CS	SBR	FA	FR	G/POS	TPR
1997	Col-N	35	93	13	26	2	1	5	11	8	11	.280	.337	.484	821	91	-1	0	1	-0	1.000	1	O-15(13-0-2)/1-8	-0.2
1998	Col-N	152	530	78	167	37	1	25	97	53	54	.315	.384	.530	914	113	11	3	3	-0	.995	16	*1-146	1.2
1999	Col-N	159	578	114	185	39	5	35	113	68	77	.320	.397	.587	984	114	13	7	6	-1	.993	3	*1-156	0.0
2000	Col-N★	160	580	138	**216**	**59**	2	42	**147**	103	61	**.372**	**.470**	**.698**	**1168**	148	46	5	3	0	.995	19	*1-160	4.6
Total	4	506	1781	343	594	137	9	107	368	232	203	.334	.415	.601	1016	124	68	15	13	-1	.995	38	1-470/O-15(13-0-2)	5.6

■ HEINIE HELTZEL

Heltzel, William Wade b: 12/21/13, York, Pa. d: 5/1/98, York, Pa. BR/TR, 5'10", 150 lbs. Deb: 7/27/43

YEAR	TM/L	G	AB	R	H	2B	3B	HR	RBI	BB	SO	AVG	OBP	SLG	OPS	OPS+	BR+	SB	CS	SBR	FA	FR	G/POS	TPR
1943	Bos-N	29	86	6	13	3	0	0	5	7	13	.151	.215	.186	401	17	-9	0			.880	-3	3-29	-1.3
1944	Phi-N	11	22	1	4	1	0	0	0	2	3	.182	.280	.227	507	45	-2	0			.919	-2	S-10	-0.3
Total	2	40	108	7	17	4	0	0	5	9	16	.157	.229	.194	423	23	-11	0			.880	-5	/3-29,S-10	-1.6

■ ED HEMINGWAY

Hemingway, Edson Marshall b: 5/8/1893, Sheridan, Mich. d: 7/5/69, Grand Rapids, Mich BB/TR, 5'11.5", 165 lbs. Deb: 9/17/14

YEAR	TM/L	G	AB	R	H	2B	3B	HR	RBI	BB	SO	AVG	OBP	SLG	OPS	OPS+	BR+	SB	CS	SBR	FA	FR	G/POS	TPR
1914	StL-A	3	5	0	0	0	0	0	0	1	1	.000	.167	.000	167	-51	-1	1						
1917	NY-N	7	25	3	8	1	1	0	1	2	1	.320	.370	.440	810	153	2	2			1.000	0	/3-3	-0.1
1918	Phi-N	33	108	7	23	4	1	0	12	7	9	.213	.267	.269	536	59	-5	4			.958	1	/3-7	0.3
Total	3	43	138	10	31	5	2	0	13	10	11	.225	.282	.290	572	71	-5	7			.955	2	2-25/3-3,1-1	-0.3
																					.952	3	/2-25,3-13,1-1	-0.1

YEAR	TM/L	G	AB	R	H	2B	3B	HR	RBI	BB	SO	AVG	OBP	SLG	OPS	OPS+	BR+	SB	CS	SBR	FA	FR	G/POS	TPR
■ **SCOTT HEMOND**	Hemond, Scott Mathew b: 11/18/65, Taunton, Mass. BR/TR, 6', 205 lbs. Deb: 9/9/89 Career OF: (8-LF 1-CF 3-RF)																							
1989	Oak-A	4	0	2	0	0	0	0	0	0	0	—	—	—	—	—	0	0	0	0	.000	0	R	0.0
1990	Oak-A	7	13	0	2	0	0	0	1	0	5	.154	.154	.154	308	-14	-2	0	0	0	1.000	-1	/3-7,2-1	-0.3
1991	Oak-A	23	23	4	5	0	0	0	0	1	7	.217	.250	.217	467	32	-2	1	2	-0	.947	5	/C-8,2-7,3-2,S-1,D	0.3
1992	Oak-A	17	27	7	6	1	0	0	1	3	7	.222	.300	.259	559	61	-1	1	0	0	1.000	-0	/C-8,S-3,3-2,O-2L,D	-0.1
	Chi-A	8	13	1	3	1	0	0	1	1	6	.231	.286	.308	593	67	-1	0	0	0	1.000	-0	/O-2L,C-1,3-1,D-4	-0.1
	Yr	25	40	8	9	2	0	0	2	4	13	.225	.295	.275	570	63	-2	1	0	0	1.000	-1	/C-9,D-5,O-4L,S3	-0.2
1993	Oak-A	91	215	31	55	16	0	6	26	32	55	.256	.355	.414	769	113	4	14	5	1	.991	4	C-75/O-6L,1-1,2D	1.3
1994	Oak-A	91	198	23	44	11	0	3	20	16	51	.222	.280	.323	604	60	-12	7	6	-1	1.000	7	C-39,2-25,3-12,/1OD	-0.3
1995	StL-N	57	118	11	17	1	0	3	9	12	31	.144	.235	.229	464	23	-13	0	0	0	.985	0	C-38/2-6	-1.1
Total	7	298	607	79	132	30	0	12	58	65	162	.217	.296	.326	622	69	-27	23	13	1	.991	16	C-169/2-40,3-24,DO1S	-0.3
■ **DUCKY HEMP**	Hemp, William H. b: 12/27/1867, St.Louis, Mo. d: 3/6/23, St.Louis, Mo. Deb: 10/6/1887																							
1887	Lou-a	1	4	1	2	1	0	0	0	1		.500	.500	.667	1167	219	1	0			.000	-1	/O-1(0-0-1)	0.0
1890	Pit-N	21	81	9	19	0	2	0	4	8	12	.235	.311	.284	595	83	-1	3			.867	0	O-21(2-14-5)	-0.1
	Syr-a	9	33	1	5	1	0	0	1	0		.152	.176	.182	358	6	-4	1			.947	2	/O-9(2-7-0)	-0.2
Total	2	31	118	11	26	2	2	0	5	9	12	.220	.281	.265	546	67	-5	4			.877	2	/O-31(4-21-6)	-0.3
■ **BRET HEMPHILL**	Hemphill, Bret Ryan b: 12/17/71, Santa Clara, Cal. BB/TR, 6'3", 200 lbs. Deb: 6/28/99																							
1999	Ana-A	12	21	3	3	0	0	0	2	4	4	.143	.280	.143	423	12	-3	0	0	0	.955	-0	C-12	-0.2
■ **CHARLIE HEMPHILL**	Hemphill, Charles Judson "Eagle Eye" b: 4/20/1876, Greenville, Mich. d: 6/22/53, Detroit, Mich. BL/TL, 5'9", 160 lbs. Deb: 6/27/1899 F Career OF: (45-LF 607-CF 525-RF)																							
1899	StL-N	11	37	4	9	0	0	1	3	6		.243	.364	.324	688	87	-0	0			.750	-2	O-10(0-10-0)	-0.3
	Cle-N	55	202	23	56	3	5	2	23	6		.277	.301	.371	673	91	-3	3			.859	-8	O-54(0-0-54)	-1.3
	Yr	66	239	27	65	3	5	3	26	12		.272	.312	.364	676	90	-4	3			.837	-10	O-64(0-10-54)	-1.6
1901	Bos-A	136	545	71	142	10	10	3	62	39		.261	.312	.332	644	80	-14	11			.925	-4	*O-136(0-2-134)	-2.2
1902	Cle-A	25	94	14	25	2	0	0	11	5		.266	.303	.287	590	67	-4	4			.860	-1	O-19(17-1-1)	-0.6
	StL-A	103	416	67	132	14	11	6	58	44		.317	.383	.447	830	131	18	23			.952	-3	*O-101(1-31-71)/2-2	1.0
	Yr	128	510	81	157	16	11	6	69	49		.308	.369	.418	786	120	14	27			.935	-3	*O-120(18-32-72)/2-2	0.4
1903	StL-A	105	383	36	94	6	3	3	29	23		.245	.292	.300	592	80	-9	16			.961	2	*O-104(4-18-82)	-1.2
1904	StL-A	114	438	47	112	13	2	2	45	35		.256	.311	.308	619	102	2	23			.926	-2	*O-108(6-26-76)/2-1	-0.6
1906	StL-A	154	585	90	169	19	12	4	62	43		.289	.338	.383	720	131	20	33			.961	1	*O-154(0-114-40)	1.4
1907	StL-A	153	603	66	156	20	9	0	38	51		.259	.319	.322	640	105	3	14			.957	-2	*O-153(0-134-19)	-0.6
1908	NY-A	142	505	62	150	12	9	0	44	59		.297	.374	.356	730	136	22	42			.937	-2	*O-142(4-130-8)	1.5
1909	NY-A	73	181	23	44	5	1	0	10	32		.243	.357	.282	639	101	2	10			.976	-1	O-45(13-32-0)	-0.1
1910	NY-A	102	351	45	84	9	4	0	21	55		.239	.350	.288	638	95	0	19			.971	-2	O-94(0-63-31)	-0.7
1911	NY-A	69	201	32	57	4	2	1	15	37		.284	.397	.338	736	99	2	9			.952	-7	O-55(0-46-9)	-0.9
Total	11	1242	4541	580	1230	117	68	22	421	435		.271	.337	.341	678	106	38	207			.944	-29	*O-1175C/2-3	-4.6
■ **FRANK HEMPHILL**	Hemphill, Frank Vernon b: 5/13/1878, Greenville, Mich. d: 11/16/50, Chicago, Ill. BR/TR, 5'11", 165 lbs. Deb: 4/17/06 F																							
1906	Chi-A	13	40	0	3	0	0	0	2	9		.075	.275	.075	350	11	-3	1			.970	1	O-13(13-0-0)	-0.4
1909	Was-A	1	3	0	0	0	0	0	0	0		.000	.000	.000	0	-99	-1	0			1.000	0	/O-1(1-0-0)	-0.1
Total	2	14	43	0	3	0	0	0	2	9		.070	.259	.070	329	5	-4	1			.971	1	/O-14(14-0-0)	-0.5
■ **ROLLIE HEMSLEY**	Hemsley, Ralston Burdett b: 6/24/07, Syracuse, Ohio d: 7/31/72, Washington, D.C. BR/TR, 5'10", 170 lbs. Deb: 4/13/28 C Career OF: (6-LF 1-CF 0-RF)																							
1928	Pit-N	50	133	14	36	2	3	0	18	4	10	.271	.292	.331	623	60	-8	1			.962	1	C-49	-0.5
1929	Pit-N	88	235	31	68	13	7	0	37	11	22	.289	.321	.404	725	77	-9	1			.954	8	C-80	0.3
1930	Pit-N	104	324	45	82	19	6	2	45	22	21	.253	.301	.367	668	60	-21	3			.979	3	C-98	-1.1
1931	Pit-N	10	35	3	6	3	0	0	1	3	3	.171	.237	.257	494	33	-3	0			1.000	1	/C-9	-0.2
	Chi-N	66	204	28	63	17	4	3	31	17	30	.309	.362	.475	837	121	6	4			.975	5	C-53	1.4
	Yr	76	239	31	69	20	4	3	32	20	33	.289	.344	.444	787	109	3	4			.978	6	C-62	1.2
1932	*Chi-N	60	151	27	36	10	3	4	20	10	16	.238	.286	.424	710	89	-3	2			.974	2	C-47/O-1(0-1-0)	0.1
1933	Cin-N	49	116	9	22	8	0	0	7	6	8	.190	.230	.259	488	40	-9	0			.970	5	C-41	-0.2
	StL-A	32	95	7	23	2	1	1	15	11	12	.242	.321	.316	637	65	-5	0	0	0	.965	-3	C-27	-0.5
1934	StL-A	123	431	47	133	31	7	2	52	29	37	.309	.355	.427	782	93	-5	6	2	1	.973	23	*C-114/O-6(6-0-0)	2.4
1935	StL-A★	144	504	57	146	32	7	0	48	44	41	.290	.349	.381	730	85	-11	3	2	-0	.979	10	*C-141	0.6
1936	StL-A☆	116	377	43	99	24	2	2	39	46	30	.263	.343	.353	696	70	-18	2	3	-1	.969	-11	*C-114	-2.0
1937	StL-A	100	334	30	74	12	3	3	28	25	29	.222	.276	.302	578	45	-29	0	0	0	.969	-5	C-94/1-2	-2.6
1938	Cle-A	66	203	27	60	11	3	2	28	23	14	.296	.367	.409	776	96	-1	1	1	-0	.980	15	C-58	1.5
1939	Cle-A☆	107	395	58	104	17	4	2	36	26	26	.263	.309	.342	651	69	-19	2	4	-1	.984	6	*C-106	-0.7
1940	Cle-A★	119	416	46	111	20	5	4	42	22	25	.267	.304	.368	671	75	-16	1	3	-1	**.994**	9	*C-117	-0.1
1941	Cle-A	98	288	29	69	10	5	2	24	18	19	.240	.284	.330	614	65	-15	2	0	0	.980	-2	C-96	-1.1
1942	Cin-N	36	115	7	13	1	2	0	7	4	11	.113	.143	.157	299	-12	-16	0			.982	11	C-34	-0.4
	NY-A	31	85	12	25	3	1	0	15	5	9	.294	.333	.353	686	95	-1	1	0	0	.991	1	C-29	0.2
1943	NY-A	62	180	12	43	6	3	2	24	13	9	.239	.290	.339	629	83	-4	0	1	-0	.981	2	C-52	0.0
1944	NY-A★	81	284	23	76	12	5	2	26	9	13	.268	.290	.366	656	84	-7	0	2	-1	.983	-2	C-76	-0.5
1946	Phi-N	49	139	7	31	4	1	0	11	9	10	.223	.270	.266	536	54	-9	0			.977	11	C-45	0.4
1947	Phi-N	2	3	0	1	0	0	0	1	0	0	.333	.333	.333	667	80	-0	0			1.000	-0	/C-2	0.0
Total	19	1593	5047	562	1321	257	72	31	555	357	395	.262	.311	.360	671	74	-204	29	18		.978	90	*C-1482/O-7L,1-2	-3.0
■ **SOLLY HEMUS**	Hemus, Solomon Joseph b: 4/17/23, Phoenix, Ariz. BL/TR, 5'9", 175 lbs. Deb: 4/27/49 MC																							
1949	StL-N	20	33	8	11	1	0	0	2	7	3	.333	.450	.364	814	115	1	0			.981	2	2-16	0.4
1950	StL-N	11	15	1	2	1	0	0	0	2	4	.133	.235	.200	435	15	-2	0			1.000	1	/3-5	-0.1
1951	StL-N	120	420	68	118	18	9	2	32	75	31	.281	.395	.381	776	109	9	7	7	-1	.965	13	*S-105,2-12	2.8
1952	StL-N	151	570	**105**	153	28	8	15	52	96	55	.268	.392	.425	817	126	24	1	5	-2	.960	4	*S-148/3-2	3.7
1953	StL-N	154	585	110	163	32	11	14	61	86	40	.279	.382	.443	825	114	15	2	1	0	.964	7	*S-150/2-3	3.3
1954	StL-N	124	214	43	65	15	3	2	27	55	27	.304	.456	.430	886	131	14	5	1	1	.944	-20	S-66,3-27,2-12	-0.1
1955	StL-N	96	206	36	50	10	2	5	21	27	22	.243	.336	.383	720	91	-3	1	1	-0	.956	-4	3-43,2-10/S-2	-0.6
1956	StL-N	8	5	1	1	0	0	0	2	1	0	.200	.429	.200	629	77	-0	0	0	0	.000	0	H	0.0
	Phi-N	78	187	24	54	10	4	5	24	28	21	.289	.401	.465	866	134	10	1	1	-0	.974	-25	2-49/3-1	-1.1
	Yr	86	192	25	55	10	4	5	26	29	21	.286	.402	.458	860	133	10	1	1	-0	.974	-25	2-49/3-1	-1.1
1957	Phi-N	70	108	8	20	6	1	0	5	20	8	.185	.323	.259	582	61	-5	1	1	-0	.980	-3	2-24	-0.8
1958	Phi-N	105	334	53	95	14	3	8	36	51	34	.284	.392	.416	808	116	10	3	1	0	.969	-14	2-85/3-1	0.2
1959	StL-N	24	17	2	4	2	0	0	1	8	2	.235	.500	.353	853	124	1	0	0	0	1.000	1	/2-1,3-1,M	0.2
Total	11	961	2694	459	736	137	41	51	263	456	247	.273	.390	.411	802	115	75	21	18		.962	-38	S-471,2-212/3-80	7.9
■ **DAVE HENDERSON**	Henderson, David Lee b: 7/21/58, Merced, Cal. BR/TR, 6'2", 220 lbs. Deb: 4/9/81 Career OF: (36-LF 1157-CF 229-RF)																							
1981	Sea-A	59	126	17	21	3	0	6	13	16	24	.167	.266	.333	599	69	-5	2	1	0	1.000	-7	O-58(2-33-31)	-1.5
1982	Sea-A	104	324	47	82	17	1	14	48	36	67	.253	.328	.441	769	106	2	2	5	-1	.985	7	*O-101(2-99-2)	0.7
1983	Sea-A	137	484	50	130	24	5	17	55	28	93	.269	.310	.444	754	101	-1	9	3	1	.982	12	*O-133(0-80-56)/D-3	0.9
1984	Sea-A	112	350	42	98	23	0	14	43	19	56	.280	.321	.466	786	116	6	5	5	-1	.988	8	O-97(0-88-11),D-10	1.2
1985	Sea-A	139	502	70	121	28	2	14	68	48	104	.241	.311	.388	699	90	-7	6	1	1	.986	-4	*O-138(1-126-27)	-1.3
1986	Sea-A	103	337	51	93	19	4	14	44	37	95	.276	.351	.481	832	123	10	1	3	-1	.979	5	O-80(0-51-31),D-22	1.1
	*Bos-A	36	51	8	10	3	0	1	3	2	15	.196	.226	.314	540	45	-4	1	0	0	.981	-5	O-32(0-32-0)	-0.8
	Yr	139	388	59	103	22	4	15	47	39	110	.265	.336	.459	794	113	6	2	3	-1	.980	0	*O-112(0-83-31),D-22	0.3
1987	Bos-A	75	184	30	43	10	0	8	25	22	48	.234	.316	.418	734	90	-3	1	1	-0	.958	-5	O-64(5-29-30)/D-1	-0.9
	SF-N	15	21	2	5	2	0	0	1	8	5	.238	.448	.333	782	117	1	2	0	0	1.000	-1	/O-9(1-8-1)	0.0
1988	*Oak-A	146	507	100	154	38	1	24	94	47	92	.304	.367	.525	892	152	34	2	4	-1	.982	5	*O-143(1-142-0)	3.7
1989	*Oak-A	152	579	77	145	24	3	15	80	54	131	.250	.318	.380	698	99	-1	8	5	0	.977	5	*O-149(0-149-0)/D-2	0.2
1990	*Oak-A	127	450	65	122	28	0	20	63	40	105	.271	.332	.467	799	126	14	3	1	0	.988	9	*O-116(1-110-5)/D-6	2.2

YEAR	TM/L	G	AB	R	H	2B	3B	HR	RBI	BB	SO	AVG	OBP	SLG	OPS	OPS+	BR+	SB	CS	SBR	FA	FR	G/POS	TPR
1991	Oak-A★	150	572	86	158	33	0	25	85	58	113	.276	.347	.465	812	130	22	6	6	-1	.997	11	*O-140C/2-1,D-7	3.1
1992	Oak-A	20	63	1	9	1	0	0	2	2	16	.143	.169	.159	328	-8	-9	0	0	0	.950	-3	O-12(0-9-3)/D-4	-1.2
1993	Oak-A	107	382	37	84	19	0	20	53	32	113	.220	.280	.427	707	93	-6	0	3	-1	.991	9	O-76(2-60-14),D-28	0.0
1994	KC-A	56	198	27	49	14	1	5	31	16	28	.247	.307	.404	711	78	-7	2	0	0	.962	-0	O-40(17-6-17),D-16	-0.8
Total	14	1538	5130	710	1324	286	17	197	708	465	1105	.258	.322	.436	758	108	47	50	38	-2	.984	44	*O-1388C/D-99,2-1	6.6
■ KEN HENDERSON	Henderson, Kenneth Joseph b: 6/15/46, Carroll, Iowa BB/TR, 6'2", 180 lbs. Deb: 4/23/65 Career OF: (434-LF 544-CF 360-RF)																							
1965	SF-N	63	73	10	14	1	1	0	7	9	19	.192	.280	.233	513	45	-5	1	1	-0	.980	-9	O-48(5-31-16)	-1.6
1966	SF-N	11	29	4	9	1	1	1	1	2	3	.310	.375	.517	892	141	2	0	0	0	.917	-3	O-10(1-7-4)	-0.2
1967	SF-N	65	179	15	34	3	0	4	14	19	52	.190	.275	.274	549	58	-9	0	1	-0	.947	-5	O-52(8-33-18)	-1.9
1968	SF-N	3	3	1	1	0	0	0	0	2	1	.333	.600	.333	933	186	1	0	0	0	1.000	-0	/O-2(1-1-0)	0.0
1969	SF-N	113	374	42	84	14	4	6	44	42	64	.225	.311	.332	643	82	-9	6	4	-0	.969	-3	*O-111(64-5-57)/3-3	-1.9
1970	SF-N	148	554	104	163	35	3	17	88	87	78	.294	.395	.460	855	130	26	20	3	3	.966	2	*O-146(113-25-35)	2.3
1971	*SF-N	141	504	80	133	26	6	15	65	84	76	.264	.372	.429	801	128	21	18	3	3	.966	-1	*O-138(109-14-26)/1-1	1.5
1972	SF-N	130	439	60	113	21	2	18	51	38	66	.257	.319	.437	757	112	5	14	7	1	.974	9	*O-123(95-26-2)	0.9
1973	Chi-A	73	262	32	68	13	0	6	32	27	49	.260	.331	.378	709	96	-1	3	4	-1	.972	-1	O-44(8-36-0),D-26	-0.6
1974	Chi-A	162	602	76	176	35	5	20	95	66	112	.292	.364	.467	831	134	26	12	7	0	.987	9	*O-162(0-162-0)	3.2
1975	Chi-A	140	513	65	129	20	3	9	53	74	65	.251	.350	.355	705	98	1	5	3	0	.990	13	*O-137(0-137-0)/D-1	1.0
1976	Atl-N	133	435	52	114	19	0	13	61	62	68	.262	.355	.395	751	106	5	5	7	-1	.987	-12	*O-122(0-20-115)	-1.6
1977	Tex-A	75	244	23	63	14	0	5	23	18	37	.258	.317	.377	694	87	-4	2	1	0	.983	-6	O-65(0-8-61)/D-3	-1.3
1978	NY-N	7	22	2	5	2	0	1	4	4	4	.227	.346	.455	801	127	1	0	1	-0	1.000	0	/O-7(0-0-7)	0.0
	Cin-N	64	144	10	24	6	1	3	19	23	32	.167	.281	.285	566	59	-8	0	0	0	1.000	-2	O-38(0-30-9)	-1.1
	Yr	71	166	12	29	8	1	4	23	27	36	.175	.290	.307	597	67	-7	0	1	-0	1.000	-2	O-45(0-30-16)	-1.1
1979	Cin-N	10	13	1	3	1	0	0	2	0	2	.231	.231	.308	538	45	-1	0	0	0	1.000	-0	/O-2(1-0-1)	-0.2
	Chi-N	62	81	11	19	2	0	2	8	15	16	.235	.361	.333	694	83	-1	0	0	0	.950	-6	O-23(14-9-0)	-0.8
	Yr	72	94	12	22	3	0	2	10	15	18	.234	.345	.330	675	79	-2	0	0	0	.955	-6	O-25(15-9-1)	-1.0
1980	Chi-N	44	82	7	16	3	0	2	9	17	19	.195	.333	.305	638	74	-2	0	0	0	.944	-1	O-22(15-0-9)	-0.4
Total	16	1444	4553	595	1168	216	26	122	576	589	763	.257	.346	.396	741	106	45	86	42	4	.977	-19	*O-1252C/D-30,3-3,1	-2.7
■ RICKEY HENDERSON	Henderson, Rickey Henley b: 12/25/58, Chicago, Ill. BR/TL, 5'10", 195 lbs. Deb: 6/24/79 Career OF: (2250-LF 444-CF 26-RF)																							
1979	Oak-A	89	351	49	96	13	3	1	26	34	39	.274	.341	.336	677	88	-5	33	11	3	.973	3	O-88(62-32-1)	-0.2
1980	Oak-A★	158	591	111	179	22	4	9	53	117	54	.303	.422	.399	821	136	37	**100**	26	13	.984	23	*O-157(157-1-0)/D-1	6.4
1981	*Oak-A	108	423	**89**	**135**	18	7	6	35	64	68	.319	.411	.437	848	152	31	**56**	22	5	.979	20	*O-107(107-1-0)	**5.2**
1982	Oak-A★	149	536	119	143	24	4	10	51	**116**	94	.267	.399	.382	782	121	22	**130**	42	**14**	.977	9	*O-144(138-10-0)/D-4	3.8
1983	Oak-A★	145	513	105	150	25	7	9	48	**103**	80	.292	.415	.421	836	139	33	**108**	19	**17**	.992	9	*O-142(138-10-0)/D-1	5.2
1984	Oak-A★	142	502	113	147	27	4	16	58	86	81	.293	.401	.458	860	147	36	**66**	18	8	.969	8	*O-140(140-6-0)	4.5
1985	NY-A★	143	547	**146**	172	28	5	24	72	99	65	.314	.422	.516	938	159	48	**80**	10	**14**	.980	16	*O-141(6-141-0)/D-1	**7.4**
1986	NY-A★	153	608	**130**	160	31	5	28	74	89	81	.263	.359	.469	828	125	21	**87**	18	**13**	.986	12	*O-146(11-138-0)/D-5	4.3
1987	NY-A★	95	358	78	104	17	3	17	37	80	52	.291	.423	.497	920	144	27	41	8	6	.980	7	O-69(34-39-0),D-24	3.5
1988	NY-A★	140	554	118	169	30	2	6	50	82	54	.305	.397	.399	796	125	22	**93**	13	**16**	.965	10	*O-136(135-3-0)/D-3	4.3
1989	NY-A	65	235	41	58	13	1	3	22	56	29	.247	.394	.349	743	112	7	25	8	3	.993	4	O-65(65-0-0)	1.1
	*Oak-A	85	306	72	90	13	2	9	35	70	39	.294	.429	.438	866	150	25	52	6	9	.985	7	O-82(82-0-0)/D-3	3.8
	Yr	150	541	**113**	148	26	3	12	57	**126**	68	.274	.413	.399	813	133	31	**77**	14	**12**	.988	11	*O-147(147-0-0)/D-3	**4.9**
1990	*Oak-A★	136	489	**119**	159	33	3	28	61	97	60	.325	**.441**	.577	**1017**	**190**	**63**	**65**	10	**11**	.983	11	*O-118(119-0-0),D-15	**7.9**
1991	Oak-A★	134	470	105	126	17	1	18	57	98	73	.268	.402	.423	825	136	28	**58**	18	6	.970	10	*O-119(119-0-0),D-10	4.0
1992	*Oak-A	117	396	77	112	18	3	15	46	95	56	.283	.429	.457	886	156	36	48	11	7	.984	6	*O-108(108-0-0)/D-6	4.5
1993	Oak-A	90	318	77	104	19	1	17	47	85	46	.327	.472	.553	1025	186	44	31	6	5	.974	9	O-74(74-0-0),D-16	5.2
	*Tor-A	44	163	37	35	3	1	4	12	35	19	.215	.360	.319	679	84	-2	22	2	4	.975	-2	O-44(44-0-0)	-0.1
	Yr	134	481	114	139	22	2	21	59	120	65	.289	.435	.474	909	150	41	53	8	9	.974	7	*O-118(118-0-0),D-16	5.1
1994	Oak-A	87	296	66	77	13	0	6	20	72	45	.260	.413	.365	778	112	10	22	7	2	.977	4	O-71(66-10-0),D-13	1.3
1995	Oak-A	112	407	67	122	31	1	9	54	72	66	.300	.410	.447	857	130	21	32	10	4	.988	1	O-90(90-0-0),D-19	2.0
1996	*SD-N	148	465	110	112	17	2	9	29	125	90	.241	.412	.344	756	108	14	37	15	3	.975	-3	*O-134(114-10-17)	1.0
1997	SD-N	88	288	63	79	11	0	6	27	71	62	.274	.424	.375	799	120	13	29	4	5	.959	4	O-78(55-17-8)/D-2	2.0
	Ana-A	32	115	21	21	3	0	2	7	26	23	.183	.343	.261	604	61	-6	16	4	2	1.000	-0	D-19,O-13(11-2-0)	-0.5
1998	Oak-A	152	542	101	128	16	1	14	57	**118**	114	.236	.377	.347	724	92	-1	**66**	13	**10**	.988	-2	*O-151(142-24-0)	0.3
1999	*NY-N	121	438	89	138	30	0	12	42	82	82	.315	.425	.466	891	129	23	37	14	3	.988	-7	*O-116(116-0-0)/D-1	1.5
2000	NY-N	31	96	17	21	1	0	0	2	25	20	.219	.390	.229	619	64	-4	5	2	0	.946	-3	O-29(29-0-0)	-0.7
	*Sea-A	92	324	58	77	13	2	4	30	63	55	.238	.365	.327	692	79	-8	31	9	4	.984	-0	O-88(88-0-0)	-0.7
Total	22	2856	10331	2178	2914	486	62	282	1052	2060	1547	.282	.406	.423	829	130	536	1370	326	187	.980	154	*O-2650L,D-143	77.0
■ STEVE HENDERSON	Henderson, Stephen Curtis b: 11/18/52, Houston, Tex. BR/TR, 6'2", 190 lbs. Deb: 6/16/77 C Career OF: (856-LF 0-CF 43-RF)																							
1977	NY-N	99	350	67	104	16	6	12	65	43	79	.297	.376	.480	856	134	17	6	3	0	.980	6	O-97(97-0-0)	1.9
1978	NY-N	157	587	83	156	30	9	10	65	60	109	.266	.336	.399	735	108	6	13	7	0	.968	16	*O-155(155-0-0)	1.6
1979	NY-N	98	350	42	107	16	8	5	39	38	58	.306	.380	.440	820	128	14	13	5	1	.990	9	O-94(94-0-0)	2.1
1980	NY-N	143	513	75	149	17	8	8	58	62	90	.290	.370	.402	772	119	14	23	12	1	.981	13	*O-136(136-0-0)	2.3
1981	Chi-N	82	287	32	84	9	5	5	35	42	61	.293	.387	.411	798	121	9	5	7	-1	.951	1	O-77(77-0-0)	0.6
1982	Chi-N	92	257	23	60	12	4	2	29	22	64	.233	.294	.335	629	73	-9	6	5	-0	.956	0	O-70(70-0-0)	-1.3
1983	Sea-A	121	436	50	128	32	3	10	54	44	82	.294	.358	.450	808	116	10	10	14	-3	.970	1	*O-112(112-0-0)/D-6	0.3
1984	Sea-A	109	325	42	85	12	3	10	35	38	62	.262	.341	.409	750	108	4	2	4	-1	.936	-2	O-53(52-0-0),D-51	-0.3
1985	Oak-A	85	193	25	58	8	3	3	31	18	34	.301	.360	.420	780	122	6	0	0	0	.953	-7	O-58(47-0-11)/D-1	-0.3
1986	Oak-A	11	26	2	2	1	0	0	3	0	5	.077	.077	.115	192	-52	-5	0	0	0	.800	-2	/O-7(7-0-0),D-1	-0.7
1987	Oak-A	46	114	14	33	7	0	3	9	12	19	.289	.357	.430	787	115	3	0	0	0	.943	-7	O-31(5-0-28)/D-9	-0.5
1988	Hou-N	42	46	4	10	2	0	0	5	7	14	.217	.321	.261	582	72	-1	1	1	-0	1.000	0	/O-8(4-0-4),1-1	-0.2
Total	12	1085	3484	459	976	162	49	68	428	386	677	.280	.354	.413	767	113	67	79	58	-3	.968	29	O-898L/D-68,1-1	5.5
■ GEORGE HENDRICK	Hendrick, George Andrew b: 10/18/49, Los Angeles, Cal. BR/TR, 6'3", 195 lbs. Deb: 6/4/71 C Career OF: (246-LF 749-CF 897-RF)																							
1971	Oak-A	42	114	8	27	4	1	0	8	3	20	.237	.256	.289	546	55	-7	0	1	-0	.981	-7	O-36(18-16-10)	-1.7
1972	*Oak-A	58	121	10	22	1	1	4	15	3	22	.182	.208	.306	514	54	-7	3	2	-0	1.000	-7	O-41(5-28-12)	-1.8
1973	Cle-A	113	440	64	118	18	0	21	61	25	71	.268	.310	.452	763	111	4	7	6	-1	.988	-3	*O-110(0-107-3)	-0.2
1974	Cle-A★	139	495	65	138	23	1	19	67	33	73	.279	.325	.444	770	121	11	6	4	-0	.989	3	*O-133(2-131-0)/D-1	1.1
1975	Cle-A★	145	561	82	145	21	2	24	86	40	78	.258	.308	.431	739	107	3	6	7	-1	.983	1	*O-143(1-89-53)	-0.3
1976	Cle-A	149	551	72	146	20	3	25	81	51	82	.265	.327	.448	776	127	17	4	4	-1	.987	3	*O-146(136-13-3)/D-3	1.2
1977	SD-N	152	541	75	168	25	2	23	81	61	74	.311	.382	.492	874	148	36	11	6	0	.983	8	*O-142(24-131-9)	4.2
1978	SD-N	36	111	9	27	4	0	3	8	12	16	.243	.317	.360	677	96	-1	1	1	-0	.986	-0	O-33(1-26-6)	-0.2
	StL-N	102	382	55	110	27	1	17	67	28	44	.288	.340	.497	837	133	15	1	0	0	.996	6	*O-101(2-87-12)	2.1
	Yr	138	493	64	137	31	1	20	75	40	60	.278	.335	.467	801	126	15	2	1	0	.994	6	*O-134(3-113-18)	1.9
1979	StL-N	140	493	67	148	27	1	16	75	49	62	.300	.363	.456	820	121	14	2	3	-1	.993	6	*O-138(0-14-124)	1.3
1980	StL-N★	150	572	73	173	33	2	25	109	32	67	.302	.344	.498	842	128	20	6	1	1	.994	-6	*O-149(0-54-121)	0.9
1981	StL-N	101	394	67	112	19	3	18	61	41	44	.284	.358	.485	842	134	17	4	2	0	.983	-4	*O-101(0-51-59)	1.1
1982	*StL-N	136	515	65	145	20	5	19	104	37	80	.282	.331	.450	781	115	9	3	2	-0	.980	-2	*O-134(0-0-134)	0.0
1983	StL-N☆	144	529	73	168	33	3	18	97	51	76	.318	.380	.493	873	140	28	3	4	-1	.992	1	1-92,O-51(0-0-51)	2.1
1984	StL-N	120	441	57	122	28	1	9	69	32	75	.277	.327	.406	733	108	3	0	2	-1	.990	-1	*O-116(0-0-116)/1-1	-0.4
1985	Pit-N	69	256	23	59	15	0	2	25	18	42	.230	.281	.313	594	66	-12	1	0	0	.971	3	O-65(0-0-65)	-1.3
	Cal-A	16	41	5	5	1	0	2	6	4	8	.122	.200	.293	493	33	-4	0	0	0	1.000	-1	O-12(0-0-12)/D-1	-0.5
1986	*Cal-A	102	283	45	77	13	1	14	47	26	41	.272	.335	.473	809	119	7	1	1	-0	.968	-6	O-93(0-2-92)/1-7,D-4	-0.3
1987	Cal-A	65	162	14	39	10	0	5	25	14	18	.241	.301	.395	696	85	-4	0	0	0	.967	-8	O-45(37-0-11)/1-9,D-5	-1.3
1988	Cal-A	69	127	12	31	1	0	3	19	7	20	.244	.289	.323	612	73	-5	0	1	-0	.933	-1	O-24(20-0-4),1-12/D-3	-0.7
Total	18	2048	7129	941	1980	343	27	267	1111	567	1013	.278	.333	.446	779	117	146	59	47	-3	.985	-17	*O-1813R,1-121/D-17	5.3

YEAR	TM/L	G	AB	R	H	2B	3B	HR	RBI	BB	SO	AVG	OBP	SLG	OPS	OPS+	BR+	SB	CS	SBR	FA	FR	G/POS	TPR
■ HARVEY HENDRICK	Hendrick, Harvey "Gink" b: 11/9/1897, Mason, Tenn. d: 10/29/41, Covington, Tenn. BL/TR, 6'2", 190 lbs. Deb: 4/20/23 Career OF: (128-LF 21-CF 86-RF)																							
1923	*NY-A	37	66	9	18	3	1	3	12	2	8	.273	.294	.485	779	101	-1	3	0	1	.947	-2	O-13(11-2-0)	-0.3
1924	NY-A	40	76	7	20	0	0	1	11	2	7	.263	.291	.303	594	53	-5	1	0	0	.975	0	O-17(15-0-2)	-0.6
1925	Cle-A	25	28	2	8	1	2	0	9	3	5	.286	.355	.464	819	106	0	0	0	0	1.000	0	/1-3	0.0
1927	Bro-N	128	458	55	142	18	11	4	50	24	40	.310	.350	.424	773	106	3	29			.969	-16	O-64R,1-53/2-1	-2.1
1928	Bro-N	126	425	83	135	15	10	11	59	54	34	.318	.397	.478	875	129	19	16			.913	3	3-91,O-17(6-11-0)	2.6
1929	Bro-N	110	384	69	136	25	6	14	82	31	20	.354	.404	.560	964	139	22	14			.975	0	O-42L,1-39/3-7,S-4	1.6
1930	Bro-N	68	167	29	43	10	1	5	28	20	19	.257	.344	.419	763	84	-4	2			.947	-3	O-42(36-6-0)/1-7	-0.9
1931	Bro-N	1	1	0	0	0	0	0	0	0	0	.000	.000	.000	0	-99	-0	0			.000	0	H	0.0
	Cin-N	137	530	74	167	32	9	1	75	53	40	.315	.379	.415	795	121	16	3			.987	-5	*1-137	-0.2
	Yr	138	531	74	167	32	9	1	75	53	40	.315	.379	.414	793	120	16	3			.987	-5	*1-137	-0.2
1932	StL-N	28	72	8	18	2	0	1	5	5	9	.250	.299	.319	618	64	-4	0			.862	-3	3-12/O-5(0-0-5)	-0.6
	Cin-N	94	398	56	120	30	3	4	40	23	29	.302	.341	.422	763	107	4	3			.986	-4	1-94	-0.9
	Yr	122	470	64	138	32	3	5	45	28	38	.294	.335	.406	741	100	-0	3			.986	-7	1-94,3-12/O-5(0-0-5)	-1.5
1933	Chi-N	69	189	30	55	13	3	4	23	13	17	.291	.346	.455	801	128	6	4			.983	-1	1-38/O-8(4-0-4),3-1	0.2
1934	Phi-N	59	116	12	34	8	0	0	19	9	15	.293	.344	.362	706	79	-3	0			.962	-3	O-12(11-0-1)/1-7,3-7	-0.7
Total	11	922	2910	434	896	157	46	48	413	239	243	.308	.364	.443	807	113	54	75	0		.986	-32	1-378,O-220L,3/S2	-1.9
■ ELLIE HENDRICKS	Hendricks, Elrod Jerome b: 12/22/40, Charlotte Amalie, V.I. BL/TR, 6'1", 175 lbs. Deb: 4/13/68 C																							
1968	Bal-A	79	183	19	37	8	1	7	23	19	51	.202	.281	.372	652	96	-1	0	0	0	.991	-5	C-53	-0.4
1969	*Bal-A	105	295	36	72	5	0	12	38	39	44	.244	.336	.383	719	100	0	0	1	-0	**.998**	5	C-87/1-4	0.9
1970	*Bal-A	106	322	32	78	9	0	12	41	33	44	.242	.320	.382	702	92	-4	1	0	0	.986	-8	C-95	-0.7
1971	*Bal-A	101	316	33	79	14	1	9	42	39	38	.250	.336	.386	722	105	2	0	0	0	.985	-8	C-90/1-3	-0.2
1972	Bal-A	33	84	6	13	4	0	0	4	12	19	.155	.260	.202	463	38	-6	0	1	-0	.986	2	C-28	-0.4
	Chi-N	17	43	7	5	1	0	2	6	13	8	.116	.321	.279	600	65	-2	0	1	-0	.978	1	C-16	-0.1
1973	Bal-A	41	101	9	18	5	1	3	15	10	22	.178	.259	.337	596	67	-5	0	0	0	.994	4	C-38/D-1	0.1
1974	*Bal-A	66	159	18	33	8	2	3	8	17	25	.208	.288	.340	628	83	-4	0	0	0	1.000	-4	C-54/1-1,D-1	-0.6
1975	Bal-A	85	223	32	48	8	2	8	38	34	40	.215	.322	.377	698	103	1	0	1	-0	**.995**	-1	C-83	0.4
1976	Bal-A	28	79	2	11	1	0	1	4	7	13	.139	.209	.190	399	19	-8	0	1	-0	.971	-5	C-27	-1.3
	*NY-A	26	53	6	12	1	0	3	5	3	10	.226	.268	.415	683	99	-0	0	0	0	1.000	1	C-18	0.1
	Yr	54	132	8	23	2	0	4	9	10	23	.174	.232	.280	513	52	-8	0	1	-0	.982	-4	C-45	-1.2
1977	NY-A	10	11	1	3	1	0	1	5	0	2	.273	.273	.636	909	140	0	0	0	0	1.000	0	/C-6	0.1
1978	Bal-A	13	18	4	6	1	0	1	1	3	3	.333	.429	.556	984	186	2	0	0	0	.955	0	/C-6,P-1,D-1	0.2
1979	Bal-A	1	1	0	0	0	0	0	0	0	0	.000	.000	.000	0	-99	-0	0	0	0	.500	-1	/C-1	-0.1
Total	12	711	1888	205	415	66	7	62	230	229	319	.220	.308	.361	669	90	-24	1	5	-2	.990	-17	C-602/1-8,D-3,P-1	-2.0
■ JACK HENDRICKS	Hendricks, John Charles b: 4/9/1875, Joliet, Ill. d: 5/13/43, Chicago, Ill. BL/TL, 5'11.5", 160 lbs. Deb: 6/12/02 M																							
1902	NY-N	8	26	1	6	2	0	0	0	2		.231	.286	.308	593	84	-1	2			.929	0	/O-7(0-0-7)	-0.1
	Chi-N	2	7	0	4	0	1	0	0	0		.571	.571	.857	1429	350	2	0			1.000	0	/O-2(0-0-2)	0.2
	Yr	10	33	1	10	2	1	0	0	2		.303	.343	.424	767	138	1	2			.950	1	/O-9(0-0-9)	0.1
1903	Was-A	32	112	10	20	1	3	0	4	13		.179	.264	.241	505	51	-6	3			.891	-4	O-32(0-0-32)	-1.3
Total	2	42	145	11	30	3	4	0	4	15		.207	.281	.283	564	70	-5	5			.909	-3	/O-41(0-0-41)	-1.2
■ TIM HENDRYX	Hendryx, Timothy Green b: 1/31/1891, LeRoy, Ill. d: 8/14/57, Corpus Christi, Tex. BR/TR, 5'9", 170 lbs. Deb: 9/4/11																							
1911	Cle-A	4	7	0	2	0	0	0	0	0		.286	.286	.286	571	59	-0	0			1.000	0	/3-3	0.0
1912	Cle-A	23	70	9	17	2	4	1	14	8		.243	.329	.429	758	113	1	3			1.000	-2	O-22(0-22-0)	-0.2
1915	NY-A	13	40	4	8	2	0	0	1	4	2	.200	.289	.250	539	61	-2	0	3	-1	.968	1	O-12(0-12-0)	-0.3
1916	NY-A	15	62	10	18	7	1	0	5	8	6	.290	.380	.435	816	142	3	4			1.000	-2	O-15(0-0-15)	0.1
1917	NY-A	125	393	43	98	14	7	5	44	62	45	.249	.359	.359	717	118	10	6			.955	5	*O-107(0-30-77)	0.9
1918	StL-A	88	219	22	61	14	3	0	33	37	35	.279	.388	.370	757	133	10	5			.982	-9	O-65(28-20-18)	-0.2
1920	Bos-A	99	363	54	119	21	5	0	73	42	27	.328	.400	.413	814	121	13	7	9	-2	.964	-10	O-98(0-98-0)	-0.5
1921	Bos-A	49	137	10	33	8	2	0	22	24	13	.241	.362	.328	690	79	-3	1	1	-0	.958	-4	O-41(2-2-37)	-1.0
Total	8	416	1291	152	356	68	22	6	192	185	128	.276	.372	.376	749	115	31	26	13		.966	-21	O-360(30-184-147)/3-3	-1.2
■ DAVE HENGEL	Hengel, David Lee b: 12/18/61, Oakland, Cal. BR/TR, 6', 185 lbs. Deb: 9/3/86																							
1986	Sea-A	21	63	3	12	1	0	1	6	1	13	.190	.215	.254	469	27	-6	0	0	0	1.000	-1	D-11/O-8(6-0-2)	-0.8
1987	Sea-A	10	19	2	6	0	0	1	4	0	4	.316	.316	.474	789	100	-0	0	0	0	.875	-2	/O-7(2-0-7),D-1	-0.3
1988	Sea-A	26	60	3	10	1	0	2	7	1	15	.167	.180	.283	464	27	-6	0	0	0	.952	-1	O-12(4-0-8),D-12	-0.8
1989	Cle-A	12	25	2	3	1	0	0	1	2	4	.120	.185	.160	345	-2	-3	0	0	0	1.000	-1	/O-9(9-0-0),D-3	-0.4
Total	4	69	167	10	31	3	0	4	18	4	36	.186	.209	.275	485	31	-16	0	0	0	.962	-5	/O-36(21-0-17),D-27	-2.3
■ MOXIE HENGLE	Hengle, Emery J. b: 10/7/1857, Chicago, Ill. d: 12/11/24, River Forest, Ill. BR, 5'8", 144 lbs. Deb: 4/20/1884																							
1884	CP-U	19	74	9	15	2	1	0		3		.203	.234	.257	491	49	-7				.840	-7	2-19	-1.2
	StP-U	9	33	2	5	1	1	0		0		.152	.152	.242	394	32	-4				.923	1	/2-9	-0.2
	Yr	28	107	11	20	3	2	0		3		.187	.209	.252	461	46	-10				.870	-6	2-28	-1.4
1885	Buf-N	7	26	2	4	0	0	0	0	1	2	.154	.185	.154	339	10	-3				.864	-3	/2-5,O-3(0-2-1)	-0.5
Total	2	35	133	13	24	3	2	0	0	4	2	.180	.204	.233	437	38	-13				.869	-9	/2-33,O-3(0-2-1)	-1.9
■ GAIL HENLEY	Henley, Gail Curtice b: 10/15/28, Wichita, Kan. BL/TR, 5'9", 180 lbs. Deb: 4/13/54																							
1954	Pit-N	14	30	7	9	1	0	1	2	4	4	.300	.382	.433	816	114	1	0	0	0	1.000	-0	/O-9(1-0-8)	0.0
■ BOB HENLEY	Henley, Robert Clifton b: 1/30/73, Mobile, Ala. BR/TR, 6'2", 190 lbs. Deb: 7/19/98																							
1998	Mon-N	41	115	16	35	8	1	3	18	11	26	.304	.380	.470	849	124	4	3	0	1	.995	-6	C-35	0.1
■ BUTCH HENLINE	Henline, Walter John b: 12/20/1894, Ft.Wayne, Ind. d: 10/9/57, Sarasota, Fla. BR/TR, 5'10", 175 lbs. Deb: 4/13/21 U																							
1921	NY-N	1	1	0	0	0	0	0	0	0	1	.000	.000	.000	0	-99	-0	0	0	0	.000	0	H	0.0
	Phi-N	33	111	8	34	2	0	0	8	2	6	.306	.319	.324	643	65	-5	1	0	0	.987	9	C-32	0.6
	Yr	34	112	8	34	2	0	0	8	2	7	.304	.316	.321	637	64	-6	1	0	0	.987	9	C-32	0.6
1922	Phi-N	125	430	57	136	20	4	14	64	36	33	.316	.380	.479	859	110	6	2	2	-0	**.983**	2	*C-119	1.5
1923	Phi-N	111	330	45	107	14	3	7	46	37	33	.324	.407	.448	855	112	7	7	5	-0	.978	-16	C-96/O-1(1-0-0)	-0.2
1924	Phi-N	115	289	41	82	18	4	5	35	27	15	.284	.361	.426	787	98	-0	1	2	-0	.973	-1	C-83/O-2(1-1-0)	0.3
1925	Phi-N	93	263	43	80	12	5	8	48	24	16	.304	.380	.479	859	108	3	3	1	0	.956	-2	C-68/O-1(1-0-0)	0.5
1926	Phi-N	99	283	32	80	14	1	2	30	21	18	.283	.339	.360	699	84	-6	1			.970	-10	C-77/1-4,O-2(2-0-0)	-1.1
1927	Bro-N	67	177	12	47	10	3	1	18	17	10	.266	.337	.373	710	90	-3	1			.947	1	C-60	0.2
1928	Bro-N	55	132	12	28	3	1	2	8	17	8	.212	.302	.295	597	58	-8	2			.976	-4	C-45	-0.9
1929	Bro-N	27	62	5	15	2	0	1	7	9	9	.242	.338	.323	661	66	-3	0			.967	1	C-21	-0.1
1930	Chi-A	3	8	1	1	0	0	0	2	0	3	.125	.125	.125	250	-38	-2	0	0	0	1.000	0	/C-3	-0.1
1931	Chi-A	11	15	2	1	1	0	0	2	2	4	.067	.176	.133	310	-19	-3	0	0	0	.889	0	/C-4	-0.2
Total	11	740	2101	258	611	96	21	40	268	192	156	.291	.361	.414	774	96	-13	18	10		.971	-20	C-608/O-6(5-1-0),1-4	0.5
■ LES HENNESSEY	Hennessey, Lester Baker b: 12/12/1893, Lynn, Mass. d: 11/20/76, New York, N.Y. BR/TR, 6', 190 lbs. Deb: 6/4/13																							
1913	Det-A	14	22	2	3	0	0	0	0	3	6	.136	.240	.136	376	11	-2	2			.880	-2	2-10	-0.5
■ FRITZ HENRICH	Henrich, Frank Wilde b: 5/8/1899, Cincinnati, Ohio d: 5/1/59, Philadelphia, Pa. BL/TL, 5'10", 160 lbs. Deb: 4/21/24																							
1924	Phi-N	36	90	4	19	4	0	0	4	2	12	.211	.228	.256	484	26	-9	0	0	0	.978	-9	O-32(12-14-10)	-2.0
■ BOBBY HENRICH	Henrich, Robert Edward b: 12/24/38, Lawrence, Kan. BR/TR, 6'1", 185 lbs. Deb: 5/3/57 Career OF: (4-LF 2-CF 0-RF)																							
1957	Cin-N	29	10	8	2	0	0	0	1	1	4	.200	.273	.200	473	28	-1	0	0	0	.875	0	/S-7,O-6L,3-2,2-1	-0.1
1958	Cin-N	5	3	2	0	0	0	0	0	0	2	.000	.000	.000	0	-95	-1	0	0	0	1.000	1	/S-2	0.0
1959	Cin-N	14	3	3	0	0	0	0	0	0	1	.000	.000	.000	0	-97	-1	0	0	0	1.000	0	/S-5,3-1	-0.1
Total	3	48	16	13	2	0	0	0	1	1	7	.125	.176	.125	301	-17	-3	0	0	0	.929	1	/S-14,O-6L,3-3,2-1	-0.2

YEAR	TM/L	G	AB	R	H	2B	3B	HR	RBI	BB	SO	AVG	OBP	SLG	OPS	OPS+	BR+	SB	CS	SBR	FA	FR	G/POS	TPR
■ TOMMY HENRICH Henrich, Thomas David "The Clutch" or "Old Reliable" b: 2/20/13, Massillon, Ohio BL/TL, 6', 180 lbs. Deb: 5/11/37 C Career OF: (38-LF 92-CF 894-RF)																								
1937	NY-A	67	206	39	66	14	5	8	42	35	17	.320	.419	.553	972	142	14	4	0	1	.970	-4	O-59(30-0-29)	0.7
1938	*NY-A	131	471	109	127	24	7	22	91	92	32	.270	.391	.490	882	120	15	6	2	1	.984	-1	*O-130(0-0-130)	0.6
1939	NY-A	99	347	64	96	18	4	9	57	51	23	.277	.371	.429	800	106	3	7	0	2	.991	2	O-88(1-38-50)/1-1	0.2
1940	NY-A	90	293	57	90	28	5	10	53	48	30	.307	.408	.539	947	149	22	1	2	-0	.969	-1	O-76(1-24-52)/1-2	1.5
1941	*NY-A	144	538	106	149	27	5	31	85	81	40	.277	.377	.519	895	137	28	3	1	0	.980	-1	*O-139(0-19-121)	1.8
1942	NY-A★	127	483	77	129	30	5	13	67	58	42	.267	.352	.431	782	122	13	4	4	-1	.987	-1	*O-119(0-0-119)/1-7	0.4
1946	NY-A	150	565	92	142	25	4	19	83	87	63	.251	.358	.411	769	113	11	5	2	0	.992	2	*O-111(0-0-111),1-41	0.9
1947	*NY-A★	142	550	109	158	35	**13**	16	98	71	54	.287	.372	.485	857	139	27	3	2	-0	.983	6	*O-132(0-8-125)/1-6	3.0
1948	NY-A★	146	588	**138**	181	42	**14**	25	100	76	42	.308	.391	.554	945	151	40	2	3	-1	.978	-0	*O-102(6-3-96),1-46	3.3
1949	*NY-A☆	115	411	90	118	20	3	24	85	86	34	.287	.416	.526	942	148	30	2	2	-0	.958	-4	O-61(0-0-61),1-52	2.1
1950	NY-A★	73	151	20	41	6	8	6	34	27	6	.272	.382	.536	918	137	8	0	1	-0	.987	-5	1-34	0.1
Total	11	1284	4603	901	1297	269	73	183	795	712	383	.282	.382	.491	873	132	212	37	19	1	.981	-7	*O-1017R,1-189	14.6
■ OLAF HENRIKSEN Henriksen, Olaf "Swede" b: 4/26/1888, Kirkerup, Denmark d: 10/17/62, Norwood, Mass. BL/TL, 5'7.5", 158 lbs. Deb: 8/11/11																								
1911	Bos-A	27	93	17	34	2	1	0	8	14		.366	.449	.409	857	141	6	4			.953	-0	O-25(5-0-20)	0.5
1912	*Bos-A	44	56	20	18	3	1	0	8	14		.321	.457	.411	868	142	4	0			.909	-2	O-11(0-0-10)	0.1
1913	Bos-A	31	40	8	15	1	0	0	2	7	5	.375	.468	.400	868	151	3	3			1.000	-1	/O-7(6-1-0)	0.2
1914	Bos-A	63	95	16	25	2	1	1	5	22	12	.263	.407	.337	744	124	4	5	4	-0	.947	-5	O-29(8-10-10)	-0.3
1915	*Bos-A	73	92	9	18	2	2	0	13	18	7	.196	.333	.261	594	80	-1	1	5	-2	.967	-4	O-25(9-4-12)	-0.8
1916	*Bos-A	68	99	13	20	2	2	0	11	19	15	.202	.331	.263	593	78	-2	2			1.000	-4	O-31(14-7-9)	-0.8
1917	Bos-A	15	12	1	1	0	0	0	1	3	4	.083	.267	.083	350	7	-1	0			.000	0	H	-0.1
Total	7	321	487	84	131	12	7	1	48	97	43	.269	.392	.329	721	112	13	15	9		.966	-17	O-128(42-22-61)	-1.2
■ SNAKE HENRY Henry, Frederick Marshall b: 7/19/1895, Waynesville, N.C. d: 10/12/87, Wendell, N.C. BL/TL, 6', 170 lbs. Deb: 9/15/22																								
1922	Bos-N	18	66	5	13	4	1	0	5	2	8	.197	.221	.288	508	32	-7	2	2	-0	.995	1	1-18	-0.7
1923	Bos-N	11	9	1	1	0	0	0	2	1	1	.111	.200	.111	311	-17	-2	0	0	0	.000	0	H	-0.1
Total	2	29	75	6	14	4	1	0	7	3	9	.187	.218	.267	485	26	-8	2	2	-0	.995	1	/1-18	-0.8
■ GEORGE HENRY Henry, George Washington b: 8/10/1863, Philadelphia, Pa. d: 12/30/34, Lynn, Mass. BR/TR, 5'9", 180 lbs. Deb: 4/27/1893																								
1893	Cin-N	21	83	11	23	3	0	0	13	11	12	.277	.375	.313	688	82	-2	2			.965	5	O-21(10-0-11)	0.1
■ JOHN HENRY Henry, John Michael b: 9/2/1863, Springfield, Mass. d: 6/11/39, Hartford, Conn. TL, Deb: 8/13/1884																								
1884	Cle-N	9	26	2	4	0	0	0	0	0	12	.154	.154	.154	308	-3	-3				1.000	0	/P-5,O-4(0-0-4)	-0.1
1885	Bal-a	10	34	4	9	3	0	0	3	1		.265	.286	.353	639	102	0				.931	2	/P-9,O-1(1-0-0)	0.0
1886	Was-N	4	14	3	5	0	0	0	0	0	3	.357	.357	.357	714	125	0	0			.833	-0	/P-4	0.0
1890	NY-N	37	144	19	35	6	0	0	16	7	12	.243	.283	.285	568	65	-7	12			.870	-3	O-37(34-1-3)	-0.9
Total	4	60	218	28	53	9	0	0	19	8	27	.243	.273	.284	558	66	-9	12			.867	-1	/O-42(35-1-7),P-18	-1.0
■ JOHN HENRY Henry, John Park "Bull" b: 12/26/1889, Amherst, Mass. d: 11/24/41, Fort Huachuca, Ariz. BR/TR, 6', 180 lbs. Deb: 7/8/10																								
1910	Was-A	28	87	2	13	1	1	0	5	2		.149	.169	.184	352	11	-9	2			.989	2	C-18,1-10	-0.7
1911	Was-A	85	261	24	53	5	0	0	21	25		.203	.273	.222	495	39	-21	8			.969	9	C-51,1-30	-0.9
1912	Was-A	66	191	23	37	4	1	0	9	31		.194	.309	.225	535	53	-11	10			.977	8	C-65	0.3
1913	Was-A	96	273	26	61	8	4	1	26	30	43	.223	.309	.293	602	75	-8	5			**.982**	3	C-96	0.2
1914	Was-A	92	261	22	44	7	4	0	20	37	47	.169	.274	.226	500	49	-16	7	3	0	.980	6	C-92	-0.2
1915	Was-A	95	277	20	61	9	2	1	22	36	28	.220	.323	.278	601	78	-6	10	2	2	.972	4	C-94	0.8
1916	Was-A	117	305	28	76	12	3	0	46	49	40	.249	.364	.308	672	103	4	12			.981	-4	*C-116	0.9
1917	Was-A	65	163	10	31	6	0	0	18	24	16	.190	.302	.227	529	62	-6	1			.988	1	C-59	-0.1
1918	Bos-N	43	102	6	21	2	0	0	4	10	15	.206	.283	.225	509	58	-5	0			.964	1	C-38	-0.1
Total	9	687	1920	161	397	54	15	2	171	244	189	.207	.303	.254	557	65	-78	55	5		.978	31	C-629/1-40	0.2
■ RON HENRY Henry, Ronald Baxter b: 8/7/36, Chester, Pa. BR/TR, 6'1", 180 lbs. Deb: 4/15/61																								
1961	Min-A	20	28	1	4	0	0	0	3	2	7	.143	.200	.143	343	-6	-4	0	0	0	1.000	-1	/C-5,1-1	-0.5
1964	Min-A	22	41	4	5	1	1	2	5	2	17	.122	.163	.341	504	36	-4	0	0	0	.984	-0	C-13	-0.4
Total	2	42	69	5	9	1	1	2	8	4	24	.130	.178	.261	439	18	-8	0	0	0	.988	-1	/C-18,1-1	-0.9
■ BABE HERMAN Herman, Floyd Caves b: 6/26/03, Buffalo, N.Y. d: 11/27/87, Glendale, Cal. BL/TL, 6'4", 190 lbs. Deb: 4/14/26 C Career OF: (191-LF 0-CF 994-RF)																								
1926	Bro-N	137	496	64	158	35	11	11	81	44	53	.319	.375	.500	875	136	24	8			.986	-1	*1-101,O-35(6-0-29)	1.4
1927	Bro-N	130	412	65	112	26	9	14	73	39	41	.272	.336	.481	817	116	8	4			.980	0	*1-105/O-1(1-0-0)	0.1
1928	Bro-N	134	486	64	165	37	6	12	91	38	36	.340	.390	.514	904	136	25	1			.937	-7	*O-127(0-0-127)	0.8
1929	Bro-N	146	569	105	217	42	13	21	113	55	45	.381	.436	.612	1047	160	52	21			.941	-17	*O-141(0-0-141)/1-2	2.2
1930	Bro-N	153	614	143	241	48	11	35	130	66	56	.393	.455	.678	1132	171	71	18			.978	-20	*O-153(0-0-153)	3.3
1931	Bro-N	151	610	93	191	43	16	18	97	50	65	.313	.365	.525	890	137	30	17			.960	-1	*O-150(0-0-150)	2.0
1932	Cin-N	148	577	87	188	38	**19**	16	87	60	45	.326	.389	.541	930	152	42	7			.969	16	*O-146(0-0-146)	4.7
1933	Chi-N	137	508	77	147	36	12	16	93	50	57	.289	.353	.502	855	142	27	6			.957	-5	*O-131(0-0-131)	1.4
1934	Chi-N	125	467	65	142	34	5	14	84	35	71	.304	.353	.488	841	125	15	1			.971	-10	*O-113(0-0-113)/1-7	-0.2
1935	Pit-N	26	81	8	19	8	1	0	7	3	10	.235	.271	.358	629	65	-4	0			.958	-3	O-15(15-0-0)/1-3	-0.8
	Cin-N	92	349	44	117	23	5	10	58	35	25	.335	.396	.516	912	147	23	5			.976	-1	O-76(76-0-0),1-14	1.6
	Yr	118	430	52	136	31	6	10	65	38	35	.316	.373	.486	859	131	19	5			.974	-4	O-91(91-0-0),1-17	0.8
1936	Cin-N	119	380	59	106	25	2	13	71	39	36	.279	.348	.458	806	123	11	4			.967	-7	O-92(91-0-1)/1-4	0.0
1937	Det-A	17	20	2	6	3	0	0	3	1	6	.300	.364	.450	814	102	0	2	0	0	1.000	-0	/O-2(2-0-0)	0.0
1945	Bro-N	37	34	6	9	1	0	1	9	5	7	.265	.359	.382	741	107	0	0			.000	-1	/O-3(0-0-3)	-0.1
Total	13	1552	5603	882	1818	399	110	181	997	520	553	.324	.383	.532	915	141	324	94	0		.961	-56	*O-1185R,1-236	16.4
■ BILLY HERMAN Herman, William Jennings Bryan b: 7/7/09, New Albany, Ind. d: 9/5/92, W.Palm Beach, Fla. BR/TR, 5'11", 180 lbs. Deb: 8/29/31 MCH																								
1931	Chi-N	25	98	14	32	7	0	0	16	13	6	.327	.405	.398	803	115	3	2			.939	3	2-25	0.7
1932	*Chi-N	154	656	102	206	42	7	1	51	40	33	.314	.358	.404	762	105	6	14			.961	17	*2-154	3.2
1933	Chi-N	153	619	82	173	35	2	0	44	45	34	.279	.332	.342	675	93	-5	5			.956	29	*2-153	3.6
1934	Chi-N★	113	456	79	138	21	6	3	42	34	31	.303	.355	.395	750	102	2	6			.975	16	*2-111	2.4
1935	*Chi-N★	154	666	113	**227**	**57**	6	7	83	42	29	.341	.383	.476	859	128	26	6			**.964**	19	*2-154	5.3
1936	Chi-N★	153	632	101	211	57	7	5	93	59	30	.334	.392	.470	862	128	25	5			**.975**	15	*2-153	4.8
1937	Chi-N★	138	564	106	189	35	11	8	65	56	22	.335	.396	.479	875	131	25	2			.954	19	*2-137	5.1
1938	*Chi-N★	152	624	86	173	34	7	1	56	59	31	.277	.342	.359	701	90	-7	3			**.981**	25	*2-151	2.7
1939	Chi-N★	156	623	111	191	34	**18**	7	70	66	31	.307	.378	.453	830	120	18	9			.967	-3	*2-156	2.5
1940	Chi-N★	135	558	77	163	24	4	5	57	47	30	.292	.347	.376	723	101	1	1			.974	19	*2-135	2.9
1941	Chi-N	11	36	4	7	0	1	0	0	9	5	.194	.356	.250	606	75	-1	0			.898	-5	2-11	-0.5
	*Bro-N★	133	536	77	156	30	4	3	41	58	38	.291	.361	.379	740	104	4	1			.970	-27	*2-133	-1.5
	Yr	144	572	81	163	30	5	3	41	67	43	.285	.361	.371	732	103	3	1			.964	-32	*2-144	-2.0
1942	Bro-N★	155	571	76	146	34	2	2	65	72	52	.256	.339	.333	672	95	-2	6			.973	-11	*2-153/1-3	-0.4
1943	Bro-N★	153	585	76	193	41	2	2	100	66	26	.330	.398	.417	815	135	28	4			.971	-17	*2-117,3-37	1.9
1946	Bro-N	47	184	24	53	8	4	0	28	26	10	.288	.376	.375	751	112	4	2			.945	-2	3-29,2-16	0.3
	Bos-N	75	252	32	77	23	1	3	22	43	13	.306	.409	.440	849	139	14	1			.956	-16	2-44,1-22/3-5	0.0
	Yr	122	436	56	130	31	5	3	50	69	23	.298	.395	.413	808	128	18	3			.968	-18	2-60,3-34,1-22	0.3
1947	Pit-N	15	47	3	10	4	0	0	6	2	7	.213	.245	.298	543	42	-4	0			1.000	-9	2-10/1-2,M	-1.2
Total	15	1922	7707	1163	2345	486	82	47	839	737	428	.304	.367	.407	774	112	139	67			.967	71	*2-1813/3-71,1-27	31.8
■ AL HERMANN Hermann, Albert Bartel b: 3/28/1899, Milltown, N.J. d: 8/20/80, Lewes, Del. BR/TR, 6', 180 lbs. Deb: 7/17/23																								
1923	Bos-N	31	93	2	22	4	0	0	11	0	7	.237	.237	.280	516	37	-9	3	2	-0	.957	-6	2-15/3-5,1-4	-1.4
1924	Bos-N	1	1	0	0	0	0	0	0	0	1	.000	.000	.000	0	-99	-0	0	0	0	.000	0	H	0.0
Total	2	32	94	2	22	4	0	0	11	0	8	.234	.234	.277	511	36	-9	3	2	-0	.957	-6	/2-15,3-5,1-4	-1.4

YEAR	TM/L	G	AB	R	H	2B	3B	HR	RBI	BB	SO	AVG	OBP	SLG	OPS	OPS+	BR+	SB	CS	SBR	FA	FR	G/POS	TPR
■ CHAD HERMANSEN	Hermansen, Chad Bruce b: 9/10/77, Salt Lake City, Utah BR/TR, 6'2", 185 lbs. Deb: 9/7/99																							
1999	Pit-N	19	60	5	14	3	0	1	1	7	19	.233	.324	.333	657	67	-3	2	2	-0	1.000	-2	O-18(3-9-6)	-0.5
2000	Pit-N	33	108	12	20	4	1	2	8	6	37	.185	.228	.296	524	31	-12	0	0	0	.979	-4	O-31(0-27-4)	-1.5
Total	2	52	168	17	34	7	1	3	9	13	56	.202	.264	.310	573	44	-15	2	2	-0	.987	-6	/O-49(3-36-10)	-2.0
■ GENE HERMANSKI	Hermanski, Eugene Victor b: 5/11/20, Pittsfield, Mass. BL/TR, 5'11.5", 185 lbs. Deb: 8/15/43																							
1943	Bro-N	18	60	6	18	2	1	0	12	11	7	.300	.417	.367	783	127	3	1			.976	3	O-17(11-0-6)	0.5
1946	Bro-N	64	110	15	22	2	2	0	8	17	10	.200	.313	.255	567	61	-5	2			.938	-7	O-34(12-4-17)	-1.4
1947	*Bro-N	79	189	36	52	7	1	7	39	28	7	.275	.377	.434	811	111	3	5			.982	-7	O-66(64-1-3)	-0.7
1948	Bro-N	133	400	63	116	22	7	15	60	64	46	.290	.391	.493	883	133	19	15			.971	4	*O-119(6-0-113)	1.9
1949	*Bro-N	87	224	48	67	12	3	8	42	47	21	.299	.431	.487	918	140	15	12			.980	-4	O-77(64-0-17)	0.7
1950	Bro-N	94	289	36	86	17	3	7	34	36	26	.298	.381	.450	831	115	7	2			.989	3	O-78(76-0-3)	0.5
1951	Bro-N	31	80	8	20	4	0	1	5	10	12	.250	.333	.338	671	79	-2	0	2	-1	.977	1	O-19(18-0-1)	-0.3
	Chi-N	75	231	28	65	12	1	3	20	35	30	.281	.385	.381	766	105	3	3	0	1	.966	5	O-63(3-0-60)	0.6
	Yr	106	311	36	85	16	1	4	25	45	42	.273	.372	.370	742	98	1	3	2	-0	.969	6	O-82(21-0-61)	0.3
1952	Chi-N	99	275	28	70	6	0	4	34	29	32	.255	.330	.320	650	80	-7	2	0	0	.981	2	O-76(3-0-73)	-0.7
1953	Chi-N	18	40	1	6	1	0	0	1	4	7	.150	.227	.175	402	7	-5	1	0	0	1.000	-2	O-13(3-0-10)	-0.7
	Pit-N	41	62	7	11	0	0	1	4	8	14	.177	.282	.226	507	35	-6	0	0	0	1.000	-0	O-13(5-0-8)	-0.6
	Yr	59	102	8	17	1	0	1	5	12	21	.167	.261	.206	467	24	-11	1	0	0	1.000	-2	O-26(8-0-18)	-1.3
Total	9	739	1960	276	533	85	18	46	259	289	212	.272	.372	.404	776	107	25	43	2		.977	-1	O-575(265-5-311)	-0.2
■ REMY HERMOSO	Hermoso, Angel Remigio b: 10/1/46, Carabobo, Venezuela BR/TR, 5'8", 155 lbs. Deb: 9/14/67																							
1967	Atl-N	11	26	3	8	0	0	0	0	2	4	.308	.357	.308	665	93	-0	1	0	0	.952	1	/S-9,2-2	0.2
1969	Mon-N	28	74	6	12	0	0	0	3	5	10	.162	.225	.162	387	10	-9	3	1	0	.968	4	2-18/S-6	-0.4
1970	Mon-N	4	1	1	0	0	0	0	0	0	0	.000	.000	.000	0	-99	-0	0	0	0	1.000	0	/2-1,3-1	0.0
1974	Cle-A	48	122	15	27	3	1	0	5	7	7	.221	.264	.262	526	52	-8	2	2	-0	.967	7	2-45	0.2
Total	4	91	223	25	47	3	1	0	8	14	21	.211	.261	.233	494	42	-17	6	3	0	.968	12	/2-66,S-15,3-1	0.0
■ ALEX HERNANDEZ	Hernandez, Alexander (Vargas) b: 5/28/77, San Juan, P.R. BL/TL, 6'4", 190 lbs. Deb: 9/1/2000																							
2000	Pit-N	20	60	4	12	3	0	1	5	0	13	.200	.200	.300	500	24	-7	1	1	-0	.992	-2	1-12/O-5(3-0-2)	-0.9
■ CARLOS HERNANDEZ	Hernandez, Carlos Alberto (Almeida) b: 5/24/67, San Felix, Venez. BR/TR, 5'11", 218 lbs. Deb: 4/20/90																							
1990	LA-N	10	20	2	4	1	0	0	1	0	2	.200	.200	.250	450	24	-2	0	0	0	1.000	1	C-10	-0.1
1991	LA-N	15	14	1	3	1	0	0	1	0	5	.214	.267	.286	552	57	-1	1	0	0	.966	1	C-13/3-1	0.0
1992	LA-N	69	173	11	45	4	0	3	17	11	21	.260	.319	.335	654	87	-3	0	1	-0	.979	2	C-63	0.2
1993	LA-N	50	99	6	25	5	0	2	7	2	11	.253	.267	.364	631	71	-4	0	0	0	.966	7	C-43	0.4
1994	LA-N	32	64	6	14	2	0	2	6	1	14	.219	.231	.344	575	51	-5	0	0	0	1.000	5	C-27	0.1
1995	LA-N	45	94	3	14	1	0	2	8	7	25	.149	.216	.223	439	18	-11	0	0	0	.983	12	C-41	0.2
1996	LA-N	13	14	1	4	0	0	0	0	2	2	.286	.375	.286	661	84	-0	0	0	0	1.000	2	/C-9	0.2
1997	SD-N	50	134	15	42	7	1	3	14	3	27	.313	.328	.448	776	109	1	0	2	-1	.989	3	C-44/1-4	0.5
1998	*SD-N	129	390	34	102	15	0	9	52	16	54	.262	.306	.369	675	83	-11	2	2	-0	.992	11	*C-122/1-1	0.6
2000	SD-N	58	191	16	48	11	0	2	25	16	26	.251	.319	.340	659	71	-9	1	3	-1	.987	3	C-54/1-1	-0.3
	*StL-N	17	51	7	14	4	0	1	10	5	9	.275	.351	.412	763	91	-1	1	0	0	.963	-2	C-16	-0.2
	Yr	75	242	23	62	15	0	3	35	21	35	.256	.326	.355	681	75	-9	2	3	-1	.982	1	C-70/1-1	-0.5
Total	10	488	1244	102	315	51	1	24	141	63	196	.253	.299	.354	653	76	-46	5	8	-2	.985	44	C-442/1-6,3-1	1.6
■ CARLOS HERNANDEZ	Hernandez, Carlos Eduardo b: 12/12/75, Caracas, Venez. BR/TR, 5'9", 175 lbs. Deb: 5/26/99																							
1999	Hou-N	16	14	4	2	0	0	0	1	0	0	.143	.143	.143	286	-28	-3	3	1	0	1.000	4	/2-7,S-2	0.1
2000	Sea-A	2	1	0	0	0	0	0	0	0	1	.000	.000	.000	0	-99	-0	0	1	-0	1.000	0	/3-2	-0.1
Total	2	18	15	4	2	0	0	0	1	0	1	.133	.133	.133	267	-33	-3	3	2	-0	1.000	4	/2-7,3-2,S-2	0.0
■ CESAR HERNANDEZ	Hernandez, Cesar Dario (Perez) b: 9/28/66, Yamasa, D.R. BR/TR, 6', 160 lbs. Deb: 7/19/92																							
1992	Cin-N	34	51	6	14	4	0	0	4	0	10	.275	.275	.353	627	74	-2	3	1	0	.952	-2	O-18(12-6-1)	-0.4
1993	Cin-N	27	24	3	2	0	0	0	1	1	8	.083	.120	.083	203	-44	-5	1	2	-0	.970	-2	O-23(17-7-0)	-0.8
Total	2	61	75	9	16	4	0	0	5	1	18	.213	.224	.267	490	35	-7	4	3	-0	.963	-5	/O-41(29-13-1)	-1.2
■ ENZO HERNANDEZ	Hernandez, Enzo Octavio b: 2/12/49, Valle De Guanape, Venez. BR/TR, 5'8", 155 lbs. Deb: 4/17/71																							
1971	SD-N	143	549	58	122	9	3	0	12	54	34	.222	.295	.250	545	60	-28	21	5	3	.955	-11	*S-143	-2.0
1972	SD-N	114	329	33	64	11	2	1	15	22	25	.195	.245	.249	494	44	-25	24	3	4	.963	5	*S-107/O-3(2-0-1)	-0.4
1973	SD-N	70	247	26	55	2	1	0	9	17	14	.223	.273	.239	512	47	-18	15	4	2	.977	-1	S-67	-1.0
1974	SD-N	147	512	55	119	19	2	0	34	38	36	.232	.285	.277	563	60	-27	37	10	5	.966	-8	*S-145	-1.4
1975	SD-N	116	344	37	75	12	2	0	19	26	25	.218	.277	.265	541	54	-21	20	4	3	.965	8	*S-111	0.1
1976	SD-N	113	340	31	87	13	3	1	24	32	16	.256	.320	.321	640	89	-5	12	7	0	.964	4	*S-101	1.2
1977	SD-N	7	3	1	0	0	0	0	0	0	0	.000	.000	.000	0	-99	-1	0	0	0	1.000	2	/S-7	0.1
1978	LA-N	4	3	0	0	0	0	0	0	0	1	.000	.000	.000	0	-99	-1	0	0	0	.000	0	/S-2	-0.1
Total	8	714	2327	241	522	66	13	2	113	189	151	.224	.284	.266	550	59	-126	129	33	17	.964	-1	S-683/O-3(2-0-1)	-3.5
■ JACKIE HERNANDEZ	Hernandez, Jacinto (Zulueta) b: 9/11/40, Central Tinguaro, Cuba BR/TR, 6', 175 lbs. Deb: 9/14/65																							
1965	Cal-A	6	6	2	2	1	0	0	1	0	1	.333	.333	.500	833	137	0	1	0	0	1.000	-0	/S-2,3-1	0.0
1966	Cal-A	58	23	19	1	0	0	0	2	1	4	.043	.083	.043	127	-64	-5	1	1	-0	.857	13	3-11/2-8,S-8,O-3R	0.9
1967	Min-A	29	28	1	4	0	0	0	3	0	6	.143	.143	.143	286	-14	-4	0	0	0	.974	6	S-15,3-13	0.3
1968	Min-A	83	199	13	35	3	0	2	17	9	52	.176	.219	.221	440	32	-16	5	2	0	.927	9	S-79/1-1	-0.2
1969	KC-A	145	504	54	112	14	2	4	40	38	111	.222	.279	.282	561	57	-29	17	7	1	.954	-15	*S-144	-2.8
1970	KC-A	83	238	14	55	4	1	2	10	15	50	.231	.282	.282	564	56	-14	1	3	-1	.951	-5	S-77	-1.3
1971	*Pit-N	88	233	30	48	7	3	3	26	17	45	.206	.260	.300	560	59	-13	0	2	-1	.950	12	S-75/3-9	0.6
1972	Pit-N	72	176	12	33	7	1	1	14	9	43	.188	.227	.256	483	38	-15	0	0	0	.929	17	S-68/3-4	0.8
1973	Pit-N	54	73	8	18	1	2	0	8	4	12	.247	.286	.315	601	68	-3	0	0	0	.940	17	S-49	1.6
Total	9	618	1480	153	308	37	9	12	121	93	324	.208	.258	.270	527	49	-99	25	15	0	.945	53	S-517/3-38,2-8,O1	-0.1
■ JOSE HERNANDEZ	Hernandez, Jose Antonio (Figueroa) b: 7/14/69, Rio Piedras, P.R. BR/TR, 6'1", 180 lbs. Deb: 8/9/91 Career OF: (46-LF 47-CF 4-RF)																							
1991	Tex-A	45	98	8	18	2	1	0	4	3	31	.184	.208	.224	432	20	-11	0	1	-0	.975	9	S-44/3-1	0.0
1992	Cle-A	3	4	0	0	0	0	0	0	0	2	.000	.000	.000	0	-99	-1	0	0	0	.857	-0	/S-3	-0.1
1994	Chi-N	56	132	18	32	2	3	1	9	8	29	.242	.291	.326	617	61	-8	2	2	-0	.938	0	3-28,S-21/2-8,O-1C	-0.6
1995	Chi-N	93	245	37	60	11	4	13	40	13	69	.245	.283	.482	765	99	-2	1	0	0	.961	10	S-43,2-29,3-20	1.2
1996	Chi-N	131	331	52	80	14	1	10	41	24	97	.242	.295	.381	676	75	-13	4	0	1	.948	-7	S-87,3-43/2-1,O-1C	-1.2
1997	Chi-N	121	183	33	50	8	5	7	26	14	42	.273	.325	.486	811	106	1	2	5	-1	.922	-3	3-47,S-21,2-20,/O1D	-0.2
1998	*Chi-N	149	488	76	124	23	7	23	75	40	140	.254	.312	.471	783	99	-2	4	6	-1	.958	3	3-72,O-54L,S-45,/12	0.2
1999	Chi-N	99	342	57	93	12	2	15	43	40	101	.272	.357	.450	807	104	2	7	2	1	.971	3	S-92,O-20(6-14-2)/1-1	1.2
	*Atl-N	48	166	22	42	8	0	4	19	12	44	.253	.303	.373	677	70	-8	4	1	1	.964	-2	S-45/1-1,O-1(1-0-0)	-0.5
	Yr	147	508	79	135	20	2	19	62	52	145	.266	.340	.425	765	93	-6	11	3	1	.969	2	*S-137,O-21C/1-2	0.7
2000	Mil-N	124	446	51	109	22	1	11	59	41	125	.244	.316	.372	689	75	-18	3	7	-2	.950	10	3-95,S-37/O-2(2-0-0)	-0.6
Total	9	869	2435	354	608	102	24	84	316	195	680	.250	.309	.415	724	85	-59	27	24	-2	.964	23	S-438,3-306/O21D	-0.6
■ KEITH HERNANDEZ	Hernandez, Keith b: 10/20/53, San Francisco, Cal. BL/TL, 6', 195 lbs. Deb: 8/30/74																							
1974	StL-N	14	34	3	10	1	2	0	2	7	8	.294	.415	.441	856	141	2	0	0	0	.973	-2	/1-9	-0.1
1975	StL-N	64	188	20	47	8	2	3	20	17	26	.250	.312	.362	674	84	-4	0	1	-0	.996	3	1-56	-0.6
1976	StL-N	129	374	54	108	21	5	7	46	49	53	.289	.376	.428	803	126	14	4	2	0	.990	16	*1-110	2.3
1977	StL-N	161	560	90	163	41	4	15	91	79	88	.291	.380	.459	839	126	22	7	7	-1	.992	5	*1-158	1.6
1978	StL-N	159	542	90	138	32	4	11	64	82	68	.255	.355	.389	744	109	8	13	5	1	.994	3	*1-158	0.3
1979	StL-N★	161	610	**116**	210	**48**	11	11	105	80	78	**.344**	**.421**	.513	934	152	46	11	6	0	.995	19	*1-160	5.6
1980	StL-N★	159	595	**111**	191	39	8	16	99	86	73	.321	**.410**	.494	904	147	40	14	8	0	.995	5	*1-157	3.6

YEAR	TM/L	G	AB	R	H	2B	3B	HR	RBI	BB	SO	AVG	OBP	SLG	OPS	OPS+	BR+	SB	CS	SBR	FA	FR	G/POS	TPR
1981	StL-N	103	376	65	115	27	4	8	48	61	45	.306	.405	.463	868	142	23	12	5	1	.997	6	1-98/O-3(3-0-0)	2.5
1982	*StL-N	160	579	79	173	33	6	7	94	100	67	.299	.404	.413	817	128	26	19	11	0	.994	6	*1-158/O-4(2-0-2)	2.4
1983	StL-N	55	218	34	62	15	4	3	26	24	30	.284	.355	.431	787	117	5	1	1	-0	.991	3	1-54	0.5
	NY-N	95	320	43	98	8	3	9	37	64	42	.306	.425	.434	859	140	21	8	4	0	.993	11	1-90	2.7
	Yr	150	538	77	160	23	7	12	63	88	72	.297	.398	.433	831	131	26	9	5	0	.992	14	*1-144	3.2
1984	NY-N★	154	550	83	171	31	0	15	94	97	89	.311	.415	.449	864	145	37	2	3	-1	.994	18	*1-153	4.6
1985	NY-N	158	593	87	183	34	4	10	91	77	59	.309	.390	.430	820	132	28	3	3	-0	**.997**	16	*1-157	3.4
1986	*NY-N★	149	551	94	171	34	1	13	83	**94**	69	.310	.414	.446	861	141	35	2	1	0	**.996**	18	*1-149	4.5
1987	NY-N★	154	587	87	170	28	2	18	89	81	104	.290	.379	.436	816	122	20	0	2	-1	.993	18	*1-154	2.7
1988	*NY-N	95	348	43	96	16	0	11	55	31	57	.276	.337	.417	754	121	9	2	1	0	.998	8	1-93	1.1
1989	NY-N	75	215	18	50	8	0	4	19	27	39	.233	.324	.326	649	90	-2	0	3	-1	.991	-2	1-58	-0.9
1990	Cle-A	43	130	7	26	2	0	1	8	14	17	.200	.283	.238	521	47	-9	0	0	0	.994	-2	1-42	-1.4
Total	17	2088	7370	1124	2182	426	60	162	1071	1070	1012	.296	.388	.436	824	129	321	98	63	-0	.994	148	*1-2014/O-7(5-0-2)	34.8

■ LEO HERNANDEZ

Hernandez, Leonardo Jesus b: 11/6/59, Santa Lucia, Venez. BR/TR, 5'11", 170 lbs. Deb: 9/19/82

YEAR	TM/L	G	AB	R	H	2B	3B	HR	RBI	BB	SO	AVG	OBP	SLG	OPS	OPS+	BR+	SB	CS	SBR	FA	FR	G/POS	TPR
1982	Bal-A	2	2	0	0	0	0	0	0	0	2	.000	.000	.000	0	-99	-1	0	0	0	.000	0	/H	-0.1
1983	Bal-A	64	203	21	50	6	1	6	26	12	19	.246	.288	.374	663	82	-5	1	0	0	.922	-12	3-64	-1.8
1985	Bal-A	12	21	0	1	0	0	0	0	0	4	.048	.048	.048	95	-76	-5	0	0	0	1.000	-1	/1-1,O-1(1-0-0),D-8	-0.6
1986	NY-A	7	22	2	5	2	0	1	4	1	8	.227	.261	.455	715	91	-0	0	0	0	1.000	-1	/3-7,2-1	-0.1
Total	4	85	248	23	56	8	1	7	30	13	33	.226	.264	.351	615	69	-11	1	0	0	.927	-13	/3-71,D-8,2-1,O1	-2.6

■ PEDRO HERNANDEZ

Hernandez, Pedro Julio (b: Pedro Julio Montas (Hernandez)) b: 4/4/59, LaRomana, D.R. BR/TR, 6'1", 160 lbs. Deb: 9/8/79

YEAR	TM/L	G	AB	R	H	2B	3B	HR	RBI	BB	SO	AVG	OBP	SLG	OPS	OPS+	BR+	SB	CS	SBR	FA	FR	G/POS	TPR
1979	Tor-A	3	0	1	0	0	0	0	0	0	0	—	—	—	—	—	0	0	0	0	.000	0	/R	0.0
1982	Tor-A	8	9	1	0	0	0	0	0	0	3	.000	.000	.000	0	-92	-2	0	0	0	.000	-1	/3-2,O-1(1-0-0),D-3	-0.3
Total	2	11	9	2	0	0	0	0	0	0	3	.000	.000	.000	0	-92	-2	0	0	0	—	-1	/D-3,3-2,O-1(1-0-0)	-0.3

■ TOBY HERNANDEZ

Hernandez, Rafael Tobias (Alvarado) b: 11/30/58, Calabozo, Venez. BR/TR, 6'1", 160 lbs. Deb: 6/22/84

YEAR	TM/L	G	AB	R	H	2B	3B	HR	RBI	BB	SO	AVG	OBP	SLG	OPS	OPS+	BR+	SB	CS	SBR	FA	FR	G/POS	TPR
1984	Tor-A	3	2	1	1	0	0	0	0	0	0	.500	.500	.500	1000	171	0	0	0	0	1.000	-1	/C-3	0.0

■ RAMON HERNANDEZ

Hernandez, Ramon Jose (Marin) b: 5/20/76, Caracas, Venez. BR/TR, 6', 203 lbs. Deb: 6/29/99

YEAR	TM/L	G	AB	R	H	2B	3B	HR	RBI	BB	SO	AVG	OBP	SLG	OPS	OPS+	BR+	SB	CS	SBR	FA	FR	G/POS	TPR
1999	Oak-A	40	136	13	38	7	0	3	21	18	11	.279	.368	.397	765	99	0	1	0	0	.980	4	C-40	0.7
2000	*Oak-A	143	419	52	101	19	0	14	62	38	64	.241	.315	.387	701	78	-14	1	0	0	.984	-2	*C-142	-0.8
Total	2	183	555	65	139	26	0	17	83	56	75	.250	.328	.389	717	83	-14	2	0	0	.983	2	C-182	-0.1

■ RUDY HERNANDEZ

Hernandez, Rodolfo (Acosta) b: 10/18/51, Empalme, Mexico BR/TR, 5'9", 150 lbs. Deb: 9/6/72

YEAR	TM/L	G	AB	R	H	2B	3B	HR	RBI	BB	SO	AVG	OBP	SLG	OPS	OPS+	BR+	SB	CS	SBR	FA	FR	G/POS	TPR
1972	Chi-A	8	21	0	4	0	0	0	1	0	3	.190	.190	.190	381	13	-2	0	0	0	1.000	1	/S-6	-0.1

■ CHICO HERNANDEZ

Hernandez, Salvador Jose (Ramos) b: 1/3/16, Havana, Cuba d: 1/3/86, Havana, Cuba BR/TR, 6', 195 lbs. Deb: 4/16/42

YEAR	TM/L	G	AB	R	H	2B	3B	HR	RBI	BB	SO	AVG	OBP	SLG	OPS	OPS+	BR+	SB	CS	SBR	FA	FR	G/POS	TPR
1942	Chi-N	47	118	6	27	5	0	0	7	11	13	.229	.295	.271	566	69	-5	0			.975	-2	C-43	-0.5
1943	Chi-N	43	126	10	34	4	0	0	9	9	9	.270	.324	.302	625	82	-3	0			.981	-3	C-41	-0.4
Total	2	90	244	16	61	9	0	0	16	20	22	.250	.309	.287	596	76	-7	0			.978	-5	/C-84	-0.9

■ LARRY HERNDON

Herndon, Larry Darnell b: 11/3/53, Sunflower, Miss. BR/TR, 6'3", 195 lbs. Deb: 9/4/74 C Career OF: (847-LF 448-CF 76-RF)

YEAR	TM/L	G	AB	R	H	2B	3B	HR	RBI	BB	SO	AVG	OBP	SLG	OPS	OPS+	BR+	SB	CS	SBR	FA	FR	G/POS	TPR
1974	StL-N	12	1	3	1	0	0	0	0	0	0	1.000	1.000	1.000	2000	465	0	0	0	0	1.000	-0	/O-1(0-1-0)	0.0
1976	SF-N	115	337	42	97	11	3	2	23	23	45	.288	.337	.356	693	94	-2	12	10	-1	.967	-6	*O-110(0-110-0)	-1.2
1977	SF-N	49	109	13	26	4	3	1	5	5	20	.239	.278	.358	636	69	-5	4	2	0	.957	-3	O-44(0-44-0)	-0.8
1978	SF-N	151	471	52	122	15	9	1	32	35	71	.259	.312	.335	647	84	-10	13	8	0	.974	4	*O-149(0-149-0)	-0.8
1979	SF-N	132	354	35	91	14	5	7	36	29	70	.257	.315	.384	699	96	-3	8	6	-0	.963	-15	*O-122(40-84-12)	-2.0
1980	SF-N	139	493	54	127	17	11	8	49	19	91	.258	.287	.385	672	88	-10	8	8	-1	.959	-4	*O-122(53-53-28)	-2.0
1981	SF-N	96	364	48	105	15	8	5	41	20	55	.288	.327	.415	742	111	4	15	6	1	.977	5	O-93(82-7-10)	0.7
1982	Det-A	157	614	92	179	21	13	23	88	38	92	.292	.334	.480	814	120	15	12	9	-1	.983	6	*O-155(155-0-0)/D-3	1.4
1983	Det-A	153	603	88	182	28	9	20	92	46	95	.302	.354	.478	832	130	24	9	3	1	.951	1	*O-133(133-0-0),D-19	1.9
1984	*Det-A	125	407	52	114	18	5	7	43	32	63	.280	.336	.400	736	103	2	6	2	1	.986	-5	*O-117(118-0-0)/D-4	-0.7
1985	Det-A	137	442	45	108	12	7	12	37	33	79	.244	.298	.385	683	86	-9	2	1	0	.976	5	*O-136(136-0-0)	-0.9
1986	Det-A	106	283	33	70	13	1	8	37	27	40	.247	.315	.385	700	90	-4	2	1	0	.988	-1	O-83(83-0-0),D-18	-0.9
1987	*Det-A	89	225	32	73	13	2	9	47	23	35	.324	.387	.520	907	144	14	1	0	0	.989	-4	O-57(32-0-26),D-23	0.8
1988	Det-A	76	174	16	39	5	0	4	20	23	37	.224	.318	.322	640	83	-4	0	1	-0	1.000	-2	D-53,O-15(15-0-0)	-0.8
Total	14	1537	4877	605	1334	186	76	107	550	353	793	.274	.325	.409	733	103	12	92	57	0	.972	-19	*O-1337L,D-120	-5.3

■ TOM HERNON

Hernon, Thomas H. b: 11/4/1866, E.Bridgewater, Mass d: 2/4/02, New Bedford, Mass. BR/TR, Deb: 9/13/1897

YEAR	TM/L	G	AB	R	H	2B	3B	HR	RBI	BB	SO	AVG	OBP	SLG	OPS	OPS+	BR+	SB	CS	SBR	FA	FR	G/POS	TPR
1897	Chi-N	4	16	2	1	0	0	0	2	0		.063	.063	.063	125	-64	-4	1			1.000	0	/O-4(4-0-0)	-0.4

■ JOE HERR

Herr, Edward Joseph b: 5/18/1862, St.Louis, Mo. d: 7/18/43, St.Louis, Mo. BR/TR, 5'9.5", 179 lbs. Deb: 4/16/1887 Career OF: (4-LF 8-CF 3-RF)

YEAR	TM/L	G	AB	R	H	2B	3B	HR	RBI	BB	SO	AVG	OBP	SLG	OPS	OPS+	BR+	SB	CS	SBR	FA	FR	G/POS	TPR
1887	Cle-a	11	50	6	18	2	0	0	6	6		.360	.360	.318	678	93	-0	2			.729	-3	3-11	-0.2
1888	*StL-a	43	172	21	46	7	1	3	43	11		.267	.323	.372	695	110	1	9			.872	-9	S-28,O-11(4-4-3)/3-4	-0.6
1890	StL-a	12	41	5	9	2	1	0	1	5		.220	.347	.317	664	84	-1	2			.793	-7	/2-7,O-4(0-4-0),3-1	-0.7
Total	3	66	263	32	73	11	2	3	50	22		.278	.333	.354	687	102	0	13			.762	-18	/S-28,3-16,O-15C,2	-1.5

■ TOM HERR

Herr, Thomas Mitchell b: 4/4/56, Lancaster, Pa. BB/TR, 6', 185 lbs. Deb: 8/13/79 Career OF: (0-LF 1-CF 0-RF)

YEAR	TM/L	G	AB	R	H	2B	3B	HR	RBI	BB	SO	AVG	OBP	SLG	OPS	OPS+	BR+	SB	CS	SBR	FA	FR	G/POS	TPR
1979	StL-N	14	10	4	2	0	0	0	1	2	2	.200	.333	.200	533	49	-1	1	0	0	1.000	6	/2-6	0.5
1980	StL-N	76	222	29	55	12	5	0	15	16	21	.248	.301	.347	648	78	-7	9	2	1	.984	2	2-58,S-14	0.0
1981	StL-N	103	411	50	110	14	9	0	46	39	30	.268	.333	.345	678	90	-5	23	7	3	**.992**	4	*2-103	0.8
1982	*StL-N	135	493	83	131	19	4	0	36	57	56	.266	.344	.320	665	86	-7	25	12	1	.987	4	*2-128	0.5
1983	StL-N	89	313	43	101	14	4	2	31	43	27	.323	.406	.412	818	127	13	6	8	-1	.986	-19	2-86	-0.2
1984	StL-N	145	558	67	154	23	2	4	49	49	56	.276	.337	.346	682	94	-3	13	7	0	.992	-1	*2-144	0.4
1985	*StL-N★	159	596	97	180	38	3	8	110	80	55	.302	.386	.416	803	126	23	31	3	6	.985	-31	*2-158	0.7
1986	StL-N	152	559	48	141	30	4	2	61	73	75	.252	.344	.331	675	88	-7	22	8	2	.988	-22	*2-152	-2.0
1987	*StL-N	141	510	73	134	29	0	2	83	68	62	.263	.353	.331	684	81	-12	19	4	3	.989	-17	*2-137	-1.9
1988	StL-N	15	50	4	13	0	0	1	3	11	4	.260	.393	.320	713	106	1	3	0	1	.984	-6	2-15	-0.4
	Min-A	86	304	42	80	16	0	1	21	40	47	.263	.349	.326	674	88	-4	10	3	1	.988	-8	2-73/S-2,D-3	-0.9
1989	Phi-N	151	561	65	161	25	6	2	37	54	63	.287	.353	.364	716	105	5	10	7	-0	.990	2	*2-144	1.2
1990	Phi-N	119	447	39	118	21	3	4	50	36	47	.264	.322	.351	673	85	-9	7	1	1	.991	-3	*2-114	-0.8
	NY-N	27	100	9	25	5	0	1	10	14	11	.250	.342	.330	672	86	-2	0	0	0	.979	-5	2-26	-0.6
	Yr	146	547	48	143	26	3	5	60	50	58	.261	.326	.347	673	85	-10	7	1	1	.989	-8	*2-140	-1.4
1991	NY-N	70	155	17	30	7	0	1	14	32	21	.194	.332	.258	590	68	-5	7	2	1	1.000	7	2-57/O-1(0-1-0)	0.3
	SF-N	32	60	6	15	1	1	0	7	13	7	.250	.384	.300	684	98	1	2	0	0	1.000	-6	2-15/3-3	-0.5
	Yr	102	215	23	45	8	1	1	21	45	28	.209	.346	.270	616	77	-5	9	2	1	1.000	1	2-72/3-3,O-1(0-1-0)	-0.2
Total	13	1514	5349	676	1450	254	41	28	574	627	584	.271	.350	.350	700	95	-18	188	64	19	.989	-94	*2-1416/S-16,3-3,DO	-2.9

■ JOSE HERRERA

Herrera, Jose Concepcion (Ontiveros) "Loco" b: 4/8/42, San Lorenzo, Venez. BR/TR, 5'8", 165 lbs. Deb: 6/3/67 Career OF: (25-LF 13-CF 12-RF)

YEAR	TM/L	G	AB	R	H	2B	3B	HR	RBI	BB	SO	AVG	OBP	SLG	OPS	OPS+	BR+	SB	CS	SBR	FA	FR	G/POS	TPR
1967	Hou-N	5	4	0	1	0	0	0	1	0	1	.250	.250	.250	500	45	-0	0	0	0	.000	0	H	0.0
1968	Hou-N	27	100	9	24	5	0	0	7	4	12	.240	.269	.290	559	69	-4	0	2	-1	.958	-2	O-17(5-0-12)/2-7	-0.9
1969	Mon-N	47	126	7	36	5	0	2	12	3	14	.286	.302	.373	675	88	-2	1	2	-0	.980	-2	O-31(20-13-0)/2-2,3-1	-0.6
1970	Mon-N	1	1	0	0	0	0	0	0	0	1	.000	.000	.000	0	-99	-0	0	0	0	.000	0	H	0.0
Total	4	80	231	16	61	10	0	2	20	7	28	.264	.286	.333	619	79	-7	1	4	-1	.973	-4	/O-48L,2-9,3-1	-1.5

■ JOSE HERRERA

Herrera, Jose Ramon (Catalino) b: 8/30/72, Santo Domingo, D.R. BL/TL, 6', 165 lbs. Deb: 8/12/95

YEAR	TM/L	G	AB	R	H	2B	3B	HR	RBI	BB	SO	AVG	OBP	SLG	OPS	OPS+	BR+	SB	CS	SBR	FA	FR	G/POS	TPR
1995	Oak-A	33	70	9	17	1	2	0	2	6	11	.243	.303	.314	617	64	-4	1	3	-1	.956	-3	O-25(0-22-5)/D-5	-0.7
1996	Oak-A	108	320	44	86	15	1	6	30	20	59	.269	.318	.378	696	77	-12	8	2	1	.970	-10	*O-100(0-18-92)/D-1	-2.2
Total	2	141	390	53	103	16	3	6	32	26	70	.264	.315	.367	682	74	-15	9	5	0	.967	-13	O-125(0-40-97)/D-6	-2.9

YEAR	TM/L	G	AB	R	H	2B	3B	HR	RBI	BB	SO	AVG	OBP	SLG	OPS	OPS+	BR+	SB	CS	SBR	FA	FR	G/POS	TPR
■ PANCHO HERRERA Herrera, Juan Francisco (Willavicencio) b: 6/16/34, Santiago De Cuba, Cuba BR/TR, 6'3", 220 lbs. Deb: 4/15/58																								
1958	Phi-N	29	63	5	17	3	0	1	6	7	15	.270	.352	.365	717	92	-1	1	2	-0	.980	2	3-16,1-11	0.0
1960	Phi-N	145	512	61	144	26	6	17	71	51	136	.281	.352	.455	807	119	13	2	3	-1	.988	10	*1-134,2-17	1.7
1961	Phi-N	126	400	56	103	17	2	13	51	55	120	.257	.353	.408	760	102	2	5	1	1	.993	6	*1-115	0.2
Total	3	300	975	122	264	46	8	31	128	113	271	.271	.352	.430	782	110	15	8	6	-0	.990	18	1-260/2-17,3-16	1.9
■ MIKE HERRERA Herrera, Ramon b: 12/19/1897, Havana, Cuba d: 2/3/78, Havana, Cuba BR/TR, 5'6", 147 lbs. Deb: 9/22/25																								
1925	Bos-A	10	39	2	15	0	0	0	8	2	2	.385	.415	.385	799	104	0	1	0	0	.958	3	2-10	0.4
1926	Bos-A	74	237	20	61	14	1	0	19	15	13	.257	.304	.325	629	66	-12	0	5	-2	.962	5	2-48,3-16/S-4	-0.7
Total	2	84	276	22	76	14	1	0	27	17	15	.275	.320	.333	653	72	-12	1	5	-2	.961	8	/2-58,3-16,S-4	-0.3
■ LEFTY HERRING Herring, Silas Clarke b: 3/4/1880, Philadelphia, Pa. d: 2/11/65, Massapequa, N.Y. BL/TL, 5'11", 160 lbs. Deb: 5/16/1899																								
1899	Was-N	2	1	1	1	0	0	0	0	1		1.000	1.000	1.000	2000	454	1	0			1.000	0	/P-2	0.0
1904	Was-A	15	46	3	8	1	0	0	2	7		.174	.283	.196	479	54	-2	0			.991	1	1-10/O-5(0-5-0)	-0.2
Total	2	17	47	4	9	1	0	0	2	8		.191	.309	.213	522	67	-1	0			.991	1	/1-10,O-5(0-5-0),P-2	-0.2
■ ED HERRMANN Herrmann, Edward Martin b: 8/27/46, San Diego, Cal. BL/TR, 6'1", 210 lbs. Deb: 9/1/67 F																								
1967	Chi-A	2	3	1	2	1	0	0	1	1	0	.667	.750	1.000	1750	429	1	0	0	0	1.000	1	/C-2	0.3
1969	Chi-A	102	290	31	67	8	0	8	31	30	35	.231	.320	.341	662	81	-7	0	2	-1	.983	-3	C-92	-0.7
1970	Chi-A	96	297	42	84	9	0	19	52	31	41	.283	.356	.505	862	130	12	0	1	-0	.988	5	C-88	2.0
1971	Chi-A	101	294	32	63	6	0	11	35	44	48	.214	.321	.347	668	86	-5	2	0	0	.995	9	C-97	0.9
1972	Chi-A	116	354	23	88	9	0	10	40	43	37	.249	.337	.359	695	105	3	0	0	0	.989	0	*C-112	0.9
1973	Chi-A	119	379	42	85	17	1	10	39	31	55	.224	.295	.354	649	79	-11	2	4	-1	.984	5	*C-114/D-2	-0.2
1974	Chi-A†	107	367	32	95	13	1	10	39	16	49	.259	.290	.381	671	90	-6	1	0	0	.987	3	*C-107	0.2
1975	NY-A	80	200	16	51	9	2	6	30	16	23	.255	.310	.410	720	104	0	0	0	0	.979	7	D-35,C-24	0.8
1976	Cal-A	29	46	5	8	3	0	2	8	7	8	.174	.283	.370	653	96	-0	0	0	0	.954	-6	C-27	-0.6
	Hou-N	79	265	14	54	8	0	3	25	22	40	.204	.275	.268	543	60	-14	0	0	0	.987	0	C-79	-1.1
1977	Hou-N	56	158	7	46	7	0	1	17	15	18	.291	.356	.354	711	100	0	1	1	-0	.990	9	C-49	1.1
1978	Hou-N	16	36	1	4	1	0	0	0	3	3	.111	.179	.139	318	-11	-5	0	0	0	1.000	-1	C-14	-0.6
	Mon-N	19	40	1	7	1	0	0	3	1	4	.175	.195	.200	395	11	-5	0	0	0	.977	-1	C-12	-0.6
	Yr	35	76	2	11	2	0	0	3	4	7	.145	.188	.171	359	1	-10	0	0	0	.991	-2	C-26	-1.2
Total	11	922	2729	247	654	92	4	80	320	260	361	.240	.312	.364	677	91	-36	6	8	-1	.987	29	C-817/D-37	2.4
■ JOHN HERRNSTEIN Herrnstein, John Ellett b: 3/31/38, Hampton, Va. BL/TL, 6'3", 215 lbs. Deb: 9/15/62																								
1962	Phi-N	6	5	0	1	0	0	0	1	1	3	.200	.333	.200	533	48	-0	0	0	0	.000	-0	/O-1(0-0-1)	-0.1
1963	Phi-N	15	12	1	2	0	0	1	1	1	5	.167	.231	.417	647	83	-0	0	0	0	1.000	-1	/O-2(2-0-0),1-1	-0.1
1964	Phi-N	125	303	38	71	12	4	6	25	22	67	.234	.291	.360	650	83	-7	1	2	-0	.977	-20	O-69(63-4-3),1-68	-3.5
1965	Phi-N	63	85	8	17	2	0	1	5	2	18	.200	.227	.259	486	37	-7	0	0	0	.984	-3	1-18,O-14(11-2-1)	-1.1
1966	Phi-N	4	10	0	1	0	0	0	1	0	7	.100	.100	.100	200	-44	-2	0	0	0	1.000	-0	/O-2(2-0-0)	-0.2
	Chi-N	9	17	3	3	0	0	0	0	3	8	.176	.300	.176	476	36	-1	0	0	0	.975	-1	/1-4,O-1(1-0-0)	-0.3
	Atl-N	17	18	2	4	0	0	0	1	0	7	.222	.222	.222	444	24	-2	0	0	0	1.000	-1	/O-5(5-0-0)	-0.3
	Yr	30	45	5	8	0	0	0	2	3	22	.178	.229	.178	407	15	-5	0	0	0	1.000	-2	/O-8(8-0-0),1-4	-0.8
Total	5	239	450	52	99	14	4	8	34	29	115	.220	.272	.322	594	67	-20	1	2	-0	.983	-26	/O-94(84-6-5),1-91	-5.6
■ RICK HERRSCHER Herrscher, Richard Franklin b: 11/3/36, St.Louis, Mo. BR/TR, 6'2.5", 187 lbs. Deb: 8/1/62																								
1962	NY-N	35	50	5	11	3	0	1	6	5	11	.220	.291	.340	631	68	-2	0	0	0	1.000	2	1-10/3-6,O-4L,S-3	0.0
■ EARL HERSH Hersh, Earl Walter b: 5/21/32, Ebbvale, Md. BL/TL, 6', 205 lbs. Deb: 9/4/56																								
1956	Mil-N	7	13	0	3	3	0	0	0	0	5	.231	.231	.462	692	85	-0	0	0	0	.000	-1	/O-2(2-0-0)	-0.2
■ MIKE HERSHBERGER Hershberger, Norman Michael b: 10/9/39, Massillon, Ohio BR/TR, 5'10", 175 lbs. Deb: 9/5/61																								
1961	Chi-A	15	55	9	17	3	0	0	5	2	2	.309	.333	.364	697	88	-1	1	1	-0	1.000	2	O-13(1-9-3)	0.0
1962	Chi-A	148	427	54	112	14	2	4	46	37	36	.262	.325	.333	658	78	-13	10	6	0	.984	-7	*O-135(1-52-90)	-2.6
1963	Chi-A	135	476	64	133	26	2	3	45	39	39	.279	.339	.361	700	98	-1	9	3	1	.976	-5	*O-119(1-73-67)	-1.1
1964	Chi-A	141	452	55	104	15	3	2	31	48	47	.230	.310	.290	599	70	-17	8	6	-0	.984	-8	*O-134(0-64-85)	-3.4
1965	KC-A	150	494	43	114	15	5	5	48	37	42	.231	.291	.312	603	72	-18	7	3	0	.988	4	*O-144(5-9-134)	-2.4
1966	KC-A	146	538	55	136	27	7	2	57	47	37	.253	.316	.340	656	92	-6	13	5	1	.977	12	*O-143(12-3-130)	-0.2
1967	KC-A	142	480	55	122	25	1	1	49	38	40	.254	.318	.317	635	91	-5	10	3	1	.982	7	*O-130(10-0-122)	-0.6
1968	Oak-A	99	246	23	67	9	2	5	32	21	22	.272	.332	.386	718	123	6	8	3	1	.978	-7	O-90(71-6-27)	-0.4
1969	Oak-A	51	129	11	26	2	0	1	10	10	15	.202	.259	.240	499	42	-10	1	2	-0	.980	-5	O-35(16-8-13)	-1.8
1970	Mil-A	49	98	7	23	5	0	1	6	10	8	.235	.306	.316	622	71	-4	1	2	-0	.946	-6	O-35(0-0-35)	-1.2
1971	Chi-A	74	177	22	46	9	0	2	15	30	23	.260	.379	.345	724	103	2	6	2	1	.960	-8	O-59(0-58-2)	-0.7
Total	11	1150	3572	398	900	150	22	26	344	319	311	.252	.319	.328	647	85	-65	74	36	4	.980	-21	*O-1037(117-282-708)	-14.4
■ WILLARD HERSHBERGER Hershberger, Willard McKee "Bill" b: 5/28/10, Lemoncove, Cal. d: 8/3/40, Boston, Mass. BR/TR, 5'10.5", 167 lbs. Deb: 4/19/38																								
1938	Cin-N	49	105	12	29	3	1	0	12	5	6	.276	.315	.324	639	78	-3	1			.960	-1	C-39/2-1	-0.2
1939	*Cin-N	63	174	23	60	9	2	0	32	9	4	.345	.384	.420	803	115	4	1			.987	-2	C-60	0.5
1940	Cin-N	48	123	6	38	4	2	0	26	6	6	.309	.351	.374	725	99	-0	0			.985	-2	C-37	-0.1
Total	3	160	402	41	127	16	5	0	70	20	16	.316	.356	.381	737	101	1	2			.980	-5	C-136/2-1	0.2
■ NEAL HERTWECK Hertweck, Neal Charles b: 11/22/31, St.Louis, Mo. BL/TL, 6'1.5", 175 lbs. Deb: 9/27/52																								
1952	StL-N	2	6	0	0	0	0	0	0	1	1	.000	.143	.000	143	-57	-1	0	0	0	1.000	-0	/1-2	-0.2
■ STEVE HERTZ Hertz, Stephen Allan b: 2/26/45, Fairfield, Ohio BR/TR, 6'1", 195 lbs. Deb: 4/21/64																								
1964	Hou-N	5	4	2	0	0	0	0	0	0	3	.000	.000	.000	0	-99	-1	0	0	0	1.000	0	/3-2	-0.1
■ BUCK HERZOG Herzog, Charles Lincoln b: 7/9/1885, Baltimore, Md. d: 9/4/53, Baltimore, Md. BR/TR, 5'11", 160 lbs. Deb: 4/17/08 M Career OF: (28-LF 0-CF 4-RF)																								
1908	NY-N	64	160	38	48	6	2	0	11	36		.300	.448	.363	811	152	13	16			.921	1	2-42,S-12/3-4,O-1L	1.7
1909	NY-N	42	130	16	24	2	0	0	8	13		.185	.264	.200	464	43	-8	2			.914	-2	O-29L/2-6,3-4,S-1	-1.4
1910	Bos-N	106	380	51	95	20	3	3	32	30	34	.250	.329	.342	672	92	-4	13			.915	4	*3-105	0.3
1911	Bos-N	79	294	53	91	19	5	5	41	33	21	.310	.398	.459	857	129	12	26			.934	8	S-74/3-4	2.5
	*NY-N	69	247	37	66	14	4	1	26	14	19	.267	.325	.368	693	91	-4	22			.926	10	3-65/2-3,S-1	0.8
	Yr	148	541	90	157	33	9	6	67	47	40	.290	.365	.418	783	112	8	48			.935	18	S-75,3-69/2-3	3.3
1912	*NY-N	140	482	72	127	20	9	2	47	57	34	.263	.350	.355	705	90	-6	37			.942	19	*3-140	1.7
1913	*NY-N	96	290	46	83	15	3	3	31	22	12	.286	.349	.390	739	110	4	23			.947	1	3-84/2-2	0.7
1914	Cin-N	138	498	54	140	14	8	1	40	42	27	.281	.348	.347	695	104	3	46			.939	31	*S-137/1-2,M	4.6
1915	Cin-N	155	579	61	153	14	10	1	42	34	21	.264	.314	.328	642	93	-5	35	16	2	.945	31	*S-153/1-2,M	4.2
1916	Cin-N	79	281	30	75	14	2	1	24	21	12	.267	.329	.342	671	109	3	15	12	-1	.931	-2	S-65,3-12/O-1L,M	0.6
	NY-N	77	280	40	73	10	4	0	25	22	24	.261	.326	.325	651	106	2	19	16	-1	.978	14	2-44,3-27/S-9	2.1
	Yr	156	561	70	148	24	6	1	49	43	36	.264	.327	.333	661	107	5	34	28	-2	.926	12	S-74,2-44,3-39,/O-1L	2.7
1917	*NY-N	114	417	69	98	10	8	2	31	31	36	.235	.308	.312	620	93	-3	12			.948	-9	*2-113	-1.1
1918	Bos-N	118	473	57	108	12	6	0	26	29	28	.228	.280	.279	559	74	-15	10			.961	4	2-99,1-12/S-7	-1.1
1919	Bos-N	73	275	27	77	8	5	1	25	13	11	.280	.327	.356	683	110	3	16			.953	-14	2-70/1-1	-1.1
	Chi-N	52	193	15	53	4	4	0	17	10	7	.275	.336	.337	673	102	1	12			.987	-11	2-52	-1.0
	Yr	125	468	42	130	12	9	1	42	23	18	.278	.331	.348	679	106	4	28			.967	-25	*2-122/1-1	-2.1
1920	Chi-N	91	305	39	59	9	2	0	19	20	21	.193	.261	.236	497	43	-22	8	9	-1	.938	-6	2-59,3-28/1-1	-3.1
Total	13	1493	5284	705	1370	191	75	20	445	427	307	.259	.329	.335	664	96	-26	312	53		.954	77	2-490,3-473,S/O1	10.4
■ WHITEY HERZOG Herzog, Dorrel Norman Elvert b: 11/9/31, New Athens, Ill. BL/TL, 5'11", 182 lbs. Deb: 4/17/56 MC Career OF: (117-LF 137-CF 206-RF)																								
1956	Was-A	117	421	49	103	13	7	4	35	35	74	.245	.303	.337	640	69	-20	8	5	0	.980	1	*O-103(15-84-7)/1-5	-2.3
1957	Was-A	36	78	7	13	3	0	0	4	13	12	.167	.301	.205	506	41	-6	1	2	-0	.981	-3	O-28(2-26-0)	-1.1
1958	Was-A	8	5	0	0	0	0	0	0	1	5	.000	.167	.000	167	-51	-1	0	0	0	1.000	-2	/O-7(0-5-2)	-0.3

YEAR	TM/L	G	AB	R	H	2B	3B	HR	RBI	BB	SO	AVG	OBP	SLG	OPS	OPS+	BR+	SB	CS	SBR	FA	FR	G/POS	TPR
	KC-A	88	96	11	23	1	2	0	9	16	21	.240	.348	.292	640	77	-2	0	3	-1	.968	-10	O-37(29-7-1),1-22	-1.5
	Yr	96	101	11	23	1	2	0	9	17	26	.228	.339	.277	616	71	-3	0	3	-1	.972	-12	O-44(29-12-3),1-22	-1.8
1959	KC-A	38	123	25	36	7	1	1	9	34	23	.293	.446	.390	836	129	7	1	0	0	.963	2	O-34(1-13-20)/1-1	0.8
1960	KC-A	83	252	43	67	10	2	8	38	40	32	.266	.366	.417	783	111	4	0	1	-0	.985	1	O-69(29-0-42)/1-2	0.2
1961	Bal-A	113	323	39	94	11	6	5	35	50	41	.291	.388	.409	796	117	10	1	4	-1	1.000	-11	O-98(27-0-73)	-0.8
1962	Bal-A	99	263	34	70	13	1	7	35	41	36	.266	.371	.403	774	116	7	2	3	-1	.978	0	O-70(13-1-59)	0.2
1963	Det-A	52	53	5	8	2	1	0	7	11	17	.151	.308	.226	534	51	-3	0	0	0	.976	-2	/1-7,O-4(1-1-2)	-0.6
Total	8	634	1614	213	414	60	20	25	172	241	261	.257	.356	.365	720	96	-4	13	18	-3	.982	-23	O-450R/1-37	-5.4
■ OTTO HESS	Hess, Otto C. b: 10/10/1878, Bern, Switzerland d: 2/25/26, Tucson, Ariz. BL/TL, 6'1", 170 lbs. Deb: 8/3/02 Career OF: (36-LF 10-CF 5-RF)																							
1902	Cle-A	7	14	2	1	0	0	0	1	2		.071	.188	.071	259	-27	-2	0			.870	1	/P-7	0.0
1904	Cle-A	34	100	4	12	2	1	0	5	3		.120	.146	.160	306	-3	-12	0			.951	-1	P-21,O-12(7-5-0)	-0.5
1905	Cle-A	54	173	15	44	8	1	2	13	7		.254	.291	.347	638	101	-0	2			.950	3	O-28(27-0-1),P-26	0.1
1906	Cle-A	53	154	13	31	5	2	0	11	2		.201	.212	.260	471	48	-10	1			.949	-3	P-43/O-5(0-5-0)	-0.2
1907	Cle-A	19	30	4	4	0	0	0	0	4		.133	.278	.133	411	31	-2	1			.941	-1	P-17/O-2(2-0-0)	-0.1
1908	Cle-A	9	14	0	0	0	0	0	0	1		.000	.067	.000	67	-78	-3	0			1.000	-1	/P-4,O-4(0-0-4)	-0.4
1912	Bos-N	33	94	10	23	4	4	0	10	0	26	.245	.245	.372	617	66	-5	0			.951	-3	P-33	0.0
1913	Bos-N	35	83	9	26	0	1	2	11	7	15	.313	.367	.410	776	119	2	0			.945	1	P-29	0.0
1914	Bos-N	31	47	5	11	1	0	1	6	1	11	.234	.250	.319	569	69	-2	0			.947	1	P-14/1-5	-0.1
1915	Bos-N	5	5	1	2	1	0	0	1	0	2	.400	.400	.600	1000	210	1	0			.800	-0	/P-4,1-1	0.0
Total	10	280	714	63	154	21	9	5	58	27	54	.216	.248	.291	540	63	-33	4			.941	-3	P-198/O-51L,1-6	-1.2
■ TOM HESS	Hess, Thomas (b: Thomas Heslin) b: 8/15/1875, Brooklyn, N.Y. d: 12/15/45, Albany, N.Y. Deb: 6/6/1892																							
1892	Bal-N	1	2	0	0	0	0	0	0	0	0	.000	.000	.000	0	-97	-0	0			.000	0	/C-1	0.0
■ GUS HETLING	Hetling, August Julius b: 11/21/1885, St.Louis, Mo. d: 10/13/62, Wichita, Kan. BR/TR, 5'10", 165 lbs. Deb: 10/6/06																							
1906	Det-A	2	7	0	1	0	0	0	0	0		.143	.143	.143	286	-10	-1	0			1.000	-0	/3-2	-0.1
■ GEORGE HEUBEL	Heubel, George A. b: 1849, Paterson, N.J. d: 1/22/1896, Philadelphia, Pa. 5'11.5", 178 lbs. Deb: 5/20/1871 U																							
1871	Ath-n	17	75	18	23	4	2	0	13	2	0	.307	.325	.413	738	112	1	1	0	0	.758	1	O-16(0-0-16)/1-1	0.2
1872	Oly-n	5	23	2	3	0	0	0	1	0	0	.130	.130	.130	261	-21	-3	0	0	0	.800	-1	/O-5(0-5-0)	-0.3
1876	NY-N	1	4	0	0	0	0	0	0	0	0	.000	.000	.000	0	-99	-1				.750	-0	/1-1	-0.1
Total	2 n	22	98	20	26	4	2	0	14	2	0	.265	.280	.347	627	83	-2	1	0	0	.767	0	/O-21(0-5-16),1-1	-0.1
■ JOHNNIE HEVING	Heving, John Aloysius b: 4/29/1896, Covington, Ky. d: 12/24/68, Salisbury, N.C. BR/TR, 6', 175 lbs. Deb: 9/24/20 F																							
1920	StL-A	1	1	0	0	0	0	0	0	0	0	.000	.000	.000	0	-97	-0	0	0	0	.000	0	H	0.0
1924	Bos-A	45	109	15	31	5	1	0	11	10	7	.284	.345	.349	693	79	-3	0	0	0	.969	4	C-29	0.2
1925	Bos-A	45	119	14	20	7	0	0	6	12	7	.168	.244	.227	471	20	-15	0	1	-0	.958	3	C-34	-1.0
1928	Bos-A	82	158	11	41	7	2	0	11	11	10	.259	.308	.329	637	69	-7	1	1	-0	.967	-4	C-62	-0.8
1929	Bos-A	76	188	26	60	4	3	0	23	8	7	.319	.354	.372	726	89	-3	1	2	-0	.988	5	C-55	0.5
1930	Bos-A	75	220	15	61	5	3	0	17	11	14	.277	.312	.327	639	65	-12	2	0	0	.987	-4	C-71	-1.0
1931	*Phi-A	42	113	8	27	3	2	1	12	6	8	.239	.277	.327	605	55	-8	0	0	0	.993	2	C-40	-0.3
1932	Phi-A	33	77	14	21	6	1	0	10	7	6	.273	.333	.377	710	81	-2	0	0	0	1.000	-1	C-28	-0.2
Total	8	399	985	103	261	37	12	1	90	65	59	.265	.312	.330	642	66	-50	4	4	-1	.981	4	C-319	-2.6
■ MIKE HEYDON	Heydon, Michael Edward "Ed" b: 7/15/1874, Missouri d: 10/13/13, Indianapolis, Ind. BL/TR, 6', Deb: 10/12/1898																							
1898	Bal-N	3	9	2	1	0	0	0	1	2		.111	.333	.111	444	28	-1	0			.917	-1	/C-3	-0.1
1899	Was-N	3	3	0	0	0	0	0	0	2		.000	.400	.000	400	14	-0	0			.833	-0	/C-2	0.0
1901	StL-N	16	43	2	9	1	1	1	6	5		.209	.292	.349	641	90	-1	2			.941	-3	C-13/O-1(0-1-0)	-0.2
1904	Chi-A	4	10	0	1	1	0	0	1	1		.100	.250	.200	450	45	-1	0			1.000	1	/C-4	0.1
1905	Was-A	77	245	20	47	7	4	1	26	21		.192	.261	.265	527	70	-8	5			.955	12	C-77	1.2
1906	Was-A	49	145	14	23	7	1	0	10	14		.159	.237	.221	458	46	-9	2			.937	-2	C-49	-0.7
1907	Was-A	62	164	14	30	3	0	0	9	25		.183	.302	.201	503	66	-5	3			.961	-8	C-57	-0.8
Total	7	214	619	52	111	19	6	2	53	70		.179	.271	.239	510	64	-24	12			.952	-0	C-205/O-1(0-1-0)	-0.5
■ JACK HIATT	Hiatt, Jack E b: 7/27/42, Bakersfield, Cal. BR/TR, 6'2", 190 lbs. Deb: 9/7/64 C																							
1964	LA-A	9	16	2	6	0	0	0	2	2	3	.375	.444	.375	819	145	1	0	0	0	.889	-1	/C-3,1-2	0.0
1965	SF-N	40	67	5	19	4	0	1	7	12	14	.284	.392	.388	780	118	2	0	0	0	.987	-2	C-21/1-7	0.0
1966	SF-N	18	23	2	7	2	0	0	1	4	5	.304	.407	.391	799	120	1	0	0	0	.982	1	/1-7	0.2
1967	SF-N	73	153	24	42	6	0	6	26	27	37	.275	.387	.431	818	136	8	0	0	0	.990	-3	1-36/C-3,O-2(2-0-0)	0.4
1968	SF-N	90	224	14	52	10	2	4	34	41	61	.232	.353	.348	702	111	5	0	0	0	.994	-1	C-58,1-10	0.7
1969	SF-N	69	194	18	38	4	0	7	34	48	58	.196	.355	.325	680	93	0	0	0	0	.992	0	C-60/1-3	0.3
1970	Mon-N	17	43	4	14	2	0	0	7	14	14	.326	.491	.372	863	135	3	0	0	0	.961	-4	C-12/1-2	0.0
	Chi-N	66	178	19	43	12	1	2	22	31	48	.242	.354	.354	708	81	-4	0	0	0	.990	5	C-63/1-2	0.3
	Yr	83	221	23	57	14	1	2	29	45	62	.258	.383	.357	741	91	-1	0	0	0	.986	2	C-75/1-4	0.3
1971	Hou-N	69	174	16	48	8	1	1	16	35	39	.276	.403	.351	753	118	6	0	1	-0	.991	-1	C-65/1-1	0.8
1972	Hou-N	10	25	2	5	3	0	0	0	5	5	.200	.333	.320	653	88	-0	0	0	0	1.000	-3	C-10	-0.3
	Cal-A	22	45	4	13	0	1	1	5	5	11	.289	.360	.400	760	133	2	0	0	0	1.000	-8	C-17	-0.7
Total	9	483	1142	110	287	51	5	22	154	224	295	.251	.376	.363	738	109	24	0	1	-0	.990	-16	C-312/1-70,O-2(2-0-0)	1.7
■ PHIL HIATT	Hiatt, Philip Farrell b: 5/1/69, Pensacola, Fla. BR/TR, 6'3", 200 lbs. Deb: 4/7/93 Career OF: (2-LF 2-CF 46-RF)																							
1993	KC-A	81	238	30	52	12	1	7	36	16	82	.218	.287	.366	653	70	-10	6	3	0	.909	-1	3-70/D-9	-1.1
1995	KC-A	52	113	11	23	6	0	4	12	9	37	.204	.262	.363	625	60	-7	1	0	0	.957	-4	O-47(1-2-45)/D-2	-1.2
1996	Det-A	7	21	3	4	0	1	0	1	2	11	.190	.261	.286	547	38	-2	0	0	0	1.000	1	/3-3,O-2(1-0-1),D-1	-0.1
Total	3	140	372	44	79	18	2	11	49	27	130	.212	.278	.360	639	65	-20	7	3	0	.913	-5	/3-73,O-49R,D-12	-2.4
■ JIM HIBBS	Hibbs, James Kerr b: 9/10/44, Klamath Falls, Ore. BR/TR, 6', 190 lbs. Deb: 4/12/67																							
1967	Cal-A	3	3	0	0	0	0	0	0	0	2	.000	.000	.000	0	-99	-1	0	0	0	.000	0	H	-0.1
■ EDDIE HICKEY	Hickey, Edward A. b: 8/18/1872, Cleveland, Ohio d: 3/25/41, Tacoma, Wash. Deb: 9/3/01																							
1901	Chi-N	10	37	4	6	0	0	0	3	2		.162	.225	.162	387	14	-4	1			.743	-2	3-10	-0.5
■ MIKE HICKEY	Hickey, Michael Francis b: 12/25/1871, Chicopee, Mass. d: 6/11/18, Springfield, Mass BR/TR, 5'10.5", 150 lbs. Deb: 9/14/1899																							
1899	Bos-N	1	3	0	1	0	0	0	0	0		.333	.333	.333	667	76	-0	0			.889	1	/2-1	0.1
■ CHARLIE HICKMAN	Hickman, Charles Taylor "Cheerful Charlie" or "Piano Legs" b: 3/4/1876, Taylortown, Dunkard Township, Pa. d: 4/19/34, Morgantown, W.Va. BR/TR, 5'11.5", 215 lbs. Deb: 9/8/1897 Career OF: (46-LF 3-CF 242-RF)																							
1897	*Bos-N	2	3	1	2	0	0	1	2	0		.667	.667	1.667	2333	476	1	0			1.000	0	/P-2	0.0
1898	Bos-N	19	58	4	15	2	0	0	7	1		.259	.283	.293	576	62	-3	0			1.000	-1	/O-7(6-1-0),1-6,P-6	-0.3
1899	Bos-N	19	63	15	25	2	7	0	15	2		.397	.433	.651	1084	178	6	1			.941	-2	P-11/O-7(6-1-0),1-1	0.1
1900	NY-N	127	473	65	148	19	17	9	91	17		.313	.359	.482	841	137	22	10			.842	-4	*3-120/O-7(0-0-7)	1.7
1901	NY-N	112	406	44	113	20	6	4	62	15		.278	.315	.387	702	107	2	5			.904	-7	O-50R,S-23,3-15,/P21	-0.6
1902	Bos-A	28	108	13	32	5	2	3	16	3		.296	.339	.463	802	118	2	1			.939	1	O-27(27-0-0)	0.1
	Cle-A	102	426	61	161	31	11	8	94	12		.378	.399	.559	958	170	38	8			.966	-7	1-98/2-3,P-1	2.7
	Yr	130	534	74	**193**	36	13	11	110	15		.361	.387	.539	926	159	39	9			.966	-6	1-98,O-27L/2-3,P-1	2.8
1903	Cle-A	131	522	64	154	31	11	12	97	17		.295	.325	.466	790	137	21	14			.972	-7	*1-125/2-7	1.3
1904	Cle-A	86	337	34	97	22	10	4	45	13		.288	.318	.448	766	142	14	9			.943	-0	2-45,1-40/O-1(1-0-0)	1.5
	Det-A	42	144	18	35	6	6	2	22	11		.243	.297	.410	706	126	4	3			.970	-2	1-39	0.1
	Yr	128	481	52	132	28	16	6	67	24		.274	.312	.437	748	137	18	12			.969	-3	1-79,2-45/O-1(1-0-0)	1.6
1905	Det-A	59	213	21	47	12	3	2	20	12		.221	.278	.333	612	93	-2	3			.940	3	O-47(0-0-47),1-12	-0.2
	Was-A	88	360	48	112	25	9	2	46	9		.311	.332	.447	779	152	19	3			.922	8	2-85/1-3	2.9
	Yr	147	573	69	159	37	12	4	66	21		.277	.311	.405	716	129	16	6			.922	10	2-85,O-47R,1-15	2.7

YEAR	TM/L	G	AB	R	H	2B	3B	HR	RBI	BB	SO	AVG	OBP	SLG	OPS	OPS+	BR+	SB	CS	SBR	FA	FR	G/POS	TPR
1906	Was-A	120	451	53	128	25	5	9	57	14		.284	.311	.421	733	135	15	9			.955	-1	O-95R,1-18/3-5,2-1	1.1
1907	Was-A	60	198	20	55	9	3	1	23	14		.278	.338	.369	707	136	8	4			.965	-4	1-30,O-18R/2-3,P-1	0.3
	Chi-A	21	23	1	6	2	0	0	1	4		.261	.370	.348	718	134	1	0			.667	-1	/O-3(0-0-3)	0.0
	Yr	81	221	21	61	11	3	1	24	18		.276	.342	.367	708	135	9	4			.965	-5	1-30,O-21R/2-3,P-1	0.3
1908	Cle-A	65	197	16	46	6	1	2	16	9		.234	.271	.305	575	86	-3	2			.907	-0	O-28(0-0-28),1-20/2-1	-0.6
Total	12	1081	3982	478	1176	217	91	59	614	153		.295	.331	.440	771	133	145	72			.968	-25	1-394,O-290R,23/PS	10.1
■ **JIM HICKMAN**	Hickman, David James b: 5/19/1892, Johnson City, Tenn d: 12/30/58, Brooklyn, N.Y. BR/TR, 5'7.5", 170 lbs. Deb: 9/17/15																							
1915	Bal-F	20	81	7	17	4	1	1	7	4	14	.210	.256	.321	577	60	-6	5			.963	4	O-20(0-20-0)	-0.3
1916	Bro-N	9	5	3	1	0	0	0	0	2	0	.200	.429	.200	629	94	0	1			1.000	-1	/O-3(2-1-0)	-0.1
1917	Bro-N	114	370	46	81	15	4	6	36	17	66	.219	.253	.330	583	76	-11	14			.942	7	*O-101(26-71-3)	-1.1
1918	Bro-N	53	167	14	39	4	7	1	16	8	31	.234	.281	.359	640	95	-2	5			.914	-3	O-46(0-10-42)	-0.8
1919	Bro-N	57	104	14	20	3	1	0	11	6	17	.192	.236	.240	477	43	-7	2			.962	-4	O-29(4-6-22)	-1.4
Total	5	253	727	84	158	26	13	8	70	37	128	.217	.259	.322	581	74	-26	27			.941	4	O-199(32-108-67)	-3.7
■ **JIM HICKMAN**	Hickman, James Lucius b: 5/10/37, Henning, Tenn. BR/TR, 6'4", 205 lbs. Deb: 4/14/62 Career OF: (144-LF 365-CF 421-RF)																							
1962	NY-N	140	392	54	96	18	2	13	46	47	96	.245	.330	.401	731	94	-3	4	4	-1	.971	1	*O-124(7-84-33)	-0.8
1963	NY-N	146	494	53	113	21	6	17	51	44	120	.229	.293	.399	692	96	-3	0	5	-2	.963	-0	O-82(19-42-22),3-59	-1.0
1964	NY-N	139	409	48	105	14	1	11	57	36	90	.257	.320	.377	696	98	-1	0	1	-0	.976	-9	*O-113(39-89-19)/3-1	-1.5
1965	NY-N	141	369	32	87	18	0	15	40	27	76	.236	.291	.407	698	98	-2	3	1	0	.965	-8	O-91C,1-30,3-14	-1.6
1966	NY-N	58	160	15	38	7	0	4	16	13	34	.237	.299	.356	655	83	-4	2	1	0	.986	1	O-45(16-8-23),1-17	-0.6
1967	LA-N	65	98	7	16	6	1	0	10	14	28	.163	.268	.245	513	52	-6	1	1	-0	1.000	-3	O-37L/1-2,3-2,P-1	-1.1
1968	Chi-N	75	188	22	42	6	3	5	23	18	38	.223	.295	.367	662	91	-2	1	1	-0	.975	-4	O-66(3-20-49)	-1.1
1969	Chi-N	134	338	38	80	11	2	21	54	47	74	.237	.330	.467	797	107	3	2	1	0	.981	-14	*O-125(5-9-116)	-1.7
1970	Chi-N★	149	514	102	162	33	4	32	115	93	99	.315	.421	.582	1003	148	36	0	1	-0	.974	6	O-79(2-53-28),1-74	3.3
1971	Chi-N	117	383	50	98	13	2	19	60	50	61	.256	.346	.449	795	108	5	0	1	-0	.982	-4	O-69(1-3-66),1-44	-0.7
1972	Chi-N	115	368	65	100	15	2	17	64	52	64	.272	.365	.462	827	121	11	3	1	0	.992	7	1-77,O-27(1-0-26)	1.1
1973	Chi-N	92	201	27	49	1	2	3	20	42	42	.244	.374	.313	688	86	-2	1	1	-0	.988	-2	1-51,O-13(3-0-11)	-0.9
1974	StL-N	50	60	5	16	0	0	2	4	8	10	.267	.353	.367	720	102	0	0	0	0	.986	1	1-14/3-1	0.1
Total	13	1421	3974	518	1002	163	25	159	560	491	832	.252	.337	.426	763	106	31	17	19	-3	.976	-29	O-871R,1-309/3-77,P	-6.5
■ **BUDDY HICKS**	Hicks, Clarence Walter b: 2/15/27, Belvedere, Cal. BB/TR, 5'10", 170 lbs. Deb: 4/17/56																							
1956	Det-A	26	47	5	10	2	0	0	5	3	2	.213	.260	.255	515	36	-4	0	1	-0	1.000	-1	S-16/2-6,3-1	-0.5
■ **JIM HICKS**	Hicks, James Edward b: 5/18/40, East Chicago, Ind. BR/TR, 6'3", 205 lbs. Deb: 10/2/64																							
1964	Chi-A	2	0	0	0	0	0	0	0	0	0	—	—	—	—	—	0	0	0	0	.000	0	R	0.0
1965	Chi-A	13	19	2	5	1	0	1	2	0	9	.263	.263	.474	737	112	0	0	0	0	.750	-2	/O-5(3-0-2)	-0.2
1966	Chi-A	18	26	3	5	0	1	0	1	1	5	.192	.222	.269	491	43	-2	0	0	0	1.000	-1	O-10(2-0-8)/1-2	-0.4
1969	StL-N	19	44	5	8	0	2	1	3	4	14	.182	.250	.341	591	64	-2	0	0	0	1.000	1	O-15(0-0-15)	-0.2
	Cal-A	37	48	6	4	0	0	3	8	13	18	.083	.279	.271	550	57	-3	0	1	-0	1.000	-3	O-10(4-3-3)/1-8	-0.7
1970	Cal-A	4	4	0	1	0	0	0	0	0	2	.250	.250	.250	500	40	-0	0	0	0	.000	0	H	0.0
Total	5	93	141	16	23	1	3	5	14	18	48	.163	.258	.319	577	64	-7	0	1	-0	.981	-6	/O-40(9-3-28),1-10	-1.5
■ **NAT HICKS**	Hicks, Nathan Woodhull b: 4/19/1845, Hempstead, N.Y. d: 4/21/07, Hoboken, N.J. BR/TR, 6'1", 186 lbs. Deb: 4/22/1872 M																							
1872	Mut-n	56	268	55	82	12	2	0	33	5	3	.306	.319	.366	684	117	7	3	0	1	.875	5	*C-54/O-3(0-0-3)	0.9
1873	Mut-n	28	121	12	29	1	2	1	14	7	0	.240	.281	.306	587	75	-3	2	0	0	.788	4	C-28	0.1
1874	Phi-n	58	266	51	73	8	1	0	30	5	4	.274	.288	.312	600	89	-4	3	2	-0	.823	6	*C-57/O-4C,2-1,M	0.2
1875	Mut-n	62	269	32	67	10	0	0	22	2	10	.249	.255	.286	541	83	-5	1	0	0	.819	6	*C-60/O-5(0-1-4),M	0.1
1876	NY-N	45	191	20	44	4	1	0	15	3	4	.230	.246	.266	512	81	-2				.741	-6	C-45	-0.6
1877	Cin-N	8	32	3	6	0	0	0	3	1	2	.188	.212	.188	400	30	-2				.868	0	/C-8	-0.2
Total	4 n	204	924	150	251	31	5	1	99	19	17	.272	.286	.319	606	93	-5	9	2	1	.829	22	C-199/O-12(0-5-7),2-1	1.3
Total	2	53	223	23	50	4	1	0	18	4	6	.224	.241	.255	496	73	-4				.757	-5	/C-53	-0.8
■ **JOE HICKS**	Hicks, William Joseph b: 4/7/33, Ivy, Va. BL/TR, 6', 180 lbs. Deb: 9/18/59																							
1959	Chi-A	6	7	0	3	0	0	0	0	1	1	.429	.500	.429	929	160	1	0	1	-0	1.000	-0	/O-4(1-2-1)	0.0
1960	Chi-A	36	47	3	9	1	0	0	2	6	3	.191	.296	.213	509	40	-4	0	1	-0	1.000	-4	O-14(3-11-0)	-0.8
1961	Was-A	12	29	2	5	0	0	1	1	0	4	.172	.172	.276	448	18	-3	0	1	-0	1.000	1	/O-7(3-0-4)	-0.4
1962	Was-A	102	174	20	39	4	2	6	14	15	34	.224	.286	.374	659	76	-6	3	1	0	.962	-3	O-42(5-22-16)	-1.1
1963	NY-N	56	159	16	36	6	1	5	22	7	31	.226	.272	.371	643	82	-4	0	2	-1	.966	-2	O-41(5-33-5)	-0.8
Total	5	212	416	41	92	11	3	12	39	29	73	.221	.278	.349	627	72	-17	3	6	-1	.970	-8	O-108(17-68-26)	-3.1
■ **RICHARD HIDALGO**	Hidalgo, Richard Jose b: 7/2/75, Caracas, Venez. BR/TR, 6'3", 190 lbs. Deb: 9/1/97																							
1997	*Hou-N	19	62	8	19	5	0	2	6	4	18	.306	.358	.484	842	123	2	1	0	0	1.000	-2	O-19(1-17-1)	0.0
1998	*Hou-N	74	211	31	64	15	0	7	35	17	37	.303	.361	.474	835	121	6	3	3	-0	.978	-5	O-72(9-57-14)	0.0
1999	Hou-N	108	383	49	87	25	2	15	56	56	73	.227	.332	.420	752	90	-6	8	5	0	.991	7	*O-108(97-30-3)	-0.1
2000	Hou-N	153	558	118	175	42	3	44	122	56	110	.314	.397	.636	1033	147	39	13	6	1	.984	5	*O-150(36-125-37)	4.0
Total	4	354	1214	206	345	87	5	68	219	133	238	.284	.368	.532	900	124	41	25	14	1	.986	4	O-349(143-229-55)	3.9
■ **MAHLON HIGBEE**	Higbee, Mahlon Jesse b: 8/16/01, Louisville, Ky. d: 4/7/68, Depauw, Ind. BR/TR, 5'11", 165 lbs. Deb: 9/27/22																							
1922	NY-N	3	10	2	4	0	0	1	5	0	2	.400	.400	.700	1100	177	1	0	0	0	1.000	-1	/O-3(2-0-1)	0.0
■ **HIGBY**	Higby Deb: 9/18/1872																							
1872	Atl-n	1	4	0	0	0	0	0	0	0	0	.000	.000	.000	0	-85	-1	0	0	0	.667	0	/O-1(0-0-1)	-0.1
■ **BILL HIGDON**	Higdon, William Travis b: 4/27/24, Camp Hill, Ala. d: 8/30/86, Pascagoula, Miss. BL/TR, 6'1", 193 lbs. Deb: 9/10/49																							
1949	Chi-A	11	23	3	7	3	0	0	1	6	3	.304	.448	.435	883	139	2	1	0	0	1.000	-1	/O-6(0-6-0)	0.1
■ **KEVIN HIGGINS**	Higgins, Kevin Wayne b: 1/22/67, San Gabriel, Cal. BL/TR, 5'11", 170 lbs. Deb: 5/29/93																							
1993	SD-N	71	181	17	40	4	1	0	13	16	17	.221	.295	.254	549	48	-13	0	1	-0	.983	-3	C-59/3-4,1-3,O-3R,2	-1.3
■ **MARK HIGGINS**	Higgins, Mark Douglas b: 7/9/63, Miami, Fla. BR/TR, 6'2", 210 lbs. Deb: 9/7/89																							
1989	Cle-A	6	10	1	1	0	0	0	0	1	6	.100	.182	.100	282	-18	-2	0	0	0	1.000	1	/1-5	-0.1
■ **PINKY HIGGINS**	Higgins, Michael Franklin "Mike" b: 5/27/09, Red Oak, Tex. d: 3/21/69, Dallas, Tex. BR/TR, 6'1", 185 lbs. Deb: 6/25/30 M																							
1930	Phi-A	14	24	1	6	2	0	0	0	4	5	.250	.357	.333	690	73	-1	0	0	0	1.000	-2	/3-5,2-2,S-1	-0.2
1933	Phi-A	152	567	85	178	34	12	13	99	61	53	.314	.383	.485	868	127	22	2	7	-2	.947	-6	*3-152	1.8
1934	Phi-A☆	144	543	89	179	37	6	16	90	56	70	.330	.392	.508	901	136	28	9	2	1	.914	-19	*3-144	1.4
1935	Phi-A	133	524	69	155	32	4	23	94	42	62	.296	.350	.504	854	120	12	6	2	1	.947	-14	*3-131	0.3
1936	Phi-A★	146	550	89	159	32	2	12	80	67	61	.289	.366	.420	786	96	-4	7	4	0	.941	-14	*3-145	-1.1
1937	Bos-A	153	570	88	172	33	5	9	106	76	51	.302	.385	.425	809	100	1	2	6	-2	.935	-17	*3-152	-1.0
1938	Bos-A	139	524	77	159	29	5	5	106	71	55	.303	.388	.406	794	95	-3	10	9	-1	.914	-10	*3-138	-0.7
1939	Det-A	132	489	57	135	23	2	8	76	56	41	.276	.353	.380	733	81	-13	7	4	0	.914	-11	*3-130	-1.8
1940	*Det-A	131	480	70	130	24	3	13	76	61	31	.271	.357	.415	771	91	-6	4	2	0	.928	-11	*3-129	-1.2
1941	Det-A	147	540	79	161	28	3	11	73	67	45	.298	.378	.422	800	101	2	5	4	-0	.946	1	*3-145	0.8
1942	Det-A	143	499	65	133	34	2	11	79	72	21	.267	.362	.409	771	108	6	3	7	-2	.926	-14	*3-137	-0.4
1943	Det-A	138	523	62	145	20	1	10	84	57	31	.277	.349	.377	726	104	3	2	5	-1	.940	-7	*3-138	-0.3
1944	Det-A★	148	543	79	161	32	4	7	76	81	34	.297	.392	.409	801	122	18	4	4	-1	.954	-7	*3-146	1.3
1946	Det-A	18	60	2	13	3	1	0	8	5	6	.217	.277	.300	577	58	-3	0	1	-0	.949	-2	3-17	-0.6
	*Bos-A	64	200	18	55	11	1	2	28	24	24	.275	.356	.370	726	97	-0	0	2	-1	.947	0	3-59	-0.1
	Yr	82	260	20	68	14	2	2	36	29	30	.262	.338	.354	692	88	-4	0	3	-1	.947	-2	3-76	-0.7
Total	14	1802	6636	930	1941	374	51	140	1075	800	590	.292	.370	.428	798	106	63	61	59	-7	.935	-131	*3-1768/2-2,S-1	-1.8

■ BOB HIGGINS
Higgins, Robert Stone b: 9/23/1886, Fayetteville, Tenn. d: 5/25/41, Chattanooga, Tenn. BR/TR, 5'8", 176 lbs. Deb: 9/13/09

YEAR	TM/L	G	AB	R	H	2B	3B	HR	RBI	BB	SO	AVG	OBP	SLG	OPS	OPS+	BR+	SB	CS	SBR	FA	FR	G/POS	TPR
1909	Cle-A	8	23	0	2	0	0	0	0	0		.087	.087	.087	174	-43	-4	0			1.000	3	/C-8	0.0
1911	Bro-N	4	10	1	3	0	0	0	2	1	0	.300	.364	.300	664	90	-0	1			.933	0	/C-2,3-1	0.0
1912	Bro-N	1	2	0	0	0	0	0	0	0	1	.000	.000	.000	0	-99	-1	0			.750	-0	/C-1	-0.1
Total	3	13	35	1	5	0	0	0	2	1	1	.143	.167	.143	310	-6	-4	1			.970	3	/C-11,3-1	-0.1

■ BILL HIGGINS
Higgins, William Edward b: 9/8/1861, Wilmington, Del. d: 4/25/19, Wilmington, Del. TR, 5'9", 155 lbs. Deb: 8/9/1888

YEAR	TM/L	G	AB	R	H	2B	3B	HR	RBI	BB	SO	AVG	OBP	SLG	OPS	OPS+	BR+	SB	CS	SBR	FA	FR	G/POS	TPR
1888	Bos-N	14	54	5	10	1	0	0	4	1	3	.185	.200	.204	404	28	-4	1			.906	5	2-14	0.2
1890	StL-a	67	258	39	65	6	2	0	35	24		.252	.316	.291	606	69	-11	7			.951	13	2-67	0.4
	Syr-a	1	4	1	1	1	0	0	1	0		.250	.250	.500	750	135	0	0			1.000	1	/2-1	0.1
	Yr	68	262	40	66	7	2	0	36	24		.252	.315	.294	609	70	-11	7			.952	14	2-68	0.5
Total	2	82	316	45	76	8	2	0	40	25	3	.241	.296	.278	575	64	-15	8			.943	20	/2-82	0.7

■ BOBBY HIGGINSON
Higginson, Robert Leigh b: 8/18/70, Philadelphia, Pa. BL/TR, 5'11", 180 lbs. Deb: 4/26/95 Career OF: (394-LF 21-CF 405-RF)

YEAR	TM/L	G	AB	R	H	2B	3B	HR	RBI	BB	SO	AVG	OBP	SLG	OPS	OPS+	BR+	SB	CS	SBR	FA	FR	G/POS	TPR
1995	Det-A	131	410	61	92	17	5	14	43	62	107	.224	.333	.393	726	89	-7	6	4	-0	.985	6	*O-123(65-0-67)/D-2	-0.6
1996	Det-A	130	440	75	141	35	0	26	81	65	66	.320	.409	.577	986	146	32	6	3	0	.963	-7	*O-123(63-19-57)/D-4	1.9
1997	Det-A	146	546	94	163	30	5	27	101	70	85	.299	.381	.520	901	133	27	12	7	0	.972	6	*O-143(104-2-57)/D-2	2.6
1998	Det-A	157	612	92	174	37	4	25	85	63	101	.284	.357	.480	837	114	13	3	3	-0	.982	9	*O-153(17-0-136)/D-2	1.3
1999	Det-A	107	377	51	90	18	0	12	46	64	66	.239	.352	.382	734	88	-6	4	6	-1	.983	-0	O-88(0-0-88),D-17	-1.2
2000	Det-A	154	597	104	179	44	4	30	102	74	99	.300	.379	.538	917	133	29	15	3	2	.979	16	*O-145(145-0-0),D-10	3.9
Total	6	825	2982	477	839	181	18	134	458	398	524	.281	.370	.489	858	119	88	46	26	1	.977	30	O-775R/D-37	7.9

■ ANDY HIGH
High, Andrew Aird "Handy Andy" b: 11/21/1897, Ava, Ill. d: 2/22/81, Sylvania, Ohio BL/TR, 5'6", 155 lbs. Deb: 4/12/22 FC

YEAR	TM/L	G	AB	R	H	2B	3B	HR	RBI	BB	SO	AVG	OBP	SLG	OPS	OPS+	BR+	SB	CS	SBR	FA	FR	G/POS	TPR
1922	Bro-N	153	579	82	164	27	10	6	65	59	26	.283	.354	.396	749	94	-5	3	12	-4	.958	-5	*3-130,S-22/2-1	-0.3
1923	Bro-N	123	426	51	115	23	9	3	37	47	13	.270	.344	.387	731	95	-3	4	1	1	.969	-9	3-80,S-45/2-5	-0.1
1924	Bro-N	144	582	98	191	26	13	6	61	57	16	.328	.390	.448	838	128	24	3	6	-1	.964	-10	*2-133,S-17/3-1	1.7
1925	Bro-N	44	115	11	23	4	1	0	6	14	5	.200	.287	.252	539	40	-10	0	1	-0	.938	-5	2-11,3-11/S-3	-1.4
	Bos-N	60	219	31	63	11	1	4	28	24	2	.288	.361	.402	762	104	2	3	5	-1	.979	-9	3-60/2-1	-0.5
	Yr	104	334	42	86	15	2	4	34	38	7	.257	.335	.350	685	80	-9	3	6	-1	.963	-14	3-71,2-12/S-3	-1.9
1926	Bos-N	130	476	55	141	17	10	2	66	39	9	.296	.351	.387	737	108	5	4			.962	-6	3-81,2-49	0.6
1927	Bos-N	113	384	59	116	15	9	4	46	26	11	.302	.350	.419	769	114	7	4			.915	-21	3-89/2-8,S-2	-0.8
1928	*StL-N	111	368	58	105	14	3	6	37	37	10	.285	.355	.389	744	93	-3	2			.935	-19	3-73,2-19	-1.8
1929	StL-N	146	603	95	178	32	4	10	63	38	18	.295	.340	.411	751	84	-15	7			**.967**	-19	*3-123,2-22	-2.4
1930	*StL-N	72	215	34	60	12	2	2	29	23	6	.279	.349	.381	730	74	-9	1			.990	-7	3-48/2-3	-1.1
1931	*StL-N	63	131	20	35	6	1	0	19	24	4	.267	.389	.328	717	91	-0	0			1.000	-5	3-23,2-19	-0.3
1932	Cin-N	84	191	16	36	4	2	0	12	23	6	.188	.276	.230	506	39	-16	1			.950	-10	3-46,2-12	-2.4
1933	Cin-N	24	43	4	9	2	0	1	6	5	1	.209	.292	.326	617	77	-1	0			.966	1	3-11/2-2	0.0
1934	Phi-N	47	68	4	14	2	0	0	7	9	3	.206	.299	.235	534	40	-6	1			.906	-2	3-14/2-2	-0.7
Total	13	1314	4400	618	1250	195	65	44	482	425	130	.284	.350	.388	738	94	-31	33	25		.956	-126	3-790,2-287/S-89	-9.5

■ CHARLIE HIGH
High, Charles Edwin b: 12/1/1898, Ava, Ill. d: 9/11/60, Oak Grove, Ore. BL/TR, 5'9", 170 lbs. Deb: 9/5/19 F

YEAR	TM/L	G	AB	R	H	2B	3B	HR	RBI	BB	SO	AVG	OBP	SLG	OPS	OPS+	BR+	SB	CS	SBR	FA	FR	G/POS	TPR
1919	Phi-A	11	29	2	2	0	0	0	1	3	4	.069	.182	.069	251	-28	-5	2			.944	-0	/O-9(0-1-8)	-0.6
1920	Phi-A	17	65	7	20	2	1	1	6	3	6	.308	.375	.415	790	108	1	0	2	-1	.882	-1	O-17(0-2-15)	-0.1
Total	2	28	94	9	22	2	1	1	7	6	10	.234	.314	.309	623	68	-4	2	2		.904	-1	/O-26(0-3-23)	-0.7

■ HUGH HIGH
High, Hugh Jenken "Bunny" b: 10/24/1887, Pottstown, Pa. d: 11/16/62, St.Louis, Mo. BL/TL, 5'7.5", 155 lbs. Deb: 4/11/13 F

YEAR	TM/L	G	AB	R	H	2B	3B	HR	RBI	BB	SO	AVG	OBP	SLG	OPS	OPS+	BR+	SB	CS	SBR	FA	FR	G/POS	TPR
1913	Det-A	87	183	18	42	6	1	0	16	28	24	.230	.335	.273	608	80	-4	6			.982	1	O-52(3-39-7)	-0.6
1914	Det-A	84	184	25	49	5	3	0	17	26	21	.266	.363	.326	689	104	2	7	6	-1	.959	-7	O-53(13-39-1)	-1.0
1915	NY-A	119	427	51	110	19	7	1	43	62	47	.258	.356	.342	698	109	6	22	13	0	**.981**	-1	*O-117(44-71-1)	-0.2
1916	NY-A	116	377	44	99	13	4	1	28	47	44	.263	.349	.326	675	101	-1	13			.950	-1	*O-110(107-2-1)	-0.5
1917	NY-A	103	365	37	86	11	6	1	19	48	31	.236	.329	.307	636	93	-2	8			.986	0	*O-100(99-1-0)	-0.7
1918	NY-A	7	10	1	0	0	0	0	0	1	1	.000	.091	.000	91	-71	-2	0			1.000	0	/O-4(2-1-1)	-0.2
Total	6	516	1546	176	386	54	21	3	123	212	168	.250	.345	.318	662	98	2	56	19		.972	-8	O-436(268-153-11)	-3.2

■ DICK HIGHAM
Higham, Richard b: 7/24/1851, Ipswich, England
d: 3/18/05, Chicago, Ill. BL/TR, 5'8.5", 171 lbs. Deb: 6/1/1871 MU NA OF: (0-LF 9-CF 93-RF) Career OF: (0-LF 0-CF 122-RF)

YEAR	TM/L	G	AB	R	H	2B	3B	HR	RBI	BB	SO	AVG	OBP	SLG	OPS	OPS+	BR+	SB	CS	SBR	FA	FR	G/POS	TPR
1871	Mut-n	21	94	21	34	3	1	0	9	2	0	.362	.375	.415	790	139	6	3	2	-0	.747	-5	2-12/O-8(0-0-8),C-1	0.0
1872	Bal-n	50	245	72	84	10	1	2	38	2	3	.343	.348	.416	765	128	7	3	5	-1	.847	-3	C-25,O-24R/2-5,31	0.3
1873	Mut-n	49	245	57	77	5	4	0	34	2	1	.314	.320	.367	687	104	1	1	3	-1	.714	-14	O-19R,2-18,C-17	-1.0
1874	Mut-n	65	333	58	87	14	3	1	38	4	0	.261	.270	.330	600	89	-5	5	3	0	**.852**	8	*C-48,O-33R/2-1,M	0.4
1875	Chi-n	42	208	44	49	5	3	0	12	0	0	.236	.236	.288	524	80	-4	6	2	-1	.821	-7	C-24,O-14R,2-13	-0.9
	Mut-n	15	64	12	25	5	0	0	10	0	1	.391	.391	.469	859	187	5	0	0	0	.739	-3	/C-8,2-6,O-3R,1-2	0.2
	Yr	57	272	56	74	10	3	0	22	0	1	.272	.272	.331	603	106	1	6	2	1	.802	-10	C-32,2-19,O-17R,/1	-0.7
1876	Har-N	67	314	59	102	**21**	2	0	35	2	7	.325	.331	.407	738	134	9				.869	-2	*O-59R,C-13/S-1,2-1	0.7
1878	Pro-N	62	281	**60**	90	**22**	1	1	29	5	16	.320	.332	.416	749	145	13				.811	3	*O-62(0-0-62)/C-1	1.5
1880	Tro-N	1	5	1	1	0	0	0	0	0	0	.200	.200	.200	400	34	-0				.000	-2	/O-1(0-0-1),C-1	-0.3
Total	5 n	242	1189	264	356	42	12	3	141	10	5	.299	.305	.362	668	108	10	18	15	-1	.837	-24	C-123,O-101R/2-55,13	-1.0
Total	3	130	600	120	193	43	3	1	64	7	23	.322	.331	.410	740	138	22				.834	-2	O-122R/C-15,2-1,S-1	1.9

■ JOHN HILAND
Hiland, John William b: 9/1860, Baltic, R.I. d: 4/10/01, Philadelphia, Pa. BL/TL, 5'8.5", 165 lbs. Deb: 8/20/1885

YEAR	TM/L	G	AB	R	H	2B	3B	HR	RBI	BB	SO	AVG	OBP	SLG	OPS	OPS+	BR+	SB	CS	SBR	FA	FR	G/POS	TPR
1885	Phi-N	3	9	0	0	0	0	0	0	0	4	.000	.000	.000	0	-99	-2				.833	-2	/2-3	-0.4

■ HILDEBRAND
Hildebrand Deb: 8/29/02

YEAR	TM/L	G	AB	R	H	2B	3B	HR	RBI	BB	SO	AVG	OBP	SLG	OPS	OPS+	BR+	SB	CS	SBR	FA	FR	G/POS	TPR
1902	Chi-N	1	4	1	0	0	0	0	0	1		.000	.200	.000	200	-39	-1	0			1.000	-0	/O-1(0-0-1)	-0.1

■ GEORGE HILDEBRAND
Hildebrand, George Albert b: 9/6/1878, San Francisco, Cal d: 5/30/60, Reseda, Cal. BR/TR, 5'8", 170 lbs. Deb: 4/17/02 U

YEAR	TM/L	G	AB	R	H	2B	3B	HR	RBI	BB	SO	AVG	OBP	SLG	OPS	OPS+	BR+	SB	CS	SBR	FA	FR	G/POS	TPR
1902	Bro-N	11	41	3	9	1	0	0	5	3		.220	.289	.244	533	64	-2	0			1.000	2	O-11(11-0-0)	0.0

■ PALMER HILDEBRAND
Hildebrand, Palmer Marion "Pete" b: 12/23/1884, Shauck, Ohio d: 1/25/60, N.Canton, Ohio BR/TR, 5'10", 170 lbs. Deb: 5/14/13

YEAR	TM/L	G	AB	R	H	2B	3B	HR	RBI	BB	SO	AVG	OBP	SLG	OPS	OPS+	BR+	SB	CS	SBR	FA	FR	G/POS	TPR
1913	StL-N	26	55	3	9	2	0	0	1	1	10	.164	.207	.200	407	17	-6	1			.968	0	C-22/O-1(1-0-0)	-0.5

■ BELDEN HILL
Hill, Belden L. b: 8/24/1864, Kewanee, Ill. d: 10/22/34, Cedar Rapids, Iowa BR/TR, 6', Deb: 8/27/1890

YEAR	TM/L	G	AB	R	H	2B	3B	HR	RBI	BB	SO	AVG	OBP	SLG	OPS	OPS+	BR+	SB	CS	SBR	FA	FR	G/POS	TPR
1890	Bal-a	9	30	3	5	2	0	0	2	3		.167	.306	.233	539	56	-2	6			.857	1	/3-9	0.0

■ DONNIE HILL
Hill, Donald Earl b: 11/12/60, Pomona, Cal. BB/TR, 5'10", 160 lbs. Deb: 7/25/83 Career OF: (0-LF 0-CF 1-RF)

YEAR	TM/L	G	AB	R	H	2B	3B	HR	RBI	BB	SO	AVG	OBP	SLG	OPS	OPS+	BR+	SB	CS	SBR	FA	FR	G/POS	TPR
1983	Oak-A	53	158	20	42	7	0	2	15	4	21	.266	.284	.348	632	77	-5	1	1	-0	.961	0	S-53	0.0
1984	Oak-A	73	174	21	40	6	0	2	16	5	12	.230	.251	.299	550	55	-11	1	1	-0	.949	-12	S-66/2-4,3-2,D-2	-1.7
1985	Oak-A	123	393	45	112	13	2	3	48	23	33	.285	.325	.351	676	92	-4	9	4	1	.973	-41	*2-122	-3.8
1986	Oak-A	108	339	37	96	16	2	4	29	23	38	.283	.329	.378	706	99	-1	5	2	0	.984	-12	2-68,3-33/S-2,D-3	-1.0
1987	Chi-A	111	410	57	98	14	6	9	46	30	35	.239	.293	.368	661	72	-17	1	0	0	.987	-29	2-84,3-32/D-1	-4.0
1988	Chi-A	83	221	17	48	6	1	2	20	26	32	.217	.300	.281	580	64	-10	3	1	0	.975	-11	2-59,3-12/D-5	-2.0
1990	Cal-A	103	352	36	93	18	2	3	32	29	27	.264	.322	.352	674	90	-5	1	2	-0	.990	3	2-60,S-24,3-21,/1PD	0.1
1991	Cal-A	77	209	36	50	8	1	1	20	30	21	.239	.335	.301	636	77	-5	1	0	0	.971	-3	2-39,S-29/1-3	-0.5
1992	Min-A	25	51	7	15	3	0	0	2	5	6	.294	.368	.353	721	100	0	0	0	0	.944	-3	S-10/2-7,3-5,O-1R	-0.2
Total	9	756	2307	276	594	91	14	26	228	175	225	.257	.311	.343	654	81	-58	22	11		.980	-107	2-443,S-184,3/D1OP	-13.1

■ GLENALLEN HILL
Hill, Glenallen b: 3/22/65, Santa Cruz, Cal. BR/TR, 6'2", 210 lbs. Deb: 9/1/89 Career OF: (336-LF 73-CF 452-RF)

YEAR	TM/L	G	AB	R	H	2B	3B	HR	RBI	BB	SO	AVG	OBP	SLG	OPS	OPS+	BR+	SB	CS	SBR	FA	FR	G/POS	TPR
1989	Tor-A	19	52	4	15	0	0	1	7	3	12	.288	.327	.346	673	92	-1	2	1	0	.964	-2	O-16(3-0-13)/D-3	-0.3
1990	Tor-A	84	260	47	60	11	3	12	32	18	62	.231	.281	.435	715	95	-3	8	3	1	.983	0	O-60(27-1-34),D-20	-0.4
1991	Tor-A	35	99	14	25	5	2	3	11	7	24	.253	.302	.434	736	97	-1	2	2	-0	.967	1	D-16,O-13(9-0-4)	-0.1
	Cle-A	37	122	15	32	3	0	5	14	16	30	.262	.348	.410	758	108	1	4	2	0	.978	-1	O-33(12-26-1)/D-1	0.0
	Yr	72	221	29	57	8	2	8	25	23	54	.258	.328	.421	749	103	1	6	4	-0	.975	-0	O-46(21-26-5),D-17	-0.1

YEAR	TM/L	G	AB	R	H	2B	3B	HR	RBI	BB	SO	AVG	OBP	SLG	OPS	OPS+	BR+	SB	CS	SBR	FA	FR	G/POS	TPR
1992	Cle-A	102	369	38	89	16	1	18	49	20	73	.241	.288	.436	724	102	-1	9	6	-0	.956	2	O-59(50-1-8),D-34	-0.2
1993	Cle-A	66	174	19	39	7	2	5	25	11	50	.224	.274	.374	648	73	-7	7	3	0	.940	-4	O-39(9-0-30),D-18	-1.3
	Chi-N	31	87	14	30	7	0	10	22	6	21	.345	.387	.770	1157	204	12	1	0	0	.957	1	O-21(18-0-4)	1.2
1994	Chi-N	89	269	48	80	12	1	10	38	29	57	.297	.366	.461	827	115	6	19	6	2	.987	-6	O-78(31-44-7)	0.2
1995	SF-N	132	497	71	131	29	4	24	86	39	98	.264	.318	.483	801	111	6	25	5	4	.959	-1	*O-125(0-1-124)	0.2
1996	SF-N	98	379	56	106	26	0	19	67	33	95	.280	.347	.499	846	125	12	6	3	0	.960	-2	O-98(0-0-98)	0.5
1997	*SF-N	128	398	47	104	28	4	11	64	19	87	.261	.302	.435	736	93	-6	7	4	0	.947	-6	O-97(0-0-97)/D-7	-1.6
1998	Sea-A	74	259	37	75	20	2	12	33	14	45	.290	.333	.521	855	118	6	1	1	-0	.965	-4	O-71(71-0-0)	-0.1
	*Chi-N	48	131	26	46	5	0	8	23	14	34	.351	.414	.573	986	151	10	0	0	0	.984	3	O-34(28-0-6)	1.1
1999	Chi-N	99	253	43	76	9	1	20	55	22	61	.300	.356	.581	937	134	12	5	1	1	.955	-6	O-62(37-0-26)/D-4	0.4
2000	Chi-N	64	168	23	44	4	1	11	29	10	43	.262	.303	.494	797	99	-1	0	1	-0	.955	1	O-29(29-0-0)/D-9	-0.2
	*NY-A	40	132	22	44	5	0	16	29	9	33	.333	.380	.735	1115	176	14	0	0	0	1.000	-1	D-24,O-12(12-0-0)	1.0
Total	12	1146	3649	524	996	187	21	185	584	270	825	.273	.326	.488	814	114	60	96	38	8	.964	-26	O-847R,D-136	0.4

■ HERMAN HILL Hill, Herman Alexander b: 10/12/45, Tuskegee, Ala. d: 12/14/70, Valencia, Venez. BL/TR, 6'2", 190 lbs. Deb: 9/2/69

YEAR	TM/L	G	AB	R	H	2B	3B	HR	RBI	BB	SO	AVG	OBP	SLG	OPS	OPS+	BR+	SB	CS	SBR	FA	FR	G/POS	TPR
1969	Min-A	16	2	4	0	0	0	0	0	0	1	.000	.000	.000	0	-98	-1	1	2	-0	.000	-1	/O-2(0-2-0)	-0.2
1970	Min-A	27	22	8	2	0	0	0	0	0	6	.091	.091	.091	182	-49	-4	0	0	0	1.000	-2	O-14(2-10-2)	-0.7
Total	2	43	24	12	2	0	0	0	0	0	7	.083	.083	.083	167	-53	-5	1	2	-0	1.000	-3	/O-16(2-12-2)	-0.9

■ HUGH HILL Hill, Hugh Ellis b: 7/21/1879, Ringgold, Ga. d: 9/6/58, Cincinnati, Ohio BL/TR, 5'11.5", 168 lbs. Deb: 5/1/03 F

YEAR	TM/L	G	AB	R	H	2B	3B	HR	RBI	BB	SO	AVG	OBP	SLG	OPS	OPS+	BR+	SB	CS	SBR	FA	FR	G/POS	TPR
1903	Cle-A	1	1	0	0	0	0	0	0	0		.000	.000	.000	0	-99	-0	0			.000	0	H	0.0
1904	StL-N	23	93	13	21	2	1	3	4	2		.226	.242	.366	608	91	-2	3			1.000	0	O-23(23-0-0)	-0.3
Total	2	24	94	13	21	2	1	3	4	2		.223	.240	.362	601	89	-2	3			1.000	0	/O-23(23-0-0)	-0.3

■ HUNTER HILL Hill, Hunter Benjamin b: 6/21/1879, Austin, Tex. d: 2/22/59, Austin, Tex. BR/TR, Deb: 7/1/03

YEAR	TM/L	G	AB	R	H	2B	3B	HR	RBI	BB	SO	AVG	OBP	SLG	OPS	OPS+	BR+	SB	CS	SBR	FA	FR	G/POS	TPR
1903	StL-A	86	317	30	77	11	3	0	25	8		.243	.264	.297	560	70	-12	2			.923	-1	3-86	-1.1
1904	StL-A	58	219	19	47	3	0	0	14	6		.215	.246	.228	474	54	-11	4			.826	-16	3-56/O-1(1-0-0)	-3.0
	Was-A	77	290	18	57	6	1	0	17	11		.197	.228	.224	453	44	-18	10			.895	-6	3-71/O-5(0-0-5)	-2.6
	Yr	135	509	37	104	9	1	0	31	17		.204	.236	.226	462	48	-30	14			.864	-23	*3-127/O-6(1-0-5)	-5.6
1905	Was-A	104	374	37	78	12	1	1	24	32		.209	.278	.254	532	72	-11	10			.908	-1	*3-103	-1.0
Total	3	325	1200	104	259	32	5	1	80	57		.216	.257	.253	510	62	-53	26			.895	-24	3-316/O-6(1-0-5)	-7.7

■ JESSE HILL Hill, Jesse Terrill b: 1/20/07, Yates, Mo. d: 8/31/93, Pasadena, Cal. BR/TR, 5'9", 165 lbs. Deb: 4/17/35

YEAR	TM/L	G	AB	R	H	2B	3B	HR	RBI	BB	SO	AVG	OBP	SLG	OPS	OPS+	BR+	SB	CS	SBR	FA	FR	G/POS	TPR
1935	NY-A	107	392	69	115	20	3	4	33	42	32	.293	.362	.390	752	100	0	14	4	2	.951	2	O-94(94-0-0)	-0.1
1936	Was-A	85	233	50	71	19	5	0	34	29	23	.305	.384	.429	813	106	3	11	0	2	.967	-8	O-60(54-4-2)	-0.5
1937	Was-A	33	92	24	20	2	1	1	4	13	16	.217	.314	.293	608	57	-6	2	0	0	.986	2	O-21(3-18-0)	-0.4
	Phi-A	70	242	32	71	12	3	1	37	31	20	.293	.374	.380	754	92	-2	16	3	2	.954	-5	O-68(3-65-0)	-0.6
	Yr	103	334	56	91	14	4	2	41	44	36	.272	.357	.356	713	82	-8	18	4	3	.964	-3	O-89(6-83-0)	-1.0
Total	3	295	959	175	277	53	12	6	108	115	91	.289	.366	.388	753	95	-5	43	8	7	.959	-8	O-243(154-87-2)	-1.6

■ MARC HILL Hill, Marc Kevin b: 2/18/52, Elsberry, Mo. BR/TR, 6'3", 210 lbs. Deb: 9/28/73 C

YEAR	TM/L	G	AB	R	H	2B	3B	HR	RBI	BB	SO	AVG	OBP	SLG	OPS	OPS+	BR+	SB	CS	SBR	FA	FR	G/POS	TPR
1973	StL-N	1	3	0	0	0	0	0	0	0	1	.000	.000	.000	0	-99	-1	0	0	0	1.000	0	/C-1	-0.1
1974	StL-N	10	21	2	5	1	0	0	2	4	5	.238	.360	.286	646	83	-0	0	0	0	1.000	3	/C-9	0.3
1975	SF-N	72	182	14	39	4	0	5	23	25	27	.214	.309	.319	628	71	-7	0	0	0	.994	1	C-60/3-1	-0.4
1976	SF-N	54	131	11	24	5	0	3	15	10	19	.183	.246	.290	537	50	-9	0	1	-0	.995	1	C-49/1-1	-0.7
1977	SF-N	108	320	28	80	10	0	9	50	34	34	.250	.322	.366	688	84	-7	0	1	-0	.989	-3	*C-102	-0.6
1978	SF-N	117	358	20	87	15	1	3	36	45	39	.243	.329	.316	645	84	-7	1	2	-0	.986	0	*C-116/1-2	-0.2
1979	SF-N	63	169	20	35	3	0	3	15	26	25	.207	.313	.278	591	67	-7	0	1	-0	.991	-6	C-58/1-1	-1.1
1980	SF-N	17	41	1	7	2	0	0	0	1	7	.171	.190	.220	410	14	-5	0	0	0	.972	2	C-14	-0.3
	Sea-A	29	70	8	16	2	1	2	9	3	10	.229	.260	.371	632	70	-3	0	0	0	.991	-0	C-29	-0.2
1981	Chi-A	16	6	0	0	0	0	0	0	0	1	.000	.000	.000	0	-99	-2	0	0	0	1.000	0	C-14/1-1,3-1	-0.1
1982	Chi-A	53	88	9	23	2	0	3	13	6	13	.261	.316	.386	702	92	-1	0	0	0	.993	6	C-49/1-1,3-1	0.5
1983	Chi-A	58	133	11	30	6	0	1	11	9	24	.226	.275	.293	568	54	-8	0	1	-0	.991	5	C-55/1-1,D-2	-0.2
1984	Chi-A	77	193	15	45	10	1	5	20	9	26	.233	.275	.373	648	74	-7	0	1	-0	.991	4	C-72/1-2	-0.1
1985	Chi-A	40	75	5	10	2	0	0	4	12	9	.133	.253	.160	413	16	-9	0	0	0	.985	9	C-37/3-1	0.1
1986	Chi-A	22	19	2	3	0	0	0	0	1	3	.158	.238	.158	396	10	-2	0	0	0	1.000	7	C-22	0.5
Total	14	737	1809	146	404	62	3	34	198	185	243	.223	.298	.317	615	69	-74	1	7	-2	.990	30	C-687/1-9,3-4,D-2	-2.6

■ OLIVER HILL Hill, Oliver Clinton b: 10/16/09, Powder Springs, Ga d: 9/20/70, Decatur, Ga. BL/TR, 5'11", 178 lbs. Deb: 4/19/39

YEAR	TM/L	G	AB	R	H	2B	3B	HR	RBI	BB	SO	AVG	OBP	SLG	OPS	OPS+	BR+	SB	CS	SBR	FA	FR	G/POS	TPR
1939	Bos-N	2	2	1	1	1	0	0	0	0	0	.500	.500	1.000	1500	317	1	0			.000	0	H	0.1

■ HOMER HILLEBRAND Hillebrand, Homer Hiller Henry b: 10/10/1879, Freeport, Ill. d: 1/20/74, Elsinore, Cal. BR/TL, 5'8", 165 lbs. Deb: 4/24/05 Career OF: (1-LF 0-CF 6-RF)

YEAR	TM/L	G	AB	R	H	2B	3B	HR	RBI	BB	SO	AVG	OBP	SLG	OPS	OPS+	BR+	SB	CS	SBR	FA	FR	G/POS	TPR
1905	Pit-N	39	110	9	26	3	2	0	7	6		.236	.282	.300	582	72	-4	1			.978	-3	1-16,P-10/O-7R,C-3	-0.6
1906	Pit-N	7	21	1	5	1	0	0	3	1		.238	.273	.286	558	71	-1	0			1.000	1	/P-7	0.0
1908	Pit-N	1	0	0	0	0	0	0	0	0		—	—	—	—	—	0	0			.000	-0	/P-1	0.0
Total	3	47	131	10	31	4	2	0	10	7		.237	.281	.298	578	71	-5	1			1.000	-1	/P-18,1-16,O-7R,C-3	-0.6

■ CHUCK HILLER Hiller, Charles Joseph b: 10/1/34, Johnsburg, Ill. BL/TR, 5'11", 170 lbs. Deb: 4/11/61 C Career OF: (12-LF 0-CF 1-RF)

YEAR	TM/L	G	AB	R	H	2B	3B	HR	RBI	BB	SO	AVG	OBP	SLG	OPS	OPS+	BR+	SB	CS	SBR	FA	FR	G/POS	TPR
1961	SF-N	70	240	38	57	12	1	2	12	32	30	.237	.330	.321	651	76	-7	4	4	-1	.973	-14	2-67	-1.7
1962	*SF-N	161	602	94	166	22	2	3	48	55	49	.276	.344	.334	678	84	-12	5	4	-0	.964	-18	*2-161	-1.6
1963	SF-N	111	417	44	93	10	2	6	33	20	23	.223	.262	.300	562	62	-21	3	2	-0	.963	-15	*2-109	-3.0
1964	SF-N	80	205	21	37	8	1	1	17	17	23	.180	.247	.244	491	38	-17	1	1	-0	.977	2	2-60/3-1	-1.1
1965	SF-N	7	7	1	1	0	0	1	1	0	1	.143	.143	.571	714	88	-0	0	0	0	1.000	-1	/2-2	-0.1
	NY-N	100	286	24	68	11	1	5	21	14	24	.238	.276	.336	611	74	-10	1	1	-0	.959	-12	2-80/O-4(3-0-1),3-2	-1.8
	Yr	107	293	25	69	11	1	6	22	14	25	.235	.273	.341	614	74	-11	1	1	-0	.959	-13	2-82/O-4(3-0-1),3-2	-1.9
1966	NY-N	108	254	25	71	8	2	2	14	15	22	.280	.332	.350	683	92	-2	0	0	0	.981	11	2-45,3-14/O-9(9-0-0)	1.1
1967	NY-N	25	54	0	5	3	0	0	3	2	11	.093	.125	.148	273	-22	-9	0	0	0	.968	2	2-14	-0.6
	Phi-N	31	43	4	13	1	0	0	2	2	4	.302	.333	.326	659	88	-1	0	2	-1	.947	-3	/2-6	-0.4
	Yr	56	97	4	18	4	0	0	5	4	15	.186	.218	.227	445	27	-9	0	2	-1	.963	-0	2-20	-1.0
1968	Pit-N	11	13	2	5	1	0	0	1	0	0	.385	.385	.462	846	155	1	0	0	0	.857	-0	/2-2	0.1
Total	8	704	2121	253	516	76	9	20	152	157	187	.243	.301	.316	617	72	-78	14	14	-2	.967	-49	2-546/3-17,O-13L	-9.1

■ HOB HILLER Hiller, Harvey Max b: 5/12/1893, E.Mauch Chunk, Pa. d: 12/27/56, Lehighton, Pa. BR/TR, 5'8", 162 lbs. Deb: 4/22/20 Career OF: (0-LF 0-CF 1-RF)

YEAR	TM/L	G	AB	R	H	2B	3B	HR	RBI	BB	SO	AVG	OBP	SLG	OPS	OPS+	BR+	SB	CS	SBR	FA	FR	G/POS	TPR
1920	Bos-A	17	29	4	5	1	1	0	2	2	5	.172	.226	.276	502	34	-3	0	3	-1	.905	1	/3-6,S-5,2-2,O-1R	-0.3
1921	Bos-A	1	1	0	0	0	0	0	0	0	0	.000	.000	.000	0	-99	-0	0	0	0	.000	0	H	0.0
Total	2	18	30	4	5	1	1	0	2	2	5	.167	.219	.267	485	29	-3	0	3	-1	.905	1	/3-6,S-5,2-2,O-1R	-0.3

■ ED HILLEY Hilley, Edward Garfield "Whitey" b: 6/17/1879, Cleveland, Ohio d: 11/14/56, Cleveland, Ohio BR/TR, 5'10.5", 170 lbs. Deb: 9/29/03

YEAR	TM/L	G	AB	R	H	2B	3B	HR	RBI	BB	SO	AVG	OBP	SLG	OPS	OPS+	BR+	SB	CS	SBR	FA	FR	G/POS	TPR
1903	Phi-A	1	3	1	1	0	0	0	0	1		.333	.500	.333	833	147	0	0			.800	-0	/3-1	0.0

■ MACK HILLIS Hillis, Malcolm David b: 7/23/01, Cambridge, Mass. d: 6/16/61, Cambridge, Mass. BR/TR, 5'10", 165 lbs. Deb: 9/13/24

YEAR	TM/L	G	AB	R	H	2B	3B	HR	RBI	BB	SO	AVG	OBP	SLG	OPS	OPS+	BR+	SB	CS	SBR	FA	FR	G/POS	TPR
1924	NY-A	1	1	1	0	0	0	0	0	0	0	.000	.000	.000	0	-99	-0	0	0	0	.000	0	/2-1	0.0
1928	Pit-N	11	36	6	9	2	3	1	7	0	6	.250	.250	.556	806	101	-0	1			.973	-1	/2-8,3-1	-0.1
Total	2	12	37	7	9	2	3	1	7	0	6	.243	.243	.541	784	96	-1	1	0		.973	-1	/2-9,3-1	-0.1

■ PAT HILLY Hilly, William Edward (b: William Edward Hilgerink) b: 2/24/1887, Fostoria, Ohio d: 7/25/53, Eureka, Mo. BR/TR, 5'11", 180 lbs. Deb: 5/7/14

YEAR	TM/L	G	AB	R	H	2B	3B	HR	RBI	BB	SO	AVG	OBP	SLG	OPS	OPS+	BR+	SB	CS	SBR	FA	FR	G/POS	TPR
1914	Phi-N	8	10	2	3	0	0	0	1	1	5	.300	.364	.300	664	92	-0	0			1.000	-1	/O-4(0-0-4)	-0.1

■ CHARLIE HILSEY Hilsey, Charles T. b: 3/23/1864, Philadelphia, Pa. d: 10/31/18, Philadelphia, Pa. 5'7", 180 lbs. Deb: 9/27/1883

YEAR	TM/L	G	AB	R	H	2B	3B	HR	RBI	BB	SO	AVG	OBP	SLG	OPS	OPS+	BR+	SB	CS	SBR	FA	FR	G/POS	TPR
1883	Phi-N	3	10	0	1	0	0	0	1	0	4	.100	.100	.100	200	-43	-2				.714	-0	/P-3	0.0
1884	Phi-a	6	24	5	5	1	1	0		0		.208	.208	.333	542	69	-1				.250	-0	/O-3(1-2-0),P-3	-0.1
Total	2	9	34	5	6	1	1	0	1	0	4	.176	.176	.265	441	38	-2				.824	-1	/P-6,O-3(1-2-0)	-0.1

YEAR	TM/L	G	AB	R	H	2B	3B	HR	RBI	BB	SO	AVG	OBP	SLG	OPS	OPS+	BR+	SB	CS	SBR	FA	FR	G/POS	TPR
■ **DAVE HILTON**	Hilton, John David b: 9/15/50, Uvalde, Tex. BR/TR, 5'11", 191 lbs. Deb: 9/10/72 C																							
1972	SD-N	13	47	2	10	2	1	0	5	3	6	.213	.260	.298	558	63	-2	1	0	0	.939	-3	3-13	-0.5
1973	SD-N	70	234	21	46	9	0	5	16	19	35	.197	.260	.299	559	59	-14	2	1	0	.970	-4	3-47,2-23	-1.7
1974	SD-N	74	217	17	52	8	2	1	12	13	28	.240	.283	.309	591	68	-10	3	5	-1	.948	-5	3-55,2-15	-1.6
1975	SD-N	4	8	0	0	0	0	0	0	0	0	.000	.000	.000	0	-99	-2	0	0	0	.900	1	/3-4	-0.1
Total	4	161	506	40	108	19	3	6	33	35	69	.213	.266	.298	564	61	-28	6	6	-1	.954	-11	3-119/2-38	-3.9
■ **JACK HIMES**	Himes, John Herb b: 9/22/1878, Bryan, Ohio d: 12/16/49, Joliet, Ill. BL/TR, 6'2", 180 lbs. Deb: 9/18/05																							
1905	StL-N	12	41	3	6	0	0	0	0	1		.146	.167	.146	313	-7	-5	0			1.000	-1	O-11(1-0-11)	-0.7
1906	StL-N	40	155	10	42	5	2	0	14	7		.271	.307	.329	636	102	-0	4			.977	5	O-40(0-32-8)	0.3
Total	2	52	196	13	48	5	2	0	14	8		.245	.278	.291	569	79	-5	4			.981	4	/O-51(1-32-19)	-0.4
■ **A.J. HINCH**	Hinch, Andrew Jay b: 5/15/74, Waverly, Iowa BR/TR, 6'1", 195 lbs. Deb: 4/1/98																							
1998	Oak-A	120	337	34	78	10	0	9	35	30	89	.231	.302	.341	643	69	-16	3	0	1	.986	-6	*C-118	-1.4
1999	Oak-A	76	205	26	44	4	1	7	24	11	41	.215	.261	.346	608	56	-14	6	2	1	.987	-2	C-73	-1.1
2000	Oak-A	6	8	1	2	0	0	0	0	1	1	.250	.333	.250	583	52	-1	0	0	0	.900	-1	/C-5,D-1	-0.1
Total	3	202	550	61	124	14	1	16	59	42	131	.225	.288	.342	629	64	-30	9	2	1	.986	-10	C-196/D-1	-2.6
■ **HARRY HINCHMAN**	Hinchman, Harry Sibley b: 8/4/1878, Philadelphia, Pa. d: 1/19/33, Toledo, Ohio BB/TR, 5'11", 165 lbs. Deb: 7/29/07 F																							
1907	Cle-A	15	51	3	11	3	1	0	9	5		.216	.286	.314	599	90	-1	2			.904	4	2-15	0.4
■ **BILL HINCHMAN**	Hinchman, William White b: 4/4/1883, Philadelphia, Pa. d: 2/20/63, Columbus, Ohio BR/TR, 5'11", 190 lbs. Deb: 9/24/05 FC Career OF: (330-LF 61-CF 357-RF)																							
1905	Cin-N	17	51	10	13	4	1	0	10	13		.255	.415	.373	788	122	2	4			.905	-3	O-12(12-0-0)/3-4,1-1	-0.1
1906	Cin-N	18	54	7	11	1	1	0	1	8		.204	.306	.259	566	73	-1	2			.963	1	O-16(8-0-8)	-0.2
1907	Cle-A	152	514	62	117	19	9	1	50	47		.228	.311	.305	616	96	-1	15			.958	-5	*O-148L/1-4,2-1	-1.6
1908	Cle-A	137	464	55	107	23	8	6	59	38		.231	.301	.353	655	112	6	9			.975	-6	O-75R,S-51/1-4	-0.2
1909	Cle-A	139	457	57	118	20	13	2	53	41		.258	.331	.372	703	117	9	22			.918	1	*O-131(87-38-6)/S-6	0.4
1915	Pit-N	156	577	72	177	33	14	5	77	48	75	.307	.368	.438	807	146	31	17	17	-2	.969	3	*O-156(6-0-151)	2.6
1916	Pit-N	152	555	64	175	18	**16**	4	76	54	61	.315	.378	.427	805	146	30	10			.962	-4	*O-124(23-0-101),1-31	2.2
1917	Pit-N	69	244	27	46	5	5	2	29	33	27	.189	.288	.275	562	71	-8	5			.945	-1	O-48(41-8-0),1-20	-1.4
1918	Pit-N	50	111	10	26	5	2	0	13	15	8	.234	.336	.315	651	96	0	1			1.000	-4	O-40(2-0-32)/1-3	-0.6
1920	Pit-N	18	16	0	3	0	0	0	1	1	3	.188	.278	.188	465	34	-1	0	0	0	.000	0	H	-0.1
Total	10	908	3043	364	793	128	69	20	369	298	174	.261	.336	.368	704	118	67	85	17		.954	-17	O-750R/1-63,S-57,32	1.0
■ **HUNKEY HINES**	Hines, Henry Fred b: 9/29/1867, Elgin, Ill. d: 1/2/28, Rockford, Ill. BR/TR, 5'7", 165 lbs. Deb: 5/16/1895																							
1895	Bro-N	2	8	3	2	0	0	0	1	2	0	.250	.400	.250	650	76	-0	0			1.000	0	/O-2(0-0-2)	0.0
■ **MIKE HINES**	Hines, Michael P. b: 9/1862, Ireland d: 3/14/10, New Bedford, Mass. BR/TL, 5'10", 176 lbs. Deb: 5/1/1883																							
1883	Bos-N	63	231	38	52	13	1	0	16	7	36	.225	.248	.290	538	61	-11				.887	8	C-59/O-7(0-2-5)	0.2
1884	Bos-N	35	132	16	23	3	0	0	3	3	24	.174	.193	.197	390	23	-11				.919	6	C-35	-0.2
1885	Bos-N	14	56	11	13	4	0	0	4	4	5	.232	.283	.304	587	93	-0				.857	-3	O-14(0-0-14)	-0.3
	Bro-a	3	13	1	1	0	1	0	1	0		.077	.077	.231	308	-6	-2				1.000	-1	/C-3	-0.2
	Pro-N	1	3	0	0	0	0	0	0	0	2	.000	.000	.000	0	-99	-1				.636	-0	/C-1	-0.1
1888	Bos-N	4	16	3	2	0	1	0	2	2	0	.125	.222	.250	472	49	-1	0			1.000	-0	/O-3(2-0-1),C-1	-0.1
Total	4	120	451	69	91	20	3	0	26	16	67	.202	.229	.259	489	51	-25	0			.896	9	/C-99,O-24(2-2-20)	-0.7
■ **PAUL HINES**	Hines, Paul A. b: 3/1/1852, Washington, D.C. d: 7/10/35, Hyattsville, Md. BR/TR, 5'9.5", 173 lbs. Deb: 4/20/1872 NA OF: (41-LF 85-CF 0-RF) Career OF: (27-LF 1218-CF 7-RF)																							
1872	Nat-n	11	49	9	12	1	0	0	5	0	0	.245	.245	.265	510	49	-4	0	0	0	.862	-3	/1-9,3-2,C-1	-0.5
1873	Was-n	39	181	33	60	6	3	1	29	1	1	.331	.335	.414	750	125	6	0	1	-0	.798	-0	*O-36(36-0-0)/2-2,C-1	0.4
1874	Chi-n	59	271	47	80	10	2	0	34	4	4	.295	.305	.347	652	108	2	4	1		.877	5	*O-50C,2-11/S-2	0.6
1875	Chi-n	69	308	45	101	14	4	0	36	1	0	.328	.330	.399	729	151	15	6	9	-2	.889	9	O-39C,2-30/C-1,S-1	1.7
1876	Chi-N	64	306	62	101	**21**	3	2	59	1	3	.330	.333	.439	773	139	10				**.923**	5	*O-64(0-64-0)/2-1	1.1
1877	Chi-N	60	261	44	73	11	7	0	23	1	8	.280	.282	.375	658	94	-3				.806	-10	*O-49(24-18-7),2-11	-1.3
1878	Pro-N	62	257	42	92	13	4	**4**	**50**	2	10	.358	.363	**.486**	**849**	178	20				.849	3	*O-61(0-61-0)/S-1	1.9
1879	Pro-N	85	409	81	**146**	25	10	2	52	8	16	.357	.369	.482	851	181	**34**				.867	7	*O-85(0-85-0)	3.4
1880	Pro-N	85	374	64	115	20	2	3	35	13	17	.307	.331	.396	726	150	19				**.927**	8	*O-75(0-75-0)/2-6,1-4	2.3
1881	Pro-N	80	361	65	103	**27**	5	2	31	13	12	.285	.310	.404	715	125	10				.897	-1	*O-78(0-78-0)/2-4,1-1	0.5
1882	Pro-N	84	379	73	117	28	10	4	34	10	14	.309	.326	.467	793	151	21				.861	1	*O-82(0-82-0)/1-2	1.6
1883	Pro-N	97	442	94	132	32	4	4	45	18	23	.299	.326	.416	742	120	10				.905	7	*O-89(0-89-0)/1-9	1.1
1884	*Pro-N	114	490	94	148	**36**	10	3	41	44	28	.302	.360	.435	794	151	30				.895	2	*O-108C/1-7,P-1	2.4
1885	Pro-N	98	411	63	111	20	4	1	35	19	18	.270	.302	.345	648	112	6				.865	4	*O-92C/1-4,S-1,32	0.6
1886	Was-N	121	487	80	152	30	8	9	56	35	21	.312	.358	.462	820	157	33	21			.899	3	*O-92C,3-15,1-10,/S2	3.0
1887	Was-N	123	526	83	195	32	5	10	72	48	24	.371	.380	.458	838	139	27	46			.886	-14	*O-109C/1-7,2-5,S-4	0.8
1888	Ind-N	133	513	84	144	26	3	4	58	41	45	.281	.343	.366	710	124	15	31			.912	-7	*O-125C/1-6,S-2	0.3
1889	Ind-N	121	486	77	148	27	1	6	72	49	22	.305	.374	.401	775	114	10	34			.964	4	*1-109,O-12(0-12-0)	0.2
1890	Pit-N	31	121	11	22	1	0	0	9	11	7	.182	.256	.190	446	34	-9	6			.973	2	1-17,O-14(0-14-0)	-0.8
	Bos-N	69	273	41	72	12	3	2	48	32	20	.264	.350	.352	701	97	-1	9			.881	-12	O-69(2-68-0)/1-1	-1.4
	Yr	100	394	52	94	13	3	2	57	43	27	.239	.321	.302	623	80	-9	15			.871	-10	O-83(2-82-0),1-18	-2.2
1891	Was-a	54	206	25	58	7	5	0	31	21	16	.282	.376	.364	740	117	6	6			.856	-3	O-47(0-47-0)/1-8	0.0
Total	4 n	178	809	134	253	31	9	1	104	6	5	.313	.318	.377	695	123	19	10	11	-2	.857	11	O-125C/2-43,1-9,SC3	2.2
Total	16	1481	6302	1083	1929	368	84	56	751	366	304	.306	.343	.413	756	132	237	153			.887	-3	*O-1251C,1-185/23SP	15.7
■ **GORDIE HINKLE**	Hinkle, Daniel Gordon b: 4/3/05, Toronto, Ohio d: 3/19/72, Houston, Tex. BR/TR, 6', 185 lbs. Deb: 4/19/34																							
1934	Bos-A	27	75	7	13	6	1	0	9	7	23	.173	.244	.280	524	33	-8	0	0	0	.992	4	C-26	-0.2
■ **GEORGE HINSHAW**	Hinshaw, George Addison b: 10/23/59, Los Angeles, Cal. BR/TR, 6', 185 lbs. Deb: 9/19/82																							
1982	SD-N	6	15	1	4	0	0	0	1	3	5	.267	.389	.267	656	91	0	0	0	0	1.000	0	/O-6(1-0-5)	0.0
1983	SD-N	7	16	1	7	1	0	0	4	0	4	.438	.438	.500	938	165	1	1	0	0	1.000	-0	/3-5	0.1
Total	2	13	31	2	11	1	0	0	5	3	9	.355	.412	.387	799	129	1	1	0	0	1.000	0	/O-6(1-0-5),3-5	0.1
■ **PAUL HINSON**	Hinson, James Paul b: 5/9/04, Vanleer, Tenn. d: 9/23/60, Muskogee, Okla. BR/TR, 5'10", 150 lbs. Deb: 4/19/28																							
1928	Bos-A	3	0	1	0	0	0	0	0	0	0	—	—	—	—	—	0	0	0	0	.000	0	R	0.0
■ **CHUCK HINTON**	Hinton, Charles Edward b: 5/3/34, Rocky Mount, N.C. BR/TR, 6'1", 197 lbs. Deb: 5/14/61 Career OF: (525-LF 201-CF 299-RF)																							
1961	Was-A	106	339	51	88	13	5	6	34	40	81	.260	.339	.381	720	93	-3	22	5	3	.963	0	O-92(72-2-20)	-0.5
1962	Was-A	151	542	73	168	25	6	17	75	47	66	.310	.365	.472	837	124	18	28	10	3	.988	-10	*O-136R,2-12/S-1	0.4
1963	Was-A	150	566	80	152	20	12	15	55	64	79	.269	.344	.426	770	115	11	25	9	2	.989	-1	*O-125L,3-19/1-6,S	0.5
1964	Was-A★	138	514	71	141	25	7	11	53	57	77	.274	.348	.414	762	112	8	17	6	2	.985	10	*O-131(131-1-1)/3-2	1.3
1965	Cle-A	133	431	59	110	17	6	18	54	53	65	.255	.338	.448	786	120	11	17	3	3	.966	-9	O-72C,1-40,2-23,/3	0.2
1966	Cle-A	123	348	46	89	9	3	12	50	35	66	.256	.326	.402	728	108	3	10	6	0	.973	-8	*O-104C/1-6,2-2	-0.9
1967	Cle-A	147	498	55	122	19	3	10	37	43	100	.245	.306	.355	662	94	-4	6	8	-1	.976	-13	*O-136(26-53-92)/2-5	-2.7
1968	Cal-A	116	267	28	52	10	3	7	23	24	61	.195	.261	.333	595	82	-6	3	1	0	.987	-6	1-48,O-37R,3-13,/2	-1.7
1969	Cle-A	94	121	18	31	3	2	3	19	8	22	.256	.308	.388	696	91	-2	2	0	0	.941	-10	O-40(28-4-9),3-14	-1.2
1970	Cle-A	107	195	24	62	4	0	9	29	25	34	.318	.395	.477	872	133	9	0	2	-1	.994	-6	1-40,O-35R/C-4,23	0.0
1971	Cle-A	88	147	13	33	7	0	5	14	20	34	.224	.317	.374	692	87	-2	0	0	0	1.000	-7	1-20,O-20(15-0-5)/C-5	-1.2
Total	11	1353	3968	518	1048	152	47	113	443	416	685	.264	.335	.412	747	108	45	130	50	11	.979	-59	O-928L,1-160/23CS	-5.8
■ **JOHN HINTON**	Hinton, John Robert "Red" b: 6/20/1876, Pittsburgh, Pa. d: 7/19/20, Braddock, Pa. BR/TR, 6', 200 lbs. Deb: 6/3/01																							
1901	Bos-N	4	13	0	1	0	0	0	0	2		.077	.200	.077	277	-17	-2	0			.750	-2	/3-4	-0.4

■ TOMMY HINZO
Hinzo, Thomas Lee b: 6/18/64, San Diego, Cal. BB/TR, 5'10", 170 lbs. Deb: 7/16/87

YEAR	TM/L	G	AB	R	H	2B	3B	HR	RBI	BB	SO	AVG	OBP	SLG	OPS	OPS+	BR+	SB	CS	SBR	FA	FR	G/POS	TPR
1987	Cle-A	67	257	31	68	9	3	3	21	10	47	.265	.297	.358	655	72	-10	9	4	1	.973	-4	2-67	-1.0
1989	Cle-A	18	17	4	0	0	0	0	0	2	6	.000	.105	.000	105	-67	-4	1	2	-0	.867	0	/2-6,S-1,D-1	-0.4
Total	2	85	274	35	68	9	3	3	21	12	53	.248	.285	.336	620	64	-14	10	6	0	.968	-4	/2-73,D-1,S-1	-1.4

■ GENE HISER
Hiser, Gene Taylor b: 12/11/48, Baltimore, Md. BL/TL, 5'11", 175 lbs. Deb: 8/20/71

YEAR	TM/L	G	AB	R	H	2B	3B	HR	RBI	BB	SO	AVG	OBP	SLG	OPS	OPS+	BR+	SB	CS	SBR	FA	FR	G/POS	TPR
1971	Chi-N	17	29	4	6	0	0	0	1	4	8	.207	.303	.207	510	41	-2	1	0	0	1.000	-0	/O-9(0-4-5)	-0.2
1972	Chi-N	32	46	2	9	0	0	0	4	6	8	.196	.288	.196	484	36	-4	1	0	0	1.000	-0	O-15(4-2-9)	-0.4
1973	Chi-N	100	109	15	19	3	0	1	6	11	17	.174	.256	.229	486	33	-10	4	5	-1	.980	-18	O-64(25-22-18)	-3.1
1974	Chi-N	12	17	2	4	1	0	0	1	0	3	.235	.235	.294	529	46	-1	0	0	0	1.000	-2	/O-8(6-1-1)	-0.3
1975	Chi-N	45	62	11	15	3	0	0	6	11	7	.242	.356	.290	646	77	-1	0	1	-0	1.000	-3	O-18(7-6-5)/1-1	-0.5
Total	5	206	263	34	53	7	0	1	18	32	43	.202	.291	.240	530	46	-18	6	6	-1	.992	-22	O-114(42-35-38)/1-1	-4.5

■ LARRY HISLE
Hisle, Larry Eugene b: 5/5/47, Portsmouth, Ohio BR/TR, 6'2", 195 lbs. Deb: 4/10/68 C Career OF: (460-LF 502-CF 99-RF)

YEAR	TM/L	G	AB	R	H	2B	3B	HR	RBI	BB	SO	AVG	OBP	SLG	OPS	OPS+	BR+	SB	CS	SBR	FA	FR	G/POS	TPR
1968	Phi-N	7	11	1	4	1	0	0	1	1	4	.364	.417	.455	871	161	1	0	0	0	1.000	-1	/O-6(0-6-0)	0.0
1969	Phi-N	145	482	75	128	23	5	20	56	48	152	.266	.338	.459	797	125	15	18	8	1	.977	11	*O-140(1-139-0)	2.4
1970	Phi-N	126	405	52	83	22	4	10	44	53	139	.205	.302	.353	655	77	-14	5	5	-1	.978	5	*O-121(0-86-36)	-1.3
1971	Phi-N	36	76	7	15	3	0	0	3	6	22	.197	.256	.237	493	40	-6	1	0	0	.962	-0	O-27(19-8-0)	-0.7
1973	Min-A	143	545	88	148	25	6	15	64	64	128	.272	.352	.422	774	113	10	11	4	1	.975	6	*O-143(49-93-3)	1.2
1974	Min-A	143	510	68	146	20	7	19	79	48	112	.286	.357	.465	822	131	20	12	6	0	.979	-8	*O-137(74-52-26)	0.6
1975	Min-A	80	255	37	80	9	2	11	51	27	39	.314	.382	.494	876	144	15	17	3	3	.976	-7	O-58(37-26-9),D-14	0.7
1976	Min-A	155	581	81	158	19	5	14	96	56	93	.272	.340	.394	734	112	9	31	18	1	.984	14	*O-154(135-5-18)	1.5
1977	Min-A★	141	546	95	165	36	3	28	**119**	56	106	.302	.373	.533	906	146	34	21	10	1	.974	1	*O-134(68-65-6)/D-6	3.1
1978	Mil-A★	142	520	96	151	24	0	34	115	67	90	.290	.377	.533	909	153	36	10	6	0	.978	-2	O-87(67-22-1),D-51	3.0
1979	Mil-A	26	96	18	27	7	0	3	14	11	19	.281	.355	.448	803	115	2	1	0	0	1.000	1	D-15,O-10(10-0-0)	0.2
1980	Mil-A	17	60	16	17	0	0	6	16	14	7	.283	.427	.583	1010	180	7	1	1	-0	.000	0	D-17	0.6
1981	Mil-A	27	87	11	20	4	0	4	11	6	17	.230	.295	.414	709	108	1	0	0	0	.000	0	D-24	0.0
1982	Mil-A	9	31	7	4	0	0	2	5	5	13	.129	.250	.323	573	60	-2	0	0	0	.000	0	/D-8	-0.2
Total	14	1197	4205	652	1146	193	32	166	674	462	941	.273	.350	.452	802	123	126	128	61	7	.978	19	*O-1017C,D-135	11.1

■ JIM HITCHCOCK
Hitchcock, James Franklin b: 6/28/11, Inverness, Ala. d: 6/23/59, Montgomery, Ala. BR/TR, 5'11", 175 lbs. Deb: 8/24/38 F

YEAR	TM/L	G	AB	R	H	2B	3B	HR	RBI	BB	SO	AVG	OBP	SLG	OPS	OPS+	BR+	SB	CS	SBR	FA	FR	G/POS	TPR
1938	Bos-N	28	76	2	13	0	0	0	7	2	11	.171	.192	.171	363	1	-10	1			.881	-2	S-24/3-2	-1.1

■ BILLY HITCHCOCK
Hitchcock, William Clyde b: 7/31/16, Inverness, Ala. BR/TR, 6'1.5", 185 lbs. Deb: 4/14/42 FMC

YEAR	TM/L	G	AB	R	H	2B	3B	HR	RBI	BB	SO	AVG	OBP	SLG	OPS	OPS+	BR+	SB	CS	SBR	FA	FR	G/POS	TPR
1942	Det-A	85	280	27	59	8	1	0	29	26	21	.211	.280	.246	527	45	-20	2	2	-0	.944	-3	S-80/3-1	-1.8
1946	Det-A	3	3	0	0	0	0	0	0	1	0	.000	.250	.000	250	-25	-0	0	0	0	1.000	0	/2-1	0.0
	Was-A	98	354	27	75	8	3	0	25	26	52	.212	.268	.251	519	48	-25	2	4	-1	.966	-4	S-53,3-46	-2.8
	Yr	101	357	27	75	8	3	0	25	27	52	.210	.268	.249	517	48	-25	2	4	-1	.966	-3	S-53,3-46/2-1	-2.8
1947	StL-A	80	275	25	61	2	2	1	28	21	34	.222	.277	.255	532	47	-19	3	0	1	.977	11	2-46,3-17/S-7,1-5	-0.5
1948	Bos-A	49	124	15	37	3	2	1	20	7	9	.298	.341	.379	720	87	-2	0	0	0	.951	6	2-15,3-15	0.4
1949	Bos-A	55	147	22	30	6	1	0	9	17	11	.204	.291	.259	549	43	-12	2	3	-1	.993	-8	1-29/2-8	-2.1
1950	Phi-A	115	399	35	109	22	5	1	54	45	32	.273	.347	.361	708	83	-10	3	1	0	.967	-3	*2-107/S-1	-0.6
1951	Phi-A	77	222	27	68	10	4	1	36	21	23	.306	.371	.401	772	107	2	2	0	0	.929	7	3-45,2-23/1-1	1.1
1952	Phi-A	119	407	45	100	8	4	1	56	39	45	.246	.318	.292	610	66	-17	1	1	-0	.942	-1	*3-104,1-13	-2.0
1953	Det-A	22	38	8	8	0	0	0	0	3	3	.211	.268	.211	479	31	-4	0	0	0	.929	0	3-12/2-1,S-1	-0.3
Total	9	703	2249	231	547	67	22	5	257	206	230	.243	.310	.299	609	65	-108	15	11	-1	.938	7	3-240,2-201,S-142,/1	-8.6

■ MYRIL HOAG
Hoag, Myril Oliver b: 3/9/08, Davis, Cal. d: 7/28/71, High Springs, Fla BR/TR, 5'11", 180 lbs. Deb: 4/15/31 Career OF: (254-LF 334-CF 322-RF)

YEAR	TM/L	G	AB	R	H	2B	3B	HR	RBI	BB	SO	AVG	OBP	SLG	OPS	OPS+	BR+	SB	CS	SBR	FA	FR	G/POS	TPR
1931	NY-A	44	28	6	4	2	0	0	3	1	8	.143	.172	.214	387	1	-4	0	0	0	1.000	-7	O-23(11-2-10)/3-1	-1.0
1932	*NY-A	46	54	18	20	5	0	1	7	7	13	.370	.443	.519	961	156	5	1	1	-0	.962	-10	O-35(27-2-9)/1-1	-0.6
1934	NY-A	97	251	45	67	8	2	3	34	21	21	.267	.324	.351	674	79	-8	1	3	-1	.974	-9	O-86(29-17-50)	-1.9
1935	NY-A	48	110	13	28	4	1	1	13	12	19	.255	.328	.336	664	76	-4	4	2	0	.986	-2	O-37(2-3-32)/3-1	-0.6
1936	NY-A	45	156	23	47	9	4	3	34	7	16	.301	.343	.468	811	102	-0	3	1	0	.955	-4	O-39(2-26-12)	-0.5
1937	*NY-A	106	362	48	109	19	8	3	46	33	33	.301	.364	.423	787	97	-2	4	7	-2	.955	-6	O-99(24-9-70)	-1.3
1938	*NY-A	85	267	28	74	14	3	0	48	25	31	.277	.344	.352	696	75	-10	4	3	-0	.965	-4	O-70(31-13-28)	-1.7
1939	StL-A★	129	482	58	142	23	4	10	75	24	35	.295	.329	.421	751	89	-10	9	5	0	.971	-8	*O-117(11-49-60)/P-1	-2.1
1940	StL-A	76	191	20	50	11	0	3	26	13	30	.262	.309	.366	675	73	-8	2	0	0	.971	-6	O-46(1-1-44)	-1.5
1941	StL-A	1	1	0	0	0	0	0	0	0	0	.000	.000	.000	0	-97	-0	0	0	0	.000	0	H	0.0
	Chi-A	106	380	30	97	13	3	1	44	27	29	.255	.306	.313	620	65	-19	6	10	-2	.957	-6	O-99(75-25-0)	-3.1
	Yr	107	381	30	97	13	3	1	44	27	29	.255	.306	.312	618	65	-20	6	10	-2	.957	-6	O-99(75-25-0)	-3.1
1942	Chi-A	113	412	47	99	18	2	2	37	36	21	.240	.301	.308	610	73	-15	17	8	1	.972	-4	*O-112(41-81-0)	-2.3
1944	Chi-A	17	48	5	11	1	0	0	4	10	1	.229	.362	.250	612	77	-1	1	3	-1	.969	-1	O-14(0-13-1)	-0.3
	Cle-A	67	277	33	79	9	3	1	27	25	23	.285	.347	.350	697	103	1	6	4	-0	.947	-1	O-66(0-66-0)	-0.2
	Yr	84	325	38	90	10	3	1	31	35	24	.277	.349	.335	684	99	0	7	7	-1	.950	-2	O-80(0-79-1)	-0.5
1945	Cle-A	40	128	10	27	5	3	0	3	11	18	.211	.279	.297	575	70	-5	1	2	-0	.987	0	O-33(0-27-6)/P-2	-0.7
Total	13	1020	3147	384	854	141	33	28	401	252	298	.271	.328	.364	692	83	-80	59	49	-4	.965	-67	O-876C/P-3,3-2,1-1	-17.8

■ DON HOAK
Hoak, Donald Albert "Tiger" b: 2/5/28, Roulette, Pa. d: 10/9/69, Pittsburgh, Pa. BR/TR, 6', 175 lbs. Deb: 4/18/54 C

YEAR	TM/L	G	AB	R	H	2B	3B	HR	RBI	BB	SO	AVG	OBP	SLG	OPS	OPS+	BR+	SB	CS	SBR	FA	FR	G/POS	TPR
1954	Bro-N	88	261	41	64	9	5	7	26	25	39	.245	.321	.398	719	83	-7	8	3	1	.950	4	3-75	-0.2
1955	*Bro-N	94	279	50	67	13	3	5	19	46	50	.240	.350	.362	712	87	-4	9	5	0	.960	17	3-78	1.3
1956	Chi-N	121	424	51	91	18	4	5	37	41	46	.215	.285	.311	597	61	-23	8	3	1	.949	-18	*3-110	-4.3
1957	Cin-N★	149	529	78	155	**39**	2	19	89	74	54	.293	.384	.482	866	122	18	8	15	-3	**.971**	-0	*3-149/2-1	1.4
1958	Cin-N	114	417	51	109	30	0	6	50	43	36	.261	.333	.376	710	83	-9	6	8	-1	.964	4	*3-112/S-1	-0.8
1959	Pit-N	155	564	60	166	29	3	8	65	71	75	.294	.377	.399	776	108	9	9	2	1	.961	9	*3-155	1.9
1960	*Pit-N	155	553	97	156	24	9	16	79	74	74	.282	.368	.445	813	120	17	3	2	-0	.948	4	*3-155	2.1
1961	Pit-N	145	503	72	150	27	7	12	61	73	53	.298	.390	.451	842	122	18	4	2	0	.953	-3	*3-143	1.4
1962	Pit-N	121	411	63	99	14	8	5	48	49	49	.241	.323	.350	674	81	-11	4	2	0	**.969**	-3	*3-116	-1.4
1963	Phi-N	115	377	35	87	11	3	6	24	27	52	.231	.284	.324	608	75	-12	5	5	-1	.958	6	*3-106	-0.7
1964	Phi-N	6	4	0	0	0	0	0	0	0	2	.000	.000	.000	0	-99	-1	0	0	0	.000	0	H	-0.1
Total	11	1263	4322	598	1144	214	44	89	498	523	530	.265	.347	.396	743	98	-5	64	47	-2	.959	20	*3-1199/S-1,2-1	0.6

■ BILL HOBBS
Hobbs, William Lee "Smokey" b: 5/7/1893, Grants Lick, Ky. d: 1/5/45, Hamilton, Ohio BR/TR, 5'9.5", 155 lbs. Deb: 8/9/13

YEAR	TM/L	G	AB	R	H	2B	3B	HR	RBI	BB	SO	AVG	OBP	SLG	OPS	OPS+	BR+	SB	CS	SBR	FA	FR	G/POS	TPR
1913	Cin-N	4	4	0	0	0	0	0	0	0	3	.000	.000	.000	0	-99	-1	0			1.000	1	/2-1,3-1	0.0
1916	Cin-N	6	11	1	2	1	0	0	1	2	0	.182	.308	.273	580	81	-0	1			.947	6	/S-6	0.6
Total	2	10	15	1	2	1	0	0	1	2	3	.133	.235	.200	435	32	-1	1			.947	6	/S-6,3-1,2-1	0.6

■ DICK HOBLITZEL
Hoblitzel, Richard Carleton "Doc" (b: Richard Carleton Hoblitzell)
b: 10/26/1888, Waverly, W.Va. d: 11/14/62, Parkersburg, W.Va. BL/TL, 6', 172 lbs. Deb: 9/5/08

YEAR	TM/L	G	AB	R	H	2B	3B	HR	RBI	BB	SO	AVG	OBP	SLG	OPS	OPS+	BR+	SB	CS	SBR	FA	FR	G/POS	TPR
1908	Cin-N	32	114	8	29	3	2	0	8	7		.254	.309	.316	625	102	0	2			.985	2	1-32	0.1
1909	Cin-N	142	517	59	159	23	11	4	67	44		.308	.364	.418	782	144	25	17			.982	-3	*1-142	2.1
1910	Cin-N	155	611	85	170	24	13	4	70	47	32	.278	.332	.380	712	112	7	28			.984	-8	*1-148/2-7	-0.3
1911	Cin-N	158	622	81	180	19	13	11	91	42	44	.289	.342	.415	757	116	10	32			.990	2	*1-158	0.8
1912	Cin-N	148	558	73	164	32	12	2	85	48	28	.294	.352	.405	757	110	7	23			.985	2	*1-147	0.5
1913	Cin-N	137	502	59	143	23	7	3	62	35	26	.285	.334	.376	710	103	1	18			.988	-5	*1-134	-0.8
1914	Cin-N	78	248	31	52	8	7	0	26	26	26	.210	.287	.298	586	72	-9	7			.988	-4	1-75	-1.6
	Bos-A	69	229	31	73	10	3	0	33	19	21	.319	.386	.389	774	133	9	12	12	-2	.979	-5	1-68	0.1
1915	*Bos-A	124	399	54	113	15	12	2	61	38	26	.283	.351	.396	747	128	13	9	14	-3	.987	-1	*1-117	0.6
1916	*Bos-A	130	417	57	108	17	1	0	39	47	28	.259	.338	.305	643	93	-3	10			.989	-1	*1-126	-0.8
1917	Bos-A	120	420	49	108	19	7	1	47	46	22	.257	.336	.343	679	108	4	12			.990	-8	*1-118	-0.7
1918	Bos-A	25	69	4	11	1	0	0	4	8	3	.159	.266	.174	440	33	-5	3			.996	1	1-19	-0.5
Total	11	1318	4706	591	1310	194	88	27	593	407	256	.278	.341	.374	715	111	61	173	26		.987	-29	*1-1284/2-7	-0.5

YEAR	TM/L	G	AB	R	H	2B	3B	HR	RBI	BB	SO	AVG	OBP	SLG	OPS	OPS+	BR+	SB	CS	SBR	FA	FR	G/POS	TPR
■ BUTCH HOBSON	Hobson, Clell Lavern b: 8/17/51, Tuscaloosa, Ala. BR/TR, 6'1", 193 lbs. Deb: 9/7/75 M																							
1975	Bos-A	2	4	0	1	0	0	0	0	0	2	.250	.250	.250	500	38	-0	0	0	0	1.000	1	/3-1	0.0
1976	Bos-A	76	269	34	63	7	5	8	34	15	62	.234	.275	.387	661	82	-7	0	1	-0	.936	-7	3-76	-1.6
1977	Bos-A	159	593	77	157	33	5	30	112	27	162	.265	.301	.489	790	100	-2	5	4	-0	.946	-28	*3-159	-3.3
1978	Bos-A	147	512	65	128	26	2	17	80	50	122	.250	.317	.408	725	92	-5	1	0	0	.899	-14	*3-133,D-14	-2.2
1979	Bos-A	146	528	74	138	26	7	28	93	30	78	.261	.301	.496	797	105	1	3	2	-0	.935	-21	*3-142/2-1	-2.2
1980	Bos-A	93	324	35	74	6	0	11	39	25	69	.228	.284	.349	632	69	-14	1	1	-0	.910	-9	3-57,D-36	-2.5
1981	Cal-A	85	268	27	63	7	4	4	36	35	60	.235	.326	.336	661	91	-2	1	1	-0	.929	-11	3-83/D-2	-1.6
1982	NY-A	30	58	2	10	2	0	0	3	1	14	.172	.186	.207	393	8	-7	0	0	0	.951	-1	D-15,1-11	-0.9
Total	8	738	2556	314	634	107	23	98	397	183	569	.248	.300	.423	722	91	-38	11	9	-1	.926	-90	3-651/D-67,1-11,2-1	-14.3
■ ED HOCK	Hock, Edward Francis b: 3/27/1899, Franklin Furnace, Ohio d: 11/21/63, Portsmouth, Ohio BL/TL, 5'10.5", 165 lbs. Deb: 7/8/20																							
1920	StL-N	1	0	0	0	0	0	0	0	0	0	—	—	—	—	—	0	0	0	0	.000	-1	/O-1(1-0-0)	-0.1
1923	Cin-N	2	0	0	0	0	0	0	0	0	0	—	—	—	—	—	0	0	0	0	.000	0	R	0.0
1924	Cin-N	16	10	7	1	0	0	0	0	0	2	.100	.182	.100	282	-23	-2	0	0	0	1.000	-0	/O-2(1-2-0)	-0.2
Total	3	19	10	7	1	0	0	0	0	0	2	.100	.182	.100	282	-23	-2	0	0	0	1.000	-1	/O-3(2-2-0)	-0.3
■ ORIS HOCKETT	Hockett, Oris Leon "Brown" b: 9/29/09, Amboy, Ind. d: 3/23/69, Torrance, Cal. BL/TR, 5'9", 182 lbs. Deb: 9/4/38																							
1938	Bro-N	21	70	8	23	5	1	1	8	4	9	.329	.365	.471	836	126	2	0			.893	-4	O-17(4-13-0)	-0.2
1939	Bro-N	9	13	3	3	0	0	0	1	1	1	.231	.286	.231	516	39	-1	0			1.000	1	/O-1(1-0-0)	-0.1
1941	Cle-A	2	6	0	2	0	0	0	1	2	0	.333	.500	.333	833	131	0	0	0	0	1.000	-1	/O-2(0-2-0)	0.0
1942	Cle-A	148	601	85	150	22	7	7	48	45	45	.250	.305	.344	650	88	-12	12	12	-2	.980	-2	*O-145(0-2-144)	-2.5
1943	Cle-A	141	601	70	166	33	4	2	51	45	45	.276	.331	.354	685	107	4	13	18	-3	.960	1	*O-139(35-81-26)	-0.5
1944	Cle-A☆	124	457	47	132	29	5	1	50	35	27	.289	.339	.381	720	110	5	8	9	-1	.986	-4	*O-110(45-65-1)	-0.5
1945	Chi-A	106	417	46	122	23	4	2	55	27	30	.293	.340	.381	721	112	5	10	9	-1	.982	1	*O-106(0-106-0)	0.3
Total	7	551	2165	259	598	112	21	13	214	159	157	.276	.329	.365	694	103	4	43	48		.974	-6	O-520(85-269-171)	-3.5
■ DENNY HOCKING	Hocking, Dennis Lee b: 4/2/70, Torrance, Cal. BB/TR, 5'10", 176 lbs. Deb: 9/10/93 Career OF: (57-LF 35-CF 84-RF)																							
1993	Min-A	15	36	7	5	1	0	0	0	6	8	.139	.262	.167	429	18	-4	1	0	0	.971	-2	S-12/2-1	-0.5
1994	Min-A	11	31	3	10	3	0	0	2	0	4	.323	.323	.419	742	89	-1	2	0	0	1.000	1	S-10	0.1
1995	Min-A	9	25	4	5	0	2	0	3	2	2	.200	.259	.360	619	59	-2	1	0	0	.971	1	/S-6	0.0
1996	Min-A	49	127	16	25	6	0	1	10	8	24	.197	.244	.268	512	29	-14	3	3	-0	.985	1	O-33R/S-6,2-2,1D	-1.3
1997	Min-A	115	253	28	65	12	4	2	25	18	51	.257	.309	.360	669	73	-10	3	5	-1	.975	3	S-44,3-39,O-20R,2/1D	-0.5
1998	Min-A	110	198	32	40	6	1	3	15	16	44	.202	.262	.288	550	42	-17	2	1	0	1.000	3	2-47,S-28,O-24L,3/1D	-1.1
1999	Min-A	136	386	47	103	18	2	7	41	22	54	.267	.311	.378	690	72	-16	11	7	-0	.987	-23	S-61,2-56,O-38L,/31	-3.3
2000	Min-A	134	373	52	111	24	4	4	47	48	77	.298	.378	.416	793	96	-1	7	5	-0	1.000	-15	O-51C,2-47,3-16,S1/D	-1.4
Total	8	579	1429	189	364	70	13	17	143	120	264	.255	.314	.358	672	70	-65	30	21	-1	.979	-31	S-182,2-168,O/31D	-8.0
■ JOHNNY HODAPP	Hodapp, Urban John b: 9/26/05, Cincinnati, Ohio d: 6/14/80, Cincinnati, Ohio BR/TR, 6', 185 lbs. Deb: 8/19/25 Career OF: (29-LF 0-CF 2-RF)																							
1925	Cle-A	37	130	12	31	5	1	0	14	11	7	.238	.298	.292	590	50	-10	2	3	-1	.960	3	3-37	-0.5
1926	Cle-A	3	5	0	1	0	0	0	0	0	1	.200	.200	.200	400	5	-1	0	0	0	.750	-1	/3-3	-0.1
1927	Cle-A	79	240	25	73	15	3	5	40	14	23	.304	.343	.454	797	105	1	2	2	-0	.935	1	3-67/1-4	0.4
1928	Cle-A	116	449	51	145	31	6	2	73	20	20	.323	.352	.432	784	104	2	2	1	0	.944	-2	*3-101,1-13	0.5
1929	Cle-A	90	294	30	96	12	7	4	51	15	14	.327	.361	.456	817	105	2	3	3	-0	.977	5	2-72	0.8
1930	Cle-A	154	635	111	**225**	**51**	8	9	121	32	29	.354	.386	.502	889	119	17	6	5	-0	.970	12	*2-154	3.0
1931	Cle-A	122	468	71	138	19	4	2	56	27	23	.295	.336	.365	701	80	-14	1	5	-2	.969	16	*2-121	0.8
1932	Cle-A	7	16	2	2	1	0	0	0	0	2	.125	.125	.188	313	-19	-3	0	0	0	1.000	-2	/2-7	-0.4
	Chi-A	68	176	21	40	8	0	3	20	11	3	.227	.273	.324	597	58	-12	1	0	0	.967	-5	O-31(29-0-2)/2-5,3-4	-1.6
	Yr	75	192	23	42	9	0	3	20	11	5	.219	.261	.313	574	51	-15	1	0	0	.967	-7	O-31(29-0-2),2-12/3-4	-2.0
1933	Bos-A	115	413	55	129	27	5	3	54	33	14	.312	.365	.424	788	109	5	1	1	-0	.960	3	*2-101,1-10	1.3
Total	9	791	2826	378	880	169	34	28	429	163	136	.311	.350	.425	775	98	-12	18	20	-3	.967	30	2-460,3-212/O-31L,1	4.2
■ MEL HODERLEIN	Hoderlein, Melvin Anthony b: 6/26/23, Mt.Carmel, Ohio BB/TR, 5'10", 185 lbs. Deb: 8/16/51																							
1951	Bos-A	9	14	1	5	1	1	0	1	6	2	.357	.550	.571	1121	185	2	0	1	-0	1.000	1	/2-3,3-3	0.3
1952	Was-A	72	208	16	56	8	2	0	17	18	22	.269	.333	.327	660	87	-3	2	0	0	.978	-2	2-58	-0.1
1953	Was-A	23	47	5	9	0	0	0	5	6	9	.191	.283	.191	475	31	-4	0	0	0	.953	-3	2-11/S-2	-0.7
1954	Was-A	14	25	0	4	1	0	0	1	1	4	.160	.192	.200	392	8	-3	0	0	0	.939	1	/S-6,2-5	-0.1
Total	4	118	294	22	74	10	3	0	24	31	37	.252	.327	.306	633	78	-9	2	1	0	.973	-3	/2-77,S-8,3-3	-0.6
■ CHARLIE HODES	Hodes, Charles b: 1848, New York, N.Y. d: 2/14/1875, Brooklyn, N.Y. TR, 5'11.5", 175 lbs. Deb: 5/8/1871 Career OF: (0-LF 20-CF 6-RF)																							
1871	Chi-n	28	130	32	36	4	1	2	25	7	0	.277	.314	.369	683	86	-4	3	0	1	.796	3	*C-20,3-10/O-4C,S-1	0.0
1872	Tro-n	13	61	17	15	3	0	0	12	1	0	.246	.258	.295	553	69	-2	0	0	0	.759	0	/S-5,O-4C,C-3,3-1	-0.2
1874	Atl-n	21	81	8	12	3	0	0	7	0	2	.148	.148	.185	333	7	-7	0	0	0	.825	-4	O-18C/C-3,2-3,1-1	-0.8
Total	3 n	62	272	57	63	10	1	2	44	8	2	.232	.254	.298	551	64	-13	3	0	1	.820	-0	/O-26C,C-26,3-11,S21	-1.0
■ BERT HODGE	Hodge, Edward Burton b: 5/25/17, Knoxville, Tenn. BL/TR, 5'11", 170 lbs. Deb: 4/14/42																							
1942	Phi-N	8	11	0	2	0	0	0	0	1	0	.182	.250	.182	432	29	-1	0			1.000	-1	/3-2	-0.2
■ GOMER HODGE	Hodge, Harold Morris b: 4/3/44, Rutherfordton, N.C. BB/TR, 6'2", 185 lbs. Deb: 4/6/71																							
1971	Cle-A	80	83	3	17	3	0	1	9	4	19	.205	.258	.277	536	47	-6	0	0	0	1.000	-2	/1-3,3-3,2-2	-0.8
■ GIL HODGES	Hodges, Gilbert Raymond (b: Gilbert Ray Hodge) b: 4/4/24, Princeton, Ind. d: 4/2/72, West Palm Beach, Fla BR/TR, 6'1.5", 200 lbs. Deb: 10/3/43 M Career OF: (53-LF 1-CF 25-RF)																							
1943	Bro-N	1	2	0	0	0	0	0	0	1	2	.000	.333	.000	333	0	-0	1			.600	0	/3-1	0.0
1947	*Bro-N	28	77	9	12	3	1	1	7	14	19	.156	.286	.260	545	44	-6	0			.958	-2	C-24	-0.7
1948	Bro-N	134	481	48	120	18	5	11	70	43	61	.249	.311	.376	687	82	-12	7			.986	-1	1-96,C-38	-1.5
1949	*Bro-N★	156	596	94	170	23	4	23	115	66	64	.285	.360	.453	813	112	10	10			**.995**	-4	*1-156	0.1
1950	Bro-N☆	153	561	98	159	26	2	32	113	73	73	.283	.367	.508	875	125	20	6			**.994**	1	*1-153	1.4
1951	Bro-N★	158	582	118	156	25	3	40	103	93	99	.268	.374	.527	901	137	30	9	7	-0	.992	7	*1-158	3.1
1952	*Bro-N☆	153	508	87	129	27	1	32	102	107	90	.254	.386	.500	886	142	31	2	4	-1	.992	5	*1-153	3.1
1953	*Bro-N★	141	520	101	157	22	7	31	122	75	84	.302	.393	.550	943	139	31	1	4	-1	.993	8	*1-127,O-24(18-0-6)	2.8
1954	Bro-N★	154	579	106	176	23	5	42	130	74	84	.304	.384	.579	962	142	35	3	3	-0	.995	9	*1-154	3.3
1955	*Bro-N★	150	546	75	158	24	5	27	102	80	91	.289	.383	.500	883	128	23	2	1	0	.991	1	*1-139,O-16(9-1-6)	1.6
1956	*Bro-N	153	550	86	146	29	4	32	87	76	91	.265	.355	.507	862	119	15	3	3	-0	.992	1	*1-138,O-30L/C-1	0.7
1957	Bro-N★	150	579	94	173	28	7	27	98	63	91	.299	.370	.511	881	122	18	5	3	0	.990	2	*1-150/3-2,2-1	1.1
1958	LA-N	141	475	68	123	15	1	22	64	52	87	.259	.332	.434	766	98	-2	8	2	1	.992	1	*1-122,3-15/O-9R,C	-0.7
1959	*LA-N	124	413	57	114	19	2	25	80	58	92	.276	.369	.513	883	123	14	3	2	-0	**.992**	0	*1-113/3-4	0.8
1960	LA-N	101	197	22	39	8	1	8	30	26	37	.198	.295	.371	665	76	-7	0	1	-0	.995	1	1-92,3-10	-0.9
1961	LA-N	109	215	25	52	4	0	8	31	24	43	.242	.318	.372	690	76	-7	3	1	0	.998	0	*1-100	-1.0
1962	NY-N	54	127	15	32	1	0	9	17	15	27	.252	.331	.472	803	111	2	0	0	0	.986	3	1-47	0.3
1963	NY-N	11	22	2	5	0	0	0	3	3	2	.227	.320	.227	547	60	-1	0	0	0	1.000	2	1-10	0.0
Total	18	2071	7030	1105	1921	295	48	370	1274	943	1137	.273	.361	.487	848	119	193	63	31		.992	34	*1-1908/O-79L,C32	13.5
■ RON HODGES	Hodges, Ronald Wray b: 6/22/49, Rocky Mount, Va. BL/TR, 6'1", 185 lbs. Deb: 6/13/73																							
1973	*NY-N	45	127	5	33	2	0	1	18	11	19	.260	.319	.299	618	73	-4	0	1	-0	.992	2	C-40	-0.1
1974	NY-N	59	136	16	30	4	0	4	14	19	11	.221	.316	.338	654	84	-3	0	0	0	.953	-2	C-44	-0.3
1975	NY-N	9	34	3	7	1	0	2	4	1	6	.206	.229	.412	640	79	-1	0	0	0	1.000	0	/C-9	-0.1
1976	NY-N	56	155	21	35	6	0	4	24	27	16	.226	.341	.342	683	100	1	2	0	0	.976	-9	C-52	-0.6
1977	NY-N	66	117	6	31	4	0	1	5	9	17	.265	.317	.325	642	76	-4	0	2	-1	.992	-0	C-27	-0.4
1978	NY-N	47	102	4	26	4	1	0	7	10	11	.255	.327	.314	641	83	-2	1	2	-0	.982	6	C-30	0.4
1979	NY-N	59	86	4	14	4	0	0	5	19	16	.163	.314	.209	524	47	-6	0	0	0	.980	1	C-22	-0.4

YEAR	TM/L	G	AB	R	H	2B	3B	HR	RBI	BB	SO	AVG	OBP	SLG	OPS	OPS+	BR+	SB	CS	SBR	FA	FR	G/POS	TPR
1980	NY-N	36	42	4	10	2	0	0	5	10	13	.238	.385	.286	670	92	0	1	1	-0	.982	4	/C-9	0.4
1981	NY-N	35	43	5	13	2	0	1	6	5	8	.302	.375	.419	794	127	2	1	0	0	1.000	-1	/C-7	0.1
1982	NY-N	80	228	26	56	12	1	5	27	41	40	.246	.361	.373	733	106	3	4	3	-0	.980	-0	C-74	0.6
1983	NY-N	110	250	20	65	12	0	0	21	49	42	.260	.385	.308	693	95	1	0	3	-1	.971	-10	C-96	-0.7
1984	NY-N	64	106	5	22	3	0	1	11	23	18	.208	.354	.264	618	77	-2	1	1	-0	.979	-1	C-35	-0.2
Total	12	666	1426	119	342	56	2	19	147	224	217	.240	.345	.322	666	88	-15	10	13	-2	.978	-9	C-445	-1.3
■ RALPH HODGIN	Hodgin, Elmer Ralph b: 2/10/16, Greensboro, N.C. BL/TR, 5'10", 170 lbs. Deb: 4/19/39																							
1939	Bos-N	32	48	4	10	1	0	0	4	3	4	.208	.255	.229	484	33	-5	0			1.000	-1	/O-9(2-0-7)	-0.6
1943	Chi-A	117	407	52	128	22	8	1	50	20	24	.314	.356	.415	771	125	12	3	5	-1	.945	-7	3-56,O-42(17-0-25)	0.2
1944	Chi-A	121	465	56	137	25	7	1	51	21	14	.295	.333	.385	718	106	2	3	1	0	.942	12	3-82,O-33(33-0-0)	1.5
1946	Chi-A	87	258	32	65	10	1	0	25	19	6	.252	.308	.298	607	73	-9	0	1	-0	.983	-2	O-57(49-0-8)	-1.7
1947	Chi-A	59	180	26	53	10	3	1	24	13	4	.294	.352	.400	752	113	3	1	0	0	.990	1	O-41(40-0-1)	0.1
1948	Chi-A	114	331	28	88	11	5	1	34	21	11	.266	.310	.338	648	75	-13	0	3	-1	.970	5	O-79(39-2-40)	-1.3
Total	6	530	1689	198	481	79	24	4	188	97	63	.285	.330	.367	697	98	-10	7	10		.985	7	O-261(180-2-81),3-138	-1.8
■ PAUL HODGSON	Hodgson, Paul Joseph Denis b: 4/14/60, Montreal, Que., Can. BR/TR, 6'2", 190 lbs. Deb: 8/31/80																							
1980	Tor-A	20	41	5	9	0	1	1	5	3	12	.220	.273	.341	614	64	-2	0	1	-0	1.000	-0	O-11(10-1-0)/D-3	-0.3
■ ART HOELSKOETTER	Hoelskoetter, Arthur "Holley" or "Hoss" (a.k.a. Arthur H. Hostetter) b: 9/30/1882, St.Louis, Mo. d: 8/3/54, St.Louis, Mo. BR/TR, 6'2", Deb: 9/10/05 Career OF: (1-LF 7-CF 13-RF)																							
1905	StL-N	24	83	7	20	2	1	0	5	3		.241	.267	.289	557	68	-3	1			.972	1	3-20/2-3,P-1	-0.2
1906	StL-N	94	317	21	71	6	3	0	14	4		.224	.238	.262	500	58	-17	2			.943	-6	3-53,S-16,P-12,O/2	-2.1
1907	StL-N	119	397	21	98	6	3	2	28	27		.247	.298	.292	590	88	-6	5			.927	10	2-73,1-27/C-8,OP3	0.5
1908	StL-N	62	155	10	36	7	1	0	6	6		.232	.265	.290	556	81	-4	1			.948	0	C-41/3-2,1-1,2-1	0.1
Total	4	299	952	59	225	21	8	2	53	40		.236	.271	.282	552	75	-30	9			.924	5	/2-78,3-77,C-49,1OSP	-1.7
■ JACK HOEY	Hoey, John Bernard b: 11/10/1881, Watertown, Mass. d: 11/14/47, Waterbury, Conn. BL/TL, 5'9", 185 lbs. Deb: 6/27/06																							
1906	Bos-A	94	361	27	88	8	4	0	24	14		.244	.274	.288	562	76	-10	10			.915	-8	O-94(94-0-0)	-2.6
1907	Bos-A	39	96	7	21	2	1	0	8	1		.219	.227	.260	487	56	-5	2			.857	-5	O-21(17-4-0)	-1.3
1908	Bos-A	13	43	5	7	0	0	0	3	0		.163	.163	.163	326	6	-4	1			1.000	-0	O-11(0-0-11)	-0.6
Total	3	146	500	39	116	10	5	0	35	15		.232	.256	.272	528	66	-20	13			.913	-13	O-126(111-4-11)	-4.5
■ STEW HOFFERTH	Hofferth, Stewart Edward b: 1/27/13, Logansport, Ind. d: 3/7/94, Valparaiso, Ind. BR/TR, 6'2", 195 lbs. Deb: 4/19/44																							
1944	Bos-N	66	180	14	36	8	0	1	26	11	5	.200	.246	.261	507	41	-14	0			.984	0	C-47	-1.1
1945	Bos-N	50	170	13	40	2	0	3	15	14	11	.235	.297	.300	597	66	-8	1			.980	6	C-45	0.1
1946	Bos-N	20	58	3	12	1	1	0	10	3	6	.207	.246	.259	505	43	-4	0			1.000	-1	C-15	-0.5
Total	3	136	408	30	88	11	1	4	51	28	22	.216	.268	.277	545	52	-26	1			.985	6	C-107	-1.5
■ DUTCH HOFFMAN	Hoffman, Clarence Casper "Red" b: 1/28/04, Freeburg, Ill. d: 12/6/62, Belleville, Ill. BR/TR, 6', 175 lbs. Deb: 4/23/29																							
1929	Chi-A	107	337	27	87	16	5	3	37	24	28	.258	.307	.362	669	73	-14	6	3	0	.984	-1	O-88(2-74-12)	-1.8
■ DANNY HOFFMAN	Hoffman, Daniel John b: 3/2/1880, Canton, Conn. d: 3/14/22, Manchester, Conn. BL/TL, 5'9", 175 lbs. Deb: 4/20/03																							
1903	Phi-A	74	248	29	61	5	7	2	22	6		.246	.267	.347	613	79	-7	7			.950	0	O-62(43-0-19)/P-1	-1.0
1904	Phi-A	53	204	31	61	7	5	3	24	5		.299	.329	.426	755	131	7	9			.936	0	O-51(14-14-23)	0.5
1905	*Phi-A	120	459	66	120	10	10	1	35	33		.261	.312	.333	646	103	1	**46**			.942	-2	*O-118(14-102-2)	-0.7
1906	Phi-A	7	22	4	5	0	0	0	0	3		.227	.320	.227	547	70	-1	1			1.000	1	/O-7(0-7-0)	0.0
	NY-A	100	320	34	82	10	6	0	23	27		.256	.318	.325	643	92	-3	32			.938	-9	O-98(0-98-0)	-1.8
	Yr	107	342	38	87	10	6	0	23	30		.254	.318	.319	637	91	-3	33			.943	-8	*O-105(0-105-0)	-1.8
1907	NY-A	136	517	81	131	10	3	5	46	42		.253	.325	.313	639	96	-1	30			.953	8	*O-135(0-135-0)	0.0
1908	StL-A	99	363	41	91	9	7	1	25	23		.251	.304	.322	627	103	1	17			.962	11	O-99(6-46-47)	0.8
1909	StL-A	110	387	44	104	6	7	2	26	41		.269	.349	.336	685	125	13	24			.968	2	*O-110(0-109-1)	1.1
1910	StL-A	106	380	20	90	11	5	0	27	34		.237	.306	.292	598	93	-3	16			.960	1	*O-106(0-102-4)	-0.8
1911	StL-A	24	81	11	17	3	2	0	7	12		.210	.326	.296	623	77	-2	3			.908	3	O-23(0-23-0)	-0.1
Total	9	829	2981	361	762	71	52	14	235	226		.256	.316	.328	645	101	5	185			.951	15	O-809(77-636-96)/P-1	-2.0
■ TEX HOFFMAN	Hoffman, Edward Adolph b: 11/30/1893, San Antonio, Tex. d: 5/19/47, New Orleans, La. BL/TR, 5'9", 195 lbs. Deb: 7/11/15																							
1915	Cle-A	9	13	1	2	0	0	0	2	1	5	.154	.214	.154	368	10	-1	0			.750	-2	/3-3	-0.3
■ GLENN HOFFMAN	Hoffman, Glenn Edward b: 7/7/58, Orange, Cal. BR/TR, 6'2", 190 lbs. Deb: 4/12/80 FMC																							
1980	Bos-A	114	312	37	89	15	4	4	42	19	41	.285	.330	.397	728	94	-3	2	4	-1	.946	-0	*3-110/S-5,2-2	-0.5
1981	Bos-A	78	242	28	56	10	0	1	20	12	25	.231	.271	.285	556	57	-13	0	1	-0	.960	5	S-78/3-1	-0.1
1982	Bos-A	150	469	53	98	23	2	7	49	30	69	.209	.264	.311	575	54	-30	0	4	-1	.972	13	*S-150	-0.3
1983	Bos-A	143	473	56	123	24	1	4	41	30	76	.260	.307	.340	647	73	-17	1	1	-0	.962	-6	*S-143	-0.9
1984	Bos-A	64	74	8	14	4	0	0	4	5	10	.189	.241	.243	484	33	-7	0	1	-0	.957	5	S-56/3-4,2-2	0.1
1985	Bos-A	96	279	40	77	17	2	6	34	25	40	.276	.346	.416	762	103	1	2	2	-0	.975	-1	S-93/2-3,3-3	0.9
1986	Bos-A	12	23	1	5	2	0	0	1	2	3	.217	.280	.304	584	59	-1	0	0	0	.923	-2	S-11/3-1	-0.3
1987	Bos-A	21	55	5	11	3	0	0	6	3	9	.200	.267	.255	521	38	-5	0	0	0	.984	2	S-16/3-3,2-2	-0.1
	LA-N	40	132	10	29	5	0	0	10	7	23	.220	.270	.258	527	42	-11	0	1	-0	.966	1	S-40	-0.6
1989	Cal-A	48	104	9	22	3	0	1	3	3	13	.212	.241	.269	510	44	-8	0	2	-1	.982	3	S-23,3-18/2-4,1D	-0.5
Total	9	766	2163	247	524	106	9	23	210	136	309	.242	.293	.331	625	68	-93	5	16	-5	.966	21	S-615,3-140/2-13,D1	-2.3
■ IZZY HOFFMAN	Hoffman, Harry C. b: 1/5/1875, Bridgeport, N.J. d: 11/13/42, Philadelphia, Pa. BL/TL, 5'9", 160 lbs. Deb: 4/14/04																							
1904	Was-A	10	30	1	3	1	0	0	1	2		.100	.156	.133	290	-8	-4	0			1.000	1	/O-9(0-9-0)	-0.4
1907	Bos-N	19	86	17	24	3	1	0	3	6		.279	.326	.337	663	108	1	2			.897	-2	O-19(3-1-16)	-0.2
Total	2	29	116	18	27	4	1	0	4	8		.233	.282	.284	567	79	-3	2			.939	-1	/O-28(3-10-16)	-0.6
■ JOHN HOFFMAN	Hoffman, John Edward "Pork Chop" b: 10/31/43, Aberdeen, S.D. BL/TR, 6', 190 lbs. Deb: 7/30/64																							
1964	Hou-N	6	15	1	1	0	0	0	0	1	7	.067	.125	.067	192	-47	-3	0	0	0	1.000	-2	/C-5	-0.5
1965	Hou-N	2	6	1	2	0	0	0	1	0	3	.333	.333	.333	667	95	-0	0	0	0	1.000	-1	/C-2	-0.1
Total	2	8	21	2	3	0	0	0	1	1	10	.143	.182	.143	325	-8	-3	0	0	0	1.000	-2	/C-7	-0.6
■ LARRY HOFFMAN	Hoffman, Lawrence Charles b: 7/18/1878, Chicago, Ill. d: 12/29/48, Chicago, Ill. BR/TR, Deb: 7/4/01																							
1901	Chi-N	6	22	2	7	1	0	0	6	0		.318	.348	.364	711	111	0	1			.800	-2	/3-5,2-1	-0.1
■ HICKEY HOFFMAN	Hoffman, Otto Charles b: 10/27/1856, Cleveland, Ohio d: 10/27/15, Peoria, Ill. Deb: 5/10/1879																							
1879	Cle-N	2	6	0	0	0	0	0	0	0	3	.000	.000	.000	0	-99	-1				.857	0	/C-2,O-1(0-0-1)	-0.1
■ RAY HOFFMAN	Hoffman, Raymond Lamont b: 6/14/17, Detroit, Mich. BL/TR, 6'0.5", 175 lbs. Deb: 8/30/42																							
1942	Was-A	7	19	2	1	0	0	0	2	1	1	.053	.100	.053	153	-57	-4	0	0	0	.815	2	/3-6	-0.2
■ JESSE HOFFMEISTER	Hoffmeister, Jesse H. b: Toledo, Ohio TR, Deb: 7/24/1897																							
1897	Pit-N	48	188	33	58	6	9	3	36	8		.309	.337	.484	821	120	4	6			.792	-12	3-48	-0.7
■ SOLLY HOFMAN	Hofman, Arthur Frederick "Circus Solly" b: 10/29/1882, St.Louis, Mo. d: 3/10/56, St.Louis, Mo. BR/TR, 6', 160 lbs. Deb: 7/28/03 Career OF: (77-LF 557-CF 79-RF)																							
1903	Pit-N	3	2	1	0	0	0	0	0	0		.000	.000	.000	0	-97	-1	0			.000	-1	/O-2(1-1-0)	-0.1
1904	Chi-N	7	26	7	7	0	0	1	4	1		.269	.296	.385	681	110	0	2			1.000	0	/O-6(1-3-2),S-1	0.0
1905	Chi-N	86	287	43	68	14	4	1	38	20		.237	.289	.324	613	79	-8	15			.955	4	2-59/1-9,S-9,3-3,O	-0.4
1906	*Chi-N	64	195	30	50	2	3	2	20	20		.256	.326	.328	654	98	-0	13			.976	-1	O-23C,1-21/S-9,23	-0.3
1907	Chi-N	134	470	67	126	11	3	1	36	41		.268	.328	.311	639	94	-3	29			.938	2	O-69R,S-42,1-18,/32	-0.4
1908	*Chi-N	120	411	55	100	15	5	2	42	33		.243	.309	.319	628	96	-1	15			.955	5	O-50C,1-37,2-22,/3	0.1
1909	Chi-N	153	527	60	150	21	4	2	58	53		.285	.351	.351	702	115	10	20			.965	5	*O-153(0-143-11)	0.9

YEAR	TM/L	G	AB	R	H	2B	3B	HR	RBI	BB	SO	AVG	OBP	SLG	OPS	OPS+	BR+	SB	CS	SBR	FA	FR	G/POS	TPR
1910	*Chi-N	136	477	83	155	24	16	3	86	65	34	.325	.406	.461	867	154	33	29			.975	5	*O-110C,1-24/3-1	3.4
1911	Chi-N	143	512	66	129	17	2	2	70	66	40	.252	.341	.305	645	81	-11	30			.968	-6	*O-107(2-107-0),1-36	-2.6
1912	Chi-N	36	125	28	34	11	0	0	18	22	13	.272	.385	.360	745	105	2	5			.987	4	O-27(0-27-0)/1-9	0.3
	Pit-N	17	53	7	15	4	1	0	2	5	6	.283	.345	.396	741	104	0	0			1.000	2	O-15(0-15-0)	0.1
	Yr	53	178	35	49	15	1	0	20	27	19	.275	.374	.371	745	105	2	5			.991	6	O-42(0-42-0)/1-9	0.4
1913	Pit-N	28	83	11	19	5	2	0	7	8	6	.229	.297	.337	634	84	-2	3			.964	-1	O-24(0-23-2)	-0.4
1914	Bro-F	147	515	65	148	25	12	5	83	54	41	.287	.357	.412	769	110	-1	34			.951	5	*2-108,1-22,O-21L/S	0.4
1915	Buf-F	109	346	29	81	10	6	0	27	30	28	.234	.295	.298	593	66	-21	12			.961	1	O-82L,1-11/3-4,2S	-2.6
1916	NY-A	6	27	0	8	1	1	0	2	1	1	.296	.321	.407	729	116	0	1			1.000	2	/O-6(0-6-0)	0.2
	Chi-N	5	16	2	5	2	1	0	2	2	2	.313	.389	.563	951	172	1	0			1.000	0	/O-4(4-0-0)	0.2
Total	14	1194	4072	554	1095	162	60	19	495	421	171	.269	.340	.352	692	102	-1	208			.967	25	O-702C,2-198,1/S3	-1.2
■ BOBBY HOFMAN	Hofman, Robert George b: 10/5/25, St.Louis, Mo. d: 4/5/94, Chesterfield, Mo. BR/TR, 5'11", 175 lbs. Deb: 4/19/49 C																							
1949	NY-N	19	48	4	10	0	0	0	3	5	6	.208	.296	.208	505	38	-4	0			.939	-0	2-16	-0.3
1952	NY-N	32	63	11	18	2	2	2	4	8	10	.286	.375	.476	851	134	3	0	0	0	.964	3	2-21/3-2,1-1	0.7
1953	NY-N	74	169	21	45	7	2	12	34	12	23	.266	.315	.544	859	117	3	1	1	-0	.918	2	3-23,2-17	0.5
1954	NY-N	71	125	12	28	5	0	8	30	17	15	.224	.322	.456	778	99	-1	0	0	0	.994	-4	1-21,2-10/3-8	-0.5
1955	NY-N	96	207	32	55	7	2	10	28	22	31	.266	.339	.464	803	110	3	0	2	-1	1.000	-5	1-24,C-19,2-19,/3-5	-0.3
1956	NY-N	47	56	1	10	1	0	0	2	6	8	.179	.270	.196	466	28	-6	0	0	0	1.000	1	/C-7,3-7,1-3,2-2	-0.4
1957	NY-N	2	2	0	0	0	0	0	0	0	1	.000	.000	.000	0	-99	-1	0	0	0	.000	0	H	-0.1
Total	7	341	670	81	166	22	6	32	101	70	94	.248	.323	.442	765	100	-2	1	3		.969	-3	/2-85,1-49,3-45,C	-0.4
■ FRED HOFMANN	Hofmann, Fred "Bootnose" b: 6/10/1894, St.Louis, Mo. d: 11/19/64, St.Helena, Cal. BR/TR, 5'11.5", 175 lbs. Deb: 9/26/19 C																							
1919	NY-A	1	1	0	0	0	0	0	0	0	0	.000	.000	.000	0	-99	-0	0			1.000	0	/C-1	0.0
1920	NY-A	15	24	3	7	0	0	0	1	1	2	.292	.346	.292	638	68	-1	0	0	0	.905	-4	C-14	-0.4
1921	NY-A	23	62	7	11	1	1	1	5	5	13	.177	.250	.274	524	33	-6	0	0	0	.952	-0	C-18/1-1	-0.5
1922	NY-A	37	91	13	27	5	3	2	10	9	12	.297	.360	.484	844	116	2	0	0	0	.962	-4	C-29	0.0
1923	*NY-A	72	238	24	69	10	4	3	26	18	27	.290	.350	.403	753	96	-2	2	1	0	.979	-3	C-70	0.0
1924	NY-A	62	166	17	29	6	1	1	11	12	15	.175	.239	.241	480	24	-19	2	1	0	.991	2	C-54	-1.4
1925	NY-A	3	2	0	0	0	0	0	0	0	0	.000	.000	.000	0	-99	-1	0	0	0	1.000	0	/C-1	0.0
1927	Bos-A	87	217	20	59	19	1	0	24	21	26	.272	.342	.369	710	86	-4	2	0	0	.943	-2	C-81	-0.1
1928	Bos-A	78	199	14	45	8	1	0	16	11	25	.226	.270	.276	547	45	-16	0	1	-0	.982	4	C-71	-0.8
Total	9	378	1000	98	247	49	11	7	93	77	120	.247	.308	.339	647	68	-48	6	3		.969	-7	C-339/1-1	-3.2
■ HARRY HOGAN	Hogan, Harry S. b: 11/1/1875, Syracuse, N.Y. d: 1/24/34, Syracuse, N.Y. Deb: 8/13/01																							
1901	Cle-A	1	4	0	0	0	0	0	0	0		.000	.000	.000	0	-99	-1	0			.000	-0	/O-1(0-0-1)	-0.1
■ SHANTY HOGAN	Hogan, James Francis b: 3/21/06, Somerville, Mass. d: 4/7/67, Boston, Mass. BR/TR, 6'1", 240 lbs. Deb: 6/23/25																							
1925	Bos-N	9	21	2	6	1	1	0	3	1	3	.286	.318	.429	747	97	-0	0	0	0	1.000	-1	/O-5(2-0-3)	-0.1
1926	Bos-N	4	14	1	4	1	1	0	5	0	0	.286	.286	.500	786	119	0	0			.852	1	/C-4	0.2
1927	Bos-N	71	229	24	66	17	1	3	32	9	23	.288	.324	.410	734	104	0	2			.985	1	C-61	0.6
1928	NY-N	131	411	48	137	25	2	10	71	42	25	.333	.406	.477	883	129	19	0			.978	-10	*C-124	1.6
1929	NY-N	102	317	19	95	13	0	5	45	25	22	.300	.362	.388	750	86	-6	1			.979	-4	C-93	-0.4
1930	NY-N	122	389	60	132	26	2	13	75	21	24	.339	.378	.517	894	116	9	2			.982	-3	C-96	1.1
1931	NY-N	123	396	42	119	17	1	12	65	29	29	.301	.354	.439	794	115	8	1			**.996**	-0	*C-113	1.4
1932	NY-N	140	502	36	144	18	2	8	77	26	22	.287	.323	.378	702	90	-7	0			.983	-8	*C-136	-0.7
1933	Bos-N	96	328	15	83	7	0	3	30	13	9	.253	.288	.302	590	75	-11	0			**.997**	-1	C-95	-0.7
1934	Bos-N	92	279	20	73	5	2	4	34	16	13	.262	.316	.337	653	81	-8	0			.986	-2	C-90	-0.5
1935	Bos-N	59	163	9	49	8	0	2	25	21	8	.301	.394	.387	780	120	6	0			.990	-4	C-56	0.5
1936	Was-A	19	65	8	21	4	0	1	7	11	2	.323	.421	.431	852	117	2	0	1	-0	.989	2	C-19	0.5
1937	Was-A	21	66	4	10	4	0	0	5	6	8	.152	.222	.212	434	10	-9	0	1	-0	.979	2	C-21	-0.6
Total	13	989	3180	288	939	146	12	61	474	220	188	.295	.348	.406	754	101	2	6	2		.985	-27	C-908/O-5(2-0-3)	2.9
■ KENNY HOGAN	Hogan, Kenneth Sylvester b: 10/9/02, Cleveland, Ohio d: 1/2/80, Cleveland, Ohio BL/TR, 5'9", 145 lbs. Deb: 10/2/21																							
1921	Cin-N	1	2	0	0	0	0	0	0	0	1	.000	.000	.000	0	-99	-1	0	0	0	.000	-1	/O-1(0-1-0)	-0.1
1923	Cle-A	1	0	0	0	0	0	0	0	0	0	—	—	—	—	—	0	0	0	0	.000	0	R	0.0
1924	Cle-A	2	1	0	0	0	0	0	0	0	0	.000	.000	.000	0	-99	-0	0	0	0	.000	0	H	0.0
Total	3	4	3	0	0	0	0	0	0	0	1	.000	.000	.000	0	-99	-1	0	0	0	—	-1	/O-1(0-1-0)	-0.1
■ MARTY HOGAN	Hogan, Martin F. b: 10/15/1869, Wensbury, England d: 8/15/23, Youngstown, Ohio BR, 5'8", 145 lbs. Deb: 8/6/1894																							
1894	Cin-N	6	23	4	3	0	0	0	3	1	4	.130	.167	.130	297	-27	-5	2			.846	-0	/O-6(0-0-6)	-0.4
	StL-N	29	100	11	28	3	4	0	13	3	13	.280	.308	.390	698	67	-6	7			.887	-1	O-29(1-1-28)	-0.7
	Yr	35	123	15	31	3	4	0	16	4	17	.252	.281	.341	623	49	-11	9			.879	-2	O-35(1-1-34)	-1.1
1895	StL-N	5	18	2	3	1	0	0	2	3	0	.167	.286	.222	508	32	-2	2			.833	1	/O-5(0-5-0)	-0.1
Total	2	40	141	17	34	4	4	0	18	7	17	.241	.282	.326	608	47	-12	11			.869	-1	/O-40(1-6-34)	-1.2
■ EDDIE HOGAN	Hogan, Robert Edward b: 4/1860, St.Louis, Mo. BR, 5'7", 153 lbs. Deb: 7/5/1882 Career OF: (27-LF 2-CF 89-RF)																							
1882	StL-a	1	3	1	1	0	0	0		0		.333	.333	.333	667	121	0				.333	-1	/P-1	0.0
1884	Mil-U	11	37	6	3	1	0	0		7		.081	.227	.108	335	9	-4				.806	7	O-11(0-0-11)	0.2
1887	NY-a	32	150	22	54	6	1	0	5	30		.360	.373	.267	639	84	-0	12			.750	-7	O-29(1-2-26)/S-4,3-1	-0.6
1888	Cle-a	78	269	60	61	16	6	0	24	50		.227	.368	.331	699	128	12	30			.896	-5	O-78(26-0-52)	0.6
Total	4	122	459	89	119	23	7	0	29	87		.259	.357	.294	651	106	8	42			.844	-6	O-118R/S-4,3-1,P-1	0.2
■ WILLIE HOGAN	Hogan, William Henry b: 9/14/1884, N.San Juan, Cal. d: 9/28/74, San Jose, Cal. BR/TR, 5'10", 175 lbs. Deb: 4/12/11 F																							
1911	Phi-A	7	19	1	2	1	0	0	2	0		.105	.105	.158	263	-27	-3	0			.900	0	/O-6(6-0-0)	-0.3
	StL-A	123	443	53	115	17	8	2	62	43		.260	.328	.348	675	92	-5	18			.929	13	*O-117(115-0-2)/1-5	0.3
	Yr	130	462	54	117	18	8	2	64	43		.253	.320	.340	659	87	-8	18			.928	13	*O-123(121-0-2)/1-5	0.0
1912	StL-A	108	360	32	77	10	2	1	36	34		.214	.284	.261	545	58	-19	17			.972	11	*O-100(91-4-4)	-1.3
Total	2	238	822	86	194	28	10	3	100	77		.236	.304	.305	609	75	-27	35			.947	24	O-223(212-4-6)/1-5	-1.3
■ BERT HOGG	Hogg, Wilbert George "Sonny" b: 4/21/13, Detroit, Mich. d: 11/5/73, Detroit, Mich. BR/TR, 5'11.5", 162 lbs. Deb: 6/1/34																							
1934	Bro-N	2	1	0	0	0	0	0	0	0	0	.000	.000	.000	0	-99	-0	0			.000	0	/3-1	0.0
■ GEORGE HOGRIEVER	Hogriever, George C. b: 3/17/1869, Cincinnati, Ohio d: 1/26/61, Appleton, Wis. BR/TR, 5'8", 160 lbs. Deb: 4/24/1895																							
1895	Cin-N	69	239	61	65	8	7	2	34	36	17	.272	.374	.389	763	93	-2	41			.934	2	O-66(10-48-8)/2-3	-0.3
1901	Mil-A	54	221	25	52	10	2	0	16	30		.235	.329	.299	628	79	-5	7			.901	2	O-54(49-5-0)	-0.6
Total	2	123	460	86	117	18	9	2	50	66	17	.254	.353	.346	698	87	-7	48			.920	4	O-120(59-53-8)/2-3	-0.9
■ BILL HOHMAN	Hohman, William Henry b: 11/27/03, Brooklyn, Md. d: 10/29/68, Baltimore, Md. BR/TR, 6', 178 lbs. Deb: 8/24/27																							
1927	Phi-N	7	18	1	5	0	0	0	0	2	3	.278	.350	.278	628	69	-1	0			.917	-0	/O-6(6-0-0)	-0.1
■ EDDIE HOHNHORST	Hohnhorst, Edward Hicks b: 1/31/1885, Covington, Ky. d: 3/28/16, Covington, Ky. BL/TL, 6'1", 175 lbs. Deb: 9/10/10																							
1910	Cle-A	18	63	8	20	3	1	0	6	4		.317	.358	.397	755	135	2	3			.972	-1	1-18	0.1
1912	Cle-A	15	54	5	11	1	0	0	2	2		.204	.232	.222	454	29	-5	5			.963	-1	1-15	-0.6
Total	2	33	117	13	31	4	1	0	8	6		.265	.301	.316	617	83	-3	8			.968	-2	/1-33	-0.5
■ CHRIS HOILES	Hoiles, Christopher Allen b: 3/20/65, Bowling Green, O. BR/TR, 6', 213 lbs. Deb: 4/25/89																							
1989	Bal-A	6	9	0	1	1	0	0	1	1	3	.111	.200	.222	422	19	-1	0	0	0	1.000	1	/C-3,D-3	0.0
1990	Bal-A	23	63	7	12	3	0	1	6	5	12	.190	.250	.286	536	51	-4	0	0	0	1.000	-1	/C-7,1-6,D-7	-0.5
1991	Bal-A	107	341	36	83	15	0	11	31	29	61	.243	.305	.384	689	93	-4	0	2	-1	**.998**	-14	C-89,D-13/1-2	-1.4
1992	Bal-A	96	310	49	85	10	1	20	40	55	60	.274	.387	.506	893	145	19	0	2	-1	.994	-10	C-95/D-1	1.5
1993	Bal-A	126	419	80	130	28	0	29	82	69	94	.310	.419	.585	1003	160	37	1	1	-0	.993	-0	*C-124/D-2	4.2

YEAR	TM/L	G	AB	R	H	2B	3B	HR	RBI	BB	SO	AVG	OBP	SLG	OPS	OPS+	BR+	SB	CS	SBR	FA	FR	G/POS	TPR
1994	Bal-A	99	332	45	82	10	0	19	53	63	73	.247	.375	.449	824	106	4	2	0	0	.989	5	C-98	1.4
1995	Bal-A	114	352	53	88	15	1	19	58	67	80	.250	.376	.460	836	114	9	1	0	0	**.996**	-3	*C-107/D-6	1.1
1996	*Bal-A	127	407	64	105	13	0	25	73	57	97	.258	.362	.474	836	110	6	0	1	-0	.992	-10	*C-126/1-1	0.3
1997	*Bal-A	99	320	45	83	15	0	12	49	51	86	.259	.378	.419	797	111	7	1	0	0	**1.000**	-3	C-87/1-4,3-1,D-8	0.9
1998	Bal-A	97	267	36	70	12	0	15	56	38	50	.262	.362	.476	838	117	7	0	1	-0	**.995**	1	C-83/1-6,D-6	1.2
Total	10	894	2820	415	739	122	2	151	449	435	616	.262	.369	.467	837	119	80	5	7	-1	.994	-34	C-819/D-46,1-19,3-1	8.7

■ AARON HOLBERT
Holbert, Aaron Keith b: 1/9/73, Torrance, Cal. BR/TR, 6', 160 lbs. Deb: 4/14/96 F

YEAR	TM/L	G	AB	R	H	2B	3B	HR	RBI	BB	SO	AVG	OBP	SLG	OPS	OPS+	BR+	SB	CS	SBR	FA	FR	G/POS	TPR
1996	StL-N	1	3	0	0	0	0	0	0	0	0	.000	.000	.000	0	-99	-1	0	0	0	1.000	-1	/2-1	-0.2

■ RAY HOLBERT
Holbert, Ray Arthur b: 9/25/70, Torrance, Cal. BR/TR, 6', 170 lbs. Deb: 5/2/94 F Career OF: (0-LF 0-CF 1-RF)

YEAR	TM/L	G	AB	R	H	2B	3B	HR	RBI	BB	SO	AVG	OBP	SLG	OPS	OPS+	BR+	SB	CS	SBR	FA	FR	G/POS	TPR
1994	SD-N	5	5	1	1	0	0	0	0	0	4	.200	.200	.200	400	5	-1	0	0	0	.000	0	/S-1	-0.1
1995	SD-N	63	73	11	13	2	1	2	5	8	20	.178	.277	.315	592	58	-5	4	0	1	.940	6	S-30/2-7,O-1(0-0-1)	0.3
1998	Atl-N	8	15	2	2	0	0	0	1	2	4	.133	.235	.133	369	0	-2	0	0	0	.952	2	/S-7	0.0
	Mon-N	2	5	0	0	0	0	0	0	0	1	.000	.000	.000	0	-99	-1	0	0	0	1.000	-0	/2-1	-0.2
	Yr	10	20	2	2	0	0	0	1	2	5	.100	.182	.100	282	-23	-4	0	0	0	.952	2	/S-7,2-1	-0.2
1999	KC-A	34	100	14	28	3	0	0	5	8	20	.280	.333	.310	643	64	-5	7	4	0	.987	-11	S-22,2-11/3-1	-1.3
2000	KC-A	3	4	0	1	0	0	0	0	0	2	.250	.250	.250	500	27	-0	0	0	0	1.000	1	/2-1,3-1,S-1	0.1
Total	5	115	202	28	45	5	1	2	11	18	51	.223	.293	.287	580	51	-14	11	4	1	.962	-2	/S-61,2-20,3-2,O-1R	-1.2

■ BILL HOLBERT
Holbert, William Henry b: 3/14/1855, Baltimore, Md. d: 3/20/35, Laurel, Md. BR/TR, 197 lbs. Deb: 9/5/1876 MU Career OF: (12-LF 19-CF 38-RF)

YEAR	TM/L	G	AB	R	H	2B	3B	HR	RBI	BB	SO	AVG	OBP	SLG	OPS	OPS+	BR+	SB	CS	SBR	FA	FR	G/POS	TPR
1876	Lou-N	12	43	3	11	0	0	0	5	0	3	.256	.256	.256	512	60	-2				.843	7	C-12	0.5
1878	Mil-N	45	173	10	32	2	0	0	12	3	14	.185	.199	.197	395	28	-13				.818	7	O-30(0-0-30),C-21	-0.6
1879	Syr-N	59	229	11	46	0	0	0	21	1	20	.201	.204	.201	405	39	-14				.897	-1	*C-56/O-4(0-3-1),M	-1.2
	Tro-N	4	15	1	4	0	0	0	2	0	1	.267	.267	.267	533	82	-0				.893	1	/C-4	0.0
	Yr	63	244	12	50	0	0	0	23	1	21	.205	.208	.205	413	41	-14				.897	0	C-60/O-4(0-3-1)	-1.2
1880	Tro-N	60	212	18	40	5	1	0	8	9	18	.189	.222	.222	443	48	-11				.911	12	*C-58/O-3(0-0-3)	0.2
1881	Tro-N	46	180	16	49	3	0	0	14	3	13	.272	.284	.289	573	77	-5				.918	7	C-43/O-3(0-0-3)	0.3
1882	Tro-N	71	251	24	46	5	0	0	23	11	22	.183	.218	.203	421	38	-16				.892	16	*C-58,3-12/O-3(0-3-0)	0.4
1883	NY-a	73	299	26	71	9	1	0		1		.237	.240	.274	514	62	-13				.920	**34**	*C-68/O-5(0-5-0),2-1	2.4
1884	*NY-a	65	255	28	53	5	0	0		7		.208	.235	.227	462	53	-13				.920	20	C-59/O-5(4-0-1),S-1	1.1
1885	NY-a	56	202	13	35	3	0	0	13	8		.173	.205	.188	393	27	-16				.900	12	C-39,O-13(8-5-0)/3-5	0.0
1886	NY-a	48	171	8	35	4	2	0	13	6		.205	.232	.251	483	54	-9	4			.922	19	C-45/O-3(0-3-0),S-1	1.2
1887	NY-a	69	262	20	65	4	3	0	32	7		.248	.248	.267	515	46	-18	12			.894	2	C-60/1-8,S-2,2-1	-1.0
1888	Bro-a	15	50	4	6	1	0	0	1	2		.120	.170	.140	310	-0	-6	0			.926	2	C-15	-0.2
Total	12	623	2342	182	493	41	7	0	144	58	91	.211	.228	.232	460	47	-136	16			.907	138	C-538/O-69R,3-17,1S2	3.1

■ SAMMY HOLBROOK
Holbrook, James Marbury b: 7/17/10, Meridian, Miss. d: 4/10/91, Jackson, Miss. BR/TR, 5'11", 189 lbs. Deb: 4/25/35

YEAR	TM/L	G	AB	R	H	2B	3B	HR	RBI	BB	SO	AVG	OBP	SLG	OPS	OPS+	BR+	SB	CS	SBR	FA	FR	G/POS	TPR
1935	Was-A	52	135	20	35	2	2	2	25	30	16	.259	.408	.348	756	101	2	0	0	0	.952	-11	C-47	-0.6

■ JOE HOLDEN
Holden, Joseph Francis "Socks" b: 6/4/13, St.Clair, Pa. d: 5/10/96, St.Clair, Pa. BL/TR, 5'8", 175 lbs. Deb: 6/14/34

YEAR	TM/L	G	AB	R	H	2B	3B	HR	RBI	BB	SO	AVG	OBP	SLG	OPS	OPS+	BR+	SB	CS	SBR	FA	FR	G/POS	TPR
1934	Phi-N	10	14	1	1	0	0	0	0	0	2	.071	.071	.071	143	-54	-3	0			1.000	2	/C-6	-0.1
1935	Phi-N	6	9	0	1	0	0	0	0	0	3	.111	.111	.111	222	-36	-2	1			1.000	-1	/C-4	-0.2
1936	Phi-N	1	1	0	0	0	0	0	0	0	0	.000	.000	.000	0	-91	-0	0			.000	0	H	0.0
Total	3	17	24	1	2	0	0	0	0	0	5	.083	.083	.083	167	-49	-5	1			1.000	2	/C-10	-0.3

■ BILL HOLDEN
Holden, William Paul b: 9/7/1889, Birmingham, Ala. d: 9/14/71, Pensacola, Fla. BR/TR, 6', 170 lbs. Deb: 9/11/13

YEAR	TM/L	G	AB	R	H	2B	3B	HR	RBI	BB	SO	AVG	OBP	SLG	OPS	OPS+	BR+	SB	CS	SBR	FA	FR	G/POS	TPR
1913	NY-A	18	53	6	16	3	1	0	8	8	5	.302	.393	.396	790	131	2	0			.977	3	O-16(0-16-0)	0.4
1914	NY-A	50	165	12	30	3	2	0	12	16	26	.182	.254	.224	478	44	-11	2	4	-1	.981	-1	O-45(3-37-6)	-1.8
	Cin-N	11	28	2	6	0	0	0	1	3	5	.214	.290	.214	505	49	-2	0			1.000	-2	O-10(7-3-1)	-0.4
Total	2	79	246	20	52	6	3	0	21	27	36	.211	.289	.260	550	64	-11	2	4		.981	0	/O-71(10-56-7)	-1.8

■ JIM HOLDSWORTH
Holdsworth, James "Long Jim" b: 7/14/1850, New York, N.Y. d: 3/22/18, New York, N.Y. BR/TR, Deb: 5/14/1872 NA OF: (0-LF 46-CF 5-RF)

YEAR	TM/L	G	AB	R	H	2B	3B	HR	RBI	BB	SO	AVG	OBP	SLG	OPS	OPS+	BR+	SB	CS	SBR	FA	FR	G/POS	TPR
1872	Cle-n	22	110	19	33	5	0	0	11	1	2	.300	.306	.345	652	106	1	3	2	-0	.765	-1	S-22	0.0
	Eck-n	2	7	1	2	0	0	0	0	0	0	.286	.286	.286	571	90	0	0	0	0	.933	2	/S-2	0.1
	Yr	24	117	20	35	5	0	0	11	1	2	.299	.305	.342	647	105	1	3	2	-0	.780	1	S-24	0.1
1873	Mut-n	53	233	46	75	4	8	0	28	0	3	.322	.322	.408	730	116	4	1	0	0	.775	-14	*S-53	-0.8
1874	Phi-n	57	285	60	97	8	9	0	37	1	0	.340	.343	.432	774	142	12	1	2	-0	.694	-25	3-31,S-21/O-6C,21	-1.2
1875	Mut-n	71	324	45	92	12	1	0	23	1	3	.284	.286	.327	613	107	1	3	3	-0	.780	1	O-45(0-43-2),S-26	0.0
1876	NY-N	52	242	23	64	3	2	0	19	1	2	.264	.269	.295	563	101	2				.902	1	*O-49(0-49-0)/2-3	0.0
1877	Har-N	55	260	26	66	5	2	0	20	2	8	.254	.260	.288	548	81	-4				.833	-3	*O-55(0-55-0)	-0.8
1882	Tro-N	1	3	0	0	0	0	0	0	0	1	.000	.000	.000	0	-99	-1				1.000	1	/O-1(0-1-0)	0.0
1884	Ind-a	5	18	1	2	0	0	0		2		.111	.200	.111	311	4	-2				.929	1	/O-5(0-5-0)	-0.1
Total	4 n	205	959	171	299	29	18	0	99	3	8	.312	.314	.380	693	119	18	8	7	-1	.750	-38	S-124/O-51C,3-31,21	-1.9
Total	4	113	523	50	132	8	4	0	39	5	11	.252	.260	.284	543	85	-5				.875	0	O-110(0-110-0)/2-3	-0.9

■ WALTER HOLKE
Holke, Walter Henry "Union Man" b: 12/25/1892, St.Louis, Mo. d: 10/12/54, St.Louis, Mo. BB/TL, 6'1.5", 185 lbs. Deb: 10/6/14 C

YEAR	TM/L	G	AB	R	H	2B	3B	HR	RBI	BB	SO	AVG	OBP	SLG	OPS	OPS+	BR+	SB	CS	SBR	FA	FR	G/POS	TPR
1914	NY-N	2	6	0	2	0	0	0	0	0	0	.333	.333	.333	667	102	-0	0			.950	0	/1-2	0.0
1916	NY-N	34	111	16	39	4	2	0	13	6	16	.351	.390	.423	813	158	7	10			.997	-0	1-34	0.7
1917	*NY-N	153	527	55	146	12	7	2	55	34	54	.277	.327	.338	665	107	4	13			.989	-5	*1-153	-0.6
1918	NY-N	88	326	38	82	17	4	1	27	10	26	.252	.276	.337	613	88	-6	10			.990	5	1-88	-0.3
1919	Bos-N	137	518	48	151	14	6	0	48	21	25	.292	.325	.342	667	105	2	19			.993	6	*1-136	0.6
1920	Bos-N	144	551	53	162	15	11	3	64	28	31	.294	.329	.377	707	107	4	4	11	-3	.991	-3	*1-143	-0.6
1921	Bos-N	150	579	60	151	15	10	3	63	17	41	.261	.284	.337	621	67	-28	8	11	-2	**.997**	3	*1-150	-3.8
1922	Bos-N	105	395	35	115	9	4	0	46	14	23	.291	.317	.334	651	71	-17	6	8	-1	.993	-4	*1-105	-2.8
1923	Phi-N	147	562	64	175	31	4	7	70	16	37	.311	.330	.418	749	86	-12	7	9	-2	.991	-1	*1-146/P-1	-2.3
1924	Phi-N	148	563	60	169	23	6	6	64	25	33	.300	.330	.394	724	83	-13	3	8	-2	.993	4	*1-148	-2.1
1925	Phi-N	39	86	11	21	5	0	1	17	3	6	.244	.270	.337	607	50	-7	0	0	0	.994	1	1-23	-0.6
	Cin-N	65	232	24	65	8	4	1	20	17	12	.280	.329	.362	691	78	-7	1	3	-1	.997	1	1-65	-1.1
	Yr	104	318	35	86	13	4	2	37	20	18	.270	.314	.355	669	69	-15	1	3	-1	.996	2	1-88	-1.7
Total	11	1212	4456	464	1278	153	58	24	487	191	304	.287	.318	.363	682	89	-72	81	50		.993	7	*1-1193/P-1	-12.9

■ BILL HOLLAHAN
Hollahan, William James "Happy" b: 11/22/1896, New York, N.Y. d: 11/27/65, New York, N.Y. BR/TR, 5'8", 165 lbs. Deb: 9/27/20

YEAR	TM/L	G	AB	R	H	2B	3B	HR	RBI	BB	SO	AVG	OBP	SLG	OPS	OPS+	BR+	SB	CS	SBR	FA	FR	G/POS	TPR
1920	Was-A	3	4	0	1	0	0	0	1	1	2	.250	.400	.250	650	77	-0	1	0	0	1.000	0	/3-3	0.0

■ DUTCH HOLLAND
Holland, Robert Clyde b: 10/12/03, Middlesex, N.C. d: 6/16/67, Lumberton, N.C. BR/TR, 6'1", 190 lbs. Deb: 8/16/32

YEAR	TM/L	G	AB	R	H	2B	3B	HR	RBI	BB	SO	AVG	OBP	SLG	OPS	OPS+	BR+	SB	CS	SBR	FA	FR	G/POS	TPR
1932	Bos-N	39	156	15	46	11	1	1	18	12	20	.295	.345	.397	743	103	1	0			.990	2	O-39(39-0-0)	0.0
1933	Bos-N	13	31	3	8	3	0	0	3	3	8	.258	.324	.355	678	102	0	1			.867	-1	/O-7(7-0-0)	-0.2
1934	Cle-A	50	128	19	32	12	1	2	13	13	11	.250	.319	.406	725	85	-3	0	0	0	.957	-4	O-31(15-0-16)	-0.9
Total	3	102	315	37	86	26	2	3	34	28	39	.273	.332	.397	729	95	-3	1	0		.969	-3	/O-77(61-0-16)	-1.1

■ WILL HOLLAND
Holland, Willard A. b: Georgetown, Del. d: 7/19/30, Philadelphia, Pa. 5'10", 180 lbs. Deb: 7/10/1889

YEAR	TM/L	G	AB	R	H	2B	3B	HR	RBI	BB	SO	AVG	OBP	SLG	OPS	OPS+	BR+	SB	CS	SBR	FA	FR	G/POS	TPR
1889	Bal-a	40	143	13	27	1	2	0	16	9	28	.189	.247	.224	471	34	-13	4			.853	-15	S-39/O-1(1-0-0)	-2.3

■ TODD HOLLANDSWORTH
Hollandsworth, Todd Mathew b: 4/20/73, Dayton, Ohio BL/TL, 6'2", 195 lbs. Deb: 4/25/95 Career OF: (326-LF 189-CF 45-RF)

YEAR	TM/L	G	AB	R	H	2B	3B	HR	RBI	BB	SO	AVG	OBP	SLG	OPS	OPS+	BR+	SB	CS	SBR	FA	FR	G/POS	TPR
1995	*LA-N	41	103	16	24	2	0	5	13	10	29	.233	.307	.398	705	92	-1	2	1	0	.938	-3	O-37(9-25-3)	-0.4
1996	*LA-N	149	478	64	139	26	4	12	59	41	93	.291	.349	.437	787	115	10	21	6	3	.978	-3	*O-142(122-18-9)	0.6
1997	LA-N	106	296	39	73	20	2	4	31	17	60	.247	.288	.368	656	76	-11	5	5	-1	.984	-3	O-99(80-30-4)	-1.6
1998	LA-N	55	175	23	47	6	4	3	20	9	42	.269	.308	.400	708	90	-3	4	3	-0	.957	-3	O-51(48-10-1)	-0.7
1999	LA-N	92	261	39	74	12	2	9	32	24	61	.284	.346	.448	794	105	2	5	2	0	.984	-3	O-67(27-34-9),1-13	-0.2
2000	LA-N	81	261	42	61	12	0	8	24	30	61	.234	.315	.372	687	76	-10	11	4	1	.987	-1	O-77(9-68-1)	-0.9
	Col-N	56	167	39	54	8	0	11	23	11	38	.323	.365	.569	934	102	1	7	3	0	.988	-0	O-48(31-4-18)	0.0

YEAR	TM/L	G	AB	R	H	2B	3B	HR	RBI	BB	SO	AVG	OBP	SLG	OPS	OPS+	BR+	SB	CS	SBR	FA	FR	G/POS	TPR
	Yr	137	428	81	115	20	0	19	47	41	99	.269	.334	.449	783	88	-8	18	7	2	.987	-2	*O-125(40-72-19)	-0.9
Total	6	580	1741	262	472	86	12	52	202	142	384	.271	.328	.424	752	96	-14	55	24	4	.977	-16	O-521L/1-13	-3.2
■ **GARY HOLLE**	Holle, Gary Charles b: 8/11/54, Albany, N.Y. BR/TL, 6'6", 210 lbs. Deb: 6/2/79																							
1979	Tex-A	5	6	0	1	1	0	0	0	1	0	.167	.286	.333	619	67	-0	0	0	0	1.000	-0	/1-1	-0.1
■ **BUG HOLLIDAY**	Holliday, James Wear b: 2/8/1867, St.Louis, Mo. d: 2/15/10, Cincinnati, Ohio BR/TR, 5'11", 151 lbs. Deb: 4/17/1889 U Career OF: (211-LF 598-CF 92-RF)																							
1889	Cin-a	135	563	107	181	28	7	**19**	104	43	59	.321	.372	.497	869	142	27	46			.923	-7	*O-135(0-135-0)	1.3
1890	Cin-N	131	518	93	140	18	14	4	75	49	36	.270	.341	.382	724	111	7	50			.948	-2	*O-131(0-131-0)	0.0
1891	Cin-N	111	442	74	141	21	10	9	84	37	28	.319	.376	.473	848	145	24	30			.939	-8	*O-111(49-62-0)	1.1
1892	Cin-N	152	602	114	177	23	16	**13**	91	57	39	.294	.356	.450	806	145	31	43			.933	-4	*O-152(1-78-77)/P-1	1.7
1893	Cin-N	126	500	108	155	24	10	5	89	73	22	.310	.401	.428	829	117	13	32			.944	-10	*O-125(1-125-0)/1-1	-0.4
1894	Cin-N	123	521	126	196	24	8	13	123	41	20	.376	.424	.528	952	123	19	33			.912	0	*O-121(111-5-8)/1-1	0.6
1895	Cin-N	32	127	25	38	9	2	0	20	10	3	.299	.350	.402	752	90	-2	6			.940	-4	O-32(5-27-0)	-0.7
1896	Cin-N	29	84	17	27	4	0	0	8	9	4	.321	.394	.369	763	95	-0	1			.925	-2	O-16L/1-5,S-1,P-1	-0.3
1897	Cin-N	61	195	50	61	9	4	2	20	27		.313	.399	.431	830	112	4	6			.940	-6	O-42L/S-4,2-3,1-3	-0.5
1898	Cin-N	30	106	21	25	2	1	0	7	14		.236	.325	.274	599	67	-4	5			.969	-2	O-28(2-26-0)	-0.8
Total	10	930	3658	735	1141	162	72	65	621	360	211	.312	.377	.449	826	125	118	252			.934	-45	O-893C/1-10,S-5,2P	2.0
■ **HOLLY HOLLINGSHEAD**	Hollingshead, John Samuel (a.k.a. Samuel John Holly) b: 1/17/1853, Washington, D.C. d: 10/6/26, Washington, D.C. Deb: 4/20/1872 M																							
1872	Nat-n	9	44	12	15	1	1	0	6	1	0	.341	.356	.409	765	115	0	0	0	0	.778	-3	/2-9	-0.2
1873	Was-n	30	136	25	35	2	2	0	22	0	6	.257	.257	.301	559	68	-5	0	0	0	.833	2	O-30(0-30-0)/2-2	-0.3
1875	Was-n	19	81	8	20	1	1	0	5	1	2	.247	.256	.284	540	91	-1	2	1	0	.826	2	O-19(4-13-3),M	0.2
Total	3 n	58	261	45	70	4	4	0	33	2	8	.268	.274	.314	588	83	-5	2	1	0	.831	1	/O-49(4-43-3),2-11	-0.3
■ **DAMON HOLLINS**	Hollins, Damon Jamall b: 6/12/74, Fairfield, Cal. BR/TL, 5'11", 180 lbs. Deb: 4/24/98																							
1998	Atl-N	3	6	0	1	0	0	0	0	0	1	.167	.167	.167	333	-12	-1	0	0	0	1.000	-1	/O-3(2-0-1)	-0.2
	LA-N	5	9	1	2	0	0	0	2	0	2	.222	.222	.222	444	18	-1	0	1	-0	1.000	-0	/O-4(1-0-3)	-0.2
	Yr	8	15	1	3	0	0	0	2	0	3	.200	.200	.200	400	6	-2	0	1	-0	1.000	-1	/O-7(3-0-4)	-0.4
■ **DAVE HOLLINS**	Hollins, David Michael b: 5/25/66, Buffalo, N.Y. BB/TR, 6'1", 207 lbs. Deb: 4/12/90																							
1990	Phi-N	72	114	14	21	0	0	5	15	10	28	.184	.256	.316	572	57	-7	0	0	0	.932	-1	3-30/1-1	-0.9
1991	Phi-N	56	151	18	45	10	2	6	21	17	26	.298	.380	.510	890	150	10	1	1	-0	.922	-3	3-36/1-6	0.7
1992	Phi-N	156	586	104	158	28	4	27	93	76	110	.270	.372	.469	841	137	30	9	6	-0	.954	-20	*3-156/1-1	1.1
1993	*Phi-N★	143	543	104	148	30	4	18	93	85	109	.273	.376	.442	818	120	17	2	3	-1	.914	-29	*3-143	-1.1
1994	Phi-N	44	162	28	36	7	1	4	26	23	32	.222	.333	.352	685	77	-5	1	0	0	.887	-15	3-43/O-1(0-0-1)	-2.0
1995	Phi-N	65	205	46	47	12	2	7	25	53	38	.229	.399	.410	809	113	6	1	1	-0	.988	-6	1-61	-0.5
	Bos-A	5	13	2	2	0	0	0	1	4	7	.154	.353	.154	507	37	-1	0	0	0	1.000	-0	/O-2(0-0-2),D-3	-0.1
1996	Min-A	121	422	71	102	26	0	13	53	71	102	.242	.364	.396	760	91	-5	6	4	-0	.953	-4	*3-116/S-1,D-3	-0.7
	Sea-A	28	94	17	33	3	0	3	25	13	15	.351	.445	.479	924	134	6	0	2	-1	.961	2	3-28/1-1	0.6
	Yr	149	516	88	135	29	0	16	78	84	117	.262	.378	.411	789	98	1	6	6	-1	.955	-2	*3-144/D-3,S-1,1-1	-0.1
1997	Ana-A	149	572	101	165	29	2	16	85	62	124	.288	.366	.430	796	107	7	16	6	1	.922	-11	*3-135,1-14	-0.2
1998	Ana-A	101	363	60	88	16	2	11	39	44	69	.242	.336	.388	724	87	-6	11	3	1	.929	-7	3-91/1-7,D-2	-1.2
1999	Tor-A	27	99	12	22	5	0	2	6	6	22	.222	.260	.333	593	49	-8	0	0	0	.000	0	D-25	-0.9
Total	10	967	3324	577	867	166	17	112	482	463	682	.261	.362	.422	784	107	44	47	26	1	.933	-93	3-778/1-91,D-33,OS	-5.2
■ **STAN HOLLMIG**	Hollmig, Stanley Ernest "Hondo" b: 1/2/26, Fredericksburg, Tex d: 12/4/81, San Antonio, Tex. BR/TR, 6'2.5", 190 lbs. Deb: 4/19/49																							
1949	Phi-N	81	251	28	64	11	6	2	26	20	43	.255	.315	.371	686	85	-6	1			.958	-6	O-66(0-0-66)	-1.3
1950	Phi-N	11	12	1	3	2	0	0	1	0	3	.250	.250	.417	667	73	-1	0			1.000	-1	/O-3(2-0-1)	-0.1
1951	Phi-N	2	2	0	0	0	0	0	0	0	0	.000	.000	.000	0	-99	-1	0	0	0	.000	0	H	-0.1
Total	3	94	265	29	67	13	6	2	27	20	46	.253	.310	.370	680	84	-7	1	0		.959	-6	/O-69(2-0-67)	-1.5
■ **CHARLIE HOLLOCHER**	Hollocher, Charles Jacob b: 6/11/1896, St.Louis, Mo. d: 8/14/40, Frontenac, Mo. BL/TR, 5'7", 154 lbs. Deb: 4/16/18																							
1918	*Chi-N	131	509	72	**161**	23	6	2	38	47	30	.316	.379	.397	775	133	21	26			.929	-19	*S-131	1.2
1919	Chi-N	115	430	51	116	14	5	3	26	44	19	.270	.347	.347	694	108	6	16			.941	6	*S-115	2.2
1920	Chi-N	80	301	53	96	17	2	0	22	41	15	.319	.406	.389	795	126	12	20	14	-1	.954	9	S-80	2.7
1921	Chi-N	140	558	71	161	28	8	3	37	43	13	.289	.342	.384	725	91	-6	5	16	-5	**.963**	3	*S-137	0.7
1922	Chi-N	152	592	90	201	37	8	3	69	58	5	.340	.403	.444	847	116	16	19	29	-6	**.965**	-5	*S-152	2.0
1923	Chi-N	66	260	46	89	14	2	1	28	26	5	.342	.410	.423	833	120	9	9	10	-2	.963	-9	S-65	0.5
1924	Chi-N	76	286	28	70	12	4	2	21	18	7	.245	.292	.336	627	67	-14	4	11	-3	.969	4	S-71	-0.5
Total	7	760	2936	411	894	145	35	14	241	277	94	.304	.370	.392	762	110	44	99	80		.954	-13	S-751	8.8
■ **ED HOLLY**	Holly, Edward William (b: Edward William Ruthlavy) b: 7/6/1879, Chicago, Ill. d: 11/27/73, Williamsport, Pa. BR/TR, 5'10", 165 lbs. Deb: 7/18/06 Career OF: (1-LF 0-CF 1-RF)																							
1906	StL-N	10	34	1	2	0	0	0	7	5		.059	.179	.059	238	-27	-5	0			.939	-3	S-10	-0.8
1907	StL-N	150	545	55	125	18	3	1	40	36		.229	.283	.279	562	79	-14	16			.927	11	*S-147/2-3	0.2
1914	Pit-F	100	350	28	86	9	4	0	26	17	52	.246	.281	.294	575	57	-27	14			.942	-2	S-94/O-2(1-0-1),2-1	-2.4
1915	Pit-F	16	42	8	11	2	0	0	5	5	6	.262	.354	.310	664	88	-1	3			.865	-4	S-11/3-3	-0.5
Total	4	276	971	92	224	29	7	1	78	63	58	.231	.282	.278	560	67	-46	33			.931	1	S-262/2-4,3-3,O-2L	-3.5
■ **WATTIE HOLM**	Holm, Roscoe Albert b: 12/28/01, Peterson, Iowa d: 5/19/50, Everly, Iowa BR/TR, 5'9.5", 160 lbs. Deb: 4/15/24 Career OF: (93-LF 92-CF 85-RF)																							
1924	StL-N	81	293	40	86	10	4	0	23	8	16	.294	.317	.355	672	81	-8	1	4	-1	.988	2	O-64(1-63-0)/C-9,3-4	-1.0
1925	StL-N	13	58	10	12	1	1	0	2	3	1	.207	.246	.259	505	28	-6	1	0	0	.976	2	O-13(3-0-11)	-0.5
1926	*StL-N	55	144	18	41	5	1	0	21	18	14	.285	.364	.333	698	85	-2	3			.962	-3	O-39(26-0-13)	-0.8
1927	StL-N	110	419	55	120	27	8	3	66	24	29	.286	.327	.411	737	93	-5	4			.967	-8	O-97(55-25-18)/3-9	-1.9
1928	*StL-N	102	386	61	107	24	6	3	47	32	17	.277	.334	.394	728	88	-7	1			.918	-10	3-83/O-7(0-0-7)	-1.2
1929	StL-N	64	176	21	41	5	6	0	14	12	8	.233	.282	.330	611	50	-14	1			.944	3	O-44(6-4-34)/3-1	-1.3
1932	StL-N	11	17	2	3	1	0	0	1	3	1	.176	.333	.235	569	55	-1	0			1.000	0	/O-4(2-0-2)	-0.1
Total	7	436	1493	207	410	73	26	6	174	100	86	.275	.322	.370	693	81	-43	11	4		.970	-15	O-268L/3-97,C-9	-6.8
■ **BILLY HOLM**	Holm, William Frederick Henry b: 7/21/12, Chicago, Ill. d: 7/27/77, East Chicago, Ind BR/TR, 5'10.5", 168 lbs. Deb: 9/24/43																							
1943	Chi-N	7	15	0	1	0	0	0	0	2	4	.067	.176	.067	243	-29	-2	0			1.000	1	/C-7	-0.1
1944	Chi-N	54	132	10	18	2	0	0	6	16	19	.136	.235	.152	386	10	-15	1			.979	-2	C-50	-1.6
1945	Bos-A	58	135	12	25	2	1	0	9	23	17	.185	.317	.215	532	54	-7	1	1	-0	.980	-4	C-57	-0.8
Total	3	119	282	22	44	4	1	0	15	41	40	.156	.272	.177	449	30	-25	2	1		.981	-4	C-114	-2.5
■ **GARY HOLMAN**	Holman, Gary Richard b: 1/25/44, Long Beach, Cal. BL/TL, 6'1", 200 lbs. Deb: 6/26/68																							
1968	Was-A	75	85	10	25	5	1	0	7	13	15	.294	.388	.376	764	137	4	0	0	0	1.000	2	1-33,O-10(3-0-8)	0.6
1969	Was-A	41	31	1	5	1	0	0	2	4	7	.161	.257	.194	451	29	-3	0	0	0	1.000	-1	1-11/O-3(1-0-2)	-0.5
Total	2	116	116	11	30	6	1	0	9	17	22	.259	.353	.328	681	107	1	0	0	0	1.000	1	/1-44,O-13(4-0-10)	0.1
■ **FRED HOLMES**	Holmes, Frederick C. b: 7/1/1878, Chicago, Ill. d: 2/13/56, Norwood Park, Ill. BR/TR, Deb: 8/23/03																							
1903	NY-A	1	0	0	0	0	0	0	0	1		—	1.000	—	1000	207	0	0			.833	-0	/1-1	0.0
1904	Chi-N	1	3	1	1	1	0	0	0	0		.333	.333	.667	1000	206	0	0			1.000	0	/C-1	0.0
Total	2	2	3	1	1	1	0	0	0	1		.333	.500	.667	1167	255	1	0			1.000	-0	/C-1,1-1	0.0
■ **DUCKY HOLMES**	Holmes, Howard Elbert b: 7/8/1883, Dayton, Ohio d: 9/18/45, Dayton, Ohio BR/TR, 5'10", 160 lbs. Deb: 4/18/06 U																							
1906	StL-N	9	27	2	5	0	0	0	2	2		.185	.267	.185	452	43	-2	0			.979	-0	/C-9	-0.2
■ **DUCKY HOLMES**	Holmes, James William b: 1/28/1869, Des Moines, Iowa d: 8/6/32, Truro, Iowa BL/TR, 5'6", 170 lbs. Deb: 8/8/1895 Career OF: (564-LF 37-CF 285-RF)																							
1895	Lou-N	40	161	33	60	10	2	3	20	12	9	.373	.426	.516	942	152	13	9			.780	-11	O-29R/S-8,3-4,P-2	0.0
1896	Lou-N	47	141	22	38	3	2	0	18	13	5	.270	.360	.319	679	83	-3	8			.790	-7	O-33C/P-2,S-1,2-1	-1.0
1897	Lou-N	2	4	0	0	0	0	0	0	1		.000	.200	.000	200	-46	-1	0			1.000	1	/S-1	0.0

YEAR	TM/L	G	AB	R	H	2B	3B	HR	RBI	BB	SO	AVG	OBP	SLG	OPS	OPS+	BR+	SB	CS	SBR	FA	FR	G/POS	TPR
	NY-N	80	310	52	82	8	6	1	45	18		.265	.313	.339	652	74	-12	30			.905	-7	O-78(78-0-0)/S-1	-2.3
	Yr	82	314	52	82	8	6	1	45	19		.261	.312	.334	646	73	-13	30			.905	-6	O-78(78-0-0)/S-2	-2.3
1898	StL-N	23	101	9	24	1	1	0	0	2		.238	.260	.267	527	50	-7	4			.900	2	O-22(11-2-9)	-0.6
	Bal-N	113	442	54	126	10	9	1	64	23		.285	.333	.355	689	96	-3	25			.935	4	*O-113(113-0-0)	-0.9
	Yr	136	543	63	150	11	10	1	64	25		.276	.320	.339	659	87	-10	29			.930	6	*O-135(124-2-9)	-1.5
1899	Bal-N	138	553	80	177	31	7	4	66	39		.320	.381	.423	804	114	10	50			.927	6	*O-138(137-0-1)	0.3
1901	Det-A	131	537	90	158	28	10	4	62	37		.294	.347	.406	753	103	2	35			.907	-2	*O-131(2-0-131)	-0.6
1902	Det-A	92	362	50	93	15	4	2	33	28		.257	.319	.337	656	80	-9	16			.950	6	O-92(1-0-91)	-0.8
1903	Was-A	21	71	13	16	3	1	1	8	5		.225	.286	.338	624	85	-1	10			.912	1	O-14(0-3-11)/3-4,2-2	-0.1
	Chi-A	86	344	53	96	7	5	0	18	25		.279	.335	.328	664	104	3	25			.965	2	O-82(82-0-0)/3-3	0.0
	Yr	107	415	66	112	10	6	1	26	30		.270	.327	.330	657	101	1	35			.956	3	O-96(82-3-11)/3-7,2-2	-0.1
1904	Chi-A	68	251	42	78	11	9	1	19	14		.311	.354	.438	793	156	15	13			.975	2	O-63(53-2-8)	1.5
1905	Chi-A	92	328	42	66	15	2	0	22	19		.201	.258	.259	517	67	-12	11			.936	-1	O-89(87-1-1)	-2.1
Total	10	933	3605	540	1014	142	58	17	375	236	14	.281	.336	.367	703	99	-6	236			.924	-5	O-884L/3-11,S-11,P2	-6.6

■ **TOMMY HOLMES** Holmes, Thomas Francis "Kelly" b: 3/29/17, Brooklyn, N.Y. BL/TL, 5'10", 180 lbs. Deb: 4/14/42 M

YEAR	TM/L	G	AB	R	H	2B	3B	HR	RBI	BB	SO	AVG	OBP	SLG	OPS	OPS+	BR+	SB	CS	SBR	FA	FR	G/POS	TPR
1942	Bos-N	141	558	56	155	24	4	4	41	64	10	.278	.353	.357	710	110	8	2			.990	15	*O-140(0-137-3)	2.1
1943	Bos-N	152	629	75	170	33	10	5	41	58	20	.270	.334	.378	712	107	5	7			.993	8	*O-152(2-149-1)	0.9
1944	Bos-N	155	631	93	195	42	6	13	73	61	11	.309	.372	.456	828	127	22	4			.991	6	*O-155(2-154-0)	2.4
1945	Bos-N†	154	636	125	**224**	**47**	6	**28**	117	70	9	.352	.420	**.577**	**997**	**175**	**62**	15			.983	1	*O-154(32-2-121)	**5.2**
1946	Bos-N	149	568	80	176	35	6	6	79	58	14	.310	.377	.424	801	126	19	7			.987	8	*O-146(0-0-146)	2.3
1947	Bos-N	150	618	90	**191**	33	3	9	53	44	16	.309	.360	.416	776	108	7	3			.989	10	*O-147(0-0-147)	1.1
1948	*Bos-N★	139	585	85	190	35	7	6	61	46	20	.325	.375	.439	814	122	17	1			.983	3	*O-137(0-0-137)	1.6
1949	Bos-N	117	380	47	101	20	4	8	59	39	6	.266	.337	.403	740	103	1	1			.987	5	*O-103(0-0-103)	0.3
1950	Bos-N	105	322	44	96	20	1	9	51	33	8	.298	.370	.450	821	122	11	0			1.000	-0	O-88(0-0-88)	0.7
1951	Bos-N	27	29	1	5	2	0	0	5	3	4	.172	.250	.241	491	35	-3	0	0	0	1.000	-1	/O-3(2-0-1),M	-0.4
1952	*Bro-N	31	36	2	4	1	0	0	1	4	4	.111	.200	.139	339	-4	-5	0	0	0	1.000	-1	/O-6(0-0-6)	-0.6
Total	11	1320	4992	698	1507	292	47	88	581	480	122	.302	.366	.432	798	122	145	40	0		.989	53	*O-1231(38-442-753)	15.6

■ **RED HOLT** Holt, James Emmett Madison b: 7/25/1894, Dayton, Tenn. d: 2/2/61, Birmingham, Ala. BL/TL, 5'11", 175 lbs. Deb: 9/5/25

YEAR	TM/L	G	AB	R	H	2B	3B	HR	RBI	BB	SO	AVG	OBP	SLG	OPS	OPS+	BR+	SB	CS	SBR	FA	FR	G/POS	TPR
1925	Phi-A	27	88	13	24	7	0	1	8	12	9	.273	.360	.386	746	84	-2	0	0	0	.986	0	1-25	-0.3

■ **JIM HOLT** Holt, James William b: 5/27/44, Graham, N.C. BL/TR, 6', 195 lbs. Deb: 4/17/68 Career OF: (198-LF 143-CF 63-RF)

YEAR	TM/L	G	AB	R	H	2B	3B	HR	RBI	BB	SO	AVG	OBP	SLG	OPS	OPS+	BR+	SB	CS	SBR	FA	FR	G/POS	TPR
1968	Min-A	70	106	9	22	2	1	0	8	4	20	.208	.236	.245	482	44	-7	0	1	-0	.973	-5	O-38(23-2-14)/1-1	-1.6
1969	Min-A	12	14	3	5	0	0	1	2	0	4	.357	.357	.571	929	153	1	0	0	0	1.000	-2	/O-5(1-0-4),1-1	-0.1
1970	*Min-A	142	319	37	85	9	3	3	40	17	32	.266	.304	.342	645	77	-10	3	1	0	.995	-11	*O-130(76-52-4)/1-2	-2.6
1971	Min-A	126	340	35	88	11	3	1	29	16	28	.259	.294	.318	612	71	-13	5	1	1	.986	-5	*O-106(12-86-12)/1-3	-2.1
1972	Min-A	10	27	6	12	1	0	1	6	0	1	.444	.444	.593	1037	197	3	0	0	0	.917	0	/O-7(2-0-5),1-1	0.3
1973	Min-A	132	441	52	131	25	3	11	58	29	43	.297	.343	.442	785	115	8	0	3	-1	.990	5	*O-102(80-3-21),1-33	0.4
1974	Min-A	79	197	24	50	11	0	0	16	14	16	.254	.307	.310	616	75	-6	0	0	0	.996	5	1-67/O-5(2-0-3)	-0.5
	*Oak-A	30	42	1	6	0	0	0	0	1	9	.143	.182	.143	325	-6	-6	0	0	0	1.000	1	1-17/D-3	-0.5
	Yr	109	239	25	56	11	0	0	16	15	25	.234	.285	.280	565	63	-11	0	0	0	.996	6	1-84/O-5(2-0-3),D-3	-1.0
1975	*Oak-A	102	123	7	27	3	0	2	16	11	11	.220	.294	.293	587	68	-5	0	0	0	.991	1	1-52/O-2L,C-1,D-4	-0.6
1976	Oak-A	4	7	0	2	2	0	0	2	1	2	.286	.375	.571	946	182	1	0	0	0	.000	0	/D-2	0.1
Total	9	707	1616	174	428	64	10	19	177	93	166	.265	.308	.352	660	84	-35	8	6	-0	.988	-11	O-395L,1-177/D-9,C	-7.2

■ **ROGER HOLT** Holt, Roger Boyd b: 4/8/56, Daytona Beach, Fla. BB/TR, 5'11", 165 lbs. Deb: 10/4/80

YEAR	TM/L	G	AB	R	H	2B	3B	HR	RBI	BB	SO	AVG	OBP	SLG	OPS	OPS+	BR+	SB	CS	SBR	FA	FR	G/POS	TPR
1980	NY-A	2	6	0	1	0	0	0	1	1	2	.167	.286	.167	452	28	-1	0	0	0	1.000	1	/2-2	0.0

■ **MARTY HONAN** Honan, Martin Weldon b: 5/29/1869, Chicago, Ill. d: 8/20/08, Chicago, Ill. Deb: 10/3/1890

YEAR	TM/L	G	AB	R	H	2B	3B	HR	RBI	BB	SO	AVG	OBP	SLG	OPS	OPS+	BR+	SB	CS	SBR	FA	FR	G/POS	TPR
1890	Chi-N	1	3	0	0	0	0	0	1	0	2	.000	.000	.000	0	-96	-1	0			.857	-0	/C-1	-0.1
1891	Chi-N	5	12	1	2	0	1	0	3	1	3	.167	.231	.333	564	64	-1	0			.963	2	/C-5	0.1
Total	2	6	15	1	2	0	1	0	4	1	5	.133	.188	.267	454	32	-1	0			.941	1	/C-6	0.0

■ **ABIE HOOD** Hood, Albie Larrison b: 1/31/03, Sanford, N.C. d: 10/14/88, Chesapeake, Va. BL/TR, 5'7", 152 lbs. Deb: 7/15/25

YEAR	TM/L	G	AB	R	H	2B	3B	HR	RBI	BB	SO	AVG	OBP	SLG	OPS	OPS+	BR+	SB	CS	SBR	FA	FR	G/POS	TPR
1925	Bos-N	5	21	2	6	2	0	1	2	1	0	.286	.318	.524	842	122	1	0	0	0	.920	-4	/2-5	-0.3

■ **WALLY HOOD** Hood, Wallace James Sr. b: 2/9/1895, Whittier, Cal. d: 5/2/65, Hollywood, Cal. BR/TR, 5'11.5", 160 lbs. Deb: 4/15/20 F

YEAR	TM/L	G	AB	R	H	2B	3B	HR	RBI	BB	SO	AVG	OBP	SLG	OPS	OPS+	BR+	SB	CS	SBR	FA	FR	G/POS	TPR
1920	Bro-N	7	14	4	2	1	0	0	1	4	4	.143	.333	.214	548	58	-1	2	0	0	.944	1	/O-5(0-2-3)	0.1
	Pit-N	2	1	1	0	0	0	0	0	1	0	.000	.500	.000	500	50	0	1	0	0	.000	0	H	0.0
	Yr	9	15	5	2	1	0	0	1	5	4	.133	.350	.200	550	59	-1	3	0	1	.944	1	/O-5(0-2-3)	0.1
1921	Bro-N	56	65	16	17	1	2	1	4	9	14	.262	.360	.385	745	94	-0	2	2	-0	.957	-6	O-20(3-9-7)	-0.7
1922	Bro-N	2	0	2	0	0	0	0	0	0	0	—	—	—	—	—	0	0	0	0	.000	0	R	0.0
Total	3	67	80	23	19	2	2	1	5	14	18	.237	.358	.350	708	88	-1	5	2	0	.951	-4	/O-25(3-11-10)	-0.6

■ **ALEX HOOKS** Hooks, Alexander Marcus b: 8/29/06, Edgewood, Tex. d: 6/19/93, Edgewood, Tex. BL/TL, 6'1", 183 lbs. Deb: 4/17/35

YEAR	TM/L	G	AB	R	H	2B	3B	HR	RBI	BB	SO	AVG	OBP	SLG	OPS	OPS+	BR+	SB	CS	SBR	FA	FR	G/POS	TPR
1935	Phi-A	15	44	4	10	3	0	0	4	3	10	.227	.277	.295	572	48	-3	0	0	0	1.000	0	1-10	-0.4

■ **HARRY HOOPER** Hooper, Harry Bartholomew b: 8/24/1887, Bell Station, Cal. d: 12/18/74, Santa Cruz, Cal. BL/TR, 5'10", 168 lbs. Deb: 4/16/09 H Career OF: (74-LF 18-CF 2192-RF)

YEAR	TM/L	G	AB	R	H	2B	3B	HR	RBI	BB	SO	AVG	OBP	SLG	OPS	OPS+	BR+	SB	CS	SBR	FA	FR	G/POS	TPR
1909	Bos-A	81	255	29	72	3	4	0	12	16		.282	.337	.325	662	107	2	15			.952	4	O-74(62-4-8)	0.2
1910	Bos-A	155	584	81	156	9	10	2	27	62		.267	.346	.327	673	108	7	40			.938	11	*O-155(9-4-142)	1.2
1911	Bos-A	130	524	93	163	20	6	4	45	73		.311	.399	.395	794	123	19	38			.954	6	*O-130(0-0-130)	1.7
1912	*Bos-A	147	590	98	143	20	12	2	53	66		.242	.326	.327	653	83	-13	29			.964	2	*O-147(0-0-147)	-1.9
1913	Bos-A	148	586	100	169	29	12	4	40	60	51	.288	.359	.399	759	119	14	26			.968	9	*O-147(1-9-137)/P-1	1.6
1914	Bos-A	142	530	85	137	23	15	1	41	58	47	.258	.336	.364	700	110	6	19	14	-1	.973	11	*O-140(0-1-139)	1.0
1915	*Bos-A	149	566	90	133	20	13	2	51	89	36	.235	.342	.327	669	103	4	22	20	-2	.972	11	*O-149(0-0-149)	0.5
1916	*Bos-A	151	575	75	156	20	11	1	37	80	35	.271	.361	.350	711	113	11	27	11	2	.966	8	*O-151(0-0-151)	1.4
1917	Bos-A	151	559	89	143	21	11	3	45	80	40	.256	.355	.349	704	116	13	21			.971	-1	*O-151(0-0-151)	0.4
1918	*Bos-A	126	474	81	137	26	13	1	44	75	25	.289	.391	.405	796	143	27	24			.963	-0	*O-126(0-0-126)	2.2
1919	Bos-A	128	491	76	131	25	6	3	49	79	28	.267	.374	.360	734	113	12	23			.979	10	*O-128(0-0-128)	1.5
1920	Bos-A	139	536	91	167	30	17	7	53	88	27	.312	.411	.470	881	139	33	16	18	-3	.963	7	*O-139(2-0-137)	2.8
1921	Chi-A	108	419	74	137	26	5	8	58	55	21	.327	.406	.470	876	125	17	13	7	0	.975	-3	*O-108(0-0-108)	0.5
1922	Chi-A	152	602	111	183	35	8	11	80	68	33	.304	.379	.444	823	114	13	16	12	-1	.962	7	*O-149(0-0-149)	0.7
1923	Chi-A	145	576	87	166	32	4	10	65	68	22	.288	.370	.410	780	106	6	18	18	-2	.960	-4	*O-143(0-0-143)	-1.2
1924	Chi-A	130	476	107	156	27	8	10	62	65	26	.328	.413	.481	894	134	25	16	13	-1	.986	11	*O-123(0-0-123)	2.3
1925	Chi-A	127	442	62	117	23	5	6	55	54	21	.265	.351	.380	731	90	-6	12	8	-0	.976	4	*O-124(0-0-124)	-1.1
Total	17	2309	8785	1429	2466	389	160	75	817	1136	412	.281	.368	.387	755	114	189	375	121		.966	91	*O-2284R/P-1	13.8

■ **MIKE HOOPER** Hooper, Michael H. b: 2/7/1850, Baltimore, Md. d: 12/2/17, Baltimore, Md. 5'6", 165 lbs. Deb: 6/27/1873

YEAR	TM/L	G	AB	R	H	2B	3B	HR	RBI	BB	SO	AVG	OBP	SLG	OPS	OPS+	BR+	SB	CS	SBR	FA	FR	G/POS	TPR
1873	Mar-n	3	14	3	3	1	0	0	2	0	0	.214	.214	.286	500	62	-0	0	0	0	.833	-1	/O-2(2-0-0),C-1	-0.1

■ **CHARLIE HOOVER** Hoover, Charles E. b: 9/21/1865, Mound City, Ill. BL/TR, 5'8", Deb: 10/9/1888

YEAR	TM/L	G	AB	R	H	2B	3B	HR	RBI	BB	SO	AVG	OBP	SLG	OPS	OPS+	BR+	SB	CS	SBR	FA	FR	G/POS	TPR
1888	KC-a	3	10	0	3	0	0	0	1	0		.300	.300	.300	600	87	-0	0			.857	0	/C-3	0.0
1889	KC-a	71	258	44	64	2	5	1	25	29	38	.248	.329	.306	635	77	-8	9			.916	-4	C-66/3-4,O-3(3-0-0)	-0.6
Total	2	74	268	44	67	2	5	1	26	29	38	.250	.328	.306	634	77	-8	9			.913	-4	/C-69,3-4,O-3(3-0-0)	-0.6

■ **JOE HOOVER** Hoover, Robert Joseph b: 4/15/15, Brawley, Cal. d: 9/2/65, Los Angeles, Cal. BR/TR, 5'11", 175 lbs. Deb: 4/21/43

YEAR	TM/L	G	AB	R	H	2B	3B	HR	RBI	BB	SO	AVG	OBP	SLG	OPS	OPS+	BR+	SB	CS	SBR	FA	FR	G/POS	TPR
1943	Det-A	144	575	78	140	15	8	4	38	36	101	.243	.289	.318	607	72	-21	6	5	-0	.944	-6	*S-144	-1.7
1944	Det-A	120	441	67	104	20	2	0	29	35	66	.236	.301	.290	591	66	-19	7	10	-2	.932	15	*S-119/2-1	0.4
1945	*Det-A	74	222	33	57	10	5	1	17	21	35	.257	.324	.360	684	92	-2	6	2	1	.944	-7	S-68	-0.4
Total	3	338	1238	178	301	45	15	5	84	92	202	.243	.300	.316	616	73	-42	19	17	-2	.939	3	S-331/2-1	-1.7

YEAR	TM/L	G	AB	R	H	2B	3B	HR	RBI	BB	SO	AVG	OBP	SLG	OPS	OPS+	BR+	SB	CS	SBR	FA	FR	G/POS	TPR
■ **BUSTER HOOVER**	Hoover, William James b: 4/12/1863, Philadelphia, Pa. d: 4/16/24, Jersey City, N.J. BR/TR, 6'1", 178 lbs. Deb: 4/17/1884 Career OF: (55-LF 45-CF 2-RF)																							
1884	Phi-U	63	275	76	100	20	8	0		12		.364	.390	.495	885	180	19				.780	-1	O-37L,S-15/1-6,23	1.5
	Phi-N	10	42	6	8	1	0	1	4	4	9	.190	.261	.286	547	75	-1				.929	-1	O-10(6-4-0)	-0.2
1886	Bal-a	40	157	25	34	2	6	0	10	16		.217	.297	.306	603	91	-1	15			.839	-1	O-40(0-40-0)	-0.3
1892	Cin-N	14	51	7	9	0	0	0	2	5	4	.176	.250	.176	426	30	-4	1			.966	1	O-14(12-1-2)	-0.4
Total	3	127	525	114	151	23	14	1	16	37	13	.288	.337	.390	727	129	13	16			.840	-3	O-101L/S-15,2-6,13	0.6
■ **DON HOPKINS**	Hopkins, Donald b: 1/9/52, West Point, Miss. BL/TR, 6', 175 lbs. Deb: 4/8/75																							
1975	*Oak-A	82	6	25	1	0	0	0	0	2	0	.167	.375	.167	542	59	-0	21	9	1	1.000	-2	D-20/O-5(1-2-2)R-0	-0.1
1976	Oak-A	3	0	0	0	0	0	0	0	0	0	—	—	—	—	—	0	0	1	-0	.000	0	R	0.0
Total	2	85	6	25	1	0	0	0	0	2	0	.167	.375	.167	542	59	-0	21	10	1	1.000	-2	/D-20,O-5(1-2-2)	-0.1
■ **GAIL HOPKINS**	Hopkins, Gail Eason b: 2/19/43, Tulsa, Okla. BL/TR, 5'10", 200 lbs. Deb: 6/29/68																							
1968	Chi-A	29	37	4	8	2	0	0	2	6	3	.216	.326	.270	596	81	-1	0	0	0	1.000	-1	/1-7	-0.2
1969	Chi-A	124	373	52	99	13	3	8	46	50	28	.265	.354	.381	734	100	1	2	1	0	.994	-3	*1-101	-1.0
1970	Chi-A	116	287	32	82	8	1	6	29	28	19	.286	.351	.383	735	99	-0	0	0	0	.987	-2	1-77/C-8	-0.7
1971	KC-A	103	295	35	82	16	1	9	47	37	13	.278	.366	.431	797	126	11	3	1	0	.990	3	1-83	0.8
1972	KC-A	53	71	1	15	2	0	0	5	7	4	.211	.282	.239	521	56	-4	0	0	0	.990	-2	1-13/3-1	-0.7
1973	KC-A	74	138	17	34	6	1	2	16	29	15	.246	.385	.348	732	100	1	1	2	-0	1.000	0	D-36,1-10	0.0
1974	LA-N	15	18	1	4	0	0	0	0	3	1	.222	.333	.222	556	60	-1	0	0	0	1.000	1	/C-2,1-2	0.0
Total	7	514	1219	142	324	47	6	25	145	160	83	.266	.355	.376	730	103	8	6	4	-0	.991	-4	1-293/D-36,C-10,3-1	-1.8
■ **BUCK HOPKINS**	Hopkins, John Winton "Sis" b: 1/3/1883, Grafton, Va. d: 10/2/29, Phoebus, Va. BL/TL, 5'10", 165 lbs. Deb: 7/22/07																							
1907	StL-N	15	44	7	6	3	0	0	3	10		.136	.333	.205	538	71	-1	2			.875	-4	O-15(0-15-0)	-0.6
■ **MARTY HOPKINS**	Hopkins, Meredith Hilliard b: 2/22/07, Wolfe City, Tex. d: 11/20/63, Dallas, Tex. BR/TR, 5'11", 175 lbs. Deb: 4/17/34																							
1934	Phi-N	10	25	6	3	2	0	0	3	7	5	.120	.313	.200	513	36	-2	0			1.000	-1	/3-9	-0.3
	Chi-A	67	210	22	45	7	0	2	28	42	26	.214	.348	.276	624	61	-11	0	3	-1	.957	4	3-63	-0.5
1935	Chi-A	59	144	20	32	3	0	2	17	36	23	.222	.378	.285	663	72	-4	1	0	0	.960	-7	3-49/2-5	-0.9
Total	2	136	379	48	80	12	0	4	48	85	54	.211	.357	.274	631	63	-18	1	3		.960	-4	3-121/2-5	-1.7
■ **MIKE HOPKINS**	Hopkins, Michael Joseph "Skinner" b: 11/1/1872, Glasgow, Scotland d: 2/5/52, Pittsburgh, Pa. BR/TR, 5'8", 160 lbs. Deb: 8/24/02																							
1902	Pit-N	1	2	0	2	1	0	0	0	0		1.000	1.000	1.500	2500	648	1	0			1.000	0	/C-1	0.1
■ **JOHNNY HOPP**	Hopp, John Leonard "Hippity" b: 7/18/16, Hastings, Neb. BL/TL, 5'10", 175 lbs. Deb: 9/18/39 C Career OF: (132-LF 471-CF 127-RF)																							
1939	StL-N	6	4	1	2	1	0	0	2	1	1	.500	.600	.750	1350	246	1	0			1.000	0	/1-2	0.1
1940	StL-N	80	152	24	41	7	4	1	14	9	21	.270	.315	.388	703	88	-3	3			.967	-2	O-39(12-27-0),1-10	-0.6
1941	StL-N	134	445	83	135	25	11	4	50	50	63	.303	.378	.436	813	121	13	15			.982	1	O-91(58-23-10),1-39	0.7
1942	*StL-N	95	314	41	81	16	7	3	37	36	40	.258	.334	.382	716	102	1	14			.983	-4	1-88	-1.1
1943	*StL-N	91	241	33	54	10	2	2	25	24	22	.224	.297	.307	604	71	-9	8			.950	-2	O-52(40-12-0),1-27	-1.5
1944	*StL-N	139	527	106	177	35	9	11	72	58	47	.336	.404	.499	903	150	35	15			**.997**	-10	*O-131(1-130-0)/1-6	2.2
1945	StL-N	124	446	67	129	22	8	3	44	49	24	.289	.363	.395	758	108	5	14			.980	-7	*O-104(2-26-89),1-15	-0.8
1946	Bos-N★	129	445	71	148	23	8	3	48	34	34	.333	.386	.440	827	133	19	21			.981	-1	1-68,O-58(1-57-0)	1.5
1947	Bos-N	134	430	74	124	20	2	2	32	58	30	.288	.376	.358	734	98	1	13			.980	-6	*O-125(0-123-2)	-0.8
1948	Pit-N	120	392	64	109	15	12	1	31	40	25	.278	.345	.385	730	95	-2	5			1.000	1	O-80(1-71-8),1-25	-0.4
1949	Pit-N	20	55	5	12	3	1	0	3	7	3	.218	.306	.309	616	64	-3	0			.929	-1	/O-7(2-0-5),1-6	-0.4
	Bro-N	8	14	0	0	0	0	0	0	0	3	.000	.000	.000	0	-96	-4	0			1.000	1	/O-4(1-0-3),1-2	-0.3
	Pit-N	85	316	50	106	11	4	5	36	30	26	.335	.393	.443	836	121	10	9			.994	-0	1-71/O-9(2-0-7)	0.7
	Yr	113	385	55	118	14	5	5	39	37	32	.306	.367	.408	775	105	3	9			.990	-0	1-79,O-20(5-0-15)	-0.0
1950	Pit-N	106	318	51	108	24	5	8	47	43	17	.340	.420	.522	942	141	20	7			.990	-6	1-70/O-7(2-2-3)	1.1
	*NY-A	19	27	9	9	2	1	1	8	8	1	.333	.486	.593	1078	180	4	0	1	-0	1.000	-1	1-12/O-6(6-0-0)	0.2
1951	*NY-A	46	63	10	13	1	0	2	4	9	11	.206	.306	.317	623	71	-3	2	0	0	.992	-1	1-25	-0.4
1952	NY-A	15	25	4	4	0	0	0	2	2	3	.160	.250	.160	410	17	-3	2	0	0	1.000	1	1-12	-0.2
	Det-A	42	46	5	10	1	0	0	3	6	7	.217	.308	.239	547	53	-3	0	0	0	1.000	-1	/O-4(4-0-0),1-1	-0.4
	Yr	57	71	9	14	1	0	0	5	8	10	.197	.287	.211	499	41	-5	2	0	0	1.000	-0	1-13/O-4(4-0-0)	-0.6
Total	14	1393	4260	698	1262	216	74	46	458	464	378	.296	.368	.414	782	113	80	128	1		.985	-36	O-717C,1-479	-0.4
■ **SHAGS HORAN**	Horan, Joseph Patrick b: 9/6/1895, St.Louis, Mo. d: 2/13/69, Torrance, Cal. BR/TR, 5'10", 170 lbs. Deb: 7/14/24																							
1924	NY-A	22	31	4	9	1	0	0	7	1	5	.290	.313	.323	635	64	-2	0	0	0	1.000	-4	O-14(4-1-9)	-0.6
■ **SAM HORN**	Horn, Samuel Lee b: 11/2/63, Dallas, Tex. BL/TL, 6'5", 250 lbs. Deb: 7/25/87																							
1987	Bos-A	46	158	31	44	7	0	14	34	17	55	.278	.356	.589	945	141	9	0	1	-0	.000	0	D-40	0.7
1988	Bos-A	24	61	4	9	0	0	2	8	11	20	.148	.278	.246	524	46	-4	0	0	0	.000	0	D-16	-0.5
1989	Bos-A	33	54	1	8	2	0	0	4	8	16	.148	.258	.185	443	25	-5	0	0	0	1.000	-0	D-14/1-2	-0.6
1990	Bal-A	79	246	30	61	13	0	14	45	32	62	.248	.335	.472	806	127	8	0	0	0	.970	-0	D-63,1-10	0.5
1991	Bal-A	121	317	45	74	16	0	23	61	41	99	.233	.327	.502	828	131	12	0	0	0	.000	0	*D-102	0.9
1992	Bal-A	63	162	13	38	10	1	5	19	21	60	.235	.326	.401	727	100	0	0	0	0	.000	0	D-46	-0.1
1993	Cle-A	12	33	8	15	1	0	4	8	1	5	.455	.486	.848	1334	252	7	0	0	0	.000	0	D-11	0.6
1995	Tex-A	11	9	0	1	0	0	0	0	1	6	.111	.200	.111	311	-16	-2	0	0	0	.000	0	/D-1	-0.2
Total	8	389	1040	132	250	49	1	62	179	132	323	.240	.330	.468	798	118	25	0	1	-0	.972	-0	D-293/1-12	1.3
■ **BOB HORNER**	Horner, James Robert b: 8/6/57, Junction City, Kan. BR/TR, 6'1", 210 lbs. Deb: 6/16/78																							
1978	Atl-N	89	323	50	86	17	1	23	63	24	42	.266	.321	.539	860	123	8	0	0	0	.956	6	3-89	1.3
1979	Atl-N	121	487	66	153	15	1	33	98	22	74	.314	.348	.552	900	132	19	0	2	-1	.930	-7	3-82,1-45	0.8
1980	Atl-N	124	463	81	124	14	1	35	89	27	50	.268	.310	.529	839	126	13	3	1	0	.935	5	*3-121/1-1	1.7
1981	Atl-N	79	300	42	83	10	0	15	42	32	39	.277	.348	.460	808	125	9	2	3	-1	.938	-15	3-79	-0.8
1982	*Atl-N★	140	499	85	130	24	0	32	97	66	75	.261	.351	.501	852	131	20	3	5	-1	.970	-17	*3-137	-0.1
1983	Atl-N	104	386	75	117	25	1	20	68	50	63	.303	.384	.528	913	140	21	4	2	0	.958	-13	*3-104/1-1	0.7
1984	Atl-N	32	113	15	31	8	0	3	19	14	17	.274	.354	.425	779	110	2	0	0	0	.965	-1	3-32	0.1
1985	Atl-N	130	483	61	129	25	3	27	89	50	57	.267	.337	.499	836	123	14	1	1	-0	1.000	-10	1-87,3-40	-0.3
1986	Atl-N	141	517	70	141	22	0	27	87	52	72	.273	.342	.472	813	116	10	1	4	-1	.995	2	*1-139	0.2
1988	StL-N	60	206	15	53	9	1	3	33	32	23	.257	.360	.354	714	105	2	0	0	0	.990	-1	1-57	-0.3
Total	10	1020	3777	560	1047	169	8	218	685	369	512	.277	.344	.499	843	125	119	14	18	-3	.946	-50	3-684,1-330	3.3
■ **ROGERS HORNSBY**	Hornsby, Rogers "Rajah" b: 4/27/1896, Winters, Tex. d: 1/5/63, Chicago, Ill. BR/TR, 5'11", 175 lbs. Deb: 9/10/15 MCH Career OF: (6-LF 1-CF 13-RF)																							
1915	StL-N	18	57	5	14	2	0	0	4	2	6	.246	.271	.281	552	67	-2	0	2	-1	.922	1	S-18	-0.2
1916	StL-N	139	495	63	155	17	15	6	65	40	63	.313	.369	.444	814	150	29	17			.928	-2	3-83,S-45,1-15,/2-1	3.6
1917	StL-N	145	523	86	171	24	**17**	8	66	45	34	.327	.385	**.484**	**868**	**170**	**42**	17			.939	21	*S-144	**8.0**
1918	StL-N	115	416	51	117	19	11	5	60	40	43	.281	.349	.416	764	138	18	8			.933	10	*S-109/O-3(0-1-2)	**3.9**
1919	StL-N	138	512	68	163	15	9	8	71	48	41	.318	.384	.430	814	**154**	**34**	17			.933	2	3-72,S-37,2-25,/1-5	4.4
1920	StL-N	149	589	96	**218**	**44**	20	9	**94**	60	50	**.370**	**.431**	**.559**	**990**	**190**	**68**	12	15	-3	.962	11	*2-149	**8.1**
1921	StL-N	154	592	**131**	**235**	**44**	**18**	21	**126**	60	48	**.397**	**.458**	**.639**	**1097**	**191**	**78**	13	13	-2	.969	-3	*2-142/O-6L,S-3,31	7.4
1922	StL-N	154	623	**141**	**250**	**46**	14	**42**	**152**	65	50	**.401**	**.459**	**.722**	**1181**	**210**	**99**	17	12	-0	**.967**	-7	*2-154	**8.7**
1923	StL-N	107	424	89	163	32	10	17	83	55	29	**.384**	**.459**	**.627**	**1086**	**188**	**54**	3	7	-2	.962	-17	2-96,1-10	3.5
1924	StL-N	143	536	**121**	**227**	**43**	14	25	94	**89**	32	**.424**	**.507**	**.696**	**1203**	**223**	**97**	5	12	-3	.965	-4	*2-143	**9.1**
1925	StL-N	138	504	133	203	41	10	**39**	**143**	83	39	**.403**	**.489**	**.756**	**1245**	**208**	**83**	5	3	0	.954	-20	*2-136,M	**6.2**
1926	*StL-N	134	527	96	167	34	5	11	93	61	39	.317	.388	.463	851	123	18	3			.962	-29	*2-134,M	-0.8
1927	NY-N	155	568	**133**	205	32	9	26	125	**86**	38	.361	**.448**	.586	**1035**	**176**	**63**	9			.972	3	*2-155,M	6.8
1928	Bos-N	140	486	99	188	42	7	21	94	**107**	41	**.387**	**.498**	**.632**	**1130**	**204**	**81**	5			.973	-24	*2-140,M	**5.8**
1929	*Chi-N	156	602	**156**	229	47	8	39	149	87	65	.380	.459	**.679**	**1139**	**178**	**74**	2			.973	1	*2-156	**7.0**
1930	Chi-N	42	104	15	32	5	1	2	18	12	12	.308	.385	.433	817	96	-0	0			.916	-3	2-25,M	-0.2

YEAR	TM/L	G	AB	R	H	2B	3B	HR	RBI	BB	SO	AVG	OBP	SLG	OPS	OPS+	BR+	SB	CS	SBR	FA	FR	G/POS	TPR
1931	Chi-N	100	357	64	118	37	1	16	90	56	23	.331	.421	.574	996	162	32	1			.951	-15	2-69,3-26,M	2.2
1932	Chi-N	19	58	10	13	2	0	1	7	10	4	.224	.357	.310	667	82	-1	0			1.000	-4	O-10(0-0-10)/3-6,M	-0.6
1933	StL-N	46	83	9	27	6	0	2	21	12	6	.325	.423	.470	893	147	6	1			.967	-7	2-17	0.0
	StL-A	11	9	2	3	1	0	1	2	2	1	.333	.455	.778	1232	208	1	0	0	0	.000	0	HM	0.1
1934	StL-A	24	23	2	7	2	0	1	11	7	4	.304	.484	.522	1006	147	2	0	0	0	1.000	0	/3-1,O-1(0-0-1),M	0.2
1935	StL-A	10	24	1	5	3	0	0	3	3	6	.208	.296	.333	630	60	-1	0	0	0	1.000	0	/1-3,2-2,3-1,M	-0.2
1936	StL-A	2	5	1	2	0	0	0	2	1	0	.400	.500	.400	900	121	0	0	0	0	1.000	-0	/1-1,M	0.0
1937	StL-A	20	56	7	18	3	0	1	11	7	5	.321	.397	.429	825	107	1	0	0	0	.947	-5	2-17,M	-0.3
Total	23	2259	8173	1579	2930	541	169	301	1584	1038	679	.358	.434	.577	1010	176	875	135	64		.965	-91	*2-1561,S-356,3/1O	82.7

■ JOE HORNUNG

Hornung, Michael Joseph "Ubbo Ubbo" b: 6/12/1857, Carthage, N.Y. d: 10/30/31, Howard Beach, N.Y. BR/TR, 5'8.5", 164 lbs. Deb: 5/1/1879 U Career OF: (1051-LF 1-CF 5-RF)

YEAR	TM/L	G	AB	R	H	2B	3B	HR	RBI	BB	SO	AVG	OBP	SLG	OPS	OPS+	BR+	SB	CS	SBR	FA	FR	G/POS	TPR
1879	Buf-N	78	319	46	85	18	7	0	38	2	27	.266	.271	.367	638	105	1				.844	-2	*O-77(76-0-1)/1-1	-0.5
1880	Buf-N	85	342	47	91	8	11	1	42	8	29	.266	.283	.363	645	115	5				.874	-0	*O-67L,1-18/2-5,P-1	0.0
1881	Bos-N	83	324	40	78	12	8	2	25	5	25	.241	.252	.346	598	90	-4				**.948**	12	*O-83(83-1-0)	0.3
1882	Bos-N	85	388	67	117	14	11	1	50	2	25	.302	.305	.402	707	124	10				**.932**	11	*O-84(84-0-0)/1-1	1.6
1883	Bos-N	98	446	**107**	124	25	13	8	66	8	54	.278	.291	.446	737	117	8				**.936**	7	*O-98(98-0-0)/3-1	1.1
1884	Bos-N	115	518	119	139	27	10	7	51	17	80	.268	.292	.400	691	116	8				.916	3	*O-110(110-0-0)/1-6	0.8
1885	Bos-N	25	109	14	22	4	1	1	7	1	20	.202	.209	.284	493	61	-5				.919	-3	O-25(25-0-0)	-0.8
1886	Bos-N	94	424	67	109	12	2	2	40	10	62	.257	.274	.309	583	80	-10	16			**.948**	7	*O-94(94-0-0)	-0.6
1887	Bos-N	98	454	85	135	10	6	5	49	17	28	.297	.302	.355	657	82	-11	41			**.935**	13	*O-98(98-0-0)	-0.1
1888	Bos-N	107	431	61	103	11	7	3	53	16	39	.239	.269	.318	587	85	-8	29			.947	-8	*O-107(106-0-1)	-1.8
1889	Bal-a	135	533	73	122	13	9	1	78	22	72	.229	.269	.293	561	59	-30	34			.913	11	*O-134(134-0-1)/3-1	-1.9
1890	NY-N	120	513	62	122	18	5	0	65	12	37	.238	.258	.292	550	60	-28	39			.931	-3	O-77L,1-36/3-5,S-2	-3.2
Total	12	1123	4801	788	1247	172	90	31	564	120	498	.260	.277	.350	627	91	-63	159			.922	49	*O-1054L/1-62,32SP	-5.1

■ TONY HORTON

Horton, Anthony Darrin b: 12/6/44, Santa Monica, Cal. BR/TR, 6'3", 210 lbs. Deb: 7/31/64

YEAR	TM/L	G	AB	R	H	2B	3B	HR	RBI	BB	SO	AVG	OBP	SLG	OPS	OPS+	BR+	SB	CS	SBR	FA	FR	G/POS	TPR
1964	Bos-A	36	126	9	28	5	0	1	8	3	20	.222	.240	.286	526	44	-10	0	0	0	1.000	1	O-24(24-0-0)/1-8	-1.1
1965	Bos-A	60	163	23	48	8	1	7	23	18	36	.294	.365	.485	849	131	7	0	2	-1	.980	-1	1-44	0.3
1966	Bos-A	6	22	0	3	0	0	0	2	0	5	.136	.136	.136	273	-19	-3	0	0	0	1.000	1	/1-6	-0.3
1967	Bos-A	21	39	2	12	3	0	0	9	0	5	.308	.308	.385	692	96	-0	0	0	0	.929	-1	/1-6	-0.2
	Cle-A	106	363	35	102	13	4	10	44	18	52	.281	.322	.421	744	117	7	3	0	1	.991	-6	1-94	-0.4
	Yr	127	402	37	114	16	4	10	53	18	57	.284	.321	.418	739	114	6	3	0	1	.987	-6	*1-100	-0.6
1968	Cle-A	133	477	57	119	29	3	14	59	34	56	.249	.304	.411	714	117	8	3	1	0	.992	-4	*1-128	-0.4
1969	Cle-A	159	625	77	174	25	4	27	93	37	91	.278	.321	.461	782	113	8	3	3	-0	.989	-0	*1-157	-0.6
1970	Cle-A	115	413	48	111	19	3	17	59	30	54	.269	.324	.453	777	107	3	3	2	-0	.994	3	*1-112	-0.3
Total	7	636	2228	251	597	102	15	76	297	140	319	.268	.315	.430	745	109	19	12	8	-0	.990	-7	1-555/O-24(24-0-0)	-3.0

■ WILLIE HORTON

Horton, Willie Watterson b: 10/18/42, Arno, Va. BR/TR, 5'11", 209 lbs. Deb: 9/10/63 C Career OF: (1117-LF 0-CF 123-RF)

YEAR	TM/L	G	AB	R	H	2B	3B	HR	RBI	BB	SO	AVG	OBP	SLG	OPS	OPS+	BR+	SB	CS	SBR	FA	FR	G/POS	TPR
1963	Det-A	15	43	6	14	2	1	1	4	0	8	.326	.326	.488	814	120	1	2	0	0	1.000	-1	/O-9(8-0-1)	0.0
1964	Det-A	25	80	6	13	1	3	1	10	11	20	.162	.272	.287	559	55	-5	0	0	0	.943	-2	O-23(20-0-3)	-0.8
1965	Det-A★	143	512	69	140	20	2	29	104	48	101	.273	.343	.490	833	132	21	5	9	-2	.988	5	*O-141(111-0-34)/3-1	1.6
1966	Det-A	146	526	72	138	22	6	27	100	44	103	.262	.323	.481	804	125	15	1	1	-0	.979	-4	*O-137(129-0-20)	0.4
1967	Det-A	122	401	47	110	20	3	19	67	36	80	.274	.340	.481	821	137	17	0	0	0	.971	-0	*O-110(109-0-1)	1.2
1968	*Det-A★	143	512	68	146	20	2	36	85	49	110	.285	.357	.543	900	165	38	0	3	-1	.973	0	*O-139(139-0-0)	3.4
1969	Det-A	141	508	66	133	17	1	28	91	52	93	.262	.334	.465	798	116	10	3	3	-0	.972	9	*O-136(135-0-3)	1.0
1970	Det-A★	96	371	53	113	18	2	17	69	28	43	.305	.357	.501	858	133	15	0	1	-0	.982	5	O-96(96-0-2)	1.5
1971	Det-A	119	450	64	130	25	1	22	72	37	75	.289	.352	.496	848	133	18	1	5	-2	.963	-10	*O-118(106-0-29)	-0.1
1972	*Det-A	108	333	44	77	9	5	11	36	27	47	.231	.295	.387	682	99	-1	0	0	0	1.000	-10	O-98(81-0-30)	-1.9
1973	Det-A★	111	411	42	130	19	3	17	53	23	57	.316	.363	.501	864	132	16	1	4	-1	.942	-10	*O-107(107-0-0)/D-1	-0.1
1974	Det-A	72	238	32	71	8	1	15	47	21	36	.298	.363	.529	892	149	14	0	1	-0	.947	-4	O-64(64-0-0)/D-1	0.7
1975	Det-A	159	615	62	169	13	1	25	92	44	109	.275	.323	.421	744	104	2	1	2	-0	.000	0	*D-159	-0.3
1976	Det-A	114	401	40	105	17	0	14	56	49	63	.262	.345	.409	754	116	8	0	0	0	.000	0	*D-105	0.6
1977	Det-A	1	4	0	1	0	0	0	0	0	0	.250	.250	.250	500	35	-0	0	0	0	1.000	-0	/O-1(1-0-0)	-0.1
	Tex-A	139	519	55	150	23	3	15	75	42	117	.289	.342	.432	774	108	6	2	3	-1	.938	-1	*D-128,O-10(10-0-0)	-0.1
	Yr	140	523	55	151	23	3	15	75	42	117	.289	.342	.430	772	108	5	2	3	-1	.941	-2	*D-128,O-11(11-0-0)	-0.2
1978	Cle-A	50	169	15	42	7	0	5	22	15	25	.249	.314	.379	692	95	-1	3	0	1	.000	0	D-48	-0.2
	Oak-A	32	102	11	32	8	0	3	19	9	15	.314	.369	.480	850	145	6	0	1	-0	.333	-1	D-27/O-1(1-0-0)	0.4
	Tor-A	33	122	12	25	6	0	3	19	4	29	.205	.230	.328	558	54	-8	0	0	0	.000	0	D-30	-0.9
	Yr	115	393	38	99	21	0	11	60	28	69	.252	.303	.389	693	95	-4	3	1	0	.842	-1	*D-105/O-1(1-0-0)	-0.7
1979	Sea-A	162	646	77	180	19	5	29	106	42	112	.279	.327	.458	785	107	5	1	1	-0	.000	0	*D-162	0.0
1980	Sea-A	97	335	32	74	10	1	8	36	39	70	.221	.310	.328	638	74	-11	0	4	-1	.000	0	D-92	-1.6
Total	18	2028	7298	873	1993	284	40	325	1163	620	1313	.273	.335	.457	791	119	166	20	38	-9	.972	-24	*O-1190L,D-753/3-1	4.7

■ DWAYNE HOSEY

Hosey, Dwayne Samuel b: 3/11/67, Sharon, Pa. BB/TR, 5'10", 175 lbs. Deb: 9/1/95

YEAR	TM/L	G	AB	R	H	2B	3B	HR	RBI	BB	SO	AVG	OBP	SLG	OPS	OPS+	BR+	SB	CS	SBR	FA	FR	G/POS	TPR
1995	*Bos-A	24	68	20	23	8	1	3	7	8	16	.338	.408	.618	1026	157	6	6	0	1	1.000	-1	O-21(2-19-1)/D-1	0.6
1996	Bos-A	28	78	13	17	2	2	1	3	7	17	.218	.282	.333	616	54	-6	6	3	0	.984	1	O-26(7-20-0)/D-2	-0.4
Total	2	52	146	33	40	10	3	4	10	15	33	.274	.342	.466	807	102	-0	12	3	2	.991	1	/O-47(9-39-1),D-3	0.2

■ STEVE HOSEY

Hosey, Steven Bernard b: 4/2/69, Oakland, Cal. BR/TR, 6'3", 215 lbs. Deb: 8/29/92

YEAR	TM/L	G	AB	R	H	2B	3B	HR	RBI	BB	SO	AVG	OBP	SLG	OPS	OPS+	BR+	SB	CS	SBR	FA	FR	G/POS	TPR
1992	SF-N	21	56	6	14	1	0	1	6	0	15	.250	.250	.321	571	64	-3	1	1	-0	.960	-2	O-18(0-0-18)	-0.6
1993	SF-N	3	2	0	1	1	0	0	1	1	1	.500	.667	1.000	1667	350	1	0	0	0	.000	-0	/O-1(0-0-1)	0.0
Total	2	24	58	6	15	2	0	1	7	1	16	.259	.271	.345	616	77	-2	1	1	-0	.960	-3	/O-19(0-0-19)	-0.6

■ TIM HOSLEY

Hosley, Timothy Kenneth b: 5/10/47, Spartanburg, S.C. BR/TR, 5'10", 195 lbs. Deb: 9/8/70

YEAR	TM/L	G	AB	R	H	2B	3B	HR	RBI	BB	SO	AVG	OBP	SLG	OPS	OPS+	BR+	SB	CS	SBR	FA	FR	G/POS	TPR
1970	Det-A	7	12	1	2	0	0	1	2	0	6	.167	.167	.417	583	55	-1	0	0	0	1.000	2	/C-4	0.1
1971	Det-A	7	16	2	3	0	0	2	6	0	1	.188	.188	.563	750	102	-0	0	0	0	1.000	-0	/C-4,1-1	0.0
1973	Oak-A	13	14	3	3	0	0	0	2	2	3	.214	.313	.214	527	53	-1	0	0	0	.952	-1	C-13	-0.2
1974	Oak-A	11	7	3	2	0	0	0	1	1	2	.286	.375	.286	661	99	0	0	0	0	1.000	0	/C-8,1-1	0.0
1975	Chi-N	62	141	22	36	7	0	6	20	27	25	.255	.382	.433	815	120	5	1	1	-0	.968	-2	C-53	0.5
1976	Oak-A	37	55	4	9	2	0	1	4	8	12	.164	.270	.255	524	56	-3	0	0	0	.968	-1	C-37	-0.3
	Chi-N	1	1	0	0	0	0	0	0	0	0	.000	.000	.000	0	-92	-0	0	0	0	.000	0	H	0.0
1977	Oak-A	39	78	5	15	0	0	1	10	16	13	.192	.337	.231	568	59	-4	0	0	0	.955	3	C-19,D-12/1-3	-0.1
1978	Oak-A	13	23	1	7	2	0	0	3	1	6	.304	.360	.391	751	117	1	0	0	0	.962	0	/C-6,D-1	0.1
1981	Oak-A	18	21	2	2	0	0	1	5	2	5	.095	.174	.238	412	19	-2	0	0	0	.750	-0	/1-1,D-4	-0.3
Total	9	208	368	43	79	11	0	12	53	57	73	.215	.326	.342	669	87	-6	1	1	-0	.968	0	C-144/D-17,1-6	-0.2

■ CHUCK HOSTETLER

Hostetler, Charles Cloyd b: 9/22/03, McClellandtown, Pa. d: 2/18/71, Fort Collins, Colo BL/TR, 6', 175 lbs. Deb: 4/18/44

YEAR	TM/L	G	AB	R	H	2B	3B	HR	RBI	BB	SO	AVG	OBP	SLG	OPS	OPS+	BR+	SB	CS	SBR	FA	FR	G/POS	TPR
1944	Det-A	90	265	42	79	9	2	0	20	21	31	.298	.350	.347	697	94	-2	4	4	-1	.985	0	O-65(1-4-61)	-0.6
1945	*Det-A	42	44	3	7	3	0	0	2	7	8	.159	.275	.227	502	43	-3	0	0	0	.889	-3	/O-8(6-1-1)	-0.6
Total	2	132	309	45	86	12	2	0	22	28	39	.278	.338	.330	668	87	-5	4	4	-1	.979	-2	/O-73(7-5-62)	-1.2

■ DAVE HOSTETLER

Hostetler, David Alan b: 3/27/56, Pasadena, Cal. BR/TR, 6'4", 215 lbs. Deb: 9/15/81

YEAR	TM/L	G	AB	R	H	2B	3B	HR	RBI	BB	SO	AVG	OBP	SLG	OPS	OPS+	BR+	SB	CS	SBR	FA	FR	G/POS	TPR
1981	Mon-N	5	6	1	3	0	0	1	1	0	2	.500	.500	1.000	1500	314	2	0	0	0	1.000	-0	/1-2	0.1
1982	Tex-A	113	418	53	97	12	3	22	67	42	113	.232	.304	.433	737	105	2	2	2	-0	.990	-11	*1-109/D-3	-1.7
1983	Tex-A	94	304	31	67	9	2	11	46	42	103	.220	.325	.372	696	93	-2	0	2	-1	1.000	-0	D-88/1-2	-0.6
1984	Tex-A	37	82	7	18	2	1	3	10	13	27	.220	.326	.378	704	91	-1	0	0	0	1.000	1	1-14,D-13	-0.1
1988	Pit-N	6	8	0	2	0	0	0	0	0	3	.250	.250	.250	500	45	-1	0	0	0	.944	-0	/1-4,C-1	-0.1
Total	5	255	818	92	187	23	6	37	124	97	248	.229	.315	.407	722	100	-1	2	4	-1	.990	-11	1-131,D-104/C-1	-2.4

YEAR	TM/L	G	AB	R	H	2B	3B	HR	RBI	BB	SO	AVG	OBP	SLG	OPS	OPS+	BR+	SB	CS	SBR	FA	FR	G/POS	TPR
■ PETE HOTALING	Hotaling, Peter James "Monkey" b: 12/16/1856, Mohawk, N.Y. d: 7/3/28, Cleveland, Ohio BL/TR (BR 1880 (1 GAME)), 5'8", 166 lbs. Deb: 5/1/1879 Career OF: (7-LF 816-CF 4-RF)																							
1879	Cin-N	81	369	64	103	20	9	1	27	12	17	.279	.302	.390	692	133	13				.843	-0	*O-69C/C-8,2-6,3-3	1.0
1880	Cle-N	78	325	40	78	17	8	0	41	10	30	.240	.263	.342	604	105	2				.896	-2	*O-78(2-76-0)/C-2	-0.4
1881	Wor-N	77	317	51	98	15	3	1	35	18	12	.309	.346	.385	731	123	8				.862	-3	*O-74(2-72-1)/C-3	0.1
1882	Bos-N	84	378	64	98	16	5	0	28	16	21	.259	.289	.328	617	97	-1				.865	2	*O-84(0-84-1)	-0.1
1883	Cle-N	100	417	54	108	20	8	0	30	12	31	.259	.280	.345	625	90	-5				.829	1	*O-100(0-100-0)	-0.6
1884	Cle-N	102	408	69	99	16	6	3	27	28	50	.243	.291	.333	625	93	-4				.849	-1	*O-102(3-99-0)/2-1	-0.7
1885	Bro-a	94	370	73	95	9	5	1	34	49		.257	.350	.316	666	111	7				.893	0	*O-94(0-94-0)	0.4
1887	Cle-a	126	558	108	204	28	13	3	94	53		.366	.373	.424	797	126	19	43			.903	1	*O-126(0-126-0)	1.2
1888	Cle-a	98	403	67	101	7	6	0	55	26		.251	.307	.298	605	97	-0	35			.878	-9	*O-98(0-98-0)	-1.2
Total	9	840	3545	590	984	148	63	9	371	224	161	.278	.314	.353	667	108	39	78			.869	-11	O-825C/C-13,2-7,3-3	-0.3
■ KEN HOTTMAN	Hottman, Kenneth Roger b: 5/7/48, Stockton, Cal. BR/TR, 5'11", 190 lbs. Deb: 9/11/71																							
1971	Chi-A	6	16	1	2	0	0	0	0	1	2	.125	.176	.125	301	-13	-2	0	0	0	1.000	-1	/O-5(5-0-0)	-0.4
■ SADIE HOUCK	Houck, Sargent Perry b: 3/1856, Washington, D.C. d: 5/26/19, Washington, D.C. BR/TR, 5'7", 151 lbs. Deb: 5/1/1879 Career OF: (39-LF 20-CF 54-RF)																							
1879	Bos-N	80	356	69	95	24	9	2	49	4	11	.267	.275	.402	677	117	6				.814	-8	O-47(1-5-42),S-33	0.0
1880	Bos-N	12	47	2	7	0	0	0	2	0	6	.149	.149	.149	298	1	-5				.786	-1	O-12(0-2-10)	-0.6
	Pro-N	49	184	27	37	7	7	1	22	3	6	.201	.214	.332	545	85	-3				.873	-1	O-49(38-12-2)	-0.6
	Yr	61	231	29	44	7	7	1	24	3	12	.190	.201	.294	495	68	-7				.855	-3	O-61(38-14-12)	-1.2
1881	Det-N	75	308	43	86	16	6	1	36	6	6	.279	.293	.380	673	106	1				.868	1	*S-75	0.5
1883	Det-N	101	416	52	105	18	12	0	40	9	18	.252	.268	.353	622	91	-4				.852	5	*S-101	0.4
1884	Phi-a	108	472	93	140	19	14	0		7		.297	.318	.396	714	124	10				**.893**	23	*S-108/2-1	3.3
1885	Phi-a	93	388	74	99	10	9	0	54	10		.255	.286	.327	614	88	-6				.863	22	*S-93	1.6
1886	Bal-a	61	260	29	50	8	1	0	17	4		.192	.216	.231	447	41	-18	25			.849	-5	S-55/2-5,O-1(0-1-0)	-1.9
	Was-N	52	195	14	42	3	0	0	14	2	28	.215	.223	.231	454	41	-13	4			.858	0	S-51/2-1	-1.1
1887	NY-a	10	36	3	8	1	0	0	0	3		.222	.243	.182	425	20	-3	2			.831	4	S-10/2-1	0.1
Total	8	641	2662	406	669	106	58	4	234	48	75	.251	.269	.338	608	91	-35	31			.863	39	S-526,O-109R/2-8	1.7
■ RALPH HOUK	Houk, Ralph George "Major" b: 8/9/19, Lawrence, Kan. BR/TR, 5'11", 193 lbs. Deb: 4/26/47 MC																							
1947	*NY-A	41	92	7	25	3	1	0	12	11	5	.272	.356	.326	682	91	-1	0	0	0	.987	2	C-41	0.2
1948	NY-A	14	29	3	8	2	0	0	3	0	0	.276	.276	.345	621	65	-2	0	0	0	1.000	5	C-14	0.3
1949	NY-A	5	7	0	4	0	0	0	1	0	1	.571	.571	.571	1143	203	1	0	0	0	.889	-1	/C-5	0.1
1950	NY-A	10	9	0	1	1	0	0	1	0	2	.111	.111	.222	333	-17	-2	0	0	0	.929	1	/C-9	-0.1
1951	NY-A	3	5	0	1	0	0	0	2	0	1	.200	.200	.200	400	9	-1	0	0	0	1.000	-1	/C-3	-0.1
1952	*NY-A	9	6	0	2	0	0	0	0	1	0	.333	.429	.333	762	121	0	0	0	0	.917	1	/C-9	0.1
1953	NY-A	8	9	2	2	0	0	0	1	0	1	.222	.222	.222	444	21	-1	0	0	0	1.000	-0	/C-8	-0.1
1954	NY-A	1	1	0	0	0	0	0	0	0	0	.000	.000	.000	0	-99	-0	0	0	0	.000	0	H	0.0
Total	8	91	158	12	43	6	1	0	20	12	10	.272	.327	.323	650	79	-5	0	0	0	.981	6	/C-89	0.4
■ FRANK HOUSE	House, Henry Franklin "Pig" b: 2/18/30, Bessemer, Ala. BL/TR, 6'2", 190 lbs. Deb: 7/21/50																							
1950	Det-A	5	5	1	2	1	0	0	0	0	1	.400	.400	.600	1000	148	0	0	0	0	1.000	0	/C-5	0.0
1951	Det-A	18	41	3	9	2	0	1	4	6	2	.220	.319	.341	661	78	-1	1	1	-0	.957	1	C-18	0.1
1954	Det-A	114	352	35	88	12	1	9	38	31	34	.250	.313	.366	679	87	-7	2	1	0	.992	-1	*C-107	-0.3
1955	Det-A	102	328	37	85	11	1	15	53	22	25	.259	.312	.436	748	102	-1	0	0	0	.987	2	C-93	0.5
1956	Det-A	94	321	44	77	6	2	10	44	21	19	.240	.293	.364	657	72	-14	1	1	-0	.986	-6	C-88	-1.6
1957	Det-A	106	348	31	90	9	0	7	36	35	26	.259	.328	.345	673	82	-8	1	1	-0	.997	9	C-97	0.5
1958	KC-A	76	202	16	51	6	3	4	24	12	13	.252	.298	.371	669	81	-5	1	0	0	.992	-7	C-55	-1.0
1959	KC-A	98	347	32	82	14	3	1	30	20	23	.236	.282	.303	584	59	-19	0	3	-1	.982	-8	C-95	-2.5
1960	Cin-N	23	28	0	5	2	0	0	3	0	2	.179	.179	.250	429	16	-3	0	0	0	1.000	1	/C-8	-0.2
1961	Det-A	17	22	3	5	1	1	0	3	4	2	.227	.346	.364	710	87	-0	0	0	0	.974	-1	C-14	-0.1
Total	10	653	1994	202	494	64	11	47	235	151	147	.248	.304	.362	666	80	-60	6	7	-1	.988	-10	C-580	-4.6
■ CHARLIE HOUSEHOLDER	Householder, Charles F. b: 1856, Harrisburg, Pa. BR/TR, 5'7", 150 lbs. Deb: 4/20/1884																							
1884	CP-U	83	310	32	74	12	5	1		12		.239	.267	.319	586	77	-18				.796	-6	3-41,O-40L/S-3,P-2	-2.1
■ CHARLIE HOUSEHOLDER	Householder, Charles W. b: 1856, Harrisburg, Pa. d: 12/26/08, Harrisburg, Pa. BL/TL, 5'11", 158 lbs. Deb: 5/2/1882 Career OF: (2-LF 2-CF 1-RF)																							
1882	Bal-a	74	307	42	78	10	7	1		4		.254	.264	.342	606	111	4				.971	3	*1-74/C-3	0.0
1884	Bro-a	76	273	28	66	15	3	3		12		.242	.279	.352	630	104	1				.959	-5	1-40,C-31/O-6L,2-1	-0.5
Total	2	150	580	70	144	25	10	4		16		.248	.271	.347	617	108	5				.967	-2	1-114/C-34,O-6L,2-1	-0.5
■ ED HOUSEHOLDER	Householder, Edward H. b: 10/12/1869, Pittsburgh, Pa. d: 7/3/24, Los Angeles, Cal. BL/TL, Deb: 4/17/03																							
1903	Bro-N	12	43	5	9	0	0	0	9	2		.209	.244	.209	454	31	-4	3			.967	1	O-12(0-12-0)	-0.4
■ PAUL HOUSEHOLDER	Householder, Paul Wesley b: 9/4/58, Columbus, Ohio BB/TR, 6', 180 lbs. Deb: 8/26/80																							
1980	Cin-N	20	45	3	11	1	1	0	7	1	13	.244	.261	.311	572	59	-3	1	0	0	1.000	-1	O-14(0-1-13)	-0.4
1981	Cin-N	23	69	12	19	4	0	2	9	10	16	.275	.367	.420	787	121	2	3	1	0	1.000	-1	O-19(1-6-13)	0.1
1982	Cin-N	138	417	40	88	11	5	9	34	30	77	.211	.267	.326	593	64	-21	17	11	-0	.992	6	*O-131(0-9-123)	-2.1
1983	Cin-N	123	380	40	97	24	4	6	43	44	60	.255	.336	.387	723	96	-2	12	12	-2	**.991**	-1	*O-112(6-36-80)	-0.8
1984	Cin-N	14	12	3	1	1	0	0	0	3	3	.083	.267	.167	433	23	-1	1	1	-0	1.000	-2	O-10(3-1-6)	-0.4
	StL-N	13	14	1	2	0	0	0	0	0	3	.143	.143	.143	286	-20	-2	0	0	0	1.000	-3	/O-8(4-1-4)	-0.6
	Yr	27	26	4	3	1	0	0	0	3	6	.115	.207	.154	361	3	-3	1	1	-0	1.000	-5	O-18(7-2-10)	-1.0
1985	Mil-A	95	299	41	77	15	0	11	34	27	60	.258	.321	.418	739	101	0	1	2	-0	.986	-1	O-91(7-32-59)/D-3	-0.5
1986	Mil-A	26	78	4	17	3	1	1	16	7	16	.218	.291	.321	611	64	-4	1	2	-0	1.000	-3	O-22(12-5-8)/D-3	-0.8
1987	Hou-N	14	12	2	1	1	0	0	1	4	2	.083	.313	.167	479	33	-1	0	0	0	1.000	-2	/O-7(0-6-1)	-0.3
Total	8	466	1326	146	313	60	11	29	144	126	250	.236	.305	.363	669	83	-31	36	29	-2	.991	-7	O-414(33-97-307)/D-6	-5.8
■ JOHN HOUSEMAN	Houseman, John Franklin b: 1/10/1870, Netherlands d: 11/4/22, Chicago, Ill. 160 lbs. Deb: 9/11/1894 Career OF: (7-LF 7-CF 19-RF)																							
1894	Chi-N	4	15	5	6	3	1	0	4	5	3	.400	.571	.733	1305	202	3	2			.950	-0	/S-3,2-1	0.2
1897	StL-N	80	278	34	68	6	6	0	21	28		.245	.329	.309	638	70	-11	16			.918	-2	2-41,O-33R/S-5,3-3	-1.1
Total	2	84	293	39	74	9	7	0	25	33	3	.253	.344	.331	675	79	-8	18			.916	-3	/2-42,O-33R,S-8,3-3	-0.9
■ BEN HOUSER	Houser, Benjamin Franklin b: 11/30/1883, Shenandoah, Pa. d: 1/15/52, Augusta, Maine BL/TL, 6'1", 185 lbs. Deb: 5/2/10																							
1910	Phi-A	34	69	9	13	3	2	0	7	7		.188	.263	.290	553	74	-2	0			1.000	-0	1-26	-0.3
1911	Bos-N	20	71	11	18	1	0	1	9	8	6	.254	.329	.310	639	73	-2	2			.988	0	1-20	-0.3
1912	Bos-N	108	332	38	95	17	3	8	52	22	29	.286	.332	.428	760	105	1	1			.986	-3	1-83	-0.4
Total	3	162	472	58	126	21	5	9	68	37	35	.267	.322	.390	711	96	-4	3			.989	-3	1-129	-1.0
■ WAYNE HOUSIE	Housie, Wayne Tyrone b: 5/20/65, Hampton, Va. BB/TR, 5'9", 165 lbs. Deb: 9/17/91																							
1991	Bos-A	11	8	2	2	1	0	0	0	1	3	.250	.333	.375	708	91	-0	1	0	0	1.000	-1	/O-4(0-4-0),D-2	-0.1
1993	NY-N	18	16	2	3	1	0	0	1	1	1	.188	.235	.250	485	30	-2	0	0	0	.000	-1	/O-2(0-0-2)	-0.2
Total	2	29	24	4	5	2	0	0	1	2	4	.208	.269	.292	561	51	-2	1	0	0	1.000	-2	/O-6(0-4-2),D-2	-0.3
■ TYLER HOUSTON	Houston, Tyler Sam b: 1/17/71, Las Vegas, Nev. BL/TR, 6'2", 210 lbs. Deb: 4/3/96 Career OF: (1-LF 0-CF 1-RF)																							
1996	Atl-N	33	27	3	6	2	1	1	8	1	9	.222	.250	.481	731	83	-1	0	0	0	1.000	0	1-11	-0.1
	Chi-N	46	115	18	39	7	0	2	19	8	18	.339	.382	.452	834	116	3	3	2	-0	.986	-3	C-27/3-9,2-2,1-1,O	0.1
	Yr	79	142	21	45	9	1	3	27	9	27	.317	.358	.458	815	109	2	3	2	-0	.986	-3	C-27,1-12/3-9,2O	0.0
1997	Chi-N	72	196	15	51	10	0	2	28	9	35	.260	.293	.342	635	64	-10	1	0	0	.986	-4	C-41,3-12/1-2,2S	-1.1
1998	*Chi-N	95	255	26	65	7	1	9	33	13	53	.255	.291	.396	687	76	-9	2	2	-0	.993	2	C-63,3-12/1-7	-0.5
1999	Chi-N	100	249	26	58	9	1	9	27	28	67	.233	.310	.386	696	76	-10	1	1	-0	.901	-12	3-63,C-18/1-2,O-1R	-2.0

YEAR	TM/L	G	AB	R	H	2B	3B	HR	RBI	BB	SO	AVG	OBP	SLG	OPS	OPS+	BR+	SB	CS	SBR	FA	FR	G/POS	TPR
	Cle-A	13	27	2	4	1	0	1	3	3	11	.148	.233	.296	530	32	-3	0	0	0	1.000	-0	3-10/C-1	-0.3
2000	Mil-N	101	284	30	71	15	0	18	43	17	72	.250	.292	.493	785	95	-4	2	1	0	.982	3	1-35,3-28,C-23	-0.2
Total	5	460	1153	120	294	51	3	42	161	79	265	.255	.303	.414	716	82	-34	9	6	-0	.984	-13	C-173,3-134/1-58,2OS	-4.1

■ LEFTY HOUTZ

Houtz, Fred Fritz b: 9/4/1875, Connersville, Ind. d: 2/15/59, St.Marys, Ohio BL/TL, 5'10", 170 lbs. Deb: 7/23/1899

YEAR	TM/L	G	AB	R	H	2B	3B	HR	RBI	BB	SO	AVG	OBP	SLG	OPS	OPS+	BR+	SB	CS	SBR	FA	FR	G/POS	TPR
1899	Cin-N	5	17	1	4	0	1	0	0	4		.235	.381	.353	734	100	0	1			1.000	4	/O-5(1-4-0)	0.4

■ STEVE HOVLEY

Hovley, Stephen Eugene b: 12/18/44, Ventura, Cal. BL/TL, 5'10", 188 lbs. Deb: 6/26/69 Career OF: (26-LF 118-CF 190-RF)

YEAR	TM/L	G	AB	R	H	2B	3B	HR	RBI	BB	SO	AVG	OBP	SLG	OPS	OPS+	BR+	SB	CS	SBR	FA	FR	G/POS	TPR
1969	Sea-A	91	329	41	91	14	3	3	20	30	34	.277	.339	.365	704	98	-1	10	4	1	.989	7	O-84(3-35-49)	0.4
1970	Mil-A	40	135	17	38	9	0	0	16	17	11	.281	.366	.348	714	97	0	5	1	1	.958	-2	O-38(0-4-38)	-0.3
	Oak-A	72	100	8	19	1	0	0	1	5	11	.190	.229	.200	429	20	-11	3	0	1	1.000	-6	O-42(10-26-7)	-1.8
	Yr	112	235	25	57	10	0	0	17	22	22	.243	.310	.285	595	67	-10	8	1	1	.977	-8	O-80(10-30-45)	-2.1
1971	Oak-A	24	27	3	3	2	0	0	3	7	9	.111	.314	.185	499	45	-2	2	0	0	1.000	-1	O-11(4-3-4)	-0.2
1972	KC-A	105	196	24	53	5	1	3	24	24	29	.270	.353	.352	705	111	3	3	3	-0	.982	-5	O-68(5-25-39)	-0.4
1973	KC-A	104	232	29	59	8	1	2	24	33	34	.254	.347	.323	670	83	-4	6	4	-0	.975	-10	O-79(4-25-53),D-15	-1.7
Total	5	436	1019	122	263	39	5	8	88	116	128	.258	.336	.330	666	88	-14	29	12	2	.982	-16	O-322R/D-15	-4.0

■ CHRIS HOWARD

Howard, Christopher Hugh b: 2/27/66, San Diego, Cal. BR/TR, 6'2", 200 lbs. Deb: 9/15/91

YEAR	TM/L	G	AB	R	H	2B	3B	HR	RBI	BB	SO	AVG	OBP	SLG	OPS	OPS+	BR+	SB	CS	SBR	FA	FR	G/POS	TPR
1991	Sea-A	9	6	1	1	1	0	0	0	1	2	.167	.286	.333	619	71	-0	0	0	0	1.000	1	/C-9	0.1
1993	Sea-A	4	1	0	0	0	0	0	0	0	0	.000	.000	.000	0	-99	-0	0	0	0	1.000	1	/C-4	0.0
1994	Sea-A	9	25	2	5	1	0	0	2	1	6	.200	.259	.240	499	29	-3	0	0	0	1.000	-3	/C-9	-0.5
Total	3	22	32	3	6	2	0	0	2	2	8	.188	.257	.250	507	33	-3	0	0	0	1.000	-1	/C-22	-0.4

■ DAVE HOWARD

Howard, David Austin "Del" b: 5/1/1889, Washington, D.C. d: 1/26/56, Dallas, Tex. BR/TR, 5'11", 165 lbs. Deb: 5/8/12 Career OF: (0-LF 1-CF 1-RF)

YEAR	TM/L	G	AB	R	H	2B	3B	HR	RBI	BB	SO	AVG	OBP	SLG	OPS	OPS+	BR+	SB	CS	SBR	FA	FR	G/POS	TPR
1912	Was-A	1	0	1	0	0	0	0	0	0		—	—	—	—	—	0	0			.000	-0	R	0.0
1915	Bro-F	24	36	5	8	1	0	0	1	1	8	.222	.243	.250	493	39	-4	0			.925	3	2-12/O-2C,S-1,3-1	-0.1
Total	2	25	36	6	8	1	0	0	1	1	8	.222	.243	.250	493	39	-4	0			.925	3	/2-12,O-2C,3-1,S-1	-0.1

■ DAVID HOWARD

Howard, David Wayne b: 2/26/67, Sarasota, Fla. BB/TR (BL 1996-98), 6', 175 lbs. Deb: 4/14/91 F Career OF: (20-LF 25-CF 28-RF)

YEAR	TM/L	G	AB	R	H	2B	3B	HR	RBI	BB	SO	AVG	OBP	SLG	OPS	OPS+	BR+	SB	CS	SBR	FA	FR	G/POS	TPR
1991	KC-A	94	236	20	51	7	0	1	17	16	45	.216	.269	.258	527	46	-17	3	2	-0	.962	19	S-63,2-26/3-1,OD	0.7
1992	KC-A	74	219	19	49	6	2	1	18	15	43	.224	.274	.283	557	55	-13	3	4	-1	.976	-3	S-74/O-2(0-2-0)	-1.2
1993	KC-A	15	24	5	8	0	1	0	2	2	5	.333	.385	.417	801	109	0	1	0	0	.927	2	/2-7,S-3,3-2,O-1C	0.3
1994	KC-A	46	83	9	19	4	0	1	13	11	23	.229	.319	.313	632	61	-5	3	2	-0	1.000	8	3-25,S-15/2-3,OPD	0.4
1995	KC-A	95	255	23	62	13	4	0	19	24	41	.243	.311	.325	636	65	-13	6	1	1	.994	15	2-41,S-33,O-30C,/1D	0.6
1996	KC-A	143	420	51	92	14	5	4	48	40	74	.219	.293	.305	598	52	-31	5	6	-1	**.982**	19	*S-135/2-3,1-2,O-1C	-0.3
1997	KC-A	80	162	24	39	8	1	1	13	10	31	.241	.289	.321	610	58	-10	2	2	-0	.973	7	2-34,O-23R/S-9,3D	-0.2
1998	StL-N	46	102	15	25	1	1	2	12	12	22	.245	.325	.333	658	74	-4	0	0	0	1.000	4	2-19,S-16,3-14,/O-2C	0.1
1999	StL-N	52	82	3	17	4	0	1	6	7	27	.207	.286	.293	578	47	-7	0	2	-1	.966	2	S-13/1-9,2-9,O-5L,3	-0.5
Total	9	645	1583	169	362	57	14	11	148	137	311	.229	.294	.303	597	57	-99	23	19	-2	.976	72	S-361,2-142/O31DP	-0.1

■ DOUG HOWARD

Howard, Douglas Lynn b: 2/6/48, Salt Lake City, Utah BR/TR, 6'3", 185 lbs. Deb: 9/6/72 Career OF: (16-LF 6-CF 2-RF)

YEAR	TM/L	G	AB	R	H	2B	3B	HR	RBI	BB	SO	AVG	OBP	SLG	OPS	OPS+	BR+	SB	CS	SBR	FA	FR	G/POS	TPR
1972	Cal-A	11	38	4	10	1	0	0	2	1	3	.263	.300	.289	589	81	-1	0	0	0	1.000	-1	/O-8(8-0-0),1-1,3-1	-0.3
1973	Cal-A	8	21	2	2	0	0	0	1	1	6	.095	.136	.095	232	-37	-4	0	0	0	1.000	-1	/O-6(6-0-0),1-1,3-1	-0.5
1974	Cal-A	22	39	5	9	0	1	0	5	2	1	.231	.268	.282	550	62	-2	1	0	0	1.000	-2	/O-8(2-6-0),1-5,D-3	-0.4
1975	StL-N	17	29	1	6	0	0	1	1	0	7	.207	.207	.310	517	41	-2	0	0	0	1.000	1	/1-7	-0.1
1976	Cle-A	39	90	7	19	4	0	0	13	3	13	.211	.245	.256	500	47	-6	1	1	-0	.991	1	1-32/O-2(0-0-2),D-4	-0.7
Total	5	97	217	19	46	5	1	1	22	7	30	.212	.243	.258	501	46	-15	2	1	0	.994	-1	/1-46,O-24L,D-7,3-2	-2.0

■ ELSTON HOWARD

Howard, Elston Gene b: 2/23/29, St.Louis, Mo. d: 12/14/80, New York, N.Y. BR/TR, 6'2", 200 lbs. Deb: 4/14/55 C Career OF: (230-LF 0-CF 40-RF)

YEAR	TM/L	G	AB	R	H	2B	3B	HR	RBI	BB	SO	AVG	OBP	SLG	OPS	OPS+	BR+	SB	CS	SBR	FA	FR	G/POS	TPR
1955	*NY-A	97	279	33	81	8	7	10	43	20	36	.290	.340	.477	817	120	6	0	0	0	.978	2	O-75(62-0-15)/C-9	0.4
1956	*NY-A	98	290	35	76	8	3	5	34	21	30	.262	.314	.362	676	81	-9	0	1	-0	.990	-5	O-65(62-0-5),C-26	-1.5
1957	*NY-A☆	110	356	33	90	13	4	8	44	16	43	.253	.285	.379	664	81	-11	2	5	-1	.961	-12	O-71(69-0-2),C-32/1-2	-2.6
1958	*NY-A☆	103	376	45	118	19	5	11	66	22	60	.314	.352	.479	830	131	14	1	1	-0	.997	2	C-67,O-24(17-0-8)/1-5	1.9
1959	NY-A☆	125	443	59	121	24	6	18	73	20	57	.273	.309	.476	785	116	7	0	1	-0	.985	-2	1-50,C-43,O-28L	0.3
1960	*NY-A★	107	323	29	79	11	3	6	39	28	43	.245	.305	.353	658	82	-9	3	0	1	.987	2	C-91/O-1(1-0-0)	-0.2
1961	*NY-A★	129	446	64	155	17	5	21	77	28	65	.348	.390	.549	939	156	34	0	3	-1	.993	7	*C-111/1-9	4.3
1962	*NY-A★	136	494	63	138	23	5	21	91	31	76	.279	.323	.474	797	115	8	1	1	-0	.995	-1	*C-129	1.4
1963	*NY-A★	135	487	75	140	21	6	28	85	35	68	.287	.343	.528	871	141	25	0	0	0	.994	-3	*C-132	2.9
1964	*NY-A★	150	550	63	172	27	3	15	84	48	73	.313	.373	.455	828	127	20	1	1	-0	**.998**	11	*C-146	4.0
1965	NY-A☆	110	391	38	91	15	1	9	45	24	65	.233	.279	.345	624	77	-13	0	0	0	.991	-5	C-95/1-5,O-1(1-0-0)	-1.3
1966	NY-A	126	410	38	105	19	2	6	35	37	65	.256	.319	.356	675	97	-1	0	0	0	.985	-4	*C-100,1-13	-0.1
1967	NY-A	66	199	13	39	6	0	3	17	12	36	.196	.249	.271	520	56	-11	0	0	0	.984	-1	C-48/1-1	-1.1
	*Bos-A	42	116	9	17	3	0	1	11	9	24	.147	.214	.198	413	21	-11	0	0	0	.996	2	C-41	-0.8
	Yr	108	315	22	56	9	0	4	28	21	60	.178	.236	.244	480	42	-23	0	0	0	.990	1	C-89/1-1	-1.9
1968	Bos-A	71	203	22	49	4	0	5	18	22	45	.241	.319	.335	654	92	-1	1	1	-0	.995	-3	C-68	-0.2
Total	14	1605	5363	619	1471	218	50	167	762	373	786	.274	.325	.427	752	108	49	9	14	-3	.993	-9	*C-1138,O-265L/1-85	7.4

■ FRANK HOWARD

Howard, Frank Oliver "Hondo" or "The Capital Punisher"
b: 8/8/36, Columbus, Ohio BR/TR, 6'7", 255 lbs. Deb: 9/10/58 MC Career OF: (923-LF 0-CF 530-RF)

YEAR	TM/L	G	AB	R	H	2B	3B	HR	RBI	BB	SO	AVG	OBP	SLG	OPS	OPS+	BR+	SB	CS	SBR	FA	FR	G/POS	TPR
1958	LA-N	8	29	3	7	1	0	1	2	1	11	.241	.267	.379	646	66	-1	0	0	0	1.000	0	/O-8(3-0-5)	-0.2
1959	LA-N	9	21	2	3	0	1	1	6	2	9	.143	.217	.381	598	52	-2	0	0	0	1.000	-0	/O-6(4-0-2)	-0.2
1960	LA-N	117	448	54	120	15	2	23	77	32	108	.268	.321	.464	785	105	2	0	1	-0	.984	-2	*O-115(22-0-94)/1-4	-0.5
1961	LA-N	92	267	36	79	10	2	15	45	21	50	.296	.349	.517	866	116	6	0	1	-0	.934	-4	O-65(20-0-46)/1-7	-0.3
1962	LA-N	141	493	80	146	25	6	31	119	39	108	.296	.349	.560	909	148	31	1	0	0	.972	2	*O-131(9-0-128)	2.4
1963	*LA-N	123	417	58	114	16	1	28	64	33	116	.273	.333	.518	851	151	25	1	2	-0	.960	-1	*O-111(6-0-107)	1.7
1964	LA-N	134	433	60	98	13	2	24	69	51	113	.226	.308	.432	740	114	7	1	0	0	.979	-7	*O-122(0-0-122)	-0.8
1965	Was-A	149	516	53	149	22	6	21	84	55	112	.289	.360	.477	836	138	25	0	0	0	.981	-8	*O-138(138-0-5)	1.0
1966	Was-A	146	493	52	137	19	4	18	71	53	104	.278	.349	.442	791	127	17	1	1	-0	.982	-2	*O-135(135-0-0)	0.8
1967	Was-A	149	519	71	133	20	2	36	89	60	155	.256	.339	.511	850	154	33	0	1	-0	.986	-7	*O-141(141-0-3)/1-4	2.0
1968	Was-A★	158	598	79	164	28	3	**44**	106	54	141	.274	.340	**.552**	892	**172**	49	0	0	0	.955	2	*O-107(107-0-0),1-55	4.7
1969	Was-A★	161	592	111	175	17	2	48	111	102	96	.296	.403	.574	978	180	64	1	0	0	.974	-18	*O-114(108-0-6),1-70	3.7
1970	Was-A★	161	566	90	160	15	1	**44**	**126**	**132**	125	.283	.420	.546	966	173	61	1	2	-0	.973	-9	*O-120(114-0-6),1-48	4.2
1971	Was-A★	153	549	60	153	25	2	26	83	77	121	.279	.369	.474	843	146	33	1	0	0	.993	3	*O-100(95-0-5),1-68	2.8
1972	Tex-A	95	287	28	70	9	0	9	31	42	55	.244	.342	.369	712	117	7	1	0	0	.981	-6	1-66,O-21(20-0-1)	-0.6
	Det-A	14	33	1	8	1	0	1	7	4	8	.242	.324	.364	688	101	0	0	0	0	.952	-1	1-10/O-1(1-0-0)	-0.1
	Yr	109	320	29	78	10	0	10	38	46	63	.244	.341	.369	709	115	7	1	0	0	.978	-7	1-76,O-22(21-0-1)	-0.7
1973	Det-A	85	227	26	58	9	1	12	29	24	28	.256	.327	.463	789	113	3	0	1	-0	.923	-1	D-76/1-2	0.0
Total	16	1895	6488	864	1774	245	35	382	1119	782	1460	.273	.355	.499	853	143	360	8	9	-1	.975	-57	*O-1435L,1-334/D-76	20.6

■ DEL HOWARD

Howard, George Elmer b: 12/24/1877, Kenney, Ill. d: 12/24/56, Seattle, Wash. BL/TR, 6', 180 lbs. Deb: 4/15/05 F Career OF: (137-LF 34-CF 85-RF)

YEAR	TM/L	G	AB	R	H	2B	3B	HR	RBI	BB	SO	AVG	OBP	SLG	OPS	OPS+	BR+	SB	CS	SBR	FA	FR	G/POS	TPR
1905	Pit-N	123	435	56	127	18	5	2	63	27		.292	.345	.370	715	110	5	19			.978	-7	1-90,O-28(1-0-27)/P-1	-0.4
1906	Bos-N	147	545	46	142	19	8	1	54	26		.261	.306	.330	637	101	-1	17			.911	-12	O-87L,2-45,S-14,/1	-1.9
1907	Bos-N	50	187	20	51	4	2	1	13	11		.273	.330	.332	662	108	2	11			.969	-3	O-45(45-0-0)/2-3	-0.4
	*Chi-N	51	148	10	34	2	2	0	13	6		.230	.269	.270	540	65	-6	3			.972	-4	1-33/O-8(0-3-6)	-1.2
	Yr	101	335	30	85	6	4	1	26	17		.254	.304	.304	608	88	-5	14			.961	-6	O-53(45-3-6),1-33/2-3	-1.6
1908	*Chi-N	96	315	42	88	7	3	1	26	23		.279	.338	.330	668	109	4	11			.965	-5	O-81(4-31-52)/1-5	-0.7
1909	Chi-N	69	203	25	40	4	2	1	24	18		.197	.282	.251	533	64	-8	6			.980	0	1-57	-1.0
Total	5	536	1833	199	482	54	22	6	193	111		.263	.318	.326	644	98	-5	67			.946	-30	O-249L,1-187/2-48,SP	-5.6

■ IVAN HOWARD

Howard, Ivan Chester b: 10/12/1882, Kenney, Ill. d: 3/30/67, Medford, Ore. BB/TR, 5'10", 170 lbs. Deb: 4/25/14 F

YEAR	TM/L	G	AB	R	H	2B	3B	HR	RBI	BB	SO	AVG	OBP	SLG	OPS	OPS+	BR+	SB	CS	SBR	FA	FR	G/POS	TPR
1914	StL-A	81	209	21	51	6	2	0	20	28	42	.244	.342	.292	634	94	-0	14	10	-0	.936	-7	3-34,1-28/O-3L,S-1	-0.9
1915	StL-A	113	324	43	90	10	7	2	43	43	48	.278	.368	.370	738	126	11	29	12	2	.992	5	1-48,3-23,O-17R,/2S	1.7

YEAR	TM/L	G	AB	R	H	2B	3B	HR	RBI	BB	SO	AVG	OBP	SLG	OPS	OPS+	BR+	SB	CS	SBR	FA	FR	G/POS	TPR
1916	Cle-A	81	246	20	46	11	5	0	23	30	34	.187	.298	.272	571	68	-9	9			.970	7	2-65/1-7	-0.2
1917	Cle-A	27	39	7	4	0	0	0	0	3	5	.103	.167	.103	269	-17	-5	1			.833	2	/3-6,2-4,O-4(0-4-0)	-0.4
Total	4	302	818	91	191	27	14	2	86	104	129	.233	.331	.308	639	92	-4	53	22		.990	6	/1-83,2-71,3-63,OS	0.2
■ **LARRY HOWARD** Howard, Lawrence Rayford b: 6/6/45, Columbus, Ohio BR/TR, 6'3", 200 lbs. Deb: 8/9/70																								
1970	Hou-N	31	88	11	27	6	0	2	16	10	23	.307	.378	.443	821	124	3	0	0	0	.993	-5	C-26/1-2,O-1(0-0-1)	-0.1
1971	Hou-N	24	64	6	15	3	0	2	14	3	17	.234	.269	.375	644	83	-2	0	1	-0	.992	2	C-22	0.1
1972	Hou-N	54	157	16	35	7	0	2	13	17	30	.223	.299	.306	605	74	-5	0	0	0	.980	0	C-53/O-1(1-0-0)	-0.4
1973	Hou-N	20	48	3	8	3	0	0	4	5	12	.167	.245	.229	474	32	-4	0	0	0	.989	-1	C-20	-0.5
	Atl-N	4	8	0	1	0	0	0	0	2	3	.125	.300	.125	425	20	-1	0	0	0	1.000	-0	/C-2	-0.1
	Yr	24	56	3	9	3	0	0	4	7	15	.161	.254	.214	468	31	-5	0	0	0	.990	-1	C-22	-0.6
Total	4	133	365	36	86	19	0	6	47	37	85	.236	.306	.337	643	81	-9	0	1	-0	.986	-4	C-123/O-2(1-0-1),1-2	-1.0
■ **MATT HOWARD** Howard, Matthew Christopher b: 9/22/67, Fall River, Mass. BR/TR, 5'10", 170 lbs. Deb: 5/17/96																								
1996	NY-A	35	54	9	11	1	0	1	9	2	8	.204	.232	.278	510	28	-6	1	0	0	.976	-5	2-30/3-6	-0.9
■ **MIKE HOWARD** Howard, Michael Fredric b: 4/2/58, Seattle, Wash. BB/TR, 6'2", 185 lbs. Deb: 9/12/81																								
1981	NY-N	14	24	4	4	1	0	0	3	4	6	.167	.286	.208	494	43	-2	2	0	0	.952	-1	O-14(6-1-7)	-0.2
1982	NY-N	33	39	5	7	0	0	1	3	6	7	.179	.304	.256	561	59	-2	2	0	0	1.000	-3	O-22(9-7-8)/2-3	-0.5
1983	NY-N	1	3	0	1	0	0	0	1	0	1	.333	.333	.333	667	86	-0	0	0	0	.000	-0	/O-1(0-0-1)	0.0
Total	3	48	66	9	12	1	0	1	7	10	14	.182	.299	.242	541	54	-4	4	0	1	.980	-4	/O-37(15-8-16),2-3	-0.7
■ **PAUL HOWARD** Howard, Paul Joseph "Del" b: 5/20/1884, Boston, Mass. d: 8/29/68, Miami, Fla. BR/TR, 5'8", 170 lbs. Deb: 9/16/09																								
1909	Bos-A	6	15	2	3	1	0	0	2	3		.200	.368	.267	635	99	0	0			1.000	-1	/O-6(4-0-2)	-0.1
■ **STEVE HOWARD** Howard, Steven Bernard b: 12/7/63, Oakland, Cal. BR/TR, 6'2", 205 lbs. Deb: 6/16/90																								
1990	Oak-A	21	52	5	12	4	0	0	1	4	17	.231	.286	.308	593	69	-2	0	0	0	.933	-4	O-14(4-3-8)/D-7	-0.7
■ **THOMAS HOWARD** Howard, Thomas Sylvester b: 12/11/64, Middletown, Ohio BB/TR (BL 1996-98), 6'2", 205 lbs. Deb: 7/3/90 Career OF: (305-LF 228-CF 206-RF)																								
1990	SD-N	20	44	4	12	2	0	0	0	0	11	.273	.273	.318	591	61	-2	0	1	-0	.950	-2	O-13(9-2-2)	-0.5
1991	SD-N	106	281	30	70	12	3	4	22	24	57	.249	.310	.356	666	84	-6	10	7	-0	.995	3	O-86(34-41-14)	-0.5
1992	SD-N	5	3	1	1	0	0	0	0	0	0	.333	.333	.333	667	88	-0	0	0	0	.000	0	/H	0.0
	Cle-A	117	358	36	99	15	2	2	32	17	60	.277	.309	.346	656	85	-8	15	8	1	.990	-7	O-97(68-22-13)/D-2	-1.7
1993	Cle-A	74	178	26	42	7	0	3	23	12	42	.236	.284	.326	610	64	-9	5	1	1	.977	-3	O-47(9-11-28)/D-7	-1.2
	Cin-N	38	141	22	39	8	3	4	13	12	21	.277	.333	.461	794	110	2	5	6	-1	.987	2	O-37(27-12-0)	0.2
1994	Cin-N	83	178	24	47	11	0	5	24	10	30	.264	.303	.410	713	85	-4	4	2	0	.965	-5	O-57(41-7-12)	-1.0
1995	*Cin-N	113	281	42	85	15	2	3	26	20	37	.302	.351	.402	753	98	-1	17	8	1	.985	-9	O-82(36-39-14)	-0.9
1996	Cin-N	121	360	50	98	19	10	6	42	17	51	.272	.311	.431	741	93	-5	6	5	-0	.982	-9	*O-103(51-40-32)	-1.6
1997	*Hou-N	107	255	24	63	16	1	3	22	26	48	.247	.324	.353	677	80	-7	1	2	-0	1.000	-2	O-62(10-41-18)	-1.0
1998	LA-N	47	76	9	14	4	0	2	4	3	15	.184	.215	.316	531	40	-7	1	0	0	1.000	-3	O-29(11-13-6)/D-1	-1.0
1999	StL-N	98	195	16	57	10	0	6	28	17	26	.292	.355	.436	791	98	-1	1	1	-0	.987	-4	O-48(3-0-45)/D-1	-0.6
2000	StL-N	86	133	13	28	4	1	6	28	7	34	.211	.255	.391	646	60	-9	1	0	0	.960	-5	O-27(6-0-22)/1-1,D-3	-1.4
Total	11	1015	2483	297	655	123	22	44	264	165	432	.264	.313	.384	697	85	-57	66	41	0	.986	-44	O-688L/D-14,1-1	-11.2
■ **WILBUR HOWARD** Howard, Wilbur Leon b: 1/8/49, Lowell, N.C. BB/TR, 6'2", 175 lbs. Deb: 9/4/73 Career OF: (214-LF 69-CF 50-RF)																								
1973	Mil-A	16	39	3	8	0	0	0	1	2	10	.205	.244	.205	449	28	-4	0	1	-0	.969	2	O-12(5-0-7)/D-1	-0.2
1974	Hou-N	64	111	19	24	4	0	2	5	5	18	.216	.250	.306	556	57	-7	4	5	-1	1.000	-4	O-50(43-4-3)	-1.4
1975	Hou-N	121	392	62	111	16	8	0	21	21	67	.283	.325	.365	689	98	-2	32	11	3	.995	1	O-95(53-34-12)	-0.2
1976	Hou-N	94	191	26	42	7	2	1	18	7	28	.220	.247	.293	541	58	-11	7	5	-0	.961	-8	O-63(37-11-20)/2-2	-2.3
1977	Hou-N	87	187	22	48	6	0	2	13	5	30	.257	.276	.321	597	65	-10	11	1	2	.990	-4	O-62(46-15-4)/2-4	-1.4
1978	Hou-N	84	148	17	34	4	1	1	13	5	22	.230	.269	.291	560	61	-8	6	2	1	1.000	-7	O-38(30-5-4)/C-3,2-1	-1.6
Total	6	466	1068	149	267	37	11	6	71	45	175	.250	.284	.322	606	73	-42	60	25	4	.987	-20	O-320L/2-7,C-3,D-1	-7.1
■ **JIM HOWARTH** Howarth, James Eugene b: 3/7/47, Biloxi, Miss. BL/TL, 5'11", 175 lbs. Deb: 9/5/71																								
1971	SF-N	7	13	3	3	1	0	0	2	3	3	.231	.375	.308	683	97	0	0	0	0	1.000	-1	/O-6(2-1-3)	-0.1
1972	SF-N	74	119	16	28	4	0	1	7	16	18	.235	.326	.294	620	76	-3	3	2	-0	1.000	-3	O-25(8-17-0)/1-4	-0.8
1973	SF-N	65	90	8	18	1	1	0	7	7	8	.200	.258	.233	491	36	-8	0	0	0	1.000	-5	O-33(5-21-7)/1-1	-1.4
1974	SF-N	6	4	0	0	0	0	0	0	0	0	.000	.000	.000	0	-96	-1	0	0	0	.000	-0	/O-1(1-0-0)	-0.1
Total	4	152	226	27	49	6	1	1	16	26	29	.217	.298	.265	563	58	-12	3	2	-0	1.000	-9	/O-65(16-39-10),1-5	-2.4
■ **ART HOWE** Howe, Arthur Henry b: 12/15/46, Pittsburgh, Pa. BR/TR, 6'2", 190 lbs. Deb: 7/10/74 MC																								
1974	*Pit-N	29	74	10	18	4	1	1	5	9	13	.243	.325	.365	690	96	-0	0	0	0	.937	4	3-20/S-2	0.3
1975	Pit-N	63	146	13	25	9	0	1	10	15	15	.171	.248	.253	502	40	-12	1	0	0	.938	3	3-42/S-3	-0.9
1976	Hou-N	21	29	0	4	1	0	0	0	6	6	.138	.286	.172	458	35	-2	0	0	0	.938	2	/3-8,2-2	-0.1
1977	Hou-N	125	413	44	109	23	7	8	58	41	60	.264	.338	.412	749	110	5	0	1	-0	.985	6	2-96,3-19,S-11	1.6
1978	Hou-N	119	420	46	123	33	3	7	55	34	41	.293	.347	.436	783	127	14	2	3	-1	.977	-4	*2-107,3-11/1-1	1.6
1979	Hou-N	118	355	32	88	15	2	6	33	36	37	.248	.319	.352	671	88	-6	3	1	0	.991	6	2-68,3-59/1-3	0.2
1980	*Hou-N	110	321	34	91	12	5	10	46	34	29	.283	.354	.445	799	132	13	1	0	0	.986	1	1-77,3-25/S-5,2-3	1.1
1981	*Hou-N	103	361	43	107	22	4	3	36	41	23	.296	.368	.404	773	125	12	1	3	-1	.966	5	3-98/1-2	1.6
1982	Hou-N	110	365	29	87	15	1	5	38	41	45	.238	.317	.326	643	87	-6	2	0	0	.972	8	3-72,1-35	-0.1
1984	StL-N	89	139	17	30	5	0	2	12	18	18	.216	.306	.295	601	71	-5	0	2	-1	.979	8	3-45,1-11/2-8,S-5	0.1
1985	StL-N	4	3	0	0	0	0	0	0	0	0	.000	.000	.000	0	-99	-1	0	0	0	1.000	0	/1-1,3-1	-0.1
Total	11	891	2626	268	682	139	23	43	293	275	287	.260	.332	.379	711	103	12	10	10	-1	.965	38	3-400,2-284,1-130,/S	5.3
■ **SHORTY HOWE** Howe, John b: New York, N.Y. Deb: 6/17/1890																								
1890	NY-N	19	64	4	11	0	0	0	4	3	2	.172	.221	.172	392	15	-7	3			.887	3	2-18/3-1	-0.3
1893	NY-N	1	5	1	3	0	0	0	2	0	0	.600	.600	.600	1200	219	1	1			.400	-1	/3-1	0.0
Total	2	20	69	5	14	0	0	0	6	3	2	.203	.247	.203	449	30	-6	4			.400	2	/2-18,3-2	-0.3
■ **HARRY HOWELL** Howell, Henry Harry b: 11/14/1876, New Jersey d: 5/22/56, Spokane, Wash. BR/TR, 5'9", Deb: 10/10/1898 U Career OF: (10-LF 17-CF 6-RF)																								
1898	Bro-N	2	8	1	2	0	0	0	1	1		.250	.333	.250	583	68	-0	0			1.000	0	/P-2	0.0
1899	Bal-N	28	82	4	12	2	2	0	3	3		.146	.195	.220	415	13	-10	0			.940	1	P-28	0.0
1900	*Bro-N	22	42	6	12	2	0	1	6	6		.286	.388	.405	793	112	1	1			.949	1	P-21	0.0
1901	Bal-A	53	188	26	41	10	5	2	26	5		.218	.242	.356	599	62	-11	6			.905	-3	P-37/O-9L,S-6,12	-0.5
1902	Bal-A	96	347	42	93	16	11	2	42	18		.268	.312	.395	706	91	-5	7			.951	-9	P-26,2-26,O-18C,3S/1	-1.7
1903	NY-A	40	106	14	23	3	2	1	12	5		.217	.259	.311	570	66	-4	1			**1.000**	1	P-25/3-7,S-5,1-1,2	-0.4
1904	StL-A	36	113	9	25	5	2	1	6	4		.221	.261	.327	588	91	-1	0			.971	9	P-34	0.0
1905	StL-A	42	135	9	26	6	2	1	10	3		.193	.216	.289	505	63	-6	0			.966	18	P-38/O-3(1-2-0)	-0.1
1906	StL-A	35	103	5	13	3	1	0	6	6		.126	.174	.175	349	10	-11	2			.934	8	P-35	0.0
1907	StL-A	44	114	12	27	5	0	2	7	7		.237	.281	.333	614	96	-1	2			.982	9	P-42/O-2(0-2-0)	0.1
1908	StL-A	41	120	10	22	7	0	1	9	4		.183	.210	.267	476	54	-6	0			.961	0	P-41	0.0
1909	StL-A	18	34	5	6	1	0	0	3	2		.176	.222	.206	428	38	-2	0			.938	1	P-10/3-7,O-1(0-1-0)	0.0
1910	StL-A	1	2	0	0	0	0	0	0	0		.000	.000	.000	0	-99	-0	0			1.000	0	/P-1	0.0
Total	13	458	1394	143	302	60	25	11	131	64		.217	.257	.319	576	69	-58	19			.958	36	P-340/O-33C,3-29,2S1	-2.6
■ **DIXIE HOWELL** Howell, Homer Elliott b: 4/24/20, Louisville, Ky. d: 10/5/90, Binghamton, N.Y. BR/TR, 5'11", 195 lbs. Deb: 5/6/47																								
1947	Pit-N	76	214	23	59	11	0	4	25	27	34	.276	.357	.383	740	94	-1	1			.974	-3	C-74	-0.1
1949	Cin-N	64	172	17	42	6	1	2	18	8	21	.244	.286	.326	611	63	-9	0			.987	5	C-56	-0.1
1950	Cin-N	82	224	30	50	9	1	2	22	32	31	.223	.326	.299	625	65	-11	0			.986	-4	C-81	-1.0
1951	Cin-N	77	207	22	52	6	1	2	18	15	34	.251	.302	.319	621	66	-10	0	2	-1	.987	4	C-73	-0.4
1952	Cin-N	17	37	4	7	1	1	2	4	3	9	.189	.250	.432	682	86	-1	0	0	0	.981	1	C-16	0.0
1953	Bro-N	1	1	0	0	0	0	0	0	0	1	.000	.000	.000	0	-98	-0	0	0	0	.000	0	H	0.0

YEAR	TM/L	G	AB	R	H	2B	3B	HR	RBI	BB	SO	AVG	OBP	SLG	OPS	OPS+	BR+	SB	CS	SBR	FA	FR	G/POS	TPR
1955	Bro-N	16	42	2	11	4	0	0	5	1	7	.262	.279	.357	636	66	-2	0	0	0	.981	-2	C-13	-0.3
1956	Bro-N	7	13	0	3	2	0	0	1	1	3	.231	.286	.385	670	72	-1	0	0	0	1.000	-0	/C-6	-0.1
Total	8	340	910	98	224	39	4	12	93	87	140	.246	.315	.337	652	73	-35	1	2		.984	2	C-319	-2.0
■ **JACK HOWELL** Howell, Jack Robert b: 8/18/61, Tucson, Ariz. BL/TR, 6', 201 lbs. Deb: 5/20/85 Career OF: (88-LF 1-CF 23-RF)																								
1985	Cal-A	43	137	19	27	4	0	5	18	16	33	.197	.281	.336	617	68	-6	1	1	-0	.931	-1	3-42	-0.8
1986	*Cal-A	63	151	26	41	14	2	4	21	19	28	.272	.353	.470	823	123	5	2	0	0	.977	-1	3-39/O-8(7-0-1),D-2	0.4
1987	Cal-A	138	449	64	110	18	5	23	64	57	118	.245	.333	.461	794	111	7	4	3	-0	.987	-8	O-89L,3-48,2-13	-0.5
1988	Cal-A	154	500	59	127	32	2	16	63	46	130	.254	.324	.422	746	110	6	2	6	-2	.953	-20	*3-152/O-2(1-1-0)	-1.5
1989	Cal-A	144	474	56	108	19	4	20	52	52	125	.228	.308	.411	720	103	1	0	3	-1	**.974**	23	*3-142/O-4(1-0-3)	2.3
1990	Cal-A	105	316	35	72	19	1	8	33	46	61	.228	.328	.370	698	97	-1	3	0	1	.939	7	*3-102/1-1,S-1	0.7
1991	Cal-A	32	81	11	17	2	0	2	7	11	11	.210	.304	.309	613	70	-3	1	1	-0	.968	2	2-12/3-8,O-5R,1D	-0.2
	SD-N	58	160	24	33	3	1	6	16	18	33	.206	.287	.350	637	76	-5	0	0	0	.985	6	3-54	0.1
1996	Cal-A	66	126	20	34	4	1	8	21	10	30	.270	.324	.508	831	106	0	0	1	-0	.884	-2	3-43/1-2,2-1,D-4	-0.2
1997	Ana-A	77	174	25	45	7	0	14	34	13	36	.259	.310	.540	850	117	3	1	0	0	.976	1	3-24,D-22,1-12	0.2
1998	Hou-N	24	38	4	11	5	0	1	7	4	12	.289	.357	.500	857	126	1	0	0	0	1.000	2	1-10/3-2	0.3
1999	Hou-N	37	33	2	7	2	0	1	1	8	9	.212	.366	.364	729	87	-0	0	0	0	1.000	1	/1-5,3-3,D-2	0.0
Total	11	941	2639	345	632	129	16	108	337	300	626	.239	.320	.423	743	103	8	14	15	-2	.958	9	3-659,O-108L/1D2S	0.8
■ **RED HOWELL** Howell, Murray Donald "Porky" b: 1/29/09, Atlanta, Ga. d: 10/1/50, Travelers Rest, S.C BR/TR, 6', 215 lbs. Deb: 4/24/41																								
1941	Cle-A	11	7	0	2	0	0	0	2	4	2	.286	.545	.286	831	132	1	0	0	0	.000	0	H	0.1
■ **PAT HOWELL** Howell, Patrick O'Neal b: 8/31/68, Mobile, Ala. BB/TR, 5'11", 155 lbs. Deb: 7/10/92																								
1992	NY-N	31	75	9	14	1	0	0	1	2	15	.187	.218	.200	418	19	-8	4	2	0	1.000	-0	O-28(0-28-0)	-0.9
■ **ROY HOWELL** Howell, Roy Lee b: 12/18/53, Lompoc, Cal. BL/TR, 6'1", 190 lbs. Deb: 9/9/74																								
1974	Tex-A	13	44	2	11	1	0	1	3	2	10	.250	.283	.341	624	81	-1	0	0	0	.906	-2	3-12	-0.3
1975	Tex-A	125	383	43	96	15	2	10	51	39	79	.251	.325	.379	703	99	-1	2	2	-0	.933	-7	*3-115/D-5	-0.8
1976	Tex-A	140	491	55	124	28	2	8	53	30	106	.253	.297	.367	664	92	-6	1	0	0	.926	-8	*3-130/D-8	-1.5
1977	Tex-A	7	17	0	0	0	0	0	0	2	4	.000	.105	.000	105	-68	-4	0	0	0	1.000	-0	/O-2L,1-1,3-1,D-2	-0.4
	Tor-A	96	364	41	115	17	1	10	44	42	76	.316	.388	.451	839	126	14	4	1	1	.953	-7	3-87/D-8	0.6
	Yr	103	381	41	115	17	1	10	44	44	80	.302	.376	.430	806	117	10	4	1	1	.954	-7	3-88,D-10/O-2L,1-1	0.2
1978	Tor-A★	140	551	67	149	28	3	8	61	44	78	.270	.326	.376	701	95	-4	0	1	-0	.950	11	*3-131/O-5(0-0-5),D-1	0.4
1979	Tor-A	138	511	60	126	28	4	15	72	42	91	.247	.311	.405	716	90	-8	1	4	-1	.952	-1	*3-133/D-4	-1.2
1980	Tor-A	142	528	51	142	28	9	10	57	50	92	.269	.338	.413	751	100	0	0	0	0	.958	-18	*3-138/D-2	-2.0
1981	*Mil-A	76	244	37	58	13	1	6	33	23	39	.238	.309	.373	682	101	-0	0	0	0	.958	-6	3-53,D-13/1-3,O-1R	-0.8
1982	*Mil-A	98	300	31	78	11	2	4	38	21	39	.260	.308	.350	658	86	-6	0	2	-1	.933	-1	D-84/1-4,O-2(0-0-2)	-1.0
1983	Mil-A	69	194	23	54	9	6	4	25	15	29	.278	.330	.448	779	121	5	1	3	-1	.960	1	D-54/1-2	0.3
1984	Mil-A	68	164	12	38	5	1	4	17	8	32	.232	.284	.348	632	77	-5	0	1	-0	.907	1	3-46/1-4,D-8	-0.5
Total	11	1112	3791	422	991	183	31	80	454	318	675	.261	.322	.389	712	97	-16	9	14	-3	.944	-35	3-846,D-189/1-14,O	-7.2
■ **BILL HOWERTON** Howerton, William Ray "Hopalong" b: 12/12/21, Lompoc, Cal. BL/TR, 5'11", 185 lbs. Deb: 9/11/49																								
1949	StL-N	9	13	1	4	1	0	0	1	0	2	.308	.308	.385	692	81	-0	0			.900	-1	/O-6(2-3-1)	-0.2
1950	StL-N	110	313	50	88	20	8	10	59	47	60	.281	.375	.492	867	120	9	0			.969	-11	O-94(32-54-11)	-0.5
1951	StL-N	24	65	10	17	4	1	1	4	10	12	.262	.360	.400	760	104	1	0	1	-0	.949	1	O-17(3-0-14)	0.0
	Pit-N	80	219	29	60	12	2	11	37	26	44	.274	.351	.498	849	122	6	1	0	0	.950	-8	O-53(4-38-11)/3-4	-0.3
	Yr	104	284	39	77	16	3	12	41	36	56	.271	.353	.475	828	118	7	1	1	-0	.950	-8	O-70(7-38-25)/3-4	-0.3
1952	Pit-N	13	25	3	8	1	1	0	4	6	5	.320	.452	.440	892	144	2	0	0	0	.900	-2	/O-5(0-2-3),3-1	0.0
	NY-N	11	15	2	1	1	0	0	1	3	2	.067	.222	.133	356	1	-2	0	0	0	1.000	-0	/O-3(0-1-2)	-0.2
	Yr	24	40	5	9	2	1	0	5	9	7	.225	.367	.325	692	92	-0	0	0	0	.938	-2	/O-8(0-3-5),3-1	-0.2
Total	4	247	650	95	178	39	12	22	106	92	125	.274	.364	.472	836	117	16	1	1		.958	-22	O-178(41-98-42)/3-5	-1.2
■ **DANN HOWITT** Howitt, Dann Paul John b: 2/13/64, Battle Creek, Mich. BL/TR, 6'5", 205 lbs. Deb: 9/15/89 Career OF: (36-LF 19-CF 52-RF)																								
1989	Oak-A	3	3	0	0	0	0	0	0	0	2	.000	.000	.000	0	-99	-1	0	0	0	1.000	-1	/1-1,O-1(0-0-1)	-0.1
1990	Oak-A	14	22	3	3	0	1	0	1	3	12	.136	.240	.227	467	33	-2	0	0	0	1.000	-2	O-11(0-0-11)/1-5,3-1	-0.4
1991	Oak-A	21	42	5	7	1	0	1	3	1	12	.167	.186	.262	448	24	-4	0	0	0	1.000	-4	O-20(5-7-10)/1-1	-0.9
1992	Oak-A	22	48	1	6	0	0	1	2	5	4	.125	.208	.188	395	12	-6	0	0	0	.951	1	O-19(4-5-12)/1-4,D-1	-0.6
	Sea-A	13	37	6	10	4	1	1	8	3	5	.270	.325	.514	839	131	1	1	1	-0	1.000	1	O-11(10-0-1)	0.2
	Yr	35	85	7	16	4	1	2	10	8	9	.188	.258	.329	587	66	-4	1	1	-0	.970	2	O-30(14-5-13)/1-4,D-1	-0.4
1993	Sea-A	32	76	6	16	3	1	2	8	4	18	.211	.250	.355	605	60	-5	0	0	0	1.000	-5	O-29(16-6-12)/D-2	-1.0
1994	Chi-A	10	14	4	5	3	0	0	0	1	7	.357	.400	.571	971	149	1	0	0	0	1.000	-2	/O-7(1-1-5),1-4	-0.1
Total	6	115	242	25	47	11	3	5	22	17	60	.194	.247	.326	574	57	-15	1	1	-0	.987	-12	/O-98R,1-15,D-3,3-1	-2.9
■ **DAN HOWLEY** Howley, Daniel Philip "Howling Dan" or "Dapper Dan" b: 10/16/1885, Weymouth, Mass. d: 3/10/44, Weymouth, Mass. BR/TR, 6', 187 lbs. Deb: 5/15/13 MC																								
1913	Phi-N	26	32	5	4	2	0	0	2	4	4	.125	.222	.188	410	17	-3	3			.954	1	C-22	-0.2
■ **DICK HOWSER** Howser, Richard Dalton b: 5/14/36, Miami, Fla. d: 6/17/87, Kansas City, Mo. BR/TR, 5'8", 155 lbs. Deb: 4/11/61 MC																								
1961	KC-A★	158	611	108	171	29	6	3	45	92	38	.280	.379	.362	740	97	1	37	9	5	.950	-17	*S-157	0.3
1962	KC-A	83	286	53	68	8	3	6	34	38	8	.238	.329	.350	679	79	-8	19	2	3	.962	-8	S-72	-0.6
1963	KC-A	15	41	4	8	0	0	0	1	7	3	.195	.313	.195	508	44	-3	0	0	0	.957	-4	S-10	-0.6
	Cle-A	49	162	25	40	5	0	1	10	22	18	.247	.337	.296	633	80	-4	9	3	1	.950	-17	S-44	-1.7
	Yr	64	203	29	48	5	0	1	11	29	21	.236	.332	.276	608	72	-7	9	3	1	.951	-20	S-54	-2.3
1964	Cle-A	162	637	101	163	23	4	3	52	76	39	.256	.337	.319	656	84	-11	20	7	2	.974	3	*S-162	0.9
1965	Cle-A	107	307	47	72	8	2	1	6	57	25	.235	.356	.283	640	83	-4	17	4	2	.977	-6	S-73,2-17	0.0
1966	Cle-A	67	140	18	32	9	1	2	4	15	23	.229	.303	.350	653	87	-2	2	4	-1	.986	-7	2-26,S-26	-0.7
1967	NY-A	63	149	18	40	6	0	0	10	25	15	.268	.381	.309	689	110	3	1	4	-1	.990	-6	2-22,3-12/S-3	-0.2
1968	NY-A	85	150	24	23	2	1	0	3	35	17	.153	.321	.180	501	57	-6	0	1	-0	.982	5	2-29/3-2,S-1	0.1
Total	8	789	2483	398	617	90	17	16	165	367	186	.248	.348	.318	666	86	-33	105	34	11	.963	-56	S-548/2-94,3-14	-2.5
■ **DUMMY HOY** Hoy, William Ellsworth b: 5/23/1862, Houcktown, Ohio d: 12/15/61, Cincinnati, Ohio BL/TR, 5'6", 160 lbs. Deb: 4/20/1888 Career OF: (66-LF 1727-CF 5-RF)																								
1888	Was-N	136	503	77	138	10	8	2	29	69	48	.274	.374	.338	712	136	26	**82**			.897	7	*O-136(0-136-1)	2.7
1889	Was-N	127	507	98	139	11	6	0	39	75	30	.274	.374	.320	694	101	6	35			.890	-4	*O-127(1-126-0)	-0.2
1890	Buf-P	122	493	107	147	17	8	1	53	94	36	.298	.418	.371	790	122	24	39			.912	6	*O-122(0-122-0)/2-1	2.0
1891	StL-a	139	559	134	163	13	5	5	64	**117**	25	.292	.424	.360	784	108	9	59			.911	-1	*O-139(0-139-0)	0.3
1892	Was-N	152	593	108	167	19	8	3	75	86	23	.282	.376	.356	732	125	22	60			.884	-12	*O-152(3-150-0)	-0.1
1893	Was-N	130	564	106	138	12	6	0	45	66	9	.245	.337	.287	625	68	-23	48			.892	-1	*O-130(0-130-0)	-2.7
1894	Cin-N	128	503	118	153	23	13	5	71	90	19	.304	.421	.431	853	102	4	28			.895	3	*O-128(0-128-0)	-0.1
1895	Cin-N	107	429	93	119	21	12	3	55	52	8	.277	.363	.403	767	94	-5	50			.883	-3	*O-107(62-41-4)	-1.3
1896	Cin-N	121	443	120	132	23	7	4	57	65	13	.298	.403	.409	812	107	6	50			.946	5	*O-120(0-120-0)	0.3
1897	Cin-N	128	497	87	145	24	6	2	42	54		.292	.375	.376	751	92	-5	37			.934	7	*O-128(0-128-0)	-0.5
1898	Lou-N	148	582	104	177	15	16	6	66	49		.304	.367	.416	783	126	19	37			.946	6	*O-148(0-148-0)	1.4
1899	Lou-N	155	636	117	194	17	13	5	49	62		.305	.376	.396	772	112	11	33			.928	-6	*O-155(0-155-0)	-0.4
1901	Chi-A	132	527	112	155	28	11	2	60	**86**		.294	.407	.400	807	128	25	27			.958	2	*O-132(0-132-0)	1.8
1902	Cin-N	72	279	48	81	15	2	2	20	41		.290	.389	.380	769	125	10	11			.933	-5	O-72(0-72-0)	0.1
Total	14	1797	7115	1429	2048	248	121	40	725	1006	211	.288	.386	.374	760	109	130	596			.915	3	*O-1796C/2-1	3.3
■ **KENT HRBEK** Hrbek, Kent Alan b: 5/21/60, Minneapolis, Minn. BL/TR, 6'4", 235 lbs. Deb: 8/24/81																								
1981	Min-A	24	67	5	16	5	0	1	7	5	9	.239	.301	.358	660	84	-1	0	0	0	1.000	-2	1-13/D-8	-0.4
1982	Min-A★	140	532	82	160	21	4	23	92	54	80	.301	.365	.485	850	128	20	3	1	0	.993	-0	*1-138/D-2	1.1
1983	Min-A	141	515	75	153	41	5	16	84	57	71	.297	.370	.489	860	130	21	4	6	-1	.990	-2	*1-137/D-2	0.9
1984	Min-A	149	559	80	174	31	3	27	107	65	87	.311	.387	.522	909	142	33	1	1	-0	.990	-6	*1-148/D-1	1.7
1985	Min-A	158	593	78	165	31	2	21	93	67	87	.278	.353	.444	797	110	9	1	1	-0	.995	1	*1-156/D-2	0.0

YEAR	TM/L	G	AB	R	H	2B	3B	HR	RBI	BB	SO	AVG	OBP	SLG	OPS	OPS+	BR+	SB	CS	SBR	FA	FR	G/POS	TPR
1986	Min-A	149	550	85	147	27	1	29	91	71	81	.267	.357	.478	835	122	17	2	2	-0	.992	-2	*1-147/D-1	0.5
1987	*Min-A	143	477	85	136	20	1	34	90	84	60	.285	.392	.545	937	140	29	5	2	0	.996	-10	*1-137/D-1	1.0
1988	Min-A	143	510	75	159	31	0	25	76	67	54	.312	.392	.520	911	149	34	0	3	-1	.997	-6	*1-105,D-37	1.8
1989	Min-A	109	375	59	102	17	0	25	84	53	35	.272	.364	.517	881	136	18	3	0	1	.995	1	1-89,D-18	1.3
1990	Min-A	143	492	61	141	26	0	22	79	69	45	.287	.382	.474	856	129	21	5	2	0	**.997**	1	*1-120,D-20/3-1	1.2
1991	*Min-A	132	462	72	131	20	1	20	89	67	48	.284	.374	.461	835	124	16	4	4	-1	.994	4	*1-128	1.1
1992	Min-A	112	394	52	96	20	0	15	58	71	56	.244	.359	.409	768	111	7	5	2	0	.997	-1	*1-104/D-8	-0.1
1993	Min-A	123	392	60	95	11	1	25	83	71	57	.242	.360	.467	827	120	12	4	2	0	.995	3	*1-115/D-2	0.4
1994	Min-A	81	274	34	74	11	0	10	53	37	28	.270	.359	.420	779	100	0	0	0	0	.997	-2	1-72/D-4	-0.7
Total	14	1747	6192	903	1749	312	18	293	1086	838	798	.282	.370	.481	851	127	234	37	26	-1	.994	-21	*1-1609,D-106/3-1	9.8

■ WALT HRINIAK

Hriniak, Walter John b: 5/22/43, Natick, Mass. BL/TR, 5'11", 180 lbs. Deb: 9/10/68 C

YEAR	TM/L	G	AB	R	H	2B	3B	HR	RBI	BB	SO	AVG	OBP	SLG	OPS	OPS+	BR+	SB	CS	SBR	FA	FR	G/POS	TPR
1968	Atl-N	9	26	0	9	0	0	0	3	0	3	.346	.346	.346	692	108	0	0	0	0	.967	3	/C-9	0.3
1969	Atl-N	7	7	0	1	0	0	0	0	2	1	.143	.333	.143	476	38	-0	0	0	0	1.000	-1	/C-6	-0.1
	SD-N	31	66	4	15	0	0	0	1	8	11	.227	.329	.227	556	61	-3	0	0	0	.981	-2	C-19	-0.4
	Yr	38	73	4	16	0	0	0	1	10	12	.219	.329	.219	549	58	-4	0	0	0	.982	-3	C-25	-0.5
Total	2	47	99	4	25	0	0	0	4	10	15	.253	.333	.253	586	71	-3	0	0	0	.977	-0	/C-34	-0.2

■ AL HUBBARD

Hubbard, Allen (a.k.a. Al West For 1 Game In 1883) b: 12/9/1860, Westfield, Mass. d: 12/14/30, Newton, Mass. Deb: 9/13/1883

YEAR	TM/L	G	AB	R	H	2B	3B	HR	RBI	BB	SO	AVG	OBP	SLG	OPS	OPS+	BR+	SB	CS	SBR	FA	FR	G/POS	TPR
1883	Phi-a	2	6	2	2	0	0	0	2	1		.333	.429	.333	762	136	0				.750	-0	/S-1,C-1	0.0

■ GLENN HUBBARD

Hubbard, Glenn Dee b: 9/25/57, Hahn Air Force Base, W.Germany BR/TR, 5'7", 180 lbs. Deb: 7/14/78 C

YEAR	TM/L	G	AB	R	H	2B	3B	HR	RBI	BB	SO	AVG	OBP	SLG	OPS	OPS+	BR+	SB	CS	SBR	FA	FR	G/POS	TPR
1978	Atl-N	44	163	15	42	4	0	2	13	10	20	.258	.309	.319	628	68	-7	2	1	0	.979	3	2-44	-0.1
1979	Atl-N	97	325	34	75	12	0	3	29	27	43	.231	.292	.295	587	56	-19	0	6	-2	.968	5	2-91	-1.2
1980	Atl-N	117	431	55	107	21	3	9	43	49	69	.248	.325	.374	699	91	-5	7	5	-0	.978	19	*2-117	2.2
1981	Atl-N	99	361	39	85	13	5	6	33	33	59	.235	.303	.349	652	82	-8	4	2	0	.991	-4	2-98	-0.7
1982	*Atl-N	145	532	75	132	25	1	9	59	59	62	.248	.327	.350	676	86	-9	4	3	-0	.983	20	*2-144	1.9
1983	Atl-N★	148	517	65	136	24	6	12	70	55	71	.263	.339	.402	741	97	-1	3	8	-2	.985	22	*2-148	2.7
1984	Atl-N	120	397	53	93	27	2	9	43	55	61	.234	.333	.380	714	93	-3	4	1	1	.988	20	*2-117	2.5
1985	Atl-N	142	439	51	102	21	0	5	39	56	54	.232	.325	.314	639	75	-13	4	3	-0	.989	**62**	*2-140	5.7
1986	Atl-N	143	408	42	94	16	1	4	36	66	74	.230	.343	.304	647	76	-11	3	2	-0	.976	**41**	*2-142	3.8
1987	Atl-N	141	443	69	117	33	2	5	38	77	57	.264	.380	.381	762	98	1	1	1	-0	.986	**28**	*2-139	3.6
1988	*Oak-A	105	294	35	75	12	2	3	33	33	50	.255	.336	.340	676	93	-2	1	3	-1	.987	4	*2-104/D-1	0.3
1989	Oak-A	53	131	12	26	6	0	3	12	19	20	.198	.300	.313	613	76	-4	2	0	0	.968	10	2-48/D-3	0.8
Total	12	1354	4441	545	1084	214	22	70	448	539	640	.244	.330	.349	680	85	-81	35	35	-5	.983	229	*2-1332/D-4	21.5

■ MIKE HUBBARD

Hubbard, Michael Wayne b: 2/16/71, Lynchburg, Va. BR/TR, 6'1", 180 lbs. Deb: 7/13/95

YEAR	TM/L	G	AB	R	H	2B	3B	HR	RBI	BB	SO	AVG	OBP	SLG	OPS	OPS+	BR+	SB	CS	SBR	FA	FR	G/POS	TPR
1995	Chi-N	15	23	2	4	0	0	0	1	2	2	.174	.240	.174	414	12	-3	0	0	0	.971	-1	/C-9	-0.4
1996	Chi-N	21	38	1	4	0	0	1	4	0	15	.105	.105	.184	289	-25	-7	0	0	0	1.000	-0	C-14	-0.6
1997	Chi-N	29	64	4	13	0	0	1	2	2	21	.203	.227	.250	477	24	-7	0	0	0	.992	3	C-20/3-1	-0.3
1998	Mon-N	32	55	3	8	1	0	1	3	0	17	.145	.161	.218	379	-2	-8	0	0	0	1.000	-1	C-24/2-1	-0.8
2000	Atl-N	2	1	0	0	0	0	0	0	0	1	.000	.000	.000	0	-99	-0	0	0	0	1.000	0	/C-1	0.0
Total	5	99	181	10	29	1	0	3	10	4	56	.160	.183	.215	398	4	-25	0	0	0	.994	1	/C-68,2-1,3-1	-2.1

■ TRENIDAD HUBBARD

Hubbard, Trenidad Aviel (b: Trent Hubbard) b: 5/11/64, Chicago, Ill. BR/TR, 5'8", 180 lbs. Deb: 7/7/94 Career OF: (132-LF 100-CF 31-RF)

YEAR	TM/L	G	AB	R	H	2B	3B	HR	RBI	BB	SO	AVG	OBP	SLG	OPS	OPS+	BR+	SB	CS	SBR	FA	FR	G/POS	TPR
1994	Col-N	18	25	3	7	1	1	1	3	3	4	.280	.357	.520	877	107	0	0	0	0	1.000	-1	/O-5(2-3-0)	-0.1
1995	*Col-N	24	58	13	18	4	0	3	9	8	6	.310	.394	.534	928	110	1	2	1	0	1.000	-4	O-16(4-14-0)	-0.3
1996	Col-N	45	60	12	13	5	1	1	12	9	22	.217	.329	.383	712	70	-2	2	0	0	1.000	-2	O-19(3-16-0)	-0.4
	SF-N	10	29	3	6	0	1	1	2	2	5	.207	.258	.379	637	68	-1	0	0	0	1.000	1	/O-9(8-1-0)	0.0
	Yr	55	89	15	19	5	2	2	14	11	27	.213	.307	.382	689	68	-4	2	0	0	1.000	-0	O-28(11-17-0)	-0.4
1997	Cle-A	7	12	3	3	1	0	0	0	1	3	.250	.308	.333	641	65	-1	2	0	0	1.000	-2	/O-6(5-1-0)	-0.2
1998	LA-N	94	208	29	62	9	1	7	18	18	46	.298	.362	.452	814	120	6	9	5	0	.991	-9	O-81(34-46-4)/3-1	-0.3
1999	LA-N	82	105	23	33	5	0	1	13	13	24	.314	.390	.390	780	104	1	4	3	-0	.980	-11	O-51(29-19-3)/C-1,2-1	-1.0
2000	Atl-N	61	81	15	15	2	1	1	6	11	20	.185	.290	.272	562	44	-7	2	1	0	1.000	-7	O-44(36-0-10)	-1.4
	Bal-A	31	27	3	5	0	1	0	0	0	3	.185	.185	.259	444	11	-4	2	1	0	.929	-7	O-24(11-0-14)/D-6	-1.0
Total	7	372	605	104	162	27	6	15	63	65	133	.268	.344	.407	750	91	-7	23	11	1	.990	-41	O-255L/D-6,2-1,C3	-4.7

■ KEN HUBBS

Hubbs, Kenneth Douglas b: 12/23/41, Riverside, Cal. d: 2/13/64, Provo, Utah BR/TR, 6'2", 175 lbs. Deb: 9/10/61

YEAR	TM/L	G	AB	R	H	2B	3B	HR	RBI	BB	SO	AVG	OBP	SLG	OPS	OPS+	BR+	SB	CS	SBR	FA	FR	G/POS	TPR
1961	Chi-N	10	28	4	5	1	1	1	2	0	8	.179	.179	.393	571	46	-2	0	0	0	1.000	-2	/2-8	-0.3
1962	Chi-N	160	661	90	172	24	9	5	49	35	129	.260	.300	.346	647	71	-28	3	7	-2	.983	4	*2-159	-1.1
1963	Chi-N	154	566	54	133	19	3	8	47	39	93	.235	.287	.322	608	71	-21	8	9	-1	.974	20	*2-152	1.2
Total	3	324	1255	148	310	44	13	14	98	74	230	.247	.292	.336	628	70	-51	11	16	-3	.979	23	2-319	-0.2

■ CLARENCE HUBER

Huber, Clarence Bill "Gilly" b: 10/27/1896, Tyler, Tex. d: 2/22/65, Laredo, Tex. BR/TR, 5'10", 165 lbs. Deb: 9/17/20

YEAR	TM/L	G	AB	R	H	2B	3B	HR	RBI	BB	SO	AVG	OBP	SLG	OPS	OPS+	BR+	SB	CS	SBR	FA	FR	G/POS	TPR
1920	Det-A	11	42	4	9	2	1	0	5	0	5	.214	.214	.310	524	39	-4	0	0	0	.907	2	3-11	-0.1
1921	Det-A	1	0	0	0	0	0	0	0	0	0	—	—	—	—	—	-0	0	0	0	1.000	-0	/3-1	0.0
1925	Phi-N	124	436	46	124	28	5	5	54	17	33	.284	.311	.406	717	75	-17	3	5	-1	.947	-9	*3-120	-1.9
1926	Phi-N	118	376	45	92	17	7	1	34	42	29	.245	.324	.335	659	74	-13	9			.956	8	*3-115	0.1
Total	4	254	854	95	225	47	13	6	93	59	67	.263	.313	.370	683	73	-34	12	5		.948	1	3-247	-1.9

■ OTTO HUBER

Huber, Otto b: 3/12/14, Garfield, N.J. d: 4/9/89, Passaic, N.J. BR/TR, 5'10", 165 lbs. Deb: 6/10/39

YEAR	TM/L	G	AB	R	H	2B	3B	HR	RBI	BB	SO	AVG	OBP	SLG	OPS	OPS+	BR+	SB	CS	SBR	FA	FR	G/POS	TPR
1939	Bos-N	11	22	2	6	1	0	0	3	0	1	.273	.273	.318	591	63	-1	0			1.000	-0	/2-4,3-4	-0.1

■ DAVE HUDGENS

Hudgens, David Mark b: 12/5/56, Oroville, Cal. BL/TL, 6'2", 210 lbs. Deb: 9/4/83 C

YEAR	TM/L	G	AB	R	H	2B	3B	HR	RBI	BB	SO	AVG	OBP	SLG	OPS	OPS+	BR+	SB	CS	SBR	FA	FR	G/POS	TPR
1983	Oak-A	6	7	0	1	0	0	0	0	0	3	.143	.143	.143	286	-22	-1	0	0	0	1.000	-0	/1-3,D-1	-0.1

■ JIMMY HUDGENS

Hudgens, James Price b: 8/24/02, Newburg, Mo. d: 8/26/55, St.Louis, Mo. BL/TR, 6', 180 lbs. Deb: 9/14/23

YEAR	TM/L	G	AB	R	H	2B	3B	HR	RBI	BB	SO	AVG	OBP	SLG	OPS	OPS+	BR+	SB	CS	SBR	FA	FR	G/POS	TPR
1923	StL-N	6	12	2	3	1	0	0	0	3	3	.250	.400	.333	733	97	0	0	0	0	1.000	1	/1-3,2-1	0.1
1925	Cin-N	3	7	0	3	1	1	0	0	1	1	.429	.500	.857	1357	245	2	0	0	0	1.000	0	/1-3	0.1
1926	Cin-N	17	20	2	5	1	0	0	1	1	0	.250	.286	.300	586	59	-1	0			1.000	0	/1-6	-0.1
Total	3	26	39	4	11	3	1	0	1	5	4	.282	.364	.410	774	107	0	0	0		1.000	1	/1-12,2-1	0.1

■ REX HUDLER

Hudler, Rex Allen b: 9/2/60, Tempe, Ariz. BR/TR, 6', 180 lbs. Deb: 9/9/84 Career OF: (124-LF 65-CF 64-RF)

YEAR	TM/L	G	AB	R	H	2B	3B	HR	RBI	BB	SO	AVG	OBP	SLG	OPS	OPS+	BR+	SB	CS	SBR	FA	FR	G/POS	TPR
1984	NY-A	9	7	2	1	1	0	0	0	1	5	.143	.333	.286	619	76	-0	0	0	0	1.000	0	/2-9	0.0
1985	NY-A	20	51	4	8	0	1	0	1	1	9	.157	.173	.196	369	1	-7	0	1	-0	.977	7	2-16/1-1,S-1	0.1
1986	Bal-A	14	1	1	0	0	0	0	0	0	0	.000	.000	.000	0	-99	-0	1	0	0	.800	1	2-13/3-1	0.1
1988	Mon-N	77	216	38	59	14	2	4	14	10	34	.273	.305	.412	717	100	-1	29	7	4	.978	-1	2-41,S-27/O-4(2-0-2)	0.5
1989	Mon-N	92	155	21	38	7	0	6	13	6	23	.245	.278	.406	684	92	-2	15	4	2	.958	-14	2-38,O-23L,S-18	-1.4
1990	Mon-N	4	3	1	1	0	0	0	0	0	1	.333	.333	.333	667	87	-0	0	0	0	.000	0	/H	0.0
	StL-N	89	217	30	61	11	2	7	22	12	31	.281	.325	.447	772	110	2	18	10	0	.979	0	O-45R,2-10/1-6,3S	0.2
	Yr	93	220	31	62	11	2	7	22	12	32	.282	.325	.445	770	109	2	18	10	0	.979	0	O-45R,2-10/1-6,3S	0.2
1991	StL-N	101	207	21	47	10	2	1	15	10	29	.227	.263	.309	572	60	-11	12	8	-0	.981	-3	O-58L,1-12/2-5	-1.7
1992	StL-N	61	98	17	24	4	0	3	5	2	23	.245	.267	.378	645	83	-3	2	6	-2	.957	-8	2-16,O-12(5-1-7)/1-8	-1.3
1994	Cal-A	56	124	17	37	8	0	8	20	6	28	.298	.331	.556	887	122	3	2	2	-0	.971	-2	2-22,O-18L/3-4,1D	0.2
1995	Cal-A	84	223	30	59	16	0	6	27	10	48	.265	.311	.417	728	88	-4	13	0	3	.986	-12	2-52,O-22L/1-2,D-3	-1.1
1996	Cal-A	92	302	60	94	20	3	16	40	9	54	.311	.338	.556	894	120	8	14	5	1	.982	-7	2-53,O-21C/1-7,D-8	0.4
1997	Phi-N	50	122	17	27	4	0	5	10	6	28	.221	.264	.377	641	65	-7	1	0	0	.962	-3	O-35(11-16-8)/2-6	-1.0
1998	Phi-N	25	41	2	5	1	0	0	2	4	12	.122	.200	.146	346	-7	-6	0	0	0	1.000	1	/O-9(3-1-5),1-1	-0.6
Total	13	774	1767	261	461	96	10	56	169	77	325	.261	.297	.422	719	91	-28	107	43	8	.975	-42	2-281,O-247L/S1D3	-5.6

■ JOHNNY HUDSON

Hudson, John Wilson "Mr. Chips" b: 6/30/12, Bryan, Tex. d: 11/7/70, Bryan, Tex. BR/TR, 5'10", 160 lbs. Deb: 6/20/36

YEAR	TM/L	G	AB	R	H	2B	3B	HR	RBI	BB	SO	AVG	OBP	SLG	OPS	OPS+	BR+	SB	CS	SBR	FA	FR	G/POS	TPR
1936	Bro-N	6	12	1	2	0	0	0	0	2	1	.167	.286	.167	452	24	-1	0			.889	-1	/S-4,2-1	-0.2

YEAR	TM/L	G	AB	R	H	2B	3B	HR	RBI	BB	SO	AVG	OBP	SLG	OPS	OPS+	BR+	SB	CS	SBR	FA	FR	G/POS	TPR
1937	Bro-N	13	27	3	5	4	0	0	2	3	9	.185	.267	.333	600	61	-2	0			.867	-4	S-11/2-1	-0.5
1938	Bro-N	135	498	59	130	21	5	2	37	39	76	.261	.315	.335	650	77	-15	7			.963	-4	*2-132/S-3	-1.1
1939	Bro-N	109	343	46	87	17	3	2	32	30	36	.254	.317	.338	656	74	-12	5			.959	-18	S-50,2-45/3-1	-2.5
1940	Bro-N	85	179	13	39	4	3	0	19	9	26	.218	.255	.274	529	43	-14	2			.921	0	S-38,2-27/3-1	-1.1
1941	Chi-N	50	99	8	20	4	0	0	6	3	15	.202	.225	.242	468	33	-9	3			.907	-1	S-17,2-13,3-10	-0.8
1945	NY-N	28	11	8	0	0	0	0	0	1	1	.000	.083	.000	83	-75	-3	0			.875	3	/3-5,2-2	0.0
Total	7	426	1169	138	283	50	11	4	96	87	164	.242	.296	.314	610	65	-56	17			.962	-25	2-221,S-123/3-17	-6.2
■ FRANK HUELSMAN Huelsman, Frank Elmer b: 6/5/1874, St.Louis, Mo. d: 6/9/59, Affton, Mo. BR/TR, 6'2", 210 lbs. Deb: 10/3/1897																								
1897	StL-N	2	7	0	2	1	0	0	0	0		.286	.286	.429	714	89	-0	0			.000	-1	/O-2(2-0-0)	-0.1
1904	Chi-A	3	6	0	1	1	0	0	0	0		.167	.167	.333	500	58	-0	0			.000	-1	/O-1(0-1-0)	-0.1
	Det-A	4	18	1	6	1	0	0	4	1		.333	.368	.389	757	144	1	1			1.000	-1	/O-4(4-0-0)	0.0
	Chi-A	1	1	0	0	0	0	0	0	0		.000	.000	.000	0	-99	-0	0			.000	0	H	0.0
	StL-A	20	68	6	15	2	1	0	1	6		.221	.303	.279	582	90	-1	0			1.000	-3	O-18(0-0-18)	-0.5
	Was-A	84	303	21	75	19	4	2	30	24		.248	.313	.356	670	113	5	6			.960	-3	O-84(82-2-0)	-0.4
	Yr	112	396	28	97	23	5	2	35	31		.245	.311	.343	654	110	5	7			.960	-8	*O-107(86-3-18)	-1.0
1905	Was-A	121	421	48	114	28	8	3	62	31		.271	.333	.397	729	136	17	11			.929	-9	*O-116(115-0-1)	0.1
Total	3	235	824	76	213	52	13	5	97	62		.258	.322	.371	693	123	21	18			.941	-17	O-225(203-3-19)	-1.0
■ AUBREY HUFF Huff, Aubrey L. b: 12/20/76, Marion, Ohio BL/TR, 6'4", 220 lbs. Deb: 8/2/2000																								
2000	TB-A	39	122	12	35	7	0	4	14	5	18	.287	.320	.443	763	91	-2	0	0	0	.939	-2	3-37	-0.4
■ MIKE HUFF Huff, Michael Kale b: 8/11/63, Honolulu, Hawaii BR/TR, 6'1", 190 lbs. Deb: 8/7/89 Career OF: (132-LF 121-CF 121-RF)																								
1989	LA-N	12	25	4	5	1	0	1	2	3	6	.200	.310	.360	670	93	-0	0	1	-0	1.000	-0	/O-9(7-1-2)	-0.1
1991	Cle-A	51	146	28	35	6	1	2	10	25	30	.240	.366	.336	701	95	0	11	2	2	.990	-3	O-48(8-39-5)/2-2	-0.2
	Chi-A	51	97	14	26	4	1	1	15	12	18	.268	.360	.361	721	103	1	3	2	-0	.986	-11	O-48(9-14-35)/2-2,D-2	-1.1
	Yr	102	243	42	61	10	2	3	25	37	48	.251	.364	.346	709	98	1	14	4	2	.988	-14	O-96C/2-4,D-2	-1.3
1992	Chi-A	60	115	13	24	5	0	0	8	10	24	.209	.278	.252	530	50	-8	1	2	-0	1.000	-10	O-56(10-3-45)/D-1	-2.0
1993	Chi-A	43	44	4	8	2	0	1	6	9	15	.182	.333	.295	629	72	-1	1	0	0	1.000	-12	O-43(31-8-7)	-1.3
1994	Tor-A	80	207	31	63	15	3	3	25	27	27	.304	.392	.449	842	116	6	2	1	0	.992	-6	O-76(57-19-8)	-0.2
1995	Tor-A	61	138	14	32	9	1	1	9	22	21	.232	.342	.333	675	77	-4	1	1	-0	.980	-5	O-55(9-33-15)	-0.9
1996	Tor-A	11	29	5	5	0	1	0	0	1	5	.172	.200	.241	441	11	-4	0	0	0	1.000	-2	/O-9(1-4-4),3-3	-0.5
Total	7	369	801	113	198	42	7	9	75	109	146	.247	.347	.351	698	88	-11	19	9	1	.991	-48	O-344L/2-4,3-3,D-3	-6.3
■ BEN HUFFMAN Huffman, Bennie F b: 7/18/14, Rileyville, Va. BL/TR, 5'11.5", 175 lbs. Deb: 4/23/37																								
1937	StL-A	76	176	18	48	9	0	1	24	10	7	.273	.323	.341	664	67	-9	1	0	0	.970	-8	C-42	-1.3
■ ED HUG Hug, Edward Ambrose b: 7/14/1880, Fayetteville, O. d: 5/11/53, Cincinnati, Ohio BR/TR, Deb: 7/6/03																								
1903	Bro-N	1	0	0	0	0	0	0	0	1		—	1.000	—	1000	199	0	0			.000	0	/C-1	0.0
■ MILLER HUGGINS Huggins, Miller James "Hug" or "Mighty Mite" b: 3/27/1879, Cincinnati, Ohio d: 9/25/29, New York, N.Y. BB/TR, 5'6.5", 140 lbs. Deb: 4/15/04 MH																								
1904	Cin-N	140	491	96	129	12	7	2	30	88		.263	.377	.328	705	108	9	13			.945	1	*2-140	1.2
1905	Cin-N	149	564	117	154	11	8	1	38	**103**		.273	.392	.326	718	103	8	27			.945	**36**	*2-149	4.6
1906	Cin-N	146	545	81	159	11	7	0	26	71		.292	.376	.338	714	118	14	41			.948	22	*2-146	4.0
1907	Cin-N	156	561	64	139	12	4	1	31	**83**		.248	.346	.289	635	95	0	28			.961	0	*2-156	0.2
1908	Cin-N	135	498	65	119	14	5	0	23	58		.239	.321	.287	608	97	0	30			.959	4	*2-135	0.6
1909	Cin-N	57	159	18	34	3	1	0	6	28		.214	.335	.245	580	81	-2	11			.933	4	2-31,3-15	0.3
1910	StL-N	151	547	101	145	15	6	1	36	**116**	46	.265	.399	.320	719	114	18	34			.963	3	*2-151	2.3
1911	StL-N	138	509	106	133	19	2	1	24	96	52	.261	.385	.312	697	99	5	37			.961	11	*2-136	1.8
1912	StL-N	120	431	82	131	15	4	0	29	87	31	.304	.422	.357	779	117	16	35			.943	-7	*2-114	1.1
1913	StL-N	121	382	74	109	12	0	0	27	92	49	.285	**.432**	.317	749	117	17	23			**.977**	0	*2-113,M	1.9
1914	StL-N	148	509	85	134	17	4	1	24	**105**	63	.263	.396	.318	714	115	16	32			.964	-5	*2-147,M	1.5
1915	StL-N	107	353	57	85	5	2	2	24	74	68	.241	.377	.283	660	101	5	13	12	-1	.957	3	*2-105,M	0.9
1916	StL-N	18	9	2	3	0	0	0	0	2	3	.333	.500	.333	833	159	1	0			1.000	4	/2-7,M	0.6
Total	13	1586	5558	948	1474	146	50	9	318	1003	312	.265	.382	.314	696	107	106	324	12		.956	77	*2-1530/3-15	21.0
■ ED HUGHES Hughes, Edward J. b: 10/5/1880, Chicago, Ill. d: 10/11/27, McHenry, Ill. BR/TR, 6'1", 180 lbs. Deb: 8/29/02 F																								
1902	Chi-A	1	4	0	1	0	0	0	0	0		.250	.250	.250	500	41	-0	0			.778	0	/C-1	0.0
1905	Bos-A	6	14	2	3	0	0	0	2	0		.214	.214	.214	429	36	-1	0			.500	-2	/P-6	0.0
1906	Bos-A	2	3	0	0	0	0	0	0	0		.000	.000	.000	0	-99	-1	0			.750	-0	/P-2	0.0
Total	3	9	21	2	4	0	0	0	2	0		.190	.190	.190	381	17	-2	0			.571	-2	/P-8,C-1	0.0
■ JOE HUGHES Hughes, Joseph Thompson b: 2/21/1880, Pardoe, Pa. d: 3/13/51, Cleveland, Ohio BR/TR, 5'10", 165 lbs. Deb: 8/30/02																								
1902	Chi-N	1	3	0	0	0	0	0	0	0		.000	.000	.000	0	-99	-1	0			.000	-0	/O-1(0-0-1)	-0.1
■ KEITH HUGHES Hughes, Keith Wills b: 9/12/63, Bryn Mawr, Pa. BL/TL, 6'3", 210 lbs. Deb: 5/19/87																								
1987	NY-A	4	4	0	0	0	0	0	0	0	2	.000	.000	.000	0	-99	-1	0	0	0	.000	0	/H	-0.1
	Phi-N	37	76	8	20	2	0	0	10	7	11	.263	.333	.289	623	65	-4	0	0	0	.963	-2	O-19(13-0-6)	-0.7
1988	Bal-A	41	108	10	21	4	2	2	14	16	27	.194	.298	.324	622	76	-3	1	0	0	.969	2	O-31(0-0-31)/D-1	-0.2
1990	NY-N	8	9	0	0	0	0	0	0	0	4	.000	.000	.000	0	-99	-2	0	0	0	1.000	-1	/O-5(4-1-0)	-0.4
1993	Cin-N	3	4	0	0	0	0	0	0	0	0	.000	.000	.000	0	-99	-1	0	0	0	.000	-1	/O-2(2-0-0)	-0.2
Total	4	93	201	18	41	6	2	2	24	23	44	.204	.289	.284	572	57	-11	1	0	0	.969	-2	/O-57(19-1-37),D-1	-1.6
■ BOBBY HUGHES Hughes, Robert E. b: 3/10/71, Burbank, Cal. BR/TR, 6'4", 237 lbs. Deb: 4/2/98																								
1998	Mil-N	85	218	28	50	7	2	9	29	16	54	.229	.285	.404	689	78	-7	1	2	-0	.995	2	C-72/O-3(0-0-3)	-0.3
1999	Mil-N	48	101	10	26	2	0	3	8	5	28	.257	.292	.366	659	66	-5	0	0	0	.988	-1	C-44/D-1	-0.4
Total	2	133	319	38	76	9	2	12	37	21	82	.238	.287	.392	679	74	-13	1	2	-0	.993	1	C-116/O-3(0-0-3),D-1	-0.7
■ ROY HUGHES Hughes, Roy John "Jeep" or "Sage" b: 1/11/11, Cincinnati, Ohio d: 3/5/95, Asheville, N.C. BR/TR, 5'10.5", 167 lbs. Deb: 4/16/35																								
1935	Cle-A	82	266	40	78	15	3	0	14	18	17	.293	.340	.372	713	83	-7	13	3	2	.987	-1	2-40,S-29/3-1	-0.2
1936	Cle-A	152	638	112	188	35	9	0	63	57	40	.295	.356	.378	734	81	-19	20	9	1	.973	5	*2-152	-0.3
1937	Cle-A	104	346	57	96	12	6	1	40	40	22	.277	.352	.355	708	78	-11	11	6	0	.939	12	3-58,2-32	0.5
1938	StL-A	58	96	16	27	3	0	2	13	12	11	.281	.361	.375	736	85	-2	3	0	1	.957	4	2-21/3-5,S-2	0.4
1939	StL-A	17	23	6	2	0	0	0	1	4	4	.087	.222	.087	309	-18	-4	0	0	0	1.000	1	/2-6,S-1	-0.3
	Phi-N	65	237	22	54	5	1	1	16	21	18	.228	.291	.270	561	53	-15	4			.984	0	2-65	-1.1
1940	Phi-N	1	0	0	0	0	0	0	0	0	0	—	—	—	—	—	0	0			1.000	-0	/2-1	0.0
1944	Chi-N	126	478	86	137	16	6	1	28	35	30	.287	.337	.351	688	94	-3	16			.951	11	3-66,S-52	1.3
1945	*Chi-N	69	222	34	58	8	1	0	8	16	18	.261	.311	.306	617	73	-8	6			.931	-8	S-36,2-21/3-9,1-2	-1.2
1946	Phi-N	89	276	23	65	11	1	0	22	19	15	.236	.287	.283	570	64	-13	7			.942	-12	S-34,3-31/2-7,1-1	-2.5
Total	9	763	2582	396	705	105	27	5	205	222	175	.273	.332	.340	673	78	-83	80	18		.980	12	2-345,3-170,S-154,/1	-3.4
■ TERRY HUGHES Hughes, Terry Wayne b: 5/13/49, Spartanburg, S.C. BR/TR, 6'1", 185 lbs. Deb: 9/2/70 Career OF: (0-LF 0-CF 1-RF)																								
1970	Chi-N	2	3	0	1	0	0	0	0	0	0	.333	.333	.333	667	71	-0	0	0	0	.000	-0	/3-1,O-1(0-0-1)	0.0
1973	StL-N	11	14	1	3	1	0	0	1	1	4	.214	.267	.286	552	53	-1	0	0	0	1.000	0	/3-5,1-1	-0.1
1974	Bos-A	41	69	5	14	2	0	1	6	6	18	.203	.286	.275	561	58	-4	0	0	0	.958	4	3-36/D-1	0.0
Total	3	54	86	6	18	3	0	1	7	7	22	.209	.284	.279	563	58	-5	0	0	0	.961	3	/3-42,D-1,1-1,O-1R	-0.1
■ TOM HUGHES Hughes, Thomas Franklin b: 8/6/07, Emmet, Ark. d: 8/10/89, Beaumont, Tex. BL/TR, 6'1", 190 lbs. Deb: 9/9/30																								
1930	Det-A	17	59	8	22	2	3	0	5	4	8	.373	.413	.508	921	130	3	0	1	-0	.897	-3	O-16(4-12-0)	-0.2
■ BILL HUGHES Hughes, William R. b: 11/25/1866, Blandinsville, Ill. d: 8/25/43, Santa Ana, Cal. BL/TL, Deb: 9/28/1884																								
1884	Was-U	14	49	5	6	0	0	0		2		.122	.157	.122	279	-15	-8				.955	0	/1-9,O-6(0-1-5)	-0.8

YEAR	TM/L	G	AB	R	H	2B	3B	HR	RBI	BB	SO	AVG	OBP	SLG	OPS	OPS+	BR+	SB	CS	SBR	FA	FR	G/POS	TPR
1885	Phi-a	4	16	3	3	1	1	0	1	1		.188	.278	.375	653	99	-0				1.000	-0	/O-2(0-0-2),P-2	0.0
Total	2	18	65	8	9	1	1	0	1	3		.138	.188	.185	373	15	-8				.813	-0	/1-9,O-8(0-1-7),P-2	-0.8

■ EMIL HUHN Huhn, Emil Hugo "Hap" b: 3/10/1892, North Vernon, Ind. d: 9/5/25, Camden, S.C. BR/TR, 6', 180 lbs. Deb: 4/10/15

YEAR	TM/L	G	AB	R	H	2B	3B	HR	RBI	BB	SO	AVG	OBP	SLG	OPS	OPS+	BR+	SB	CS	SBR	FA	FR	G/POS	TPR
1915	New-F	124	415	34	94	18	1	1	41	28	40	.227	.279	.282	561	61	-29	13			.985	-2	*1-101,C-16	-3.5
1916	Cin-N	37	94	4	24	3	2	0	3	2	11	.255	.271	.330	601	86	-2	0			.989	1	C-18,1-14/O-1(0-0-1)	0.0
1917	Cin-N	23	51	2	10	1	2	0	3	2	5	.196	.226	.294	521	62	-2	1			.969	-2	C-15/1-1	-0.4
Total	3	184	560	40	128	22	5	1	47	32	56	.229	.273	.291	564	65	-33	14			.986	-3	1-116/C-49,O-1(0-0-1)	-3.9

■ BILLY HULEN Hulen, William Franklin b: 3/12/1870, Dixon, Cal. d: 10/2/47, Santa Rosa, Cal. BL/TL, 5'8", 148 lbs. Deb: 5/2/1896 Career OF: (0-LF 12-CF 0-RF)

YEAR	TM/L	G	AB	R	H	2B	3B	HR	RBI	BB	SO	AVG	OBP	SLG	OPS	OPS+	BR+	SB	CS	SBR	FA	FR	G/POS	TPR
1896	Phi-N	88	339	87	90	18	7	0	38	55	20	.265	.368	.360	728	93	-2	23			.874	-21	S-73,O-12(0-12-0)/2-2	-1.6
1899	Was-N	19	68	10	10	1	0	0	3	10		.147	.256	.162	418	16	-8	5			.902	-4	S-19	-1.0
Total	2	107	407	97	100	19	7	0	41	65	20	.246	.350	.327	676	81	-9	28			.880	-25	/S-92,O-12C,2-2	-2.6

■ TIM HULETT Hulett, Timothy Craig b: 1/12/60, Springfield, Ill. BR/TR, 6', 195 lbs. Deb: 9/15/83 Career OF: (1-LF 0-CF 0-RF)

YEAR	TM/L	G	AB	R	H	2B	3B	HR	RBI	BB	SO	AVG	OBP	SLG	OPS	OPS+	BR+	SB	CS	SBR	FA	FR	G/POS	TPR
1983	Chi-A	6	5	0	1	0	0	0	0	0	0	.200	.200	.200	400	10	-1	1	0	0	.875	2	/2-6	0.1
1984	Chi-A	8	7	1	0	0	0	0	0	1	4	.000	.125	.000	125	-59	-2	1	0	0	1.000	4	/3-4,2-3	0.3
1985	Chi-A	141	395	52	106	19	4	5	37	30	81	.268	.326	.375	701	88	-6	6	4	-0	.924	8	*3-115,2-28/O-1L	0.1
1986	Chi-A	150	520	53	120	16	5	17	44	21	91	.231	.262	.379	641	70	-23	4	1	1	.951	-6	3-89,2-66	-2.6
1987	Chi-A	68	240	20	52	10	0	7	28	10	41	.217	.248	.346	594	54	-16	0	2	-1	.953	-3	3-61/2-8	-2.0
1989	Bal-A	33	97	12	27	5	0	3	18	10	17	.278	.346	.423	768	119	2	0	0	0	.976	-5	2-23,3-11	-0.2
1990	Bal-A	53	153	16	39	7	1	3	16	15	41	.255	.321	.373	694	97	-1	1	0	0	.961	6	3-24,2-16/D-8	0.5
1991	Bal-A	79	206	29	42	9	0	7	18	13	49	.204	.255	.350	604	68	-10	0	0	-0	.976	-8	3-39,2-26,D-15,/S-1	-1.8
1992	Bal-A	57	142	11	41	7	2	2	21	10	31	.289	.340	.408	748	106	1	0	1	-0	.935	10	3-27,D-13,2-10,/S-5	1.0
1993	Bal-A	85	260	40	78	15	0	2	23	23	56	.300	.364	.381	744	96	-1	1	2	-0	.963	19	3-75/S-8,2-4,D-2	1.7
1994	Bal-A	36	92	11	21	2	1	2	15	12	24	.228	.317	.337	654	66	-5	0	0	0	.992	13	2-23/3-9,S-6	0.9
1995	StL-N	4	11	0	2	0	0	0	0	0	3	.182	.182	.182	364	-4	-2	0	0	0	.941	2	/2-2,S-1	0.1
Total	12	720	2128	245	529	90	13	48	220	145	438	.249	.300	.371	670	80	-62	14	11	-1	.947	43	3-454,2-215/D-38,SO	-1.9

■ DAVID HULSE Hulse, David Lindsey b: 2/25/68, San Angelo, Tex. BL/TL, 5'11", 170 lbs. Deb: 8/11/92

YEAR	TM/L	G	AB	R	H	2B	3B	HR	RBI	BB	SO	AVG	OBP	SLG	OPS	OPS+	BR+	SB	CS	SBR	FA	FR	G/POS	TPR
1992	Tex-A	32	92	14	28	4	0	0	2	3	18	.304	.326	.348	674	92	-1	3	1	0	.984	-4	O-31(0-29-2)/D-1	-0.5
1993	Tex-A	114	407	71	118	9	10	1	29	26	57	.290	.334	.369	703	92	-5	29	9	3	.988	-6	*O-112(0-112-0)/D-2	-0.5
1994	Tex-A	77	310	58	79	8	4	1	19	21	53	.255	.306	.316	622	61	-18	18	2	3	.978	-4	O-76(0-76-0)/D-1	-1.6
1995	Mil-A	119	339	46	85	11	6	3	47	18	60	.251	.289	.345	634	61	-20	15	3	2	.984	-26	*O-115(67-52-17)	-4.3
1996	Mil-A	81	117	18	26	3	0	0	6	8	16	.222	.272	.248	520	32	-12	4	1	1	.990	-14	O-68(24-37-11)/D-4	-2.4
Total	5	423	1265	207	336	35	20	5	103	76	204	.266	.309	.337	646	69	-55	69	16	10	.985	-53	O-402(91-306-30)/D-8	-9.3

■ RUDY HULSWITT Hulswitt, Rudolph Edward b: 2/23/1877, Newport, Ky. d: 1/16/50, Louisville, Ky. BR/TR, 5'8.5", 165 lbs. Deb: 6/16/1899 C

YEAR	TM/L	G	AB	R	H	2B	3B	HR	RBI	BB	SO	AVG	OBP	SLG	OPS	OPS+	BR+	SB	CS	SBR	FA	FR	G/POS	TPR
1899	Lou-N	1	0	0	0	0	0	0	0	0		—	—	—	—	—	0	0			.333	-1	/S-1	-0.1
1902	Phi-N	128	497	59	135	11	7	0	38	30		.272	.316	.322	638	97	-2	12			.917	8	*S-125/3-3	1.0
1903	Phi-N	138	519	56	128	22	9	1	58	28		.247	.288	.329	617	78	-16	10			.906	-3	*S-138	-1.4
1904	Phi-N	113	406	36	99	11	4	1	36	16		.244	.276	.298	574	80	-10	8			.912	-13	*S-113	-2.0
1908	Cin-N	119	386	27	88	5	7	1	28	30		.228	.287	.285	572	85	-6	7			.936	-6	*S-118/2-1	-1.0
1909	StL-N	82	289	21	81	8	3	0	29	19		.280	.329	.329	658	111	3	7			.930	-6	S-65,2-12	0.0
1910	StL-N	63	133	9	33	7	2	0	14	13	10	.248	.320	.331	651	93	-1	5			.854	-13	S-30/2-2	-1.4
Total	7	644	2230	208	564	64	32	3	203	136	10	.253	.299	.314	613	89	-33	49			.915	-33	S-590/2-15,3-3	-4.9

■ JOHN HUMMEL Hummel, John Edwin "Silent John" b: 4/4/1883, Bloomsburg, Pa. d: 5/18/59, Springfield, Mass. BR/TR, 5'11", 160 lbs. Deb: 9/12/05 Career OF: (145-LF 26-CF 125-RF)

YEAR	TM/L	G	AB	R	H	2B	3B	HR	RBI	BB	SO	AVG	OBP	SLG	OPS	OPS+	BR+	SB	CS	SBR	FA	FR	G/POS	TPR
1905	Bro-N	30	109	19	29	3	4	0	7	9		.266	.322	.367	689	114	2	6			.962	0	2-30	0.2
1906	Bro-N	97	286	20	57	6	4	1	21	36		.199	.289	.259	548	77	-7	10			.953	1	2-50,O-21L,1-15	-0.8
1907	Bro-N	107	342	41	80	12	3	3	31	26		.234	.294	.313	607	98	-2	8			.951	13	2-44,O-33L,1-12,/S	1.1
1908	Bro-N	154	594	51	143	11	12	4	41	34		.241	.284	.320	604	97	-4	20			.973	8	O-95L,2-43/S-9,1-8	-0.1
1909	Bro-N	146	542	54	152	15	9	4	52	22		.280	.311	.363	674	113	6	16			.987	-17	1-54,2-38,S-36,O-17R	-1.4
1910	Bro-N	153	578	67	141	21	13	5	74	57	81	.244	.314	.351	665	97	-4	21			**.965**	-14	*2-153	-1.8
1911	Bro-N	137	477	54	129	21	11	5	58	67	66	.270	.360	.392	752	115	10	16			**.972**	-5	*2-127/1-4,S-2	0.7
1912	Bro-N	122	411	55	116	21	7	5	54	49	55	.282	.359	.404	763	113	7	7			.969	-16	2-58,O-44R,1-11	-0.9
1913	Bro-N	67	198	20	48	7	7	2	24	13	23	.242	.292	.379	671	88	-4	4			.938	-1	O-28R,S-17/1-6,2-3	-0.5
1914	Bro-N	73	208	25	55	8	9	0	20	16	25	.264	.317	.389	706	107	1	5			.982	-2	1-36,O-19R/2-1,S-1	-0.2
1915	Bro-N	53	100	6	23	2	3	0	8	6	11	.230	.274	.310	584	75	-3	1	1	-0	1.000	-4	O-21(2-1-18),1-11/S-1	-0.9
1918	NY-A	22	61	9	18	1	2	0	4	11	8	.295	.411	.377	788	135	3	3			.960	-3	O-15(6-7-1)/1-3,2-1	-0.1
Total	12	1161	3906	421	991	128	84	29	394	346	269	.254	.316	.352	668	103	6	117	1		.963	-40	2-548,O-293L,1-160,/S	-4.7

■ AL HUMPHREY Humphrey, Albert b: 2/28/1886, Ashtabula, Ohio d: 5/13/61, Ashtabula, Ohio BL/TR, 5'11", 180 lbs. Deb: 9/1/11

YEAR	TM/L	G	AB	R	H	2B	3B	HR	RBI	BB	SO	AVG	OBP	SLG	OPS	OPS+	BR+	SB	CS	SBR	FA	FR	G/POS	TPR
1911	Bro-N	8	27	4	5	0	0	0	0	3	7	.185	.267	.185	452	29	-2	0			.923	-2	/O-8(0-7-1)	-0.5

■ TERRY HUMPHREY Humphrey, Terryal Gene b: 8/4/49, Chickasha, Okla. BR/TR, 6'3", 190 lbs. Deb: 9/5/71

YEAR	TM/L	G	AB	R	H	2B	3B	HR	RBI	BB	SO	AVG	OBP	SLG	OPS	OPS+	BR+	SB	CS	SBR	FA	FR	G/POS	TPR
1971	Mon-N	9	26	1	5	1	0	0	1	0	4	.192	.192	.231	423	19	-3	0	0	0	.981	2	/C-9	0.0
1972	Mon-N	69	215	13	40	8	0	1	9	16	38	.186	.249	.237	486	38	-17	4	1	1	.986	-3	C-65	-1.9
1973	Mon-N	43	90	5	15	2	0	1	9	5	16	.167	.211	.222	433	19	-10	0	1	-0	1.000	5	C-35	-0.5
1974	Mon-N	20	52	3	10	3	0	0	3	4	9	.192	.250	.250	500	38	-4	0	0	0	.990	6	C-17	0.2
1975	Det-A	18	41	0	10	0	0	0	1	2	6	.244	.279	.244	523	47	-3	0	0	0	1.000	1	C-18	-0.1
1976	Cal-A	71	196	17	48	10	0	1	19	13	30	.245	.308	.311	620	87	-3	0	1	-0	.980	1	C-71	0.0
1977	Cal-A	123	304	17	69	11	0	2	34	21	58	.227	.286	.283	569	58	-17	1	1	-0	.989	-0	*C-123	-1.3
1978	Cal-A	53	114	11	25	4	1	1	9	6	12	.219	.270	.298	569	62	-6	0	1	-0	.978	11	C-52/2-1,3-1	0.6
1979	Cal-A	9	17	2	1	0	0	0	0	1	2	.059	.111	.059	170	-55	-4	0	0	0	.983	6	/C-9	0.2
Total	9	415	1055	69	223	39	1	6	85	68	175	.211	.268	.267	535	51	-67	5	5	-1	.986	28	C-399/3-1,2-1	-2.8

■ MIKE HUMPHREYS Humphreys, Michael Butler b: 4/10/67, Dallas, Tex. BR/TR, 6', 185 lbs. Deb: 7/29/91 Career OF: (21-LF 5-CF 9-RF)

YEAR	TM/L	G	AB	R	H	2B	3B	HR	RBI	BB	SO	AVG	OBP	SLG	OPS	OPS+	BR+	SB	CS	SBR	FA	FR	G/POS	TPR
1991	NY-A	25	40	9	8	0	0	0	3	9	7	.200	.347	.200	547	55	-2	2	0	0	1.000	-2	/O-9(8-0-2),3-6,D-7	-0.4
1992	NY-A	4	10	0	1	0	0	0	0	0	1	.100	.100	.100	200	-44	-2	0	0	0	1.000	1	/O-2(2-0-0),D-1	-0.1
1993	NY-A	25	35	6	6	2	1	1	6	4	11	.171	.256	.371	628	69	-2	2	1	0	1.000	-7	O-21(11-5-7)/D-3	-0.9
Total	3	54	85	15	15	2	1	1	9	13	19	.176	.286	.259	545	51	-6	4	1	1	1.000	-8	/O-32L,D-11,3-6	-1.4

■ JOHN HUMPHRIES Humphries, John Henry b: 11/12/1861, N.Gower, Ont., Can. d: 11/29/33, Salinas, Cal. BL/TL, 6', 185 lbs. Deb: 7/7/1883 Career OF: (1-LF 4-CF 19-RF)

YEAR	TM/L	G	AB	R	H	2B	3B	HR	RBI	BB	SO	AVG	OBP	SLG	OPS	OPS+	BR+	SB	CS	SBR	FA	FR	G/POS	TPR
1883	NY-N	29	107	5	12	1	0	0	4	1	22	.112	.120	.121	242	-26	-16				.815	-5	C-20,O-12(0-1-11)	-1.8
1884	Was-a	49	193	23	34	2	0	0		9		.176	.217	.187	403	37	-12				.890	-6	C-35,O-12(1-3-8)/1-4	-1.4
	NY-N	20	64	6	6	0	0	0	2	9	19	.094	.205	.094	299	-2	-7				.896	11	C-20	0.4
Total	2	98	364	34	52	3	0	0	6	19	41	.143	.188	.151	339	9	-35				.876	-0	/C-75,O-24R,1-4	-2.8

■ RANDY HUNDLEY Hundley, Cecil Randolph b: 6/1/42, Martinsville, Va. BR/TR, 6', 175 lbs. Deb: 9/27/64 FC

YEAR	TM/L	G	AB	R	H	2B	3B	HR	RBI	BB	SO	AVG	OBP	SLG	OPS	OPS+	BR+	SB	CS	SBR	FA	FR	G/POS	TPR
1964	SF-N	2	1	1	0	0	0	0	0	0	1	.000	.000	.000	0	-98	-0	0	0	0	.000	0	/C-2	0.0
1965	SF-N	6	15	0	1	0	0	0	0	0	4	.067	.067	.067	133	-61	-3	0	0	0	1.000	4	/C-6	0.1
1966	Chi-N	149	526	50	124	22	3	19	63	35	113	.236	.287	.397	685	87	-10	1	3	-1	.986	-11	*C-149	-1.6
1967	Chi-N	152	539	68	144	25	3	14	60	44	75	.267	.325	.403	727	102	2	2	4	-1	.996	-12	*C-152	-0.4
1968	Chi-N	160	553	41	125	18	4	7	65	39	69	.226	.282	.311	593	73	-18	1	0	0	.995	-13	*C-160	-2.6
1969	Chi-N★	151	522	67	133	15	1	18	64	61	90	.255	.336	.391	727	91	-5	2	3	-1	.992	12	*C-151	1.4
1970	Chi-N	73	250	13	61	5	0	7	36	16	52	.244	.289	.348	637	62	-13	0	1	-0	.990	-1	C-73	-1.1
1971	Chi-N	9	21	1	7	1	0	0	2	0	2	.333	.333	.381	714	89	-0	0	0	0	.979	3	/C-8	0.3
1972	Chi-N	114	357	23	78	12	0	5	30	22	62	.218	.264	.294	558	53	-22	1	0	0	**.995**	7	*C-113	-1.0
1973	Chi-N	124	368	35	83	11	1	10	43	30	51	.226	.284	.342	626	68	-16	5	6	-1	.993	11	*C-122	-0.1
1974	Min-A	32	88	2	17	2	0	0	3	4	12	.193	.228	.216	444	27	-8	0	0	0	.965	1	C-28	-0.6

YEAR	TM/L	G	AB	R	H	2B	3B	HR	RBI	BB	SO	AVG	OBP	SLG	OPS	OPS+	BR+	SB	CS	SBR	FA	FR	G/POS	TPR
1975	SD-N	74	180	7	37	5	1	2	14	19	29	.206	.285	.278	563	60	-10	0	0	0	.970	1	C-51	-0.7
1976	Chi-N	13	18	3	3	2	0	0	1	1	4	.167	.211	.278	488	35	-2	0	0	0	.923	-0	/C-9	-0.2
1977	Chi-N	2	4	0	0	0	0	0	0	0	1	.000	.000	.000	0	-90	-1	0	0	0	1.000	0	/C-2	-0.1
Total	14	1061	3442	311	813	118	13	82	381	271	565	.236	.294	.350	644	76	-107	12	17	-3	.990	2	*C-1026	-6.6

■ TODD HUNDLEY

Hundley, Todd Randolph b: 5/27/69, Martinsville, Va. BB/TR (BL 1999 (part), 2000 (PART)), 5'11", 185 lbs. Deb: 5/18/90 F Career OF: (34-LF 0-CF 0-RF)

YEAR	TM/L	G	AB	R	H	2B	3B	HR	RBI	BB	SO	AVG	OBP	SLG	OPS	OPS+	BR+	SB	CS	SBR	FA	FR	G/POS	TPR
1990	NY-N	36	67	8	14	6	0	0	2	6	18	.209	.274	.299	572	58	-4	0	0	0	.988	2	C-36	-0.1
1991	NY-N	21	60	5	8	0	1	1	7	6	14	.133	.224	.217	441	25	-6	0	0	0	1.000	-6	C-20	-1.1
1992	NY-N	123	358	32	75	17	0	7	32	19	76	.209	.257	.316	573	62	-18	3	0	1	.996	2	*C-121	-1.0
1993	NY-N	130	417	40	95	17	2	11	53	23	62	.228	.271	.357	629	68	-20	1	1	-0	.988	-6	*C-123	-1.9
1994	NY-N	91	291	45	69	10	1	16	42	25	73	.237	.304	.443	747	93	-4	2	1	0	.990	-4	C-82	-0.3
1995	NY-N	90	275	39	77	11	0	15	51	42	64	.280	.385	.484	869	131	13	1	0	0	.987	-12	C-89	0.6
1996	NY-N★	153	540	85	140	32	1	41	112	79	146	.259	.357	.550	907	141	31	1	3	-1	.992	-7	*C-150	3.1
1997	NY-N†	132	417	78	114	21	2	30	86	83	116	.273	.398	.549	947	150	32	2	3	-1	.987	-19	*C-122/D-1	1.9
1998	NY-N	53	124	8	20	4	0	3	12	16	55	.161	.262	.266	529	40	-11	1	1	-0	.898	-1	O-34(34-0-0)/C-2	-1.2
1999	LA-N	114	376	49	78	14	0	24	55	44	113	.207	.297	.436	733	87	-9	3	0	1	.979	-8	*C-108	-1.0
2000	LA-N	90	299	49	85	16	0	24	70	45	69	.284	.382	.579	960	145	20	0	1	-0	.979	-12	C-84/D-1	1.2
Total	11	1033	3224	438	775	148	7	172	522	388	806	.240	.327	.451	778	106	23	14	10	-0	.988	-70	C-937/O-34L,D-2	0.2

■ BERNIE HUNGLING

Hungling, Bernard Herman "Bud" b: 3/5/1896, Dayton, Ohio d: 3/30/68, Dayton, Ohio BR/TR, 6'2", 180 lbs. Deb: 4/14/22

YEAR	TM/L	G	AB	R	H	2B	3B	HR	RBI	BB	SO	AVG	OBP	SLG	OPS	OPS+	BR+	SB	CS	SBR	FA	FR	G/POS	TPR
1922	Bro-N	39	102	9	23	1	2	1	13	6	20	.225	.269	.304	572	48	-8	2	0	0	.968	1	C-36	-0.4
1923	Bro-N	2	4	0	0	0	0	0	0	0	2	.000	.000	.000	0	-99	-1	0	1	-0	.667	-1	/C-1	-0.2
1930	StL-A	10	31	4	10	2	0	0	2	5	3	.323	.417	.387	804	102	0	0	1	-0	1.000	-4	C-10	-0.3
Total	3	51	137	13	33	3	2	1	15	11	25	.241	.297	.314	611	57	-9	2	2	-0	.968	-3	/C-47	-0.9

■ BILL HUNNEFIELD

Hunnefield, William Fenton "Wild Bill" b: 1/5/1899, Dedham, Mass. d: 8/28/76, Nantucket, Mass. BB/TR, 5'10", 165 lbs. Deb: 4/17/26

YEAR	TM/L	G	AB	R	H	2B	3B	HR	RBI	BB	SO	AVG	OBP	SLG	OPS	OPS+	BR+	SB	CS	SBR	FA	FR	G/POS	TPR
1926	Chi-A	131	470	81	129	26	4	3	48	37	28	.274	.329	.366	695	84	-12	24	9	2	.931	-8	S-98,3-17,2-15	-0.6
1927	Chi-A	112	365	45	104	25	1	2	36	25	24	.285	.332	.375	708	85	-8	15	13	-1	.933	-20	S-79,2-17/3-1	-2.0
1928	Chi-A	94	333	42	98	8	3	2	24	26	24	.294	.351	.354	705	87	-6	16	6	1	.967	-12	2-82/S-3,3-1	-1.3
1929	Chi-A	47	127	13	23	5	0	0	9	7	3	.181	.224	.220	444	15	-16	5	2	0	.969	-4	2-29/3-4,S-2	-1.8
1930	Chi-A	31	81	11	22	2	0	1	5	4	10	.272	.314	.333	647	67	-4	1	1	-0	.932	-11	S-22/1-1	-1.2
1931	Cle-A	21	71	13	17	4	1	0	4	9	4	.239	.325	.324	649	67	-3	3	1	0	.853	-10	S-21/2-1	-1.0
	Bos-N	11	21	2	6	0	0	0	1	0	2	.286	.286	.286	571	56	-1	0			.864	2	/3-5,2-4	0.1
	NY-N	64	196	23	53	5	0	1	17	9	16	.270	.302	.311	614	67	-9	3			.951	-5	2-56/S-5	-1.1
	Yr	75	217	25	59	5	0	1	18	9	18	.272	.301	.309	610	66	-10	3			.951	-3	2-60/3-5,S-5	-1.0
Total	6	511	1664	230	452	75	9	9	144	117	111	.272	.322	.344	666	76	-60	67	32		.925	-67	S-230,2-204/3-28,1	-8.9

■ RANDY HUNT

Hunt, James Randall b: 1/3/60, Prattville, Ala. BR/TR, 6', 185 lbs. Deb: 6/4/85

YEAR	TM/L	G	AB	R	H	2B	3B	HR	RBI	BB	SO	AVG	OBP	SLG	OPS	OPS+	BR+	SB	CS	SBR	FA	FR	G/POS	TPR
1985	StL-N	14	19	1	3	0	0	0	1	0	5	.158	.158	.158	316	-12	-3	0	1	-0	1.000	1	C-13	-0.2
1986	Mon-N	21	48	4	10	0	0	2	5	5	16	.208	.283	.333	616	70	-2	0	0	0	.960	6	C-21	0.5
Total	2	35	67	5	13	0	0	2	6	5	21	.194	.250	.284	534	48	-5	0	1	-0	.967	7	/C-34	0.3

■ KEN HUNT

Hunt, Kenneth Lawrence b: 7/13/34, Grand Forks, N.Dak d: 6/8/97, Gardena, Cal. BR/TR, 6'1", 205 lbs. Deb: 9/10/59 Career OF: (52-LF 151-CF 58-RF)

YEAR	TM/L	G	AB	R	H	2B	3B	HR	RBI	BB	SO	AVG	OBP	SLG	OPS	OPS+	BR+	SB	CS	SBR	FA	FR	G/POS	TPR
1959	NY-A	6	12	2	4	1	0	0	1	0	3	.333	.333	.417	750	108	0	0	0	0	1.000	0	/O-5(0-0-5)	0.0
1960	NY-A	25	22	4	6	2	0	0	1	4	4	.273	.407	.364	771	117	1	0	0	0	.957	-6	O-24(17-5-2)	-0.5
1961	LA-A	149	479	70	122	29	3	25	84	49	120	.255	.329	.484	813	103	1	8	2	1	.950	-6	*O-134(8-108-23)/2-1	-0.9
1962	LA-A	13	11	4	2	0	0	1	1	1	5	.182	.250	.455	705	88	-0	1	0	0	.867	-1	/1-3	-0.1
1963	LA-A	59	142	17	26	6	1	5	16	15	49	.183	.261	.345	606	72	-6	0	1	-0	.972	-6	O-50(22-2-27)	-1.6
	Was-A	7	20	1	4	0	0	1	4	2	6	.200	.273	.350	623	73	-1	0	0	0	1.000	0	/O-5(1-3-1)	-0.1
	Yr	66	162	18	30	6	1	6	20	17	55	.185	.263	.346	608	73	-6	0	1	-0	.976	-6	O-55(23-5-28)	-1.7
1964	Was-A	51	96	9	13	4	0	1	4	14	35	.135	.245	.208	454	28	-9	0	1	-0	1.000	-2	O-37(4-33-0)	-1.4
Total	6	310	782	107	177	42	4	33	111	85	222	.226	.306	.417	723	89	-14	9	4	1	.964	-21	O-255C/1-3,2-1	-4.6

■ JOEL HUNT

Hunt, Oliver Joel "Jodie" b: 10/11/05, Texico, N.Mex. d: 7/24/78, Teague, Tex. BR/TR, 5'10", 165 lbs. Deb: 4/27/31

YEAR	TM/L	G	AB	R	H	2B	3B	HR	RBI	BB	SO	AVG	OBP	SLG	OPS	OPS+	BR+	SB	CS	SBR	FA	FR	G/POS	TPR
1931	StL-N	4	1	2	0	0	0	0	0	0	1	.000	.000	.000	0	-96	-0	0			.000	-1	/O-1(0-0-1)	-0.1
1932	StL-N	12	21	0	4	1	0	0	3	4	3	.190	.320	.238	558	51	-1	0			1.000	0	/O-5(0-0-5)	-0.1
Total	2	16	22	2	4	1	0	0	3	4	4	.182	.308	.227	535	45	-2	0			1.000	-0	/O-6(0-0-6)	-0.2

■ DICK HUNT

Hunt, Richard M. b: 1847, New York d: 11/20/1895, Brooklyn, N.Y. 5'9", 145 lbs. Deb: 5/7/1872

YEAR	TM/L	G	AB	R	H	2B	3B	HR	RBI	BB	SO	AVG	OBP	SLG	OPS	OPS+	BR+	SB	CS	SBR	FA	FR	G/POS	TPR
1872	Eck-n	11	48	11	15	1	1	0	5	1	0	.313	.327	.375	702	136	3	0	1	-0	.636	-3	/O-8(0-0-8),2-3	0.0

■ RON HUNT

Hunt, Ronald Kenneth b: 2/23/41, St.Louis, Mo. BR/TR, 6', 186 lbs. Deb: 4/16/63

YEAR	TM/L	G	AB	R	H	2B	3B	HR	RBI	BB	SO	AVG	OBP	SLG	OPS	OPS+	BR+	SB	CS	SBR	FA	FR	G/POS	TPR
1963	NY-N	143	533	64	145	28	4	10	42	40	50	.272	.338	.396	734	109	6	5	4	-0	.967	2	*2-142/3-1	2.2
1964	NY-N★	127	475	59	144	19	6	6	42	29	30	.303	.357	.406	764	117	11	6	2	1	.979	-8	*2-109,3-12	1.4
1965	NY-N	57	196	21	47	12	1	1	10	14	19	.240	.310	.327	637	82	-4	2	7	-2	.979	-5	2-46/3-6	-0.8
1966	NY-N★	132	479	63	138	19	2	3	33	41	34	.288	.358	.355	713	101	2	8	10	-2	.970	7	*2-123/S-1,3-1	1.9
1967	LA-N	110	388	44	102	17	3	3	33	39	24	.263	.346	.345	691	107	5	2	1	0	.980	-16	2-90/3-8	-0.4
1968	SF-N	148	529	79	132	19	0	2	28	78	41	.250	.372	.297	669	103	7	6	6	-1	.972	-17	*2-147	0.2
1969	SF-N	128	478	72	125	23	3	3	41	51	47	.262	.363	.341	704	100	3	9	2	1	.979	-9	*2-125/3-1	0.3
1970	SF-N	117	367	70	103	17	1	6	41	44	29	.281	.396	.381	777	111	9	1	2	-0	.968	-28	2-85,3-16	-1.5
1971	Mon-N	152	520	89	145	20	3	5	38	58	41	.279	.403	.358	761	116	17	5	7	-1	.979	-9	*2-133,3-19	1.6
1972	Mon-N	129	443	56	112	20	0	0	18	51	29	.253	.363	.298	661	88	-3	9	2	1	.982	-7	*2-122/3-5	-0.1
1973	Mon-N	113	401	61	124	14	0	0	18	52	19	.309	.419	.344	763	110	10	10	7	-0	.982	-21	*2-102,3-14	-0.5
1974	Mon-N	115	403	66	108	15	0	0	26	55	17	.268	.375	.305	680	87	-4	2	5	-1	.941	-14	3-75,2-31/S-1	-1.8
	StL-N	12	23	1	4	0	0	0	0	3	2	.174	.321	.174	495	42	-2	0	0	0	1.000	-1	/2-5	-0.3
	Yr	127	426	67	112	15	0	0	26	58	19	.263	.372	.298	670	85	-5	2	5	-1	.941	-16	3-75,2-36/S-1	-2.1
Total	12	1483	5235	745	1429	223	23	39	370	555	382	.273	.369	.347	716	104	58	65	55	-5	.976	-126	*2-1260,3-158/S-2	2.2

■ BRIAN HUNTER

Hunter, Brian Lee b: 3/5/71, Portland, Ore. BR/TR, 6'4", 180 lbs. Deb: 6/27/94

YEAR	TM/L	G	AB	R	H	2B	3B	HR	RBI	BB	SO	AVG	OBP	SLG	OPS	OPS+	BR+	SB	CS	SBR	FA	FR	G/POS	TPR
1994	Hou-N	6	24	2	6	1	0	0	0	1	6	.250	.280	.292	572	52	-2	2	1	0	.938	1	/O-6(0-6-0)	-0.1
1995	Hou-N	78	321	52	97	14	5	2	28	21	52	.302	.349	.396	744	103	1	24	7	3	.955	9	O-74(0-74-0)	1.3
1996	Hou-N	132	526	74	145	27	2	5	35	17	92	.276	.301	.363	664	80	-16	35	9	5	.960	9	*O-127(0-127-0)	-0.1
1997	Det-A	162	658	112	177	29	7	4	45	66	121	.269	.337	.353	689	81	-17	**74**	18	10	.990	8	*O-162(0-162-0)	0.2
1998	Det-A	142	595	67	151	29	3	4	36	36	94	.254	.299	.333	631	64	-32	42	12	5	.988	14	*O-139(0-139-0)	-1.0
1999	Det-A	18	55	8	13	2	1	0	0	5	11	.236	.311	.309	621	60	-3	0	3	-1	1.000	2	O-18(0-18-0)	-0.2
	Sea-A	121	484	71	112	11	5	4	34	32	80	.231	.280	.300	580	49	-37	44	5	8	.985	4	*O-121(119-19-0)	-2.7
	Yr	139	539	79	125	13	6	4	34	37	91	.232	.284	.301	584	50	-40	**44**	8	**7**	.988	5	*O-139(119-37-0)	-2.9
2000	Col-N	72	200	36	55	4	1	1	13	21	31	.275	.347	.320	667	55	-13	15	3	2	.981	1	O-63(27-34-12)	-1.0
	Cin-N	32	40	11	9	1	0	0	1	6	9	.225	.326	.250	576	46	-3	5	0	1	.971	-10	O-25(9-16-0)	-1.2
	Yr	104	240	47	64	5	1	1	14	27	40	.267	.343	.308	652	55	-16	20	3	3	.979	-9	O-88(36-50-12)	-2.2
Total	7	763	2903	433	765	118	24	20	192	205	496	.264	.314	.341	656	71	-122	241	58	33	.979	36	O-735(155-595-12)	-4.8

■ BRIAN HUNTER

Hunter, Brian Ronald b: 3/4/68, Torrance, Cal. BR/TL, 6', 195 lbs. Deb: 5/31/91 Career OF: (74-LF 0-CF 29-RF)

YEAR	TM/L	G	AB	R	H	2B	3B	HR	RBI	BB	SO	AVG	OBP	SLG	OPS	OPS+	BR+	SB	CS	SBR	FA	FR	G/POS	TPR
1991	*Atl-N	97	271	32	68	16	1	12	50	17	48	.251	.298	.450	748	101	-0	0	2	-1	.988	-4	1-85/O-6(5-0-1)	-1.1
1992	*Atl-N	102	238	34	57	13	2	14	41	21	50	.239	.301	.487	789	113	3	1	2	-0	.997	3	1-92/O-6(1-0-5)	0.2
1993	Atl-N	37	80	4	11	3	1	0	8	2	15	.138	.159	.200	359	-5	-12	0	0	0	.994	0	1-29/O-2(0-0-2)	-1.4
1994	Pit-N	76	233	28	53	15	1	11	47	15	55	.227	.274	.442	716	82	-7	0	0	0	.991	-1	1-59/O-5(5-0-0)	-1.3
	Cin-N	9	23	6	7	1	0	4	10	2	1	.304	.360	.870	1230	209	3	0	0	0	1.000	-0	/O-5(1-0-4),1-1	0.3
	Yr	85	256	34	60	16	1	15	57	17	56	.234	.282	.480	763	93	-4	0	0	0	.991	-1	1-60,O-10(6-0-4)	-1.0
1995	Cin-N	40	79	9	17	6	0	1	9	11	21	.215	.319	.329	648	72	-3	2	1	0	.983	0	1-23/O-4(3-0-1)	-0.4
1996	Sea-A	75	198	21	53	10	0	7	28	15	43	.268	.332	.424	756	89	-3	0	1	-0	.991	-2	1-41,O-29(29-0-2)/D-2	-0.9
1998	StL-N	62	112	11	23	9	1	4	13	7	23	.205	.258	.411	669	73	-5	1	1	-0	.938	-1	O-25L,1-10/D-1	-0.8

YEAR	TM/L	G	AB	R	H	2B	3B	HR	RBI	BB	SO	AVG	OBP	SLG	OPS	OPS+	BR+	SB	CS	SBR	FA	FR	G/POS	TPR
1999	*Atl-N	114	181	28	45	12	1	6	30	31	40	.249	.370	.425	796	101	1	0	1	-0	.991	1	*1-101/O-8(8-0-0)	-0.3
2000	Atl-N	2	2	1	1	0	0	1	1	0	0	.500	.500	2.000	2500	496	1	0	0	0	.000	0	/H	0.1
	Phi-N	85	138	13	29	5	0	7	22	20	39	.210	.310	.399	709	76	-5	0	1	-0	.994	-1	1-40/O-9(6-0-3),D-1	-0.9
	Yr	87	140	14	30	5	0	8	23	20	39	.214	.313	.421	734	82	-4	0	1	-0	.994	-1	1-40/O-9(6-0-3),D-1	-0.8
Total	9	699	1555	187	364	90	7	67	259	141	335	.234	.302	.430	733	89	-28	4	9	-2	.991	-5	1-481/O-99L,D-4	-6.5
■ EDDIE HUNTER Hunter, Edison Franklin b: 2/6/05, Bellevue, Ky. d: 3/14/67, Colerain, Ohio BR/TR, 5′7.5″, 150 lbs. Deb: 8/5/33																								
1933	Cin-N	1	0	0	0	0	0	0	0	0	0	—	—	—	—	—	0	0			.000	0	/3-1	0.0
■ NEWT HUNTER Hunter, Frederick Creighton b: 1/5/1880, Chillicothe, Ohio d: 10/26/63, Columbus, Ohio BR/TR, 6′, 180 lbs. Deb: 4/12/11 C																								
1911	Pit-N	65	209	35	53	10	6	2	24	25	43	.254	.345	.388	732	101	0	9			.989	-2	1-61	-0.3
■ GEORGE HUNTER Hunter, George Henry b: 7/8/1887, Buffalo, N.Y. d: 1/11/68, Harrisburg, Pa. BB/TL, 5′8.5″, 165 lbs. Deb: 5/4/09 F																								
1909	Bro-N	44	123	8	28	7	0	0	8	9		.228	.286	.285	570	80	-3	1			.871	-4	O-23(4-1-18),P-16	-0.8
1910	Bro-N	1	0	0	0	0	0	0	0	0	0	—	—	—	—	—	0	0			.000	-0	/O-1(0-0-1)	0.0
Total	2	45	123	8	28	7	0	0	8	9	0	.228	.286	.285	570	80	-3	1			.871	-5	/O-24(4-1-19),P-16	-0.8
■ BILLY HUNTER Hunter, Gordon William b: 6/4/28, Punxsutawney, Pa. BR/TR, 6′, 180 lbs. Deb: 4/14/53 MC																								
1953	StL-A★	154	567	50	124	18	1	1	37	24	45	.219	.253	.259	512	38	-50	3	1	0	.970	15	*S-152	-2.2
1954	Bal-A	125	411	28	100	9	5	2	27	21	38	.243	.283	.304	588	66	-21	5	4	-0	.948	1	*S-124	-1.1
1955	NY-A	98	255	14	58	7	1	3	20	15	18	.227	.270	.298	568	54	-17	9	2	1	.958	1	S-98	-0.9
1956	NY-A	39	75	8	21	3	4	0	11	2	4	.280	.299	.427	725	93	-1	0	1	-0	1.000	10	S-32/3-4	0.9
1957	KC-A	116	319	39	61	10	4	8	29	27	43	.191	.261	.323	584	58	-19	1	2	-0	.974	-5	2-64,S-35,3-17	-2.0
1958	KC-A	22	58	6	9	1	1	2	11	5	7	.155	.222	.310	533	44	-5	1	1	-0	.933	-3	S-12/2-8,3-1	-0.6
	Cle-A	76	190	21	37	10	2	0	9	17	37	.195	.264	.268	533	48	-13	4	1	1	.948	1	S-75/3-2	-0.7
	Yr	98	248	27	46	11	3	2	20	22	44	.185	.255	.278	533	47	-18	5	2	0	.946	-1	S-87/2-8,3-3	-1.3
Total	6	630	1875	166	410	58	18	16	144	111	192	.219	.265	.294	560	53	-126	23	12	1	.958	19	S-528/2-72,3-24	-6.6
■ BUDDY HUNTER Hunter, Harold James b: 8/9/47, Omaha, Neb. BR/TR, 5′10″, 170 lbs. Deb: 7/1/71																								
1971	Bos-A	8	9	2	2	1	0	0	0	2	1	.222	.364	.333	697	92	-0	0	0	0	1.000	1	/2-6	0.1
1973	Bos-A	13	7	3	3	1	0	0	2	3	1	.429	.636	.571	1208	229	2	0	0	0	1.000	3	/3-3,2-2,D-1	0.5
1975	Bos-A	1	1	0	0	0	0	0	0	0	0	.000	.000	.000	0	-92	-0	0	0	0	.750	0	/2-1	0.0
Total	3	22	17	5	5	2	0	0	2	5	2	.294	.478	.412	890	144	1	0	0	0	.968	5	/2-9,3-3,D-1	0.6
■ HERB HUNTER Hunter, Herbert Harrison b: 12/25/1896, Boston, Mass. d: 7/25/70, Orlando, Fla. BL/TR, 6′0.5″, 165 lbs. Deb: 4/29/16 Career OF: (3-LF 1-CF 0-RF)																								
1916	NY-N	21	28	3	7	0	0	1	4	0	5	.250	.250	.357	607	90	-1	0			1.000	0	/3-6,1-2	0.0
	Chi-N	2	4	0	0	0	0	0	0	0	0	.000	.000	.000	0	-90	-1	0			.750	0	/3-1	-0.1
	Yr	23	32	3	7	0	0	1	4	0	5	.219	.219	.313	531	65	-1	0			.941	1	/3-7,1-2	-0.1
1917	Chi-N	3	3	0	0	0	0	0	0	0	0	.000	.000	.000	0	-93	-1	0			1.000	0	/2-1,3-1	0.0
1920	Bos-A	4	12	2	1	0	0	0	0	1	1	.083	.154	.083	237	-38	-2	0	0	0	.857	-1	/O-4(3-1-0)	-0.3
1921	StL-N	9	2	3	0	0	0	0	0	1	0	.000	.333	.000	333	-4	-0	0	3	-1	1.000	0	/1-1	-0.1
Total	4	39	49	8	8	0	0	1	4	2	6	.163	.196	.224	421	24	-5	0	3		.905	0	/3-8,O-4L,1-3,2-1	-0.5
■ LEM HUNTER Hunter, Robert Lemuel b: 1/16/1863, Warren, Ohio d: 11/9/56, W.Lafayette, Ohio Deb: 9/1/1883																								
1883	Cle-N	1	4	1	1	0	0	0	0	0	2	.250	.250	.250	500	53	-0				.000	-1	/O-1(0-0-1),P-1	0.0
■ TORII HUNTER Hunter, Torii Kedar b: 7/18/75, Pine Bluff, Ark. BR/TR, 6′2″, 205 lbs. Deb: 8/22/97																								
1997	Min-A	1	0	0	0	0	0	0	0	0	0	—	—	—	—	—	0	0	0	0	.000	0	/R	0.0
1998	Min-A	6	17	0	4	1	0	0	2	2	6	.235	.316	.294	610	59	-1	0	1	-0	1.000	-2	/O-6(0-6-0)	-0.3
1999	Min-A	135	384	52	98	17	2	9	35	26	72	.255	.313	.380	693	73	-16	10	6	-0	.997	-3	*O-130(16-107-14)	-1.8
2000	Min-A	99	336	44	94	14	7	5	44	18	68	.280	.320	.408	728	78	-11	4	3	-0	.989	16	O-99(1-98-0)	0.5
Total	4	241	737	96	196	32	9	14	81	46	146	.266	.316	.391	707	75	-28	14	10	-0	.993	11	O-235(17-211-14)	-1.6
■ BILL HUNTER Hunter, William Ellsworth b: 7/8/1887, Buffalo, N.Y. d: 4/10/34, Buffalo, N.Y. BL/TL, 5′7.5″, 155 lbs. Deb: 8/6/12 F																								
1912	Cle-A	21	55	6	9	2	0	0	2	10		.164	.303	.200	503	43	-4	0			1.000	-0	O-16(0-16-0)	-0.5
■ BILL HUNTER Hunter, William Robert b: 1855, St.Thomas, Ont., Can. 5′7.5″, 160 lbs. Deb: 5/2/1884																								
1884	Lou-a	2	7	1	1	0	0	0		0		.143	.143	.143	286	-7	-1				.667	-2	/C-2	-0.3
■ STEVE HUNTZ Huntz, Stephen Michael b: 12/3/45, Cleveland, Ohio BB/TR, 6′1″, 204 lbs. Deb: 9/19/67																								
1967	StL-N	3	6	1	1	0	0	0	0	1	2	.167	.286	.167	452	33	-0	0	0	0	1.000	-1	/2-2	-0.2
1969	StL-N	71	139	13	27	4	0	3	13	27	34	.194	.325	.288	613	73	-4	0	0	0	.945	-6	S-52,2-12/3-6	-0.6
1970	SD-N	106	352	54	77	8	0	11	37	66	69	.219	.344	.335	679	86	-5	0	3	-1	.958	-12	S-57,3-51	-1.2
1971	Chi-A	35	86	10	18	3	1	2	6	7	9	.209	.269	.337	606	69	-4	1	0	0	1.000	-1	2-14/S-7,3-6	-0.3
1975	SD-N	22	53	3	8	4	0	0	4	7	8	.151	.250	.226	476	35	-5	0	0	0	.939	1	3-16/2-2	-0.4
Total	5	237	636	81	131	19	1	16	60	108	122	.206	.322	.314	637	76	-19	1	3	-1	.955	-18	S-116/3-79,2-30	-2.7
■ DAVE HUPPERT Huppert, David Blain b: 4/17/57, South Gate, Cal. BR/TR, 6′1″, 190 lbs. Deb: 9/15/83																								
1983	Bal-A	2	0	0	0	0	0	0	0	0	0	—	—	—	—	—	0	0	0	0	1.000	0	/C-2	0.0
1985	Mil-A	15	21	1	1	0	0	0	0	2	7	.048	.130	.048	178	-49	-4	0	0	0	.960	2	C-15	-0.2
Total	2	17	21	1	1	0	0	0	0	2	7	.048	.130	.048	178	-49	-4	0	0	0	.962	3	/C-17	-0.2
■ CLINT HURDLE Hurdle, Clinton Merrick b: 7/30/57, Big Rapids, Mich. BL/TR, 6′3″, 195 lbs. Deb: 9/18/77 C Career OF: (97-LF 0-CF 238-RF)																								
1977	KC-A	9	26	5	8	0	0	2	7	2	7	.308	.357	.538	896	139	1	0	0	0	1.000	-0	/O-9(0-0-9)	0.1
1978	*KC-A	133	417	48	110	25	5	7	56	56	84	.264	.352	.398	750	108	5	1	3	-1	.958	-11	O-78R,1-52/3-1,D-1	-1.3
1979	KC-A	59	171	16	41	10	3	3	30	28	24	.240	.350	.386	736	96	-0	0	1	-0	.968	-3	O-50(30-0-20)/3-1,D-4	-0.6
1980	*KC-A	130	395	50	116	31	2	10	60	34	61	.294	.353	.458	811	119	10	0	0	0	.960	-3	*O-126(0-0-126)	0.1
1981	*KC-A	28	76	12	25	3	1	4	15	13	10	.329	.427	.553	980	182	8	0	0	0	1.000	1	O-28(2-0-26)	0.8
1982	Cin-N	19	34	2	7	1	0	0	1	2	6	.206	.270	.235	506	42	-3	0	1	-0	.950	-2	O-17(17-0-1)	-0.6
1983	NY-N	13	33	3	6	2	0	0	2	2	10	.182	.229	.242	471	31	-3	0	0	0	.800	-2	/3-9,O-1(0-0-1)	-0.5
1985	NY-N	43	82	7	16	4	0	3	7	13	20	.195	.313	.354	666	88	-1	0	1	-0	1.000	-2	C-17,O-10(2-0-8)	-0.3
1986	StL-N	78	154	18	30	5	1	3	15	26	38	.195	.315	.299	614	71	-6	0	0	0	.994	-2	1-39,O-10L/C-5,3-4	-0.9
1987	NY-N	3	3	1	1	0	0	0	0	0	1	.333	.333	.333	667	82	-0	0	0	0	1.000	-0	/1-1	0.0
Total	10	515	1391	162	360	81	12	32	193	176	261	.259	.345	.403	748	106	12	1	6	-2	.965	-23	O-329R/1-92,C-22,3D	-3.2
■ JERRY HURLEY Hurley, Jeremiah b: 4/1875, New York, N.Y. d: 12/27/19, New York, N.Y. BR/TR, Deb: 9/23/01																								
1901	Cin-N	9	21	1	1	0	0	0	0	1		.048	.130	.048	178	-51	-4	1			.938	1	/C-7	-0.3
1907	Bro-N	1	2	0	0	0	0	0	0	1		.000	.333	.000	333	5	-0	0			1.000	-0	/C-1	0.0
Total	2	10	23	1	1	0	0	0	0	2		.043	.154	.043	197	-44	-4	1			.943	1	/C-8	-0.3
■ JERRY HURLEY Hurley, Jeremiah Joseph b: 6/15/1863, Boston, Mass. d: 9/17/50, Boston, Mass. BR/TR, 6′, 190 lbs. Deb: 5/1/1889																								
1889	Bos-N	1	4	0	0	0	0	0	0	0	0	.000	.000	.000	0	-94	-1	0			.000	-1	/O-1(0-0-1),C-1	-0.2
1890	Pit-P	8	22	5	6	1	0	0	2	2	5	.273	.333	.318	652	81	-0	0			.906	-0	/C-7,O-1(1-0-0)	0.0
1891	Cin-a	24	66	10	14	3	2	0	6	12	13	.212	.333	.318	652	80	-2	2			.862	-3	C-24/O-1(0-0-1),1-1	-0.3
Total	3	33	92	15	20	4	2	0	8	14	18	.217	.321	.304	625	72	-3	2			.870	-5	/C-32,O-3(1-0-2),1-1	-0.5
■ DICK HURLEY Hurley, William H. b: 1847, Honesdale, Pa. 5′7″, 160 lbs. Deb: 4/18/1872																								
1872	Oly-n	2	7	0	0	0	0	0	0	0	1	.000	.000	.000	0	-99	-2	0	0	0	.667	-0	/O-2(0-0-2)	-0.1
■ DON HURST Hurst, Frank O'Donnell b: 8/12/05, Maysville, Ky. d: 12/6/52, Los Angeles, Cal. BL/TL, 6′, 215 lbs. Deb: 5/13/28																								
1928	Phi-N	107	396	73	113	23	4	19	64	68	40	.285	.391	.508	899	129	17	3			.989	4	*1-104	1.4
1929	Phi-N	154	589	100	179	29	4	31	125	80	36	.304	.390	.525	914	117	15	10			.985	5	*1-154	0.9
1930	Phi-N	119	391	78	128	19	3	17	78	46	22	.327	.401	.522	923	113	8	6			.984	-3	1-96/O-7(0-7-0)	-0.1

YEAR	TM/L	G	AB	R	H	2B	3B	HR	RBI	BB	SO	AVG	OBP	SLG	OPS	OPS+	BR+	SB	CS	SBR	FA	FR	G/POS	TPR
1931	Phi-N	137	489	63	149	37	5	11	91	64	28	.305	.386	.468	855	119	14	8			.986	11	*1-135	1.3
1932	Phi-N	150	579	109	196	41	4	24	**143**	65	27	.339	.412	.547	959	139	33	10			**.993**	-3	*1-150	1.6
1933	Phi-N	147	550	58	147	27	8	8	76	48	32	.267	.327	.389	716	92	-5	3			.985	7	*1-142	-1.2
1934	Phi-N	40	130	16	34	9	0	2	21	12	7	.262	.324	.377	701	77	-4	1			.994	-1	1-34	-0.8
	Chi-N	51	151	13	30	5	0	3	12	8	18	.199	.239	.291	530	42	-13	0			.986	-2	1-48	-1.9
	Yr	91	281	29	64	14	0	5	33	20	25	.228	.279	.331	610	60	-16	1			.990	-3	1-82	-2.7
Total	7	905	3275	510	976	190	28	115	610	391	210	.298	.375	.478	854	113	66	41			.987	19	1-863/O-7(0-7-0)	1.2
■ JIMMY HURST Hurst, Jimmy O'Neal b: 3/1/72, Tuscaloosa, Ala. BR/TR, 6'6", 225 lbs. Deb: 9/10/97																								
1997	Det-A	13	17	1	3	1	0	1	1	2	6	.176	.263	.412	675	73	-1	0	0	0	1.000	-3	O-12(1-1-10)/D-1	-0.3
■ BUTCH HUSKEY Huskey, Robert Leon b: 11/10/71, Anadarko, Okla. BR/TR, 6'3", 244 lbs. Deb: 9/8/93 Career OF: (78-LF 0-CF 264-RF)																								
1993	NY-N	13	41	2	6	1	0	0	3	1	13	.146	.167	.171	337	-10	-6	0	0	0	.923	3	3-13	-0.3
1995	NY-N	28	90	8	17	1	0	3	11	10	16	.189	.270	.300	570	52	-6	1	0	0	.925	5	3-27/O-1(1-0-0)	-0.1
1996	NY-N	118	414	43	115	16	2	15	60	27	77	.278	.322	.435	757	102	-0	1	2	-0	.984	-6	1-75,O-40(0-0-40)/3-6	-1.4
1997	NY-N	142	471	61	135	26	2	24	81	25	84	.287	.324	.503	827	117	9	8	5	0	.968	-3	O-92R,1-22,3-15,/D	0.1
1998	NY-N	113	369	43	93	18	0	13	59	26	66	.252	.303	.407	710	86	-9	7	6	-1	.978	1	*O-103(0-0-103)/D-1	-1.3
1999	Sea-A	74	262	44	76	9	0	15	49	27	45	.290	.356	.496	853	117	6	3	1	0	1.000	-3	O-53L/1-10,3-1,D-7	0.0
	*Bos-A	45	124	18	33	6	0	7	28	7	20	.266	.305	.484	789	94	-2	0	0	0	1.000	-1	D-37/O-4(2-0-2),3-2	-0.4
	Yr	119	386	62	109	15	0	22	77	34	65	.282	.340	.492	833	109	4	3	1	0	1.000	-4	O-57L,D-44,1-10,/3	-0.4
2000	Min-A	64	215	22	48	13	0	5	27	25	49	.223	.310	.353	663	64	-12	0	2	-1	.975	3	D-39,O-15(0-0-15)/1-9	-1.3
	Col-N	45	92	18	32	8	0	4	18	16	14	.348	.444	.565	1010	119	3	1	1	-0	1.000	-1	O-23(15-0-8)/1-8	0.1
Total	7	642	2078	259	555	98	4	86	336	164	384	.267	.322	.442	764	96	-16	21	17	-1	.976	-2	O-331R,1-124/D-88,3	-4.6
■ JEFF HUSON Huson, Jeffrey Kent b: 8/15/64, Scottsdale, Ariz. BL/TR, 6'3", 180 lbs. Deb: 9/2/88 Career OF: (10-LF 3-CF 3-RF)																								
1988	Mon-N	20	42	7	13	2	0	0	3	4	3	.310	.370	.357	727	105	0	2	1	0	.932	1	S-15/2-2,3-1,O-1C	0.2
1989	Mon-N	32	74	1	12	5	0	0	2	6	6	.162	.225	.230	455	30	-7	3	0	1	.886	4	S-20/2-9,3-1	-0.1
1990	Tex-A	145	396	57	95	12	2	0	28	46	54	.240	.322	.280	602	70	-15	12	4	1	.960	-13	*S-119,3-36,2-12	-1.9
1991	Tex-A	119	268	36	57	8	3	2	26	39	32	.213	.313	.287	600	68	-11	8	3	1	.965	-0	*S-116/2-2,3-1	-0.3
1992	Tex-A	123	318	49	83	14	3	4	24	41	43	.261	.347	.362	709	102	2	18	6	2	.968	-9	S-82,2-47/O-2C,D-1	0.1
1993	Tex-A	23	45	3	6	1	1	0	2	0	10	.133	.133	.200	333	-12	-7	0	0	0	.909	5	S-12/2-5,3-2,D-2	-0.1
1995	Bal-A	66	161	24	40	4	2	1	19	15	20	.248	.316	.317	633	64	-8	5	4	-0	1.000	2	3-33,2-21/S-1,D-3	-0.5
1996	Bal-A	17	28	5	9	1	0	0	2	1	3	.321	.345	.357	702	78	-1	0	0	0	.973	1	2-12/3-3,O-1(0-0-1)	0.0
1997	Mil-A	84	143	12	29	3	0	0	11	5	15	.203	.240	.224	464	22	-16	3	0	1	.989	-2	2-32,1-21/O-9L,3D	-1.7
1998	Sea-A	31	49	8	8	1	0	1	4	5	6	.163	.241	.245	486	27	-5	1	1	-0	1.000	-2	/2-8,3-8,1-7,SOD	-0.7
1999	Ana-A	97	225	21	59	7	1	0	18	16	27	.262	.311	.302	613	58	-14	10	1	2	.993	-2	2-41,S-22,D-10,/31O	-1.1
2000	Chi-N	70	130	19	28	7	1	0	11	13	9	.215	.287	.285	571	46	-11	2	1	0	1.000	3	3-18,2-17,S-17,/1-1	-0.6
Total	12	827	1879	242	439	65	13	8	150	191	228	.234	.306	.295	601	64	-92	64	21	7	.956	-12	S-405,2-208,3/1DO	-6.7
■ CARL HUSTA Husta, Carl Lawrence "Sox" b: 4/8/02, Egg Harbor City, N.J. d: 11/6/51, Kingston, N.Y. BR/TR, 5'11", 176 lbs. Deb: 9/24/25																								
1925	Phi-A	6	22	2	3	0	0	0	2	2	3	.136	.208	.136	345	-11	-4	0	0	0	.976	2	/S-6	-0.1
■ HARRY HUSTON Huston, Harry Emanuel Kress b: 10/14/1883, Bellefontaine, O. d: 10/13/69, Blackwell, Okla. BR/TR, 5'9", 168 lbs. Deb: 9/3/06																								
1906	Phi-N	2	4	0	0	0	0	0	0	1		.000	.200	.000	200	-37	-1	0			1.000	-0	/C-2	-0.1
■ WARREN HUSTON Huston, Warren Llewellyn b: 10/31/13, Newtonville, Mass. d: 8/30/99, Wareham, Mass. BR/TR, 6', 170 lbs. Deb: 6/24/37																								
1937	Phi-A	38	54	5	7	3	0	0	3	2	9	.130	.161	.185	346	-13	-10	0	1	-0	.918	8	2-16,S-15/3-2	-0.1
1944	Bos-N	33	55	7	11	1	0	0	1	8	5	.200	.313	.218	531	49	-3	0			.979	3	3-20/2-5,S-4	0.0
Total	2	71	109	12	18	4	0	0	4	10	14	.165	.242	.202	444	19	-13	0	1		.964	11	/3-22,2-21,S-19	-0.1
■ JOE HUTCHESON Hutcheson, Joseph Johnson "Slug" or "Poodles" b: 2/5/05, Springtown, Tex. d: 2/23/93, Tyler, Tex. BL/TR, 6'2", 200 lbs. Deb: 7/8/33																								
1933	Bro-N	55	184	19	43	4	1	6	21	15	13	.234	.295	.364	659	91	-2	1			.989	1	O-45(0-0-45)	-0.4
■ ED HUTCHINSON Hutchinson, Edwin Forrest b: 5/19/1867, Pittsburgh, Pa. d: 7/19/34, Colfax, Cal. BL/TR, 5'11", 175 lbs. Deb: 6/17/1890																								
1890	Chi-N	4	17	0	1	1	0	0	0	0	0	.059	.059	.118	176	-47	-3	0			1.000	6	/2-4	0.2
■ FRED HUTCHINSON Hutchinson, Frederick Charles b: 8/12/19, Seattle, Wash. d: 11/12/64, Bradenton, Fla. BL/TR, 6'2", 200 lbs. Deb: 5/2/39 M																								
1939	Det-A	13	34	5	13	1	0	0	6	2	0	.382	.417	.412	828	105	0	0	0	0	1.000	-0	P-13	0.0
1940	*Det-A	17	30	1	8	1	0	0	2	0	0	.267	.267	.300	567	43	-2	0	0	0	.900	0	P-17	0.0
1941	Det-A	2	2	0	0	0	0	0	0	0	2	.000	.000	.000	0	-91	-1	0	0	0	.000	0	H	-0.1
1946	Det-A	40	89	11	28	4	0	0	13	6	1	.315	.358	.360	717	95	-0	0	0	0	.983	3	P-28	0.0
1947	Det-A	56	106	8	32	5	2	2	15	6	6	.302	.339	.443	783	113	1	2	0	0	.982	2	P-33	0.0
1948	Det-A	76	112	11	23	1	0	1	12	22	9	.205	.341	.241	582	55	-6	3	0	1	**1.000**	3	P-33	0.0
1949	Det-A	38	73	12	18	2	1	0	7	8	5	.247	.329	.301	631	67	-3	1	0	0	.983	2	P-33	0.0
1950	Det-A	44	95	15	31	7	0	0	20	12	3	.326	.407	.400	807	104	1	0	0	0	.944	2	P-39	0.0
1951	Det-A★	47	85	7	16	2	0	0	7	7	4	.188	.250	.212	462	26	-9	0	1	-0	.939	2	P-31	0.0
1952	Det-A	17	18	0	1	0	0	0	0	3	0	.056	.190	.056	246	-29	-3	0	0	0	1.000	2	P-12,M	0.0
1953	Det-A	4	6	1	1	0	0	1	1	0	0	.167	.167	.667	833	118	0	0	0	0	1.000	-0	/P-3,1-1,M	0.0
Total	11	354	650	71	171	23	3	4	83	66	30	.263	.334	.326	660	75	-22	6	1	1	.970	15	P-242/1-1	-0.1
■ ROY HUTSON Hutson, Roy Lee b: 2/27/02, Luray, Mo. d: 5/20/57, LaMesa, Cal. BL/TR, 5'9", 165 lbs. Deb: 9/20/25																								
1925	Bro-N	7	8	1	4	0	0	0	1	1	1	.500	.556	.500	1056	177	1	0	0	0	1.000	-1	/O-4(3-0-1)	0.0
■ JIM HUTTO Hutto, James Neamon b: 10/17/47, Norfolk, Va. BR/TR, 5'11", 195 lbs. Deb: 4/17/70 Career OF: (16-LF 0-CF 6-RF)																								
1970	Phi-N	57	92	7	17	2	0	3	12	5	20	.185	.227	.304	531	42	-8	0	0	0	1.000	-3	O-22L,1-12/C-5,3-1	-1.2
1975	Bal-A	4	5	0	0	0	0	0	0	0	2	.000	.000	.000	0	-99	-1	0	0	0	1.000	-0	/C-3	-0.1
Total	2	61	97	7	17	2	0	3	12	5	22	.175	.216	.289	504	35	-9	0	0	0	1.000	-3	/O-22L,1-12,C-8,3-1	-1.3
■ TOM HUTTON Hutton, Thomas George b: 4/20/46, Los Angeles, Cal. BL/TL, 5'11", 180 lbs. Deb: 9/16/66 Career OF: (82-LF 5-CF 91-RF)																								
1966	LA-N	3	2	0	0	0	0	0	0	0	0	.000	.000	.000	0	-99	-1	0	0	0	1.000	-0	/1-3	-0.1
1969	LA-N	16	48	2	13	0	0	0	4	5	7	.271	.340	.271	610	78	-1	0	0	0	.993	4	1-16	0.2
1972	Phi-N	134	381	40	99	16	2	4	38	56	24	.260	.355	.344	699	97	0	5	8	-2	.992	1	1-87,O-48(5-4-39)	-0.9
1973	Phi-N	106	247	31	65	11	0	5	29	32	31	.263	.348	.368	716	96	-1	3	1	0	.998	4	1-71	-0.1
1974	Phi-N	96	208	32	50	6	3	4	33	30	13	.240	.336	.356	692	90	-2	2	2	-0	.996	-3	1-39,O-33(33-0-0)	-1.0
1975	Phi-N	113	165	24	41	6	0	3	24	27	10	.248	.354	.339	694	90	-2	2	5	-1	.994	3	1-71,O-12(0-0-12)	-0.3
1976	*Phi-N	95	124	15	25	5	1	1	13	27	11	.202	.344	.282	627	77	-3	1	2	-0	1.000	4	1-72/O-1(0-0-1)	-0.2
1977	*Phi-N	107	81	12	25	3	0	2	11	12	10	.309	.398	.420	818	114	2	1	1	-0	.993	1	1-73/O-9(7-0-2)	0.2
1978	Tor-A	64	173	19	44	9	0	2	9	19	11	.254	.328	.341	669	87	-3	1	2	-0	1.000	-5	O-55(32-0-23)/1-9	-1.1
	Mon-N	39	59	4	12	3	0	0	5	10	5	.203	.319	.254	573	63	-3	0	0	0	1.000	-3	1-17/O-5(3-1-1)	-0.7
1979	Mon-N	86	83	14	21	2	1	1	13	10	7	.253	.333	.337	671	84	-2	0	0	0	1.000	1	1-25/O-9(0-0-9)	-0.1
1980	Mon-N	62	55	2	12	2	0	0	5	4	10	.218	.271	.255	526	47	-4	0	0	0	1.000	-2	/1-7,O-4(1-0-3),P-1	-0.6
1981	Mon-N	31	29	1	3	0	0	0	2	2	1	.103	.161	.103	265	-23	-5	0	0	0	1.000	-0	/1-9,O-2(1-0-1)	-0.6
Total	12	952	1655	196	410	63	7	22	186	234	140	.248	.341	.334	675	87	-22	15	21	-4	.995	5	1-499,O-178R/P-1	-5.3
■ HAM HYATT Hyatt, Robert Hamilton b: 11/1/1884, Buncombe Co., N.C. d: 9/11/63, Liberty Lake, Wash. BL/TR, 6'1", 185 lbs. Deb: 4/15/09 Career OF: (27-LF 7-CF 49-RF)																								
1909	*Pit-N	49	67	9	20	3	4	0	7	3		.299	.329	.463	791	134	2	1			.933	3	/O-6(5-0-1),1-2	0.5
1910	Pit-N	74	175	19	46	5	6	1	30	8	14	.263	.306	.377	684	94	-2	3			.986	-2	1-38/O-4(0-3-1)	-0.5
1912	Pit-N	46	97	13	28	3	1	0	22	6	8	.289	.330	.340	670	85	-2	2			.955	-2	O-15(0-1-14)/1-3	-0.5
1913	Pit-N	63	81	8	27	6	2	4	16	3	8	.333	.372	.605	977	184	8	0			1.000	-2	/1-5,O-5(1-0-5)	0.6
1914	Pit-N	74	79	2	17	3	1	1	15	7	14	.215	.295	.316	612	86	-1	1			.980	-2	/1-7,C-1	-0.4
1915	StL-N	106	295	23	79	8	9	2	46	28	24	.268	.337	.376	714	116	6	3	3	-0	.991	-6	1-64,O-25(0-1-26)	-0.3

YEAR	TM/L	G	AB	R	H	2B	3B	HR	RBI	BB	SO	AVG	OBP	SLG	OPS	OPS+	BR+	SB	CS	SBR	FA	FR	G/POS	TPR
1918	NY-A	53	131	11	30	8	0	2	10	8	8	.229	.273	.336	609	82	-4	1			1.000	-1	O-25(21-2-2)/1-5	-0.7
Total	7	465	925	85	247	36	23	10	146	63	76	.267	.321	.388	709	108	7	11	3		.989	-11	1-124/O-80R,C-1	-1.3
■ TIM HYERS	Hyers, Timothy James b: 10/3/71, Atlanta, Ga. BL/TL, 6'1", 185 lbs. Deb: 4/4/94 Career OF: (13-LF 0-CF 6-RF)																							
1994	SD-N	52	118	13	30	3	0	0	7	9	15	.254	.307	.280	587	56	-7	3	0	1	.986	0	1-41/O-2(0-0-2)	-0.9
1995	SD-N	6	5	0	0	0	0	0	0	0	1	.000	.000	.000	0	-99	-1	0	0	0	1.000	0	/1-1	-0.1
1996	Det-A	17	26	1	2	1	0	0	0	4	5	.077	.200	.115	315	-18	-5	0	0	0	1.000	-0	/1-9,O-1(1-0-0),D-2	-0.5
1999	Fla-N	58	81	8	18	4	1	2	12	14	11	.222	.337	.370	707	84	-2	0	0	0	1.000	-4	O-15(12-0-4),1-14/D-1	-0.6
Total	4	133	230	22	50	8	1	2	19	27	32	.217	.300	.287	587	54	-16	3	0	1	.990	-3	/1-65,O-18L,D-3	-2.1
■ JIM HYNDMAN	Hyndman, James Harvey b: 7/9/1866, Hamilton, Ontario, Canada d: 1/16/34, Alamosa, Colo. Deb: 7/23/1886																							
1886	Phi-a	1	4	0	0	0	0	0	0	0		.000	.000	.000	0	-99	-1	0			1.000	0	/O-1(0-0-1),P-1	-0.1
■ PAT HYNES	Hynes, Patrick J. b: 3/12/1884, St.Louis, Mo. d: 3/12/07, St.Louis, Mo. TL, Deb: 9/27/03																							
1903	StL-N	1	3	0	0	0	0	0	0	0		.000	.000	.000	0	-99	-1	0			.500	-1	/P-1	0.0
1904	StL-A	66	254	23	60	7	3	0	15	3		.236	.248	.287	535	74	-8	3			.901	-12	O-63(0-0-63)/P-5	-2.4
Total	2	67	257	23	60	7	3	0	15	3		.233	.245	.284	529	71	-9	3			.857	-12	/O-63(0-0-63),P-6	-2.4
■ ADAM HYZDU	Hyzdu, Adam Davis b: 12/6/71, San Jose, Cal. BR/TR, 6'2", 210 lbs. Deb: 9/8/2000																							
2000	Pit-N	12	18	2	7	2	0	1	4	0	4	.389	.389	.667	1056	161	2	0	0	0	1.000	-1	/O-5(1-0-4)	0.0
■ RAUL IBANEZ	Ibanez, Raul Javier b: 6/2/72, New York, N.Y. BL/TR, 6'2", 210 lbs. Deb: 8/1/96 Career OF: (65-LF 0-CF 101-RF)																							
1996	Sea-A	4	5	0	0	0	0	0	0	0	1	.000	.167	.000	167	-53	-1	0	0	0	.000	0	/D-2	-0.1
1997	Sea-A	11	26	3	4	0	1	1	4	0	6	.154	.154	.346	500	26	-3	0	0	0	1.000	-1	/O-8(2-0-6),D-1	-0.4
1998	Sea-A	37	98	12	25	7	1	2	12	5	22	.255	.291	.408	699	79	-3	0	0	0	1.000	-5	O-17(6-0-12),1-16/D-1	-1.0
1999	Sea-A	87	209	23	54	7	0	9	27	17	32	.258	.314	.421	735	87	-4	5	1	1	.988	-9	O-57R,1-21/C-1,D-1	-1.4
2000	*Sea-A	92	140	21	32	8	0	2	15	14	25	.229	.303	.329	632	62	-8	2	0	0	.978	-14	O-76(35-0-44)/1-3,D-4	-2.2
Total	5	231	478	59	115	22	2	14	58	36	86	.241	.297	.383	679	73	-20	7	1	1	.985	-30	O-158R/1-40,D-9,C-1	-5.1
■ PETE INCAVIGLIA	Incaviglia, Peter Joseph b: 4/2/64, Pebble Beach, Cal. BR/TR, 6'1", 230 lbs. Deb: 4/8/86 Career OF: (825-LF 37-CF 189-RF)																							
1986	Tex-A	153	540	82	135	21	2	30	88	55	185	.250	.324	.463	787	108	5	3	2	-0	.921	-11	*O-114(1-0-112),D-36	-1.3
1987	Tex-A	139	509	85	138	26	4	27	80	48	168	.271	.335	.497	832	116	11	9	3	1	.945	-3	*O-132(132-0-0)/D-6	0.2
1988	Tex-A	116	418	59	104	19	3	22	54	39	153	.249	.323	.467	790	116	8	6	4	-0	.989	6	O-93(93-0-0),D-21	1.0
1989	Tex-A	133	453	48	107	27	4	21	81	32	136	.236	.295	.453	748	106	2	5	7	-1	.973	-3	*O-125(120-10-0)/D-5	-0.6
1990	Tex-A	153	529	59	123	27	0	24	85	45	146	.233	.304	.420	723	100	-1	3	4	-1	.974	-0	*O-145(135-27-1)/D-2	-0.7
1991	Det-A	97	337	38	72	12	1	11	38	36	92	.214	.291	.353	645	76	-11	1	3	-1	.973	2	O-54(50-0-4),D-41	-1.3
1992	Hou-N	113	349	31	93	22	1	11	44	25	99	.266	.321	.430	751	116	6	2	2	-0	.970	4	O-98(57-0-48)	0.7
1993	*Phi-N	116	368	60	101	16	3	24	89	21	82	.274	.324	.530	854	126	11	1	1	-0	.971	-2	O-97(89-0-8)	0.7
1994	Phi-N	80	244	28	56	10	1	13	32	16	71	.230	.280	.439	718	82	-8	1	0	0	.979	-2	O-63(63-0-0)	-1.1
1996	Phi-N	99	269	33	63	7	2	16	42	30	82	.234	.318	.454	771	99	-1	2	0	0	.969	-3	O-71(70-0-2)	-0.6
	*Bal-A	12	33	4	10	2	0	2	8	0	7	.303	.324	.545	869	115	1	0	0	0	1.000	-0	/O-7(7-0-0),D-4	0.0
1997	Bal-A	48	138	18	34	4	0	5	12	11	43	.246	.316	.384	700	84	-3	0	0	0	.952	-3	D-26,O-18(4-0-14)	-0.8
	NY-A	5	16	1	4	0	0	0	0	0	3	.250	.250	.250	500	31	-2	0	0	0	.000	0	/D-5	-0.2
	Yr	53	154	19	38	4	0	5	12	11	46	.247	.310	.370	680	79	-5	0	0	0	.952	-3	D-31,O-18(4-0-14)	-1.0
1998	Det-A	7	14	0	1	0	0	0	0	1	6	.071	.133	.071	205	-44	-3	0	0	0	.000	-0	/O-1(1-0-0),D-4	-0.3
	*Hou-N	13	16	0	2	1	0	0	2	1	4	.125	.176	.188	364	-4	-2	0	0	0	1.000	-0	/O-3(3-0-0)	-0.3
Total	12	1284	4233	546	1043	194	21	206	655	360	1277	.246	.312	.448	760	104	12	33	26	-2	.966	-19	*O-1021L,D-150	-4.6
■ ALEXIS INFANTE	Infante, Fermin Alexis (Carpio) b: 12/4/61, Barquisimeto, Venez. BR/TR, 5'10", 175 lbs. Deb: 9/27/87																							
1987	Tor-A	1	0	0	0	0	0	0	0	0	0	—	—	—	—	—	0	0	0	0	.000	0	/R	0.0
1988	Tor-A	19	15	7	3	0	0	0	0	2	4	.200	.294	.200	494	41	-1	0	0	0	.909	1	/3-9,S-2,D-7	0.0
1989	Tor-A	20	12	1	2	0	0	0	0	0	1	.167	.167	.167	333	-6	-2	1	0	0	1.000	4	/S-9,3-4,2-1,D-4	0.3
1990	Atl-N	20	28	3	1	1	0	0	0	0	7	.036	.069	.071	140	-58	-6	0	0	0	.964	4	2-10/3-4,S-3	-0.2
Total	4	60	55	11	6	1	0	0	0	2	12	.109	.155	.127	282	-20	-9	1	0	0	.933	9	/3-17,S-14,2-11,D	0.1
■ SCOTTY INGERTON	Ingerton, William John b: 4/19/1886, Peninsula, Ohio d: 6/15/56, Cleveland, Ohio BR/TR, 6'1", 172 lbs. Deb: 4/12/11																							
1911	Bos-N	136	521	63	130	24	4	5	61	39	68	.250	.304	.340	644	74	-19	6			.942	18	3-58,O-43L,1-17,2/S	-0.1
■ CHARLIE INGRAHAM	Ingraham, Charles W. b: 4/8/1860, Illinois d: 2/18/06, Chicago, Ill. 5'11", 170 lbs. Deb: 7/4/1883																							
1883	Bal-a	1	4	0	1	0	0	0		0		.250	.250	.250	500	60	-0				.833	-1	/C-1	-0.1
■ GAREY INGRAM	Ingram, Garey Lamar b: 7/25/70, Columbus, Ga. BR/TR, 5'11", 180 lbs. Deb: 5/15/94 Career OF: (10-LF 1-CF 0-RF)																							
1994	LA-N	26	78	10	22	1	0	3	8	7	22	.282	.341	.410	751	101	0	0	0	0	.982	6	2-23	0.7
1995	LA-N	44	55	5	11	2	0	0	3	9	8	.200	.313	.236	549	52	-4	3	0	1	.750	0	3-12/2-7,O-4(4-0-0)	-0.3
1997	LA-N	12	9	2	4	0	0	0	1	1	3	.444	.500	.444	944	162	1	1	0	0	1.000	-2	/O-7(6-1-0)	-0.1
Total	3	82	142	17	37	3	0	3	12	17	33	.261	.340	.345	685	87	-3	4	0	1	.985	5	/2-30,3-12,O-11L	0.3
■ MEL INGRAM	Ingram, Melvin David b: 7/4/04, Asheville, N.C. d: 10/28/79, Medford, Ore. BR/TR, 5'11.5", 175 lbs. Deb: 7/24/29																							
1929	Pit-N	3	0	1	0	0	0	0	0	0	0	—	—	—	—	—	0	0			.000	0	R	0.0
■ RICCARDO INGRAM	Ingram, Riccardo Benay b: 9/10/66, Douglas, Ga. BR/TR, 6', 205 lbs. Deb: 6/26/94																							
1994	Det-A	12	23	3	5	0	0	0	2	1	2	.217	.250	.217	467	22	-3	0	1	-0	1.000	-0	/O-8(7-1-0),D-1	-0.3
1995	Min-A	4	8	0	1	0	0	0	1	2	1	.125	.300	.125	425	16	-1	0	0	0	.000	0	/D-3	-0.1
Total	2	16	31	3	6	0	0	0	3	3	3	.194	.265	.194	458	21	-4	0	1	-0	1.000	-0	/O-8(7-1-0),D-4	-0.4
■ DANE IORG	Iorg, Dane Charles b: 5/11/50, Eureka, Cal. BL/TR, 6', 180 lbs. Deb: 4/9/77 F Career OF: (223-LF 0-CF 124-RF)																							
1977	Phi-N	12	30	3	5	1	0	0	2	1	3	.167	.194	.200	394	6	-4	0	0	0	.986	-0	/1-9	-0.5
	StL-N	30	32	2	10	1	0	0	4	5	4	.313	.405	.344	749	105	1	0	1	-0	.875	-2	/O-7(4-0-3)	-0.2
	Yr	42	62	5	15	2	0	0	6	6	7	.242	.309	.274	583	58	-4	0	1	-0	.986	-2	/1-9,O-7(4-0-3)	-0.7
1978	StL-N	35	85	6	23	4	1	0	4	4	10	.271	.303	.341	645	81	-2	0	0	0	1.000	0	O-25(8-0-18)	-0.3
1979	StL-N	79	179	12	52	11	1	1	21	12	28	.291	.339	.380	718	95	-1	1	2	-0	.964	-6	O-39(22-0-20),1-10	-1.0
1980	StL-N	105	251	33	76	23	1	3	36	20	34	.303	.354	.438	792	116	5	1	1	-0	.991	-3	O-63(49-0-14)/1-5,3-1	-0.1
1981	StL-N	75	217	23	71	11	2	2	39	7	9	.327	.348	.424	772	115	4	2	0	0	.963	-11	O-57(46-0-14)/1-8,3-2	-1.0
1982	*StL-N	102	238	17	70	14	1	0	34	23	23	.294	.356	.361	718	100	1	0	1	-0	.971	-5	O-63L,1-10/3-2	-0.8
1983	StL-N	58	116	6	31	9	1	0	11	10	11	.267	.331	.362	693	92	-1	1	0	0	.974	-3	O-22(10-0-13),1-11	-0.6
1984	StL-N	15	28	3	4	2	0	0	3	2	6	.143	.200	.214	414	17	-3	0	0	0	1.000	-1	/1-6,O-5(3-0-2)	-0.4
	*KC-A	78	235	27	60	16	2	5	30	13	15	.255	.294	.404	699	90	-4	0	1	-0	.995	-4	1-43,O-22L/3-1,D-5	-1.2
1985	*KC-A	64	130	7	29	9	1	1	21	8	16	.223	.268	.331	599	63	-7	0	1	-0	1.000	-5	O-32R/1-2,3-1,D-2	-1.3
1986	SD-N	90	106	10	24	2	1	2	11	2	21	.226	.241	.321	561	55	-7	0	0	0	1.000	-2	1-10/3-6,O-3L,P-2	-0.9
Total	10	743	1647	149	455	103	11	14	216	107	180	.276	.321	.378	699	92	-19	5	7	-1	.977	-41	O-338L,1-114/3-13,DP	-8.3
■ GARTH IORG	Iorg, Garth Ray b: 10/12/54, Arcata, Cal. BR/TR, 5'11", 170 lbs. Deb: 4/9/78 F Career OF: (13-LF 1-CF 0-RF)																							
1978	Tor-A	19	49	3	8	0	0	0	3	3	4	.163	.226	.163	390	11	-6	0	0	0	.966	4	2-18	-0.1
1980	Tor-A	80	222	24	55	10	1	2	14	12	39	.248	.286	.329	615	65	-11	2	1	0	.988	8	2-32,3-20,O-14L,1/SD	-0.2
1981	Tor-A	70	215	17	52	11	0	0	10	7	31	.242	.269	.293	562	58	-12	2	3	-1	.963	-0	2-46,3-17/S-2,1D	-1.1
1982	Tor-A	129	417	45	119	20	5	1	36	12	38	.285	.312	.365	676	78	-13	3	2	-0	.946	-4	*3-100,2-30/D-1	-1.7
1983	Tor-A	122	375	40	103	22	5	2	39	13	45	.275	.301	.376	677	80	-10	7	0	2	.976	-3	3-85,2-39/S-1	-1.2
1984	Tor-A	121	247	24	56	10	3	1	25	5	16	.227	.245	.304	549	49	-17	1	3	-1	.945	1	*3-112/2-7,S-2,D-1	-1.8
1985	*Tor-A	131	288	33	90	22	1	7	37	21	26	.313	.359	.469	828	122	8	3	6	-1	.951	11	*3-104,2-23	1.7
1986	Tor-A	137	327	30	85	19	1	3	44	20	47	.260	.305	.352	656	76	-11	3	0	1	.955	-15	3-90,2-52/S-2	-2.4
1987	Tor-A	122	310	35	65	11	0	4	30	21	52	.210	.264	.284	548	45	-25	2	2	-0	.982	-13	2-91,3-28/D-5	-3.3
Total	9	931	2450	251	633	125	16	20	238	114	298	.258	.294	.347	641	72	-95	23	17	-1	.955	-12	3-556,2-338/O1DS	-10.1

YEAR	TM/L	G	AB	R	H	2B	3B	HR	RBI	BB	SO	AVG	OBP	SLG	OPS	OPS+	BR+	SB	CS	SBR	FA	FR	G/POS	TPR
■ HAPPY IOTT	Iott, Frederick "Happy Jack" or "Biddo" (b: Frederick Hoyot) b: 7/7/1876, Houlton, Me. d: 2/17/41, Island Falls, Me. BR/TR, 5'10", 175 lbs. Deb: 9/16/03																							
1903	Cle-A	3	10	1	2	0	0	0	0	2		.200	.333	.200	533	64	-0	1			.875	-0	/O-3(0-3-0)	-0.1
■ HAL IRELAN	Irelan, Harold "Grump" b: 8/5/1890, Burnettsville, Ind. d: 7/16/44, Carmel, Ind. BB/TR, 5'7", 165 lbs. Deb: 4/23/14																							
1914	Phi-N	67	165	16	39	8	0	1	16	21	22	.236	.326	.303	629	82	-3	3			.909	11	2-44/S-3,1-2,3-2	0.9
■ TIM IRELAND	Ireland, Timothy Neal b: 3/14/53, Oakland, Cal. BR/TR (BB 1981), 6', 180 lbs. Deb: 9/20/81 Career OF: (0-LF 0-CF 2-RF)																							
1981	KC-A	4	0	1	0	0	0	0	0	0	0	—	—	—	—	—	0	0	1	-0	1.000	-0	/1-4	0.0
1982	KC-A	7	7	2	1	0	0	0	0	1	1	.143	.250	.143	393	11	-1	0	0	0	1.000	0	/2-4,O-2(0-0-2),3-1	-0.1
Total	2	11	7	3	1	0	0	0	0	1	1	.143	.250	.143	393	11	-1	0	1	-0	1.000	0	/2-4,1-4,O-2R,3-1	-0.1
■ MONTE IRVIN	Irvin, Monford b: 2/25/19, Columbia, Ala. BR/TR, 6'1", 195 lbs. Deb: 7/8/49 H Career OF: (507-LF 1-CF 87-RF)																							
1949	NY-N	36	76	7	17	3	2	0	7	17	11	.224	.366	.316	681	84	-1	0			1.000	0	O-10(0-0-10)/1-5,3-5	-0.1
1950	NY-N	110	374	61	112	19	5	15	66	52	41	.299	.392	.497	889	131	18	3			.979	5	1-59,O-49R/3-1	1.8
1951	*NY-N	151	558	94	174	19	11	24	**121**	89	44	.312	.415	.514	929	147	40	12	2	2	.996	11	*O-112(89-0-27),1-39	4.3
1952	NY-N†	46	126	10	39	2	1	4	21	10	11	.310	.365	.437	801	120	3	0	1	-0	1.000	-2	O-32(30-1-1)	-0.1
1953	NY-N	124	444	72	146	21	5	21	97	55	34	.329	.406	.541	947	142	28	2	0	0	.973	8	*O-113(102-0-13)	2.8
1954	*NY-N	135	432	62	113	13	3	19	64	70	23	.262	.367	.438	805	108	6	7	4	0	.976	4	*O-128L/1-1,3-1	0.3
1955	NY-N	51	150	16	38	7	1	1	17	17	15	.253	.341	.333	675	80	-4	3	0	1	.961	1	O-45(44-0-4)	-0.4
1956	Chi-N	111	339	44	92	13	3	15	50	41	41	.271	.350	.460	810	118	8	1	0	0	.991	11	O-96(96-0-0)	1.4
Total	8	764	2499	366	731	97	31	99	443	351	220	.293	.385	.475	860	126	99	28	7		.983	38	O-585L,1-104/3-7	10.0
■ ED IRVIN	Irvin, William Edward b: 1882, Philadelphia, Pa. d: 2/18/16, Philadelphia, Pa. BR/TR, Deb: 5/18/12																							
1912	Det-A	1	3	0	2	0	2	0	0	0		.667	.667	2.000	2667	675	2	0			.500	-1	/3-1	0.1
■ ARTHUR IRWIN	Irwin, Arthur Albert "Doc" or "Sandy" b: 2/14/1858, Toronto, Ont., Can. d: 7/16/21, AtSea Atlantic Ocean N.Y. To Boston BL/TR, 5'8.5", 158 lbs. Deb: 5/1/1880 FMU																							
1880	Wor-N	85	352	53	91	19	4	1	35	11	27	.259	.281	.344	625	102	-0				.895	**31**	*S-82/3-3,C-1	**3.3**
1881	Wor-N	50	206	27	55	8	2	0	24	7	4	.267	.291	.325	616	88	-3				.851	-8	S-50	-0.8
1882	Wor-N	84	333	30	73	12	4	0	30	14	34	.219	.251	.279	530	68	-12				.837	21	3-51,S-33	1.0
1883	Pro-N	98	406	67	116	22	7	0	44	12	38	.286	.306	.374	681	103	1				.856	-7	*S-94/2-4	-0.3
1884	*Pro-N	102	404	73	97	14	3	2	44	28	52	.240	.289	.304	594	89	-4				.881	-6	*S-102/P-1	-0.6
1885	Pro-N	59	218	16	39	2	1	0	14	14	29	.179	.228	.197	426	40	-14				.875	4	S-58/3-1,2-1	-0.7
1886	Phi-N	101	373	51	87	6	6	0	34	35	39	.233	.299	.282	581	77	-10	24			.891	4	*S-100/3-1	-0.2
1887	Phi-N	100	422	65	143	14	8	2	56	48	26	.339	.344	.350	694	88	-6	19			.892	-10	*S-100	-1.0
1888	Phi-N	125	448	51	98	12	4	0	28	33	56	.219	.277	.263	540	69	-15	19			.900	12	*S-122/2-3	0.0
1889	Phi-N	18	73	9	16	5	0	0	10	6	6	.219	.278	.288	566	54	-5	6			.845	-6	S-18	-0.9
	Was-N	85	313	49	73	10	5	0	32	42	37	.233	.326	.297	623	80	-7	9			.895	12	S-85/P-1,2-1,M	0.7
	Yr	103	386	58	89	15	5	0	42	48	43	.231	.317	.295	613	74	-12	15			.888	6	*S-103/P-1,2-1	-0.2
1890	Bos-P	96	354	60	92	17	1	0	45	57	29	.260	.364	.314	678	77	-11	16			.878	3	*S-96	-0.4
1891	Bos-a	6	17	1	2	0	0	0	0	2	1	.118	.286	.118	403	16	-2	0			.778	-1	/S-6,M	-0.2
1894	Phi-N	1	0	0	0	0	0	0	0	0	0	—	—	—	—	—	0	0			.000	0	/S-1,M	0.0
Total	13	1010	3919	552	982	141	45	5	396	309	378	.251	.299	.305	604	81	-87	93			.881	49	S-947/3-56,2-9,PC	-0.1
■ CHARLIE IRWIN	Irwin, Charles Edwin b: 2/15/1869, Clinton, Ill. d: 9/21/25, Chicago, Ill. BL/TR, 5'10", 160 lbs. Deb: 9/3/1893 Career OF: (1-LF 0-CF 5-RF)																							
1893	Chi-N	21	82	14	25	6	2	0	13	10	1	.305	.394	.427	820	120	3	4			.910	-1	S-21	0.2
1894	Chi-N	130	504	85	149	25	9	8	100	64	23	.296	.386	.429	814	91	-8	35			.819	-10	3-68,S-62	-1.1
1895	Chi-N	3	10	4	2	0	0	0	0	2	1	.200	.333	.200	533	37	-1	0			.900	-2	/S-3	-0.2
1896	Cin-N	127	476	77	141	16	6	1	67	26	17	.296	.338	.361	699	79	-15	31			**.931**	7	*3-127	-0.6
1897	Cin-N	134	505	89	146	26	6	0	74	47		.289	.360	.364	724	86	-10	27			.940	-6	*3-134	-1.2
1898	Cin-N	136	501	77	120	14	5	3	55	31		.240	.297	.305	602	68	-22	18			.940	14	*3-136	-0.6
1899	Cin-N	90	314	42	73	4	8	1	52	26		.232	.295	.306	601	64	-16	26			.909	-13	3-78/S-6,2-3,1-1	-2.5
1900	Cin-N	87	333	59	91	15	6	1	44	14		.273	.314	.363	678	89	-6	9			.931	-11	3-61,S-16/O-6R,2-3	-1.4
1901	Cin-N	67	260	25	62	12	2	0	25	14		.238	.285	.300	585	75	-8	13			.893	4	3-67	-0.2
	Bro-N	65	242	25	52	13	2	0	20	14		.215	.269	.285	554	59	-13	4			.956	-2	3-65	-1.3
	Yr	132	502	50	114	25	4	0	45	28		.227	.277	.293	570	67	-21	17			.921	2	*3-132	-1.5
1902	Bro-N	131	458	59	125	14	0	2	43	39		.273	.346	.317	662	104	4	13			.927	-10	*3-130/S-1	-0.3
Total	10	991	3685	556	986	145	46	16	493	287	42	.268	.331	.345	676	82	-93	180			.921	-31	3-866,S-109/O-6R,21	-9.2
■ JOHN IRWIN	Irwin, John b: 7/21/1861, Toronto, Ont., Can d: 2/28/34, Boston, Mass. BL/TR, 5'10", 168 lbs. Deb: 5/31/1882 F Career OF: (9-LF 0-CF 9-RF)																							
1882	Wor-N	1	4	0	0	0	0	0	0	0	2	.000	.000	.000	0	-98	-1				.636	-1	/1-1	-0.2
1884	Bos-U	105	432	81	101	22	6	1		15		.234	.260	.319	579	76	-26				.780	4	*3-105	-1.8
1886	Phi-a	3	13	4	3	1	0	0	1	0		.231	.231	.308	538	67	-1	0			.714	-1	/S-2,3-1	-0.2
1887	Was-N	8	34	6	14	2	0	2	3	3	6	.412	.429	.613	1041	196	4	6			.875	-2	/S-5,3-4	0.2
1888	Was-N	37	126	14	28	5	2	0	8	5	18	.222	.263	.294	557	82	-2	15			.860	-1	S-27,3-10	-0.3
1889	Was-N	58	228	42	66	11	4	0	25	25	14	.289	.370	.373	742	115	6	10			.868	0	3-58	0.6
1890	Buf-P	77	308	62	72	11	4	0	34	43	19	.234	.335	.295	631	75	-8	18			.883	4	3-64,1-12/2-1	-0.3
1891	Bos-a	19	72	6	16	2	2	0	15	6	9	.222	.282	.306	588	69	-3	6			.882	0	O-17(9-0-9)/3-2,S-1	-0.3
	Lou-a	14	55	7	15	1	1	0	7	5	6	.273	.344	.327	672	94	-0	1			.795	-7	3-14	-0.6
	Yr	33	127	13	31	3	3	0	22	11	15	.244	.309	.315	624	80	-4	7			.882	-6	O-17(9-0-9),3-16/S-1	-0.9
Total	8	322	1272	222	315	55	19	3	93	102	74	.248	.308	.326	634	87	-31	56			.829	-4	3-258/S-35,O-17L,12	-2.9
■ TOMMY IRWIN	Irwin, Thomas Andrew b: 12/20/12, Altoona, Pa. d: 4/25/96, Altoona, Pa. BR/TR, 5'11", 165 lbs. Deb: 10/1/38																							
1938	Cle-A	3	9	1	1	0	0	0	0	3	1	.111	.333	.111	444	16	-1	0	0	0	1.000	0	/S-3	-0.1
■ WALT IRWIN	Irwin, Walter Kingsley b: 9/23/1897, Henrietta, Pa. d: 8/18/76, Spring Lake, Mich. BR/TR, 5'10.5", 170 lbs. Deb: 4/24/21																							
1921	StL-N	4	1	1	0	0	0	0	0	0	1	.000	.000	.000	0	-99	-0	0	0	0	.000	0	H	0.0
■ ORLANDO ISALES	Isales, Orlando (Pizarro) b: 12/22/59, Santurce, P.R. BR/TR, 5'9", 175 lbs. Deb: 9/11/80																							
1980	Phi-N	3	5	1	2	0	1	0	3	1	0	.400	.500	.800	1300	244	1	0	0	0	1.000	-0	/O-2(0-0-2)	0.1
■ FRANK ISBELL	Isbell, William Frank "Bald Eagle" b: 8/21/1875, Delevan, N.Y. d: 7/15/41, Wichita, Kan. BL/TR, 5'11", 190 lbs. Deb: 5/1/1898 Career OF: (15-LF 33-CF 54-RF)																							
1898	Chi-N	45	159	17	37	4	0	0	8	3		.233	.252	.258	509	46	-11	3			.956	-7	O-28C,P-13/3-3,2S	-1.6
1901	Chi-A	137	556	93	143	15	8	3	70	36		.257	.311	.329	640	79	-15	**52**			.980	13	*1-137/2-2,P-1,S3	-0.4
1902	Chi-A	137	515	62	130	14	4	4	59	14		.252	.276	.318	595	68	-23	38			.986	10	*1-133/S-4,P-1,C-1	-1.5
1903	Chi-A	138	546	52	132	25	9	2	59	12		.242	.266	.332	597	82	-13	26			.984	7	*1-117,3-19/2-2,SO	-0.8
1904	Chi-A	96	314	27	66	10	3	1	34	16		.210	.255	.271	526	69	-11	19			.986	0	1-57,2-27/O-5R,S-4	-1.3
1905	Chi-A	94	341	55	101	21	11	2	45	15		.296	.335	.440	775	151	18	15			.964	-1	2-43,O-41R/1-9,S-2	1.6
1906	*Chi-A	143	549	71	153	18	11	0	57	30		.279	.324	.352	676	115	9	37			.949	-22	*2-132,O-14C/P-1,C	-1.4
1907	Chi-A	125	486	60	118	19	7	0	41	22		.243	.281	.311	592	92	-6	22			.957	10	*2-119/O-5L,P-1,S-1	0.5
1908	Chi-A	84	320	31	79	15	3	1	49	19		.247	.297	.322	619	103	1	18			.990	2	1-65,2-18	0.2
1909	Chi-A	120	433	33	97	17	6	0	33	23		.224	.265	.291	556	79	-12	23			.994	1	*1-101/O-9(0-9-0),2-5	-1.4
Total	10	1119	4219	501	1056	158	62	13	455	190		.250	.289	.326	616	89	-64	253			.986	13	1-619,2-351,O/3PSC	-6.1
■ MIKE IVIE	Ivie, Michael Wilson b: 8/8/52, Atlanta, Ga. BR/TR, 6'3", 205 lbs. Deb: 9/4/71																							
1971	SD-N	6	17	0	8	0	0	0	3	1	1	.471	.526	.471	997	198	2	0	0	0	1.000	-2	/C-6	0.1
1974	SD-N	12	34	1	3	0	0	1	3	2	8	.088	.139	.176	315	-13	-5	0	0	0	.986	-0	1-11	-0.6
1975	SD-N	111	377	36	94	16	2	8	46	20	63	.249	.294	.366	660	88	-8	4	4	-1	.989	-5	1-78,3-61/C-1	-1.9
1976	SD-N	140	405	51	118	19	5	7	70	30	41	.291	.348	.415	763	126	13	6	6	-1	.995	1	*1-135/C-2,3-2	0.5
1977	SD-N	134	489	66	133	29	2	9	66	39	57	.272	.328	.395	723	104	1	3	2	-0	.992	-5	*1-105,3-25	-1.0
1978	SF-N	117	318	34	98	14	3	11	55	27	45	.308	.366	.475	841	139	16	3	0	1	.995	-10	1-76,O-22(22-0-0)	0.1

YEAR	TM/L	G	AB	R	H	2B	3B	HR	RBI	BB	SO	AVG	OBP	SLG	OPS	OPS+	BR+	SB	CS	SBR	FA	FR	G/POS	TPR
1979	SF-N	133	402	58	115	18	3	27	89	47	80	.286	.362	.547	909	155	29	5	1	1	.995	-6	1-98,O-24L/3-4,2-1	1.9
1980	SF-N	79	286	21	69	16	1	4	25	19	40	.241	.289	.346	635	78	-9	1	2	-0	.993	-6	1-72	-2.2
1981	SF-N	7	17	1	5	2	0	0	3	0	1	.294	.294	.412	706	100	-0	0	0	0	1.000	1	/1-5	0.0
	Hou-N	19	42	2	10	3	0	0	6	2	11	.238	.273	.310	582	68	-2	0	1	-0	.989	2	1-10	-0.1
	Yr	26	59	3	15	5	0	0	9	2	12	.254	.279	.339	618	78	-2	0	1	-0	.992	3	1-15	-0.1
1982	Hou-N	7	6	0	2	0	0	0	0	1	0	.333	.429	.333	762	125	0	0	0	0	.000	0	/H	0.0
	Det-A	80	259	35	60	12	1	14	38	24	51	.232	.302	.448	750	102	0	0	0	0	.000	0	D-79	-0.2
1983	Det-A	12	42	4	9	4	0	0	7	2	4	.214	.250	.310	560	54	-3	0	0	0	1.000	-0	1-12	-0.4
Total	11	857	2694	309	724	133	17	81	411	214	402	.269	.326	.421	747	112	35	22	16	-1	.993	-31	1-602/3-92,D-79,OC2	-3.8

■ HANK IZQUIERDO Izquierdo, Enrique Roberto (Valdes) b: 3/20/31, Matanzas, Cuba BR/TR, 5'11", 175 lbs. Deb: 8/9/67

YEAR	TM/L	G	AB	R	H	2B	3B	HR	RBI	BB	SO	AVG	OBP	SLG	OPS	OPS+	BR+	SB	CS	SBR	FA	FR	G/POS	TPR
1967	Min-A	16	26	4	7	2	0	0	2	1	2	.269	.296	.346	642	83	-1	0	0	0	.986	3	C-16	0.3

■ RAY JABLONSKI Jablonski, Raymond Leo "Jabbo" b: 12/17/26, Chicago, Ill. d: 11/25/85, Chicago, Ill. BR/TR, 5'10", 183 lbs. Deb: 4/14/53 Career OF: (29-LF 0-CF 0-RF)

YEAR	TM/L	G	AB	R	H	2B	3B	HR	RBI	BB	SO	AVG	OBP	SLG	OPS	OPS+	BR+	SB	CS	SBR	FA	FR	G/POS	TPR
1953	StL-N	157	604	64	162	23	5	21	112	34	61	.268	.308	.427	735	89	-11	2	2	-0	.932	-16	*3-157	-2.7
1954	StL-N★	152	611	80	181	33	3	12	104	49	42	.296	.350	.419	769	99	-1	9	4	1	.925	-7	*3-149/1-1	-0.8
1955	Cin-N	74	221	28	53	9	0	9	28	13	35	.240	.291	.403	694	77	-8	0	1	-0	.872	-10	3-28,O-28(28-0-0)	-2.0
1956	Cin-N	130	407	42	104	25	1	15	66	37	57	.256	.328	.432	761	96	-2	2	4	-1	.970	-25	*3-127/2-1	-3.0
1957	NY-N	107	305	37	88	15	1	9	57	31	47	.289	.354	.433	787	110	5	0	2	-1	.941	-3	3-70/1-6,O-1(1-0-0)	0.1
1958	SF-N	82	230	28	53	15	1	12	46	17	50	.230	.289	.461	750	97	-2	2	0	0	.946	-8	3-57	-1.0
1959	StL-N	60	87	11	22	4	0	3	14	8	19	.253	.316	.402	718	84	-2	1	0	0	.900	-3	3-19/S-1	-0.5
	KC-A	25	65	4	17	1	0	2	8	3	11	.262	.294	.369	663	79	-2	0	0	0	.947	-3	3-17	-0.5
1960	KC-A	21	32	3	7	1	0	0	3	4	8	.219	.306	.250	556	52	-2	0	0	0	.944	0	/3-6	-0.2
Total	8	808	2562	297	687	126	11	83	438	196	330	.268	.324	.423	747	94	-26	16	13	-1	.936	-75	3-630/O-29L,1-7,S2	-10.6

■ FRED JACKLITSCH Jacklitsch, Frederick Lawrence b: 5/24/1876, Brooklyn, N.Y. d: 7/18/37, Brooklyn, N.Y. BR/TR, 5'9", 180 lbs. Deb: 6/6/00

YEAR	TM/L	G	AB	R	H	2B	3B	HR	RBI	BB	SO	AVG	OBP	SLG	OPS	OPS+	BR+	SB	CS	SBR	FA	FR	G/POS	TPR
1900	Phi-N	5	11	0	2	1	0	0	3	0		.182	.182	.273	455	25	-1	0			1.000	-2	/C-3	-0.2
1901	Phi-N	33	120	14	30	4	3	0	24	12		.250	.328	.333	662	90	-1	2			.971	-1	C-30/3-1	0.1
1902	Phi-N	38	114	8	23	4	0	0	8	9		.202	.278	.237	515	59	-5	2			.927	-9	C-29/O-1(0-1-0)	-1.2
1903	Bro-N	60	176	31	47	8	3	1	21	33		.267	.389	.364	752	118	6	4			.975	-9	C-53/2-1,O-1(0-1-0)	0.2
1904	Bro-N	26	77	8	18	3	1	0	8	7		.234	.322	.299	621	94	-0	7			.957	-7	1-11/2-8,C-5	-0.7
1905	NY-A	1	3	1	0	0	0	0	1	1		.000	.250	.000	250	-17	-0	0			1.000	-0	/C-1	0.0
1907	Phi-N	73	202	19	43	7	0	0	17	27		.213	.312	.248	559	76	-4	7			.984	11	C-58/1-6,O-1(0-0-1)	1.4
1908	Phi-N	37	86	6	19	3	0	0	7	14		.221	.337	.256	592	87	-1	3			.976	3	C-30	0.6
1909	Phi-N	20	32	6	10	1	1	0	1	10		.313	.476	.406	882	173	4	1			.964	-2	C-11/2-1	0.3
1910	Phi-N	25	51	7	10	3	0	0	2	5	9	.196	.268	.255	523	51	-3	0			.989	5	C-13/1-2,2-1,3-1	0.3
1914	Bal-F	122	337	40	93	21	4	2	48	52	66	.276	.376	.380	756	103	-2	7			**.988**	2	*C-118	1.1
1915	Bal-F	49	135	20	32	9	0	2	13	31	25	.237	.387	.348	735	104	0	2			.992	-7	C-45/S-1	-0.3
1917	Bos-N	1	0	0	0	0	0	0	0	0	0	—	—	—	—	—	0	0			1.000	-0	/C-1	0.0
Total	13	490	1344	160	327	64	12	5	153	201	100	.243	.349	.320	669	95	-8	35			.978	-14	C-397/1-19,2-11,O3S	1.6

■ CHARLIE JACKSON Jackson, Charles Herbert "Lefty" b: 2/7/1894, Granite City, Ill. d: 5/27/68, Radford, Va. BL/TL, 5'9", 150 lbs. Deb: 8/20/15

YEAR	TM/L	G	AB	R	H	2B	3B	HR	RBI	BB	SO	AVG	OBP	SLG	OPS	OPS+	BR+	SB	CS	SBR	FA	FR	G/POS	TPR
1915	Chi-A	1	1	0	0	0	0	0	0	0	1	.000	.000	.000	0	-97	-0	0			.000	0	H	0.0
1917	Pit-N	41	121	7	29	3	2	0	1	10	22	.240	.303	.298	601	82	-2	4			.986	0	O-36(20-1-15)	-0.4
Total	2	42	122	7	29	3	2	0	1	10	23	.238	.301	.295	596	80	-3	4			.986	0	/O-36(20-1-15)	-0.4

■ CHUCK JACKSON Jackson, Charles Leo b: 3/19/63, Seattle, Wash. BR/TR, 6', 185 lbs. Deb: 5/26/87 Career OF: (1-LF 13-CF 2-RF)

YEAR	TM/L	G	AB	R	H	2B	3B	HR	RBI	BB	SO	AVG	OBP	SLG	OPS	OPS+	BR+	SB	CS	SBR	FA	FR	G/POS	TPR
1987	Hou-N	35	71	3	15	3	0	1	6	7	19	.211	.282	.296	578	55	-5	1	1	-0	.957	-1	3-16,O-13(1-12-0)/S-1	-0.6
1988	Hou-N	46	83	7	19	5	1	1	8	7	16	.229	.289	.349	638	86	-2	1	1	-0	.908	1	3-32/S-3,O-3(0-1-2)	0.0
1994	Tex-A	1	2	0	0	0	0	0	0	0	0	.000	.000	.000	0	-99	-1	0	0	0	.000	0	/3-1	-0.1
Total	3	82	156	10	34	8	1	2	14	14	35	.218	.282	.321	603	69	-7	2	2	-0	.928	1	/3-49,O-16C,S-4	-0.7

■ DAMIAN JACKSON Jackson, Damian Jacques b: 8/16/73, Los Angeles, Cal. BR/TR, 5'10", 160 lbs. Deb: 9/12/96 Career OF: (22-LF 0-CF 2-RF)

YEAR	TM/L	G	AB	R	H	2B	3B	HR	RBI	BB	SO	AVG	OBP	SLG	OPS	OPS+	BR+	SB	CS	SBR	FA	FR	G/POS	TPR
1996	Cle-A	5	10	2	3	2	0	0	1	1	4	.300	.364	.500	864	116	0	0	0	0	1.000	2	/S-5	0.3
1997	Cle-A	8	9	2	1	0	0	0	0	0	1	.111	.200	.111	311	-15	-2	1	0	0	1.000	1	/S-5,2-1	0.0
	Cin-N	12	27	6	6	2	1	1	2	4	7	.222	.323	.481	804	106	0	1	1	-0	1.000	0	/S-6,2-3	0.1
1998	Cin-N	13	38	4	12	5	0	0	7	6	4	.316	.409	.447	856	124	2	2	0	0	.972	-1	S-10/O-3(3-0-1)	0.2
1999	SD-N	133	388	56	87	20	2	9	39	53	105	.224	.322	.356	678	77	-14	34	10	4	.940	-5	*S-100,2-21/O-3L	-0.5
2000	SD-N	138	470	68	120	27	6	6	37	62	108	.255	.346	.377	722	88	-8	28	6	4	.955	12	S-88,2-36,O-17L	1.5
Total	5	309	942	138	229	56	9	16	86	126	229	.243	.337	.373	709	85	-21	66	17	9	.951	11	S-214/2-61,O-23L	1.6

■ DARRIN JACKSON Jackson, Darrin Jay b: 8/22/62, Los Angeles, Cal. BR/TR, 6', 185 lbs. Deb: 6/17/85 Career OF: (185-LF 510-CF 187-RF)

YEAR	TM/L	G	AB	R	H	2B	3B	HR	RBI	BB	SO	AVG	OBP	SLG	OPS	OPS+	BR+	SB	CS	SBR	FA	FR	G/POS	TPR
1985	Chi-N	5	11	0	1	0	0	0	0	0	3	.091	.091	.091	182	-44	-2	0	0	0	1.000	-1	/O-4(0-4-0)	-0.3
1987	Chi-N	7	5	2	4	1	0	0	0	0	0	.800	.800	1.000	1800	359	2	0	0	0	1.000	-2	/O-5(2-3-0)	0.0
1988	Chi-N	100	188	29	50	11	3	6	20	5	28	.266	.289	.452	741	105	0	4	1	1	.983	-10	O-74(11-46-20)	-1.1
1989	Chi-N	45	83	7	19	4	0	1	8	6	17	.229	.281	.313	594	65	-4	1	2	-0	.970	-1	O-39(10-9-20)	-0.7
	SD-N	25	87	10	18	3	0	3	12	7	17	.207	.266	.345	611	73	-3	0	2	-1	.954	2	O-24(0-24-0)	-0.2
	Yr	70	170	17	37	7	0	4	20	13	34	.218	.273	.329	603	68	-7	1	4	-1	.962	1	O-63(10-33-20)	-0.9
1990	SD-N	58	113	10	29	3	0	3	9	5	24	.257	.288	.363	651	77	-4	3	0	1	.985	-5	O-39(4-30-5)	-0.9
1991	SD-N	122	359	51	94	12	1	21	49	27	66	.262	.317	.476	793	117	7	5	3	0	.992	7	O-98(21-79-0)/P-1	1.3
1992	SD-N	155	587	72	146	23	5	17	70	26	106	.249	.285	.392	677	88	-11	14	3	2	.996	24	*O-153(5-152-2)	1.5
1993	Tor-A	46	176	15	38	8	0	5	19	8	53	.216	.250	.347	597	58	-11	0	2	-1	.989	-2	O-46(0-10-37)	-1.5
	NY-N	31	87	4	17	1	0	1	7	2	22	.195	.213	.241	455	22	-10	0	0	0	1.000	2	O-26(10-16-0)	-0.8
1994	Chi-A	104	369	43	115	17	3	10	51	27	56	.312	.363	.455	819	111	6	7	1	1	.996	0	*O-102(0-16-92)	0.3
1997	Min-A	49	130	19	33	2	1	3	21	4	21	.254	.276	.354	630	62	-7	2	0	0	.990	0	O-44(0-44-0)	-0.6
	Mil-A	26	81	7	22	7	0	2	15	2	10	.272	.289	.432	721	84	-2	2	1	0	1.000	-1	O-26(21-9-3)	-0.3
	Yr	75	211	26	55	9	1	5	36	6	31	.261	.281	.384	665	70	-10	4	1	1	.994	-1	O-70(21-53-3)	-0.9
1998	Mil-N	114	204	20	49	13	1	4	20	9	37	.240	.276	.373	648	68	-10	1	1	-0	.982	-17	O-94(55-43-5)/D-2	-2.7
1999	Chi-A	73	149	22	41	9	1	4	16	3	20	.275	.289	.430	719	80	-5	4	1	1	.972	-11	O-64(46-25-3)/D-3	-1.5
Total	12	960	2629	311	676	114	15	80	317	131	480	.257	.295	.403	698	87	-53	43	17	4	.989	-14	O-838C/D-5,P-1	-7.5

■ GEORGE JACKSON Jackson, George Christopher "Hickory" b: 10/14/1882, Springfield, Mo. d: 11/25/72, Cleburne, Tex. BR/TR, 6'0.5", 180 lbs. Deb: 8/2/11

YEAR	TM/L	G	AB	R	H	2B	3B	HR	RBI	BB	SO	AVG	OBP	SLG	OPS	OPS+	BR+	SB	CS	SBR	FA	FR	G/POS	TPR
1911	Bos-N	39	147	28	51	11	2	0	25	12	21	.347	.404	.449	853	128	5	12			.929	-2	O-39(38-1-0)	0.2
1912	Bos-N	110	397	55	104	13	5	4	48	38	72	.262	.342	.350	692	88	-6	22			.943	2	*O-107(96-11-0)	-0.9
1913	Bos-N	3	10	0	3	0	0	0	0	0	2	.300	.300	.300	600	70	-0	0			.875	0	/O-3(0-3-0)	0.0
Total	3	152	554	85	158	24	7	4	73	50	95	.285	.357	.375	733	98	-1	34			.938	0	O-149(134-15-0)	-0.7

■ HENRY JACKSON Jackson, Henry Everett b: 6/23/1861, Union City, Ind. d: 9/14/32, Chicago, Ill. BR/TR, 6'2", 185 lbs. Deb: 9/13/1887

YEAR	TM/L	G	AB	R	H	2B	3B	HR	RBI	BB	SO	AVG	OBP	SLG	OPS	OPS+	BR+	SB	CS	SBR	FA	FR	G/POS	TPR
1887	Ind-N	10	38	1	10	1	0	0	3	0	12	.263	.263	.289	553	55	-2	2			.933	-1	1-10	-0.4

■ JIM JACKSON Jackson, James Benner b: 11/28/1877, Philadelphia, Pa. d: 10/9/55, Philadelphia, Pa. BR/TR (BL 1906 (1 GAME)), Deb: 4/26/01

YEAR	TM/L	G	AB	R	H	2B	3B	HR	RBI	BB	SO	AVG	OBP	SLG	OPS	OPS+	BR+	SB	CS	SBR	FA	FR	G/POS	TPR
1901	Bal-A	99	364	42	91	17	3	2	50	20		.250	.291	.330	621	69	-16	11			**.971**	3	O-96(35-59-2)	-1.7
1902	NY-N	37	116	14	21	5	1	0	15	16		.181	.280	.241	522	62	-5	6			.899	-3	O-36(32-2-2)	-1.0
1905	Cle-A	109	426	60	109	12	4	2	31	34		.256	.317	.317	634	100	0	15			.951	5	*O-106(104-0-2)/3-3	-0.1
1906	Cle-A	105	374	44	80	13	2	0	38	38		.214	.290	.259	549	73	-10	25			.975	-6	*O-104(103-1-0)	-2.5
Total	4	350	1280	160	301	47	10	4	134	108		.235	.298	.297	595	79	-31	57			.959	-2	O-342(274-62-6)/3-3	-5.3

■ JOE JACKSON Jackson, Joseph Jefferson "Shoeless Joe" b: 7/16/1889, Pickens Co., S.C. d: 12/5/51, Greenville, S.C. BL/TR, 6'1", 200 lbs. Deb: 8/25/08 Career OF: (584-LF 145-CF 559-RF)

YEAR	TM/L	G	AB	R	H	2B	3B	HR	RBI	BB	SO	AVG	OBP	SLG	OPS	OPS+	BR+	SB	CS	SBR	FA	FR	G/POS	TPR
1908	Phi-A	5	23	0	3	0	0	0	3	0		.130	.130	.130	261	-14	-3	0			.875	-1	/O-5(0-5-0)	-0.4
1909	Phi-A	5	17	3	3	0	0	0	3	1		.176	.222	.176	399	26	-1	0			.833	-0	/O-4(3-1-0)	-0.2
1910	Cle-A	20	75	15	29	2	5	1	11	8		.387	.446	.587	1032	220	10	4			.977	0	O-20(0-15-5)	1.0

YEAR	TM/L	G	AB	R	H	2B	3B	HR	RBI	BB	SO	AVG	OBP	SLG	OPS	OPS+	BR+	SB	CS	SBR	FA	FR	G/POS	TPR
1911	Cle-A	147	571	126	233	45	19	7	83	56		.408	**.468**	.590	1058	192	70	41			.958	8	*O-147(0-47-100)	6.7
1912	Cle-A	154	572	121	**226**	44	**26**	3	90	54		.395	.458	.579	1036	190	66	35			.950	13	*O-150(0-19-131)	6.8
1913	Cle-A	148	528	109	**197**	**39**	17	7	71	80	26	.373	.460	**.551**	**1011**	190	**62**	26			.930	2	*O-148(0-0-148)	5.8
1914	Cle-A	122	453	61	153	22	13	3	53	41	34	.338	.399	.464	862	153	29	22	15	-0	.967	2	*O-119(0-31-88)	2.5
1915	Cle-A	83	303	42	99	16	9	3	45	28	11	.327	.389	.469	858	154	19	10	10	-1	.961	-3	O-50(5-0-44),1-30	1.2
	Chi-A	45	158	21	43	4	5	2	36	24	12	.272	.378	.399	777	129	6	6	10	-2	.947	-2	O-45(19-26-0)	0.0
	Yr	128	461	63	142	20	14	5	81	52	23	.308	.385	.445	830	145	25	16	20	-3	.953	-5	O-95(24-26-44),1-30	1.2
1916	Chi-A	155	592	91	202	40	**21**	3	78	46	25	.341	.393	.495	888	165	44	24	14	0	.975	-1	*O-155(131-1-23)	3.9
1917	*Chi-A	146	538	91	162	20	17	5	75	57	25	.301	.375	.429	805	142	27	13			.984	9	*O-145(134-0-11)	3.3
1918	Chi-A	17	65	9	23	2	2	1	20	8	1	.354	.425	.492	917	175	6	3			1.000	-0	O-17(14-0-3)	0.5
1919	*Chi-A	139	516	79	181	31	14	7	96	60	10	.351	.422	.506	928	159	41	9			.967	-4	*O-139(133-0-6)	3.2
1920	Chi-A	146	570	105	218	42	**20**	12	121	56	14	.382	.444	.589	1033	172	58	9	12	-2	.965	-1	*O-145(145-0-0)	4.7
Total	13	1332	4981	873	1772	307	168	54	785	519	158	.356	.423	.517	940	169	433	202	61		.962	23	*O-1289L/1-30	39.0
■ **KEN JACKSON**	Jackson, Kenneth Bernard b: 8/21/63, Shreveport, La. BR/TR, 5'9", 170 lbs. Deb: 9/12/87																							
1987	Phi-N	8	16	1	4	2	0	0	2	1	4	.250	.333	.375	708	85	-0	0	0	0	.955	-1	/S-8	-0.1
■ **LOU JACKSON**	Jackson, Louis Clarence b: 7/26/35, Riverton, La. d: 5/27/69, Tokyo, Japan BL/TR, 5'10", 168 lbs. Deb: 7/23/58																							
1958	Chi-N	24	35	5	6	2	1	1	6	1	9	.171	.194	.371	566	46	-3	0	1	-0	1.000	-4	O-12(4-4-6)	-0.8
1959	Chi-N	6	4	2	1	0	0	0	1	0	2	.250	.250	.250	500	34	-0	0	0	0	.000	0	H	0.0
1964	Bal-A	4	8	0	3	0	0	0	0	0	2	.375	.375	.375	750	110	0	0	0	0	1.000	1	/O-1(1-0-0)	0.1
Total	3	34	47	7	10	2	1	1	7	1	13	.213	.229	.362	591	55	-3	0	1	-0	1.000	-4	/O-13(5-4-6)	-0.7
■ **RANDY JACKSON**	Jackson, Ransom Joseph "Handsome Ransom" b: 2/10/26, Little Rock, Ark. BR/TR, 6'1.5", 180 lbs. Deb: 5/2/50																							
1950	Chi-N	34	111	13	25	4	3	3	6	7	25	.225	.271	.396	668	74	-5	4			.911	-4	3-27	-0.9
1951	Chi-N	145	557	78	153	24	6	16	76	47	44	.275	.332	.425	758	101	-1	14	3	2	.956	8	*3-143	0.9
1952	Chi-N	116	379	44	88	8	5	9	34	27	42	.232	.285	.351	636	75	-14	6	5	-0	.958	-3	*3-104/O-1(1-0-0)	-1.8
1953	Chi-N	139	498	61	142	22	8	19	66	42	61	.285	.341	.476	817	108	5	8	4	0	.949	3	*3-133	0.7
1954	Chi-N★	126	484	77	132	17	6	19	67	44	55	.273	.336	.450	786	102	0	2	1	0	.955	-1	*3-124	-0.1
1955	Chi-N★	138	499	73	132	13	7	21	70	58	58	.265	.342	.445	787	107	5	0	2	-1	.949	-13	*3-134	-1.0
1956	*Bro-N	101	307	37	84	15	7	8	53	28	38	.274	.338	.446	785	101	0	2	1	0	.993	21	3-80	2.2
1957	Bro-N	48	131	7	26	1	0	2	16	9	20	.198	.250	.252	502	32	-12	0	0	0	.976	-2	3-34	-1.5
1958	LA-N	35	65	8	12	3	0	1	4	5	10	.185	.243	.277	520	36	-6	0	0	0	.964	7	3-17	0.1
	Cle-A	29	91	7	22	3	1	4	13	3	18	.242	.266	.429	695	90	-2	0	0	0	.901	5	3-24	0.3
1959	Cle-A	3	7	0	1	0	0	0	0	0	1	.143	.143	.143	286	-22	-1	0	0	0	1.000	-1	/3-2	-0.2
	Chi-N	41	74	7	18	5	1	1	10	11	10	.243	.341	.378	720	92	-1	0	0	0	.941	-3	3-22/O-1(1-0-0)	-0.4
Total	10	955	3203	412	835	115	44	103	415	281	382	.261	.322	.421	742	94	-31	36	16		.955	18	3-844/O-2(2-0-0)	-1.7
■ **REGGIE JACKSON**	Jackson, Reginald Martinez b: 5/18/46, Wyncote, Pa. BL/TL, 6', 200 lbs. Deb: 6/9/67 H Career OF: (20-LF 186-CF 1939-RF)																							
1967	KC-A	35	118	13	21	4	4	1	6	10	46	.178	.271	.305	576	72	-4	1	1	-0	.933	-2	O-34(19-3-14)	-0.9
1968	Oak-A	154	553	82	138	13	6	29	74	50	171	.250	.317	.452	770	138	23	14	4	2	.959	8	*O-151(1-9-147)	2.5
1969	Oak-A★	152	549	**123**	151	36	3	47	118	114	142	.275	.410	**.608**	**1019**	**190**	**68**	13	5	1	.964	5	*O-150(0-10-144)	6.7
1970	Oak-A	149	426	57	101	21	2	23	66	75	135	.237	.361	.458	819	129	18	26	17	-0	.956	-11	*O-142(0-49-113)	0.1
1971	*Oak-A★	150	567	87	157	29	3	32	80	63	161	.277	.355	.508	863	145	32	16	10	0	.977	9	*O-145(0-3-145)	3.5
1972	*Oak-A★	135	499	72	132	25	2	25	75	59	125	.265	.352	.473	825	152	31	9	8	-1	.971	2	*O-135(0-92-43)	3.0
1973	*Oak-A★	151	539	**99**	158	28	2	**32**	**117**	76	111	.293	.387	**.531**	**918**	**165**	**47**	22	8	2	.971	4	*O-145(0-1-144)/D-3	4.5
1974	*Oak-A★	148	506	90	146	25	1	29	93	86	105	.289	.396	.514	910	**171**	**48**	25	5	**4**	.968	9	*O-127(0-3-126),D-19	5.5
1975	*Oak-A★	157	593	91	150	39	3	**36**	104	67	133	.253	.332	.511	843	138	27	17	8	1	.965	9	*O-147(0-0-147)/D-9	2.9
1976	Bal-A	134	498	84	138	27	2	27	91	54	108	.277	.353	**.502**	855	**158**	35	28	7	4	.964	2	*O-121(0-16-111),D-11	3.6
1977	*NY-A★	146	525	93	150	39	2	32	110	74	129	.286	.377	.550	928	151	37	17	3	3	.949	-1	*O-127(0-0-127),D-18	3.1
1978	*NY-A†	139	511	82	140	13	5	27	97	58	133	.274	.358	.477	836	136	24	14	11	-1	.986	3	*O-104(0-0-104),D-35	2.0
1979	NY-A★	131	465	78	138	24	2	29	89	65	107	.297	.385	.544	929	151	33	9	8	-1	.986	7	*O-125(0-0-125)/D-3	3.1
1980	*NY-A★	143	514	94	154	22	4	**41**	111	83	122	.300	.399	.597	996	172	51	1	2	-0	.962	-2	O-94(0-0-94),D-46	4.1
1981	*NY-A★	94	334	33	79	17	1	15	54	46	82	.237	.331	.428	759	119	8	0	3	-1	.974	0	O-61(0-0-61),D-33	0.3
1982	*Cal-A★	153	530	92	146	17	1	**39**	101	85	156	.275	.378	.532	910	147	35	4	5	-1	.972	-18	*O-139(0-0-139)/D-5	0.9
1983	Cal-A†	116	397	43	77	14	1	14	49	52	140	.194	.294	.340	634	74	-14	0	2	-1	.986	-5	D-62,O-47(0-0-47)	-2.3
1984	Cal-A★	143	525	67	117	17	2	25	81	55	141	.223	.300	.406	706	94	-5	8	4	0	1.000	0	*D-134/O-3(0-0-3)	-0.9
1985	Cal-A	143	460	64	116	27	0	27	85	78	138	.252	.362	.487	849	130	20	1	2	-0	.944	-9	O-81(0-0-81),D-52	0.6
1986	*Cal-A	132	419	65	101	12	2	18	58	92	115	.241	.381	.408	789	116	13	1	1	-0	.833	-0	*D-121/O-4(0-0-4)	0.9
1987	Oak-A	115	336	42	74	14	1	15	43	33	97	.220	.298	.402	699	89	-6	2	1	0	1.000	-2	D-79,O-20(0-0-20)	-1.0
Total	21	2820	9864	1551	2584	463	49	563	1702	1375	2597	.262	.358	.490	848	140	520	228	115	10	.967	8	*O-2102R,D-630	42.2
■ **SONNY JACKSON**	Jackson, Roland Thomas b: 7/9/44, Washington, D.C. BL/TR, 5'9", 155 lbs. Deb: 9/27/63 C Career OF: (48-LF 158-CF 6-RF)																							
1963	Hou-N	1	3	0	0	0	0	0	0	0	1	.000	.000	.000	0	-99	-1	0	0	0	.833	1	/S-1	0.0
1964	Hou-N	9	23	3	8	1	0	0	1	2	3	.348	.400	.391	791	131	1	1	0	0	.870	-4	/S-7	-0.2
1965	Hou-N	10	23	1	3	0	0	0	0	1	1	.130	.167	.130	297	-16	-4	1	1	-0	.969	-1	/S-8,3-1	-0.4
1966	Hou-N	150	596	80	174	6	5	3	25	42	53	.292	.342	.334	676	95	-3	49	14	6	.951	-13	*S-150	0.4
1967	Hou-N	129	520	67	123	18	3	0	25	36	45	.237	.286	.283	569	66	-23	22	9	2	.943	-8	*S-128	-2.0
1968	Atl-N	105	358	37	81	8	2	1	19	25	35	.226	.282	.268	551	66	-14	16	6	1	.952	-17	S-99	-2.6
1969	*Atl-N	98	318	41	76	3	5	1	27	35	33	.239	.318	.289	608	71	-11	12	7	0	.961	-23	S-97	-2.4
1970	Atl-N	103	328	60	85	14	3	0	20	45	27	.259	.350	.320	670	76	-9	11	4	1	.933	-23	S-87	-2.1
1971	Atl-N	149	547	58	141	20	5	2	25	35	45	.258	.304	.324	627	73	-19	7	6	-1	.980	3	*O-145(0-145-0)	-2.2
1972	Atl-N	60	126	20	30	6	3	0	8	7	9	.238	.278	.333	612	67	-5	1	0	0	.976	-6	S-17,O-10(0-9-1)/3-6	-1.0
1973	Atl-N	117	206	29	43	5	2	0	12	22	13	.209	.288	.252	541	47	-14	6	3	0	.981	-14	O-56(48-4-4),S-36	-2.7
1974	Atl-N	5	7	0	3	0	0	0	0	0	0	.429	.429	.429	857	134	0	0	1	-0	1.000	0	/O-1(0-0-1)	0.0
Total	12	936	3055	396	767	81	28	7	162	250	265	.251	.310	.303	613	73	-103	126	51	10	.949	-104	S-630,O-212C/3-7	-15.2
■ **RON JACKSON**	Jackson, Ronald Harris b: 10/22/33, Kalamazoo, Mich. BR/TR, 6'7", 225 lbs. Deb: 6/15/54																							
1954	Chi-A	40	93	10	26	4	0	4	10	6	20	.280	.337	.452	788	111	1	2	1	0	.988	-3	1-35	-0.3
1955	Chi-A	40	74	10	15	1	1	2	7	8	22	.203	.280	.324	605	61	-4	1	0	0	.988	-1	1-29	-0.6
1956	Chi-A	22	56	7	12	3	0	1	4	10	13	.214	.333	.321	655	73	-2	1	0	0	1.000	1	1-19	-0.2
1957	Chi-A	13	60	4	19	3	0	2	8	1	12	.317	.328	.467	795	114	1	0	0	0	.992	-1	1-13	-0.1
1958	Chi-A	61	146	19	34	4	0	7	21	18	46	.233	.325	.404	729	101	0	2	0	0	.997	-2	1-38	-0.3
1959	Chi-A	10	14	3	3	1	0	1	2	1	0	.214	.313	.500	813	121	0	0	0	0	1.000	-0	/1-5	0.0
1960	Bos-A	10	31	1	7	2	0	0	0	1	6	.226	.250	.290	540	44	-2	0	0	0	.973	-0	/1-9	-0.3
Total	7	196	474	54	116	18	1	17	52	45	119	.245	.317	.395	711	92	-6	6	1	1	.992	-6	1-148	-1.8
■ **RON JACKSON**	Jackson, Ronnie Damien b: 5/9/53, Birmingham, Ala. BR/TR, 6', 205 lbs. Deb: 9/12/75 C Career OF: (51-LF 1-CF 4-RF)																							
1975	Cal-A	13	39	2	9	2	0	0	2	2	10	.231	.268	.282	550	60	-2	1	1	-0	.947	-0	/O-9(9-0-0),3-3,D-1	-0.3
1976	Cal-A	127	410	44	93	18	3	8	40	30	58	.227	.291	.344	635	91	-5	5	4	-0	.950	1	*3-114/2-7,O-4L,D-6	-0.6
1977	Cal-A	106	292	38	71	15	2	8	28	24	42	.243	.303	.390	693	91	-4	3	2	-0	.990	2	1-43,3-30,D-20,/OS	-0.6
1978	Cal-A	105	387	49	115	18	6	6	57	16	31	.297	.340	.421	761	117	8	2	3	-1	.994	-3	1-75,3-31/O-1R,D-1	-0.1
1979	Min-A	159	583	85	158	40	5	14	68	51	59	.271	.339	.429	768	102	1	3	1	0	.994	11	*1-157/S-1,3-1,O-1L	0.3
1980	Min-A	131	396	48	105	29	3	5	42	28	41	.265	.319	.391	710	87	-7	1	8	-3	.991	-1	*1-119,O-15L/3-2,D	-1.7
1981	Min-A	54	175	17	46	9	0	4	28	10	15	.263	.306	.383	689	91	-2	2	2	-0	.988	1	1-36/O-7L,3-3,D-6	-0.4
	Det-A	31	95	12	27	8	1	1	12	8	11	.284	.340	.421	761	114	2	4	1	1	1.000	-1	1-29	0.0
	Yr	85	270	29	73	17	1	5	40	18	26	.270	.318	.396	715	99	-1	6	3	0	.993	1	1-65/O-7L,D-6,3-3	-0.4
1982	*Cal-A	53	142	15	47	6	0	2	19	10	12	.331	.383	.415	799	119	4	0	1	-0	.994	0	1-37/3-9	0.2
1983	Cal-A	102	348	41	80	16	1	8	39	27	33	.230	.291	.351	642	76	-12	2	2	-0	.957	2	3-38,1-35,D-16,O-15L	-1.4
1984	Cal-A	33	91	5	15	2	1	0	5	7	13	.165	.224	.209	433	21	-10	0	0	0	.990	-0	1-21/3-9,O-1(1-0-0)	-1.1
	Bal-A	12	28	0	8	2	0	0	2	0	4	.286	.286	.357	643	78	-1	0	2	-1	.960	2	3-10	0.0

YEAR	TM/L	G	AB	R	H	2B	3B	HR	RBI	BB	SO	AVG	OBP	SLG	OPS	OPS+	BR+	SB	CS	SBR	FA	FR	G/POS	TPR
	Yr	45	119	5	23	4	1	0	7	7	17	.193	.238	.244	482	34	-11	0	2	-1	.990	1	1-21,3-19/O-1(1-0-0)	-1.1
Total	10	926	2986	356	774	165	22	56	342	213	329	.259	.316	.385	701	94	-29	23	27	-4	.993	14	1-552,3-250/OD2S	-5.7
■ RYAN JACKSON	Jackson, Ryan Dewitte b: 11/15/71, Orlando, Fla. BL/TL, 6'2", 195 lbs. Deb: 3/31/98 Career OF: (11-LF 0-CF 23-RF)																							
1998	Fla-N	111	260	26	65	15	1	5	31	20	73	.250	.306	.373	679	82	-7	1	1	-0	.973	-7	1-44,O-32R/D-5	-1.9
1999	Sea-A	32	68	4	16	3	0	0	10	6	19	.235	.307	.279	586	52	-5	3	3	-0	.989	-0	1-29/O-1(1-0-0)	-0.7
Total	2	143	328	30	81	18	1	5	41	26	92	.247	.306	.354	660	75	-12	4	4	-1	.978	-7	/1-73,O-33R,D-5	-2.6
■ SAM JACKSON	Jackson, Samuel b: 3/24/1849, Ripon, England d: 8/4/1893, Clifton Springs, N.Y. BR/TR, 5'5.5", 160 lbs. Deb: 5/16/1871 Career OF: (3-LF 1-CF 0-RF)																							
1871	Bos-n	16	76	17	17	5	3	0	11	1	4	.224	.234	.368	602	68	-3	0	1	-0	.818	-1	2-14/S-1,O-1(0-1-0)	-0.4
1872	Atl-n	4	12	0	2	0	0	0	0	0	0	.167	.167	.167	333	2	-1	0	0	0	.667	-3	/O-3(3-0-0),2-1,3-1	-0.3
Total	2 n	20	88	17	19	5	3	0	11	1	4	.216	.225	.341	566	58	-5	0	1	-0	.810	-5	/2-15,O-4L,3-1,S-1	-0.7
■ TRAVIS JACKSON	Jackson, Travis Calvin "Stonewall" b: 11/2/03, Waldo, Ark. d: 7/27/87, Waldo, Ark. BR/TR, 5'10.5", 160 lbs. Deb: 9/27/22 CH Career OF: (0-LF 0-CF 1-RF)																							
1922	NY-N	3	8	1	0	0	0	0	0	0	2	.000	.000	.000	0	-99	-2	0	0	0	.909	0	/S-3	-0.2
1923	*NY-N	96	327	45	90	12	7	4	37	22	40	.275	.321	.391	712	88	-6	3	3	-0	.943	-4	S-60,3-31/2-1	-0.2
1924	*NY-N	151	596	81	180	26	8	11	76	21	56	.302	.326	.428	754	103	1	6	7	-1	.937	-0	*S-151	1.6
1925	NY-N	112	411	51	117	15	2	9	59	24	43	.285	.327	.397	724	87	-8	8	3	1	.942	4	*S-110	0.7
1926	NY-N	111	385	64	126	24	8	8	51	20	26	.327	.362	.494	856	130	14	2			.962	1	*S-108/O-1(0-0-1)	2.6
1927	NY-N	127	469	67	149	29	4	14	98	32	30	.318	.363	.486	849	126	16	8			.952	28	*S-124/3-2	5.5
1928	NY-N	150	537	73	145	35	6	14	77	56	46	.270	.339	.436	775	101	-1	8			.952	28	*S-149	4.2
1929	NY-N	149	551	92	162	21	12	21	94	64	56	.294	.367	.490	857	111	8	10			**.969**	19	*S-149	3.9
1930	NY-N	116	431	70	146	27	8	13	82	32	25	.339	.386	.529	915	121	14	6			.956	11	*S-115	3.3
1931	NY-N	145	555	65	172	26	10	5	71	36	23	.310	.353	.420	773	110	7	13			**.970**	10	*S-145	2.7
1932	NY-N	52	195	23	50	17	1	4	38	13	16	.256	.310	.415	725	95	-2	1			.925	-5	S-52	-0.2
1933	*NY-N	53	122	11	30	5	0	0	12	8	11	.246	.292	.287	579	67	-5	2			.890	7	S-21,3-21	0.3
1934	NY-N★	137	523	75	140	26	7	16	101	37	71	.268	.316	.436	752	102	-0	1			.945	12	*S-130/3-9	2.0
1935	NY-N	128	511	74	154	20	12	9	80	29	64	.301	.340	.440	780	110	6	3			.947	-7	*3-128	0.4
1936	*NY-N	126	465	41	107	8	1	7	53	18	56	.230	.260	.297	557	50	-33	0			.952	-1	*3-116/S-9	-2.9
Total	15	1656	6086	833	1768	291	86	135	929	412	565	.291	.337	.433	770	102	8	71	13		.952	104	*S-1326,3-307/O-1R,2	23.7
■ BO JACKSON	Jackson, Vincent Edward b: 11/30/62, Bessemer, Ala. BR/TR, 6'1", 225 lbs. Deb: 9/2/86 Career OF: (415-LF 88-CF 63-RF)																							
1986	KC-A	25	82	9	17	2	1	2	9	7	34	.207	.286	.329	615	66	-4	3	1	0	.886	-3	O-23(0-0-23)/D-1	-0.8
1987	KC-A	116	396	46	93	17	2	22	53	30	158	.235	.297	.455	752	93	-5	10	4	1	.955	-7	*O-113(95-21-3)/D-1	-1.5
1988	KC-A	124	439	63	108	16	4	25	68	25	146	.246	.288	.472	760	108	2	27	6	4	.973	6	*O-121(103-5-15)/D-2	0.9
1989	KC-A★	135	515	86	132	15	6	32	105	39	172	.256	.312	.495	808	125	14	26	9	3	.967	7	*O-110(110-1-0),D-24	2.0
1990	KC-A	111	405	74	110	16	1	28	78	44	128	.272	.346	.523	869	142	21	15	9	0	.952	8	O-97(36-61-0),D-10	2.7
1991	Chi-A	23	71	8	16	4	0	3	14	12	25	.225	.337	.408	746	108	1	0	1	-0	.000	0	D-21	0.0
1993	*Chi-A	85	284	32	66	9	0	16	45	23	106	.232	.290	.433	723	94	-4	0	2	-1	.989	3	O-47(28-0-19),D-36	-0.6
1994	Cal-A	75	201	23	56	7	0	13	43	20	72	.279	.347	.507	854	115	4	1	0	0	.964	-2	O-46(43-0-3)/D-9	0.1
Total	8	694	2393	341	598	86	14	141	415	200	841	.250	.311	.474	786	112	30	82	32	7	.962	12	O-557L,D-104	2.8
■ BILL JACKSON	Jackson, William Riley b: 4/4/1881, Pittsburgh, Pa. d: 9/24/58, Peoria, Ill. BL/TL, 5'11.5", 160 lbs. Deb: 4/30/14																							
1914	Chi-F	26	25	2	1	0	0	0	1	3	5	.040	.143	.040	183	-52	-6	0			.917	0	/O-6(2-2-2),1-4	-0.6
1915	Chi-F	50	98	15	16	1	0	1	12	14	15	.163	.268	.204	472	36	-10	3			.983	0	1-36/O-1(0-1-0)	-1.2
Total	2	76	123	17	17	1	0	1	13	17	20	.138	.243	.171	414	18	-16	3			.984	0	/1-40,O-7(2-3-2)	-1.8
■ SPOOK JACOBS	Jacobs, Robert Forrest Vandergrift b: 11/4/25, Cheswold, Del. BR/TR, 5'8.5", 155 lbs. Deb: 4/13/54																							
1954	Phi-A	132	508	63	131	11	1	0	26	60	22	.258	.336	.283	620	71	-18	17	3	3	.974	-19	*2-131	-2.6
1955	KC-A	13	23	7	6	0	0	0	1	3	0	.261	.370	.261	631	71	-1	1	2	-0	1.000	-3	/2-7	-0.4
1956	KC-A	32	97	13	21	3	0	0	5	15	5	.216	.321	.247	569	52	-6	4	1	1	.968	-4	2-31	-0.7
	Pit-N	11	37	4	6	2	0	0	1	2	5	.162	.225	.216	441	20	-4	0	2	-1	.926	-4	2-11	-0.9
Total	3	188	665	87	164	16	1	0	33	80	32	.247	.329	.274	603	65	-30	22	8	2	.971	-29	2-180	-4.6
■ JAKE JACOBS	Jacobs, Lamar Gary b: 6/9/37, Youngstown, Ohio BR/TR, 6', 175 lbs. Deb: 9/13/60																							
1960	Was-A	6	2	0	0	0	0	0	0	0	0	.000	.000	.000	0	-99	-1	0	0	0	.000	0	H	-0.1
1961	Min-A	4	8	0	2	0	0	0	0	0	2	.250	.250	.250	500	32	-1	0	0	0	1.000	-1	/O-3(0-3-0)	-0.2
Total	2	10	10	0	2	0	0	0	0	0	2	.200	.200	.200	400	7	-1	0	0	0	1.000	-1	/O-3(0-3-0)	-0.3
■ MIKE JACOBS	Jacobs, Morris Elmore b: 12/1877, Louisville, Ky. d: 3/21/49, Louisville, Ky. Deb: 7/16/02																							
1902	Chi-N	5	19	1	4	0	0	0	2	0		.211	.211	.211	421	31	-2	0			.880	-2	/S-5	-0.3
■ OTTO JACOBS	Jacobs, Otto Albert b: 4/19/1889, Chicago, Ill. d: 11/19/55, Chicago, Ill. BR/TR, 5'9", 180 lbs. Deb: 6/13/18																							
1918	Chi-A	29	73	4	15	3	1	0	3	5	8	.205	.256	.274	530	59	-4	0			.955	-4	C-21	-0.7
■ RAY JACOBS	Jacobs, Raymond Frederick b: 1/2/02, Salt Lake City, Utah d: 4/5/52, Los Angeles, Cal. BR/TR, 6', 160 lbs. Deb: 4/20/28																							
1928	Chi-N	2	2	0	0	0	0	0	0	0	1	.000	.000	.000	0	-99	-1	0			.000	0	H	-0.1
■ MERWIN JACOBSON	Jacobson, Merwin John William "Jake" b: 3/7/1894, New Britain, Conn. d: 1/13/78, Baltimore, Md. BL/TL, 5'11.5", 165 lbs. Deb: 9/8/15																							
1915	NY-N	8	24	0	2	0	0	0	0	1	5	.083	.120	.083	203	-40	-4	0			.909	0	/O-5(0-2-3)	-0.5
1916	Chi-N	4	13	2	3	0	0	0	0	1	4	.231	.286	.231	516	54	-1	2			1.000	0	/O-4(0-0-4)	-0.1
1926	Bro-N	110	288	41	71	9	2	0	23	36	24	.247	.330	.292	622	70	-11	5			.975	-3	O-86(2-53-32)	-1.8
1927	Bro-N	11	6	4	0	0	0	0	1	0	1	.000	.000	.000	0	-99	-2	0			1.000	-1	/O-3(0-0-3)	-0.3
Total	4	133	331	47	76	9	2	0	24	38	34	.230	.309	.269	578	59	-18	7			.973	-4	/O-98(2-55-42)	-2.7
■ BABY DOLL JACOBSON	Jacobson, William Chester b: 8/16/1890, Cable, Ill. d: 1/16/77, Orion, Ill. BR/TR, 6'3", 215 lbs. Deb: 4/14/15 Career OF: (88-LF 1098-CF 194-RF)																							
1915	Det-A	37	65	5	14	6	2	0	4	5	14	.215	.282	.369	651	90	-1	0	2	-1	.983	-2	1-10/O-7(3-5-0)	-0.5
	StL-A	34	115	13	24	6	1	1	9	10	26	.209	.295	.304	599	82	-3	3	3	-0	.981	-1	O-32(3-3-26)	-0.7
	Yr	71	180	18	38	12	3	1	13	15	40	.211	.290	.328	618	84	-4	3	5	-1	.984	-4	O-39(6-8-26),1-10	-1.2
1917	StL-A	148	529	53	131	23	7	4	55	31	67	.248	.294	.340	635	97	-4	10			.975	7	*O-131(0-54-77),1-11	-0.6
1919	StL-A	120	455	70	147	31	8	4	51	24	47	.323	.362	.453	815	125	13	9			.949	1	*O-106(17-73-16)/1-8	0.7
1920	StL-A	154	609	97	216	34	14	9	122	46	37	.355	.402	.501	903	134	29	11	7	-0	.979	11	*O-154(0-120-34)/1-1	2.8
1921	StL-A	151	599	90	211	38	14	5	90	42	30	.352	.398	.487	885	118	16	8	8	-1	.982	5	*O-142(0-141-1),1-10	1.2
1922	StL-A	145	555	88	176	22	16	9	102	46	36	.317	.379	.463	842	114	11	19	6	2	.969	4	*O-137(11-125-1)/1-7	1.1
1923	StL-A	147	592	76	183	29	6	8	81	29	27	.309	.343	.419	762	95	-6	6	6	-1	.974	9	*O-146(0-146-0)	-0.4
1924	StL-A	152	579	103	184	41	12	19	97	35	45	.318	.361	.528	889	120	13	6	8	-1	.986	16	*O-152(0-152-0)	2.0
1925	StL-A	142	540	103	184	30	9	15	76	45	26	.341	.392	.513	905	122	17	8	11	-2	.965	1	*O-139(0-139-0)	0.9
1926	StL-A	50	182	18	52	15	1	2	21	9	14	.286	.319	.412	731	86	-4	1	2	-0	.964	-6	O-50(0-50-0)	-1.3
	Bos-A	98	394	44	120	36	1	6	69	22	22	.305	.344	.447	791	109	3	4	1	1	.980	-8	O-98(6-57-36)	-1.0
	Yr	148	576	62	172	51	2	8	90	31	36	.299	.337	.436	772	101	-2	5	3	0	.975	-15	*O-148(6-107-36)	-2.3
1927	Bos-A	45	155	11	38	9	3	0	24	5	12	.245	.278	.342	620	61	-9	1	0	0	.979	1	O-39(39-0-0)	-1.1
	Cle-A	32	103	13	26	5	0	0	13	6	4	.252	.300	.301	601	56	-7	0	0	0	.932	-1	O-31(0-31-0)	-0.9
	Phi-A	17	35	3	8	3	0	1	5	0	3	.229	.229	.400	629	57	-2	0	0	0	1.000	-5	O-14(9-2-3)	-0.8
	Yr	94	293	27	72	17	3	1	42	11	19	.246	.280	.334	615	59	-19	1	0	0	.959	-5	O-84(48-33-3)	-2.8
Total	11	1472	5507	787	1714	328	94	83	819	355	410	.311	.357	.450	807	111	65	86	54		.973	31	*O-1378C/1-47	1.4
■ BROOK JACOBY	Jacoby, Brook Wallace b: 11/23/59, Philadelphia, Pa. BR/TR, 5'11", 195 lbs. Deb: 9/13/81																							
1981	Atl-N	11	10	0	2	0	0	0	1	0	3	.200	.200	.200	400	13	-1	0	0	0	1.000	2	/3-3	0.1
1983	Atl-N	4	8	0	0	0	0	0	0	0	1	.000	.000	.000	0	-93	-2	0	0	0	1.000	-1	/3-2	-0.3
1984	Cle-A	126	439	64	116	19	3	7	40	32	73	.264	.319	.369	688	88	-7	3	2	-0	.951	-20	*3-126/S-1	-2.9
1985	Cle-A	161	606	72	166	26	3	20	87	48	120	.274	.327	.426	753	105	3	2	3	-1	.958	-7	*3-161/2-1	-0.7

YEAR	TM/L	G	AB	R	H	2B	3B	HR	RBI	BB	SO	AVG	OBP	SLG	OPS	OPS+	BR+	SB	CS	SBR	FA	FR	G/POS	TPR
1986	Cle-A★	158	583	83	168	30	4	17	80	56	137	.288	.351	.441	791	116	13	2	1	0	.941	-13	*3-158	-0.2
1987	Cle-A	155	540	73	162	26	4	32	69	75	73	.300	.388	.541	929	142	33	2	3	-1	.946	-7	*3-144/1-7,D-4	2.2
1988	Cle-A	152	552	59	133	25	0	9	49	48	101	.241	.303	.335	638	76	-17	2	3	-1	.975	1	*3-151	-1.7
1989	Cle-A	147	519	49	141	26	5	13	64	62	90	.272	.353	.416	769	114	10	2	5	-1	.955	-10	*3-144/D-3	-0.1
1990	Cle-A★	155	553	77	162	24	4	14	75	63	58	.293	.367	.427	794	122	17	1	4	-1	.981	-12	3-99,1-78	-0.1
1991	Cle-A	66	231	14	54	9	1	4	24	16	32	.234	.289	.333	622	71	-9	0	1	-0	.988	-0	1-55,3-15	-1.3
	Oak-A	56	188	14	40	12	0	0	20	11	22	.213	.260	.277	537	51	-13	2	0	0	.982	-8	3-52/1-3	-2.1
	Yr	122	419	28	94	21	1	4	44	27	54	.224	.276	.308	584	63	-22	2	1	0	.987	-8	3-67,1-58	-3.4
1992	Cle-A	120	291	30	76	7	0	4	36	28	54	.261	.328	.326	655	85	-5	0	3	-1	.957	3	*3-111,1-10	-0.4
Total	11	1311	4520	535	1220	204	24	120	545	439	764	.270	.337	.405	742	104	22	16	25	-5	.958	-71	*3-1166,1-153/D-7,2S	-7.5

■ **HARRY JACOBY** Jacoby, Harry b: Philadelphia, Pa. Deb: 5/2/1882 Career OF: (0-LF 0-CF 13-RF)

YEAR	TM/L	G	AB	R	H	2B	3B	HR	RBI	BB	SO	AVG	OBP	SLG	OPS	OPS+	BR+	SB	CS	SBR	FA	FR	G/POS	TPR
1882	Bal-a	31	121	17	21	1	1	1		7		.174	.219	.223	442	53	-5				.776	8	3-19,O-13(0-0-13)	0.3
1885	Bal-a	11	43	4	6	2	0	0	1	2		.140	.178	.186	364	15	-4				.896	-8	2-11	-1.1
Total	2	42	164	21	27	3	1	1	1	9		.165	.208	.213	422	43	-9				.776	-0	/3-19,O-13R,2-11	-0.8

■ **JOHN JAHA** Jaha, John Emil b: 5/27/66, Portland, Ore. BR/TR, 6'1", 205 lbs. Deb: 7/9/92 Career OF: (1-LF 0-CF 0-RF)

YEAR	TM/L	G	AB	R	H	2B	3B	HR	RBI	BB	SO	AVG	OBP	SLG	OPS	OPS+	BR+	SB	CS	SBR	FA	FR	G/POS	TPR
1992	Mil-A	47	133	17	30	3	1	2	10	12	30	.226	.299	.308	608	72	-5	10	0	2	1.000	-0	1-38/O-1(1-0-0),D-8	-0.5
1993	Mil-A	153	515	78	136	21	0	19	70	51	109	.264	.340	.416	755	103	2	13	9	-0	.992	9	*1-150/2-1,3-1	-0.3
1994	Mil-A	84	291	45	70	14	0	12	39	32	75	.241	.336	.412	749	88	-5	3	3	-0	.989	-1	1-73,D-11	-1.3
1995	Mil-A	88	316	59	99	20	2	20	65	36	66	.313	.390	.579	970	140	18	2	1	0	.997	3	1-81/D-6	1.3
1996	Mil-A	148	543	108	163	28	1	34	118	85	118	.300	.400	.543	943	130	26	3	1	0	.992	1	1-85,D-63	1.4
1997	Mil-A	46	162	25	40	7	0	11	26	25	40	.247	.358	.494	852	118	4	1	0	0	.992	-1	1-27,D-20	0.0
1998	Mil-N	73	216	29	45	6	1	7	38	49	66	.208	.369	.343	712	89	-2	1	3	-1	.994	-6	1-57/D-8	-1.3
1999	Oak-A★	142	457	93	126	23	0	35	111	101	129	.276	.416	.556	972	151	39	2	0	0	1.000	0	*D-130/1-8	2.9
2000	Oak-A	33	97	14	17	1	0	1	5	33	38	.175	.398	.216	615	63	-3	1	0	0	.000	0	D-30	-0.5
Total	9	814	2730	468	726	123	5	141	482	424	671	.266	.375	.470	844	117	75	36	17	2	.993	3	1-519,D-276/3-1,2O	1.7

■ **ART JAHN** Jahn, Arthur Charles b: 12/2/1895, Struble, Iowa d: 1/9/48, Little Rock, Ark. BR/TR, 6', 180 lbs. Deb: 7/2/25

YEAR	TM/L	G	AB	R	H	2B	3B	HR	RBI	BB	SO	AVG	OBP	SLG	OPS	OPS+	BR+	SB	CS	SBR	FA	FR	G/POS	TPR
1925	Chi-N	58	226	30	68	10	8	0	37	11	20	.301	.336	.416	752	90	-4	2	2	-0	.985	2	O-58(58-0-0)	-0.6
1928	NY-N	10	29	7	8	1	0	1	7	2	5	.276	.323	.414	736	91	-0	0			1.000	1	/O-8(7-1-0)	0.0
	Phi-N	36	94	8	21	4	0	0	11	4	11	.223	.270	.266	536	39	-8	0			.978	-4	O-29(2-0-27)	-1.4
	Yr	46	123	15	29	5	0	1	18	6	16	.236	.282	.301	583	51	-9	0			.985	-3	O-37(9-1-27)	-1.4
Total	2	104	349	45	97	15	8	1	55	17	36	.278	.317	.375	692	76	-13	2	2		.985	-1	/O-95(67-1-27)	-2.0

■ **ART JAMES** James, Arthur b: 8/2/52, Detroit, Mich. BL/TL, 6', 170 lbs. Deb: 4/10/75

YEAR	TM/L	G	AB	R	H	2B	3B	HR	RBI	BB	SO	AVG	OBP	SLG	OPS	OPS+	BR+	SB	CS	SBR	FA	FR	G/POS	TPR
1975	Det-A	11	40	2	9	2	0	0	1	1	3	.225	.244	.275	519	44	-3	1	2	-0	1.000	2	O-11(0-4-7)	-0.2

■ **BERT JAMES** James, Berton Hulon "Jesse" b: 7/7/1886, Coopertown, Tenn. d: 1/2/59, Adairville, Ky. BL/TR, 5'11", 175 lbs. Deb: 9/18/09

YEAR	TM/L	G	AB	R	H	2B	3B	HR	RBI	BB	SO	AVG	OBP	SLG	OPS	OPS+	BR+	SB	CS	SBR	FA	FR	G/POS	TPR
1909	StL-N	6	21	1	6	0	0	0	0	4		.286	.400	.286	686	120	1	1			.909	0	/O-6(0-0-6)	0.1

■ **CHARLIE JAMES** James, Charles Wesley b: 12/22/37, St.Louis, Mo. BR/TR, 6'1", 195 lbs. Deb: 8/2/60

YEAR	TM/L	G	AB	R	H	2B	3B	HR	RBI	BB	SO	AVG	OBP	SLG	OPS	OPS+	BR+	SB	CS	SBR	FA	FR	G/POS	TPR
1960	StL-N	43	50	5	9	1	0	2	5	1	12	.180	.196	.320	516	35	-4	0	0	0	.917	-10	O-37(23-7-9)	-1.6
1961	StL-N	108	349	43	89	19	2	4	44	15	59	.255	.292	.355	647	64	-18	2	2	-0	.962	-6	O-90(39-4-56)	-2.9
1962	StL-N	129	388	50	107	13	4	8	59	10	58	.276	.301	.392	693	77	-13	3	4	-1	.988	-10	*O-116(17-1-104)	-3.0
1963	StL-N	116	347	34	93	14	2	10	45	10	64	.268	.292	.406	699	91	-5	2	1	0	.994	1	*O-101(82-1-25)	-1.0
1964	*StL-N	88	233	24	52	9	1	5	17	11	58	.223	.261	.335	596	61	-12	0	0	0	.963	-3	O-60(46-0-14)	-1.9
1965	Cin-N	26	39	2	8	0	0	0	2	1	9	.205	.225	.205	430	21	-4	0	0	0	.909	-1	/O-7(3-0-4)	-0.5
Total	6	510	1406	158	358	56	9	29	172	48	260	.255	.284	.369	653	71	-55	7	7	-1	.976	-29	O-411(210-13-212)	-10.9

■ **CLEO JAMES** James, Cleo Joel b: 8/31/40, Clarksdale, Miss. BR/TR, 5'10", 176 lbs. Deb: 4/15/68

YEAR	TM/L	G	AB	R	H	2B	3B	HR	RBI	BB	SO	AVG	OBP	SLG	OPS	OPS+	BR+	SB	CS	SBR	FA	FR	G/POS	TPR
1968	LA-N	10	10	2	2	1	0	0	0	0	6	.200	.200	.300	500	52	-1	0	0	0	1.000	-0	/O-2(2-0-0)	-0.1
1970	Chi-N	100	176	33	37	7	2	3	14	17	24	.210	.298	.324	622	59	-10	5	0	1	1.000	-10	O-90(5-83-2)	-2.0
1971	Chi-N	54	150	25	43	7	0	2	13	10	16	.287	.355	.373	729	93	-1	6	2	1	.979	-1	O-48(1-35-14)/3-2	-0.3
1973	Chi-N	44	45	9	5	0	0	0	0	1	6	.111	.130	.111	242	-30	-8	5	0	1	.960	-4	O-22(14-8-1)	-1.2
Total	4	208	381	69	87	15	2	5	27	28	52	.228	.300	.318	618	63	-19	16	2	3	.988	-15	O-162(22-126-17)/3-2	-3.6

■ **DION JAMES** James, Dion b: 11/9/62, Philadelphia, Pa. BL/TL, 6'1", 170 lbs. Deb: 9/16/83 Career OF: (322-LF 242-CF 155-RF)

YEAR	TM/L	G	AB	R	H	2B	3B	HR	RBI	BB	SO	AVG	OBP	SLG	OPS	OPS+	BR+	SB	CS	SBR	FA	FR	G/POS	TPR
1983	Mil-A	11	20	1	2	0	0	0	1	2	2	.100	.182	.100	282	-22	-3	1	0	0	1.000	-3	/O-9(4-8-1),D-2	-0.7
1984	Mil-A	128	387	52	114	19	5	1	30	32	41	.295	.353	.377	730	106	4	10	10	-1	.989	-1	*O-118(2-30-93)	-0.3
1985	Mil-A	18	49	5	11	1	0	0	3	6	6	.224	.309	.245	554	54	-3	0	0	0	1.000	-2	O-11(0-11-0)/D-3	-0.5
1987	Atl-N	134	494	80	154	37	6	10	61	70	63	.312	.399	.472	871	124	19	10	8	-1	**.996**	1	*O-126(29-99-0)	1.7
1988	Atl-N	132	386	46	99	17	5	3	30	58	59	.256	.355	.350	705	98	1	9	9	-1	.987	-12	*O-120(86-49-3)	-1.6
1989	Atl-N	63	170	15	44	7	0	1	11	25	23	.259	.357	.318	675	92	-1	1	3	-1	1.000	-0	O-46(26-1-23)/1-8	-0.4
	Cle-A	71	245	26	75	11	0	4	29	24	26	.306	.368	.400	768	114	5	1	4	-1	.976	0	O-37L,D-27/1-2	0.2
1990	Cle-A	87	248	28	68	15	2	1	22	27	23	.274	.348	.363	711	99	0	5	3	0	.996	-5	1-35,O-33L,D-10	-0.8
1992	NY-A	67	145	24	38	8	0	3	17	22	15	.262	.363	.379	742	109	2	1	0	0	1.000	-8	O-46(8-12-27)/D-5	-0.7
1993	NY-A	115	343	62	114	21	2	7	36	31	31	.332	.391	.466	857	134	17	0	0	0	.966	-14	*O-103L/1-1,D-1	0.0
1995	*NY-A	85	209	22	60	6	1	2	26	20	16	.287	.349	.354	703	85	-4	4	1	1	.968	-5	O-29(23-0-6),D-27/1-6	-1.1
1996	NY-A	6	12	1	2	0	0	0	0	1	2	.167	.231	.167	397	3	-2	1	0	0	1.000	-1	/O-4(3-0-1),D-1	-0.2
Total	11	917	2708	362	781	142	21	32	266	318	307	.288	.365	.392	757	107	35	43	38	-4	.986	-51	O-682L/D-76,1-52	-4.4

■ **CHRIS JAMES** James, Donald Chris b: 10/4/62, Rusk, Tex. BR/TR, 6'1", 190 lbs. Deb: 4/23/86 Career OF: (322-LF 51-CF 229-RF)

YEAR	TM/L	G	AB	R	H	2B	3B	HR	RBI	BB	SO	AVG	OBP	SLG	OPS	OPS+	BR+	SB	CS	SBR	FA	FR	G/POS	TPR
1986	Phi-N	16	46	5	13	3	0	1	5	1	13	.283	.298	.413	711	91	-1	0	0	0	1.000	-1	O-11(4-7-0)	-0.2
1987	Phi-N	115	358	48	105	20	6	17	54	27	67	.293	.346	.525	871	123	11	3	1	0	.990	-2	*O-108(96-16-5)	0.6
1988	Phi-N	150	566	57	137	24	1	19	66	31	73	.242	.285	.389	674	90	-9	7	4	0	.989	-4	*O-116(8-27-101)/3-31	-1.7
1989	Phi-N	45	179	14	37	4	0	2	19	4	23	.207	.224	.263	487	39	-14	3	1	0	.985	-1	O-37(37-0-0),3-11	-1.8
	SD-N	87	303	41	80	13	2	11	46	22	45	.264	.316	.429	745	111	3	2	1	0	.987	-0	O-79(50-0-29)/3-6	0.1
	Yr	132	482	55	117	17	2	13	65	26	68	.243	.283	.367	650	84	-11	5	2	0	.986	-1	*O-116(87-0-29),3-17	-1.7
1990	Cle-A	140	528	62	158	32	4	12	70	31	71	.299	.343	.443	786	119	12	4	3	-0	1.000	0	*D-124,O-14(12-1-1)	0.8
1991	Cle-A	115	437	31	104	16	2	5	41	18	61	.238	.275	.318	593	63	-22	3	4	-1	1.000	0	D-60,O-39L,1-15	-2.7
1992	SF-N	111	248	25	60	10	4	5	32	14	45	.242	.288	.375	663	91	-4	2	3	-1	.974	1	O-62(60-0-2)	-0.6
1993	Hou-N	65	129	19	33	10	1	6	19	15	34	.256	.338	.488	826	122	4	2	0	0	.958	3	O-34(16-0-18)	0.6
	Tex-A	8	31	5	11	1	0	3	7	3	6	.355	.412	.677	1089	195	4	0	0	0	1.000	-1	/O-7(4-0-4)	0.3
1994	Tex-A	52	133	28	34	8	4	7	19	20	38	.256	.365	.534	899	128	6	0	0	0	1.000	-6	O-48(1-0-47)	-0.2
1995	KC-A	26	58	6	18	3	0	2	7	6	10	.310	.385	.466	850	118	2	1	0	0	1.000	-0	D-14/O-5(5-0-0)	0.1
	Bos-A	16	24	2	4	1	0	0	1	1	4	.167	.200	.208	408	6	-3	0	0	0	1.000	-0	/O-8(4-0-4),D-6	-0.4
	Yr	42	82	8	22	4	0	2	8	7	14	.268	.333	.390	724	86	-2	1	0	0	1.000	-1	D-20,O-13(9-0-4)	-0.3
Total	10	946	3040	343	794	145	24	90	386	193	490	.261	.310	.413	723	99	-12	27	17	-0	.987	-12	O-568L,D-204/3-48,1	-5.1

■ **SKIP JAMES** James, Philip Robert b: 10/21/49, Elmhurst, Ill. BL/TL, 6', 185 lbs. Deb: 9/12/77

YEAR	TM/L	G	AB	R	H	2B	3B	HR	RBI	BB	SO	AVG	OBP	SLG	OPS	OPS+	BR+	SB	CS	SBR	FA	FR	G/POS	TPR
1977	SF-N	10	15	3	4	1	0	0	3	2	3	.267	.353	.333	686	86	-0	0	0	0	1.000	1	/1-9	0.0
1978	SF-N	41	21	5	2	1	0	0	3	4	5	.095	.240	.143	383	10	-2	1	0	0	1.000	2	1-27	-0.1
Total	2	51	36	8	6	2	0	0	6	6	8	.167	.286	.222	508	42	-3	1	0	0	1.000	3	/1-36	-0.1

■ **BERNIE JAMES** James, Robert Byrne b: 9/2/05, Angleton, Tex. d: 8/1/94, San Antonio, Tex. BB/TR, 5'9.5", 150 lbs. Deb: 5/6/29 Career OF: (0-LF 1-CF 0-RF)

YEAR	TM/L	G	AB	R	H	2B	3B	HR	RBI	BB	SO	AVG	OBP	SLG	OPS	OPS+	BR+	SB	CS	SBR	FA	FR	G/POS	TPR
1929	Bos-N	46	101	12	31	3	2	0	9	9	13	.307	.369	.376	746	89	-1	3			.940	-9	2-32/O-1(0-1-0)	-0.9
1930	Bos-N	8	11	1	2	1	0	0	1	0	1	.182	.182	.273	455	8	-2	0			.941	0	/2-7	-0.1
1933	NY-N	60	125	22	28	2	1	1	10	8	12	.224	.271	.280	551	58	-7	5			.948	2	2-26/S-6,3-5	-0.3
Total	3	114	237	35	61	6	3	1	20	17	26	.257	.310	.321	630	70	-10	8			.944	-7	/2-65,S-6,3-5,O-1C	-1.3

YEAR	TM/L	G	AB	R	H	2B	3B	HR	RBI	BB	SO	AVG	OBP	SLG	OPS	OPS+	BR+	SB	CS	SBR	FA	FR	G/POS	TPR
■ **CHARLIE JAMIESON**	Jamieson, Charles Devine "Cuckoo" b: 2/7/1893, Paterson, N.J. d: 10/27/69, Paterson, N.J. BL/TL, 5'8.5", 165 lbs. Deb: 9/20/15 Career OF: (1408-LF 34-CF 203-RF)																							
1915	Was-A	17	68	9	19	3	2	0	7	6	9	.279	.338	.382	720	113	1	0			1.000	4	O-17(17-0-0)	0.4
1916	Was-A	64	145	16	36	4	0	0	13	18	18	.248	.331	.276	607	83	-2	5			.913	-4	O-41(24-2-15)/1-4,P-1	-0.9
1917	Was-A	20	35	4	6	2	0	0	2	6	5	.171	.293	.229	521	60	-2	0			.875	-2	/O-9(9-0-0),P-1	-0.4
	Phi-A	85	345	41	92	6	2	0	27	37	36	.267	.341	.296	637	96	-1	8			.937	-2	O-83(0-0-83)	-0.8
	Yr	105	380	45	98	8	2	0	29	43	41	.258	.336	.289	626	92	-2	8			.930	-4	O-92(9-0-83)/P-1	-1.2
1918	Phi-A	110	416	50	84	11	2	0	11	54	30	.202	.297	.238	535	61	-18	11			.970	-0	*O-102(0-1-101)/P-5	-2.6
1919	Cle-A	26	17	3	6	2	1	0	2	0	2	.353	.353	.588	941	153	1	2			.750	-1	/P-4,O-3(0-2-1)	0.0
1920	*Cle-A	108	370	69	118	17	7	1	40	41	26	.319	.388	.411	799	108	5	2	9	-3	.966	-2	O-98(93-5-0)/1-4	-0.4
1921	Cle-A	140	536	94	166	33	10	1	46	67	27	.310	.387	.414	802	103	4	8	4	0	.974	-6	*O-137(125-19-0)	-1.1
1922	Cle-A	145	567	87	183	29	11	3	57	54	22	.323	.388	.429	816	112	11	15	9	0	.978	-2	*O-144(141-2-1)/P-2	-0.2
1923	Cle-A	152	644	130	**222**	36	12	2	51	80	37	.345	.422	.447	869	129	30	18	14	-1	.974	7	*O-152(152-0-0)	2.3
1924	Cle-A	143	594	98	213	34	8	3	54	47	15	.359	.407	.458	865	121	19	21	12	0	.974	4	*O-139(139-0-0)	1.2
1925	Cle-A	138	557	109	165	24	5	4	42	72	26	.296	.380	.379	759	92	-5	14	18	-3	.955	7	*O-135(135-0-0)	-1.1
1926	Cle-A	143	555	89	166	33	7	2	45	53	22	.299	.361	.395	756	96	-3	9	7	-0	.960	-0	*O-143(143-0-0)	-1.5
1927	Cle-A	127	489	73	151	23	6	0	36	64	14	.309	.394	.380	775	101	4	7	9	-2	.969	5	*O-127(127-0-0)	-0.3
1928	Cle-A	112	433	63	133	18	4	1	37	56	20	.307	.388	.374	762	100	2	3	12	-4	.984	20	*O-111(111-0-0)	0.9
1929	Cle-A	102	364	56	106	22	1	0	26	50	12	.291	.378	.357	735	87	-5	2	13	-4	.980	-2	O-93(93-0-0)	-1.7
1930	Cle-A	103	366	64	110	22	1	1	52	36	20	.301	.368	.374	742	85	-7	5	2	0	.955	-5	O-95(93-2-0)	-1.7
1931	Cle-A	28	43	7	13	2	1	0	4	5	1	.302	.375	.395	770	97	-0	1	1	-0	.833	-2	/O-7(6-1-0)	-0.2
1932	Cle-A	16	16	0	1	1	0	0	0	2	3	.063	.211	.125	336	-10	-3	0	0	0	1.000	1	/O-2(0-0-2)	-0.2
Total	18	1779	6560	1062	1990	322	80	18	552	748	345	.303	.378	.385	763	101	32	131	110		.967	19	*O-1638L/P-13,1-8	-8.3
■ **VIC JANOWICZ**	Janowicz, Victor Felix b: 2/26/30, Elyria, Ohio d: 2/27/96, Columbus, Ohio BR/TR, 5'9", 185 lbs. Deb: 5/31/53																							
1953	Pit-N	42	123	10	31	3	1	2	8	5	31	.252	.287	.341	628	63	-7	0	1	-0	.937	-12	C-35	-1.7
1954	Pit-N	41	73	10	11	3	0	0	2	7	23	.151	.235	.192	426	13	-9	0	0	0	.904	1	3-18/O-1(1-0-0)	-0.9
Total	2	83	196	20	42	6	1	2	10	12	54	.214	.267	.286	552	44	-16	0	1	-0	.937	-11	/C-35,3-18,O-1(1-0-0)	-2.6
■ **RAY JANSEN**	Jansen, Raymond William b: 1/16/1889, St.Louis, Mo. d: 3/19/34, St.Louis, Mo. BR/TR, 5'11", 155 lbs. Deb: 9/30/10																							
1910	StL-A	1	5	0	4	0	0	0	0	0		.800	.800	.800	1600	428	2	0			.700	0	/3-1	0.2
■ **HEINIE JANTZEN**	Jantzen, Walter C. b: 4/9/1890, Chicago, Ill. d: 4/1/48, Hines, Ill. BR/TR, 5'11.5", 170 lbs. Deb: 6/29/12																							
1912	StL-A	31	119	10	22	0	1	1	8	4		.185	.218	.227	445	28	-11	3			1.000	3	O-31(0-0-31)	-1.0
■ **HAL JANVRIN**	Janvrin, Harold Chandler "Childe Harold" b: 8/27/1892, Haverhill, Mass. d: 3/1/62, Boston, Mass. BR/TR, 5'11.5", 168 lbs. Deb: 7/9/11 Career OF: (17-LF 4-CF 1-RF)																							
1911	Bos-A	9	27	2	4	1	0	0	1	3		.148	.258	.185	443	25	-3	0			.733	-2	/3-5,1-4	-0.5
1913	Bos-A	87	276	18	57	5	1	3	25	23	27	.207	.272	.264	537	56	-16	17			.923	-10	S-48,3-19/2-8,1-6	-2.4
1914	Bos-A	145	492	65	117	18	6	1	51	38	50	.238	.296	.305	601	81	-12	29	20	-1	.919	-22	2-59,1-57,S-20,/3-6	-3.8
1915	*Bos-A	99	316	41	85	9	1	0	37	14	27	.269	.317	.304	620	88	-5	8	14	-3	.917	-20	S-64,3-20/2-8	-2.5
1916	*Bos-A	117	310	32	69	11	4	0	26	32	32	.223	.299	.284	583	75	-9	6			.921	-19	S-59,2-39/1-4,3-4	-2.7
1917	Bos-A	55	127	21	25	3	0	0	8	11	13	.197	.266	.220	487	49	-8	2			.940	1	2-38,S-10/1-1	-0.6
1919	Was-A	61	208	17	37	4	1	1	13	19	17	.178	.253	.221	474	34	-18	8			.927	-27	2-56/S-2	-4.8
	StL-N	7	14	1	3	1	0	0	1	2	2	.214	.313	.286	598	86	-0	0			1.000	-2	/2-2,S-1,3-1	-0.2
1920	StL-N	87	270	33	74	8	4	1	28	17	19	.274	.317	.344	662	93	-3	5	6	-1	.926	-2	S-27,1-25,O-20L,/2	-0.7
1921	StL-N	18	32	5	9	1	0	0	5	1	0	.281	.303	.313	616	65	-2	1	0	0	.968	0	/1-9,2-1	-0.2
	Bro-N	44	92	8	18	4	0	0	14	7	6	.196	.253	.239	492	30	-9	3	1	0	.922	-4	S-17,2-10/1-8,3O	-1.2
	Yr	62	124	13	27	5	0	0	19	8	6	.218	.265	.258	523	38	-11	4	1	1	.922	-3	1-17,S-17,2-11,/3O	-1.4
1922	Bro-N	30	57	7	17	3	1	0	1	4	4	.298	.344	.386	730	89	-1	0	0	0	.889	-4	2-15/S-4,3-2,1-1,O	-0.4
Total	10	759	2221	250	515	68	18	6	210	171	197	.232	.292	.287	579	70	-85	79	41		.907	-110	S-252,2-242,1/3O	-20.0
■ **ROY JARVIS**	Jarvis, Leroy Gilbert b: 6/27/26, Shawnee, Okla. d: 1/13/90, Oklahoma City, Okla. BR/TR, 5'9", 160 lbs. Deb: 4/30/44																							
1944	Bro-N	1	1	0	0	0	0	0	0	0	1	.000	.000	.000	0	-99	-0	0			1.000	-0	/C-1	0.0
1946	Pit-N	2	4	0	1	0	0	0	0	1	1	.250	.400	.250	650	84	-0	0			.800	-0	/C-1	0.0
1947	Pit-N	18	45	4	7	1	0	1	4	6	5	.156	.255	.244	499	32	-4	0			.967	-0	C-15	-0.4
Total	3	21	50	4	8	1	0	1	4	7	7	.160	.263	.240	503	34	-5	0			.955	-1	/C-17	-0.4
■ **PAUL JATA**	Jata, Paul b: 9/4/49, Astoria, N.Y. BR/TR, 6'1", 190 lbs. Deb: 4/19/72																							
1972	Det-A	32	74	8	17	2	0	0	3	7	14	.230	.296	.257	553	64	-3	0	1	-0	.991	-1	1-12,O-10(5-0-5)/C-1	-0.7
■ **AL JAVIER**	Javier, Ignacio Alfredo (b: Ignacio Alfredo Wilkes (Javier)) b: 2/4/54, San Pedro De Macoris, D.R. BR/TR, 5'11", 170 lbs. Deb: 9/9/76																							
1976	Hou-N	8	24	1	5	0	0	0	0	2	5	.208	.269	.208	478	41	-2	0	0	0	1.000	-2	/O-7(4-0-4)	-0.4
■ **JULIAN JAVIER**	Javier, Manuel Julian (Liranzo) b: 8/9/36, San Francisco De Macoris, D.R. BR/TR, 6'1", 175 lbs. Deb: 5/28/60 F																							
1960	StL-N	119	451	55	107	19	8	4	21	21	72	.237	.273	.341	614	62	-24	19	4	3	.962	5	*2-119	-0.8
1961	StL-N	113	445	58	124	14	3	2	41	30	51	.279	.327	.337	664	70	-18	11	4	1	.966	-0	*2-113	-0.8
1962	StL-N	155	598	97	157	25	5	7	39	47	73	.263	.317	.356	674	73	-22	26	9	3	.977	1	*2-151/S-4	-0.6
1963	StL-N★	161	609	82	160	27	9	9	46	24	86	.263	.297	.381	678	86	-11	18	10	0	.969	-14	*2-161	-1.2
1964	*StL-N	155	535	66	129	19	5	12	65	30	82	.241	.283	.363	645	74	-18	9	7	-0	.966	-7	*2-154	-1.4
1965	StL-N	77	229	34	52	6	4	2	23	8	44	.227	.262	.314	577	56	-13	5	5	-1	.975	-6	2-69	-1.5
1966	StL-N	147	460	52	105	13	5	7	31	26	63	.228	.271	.324	595	64	-22	11	5	1	.981	2	*2-145	-0.9
1967	*StL-N	140	520	68	146	16	3	14	64	25	92	.281	.315	.404	719	106	2	6	7	-1	.965	-19	*2-138	-0.7
1968	*StL-N★	139	519	54	135	25	4	4	52	24	61	.260	.294	.347	641	93	-5	10	3	1	.976	-24	*2-139	-1.9
1969	StL-N	143	493	59	139	28	2	10	42	40	74	.282	.337	.408	745	107	4	8	4	0	.967	-18	*2-141	-0.4
1970	StL-N	139	513	62	129	16	3	2	42	24	70	.251	.286	.306	592	58	-31	6	4	-0	.980	13	*2-137	-0.9
1971	StL-N	90	259	32	67	6	4	3	28	9	33	.259	.289	.347	636	76	-8	5	1	1	.978	2	2-80/3-1	-0.2
1972	*Cin-N	44	91	3	19	2	0	2	12	6	11	.209	.258	.297	554	61	-5	1	0	0	.896	-3	3-19/2-5,1-1	-0.8
Total	13	1622	5722	722	1469	216	55	78	506	314	812	.257	.298	.355	652	78	-172	135	63	8	.972	-68	*2-1552/3-20,S-4,1	-12.1
■ **STAN JAVIER**	Javier, Stanley Julian Antonio (De Javier) b: 1/9/64, San Francisco De Macoris, D.R. BB/TR, 6', 185 lbs. Deb: 4/15/84 F Career OF: (403-LF 678-CF 481-RF)																							
1984	NY-A	7	7	1	1	0	0	0	0	0	1	.143	.143	.143	286	-22	-1	0	0	0	1.000	-2	/O-5(0-3-3)	-0.3
1986	Oak-A	59	114	13	23	8	0	0	8	16	27	.202	.305	.272	577	63	-5	8	0	2	1.000	-1	O-51(3-49-0)/D-2	-0.5
1987	Oak-A	81	151	22	28	3	1	2	9	19	33	.185	.276	.258	535	46	-12	3	2	-0	.983	-9	O-71(8-52-15)/1-6,D-1	-2.1
1988	*Oak-A	125	397	49	102	13	3	2	35	32	63	.257	.316	.320	635	81	-10	20	1	4	.980	-13	*O-115L/1-4,D-2	-2.1
1989	*Oak-A	112	310	42	77	12	3	1	28	31	45	.248	.319	.316	635	82	-7	12	2	2	.991	-8	*O-107R/1-1,2-1	-1.5
1990	Oak-A	19	33	4	8	0	2	0	3	3	6	.242	.306	.364	669	90	-0	0	0	0	1.000	-2	O-13(4-4-5)/D-2	-0.3
	LA-N	104	276	56	84	9	4	3	24	37	44	.304	.387	.399	785	120	9	15	7	1	1.000	2	O-87(9-70-12)	1.1
1991	LA-N	121	176	21	36	5	3	1	11	16	36	.205	.271	.284	555	57	-10	7	1	1	.986	-14	O-69(49-7-18)/1-2	-2.5
1992	LA-N	56	58	6	11	3	0	1	5	6	11	.190	.277	.293	570	63	-3	1	2	-0	1.000	-7	O-27(15-2-11)	-1.2
	Phi-N	74	276	36	72	14	1	0	24	31	43	.261	.340	.319	659	88	-3	17	1	3	.986	13	O-74(27-49-1)	1.2
	Yr	130	334	42	83	17	1	1	29	37	54	.249	.329	.314	643	84	-6	18	3	3	.987	5	*O-101(42-51-12)	0.0
1993	Cal-A	92	237	33	69	10	4	3	28	27	33	.291	.366	.405	771	104	2	12	2	2	.981	-11	O-64L,1-12/2-2,D-1	-0.9
1994	Oak-A	109	419	75	114	23	0	10	44	49	76	.272	.351	.399	750	101	2	24	7	3	.986	0	*O-108C/1-1,3-1	0.5
1995	Oak-A	130	442	81	123	20	2	8	56	49	63	.278	.356	.387	742	98	0	36	5	6	**1.000**	7	*O-124(32-101-1)/3-1	1.2
1996	SF-N	71	274	44	74	25	0	2	22	25	51	.270	.336	.383	719	93	-3	14	2	2	.984	7	O-71(0-53-18)	0.6
1997	*SF-N	142	440	69	126	16	4	8	50	56	70	.286	.373	.395	769	104	4	25	3	4	.977	-6	*O-130(5-46-94)/1-3	-0.1
1998	SF-N	135	417	63	121	13	5	4	49	65	63	.290	.387	.374	761	108	7	21	5	3	.986	-9	*O-121(6-29-95)	-0.2
1999	SF-N	112	333	49	92	15	1	3	30	29	55	.276	.336	.354	690	81	-10	13	6	1	.976	-2	O-94(51-3-42)	-1.3
	*Hou-N	20	64	12	21	4	1	0	4	9	8	.328	.411	.422	833	113	2	3	1	0	1.000	-2	O-18(7-6-10)/D-1	0.0
	Yr	132	397	61	113	19	2	3	34	38	63	.285	.349	.365	714	86	-8	16	7	1	.980	-3	*O-112(58-9-52)/D-1	-1.3

YEAR	TM/L	G	AB	R	H	2B	3B	HR	RBI	BB	SO	AVG	OBP	SLG	OPS	OPS+	BR+	SB	CS	SBR	FA	FR	G/POS	TPR
2000	*Sea-A	105	342	61	94	18	5	5	40	42	64	.275	.354	.401	755	93	-3	4	3	-0	.993	-8	O-88L/1-3,D-4	-1.3
Total	16	1674	4766	737	1276	211	39	53	470	542	792	.268	.345	.362	707	92	-41	235	50	34	.988	-65	*O-1437C/1-32,D23	-9.7

■ TEX JEANES Jeanes, Ernest Lee b: 12/19/1900, Maypearl, Tex. d: 4/5/73, Longview, Tex. BR/TR, 6', 176 lbs. Deb: 4/20/21

YEAR	TM/L	G	AB	R	H	2B	3B	HR	RBI	BB	SO	AVG	OBP	SLG	OPS	OPS+	BR+	SB	CS	SBR	FA	FR	G/POS	TPR
1921	Cle-A	5	3	2	2	1	0	0	4	1	0	.667	.750	1.000	1750	338	1	0	0	0	1.000	-1	/O-5(1-2-1)	0.0
1922	Cle-A	1	1	0	0	0	0	0	0	1	0	.000	.500	.000	500	39	0	0	0	0	.000	-1	/P-1,O-1(1-0-0)	0.0
1925	Was-A	15	19	2	5	1	0	1	4	3	2	.263	.364	.474	837	113	0	1	0	0	1.000	-5	O-13(1-10-2)	-0.5
1926	Was-A	21	30	6	7	2	0	0	3	0	3	.233	.233	.300	533	39	-3	0	0	0	1.000	-3	O-14(3-10-1)	-0.6
1927	NY-N	11	20	5	6	0	0	0	0	2	2	.300	.364	.300	664	79	-0	0			1.000	1	/O-6(4-0-2),P-1	0.0
Total	5	53	73	15	20	4	0	1	11	7	7	.274	.338	.370	707	85	-2	1	0		1.000	-9	/O-39(10-22-6),P-2	-1.1

■ HAL JEFFCOAT Jeffcoat, Harold Bentley b: 9/6/24, W.Columbia, S.C. BR/TR, 5'10.5", 185 lbs. Deb: 4/20/48 F Career OF: (29-LF 435-CF 97-RF)

YEAR	TM/L	G	AB	R	H	2B	3B	HR	RBI	BB	SO	AVG	OBP	SLG	OPS	OPS+	BR+	SB	CS	SBR	FA	FR	G/POS	TPR
1948	Chi-N	134	473	53	132	16	4	4	42	24	68	.279	.315	.355	670	85	-11	8			.976	9	*O-119(0-119-0)	-0.6
1949	Chi-N	108	363	43	89	18	6	2	26	20	48	.245	.286	.344	631	70	-16	12			.963	7	*O-101(1-68-32)	-1.2
1950	Chi-N	66	179	21	42	13	1	2	18	6	23	.235	.259	.352	611	60	-11	7			.967	-3	O-53(12-11-31)	-1.6
1951	Chi-N	113	278	44	76	20	2	4	27	16	23	.273	.315	.403	718	90	-4	8	4	0	.989	-2	O-87(14-39-34)	-0.8
1952	Chi-N	102	297	29	65	17	2	4	30	15	40	.219	.259	.330	589	61	-16	7	2	1	.996	3	O-95(0-95-0)	-1.5
1953	Chi-N	106	183	22	43	3	1	4	22	21	26	.235	.314	.328	642	66	-9	5	0	1	.973	-17	*O-100(2-99-0)	-2.7
1954	Chi-N	56	31	13	8	2	1	1	6	1	7	.258	.281	.484	765	94	-0	2	0	0	.889	-1	P-43/O-3(0-3-0)	-0.1
1955	Chi-N	52	23	3	4	0	0	1	1	2	9	.174	.240	.304	544	43	-2	0	0	0	.903	1	P-50	0.0
1956	Cin-N	49	54	5	8	2	0	0	5	3	20	.148	.193	.185	378	2	-7	0	1	-0	.969	3	P-38	0.0
1957	Cin-N	53	69	13	14	3	1	4	11	5	20	.203	.267	.449	716	82	-2	0	0	0	.958	-1	P-37	0.0
1958	Cin-N	50	9	2	5	0	0	0	0	1	2	.556	.600	.556	1156	198	1	0	0	0	1.000	2	P-49/O-1(0-1-0)	0.0
1959	Cin-N	17	1	1	1	1	0	0	0	0	0	1.000	1.000	2.000	3000	655	1	0	0	0	1.000	0	P-17	0.0
	StL-N	12	3	0	0	0	0	0	0	0	3	.000	.000	.000	0	-94	-1	0	0	0	1.000	0	P-11	0.0
	Yr	29	4	1	1	1	0	0	0	0	3	.250	.250	.500	750	90	-0	0	0	0	1.000	0	P-28	0.0
Total	12	918	1963	249	487	95	18	26	188	114	289	.248	.291	.355	646	73	-78	49	7		.978	0	O-559C,P-245	-8.5

■ GREGG JEFFERIES Jefferies, Gregory Scott b: 8/1/67, Burlingame, Cal. BB/TR, 5'10", 185 lbs. Deb: 9/6/87 Career OF: (369-LF 0-CF 0-RF)

YEAR	TM/L	G	AB	R	H	2B	3B	HR	RBI	BB	SO	AVG	OBP	SLG	OPS	OPS+	BR+	SB	CS	SBR	FA	FR	G/POS	TPR
1987	NY-N	6	6	0	3	1	0	0	2	0	0	.500	.500	.667	1167	217	1	0	0	0	.000	0	/H	0.1
1988	*NY-N	29	109	19	35	8	2	6	17	8	10	.321	.368	.596	964	181	11	5	1	1	.979	-3	3-20,2-10	0.9
1989	NY-N	141	508	72	131	28	2	12	56	39	46	.258	.317	.392	709	107	3	21	6	3	.975	-31	*2-123,3-20	-2.4
1990	NY-N	153	604	96	171	**40**	3	15	68	46	40	.283	.339	.434	773	111	8	11	2	2	.976	-9	*2-118,3-34	0.4
1991	NY-N	136	486	59	132	19	2	9	62	47	38	.272	.338	.374	713	101	1	26	5	4	.982	-16	2-77,3-51	-0.9
1992	KC-A	152	604	66	172	36	3	10	75	43	29	.285	.333	.404	737	103	2	19	9	1	.939	-2	*3-146/2-1,D-1	0.1
1993	StL-N★	142	544	89	186	24	3	16	83	62	32	.342	.411	.485	896	142	34	46	9	7	.993	-11	*1-140/2-1	1.6
1994	StL-N★	103	397	52	129	27	1	12	55	45	26	.325	.395	.489	884	131	19	12	5	1	.993	-9	*1-102	0.1
1995	Phi-N	114	480	69	147	31	2	11	56	35	26	.306	.353	.448	801	109	6	9	5	0	.994	-2	1-59,O-55(55-0-0)	-0.3
1996	Phi-N	104	404	59	118	17	3	7	51	36	21	.292	.351	.401	752	97	-1	20	6	2	.998	6	1-53,O-51(51-0-0)	0.0
1997	Phi-N	130	476	68	122	25	3	11	48	53	27	.256	.333	.391	724	89	-8	12	6	1	.986	5	*O-124(124-0-0)	-0.6
1998	Phi-N	125	483	65	142	22	3	8	48	29	27	.294	.335	.402	737	91	-6	11	3	1	.994	-1	*O-121(121-0-0)	-0.9
	Ana-A	19	72	7	25	6	0	1	10	0	5	.347	.347	.472	819	110	1	1	0	0	1.000	-1	O-15(15-0-0)/1-3	0.0
1999	Det-A	70	205	22	41	8	0	6	18	13	11	.200	.261	.327	588	49	-16	3	4	-1	1.000	-2	D-45/1-3,2-2,O-2L	-2.1
2000	Det-A	41	142	18	39	8	0	2	14	16	10	.275	.348	.373	721	85	-3	0	2	-1	.994	-3	1-20,2-14/3-6,OD	-0.7
Total	14	1465	5520	761	1593	300	27	126	663	472	348	.289	.347	.421	768	107	51	196	63	21	.994	-79	1-380,O-369L,23/D	-4.7

■ REGGIE JEFFERSON Jefferson, Reginald Jirod b: 9/25/68, Tallahassee, Fla. BL/TL (BB 1991-93), 6'4", 215 lbs. Deb: 5/18/91 Career OF: (49-LF 0-CF 0-RF)

YEAR	TM/L	G	AB	R	H	2B	3B	HR	RBI	BB	SO	AVG	OBP	SLG	OPS	OPS+	BR+	SB	CS	SBR	FA	FR	G/POS	TPR
1991	Cin-N	5	7	1	1	0	0	1	1	1	2	.143	.250	.571	821	120	0	0	0	0	1.000	0	/1-2	0.0
	Cle-A	26	101	10	20	3	0	2	12	3	22	.198	.221	.287	508	39	-8	0	0	0	.993	2	1-26	-0.8
1992	Cle-A	24	89	8	30	6	2	1	6	1	17	.337	.352	.483	835	134	4	0	0	0	.993	1	1-15/D-7	0.3
1993	Cle-A	113	366	35	91	11	2	10	34	28	78	.249	.311	.372	682	83	-9	1	3	-1	.976	-0	D-88,1-15	-1.6
1994	Sea-A	63	162	24	53	11	0	8	32	17	32	.327	.394	.543	938	136	9	0	0	0	.981	1	D-32,1-13/O-2(2-0-0)	0.6
1995	*Bos-A	46	121	21	35	8	0	5	26	9	24	.289	.338	.479	818	106	1	0	0	0	1.000	0	D-32/1-7,O-2(2-0-0)	-0.1
1996	Bos-A	122	386	67	134	30	4	19	74	25	89	.347	.391	.593	985	141	23	0	0	0	.969	-3	D-49,O-45L,1-16	1.4
1997	Bos-A	136	489	74	156	33	1	13	67	24	93	.319	.360	.470	830	112	8	1	2	-0	.975	-1	*D-119,1-12	-0.1
1998	Bos-A	62	196	24	60	16	1	8	31	21	40	.306	.376	.520	897	127	8	0	0	0	.953	-0	D-48/1-7	0.4
1999	Bos-A	83	206	21	57	13	1	5	17	17	54	.277	.338	.422	760	90	-3	0	0	0	1.000	0	D-58/1-2	-0.6
Total	9	680	2123	285	637	131	11	72	300	146	451	.300	.351	.474	825	111	31	2	5	-1	.986	-0	D-433,1-115/O-49L	-0.5

■ STAN JEFFERSON Jefferson, Stanley b: 12/4/62, New York, N.Y. BB/TR, 5'11", 175 lbs. Deb: 9/7/86

YEAR	TM/L	G	AB	R	H	2B	3B	HR	RBI	BB	SO	AVG	OBP	SLG	OPS	OPS+	BR+	SB	CS	SBR	FA	FR	G/POS	TPR
1986	NY-N	14	24	6	5	1	0	1	3	2	8	.208	.296	.375	671	86	-0	0	0	0	1.000	-1	/O-7(1-7-0)	-0.1
1987	SD-N	116	422	59	97	8	7	8	29	39	92	.230	.298	.339	637	71	-18	34	11	4	.987	-10	*O-107(61-83-0)	-2.7
1988	SD-N	49	111	16	16	1	2	1	4	9	22	.144	.215	.216	431	25	-11	5	1	1	1.000	-4	O-38(10-27-0)	-1.6
1989	NY-A	10	12	1	1	0	0	0	1	0	4	.083	.083	.083	167	-54	-2	1	1	-0	1.000	-3	/O-7(0-2-6),D-1	-0.6
	Bal-A	35	127	19	33	7	0	4	20	4	22	.260	.288	.409	697	97	-1	9	3	1	.988	2	O-32(1-8-26)/D-2	0.1
	Yr	45	139	20	34	7	0	4	21	4	26	.245	.271	.381	652	84	-3	10	4	1	.988	-2	O-39(1-10-32)/D-3	-0.5
1990	Bal-A	10	19	1	0	0	0	0	0	2	8	.000	.095	.000	95	-74	-4	1	0	0	1.000	-2	/O-5(0-3-5),D-1	-0.6
	Cle-A	49	98	21	27	8	0	2	10	8	18	.276	.343	.418	761	112	2	8	4	0	.985	0	O-34(23-11-1)/D-5	0.2
	Yr	59	117	22	27	8	0	2	10	10	26	.231	.302	.350	653	83	-3	9	4	1	.987	-2	O-39(23-14-6)/D-6	-0.4
1991	Cin-N	13	19	2	1	0	0	0	0	1	3	.053	.100	.053	153	-54	-4	2	0	0	1.000	-2	/O-5(4-1-1)	-0.5
Total	6	296	832	125	180	25	9	16	67	65	177	.216	.279	.326	604	66	-40	60	20	6	.990	-20	O-235(100-142-39)/D-9	-5.8

■ IRV JEFFRIES Jeffries, Irvine Franklin b: 9/10/05, Louisville, Ky. d: 6/8/82, Louisville, Ky. BR/TR, 5'10", 175 lbs. Deb: 4/30/30 Career OF: (0-LF 1-CF 0-RF)

YEAR	TM/L	G	AB	R	H	2B	3B	HR	RBI	BB	SO	AVG	OBP	SLG	OPS	OPS+	BR+	SB	CS	SBR	FA	FR	G/POS	TPR
1930	Chi-A	40	97	14	23	3	0	2	11	3	2	.237	.275	.330	604	54	-7	1	2	-0	.976	-3	3-20,S-13	-0.7
1931	Chi-A	79	223	29	50	10	0	2	16	14	9	.224	.270	.296	566	52	-16	3	0	1	.949	2	3-61/2-6,S-5,O-1C	-1.0
1934	Phi-N	56	175	28	43	6	0	4	19	15	10	.246	.305	.349	654	66	-8	2			.962	4	2-52/3-1	-0.2
Total	3	175	495	71	116	19	0	8	46	32	21	.234	.284	.321	605	58	-31	6	2		.955	3	/3-82,2-58,S-18,O-1C	-1.9

■ CHRIS JELIC Jelic, Christopher John b: 12/16/63, Bethlehem, Pa. BR/TR, 5'11", 180 lbs. Deb: 9/30/90

YEAR	TM/L	G	AB	R	H	2B	3B	HR	RBI	BB	SO	AVG	OBP	SLG	OPS	OPS+	BR+	SB	CS	SBR	FA	FR	G/POS	TPR
1990	NY-N	4	11	2	1	0	0	1	1	0	3	.091	.091	.364	455	19	-1	0	0	0	1.000	-1	/O-4(4-0-0)	-0.3

■ FRANK JELINCICH Jelincich, Frank Anthony "Jelly" b: 9/3/19, San Jose, Cal. d: 6/27/92, Rochester, Minn. BR/TR, 6'2", 198 lbs. Deb: 9/6/41

YEAR	TM/L	G	AB	R	H	2B	3B	HR	RBI	BB	SO	AVG	OBP	SLG	OPS	OPS+	BR+	SB	CS	SBR	FA	FR	G/POS	TPR
1941	Chi-N	4	8	0	1	0	0	0	2	1	2	.125	.222	.125	347	-1	-1	0			1.000	-1	/O-2(2-0-0)	-0.2

■ GREG JELKS Jelks, Gregory Dion b: 8/16/61, Cherokee, Ala. BR/TR, 6'2", 190 lbs. Deb: 8/20/87

YEAR	TM/L	G	AB	R	H	2B	3B	HR	RBI	BB	SO	AVG	OBP	SLG	OPS	OPS+	BR+	SB	CS	SBR	FA	FR	G/POS	TPR
1987	Phi-N	10	11	2	1	1	0	0	0	3	4	.091	.286	.182	468	26	-1	0	0	0	.750	0	/3-4,1-2,O-1(1-0-0)	-0.1

■ STEVE JELTZ Jeltz, Larry Steven b: 5/28/59, Paris, France BB/TR (BR 1983-85), 5'11", 180 lbs. Deb: 7/17/83

YEAR	TM/L	G	AB	R	H	2B	3B	HR	RBI	BB	SO	AVG	OBP	SLG	OPS	OPS+	BR+	SB	CS	SBR	FA	FR	G/POS	TPR
1983	Phi-N	13	8	0	1	0	1	0	1	1	2	.125	.222	.375	597	63	-0	0	0	0	1.000	1	/2-4,S-2,3-2	0.0
1984	Phi-N	28	68	7	14	0	1	1	7	7	11	.206	.280	.279	559	57	-4	2	1	0	.992	11	S-27/3-1	1.0
1985	Phi-N	89	196	17	37	4	1	0	12	26	55	.189	.284	.219	503	41	-15	1	1	-0	.958	6	S-86	-0.2
1986	Phi-N	145	439	44	96	11	4	0	36	65	97	.219	.321	.262	583	60	-22	6	3	0	.967	-2	*S-141	-0.9
1987	Phi-N	114	293	37	68	9	6	0	12	39	54	.232	.324	.304	628	66	-14	1	2	-0	.971	3	*S-114/O-1(1-0-0)	-0.1
1988	Phi-N	148	379	39	71	11	4	0	27	59	58	.187	.297	.237	534	54	-21	3	0	1	.976	-1	*S-148	-1.3
1989	Phi-N	116	263	28	64	7	3	4	25	45	44	.243	.356	.338	694	99	1	4	2	0	.985	1	S-63,3-30,2-23,/O-1C	0.7
1990	KC-A	74	103	11	16	4	0	0	10	6	21	.155	.202	.194	396	11	-12	1	1	-0	.977	9	2-34,S-23,O-13R,/3D	-0.3
Total	8	727	1749	183	367	46	20	5	130	248	342	.210	.309	.268	577	61	-86	18	10	0	.971	28	S-604/2-61,3-36,OD	-1.1

■ GEOFF JENKINS Jenkins, Geoffrey Scott b: 7/21/74, Olympia, Wash. BL/TR, 6'1", 205 lbs. Deb: 4/24/98

YEAR	TM/L	G	AB	R	H	2B	3B	HR	RBI	BB	SO	AVG	OBP	SLG	OPS	OPS+	BR+	SB	CS	SBR	FA	FR	G/POS	TPR
1998	Mil-N	84	262	33	60	12	1	9	28	20	61	.229	.289	.385	674	75	-10	1	3	-1	.968	0	O-81(81-0-1)	-1.3
1999	Mil-N	135	447	70	140	43	3	21	82	35	87	.313	.372	.564	936	134	22	5	1	1	.974	14	*O-128(128-0-0)	3.1

YEAR	TM/L	G	AB	R	H	2B	3B	HR	RBI	BB	SO	AVG	OBP	SLG	OPS	OPS+	BR+	SB	CS	SBR	FA	FR	G/POS	TPR
2000	Mil-N	135	512	100	155	36	4	34	94	33	135	.303	.363	.588	950	137	27	11	1	2	.975	15	*O-131(131-0-0)	3.7
Total	3	354	1221	203	355	91	8	64	204	88	283	.291	.350	.536	886	123	39	17	5	2	.973	29	O-340(340-0-1)	5.5

■ JOHN JENKINS

Jenkins, John Robert b: 7/7/1896, Bosworth, Mo. d: 8/3/68, Columbia, Mo. BR/TR, 5′8″, 160 lbs. Deb: 8/5/22

YEAR	TM/L	G	AB	R	H	2B	3B	HR	RBI	BB	SO	AVG	OBP	SLG	OPS	OPS+	BR+	SB	CS	SBR	FA	FR	G/POS	TPR
1922	Chi-A	5	3	0	0	0	0	0	1	0	2	.000	.000	.000	0	-99	-1	0	0	0	.000	-0	/2-1,S-1	-0.1

■ JOE JENKINS

Jenkins, Joseph Daniel b: 10/12/1890, Shelbyville, Tenn. d: 6/21/74, Fresno, Cal. BR/TR, 5′11″, 170 lbs. Deb: 4/30/14

YEAR	TM/L	G	AB	R	H	2B	3B	HR	RBI	BB	SO	AVG	OBP	SLG	OPS	OPS+	BR+	SB	CS	SBR	FA	FR	G/POS	TPR
1914	StL-A	19	32	0	4	1	1	0	0	1	11	.125	.152	.219	370	12	-4	2			.931	-4	/C-9	-0.8
1917	Chi-A	10	9	0	1	0	0	0	2	0	5	.111	.111	.111	222	-32	-1	0			.000	0	/C-1	-0.2
1919	Chi-A	11	19	0	3	1	0	0	1	1	1	.158	.200	.211	411	15	-2	1			.824	-2	/C-4	-0.4
Total	3	40	60	0	8	2	1	0	3	2	17	.133	.161	.200	361	6	-7	3			.891	-6	/C-14	-1.4

■ TOM JENKINS

Jenkins, Thomas Griffith "Tut" b: 4/10/1898, Camden, Ala. d: 5/3/79, Weymouth, Mass. BL/TR, 6′1.5″, 174 lbs. Deb: 9/15/25

YEAR	TM/L	G	AB	R	H	2B	3B	HR	RBI	BB	SO	AVG	OBP	SLG	OPS	OPS+	BR+	SB	CS	SBR	FA	FR	G/POS	TPR
1925	Bos-A	15	64	9	19	2	1	0	5	3	4	.297	.338	.359	698	77	-2	0	0	0	.938	-2	O-15(15-0-0)	-0.5
1926	Bos-A	21	50	3	9	1	1	0	6	3	7	.180	.226	.240	466	22	-6	0	0	0	1.000	-1	O-13(12-1-0)	-0.8
	Phi-A	6	23	3	4	2	0	0	0	0	2	.174	.174	.261	435	12	-3	0	0	0	1.000	0	/O-6(5-0-1)	-0.3
	Yr	27	73	6	13	3	1	0	6	3	9	.178	.211	.247	457	19	-9	0	0	0	1.000	-1	O-19(17-1-1)	-1.1
1929	StL-A	21	22	1	4	0	1	0	0	4	8	.182	.308	.273	580	49	-2	0	0	0	1.000	-1	/O-3(0-1-2)	-0.3
1930	StL-A	2	8	1	2	1	1	0	3	0	1	.250	.250	.625	875	110	0	0	0	0	1.000	-0	/O-2(0-0-2)	0.0
1931	StL-A	81	230	20	61	7	2	3	25	17	25	.265	.316	.352	668	73	-9	1	3	-1	.952	-4	O-58(0-0-58)	-1.6
1932	StL-A	25	62	5	20	1	0	0	5	1	6	.323	.333	.339	672	70	-3	0	0	0	.939	2	O-12(0-0-12)	-0.1
Total	6	171	459	42	119	14	6	3	44	28	53	.259	.303	.336	639	64	-25	1	3	-1	.958	-6	O-109(32-2-75)	-3.6

■ ALAMAZOO JENNINGS

Jennings, Alfred Gorden b: 11/30/1850, Newport, Ky. d: 11/2/1894, Cincinnati, Ohio Deb: 8/15/1878 U

YEAR	TM/L	G	AB	R	H	2B	3B	HR	RBI	BB	SO	AVG	OBP	SLG	OPS	OPS+	BR+	SB	CS	SBR	FA	FR	G/POS	TPR
1878	Mil-N	1	2	0	0	0	0	0	0	1	0	.000	.333	.000	333	16	-0				.429	-2	/C-1	-0.2

■ HUGHIE JENNINGS

Jennings, Hugh Ambrose "Ee-Yah" b: 4/2/1869, Pittston, Pa. d: 2/1/28, Scranton, Pa. BR/TR, 5′8.5″, 165 lbs. Deb: 6/1/1891 MCH

YEAR	TM/L	G	AB	R	H	2B	3B	HR	RBI	BB	SO	AVG	OBP	SLG	OPS	OPS+	BR+	SB	CS	SBR	FA	FR	G/POS	TPR
1891	Lou-a	88	351	51	103	10	8	1	58	17	35	.293	.342	.376	718	107	2	12			.891	4	S-68,1-17/3-3	0.6
1892	Lou-N	152	594	65	133	16	4	2	61	30	30	.224	.272	.274	546	71	-21	28			.907	15	*S-152	0.2
1893	Lou-N	23	88	6	12	3	0	0	9	3	3	.136	.174	.170	344	-9	-14	0			.899	6	S-23	-0.6
	Bal-N	16	55	6	14	0	0	1	6	4	3	.255	.339	.309	648	71	-2	0			.886	-2	S-15/O-1(0-0-1)	-0.3
	Yr	39	143	12	26	3	0	1	15	7	6	.182	.240	.224	464	25	-16	0			.895	4	S-38/O-1(0-0-1)	-0.9
1894	*Bal-N	128	501	134	168	28	16	4	109	37	17	.335	.411	.479	890	109	7	37			**.928**	33	*S-128	3.5
1895	*Bal-N	131	529	159	204	41	7	4	125	24	17	.386	.444	.512	957	142	34	53			**.940**	**36**	*S-131	**6.1**
1896	*Bal-N	130	521	125	209	27	9	0	121	19	11	.401	.472	.488	960	151	42	70			**.928**	34	*S-130	**6.9**
1897	*Bal-N	117	439	133	156	26	9	2	79	42		.355	.463	.469	932	146	35	60			**.933**	27	*S-116	**5.7**
1898	Bal-N	143	534	135	175	25	11	1	87	78		.328	.454	.421	876	149	42	28			.929	-0	*S-115,2-27/O-1R	4.5
1899	Bro-N	16	41	7	7	0	2	0	6	9		.171	.346	.268	614	68	-1	4			.825	-6	S-11/1-4	-0.6
	Bal-N	2	8	2	3	0	2	0	2	0		.375	.375	.875	1250	227	1	0			1.000	-1	/2-2	0.0
	Bro-N	51	175	35	57	3	8	0	34	13		.326	.424	.434	859	133	9	14			.987	-1	1-46/2-1,S-1	0.7
	Yr	69	224	44	67	3	12	0	42	22		.299	.408	.420	827	124	9	18			.985	-8	1-50,S-12/2-3	0.1
1900	*Bro-N	115	441	61	120	18	6	1	69	31		.272	.348	.347	694	87	-8	31			.982	5	*1-112/2-2	-0.3
1901	Phi-N	82	302	38	79	21	2	1	39	25		.262	.342	.354	696	100	1	13			.979	-3	1-80/2-1,S-1	-0.4
1902	Phi-N	78	290	32	79	13	4	1	32	14		.272	.330	.355	685	111	4	8			.983	1	1-69/S-5,2-4	0.4
1903	Bro-N	6	17	2	4	0	0	0	1	1		.235	.316	.235	551	60	-1	1			1.000	-0	/O-4(1-0-3)	-0.1
1907	Det-A	1	4	0	1	1	0	0	0	0		.250	.250	.500	750	133	0	0			.750	-1	/2-1,S-1,M	-0.1
1909	Det-A	2	4	1	2	0	0	0	2	0		.500	.500	.500	1000	207	0	0			1.000	0	/1-2,M	0.1
1912	Det-A	1	1	0	0	0	0	0	0	0		.000	.000	.000	0	-99	-0	0			.000	0	HM	0.0
1918	Det-A	1	0	0	0	0	0	0	0	0	0	—	—	—	—	—	0	0			1.000	-0	/1-1,M	0.0
Total	17	1283	4895	992	1526	232	88	18	840	347	116	.312	.391	.406	797	118	130	359			.922	147	S-897,1-331/2-38,O3	26.3

■ DOUG JENNINGS

Jennings, James Douglas b: 9/30/64, Atlanta, Ga. BL/TL, 5′10″, 170 lbs. Deb: 4/8/88 Career OF: (58-LF 0-CF 22-RF)

YEAR	TM/L	G	AB	R	H	2B	3B	HR	RBI	BB	SO	AVG	OBP	SLG	OPS	OPS+	BR+	SB	CS	SBR	FA	FR	G/POS	TPR
1988	Oak-A	71	101	9	21	6	0	1	15	21	28	.208	.355	.297	652	88	-1	0	1	-0	1.000	-3	O-23(16-0-7),1-14/D-2	-0.5
1989	Oak-A	4	4	0	0	0	0	0	0	0	2	.000	.000	.000	0	-99	-1	0	0	0	1.000	-1	/O-3(3-0-0)	-0.2
1990	*Oak-A	64	156	19	30	7	2	2	14	17	48	.192	.280	.301	581	65	-7	0	3	-1	.984	-8	O-45(33-0-15)/1-4,D-8	-1.8
1991	Oak-A	8	9	0	1	0	0	0	0	2	2	.111	.273	.111	384	11	-1	0	1	-0	1.000	-1	/O-6(6-0-0)	-0.2
1993	Chi-N	42	52	8	13	3	1	2	8	3	10	.250	.316	.462	777	107	0	0	0	0	1.000	-1	1-10	-0.1
Total	5	189	322	36	65	16	3	5	37	43	90	.202	.307	.317	624	76	-10	0	5	-2	.991	-13	/O-77L,1-28,D-10	-2.8

■ ROBIN JENNINGS

Jennings, Robin Christopher b: 4/11/72, Singapore, Singapore BL/TL, 6′2″, 205 lbs. Deb: 4/18/96

YEAR	TM/L	G	AB	R	H	2B	3B	HR	RBI	BB	SO	AVG	OBP	SLG	OPS	OPS+	BR+	SB	CS	SBR	FA	FR	G/POS	TPR
1996	Chi-N	31	58	7	13	5	0	0	4	3	9	.224	.274	.310	585	52	-4	1	0	0	1.000	1	O-11(0-0-11)	-0.3
1997	Chi-N	9	18	1	3	1	0	0	2	0	2	.167	.167	.222	389	1	-3	0	0	0	1.000	-1	/O-5(4-2-0)	-0.4
1999	Chi-N	5	5	0	1	0	0	0	0	0	2	.200	.200	.200	400	2	-1	0	0	0	.000	0	-0,-0	-0.1
Total	3	45	81	8	17	6	0	0	6	3	13	.210	.247	.284	531	38	-7	1	0	0	1.000	-0	/O-16(4-2-11)	-0.8

■ BILL JENNINGS

Jennings, William Lee b: 9/28/25, St.Louis, Mo. BR/TR, 6′2″, 175 lbs. Deb: 7/19/51

YEAR	TM/L	G	AB	R	H	2B	3B	HR	RBI	BB	SO	AVG	OBP	SLG	OPS	OPS+	BR+	SB	CS	SBR	FA	FR	G/POS	TPR
1951	StL-A	64	195	20	35	10	2	0	13	26	42	.179	.276	.251	527	42	-16	1	0	0	.953	-5	S-64	-1.7

■ WOODY JENSEN

Jensen, Forrest Docenus b: 8/11/07, Bremerton, Wash. BL/TL, 5′10.5″, 160 lbs. Deb: 4/20/31

YEAR	TM/L	G	AB	R	H	2B	3B	HR	RBI	BB	SO	AVG	OBP	SLG	OPS	OPS+	BR+	SB	CS	SBR	FA	FR	G/POS	TPR
1931	Pit-N	73	267	43	65	5	4	3	17	10	18	.243	.276	.326	602	62	-15	4			.974	5	O-67(64-3-0)	-1.3
1932	Pit-N	7	5	2	0	0	0	0	0	0	2	.000	.000	.000	0	-99	-1	0			.000	-1	/O-1(1-0-0)	-0.2
1933	Pit-N	70	196	29	58	7	3	0	15	8	2	.296	.330	.362	692	98	-1	1			.980	-0	O-40(40-0-0)	-0.3
1934	Pit-N	88	283	34	82	13	4	0	27	4	13	.290	.304	.364	668	76	-10	2			.993	-3	O-66(46-17-4)	-1.5
1935	Pit-N	143	627	97	203	28	7	8	62	15	14	.324	.344	.429	773	103	2	9			.977	-4	*O-140(138-0-2)	-1.0
1936	Pit-N	153	696	98	197	34	10	10	58	16	19	.283	.305	.404	709	87	-14	2			.975	1	*O-153(152-1-0)	-2.2
1937	Pit-N	124	509	77	142	23	9	5	45	15	29	.279	.301	.389	690	86	-11	2			.963	-0	*O-120(88-32-0)	-1.7
1938	Pit-N	68	125	12	25	4	0	0	10	1	3	.200	.213	.232	445	22	-13	0			.900	-11	O-38(15-21-2)	-2.6
1939	Pit-N	12	12	0	2	0	0	0	1	0	0	.167	.167	.167	333	-10	-2	0			1.000	-1	/O-3(0-1-2)	-0.3
Total	9	738	2720	392	774	114	37	26	235	69	100	.285	.307	.382	689	84	-65	20			.972	-13	O-628(544-75-10)	-11.1

■ JACKIE JENSEN

Jensen, Jack Eugene b: 3/9/27, San Francisco, Cal. d: 7/14/82, Charlottesville, Va. BR/TR, 5′11″, 190 lbs. Deb: 4/18/50

YEAR	TM/L	G	AB	R	H	2B	3B	HR	RBI	BB	SO	AVG	OBP	SLG	OPS	OPS+	BR+	SB	CS	SBR	FA	FR	G/POS	TPR
1950	*NY-A	45	70	13	12	2	2	1	5	7	8	.171	.247	.300	547	41	-7	4	0	1	.947	-4	O-23(17-0-7)	-1.0
1951	NY-A	56	168	30	50	8	1	8	25	18	18	.298	.369	.500	869	138	8	8	2	1	.974	1	O-48(21-27-1)	0.8
1952	NY-A	7	19	3	2	1	1	0	2	4	4	.105	.261	.263	524	49	-1	1	0	0	1.000	-1	/O-5(0-5-0)	-0.3
	Was-A★	144	570	80	163	29	5	10	80	63	40	.286	.360	.407	767	117	13	17	6	2	.977	6	*O-143(0-7-142)	1.6
	Yr	151	589	83	165	30	6	10	82	67	44	.280	.357	.402	759	115	12	18	6	**2**	.978	5	*O-148(0-12-142)	1.3
1953	Was-A	147	552	87	147	32	8	10	84	73	51	.266	.357	.408	765	109	7	18	8	1	.983	-4	*O-146(0-1-145)	-0.1
1954	Bos-A	152	580	92	160	25	7	25	117	79	52	.276	.365	.472	837	115	12	**22**	7	2	.986	-7	*O-151(8-106-44)	0.1
1955	Bos-A★	152	574	95	158	27	6	26	**116**	89	63	.275	.375	.479	854	118	15	16	7	1	.977	1	*O-150(0-0-150)	1.1
1956	Bos-A	151	578	80	182	23	**11**	20	97	89	43	.315	.407	.497	904	123	20	11	3	1	.962	2	*O-151(0-0-151)	1.7
1957	Bos-A	145	544	82	153	29	2	23	103	75	66	.281	.370	.469	839	121	16	8	5	0	.960	4	*O-144(4-0-143)	1.6
1958	Bos-A★	154	548	83	157	31	0	35	**122**	99	65	.286	.398	.535	933	144	35	9	4	1	.981	3	*O-153(2-0-153)	3.4
1959	Bos-A	148	535	101	148	31	0	28	**112**	88	67	.277	.379	.492	870	131	24	20	5	3	.982	15	*O-146(0-7-142)	3.6
1961	Bos-A	137	498	64	131	21	2	13	66	66	69	.263	.353	.392	744	96	-2	9	8	-1	.986	11	*O-131(2-0-129)	0.0
Total	11	1438	5236	810	1463	259	45	199	929	750	546	.279	.372	.460	832	119	142	143	55	12	.977	28	*O-1391(54-153-1207)	12.5

■ MARCUS JENSEN

Jensen, Marcus Christian b: 12/14/72, Oakland, Cal. BB/TR, 6′4″, 195 lbs. Deb: 4/14/96

YEAR	TM/L	G	AB	R	H	2B	3B	HR	RBI	BB	SO	AVG	OBP	SLG	OPS	OPS+	BR+	SB	CS	SBR	FA	FR	G/POS	TPR
1996	SF-N	9	19	4	4	1	0	0	4	8	7	.211	.444	.263	708	96	1	0	0	0	.955	-0	/C-7	0.1
1997	SF-N	30	74	5	11	2	0	1	3	7	23	.149	.222	.216	438	16	-9	0	0	0	.983	-7	C-28	-1.5
	Det-A	8	11	1	2	0	0	0	1	1	5	.182	.250	.182	432	15	-1	0	0	0	.964	1	/C-8	0.0
1998	Mil-N	2	2	0	0	0	0	0	0	0	2	.000	.000	.000	0	-99	-1	0	0	0	1.000	-0	/C-1	-0.1
1999	StL-N	16	34	5	8	5	0	1	1	6	12	.235	.350	.471	821	105	0	0	0	0	.988	2	C-14	0.2

YEAR	TM/L	G	AB	R	H	2B	3B	HR	RBI	BB	SO	AVG	OBP	SLG	OPS	OPS+	BR+	SB	CS	SBR	FA	FR	G/POS	TPR
2000	Min-A	52	139	16	29	7	1	3	14	24	36	.209	.325	.338	663	65	-7	0	1	-0	.993	-6	C-49/D-1	-1.1
Total	5	117	279	31	54	15	1	5	23	46	85	.194	.308	.308	616	58	-18	0	1	-0	.985	-11	C-107/D-1	-2.4
■ **DAN JESSEE**	Jessee, Daniel Edward b: 2/22/01, Olive Hill, Ky. d: 4/30/70, Venice, Fla. BL/TR, 5'10", 165 lbs. Deb: 8/14/29																							
1929	Cle-A	1	0	0	0	0	0	0	0	0	0	—	—	—	—	—	0	0	0	0	.000	0	R	0.0
■ **GARRY JESTADT**	Jestadt, Garry Arthur b: 3/19/47, Chicago, Ill. BR/TR, 6'2", 188 lbs. Deb: 9/17/69																							
1969	Mon-N	6	6	1	0	0	0	0	1	0	0	.000	.000	.000	0	-99	-2	0	0	0	.667	-0	/S-1	-0.2
1971	Chi-N	3	3	0	0	0	0	0	0	0	0	.000	.000	.000	0	-87	-1	0	0	0	.000	0	/3-1	-0.1
	SD-N	75	189	17	55	13	0	0	13	11	24	.291	.330	.360	690	102	0	1	3	-1	.935	11	3-49,2-23/S-1	1.2
	Yr	78	192	17	55	13	0	0	13	11	24	.286	.325	.354	679	98	-1	1	3	-1	.935	11	3-50,2-23/S-1	1.1
1972	SD-N	92	256	15	63	5	1	6	22	13	21	.246	.283	.344	626	83	-7	0	0	0	.944	-17	2-48,3-25/S-3	-2.3
Total	3	176	454	33	118	18	1	6	36	24	45	.260	.297	.344	641	87	-9	1	3	-1	.942	-7	/3-75,2-71,S-5	-1.4
■ **DEREK JETER**	Jeter, Derek Sanderson b: 6/26/74, Pequannock, N.J. BR/TR, 6'3", 175 lbs. Deb: 5/29/95																							
1995	NY-A	15	48	5	12	4	1	0	7	3	11	.250	.294	.375	669	73	-2	0	0	0	.962	-1	S-15	-0.2
1996	*NY-A	157	582	104	183	25	6	10	78	48	102	.314	.376	.430	805	103	4	14	7	1	.969	-3	*S-157	1.4
1997	*NY-A	159	654	116	190	31	7	10	70	74	125	.291	.371	.405	776	103	5	23	12	1	.975	-0	*S-159	1.8
1998	*NY-A★	149	626	**127**	203	25	8	19	84	57	119	.324	.385	.481	866	128	27	30	6	5	.986	-24	*S-148	1.9
1999	*NY-A★	158	627	134	**219**	37	9	24	102	91	116	.349	.441	.552	993	153	54	19	8	1	.978	-34	*S-158	3.2
2000	*NY-A★	148	593	119	201	31	4	15	73	68	99	.339	.418	.481	898	129	29	22	4	3	.961	-41	*S-148	0.4
Total	6	786	3130	605	1008	153	35	78	414	341	572	.322	.397	.468	865	123	117	108	37	11	.973	-103	S-785	8.5
■ **JOHNNY JETER**	Jeter, John b: 10/24/44, Shreveport, La. BR/TR, 6'1", 180 lbs. Deb: 6/14/69 F																							
1969	Pit-N	28	29	7	9	1	1	1	6	3	15	.310	.375	.517	892	151	2	1	1	-0	1.000	-4	O-20(16-1-4)	-0.2
1970	*Pit-N	85	126	27	30	3	2	2	12	13	34	.238	.314	.341	656	77	-4	9	5	0	1.000	-8	O-56(35-10-11)	-1.3
1971	SD-N	18	75	8	24	4	0	1	3	2	16	.320	.338	.413	751	120	2	2	0	0	.967	4	O-17(0-17-0)	0.6
1972	SD-N	110	326	25	72	4	3	7	21	18	92	.221	.266	.316	582	70	-14	11	5	1	.987	1	O-91(0-91-0)	-1.5
1973	Chi-A	89	300	38	72	14	4	7	26	9	74	.240	.262	.383	645	77	-10	4	3	-0	.955	-3	O-72(19-27-29)/D-3	-1.7
1974	Cle-A	6	17	3	6	1	0	0	1	1	6	.353	.389	.412	801	132	1	1	2	-0	.833	-2	/O-6(5-1-0)	-0.2
Total	6	336	873	108	213	27	10	18	69	46	237	.244	.284	.360	644	82	-24	28	16	1	.975	-11	O-262(75-147-44)/D-3	-4.3
■ **SHAWN JETER**	Jeter, Shawn Darrell b: 6/28/66, Shreveport, La. BL/TR, 6'2", 185 lbs. Deb: 6/13/92 F																							
1992	Chi-A	13	18	1	2	0	0	0	0	0	7	.111	.111	.111	222	-38	-3	0	0	0	.909	-2	/O-8(1-1-6),D-3	-0.5
■ **SAM JETHROE**	Jethroe, Samuel "Jet" b: 1/20/18, E.St.Louis, Ill. BB/TR, 6'1", 178 lbs. Deb: 4/18/50																							
1950	Bos-N	141	582	100	159	28	8	18	58	52	93	.273	.338	.442	780	110	7	**35**			.969	8	*O-141(0-141-0)	1.1
1951	Bos-N	148	572	101	160	29	10	18	65	57	88	.280	.356	.460	816	127	21	**35**	5	**6**	.974	7	*O-140(13-127-2)	2.8
1952	Bos-N	151	608	79	141	23	7	13	58	68	112	.232	.318	.357	675	90	-8	28	9	3	.970	4	*O-151(1-150-0)	-0.5
1954	Pit-N	2	1	0	0	0	0	0	0	0	0	.000	.000	.000	0	-99	-0	0	0	0	1.000	-0	/O-1(0-0-1)	-0.1
Total	4	442	1763	280	460	80	25	49	181	177	293	.261	.337	.418	755	108	19	98	14		.971	19	O-433(14-418-3)	3.3
■ **NAT JEWETT**	Jewett, Nathan W. b: 12/25/1842, New York, N.Y. d: 2/23/14, Bronx, N.Y. 5'6", 137 lbs. Deb: 7/4/1872																							
1872	Eck-n	2	8	1	1	0	0	0	0	0	0	.125	.125	.125	250	-27	-1	0	0	0	.700	-2	/C-2	-0.2
■ **HOUSTON JIMENEZ**	Jimenez, Alfonso (Gonzales) b: 10/30/57, Navojoa, Mexico BR/TR, 5'8", 144 lbs. Deb: 6/13/83																							
1983	Min-A	36	86	5	15	5	1	0	9	4	11	.174	.211	.256	467	27	-9	0	1	-0	.969	4	S-36	-0.2
1984	Min-A	108	298	28	60	11	1	0	19	15	34	.201	.240	.245	485	33	-27	0	1	-0	.959	-5	*S-107	-2.3
1987	Pit-N	5	6	0	0	0	0	0	0	1	2	.000	.143	.000	143	-58	-1	0	0	0	1.000	1	/2-2,S-2	0.0
1988	Cle-A	9	21	1	1	0	0	0	1	0	2	.048	.048	.048	95	-71	-5	0	0	0	.973	6	/2-7,S-2	0.1
Total	4	158	411	34	76	16	2	0	29	20	49	.185	.223	.234	456	25	-42	0	2	-1	.962	7	S-147/2-9	-2.4
■ **D'ANGELO JIMENEZ**	Jimenez, D'Angelo b: 12/21/77, Santo Domingo, D.R. BB/TR, 6', 160 lbs. Deb: 9/15/99																							
1999	NY-A	7	20	3	8	2	0	0	4	3	4	.400	.478	.500	978	152	2	0	0	0	1.000	-2	/3-6,2-1	0.0
■ **ELVIO JIMENEZ**	Jimenez, Felix Elvio (Rivera) b: 1/6/40, San Pedro De Macoris, D.R. BR/TR, 5'9", 170 lbs. Deb: 10/4/64 F																							
1964	NY-A	1	6	0	2	0	0	0	0	0	0	.333	.333	.333	667	85	-0	0	0	0	1.000	0	/O-1(1-0-0)	0.0
■ **MANNY JIMENEZ**	Jimenez, Manuel Emilio (Rivera) b: 11/19/38, San Pedro De Macoris, D.R. BL/TR, 6'1", 195 lbs. Deb: 4/11/62 F																							
1962	KC-A	139	479	48	144	24	2	11	69	31	34	.301	.357	.428	785	105	4	0	1	-0	.985	-5	*O-122(116-0-6)	-0.8
1963	KC-A	60	157	12	44	9	0	0	15	16	14	.280	.365	.338	703	93	-1	0	1	-0	.960	1	O-40(33-0-8)	-0.2
1964	KC-A	95	204	19	46	7	0	12	38	15	24	.225	.295	.436	731	97	-1	0	0	0	.939	-4	O-49(46-0-4)	-0.8
1966	KC-A	13	35	1	4	0	1	0	1	6	4	.114	.244	.171	415	22	-3	0	0	0	.909	-2	O-12(8-0-4)	-0.7
1967	Pit-N	50	56	3	14	2	0	2	10	1	4	.250	.276	.393	669	89	-1	0	0	0	1.000	-1	/O-6(6-0-0)	-0.3
1968	Pit-N	66	66	7	20	1	1	1	11	6	15	.303	.403	.394	797	142	4	0	0	0	.857	-1	/O-5(5-0-0)	0.3
1969	Chi-N	6	6	0	1	0	0	0	0	0	2	.167	.167	.167	333	-6	-1	0	0	0	.000	0	H	-0.1
Total	7	429	1003	90	273	43	4	26	144	75	97	.272	.339	.401	740	100	1	0	2	-1	.966	-11	O-234(214-0-22)	-2.6
■ **KEITH JOHNS**	Johns, Robert Keith b: 7/19/71, Callahan, Fla. BR/TR, 6'1", 175 lbs. Deb: 5/23/98																							
1998	Bos-A	2	0	0	0	0	0	0	0	1	0	—	1.000	—	1000	188	0	0	0	0	1.000	0	/2-1,D-1	0.1
■ **TOMMY JOHNS**	Johns, Thomas Pearce b: 9/7/1851, Baltimore, Md. d: 4/13/27, Baltimore, Md. Deb: 5/14/1873																							
1873	Mar-n	1	4	0	0	0	0	0	0	0	0	.000	.000	.000	0	-99	-1	0	0	0	.000	-1	/O-1(1-0-0)	-0.1
■ **PETE JOHNS**	Johns, William R. b: 1/17/1889, Cleveland, Ohio d: 8/9/64, Cleveland, Ohio BR/TR, 5'10", 165 lbs. Deb: 8/25/15 Career OF: (1-LF 3-CF 0-RF)																							
1915	Chi-A	28	100	7	21	2	1	0	11	8	11	.210	.275	.250	525	56	-5	2	7	-2	.943	4	3-28	-0.3
1918	StL-A	46	89	5	16	1	1	0	11	4	6	.180	.215	.213	429	30	-8	0			.990	-1	1-10/S-4,3-4,O-4C,2	-1.0
Total	2	74	189	12	37	3	2	0	22	12	17	.196	.248	.233	480	44	-13	2	7		.929	2	/3-32,1-10,O-4C,S2	-1.3
■ **ABBIE JOHNSON**	Johnson, Albert L. b: 1875, Chicago, Ill. d: 11/28/60, Detroit, Mich. 5'9.5", 165 lbs. Deb: 9/1/1896																							
1896	Lou-N	25	87	10	20	2	1	0	14	4	6	.230	.264	.276	540	44	-7	0			.937	-5	2-25	-0.9
1897	Lou-N	49	165	16	40	6	1	0	23	13		.242	.302	.291	593	59	-10	2			.882	-10	2-34,S-12	-1.5
Total	2	74	252	26	60	8	2	0	37	17	6	.238	.289	.286	575	54	-17	2			.904	-14	/2-59,S-12	-2.4
■ **ALEX JOHNSON**	Johnson, Alexander b: 12/7/42, Helena, Ark. BR/TR, 6', 205 lbs. Deb: 7/25/64 Career OF: (937-LF 16-CF 54-RF)																							
1964	Phi-N	43	109	18	33	7	1	4	18	6	26	.303	.345	.495	840	135	5	1	2	-0	.980	-1	O-35(34-0-1)	0.2
1965	Phi-N	97	262	27	77	9	3	8	28	15	60	.294	.337	.443	780	120	6	4	4	-1	.966	-5	O-82(76-9-1)	-0.2
1966	StL-N	25	86	7	16	0	1	2	6	5	18	.186	.231	.279	510	41	-7	1	1	-0	.962	-1	O-22(22-0-0)	-1.0
1967	StL-N	81	175	20	39	9	2	1	12	9	26	.223	.273	.314	587	68	-7	6	3	0	.970	0	O-57(5-6-48)	-1.0
1968	Cin-N	149	603	79	188	32	6	2	58	26	71	.312	.343	.395	738	114	10	16	6	1	.947	5	*O-140(140-0-1)	0.9
1969	Cin-N	139	523	86	165	18	4	17	88	25	69	.315	.357	.463	820	122	14	11	8	-0	.927	1	*O-132(132-0-0)	0.8
1970	Cal-A★	156	614	85	202	26	6	14	86	35	68	**.329**	.372	.459	831	133	26	17	2	3	.959	5	*O-156(155-0-1)	2.5
1971	Cal-A	65	242	19	63	8	0	2	21	15	34	.260	.309	.318	627	84	-6	5	2	0	.926	-6	O-61(61-0-0)	-1.6
1972	Cle-A	108	356	31	85	10	1	8	37	22	40	.239	.285	.340	625	83	-8	6	8	-1	.955	-5	O-95(95-0-0)	-2.3
1973	Tex-A	158	624	62	179	26	3	8	68	32	82	.287	.324	.377	700	101	-1	10	5	0	.987	1	*D-116,O-41(40-1-0)	-0.4
1974	Tex-A	114	453	57	132	14	3	4	41	28	59	.291	.338	.362	700	104	2	20	9	1	.956	6	O-81(81-0-0),D-32	0.4
	NY-A	10	28	3	6	1	0	1	2	0	3	.214	.214	.357	571	63	-1	0	0	0	.000	-0	/O-1(1-0-0),D-4	-0.2
	Yr	124	481	60	138	15	3	5	43	28	62	.287	.331	.362	693	102	1	20	9	1	.956	5	O-82(82-0-0),D-36	0.2
1975	NY-A	52	119	15	31	5	1	1	15	7	21	.261	.302	.345	646	84	-3	2	3	-1	1.000	-1	D-28/O-7(5-0-2)	-0.6
1976	Det-A	125	429	41	115	15	2	6	45	19	49	.268	.302	.354	657	88	-7	14	10	-0	.954	-3	O-90(90-0-0),D-19	-1.8
Total	13	1322	4623	550	1331	180	33	78	525	244	626	.288	.329	.392	720	105	23	113	63	3	.953	-5	O-1000L,D-199	-4.3

■ TONY JOHNSON

Johnson, Anthony Clair b: 6/23/56, Memphis, Tenn. BR/TR, 6'3", 145 lbs. Deb: 9/28/81

YEAR	TM/L	G	AB	R	H	2B	3B	HR	RBI	BB	SO	AVG	OBP	SLG	OPS	OPS+	BR+	SB	CS	SBR	FA	FR	G/POS	TPR
1981	Mon-N	2	1	0	0	0	0	0	0	0	0	.000	.000	.000	0	-99	-0	0	0	0	.000	-0	/O-1(1-0-0)	-0.1
1982	Tor-A	70	98	17	23	2	1	3	14	11	26	.235	.312	.367	679	79	-3	3	13	-4	.979	-2	O-28(25-2-2),D-28	-1.0
Total	2	72	99	17	23	2	1	3	14	11	26	.232	.309	.364	673	77	-3	3	13	-4	.979	-3	/O-29(26-2-2),D-28	-1.1

■ BOB JOHNSON

Johnson, Bobby Earl b: 7/31/59, Dallas, Tex. BR/TR, 6'3", 195 lbs. Deb: 9/1/81

YEAR	TM/L	G	AB	R	H	2B	3B	HR	RBI	BB	SO	AVG	OBP	SLG	OPS	OPS+	BR+	SB	CS	SBR	FA	FR	G/POS	TPR
1981	Tex-A	6	18	2	5	0	0	2	4	1	3	.278	.316	.611	927	171	1	0	0	0	1.000	-1	/C-5,1-1	0.1
1982	Tex-A	20	56	4	7	2	0	2	7	3	22	.125	.183	.268	451	23	-6	0	1	-0	1.000	0	C-14/1-3	-0.6
1983	Tex-A	72	175	18	37	6	1	5	16	16	55	.211	.281	.343	624	72	-7	3	0	1	1.000	3	C-62,1-10	-0.2
Total	3	98	249	24	49	8	1	9	27	20	80	.197	.262	.345	607	68	-11	3	1	0	1.000	3	/C-81,1-14	-0.7

■ BRIAN JOHNSON

Johnson, Brian David b: 1/8/68, Oakland, Cal. BR/TR, 6'2", 210 lbs. Deb: 4/5/94

YEAR	TM/L	G	AB	R	H	2B	3B	HR	RBI	BB	SO	AVG	OBP	SLG	OPS	OPS+	BR+	SB	CS	SBR	FA	FR	G/POS	TPR
1994	SD-N	36	93	7	23	4	1	3	16	5	21	.247	.286	.409	694	81	-3	0	0	0	1.000	2	C-24/1-5	0.1
1995	SD-N	68	207	20	52	9	0	3	29	11	39	.251	.292	.338	630	68	-10	0	0	0	.993	1	C-55/1-2	-0.5
1996	*SD-N	82	243	18	66	13	1	8	35	4	36	.272	.295	.432	727	94	-3	0	0	0	.989	0	C-66/1-1,3-1	0.1
1997	Det-A	45	139	13	33	6	1	2	18	5	19	.237	.264	.338	602	56	-9	1	0	0	.987	-6	C-43/D-2	-1.2
	*SF-N	56	179	19	50	7	2	11	27	14	26	.279	.338	.525	864	125	6	0	1	-0	.995	0	C-55/1-2	0.9
1998	SF-N	99	308	34	73	8	1	13	34	28	67	.237	.311	.396	707	90	-5	0	2	-1	.994	-2	C-95/O-1(1-0-0)	-0.2
1999	Cin-N	45	117	12	27	7	0	5	18	9	31	.231	.286	.419	705	73	-5	0	0	0	.995	1	C-39	-0.3
2000	KC-A	37	125	9	26	6	0	4	18	4	28	.208	.233	.352	585	45	-11	0	0	0	.991	2	C-37	-0.6
Total	7	468	1411	132	350	60	6	49	195	80	267	.248	.294	.403	697	82	-41	1	3	-1	.993	-2	C-414/1-10,D-2,O3	-1.7

■ CALEB JOHNSON

Johnson, Caleb Clark b: 5/23/1844, Fulton, Ill. d: 3/7/25, Sterling, Ill. Deb: 5/24/1871

YEAR	TM/L	G	AB	R	H	2B	3B	HR	RBI	BB	SO	AVG	OBP	SLG	OPS	OPS+	BR+	SB	CS	SBR	FA	FR	G/POS	TPR
1871	Cle-n	16	67	10	15	1	0	0	7	0	1	.224	.224	.239	463	35	-5	1	0	0	.736	-5	2-10/O-6(0-0-6)	-0.6

■ CHARLIE JOHNSON

Johnson, Charles Cleveland "Home Run" b: 3/12/1885, Slatington, Pa. d: 8/28/40, Marcus Hook, Pa. BL/TL, 5'9", 150 lbs. Deb: 9/21/08

YEAR	TM/L	G	AB	R	H	2B	3B	HR	RBI	BB	SO	AVG	OBP	SLG	OPS	OPS+	BR+	SB	CS	SBR	FA	FR	G/POS	TPR
1908	Phi-N	6	16	2	4	0	1	0	2	1		.250	.333	.375	708	122	0	0			1.000	-0	/O-4(1-3-0)	0.0

■ CHARLES JOHNSON

Johnson, Charles Edward b: 7/20/71, Fort Pierce, Fla. BR/TR, 6'2", 215 lbs. Deb: 5/6/94

YEAR	TM/L	G	AB	R	H	2B	3B	HR	RBI	BB	SO	AVG	OBP	SLG	OPS	OPS+	BR+	SB	CS	SBR	FA	FR	G/POS	TPR
1994	Fla-N	4	11	5	5	1	0	1	4	1	4	.455	.500	.818	1318	229	2	0	0	0	1.000	0	/C-4	0.2
1995	Fla-N	97	315	40	79	15	1	11	39	46	71	.251	.353	.410	763	100	1	0	2	-1	.992	-2	C-97	0.4
1996	Fla-N	120	386	34	84	13	1	13	37	40	91	.218	.294	.358	652	73	-16	1	0	0	**.995**	7	*C-120	-0.2
1997	*Fla-N★	124	416	43	104	26	1	19	63	60	109	.250	.349	.454	803	113	8	0	2	-1	**1.000**	8	*C-123	2.2
1998	Fla-N	31	113	13	25	5	0	7	23	16	30	.221	.318	.451	769	105	0	0	1	-0	.990	-7	C-31	-0.5
	LA-N	102	346	31	75	13	0	12	35	29	99	.217	.279	.358	638	70	-16	0	1	-0	.992	2	*C-100	-0.8
	Yr	133	459	44	100	18	0	19	58	45	129	.218	.289	.381	670	79	-16	0	2	-1	.992	-5	*C-131	-1.3
1999	Bal-A	135	426	58	107	19	1	16	54	55	107	.251	.342	.413	755	95	-3	0	0	0	.994	-5	*C-135	0.1
2000	Bal-A	84	286	52	84	16	0	21	55	32	69	.294	.365	.570	935	136	15	2	0	0	.994	-11	C-83/D-1	0.9
	*Chi-A	44	135	24	44	8	0	10	36	20	37	.326	.417	.607	1024	153	11	0	0	0	.987	-11	C-43	0.3
	Yr	128	421	76	128	24	0	31	91	52	106	.304	.382	.582	964	142	26	2	0	0	.932	-22	*C-126/D-1	1.2
Total	7	741	2434	300	607	116	4	110	346	299	617	.249	.335	.436	771	102	3	3	6	-1	.994	-19	C-736/D-1	2.6

■ CLIFF JOHNSON

Johnson, Clifford b: 7/22/47, San Antonio, Tex. BR/TR, 6'4", 225 lbs. Deb: 9/13/72

YEAR	TM/L	G	AB	R	H	2B	3B	HR	RBI	BB	SO	AVG	OBP	SLG	OPS	OPS+	BR+	SB	CS	SBR	FA	FR	G/POS	TPR
1972	Hou-N	5	4	0	1	0	0	0	0	2	0	.250	.500	.250	750	121	0	0	0	0	1.000	1	/C-1	0.1
1973	Hou-N	7	20	6	6	2	0	2	6	1	7	.300	.364	.700	1064	189	2	0	0	0	1.000	-0	/1-5	0.2
1974	Hou-N	83	171	26	39	4	1	10	29	33	45	.228	.362	.439	801	129	7	0	1	-0	.978	-4	C-28,1-21	0.3
1975	Hou-N	122	340	52	94	16	1	20	65	46	64	.276	.371	.506	877	152	23	1	0	0	.991	-12	1-47,C-41/O-1(1-0-0)	1.0
1976	Hou-N	108	318	36	72	21	2	10	49	62	59	.226	.359	.399	759	126	13	0	0	0	.977	-12	C-66,O-20L,1-16	0.2
1977	Hou-N	51	144	22	43	8	0	10	23	23	30	.299	.409	.563	972	173	15	0	1	-0	.946	-0	O-34(33-0-4),1-10	1.3
	*NY-A	56	142	24	42	8	0	12	31	20	23	.296	.405	.606	1010	173	15	0	1	-0	1.000	3	D-25,C-15,1-11	1.6
1978	*NY-A	76	174	20	32	9	1	6	19	30	32	.184	.307	.351	658	87	-3	0	0	0	.975	0	D-39,C-22/1-1	-0.3
1979	NY-A	28	64	11	17	6	0	2	6	10	7	.266	.365	.453	818	122	2	0	0	0	1.000	-0	D-22/C-4	0.1
	Cle-A	72	240	37	65	10	0	18	61	24	39	.271	.349	.538	887	135	11	2	0	0	.000	-0	D-62/C-1	0.9
	Yr	100	304	48	82	16	0	20	67	34	46	.270	.353	.520	873	132	13	2	0	0	1.000	-1	D-84/C-5	1.0
1980	Cle-A	54	174	25	40	3	1	6	28	25	30	.230	.327	.362	689	88	-3	0	1	-0	.000	0	D-45	-0.4
	Chi-N	68	196	28	46	8	0	10	34	29	35	.235	.336	.429	765	104	1	0	0	0	.992	-6	1-46/O-3(3-0-0),C-1	-0.8
1981	*Oak-A	84	273	40	71	8	0	17	59	28	60	.260	.336	.476	812	138	13	5	3	0	1.000	-1	D-68/1-9	0.9
1982	Oak-A	73	214	19	51	10	0	7	31	26	41	.238	.326	.383	710	98	-0	1	2	-0	.987	1	D-48,1-11	-0.2
1983	Tor-A	142	407	59	108	23	1	22	76	67	69	.265	.376	.489	865	128	17	0	1	-0	1.000	0	*D-130/1-6	1.2
1984	Tor-A	127	359	51	109	23	1	16	61	50	62	.304	.393	.507	900	142	21	0	1	-0	1.000	-1	*D-109/1-2	1.7
1985	Tex-A	82	296	31	76	17	1	12	56	31	44	.257	.333	.443	776	109	3	0	0	0	.000	0	D-82	0.1
	*Tor-A	24	73	4	20	0	0	1	10	9	15	.274	.354	.315	669	83	-1	0	0	0	.947	-1	D-21/1-3	-0.3
	Yr	106	369	35	96	17	1	13	66	40	59	.260	.337	.417	755	104	2	0	0	0	.947	-1	*D-103/1-3	-0.2
1986	Tor-A	107	336	48	84	12	1	15	55	52	57	.250	.357	.426	783	109	5	0	1	-0	1.000	0	D-95/1-1	0.2
Total	15	1369	3945	539	1016	188	10	196	699	568	719	.258	.358	.459	817	125	143	9	12	-2	.993	-33	D-746,1-189,C-179,/O	7.8

■ DARRELL JOHNSON

Johnson, Darrell Dean b: 8/25/28, Horace, Neb. BR/TR, 6'1", 180 lbs. Deb: 4/20/52 MC

YEAR	TM/L	G	AB	R	H	2B	3B	HR	RBI	BB	SO	AVG	OBP	SLG	OPS	OPS+	BR+	SB	CS	SBR	FA	FR	G/POS	TPR
1952	StL-A	29	78	9	22	2	1	0	9	11	4	.282	.371	.333	704	94	-0	0	0	0	.990	1	C-22	0.2
	Chi-A	22	37	3	4	0	0	0	1	5	9	.108	.214	.108	322	-8	-5	1	0	0	.955	5	C-21	0.0
	Yr	51	115	12	26	2	1	0	10	16	13	.226	.321	.261	581	62	-5	1	0	0	.974	6	C-43	0.2
1957	NY-A	21	46	4	10	1	0	1	8	3	10	.217	.280	.304	584	61	-3	0	0	0	1.000	4	C-20	0.2
1958	NY-A	5	16	1	4	0	0	0	0	0	2	.250	.250	.250	500	39	-1	0	0	0	1.000	1	/C-4	0.0
1960	StL-N	8	2	0	0	0	0	0	0	1	0	.000	.333	.000	333	1	-0	0	0	0	1.000	1	/C-8	0.1
1961	Phi-N	21	61	4	14	1	0	0	3	3	8	.230	.277	.246	523	41	-5	0	0	0	.982	2	C-21	-0.2
	*Cin-N	20	54	3	17	2	0	1	6	1	2	.315	.327	.407	735	92	-1	0	0	0	1.000	4	C-20	0.4
	Yr	41	115	7	31	3	0	1	9	4	10	.270	.300	.322	622	65	-6	0	0	0	.991	6	C-41	0.2
1962	Cin-N	2	4	0	0	0	0	0	0	2	0	.000	.333	.000	333	-2	-0	0	0	0	1.000	2	/C-2	0.1
	Bal-A	6	22	0	4	0	0	0	1	0	4	.182	.182	.182	364	-2	-3	0	0	0	1.000	-1	/C-6	-0.4
Total	6	134	320	24	75	6	1	2	28	26	39	.234	.296	.278	574	57	-19	1	0	0	.988	20	C-124	0.4

■ DAVEY JOHNSON

Johnson, David Allen b: 1/30/43, Orlando, Fla. BR/TR, 6'1", 180 lbs. Deb: 4/13/65 M

YEAR	TM/L	G	AB	R	H	2B	3B	HR	RBI	BB	SO	AVG	OBP	SLG	OPS	OPS+	BR+	SB	CS	SBR	FA	FR	G/POS	TPR
1965	Bal-A	20	47	5	8	3	0	0	1	5	6	.170	.250	.234	484	38	-4	3	0	1	.929	3	/3-9,2-3,S-2	0.0
1966	*Bal-A	131	501	47	129	20	3	7	56	31	64	.257	.302	.351	653	88	-8	3	4	-1	.971	2	*2-126/S-3	0.5
1967	Bal-A	148	510	62	126	30	3	10	64	59	82	.247	.330	.376	706	109	6	4	5	-1	.981	0	*2-144/3-3	1.9
1968	Bal-A★	145	504	50	122	24	4	9	56	44	80	.242	.309	.359	668	102	1	7	3	0	.978	4	*2-127,S-34	1.9
1969	*Bal-A†	142	511	52	143	34	1	7	57	57	52	.280	.356	.391	747	108	6	3	4	-1	.984	-3	*2-142/S-2	1.2
1970	*Bal-A★	149	530	68	149	27	1	10	53	66	68	.281	.361	.392	753	106	6	2	1	0	.990	1	*2-149/S-2	1.7
1971	*Bal-A	142	510	67	144	26	1	18	72	51	55	.282	.353	.443	796	125	17	3	1	0	.984	-1	*2-140	2.7
1972	Bal-A	118	376	31	83	22	3	5	32	52	68	.221	.322	.335	657	93	-2	1	1	-0	**.990**	10	*2-116	1.7
1973	Atl-N★	157	559	84	151	25	0	43	99	81	93	.270	.371	.546	917	140	30	5	3	0	.966	-3	*2-156	3.9
1974	Atl-N	136	454	56	114	18	0	15	62	75	59	.251	.361	.390	751	105	5	1	2	-0	.993	7	1-73,2-71	1.0
1975	Atl-N	1	1	0	1	1	0	0	1	0	0	1.000	1.000	2.000	3000	691	1	0	0	0	.000	0	H	0.1
1977	*Phi-N	78	156	23	50	9	1	8	36	23	20	.321	.414	.545	959	148	11	1	1	-0	1.000	-2	1-43/2-9,3-6	0.8
1978	Phi-N	44	89	14	17	2	0	2	14	10	19	.191	.287	.281	568	59	-5	0	0	0	.930	-6	2-15/3-9,1-7	-1.2
	Chi-N	24	49	5	15	1	1	2	6	5	9	.306	.393	.490	883	130	2	0	0	0	.839	-3	3-12	-0.1
	Yr	68	138	19	32	3	1	4	20	15	28	.232	.325	.355	680	86	-2	0	0	0	.844	-9	3-21,2-15/1-7	-1.3
Total	13	1435	4797	564	1252	242	18	136	609	559	675	.261	.343	.404	747	110	67	33	25	-1	.980	10	*2-1198,1-123/S-43,3	16.1

■ DERON JOHNSON

Johnson, Deron Roger b: 7/17/38, San Diego, Cal. d: 4/23/92, Poway, Cal. BR/TR, 6'2", 209 lbs. Deb: 9/20/60 C

YEAR	TM/L	G	AB	R	H	2B	3B	HR	RBI	BB	SO	AVG	OBP	SLG	OPS	OPS+	BR+	SB	CS	SBR	FA	FR	G/POS	TPR
1960	NY-A	6	4	0	2	1	0	0	0	0	0	.500	.500	.750	1250	247	1	0	0	0	.750	0	/3-5	0.1
1961	NY-A	13	19	1	2	0	0	0	2	2	5	.105	.190	.105	296	-20	-3	0	0	0	1.000	2	/3-8	-0.1

YEAR	TM/L	G	AB	R	H	2B	3B	HR	RBI	BB	SO	AVG	OBP	SLG	OPS	OPS+	BR+	SB	CS	SBR	FA	FR	G/POS	TPR
	KC-A	83	283	31	61	11	3	8	42	14	44	.216	.255	.360	615	61	-16	0	1	-0	.948	3	O-59R,3-19/1-3	-1.8
	Yr	96	302	32	63	11	3	8	44	16	49	.209	.251	.344	595	57	-19	0	1	-0	.948	5	O-59R,3-27/1-3	-1.9
1962	KC-A	17	19	1	2	1	0	0	0	3	8	.105	.227	.158	385	6	-3	0	0	0	1.000	-1	/1-2,3-2,O-2(0-0-2)	-0.4
1964	Cin-N	140	477	63	130	24	4	21	79	37	98	.273	.328	.472	799	118	10	4	3	-0	.990	3	*1-131,O-10L/3-1	0.6
1965	Cin-N	159	616	92	177	30	7	32	**130**	52	97	.287	.345	.515	859	129	23	0	4	-1	.948	-12	*3-159	0.9
1966	Cin-N	142	505	75	130	25	3	24	81	39	87	.257	.313	.461	775	103	2	1	2	-0	.980	-8	*O-106L,1-71,3-18	-1.4
1967	Cin-N	108	361	39	81	18	1	13	53	22	104	.224	.273	.388	661	78	-11	0	1	-0	.997	-4	1-81,3-24	-2.1
1968	Atl-N	127	342	29	71	11	1	8	33	35	79	.208	.287	.316	603	81	-8	0	1	-0	.996	-1	1-97,3-21	-1.6
1969	Phi-N	138	475	51	121	19	4	17	80	60	111	.255	.338	.419	757	114	9	4	2	0	1.000	-14	O-72L,3-50,1-18	-1.1
1970	Phi-N	159	574	66	147	28	3	27	93	72	132	.256	.339	.456	795	114	10	0	0	0	.995	-11	*1-154/3-3	-1.2
1971	Phi-N	158	582	74	154	29	0	34	95	72	146	.265	.348	.490	837	135	26	0	1	-0	.995	-4	*1-136,3-22	1.1
1972	Phi-N	96	230	19	49	4	1	9	31	26	69	.213	.301	.357	658	84	-5	0	1	-0	.982	-4	1-62	-1.5
1973	Phi-N	12	36	3	6	2	0	1	5	5	10	.167	.286	.306	591	62	-2	0	0	0	.976	-0	1-10	-0.3
	*Oak-A	131	464	61	114	14	2	19	81	59	116	.246	.332	.407	739	113	8	0	1	-0	.994	-3	*D-107,1-23	0.0
1974	Oak-A	50	174	16	34	1	2	7	23	11	37	.195	.243	.345	588	72	-7	1	0	0	.991	-2	1-28,D-23	-1.3
	Mil-A	49	152	14	23	3	0	6	18	21	41	.151	.254	.289	544	56	-9	1	0	0	.833	-0	D-46/1-2	-1.1
	Bos-A	11	25	0	3	0	0	0	2	0	6	.120	.120	.120	240	-29	-4	0	0	0	.000	0	/D-8	-0.5
	Yr	110	351	30	60	4	2	13	43	32	84	.171	.240	.305	545	57	-20	2	0	0	.983	-3	D-77,1-30	-2.9
1975	Chi-A	148	555	66	129	25	1	18	72	48	117	.232	.295	.378	673	88	-10	0	1	-0	.994	-4	D-93,1-55	-2.2
	Bos-A	3	10	2	6	0	0	1	3	2	0	.600	.667	.900	1567	313	3	0	0	0	1.000	-1	/1-2,D-1	0.2
	Yr	151	565	68	135	25	1	19	75	50	117	.239	.302	.388	690	92	-7	0	1	-0	.994	-5	D-94,1-57	-2.0
1976	Bos-A	15	38	3	5	1	1	0	0	5	11	.132	.233	.211	443	27	-3	0	0	0	1.000	-0	/1-5,D-9	-0.4
Total	16	1765	5941	706	1447	247	33	245	923	585	1318	.244	.313	.420	733	102	10	11	18	-4	.993	-63	1-880,3-332,D-2872,O	-14.1
■ DON JOHNSON	Johnson, Donald Spore "Pep" b: 12/7/11, Chicago, Ill. d: 4/6/2000, Laguna Beach, Cal. BR/TR, 6′, 170 lbs. Deb: 9/26/43 F																							
1943	Chi-N	10	42	5	8	2	0	0	1	2	4	.190	.227	.238	465	35	-4	0			.957	3	2-10	0.0
1944	Chi-N☆	154	608	50	169	37	1	2	71	28	48	.278	.311	.352	663	87	-12	8			.947	1	*2-154	-0.3
1945	*Chi-N†	138	557	94	168	23	2	2	58	32	34	.302	.343	.361	704	98	-2	9			.975	10	*2-138	1.6
1946	Chi-N	83	314	37	76	10	1	1	19	26	39	.242	.306	.290	596	71	-12	6			.981	-10	2-83	-1.8
1947	Chi-N	120	402	33	104	17	2	3	26	24	45	.259	.302	.333	635	71	-17	2			.970	-4	*2-108/3-6	-1.5
1948	Chi-N	6	12	0	3	0	0	0	0	0	1	.250	.250	.250	500	37	-1	1			1.000	-2	/2-2,3-2	-0.3
Total	6	511	1935	219	528	89	6	8	175	112	171	.273	.315	.337	653	83	-47	26			.966	-2	2-495/3-8	-2.3
■ ED JOHNSON	Johnson, Edwin Cyril b: 3/31/1899, Morganfield, Ky. d: 7/3/75, Morganfield, Ky. BL/TR, 5′9″, 160 lbs. Deb: 9/26/20																							
1920	Was-A	4	13	1	3	0	0	0	2	3	2	.231	.375	.231	606	65	-0	0	0	0	.625	-1	/O-4(0-0-2)	-0.1
■ ELMER JOHNSON	Johnson, Elmer Ellsworth "Hickory" b: 6/12/1884, Beard, Ind. d: 10/31/66, Hollywood, Fla. BR/TR, 5′9″, 185 lbs. Deb: 4/24/14																							
1914	NY-N	11	12	0	2	1	0	0	0	1	3	.167	.231	.250	481	44	-1	0			.947	-1	C-11	-0.2
■ ERIK JOHNSON	Johnson, Erik Anthony b: 10/11/65, Oakland, Cal. BR/TR, 5′11″, 175 lbs. Deb: 7/8/93																							
1993	SF-N	4	5	1	2	2	0	0	0	0	1	.400	.400	.800	1200	219	1	0	0	0	1.000	-1	/2-2,3-1,S-1	0.0
1994	SF-N	5	13	0	2	0	0	0	0	0	4	.154	.154	.154	308	-20	-2	0	0	0	1.000	1	/2-2,S-1	-0.1
Total	2	9	18	1	4	2	0	0	0	0	5	.222	.222	.333	556	45	-2	0	0	0	1.000	-0	/2-4,S-2,3-1	-0.1
■ ERNIE JOHNSON	Johnson, Ernest Rudolph b: 4/29/1888, Chicago, Ill. d: 5/1/52, Monrovia, Cal. BL/TR, 5′9″, 151 lbs. Deb: 8/5/12 F																							
1912	Chi-A	21	42	7	11	0	1	0	5	1		.262	.279	.310	589	70	-2	0			.984	3	S-16	0.2
1915	StL-F	152	512	58	123	18	10	7	67	46	35	.240	.305	.355	661	81	-21	32			.942	18	*S-152	0.8
1916	StL-A	74	236	29	54	9	3	0	19	30	23	.229	.323	.292	616	89	-2	13			.936	-8	S-60,3-12	-0.7
1917	StL-A	80	199	28	49	6	2	2	20	12	16	.246	.296	.327	622	93	-2	13			.924	11	S-39,2-18,3-14	1.3
1918	StL-A	29	34	7	9	1	0	0	0	0	2	.265	.286	.294	580	77	-1	4			.821	-2	S-11/3-1	-0.3
1921	Chi-A	142	613	93	181	28	7	1	51	29	24	.295	.328	.369	697	78	-21	22	13	0	.947	18	*S-141	1.2
1922	Chi-A	144	603	85	153	17	3	0	56	40	30	.254	.304	.292	596	56	-38	21	18	-2	.952	2	*S-141	-2.2
1923	Chi-A	12	53	5	10	2	0	0	1	3	5	.189	.246	.226	472	25	-6	2	1	0	.922	-0	S-12	-0.5
	*NY-A	19	38	6	17	1	1	1	8	1	1	.447	.462	.605	1067	176	4	0	0	0	.977	-1	S-15/3-1	0.4
	Yr	31	91	11	27	3	1	1	9	4	6	.297	.333	.385	718	88	-2	2	1	0	.944	-1	S-27/3-1	-0.1
1924	NY-A	64	119	24	42	4	8	3	12	11	7	.353	.412	.597	1009	158	10	1	6	-2	.955	-1	2-27/S-9,3-2	0.7
1925	NY-A	76	170	30	48	5	1	5	17	8	10	.282	.315	.412	726	85	-5	6	3	0	.955	-10	2-34,S-28/3-2	-1.1
Total	10	813	2619	372	697	91	36	19	256	181	153	.266	.317	.350	667	80	-84	114	41		.944	29	S-624/2-79,3-32	-0.2
■ FRANK JOHNSON	Johnson, Frank Herbert b: 7/22/42, ElPaso, Tex. BR/TR, 6′1″, 155 lbs. Deb: 9/7/66 Career OF: (51-LF 10-CF 14-RF)																							
1966	SF-N	15	32	2	7	0	0	0	0	2	7	.219	.265	.219	483	35	-3	0	1	-0	1.000	-3	O-13(8-2-7)	-0.7
1967	SF-N	8	10	3	3	0	0	0	0	1	2	.300	.364	.300	664	93	-0	0	0	0	.889	-0	/O-3(2-1-1)	0.0
1968	SF-N	67	174	11	33	2	0	1	7	12	23	.190	.246	.218	464	40	-12	1	0	0	.944	3	3-36/O-8C,S-5,2-3	-1.1
1969	SF-N	7	10	2	1	0	0	0	0	0	1	.100	.100	.100	200	-45	-2	0	0	0	1.000	-1	/O-7(5-1-1)	-0.3
1970	SF-N	67	161	25	44	1	2	3	31	19	18	.273	.357	.360	717	94	-1	1	1	-0	.979	-2	O-33(29-1-4),1-27	-0.6
1971	SF-N	32	49	4	4	1	0	0	5	3	9	.082	.135	.102	237	-33	-9	0	0	0	.975	-3	/1-9,O-4(3-0-1)	-1.3
Total	6	196	436	47	92	4	2	4	43	37	60	.211	.277	.257	534	52	-26	2	2	-0	.979	-6	/O-68L,1-36,3-36,S2	-4.0
■ HOWARD JOHNSON	Johnson, Howard Michael b: 11/29/60, Clearwater, Fla. BB/TR, 5′11″, 178 lbs. Deb: 4/14/82 Career OF: (99-LF 86-CF 36-RF)																							
1982	Det-A	54	155	23	49	5	0	4	14	16	30	.316	.384	.426	810	122	5	7	4	0	.901	-9	3-33,D-10/O-9(3-1-5)	-0.5
1983	Det-A	27	66	11	14	0	0	3	5	7	10	.212	.297	.348	646	79	-2	0	0	0	.851	-6	3-21/D-2	-0.8
1984	*Det-A	116	355	43	88	14	1	12	50	40	67	.248	.326	.394	720	99	-0	10	6	0	.944	-18	*3-108/S-9,1-1,OD	-2.0
1985	NY-N	126	389	38	94	18	4	11	46	34	78	.242	.303	.393	696	96	-3	6	4	-0	.941	-13	*3-113/S-7,O-1(1-0-0)	-1.8
1986	*NY-N	88	220	30	54	14	0	10	39	31	64	.245	.341	.445	787	119	5	8	1	1	.903	-2	3-45,S-34/O-1(1-0-0)	0.7
1987	NY-N	157	554	93	147	22	1	36	99	83	113	.265	.366	.504	870	135	28	32	10	4	.938	-18	*3-140,S-38/O-2L	1.4
1988	*NY-N	148	495	85	114	21	1	24	68	86	104	.230	.348	.422	770	126	18	23	7	3	.951	-14	*3-131/S-52	1.1
1989	NY-N★	153	571	**104**	164	41	3	36	101	77	126	.287	.373	.559	932	171	51	41	8	6	.910	-33	*3-143,S-31	2.8
1990	NY-N	154	590	89	144	37	3	23	90	69	100	.244	.323	.434	757	107	4	34	8	5	.913	-5	3-92,S-73	1.0
1991	NY-N★	156	564	108	146	34	4	**38**	**117**	78	120	.259	.350	.535	885	147	33	30	16	1	.927	-4	*3-104,O-30R,S-28	3.3
1992	NY-N	100	350	48	78	19	0	7	43	55	79	.223	.332	.337	669	91	-3	22	5	3	.981	-4	O-98(16-84-1)	-0.6
1993	NY-N	72	235	32	56	8	2	7	26	43	43	.238	.356	.379	735	98	0	6	4	-0	.944	5	3-67	0.6
1994	Col-N	93	227	30	48	10	2	10	40	39	73	.211	.327	.405	732	77	-8	11	3	1	.979	-2	O-62(62-0-0)/1-1	-1.0
1995	Chi-N	87	169	26	33	4	1	7	22	34	46	.195	.333	.355	688	83	-4	1	1	-0	.926	-8	3-34,O-13L/2-8,1S	-1.2
Total	14	1531	4940	760	1229	247	22	228	760	692	1053	.249	.343	.446	789	118	126	231	77	24	.929	-129	*3-1031,S-273,O/D21	3.0
■ SPUD JOHNSON	Johnson, John Ralph b: 1860, Canada BL/TL, 5′9″, 175 lbs. Deb: 4/18/1889 Career OF: (96-LF 0-CF 187-RF)																							
1889	Col-a	116	459	91	130	14	10	2	79	39	47	.283	.355	.370	725	112	9	34			.879	-11	O-69R,3-44/1-2,S-1	-0.2
1890	Col-a	135	538	106	186	23	18	1	**113**	48		.346	.409	.461	870	168	46	43			.926	-16	*O-135(96-0-39)	2.4
1891	Cle-N	80	327	49	84	8	3	1	46	22	23	.257	.319	.309	628	80	-9	16			.872	-5	O-79(0-0-79)/1-1	-1.3
Total	3	331	1324	246	400	45	31	4	238	109	70	.302	.368	.392	760	125	47	93			.899	-32	O-283R/3-44,1-3,S-1	0.9
■ KEITH JOHNSON	Johnson, Keith b: 4/17/71, Hanford, Cal. BR/TR, 5′11″, 200 lbs. Deb: 4/17/2000																							
2000	Ana-A	6	4	2	2	0	0	0	0	2	0	.500	.667	.500	1167	201	1	0	0	0	1.000	3	/1-3,2-2,S-1	0.3
■ LANCE JOHNSON	Johnson, Kenneth Lance b: 7/6/63, Cincinnati, Ohio BL/TL, 5′11″, 160 lbs. Deb: 7/10/87 Career OF: (53-LF 1327-CF 21-RF)																							
1987	*StL-N	33	59	4	13	2	1	0	7	4	6	.220	.270	.288	558	47	-4	6	1	1	.931	-6	O-25(3-6-17)	-1.0
1988	Chi-A	33	124	11	23	4	1	0	6	6	11	.185	.223	.234	457	28	-12	6	2	1	.970	-4	O-31(0-31-0)/D-1	-1.6
1989	Chi-A	50	180	28	54	8	2	0	16	17	24	.300	.360	.367	727	108	2	16	3	2	.983	0	O-45(42-8-0)/D-1	0.4
1990	Chi-A	151	541	76	154	18	9	1	51	33	45	.285	.327	.357	684	93	-5	36	22	0	.973	-2	*O-148(6-148-0)/D-1	-0.9
1991	Chi-A	159	588	72	161	14	**13**	0	49	26	58	.274	.306	.342	648	81	-16	26	11	2	.995	13	*O-157(0-157-2)	-0.2
1992	Chi-A	157	567	67	158	15	**12**	3	47	34	33	.279	.321	.363	684	92	-6	41	14	4	.987	8	*O-157(0-157-0)	0.5
1993	*Chi-A	147	540	75	168	18	**14**	0	47	36	33	.311	.354	.396	750	104	3	35	7	5	.980	16	*O-146(0-146-0)	2.4

YEAR	TM/L	G	AB	R	H	2B	3B	HR	RBI	BB	SO	AVG	OBP	SLG	OPS	OPS+	BR+	SB	CS	SBR	FA	FR	G/POS	TPR
1994	Chi-A	106	412	56	114	11	**14**	3	54	26	23	.277	.323	.393	716	85	-10	26	6	4	**1.000**	13	*O-103(0-103-0)/D-1	0.8
1995	Chi-A	142	607	98	**186**	18	12	10	57	32	31	.306	.342	.425	767	103	2	40	6	**7**	.991	6	*O-140(0-140-0)/D-1	1.5
1996	NY-N★	160	682	117	**227**	31	**21**	9	69	33	40	.333	.365	.479	844	126	24	50	12	**7**	.971	14	*O-157(0-157-0)	4.5
1997	NY-N	72	265	43	82	10	6	1	24	33	21	.309	.386	.404	790	111	5	15	10	-0	.975	4	O-66(0-66-0)	1.0
	Chi-N	39	145	17	44	6	2	4	15	9	10	.303	.344	.455	799	105	1	5	2	0	.963	-1	O-39(0-39-0)/D-1	0.1
	Yr	111	410	60	126	16	8	5	39	42	31	.307	.372	.422	794	109	6	20	12	0	.971	3	*O-105(0-105-0)/D-1	1.1
1998	*Chi-N	85	304	51	85	8	4	2	21	26	22	.280	.336	.352	688	79	-9	10	6	0	.975	-0	O-78(0-78-0)	-0.8
1999	Chi-N	95	335	46	87	11	6	1	21	37	20	.260	.333	.337	671	71	-14	13	3	2	.988	10	O-91(0-91-0)	-0.1
2000	NY-A	18	30	6	9	1	0	0	2	0	7	.300	.300	.333	633	61	-2	2	0	0	1.000	-1	/O-4(2-0-2),D-2	-0.2
Total	14	1447	5379	767	1565	175	117	34	486	352	384	.291	.335	.386	721	95	-42	327	105	35	.983	71	*O-1387C/D-8	6.4

■ LAMAR JOHNSON

Johnson, Lamar b: 9/2/50, Bessemer, Ala. BR/TR, 6'2", 225 lbs. Deb: 5/18/74 Career OF: (1-LF 0-CF 0-RF)

YEAR	TM/L	G	AB	R	H	2B	3B	HR	RBI	BB	SO	AVG	OBP	SLG	OPS	OPS+	BR+	SB	CS	SBR	FA	FR	G/POS	TPR
1974	Chi-A	10	29	1	10	0	0	0	2	0	3	.345	.345	.345	690	97	-0	0	0	0	1.000	-0	/1-7,D-3	-0.1
1975	Chi-A	8	30	2	6	3	0	1	1	1	5	.200	.226	.400	626	73	-1	0	0	0	.960	-1	/1-6,D-2	-0.3
1976	Chi-A	82	222	29	71	11	1	4	33	19	37	.320	.379	.432	811	136	10	2	1	0	.983	-1	D-35,1-34/O-1(1-0-0)	0.7
1977	Chi-A	118	374	52	113	12	5	18	65	24	53	.302	.344	.505	850	128	13	1	1	-0	.990	1	D-68,1-45	1.0
1978	Chi-A	148	498	52	136	23	2	8	72	43	46	.273	.333	.376	709	98	-1	6	5	-0	.992	2	*1-108,D-36	-0.7
1979	Chi-A	133	479	60	148	29	1	12	74	41	56	.309	.366	.449	815	118	12	8	2	1	.987	-1	1-94,D-37	0.6
1980	Chi-A	147	541	51	150	26	3	13	81	47	53	.277	.335	.409	744	103	2	2	3	-1	.990	2	1-80,D-66	-0.3
1981	Chi-A	41	134	10	37	7	0	1	15	5	14	.276	.302	.351	653	89	-2	0	2	-1	.989	-2	1-36/D-2	-0.7
1982	Tex-A	105	324	37	84	11	0	7	38	31	40	.259	.326	.358	684	92	-3	3	5	-1	.982	-2	D-77,1-12	-0.9
Total	9	792	2631	294	755	122	12	64	381	211	307	.287	.342	.415	757	109	30	22	19	-2	.989	-1	1-422,D-326/O-1L	-0.7

■ LARRY JOHNSON

Johnson, Larry Doby b: 8/17/50, Cleveland, Ohio BR/TR, 6', 185 lbs. Deb: 10/3/72

YEAR	TM/L	G	AB	R	H	2B	3B	HR	RBI	BB	SO	AVG	OBP	SLG	OPS	OPS+	BR+	SB	CS	SBR	FA	FR	G/POS	TPR
1972	Cle-A	1	2	0	1	0	0	0	0	0	1	.500	.500	.500	1000	192	0	0	0	0	1.000	0	/C-1	0.1
1974	Cle-A	1	0	1	0	0	0	0	0	0	0	—	—	—	—	—	0	0	0	0	.000	0	R	0.0
1975	Mon-N	1	3	0	1	1	0	0	1	1	1	.333	.500	.667	1167	212	1	0	0	0	1.000	-0	/C-1	0.0
1976	Mon-N	6	13	0	2	1	0	0	0	0	2	.154	.154	.231	385	8	-2	0	0	0	1.000	1	/C-5	-0.1
1978	Chi-A	3	8	0	1	0	0	0	0	1	4	.125	.222	.125	347	0	-1	0	0	0	.857	-0	/C-2,D-1	-0.2
Total	5	12	26	1	5	2	0	0	1	2	8	.192	.250	.269	519	46	-2	0	0	0	.975	1	/C-9,D-1	-0.2

■ LOU JOHNSON

Johnson, Louis Brown "Slick" b: 9/22/34, Lexington, Ky. BR/TR, 5'11", 175 lbs. Deb: 4/17/60

YEAR	TM/L	G	AB	R	H	2B	3B	HR	RBI	BB	SO	AVG	OBP	SLG	OPS	OPS+	BR+	SB	CS	SBR	FA	FR	G/POS	TPR
1960	Chi-N	34	68	6	14	2	1	0	1	5	19	.206	.270	.265	535	48	-5	3	1	0	1.000	1	O-25(8-4-13)	-0.4
1961	LA-A	1	0	0	0	0	0	0	0	0	0	—	—	—	—	—	0	0	0	0	.000	-0	/O-1(1-0-0)	0.0
1962	Mil-N	61	117	22	33	4	5	2	13	11	27	.282	.349	.453	802	116	3	6	1	1	1.000	-9	O-55(38-20-1)	-0.7
1965	*LA-N	131	468	57	121	24	1	12	58	24	81	.259	.317	.391	708	105	2	15	6	1	.985	-3	*O-128(124-11-3)	-0.7
1966	*LA-N	152	526	71	143	20	2	17	73	21	75	.272	.317	.414	732	110	6	8	10	-2	.985	-2	*O-148(104-2-65)	-0.6
1967	LA-N	104	330	39	89	14	1	11	41	24	52	.270	.332	.418	751	124	9	4	3	-0	.976	2	O-91(81-1-11)	0.7
1968	Chi-N	62	205	14	50	14	3	1	14	6	23	.244	.289	.356	645	87	-3	3	1	0	.970	-4	O-57(1-0-56)	-1.3
	Cle-A	65	202	25	52	11	1	5	23	9	24	.257	.302	.396	698	112	2	6	1	1	.989	1	O-57(41-0-20)	0.2
1969	Cal-A	67	133	10	27	8	0	0	9	10	19	.203	.274	.263	537	53	-8	5	1	1	.935	-5	O-44(23-0-23)	-1.5
Total	8	677	2049	244	529	97	14	48	232	110	320	.258	.313	.389	702	103	6	50	24	3	.981	-19	O-606(421-38-192)	-4.3

■ MARK JOHNSON

Johnson, Mark Landon b: 9/12/75, Wheat Ridge, Colo. BL/TR, 6', 185 lbs. Deb: 9/14/98

YEAR	TM/L	G	AB	R	H	2B	3B	HR	RBI	BB	SO	AVG	OBP	SLG	OPS	OPS+	BR+	SB	CS	SBR	FA	FR	G/POS	TPR
1998	Chi-A	7	23	2	2	0	2	0	1	1	8	.087	.125	.261	386	-3	-4	0	0	0	1.000	-1	/C-7	-0.4
1999	Chi-A	73	207	27	47	11	0	4	16	36	58	.227	.347	.338	685	76	-7	3	1	0	.993	4	C-72/D-2	0.1
2000	Chi-A	75	213	29	48	11	0	3	23	27	40	.225	.315	.319	635	61	-13	3	2	-0	.992	8	C-74/D-1	0.0
Total	3	155	443	58	97	22	2	7	40	64	106	.219	.322	.325	647	65	-23	6	3	0	.993	11	C-153/D-3	-0.3

■ MARK JOHNSON

Johnson, Mark Patrick b: 10/17/67, Worcester, Mass. BL/TL, 6'4", 230 lbs. Deb: 4/26/95

YEAR	TM/L	G	AB	R	H	2B	3B	HR	RBI	BB	SO	AVG	OBP	SLG	OPS	OPS+	BR+	SB	CS	SBR	FA	FR	G/POS	TPR
1995	Pit-N	79	221	32	46	6	1	13	28	37	66	.208	.327	.421	748	94	-2	5	2	0	.986	-4	1-70	-1.1
1996	Pit-N	127	343	55	94	24	0	13	47	44	64	.274	.365	.458	823	112	7	6	4	-0	.994	5	*1-100/O-1(1-0-0)	0.3
1997	Pit-N	78	219	30	47	10	0	4	29	43	78	.215	.348	.315	664	74	-7	1	1	-0	.992	1	1-63/D-1	-1.2
1998	Ana-A	10	14	1	1	0	0	0	0	0	6	.071	.071	.071	143	-62	-3	0	0	0	1.000	0	/1-5,D-2	-0.3
2000	NY-N	21	22	2	4	0	0	1	6	5	9	.182	.333	.318	652	68	-1	0	0	0	1.000	0	/1-4,O-1(1-0-0),D-1	-0.1
Total	5	315	819	120	192	40	1	31	110	129	223	.234	.345	.399	744	93	-7	12	7	0	.991	2	1-242/D-4,O-2(2-0-0)	-2.4

■ OTIS JOHNSON

Johnson, Otis L. b: 11/5/1883, Fowler, Ind. d: 11/9/15, Johnson City, N.Y. BB/TR, 5'9", 185 lbs. Deb: 4/12/11

YEAR	TM/L	G	AB	R	H	2B	3B	HR	RBI	BB	SO	AVG	OBP	SLG	OPS	OPS+	BR+	SB	CS	SBR	FA	FR	G/POS	TPR
1911	NY-A	71	209	21	49	9	6	3	36	39		.234	.363	.378	741	100	1	12			.907	-9	S-47,2-15/3-3	-0.5

■ PAUL JOHNSON

Johnson, Paul Oscar b: 9/2/1896, N.Grosvenor Dale, Conn. d: 2/14/73, McAllen, Tex. BR/TR, 5'8", 160 lbs. Deb: 9/13/20

YEAR	TM/L	G	AB	R	H	2B	3B	HR	RBI	BB	SO	AVG	OBP	SLG	OPS	OPS+	BR+	SB	CS	SBR	FA	FR	G/POS	TPR
1920	Phi-A	18	72	6	15	0	0	0	5	4	8	.208	.250	.208	458	22	-8	1	1	-0	.933	-3	O-18(13-4-1)	-1.2
1921	Phi-A	48	127	17	40	6	2	1	10	9	17	.315	.360	.417	778	97	-1	0	2	-1	.969	-5	O-32(6-24-2)	-0.7
Total	2	66	199	23	55	6	2	1	15	13	25	.276	.321	.342	662	71	-9	1	3	-1	.958	-7	/O-50(19-28-3)	-1.9

■ RANDY JOHNSON

Johnson, Randall Glenn b: 6/10/56, Escondido, Cal. BR/TR, 6'1", 190 lbs. Deb: 4/27/82

YEAR	TM/L	G	AB	R	H	2B	3B	HR	RBI	BB	SO	AVG	OBP	SLG	OPS	OPS+	BR+	SB	CS	SBR	FA	FR	G/POS	TPR
1982	Atl-N	27	46	5	11	5	0	0	6	6	4	.239	.352	.348	700	93	-0	0	1	-0	.955	5	2-13/3-4	0.5
1983	Atl-N	86	144	22	36	3	0	1	17	20	27	.250	.345	.292	637	73	-4	1	3	-1	.991	10	3-53/2-4	0.4
1984	Atl-N	91	294	28	82	13	0	5	30	21	21	.279	.329	.374	703	91	-3	4	7	-2	.939	5	3-81	-0.1
Total	3	204	484	55	129	21	0	6	53	47	52	.267	.336	.347	684	85	-8	5	11	-3	.956	20	3-138/2-17	0.8

■ RANDY JOHNSON

Johnson, Randall Stuart b: 8/15/58, Miami, Fla. BL/TL, 6'2", 195 lbs. Deb: 7/5/80

YEAR	TM/L	G	AB	R	H	2B	3B	HR	RBI	BB	SO	AVG	OBP	SLG	OPS	OPS+	BR+	SB	CS	SBR	FA	FR	G/POS	TPR
1980	Chi-A	12	20	0	4	0	0	0	3	2	4	.200	.304	.200	504	41	-1	0	0	0	.000	-0	/1-1,O-1(1-0-0),D-4	-0.2
1982	Min-A	89	234	26	58	10	0	10	33	30	46	.248	.333	.419	752	102	1	0	0	0	1.000	-0	D-67/O-2(0-0-2)	-0.2
Total	2	101	254	26	62	10	0	10	36	32	50	.244	.331	.402	733	98	-1	0	0	0	1.000	-1	/D-71,O-3(1-0-2),1-1	-0.4

■ FOOTER JOHNSON

Johnson, Richard Allan "Treads" b: 2/15/32, Dayton, Ohio BL/TL, 5'11", 175 lbs. Deb: 6/22/58

YEAR	TM/L	G	AB	R	H	2B	3B	HR	RBI	BB	SO	AVG	OBP	SLG	OPS	OPS+	BR+	SB	CS	SBR	FA	FR	G/POS	TPR
1958	Chi-N	8	5	1	0	0	0	0	0	0	1	.000	.000	.000	0	-99	-1	0	0	0	.000	0	H	-0.1

■ BOB JOHNSON

Johnson, Robert Lee "Indian Bob" b: 11/26/06, Pryor, Okla.
d: 7/6/82, Tacoma, Wash. BR/TR, 6', 180 lbs. Deb: 4/12/33 F Career OF: (1592-LF 162-CF 24-RF)

YEAR	TM/L	G	AB	R	H	2B	3B	HR	RBI	BB	SO	AVG	OBP	SLG	OPS	OPS+	BR+	SB	CS	SBR	FA	FR	G/POS	TPR
1933	Phi-A	142	535	103	155	44	4	21	93	85	74	.290	.387	.505	892	133	26	8	3	1	.952	2	*O-142(127-1-15)	1.9
1934	Phi-A	141	547	111	168	26	6	34	92	58	60	.307	.375	.563	938	144	33	12	8	-0	.967	10	*O-139(139-0-0)	3.2
1935	Phi-A★	147	582	103	174	29	5	28	109	78	76	.299	.384	.510	894	130	25	2	4	-1	.946	4	*O-147(147-0-0)	1.9
1936	Phi-A	153	566	91	165	29	14	25	121	88	71	.292	.389	.525	913	126	22	6	6	-1	.962	3	*O-131L,2-22/1-1	1.6
1937	Phi-A	138	477	91	146	32	6	25	108	98	65	.306	.425	.556	981	148	37	9	7	-0	.976	9	*O-133(129-6-0)/2-2	3.5
1938	Phi-A★	152	563	114	176	27	9	30	113	87	73	.313	.406	.552	959	142	36	9	8	-1	.963	10	*O-150C/2-3,3-1	3.6
1939	Phi-A☆	150	544	115	184	30	9	23	114	99	59	.338	.440	.553	993	156	49	15	5	2	.967	7	*O-150(138-14-0)/2-1	4.5
1940	Phi-A☆	138	512	93	137	25	4	31	103	83	64	.268	.374	.514	888	130	23	8	2	1	.962	5	*O-136(116-13-8)	2.1
1941	Phi-A	149	552	98	152	30	8	22	107	95	75	.275	.385	.478	863	130	25	6	4	-0	.990	7	*O-122(118-4-0),1-28	2.1
1942	Phi-A★	149	550	78	160	35	7	13	80	82	61	.291	.384	.451	835	135	26	3	2	-0	.963	5	*O-149(148-0-1)	2.4
1943	Was-A★	117	438	65	116	22	8	7	63	64	50	.265	.362	.400	762	127	16	11	5	1	.996	9	O-88L,3-19,1-10	2.1
1944	Bos-A★	144	525	106	170	40	8	17	106	95	67	.324	**.431**	.528	**959**	**175**	**54**	2	7	-2	.977	4	*O-142(142-0-0)	4.9
1945	Bos-A†	143	529	71	148	27	7	12	74	63	56	.280	.358	.425	783	124	16	5	3	0	.975	3	*O-140(140-1-0)	1.1
Total	13	1863	6920	1239	2051	396	95	288	1283	1075	851	.296	.393	.506	899	139	388	96	64	-1	.968	79	*O-1769L/1-39,2-28,3	34.9

■ BOB JOHNSON

Johnson, Robert Wallace b: 3/4/36, Omaha, Neb. BR/TR, 5'10", 175 lbs. Deb: 4/19/60 Career OF: (2-LF 0-CF 0-RF)

YEAR	TM/L	G	AB	R	H	2B	3B	HR	RBI	BB	SO	AVG	OBP	SLG	OPS	OPS+	BR+	SB	CS	SBR	FA	FR	G/POS	TPR
1960	KC-A	76	146	12	30	4	0	1	9	19	23	.205	.301	.253	555	51	-10	2	0	0	.947	12	S-30,2-27,3-11	0.5
1961	Was-A	61	224	27	66	13	1	6	28	19	26	.295	.352	.442	794	113	4	4	2	0	.956	-2	S-57/2-2,3-2	0.7
1962	Was-A	135	466	58	134	20	2	12	43	32	50	.288	.335	.416	751	102	0	9	6	-0	.944	-4	3-72,S-50/2-3,O-1L	0.0
1963	Bal-A	82	254	34	75	10	0	8	32	18	35	.295	.347	.429	776	120	7	5	1	1	.987	-2	2-50/1-8,S-7,3-5	1.0
1964	Bal-A	93	210	18	52	8	2	3	29	9	37	.248	.282	.348	629	74	-8	0	0	0	.964	-12	S-18,1-15,2-15,/3O	-1.9

YEAR	TM/L	G	AB	R	H	2B	3B	HR	RBI	BB	SO	AVG	OBP	SLG	OPS	OPS+	BR+	SB	CS	SBR	FA	FR	G/POS	TPR
1965	Bal-A	87	273	36	66	13	2	5	27	15	34	.242	.284	.359	643	80	-8	1	0	0	.996	-11	1-34,S-23,3-13,/2-5	-1.9
1966	Bal-A	71	157	13	34	5	0	1	10	12	24	.217	.276	.268	544	58	-8	0	1	-0	.966	0	2-20,1-17/3-3	-0.8
1967	Bal-A	4	3	1	1	0	0	0	0	1	1	.333	.500	.333	833	152	0	0	0	0	.000	0	H	0.0
	NY-N	90	230	26	80	8	3	5	27	12	29	.348	.380	.474	854	145	13	1	1	-0	.987	-7	2-39,1-23,S-14,/3-1	0.8
1968	Cin-N	16	15	2	4	0	0	0	1	1	2	.267	.313	.267	579	71	-0	0	0	0	.500	-1	/S-2,1-1	-0.1
	Atl-N	59	187	15	49	5	1	0	11	10	20	.262	.299	.299	599	80	-5	0	0	0	.948	1	3-48/2-4	-0.4
	Yr	75	202	17	53	5	1	0	12	11	22	.262	.300	.297	597	79	-5	0	0	0	.948	1	3-48/2-4,S-2,1-1	-0.5
1969	StL-N	19	29	1	6	0	0	1	2	2	4	.207	.258	.310	568	58	-2	0	0	0	.833	-1	/3-4,1-1	-0.3
	Oak-A	51	67	5	23	1	0	1	9	3	4	.343	.380	.403	783	125	2	0	0	0	1.000	0	/1-7,2-2	0.2
1970	Oak-A	30	46	6	8	1	0	1	2	3	2	.174	.240	.261	501	39	-4	2	1	0	.952	1	/3-6,1-1	-0.3
Total	11	874	2307	254	628	88	11	44	230	156	291	.272	.321	.377	698	95	-18	24	12	1	.956	-26	S-201,2-167,31/O	-2.5

■ RON JOHNSON

Johnson, Ronald David b: 3/23/56, Long Beach, Cal. BR/TR, 6'3", 215 lbs. Deb: 9/12/82

YEAR	TM/L	G	AB	R	H	2B	3B	HR	RBI	BB	SO	AVG	OBP	SLG	OPS	OPS+	BR+	SB	CS	SBR	FA	FR	G/POS	TPR
1982	KC-A	8	14	2	4	2	0	0	0	4	3	.286	.444	.429	873	141	1	0	0	0	.976	-0	/1-7	0.0
1983	KC-A	9	27	2	7	0	0	0	1	3	1	.259	.333	.259	593	66	-1	0	0	0	.971	-1	/1-7,C-2	-0.3
1984	Mon-N	5	5	0	1	0	0	0	1	0	2	.200	.200	.200	400	13	-1	0	0	0	1.000	-1	/1-2,O-1(0-0-1)	-0.1
Total	3	22	46	4	12	2	0	0	2	7	6	.261	.358	.304	663	85	-1	0	0	0	.974	-2	/1-16,C-2,O-1(0-0-1)	-0.4

■ RONDIN JOHNSON

Johnson, Rondin Allen b: 12/16/58, Bremerton, Wash. BB/TR, 5'10", 160 lbs. Deb: 9/3/86

YEAR	TM/L	G	AB	R	H	2B	3B	HR	RBI	BB	SO	AVG	OBP	SLG	OPS	OPS+	BR+	SB	CS	SBR	FA	FR	G/POS	TPR
1986	KC-A	11	31	1	8	0	1	0	2	0	3	.258	.258	.323	581	56	-2	0	0	0	1.000	4	2-11	0.2

■ ROY JOHNSON

Johnson, Roy Cleveland b: 2/23/03, Pryor, Okla. d: 9/10/73, Tacoma, Wash. BL/TR, 5'9", 175 lbs. Deb: 4/18/29 F Career OF: (527-LF 70-CF 483-RF)

YEAR	TM/L	G	AB	R	H	2B	3B	HR	RBI	BB	SO	AVG	OBP	SLG	OPS	OPS+	BR+	SB	CS	SBR	FA	FR	G/POS	TPR
1929	Det-A	148	640	128	201	**45**	14	10	69	67	60	.314	.379	.475	854	118	17	20	15	-1	.928	14	*O-146(91-37-23)	1.8
1930	Det-A	125	462	84	127	30	13	2	35	40	46	.275	.333	.409	742	85	-11	17	10	0	.936	4	*O-118(7-2-110)	-1.4
1931	Det-A	151	621	107	173	37	**19**	8	55	72	51	.279	.355	.438	793	104	3	33	21	-0	.960	15	*O-150(0-5-148)	0.8
1932	Det-A	49	195	33	49	14	2	3	22	20	26	.251	.324	.390	714	81	-6	7	2	1	.929	0	O-48(0-0-48)	-0.7
	Bos-A	94	349	70	104	24	4	11	47	44	41	.298	.378	.484	862	125	13	13	4	1	.930	-6	O-85(14-16-56)	0.4
	Yr	143	544	103	153	38	6	14	69	64	67	.281	.359	.450	809	109	7	20	6	2	.930	-5	*O-133(14-16-104)	-0.3
1933	Bos-A	133	483	88	151	30	7	10	95	55	36	.313	.387	.466	853	126	19	13	10	-1	.922	4	*O-125(26-10-95)	1.4
1934	Bos-A	143	569	85	182	43	10	7	119	54	36	.320	.379	.467	846	109	7	11	5	1	.948	-3	*O-137(137-0-0)	-0.3
1935	Bos-A	145	553	70	174	33	9	3	66	74	34	.315	.398	.423	822	105	7	11	12	-2	.944	-2	*O-142(142-0-0)	-0.4
1936	*NY-A	63	147	21	39	8	2	1	19	21	14	.265	.361	.367	728	83	-4	3	1	0	.944	0	O-33(28-0-3)	-0.4
1937	NY-A	12	51	5	15	3	0	0	6	3	2	.294	.333	.353	686	73	-2	1	0	0	.840	-2	O-12(12-0-0)	-0.4
	Bos-N	85	260	24	72	8	3	3	22	38	29	.277	.369	.365	735	110	5	5			.965	-1	O-63(63-0-0)/3-1	0.1
1938	Bos-N	7	29	2	5	0	0	0	1	1	5	.172	.200	.172	372	4	-4	1			.769	-2	/O-7(7-0-0)	-0.7
Total	10	1155	4359	717	1292	275	83	58	556	489	380	.296	.369	.437	806	107	44	135	80		.938	22	*O-1066L/3-1	0.2

■ ROY JOHNSON

Johnson, Roy Edward b: 6/27/59, Parkin, Ark. BL/TL, 6'4", 205 lbs. Deb: 7/3/82

YEAR	TM/L	G	AB	R	H	2B	3B	HR	RBI	BB	SO	AVG	OBP	SLG	OPS	OPS+	BR+	SB	CS	SBR	FA	FR	G/POS	TPR
1982	Mon-N	17	32	2	7	2	0	0	2	1	6	.219	.242	.281	524	45	-2	0	0	0	1.000	-2	O-11(0-9-3)	-0.4
1984	Mon-N	16	33	2	5	2	0	1	2	7	10	.152	.300	.303	603	73	-1	1	0	0	.938	-1	O-10(9-0-1)	-0.2
1985	Mon-N	3	5	0	0	0	0	0	0	0	3	.000	.000	.000	0	-99	-1	0	0	0	.000	-1	/O-3(0-1-2)	-0.3
Total	3	36	70	4	12	4	0	1	4	8	19	.171	.256	.271	528	49	-5	1	0	0	.971	-4	/O-24(9-10-6)	-0.9

■ STAN JOHNSON

Johnson, Stanley Lucius b: 2/12/37, Dallas, Tex. BL/TL, 5'10", 180 lbs. Deb: 9/18/60

YEAR	TM/L	G	AB	R	H	2B	3B	HR	RBI	BB	SO	AVG	OBP	SLG	OPS	OPS+	BR+	SB	CS	SBR	FA	FR	G/POS	TPR
1960	Chi-A	5	6	1	1	0	0	1	1	0	1	.167	.167	.667	833	116	0	0	1	-0	1.000	-1	/O-2(2-0-0)	-0.1
1961	KC-A	3	3	1	0	0	0	0	0	2	1	.000	.400	.000	400	17	-0	0	0	0	.000	-1	/O-2(0-0-2)	-0.1
Total	2	8	9	2	1	0	0	1	1	2	2	.111	.273	.444	717	89	-0	0	1	-0	1.000	-2	/O-4(2-0-2)	-0.2

■ TIM JOHNSON

Johnson, Timothy Evald b: 7/22/49, Grand Forks, N.D. BL/TR, 6'1", 170 lbs. Deb: 4/24/73 MC Career OF: (2-LF 0-CF 0-RF)

YEAR	TM/L	G	AB	R	H	2B	3B	HR	RBI	BB	SO	AVG	OBP	SLG	OPS	OPS+	BR+	SB	CS	SBR	FA	FR	G/POS	TPR
1973	Mil-A	136	465	39	99	10	2	0	32	29	93	.213	.261	.243	504	44	-35	6	3	0	.962	-18	*S-135	-3.8
1974	Mil-A	93	245	25	60	7	7	0	25	11	48	.245	.280	.331	611	76	-8	4	3	-0	.970	-2	S-64,2-26/3-1,OD	-0.3
1975	Mil-A	38	85	6	12	1	0	0	2	6	17	.141	.198	.153	351	0	-11	3	0	1	1.000	1	2-11,3-11,S-10,/1D	-0.8
1976	Mil-A	105	273	25	75	4	3	0	14	19	32	.275	.327	.311	638	89	-3	4	1	1	.980	-18	*2-100,3-17/1-1,S-1	-1.7
1977	Mil-A	30	33	5	2	1	0	0	2	5	10	.061	.184	.091	275	-22	-6	1	0	0	.929	3	2-10/S-6,3-4,O-1L,D	-0.3
1978	Mil-A	3	3	1	0	0	0	0	0	2	0	.000	.400	.000	400	22	-0	0	0	0	1.000	-1	/S-2	-0.2
	Tor-A	68	79	9	19	2	0	0	3	8	16	.241	.318	.266	584	65	-3	0	1	-0	.975	5	S-49,2-13	0.4
	Yr	71	82	10	19	2	0	0	3	10	16	.232	.323	.256	579	63	-4	0	1	-0	.975	4	S-51,2-13	0.2
1979	Tor-A	43	86	6	16	2	1	0	6	8	15	.186	.255	.233	488	32	-8	0	1	-0	.958	6	2-25/3-9,1-7	-0.2
Total	7	516	1269	116	283	27	13	0	84	88	231	.223	.276	.265	541	55	-75	18	9	1	.965	-25	S-267,2-185/3-42,1DO	-6.9

■ WALLACE JOHNSON

Johnson, Wallace Darnell b: 12/25/56, Gary, Ind. BB/TR, 5'11", 185 lbs. Deb: 9/8/81 C

YEAR	TM/L	G	AB	R	H	2B	3B	HR	RBI	BB	SO	AVG	OBP	SLG	OPS	OPS+	BR+	SB	CS	SBR	FA	FR	G/POS	TPR
1981	*Mon-N	11	9	1	2	0	1	0	3	1	1	.222	.300	.444	744	108	0	1	1	-0	1.000	1	/2-1	0.1
1982	Mon-N	36	57	5	11	0	2	0	2	5	5	.193	.258	.263	521	45	-4	4	1	1	.952	-6	2-13	-0.9
1983	Mon-N	3	2	1	1	0	0	0	0	1	0	.500	.667	.500	1167	229	1	1	0	0	.000	0	/H	0.1
	SF-N	7	8	0	1	0	0	0	1	0	0	.125	.125	.125	250	-32	-1	0	0	0	1.000	1	/2-1	-0.1
	Yr	10	10	1	2	0	0	0	1	1	0	.200	.273	.200	473	34	-1	1	0	0	1.000	1	/2-1	0.0
1984	Mon-N	17	24	3	5	0	0	0	4	5	4	.208	.345	.208	553	61	-1	0	0	0	.968	0	/1-4	-0.1
1986	Mon-N	61	127	13	36	3	1	1	10	7	9	.283	.321	.346	667	85	-3	6	3	0	.991	-0	1-27	-0.4
1987	Mon-N	75	85	7	21	5	0	1	14	7	6	.247	.304	.341	646	69	-4	5	0	1	.972	-1	/1-9	-0.5
1988	Mon-N	86	94	7	29	5	1	0	3	12	15	.309	.387	.383	770	116	2	0	2	-1	.989	1	1-13/2-1	0.2
1989	Mon-N	85	114	9	31	3	1	2	17	7	12	.272	.314	.368	682	93	-1	1	0	0	.972	-1	1-18	-0.3
1990	Mon-N	47	49	6	8	1	0	1	5	7	6	.163	.281	.245	526	48	-3	1	0	0	1.000	-1	/1-7	-0.5
Total	9	428	569	52	145	17	6	5	59	52	58	.255	.318	.332	650	81	-15	19	7	2	.983	-7	/1-78,2-16	-2.4

■ WALTER JOHNSON

Johnson, Walter Perry "Barney" or "The Big Train"
b: 11/6/1887, Humboldt, Kan. d: 12/10/46, Washington, D.C. BR/TR, 6'1", 200 lbs. Deb: 8/2/07 MH

YEAR	TM/L	G	AB	R	H	2B	3B	HR	RBI	BB	SO	AVG	OBP	SLG	OPS	OPS+	BR+	SB	CS	SBR	FA	FR	G/POS	TPR
1907	Was-A	14	36	3	4	0	1	0	1	1		.111	.135	.167	302	-4	-4	0			.893	-2	P-14	0.0
1908	Was-A	36	79	7	13	3	2	0	5	6		.165	.250	.253	503	69	-3	0			.938	-4	P-36	0.0
1909	Was-A	40	101	6	13	3	0	1	6	1		.129	.137	.188	325	3	-11	0			.926	-2	P-40	0.0
1910	Was-A	45	137	14	24	6	1	2	12	4		.175	.199	.277	476	51	-8	2			.950	-1	P-45	0.0
1911	Was-A	42	128	18	30	5	3	1	15	0		.234	.234	.344	578	62	-7	1			.965	4	P-40	0.0
1912	Was-A	55	144	16	38	6	4	2	20	7		.264	.298	.403	701	99	-1	2			.964	1	P-50	0.0
1913	Was-A	55	134	12	35	5	6	2	14	5	14	.261	.293	.433	726	109	0	2			**1.000**	-0	P-48/O-1(0-1-0)	0.0
1914	Was-A	55	136	23	30	4	1	3	16	10	27	.221	.274	.331	605	79	-4	2	1	0	.964	2	P-51/O-1(1-0-0)	-0.1
1915	Was-A	64	147	14	34	7	4	2	17	8	34	.231	.276	.374	650	93	-2	0	2	-1	.951	0	P-47/O-4(1-0-3)	-0.2
1916	Was-A	58	142	13	32	2	4	1	7	11	28	.225	.286	.317	603	82	-4	0			.937	-5	P-48	0.0
1917	Was-A	57	130	15	33	12	1	0	15	9	30	.254	.312	.362	674	107	1	1			**1.000**	-1	P-47	0.0
1918	Was-A	65	150	10	40	4	4	1	18	9	18	.267	.321	.367	688	109	1	2			.988	-3	P-39/O-4(0-4-0)	0.0
1919	Was-A	56	125	13	24	1	3	1	8	12	17	.192	.263	.272	535	51	-8	1			.988	-0	P-39/O-3(0-2-1)	-0.1
1920	Was-A	33	64	6	17	1	3	1	7	3	10	.266	.299	.422	720	92	-1	0	0	0	.971	-1	P-21	0.0
1921	Was-A	38	111	10	30	7	0	0	10	6	14	.270	.308	.333	641	67	-6	0	0	0	.982	-3	P-35	0.0
1922	Was-A	43	108	8	22	3	0	1	15	2	12	.204	.218	.259	477	25	-12	0	0	0	**1.000**	1	P-41	0.0
1923	Was-A	42	93	11	18	3	3	0	13	4	15	.194	.227	.290	517	37	-9	0	0	0	.970	-2	P-42	0.0
1924	*Was-A	39	113	18	32	9	0	1	14	3	11	.283	.308	.389	697	82	-4	0	0	0	**1.000**	-1	P-38	0.0
1925	*Was-A	36	97	12	42	6	1	2	20	3	6	.433	.455	.577	1033	164	9	0	1	-0	**1.000**	-4	P-30	0.0
1926	Was-A	35	103	6	20	5	0	1	12	3	11	.194	.217	.272	489	28	-11	0	0	0	.980	-5	P-33	0.0
1927	Was-A	26	46	6	16	2	0	2	10	3	4	.348	.388	.522	909	136	2	0	0	0	1.000	0	P-18	0.0
Total	21	934	2324	241	547	94	41	24	255	110	251	.235	.274	.342	616	76	-83	13	4		.969	-25	P-802/O-13(2-7-4)	-0.4

■ BILL JOHNSON

Johnson, William F. "Sleepy Bill" b: 9/1862, New Jersey d: 7/17/42, Chester, Pa. BL/TL, 140 lbs. Deb: 6/27/1884

YEAR	TM/L	G	AB	R	H	2B	3B	HR	RBI	BB	SO	AVG	OBP	SLG	OPS	OPS+	BR+	SB	CS	SBR	FA	FR	G/POS	TPR
1884	Phi-U	1	4	0	0	0	0	0		0		.000	.000	.000	0	-99	-1				.000	-0	/O-1(1-0-0)	-0.1

YEAR	TM/L	G	AB	R	H	2B	3B	HR	RBI	BB	SO	AVG	OBP	SLG	OPS	OPS+	BR+	SB	CS	SBR	FA	FR	G/POS	TPR
1887	Ind-N	11	42	3	8	0	0	0	3	0	6	.190	.209	.190	400	12	-5	5			.765	-2	O-11(0-0-11)	-0.6
1890	Bal-a	24	95	15	28	2	3	0	6	7		.295	.350	.379	728	110	1	8			.865	2	O-24(0-0-24)	0.2
1891	Bal-a	129	480	101	130	13	14	2	79	89	55	.271	.389	.369	758	116	13	32			.877	6	*O-129(60-24-46)	1.4
1892	Bal-N	4	15	2	2	0	0	0	2	2	0	.133	.235	.133	369	12	-2	0			.667	-1	/O-4(1-0-3)	-0.3
Total	5	169	636	121	168	15	17	2	90	98	61	.264	.368	.351	718	105	6	45			.867	5	O-169(62-24-84)	0.6

■ BILL JOHNSON

Johnson, William Lawrence b: 10/18/1892, Chicago, Ill. d: 11/3/50, Los Angeles, Cal. BL/TR, 5'11", 170 lbs. Deb: 9/22/16

YEAR	TM/L	G	AB	R	H	2B	3B	HR	RBI	BB	SO	AVG	OBP	SLG	OPS	OPS+	BR+	SB	CS	SBR	FA	FR	G/POS	TPR
1916	Phi-A	4	15	1	4	1	0	0	1	0	4	.267	.267	.333	600	84	-0	0			1.000	-1	/O-4(0-4-0)	-0.2
1917	Phi-A	48	109	7	19	2	2	1	8	8	14	.174	.237	.257	494	51	-7	4			.900	-3	O-30(2-1-27)	-1.2
Total	2	52	124	8	23	3	2	1	9	8	18	.185	.241	.266	507	55	-7	4			.909	-4	/O-34(2-5-27)	-1.4

■ BILLY JOHNSON

Johnson, William Russell "Bull" b: 8/30/18, Montclair, N.J. BR/TR, 5'10", 180 lbs. Deb: 4/22/43

YEAR	TM/L	G	AB	R	H	2B	3B	HR	RBI	BB	SO	AVG	OBP	SLG	OPS	OPS+	BR+	SB	CS	SBR	FA	FR	G/POS	TPR
1943	*NY-A	155	592	70	166	24	6	5	94	53	30	.280	.344	.367	710	107	5	3	5	-1	.966	12	*3-155	1.9
1946	NY-A	85	296	51	77	14	5	4	35	31	42	.260	.334	.382	716	98	-1	1	0	0	.955	7	3-74	0.7
1947	*NY-A★	132	494	67	141	19	8	10	95	44	43	.285	.351	.417	768	114	8	1	2	-0	.952	-17	*3-132	-1.0
1948	NY-A	127	446	59	131	20	6	12	64	41	30	.294	.358	.446	805	114	8	0	0	0	.947	6	*3-118	1.3
1949	*NY-A	113	329	48	82	11	3	8	56	48	44	.249	.348	.374	722	91	-4	1	0	0	.951	-2	3-81,1-21/2-1	-0.7
1950	*NY-A	108	327	44	85	16	2	6	40	42	30	.260	.346	.376	722	87	-6	1	0	0	.958	-1	*3-100/1-5	-0.7
1951	NY-A	15	40	5	12	3	0	0	4	7	0	.300	.404	.375	779	116	1	0	1	-0	.960	-3	3-13	-0.2
	StL-N	124	442	52	116	23	1	14	64	46	49	.262	.340	.414	754	101	1	5	3	0	**.976**	11	*3-124	1.2
1952	StL-N	94	282	23	71	10	2	2	34	34	21	.252	.339	.323	661	84	-5	1	0	0	.951	2	3-89	-0.4
1953	StL-N	11	5	0	1	0	0	0	1	1	1	.200	.333	.400	733	90	-0	0	0	0	1.000	2	3-11	0.2
Total	9	964	3253	419	882	141	33	61	487	347	290	.271	.346	.391	737	102	6	13	11	-1	.959	18	3-897/1-26,2-1	2.3

■ RUSS JOHNSON

Johnson, William Russell b: 2/22/73, Baton Rouge, La. BR/TR, 5'10", 185 lbs. Deb: 4/8/97

YEAR	TM/L	G	AB	R	H	2B	3B	HR	RBI	BB	SO	AVG	OBP	SLG	OPS	OPS+	BR+	SB	CS	SBR	FA	FR	G/POS	TPR
1997	*Hou-N	21	60	7	18	1	0	2	9	6	14	.300	.364	.417	780	108	1	1	1	-0	.963	-2	3-14/2-3	-0.1
1998	Hou-N	8	13	2	3	1	0	0	0	1	5	.231	.333	.308	641	72	-0	1	0	0	1.000	4	/3-5,2-1	0.4
1999	*Hou-N	83	156	24	44	10	0	5	23	20	31	.282	.364	.442	806	104	1	2	3	-1	.944	6	3-36,2-15/S-2	0.7
2000	Hou-N	26	45	4	8	0	0	0	3	2	10	.178	.213	.178	391	-0	-7	1	1	-0	1.000	-3	/S-5,3-4,2-3	-0.9
	TB-A	74	185	28	47	8	0	2	17	25	30	.254	.346	.330	676	73	-7	4	1	1	.967	4	3-49,2-18,S-11	-0.1
Total	4	212	459	65	120	20	0	9	52	54	90	.261	.342	.364	706	80	-12	9	6	-0	.961	9	3-108/2-40,S-18	0.0

■ GREG JOHNSTON

Johnston, Gregory Bernard b: 2/12/55, Los Angeles, Cal. BL/TL, 6', 175 lbs. Deb: 7/27/79

YEAR	TM/L	G	AB	R	H	2B	3B	HR	RBI	BB	SO	AVG	OBP	SLG	OPS	OPS+	BR+	SB	CS	SBR	FA	FR	G/POS	TPR
1979	SF-N	42	74	5	15	2	0	1	7	2	17	.203	.224	.270	494	37	-7	0	0	0	.966	-1	O-17(13-1-5)	-0.9
1980	Min-A	14	27	3	5	3	0	0	1	2	4	.185	.241	.296	538	43	-2	0	0	0	1.000	-3	O-14(0-14-0)	-0.5
1981	Min-A	7	16	2	2	0	0	0	0	2	5	.125	.222	.125	347	2	-2	0	0	0	1.000	0	/O-6(0-6-0)	-0.2
Total	3	63	117	10	22	5	0	1	8	6	26	.188	.228	.256	484	33	-11	0	0	0	.985	-4	/O-37(13-21-5)	-1.6

■ JIMMY JOHNSTON

Johnston, James Harle b: 12/10/1889, Cleveland, Tenn.
d: 2/14/67, Chattanooga, Tenn. BR/TR, 5'10", 160 lbs. Deb: 5/3/11 FC Career OF: (72-LF 112-CF 177-RF)

YEAR	TM/L	G	AB	R	H	2B	3B	HR	RBI	BB	SO	AVG	OBP	SLG	OPS	OPS+	BR+	SB	CS	SBR	FA	FR	G/POS	TPR
1911	Chi-A	1	2	0	0	0	0	0	2	0		.000	.000	.000	0	-99	-1	0			1.000	-0	/O-1(0-1-0)	-0.1
1914	Chi-N	50	101	9	23	3	2	1	8	4	9	.228	.264	.327	591	76	-3	3			.929	4	O-28(2-22-4)/2-4	0.0
1916	*Bro-N	118	425	58	107	13	8	1	26	35	38	.252	.313	.327	640	94	-3	22	19	-2	.964	7	*O-106(8-45-55)	-0.4
1917	Bro-N	103	330	33	89	10	4	0	25	23	28	.270	.321	.324	645	96	-1	16			.958	4	O-66L,1-14/S-4,23	-0.2
1918	Bro-N	123	484	54	136	16	8	0	27	33	31	.281	.328	.347	675	106	3	22			.956	8	O-96R,1-21/3-4,2-1	0.6
1919	Bro-N	117	405	56	114	11	4	1	23	29	26	.281	.334	.336	670	100	0	11			.960	-6	2-87,O-14C/1-2,S-1	-0.5
1920	*Bro-N	155	635	87	185	17	12	1	52	43	23	.291	.338	.361	699	98	-1	19	15	-1	.934	-6	*3-146/O-7(0-0-7),S-3	-0.5
1921	Bro-N	152	624	104	203	41	14	5	56	45	26	.325	.372	.460	832	115	13	28	16	1	.935	8	*3-150/S-3	3.1
1922	Bro-N	138	567	110	181	20	7	4	49	38	17	.319	.364	.400	764	98	-1	18	9	1	.947	7	2-62,S-50,3-26	1.4
1923	Bro-N	151	625	111	203	29	11	4	60	53	15	.325	.378	.426	803	115	14	16	13	-1	.948	**25**	2-84,S-52,3-14	**4.4**
1924	Bro-N	86	315	51	94	11	2	2	29	27	10	.298	.356	.365	721	97	-1	5	6	-1	.939	-4	S-63,3-10/1-4,O-1R	0.2
1925	Bro-N	123	431	63	128	13	3	2	43	45	15	.297	.369	.355	724	88	-6	7	5	-0	.886	-23	3-81,O-20R/1-8,S-2	-2.4
1926	Bos-N	23	57	7	14	1	0	1	5	10	3	.246	.358	.316	674	91	-0	2			.865	-4	3-14/2-2,O-1(1-0-0)	-0.3
	NY-N	37	69	11	16	0	0	0	5	6	5	.232	.293	.232	525	43	-5	0			1.000	-5	O-14(1-7-6)	-1.1
	Yr	60	126	18	30	1	0	1	10	16	8	.238	.324	.270	594	64	-6	2			1.000	-8	O-15(2-7-6),3-14/2-2	-1.4
Total	13	1377	5070	754	1493	185	75	22	410	391	246	.294	.347	.374	721	100	7	169	83		.926	15	3-448,O-354R,2S/1	4.2

■ JOHNNY JOHNSTON

Johnston, John Thomas b: 3/28/1890, Longview, Tex. d: 3/7/40, San Diego, Cal. BL/TR, 5'11", 172 lbs. Deb: 4/10/13

YEAR	TM/L	G	AB	R	H	2B	3B	HR	RBI	BB	SO	AVG	OBP	SLG	OPS	OPS+	BR+	SB	CS	SBR	FA	FR	G/POS	TPR
1913	StL-A	111	380	37	85	14	4	2	27	42	51	.224	.308	.297	605	79	-10	11			.965	12	*O-107(106-0-0)	-0.3

■ REX JOHNSTON

Johnston, Rex David b: 11/8/37, Colton, Cal. BB/TR, 6'1.5", 202 lbs. Deb: 4/15/64

YEAR	TM/L	G	AB	R	H	2B	3B	HR	RBI	BB	SO	AVG	OBP	SLG	OPS	OPS+	BR+	SB	CS	SBR	FA	FR	G/POS	TPR
1964	Pit-N	14	7	1	0	0	0	0	0	3	0	.000	.300	.000	300	-7	-1	0	0	0	1.000	-2	/O-8(6-2-0)	-0.3

■ DICK JOHNSTON

Johnston, Richard Frederick b: 4/6/1863, Kingston, N.Y. d: 4/4/34, Detroit, Mich. BR/TR, 5'8", 155 lbs. Deb: 8/12/1884

YEAR	TM/L	G	AB	R	H	2B	3B	HR	RBI	BB	SO	AVG	OBP	SLG	OPS	OPS+	BR+	SB	CS	SBR	FA	FR	G/POS	TPR
1884	Ric-a	39	146	23	41	5	5	2		2		.281	.291	.425	715	132	5				.865	9	O-37(0-37-0)/S-2	1.1
1885	Bos-N	26	111	17	26	6	3	1	23	0	15	.234	.234	.369	604	96	-1				.842	1	O-26(0-26-0)	0.0
1886	Bos-N	109	413	48	99	18	9	1	57	3	70	.240	.245	.334	579	78	-12	11			.892	17	*O-109(0-109-0)	0.1
1887	Bos-N	127	523	87	147	13	20	5	77	16	35	.281	.281	.393	674	85	-12	52			.933	25	*O-127(0-127-0)	0.8
1888	Bos-N	135	585	102	173	31	**18**	12	68	15	33	.296	.314	.472	786	145	27	35			.898	7	*O-135(0-135-0)	2.8
1889	Bos-N	132	539	80	123	16	4	5	67	41	60	.228	.285	.301	586	60	-30	34			.917	-7	*O-132(0-132-0)	-3.7
1890	Bos-P	2	9	0	1	0	0	0	0	0	1	.111	.111	.111	222	-38	-2	0			.800	0	/O-2(0-2-0)	-0.1
	NY-P	77	306	37	74	9	7	1	43	18	25	.242	.288	.327	615	59	-20	7			.897	3	O-76(12-62-2)/S-2	-1.5
	Yr	79	315	37	75	9	7	1	43	18	26	.238	.284	.321	604	56	-22	7			.894	3	O-78(12-64-2)/S-2	-1.6
1891	Cin-a	99	376	59	83	11	2	6	51	38	44	.221	.301	.309	609	68	-17	12			.895	-1	*O-99(0-99-1)	-1.9
Total	8	746	3008	453	767	109	68	33	386	133	283	.255	.285	.366	651	87	-62	151			.903	54	O-743(12-729-3)/S-4	-2.4

■ DOC JOHNSTON

Johnston, Wheeler Roger b: 9/9/1887, Cleveland, Tenn. d: 2/17/61, Chattanooga, Tenn. BL/TL, 6', 170 lbs. Deb: 10/3/09 F

YEAR	TM/L	G	AB	R	H	2B	3B	HR	RBI	BB	SO	AVG	OBP	SLG	OPS	OPS+	BR+	SB	CS	SBR	FA	FR	G/POS	TPR
1909	Cin-N	3	10	1	0	0	0	0	1	0		.000	.000	.000	0	-99	-2	0			1.000	0	/1-3	-0.2
1912	Cle-A	43	164	22	46	7	4	1	11	11		.280	.326	.390	716	101	-0	8			.991	-2	1-41	-0.3
1913	Cle-A	133	530	74	135	19	12	2	39	35	65	.255	.309	.347	657	89	-8	19			.989	-1	*1-133	-1.4
1914	Cle-A	104	340	43	83	15	1	0	23	28	46	.244	.311	.294	605	79	-9	14	9	-0	.987	-7	1-90/O-2(0-2-0)	-2.0
1915	Pit-N	147	543	71	144	19	12	5	64	38	40	.265	.328	.372	700	113	8	26	17	-0	.991	-12	*1-147	-0.9
1916	Pit-N	114	404	33	86	10	10	0	39	20	42	.213	.262	.287	549	68	-16	17			.987	-2	*1-110	-2.4
1918	Cle-A	74	273	30	62	12	2	0	25	26	19	.227	.301	.286	587	70	-10	12			.989	-3	1-73	-1.6
1919	Cle-A	102	331	42	101	17	3	1	33	25	18	.305	.359	.384	743	102	1	21			.984	-3	1-98	-0.5
1920	*Cle-A	147	535	68	156	24	10	2	71	28	32	.292	.333	.385	718	87	-11	13	7	0	.992	-1	*1-147	-1.4
1921	Cle-A	118	384	53	114	20	7	2	46	29	15	.297	.353	.401	754	90	-6	2	9	-3	.988	-1	*1-116	-1.5
1922	Phi-A	71	260	41	65	11	7	1	29	24	15	.250	.316	.358	673	73	-10	7	6	-1	.990	-5	1-65	-2.0
Total	11	1056	3774	478	992	154	68	14	381	264	292	.263	.319	.351	670	88	-62	139	48		.989	-37	*1-1023/O-2(0-2-0)	-14.2

■ FRED JOHNSTON

Johnston, Wilfred Ivy b: 7/9/1899, Charlotte, N.C. d: 7/14/59, Tyler, Tex. BR/TR, 5'11.5", 170 lbs. Deb: 6/29/24

YEAR	TM/L	G	AB	R	H	2B	3B	HR	RBI	BB	SO	AVG	OBP	SLG	OPS	OPS+	BR+	SB	CS	SBR	FA	FR	G/POS	TPR
1924	Bro-N	4	4	1	1	0	0	0	0	0	1	.250	.250	.250	500	35	-0	0	0	0	.667	0	/2-1,3-1	0.0

■ JAY JOHNSTONE

Johnstone, John William b: 11/20/45, Manchester, Conn. BL/TR, 6'1", 175 lbs. Deb: 7/30/66 Career OF: (258-LF 521-CF 572-RF)

YEAR	TM/L	G	AB	R	H	2B	3B	HR	RBI	BB	SO	AVG	OBP	SLG	OPS	OPS+	BR+	SB	CS	SBR	FA	FR	G/POS	TPR
1966	Cal-A	61	254	35	67	12	4	3	17	11	36	.264	.297	.378	675	95	-2	3	3	-0	.975	-2	O-61(41-12-13)	-0.8
1967	Cal-A	79	230	18	48	7	1	2	10	5	37	.209	.226	.274	499	49	-15	3	2	-0	.973	2	O-63(0-62-1)	-1.6
1968	Cal-A	41	115	11	30	4	1	0	3	7	15	.261	.303	.313	616	90	-1	2	1	0	.984	2	O-29(1-21-7)	-0.1
1969	Cal-A	148	540	64	146	20	5	10	59	38	75	.270	.324	.381	706	102	0	3	9	-2	.983	12	*O-144(0-144-0)	0.6
1970	Cal-A	119	320	34	76	10	5	11	39	24	53	.237	.293	.403	696	93	-4	1	0	0	.981	-1	*O-100(2-88-10)	-0.8
1971	Chi-A	124	388	53	101	14	1	16	40	38	50	.260	.331	.425	756	109	4	10	5	0	.968	-3	*O-119(11-92-23)	-0.2
1972	Chi-A	113	261	27	49	9	0	4	17	25	42	.188	.259	.268	527	56	-14	2	1	0	.988	-12	O-97(13-85-6)	-3.2
1973	Oak-A	23	28	1	3	1	0	0	3	2	4	.107	.167	.143	310	-13	-4	0	1	-0	1.000	-2	/O-7(3-1-3),2-2,D-4	-0.7

YEAR	TM/L	G	AB	R	H	2B	3B	HR	RBI	BB	SO	AVG	OBP	SLG	OPS	OPS+	BR+	SB	CS	SBR	FA	FR	G/POS	TPR
1974	Phi-N	64	200	30	59	10	4	6	30	24	28	.295	.371	.475	846	130	8	5	5	-1	.968	-7	O-59(31-1-40)	-0.3
1975	Phi-N	122	350	50	115	19	2	7	54	42	39	.329	.401	.454	855	132	16	7	3	0	.976	-2	*O-101(0-3-100)	1.0
1976	*Phi-N	129	440	62	140	38	4	5	53	41	39	.318	.379	.457	836	132	19	5	5	-1	.982	8	*O-122(2-0-120)/1-6	2.0
1977	*Phi-N	112	363	64	103	18	4	15	59	38	38	.284	.355	.479	834	116	8	3	7	-2	1.000	3	O-91(4-0-87),1-19	0.4
1978	Phi-N	35	56	3	10	2	0	0	4	6	9	.179	.258	.214	472	33	-5	0	2	-1	.988	-1	/1-8,O-7(3-0-4)	-0.8
	*NY-A	36	65	6	17	0	0	1	6	4	10	.262	.333	.308	641	83	-1	0	1	-0	1.000	-3	O-22(8-0-14)/D-5	-0.5
1979	NY-A	23	48	7	10	1	0	1	7	2	7	.208	.240	.292	532	44	-4	1	0	0	1.000	-2	O-19(14-4-1)/D-3	-0.6
	SD-N	75	201	10	59	8	2	0	32	18	21	.294	.352	.353	705	99	-0	1	3	-1	.985	-3	O-45(35-7-4),1-22	-0.6
1980	LA-N	109	251	31	77	15	2	2	20	24	29	.307	.372	.406	778	119	7	3	2	-0	.965	1	O-61(5-0-57)	0.5
1981	*LA-N	61	83	8	17	3	0	3	6	7	13	.205	.267	.349	616	76	-3	0	1	-0	.957	-0	O-16(8-0-8)/1-2	-0.4
1982	LA-N	21	13	1	1	1	0	0	2	5	2	.077	.333	.154	487	41	-1	0	0	0	.000	0	H	-0.1
	Chi-N	98	269	39	67	13	1	10	43	40	41	.249	.346	.416	763	109	4	0	2	-1	.982	1	O-86(34-0-58)	0.0
	Yr	119	282	40	68	14	1	10	45	45	43	.241	.346	.404	750	107	3	0	2	-1	.982	1	O-86(34-0-58)	-0.1
1983	Chi-N	86	140	16	36	7	0	6	22	20	24	.257	.362	.436	798	115	3	1	1	-0	.935	-4	O-44(36-0-8)	-0.3
1984	Chi-N	52	73	8	21	2	2	0	3	7	18	.288	.350	.370	720	94	-0	0	0	0	1.000	-4	O-15(7-1-8)	-0.5
1985	*LA-N	17	15	0	2	1	0	0	2	1	2	.133	.188	.200	388	9	-2	0	0	0	.000	0	H	-0.3
Total	20	1748	4703	578	1254	215	38	102	531	429	632	.267	.331	.394	724	103	11	50	54	-8	.979	-17	*O-1308R/1-57,D-12,2	-7.3

■ **STAN JOK** Jok, Stanley Edward "Tucker" b: 5/3/26, Buffalo, N.Y. d: 3/6/72, Buffalo, N.Y. BR/TR, 6', 190 lbs. Deb: 4/13/54

YEAR	TM/L	G	AB	R	H	2B	3B	HR	RBI	BB	SO	AVG	OBP	SLG	OPS	OPS+	BR+	SB	CS	SBR	FA	FR	G/POS	TPR
1954	Phi-N	3	3	0	0	0	0	0	0	0	2	.000	.000	.000	0	-99	-1	0	0	0	.000	0	H	-0.1
	Chi-A	3	12	1	2	0	0	0	2	1	2	.167	.231	.167	397	10	-1	0	0	0	1.000	-0	/3-3	-0.2
1955	Chi-A	6	4	3	1	0	0	1	2	1	1	.250	.400	1.000	1400	260	1	0	0	0	.857	1	/3-3,O-1(1-0-0)	0.1
Total	2	12	19	4	3	0	0	1	4	2	5	.158	.238	.316	554	47	-2	0	0	0	.941	0	/3-6,O-1(1-0-0)	-0.2

■ **SMEAD JOLLEY** Jolley, Smead Powell "Guinea" or "Smudge" b: 1/14/02, Wesson, Ark. d: 11/17/91, Alameda, Cal. BL/TR, 6'3.5", 210 lbs. Deb: 4/17/30

YEAR	TM/L	G	AB	R	H	2B	3B	HR	RBI	BB	SO	AVG	OBP	SLG	OPS	OPS+	BR+	SB	CS	SBR	FA	FR	G/POS	TPR
1930	Chi-A	152	616	76	193	38	12	16	114	28	52	.313	.346	.492	838	114	10	3	1	0	.950	-3	*O-151(68-0-83)	-0.4
1931	Chi-A	54	110	5	33	11	0	3	28	7	4	.300	.353	.482	835	125	3	0	0	0	.857	-5	O-23(8-0-15)	-0.2
1932	Chi-A	12	42	3	15	3	0	0	7	3	0	.357	.413	.429	842	127	2	1	0	0	.923	-2	O-11(7-0-4)	-0.1
	Bos-A	137	531	57	164	27	5	18	99	27	29	.309	.345	.480	825	115	9	0	5	-2	.943	-5	*O-126(120-0-6)/C-5	-0.4
	Yr	149	573	60	179	30	5	18	106	30	29	.312	.350	.476	826	116	11	1	5	-2	.942	-8	*O-137(127-0-10)/C-5	-0.5
1933	Bos-A	118	411	47	116	32	4	9	65	24	20	.282	.325	.445	770	103	0	1	1	-0	.955	-4	*O-102(87-0-15)	-0.9
Total	4	473	1710	188	521	111	21	46	313	89	105	.305	.343	.475	818	112	24	5	7	-1	.944	-19	O-413(290-0-123)/C-5	-2.0

■ **JONES** Jones Deb: 5/14/1873

YEAR	TM/L	G	AB	R	H	2B	3B	HR	RBI	BB	SO	AVG	OBP	SLG	OPS	OPS+	BR+	SB	CS	SBR	FA	FR	G/POS	TPR
1873	Mar-n	1	4	0	3	0	0	0	1	0	0	.750	.750	.750	1500	452	2	0	0	0	.800	0	/O-1(0-1-0)	0.1
1874	Bal-n	2	7	0	1	0	0	0	1	0	0	.143	.143	.143	286	-8	-1	0	0	0	.875	-1	/C-1,O-1(0-0-1)	-0.1
Total	2 n	3	11	0	4	0	0	0	2	0	0	.364	.364	.364	727	140	1	0	0	0	.800	-0	/O-2(0-1-1),C-1	0.0

■ **JONES** Jones b: Johnstown, Pa. Deb: 7/14/1884

YEAR	TM/L	G	AB	R	H	2B	3B	HR	RBI	BB	SO	AVG	OBP	SLG	OPS	OPS+	BR+	SB	CS	SBR	FA	FR	G/POS	TPR
1884	Was-a	4	17	2	5	0	0	0		1		.294	.333	.294	627	120	0				1.000	-0	/O-4(4-0-0)	0.0

■ **JONES** Jones Deb: 4/30/1885

YEAR	TM/L	G	AB	R	H	2B	3B	HR	RBI	BB	SO	AVG	OBP	SLG	OPS	OPS+	BR+	SB	CS	SBR	FA	FR	G/POS	TPR
1885	NY-a	1	4	0	1	0	0	0	0	0		.250	.250	.250	500	63	-0				1.000	1	/3-1	0.1

■ **ANDRUW JONES** Jones, Andruw Rudolf b: 4/23/77, Willemstad, Curacao BR/TR, 6'1", 170 lbs. Deb: 8/15/96

YEAR	TM/L	G	AB	R	H	2B	3B	HR	RBI	BB	SO	AVG	OBP	SLG	OPS	OPS+	BR+	SB	CS	SBR	FA	FR	G/POS	TPR
1996	*Atl-N	31	106	11	23	7	1	5	13	7	29	.217	.265	.443	709	78	-4	3	0	1	.975	5	O-29(0-12-20)	0.1
1997	*Atl-N	153	399	60	92	18	1	18	70	56	107	.231	.331	.416	747	92	-5	20	11	1	.977	8	*O-147(2-57-95)	0.1
1998	*Atl-N	159	582	89	158	33	8	31	90	40	129	.271	.323	.515	838	116	11	27	4	5	.995	**32**	*O-159(0-159-0)	4.7
1999	*Atl-N	162	592	97	163	35	5	26	84	76	103	.275	.366	.483	849	113	11	24	12	1	.981	35	*O-162(0-162-0)	4.6
2000	*Atl-N★	161	656	122	199	36	6	36	104	59	100	.303	.369	.541	910	127	26	21	6	3	.996	20	*O-161(0-161-0)	4.7
Total	5	666	2335	379	635	129	21	116	361	238	468	.272	.346	.494	840	112	40	95	33	9	.987	100	O-658(2-551-115)	14.2

■ **CHARLIE JONES** Jones, Charles Claude "Casey" b: 6/2/1876, Butler, Pa. d: 4/2/47, Two Harbors, Minn. BR/TR, 6'1", 165 lbs. Deb: 5/2/01 Career OF: (12-LF 443-CF 12-RF)

YEAR	TM/L	G	AB	R	H	2B	3B	HR	RBI	BB	SO	AVG	OBP	SLG	OPS	OPS+	BR+	SB	CS	SBR	FA	FR	G/POS	TPR
1901	Bos-A	10	41	6	6	2	0	0	6	1		.146	.167	.195	362	0	-6	2			.929	-2	O-10(0-8-2)	-0.8
1904	Chi-A	5	17	2	4	0	1	0	1	1		.235	.278	.353	631	103	0	0			1.000	1	/O-5(0-5-0)	0.1
1905	Was-A	142	544	68	113	18	4	2	41	31		.208	.254	.267	521	68	-20	24			.971	17	*O-142(0-142-0)	-1.2
1906	Was-A	131	497	56	120	11	11	3	42	24		.241	.283	.326	609	95	-4	34			.961	8	*O-128(0-128-0)/2-1	-0.2
1907	Was-A	121	437	48	116	14	10	0	37	22		.265	.304	.343	647	115	6	26			.967	-1	*O-111C/2-5,1-4,S-2	0.0
1908	StL-A	74	263	37	61	11	2	0	17	14		.232	.279	.289	568	84	-5	14			.963	-1	O-72(0-70-2)	-1.1
Total	6	483	1799	217	420	56	28	5	144	93		.233	.276	.304	580	87	-29	100			.966	21	O-468C/2-6,1-4,S-2	-3.2

■ **CHARLIE JONES** Jones, Charles F. b: New York, N.Y. Deb: 6/28/1884

YEAR	TM/L	G	AB	R	H	2B	3B	HR	RBI	BB	SO	AVG	OBP	SLG	OPS	OPS+	BR+	SB	CS	SBR	FA	FR	G/POS	TPR
1884	Bro-a	25	90	10	16	1	0	0		5		.178	.221	.189	410	35	-6				.871	-7	2-13,3-11/O-2(1-0-1)	-1.2

■ **CHARLEY JONES** Jones, Charles Wesley "Baby" (b: Benjamin Wesley Rippay) b: 4/30/1850, Alamance Co., N.C. BR/TR, 5'11.5", 202 lbs. Deb: 5/4/1875 U Career OF: (624-LF 246-CF 8-RF)

YEAR	TM/L	G	AB	R	H	2B	3B	HR	RBI	BB	SO	AVG	OBP	SLG	OPS	OPS+	BR+	SB	CS	SBR	FA	FR	G/POS	TPR
1875	Wes-n	12	47	4	13	2	4	0	10	0	5	.277	.277	.489	766	152	2	1	1	-0	.800	-2	O-12(12-0-0)	0.1
	Har-n	1	4	1	0	0	0	0	0	0	1	.000	.000	.000	0	-95	-1	0	0	0	.667	-0	/O-1(0-1-0)	-0.1
	Yr	13	51	5	13	2	4	0	10	0	6	.255	.255	.451	706	133	1	1	1	-0	.778	-2	O-13(12-1-0)	0.0
1876	Cin-N	64	283	40	79	17	4	4	38	7	17	.279	.304	.420	724	162	20				.857	3	*O-64(10-53-1)	1.7
1877	Cin-N	17	69	16	21	3	3	1	10	4	8	.304	.342	.478	821	175	6				.920	1	1-10/O-8(5-3-0)	0.5
	Chi-N	2	8	1	3	1	0	0	2	1	0	.375	.444	.500	944	176	1				1.000	1	/O-2(0-2-0)	0.1
	Cin-N	38	163	36	51	8	7	1	26	10	17	.313	.353	.466	819	175	15				.838	10	O-38(38-0-0)	2.0
	Yr	57	240	53	75	12	10	2	38	15	25	.313	.353	.471	824	175	22				.845	12	O-48(43-5-0),1-10	**2.6**
1878	Cin-N	61	261	50	81	11	7	3	39	4	17	.310	.321	.441	761	163	18				.896	6	*O-61(51-10-0)	1.8
1879	Bos-N	83	355	**85**	112	22	10	**9**	**62**	**29**	38	.315	.367	.510	877	182	31				**.933**	12	*O-83(83-0-0)	3.4
1880	Bos-N	66	280	44	84	15	3	5	37	11	27	.300	.326	.429	755	159	17				.826	-4	*O-66(66-1-0)	0.8
1883	Cin-a	90	391	84	115	15	12	10	80	20		.294	.328	.471	799	146	18				.876	2	*O-90(16-75-0)	1.5
1884	Cin-a	112	472	117	148	19	17	7	71	37		.314	**.376**	.470	846	166	34				.887	3	*O-112(63-51-0)	3.0
1885	Cin-a	112	487	108	157	19	17	5	35	21		.322	.362	.462	824	156	29				.891	12	*O-112(112-0-0)	3.4
1886	Cin-a	127	500	87	135	22	10	6	68	61		.270	.356	.390	746	130	17	3			.879	3	*O-127(127-0-0)	1.5
1887	Cin-a	41	172	28	67	7	4	2	40	19		.390	.400	.451	851	134	7	7			.900	-0	O-41(41-1-0)	0.5
	NY-a	62	259	30	75	11	3	3	29	12		.290	.306	.360	666	89	-4	8			.917	4	O-62(6-50-7)/P-2,1-1	-0.1
	Yr	103	431	58	142	18	7	5	69	31		.329	.343	.395	738	107	4	15			.910	4	*O-103C/P-2,1-1	0.4
1888	KC-a	6	25	2	4	0	1	0	5	1		.160	.192	.240	432	36	-2	1			.750	-1	/O-6(6-0-0)	-0.2
Total	11	881	3725	728	1132	170	98	56	542	237	124	.304	.347	.443	790	150	208	19	0		.882	51	O-872L/1-11,P-2	19.9

■ **CHRIS JONES** Jones, Christopher Carlos b: 12/16/65, Utica, N.Y. BR/TR, 6'2", 205 lbs. Deb: 4/21/91 Career OF: (127-LF 100-CF 168-RF)

YEAR	TM/L	G	AB	R	H	2B	3B	HR	RBI	BB	SO	AVG	OBP	SLG	OPS	OPS+	BR+	SB	CS	SBR	FA	FR	G/POS	TPR
1991	Cin-N	52	89	14	26	1	2	2	6	2	31	.292	.308	.416	723	98	-1	2	1	0	1.000	-5	O-26(18-3-9)	-0.6
1992	Hou-N	54	63	7	12	2	1	1	4	7	21	.190	.271	.302	573	65	-3	3	0	1	.931	-13	O-43(17-5-25)	-1.8
1993	Col-N	86	209	29	57	11	4	6	31	10	48	.273	.306	.450	756	85	-5	9	4	1	.983	-9	O-70(16-52-4)	-1.3
1994	Col-N	21	40	6	12	2	1	0	2	2	14	.300	.333	.400	733	77	-1	0	1	-0	.941	-5	O-14(4-13-0)	-0.6
1995	NY-N	79	182	33	51	6	2	8	31	13	45	.280	.332	.467	799	111	2	2	1	0	.976	-2	O-52(25-0-28)/1-5	-0.1
1996	NY-N	89	149	22	36	7	0	4	18	12	42	.242	.307	.369	676	81	-4	1	0	0	.957	-14	O-66(17-8-44)/1-5	-1.9
1997	SD-N	92	152	24	37	9	0	7	25	16	45	.243	.324	.441	764	105	1	7	2	1	.951	-9	O-61(24-19-25)	-0.8
1998	Ari-N	20	31	3	6	1	0	0	3	3	9	.194	.265	.226	491	31	-3	0	0	0	1.000	-1	/O-8(1-0-7)	-0.4
	SF-N	43	90	14	17	2	1	2	10	8	28	.189	.255	.300	555	48	-7	2	1	0	.941	-4	O-29(5-0-24)/D-2	-1.2
	Yr	63	121	17	23	3	1	2	13	11	37	.190	.258	.281	539	43	-10	2	1	0	.956	-5	O-37(6-0-31)/D-2	-1.6
2000	Mil-N	12	16	3	3	2	0	0	1	1	4	.188	.235	.313	548	37	-2	0	0	0	1.000	0	/O-2(0-0-2)	-0.1
Total	9	548	1021	155	257	43	11	30	131	74	287	.252	.305	.404	709	86	-22	26	10	2	.967	-62	O-371R/1-10,D-2	-8.8

YEAR	TM/L	G	AB	R	H	2B	3B	HR	RBI	BB	SO	AVG	OBP	SLG	OPS	OPS+	BR+	SB	CS	SBR	FA	FR	G/POS	TPR
■ CHRIS JONES	Jones, Christopher Dale b: 7/13/57, Los Angeles, Cal. BL/TL, 6', 183 lbs. Deb: 6/8/85																							
1985	Hou-N	31	25	0	5	0	0	0	1	3	7	.200	.286	.200	486	39	-2	0	0	0	1.000	-3	O-15(2-9-4)	-0.6
1986	SF-N	3	1	0	0	0	0	0	0	0	0	.000	.000	.000	0	-99	-0	1	0	0	.000	0	/H	0.0
Total	2	34	26	0	5	0	0	0	1	3	7	.192	.276	.192	468	34	-2	1	0	0	1.000	-3	/O-15(2-9-4)	-0.6
■ CLARENCE JONES	Jones, Clarence Woodrow b: 11/7/41, Zanesville, Ohio BL/TL, 6'2", 185 lbs. Deb: 4/20/67 C																							
1967	Chi-N	53	135	13	34	7	0	2	16	14	33	.252	.322	.348	670	88	-2	0	0	0	.978	-4	O-31(2-0-29),1-13	-0.9
1968	Chi-N	5	2	0	0	0	0	0	0	2	1	.000	.500	.000	500	56	0	0	0	0	1.000	-0	/1-1	0.0
Total	2	58	137	13	34	7	0	2	16	16	34	.248	.327	.343	670	88	-2	0	0	0	.979	-4	/O-31(2-0-29),1-14	-0.9
■ CLEON JONES	Jones, Cleon Joseph b: 8/4/42, Plateau, Ala. BR/TL, 6', 200 lbs. Deb: 9/14/63 Career OF: (802-LF 273-CF 103-RF)																							
1963	NY-N	6	15	1	2	0	0	0	1	0	4	.133	.133	.133	267	-23	-2	0	0	0	1.000	-1	/O-5(1-5-0)	-0.4
1965	NY-N	30	74	2	11	1	0	1	9	2	23	.149	.171	.203	374	5	-9	1	0	0	1.000	-1	O-23(2-18-3)	-1.1
1966	NY-N	139	495	74	136	16	4	8	57	30	62	.275	.320	.372	692	94	-4	16	8	1	.979	-2	*O-129(3-107-35)	-1.1
1967	NY-N	129	411	46	101	10	5	5	30	19	57	.246	.286	.331	617	77	-13	12	2	2	.977	-6	*O-115(20-86-21)	-2.3
1968	NY-N	147	509	63	151	29	4	14	55	31	98	.297	.343	.452	795	136	21	23	12	1	.963	-10	*O-139(117-28-18)	0.6
1969	*NY-N★	137	483	92	164	25	4	12	75	64	60	.340	.424	.482	907	150	35	16	8	1	.991	8	*O-122(121-1-0),1-15	3.7
1970	NY-N	134	506	71	140	25	8	10	63	57	87	.277	.356	.417	773	106	5	12	3	2	.981	12	*O-130(125-6-1)	1.1
1971	NY-N	136	505	63	161	24	6	14	69	53	87	.319	.386	.473	859	144	29	6	5	-0	.981	7	*O-132(132-1-0)	3.0
1972	NY-N	106	375	39	92	15	1	5	52	30	83	.245	.308	.331	639	84	-8	1	6	-2	.986	-1	O-84(71-5-14),1-20	-1.8
1973	*NY-N	92	339	48	88	13	0	11	48	28	51	.260	.322	.395	717	99	-1	1	1	-0	.967	1	O-92(73-13-8)	-0.6
1974	NY-N	124	461	62	130	23	1	13	60	38	79	.282	.345	.421	765	115	8	3	3	-0	.970	3	*O-120(117-3-3)	0.4
1975	NY-N	21	50	2	12	1	0	0	2	3	6	.240	.283	.260	543	54	-3	0	0	0	1.000	-3	O-12(12-0-0)	-0.7
1976	Chi-A	12	40	2	8	1	0	0	3	5	5	.200	.304	.225	529	56	-2	0	0	0	1.000	-2	/O-8(8-0-0),D-3	-0.5
Total	13	1213	4263	565	1196	183	33	93	524	360	702	.281	.342	.404	747	111	56	91	48	3	.978	6	*O-1111L/1-35,D-3	0.3
■ COBE JONES	Jones, Coburn Dyas b: 8/21/07, Denver, Colo. d: 6/3/69, Denver, Colo. BB/TR, 5'7", 155 lbs. Deb: 9/27/28																							
1928	Pit-N	1	2	0	1	0	0	0	0	0	0	.500	.500	.500	1000	156	0	0			1.000	-0	/S-1	0.0
1929	Pit-N	25	63	6	16	5	1	0	4	1	5	.254	.266	.365	631	53	-5	1			.919	-8	S-15	-1.1
Total	2	26	65	6	17	5	1	0	4	1	5	.262	.273	.369	642	56	-5	1			.921	-8	/S-16	-1.1
■ DARRYL JONES	Jones, Darryl Lee b: 6/5/51, Meadville, Pa. BR/TR, 5'10", 175 lbs. Deb: 6/6/79 F																							
1979	NY-A	18	47	6	12	5	1	0	6	2	7	.255	.286	.404	690	86	-1	0	0	0	1.000	-1	D-15/O-2(1-0-1)	-0.2
■ DAVY JONES	Jones, David Jefferson "Kangaroo" b: 6/30/1880, Cambria, Wis. d: 3/31/72, Mankato, Minn. BL/TR, 5'10", 165 lbs. Deb: 9/15/01																							
1901	Mil-A	14	52	12	9	0	0	3	5	11		.173	.328	.346	674	91	-0	4			.911	1	O-14(14-0-0)	0.0
1902	StL-A	15	49	4	11	1	1	0	3	6		.224	.309	.286	595	67	-2	5			.973	5	O-15(0-0-15)	0.2
	Chi-N	64	243	41	74	12	3	0	14	38		.305	.399	.379	777	144	15	12			.955	-1	O-64(0-47-17)	1.1
1903	Chi-N	130	497	64	140	18	3	1	62	53		.282	.352	.336	688	99	1	15			.970	0	*O-130(0-97-33)	-0.5
1904	Chi-N	98	336	44	82	11	5	3	39	41		.244	.330	.333	663	105	3	14			.932	-10	O-97(0-1-97)	-1.2
1906	Det-A	84	323	41	84	12	2	0	24	41		.260	.347	.310	657	103	3	21			.981	4	O-83(0-82-1)	0.3
1907	*Det-A	126	491	101	134	10	6	0	27	60		.273	.357	.318	674	111	9	30			.971	13	*O-125(121-4-0)	1.6
1908	*Det-A	56	121	17	25	2	1	0	10	13		.207	.284	.240	523	68	-4	11			.960	2	O-32(4-26-2)	-0.3
1909	*Det-A	69	204	44	57	2	2	0	10	28		.279	.369	.309	678	110	4	12			.982	-2	O-57(42-13-2)	-0.2
1910	Det-A	113	377	77	100	6	6	0	24	51		.265	.362	.313	675	105	4	25			.956	1	*O-101(95-6-0)	0.0
1911	Det-A	98	341	78	93	10	0	0	19	41		.273	.354	.302	656	80	-8	25			.950	-1	O-92(92-0-0)	-1.3
1912	Det-A	99	316	54	93	5	2	0	24	38		.294	.370	.323	693	102	2	16			.962	-1	O-81(72-5-4)	-0.2
1913	Chi-A	12	21	2	6	0	0	0	0	9	0	.286	.500	.286	786	132	2	1			.867	-1	/O-9(9-0-0)	0.1
1914	Pit-F	97	352	58	96	9	8	2	24	42	16	.273	.355	.361	716	96	-6	15			.970	8	O-93(93-0-0)	-0.3
1915	Pit-F	14	49	6	16	0	1	0	4	6	0	.327	.400	.367	767	118	1	1			.926	-1	O-13(13-0-0)	-0.1
Total	14	1089	3772	643	1020	98	40	9	289	478	16	.270	.356	.325	681	102	23	207			.962	18	*O-1006(555-281-171)	-0.8
■ DAX JONES	Jones, Dax Xenos b: 8/4/70, Pittsburgh, Pa. BR/TR, 6', 170 lbs. Deb: 7/11/96																							
1996	SF-N	34	58	7	10	0	2	1	7	8	12	.172	.273	.293	566	51	-4	2	2	-0	1.000	-4	O-33(0-29-4)	-0.9
■ FIELDER JONES	Jones, Fielder Allison b: 8/13/1871, Shinglehouse, Pa. d: 3/13/34, Portland, Ore. BL/TR, 5'11", 180 lbs. Deb: 4/18/1896 M Career OF: (4-LF 1255-CF 516-RF)																							
1896	Bro-N	104	395	82	140	10	8	3	46	48	15	.354	.427	.443	870	137	24	18						
1897	Bro-N	135	548	134	172	15	10	1	49	61		.314	.392	.383	775	111	12	48			.928	-4	*O-103(0-0-103)	1.3
1898	Bro-N	146	596	89	181	15	9	1	69	46		.304	.362	.364	726	108	7	36			.941	4	*O-135(2-0-133)	0.8
1899	Bro-N	102	365	75	104	8	2	2	38	54		.285	.390	.334	724	97	2	18			.946	-7	*O-144(0-4-144)/S-2	-0.7
1900	*Bro-N	136	552	106	171	26	4	4	54	57		.310	.383	.393	777	108	7	33			.946	-3	O-96(2-89-6)	-0.7
1901	Chi-A	133	521	120	162	16	3	2	65	84		.311	.412	.365	777	120	20	38			.957	0	*O-136(0-136-0)	-0.2
1902	Chi-A	135	532	98	171	16	5	0	54	57		.321	.390	.370	761	117	15	33			.937	1	*O-133(0-5-128)	1.4
1903	Chi-A	136	530	71	152	18	5	0	45	47		.287	.348	.340	688	112	9	21			.972	13	*O-135(0-135-0)	2.0
1904	Chi-A	149	547	72	133	14	5	3	42	53		.243	.316	.303	619	100	2	25			**.985**	0	*O-136(0-136-0)	0.3
1905	Chi-A	153	568	91	139	17	12	2	38	73		.245	.335	.327	662	115	12	20			.977	5	*O-149(0-149-0),M	-0.1
1906	*Chi-A	144	496	77	114	22	4	2	34	83		.230	.346	.302	648	106	8	26			.970	8	*O-153(0-153-0),M	1.3
1907	Chi-A	154	559	72	146	18	1	0	47	67		.261	.345	.297	642	109	9	17			**.988**	8	*O-144(0-144-0),M	1.0
1908	Chi-A	149	529	92	134	11	7	1	50	86		.253	.366	.306	672	121	17	26			.973	3	*O-154(0-154-0),M	0.4
1914	StL-F	5	3	0	1	0	0	0	0	1	0	.333	.500	.333	833	123	0	0			.968	-2	*O-149(0-149-0),M	1.0
1915	StL-F	7	6	1	0	0	0	0	0	0	0	.000	.000	.000	0	-95	-2	0			.000	0	HM	0.0
Total	15	1788	6747	1180	1920	206	75	21	631	817	15	.285	.368	.347	715	112	143	359			1.000	-1	/O-3(0-1-2),M	-0.3
																					.964	26	*O-1770C/S-2	7.5
■ FRANK JONES	Jones, Frank M. b: 8/25/1858, Princeton, Ill. d: 2/4/36, Marietta, Ohio BL, Deb: 7/2/1884																							
1884	Det-N	2	8	0	1	0	0	0	0	0	1	.125	.125	.125	250	-22	-1				.667	-1	/S-1,O-1(0-0-1)	-0.2
■ DEACON JONES	Jones, Grover William b: 4/18/34, White Plains, N.Y. BL/TR, 5'10", 185 lbs. Deb: 9/8/62 C																							
1962	Chi-A	18	28	3	9	2	0	0	8	4	6	.321	.406	.393	799	117	1	0	0	0	.962	-0	/1-6	0.0
1963	Chi-A	17	16	4	3	0	1	1	2	2	2	.188	.316	.500	816	127	1	0	0	0	1.000	-0	/1-1	0.1
1966	Chi-A	5	5	0	2	0	0	0	0	0	0	.400	.400	.400	800	140	0	0	0	0	.000	0	H	0.0
Total	3	40	49	7	14	2	1	1	10	6	8	.286	.375	.429	804	122	2	0	0	0	.966	-0	/1-7	0.1
■ HAL JONES	Jones, Harold Marion b: 4/9/36, Louisiana, Mo. BR/TR, 6'2", 194 lbs. Deb: 4/25/61																							
1961	Cle-A	12	35	2	6	0	0	2	4	2	12	.171	.216	.343	559	48	-3	0	0	0	.974	-2	1-10	-0.5
1962	Cle-A	5	16	2	5	1	0	0	1	0	4	.313	.353	.375	728	99	-0	0	0	0	.969	0	/1-4	0.0
Total	2	17	51	4	11	1	0	2	5	2	16	.216	.259	.353	612	64	-3	0	0	0	.973	-2	/1-14	-0.5
■ HENRY JONES	Jones, Henry Monroe b: 5/10/1857, New York d: 5/31/55, Manistee, Mich. BB, 5'6", 149 lbs. Deb: 8/20/1884																							
1884	Det-N	34	127	24	28	3	1	0	3	16	18	.220	.308	.260	568	86	-1				.897	-2	2-16,O-11(0-0-11)/S-7	-0.2
■ HOWIE JONES	Jones, Howard "Cotton" (b: Howard Painter) b: 3/1/1897, Irwin, Pa. d: 7/15/72, Jeannette, Pa. BL/TL, 5'11", 165 lbs. Deb: 9/5/21																							
1921	StL-N	3	2	0	0	0	0	0	0	0	1	.000	.000	.000	0	-99	-1	0	0	0	.000	-1	/O-1(1-0-0)	-0.1
■ JACQUE JONES	Jones, Jacque Dewayne b: 4/25/75, San Diego, Cal. BL/TL, 5'10", 175 lbs. Deb: 6/9/99																							
1999	Min-A	95	322	54	93	24	2	9	44	17	63	.289	.332	.460	792	96	-3	3	4	-1	.980	3	O-93(1-82-19)	0.0
2000	Min-A	154	523	66	149	26	5	19	76	26	111	.285	.319	.463	781	90	-9	7	5	-0	.994	7	*O-147(90-63-1)	-0.4
Total	2	249	845	120	242	50	7	28	120	43	174	.286	.324	.462	786	92	-12	10	9	-1	.988	10	O-240(91-145-20)	-0.4
■ DALTON JONES	Jones, James Dalton b: 12/10/43, McComb, Miss. BL/TR, 6'1", 180 lbs. Deb: 4/17/64 Career OF: (12-LF 0-CF 8-RF)																							
1964	Bos-A	118	374	37	86	16	4	6	39	22	38	.230	.275	.342	617	67	-17	6	3	0	.959	-8	2-85/S-1,3-1	-1.9
1965	Bos-A	112	367	41	99	13	5	5	37	28	45	.270	.325	.373	698	92	-3	8	1	1	.930	-3	3-81/2-8	-0.5

YEAR	TM/L	G	AB	R	H	2B	3B	HR	RBI	BB	SO	AVG	OBP	SLG	OPS	OPS+	BR+	SB	CS	SBR	FA	FR	G/POS	TPR
1966	Bos-A	115	252	26	59	11	5	4	23	22	27	.234	.303	.365	668	83	-5	1	2	-0	.962	-15	2-70/3-3	-1.7
1967	*Bos-A	89	159	18	46	6	2	3	25	11	23	.289	.335	.409	744	110	2	0	1	-0	.912	-4	3-30,2-19/1-1	-0.3
1968	Bos-A	111	354	38	83	13	0	5	29	17	53	.234	.272	.314	585	72	-12	1	1	-0	.996	-6	1-56,2-26/3-8	-2.3
1969	Bos-A	111	336	50	74	18	3	3	33	39	36	.220	.305	.318	623	71	-13	1	1	-0	.992	-1	1-81/3-9,2-1	-2.1
1970	Det-A	89	191	29	42	7	0	6	21	33	33	.220	.338	.351	689	90	-2	1	1	-0	.985	-3	2-35,3-18,1-10	-0.4
1971	Det-A	83	138	15	35	5	0	5	11	9	21	.254	.304	.399	703	94	-1	1	3	-1	1.000	-7	O-16L,3-13/1-3,2-1	-1.0
1972	Det-A	7	7	0	0	0	0	0	0	0	2	.000	.000	.000	0	-97	-2	0	0	0	.000	0	H	-0.2
	Tex-A	72	151	14	24	2	0	4	19	10	31	.159	.211	.252	463	39	-12	1	0	0	.979	-7	3-23,2-17/1-7,O-2L	-2.1
	Yr	79	158	14	24	2	0	4	19	10	33	.152	.202	.241	443	33	-14	1	0	0	.979	-7	3-23,2-17/1-7,O-2L	-2.3
Total	9	907	2329	268	548	91	19	41	237	191	309	.235	.296	.343	640	79	-65	20	13	-0	.967	-54	2-262,3-186,1/OS	-12.5

■ JAKE JONES Jones, James Murrell b: 11/23/20, Epps, La. BR/TR, 6'3", 197 lbs. Deb: 9/20/41

YEAR	TM/L	G	AB	R	H	2B	3B	HR	RBI	BB	SO	AVG	OBP	SLG	OPS	OPS+	BR+	SB	CS	SBR	FA	FR	G/POS	TPR
1941	Chi-A	3	11	0	0	0	0	0	0	0	4	.000	.000	.000	0	-99	-3	0	0	0	1.000	-1	/1-3	-0.4
1942	Chi-A	7	20	2	3	1	0	0	0	2	2	.150	.227	.200	427	21	-2	1	0	0	.961	-1	/1-5	-0.3
1946	Chi-A	24	79	10	21	5	1	3	13	2	13	.266	.284	.468	752	112	0	0	0	0	.986	-3	1-20	-0.4
1947	Chi-A	45	171	15	41	7	1	3	20	13	25	.240	.297	.345	642	81	-5	1	0	0	.988	-1	1-43	-0.7
	Bos-A	109	404	50	95	14	3	16	76	41	60	.235	.310	.403	714	91	-6	5	4	-0	.991	-2	*1-109	-1.3
	Yr	154	575	65	136	21	4	19	96	54	85	.237	.306	.386	693	88	-11	6	4	-0	.990	-3	*1-152	-2.0
1948	Bos-A	36	105	3	21	4	0	1	8	11	26	.200	.276	.267	543	43	-9	1	0	0	.993	2	1-31	-0.7
Total	5	224	790	80	181	31	5	23	117	69	130	.229	.294	.368	663	80	-25	8	4	0	.989	-6	1-211	-3.8

■ JIM JONES Jones, James Tilford "Sheriff" b: 12/25/1876, London, Ky. d: 5/6/53, London, Ky. BR/TR, 5'10", 162 lbs. Deb: 6/29/1897

YEAR	TM/L	G	AB	R	H	2B	3B	HR	RBI	BB	SO	AVG	OBP	SLG	OPS	OPS+	BR+	SB	CS	SBR	FA	FR	G/POS	TPR
1897	Lou-N	2	4	2	1	1	0	0	0	1		.250	.400	.500	900	142	0	0			.000	-0	/P-1	0.0
1901	NY-N	21	91	10	19	4	3	0	5	4		.209	.250	.319	569	67	-4	2			.900	1	O-20(0-0-20)/P-1	-0.4
1902	NY-N	67	249	16	59	11	1	0	19	13		.237	.275	.289	564	75	-8	7			.897	-1	O-67(49-3-15)	-1.3
Total	3	90	344	28	79	16	4	0	24	18		.230	.270	.299	569	74	-12	9			.898	0	/O-87(49-3-35),P-2	-1.7

■ JEFF JONES Jones, Jeffrey Raymond b: 10/22/57, Philadelphia, Pa. BR/TR, 6'2", 200 lbs. Deb: 4/4/83

YEAR	TM/L	G	AB	R	H	2B	3B	HR	RBI	BB	SO	AVG	OBP	SLG	OPS	OPS+	BR+	SB	CS	SBR	FA	FR	G/POS	TPR
1983	Cin-N	16	44	6	10	3	0	0	5	11	13	.227	.393	.295	688	90	0	2	0	0	1.000	1	O-13(8-0-5)/1-1	0.1

■ BINKY JONES Jones, John Joseph b: 7/11/1899, St.Louis, Mo. d: 5/13/61, St.Louis, Mo. BR/TR, 5'9", 154 lbs. Deb: 4/15/24

YEAR	TM/L	G	AB	R	H	2B	3B	HR	RBI	BB	SO	AVG	OBP	SLG	OPS	OPS+	BR+	SB	CS	SBR	FA	FR	G/POS	TPR
1924	Bro-N	10	37	0	4	1	0	0	2	0	3	.108	.108	.135	243	-36	-7	0	0	0	.898	-1	S-10	-0.7

■ JOHN JONES Jones, John William "Skins" b: 5/13/01, Coatesville, Pa. d: 11/3/56, Baltimore, Md. BL/TL, 5'11", 185 lbs. Deb: 9/26/23

YEAR	TM/L	G	AB	R	H	2B	3B	HR	RBI	BB	SO	AVG	OBP	SLG	OPS	OPS+	BR+	SB	CS	SBR	FA	FR	G/POS	TPR
1923	Phi-A	1	4	0	1	0	0	0	1	0	1	.250	.250	.250	500	31	-0	0	0	0	1.000	0	/O-1(0-1-0)	0.0
1932	Phi-A	4	6	0	1	0	0	0	0	0	3	.167	.167	.167	333	-13	-1	0	0	0	1.000	-0	/O-1(0-0-1)	-0.1
Total	2	5	10	0	2	0	0	0	1	0	4	.200	.200	.200	400	4	-1	0	0	0	1.000	0	/O-2(0-1-1)	-0.1

■ CHIPPER JONES Jones, Larry Wayne b: 4/24/72, DeLand, Fla. BB/TR, 6'3", 185 lbs. Deb: 9/11/93 Career OF: (18-LF 0-CF 9-RF)

YEAR	TM/L	G	AB	R	H	2B	3B	HR	RBI	BB	SO	AVG	OBP	SLG	OPS	OPS+	BR+	SB	CS	SBR	FA	FR	G/POS	TPR
1993	Atl-N	8	3	2	2	1	0	0	0	1	1	.667	.750	1.000	1750	360	1	0	0	0	1.000	1	/S-3	0.2
1995	*Atl-N	140	524	87	139	22	3	23	86	73	99	.265	.355	.450	805	107	6	8	4	0	.931	3	*3-123,O-20(15-0-5)	0.9
1996	*Atl-N★	157	598	114	185	32	5	30	110	87	88	.309	.397	.530	927	134	31	14	1	3	.947	-24	*3-118,S-38/O-1R	1.4
1997	*Atl-N★	157	597	100	176	41	3	21	111	76	88	.295	.374	.479	854	119	17	20	5	3	.955	-21	*3-152/O-5(3-0-3)	0.0
1998	*Atl-N★	160	601	123	188	29	5	34	107	96	93	.313	.408	.547	956	148	44	16	6	1	.971	-2	*3-158	4.3
1999	*Atl-N	157	567	116	181	41	1	45	110	126	94	.319	.445	.633	1078	169	63	25	3	4	.950	-26	*3-156/S-1	4.0
2000	*Atl-N★	156	579	118	180	38	1	36	111	95	64	.311	.410	.566	976	145	41	14	7	1	.944	-3	*3-152/S-6	3.8
Total	7	935	3469	660	1051	204	18	189	635	554	527	.303	.400	.536	935	138	204	97	26	12	.950	-71	3-859/S-48,O-26L	14.6

■ LYNN JONES Jones, Lynn Morris b: 1/1/53, Meadville, Pa. BR/TR, 5'9", 175 lbs. Deb: 4/13/79 FC Career OF: (154-LF 85-CF 237-RF)

YEAR	TM/L	G	AB	R	H	2B	3B	HR	RBI	BB	SO	AVG	OBP	SLG	OPS	OPS+	BR+	SB	CS	SBR	FA	FR	G/POS	TPR
1979	Det-A	95	213	33	63	8	0	4	26	17	22	.296	.351	.390	740	96	-1	9	6	-0	.980	-10	O-84(20-42-25)/D-6	-1.3
1980	Det-A	30	55	9	14	2	2	0	6	10	5	.255	.369	.364	733	99	0	1	0	0	1.000	-2	O-17(4-4-9)/D-6	-0.1
1981	Det-A	71	174	19	45	5	0	2	19	18	10	.259	.332	.322	653	86	-3	1	2	-0	.989	-4	O-60(9-0-52)/D-4	-1.0
1982	Det-A	58	139	15	31	3	1	0	14	7	14	.223	.260	.259	519	43	-11	0	2	-1	1.000	-5	O-56(5-2-49)/D-1	-1.8
1983	Det-A	49	64	9	17	1	2	0	6	3	6	.266	.299	.344	642	78	-2	1	0	0	.968	-7	O-31(9-1-22)/D-6	-0.9
1984	*KC-A	47	103	11	31	6	0	1	10	4	9	.301	.333	.388	722	98	-0	1	3	-1	.962	-12	O-45(13-7-29)	-1.5
1985	*KC-A	110	152	12	32	7	0	0	9	8	15	.211	.264	.257	520	43	-12	0	1	-0	.983	-24	*O-100(57-21-32)/D-2	-3.8
1986	KC-A	67	47	1	6	2	0	0	1	6	5	.128	.226	.170	397	10	-6	0	0	0	.971	-21	O-62(37-8-19)/2-1,D-3	-2.7
Total	8	527	947	109	239	34	5	7	91	73	86	.252	.310	.321	631	73	-34	13	14	-2	.983	-84	O-455R/D-28,2-1	-13.1

■ MACK JONES Jones, Mack "Mack The Knife" b: 11/6/38, Atlanta, Ga. BL/TR, 6'1", 180 lbs. Deb: 7/13/61

YEAR	TM/L	G	AB	R	H	2B	3B	HR	RBI	BB	SO	AVG	OBP	SLG	OPS	OPS+	BR+	SB	CS	SBR	FA	FR	G/POS	TPR
1961	Mil-N	28	104	13	24	3	2	0	12	12	28	.231	.322	.298	620	70	-4	4	4	-1	1.000	-2	O-26(0-26-0)	-0.8
1962	Mil-N	91	333	51	85	17	4	10	36	44	100	.255	.354	.420	775	110	5	5	1	1	.973	-8	O-91(0-9-85)	-0.8
1963	Mil-N	93	228	36	50	11	4	3	22	26	59	.219	.318	.342	660	91	-2	8	4	0	.978	-8	O-80(12-69-0)	-1.3
1965	Mil-N	143	504	78	132	18	7	31	75	29	122	.262	.314	.510	824	127	16	8	2	1	.980	-10	*O-133(31-119-0)	0.2
1966	Atl-N	118	417	60	110	14	1	23	66	39	85	.264	.338	.468	806	120	11	16	10	0	.981	-3	*O-112(1-112-3)/1-1	0.5
1967	Atl-N	140	454	72	115	23	4	17	50	64	108	.253	.357	.434	791	127	17	10	6	0	.985	2	*O-126(26-100-0)	1.6
1968	Cin-N	103	234	40	59	9	1	10	34	28	46	.252	.345	.427	772	123	7	2	3	-1	.988	-8	O-60(24-34-3)	-0.4
1969	Mon-N	135	455	73	123	23	5	22	79	67	110	.270	.382	.488	870	142	27	6	7	-1	.959	7	*O-129(125-5-0)	2.6
1970	Mon-N	108	271	51	65	11	3	14	32	59	74	.240	.399	.458	857	129	14	5	3	0	.968	-4	O-87(85-2-0)	0.5
1971	Mon-N	43	91	11	15	3	0	3	9	15	24	.165	.296	.297	593	68	-4	1	0	0	.952	-2	O-27(27-0-0)	-0.7
Total	10	1002	3091	485	778	132	31	133	415	383	756	.252	.349	.444	792	120	87	65	40	0	.976	-35	O-871(331-476-91)/1-1	1.4

■ RED JONES Jones, Maurice Morris b: 11/2/14, Timpson, Tex. d: 6/30/75, Lincoln, Cal. BL/TR, 6'3", 190 lbs. Deb: 4/16/40

YEAR	TM/L	G	AB	R	H	2B	3B	HR	RBI	BB	SO	AVG	OBP	SLG	OPS	OPS+	BR+	SB	CS	SBR	FA	FR	G/POS	TPR
1940	StL-N	12	11	0	1	0	0	0	1	1	2	.091	.167	.091	258	-26	-2	0			1.000	-0	/O-1(1-0-0)	-0.2

■ RICKY JONES Jones, Ricky Miron b: 6/4/58, Tupelo, Miss. BR/TR, 6'3", 186 lbs. Deb: 9/3/86

YEAR	TM/L	G	AB	R	H	2B	3B	HR	RBI	BB	SO	AVG	OBP	SLG	OPS	OPS+	BR+	SB	CS	SBR	FA	FR	G/POS	TPR
1986	Bal-A	16	33	2	6	2	0	0	4	6	8	.182	.308	.242	550	53	-2	0	0	0	1.000	7	2-11/3-6	0.5

■ BOB JONES Jones, Robert Oliver b: 10/11/49, Elkton, Md. BL/TL, 6'2", 195 lbs. Deb: 10/1/74 Career OF: (53-LF 27-CF 73-RF)

YEAR	TM/L	G	AB	R	H	2B	3B	HR	RBI	BB	SO	AVG	OBP	SLG	OPS	OPS+	BR+	SB	CS	SBR	FA	FR	G/POS	TPR
1974	Tex-A	2	5	0	0	0	0	0	0	0	1	.000	.000	.000	0	-99	-1	0	0	0	1.000	0	/O-2(2-0-0)	-0.1
1975	Tex-A	9	11	2	1	0	0	0	0	3	3	.091	.286	.091	377	11	-1	0	0	0	1.000	-1	/O-5(3-1-1),D-1	-0.2
1976	Cal-A	78	166	22	35	6	0	6	17	14	30	.211	.276	.355	632	90	-3	3	0	1	.990	-5	O-62(17-25-21)/D-2	-0.9
1977	Cal-A	14	17	3	3	0	0	1	3	4	5	.176	.333	.353	686	91	-0	0	0	0	.000	0	/D-6	0.0
1981	Tex-A	10	34	4	9	1	0	3	7	1	7	.265	.286	.559	845	146	2	0	1	-0	1.000	3	O-10(1-0-9)	0.4
1983	Tex-A	41	72	5	16	4	0	1	11	5	17	.222	.291	.319	611	69	-3	0	2	-1	1.000	0	O-11(6-0-5),D-11/1-1	-0.4
1984	Tex-A	64	143	14	37	4	0	4	22	10	19	.259	.312	.371	682	85	-3	1	1	-0	1.000	-0	O-22L,1-15/D-4	-0.5
1985	Tex-A	83	134	14	30	2	0	5	23	11	30	.224	.288	.351	638	73	-5	1	0	0	1.000	-7	O-30(8-1-22),D-10/1-4	-1.3
1986	Tex-A	13	21	1	2	0	0	0	3	2	5	.095	.174	.095	269	-24	-4	0	0	0	.909	-2	/O-9(5-0-4),1-2	-0.6
Total	9	314	603	65	133	17	0	20	86	50	117	.221	.286	.348	634	78	-18	5	4	-0	.992	-11	O-151R/D-34,1-22	-3.6

■ BOB JONES Jones, Robert Walter "Ducky" b: 12/2/1889, Clayton, Cal. d: 8/30/64, San Diego, Cal. BL/TR, 6', 170 lbs. Deb: 4/11/17 Career OF: (53-LF 27-CF 73-RF)

YEAR	TM/L	G	AB	R	H	2B	3B	HR	RBI	BB	SO	AVG	OBP	SLG	OPS	OPS+	BR+	SB	CS	SBR	FA	FR	G/POS	TPR
1917	Det-A	46	77	16	12	1	2	0	2	4	8	.156	.198	.221	418	28	-7	3			.938	-1	2-18/3-8	-0.8
1918	Det-A	74	287	43	79	14	4	0	21	17	16	.275	.320	.352	672	107	1	7			.947	-8	3-63/1-6,O-1	-0.6
1919	Det-A	127	439	37	114	18	6	1	57	34	39	.260	.314	.335	649	84	-10	11			.944	-24	*3-127	-3.2
1920	Det-A	81	265	35	66	6	3	1	18	22	13	.249	.309	.306	615	65	-13	3	4	-1	.942	-5	3-67/2-5,S-1	-1.7
1921	Det-A	141	554	82	168	23	9	1	72	37	24	.303	.348	.383	731	87	-11	8	9	-1	.950	10	*3-141	0.6
1922	Det-A	124	455	65	117	10	6	3	44	36	18	.257	.314	.325	640	69	-21	8	5	0	**.962**	11	*3-119	-0.2
1923	Det-A	100	372	51	93	15	4	1	40	29	13	.250	.306	.320	626	66	-19	7	6	-1	.954	5	3-97	-0.8
1924	Det-A	110	393	52	107	27	4	0	47	20	20	.272	.308	.361	669	73	-17	1	5	-2	.956	-2	*3-106	-1.3
1925	Det-A	50	148	18	35	6	0	0	15	9	5	.236	.280	.277	557	42	-13	1	1	-0	.985	9	3-46	-0.2
Total	9	853	2990	399	791	120	38	7	316	208	156	.265	.314	.337	651	75	-109	49	30		.953	-4	3-774/2-23,1-6,SO	-8.2

YEAR	TM/L	G	AB	R	H	2B	3B	HR	RBI	BB	SO	AVG	OBP	SLG	OPS	OPS+	BR+	SB	CS	SBR	FA	FR	G/POS	TPR
■ **RON JONES**	Jones, Ronald Glen b: 6/11/64, Seguin, Tex. BL/TR, 5'10", 195 lbs. Deb: 8/26/88																							
1988	Phi-N	33	124	15	36	6	1	8	26	2	14	.290	.302	.548	850	136	5	0	0	0	1.000	2	O-32(0-0-32)	0.7
1989	Phi-N	12	31	7	9	0	0	2	4	9	1	.290	.450	.484	934	167	3	1	0	0	1.000	2	O-12(3-0-10)	0.5
1990	Phi-N	24	58	5	16	2	0	3	7	9	9	.276	.373	.466	839	130	2	0	1	-0	1.000	-1	O-16(8-0-8)	0.1
1991	Phi-N	28	26	0	4	2	0	0	3	2	9	.154	.214	.231	445	25	-3	0	0	0	.000	0	H	-0.4
Total	4	97	239	27	65	10	1	13	40	22	33	.272	.333	.485	819	128	8	1	1	-0	1.000	3	/O-60(11-0-50)	0.9
■ **ROSS JONES**	Jones, Ross A. b: 1/14/60, Miami, Fla. BR/TR, 6'2", 185 lbs. Deb: 4/2/84																							
1984	NY-N	17	10	2	1	1	0	0	1	3	4	.100	.308	.200	508	46	-1	0	0	0	.833	1	/S-6,2-1,3-1	0.1
1986	Sea-A	11	21	0	2	0	0	0	0	0	4	.095	.095	.095	190	-48	-4	0	1	-0	1.000	1	/S-4,2-3,3-2,D-1	-0.3
1987	KC-A	39	114	10	29	4	2	0	10	5	15	.254	.292	.325	616	62	-6	1	0	0	.974	1	S-36/2-3	-0.1
Total	3	67	145	12	32	5	2	0	11	8	23	.221	.266	.283	549	46	-11	1	1	-0	.971	3	/S-46,2-7,3-3,D-1	-0.3
■ **RUPPERT JONES**	Jones, Ruppert Sanderson b: 3/12/55, Dallas, Tex. BL/TL, 5'10", 175 lbs. Deb: 8/1/76 Career OF: (174-LF 917-CF 157-RF)																							
1976	KC-A	28	51	9	11	1	1	1	7	3	16	.216	.259	.333	593	72	-2	0	2	-1	1.000	-5	O-17(2-7-9)/D-3	-0.8
1977	Sea-A★	160	597	85	157	26	8	24	76	55	120	.263	.327	.454	781	111	8	13	9	-0	.981	22	*O-155(0-155-0)/D-4	2.8
1978	Sea-A	129	472	48	111	24	3	6	46	55	85	.235	.315	.337	652	84	-10	22	6	3	.985	16	*O-128(0-128-0)	0.8
1979	Sea-A	162	622	109	166	29	9	21	78	85	78	.267	.358	.444	801	113	12	33	12	3	.989	14	*O-161(0-161-0)	2.7
1980	NY-A	83	328	38	73	11	3	9	42	34	50	.223	.301	.357	658	81	-9	18	8	1	.988	8	O-82(0-82-0)	0.0
1981	SD-N	105	397	53	99	34	1	4	39	43	66	.249	.323	.370	693	104	1	7	9	-2	.993	10	*O-104(0-104-0)	1.0
1982	SD-N★	116	424	69	120	20	2	12	61	62	90	.283	.376	.425	800	130	19	18	15	-1	.984	8	*O-114(0-114-0)	2.5
1983	SD-N	133	335	42	78	12	3	12	49	35	58	.233	.305	.394	699	96	-3	11	11	-1	.981	-2	*O-111(0-111-0)/1-5	-0.8
1984	*Det-A	79	215	26	61	12	1	12	37	21	47	.284	.347	.516	864	136	10	2	4	-1	1.000	-5	O-73(61-24-0)/D-2	0.2
1985	Cal-A	125	389	66	90	17	2	21	67	57	82	.231	.330	.447	777	111	6	7	4	0	.995	10	O-73(31-18-31),D-43	1.2
1986	*Cal-A	126	393	73	90	21	3	17	49	64	87	.229	.341	.427	769	109	6	10	3	1	.981	-12	*O-121(28-10-96)	-1.0
1987	Cal-A	85	192	25	47	8	2	8	28	20	38	.245	.316	.432	748	99	-1	2	1	0	.965	-15	O-66(52-3-21)/D-3	-1.7
Total	12	1331	4415	643	1103	215	38	147	579	534	817	.250	.332	.416	748	106	38	143	84	2	.986	51	*O-1205C/D-55,1-5	6.9
■ **JACK JONES**	Jones, Ryerson L. "Ri" or "Angel Sleeves" b: Cincinnati, Ohio TR, Deb: 8/13/1883 Career OF: (0-LF 2-CF 0-RF)																							
1883	Lou-a	2	7	1	0	0	0	0		0		.000	.000	.000	0	-99	-2				.500	-1	/O-2(0-2-0),S-1	-0.2
1884	Cin-U	69	272	36	71	5	1	2		12		.261	.292	.309	601	76	-16				.858	2	S-41,2-19,3-10	-1.0
Total	2	71	279	37	71	5	1	2		12		.254	.285	.301	586	73	-17				.857	1	/S-42,2-19,3-10,O-2C	-1.2
■ **TERRY JONES**	Jones, Terry Lee b: 2/15/71, Birmingham, Ala. BB/TR, 5'10", 160 lbs. Deb: 9/9/96																							
1996	Col-N	12	10	6	3	0	0	0	1	0	3	.300	.300	.300	600	48	-1	0	0	0	1.000	-1	/O-4(0-4-0)	-0.1
1998	Mon-N	60	212	30	46	7	2	1	15	21	46	.217	.288	.283	571	52	-15	16	4	2	.988	9	O-60(0-60-0)	-0.3
1999	Mon-N	17	63	4	17	1	1	0	3	3	14	.270	.303	.317	620	59	-4	1	2	-0	1.000	4	O-17(5-12-0)	-0.1
2000	Mon-N	108	168	30	42	8	2	0	13	10	32	.250	.292	.321	614	54	-12	7	2	1	.970	-12	O-78(55-26-7)	-2.3
Total	4	197	453	70	108	16	5	1	32	34	95	.238	.292	.302	594	54	-31	24	8	2	.984	-1	O-159(60-102-7)	-2.8
■ **TOM JONES**	Jones, Thomas b: 1/22/1877, Honesdale, Pa. d: 6/21/23, Danville, Pa. BR/TR, 6'1", 195 lbs. Deb: 8/25/02 Career OF: (0-LF 0-CF 4-RF)																							
1902	Bal-A	37	159	22	45	8	4	0	14	2		.283	.292	.384	676	83	-4	1			.955	-2	1-37/2-1	-0.6
1904	StL-A	156	625	53	152	15	10	2	68	15		.243	.270	.309	579	88	-10	16			.988	0	*1-134,2-23/O-4R	-1.4
1905	StL-A	135	504	44	122	16	2	0	48	30		.242	.290	.282	572	86	-8	5			.985	7	*1-135	-0.4
1906	StL-A	144	539	51	136	22	6	0	30	24		.252	.290	.315	606	94	-5	27			.985	11	*1-143	0.4
1907	StL-A	155	549	52	137	17	3	0	34	34		.250	.298	.291	590	88	-7	24			.983	2	*1-155	-1.0
1908	StL-A	155	549	43	135	14	2	1	50	30		.246	.290	.284	574	86	-8	18			.986	-2	*1-155	-1.5
1909	StL-A	97	337	30	84	9	3	0	29	18		.249	.299	.294	593	94	-2	13			.989	7	1-95/3-2	0.3
	*Det-A	44	153	13	43	9	0	0	18	5		.281	.317	.340	657	103	0	9			.984	2	1-44	0.2
	Yr	141	490	43	127	18	3	0	47	23		.259	.305	.308	613	97	-2	22			.988	9	*1-139/3-2	0.5
1910	Det-A	135	432	32	110	12	4	1	45	35		.255	.325	.308	633	92	-3	22			.985	-4	*1-135	-1.1
Total	8	1058	3847	340	964	122	34	4	336	193		.251	.294	.303	597	90	-48	135			.984	22	*1-1033/2-24,O-4R,3	-5.1
■ **TRACY JONES**	Jones, Tracy Donald b: 3/31/61, Hawthorne, Cal. BR/TR, 6'3", 220 lbs. Deb: 4/7/86 Career OF: (231-LF 52-CF 83-RF)																							
1986	Cin-N	46	86	16	30	3	0	2	10	9	5	.349	.411	.453	864	132	4	7	1	1	1.000	-0	O-24(23-3-0)/1-2	0.4
1987	Cin-N	117	359	53	104	17	3	10	44	23	40	.290	.338	.437	775	99	-1	31	8	4	.990	-3	O-95(56-34-17)	-0.3
1988	Cin-N	37	83	9	19	1	0	1	9	8	6	.229	.304	.277	581	65	-3	9	0	2	.955	-2	O-25(3-0-23)	-0.5
	Mon-N	53	141	20	47	5	1	2	15	12	12	.333	.390	.426	815	128	5	9	6	-0	1.000	-8	O-43(26-9-15)	-0.4
	Yr	90	224	29	66	6	1	3	24	20	18	.295	.358	.371	728	105	2	18	6	2	.980	-10	O-68(29-9-38)	-0.9
1989	SF-N	40	97	5	18	4	0	0	12	5	14	.186	.233	.227	460	33	-8	2	1	0	1.000	-8	O-30(9-5-22)	-1.8
	Det-A	46	158	17	41	10	0	3	26	16	16	.259	.331	.380	711	102	1	1	1	-0	.986	-1	O-36(34-0-3)/D-8	-0.2
1990	Det-A	50	118	15	27	4	1	4	9	6	13	.229	.283	.381	665	84	-3	1	1	-0	.952	-2	O-27(27-0-0),D-20	-0.6
	Sea-A	25	86	8	26	4	0	2	15	3	12	.302	.341	.419	759	110	1	0	1	-0	1.000	-1	O-18(18-1-0)/D-5	-0.1
	Yr	75	204	23	53	8	1	6	24	9	25	.260	.307	.397	704	95	-2	1	2	-0	.973	-3	O-45(45-1-0),D-25	-0.7
1991	Sea-A	79	175	30	44	8	1	3	24	18	22	.251	.325	.360	685	89	-2	2	0	0	1.000	-5	D-37,O-36(35-0-3)	-0.9
Total	6	493	1303	173	356	56	6	27	164	100	140	.273	.331	.388	719	96	-7	62	19	7	.988	-31	O-334L/D-70,1-2	-4.4
■ **NIPPY JONES**	Jones, Vernal Leroy b: 6/29/25, Los Angeles, Cal. d: 10/3/95, Sacramento, Cal. BR/TR, 6'1", 185 lbs. Deb: 6/8/46																							
1946	*StL-N	16	12	3	4	0	0	0	1	2	2	.333	.429	.333	762	113	0	0			.800	-1	/2-3	0.1
1947	StL-N	23	73	6	18	4	0	1	5	2	10	.247	.267	.342	609	58	-5	0			.935	-2	2-13/O-2(0-0-2)	-0.5
1948	StL-N	132	481	58	122	21	9	10	81	36	45	.254	.307	.397	704	84	-11	2			.986	-9	*1-128	-2.5
1949	StL-N	110	380	51	114	20	2	8	62	16	20	.300	.330	.426	756	97	-3	1			.984	-8	1-98	-1.4
1950	StL-N	13	26	0	6	1	0	0	6	3	1	.231	.310	.269	580	52	-2	0			.983	-1	/1-8	-0.2
1951	StL-N	80	300	20	79	12	0	3	41	9	13	.263	.287	.333	620	66	-15	1	2	-0	.991	-1	1-71	-1.9
1952	Phi-N	8	30	3	5	0	0	1	5	0	4	.167	.167	.267	433	19	-3	0	0	0	.976	0	/1-8	-0.3
1957	*Mil-N	30	79	5	21	2	1	2	8	3	7	.266	.293	.392	685	88	-2	0	0	0	.994	-0	1-20/O-1(0-0-1)	-0.3
Total	8	412	1381	146	369	60	12	25	209	71	102	.267	.304	.382	687	81	-40	4	2		.987	-19	1-333/2-16,O-3(0-0-3)	-7.0
■ **BILL JONES**	Jones, William b: Syracuse, N.Y. Deb: 5/17/1882																							
1882	Bal-a	4	15	1	1	0	0	0		0		.067	.067	.067	133	-59	-2				1.000	0	/O-2(0-1-1),C-2	-0.2
1884	Phi-U	4	14	2	2	0	0	0		1		.143	.200	.143	343	6	-2				.862	0	/C-4,O-1(0-0-1)	-0.1
Total	2	8	29	3	3	0	0	0		1		.103	.133	.103	237	-25	-4				.857	1	/C-6,O-3(0-1-2)	-0.3
■ **BILL JONES**	Jones, William Dennis "Midget" b: 4/8/1887, Hartland, N.B., Can. d: 10/10/46, Boston, Mass. BL/TR, 5'6.5", 157 lbs. Deb: 6/20/11																							
1911	Bos-N	24	51	6	11	2	1	0	3	15	7	.216	.394	.294	688	87	-0	1			.867	-1	O-18(0-18-0)	-0.3
1912	Bos-N	3	2	0	1	0	0	0	2	0	1	.500	.500	.500	1000	171	0	0			.000	0	H	0.0
Total	2	27	53	6	12	2	1	0	5	15	8	.226	.397	.302	699	89	0	1			.867	-1	/O-18(0-18-0)	-0.3
■ **TEX JONES**	Jones, William Roderick b: 8/4/1885, Marion, Kan. d: 2/26/38, Wichita, Kan. BR/TR, 6', 192 lbs. Deb: 4/13/11																							
1911	Chi-A	9	31	4	6	1	0	0	4	3		.194	.265	.226	491	39	-3	1			1.000	3	/1-9	0.0
■ **TIM JONES**	Jones, William Timothy b: 12/1/62, Sumter, S.C. BL/TR, 5'10", 175 lbs. Deb: 7/26/88																							
1988	StL-N	31	52	2	14	0	0	0	3	4	10	.269	.321	.269	591	70	-2	4	1	1	.955	5	/S-9,2-8,3-1	0.4
1989	StL-N	42	75	11	22	6	0	0	7	7	8	.293	.361	.373	735	107	1	1	0	0	1.000	-2	2-12,S-12/3-5,CO	0.0
1990	StL-N	67	128	9	28	7	1	1	12	12	20	.219	.291	.313	603	66	-6	3	4	-1	.944	2	S-29,2-19/3-6,P-1	-0.3
1991	StL-N	16	24	1	4	2	0	0	2	2	6	.167	.231	.250	481	35	-2	0	1	-0	1.000	-2	S-14/2-4	-0.5
1992	StL-N	67	145	9	29	4	0	0	3	11	29	.200	.256	.228	484	39	-11	5	2	0	.972	2	S-34,2-28/3-2,O-1C	-0.7
1993	StL-N	29	61	13	16	6	0	0	1	9	8	.262	.366	.361	727	97	0	2	2	-0	.976	5	S-21/2-7	0.6
Total	6	252	485	45	113	25	1	1	28	45	81	.233	.302	.295	597	68	-20	15	10	-0	.964	10	S-119/2-78,3-14,OPC	-0.5
■ **WILLIE JONES**	Jones, Willie Edward "Puddin' Head" b: 8/16/25, Dillon, S.C. d: 10/18/83, Cincinnati, Ohio BR/TR, 6'1", 192 lbs. Deb: 9/10/47																							
1947	Phi-N	18	62	5	14	0	1	0	10	7	0	.226	.304	.258	562	53	-4	2			.909	2	3-17	-0.2

YEAR	TM/L	G	AB	R	H	2B	3B	HR	RBI	BB	SO	AVG	OBP	SLG	OPS	OPS+	BR+	SB	CS	SBR	FA	FR	G/POS	TPR
1948	Phi-N	17	60	9	20	2	0	2	9	3	5	.333	.365	.467	832	126	2	0			.926	2	3-17	0.4
1949	Phi-N	149	532	71	130	35	1	19	77	65	66	.244	.328	.421	749	102	1	3			.948	-4	*3-145	-0.4
1950	*Phi-N★	157	610	100	163	28	6	25	88	61	40	.267	.337	.456	793	108	6	5			.954	-6	*3-157	-0.1
1951	Phi-N★	148	564	79	161	28	5	22	81	60	47	.285	.358	.470	828	123	17	6	2	1	.966	-9	*3-147	0.9
1952	Phi-N	147	541	60	135	12	3	18	72	53	36	.250	.323	.383	706	96	-3	5	3	0	**.969**	4	*3-147	0.0
1953	Phi-N	149	481	61	108	16	2	19	70	85	45	.225	.342	.385	727	90	-6	1	1	-0	**.975**	-3	*3-147	-0.9
1954	Phi-N	142	535	64	145	28	3	12	56	61	54	.271	.346	.402	748	94	-4	4	1	1	**.968**	-2	*3-141	-0.6
1955	Phi-N	146	516	65	133	20	3	16	81	77	51	.258	.357	.401	759	103	4	6	2	1	**.960**	-13	*3-146	-0.9
1956	Phi-N	149	520	88	144	20	4	17	78	92	49	.277	.387	.429	815	121	19	5	4	-0	**.973**	1	*3-149	1.9
1957	Phi-N	133	440	58	96	19	2	9	47	61	41	.218	.313	.332	645	76	-14	1	0	0	.966	-7	*3-126	-2.2
1958	Phi-N	118	398	52	108	15	1	14	60	49	45	.271	.354	.420	774	105	4	1	2	-0	**.967**	-13	*3-110/1-1	-1.1
1959	Phi-N	47	160	23	43	9	1	7	24	19	14	.269	.346	.469	815	113	3	0	0	0	.975	-3	3-46	-0.1
	Cle-A	11	18	1	4	1	0	0	1	1	3	.222	.263	.278	541	51	-1	0	0	0	.929	2	/3-4	0.0
	Cin-N	72	233	33	58	12	1	7	31	28	26	.249	.332	.399	731	91	-3	0	2	-1	.966	-3	3-68	-0.6
1960	Cin-N	79	149	16	40	7	0	3	27	31	16	.268	.394	.376	770	110	4	1	0	0	.962	-3	3-46/2-1	0.0
1961	Cin-N	9	7	1	0	0	0	0	0	2	3	.000	.222	.000	222	-34	-1	0	0	0	.000	-0	/3-1	-0.2
Total	15	1691	5826	786	1502	252	33	190	812	755	541	.258	.345	.410	755	102	20	40	17		.963	-55	*3-1614/2-1,1-1	-4.1

■ BUBBER JONNARD Jonnard, Clarence James b: 11/23/1897, Nashville, Tenn. d: 8/23/77, New York, N.Y. BR/TR, 6'1", 185 lbs. Deb: 10/1/20 FC

YEAR	TM/L	G	AB	R	H	2B	3B	HR	RBI	BB	SO	AVG	OBP	SLG	OPS	OPS+	BR+	SB	CS	SBR	FA	FR	G/POS	TPR
1920	Chi-A	2	5	0	0	0	0	0	0	0	1	.000	.000	.000	0	-99	-1	0	0	0	.857	0	/C-1	-0.1
1922	Pit-N	10	21	4	5	0	1	0	2	2	4	.238	.304	.333	638	64	-1	0	0	0	.974	2	C-10	0.1
1926	Phi-N	19	34	3	4	1	0	0	2	3	4	.118	.189	.147	336	-8	-5	0			.949	0	C-15	-0.4
1927	Phi-N	53	143	18	42	6	0	0	14	7	7	.294	.327	.336	662	77	-5	0			.967	-9	C-41	-1.1
1929	StL-N	18	31	1	3	0	0	0	2	0	6	.097	.097	.097	194	-51	-7	0			.957	1	C-18	-0.5
1935	Phi-N	1	1	0	0	0	0	0	0	0	1	.000	.000	.000	0	-91	-0	0			1.000	-0	/C-1	0.0
Total	6	103	235	26	54	7	1	0	20	12	23	.230	.267	.268	535	41	-20	0	0		.960	-6	/C-86	-2.0

■ EDDIE JOOST Joost, Edwin David b: 6/5/16, San Francisco, Cal BR/TR, 6', 175 lbs. Deb: 9/11/36 M

YEAR	TM/L	G	AB	R	H	2B	3B	HR	RBI	BB	SO	AVG	OBP	SLG	OPS	OPS+	BR+	SB	CS	SBR	FA	FR	G/POS	TPR
1936	Cin-N	13	26	1	4	1	0	0	1	2	5	.154	.214	.192	407	11	-3	0			.947	-1	/S-7,2-5	-0.4
1937	Cin-N	6	12	0	1	0	0	0	0	0	0	.083	.083	.083	167	-57	-3	0			.875	0	/2-6	-0.2
1939	Cin-N	42	143	23	36	6	3	0	14	12	15	.252	.310	.336	645	73	-5	1			.957	-3	2-32/S-6	-0.6
1940	*Cin-N	88	278	24	60	7	2	1	24	32	40	.216	.301	.266	567	57	-15	4			.960	-1	S-78/2-7,3-4	-1.0
1941	Cin-N	152	537	67	136	25	4	4	40	69	59	.253	.340	.337	678	91	-5	9			.942	-6	*S-147/2-4,1-2,3-1	0.0
1942	Cin-N	142	562	65	126	30	3	6	41	62	57	.224	.307	.320	627	84	-11	9			.933	-10	*S-130,2-15	-1.2
1943	Bos-N	124	421	34	78	16	3	2	20	68	80	.185	.299	.252	550	61	-20	5			.945	13	3-67,2-60/S-1	-0.4
1945	Bos-N	35	141	16	35	7	1	0	9	13	7	.248	.312	.312	624	73	-5	0			.945	-7	2-19,3-16	-1.1
1947	Phi-A	151	540	76	111	22	3	13	64	114	110	.206	.348	.330	678	87	-6	6	6	-1	.956	-3	*S-151	-0.1
1948	Phi-A	135	509	99	127	22	2	16	55	119	87	.250	.393	.395	788	110	11	2	4	-1	.973	5	*S-135	2.2
1949	Phi-A★	144	525	128	138	25	3	23	81	149	80	.263	.429	.453	883	138	36	2	1	0	.969	8	*S-144	5.1
1950	Phi-A	131	476	79	111	12	3	18	58	103	68	.233	.373	.384	757	96	-1	5	1	1	.956	-7	*S-131	0.1
1951	Phi-A	140	553	107	160	28	5	19	78	106	70	.289	.409	.461	870	132	28	10	8	-1	.974	4	*S-140	3.9
1952	Phi-A☆	146	540	94	132	26	3	20	75	122	94	.244	.388	.415	803	116	16	5	8	-2	.962	-7	*S-146	1.7
1953	Phi-A	51	177	39	44	6	0	6	15	45	24	.249	.401	.384	785	109	4	3	2	-0	.958	-6	S-51	0.2
1954	Phi-A	19	47	7	17	3	0	1	9	10	10	.362	.474	.489	963	163	5	0	1	-0	.963	-3	/S-9,3-5,2-1,M	0.2
1955	Bos-A	55	119	15	23	2	0	5	17	17	21	.193	.299	.336	635	65	-6	0	0	0	.932	5	S-20,2-17/3-2	0.1
Total	17	1574	5606	874	1339	238	35	134	601	1043	827	.239	.361	.366	727	99	19	61	31		.958	-20	*S-1296,2-166/3-95,1	8.5

■ DUTCH JORDAN Jordan, Adolf Otto b: 1/5/1880, Pittsburgh, Pa. d: 12/23/72, W.Allegheny, Pa. BR/TR, 5'10", 185 lbs. Deb: 4/25/03 Career OF: (1-LF 0-CF 3-RF)

YEAR	TM/L	G	AB	R	H	2B	3B	HR	RBI	BB	SO	AVG	OBP	SLG	OPS	OPS+	BR+	SB	CS	SBR	FA	FR	G/POS	TPR
1903	Bro-N	78	267	27	63	11	1	0	21	19		.236	.289	.285	574	66	-12	9			.928	-14	2-54,3-18/O-4R,1-1	-2.4
1904	Bro-N	87	252	21	45	10	2	0	19	13		.179	.225	.234	459	43	-17	7			.958	-17	2-70,3-11/1-4	-3.6
Total	2	165	519	48	108	21	3	0	40	32		.208	.258	.260	518	55	-29	16			.945	-31	2-124/3-29,1-5,O-4R	-6.0

■ BUCK JORDAN Jordan, Baxter Byerly b: 1/16/07, Cooleemee, N.C. d: 3/18/93, Salisbury, N.C. BL/TR, 6', 170 lbs. Deb: 9/15/27

YEAR	TM/L	G	AB	R	H	2B	3B	HR	RBI	BB	SO	AVG	OBP	SLG	OPS	OPS+	BR+	SB	CS	SBR	FA	FR	G/POS	TPR
1927	NY-N	5	5	0	1	0	0	0	0	0	3	.200	.200	.200	400	7	-1	0			.000	0	H	-0.1
1929	NY-N	2	2	1	1	1	0	0	0	0	0	.500	.500	1.000	1500	262	0	0			1.000	-0	/1-1	0.0
1931	Was-A	9	18	3	4	2	0	0	1	1	3	.222	.263	.333	596	56	-1	0	0	0	.978	-1	/1-7	-0.2
1932	Bos-N	49	212	27	68	12	3	2	29	4	5	.321	.333	.434	767	109	2	1			.991	-1	1-49	-0.4
1933	Bos-N	152	588	77	168	29	9	4	46	34	22	.286	.327	.386	713	112	8	4			.991	-3	*1-150	-1.0
1934	Bos-N	124	489	68	152	26	9	2	58	35	19	.311	.358	.413	771	114	10	3			.989	-3	*1-117	-0.4
1935	Bos-N	130	470	62	131	24	5	5	35	19	17	.279	.307	.383	690	91	-7	3			.983	1	1-95/3-8,O-2(0-0-2)	-1.4
1936	Bos-N	138	555	81	179	27	5	3	66	45	22	.323	.375	.405	781	118	15	2			.993	1	*1-136	0.3
1937	Bos-N	8	8	1	2	0	0	0	0	0	0	.250	.250	.250	500	40	-1	0			.000	0	H	-0.1
	Cin-N	98	316	45	89	14	3	1	28	25	14	.282	.334	.354	689	92	-4	6			.989	-2	1-76	-1.2
	Yr	106	324	46	91	14	3	1	28	25	14	.281	.332	.352	684	91	-4	6			.989	-2	1-76	-1.3
1938	Cin-N	9	7	0	2	0	0	0	0	2	0	.286	.444	.286	730	107	0	0			.000	0	H	0.0
	Phi-N	87	310	31	93	18	1	0	18	17	4	.300	.336	.365	701	95	-2	1			.973	-4	3-58,1-17	-0.5
	Yr	96	317	31	95	18	1	0	18	19	4	.300	.339	.363	702	96	-2	1			.973	-4	3-58,1-17	-0.5
Total	10	811	2980	396	890	153	35	17	281	182	109	.299	.340	.391	731	106	20	20	0		.990	-12	1-648/3-66,O-2(0-0-2)	-5.0

■ BRIAN JORDAN Jordan, Brian O'Neal b: 3/29/67, Baltimore, Md. BR/TR, 6'1", 205 lbs. Deb: 4/8/92 Career OF: (68-LF 128-CF 732-RF)

YEAR	TM/L	G	AB	R	H	2B	3B	HR	RBI	BB	SO	AVG	OBP	SLG	OPS	OPS+	BR+	SB	CS	SBR	FA	FR	G/POS	TPR
1992	StL-N	55	193	17	40	9	4	5	22	10	48	.207	.250	.373	623	77	-7	7	2	1	.991	-1	O-53(27-9-21)	-0.9
1993	StL-N	67	223	33	69	10	6	10	44	12	35	.309	.356	.543	898	139	11	6	6	-1	.973	-3	O-65(23-37-12)	0.6
1994	StL-N	53	178	14	46	8	2	5	15	16	40	.258	.323	.410	733	91	-3	4	3	-0	.991	5	O-46(18-9-22)/1-1	0.1
1995	StL-N	131	490	83	145	20	4	22	81	22	79	.296	.340	.488	828	116	9	24	9	2	.996	4	*O-126(0-13-116)	0.9
1996	*StL-N	140	513	82	159	36	1	17	104	29	84	.310	.355	.483	839	120	14	22	5	3	.994	13	*O-136(0-13-128)/1-1	2.3
1997	StL-N	47	145	17	34	5	0	0	10	10	21	.234	.311	.269	580	54	-9	6	1	1	1.000	1	O-44(0-14-30)	-0.9
1998	StL-N	150	564	100	178	34	7	25	91	40	66	.316	.370	.534	904	135	28	17	5	2	.970	1	*O-141R/3-1,D-3	2.5
1999	*Atl-N★	153	576	100	163	28	4	23	115	51	81	.283	.351	.465	816	104	3	13	8	0	.990	9	*O-150(0-0-150)	0.3
2000	*Atl-N	133	489	71	129	26	0	17	77	38	80	.264	.323	.421	745	87	-11	10	2	2	.990	11	*O-130(0-0-130)	-0.4
Total	9	929	3371	517	963	176	28	124	559	228	534	.286	.341	.465	805	109	36	109	41	10	.988	40	O-891R/D-3,1-2,3-1	4.5

■ SLATS JORDAN Jordan, Clarence Veasey b: 9/26/1879, Baltimore, Md. d: 12/7/53, Catonsville, Md. BL/TL, 6'1", 190 lbs. Deb: 9/28/01

YEAR	TM/L	G	AB	R	H	2B	3B	HR	RBI	BB	SO	AVG	OBP	SLG	OPS	OPS+	BR+	SB	CS	SBR	FA	FR	G/POS	TPR
1901	Bal-A	1	3	0	0	0	0	0	0	0		.000	.000	.000	0	-96	-1	0			.867	-1	/1-1	-0.1
1902	Bal-A	1	4	0	0	0	0	0	0	0		.000	.000	.000	0	-96	-1	0			.000	-0	/O-1(0-0-1)	-0.1
Total	2	2	7	0	0	0	0	0	0	0		.000	.000	.000	0	-96	-2	0			—	-1	/O-1(0-0-1),1-1	-0.2

■ JIMMY JORDAN Jordan, James William "Lord" b: 1/13/08, Tucapau, S.C. d: 12/4/57, Gastonia, N.C. BR/TR, 5'9", 157 lbs. Deb: 4/20/33

YEAR	TM/L	G	AB	R	H	2B	3B	HR	RBI	BB	SO	AVG	OBP	SLG	OPS	OPS+	BR+	SB	CS	SBR	FA	FR	G/POS	TPR
1933	Bro-N	70	211	16	54	12	1	0	17	4	6	.256	.270	.322	592	71	-8	3			.969	12	S-51,2-11	0.8
1934	Bro-N	97	369	34	98	17	2	0	43	9	32	.266	.285	.322	607	66	-18	1			.956	-13	S-51,2-41/3-9	-2.5
1935	Bro-N	94	295	26	82	7	0	0	30	9	17	.278	.302	.302	603	64	-15	3			.983	27	2-46,S-28/3-5	1.6
1936	Bro-N	115	398	26	93	15	1	2	28	15	21	.234	.262	.291	553	48	-29	1			.970	-17	2-98/S-9,3-6	-4.0
Total	4	376	1273	102	327	51	4	2	118	37	76	.257	.279	.308	587	60	-71	8			.969	8	2-196,S-139/3-20	-4.1

■ KEVIN JORDAN Jordan, Kevin Wayne b: 10/9/69, San Francisco, Cal. BR/TR, 6'1", 185 lbs. Deb: 8/8/95

YEAR	TM/L	G	AB	R	H	2B	3B	HR	RBI	BB	SO	AVG	OBP	SLG	OPS	OPS+	BR+	SB	CS	SBR	FA	FR	G/POS	TPR
1995	Phi-N	24	54	6	10	1	0	2	6	2	9	.185	.228	.315	543	41	-5	0	0	0	.984	6	/2-9,3-1	0.1
1996	Phi-N	43	131	15	37	10	0	3	12	5	20	.282	.314	.427	741	92	-2	2	1	0	1.000	-2	1-30/2-7,3-1	-0.5
1997	Phi-N	84	177	19	47	8	0	6	30	3	26	.266	.278	.412	690	78	-6	0	1	-0	.987	-5	1-25,3-12/2-6,D-1	-1.4
1998	Phi-N	112	250	23	69	13	0	2	27	8	30	.276	.304	.352	656	71	-11	0	0	0	1.000	0	1-24,2-22/3-6,D-8	-1.1
1999	Phi-N	120	347	36	99	17	3	4	51	24	34	.285	.342	.386	728	81	-9	0	0	0	.943	1	3-62,2-33,1-13	-0.7
2000	Phi-N	109	337	30	74	16	2	5	36	17	41	.220	.259	.323	583	45	-29	0	1	-0	.988	-8	2-47,3-39/1-9	-3.4
Total	6	492	1296	129	336	65	5	22	162	59	160	.259	.297	.368	665	69	-62	2	3	-1	.980	-8	2-124,3-121,1-101,/D	-7.0

YEAR	TM/L	G	AB	R	H	2B	3B	HR	RBI	BB	SO	AVG	OBP	SLG	OPS	OPS+	BR+	SB	CS	SBR	FA	FR	G/POS	TPR
■ MIKE JORDAN	Jordan, Michael Henry "Mitty" b: 2/7/1863, Lawrence, Mass. d: 9/25/40, Lawrence, Mass. 5'7.5", 155 lbs. Deb: 8/21/1890																							
1890	Pit-N	37	125	8	12	1	0	0	6	15	19	.096	.210	.104	314	-9	-16	5			.947	2	O-37(29-8-0)	-1.4
■ RICKY JORDAN	Jordan, Paul Scott b: 5/26/65, Richmond, Cal. BR/TR, 6'3", 209 lbs. Deb: 7/17/88 Career OF: (11-LF 0-CF 0-RF)																							
1988	Phi-N	69	273	41	84	15	1	11	43	7	39	.308	.325	.491	816	128	9	1	1	-0	.992	-5	1-69	-0.2
1989	Phi-N	144	523	63	149	22	3	12	75	23	62	.285	.325	.407	728	107	3	4	3	-0	.993	-11	*1-140	-1.9
1990	Phi-N	92	324	32	78	21	0	5	44	13	39	.241	.281	.352	633	73	-13	2	0	0	.995	-8	1-84	-2.7
1991	Phi-N	101	301	38	82	21	3	9	49	14	49	.272	.309	.452	761	113	4	0	2	-1	.987	-6	1-72	-0.8
1992	Phi-N	94	276	33	84	19	0	4	34	5	44	.304	.317	.417	733	106	1	3	0	1	.995	-6	1-54,O-11(11-0-0)	-0.9
1993	*Phi-N	90	159	21	46	4	1	5	18	8	32	.289	.327	.421	749	100	-0	0	0	0	.990	-5	1-33	-0.8
1994	Phi-N	72	220	29	62	14	2	8	37	6	32	.282	.304	.473	777	96	-2	0	0	0	.993	-8	1-49	-1.4
1996	Sea-A	15	28	4	7	0	0	1	4	1	6	.250	.300	.357	657	65	-2	0	0	0	1.000	-1	/1-9,D-2	-0.3
Total	8	677	2104	261	592	116	10	55	304	77	303	.281	.311	.424	736	103	1	10	6	0	.993	-49	1-510/O-11L,D-2	-9.0
■ SCOTT JORDAN	Jordan, Scott Allan b: 5/27/63, Waco, Tex. BR/TR, 6', 175 lbs. Deb: 9/2/88																							
1988	Cle-A	7	9	0	1	0	0	0	1	0	3	.111	.111	.111	222	-37	-2	0	0	0	1.000	-1	/O-6(0-5-1)	-0.3
■ TOM JORDAN	Jordan, Thomas Jefferson b: 9/5/19, Lawton, Okla. BR/TR, 6'1.5", 195 lbs. Deb: 9/4/44																							
1944	Chi-A	14	45	2	12	1	1	0	3	1	0	.267	.283	.333	616	77	-2	0	0	0	.947	-1	C-14	-0.2
1946	Chi-A	10	15	1	4	2	1	0	0	0	1	.267	.267	.533	800	124	0	0	0	0	1.000	1	/C-2	0.1
	Cle-A	14	35	2	7	1	0	1	3	3	1	.200	.263	.314	577	65	-2	1	1	-0	.974	-6	C-13	-0.8
	Yr	24	50	3	11	3	1	1	3	3	2	.220	.264	.380	644	83	-1	1	1	-0	.980	-5	C-15	-0.7
1948	StL-A	1	1	0	0	0	0	0	0	0	0	.000	.000	.000	0	-97	-0	0	0	0	.000	0	H	0.0
Total	3	39	96	5	23	4	2	1	6	4	2	.240	.270	.354	624	78	-3	1	1	-0	.963	-6	/C-29	-0.9
■ TIM JORDAN	Jordan, Timothy Joseph b: 2/14/1879, New York, N.Y. d: 9/13/49, Bronx, N.Y. BL/TL, 6'1", 170 lbs. Deb: 8/10/01																							
1901	Was-A	6	20	2	4	1	0	0	2	3		.200	.304	.250	554	56	-1	0			.941	-1	/1-6	-0.2
1903	NY-A	2	8	2	1	0	0	0	0	0		.125	.125	.125	250	-23	-1	0			.889	-1	/1-2	-0.2
1906	Bro-N	129	450	67	118	20	8	**12**	78	59		.262	.352	.422	774	153	27	16			.978	-9	*1-126	1.7
1907	Bro-N	147	485	43	133	15	8	4	53	74		.274	.371	.363	734	141	26	10			.980	-6	*1-143	2.0
1908	Bro-N	148	515	58	127	18	5	**12**	60	59		.247	.328	.371	698	128	16	9			.982	-15	*1-146	-0.2
1909	Bro-N	103	330	47	90	20	3	3	36	59		.273	.386	.379	765	142	19	13			.983	-9	1-95	0.9
1910	Bro-N	5	5	1	1	0	0	1	3	0	2	.200	.200	.800	1000	195	0	0			.000	0	H	0.0
Total	7	540	1813	220	474	74	24	32	232	254	2	.261	.355	.382	737	139	87	48			.980	-41	1-518	4.0
■ ART JORGENS	Jorgens, Arndt Ludwig b: 5/18/05, Modum, Norway d: 3/1/80, Evanston, Ill. BR/TR, 5'9", 160 lbs. Deb: 4/26/29 F																							
1929	NY-A	18	34	6	11	3	0	0	4	6	7	.324	.425	.412	837	125	2	0	2	-1	.979	-0	C-15	0.1
1930	NY-A	16	30	7	11	3	0	0	1	2	4	.367	.406	.467	873	126	1	0	0	0	.960	-0	C-16	0.1
1931	NY-A	46	100	12	27	1	2	0	14	9	3	.270	.330	.320	650	76	-3	0	1	-0	.962	-1	C-40	-0.3
1932	NY-A	56	151	13	33	7	1	2	19	14	11	.219	.285	.318	603	59	-9	0	0	0	.967	0	C-56	-0.6
1933	NY-A	21	50	9	11	3	0	2	13	12	3	.220	.371	.400	771	111	1	1	0	0	.982	2	C-19	0.4
1934	NY-A	58	183	14	38	6	1	0	20	23	24	.208	.296	.251	547	45	-15	2	0	0	.984	6	C-56	-0.4
1935	NY-A	36	84	6	20	2	0	0	8	12	10	.238	.333	.262	595	59	-5	0	0	0	1.000	6	C-33	0.2
1936	NY-A	31	66	5	18	3	1	0	5	2	3	.273	.294	.348	643	60	-4	0	0	0	.990	3	C-30	0.0
1937	NY-A	13	23	3	3	1	0	0	3	2	5	.130	.200	.174	374	-5	-4	0	0	0	1.000	0	C-11	-0.3
1938	NY-A	9	17	3	4	2	0	0	2	3	3	.235	.350	.353	703	77	-1	0	0	0	.923	1	/C-8	0.0
1939	NY-A	3	0	1	0	0	0	0	0	0	0	—	—	—	—	—	0	0	0	0	1.000	0	/C-2	0.0
Total	11	307	738	79	176	31	5	4	89	85	73	.238	.317	.310	627	66	-37	3	3	-0	.978	17	C-286	-0.8
■ PINKY JORGENSEN	Jorgensen, Carl b: 11/21/14, Laton, Cal. d: 5/2/96, Santa Cruz, Cal. BR/TR, 6'1", 195 lbs. Deb: 9/14/37																							
1937	Cin-N	6	14	1	4	0	0	0	1	1	2	.286	.333	.286	619	73	-0	0			.875	0	/O-4(4-0-0)	-0.1
■ SPIDER JORGENSEN	Jorgensen, John Donald b: 11/3/19, Folsom, Cal. BL/TR, 5'9", 155 lbs. Deb: 4/15/47																							
1947	*Bro-N	129	441	57	121	29	8	5	67	58	45	.274	.360	.410	770	100	1	4			.949	-5	*3-128	-0.4
1948	Bro-N	31	90	15	27	6	2	1	13	16	13	.300	.411	.444	856	127	4	1			.887	-6	3-24	-0.2
1949	*Bro-N	53	134	15	36	5	1	1	14	23	13	.269	.376	.343	719	90	-1	0			.946	-5	3-36	-0.6
1950	Bro-N	2	2	0	0	0	0	0	1	1	0	.000	.333	.000	333	-4	-0	0			1.000	-0	/3-1	0.0
	NY-N	24	37	5	5	0	0	0	4	5	2	.135	.238	.135	373	1	-5	0			.913	1	/3-5	-0.4
	Yr	26	39	5	5	0	0	0	5	6	2	.128	.244	.128	373	1	-6	0			.917	1	/3-6	-0.4
1951	NY-N	28	51	5	12	0	0	2	8	3	2	.235	.291	.353	644	72	-2	0	0	0	1.000	-2	O-11(0-0-11)/3-1	-0.5
Total	5	267	755	97	201	40	11	9	107	106	75	.266	.359	.384	743	95	-4	5	0		.940	-17	3-195/O-11(0-0-11)	-2.1
■ MIKE JORGENSEN	Jorgensen, Michael b: 8/16/48, Passaic, N.J. BL/TL, 6', 195 lbs. Deb: 9/10/68 M Career OF: (108-LF 76-CF 102-RF)																							
1968	NY-N	8	14	0	2	1	0	0	0	0	4	.143	.143	.214	357	6	-2	0	0	0	1.000	-0	/1-4	-0.2
1970	NY-N	76	87	15	17	3	1	3	4	10	23	.195	.278	.356	635	69	-4	2	2	-0	.992	3	1-50,O-10(0-9-1)	-0.2
1971	NY-N	45	118	16	26	1	1	5	11	11	24	.220	.303	.373	676	92	-1	1	2	-0	.951	-2	O-31(4-25-4)/1-1	-0.5
1972	Mon-N	113	372	48	86	12	3	13	47	53	75	.231	.333	.384	718	102	1	12	13	-2	.995	0	1-76,O-28(2-26-0)	-0.8
1973	Mon-N	138	413	49	95	16	2	9	47	64	49	.230	.338	.344	681	86	-6	16	7	1	**.995**	4	*1-123,O-11(9-2-0)	-1.0
1974	Mon-N	131	287	45	89	16	1	11	59	70	39	.310	.448	.488	936	153	24	3	5	-1	.998	7	1-91,O-29(28-1-0)	2.5
1975	Mon-N	144	445	58	116	18	0	18	67	79	75	.261	.380	.422	803	117	13	3	3	-0	.994	3	*1-133/O-6(5-1-0)	0.6
1976	Mon-N	125	343	36	87	13	0	6	23	52	48	.254	.352	.344	696	94	-1	7	1	1	.989	0	1-81,O-41(25-0-16)	-0.7
1977	Mon-N	19	20	3	4	1	0	0	0	3	4	.200	.304	.250	554	52	-1	0	0	0	1.000	1	/1-5	0.0
	Oak-A	66	203	18	50	4	1	8	32	25	44	.246	.335	.394	729	99	0	3	2	-0	.989	1	1-48,O-20(6-1-13)/D-2	-0.3
1978	Tex-A	96	97	20	19	3	0	1	9	18	10	.196	.322	.258	579	65	-4	3	1	0	.994	6	1-78/O-9(2-4-4),D-1	0.1
1979	Tex-A	90	157	21	35	7	0	6	16	14	29	.223	.295	.382	677	82	-4	0	2	-1	.988	2	1-60,O-20(4-7-9)/D-2	-0.5
1980	NY-N	119	321	43	82	11	0	7	43	46	55	.255	.349	.355	704	100	1	0	3	-1	.995	-1	1-72,O-31(9-0-22)	-0.7
1981	NY-N	86	122	8	25	5	2	3	15	12	24	.205	.276	.352	629	79	-4	4	0	1	.991	1	1-40,O-19(4-0-15)	-0.4
1982	NY-N	120	114	16	29	6	0	2	14	21	24	.254	.370	.360	730	106	2	2	0	0	.991	-3	1-56,O-16(1-0-15)	-0.2
1983	NY-N	38	24	5	6	3	0	1	3	2	4	.250	.333	.500	833	129	1	0	1	-0	1.000	1	1-19	0.1
	Atl-N	57	48	5	12	1	0	1	8	8	8	.250	.357	.333	690	86	-1	0	0	0	1.000	-0	1-19/O-6(6-0-0)	-0.1
	Yr	95	72	10	18	4	0	2	11	10	12	.250	.349	.389	738	100	0	0	1	-0	1.000	1	1-38/O-6(6-0-0)	0.0
1984	Atl-N	31	26	4	7	1	0	0	5	3	6	.269	.345	.308	653	79	-1	0	1	-0	1.000	-1	/1-8,O-4(1-0-3)	-0.3
	StL-N	59	98	5	24	4	2	1	12	10	17	.245	.315	.357	672	91	-1	0	0	0	.991	2	1-39	-0.1
	Yr	90	124	9	31	5	2	1	17	13	23	.250	.321	.347	668	87	-2	0	1	-0	.992	0	1-47/O-4(1-0-3)	-0.4
1985	*StL-N	72	112	14	22	6	0	0	11	31	27	.196	.375	.250	625	79	-1	2	1	0	.994	-2	1-49/O-2(2-0-0)	-0.6
Total	17	1633	3421	429	833	132	13	95	426	532	589	.243	.349	.373	722	100	11	58	44	-3	.994	22	*1-1052,O-283L/D-5	-3.3
■ TERRY JORGENSEN	Jorgensen, Terry Allen b: 9/2/66, Kewaunee, Wis. BR/TR, 6'4", 208 lbs. Deb: 9/10/89																							
1989	Min-A	10	23	1	4	1	0	0	2	4	5	.174	.296	.217	514	44	-2	0	0	0	.958	3	/3-9	0.2
1992	Min-A	22	58	5	18	1	0	0	5	3	11	.310	.355	.328	682	89	-1	1	2	-0	1.000	2	1-13/3-9,S-2	0.1
1993	Min-A	59	152	15	34	7	0	1	12	10	21	.224	.272	.289	561	51	-11	1	0	0	.982	8	3-45/1-9,S-6	-0.2
Total	3	91	233	21	56	9	0	1	19	17	37	.240	.295	.292	587	60	-13	2	2	-0	.975	14	/3-63,1-22,S-8	0.1
■ FELIX JOSE	Jose, Domingo Felix Andujar (b: Domingo Felix Andujar (Jose)) b: 5/2/65, Santo Domingo, D.R. BB/TR, 6'1", 190 lbs. Deb: 9/2/88																							
1988	Oak-A	8	6	2	2	1	0	0	1	0	1	.333	.333	.500	833	135	0	1	0	0	1.000	-1	/O-6(1-0-5)	-0.1
1989	Oak-A	20	57	3	11	2	0	0	5	4	13	.193	.246	.228	474	36	-5	0	1	-0	.974	-0	O-19(4-0-16)	-0.6
1990	Oak-A	101	341	42	90	12	0	8	39	16	65	.264	.307	.370	676	92	-4	8	2	1	.977	0	O-92(26-24-53)/D-7	-0.5
	StL-N	25	85	12	23	4	1	3	13	8	16	.271	.333	.447	780	112	1	4	4	-1	1.000	-2	O-23(1-2-21)	-0.2
1991	StL-N★	154	568	69	173	40	6	8	77	50	113	.305	.363	.438	801	123	18	20	12	0	.990	4	*O-153(0-0-153)	1.8
1992	StL-N	131	509	62	150	22	3	14	75	40	100	.295	.347	.432	779	123	15	28	12	2	.979	11	*O-127(0-0-127)	2.5
1993	KC-A	149	499	64	126	24	3	6	43	36	95	.253	.304	.349	653	71	-21	31	13	2	.972	-10	*O-144(0-10-136)/D-1	-3.5

YEAR	TM/L	G	AB	R	H	2B	3B	HR	RBI	BB	SO	AVG	OBP	SLG	OPS	OPS+	BR+	SB	CS	SBR	FA	FR	G/POS	TPR
1994	KC-A	99	366	56	111	28	1	11	55	35	75	.303	.364	.475	839	110	5	10	12	-2	.980	2	O-98(0-0-98)	0.0
1995	KC-A	9	30	2	4	1	0	0	1	2	9	.133	.188	.167	354	-7	-5	0	0	0	1.000	2	/O-7(0-0-7)	-0.3
2000	NY-A	20	29	4	7	0	0	1	5	2	9	.241	.290	.345	635	61	-2	0	1	-0	.929	-3	O-14(6-0-8)/D-2	-0.5
Total	9	716	2490	316	697	134	14	51	314	193	496	.280	.334	.406	740	101	2	102	57	2	.980	3	O-683(38-36-624)/D-10	-1.4

■ RICK JOSEPH

Joseph, Ricardo Emelindo (Harrigan) b: 8/24/39, San Pedro De Macoris, D.R. d: 9/8/79, Santiago, D.R. BR/TR, 6'1", 195 lbs. Deb: 6/18/64 Career OF: (13-LF 0-CF 0-RF)

YEAR	TM/L	G	AB	R	H	2B	3B	HR	RBI	BB	SO	AVG	OBP	SLG	OPS	OPS+	BR+	SB	CS	SBR	FA	FR	G/POS	TPR
1964	KC-A	17	54	3	12	2	0	0	1	3	11	.222	.263	.259	522	45	-4	0	1	-0	.981	-1	1-12/3-3	-0.7
1967	Phi-N	17	41	4	9	2	0	1	5	4	10	.220	.289	.341	630	79	-1	0	0	0	1.000	1	1-13	0.0
1968	Phi-N	66	155	20	34	5	0	3	12	16	35	.219	.297	.310	606	82	-3	0	1	-0	.992	1	1-30,3-14/O-1(1-0-0)	-0.5
1969	Phi-N	99	264	35	72	15	0	6	37	22	57	.273	.331	.398	729	106	2	2	1	0	.956	7	3-58,1-17/2-1	0.8
1970	Phi-N	71	119	7	27	2	1	3	10	6	28	.227	.264	.336	600	61	-7	0	0	0	.917	-5	O-12(12-0-0),1-10/3-9	-1.3
Total	5	270	633	69	154	26	1	13	65	51	141	.243	.302	.349	651	85	-13	2	3	-1	.933	2	/3-84,1-82,O-13L,2	-1.7

■ DUANE JOSEPHSON

Josephson, Duane Charles b: 6/3/42, New Hampton, Iowa d: 1/30/97, New Hampton, Iowa BR/TR, 6', 195 lbs. Deb: 9/15/65

YEAR	TM/L	G	AB	R	H	2B	3B	HR	RBI	BB	SO	AVG	OBP	SLG	OPS	OPS+	BR+	SB	CS	SBR	FA	FR	G/POS	TPR
1965	Chi-A	4	9	2	1	0	0	0	0	2	4	.111	.273	.111	384	14	-1	0	0	0	1.000	1	/C-4	0.0
1966	Chi-A	11	38	3	9	1	0	0	3	3	3	.237	.293	.263	556	65	-2	0	0	0	.974	3	C-11	0.1
1967	Chi-A	62	189	11	45	5	1	1	9	6	24	.238	.262	.291	553	65	-8	0	3	-1	1.000	-6	C-59	-1.4
1968	Chi-A★	128	434	35	107	16	6	6	45	18	52	.247	.286	.353	639	92	-5	2	4	-1	.990	12	*C-122	1.4
1969	Chi-A	52	162	19	39	6	2	1	20	13	17	.241	.301	.321	622	71	-6	0	0	0	.984	-1	C-47	-0.5
1970	Chi-A	96	285	28	90	12	1	4	41	24	28	.316	.375	.407	782	111	5	0	1	-0	.985	-11	C-84	-0.3
1971	Bos-A	91	306	38	75	14	1	10	39	22	35	.245	.296	.395	691	88	-5	2	0	0	.989	-4	C-87	-0.6
1972	Bos-A	26	82	11	22	4	1	1	7	4	11	.268	.310	.378	688	99	-0	0	2	-1	.980	-1	1-16/C-6	-0.3
Total	8	470	1505	147	388	58	12	23	164	92	174	.258	.305	.358	663	89	-23	4	10	-3	.989	-7	C-420/1-16	-1.6

■ VON JOSHUA

Joshua, Von Everett b: 5/1/48, Oakland, Cal. BL/TL, 5'10", 170 lbs. Deb: 9/2/69 C Career OF: (129-LF 419-CF 57-RF)

YEAR	TM/L	G	AB	R	H	2B	3B	HR	RBI	BB	SO	AVG	OBP	SLG	OPS	OPS+	BR+	SB	CS	SBR	FA	FR	G/POS	TPR
1969	LA-N	14	8	2	2	0	0	0	0	0	2	.250	.250	.250	500	43	-1	1	0	0	.800	-2	/O-8(7-0-2)	-0.3
1970	LA-N	72	109	23	29	1	3	1	8	6	24	.266	.304	.358	662	80	-3	2	2	-0	.941	-8	O-41(21-10-16)	-1.3
1971	LA-N	11	7	2	0	0	0	0	0	0	1	.000	.000	.000	0	-99	-2	0	0	0	1.000	-1	/O-5(4-1-0)	-0.3
1973	LA-N	75	159	19	40	4	1	2	17	8	29	.252	.292	.327	619	74	-6	7	2	1	.984	-5	O-46(42-1-4)	-1.2
1974	*LA-N	81	124	11	29	5	1	1	16	7	17	.234	.280	.315	595	69	-5	3	2	-0	.943	-9	O-35(12-17-6)	-1.6
1975	SF-N	129	507	75	161	25	10	7	43	32	75	.318	.359	.448	807	118	11	20	10	1	**.993**	6	*O-117(0-117-0)	1.6
1976	SF-N	42	156	13	41	5	2	0	2	4	20	.263	.281	.321	602	68	-7	1	3	-1	.948	-3	O-35(3-33-0)	-1.2
	Mil-A	107	423	44	113	13	5	5	28	18	58	.267	.297	.357	654	93	-5	8	10	-2	.982	6	*O-105(26-82-0)/D-1	-0.5
1977	Mil-A	144	536	58	140	25	7	9	49	21	74	.261	.289	.384	673	82	-15	12	9	-1	.970	-6	*O-140(0-140-0)	-2.2
1979	LA-N	94	142	22	40	7	1	3	14	7	23	.282	.315	.408	724	97	-1	1	1	-0	.967	-9	O-46(11-10-28)	-1.1
1980	SD-N	53	63	8	15	2	1	2	7	5	15	.238	.294	.397	691	97	-1	0	1	-0	1.000	-2	O-12(3-8-1)/1-2	-0.3
Total	10	822	2234	277	610	87	31	30	184	108	338	.273	.307	.380	687	91	-34	55	40	-2	.975	-31	O-590C/1-2,D-1	-8.4

■ TED JOURDAN

Jourdan, Theodore Charles b: 9/5/1895, New Orleans, La. d: 9/23/61, New Orleans, La. BL/TL, 6', 175 lbs. Deb: 9/18/16

YEAR	TM/L	G	AB	R	H	2B	3B	HR	RBI	BB	SO	AVG	OBP	SLG	OPS	OPS+	BR+	SB	CS	SBR	FA	FR	G/POS	TPR
1916	Chi-A	3	2	0	0	0	0	0	0	1	1	.000	.333	.000	333	1	-0	2			.000	0	H	0.0
1917	Chi-A	17	34	2	5	0	1	0	2	1	3	.147	.171	.206	377	15	-4	0			.973	-0	1-14	-0.5
1918	Chi-A	7	10	1	1	0	0	0	1	0	0	.100	.100	.100	200	-39	-2	0			1.000	-0	/1-2	-0.2
1920	Chi-A	48	150	16	36	5	2	0	8	17	17	.240	.337	.300	637	70	-6	3	2	-0	.982	-4	1-40	-1.1
Total	4	75	196	19	42	5	3	0	11	19	21	.214	.300	.270	570	56	-11	5	2		.981	-4	/1-56	-1.8

■ POP JOY

Joy, Aloysius C. b: 6/11/1860, Washington, D.C. d: 6/28/37, Washington, D.C. Deb: 6/3/1884

YEAR	TM/L	G	AB	R	H	2B	3B	HR	RBI	BB	SO	AVG	OBP	SLG	OPS	OPS+	BR+	SB	CS	SBR	FA	FR	G/POS	TPR
1884	Was-U	36	130	12	28	0	0	0		2		.215	.227	.215	443	36	-14				.966	0	1-36	-1.5

■ JOYCE

Joyce Deb: 8/14/1886

YEAR	TM/L	G	AB	R	H	2B	3B	HR	RBI	BB	SO	AVG	OBP	SLG	OPS	OPS+	BR+	SB	CS	SBR	FA	FR	G/POS	TPR
1886	Was-N	1	0	0	0	0	0	0	0	0	0	—	—	—	—	—	0	0			.000	-0	/O-1(0-1-0)	0.0

■ BILL JOYCE

Joyce, William Michael "Scrappy Bill" b: 9/21/1865, St.Louis, Mo. d: 5/8/41, St.Louis, Mo. BL/TR, 5'11", 185 lbs. Deb: 4/19/1890 M

YEAR	TM/L	G	AB	R	H	2B	3B	HR	RBI	BB	SO	AVG	OBP	SLG	OPS	OPS+	BR+	SB	CS	SBR	FA	FR	G/POS	TPR
1890	Bro-P	133	489	121	123	18	18	1	78	**123**	77	.252	.413	.368	782	103	7	43			.811	-11	*3-133	-0.1
1891	Bos-a	65	243	76	75	9	15	3	51	63	27	.309	.460	.506	966	179	29	36			.849	-1	3-64/1-1	2.5
1892	Bro-N	97	372	89	91	15	12	6	45	82	55	.245	.392	.398	790	144	25	23			.862	-19	3-94/O-3(3-0-0)	0.7
1894	Was-N	99	355	103	126	25	14	17	89	87	33	.355	.496	.648	1143	179	51	21			.866	-3	*3-99	3.8
1895	Was-N	127	479	110	149	26	13	17	97	**96**	56	.311	.440	.526	966	150	40	29			.846	-7	*3-127	2.8
1896	Was-N	81	310	85	97	16	10	8	51	67	20	.313	.454	.506	960	153	28	32			.888	-7	3-48,2-33	1.9
	NY-N	49	165	36	61	9	2	5	43	34	14	.370	.500	.539	1039	179	22	13			.883	0	3-49,M	2.0
	Yr	130	475	121	158	25	12	**13**	94	101	34	.333	.470	.518	988	162	50	45			.885	-7	3-97,2-33	3.9
1897	NY-N	110	389	111	118	15	13	3	64	81		.303	.444	.432	875	135	26	35			.851	-1	*3-107/1-2,M	2.3
1898	NY-N	145	508	91	131	20	9	10	91	88		.258	.386	.392	778	127	22	34			.966	8	*1-130,3-14/2-2,M	2.8
Total	8	906	3310	822	971	153	106	70	609	721	282	.293	.435	.467	902	144	250	266			.851	-40	3-735,1-133/2-35,O	18.7

■ WALLY JOYNER

Joyner, Wallace Keith b: 6/16/62, Atlanta, Ga. BL/TL, 6'2", 203 lbs. Deb: 4/8/86

YEAR	TM/L	G	AB	R	H	2B	3B	HR	RBI	BB	SO	AVG	OBP	SLG	OPS	OPS+	BR+	SB	CS	SBR	FA	FR	G/POS	TPR
1986	*Cal-A★	154	593	82	172	27	3	22	100	57	58	.290	.354	.457	811	120	16	5	2	0	.989	9	*1-152	1.6
1987	Cal-A	149	564	100	161	33	1	34	117	72	64	.285	.371	.528	900	140	32	8	2	1	.993	-7	*1-149	1.7
1988	Cal-A	158	597	81	176	31	2	13	85	55	51	.295	.359	.419	778	120	17	8	2	1	.995	12	*1-156	1.9
1989	Cal-A	159	593	78	167	30	2	16	79	46	58	.282	.340	.420	759	115	11	3	2	-0	**.997**	-4	*1-159	-0.4
1990	Cal-A	83	310	35	83	15	0	8	41	41	34	.268	.355	.394	749	111	5	2	1	0	.995	2	1-83	0.1
1991	Cal-A	143	551	79	166	34	3	21	96	52	66	.301	.363	.488	851	133	24	2	0	0	.994	1	*1-141	1.5
1992	KC-A	149	572	66	154	36	2	9	66	55	50	.269	.338	.386	724	100	-0	11	5	1	.993	14	*1-145/D-4	0.4
1993	KC-A	141	497	83	145	36	3	15	65	66	67	.292	.378	.467	845	119	14	5	9	-2	.994	20	*1-140	1.8
1994	KC-A	97	363	52	113	20	3	8	57	47	43	.311	.390	.449	839	111	7	3	2	-0	.991	3	1-86,D-11	0.1
1995	KC-A	131	465	69	144	28	0	12	83	69	65	.310	.401	.447	848	119	15	3	2	-0	**.998**	12	*1-126/D-2	1.5
1996	*SD-N	121	433	59	120	29	1	8	65	69	71	.277	.380	.404	784	114	11	5	3	0	**.997**	4	*1-119	0.4
1997	SD-N	135	455	59	149	29	2	13	83	51	51	.327	.398	.486	883	140	27	3	5	-1	**.996**	1	*1-131	1.5
1998	*SD-N	131	439	58	131	30	1	12	80	51	44	.298	.373	.453	826	125	17	1	2	-0	.993	-1	*1-127	0.4
1999	SD-N	110	323	34	80	14	2	5	43	58	54	.248	.366	.350	715	89	-3	0	1	-0	.995	6	*1-105/D-1	-0.6
2000	*Atl-N	119	224	24	63	12	0	5	32	31	31	.281	.371	.402	773	96	-1	0	0	0	.992	1	1-55/D-7	-0.3
Total	15	1980	6979	959	2024	404	25	201	1092	820	807	.290	.368	.441	809	118	193	59	38	-0	.994	72	*1-1874/D-25	11.6

■ FRANK JUDE

Jude, Frank b: 1884, Libby, Minn. d: 5/4/61, Brownsville, Tex. BR/TR, 5'7", 150 lbs. Deb: 7/9/06

YEAR	TM/L	G	AB	R	H	2B	3B	HR	RBI	BB	SO	AVG	OBP	SLG	OPS	OPS+	BR+	SB	CS	SBR	FA	FR	G/POS	TPR
1906	Cin-N	80	308	31	64	6	4	1	31	16		.208	.261	.263	524	61	-14	7			.965	-3	O-80(0-0-80)	-2.3

■ JOE JUDGE

Judge, Joseph Ignatius b: 5/25/1894, Brooklyn, N.Y. d: 3/11/63, Washington, D.C. BL/TL, 5'8.5", 155 lbs. Deb: 9/20/15 C

YEAR	TM/L	G	AB	R	H	2B	3B	HR	RBI	BB	SO	AVG	OBP	SLG	OPS	OPS+	BR+	SB	CS	SBR	FA	FR	G/POS	TPR
1915	Was-A	12	41	7	17	2	0	0	9	4	6	.415	.500	.463	963	185	5	2	3	-1	.990	-1	1-10/O-2(0-0-2)	0.3
1916	Was-A	103	336	42	74	10	8	0	28	54	44	.220	.333	.298	631	91	-2	18			.986	4	*1-103	-0.1
1917	Was-A	102	393	62	112	15	15	2	30	50	40	.285	.369	.415	783	141	19	17			.988	-1	*1-100	1.7
1918	Was-A	130	502	56	131	23	7	1	46	49	32	.261	.332	.341	672	105	3	20			.985	2	*1-130	0.1
1919	Was-A	135	521	83	150	33	12	2	31	81	35	.288	.386	.409	795	124	19	23			.988	-4	*1-133	1.3
1920	Was-A	126	493	103	164	19	15	5	51	65	34	.333	.416	.462	878	136	28	12	12	-2	.992	-8	*1-124	1.5
1921	Was-A	153	622	87	187	26	11	7	72	68	35	.301	.372	.412	784	105	5	21	6	3	.996	-3	*1-152	-0.5
1922	Was-A	148	591	84	174	32	15	10	81	50	20	.294	.355	.450	806	114	11	5	15	-4	.996	3	*1-147	0.0
1923	Was-A	113	405	56	127	24	6	2	63	58	20	.314	.406	.417	823	123	16	11	7	-0	**.993**	8	*1-112	1.6
1924	*Was-A	140	516	71	167	38	9	3	79	53	21	.324	.393	.450	843	121	16	13	8	0	.994	-2	*1-140	0.4
1925	*Was-A	112	376	65	118	31	5	8	66	55	21	.314	.406	.487	892	128	17	7	12	-3	**.993**	3	*1-109	1.0
1926	Was-A	134	453	70	132	25	11	7	92	53	25	.291	.367	.442	808	113	8	7	5	-0	.994	10	*1-128	1.0
1927	Was-A	137	522	68	161	29	11	2	71	45	22	.308	.366	.418	783	104	3	10	5	0	**.996**	-6	*1-136	-1.1
1928	Was-A	153	542	78	166	31	10	3	93	80	19	.306	.396	.417	813	115	14	16	4	2	.996	1	*1-149	0.7
1929	Was-A	143	543	83	171	35	8	6	71	73	33	.315	.397	.442	839	115	14	12	5	1	**.996**	3	*1-142	0.8

YEAR	TM/L	G	AB	R	H	2B	3B	HR	RBI	BB	SO	AVG	OBP	SLG	OPS	OPS+	BR+	SB	CS	SBR	FA	FR	G/POS	TPR
1930	Was-A	126	442	83	144	29	11	10	80	60	29	.326	.410	.509	919	131	22	13	6	1	**.998**	2	*1-117	1.6
1931	Was-A	35	74	11	21	3	0	0	9	8	8	.284	.354	.324	678	79	-2	0	0	0	.994	1	1-15	-0.2
1932	Was-A	82	291	45	75	16	3	3	29	37	19	.258	.343	.364	708	84	-6	3	3	-0	.997	1	1-78	-1.1
1933	Bro-N	42	112	7	24	2	1	0	9	7	10	.214	.261	.250	511	48	-7	1			.989	0	1-28	-1.1
	Bos-A	35	108	20	32	8	1	0	22	13	4	.296	.372	.389	761	103	1	2	1	0	1.000	-0	1-29	-0.2
1934	Bos-A	10	15	3	5	2	0	0	2	2	1	.333	.412	.467	878	118	0	0	0	0	1.000	0	/1-2	0.0
Total	20	2171	7898	1184	2352	433	159	71	1034	965	478	.298	.378	.420	798	115	183	213	92		.993	13	*1-2084/O-2(0-0-2)	7.7
■ WALLY JUDNICH	Judnich, Walter Franklin b: 1/24/17, San Francisco, Cal d: 7/12/71, Glendale, Cal. BL/TL, 6'1", 205 lbs. Deb: 4/16/40																							
1940	StL-A	137	519	97	157	27	7	24	89	54	71	.303	.368	.520	888	125	18	8	5	0	**.989**	-1	*O-133(0-133-0)	1.3
1941	StL-A	146	546	90	155	40	6	14	83	80	45	.284	.377	.456	833	116	13	5	5	-1	.980	3	*O-140(0-140-0)	1.1
1942	StL-A	132	457	78	143	22	6	17	82	74	41	.313	.413	.499	912	153	34	3	2	-0	**.991**	-2	*O-122(0-122-0)	2.9
1946	StL-A	142	511	60	134	23	4	15	72	60	54	.262	.340	.411	751	104	2	0	4	-1	**.995**	11	*O-137(6-131-1)	0.9
1947	StL-A	144	500	58	129	24	3	18	64	60	62	.258	.338	.426	764	109	5	2	5	-1	.989	-6	*1-129,O-15(0-14-1)	-0.7
1948	*Cle-A	79	218	36	56	13	3	2	29	56	23	.257	.411	.372	782	112	7	2	3	-1	.970	-8	O-49(0-35-14),1-20	-0.3
1949	Pit-N	10	35	5	8	1	0	0	1	1	2	.229	.250	.257	507	35	-3	0			1.000	1	/O-8(0-8-0)	-0.2
Total	7	790	2786	424	782	150	29	90	420	385	298	.281	.369	.452	822	119	76	20	24		.988	-2	O-604(6-583-16),1-149	5.0
■ LYLE JUDY	Judy, Lyle Leroy "Punch" b: 11/15/13, Lawrenceville, Ill d: 1/15/91, Ormond Beach, Fla. BR/TR, 5'10", 150 lbs. Deb: 9/17/35																							
1935	StL-N	8	11	2	0	0	0	0	0	2	2	.000	.154	.000	154	-53	-2	2			1.000	1	/2-5	-0.2
■ RED JUELICH	Juelich, John Samuel b: 9/20/16, St.Louis, Mo. d: 12/25/70, St.Louis, Mo. BR/TR, 5'11.5", 170 lbs. Deb: 5/30/39																							
1939	Pit-N	17	46	5	11	0	2	0	4	2	4	.239	.271	.326	597	61	-3	0			.935	-5	2-10/3-2	-0.7
■ GEORGE JUMONVILLE	Jumonville, George Benedict b: 5/16/17, Mobile, Ala. d: 12/12/96, Mobile, Ala. BR/TR, 6', 175 lbs. Deb: 9/13/40																							
1940	Phi-N	11	34	0	3	0	0	0	0	1	6	.088	.139	.088	227	-38	-6	0			.952	-4	S-10/3-1	-1.0
1941	Phi-N	6	7	1	3	0	0	1	2	0	0	.429	.429	.857	1286	266	1	0			1.000	1	/2-1,S-1	0.2
Total	2	17	41	1	6	0	0	1	2	1	6	.146	.186	.220	406	12	-5	0			.953	-4	/S-11,2-1,3-1	-0.8
■ ED JURAK	Jurak, Edward James b: 10/24/57, Los Angeles, Cal. BR/TR, 6'2", 185 lbs. Deb: 6/30/82 Career OF: (2-LF 1-CF 1-RF)																							
1982	Bos-A	12	21	3	7	0	0	0	7	2	4	.333	.391	.333	725	96	-0	0	0	0	.923	2	3-11/O-1(0-1-0)	0.1
1983	Bos-A	75	159	19	44	8	4	0	18	18	25	.277	.354	.377	731	95	-1	1	2	-0	.943	9	S-38,1-19,3-12,/2D	0.9
1984	Bos-A	47	66	6	16	3	1	1	7	12	12	.242	.359	.364	723	96	0	0	2	-1	1.000	5	1-19,2-14/3-9,S-2	0.4
1985	Bos-A	26	13	4	3	0	0	0	0	1	3	.231	.286	.231	516	42	-1	0	0	0	.833	4	/3-7,S-3,1-1,O-1L,D	0.2
1988	Oak-A	3	1	1	0	0	0	0	0	0	0	.000	.000	.000	0	-99	-0	0	0	0	.000	-0	/3-1,D-1	0.0
1989	SF-N	30	42	2	10	0	0	0	1	5	5	.238	.319	.238	557	63	-2	0	0	0	.875	-2	/S-6,3-5,2-4,O-2L,1	-0.4
Total	6	193	302	35	80	11	5	1	33	38	49	.265	.349	.344	693	88	-4	1	4	-1	.941	17	/S-49,3-45,1-40,2DO	1.2
■ BILLY JURGES	Jurges, William Frederick b: 5/9/08, Bronx, N.Y. d: 3/3/97, Clearwater, Fla. BR/TR, 5'11", 175 lbs. Deb: 5/4/31 MC																							
1931	Chi-N	88	293	34	59	15	5	0	23	25	41	.201	.264	.287	551	47	-22	2			.963	11	3-54,2-33/S-3	-0.7
1932	*Chi-N	115	396	40	100	24	4	2	52	19	26	.253	.288	.348	637	71	-16	1			**.964**	**32**	*S-108/3-5	2.2
1933	Chi-N	143	487	49	131	17	6	5	50	26	39	.269	.313	.359	672	92	-6	3			.958	20	*S-143	2.6
1934	Chi-N	100	358	43	88	15	2	8	33	19	34	.246	.289	.366	655	76	-13	1			.966	14	S-98	0.8
1935	*Chi-N	146	519	69	125	33	1	1	59	42	39	.241	.304	.314	618	66	-24	3			**.964**	**30**	*S-146	1.6
1936	Chi-N	118	429	51	120	25	1	1	42	23	25	.280	.321	.350	671	79	-13	4			.960	17	*S-116	1.2
1937	Chi-N☆	129	450	53	134	18	10	1	65	42	41	.298	.365	.389	754	101	2	2			**.975**	-7	*S-128	0.4
1938	*Chi-N	137	465	53	114	18	3	1	47	58	53	.245	.335	.303	638	75	-14	3			.953	-0	*S-136	-0.5
1939	NY-N☆	138	543	84	155	21	11	6	63	47	34	.285	.349	.398	747	99	-0	3			**.965**	15	*S-137	2.5
1940	NY-N†	63	214	23	54	3	3	2	36	25	14	.252	.347	.322	669	85	-3	2			.967	-1	S-63	0.1
1941	NY-N	134	471	50	138	25	2	5	61	47	36	.293	.361	.386	747	108	6	0			.957	7	*S-134	2.3
1942	NY-N	127	464	45	119	7	1	2	30	43	42	.256	.324	.289	612	79	-11	1			.978	7	*S-124	0.6
1943	NY-N	136	481	46	110	8	2	4	29	53	38	.229	.310	.279	589	70	-17	2			.955	1	S-99,3-28	-0.9
1944	NY-N	85	246	28	52	2	1	1	23	23	20	.211	.279	.240	519	47	-17	4			.961	-1	3-61,S-10/2-1	-1.7
1945	NY-N	61	176	22	57	3	1	3	24	24	11	.324	.405	.403	808	123	6	2			.937	2	3-44/S-8	0.9
1946	Chi-N	82	221	26	49	9	2	0	17	43	28	.222	.351	.281	631	82	-3	3			.976	-3	S-73/3-7,2-2	-0.3
1947	Chi-N	14	40	5	8	2	0	1	2	9	9	.200	.347	.325	672	83	-1	0			.925	-4	S-14	-0.4
Total	17	1816	6253	721	1613	245	55	43	656	568	530	.258	.325	.335	660	82	-147	36			.964	140	*S-1540,3-199/2-36	10.7
■ JOE JUST	Just, Joseph Erwin (b: Joseph Erwin Juszczak) b: 1/8/16, Milwaukee, Wis. BR/TR, 5'11", 185 lbs. Deb: 5/13/44																							
1944	Cin-N	11	11	0	2	0	0	0	0	0	2	.182	.250	.182	432	24	-1	0			.923	0	C-10	-0.1
1945	Cin-N	14	34	2	5	0	0	0	2	4	7	.147	.237	.147	384	8	-4	0			.947	-2	C-14	-0.5
Total	2	25	45	2	7	0	0	0	2	4	9	.156	.240	.156	396	12	-5	0			.941	-1	/C-24	-0.6
■ DAVID JUSTICE	Justice, David Christopher b: 4/14/66, Cincinnati, Ohio BL/TL, 6'3", 200 lbs. Deb: 5/24/89 Career OF: (243-LF 3-CF 808-RF)																							
1989	Atl-N	16	51	7	12	3	0	1	3	3	9	.235	.291	.353	644	81	-1	2	1	0	1.000	-1	O-16(3-0-13)	-0.3
1990	Atl-N	127	439	76	124	23	2	28	78	64	92	.282	.374	.535	909	139	23	11	6	0	.981	-2	1-69,O-61(0-0-60)	1.5
1991	*Atl-N	109	396	67	109	25	1	21	87	65	81	.275	.381	.503	884	138	21	8	8	-1	.968	5	*O-106(0-0-106)	2.3
1992	*Atl-N	144	484	78	124	19	5	21	72	79	85	.256	.363	.446	809	121	15	2	4	-1	.976	14	*O-140(0-0-140)	2.5
1993	*Atl-N★	157	585	90	158	15	4	40	120	78	90	.270	.359	.515	873	129	24	3	5	-1	.985	9	*O-157(0-0-157)	2.3
1994	Atl-N★	104	352	61	110	16	2	19	59	69	45	.313	.428	.531	959	145	26	2	4	-1	.947	2	*O-102(0-0-102)	2.1
1995	*Atl-N	120	411	73	104	17	2	24	78	73	68	.253	.368	.479	848	118	11	4	2	0	.984	6	*O-120(0-0-120)	1.1
1996	Atl-N	40	140	23	45	9	0	6	25	21	22	.321	.414	.514	928	135	8	1	1	-0	1.000	5	O-40(0-0-40)	1.1
1997	*Cle-A†	139	495	84	163	31	1	33	101	80	79	.329	.423	.596	1019	156	42	3	5	-1	.984	-5	O-78(74-0-5),D-61	2.8
1998	*Cle-A	146	540	94	151	39	2	21	88	76	98	.280	.369	.476	844	114	12	9	3	1	1.000	-1	*D-123,O-21(19-0-2)	0.4
1999	*Cle-A	133	429	75	123	18	0	21	88	94	90	.287	.417	.476	893	121	17	1	3	-1	.977	0	O-93(79-0-15),D-36	1.1
2000	Cle-A	68	249	46	66	14	1	21	58	38	49	.265	.362	.582	945	130	11	1	1	-0	.977	-1	O-47(25-2-23),D-20	0.6
	*NY-A	78	275	43	84	17	0	20	60	39	42	.305	.394	.585	979	146	19	1	0	0	.985	3	O-60(43-1-25),D-18	1.7
	Yr	146	524	89	150	31	1	41	118	77	91	.286	.379	.584	963	138	30	2	1	0	.982	2	*O-107(68-3-48),D-38	2.3
Total	12	1381	4846	817	1373	246	20	276	917	779	850	.283	.384	.513	898	131	228	48	43	-4	.977	34	*O-1041R,D-258/1-69	19.2
■ SKIP JUTZE	Jutze, Alfred Henry b: 5/28/46, Bayside, N.Y. BR/TR, 5'11", 195 lbs. Deb: 9/1/72																							
1972	StL-N	21	71	1	17	2	0	0	5	1	16	.239	.250	.268	518	48	-5	0	1	-0	.964	0	C-17	-0.5
1973	Hou-N	90	278	18	62	6	0	0	18	19	37	.223	.275	.245	520	45	-20	0	1	-0	.984	-6	C-86	-2.5
1974	Hou-N	8	13	0	3	0	0	0	1	1	1	.231	.286	.231	516	48	-1	0	0	0	1.000	-0	/C-7	-0.1
1975	Hou-N	51	93	9	21	2	0	0	6	2	4	.226	.242	.247	489	39	-8	1	0	0	.988	3	C-47	-0.3
1976	Hou-N	42	92	7	14	2	3	0	6	4	16	.152	.188	.239	427	22	-10	0	0	0	.986	2	C-42	-0.8
1977	Sea-A	42	109	10	24	2	0	3	15	7	12	.220	.267	.321	588	60	-6	0	4	-1	.984	-2	C-40	-0.8
Total	6	254	656	45	141	14	3	3	51	34	86	.215	.255	.259	514	44	-50	1	6	-2	.983	-3	C-239	-5.0
■ HERB JUUL	Juul, Herbert Victor b: 2/2/1886, Chicago, Ill. d: 11/14/28, Chicago, Ill. BL/TL, 5'11", 150 lbs. Deb: 7/11/11																							
1911	Cin-N	2	2	0	0	0	0	0	0	0	0	.000	.000	.000	0	-99	-1	0			.000	-0	/P-1	0.0
■ JIM KAAT	Kaat, James Lee b: 11/7/38, Zeeland, Mich. BL/TL, 6'4", 217 lbs. Deb: 8/2/59 C																							
1959	Was-A	3	1	0	0	0	0	0	0	0	1	.000	.000	.000	0	-99	-0	0	0	0	1.000	0	/P-3	0.0
1960	Was-A	13	14	0	2	0	0	0	0	0	6	.143	.143	.143	286	-23	-2	0	0	0	1.000	0	P-13	0.0
1961	Min-A	47	63	10	15	3	1	0	1	4	13	.238	.294	.317	612	60	-4	0	0	0	.968	3	P-36	0.0
1962	Min-A☆	48	100	9	18	3	1	1	10	8	40	.180	.241	.260	501	33	-9	0	0	0	.967	6	P-39	0.0
1963	Min-A	36	61	2	8	1	0	1	8	2	19	.131	.185	.197	381	7	-8	0	0	0	.984	4	P-31	0.0
1964	Min-A	46	83	11	14	1	0	3	11	11	31	.169	.266	.289	555	54	-5	0	0	0	.928	3	P-36	0.0
1965	*Min-A	56	93	6	23	4	0	1	9	3	29	.247	.271	.323	593	65	-4	2	0	0	.929	3	P-45	0.0
1966	Min-A★	47	118	12	23	2	1	2	13	5	41	.195	.228	.280	507	42	-9	0	0	0	.956	0	P-41	0.0
1967	Min-A	45	99	7	17	3	1	1	4	7	26	.172	.226	.253	479	38	-8	0	0	0	.952	1	P-42	0.0

YEAR	TM/L	G	AB	R	H	2B	3B	HR	RBI	BB	SO	AVG	OBP	SLG	OPS	OPS+	BR+	SB	CS	SBR	FA	FR	G/POS	TPR
1968	Min-A	36	77	7	12	3	0	0	5	2	18	.156	.177	.195	372	12	-8	0	0	0	.976	-0	P-30	0.0
1969	Min-A	43	87	8	18	8	0	2	10	4	20	.207	.250	.368	618	69	-4	0	0	0	.826	-3	P-40	0.0
1970	*Min-A	56	76	17	15	1	0	1	8	6	20	.197	.265	.250	515	42	-6	0	0	0	.935	2	P-45	0.0
1971	Min-A	54	93	6	15	3	0	0	5	2	16	.161	.179	.194	372	5	-12	2	0	0	.982	-0	P-39	0.0
1972	Min-A	24	45	3	13	3	0	2	4	1	16	.289	.304	.489	793	127	1	0	1	-0	.923	-0	P-15	0.0
1973	Min-A	31	0	1	0	0	0	0	0	0	0	—	—	—	—	—	0	0	0	0	.969	-1	P-29	0.0
	Chi-A	7	0	0	0	0	0	0	0	0	0	—	—	—	—	—	0	0	0	0	1.000	-0	/P-7	0.0
	Yr	38	0	1	0	0	0	0	0	0	0	—	—	—	—	—	0	0	0	0	.973	-2	P-36	0.0
1974	Chi-A	42	1	0	0	0	0	0	0	0	0	.000	.000	.000	0	-98	-0	0	0	0	.959	-2	P-42	0.0
1975	Chi-A★	43	0	0	0	0	0	0	0	0	0	—	—	—	—	—	0	0	0	0	.982	-2	P-43	0.0
1976	*Phi-N	42	79	4	14	3	1	1	8	2	24	.177	.198	.278	476	33	-7	0	0	0	.949	-3	P-38	0.0
1977	Phi-N	36	53	4	10	3	0	0	2	2	12	.189	.218	.245	463	23	-6	0	0	0	.897	-2	P-35	0.0
1978	Phi-N	26	48	4	7	1	0	0	4	0	15	.146	.163	.167	330	-8	-7	0	0	0	1.000	-2	P-26	0.0
1979	Phi-N	3	1	0	0	0	0	0	0	0	1	.000	.500	.000	500	47	0	0	0	0	1.000	-0	/P-3	0.0
	NY-A	40	0	0	0	0	0	0	0	0	0	—	—	—	—	—	0	0	0	0	.909	-1	P-40	0.0
1980	NY-A	4	0	0	0	0	0	0	0	0	0	—	—	—	—	—	0	0	0	0	.800	1	/P-4	0.0
	StL-N	49	35	4	5	1	0	1	2	2	13	.143	.189	.257	446	23	-4	1	0	0	.952	-2	P-49	0.0
1981	StL-N	41	8	2	3	1	0	0	2	1	0	.375	.444	.500	944	163	1	0	0	0	.895	1	P-41	0.0
1982	*StL-N	62	12	0	0	0	0	0	0	1	4	.000	.077	.000	77	-76	-3	0	0	0	.917	1	P-62	0.0
1983	StL-N	24	4	0	0	0	0	0	0	0	2	.000	.000	.000	0	-99	-1	0	0	0	.889	0	P-24	0.0
Total	25	1004	1251	117	232	44	5	16	106	63	367	.185	.229	.267	496	38	-104	5	1	1	.947	6	P-898	0.0
■ JACK KADING	Kading, John Frederick b: 11/17/1884, Waukesha, Wis. d: 6/2/64, Chicago, Ill. BR/TR, 6'3", 190 lbs. Deb: 9/12/10																							
1910	Pit-N	8	23	5	7	2	1	0	4	4	5	.304	.407	.478	886	149	1	0			1.000	1	/1-8	0.3
1914	Chi-F	3	3	0	0	0	0	0	0	0	0	.000	.000	.000	0	-99	-1	0			.000	0	H	-0.1
Total	2	11	26	5	7	2	1	0	4	4	5	.269	.367	.423	790	123	1	0			1.000	1	/1-8	0.2
■ JAKE KAFORA	Kafora, Frank Jacob "Tomatoes" b: 10/16/1888, Chicago, Ill. d: 3/23/28, Chicago, Ill. BR/TR, 6', 180 lbs. Deb: 10/5/13																							
1913	Pit-N	1	1	1	0	0	0	0	0	0	1	.000	.500	.000	500	52	0	0			1.000	-1	/C-1	-0.1
1914	Pit-N	21	23	2	3	0	0	0	0	0	6	.130	.200	.130	330	-1	-3	0			1.000	-1	C-17	-0.4
Total	2	22	24	3	3	0	0	0	0	0	7	.125	.222	.125	347	4	-3	0			1.000	-2	/C-18	-0.5
■ IKE KAHDOT	Kahdot, Isaac Leonard "Chief" b: 10/22/01, Georgetown, Okla. d: 3/31/99, Oklahoma City, Okla. BR/TR, 5'5.5", 145 lbs. Deb: 9/5/22																							
1922	Cle-A	4	2	0	0	0	0	0	0	0	1	.000	.000	.000	0	-99	-1	0	0	0	1.000	1	/3-2	0.0
■ NICK KAHL	Kahl, Nicholas Alexander b: 4/10/1879, Coulterville, Ill. d: 7/13/59, Sparta, Ill. BR/TR, 5'9", 185 lbs. Deb: 5/2/05																							
1905	Cle-A	40	135	16	29	4	1	0	21	4		.215	.248	.259	507	60	-6	1			.940	-2	2-32/S-1,O-1(0-1-0)	-0.9
■ BOB KAHLE	Kahle, Robert Wayne b: 11/23/15, New Castle, Ind. d: 12/16/88, Inglewood, Cal. BR/TR, 6', 170 lbs. Deb: 4/21/38																							
1938	Bos-N	8	3	2	1	0	0	0	0	0	0	.333	.333	.333	667	93	-0	0			.000	0	H	0.0
■ OWEN KAHN	Kahn, Owen Earle "Jack" b: 6/5/05, Richmond, Va. d: 1/17/81, Richmond, Va. BR/TR, 5'11", 160 lbs. Deb: 5/24/30																							
1930	Bos-N	1	0	1	0	0	0	0	0	0	0	—	—	—	—	—	0	0			.000	0	R	0.0
■ MIKE KAHOE	Kahoe, Michael Joseph b: 9/3/1873, Yellow Springs, O d: 5/14/49, Akron, Ohio BR/TR, 6', 185 lbs. Deb: 9/22/1895 Career OF: (0-LF 1-CF 1-RF)																							
1895	Cin-N	3	4	0	0	0	0	0	0	0	0	.000	.000	.000	0	-96	-1	0			1.000	-1	/C-3	-0.1
1899	Cin-N	14	42	2	7	1	1	0	4	0		.167	.167	.238	405	10	-5	1			.957	4	C-13	0.0
1900	Cin-N	52	175	18	33	3	3	1	9	4		.189	.215	.257	473	31	-17	3			.963	5	C-51/S-1	-0.7
1901	Cin-N	4	13	0	4	0	0	0	0	1		.308	.357	.308	665	100	0	0			1.000	-2	/C-4	-0.2
	Chi-N	67	237	21	53	12	2	1	21	8		.224	.249	.304	553	62	-12	5			.974	9	C-63/1-6	0.3
	Yr	71	250	21	57	12	2	1	21	9		.228	.255	.304	559	64	-12	5			.974	7	C-67/1-6	0.1
1902	Chi-N	7	18	0	4	1	0	0	2	0		.222	.222	.278	500	56	-1	0			.875	-1	/C-4,3-2,S-1	-0.1
	StL-A	55	197	21	48	9	2	2	28	6		.244	.270	.340	610	69	-9	4			.967	-0	C-53	-0.3
1903	StL-A	77	244	26	46	7	5	0	23	11		.189	.227	.258	485	46	-16	1			.971	-3	C-71/O-2(0-1-1)	-1.3
1904	StL-A	72	236	9	51	6	1	0	12	8		.216	.242	.250	492	59	-11	4			.968	1	C-69	-0.4
1905	Phi-N	16	51	2	13	2	0	0	4	1		.255	.269	.294	563	70	-2	1			.975	0	C-15	-0.1
1907	Chi-N	5	10	0	4	0	0	0	1	0		.400	.400	.400	800	142	0	0			1.000	-1	/C-3,1-1	-0.1
	Was-A	17	47	3	9	1	0	0	1	0		.191	.191	.213	404	31	-4	0			.976	0	C-15	-0.2
1908	Was-A	17	27	1	5	1	0	0	0	0		.185	.185	.222	407	35	-2	0			.983	4	C-11	0.3
1909	Was-A	4	8	0	1	0	0	0	0	0		.125	.125	.125	250	-22	-1	2			.867	-0	/C-3	-0.1
Total	11	410	1309	103	278	43	14	4	105	39	0	.212	.237	.276	513	52	-81	21			.968	15	C-378/1-7,O-2C,3S	-3.0
■ AL KAISER	Kaiser, Alfred Edward "Deerfoot" b: 8/3/1886, Cincinnati, Ohio d: 4/11/69, Cincinnati, Ohio BR/TR, 5'9", 165 lbs. Deb: 4/18/11																							
1911	Chi-N	26	84	16	21	0	5	0	7	7	12	.250	.308	.369	677	89	-2	6			.905	-3	O-22(1-21-0)	-0.6
	Bos-N	66	197	20	40	5	2	2	15	10	26	.203	.249	.279	528	44	-15	4			.922	-6	O-58(35-21-2)	-2.4
	Yr	92	281	36	61	5	7	2	22	17	38	.217	.267	.306	573	57	-17	10			.918	-9	O-80(36-42-2)	-3.0
1912	Bos-N	4	13	0	0	0	0	0	0	0	3	.000	.000	.000	0	-98	-4	0			.900	0	/O-4(4-0-0)	-0.4
1914	Ind-F	59	187	22	43	10	0	1	16	17	41	.230	.301	.299	600	58	-13	6			.918	-3	O-50(40-10-0)/1-1	-2.0
Total	3	155	481	58	104	15	7	3	38	34	82	.216	.274	.295	569	53	-34	16			.917	-12	O-134(80-52-2)/1-1	-5.4
■ JOHN KALAHAN	Kalahan, John Joseph b: 9/30/1878, Philadelphia, Pa. d: 6/20/52, Philadelphia, Pa. BR/TR, 6', 165 lbs. Deb: 9/29/03																							
1903	Phi-A	1	5	0	0	0	0	0	0	0		.000	.000	.000	0	-96	-1	0			1.000	-1	/C-1	-0.2
■ CHARLIE KALBFUS	Kalbfus, Charles Henry "Skinny" b: 12/28/1864, Washington, D.C. d: 11/18/41, Washington, D.C. BR/TR, 5'11", 145 lbs. Deb: 4/18/1884																							
1884	Was-U	1	5	1	1	0	0	0		0		.200	.200	.200	400	22	-1				.000	-0	/O-1(0-0-1)	-0.1
■ FRANK KALIN	Kalin, Frank Bruno "Fats" (b: Frank Bruno Kalinkiewicz) b: 10/3/17, Steubenville, Ohio d: 1/12/75, Weirton, W.Va. BR/TR, 6', 200 lbs. Deb: 9/25/40																							
1940	Pit-N	3	3	0	0	0	0	0	1	2	0	.000	.400	.000	400	19	-0	0			.667	-1	/O-2(1-0-1)	-0.1
1943	Chi-A	4	4	0	0	0	0	0	0	0	0	.000	.000	.000	0	-99	-1	0	0	0	.000	0	H	-0.1
Total	2	7	7	0	0	0	0	0	1	2	0	.000	.222	.000	222	-34	-1	0	0		.667	-1	/O-2(1-0-1)	-0.2
■ AL KALINE	Kaline, Albert William b: 12/19/34, Baltimore, Md. BR/TR, 6'2", 180 lbs. Deb: 6/25/53 H Career OF: (16-LF 484-CF 2040-RF)																							
1953	Det-A	30	28	9	7	0	0	1	2	1	5	.250	.300	.357	657	78	-1	1	0	0	1.000	-7	O-20(5-11-4)	-0.8
1954	Det-A	138	504	42	139	18	3	4	43	22	45	.276	.306	.347	653	80	-15	9	5	0	.971	11	*O-135(0-0-135)	-0.9
1955	Det-A★	152	588	121	**200**	24	8	27	102	82	57	**.340**	.425	.546	971	163	53	6	8	-1	.979	7	*O-152(0-0-152)	5.3
1956	Det-A★	153	617	96	194	32	10	27	128	70	55	.314	.385	.530	915	139	33	7	1	1	.984	17	*O-153(1-12-142)	4.4
1957	Det-A★	149	577	83	170	29	4	23	90	43	38	.295	.347	.478	825	120	14	11	9	-1	.985	7	*O-145(5-21-137)	1.5
1958	Det-A★	146	543	84	170	34	7	16	85	54	47	.313	.377	.490	867	127	21	7	4	0	.994	**23**	*O-145(0-0-145)	3.9
1959	Det-A★	136	511	86	167	19	2	27	94	72	42	.327	.414	**.530**	**944**	149	36	10	4	1	.989	11	*O-136(0-122-15)	4.1
1960	Det-A★	147	551	77	153	29	4	15	68	65	47	.278	.357	.426	784	108	7	19	4	3	.987	9	*O-142(0-142-0)	1.2
1961	Det-A★	153	586	116	190	**41**	7	19	82	66	42	.324	.396	.515	912	138	32	14	1	3	.990	12	*O-147(1-22-141)/3-1	3.6
1962	Det-A★	100	398	78	121	16	6	29	94	47	39	.304	.379	.593	972	152	28	4	0	1	.983	12	*O-100(0-0-100)	3.3
1963	Det-A★	145	551	89	172	24	3	27	101	54	48	.312	.378	.514	891	142	31	6	4	-0	.992	-2	*O-140(0-2-140)	2.0
1964	Det-A†	146	525	77	154	31	5	17	68	75	51	.293	.385	.469	853	134	26	4	1	1	.990	11	*O-136(0-0-136)	2.8
1965	Det-A★	125	399	72	112	18	2	18	72	72	49	.281	.391	.471	862	142	24	6	0	1	.985	-4	*O-112(0-62-51)/3-1	1.7
1966	Det-A★	142	479	85	138	29	1	29	88	81	66	.288	.396	.534	931	161	40	5	5	-1	**.993**	5	*O-136(0-86-53)	4.0
1967	Det-A†	131	458	94	141	28	2	25	78	83	47	.308	.415	.541	957	176	46	8	2	1	.983	8	*O-130(0-1-130)	4.9
1968	*Det-A	102	327	49	94	14	1	10	53	55	39	.287	.395	.428	823	145	20	6	4	-0	.978	-1	O-74(4-0-75),1-22	1.5
1969	Det-A	131	456	74	124	17	0	21	69	54	61	.272	.350	.447	798	117	10	1	2	-0	.966	1	*O-118(0-0-118)/1-9	0.4
1970	Det-A	131	467	64	130	24	4	16	71	77	49	.278	.382	.450	831	127	19	2	2	-0	.988	1	O-91(0-0-91),1-52	1.2
1971	Det-A★	133	405	69	119	19	2	15	54	82	57	.294	.421	.462	883	144	28	4	6	-1	**1.000**	-6	*O-129(0-3-128)/1-5	1.5

YEAR	TM/L	G	AB	R	H	2B	3B	HR	RBI	BB	SO	AVG	OBP	SLG	OPS	OPS+	BR+	SB	CS	SBR	FA	FR	G/POS	TPR
1972	*Det-A	106	278	46	87	11	2	10	32	28	33	.313	.380	.475	855	148	17	1	0	0	.991	-6	O-84(0-0-84),1-11	0.8
1973	Det-A	91	310	40	79	13	0	10	45	29	28	.255	.325	.394	718	95	-2	4	1	1	1.000	-5	O-63(0-0-63),1-36	-1.3
1974	Det-A★	147	558	71	146	28	2	13	64	65	75	.262	.340	.389	729	105	5	2	2	-0	.000	0	*D-146	0.1
Total	22	2834	10116	1622	3007	498	75	399	1583	1277	1020	.297	.379	.480	859	134	470	137	65	7	.986	103	*O-2488R,D-146,1/3	45.2

■ WILLIE KAMM Kamm, William Edward b: 2/2/1900, San Francisco, Cal. d: 12/21/88, Belmont, Cal. BR/TR, 5'10.5", 170 lbs. Deb: 4/18/23

YEAR	TM/L	G	AB	R	H	2B	3B	HR	RBI	BB	SO	AVG	OBP	SLG	OPS	OPS+	BR+	SB	CS	SBR	FA	FR	G/POS	TPR
1923	Chi-A	149	544	57	159	39	9	6	87	62	82	.292	.366	.430	796	110	8	18	13	-1	.960	8	*3-149	2.3
1924	Chi-A	147	528	58	134	28	6	6	93	64	59	.254	.337	.364	700	83	-14	10	9	-1	**.971**	8	*3-146	0.3
1925	Chi-A	152	509	82	142	32	4	6	83	**90**	36	.279	.391	.393	784	105	7	11	13	-2	**.957**	-0	*3-152	1.3
1926	Chi-A	143	480	63	141	24	10	0	62	77	24	.294	.396	.385	781	108	9	12	4	1	**.978**	14	*3-142	3.1
1927	Chi-A	148	540	85	146	32	13	0	59	70	18	.270	.354	.378	732	92	-5	8	9	-1	**.972**	1	*3-146	0.3
1928	Chi-A	155	552	70	170	30	12	1	84	73	22	.308	.391	.411	802	112	12	17	9	1	**.977**	-3	*3-155	1.9
1929	Chi-A	147	523	72	140	33	6	3	63	75	23	.268	.363	.371	734	90	-6	12	5	1	**.978**	4	*3-145	0.7
1930	Chi-A	112	331	49	89	21	6	3	47	51	20	.269	.368	.396	764	97	-0	5	4	-0	.939	15	*3-106	1.8
1931	Chi-A	18	59	9	15	4	1	0	9	7	6	.254	.333	.356	689	86	-1	1	1	-0	.938	2	3-18	0.1
	Cle-A	114	410	68	121	31	4	0	66	64	13	.295	.392	.390	782	100	2	13	9	-0	.947	1	*3-114	0.6
	Yr	132	469	77	136	35	5	0	75	71	19	.290	.384	.386	770	99	2	14	10	-0	.945	3	*3-132	0.7
1932	Cle-A	148	524	76	150	34	9	3	83	75	36	.286	.379	.403	781	96	-1	6	3	0	.967	7	*3-148	1.0
1933	Cle-A	133	447	59	126	17	2	1	47	54	27	.282	.359	.336	695	81	-10	6	3	0	**.984**	1	*3-131	-0.5
1934	Cle-A	121	386	52	104	23	3	0	42	62	38	.269	.372	.345	716	84	-7	7	1	1	**.978**	11	*3-118	0.9
1935	Cle-A	6	18	2	6	0	0	0	1	0	1	.333	.333	.333	667	72	-1	0	1	-0	.875	-2	/3-4	-0.2
Total	13	1693	5851	802	1643	348	85	29	826	824	405	.281	.372	.384	756	97	-6	126	84	-2	.967	66	*3-1674	13.6

■ ALEX KAMPOURIS Kampouris, Alexis William b: 11/13/12, Sacramento, Cal. d: 5/29/93, Sacramento, Cal. BR/TR, 5'8", 155 lbs. Deb: 7/31/34 Career OF: (1-LF 0-CF 1-RF)

YEAR	TM/L	G	AB	R	H	2B	3B	HR	RBI	BB	SO	AVG	OBP	SLG	OPS	OPS+	BR+	SB	CS	SBR	FA	FR	G/POS	TPR
1934	Cin-N	19	66	6	13	1	0	0	3	3	18	.197	.254	.212	466	27	-7	2			.946	-1	2-16	-0.7
1935	Cin-N	148	499	46	123	26	5	7	62	32	84	.246	.295	.361	655	77	-17	8			.957	-1	*2-141/S-6	-0.8
1936	Cin-N	122	355	43	85	10	4	5	46	24	46	.239	.289	.332	622	72	-15	3			.969	28	*2-119/O-1(1-0-0)	1.9
1937	Cin-N	146	458	62	114	21	4	17	71	60	65	.249	.342	.424	766	112	8	2			.961	3	*2-146	2.0
1938	Cin-N	21	74	13	19	1	0	2	7	10	13	.257	.353	.351	704	97	-0	0			.973	0	2-21	0.2
	NY-N	82	268	35	66	9	1	5	37	27	50	.246	.318	.343	661	81	-7	0			.972	13	2-79	1.1
	Yr	103	342	48	85	10	1	7	44	37	63	.249	.325	.345	670	84	-7	0			.972	14	*2-100	1.3
1939	NY-N	74	201	23	50	12	2	5	29	30	41	.249	.349	.403	752	101	1	0			.973	10	2-62,3-11	1.4
1941	Bro-N	16	51	8	16	4	2	2	9	11	8	.314	.444	.588	1033	181	6	0			.987	0	2-15	0.7
1942	Bro-N	10	21	3	5	2	1	0	3	0	4	.238	.238	.429	667	92	-0	0			.970	2	/2-9	0.2
1943	Bro-N	19	44	9	10	4	1	0	4	17	6	.227	.452	.364	815	136	4	0			.946	-1	2-18	0.3
	Was-A	51	145	24	30	4	0	2	13	30	25	.207	.361	.276	637	91	0	7	1	1	.936	-3	3-33,2-10/O-1(0-0-1)	-0.1
Total	9	708	2182	272	531	94	20	45	284	244	360	.243	.325	.367	692	91	-27	22	1		.964	50	2-636/3-44,S-6,O-2L	6.2

■ FRANK KANE Kane, Francis Thomas "Sugar" (a.k.a. Frank Thomas Kiley In 1915) b: 3/9/1895, Whitman, Mass. d: 12/2/62, Brockton, Mass. BL/TR, 5'11.5", 175 lbs. Deb: 9/13/15

YEAR	TM/L	G	AB	R	H	2B	3B	HR	RBI	BB	SO	AVG	OBP	SLG	OPS	OPS+	BR+	SB	CS	SBR	FA	FR	G/POS	TPR
1915	Bro-F	3	10	2	2	0	1	0	2	0	0	.200	.200	.400	600	67	-1	0			1.000	1	/O-2(2-0-0)	0.0
1919	NY-A	1	1	0	0	0	0	0	0	0	0	.000	.000	.000	0	-99	-0	0			.000	0	H	0.0
Total	2	4	11	2	2	0	1	0	2	0	0	.182	.182	.364	545	52	-1	0			1.000	1	/O-2(2-0-0)	0.0

■ JIM KANE Kane, James Joseph "Shamus" b: 11/27/1881, Scranton, Pa. d: 10/2/47, Omaha, Neb. BL/TL, 6'2", 225 lbs. Deb: 4/21/08

YEAR	TM/L	G	AB	R	H	2B	3B	HR	RBI	BB	SO	AVG	OBP	SLG	OPS	OPS+	BR+	SB	CS	SBR	FA	FR	G/POS	TPR
1908	Pit-N	55	145	16	35	3	3	0	22	12		.241	.299	.303	603	93	-1	5			.966	-2	1-40	-0.4

■ JOHN KANE Kane, John Francis b: 9/24/1882, Chicago, Ill. d: 1/28/34, St.Anthony, Idaho BR/TR, 5'6", 138 lbs. Deb: 4/11/07 Career OF: (53-LF 130-CF 13-RF)

YEAR	TM/L	G	AB	R	H	2B	3B	HR	RBI	BB	SO	AVG	OBP	SLG	OPS	OPS+	BR+	SB	CS	SBR	FA	FR	G/POS	TPR
1907	Cin-N	79	262	40	65	9	4	3	19	22		.248	.325	.347	673	106	2	20			.959	-1	O-42L,3-25/S-6,2-2	0.0
1908	Cin-N	130	455	61	97	11	7	3	23	43		.213	.299	.288	587	90	-4	30			**.981**	4	*O-127(0-120-7)/2-1	-0.7
1909	Chi-N	20	45	6	4	1	0	0	5	2		.089	.146	.111	257	-20	-6	1			.917	3	/O-8L,S-3,3-3,2-2	-0.4
1910	*Chi-N	32	62	11	15	0	0	1	12	9	10	.242	.338	.290	628	84	-1	2			1.000	-7	O-18L/2-6,3-4,S-2	-0.8
Total	4	261	824	118	181	21	11	7	59	76	10	.220	.303	.297	600	89	-9	53			.975	-0	O-195C/3-32,2-11,S	-1.9

■ JOHN KANE Kane, John Francis b: 2/19/1900, Chicago, Ill. d: 7/25/56, Chicago, Ill. BB/TR, 5'10.5", 162 lbs. Deb: 9/3/25

YEAR	TM/L	G	AB	R	H	2B	3B	HR	RBI	BB	SO	AVG	OBP	SLG	OPS	OPS+	BR+	SB	CS	SBR	FA	FR	G/POS	TPR
1925	Chi-A	14	56	6	10	1	0	0	3	0	3	.179	.193	.196	389	-1	-9	0	0	0	.935	1	/S-8,2-6	-0.6

■ TOM KANE Kane, Thomas Joseph "Sugar" b: 12/15/06, Chicago, Ill. d: 11/26/73, Chicago, Ill. BR/TR, 5'10.5", 160 lbs. Deb: 8/3/38

YEAR	TM/L	G	AB	R	H	2B	3B	HR	RBI	BB	SO	AVG	OBP	SLG	OPS	OPS+	BR+	SB	CS	SBR	FA	FR	G/POS	TPR
1938	Bos-N	2	2	0	0	0	0	0	0	2	0	.000	.500	.000	500	53	0	0			1.000	-1	/2-2	-0.1

■ JERRY KANE Kane, William Jeremiah b: 4/1869, Baltimore, Md. d: 6/16/49, E.St.Louis, Ill. BR/TR, 6', 175 lbs. Deb: 5/2/1890

YEAR	TM/L	G	AB	R	H	2B	3B	HR	RBI	BB	SO	AVG	OBP	SLG	OPS	OPS+	BR+	SB	CS	SBR	FA	FR	G/POS	TPR
1890	StL-a	8	25	3	5	0	0	0	2	2		.200	.259	.200	459	31	-2	0			.907	-1	/1-5,C-4	-0.3

■ ROD KANEHL Kanehl, Roderick Edwin "Hot Rod" b: 4/1/34, Wichita, Kan. BR/TR, 6'1", 180 lbs. Deb: 4/15/62 Career OF: (42-LF 56-CF 7-RF)

YEAR	TM/L	G	AB	R	H	2B	3B	HR	RBI	BB	SO	AVG	OBP	SLG	OPS	OPS+	BR+	SB	CS	SBR	FA	FR	G/POS	TPR
1962	NY-N	133	351	52	87	10	2	4	27	23	36	.248	.296	.322	618	65	-17	8	6	-0	.944	15	2-62,3-30,O-20L,/1S	0.1
1963	NY-N	109	191	26	46	6	0	1	9	5	26	.241	.268	.288	556	59	-10	6	3	0	.974	-7	O-58L,3-13,2-12,/1	-1.9
1964	NY-N	98	254	25	59	7	1	1	11	7	18	.232	.256	.280	535	52	-16	3	1	0	.988	19	2-34,O-25C,3-19,/1	0.5
Total	3	340	796	103	192	23	3	6	47	35	80	.241	.277	.300	577	60	-44	17	10	0	.950	27	2-108,O-103C/3-62,1S	-1.3

■ GABE KAPLER Kapler, Gabriel Stefan b: 8/31/75, Hollywood, Cal. BR/TR, 6'2", 190 lbs. Deb: 9/20/98

YEAR	TM/L	G	AB	R	H	2B	3B	HR	RBI	BB	SO	AVG	OBP	SLG	OPS	OPS+	BR+	SB	CS	SBR	FA	FR	G/POS	TPR
1998	Det-A	7	25	3	5	0	1	0	0	1	4	.200	.231	.280	511	32	-3	2	0	0	1.000	-1	/O-6(0-0-6),D-1	-0.3
1999	Det-A	130	416	60	102	22	4	18	49	42	74	.245	.317	.447	765	93	-6	11	5	1	.981	-7	*O-128(0-114-32)/D-2	-1.1
2000	Tex-A	116	444	59	134	32	1	14	66	42	57	.302	.362	.473	835	106	4	8	4	0	.969	6	*O-116(0-84-40)	0.8
Total	3	253	885	122	241	54	6	32	115	85	135	.272	.337	.455	793	98	-5	21	9	1	.975	-1	O-250(0-198-78)/D-3	-0.6

■ HEINIE KAPPEL Kappel, Henry b: 9/1863, Philadelphia, Pa. d: 8/27/05, Philadelphia, Pa. BR/TR, 5'8", 160 lbs. Deb: 5/22/1887 F Career OF: (2-LF 0-CF 5-RF)

YEAR	TM/L	G	AB	R	H	2B	3B	HR	RBI	BB	SO	AVG	OBP	SLG	OPS	OPS+	BR+	SB	CS	SBR	FA	FR	G/POS	TPR
1887	Cin-a	23	80	11	24	3	2	0	15	2		.300	.309	.372	680	87	-2	3			.667	-3	/3-9,O-7R,2-6,S-1	-0.4
1888	Cin-a	36	143	18	37	4	4	1	15	2		.259	.274	.364	638	98	-1	20			.790	-12	S-25,2-10/3-1	-1.1
1889	Col-a	46	173	25	47	7	5	3	21	21	28	.272	.354	.422	776	127	6	10			.791	-2	S-23,3-23	0.5
Total	3	105	396	54	108	14	11	4	51	25	28	.273	.318	.391	708	109	3	33			.796	-17	/S-49,3-33,2-16,O-7R	-1.0

■ JOE KAPPEL Kappel, Joseph b: 4/27/1857, Philadelphia, Pa. d: 7/8/29, Philadelphia, Pa. BR, 5'11", 175 lbs. Deb: 5/26/1884 F Career OF: (11-LF 8-CF 5-RF)

YEAR	TM/L	G	AB	R	H	2B	3B	HR	RBI	BB	SO	AVG	OBP	SLG	OPS	OPS+	BR+	SB	CS	SBR	FA	FR	G/POS	TPR
1884	Phi-N	4	15	1	1	0	0	0	0	0	2	.067	.067	.067	133	-61	-3				.727	-3	/C-4	-0.5
1890	Phi-a	56	208	29	50	8	1	1	22	20		.240	.310	.303	613	81	-5	12			.851	-5	O-23L,S-18,3-11,/C2	-0.9
Total	2	60	223	30	51	8	1	1	22	20	2	.229	.295	.287	582	73	-8	12			.773	-8	/O-23L,S-18,3-11,C2	-1.4

■ RON KARKOVICE Karkovice, Ronald Joseph b: 8/8/63, Union, N.J. BR/TR, 6'1", 215 lbs. Deb: 8/17/86

YEAR	TM/L	G	AB	R	H	2B	3B	HR	RBI	BB	SO	AVG	OBP	SLG	OPS	OPS+	BR+	SB	CS	SBR	FA	FR	G/POS	TPR
1986	Chi-A	37	97	13	24	7	0	4	13	9	37	.247	.318	.443	761	101	-0	1	0	0	.996	14	C-37	1.5
1987	Chi-A	39	85	7	6	0	0	2	7	7	40	.071	.160	.141	301	-19	-15	3	0	1	.982	10	C-37/D-1	-0.3
1988	Chi-A	46	115	10	20	4	0	3	9	7	30	.174	.228	.287	515	43	-9	4	2	0	.995	9	C-46	0.2
1989	Chi-A	71	182	21	48	9	2	3	24	10	56	.264	.309	.385	694	97	-1	0	0	0	.986	17	C-68/D-2	1.9
1990	Chi-A	68	183	30	45	10	0	6	20	16	52	.246	.310	.399	709	99	-1	2	0	0	.994	6	C-64/D-2	0.9
1991	Chi-A	75	167	25	41	13	0	5	22	15	42	.246	.311	.413	725	101	-0	0	0	0	.988	11	C-69/O-1(1-0-0)	1.4
1992	Chi-A	123	342	39	81	12	1	13	50	30	89	.237	.304	.392	696	95	-3	10	4	1	.990	5	*C-119/O-1(0-0-1)	0.9
1993	*Chi-A	128	403	60	92	17	1	20	54	29	126	.228	.290	.424	714	91	-7	2	2	-0	.994	13	*C-127	1.3
1994	Chi-A	77	207	33	44	9	1	11	29	36	68	.213	.329	.425	754	94	-2	0	3	-1	.993	-4	C-76	-0.2
1995	Chi-A	113	323	44	70	14	1	13	51	39	84	.217	.311	.387	698	84	-8	2	3	-1	.991	-8	*C-113	-1.0
1996	Chi-A	111	355	44	78	22	0	10	38	24	93	.220	.271	.366	637	62	-22	0	0	0	.993	12	*C-111	-0.4
1997	Chi-A	51	138	10	25	3	0	6	18	11	32	.181	.257	.333	590	55	-10	0	0	0	.996	-3	C-51	-1.0
Total	12	939	2597	336	574	120	6	96	335	233	749	.221	.292	.383	674	81	-77	24	14	0	.992	83	C-918/D-5,O-2(1-0-1)	5.2

■ BILL KARLON Karlon, William John "Hank" b: 1/21/09, Palmer, Mass. d: 12/7/64, Ware, Mass. BR/TR, 6'1", 190 lbs. Deb: 4/28/30

YEAR	TM/L	G	AB	R	H	2B	3B	HR	RBI	BB	SO	AVG	OBP	SLG	OPS	OPS+	BR+	SB	CS	SBR	FA	FR	G/POS	TPR
1930	NY-A	2	5	0	0	0	0	0	0	0	1	.000	.000	.000	0	-99	-2	0	0	0	1.000	-0	/O-1(1-0-0)	-0.2

YEAR	TM/L	G	AB	R	H	2B	3B	HR	RBI	BB	SO	AVG	OBP	SLG	OPS	OPS+	BR+	SB	CS	SBR	FA	FR	G/POS	TPR
■ **MARTY KAROW**	Karow, Martin Gregory (b: Martin Gregory Karowsky) b: 7/18/04, Braddock, Pa. d: 4/27/86, Bryan, Texas BR/TR, 5'10.5", 170 lbs. Deb: 6/21/27																							
1927	Bos-A	6	10	0	2	1	0	0	0	0	2	.200	.200	.300	500	29	-1	0	0	0	1.000	0	/S-3,3-2	-0.1
■ **ERIC KARROS**	Karros, Eric Peter b: 11/4/67, Hackensack, N.J. BR/TR, 6'4", 216 lbs. Deb: 9/1/91																							
1991	LA-N	14	14	0	1	1	0	0	1	1	6	.071	.133	.143	276	-23	-2	0	0	0	1.000	0	1-10	-0.3
1992	LA-N	149	545	63	140	30	1	20	88	37	103	.257	.307	.426	732	107	3	2	4	-1	.993	11	*1-143	0.3
1993	LA-N	158	619	74	153	27	2	23	80	34	82	.247	.289	.409	697	89	-12	0	1	-0	.992	15	*1-157	-1.2
1994	LA-N	111	406	51	108	21	1	14	46	29	53	.266	.318	.426	744	98	-2	2	0	0	.991	16	*1-109	0.4
1995	*LA-N	143	551	83	164	29	3	32	105	61	115	.298	.372	.535	907	149	38	4	4	-1	.995	4	*1-143	2.6
1996	*LA-N	154	608	84	158	29	1	34	111	53	121	.260	.320	.479	799	116	11	8	0	2	.990	3	*1-154	0.1
1997	LA-N	162	628	86	167	28	0	31	104	61	116	.266	.333	.459	791	113	10	15	7	1	.992	1	*1-162	-0.3
1998	LA-N	139	507	59	150	20	1	23	87	47	93	.296	.359	.475	834	124	17	7	2	1	.991	6	*1-136/D-2	1.2
1999	LA-N	153	578	74	176	40	0	34	112	53	119	.304	.365	.550	915	135	29	8	5	0	.991	12	*1-151	2.5
2000	LA-N	155	584	84	146	29	0	31	106	63	122	.250	.327	.459	786	100	-2	4	3	-0	.995	17	*1-153/D-1	0.1
Total	10	1338	5040	658	1363	254	9	242	840	439	930	.270	.332	.468	800	114	90	50	26	2	.992	86	*1-1318/D-3	5.4
■ **JOHN KARST**	Karst, John Gottlieb "King" b: 10/15/1893, Philadelphia, Pa. d: 5/21/76, Cape May Court House, N.J. BL/TR, 5'11.5", 175 lbs. Deb: 10/6/15																							
1915	Bro-N	1	0	0	0	0	0	0	0	0	0	—	—	—	—	—	0	0			1.000	0	/3-1	0.0
■ **EDDIE KASKO**	Kasko, Edward Michael b: 6/27/32, Linden, N.J. BR/TR, 6', 180 lbs. Deb: 4/18/57 M																							
1957	StL-N	134	479	59	131	16	5	1	35	33	53	.273	.320	.334	654	75	-16	6	1	1	.961	-7	*3-120,S-13/2-1	-2.3
1958	StL-N	104	259	20	57	8	1	2	22	21	25	.220	.279	.282	560	47	-19	1	2	-0	.961	6	S-77,2-12/3-1	-0.8
1959	Cin-N	118	329	39	93	14	1	2	31	14	38	.283	.312	.350	661	74	-12	2	2	-0	.976	12	S-84,3-31/2-2	0.6
1960	Cin-N	126	479	56	140	21	1	6	51	46	37	.292	.362	.378	739	101	2	9	9	-1	.966	0	3-86,2-33,S-15	0.4
1961	*Cin-N★	126	469	64	127	22	1	2	27	32	36	.271	.323	.335	658	74	-17	4	3	-0	.964	-18	*S-112,3-12/2-6	-2.6
1962	Cin-N	134	533	74	148	26	2	4	41	35	44	.278	.328	.356	685	81	-14	3	3	-0	.941	-8	*3-114,S-21	-2.1
1963	Cin-N	76	199	25	48	9	0	3	10	21	29	.241	.314	.332	645	83	-4	0	2	-1	.959	-1	3-48,S-15/2-1	-0.5
1964	Hou-N	133	448	45	109	16	1	0	22	37	52	.243	.302	.283	586	70	-17	4	6	-1	**.978**	10	*S-128/3-2	0.2
1965	Hou-N	68	215	18	53	7	1	1	10	11	20	.247	.296	.302	598	74	-8	1	3	-1	.976	-10	S-59/3-2	-1.5
1966	Bos-A	58	136	11	29	7	0	1	12	15	19	.213	.291	.287	578	61	-7	1	0	0	.976	8	S-20,3-10/2-8	0.3
Total	10	1077	3546	411	935	146	13	22	261	265	353	.264	.318	.331	649	76	-112	31	31	-4	.971	-9	S-544,3-426/2-63	-8.3
■ **RAY KATT**	Katt, Raymond Frederick b: 5/9/27, New Braunfels, Tex. d: 10/19/99, New Braunfels, Tex BR/TR, 6'2", 200 lbs. Deb: 9/16/52 C																							
1952	NY-N	9	27	4	6	0	0	0	1	1	5	.222	.250	.222	472	32	-2	0	0	0	1.000	1	/C-8	-0.1
1953	NY-N	8	29	2	5	1	0	0	1	1	3	.172	.200	.207	407	6	-4	0	0	0	.975	-1	/C-8	-0.4
1954	NY-N	86	200	26	51	7	1	9	33	19	29	.255	.320	.435	755	94	-2	1	0	0	.973	-7	C-82	-0.6
1955	NY-N	124	326	27	70	7	2	7	28	22	38	.215	.269	.313	581	54	-22	0	0	0	.987	-8	*C-122	-2.5
1956	NY-N	37	101	10	23	4	0	7	14	6	16	.228	.278	.475	753	98	-1	0	1	-0	.978	0	C-37	0.1
	StL-N	47	158	11	41	4	0	6	20	6	24	.259	.291	.399	690	83	-4	0	1	-0	.984	-2	C-47	-0.4
	Yr	84	259	21	64	8	0	13	34	12	40	.247	.286	.429	714	89	-5	0	2	-1	.982	-1	C-84	-0.3
1957	NY-N	72	165	11	38	3	1	2	17	15	35	.230	.302	.297	599	62	-9	1	0	0	.981	-6	C-68	-1.2
1958	StL-N	19	41	1	7	1	0	1	4	4	6	.171	.244	.268	513	34	-4	0	0	0	.971	0	C-14	-0.3
1959	StL-N	15	24	0	7	2	0	0	2	0	8	.292	.292	.375	667	71	-1	0	0	0	.976	-0	C-14	-0.1
Total	8	417	1071	92	248	29	4	32	120	74	164	.232	.285	.356	641	69	-49	2	2	-0	.981	-22	C-400	-5.5
■ **BENNY KAUFF**	Kauff, Benjamin Michael b: 1/5/1890, Pomeroy, Ohio d: 11/17/61, Columbus, Ohio BL/TL, 5'8", 157 lbs. Deb: 4/20/12																							
1912	NY-A	5	11	4	3	0	0	0	2	3		.273	.429	.273	701	96	0	1			1.000	-1	/O-4(0-4-0)	-0.1
1914	Ind-F	154	571	**120**	**211**	**44**	13	8	95	72	55	**.370**	**.447**	.534	**981**	150	35	**75**			.953	16	*O-154(33-54-68)	4.3
1915	Bro-F	136	483	92	165	23	11	12	83	85	50	**.342**	**.446**	**.509**	**955**	**170**	**42**	**55**			.959	15	*O-136(0-136-0)	**5.0**
1916	NY-N	154	552	71	146	22	15	9	74	68	65	.264	.348	.408	756	139	26	40	26	-0	.962	2	*O-154(0-154-0)	2.0
1917	*NY-N	153	559	89	172	22	4	5	68	59	54	.308	.379	.388	767	140	28	30			.976	-4	*O-153(3-150-0)	1.4
1918	NY-N	67	270	41	85	19	4	2	39	16	30	.315	.355	.437	792	144	13	9			.952	-1	O-67(0-67-0)	0.9
1919	NY-N	135	491	73	136	27	7	10	67	39	45	.277	.334	.422	756	128	16	21			.950	-3	*O-134(0-134-0)	0.4
1920	NY-N	55	157	31	43	12	3	3	26	25	14	.274	.380	.446	826	138	8	3	7	-2	.960	-1	O-51(0-51-0)	0.3
Total	8	859	3094	521	961	169	57	49	454	367	313	.311	.389	.450	838	146	168	234	33		.960	23	O-853(36-750-68)	14.2
■ **DICK KAUFFMAN**	Kauffman, Howard Richard b: 6/22/1888, E.Lewisburg, Pa. d: 4/16/48, Mifflinburg, Pa. BB/TR, 6'3", 190 lbs. Deb: 9/17/14																							
1914	StL-A	7	15	1	4	1	0	0	2	0	3	.267	.267	.333	600	83	-0	0			.967	-1	/1-7	-0.2
1915	StL-A	37	124	9	32	8	2	0	14	5	27	.258	.298	.355	653	99	-1	0	3	-1	.984	-1	1-32/O-1(0-0-1)	-0.4
Total	2	44	139	10	36	9	2	0	16	5	30	.259	.295	.353	647	97	-1	0	3		.982	-2	/1-39,O-1(0-0-1)	-0.6
■ **TONY KAUFMANN**	Kaufmann, Anthony Charles b: 12/16/1900, Chicago, Ill. d: 6/4/82, Elgin, Ill. BR/TR, 5'11", 165 lbs. Deb: 9/23/21 C																							
1921	Chi-N	2	5	0	2	1	0	0	0	0	1	.400	.400	.600	1000	161	0	0	0	0	1.000	-1	/P-2	0.0
1922	Chi-N	38	45	4	9	2	1	1	4	2	14	.200	.234	.356	590	49	-4	0	0	0	.933	-1	P-37	0.0
1923	Chi-N	33	74	10	16	2	0	2	10	7	17	.216	.284	.324	608	60	-4	0	0	0	.962	-1	P-33	0.0
1924	Chi-N	35	76	6	24	5	0	1	14	3	10	.316	.342	.421	763	102	0	0	0	0	.981	-1	P-34	0.0
1925	Chi-N	31	78	8	15	7	0	2	13	2	17	.192	.213	.359	571	42	-7	0	0	0	.981	-0	P-31	0.0
1926	Chi-N	30	60	9	15	2	0	1	7	2	10	.250	.274	.333	608	62	-3	1			**1.000**	-2	P-26	0.0
1927	Chi-N	9	16	2	5	0	0	1	6	4	4	.313	.450	.500	950	154	1	0			1.000	2	/P-9	0.0
	Phi-N	8	7	1	1	0	0	1	2	0	1	.143	.143	.571	714	83	-0	0			1.000	-1	/P-5,O-1(1-0-0)	0.0
	StL-N	1	0	0	0	0	0	0	0	0	0	—	—	—	—	—	0	0			.000	0	/P-1	0.0
	Yr	18	23	3	6	0	0	2	8	4	5	.261	.370	.522	892	136	1	0			1.000	1	P-15/O-1(1-0-0)	0.0
1928	StL-N	5	0	0	0	0	0	0	0	0	0	—	—	—	—	—	0	0			1.000	-0	/P-4	0.0
1929	NY-N	39	32	18	1	0	0	0	1	6	4	.031	.184	.031	215	-43	-7	3			.964	-4	O-16(4-8-4)	-1.0
1930	StL-N	2	3	1	1	0	0	0	0	1	1	.333	.500	.333	833	103	0	0			1.000	-0	/P-2	0.0
1931	StL-N	20	18	1	2	0	0	0	0	1	3	.111	.158	.111	269	-26	-3	0			.929	-1	P-15/O-1(1-0-0)	-0.1
1935	StL-N	7	0	2	0	0	0	0	0	0	0	—	—	—	—	—	0	0			1.000	0	/P-3	0.0
Total	12	260	414	62	91	19	1	9	57	28	82	.220	.269	.336	605	57	-27	4	0		.972	-9	P-202/O-18(6-8-4)	-1.1
■ **CHARLIE KAVANAGH**	Kavanagh, Charles Hugh "Silk" b: 6/9/1893, Chicago, Ill. d: 9/6/73, Reedsburg, Wis. BR/TR, 5'9", 165 lbs. Deb: 6/11/14																							
1914	Chi-A	6	5	0	1	0	0	0	0	0	2	.200	.333	.200	533	62	-0	0			.000	0	H	0.0
■ **LEO KAVANAGH**	Kavanagh, Leo Daniel b: 8/9/1894, Chicago, Ill. d: 8/10/50, Chicago, Ill. BR/TR, 5'9", 180 lbs. Deb: 4/22/14																							
1914	Chi-F	5	11	0	3	0	0	0	1	1	0	.273	.333	.273	606	70	-1	0			1.000	-1	/S-5	-0.1
■ **MARTY KAVANAGH**	Kavanagh, Martin Joseph b: 6/13/1891, Harrison, N.J. d: 7/28/60, Eloise, Mich. BR/TR, 6', 187 lbs. Deb: 4/18/14 Career OF: (3-LF 2-CF 18-RF)																							
1914	Det-A	128	439	60	109	21	6	4	35	41	42	.248	.318	.351	669	98	-2	16	14	-1	.929	-7	*2-115/1-4	-0.9
1915	Det-A	113	332	55	98	14	13	4	49	42	44	.295	.378	.452	829	141	16	8	8	-1	.987	-15	1-44,2-42/S-2,O3	0.0
1916	Det-A	58	78	6	11	4	0	0	5	9	15	.141	.239	.192	431	29	-7	0			1.000	0	O-11(1-0-10)/2-2,3-1	-0.8
	Cle-A	19	44	4	11	2	1	1	10	2	5	.250	.283	.409	692	102	-0	0			.894	-0	/2-9,1-1,3-1	0.0
	Yr	77	122	10	22	6	1	1	15	11	20	.180	.254	.270	524	55	-7	0			1.000	-0	O-11R,2-11/3-2,1-1	-0.8
1917	Cle-A	14	14	1	0	0	0	0	0	3	2	.000	.176	.000	176	-43	-2	0			1.000	0	/O-2(0-2-0)	-0.2
1918	Cle-A	13	38	4	8	2	0	0	6	7	7	.211	.348	.263	611	77	-1	1			.967	-1	1-12	-0.3
	StL-N	12	44	6	8	1	0	1	8	3	1	.182	.234	.273	507	56	-2	1			1.000	-2	/O-8(0-0-8),2-4	-0.5
	Det-A	13	44	2	12	3	0	0	9	11	6	.273	.418	.341	759	135	3	0			.964	-1	1-12	0.1
Total	5	370	1033	138	257	47	20	10	122	118	122	.249	.330	.362	693	104	4	26	22		.926	-26	2-172/1-73,O-23R,3S	-2.6
■ **KAVANAUGH**	Kavanaugh Deb: 9/11/1872																							
1872	Eck-n	5	23	3	6	1	0	0	2	0	1	.261	.261	.304	565	86	0	0	0	0	.921	-1	/1-4,O-2(0-0-2)	0.0
■ **BILL KAY**	Kay, Walter Brocton "King Bill" b: 2/14/1878, New Castle, Va. d: 12/3/45, Roanoke, Va. BL/TR, 6'2", 180 lbs. Deb: 8/12/07																							
1907	Was-A	25	60	8	20	1	1	0	7	0		.333	.333	.383	717	139	2	0			1.000	-0	O-12(0-1-11)	0.2

YEAR	TM/L	G	AB	R	H	2B	3B	HR	RBI	BB	SO	AVG	OBP	SLG	OPS	OPS+	BR+	SB	CS	SBR	FA	FR	G/POS	TPR
■ **EDDIE KAZAK**	Kazak, Edward Terrance (b: Edward Terrance Tkaczuk) b: 7/18/20, Steubenville, O. d: 12/15/99, Austin, Tex. BR/TR, 6′, 175 lbs. Deb: 9/29/48																							
1948	StL-N	6	22	1	6	3	0	0	2	0	2	.273	.273	.409	682	78	-1	0			.900	1	/3-6	0.0
1949	StL-N★	92	326	43	99	15	3	6	42	29	17	.304	.362	.423	786	105	3	0			.926	-4	3-80/2-5	-0.1
1950	StL-N	93	207	21	53	2	2	5	23	18	19	.256	.319	.357	676	74	-8	0			.936	1	3-48	-0.6
1951	StL-N	11	33	2	6	2	0	0	4	5	5	.182	.289	.242	532	44	-3	0	0	0	.933	-1	3-10	-0.4
1952	StL-N	3	2	1	0	0	0	0	0	0	0	.000	.000	.000	0	-99	-1	0	0	0	1.000	0	/3-1	0.0
	Cin-N	13	15	1	1	0	1	0	0	0	2	.067	.067	.200	267	-29	-3	0	0	0	.667	-1	/3-3,1-1	-0.3
	Yr	16	17	2	1	0	1	0	0	0	2	.059	.059	.176	235	-37	-3	0	0	0	.750	-0	/3-4,1-1	-0.3
Total	5	218	605	69	165	22	6	11	71	52	45	.273	.332	.383	716	87	-12	0	0		.927	-3	3-148/2-5,1-1	-1.4
■ **TED KAZANSKI**	Kazanski, Theodore Stanley b: 1/25/34, Hamtramck, Mich. BR/TR, 6′1″, 175 lbs. Deb: 6/25/53																							
1953	Phi-N	95	360	39	78	17	5	2	27	26	53	.217	.275	.308	583	52	-26	1	1	-0	.949	-19	S-95	-3.6
1954	Phi-N	39	104	7	14	2	0	1	8	4	14	.135	.167	.183	349	-9	-17	0	1	-0	.945	-7	S-38	-2.2
1955	Phi-N	9	12	1	1	0	0	1	1	1	1	.083	.154	.333	487	25	-1	0	0	0	1.000	1	/S-4,3-4	-0.1
1956	Phi-N	117	379	35	80	11	1	4	34	20	41	.211	.253	.277	530	43	-31	0	2	-1	.979	-10	*2-116/S-1	-3.5
1957	Phi-N	62	185	15	49	7	1	3	11	17	20	.265	.327	.362	689	88	-3	1	1	-0	.968	-3	3-36,2-22/S-3	-0.5
1958	Phi-N	95	289	21	66	12	2	3	35	22	34	.228	.292	.315	607	62	-16	2	3	-1	.988	-13	2-59,S-22,3-16	-2.5
Total	6	417	1329	118	288	49	9	14	116	90	163	.217	.270	.299	569	51	-94	4	8	-2	.981	-51	2-197,S-163/3-56	-12.4
■ **BOB KEARNEY**	Kearney, Robert Henry b: 10/3/56, San Antonio, Tex. BR/TR, 6′, 190 lbs. Deb: 9/25/79																							
1979	SF-N	2	0	0	0	0	0	0	0	1	0	—	1.000	—	1000	211	0	0	0	0	.000	0	/C-1	0.0
1981	Oak-A	1	0	0	0	0	0	0	0	0	0	—	—	—	—	—	0	0	0	0	.000	0	/C-1	0.0
1982	Oak-A	22	71	7	12	3	0	0	5	3	10	.169	.224	.211	435	21	-8	0	0	0	.970	5	C-22	-0.2
1983	Oak-A	108	298	33	76	11	0	8	32	21	50	.255	.313	.372	685	93	-3	1	4	-1	.982	5	*C-101/D-3	0.5
1984	Sea-A	133	431	39	97	24	1	7	43	18	72	.225	.259	.334	594	64	-22	7	5	-0	.988	5	*C-133	-1.2
1985	Sea-A	108	305	24	74	14	1	6	27	11	59	.243	.278	.354	632	71	-12	1	1	-0	**.995**	6	*C-108	-0.3
1986	Sea-A	81	204	23	49	10	0	6	25	12	35	.240	.282	.377	660	77	-7	0	2	-1	.989	14	C-79	0.9
1987	Sea-A	24	47	5	8	4	1	0	1	1	9	.170	.188	.298	485	25	-5	0	0	0	.981	6	C-24	0.1
Total	8	479	1356	131	316	66	3	27	133	67	235	.233	.275	.346	621	70	-57	9	12	-2	.987	41	C-469/D-3	-0.2
■ **TEDDY KEARNS**	Kearns, Edward Joseph b: 1/1/1900, Trenton, N.J. d: 12/21/49, Trenton, N.J. BR/TR, 5′11″, 180 lbs. Deb: 10/1/20																							
1920	Phi-A	1	1	0	0	0	0	0	0	0	0	.000	.000	.000	0	-99	-0	0	0	0	.000	0	H	0.0
1924	Chi-N	4	16	0	4	0	1	0	1	1	1	.250	.294	.375	669	77	-1	0	0	0	1.000	-0	/1-4	-0.1
1925	Chi-N	3	2	0	1	0	0	0	0	0	0	.500	.500	.500	1000	154	0	0	0	0	1.000	-0	/1-3	0.0
Total	3	8	19	0	5	0	1	0	1	1	1	.263	.300	.368	668	76	-1	0	0	0	1.000	-0	/1-7	-0.1
■ **TOM KEARNS**	Kearns, Thomas J. "Dasher" b: 11/9/1859, Rochester, N.Y. d: 12/7/38, Buffalo, N.Y. BR/TR, 5′7″, 160 lbs. Deb: 8/26/1880																							
1880	Buf-N	2	7	0	0	0	0	0	0	0	0	.000	.000	.000	0	-98	-1				.667	-1	/C-2	-0.3
1882	Det-N	4	13	2	4	2	0	0	1	0	4	.308	.308	.462	769	143	1				.733	-3	/2-4	-0.2
1884	Det-N	21	79	9	16	0	1	0	7	2	10	.203	.222	.228	450	45	-5				.810	-10	2-21	-1.3
Total	3	27	99	11	20	2	1	0	8	2	14	.202	.218	.242	460	48	-6				.801	-14	/2-25,C-2	-1.8
■ **EDDIE KEARSE**	Kearse, Edward Paul "Truck" b: 2/23/16, San Francisco, Cal d: 7/15/68, Eureka, Cal. BR/TR, 6′1″, 195 lbs. Deb: 6/13/42																							
1942	NY-A	11	26	2	5	0	0	0	2	3	1	.192	.276	.192	468	34	-2	1	0	0	1.000	3	C-11	0.2
■ **CHICK KEATING**	Keating, Walter Francis b: 8/8/1891, Philadelphia, Pa. d: 7/13/59, Philadelphia, Pa. BR/TR, 5′9.5″, 155 lbs. Deb: 9/26/13																							
1913	Chi-N	2	5	1	1	1	0	0	0	0	1	.200	.200	.400	600	69	-0	0			1.000	-1	/S-2	-0.1
1914	Chi-N	20	30	3	3	0	1	0	0	6	9	.100	.250	.167	417	25	-3	0			.951	0	S-14	-0.2
1915	Chi-N	4	8	1	0	0	0	0	0	0	3	.000	.000	.000	0	-99	-2	1			.750	-0	/S-2	-0.2
1926	Phi-N	4	2	0	0	0	0	0	0	0	0	.000	.000	.000	0	-95	-1	0			1.000	-0	/2-2,S-2,3-1	-0.1
Total	4	30	45	5	4	1	1	0	0	6	13	.089	.196	.156	352	4	-5	1			.903	-1	/S-20,2-2,3-1	-0.6
■ **GREG KEATLEY**	Keatley, Gregory Steven b: 9/12/53, Princeton, W.Va. BR/TR, 6′2″, 200 lbs. Deb: 9/27/81																							
1981	KC-A	2	0	0	0	0	0	0	0	0	0	—	—	—	—	—	0	0	0	0	1.000	-0	/C-2	0.0
■ **PAT KEEDY**	Keedy, Charles Patrick b: 1/10/58, Birmingham, Ala. BR/TR, 6′4″, 205 lbs. Deb: 9/10/85 Career OF: (5-LF 0-CF 0-RF)																							
1985	Cal-A	3	4	1	2	1	0	1	1	0	0	.500	.500	1.500	2000	424	2	0	1	-0	.000	-0	/3-2,O-1(1-0-0)	0.1
1987	Chi-A	17	41	6	7	1	0	2	2	2	14	.171	.209	.341	551	42	-4	1	0	0	.943	4	3-11/1-2,2-1,SOD	0.1
1989	Cle-A	9	14	3	3	2	0	0	1	2	5	.214	.313	.357	670	87	-0	0	0	0	1.000	-0	/O-3L,3-2,1-1,SD	0.0
Total	3	29	59	10	12	4	0	3	4	4	19	.203	.254	.424	678	77	-2	1	1	-0	.929	3	/3-15,O-5L,1-3,DS2	0.2
■ **WILLIE KEELER**	Keeler, William Henry "Wee Willie" (b: William Henry O'Kelleher) b: 3/3/1872, Brooklyn, N.Y. d: 1/1/23, Brooklyn, N.Y. BL/TL, 5′4.5″, 140 lbs. Deb: 9/30/1892 H Career OF: (147-LF 10-CF 1882-RF)																							
1892	NY-N	14	53	7	17	3	0	0	6	3	3	.321	.368	.377	746	128	2	5			.878	-3	3-14	-0.1
1893	NY-N	7	24	5	8	2	1	1	7	5	1	.333	.448	.625	1073	183	3	3			.667	-5	/O-3(0-3-0),2-2,S-2	-0.2
	Bro-N	20	80	14	25	1	1	1	9	4	4	.313	.353	.387	740	101	0	2			.833	-1	3-12/O-8(8-0-0)	-0.1
	Yr	27	104	19	33	3	2	2	16	9	5	.317	.377	.442	820	121	3	5			.833	-6	3-12,O-11L/2-2,S-2	-0.3
1894	*Bal-N	129	590	165	219	27	22	5	94	40	6	.371	.427	.517	944	121	20	32			.938	3	*O-128(0-0-128)/2-1	1.3
1895	*Bal-N	131	565	162	213	24	15	4	78	37	12	.377	.429	.494	922	134	28	47			.946	0	*O-131(130-1-0)	1.3
1896	*Bal-N	126	544	153	210	22	13	4	82	37	9	.386	.432	.496	928	142	33	67			.969	6	*O-126(2-0-124)	2.7
1897	*Bal-N	129	564	145	**239**	27	19	0	74	35		**.424**	.464	.539	**1003**	164	52	64			.970	-2	*O-129(0-0-129)	3.7
1898	Bal-N	129	561	126	**216**	7	2	1	44	31		**.385**	.420	.410	830	136	26	28			.961	0	*O-128(0-0-128)/3-1	1.9
1899	Bro-N	141	570	**140**	216	12	13	1	61	37		.379	.425	.451	876	137	30	45			.979	-2	*O-141(0-0-141)	1.9
1900	*Bro-N	136	563	106	**204**	13	12	4	68	30		.362	.402	.449	851	127	20	41			.940	5	*O-136(0-0-136)/2-1	1.6
1901	Bro-N	136	595	123	202	18	12	2	43	21		.339	.369	.420	789	125	18	23			**.985**	-6	*O-125R,3-10/2-3	0.7
1902	Bro-N	133	559	86	186	20	5	0	38	21		.333	.365	.386	751	131	19	19			**.978**	2	*O-133(0-0-133)	1.6
1903	NY-A	132	512	95	160	14	7	0	32	32		.313	.368	.367	735	114	10	24			.935	-9	*O-128(0-5-123)/3-4	-0.6
1904	NY-A	143	543	78	186	14	8	2	40	35		.343	.390	.409	799	146	29	21			.935	-3	*O-142(0-0-142)	2.1
1905	NY-A	149	560	81	169	14	4	4	38	43		.302	.357	.363	719	115	10	19			.968	-3	*O-137R,2-12/3-3	0.1
1906	NY-A	152	592	96	180	8	3	2	33	40		.304	.353	.338	691	106	5	23			.987	-2	*O-152(1-0-151)	-0.5
1907	NY-A	107	423	50	99	5	2	0	17	15		.234	.265	.255	521	61	-19	7			.969	-3	*O-107(0-0-107)	-3.0
1908	NY-A	91	323	38	85	3	1	1	14	31		.263	.337	.288	625	102	2	14			.936	-1	O-88(2-0-86)	-0.3
1909	NY-A	99	360	44	95	7	5	1	32	24		.264	.327	.319	647	104	2	10			.968	-5	O-95(0-0-95)	-0.9
1910	NY-N	19	10	5	3	0	0	0	0	3	1	.300	.462	.300	762	123	1	1			1.000	-1	/O-2(1-1-0)	0.0
Total	19	2123	8591	1719	2932	241	145	33	810	524	36	.341	.388	.415	802	125	289	495			.960	-29	*O-2039R/3-44,2-19,S	13.2
■ **BOB KEELY**	Keely, Robert William b: 8/22/09, St.Louis, Mo. BR/TR, 6′, 175 lbs. Deb: 7/25/44 C																							
1944	StL-N	1	0	0	0	0	0	0	0	0	0	—	—	—	—	—	0	0			1.000	-0	/C-1	0.0
1945	StL-N	1	1	0	0	0	0	0	0	0	0	.000	.000	.000	0	-98	-0	0			1.000	-0	/C-1	0.0
Total	2	2	1	0	0	0	0	0	0	0	0	.000	.000	.000	0	-98	-0	0			1.000	-0	/C-2	0.0
■ **BILL KEEN**	Keen, William Brown "Buster" b: 8/16/1892, Oglethorpe, Ga. d: 7/16/47, South Point, Ohio BR/TR, 6′, 181 lbs. Deb: 8/8/11																							
1911	Pit-N	6	7	0	0	0	0	0	0	1	4	.000	.125	.000	125	-61	-2	0			1.000	-0	/1-1	-0.2
■ **JIM KEENAN**	Keenan, James William b: 2/10/1858, New Haven, Conn. d: 9/21/26, Cincinnati, Ohio BR/TR, 5′10″, 186 lbs. Deb: 5/17/1875 Career OF: (0-LF 1-CF 15-RF)																							
1875	NH-n	5	13	1	1	0	0	0	0	0	0	.077	.077	.077	154	-53	-2	0	0	0	.800	-3	/C-3,3-2,O-1(1-0-0)	-0.5
1880	Buf-N	2	7	1	1	0	0	0	0	1	1	.143	.250	.143	393	36	-0				.947	3	/C-2	0.2
1882	Pit-a	25	96	10	21	7	0	1		1		.219	.227	.323	550	87	-1				.906	1	C-22/O-3(0-1-2),S-1	0.2
1884	Ind-a	68	249	36	73	14	4	3		16		.293	.343	.418	761	151	14				.923	-2	C-59/1-6,O-2R,SP	1.5
1885	Cin-a	36	132	16	35	2	2	1	15	8		.265	.307	.333	640	100	-0				.926	-1	C-33/1-4,P-1	0.1
1886	Cin-a	44	148	31	40	4	3	3	24	18		.270	.357	.399	756	132	6	0			.915	0	C-30/O-7R,3-5,1P	0.7
1887	Cin-a	47	185	19	55	4	1	0	17	11		.297	.301	.287	588	63	-9	7			.934	9	C-38,1-11	0.2

YEAR	TM/L	G	AB	R	H	2B	3B	HR	RBI	BB	SO	AVG	OBP	SLG	OPS	OPS+	BR+	SB	CS	SBR	FA	FR	G/POS	TPR
1888	Cin-a	85	313	38	73	9	8	1	40	22		.233	.294	.323	617	93	-3	9			.946	3	C-69,1-16	0.4
1889	Cin-a	87	300	52	86	10	11	6	60	48	35	.287	.395	.453	849	137	15	18			.962	1	C-66,1-21/3-1	1.7
1890	Cin-N	54	202	21	28	4	2	3	19	19	36	.139	.216	.223	439	28	-19	5			.950	4	C-50/1-2,O-1R,3-1	-1.0
1891	Cin-N	75	252	30	51	7	5	4	33	33	39	.202	.302	.317	620	80	-6	2			.974	-4	1-41,C-34/3-1	-1.0
Total	10	523	1884	254	463	61	36	22	208	177	111	.246	.314	.348	661	99	-4	41	0		.935	14	C-403,1-105/O3PS	3.0
■ GEORGE KEERL	Keerl, George Henry b: 4/10/1847, Baltimore, Md. d: 9/9/23, Menominee, Mich. BR/TR, 5'7", 145 lbs. Deb: 5/5/1875																							
1875	Chi-n	6	23	2	3	0	0	0	3	0	2	.130	.130	.130	261	-9	-2	0	0	0	.815	-2	/2-6	-0.5
■ JIM KEESEY	Keesey, James Ward b: 10/27/02, Perryville, Md. d: 9/5/51, Boise, Idaho BR/TR, 6'0.5", 170 lbs. Deb: 9/6/25																							
1925	Phi-A	5	5	1	2	0	0	0	1	0	2	.400	.400	.400	800	97	-0	0	0	0	1.000	-0	/1-2	0.0
1930	Phi-A	11	12	2	3	1	0	0	2	1	2	.250	.308	.333	641	60	-1	0	0	0	.909	-0	/1-3	-0.1
Total	2	16	17	3	5	1	0	0	3	1	4	.294	.333	.353	686	71	-1	0	0	0	.923	-1	/1-5	-0.1
■ BILL KEISTER	Keister, William Hoffman "Wagon Tongue" b: 8/17/1874, Baltimore, Md. d: 8/19/24, Baltimore, Md. BL/TR, 5'5.5", 168 lbs. Deb: 5/20/1896 Career OF: (1-LF 12-CF 154-RF)																							
1896	Bal-N	15	58	8	14	3	0	0	5	3	5	.241	.302	.293	595	56	-4	4			.923	-5	/2-8,3-6	-0.7
1898	Bos-N	10	30	5	5	2	0	0	4	0		.167	.167	.233	400	14	-3	0			1.000	1	/S-4,2-4,O-1(0-0-1)	-0.2
1899	Bal-N	136	523	96	172	22	16	3	73	16		.329	.368	.449	817	117	10	33			.895	-30	S-90,2-46/O-1(1-0-0)	-1.2
1900	StL-N	126	497	78	149	26	10	1	72	25		.300	.347	.398	745	106	3	32			.927	-23	*2-116/S-7,3-3	-1.3
1901	Bal-A	115	442	78	145	20	**21**	2	93	18		.328	.365	.482	847	128	15	24			.851	-23	*S-112	-0.4
1902	Was-A	119	483	82	145	33	9	9	90	14		.300	.329	.462	791	117	8	27			.912	-4	O-65R,2-40,3-14,/S	0.2
1903	Phi-N	100	400	53	128	27	7	3	63	14		.320	.352	.445	797	131	14	11			.940	3	*O-100(0-0-100)	1.2
Total	7	621	2433	400	758	133	63	18	400	90	5	.312	.349	.440	789	116	44	131			.870	-80	S-215,2-214,O-167R,/3	-2.4
■ MICKEY KELIHER	Keliher, Maurice Michael b: 1/11/1890, Washington, D.C. d: 9/7/30, Washington, D.C. BL/TL, 6', 175 lbs. Deb: 9/10/11																							
1911	Pit-N	3	7	0	0	0	0	0	0	0	5	.000	.000	.000	0	-96	-2	0			.875	-0	/1-3	-0.2
1912	Pit-N	2	0	1	0	0	0	0	0	0	0	—	—	—	—	—	0	0			.000	0	R	0.0
Total	2	5	7	1	0	0	0	0	0	0	5	.000	.000	.000	0	-96	-2	0			.875	-0	/1-3	-0.2
■ SKEETER KELL	Kell, Everett Lee b: 10/11/29, Swifton, Ark. BR/TR, 5'9", 160 lbs. Deb: 4/19/52 F																							
1952	Phi-A	75	213	24	47	8	3	0	17	14	18	.221	.275	.286	561	53	-14	5	1	1	.963	-5	2-68	-1.5
■ GEORGE KELL	Kell, George Clyde b: 8/23/22, Swifton, Ark. BR/TR, 5'9", 175 lbs. Deb: 9/28/43 FH Career OF: (10-LF 0-CF 1-RF)																							
1943	Phi-A	1	5	1	1	0	1	0	1	0	0	.200	.200	.600	800	131	0	0	0	0	1.000	0	/3-1	0.0
1944	Phi-A	139	514	51	138	15	3	0	44	22	23	.268	.300	.309	609	75	-17	5	2	0	.958	-5	*3-139	-2.1
1945	Phi-A	147	567	50	154	30	3	4	56	27	15	.272	.306	.356	662	92	-8	2	0	0	**.964**	22	*3-147	1.7
1946	Phi-A	26	87	3	26	6	1	0	11	10	6	.299	.378	.391	768	116	2	0	0	0	.979	3	3-26	0.5
	Det-A	105	434	67	142	19	9	4	41	30	14	.327	.371	.440	811	119	10	3	2	-0	.984	5	*3-105/1-1	1.6
	Yr	131	521	70	168	25	10	4	52	40	20	.322	.372	.432	804	118	13	3	2	-0	**.983**	8	*3-131/1-1	2.1
1947	Det-A★	152	588	75	188	29	5	5	93	61	16	.320	.387	.412	798	118	16	9	11	-2	.962	18	*3-152	3.2
1948	Det-A☆	92	368	47	112	24	3	2	44	33	15	.304	.369	.402	772	102	1	2	2	-0	.969	-8	3-92	-0.7
1949	Det-A★	134	522	97	179	38	9	3	59	71	13	**.343**	.424	.467	892	136	28	7	5	-0	.975	1	*3-134	2.7
1950	Det-A★	157	641	114	**218**	**56**	6	8	101	66	18	.340	.403	.484	886	122	21	3	3	-0	**.982**	-3	*3-157	1.6
1951	Det-A★	147	598	92	**191**	**36**	3	2	59	61	18	.319	.386	.400	786	112	12	10	3	1	**.960**	9	*3-147	2.1
1952	Det-A	39	152	11	45	8	0	1	17	15	13	.296	.359	.368	728	102	1	0	1	-0	.959	-2	3-39	-0.2
	Bos-A†	75	276	41	88	15	2	6	40	31	10	.319	.390	.453	843	124	9	0	1	-0	.959	-7	3-73	0.2
	Yr	114	428	52	133	23	2	7	57	46	23	.311	.379	.423	802	117	10	0	2	-1	.959	-9	*3-112	0.0
1953	Bos-A★	134	460	68	141	41	2	12	73	52	22	.307	.383	.483	866	126	17	5	2	0	**.972**	-14	*3-124/O-7(7-0-0)	0.2
1954	Bos-A	26	93	15	24	3	0	0	10	15	3	.258	.361	.290	651	72	-3	0	0	0	.920	-3	3-25	-0.6
	Chi-A†	71	233	25	66	10	0	5	48	18	12	.283	.335	.391	725	95	-2	1	1	-0	.996	-11	1-32,3-31/O-2(2-0-1)	-1.6
	Yr	97	326	40	90	13	0	5	58	33	15	.276	.343	.362	705	88	-5	1	1	-0	.936	-14	3-56,1-32/O-2(2-0-1)	-2.2
1955	Chi-A	128	429	44	134	24	1	8	81	51	36	.312	.393	.429	822	118	12	2	2	-0	**.976**	-19	*3-105,1-24/O-1L	-0.8
1956	Chi-A	21	80	7	25	5	0	1	11	8	6	.313	.375	.412	788	106	1	0	0	0	1.000	-4	3-18/1-4	-0.3
	Bal-A★	102	345	45	90	17	2	8	37	25	31	.261	.316	.391	708	93	-5	0	1	-0	.974	-7	3-97/1-2,2-1	-1.2
	Yr	123	425	52	115	22	2	9	48	33	37	.271	.328	.395	723	96	-4	0	1	-0	**.978**	-11	*3-115/1-6,2-1	-1.5
1957	Bal-A★	99	310	28	92	9	0	9	44	25	16	.297	.353	.413	766	116	6	2	0	0	.979	-4	3-80,1-22	0.1
Total	15	1795	6702	881	2054	385	50	78	870	621	287	.306	.368	.414	782	111	102	51	36	-1	.969	-29	*3-1692/1-85,O-10L,2	6.4
■ DUKE KELLEHER	Kelleher, Albert Aloysius b: 9/30/1893, New York, N.Y. d: 9/28/47, Staten Island, N.Y. TR, Deb: 8/18/16																							
1916	NY-N	1	0	0	0	0	0	0	0	0	0	—	—	—	—	—	0	0			.000	0	/C-1	0.0
■ FRANKIE KELLEHER	Kelleher, Francis Eugene b: 8/22/16, San Francisco, Cal d: 4/13/79, Stockton, Cal. BR/TR, 6'1", 195 lbs. Deb: 7/18/42																							
1942	Cin-N	38	110	13	20	3	1	3	12	16	20	.182	.286	.309	595	74	-4	0			.986	0	O-30(30-0-0)	-0.5
1943	Cin-N	9	10	1	0	0	0	0	0	2	0	.000	.167	.000	167	-51	-2	0			1.000	-0	/O-1(0-0-1)	-0.2
Total	2	47	120	14	20	3	1	3	12	18	20	.167	.275	.283	559	64	-6	0			.986	0	/O-31(30-0-1)	-0.7
■ JOHN KELLEHER	Kelleher, John Patrick b: 9/13/1893, Brookline, Mass. d: 8/21/60, Brighton, Mass. BR/TR, 5'11", 150 lbs. Deb: 7/31/12 Career OF: (1-LF 0-CF 0-RF)																							
1912	StL-N	8	12	0	4	1	0	0	1	0	2	.333	.333	.417	750	107	0	0			1.000	1	/3-3	0.1
1916	Bro-N	2	3	0	0	0	0	0	0	0	0	.000	.000	.000	0	-97	-1	0			1.000	-1	/S-1,3-1	-0.2
1921	Chi-N	95	301	31	93	11	7	4	47	16	16	.309	.346	.432	778	104	2	2	5	-1	.947	3	3-37,2-27,1-11,S/O	0.6
1922	Chi-N	63	193	23	50	7	1	0	20	15	14	.259	.316	.306	621	60	-11	5	7	-1	.932	4	3-46/S-7,1-4	-0.6
1923	Chi-N	66	193	27	59	10	0	6	21	14	9	.306	.353	.451	803	110	2	2	4	-1	.975	-7	1-22,S-14,3-11,/2-6	-0.4
1924	Bos-N	1	1	0	0	0	0	0	0	0	1	.000	.000	.000	0	-99	-0	0	0	0	.000	0	H	0.0
Total	6	235	703	81	206	29	8	10	89	45	42	.293	.337	.400	737	92	-8	9	16		.924	-0	/3-98,1-37,2-33,SO	-0.5
■ MICK KELLEHER	Kelleher, Michael Dennis b: 7/25/47, Seattle, Wash. BR/TR, 5'9", 176 lbs. Deb: 9/1/72 C																							
1972	StL-N	23	63	5	10	2	1	0	1	6	15	.159	.232	.222	454	30	-6	0	0	0	.984	5	S-23	0.2
1973	StL-N	43	38	4	7	2	0	0	2	4	11	.184	.279	.237	516	44	-3	0	0	0	.955	9	S-42	0.8
1974	Hou-N	19	57	4	9	0	0	0	2	5	10	.158	.226	.158	384	9	-7	1	1	-0	.944	4	S-18	-0.1
1975	StL-N	7	4	0	0	0	0	0	0	0	1	.000	.000	.000	0	-97	-1	0	0	0	.909	2	/S-7	0.1
1976	Chi-N	124	337	28	77	12	1	0	22	15	32	.228	.266	.270	536	48	-23	0	4	-1	.980	12	*S-101,3-22/2-5	-0.2
1977	Chi-N	63	122	14	28	5	2	0	11	9	12	.230	.288	.303	591	53	-8	0	0	0	.976	18	2-40,S-14/3-1	1.2
1978	Chi-N	68	95	8	24	1	0	0	6	7	11	.253	.304	.263	567	53	-6	4	1	1	1.000	18	3-37,2-17,S-10	1.4
1979	Chi-N	73	142	14	36	4	1	0	10	7	9	.254	.298	.296	594	57	-8	2	0	0	.966	22	3-32,2-29,S-14	1.6
1980	Chi-N	105	96	12	14	1	1	0	4	9	17	.146	.219	.177	396	11	-11	1	3	-1	.974	25	2-57,3-31,S-17	1.5
1981	Det-A	61	77	10	17	4	0	0	6	7	10	.221	.286	.273	558	59	-4	0	0	0	.930	6	3-39,2-11/S-9	0.3
1982	Det-A	2	1	0	0	0	0	0	0	0	0	.000	.000	.000	0	-99	-0	0	0	0	1.000	-0	/2-1,3-1	-0.1
	Cal-A	34	49	9	8	1	0	0	1	5	5	.163	.255	.184	438	23	-5	1	1	-0	.965	7	S-28/3-6	0.3
	Yr	36	50	9	8	1	0	0	1	5	5	.160	.250	.180	430	20	-5	1	1	-0	.965	7	S-28/3-7,2-1	0.2
Total	11	622	1081	108	230	32	6	0	65	74	133	.213	.268	.253	521	43	-81	9	10	-2	.976	128	S-283,3-169,2-160	7.0
■ CHARLIE KELLER	Keller, Charles Ernest "King Kong" b: 9/12/16, Middletown, Md. d: 5/23/90, Frederick, Md. BL/TR, 5'10", 190 lbs. Deb: 4/22/39 F																							
1939	*NY-A	111	398	87	133	21	6	11	83	81	49	.334	.447	.500	947	144	30	6	3	0	.969	-3	*O-105(47-0-58)	2.0
1940	NY-A★	138	500	102	143	18	15	21	93	**106**	65	.286	.411	.508	919	142	35	8	2	1	.967	2	*O-136(65-0-71)	2.7
1941	*NY-A★	140	507	102	151	24	10	33	122	102	65	.298	.416	.580	996	163	47	6	4	-0	.980	4	*O-137(137-0-0)	4.2
1942	*NY-A	152	544	106	159	24	9	26	108	114	61	.292	.417	.513	930	164	49	14	2	2	.985	-0	*O-152(152-0-0)	4.3
1943	*NY-A†	141	512	97	139	15	11	31	86	**106**	60	.271	.396	.525	**922**	**167**	**45**	7	5	-0	.994	4	*O-141(141-0-0)	4.2
1945	NY-A	44	163	26	49	7	4	10	34	31	21	.301	.412	.577	989	178	16	0	2	-1	1.000	4	O-44(44-0-0)	1.8
1946	NY-A★	150	538	98	148	29	10	30	101	113	101	.275	.405	.533	938	158	44	1	4	-1	.979	-1	*O-149(149-0-0)	3.2
1947	NY-A†	45	151	36	36	6	1	13	36	41	18	.238	.404	.550	954	165	14	0	0	0	.967	-2	O-43(43-0-0)	0.9
1948	NY-A	83	247	41	66	15	2	6	44	41	25	.267	.372	.417	789	111	4	1	1	-0	.977	-5	O-66(66-0-0)	-0.6

YEAR	TM/L	G	AB	R	H	2B	3B	HR	RBI	BB	SO	AVG	OBP	SLG	OPS	OPS+	BR+	SB	CS	SBR	FA	FR	G/POS	TPR
1949	NY-A	60	116	17	29	4	1	3	16	25	15	.250	.392	.379	771	104	2	2	0	0	.976	-6	O-31(31-0-0)	-0.6
1950	Det-A	50	51	7	16	1	3	2	16	13	6	.314	.453	.569	1022	155	5	0	0	0	1.000	-1	/O-6(1-0-5)	0.3
1951	Det-A	54	62	6	16	2	0	3	21	11	12	.258	.370	.435	805	117	2	0	0	0	1.000	1	/O-8(4-0-4)	0.2
1952	NY-A	2	1	0	0	0	0	0	0	0	1	.000	.000	.000	0	-99	-0	0	0	0	.000	-0	/O-1(1-0-0)	-0.1
Total	13	1170	3790	725	1085	166	72	189	760	784	499	.286	.410	.518	928	152	293	45	23	2	.980	-4	*O-1019(881-0-138)	22.5
■ **HAL KELLER**	Keller, Harold Kefauver b: 7/7/27, Middletown, Md. BL/TR, 6'1", 200 lbs. Deb: 9/13/49 F																							
1949	Was-A	3	3	1	1	0	0	0	0	0	0	.333	.333	.333	667	78	-0	0	0	0	.000	0	H	0.0
1950	Was-A	11	28	1	6	3	0	1	5	2	2	.214	.267	.429	695	79	-1	0	0	0	1.000	-2	/C-8	-0.2
1952	Was-A	11	23	2	4	2	0	0	0	1	1	.174	.208	.261	469	31	-2	0	0	0	.967	-0	C-11	-0.2
Total	3	25	54	4	11	5	0	1	5	3	3	.204	.246	.352	597	60	-4	0	0	0	.982	-2	/C-19	-0.4
■ **FRANK KELLERT**	Kellert, Frank William b: 7/6/24, Oklahoma City, Okla. d: 11/19/76, Oklahoma City, Okla. BR/TR, 6'2.5", 185 lbs. Deb: 4/18/53																							
1953	StL-A	2	4	0	0	0	0	0	0	0	0	.000	.000	.000	0	-98	-1	0	0	0	1.000	-0	/1-1	-0.1
1954	Bal-A	10	34	3	7	2	0	0	1	5	4	.206	.308	.265	572	62	-2	0	0	0	1.000	-1	/1-9	-0.4
1955	*Bro-N	39	80	12	26	4	2	4	19	9	10	.325	.393	.575	968	149	6	0	1	-0	.983	-0	1-22	0.4
1956	Chi-N	.71	129	10	24	3	1	4	17	12	22	.186	.255	.318	573	54	-9	0	0	0	.991	3	1-27	-0.8
Total	4	122	247	25	57	9	3	8	37	26	36	.231	.304	.389	693	85	-6	0	1	-0	.990	1	/1-59	-0.9
■ **RED KELLETT**	Kellett, Donald Stafford b: 7/15/09, Brooklyn, N.Y. d: 11/3/70, Ft.Lauderdale, Fla. BR/TR, 6', 185 lbs. Deb: 7/2/34																							
1934	Bos-A	9	9	0	0	0	0	0	0	1	5	.000	.100	.000	100	-68	-2	0	0	0	.778	1	/S-4,2-2,3-1	-0.1
■ **JOE KELLEY**	Kelley, Joseph James b: 12/9/1871, Cambridge, Mass. d: 8/14/43, Baltimore, Md. BR/TR, 5'11", 190 lbs. Deb: 7/27/1891 MCH Career OF: (1001-LF 327-CF 139-RF)																							
1891	Bos-N	12	45	7	11	1	1	0	3	2	7	.244	.277	.311	588	63	-2	0			.852	-1	O-12(12-1-0)	-0.3
1892	Pit-N	56	205	26	49	7	7	0	28	17	21	.239	.297	.341	639	93	-2	8			.919	2	O-56(0-56-0)	-0.4
	Bal-N	10	33	3	7	0	0	0	4	4	7	.212	.316	.212	528	59	-1	2			.824	-3	O-10(0-10-0)	-0.4
	Yr	66	238	29	56	7	7	0	32	21	28	.235	.300	.324	624	88	-4	10			.908	-1	O-66(0-66-0)	-0.8
1893	Bal-N	125	502	120	153	27	16	9	76	77	44	.305	.401	.476	877	131	22	33			.940	7	*O-125(18-107-1)	1.7
1894	*Bal-N	129	507	165	199	48	20	6	111	107	36	.393	.502	.602	1104	158	53	46			.951	2	*O-129(129-0-0)	3.3
1895	*Bal-N	131	518	148	189	26	19	10	134	77	29	.365	.456	.546	1003	154	43	54			.964	11	*O-131(0-0-131)	3.8
1896	*Bal-N	131	519	148	189	31	19	8	100	91	19	.364	.469	.543	1013	164	53	**87**			.958	4	*O-131(129-0-2)	3.7
1897	*Bal-N	131	505	113	183	31	9	5	118	70		.362	.447	.489	936	147	37	44			.959	-2	*O-130L/S-3,3-2	2.0
1898	Bal-N	124	464	71	149	18	15	2	110	56		.321	.398	.438	835	137	23	24			.969	1	*O-122(39-83-0)/3-2	1.4
1899	Bro-N	143	538	108	175	21	14	6	93	70		.325	.410	.450	860	133	26	31			.977	8	*O-143(143-0-0)	1.9
1900	*Bro-N	121	454	90	145	23	17	6	91	53		.319	.398	.485	882	135	21	26			.959	1	O-77L,1-32,3-13	1.3
1901	Bro-N	120	492	77	151	22	12	4	65	40		.307	.363	.425	787	124	15	18			.975	7	*1-115/3-5	1.9
1902	Bal-A	60	222	50	69	17	7	1	34	34		.311	.405	.464	869	134	11	12			.973	-0	O-48(1-47-0)/3-8,1-5	0.8
	Cin-N	40	156	24	50	9	2	1	12	15		.321	.380	.423	803	135	6	3			.971	3	O-20L,2-10/3-9,SM	0.9
1903	Cin-N	105	383	85	121	22	4	3	45	51		.316	.402	.418	820	120	11	18			.947	-7	O-67L,S-12,2-11,/31M	0.1
1904	Cin-N	123	449	75	126	21	13	0	63	49		.281	.359	.385	744	119	11	15			.988	0	*1-117/O-6C,2-1,M	0.9
1905	Cin-N	90	321	43	89	7	6	1	37	27		.277	.346	.346	692	96	-1	8			.974	-3	O-85(84-0-1)/1-2,M	-0.9
1906	Cin-N	129	465	43	106	19	11	1	53	44		.228	.300	.323	623	90	-6	9			.966	-5	*O-122L/1-3,S-1,3-1	-2.0
1908	Bos-N	73	228	25	59	8	2	2	17	27		.259	.342	.338	680	119	6	5			.938	-4	O-51(38-12-1),1-11,M	-0.1
Total	17	1853	7006	1421	2220	358	194	65	1194	911	163	.317	.402	.451	853	132	324	443			.955	21	*O-1465L,1-291/32S	19.6
■ **MIKE KELLEY**	Kelley, Michael Joseph b: 12/2/1875, Templeton, Mass. d: 6/6/55, Minneapolis, Minn. BR/TR, 6', 210 lbs. Deb: 7/15/1899																							
1899	Lou-N	76	282	48	68	11	2	3	33	21		.241	.307	.326	634	74	-10	10			.974	-0	1-76	-1.0
■ **FRANK KELLIHER**	Kelliher, Francis Mortimer "Yucka" b: 5/23/1899, Somerville, Mass. d: 3/4/56, Somerville, Mass. BL/TL, 5'9.5", 175 lbs. Deb: 9/19/19																							
1919	Was-A	1	1	0	0	0	0	0	0	0	0	.000	.000	.000	0	-99	-0	0			.000	0	H	0.0
■ **NATE KELLOGG**	Kellogg, Nathaniel Monroe b: 9/28/1858, Rochester, Iowa d: 15, 5'9", 175 lbs. Deb: 8/27/1885																							
1885	Det-N	5	17	4	2	1	0	0	0	1	5	.118	.167	.176	343	11	-2				.783	-2	/S-5	-0.3
■ **BILL KELLOGG**	Kellogg, William Dearstyne b: 5/25/1884, Albany, N.Y. d: 12/12/71, Baltimore, Md. BR/TR, 5'10", 153 lbs. Deb: 4/14/14																							
1914	Cin-N	71	126	14	22	0	1	0	7	14	28	.175	.262	.190	453	34	-10	7			.988	-1	1-38,2-11/O-2C,3-1	-1.2
■ **RED KELLY**	Kelly, Albert Michael b: 11/15/1884, Union, Ill. d: 2/4/61, Zephyrhills, Fla. BR/TR, 5'11.5", 165 lbs. Deb: 6/18/10																							
1910	Chi-A	14	45	6	7	0	1	0	1	7		.156	.296	.200	496	58	-2	0			1.000	-1	O-14(0-0-14)	-0.3
■ **CHARLIE KELLY**	Kelly, Charles H. Deb: 6/14/1883																							
1883	Phi-N	2	7	1	1	0	1	0	0	0	3	.143	.143	.429	571	71	-0				.700	0	/3-2	0.0
1886	Phi-a	1	3	0	0	0	0	0	0	0		.000	.000	.000	0	-99	-1	0			.333	-1	/S-1	-0.2
Total	2	3	10	1	1	0	1	0	0	0	3	.100	.100	.300	400	19	-1	0			.700	-1	/3-2,S-1	-0.2
■ **PAT KELLY**	Kelly, Dale Patrick b: 8/27/55, Santa Maria, Cal. BR/TR, 6'3", 210 lbs. Deb: 5/28/80																							
1980	Tor-A	3	7	0	2	0	0	0	0	0	4	.286	.286	.286	571	55	-0	0	0	0	1.000	1	/C-3	0.1
■ **GEORGE KELLY**	Kelly, George Lange "Highpockets" b: 9/10/1895, San Francisco, Cal. d: 10/13/84, Burlingame, Cal. BR/TR, 6'4", 190 lbs. Deb: 8/18/15 FCH Career OF: (27-LF 16-CF 19-RF)																							
1915	NY-N	17	38	2	6	0	0	1	4	1	9	.158	.179	.237	416	27	-3	0	1	-0	.983	-0	/1-9,O-4(0-4-0)	-0.5
1916	NY-N	49	76	4	12	2	1	0	3	6	24	.158	.220	.211	430	34	-6	1			.981	-3	1-13,O-12(0-2-5)/3-1	-1.1
1917	NY-N	11	7	0	0	0	0	0	0	0	3	.000	.000	.000	0	-99	-2	0			1.000	-1	/O-4L,P-1,1-1,2-1	-0.2
	Pit-N	8	23	2	2	0	1	0	0	1	9	.087	.125	.174	299	-9	-3	0			.971	-1	/1-8	-0.4
	Yr	19	30	2	2	0	1	0	0	1	12	.067	.097	.133	230	-30	-5	0			.972	-1	/1-9,O-4L,P-1,2-1	-0.6
1919	NY-N	32	107	12	31	6	2	1	14	3	15	.290	.315	.411	727	119	2	1			.994	-3	1-32	-0.2
1920	NY-N	155	590	69	157	22	11	11	**94**	41	92	.266	.320	.397	717	106	4	6	16	-4	.994	4	*1-155	-0.1
1921	*NY-N	149	587	95	181	42	9	**23**	122	40	73	.308	.356	.528	884	131	23	4	12	-3	.990	12	*1-149	2.1
1922	*NY-N	151	592	96	194	33	8	17	107	30	65	.328	.363	.497	860	119	14	12	3	2	.993	10	*1-151	1.4
1923	*NY-N	145	560	82	172	23	5	16	103	47	64	.307	.362	.452	814	115	11	14	7	1	.993	-6	*1-145	-0.4
1924	*NY-N	144	571	91	185	37	9	21	**136**	38	52	.324	.371	.531	902	143	32	7	2	1	.993	-1	*1-125,O-14C/2-5,3	2.3
1925	NY-N	147	586	87	181	29	3	20	99	35	54	.309	.350	.471	821	112	9	5	2	0	.981	16	*2-108,1-25,O-17R	2.4
1926	NY-N	136	499	70	151	24	4	13	80	36	52	.303	.352	.445	797	115	9	4			**.993**	8	*1-114,2-18	1.0
1927	Cin-N	61	222	27	60	16	4	5	21	11	23	.270	.308	.446	754	103	-0	1			.992	-3	1-49,2-13/O-2(2-0-0)	-0.6
1928	Cin-N	116	402	46	119	33	7	3	58	28	35	.296	.345	.435	780	104	2	2			.991	9	1-99,O-13(9-0-4)	0.3
1929	Cin-N	147	577	73	169	45	9	5	103	33	61	.293	.332	.428	760	91	-10	7			.993	4	*1-147	-1.4
1930	Cin-N	51	188	18	54	10	1	5	35	7	20	.287	.313	.431	744	81	-6	1			.993	2	1-50	-0.7
	Chi-N	39	166	22	55	6	1	3	19	7	16	.331	.362	.434	796	91	-2	0			.998	4	1-39	-0.1
	Yr	90	354	40	109	16	2	8	54	14	36	.308	.336	.432	768	86	-8	1			.995	5	1-89	-0.8
1932	Bro-N	64	202	23	49	9	1	4	22	22	27	.243	.317	.356	673	82	-5	0			.984	-2	1-62/O-1(0-1-0)	-1.2
Total	16	1622	5993	819	1778	337	76	148	1020	386	694	.297	.342	.452	794	110	69	65	43		.992	49	*1-1373,2-145/O3P	2.6
■ **PAT KELLY**	Kelly, Harold Patrick b: 7/30/44, Philadelphia, Pa. BL/TL, 6'1", 185 lbs. Deb: 9/6/67 Career OF: (244-LF 60-CF 715-RF)																							
1967	Min-A	8	1	1	0	0	0	0	0	0	1	.000	.000	.000	0	-93	-0	0	0	0	.000	0	H	0.0
1968	Min-A	12	35	2	4	2	0	1	2	3	10	.114	.205	.257	462	37	-3	0	2	-1	.955	0	O-10(2-5-4)	-0.4
1969	KC-A	112	417	61	110	20	4	8	32	49	70	.264	.348	.388	737	105	3	40	13	4	.980	12	*O-107(2-44-63)	1.6
1970	KC-A	136	452	56	106	16	1	6	38	76	105	.235	.347	.314	661	84	-8	34	16	2	.963	11	*O-118(1-3-115)	-0.1
1971	Chi-A	67	213	32	62	6	3	3	22	36	29	.291	.396	.390	786	119	7	14	9	-0	.991	1	O-61(0-1-61)	0.5
1972	Chi-A	119	402	57	105	14	7	5	24	55	69	.261	.356	.368	724	113	8	32	9	4	.968	-2	*O-109(0-0-109)	0.5
1973	Chi-A★	144	550	77	154	24	5	1	44	65	91	.280	.358	.347	705	96	-1	22	15	-0	.978	2	*O-141(0-3-138)/D-1	-0.7
1974	Chi-A	122	424	60	119	16	3	4	21	46	58	.281	.354	.361	715	103	3	18	11	0	.976	-5	D-67,O-53(1-0-52)	-0.6

YEAR	TM/L	G	AB	R	H	2B	3B	HR	RBI	BB	SO	AVG	OBP	SLG	OPS	OPS+	BR+	SB	CS	SBR	FA	FR	G/POS	TPR
1975	Chi-A	133	471	73	129	21	7	9	45	58	69	.274	.356	.406	761	113	9	18	10	0	**.991**	-3	*O-115(0-0-115),D-14	0.0
1976	Chi-A	107	311	42	79	20	3	5	34	45	45	.254	.354	.386	740	116	7	15	7	1	.950	-4	D-63,O-26(14-0-12)	0.2
1977	Bal-A	120	360	50	92	13	0	10	49	53	75	.256	.357	.375	732	106	5	25	7	3	.984	-14	*O-109(91-1-33)/D-1	-1.1
1978	Bal-A	100	274	38	75	12	1	11	40	34	58	.274	.358	.445	803	133	12	10	8	-1	.969	-6	O-80(73-1-7)/D-2	0.2
1979	*Bal-A	68	153	25	44	11	0	9	25	20	25	.288	.374	.536	910	147	10	4	5	-1	1.000	-3	O-24(23-0-1),D-18	0.5
1980	Bal-A	89	200	38	52	10	1	3	26	34	54	.260	.368	.365	733	102	2	16	2	3	1.000	-3	O-36(34-2-0),D-30	0.0
1981	Cle-A	48	75	8	16	4	0	1	16	14	9	.213	.337	.307	644	88	-1	2	4	-1	1.000	-2	D-18/O-8(3-0-5)	-0.5
Total	15	1385	4338	620	1147	189	35	76	418	588	768	.264	.356	.377	733	107	55	250	118	14	.978	-15	O-997R,D-214	0.1
■ JIM KELLY Kelly, James Robert (Also Played Under Real Name Of Robert John Taggert In 1918) b: 2/1/1884, Bloomfield, N.J. d: 4/10/61, Kingsport, Tenn. BL/TR, 5'10.5", 180 lbs. Deb: 4/26/14																								
1914	Pit-N	32	44	4	10	2	1	0	3	2	3	.227	.261	.318	579	75	-2	0			1.000	0	/O-7(1-0-6)	-0.2
1915	Pit-F	148	524	68	154	12	17	4	50	35	46	.294	.340	.405	745	110	-2	38			.952	14	*O-148(14-4-133)	0.5
1918	Bos-N	35	146	19	48	1	4	0	4	9	9	.329	.376	.390	766	140	7	4			.955	1	O-35(35-0-0)	0.7
Total	3	215	714	91	212	15	22	4	57	46	58	.297	.343	.396	739	114	3	42			.954	15	O-190(50-4-139)	1.0
■ TOM KELLY Kelly, Jay Thomas b: 8/15/50, Graceville, Minn. BL/TL, 5'11", 188 lbs. Deb: 5/11/75 M																								
1975	Min-A	49	127	11	23	5	0	1	11	15	22	.181	.268	.244	512	45	-9	0	0	0	.985	1	1-43/O-2(1-0-1)	-1.1
■ JOHN KELLY Kelly, John B. b: 3/13/1879, Clifton Heights, Pa. d: 3/19/44, Baltimore, Md. 5'9", 165 lbs. Deb: 4/11/07																								
1907	StL-N	53	197	12	37	5	0	0	6	13		.188	.245	.213	458	45	-12	7			.968	-1	O-52(0-16-36)	-1.8
■ JOHN KELLY Kelly, John Francis "Honest John" or "Father" b: 3/3/1859, Paterson, N.J. d: 4/13/08, Paterson, N.J. BR/TR, 6', 185 lbs. Deb: 6/7/1879 Career OF: (0-LF 3-CF 14-RF)																								
1879	Cle-N	1	4	0	1	0	0	0	0	0	0	.250	.250	.250	500	66	-0				.571	-1	/C-1,1-1	-0.1
1882	Cle-N	30	104	6	14	2	0	0	5	1	24	.135	.143	.154	297	-5	-12				.800	-14	C-30	-2.2
1883	Bal-a	48	202	18	46	9	2	0		3		.228	.239	.292	531	68	-7				.803	-16	C-38,O-13(0-1-12)	-1.9
	Phi-N	1	3	0	0	0	0	0	0	0	2	.000	.000	.000	0	-99	-1				1.000	1	/O-1(0-1-0)	0.0
1884	Cin-U	38	142	23	40	5	1	1		6		.282	.311	.352	663	93	-5				.865	-1	C-37/O-2(0-1-1)	-0.3
	Was-U	4	14	1	5	1	0	0		0		.357	.357	.429	786	142	0				.967	1	/C-3,O-1(0-0-1)	0.1
	Yr	42	156	24	45	6	1	1		6		.288	.315	.359	674	97	-5				.874	-1	C-40/O-3(0-1-2)	-0.2
Total	4	122	469	48	106	17	3	1	5	10	26	.226	.242	.281	524	63	-25				.831	-32	C-109/O-17R,1-1	-4.4
■ KICK KELLY Kelly, John O. "Diamond John" b: 10/31/1856, New York, N.Y. d: 3/27/26, Malba, N.Y. 6'0.5", 185 lbs. Deb: 5/1/1879 MU																								
1879	Syr-N	10	36	4	4	1	0	0	2	0	6	.111	.111	.139	250	-20	-4				.827	-1	/C-8,1-2	-0.5
	Tro-N	6	22	1	5	0	0	0	0	0	1	.227	.227	.227	455	54	-1				.789	-3	/C-3,O-2(0-0-2),3-1	-0.3
	Yr	16	58	5	9	1	0	0	2	0	7	.155	.155	.172	328	9	-5				.817	-4	C-11/1-2,O-2R,3-1	-0.8
■ JOE KELLY Kelly, Joseph Henry b: 9/23/1886, Weir City, Kan. d: 8/16/77, St.Joseph, Mo. BR/TR, 5'10", 175 lbs. Deb: 4/14/14																								
1914	Pit-N	141	508	47	113	19	9	1	48	39	59	.222	.283	.301	584	77	-15	21			.946	4	*O-139(0-139-0)	-2.3
1916	Chi-N	54	169	18	43	7	1	2	15	9	16	.254	.296	.343	639	87	-3	10			.953	-1	O-46(16-25-6)	-0.7
1917	Bos-N	116	445	41	99	9	8	3	36	26	45	.222	.268	.299	567	78	-12	21			.946	14	*O-116(82-29-0)	-0.5
1918	Bos-N	47	155	20	36	2	4	0	15	6	12	.232	.265	.297	562	74	-5	12			.933	-0	O-45(22-18-0)	-0.8
1919	Bos-N	18	64	3	9	1	0	0	3	0	11	.141	.154	.156	310	-7	-8	2			.943	0	O-16(16-0-0)	-1.0
Total	5	376	1341	129	300	38	22	6	117	80	143	.224	.272	.298	570	75	-43	66			.945	16	O-362(136-211-6)	-5.3
■ JOE KELLY Kelly, Joseph James b: 4/23/1900, New York, N.Y. d: 11/24/67, Lynbrook, N.Y. BL/TL, 6', 180 lbs. Deb: 4/13/26																								
1926	Chi-N	65	176	16	59	15	3	0	32	7	11	.335	.361	.455	815	117	4	0			.953	-5	O-39(25-0-14)	-0.4
1928	Chi-N	32	52	3	11	1	0	1	7	1	3	.212	.255	.288	543	42	-4	0			.974	0	1-10	-0.5
Total	2	97	228	19	70	16	3	1	39	8	14	.307	.336	.417	753	100	-1	0			.953	-4	/O-39(25-0-14),1-10	-0.9
■ KENNY KELLY Kelly, Kenneth Alphonso b: 1/26/79, Plant City, Fla. BR/TR, 6'3", 180 lbs. Deb: 9/7/2000																								
2000	TB-A	2	1	0	0	0	0	0	0	0	0	.000	.000	.000	0	-99	-0	0	0	0	.000	0	/D-1	0.0
■ KING KELLY Kelly, Michael Joseph b: 12/31/1857, Troy, N.Y. d: 11/8/1894, Boston, Mass. BR/TR, 5'10", 170 lbs. Deb: 5/1/1878 MH Career OF: (2-LF 8-CF 742-RF)																								
1878	Cin-N	60	237	29	67	7	1	0	27	7	7	.283	.303	.321	624	116	5				.765	11	*O-47R,C-17/3-2	1.5
1879	Cin-N	77	345	78	120	20	12	2	47	8	14	.348	.363	.493	855	**188**	32				.832	12	3-33,O-29R,C-21,/2	**4.1**
1880	Chi-N	84	344	72	100	17	9	1	60	12	22	.291	.315	.401	716	133	11				.779	-3	*O-64R,C-17,3/S2P	0.9
1881	Chi-N	82	353	84	114	**27**	3	2	55	16	14	.323	.352	.433	786	139	15				.841	-0	*O-72R,C-11/3-8	1.4
1882	Chi-N	84	377	81	115	**37**	4	1	55	10	27	.305	.323	.432	755	134	13				.810	-1	S-42,O-38R,C-12,/31	1.2
1883	Chi-N	98	428	92	109	28	10	3	61	16	35	.255	.282	.388	669	93	-5				.813	3	*O-82R,C-38/2-3,3P	0.0
1884	Chi-N	108	452	**120**	160	28	5	13	95	46	24	.354	**.414**	.524	938	178	**40**				.794	-6	O-63R,C-28,S3/1P2	3.2
1885	*Chi-N	107	438	**124**	126	24	7	9	75	46	24	.288	.355	.436	791	136	16				.867	3	O-69R,C-37/2-6,31	2.0
1886	*Chi-N	118	451	**155**	175	32	11	4	79	83	33	**.388**	**.483**	.534	1018	183	47	53			.811	2	O-56R,C-53/1-9,32S	4.7
1887	Bos-N	116	539	120	211	34	11	8	63	55	40	.391	.393	.488	880	143	29	84			.856	-11	O-61R,2-30,C/PS3M	1.7
1888	Bos-N	107	440	85	140	22	11	9	71	31	39	.318	.368	.480	848	166	32	56			.905	-3	C-76,O-34(0-0-34)	3.4
1889	Bos-N	125	507	120	149	**41**	5	9	78	65	40	.294	.376	.448	824	122	14	68			.848	-9	*O-113(0-0-113),C-23	0.5
1890	Bos-P	89	340	83	111	18	6	4	66	52	22	.326	.419	.450	869	124	12	51			.915	-3	C-56,S-27/O-6R,13PM	1.1
1891	Cin-a	82	283	56	84	15	7	1	53	51	28	.297	.408	.410	818	123	9	22			.904	14	C-66/3-8,O-7R,21PS	2.3
	Bos-a	4	15	2	4	0	0	1	4	0	2	.267	.267	.467	733	111	-0	1			.950	-1	/C-4	0.0
	Yr	86	298	58	88	15	7	2	57	51	30	.295	.402	.413	814	123	9	23			.906	13	C-70/3-8,O-7R,21PS	2.3
	Bos-N	16	52	7	12	1	0	0	5	6	10	.231	.322	.250	572	60	-3	6			.844	-5	C-11/O-6(0-0-6)	-0.6
1892	*Bos-N	78	281	40	53	7	0	2	41	39	32	.189	.287	.235	522	53	-16	24			.912	0	C-72/O-2L,3-2,1P	-0.8
1893	NY-N	20	67	9	18	1	0	0	15	6	5	.269	.329	.284	612	63	-3	3			.895	-4	C-17/O-1(0-0-1)	-0.5
Total	16	1455	5949	1357	1868	359	102	69	950	549	418	.314	.368	.438	806	136	247	368			.820	0	O-750R,C-583/3S21P	26.1
■ MIKE KELLY Kelly, Michael Raymond b: 6/2/70, Los Angeles, Cal. BR/TR, 6'4", 195 lbs. Deb: 4/5/94																								
1994	Atl-N	30	77	14	21	10	1	2	9	2	17	.273	.300	.506	806	103	-0	0	1	-0	.962	-5	O-25(19-6-1)	-0.5
1995	Atl-N	97	137	26	26	6	1	3	17	11	49	.190	.260	.314	574	49	-10	7	3	0	.940	-16	O-83(58-8-17)	-2.7
1996	Cin-N	19	49	5	9	4	0	1	7	9	11	.184	.333	.327	660	75	-2	4	0	1	.972	1	O-17(6-10-1)	0.0
1997	Cin-N	73	140	27	41	13	2	6	19	10	30	.293	.340	.543	883	125	4	6	1	1	.978	-3	O-59(17-11-31)/D-1	0.1
1998	TB-A	106	279	39	67	11	2	10	33	22	80	.240	.296	.401	697	78	-10	13	6	1	1.000	-8	O-93(43-0-51)/D-6	-1.9
1999	Col-N	2	2	0	1	1	0	0	1	0	0	.500	.500	1.000	1500	210	0	0	0	0	.000	-0	/O-1(0-0-1)	0.0
Total	6	327	684	111	165	45	6	22	86	54	187	.241	.301	.421	723	85	-17	30	11	3	.978	-31	O-278(143-35-102)/D-7	-5.0
■ PAT KELLY Kelly, Patrick Franklin b: 10/14/67, Philadelphia, Pa. BR/TR, 6', 182 lbs. Deb: 5/20/91																								
1991	NY-A	96	298	35	72	12	4	3	23	15	52	.242	.289	.339	628	73	-11	12	1	2	.926	7	3-80,2-19	-0.1
1992	NY-A	106	318	38	72	22	2	7	27	25	72	.226	.303	.374	677	89	-5	8	5	0	.978	6	*2-101/D-1	0.4
1993	NY-A	127	406	49	111	24	1	7	51	24	68	.273	.322	.389	711	93	-4	14	11	-1	.978	9	*2-125	0.9
1994	NY-A	93	286	35	80	21	2	3	41	19	51	.280	.335	.399	734	92	-3	6	5	-0	.978	1	2-93	0.1
1995	*NY-A	89	270	32	64	12	1	4	29	23	65	.237	.309	.333	642	68	-13	8	3	1	.983	6	2-87/D-1	-0.2
1996	NY-A	13	21	4	3	0	0	0	2	2	9	.143	.217	.143	360	-6	-3	0	1	-0	.970	5	2-10/D-3	0.1
1997	NY-A	67	120	25	29	6	1	2	10	14	37	.242	.326	.358	684	79	-4	8	1	1	.981	14	2-48,D-16	1.2
1998	StL-N	53	153	18	33	5	0	4	14	13	48	.216	.286	.327	613	61	-9	5	1	1	.964	-1	2-41/O-3(3-0-0),S-2	-0.7
1999	Tor-A	37	116	17	31	7	0	6	20	10	23	.267	.325	.483	808	101	-0	0	1	-0	.962	-1	2-35/D-2	0.0
Total	9	681	1988	253	495	109	11	36	217	145	425	.249	.311	.369	680	82	-53	61	29	3	.977	47	2-559/3-80,D-23,OS	1.7
■ SPEED KELLY Kelly, Robert Brown b: 8/19/1884, Bryan, Ohio d: 5/6/49, Goshen, Ind. BR/TR, 6'2", 185 lbs. Deb: 7/13/09																								
1909	Was-A	17	42	3	6	2	1	0	1	3		.143	.200	.238	438	40	-3	1			.852	-1	3-10/2-3,O-1(0-1-0)	-0.5
■ ROBERTO KELLY Kelly, Roberto Conrado (Gray) "Bobby" b: 10/1/64, Panama City, Pan. BR/TR, 6'2", 192 lbs. Deb: 7/29/87 Career OF: (246-LF 886-CF 184-RF)																								
1987	NY-A	23	52	12	14	3	0	1	7	5	15	.269	.333	.385	718	91	-1	9	3	1	.955	-0	O-17(0-16-1)/D-2	0.0

YEAR	TM/L	G	AB	R	H	2B	3B	HR	RBI	BB	SO	AVG	OBP	SLG	OPS	OPS+	BR+	SB	CS	SBR	FA	FR	G/POS	TPR
1988	NY-A	38	77	9	19	4	1	1	7	3	15	.247	.275	.364	639	78	-2	5	2	0	.986	-2	O-30(1-28-2)/D-3	-0.4
1989	NY-A	137	441	65	133	18	3	9	48	41	89	.302	.369	.417	786	123	14	35	12	4	.984	7	*O-137(0-137-0)	2.3
1990	NY-A	162	641	85	183	32	4	15	61	33	148	.285	.324	.418	743	106	3	42	17	3	.988	8	*O-160(11-151-0)/D-1	1.4
1991	NY-A	126	486	68	130	22	2	20	69	45	77	.267	.336	.444	780	114	8	32	9	4	.986	3	*O-125(52-73-0)	1.3
1992	NY-A★	152	580	81	158	31	2	10	66	41	96	.272	.325	.384	709	99	-2	28	5	4	.983	10	*O-146(47-99-0)	1.0
1993	Cin-N★	78	320	44	102	17	3	9	35	17	43	.319	.357	.475	832	120	9	21	5	3	.995	5	O-77(0-77-0)	1.7
1994	Cin-N	47	179	29	54	8	0	3	21	11	35	.302	.352	.397	749	96	-1	9	8	-1	.992	3	O-47(0-47-0)	0.1
	Atl-N	63	255	44	73	15	3	6	24	24	36	.286	.348	.439	787	101	0	10	3	1	.985	-2	O-63(0-63-0)	0.1
	Yr	110	434	73	127	23	3	9	45	35	71	.293	.350	.422	771	99	-0	19	11	0	.988	1	*O-110(0-110-0)	0.2
1995	Mon-N	24	95	11	26	4	0	1	9	7	14	.274	.337	.347	684	78	-3	4	3	-0	1.000	-1	O-24(0-24-0)	-0.4
	*LA-N	112	409	47	114	19	2	6	48	15	65	.279	.311	.379	690	89	-8	15	7	1	.969	-4	*O-110(61-48-2)	-1.2
	Yr	136	504	58	140	23	2	7	57	22	79	.278	.316	.373	689	87	-11	19	10	1	.974	-5	*O-134(61-72-2)	-1.6
1996	Min-A	98	322	41	104	17	4	6	47	23	53	.323	.381	.457	837	109	5	10	2	2	.990	-1	O-93(6-40-54)/D-2	0.3
1997	Min-A	75	247	39	71	19	2	5	37	17	50	.287	.338	.441	780	100	-0	7	4	0	1.000	-4	O-59(1-1-57),D-12	-0.7
	*Sea-A	30	121	19	36	7	0	7	22	5	17	.298	.331	.529	860	121	3	2	1	0	1.000	0	O-29(28-1-0)/D-1	0.2
	Yr	105	368	58	107	26	2	12	59	22	67	.291	.336	.470	806	107	3	9	5	0	1.000	-4	O-88(29-2-57),D-13	-0.5
1998	*Tex-A	75	257	48	83	7	3	16	46	8	46	.323	.351	.560	911	127	9	0	2	-1	.976	-4	O-71(14-41-31)/D-2	0.3
1999	*Tex-A	87	290	41	87	17	1	8	37	21	57	.300	.358	.448	806	99	-0	6	1	1	.981	-7	O-85(18-37-37)	-0.7
2000	NY-A	10	25	4	3	1	0	1	1	1	6	.120	.185	.280	465	16	-3	0	0	0	1.000	-1	O-10(7-3-0)	-0.4
Total	14	1337	4797	687	1390	241	30	124	585	317	862	.290	.340	.430	770	106	31	235	84	22	.985	12	*O-1283C/D-23	4.9

■ VAN KELLY
Kelly, Van Howard b: 3/18/46, Charlotte, N.C. BL/TR, 5′11″, 180 lbs. Deb: 6/13/69

YEAR	TM/L	G	AB	R	H	2B	3B	HR	RBI	BB	SO	AVG	OBP	SLG	OPS	OPS+	BR+	SB	CS	SBR	FA	FR	G/POS	TPR
1969	SD-N	73	209	16	51	7	1	3	15	12	24	.244	.285	.330	615	75	-8	0	1	-0	.971	-3	3-49,2-10	-1.2
1970	SD-N	38	89	9	15	3	0	1	9	15	21	.169	.288	.236	524	44	-7	0	1	-0	.971	1	3-27/2-1	-0.7
Total	2	111	298	25	66	10	1	4	24	27	45	.221	.286	.302	588	65	-14	0	2	-1	.971	-3	/3-76,2-11	-1.9

■ BILL KELLY
Kelly, William Henry "Big Bill" b: 12/28/1898, Syracuse, N.Y. d: 4/8/90, Syracuse, N.Y. BR/TR, 6′, 190 lbs. Deb: 9/6/20

YEAR	TM/L	G	AB	R	H	2B	3B	HR	RBI	BB	SO	AVG	OBP	SLG	OPS	OPS+	BR+	SB	CS	SBR	FA	FR	G/POS	TPR
1920	Phi-A	9	13	0	3	1	0	0	0	0	2	.231	.231	.308	538	41	-1	0	0	0	1.000	0	/1-2	-0.1
1928	Phi-N	23	71	6	12	1	1	0	5	7	20	.169	.244	.211	455	19	-8	0			.991	1	1-23	-0.8
Total	2	32	84	6	15	2	1	0	5	7	22	.179	.242	.226	468	22	-10	0	0		.992	2	/1-25	-0.9

■ BILL KELLY
Kelly, William J. b: New York, N.Y. Deb: 5/4/1871

YEAR	TM/L	G	AB	R	H	2B	3B	HR	RBI	BB	SO	AVG	OBP	SLG	OPS	OPS+	BR+	SB	CS	SBR	FA	FR	G/POS	TPR
1871	Kek-n	18	67	16	15	1	1	0	7	6	1	.224	.288	.269	556	60	-3	0	0	0	.833	1	O-18(1-4-14)	-0.1

■ BILLY KELLY
Kelly, William Joseph b: 5/1/1886, Baltimore, Md. d: 6/3/40, Detroit, Mich. BR/TR, 6′0.5″, 183 lbs. Deb: 5/2/10

YEAR	TM/L	G	AB	R	H	2B	3B	HR	RBI	BB	SO	AVG	OBP	SLG	OPS	OPS+	BR+	SB	CS	SBR	FA	FR	G/POS	TPR
1910	StL-N	2	2	1	0	0	0	0	0	1	0	.000	.333	.000	333	-1	-0	0			.000	0	/C-1	0.0
1911	Pit-N	6	8	0	1	0	0	0	0	0	2	.125	.125	.125	250	-29	-1	0			1.000	1	/C-1	0.0
1912	Pit-N	48	132	20	42	3	2	1	11	2	16	.318	.328	.394	722	99	-1	8			.990	-9	C-39	-0.7
1913	Pit-N	48	82	11	22	2	2	0	9	2	12	.268	.302	.341	644	87	-2	1			.960	4	C-40	0.4
Total	4	104	224	32	65	5	4	1	20	5	30	.290	.312	.362	673	89	-4	9			.977	-5	/C-81	-0.3

■ BILLY KELSEY
Kelsey, George William b: 8/24/1881, Covington, Ohio d: 4/25/68, Springfield, Ohio BR/TR, 5′10″, 150 lbs. Deb: 10/4/07

YEAR	TM/L	G	AB	R	H	2B	3B	HR	RBI	BB	SO	AVG	OBP	SLG	OPS	OPS+	BR+	SB	CS	SBR	FA	FR	G/POS	TPR
1907	Pit-N	2	5	1	2	0	0	0	0	0		.400	.400	.400	800	149	0	0			1.000	-1	/C-2	0.0

■ KEN KELTNER
Keltner, Kenneth Frederick "Butch" b: 10/31/16, Milwaukee, Wis. d: 12/12/91, New Berlin, Wis. BR/TR, 6′, 190 lbs. Deb: 10/2/37

YEAR	TM/L	G	AB	R	H	2B	3B	HR	RBI	BB	SO	AVG	OBP	SLG	OPS	OPS+	BR+	SB	CS	SBR	FA	FR	G/POS	TPR
1937	Cle-A	1	1	0	0	0	0	0	1	0	0	.000	.000	.000	0	-99	-0	0	0	0	1.000	0	/3-1	0.0
1938	Cle-A	149	576	86	159	31	9	26	113	33	75	.276	.319	.497	815	103	-2	4	3	-0	.956	-10	*3-149	-0.6
1939	Cle-A	154	587	84	191	35	11	13	97	51	41	.325	.379	.489	868	125	21	6	6	-1	**.974**	6	*3-154	2.8
1940	Cle-A★	149	543	67	138	24	10	15	77	51	56	.254	.322	.418	740	93	-7	10	5	0	.953	-6	*3-148	-0.7
1941	Cle-A★	149	581	83	156	31	13	23	84	51	56	.269	.330	.485	815	119	12	2	2	-0	**.971**	23	*3-149	3.8
1942	Cle-A★	152	624	72	179	34	4	6	78	20	36	.287	.312	.383	695	101	-3	4	3	-0	**.945**	16	*3-151	1.9
1943	Cle-A★	110	427	47	111	31	3	4	39	36	20	.260	.317	.375	692	109	3	2	2	-0	.969	6	*3-107	1.0
1944	Cle-A★	149	573	74	169	41	9	13	91	53	29	.295	.355	.466	821	139	26	4	3	-0	.968	15	*3-149	4.4
1946	Cle-A★	116	398	47	96	17	1	13	45	30	38	.241	.294	.387	681	95	-5	0	3	-1	.965	-2	*3-112	-0.9
1947	Cle-A	151	541	49	139	29	3	11	76	59	45	.257	.331	.383	714	101	-0	5	4	-0	.972	-9	*3-150	-1.0
1948	*Cle-A★	153	558	91	166	24	4	31	119	89	52	.297	.395	.522	917	146	36	2	1	0	.969	0	*3-153	3.4
1949	Cle-A	80	246	35	57	9	2	8	30	38	26	.232	.335	.382	717	91	-4	0	1	-0	.980	-1	3-69	-0.6
1950	Bos-A	13	28	2	9	2	0	0	2	3	6	.321	.387	.393	780	91	-0	0	0	0	.947	-2	/3-8,1-1	-0.2
Total	13	1526	5683	737	1570	308	69	163	852	514	480	.276	.338	.441	778	113	77	39	33	-3	.965	36	*3-1500/1-1	13.3

■ JOHN KELTY
Kelty, John James "Chief" b: 3/10/1871, Jersey City, N.J. d: 4/13/29, Jersey City, N.J. 5′10″, 175 lbs. Deb: 4/19/1890

YEAR	TM/L	G	AB	R	H	2B	3B	HR	RBI	BB	SO	AVG	OBP	SLG	OPS	OPS+	BR+	SB	CS	SBR	FA	FR	G/POS	TPR
1890	Pit-N	59	207	24	49	10	2	1	27	22	42	.237	.322	.319	641	98	1	10			.898	-3	O-59(59-0-0)	-0.4

■ BILL KEMMER
Kemmer, William Edward (b: William Edward Kemmerer) b: 11/15/1873, Pennsylvania d: 6/8/45, Washington, D.C. BR/TR, 6′2″, Deb: 6/3/1895

YEAR	TM/L	G	AB	R	H	2B	3B	HR	RBI	BB	SO	AVG	OBP	SLG	OPS	OPS+	BR+	SB	CS	SBR	FA	FR	G/POS	TPR
1895	Lou-N	11	38	5	7	0	0	1	3	2	4	.184	.225	.263	488	27	-4	0			.809	2	/3-9,1-2	-0.1

■ RUDY KEMMLER
Kemmler, Rudolph (b: Rudolph Kemler) b: 1860, Chicago, Ill. d: 6/20/09, Chicago, Ill. BR/TR, Deb: 7/26/1879

YEAR	TM/L	G	AB	R	H	2B	3B	HR	RBI	BB	SO	AVG	OBP	SLG	OPS	OPS+	BR+	SB	CS	SBR	FA	FR	G/POS	TPR
1879	Pro-N	2	7	0	1	0	0	0	0	0	1	.143	.143	.143	286	-6	-1				.833	2	/C-2	0.1
1881	Cle-N	1	3	0	0	0	0	0	0	0	1	.000	.000	.000	0	-99	-1				1.000	1	/C-1	0.0
1882	Cin-a	3	11	0	1	1	0	0		0		.091	.091	.182	273	-10	-1				.909	-1	/C-3,O-1(0-0-1)	-0.2
	Pit-a	24	99	7	25	4	0	0		1		.253	.260	.293	553	90	-1				.920	3	C-23/O-1(0-0-1)	0.3
	Yr	27	110	7	26	5	0	0		1		.236	.243	.282	525	79	-2				.919	1	C-26/O-2(0-0-2)	0.1
1883	Col-a	84	318	27	66	6	2	0		13		.208	.239	.239	478	59	-13				.872	-9	*C-82/O-2(0-2-0)	-1.3
1884	Col-a	61	211	28	42	3	3	0		15		.199	.252	.242	494	67	-6				.906	-19	C-58/1-2,O-1(1-0-0)	-1.9
1885	Pit-a	18	64	2	13	2	1	0	5	2		.203	.239	.266	504	60	-3				.870	-3	C-18	-0.4
1886	StL-a	35	123	13	17	2	0	0	6	8		.138	.197	.154	351	10	-13	0			.914	4	C-32/1-3	-0.6
1889	Col-a	8	26	2	3	0	0	0	0	3	3	.115	.207	.115	322	-8	-4	0			.930	1	/C-8	-0.2
Total	8	236	862	79	168	18	6	0	11	42	5	.195	.234	.230	464	52	-42	0			.894	-22	C-227/1-5,O-5(1-2-2)	-4.2

■ STEVE KEMP
Kemp, Steven F b: 8/7/54, San Angelo, Tex. BL/TL, 6′, 195 lbs. Deb: 4/7/77 Career OF: (925-LF 0-CF 90-RF)

YEAR	TM/L	G	AB	R	H	2B	3B	HR	RBI	BB	SO	AVG	OBP	SLG	OPS	OPS+	BR+	SB	CS	SBR	FA	FR	G/POS	TPR
1977	Det-A	151	552	75	142	29	4	18	88	71	93	.257	.347	.422	769	103	3	3	3	-0	.981	-3	*O-148(148-0-0)	-0.7
1978	Det-A	159	582	75	161	18	4	15	79	97	87	.277	.381	.399	780	116	16	2	3	-1	.977	8	*O-157(157-0-0)	1.6
1979	Det-A★	134	490	88	156	26	3	26	105	68	70	.318	.404	.543	946	148	34	5	6	-1	.976	6	*O-120(117-0-3),D-11	3.1
1980	Det-A	135	508	88	149	23	3	21	101	69	64	.293	.382	.474	857	130	22	5	1	1	.995	6	O-85(85-0-0),D-46	2.3
1981	Det-A	105	372	52	103	18	4	9	49	70	48	.277	.393	.419	812	129	17	9	3	1	.986	3	O-92(92-0-0),D-12	1.6
1982	Chi-A	160	580	91	166	23	1	19	98	89	83	.286	.384	.428	812	123	21	7	7	-1	.976	-7	*O-154(154-0-0)/D-2	0.6
1983	NY-A	109	373	53	90	17	3	12	49	41	37	.241	.320	.399	719	100	-0	1	0	0	.987	1	*O-101(25-0-86)/D-2	-0.4
1984	NY-A	94	313	37	91	12	1	7	41	40	54	.291	.373	.403	775	119	9	4	1	1	.972	-2	O-75(75-0-0),D-12	0.4
1985	Pit-N	92	236	19	59	13	2	2	21	25	54	.250	.322	.347	669	88	-4	1	0	0	1.000	-1	O-63(63-0-0)	-0.7
1986	Pit-N	13	16	1	3	0	0	1	1	4	6	.188	.350	.375	725	98	0	1	0	0	1.000	0	/O-4(4-0-0)	0.1
1988	Tex-A	16	36	2	8	0	0	0	2	2	9	.222	.263	.222	485	36	-3	1	0	0	1.000	-2	/O-5(5-0-1),1-1,D-7	-0.5
Total	11	1168	4058	581	1128	179	25	130	634	576	605	.278	.370	.431	801	119	115	39	24	0	.982	10	*O-1004L/D-92,1-1	7.4

■ FRED KENDALL
Kendall, Fred Lyn b: 1/31/49, Torrance, Cal. BR/TR, 6′1″, 190 lbs. Deb: 9/8/69 FC Career OF: (1-LF 0-CF 0-RF)

YEAR	TM/L	G	AB	R	H	2B	3B	HR	RBI	BB	SO	AVG	OBP	SLG	OPS	OPS+	BR+	SB	CS	SBR	FA	FR	G/POS	TPR
1969	SD-N	10	26	2	4	0	0	0	0	2	5	.154	.214	.154	368	5	-3	0	0	0	1.000	-1	/C-9	-0.4
1970	SD-N	4	9	0	0	0	0	0	1	0	0	.000	.000	.000	0	-99	-3	0	0	0	1.000	-1	/C-2,1-1,O-1(1-0-0)	-0.4
1971	SD-N	49	111	2	19	1	0	1	7	7	16	.171	.220	.207	428	23	-11	1	0	0	1.000	1	C-39/1-1,3-1	-1.0
1972	SD-N	91	273	18	59	3	4	6	18	11	42	.216	.249	.322	571	66	-13	0	0	0	.995	3	C-82/1-1	-0.8
1973	SD-N	145	507	39	143	22	3	10	59	30	35	.282	.323	.396	720	107	3	3	1	0	.984	-17	*C-138	-0.7
1974	SD-N	141	424	32	98	15	2	8	45	49	33	.231	.311	.333	643	84	-10	0	1	-0	.983	-23	*C-133	-2.9
1975	SD-N	103	286	16	57	12	1	0	24	26	28	.199	.266	.248	514	46	-21	0	1	-0	.977	-8	C-85	-2.7
1976	SD-N	146	456	30	112	17	0	2	39	36	42	.246	.305	.296	601	77	-14	1	1	-0	.994	-19	*C-146	-2.8

YEAR	TM/L	G	AB	R	H	2B	3B	HR	RBI	BB	SO	AVG	OBP	SLG	OPS	OPS+	BR+	SB	CS	SBR	FA	FR	G/POS	TPR
1977	Cle-A	103	317	18	79	13	1	3	39	16	27	.249	.287	.325	612	69	-14	0	1	-0	.991	-13	*C-102/D-1	-2.3
1978	Bos-A	20	41	3	8	1	0	0	4	1	2	.195	.214	.220	434	20	-4	0	0	0	1.000	3	1-13/C-5,D-1	-0.2
1979	SD-N	46	102	8	17	2	0	1	6	11	7	.167	.248	.216	463	29	-10	0	0	0	.977	5	C-40/1-2	-0.4
1980	SD-N	19	24	2	7	0	0	0	2	0	3	.292	.292	.292	583	67	-1	0	0	0	.938	0	C-14/1-1	-0.1
Total	12	877	2576	170	603	86	11	31	244	189	240	.234	.288	.312	600	72	-101	5	5	-1	.987	-71	C-795/1-19,D-2,3O	-14.7
■ **JASON KENDALL** Kendall, Jason Daniel b: 6/26/74, San Diego, Cal. BR/TR, 6', 180 lbs. Deb: 4/1/96 F																								
1996	Pit-N★	130	414	54	124	23	5	3	42	35	30	.300	.375	.401	776	102	3	5	2	0	.980	-0	*C-129	1.0
1997	Pit-N	144	486	71	143	36	4	8	49	49	53	.294	.394	.434	828	115	13	18	6	2	.990	13	*C-142	3.6
1998	Pit-N★	149	535	95	175	36	3	12	75	51	51	.327	.417	.473	889	132	28	26	5	4	.992	4	*C-144	4.3
1999	Pit-N	78	280	61	93	20	3	8	41	38	32	.332	.433	.511	944	138	18	22	3	4	.988	4	C-75	2.9
2000	Pit-N★	152	579	112	185	33	6	14	58	79	79	.320	.415	.470	884	124	25	22	12	1	.991	-0	*C-147	3.2
Total	5	653	2294	393	720	148	21	45	265	252	245	.314	.406	.456	862	122	87	93	28	11	.988	20	C-637	15.0
■ **AL KENDERS** Kenders, Albert Daniel George b: 4/4/37, Barrington, N.J. BR/TR, 6', 185 lbs. Deb: 8/14/61																								
1961	Phi-N	10	23	0	4	1	0	0	1	1	0	.174	.208	.217	426	13	-3	0	0	0	1.000	-2	C-10	-0.4
■ **EDDIE KENNA** Kenna, Edward Aloysius "Scrap Iron" b: 9/30/1897, San Francisco, Cal. d: 8/21/72, San Francisco, Cal BR/TR, 5'7.5", 150 lbs. Deb: 6/2/28																								
1928	Was-A	41	118	14	35	4	2	1	20	14	8	.297	.376	.390	766	102	1	1	5	-2	.942	-3	C-33	-0.2
■ **ADAM KENNEDY** Kennedy, Adam Thomas b: 1/10/76, Riverside, Cal. BL/TR, 6'1", 180 lbs. Deb: 8/21/99																								
1999	StL-N	33	102	12	26	10	1	1	16	3	8	.255	.290	.402	692	72	-5	0	1	-0	.971	-3	2-29	-0.7
2000	Ana-A	156	598	82	159	33	11	9	72	28	73	.266	.302	.403	705	76	-23	22	8	2	.976	-18	*2-155	-2.9
Total	2	189	700	94	185	43	12	10	88	31	81	.264	.300	.403	703	76	-28	22	9	2	.975	-22	2-184	-3.6
■ **ED KENNEDY** Kennedy, Edward b: 4/1/1856, Carbondale, Pa. d: 5/20/05, New York, N.Y. 5'6", 150 lbs. Deb: 5/1/1883 Career OF: (291-LF 6-CF 0-RF)																								
1883	NY-a	94	356	57	78	6	7	2		17		.219	.255	.292	547	72	-11				.884	-7	*O-94(94-0-0)	-1.8
1884	*NY-a	103	378	49	72	6	2	1		16		.190	.225	.225	450	49	-20				.915	7	*O-100L/S-1,2-1,C-1	-1.5
1885	NY-a	96	349	35	71	8	4	2	21	12		.203	.238	.266	505	64	-13				.841	2	*O-96(95-1-0)	-1.2
1886	Bro-a	6	22	1	4	0	0	0	2	2		.182	.250	.182	432	36	-2	1			.909	-1	/O-6(3-4-0)	-0.3
Total	4	299	1105	142	225	20	13	5	23	47		.204	.239	.259	498	61	-46	1			.878	0	O-296L/C-1,2-1,S-1	-4.8
■ **JIM KENNEDY** Kennedy, James Earl b: 11/1/46, Tulsa, Okla. BL/TR, 5'9", 160 lbs. Deb: 6/14/70 F																								
1970	StL-N	12	24	1	3	0	0	0	0	0	0	.125	.125	.125	250	-32	-4	0	0	0	.909	1	/S-7,2-5	-0.3
■ **JOHN KENNEDY** Kennedy, John Edward b: 5/29/41, Chicago, Ill. BR/TR, 6', 185 lbs. Deb: 9/5/62																								
1962	Was-A	14	42	6	11	0	1	1	2	2	7	.262	.295	.381	676	81	-1	0	1	-0	.974	0	/S-9,3-2	-0.1
1963	Was-A	36	62	3	11	1	1	0	4	6	22	.177	.261	.226	487	38	-5	2	0	0	.954	6	3-26/S-2	0.2
1964	Was-A	148	482	55	111	16	4	7	35	29	119	.230	.281	.324	605	68	-21	3	3	-0	.941	9	*3-106,S-49/2-2	-1.0
1965	*LA-N	104	105	12	18	3	0	1	5	8	33	.171	.243	.229	472	36	-9	1	0	0	.971	11	3-95/S-5	0.3
1966	*LA-N	125	274	15	55	9	2	3	24	10	64	.201	.242	.281	523	49	-19	1	2	-0	.965	13	3-87,S-28,2-15	-0.5
1967	NY-A	78	179	22	35	4	0	1	17	17	35	.196	.269	.235	504	52	-10	2	1	0	.915	7	S-36,3-34/2-2	-0.1
1969	Sea-A	61	128	18	30	3	1	4	14	14	25	.234	.315	.367	682	92	-2	4	0	1	.916	-4	S-33,3-23	-0.2
1970	Mil-A	25	55	8	14	2	0	2	6	5	9	.255	.317	.400	717	96	-0	0	1	-0	.921	-1	2-16/3-5,S-4,1-1	-0.1
	Bos-A	43	129	15	33	7	1	4	17	6	14	.256	.294	.419	713	88	-2	0	0	0	.960	3	3-33/2-2	0.0
	Yr	68	184	23	47	9	1	6	23	11	23	.255	.301	.413	714	91	-3	0	1	-0	.962	1	3-38,2-18/S-4,1-1	-0.1
1971	Bos-A	74	272	41	75	12	5	5	22	14	42	.276	.321	.412	732	99	-1	1	1	-0	.974	-18	2-37,S-33/3-5	-1.4
1972	Bos-A	71	212	22	52	11	1	2	22	18	40	.245	.313	.335	648	88	-3	0	1	-0	.962	-6	2-32,S-27,3-11	-0.5
1973	Bos-A	67	155	17	28	9	1	1	16	12	45	.181	.249	.271	519	44	-12	0	0	0	.980	7	2-31,3-24/D-9	-0.3
1974	Bos-A	10	15	3	2	0	0	1	1	1	6	.133	.188	.333	521	44	-1	0	0	0	.778	-1	/2-6,3-4	-0.2
Total	12	856	2110	237	475	77	17	32	185	142	461	.225	.282	.323	605	70	-87	14	10	-0	.953	26	3-455,S-226,2/D1	-3.9
■ **JOHN KENNEDY** Kennedy, John Irvin b: 10/12/26, Jacksonville, Fla. d: 4/27/98, Jacksonville, Fla. BR/TR, 5'10", 175 lbs. Deb: 4/22/57																								
1957	Phi-N	5	2	1	0	0	0	0	0	0	1	.000	.000	.000	0	-99	-1	0	0	0	.500	0	/3-2	0.0
■ **JUNIOR KENNEDY** Kennedy, Junior Raymond b: 8/9/50, Fort Gibson, Okla. BR/TR, 6', 185 lbs. Deb: 8/9/74 F																								
1974	Cin-N	22	19	2	3	0	0	0	0	6	4	.158	.360	.158	518	49	-1	0	0	0	.909	-1	2-17/3-5	-0.2
1978	Cin-N	89	157	22	40	2	2	0	11	31	28	.255	.381	.293	674	91	-0	4	1	1	.979	13	2-71/3-4	1.6
1979	Cin-N	83	220	29	60	7	0	1	17	28	31	.273	.355	.318	673	85	-4	4	3	-0	.980	-1	2-59/S-5,3-4	-0.1
1980	Cin-N	104	337	31	88	16	3	1	34	36	34	.261	.332	.335	668	87	-5	3	1	0	.988	2	*2-103	0.2
1981	Cin-N	27	44	5	11	1	0	0	5	1	5	.250	.267	.273	539	52	-3	0	0	0	.980	2	2-16/3-5	0.0
1982	Chi-N	105	242	22	53	3	1	2	25	21	34	.219	.281	.264	546	52	-15	1	4	-1	.978	13	2-71,S-28/3-7	0.1
1983	Chi-N	17	22	3	3	0	0	0	3	1	6	.136	.174	.136	310	-12	-3	0	0	0	1.000	2	/2-7,3-4,S-1	-0.1
Total	7	447	1041	114	258	29	6	4	95	124	142	.248	.328	.299	627	75	-31	12	9	-1	.982	30	2-344/S-34,3-29	1.5
■ **DOC KENNEDY** Kennedy, Michael Joseph b: 8/11/1853, Brooklyn, N.Y. d: 5/23/20, Grove, N.Y. BR/TR, 5'9.5", 185 lbs. Deb: 5/1/1879 Career OF: (4-LF 5-CF 0-RF)																								
1879	Cle-N	49	193	19	56	8	2	1	18	2	10	.290	.297	.368	665	119	4				.891	3	C-46/1-4	0.7
1880	Cle-N	66	250	26	50	10	1	0	18	5	12	.200	.216	.248	464	58	-10				.899	-1	*C-65/O-2(1-1-0)	-1.0
1881	Cle-N	39	150	19	47	7	1	0	15	5	13	.313	.335	.373	709	129	5				.920	5	C-35/O-3(2-1-0),3-1	1.0
1882	Cle-N	1	3	0	1	0	0	0	0	1	0	.333	.500	.333	833	180	0				.857	3	/C-1	0.3
1883	Buf-N	5	19	3	6	0	0	0	2	2	2	.316	.381	.316	697	113	0				.583	-2	/O-4(1-3-0),1-1	-0.1
Total	5	160	615	67	160	25	4	1	53	15	37	.260	.278	.319	596	98	-1				.901	9	C-147/O-9C,1-5,3-1	0.9
■ **RAY KENNEDY** Kennedy, Raymond Lincoln b: 5/19/1895, Pittsburgh, Pa. d: 1/18/69, Casselberry, Fla. BR/TR, 5'9", 165 lbs. Deb: 9/8/16																								
1916	StL-A	1	1	0	0	0	0	0	0	0	0	.000	.000	.000	0	-99	-0	0			.000	0	H	0.0
■ **BOB KENNEDY** Kennedy, Robert Daniel b: 8/18/20, Chicago, Ill. BR/TR, 6'2", 193 lbs. Deb: 9/14/39 FMC Career OF: (203-LF 30-CF 601-RF)																								
1939	Chi-A	3	8	0	2	0	0	0	1	0	0	.250	.250	.250	500	27	-1	0	0	0	.750	-1	/3-2	-0.2
1940	Chi-A	154	606	74	153	23	3	3	52	42	58	.252	.301	.315	616	59	-36	3	7	-2	.938	-3	*3-154	-3.4
1941	Chi-A	76	257	16	53	9	3	1	29	17	23	.206	.255	.276	532	41	-22	5	3	0	.934	3	3-71	-1.6
1942	Chi-A	113	412	37	95	18	5	0	38	22	41	.231	.270	.299	568	61	-22	11	7	-0	.956	4	3-96,O-16(13-0-3)	-1.6
1946	Chi-A	113	411	43	106	13	5	5	34	24	42	.258	.300	.350	651	85	-10	6	8	-1	.965	4	O-75(59-12-4),3-29	-1.3
1947	Chi-A	115	428	47	112	19	3	6	48	18	38	.262	.291	.362	654	84	-11	3	4	-1	.968	-3	*O-106(14-1-91)/3-1	-2.0
1948	Chi-A	30	113	4	28	8	1	0	14	4	17	.248	.274	.336	610	64	-6	0	2	-1	.970	-0	O-30(25-0-5)	-0.9
	*Cle-A	66	73	10	22	3	2	0	5	4	6	.301	.338	.397	735	98	-1	0	0	0	1.000	-13	O-50(2-0-48)/2-2,1-1	-1.4
	Yr	96	186	14	50	11	3	0	19	8	23	.269	.299	.360	659	77	-7	0	2	-1	.981	-13	O-80(27-0-53)/2-2,1-1	-2.3
1949	Cle-A	121	424	49	117	23	5	9	57	37	40	.276	.334	.417	752	100	-2	5	5	-1	.990	3	O-98(1-0-98),3-21	-0.3
1950	Cle-A	146	540	79	157	27	5	9	54	53	31	.291	.355	.409	764	99	-2	3	4	-1	.987	1	*O-144(0-10-138)	-0.6
1951	Cle-A	108	321	30	79	15	4	7	29	34	33	.246	.320	.383	703	95	-3	4	2	0	.968	-1	*O-106(1-0-105)	-0.7
1952	Cle-A	22	40	6	12	3	1	0	12	9	5	.300	.429	.425	854	148	3	1	0	0	1.000	0	O-13(1-5-8)/3-3	0.3
1953	Cle-A	100	161	22	38	5	0	3	22	19	11	.236	.320	.323	643	76	-5	0	2	-1	1.000	-21	O-89(42-2-52)	-3.0
1954	Cle-A	1	0	0	0	0	0	0	0	0	0	—	—	—	—	—	0	0	0	0	.000	-0	/O-1(1-0-0)	0.0
	Bal-A	106	323	37	81	13	2	6	45	28	43	.251	.311	.359	670	90	-6	2	1	0	.938	-6	3-71,O-21(12-0-9)	-1.3
	Yr	107	323	37	81	13	2	6	45	28	43	.251	.311	.359	670	90	-6	2	1	0	.938	-7	3-71,O-22(13-0-9)	-1.3
1955	Bal-A	26	70	10	10	1	0	0	5	10	10	.143	.250	.157	407	12	-9	0	1	-0	1.000	-1	O-14(0-0-14)/1-6,3-1	-1.1
	Chi-A	83	214	28	65	10	2	9	43	16	16	.304	.352	.495	848	122	6	0	2	-1	.938	-13	3-55,O-20(4-0-16)/1-3	-0.8
	Yr	109	284	38	75	11	2	9	48	26	26	.264	.326	.412	738	97	-2	0	3	-1	.938	-13	3-56,O-34(4-0-30)/1-9	-1.9
1956	Chi-A	8	13	0	1	0	0	0	0	2	4	.077	.200	.077	277	-24	-2	0	0	0	1.000	-1	/3-6	-0.3
	Det-A	69	177	17	41	5	0	4	22	24	19	.232	.330	.328	658	74	-6	2	2	-0	.931	-3	O-29(20-0-9),3-27	-1.1
	Yr	77	190	17	42	5	0	4	22	26	23	.221	.321	.311	632	67	-9	2	2	-0	.909	-4	3-33,O-29(20-0-9)	-1.4
1957	Chi-A	4	2	0	0	0	0	0	0	0	1	.000	.000	.000	0	-99	-1	0	0	0	.000	0	H	-0.1

YEAR	TM/L	G	AB	R	H	2B	3B	HR	RBI	BB	SO	AVG	OBP	SLG	OPS	OPS+	BR+	SB	CS	SBR	FA	FR	G/POS	TPR
	Bro-N	19	31	5	4	1	0	1	4	1	5	.129	.156	.258	414	8	-4	0	0	0	1.000	-4	/O-9(8-0-1),3-3	-0.9
Total	16	1483	4624	514	1176	196	41	63	514	364	443	.254	.310	.355	665	80	-141	45	50	-8	.978	-55	O-821R,3-540/1-10,2	-22.3
■ SNAPPER KENNEDY Kennedy, Sherman Montgomery b: 11/1/1878, Conneaut, Ohio d: 8/15/45, Pasadena, Tex. BB/TR, 5'10", 165 lbs. Deb: 5/1/02																								
1902	Chi-N	1	5	0	0	0	0	0	0	0	0	.000	.000	.000	0	-99	-1	0			1.000	1	/O-1(0-1-0)	-0.1
■ TERRY KENNEDY Kennedy, Terrence Edward b: 6/4/56, Euclid, Ohio BL/TR, 6'3", 220 lbs. Deb: 9/4/78 F Career OF: (28-LF 0-CF 0-RF)																								
1978	StL-N	10	29	0	5	0	0	0	2	4	3	.172	.273	.172	445	27	-3	0	0	0	.980	0	C-10	-0.2
1979	StL-N	33	109	11	31	7	0	2	17	6	20	.284	.322	.404	725	96	-1	0	0	0	.993	-4	C-32	-0.4
1980	StL-N	84	248	28	63	12	3	4	34	28	34	.254	.330	.375	705	93	-2	0	0	0	.967	-3	C-41,O-28(28-0-0)	-0.5
1981	SD-N★	101	382	32	115	24	1	2	41	22	53	.301	.342	.385	727	114	6	0	2	-1	.964	-8	*C-100	0.2
1982	SD-N	153	562	75	166	42	1	21	97	26	91	.295	.332	.486	818	133	22	1	0	0	.990	-18	*C-139,1-12	0.9
1983	SD-N☆	149	549	47	156	27	2	17	98	51	89	.284	.347	.434	781	119	13	1	3	-1	.986	-8	*C-143/1-4	1.1
1984	*SD-N	148	530	54	127	16	1	14	57	33	99	.240	.287	.353	640	79	-16	1	2	-0	.982	-14	*C-147	-2.6
1985	SD-N★	143	532	54	139	27	1	10	74	31	102	.261	.302	.372	674	89	-9	0	0	0	.986	0	*C-140/1-5	-0.3
1986	SD-N	141	432	46	114	22	1	12	57	37	74	.264	.325	.403	728	102	0	0	3	-1	.990	-0	*C-123	0.4
1987	Bal-A★	143	512	51	128	13	1	18	62	35	112	.250	.299	.385	684	82	-14	1	0	0	.993	-16	*C-142	-2.3
1988	Bal-A	85	265	20	60	10	0	3	16	15	53	.226	.270	.298	569	61	-14	0	0	0	.994	-8	*C-79	-1.8
1989	*SF-N	125	355	19	85	15	0	5	34	35	56	.239	.308	.324	632	83	-8	1	3	-1	.986	-3	*C-121/1-2	-0.6
1990	SF-N	107	303	25	84	22	0	2	26	31	38	.277	.344	.370	714	100	0	1	2	-0	.991	-12	*C-103	-0.8
1991	SF-N	69	171	12	40	7	1	3	13	11	31	.234	.284	.339	623	77	-6	0	0	0	.978	-3	C-58/1-2	-0.7
Total	14	1491	4979	474	1313	244	12	113	628	365	855	.264	.316	.386	702	97	-30	6	15	-4	.985	-100	*C-1378/O-28L,1-25	-7.6
■ ED KENNEDY Kennedy, William Edward b: 4/5/1861, Bellevue, Ky. d: 12/22/12, Cheyenne, Wyoming BR/TR, 5'7", 160 lbs. Deb: 5/17/1884																								
1884	Cin-U	13	48	6	10	1	1	0		1		.208	.224	.271	495	46	-5				.857	0	/3-8,S-4,O-1(0-0-1)	-0.4
■ JERRY KENNEY Kenney, Gerald T b: 6/30/45, St.Louis, Mo. BL/TR, 6'1", 170 lbs. Deb: 9/5/67 Career OF: (0-LF 31-CF 0-RF)																								
1967	NY-A	20	58	4	18	2	0	1	5	10	8	.310	.412	.397	808	145	4	2	1	0	.952	-4	S-18	0.2
1969	NY-A	130	447	49	115	14	2	2	34	48	36	.257	.331	.311	642	83	-9	25	14	1	.975	11	3-83,O-31C,S-10	0.3
1970	NY-A	140	404	46	78	10	7	4	35	52	44	.193	.285	.282	567	60	-22	20	6	2	.960	15	*3-135/2-2	-0.5
1971	NY-A	120	325	50	85	10	3	0	20	56	38	.262	.372	.311	682	101	3	9	8	-1	.953	11	*3-109/S-5,1-1	1.4
1972	NY-A	50	119	16	25	2	0	0	7	16	13	.210	.304	.227	531	62	-5	3	0	1	.969	5	S-45/3-1	0.5
1973	Cle-A	5	16	0	4	0	1	0	2	2	0	.250	.333	.375	708	97	-0	0	0	0	1.000	-2	/2-5	-0.1
Total	6	465	1369	165	325	38	13	7	103	184	139	.237	.329	.299	628	82	-29	59	29	3	.962	36	3-328/S-78,O-31C,21	1.8
■ JOHN KENNEY Kenney, John Deb: 5/2/1872																								
1872	Atl-n	5	19	0	0	0	0	0	1	0	1	.000	.000	.000	0	-85	-4	0	0	0	.692	-2	/2-3,O-3(2-0-1)	-0.5
■ JEFF KENT Kent, Jeffrey Franklin b: 3/7/68, Bellflower, Cal. BR/TR, 6'1", 185 lbs. Deb: 4/12/92																								
1992	Tor-A	65	192	36	46	13	1	8	35	20	47	.240	.330	.443	773	110	2	2	1	0	.915	-3	3-49,2-17/1-3	0.0
	NY-N	37	113	16	27	8	1	3	15	7	29	.239	.289	.407	696	97	-1	0	2	-1	.980	8	2-34/3-1,S-1	0.7
1993	NY-N	140	496	65	134	24	0	21	80	30	88	.270	.322	.446	768	104	2	4	4	-1	.969	-19	*2-127,3-12/S-2	-1.1
1994	NY-N	107	415	53	121	24	5	14	68	23	84	.292	.344	.475	818	112	6	1	4	-1	.976	0	*2-107	1.0
1995	NY-N	125	472	65	131	22	3	20	65	29	89	.278	.330	.464	794	110	5	3	3	-0	.984	-8	*2-122	0.3
1996	NY-N	89	335	45	97	20	1	9	39	21	56	.290	.333	.436	769	106	2	4	3	-1	.925	6	3-89	0.9
	*Cle-A	39	102	16	27	7	0	3	16	10	22	.265	.336	.422	758	90	-2	2	1	-0	.992	3	1-20/2-9,3-6,D-5	0.1
1997	*SF-N	155	580	90	145	38	2	29	121	48	133	.250	.321	.472	794	108	4	11	3	1	.979	11	*2-148,1-13	2.2
1998	SF-N	137	526	94	156	37	3	31	128	48	110	.297	.365	.555	920	146	34	9	4	1	.972	11	*2-134/1-1	4.9
1999	SF-N★	138	511	86	148	40	2	23	101	61	112	.290	.371	.511	882	129	22	13	6	1	.984	-8	*2-133/1-1	2.0
2000	*SF-N★	159	587	114	196	41	7	33	125	90	107	.334	.430	.596	1026	167	63	12	9	-1	.986	3	*2-150,1-16	6.6
Total	9	1191	4329	680	1228	274	25	194	793	387	877	.284	.352	.493	845	123	138	61	40	-1	.979	47	2-981,3-157/1-54,DS	17.6
■ DICK KENWORTHY Kenworthy, Richard Lee b: 4/1/41, Red Oak, Iowa BR/TR, 5'9", 170 lbs. Deb: 9/8/62																								
1962	Chi-A	3	4	0	0	0	0	0	0	0	3	.000	.000	.000	0	-99	-1	0	0	0	1.000	1	/2-2	0.0
1964	Chi-A	2	2	0	0	0	0	0	0	0	1	.000	.000	.000	0	-99	-1	0	0	0	.000	0	H	-0.1
1965	Chi-A	3	1	0	0	0	0	0	0	1	0	.000	.667	.000	667	113	0	0	0	0	.000	0	H	0.0
1966	Chi-A	9	25	1	5	0	0	0	0	0	0	.200	.200	.200	400	16	-3	0	0	0	.875	-3	/3-6	-0.6
1967	Chi-A	50	97	9	22	4	1	4	11	4	17	.227	.265	.412	677	101	-0	0	2	-1	.971	1	3-35	0.0
1968	Chi-A	58	122	2	27	2	0	0	2	5	21	.221	.252	.238	490	49	-8	0	1	-0	.938	4	3-38	-0.4
Total	6	125	251	12	54	6	1	4	13	10	42	.215	.251	.295	546	63	-12	0	3	-1	.948	4	/3-79,2-2	-1.1
■ BILL KENWORTHY Kenworthy, William Jennings "Duke" b: 7/4/1886, Cambridge, Ohio d: 9/21/50, Eureka, Cal. BR/TR, 5'7", 165 lbs. Deb: 8/28/12																								
1912	Was-A	12	38	6	9	1	0	0	2	2		.237	.293	.263	556	59	-2	3			1.000	-0	O-12(7-5-0)	-0.3
1914	KC-F	146	545	93	173	40	14	15	91	36	44	.317	.372	.525	896	148	25	37			.952	21	*2-145	**4.9**
1915	KC-F	122	396	59	118	30	7	3	52	28	32	.298	.355	.432	787	126	7	20			.936	-7	*2-108/O-7(0-0-7)	0.1
1917	StL-A	5	10	1	1	0	0	0	1	1	1	.100	.182	.100	282	-14	-1	1			.889	1	/2-4	-0.1
Total	4	285	989	159	301	71	21	18	146	67	77	.304	.360	.473	833	135	28	61			.945	14	2-257/O-19(7-5-7)	4.6
■ JOE KEOUGH Keough, Joseph William b: 1/7/46, Pomona, Cal. BL/TL, 6', 185 lbs. Deb: 8/7/68 F																								
1968	Oak-A	34	98	7	21	2	1	2	18	8	11	.214	.274	.316	590	82	-2	1	0	0	.962	1	O-29(28-0-1)/1-1	-0.3
1969	KC-A	70	166	17	31	2	0	0	7	13	13	.187	.254	.199	453	28	-16	5	2	0	1.000	-3	O-49(3-26-21)/1-1	-2.1
1970	KC-A	57	183	28	59	6	2	4	21	23	18	.322	.398	.443	841	132	8	1	1	-0	.985	2	O-34(18-1-15),1-18	0.7
1971	KC-A	110	351	34	87	14	2	3	30	35	26	.248	.318	.325	643	83	-8	0	6	-2	.982	-6	*O-100(1-7-93)	-2.2
1972	KC-A	56	64	8	14	2	0	0	5	8	7	.219	.324	.250	574	73	-2	2	0	0	1.000	-3	O-16(9-2-5)	-0.5
1973	Chi-A	5	1	1	0	0	0	0	0	0	0	.000	.000	.000	0	-97	-0	0	0	0	.000	0	H	0.0
Total	6	332	863	95	212	26	5	9	81	87	75	.246	.318	.319	637	82	-19	9	9	-1	.984	-9	O-228(59-36-135)/1-20	-4.4
■ MARTY KEOUGH Keough, Richard Martin b: 4/14/34, Oakland, Cal. BL/TL, 6', 180 lbs. Deb: 4/21/56 F Career OF: (127-LF 203-CF 148-RF)																								
1956	Bos-A	3	2	1	0	0	0	0	0	1	0	.000	.333	.000	333	-5	-0	0	0	0	.000	0	H	0.0
1957	Bos-A	9	17	1	1	0	0	0	0	4	3	.059	.238	.059	297	-14	-3	0	0	0	1.000	0	/O-7(0-2-5)	-0.3
1958	Bos-A	68	118	21	26	3	3	1	9	7	29	.220	.264	.322	586	57	-7	1	1	-0	.974	-5	O-25(1-21-3)/1-2	-1.4
1959	Bos-A	96	251	40	61	13	5	7	27	26	40	.243	.321	.418	740	97	-1	3	1	0	.993	-1	O-69(0-69-0)/1-3	-0.5
1960	Bos-A	38	105	15	26	6	1	1	9	8	8	.248	.301	.352	653	73	-4	2	2	-0	1.000	1	O-29(1-28-0)	-0.5
	Cle-A	65	149	19	37	5	0	3	11	9	23	.248	.296	.342	638	74	-6	2	3	-1	.986	-4	O-42(2-25-16)	-1.2
	Yr	103	254	34	63	11	1	4	20	17	31	.248	.298	.346	644	74	-10	4	5	-1	.992	-3	O-71(3-53-16)	-1.7
1961	Was-A	135	390	57	97	18	9	9	34	32	60	.249	.309	.410	719	92	-6	12	5	1	.978	2	*O-100(63-25-18),1-10	-0.8
1962	Cin-N	111	230	34	64	8	2	7	27	21	31	.278	.349	.422	771	102	1	3	1	0	.968	-5	O-71(48-17-10),1-29	-0.7
1963	Cin-N	95	172	21	39	8	2	6	21	25	37	.227	.338	.401	739	109	2	1	4	-1	.992	-3	1-46,O-28(4-3-22)	-0.5
1964	Cin-N	109	276	29	71	9	1	9	28	22	58	.257	.314	.395	709	95	-2	1	2	-0	.991	-6	O-81(1-11-71)/1-4	-1.3
1965	Cin-N	62	43	14	5	0	0	0	3	3	14	.116	.191	.116	308	-10	-6	0	0	0	.988	-1	1-32/O-4(3-0-1)	-0.7
1966	Atl-N	17	17	1	1	0	0	0	1	1	6	.059	.111	.059	170	-50	-3	0	0	0	1.000	-2	/1-4,O-3(2-0-1)	-0.6
	Chi-N	33	26	3	6	1	0	0	5	5	9	.231	.375	.269	644	82	-0	1	0	0	1.000	-2	/O-5(2-2-1)	-0.2
	Yr	50	43	4	7	1	0	0	6	6	15	.163	.280	.186	466	32	-4	1	0	0	.667	-3	/O-8(4-2-2),1-4	-0.8
Total	11	841	1796	256	434	71	23	43	176	164	318	.242	.311	.379	690	86	-35	26	19	-1	.984	-25	O-464C,1-130	-8.7
■ JOHN KERINS Kerins, John Nelson b: 7/15/1858, Indianapolis, Ind d: 9/8/19, Louisville, Ky. BR/TR, 5'10", 177 lbs. Deb: 5/1/1884 MU Career OF: (13-LF 9-CF 49-RF)																								
1884	Ind-a	94	364	58	78	10	3	6		6		.214	.229	.308	537	76	-10				**.972**	6	*1-87/C-5,O-5R,3-1	-1.1
1885	Lou-a	112	456	65	111	9	16	3	51	20		.243	.281	.353	634	100	-1				.947	3	*1-96,C-19/O-3R,3-1	-0.4
1886	Lou-a	120	487	113	131	19	9	4	50	66		.269	.360	.370	729	122	13	26			.933	**39**	C-65,1-47/O-7R,S-1	**4.6**
1887	Lou-a	112	514	101	178	18	**19**	5	57	38		.346	.349	.443	792	118	9	49			.970	25	1-74,C-35/O-5(1-1-3)	2.5
1888	Lou-a	83	319	38	75	11	4	2	41	25		.235	.297	.313	610	98	-0	16			.844	2	O-47R,C-33/1-4,32M	0.3
1889	Lou-a	2	9	2	3	1	0	0	3	0	1	.333	.333	.444	778	123	0	0			.500	-1	/O-2(0-0-2),C-1	-0.1

YEAR	TM/L	G	AB	R	H	2B	3B	HR	RBI	BB	SO	AVG	OBP	SLG	OPS	OPS+	BR+	SB	CS	SBR	FA	FR	G/POS	TPR
	Bal-a	16	53	7	15	2	0	0	12	2	4	.283	.321	.321	642	82	-1	2			.981	-2	/1-9,C-4,O-2C,S-1	-0.3
	Yr	18	62	9	18	3	0	0	15	2	5	.290	.323	.339	662	87	-1	2			.981	-2	/1-9,C-5,O-4C,S-1	-0.4
1890	StL-a	18	63	8	8	2	0	0	3	8		.127	.225	.159	384	12	-7	2			.968	1	1-17/C-1,M	-0.7
Total	7	557	2265	392	599	72	51	20	217	165	5	.264	.308	.357	665	102	3	95			.963	73	1-334,C-163/O3S2	4.8
■ ORIE KERLIN	Kerlin, Orie Milton "Cy" b: 1/23/1891, Summerfield, La. d: 10/29/74, Shreveport, La. BL/TR, 5'7", 149 lbs. Deb: 6/6/15																							
1915	Pit-F	3	1	0	0	0	0	0	0	0	0	.000	.000	.000	0	-99	-0	0			.000	-0	/C-3	0.0
■ BILL KERN	Kern, William George b: 2/28/33, Coplay, Pa. BR/TR, 6'2", 184 lbs. Deb: 9/19/62																							
1962	KC-A	8	16	1	4	0	0	1	1	0	3	.250	.250	.438	688	77	-1	0	0	0	1.000	1	/O-3(3-0-0)	0.0
■ JOE KERNAN	Kernan, Joseph b: Baltimore, Md. Deb: 4/14/1873																							
1873	Mar-n	2	8	1	3	0	0	0	1	0	0	.375	.375	.375	750	161	1	0	0	0	.700	1	/2-1,O-1(0-1-0)	0.1
■ GEORGE KERNEK	Kernek, George Boyd b: 1/12/40, Holdenville, Okla. BL/TL, 6'3", 170 lbs. Deb: 9/5/65																							
1965	StL-N	10	31	6	9	3	1	0	3	2	4	.290	.333	.452	785	109	0	0	0	0	.972	-0	/1-7	0.0
1966	StL-N	20	50	5	12	0	1	0	3	4	9	.240	.309	.280	589	65	-2	1	0	0	.984	-0	1-16	-0.3
Total	2	30	81	11	21	3	2	0	6	6	13	.259	.318	.346	664	82	-2	1	0	0	.980	-0	/1-23	-0.3
■ RUSS KERNS	Kerns, Russell Eldon b: 11/10/20, Fremont, Ohio d: 8/21/2000, Placerville, Cal. BL/TR, 6', 188 lbs. Deb: 8/18/45																							
1945	Det-A	1	1	0	0	0	0	0	0	0	0	.000	.000	.000	0	-94	-0	0	0	0	.000	0	H	0.0
■ JOHN KERR	Kerr, John Francis b: 11/26/1898, San Francisco, Cal. d: 10/19/93, Long Beach, Cal. BR/TR (BB 1923-24), 5'8", 158 lbs. Deb: 5/1/23																							
1923	Det-A	19	42	4	9	1	0	0	1	4	5	.214	.283	.238	521	39	-4	0	0	0	.877	4	S-15	0.2
1924	Det-A	17	11	3	3	0	0	0	1	0	0	.273	.273	.273	545	42	-1	0	0	0	.000	-0	/3-3,O-2	-0.1
1929	Chi-A	127	419	50	108	20	4	1	39	31	24	.258	.310	.332	642	66	-21	9	8	-1	.971	24	*2-122/S-1	0.5
1930	Chi-A	70	266	37	77	11	6	3	27	21	23	.289	.351	.410	760	95	-2	4	2	0	.980	0	2-52,S-20	0.2
1931	Chi-A	128	444	51	119	17	2	2	50	35	22	.268	.324	.329	653	77	-15	9	3	1	.968	8	*2-117/3-7,S-1	0.1
1932	Was-A	51	132	14	36	6	1	0	15	13	3	.273	.338	.333	671	75	-5	3	2	-0	.954	-1	2-17,S-14/3-8	-0.3
1933	*Was-A	28	40	5	8	0	0	0	0	3	2	.200	.256	.200	456	22	-4	0	0	0	.966	3	2-16/3-1	-0.1
1934	Was-A	31	103	8	28	4	0	0	12	8	13	.272	.324	.311	635	67	-5	1	1	-0	.971	10	3-17,2-13	0.5
Total	8	471	1457	172	388	59	13	6	145	115	92	.266	.323	.337	660	73	-56	26	16	0	.970	48	2-337/S-51,3-36,O-2	1.0
■ DOC KERR	Kerr, John Jonas b: 1/17/1882, Dellroy, Ohio d: 6/9/37, Baltimore, Md. BB/TR, 5'10.5", 190 lbs. Deb: 4/22/14																							
1914	Pit-F	42	71	3	17	4	2	1	7	10	13	.239	.333	.394	728	99	-1	0			.970	1	C-18	0.1
	Bal-F	14	34	4	9	1	1	0	1	1	6	.265	.286	.353	639	71	-2	1			.979	5	C-13/1-1	0.3
	Yr	56	105	7	26	5	3	1	8	11	19	.248	.319	.381	700	90	-3	1			.974	5	C-31/1-1	0.4
1915	Bal-F	3	6	1	2	0	0	0	0	1	0	.333	.429	.333	762	112	0	0			1.000	-1	/C-2,1-1	-0.1
Total	2	59	111	8	28	5	3	1	8	12	19	.252	.325	.378	704	91	-3	1			.975	4	/C-33,1-2	0.3
■ BUDDY KERR	Kerr, John Joseph b: 11/6/22, Astoria, N.Y. BR/TR, 6'2", 180 lbs. Deb: 9/8/43																							
1943	NY-N	27	98	14	28	3	0	2	12	8	5	.286	.352	.378	729	110	1	1			.955	5	S-27	0.8
1944	NY-N	150	548	68	146	31	4	9	63	37	32	.266	.316	.387	703	97	-3	14			.954	**17**	*S-149	2.6
1945	NY-N	149	546	53	136	20	3	4	40	41	34	.249	.304	.319	623	72	-21	5			.964	**28**	*S-148	1.9
1946	NY-N	145	497	50	124	20	3	6	40	53	31	.249	.324	.338	662	87	-8	7			**.982**	6	*S-126,3-18	0.7
1947	NY-N	138	547	73	157	23	5	7	49	36	49	.287	.331	.386	717	89	-9	2			.977	12	*S-138	1.1
1948	NY-N★	144	496	41	119	16	4	0	46	56	36	.240	.317	.288	605	64	-23	9			.967	3	*S-143	-1.1
1949	NY-N	90	220	16	46	4	0	0	19	21	23	.209	.284	.227	511	39	-19	0			.959	6	S-89	-0.9
1950	Bos-N	155	507	45	115	24	6	2	46	50	50	.227	.296	.310	606	64	-27	0			.965	2	*S-155	-1.5
1951	Bos-N	69	172	18	32	4	0	1	18	22	20	.186	.282	.227	509	41	-14	0	0	0	.969	13	S-63/2-5	0.3
Total	9	1067	3631	378	903	145	25	31	333	324	280	.249	.312	.328	640	76	-123	38	0		.967	92	*S-1038/3-18,2-5	3.9
■ MEL KERR	Kerr, John Melville b: 5/22/03, Souris, Man., Can. d: 8/9/80, Vero Beach, Fla. BL/TL, 5'11.5", 155 lbs. Deb: 9/16/25 C																							
1925	Chi-N	1	0	1	0	0	0	0	0	0	0	—	—	—	—	—	0	0	0	0	.000	0	R	0.0
■ DAN KERWIN	Kerwin, Daniel Patrick (b: Daniel Patrick Kervin) b: 7/9/1879, Philadelphia, Pa. d: 7/13/60, Philadelphia, Pa. BL/TL, 5'9", 164 lbs. Deb: 9/27/03																							
1903	Cin-N	2	6	1	4	1	0	0	1	2		.667	.778	.833	1611	323	2	0			.500	-1	/O-2(2-0-0)	0.1
■ DON KESSINGER	Kessinger, Donald Eulon b: 7/17/42, Forrest City, Ark. BB/TR (BR 1964-65), 6'1", 175 lbs. Deb: 9/7/64 FM																							
1964	Chi-N	4	12	1	2	0	0	0	0	0	1	.167	.167	.167	333	-6	-2	0	0	0	1.000	-1	/S-4	-0.3
1965	Chi-N	106	309	19	62	4	3	0	14	20	44	.201	.254	.233	487	37	-25	1	2	-0	.948	21	*S-105	0.3
1966	Chi-N	150	533	50	146	8	2	1	43	26	46	.274	.308	.302	610	70	-21	13	7	0	.951	-10	*S-148	-1.9
1967	Chi-N	145	580	61	134	10	7	0	42	33	80	.231	.277	.272	550	55	-33	6	13	-3	.973	-3	*S-143	-3.0
1968	Chi-N★	160	655	63	157	14	7	1	32	38	86	.240	.283	.287	570	67	-25	9	9	-1	.962	18	*S-159	0.6
1969	Chi-N★	158	664	109	181	38	6	4	53	61	70	.273	.335	.366	701	85	-12	11	8	-0	**.976**	25	*S-157	3.3
1970	Chi-N★	154	631	100	168	21	14	1	39	66	59	.266	.338	.349	686	75	-21	12	6	1	.972	9	*S-154	0.8
1971	Chi-N★	155	617	77	159	18	6	2	38	52	54	.258	.318	.316	634	70	-22	15	8	1	.966	4	*S-154	0.1
1972	Chi-N★	149	577	77	158	20	6	1	39	67	44	.274	.351	.334	686	87	-8	8	7	-1	.965	8	*S-146	1.9
1973	Chi-N	160	577	52	151	22	3	0	43	57	44	.262	.328	.310	638	72	-20	6	6	-1	.964	17	*S-158	1.6
1974	Chi-N★	153	599	83	155	20	7	1	42	62	54	.259	.332	.321	653	80	-15	7	7	-1	.958	2	*S-150	0.4
1975	Chi-N	154	601	77	146	26	10	0	46	68	47	.243	.321	.319	640	75	-19	4	7	-2	.967	-2	*S-140,3-13	-0.7
1976	StL-N	145	502	55	120	22	6	1	40	61	51	.239	.323	.313	635	80	-12	3	0	1	.969	-4	*S-113,2-31/3-2	0.0
1977	StL-N	59	134	14	32	4	0	0	7	14	26	.239	.311	.269	579	58	-8	0	0	0	.978	2	S-26,2-24/3-4	-0.3
	Chi-A	39	119	12	28	3	2	0	11	13	7	.235	.311	.294	605	66	-5	2	1	0	.959	-4	S-21,2-13/3-9	-0.7
1978	Chi-A	131	431	35	110	18	1	1	31	36	34	.255	.313	.309	621	75	-14	2	4	-1	.974	-19	*S-123/2-9	-2.2
1979	Chi-A	56	110	14	22	6	0	1	7	10	12	.200	.267	.282	548	48	-8	1	0	0	.988	-1	S-54/1-1,2-1,M	-0.5
Total	16	2078	7651	899	1931	254	80	14	527	684	759	.252	.316	.312	628	72	-268	100	85	-8	.966	61	*S-1955/2-78,3-28,1	-0.6
■ KEITH KESSINGER	Kessinger, Robert Keith b: 2/19/67, Forrest City, Ark. BB/TR, 6'2", 185 lbs. Deb: 9/15/93 F																							
1993	Cin-N	11	27	4	7	1	0	1	3	4	4	.259	.355	.407	762	103	0	0	0	0	.935	-1	S-11	0.0
■ HENRY KESSLER	Kessler, Henry "Lucky" b: 1847, Brooklyn, N.Y. d: 1/9/1900, Franklin, Pa. BR/TR, 5'10", 144 lbs. Deb: 8/4/1873 NA OF: (2-LF 6-CF 3-RF) Career OF: (0-LF 2-CF 14-RF)																							
1873	Atl-n	1	5	0	1	0	0	0	1	0	0	.200	.200	.200	400	21	-0	0	0	0	.882	0	/1-1	0.0
1874	Atl-n	14	56	8	17	1	0	0	4	0	2	.304	.304	.321	625	114	1	0	0	0	.737	-3	/C-9,2-4,O-4L,3-1	-0.1
1875	Atl-n	25	105	17	26	2	0	0	7	1	2	.248	.255	.267	521	93	0	0	2	-1	.794	-1	S-18/O-7C,C-3,12	-0.1
1876	Cin-N	59	255	26	64	5	0	0	11	7	10	.251	.278	.278	557	100	2				.788	-8	S-46,O-16(0-2-14)	-0.4
1877	Cin-N	6	20	0	2	0	0	0	0	2	1	.100	.182	.100	282	-10	-2				.500	-5	/C-5,1-1	-0.7
Total	3 n	40	166	25	44	3	0	0	12	1	4	.265	.269	.283	553	98	1	0	2	-1	.739	-4	/S-18,C-12,O-11C,213	-0.2
Total	2	65	275	26	66	5	0	0	11	9	11	.240	.271	.265	536	91	0				.788	-14	/S-46,O-16R,C-5,1-1	-1.1
■ FRED KETCHUM	Ketchum, Frederick L. b: 7/27/1875, Elmira, N.Y. d: 3/12/08, Cortland, N.Y. BL/TR, 5'8", 157 lbs. Deb: 9/12/1899																							
1899	Lou-N	15	61	13	18	1	0	0	5	0		.295	.306	.311	618	70	-3	2			1.000	-4	O-15(4-1-10)	-0.7
1901	Phi-A	5	22	5	5	0	0	0	2	0		.227	.227	.227	455	25	-2	0			.875	-1	/O-5(5-0-0)	-0.3
Total	2	20	83	18	23	1	0	0	7	0		.277	.286	.289	575	58	-5	2			.960	-5	/O-20(9-1-10)	-1.0
■ PHIL KETTER	Ketter, Philip (b: Philip Ketterer) b: 4/13/1884, St.Louis, Mo. d: 4/9/65, St.Louis, Mo. TR, Deb: 5/23/12																							
1912	StL-A	2	6	1	2	0	0	0	0	0		.333	.333	.333	667	94	-0	0			1.000	-1	/C-2	-0.1
■ SAM KHALIFA	Khalifa, Sam b: 12/5/63, Fontana, Cal. BR/TR, 5'11", 170 lbs. Deb: 6/25/85																							
1985	Pit-N	95	320	30	76	14	3	2	31	34	56	.237	.311	.319	629	77	-9	5	2	0	.967	13	S-95	1.4
1986	Pit-N	64	151	8	28	6	0	0	4	19	28	.185	.276	.225	502	39	-12	0	2	-1	.961	14	S-60/2-6	0.6

YEAR	TM/L	G	AB	R	H	2B	3B	HR	RBI	BB	SO	AVG	OBP	SLG	OPS	OPS+	BR+	SB	CS	SBR	FA	FR	G/POS	TPR
1987	Pit-N	5	17	1	3	0	0	0	2	0	2	.176	.176	.176	353	-6	-3	0	0	0	.917	-5	/S-5	-0.7
Total	3	164	488	39	107	20	3	2	37	53	86	.219	.296	.285	581	62	-24	5	4	-0	.964	22	S-160/2-6	1.3

■ HOD KIBBIE
Kibbie, Horace Kent b: 7/18/03, Ft.Worth, Tex. d: 10/19/75, Ft.Worth, Tex. BR/TR, 5'10", 150 lbs. Deb: 6/13/25

YEAR	TM/L	G	AB	R	H	2B	3B	HR	RBI	BB	SO	AVG	OBP	SLG	OPS	OPS+	BR+	SB	CS	SBR	FA	FR	G/POS	TPR
1925	Bos-N	11	41	5	11	2	0	0	2	5	6	.268	.348	.317	665	78	-1	0	0	0	.904	-0	/2-8,S-3	-0.1

■ JACK KIBBLE
Kibble, John Westly "Happy" b: 1/2/1892, Seatonville, Ill. d: 12/13/69, Roundup, Mont. BB/TR, 5'9.5", 154 lbs. Deb: 9/10/12

YEAR	TM/L	G	AB	R	H	2B	3B	HR	RBI	BB	SO	AVG	OBP	SLG	OPS	OPS+	BR+	SB	CS	SBR	FA	FR	G/POS	TPR
1912	Cle-A	5	8	1	0	0	0	0	0	0		.000	.111	.000	111	-65	-2	0			1.000	4	/3-4,2-1	0.2

■ STEVE KIEFER
Kiefer, Steven George b: 10/18/60, Chicago, Ill. BR/TR, 6'1", 180 lbs. Deb: 9/3/84 F

YEAR	TM/L	G	AB	R	H	2B	3B	HR	RBI	BB	SO	AVG	OBP	SLG	OPS	OPS+	BR+	SB	CS	SBR	FA	FR	G/POS	TPR
1984	Oak-A	23	40	7	7	1	2	0	2	2	10	.175	.214	.300	514	43	-3	2	1	0	.904	1	S-17/3-2,D-3	-0.2
1985	Oak-A	40	66	8	13	1	1	1	10	1	18	.197	.209	.288	497	37	-6	0	0	0	.881	3	3-34/D-2	-0.3
1986	Mil-A	2	6	0	0	0	0	0	0	0	4	.000	.000	.000	0	-97	-2	0	0	0	1.000	3	/S-2	0.1
1987	Mil-A	28	99	17	20	4	0	5	17	7	28	.202	.262	.394	656	69	-5	0	0	0	.966	-3	3-26/2-4	-0.7
1988	Mil-A	7	10	2	3	1	0	1	1	2	3	.300	.462	.700	1162	219	2	0	0	0	1.000	-1	/2-4,3-4	0.1
1989	NY-A	5	8	0	1	0	0	0	0	0	5	.125	.125	.125	250	-30	-1	0	0	0	1.000	-1	/3-5	-0.3
Total	6	105	229	34	44	7	3	7	30	12	68	.192	.239	.341	579	56	-15	2	1	0	.920	1	/3-71,S-19,2-8,D-5	-1.3

■ BILL KIENZLE
Kienzle, William H. b: Philadelphia, Pa. BL/TL, Deb: 9/15/1882

YEAR	TM/L	G	AB	R	H	2B	3B	HR	RBI	BB	SO	AVG	OBP	SLG	OPS	OPS+	BR+	SB	CS	SBR	FA	FR	G/POS	TPR
1882	Phi-a	9	33	8	11	3	2	0	9	5		.333	.421	.545	967	200	3				.842	-1	/O-9(0-9-0)	0.2
1884	Phi-U	67	299	76	76	13	8	0		21		.254	.303	.351	654	106	-6				.772	-2	O-67(0-67-0)	-0.9
Total	2	76	332	84	87	16	10	0	9	26		.262	.316	.370	686	116	-3				.781	-3	/O-76(0-76-0)	-0.7

■ BROOKS KIESCHNICK
Kieschnick, Michael Brooks b: 6/6/72, Robstown, Tex. BL/TR, 6'4", 225 lbs. Deb: 4/3/96

YEAR	TM/L	G	AB	R	H	2B	3B	HR	RBI	BB	SO	AVG	OBP	SLG	OPS	OPS+	BR+	SB	CS	SBR	FA	FR	G/POS	TPR
1996	Chi-N	25	29	6	10	2	0	1	6	3	8	.345	.406	.517	923	138	2	0	0	0	.833	-3	/O-8(4-0-5)	-0.1
1997	Chi-N	39	90	9	18	2	0	4	12	12	21	.200	.294	.356	650	67	-4	1	0	0	.952	-1	O-27(26-0-1)	-0.6
2000	Cin-N	14	12	0	0	0	0	0	0	1	5	.000	.077	.000	77	-75	-3	0	0	0	1.000	0	/1-1	-0.3
Total	3	78	131	15	28	4	0	5	18	16	34	.214	.299	.359	658	69	-6	1	0	0	.938	-4	/O-35(30-0-6),1-1	-1.0

■ PETE KILDUFF
Kilduff, Peter John b: 4/4/1893, Weir City, Kan. d: 2/14/30, Pittsburg, Kan. BR/TR, 5'7", 155 lbs. Deb: 4/18/17

YEAR	TM/L	G	AB	R	H	2B	3B	HR	RBI	BB	SO	AVG	OBP	SLG	OPS	OPS+	BR+	SB	CS	SBR	FA	FR	G/POS	TPR
1917	NY-N	31	78	12	16	3	0	1	12	4	11	.205	.253	.282	535	66	-3	2			.954	-2	2-21/S-5,3-1	-0.5
	Chi-N	56	202	23	56	9	5	0	15	12	19	.277	.324	.371	695	105	1	11			.920	-14	S-51/2-5	-1.1
	Yr	87	280	35	72	12	5	1	27	16	30	.257	.304	.346	651	95	-2	13			.917	-16	S-56,2-26/3-1	-1.6
1918	Chi-N	30	93	7	19	2	2	0	13	7	7	.204	.267	.269	536	62	-4	1			.935	-3	2-30	-0.8
1919	Chi-N	31	88	5	24	4	2	0	8	10	5	.273	.360	.364	724	117	2	1			.974	-4	3-14/2-8,S-7	-0.1
	Bro-N	32	73	9	22	3	1	0	8	12	11	.301	.407	.370	777	132	4	5			.862	-4	3-26/2-1	0.0
	Yr	63	161	14	46	7	3	0	16	22	16	.286	.382	.366	748	124	6	6			.903	-8	3-40/2-9,S-7	-0.1
1920	*Bro-N	141	478	62	130	26	8	0	58	58	43	.272	.351	.360	711	101	2	2	9	-3	.967	8	*2-134/3-5	1.0
1921	Bro-N	107	372	45	107	15	10	3	45	31	36	.288	.344	.406	750	94	-3	6	6	-1	.963	13	*2-105/3-1	1.2
Total	5	428	1384	163	374	62	28	4	159	134	132	.270	.338	.364	702	98	-1	28	15		.963	-7	2-304/S-63,3-47	-0.3

■ JOHN KILEY
Kiley, John Frederick b: 7/1/1859, Dedham, Mass. d: 12/18/40, Norwood, Mass. BL/TL, 5'7", 147 lbs. Deb: 5/1/1884

YEAR	TM/L	G	AB	R	H	2B	3B	HR	RBI	BB	SO	AVG	OBP	SLG	OPS	OPS+	BR+	SB	CS	SBR	FA	FR	G/POS	TPR
1884	Was-a	14	56	9	12	2	2	0		3		.214	.267	.321	588	103	1				.571	-4	O-14(13-1-1)	-0.3
1891	Bos-N	1	2	0	0	0	0	0	0	1	1	.000	.500	.000	500	45	0	0			1.000	0	/P-1	0.0
Total	2	15	58	9	12	2	2	0	0	4	1	.207	.281	.310	592	102	1	0			.571	-4	/O-14(13-1-1),P-1	-0.3

■ PAT KILHULLEN
Kilhullen, Joseph Isadore b: 8/10/1890, Carbondale, Pa. d: 11/2/22, Oakland, Cal. BR/TR, 5'9", 175 lbs. Deb: 6/10/14

YEAR	TM/L	G	AB	R	H	2B	3B	HR	RBI	BB	SO	AVG	OBP	SLG	OPS	OPS+	BR+	SB	CS	SBR	FA	FR	G/POS	TPR
1914	Pit-N	1	1	0	0	0	0	0	0	0	0	.000	.000	.000	0	-99	-0	0			.000	0	/C-1	0.0

■ HARMON KILLEBREW
Killebrew, Harmon Clayton "Killer" b: 6/29/36, Payette, Idaho BR/TR, 5'11", 213 lbs. Deb: 6/23/54 H Career OF: (470-LF 0-CF 1-RF)

YEAR	TM/L	G	AB	R	H	2B	3B	HR	RBI	BB	SO	AVG	OBP	SLG	OPS	OPS+	BR+	SB	CS	SBR	FA	FR	G/POS	TPR
1954	Was-A	9	13	1	4	1	0	0	3	2	3	.308	.400	.385	785	122	0	0	0	0	1.000	-2	/2-3	-0.2
1955	Was-A	38	80	12	16	1	0	4	7	9	31	.200	.281	.363	643	76	-3	0	0	0	.935	5	3-23/2-3	0.2
1956	Was-A	44	99	10	22	2	0	5	13	10	39	.222	.294	.394	688	80	-3	0	0	0	.951	-0	3-20/2-4	-0.3
1957	Was-A	9	31	4	9	2	0	2	5	2	8	.290	.333	.548	882	139	1	0	0	0	.947	-1	/3-7,2-1	0.0
1958	Was-A	13	31	2	6	0	0	0	2	0	12	.194	.219	.194	412	15	-4	0	0	0	1.000	0	/3-9	-0.4
1959	Was-A★	153	546	98	132	20	2	**42**	105	90	116	.242	.356	.516	873	137	28	3	2	-0	.938	-8	*3-150/O-4(4-0-0)	1.9
1960	Was-A	124	442	84	122	19	1	31	80	71	106	.276	.377	.534	911	145	28	1	0	0	.987	-9	1-71,3-65	1.5
1961	Min-A★	150	541	94	156	20	7	46	122	107	109	.288	.409	.606	1015	159	46	1	2	-0	.987	-10	*1-119,3-45/O-2L	2.8
1962	Min-A	155	552	85	134	21	1	**48**	**126**	106	142	.243	.369	.545	914	137	29	1	2	-0	.967	-10	*O-151(151-0-0)/1-4	1.0
1963	Min-A★	142	515	88	133	18	0	**45**	96	72	105	.258	.353	**.555**	908	147	32	0	0	0	.987	-3	*O-137(137-0-0)	2.1
1964	Min-A★	158	577	95	156	11	1	**49**	111	93	135	.270	.379	.548	927	153	42	0	0	0	.971	-7	*O-157(157-0-1)	2.8
1965	*Min-A★	113	401	78	108	16	1	25	75	72	69	.269	.386	.501	887	144	25	0	0	0	.988	-9	1-72,3-44/O-1(1-0-0)	1.2
1966	Min-A★	162	569	89	160	27	1	39	110	**103**	98	.281	.393	.538	931	155	43	0	2	-1	.951	-17	*3-107,1-42,O-18L	2.3
1967	Min-A★	163	547	105	147	24	1	**44**	113	**131**	111	.269	.413	.558	970	170	53	1	0	0	.992	-8	*1-160/3-3	3.8
1968	Min-A★	100	295	40	62	7	2	17	40	70	70	.210	.365	.420	785	131	13	0	0	0	.994	3	1-77,3-11	1.4
1969	*Min-A★	162	555	106	153	20	2	**49**	**140**	**145**	84	.276	**.430**	.584	1014	177	63	8	2	1	.929	-21	*3-105,1-80	3.8
1970	*Min-A★	157	527	96	143	20	1	41	113	128	84	.271	.416	.546	962	161	48	0	3	-1	.948	-29	*3-138,1-28	1.6
1971	Min-A★	147	500	61	127	19	1	28	**119**	**114**	96	.254	.393	.464	857	137	28	3	2	-0	.997	-15	1-90,3-64	0.6
1972	Min-A	139	433	53	100	13	2	26	74	94	91	.231	.369	.450	820	136	22	0	1	-0	.992	11	*1-130	2.6
1973	Min-A	69	248	29	60	9	1	5	32	41	59	.242	.352	.347	698	94	-1	0	0	0	.998	4	1-57/D-9	-0.1
1974	Min-A	122	333	28	74	7	0	13	54	45	61	.222	.315	.360	675	91	-4	0	0	0	.992	2	D-57,1-33	-0.6
1975	KC-A	106	312	25	62	13	0	14	44	54	70	.199	.319	.375	694	93	-3	1	2	-0	1.000	-1	D-92/1-6	-0.7
Total	22	2435	8147	1283	2086	290	24	573	1584	1559	1699	.256	.379	.509	887	142	484	19	18	-2	.992	-123	1-969,3-791,OD/2	27.3

■ RED KILLEFER
Killefer, Wade Hampton b: 4/13/1885, Bloomingdale, Mich
d: 9/4/58, Los Angeles, Cal. BR/TR, 5'9", 175 lbs. Deb: 9/16/07 F Career OF: (135-LF 135-CF 27-RF)

YEAR	TM/L	G	AB	R	H	2B	3B	HR	RBI	BB	SO	AVG	OBP	SLG	OPS	OPS+	BR+	SB	CS	SBR	FA	FR	G/POS	TPR
1907	Det-A	1	4	0	0	0	0	0	0	0		.000	.000	.000	0	-97	-1	0			1.000	0	/O-1(0-0-1)	-0.1
1908	Det-A	28	75	9	16	1	0	0	11	3		.213	.253	.227	480	54	-4	4			.956	-5	2-16/S-7,3-4	-1.0
1909	Det-A	23	61	6	17	2	2	1	4	3		.279	.343	.426	770	137	2	2			.912	-1	2-17/O-1(0-0-1)	0.1
	Was-A	40	121	11	21	1	0	0	5	13		.174	.265	.182	447	43	-7	4			.957	-3	O-24C/3-6,C-3,2S	-1.2
	Yr	63	182	17	38	3	2	1	9	16		.209	.291	.264	554	76	-4	6			.957	-4	O-25C,2-20/3-6,CS	-1.1
1910	Was-A	106	345	35	79	17	1	0	24	29		.229	.318	.284	602	93	-1	17			.940	-5	2-88,O-12(6-0-6)	-0.7
1914	Cin-N	42	141	16	39	6	1	0	12	20	18	.277	.386	.333	719	111	3	11			.968	-4	O-37(1-18-18)/2-5,3-1	-0.4
1915	Cin-N	155	555	75	151	25	11	1	41	38	33	.272	.340	.362	702	110	8	12	18	-4	.970	5	*O-150(79-73-0)/1-2	0.0
1916	Cin-N	70	234	29	57	9	1	1	18	21	8	.244	.327	.303	630	96	-0	7			.966	-2	O-68(43-27-0)	-0.6
	NY-N	2	1	0	1	0	0	0	1	1	0	1.000	1.000	1.000	2000	544	1	0			.000	0	H	0.1
	Yr	72	235	29	58	9	1	1	19	22	8	.247	.332	.306	638	99	1	7			.966	-2	O-68(43-27-0)	-0.5
Total	7	467	1537	181	381	61	16	3	116	128	59	.248	.328	.314	642	98	1	57	18		.965	-15	O-293L,2-129/3SC1	-3.8

■ BILL KILLEFER
Killefer, William Lavier "Reindeer Bill"
b: 10/10/1887, Bloomingdale, Mich d: 7/3/60, Elsmere, Del. BR/TR, 5'10.5", 200 lbs. Deb: 9/13/09 FMC Career OF: (1-LF 0-CF 0-RF)

YEAR	TM/L	G	AB	R	H	2B	3B	HR	RBI	BB	SO	AVG	OBP	SLG	OPS	OPS+	BR+	SB	CS	SBR	FA	FR	G/POS	TPR
1909	StL-A	11	29	0	4	0	0	0	1	0		.138	.138	.138	276	-14	-4	2			.905	2	C-11	-0.1
1910	StL-A	74	193	14	24	2	2	0	7	12		.124	.184	.155	339	7	-21	0			.938	12	C-73	-0.3
1911	Phi-N	6	16	3	3	0	0	0	2	0	2	.188	.188	.188	375	5	-2	0			.975	2	/C-6	0.0
1912	Phi-N	85	268	18	60	6	3	1	21	4	14	.224	.241	.280	521	40	-23	6			.973	17	C-85	0.2
1913	Phi-N	120	360	25	88	14	3	0	24	4	17	.244	.255	.300	555	56	-21	2			.988	13	*C-118/1-1	0.1
1914	Phi-N	98	299	27	70	10	1	0	27	8	17	.234	.261	.274	536	56	-17	3			.978	18	C-90	0.9
1915	*Phi-N	105	320	26	76	9	2	0	24	18	14	.237	.287	.278	565	70	-11	5	3	0	.972	14	*C-104	1.2
1916	Phi-N	97	286	22	62	5	4	3	27	8	14	.217	.246	.294	539	63	-13	2			**.985**	-1	C-91	-0.7
1917	Phi-N	125	409	28	112	12	0	0	31	15	21	.274	.306	.303	609	84	-8	4			**.984**	10	*C-120/O-1(1-0-0)	1.4
1918	*Chi-N	104	331	30	77	10	3	0	22	17	10	.233	.276	.281	557	68	-13	5			.982	9	*C-104	0.6
1919	Chi-N	103	315	17	90	10	2	0	22	15	8	.286	.322	.330	652	96	-2	5			**.987**	17	*C-100	2.7

YEAR	TM/L	G	AB	R	H	2B	3B	HR	RBI	BB	SO	AVG	OBP	SLG	OPS	OPS+	BR+	SB	CS	SBR	FA	FR	G/POS	TPR
1920	Chi-N	62	191	16	42	7	1	0	16	8	5	.220	.280	.267	547	56	-10	2	2	-0	.977	18	C-61	1.3
1921	Chi-N	45	133	11	43	1	0	0	16	4	4	.323	.357	.331	688	83	-3	3	3	-0	.964	-1	C-42,M	-0.2
Total	13	1035	3150	237	751	86	21	4	240	113	126	.238	.273	.283	555	63	-147	39	8		.976	131	*C-1005/O-1L,1-1	7.1
■ GENE KIMBALL Kimball, Eugene Boynton b: 8/31/1850, Rochester, N.Y. d: 8/2/1882, Rochester, N.Y. 5'10", 160 lbs. Deb: 5/4/1871																								
1871	Cle-n	29	131	18	25	1	0	0	9	3	2	.191	.209	.198	407	19	-12	5	1	1	.743	-7	2-17/O-9R,S-6,3-2	-1.3
■ DICK KIMBLE Kimble, Richard Lewis b: 7/27/15, Buchtel, Ohio BL/TR, 5'9", 160 lbs. Deb: 8/20/45																								
1945	Was-A	20	49	5	12	1	1	0	1	5	2	.245	.315	.306	621	88	-1	0	0	0	.950	-3	S-15	-0.3
■ BRUCE KIMM Kimm, Bruce Edward b: 6/29/51, Cedar Rapids, Iowa BR/TR, 5'11", 175 lbs. Deb: 5/4/76 C																								
1976	Det-A	63	152	13	40	8	0	1	6	15	20	.263	.329	.336	665	91	-1	4	3	-0	.970	4	C-61/D-2	0.5
1977	Det-A	14	25	2	2	1	0	0	1	0	4	.080	.115	.120	235	-34	-5	0	1	-0	.958	3	C-12/D-2	-0.2
1979	Chi-N	9	11	0	1	0	0	0	0	0	0	.091	.091	.091	182	-46	-2	0	1	-0	.969	2	/C-9	0.0
1980	Chi-A	100	251	20	61	10	1	0	19	17	26	.243	.291	.291	582	60	-13	1	3	-1	.985	-1	C-98	-1.2
Total	4	186	439	35	104	19	1	1	26	32	50	.237	.290	.292	582	62	-22	5	8	-2	.977	8	C-180/D-4	-0.9
■ WALLY KIMMICK Kimmick, Walter Lyons b: 5/30/1897, Turtle Creek, Pa. d: 7/24/89, Boswell, Pa. BR/TR, 5'11", 174 lbs. Deb: 9/13/19																								
1919	StL-N	2	1	0	0	0	0	0	0	1	0	.000	.500	.000	500	61	0	1			1.000	0	/S-1	0.0
1921	Cin-N	3	6	0	1	0	0	0	1	0	1	.167	.167	.167	333	-12	-1	0	0	0	.667	-0	/3-2	-0.1
1922	Cin-N	39	89	11	22	2	1	0	12	3	12	.247	.272	.292	564	46	-7	0	0	0	.965	2	S-30/2-3,3-1	-0.3
1923	Cin-N	29	80	11	18	2	1	0	6	5	15	.225	.271	.275	546	45	-6	3	0	0	.972	8	2-17/3-4,S-1	0.3
1925	Phi-N	70	141	16	43	3	2	1	10	22	26	.305	.399	.376	775	91	-1	0	3	-1	.904	-3	S-28,3-21,2-13	-0.2
1926	Phi-N	20	28	0	6	2	1	0	2	3	7	.214	.290	.357	647	70	-1	0	0	0	1.000	-2	/1-5,S-4,3-4,2-1	-0.3
Total	6	163	345	39	90	9	5	1	31	34	61	.261	.327	.325	652	67	-17	4	3		.933	4	/S-64,2-34,3-32,1-5	-0.6
■ JERRY KINDALL Kindall, Gerald Donald "Slim" b: 5/27/35, St.Paul, Minn. BR/TR (BB 1960 (part)), 6'2.5", 175 lbs. Deb: 7/1/56																								
1956	Chi-N	32	55	7	9	1	1	0	0	6	17	.164	.246	.218	464	27	-6	1	0	0	.956	2	S-18	-0.2
1957	Chi-N	72	181	18	29	3	0	6	12	8	48	.160	.196	.276	472	25	-19	1	0	0	.920	-4	2-28,3-19/S-9	-2.2
1958	Chi-N	3	6	0	1	1	0	0	0	0	3	.167	.167	.333	500	29	-1	0	0	0	1.000	1	/2-3	0.1
1960	Chi-N	89	246	17	59	16	2	2	23	5	52	.240	.255	.346	601	63	-13	4	3	-0	.966	14	2-82/S-2	0.6
1961	Chi-N	96	310	37	75	22	3	9	44	18	89	.242	.288	.419	707	84	-8	2	2	-0	.950	7	2-50,S-47	0.5
1962	Cle-A	154	530	51	123	21	1	13	55	45	107	.232	.292	.349	641	74	-20	4	3	-0	.978	21	*2-154	1.4
1963	Cle-A	86	234	27	48	4	1	5	20	18	71	.205	.268	.295	563	58	-13	3	1	0	.958	3	S-46,2-37/1-4	-0.5
1964	Cle-A	23	25	5	9	1	0	2	2	2	7	.360	.407	.640	1047	188	3	0	0	0	.989	3	1-23	0.5
	Min-A	62	128	8	19	2	0	1	6	7	44	.148	.199	.188	386	8	-16	0	0	0	.969	5	2-51/S-7,1-1	-0.8
	Yr	85	153	13	28	3	0	3	8	9	51	.183	.233	.261	495	37	-13	0	0	0	.969	8	2-51,1-24/S-7	-0.3
1965	Min-A	125	342	41	67	12	1	6	36	36	97	.196	.278	.289	568	59	-18	2	2	-0	.963	-1	*2-106,3-10/S-7	-1.1
Total	9	742	2057	211	439	83	9	44	198	145	535	.213	.268	.327	595	62	-111	17	11	-0	.967	50	2-511,S-136/3-29,1	-1.7
■ RALPH KINER Kiner, Ralph McPherran b: 10/27/22, Santa Rita, N.Mex. BR/TR, 6'2", 195 lbs. Deb: 4/16/46 H Career OF: (1306-LF 76-CF 0-RF)																								
1946	Pit-N	144	502	63	124	17	3	**23**	81	74	109	.247	.345	.430	775	116	10	3			.969	1	*O-140(64-76-0)	0.5
1947	Pit-N	152	565	118	177	23	4	**51**	127	98	81	.313	.417	**.639**	**1055**	**172**	**58**	1			.983	13	*O-152(152-0-0)	**5.7**
1948	Pit-N★	156	555	104	147	19	5	**40**	123	112	61	.265	.391	.533	924	145	36	1			.975	7	*O-154(154-0-0)	3.1
1949	Pit-N★	152	549	116	170	19	5	**54**	**127**	**117**	61	.310	.432	**.658**	**1089**	**183**	**66**	6			.979	-1	*O-152(152-0-0)	**5.2**
1950	Pit-N★	150	547	112	149	21	6	**47**	118	122	79	.272	.408	.590	998	154	45	2			.965	-3	*O-150(150-0-0)	2.9
1951	Pit-N★	151	531	**124**	164	31	6	**42**	109	**137**	57	.309	**.452**	**.627**	**1079**	182	67	2	1	0	.967	-5	O-94(94-0-0),1-58	5.1
1952	Pit-N☆	149	516	90	126	17	2	**37**	87	**110**	77	.244	.384	.500	884	140	30	3	0	1	.970	-6	*O-149(149-0-0)	1.4
1953	Pit-N	41	148	27	40	6	1	7	29	25	21	.270	.383	.466	849	121	5	1	0	0	1.000	1	O-41(41-0-0)	0.3
	Chi-N★	117	414	73	117	14	2	28	87	75	67	.283	.394	.529	923	135	22	1	1	-0	.964	-4	*O-116(116-0-0)	1.1
	Yr	158	562	100	157	20	3	35	116	100	88	.279	.391	.512	903	131	28	2	1	0	.973	-3	*O-157(157-0-0)	1.4
1954	Chi-N	147	557	88	159	36	5	22	73	76	90	.285	.373	.487	860	121	17	2	0	0	.971	-0	*O-147(147-0-0)	0.8
1955	Cle-A	113	321	56	78	13	0	18	54	65	46	.243	.370	.452	822	116	8	0	0	0	.986	-5	O-87(87-0-0)	-0.2
Total	10	1472	5205	971	1451	216	39	369	1015	1011	749	.279	.398	.548	946	148	364	22	2		.974	-2	*O-1382L/1-58	25.9
■ CHICK KING King, Charles Gilbert b: 11/10/30, Paris, Tenn. BR/TR, 6'2", 190 lbs. Deb: 8/27/54																								
1954	Det-A	11	28	4	6	0	1	0	3	3	8	.214	.290	.286	576	59	-2	0	0	0	.958	1	/O-7(0-7-0)	-0.1
1955	Det-A	7	21	3	5	0	0	0	0	1	2	.238	.273	.238	511	39	-2	0	0	0	.923	-0	/O-6(6-0-0)	-0.2
1956	Det-A	7	9	0	2	0	0	0	0	1	4	.222	.300	.222	522	40	-1	0	0	0	.800	-1	/O-4(4-0-0)	-0.2
1958	Chi-N	8	8	1	2	0	0	0	1	3	1	.250	.455	.250	705	95	0	0	0	0	1.000	-2	/O-7(0-7-0)	-0.2
1959	Chi-N	7	3	3	0	0	0	0	0	0	1	.000	.000	.000	0	-99	-1	0	0	0	1.000	-0	/O-1(0-1-0)	-0.1
	StL-N	5	7	0	3	0	0	0	1	0	2	.429	.429	.429	857	121	0	0	0	0	1.000	-0	/O-4(1-3-0)	0.0
	Yr	12	10	3	3	0	0	0	1	0	3	.300	.300	.300	600	59	-1	0	0	0	1.000	-0	/O-5(1-4-0)	-0.1
Total	5	45	76	11	18	0	1	0	5	8	18	.237	.310	.263	573	56	-5	0	0	0	.947	-3	/O-29(11-18-0)	-0.8
■ LEE KING King, Edward Lee b: 3/28/1894, Waltham, Mass. d: 9/7/38, Newton Center, Mass. BR/TR, 5'10", 160 lbs. Deb: 6/24/16 Career OF: (21-LF 2-CF 1-RF)																								
1916	Phi-A	42	144	13	27	1	2	0	8	7	15	.188	.230	.222	452	38	-11	4			1.000	-10	O-22L,S-11/3-5,2-2	-2.5
1919	Bos-N	2	1	0	0	0	0	0	0	0	0	.000	.000	.000	0	-99	-0	0			.000	0	H	0.0
Total	2	44	145	13	27	1	2	0	8	7	15	.186	.229	.221	449	37	-12	4			1.000	-10	/O-22L,S-11,3-5,2-2	-2.5
■ HAL KING King, Harold b: 2/1/44, Oviedo, Fla. BL/TR, 6'1", 200 lbs. Deb: 9/6/67																								
1967	Hou-N	15	44	2	11	1	2	0	6	2	9	.250	.283	.364	646	87	-1	0	0	0	1.000	-2	C-11	-0.3
1968	Hou-N	27	55	4	8	2	1	0	2	7	16	.145	.242	.218	460	40	-4	0	0	0	.968	-4	C-19	-0.8
1970	Atl-N	89	204	29	53	8	0	11	30	32	41	.260	.366	.461	826	113	4	1	0	0	.985	-11	C-62	-0.4
1971	Atl-N	86	198	14	41	9	0	5	19	29	43	.207	.320	.328	649	79	-5	0	0	0	.983	-2	C-60	-0.4
1972	Tex-A	50	122	12	22	5	0	4	12	25	35	.180	.333	.320	653	99	1	0	0	0	.970	-7	C-38	-0.5
1973	*Cin-N	35	43	5	8	0	0	4	10	6	10	.186	.286	.465	751	110	0	0	0	0	1.000	-1	/C-9	0.0
1974	Cin-N	20	17	1	3	1	0	0	3	3	4	.176	.300	.235	535	52	-1	0	0	0	1.000	0	/C-5	-0.1
Total	7	322	683	67	146	26	3	24	82	104	158	.214	.325	.366	691	93	-5	1	0	0	.982	-26	C-204	-2.5
■ JIM KING King, James Hubert b: 8/27/32, Elkins, Ark. BL/TR, 6', 185 lbs. Deb: 4/17/55																								
1955	Chi-N	113	301	43	77	12	3	11	45	24	39	.256	.315	.425	740	95	-3	2	1	0	.990	5	O-93(17-0-76)	-0.1
1956	Chi-N	118	317	32	79	13	2	15	54	30	40	.249	.316	.445	761	103	1	1	2	-0	.990	14	O-82(69-0-14)	1.0
1957	StL-N	22	35	1	11	0	0	0	2	4	2	.314	.385	.314	699	89	-0	0	0	0	1.000	-2	/O-8(1-3-4)	-0.3
1958	SF-N	34	56	8	12	2	1	2	8	10	8	.214	.343	.393	736	96	-0	0	1	-0	1.000	-2	O-15(9-0-6)	-0.3
1961	Was-A	110	263	43	71	12	1	11	46	38	45	.270	.366	.449	815	118	7	4	0	1	.980	-6	O-91(25-0-67)/C-1	-0.3
1962	Was-A	132	333	39	81	15	0	11	35	55	37	.243	.355	.387	743	101	2	4	2	0	.979	2	*O-101(20-0-81)	-0.2
1963	Was-A	136	459	61	106	16	5	24	62	45	43	.231	.301	.444	745	106	2	3	0	1	.987	1	*O-123(2-0-122)	-0.5
1964	Was-A	134	415	46	100	15	1	18	56	55	65	.241	.337	.412	749	108	5	3	1	0	.973	8	*O-121(0-0-121)	0.6
1965	Was-A	120	258	46	55	10	2	14	49	44	50	.213	.339	.430	769	119	7	1	0	0	.993	-2	O-88(1-0-87)	0.1
1966	Was-A	117	310	41	77	14	2	10	30	38	41	.248	.330	.403	734	111	4	4	0	1	.987	0	O-85(0-0-85)	0.0
1967	Was-A	47	100	10	21	2	2	1	12	15	13	.210	.331	.300	631	91	-1	1	1	-0	.962	-3	O-31(0-0-31)/C-1	-0.6
	Chi-A	23	50	2	6	1	0	0	2	4	16	.120	.185	.140	325	-3	-6	0	0	0	1.000	-2	O-12(1-0-12)	-1.0
	Cle-A	19	21	2	3	0	0	0	0	1	2	.143	.182	.143	325	-3	-3	0	0	0	1.000	-0	/O-1(0-0-1)	-0.3
	Yr	89	171	14	30	3	2	1	14	20	31	.175	.273	.234	507	53	-10	1	1	-0	.971	-5	O-44(1-0-44)/C-1	-1.9
Total	11	1125	2918	374	699	112	19	117	401	363	401	.240	.328	.411	740	104	15	23	8	2	.984	13	O-851(145-3-707)/C-2	-1.9
■ JEFF KING King, Jeffrey Wayne b: 12/26/64, Marion, Ind. BR/TR, 6'1", 180 lbs. Deb: 6/2/89 Career OF: (0-LF 0-CF 1-RF)																								
1989	Pit-N	75	215	31	42	13	3	5	19	20	34	.195	.270	.353	624	80	-6	4	2	0	.995	-2	1-46,3-13/2-7,S-1	-1.1
1990	*Pit-N	127	371	46	91	17	1	14	53	21	50	.245	.288	.410	697	93	-5	3	3	-0	.938	16	*3-115/1-1	1.1
1991	Pit-N	33	109	16	26	1	1	4	18	14	15	.239	.331	.376	707	100	0	3	1	0	.975	1	3-33	0.1
1992	*Pit-N	130	480	56	111	21	2	14	65	27	56	.231	.275	.371	646	82	-13	4	6	-1	.953	-4	3-73,1-32,2-32,/SO	-2.1

YEAR	TM/L	G	AB	R	H	2B	3B	HR	RBI	BB	SO	AVG	OBP	SLG	OPS	OPS+	BR+	SB	CS	SBR	FA	FR	G/POS	TPR
1993	Pit-N	158	611	82	180	35	3	9	98	59	54	.295	.361	.406	766	105	5	8	6	-0	.964	21	*3-156/2-2,S-2	2.6
1994	Pit-N	94	339	36	89	23	0	5	42	30	38	.263	.322	.375	697	80	-10	3	2	-0	.955	11	3-91/2-1	0.2
1995	Pit-N	122	445	61	118	27	2	18	87	55	63	.265	.347	.456	803	108	5	7	4	0	.942	-1	3-84,1-35/2-8,S-2	0.1
1996	Pit-N	155	591	91	160	36	4	30	111	70	95	.271	.350	.497	847	117	14	15	1	3	.997	-2	1-92,2-71,3-17	1.0
1997	KC-A	155	543	84	129	30	1	28	112	89	96	.238	.347	.451	798	104	3	16	5	2	**.996**	20	*1-150/D-2	1.0
1998	KC-A	131	486	83	128	17	1	24	93	42	73	.263	.325	.451	775	96	-4	10	2	2	.995	7	*1-112,D-16/3-4	-0.6
1999	KC-A	21	72	14	17	2	0	3	11	15	10	.236	.389	.389	778	97	0	2	0	0	.990	1	1-20/D-1	-0.1
Total	11	1201	4262	600	1091	222	18	154	709	442	584	.256	.329	.425	754	99	-10	75	32	5	.953	66	3-586,1-488,2/DSO	2.2
■ **LEE KING**	King, Lee b: 12/26/1892, Hundred, W.Va. d: 9/16/67, Shinnston, W.Va. BR/TR, 5'8", 160 lbs. Deb: 9/20/16 Career OF: (109-LF 114-CF 125-RF)																							
1916	Pit-N	8	18	0	2	0	0	0	1	0	7	.111	.111	.111	222	-31	-3	0			.714	-1	/O-8(2-0-4)	-0.5
1917	Pit-N	111	381	32	95	14	5	1	35	15	58	.249	.281	.320	602	82	-9	8			.968	9	*O-102(7-0-95)	-0.6
1918	Pit-N	36	112	9	26	3	2	1	11	11	15	.232	.301	.321	622	87	-2	3			.909	-8	O-36(32-0-4)	-1.2
1919	NY-N	21	20	5	2	1	0	0	1	1	6	.100	.143	.150	293	-12	-3	0			.667	-3	/O-7(2-1-3)	-0.6
1920	NY-N	93	261	32	72	11	4	7	42	21	38	.276	.335	.429	764	120	6	3	7	-2	.951	-11	O-84(0-83-1)	-1.2
1921	NY-N	39	94	17	21	4	2	0	7	13	6	.223	.324	.309	633	68	-4	0	2	-1	.921	-5	O-35(0-24-12)/1-1	-1.1
	Phi-N	64	216	25	58	19	4	4	32	8	37	.269	.298	.449	747	88	-4	1	4	-1	.911	-2	O-57(55-1-2)	-1.2
	Yr	103	310	42	79	23	6	4	39	21	43	.255	.306	.406	713	83	-8	1	6	-2	.914	-7	O-92(55-25-14)/1-1	-2.3
1922	Phi-N	19	53	8	12	5	1	2	13	8	6	.226	.328	.472	800	95	-1	0	0	0	.946	-0	O-15(11-4-0)	-0.2
	*NY-N	20	34	6	6	3	0	0	2	5	2	.176	.282	.265	547	41	-3	1	0	0	1.000	0	/1-5,O-5(0-1-4)	-0.3
	Yr	39	87	14	18	8	1	2	15	13	8	.207	.310	.391	701	76	-3	1	0	0	.961	-0	O-20(11-5-4)/1-5	-0.5
Total	7	411	1189	134	294	60	18	15	144	82	175	.247	.299	.366	665	87	-22	16	13		.940	-21	O-349R/1-6	-6.9
■ **LYNN KING**	King, Lynn Paul "Dig" b: 11/28/07, Villisca, Iowa d: 5/11/72, Atlantic, Iowa BL/TR, 5'9", 165 lbs. Deb: 9/21/35																							
1935	StL-N	8	22	6	4	0	0	0	0	4	1	.182	.308	.182	490	34	-2	2			1.000	2	/O-6(0-6-0)	0.0
1936	StL-N	78	100	12	19	2	1	0	10	9	14	.190	.257	.230	487	32	-9	2			.984	-4	O-34(7-12-15)	-1.4
1939	StL-N	89	85	10	20	2	0	0	11	15	3	.235	.350	.259	609	62	-4	2			.982	-10	O-44(14-29-1)	-1.4
Total	3	175	207	28	43	4	1	0	21	28	18	.208	.302	.237	539	45	-15	6			.986	-12	/O-84(21-47-16)	-2.8
■ **MART KING**	King, Marshal Ney b: 12/1849, Troy, N.Y. d: 10/19/11, Troy, N.Y. TR, 5'9.5", 176 lbs. Deb: 5/8/1871 Career OF: (1-LF 13-CF 0-RF)																							
1871	Chi-n	20	101	23	21	1	0	2	16	8	1	.208	.266	.277	543	51	-7	5	0	1	.786	-3	O-11C/C-9,S-3,3-1	-0.6
1872	Tro-n	3	11	0	0	0	0	0	1	0	1	.000	.000	.000	0	-99	-2	0	0	0	.857	-0	/O-3(0-3-0)	-0.2
Total	2 n	23	112	23	21	1	0	2	17	8	2	.188	.242	.250	492	39	-10	5	0	1	.810	-3	/O-14C,C-9,S-3,3-1	-0.8
■ **SAM KING**	King, Samuel Warren b: 5/17/1852, Peabody, Mass. d: 8/11/22, Peabody, Mass. TL, 6', Deb: 5/1/1884																							
1884	Was-a	12	45	3	8	2	0	0		1		.178	.213	.222	435	48	-2				.912	-1	1-12	-0.4
■ **STEVE KING**	King, Stephen F. b: 1842, Troy, N.Y. d: 7/8/1895, Troy, N.Y. 5'9", 175 lbs. Deb: 5/9/1871																							
1871	Tro-n	29	144	45	57	10	6	0	34	1	1	.396	.400	.549	949	167	12	3	3	-0	.833	3	*O-29(29-0-0)	1.0
1872	Tro-n	25	128	33	39	8	0	0	21	1	2	.305	.310	.367	677	106	1	1	1	-0	.776	1	O-25(25-0-0)	0.1
Total	2 n	54	272	78	96	18	6	0	55	2	3	.353	.358	.463	821	139	12	4	4	-1	.807	4	/O-54(54-0-0)	1.1
■ **WES KINGDON**	Kingdon, Westcott William b: 7/4/1900, Los Angeles, Cal. d: 4/19/75, Capistrano, Cal. BR/TR, 5'8", 148 lbs. Deb: 6/12/32																							
1932	Was-A	18	34	10	11	3	1	0	3	5	2	.324	.410	.471	881	129	2	0	0	0	.929	-2	/3-8,S-4	0.0
■ **MIKE KINGERY**	Kingery, Michael Scott b: 3/29/61, St.James, Minn. BL/TL, 6', 180 lbs. Deb: 7/7/86 Career OF: (68-LF 329-CF 292-RF)																							
1986	KC-A	62	209	25	54	8	5	3	14	12	30	.258	.299	.388	686	83	-5	7	3	0	.973	-3	O-59(1-13-51)	-1.0
1987	Sea-A	120	354	38	99	25	4	9	52	27	43	.280	.334	.449	783	100	-0	7	9	-2	.992	10	*O-114(0-6-111)/D-4	0.3
1988	Sea-A	57	123	21	25	6	0	1	9	19	23	.203	.315	.276	591	64	-5	3	1	0	.989	-1	O-44(9-24-13),1-10	-0.7
1989	Sea-A	31	76	14	17	3	0	2	6	7	14	.224	.289	.342	631	75	-3	1	1	-0	1.000	3	O-23(2-20-1)	0.0
1990	SF-N	105	207	24	61	7	1	0	24	12	19	.295	.336	.338	675	89	-3	6	1	1	.978	-12	O-95(15-9-74)	-1.6
1991	SF-N	91	110	13	20	2	2	0	8	15	21	.182	.280	.236	516	48	-7	1	0	0	.975	-7	O-38(14-2-22)/1-6	-1.6
1992	Oak-A	12	28	3	3	0	0	0	1	1	3	.107	.138	.107	245	-32	-5	0	0	0	1.000	-2	O-10(2-6-2)	-0.8
1994	Col-N	105	301	56	105	27	8	4	41	30	26	.349	.411	.532	943	123	11	5	7	-1	.979	-5	O-98(20-77-2)/1-1	0.5
1995	*Col-N	119	350	66	94	18	4	8	37	45	40	.269	.352	.411	763	78	-10	13	5	1	.979	-11	*O-108(0-108-0)/1-5	-1.9
1996	Pit-N	117	276	32	68	12	2	3	27	23	29	.246	.307	.337	644	68	-13	2	1	0	.985	-8	O-83(5-64-16)	-2.1
Total	10	819	2034	292	546	108	26	30	219	191	248	.268	.333	.391	725	86	-40	45	28	0	.984	-37	O-672C/1-22,D-4	-8.9
■ **DAVE KINGMAN**	Kingman, David Arthur b: 12/21/48, Pendleton, Ore. BR/TR, 6'6", 210 lbs. Deb: 7/30/71 Career OF: (508-LF 0-CF 144-RF)																							
1971	*SF-N	41	115	17	32	10	2	6	24	9	35	.278	.336	.557	893	151	7	5	0	1	.981	-4	1-20,O-14(7-0-7)	0.3
1972	SF-N	135	472	65	106	17	4	29	83	51	140	.225	.306	.462	767	114	7	16	6	1	.932	3	3-59,1-56,O-22L	0.6
1973	SF-N	112	305	54	62	10	1	24	55	41	122	.203	.302	.479	780	109	2	8	5	0	.910	3	3-60,1-46/P-2	0.3
1974	SF-N	121	350	41	78	18	2	18	55	37	125	.223	.303	.440	743	101	-1	8	8	-1	.983	2	1-91,3-21/O-2(0-0-2)	-0.6
1975	NY-N	134	502	65	116	22	1	36	88	34	153	.231	.285	.494	779	119	7	7	5	-0	.958	4	O-71L,1-58,3-12	0.3
1976	NY-N★	123	474	70	113	14	1	37	86	28	135	.238	.288	.506	794	130	14	7	4	0	.959	3	*O-111(5-0-106),1-16	1.1
1977	NY-N	58	211	22	44	7	0	9	28	13	66	.209	.264	.370	634	71	-9	3	2	-0	.974	-2	O-45(26-0-20),1-17	-1.5
	SD-N	56	168	16	40	9	0	11	39	12	48	.238	.297	.488	785	119	3	2	3	-1	.964	2	O-28(28-0-0),1-13/3-2	0.3
	Yr	114	379	38	84	16	0	20	67	25	114	.222	.279	.422	701	92	-7	5	5	-1	.970	-0	O-73L,1-30/3-2	-1.2
	Cal-A	10	36	4	7	2	0	2	4	1	16	.194	.237	.417	654	77	-1	0	0	0	.974	-1	/1-8,O-2(2-0-0)	-0.3
	NY-A	8	24	5	6	2	0	4	7	2	13	.250	.333	.833	1167	208	3	0	1	-0	.000	0	/D-6	0.3
	Yr	18	60	9	13	4	0	6	11	3	29	.217	.277	.583	860	131	2	0	1	-0	.974	-1	/1-8,D-6,O-2(2-0-0)	0.0
1978	Chi-N	119	395	65	105	17	4	28	79	39	111	.266	.341	.542	883	128	13	3	4	-1	.978	0	*O-100(100-0-0)/1-6	0.9
1979	Chi-N†	145	532	97	153	19	5	**48**	115	45	131	.288	.348	**.613**	**960**	143	29	4	2	0	.954	5	*O-139(139-0-0)	2.8
1980	Chi-N★	81	255	31	71	8	0	18	57	21	44	.278	.333	.522	855	126	8	2	2	-0	.941	1	O-61(63-0-1)/1-2	0.6
1981	NY-N	100	353	40	78	11	3	22	59	55	105	.221	.328	.456	784	122	10	6	0	1	.974	-6	1-56,O-48(48-0-0)	0.0
1982	NY-N	149	535	80	109	9	1	**37**	99	59	156	.204	.288	.432	719	99	-3	4	0	1	.986	-14	*1-143	-2.6
1983	NY-N	100	248	25	49	7	0	13	29	22	57	.198	.266	.383	649	79	-8	2	1	0	.994	-5	1-50/O-5(0-0-5)	-1.7
1984	Oak-A	147	549	68	147	23	1	35	118	44	119	.268	.329	.505	833	136	24	2	1	0	1.000	-2	*D-139/1-9	1.8
1985	Oak-A	158	592	66	141	16	0	30	91	62	114	.238	.313	.417	730	105	4	3	2	-0	1.000	-1	*D-149/1-9	-0.3
1986	Oak-A	144	561	70	118	19	0	35	94	33	126	.210	.258	.431	689	90	-11	3	3	-0	.895	-1	*D-140/1-3	-1.6
Total	16	1941	6677	901	1575	240	25	442	1210	608	1816	.236	.305	.478	783	115	97	85	49	2	.957	-11	O-648L,1-603,D3/P	0.7
■ **HARRY KINGMAN**	Kingman, Henry Lees b: 4/3/1892, Tientsin, China d: 12/27/82, Oakland, Cal. BL/TL, 6'1.5", 165 lbs. Deb: 7/1/14																							
1914	NY-A	4	3	0	0	0	0	0	0	1	2	.000	.250	.000	250	-24	-0	0			1.000	-0	/1-1	-0.1
■ **EUGENE KINGSALE**	Kingsale, Eugene Humphrey b: 8/20/76, Solito, Aruba BB/TR, 6'3", 170 lbs. Deb: 9/3/96																							
1996	Bal-A	3	0	0	0	0	0	0	0	0	0	—	—	—	—	—	0	0	0	0	1.000	-1	/O-2(0-2-0)	-0.1
1998	Bal-A	11	2	1	0	0	0	0	0	0	1	.000	.000	.000	0	-99	-1	0	0	0	1.000	-2	/O-4(0-4-0)	-0.2
1999	Bal-A	28	85	9	21	2	0	0	7	5	13	.247	.304	.271	575	50	-6	1	3	-1	.980	-2	O-24(0-24-0)/D-2	-0.8
2000	Bal-A	26	88	13	21	2	1	0	9	2	14	.239	.256	.284	540	38	-8	1	2	-0	.954	1	O-24(0-24-0)/D-1	-0.7
Total	4	68	175	23	42	4	1	0	16	7	28	.240	.277	.274	551	42	-15	2	5	-1	.966	-3	/O-54(0-54-0),D-3	-1.8
■ **MIKE KINKADE**	Kinkade, Michael A. b: 5/6/73, Livonia, Mich. BR/TR, 6'1", 210 lbs. Deb: 9/8/98 Career OF: (12-LF 0-CF 9-RF)																							
1998	NY-N	3	2	2	0	0	0	0	0	0	0	.000	.000	.000	0	-99	-1	0	0	0	.000	0	/3-1	-0.1
1999	NY-N	28	46	3	9	2	1	2	6	3	9	.196	.275	.413	688	73	-2	1	0	0	1.000	-4	O-17L/3-3,C-1,1-1	-0.6
2000	NY-N	2	2	0	0	0	0	0	0	0	1	.000	.000	.000	0	-99	-1	0	0	0	.000	-0	/O-1(0-0-1)	-0.1
	Bal-A	3	7	0	3	1	0	0	1	0	0	.429	.500	.571	1071	176	1	0	0	0	1.000	-0	/1-1,D-2	0.1
Total	3	36	57	5	12	3	1	2	7	3	10	.211	.286	.404	689	74	-2	1	0	0	1.000	-5	/O-18L,3-4,D-2,1C	-0.7
■ **WALT KINLOCK**	Kinlock, Walter b: 1878, St.Joseph, Mo. Deb: 8/1/1895																							
1895	StL-N	1	3	0	1	0	0	0	0	0	2	.333	.333	.333	667	73	-0	0			1.000	1	/3-1	0.0

YEAR	TM/L	G	AB	R	H	2B	3B	HR	RBI	BB	SO	AVG	OBP	SLG	OPS	OPS+	BR+	SB	CS	SBR	FA	FR	G/POS	TPR
■ **BOB KINSELLA**	Kinsella, Robert Francis "Red" b: 1/5/1899, Springfield, Ill. d: 12/30/51, Los Angeles, Cal. BL/TR, 5'9.5", 165 lbs. Deb: 9/20/19																							
1919	NY-N	3	9	1	2	0	0	0	0	0	3	.222	.222	.222	444	34	-1	1			.500	-2	/O-3(2-0-1)	-0.3
1920	NY-N	1	3	0	1	0	0	0	1	0	2	.333	.333	.333	667	93	-0	0	0	0	.500	-1	/O-1(0-0-1)	-0.1
Total	2	4	12	1	3	0	0	0	1	0	5	.250	.250	.250	500	49	-1	1	0		.500	-2	/O-4(2-0-2)	-0.4
■ **KINSLER**	Kinsler b: Staten Island, N.Y. Deb: 6/8/1893																							
1893	NY-N	1	3	1	0	0	0	0	0	1	1	.000	.250	.000	250	-31	-1	0			1.000	-0	/O-1(0-0-1)	-0.1
■ **TOM KINSLOW**	Kinslow, Thomas F. b: 1/12/1866, Washington, D.C. d: 2/22/01, Washington, D.C. BR/TR, 5'10", 160 lbs. Deb: 6/4/1886																							
1886	Was-N	3	8	1	2	0	0	0	1	0	1	.250	.250	.250	500	56	-0	0			1.000	-0	/C-3	0.0
1887	NY-a	2	6	0	0	0	0	0	0	0		.000	.000	.000	0	-99	-2	0			1.000	-0	/C-2	-0.1
1890	Bro-P	64	242	30	64	11	6	4	46	10	22	.264	.299	.409	708	83	-8	2			.909	11	C-64	0.7
1891	Bro-N	61	228	22	54	6	0	0	33	9	22	.237	.266	.263	529	55	-13	3			.922	-9	C-61	-1.6
1892	Bro-N	66	246	37	75	6	11	2	40	13	17	.305	.342	.443	785	142	11	4			.933	5	C-66	2.0
1893	Bro-N	78	312	38	76	8	4	4	45	11	13	.244	.272	.333	605	63	-18	4			.932	-2	C-76/O-2(0-0-2)	-1.0
1894	Bro-N	62	223	39	68	5	6	2	41	20	11	.305	.362	.408	770	92	-3	4			.907	-9	C-61/1-1	-0.5
1895	Pit-N	19	62	10	14	2	0	0	5	2	2	.226	.250	.258	508	33	-6	1			.962	-2	C-18	-0.6
1896	Lou-N	8	25	4	7	0	1	0	7	1	5	.280	.308	.360	668	79	-1	0			.810	-2	/C-5,1-1	-0.2
1898	Was-N	3	9	0	1	0	0	0	0	0		.111	.111	.111	222	-36	-2	0			.800	-1	/C-3,1-1	-0.2
	StL-N	14	53	5	15	2	1	0	4	1		.283	.309	.358	668	89	-1	0			.925	1	C-14	0.1
	Yr	17	62	5	16	2	1	0	4	1		.258	.281	.323	604	72	-3	0			.909	0	C-17/1-1	-0.1
Total	10	380	1414	186	376	40	29	12	222	67	93	.266	.301	.361	662	81	-42	18			.923	-7	C-373/1-3,O-2(0-0-2)	-1.4
■ **WALT KINZIE**	Kinzie, Walter Harris b: 3/1858, Chicago, Ill. d: 11/5/09, Chicago, Ill. BR/TR, 5'10.5", 161 lbs. Deb: 7/17/1882																							
1882	Det-N	13	53	5	5	0	1	0	2	0	8	.094	.094	.132	226	-28	-7				.852	-4	S-13	-1.0
1884	Chi-N	19	82	4	13	3	0	2	8	0	13	.159	.159	.268	427	29	-7				.831	-3	S-17/3-2	-0.8
	StL-a	2	9	0	1	0	0	0		0		.111	.111	.111	222	-26	-1				.727	-3	/2-2	-0.4
Total	2	34	144	9	19	3	1	2	10	0	21	.132	.132	.208	340	6	-15				.840	-9	/S-30,2-2,3-2	-2.2
■ **ED KIPPERT**	Kippert, Edward August "Kickapoo" b: 1/3/1880, Detroit, Mich. d: 6/3/60, Detroit, Mich. BR/TR, 5'10.5", 180 lbs. Deb: 4/14/14																							
1914	Cin-N	2	2	0	0	0	0	0	0	0	0	.000	.000	.000	0	-97	-0	0			1.000	-1	/O-2(1-1-0)	-0.1
■ **JIM KIRBY**	Kirby, James Herschel b: 5/5/23, Nashville, Tenn. BR/TR, 5'11", 175 lbs. Deb: 5/1/49																							
1949	Chi-N	3	2	0	1	0	0	0	0	0	0	.500	.500	.500	1000	174	0	0			.000	0	H	0.0
■ **LA RUE KIRBY**	Kirby, La Rue b: 12/30/1889, Eureka, Mich. d: 6/10/61, Lansing, Mich. BB/TR, 6', 185 lbs. Deb: 8/7/12																							
1912	NY-N	3	5	1	1	1	0	0	0	0	0	.200	.200	.400	600	60	-0	0			1.000	0	/P-3	0.0
1914	StL-F	52	195	21	48	6	3	2	18	14	30	.246	.303	.338	642	71	-11	5			.973	2	O-50(0-49-1)	-1.3
1915	StL-F	61	178	15	38	7	2	0	16	17	31	.213	.282	.275	557	54	-13	3			.969	-3	O-52(9-40-4)/P-1	-2.0
Total	3	116	378	37	87	14	5	2	34	31	61	.230	.292	.310	601	63	-25	8			.971	-1	O-102(9-89-5)/P-4	-3.3
■ **WAYNE KIRBY**	Kirby, Wayne Leonard b: 1/22/64, Williamsburg, Va. BL/TR, 5'10", 185 lbs. Deb: 9/12/91 Career OF: (39-LF 128-CF 246-RF)																							
1991	Cle-A	21	43	4	9	2	0	0	5	2	6	.209	.244	.256	500	38	-4	1	2	-0	1.000	-1	O-21(5-1-17)	-0.5
1992	Cle-A	21	18	9	3	1	0	1	1	3	2	.167	.286	.389	675	89	-0	0	3	-1	1.000	-0	/O-2(1-0-1),D-4	-0.2
1993	Cle-A	131	458	71	123	19	5	6	60	37	58	.269	.327	.371	698	88	-8	17	5	2	.983	13	*O-123(2-15-113)/D-5	0.1
1994	Cle-A	78	191	33	56	6	0	5	23	13	30	.293	.341	.403	745	91	-3	11	4	1	.959	-11	O-68(8-6-55)/D-2	-1.3
1995	*Cle-A	101	188	29	39	10	2	1	14	13	32	.207	.262	.298	560	45	-16	10	3	1	.990	-10	O-68(1-34-35)/D-7	-2.4
1996	Cle-A	27	16	3	4	1	0	0	1	2	2	.250	.333	.313	646	65	-1	0	1	-0	1.000	-6	O-18(2-5-11)	-0.7
	*LA-N	65	188	23	51	10	1	1	11	17	17	.271	.335	.351	686	88	-3	4	2	0	.969	-3	O-53(8-47-0)	-0.5
1997	LA-N	46	65	6	11	2	0	0	4	10	12	.169	.280	.200	480	31	-6	0	0	0	1.000	-2	O-26(9-16-2)	-0.9
1998	NY-N	26	31	5	6	0	1	0	0	1	9	.194	.219	.258	477	25	-3	1	1	-0	1.000	-3	O-19(3-4-12)	-0.7
Total	8	516	1198	183	302	51	9	14	119	98	168	.252	.312	.345	657	75	-44	44	21	2	.981	-24	O-398R/D-18	-7.1
■ **TOM KIRK**	Kirk, Thomas Daniel b: 9/27/27, Philadelphia, Pa. d: 8/1/74, Philadelphia, Pa. BL/TL, 5'10.5", 182 lbs. Deb: 6/24/47																							
1947	Phi-A	1	1	0	0	0	0	0	0	0	0	.000	.000	.000	0	-98	-0	0	0	0	.000	0	H	0.0
■ **JAY KIRKE**	Kirke, Judson Fabian b: 6/16/1888, Fleischmanns, N.Y d: 8/31/68, New Orleans, La. BL/TR, 6', 195 lbs. Deb: 9/28/10 Career OF: (102-LF 2-CF 38-RF)																							
1910	Det-A	8	25	3	5	1	0	0	3	1		.200	.231	.240	471	44	-2	1			.917	-3	/2-7,O-1(1-0-0)	-0.5
1911	Bos-N	20	89	9	32	5	5	0	12	2	6	.360	.380	.528	909	142	4	3			.929	-1	O-14L/1-3,2-1,S3	0.3
1912	Bos-N	103	359	53	115	11	4	4	62	9	46	.320	.339	.407	745	102	-1	7			.903	-1	O-72L,3-14/S-2,1-1	-0.4
1913	Bos-N	18	38	3	9	2	0	0	3	1	6	.237	.293	.289	582	65	-2	0			.923	2	O-13(3-2-8)	-0.1
1914	Cle-A	67	242	18	66	10	2	1	25	7	30	.273	.296	.343	639	89	-4	5	10	-2	.974	0	O-42(22-0-20),1-18	-1.0
1915	Cle-A	87	339	35	105	19	2	2	40	14	21	.310	.346	.395	742	120	6	5	6	-1	.986	-1	1-87	0.3
1918	NY-N	17	56	1	14	1	0	0	3	1	3	.250	.263	.268	531	63	-3	0			.978	1	1-16	-0.3
Total	7	320	1148	122	346	49	13	7	148	35	112	.301	.328	.385	713	103	-0	21	16		.927	-3	O-142L,1-125/3-15,2S	-1.7
■ **WILLIE KIRKLAND**	Kirkland, Willie Charles b: 2/17/34, Siluria, Ala. BL/TR, 6'1", 206 lbs. Deb: 4/15/58																							
1958	SF-N	122	418	48	108	25	6	14	56	43	69	.258	.335	.447	782	107	4	3	2	-0	.961	-0	*O-115(5-0-112)	-0.1
1959	SF-N	126	463	64	126	22	3	22	68	42	84	.272	.337	.475	812	116	9	5	3	0	.969	1	*O-117(13-0-109)	0.5
1960	SF-N	146	515	59	130	21	10	21	65	44	86	.252	.316	.454	771	115	9	12	7	0	.978	4	*O-143(3-0-143)	0.7
1961	Cle-A	146	525	84	136	22	5	27	95	48	77	.259	.322	.474	797	113	7	7	0	2	.974	8	*O-138(0-0-138)	0.8
1962	Cle-A	137	419	56	84	9	1	21	72	43	62	.200	.275	.377	652	76	-16	9	1	2	.972	0	*O-125(0-12-121)	-2.1
1963	Cle-A	127	427	51	98	13	2	15	47	45	99	.230	.304	.375	679	90	-6	8	2	1	.984	7	*O-112(5-64-45)	-0.3
1964	Bal-A	66	150	14	30	5	0	3	22	17	26	.200	.286	.293	579	62	-8	3	2	-0	.989	0	O-58(2-10-48)	-1.1
	Was-A	32	102	8	22	6	0	5	13	6	30	.216	.259	.422	681	86	-2	0	0	0	.907	-3	O-27(12-1-15)	-0.8
	Yr	98	252	22	52	11	0	8	35	23	56	.206	.275	.345	621	72	-10	3	2	-0	.964	-3	O-85(14-11-63)	-1.9
1965	Was-A	123	312	38	72	9	1	14	54	19	65	.231	.275	.401	676	91	-5	3	2	-0	.987	-6	O-92(32-5-67)	-1.7
1966	Was-A	124	163	21	31	2	1	6	17	16	50	.190	.263	.325	588	68	-7	2	0	0	.983	-12	O-68(50-0-19)	-2.2
Total	9	1149	3494	443	837	134	29	148	509	323	648	.240	.307	.422	728	99	-15	52	19	5	.974	-2	O-995(122-92-817)	-6.3
■ **ED KIRKPATRICK**	Kirkpatrick, Edgar Leon b: 10/8/44, Spokane, Wash. BL/TR, 5'11.5", 195 lbs. Deb: 9/13/62 Career OF: (236-LF 62-CF 291-RF)																							
1962	LA-A	3	6	0	0	0	0	0	0	0	2	.000	.000	.000	0	-99	-2	0	0	0	1.000	1	/C-1	-0.1
1963	LA-A	34	77	4	15	5	0	2	7	6	19	.195	.262	.338	600	71	-3	1	0	0	.986	-0	C-14,O-10(10-0-0)	-0.3
1964	LA-A	75	219	20	53	13	3	2	22	23	30	.242	.320	.356	676	97	-1	2	2	-0	.969	-2	O-63(63-0-1)	-0.7
1965	Cal-A	19	73	8	19	5	0	3	8	3	9	.260	.289	.452	742	110	1	1	2	-0	.969	1	O-19(0-0-19)	-0.1
1966	Cal-A	117	312	31	60	7	4	9	44	51	67	.192	.315	.327	642	87	-4	7	4	0	.994	-6	*O-102(17-0-86)/1-3	-1.7
1967	Cal-A	3	8	0	0	0	0	0	0	0	2	.000	.000	.000	0	-99	-2	0	0	0	1.000	-2	/C-2,O-1(1-0-0)	-0.5
1968	Cal-A	89	161	23	37	4	0	1	15	25	32	.230	.337	.273	610	90	-1	1	3	-1	.982	-5	O-45(12-1-34)/C-4,1-2	-1.0
1969	KC-A	120	315	40	81	11	4	14	49	43	42	.257	.352	.451	803	122	9	3	5	-1	.995	8	O-82R/C-8,1-2,32	1.4
1970	KC-A	134	424	59	97	17	2	18	62	55	65	.229	.319	.406	724	98	-1	4	4	-1	.978	-8	C-89,O-19(8-3-8),1-16	-0.8
1971	KC-A	120	365	46	80	12	1	9	46	48	60	.219	.313	.332	645	83	-8	3	4	-1	.992	-1	O-61(30-16-18),C-59	-0.9
1972	KC-A	113	364	43	100	15	1	9	43	51	50	.275	.368	.396	764	128	14	3	5	-1	.991	-5	*C-108/1-1	1.5
1973	KC-A	126	429	61	113	24	3	6	45	46	48	.263	.336	.375	711	93	-4	3	7	-2	.990	-5	*O-108R,C-14/D-8	-1.6
1974	*Pit-N	116	271	32	67	9	0	6	38	51	30	.247	.370	.347	717	105	4	1	2	-0	.993	-4	1-59,O-14(0-2-12)/C-6	-0.5
1975	*Pit-N	89	144	15	34	5	0	5	16	18	22	.236	.321	.375	696	93	-1	1	0	0	1.000	-1	1-28,O-14(8-0-6)	-0.4
1976	Pit-N	83	146	14	34	9	0	0	16	14	15	.233	.300	.295	595	69	-6	1	0	0	.990	-1	1-25/O-9(3-4-2),3-1	-0.9
1977	Pit-N	21	28	5	4	2	0	1	4	8	6	.143	.333	.321	655	75	-1	1	0	0	.972	-1	1-10/O-2(1-1-0),3-1	-0.2
	Tex-A	20	48	2	9	1	0	0	3	4	11	.188	.250	.208	458	26	-5	2	0	0	1.000	1	/O-6L,1-3,C-1,D-5	-0.4
	Mil-A	29	77	8	21	4	0	0	6	10	8	.273	.364	.325	688	89	-1	0	1	-0	.973	-2	O-22(22-0-0)/3-1,D-3	-0.4
	Yr	49	125	10	30	5	0	0	9	14	19	.240	.321	.280	601	65	-6	2	1	0	.980	-2	O-28L/D-8,1-3,C3	-0.8
Total	16	1311	3467	411	824	143	18	85	424	456	518	.238	.330	.363	693	97	-11	34	39	-6	.989	-32	O-577R,C-306,1/D32	-7.6

YEAR	TM/L	G	AB	R	H	2B	3B	HR	RBI	BB	SO	AVG	OBP	SLG	OPS	OPS+	BR+	SB	CS	SBR	FA	FR	G/POS	TPR
■ ENOS KIRKPATRICK	Kirkpatrick, Enos Claire b: 12/8/1885, Pittsburgh, Pa. d: 4/14/64, Pittsburgh, Pa. BR/TR, 5'10", 175 lbs. Deb: 8/24/12 Career OF: (2-LF 0-CF 1-RF)																							
1912	Bro-N	32	94	13	18	1	1	0	6	9	15	.191	.269	.223	493	37	-8	5			.968	6	3-29/S-3	-0.1
1913	Bro-N	48	89	13	22	4	1	1	5	3	18	.247	.287	.348	636	79	-3	5			.897	-1	S-10/1-8,2-6,3-4	-0.4
1914	Bal-F	55	174	22	44	7	2	2	16	18	30	.253	.330	.351	680	83	-7	10			.932	-5	3-36,S-11/O-3L,1-1	-1.0
1915	Bal-F	68	171	22	41	8	2	0	19	24	15	.240	.337	.310	647	80	-6	12			.911	-3	3-28,2-21/1-5,S-5	-0.9
Total	4	203	528	70	125	20	6	3	46	54	78	.237	.315	.314	629	74	-24	32			.936	-2	/3-97,S-29,2-27,10	-2.4
■ JOE KIRRENE	Kirrene, Joseph John b: 10/4/31, San Francisco, Cal. BR/TR, 6'2", 195 lbs. Deb: 10/1/50																							
1950	Chi-A	1	4	0	1	0	0	0	0	0	1	.250	.250	.250	500	29	-0	0	0	0	1.000	-1	/3-1	-0.1
1954	Chi-A	9	23	4	7	1	0	0	4	5	2	.304	.448	.348	796	116	1	1	0	0	.947	-2	/3-9	-0.1
Total	2	10	27	4	8	1	0	0	4	5	3	.296	.424	.333	758	105	1	1	0	0	.952	-3	/3-10	-0.2
■ ERNIE KISH	Kish, Ernest Alexander b: 2/6/18, Washington, D.C. d: 12/21/93, Kirtland, Ohio BL/TR, 5'9.5", 170 lbs. Deb: 7/29/45																							
1945	Phi-A	43	110	10	27	5	1	0	10	9	9	.245	.320	.309	629	83	-2	0	3	-1	.932	-4	O-30(13-8-11)	-0.9
■ BILL KISSINGER	Kissinger, William Francis "Shang" b: 8/15/1871, Dayton, Ky. d: 4/20/29, Cincinnati, Ohio BR/TR, 185 lbs. Deb: 5/30/1895 Career OF: (10-LF 1-CF 3-RF)																							
1895	Bal-N	2	5	1	1	0	0	0	0	0	1	.200	.200	.200	400	3	-1	0			1.000	0	/P-2	0.0
	StL-N	33	97	8	24	6	1	0	8	0	11	.247	.247	.330	577	49	-8	1			.975	-4	P-24/S-4,O-4R,3-1	-0.6
	Yr	35	102	9	25	6	1	0	8	0	12	.245	.245	.324	569	46	-9	1			**.976**	-5	P-26/S-4,O-4R,3-1	-0.6
1896	StL-N	23	73	8	22	4	0	0	12	0	4	.301	.301	.356	658	76	-3	0			.906	0	P-20/O-3(3-0-0),3-1	-0.2
1897	StL-N	14	39	7	13	3	2	0	6	3		.333	.381	.513	894	138	2	0			.786	-2	/O-7(6-1-0),P-7	-0.1
Total	3	72	214	24	60	13	3	0	26	3	16	.280	.290	.369	659	73	-9	1			.935	-6	/P-53,O-14L,S-4,3-2	-0.9
■ CHRIS KITSOS	Kitsos, Christopher Anestos b: 2/11/28, New York, N.Y. BB/TR, 5'9", 165 lbs. Deb: 4/21/54																							
1954	Chi-N	1	0	0	0	0	0	0	0	0	0	—	—	—	—	—	0	0	0	0	1.000	0	/S-1	0.0
■ RON KITTLE	Kittle, Ronald Dale b: 1/5/58, Gary, Indiana BR/TR, 6'4", 220 lbs. Deb: 9/2/82 Career OF: (348-LF 0-CF 5-RF)																							
1982	Chi-A	20	29	3	7	2	0	1	7	3	12	.241	.313	.414	726	97	-0	0	0	0	1.000	-2	/O-5(0-0-5),D-3	-0.2
1983	*Chi-A★	145	520	75	132	19	3	35	100	39	150	.254	.316	.504	820	117	10	8	3	1	.964	-9	*O-139(139-0-0)/D-2	-0.4
1984	Chi-A	139	466	67	100	15	0	32	74	49	137	.215	.298	.453	750	100	-1	3	6	-1	.972	3	*O-124(124-0-0)/D-7	-0.5
1985	Chi-A	116	379	51	87	12	0	26	58	31	92	.230	.296	.467	763	101	-1	1	4	-1	.989	-3	O-57(57-0-0),D-57	-0.8
1986	Chi-A	86	296	34	63	11	0	17	48	28	87	.213	.287	.422	710	87	-6	2	1	0	1.000	2	D-62,O-20(20-0-0)	-0.7
	NY-A	30	80	8	19	2	0	4	12	7	23	.237	.299	.412	711	92	-1	2	0	0	1.000	0	D-24/O-1(1-0-0)	-0.1
	Yr	116	376	42	82	13	0	21	60	35	110	.218	.290	.420	710	89	-7	4	1	1	.851	2	D-86,O-21(21-0-0)	-0.8
1987	NY-A	59	159	21	44	5	0	12	28	10	36	.277	.324	.535	858	123	5	0	1	-0	1.000	1	D-49/O-2(2-0-0)	0.3
1988	Cle-A	75	225	31	58	8	0	18	43	16	65	.258	.329	.533	863	134	9	0	0	0	.000	0	D-63	0.7
1989	Chi-A	51	169	26	51	10	0	11	37	22	42	.302	.385	.556	942	166	15	0	1	-0	.982	-3	1-27,D-17/O-5(5-0-0)	0.9
1990	Chi-A	83	277	29	68	14	0	16	43	24	77	.245	.313	.469	782	118	6	0	0	0	.987	-4	D-54,1-25	-0.2
	Bal-A	22	61	4	10	2	0	2	3	2	14	.164	.203	.295	498	39	-5	0	0	0	1.000	-1	D-13/1-5	-0.7
	Yr	105	338	33	78	16	0	18	46	26	91	.231	.293	.438	731	104	0	0	0	0	.989	-5	D-67,1-30	-0.9
1991	Chi-A	17	47	7	9	0	0	2	7	5	9	.191	.296	.319	615	72	-2	0	0	0	.982	-1	1-15	-0.4
Total	10	843	2708	356	648	100	3	176	460	236	744	.239	.309	.473	783	110	28	16	16	-2	.974	-17	O-353L,D-351/1-72	-2.1
■ MALACHI KITTRIDGE	Kittridge, Malachi Jeddidah "Jeddidah" b: 10/12/1869, Clinton, Mass. d: 6/23/28, Gary, Ind. BR/TR, 5'7", 170 lbs. Deb: 4/19/1890 M																							
1890	Chi-N	96	333	46	67	8	3	3	35	39	53	.201	.287	.270	557	60	-17	7			.944	2	*C-96	-0.6
1891	Chi-N	79	296	26	62	8	5	2	27	17	28	.209	.252	.291	543	58	-17	4			.940	-0	C-79	-0.9
1892	Chi-N	69	229	19	41	5	0	0	10	11	27	.179	.217	.201	418	26	-21	2			.946	15	C-69	0.0
1893	Chi-N	70	255	32	59	9	5	2	30	17	15	.231	.279	.329	609	62	-15	3			.939	6	C-70	-0.2
1894	Chi-N	51	168	36	53	8	2	0	23	26	20	.315	.407	.387	794	87	-3	2			.925	2	C-51	0.2
1895	Chi-N	60	212	30	48	6	3	3	29	16	9	.226	.284	.325	609	53	-16	6			.976	-2	C-59	-1.0
1896	Chi-N	65	215	17	48	4	1	1	19	14	14	.223	.274	.265	539	41	-19	6			.962	1	C-64/P-1	-1.0
1897	Chi-N	79	262	25	53	5	5	1	30	22		.202	.264	.271	535	40	-23	9			.952	3	C-79	-1.1
1898	Lou-N	86	287	27	70	8	5	1	31	15		.244	.281	.317	599	73	-11	9			.944	-11	C-86	-1.3
1899	Lou-N	46	131	11	26	2	1	0	13	26		.198	.335	.229	564	56	-7	3			.975	8	C-44	0.4
	Was-N	44	133	14	20	3	0	0	11	10		.150	.215	.173	388	7	-17	2			.949	4	C-43	-0.8
	Yr	90	264	25	46	5	1	0	24	36		.174	.278	.201	479	32	-24	5			.962	12	C-87	-0.4
1901	Bos-N	114	381	24	96	14	0	2	40	32		.252	.312	.304	616	72	-13	2			**.984**	12	*C-113	1.0
1902	Bos-N	80	255	18	60	7	2	0	30	24		.235	.304	.286	590	81	-5	4			.981	6	C-72	0.8
1903	Bos-N	32	99	10	21	2	0	0	6	11		.212	.291	.232	523	52	-6	1			.981	5	C-30	0.2
	Was-A	60	192	8	41	4	1	0	16	10		.214	.252	.245	497	49	-12	1			.978	-3	C-60	-1.0
1904	Was-A	81	265	11	64	7	0	0	24	8		.242	.266	.268	534	70	-9	2			.982	1	C-79,M	-0.1
1905	Was-A	77	238	16	39	8	0	0	14	15		.164	.213	.197	411	32	-18	1			.978	4	C-76	-0.7
1906	Was-A	22	68	5	13	0	0	0	3	1		.191	.203	.191	394	25	-6	0			.946	2	C-22	-0.7
	Cle-A	5	10	0	1	0	0	0	0	0		.100	.100	.100	200	-38	-2	0			.938	-1	/C-5	-0.2
	Yr	27	78	5	14	0	0	0	3	1		.179	.190	.179	369	16	-8	0			.945	-3	C-27	-0.9
Total	16	1216	4029	375	882	108	31	17	391	314	166	.219	.277	.274	550	56	-236	64			.961	47	*C-1197/P-1	-7.0
■ DANNY KLASSEN	Klassen, Daniel Victor b: 9/22/75, Leamington, Ont., Can. BR/TR, 6', 175 lbs. Deb: 7/4/98																							
1998	Ari-N	29	108	12	21	2	1	3	8	9	33	.194	.263	.315	578	51	-8	1	1	-0	.964	-5	2-29	-1.1
1999	Ari-N	1	1	0	1	0	0	0	0	0	0	1.000	1.000	1.000	2000	406	0	0	0	0	.000	0	-0,-0	0.0
2000	Ari-N	29	76	13	18	3	0	2	8	8	24	.237	.318	.355	673	69	-4	1	1	-0	.962	1	3-25/S-3	-0.3
Total	3	59	185	25	40	5	1	5	16	17	57	.216	.289	.335	624	61	-11	2	2	-0	.964	-4	/2-29,3-25,S-3	-1.4
■ BOBBY KLAUS	Klaus, Robert Francis b: 12/27/37, Spring Grove, Ill. BR/TR, 5'10", 170 lbs. Deb: 4/21/64 F																							
1964	Cin-N	40	93	10	17	5	1	2	6	4	13	.183	.216	.323	539	48	-7	1	0	0	.972	4	2-18,3-11/S-3	-0.2
	NY-N	56	209	25	51	8	3	2	11	25	30	.244	.325	.340	664	90	-2	3	4	-1	.986	-4	2-25,3-28/S-5	-0.5
	Yr	96	302	35	68	13	4	4	17	29	43	.225	.293	.334	627	76	-9	4	4	-1	.981	0	2-43,3-39/S-8	-0.7
1965	NY-N	119	288	30	55	12	0	2	12	45	49	.191	.302	.253	556	61	-14	1	6	-2	.968	15	2-72,S-28,3-25	0.5
Total	2	215	590	65	123	25	4	6	29	74	92	.208	.298	.295	593	69	-23	5	10	-2	.973	16	2-115/3-64,S-36	-0.2
■ BILLY KLAUS	Klaus, William Joseph b: 12/9/28, Spring Grove, Ill. BL/TR, 5'10", 165 lbs. Deb: 4/16/52 F																							
1952	Bos-N	7	4	3	0	0	0	0	0	1	1	.000	.200	.000	200	-42	-1	0	0	0	.500	-1	/S-4	-0.2
1953	Mil-N	2	2	1	0	0	0	0	1	0	0	.000	.000	.000	0	-99	-1	0	0	0	.000	0	H	-0.1
1955	Bos-A	135	541	83	153	26	2	7	60	60	44	.283	.354	.377	731	89	-8	6	0	1	.955	-7	*S-126/3-8	-0.3
1956	Bos-A	135	520	91	141	29	5	7	59	90	43	.271	.380	.387	766	92	-4	1	0	0	.945	-4	*3-106,S-26	-0.6
1957	Bos-A	127	477	76	120	18	4	10	42	55	53	.252	.329	.369	698	85	-9	2	0	0	.961	11	*S-118	1.3
1958	Bos-A	61	88	5	14	4	0	1	7	5	16	.159	.204	.239	443	20	-10	0	0	0	.883	-6	S-27	-1.6
1959	Bal-A	104	321	33	80	11	0	3	25	51	38	.249	.352	.312	664	86	-4	2	4	-1	.970	-12	S-59,3-49/2-1	-1.4
1960	Bal-A	46	43	8	9	2	0	1	6	9	9	.209	.346	.326	672	84	-1	0	0	0	.960	8	2-30,S-12/3-2	0.8
1961	Was-A	91	251	26	57	8	2	7	30	30	34	.227	.314	.359	673	81	-7	2	2	-0	.961	-5	3-51,S-18/2-1,O-1L	-1.1
1962	Phi-N	102	248	30	51	8	2	4	20	29	43	.206	.291	.302	594	61	-13	1	1	-0	.983	-6	3-53,S-30,2-11	-1.7
1963	Phi-N	11	18	1	1	0	0	0	0	1	4	.056	.105	.056	161	-53	-4	0	0	0	1.000	-2	/S-5,3-3	-0.6
Total	11	821	2513	357	626	106	15	40	250	331	285	.249	.337	.351	688	82	-60	14	7	1	.955	-24	S-425,3-272/2-43,O	-5.5
■ OLLIE KLEE	Klee, Ollie Chester "Babe" b: 5/20/1900, Piqua, Ohio d: 2/9/77, Toledo, Ohio BL/TL, 5'9.5", 160 lbs. Deb: 8/10/25																							
1925	Cin-N	3	1	0	0	0	0	0	0	0	1	.000	.000	.000	0	-99	-0	0	0	0	.000	-1	/O-1(0-1-0)	-0.1
■ CHUCK KLEIN	Klein, Charles Herbert b: 10/7/04, Indianapolis, Ind. d: 3/28/58, Indianapolis, Ind. BL/TR, 6', 185 lbs. Deb: 7/30/28 CH Career OF: (261-LF 44-CF 1305-RF)																							
1928	Phi-N	64	253	41	91	14	4	11	34	14	22	.360	.396	.577	973	146	16	0			.978	1	O-63(0-0-63)	1.2
1929	Phi-N	149	616	126	219	45	6	**43**	145	54	61	.356	.407	.657	1065	149	44	5			.966	-2	*O-149(0-25-123)	2.8
1930	Phi-N	156	648	**158**	250	**59**	8	40	170	54	50	.386	.436	.687	1123	155	56	4			.960	23	*O-156(0-0-156)	**5.7**

YEAR	TM/L	G	AB	R	H	2B	3B	HR	RBI	BB	SO	AVG	OBP	SLG	OPS	OPS+	BR+	SB	CS	SBR	FA	FR	G/POS	TPR
1931	Phi-N	148	594	**121**	200	34	10	**31**	**121**	59	49	.337	.398	**.584**	**982**	149	40	7			.971	-5	*O-148(90-17-43)	2.6
1932	Phi-N	154	650	**152**	**226**	50	15	**38**	137	60	49	.348	.404	**.646**	**1050**	158	52	**20**			.960	9	*O-154(0-0-154)	5.0
1933	Phi-N★	152	606	101	**223**	**44**	7	**28**	**120**	56	36	**.368**	**.422**	**.602**	**1025**	168	**53**	15			.986	9	*O-152(0-1-152)	**5.4**
1934	Chi-N★	115	435	78	131	27	2	20	80	47	38	.301	.372	.510	882	136	22	3			.962	-3	*O-110(97-1-15)	1.3
1935	*Chi-N	119	434	71	127	14	4	21	73	41	42	.293	.355	.488	844	123	14	4			.958	-1	*O-111(0-0-111)	0.6
1936	Chi-N	29	109	19	32	5	0	5	18	16	14	.294	.384	.477	861	128	4	0			.917	1	O-29(0-0-29)	0.3
	Phi-N	117	492	83	152	30	7	20	86	33	45	.309	.352	.520	873	120	12	6			.930	-4	*O-117(2-0-115)	0.1
	Yr	146	601	102	184	35	7	25	104	49	59	.306	.358	.512	871	122	17	6			.927	-4	*O-146(2-0-144)	0.4
1937	Phi-N	115	406	74	132	20	2	15	57	39	21	.325	.386	.495	881	127	15	3			.949	-4	*O-102(29-0-75)	0.5
1938	Phi-N	129	458	53	113	22	2	8	61	38	30	.247	.304	.356	660	83	-11	7			.960	-3	*O-119(3-0-118)	-2.1
1939	Phi-N	25	47	8	9	2	1	1	9	10	4	.191	.333	.340	674	84	-1	1			1.000	-0	O-11(0-0-11)/1-1	-0.2
	Pit-N	85	270	37	81	16	4	11	47	26	17	.300	.361	.511	873	134	12	1			.951	-2	O-66(30-0-37)	0.6
	Yr	110	317	45	90	18	5	12	56	36	21	.284	.357	.486	843	127	11	2			.958	-2	O-77(30-0-48)/1-1	0.4
1940	Phi-N	116	354	39	77	16	2	7	37	44	30	.218	.304	.333	637	79	-10	2			.984	-3	O-96(6-0-90)	-1.9
1941	Phi-N	50	73	6	9	0	0	1	3	10	6	.123	.229	.164	393	12	-8	0			.958	-1	O-14(2-0-12)	-1.0
1942	Phi-N	14	14	0	1	0	0	0	0	0	2	.071	.071	.071	143	-61	-3	0			.000	0	H	-0.3
1943	Phi-N	12	20	0	2	0	0	0	3	0	3	.100	.100	.100	200	-44	-4	1			.000	-1	/O-2(2-0-0)	-0.5
1944	Phi-N	4	7	1	1	0	0	0	0	0	2	.143	.143	.143	286	-20	-1	0			1.000	1	/O-1(0-0-1)	-0.1
Total	17	1753	6486	1168	2076	398	74	300	1201	601	521	.320	.379	.543	922	135	303	79			.962	16	*O-1600R/1-1	20.0

■ **LOU KLEIN** Klein, Louis Frank b: 10/22/18, New Orleans, La. d: 6/20/76, Metairie, La. BR/TR, 5′11″, 170 lbs. Deb: 4/21/43 MC Career OF: (4-LF 0-CF 3-RF)

YEAR	TM/L	G	AB	R	H	2B	3B	HR	RBI	BB	SO	AVG	OBP	SLG	OPS	OPS+	BR+	SB	CS	SBR	FA	FR	G/POS	TPR
1943	*StL-N	154	627	91	180	28	14	7	62	50	70	.287	.342	.410	752	112	8	9			.973	-19	*2-126,S-51	-0.1
1945	StL-N	19	57	12	13	4	1	1	6	14	9	.228	.389	.386	775	113	2	0			.929	-0	/S-7,O-7L,3-4,2-2	0.1
1946	StL-N	23	93	12	18	3	0	1	4	9	7	.194	.265	.258	523	47	-7	1			.975	-3	2-23	-0.9
1949	StL-N	58	114	25	25	6	0	2	12	22	20	.219	.355	.325	680	80	-3	0			.890	-4	S-21/2-9,3-7	-0.6
1951	Cle-A	2	2	0	0	0	0	0	0	0	1	.000	.000	.000	0	-99	-1	0	0	0	.000	0	H	-0.1
	Phi-A	49	144	22	33	7	0	5	17	10	12	.229	.279	.382	661	76	-6	0	0	0	.975	-4	2-42	-0.7
	Yr	51	146	22	33	7	0	5	17	10	13	.226	.276	.377	652	74	-6	0	0	0	.975	-4	2-42	-0.8
Total	5	305	1037	162	269	48	15	16	101	105	119	.259	.330	.381	711	97	-5	10	0		.975	-30	2-202/S-79,3-11,O-7L	-2.3

■ **RED KLEINOW** Kleinow, John Peter b: 7/20/1879, Milwaukee, Wis. d: 10/9/29, New York, N.Y. BR/TR, 5′10″, 165 lbs. Deb: 5/3/04 Career OF: (0-LF 0-CF 1-RF)

YEAR	TM/L	G	AB	R	H	2B	3B	HR	RBI	BB	SO	AVG	OBP	SLG	OPS	OPS+	BR+	SB	CS	SBR	FA	FR	G/POS	TPR
1904	NY-A	68	209	12	43	8	4	0	16	15		.206	.259	.282	541	68	-8	4			.966	-6	C-62/3-2,O-1(0-0-1)	-0.9
1905	NY-A	88	253	23	56	6	3	1	24	20		.221	.284	.281	564	71	-8	7			.978	-7	C-83/1-3	-0.9
1906	NY-A	96	268	30	59	9	3	0	31	24		.220	.287	.276	563	69	-9	8			.974	-1	C-95/1-1	-0.2
1907	NY-A	90	269	30	71	6	4	0	26	24		.264	.327	.316	643	97	-0	5			.970	-6	C-86/1-1	0.2
1908	NY-A	96	279	16	47	3	2	1	13	22		.168	.237	.204	441	43	-17	5			.973	-4	C-89/2-2	-1.5
1909	NY-A	78	206	24	47	11	4	0	15	25		.228	.315	.320	635	100	0	7			.966	-3	C-77	0.5
1910	NY-A	6	12	2	5	0	0	0	2	1		.417	.462	.417	878	166	1	2			1.000	0	/C-5	0.1
	Bos-A	50	147	9	22	1	0	1	8	20		.150	.251	.177	428	34	-11	3			.968	4	C-49	-0.2
	Yr	56	159	11	27	1	0	1	10	21		.170	.267	.195	462	44	-10	5			.970	4	C-54	-0.1
1911	Bos-A	8	14	0	3	0	0	0	0	2		.214	.313	.214	527	48	-1	1			1.000	0	/C-8	0.0
	Phi-N	4	8	0	1	1	0	0	0	0	1	.125	.125	.250	375	4	-1	0			1.000	-0	/C-4	-0.1
Total	8	584	1665	146	354	45	20	3	135	153	1	.213	.282	.269	551	71	-53	42			.972	-23	C-558/1-5,2-2,3O	-3.0

■ **RYAN KLESKO** Klesko, Ryan Anthony b: 6/12/71, Westminster, Cal. BL/TL, 6′3″, 220 lbs. Deb: 9/12/92 Career OF: (627-LF 0-CF 2-RF)

YEAR	TM/L	G	AB	R	H	2B	3B	HR	RBI	BB	SO	AVG	OBP	SLG	OPS	OPS+	BR+	SB	CS	SBR	FA	FR	G/POS	TPR
1992	Atl-N	13	14	0	0	0	0	0	1	0	5	.000	.067	.000	67	-75	-3	0	0	0	1.000	-1	/1-5	-0.4
1993	Atl-N	22	17	3	6	1	0	2	5	3	4	.353	.450	.765	1215	216	3	0	0	0	1.000	-1	/1-3,O-2(2-0-0)	0.2
1994	Atl-N	92	245	42	68	13	3	17	47	26	48	.278	.349	.563	913	130	10	1	0	0	.921	-11	O-74(74-0-0)/1-6	-0.2
1995	*Atl-N	107	329	48	102	25	2	23	70	47	72	.310	.399	.608	1007	156	27	5	4	-0	.942	-10	*O-102(102-0-0)/1-4	1.3
1996	*Atl-N	153	528	90	149	21	4	34	93	68	129	.282	.366	.530	897	126	19	6	3	0	.975	-5	*O-144(144-0-0)/1-2	1.0
1997	*Atl-N	143	467	67	122	23	6	24	84	48	130	.261	.335	.490	826	110	6	4	4	-1	.969	-9	*O-130(130-0-0),1-22	-0.8
1998	*Atl-N	129	427	69	117	29	1	18	70	56	66	.274	.362	.473	835	117	11	5	3	0	.994	-1	*O-120(120-0-0)/1-7	0.6
1999	*Atl-N	133	404	55	120	28	2	21	80	53	69	.297	.381	.532	913	128	17	5	2	0	.989	-9	1-75,O-53(53-0-0)/D-1	0.1
2000	SD-N	145	494	88	140	33	2	26	92	91	81	.283	.396	.516	912	136	29	23	7	3	.992	0	*1-136/O-4(2-0-2)	1.8
Total	9	937	2925	462	824	173	20	165	542	392	604	.282	.370	.524	893	128	118	49	23	3	.969	-46	O-629L,1-260/D-1	3.6

■ **JAY KLEVEN** Kleven, Jay Allen b: 12/2/49, Oakland, Cal. BR/TR, 6′2″, 190 lbs. Deb: 6/20/76

YEAR	TM/L	G	AB	R	H	2B	3B	HR	RBI	BB	SO	AVG	OBP	SLG	OPS	OPS+	BR+	SB	CS	SBR	FA	FR	G/POS	TPR
1976	NY-N	2	5	0	1	0	0	0	2	0	1	.200	.200	.200	400	15	-1	0	0	0	1.000	0	/C-2	0.0

■ **LOU KLIMCHOCK** Klimchock, Louis Stephen b: 10/15/39, Hostetter, Pa. BL/TR, 5′11″, 180 lbs. Deb: 9/27/58

YEAR	TM/L	G	AB	R	H	2B	3B	HR	RBI	BB	SO	AVG	OBP	SLG	OPS	OPS+	BR+	SB	CS	SBR	FA	FR	G/POS	TPR
1958	KC-A	2	10	2	2	0	0	1	1	0	1	.200	.200	.500	700	84	-0	0	0	0	1.000	-1	/2-2	-0.1
1959	KC-A	17	66	10	18	1	0	4	13	1	6	.273	.284	.470	753	101	-0	0	0	0	.949	-4	2-16	-0.3
1960	KC-A	10	10	0	3	0	0	0	0	0	0	.300	.300	.300	600	62	-1	0	0	0	.000	0	/2-1	-0.1
1961	KC-A	57	121	8	26	4	1	1	16	5	13	.215	.246	.289	535	42	-10	0	0	0	.976	-5	1-11/O-7L,3-6,2-1	-1.7
1962	Mil-N	8	8	0	0	0	0	0	0	0	2	.000	.000	.000	0	-99	-2	0	0	0	.000	0	H	-0.2
1963	Was-A	9	14	1	2	0	0	0	2	0	1	.143	.143	.143	286	-20	-2	0	0	0	1.000	1	/2-3	-0.1
	Mil-N	24	46	6	9	1	0	0	1	0	12	.196	.196	.217	413	19	-5	0	1	-0	.988	0	1-12	-0.6
1964	Mil-N	10	21	3	7	2	0	0	2	1	2	.333	.364	.429	792	121	1	0	0	0	1.000	-3	/3-4,2-2	-0.2
1965	Mil-N	34	39	3	3	0	0	0	3	2	8	.077	.122	.077	199	-42	-7	0	0	0	.923	1	/1-4	-0.7
1966	NY-N	5	5	0	0	0	0	0	0	0	3	.000	.000	.000	0	-99	-1	0	0	0	.000	0	H	-0.1
1968	Cle-A	11	15	0	2	0	0	0	3	1	0	.133	.188	.133	321	-2	-2	0	0	0	.500	-3	/3-4,1-1,2-1	-0.5
1969	Cle-A	90	258	26	74	13	2	6	26	18	14	.287	.333	.422	756	107	2	0	0	0	.934	-16	3-56,2-21/C-1	-1.4
1970	Cle-A	41	56	5	9	0	0	1	2	3	9	.161	.217	.214	431	18	-6	0	0	0	1.000	-1	/1-5,2-5	-0.7
Total	12	318	669	64	155	21	3	13	69	31	71	.232	.267	.330	597	63	-35	0	1	-0	.906	-30	/3-70,2-52,1-33,OC	-6.7

■ **BOBBY KLINE** Kline, John Robert b: 1/27/29, St.Petersburg, Fla BR/TR, 6′, 179 lbs. Deb: 4/11/55

YEAR	TM/L	G	AB	R	H	2B	3B	HR	RBI	BB	SO	AVG	OBP	SLG	OPS	OPS+	BR+	SB	CS	SBR	FA	FR	G/POS	TPR
1955	Was-A	77	140	12	31	5	0	0	9	11	27	.221	.288	.257	545	50	-10	0	0	0	.943	13	S-69/2-4,3-3,P-1	0.7

■ **JOHNNY KLING** Kling, John "Noisy" b: 2/25/1875, Kansas City, Mo. d: 1/31/47, Kansas City, Mo. BR/TR, 5′9.5″, 160 lbs. Deb: 9/11/00 FM Career OF: (10-LF 1-CF 13-RF)

YEAR	TM/L	G	AB	R	H	2B	3B	HR	RBI	BB	SO	AVG	OBP	SLG	OPS	OPS+	BR+	SB	CS	SBR	FA	FR	G/POS	TPR
1900	Chi-N	15	51	8	15	3	1	0	7	2		.294	.321	.392	713	100	-0	0			.901	-2	C-15	-0.1
1901	Chi-N	74	256	26	70	6	3	0	21	9		.273	.301	.320	621	83	-6	8			.952	-10	C-69/1-1,O-1(0-0-1)	-0.9
1902	Chi-N	115	436	50	126	19	3	0	59	29		.289	.333	.346	680	113	6	25			.974	8	*C-113/S-1	2.6
1903	Chi-N	132	491	67	146	29	13	3	68	22		.297	.330	.428	758	119	9	23			.969	2	*C-132	2.3
1904	Chi-N	123	452	41	110	18	0	2	46	16		.243	.271	.296	567	75	-14	7			.974	-12	*C-104,O-10L/1-6	-1.7
1905	Chi-N	111	380	26	83	8	6	1	52	28		.218	.272	.279	551	62	-18	13			.966	0	*C-106/O-4(0-0-4),1-1	-0.7
1906	*Chi-N	107	343	45	107	15	8	2	46	23		.312	.357	.420	777	134	12	14			**.982**	5	C-96/O-3(0-0-3)	2.9
1907	*Chi-N	104	334	44	95	15	8	1	43	27		.284	.342	.386	728	120	7	9			**.987**	6	C-98/1-2	2.6
1908	*Chi-N	126	424	51	117	23	5	4	59	21		.276	.315	.382	697	117	7	16			.979	2	*C-117/O-6(1-1-4),1-2	2.3
1910	*Chi-N	91	297	31	80	17	2	2	32	37	27	.269	.354	.360	714	109	4	3			.979	-5	C-86	0.8
1911	Chi-N	27	80	8	14	3	2	1	5	8	14	.175	.250	.300	550	54	-5	1			.969	5	C-25	0.1
	Bos-N	75	241	32	54	8	1	2	24	30	29	.224	.310	.290	600	63	-12	0			.951	-5	C-71/3-1	-1.1
	Yr	102	321	40	68	11	3	3	29	38	43	.212	.295	.293	588	61	-17	1			.956	-0	C-96/3-1	-1.0
1912	Bos-N	81	252	26	80	10	3	2	30	15	30	.317	.356	.405	761	106	2	3			.958	6	C-74,M	1.3
1913	Cin-N	80	209	20	57	7	6	0	23	14	14	.273	.318	.364	682	95	-2	2			.975	7	C-63	1.0
Total	13	1261	4246	475	1154	181	61	20	515	281	114	.272	.319	.357	676	100	-10	124			.971	6	*C-1169/O-24R,13S	11.4

■ **RUDY KLING** Kling, Rudolph A. b: 3/23/1870, St.Louis, Mo. d: 3/14/37, St.Louis, Mo. BR/TR, 5′10″, 178 lbs. Deb: 9/21/02

YEAR	TM/L	G	AB	R	H	2B	3B	HR	RBI	BB	SO	AVG	OBP	SLG	OPS	OPS+	BR+	SB	CS	SBR	FA	FR	G/POS	TPR
1902	StL-N	4	10	1	2	0	0	0	0	4		.200	.429	.200	629	99	0	1			.842	-2	/S-4	-0.2

■ **JOE KLINGER** Klinger, Joseph John b: 8/2/02, Canonsburg, Pa. d: 7/31/60, Little Rock, Ark. BR/TR, 6′, 190 lbs. Deb: 9/13/27

YEAR	TM/L	G	AB	R	H	2B	3B	HR	RBI	BB	SO	AVG	OBP	SLG	OPS	OPS+	BR+	SB	CS	SBR	FA	FR	G/POS	TPR
1927	NY-N	3	5	0	2	0	0	0	0	0	2	.400	.400	.400	800	115	0	0			1.000	0	/O-1(1-0-0)	0.0

YEAR	TM/L	G	AB	R	H	2B	3B	HR	RBI	BB	SO	AVG	OBP	SLG	OPS	OPS+	BR+	SB	CS	SBR	FA	FR	G/POS	TPR
1930	Chi-A	4	8	0	3	0	0	0	1	0	0	.375	.375	.375	750	94	-0	0	0	0	1.000	-1	/C-2,1-2	-0.1
Total	2	7	13	0	5	0	0	0	1	0	2	.385	.385	.385	769	102	0	0	0		1.000	-1	/1-2,C-2,O-1(1-0-0)	-0.1

■ **NAP KLOZA** Kloza, John Clarence b: 9/7/03, Poland d: 6/11/62, Milwaukee, Wis. BR/TR, 5′11″, 180 lbs. Deb: 8/16/31

YEAR	TM/L	G	AB	R	H	2B	3B	HR	RBI	BB	SO	AVG	OBP	SLG	OPS	OPS+	BR+	SB	CS	SBR	FA	FR	G/POS	TPR
1931	StL-A	3	7	1	1	0	0	0	0	1	4	.143	.250	.143	393	5	-1	0	0	0	1.000	-0	/O-3(0-0-3)	-0.1
1932	StL-A	19	13	4	2	0	1	0	2	4	4	.154	.353	.308	661	69	-1	0	0	0	1.000	-1	/O-3(1-2-0)	-0.2
Total	2	22	20	5	3	0	1	0	2	5	8	.150	.320	.250	570	48	-1	0	0	0	1.000	-2	/O-6(1-2-3)	-0.3

■ **JOE KLUGMANN** Klugmann, Josie b: 3/26/1895, St.Louis, Mo. d: 7/18/51, Moberly, Mo. BR/TR, 5′11″, 175 lbs. Deb: 9/23/21

YEAR	TM/L	G	AB	R	H	2B	3B	HR	RBI	BB	SO	AVG	OBP	SLG	OPS	OPS+	BR+	SB	CS	SBR	FA	FR	G/POS	TPR
1921	Chi-N	6	21	3	6	0	0	0	2	1	2	.286	.348	.286	634	69	-1	0	1	-0	.969	0	/2-5	-0.1
1922	Chi-N	2	2	0	0	0	0	0	0	0	0	.000	.000	.000	0	-98	-1	0	0	0	1.000	1	/2-2	0.0
1924	Bro-N	31	79	7	13	2	1	0	3	2	9	.165	.185	.215	400	7	-10	0	0	0	.929	-1	2-28/S-1	-1.1
1925	Cle-A	38	85	12	28	9	2	0	12	8	4	.329	.387	.482	869	119	2	3	1	0	.959	-3	2-29/1-4,3-2	0.0
Total	4	77	187	22	47	11	3	0	17	11	15	.251	.296	.342	639	67	-10	3	2	-0	.947	-3	/2-64,1-4,3-2,S-1	-1.2

■ **ELMER KLUMPP** Klumpp, Elmer Edward b: 8/26/06, St.Louis, Mo. d: 10/18/96, Menomonee Falls, Wis. BR/TR, 6′, 184 lbs. Deb: 4/17/34

YEAR	TM/L	G	AB	R	H	2B	3B	HR	RBI	BB	SO	AVG	OBP	SLG	OPS	OPS+	BR+	SB	CS	SBR	FA	FR	G/POS	TPR
1934	Was-A	12	15	2	2	0	0	0	0	0	1	.133	.188	.133	321	-17	-3	0	0	0	.889	-1	C-11	-0.3
1937	Bro-N	5	11	0	1	0	0	0	2	1	4	.091	.167	.091	258	-28	-2	0			1.000	1	/C-3	-0.1
Total	2	17	26	2	3	0	0	0	2	1	5	.115	.179	.115	294	-21	-5	0	0		.943	-0	/C-14	-0.4

■ **BILLY KLUSMAN** Klusman, William F. b: 3/24/1865, Cincinnati, Ohio d: 6/24/07, Cincinnati, Ohio BR/TR, 5′10.5″, 185 lbs. Deb: 6/21/1888

YEAR	TM/L	G	AB	R	H	2B	3B	HR	RBI	BB	SO	AVG	OBP	SLG	OPS	OPS+	BR+	SB	CS	SBR	FA	FR	G/POS	TPR
1888	Bos-N	28	107	9	18	4	0	2	11	5	13	.168	.205	.262	467	47	-6	3			.914	-9	2-28	-1.4
1890	StL-a	15	65	9	18	4	1	1	11	1		.277	.288	.415	703	94	-1	1			.896	-3	2-15	-0.3
Total	2	43	172	18	36	8	1	3	22	6	13	.209	.236	.320	556	67	-8	4			.908	-12	/2-43	-1.7

■ **TED KLUSZEWSKI** Kluszewski, Theodore Bernard "Big Klu" b: 9/10/24, Argo, Ill. d: 3/29/88, Cincinnati, Ohio BL/TL, 6′2″, 225 lbs. Deb: 4/18/47 C

YEAR	TM/L	G	AB	R	H	2B	3B	HR	RBI	BB	SO	AVG	OBP	SLG	OPS	OPS+	BR+	SB	CS	SBR	FA	FR	G/POS	TPR
1947	Cin-N	9	10	1	1	0	0	0	2	1	2	.100	.182	.100	282	-23	-2	0			1.000	-0	/1-2	-0.2
1948	Cin-N	113	379	49	104	23	4	12	57	18	32	.274	.307	.451	758	107	1	1			.990	1	1-98	-0.1
1949	Cin-N	136	531	63	164	26	2	8	68	19	24	.309	.333	.411	743	97	-3	3			.989	-7	*1-134	-1.4
1950	Cin-N	134	538	76	165	37	0	25	111	33	28	.307	.348	.515	863	123	16	3			.987	-11	*1-131	0.0
1951	Cin-N	154	607	74	157	35	2	13	77	35	33	.259	.301	.387	688	83	-16	6	2	1	**.997**	-6	*1-154	-2.7
1952	Cin-N	135	497	62	159	24	11	16	86	47	28	.320	.383	.509	892	146	30	3	3	-0	**.993**	-10	*1-133	1.6
1953	Cin-N★	149	570	97	180	25	0	40	108	55	34	.316	.380	.570	950	142	34	2	0	0	**.995**	-18	*1-147	0.8
1954	Cin-N★	149	573	104	187	28	3	**49**	**141**	78	35	.326	.410	.642	1052	165	53	0	2	-1	**.996**	-4	*1-149	3.9
1955	Cin-N★	153	612	116	**192**	25	0	47	113	66	40	.314	.384	.585	969	144	38	1	1	-0	**.995**	-9	*1-153	2.0
1956	Cin-N★	138	517	91	156	14	1	35	102	49	31	.302	.366	.536	901	130	22	1	0	0	.990	-5	*1-131	1.0
1957	Cin-N	69	127	12	34	7	0	6	21	5	5	.268	.301	.465	765	95	-1	0	0	0	.989	0	1-23	-0.2
1958	Pit-N	100	301	29	88	13	4	4	37	26	16	.292	.351	.402	753	101	1	0	0	0	.994	-5	1-72	-0.8
1959	Pit-N	60	122	11	32	10	1	2	17	5	14	.262	.291	.410	701	85	-3	0	0	0	1.000	-1	1-20	-0.5
	*Chi-A	31	101	11	30	2	1	2	10	9	10	.297	.355	.396	751	107	1	0	1	-0	1.000	-2	1-29	-0.3
1960	Chi-A	81	181	20	53	9	0	5	39	22	10	.293	.369	.425	795	116	4	0	1	-0	.997	-2	1-39	0.0
1961	LA-A	107	263	32	64	12	0	15	39	24	23	.243	.307	.460	767	91	-4	0	0	0	.989	-5	1-66	-1.2
Total	15	1718	5929	848	1766	290	29	279	1028	492	365	.298	.354	.498	852	122	171	20	10		.993	-82	*1-1481	1.9

■ **MICKEY KLUTTS** Klutts, Gene Ellis b: 9/20/54, Montebello, Cal. BR/TR, 5′11″, 189 lbs. Deb: 7/7/76

YEAR	TM/L	G	AB	R	H	2B	3B	HR	RBI	BB	SO	AVG	OBP	SLG	OPS	OPS+	BR+	SB	CS	SBR	FA	FR	G/POS	TPR
1976	NY-A	2	3	0	0	0	0	0	0	0	1	.000	.000	.000	0	-99	-1	0	0	0	.875	0	/S-2	0.0
1977	NY-A	5	15	3	4	1	0	1	4	2	1	.267	.389	.533	922	150	1	0	1	-0	1.000	2	/3-4,S-1	0.3
1978	NY-A	1	2	1	2	1	0	0	0	0	0	1.000	1.000	1.500	2500	608	2	0	0	0	.750	0	/3-1	0.2
1979	Oak-A	24	73	3	14	2	1	1	4	7	20	.192	.262	.288	550	51	-5	0	1	-0	.882	-2	S-10/2-8,3-6,D-2	-0.7
1980	Oak-A	75	197	20	53	14	0	4	21	13	41	.269	.314	.401	715	102	-0	1	4	-1	.947	-6	3-62/S-8,2-7,D-1	-0.8
1981	*Oak-A	15	46	9	17	0	0	5	11	2	9	.370	.396	.696	1091	220	7	0	0	0	.957	-5	3-14	0.2
1982	Oak-A	55	157	10	28	8	0	0	14	9	18	.178	.223	.229	452	26	-16	0	0	0	.946	-3	3-49	-2.0
1983	Tor-A	22	43	3	11	0	0	3	5	1	11	.256	.289	.465	754	98	-0	0	1	-0	1.000	-3	3-17/D-2	-0.3
Total	8	199	536	49	129	26	1	14	59	34	101	.241	.290	.371	661	84	-13	1	7	-2	.948	-16	3-153/S-21,2-15,D-5	-3.1

■ **CLYDE KLUTTZ** Kluttz, Clyde Franklin b: 12/12/17, Rockwell, N.C. d: 5/12/79, Salisbury, N.C. BR/TR, 6′, 198 lbs. Deb: 4/20/42

YEAR	TM/L	G	AB	R	H	2B	3B	HR	RBI	BB	SO	AVG	OBP	SLG	OPS	OPS+	BR+	SB	CS	SBR	FA	FR	G/POS	TPR
1942	Bos-N	72	210	21	56	10	1	1	31	7	13	.267	.294	.338	632	86	-4	0			.979	0	C-57	-0.1
1943	Bos-N	66	207	13	51	7	0	0	20	15	9	.246	.297	.280	577	68	-8	0			.973	2	C-55	-0.3
1944	Bos-N	81	229	20	64	12	2	2	19	13	14	.279	.318	.376	694	91	-3	0			.980	4	C-58	0.4
1945	Bos-N	25	81	9	24	4	1	0	10	2	6	.296	.313	.370	684	89	-1	0			.987	-0	C-19	0.0
	NY-N	73	222	25	62	14	0	4	21	15	10	.279	.331	.396	727	100	-1	1			.978	-6	C-57	-0.3
	Yr	98	303	34	86	18	1	4	31	17	16	.284	.326	.389	716	97	-2	1			.981	-6	C-76	-0.3
1946	NY-N	5	8	0	3	0	0	0	1	0	1	.375	.375	.375	750	112	0	0			.857	-1	/C-2	0.0
	StL-N	52	136	8	36	7	0	0	14	10	10	.265	.315	.316	631	76	-4	0			.980	2	C-49	0.0
	Yr	57	144	8	39	7	0	0	15	10	11	.271	.318	.319	638	78	-4	0			.976	1	C-51	0.0
1947	Pit-N	73	232	26	70	9	2	6	42	17	18	.302	.355	.435	790	106	2	1			.987	3	C-69	0.8
1948	Pit-N	94	271	26	60	12	2	4	20	20	19	.221	.275	.325	600	61	-15	3			.978	0	C-91	-1.1
1951	StL-A	4	4	2	2	1	0	0	1	1	0	.500	.600	.750	1350	256	1	0	0	0	1.000	1	/C-1	0.2
	Was-A	53	159	15	49	9	0	1	22	20	8	.308	.389	.384	773	111	3	0	0	0	.968	-7	C-46	-0.2
	Yr	57	163	17	51	10	0	1	23	21	8	.313	.395	.393	787	115	4	0	0	0	.968	-6	C-47	0.0
1952	Was-A	58	144	7	33	5	0	1	11	12	11	.229	.293	.285	578	63	-7	0	0	0	.979	-1	C-52	-0.6
Total	9	656	1903	172	510	90	8	19	212	132	119	.268	.318	.354	671	86	-39	5	0		.978	-3	C-556	-1.2

■ **JOE KMAK** Kmak, Joseph Robert b: 5/3/63, Napa, Cal. BR/TR, 6′, 185 lbs. Deb: 4/6/93

YEAR	TM/L	G	AB	R	H	2B	3B	HR	RBI	BB	SO	AVG	OBP	SLG	OPS	OPS+	BR+	SB	CS	SBR	FA	FR	G/POS	TPR
1993	Mil-A	51	110	9	24	5	0	0	7	14	13	.218	.317	.264	581	59	-6	6	2	1	1.000	2	C-50	-0.2
1995	Chi-N	19	53	7	13	3	0	1	6	6	12	.245	.333	.358	692	84	-1	0	0	0	1.000	-1	C-18/3-1	-0.1
Total	2	70	163	16	37	8	0	1	13	20	25	.227	.323	.294	617	67	-7	6	2	1	1.000	0	/C-68,3-1	-0.3

■ **OTTO KNABE** Knabe, Franz Otto "Dutch" b: 6/12/1884, Carrick, Pa. d: 5/17/61, Philadelphia, Pa. BR/TR, 5′8″, 175 lbs. Deb: 10/3/05 M Career OF: (2-LF 0-CF 5-RF)

YEAR	TM/L	G	AB	R	H	2B	3B	HR	RBI	BB	SO	AVG	OBP	SLG	OPS	OPS+	BR+	SB	CS	SBR	FA	FR	G/POS	TPR
1905	Pit-N	3	10	0	3	1	0	0	2	3		.300	.462	.400	862	154	1	0			.786	0	/3-3	0.1
1907	Phi-N	129	444	67	113	16	9	1	34	52		.255	.339	.338	677	114	8	18			.960	1	*2-121/O-5(1-0-3)	1.1
1908	Phi-N	151	555	63	121	26	8	0	27	49		.218	.290	.294	583	84	-10	27			.969	11	*2-151	0.3
1909	Phi-N	113	402	40	94	13	3	0	34	35		.234	.308	.281	589	82	-8	9			.938	8	*2-110/O-1(1-0-0)	0.1
1910	Phi-N	137	510	73	133	18	6	1	44	47	42	.261	.327	.325	652	87	-8	15			.954	14	*2-136	0.7
1911	Phi-N	142	528	99	125	15	6	1	42	94	35	.237	.352	.294	646	80	-10	23			.950	4	*2-142	-0.4
1912	Phi-N	126	426	56	120	11	4	0	46	55	20	.282	.366	.326	693	85	-7	16			.952	1	*2-123	-0.4
1913	Phi-N	148	571	70	150	25	7	2	53	45	26	.263	.320	.342	661	85	-11	14			.959	12	*2-148	0.3
1914	Bal-F	147	469	45	106	26	2	2	42	53	28	.226	.307	.303	610	65	-30	10			.956	1	*2-144,M	-2.8
1915	Bal-F	103	320	38	81	16	2	1	25	37	16	.253	.334	.325	659	83	-11	7			.975	7	2-94/O-1(0-0-1),M	-0.3
1916	Pit-N	28	89	4	17	3	1	0	9	6	6	.191	.258	.247	505	55	-5	1			.962	-0	2-28	-0.5
	Chi-N	51	145	17	40	8	0	0	7	9	18	.276	.327	.331	658	92	-1	3			.939	6	2-42/S-1,3-1,O-1R	0.6
	Yr	79	234	21	57	11	1	0	16	15	24	.244	.300	.299	600	79	-6	4			.948	5	2-70/S-1,3-1,O-1R	0.1
Total	11	1278	4469	572	1103	178	48	8	365	485	191	.247	.325	.313	639	84	-92	143			.957	64	*2-1239/O-8R,3-4,S	-1.2

■ **COTTON KNAUPP** Knaupp, Henry Antone b: 8/13/1889, San Antonio, Tex. d: 7/6/67, New Orleans, La. BR/TR, 5′9″, 165 lbs. Deb: 8/30/10

YEAR	TM/L	G	AB	R	H	2B	3B	HR	RBI	BB	SO	AVG	OBP	SLG	OPS	OPS+	BR+	SB	CS	SBR	FA	FR	G/POS	TPR
1910	Cle-A	18	59	3	14	3	1	0	11	8		.237	.338	.322	660	105	1	1			.884	-8	S-18	-0.8
1911	Cle-A	13	39	2	4	1	0	0	0	0		.103	.103	.128	231	-35	-7	3			.964	2	S-13	-0.5
Total	2	31	98	5	18	4	1	0	11	8		.184	.252	.245	497	48	-6	4			.913	-6	/S-31	-1.3

■ **ALAN KNICELY** Knicely, Alan Lee b: 5/19/55, Harrisonburg, Va. BR/TR, 6′0.5″, 194 lbs. Deb: 8/12/79 Career OF: (5-LF 0-CF 20-RF)

YEAR	TM/L	G	AB	R	H	2B	3B	HR	RBI	BB	SO	AVG	OBP	SLG	OPS	OPS+	BR+	SB	CS	SBR	FA	FR	G/POS	TPR
1979	Hou-N	7	6	0	0	0	0	0	0	2	3	.000	.250	.000	250	-27	-1	0	0	0	1.000	-2	/C-3,3-1	-0.3
1980	Hou-N	1	1	0	0	0	0	0	0	0	1	.000	.000	.000	0	-99	-0	0	0	0	.000	0	/H	0.0

YEAR	TM/L	G	AB	R	H	2B	3B	HR	RBI	BB	SO	AVG	OBP	SLG	OPS	OPS+	BR+	SB	CS	SBR	FA	FR	G/POS	TPR
1981	Hou-N	3	7	2	4	0	0	2	2	0	1	.571	.571	1.429	2000	477	3	0	0	0	1.000	0	/C-2,O-1(1-0-0)	0.3
1982	Hou-N	59	133	10	25	2	0	2	12	14	30	.188	.270	.248	518	50	-9	0	1	-0	.977	-9	C-23,O-16(1-0-15)/3-1	-1.8
1983	Cin-N	59	98	11	22	3	0	2	10	16	28	.224	.333	.316	650	78	-2	0	2	-1	1.000	-2	C-31/O-8(3-0-5),1-2	-0.4
1984	Cin-N	10	29	0	4	0	0	0	5	3	6	.138	.219	.138	357	2	-4	0	0	0	.984	0	/1-8,C-1	-0.4
1985	Cin-N	48	158	17	40	9	0	5	26	16	34	.253	.326	.405	731	98	-0	0	0	0	.968	-14	C-46	-1.3
	Phi-N	7	7	0	0	0	0	0	0	0	4	.000	.000	.000	0	-97	-2	0	0	0	1.000	-0	/1-1	-0.2
	Yr	55	165	17	40	9	0	5	26	16	38	.242	.313	.388	701	91	-2	0	0	0	.968	-14	C-46/1-1	-1.5
1986	StL-N	34	82	8	16	3	0	1	6	17	21	.195	.333	.268	602	68	-3	1	1	-0	.995	-1	1-29/C-2	-0.6
Total	8	228	521	48	111	17	0	12	61	68	128	.213	.306	.315	621	73	-18	1	4	-1	.979	-26	C-108/1-40,O-25R,3	-4.7

■ AUSTIN KNICKERBOCKER

Knickerbocker, Austin Jay b: 10/15/18, Bangall, N.Y. d: 2/18/97, Clinton Corners, N.Y. BR/TR, 5'11", 185 lbs. Deb: 4/19/47

YEAR	TM/L	G	AB	R	H	2B	3B	HR	RBI	BB	SO	AVG	OBP	SLG	OPS	OPS+	BR+	SB	CS	SBR	FA	FR	G/POS	TPR
1947	Phi-A	21	48	8	12	3	2	0	2	3	4	.250	.294	.396	690	89	-1	0	1	-0	.943	0	O-14(2-2-10)	-0.2

■ BILL KNICKERBOCKER

Knickerbocker, William Hart b: 12/29/11, Los Angeles, Cal. d: 9/8/63, Sebastopol, Cal. BR/TR, 5'11", 170 lbs. Deb: 4/12/33

YEAR	TM/L	G	AB	R	H	2B	3B	HR	RBI	BB	SO	AVG	OBP	SLG	OPS	OPS+	BR+	SB	CS	SBR	FA	FR	G/POS	TPR
1933	Cle-A	80	279	20	63	16	3	2	32	11	30	.226	.255	.326	581	51	-21	1	4	-1	.939	2	S-80	-1.4
1934	Cle-A	146	593	82	188	32	5	4	67	25	40	.317	.347	.408	755	93	-7	6	6	-1	.962	-7	*S-146	-0.4
1935	Cle-A	132	540	77	161	34	5	0	55	27	31	.298	.332	.380	711	82	-15	2	12	-4	.956	9	*S-128	0.0
1936	Cle-A	155	618	81	182	35	3	8	73	56	30	.294	.354	.400	754	85	-15	5	14	-4	.952	-1	*S-155	-0.7
1937	StL-A	121	491	53	128	29	5	4	61	30	32	.261	.303	.365	668	67	-26	3	2	-0	.958	-13	*S-115/2-6	-2.8
1938	NY-A	46	128	15	32	8	3	1	21	11	10	.250	.309	.383	692	73	-6	0	0	0	.982	-5	2-34/S-3	-0.5
1939	NY-A	6	13	2	2	1	0	0	1	0	0	.154	.154	.231	385	-3	-2	0	0	0	1.000	2	/2-2,S-2	0.0
1940	NY-A	45	124	17	30	8	1	1	10	14	8	.242	.333	.347	680	80	-3	1	1	-0	.985	-3	S-19,3-17	-0.4
1941	Chi-A	89	343	51	84	23	2	7	29	41	27	.245	.329	.385	714	89	-6	6	5	-0	.970	-17	2-88	-1.7
1942	Phi-A	87	289	25	73	12	0	1	19	29	30	.253	.323	.304	627	77	-8	1	2	-0	.964	-12	2-81/S-1	-1.6
Total	10	907	3418	423	943	198	27	28	368	244	238	.276	.326	.374	700	79	-109	25	46	-11	.955	-42	S-649,2-211/3-17	-9.5

■ LON KNIGHT

Knight, Alonzo P. b: 6/16/1853, Philadelphia, Pa. d: 4/23/32, Philadelphia, Pa. BR/TR, 5'11.5", 165 lbs. Deb: 9/4/1875 MU Career OF: (0-LF 7-CF 473-RF)

YEAR	TM/L	G	AB	R	H	2B	3B	HR	RBI	BB	SO	AVG	OBP	SLG	OPS	OPS+	BR+	SB	CS	SBR	FA	FR	G/POS	TPR
1875	Ath-n	13	47	5	6	2	0	0	2	0	2	.128	.128	.170	298	2	-5	2	0	0	.875	-0	P-13/S-1	-0.1
1876	Phi-N	55	242	32	60	9	3	0	24	2	2	.248	.256	.313	569	89	-3				.804	-7	P-34,1-13/O-9R,2-6	-0.6
1880	Wor-N	49	201	31	48	11	3	0	21	5	8	.239	.257	.323	581	88	-3				.863	5	O-49(0-0-49)	0.2
1881	Det-N	83	340	67	92	16	3	1	52	23	21	.271	.317	.344	661	104	1				.890	1	*O-82(0-0-82)/2-1,1-1	0.3
1882	Det-N	86	347	39	72	12	6	0	24	16	21	.207	.242	.277	519	66	-13				.867	1	*O-84(0-0-84)/1-2	-1.2
1883	Phi-a	97	429	98	108	23	9	1	53	21		.252	.287	.354	641	96	-3				.858	0	*O-93R/3-3,2-2,M	-0.3
1884	Phi-a	108	484	94	131	18	12	1		10		.271	.287	.364	651	104	0				.911	11	*O-108R/P-2,1-1,M	0.9
1885	Phi-a	29	119	17	25	1	1	0	14	9		.210	.271	.235	507	58	-6				.921	4	O-29(0-0-29)/P-1	-0.1
	Pro-N	25	81	8	13	1	0	0	8	11	17	.160	.261	.173	434	44	-4				.957	1	O-25(0-4-22)/P-1	-0.3
Total	7	532	2243	386	549	91	37	3	196	97	69	.245	.277	.323	600	89	-30				.887	17	O-479R/P-38,1-17,23	-1.1

■ RAY KNIGHT

Knight, Charles Ray b: 12/28/52, Albany, Ga. BR/TR, 6'2", 190 lbs. Deb: 9/10/74 MC Career OF: (9-LF 0-CF 1-RF)

YEAR	TM/L	G	AB	R	H	2B	3B	HR	RBI	BB	SO	AVG	OBP	SLG	OPS	OPS+	BR+	SB	CS	SBR	FA	FR	G/POS	TPR
1974	Cin-N	14	11	1	2	1	0	0	2	1	2	.182	.250	.273	523	47	-1	0	0	0	1.000	1	3-14	0.0
1977	Cin-N	80	92	8	24	5	1	1	13	9	16	.261	.327	.370	696	85	-2	1	1	-0	.941	4	3-37,2-17/O-5L,S-3	0.3
1978	Cin-N	83	65	7	13	3	0	1	4	3	13	.200	.235	.292	528	47	-5	0	0	0	.868	5	3-60/2-4,O-3L,1S	0.0
1979	*Cin-N	150	551	64	175	37	4	10	79	38	57	.318	.365	.454	819	121	16	4	4	-1	.962	-15	*3-149	-0.2
1980	Cin-N★	162	618	71	163	39	7	14	78	36	62	.264	.309	.417	726	101	-1	1	2	-0	.969	-15	*3-162	-2.0
1981	Cin-N	106	386	43	100	23	1	6	34	33	51	.259	.324	.370	694	95	-3	2	4	-1	.957	-13	*3-105	-0.8
1982	Hou-N★	158	609	72	179	36	6	6	70	48	58	.294	.350	.402	753	119	15	2	5	-1	.990	-2	1-96,3-67	0.4
1983	Hou-N	145	507	43	154	36	4	9	70	42	62	.304	.362	.444	805	130	20	0	3	-1	.993	-11	*1-143	0.0
1984	Hou-N	88	278	15	62	10	0	2	29	14	30	.223	.263	.281	543	57	-16	0	3	-1	.946	-2	3-54,1-24	-2.3
	NY-N	27	93	13	26	4	0	1	6	7	13	.280	.337	.355	691	96	-0	0	0	0	.962	-4	3-27/1-3	-0.5
	Yr	115	371	28	88	14	0	3	35	21	43	.237	.282	.299	581	67	-17	0	3	-1	.951	-6	3-81,1-27	-2.8
1985	NY-N	90	271	22	59	12	0	6	36	13	32	.218	.256	.328	585	64	-14	1	1	-0	.958	-11	3-73/2-2,1-1	-2.7
1986	*NY-N	137	486	51	145	24	2	11	76	40	63	.298	.357	.424	780	118	11	2	1	0	.948	-11	*3-132/1-1	-0.2
1987	Bal-A	150	563	46	144	24	0	14	65	39	90	.256	.311	.373	684	82	-14	0	0	0	.956	10	*3-130,D-14/1-6	-0.7
1988	Det-A	105	299	34	65	12	2	3	33	20	30	.217	.273	.301	574	63	-15	1	1	-0	.991	-3	1-64,D-25,3-11,/O-2L	-2.3
Total	13	1495	4829	490	1311	266	27	84	595	343	579	.271	.325	.390	714	99	-10	14	25	-6	.957	-67	*3-1021,1-339/D2OS	-12.2

■ JOHN KNIGHT

Knight, John Wesley "Schoolboy" b: 10/6/1885, Philadelphia, Pa. d: 12/19/65, Walnut Creek, Cal. BR/TR, 6'2.5", 180 lbs. Deb: 4/14/05 Career OF: (0-LF 0-CF 1-RF)

YEAR	TM/L	G	AB	R	H	2B	3B	HR	RBI	BB	SO	AVG	OBP	SLG	OPS	OPS+	BR+	SB	CS	SBR	FA	FR	G/POS	TPR
1905	Phi-A	88	325	28	66	12	1	3	29	9		.203	.227	.274	501	58	-16	4			.895	-28	S-79/3-4	-4.7
1906	Phi-A	74	253	29	49	7	2	3	20	19		.194	.250	.273	523	62	-11	6			.922	0	3-67/2-7	-1.0
1907	Phi-A	40	139	6	29	7	1	0	12	10		.209	.272	.273	545	72	-4	1			.862	-0	3-40	-0.4
	Bos-A	98	360	31	78	9	3	2	29	19		.217	.256	.275	531	70	-13	8			.924	7	3-92/2-4	-0.3
	Yr	138	499	37	107	16	4	2	41	29		.214	.260	.275	535	71	-17	9			.906	7	*3-132/2-4	-0.7
1909	NY-A	116	360	46	85	8	5	0	40	37		.236	.311	.286	597	88	-4	15			.901	1	S-76,1-19,2-17,/3-3	-0.2
1910	NY-A	117	414	58	129	25	4	3	45	34		.312	.372	.413	785	138	18	23			.929	-1	S-79,1-23/2-7,3O	2.1
1911	NY-A	132	470	69	126	16	7	3	62	42		.268	.342	.351	693	88	-8	18			.907	3	S-82,1-27,2-21,/3-1	0.1
1912	Was-A	32	93	10	15	2	1	0	9	16		.161	.284	.204	489	40	-7	4			.926	-5	2-27/1-5	-1.1
1913	NY-A	70	250	24	59	10	0	0	24	25	27	.236	.310	.276	586	72	-9	7			.980	8	1-50,2-21	-0.2
Total	8	767	2664	301	636	96	24	14	270	211	27	.239	.300	.309	609	84	-54	86			.909	-15	S-316,3-211,12/O	-5.7

■ JOE KNIGHT

Knight, Joseph William "Quiet Joe"
b: 9/28/1859, Port Stanley, Ont., Canada d: 10/16/38, Lynhurst, Ont., Canada BL/TL, 5'11", 185 lbs. Deb: 5/16/1884

YEAR	TM/L	G	AB	R	H	2B	3B	HR	RBI	BB	SO	AVG	OBP	SLG	OPS	OPS+	BR+	SB	CS	SBR	FA	FR	G/POS	TPR
1884	Phi-N	6	24	2	6	3	0	0	2	0	2	.250	.250	.375	625	98	-0				.789	-0	/P-6	0.0
1890	Cin-N	127	481	67	150	26	8	4	67	38	31	.312	.367	.424	791	131	18	17			.925	-6	*O-127(127-0-0)	0.7
Total	2	133	505	69	156	29	8	4	69	38	33	.309	.362	.422	784	130	18	17			.925	-6	O-127(127-0-0)/P-6	0.7

■ PETE KNISELY

Knisely, Peter Cole b: 8/11/1887, Waynesburg, Pa. d: 7/1/48, Brownsville, Pa. BR/TR, 5'9", 185 lbs. Deb: 9/4/12 Career OF: (18-LF 23-CF 22-RF)

YEAR	TM/L	G	AB	R	H	2B	3B	HR	RBI	BB	SO	AVG	OBP	SLG	OPS	OPS+	BR+	SB	CS	SBR	FA	FR	G/POS	TPR
1912	Cin-N	21	67	10	22	7	3	0	7	4	5	.328	.375	.522	897	148	4	3			.939	-3	O-13(0-13-0)/2-3,S-1	0.1
1913	Chi-N	2	2	0	0	0	0	0	0	0	1	.000	.000	.000	0	-99	-1	0			.000	0	H	-0.1
1914	Chi-N	37	69	5	9	0	1	0	5	5	6	.130	.200	.159	359	7	-8	0			.975	2	O-17(10-1-6)	-0.7
1915	Chi-N	64	134	12	33	9	0	0	17	15	18	.246	.331	.313	645	95	-0	1	2	-0	.940	-7	O-33(8-9-16)/2-9	-1.0
Total	4	124	272	27	64	16	4	0	29	24	30	.235	.307	.324	630	86	-5	4	2		.951	-7	/O-63C,2-12,S-1	-1.7

■ CHUCK KNOBLAUCH

Knoblauch, Edward Charles b: 7/7/68, Houston, Tex. BR/TR, 5'9", 181 lbs. Deb: 4/9/91

YEAR	TM/L	G	AB	R	H	2B	3B	HR	RBI	BB	SO	AVG	OBP	SLG	OPS	OPS+	BR+	SB	CS	SBR	FA	FR	G/POS	TPR
1991	*Min-A	151	565	78	159	24	6	1	50	59	40	.281	.354	.350	704	91	-5	25	5	4	.975	-1	*2-148/S-2	0.2
1992	Min-A★	155	600	104	178	19	6	2	56	88	60	.297	.391	.358	749	108	10	34	13	3	.992	-16	*2-154/S-1,D-1	0.1
1993	Min-A	153	602	82	167	27	4	2	41	65	44	.277	.357	.346	702	89	-7	29	11	3	.988	-5	*2-148/S-6,O-1(0-1-0)	-0.2
1994	Min-A★	109	445	85	139	**45**	3	5	51	41	56	.312	.383	.461	844	116	12	35	6	6	.994	-23	*2-109/S-1	-0.1
1995	Min-A	136	538	107	179	34	8	11	63	78	95	.333	.427	.487	914	137	33	46	18	4	.985	-8	*2-136/S-2	3.3
1996	Min-A★	153	578	140	197	35	**14**	13	72	98	74	.341	.452	.517	969	142	43	45	14	5	**.988**	-27	*2-151/D-2	2.6
1997	Min-A★	156	611	117	178	26	10	9	58	84	84	.291	.392	.411	803	108	11	62	10	**10**	.985	-16	*2-154/S-1,D-1	1.2
1998	*NY-A	150	603	117	160	25	4	17	64	76	70	.265	.364	.405	769	104	6	31	12	3	.981	-11	*2-149/D-1	0.4
1999	*NY-A	150	603	120	176	36	4	18	68	83	57	.292	.396	.454	850	118	19	28	9	3	.963	-24	*2-150	0.6
2000	*NY-A	102	400	75	113	22	2	5	26	46	45	.283	.368	.385	753	93	-3	15	7	1	.958	-27	2-82,D-20	-2.4
Total	10	1415	5545	1025	1646	293	61	83	549	718	625	.297	.389	.417	806	111	119	350	105	40	.982	-158	*2-1381/D-25,S-13,O	5.7

■ MIKE KNODE

Knode, Kenneth Thomson b: 11/8/1895, Westminster, Md. d: 12/20/80, South Bend, Ind. BR/TR, 5'10", 160 lbs. Deb: 6/28/20 F

YEAR	TM/L	G	AB	R	H	2B	3B	HR	RBI	BB	SO	AVG	OBP	SLG	OPS	OPS+	BR+	SB	CS	SBR	FA	FR	G/POS	TPR
1920	StL-N	42	65	11	15	1	1	0	12	5	6	.231	.306	.277	582	71	-2	0	1	-0	.824	-0	/O-9R,2-4,S-2,3-2	-0.3

■ RAY KNODE

Knode, Robert Troxell "Bob" b: 1/28/01, Westminster, Md. d: 4/13/82, Battle Creek, Mich BL/TL, 5'10", 160 lbs. Deb: 6/30/23 F

YEAR	TM/L	G	AB	R	H	2B	3B	HR	RBI	BB	SO	AVG	OBP	SLG	OPS	OPS+	BR+	SB	CS	SBR	FA	FR	G/POS	TPR
1923	Cle-A	22	38	7	11	0	0	2	4	2	4	.289	.325	.447	772	102	-0	1	0	0	.992	0	1-21	0.0
1924	Cle-A	11	37	6	9	1	0	0	4	3	0	.243	.300	.270	570	47	-3	2	1	0	.992	1	1-10	-0.2

YEAR	TM/L	G	AB	R	H	2B	3B	HR	RBI	BB	SO	AVG	OBP	SLG	OPS	OPS+	BR+	SB	CS	SBR	FA	FR	G/POS	TPR
1925	Cle-A	45	108	13	27	5	0	0	11	10	4	.250	.314	.296	610	55	-7	3	3	-0	.990	1	1-34	-0.8
1926	Cle-A	31	24	6	8	1	1	0	2	2	3	.333	.385	.458	843	118	1	0	0	0	.984	1	1-11	0.1
Total	4	109	207	32	55	7	1	2	21	17	11	.266	.321	.338	660	69	-10	6	4	-0	.990	2	/1-76	-0.9

■ PUNCH KNOLL

Knoll, Charles Elmer b: 10/7/1881, Evansville, Ind. d: 2/8/60, Evansville, Ind. BR/TR, 5'7.5", 170 lbs. Deb: 4/27/05

YEAR	TM/L	G	AB	R	H	2B	3B	HR	RBI	BB	SO	AVG	OBP	SLG	OPS	OPS+	BR+	SB	CS	SBR	FA	FR	G/POS	TPR
1905	Was-A	79	244	24	52	10	5	0	29	9		.213	.247	.295	542	75	-8	3			.927	-1	O-63(10-0-53)/C-5,1-2	-1.3

■ BOBBY KNOOP

Knoop, Robert Frank b: 10/18/38, Sioux City, Iowa BR/TR, 6'1", 170 lbs. Deb: 4/13/64 MC

YEAR	TM/L	G	AB	R	H	2B	3B	HR	RBI	BB	SO	AVG	OBP	SLG	OPS	OPS+	BR+	SB	CS	SBR	FA	FR	G/POS	TPR
1964	LA-A	162	486	42	105	8	1	7	38	46	109	.216	.291	.280	570	66	-22	3	2	-0	.978	**37**	*2-161	3.0
1965	Cal-A	142	465	47	125	24	4	7	43	31	101	.269	.315	.383	697	99	-1	3	2	-0	.971	13	*2-142	2.5
1966	Cal-A★	161	590	54	137	18	**11**	17	72	43	144	.232	.285	.386	672	94	-6	1	5	-2	**.981**	17	*2-161	2.4
1967	Cal-A	159	511	51	125	18	5	9	38	44	136	.245	.306	.352	658	98	-2	2	2	-0	.986	1	*2-159	1.3
1968	Cal-A	152	494	48	123	20	4	3	39	35	128	.249	.303	.324	627	93	-5	3	2	-0	.981	16	*2-151	2.7
1969	Cal-A	27	71	5	14	1	0	1	6	13	16	.197	.321	.254	575	66	-3	1	3	-1	.977	2	2-27	0.0
	Chi-A	104	345	34	79	14	1	6	41	35	68	.229	.304	.328	631	73	-12	2	0	0	.985	23	*2-104	1.8
	Yr	131	416	39	93	15	1	7	47	48	84	.224	.307	.315	622	72	-15	3	3	-0	.984	25	*2-131	1.8
1970	Chi-A	130	402	34	92	13	2	5	36	34	79	.229	.292	.308	601	63	-20	0	1	-0	.984	**35**	*2-126	2.3
1971	KC-A	72	161	14	33	8	1	1	11	15	36	.205	.273	.286	558	59	-9	1	0	0	.968	-1	2-52/3-1	-0.7
1972	KC-A	44	97	8	23	5	0	0	7	9	16	.237	.302	.289	591	77	-3	0	0	0	.972	8	2-33/3-4	0.7
Total	9	1153	3622	337	856	129	29	56	331	305	833	.236	.298	.334	632	83	-83	16	17	-2	.980	150	*2-1116/3-5	16.0

■ RANDY KNORR

Knorr, Randy Duane b: 11/12/68, San Gabriel, Cal. BR/TR, 6'2", 215 lbs. Deb: 9/5/91

YEAR	TM/L	G	AB	R	H	2B	3B	HR	RBI	BB	SO	AVG	OBP	SLG	OPS	OPS+	BR+	SB	CS	SBR	FA	FR	G/POS	TPR
1991	Tor-A	3	1	0	0	0	0	0	0	1	1	.000	.500	.000	500	49	0	0	0	0	1.000	1	/C-3	0.1
1992	Tor-A	8	19	1	5	0	0	1	2	1	5	.263	.300	.421	721	96	-0	0	0	0	1.000	1	/C-8	0.1
1993	*Tor-A	39	101	11	25	3	2	4	20	9	29	.248	.309	.436	745	97	-1	0	0	0	1.000	-1	C-39	0.0
1994	Tor-A	40	124	20	30	2	0	7	19	10	35	.242	.304	.427	731	86	-3	0	0	0	.993	-0	C-40	-0.1
1995	Tor-A	45	132	18	28	8	0	3	16	11	28	.212	.273	.341	614	59	-8	0	0	0	.971	-1	C-45	-0.7
1996	Hou-N	37	87	7	17	5	0	1	7	5	18	.195	.247	.287	535	44	-7	0	1	-0	1.000	8	C-33	0.2
1997	Hou-N	4	8	1	3	0	0	1	1	0	2	.375	.375	.750	1125	193	1	0	0	0	1.000	1	/C-3,1-2	0.2
1998	Fla-N	15	49	4	10	4	1	2	11	1	10	.204	.220	.449	669	74	-2	0	0	0	.989	-2	C-15	-0.3
1999	Hou-N	13	30	2	5	1	0	0	0	1	8	.167	.194	.200	394	-0	-5	0	0	0	1.000	0	C-11	-0.4
2000	Tex-A	15	34	5	10	2	0	2	2	0	3	.294	.294	.529	824	99	-0	0	0	0	.985	1	C-15	0.1
Total	10	219	585	69	133	25	3	21	78	39	139	.227	.278	.388	666	73	-26	0	1	-0	.990	7	C-212/1-2	-0.8

■ GEORGE KNOTHE

Knothe, George Bertram b: 1/12/1898, Bayonne, N.J. d: 7/3/81, Dover, N.J. BR/TR, 5'10", 165 lbs. Deb: 4/25/32 F

YEAR	TM/L	G	AB	R	H	2B	3B	HR	RBI	BB	SO	AVG	OBP	SLG	OPS	OPS+	BR+	SB	CS	SBR	FA	FR	G/POS	TPR
1932	Phi-N	6	12	2	1	1	0	0	0	0	0	.083	.083	.167	250	-31	-2	0			.923	-1	/2-5	-0.3

■ FRITZ KNOTHE

Knothe, Wilfred Edgar b: 5/1/03, Passaic, N.J. d: 3/27/63, Passaic, N.J. BR/TR, 5'10.5", 180 lbs. Deb: 4/12/32 F

YEAR	TM/L	G	AB	R	H	2B	3B	HR	RBI	BB	SO	AVG	OBP	SLG	OPS	OPS+	BR+	SB	CS	SBR	FA	FR	G/POS	TPR
1932	Bos-N	89	344	45	82	19	1	1	36	39	37	.238	.318	.308	626	72	-13	5			.947	-3	3-87	-1.3
1933	Bos-N	44	158	15	36	5	2	1	6	13	25	.228	.291	.304	594	76	-5	1			.978	-7	3-33/S-9	-1.0
	Phi-N	41	113	10	17	2	0	0	11	6	19	.150	.193	.168	361	3	-14	2			.949	15	3-32/2-4	0.2
	Yr	85	271	25	53	7	2	1	17	19	44	.196	.251	.247	498	42	-20	3			.961	8	3-65/S-9,2-4	-0.8
Total	2	174	615	70	135	26	3	2	53	58	81	.220	.289	.281	570	59	-31	8			.953	5	3-152/S-9,2-4	-2.1

■ JOE KNOTTS

Knotts, Joseph Steven b: 3/3/1884, Greensboro, Pa. d: 9/15/50, Philadelphia, Pa. BR/TR, Deb: 9/18/07

YEAR	TM/L	G	AB	R	H	2B	3B	HR	RBI	BB	SO	AVG	OBP	SLG	OPS	OPS+	BR+	SB	CS	SBR	FA	FR	G/POS	TPR
1907	Bos-N	3	8	0	0	0	0	0	0	1		.000	.111	.000	111	-65	-2	0			1.000	-0	/C-3	-0.2

■ ED KNOUFF

Knouff, Edward "Fred" b: 6/1868, Philadelphia, Pa. d: 9/14/1900, Philadelphia, Pa. BR/TR, 210 lbs. Deb: 7/1/1885

YEAR	TM/L	G	AB	R	H	2B	3B	HR	RBI	BB	SO	AVG	OBP	SLG	OPS	OPS+	BR+	SB	CS	SBR	FA	FR	G/POS	TPR
1885	Phi-a	14	48	5	9	0	0	0	2	2		.188	.220	.188	408	28	-4				.867	1	P-14/O-1(0-0-1)	0.0
1886	Bal-a	1	3	0	0	0	0	0	0	0		.000	.250	.000	250	-20	-0	0			1.000	1	/P-1	0.0
1887	Bal-a	9	32	4	10	0	0	0	3	1		.313	.313	.290	603	73	-1	1			.889	-1	/P-9,O-3(2-0-1)	-0.1
	StL-a	15	57	4	11	1	2	0	6	1		.193	.207	.268	475	29	-6	1			.800	-2	/O-9(0-4-5),P-6	-0.4
	Yr	24	89	8	21	1	2	0	9	2		.236	.244	.276	520	43	-7	2			.897	-3	P-15,O-12(2-4-6)	-0.5
1888	StL-a	9	31	1	3	0	0	0	1	3		.097	.200	.097	297	-3	-4	1			.842	-2	/P-9	0.0
	Cle-a	2	6	0	1	1	0	0	0	1		.167	.286	.333	619	101	0	0			1.000	1	/P-2,2-1	0.0
	Yr	11	37	1	4	1	0	0	1	4		.108	.214	.135	349	12	-4	1			.880	-1	P-11/2-1	0.0
1889	Phi-a	3	12	2	3	1	0	0	2	1	1	.250	.308	.333	641	84	-0	1			1.000	-1	/P-3	0.0
Total	5	53	189	16	37	3	2	0	14	9	1	.196	.236	.225	461	35	-15	4			.891	-3	/P-44,O-13(2-4-7),2-1	-0.5

■ JAKE KNOWDELL

Knowdell, Jacob Augustus b: 7/27/1840, Brooklyn, N.Y. 5'7.5", 148 lbs. Deb: 6/20/1874 Career OF: (4-LF 3-CF 1-RF)

YEAR	TM/L	G	AB	R	H	2B	3B	HR	RBI	BB	SO	AVG	OBP	SLG	OPS	OPS+	BR+	SB	CS	SBR	FA	FR	G/POS	TPR
1874	Atl-n	24	86	8	12	1	1	0	3	1	3	.140	.149	.174	324	4	-8	1	0	0	.824	-4	C-21/O-4(4-0-0)	-0.9
1875	Atl-n	43	163	17	32	2	0	0	9	1	3	.196	.201	.209	410	49	-7	0	1	-0	.781	-8	C-33,S-11/O-4C,2-1	-1.3
1878	Mil-N	4	14	2	3	1	0	0	2	0	3	.214	.214	.286	500	59	-1				.875	-2	/C-2,O-1(0-0-1),S-1	-0.3
Total	2 n	67	249	25	44	3	1	0	12	2	6	.177	.183	.197	380	32	-15	1	1	-0	.796	-12	/C-54,S-11,O-8L,2-1	-2.2

■ JIMMY KNOWLES

Knowles, James "Darby" b: 9/1856, Toronto, Ont., Can. d: 2/11/12, Jersey City, N.J. 5'9", 160 lbs. Deb: 5/2/1884

YEAR	TM/L	G	AB	R	H	2B	3B	HR	RBI	BB	SO	AVG	OBP	SLG	OPS	OPS+	BR+	SB	CS	SBR	FA	FR	G/POS	TPR
1884	Pit-a	46	182	19	42	5	7	0		5		.231	.259	.335	594	94	-1				.961	-0	1-46	-0.5
	Bro-a	41	153	19	36	5	1	1		3		.235	.255	.301	555	80	-3				.953	1	1-30,3-11	-0.5
	Yr	87	335	38	78	10	8	1		8		.233	.257	.319	577	87	-5				.958	1	1-76,3-11	-1.0
1886	Was-N	115	443	43	94	16	11	3	35	15	73	.212	.238	.318	556	72	-15	20			.899	**28**	2-62,3-53	1.5
1887	NY-a	16	61	12	16	1	1	0	6	1		.262	.262	.300	562	59	-3	6			.934	-3	2-16/3-1	-0.5
1890	Roc-a	123	491	83	138	12	8	5	84	59		.281	.359	.369	728	124	16	55			.881	7	*3-123	2.2
1892	NY-N	16	59	9	9	1	0	0	7	6	8	.153	.231	.169	400	22	-5	2			.792	-4	3-15/S-1	-0.9
Total	5	357	1389	185	335	40	28	9	132	89	81	.241	.288	.329	618	92	-12	83			.861	28	3-203/2-78,1-76,S-1	1.3

■ ANDY KNOX

Knox, Andrew Jackson "Dasher" b: 1/6/1864, Philadelphia, Pa. d: 9/14/40, Philadelphia, Pa. BR/TR, Deb: 9/19/1890

YEAR	TM/L	G	AB	R	H	2B	3B	HR	RBI	BB	SO	AVG	OBP	SLG	OPS	OPS+	BR+	SB	CS	SBR	FA	FR	G/POS	TPR
1890	Phi-a	21	75	6	19	3	0	0	8	9		.253	.333	.293	627	85	-1	5			.963	-2	1-21	-0.4

■ CLIFF KNOX

Knox, Clifford Hiram "Bud" b: 1/7/02, Coalville, Iowa d: 9/24/65, Oskaloosa, Iowa BB/TR, 5'11.5", 178 lbs. Deb: 7/1/24

YEAR	TM/L	G	AB	R	H	2B	3B	HR	RBI	BB	SO	AVG	OBP	SLG	OPS	OPS+	BR+	SB	CS	SBR	FA	FR	G/POS	TPR
1924	Pit-N	6	18	1	4	0	0	0	2	2	0	.222	.300	.222	522	41	-1	0	0	0	.917	2	/C-6	0.1

■ JOHN KNOX

Knox, John Clinton b: 7/26/48, Newark, N.J. BL/TR, 6', 170 lbs. Deb: 8/1/72

YEAR	TM/L	G	AB	R	H	2B	3B	HR	RBI	BB	SO	AVG	OBP	SLG	OPS	OPS+	BR+	SB	CS	SBR	FA	FR	G/POS	TPR
1972	*Det-A	14	13	1	1	1	0	0	0	1	2	.077	.143	.154	297	-11	-2	0	0	0	1.000	4	/2-4	0.2
1973	Det-A	12	32	1	9	1	0	0	3	3	3	.281	.343	.313	655	80	-1	1	1	-0	1.000	-3	/2-9	-0.3
1974	Det-A	55	88	11	27	1	1	0	6	6	13	.307	.351	.341	692	96	-0	5	4	-0	.956	8	2-33/3-1,D-2	0.8
1975	Det-A	43	86	8	23	1	0	0	2	10	9	.267	.344	.279	623	74	-2	1	2	-0	.980	-1	2-23/3-3,D-3	-0.3
Total	4	124	219	21	60	4	1	0	11	20	27	.274	.335	.301	636	79	-5	7	7	-1	.973	8	/2-69,D-5,3-4	0.4

■ NICK KOBACK

Koback, Nicholas Nicholie b: 7/19/35, Hartford, Conn. BR/TR, 6', 187 lbs. Deb: 7/29/53

YEAR	TM/L	G	AB	R	H	2B	3B	HR	RBI	BB	SO	AVG	OBP	SLG	OPS	OPS+	BR+	SB	CS	SBR	FA	FR	G/POS	TPR
1953	Pit-N	7	16	1	2	0	1	0	0	1	4	.125	.176	.250	426	10	-2	0	0	0	1.000	-3	/C-6	-0.5
1954	Pit-N	4	10	0	0	0	0	0	0	0	8	.000	.000	.000	0	-99	-3	0	0	0	1.000	0	/C-4	-0.3
1955	Pit-N	5	7	0	2	0	0	0	0	0	1	.286	.286	.286	571	53	-0	0	0	0	1.000	0	/C-2	0.0
Total	3	16	33	1	4	0	1	0	0	1	13	.121	.147	.182	329	-15	-6	0	0	0	1.000	-3	/C-12	-0.8

■ BARNEY KOCH

Koch, Barnett b: 3/23/23, Campbell, Neb. d: 6/6/87, Tacoma, Wash. BR/TR, 5'8", 140 lbs. Deb: 7/23/44

YEAR	TM/L	G	AB	R	H	2B	3B	HR	RBI	BB	SO	AVG	OBP	SLG	OPS	OPS+	BR+	SB	CS	SBR	FA	FR	G/POS	TPR
1944	Bro-N	33	96	11	21	2	0	0	1	3	9	.219	.242	.240	482	37	-8	0			.956	-6	2-29/S-1	-1.3

■ BRAD KOCHER

Kocher, Bradley Wilson b: 1/16/1888, White Haven, Pa. d: 1/13/65, White Haven, Pa. BR/TR, 5'11", 188 lbs. Deb: 4/24/12

YEAR	TM/L	G	AB	R	H	2B	3B	HR	RBI	BB	SO	AVG	OBP	SLG	OPS	OPS+	BR+	SB	CS	SBR	FA	FR	G/POS	TPR
1912	Det-A	29	63	5	13	3	1	0	9	2		.206	.231	.286	516	49	-4	0			.904	-3	C-24	-0.6
1915	NY-N	4	11	3	5	0	1	0	2	0	1	.455	.455	.636	1091	243	2	0			1.000	-1	/C-3	0.1
1916	NY-N	34	65	1	7	2	0	0	1	2	10	.108	.134	.138	273	-17	-9	0			.978	-7	C-30	-1.7
Total	3	67	139	9	25	5	2	0	12	4	11	.180	.203	.245	447	34	-12	0			.943	-11	/C-57	-2.2

YEAR	TM/L	G	AB	R	H	2B	3B	HR	RBI	BB	SO	AVG	OBP	SLG	OPS	OPS+	BR+	SB	CS	SBR	FA	FR	G/POS	TPR
■ PETE KOEGEL	Koegel, Peter John b: 7/31/47, Mineola, N.Y. BR/TR, 6′6.5″, 230 lbs. Deb: 9/1/70 Career OF: (2-LF 0-CF 2-RF)																							
1970	Mil-A	7	8	2	2	0	0	1	1	1	3	.250	.333	.625	958	157	1	0	0	0	1.000	-0	/O-1(1-0-0)	0.0
1971	Mil-A	2	3	0	0	0	0	0	0	2	2	.000	.400	.000	400	22	-0	0	0	0	1.000	-0	/1-1	0.0
	Phi-N	12	26	1	6	1	0	0	3	2	7	.231	.286	.269	555	58	-1	0	0	0	1.000	-1	/C-7,O-1(1-0-0)	-0.2
1972	Phi-N	41	49	3	7	2	0	0	1	6	16	.143	.236	.184	420	20	-5	0	0	0	1.000	-2	/1-8,C-5,3-4,O-2R	-0.8
Total	3	62	86	6	15	3	0	1	5	11	28	.174	.268	.244	512	45	-6	0	0	0	.971	-3	/C-12,1-9,3-4,O-4L	-1.0
■ BEN KOEHLER	Koehler, Benard James b: 1/26/1877, Schoerndorn, Germany d: 5/21/61, South Bend, Ind. BR/TR, 5′10.5″, 175 lbs. Deb: 4/23/05 Career OF: (1-LF 158-CF 17-RF)																							
1905	StL-A	142	536	55	127	14	6	2	47	32		.237	.285	.297	582	89	-7	22			.969	6	*O-124C,1-12/2-6	-0.8
1906	StL-A	66	186	27	41	1	1	0	15	24		.220	.322	.237	559	79	-3	9			.957	-4	O-52C/2-7,S-1,3-1	-1.0
Total	2	208	722	82	168	15	7	2	62	56		.233	.295	.281	576	87	-10	31			.966	2	O-176C/2-13,1-12,3S	-1.8
■ PIP KOEHLER	Koehler, Horace Levering b: 1/16/02, Gilbert, Pa. d: 12/8/86, Tacoma, Wash. BR/TR, 5′10″, 165 lbs. Deb: 4/22/25																							
1925	NY-N	12	2	1	0	0	0	0	0	0	1	.000	.000	.000	0	-99	-1	0	0	0	1.000	-1	/O-3(1-0-2)	-0.1
■ BRIAN KOELLING	Koelling, Brian Wayne b: 6/11/69, Cincinnati, Ohio BR/TR, 6′1″, 185 lbs. Deb: 8/21/93																							
1993	Cin-N	7	15	2	1	0	0	0	0	0	2	.067	.125	.067	192	-47	-3	0	0	0	.941	1	/2-3,S-2	-0.2
■ LEN KOENECKE	Koenecke, Leonard George b: 1/18/04, Baraboo, Wis. d: 9/17/35, Toronto, Ont., Can BL/TR, 5′11″, 180 lbs. Deb: 4/12/32																							
1932	NY-N	42	137	33	35	5	0	4	14	11	13	.255	.320	.380	700	89	-2	3			.924	-5	O-35(35-0-0)	-0.9
1934	Bro-N	123	460	79	147	31	7	14	73	70	38	.320	.411	.509	919	152	36	8			**.994**	2	*O-121(0-121-0)	3.3
1935	Bro-N	100	325	43	92	13	2	4	27	43	45	.283	.369	.372	741	102	2	0			.966	-4	O-91(16-68-7)	-0.4
Total	3	265	922	155	274	49	9	22	114	124	96	.297	.383	.441	824	125	36	11			.976	-7	O-247(51-189-7)	2.0
■ MARK KOENIG	Koenig, Mark Anthony b: 7/19/04, San Francisco, Cal. d: 4/22/93, Willows, Cal. BB/TR, 6′, 180 lbs. Deb: 9/8/25 Career OF: (0-LF 0-CF 1-RF)																							
1925	NY-A	28	110	14	23	6	1	0	4	5	4	.209	.243	.282	525	34	-12	0	1	-0	.944	-3	S-28	-1.1
1926	*NY-A	147	617	93	167	26	8	5	62	43	37	.271	.319	.363	682	79	-20	4	3	-0	.931	-0	*S-141	-0.5
1927	*NY-A	123	526	99	150	20	11	3	62	25	21	.285	.320	.382	702	84	-14	3	2	-0	.936	14	*S-122	1.3
1928	*NY-A	132	533	89	170	19	10	4	63	32	19	.319	.360	.415	774	106	4	3	5	-1	.923	-20	*S-125	-0.3
1929	NY-A	116	373	44	109	27	5	3	41	23	17	.292	.335	.416	751	99	-2	1	1	-0	.911	-13	S-61,3-37/2-1	-0.6
1930	NY-A	21	74	9	17	5	0	0	9	6	5	.230	.296	.297	594	53	-5	0	0	0	.905	2	S-19	-0.1
	Det-A	76	267	37	64	9	2	1	16	20	15	.240	.295	.300	595	50	-20	2	0	0	.922	-14	S-70/P-2,3-2,O-1R	-2.4
	Yr	97	341	46	81	14	2	1	25	26	20	.238	.295	.299	595	51	-25	2	0	0	.918	-13	S-89/P-2,3-2,O-1R	-2.5
1931	Det-A	106	364	33	92	24	4	1	39	14	12	.253	.282	.349	631	63	-20	8	2	1	.955	-23	2-55,S-35/P-3	-3.4
1932	*Chi-N	33	102	15	36	5	1	3	11	3	5	.353	.377	.510	887	137	5	0			.932	10	S-31	1.6
1933	Chi-N	80	218	32	62	12	1	3	25	15	9	.284	.330	.390	720	105	1	5			.922	5	3-37,S-26/2-2	0.9
1934	Cin-N	151	633	60	172	26	6	1	67	15	24	.272	.289	.336	625	68	-29	5			.930	6	3-64,S-58,2-26,/1-4	-1.5
1935	NY-N	107	396	40	112	12	0	3	37	13	18	.283	.306	.336	641	74	-15	0			.968	-11	2-64,S-21,3-15	-1.9
1936	*NY-N	42	58	7	16	4	0	1	7	8	4	.276	.373	.397	770	109	1	0			.905	-1	S-10/2-8,3-3	0.1
Total	12	1162	4271	572	1190	195	49	28	443	222	190	.279	.316	.367	683	81	-125	31	14		.927	-50	S-747,3-158,2/P1O	-7.9
■ HENRY KOHLER	Kohler, Henry C. b: 5/5/1852, Baltimore, Md. d: 8/27/34, Baltimore, Md. Deb: 7/12/1871 Career OF: (0-LF 1-CF 0-RF)																							
1871	Kek-n	3	12	0	2	1	0	0	1	0	0	.167	.167	.250	417	17	-1	0	0	0	.000	-0	/C-2,1-2,3-1	-0.1
1873	Mar-n	6	25	2	3	0	0	0	1	0	1	.120	.120	.120	240	-37	-3	0	0	0	.686	-4	/3-6,C-1,1-1,O-1C	-0.5
1874	Bal-n	2	4	0	0	0	0	0	0	0	0	.000	.000	.000	0	-99	-1	0	0	0	.714	-1	/1-1	-0.1
Total	3 n	11	41	2	5	1	0	0	2	0	1	.122	.122	.146	268	-24	-6	0	0	0	.700	-5	/3-7,1-4,C-3,O-1C	-0.7
■ DICK KOKOS	Kokos, Richard Jerome (b: Richard Jerome Kokoszka) b: 2/28/28, Chicago, Ill. d: 4/9/86, Chicago, Ill. BL/TL, 5′8.5″, 170 lbs. Deb: 7/8/48																							
1948	StL-A	71	258	40	77	15	3	4	40	28	32	.298	.374	.426	800	110	3	4	3	-0	.964	-1	O-71(0-0-71)	0.0
1949	StL-A	143	501	80	131	28	1	23	77	66	91	.261	.351	.459	810	109	4	3	5	-1	.981	8	*O-138(0-0-138)	0.7
1950	StL-A	143	490	77	128	27	5	18	67	88	73	.261	.375	.447	822	106	4	8	8	-1	.970	9	*O-127(81-0-50)	0.4
1953	StL-A	107	299	41	72	12	0	13	38	56	53	.241	.361	.411	772	106	3	0	5	-2	.963	-1	O-83(61-0-22)	-0.4
1954	Bal-A	11	10	1	2	0	0	1	1	4	3	.200	.429	.500	929	166	1	0	0	0	1.000	0	/O-1(1-0-0)	0.1
Total	5	475	1558	239	410	82	9	59	223	242	252	.263	.365	.441	806	108	16	15	21	-4	.971	16	O-420(143-0-281)	0.8
■ GARY KOLB	Kolb, Gary Alan b: 3/13/40, Rock Falls, Ill. BL/TR, 6′, 195 lbs. Deb: 9/7/60 Career OF: (57-LF 18-CF 77-RF)																							
1960	StL-N	9	3	1	0	0	0	0	0	0	0	.000	.000	.000	0	-92	-1	0	0	0	1.000	-0	/O-2(1-1-1)	-0.1
1962	StL-N	6	14	1	5	0	0	0	0	1	3	.357	.400	.357	757	96	-0	0	0	0	1.000	-1	/O-6(1-0-5)	-0.1
1963	StL-N	75	96	23	26	1	5	3	10	22	26	.271	.407	.479	886	141	6	2	1	0	.981	-11	O-58(25-0-35)/C-1,3-1	-0.7
1964	Mil-N	36	64	7	12	1	0	0	2	6	10	.188	.257	.203	460	31	-6	3	2	-0	1.000	-6	O-14R/3-7,2-6,C-2	-1.2
1965	Mil-N	24	27	3	7	0	0	0	1	1	6	.259	.286	.259	545	54	-2	0	0	0	1.000	-3	O-13(9-3-2)	-0.5
	NY-N	40	90	8	15	2	0	1	7	3	28	.167	.194	.222	416	17	-10	3	0	1	.976	-1	O-29(10-10-9)/1-1,3-1	-1.2
	Yr	64	117	11	22	2	0	1	8	4	34	.188	.215	.231	446	26	-11	3	0	1	.981	-4	O-42L/1-1,3-1	-1.7
1968	Pit-N	74	119	16	26	4	1	2	6	11	17	.218	.285	.319	604	82	-3	2	1	0	.900	-2	O-25R,C-10/3-4,2-1	-0.6
1969	Pit-N	29	37	4	3	1	0	0	3	2	14	.081	.128	.108	236	-34	-7	0	0	0	1.000	0	/C-7	-0.7
Total	7	293	450	63	94	9	6	6	29	46	104	.209	.282	.296	578	65	-21	10	4	1	.965	-23	O-147R/C-20,3-13,21	-5.1
■ DON KOLLOWAY	Kolloway, Donald Martin "Butch" or "Cab" b: 8/4/18, Posen, Ill. d: 6/30/94, Blue Island, Ill. BR/TR, 6′3″, 200 lbs. Deb: 9/16/40																							
1940	Chi-A	10	40	5	9	1	0	0	3	0	3	.225	.225	.250	475	23	-5	1	0	0	.922	-2	2-10	-0.5
1941	Chi-A	71	280	33	76	8	3	3	24	6	12	.271	.292	.354	645	71	-13	11	4	1	.955	-7	2-62/1-4	-1.5
1942	Chi-A	147	601	72	164	**40**	4	3	60	30	39	.273	.311	.368	678	92	-8	16	14	-1	.966	-9	*2-116,1-33	-1.4
1943	Chi-A	85	348	29	75	14	4	1	33	9	30	.216	.235	.287	523	53	-22	11	7	-0	.968	-1	2-85	-2.0
1946	Chi-A	123	482	45	135	23	4	3	53	9	29	.280	.293	.363	656	86	-11	14	6	1	.972	3	2-90,3-31	-0.2
1947	Chi-A	124	485	49	135	25	4	2	35	17	34	.278	.303	.359	662	87	-11	11	4	1	.962	5	2-99,1-11/3-8	0.0
1948	Chi-A	119	417	60	114	14	4	6	38	18	18	.273	.303	.369	673	81	-13	2	4	-1	.966	11	2-83,3-18	0.1
1949	Chi-A	4	4	0	0	0	0	0	0	0	1	.000	.000	.000	0	-99	-1	0	0	0	.000	0	/3-2	-0.1
	Det-A	126	483	71	142	19	3	2	47	49	25	.294	.361	.358	720	91	-6	7	7	-1	.956	-21	2-62,1-57/3-7	-2.6
	Yr	130	487	71	142	19	3	2	47	49	26	.292	.359	.355	714	89	-7	7	7	-1	.956	-21	2-62,1-57/3-9	-2.7
1950	Det-A	125	467	55	135	20	4	6	62	29	28	.289	.331	.388	718	81	-15	1	3	-1	.989	3	*1-118/2-1	-1.6
1951	Det-A	78	212	28	54	7	0	1	17	15	12	.255	.307	.302	609	65	-10	2	3	-1	.992	6	1-59	-0.7
1952	Det-A	65	173	19	42	9	0	2	21	7	19	.243	.280	.329	610	69	-8	0	2	-1	.979	-1	1-32/2-8	-1.0
1953	Phi-A	2	1	0	0	0	0	0	0	0	1	.000	.000	.000	0	-96	-0	0	0	0	.000	0	/3-1	0.0
Total	12	1079	3993	466	1081	180	30	29	393	189	251	.271	.305	.353	658	80	-123	76	54	-2	.964	-13	2-616,1-314/3-67	-11.5
■ KARL KOLSETH	Kolseth, Karl Dickey "Koley" b: 12/25/1892, Cambridge, Mass. d: 5/3/56, Cumberland, Md. BL/TR, 6′, 182 lbs. Deb: 9/30/15																							
1915	Bal-F	6	23	1	6	1	1	0	1	1	0	.261	.292	.391	683	89	-1	0			.915	-2	/1-6	-0.3
■ FRED KOMMERS	Kommers, Frederick Raymond "Bugs" b: 3/31/1886, Chicago, Ill. d: 6/14/43, Chicago, Ill. BL/TR, 6′, 175 lbs. Deb: 6/25/13																							
1913	Pit-N	40	155	14	36	5	4	0	22	10	29	.232	.279	.316	595	73	-6	1			.979	-2	O-40(0-40-0)	-1.1
1914	StL-F	76	244	33	75	9	8	3	41	24	33	.307	.376	.447	823	117	3	7			.908	-2	O-67(3-36-28)	-0.3
	Bal-F	16	42	5	9	1	0	1	1	7	10	.214	.340	.310	650	75	-2	0			.938	-2	O-12(11-1-0)	-0.5
	Yr	92	286	38	84	10	8	4	42	31	43	.294	.371	.427	797	111	1	7			.911	-4	O-79(14-37-28)	-0.8
Total	2	132	441	52	120	15	12	4	64	41	72	.272	.340	.388	727	99	-5	8			.938	-6	O-119(14-77-28)	-1.9
■ BRAD KOMMINSK	Komminsk, Brad Lynn b: 4/4/61, Lima, Ohio BR/TR, 6′2″, 205 lbs. Deb: 8/14/83 Career OF: (74-LF 91-CF 171-RF)																							
1983	Atl-N	19	36	2	8	2	0	0	4	5	7	.222	.317	.278	595	62	-2	0	0	0	.944	-1	O-13(1-0-12)	-0.3
1984	Atl-N	90	301	37	61	10	0	8	36	29	77	.203	.277	.316	593	62	-15	18	8	1	.993	-2	O-80(28-2-50)	-2.1
1985	Atl-N	106	300	52	68	12	3	4	21	38	71	.227	.316	.327	642	75	-9	10	8	-1	.959	-4	O-92(28-1-63)	-1.9
1986	Atl-N	5	5	1	2	0	0	0	1	0	1	.400	.400	.400	800	115	0	0	1	-0	1.000	-0	/3-2,O-2(0-0-2)	0.0
1987	Mil-A	7	15	0	1	0	0	0	0	1	7	.067	.125	.067	192	-46	-3	1	0	0	1.000	0	/O-5(0-0-5),D-1	-0.3
1989	Cle-A	71	198	27	47	8	2	8	33	24	55	.237	.323	.419	742	106	1	8	2	1	.995	3	O-68(2-66-2)	0.5

YEAR	TM/L	G	AB	R	H	2B	3B	HR	RBI	BB	SO	AVG	OBP	SLG	OPS	OPS+	BR+	SB	CS	SBR	FA	FR	G/POS	TPR
1990	SF-N	8	5	2	1	0	0	0	0	1	2	.200	.333	.200	533	52	-0	0	0	0	1.000	-3	/O-7(2-2-3)	-0.3
	Bal-A	46	101	18	24	4	0	3	8	14	29	.238	.342	.366	708	101	1	1	1	-0	1.000	-5	O-40(6-12-26)/D-2	-0.5
1991	Oak-A	24	25	1	3	1	0	0	2	2	9	.120	.185	.160	345	-4	-4	1	0	0	1.000	-6	O-22(7-8-8)	-0.9
Total	8	376	986	140	215	37	5	23	105	114	258	.218	.303	.336	639	75	-31	39	20	2	.984	-17	O-329R/D-3,3-2	-5.8
■ PAUL KONERKO	Konerko, Paul Henry b: 3/5/76, Providence, R.I. BR/TR, 6'3", 205 lbs. Deb: 9/8/97																							
1997	LA-N	6	7	0	1	0	0	0	0	1	2	.143	.250	.143	393	7	-1	0	0	0	1.000	-1	/1-1,3-1	-0.1
1998	LA-N	49	144	14	31	1	0	4	16	10	30	.215	.276	.306	581	56	-9	0	1	-0	.995	-1	1-23,3-11,O-11L	-1.3
	Cin-N	26	73	7	16	3	0	3	13	6	10	.219	.287	.384	671	74	-3	0	0	0	1.000	1	/3-9,1-7,O-7L,D-3	-0.3
	Yr	75	217	21	47	4	0	7	29	16	40	.217	.280	.332	611	62	-12	0	1	-0	.996	-0	1-30,3-20,O-18L/D	-1.6
1999	Chi-A	142	513	71	151	31	4	24	81	45	68	.294	.354	.511	864	117	12	1	0	0	.995	3	1-92,D-54/3-1	0.4
2000	*Chi-A	143	524	84	156	31	1	21	97	47	72	.298	.367	.481	848	111	9	1	0	0	.991	-8	*1-122/3-7,D-7	-0.9
Total	4	366	1261	176	355	66	5	52	207	109	182	.282	.346	.466	811	105	7	2	1	0	.993	-5	1-245/D-64,3-29,O	-2.2
■ ED KONETCHY	Konetchy, Edward Joseph "Big Ed" b: 9/3/1885, LaCrosse, Wis. d: 5/27/47, Ft.Worth, Tex. BR/TR, 6'2.5", 195 lbs. Deb: 6/29/07 Career OF: (2-LF 4-CF 1-RF)																							
1907	StL-N	91	331	34	83	11	9	2	30	26		.251	.317	.356	673	115	5	13			.975	4	1-91	0.8
1908	StL-N	154	545	46	135	19	12	5	50	38		.248	.309	.354	663	117	9	16			.986	11	*1-154	2.0
1909	StL-N	152	576	88	165	23	14	4	80	65		.286	.366	.396	762	145	31	25			.985	5	*1-152	3.6
1910	StL-N	144	520	87	157	23	16	3	78	78	59	.302	.397	.425	822	145	32	18			**.991**	8	*1-144/P-1	**3.9**
1911	StL-N	158	571	90	165	**38**	13	6	88	81	63	.289	.384	.433	816	132	26	27			**.991**	-6	*1-158	1.5
1912	StL-N	143	538	81	169	26	13	8	82	62	66	.314	.389	.455	844	134	25	25			.991	6	*1-142/O-1(1-0-0)	2.6
1913	StL-N	140	504	75	139	18	17	8	68	53	41	.276	.353	.427	779	124	15	27			**.995**	7	*1-140/P-1	2.0
1914	Pit-N	154	563	56	140	23	9	4	51	32	48	.249	.291	.343	634	92	-7	20			**.995**	5	*1-154	-0.7
1915	Pit-F	152	576	79	181	31	18	10	93	41	52	.314	.363	.483	846	138	18	27			**.994**	-0	*1-152	1.5
1916	Bos-N	158	566	76	147	29	13	3	70	43	46	.260	.320	.373	693	117	11	13			.990	9	*1-158	1.7
1917	Bos-N	130	474	56	129	19	13	2	54	36	40	.272	.330	.380	710	125	13	16			**.994**	2	*1-129	1.3
1918	Bos-N	119	437	33	103	15	5	2	56	32	35	.236	.291	.307	598	86	-8	5			**.992**	-2	*1-112/O-6(1-4-1),P-1	-1.4
1919	Bro-N	132	486	46	145	24	9	1	47	29	39	.298	.342	.391	733	117	10	14			**.994**	7	*1-132	1.4
1920	*Bro-N	131	497	62	153	22	12	5	63	33	18	.308	.352	.431	783	120	12	3	2	-0	.990	1	*1-130	1.0
1921	Bro-N	55	197	25	53	6	5	3	23	19	21	.269	.336	.396	732	90	-3	3	3	-0	.987	-1	1-54	-0.8
	Phi-N	72	268	38	86	17	4	8	59	21	17	.321	.379	.504	883	122	8	3	0	1	.986	6	1-71	1.0
	Yr	127	465	63	139	23	9	11	82	40	38	.299	.361	.458	819	109	6	6	3	0	.986	4	*1-125	0.2
Total	15	2085	7649	972	2150	344	182	74	992	689	545	.281	.346	.403	749	122	198	255	5		.990	59	*1-2073/O-7C,P-3	21.4
■ MIKE KONNICK	Konnick, Michael Aloysius b: 1/13/1889, Glen Lyon, Pa. d: 7/9/71, Wilkes-Barre, Pa. BR/TR, 5'9", 180 lbs. Deb: 10/3/09																							
1909	Cin-N	2	5	0	2	1	0	0	1	0		.400	.400	.600	1000	211	1	0			1.000	-1	/C-2	0.0
1910	Cin-N	1	3	0	0	0	0	0	0	1	0	.000	.250	.000	250	-27	-0	0			1.000	-1	/S-1	-0.1
Total	2	3	8	0	2	1	0	0	1	1	0	.250	.333	.375	708	117	0	0			1.000	-1	/C-2,S-1	-0.1
■ BRUCE KONOPKA	Konopka, Bruno Bruce b: 9/16/19, Hammond, Ind. d: 9/27/96, Denver, Colo. BL/TL, 6'2", 190 lbs. Deb: 6/7/42																							
1942	Phi-A	5	10	2	3	0	0	0	1	1	0	.300	.364	.300	664	88	-0	0	0	0	1.000	-0	/1-3	0.0
1943	Phi-A	2	2	0	0	0	0	0	0	0	1	.000	.000	.000	0	-99	-0	0	0	0	.000	0	H	-0.1
1946	Phi-A	38	93	7	22	4	1	0	9	4	8	.237	.268	.301	569	59	-5	0	0	0	.994	1	1-20/O-1(1-0-0)	-0.5
Total	3	45	105	9	25	4	1	0	10	5	9	.238	.273	.295	568	59	-6	0	0	0	.995	1	/1-23,O-1(1-0-0)	-0.6
■ HARRY KOONS	Koons, Henry M. b: 1863, Philadelphia, Pa. BR/TR, 5'8", 174 lbs. Deb: 4/17/1884																							
1884	Alt-U	21	78	8	18	2	1	0	2			.231	.250	.282	532	60	-6				.866	5	3-21/C-1	-0.1
	CP-U	1	3	0	0	0	0	0	0			.000	.000	.000	0	-99	-1				.000	0	/3-1	-0.1
	Yr	22	81	8	18	2	1	0	2			.222	.241	.272	513	54	-7				.866	5	3-22/C-1	-0.2
■ GEORGE KOPACZ	Kopacz, George Felix "Sonny" b: 2/26/41, Chicago, Ill. BL/TL, 6'1", 195 lbs. Deb: 9/18/66																							
1966	Atl-N	6	9	1	0	0	0	0	0	1	5	.000	.100	.000	100	-68	-2	0	0	0	.909	-1	/1-2	-0.3
1970	Pit-N	10	16	1	3	0	0	0	0	0	5	.188	.188	.188	375	1	-2	0	0	0	1.000	-1	/1-3	-0.3
Total	2	16	25	2	3	0	0	0	0	1	10	.120	.154	.120	274	-25	-4	0	0	0	.964	-1	/1-5	-0.6
■ WALLY KOPF	Kopf, Walter Henry b: 7/10/1899, Stonington, Conn. d: 4/30/79, Hamilton Co., Ohio BB/TR, 5'11", 168 lbs. Deb: 10/1/21 F																							
1921	NY-N	2	3	0	1	0	0	0	0	1	1	.333	.500	.333	833	125	0	0	0	0	1.000	2	/3-2	0.2
■ LARRY KOPF	Kopf, William Lorenz (a.k.a. Fred Brady In 1913) b: 11/3/1890, Bristol, Conn. d: 10/15/86, Anderson Twp., O. BB/TR, 5'9", 160 lbs. Deb: 9/2/13 F Career OF: (1-LF 1-CF 0-RF)																							
1913	Cle-A	6	10	2	3	1	0	0	1	0	0	.300	.300	.400	700	102	-0	0			.923	2	/2-4,3-1	0.2
1914	Phi-A	37	69	8	13	2	2	0	12	8	14	.188	.300	.275	575	76	-2	6			.899	1	S-13/3-8,2-5	0.2
1915	Phi-A	118	386	39	87	10	2	1	33	41	45	.225	.314	.269	584	77	-10	5	9	-2	.920	-8	S-74,3-42/2-2	-1.5
1916	Cin-N	11	40	2	11	2	0	0	5	1	8	.275	.293	.325	618	92	-1	1			.942	-2	S-11	-0.2
1917	Cin-N	148	573	81	146	19	8	2	26	28	48	.255	.297	.326	623	95	-5	17			.916	-11	*S-145	-0.6
1919	*Cin-N	135	503	51	136	18	5	0	58	28	27	.270	.313	.326	639	95	-4	18			.943	-34	*S-135	-3.2
1920	Cin-N	126	458	56	112	15	6	0	59	35	24	.245	.305	.303	609	76	-13	14	13	-1	.929	-33	*S-123/2-2,3-2,O-1C	-4.2
1921	Cin-N	107	367	36	80	8	3	1	25	43	20	.218	.310	.264	574	56	-22	3	14	-4	.947	-15	S-93/2-4,3-3,O-1L	-3.1
1922	Bos-N	126	466	59	124	6	3	1	37	45	22	.266	.332	.298	630	67	-22	8	9	-1	.944	-14	2-78,S-33,3-13	-2.9
1923	Bos-N	39	138	15	38	3	1	0	10	13	6	.275	.338	.312	649	75	-4	0	3	-1	.905	-8	S-37/2-4	-0.9
Total	10	853	3010	349	750	84	30	5	266	242	214	.249	.312	.302	614	78	-81	72	48		.928	-122	S-664/2-99,3-69,O-2L	-16.2
■ MERLIN KOPP	Kopp, Merlin Henry "Manny" b: 1/2/1892, Toledo, Ohio d: 5/6/60, Sacramento, Cal. BB/TR (BR 1915), 5'8", 158 lbs. Deb: 8/2/15																							
1915	Was-A	16	32	2	8	0	0	0	0	5	7	.250	.351	.250	601	79	-1	1			.933	-1	/O-9(8-0-1)	-0.2
1918	Phi-A	96	363	60	85	7	7	0	18	42	55	.234	.320	.292	612	84	-6	22			.972	12	O-96(96-0-0)	0.2
1919	Phi-A	75	235	34	53	2	4	1	12	42	43	.226	.348	.281	629	77	-6	16			.924	-2	O-65(58-7-0)	-1.2
Total	3	187	630	96	146	9	11	1	30	89	105	.232	.332	.286	618	81	-12	39			.953	8	O-170(162-7-1)	-1.2
■ JOE KOPPE	Koppe, Joseph (b: Joseph Kopchia) b: 10/19/30, Detroit, Mich. BR/TR, 5'10", 165 lbs. Deb: 8/9/58 Career OF: (0-LF 0-CF 3-RF)																							
1958	Mil-N	16	9	3	4	0	0	0	0	1	1	.444	.500	.444	944	167	1	0	0	0	.833	5	/S-3	0.6
1959	Phi-N	126	422	68	110	18	7	7	28	41	80	.261	.329	.386	715	88	-7	7	7	-1	.954	5	*S-113,2-11	0.7
1960	Phi-N	58	170	13	29	6	1	1	13	23	47	.171	.273	.235	508	41	-14	3	2	-0	.956	-12	S-55/3-2	-2.2
1961	Phi-N	6	3	1	0	0	0	0	0	0	0	.000	.000	.000	0	-99	-1	0	0	0	.800	0	/S-5	-0.1
	LA-A	91	338	46	85	12	2	5	40	45	77	.251	.341	.343	684	75	-11	3	3	-0	.947	-6	S-88/2-3,3-1	-0.9
1962	LA-A	128	375	47	85	16	0	4	40	73	84	.227	.356	.301	657	81	-7	2	1	0	.957	4	*S-118/2-5,3-4	0.8
1963	LA-A	76	143	11	30	4	1	1	12	9	30	.210	.261	.273	534	53	-9	0	0	0	.962	8	S-19,3-18,2-14,/O-3R	0.0
1964	LA-A	54	113	10	29	4	1	0	6	14	16	.257	.339	.310	648	91	-1	0	0	0	.945	15	S-31,2-13/3-3	1.7
1965	Cal-A	23	33	3	7	1	0	1	2	3	10	.212	.278	.333	611	75	-1	1	0	0	.979	9	2-10/S-4,3-4	0.9
Total	8	578	1606	202	379	61	12	19	141	209	345	.236	.327	.324	651	76	-50	16	13	-1	.952	29	S-436/2-56,3-32,O-3R	1.5
■ GEORGE KOPSHAW	Kopshaw, George Karl b: 7/5/1895, Passaic, N.J. d: 12/26/34, Lynchburg, Va. BR/TR, 5'11.5", 176 lbs. Deb: 8/4/23																							
1923	StL-N	2	5	1	1	1	0	0	0	0	1	.200	.200	.400	600	56	-0	0	0	0	1.000	-1	/C-1	-0.1
■ STEVE KORCHECK	Korcheck, Stephen Joseph "Hoss" b: 8/11/32, McClellandtown, Pa. BR/TR, 6'1", 205 lbs. Deb: 9/6/54																							
1954	Was-A	2	7	0	1	0	0	0	0	0	2	.143	.143	.143	286	-23	-1	0	0	0	.857	-1	/C-2	-0.2
1955	Was-A	13	36	3	10	2	0	0	2	0	5	.278	.297	.333	631	73	-1	0	0	0	1.000	1	C-12	0.0
1958	Was-A	21	51	6	4	2	1	0	1	1	16	.078	.096	.157	253	-32	-9	0	0	0	.975	0	C-20	-0.9
1959	Was-A	22	51	3	8	2	0	0	4	5	13	.157	.232	.196	428	19	-6	0	0	0	.974	6	C-22	0.1
Total	4	58	145	12	23	6	1	0	7	6	36	.159	.197	.214	411	13	-18	0	0	0	.976	7	/C-56	-1.0
■ ART KORES	Kores, Arthur Emil "Dutch" b: 7/22/1886, Milwaukee, Wis. d: 3/26/74, Milwaukee, Wis. BR/TR, 5'9", 167 lbs. Deb: 7/24/15																							
1915	StL-F	60	201	18	47	9	2	1	22	21	13	.234	.306	.313	620	71	-11	6			.960	19	3-60	1.1

YEAR	TM/L	G	AB	R	H	2B	3B	HR	RBI	BB	SO	AVG	OBP	SLG	OPS	OPS+	BR+	SB	CS	SBR	FA	FR	G/POS	TPR
■ **ANDY KOSCO** Kosco, Andrew John b: 10/5/41, Youngstown, Ohio BR/TR, 6'3", 207 lbs. Deb: 8/13/65 Career OF: (136-LF 14-CF 312-RF)																								
1965	Min-A	23	55	3	13	4	0	1	6	1	15	.236	.250	.364	614	69	-2	0	0	0	1.000	0	O-14(0-0-14)/1-2	-0.3
1966	Min-A	57	158	11	35	5	0	2	13	7	31	.222	.255	.291	546	53	-10	0	1	-0	.986	-1	O-40(31-7-5)/1-5	-1.4
1967	Min-A	9	28	4	4	1	0	0	4	2	4	.143	.200	.179	379	12	-3	0	0	0	.923	-0	/O-7(0-0-7)	-0.4
1968	NY-A	131	466	47	112	19	1	15	59	16	71	.240	.270	.382	652	99	-3	2	2	-0	.960	3	O-95(1-0-94),1-28	-1.0
1969	LA-N	120	424	51	105	13	2	19	74	21	66	.248	.285	.422	707	103	-1	0	1	-0	.981	-6	*O-109(38-0-76)/1-3	-1.4
1970	LA-N	74	224	21	51	12	0	8	27	1	40	.228	.231	.388	620	66	-12	1	1	-0	.981	-2	O-58(3-0-55)/1-1	-1.7
1971	Mil-A	98	264	27	60	6	2	10	39	24	57	.227	.292	.379	670	90	-4	1	3	-1	.988	-3	O-45L,1-29,3-12	-1.3
1972	Cal-A	49	142	15	34	4	2	6	13	5	23	.239	.270	.423	693	110	1	1	0	0	.985	0	O-36(24-0-13)	-0.1
	Bos-A	17	47	5	10	2	1	3	6	2	9	.213	.260	.489	749	113	0	0	0	0	1.000	0	O-12(12-0-0)	0.0
	Yr	66	189	20	44	6	3	9	19	7	32	.233	.268	.439	707	111	1	1	0	0	.988	1	O-48(36-0-13)	-0.1
1973	*Cin-N	47	118	17	33	7	0	9	21	13	26	.280	.351	.568	919	159	9	0	0	0	1.000	-5	O-36(1-7-28)/1-1	0.2
1974	Cin-N	33	37	3	7	2	0	0	5	7	8	.189	.318	.243	561	59	-2	0	0	0	.846	-2	/3-8,O-1(0-0-1)	-0.4
Total	10	658	1963	204	464	75	8	73	267	99	350	.236	.275	.394	669	92	-28	5	8	-2	.979	-16	O-453R/1-69,3-20	-7.8
■ **CLEM KOSHOREK** Koshorek, Clement John "Scooter" b: 6/20/25, Royal Oak, Mich. d: 9/8/91, Royal Oak, Mich. BR/TR, 5'4.5", 165 lbs. Deb: 4/15/52																								
1952	Pit-N	98	322	27	84	17	0	0	15	26	39	.261	.320	.314	634	74	-11	4	7	-2	.949	1	S-33,2-27,3-26	-0.8
1953	Pit-N	1	1	0	0	0	0	0	0	0	1	.000	.000	.000	0	-99	-0	0	0	0	.000	0	H	0.0
Total	2	99	323	27	84	17	0	0	15	26	40	.260	.319	.313	632	74	-11	4	7	-2	.949	1	/S-33,2-27,3-26	-0.8
■ **COREY KOSKIE** Koskie, Cordel Leonard b: 6/28/73, Anola, Man., Can. BL/TR, 6'3", 215 lbs. Deb: 9/9/98 Career OF: (0-LF 0-CF 25-RF)																								
1998	Min-A	11	29	2	4	0	0	1	2	2	10	.138	.194	.241	435	12	-4	0	0	0	.941	-1	3-10	-0.5
1999	Min-A	117	342	42	106	21	0	11	58	40	72	.310	.390	.468	858	114	8	4	4	-1	.962	1	3-79,O-25R,D-12	0.7
2000	Min-A	146	474	79	142	32	4	9	65	77	104	.300	.402	.441	843	107	8	5	4	-0	.966	-0	*3-139/D-1	0.8
Total	3	274	845	123	252	53	4	21	125	119	186	.298	.391	.445	836	107	12	9	8	-1	.964	0	3-228/O-25R,D-13	1.0
■ **KEVIN KOSLOFSKI** Koslofski, Kevin Craig b: 9/24/66, Decatur, Ill. BL/TR, 5'8", 165 lbs. Deb: 6/28/92																								
1992	KC-A	55	133	20	33	0	2	3	13	12	23	.248	.315	.346	661	83	-3	2	1	0	.991	-1	O-52(15-18-23)	-0.5
1993	KC-A	15	26	4	7	0	0	1	2	4	5	.269	.387	.385	772	102	0	0	1	-0	1.000	-0	O-13(3-4-7)/D-1	0.0
1994	KC-A	2	4	2	1	0	0	0	0	2	1	.250	.500	.250	750	97	0	0	0	0	.750	0	/O-2(0-1-1)	0.0
1996	Mil-A	25	42	5	9	3	2	0	6	4	12	.214	.298	.381	679	67	-2	0	0	0	.972	-4	O-22(6-14-2)/D-1	-0.6
Total	4	97	205	31	50	3	4	4	21	22	41	.244	.326	.356	682	83	-5	2	2	-0	.983	-5	/O-89(24-37-33),D-2	-1.1
■ **MIKE KOSMAN** Kosman, Michael Thomas b: 12/10/17, Hamtramck, Mich. BR/TR, 5'9", 160 lbs. Deb: 4/20/44																								
1944	Cin-N	1	0	0	0	0	0	0	0	0	0	—	—	—	—	—	0	0			.000	0	R	0.0
■ **FRED KOSTER** Koster, Frederick Charles "Fritz" b: 12/21/05, Louisville, Ky. d: 4/24/79, St.Matthews, Ky. BL/TL, 5'10.5", 165 lbs. Deb: 4/27/31																								
1931	Phi-N	76	151	21	34	2	2	0	8	14	21	.225	.291	.265	556	47	-11	4			.923	-4	O-41(6-14-22)	-1.7
■ **FRANK KOSTRO** Kostro, Frank Jerry b: 8/4/37, Windber, Pa. BR/TR, 6'2", 190 lbs. Deb: 9/2/62 Career OF: (21-LF 0-CF 16-RF)																								
1962	Det-A	16	41	5	11	3	0	0	3	1	6	.268	.286	.341	627	66	-2	0	0	0	.967	1	3-11	-0.2
1963	Det-A	31	52	4	12	1	0	0	0	9	13	.231	.344	.250	594	67	-2	0	0	0	.929	-1	/3-6,1-3,O-3(1-0-2)	-0.3
	LA-A	43	99	6	22	2	1	2	10	6	17	.222	.267	.323	590	68	-4	0	0	0	.960	-2	3-19/1-5,O-3(1-0-2)	-0.7
	Yr	74	151	10	34	3	1	2	10	15	30	.225	.295	.298	593	68	-6	0	0	0	.953	-3	3-25/1-8,O-6(2-0-4)	-1.0
1964	Min-A	59	103	10	28	5	0	3	12	4	21	.272	.306	.408	713	96	-1	0	0	0	.912	-3	3-12/2-7,O-2L,1-1	-0.4
1965	Min-A	20	31	2	5	2	0	0	1	4	5	.161	.257	.226	483	37	-3	0	0	0	.923	-1	/2-7,3-6,O-2(1-0-1)	-0.3
1967	Min-A	32	31	4	10	0	0	0	2	3	2	.323	.382	.323	705	102	0	0	0	0	1.000	-1	/O-3(2-0-1),3-1	-0.1
1968	Min-A	63	108	9	26	4	1	0	9	6	20	.241	.281	.296	577	71	-4	0	0	0	1.000	-1	O-24(14-0-10)/1-5	-0.7
1969	Min-A	2	2	0	0	0	0	0	0	0	1	.000	.000	.000	0	-98	-1	0	0	0	.000	0	H	-0.1
Total	7	266	467	40	114	17	2	5	37	33	85	.244	.295	.321	617	74	-16	0	0	0	.926	-8	/3-55,O-37L,2-14,1	-2.8
■ **MARK KOTSAY** Kotsay, Mark Steven b: 12/2/75, Whittier, Cal. BL/TL, 6', 180 lbs. Deb: 7/11/97																								
1997	Fla-N	14	52	5	10	1	1	0	4	4	7	.192	.250	.250	500	33	-5	3	0	1	1.000	2	O-14(0-14-0)	-0.2
1998	Fla-N	154	578	72	161	25	7	11	68	34	61	.279	.320	.403	723	93	-7	10	5	0	.984	22	*O-145(0-46-107)/1-3	1.0
1999	Fla-N	148	495	57	134	23	9	8	50	29	50	.271	.311	.402	713	83	-14	7	6	-1	.981	12	*O-129(0-0-129),1-19	-1.0
2000	Fla-N	152	530	87	158	31	5	12	57	42	46	.298	.350	.443	793	104	2	19	9	1	.990	9	*O-142(0-9-139)/1-2	0.6
Total	4	468	1655	221	463	80	22	31	179	109	164	.280	.325	.411	736	92	-24	39	20	2	.986	45	O-430(0-69-375)/1-24	0.4
■ **BRIAN KOWITZ** Kowitz, Brian Mark b: 8/7/69, Baltimore, Md. BL/TL, 5'10", 180 lbs. Deb: 6/4/95																								
1995	Atl-N	10	24	3	4	1	0	0	3	2	5	.167	.259	.208	468	24	-3	0	1	-0	1.000	-2	/O-8(2-1-5)	-0.5
■ **ERNIE KOY** Koy, Ernest Anyz "Chief" b: 9/17/09, Sealy, Tex. BR/TR, 6', 200 lbs. Deb: 4/19/38																								
1938	Bro-N	142	521	78	156	29	13	11	76	38	76	.299	.352	.468	820	121	14	15			.984	-1	*O-135(54-64-18)/3-1	0.7
1939	Bro-N	125	425	57	118	37	5	8	67	39	64	.278	.338	.445	783	105	2	11			.962	-0	*O-114(110-3-3)	-0.4
1940	Bro-N	24	48	9	11	2	1	1	8	3	3	.229	.275	.375	650	73	-2	1			1.000	-4	O-19(11-5-2)	-0.6
	StL-N	93	348	44	108	19	5	8	52	28	59	.310	.368	.463	831	121	10	12			.970	-3	O-91(91-0-0)	0.2
	Yr	117	396	53	119	21	6	9	60	31	62	.301	.357	.452	809	115	8	13			.973	-6	*O-110(102-5-2)	-0.4
1941	StL-N	13	40	5	8	1	0	2	4	1	8	.200	.220	.375	595	61	-2	0			1.000	-2	O-12(12-0-0)	-0.5
	Cin-N	67	204	24	51	11	2	2	27	14	22	.250	.301	.353	654	84	-5	1			.990	-1	O-49(42-1-6)	-0.9
	Yr	80	244	29	59	12	2	4	31	15	30	.242	.288	.357	645	80	-7	1			.991	-3	O-61(54-1-6)	-1.4
1942	Cin-N	3	2	0	0	0	0	0	0	0	2	.000	.000	.000	0	-99	-0	0			.000	0	H	-0.1
	Phi-N	91	258	21	63	9	3	4	26	14	50	.244	.283	.349	632	89	-5	0			.981	-9	O-78(28-52-4)	-1.7
	Yr	94	260	21	63	9	3	4	26	14	52	.242	.281	.346	627	87	-5	0			.981	-9	O-78(28-52-4)	-1.8
Total	5	558	1846	238	515	108	29	36	260	137	284	.279	.332	.427	759	107	11	40			.977	-20	O-498(348-125-33)/3-1	-3.3
■ **AL KOZAR** Kozar, Albert Kenneth b: 7/5/21, McKees Rocks, Pa. BR/TR, 5'9.5", 173 lbs. Deb: 4/19/48																								
1948	Was-A	150	577	61	144	25	8	1	58	66	52	.250	.327	.326	652	76	-20	4	2	0	.967	-21	*2-149	-3.2
1949	Was-A	105	350	46	94	15	2	4	31	25	23	.269	.321	.357	678	81	-11	2	1	0	.977	-7	*2-102	-1.3
1950	Was-A	20	55	7	11	1	0	0	3	5	8	.200	.267	.218	485	27	-6	0	0	0	.962	-0	2-15	-0.5
	Chi-A	10	10	4	3	0	0	1	2	0	3	.300	.300	.600	900	129	0	0	0	0	1.000	3	/2-4,3-1	0.3
	Yr	30	65	11	14	1	0	1	5	5	11	.215	.271	.277	548	42	-6	0	0	0	.968	2	2-19/3-1	-0.2
Total	3	285	992	118	252	41	10	6	94	96	86	.254	.321	.334	655	76	-36	6	3	0	.971	-26	2-270/3-1	-4.7
■ **JOE KRACHER** Kracher, Joseph Peter "Jug" b: 11/4/15, Philadelphia, Pa. d: 12/24/81, San Angelo, Tex. BR/TR, 5'11", 185 lbs. Deb: 9/17/39																								
1939	Phi-N	5	5	1	1	0	0	0	0	2	1	.200	.429	.200	629	76	0	0			1.000	-1	/C-2	-0.1
■ **CLARENCE KRAFT** Kraft, Clarence Otto "Big Boy" b: 6/9/1887, Evansville, Ind. d: 3/26/58, Fort Worth, Tex. BR/TR, 6', 190 lbs. Deb: 5/1/14																								
1914	Bos-N	3	3	0	1	0	0	0	0	0	1	.333	.333	.333	667	99	-0	0			1.000	0	/1-1	0.0
■ **ED KRANEPOOL** Kranepool, Edward Emil b: 11/8/44, New York, N.Y. BL/TL, 6'3", 215 lbs. Deb: 9/22/62 Career OF: (132-LF 1-CF 118-RF)																								
1962	NY-N	3	6	0	1	1	0	0	0	0	1	.167	.167	.333	500	30	-1	0	0	0	1.000	1	/1-3	0.0
1963	NY-N	86	273	22	57	12	2	2	14	18	50	.209	.258	.289	547	56	-15	4	2	0	.954	-2	O-55(6-0-50),1-20	-2.4
1964	NY-N	119	420	47	108	19	4	10	45	32	50	.257	.313	.393	706	100	-1	0	1	-0	.991	3	*1-104/O-6(0-1-5)	-0.5
1965	NY-N☆	153	525	44	133	24	4	10	53	39	71	.253	.307	.371	679	94	-5	1	4	-1	.992	-2	*1-147	-1.8
1966	NY-N	146	464	51	118	15	2	16	57	41	66	.254	.319	.399	718	100	-0	1	1	-0	.992	5	*1-132,O-11(11-0-0)	-0.3
1967	NY-N	141	469	37	126	17	1	10	54	37	51	.269	.323	.373	697	100	0	0	4	-1	.992	4	*1-139	-0.5
1968	NY-N	127	373	29	86	13	1	3	20	19	39	.231	.272	.295	566	70	-14	0	3	-1	.994	5	*1-113/O-2(2-0-0)	-1.9
1969	*NY-N	112	353	36	84	9	2	11	49	37	32	.238	.310	.368	679	88	-6	3	2	-0	.993	3	*1-106/O-2(2-0-0)	-1.2
1970	NY-N	43	47	2	8	0	0	0	3	5	2	.170	.250	.170	420	15	-6	0	0	0	1.000	0	/1-8	-0.6
1971	NY-N	122	421	61	118	20	4	14	58	38	33	.280	.341	.447	788	123	12	0	4	-1	**.998**	-3	*1-108,O-11(6-0-5)	-0.1
1972	NY-N	122	327	28	88	15	1	8	34	34	35	.269	.340	.394	734	111	5	1	0	0	.996	-1	*1-108/O-1(0-0-1)	-0.3
1973	*NY-N	100	284	28	68	12	2	1	35	30	28	.239	.312	.306	618	73	-10	1	0	0	.998	-0	1-51,O-32(31-0-1)	-1.6

YEAR	TM/L	G	AB	R	H	2B	3B	HR	RBI	BB	SO	AVG	OBP	SLG	OPS	OPS+	BR+	SB	CS	SBR	FA	FR	G/POS	TPR
1974	NY-N	94	217	20	65	11	1	4	24	18	14	.300	.353	.415	768	116	4	1	0	0	.977	-6	O-33(32-0-1),1-24	-0.5
1975	NY-N	106	325	42	105	16	0	4	43	27	21	.323	.375	.409	784	123	10	1	1	-0	.997	-0	1-82/O-4(4-0-0)	0.3
1976	NY-N	123	415	47	121	17	1	10	49	35	38	.292	.347	.410	756	121	11	1	0	0	.996	-6	1-86,O-31(23-0-8)	-0.4
1977	NY-N	108	281	28	79	17	0	10	40	23	20	.281	.336	.448	784	113	5	1	4	-1	.984	-1	O-42(10-0-32),1-41	-0.1
1978	NY-N	66	81	7	17	2	0	3	19	8	12	.210	.289	.346	635	79	-2	0	0	0	1.000	-2	O-12(3-0-9)/1-3	-0.5
1979	NY-N	82	155	7	36	5	0	2	17	13	18	.232	.296	.303	599	66	-7	0	1	-0	1.000	0	1-29/O-8(2-0-6)	-0.9
Total	18	1853	5436	536	1418	225	25	118	614	454	581	.261	.319	.377	696	97	-21	15	27	-6	.994	-2	*1-1304,O-250L	-13.3

■ CHARLIE KRAUSE Krause, Charles b: 10/2/1873, Detroit, Mich. d: 3/30/48, Eloise, Mich. TR, Deb: 7/27/01

YEAR	TM/L	G	AB	R	H	2B	3B	HR	RBI	BB	SO	AVG	OBP	SLG	OPS	OPS+	BR+	SB	CS	SBR	FA	FR	G/POS	TPR
1901	Cin-N	1	4	0	1	0	0	0	0	0		.250	.250	.250	500	48	-0	0			.000	0	/2-1	0.0

■ DANNY KRAVITZ Kravitz, Daniel "Dusty" or "Beak" b: 12/21/30, Lopez, Pa. BL/TR, 5'11", 195 lbs. Deb: 4/17/56

YEAR	TM/L	G	AB	R	H	2B	3B	HR	RBI	BB	SO	AVG	OBP	SLG	OPS	OPS+	BR+	SB	CS	SBR	FA	FR	G/POS	TPR
1956	Pit-N	32	68	6	18	2	2	2	10	5	9	.265	.315	.441	756	103	0	1	1	-0	.944	0	C-26/3-2	0.1
1957	Pit-N	19	41	2	6	1	0	0	4	2	10	.146	.186	.171	357	-3	-6	0	0	0	1.000	0	C-15	-0.5
1958	Pit-N	45	100	9	24	3	2	1	5	11	10	.240	.315	.340	655	76	-3	0	0	0	.967	-6	C-37	-0.8
1959	Pit-N	52	162	18	41	9	1	3	21	5	14	.253	.275	.377	652	72	-7	0	1	-0	.986	-1	C-45	-0.6
1960	Pit-N	8	6	0	0	0	0	0	0	1	2	.000	.143	.000	143	-57	-1	0	0	0	1.000	-0	/C-1	-0.1
	KC-A	59	175	17	41	7	2	4	14	11	19	.234	.280	.366	645	73	-7	0	0	0	.971	-4	C-47	-0.9
Total	5	215	552	52	130	22	7	10	54	35	64	.236	.281	.355	636	70	-25	1	2	-0	.973	-10	C-171/3-2	-2.8

■ FRANK KREEGER Kreeger, Frank d: 7/14/1899, Shelby Co., Ill. Deb: 7/28/1884

YEAR	TM/L	G	AB	R	H	2B	3B	HR	RBI	BB	SO	AVG	OBP	SLG	OPS	OPS+	BR+	SB	CS	SBR	FA	FR	G/POS	TPR
1884	KC-U	1	3	0	0	0	0	0		0		.000	.000	.000	0	-99	-1				.000	-1	/O-1(0-1-0),P-1	-0.1

■ MIKE KREEVICH Kreevich, Michael Andreas b: 6/10/08, Mt.Olive, Ill. d: 4/25/94, Pana, Ill. BR/TR, 5'7.5", 168 lbs. Deb: 9/7/31 Career OF: (27-LF 1095-CF 69-RF)

YEAR	TM/L	G	AB	R	H	2B	3B	HR	RBI	BB	SO	AVG	OBP	SLG	OPS	OPS+	BR+	SB	CS	SBR	FA	FR	G/POS	TPR
1931	Chi-N	5	12	0	2	0	0	0	0	0	6	.167	.167	.167	333	-10	-2	1			1.000	-0	/O-4(1-1-2)	-0.2
1935	Chi-A	6	23	3	10	2	0	0	2	1	0	.435	.458	.522	980	149	2	1	1	-0	1.000	-2	/3-6	-0.1
1936	Chi-A	137	550	99	169	32	11	5	69	61	46	.307	.378	.433	811	96	-3	10	5	0	.964	-2	*O-133(17-65-57)	-0.9
1937	Chi-A	144	583	94	176	29	**16**	12	73	43	45	.302	.350	.468	818	104	2	10	1	2	**.988**	7	*O-138(6-138-1)	0.7
1938	Chi-A★	129	489	73	145	26	12	6	73	55	23	.297	.371	.436	807	99	-1	13	5	1	.975	4	*O-127(0-127-1)	0.1
1939	Chi-A	145	541	85	175	30	8	5	77	59	40	.323	.390	.436	826	108	8	23	10	2	.975	16	*O-139(0-139-0)/3-4	2.0
1940	Chi-A	144	582	86	154	27	10	8	55	34	49	.265	.305	.387	692	77	-21	15	7	1	.982	12	*O-144(0-144-0)	-1.1
1941	Chi-A	121	436	44	101	16	8	0	37	35	26	.232	.289	.305	594	58	-27	17	5	2	**.994**	0	*O-113(0-113-0)	-2.7
1942	Phi-A	116	444	57	113	19	1	1	30	47	31	.255	.326	.309	634	79	-11	7	9	-2	.981	4	*O-107(0-107-0)	-1.2
1943	StL-A	60	161	24	41	6	0	0	10	26	13	.255	.358	.292	650	89	1	4	1	1	.993	5	O-51(3-47-1)	0.3
1944	*StL-A	105	402	55	121	15	6	5	44	27	24	.301	.348	.405	754	108	4	3	3	-0	.986	-1	*O-100(0-93-7)	0.0
1945	StL-A	84	295	34	70	11	1	2	21	37	27	.237	.322	.302	624	78	-8	4	1	1	.991	4	O-81(0-81-0)	-0.6
	Was-A	45	158	22	44	8	2	1	23	21	9	.278	.363	.373	737	124	5	7	5	-0	.971	-2	O-40(0-40-0)	0.2
	Yr	129	453	56	114	19	3	3	44	58	36	.252	.337	.327	663	92	-3	11	6	0	.985	2	*O-121(0-121-0)	-0.4
Total	12	1241	4676	676	1321	221	75	45	514	446	339	.283	.346	.391	737	92	-53	115	53		.982	46	*O-1177C/3-10	-3.5

■ CHARLIE KREHMEYER Krehmeyer, Charles L. b: 7/5/1863, St.Louis, Mo. d: 2/10/26, St.Louis, Mo. BL/TL, 5'11", 179 lbs. Deb: 7/8/1884

YEAR	TM/L	G	AB	R	H	2B	3B	HR	RBI	BB	SO	AVG	OBP	SLG	OPS	OPS+	BR+	SB	CS	SBR	FA	FR	G/POS	TPR
1884	StL-a	21	70	3	16	0	1	0	5	2		.229	.250	.257	507	64	-3				.619	-5	O-15(5-9-1)/C-7,1-1	-0.7
1885	Lou-a	7	31	4	7	1	1	0	5	1		.226	.250	.323	573	80	-1				.909	-1	/C-4,O-2(1-0-1),1-1	-0.1
	StL-N	1	3	0	0	0	0	0	0	0	2	.000	.000	.000	0	-99	-1				.429	-2	/C-1	-0.2
Total	2	29	104	7	23	1	2	0	10	3	2	.221	.243	.269	512	64	-4				.571	-7	/O-17(6-9-2),C-12,1-2	-1.0

■ MICKEY KREITNER Kreitner, Albert Joseph b: 10/10/22, Nashville, Tenn. BR/TR, 6'3", 190 lbs. Deb: 9/28/43

YEAR	TM/L	G	AB	R	H	2B	3B	HR	RBI	BB	SO	AVG	OBP	SLG	OPS	OPS+	BR+	SB	CS	SBR	FA	FR	G/POS	TPR
1943	Chi-N	3	8	0	3	0	0	0	2	1	2	.375	.444	.375	819	140	0	0			1.000	-1	/C-3	0.0
1944	Chi-N	39	85	3	13	2	0	0	1	8	16	.153	.234	.176	411	17	-9	0			.992	-1	C-39	-0.9
Total	2	42	93	3	16	2	0	0	3	9	18	.172	.252	.194	446	27	-9	0			.992	-1	/C-42	-0.9

■ RALPH KREITZ Kreitz, Ralph Wesley "Red" b: 11/13/1885, Plum Creek, Neb. d: 7/20/41, Portland, Ore. BR/TR, 5'9.5", 175 lbs. Deb: 8/1/11

YEAR	TM/L	G	AB	R	H	2B	3B	HR	RBI	BB	SO	AVG	OBP	SLG	OPS	OPS+	BR+	SB	CS	SBR	FA	FR	G/POS	TPR
1911	Chi-A	7	17	0	4	1	0	0	0	2		.235	.316	.294	610	73	-1	0			1.000	-3	/C-7	-0.3

■ JIMMY KREMERS Kremers, James Edward b: 10/8/65, Little Rock, Ark. BL/TR, 6'3", 205 lbs. Deb: 6/5/90

YEAR	TM/L	G	AB	R	H	2B	3B	HR	RBI	BB	SO	AVG	OBP	SLG	OPS	OPS+	BR+	SB	CS	SBR	FA	FR	G/POS	TPR
1990	Atl-N	29	73	7	8	1	1	1	2	6	27	.110	.177	.192	369	1	-10	0	0	0	.992	-3	C-27	-1.3

■ WAYNE KRENCHICKI Krenchicki, Wayne Richard b: 9/17/54, Trenton, N.J. BL/TR, 6'1", 180 lbs. Deb: 6/15/79 Career OF: (1-LF 0-CF 0-RF)

YEAR	TM/L	G	AB	R	H	2B	3B	HR	RBI	BB	SO	AVG	OBP	SLG	OPS	OPS+	BR+	SB	CS	SBR	FA	FR	G/POS	TPR
1979	Bal-A	16	21	1	4	1	0	0	0	0	0	.190	.190	.238	429	15	-2	0	0	0	.875	1	/3-7,2-6	-0.2
1980	Bal-A	9	14	1	2	0	0	0	0	1	3	.143	.200	.143	343	-4	-2	0	0	0	1.000	0	/S-6,2-1,D-1	-0.2
1981	Bal-A	33	56	7	12	4	0	0	6	4	9	.214	.267	.286	552	59	-3	0	0	0	.964	4	S-16/2-7,3-6,D-1	0.3
1982	Cin-N	94	187	19	53	6	1	2	21	13	23	.283	.330	.358	688	91	-2	5	3	0	.955	7	3-70/2-9	0.4
1983	Cin-N	51	77	6	21	2	0	0	11	8	4	.273	.349	.299	648	78	-2	0	0	0	.980	1	3-39/2-1	-0.1
	Det-A	59	133	18	37	7	0	1	16	11	27	.278	.338	.353	691	93	-1	0	0	0	.934	-8	3-48/2-6,S-6,1-3	-0.9
1984	Cin-N	97	181	18	54	9	2	6	22	19	23	.298	.365	.470	835	127	6	0	1	-0	.967	3	3-62/1-3,2-3	0.9
1985	Cin-N	90	173	16	47	9	0	4	25	28	20	.272	.373	.393	766	109	3	0	0	0	.967	4	3-52/2-3	0.7
1986	Mon-N	101	221	21	53	6	2	2	23	22	32	.240	.309	.312	621	72	-8	2	4	-1	.991	1	1-41,3-24/2-1,O-1L	-1.1
Total	8	550	1063	107	283	44	5	15	124	106	141	.266	.334	.359	693	92	-11	7	8	-1	.955	14	3-308/1-47,2-37,SDO	-0.2

■ CHUCK KRESS Kress, Charles Steven b: 12/9/21, Philadelphia, Pa. BL/TL, 6', 190 lbs. Deb: 4/16/47

YEAR	TM/L	G	AB	R	H	2B	3B	HR	RBI	BB	SO	AVG	OBP	SLG	OPS	OPS+	BR+	SB	CS	SBR	FA	FR	G/POS	TPR
1947	Cin-N	11	27	4	4	0	0	0	0	6	4	.148	.303	.148	451	23	-3	0			.983	1	/1-8	-0.2
1949	Cin-N	27	29	3	6	3	0	0	3	3	5	.207	.281	.310	592	58	-2	0			.974	0	1-16	-0.2
	Chi-A	97	353	45	98	17	6	1	44	39	44	.278	.349	.368	718	93	-4	6	7	-1	.994	-0	1-95	-0.8
1950	Chi-A	3	8	0	0	0	0	0	0	0	2	.000	.000	.000	0	-99	-2	0	0	0	1.000	-0	/1-2	-0.3
1954	Det-A	24	37	4	7	0	1	0	3	1	4	.189	.211	.243	454	24	-4	0	1	-0	.971	-0	/1-7,O-1(0-0-1)	-0.5
	Bro-N	13	12	1	1	0	0	0	2	0	0	.083	.083	.083	167	-55	-3	0	0	0	.500	-0	/1-1	-0.3
Total	4	175	466	57	116	20	7	1	52	49	59	.249	.320	.328	649	74	-17	6	8		.990	0	1-129/O-1(0-0-1)	-2.3

■ RED KRESS Kress, Ralph b: 1/2/07, Columbia, Cal. d: 11/29/62, Los Angeles, Cal. BR/TR, 5'11.5", 165 lbs. Deb: 9/24/27 C Career OF: (22-LF 0-CF 103-RF)

YEAR	TM/L	G	AB	R	H	2B	3B	HR	RBI	BB	SO	AVG	OBP	SLG	OPS	OPS+	BR+	SB	CS	SBR	FA	FR	G/POS	TPR
1927	StL-A	7	23	3	7	2	1	1	3	3	3	.304	.385	.609	993	150	2	0	0	0	.974	1	/S-7	0.3
1928	StL-A	150	560	78	153	26	10	3	81	48	70	.273	.332	.371	703	82	-15	5	4	-0	.929	-17	*S-150	-1.5
1929	StL-A	147	557	82	170	38	4	9	107	52	54	.305	.366	.436	802	102	1	5	8	-2	**.946**	-2	*S-146	1.3
1930	StL-A	154	614	94	192	43	8	16	112	50	56	.313	.366	.487	853	110	9	3	12	-4	.938	-12	*S-123,3-31	0.8
1931	StL-A	150	605	87	188	46	8	16	114	46	48	.311	.360	.493	853	118	14	3	16	-5	.936	-11	3-84,O-40R,S-38,1	-0.1
1932	StL-A	14	52	2	9	0	1	2	9	4	6	.173	.232	.327	559	41	-5	1	1	-0	.909	2	3-14	-0.2
	Chi-A	135	515	83	147	42	4	9	57	47	36	.285	.346	.435	781	108	5	6	3	0	.956	11	O-64R,S-53,3-19,/1	1.5
	Yr	149	567	85	156	42	5	11	66	51	42	.275	.336	.425	761	101	-0	7	4	0	.956	13	O-64R,S-53,3-33,/1	1.3
1933	Chi-A	129	467	47	116	20	5	10	78	37	40	.248	.304	.377	680	83	-13	4	4	-1	.978	-4	*1-111/O-8(0-0-8)	-2.7
1934	Chi-A	8	14	3	4	0	0	0	1	3	3	.286	.412	.286	697	80	-0	0	0	0	1.000	-4	/2-3	-0.4
	Was-A	56	171	18	39	4	3	4	24	17	19	.228	.298	.357	655	71	-8	3	0	1	.993	-2	1-30,O-10L/2-6,S3	-1.1
	Yr	64	185	21	43	4	3	4	25	20	22	.232	.307	.351	659	72	-8	3	0	1	.993	-6	1-30,O-10L/2-9,S3	-1.5
1935	Was-A	84	252	32	75	13	4	2	42	25	16	.298	.361	.405	766	101	0	3	3	-0	.964	17	S-53/1-5,P-3,O-2R,2	1.8
1936	Was-A	109	391	51	111	20	6	8	51	39	25	.284	.349	.427	776	96	-3	6	0	1	.927	9	S-64,2-33/1-5	1.2
1938	StL-A	150	566	74	171	33	3	7	79	69	47	.302	.378	.408	786	97	-1	5	4	-0	**.965**	-15	*S-150	-0.5
1939	StL-A	13	43	5	12	1	0	0	8	6	2	.279	.367	.302	670	72	-2	1	0	0	.933	-3	S-13	-0.3
	Det-A	51	157	19	38	7	0	1	22	17	16	.242	.316	.306	622	55	-10	2	1	0	.959	2	S-25,2-16/3-4	-0.5
	Yr	64	200	24	50	8	0	1	30	23	18	.250	.327	.305	632	59	-12	3	1	0	.951	-1	S-38,2-16/3-4	-0.8
1940	Det-A	33	99	13	22	3	1	1	11	10	12	.222	.294	.303	597	50	-7	0	0	0	.924	9	3-17,S-12	0.3
1946	NY-N	1	1	0	0	0	0	0	0	1	0	.000	.500	.000	500	48	0	0			1.000	1	/P-1	0.0
Total	14	1391	5087	691	1454	298	58	89	799	474	453	.286	.347	.420	767	96	-34	47	56		.944	-16	S-835,3-170,1O/2P	-0.1

■ CHAD KREUTER Kreuter, Chadden Michael b: 8/26/64, Greenbrae, Cal. BB/TR (BR 1989 (part), 90), 6′2″, 195 lbs. Deb: 9/14/88 Career OF: (1-LF 0-CF 0-RF)

YEAR	TM/L	G	AB	R	H	2B	3B	HR	RBI	BB	SO	AVG	OBP	SLG	OPS	OPS+	BR+	SB	CS	SBR	FA	FR	G/POS	TPR
1988	Tex-A	16	51	3	14	2	1	1	5	7	13	.275	.362	.412	774	113	1	0	0	0	.990	2	C-16	0.4
1989	Tex-A	87	158	16	24	3	0	5	9	27	40	.152	.276	.266	541	52	-10	0	1	-0	.992	12	C-85	0.5
1990	Tex-A	22	22	2	1	1	0	0	2	8	9	.045	.300	.091	391	14	-2	0	0	0	.977	-1	C-20/D-1	-0.3
1991	Tex-A	3	4	0	0	0	0	0	0	0	1	.000	.000	.000	0	-99	-1	0	0	0	1.000	0	/C-1	-0.1
1992	Det-A	67	190	22	48	9	0	2	16	20	38	.253	.324	.332	655	83	-4	0	1	-0	.983	5	C-62/D-1	0.4
1993	Det-A	119	374	59	107	23	3	15	51	49	92	.286	.373	.484	857	129	16	2	1	0	.988	3	*C-112/1-1,D-2	2.4
1994	Det-A	65	170	17	38	8	0	1	19	28	36	.224	.333	.288	622	62	-9	0	1	-0	.987	-2	C-64/1-1,O-1(1-0-0)	-0.7
1995	Sea-A	26	75	12	17	5	0	1	8	5	22	.227	.293	.333	626	62	-4	0	0	0	.976	0	C-23	-0.3
1996	Chi-A	46	114	14	25	8	0	3	18	13	29	.219	.310	.368	678	74	-5	0	0	0	.990	-4	C-38/1-2	-0.7
1997	Chi-A	19	37	6	8	2	1	1	3	8	9	.216	.356	.405	761	102	0	0	1	-0	.984	-2	C-13/1-2	-0.2
	Ana-A	70	218	19	51	7	1	4	18	21	57	.234	.301	.330	632	65	-11	0	2	-1	.994	7	C-67/D-2	-0.1
	Yr	89	255	25	59	9	2	5	21	29	66	.231	.310	.341	651	70	-11	0	3	-1	.992	5	C-80/1-2,D-2	-0.3
1998	Chi-A	93	245	26	62	9	1	2	33	32	45	.253	.346	.322	669	78	-7	1	0	0	.985	-10	C-91	-1.1
	Ana-A	3	7	1	1	1	0	0	0	1	4	.143	.250	.286	536	39	-1	0	0	0	.882	-0	/C-3	-0.1
	Yr	96	252	27	63	10	1	2	33	33	49	.250	.344	.321	665	77	-8	1	0	0	.981	-10	C-94	-1.2
1999	KC-A	107	324	31	73	15	0	5	35	34	65	.225	.310	.318	628	59	-20	0	0	0	.994	-9	*C-101/D-1	-2.2
2000	LA-N	80	212	32	56	13	0	6	28	54	48	.264	.418	.410	828	116	8	1	0	0	.994	3	C-78	1.5
Total	13	823	2201	260	525	106	7	46	245	307	508	.239	.337	.356	692	83	-48	4	7	-2	.989	2	C-774/D-7,1-6,O-1L	-0.6

■ PAUL KRICHELL Krichell, Paul Bernard b: 12/19/1882, New York, N.Y. d: 6/4/57, Bronx, N.Y. BR/TR, 5′7″, 150 lbs. Deb: 5/12/11

YEAR	TM/L	G	AB	R	H	2B	3B	HR	RBI	BB	SO	AVG	OBP	SLG	OPS	OPS+	BR+	SB	CS	SBR	FA	FR	G/POS	TPR
1911	StL-A	28	82	6	19	3	0	0	8	4		.232	.276	.268	544	54	-5	2			.943	-2	C-25	-0.5
1912	StL-A	59	161	19	35	6	0	0	8	19		.217	.304	.255	559	62	-7	2			.959	-1	C-59	-0.4
Total	2	87	243	25	54	9	0	0	16	23		.222	.295	.259	554	60	-12	4			.955	-3	/C-84	-0.9

■ BILL KRIEG Krieg, William Frederick b: 1/29/1859, Petersburg, Ill. d: 3/25/30, Chillicothe, Ill. BR/TR, 5′8″, 180 lbs. Deb: 4/20/1884 Career OF: (20-LF 8-CF 3-RF)

YEAR	TM/L	G	AB	R	H	2B	3B	HR	RBI	BB	SO	AVG	OBP	SLG	OPS	OPS+	BR+	SB	CS	SBR	FA	FR	G/POS	TPR
1884	CP-U	71	279	35	69	15	4	0		11		.247	.276	.330	606	83	-14				.932	15	C-53,O-20L/S-1,1-1	0.4
1885	Chi-N	1	3	0	0	0	0	0	0	0	2	.000	.000	.000	0	-88	-1				.800	2	/O-1(0-0-1)	0.1
	Bro-a	17	60	7	9	4	0	1	5	2		.150	.177	.267	444	39	-4				.910	-4	C-12/1-5	-0.7
1886	Was-N	27	98	11	25	6	3	1	15	3	12	.255	.277	.408	685	113	1	2			.975	-1	1-27	-0.2
1887	Was-N	25	102	9	31	4	1	2	17	7	5	.304	.311	.379	690	96	-0	2			.973	-3	1-16/O-9(7-2-0)	-0.4
Total	4	141	542	62	134	29	8	4	37	23	19	.247	.270	.344	614	85	-18	4			.929	9	/C-65,1-49,O-30L,S	-0.8

■ JOHN KRONER Kroner, John Harold b: 11/13/08, St.Louis, Mo. d: 8/26/68, St.Louis, Mo. BR/TR, 6′, 185 lbs. Deb: 9/29/35 Career OF: (0-LF 0-CF 1-RF)

YEAR	TM/L	G	AB	R	H	2B	3B	HR	RBI	BB	SO	AVG	OBP	SLG	OPS	OPS+	BR+	SB	CS	SBR	FA	FR	G/POS	TPR
1935	Bos-A	2	4	1	1	0	0	0	0	1	1	.250	.400	.250	650	67	-0	0	0	0	1.000	-1	/3-2	-0.1
1936	Bos-A	84	298	40	87	17	8	4	62	26	24	.292	.349	.443	792	89	-6	2	3	-1	.964	-2	2-38,3-28,S-18,/O-1R	-0.3
1937	Cle-A	86	283	29	67	14	1	2	26	22	25	.237	.292	.314	606	52	-21	1	1	-0	.969	-3	2-64,3-11	-1.9
1938	Cle-A	51	117	13	29	16	0	1	17	19	6	.248	.353	.410	763	92	-1	0	1	-0	.974	12	2-31/1-7,3-3,S-1	1.0
Total	4	223	702	83	184	47	9	7	105	68	56	.262	.327	.385	712	75	-29	3	5	-1	.968	6	2-133/3-44,S-19,1O	-1.3

■ MIKE KRSNICH Krsnich, Michael b: 9/24/31, W.Allis, Wis. BR/TR, 6′1″, 190 lbs. Deb: 4/23/60 F

YEAR	TM/L	G	AB	R	H	2B	3B	HR	RBI	BB	SO	AVG	OBP	SLG	OPS	OPS+	BR+	SB	CS	SBR	FA	FR	G/POS	TPR
1960	Mil-N	4	9	0	3	1	0	0	2	0	0	.333	.333	.444	778	120	0	0	0	0	1.000	-0	/O-3(3-0-0)	0.0
1962	Mil-N	11	12	0	1	1	0	0	2	0	4	.083	.083	.167	250	-36	-2	0	0	0	1.000	-0	/O-3(3-0-0),1-1,3-1	-0.3
Total	2	15	21	0	4	2	0	0	4	0	4	.190	.190	.286	476	28	-2	0	0	0	1.000	-0	/O-6(6-0-0),3-1,1-1	-0.3

■ ROCKY KRSNICH Krsnich, Rocco Peter b: 8/5/27, W.Allis, Wis. BR/TR, 6′1″, 174 lbs. Deb: 9/13/49 F

YEAR	TM/L	G	AB	R	H	2B	3B	HR	RBI	BB	SO	AVG	OBP	SLG	OPS	OPS+	BR+	SB	CS	SBR	FA	FR	G/POS	TPR
1949	Chi-A	16	55	7	12	3	1	1	9	6	4	.218	.295	.364	659	76	-2	0	1	-0	.935	4	3-16	0.1
1952	Chi-A	40	91	11	21	7	2	1	15	12	9	.231	.327	.385	712	97	-0	0	0	0	.959	11	3-37	1.0
1953	Chi-A	64	129	9	26	8	0	1	14	12	11	.202	.270	.287	556	49	-9	0	2	-1	.929	9	3-57	-0.1
Total	3	120	275	27	59	18	3	3	38	30	24	.215	.294	.335	629	70	-12	0	3	-1	.942	23	3-110	1.0

■ OTTO KRUEGER Krueger, Arthur William "Oom Paul" b: 9/17/1876, Chicago, Ill. d: 2/20/61, St.Louis, Mo. BR/TR, 5′7″, 165 lbs. Deb: 9/16/1899 Career OF: (51-LF 3-CF 13-RF)

YEAR	TM/L	G	AB	R	H	2B	3B	HR	RBI	BB	SO	AVG	OBP	SLG	OPS	OPS+	BR+	SB	CS	SBR	FA	FR	G/POS	TPR
1899	Cle-N	13	44	4	10	1	0	0	2	8		.227	.358	.250	608	73	-1	1			.763	-2	/3-9,S-2,2-2	-0.2
1900	StL-N	12	35	8	14	3	2	1	3	10		.400	.543	.686	1229	240	8	0			.852	-6	2-12	0.2
1901	StL-N	142	520	77	143	16	12	2	79	50		.275	.353	.363	717	114	11	19			.881	-9	*3-142	0.6
1902	StL-N	128	467	55	124	7	8	0	46	29		.266	.313	.315	627	98	-2	14			.897	0	*S-107,3-18	0.3
1903	Pit-N	80	256	42	63	6	8	1	28	21		.246	.323	.344	667	87	-4	5			.884	-5	S-29,O-28L,3-13,/2	-0.9
1904	Pit-N	86	268	34	52	6	2	1	26	29		.194	.282	.243	525	61	-11	8			.905	-5	O-33L,S-32,3-10	-1.8
1905	Phi-N	46	114	10	21	1	1	0	12	13		.184	.273	.211	484	47	-7	1			.930	-9	S-23/O-6(0-3-3),3-1	-1.7
Total	7	507	1704	230	427	40	33	5	196	160		.251	.326	.322	648	94	-7	48			.902	-36	S-193,3-193/O-67L,2	-3.5

■ ERNIE KRUEGER Krueger, Ernest George b: 12/27/1890, Chicago, Ill. d: 4/22/76, Waukegan, Ill. BR/TR, 5′10.5″, 185 lbs. Deb: 8/4/13

YEAR	TM/L	G	AB	R	H	2B	3B	HR	RBI	BB	SO	AVG	OBP	SLG	OPS	OPS+	BR+	SB	CS	SBR	FA	FR	G/POS	TPR
1913	Cle-A	5	6	0	0	0	0	0	0	0	2	.000	.000	.000	0	-97	-1	0			1.000	-0	/C-4	-0.2
1915	NY-A	10	29	3	5	1	0	0	0	0	5	.172	.200	.207	407	22	-3	0	1	-0	.905	-4	/C-8	-0.7
1917	NY-N	8	10	0	0	0	0	0	0	0	4	.000	.000	.000	0	-99	-2	0			.857	-2	/C-5	-0.5
	Bro-N	31	81	10	22	2	2	1	6	5	7	.272	.330	.383	712	115	1	1			.979	1	C-23	0.5
	Yr	39	91	10	22	2	2	1	6	5	11	.242	.296	.341	637	94	-1	1			.973	-1	C-28	0.0
1918	Bro-N	30	87	4	25	4	2	0	7	4	9	.287	.319	.379	698	113	1	2			.986	6	C-23	0.9
1919	Bro-N	80	226	24	56	7	4	5	36	19	25	.248	.312	.381	692	105	1	4			.963	5	C-66	1.4
1920	*Bro-N	52	146	21	42	4	2	1	17	16	13	.288	.358	.363	721	104	1	2	0	0	.959	-4	C-46	0.2
1921	Bro-N	65	163	18	43	11	4	3	20	14	12	.264	.322	.436	758	95	-1	2	2	-0	.969	-2	C-52	-0.1
1925	Cin-N	37	88	7	27	4	0	1	7	6	8	.307	.351	.386	737	90	-1	1	2	-0	.946	-4	C-30	-0.4
Total	8	318	836	87	220	33	14	11	93	64	85	.263	.319	.376	695	97	-4	12	5		.964	-3	C-257	1.1

■ CHRIS KRUG Krug, Everett Ben b: 12/25/39, Los Angeles, Cal. BR/TR, 6′4″, 200 lbs. Deb: 5/30/65 C

YEAR	TM/L	G	AB	R	H	2B	3B	HR	RBI	BB	SO	AVG	OBP	SLG	OPS	OPS+	BR+	SB	CS	SBR	FA	FR	G/POS	TPR
1965	Chi-N	60	169	16	34	5	0	5	24	13	52	.201	.262	.320	582	61	-9	0	1	-0	.980	1	C-58	-0.6
1966	Chi-N	11	28	1	6	1	0	0	1	1	8	.214	.241	.250	491	36	-2	0	0	0	1.000	3	C-10	0.1
1969	SD-N	8	17	0	1	0	0	0	0	1	6	.059	.111	.059	170	-53	-3	0	0	0	.938	-1	/C-7	-0.4
Total	3	79	214	17	41	6	0	5	25	15	66	.192	.248	.290	538	50	-15	0	1	-0	.980	3	/C-75	-0.9

■ GENE KRUG Krug, Gary Eugene b: 2/12/55, Garden City, Kan. BL/TL, 6′4″, 225 lbs. Deb: 4/29/81

YEAR	TM/L	G	AB	R	H	2B	3B	HR	RBI	BB	SO	AVG	OBP	SLG	OPS	OPS+	BR+	SB	CS	SBR	FA	FR	G/POS	TPR
1981	Chi-N	7	5	0	2	0	0	0	0	1	1	.400	.500	.400	900	151	0	0	0	0	.000	0	/H	0.0

■ HENRY KRUG Krug, Henry Charles b: 12/4/1876, San Francisco, Cal. d: 1/14/08, San Francisco, Cal BR/TR, Deb: 7/26/02

YEAR	TM/L	G	AB	R	H	2B	3B	HR	RBI	BB	SO	AVG	OBP	SLG	OPS	OPS+	BR+	SB	CS	SBR	FA	FR	G/POS	TPR
1902	Phi-N	53	198	20	45	3	3	0	14	7		.227	.261	.273	534	65	-9	2			.947	-7	O-28L,2-13/S-9,3-6	-1.7

■ MARTY KRUG Krug, Martin John b: 9/10/1888, Koblenz, Germany d: 6/27/66, Glendale, Cal. BR/TR, 5′9″, 165 lbs. Deb: 5/29/12

YEAR	TM/L	G	AB	R	H	2B	3B	HR	RBI	BB	SO	AVG	OBP	SLG	OPS	OPS+	BR+	SB	CS	SBR	FA	FR	G/POS	TPR
1912	Bos-A	20	39	6	12	2	1	0	7	5		.308	.386	.410	797	122	1	2			.895	-2	/S-11,2-4	0.0
1922	Chi-N	127	450	67	124	23	4	4	60	43	43	.276	.343	.371	714	82	-11	7	9	-2	.937	-6	*3-104,2-23/S-1	-1.1
Total	2	147	489	73	136	25	5	4	67	48	43	.278	.346	.374	721	85	-10	9	9		.910	-8	3-104/2-27,S-12	-1.1

■ ART KRUGER Kruger, Arthur T. b: 3/16/1881, San Antonio, Tex. d: 11/28/49, Hondo, Cal. BR/TR, 6′, 185 lbs. Deb: 4/11/07

YEAR	TM/L	G	AB	R	H	2B	3B	HR	RBI	BB	SO	AVG	OBP	SLG	OPS	OPS+	BR+	SB	CS	SBR	FA	FR	G/POS	TPR
1907	Cin-N	100	317	25	74	10	9	0	28	18		.233	.285	.322	607	87	-6	10			.972	0	O-96(26-70-1)	-1.2
1910	Cle-A	47	168	14	26	4	2	0	10	15		.155	.237	.202	439	37	-12	10			.947	2	O-47(47-0-0)	-1.5
	Bos-N	1	1	0	0	0	0	0	0	0	0	.000	.000	.000	0	-96	-0	0			.000	0	H	0.0
	Cle-A	15	55	5	12	2	1	0	4	5		.218	.295	.291	586	82	-1	2			.974	2	O-15(15-0-0)	0.0
1914	KC-F	122	441	45	114	24	7	4	47	23	59	.259	.297	.372	669	85	-18	11			.963	-7	*O-120(7-130-0)	-3.5
1915	KC-F	80	240	24	57	9	2	2	26	12	29	.237	.277	.317	593	70	-14	5			.984	0	O-66(33-3-30)	-1.8
Total	4	365	1222	113	283	49	21	6	115	73	88	.232	.281	.321	602	76	-52	38			.968	-2	O-344(128-203-31)	-8.0

YEAR	TM/L	G	AB	R	H	2B	3B	HR	RBI	BB	SO	AVG	OBP	SLG	OPS	OPS+	BR+	SB	CS	SBR	FA	FR	G/POS	TPR
■ **JOHN KRUK**	Kruk, John Martin b: 2/9/61, Charleston, W.Va. BL/TL, 5'10", 204 lbs. Deb: 4/7/86 Career OF: (303-LF 11-CF 125-RF)																							
1986	SD-N	122	278	33	86	16	2	4	38	45	58	.309	.406	.424	830	132	14	2	4	-1	.981	-5	O-74(70-0-6)/1-9	0.5
1987	SD-N	138	447	72	140	14	2	20	91	73	93	.313	.410	.488	897	142	29	18	10	0	.996	3	*1-101,O-29(29-0-0)	2.5
1988	SD-N	120	378	54	91	17	1	9	44	80	68	.241	.373	.362	736	114	10	5	3	0	.995	-2	1-63,O-55(29-0-26)	0.3
1989	SD-N	31	76	7	14	0	0	3	6	17	14	.184	.333	.303	636	83	-1	0	0	0	.962	1	O-27(2-0-25)	-0.1
	Phi-N	81	281	46	93	13	6	5	38	27	39	.331	.390	.473	863	146	17	3	0	1	.983	-4	O-72(63-0-12)/1-7	1.2
	Yr	112	357	53	107	13	6	8	44	44	53	.300	.377	.437	814	132	15	3	0	1	.977	-3	O-99(65-0-37)/1-7	1.1
1990	Phi-N	142	443	52	129	25	8	7	67	69	70	.291	.387	.431	818	125	17	10	5	0	.986	-5	O-87(68-0-21),1-61	0.7
1991	Phi-N☆	152	538	84	158	27	6	21	92	67	100	.294	.373	.483	856	141	29	7	0	2	.997	-1	*1-102,O-52(36-11-6)	2.2
1992	Phi-N★	144	507	86	164	30	4	10	70	92	88	.323	.428	.458	886	151	39	3	5	-1	.993	-12	*1-121,O-35(6-0-29)	1.8
1993	*Phi-N★	150	535	100	169	33	5	14	85	111	87	.316	.433	.475	908	145	40	6	2	1	.993	-11	*1-144	1.6
1994	Phi-N	75	255	35	77	17	0	5	38	42	51	.302	.401	.427	828	113	7	4	1	1	.995	-1	1-69	0.0
1995	Chi-A	45	159	13	49	7	0	2	23	26	33	.308	.405	.390	795	113	4	0	1	-0	.909	-1	D-42/1-1	0.1
Total	10	1200	3897	582	1170	199	34	100	592	649	701	.300	.400	.446	846	134	205	58	31	2	.995	-37	1-678,O-431L/D-42	10.8
■ **DICK KRYHOSKI**	Kryhoski, Richard David b: 3/24/25, Leonia, N.J. BL/TL, 6'2", 200 lbs. Deb: 4/19/49																							
1949	NY-A	54	177	18	52	10	3	1	27	9	17	.294	.335	.401	736	94	-2	2	4	-1	.983	-1	1-51	-0.6
1950	Det-A	53	169	20	37	10	0	4	19	8	11	.219	.258	.349	608	53	-13	0	1	-0	.991	-0	1-47	-1.4
1951	Det-A	119	421	58	121	19	4	12	57	28	29	.287	.335	.437	772	107	2	1	2	-0	.991	3	*1-112	0.1
1952	StL-A	111	342	38	83	13	1	11	42	23	42	.243	.296	.383	679	86	-8	2	0	0	.989	-5	1-86	-1.6
1953	StL-A	104	338	35	94	18	4	16	50	26	33	.278	.333	.497	830	119	7	0	5	-2	.992	5	1-88	0.6
1954	Bal-A	100	300	32	78	13	2	1	34	19	24	.260	.308	.327	635	80	-9	0	0	0	.992	3	1-69	-1.0
1955	KC-A	28	47	2	10	2	0	0	2	6	7	.213	.302	.255	557	50	-3	0	1	-0	.988	0	1-14	-0.4
Total	7	569	1794	203	475	85	14	45	231	119	163	.265	.315	.403	718	93	-25	5	13	-3	.990	5	1-467	-4.3
■ **TONY KUBEK**	Kubek, Anthony Christopher b: 10/12/36, Milwaukee, Wis. BL/TR, 6'3", 191 lbs. Deb: 4/20/57 Career OF: (80-LF 46-CF 31-RF)																							
1957	*NY-A	127	431	56	128	21	3	3	39	24	48	.297	.338	.381	719	98	-2	6	6	-1	.938	1	O-50L,S-41,3-38,/2	-0.2
1958	*NY-A☆	138	559	66	148	21	1	2	48	25	57	.265	.297	.317	614	72	-22	5	4	-0	.961	20	*S-134/O-3R,1-1,2-1	0.9
1959	NY-A★	132	512	67	143	25	7	6	51	24	46	.279	.314	.391	705	95	-4	3	3	-0	.968	-1	S-67,O-53R,3-17,/2	-0.2
1960	*NY-A	147	568	77	155	25	3	14	62	31	42	.273	.314	.401	715	98	-4	3	0	1	.968	-4	*S-136,O-29(22-6-1)	0.3
1961	*NY-A★	153	617	84	170	38	6	8	46	27	60	.276	.307	.395	702	91	-10	1	3	-1	.959	13	*S-145	1.4
1962	*NY-A	45	169	28	53	6	1	4	17	12	17	.314	.359	.432	791	115	3	2	1	0	.954	5	S-35/O-6(6-0-0)	1.2
1963	*NY-A	135	557	72	143	21	3	7	44	28	68	.257	.295	.343	638	79	-16	4	2	0	.980	10	*S-132/O-1(0-1-0)	0.6
1964	NY-A	106	415	46	95	16	3	8	31	26	55	.229	.276	.340	616	69	-18	4	1	1	.978	4	S-99	-0.5
1965	NY-A	109	339	26	74	5	3	5	35	20	48	.218	.262	.295	557	58	-19	1	3	-1	.964	-10	S-93/O-3(1-0-2),1-1	-2.3
Total	9	1092	4167	522	1109	178	30	57	373	217	441	.266	.305	.364	669	85	-92	29	23	-2	.967	39	S-882,O-145L/3-55,21	1.2
■ **TED KUBIAK**	Kubiak, Theodore Rodger b: 5/12/42, New Brunswick, N.J. BB/TR, 6', 175 lbs. Deb: 4/14/67																							
1967	KC-A	53	102	6	16	2	1	0	5	12	20	.157	.246	.196	442	33	-8	0	0	0	.984	-3	S-20,2-10/3-5	-1.1
1968	Oak-A	48	120	10	30	5	2	0	8	8	18	.250	.308	.325	633	96	-1	1	1	-0	.929	-3	2-24,S-12	-0.1
1969	Oak-A	92	305	38	76	9	1	2	27	25	35	.249	.308	.305	613	75	-10	2	0	0	.976	-0	S-42,2-33	-0.3
1970	Mil-A	158	540	63	136	9	6	4	41	72	51	.252	.340	.313	653	81	-12	4	9	-2	.989	-17	2-91,S-73	-1.8
1971	Mil-A	89	260	26	59	6	5	3	17	41	31	.227	.332	.323	655	87	-3	0	5	-2	.971	-3	2-48,S-39	-0.1
	StL-N	32	72	8	18	3	2	1	10	11	12	.250	.349	.389	738	105	1	1	0	-0	.959	-4	S-17,2-14	-0.1
1972	Tex-A	46	116	5	26	3	0	0	7	12	12	.224	.302	.250	552	69	-4	0	1	-0	.990	-3	2-25,S-15/3-1	-0.5
	*Oak-A	51	94	14	17	4	1	0	8	9	11	.181	.252	.245	497	51	-6	0	0	0	.988	2	2-49/3-1	-0.2
	Yr	97	210	19	43	7	1	0	15	21	23	.205	.280	.248	528	61	-10	0	1	-0	.989	-1	2-74,S-15/3-2	-0.7
1973	*Oak-A	106	182	15	40	6	1	3	17	12	19	.220	.268	.313	581	67	-8	1	1	-0	.973	6	2-83,S-26/3-2	0.2
1974	Oak-A	99	220	22	46	3	0	0	18	18	15	.209	.269	.223	492	46	-15	1	1	-0	.995	-9	2-71,S-19,3-14,/D-2	-2.1
1975	Oak-A	20	28	2	7	1	0	0	4	2	2	.250	.300	.286	586	68	-1	0	0	0	1.000	2	/S-7,3-7,2-6	0.2
	SD-N	87	196	13	44	5	0	0	14	24	18	.224	.309	.250	559	60	-10	3	1	0	.954	1	3-64,2-11/1-1	-0.9
1976	SD-N	96	212	16	50	5	2	0	26	25	28	.236	.316	.278	595	76	-6	0	3	-1	.971	-9	3-27,2-25/S-6,1-1	-1.6
Total	10	977	2447	238	565	61	21	13	202	271	272	.231	.309	.289	598	73	-85	13	22	-5	.981	-39	2-490,S-276,3/1D	-8.4
■ **JACK KUBISZYN**	Kubiszyn, John Henry b: 12/19/36, Buffalo, N.Y. BR/TR, 5'11", 170 lbs. Deb: 4/23/61																							
1961	Cle-A	25	42	4	9	0	0	0	0	2	5	.214	.250	.214	464	26	-4	0	0	0	1.000	3	/3-8,S-7,2-2	-0.1
1962	Cle-A	25	59	3	10	2	0	1	2	5	7	.169	.234	.254	489	32	-6	0	0	0	.964	2	S-18/3-1	-0.2
Total	2	50	101	7	19	2	0	1	2	7	12	.188	.241	.238	478	30	-10	0	0	0	.969	5	/S-25,3-9,2-2	-0.3
■ **GIL KUBSKI**	Kubski, Gilbert Thomas b: 10/12/54, Longview, Tex. BL/TR, 6'3", 185 lbs. Deb: 9/2/80																							
1980	Cal-A	22	63	11	16	3	0	0	6	6	10	.254	.319	.302	620	73	-2	1	1	-0	1.000	1	O-20(1-0-19)	-0.3
■ **STEVE KUCZEK**	Kuczek, Stanislaw Leo b: 12/28/24, Amsterdam, N.Y. BR/TR, 6', 160 lbs. Deb: 9/29/49																							
1949	Bos-N	1	1	0	1	1	0	0	0	0	0	1.000	1.000	2.000	3000	723	1	0			.000	0	H	0.1
■ **BILL KUEHNE**	Kuehne, William J. (b: William J. Knelme) b: 10/24/1858, Leipzig, Germany d: 10/27/21, Sulphur Springs, O BR/TR, 5'8", 185 lbs. Deb: 5/1/1883 Career OF: (33-LF 9-CF 30-RF)																							
1883	Col-a	95	374	38	85	8	14	1		2		.227	.231	.332	563	86	-5				.833	-5	*3-69,2-18/S-7,O-3C	-0.7
1884	Col-a	110	415	48	98	13	16	5		9		.236	.254	.381	635	113	6				.881	11	*3-110	1.8
1885	Pit-a	104	411	54	93	9	19	0	43	15		.226	.257	.341	598	89	-6				.865	-1	*3-97/S-7	-0.5
1886	Pit-a	117	481	73	98	16	17	1	48	19		.204	.237	.314	551	72	-17	26			.899	-1	O-54L,3-47,1-18	-1.8
1887	Pit-N	102	416	68	134	18	15	1	41	14	39	.322	.324	.425	749	113	7	17			.883	-13	*S-91/3-4,1-4,O-3R	-0.3
1888	Pit-N	138	524	60	123	22	11	3	62	9	68	.235	.250	.336	586	93	-5	34			.910	0	3-75,S-63	-0.2
1889	Pit-N	97	390	43	96	20	5	5	57	9	36	.246	.263	.362	625	82	-11	15			.885	-1	3-75,O-13L/2-5,S1	-1.0
1890	Pit-P	126	528	66	126	21	12	5	73	28	37	.239	.277	.352	629	74	-21	21			.850	6	*3-126	-1.0
1891	Col-a	68	261	32	56	9	0	2	22	10	22	.215	.244	.272	516	50	-18	21			.885	-2	3-68	-1.6
	Lou-a	39	152	25	41	3	1	1	17	7	13	.270	.306	.322	629	81	-4	9			.896	-2	3-39	-0.5
	Yr	107	413	57	97	12	1	3	39	17	35	.235	.267	.291	557	62	-22	30			.889	-4	*3-107	-2.1
1892	Lou-N	76	287	22	48	4	5	0	36	13	36	.167	.203	.216	419	29	-25	6			.874	-3	3-76	-2.5
	StL-N	6	24	1	4	1	0	0	0	0	3	.167	.200	.208	408	25	-2	1			.895	0	/3-5,S-1	-0.2
	Cin-N	6	24	3	5	1	0	1	4	1	5	.208	.240	.375	615	87	-1	0			.941	2	/3-4,2-2	0.1
	StL-N	1	4	0	0	0	0	0	0	0	1	.000	.000	.000	0	-99	-1	0			1.000	1	/3-1	0.0
	Yr	89	339	26	57	6	5	1	40	14	45	.168	.203	.224	428	32	-28	7			.880	-0	3-86/2-2,S-1	-2.6
Total	10	1085	4291	533	1007	145	115	25	403	136	260	.235	.258	.337	595	82	-102	150			.875	-8	3-796,S-171/O-73L,21	-8.4
■ **HARVEY KUENN**	Kuenn, Harvey Edward b: 12/4/30, W.Allis, Wis. d: 2/28/88, Peoria, Ariz. BR/TR, 6'2", 190 lbs. Deb: 9/6/52 MC Career OF: (354-LF 163-CF 343-RF)																							
1952	Det-A	19	80	2	26	2	2	0	8	2	1	.325	.349	.400	749	107	1	2	1	0	.962	2	S-19	0.4
1953	Det-A★	155	679	94	**209**	33	7	2	48	50	31	.308	.356	.386	742	101	1	6	5	-0	.973	-21	*S-155	-0.6
1954	Det-A☆	155	656	81	**201**	28	6	5	48	29	13	.306	.337	.390	727	100	-1	9	9	-1	.966	3	*S-155	1.4
1955	Det-A★	145	620	101	190	**38**	5	8	62	40	27	.306	.349	.423	772	109	6	8	3	1	.956	-28	*S-141	-0.9
1956	Det-A★	146	591	96	**196**	32	7	12	88	55	34	.332	.391	.470	862	126	22	9	5	0	**.968**	-20	*S-141/O-1(1-0-0)	1.4
1957	Det-A★	151	624	74	173	30	6	9	44	47	28	.277	.328	.388	716	92	-7	5	8	-2	.955	-49	*S-136,3-17/1-1	-4.8
1958	Det-A☆	139	561	73	179	**39**	3	8	54	51	34	.319	.376	.442	818	116	13	5	10	-2	.984	15	*O-138(0-138-0)	1.9
1959	Det-A★	139	561	99	**198**	**42**	7	9	71	48	37	**.353**	.405	.501	906	140	31	7	2	1	.988	1	*O-137(0-23-116)	2.7
1960	Cle-A★	126	474	65	146	24	0	9	54	55	25	.308	.381	.416	797	119	14	3	0	1	.966	1	*O-119(2-2-117)/3-5	1.1
1961	SF-N	131	471	60	125	22	4	5	46	47	34	.265	.333	.361	694	87	-8	5	4	-0	.988	-7	O-93L,3-32/S-1	-2.1
1962	*SF-N	130	487	73	148	23	5	10	68	49	37	.304	.369	.433	802	116	12	3	6	-1	.970	-9	*O-105(99-0-10),3-30	-0.4
1963	SF-N	120	417	61	121	13	2	6	31	44	38	.290	.361	.374	735	113	8	2	1	0	.975	-30	O-64(45-0-27),3-53	-2.8
1964	SF-N	111	351	42	92	16	2	4	22	35	32	.262	.331	.353	684	91	-4	0	1	-0	.952	-13	O-88L,1-11/3-2	-2.4
1965	SF-N	23	59	4	14	0	0	0	6	10	3	.237	.357	.237	594	69	-2	3	1	0	1.000	-1	O-14(12-0-2)/1-7	-0.4
	Chi-N	54	120	11	26	5	0	0	6	22	13	.217	.338	.258	596	69	-4	1	0	0	.975	-3	O-35(31-0-4)/1-1	-0.9

YEAR	TM/L	G	AB	R	H	2B	3B	HR	RBI	BB	SO	AVG	OBP	SLG	OPS	OPS+	BR+	SB	CS	SBR	FA	FR	G/POS	TPR
	Yr	77	179	15	40	5	0	0	12	32	16	.223	.344	.251	596	69	-6	4	1	1	.981	-4	O-49(43-0-6)/1-8	-1.3
1966	Chi-N	3	3	0	1	0	0	0	0	0	1	.333	.333	.333	667	85	-0	0	0	0	.000	-0	/O-1(1-0-0)	0.0
	Phi-N	86	159	15	47	9	0	0	15	10	16	.296	.337	.352	689	92	-2	0	0	0	1.000	-6	O-31(31-0-0),1-13/3-1	-1.0
	Yr	89	162	15	48	9	0	0	15	10	17	.296	.337	.352	689	92	-2	0	0	0	1.000	-7	O-32(32-0-0),1-13/3-1	-1.0
Total	15	1833	6913	951	2092	356	56	87	671	594	404	.303	.359	.408	767	108	81	68	56	-5	.978	-163	O-826L,S-748,3-140,/1	-7.4

■ JOE KUHEL Kuhel, Joseph Anthony b: 6/25/06, Cleveland, Ohio d: 2/26/84, Kansas City, Kan. BL/TL, 6', 180 lbs. Deb: 7/31/30 M

YEAR	TM/L	G	AB	R	H	2B	3B	HR	RBI	BB	SO	AVG	OBP	SLG	OPS	OPS+	BR+	SB	CS	SBR	FA	FR	G/POS	TPR
1930	Was-A	18	63	9	18	3	3	0	17	5	6	.286	.348	.429	776	95	-1	1	0	0	.981	-1	1-16	-0.2
1931	Was-A	139	524	70	141	34	8	8	85	47	45	.269	.335	.410	745	94	-5	7	5	-0	.991	-7	*1-139	-2.4
1932	Was-A	101	347	52	101	21	5	4	52	32	19	.291	.353	.415	768	99	-0	5	2	0	.994	-2	1-85	-0.9
1933	*Was-A	153	602	89	194	34	10	11	107	59	48	.322	.385	.467	851	126	22	17	8	1	**.996**	-7	*1-153	0.2
1934	Was-A	63	263	49	76	12	3	3	25	30	14	.289	.364	.392	756	99	-0	2	7	-2	.994	-4	1-63	-1.2
1935	Was-A	151	633	99	165	25	9	2	74	78	44	.261	.345	.338	684	80	-17	5	4	-0	.991	0	*1-151	-3.0
1936	Was-A	149	588	107	189	42	8	16	118	64	30	.321	.392	.502	893	126	23	15	7	1	.993	-2	*1-149	0.7
1937	Was-A	136	547	73	155	24	11	6	61	63	39	.283	.357	.400	758	95	-4	6	3	0	.993	3	*1-136	-1.2
1938	Chi-A	117	412	67	110	27	4	8	51	72	35	.267	.376	.410	786	95	-2	9	7	-0	.988	-7	*1-111	-1.9
1939	Chi-A	139	546	107	164	24	9	15	56	64	51	.300	.376	.460	836	110	8	18	5	2	.992	-4	*1-136	-0.6
1940	Chi-A	155	603	111	169	28	8	27	94	87	59	.280	.374	.488	861	120	18	12	5	1	.988	-5	*1-155	-0.1
1941	Chi-A	153	600	99	150	39	5	12	63	70	55	.250	.331	.392	723	92	-8	20	5	3	.994	-1	*1-151	-2.0
1942	Chi-A	115	413	60	103	14	4	4	52	60	22	.249	.347	.332	679	94	-2	22	9	2	.991	-4	*1-112	-1.5
1943	Chi-A	153	531	55	113	21	1	5	46	76	45	.213	.319	.284	604	77	-13	14	8	0	.995	1	*1-153	-2.2
1944	Was-A	139	518	90	144	26	7	4	51	68	40	.278	.364	.378	742	117	13	11	6	0	.987	-2	*1-138	0.5
1945	Was-A	142	533	73	152	29	13	2	75	79	31	.285	.378	.400	778	137	27	10	5	0	.989	-6	*1-141	1.5
1946	Was-A	14	20	2	3	0	0	0	2	5	2	.150	.320	.150	470	36	-1	0	0	0	1.000	0	/1-5	-0.1
	Chi-A	64	238	24	65	9	3	4	20	21	24	.273	.335	.387	721	105	1	4	4	-1	.994	-2	1-63	-0.3
	Yr	78	258	26	68	9	3	4	22	26	26	.264	.333	.368	702	100	-0	4	4	-1	.994	-2	1-68	-0.4
1947	Chi-A	3	3	0	0	0	0	0	0	0	3	.000	.000	.000	0	-99	-1	0	0	0	.000	0	H	-0.1
Total	18	2104	7984	1236	2212	412	111	131	1049	980	612	.277	.359	.406	765	104	57	178	90	8	.992	-48	*1-2057	-14.8

■ KENNY KUHN Kuhn, Kenneth Harold b: 3/20/37, Louisville, Ky. BL/TR, 5'10.5", 175 lbs. Deb: 7/7/55

YEAR	TM/L	G	AB	R	H	2B	3B	HR	RBI	BB	SO	AVG	OBP	SLG	OPS	OPS+	BR+	SB	CS	SBR	FA	FR	G/POS	TPR
1955	Cle-A	4	6	0	2	0	0	0	0	1	0	.333	.429	.333	762	103	0	1	0	0	1.000	-2	/S-4	-0.1
1956	Cle-A	27	22	7	6	1	0	0	2	0	4	.273	.273	.318	591	54	-1	0	1	-0	1.000	2	S-17/2-5	0.0
1957	Cle-A	40	53	5	9	0	0	0	5	4	9	.170	.228	.170	398	10	-6	0	0	0	.974	-3	2-14/3-2,S-1	-0.9
Total	3	71	81	12	17	1	0	0	7	5	13	.210	.256	.222	478	30	-8	1	1	-0	.963	-3	/S-22,2-19,3-2	-1.0

■ WALT KUHN Kuhn, Walter Charles "Red" b: 2/2/1884, Fresno, Cal. d: 6/14/35, Fresno, Cal. BR/TR, 5'7", 162 lbs. Deb: 4/18/12

YEAR	TM/L	G	AB	R	H	2B	3B	HR	RBI	BB	SO	AVG	OBP	SLG	OPS	OPS+	BR+	SB	CS	SBR	FA	FR	G/POS	TPR
1912	Chi-A	76	178	16	36	7	0	0	10	20		.202	.286	.242	528	53	-10	5			.966	9	C-75/2-1	0.3
1913	Chi-A	26	50	5	8	1	0	0	5	13	8	.160	.333	.180	513	52	-2	1			.980	-2	C-24	-0.3
1914	Chi-A	17	40	4	11	1	0	0	0	8	11	.275	.396	.300	696	111	1	2	3	-1	.987	-1	C-16	0.1
Total	3	119	268	25	55	9	0	0	15	41	19	.205	.313	.239	552	62	-12	8	3		.971	6	C-115/2-1	0.1

■ CHARLIE KUHNS Kuhns, Charles B. b: 10/27/1877, Freeport, Pa. d: 7/15/22, Pittsburgh, Pa. 5'9", 160 lbs. Deb: 6/4/1897

YEAR	TM/L	G	AB	R	H	2B	3B	HR	RBI	BB	SO	AVG	OBP	SLG	OPS	OPS+	BR+	SB	CS	SBR	FA	FR	G/POS	TPR
1897	Pit-N	1	3	0	0	0	0	0	0	1		.000	.250	.000	250	-32	-1	0			.667	0	/3-1	0.0
1899	Bos-N	7	18	2	5	0	0	0	3	2		.278	.350	.278	628	67	-1	0			.813	-1	/S-3,3-3	-0.1
Total	2	8	21	2	5	0	0	0	3	3		.238	.333	.238	571	53	-1	0			.733	-1	/3-4,S-3	-0.1

■ DUANE KUIPER Kuiper, Duane Eugene b: 6/19/50, Racine, Wis. BL/TR, 6', 175 lbs. Deb: 9/9/74

YEAR	TM/L	G	AB	R	H	2B	3B	HR	RBI	BB	SO	AVG	OBP	SLG	OPS	OPS+	BR+	SB	CS	SBR	FA	FR	G/POS	TPR
1974	Cle-A	10	22	7	11	2	0	0	4	2	2	.500	.542	.591	1133	228	4	1	1	-0	1.000	1	/2-8	0.5
1975	Cle-A	90	346	42	101	11	1	0	25	30	26	.292	.362	.329	691	97	-0	19	18	-2	.972	-14	2-87/D-1	-1.1
1976	Cle-A	135	506	47	133	13	6	0	37	30	42	.263	.305	.312	618	82	-12	10	17	-4	**.987**	20	*2-128/1-5,D-2	1.3
1977	Cle-A	148	610	62	169	15	8	1	50	37	55	.277	.326	.333	658	83	-14	11	11	-1	.985	2	*2-148	-0.5
1978	Cle-A	149	547	52	155	18	6	0	43	19	35	.283	.312	.338	650	84	-12	4	9	-2	.979	-19	*2-149	-2.6
1979	Cle-A	140	479	46	122	9	5	0	39	37	27	.255	.313	.294	608	65	-23	4	9	-2	**.988**	-4	*2-140	-2.1
1980	Cle-A	42	149	10	42	5	0	0	9	13	8	.282	.340	.315	655	80	-4	0	1	-0	.995	-8	2-42	-0.9
1981	Cle-A	72	206	15	53	6	0	0	14	8	13	.257	.285	.286	571	66	-9	1	1	-0	.983	-5	2-72	-1.2
1982	SF-N	107	218	26	61	9	1	0	17	32	24	.280	.377	.330	707	100	1	2	2	-0	.978	-7	2-51	-0.3
1983	SF-N	72	176	14	44	2	2	0	14	27	13	.250	.356	.284	640	82	-3	0	1	-0	.988	-9	2-64	-0.9
1984	SF-N	83	115	8	23	1	0	0	11	12	10	.200	.276	.209	484	39	-9	0	1	-0	.969	6	2-31/1-1	-0.3
1985	SF-N	9	5	0	3	0	0	0	0	1	0	.600	.667	.600	1267	270	1	0	0	0	.000	0	/H	0.1
Total	12	1057	3379	329	917	91	29	1	263	248	255	.271	.326	.316	643	81	-79	52	71	-13	.983	-36	2-920/1-6,D-3	-8.0

■ JEFF KUNKEL Kunkel, Jeffrey William b: 3/25/62, W.Palm Beach, Fla. BR/TR, 6'2", 180 lbs. Deb: 7/23/84 F Career OF: (14-LF 30-CF 5-RF)

YEAR	TM/L	G	AB	R	H	2B	3B	HR	RBI	BB	SO	AVG	OBP	SLG	OPS	OPS+	BR+	SB	CS	SBR	FA	FR	G/POS	TPR
1984	Tex-A	50	142	13	29	2	3	3	7	2	35	.204	.221	.324	545	47	-10	4	3	-0	.922	-1	S-48/D-1	-0.8
1985	Tex-A	2	4	1	1	0	0	0	0	0	3	.250	.250	.250	500	37	-0	0	0	0	1.000	1	/S-2	0.1
1986	Tex-A	8	13	3	3	0	0	1	2	0	2	.231	.231	.462	692	81	-0	0	0	0	.769	-0	/S-5,D-1	-0.1
1987	Tex-A	15	32	1	7	0	0	1	2	0	10	.219	.242	.313	555	46	-3	0	1	-0	.955	2	2-10/3-3,O-3C,1SD	-0.1
1988	Tex-A	55	154	14	35	8	3	2	15	4	35	.227	.252	.357	609	67	-7	0	1	-0	.949	6	2-28,S-19,3-10,/OPD	0.0
1989	Tex-A	108	293	39	79	21	2	8	29	20	75	.270	.323	.437	760	110	3	3	2	-0	.936	2	S-59,O-30C/2-8,3PD	0.9
1990	Tex-A	99	200	17	34	11	1	3	17	11	66	.170	.221	.280	501	39	-17	2	1	0	.958	9	S-67,3-15,2-13,/OD	-0.4
1992	Chi-N	20	29	0	4	2	0	0	1	0	8	.138	.138	.207	345	-3	-4	0	0	0	1.000	4	/S-6,2-3,O-3(3-0-0)	0.0
Total	8	357	867	88	192	44	9	18	73	37	234	.221	.260	.355	615	69	-38	9	8	-1	.940	22	S-207/2-62,O3DP1	-0.4

■ RUSTY KUNTZ Kuntz, Russell Jay b: 2/4/55, Orange, Cal. BR/TR, 6'3", 190 lbs. Deb: 9/1/79 C Career OF: (63-LF 117-CF 63-RF)

YEAR	TM/L	G	AB	R	H	2B	3B	HR	RBI	BB	SO	AVG	OBP	SLG	OPS	OPS+	BR+	SB	CS	SBR	FA	FR	G/POS	TPR
1979	Chi-A	5	11	0	1	0	0	0	0	2	6	.091	.231	.091	322	-9	-2	0	0	0	1.000	1	/O-5(1-1-3)	-0.1
1980	Chi-A	36	62	5	14	4	0	0	3	5	13	.226	.284	.290	574	58	-4	1	0	0	.979	-5	O-34(19-9-6)	-0.9
1981	Chi-A	67	55	15	14	2	0	0	4	6	8	.255	.339	.291	630	85	-1	1	0	0	1.000	-13	O-51(28-13-13)/D-5	-1.5
1982	Chi-A	21	26	4	5	1	0	0	3	2	8	.192	.250	.231	481	33	-2	0	0	0	1.000	-7	O-21(1-20-1)	-1.0
1983	Chi-A	28	42	6	11	1	0	0	1	6	13	.262	.354	.286	640	76	-1	1	0	0	.976	-6	O-27(2-25-0)/D-1	-0.7
	Min-A	31	100	13	19	3	0	3	5	12	28	.190	.277	.310	587	59	-6	0	0	0	.986	0	O-30(0-27-3)	-0.6
	Yr	59	142	19	30	4	0	3	6	18	41	.211	.300	.303	603	64	-7	1	0	0	.982	-6	O-57(2-52-3)/D-1	-1.3
1984	*Det-A	84	140	32	40	12	0	2	22	25	28	.286	.398	.414	812	126	6	2	2	-0	.987	-16	O-67(12-22-37),D-10	-1.2
1985	Det-A	5	5	0	0	0	0	0	0	2	2	.000	.286	.000	286	-13	-1	0	1	-0	.000	-0	/1-1,D-3	-0.1
Total	7	277	441	75	104	23	0	5	38	60	106	.236	.330	.322	652	81	-10	5	3	0	.988	-46	O-235C/D-19,1-1	-6.1

■ WHITEY KUROWSKI Kurowski, George John b: 4/19/18, Reading, Pa. d: 12/9/99, Sinking Spring, Pa. BR/TR, 5'11", 193 lbs. Deb: 9/23/41 Career OF: (1-LF 0-CF 0-RF)

YEAR	TM/L	G	AB	R	H	2B	3B	HR	RBI	BB	SO	AVG	OBP	SLG	OPS	OPS+	BR+	SB	CS	SBR	FA	FR	G/POS	TPR
1941	StL-N	5	9	1	3	2	0	0	2	0	2	.333	.400	.556	956	157	1	0			1.000	-1	/3-4	0.0
1942	*StL-N	115	366	51	93	17	3	9	42	33	60	.254	.326	.391	717	102	0	7			.944	9	*3-104/S-1,O-1(1-0-0)	1.3
1943	*StL-N☆	139	522	69	150	24	8	13	70	31	54	.287	.330	.439	768	116	8	3			.952	1	*3-137/S-2	1.2
1944	*StL-N★	149	555	95	150	25	7	20	87	58	40	.270	.341	.449	790	119	13	2			**.965**	4	*3-146/2-9,S-1	1.8
1945	StL-N†	133	511	84	165	27	3	21	102	45	45	.323	.383	.511	894	144	28	1			.964	2	*3-131/S-6	3.1
1946	*StL-N★	142	519	76	156	32	5	14	89	72	47	.301	.391	.462	853	136	25	2			**.966**	0	*3-138	2.6
1947	StL-N★	146	513	108	159	27	6	27	104	87	56	.310	.420	.544	964	148	37	4			.954	-14	*3-141	2.2
1948	StL-N	77	220	34	47	8	0	2	33	42	28	.214	.352	.277	629	68	-8	0			.939	-11	3-65	-1.9
1949	StL-N	10	14	0	2	0	0	0	0	1	0	.143	.200	.143	343	-6	-2	0			1.000	-0	/3-2	-0.2
Total	9	916	3229	518	925	162	32	106	529	369	332	.286	.366	.455	821	124	103	19			.957	-10	3-868/S-10,2-9,O-1L	10.1

■ CRAIG KUSICK Kusick, Craig Robert b: 9/30/48, Milwaukee, Wis. BR/TR, 6'3", 232 lbs. Deb: 9/8/73 Career OF: (11-LF 0-CF 0-RF)

YEAR	TM/L	G	AB	R	H	2B	3B	HR	RBI	BB	SO	AVG	OBP	SLG	OPS	OPS+	BR+	SB	CS	SBR	FA	FR	G/POS	TPR
1973	Min-A	15	48	4	12	2	0	0	4	7	9	.250	.357	.292	649	81	-1	0	0	0	.989	-1	1-11/O-2(2-0-0),D-2	-0.3
1974	Min-A	76	201	36	48	7	1	8	26	35	36	.239	.354	.403	757	114	4	0	0	0	.996	4	1-75	0.3
1975	Min-A	57	156	14	37	8	0	6	27	21	23	.237	.346	.404	750	110	2	0	0	0	.990	1	1-51	0.0
1976	Min-A	109	266	33	69	13	0	11	36	35	44	.259	.348	.432	780	125	8	5	1	1	.977	3	D-79,1-23	1.0

YEAR	TM/L	G	AB	R	H	2B	3B	HR	RBI	BB	SO	AVG	OBP	SLG	OPS	OPS+	BR+	SB	CS	SBR	FA	FR	G/POS	TPR
1977	Min-A	115	268	34	68	12	0	12	45	49	60	.254	.375	.433	808	121	9	3	1	0	.972	-2	D-85,1-23	0.5
1978	Min-A	77	191	23	33	3	2	4	20	37	38	.173	.310	.272	582	64	-8	3	2	-0	.987	2	D-35,1-27/O-9(9-0-0)	-1.0
1979	Min-A	24	54	8	13	4	0	3	6	3	11	.241	.281	.481	762	97	-0	0	0	0	1.000	-0	D-12/1-8	-0.1
	Tor-A	24	54	3	11	1	0	2	7	7	7	.204	.306	.333	640	72	-2	0	0	0	.978	1	1-20/P-1,D-1	-0.2
	Yr	48	108	11	24	5	0	5	13	10	18	.222	.294	.407	702	85	-3	0	0	0	.983	1	1-28,D-13/P-1	-0.3
Total	7	497	1238	155	291	50	3	46	171	194	228	.235	.345	.392	736	106	13	11	4	1	.988	8	1-238,D-214/O-11L,P	0.2

■ **ART KUSNYER** Kusnyer, Arthur William b: 12/19/45, Akron, Ohio BR/TR, 6'2", 198 lbs. Deb: 9/21/70 C

YEAR	TM/L	G	AB	R	H	2B	3B	HR	RBI	BB	SO	AVG	OBP	SLG	OPS	OPS+	BR+	SB	CS	SBR	FA	FR	G/POS	TPR
1970	Chi-A	4	10	0	1	0	0	0	0	0	4	.100	.100	.100	200	-43	-2	0	0	0	.941	1	/C-3	-0.1
1971	Cal-A	6	13	0	2	0	0	0	0	0	3	.154	.154	.154	308	-14	-2	0	0	0	.958	1	/C-6	-0.1
1972	Cal-A	64	179	13	37	2	1	2	13	16	33	.207	.276	.263	538	64	-8	0	0	0	.975	-3	C-63	-0.9
1973	Cal-A	41	64	5	8	2	0	0	3	2	12	.125	.152	.156	308	-14	-10	0	1	-0	.979	1	C-41	-0.9
1976	Mil-A	15	34	2	4	1	0	0	3	1	5	.118	.167	.147	314	-8	-5	1	0	0	.938	-1	C-14	-0.5
1978	KC-A	9	13	1	3	1	0	1	2	2	4	.231	.333	.538	872	138	1	0	0	0	.946	3	/C-9	0.4
Total	6	139	313	21	55	6	1	3	21	21	61	.176	.232	.230	462	37	-26	1	1	-0	.970	2	C-136	-2.1

■ **JUL KUSTUS** Kustus, Joseph J. "Joe" or "Kul" b: 9/5/1882, Detroit, Mich. d: 4/27/16, Eloise, Mich. BR/TR, 5'10", Deb: 4/17/09

YEAR	TM/L	G	AB	R	H	2B	3B	HR	RBI	BB	SO	AVG	OBP	SLG	OPS	OPS+	BR+	SB	CS	SBR	FA	FR	G/POS	TPR
1909	Bro-N	53	173	12	25	5	0	1	11	11		.145	.204	.191	395	23	-16	9			.951	0	O-50(1-18-31)	-2.0

■ **RANDY KUTCHER** Kutcher, Randy Scott b: 4/20/60, Anchorage, Alaska BR/TR, 5'11", 175 lbs. Deb: 6/19/86 Career OF: (26-LF 78-CF 52-RF)

YEAR	TM/L	G	AB	R	H	2B	3B	HR	RBI	BB	SO	AVG	OBP	SLG	OPS	OPS+	BR+	SB	CS	SBR	FA	FR	G/POS	TPR
1986	SF-N	71	186	28	44	9	1	7	16	11	41	.237	.279	.409	688	92	-3	6	5	-0	.990	-1	O-51C,S-13/3-4,2-3	-0.5
1987	SF-N	14	16	7	3	1	1	0	1	1	5	.188	.235	.375	610	61	-1	1	0	0	1.000	1	/O-6C,2-2,3-2,S-1	0.0
1988	Bos-A	19	12	2	2	1	0	0	0	0	2	.167	.167	.250	417	14	-1	0	1	-0	1.000	0	/O-7(5-0-2),3-2,D-7	-0.1
1989	Bos-A	77	160	28	36	10	3	2	18	11	46	.225	.275	.363	637	74	-6	3	0	1	.982	-3	O-57R/3-6,C-1,D-6	-0.9
1990	*Bos-A	63	74	18	17	4	1	1	5	13	18	.230	.345	.351	696	91	-1	3	3	-0	1.000	-0	O-34R,3-11/2-5,D-5	-0.1
Total	5	244	448	83	102	25	6	10	40	36	112	.228	.285	.377	662	82	-12	13	9	-0	.989	-3	O-155C/3-25,D-18,S2C	-1.6

■ **JOE KUTINA** Kutina, Joseph Peter b: 1/16/1885, Chicago, Ill. d: 4/13/45, Chicago, Ill. BR/TR, 6'2", 205 lbs. Deb: 9/6/11

YEAR	TM/L	G	AB	R	H	2B	3B	HR	RBI	BB	SO	AVG	OBP	SLG	OPS	OPS+	BR+	SB	CS	SBR	FA	FR	G/POS	TPR
1911	StL-A	26	101	12	26	6	2	3	15	2		.257	.279	.446	724	105	-0	2			.981	-1	1-26	-0.2
1912	StL-A	69	205	18	42	9	3	1	18	13		.205	.262	.293	555	61	-11	0			.985	-3	1-51/O-1(1-0-0)	-1.5
Total	2	95	306	30	68	15	5	4	33	15		.222	.268	.343	611	76	-11	2			.984	-4	/1-77,O-1(1-0-0)	-1.7

■ **AL KVASNAK** Kvasnak, Alexander b: 1/11/21, Sagamore, Pa. BR/TR, 6'1", 170 lbs. Deb: 4/15/42

YEAR	TM/L	G	AB	R	H	2B	3B	HR	RBI	BB	SO	AVG	OBP	SLG	OPS	OPS+	BR+	SB	CS	SBR	FA	FR	G/POS	TPR
1942	Was-A	5	11	3	2	0	0	0	0	2	1	.182	.308	.182	490	40	-1	0	0	0	1.000	-0	/O-3(1-0-2)	-0.1

■ **ANDY KYLE** Kyle, Andrew Ewing b: 10/29/1889, Toronto, Ont., Can. d: 9/6/71, Toronto, Ont., Can. BL/TL, 5'8", 160 lbs. Deb: 9/7/12

YEAR	TM/L	G	AB	R	H	2B	3B	HR	RBI	BB	SO	AVG	OBP	SLG	OPS	OPS+	BR+	SB	CS	SBR	FA	FR	G/POS	TPR
1912	Cin-N	9	21	3	7	1	0	0	4	4	2	.333	.440	.381	821	129	1	0			1.000	0	/O-7(2-5-0)	0.1

■ **CHET LAABS** Laabs, Chester Peter b: 4/30/12, Milwaukee, Wis. d: 1/26/83, Warren, Mich. BR/TR, 5'8", 175 lbs. Deb: 5/5/37

YEAR	TM/L	G	AB	R	H	2B	3B	HR	RBI	BB	SO	AVG	OBP	SLG	OPS	OPS+	BR+	SB	CS	SBR	FA	FR	G/POS	TPR
1937	Det-A	72	242	31	58	13	5	8	37	24	66	.240	.308	.434	742	83	-8	6	2	1	.971	-7	O-62(22-40-0)	-1.5
1938	Det-A	64	211	26	50	7	3	7	37	15	52	.237	.288	.398	686	66	-12	3	2	-0	.971	-1	O-53(22-32-0)	-1.4
1939	Det-A	5	16	1	5	1	1	0	2	2	0	.313	.389	.500	889	117	0	0	0	0	.933	1	/O-5(5-0-0)	0.1
	StL-A	95	317	52	95	20	5	10	62	33	62	.300	.368	.489	856	115	6	4	1	1	.972	-0	O-79(3-70-6)	0.4
	Yr	100	333	53	100	21	6	10	64	35	62	.300	.369	.489	858	115	7	4	1	1	.969	1	O-84(8-70-6)	0.5
1940	StL-A	105	218	32	59	11	5	10	40	34	59	.271	.372	.505	876	122	7	3	3	-0	.969	-7	O-63(25-29-10)	-0.3
1941	StL-A	118	392	64	109	23	6	15	59	51	59	.278	.361	.482	843	117	9	5	2	0	.982	-2	*O-100(21-15-64)	0.2
1942	StL-A	144	520	90	143	21	7	27	99	88	88	.275	.380	.498	878	144	30	0	3	-1	.970	-4	*O-139(36-25-80)	1.8
1943	StL-A★	151	580	83	145	27	7	17	85	73	105	.250	.338	.409	747	115	11	5	7	-1	.976	2	*O-150(125-24-6)	0.3
1944	*StL-A	66	201	28	47	10	2	5	23	29	33	.234	.330	.378	709	96	-1	3	1	0	1.000	-2	O-55(38-0-18)	-0.6
1945	StL-A	35	109	15	26	4	3	1	8	16	17	.239	.352	.358	709	101	1	0	0	0	.986	-4	O-35(34-2-2)	-0.6
1946	StL-A	80	264	40	69	13	0	16	52	20	50	.261	.316	.492	808	117	5	3	1	0	.987	1	O-72(6-0-66)	0.4
1947	Phi-A	15	32	5	7	1	0	1	5	4	4	.219	.306	.344	649	79	-1	0	0	0	1.000	1	/O-7(6-0-1)	-0.1
Total	11	950	3102	467	813	151	44	117	509	389	595	.262	.346	.452	798	113	47	32	22	-1	.977	-21	O-820(343-237-253)	-1.3

■ **COCO LABOY** Laboy, Jose Alberto b: 7/3/39, Ponce, P.R. BR/TR, 5'10", 170 lbs. Deb: 4/8/69

YEAR	TM/L	G	AB	R	H	2B	3B	HR	RBI	BB	SO	AVG	OBP	SLG	OPS	OPS+	BR+	SB	CS	SBR	FA	FR	G/POS	TPR
1969	Mon-N	157	562	53	145	29	1	18	83	40	96	.258	.312	.409	721	100	-1	0	2	-1	.944	4	*3-156	0.1
1970	Mon-N	137	432	37	86	26	1	5	53	31	81	.199	.256	.299	555	48	-33	0	2	-1	.946	-4	*3-132/2-3	-3.8
1971	Mon-N	76	151	10	38	4	0	1	14	11	19	.252	.302	.298	600	70	-6	0	1	-0	.937	1	3-65/2-2	-0.5
1972	Mon-N	28	69	6	18	2	0	3	14	10	16	.261	.354	.420	775	117	2	0	0	0	.980	-2	3-24/2-3,S-2	0.0
1973	Mon-N	22	33	2	4	1	0	1	2	5	8	.121	.237	.242	479	32	-3	0	0	0	.889	1	3-20/2-1	-0.2
Total	5	420	1247	108	291	62	2	28	166	97	220	.233	.292	.354	646	77	-41	0	5	-2	.944	-0	3-397/2-9,S-2	-4.4

■ **CANDY LaCHANCE** LaChance, George Joseph b: 2/15/1870, Putnam, Conn. d: 8/18/32, Waterville, Conn. BB/TR, 6'1", 183 lbs. Deb: 8/15/1893 Career OF: (15-LF 2-CF 7-RF)

YEAR	TM/L	G	AB	R	H	2B	3B	HR	RBI	BB	SO	AVG	OBP	SLG	OPS	OPS+	BR+	SB	CS	SBR	FA	FR	G/POS	TPR
1893	Bro-N	11	35	1	6	1	0	0	6	2	12	.171	.237	.200	437	17	-4	0			.654	-6	/C-6,O-5(4-0-1)	-0.8
1894	Bro-N	69	261	48	83	13	8	5	52	16	32	.318	.360	.487	846	110	3	20			.979	-5	1-56,C-11/O-3(0-0-3)	-0.1
1895	Bro-N	128	541	102	170	23	9	8	108	29	48	.314	.358	.434	793	113	10	37			.983	-6	*1-126/O-3(0-0-3)	0.3
1896	Bro-N	89	348	60	99	10	13	7	58	23	32	.284	.331	.448	779	110	4	17			.986	-3	*1-89	0.0
1897	Bro-N	126	520	86	160	28	16	4	90	15		.308	.333	.446	779	111	5	26			.978	-4	*1-126	0.1
1898	Bro-N	136	526	62	130	23	7	5	65	31		.247	.299	.346	645	85	-12	23			.988	-20	1-74,S-48,O-13L	-2.9
1899	Bal-N	125	472	65	145	23	10	1	75	21		.307	.350	.405	755	101	-1	31			.984	-7	*1-125	-0.7
1901	Cle-A	133	548	81	166	22	9	1	75	7		.303	.314	.381	696	96	-4	11			.979	-3	*1-133	-0.9
1902	Bos-A	138	541	60	151	13	4	6	56	18		.279	.309	.351	660	80	-15	8			.983	-11	*1-138	-2.8
1903	*Bos-A	141	522	60	134	22	6	1	53	28		.257	.303	.328	631	85	-10	12			.984	-11	*1-141	-2.4
1904	Bos-A	157	573	55	130	19	5	1	47	23		.227	.265	.283	548	69	-20	7			**.992**	-14	*1-157	-4.1
1905	Bos-A	12	41	1	6	1	0	0	5	6		.146	.255	.171	426	36	-3	0			.988	-0	1-12	-0.4
Total	12	1265	4928	681	1380	198	87	39	690	219	124	.280	.318	.379	697	94	-46	192			.984	-90	*1-1177/S-48,O-24L,C	-14.7

■ **RENE LACHEMANN** Lachemann, Rene George b: 5/4/45, Los Angeles, Cal. BR/TR, 6', 198 lbs. Deb: 5/4/65 FMC

YEAR	TM/L	G	AB	R	H	2B	3B	HR	RBI	BB	SO	AVG	OBP	SLG	OPS	OPS+	BR+	SB	CS	SBR	FA	FR	G/POS	TPR
1965	KC-A	92	216	20	49	7	1	9	29	12	57	.227	.268	.394	661	87	-5	0	0	0	.980	2	C-75	0.0
1966	KC-A	7	5	0	1	1	0	0	0	0	1	.200	.200	.400	600	70	-0	0	0	0	1.000	1	/C-6	0.1
1968	Oak-A	19	60	3	9	1	0	0	4	1	11	.150	.177	.167	344	5	-7	0	0	0	.967	-6	C-16	-1.5
Total	3	118	281	23	59	9	1	9	33	13	69	.210	.247	.345	593	70	-12	0	0	0	.978	-3	/C-97	-1.4

■ **PETE LaCOCK** LaCock, Ralph Pierre b: 1/17/52, Burbank, Cal. BL/TL, 6'3", 210 lbs. Deb: 9/6/72 Career OF: (52-LF 1-CF 65-RF)

YEAR	TM/L	G	AB	R	H	2B	3B	HR	RBI	BB	SO	AVG	OBP	SLG	OPS	OPS+	BR+	SB	CS	SBR	FA	FR	G/POS	TPR
1972	Chi-N	5	6	3	3	0	0	0	4	0	1	.500	.500	.500	1000	167	1	1	0	0	1.000	-1	/O-3(0-0-3)	0.0
1973	Chi-N	11	16	1	4	1	0	0	3	1	2	.250	.294	.313	607	63	-1	0	0	0	1.000	-0	/O-5(0-0-5)	-0.1
1974	Chi-N	35	110	9	20	4	1	1	8	12	16	.182	.268	.264	532	47	-8	0	0	0	.974	1	O-22(0-0-22),1-11	-0.9
1975	Chi-N	106	249	30	57	8	1	6	30	37	27	.229	.329	.341	670	82	-5	0	2	-1	.988	1	1-53,O-26(11-0-15)	-1.0
1976	Chi-N	106	244	34	54	9	2	8	28	42	37	.221	.338	.373	711	93	-1	1	4	-1	.975	-4	1-54,O-19(7-0-12)	-1.2
1977	*KC-A	88	218	25	66	12	1	3	29	15	25	.303	.350	.408	759	105	2	2	1	0	.990	1	1-29,D-26,O-12(8-1-3)	0.1
1978	*KC-A	118	322	44	95	21	2	5	48	21	27	.295	.338	.419	757	109	3	1	0	0	.993	-6	*1-106	-0.7
1979	KC-A	132	408	54	113	25	4	3	56	37	26	.277	.339	.380	718	92	-4	2	1	0	**.997**	1	*1-108,D-16	-1.0
1980	*KC-A	114	156	14	32	6	0	1	18	17	10	.205	.287	.263	550	51	-10	1	0	0	.997	-3	1-86,O-29(26-0-5)	-1.5
Total	9	715	1729	214	444	86	11	27	224	182	171	.257	.329	.366	695	89	-24	8	8	-1	.991	-9	1-447,O-116R/D-42	-6.3

■ **LEE LACY** Lacy, Leondaus b: 4/10/48, Longview, Tex. BR/TR, 6'1", 175 lbs. Deb: 6/30/72 Career OF: (417-LF 77-CF 594-RF)

YEAR	TM/L	G	AB	R	H	2B	3B	HR	RBI	BB	SO	AVG	OBP	SLG	OPS	OPS+	BR+	SB	CS	SBR	FA	FR	G/POS	TPR
1972	LA-N	60	243	34	63	7	3	0	12	19	37	.259	.313	.313	626	80	-6	5	3	0	.973	-8	2-58	-1.1
1973	LA-N	57	135	14	28	2	0	0	8	15	34	.207	.287	.222	509	45	-10	2	3	-1	.965	-1	2-41	-0.9
1974	*LA-N	48	78	13	22	6	0	0	8	2	14	.282	.300	.359	659	87	-2	2	0	0	.968	2	2-34/3-1	0.2
1975	LA-N	101	306	44	96	11	5	7	40	22	29	.314	.360	.451	811	129	11	5	9	-2	.935	-4	2-43,O-43(37-3-8)/S-1	0.4
1976	Atl-N	50	180	25	49	4	2	3	20	6	12	.272	.299	.367	666	83	-4	2	2	-0	.969	-10	2-44/O-5(1-4-1),3-1	-1.3

YEAR	TM/L	G	AB	R	H	2B	3B	HR	RBI	BB	SO	AVG	OBP	SLG	OPS	OPS+	BR+	SB	CS	SBR	FA	FR	G/POS	TPR
	LA-N	53	158	17	42	7	1	0	14	16	13	.266	.333	.323	656	88	-2	1	2	-0	.979	1	O-37(5-23-10)/3-3,2-2	-0.3
	Yr	103	338	42	91	11	3	3	34	22	25	.269	.316	.346	662	86	-6	3	4	-1	.970	-10	2-46,O-42C/3-4	-1.6
1977	*LA-N	75	169	28	45	7	0	6	21	10	21	.266	.307	.414	721	92	-2	4	0	1	1.000	-13	O-32L,2-22,3-12	-1.4
1978	*LA-N	103	245	29	64	16	4	13	40	27	30	.261	.337	.518	855	136	11	7	4	0	.971	-5	O-44R,2-24/3-9,S-1	0.5
1979	*Pit-N	84	182	17	45	9	3	5	15	22	36	.247	.332	.412	744	97	-1	6	1	1	.973	-2	O-41(41-0-0)/2-5	-0.3
1980	Pit-N	109	278	45	93	20	4	7	33	28	33	.335	.399	.511	910	150	19	18	9	1	.984	5	O-88(86-3-0)/3-3	2.2
1981	Pit-N	78	213	31	57	11	4	2	10	11	29	.268	.307	.385	692	92	-3	24	3	4	.977	3	O-63(34-1-29)/3-1	0.3
1982	Pit-N	121	359	66	112	16	3	5	31	32	57	.312	.370	.415	785	116	8	40	15	4	.965	-8	*O-113(40-17-71)/3-2	-0.1
1983	Pit-N	108	288	40	87	12	3	4	13	22	36	.302	.352	.406	758	107	3	31	13	2	1.000	-8	O-98(59-24-28)	-0.6
1984	Pit-N	138	474	66	152	26	3	12	70	32	61	.321	.364	.464	828	131	18	21	11	1	**.996**	4	*O-127(78-0-88)/2-2	1.8
1985	Bal-A	121	492	69	144	22	4	9	48	39	95	.293	.347	.409	756	109	6	10	3	1	.984	4	*O-115(0-1-115)/D-5	0.5
1986	Bal-A	130	491	77	141	18	0	11	47	37	71	.287	.337	.391	728	99	-1	4	6	-1	.992	6	*O-120(0-0-120)/D-3	-0.3
1987	Bal-A	87	258	35	63	13	3	7	28	32	49	.244	.328	.399	727	94	-2	3	2	-0	.973	2	O-80(1-1-79)/D-4	-0.4
Total	16	1523	4549	650	1303	207	42	91	458	372	657	.286	.342	.410	752	108	43	185	86	11	.983	-31	*O-1006R,2-275/3DS	-0.8

■ **GUY LACY** Lacy, Osceola Guy b: 6/12/1897, Cleveland, Tenn. d: 11/19/53, Cleveland, Tenn. BR/TR, 5'11.5", 170 lbs. Deb: 5/7/26

YEAR	TM/L	G	AB	R	H	2B	3B	HR	RBI	BB	SO	AVG	OBP	SLG	OPS	OPS+	BR+	SB	CS	SBR	FA	FR	G/POS	TPR
1926	Cle-A	13	24	2	4	0	0	1	2	2	2	.167	.259	.292	551	43	-2	0	0	0	.976	1	2-11/3-2	-0.1

■ **HI LADD** Ladd, Arthur Clifford b: 2/9/1870, Willimantic, Conn. d: 5/7/48, Cranston, R.I. BL/TR, 6'4", 180 lbs. Deb: 7/12/1898

YEAR	TM/L	G	AB	R	H	2B	3B	HR	RBI	BB	SO	AVG	OBP	SLG	OPS	OPS+	BR+	SB	CS	SBR	FA	FR	G/POS	TPR
1898	Pit-N	1	3	0	0	0	0	0	0	0		.000	.000	.000	0	-99	-0	0			.000	0	H	0.0
	Bos-N	1	4	1	1	0	0	0	0	0		.250	.250	.250	500	41	-0	0			1.000	-0	/O-1(1-0-0)	0.0
	Yr	2	5	1	1	0	0	0	0	0		.200	.200	.200	400	14	-1	0			1.000	-0	/O-1(1-0-0)	0.0

■ **STEVE LADEW** Ladew, Stephen b: St.Louis, Mo. Deb: 9/27/1889

YEAR	TM/L	G	AB	R	H	2B	3B	HR	RBI	BB	SO	AVG	OBP	SLG	OPS	OPS+	BR+	SB	CS	SBR	FA	FR	G/POS	TPR
1889	KC-a	2	4	0	0	0	0	0	0	0	3	.000	.000	.000	0	-95	-1	0			1.000	-0	/O-1(1-0-0),P-1	-0.1

■ **JOE LAFATA** Lafata, Joseph Joseph b: 8/3/21, Detroit, Mich. BL/TL, 6', 163 lbs. Deb: 4/17/47

YEAR	TM/L	G	AB	R	H	2B	3B	HR	RBI	BB	SO	AVG	OBP	SLG	OPS	OPS+	BR+	SB	CS	SBR	FA	FR	G/POS	TPR
1947	NY-N	62	95	13	21	1	0	2	18	15	18	.221	.333	.295	628	68	-4	1			.974	-1	O-19(20-1-0)/1-2	-0.6
1948	NY-N	1	1	0	0	0	0	0	0	0	1	.000	.000	.000	0	-99	-0	0			.000	0	H	0.0
1949	NY-N	64	140	18	33	2	2	3	16	9	23	.236	.282	.343	625	67	-7	1			.984	-4	1-47	-1.2
Total	3	127	236	31	54	3	2	5	34	24	42	.229	.303	.322	625	67	-11	2			.985	-5	/1-49,O-19(20-1-0)	-1.8

■ **FLIP LAFFERTY** Lafferty, Frank Bernard b: 5/4/1854, Scranton, Pa. d: 2/8/10, Wilmington, Del. TR, Deb: 9/15/1876

YEAR	TM/L	G	AB	R	H	2B	3B	HR	RBI	BB	SO	AVG	OBP	SLG	OPS	OPS+	BR+	SB	CS	SBR	FA	FR	G/POS	TPR
1876	Phi-N	1	3	0	0	0	0	0	0	0	0	.000	.000	.000	0	-99	-1				.750	0	/P-1	0.0
1877	Lou-N	4	17	2	1	1	0	0	0	0	4	.059	.059	.118	176	-39	-3				.750	-1	/O-4(0-4-0)	-0.4
Total	2	5	20	2	1	1	0	0	0	0	4	.050	.050	.100	150	-46	-3				.750	-1	/O-4(0-4-0),P-1	-0.4

■ **TY LaFOREST** LaForest, Biron Joseph b: 4/18/17, Edmundston, N.B., Canada d: 5/5/47, Arlington, Mass. BR/TR, 5'9", 165 lbs. Deb: 8/4/45

YEAR	TM/L	G	AB	R	H	2B	3B	HR	RBI	BB	SO	AVG	OBP	SLG	OPS	OPS+	BR+	SB	CS	SBR	FA	FR	G/POS	TPR
1945	Bos-A	52	204	25	51	7	4	2	16	10	35	.250	.285	.353	638	83	-5	4	4	-1	.966	1	3-45/O-5(3-0-2)	-0.5

■ **ROGER LaFRANCOIS** LaFrancois, Roger Victor b: 8/2/54, Norwich, Conn. BL/TR, 6'2", 215 lbs. Deb: 5/27/82

YEAR	TM/L	G	AB	R	H	2B	3B	HR	RBI	BB	SO	AVG	OBP	SLG	OPS	OPS+	BR+	SB	CS	SBR	FA	FR	G/POS	TPR
1982	Bos-A	8	10	1	4	1	0	0	1	0	0	.400	.400	.500	900	137	0	0	0	0	1.000	-0	/C-8	0.0

■ **MIKE LAGA** Laga, Michael Russell b: 6/14/60, Ridgewood, N.J. BL/TL, 6'2", 210 lbs. Deb: 9/1/82

YEAR	TM/L	G	AB	R	H	2B	3B	HR	RBI	BB	SO	AVG	OBP	SLG	OPS	OPS+	BR+	SB	CS	SBR	FA	FR	G/POS	TPR
1982	Det-A	27	88	6	23	9	0	3	11	4	23	.261	.293	.466	759	104	0	1	0	0	.994	-2	1-19/D-8	-0.3
1983	Det-A	12	21	2	4	0	0	0	2	1	9	.190	.227	.190	418	17	-2	0	0	0	1.000	-0	/1-5,D-6	-0.2
1984	Det-A	9	11	1	6	0	0	0	1	1	2	.545	.583	.545	1129	216	2	0	0	0	1.000	0	/1-4,D-4	0.2
1985	Det-A	9	36	3	6	1	0	2	6	0	9	.167	.167	.361	528	40	-3	0	0	0	.974	1	/1-4,D-5	-0.3
1986	Det-A	15	45	6	9	1	0	3	8	5	13	.200	.280	.422	702	88	-1	0	0	0	1.000	-0	1-12/D-2	-0.2
	StL-N	18	46	7	10	4	0	3	8	5	18	.217	.308	.500	808	120	1	0	0	0	1.000	2	1-16	0.2
1987	StL-N	17	29	4	4	1	0	1	4	2	7	.138	.194	.276	469	22	-3	0	0	0	.973	1	1-12	-0.3
1988	StL-N	41	100	5	13	0	0	1	4	2	21	.130	.147	.160	307	-12	-14	0	0	0	1.000	1	1-37	-1.7
1989	SF-N	17	20	1	4	1	0	1	7	1	6	.200	.238	.400	638	82	-1	0	0	0	1.000	-0	/1-4	-0.1
1990	SF-N	23	27	4	5	1	0	2	4	1	7	.185	.241	.444	686	88	-1	0	0	0	1.000	1	1-10	0.0
Total	9	188	423	39	84	18	0	16	55	22	115	.199	.242	.355	596	63	-22	1	0	0	.996	2	1-123/D-25	-2.7

■ **JOE LAHOUD** Lahoud, Joseph Michael b: 4/14/47, Danbury, Conn. BL/TL, 6', 202 lbs. Deb: 4/10/68 Career OF: (198-LF 14-CF 296-RF)

YEAR	TM/L	G	AB	R	H	2B	3B	HR	RBI	BB	SO	AVG	OBP	SLG	OPS	OPS+	BR+	SB	CS	SBR	FA	FR	G/POS	TPR
1968	Bos-A	29	78	5	15	1	0	1	6	16	16	.192	.330	.244	573	71	-2	0	2	-1	.926	-3	O-25(3-1-22)	-0.9
1969	Bos-A	101	218	32	41	5	0	9	21	40	43	.188	.317	.335	651	78	-6	2	1	0	.979	-7	O-66(24-12-33)/1-1	-1.6
1970	Bos-A	17	49	6	12	1	0	2	5	7	6	.245	.339	.388	727	93	-0	0	0	0	.963	2	O-13(9-0-5)	0.1
1971	Bos-A	107	256	39	55	9	3	14	32	40	45	.215	.330	.438	768	108	3	2	2	-0	.993	3	O-69(7-0-63)	0.3
1972	Mil-A	111	316	35	75	9	3	12	34	45	54	.237	.332	.399	731	119	8	3	4	-1	.974	-2	O-97(38-0-63)	0.0
1973	Mil-A	96	225	29	46	9	0	5	26	27	36	.204	.304	.311	615	75	-7	5	5	-1	1.000	2	D-41,O-40(2-0-39)	-0.9
1974	Cal-A	127	325	46	88	16	3	13	44	47	57	.271	.368	.458	826	145	19	4	5	-1	.976	-6	*O-106(70-0-39),D-10	0.8
1975	Cal-A	76	192	21	41	6	2	6	33	48	33	.214	.373	.359	733	116	6	2	1	0	1.000	-3	D-35,O-29(7-0-22)	0.2
1976	Cal-A	42	96	8	17	4	0	0	4	18	16	.177	.319	.219	538	63	-4	0	0	0	.962	-2	O-26(21-1-6)/D-3	-0.7
	Tex-A	38	89	10	20	3	1	1	5	10	16	.225	.303	.315	618	79	-2	1	0	0	1.000	-2	D-22/O-5(4-0-1)	-0.5
	Yr	80	185	18	37	7	1	1	9	28	32	.200	.312	.265	576	72	-6	1	0	0	.964	-4	O-31(25-1-7),D-25	-1.2
1977	*KC-A	34	65	8	17	5	0	2	8	11	16	.262	.368	.431	799	116	2	1	0	0	.952	-1	O-15(13-0-2)/D-4	0.0
1978	KC-A	13	16	0	2	0	0	0	0	0	1	.125	.125	.125	250	-29	-3	0	0	0	.000	-0	/O-1(0-0-1),D-1	-0.3
Total	11	791	1925	239	429	68	12	65	218	309	339	.223	.335	.372	707	103	14	20	20	-3	.979	-19	O-492R,D-116/1-1	-3.5

■ **DICK LAJESKIE** Lajeskie, Richard Edward b: 1/8/26, Passaic, N.J. d: 8/15/76, Ramsey, N.J. BR/TR, 5'11", 175 lbs. Deb: 9/10/46

YEAR	TM/L	G	AB	R	H	2B	3B	HR	RBI	BB	SO	AVG	OBP	SLG	OPS	OPS+	BR+	SB	CS	SBR	FA	FR	G/POS	TPR
1946	NY-N	6	10	3	2	0	0	0	0	3	2	.200	.429	.200	629	81	0	0			.964	5	/2-4	0.5

■ **NAP LAJOIE** Lajoie, Napoleon "Larry" b: 9/5/1874, Woonsocket, R.I. d: 2/7/59, Daytona Beach, Fla. BR/TR, 6'1", 195 lbs. Deb: 8/12/1896 MH Career OF: (4-LF 5-CF 18-RF)

YEAR	TM/L	G	AB	R	H	2B	3B	HR	RBI	BB	SO	AVG	OBP	SLG	OPS	OPS+	BR+	SB	CS	SBR	FA	FR	G/POS	TPR
1896	Phi-N	39	175	36	57	12	7	4	42	1	11	.326	.330	.543	872	129	5	7			.995	-3	1-39	0.2
1897	Phi-N	127	545	107	197	40	23	9	127	15		.361	.392	**.569**	960	156	39	20			.984	-6	*1-108,O-19R/3-2	2.7
1898	Phi-N	147	608	113	197	**43**	11	6	**127**	21		.324	.354	.461	814	139	26	25			.949	-1	*2-146/1-1	3.0
1899	Phi-N	77	312	70	118	19	9	6	70	12		.378	.419	.554	974	172	29	13			.954	23	2-67/O-5(0-5-0)	4.8
1900	Phi-N	102	451	95	152	33	12	7	92	10		.337	.362	.510	872	140	21	22			**.954**	30	*2-102/3-1	**5.0**
1901	Phi-A	131	544	**145**	**232**	**48**	14	**14**	**125**	24		**.426**	**.463**	**.643**	**1106**	**196**	**68**	27			**.960**	**29**	*2-119,S-12	**8.5**
1902	Phi-A	1	4	0	1	0	0	0	1	0		.250	.250	.250	500	37	-0	1			1.000	-0	/2-1	-0.1
	Cle-A	86	348	81	132	35	5	7	64	19		.379	.421	.569	990	180	36	19			.974	30	2-86	6.1
	Yr	87	352	81	133	35	5	7	65	19		.378	.419	.565	984	178	36	20			.974	29	2-87	**6.0**
1903	Cle-A	125	485	90	167	41	11	7	93	24		**.344**	.379	**.518**	**896**	**170**	**39**	21			.955	**40**	*2-122/1-1,3-1	**8.1**
1904	Cle-A	140	553	92	**208**	**49**	15	5	**102**	27		**.376**	**.413**	**.546**	**959**	**204**	**63**	29			.962	-1	2-95,S-44/1-2	**7.0**
1905	Cle-A	65	249	29	82	12	2	2	41	17		.329	.377	.418	795	150	14	11			.991	9	2-59/1-5,M	2.5
1906	Cle-A	152	602	88	**214**	**48**	9	0	91	30		.355	.392	.465	857	170	46	20			**.973**	31	*2-130,3-15/S-7,M	**8.4**
1907	Cle-A	137	509	53	152	30	6	2	63	30		.299	.345	.393	738	134	18	24			**.969**	**46**	*2-128/1-9,M	**7.0**
1908	Cle-A	157	581	77	168	32	6	2	74	47		.289	.352	.375	727	136	23	15			**.964**	**49**	*2-156/1-1,M	**8.1**
1909	Cle-A	128	469	56	152	33	7	1	47	35		.324	.378	.431	809	149	26	13			.959	19	*2-120/1-8,M	5.0
1910	Cle-A	159	591	94	**227**	**51**	7	4	76	60		.384	.445	.514	960	198	**66**	26			.966	15	*2-149,1-10	**8.8**
1911	Cle-A	90	315	36	115	20	1	2	60	26		.365	.420	.454	874	142	18	13			.990	-7	1-41,2-37	1.1
1912	Cle-A	117	448	66	165	34	4	0	90	28		.368	.414	.462	876	146	26	18			.959	5	2-97,1-20	3.1
1913	Cle-A	137	465	66	156	25	2	1	68	33	17	.335	.398	.404	802	131	19	17			**.970**	9	*2-126	3.2
1914	Cle-A	121	419	37	108	14	3	0	50	32	15	.258	.313	.305	619	83	-9	14	15	-2	.959	6	2-80,1-31	-0.5
1915	Phi-A	129	490	40	137	24	5	1	61	11	16	.280	.301	.355	656	100	-3	10	6	0	.962	14	*2-110,S-10/1-5,3-2	1.4
1916	Phi-A	113	426	33	105	14	4	2	35	14	26	.246	.272	.312	584	79	-13	15			.973	30	*2-105/1-5,O-2(2-0-0)	2.1
Total	21	2480	9589	1504	3242	657	163	82	1599	516	85	.338	.380	.466	846	150	559	380	21		.963	366	*2-2035,1-286/SO3	95.5

■ EDDIE LAKE
Lake, Edward Erving "Sparky" b: 3/18/16, Antioch, Cal. d: 6/7/95, Castro Valley, Cal. BR/TR, 5'7", 160 lbs. Deb: 9/26/39

YEAR	TM/L	G	AB	R	H	2B	3B	HR	RBI	BB	SO	AVG	OBP	SLG	OPS	OPS+	BR+	SB	CS	SBR	FA	FR	G/POS	TPR
1939	StL-N	2	4	0	1	0	0	0	0	1	0	.250	.400	.250	650	74	-0	0			.857	-1	/S-2	-0.1
1940	StL-N	32	66	12	14	3	0	2	7	12	17	.212	.342	.348	690	86	-1	1			.957	-7	2-17/S-6	-0.7
1941	StL-N	45	76	9	8	2	0	0	0	15	22	.105	.253	.132	384	10	-9	3			.903	6	S-15,3-15/2-5	-0.2
1943	Bos-A	75	216	26	43	10	0	3	16	47	35	.199	.345	.287	632	84	-2	3	6	-1	.961	3	S-63	0.4
1944	Bos-A	57	126	21	26	5	0	0	8	23	22	.206	.329	.246	575	66	-5	5	2	0	.927	-5	S-41/P-6,2-3,3-1	-0.7
1945	Bos-A	133	473	81	132	27	1	11	51	106	37	.279	**.412**	.410	822	136	27	9	7	-0	.948	19	*S-130/2-1	5.9
1946	Det-A	155	587	105	149	24	1	8	31	103	69	.254	.369	.339	708	93	-1	15	9	0	.947	-21	*S-155	-1.4
1947	Det-A	158	602	96	127	19	6	12	46	120	54	.211	.343	.322	665	83	-11	11	10	-1	.943	-29	*S-158	-3.3
1948	Det-A	64	198	51	52	6	0	2	18	57	20	.263	.427	.323	751	99	3	3	3	-0	.972	-3	2-45,3-17	0.2
1949	Det-A	94	240	38	47	9	1	1	15	61	33	.196	.359	.254	613	63	-10	2	8	-2	.959	-10	S-38,2-19,3-18	-1.9
1950	Det-A	20	7	3	0	0	0	0	1	1	3	.000	.125	.000	125	-64	-2	0	0	0	.000	0	/S-1,3-1	-0.2
Total	11	835	2595	442	599	105	9	39	193	546	312	.231	.366	.323	689	91	-11	52	45		.947	-48	S-609/2-90,3-52,P-6	-2.0

■ FRED LAKE
Lake, Frederick Lovett b: 10/16/1866, Nova Scotia, Can. d: 11/24/31, Boston, Mass. BR/TR, 5'10", 170 lbs. Deb: 5/7/1891 M Career OF: (0-LF 0-CF 1-RF)

YEAR	TM/L	G	AB	R	H	2B	3B	HR	RBI	BB	SO	AVG	OBP	SLG	OPS	OPS+	BR+	SB	CS	SBR	FA	FR	G/POS	TPR
1891	Bos-N	5	7	1	1	0	0	0	0	2	4	.143	.333	.143	476	36	-1	0			1.000	-0	/C-4,O-1(0-0-1)	-0.1
1894	Lou-N	16	42	8	12	2	0	1	10	11	6	.286	.474	.405	878	122	3	2			.864	-3	/2-6,S-5,C-5	0.0
1897	*Bos-N	19	62	2	15	4	0	0	5	1		.242	.254	.306	560	45	-5	2			.970	-1	C-18	-0.4
1898	Pit-N	5	13	1	1	0	0	0	1	2		.077	.200	.077	277	-20	-2	0			1.000	-0	/1-3	-0.2
1910	Bos-N	3	1	0	0	0	0	0	0	1	0	.000	.500	.000	500	46	0	0			.000	0	HM	0.0
Total	5	48	125	12	29	6	0	1	16	17	10	.232	.342	.304	646	68	-5	4			.930	-5	/C-27,2-6,S-5,1O	-0.7

■ STEVE LAKE
Lake, Steven Michael b: 3/14/57, Inglewood, Cal. BR/TR, 6'1", 190 lbs. Deb: 4/9/83

YEAR	TM/L	G	AB	R	H	2B	3B	HR	RBI	BB	SO	AVG	OBP	SLG	OPS	OPS+	BR+	SB	CS	SBR	FA	FR	G/POS	TPR
1983	Chi-N	38	85	9	22	4	1	1	7	2	6	.259	.284	.365	649	75	-3	0	0	0	1.000	4	C-32	0.2
1984	*Chi-N	25	54	4	12	4	0	2	7	0	7	.222	.236	.407	644	71	-2	0	0	0	.955	0	C-24	-0.1
1985	Chi-N	58	119	5	18	2	0	1	11	3	21	.151	.179	.193	372	4	-15	1	0	0	.995	6	C-55	-0.8
1986	Chi-N	10	19	4	8	1	0	0	4	1	2	.421	.450	.474	924	144	1	0	0	0	1.000	-0	C-10	0.1
	StL-N	26	49	4	12	1	0	2	10	2	5	.245	.275	.388	662	81	-1	0	0	0	.976	1	C-26	0.0
	Yr	36	68	8	20	2	0	2	14	3	7	.294	.324	.412	736	100	-0	0	0	0	.983	1	C-36	0.1
1987	*StL-N	74	179	19	45	7	2	2	19	10	18	.251	.291	.346	637	67	-9	0	0	0	.996	-2	C-59	-0.8
1988	StL-N	36	54	5	15	3	0	1	4	3	15	.278	.339	.389	728	107	1	0	0	0	.983	-1	C-19	0.0
1989	Phi-N	58	155	9	39	5	1	2	14	12	20	.252	.305	.335	641	83	-3	0	0	0	.990	3	C-55	0.3
1990	Phi-N	29	80	4	20	2	0	0	6	3	12	.250	.286	.275	561	55	-5	0	0	0	.993	4	C-28	0.0
1991	Phi-N	58	158	12	36	4	1	1	11	2	26	.228	.237	.285	522	47	-11	0	0	0	.993	2	C-58	-0.7
1992	Phi-N	20	53	3	13	2	0	1	2	1	8	.245	.259	.340	599	69	-2	0	0	0	.975	0	C-17	-0.2
1993	Chi-N	44	120	11	27	6	0	5	13	4	19	.225	.250	.400	650	72	-5	0	0	0	.985	1	C-41	-0.3
Total	11	476	1125	89	267	41	5	18	108	43	159	.237	.269	.331	600	64	-56	1	0	0	.989	18	C-424	-2.3

■ AL LAKEMAN
Lakeman, Albert Wesley "Moose" b: 12/31/18, Cincinnati, Ohio d: 5/25/76, Spartanburg, S.C. BR/TR, 6'2", 195 lbs. Deb: 4/19/42 C

YEAR	TM/L	G	AB	R	H	2B	3B	HR	RBI	BB	SO	AVG	OBP	SLG	OPS	OPS+	BR+	SB	CS	SBR	FA	FR	G/POS	TPR
1942	Cin-N	20	38	0	6	1	0	0	2	3	10	.158	.238	.184	422	24	-4	0			.970	3	C-17	0.0
1943	Cin-N	22	55	5	14	2	1	0	6	3	11	.255	.293	.327	620	80	-2	0			1.000	-2	C-21	-0.2
1944	Cin-N	1	1	0	0	0	0	0	0	0	1	.000	.000	.000	0	-99	-0	0			.000	0	H	0.0
1945	Cin-N	76	258	22	66	9	4	8	31	17	45	.256	.304	.415	719	101	-1	0			.963	-11	C-74	-0.7
1946	Cin-N	23	30	0	4	0	0	0	4	2	7	.133	.188	.133	321	-9	-4	0			1.000	-0	/C-6	-0.5
1947	Cin-N	2	2	0	0	0	0	0	0	0	1	.000	.000	.000	0	-99	-1	0			.000	0	H	-0.1
	Phi-N	55	182	11	29	3	0	6	19	5	39	.159	.186	.275	461	22	-21	0			.995	-5	1-29,C-23	-2.6
	Yr	57	184	11	29	3	0	6	19	5	40	.158	.184	.272	456	20	-22	0			.995	-5	1-29,C-23	-2.7
1948	Phi-N	32	68	2	11	2	0	1	4	5	22	.162	.219	.235	454	23	-7	0			1.000	-2	C-22/P-1	-0.9
1949	Bos-N	3	6	0	1	0	0	0	0	1	0	.167	.286	.167	452	26	-1	0			1.000	1	/1-2	0.0
1954	Det-A	5	6	0	0	0	0	0	0	0	1	.000	.000	.000	0	-99	-2	0	0	0	1.000	1	/C-4	-0.1
Total	9	239	646	40	131	17	5	15	66	36	137	.203	.248	.314	562	55	-42	0	0		.974	-16	C-167/1-31,P-1	-5.1

■ TIM LAKER
Laker, Timothy John b: 11/27/69, Encino, Cal. BR/TR, 6'3", 195 lbs. Deb: 8/18/92

YEAR	TM/L	G	AB	R	H	2B	3B	HR	RBI	BB	SO	AVG	OBP	SLG	OPS	OPS+	BR+	SB	CS	SBR	FA	FR	G/POS	TPR
1992	Mon-N	28	46	8	10	3	0	0	4	2	14	.217	.250	.283	533	51	-3	1	1	-0	.991	5	C-28	0.3
1993	Mon-N	43	86	3	17	2	1	0	7	2	16	.198	.225	.244	469	24	-9	2	0	0	.987	2	C-43	-0.5
1995	Mon-N	64	141	17	33	8	1	3	20	14	38	.234	.308	.369	676	75	-5	0	1	-0	.977	3	C-61	0.0
1997	Bal-A	7	14	0	0	0	0	0	1	2	9	.000	.125	.000	125	-66	-3	0	0	0	.966	-2	/C-7	-0.5
1998	TB-A	3	5	1	1	0	0	0	0	1	1	.200	.333	.200	533	43	-0	0	1	-0	1.000	-0	/C-2,D-1	-0.1
	Pit-N	14	24	2	9	1	0	1	2	1	3	.375	.400	.542	942	143	1	0	0	0	1.000	-1	/1-4,C-1	0.0
1999	Pit-N	6	9	0	3	0	0	0	0	0	2	.333	.333	.333	667	70	-0	0	0	0	1.000	-0	/C-2	-0.1
Total	6	165	325	31	73	14	2	4	34	22	83	.225	.278	.317	595	57	-20	3	3	-0	.982	7	C-144/1-4,D-1	-0.9

■ DAN LALLY
Lally, Daniel J. b: 8/12/1867, Jersey City, N.J. d: 4/14/36, Milwaukee, Wis. BR/TR, 5'11.5", 210 lbs. Deb: 8/19/1891

YEAR	TM/L	G	AB	R	H	2B	3B	HR	RBI	BB	SO	AVG	OBP	SLG	OPS	OPS+	BR+	SB	CS	SBR	FA	FR	G/POS	TPR
1891	Pit-N	41	143	24	32	6	2	1	17	16	20	.224	.319	.315	634	87	-2	0			.839	-7	O-41(0-4-37)	-0.8
1897	StL-N	88	359	57	102	16	5	2	42	9		.284	.315	.373	688	83	-10	12			.896	3	O-85(83-1-1)/1-3	-1.3
Total	2	129	502	81	134	22	7	3	59	25	20	.267	.316	.357	673	84	-12	12			.885	-4	O-126(83-5-38)/1-3	-2.1

■ RAY LAMANNO
Lamanno, Raymond Simond b: 11/17/19, Oakland, Cal. d: 2/9/94, Berkeley, Cal. BR/TR, 6', 185 lbs. Deb: 9/11/41

YEAR	TM/L	G	AB	R	H	2B	3B	HR	RBI	BB	SO	AVG	OBP	SLG	OPS	OPS+	BR+	SB	CS	SBR	FA	FR	G/POS	TPR
1941	Cin-N	1	0	0	0	0	0	0	0	0	0	—	1.000	—	1000	197	0	0			1.000	-0	/C-1	0.0
1942	Cin-N	111	371	40	98	12	2	12	43	31	54	.264	.324	.404	729	113	5	0			.978	-11	*C-104	0.1
1946	Cin-N★	85	239	18	58	12	0	1	30	11	26	.243	.285	.305	590	70	-10	0			.974	2	C-61	-0.5
1947	Cin-N	118	413	33	106	21	3	5	50	28	39	.257	.307	.358	665	77	-15	0			.986	9	C-109	0.0
1948	Cin-N	127	385	31	93	12	0	2	27	48	32	.242	.329	.273	601	67	-16	2			.978	-11	*C-125	-2.1
Total	5	442	1408	122	355	57	5	18	150	118	151	.252	.314	.338	653	82	-36	2			.980	-11	C-400	-2.5

■ BILL LAMAR
Lamar, William Harmong "Good Time Bill" b: 3/21/1897, Rockville, Md. d: 5/24/70, Rockport, Mass. BL/TR, 6'1", 185 lbs. Deb: 9/19/17

YEAR	TM/L	G	AB	R	H	2B	3B	HR	RBI	BB	SO	AVG	OBP	SLG	OPS	OPS+	BR+	SB	CS	SBR	FA	FR	G/POS	TPR
1917	NY-A	11	41	2	10	0	0	0	3	0	2	.244	.244	.244	488	48	-3	1			1.000	0	O-11(10-1-0)	-0.3
1918	NY-A	28	110	12	25	3	0	0	2	6	2	.227	.267	.255	522	56	-6	2			.884	-2	O-27(8-17-2)	-1.1
1919	NY-A	11	16	1	3	1	0	0	0	2	1	.188	.278	.250	528	48	-1	1			1.000	-1	/O-3(0-1-2),1-1	-0.2
	Bos-A	48	148	18	43	5	1	0	14	5	9	.291	.314	.338	652	88	-3	3			.922	-2	O-36(6-29-1)	-0.8
	Yr	59	164	19	46	6	1	0	14	7	10	.280	.310	.329	639	83	-4	4			.926	-3	O-39(6-30-3)/1-1	-1.0
1920	*Bro-N	24	44	5	12	4	0	0	4	0	1	.273	.273	.364	636	79	-1	4	0	0	1.000	-3	O-12(0-6-6)	-0.5
1921	Bro-N	3	3	2	1	0	0	0	0	0	0	.333	.333	.333	667	74	-0	0	0	0	.000	-1	/O-1(0-1-0)	-0.1
1924	Phi-A	87	367	68	121	22	5	7	48	18	21	.330	.361	.474	835	113	5	8	8	-1	.971	4	O-87(87-0-0)	0.1
1925	Phi-A	138	568	85	202	39	8	3	77	21	17	.356	.379	.468	847	107	5	2	6	-2	.953	4	*O-131(131-0-0)	-0.3
1926	Phi-A	116	419	62	119	17	6	5	50	18	15	.284	.315	.389	704	78	-14	4	5	-1	.954	-3	*O-107(107-0-0)	-2.6
1927	Phi-A	84	324	48	97	23	3	4	47	16	10	.299	.334	.426	760	91	-5	4	8	-2	.952	-3	O-79(76-3-0)	-1.6
Total	9	550	2040	303	633	114	23	19	245	86	78	.310	.339	.417	755	94	-24	25	27		.952	-6	O-494(425-58-11)/1-1	-7.4

■ DAVID LAMB
Lamb, David Christian b: 6/6/75, West Hills, Cal. BB/TR, 6'2", 165 lbs. Deb: 4/12/99

YEAR	TM/L	G	AB	R	H	2B	3B	HR	RBI	BB	SO	AVG	OBP	SLG	OPS	OPS+	BR+	SB	CS	SBR	FA	FR	G/POS	TPR
1999	TB-A	55	124	18	28	5	1	1	13	10	18	.226	.284	.306	590	50	-9	0	1	-0	.945	3	S-35,2-15/D-3	-0.4
2000	NY-N	7	5	1	1	0	0	0	0	1	1	.200	.333	.200	533	41	-0	0	0	0	1.000	-1	/3-3,2-2,S-2	-0.1
Total	2	62	129	19	29	5	1	1	13	11	19	.225	.286	.302	588	50	-10	0	1	-0	.947	2	/S-37,2-17,3-3,D-3	-0.5

■ LYMAN LAMB
Lamb, Laymon Raymond b: 3/17/1895, Lincoln, Neb. d: 10/5/55, Fayetteville, Ark. BR/TR, 5'7", 150 lbs. Deb: 9/14/20

YEAR	TM/L	G	AB	R	H	2B	3B	HR	RBI	BB	SO	AVG	OBP	SLG	OPS	OPS+	BR+	SB	CS	SBR	FA	FR	G/POS	TPR
1920	StL-A	9	24	4	9	2	0	0	4	0	7	.375	.375	.458	833	116	0	2	0	0	1.000	-2	/O-7(5-2-0)	-0.1
1921	StL-A	45	134	18	34	9	2	1	17	4	12	.254	.281	.373	654	62	-8	0	0	0	.942	-9	3-25/2-7,O-6(2-0-4)	-1.5
Total	2	54	158	22	43	11	2	1	21	4	19	.272	.294	.386	681	70	-8	2	0	0	1.000	-11	/3-25,O-13(7-2-4),2-7	-1.6

■ MIKE LAMB
Lamb, Michael Robert b: 8/9/75, West Covina, Cal. BL/TR, 6'1", 185 lbs. Deb: 4/23/2000

YEAR	TM/L	G	AB	R	H	2B	3B	HR	RBI	BB	SO	AVG	OBP	SLG	OPS	OPS+	BR+	SB	CS	SBR	FA	FR	G/POS	TPR
2000	Tex-A	138	493	65	137	25	2	6	47	34	60	.278	.330	.373	703	75	-18	0	2	-1	.913	-8	*3-135/D-2	-2.4

YEAR	TM/L	G	AB	R	H	2B	3B	HR	RBI	BB	SO	AVG	OBP	SLG	OPS	OPS+	BR+	SB	CS	SBR	FA	FR	G/POS	TPR
■ **PETE LAMERS** Lamers, Pierre b: 12/1873, New York, N.Y. d: 10/24/31, Brooklyn, N.Y. TR, 5'10", 170 lbs. Deb: 9/10/02																								
1902	Chi-N	2	9	2	2	0	0	0	0	0		.222	.222	.222	444	38	-1	0			.857	-0	/C-2	-0.1
1907	Cin-N	1	2	0	0	0	0	0	0	0		.000	.000	.000	0	-96	-0	0			1.000	-0	/C-1	-0.1
Total	2	3	11	2	2	0	0	0	0	0		.182	.182	.182	364	13	-1	0			.867	-1	/C-3	-0.2
■ **GENE LAMONT** Lamont, Gene William b: 12/25/46, Rockford, Ill. BL/TR, 6'1", 195 lbs. Deb: 9/2/70 MC																								
1970	Det-A	15	44	3	13	3	1	1	4	2	9	.295	.340	.477	818	122	1	0	0	0	1.000	1	C-15	0.3
1971	Det-A	7	15	2	1	0	0	0	1	0	5	.067	.067	.067	133	-60	-3	0	0	0	.952	2	/C-7	-0.1
1972	Det-A	1	0	0	0	0	0	0	0	0	0	—	—	—	—	—	0	0	0	0	1.000	-0	/C-1	0.0
1974	Det-A	60	92	9	20	4	0	3	8	7	19	.217	.273	.359	631	78	-3	0	0	0	.974	8	C-60	0.7
1975	Det-A	4	8	1	3	1	0	0	1	0	2	.375	.375	.500	875	139	0	1	0	0	.944	1	/C-4	0.2
Total	5	87	159	15	37	8	1	4	14	9	35	.233	.278	.371	649	80	-4	1	0	0	.977	12	/C-87	1.1
■ **BOBBY LaMOTTE** LaMotte, Robert Eugene b: 2/15/1898, Savannah, Ga. d: 11/2/70, Chatham, Ga. BR/TR, 5'11", 160 lbs. Deb: 9/1/20																								
1920	Was-A	4	3	0	0	0	0	0	0	1	1	.000	.250	.000	250	-31	-1	0	0	0	.750	0	/S-1,3-1	0.0
1921	Was-A	16	41	5	8	0	0	0	2	5	0	.195	.283	.195	478	25	-5	0	0	0	.940	2	S-12	-0.2
1922	Was-A	68	214	22	54	10	2	1	23	15	21	.252	.307	.332	639	70	-10	6	1	1	.954	8	3-62/S-6	0.3
1925	StL-A	97	356	61	97	20	4	2	51	34	22	.272	.338	.368	706	75	-14	5	5	-1	.926	2	S-93/3-3	-0.2
1926	StL-A	36	79	11	16	4	3	0	9	11	6	.203	.300	.329	629	61	-5	0	0	0	.919	-2	S-30/3-1	-0.4
Total	5	221	693	99	175	34	9	3	85	66	50	.253	.320	.341	661	69	-33	11	6	0	.927	10	S-142/3-67	-0.5
■ **KEITH LAMPARD** Lampard, Christopher Keith b: 12/20/45, Warrington, England BL/TR, 6'2", 197 lbs. Deb: 9/15/69																								
1969	Hou-N	9	12	2	3	0	0	1	2	0	3	.250	.250	.500	750	108	0	0	0	0	1.000	1	/O-1(1-0-0)	0.1
1970	Hou-N	53	72	8	17	8	1	0	5	5	24	.236	.295	.375	670	82	-2	0	0	0	1.000	-1	O-16(13-0-4)/1-2	-0.3
Total	2	62	84	10	20	8	1	1	7	5	27	.238	.289	.393	682	85	-2	0	0	0	1.000	1	/O-17(14-0-4),1-2	-0.2
■ **TOM LAMPKIN** Lampkin, Thomas Michael b: 3/4/64, Cincinnati, Ohio BL/TR, 5'11", 185 lbs. Deb: 9/10/88 Career OF: (15-LF 0-CF 2-RF)																								
1988	Cle-A	4	4	0	0	0	0	0	0	1	0	.000	.200	.000	200	-38	-1	0	0	0	1.000	-1	/C-3	-0.2
1990	SD-N	26	63	4	14	0	1	1	4	4	9	.222	.269	.302	570	56	-4	0	1	-0	.971	1	C-20	-0.3
1991	SD-N	38	58	4	11	3	1	0	3	3	9	.190	.230	.276	505	40	-5	0	0	0	1.000	0	C-11	-0.4
1992	SD-N	9	17	3	4	0	0	0	0	6	1	.235	.458	.235	694	100	1	2	0	0	1.000	-2	/C-7,O-1(1-0-0)	0.0
1993	Mil-A	73	162	22	32	8	0	4	25	20	26	.198	.286	.321	607	64	-8	7	3	0	.978	-3	C-60/O-3(2-0-1),D-1	-0.8
1995	SF-N	65	76	8	21	2	0	1	9	9	8	.276	.360	.342	703	89	-1	2	0	0	1.000	-2	C-17/O-6(6-0-0)	-0.1
1996	SF-N	66	177	26	41	8	0	6	29	20	22	.232	.327	.379	705	89	-3	1	5	-2	.992	7	C-53	0.6
1997	StL-N	108	229	28	56	8	1	7	22	28	30	.245	.337	.380	717	88	-4	2	1	0	.989	-6	C-86	-0.5
1998	StL-N	93	216	25	50	12	1	6	28	24	32	.231	.328	.380	708	86	-4	3	2	-0	.986	-3	C-62/O-5(4-0-1),1-2	-0.4
1999	Sea-A	76	206	29	60	11	2	9	34	13	32	.291	.348	.495	843	115	4	1	3	-1	.985	-6	C-56/O-2(2-0-0),D-2	0.0
2000	Sea-A	36	103	15	26	6	1	7	23	9	17	.252	.330	.534	864	117	2	0	0	0	.987	-4	C-28/D-3	0.0
Total	11	594	1311	164	315	58	7	41	177	137	186	.240	.324	.389	713	88	-22	18	15	-1	.987	-17	C-403/O-17L,D-6,1-2	-2.1
■ **RICK LANCELLOTTI** Lancellotti, Richard Anthony b: 7/5/56, Providence, R.I. BL/TL, 6'3", 195 lbs. Deb: 8/27/82																								
1982	SD-N	17	39	2	7	2	0	0	4	2	8	.179	.220	.231	450	28	-4	0	0	0	1.000	-2	/1-7,O-3(2-0-1)	-0.6
1986	SF-N	15	18	2	4	0	0	2	6	0	7	.222	.222	.556	778	113	0	0	0	0	1.000	1	/1-1,O-1(0-0-1)	0.1
1990	Bos-A	4	8	0	0	0	0	0	1	0	3	.000	.000	.000	0	-96	-2	0	0	0	1.000	0	/1-2	-0.2
Total	3	36	65	4	11	2	0	2	11	2	18	.169	.194	.292	486	35	-6	0	0	0	1.000	-0	/1-10,O-4(2-0-2)	-0.7
■ **GROVER LAND** Land, Grover Cleveland b: 9/22/1884, Frankfort, Ky. d: 7/22/58, Phoenix, Ariz. BR/TR, 6', 190 lbs. Deb: 9/2/08 C																								
1908	Cle-A	8	16	1	3	0	0	0	2	0		.188	.188	.188	375	22	-1	0			.955	-1	/C-8	-0.3
1909	Cle-A	1	4	0	2	0	0	0	1	0		.500	.500	.500	1000	207	0	0			1.000	0	/C-1	0.1
1910	Cle-A	34	111	4	23	0	0	0	7	2		.207	.228	.207	435	36	-8	1			.982	5	C-33	-0.1
1911	Cle-A	35	107	5	15	1	2	0	10	3		.140	.164	.187	351	-2	-15	2			.961	1	C-34/1-1	-1.2
1913	Cle-A	17	47	3	11	1	0	0	9	4	1	.234	.321	.255	576	67	-2	1			.924	1	C-17	0.0
1914	Bro-F	102	335	24	92	6	2	0	29	12	23	.275	.306	.304	610	67	-20	7			.970	0	C-97	-1.3
1915	Bro-F	96	290	25	75	13	2	0	22	6	20	.259	.279	.317	596	68	-17	3			.960	-6	C-81	-1.8
Total	7	293	910	62	221	21	6	0	80	27	44	.243	.271	.279	550	55	-64	14			.964	-2	C-271/1-1	-4.6
■ **DOC LAND** Land, William Gilbert (b: Doc Burrell Land) b: 5/14/03, Binnsville, Miss. d: 4/14/86, Livingston, Ala. BL/TL, 5'11", 165 lbs. Deb: 10/6/29																								
1929	Was-A	1	3	0	0	0	0	0	0	1	0	.000	.250	.000	250	-30	-1	0	0	0	1.000	-0	/O-1(0-1-0)	-0.1
■ **KEN LANDENBERGER** Landenberger, Kenneth Henry "Red" b: 7/29/28, Lyndhurst, Ohio d: 7/28/60, Cleveland, Ohio BL/TL, 6'3", 200 lbs. Deb: 9/20/52																								
1952	Chi-A	2	5	0	1	0	0	0	0	0	2	.200	.200	.200	400	11	-1	0	0	0	1.000	0	/1-1	0.0
■ **RAFAEL LANDESTOY** Landestoy, Rafael Silvialdo (Santana) b: 5/28/53, Bani, D.R. BB/TR (BR 1977), 5'10", 165 lbs. Deb: 8/27/77 C																								
1977	*LA-N	15	18	6	5	0	0	0	0	3	2	.278	.381	.278	659	80	-0	2	0	0	1.000	3	/2-8,S-3	0.3
1978	Hou-N	59	218	18	58	5	1	0	9	8	23	.266	.292	.298	590	70	-9	7	4	0	.980	-13	S-50/O-3(1-2-0),2-2	-1.8
1979	Hou-N	129	282	33	76	9	6	0	30	29	24	.270	.340	.344	684	92	-3	13	4	1	.971	-2	*2-114/S-3	0.1
1980	*Hou-N	149	393	42	97	13	8	1	27	31	37	.247	.307	.328	635	84	-9	23	12	1	.991	-6	2-94,S-65/3-3	-0.6
1981	Hou-N	35	74	6	11	1	1	0	4	16	9	.149	.300	.189	489	43	-5	4	1	1	.966	-4	2-31	-0.8
	Cin-N	12	11	2	2	0	0	0	1	1	0	.182	.250	.182	432	24	-1	1	0	0	1.000	-0	/2-3	-0.1
	Yr	47	85	8	13	1	1	0	5	17	9	.153	.294	.188	482	40	-6	5	1	1	.967	-5	2-34	-0.9
1982	Cin-N	73	111	11	21	3	0	1	9	8	14	.189	.250	.243	493	38	-9	2	0	0	1.000	4	3-21,2-16/O-3L,S-2	-0.5
1983	Cin-N	7	5	0	0	0	0	0	0	0	0	.000	.000	.000	0	-97	-1	0	0	0	1.000	-1	/1-2,3-1,O-1(1-0-0)	-0.2
	*LA-N	64	64	6	11	1	1	1	1	3	8	.172	.209	.266	475	31	-6	0	2	-1	1.000	2	2-14,3-10,O-10L,/S	-0.5
	Yr	71	69	6	11	1	1	1	1	3	8	.159	.194	.246	441	21	-7	0	2	-1	1.000	1	2-14,3-11,O-11L,/1S	-0.7
1984	LA-N	53	54	10	10	0	0	1	2	1	6	.185	.200	.241	441	24	-6	2	1	0	.886	1	2-14,3-11/O-5(1-1-4)	-0.4
Total	8	596	1230	134	291	32	17	4	83	100	123	.237	.297	.300	597	70	-49	54	24	3	.976	-17	2-296,S-124/3-46,O1	-4.5
■ **JIM LANDIS** Landis, James Henry b: 3/9/34, Fresno, Cal. BR/TR, 6'1", 180 lbs. Deb: 4/16/57																								
1957	Chi-A	96	274	38	58	11	3	2	16	45	61	.212	.329	.296	625	72	-10	14	4	2	.985	4	O-90(11-38-44)	-0.8
1958	Chi-A	142	523	72	145	23	7	15	64	52	80	.277	.352	.434	786	117	12	19	7	2	.986	6	*O-142(0-142-0)	1.3
1959	*Chi-A	149	515	78	140	26	7	5	60	78	68	.272	.376	.379	755	109	10	20	9	1	.993	16	*O-148(0-148-0)	1.9
1960	Chi-A	148	494	89	125	25	6	10	49	80	84	.253	.367	.389	756	106	6	23	6	3	.985	13	*O-147(0-147-0)	1.5
1961	Chi-A	140	534	87	151	18	8	22	85	65	71	.283	.365	.470	835	123	18	19	5	2	.988	19	*O-139(0-139-0)	3.4
1962	Chi-A★	149	534	82	122	21	6	15	61	80	105	.228	.339	.375	713	92	-5	19	7	2	.995	10	*O-144(0-144-0)	0.3
1963	Chi-A	133	396	56	89	6	6	13	45	47	75	.225	.316	.369	685	93	-3	8	6	-0	**.993**	1	*O-124(0-124-0)	-0.6
1964	Chi-A	106	298	30	62	8	4	1	18	36	64	.208	.306	.272	578	64	-14	5	0	1	.995	-4	*O-101(0-101-0)	-2.0
1965	KC-A	118	364	46	87	15	1	3	36	57	84	.239	.347	.310	657	90	-3	8	3	1	.985	6	*O-108(0-108-1)	0.0
1966	Cle-A	85	158	23	35	5	1	3	14	20	25	.222	.317	.323	639	84	-3	2	1	0	1.000	-11	O-61(18-37-17)	-1.7
1967	Det-A	25	48	4	10	0	0	2	4	7	12	.208	.309	.333	642	87	-1	0	2	-1	.952	0	O-12(6-1-6)	-0.2
	Bos-A	5	7	1	1	0	0	1	1	1	3	.143	.250	.571	821	126	0	0	0	0	1.000	-1	/O-5(0-0-5)	-0.1
	Yr	30	55	5	11	0	0	3	5	8	15	.200	.302	.364	665	92	-0	0	2	-1	.960	-1	O-17(6-1-11)	-0.3
	Hou-N	50	143	19	36	11	1	1	14	20	35	.252	.348	.364	711	107	2	2	1	0	1.000	-1	O-44(28-3-14)	-0.1
Total	11	1346	4288	625	1061	169	50	93	467	588	767	.247	.346	.375	721	100	10	139	51	13	.989	58	*O-1265(63-1132-87)	2.9
■ **KEN LANDREAUX** Landreaux, Kenneth Francis b: 12/22/54, Los Angeles, Cal. BL/TR, 5'10", 165 lbs. Deb: 9/11/77 Career OF: (198-LF 859-CF 105-RF)																								
1977	Cal-A	23	76	6	19	5	1	0	5	5	15	.250	.296	.342	638	76	-3	1	1	-0	.970	5	O-22(0-22-0)	0.2
1978	Cal-A	93	260	37	58	7	5	5	23	20	20	.223	.284	.346	630	79	-8	7	3	0	.986	-7	O-83(32-23-35)/D-1	-1.7
1979	Min-A	151	564	81	172	27	5	15	83	37	57	.305	.352	.450	802	110	8	10	3	1	.981	-8	*O-147(49-98-0)	-0.2
1980	Min-A★	129	484	56	136	23	11	7	62	39	42	.281	.337	.417	754	98	-1	8	6	-0	.976	-9	*O-120(54-68-0)/D-6	-1.4
1981	*LA-N	99	390	48	98	16	4	7	41	25	42	.251	.298	.367	665	91	-6	18	4	3	**1.000**	-4	O-95(0-95-0)	-0.8
1982	LA-N	129	461	71	131	23	7	7	50	39	54	.284	.345	.410	755	113	8	31	10	3	.986	2	*O-117(1-116-0)	1.3

YEAR	TM/L	G	AB	R	H	2B	3B	HR	RBI	BB	SO	AVG	OBP	SLG	OPS	OPS+	BR+	SB	CS	SBR	FA	FR	G/POS	TPR
1983	*LA-N	141	481	63	135	25	3	17	66	34	52	.281	.331	.451	782	115	8	30	11	3	.990	-2	*O-137(7-131-2)	0.8
1984	LA-N	134	438	39	110	11	5	11	47	29	35	.251	.299	.374	674	89	-7	10	9	-1	.986	-16	*O-129(9-105-18)	-2.8
1985	*LA-N	147	482	70	129	26	2	12	50	33	37	.268	.316	.405	720	103	1	15	5	2	.975	-7	*O-140(11-126-4)	-0.7
1986	LA-N	103	283	34	74	13	2	4	29	22	39	.261	.317	.364	681	94	-3	10	5	0	.955	-5	O-85(20-69-1)	-0.9
1987	LA-N	115	182	17	37	4	0	6	23	16	28	.203	.271	.324	596	58	-11	5	3	0	.951	-6	O-63(15-6-45)	-1.9
Total	11	1264	4101	522	1099	180	45	91	479	299	421	.268	.321	.400	721	99	-14	145	60	11	.981	-57	*O-1138C/D-7	-8.1
■ HOBIE LANDRITH	Landrith, Hobert Neal b: 3/16/30, Decatur, Ill. BL/TR, 5'10", 170 lbs. Deb: 7/30/50 C																							
1950	Cin-N	4	14	1	3	0	0	0	1	2	1	.214	.313	.214	527	41	-1	0			1.000	-1	/C-4	-0.2
1951	Cin-N	4	13	3	5	1	0	0	0	1	1	.385	.429	.462	890	137	1	0	0	0	1.000	1	/C-4	0.2
1952	Cin-N	15	50	1	13	4	0	0	4	0	4	.260	.260	.340	600	65	-2	0	1	-0	1.000	0	C-14	-0.2
1953	Cin-N	52	154	15	37	3	1	3	16	12	8	.240	.299	.331	631	64	-8	2	0	0	.985	0	C-47	-0.5
1954	Cin-N	48	81	12	16	0	0	5	14	18	9	.198	.343	.383	726	86	-1	1	0	0	.986	4	C-42	0.4
1955	Cin-N	43	87	9	22	3	0	4	7	10	14	.253	.330	.425	755	93	-1	0	1	-0	1.000	4	C-27	0.3
1956	Chi-N	111	312	22	69	10	3	4	32	39	38	.221	.310	.311	621	69	-13	0	2	-1	.975	-3	C-99	-1.2
1957	StL-N	75	214	18	52	6	0	3	26	25	27	.243	.322	.313	635	70	-8	1	2	-0	.987	5	C-67	-0.1
1958	StL-N	70	144	9	31	4	0	3	13	26	21	.215	.335	.306	641	68	-6	0	1	-0	.992	2	C-45	-0.2
1959	SF-N	109	283	30	71	14	0	3	29	43	23	.251	.350	.332	682	85	-5	0	4	-1	.992	7	*C-109	0.5
1960	SF-N	71	190	18	46	10	0	1	20	23	11	.242	.324	.311	634	79	-5	1	1	-0	.966	-5	C-70	-0.8
1961	SF-N	43	71	11	17	4	0	2	10	12	7	.239	.349	.380	730	97	-0	0	0	0	.985	2	C-30	0.2
1962	NY-N	23	45	6	13	3	0	1	7	8	3	.289	.396	.422	818	118	1	0	0	0	.968	-1	C-21	0.1
	Bal-A	60	167	18	37	4	1	4	17	19	9	.222	.305	.329	634	75	-6	0	0	0	.982	5	C-60	0.1
1963	Bal-A	2	1	0	0	0	0	0	0	0	0	.000	.000	.000	0	-99	-0	0	0	0	1.000	-0	/C-1	0.0
	Was-A	42	103	6	18	3	0	1	7	15	12	.175	.280	.233	513	46	-7	0	0	0	.978	2	C-37	-0.4
	Yr	44	104	6	18	3	0	1	7	15	12	.173	.277	.231	508	44	-7	0	0	0	.978	2	C-38	-0.4
Total	14	772	1929	179	450	69	5	34	203	253	188	.233	.323	.327	650	76	-63	5	12		.983	22	C-677	-1.8
■ CED LANDRUM	Landrum, Cedric Bernard b: 9/3/63, Butler, Ala. BL/TR, 5'7", 167 lbs. Deb: 5/28/91																							
1991	Chi-N	56	86	28	20	2	1	0	6	10	18	.233	.313	.279	592	65	-4	27	5	4	.968	-9	O-44(25-18-8)	-1.0
1993	NY-N	22	19	2	5	1	0	0	1	0	5	.263	.263	.316	579	55	-1	0	0	0	.000	-1	/O-3(3-0-0)	-0.2
Total	2	78	105	30	25	3	1	0	7	10	23	.238	.304	.286	590	63	-5	27	5	4	.968	-11	/O-47(28-18-8)	-1.2
■ DON LANDRUM	Landrum, Donald Leroy b: 2/16/36, Santa Rosa, Cal. BL/TR, 6', 180 lbs. Deb: 9/28/57																							
1957	Phi-N	2	7	1	1	1	0	0	0	2	1	.143	.333	.286	619	71	-0	0	0	0	1.000	1	/O-2(0-2-0)	0.0
1960	StL-N	13	49	7	12	0	1	2	3	4	6	.245	.315	.408	723	88	-1	3	0	1	1.000	-0	O-13(2-13-3)	-0.1
1961	StL-N	28	66	5	11	2	0	1	3	5	14	.167	.225	.242	468	22	-7	1	0	0	1.000	-3	O-25(6-20-4)/2-1	-1.1
1962	StL-N	32	35	11	11	0	0	0	3	4	2	.314	.385	.314	699	82	-1	2	0	0	1.000	-6	O-26(16-4-7)	-0.7
	Chi-N	83	238	29	67	5	2	1	15	30	31	.282	.369	.332	701	87	-3	9	2	1	.969	-1	O-59(1-41-18)	-0.5
	Yr	115	273	40	78	5	2	1	18	34	33	.286	.371	.330	701	85	-4	11	2	2	.973	-7	O-85(17-45-25)	-1.2
1963	Chi-N	84	227	27	55	4	1	1	10	13	42	.242	.295	.282	577	64	-10	6	3	0	.972	-4	O-57(0-55-3)	-1.8
1964	Chi-N	11	11	2	0	0	0	0	0	1	2	.000	.083	.000	83	-71	-2	0	0	0	1.000	1	/O-1(0-1-0)	-0.2
1965	Chi-N	131	425	60	96	20	4	6	34	36	84	.226	.301	.334	636	77	-13	14	8	0	.988	1	*O-115(3-111-1)	-1.5
1966	SF-N	72	102	9	19	4	0	1	7	9	18	.186	.259	.255	514	42	-8	1	1	-0	.968	-5	O-54(38-14-3)	-1.5
Total	8	456	1160	151	272	36	8	12	75	104	200	.234	.308	.310	618	69	-45	36	14	3	.982	-16	O-352(66-261-39)/2-1	-7.4
■ JESSE LANDRUM	Landrum, Jesse Glenn b: 7/31/12, Crockett, Tex. d: 6/27/83, Beaumont, Tex. BR/TR, 5'11.5", 175 lbs. Deb: 4/26/38																							
1938	Chi-A	4	6	0	0	0	0	0	1	0	2	.000	.000	.000	0	-98	-2	0	0	0	1.000	-1	/2-3	-0.2
■ TITO LANDRUM	Landrum, Terry Lee b: 10/25/54, Joplin, Mo. BR/TR, 5'11", 175 lbs. Deb: 7/23/80 Career OF: (199-LF 55-CF 276-RF)																							
1980	StL-N	35	77	6	19	2	2	0	7	6	17	.247	.310	.325	634	75	-3	3	2	-0	.976	-5	O-29(17-8-6)	-0.9
1981	StL-N	81	119	13	31	5	4	0	10	6	14	.261	.302	.370	671	87	-2	4	2	0	1.000	-13	O-67(43-6-24)	-1.8
1982	StL-N	79	72	12	20	3	0	2	14	8	18	.278	.358	.403	761	111	1	0	1	-0	1.000	5	O-56(24-6-29)	0.6
1983	StL-N	6	5	0	1	0	1	0	0	1	2	.200	.333	.600	933	154	0	1	0	0	1.000	-2	/O-5(4-0-1)	-0.1
	*Bal-A	26	42	8	13	2	0	1	4	1	11	.310	.326	.429	754	108	0	0	2	-1	1.000	-6	O-26(11-4-15)	-0.7
1984	StL-N	105	173	21	47	9	1	3	26	10	27	.272	.311	.387	699	98	-1	3	4	-1	.979	-21	O-88(55-20-25)	-2.6
1985	*StL-N	85	161	21	45	8	2	4	21	19	30	.280	.356	.429	784	119	4	1	4	-1	1.000	-11	O-73(10-0-67)	-1.0
1986	StL-N	96	205	24	43	7	1	2	17	20	41	.210	.283	.283	566	57	-12	3	1	0	.993	-4	O-78(9-4-70)	-1.9
1987	StL-N	30	50	5	10	1	0	0	6	7	14	.200	.298	.220	518	39	-4	1	1	-0	1.000	-2	O-23(2-7-17)/1-1	-0.7
	LA-N	51	67	8	16	3	0	1	4	3	16	.239	.282	.328	610	63	-4	1	1	-0	.971	-5	O-31(19-0-14)	-0.9
	Yr	81	117	13	26	4	0	1	10	10	30	.222	.289	.282	571	53	-8	2	2	-0	.987	-7	O-54(21-7-31)/1-1	-1.6
1988	Bal-A	13	24	2	3	0	1	0	2	4	6	.125	.250	.208	458	31	-2	0	0	0	1.000	-3	O-12(5-0-8)/D-1	-0.5
Total	9	607	995	120	248	40	12	13	111	85	196	.249	.312	.353	664	84	-22	17	18	-3	.992	-65	O-488R/D-1,1-1	-10.5
■ CHAPPY LANE	Lane, George M. b: Pittsburgh, Pa. BR, 165 lbs. Deb: 5/16/1882 Career OF: (5-LF 12-CF 5-RF)																							
1882	Pit-a	57	214	26	38	8	2	3		5		.178	.196	.276	472	60	-8				.974	5	1-43,O-13(0-12-1)/C-2	-0.6
1884	Tol-a	57	215	26	49	9	5	1		2		.228	.242	.330	572	82	-5				.948	4	1-46/O-9L,3-2,C-1	-0.5
Total	2	114	429	52	87	17	7	4		7		.203	.219	.303	522	72	-13				.961	9	/1-89,O-22C,C-3,3-2	-1.1
■ HUNTER LANE	Lane, James Hunter "Dodo" b: 7/20/1900, Pulaski, Tenn. d: 9/12/94, Memphis, Tenn. BR/TR, 5'11", 165 lbs. Deb: 5/13/24																							
1924	Bos-N	7	15	0	1	0	0	0	0	1	1	.067	.125	.067	192	-49	-3	0	0	0	.909	-1	/3-4,2-1	-0.4
■ MARVIN LANE	Lane, Marvin b: 1/18/50, Sandersville, Ga. BR/TR, 5'11", 180 lbs. Deb: 9/4/71																							
1971	Det-A	8	14	0	2	0	0	0	1	1	3	.143	.200	.143	343	-1	-2	0	0	0	1.000	-1	/O-6(3-0-3)	-0.3
1972	Det-A	8	6	2	0	0	0	0	0	0	2	.000	.000	.000	0	-97	-1	0	0	0	1.000	-1	/O-3(1-1-1)	-0.2
1973	Det-A	6	8	2	2	0	0	1	2	2	2	.250	.400	.625	1025	173	1	0	0	0	1.000	-1	/O-4(3-0-3)	0.0
1974	Det-A	50	103	16	24	4	1	2	9	19	24	.233	.352	.350	702	99	0	2	0	1	.986	-3	O-46(40-2-6)/D-1	-0.4
1976	Det-A	18	48	3	9	1	0	0	5	6	11	.188	.278	.208	486	42	-3	0	0	0	.960	-2	O-15(10-5-0)	-0.6
Total	5	90	179	23	37	5	1	3	17	28	42	.207	.314	.296	610	74	-5	2	0	0	.983	-8	/O-74(57-8-13),D-1	-1.5
■ DICK LANE	Lane, Richard Harrison b: 6/28/27, Highland Park, Mich. BR/TR, 5'11", 178 lbs. Deb: 6/20/49																							
1949	Chi-A	12	42	4	5	0	0	0	4	5	3	.119	.213	.119	332	-11	-7	0	1	-0	1.000	1	O-11(11-0-0)	-0.7
■ DON LANG	Lang, Donald Charles b: 3/15/15, Selma, Cal. BR/TR, 6', 175 lbs. Deb: 7/4/38																							
1938	Cin-N	21	50	5	13	3	1	1	11	2	7	.260	.288	.420	708	95	-1	0			.976	2	3-15/2-1,S-1	0.2
1948	StL-N	117	323	30	87	14	1	4	31	47	38	.269	.364	.356	720	90	-3	2			.964	9	3-95/2-2	0.6
Total	2	138	373	35	100	17	2	5	42	49	45	.268	.355	.365	719	91	-3	2			.966	10	3-110/2-3,S-1	0.8
■ BILL LANGE	Lange, William Alexander "Little Eva" b: 6/6/1871, San Francisco, Cal d: 7/23/50, San Francisco, Cal. BR/TR, 6'1.5", 190 lbs. Deb: 4/27/1893 Career OF: (15-LF 702-CF 2-RF)																							
1893	Chi-N	117	469	92	132	8	7	8	88	52	20	.281	.358	.380	738	98	-2	47			.888	2	2-57,O-40C/3-8,SC	0.1
1894	Chi-N	113	449	86	146	17	9	6	91	56	18	.325	.402	.443	846	98	-1	65			.912	5	*O-111C/S-2,3-1	-0.3
1895	Chi-N	123	478	120	186	27	16	10	98	55	24	.389	.456	.575	1032	155	38	67			.924	10	*O-123(0-123-0)	3.2
1896	Chi-N	122	469	114	153	21	16	4	92	65	24	.326	.414	.465	879	126	19	84			.932	10	*O-121(0-121-0)/C-1	1.7
1897	Chi-N	118	479	119	163	24	14	5	83	48		.340	.406	.480	886	129	19	**73**			.946	2	*O-118(0-118-0)	1.2
1898	Chi-N	113	442	79	141	16	11	5	69	36		.319	.377	.439	816	134	18	22			.970	10	*O-111(0-111-0)/1-2	2.0
1899	Chi-N	107	416	81	135	21	7	1	58	38		.325	.382	.416	798	122	13	41			.976	12	O-94(0-94-0),1-14	1.7
Total	7	813	3202	691	1056	134	80	39	579	350	86	.330	.400	.458	858	123	105	399			.942	50	O-718C/2-57,1-16,S3C	9.6
■ SAM LANGFORD	Langford, Elton b: 5/21/01, Briggs, Tex. d: 7/31/93, Plainview, Tex. BL/TR, 6', 180 lbs. Deb: 4/13/26																							
1926	Bos-A	1	1	1	0	0	0	0	0	0	0	.000	.000	.000	0	-99	-0	0	0	0	.000	0	H	0.0
1927	Cle-A	20	67	10	18	5	0	1	7	5	7	.269	.347	.388	735	90	-1	0	1	-0	1.000	-2	O-20(1-18-1)	-0.4

YEAR	TM/L	G	AB	R	H	2B	3B	HR	RBI	BB	SO	AVG	OBP	SLG	OPS	OPS+	BR+	SB	CS	SBR	FA	FR	G/POS	TPR
1928	Cle-A	110	427	50	118	17	8	4	50	21	35	.276	.312	.382	694	81	-13	3	7	-2	.972	-8	*O-107(32-76-0)	-2.8
Total	3	131	495	61	136	22	8	5	57	26	42	.275	.316	.382	698	81	-14	3	8	-2	.976	-11	O-127(33-94-1)	-3.2
■ BOB LANGSFORD Langsford, Robert William (b: Robert Hugo Lankswert) b: 8/5/1865, Louisville, Ky. d: 1/10/07, Louisville, Ky. BR/TR, Deb: 6/18/1899																								
1899	Lou-N	1	4	0	0	0	0	0	0	0		.000	.000	.000	0	-99	-1	0			1.000	-0	/S-1	-0.1
■ HAL LANIER Lanier, Harold Clifton b: 7/4/42, Denton, N.C. BR/TR (BB 1967 (part), 68-70), 6'2", 180 lbs. Deb: 6/18/64 FMC																								
1964	SF-N	98	383	40	105	16	3	2	28	5	44	.274	.284	.347	631	75	-13	2	1	0	.979	10	2-98/S-3	0.6
1965	SF-N	159	522	41	118	15	9	0	39	21	67	.226	.256	.289	545	52	-33	2	1	0	.976	-5	*2-158/S-1	-2.7
1966	SF-N	149	459	37	106	14	2	3	37	16	49	.231	.257	.290	547	50	-30	1	0	0	.991	28	*2-112,S-41	0.9
1967	SF-N	151	525	37	112	16	3	0	42	16	61	.213	.239	.255	495	42	-39	2	2	-0	.974	29	*S-137,2-34	0.2
1968	SF-N	151	486	37	100	14	1	0	27	12	57	.206	.225	.239	464	39	-36	2	2	-0	**.979**	14	*S-150	-1.1
1969	SF-N	150	495	37	113	9	1	0	35	25	68	.228	.265	.251	516	46	-35	0	1	-0	.969	**29**	*S-150	1.0
1970	SF-N	134	438	33	101	13	1	2	41	21	41	.231	.266	.279	544	47	-33	1	2	-0	.967	13	*S-130/2-4,1-2	-0.7
1971	*SF-N	109	206	21	48	8	0	1	13	15	26	.233	.285	.286	571	63	-10	0	0	0	.957	5	3-83,2-13/S-8,1-3	-0.4
1972	NY-A	60	103	5	22	3	0	0	6	2	13	.214	.236	.243	479	44	-7	1	2	-0	.973	9	3-47/S-9,2-3	0.2
1973	NY-A	35	86	9	18	3	0	0	5	3	10	.209	.244	.244	489	39	-7	0	0	0	.960	1	S-26/2-8,3-1	-0.4
Total	10	1196	3703	297	843	111	20	8	273	136	436	.228	.256	.275	531	50	-245	11	11	-1	.971	132	S-655,2-430,3-131,/1	-2.4
■ RIMP LANIER Lanier, Lorenzo b: 10/19/48, Tuskegee, Ala. BL/TR, 5'8", 150 lbs. Deb: 9/11/71																								
1971	Pit-N	6	4	0	0	0	0	0	0	0	1	.000	.200	.000	200	-39	-1	0	0	0	.000	0	H	-0.1
■ RAY LANKFORD Lankford, Raymond Lewis b: 6/5/67, Los Angeles, Cal. BL/TL, 5'11", 198 lbs. Deb: 8/21/90 Career OF: (221-LF 1115-CF 0-RF)																								
1990	StL-N	39	126	12	36	10	1	3	12	13	27	.286	.353	.452	805	119	3	8	2	1	.989	2	O-35(0-35-0)	0.6
1991	StL-N	151	566	83	142	23	**15**	9	69	41	114	.251	.303	.392	695	93	-6	44	20	3	.984	11	*O-149(0-149-0)	0.7
1992	StL-N	153	598	87	175	40	6	20	86	72	147	.293	.373	.480	853	144	35	42	24	1	.996	10	*O-153(0-153-0)	4.8
1993	StL-N	127	407	64	97	17	3	7	45	81	111	.238	.369	.346	715	95	0	14	14	-2	.978	3	*O-121(0-121-0)	0.3
1994	StL-N	109	416	89	111	25	5	19	57	58	113	.267	.362	.488	850	121	13	11	10	-1	.978	3	*O-104(0-104-0)	1.6
1995	StL-N	132	483	81	134	35	2	25	82	63	110	.277	.363	.513	877	128	19	24	8	2	.990	7	*O-129(0-129-0)	3.0
1996	*StL-N	149	545	100	150	36	8	21	86	79	133	.275	.370	.486	856	125	20	35	7	5	**.997**	15	*O-144(0-144-0)	4.0
1997	StL-N★	133	465	94	137	36	3	31	98	95	125	.295	.414	.585	999	160	43	21	11	1	.971	6	*O-131(0-131-0)	4.9
1998	StL-N	154	533	94	156	37	1	31	105	86	151	.293	.394	.540	934	144	35	26	5	4	.986	4	*O-145(0-145-0)/D-1	4.4
1999	StL-N	122	422	77	129	32	1	15	63	49	110	.306	.382	.493	875	119	12	14	4	2	.987	8	*O-106(105-2-0)/D-1	1.8
2000	*StL-N	128	392	73	99	16	3	26	65	70	148	.253	.371	.508	879	119	11	5	6	-1	.973	-2	*O-117(116-2-0)/D-1	0.5
Total	11	1397	4953	854	1366	307	48	207	768	707	1289	.276	.369	.483	852	125	186	244	111	15	.985	68	*O-1334C/D-3	26.6
■ RED LANNING Lanning, Lester Alfred b: 5/13/1895, Harvard, Ill. d: 6/13/62, Bristol, Conn. BL/TL, 5'9", 165 lbs. Deb: 6/20/16																								
1916	Phi-A	19	33	5	6	2	0	0	1	10	9	.182	.372	.242	615	89	0	0			.909	-4	/O-9(7-0-6),P-6	-0.4
■ CARNEY LANSFORD Lansford, Carney Ray b: 2/7/57, San Jose, Cal. BR/TR, 6'2", 195 lbs. Deb: 4/8/78 F																								
1978	Cal-A	121	453	63	133	23	2	8	52	31	67	.294	.344	.406	750	115	8	20	9	1	.942	-26	*3-117/S-2,D-1	-1.9
1979	*Cal-A	157	654	114	188	30	5	19	79	39	115	.287	.330	.436	766	108	6	20	8	2	**.983**	-24	*3-157	-1.9
1980	Cal-A	151	602	87	157	27	3	15	80	50	93	.261	.317	.390	708	95	-5	14	5	1	.955	-24	*3-150	-3.0
1981	Bos-A	102	399	61	134	23	3	4	52	34	28	**.336**	.391	.439	829	131	16	15	10	-0	.951	-0	3-86,D-16	1.5
1982	Bos-A	128	482	65	145	28	4	11	63	46	48	.301	.364	.444	808	114	10	9	4	1	.968	-13	*3-114,D-13	-0.5
1983	Oak-A	80	299	43	92	16	2	10	45	22	33	.308	.361	.475	836	136	14	3	8	-2	.957	-5	3-78/S-1	0.6
1984	Oak-A	151	597	70	179	31	5	14	74	40	62	.300	.347	.439	786	124	18	9	3	1	.957	-8	*3-151	0.9
1985	Oak-A	98	401	51	111	18	2	13	46	18	27	.277	.314	.429	743	109	4	2	3	-1	.976	-32	3-97	-3.0
1986	Oak-A	151	591	80	168	16	4	19	72	39	51	.284	.334	.421	755	112	9	16	7	1	.982	-18	*3-100,1-60/2-1,D-3	-1.3
1987	Oak-A	151	554	89	160	27	4	19	76	60	44	.289	.368	.455	822	125	21	27	8	3	**.980**	-3	*3-142,1-17/D-4	1.7
1988	*Oak-A★	150	556	80	155	20	2	7	57	35	35	.279	.329	.360	689	96	-3	29	8	4	**.979**	-12	*3-143/1-9,2-1,D-1	-1.2
1989	*Oak-A	148	551	81	185	28	2	2	52	51	25	.336	.401	.405	806	132	26	37	15	3	.957	-26	*3-136,1-15/D-3	0.2
1990	*Oak-A	134	507	58	136	15	1	3	50	45	50	.268	.335	.320	655	88	-7	16	14	-1	**.970**	-21	*3-126/1-5,D-5	-3.0
1991	Oak-A	5	16	0	1	0	0	0	1	0	2	.063	.063	.063	125	-69	-4	0	0	0	1.000	-1	/3-4,D-1	-0.5
1992	*Oak-A	135	496	65	130	30	1	7	75	43	39	.262	.330	.369	699	101	0	7	2	1	.965	-23	*3-119,1-18/S-1,D-2	-2.3
Total	15	1862	7158	1007	2074	332	40	151	874	553	719	.290	.346	.411	757	112	114	224	104	13	.966	-235	*3-1720,1-124/DS2	-13.7
■ JODY LANSFORD Lansford, Joseph Dale b: 1/15/61, San Jose, Cal. BR/TR, 6'5", 225 lbs. Deb: 7/31/82 F																								
1982	SD-N	13	22	6	4	0	0	0	3	6	4	.182	.357	.182	539	58	-1	0	1	-0	.986	-1	/1-9	-0.2
1983	SD-N	12	8	1	2	0	0	1	2	0	3	.250	.250	.625	875	140	0	0	0	0	1.000	0	/1-8	0.0
Total	2	25	30	7	6	0	0	1	5	6	7	.200	.333	.300	633	82	-1	0	1	-0	.988	-1	/1-17	-0.2
■ MIKE LANSING Lansing, Michael Thomas b: 4/3/68, Rawlins, Wyo. BR/TR, 6', 180 lbs. Deb: 4/7/93																								
1993	Mon-N	141	491	64	141	29	1	3	45	46	56	.287	.354	.369	723	90	-6	23	5	3	.942	6	3-81,S-51,2-25	0.8
1994	Mon-N	106	394	44	105	21	2	5	35	30	37	.266	.329	.368	697	81	-11	12	8	-0	.983	1	2-82,3-27,S-12	-0.5
1995	Mon-N	127	467	47	119	30	2	10	62	28	65	.255	.301	.392	693	78	-15	27	4	5	.991	7	*2-127/S-2	0.2
1996	Mon-N	159	641	99	183	40	2	11	53	44	85	.285	.341	.406	747	94	-6	23	8	2	.985	-10	*2-159/S-2	-0.5
1997	Mon-N	144	572	86	161	45	2	20	70	45	92	.281	.339	.472	811	110	7	11	5	1	.987	-6	*2-144	0.9
1998	Col-N	153	584	73	161	39	2	12	66	39	88	.276	.326	.411	737	76	-19	10	3	1	.987	5	*2-153/3-1	-0.5
1999	Col-N	35	145	24	45	9	0	4	15	7	22	.310	.346	.455	802	79	-4	2	0	0	.990	7	2-35	0.4
2000	Col-N	90	365	62	94	14	6	11	47	31	49	.258	.316	.419	735	65	-19	8	2	1	.983	-12	2-88	-2.5
	Bos-A	49	139	10	27	4	0	0	13	7	26	.194	.233	.223	456	16	-18	0	0	0	1.000	3	2-49/3-1	-1.2
Total	8	1004	3798	509	1036	231	17	76	406	277	520	.273	.328	.403	731	83	-91	116	35	13	.987	1	2-862,3-110/S-67	-2.9
■ PETE LAPAN Lapan, Peter Nelson b: 6/25/1891, Easthampton, Mass d: 1/5/53, Norwalk, Cal. BR/TR, 5'7", 165 lbs. Deb: 9/16/22																								
1922	Was-A	11	34	7	11	1	0	1	6	3	4	.324	.378	.441	820	119	1	1	0	0	.958	-0	C-11	0.2
1923	Was-A	2	2	0	0	0	0	0	0	0	0	.000	.000	.000	0	-99	-1	0	0	0	.000	0	H	-0.1
Total	2	13	36	7	11	1	0	1	6	3	4	.306	.359	.417	776	107	0	1	0	0	.958	-0	/C-11	0.1
■ RALPH LaPOINTE LaPointe, Ralph Robert b: 1/8/22, Winooski, Vt. d: 9/13/67, Burlington, Vt. BR/TR, 5'11", 185 lbs. Deb: 4/15/47																								
1947	Phi-N	56	211	33	65	7	0	1	15	17	15	.308	.362	.355	718	95	-1	8			.956	-10	S-54	-0.8
1948	StL-N	87	222	27	50	3	0	0	15	18	19	.225	.283	.239	522	40	-18	1			.965	8	2-44,S-25/3-1	-0.7
Total	2	143	433	60	115	10	0	1	30	35	34	.266	.322	.296	618	66	-19	9			.955	-2	/S-79,2-44,3-1	-1.5
■ FRANK LaPORTE LaPorte, Frank Breyfogle "Pot" b: 2/6/1880, Uhrichsville, Ohio d: 9/25/39, Newcomerstown, O. BR/TR, 5'8", 175 lbs. Deb: 9/29/05 Career OF: (39-LF 16-CF 92-RF)																								
1905	NY-A	11	40	4	16	1	0	1	12	1		.400	.415	.500	915	170	3	1			.918	-3	2-11	0.0
1906	NY-A	123	454	60	120	23	9	2	54	22		.264	.300	.368	668	99	-2	10			.904	-6	*3-114/2-5,O-1(1-0-0)	-0.5
1907	NY-A	130	470	56	127	20	11	0	48	27		.270	.317	.360	676	107	3	10			.896	-11	3-64,O-63R/1-1	-1.0
1908	Bos-A	62	156	14	37	1	3	0	15	12		.237	.296	.282	578	86	-2	3			.950	10	2-27,3-12/O-5(0-2-3)	0.9
	NY-A	39	145	7	38	3	4	1	15	8		.262	.301	.359	659	113	2	3			.934	-3	2-26,O-11(3-0-8)	-0.2
	Yr	101	301	21	75	4	7	1	30	20		.249	.298	.319	617	98	-1	6			.942	6	2-53,O-16R,3-12	0.7
1909	NY-A	89	309	35	92	19	3	0	31	18		.298	.340	.379	719	126	8	5			.938	-15	2-83	-0.7
1910	NY-A	124	432	43	114	14	6	2	67	33		.264	.321	.338	658	100	-0	16			.959	-11	2-79,O-23L,3-15	-1.3
1911	StL-A	136	507	71	159	37	12	2	82	34		.314	.361	.446	807	130	18	4			.950	-6	*2-133/3-3	1.5
1912	StL-A	80	266	32	83	11	4	1	38	20		.312	.367	.395	762	122	8	7			.944	-3	2-39,O-32(0-0-32)	0.4
	Was-A	40	136	13	42	9	1	0	17	12		.309	.365	.390	755	115	3	3			.939	3	2-37	0.6
	Yr	120	402	45	125	20	5	1	55	32		.311	.366	.393	759	120	10	10			.941	0	2-76,O-32(0-0-32)	1.0
1913	Was-A	79	242	25	61	5	4	0	18	17	16	.252	.309	.306	615	78	-7	10			.952	3	3-46,2-13,O-12(4-0-8)	-0.4
1914	Ind-F	133	505	86	157	27	12	4	**107**	36	36	.311	.361	.436	797	105	-3	15			.956	6	*2-132	0.5
1915	New-F	148	550	55	139	28	10	2	56	48	33	.253	.314	.351	665	92	-16	14			.960	5	*2-146	-0.8
Total	11	1194	4212	501	1185	198	79	15	560	288	85	.281	.331	.377	708	107	14	101			.952	-31	2-731,3-254,O-147R,/1	-1.0

■ JACK LAPP
Lapp, John Walker b: 9/10/1884, Frazer, Pa. d: 2/6/20, Philadelphia, Pa. BL/TR, 5'8", 160 lbs. Deb: 9/11/08

YEAR	TM/L	G	AB	R	H	2B	3B	HR	RBI	BB	SO	AVG	OBP	SLG	OPS	OPS+	BR+	SB	CS	SBR	FA	FR	G/POS	TPR
1908	Phi-A	13	35	4	5	0	1	0	1	5		.143	.268	.200	468	49	-2	0			.947	-3	C-13	-0.4
1909	Phi-A	21	56	8	19	3	1	0	10	3		.339	.373	.429	801	150	3	1			.938	1	C-19	0.6
1910	*Phi-A	71	192	18	45	4	3	0	17	20		.234	.310	.286	596	88	-2	0			.980	6	C-63	1.1
1911	*Phi-A	68	167	35	59	10	3	1	26	24		.353	.435	.467	902	154	13	4			.972	-6	C-57/1-4	1.1
1912	Phi-A	91	281	26	82	15	6	1	35	19		.292	.337	.399	735	114	4	3			.958	-14	C-83	-0.3
1913	*Phi-A	82	238	23	54	4	4	1	20	37	26	.227	.336	.290	626	85	-3	1			.968	-14	C-78/1-1	-1.1
1914	*Phi-A	69	199	22	46	7	2	0	19	31	14	.231	.338	.286	624	91	-1	1	4	-1	.977	-7	C-67	-0.4
1915	Phi-A	112	312	26	85	16	5	2	31	30	29	.272	.340	.375	715	118	6	5	2	0	.967	-4	C-89,1-12	1.0
1916	Chi-A	40	101	6	21	0	1	0	7	8	10	.208	.266	.228	494	48	-6	1			.989	-0	C-34	-0.4
Total	9	567	1581	168	416	59	26	5	166	177	79	.263	.340	.343	683	105	12	16	6		.969	-40	C-503/1-17	1.2

■ NORM LARKER
Larker, Norman Howard John b: 12/27/30, Beaver Meadows, Pa. BL/TL, 6', 200 lbs. Deb: 4/15/58

YEAR	TM/L	G	AB	R	H	2B	3B	HR	RBI	BB	SO	AVG	OBP	SLG	OPS	OPS+	BR+	SB	CS	SBR	FA	FR	G/POS	TPR
1958	LA-N	99	253	32	70	16	5	4	29	29	21	.277	.358	.427	785	103	2	1	1	-0	.985	-2	O-43(41-0-2),1-35	-0.4
1959	*LA-N	108	311	37	90	14	1	8	49	26	25	.289	.348	.418	766	96	-1	0	1	-0	.990	4	1-55,O-30(22-0-8)	-0.3
1960	LA-N★	133	440	56	142	26	3	5	78	36	24	.323	.375	.430	805	112	8	1	0	0	.993	4	*1-119/O-2(2-0-0)	0.6
1961	LA-N	97	282	29	76	16	1	5	38	24	22	.270	.329	.387	716	82	-7	0	0	0	.995	2	1-86/O-1(0-0-1)	-1.0
1962	Hou-N	147	506	58	133	19	5	9	63	70	47	.263	.360	.374	734	105	6	1	1	-0	.991	6	*1-135/O-6(6-0-0)	0.3
1963	Mil-N	64	147	15	26	6	0	1	14	24	24	.177	.301	.238	539	58	-7	0	2	-1	.992	4	1-42	-0.6
	SF-N	19	14	0	1	0	0	0	0	2	2	.071	.188	.071	259	-22	-2	0	0	0	.929	-0	1-11	-0.3
	Yr	83	161	15	27	6	0	1	14	26	26	.168	.291	.224	515	51	-9	0	2	-1	.987	4	1-53	-0.9
Total	6	667	1953	227	538	97	15	32	271	211	165	.275	.351	.390	741	97	-2	3	5	-1	.991	17	1-483/O-82(71-0-11)	-1.7

■ LARKIN
Larkin Deb: 5/29/1884

YEAR	TM/L	G	AB	R	H	2B	3B	HR	RBI	BB	SO	AVG	OBP	SLG	OPS	OPS+	BR+	SB	CS	SBR	FA	FR	G/POS	TPR
1884	Was-U	17	70	11	17	0	0	0		4		.243	.284	.243	527	63	-5				.726	-4	3-17	-0.8

■ BARRY LARKIN
Larkin, Barry Louis b: 4/28/64, Cincinnati, Ohio BR/TR, 6', 190 lbs. Deb: 8/13/86 F

YEAR	TM/L	G	AB	R	H	2B	3B	HR	RBI	BB	SO	AVG	OBP	SLG	OPS	OPS+	BR+	SB	CS	SBR	FA	FR	G/POS	TPR
1986	Cin-N	41	159	27	45	4	3	3	19	9	21	.283	.321	.403	724	94	-1	8	0	2	.976	-0	S-36/2-3	0.4
1987	Cin-N	125	439	64	107	16	2	12	43	36	52	.244	.308	.371	680	76	-15	21	6	3	.965	-0	*S-119	-0.1
1988	Cin-N★	151	588	91	174	32	5	12	56	41	24	.296	.350	.429	779	118	13	40	7	6	.960	10	*S-148	4.3
1989	Cin-N☆	97	325	47	111	14	4	4	36	20	23	.342	.383	.446	829	132	13	10	5	0	.976	16	S-82	3.8
1990	*Cin-N★	158	614	85	185	25	6	7	67	49	49	.301	.360	.396	755	103	4	30	5	5	.977	20	*S-156	4.1
1991	Cin-N★	123	464	88	140	27	4	20	69	55	64	.302	.379	.506	886	141	26	24	6	3	.976	18	*S-119	5.7
1992	Cin-N	140	533	76	162	32	6	12	78	63	58	.304	.382	.454	836	132	24	15	4	2	.983	8	*S-140	4.7
1993	Cin-N★	100	384	57	121	20	3	8	51	51	33	.315	.397	.445	842	125	15	14	1	3	.965	-6	S-99	2.0
1994	Cin-N†	110	427	78	119	23	5	9	52	64	58	.279	.373	.419	792	107	6	26	2	5	.980	2	*S-110	2.2
1995	*Cin-N★	131	496	98	158	29	6	15	66	61	49	.319	.396	.492	888	133	25	51	5	**9**	.980	-10	*S-130	3.4
1996	Cin-N★	152	517	117	154	32	4	33	89	96	52	.298	.415	.567	981	155	44	36	10	4	.975	1	*S-151	5.9
1997	Cin-N†	73	224	34	71	17	3	4	20	47	24	.317	.442	.473	915	138	15	14	3	2	.980	-7	S-63/D-2	1.5
1998	Cin-N	145	538	93	166	34	10	17	72	79	69	.309	.399	.504	903	134	28	26	3	5	.979	-20	*S-145	2.4
1999	Cin-N★	161	583	108	171	30	4	12	75	93	57	.293	.392	.420	813	103	6	30	8	4	.978	-6	*S-161	1.5
2000	Cin-N★	102	396	71	124	26	5	11	41	48	31	.313	.389	.487	876	115	10	14	6	1	.973	-26	*S-102/D-1	-0.6
Total	15	1809	6687	1134	2008	361	70	179	834	812	664	.300	.380	.456	836	121	211	359	71	54	.975	1	*S-1761/D-3,2-3	41.2

■ ED LARKIN
Larkin, Edward Francis b: 7/1/1885, Wyalusing, Pa. d: 3/28/34, Wyalusing, Pa. BR/TR, 5'8", Deb: 10/2/09

YEAR	TM/L	G	AB	R	H	2B	3B	HR	RBI	BB	SO	AVG	OBP	SLG	OPS	OPS+	BR+	SB	CS	SBR	FA	FR	G/POS	TPR
1909	Phi-A	2	6	0	1	0	0	0	1	1		.167	.286	.167	452	42	-0	0			.769	-2	/C-2	-0.2

■ GENE LARKIN
Larkin, Eugene Thomas b: 10/24/62, Flushing, N.Y. BB/TR, 6'3", 205 lbs. Deb: 5/21/87 Career OF: (7-LF 0-CF 193-RF)

YEAR	TM/L	G	AB	R	H	2B	3B	HR	RBI	BB	SO	AVG	OBP	SLG	OPS	OPS+	BR+	SB	CS	SBR	FA	FR	G/POS	TPR
1987	*Min-A	85	233	23	62	11	2	4	28	25	31	.266	.342	.382	724	89	-3	1	4	-1	.989	-2	D-40,1-26	-0.9
1988	Min-A	149	505	56	135	30	2	8	70	68	55	.267	.371	.382	753	108	8	3	2	-0	.994	-5	D-86,1-60	-0.4
1989	Min-A	136	446	61	119	25	1	6	46	54	57	.267	.358	.368	725	98	1	5	2	0	.992	-7	1-67,D-41,O-32R	-1.3
1990	Min-A	119	401	46	108	26	4	5	42	42	55	.269	.346	.392	738	99	0	5	3	0	1.000	-2	O-47R,D-43,1-28	-0.7
1991	*Min-A	98	255	34	73	14	1	2	19	30	21	.286	.364	.373	736	99	1	2	3	-1	.968	-10	O-47R,1-39/2-1,3D	-1.4
1992	Min-A	115	337	38	83	18	1	6	42	28	43	.246	.312	.359	671	85	-7	7	2	1	.992	-6	1-55,O-43(0-0-43)/D-4	-1.8
1993	Min-A	56	144	17	38	7	1	1	19	21	16	.264	.365	.347	712	92	-1	0	1	-0	1.000	-8	O-28R,1-18/3-2,D-3	-1.1
Total	7	758	2321	275	618	131	12	32	266	268	278	.266	.352	.374	726	97	-2	23	17	-1	.992	-40	1-293,D-221,O/32	-7.6

■ TERRY LARKIN
Larkin, Frank S. d: 9/16/1894, Brooklyn, N.Y. BR/TR, Deb: 5/20/1876 Career OF: (3-LF 2-CF 1-RF)

YEAR	TM/L	G	AB	R	H	2B	3B	HR	RBI	BB	SO	AVG	OBP	SLG	OPS	OPS+	BR+	SB	CS	SBR	FA	FR	G/POS	TPR
1876	NY-N	1	4	0	0	0	0	0	0	0	0	.000	.000	.000	0	-99	-1				.500	-0	/P-1	0.0
1877	Har-N	58	228	28	52	6	5	1	18	5	23	.228	.245	.311	556	83	-3				.885	-1	*P-56/3-2,2-1	0.0
1878	Chi-N	58	226	33	65	9	4	0	32	**17**	17	.288	.337	.363	700	122	5				.858	-4	*P-56/O-1(1-0-0),3-1	0.1
1879	Chi-N	60	228	26	50	12	2	0	18	8	24	.219	.246	.289	535	71	-7				.918	-7	*P-58/O-3(2-1-0)	-0.1
1880	Tro-N	6	20	1	3	1	0	0	1	3	4	.150	.261	.200	461	56	-1				1.000	-0	/P-5,O-2(0-1-1),S-1	-0.1
1884	Ric-a	40	139	17	28	1	4	0		9		.201	.265	.266	531	75	-3				.907	0	2-40	-0.2
Total	6	223	845	105	198	29	15	1	69	42	68	.234	.273	.308	581	88	-10				.884	-12	P-176/2-41,O-6L,3S	-0.3

■ HENRY LARKIN
Larkin, Henry E. "Ted" b: 1/12/1860, Reading, Pa. d: 1/31/42, Reading, Pa. BR/TR, 5'10", 175 lbs. Deb: 5/1/1884 M Career OF: (308-LF 124-CF 20-RF)

YEAR	TM/L	G	AB	R	H	2B	3B	HR	RBI	BB	SO	AVG	OBP	SLG	OPS	OPS+	BR+	SB	CS	SBR	FA	FR	G/POS	TPR
1884	Phi-a	85	326	59	90	21	9	3	37	15		.276	.324	.423	747	133	11				.856	-7	*O-85(30-55-0)/2-2	0.1
1885	Phi-a	108	453	114	149	**37**	14	8	88	26		.329	.372	.525	897	171	34				.882	12	*O-108(48-61-0)	3.8
1886	Phi-a	139	565	133	180	**36**	16	2	74	59		.319	**.390**	.450	839	161	40	32			.866	5	*O-139(139-0-0)	3.6
1887	Phi-a	126	545	105	202	22	12	3	88	48		.371	.380	.421	800	123	16	37			.895	3	O-93L,1-23,2-10	1.2
1888	Phi-a	135	546	92	147	28	12	7	101	33		.269	.326	.403	729	134	20	20			.967	-8	*1-122,2-14	0.1
1889	Phi-a	133	516	105	164	23	12	3	74	83	41	.318	.428	.426	854	145	36	11			.973	-4	*1-131/3-1,2-1	1.6
1890	Cle-P	125	506	93	167	32	15	5	112	65	18	.330	.419	.482	901	153	42	5			.978	-8	*1-125/O-1(0-1-0),M	1.7
1891	Phi-a	133	526	94	147	27	14	10	93	66	56	.279	.376	.441	817	133	22	2			.974	-5	*1-111,O-23(5-0-18)	0.5
1892	Was-N	119	464	76	130	13	7	8	96	39	21	.280	.346	.390	736	126	14	21			.969	1	*1-117/O-2(0-0-2)	1.4
1893	Was-N	81	319	54	101	20	3	4	73	50	5	.317	.422	.436	857	132	17	1			.963	-9	1-81	0.6
Total	10	1184	4766	925	1477	259	114	53	836	484	141	.310	.380	.440	819	141	252	129			.971	-21	1-710,O-451L/2-27,3	14.6

■ STEPHEN LARKIN
Larkin, Stephen Karari b: 7/24/73, Cincinnati, Ohio BL/TL, 6', 190 lbs. Deb: 9/27/98 F

YEAR	TM/L	G	AB	R	H	2B	3B	HR	RBI	BB	SO	AVG	OBP	SLG	OPS	OPS+	BR+	SB	CS	SBR	FA	FR	G/POS	TPR
1998	Cin-N	1	3	0	1	0	0	0	0	0	1	.333	.333	.333	667	75	-0	0	0	0	1.000	-0	/1-1	0.0

■ BOB LARMORE
Larmore, Robert McKahan "Red" b: 12/6/1896, Anderson, Ind. d: 1/15/64, St.Louis, Mo. BR/TR, 5'10.5", 185 lbs. Deb: 5/14/18

YEAR	TM/L	G	AB	R	H	2B	3B	HR	RBI	BB	SO	AVG	OBP	SLG	OPS	OPS+	BR+	SB	CS	SBR	FA	FR	G/POS	TPR
1918	StL-N	4	7	0	2	0	0	0	1	0	2	.286	.286	.286	571	77	-0				.778	-1	/S-2	-0.1

■ GREG LaROCCA
LaRocca, Gregory Mark b: 11/10/72, Oswego, N.Y. BR/TR, 5'11", 185 lbs. Deb: 9/7/2000

YEAR	TM/L	G	AB	R	H	2B	3B	HR	RBI	BB	SO	AVG	OBP	SLG	OPS	OPS+	BR+	SB	CS	SBR	FA	FR	G/POS	TPR
2000	SD-N	13	27	1	6	2	0	0	2	1	4	.222	.250	.296	546	40	-3	0	0	0	1.000	-2	/3-8,S-4,2-2	-0.4

■ SAM LaROQUE
LaRoque, Samuel H. J. b: 2/26/1864, St.Mathias, Que., Canada TR, 5'11", 190 lbs. Deb: 7/30/1888 Career OF: (1-LF 0-CF 0-RF)

YEAR	TM/L	G	AB	R	H	2B	3B	HR	RBI	BB	SO	AVG	OBP	SLG	OPS	OPS+	BR+	SB	CS	SBR	FA	FR	G/POS	TPR
1888	Det-N	2	9	1	4	0	0	0	2	1	1	.444	.500	.444	944	203	1	0			.789	0	/2-2	0.1
1890	Pit-N	111	434	59	105	20	4	1	40	35	29	.242	.316	.313	629	95	-1	27			.925	-10	2-78,S-31/1-2,O-1L	-0.7
1891	Pit-N	1	4	0	0	0	0	0	0	0	1	.000	.000	.000	0	-99	-1	0			.714	0	/3-1	-0.1
	Lou-a	10	35	6	11	2	1	1	8	5	8	.314	.429	.514	943	172	3	1			.875	-3	2-10/1-1	0.0
Total	3	124	482	66	120	22	5	2	50	41	39	.249	.326	.328	654	101	2	28			.916	-13	/2-90,S-31,1-3,3O	-0.7

■ VIC LaROSE
LaRose, Victor Raymond b: 12/23/44, Los Angeles, Cal. BR/TR, 5'11", 180 lbs. Deb: 9/13/68

YEAR	TM/L	G	AB	R	H	2B	3B	HR	RBI	BB	SO	AVG	OBP	SLG	OPS	OPS+	BR+	SB	CS	SBR	FA	FR	G/POS	TPR
1968	Chi-N	4	2	0	0	0	0	0	0	0	1	.000	.333	.000	333	6	-0	0	0	0	1.000	1	/2-2,S-2	0.1

■ HARRY LaROSS
LaRoss, Harry Raymond "Spike" b: 1/2/1888, Easton, Pa. d: 3/22/54, Chicago, Ill. BR/TR, 5'11.5", 170 lbs. Deb: 6/24/14

YEAR	TM/L	G	AB	R	H	2B	3B	HR	RBI	BB	SO	AVG	OBP	SLG	OPS	OPS+	BR+	SB	CS	SBR	FA	FR	G/POS	TPR
1914	Cin-N	22	48	7	11	1	0	0	5	2	10	.229	.260	.250	510	50	-3	4			.739	-6	O-20(10-10-0)	-1.0

YEAR	TM/L	G	AB	R	H	2B	3B	HR	RBI	BB	SO	AVG	OBP	SLG	OPS	OPS+	BR+	SB	CS	SBR	FA	FR	G/POS	TPR
■ **SWEDE LARSEN**	Larsen, Erling Adeli b: 11/15/13, Jersey City, N.J. BR/TR, 5'11", 170 lbs. Deb: 6/17/36																							
1936	Bos-N	3	1	0	0	0	0	0	0	0	0	.000	.000	.000	0	-99	-0	0			1.000	-0	/2-2	-0.1
■ **JASON LaRUE**	LaRue, Michael Jason b: 3/19/74, Houston, Tex. BR/TR, 5'11", 200 lbs. Deb: 6/15/99																							
1999	Cin-N	36	90	12	19	7	0	3	10	11	32	.211	.311	.389	700	73	-4	4	1	1	.990	4	C-35	0.3
2000	Cin-N	31	98	12	23	3	0	5	12	5	19	.235	.299	.418	717	75	-4	0	0	0	.991	9	C-31	0.6
Total	2	67	188	24	42	10	0	8	22	16	51	.223	.305	.404	709	75	-8	4	1	1	.990	14	/C-66	0.9
■ **TONY La RUSSA**	La Russa, Anthony b: 10/4/44, Tampa, Fla. BR/TR, 6'1", 190 lbs. Deb: 5/10/63 MC																							
1963	KC-A	34	44	4	11	1	1	0	1	7	12	.250	.353	.318	671	85	-1	0	0	0	.957	2	S-14/2-3	0.2
1968	Oak-A	5	3	0	1	0	0	0	0	0	0	.333	.333	.333	667	108	0	0	0	0	.000	0	H	0.0
1969	Oak-A	8	8	0	0	0	0	0	0	0	1	.000	.000	.000	0	-99	-2	0	0	0	.000	0	H	-0.2
1970	Oak-A	52	106	6	21	4	1	0	6	15	19	.198	.303	.255	558	57	-6	0	0	0	.969	-1	2-44	-0.5
1971	Oak-A	23	8	3	0	0	0	0	0	0	4	.000	.000	.000	0	-99	-2	0	0	0	.833	4	/2-7,S-4,3-2	0.2
	Atl-N	9	7	1	2	0	0	0	0	1	1	.286	.375	.286	661	84	-0	0	0	0	.933	0	/2-9	0.1
1973	Chi-N	1	0	1	0	0	0	0	0	0	0	—	—	—	—	—	0	0	0	0	.000	0	R	0.0
Total	6	132	176	15	35	5	2	0	7	23	37	.199	.295	.250	545	54	-11	0	0	0	.963	6	/2-63,S-18,3-2	-0.2
■ **AL LARY**	Lary, Alfred Allen b: 9/26/28, Northport, Ala. BR/TR, 6'3", 185 lbs. Deb: 9/6/54 F																							
1954	Chi-N	2	2	0	1	0	0	0	0	0	1	.500	.500	.500	1000	160	0	0	0	0	1.000	0	/P-1	0.0
1955	Chi-N	4	0	1	0	0	0	0	0	0	0	—	—	—	—	—	0	0	0	0	.000	0	R	0.0
1962	Chi-N	23	6	1	1	0	0	0	0	2	1	.167	.375	.167	542	49	-0	0	0	0	.857	-0	P-15	0.0
Total	3	29	8	2	2	0	0	0	0	2	2	.250	.400	.250	650	75	-0	0	0	0	.889	-0	/P-16	0.0
■ **LYN LARY**	Lary, Lynford Hobart "Broadway" b: 1/28/06, Armona, Cal. d: 1/9/73, Downey, Cal. BR/TR, 6', 165 lbs. Deb: 5/11/29 Career OF: (2-LF 0-CF 0-RF)																							
1929	NY-A	80	236	48	73	9	2	5	26	24	15	.309	.380	.428	808	115	6	4	1	1	.943	5	3-55,S-14/2-2	1.4
1930	NY-A	117	464	93	134	20	8	3	52	45	40	.289	.357	.386	743	92	-4	14	2	**2**	.940	-8	*S-113	0.2
1931	NY-A	155	610	100	171	35	9	10	107	88	54	.280	.376	.416	793	115	15	13	10	-1	.946	9	*S-155	3.3
1932	NY-A	91	280	56	65	14	4	3	39	52	28	.232	.358	.343	701	87	-4	9	3	1	.941	2	S-80/1-5,2-2,3-2,O	0.4
1933	NY-A	52	127	25	28	3	3	0	13	28	17	.220	.361	.291	653	79	-2	2	1	0	.938	2	3-28,S-16/1-3,O-1L	0.1
1934	NY-A	1	0	0	0	0	0	0	0	1	0	—	1.000	—	1000	189	0	0	0	0	.800	-0	/1-1	0.0
	Bos-A	129	419	58	101	20	4	2	54	66	51	.241	.344	.322	667	68	-19	12	5	1	**.965**	-5	*S-129	-1.3
	Yr	130	419	58	101	20	4	2	54	67	51	.241	.346	.322	668	68	-19	12	5	1	.965	-5	*S-129/1-1	-1.3
1935	Was-A	39	103	8	20	4	0	0	7	12	10	.194	.278	.233	511	35	-10	3	0	1	.953	-4	S-30	-1.0
	StL-A	93	371	78	107	25	7	2	35	64	43	.288	.396	.410	806	104	4	25	4	4	.962	13	S-93	2.6
	Yr	132	474	86	127	29	7	2	42	76	53	.268	.371	.371	743	90	-5	28	4	**5**	.960	9	*S-123	1.6
1936	StL-A	155	619	112	179	30	6	2	52	117	54	.289	.404	.367	771	89	-6	**37**	9	**5**	.956	-4	*S-155	0.7
1937	Cle-A	156	644	110	187	46	7	8	77	88	64	.290	.378	.421	799	100	2	18	8	1	.963	6	*S-156	1.9
1938	Cle-A	141	568	94	152	36	4	3	51	88	65	.268	.366	.361	727	84	-12	23	6	**3**	.964	-0	*S-141	0.1
1939	Cle-A	3	2	0	0	0	0	0	0	0	1	.000	.000	.000	0	-99	-1	0	0	0	.000	-1	/S-2	-0.1
	Bro-N	29	31	7	5	1	1	0	1	12	6	.161	.409	.258	667	80	-0	1			.947	1	S-12/3-7	0.2
	StL-N	34	75	11	14	3	0	0	9	16	15	.187	.330	.227	556	49	-5	1			.961	-6	S-30/3-3	-0.9
	Yr	63	106	18	19	4	1	0	10	28	21	.179	.356	.236	591	59	-5	2			.958	-4	S-42,3-10	-0.7
1940	StL-A	27	54	5	3	1	1	0	3	4	7	.056	.136	.111	247	-35	-11	0	0	0	.952	1	S-12/2-1	-0.9
Total	12	1302	4603	805	1239	247	56	38	526	705	470	.269	.369	.372	741	90	-46	162	49		.956	11	*S-1138/3-95,1-9,2O	6.7
■ **DON LASSETTER**	Lassetter, Donald O'Neal b: 3/27/33, Newnan, Ga. BR/TR, 6'3", 200 lbs. Deb: 9/21/57																							
1957	StL-N	4	13	2	2	0	1	0	0	1	3	.154	.214	.308	522	37	-1	0	0	0	1.000	1	/O-3(3-0-0)	-0.1
■ **CHRIS LATHAM**	Latham, Christopher Joseph b: 5/26/73, Coeur D'Alene, Idaho BB/TR, 6', 195 lbs. Deb: 4/12/97																							
1997	Min-A	15	22	4	4	1	0	0	1	0	8	.182	.182	.227	409	6	-3	0	0	0	.917	-3	O-10(0-8-3)	-0.6
1998	Min-A	34	94	14	15	1	0	1	5	13	36	.160	.262	.202	464	23	-11	4	2	0	.972	-1	O-32(13-15-5)	-1.1
1999	Min-A	14	22	1	2	0	0	0	3	0	13	.091	.091	.091	182	-52	-5	0	0	0	1.000	-4	O-14(6-5-4)	-0.9
Total	3	63	138	19	21	2	0	1	9	13	57	.152	.225	.188	414	9	-19	4	2	0	.969	-8	/O-56(19-28-12)	-2.6
■ **JUICE LATHAM**	Latham, George Warren "Jumbo" b: 9/6/1852, Utica, N.Y. d: 5/26/14, Utica, N.Y. BR/TR, 5'8", 164 lbs. Deb: 4/19/1875 M																							
1875	Bos-n	16	78	23	21	4	0	0	13	0	2	.269	.269	.321	590	100	-0	0	0	0	.927	0	1-16	0.0
	NH-n	20	76	6	15	1	0	0	5	0	4	.197	.197	.211	408	48	-3	6	0	1	.954	3	1-14/S-4,3-3,M	0.1
	Yr	36	154	29	36	5	0	0	18	0	6	.234	.234	.266	500	78	-3	6	0	1	.941	3	1-30/S-4,3-3	0.1
1877	Lou-N	59	278	42	81	10	6	0	22	5	6	.291	.304	.371	674	94	-3				.950	2	*1-59	-0.4
1882	Phi-a	74	323	47	92	10	2	0	38	10		.285	.306	.328	634	102	-1				**.972**	-0	*1-74,M	-0.7
1883	Lou-a	88	368	60	92	7	6	0		12		.250	.274	.302	575	92	-2				.956	-3	*1-67,2-14/S-9	-0.9
1884	Lou-a	77	308	31	52	3	3	0	23	8		.169	.197	.198	396	31	-22				.961	3	*1-76/3-1	-2.5
Total	4	298	1277	180	317	30	17	0	83	35	6	.248	.270	.298	568	82	-28				.960	1	1-276/2-14,S-9,3-1	-4.5
■ **ARLIE LATHAM**	Latham, Walter Arlington "The Freshest Man On Earth" b: 3/15/1860, W.Lebanon, N.H. d: 11/29/52, Garden City, N.Y. BR/TR, 5'8", 150 lbs. Deb: 7/5/1880 MUC Career OF: (2-LF 0-CF 11-RF)																							
1880	Buf-N	22	79	9	10	3	1	0	3	1	8	.127	.138	.190	327	10	-7				.887	-2	S-12,O-10(0-0-10)/C-1	-0.8
1883	StL-a	98	406	86	96	12	7	0		18		.236	.269	.300	569	79	-10				.866	22	*3-98/C-1	1.2
1884	StL-a	110	474	115	130	17	12	1		18		.274	.309	.367	676	116	7				.864	**40**	*3-110/C-1	4.3
1885	*StL-a	110	485	84	100	15	3	1	35	18		.206	.242	.256	498	55	-25				.875	1	*3-109/C-2	-2.1
1886	*StL-a	134	578	**152**	174	23	8	1	47	55		.301	.368	.374	741	127	17	60			.827	0	*3-133/2-1	1.8
1887	*StL-a	136	672	163	243	35	10	2	83	45		.362	.366	.413	779	106	2	129			.877	2	*3-132/2-5,C-2	0.5
1888	*StL-a	133	570	119	151	19	5	2	31	43		.265	.325	.326	652	98	-3	**109**			.882	3	*3-133/S-1	0.2
1889	StL-a	118	512	110	126	13	3	4	49	42	30	.246	.317	.307	623	69	-23	69			.883	9	*3-116/2-3	-1.0
1890	Chi-P	52	214	47	49	7	2	1	20	22	22	.229	.310	.294	604	59	-13	32			.880	3	3-52	-0.7
	Cin-N	41	164	35	41	6	2	0	15	23	18	.250	.346	.311	657	92	-1	20			.853	5	3-41/O-1(0-0-1)	0.4
1891	Cin-N	135	533	119	145	20	10	7	53	74	35	.272	.372	.386	759	120	15	87			.879	20	*3-135/C-1	3.4
1892	Cin-N	152	622	111	148	20	4	0	44	60	55	.238	.310	.283	593	81	-13	66			.883	-5	*3-142/2-9,O-1(1-0-0)	-1.4
1893	Cin-N	127	531	101	150	18	6	2	49	62	20	.282	.368	.350	718	89	-7	57			.892	-11	*3-127	-1.4
1894	Cin-N	131	534	132	167	23	6	4	60	61	24	.313	.392	.401	793	88	-10	62			.861	-10	*3-129/2-2	-1.3
1895	Cin-N	112	460	93	143	14	6	2	69	42	25	.311	.375	.380	755	91	-6	48			.861	-16	*3-108/1-3,2-1	-1.6
1896	StL-N	8	35	3	7	0	0	0	5	4	3	.200	.282	.200	482	29	-3	2			.744	-1	/3-8,M	-0.4
1899	Was-N	6	6	1	1	0	0	0	0	1		.167	.286	.167	452	26	-1	0			1.000	-0	/O-1(1-0-0),2-1	-0.1
1909	NY-N	4	2	1	0	0	0	0	0	0		.000	.000	.000	0	-99	-0	1			1.000	1	/2-2	0.0
Total	17	1629	6877	1481	1881	245	85	27	563	589	240	.274	.334	.341	676	91	-81	742			.870	61	*3-1573/2-24,OSC1	1.0
■ **CHICK LATHERS**	Lathers, Charles Ten Eyck b: 10/22/1888, Detroit, Mich. d: 7/26/71, Petoskey, Mich. BL/TR, 6', 180 lbs. Deb: 5/1/10																							
1910	Det-A	41	82	4	19	2	0	0	3	8		.232	.300	.256	556	70	-3	0			.926	5	3-14/2-7,S-4	0.2
1911	Det-A	29	45	5	10	1	0	0	4	5		.222	.314	.244	558	54	-3	0			.867	-3	/2-9,3-8,S-4,1-3	-0.5
Total	2	70	127	9	29	3	0	0	7	13		.228	.305	.252	557	64	-5	0			.933	2	/3-22,2-16,S-8,1-3	-0.3
■ **TACKS LATIMER**	Latimer, Clifford Wesley b: 11/30/1877, Loveland, Ohio d: 4/24/36, Loveland, Ohio BR/TR, 6', 160 lbs. Deb: 10/1/1898																							
1898	NY-N	5	17	1	5	1	0	0	1	0		.294	.294	.353	647	88	-0	0			.889	-1	/C-4,O-2(0-0-2)	-0.1
1899	Lou-N	9	29	3	8	1	0	0	4	2		.276	.323	.310	633	74	-1	1			.980	3	/C-8,1-1	0.2
1900	Pit-N	4	12	1	4	1	0	0	2	0		.333	.333	.417	750	106	0	0			.947	0	/C-4	0.0
1901	Bal-A	1	4	0	1	0	0	0	0	0		.250	.250	.250	500	37	-0	0			1.000	-0	/C-1	-0.1
1902	Bro-N	8	24	0	1	0	0	0	0	0		.042	.042	.042	83	-74	-5	0			.947	-0	/C-8	-0.5
Total	5	27	86	5	19	3	0	0	7	2		.221	.239	.256	494	41	-6	1			.949	2	/C-25,O-2(0-0-2),1-1	-0.5
■ **CHARLIE LAU**	Lau, Charles Richard b: 4/12/33, Romulus, Mich. d: 3/18/84, Key Colony Beach, Fla. BL/TR, 6', 190 lbs. Deb: 9/12/56 C																							
1956	Det-A	3	9	1	2	0	0	0	0	0	1	.222	.222	.222	444	18	-1	0	0	0	1.000	1	/C-3	0.0

YEAR	TM/L	G	AB	R	H	2B	3B	HR	RBI	BB	SO	AVG	OBP	SLG	OPS	OPS+	BR+	SB	CS	SBR	FA	FR	G/POS	TPR
1958	Det-A	30	68	8	10	1	2	0	6	12	15	.147	.293	.221	513	41	-5	0	0	0	.985	1	C-27	-0.4
1959	Det-A	2	6	0	1	0	0	0	0	0	2	.167	.167	.167	333	-8	-1	0	0	0	1.000	1	/C-2	0.0
1960	Mil-N	21	53	4	10	2	0	0	2	6	10	.189	.271	.226	498	41	-4	0	0	0	1.000	5	C-16	0.1
1961	Mil-N	28	82	3	17	5	0	0	5	14	11	.207	.330	.268	598	65	-4	1	1	-0	.968	-3	C-25	-0.5
	Bal-A	17	47	3	8	0	0	1	4	1	3	.170	.188	.234	422	12	-6	0	0	0	.990	5	C-17	-0.1
1962	Bal-A	81	197	21	58	11	2	6	37	7	11	.294	.322	.462	784	115	3	1	0	0	.996	-5	C-56	0.0
1963	Bal-A	29	48	4	9	2	0	0	6	1	5	.188	.204	.229	433	22	-5	0	0	0	.964	1	/C-8	-0.4
	KC-A	62	187	15	55	11	0	3	26	14	17	.294	.343	.401	744	102	1	1	0	0	.982	-10	C-50	-0.7
	Yr	91	235	19	64	13	0	3	32	15	22	.272	.316	.366	682	88	-4	1	0	0	.979	-9	C-58	-1.1
1964	KC-A	43	118	11	32	7	1	2	9	10	18	.271	.328	.398	726	98	-0	0	0	0	.990	-6	C-35	-0.5
	Bal-A	62	158	16	41	15	1	1	14	17	27	.259	.335	.386	721	100	-0	0	0	0	.992	-3	C-47	-0.1
	Yr	105	276	27	73	22	2	3	23	27	45	.264	.332	.391	724	99	-0	0	0	0	.991	-9	C-82	-0.6
1965	Bal-A	68	132	15	39	5	2	2	18	17	18	.295	.376	.409	785	120	4	0	0	0	.989	-6	C-35	0.0
1966	Bal-A	18	12	1	6	2	1	0	5	4	1	.500	.625	.833	1458	320	4	0	0	0	.000	0	H	0.4
1967	Bal-A	11	8	0	1	1	0	0	3	2	2	.125	.300	.250	550	65	-0	0	0	0	.000	0	H	0.0
	Atl-N	52	45	3	9	1	0	1	5	4	9	.200	.265	.289	554	59	-2	0	0	0	.000	0	H	-0.3
Total	11	527	1170	105	298	63	9	16	140	109	150	.255	.321	.365	686	89	-17	3	1	0	.988	-21	C-321	-2.5
■ BILLY LAUDER	Lauder, William b: 2/23/1874, New York, N.Y. d: 5/20/33, Norwalk, Conn. BR/TR, 5'10", 160 lbs. Deb: 6/25/1898 C																							
1898	Phi-N	97	361	42	95	14	7	2	67	19		.263	.300	.357	657	92	-5	6			.866	-17	3-97	-1.9
1899	Phi-N	151	583	74	156	17	6	3	90	34		.268	.310	.333	643	79	-17	15			.893	-14	*3-151	-2.6
1901	Phi-A	2	8	1	1	0	0	0	0	0		.125	.125	.125	250	-29	-1	0			.833	1	/3-2	-0.1
1902	NY-N	127	490	42	115	20	1	0	43	10		.235	.250	.280	530	64	-22	19			.908	4	*3-123/O-4(2-0-2)	-1.6
1903	NY-N	108	395	52	111	13	0	0	53	14		.281	.307	.314	621	74	-14	19			.908	-7	*3-108	-1.7
Total	5	485	1837	211	478	64	14	5	253	77		.260	.291	.318	610	76	-60	59			.894	-32	3-481/O-4(2-0-2)	-7.9
■ TIM LAUDNER	Laudner, Timothy Jon b: 6/7/58, Mason City, Iowa BR/TR, 6'3", 212 lbs. Deb: 8/28/81																							
1981	Min-A	14	43	4	7	2	0	2	5	3	17	.163	.234	.349	583	62	-2	0	0	0	1.000	-1	C-12/D-2	-0.3
1982	Min-A	93	306	37	78	19	1	7	33	34	74	.255	.329	.392	722	95	-2	0	2	-1	.976	-15	C-93	-1.3
1983	Min-A	62	168	20	31	9	0	6	18	15	49	.185	.251	.345	597	60	-10	0	0	0	.986	6	C-57/D-4	-0.2
1984	Min-A	87	262	31	54	16	1	10	35	18	78	.206	.260	.389	649	73	-10	0	0	0	.978	9	C-81/D-2	0.2
1985	Min-A	72	164	16	39	5	0	7	19	12	45	.238	.294	.396	690	82	-4	0	1	-0	.969	-4	C-68/1-1	-0.7
1986	Min-A	76	193	21	47	10	0	10	29	24	56	.244	.336	.451	787	109	2	1	0	0	.984	-15	C-68	-0.9
1987	*Min-A	113	288	30	55	7	1	16	43	23	80	.191	.253	.389	642	65	-16	1	0	0	.987	-8	*C-101/1-7,D-2	-1.9
1988	Min-A★	117	375	38	94	18	1	13	54	36	89	.251	.318	.408	726	99	-1	0	0	0	.992	0	*C-109/1-3,D-4	0.6
1989	Min-A	100	239	24	53	11	1	6	27	25	65	.222	.295	.351	647	76	-8	1	0	0	.991	0	C-68,D-19,1-11	-0.4
Total	9	734	2038	221	458	97	5	77	263	190	553	.225	.293	.391	684	83	-50	3	3	-0	.984	-27	C-657/D-33,1-22	-4.9
■ CHUCK LAUER	Lauer, John Charles b: 1865, Pittsburgh, Pa. TR, Deb: 7/17/1884 Career OF: (1-LF 2-CF 8-RF)																							
1884	Pit-a	13	44	5	5	0	0	0		0		.114	.114	.114	227	-26	-6				.938	-1	O-10(0-2-8)/P-3,1-1	-0.5
1889	Pit-N	4	16	2	3	0	0	0	1	0	5	.188	.188	.188	375	5	-2	0			.815	1	/C-3,O-1(1-0-0)	-0.1
1890	Chi-N	2	8	1	2	1	0	0	2	0	0	.250	.250	.375	625	78	-0	0			.833	0	/C-2	0.0
Total	3	19	68	8	10	1	0	0	3	0	5	.147	.147	.162	309	-5	-8	0			.944	-0	/O-11R,C-5,P-3,1-1	-0.6
■ BEN LAUGHLIN	Laughlin, Benjamin Deb: 4/28/1873																							
1873	Res-n	12	50	3	12	0	0	0	6	0	0	.240	.240	.240	480	47	-3	0	0	0	.725	-1	2-12	-0.3
■ BILL LAUTERBORN	Lauterborn, William Bernard b: 6/9/1879, Hornell, N.Y. d: 4/19/65, Andover, N.Y. BR/TR, 5'6", 140 lbs. Deb: 9/20/04 Career OF: (0-LF 2-CF 0-RF)																							
1904	Bos-N	20	69	7	19	2	0	0	2	1		.275	.286	.304	590	85	-1	1			.943	-3	2-20	-0.5
1905	Bos-N	67	200	11	37	1	1	0	9	12		.185	.238	.200	438	32	-17	1			.843	-7	3-29,2-23/S-3,O-2C	-2.4
Total	2	87	269	18	56	3	1	0	11	13		.208	.250	.227	477	45	-18	2			.929	-10	/2-43,3-29,S-3,O-2C	-2.9
■ COOKIE LAVAGETTO	Lavagetto, Harry Arthur b: 12/1/12, Oakland, Cal. d: 8/10/90, Orinda, Cal. BR/TR, 6', 170 lbs. Deb: 4/17/34 MC																							
1934	Pit-N	87	304	41	67	16	3	3	46	32	39	.220	.295	.322	617	64	-16	6			.961	-14	2-83	-2.4
1935	Pit-N	78	231	27	67	9	4	0	19	18	15	.290	.341	.364	705	87	-4	1			.951	-11	2-42,3-15	-1.2
1936	Pit-N	60	197	21	48	15	2	2	26	15	13	.244	.300	.371	671	78	-6	0			.951	-1	2-37,3-13/S-1	-0.5
1937	Bro-N	149	503	64	142	26	6	8	70	74	41	.282	.375	.406	781	110	9	13			.949	-7	*2-100,3-45	1.0
1938	Bro-N☆	137	487	68	133	34	6	6	79	68	31	.273	.364	.405	769	109	7	15			.929	-11	*3-132/2-4	0.1
1939	Bro-N☆	153	587	93	176	28	5	10	87	78	30	.300	.387	.416	802	112	12	14			.948	-5	*3-149	1.2
1940	Bro-N★	118	448	56	115	21	3	4	43	70	32	.257	.361	.344	705	90	-4	4			.932	-14	*3-116	-1.3
1941	*Bro-N★	132	441	75	122	24	7	1	78	80	21	.277	.388	.370	757	109	9	7			.938	-20	*3-120	-0.7
1946	Bro-N	88	242	36	57	9	1	3	27	38	17	.236	.339	.318	657	86	-3	3			.927	-5	3-67	-0.9
1947	*Bro-N	41	69	6	18	1	0	3	11	12	5	.261	.370	.406	776	102	0	0			.961	3	3-18/1-3	0.3
Total	10	1043	3509	487	945	183	37	40	486	485	244	.269	.360	.377	737	98	5	63			.936	-85	3-675,2-266/1-3,S-1	-4.4
■ MIKE LaVALLIERE	LaValliere, Michael Eugene b: 8/18/60, Charlotte, N.C. BL/TR (BB 1987 (2 GAMES)), 5'9", 190 lbs. Deb: 9/9/84																							
1984	Phi-N	6	7	0	0	0	0	0	0	2	2	.000	.222	.000	222	-32	-1	0	0	0	1.000	2	/C-6	0.1
1985	StL-N	12	34	2	5	1	0	0	6	7	3	.147	.293	.176	469	34	-3	0	0	0	1.000	-2	C-12	-0.4
1986	StL-N	110	303	18	71	10	2	3	30	36	37	.234	.318	.310	628	74	-10	0	1	-0	.988	2	*C-108	-0.4
1987	Pit-N	121	340	33	102	19	0	1	36	43	32	.300	.380	.365	745	98	1	0	0	0	.992	8	*C-112	1.3
1988	Pit-N	120	352	24	92	18	0	2	47	50	34	.261	.356	.330	686	99	2	3	2	-0	.987	-0	*C-114	0.8
1989	Pit-N	68	190	15	60	10	0	2	23	29	24	.316	.406	.400	806	136	10	0	2	-1	.991	-7	C-65	0.6
1990	*Pit-N	96	279	27	72	15	0	3	31	44	20	.258	.363	.344	707	99	1	0	3	-1	.990	2	C-95	0.8
1991	*Pit-N	108	336	25	97	11	2	3	41	33	27	.289	.356	.360	716	103	2	2	1	0	**.998**	2	*C-105	1.1
1992	*Pit-N	95	293	22	75	13	1	2	29	44	21	.256	.355	.328	683	95	-0	0	3	-1	.994	-1	C-92/3-1	0.3
1993	Pit-N	1	5	0	1	0	0	0	0	0	0	.200	.200	.200	400	7	-1	0	0	0	1.000	1	/C-1.	0.0
	*Chi-A	37	97	6	25	2	0	0	8	4	14	.258	.287	.278	565	54	-6	0	1	-0	1.000	4	C-37	-0.1
1994	Chi-A	59	139	6	39	4	0	1	24	20	15	.281	.375	.331	706	86	-2	0	2	-1	.991	4	C-57	0.4
1995	Chi-A	46	98	7	24	6	0	1	19	9	15	.245	.308	.337	645	71	-4	0	0	0	.996	6	C-46	0.3
Total	12	879	2473	185	663	109	5	18	294	321	244	.268	.354	.338	693	94	-11	5	15	-4	.992	20	C-850/3-1	4.8
■ DOC LAVAN	Lavan, John Leonard (b: John Leonard Laven) b: 10/28/1890, Grand Rapids, Mich d: 5/29/52, Detroit, Mich. BR/TR, 5'8.5", 151 lbs. Deb: 6/22/13 Career OF: (0-LF 1-CF 0-RF)																							
1913	StL-A	46	149	8	21	2	1	0	4	10	46	.141	.210	.168	378	11	-17	3			.899	-5	S-46	-2.0
	Phi-A	5	14	1	1	0	1	0	1	0	0	.071	.071	.214	286	-17	-2	0			1.000	0	/S-5	-0.2
	Yr	51	163	9	22	2	2	0	5	10	46	.135	.199	.172	371	9	-19	3			.906	-4	S-51	-2.2
1914	StL-A	75	239	21	63	7	4	1	21	17	39	.264	.318	.339	657	101	-0	6	12	-3	.916	-12	S-74	-1.1
1915	StL-A	157	514	44	112	17	7	1	48	42	83	.218	.281	.284	565	72	-19	13	19	-4	.913	5	*S-157	-0.7
1916	StL-A	110	343	32	81	13	1	0	19	32	38	.236	.305	.280	585	80	-8	7			.950	**34**	*S-106	3.5
1917	StL-A	118	355	19	85	8	5	0	30	19	34	.239	.284	.290	574	78	-10	5			.923	12	*S-110/2-7	1.0
1918	Was-A	117	464	44	129	17	2	0	45	14	21	.278	.302	.323	625	90	-8	12			.917	-10	*S-117/O-1(0-1-0)	-1.1
1919	StL-N	100	356	25	86	12	2	1	25	11	30	.242	.264	.295	559	72	-13	4			.929	9	S-99	0.3
1920	StL-N	142	516	52	149	21	10	1	63	19	38	.289	.318	.374	692	102	-0	11	14	-2	.942	16	*S-138	2.5
1921	StL-N	150	560	58	145	23	11	2	82	23	30	.259	.291	.350	641	70	-25	7	7	-1	.950	**19**	*S-150	0.9
1922	StL-N	89	264	24	60	8	1	0	27	13	10	.227	.271	.265	537	41	-23	3	1	0	.937	15	S-82/3-5	-0.1
1923	StL-N	50	111	10	22	6	0	1	12	9	7	.198	.264	.279	544	44	-9	0	3	-1	.924	1	S-40/3-4,1-3,2-1	-0.6
1924	StL-N	4	6	0	0	0	0	0	0	0	0	.000	.000	.000	0	-99	-2	0	0	0	1.000	2	/2-2,S-2	0.0
Total	12	1163	3891	338	954	134	45	7	377	209	376	.245	.288	.308	596	75	-136	71	56		.930	86	*S-1126/2-10,3-9,1O	2.4
■ ART LaVIGNE	LaVigne, Arthur David b: 1/26/1885, Worcester, Mass. d: 7/18/50, Worcester, Mass. BR/TR, 5'10", 162 lbs. Deb: 4/24/14																							
1914	Buf-F	51	90	10	14	2	0	0	4	7	25	.156	.216	.178	394	8	-13	0			.967	6	C-34/1-3	-0.5

YEAR	TM/L	G	AB	R	H	2B	3B	HR	RBI	BB	SO	AVG	OBP	SLG	OPS	OPS+	BR+	SB	CS	SBR	FA	FR	G/POS	TPR
■ **JOHNNY LAVIN**	Lavin, John b: Troy, N.Y. 5'11", 175 lbs. Deb: 9/10/1884																							
1884	StL-a	16	52	9	11	2	0	0		3		.212	.268	.250	518	68	-2				.750	-3	O-16(0-15-1)	-0.5
■ **RUDY LAW**	Law, Rudy Karl b: 10/7/56, Waco, Tex. BL/TL, 6'1", 165 lbs. Deb: 9/12/78 Career OF: (180-LF 484-CF 36-RF)																							
1978	LA-N	11	12	2	3	0	0	0	1	1	2	.250	.308	.250	558	58	-1	3	1	0	1.000	-2	/O-6(3-3-0)	-0.3
1980	LA-N	128	388	55	101	5	4	1	23	23	27	.260	.307	.302	608	72	-14	40	13	4	.988	-1	*O-106(5-102-0)	-1.3
1982	Chi-A	121	336	55	107	15	8	3	32	23	41	.318	.362	.438	800	118	8	36	10	4	.973	-5	O-94(4-90-0)/D-3	0.7
1983	*Chi-A	141	501	95	142	20	7	3	34	42	36	.283	.341	.369	711	92	-5	77	12	13	**.994**	-4	*O-132(0-132-0)/D-3	0.3
1984	Chi-A	136	487	68	122	14	7	6	37	39	42	.251	.310	.345	655	77	-15	29	17	0	.985	-2	*O-130(10-122-0)	-1.8
1985	Chi-A	125	390	62	101	21	6	4	36	27	40	.259	.312	.374	686	84	-9	29	6	4	.987	-5	*O-120(104-32-0)/D-3	-1.3
1986	KC-A	87	307	42	80	26	5	1	36	29	22	.261	.328	.388	716	92	-3	14	6	1	.987	-8	O-77(54-3-36)/D-2	-1.4
Total	7	749	2421	379	656	101	37	18	199	184	210	.271	.326	.366	691	88	-38	228	65	27	.986	-27	O-665C/D-11	-5.1
■ **VANCE LAW**	Law, Vance Aaron b: 10/1/56, Boise, Idaho BR/TR, 6'2", 190 lbs. Deb: 6/1/80 F Career OF: (6-LF 7-CF 2-RF)																							
1980	Pit-N	25	74	11	17	2	2	0	3	3	7	.230	.260	.311	571	58	-4	2	0	0	.964	-3	2-11/S-8,3-1	-0.6
1981	Pit-N	30	67	1	9	0	1	0	3	2	15	.134	.159	.164	324	-8	-9	1	1	-0	1.000	5	2-19/S-7,3-2	-0.4
1982	Chi-A	114	359	40	101	20	1	5	54	26	46	.281	.332	.384	716	96	-2	4	2	0	.953	-3	S-85,3-39,2-10,/O-1L	0.3
1983	*Chi-A	145	408	55	99	21	5	4	42	51	56	.243	.328	.348	676	83	-8	3	1	0	.966	5	*3-139/2-3,S-2,OD	-0.5
1984	Chi-A	151	481	60	121	18	2	17	59	41	75	.252	.312	.403	715	92	-6	4	1	1	.955	-12	*3-137,2-22/O-5C,S	-1.9
1985	Mon-N	147	519	75	138	30	6	10	52	86	96	.266	.372	.405	777	124	19	6	5	-0	.985	-1	*2-126,1-20,3-11,/O	2.5
1986	Mon-N	112	360	37	81	17	2	5	44	37	66	.225	.299	.325	624	73	-13	3	5	-1	.993	17	2-94,1-20,3-13,/PO	0.7
1987	Mon-N	133	436	52	119	27	1	12	56	51	62	.273	.349	.422	771	100	0	8	5	0	.980	-9	*2-106,3-22,1-17,/P	-0.4
1988	Chi-N★	151	556	73	163	29	2	11	78	55	79	.293	.360	.412	772	116	12	1	4	-1	.953	-12	*3-150/O-1(1-0-0)	0.0
1989	*Chi-N	130	408	38	96	22	3	7	42	38	73	.235	.300	.355	656	81	-10	2	2	-0	.949	-18	*3-119/O-1(1-0-0)	-3.1
1991	Oak-A	74	134	11	28	7	1	0	9	18	27	.209	.303	.276	579	65	-6	0	0	0	.951	-6	3-67/S-3,O-3L,1P	-1.2
Total	11	1212	3802	453	972	193	26	71	442	408	602	.256	.329	.376	705	94	-27	34	26	-2	.956	-37	3-700,2-391,S/1OPD	-4.6
■ **GARLAND LAWING**	Lawing, Garland Frederick "Knobby" b: 8/29/19, Gastonia, N.C. d: 9/27/96, Murrells Inlet, S.C. BR/TR, 6'1", 180 lbs. Deb: 5/29/46																							
1946	Cin-N	2	3	0	0	0	0	0	0	0	2	.000	.000	.000	0	-99	-1	0			.000	-1	/O-1(0-1-0)	-0.1
	NY-N	8	12	2	2	0	0	0	0	0	3	.167	.167	.167	333	-5	-2	0			1.000	-1	/O-4(3-0-1)	-0.3
	Yr	10	15	2	2	0	0	0	0	0	5	.133	.133	.133	267	-24	-2	0			1.000	-1	/O-5(3-1-1)	-0.4
■ **TOM LAWLESS**	Lawless, Thomas James b: 12/19/56, Erie, Pa. BR/TR, 5'11", 170 lbs. Deb: 7/15/82 Career OF: (14-LF 0-CF 12-RF)																							
1982	Cin-N	49	165	19	35	6	0	0	4	9	30	.212	.253	.248	501	40	-13	16	5	2	.978	7	2-47	-0.2
1984	Cin-N	43	80	10	20	2	0	1	2	8	12	.250	.318	.313	631	74	-3	6	3	0	1.000	-3	2-23/3-6	-0.5
	Mon-N	11	17	1	3	1	0	0	0	0	4	.176	.176	.235	412	15	-2	1	0	0	1.000	0	/2-9	-0.1
	Yr	54	97	11	23	3	0	1	2	8	16	.237	.295	.299	594	66	-4	7	3	0	1.000	-3	2-32/3-6	-0.6
1985	*StL-N	47	58	8	12	3	1	0	8	5	4	.207	.270	.293	563	58	-3	2	1	0	.971	9	3-13,2-11	0.6
1986	StL-N	46	39	5	11	1	0	0	3	2	8	.282	.317	.308	625	74	-1	8	1	1	.875	3	3-12/2-7,O-1(1-0-0)	0.3
1987	*StL-N	19	25	5	2	1	0	0	0	3	5	.080	.179	.120	299	-19	-4	2	0	0	1.000	-1	/2-7,3-3,O-1(0-0-1)	-0.5
1988	StL-N	54	65	9	10	2	1	1	3	7	9	.154	.236	.262	498	42	-5	6	0	1	1.000	2	3-24/O-6L,2-5,1-1	-0.2
1989	Tor-A	59	70	20	16	1	0	0	3	7	12	.229	.299	.243	542	55	-4	12	1	2	1.000	1	O-16R,3-12,D-12,/2C	-0.1
1990	Tor-A	15	12	1	1	0	0	0	1	0	1	.083	.083	.083	167	-52	-2	0	2	-1	.800	2	/3-4,O-2L,2-1,D-5	-0.1
Total	8	343	531	78	110	17	2	2	24	41	85	.207	.264	.258	522	46	-38	53	13	7	.988	20	2-117/3-74,O-26L,DC1	-0.8
■ **MIKE LAWLOR**	Lawlor, Michael H. b: 3/11/1854, Troy, N.Y. d: 8/3/18, Troy, N.Y. TR, 6', 180 lbs. Deb: 5/27/1880																							
1880	Tro-N	4	9	1	1	0	0	0	0	1	1	.111	.200	.111	311	8	-1				.867	1	/C-4	0.0
1884	Was-U	2	7	0	0	0	0	0		0		.000	.000	.000	0	-99	-2				1.000	1	/C-2	-0.1
Total	2	6	16	1	1	0	0	0	0	1	1	.063	.118	.063	180	-39	-3				.920	2	/C-6	-0.1
■ **JIM LAWRENCE**	Lawrence, James Ross b: 2/12/39, Hamilton, Ont., Can. BL/TR, 6'1", 185 lbs. Deb: 5/30/63																							
1963	Cle-A	2	0	0	0	0	0	0	0	0	0	—	—	—	—	—	0	0	0	0	.750	0	/C-2	0.0
■ **BILL LAWRENCE**	Lawrence, William Henry b: 3/11/06, San Mateo, Cal. d: 6/15/97, Redwood City, Cal. BR/TR, 6'4", 194 lbs. Deb: 4/13/32																							
1932	Det-A	25	46	10	10	1	0	0	3	5	5	.217	.294	.239	533	38	-4	0	2	-1	1.000	2	O-15(0-8-7)	-0.3
■ **OTIS LAWRY**	Lawry, Otis Carroll "Rabbit" b: 11/1/1893, Fairfield, Me. d: 10/23/65, China, Maine BL/TR, 5'8", 133 lbs. Deb: 6/28/16																							
1916	Phi-A	41	123	10	25	0	0	0	4	9	21	.203	.263	.203	466	42	-9	4			.905	-10	2-29/O-5(3-2-0)	-2.1
1917	Phi-A	30	55	7	9	1	0	0	1	2	9	.164	.193	.182	375	15	-6	1			.921	-3	2-17/O-1(1-0-0)	-1.0
Total	2	71	178	17	34	1	0	0	5	11	30	.191	.242	.197	439	34	-14	5			.911	-13	/2-46,O-6(4-2-0)	-3.1
■ **MARCUS LAWTON**	Lawton, Marcus Dwayne b: 8/18/65, Gulfport, Miss. BB/TR, 6'1", 160 lbs. Deb: 8/11/89 F																							
1989	NY-A	10	14	1	3	0	0	0	0	0	3	.214	.214	.214	429	21	-1	1	0	0	.818	-2	/O-8(7-0-1),D-1	-0.3
■ **MATT LAWTON**	Lawton, Matthew b: 11/3/71, Gulfport, Miss. BL/TR, 5'9", 180 lbs. Deb: 9/5/95 F Career OF: (149-LF 110-CF 420-RF)																							
1995	Min-A	21	60	11	19	4	1	1	12	7	11	.317	.414	.467	881	128	3	1	1	-0	.972	-2	O-19(1-12-8)/D-1	0.0
1996	Min-A	79	252	34	65	7	1	6	42	28	28	.258	.342	.365	707	78	-8	4	4	-1	.985	8	O-75(1-18-60)/D-1	-0.3
1997	Min-A	142	460	74	114	29	3	14	60	76	81	.248	.366	.415	782	102	3	7	4	0	.976	-1	*O-138(58-24-66)	-0.2
1998	Min-A	152	557	91	155	36	6	21	77	86	64	.278	.389	.478	867	122	20	16	8	1	.990	18	*O-151(12-47-100)	3.2
1999	Min-A	118	406	58	105	18	0	7	54	57	42	.259	.358	.355	713	80	-11	26	4	4	.982	-6	*O-109(10-6-103)/D-6	-1.7
2000	Min-A★	156	561	84	171	44	2	13	88	91	63	.305	.408	.460	868	113	14	23	7	3	.983	-3	*O-143(67-3-83)/D-9	0.8
Total	6	668	2296	352	629	138	13	62	333	345	289	.274	.379	.426	806	104	22	77	28	7	.983	14	O-635R/D-17	1.8
■ **GENE LAYDEN**	Layden, Eugene Francis b: 3/14/1894, Pittsburgh, Pa. d: 12/12/84, Pittsburgh, Pa. BL/TL, 5'10", 160 lbs. Deb: 7/29/15																							
1915	NY-A	3	7	2	2	0	0	0	0	0	1	.286	.286	.286	571	71	-0	0	1	-0	.750	-1	/O-2(0-2-0)	-0.2
■ **PETE LAYDON**	Laydon, Peter John b: 12/30/19, Dallas, Tex. d: 7/18/82, Edna, Tex. BR/TR, 5'11", 185 lbs. Deb: 4/28/48																							
1948	StL-A	41	104	11	26	2	1	0	4	6	10	.250	.297	.288	586	55	-7	4	2	0	.973	-1	O-30(1-24-5)	-0.8
■ **HERMAN LAYNE**	Layne, Herman b: 2/13/01, New Haven, W.Va. d: 8/27/73, Gallipolis, Ohio BR/TR, 5'11", 165 lbs. Deb: 4/16/27																							
1927	Pit-N	11	6	3	0	0	0	0	0	1	0	.000	.143	.000	143	-55	-1	0			.000	-1	/O-2(1-1-0)	-0.3
■ **HILLIS LAYNE**	Layne, Ivoria Hillis "Tony" b: 2/23/18, Whitwell, Tenn. BL/TR, 6', 170 lbs. Deb: 9/16/41																							
1941	Was-A	13	50	8	14	2	0	0	6	4	5	.280	.333	.320	653	77	-2	1	1	-0	.953	0	3-13	-0.1
1944	Was-A	33	87	6	17	2	0	0	8	6	10	.195	.263	.218	482	40	-7	2	0	0	.949	1	3-18/2-3	-0.5
1945	Was-A	61	147	23	44	5	4	1	14	10	7	.299	.352	.408	760	132	5	0	1	-0	.956	-5	3-33	0.1
Total	3	107	284	37	75	9	4	1	28	20	22	.264	.321	.335	656	92	-3	3	2	-0	.953	-3	/3-64,2-3	-0.5
■ **LES LAYTON**	Layton, Lester Lee b: 11/18/21, Nardin, Okla. BR/TR, 6', 165 lbs. Deb: 4/24/48																							
1948	NY-N	63	91	14	21	4	4	2	12	6	21	.231	.286	.429	714	90	-2	1			.951	-1	O-20(12-3-3)	-0.3
■ **JOHNNY LAZOR**	Lazor, John Paul b: 9/9/12, Taylor, Wash. BL/TR, 5'9.5", 180 lbs. Deb: 4/22/43																							
1943	Bos-A	83	208	21	47	10	2	0	13	21	25	.226	.297	.293	590	72	-7	5	6	-1	.979	-3	O-63(51-7-8)	-1.5
1944	Bos-A	16	24	0	2	1	0	0	0	1	0	.083	.120	.125	245	-30	-4	0	0	0	1.000	0	/O-6(1-0-5),C-1	-0.4
1945	Bos-A	101	335	35	104	19	2	5	45	18	17	.310	.346	.424	769	120	7	3	2	-0	.961	-8	O-81(12-0-73)	-0.7
1946	Bos-A	23	29	1	4	0	0	1	4	2	11	.138	.194	.241	435	20	-3	0	0	0	1.000	-2	/O-7(3-0-4)	-0.6
Total	4	223	596	57	157	30	4	6	62	42	53	.263	.312	.357	669	92	-7	8	8	-1	.971	-13	O-157(67-7-90)/C-1	-3.2
■ **TONY LAZZERI**	Lazzeri, Anthony Michael "Poosh 'Em Up Tony" b: 12/6/03, San Francisco, Cal. d: 8/6/46, San Francisco, Cal. BR/TR, 5'11.5", 170 lbs. Deb: 4/13/26 CH Career OF: (2-LF 0-CF 0-RF)																							
1926	*NY-A	155	589	79	162	28	14	18	114	54	96	.275	.338	.462	800	109	4	16	7	1	.961	-20	*2-149/S-5,3-1	-0.9
1927	*NY-A	153	570	92	176	29	8	18	102	69	82	.309	.383	.482	866	127	22	22	14	-0	.971	5	*2-113,S-38/3-9	3.2
1928	*NY-A	116	404	62	134	30	11	10	82	43	50	.332	.397	.535	932	148	27	15	5	2	.956	-11	*2-110	2.0

YEAR	TM/L	G	AB	R	H	2B	3B	HR	RBI	BB	SO	AVG	OBP	SLG	OPS	OPS+	BR+	SB	CS	SBR	FA	FR	G/POS	TPR
1929	NY-A	147	545	101	193	37	11	18	106	68	45	.354	.429	.561	991	164	53	9	10	-2	.969	-4	*2-147	4.8
1930	NY-A	143	571	109	173	34	15	9	121	60	62	.303	.372	.462	835	115	14	4	4	-1	.971	6	2-77,3-60/S-8,1O	2.3
1931	NY-A	135	484	67	129	27	7	8	83	79	80	.267	.371	.401	771	109	8	18	9	1	.958	-3	2-90,3-39	1.2
1932	*NY-A	142	510	79	153	28	16	15	113	82	64	.300	.399	.506	905	140	32	11	11	-1	.978	6	*2-134/3-5	4.1
1933	NY-A☆	139	523	94	154	22	12	18	104	73	62	.294	.383	.486	869	137	28	15	7	1	.968	-14	*2-138	2.3
1934	NY-A	123	438	59	117	24	6	14	67	71	64	.267	.369	.445	815	117	12	11	1	2	.976	-13	2-92,3-30	0.7
1935	NY-A	130	477	72	130	18	6	13	83	63	75	.273	.361	.417	778	107	5	11	5	1	.970	-21	*2-118/S-9	-0.7
1936	*NY-A	150	537	82	154	29	6	14	109	97	65	.287	.397	.441	838	110	11	8	5	0	.968	-32	*2-148/S-2	-1.0
1937	*NY-A	126	446	56	109	21	3	14	70	71	76	.244	.348	.399	747	87	-9	7	1	1	.966	-8	*2-125	-0.7
1938	*Chi-N	54	120	21	32	5	0	5	23	22	30	.267	.380	.433	814	120	4	0			.946	-8	S-25/3-7,2-4,O-1L	-0.2
1939	Bro-N	14	39	6	11	2	0	3	6	10	7	.282	.451	.564	1015	165	4	1			.914	0	2-11/3-2	0.5
	NY-N	13	44	7	13	0	0	1	8	7	6	.295	.392	.364	756	103	1	0			.889	-2	3-13	-0.1
	Yr	27	83	13	24	2	0	4	14	17	13	.289	.422	.458	879	133	5	1			.897	-2	3-15,2-11	0.4
Total	14	1740	6297	986	1840	334	115	178	1191	869	864	.292	.380	.467	846	122	215	148	79		.967	-119	*2-1456,3-166/SO1	17.5

■ FREDDY LEACH

Leach, Frederick b: 11/23/1897, Springfield, Mo. d: 12/10/81, Hagerman, Idaho BL/TR, 5'11", 183 lbs. Deb: 5/24/23 Career OF: (534-LF 325-CF 43-RF)

YEAR	TM/L	G	AB	R	H	2B	3B	HR	RBI	BB	SO	AVG	OBP	SLG	OPS	OPS+	BR+	SB	CS	SBR	FA	FR	G/POS	TPR
1923	Phi-N	52	104	5	27	4	0	1	16	3	14	.260	.280	.327	607	54	-7	1	2	-0	.950	-6	O-26(17-9-1)	-1.5
1924	Phi-N	8	28	6	13	2	1	2	7	2	1	.464	.500	.821	1321	221	5	0	0	0	1.000	-1	/O-7(7-0-0)	0.3
1925	Phi-N	65	292	47	91	15	4	5	28	5	21	.312	.323	.442	765	86	-7	1	2	-0	.952	-2	O-65(0-65-0)	-1.2
1926	Phi-N	129	492	73	162	29	7	11	71	16	33	.329	.352	.484	835	117	10	6			.979	1	*O-123(48-84-8)	0.4
1927	Phi-N	140	536	69	164	30	4	12	83	21	32	.306	.342	.444	786	108	4	2			.981	14	*O-140(18-123-5)	1.1
1928	Phi-N	145	588	83	179	36	11	13	96	30	30	.304	.342	.469	812	107	4	4			.978	11	*O-120(93-22-7),1-25	0.4
1929	NY-N	113	411	74	119	22	6	8	47	17	14	.290	.324	.431	755	85	-11	10			.974	-12	O-95(94-0-1)	-2.8
1930	NY-N	126	544	90	178	19	13	13	71	22	25	.327	.361	.482	843	104	2	3			.978	-3	*O-124(124-0-0)	-0.9
1931	NY-N	129	515	75	159	30	5	6	61	29	9	.309	.348	.421	769	109	5	4			.976	-4	*O-125(125-0-0)	-0.5
1932	Bos-N	84	223	21	55	9	2	1	29	18	10	.247	.306	.318	624	71	-9	1			.977	-2	O-50(8-22-21)	-1.3
Total	10	991	3733	543	1147	196	53	72	509	163	189	.307	.341	.446	787	101	-4	32	4		.975	-5	O-875L/1-25	-6.0

■ RICK LEACH

Leach, Richard Max b: 5/4/57, Ann Arbor, Mich. BL/TL, 6', 195 lbs. Deb: 4/30/81 Career OF: (116-LF 1-CF 177-RF)

YEAR	TM/L	G	AB	R	H	2B	3B	HR	RBI	BB	SO	AVG	OBP	SLG	OPS	OPS+	BR+	SB	CS	SBR	FA	FR	G/POS	TPR
1981	Det-A	54	83	9	16	3	1	1	11	16	15	.193	.323	.289	612	75	-2	0	1	-0	1.000	-1	1-32,O-15(0-0-15)/D-2	-0.6
1982	Det-A	82	218	23	52	7	2	3	12	21	29	.239	.305	.330	636	74	-8	4	0	1	.995	-1	1-56,O-14(4-0-10)/D-4	-1.1
1983	Det-A	99	242	22	60	17	0	3	26	19	21	.248	.305	.355	661	83	-6	2	2	-0	.994	3	1-73,O-13(2-0-11)/D-3	-0.7
1984	Tor-A	65	88	11	23	6	2	0	7	8	14	.261	.323	.375	698	89	-1	0	0	0	1.000	-1	O-23R,1-15/P-1,D-6	-0.3
1985	Tor-A	16	35	2	7	0	1	0	1	3	9	.200	.263	.257	520	42	-3	0	0	0	.987	-0	1-10/O-4(1-0-3)	-0.4
1986	Tor-A	110	246	35	76	14	1	5	39	13	24	.309	.344	.435	779	108	2	0	0	0	.978	-8	D-42,O-39R/1-7	-0.8
1987	Tor-A	98	195	26	55	13	1	3	25	25	25	.282	.372	.405	777	104	2	0	1	-0	.981	-6	O-43R,D-30/1-5	-0.7
1988	Tor-A	87	199	21	55	13	1	0	23	18	27	.276	.336	.352	688	93	-2	0	1	-0	1.000	-4	O-49R,D-25/1-4	-0.8
1989	Tex-A	110	239	32	65	14	1	1	23	32	33	.272	.360	.351	712	100	1	2	1	0	.951	-4	D-44,O-41(37-0-3)/1-4	-0.5
1990	SF-N	78	174	24	51	13	0	2	16	21	20	.293	.372	.402	775	117	5	0	2	-1	.989	-3	O-52(13-0-40)/1-7	-0.1
Total	10	799	1719	205	460	100	10	18	183	176	217	.268	.338	.369	707	94	-11	8	8	-1	.983	-26	O-293R,1-213,D-156,/P	-6.0

■ TOMMY LEACH

Leach, Thomas William b: 11/4/1877, French Creek, N.Y. d: 9/29/69, Haines City, Fla. BR/TR, 5'6.5", 150 lbs. Deb: 9/28/1898 Career OF: (74-LF 996-CF 13-RF)

YEAR	TM/L	G	AB	R	H	2B	3B	HR	RBI	BB	SO	AVG	OBP	SLG	OPS	OPS+	BR+	SB	CS	SBR	FA	FR	G/POS	TPR
1898	Lou-N	3	10	0	1	0	0	0	0	0		.100	.100	.100	200	-43	-2	0			.727	-0	/3-3,2-1	-0.2
1899	Lou-N	106	406	75	117	10	6	5	57	37		.288	.349	.379	728	100	-0	19			.908	1	3-80,S-25/2-2	0.3
1900	*Pit-N	51	160	20	34	1	2	1	16	21		.213	.304	.262	566	57	-9	8			.864	1	3-31/S-8,2-7,O-4L	-0.6
1901	Pit-N	98	374	64	114	12	13	2	44	20		.305	.347	.422	769	119	8	16			.903	9	3-92/S-4	1.9
1902	Pit-N	135	514	97	143	14	**22**	**6**	85	45		.278	.341	.426	767	132	18	25			.926	13	*3-134	3.6
1903	*Pit-N	127	507	97	151	16	17	7	87	40		.298	.352	.438	789	121	12	22			.879	7	*3-127	2.1
1904	Pit-N	146	579	92	149	15	12	2	56	45		.257	.316	.335	651	98	-1	23			.907	**36**	*3-146	4.0
1905	Pit-N	131	499	71	128	10	14	2	53	37		.257	.309	.345	654	92	-5	17			.988	11	O-71C,3-58/2-2,S-2	0.4
1906	Pit-N	133	476	66	136	10	7	1	39	33		.286	.333	.342	676	106	3	21			.929	2	3-65,O-60C/S-1	0.4
1907	Pit-N	149	547	102	166	19	12	4	43	40		.303	.352	.404	756	135	20	43			.980	11	*O-111C,3-33/S-6,2	3.0
1908	Pit-N	152	583	93	151	24	16	5	41	54		.259	.324	.381	705	125	15	24			.937	-4	*3-150/O-2(0-2-0)	1.8
1909	*Pit-N	151	587	**126**	153	29	8	6	43	66		.261	.337	.368	705	110	6	27			.969	3	*O-138(0-138-0),3-13	0.3
1910	Pit-N	135	529	83	143	24	5	4	52	38	62	.270	.319	.357	677	92	-7	18			.966	9	*O-131C/S-2,2-1	-0.5
1911	Pit-N	108	386	60	92	12	6	3	43	46	50	.238	.323	.324	646	78	-11	19			.987	2	O-89(1-89-0),S-13/3-1	-1.5
1912	Pit-N	28	97	24	29	4	2	0	19	12	9	.299	.376	.381	758	109	1	6			.986	4	O-24(0-24-0)	0.3
	Chi-N	82	265	50	64	10	3	2	32	55	20	.242	.378	.325	702	93	0	14			.975	5	O-73(0-73-0)/3-4	0.1
	Yr	110	362	74	93	14	5	2	51	67	29	.257	.377	.340	717	98	2	20			.978	9	O-97(0-97-0)/3-4	0.4
1913	Chi-N	131	456	**99**	131	23	10	6	32	77	44	.287	.391	.421	812	132	21	21			**.990**	3	*O-121(3-118-0)/3-2	1.6
1914	Chi-N	153	577	80	152	24	9	7	46	79	50	.263	.353	.373	726	116	13	16			.968	9	*O-136(0-136-0),3-16	1.4
1915	Cin-N	107	335	42	75	7	5	0	17	56	38	.224	.338	.275	613	85	-3	20	14	-1	.959	-4	O-96(17-81-0)	-1.5
1918	Pit-N	30	72	14	14	2	3	0	5	19	5	.194	.363	.306	668	101	1	2			.952	-2	O-23(18-0-4)/S-3	-0.2
Total	19	2156	7959	1355	2143	266	172	63	810	820	278	.269	.340	.370	710	108	80	361	14		.975	114	*O-1079C,3-955/S-64,2	16.7

■ DAN LEAHY

Leahy, Daniel C. b: 8/8/1870, Knoxville, Tenn. d: 12/30/03, Knoxville, Tenn. 5'9", 155 lbs. Deb: 9/2/1896

YEAR	TM/L	G	AB	R	H	2B	3B	HR	RBI	BB	SO	AVG	OBP	SLG	OPS	OPS+	BR+	SB	CS	SBR	FA	FR	G/POS	TPR
1896	Phi-N	2	6	0	2	1	0	0	1	1	2	.333	.429	.500	929	146	0	0			.857	1	/S-2	0.1

■ TOM LEAHY

Leahy, Thomas Joseph b: 6/2/1869, New Haven, Conn. d: 6/11/51, New Haven, Conn. BR/TR, 5'7.5", 168 lbs. Deb: 5/18/1897 Career OF: (11-LF 12-CF 4-RF)

YEAR	TM/L	G	AB	R	H	2B	3B	HR	RBI	BB	SO	AVG	OBP	SLG	OPS	OPS+	BR+	SB	CS	SBR	FA	FR	G/POS	TPR
1897	Pit-N	24	92	10	24	3	3	0	12	7		.261	.320	.359	679	82	-2	3			.935	-3	O-13(7-4-2)/C-6,3-6	-0.6
	Was-N	19	52	12	20	2	1	0	7	9		.385	.529	.462	991	164	6	6			.727	-4	O-10C/3-5,2-3,C-1	0.2
	Yr	43	144	22	44	5	4	0	19	16		.306	.405	.396	801	115	4	9			.881	-7	O-23C,3-11/C-7,2-3	-0.4
1898	Was-N	15	55	10	10	2	0	0	5	8		.182	.297	.218	515	48	-3	6			.913	0	3-12/2-3	-0.3
1901	Mil-A	33	99	18	24	6	2	0	10	11		.242	.348	.343	691	97	0	3			.941	-5	C-28/O-2(0-0-2),2-1	-0.2
	Phi-A	5	15	1	5	1	0	0	1	1		.333	.375	.400	775	110	0	0			1.000	-1	/O-2(2-0-0),C-1,S-1	0.0
	Yr	38	114	19	29	7	2	0	11	12		.254	.351	.351	702	99	0	3			.944	-6	C-29/O-4L,2-1,S-1	-0.2
1905	StL-N	35	97	3	22	1	3	0	7	8		.227	.286	.299	585	77	-3	0			.946	-9	C-29	-0.9
Total	4	131	410	54	105	15	9	0	42	44		.256	.348	.337	685	93	-2	18			.942	-21	/C-65,O-27C,3-23,2S	-1.8

■ FRED LEAR

Lear, Frederick Francis "King" b: 4/7/1894, New York, N.Y. d: 10/13/55, E.Orange, N.J. BR/TR, 6'0.5", 180 lbs. Deb: 6/7/15

YEAR	TM/L	G	AB	R	H	2B	3B	HR	RBI	BB	SO	AVG	OBP	SLG	OPS	OPS+	BR+	SB	CS	SBR	FA	FR	G/POS	TPR
1915	Phi-A	2	2	0	0	0	0	0	0	0	2	.000	.000	.000	0	-99	-0	0			.600	-0	/3-2	-0.1
1918	Chi-N	2	1	0	0	0	0	0	0	1	0	.000	.500	.000	500	56	0	0			.000	0	H	0.0
1919	Chi-N	40	76	8	17	3	1	1	11	8	11	.224	.306	.329	635	90	-1	2			.990	-2	/1-9,2-9,S-3	-0.3
1920	NY-N	31	87	12	22	0	1	1	7	8	15	.253	.323	.310	633	83	-2	0	2	-1	.951	-3	3-24/2-1	-0.5
Total	4	75	166	20	39	3	2	2	18	17	28	.235	.314	.313	627	84	-3	2	2		.924	-5	/3-26,2-10,1-9,S-3	-0.9

■ BILL LEARD

Leard, William Wallace "Wild Bill" b: 10/14/1885, Oneida, N.Y. d: 1/15/70, San Francisco, Cal BR/TR, 5'10", 155 lbs. Deb: 7/21/17

YEAR	TM/L	G	AB	R	H	2B	3B	HR	RBI	BB	SO	AVG	OBP	SLG	OPS	OPS+	BR+	SB	CS	SBR	FA	FR	G/POS	TPR
1917	Bro-N	3	3	0	0	0	0	0	0	0	1	.000	.000	.000	0	-97	-1	0			.000	0	/2-1	-0.1

■ JACK LEARY

Leary, John J. b: 1858, New Haven, Conn. TL, 5'11", 186 lbs. Deb: 8/21/1880 Career OF: (4-LF 15-CF 21-RF)

YEAR	TM/L	G	AB	R	H	2B	3B	HR	RBI	BB	SO	AVG	OBP	SLG	OPS	OPS+	BR+	SB	CS	SBR	FA	FR	G/POS	TPR
1880	Bos-N	1	3	1	0	0	0	0	0	1	0	.000	.250	.000	250	-7	-0				1.000	1	/O-1(0-0-1),P-1	0.0
1881	Det-N	3	11	2	3	1	1	0	4	1	1	.273	.333	.545	879	165	1				.833	0	/O-2(0-1-1),P-2	0.1
1882	Pit-a	60	257	32	75	7	3	1		5		.292	.305	.354	659	128	7				.759	-14	3-33,O-27R/P-3,12	-0.6
	Bal-a	4	18	3	4	1	0	0		0		.222	.222	.278	500	73	-0				.900	-0	/P-3,O-1(0-1-0)	0.0
	Yr	64	275	35	79	8	3	1		5		.287	.300	.349	649	124	7				.759	-14	3-33,O-28R/P-6,12	-0.6
1883	Lou-a	40	165	16	31	1	3	3		2		.188	.198	.285	482	58	-7				.816	-1	S-40	-0.6
	Bal-a	3	11	1	2	0	2	0		0		.182	.182	.545	727	122	0				.727	-1	/2-3	-0.1
	Yr	43	176	17	33	1	5	3		2		.188	.197	.301	498	62	-7				.816	-2	S-40/2-3	-0.7
1884	Alt-U	8	33	1	3	0	0	0		1		.091	.118	.091	209	-35	-6				.692	-2	/O-6(4-2-0),P-3,3-1	-0.6
	CP-U	10	40	0	7	1	0	0		0		.175	.175	.200	375	13	-5				.840	1	/2-4,3-3,O-3C,P-2	-0.3

YEAR	TM/L	G	AB	R	H	2B	3B	HR	RBI	BB	SO	AVG	OBP	SLG	OPS	OPS+	BR+	SB	CS	SBR	FA	FR	G/POS	TPR
	Yr	18	73	1	10	1	0	0		1		.137	.149	.151	299	-9	-12				.625	-1	/O-9C,P-5,3-4,2-4	-0.9
Total	5	129	538	56	125	11	9	4	4	10	1	.232	.246	.309	555	84	-11				.725	-17	/S-40,O-40R,3-37,P21	-2.1
■ JOHN LEARY Leary, John Louis "Jack" b: 5/2/1891, Waltham, Mass. d: 8/18/61, Waltham, Mass. BR/TR, 5'11.5", 180 lbs. Deb: 4/14/14																								
1914	StL-A	144	533	35	141	28	7	0	45	10	71	.265	.282	.343	625	91	-9	9	15	-3	.987	-4	*1-130,C-15	-2.1
1915	StL-A	75	227	19	55	10	0	0	15	5	36	.242	.268	.286	554	69	-10	2	4	-1	.985	-2	1-53,C-11	-1.4
Total	2	219	760	54	196	38	7	0	60	15	107	.258	.278	.326	604	85	-19	11	19	-4	.987	-7	1-183/C-26	-3.5
■ HAL LEATHERS Leathers, Harold Langford "Chuck" b: 12/2/1898, Selma, Cal. d: 4/12/77, Modesto, Cal. BL/TR, 5'8", 152 lbs. Deb: 9/13/20																								
1920	Chi-N	9	23	3	7	1	0	1	0	1	1	.304	.333	.478	812	129	1	1	0	0	.825	-1	/S-6,2-3	0.1
■ EMIL LEBER Leber, Emil Bohmiel b: 5/15/1881, Cleveland, Ohio d: 11/6/24, Cleveland, Ohio BR/TR, 5'11", 170 lbs. Deb: 9/2/05																								
1905	Cle-A	2	6	1	0	0	0	0	0	1		.000	.143	.000	143	-53	-1	0			1.000	-0	/3-2	-0.1
■ BEVO LeBOURVEAU LeBourveau, De Witt Wiley b: 8/24/1894, Dana, Cal. d: 12/10/47, Nevada City, Cal. BL/TR, 5'11", 175 lbs. Deb: 9/9/19																								
1919	Phi-N	17	63	4	17	0	0	0	0	10	8	.270	.370	.270	640	88	-0	2			1.000	2	O-15(15-0-2)	0.1
1920	Phi-N	84	261	29	67	7	2	3	12	11	36	.257	.295	.333	628	76	-8	9	6	-0	.949	3	O-72(51-17-4)	-1.0
1921	Phi-N	93	281	42	83	12	5	6	35	29	51	.295	.361	.438	799	102	1	4	5	-1	.911	-8	O-76(27-1-48)	-1.4
1922	Phi-N	74	167	24	45	8	3	2	20	24	29	.269	.368	.389	757	87	-3	0	3	-1	.920	-3	O-42(33-4-5)	-0.9
1929	Phi-A	12	16	1	5	0	1	0	2	5	1	.313	.476	.438	914	132	1	0	1	-0	1.000	0	/O-3(0-2-1)	0.1
Total	5	280	788	100	217	27	11	11	69	79	125	.275	.345	.379	725	91	-9	15	15		.935	-7	O-208(126-24-60)	-3.1
■ MATT LeCROY LeCroy, Matthew Hanks b: 12/13/75, Belton, S.C. BR/TR, 6'2", 225 lbs. Deb: 4/3/2000																								
2000	Min-A	56	167	18	29	10	0	5	17	17	38	.174	.258	.323	581	44	-15	0	0	0	.988	2	C-49/1-3,D-3	-0.9
■ RICKY LEDEE Ledee, Ricardo Alberto b: 11/22/73, Ponce, P.R. BL/TL, 6'2", 190 lbs. Deb: 6/14/98																								
1998	*NY-A	42	79	13	19	5	2	1	12	7	29	.241	.302	.392	695	82	-2	3	1	0	.981	-5	O-42(36-3-4)	-0.7
1999	*NY-A	88	250	45	69	13	5	9	40	28	73	.276	.349	.476	825	109	3	4	3	-0	.942	-2	O-77(69-6-3)/D-5	-0.1
2000	Cle-A	17	63	13	14	2	1	2	8	8	9	.222	.310	.381	691	72	-3	0	0	0	1.000	2	O-17(12-0-6)	-0.2
	NY-A	62	191	23	46	11	1	7	31	26	39	.241	.335	.419	754	91	-3	7	3	0	.979	-2	O-49(46-4-1),D-10	-0.5
	Tex-A	58	213	23	50	6	3	4	38	25	50	.235	.318	.347	665	66	-11	6	3	0	.977	-2	O-57(20-3-42)	-1.4
	Yr	137	467	59	110	19	5	13	77	59	98	.236	.324	.381	705	77	-17	13	6	1	.981	-1	*O-123(78-7-49),D-10	-2.1
Total	3	267	796	117	198	37	12	23	129	94	200	.249	.330	.412	742	87	-16	20	10	1	.968	-8	O-242(183-16-56)/D-15	-2.9
■ AARON LEDESMA Ledesma, Aaron David b: 6/3/71, Union City, Cal. BR/TR, 6'2", 200 lbs. Deb: 7/2/95																								
1995	NY-N	21	33	4	8	0	0	0	3	6	7	.242	.359	.242	601	64	-1	0	0	0	.875	-2	3-10/1-2,S-2	-0.3
1997	Bal-A	43	88	24	31	5	1	2	11	13	9	.352	.441	.500	941	149	7	1	0	0	.973	-1	2-22,3-11/1-5,S-4	0.7
1998	TB-A	95	299	30	97	16	3	0	29	9	51	.324	.346	.398	744	91	-4	9	7	-0	.971	9	S-58,2-19/3-7,1D	1.0
1999	TB-A	93	294	32	78	15	0	0	30	14	35	.265	.305	.316	622	58	-18	1	1	-0	.978	16	S-50,3-26,2-17,/1D	0.2
2000	Col-N	32	40	4	9	2	0	0	3	2	9	.225	.279	.275	554	32	-4	0	0	0	1.000	-1	/3-5,1-3	-0.4
Total	5	284	754	94	223	38	4	2	76	44	111	.296	.340	.365	704	80	-20	11	8	-0	.974	22	S-114/3-59,2-58,1D	1.2
■ MIKE LEDWITH Ledwith, Michael b: Brooklyn, N.Y. d: 1/2/29, Bronx, N.Y. Deb: 8/19/1874																								
1874	Atl-n	1	4	1	1	0	0	0	1	0	0	.250	.250	.250	500	69	-0	0	0	0	.600	-1	/C-1	-0.1
■ CARLOS LEE Lee, Carlos (Noriel) b: 6/20/76, Aguadulce, Panama BR/TR, 6'2", 200 lbs. Deb: 5/7/99 Career OF: (254-LF 0-CF 0-RF)																								
1999	Chi-A	127	492	66	144	32	2	16	84	13	72	.293	.316	.463	780	95	-5	4	2	0	.981	-1	*O-105L,D-16/1-5	-1.0
2000	*Chi-A	152	572	107	172	29	2	24	92	38	94	.301	.347	.484	832	106	4	13	4	1	.990	2	*O-149(149-0-0)/D-2	0.3
Total	2	279	1064	173	316	61	4	40	176	51	166	.297	.333	.475	808	101	-1	17	6	2	.986	1	O-254L/D-18,1-5	-0.7
■ CLIFF LEE Lee, Clifford Walker b: 8/4/1896, Lexington, Neb. d: 8/25/80, Denver, Colo. BR/TR, 6'1", 175 lbs. Deb: 5/15/19 Career OF: (148-LF 20-CF 136-RF)																								
1919	Pit-N	42	112	5	22	2	4	0	2	6	8	.196	.237	.286	523	55	-6	2			.962	-11	C-28/O-6(2-2-2)	-1.7
1920	Pit-N	37	76	9	18	2	2	0	8	4	14	.237	.275	.316	591	67	-3	0	1	-0	.974	0	C-19/O-2(1-1-0)	-0.2
1921	Phi-N	88	286	31	88	14	4	4	29	13	34	.308	.338	.427	764	94	-3	5	2	0	.987	-7	1-48,O-27(2-1-24)/C-2	-1.4
1922	Phi-N	122	422	65	136	29	6	17	77	32	43	.322	.371	.540	912	121	12	2	3	-1	.967	-5	O-89(83-0-6),1-18/3-1	-0.1
1923	Phi-N	107	355	54	114	20	4	11	47	20	39	.321	.357	.493	850	110	4	3	3	-0	.959	-11	O-83(54-0-32),1-16	-1.3
1924	Phi-N	21	56	4	14	3	2	1	7	2	5	.250	.276	.429	704	77	-2	0	1	-0	1.000	-1	O-13(0-0-13)/1-4	-0.4
	Cin-N	6	6	1	2	1	0	0	2	0	2	.333	.333	.500	833	122	0	0	0	0	.000	-0	/O-1(0-0-1)	0.0
	Yr	27	62	5	16	4	2	1	9	2	7	.258	.281	.435	717	82	-2	0	1	-0	1.000	-1	O-14(0-0-14)/1-4	-0.4
1925	Cle-A	77	230	43	74	15	6	4	42	21	33	.322	.378	.491	870	118	6	2	1	0	.951	-3	O-70(0-15-56)	-0.1
1926	Cle-A	21	40	4	7	1	0	1	2	6	8	.175	.283	.275	558	45	-3	0	0	0	1.000	0	/O-9(6-1-2),C-3	-0.4
Total	8	521	1583	216	475	87	28	38	216	104	186	.300	.344	.462	806	103	4	14	11		.960	-36	O-300L/1-86,C-52,3	-5.6
■ DEREK LEE Lee, Derek Gerald b: 7/28/66, Chicago, Ill. BL/TR, 6'1", 200 lbs. Deb: 6/27/93																								
1993	Min-A	15	33	3	5	1	0	0	4	1	4	.152	.176	.182	358	-4	-5	0	0	0	1.000	-2	O-13(9-0-4)	-0.8
■ DERREK LEE Lee, Derrek Leon b: 9/6/75, Sacramento, Cal. BR/TR, 6'5", 205 lbs. Deb: 4/28/97																								
1997	SD-N	22	54	9	14	3	0	1	4	9	24	.259	.365	.370	735	101	0	0	0	0	1.000	1	1-21	0.0
1998	Fla-N	141	454	62	106	29	1	17	74	47	120	.233	.319	.414	733	96	-4	5	2	0	.993	10	*1-132	-0.5
1999	Fla-N	70	218	21	45	9	1	5	20	17	70	.206	.264	.326	590	51	-17	2	1	0	.994	5	1-66	-1.6
2000	Fla-N	158	477	70	134	18	3	28	70	63	123	.281	.369	.507	877	125	18	0	3	-1	.993	7	*1-147	1.1
Total	4	391	1203	162	299	59	5	51	168	136	337	.249	.332	.433	765	100	-3	7	6	-1	.994	22	1-366	-1.0
■ DUD LEE Lee, Ernest Dudley (a.k.a. Ernest Dudley In 1920-21) b: 8/22/1899, Denver, Colo. d: 1/7/71, Denver, Colo. BL/TR, 5'9", 150 lbs. Deb: 10/3/20																								
1920	StL-A	1	2	2	2	0	0	0	1	0	0	1.000	1.000	1.000	2000	418	1	1	0	0	.333	-1	/S-1	0.0
1921	StL-A	72	180	18	30	4	2	0	11	14	34	.167	.235	.211	446	14	-24	1	1	-0	.922	5	S-31,2-30/3-3	-1.4
1924	Bos-A	94	288	36	73	9	4	0	29	40	17	.253	.350	.313	663	72	-11	8	4	0	.937	-8	S-90	-0.8
1925	Bos-A	84	255	22	57	7	3	0	19	34	19	.224	.315	.275	589	51	-19	2	3	-1	.924	17	S-84	0.5
1926	Bos-A	2	7	2	1	0	0	0	0	0	0	.143	.250	.143	393	4	-1	0	0	0	1.000	-1	/S-2	-0.2
Total	5	253	732	80	163	20	9	0	60	88	70	.223	.311	.275	586	50	-53	12	8	-0	.928	12	S-208/2-30,3-3	-1.9
■ HAL LEE Lee, Harold Burnham "Sheriff" b: 2/15/05, Ludlow, Miss. d: 9/4/89, Pascagoula, Miss. BR/TR, 5'11", 180 lbs. Deb: 4/19/30																								
1930	Bro-N	22	37	5	6	0	0	1	4	4	5	.162	.244	.243	487	19	-5	0			1.000	-1	O-12(10-0-1)	-0.6
1931	Phi-N	44	131	13	29	10	0	2	12	10	18	.221	.282	.344	625	62	-7	0			.967	-1	O-38(26-11-2)	-1.0
1932	Phi-N	149	595	76	180	42	10	18	85	36	45	.303	.343	.497	841	110	8	6			.965	11	*O-148(136-12-0)	1.0
1933	Phi-N	46	167	25	48	12	2	0	12	18	13	.287	.360	.383	743	100	1	1			.981	1	O-45(45-0-0)	-0.1
	Bos-N	88	312	32	69	15	9	1	28	18	26	.221	.266	.337	602	77	-10	1			.977	2	O-87(85-2-0)	-1.4
	Yr	134	479	57	117	27	11	1	40	36	39	.244	.300	.353	653	87	-9	2			.978	3	*O-132(130-2-0)	-1.5
1934	Bos-N	139	521	70	152	23	6	8	79	47	43	.292	.353	.405	758	111	8	3			.985	5	*O-128(128-0-0)/2-4	0.5
1935	Bos-N	112	422	49	128	18	6	0	39	18	25	.303	.333	.374	708	98	-2	0			.962	6	*O-110(98-0-12)	-0.2
1936	Bos-N	152	565	46	143	24	7	3	64	52	50	.253	.318	.336	655	82	-14	4			.973	-6	*O-150(150-0-0)	-2.8
Total	7	752	2750	316	755	144	40	33	323	203	225	.275	.326	.392	718	95	-22	15			.973	16	O-718(678-25-15)/2-4	-4.6
■ LEONIDAS LEE Lee, Leonidas Pyrrhus (b: Leonidas Pyrrhus Funkhouser) b: 12/13/1860, St.Louis, Mo. d: 6/11/12, Hendersonville, N.C. Deb: 7/17/1877																								
1877	StL-N	4	18	0	5	1	0	0	0	0	1	.278	.278	.333	611	97	-0				.667	-2	/O-4(1-2-1),S-1	-0.2
■ LERON LEE Lee, Leron b: 3/4/48, Bakersfield, Cal. BL/TR, 6', 196 lbs. Deb: 9/5/69																								
1969	StL-N	7	23	3	5	1	0	0	0	3	8	.217	.308	.261	569	60	-1	0	0	0	1.000	-0	/O-7(4-0-3)	-0.2
1970	StL-N	121	264	28	60	13	1	6	23	24	66	.227	.294	.352	646	71	-11	5	1	1	.969	-5	O-77(1-0-76)	-1.8
1971	StL-N	25	28	3	5	1	0	1	2	4	12	.179	.281	.321	603	68	-1	0	1	-0	.800	-3	/O-8(5-0-4)	-0.5
	SD-N	79	256	29	70	20	2	4	21	18	45	.273	.321	.414	735	115	4	4	5	-1	.920	-4	O-68(68-0-0)	-0.5
	Yr	104	284	32	75	21	2	5	23	22	57	.264	.317	.405	722	108	2	4	6	-1	.914	-6	O-76(73-0-4)	-1.0
1972	SD-N	101	370	50	111	23	7	12	47	29	58	.300	.356	.497	853	151	23	2	5	-1	.975	4	O-96(96-0-1)	2.1

YEAR	TM/L	G	AB	R	H	2B	3B	HR	RBI	BB	SO	AVG	OBP	SLG	OPS	OPS+	BR+	SB	CS	SBR	FA	FR	G/POS	TPR
1973	SD-N	118	333	36	79	7	2	3	30	33	61	.237	.308	.297	605	74	-11	4	0	1	.970	2	O-84(72-0-14)	-1.4
1974	Cle-A	79	232	18	54	13	0	5	25	15	42	.233	.279	.353	633	82	-6	3	2	-0	.958	4	O-62(60-0-2)/D-2	-0.6
1975	Cle-A	13	23	3	3	1	0	0	0	2	5	.130	.231	.174	405	16	-3	1	0	0	1.000	-1	/O-5(5-0-0),D-3	-0.3
	LA-N	48	43	2	11	4	0	0	2	3	9	.256	.304	.349	653	85	-1	0	0	0	1.000	-1	/O-4(4-0-0)	-0.3
1976	LA-N	23	45	1	6	0	1	0	2	2	9	.133	.170	.178	348	-1	-6	0	0	0	1.000	-2	O-10(0-0-10)	-0.9
Total	8	614	1617	173	404	83	13	31	152	133	315	.250	.309	.375	684	95	-14	19	14	-1	.962	-5	O-421(315-0-110)/D-5	-4.4

■ MANUEL LEE
Lee, Manuel Lora "Manny" (b: Manuel Lora (Lee)) b: 6/17/65, San Pedro De Macoris, D.R. BB/TR, 5'9", 161 lbs. Deb: 4/10/85 Career OF: (0-LF 0-CF 1-RF)

YEAR	TM/L	G	AB	R	H	2B	3B	HR	RBI	BB	SO	AVG	OBP	SLG	OPS	OPS+	BR+	SB	CS	SBR	FA	FR	G/POS	TPR
1985	*Tor-A	64	40	9	8	0	0	0	0	2	9	.200	.238	.200	438	21	-4	1	4	-1	.971	19	2-38/S-8,3-5,D-8	1.3
1986	Tor-A	35	78	8	16	0	1	1	7	4	10	.205	.244	.269	513	39	-7	0	1	-0	.990	4	2-29/S-5/3-2	-0.2
1987	Tor-A	56	121	14	31	2	3	1	11	6	13	.256	.291	.347	638	67	-6	2	0	0	.966	12	2-27,S-26/D-1	0.9
1988	Tor-A	116	381	38	111	16	3	2	38	26	64	.291	.337	.365	701	96	-2	3	3	-0	.988	10	2-98,S-23/3-8,D-2	1.1
1989	*Tor-A	99	300	27	78	9	2	3	34	20	60	.260	.306	.333	640	82	-7	4	2	0	.985	-2	2-40,S-28,3-17,D/O	-0.7
1990	Tor-A	117	391	45	95	12	4	6	41	26	90	.243	.290	.340	630	74	-14	3	1	0	**.993**	-10	*2-112/S-9	-2.0
1991	*Tor-A	138	445	41	104	18	3	0	29	24	107	.234	.276	.288	564	54	-28	7	2	1	.967	-28	*S-138	-4.5
1992	*Tor-A	128	396	49	104	10	1	3	39	50	73	.263	.345	.316	661	83	-8	6	2	1	.987	-18	*S-128	-1.6
1993	Tex-A	73	205	31	45	3	1	1	12	22	39	.220	.301	.259	560	54	-13	2	4	-1	.968	4	S-72/D-1	-0.4
1994	Tex-A	95	335	41	93	18	2	2	38	21	66	.278	.320	.361	681	76	-12	3	1	0	.967	4	S-85,2-13	0.0
1995	StL-N	1	1	1	1	0	0	0	0	0	0	1.000	1.000	1.000	2000	431	0	0	0	0	.800	1	/2-1	0.1
Total	11	922	2693	304	686	88	20	19	249	201	531	.255	.307	.323	631	73	-99	31	20	-0	.972	-4	S-522,2-358/3-32,DO	-6.0

■ TERRY LEE
Lee, Terry James b: 3/13/62, San Francisco, Cal. BR/TR, 6'5", 215 lbs. Deb: 9/3/90

YEAR	TM/L	G	AB	R	H	2B	3B	HR	RBI	BB	SO	AVG	OBP	SLG	OPS	OPS+	BR+	SB	CS	SBR	FA	FR	G/POS	TPR
1990	Cin-N	12	19	1	4	1	0	0	3	2	2	.211	.286	.263	549	50	-1	0	0	0	1.000	0	/1-6	-0.1
1991	Cin-N	3	6	0	0	0	0	0	0	0	2	.000	.000	.000	0	-96	-2	0	0	0	1.000	1	/1-2	0.0
Total	2	15	25	1	4	1	0	0	3	2	4	.160	.222	.200	422	17	-3	0	0	0	1.000	2	/1-8	-0.1

■ TRAVIS LEE
Lee, Travis Reynolds b: 5/26/75, San Diego, Cal. BL/TL, 6'3", 205 lbs. Deb: 3/31/98

YEAR	TM/L	G	AB	R	H	2B	3B	HR	RBI	BB	SO	AVG	OBP	SLG	OPS	OPS+	BR+	SB	CS	SBR	FA	FR	G/POS	TPR
1998	Ari-N	146	562	71	151	20	2	22	72	67	123	.269	.347	.429	775	103	2	8	1	1	.998	-3	*1-146	-1.4
1999	Ari-N	120	375	57	89	16	2	9	50	58	50	.237	.339	.363	702	77	-12	17	3	3	**.997**	1	*1-114/O-2(0-0-2)	-1.8
2000	Ari-N	72	224	34	52	13	0	8	40	25	46	.232	.309	.397	707	76	-9	5	1	1	.983	3	O-55(0-2-54),1-23	-0.9
	Phi-N	56	180	19	43	11	1	1	14	40	33	.239	.383	.328	711	81	-4	3	0	1	1.000	2	1-47,O-10(10-0-0)	-0.5
	Yr	128	404	53	95	24	1	9	54	65	79	.235	.344	.366	710	79	-12	8	1	1	.996	4	1-70,O-65(10-2-54)	-1.4
Total	3	394	1341	181	335	60	5	40	176	190	252	.250	.344	.391	735	88	-22	33	5	6	.997	1	1-330/O-67(10-2-56)	-4.6

■ BILLY LEE
Lee, William Joseph b: 1/9/1892, Bayonne, N.J. d: 1/6/84, West Hazleton, Pa. BR/TR, 5'9", 165 lbs. Deb: 4/15/15

YEAR	TM/L	G	AB	R	H	2B	3B	HR	RBI	BB	SO	AVG	OBP	SLG	OPS	OPS+	BR+	SB	CS	SBR	FA	FR	G/POS	TPR
1915	StL-A	18	59	2	11	1	0	0	4	6	5	.186	.262	.203	465	41	-4	1	1	-0	1.000	2	O-15(7-6-2)/3-1	-0.3
1916	StL-A	7	11	1	2	0	0	0	0	1	1	.182	.250	.182	432	31	-1	0			1.000	-1	/O-4(0-2-2)	-0.2
Total	2	25	70	3	13	1	0	0	4	7	6	.186	.260	.200	460	39	-5	1	1		1.000	2	/O-19(7-8-4),3-1	-0.5

■ WATTY LEE
Lee, Wyatt Arnold b: 8/12/1879, Lynch Station, Va. d: 3/6/36, Washington, D.C. BL/TL, 5'10.5", 171 lbs. Deb: 4/30/01

YEAR	TM/L	G	AB	R	H	2B	3B	HR	RBI	BB	SO	AVG	OBP	SLG	OPS	OPS+	BR+	SB	CS	SBR	FA	FR	G/POS	TPR
1901	Was-A	43	129	15	33	6	3	0	12	7		.256	.304	.349	653	82	-3	0			.948	0	P-36/O-7(2-1-4)	-0.2
1902	Was-A	109	391	61	100	21	5	4	45	33		.256	.319	.366	684	89	-6	8			.916	0	O-96(22-20-54),P-13	-1.0
1903	Was-A	75	231	17	48	8	4	0	13	18		.208	.265	.277	542	62	-11	5			.930	7	O-47(0-10-37),P-22	-0.5
1904	Pit-N	8	12	1	4	0	1	0	0	0		.333	.333	.500	833	152	1	0			.889	0	/P-5	0.0
Total	4	235	763	94	185	35	13	4	70	58		.242	.300	.338	638	80	-20	13			.917	8	O-150(24-31-95)/P-76	-1.7

■ GENE LEEK
Leek, Eugene Harold b: 7/15/36, San Diego, Cal. BR/TR, 6', 185 lbs. Deb: 4/22/59

YEAR	TM/L	G	AB	R	H	2B	3B	HR	RBI	BB	SO	AVG	OBP	SLG	OPS	OPS+	BR+	SB	CS	SBR	FA	FR	G/POS	TPR
1959	Cle-A	13	36	7	8	3	0	1	5	2	7	.222	.263	.389	652	80	-1	0	0	0	.955	-2	3-13/S-1	-0.3
1961	LA-A	57	199	16	45	9	1	5	20	7	54	.226	.260	.357	616	57	-13	0	1	-0	.958	18	3-49/S-7,O-1(1-0-0)	0.6
1962	LA-A	7	14	0	2	0	0	0	0	0	6	.143	.143	.143	286	-24	-2	0	0	0	1.000	0	/3-4	-0.2
Total	3	77	249	23	55	12	1	6	25	9	67	.221	.254	.349	603	55	-16	0	1	-0	.959	16	/3-66,S-8,O-1(1-0-0)	0.1

■ DAVE LEEPER
Leeper, David Dale b: 10/30/59, Santa Ana, Cal. BL/TL, 5'11", 170 lbs. Deb: 9/10/84

YEAR	TM/L	G	AB	R	H	2B	3B	HR	RBI	BB	SO	AVG	OBP	SLG	OPS	OPS+	BR+	SB	CS	SBR	FA	FR	G/POS	TPR
1984	KC-A	4	6	1	0	0	0	0	0	0	1	.000	.000	.000	0	-99	-2	0	0	0	1.000	-0	/O-2(2-0-0),D-1	-0.2
1985	KC-A	15	34	1	3	0	0	0	4	1	3	.088	.114	.088	203	-43	-7	0	0	0	.929	-1	/O-8(2-0-6)	-0.8
Total	2	19	40	2	3	0	0	0	4	1	4	.075	.098	.075	173	-52	-8	0	0	0	.944	-1	/O-10(4-0-6),D-1	-1.0

■ GEORGE LEES
Lees, George Edward b: 2/2/1895, Bethlehem, Pa. d: 1/2/80, Harrisburg, Pa. BR/TR, 5'9", 150 lbs. Deb: 5/7/21

YEAR	TM/L	G	AB	R	H	2B	3B	HR	RBI	BB	SO	AVG	OBP	SLG	OPS	OPS+	BR+	SB	CS	SBR	FA	FR	G/POS	TPR
1921	Chi-A	20	42	3	9	2	0	0	4	0	3	.214	.214	.262	476	21	-5	0	1	-0	.951	-2	C-16	-0.7

■ JIM LEFEBVRE
Lefebvre, James Kenneth b: 1/7/42, Inglewood, Cal. BB/TR, 6', 185 lbs. Deb: 4/12/65 MC

YEAR	TM/L	G	AB	R	H	2B	3B	HR	RBI	BB	SO	AVG	OBP	SLG	OPS	OPS+	BR+	SB	CS	SBR	FA	FR	G/POS	TPR
1965	*LA-N	157	544	57	136	21	4	12	69	71	92	.250	.339	.369	708	106	6	3	5	-1	.970	-12	*2-156	0.6
1966	*LA-N★	152	544	69	149	23	3	24	74	48	72	.274	.336	.460	796	129	20	1	1	-0	.980	-11	*2-119,3-40	2.0
1967	LA-N	136	494	51	129	18	5	8	50	44	64	.261	.325	.366	692	106	4	1	5	-2	.955	6	3-92,2-34/1-5	1.1
1968	LA-N	84	286	23	69	12	1	5	31	26	55	.241	.307	.343	649	102	1	0	0	0	.978	-10	2-62,3-16/O-5L,1-3	-0.6
1969	LA-N	95	275	29	65	15	2	4	44	48	37	.236	.352	.349	701	104	3	2	1	0	.985	1	3-44,2-37/1-6	0.6
1970	LA-N	109	314	33	79	15	1	4	44	29	42	.252	.317	.344	661	81	-9	1	1	-0	.988	-4	2-70,3-21/1-1	-0.9
1971	LA-N	119	388	40	95	14	2	12	68	39	55	.245	.317	.384	701	104	1	0	2	-1	.988	-17	*2-102/3-7	-1.0
1972	LA-N	70	169	11	34	8	0	5	24	17	30	.201	.274	.337	611	75	-6	0	0	0	.987	-1	2-33,3-11	-0.6
Total	8	922	3014	313	756	126	18	74	404	322	447	.251	.326	.378	704	105	19	8	15	-3	.979	-48	2-613,3-231/1-15,O	1.2

■ JOE LEFEBVRE
Lefebvre, Joseph Henry b: 2/22/56, Concord, N.H. BL/TR, 5'10", 175 lbs. Deb: 5/22/80 Career OF: (76-LF 7-CF 254-RF)

YEAR	TM/L	G	AB	R	H	2B	3B	HR	RBI	BB	SO	AVG	OBP	SLG	OPS	OPS+	BR+	SB	CS	SBR	FA	FR	G/POS	TPR
1980	*NY-A	74	150	26	34	1	1	8	21	27	30	.227	.345	.407	751	107	2	0	0	0	.975	-14	O-71(20-3-52)	-1.4
1981	SD-N	86	246	31	63	13	4	8	31	35	33	.256	.353	.439	792	133	11	6	4	-0	.994	4	O-84(0-2-83)	1.2
1982	SD-N	102	239	25	57	9	0	4	21	18	50	.238	.295	.326	621	78	-7	0	0	0	.972	-17	3-39,O-36L/C-3	-2.8
1983	SD-N	18	20	1	5	0	0	0	1	2	3	.250	.318	.250	568	61	-1	0	0	0	1.000	-2	/O-6(0-0-6),3-4,C-2	-0.3
	*Phi-N	101	258	34	80	20	8	8	38	31	46	.310	.390	.543	933	158	20	5	3	0	.990	-9	O-74(22-0-58)/3-9,C-3	0.8
	Yr	119	278	35	85	20	8	8	39	33	49	.306	.385	.522	907	151	19	5	3	0	.990	-11	O-80R,3-13/C-5	0.5
1984	Phi-N	52	160	22	40	9	0	3	18	23	37	.250	.351	.363	714	99	1	0	2	-1	.966	0	O-47(16-0-34)/3-1	-0.2
1986	Phi-N	14	18	0	2	0	0	0	0	3	5	.111	.238	.111	349	-1	-2	0	0	0	1.000	-0	/O-3(0-0-3)	-0.3
Total	6	447	1091	139	281	52	13	31	130	139	204	.258	.346	.414	760	115	22	11	9	-1	.986	-37	O-321R/3-53,C-8	-3.0

■ BILL LEFEBVRE
Lefebvre, Wilfred Henry "Lefty" b: 11/11/15, Natick, R.I. BL/TL, 5'11.5", 180 lbs. Deb: 6/10/38

YEAR	TM/L	G	AB	R	H	2B	3B	HR	RBI	BB	SO	AVG	OBP	SLG	OPS	OPS+	BR+	SB	CS	SBR	FA	FR	G/POS	TPR
1938	Bos-A	1	1	1	1	0	0	1	1	0	0	1.000	1.000	4.000	5000	1048	1	0	0	0	.000	-0	/P-1	0.0
1939	Bos-A	7	10	3	3	0	0	0	1	2	2	.300	.417	.300	717	83	-0	0	0	0	1.000	-1	/P-5	0.0
1943	Was-A	7	14	0	4	3	0	0	1	1	0	.286	.333	.500	833	148	1	0	0	0	1.000	-0	/P-6	0.0
1944	Was-A	60	62	4	16	2	2	0	8	12	9	.258	.378	.355	733	115	2	0	0	0	.933	-0	P-24/1-2	0.0
Total	4	75	87	8	24	5	2	1	11	15	11	.276	.382	.414	796	129	4	0	0	0	.960	-1	/P-36,1-2	0.0

■ AL LEFEVRE
Lefevre, Alfred Modesto b: 9/16/1898, New York, N.Y. d: 1/21/82, Glen Cove, N.Y. BR/TR, 5'10.5", 160 lbs. Deb: 6/28/20

YEAR	TM/L	G	AB	R	H	2B	3B	HR	RBI	BB	SO	AVG	OBP	SLG	OPS	OPS+	BR+	SB	CS	SBR	FA	FR	G/POS	TPR
1920	NY-N	17	27	5	4	0	1	0	0	0	13	.148	.148	.222	370	5	-3	0	0	0	1.000	3	/S-9,2-6,3-1	0.0

■ WADE LEFLER
Lefler, Wade Hampton b: 6/5/1896, Cooleemee, N.C. d: 3/6/81, Hickory, N.C. BL/TR, 5'11", 162 lbs. Deb: 4/16/24

YEAR	TM/L	G	AB	R	H	2B	3B	HR	RBI	BB	SO	AVG	OBP	SLG	OPS	OPS+	BR+	SB	CS	SBR	FA	FR	G/POS	TPR
1924	Bos-N	1	1	0	0	0	0	0	0	0	1	.000	.000	.000	0	-99	-0	0	0	0	.000	0	H	0.0
	Was-A	5	8	0	5	3	0	0	4	0	0	.625	.625	1.000	1625	325	2	0	0	0	1.000	-0	/O-1(0-0-1)	0.2
Total	1	6	9	0	5	3	0	0	4	0	1	.556	.556	.889	1444	279	2	0	0	0	1.000	-0	/O-1(0-0-1)	0.2

■ RON LeFLORE
LeFlore, Ronald b: 6/16/48, Detroit, Mich. BR/TR, 6', 200 lbs. Deb: 8/1/74 Career OF: (208-LF 833-CF 0-RF)

YEAR	TM/L	G	AB	R	H	2B	3B	HR	RBI	BB	SO	AVG	OBP	SLG	OPS	OPS+	BR+	SB	CS	SBR	FA	FR	G/POS	TPR
1974	Det-A	59	254	37	66	8	1	2	13	13	58	.260	.304	.323	627	78	-7	23	9	2	.935	3	O-59(0-59-0)	-0.4
1975	Det-A	136	550	66	142	13	6	8	37	33	139	.258	.303	.347	650	80	-15	28	20	-1	.973	6	*O-134(0-134-0)	-1.4
1976	Det-A★	135	544	93	172	23	8	4	39	51	111	.316	.377	.410	787	125	18	58	20	6	.973	16	*O-132(0-132-0)/D-1	3.8
1977	Det-A	154	652	100	212	30	10	16	57	37	121	.325	.365	.475	841	121	18	39	19	2	.972	2	*O-152(0-152-0)	2.0

YEAR	TM/L	G	AB	R	H	2B	3B	HR	RBI	BB	SO	AVG	OBP	SLG	OPS	OPS+	BR+	SB	CS	SBR	FA	FR	G/POS	TPR
1978	Det-A	155	666	**126**	198	30	3	12	62	65	104	.297	.363	.405	769	113	12	**68**	16	9	.976	9	*O-155(0-155-0)	3.0
1979	Det-A	148	600	110	180	22	10	9	57	52	95	.300	.356	.415	771	104	4	78	14	12	.990	4	*O-113(0-113-0),D-34	1.7
1980	Mon-N	139	521	95	134	21	11	4	39	62	99	.257	.337	.363	700	95	-2	**97**	19	**15**	.957	6	*O-130(130-0-0)	1.3
1981	Chi-A	82	337	46	83	10	4	0	24	28	70	.246	.306	.300	606	77	-10	36	11	4	.960	-1	O-82(76-7-0)	-1.0
1982	Chi-A	91	334	58	96	15	4	4	25	22	91	.287	.331	.392	724	98	-1	28	14	1	.939	-4	O-83(2-81-0)/D-2	-0.5
Total	9	1099	4458	731	1283	172	57	59	353	363	888	.288	.344	.392	735	103	16	455	142	50	.968	41	*O-1040C/D-37	8.5

■ LOU LEGETT Legett, Louis Alfred "Doc" b: 6/1/01, New Orleans, La. d: 3/6/88, New Orleans, La. BR/TR, 5'10", 166 lbs. Deb: 5/8/29

YEAR	TM/L	G	AB	R	H	2B	3B	HR	RBI	BB	SO	AVG	OBP	SLG	OPS	OPS+	BR+	SB	CS	SBR	FA	FR	G/POS	TPR
1929	Bos-N	39	81	7	13	2	0	0	6	3	18	.160	.190	.185	376	-7	-14	2			.914	-1	C-28	-1.3
1933	Bos-A	8	5	1	1	1	0	0	1	0	1	.200	.200	.400	600	56	-0	0	0	0	1.000	1	/C-2	0.0
1934	Bos-A	19	38	4	11	0	0	0	1	2	4	.289	.325	.289	614	56	-2	0	0	0	.977	-0	C-17	-0.2
1935	Bos-A	2	0	1	0	0	0	0	0	0	0	—	—	—	—	—	0	0	0	0	.000	0	R	0.0
Total	4	68	124	13	25	3	0	0	8	5	22	.202	.233	.226	458	16	-16	2	0	0	.938	-1	/C-47	-1.5

■ GREG LEGG Legg, Gregory Lynn b: 4/21/60, San Jose, Cal. BR/TR, 6'1", 185 lbs. Deb: 4/18/86

YEAR	TM/L	G	AB	R	H	2B	3B	HR	RBI	BB	SO	AVG	OBP	SLG	OPS	OPS+	BR+	SB	CS	SBR	FA	FR	G/POS	TPR
1986	Phi-N	11	20	2	9	1	0	0	1	0	3	.450	.450	.500	950	156	1	0	0	0	.941	2	/2-4,S-1	0.4
1987	Phi-N	3	2	1	0	0	0	0	0	0	0	.000	.000	.000	0	-97	-1	0	0	0	1.000	-0	/2-1,S-1,3-1	-0.1
Total	2	14	22	3	9	1	0	0	1	0	3	.409	.409	.455	864	132	1	0	0	0	.952	2	/2-5,S-2,3-1	0.3

■ MIKE LEHANE Lehane, Michael Patrick b: 4/15/1865, New York, N.Y. BR, 6'1.5", 180 lbs. Deb: 4/26/1884 Career OF: (1-LF 0-CF 0-RF)

YEAR	TM/L	G	AB	R	H	2B	3B	HR	RBI	BB	SO	AVG	OBP	SLG	OPS	OPS+	BR+	SB	CS	SBR	FA	FR	G/POS	TPR
1884	Was-U	3	12	1	4	2	0	0		0		.333	.333	.500	833	154	0				.688	-1	/S-3,O-1(1-0-0),3-1	0.0
1890	Col-a	140	512	54	108	19	5	0	56	43		.211	.276	.268	544	65	-22	13			**.982**	10	*1-140	-2.2
1891	Col-a	137	511	59	110	12	7	1	52	34	77	.215	.268	.272	540	58	-29	16			**.981**	7	*1-137	-3.0
Total	3	280	1035	114	222	33	12	1	108	77	77	.214	.273	.272	545	62	-50	29			.982	16	1-277/S-3,3-1,O-1L	-5.2

■ PAUL LEHNER Lehner, Paul Eugene "Peanuts" or "Gulliver" b: 7/1/20, Dolomite, Ala. d: 12/27/67, Birmingham, Ala. BL/TL, 5'9", 165 lbs. Deb: 9/10/46 Career OF: (110-LF 297-CF 37-RF)

YEAR	TM/L	G	AB	R	H	2B	3B	HR	RBI	BB	SO	AVG	OBP	SLG	OPS	OPS+	BR+	SB	CS	SBR	FA	FR	G/POS	TPR
1946	StL-A	16	45	6	10	1	2	0	5	1	5	.222	.239	.333	572	56	-3	0	0	0	.941	-3	O-12(0-11-1)	-0.6
1947	StL-A	135	483	59	120	25	9	7	48	28	29	.248	.294	.381	675	85	-12	5	5	-1	.980	-6	*O-127(2-125-0)	-2.3
1948	StL-A	103	333	23	92	15	4	2	46	30	19	.276	.336	.363	699	84	-8	0	2	-1	.974	-6	O-89(0-89-0)/1-2	-1.7
1949	StL-A	104	297	25	68	13	0	3	37	16	20	.229	.271	.303	574	50	-23	0	2	-1	.987	2	O-56(12-35-10),1-18	-2.4
1950	Phi-A	114	427	48	132	17	5	9	52	32	33	.309	.357	.436	793	104	1	1	1	-0	.981	6	*O-101(80-7-15)	0.1
1951	Phi-A	9	28	1	4	1	0	0	1	1	1	.143	.172	.179	351	-5	-4	0	0	0	1.000	1	/O-6(6-0-0)	-0.4
	Chi-A	23	72	9	15	3	1	0	3	10	4	.208	.305	.278	583	60	-4	0	0	0	.980	-4	O-20(8-13-9)	-0.8
	StL-A	21	67	2	9	5	0	1	2	6	5	.134	.205	.254	459	23	-8	0	1	-0	1.000	-1	O-18(1-17-0)	-1.0
	Cle-A	12	13	2	3	0	0	0	1	1	2	.231	.286	.231	516	43	-1	0	0	0	1.000	-0	/O-1(1-0-0)	-0.1
	Yr	65	180	14	31	9	1	1	7	18	12	.172	.247	.250	497	35	-17	0	1	-0	.991	-4	O-45(16-30-9)	-2.3
1952	Bos-A	3	3	0	2	0	0	0	2	2	0	.667	.800	.667	1467	288	1	0	0	0	1.000	-0	/O-2(0-0-2)	0.1
Total	7	540	1768	175	455	80	21	22	197	127	118	.257	.309	.364	672	78	-59	6	11	-3	.981	-11	O-432C/1-20	-9.1

■ CLARENCE LEHR Lehr, Clarence Emanuel "King" b: 5/16/1886, Escanaba, Mich. d: 1/31/48, Highland Park, Mich. BR/TR, 5'11", 165 lbs. Deb: 5/18/11

YEAR	TM/L	G	AB	R	H	2B	3B	HR	RBI	BB	SO	AVG	OBP	SLG	OPS	OPS+	BR+	SB	CS	SBR	FA	FR	G/POS	TPR
1911	Phi-N	23	27	2	4	0	0	0	2	0	7	.148	.148	.148	296	-17	-4	0			1.000	-1	/O-5(1-1-3),2-4,S-4	-0.5

■ HANK LEIBER Leiber, Henry Edward b: 1/17/11, Phoenix, Ariz. d: 11/8/93, Tucson, Ariz. BR/TR, 6'1.5", 205 lbs. Deb: 4/16/33 Career OF: (37-LF 602-CF 65-RF)

YEAR	TM/L	G	AB	R	H	2B	3B	HR	RBI	BB	SO	AVG	OBP	SLG	OPS	OPS+	BR+	SB	CS	SBR	FA	FR	G/POS	TPR
1933	NY-N	6	10	1	2	0	0	0	0	0	2	.200	.200	.200	400	15	-1	0			1.000	1	/O-1(1-0-0)	0.0
1934	NY-N	63	187	17	45	5	3	2	25	4	13	.241	.257	.332	588	58	-12	1			.971	-6	O-51(2-49-0)	-1.8
1935	NY-N	154	613	110	203	37	4	22	107	48	29	.331	.389	.512	901	143	36	0			.965	-15	*O-154(0-154-0)	1.7
1936	*NY-N	101	337	44	94	19	7	9	67	37	41	.279	.352	.457	809	118	8	1			.961	-7	O-86(7-78-1)/1-1	-0.2
1937	*NY-N	51	184	24	54	7	3	4	32	15	27	.293	.347	.429	776	108	2	1			.988	-7	O-46(1-42-3)	-0.6
1938	NY-N★	98	360	50	97	18	4	12	65	31	45	.269	.327	.442	769	109	3	0			.974	-9	O-89(2-86-4)	-0.8
1939	Chi-N	112	365	65	113	16	1	24	88	59	42	.310	.411	.556	967	155	29	1			.977	4	O-98(0-98-0)	3.0
1940	Chi-N†	117	440	68	133	24	2	17	86	45	68	.302	.371	.482	853	136	21	1			.985	-6	*O-103(0-53-52),1-12	1.0
1941	Chi-N†	53	162	20	35	5	0	7	25	16	25	.216	.291	.377	667	90	-3	0			.964	-4	O-29(23-2-5),1-15	-1.0
1942	NY-N	58	147	11	32	6	0	4	23	19	27	.218	.315	.340	656	91	-1	0			.990	-0	O-41(1-40-0)/P-1	-0.3
Total	10	813	2805	410	808	137	24	101	518	274	319	.288	.356	.462	818	122	83	5			.973	-49	O-698C/1-28,P-1	1.0

■ NEMO LEIBOLD Leibold, Harry Loran b: 2/17/1892, Butler, Ind. d: 2/4/77, Detroit, Mich. BL/TR, 5'6.5", 157 lbs. Deb: 4/12/13 Career OF: (144-LF 593-CF 381-RF)

YEAR	TM/L	G	AB	R	H	2B	3B	HR	RBI	BB	SO	AVG	OBP	SLG	OPS	OPS+	BR+	SB	CS	SBR	FA	FR	G/POS	TPR
1913	Cle-A	93	286	37	74	11	6	0	12	21	43	.259	.309	.339	649	87	-5	16			.945	-0	O-74(4-66-2)	-1.1
1914	Cle-A	115	402	46	106	13	3	0	32	54	56	.264	.354	.311	665	96	0	12	14	-2	.931	9	*O-107(0-90-17)	-0.1
1915	Cle-A	57	207	28	53	5	4	0	4	24	16	.256	.339	.319	658	95	-1	5	3	0	.969	9	O-52(0-52-0)	0.5
	Chi-A	36	74	10	17	1	0	0	11	15	11	.230	.360	.243	603	78	-1	1	3	-1	1.000	5	O-22(10-12-0)	0.1
	Yr	93	281	38	70	6	4	0	15	39	27	.249	.345	.299	644	91	-2	6	6	-1	.978	14	O-74(10-64-0)	0.6
1916	Chi-A	45	82	5	20	1	2	0	13	7	7	.244	.303	.305	608	82	-2	7			1.000	-5	O-24(2-16-6)	-0.8
1917	*Chi-A	125	428	59	101	12	6	0	29	74	34	.236	.350	.292	642	94	0	27			.961	-1	*O-122(16-4-102)	-0.7
1918	Chi-A	116	440	57	110	14	7	0	31	63	32	.250	.344	.314	658	97	0	13			.979	8	*O-114(95-7-12)	0.3
1919	*Chi-A	122	434	81	131	18	2	0	26	72	30	.302	.404	.353	756	113	11	17			.928	7	*O-122(7-1-114)	1.2
1920	Chi-A	108	413	61	91	16	3	1	28	55	30	.220	.316	.281	597	59	-23	7	15	-4	.977	6	*O-105(3-4-98)	-2.7
1921	Bos-A	123	467	88	143	26	6	0	31	41	27	.306	.363	.388	751	94	-4	13	7	0	.949	4	*O-117(0-107-10)	-0.4
1922	Bos-A	81	271	42	70	8	1	1	18	41	14	.258	.360	.306	666	76	-8	1	6	-2	.966	6	O-71(1-66-4)	-0.7
1923	Bos-A	12	18	1	2	0	0	0	0	1	2	.111	.158	.111	269	-28	-3	0	1	-0	.909	-3	O-10(0-10-0)	-0.7
	Was-A	95	315	68	96	13	4	1	22	53	16	.305	.408	.381	789	114	9	7	6	-1	.980	1	O-84(0-84-0)	0.6
	Yr	107	333	69	98	13	4	1	22	54	18	.294	.396	.366	762	106	6	7	7	-1	.977	-2	O-94(0-94-0)	-0.1
1924	*Was-A	84	246	41	72	6	4	0	20	42	10	.293	.398	.350	748	97	1	7	5	-0	.994	-3	O-70(4-52-14)	-0.5
1925	*Was-A	56	84	14	23	1	1	0	7	8	7	.274	.337	.310	646	66	-4	1	2	0	.972	-6	O-26(2-22-2)/3-1	-1.0
Total	13	1268	4167	638	1109	145	49	3	284	571	335	.266	.357	.327	683	91	-29	134	60		.961	37	*O-1120C/3-1	-6.0

■ ELMER LEIFER Leifer, Elmer Edwin b: 5/23/1893, Clarington, Ohio d: 9/26/48, Everett, Wash. BL/TR, 5'9.5", 170 lbs. Deb: 9/7/21

YEAR	TM/L	G	AB	R	H	2B	3B	HR	RBI	BB	SO	AVG	OBP	SLG	OPS	OPS+	BR+	SB	CS	SBR	FA	FR	G/POS	TPR
1921	Chi-A	9	10	0	3	0	0	0	1	0	4	.300	.300	.300	600	54	-1	0	0	0	1.000	-1	/3-1,O-1(1-0-0)	-0.1

■ JOHN LEIGHTON Leighton, John Atkinson b: 10/4/1861, Peabody, Mass. d: 10/31/56, Lynn, Mass. 5'11", 170 lbs. Deb: 7/12/1890

YEAR	TM/L	G	AB	R	H	2B	3B	HR	RBI	BB	SO	AVG	OBP	SLG	OPS	OPS+	BR+	SB	CS	SBR	FA	FR	G/POS	TPR
1890	Syr-a	7	27	6	8	2	0	0	0	3		.296	.367	.370	737	131	1	2			.938	-0	/O-7(0-7-0)	0.0

■ BILL LEINHAUSER Leinhauser, William Charles b: 11/4/1893, Philadelphia, Pa. d: 4/14/78, Elkins Park, Pa. BR/TR, 5'10", 150 lbs. Deb: 5/18/12

YEAR	TM/L	G	AB	R	H	2B	3B	HR	RBI	BB	SO	AVG	OBP	SLG	OPS	OPS+	BR+	SB	CS	SBR	FA	FR	G/POS	TPR
1912	Det-A	1	4	0	0	0	0	0	0	0		.000	.000	.000	0	-99	-1	0			1.000	0	/O-1	-0.1

■ ED LEIP Leip, Edgar Ellsworth b: 11/29/10, Trenton, N.J. d: 11/24/83, Zephyrhills, Fla. BR/TR, 5'9", 160 lbs. Deb: 9/16/39

YEAR	TM/L	G	AB	R	H	2B	3B	HR	RBI	BB	SO	AVG	OBP	SLG	OPS	OPS+	BR+	SB	CS	SBR	FA	FR	G/POS	TPR
1939	Was-A	9	32	4	11	1	0	0	2	2	4	.344	.382	.375	757	102	0	0	1	-0	.951	-1	/2-8	-0.1
1940	Pit-N	3	5	2	1	0	0	0	0	0	0	.200	.200	.200	400	11	-1	0			1.000	-1	/2-2	-0.1
1941	Pit-N	15	25	1	5	0	2	0	3	1	2	.200	.231	.360	591	65	-1	1			.889	2	/2-7,3-1	0.1
1942	Pit-N	3	0	0	0	0	0	0	0	0	0	—	—	—	—	—	0	0			.000	0	R	0.0
Total	4	30	62	7	17	1	2	0	5	3	6	.274	.308	.355	663	80	-2	1	1		.931	0	/2-17,3-1	-0.1

■ SCOTT LEIUS Leius, Scott Thomas b: 9/24/65, Yonkers, N.Y. BR/TR, 6'3", 195 lbs. Deb: 9/3/90 Career OF: (0-LF 2-CF 0-RF)

YEAR	TM/L	G	AB	R	H	2B	3B	HR	RBI	BB	SO	AVG	OBP	SLG	OPS	OPS+	BR+	SB	CS	SBR	FA	FR	G/POS	TPR
1990	Min-A	14	25	4	6	1	0	1	4	2	2	.240	.296	.400	696	87	-0	0	0	0	1.000	3	S-12/3-1	0.3
1991	*Min-A	109	199	35	57	7	2	5	20	30	35	.286	.380	.417	797	115	5	5	5	-1	.953	-2	3-79,S-19/O-2(0-2-0)	0.3
1992	Min-A	129	409	50	102	18	2	2	35	34	61	.249	.309	.318	626	73	-14	6	5	-0	.955	4	*3-125,S-10	-1.0
1993	Min-A	10	18	4	3	0	0	0	2	2	4	.167	.250	.167	417	14	-2	0	0	0	.947	4	/S-9	0.2
1994	Min-A	97	350	57	86	16	1	14	49	37	58	.246	.320	.417	737	88	-7	2	4	-1	.969	-1	3-95/S-2	-0.8
1995	Min-A	117	372	51	92	16	5	4	45	49	54	.247	.338	.349	688	79	-11	2	1	0	.945	-4	*3-112/S-7,D-3	-1.3
1996	Cle-A	27	43	3	6	4	0	1	3	2	8	.140	.178	.302	480	18	-6	0	0	0	1.000	1	/3-8,1-7,2-6,D-1	-0.5
1998	KC-A	17	46	2	8	0	0	0	4	1	6	.174	.191	.174	365	-4	-7	0	0	0	.867	-0	3-15/S-2,D-1	-0.7

YEAR	TM/L	G	AB	R	H	2B	3B	HR	RBI	BB	SO	AVG	OBP	SLG	OPS	OPS+	BR+	SB	CS	SBR	FA	FR	G/POS	TPR
1999	KC-A	37	74	8	15	1	0	1	10	4	8	.203	.253	.257	510	30	-8	1	0	0	.971	-0	1-13,3-10/S-2,2D	-0.8
Total	9	557	1536	214	375	63	10	28	172	161	236	.244	.318	.353	671	77	-50	16	15	-2	.954	4	3-445/S-63,1-20,D2O	-4.3
■ FRANK LEJA	Leja, Frank John b: 2/7/36, Holyoke, Mass. d: 5/3/91, Boston, Mass. BL/TL, 6'4", 205 lbs. Deb: 5/1/54																							
1954	NY-A	12	5	2	1	0	0	0	0	0	1	.200	.200	.200	400	10	-1	0	0	0	1.000	0	/1-6	-0.1
1955	NY-A	7	2	1	0	0	0	0	0	0	1	.000	.000	.000	0	-99	-1	0	0	0	1.000	0	/1-2	-0.1
1962	LA-A	7	16	0	0	0	0	0	0	1	6	.000	.059	.000	59	-85	-4	0	0	0	.953	-0	/1-4	-0.5
Total	3	26	23	3	1	0	0	0	0	1	8	.043	.083	.043	127	-67	-5	0	0	0	.958	-0	/1-12	-0.7
■ LARRY LeJEUNE	LeJeune, Sheldon Aldenbert b: 7/22/1885, Chicago, Ill. d: 4/21/52, Eloise, Mich. BR/TR, 6', 185 lbs. Deb: 5/10/11																							
1911	Bro-N	6	19	2	3	0	0	0	2	2	8	.158	.238	.158	396	12	-2	2			.818	-2	/O-6(0-6-0)	-0.5
1915	Pit-N	18	65	4	11	0	1	0	2	2	7	.169	.206	.200	406	23	-6	4	3	-0	.940	2	O-18(0-18-0)	-0.6
Total	2	24	84	6	14	0	1	0	4	4	15	.167	.213	.190	404	21	-8	6	3		.918	0	/O-24(0-24-0)	-1.1
■ DON LeJOHN	LeJohn, Donald Everett b: 5/13/34, Daisytown, Pa. BR/TR, 5'10", 175 lbs. Deb: 6/30/65																							
1965	*LA-N	34	78	2	20	2	0	0	7	5	13	.256	.301	.282	583	70	-3	0	1	-0	.959	1	3-26	-0.3
■ JACK LELIVELT	Lelivelt, John Frank b: 11/14/1885, Chicago, Ill. d: 1/20/41, Seattle, Wash. BL/TL, 5'11.5", 175 lbs. Deb: 6/24/09 F																							
1909	Was-A	91	318	25	93	8	6	0	24	19		.292	.334	.355	690	124	8	8			.970	8	O-91(41-35-15)	1.2
1910	Was-A	110	347	40	92	10	3	0	33	40		.265	.343	.311	654	110	5	20			.964	4	O-86(80-5-1)/1-7	0.5
1911	Was-A	72	225	29	72	12	4	0	22	22		.320	.386	.409	794	124	8	7			.939	4	O-49(36-0-13)/1-7	0.9
1912	NY-A	36	149	12	54	6	7	2	23	4		.362	.383	.537	920	153	9	7			.963	-1	O-36(0-36-0)	0.6
1913	NY-A	18	28	2	6	0	1	0	4	2	2	.214	.267	.286	552	61	-1	1			1.000	0	/O-5(0-4-0)	-0.1
	Cle-A	23	23	0	9	2	0	0	7	0	3	.391	.391	.478	870	150	1	1			.000	-1	/O-1(0-1-0)	0.1
	Yr	41	51	2	15	2	1	0	11	2	5	.294	.321	.373	693	101	-0	2			1.000	1	/O-6(0-5-0)	0.0
1914	Cle-A	34	64	6	21	5	1	0	13	2	10	.328	.348	.438	786	131	2	2	3	-1	.933	-3	O-13(0-6-6)/1-1	-0.2
Total	6	384	1154	114	347	43	22	2	126	89	15	.301	.353	.381	735	124	31	46	3		.962	13	O-281(157-87-35)/1-15	3.0
■ JOHNNIE LeMASTER	LeMaster, Johnnie Lee b: 6/19/54, Portsmouth, Ohio BR/TR, 6'2", 167 lbs. Deb: 9/2/75																							
1975	SF-N	22	74	4	14	4	0	2	9	4	15	.189	.241	.324	565	53	-5	2	1	0	.967	-1	S-22	-0.3
1976	SF-N	33	100	9	21	3	2	0	9	2	21	.210	.225	.280	505	42	-8	2	0	0	.937	11	S-31	0.7
1977	SF-N	68	134	13	20	5	1	0	8	13	27	.149	.224	.201	426	15	-16	2	1	0	.934	7	S-54/3-2	-0.5
1978	SF-N	101	272	23	64	18	3	1	14	21	45	.235	.293	.335	627	78	-9	6	6	-1	.966	2	S-96/2-2	0.1
1979	SF-N	108	343	42	87	11	2	3	29	23	55	.254	.304	.324	628	77	-11	9	5	0	.959	0	*S-106	-0.1
1980	SF-N	135	405	33	87	16	6	3	31	25	57	.215	.260	.306	567	59	-23	0	1	-0	.957	-14	*S-134	-2.6
1981	SF-N	104	324	27	82	9	1	0	28	24	46	.253	.307	.287	594	70	-12	3	7	-2	.964	-8	*S-103	-1.3
1982	SF-N	130	436	34	94	14	1	2	30	31	78	.216	.268	.266	534	50	-29	13	4	1	.963	-8	*S-130	-2.4
1983	SF-N	141	534	81	128	16	1	6	30	60	96	.240	.319	.307	626	77	-16	39	19	2	.964	-22	*S-139	-2.2
1984	SF-N	132	451	46	98	13	2	4	32	31	97	.217	.268	.282	549	56	-27	17	5	2	.964	4	*S-129	-0.8
1985	SF-N	12	16	1	0	0	0	0	0	1	5	.000	.059	.000	59	-86	-4	0	0	0	.955	-1	S-10	-0.5
	Cle-A	11	20	0	3	0	0	0	0	0	6	.150	.150	.150	300	-18	-3	0	1	-0	.949	3	S-10	0.0
	Pit-N	22	58	4	9	0	0	1	6	5	12	.155	.222	.207	429	21	-6	1	0	0	.983	13	S-21	0.9
1987	Oak-A	20	24	3	2	0	0	0	1	1	4	.083	.120	.083	203	-48	-5	0	1	-0	1.000	5	/3-8,S-7,2-5,D-1	0.0
Total	12	1039	3191	320	709	109	19	22	229	241	564	.222	.278	.289	567	60	-174	94	51	3	.961	-9	S-992/3-10,2-7,D-1	-9.0
■ STEVE LEMBO	Lembo, Stephen Neal b: 11/13/26, Brooklyn, N.Y. d: 12/4/89, Flushing, N.Y. BR/TR, 6'1", 185 lbs. Deb: 9/16/50																							
1950	Bro-N	5	6	0	1	0	0	0	0	1	0	.167	.286	.167	452	22	-1	0			1.000	2	/C-5	0.2
1952	Bro-N	2	5	0	1	0	0	0	1	0	1	.200	.200	.200	400	11	-1	0	0	0	1.000	0	/C-2	0.0
Total	2	7	11	0	2	0	0	0	1	1	1	.182	.250	.182	432	18	-1	0	0		1.000	3	/C-7	0.2
■ MARK LEMKE	Lemke, Mark Alan b: 8/13/65, Utica, N.Y. BB/TR, 5'9", 167 lbs. Deb: 9/17/88																							
1988	Atl-N	16	58	8	13	4	0	0	2	4	5	.224	.274	.293	567	60	-3	0	2	-1	.970	4	2-16	0.1
1989	Atl-N	14	55	4	10	2	1	2	10	5	7	.182	.250	.364	614	72	-2	0	1	-0	1.000	-2	2-14	-0.4
1990	Atl-N	102	239	22	54	13	0	0	21	21	22	.226	.288	.280	569	54	-15	0	1	-0	.989	23	3-45,2-44/S-1	0.9
1991	*Atl-N	136	269	36	63	11	2	2	23	29	27	.234	.309	.312	621	71	-10	1	2	-0	.978	13	*2-110,3-15	0.4
1992	*Atl-N	155	427	38	97	7	4	6	26	50	39	.227	.308	.304	613	70	-16	0	3	-1	.984	-10	*2-145,3-13	-2.5
1993	*Atl-N	151	493	52	124	19	2	7	49	65	50	.252	.339	.341	679	82	-11	1	2	-0	.982	6	*2-150	0.1
1994	Atl-N	104	350	40	103	15	0	3	31	38	37	.294	.363	.363	726	88	-5	0	3	-1	**.994**	7	*2-103	0.6
1995	*Atl-N	116	399	42	101	16	5	5	38	44	40	.253	.327	.356	683	78	-12	2	2	-0	.990	-11	*2-115	-1.7
1996	*Atl-N	135	498	64	127	17	0	5	37	53	48	.255	.327	.319	646	68	-22	5	2	0	.977	7	*2-133	-0.8
1997	Atl-N	109	351	33	86	17	1	2	26	33	51	.245	.310	.316	626	63	-19	2	0	0	.980	8	*2-104	-0.5
1998	Bos-A	31	91	10	17	4	0	0	7	6	15	.187	.237	.231	468	22	-10	0	1	-0	1.000	-6	2-31	-1.5
Total	11	1069	3230	349	795	125	15	32	270	348	341	.246	.319	.324	643	71	-125	11	19	-4	.984	40	2-965/3-73,S-1	-5.3
■ CHET LEMON	Lemon, Chester Earl b: 2/12/55, Jackson, Miss. BR/TR, 6', 195 lbs. Deb: 9/9/75 Career OF: (1-LF 1473-CF 454-RF)																							
1975	Chi-A	9	35	2	9	2	0	0	1	1	6	.257	.297	.314	612	72	-1	1	0	0	.923	-4	/3-6,O-1(0-1-0),D-2	-0.5
1976	Chi-A	132	451	46	111	15	5	4	38	28	65	.246	.300	.328	629	83	-10	13	7	0	.992	11	*O-131(1-130-0)	-0.2
1977	Chi-A	150	553	99	151	38	4	19	67	52	88	.273	.347	.459	807	118	13	8	7	-1	.978	**35**	*O-149(0-149-0)	4.5
1978	Chi-A★	105	357	51	107	24	6	13	55	39	46	.300	.381	.510	891	147	22	5	9	-2	.983	14	O-95(0-84-12),D-10	3.3
1979	Chi-A★	148	556	79	177	**44**	2	17	86	56	68	.318	.394	.496	890	138	31	7	11	-2	.977	9	*O-147(0-147-0)/D-1	3.5
1980	Chi-A	147	514	76	150	32	6	11	51	71	56	.292	.390	.442	832	128	22	6	6	-1	.981	2	*O-139C/2-1,D-6	2.2
1981	Chi-A	94	328	50	99	23	6	9	50	33	48	.302	.388	.491	879	155	24	5	8	-2	.984	2	O-93(0-93-0)	2.4
1982	Det-A	125	436	75	116	20	1	19	52	56	69	.266	.369	.447	816	122	15	1	4	-1	.984	1	*O-121(0-29-93)/D-1	0.9
1983	Det-A	145	491	78	125	21	5	24	69	54	70	.255	.352	.464	817	126	18	0	7	-2	.988	11	*O-145(0-145-0)	2.4
1984	*Det-A★	141	509	77	146	34	6	20	76	51	83	.287	.360	.495	855	135	24	5	5	-1	.995	16	*O-140(0-140-0)/D-1	3.7
1985	Det-A	145	517	69	137	28	4	18	68	45	93	.265	.336	.439	775	111	7	0	2	-1	.990	11	*O-144(0-144-0)	1.6
1986	Det-A	126	403	45	101	21	3	12	53	39	53	.251	.329	.407	736	99	-0	2	1	0	.985	3	*O-124(0-124-0)	0.2
1987	*Det-A	146	470	75	130	30	3	20	75	70	82	.277	.380	.481	860	132	23	0	0	0	.992	3	*O-145(0-145-0)	2.4
1988	Det-A	144	512	67	135	29	4	17	64	59	65	.264	.348	.436	783	123	16	1	2	-0	.974	4	*O-144(0-0-144)	1.5
1989	Det-A	127	414	45	98	19	2	7	47	46	71	.237	.325	.343	668	90	-4	1	5	-2	.985	-6	*O-111(0-0-111),D-13	-1.6
1990	Det-A	104	322	39	83	16	4	5	32	48	61	.258	.361	.379	740	106	4	3	2	-0	.973	6	O-96(0-3-94)/D-6	0.8
Total	16	1988	6868	973	1875	396	61	215	884	749	1024	.273	.357	.442	800	121	204	58	76	-14	.984	116	*O-1925C/D-40,3-6,2	27.1
■ JIM LEMON	Lemon, James Robert b: 3/23/28, Covington, Va. BR/TR, 6'4", 200 lbs. Deb: 8/20/50 MC																							
1950	Cle-A	12	34	4	6	1	0	1	1	3	12	.176	.243	.294	537	38	-3	0	0	0	.824	-2	O-10(10-0-0)	-0.5
1953	Cle-A	16	46	5	8	1	0	1	5	3	15	.174	.224	.261	485	32	-5	0	0	0	.913	-1	O-11(11-0-0)/1-2	-0.6
1954	Was-A	37	128	12	30	2	3	2	13	9	34	.234	.285	.344	628	76	-5	0	0	0	.951	-3	O-33(1-0-32)	-1.0
1955	Was-A	10	25	3	5	2	0	1	3	3	4	.200	.286	.400	686	88	-1	0	0	0	.923	-0	/O-6(1-0-5)	-0.1
1956	Was-A	146	538	77	146	21	**11**	27	96	65	138	.271	.352	.502	854	123	16	2	4	-1	.963	8	*O-141(12-0-130)	1.6
1957	Was-A	137	518	58	147	23	6	17	64	49	94	.284	.349	.450	799	118	12	1	7	-2	.971	-3	*O-131(0-0-131)/1-3	0.2
1958	Was-A	142	501	65	123	15	9	26	75	50	120	.246	.315	.467	782	114	8	2	4	-1	.978	0	*O-137(2-0-135)	0.2
1959	Was-A	147	531	73	148	18	3	33	100	46	99	.279	.337	.510	848	130	21	5	2	0	.969	3	*O-142(117-0-25)	1.5
1960	Was-A★	148	528	81	142	10	1	38	100	67	114	.269	.359	.508	866	133	23	2	0	1	.960	-1	*O-145(145-0-0)	1.5
1961	Min-A	129	423	57	109	26	1	14	52	44	98	.258	.333	.423	757	95	-3	1	1	-0	.940	-6	*O-120(120-0-1)	-1.6
1962	Min-A	12	17	1	3	0	0	1	5	3	4	.176	.300	.353	653	72	-1	0	0	0	1.000	-1	/O-3(2-0-1)	-0.2
1963	Min-A	7	17	0	2	0	0	0	1	1	5	.118	.167	.118	284	-18	-3	0	0	0	.800	-1	/O-4(4-0-0)	-0.4
	Phi-N	31	59	6	16	2	0	2	6	8	18	.271	.358	.407	765	121	2	0	0	0	.963	-2	O-18(16-0-4)	-0.1
	Chi-A	36	80	4	16	0	1	1	8	12	32	.200	.304	.262	567	62	-4	0	0	0	.979	-3	1-25	-0.8
Total	12	1010	3445	446	901	121	35	164	529	363	787	.262	.335	.460	795	114	57	13	18	-3	.961	-12	O-901(441-0-464)/1-30	-0.3
■ BOB LEMON	Lemon, Robert Granville b: 9/22/20, San Bernardino, Cal. d: 1/11/2000, Long Beach, Cal. BL/TR, 6', 185 lbs. Deb: 9/9/41 MCH Career OF: (0-LF 13-CF 1-RF)																							
1941	Cle-A	5	4	0	1	0	0	0	0	0	1	.250	.250	.250	500	34	-0	0	0	0	1.000	0	/3-1	0.0

YEAR	TM/L	G	AB	R	H	2B	3B	HR	RBI	BB	SO	AVG	OBP	SLG	OPS	OPS+	BR+	SB	CS	SBR	FA	FR	G/POS	TPR
1942	Cle-A	5	5	0	0	0	0	0	0	0	3	.000	.000	.000	0	-99	-1	0	0	0	.500	0	/3-1	-0.1
1946	Cle-A	55	89	9	16	3	0	1	4	7	18	.180	.240	.247	487	39	-8	0	1	-0	.976	6	P-32,O-12(0-12-0)	-0.3
1947	Cle-A	47	56	11	18	4	3	2	5	6	9	.321	.387	.607	994	179	5	0	0	0	.983	4	P-37/O-2(0-1-1)	-0.1
1948	*Cle-A☆	52	119	20	34	9	0	5	21	8	23	.286	.331	.487	818	119	2	0	0	0	.965	8	P-43	0.0
1949	Cle-A☆	46	108	17	29	6	2	7	19	10	20	.269	.331	.556	886	135	4	0	0	0	.963	6	P-37	0.0
1950	Cle-A★	72	136	21	37	9	1	6	26	13	25	.272	.340	.485	825	113	2	0	0	0	.957	5	P-44	0.0
1951	Cle-A★	56	102	11	21	4	1	3	13	9	22	.206	.270	.353	623	72	-5	0	0	0	.976	4	P-42	0.0
1952	Cle-A★	54	124	14	28	5	0	2	9	4	21	.226	.250	.315	565	60	-7	0	0	0	.982	7	P-42	0.0
1953	Cle-A☆	51	112	12	26	9	1	2	17	7	20	.232	.277	.384	661	79	-4	2	0	0	.972	8	P-41	0.0
1954	*Cle-A★	40	98	11	21	4	1	2	10	6	24	.214	.260	.337	596	61	-6	0	0	0	.963	4	P-36	0.0
1955	Cle-A	49	78	11	19	0	0	1	9	13	16	.244	.352	.282	634	69	-3	0	0	0	.983	2	P-35	0.0
1956	Cle-A	43	93	8	18	0	0	5	12	9	21	.194	.272	.355	627	63	-5	0	0	0	.934	4	P-39	0.0
1957	Cle-A	25	46	2	3	1	0	1	1	0	14	.065	.065	.152	217	-43	-9	0	0	0	1.000	3	P-21	0.0
1958	Cle-A	15	13	1	3	0	0	0	1	1	4	.231	.286	.231	516	45	-1	0	0	0	1.000	1	P-11	0.0
Total	15	615	1183	148	274	54	9	37	147	93	241	.232	.289	.386	675	82	-36	2	1	0	.969	62	P-460/O-14C,3-2	-0.5

■ DON LENHARDT
Lenhardt, Donald Eugene "Footsie" b: 10/4/22, Alton, Ill. BR/TR, 6'3", 190 lbs. Deb: 4/18/50 C Career OF: (291-LF 1-CF 5-RF)

YEAR	TM/L	G	AB	R	H	2B	3B	HR	RBI	BB	SO	AVG	OBP	SLG	OPS	OPS+	BR+	SB	CS	SBR	FA	FR	G/POS	TPR
1950	StL-A	139	480	75	131	22	6	22	81	90	94	.273	.390	.481	871	118	13	3	2	-0	.988	-12	1-86,O-39L,3-10	-0.4
1951	StL-A	31	103	9	27	3	0	5	18	6	13	.262	.303	.437	740	95	-1	1	0	0	.982	-2	O-27(27-0-0)/1-1	-0.5
	Chi-A	64	199	23	53	9	1	10	45	24	25	.266	.351	.472	823	124	6	1	1	-0	.983	-2	O-53(53-0-0)/1-2	0.0
	Yr	95	302	32	80	12	1	15	63	30	38	.265	.335	.460	796	114	5	2	1	0	.983	-4	O-80(80-0-0)/1-3	-0.5
1952	Bos-A	30	105	18	31	4	0	7	24	15	18	.295	.383	.533	917	142	6	0	1	-0	.981	-2	O-27(27-0-0)	0.2
	Det-A	45	144	18	27	2	1	3	13	28	18	.188	.320	.278	598	67	-6	0	1	-0	.989	3	O-43(43-0-0)	-0.6
	StL-A	18	48	5	13	4	1	1	5	4	8	.271	.327	.458	785	114	1	0	0	0	1.000	0	O-11(10-1-0)/1-2	0.0
	Yr	93	297	41	71	10	2	11	42	47	44	.239	.343	.397	740	102	1	0	2	-1	.988	2	O-81(80-1-0)/1-2	-0.4
1953	StL-A	97	303	37	96	15	0	10	35	41	41	.317	.400	.465	865	131	14	1	2	-0	.969	2	O-77(72-0-5)/3-6	1.1
1954	Bal-A	13	33	2	5	1	0	0	1	3	9	.152	.222	.182	404	12	-4	0	0	0	1.000	-1	/O-7(7-0-0),1-2	-0.5
	Bos-A	44	66	5	18	4	0	3	17	3	9	.273	.314	.470	784	101	-0	0	0	0	1.000	-3	O-13(13-0-0)/3-1	-0.4
	Yr	57	99	7	23	5	0	3	18	6	18	.232	.283	.374	657	74	-4	0	0	0	1.000	-4	O-20(20-0-0)/1-2,3-1	-0.9
Total	5	481	1481	192	401	64	9	61	239	214	235	.271	.365	.450	815	114	28	6	7	-1	.980	-15	O-297L/1-93,3-17	-1.1

■ PATRICK LENNON
Lennon, Patrick Orlando b: 4/27/68, Whiteville, N.C. BR/TR, 6'2", 200 lbs. Deb: 9/15/91 Career OF: (40-LF 1-CF 18-RF)

YEAR	TM/L	G	AB	R	H	2B	3B	HR	RBI	BB	SO	AVG	OBP	SLG	OPS	OPS+	BR+	SB	CS	SBR	FA	FR	G/POS	TPR
1991	Sea-A	9	8	2	1	1	0	0	1	3	1	.125	.364	.250	614	73	-0	0	0	0	1.000	0	/O-1(1-0-0),D-5	0.0
1992	Sea-A	1	2	0	0	0	0	0	0	0	0	.000	.000	.000	0	-99	-1	0	0	0	1.000	0	/1-1	-0.1
1996	KC-A	14	30	5	7	3	0	0	1	7	10	.233	.378	.333	712	82	-1	0	0	0	.947	-1	O-11(11-0-0)/D-1	-0.2
1997	Oak-A	56	116	14	34	6	1	1	14	15	35	.293	.374	.388	762	101	1	0	1	-0	.948	-5	O-36(23-1-12),D-17	-0.6
1998	Tor-A	2	4	1	2	2	0	0	0	0	1	.500	.500	1.000	1500	276	1	0	0	0	1.000	-0	/O-2(0-0-2)	0.1
1999	Tor-A	9	29	3	6	2	0	1	6	2	12	.207	.281	.379	661	65	-2	0	0	0	1.000	2	/O-8(5-0-4)	0.0
Total	6	91	189	25	50	14	1	2	22	27	59	.265	.359	.381	740	93	-1	0	1	-0	.962	-4	/O-58L,D-23,1-1	-0.8

■ BOB LENNON
Lennon, Robert Albert "Arch" b: 9/15/28, Brooklyn, N.Y. BL/TL, 6', 200 lbs. Deb: 9/9/54

YEAR	TM/L	G	AB	R	H	2B	3B	HR	RBI	BB	SO	AVG	OBP	SLG	OPS	OPS+	BR+	SB	CS	SBR	FA	FR	G/POS	TPR
1954	NY-N	3	3	0	0	0	0	0	0	0	0	.000	.000	.000	0	-99	-1	0	0	0	.000	0	H	-0.1
1956	NY-N	26	55	3	10	1	0	0	1	4	17	.182	.237	.200	437	19	-6	0	0	0	.885	-4	O-21(5-1-18)	-1.1
1957	Chi-N	9	21	2	3	1	0	1	3	1	9	.143	.182	.333	515	35	-2	0	0	0	1.000	-1	/O-4(0-4-0)	-0.4
Total	3	38	79	5	13	2	0	1	4	5	26	.165	.214	.228	442	19	-9	0	0	0	.900	-6	/O-25(5-5-18)	-1.6

■ BILL LENNON
Lennon, William H. b: 1848, Brooklyn, N.Y. 5'7", 145 lbs. Deb: 5/4/1871 MU Career OF: (0-LF 0-CF 1-RF)

YEAR	TM/L	G	AB	R	H	2B	3B	HR	RBI	BB	SO	AVG	OBP	SLG	OPS	OPS+	BR+	SB	CS	SBR	FA	FR	G/POS	TPR
1871	Kek-n	12	48	5	11	3	0	0	5	1	0	.229	.245	.292	537	52	-3	1	0	0	.887	-2	C-12/S-2,O-1(0-0-1),M	-0.3
1872	Nat-n	11	54	11	12	1	0	0	6	0	0	.222	.222	.241	463	36	-5	0	0	0	.765	-5	C-11/1-1	-0.7
1873	Mar-n	5	19	2	4	0	0	0	2	0	0	.211	.211	.211	421	33	-1	0	0	0	.942	-2	/1-4,C-1,3-1	-0.2
Total	3 n	28	121	18	27	4	0	0	13	1	0	.223	.230	.256	486	42	-9	1	0	0	.817	-9	/C-24,1-5,S-2,3O	-1.2

■ ED LENNOX
Lennox, James Edgar "Eggie" b: 11/3/1885, Camden, N.J. d: 10/26/39, Camden, N.J. BR/TR, 5'10", 174 lbs. Deb: 8/8/06

YEAR	TM/L	G	AB	R	H	2B	3B	HR	RBI	BB	SO	AVG	OBP	SLG	OPS	OPS+	BR+	SB	CS	SBR	FA	FR	G/POS	TPR
1906	Phi-A	6	17	1	1	1	0	0	0	1		.059	.111	.118	229	-28	-2	0			.909	5	/3-6	0.3
1909	Bro-N	126	435	33	114	18	9	2	44	47		.262	.337	.359	695	120	10	11			**.959**	-4	*3-121	1.1
1910	Bro-N	110	367	19	95	19	4	3	32	36	39	.259	.333	.357	690	104	2	7			.950	-16	*3-100	-1.2
1912	Chi-N	27	81	13	19	4	1	1	16	12	10	.235	.347	.346	693	90	-1	1			.934	-5	3-24	-0.5
1914	Pit-F	124	430	71	134	25	10	11	84	71	38	.312	.414	.493	907	148	24	19			.954	-15	*3-123	1.2
1915	Pit-F	55	53	1	16	3	1	1	9	7	12	.302	.383	.453	836	136	2	0			1.000	2	/3-3	0.5
Total	6	448	1383	138	379	70	25	18	185	174	99	.274	.361	.400	760	122	34	38			.953	-32	3-377	1.4

■ JIM LENTINE
Lentine, James Matthew b: 7/16/54, Los Angeles, Cal. BR/TR, 6', 175 lbs. Deb: 9/3/78

YEAR	TM/L	G	AB	R	H	2B	3B	HR	RBI	BB	SO	AVG	OBP	SLG	OPS	OPS+	BR+	SB	CS	SBR	FA	FR	G/POS	TPR
1978	StL-N	8	11	1	2	0	0	0	1	0	0	.182	.250	.182	432	23	-1	1	0	0	1.000	-0	/O-3(2-0-1)	-0.1
1979	StL-N	11	23	2	9	1	0	0	1	3	6	.391	.462	.435	896	145	2	0	1	-0	1.000	-0	/O-8(3-2-3)	0.1
1980	StL-N	9	10	1	1	0	0	0	1	0	2	.100	.100	.100	200	-43	-2	0	0	0	1.000	-2	/O-6(5-1-0)	-0.4
	Det-A	67	161	19	42	8	1	1	17	28	30	.261	.377	.342	719	96	0	2	1	0	.963	-3	O-55(40-10-6)/D-9	-0.4
Total	3	95	205	23	54	9	1	1	20	31	38	.263	.368	.332	700	92	-1	3	2	-0	.969	-5	/O-72(50-13-10),D-9	-0.8

■ EDDIE LEON
Leon, Eduardo Antonio b: 8/11/46, Tucson, Ariz. BR/TR, 6', 175 lbs. Deb: 9/9/68

YEAR	TM/L	G	AB	R	H	2B	3B	HR	RBI	BB	SO	AVG	OBP	SLG	OPS	OPS+	BR+	SB	CS	SBR	FA	FR	G/POS	TPR
1968	Cle-A	6	1	0	0	0	0	0	0	0	1	.000	.000	.000	0	-99	-0	0	0	0	1.000	3	/S-6	0.3
1969	Cle-A	64	213	20	51	6	0	3	19	19	37	.239	.302	.310	612	69	-9	2	2	-0	.952	9	S-64	0.7
1970	Cle-A	152	549	58	136	20	4	10	56	47	89	.248	.309	.353	663	78	-16	1	2	-0	.982	8	*2-141,S-23/3-1	0.3
1971	Cle-A	131	429	35	112	12	2	4	35	34	69	.261	.317	.326	643	76	-13	3	5	-1	.983	0	*2-107,S-24	-0.5
1972	Cle-A	89	225	14	45	2	1	4	16	20	47	.200	.268	.271	539	59	-11	0	2	-1	.993	-1	2-36,S-35	-0.8
1973	Chi-A	127	399	37	91	10	3	3	30	34	103	.228	.294	.291	584	63	-19	1	5	-2	.972	-2	*S-122/2-3	-0.2
1974	Chi-A	31	46	1	5	1	0	0	3	2	12	.109	.146	.130	276	-20	-7	0	0	0	.962	8	S-21/2-7,3-2,D-1	0.3
1975	NY-A	1	0	0	0	0	0	0	0	0	0	—	—	—	—	—	0	0	0	0	.000	0	/S-1	0.0
Total	8	601	1862	165	440	51	10	24	159	156	358	.236	.298	.313	611	69	-76	7	16	-4	.963	25	S-296,2-294/3-3,D-1	-0.6

■ LEONARD
Leonard Deb: 9/12/1892

YEAR	TM/L	G	AB	R	H	2B	3B	HR	RBI	BB	SO	AVG	OBP	SLG	OPS	OPS+	BR+	SB	CS	SBR	FA	FR	G/POS	TPR
1892	StL-N	1	0	0	0	0	0	0	0	1	0	—	1.000	—	1000	219	0	1			.000	-0	/O-1(0-0-1)	0.0

■ ANDY LEONARD
Leonard, Andrew Jackson b: 6/1/1846, County Cavan, Ireland
d: 8/21/03, Boston, Mass. BR/TR, 5'7", 168 lbs. Deb: 5/5/1871 NA OF: (218-LF 0-CF 0-RF) Career OF: (132-LF 0-CF 0-RF)

YEAR	TM/L	G	AB	R	H	2B	3B	HR	RBI	BB	SO	AVG	OBP	SLG	OPS	OPS+	BR+	SB	CS	SBR	FA	FR	G/POS	TPR
1871	Oly-n	31	148	33	43	8	3	0	30	3	1	.291	.305	.385	690	102	1	14	3	2	.863	-2	2-19,O-11(11-0-0)/S-1	0.0
1872	Bos-n	46	240	57	84	7	1	2	43	0	2	.350	.350	.412	763	127	6	8	5	0	.828	-4	*O-38L/3-6,2-4,S-1	0.2
1873	Bos-n	58	302	81	95	12	7	0	61	4	0	.315	.324	.401	724	105	-0	5	6	-1	.714	-1	*O-45L,2-12/1-2,S-1	-0.1
1874	Bos-n	71	339	68	106	18	4	0	50	2	2	.313	.317	.389	706	119	5	11	3	1	.807	1	*O-51L,2-11,S-11	0.6
1875	Bos-n	80	396	87	127	14	6	1	74	2	6	.321	.324	.394	718	143	15	14	8	0	.806	-1	*O-73L/S-3,3-3,2-2	1.5
1876	Bos-N	64	307	53	85	10	2	0	27	4	6	.277	.290	.327	617	103	1				.925	-1	O-35(35-0-0),2-30	-0.1
1877	Bos-N	58	272	46	78	5	0	0	27	5	5	.287	.300	.305	605	88	-4				.875	-4	O-37(37-0-0),S-21	-0.8
1878	Bos-N	60	262	41	68	8	5	0	16	3	19	.260	.268	.328	596	88	-4				.777	-7	*O-60(60-0-0)	-1.4
1880	Cin-N	33	133	15	28	3	0	1	17	8	11	.211	.255	.256	511	75	-3				.833	-12	S-23,3-10	-1.3
Total	5 n	286	1425	326	455	59	21	3	258	11	11	.319	.325	.396	721	121	27	52	25	3	.778	-7	O-218L/2-48,S-17,31	2.2
Total	4	215	974	155	259	26	7	1	87	20	41	.266	.282	.311	593	91	-10				.856	-23	O-132L/S-44,2-30,3	-3.6

■ JEFFREY LEONARD
Leonard, Jeffrey b: 9/22/55, Philadelphia, Pa. BR/TR, 6'2", 200 lbs. Deb: 9/2/77 Career OF: (896-LF 103-CF 171-RF)

YEAR	TM/L	G	AB	R	H	2B	3B	HR	RBI	BB	SO	AVG	OBP	SLG	OPS	OPS+	BR+	SB	CS	SBR	FA	FR	G/POS	TPR
1977	LA-N	11	10	1	3	0	1	0	2	1	4	.300	.364	.500	864	130	0	0	0	0	1.000	-2	O-10(6-0-4)	-0.2
1978	Hou-N	8	26	2	10	2	0	0	4	1	2	.385	.407	.462	869	154	2	0	1	-0	1.000	1	/O-8(4-2-2)	0.2
1979	Hou-N	134	411	47	119	15	5	0	47	46	68	.290	.364	.350	714	102	2	23	10	2	.959	-7	*O-123(4-22-100)	-0.8
1980	*Hou-N	88	216	29	46	7	5	3	20	19	46	.213	.277	.333	610	75	-8	4	1	1	.979	-2	O-56(3-9-44),1-11	-1.3
1981	Hou-N	7	18	1	3	1	1	0	3	0	4	.167	.167	.333	500	41	-2	1	0	0	1.000	-0	/1-2,O-2(0-0-2)	-0.2

YEAR	TM/L	G	AB	R	H	2B	3B	HR	RBI	BB	SO	AVG	OBP	SLG	OPS	OPS+	BR+	SB	CS	SBR	FA	FR	G/POS	TPR
	SF-N	37	127	20	39	11	3	4	26	12	21	.307	.371	.535	907	158	9	4	2	0	1.000	2	O-28(8-19-4)/1-5	1.1
	Yr	44	145	21	42	12	4	4	29	12	25	.290	.348	.510	858	145	8	5	2	0	1.000	2	O-30(8-19-6)/1-7	0.9
1982	SF-N	80	278	32	72	16	1	9	49	19	65	.259	.311	.421	732	103	0	18	5	2	.958	-5	O-74(56-17-2)/1-1	-0.5
1983	SF-N	139	516	74	144	17	7	21	87	35	116	.279	.326	.461	787	120	11	26	7	3	.975	8	*O-136(127-12-2)	1.8
1984	SF-N	136	514	76	155	27	2	21	86	47	123	.302	.360	.484	845	140	26	17	7	1	.970	6	*O-131(116-18-4)	2.9
1985	SF-N	133	507	49	122	20	3	17	62	21	107	.241	.272	.393	665	88	-11	11	6	0	.977	3	*O-126(125-3-0)	-1.4
1986	SF-N	89	341	48	95	11	3	6	42	20	62	.279	.324	.381	705	99	-1	16	3	2	.970	3	O-87(87-0-0)	0.1
1987	*SF-N★	131	503	70	141	29	4	19	63	21	68	.280	.312	.467	779	108	3	16	7	1	.966	-4	*O-127(127-1-0)	-0.5
1988	SF-N	44	160	12	41	8	1	2	20	9	24	.256	.296	.356	652	90	-2	7	5	-0	.987	-3	O-43(43-0-0)	-0.7
	Mil-A	94	374	45	88	19	0	8	44	16	68	.235	.272	.350	623	72	-14	10	4	1	.985	3	O-91(91-0-0)/D-2	-1.4
1989	Sea-A★	150	566	69	144	20	1	24	93	38	125	.254	.307	.420	728	100	-2	6	1	1	.982	2	*D-123,O-26(25-0-1)	-0.4
1990	Sea-A	134	478	39	120	20	0	10	75	37	97	.251	.309	.356	665	84	-10	4	2	0	.983	-8	O-79(74-0-6),D-48	-2.2
Total	14	1415	5045	614	1342	223	37	144	723	342	1000	.266	.316	.411	726	103	4	163	61	15	.974	-3	*O-1147L,D-173/1-19	-3.5
■ JOE LEONARD	Leonard, Joseph Howard b: 11/15/1894, W.Chicago, Ill. d: 5/1/20, Washington, D.C. BL/TR, 5'7.5", 156 lbs. Deb: 5/7/14																							
1914	Pit-N	53	126	17	25	2	2	0	4	12	21	.198	.268	.246	514	56	-7	4			.909	-8	3-38/S-1	-1.6
1916	Cle-A	3	2	1	0	0	0	0	0	0	1	.000	.000	.000	0	-94	-0	0			1.000	0	/2-1	0.0
	Was-A	42	168	20	46	7	0	0	14	22	23	.274	.358	.315	673	103	1	4			.952	-8	3-42	-0.5
	Yr	45	170	21	46	7	0	0	14	22	24	.271	.354	.312	666	101	1	4			.952	-7	3-42/2-1	-0.5
1917	Was-A	99	297	30	57	6	7	0	23	45	40	.192	.302	.259	562	72	-9	6			.925	-2	3-68,1-19/S-1,O-1R	-1.1
1919	Was-A	71	198	26	51	8	3	2	20	20	28	.258	.329	.359	687	94	-2	3			.944	-9	2-28,3-25/1-4,O-1L	-1.1
1920	Was-A	1	0	0	0	0	0	0	0	0	0	—	—	—	—	—	0	0	0	0	.000	0	R	0.0
Total	5	269	791	94	179	23	12	2	61	99	113	.226	.315	.293	608	82	-16	17	0		.937	-27	3-173/2-29,1-23,OS	-4.3
■ MARK LEONARD	Leonard, Mark David b: 8/14/64, Mountain View, Cal. BL/TR, 6', 195 lbs. Deb: 7/21/90																							
1990	SF-N	11	17	3	3	1	0	1	2	3	8	.176	.300	.412	712	97	-0	0	0	0	1.000	-1	/O-7(2-0-5)	-0.1
1991	SF-N	64	129	14	31	7	1	2	14	12	25	.240	.310	.357	666	90	-2	0	1	-0	1.000	-6	O-34(24-0-12)	-0.9
1992	SF-N	55	128	13	30	7	0	4	16	16	31	.234	.333	.383	716	108	2	0	1	-0	.984	0	O-37(33-0-4)	0.0
1993	Bal-A	10	15	1	1	1	0	0	3	3	7	.067	.222	.133	356	-2	-2	0	0	0	.833	-1	/O-4(4-0-0),D-3	-0.3
1994	SF-N	14	11	2	4	1	1	0	2	3	2	.364	.500	.636	1136	203	2	0	0	0	1.000	-1	/O-2(2-0-0)	0.1
1995	SF-N	14	21	4	4	1	0	1	4	5	2	.190	.346	.381	727	94	-0	0	0	0	1.000	-1	/O-6(1-0-5)	-0.1
Total	6	168	321	37	73	18	2	8	41	42	75	.227	.324	.371	695	97	-1	0	2	-1	.985	-9	/O-90(66-0-26),D-3	-1.3
■ JOHN LEOVICH	Leovich, John Joseph b: 5/5/18, Portland, Ore. d: 2/3/2000, Lincoln City, Ore. BR/TR, 6'0.5", 200 lbs. Deb: 5/1/41																							
1941	Phi-A	1	2	0	1	1	0	0	0	0	0	.500	.500	1.000	1500	296	1	0	0	0	.000	-0	/C-1	0.0
■ TED LEPCIO	Lepcio, Thaddeus Stanley b: 7/28/30, Utica, N.Y. BR/TR, 5'10", 177 lbs. Deb: 4/15/52																							
1952	Bos-A	84	274	34	72	17	2	5	26	24	41	.263	.329	.394	723	93	-3	3	3	-0	.972	8	2-57,3-25/S-1	0.8
1953	Bos-A	66	161	17	38	4	2	4	11	17	24	.236	.313	.360	673	77	-5	0	0	0	.981	17	2-34,S-20,3-11	1.4
1954	Bos-A	116	398	42	102	19	4	8	45	42	62	.256	.332	.384	716	86	-7	3	4	-1	.971	16	2-80,3-24,S-14	1.5
1955	Bos-A	51	134	19	31	9	0	6	15	12	36	.231	.313	.433	746	91	-2	1	1	-0	.943	6	3-45	0.4
1956	Bos-A	83	284	34	74	10	0	15	51	30	77	.261	.338	.454	792	96	-2	1	3	-1	.966	7	2-57,3-22	0.8
1957	Bos-A	79	232	24	56	10	2	9	37	29	61	.241	.328	.418	746	97	-1	0	0	0	.976	9	2-68	1.2
1958	Bos-A	50	136	10	27	3	0	6	14	12	47	.199	.268	.353	621	65	-7	0	1	-0	.980	-3	2-40	-0.7
1959	Bos-A	3	3	1	1	1	0	0	1	0	2	.333	.333	.667	1000	160	0	0	0	0	1.000	0	/2-1	0.0
	Det-A	76	215	25	60	8	0	7	24	17	49	.279	.332	.414	746	98	-1	2	0	0	.951	-6	S-35,2-24,3-11	-0.2
	Yr	79	218	26	61	9	0	7	25	17	51	.280	.332	.417	749	99	-0	2	0	0	.951	-6	S-35,2-25,3-11	-0.2
1960	Phi-N	69	141	16	32	7	0	2	8	17	41	.227	.319	.319	638	75	-4	0	3	-1	.942	-5	3-50,S-14/2-5	-1.0
1961	Chi-A	5	2	0	0	0	0	0	0	1	0	.000	.333	.000	333	-2	-0	0	0	0	.000	-0	/3-1	0.0
	Min-A	47	112	11	19	3	1	7	19	8	31	.170	.231	.402	633	62	-7	1	0	0	.919	2	3-35,2-22/S-6	-0.3
	Yr	52	114	11	19	3	1	7	19	9	31	.167	.234	.395	629	62	-7	1	0	0	.895	2	3-36,2-22/S-6	-0.3
Total	10	729	2092	233	512	91	11	69	251	209	471	.245	.319	.398	717	87	-40	11	15	-3	.972	51	2-388,3-224/S-90	3.9
■ PETE LePINE	LePine, Louis Joseph b: 9/5/1876, Montreal, Que., Can d: 12/3/49, Woonsocket, R.I. BL/TL, 5'10", 142 lbs. Deb: 7/21/02																							
1902	Det-A	30	96	8	20	3	2	1	19	8		.208	.276	.313	589	62	-5	1			1.000	-2	O-19(0-0-19)/1-8	-0.7
■ DON LEPPERT	Leppert, Don Eugene "Tiger" b: 11/20/30, Memphis, Tenn. BL/TR, 5'8", 175 lbs. Deb: 4/11/55																							
1955	Bal-A	40	70	6	8	0	1	0	2	9	10	.114	.215	.143	358	-2	-10	1	1	-0	.937	-7	2-35	-1.6
■ DON LEPPERT	Leppert, Donald George b: 10/19/31, Indianapolis, Ind. BR/TR, 6'2", 220 lbs. Deb: 6/18/61 C																							
1961	Pit-N	22	60	6	16	2	1	3	5	1	11	.267	.279	.483	762	97	-1	0	0	0	.968	1	C-21	0.1
1962	Pit-N	45	139	14	37	6	1	3	18	12	21	.266	.329	.388	717	92	-2	0	1	-0	.989	4	C-44	0.4
1963	Was-A☆	73	211	20	50	11	0	6	24	20	29	.237	.306	.374	680	90	-3	0	0	0	.984	-8	C-60	-0.8
1964	Was-A	50	122	6	19	3	0	3	12	11	32	.156	.226	.254	480	33	-11	0	0	0	.990	1	C-43	-0.9
Total	4	190	532	46	122	22	2	15	59	44	93	.229	.291	.363	653	78	-16	0	1	-0	.985	-2	C-168	-1.2
■ DUTCH LERCHEN	Lerchen, Bertram Roe b: 4/4/1889, Detroit, Mich. d: 1/7/62, Detroit, Mich. BR/TR, 5'8", 160 lbs. Deb: 8/14/10																							
1910	Bos-A	6	15	1	0	0	0	0	0	1		.000	.063	.000	63	-78	-3	0			.929	-3	/S-6	-0.8
■ GEORGE LERCHEN	Lerchen, George Edward b: 12/1/22, Detroit, Mich. BB/TR (BL 1953), 5'11", 175 lbs. Deb: 4/15/52																							
1952	Det-A	14	32	1	5	1	0	1	3	7	10	.156	.308	.281	589	64	-1	1	0	0	1.000	-0	/O-7(0-3-4)	-0.2
1953	Cin-N	22	17	2	5	1	0	0	2	5	6	.294	.455	.353	807	113	1	0	0	0	1.000	-0	/O-1(0-1-0)	0.0
Total	2	36	49	3	10	2	0	1	5	12	16	.204	.361	.306	667	82	-1	1	0	0	1.000	-1	/O-8(0-4-4)	-0.2
■ WALT LERIAN	Lerian, Walter Irvin "Peck" b: 2/10/03, Baltimore, Md. d: 10/22/29, Baltimore, Md. BR/TR, 5'11", 170 lbs. Deb: 4/16/28																							
1928	Phi-N	96	239	28	65	16	2	2	25	41	29	.272	.385	.381	766	97	1	1			.977	-3	C-74	0.3
1929	Phi-N	105	273	28	61	13	2	6	25	53	37	.223	.354	.352	705	71	-12	0			**.986**	1	*C-103	-0.4
Total	2	201	512	56	126	29	4	8	50	94	66	.246	.368	.365	733	83	-11	1			.982	-1	C-177	-0.1
■ BRIAN LESHER	Lesher, Brian Herbert b: 3/5/71, Wilrijk, Belgium BR/TL, 6'5", 205 lbs. Deb: 8/25/96 Career OF: (49-LF 0-CF 17-RF)																							
1996	Oak-A	26	82	11	19	3	0	5	16	5	17	.232	.284	.451	735	84	-2	0	0	0	.977	-3	O-25(14-0-14)/1-1	-0.6
1997	Oak-A	46	131	17	30	4	1	4	16	9	30	.229	.279	.366	645	68	-7	4	1	1	.958	2	O-32(31-0-3)/1-3,D-3	-0.5
1998	Oak-A	7	7	0	1	1	0	0	1	0	3	.143	.143	.286	429	8	-1	0	0	0	1.000	1	/O-4(4-0-0),1-1	0.0
2000	Sea-A	5	5	1	4	1	1	0	3	1	0	.800	.833	1.400	2233	463	3	1	0	0	1.000	0	/1-4	0.3
Total	4	84	225	29	54	9	2	9	36	15	50	.240	.290	.418	708	81	-7	5	1	1	.967	-0	/O-61L,1-9,D-3	-0.8
■ ROY LESLIE	Leslie, Roy Reid b: 8/23/1894, Bailey, Tex. d: 4/9/72, Sherman, Tex. BR/TR, 6'1", 175 lbs. Deb: 9/6/17																							
1917	Chi-N	7	19	1	4	0	0	0	1	1	5	.211	.250	.211	461	39	-1	1			.969	-0	/1-6	-0.2
1919	StL-N	12	24	2	5	1	0	0	4	4	3	.208	.321	.250	571	78	-0	0			.957	-0	/1-9	-0.1
1922	Phi-N	141	513	44	139	23	2	6	50	37	49	.271	.320	.359	679	68	-24	3	7	-2	.990	-4	*1-139	-3.7
Total	3	160	556	47	148	24	2	6	55	42	57	.266	.318	.349	667	68	-26	4	7		.988	-4	1-154	-4.0
■ SAM LESLIE	Leslie, Samuel Andrew "Sambo" b: 7/26/05, Moss Point, Miss. d: 1/21/79, Pascagoula, Miss. BL/TL, 6', 192 lbs. Deb: 10/6/29																							
1929	NY-N	1	1	0	0	0	0	0	1	0	0	.000	.000	.000	0	-99	-0	0			1.000	-0	/O-1(1-0-0)	-0.1
1930	NY-N	2	2	0	1	0	0	0	0	0	1	.500	.500	.500	1000	146	0	0			.000	0	H	0.0
1931	NY-N	53	53	11	16	4	0	3	5	1	2	.302	.315	.547	862	131	2	3			1.000	0	/1-6	0.2
1932	NY-N	77	75	5	22	4	0	1	15	2	5	.293	.329	.387	716	94	-1	0			1.000	-0	/1-2	-0.1
1933	NY-N	40	137	21	44	12	3	3	27	12	9	.321	.380	.518	898	157	10	0			.990	-0	1-35	0.7
	Bro-N	96	364	41	104	11	4	5	46	23	14	.286	.340	.379	719	110	5	1			.982	-6	1-95	-1.1
	Yr	136	501	62	148	23	7	8	73	35	23	.295	.351	.417	768	123	15	1			.984	-6	*1-130	-0.4
1934	Bro-N	146	546	75	181	29	6	9	102	69	34	.332	.409	.456	865	138	32	5			.993	5	*1-138	2.3
1935	Bro-N	142	520	72	160	30	7	5	93	55	19	.308	.379	.421	800	117	14	4			.989	-0	*1-138	0.1

YEAR	TM/L	G	AB	R	H	2B	3B	HR	RBI	BB	SO	AVG	OBP	SLG	OPS	OPS+	BR+	SB	CS	SBR	FA	FR	G/POS	TPR
1936	*NY-N	117	417	49	123	19	5	6	54	23	16	.295	.335	.408	743	100	-1	0			.991	0	1-99	-1.0
1937	*NY-N	72	191	25	59	7	2	3	30	20	12	.309	.380	.414	794	114	4	1			.990	3	1-44	0.3
1938	NY-N	76	154	12	39	7	1	1	16	11	6	.253	.307	.331	638	75	-5	0			.988	-3	1-32	-1.1
Total	10	822	2460	311	749	123	28	36	389	216	118	.304	.366	.421	787	117	60	14			.989	-2	1-589/O-1(1-0-0)	0.2
■ CHARLIE LETCHAS	Letchas, Charlie b: 10/3/15, Thomasville, Ga. d: 3/14/95, Tampa, Fla. BR/TR, 5'10", 150 lbs. Deb: 9/16/39																							
1939	Phi-N	12	44	2	10	2	0	1	3	1	2	.227	.244	.341	585	57	-3	0			.933	-1	2-12	-0.3
1941	Was-A	2	8	0	1	0	0	0	1	1	1	.125	.222	.125	347	-6	-1	0	0	0	.800	-1	/2-2	-0.2
1944	Phi-N	116	396	29	94	8	0	0	33	32	27	.237	.298	.258	555	59	-21	0			.968	6	2-47,3-32,S-29	-0.9
1946	Phi-N	6	13	1	3	0	0	0	0	1	1	.231	.286	.231	516	49	-1	0			1.000	1	/2-4	0.0
Total	4	136	461	32	108	10	0	1	37	35	31	.234	.291	.262	554	58	-26	0	0		.959	5	/2-65,3-32,S-29	-1.4
■ TOM LETCHER	Letcher, Frederick Thomas b: 1/1868, Bryan, Ohio BL, 6', Deb: 9/27/1891																							
1891	Mil-a	6	21	3	4	1	0	0	2	0	1	.190	.190	.238	429	19	-2	1			.857	0	/O-6(1-0-5)	-0.2
■ LEUTZ	Leutz Deb: 5/7/1872																							
1872	Eck-n	4	12	2	1	0	0	0	0	0	0	.083	.083	.083	167	-57	-2	0	0	0	.733	-3	/C-4	-0.4
■ JESSE LEVAN	Levan, Jesse Roy b: 7/15/26, Reading, Pa. d: 11/30/98, Reading, Pa. BL/TR, 6', 172 lbs. Deb: 9/27/47																							
1947	Phi-N	2	9	3	4	0	0	0	1	0	0	.444	.444	.444	889	142	1	0			1.000	-1	/O-2(2-0-0)	0.0
1954	Was-A	7	10	1	3	0	0	0	0	0	0	.300	.300	.300	600	68	-0	0	0	0	.000	-0	/3-4,1-1	-0.1
1955	Was-A	16	16	1	3	0	0	1	4	0	2	.188	.188	.375	563	51	-1	0	0	0	.000	0	H	-0.1
Total	3	25	35	5	10	0	0	1	5	0	2	.286	.286	.371	657	80	-1	0	0		—	-1	/3-4,O-2(2-0-0),1-1	-0.2
■ JIM LEVEY	Levey, James Julius b: 9/13/06, Pittsburgh, Pa. d: 3/14/70, Dallas, Tex. BB/TR (BR 1930-31), 5'10.5", 154 lbs. Deb: 9/17/30																							
1930	StL-A	8	37	7	9	2	0	0	3	3	2	.243	.300	.297	597	50	-3	0	0	0	.958	2	/S-8	0.0
1931	StL-A	139	498	53	104	19	2	5	38	35	83	.209	.264	.285	549	43	-42	13	8	0	.920	-10	*S-139	-4.0
1932	StL-A	152	568	59	159	30	8	4	63	21	48	.280	.310	.382	692	74	-23	6	4	-0	.939	-18	*S-152	-2.8
1933	StL-A	141	529	43	103	10	4	2	36	26	68	.195	.237	.240	477	25	-57	4	6	-1	.945	-6	*S-138	-5.2
Total	4	440	1632	162	375	61	14	11	140	85	201	.230	.272	.305	576	48	-125	23	18	-1	.936	-33	S-437	-12.0
■ CHARLIE LEVIS	Levis, Charles H. b: 6/21/1860, St.Louis, Mo. d: 10/16/26, St.Louis, Mo. BR, Deb: 4/17/1884																							
1884	Bal-U	87	373	59	85	11	4	5		3		.228	.234	.319	553	60	-30				.955	-0	*1-87	-3.4
	Was-U	1	3	0	0	0	0	0		0		.000	.000	.000	0	-99	-1				1.000	0	/1-1	-0.1
	Yr	88	376	59	85	11	4	5		3		.226	.232	.316	549	59	-30				.955	-0	1-88	-3.5
	Ind-a	3	10	0	2	0	0	0		0		.200	.200	.200	400	32	-1				1.000	0	/1-3	-0.1
1885	Bal-a	1	4	2	1	0	0	0	0	0		.250	.400	.250	650	110	0				.889	-0	/1-1	0.0
Total	2	92	390	61	88	11	4	5	0	3		.226	.234	.313	546	59	-31				.956	-0	/1-92	-3.6
■ JESSE LEVIS	Levis, Jesse b: 4/14/68, Philadelphia, Pa. BL/TR, 5'9", 180 lbs. Deb: 4/24/92																							
1992	Cle-A	28	43	2	12	4	0	1	3	0	5	.279	.279	.442	721	101	-0	0	0	0	.985	1	C-21/D-1	0.2
1993	Cle-A	31	63	7	11	2	0	0	4	2	10	.175	.200	.206	406	9	-8	0	0	0	.991	1	C-29	-0.6
1994	Cle-A	1	1	0	1	0	0	0	0	0	0	1.000	1.000	1.000	2000	417	0	0	0	0	.000	0	/H	0.0
1995	Cle-A	12	18	1	6	2	0	0	3	1	0	.333	.368	.444	813	109	0	0	0	0	1.000	0	C-12	0.1
1996	Mil-A	104	233	27	55	6	1	1	21	38	15	.236	.348	.283	631	60	-13	0	0	0	**.998**	3	C-90/D-6	-0.5
1997	Mil-A	99	200	19	57	7	0	1	19	24	17	.285	.364	.335	699	83	-4	1	0	0	.994	-10	C-78/D-8	-1.0
1998	Mil-N	22	37	4	13	0	0	0	4	7	6	.351	.478	.351	830	123	2	1	0	0	1.000	1	C-14	0.4
1999	Cle-A	10	26	0	4	0	0	0	3	1	6	.154	.214	.154	368	-4	-4	0	0	0	1.000	1	/C-9	-0.3
Total	8	307	621	60	159	21	1	3	57	73	59	.256	.340	.308	648	68	-27	2	0	0	.995	-3	C-253/D-15	-1.7
■ ED LEVY	Levy, Edward Clarence (b: Edward Clarence Whitner) b: 10/28/16, Birmingham, Ala. BR/TR, 6'5.5", 190 lbs. Deb: 4/16/40																							
1940	Phi-N	1	1	0	0	0	0	0	0	0	0	.000	.000	.000	0	-99	-0	0			.000	0	H	0.0
1942	NY-A	13	41	5	5	0	0	0	3	4	5	.122	.200	.122	322	-9	-6	1	0	0	.992	2	1-13	-0.5
1944	NY-A	40	153	12	37	11	2	4	29	6	19	.242	.270	.418	689	92	-3	1	1	-0	.962	-1	O-36(36-0-0)	-0.7
Total	3	54	195	17	42	11	2	4	32	10	24	.215	.254	.354	608	70	-9	2	1		.962	0	/O-36(36-0-0),1-13	-1.2
■ LEWIS	Lewis b: Brooklyn, N.Y. Deb: 7/12/1890																							
1890	Buf-P	1	5	1	1	0	0	0	0	0	0	.200	.200	.200	400	8	-1	0			.000	0	/O-1(1-0-0),P-1	-0.1
■ ALLAN LEWIS	Lewis, Allan Sydney "The Panamanian Express" b: 12/12/41, Colon, Panama BB/TR, 6', 170 lbs. Deb: 4/11/67																							
1967	KC-A	34	6	7	1	0	0	0	0	0	3	.167	.167	.167	333	-1	-1	14	5	1	.000	0	H	0.1
1968	Oak-A	26	4	9	1	0	0	0	0	1	0	.250	.400	.250	650	105	0	8	4	0	.000	-0	/O-1(1-0-0)	0.0
1969	Oak-A	12	1	2	0	0	0	0	0	0	0	.000	.000	.000	0	-99	-0	0	0	0	.000	0	H	0.0
1970	Oak-A	25	8	8	2	0	0	1	1	0	0	.250	.250	.625	875	139	0	7	1	1	1.000	-0	/O-2(2-0-0)	0.1
1972	*Oak-A	24	10	5	2	1	0	0	2	0	1	.200	.200	.300	500	50	-1	8	3	1	.900	-1	/O-6(5-0-1)	-0.1
1973	*Oak-A	35	0	16	0	0	0	0	0	0	0	—	—	—	—	—	0	7	4	0	1.000	-0	/O-1(1-0-0),D-6	0.0
Total	6	156	29	47	6	1	0	1	3	1	4	.207	.233	.345	578	69	-1	44	17	4	.923	-2	/O-10(9-0-1),D-6	0.1
■ DARREN LEWIS	Lewis, Darren Joel b: 8/28/67, Berkeley, Cal. BR/TR, 6', 189 lbs. Deb: 8/21/90 Career OF: (49-LF 993-CF 149-RF)																							
1990	Oak-A	25	35	4	8	0	0	0	1	7	4	.229	.372	.229	601	75	-1	2	0	0	1.000	-5	O-23(3-16-5)/D-2	-0.5
1991	SF-N	72	222	41	55	5	3	1	15	36	30	.248	.358	.311	669	93	-1	13	7	0	1.000	3	O-68(0-68-0)	0.3
1992	SF-N	100	320	38	74	8	1	1	18	29	46	.231	.297	.272	569	66	-14	28	8	3	1.000	0	O-94(0-94-0)	-1.2
1993	SF-N	136	522	84	132	17	7	2	48	30	40	.253	.302	.324	626	70	-22	46	15	5	**1.000**	8	*O-131(0-131-0)	-0.8
1994	SF-N	114	451	70	116	15	**9**	4	29	53	50	.257	.341	.357	698	86	-8	30	13	2	.993	3	*O-113(0-113-0)	-0.2
1995	SF-N	74	309	47	78	10	3	1	16	17	37	.252	.304	.314	618	65	-15	21	7	2	.995	8	O-73(0-73-0)	-0.5
	*Cin-N	58	163	19	40	3	0	0	8	17	20	.245	.324	.264	588	58	-9	11	11	-1	.992	1	O-57(0-57-0)	-0.9
	Yr	132	472	66	118	13	3	1	24	34	57	.250	.311	.297	608	63	-25	32	18	1	.994	8	*O-130(0-130-0)	-1.4
1996	Chi-A	141	337	55	77	12	2	4	53	45	40	.228	.325	.312	636	65	-17	21	5	3	.990	-11	*O-138(1-137-0)	-2.2
1997	Chi-A	81	77	15	18	1	0	0	5	11	14	.234	.330	.247	576	56	-5	11	4	1	1.000	-12	O-64(0-64-0)/D-6	-1.5
	LA-N	26	77	7	23	3	1	1	10	6	17	.299	.349	.403	752	104	0	3	2	-0	.980	1	O-25(23-2-1)	0.1
1998	*Bos-A	155	585	95	157	25	3	8	63	70	94	.268	.354	.362	717	85	-11	29	12	2	.992	3	*O-152(4-109-55)/D-1	-0.7
1999	*Bos-A	135	470	63	113	14	6	2	40	45	52	.240	.313	.309	622	58	-29	16	10	0	.994	3	*O-130(0-88-51)/D-2	-2.6
2000	Bos-A	97	270	44	65	12	0	2	17	22	34	.241	.305	.307	612	54	-19	10	5	0	.981	-7	O-89(18-41-37)/D-5	-2.5
Total	11	1214	3838	582	956	125	35	26	323	388	478	.249	.325	.320	645	72	-151	241	99	18	.994	-5	*O-1157C/D-16	-13.2
■ FRED LEWIS	Lewis, Frederick Miller b: 10/13/1858, Buffalo, N.Y. d: 6/5/45, Utica, N.Y. BB/TR, 5'10.5", 194 lbs. Deb: 7/2/1881																							
1881	Bos-N	27	114	17	25	6	0	0	9	7	5	.219	.264	.272	536	72	-3				.837	-2	O-27(0-3-24)	-0.5
1883	Phi-N	38	160	21	40	7	0	0	18	4	13	.250	.268	.294	562	78	-4				.814	1	O-38(0-38-0)	-0.4
	StL-a	49	209	37	63	8	4	1	33	1		.301	.305	.392	697	116	3				.848	-0	O-49(0-49-0)	0.1
1884	StL-a	73	300	59	97	25	3	0		16		.323	.366	.427	792	152	17				.853	3	O-73(0-73-0)	1.5
	StL-U	8	30	6	9	1	0	0		3		.300	.364	.333	697	109	-0				.909	-2	/O-8(0-8-0)	-0.2
1885	StL-N	45	181	12	53	9	0	1	27	9	10	.293	.326	.359	685	130	6				.957	7	O-45(9-37-0)	1.1
1886	Cin-a	77	324	72	103	14	6	2	32	20		.318	.365	.417	782	140	14	8			.884	-2	O-76(0-76-0)/3-1	0.8
Total	5	317	1318	224	390	70	13	4	119	60	28	.296	.330	.378	708	124	32	8			.866	4	O-316(9-284-24)/3-1	2.4
■ DUFFY LEWIS	Lewis, George Edward b: 4/18/1888, San Francisco, Cal d: 6/17/79, Salem, N.H. BL/TL, 5'10.5", 165 lbs. Deb: 4/16/10 C Career OF: (1415-LF 15-CF 2-RF)																							
1910	Bos-A	151	541	64	153	29	7	8	68	32		.283	.328	.407	734	127	14	10			.944	10	*O-149(149-0-0)	1.8
1911	Bos-A	130	469	64	144	32	4	7	86	25		.307	.355	.437	792	122	12	11			.939	5	*O-125(125-0-0)	1.1
1912	*Bos-A	154	581	85	165	36	9	6	109	52		.284	.346	.408	754	110	6	9			.947	7	*O-154(154-0-0)	0.6
1913	Bos-A	149	551	54	164	31	12	0	90	30	55	.298	.336	.397	734	112	6	12			.960	11	*O-142L/P-1,3-1	1.1
1914	Bos-A	146	510	53	142	37	9	2	79	57	41	.278	.357	.398	755	127	16	22	31	-6	.952	-2	*O-142(142-0-0)	0.3
1915	*Bos-A	152	557	69	162	31	7	2	76	45	63	.291	.348	.382	731	122	14	14	7	1	.952	-7	*O-152(152-0-0)	0.0

YEAR	TM/L	G	AB	R	H	2B	3B	HR	RBI	BB	SO	AVG	OBP	SLG	OPS	OPS+	BR+	SB	CS	SBR	FA	FR	G/POS	TPR
1916	*Bos-A	152	563	56	151	29	5	1	56	33	56	.268	.313	.343	656	97	-4	16			.970	-1	*O-151(136-15-0)	-1.4
1917	Bos-A	150	553	55	167	29	9	1	65	29	54	.302	.342	.392	735	125	14	8			.972	4	*O-150(150-0-0)	1.3
1919	NY-A	141	559	67	152	23	4	7	89	17	42	.272	.293	.365	658	84	-14	8			.985	-6	*O-141(141-0-0)	-2.8
1920	NY-A	107	365	34	99	8	1	4	61	24	32	.271	.320	.332	651	70	-16	2	8	-2	.961	-2	O-99(98-0-1)	-2.4
1921	Was-A	27	102	11	19	4	1	0	14	8	10	.186	.252	.245	497	29	-11	1	1	-0	.980	-2	O-27(26-0-1)	-1.5
Total	11	1459	5351	612	1518	289	68	38	793	352	353	.284	.333	.384	717	108	36	113	47		.959	16	*O-1432L/3-1,P-1	-1.9

■ **JACK LEWIS** Lewis, John David b: 2/14/1884, Pittsburgh, Pa. d: 2/25/56, Steubenville, Ohio BR/TR, 5′8″, 158 lbs. Deb: 9/16/11 Career OF: (0-LF 0-CF 6-RF)

YEAR	TM/L	G	AB	R	H	2B	3B	HR	RBI	BB	SO	AVG	OBP	SLG	OPS	OPS+	BR+	SB	CS	SBR	FA	FR	G/POS	TPR
1911	Bos-A	18	59	7	16	0	0	0	6	7		.271	.368	.271	639	80	-1	2			.931	-2	2-18	-0.2
1914	Pit-F	117	394	32	92	14	5	1	48	17	46	.234	.276	.302	578	58	-30	9			.949	9	*2-115/S-1	-2.1
1915	Pit-F	82	231	24	61	6	5	0	26	8	31	.264	.292	.333	625	76	-11	7			.962	-2	2-45,S-11/O-6R,13	-1.4
Total	3	217	684	63	169	20	10	1	80	32	77	.247	.290	.310	600	66	-42	18			.951	5	2-178/S-12,O-6R,13	-3.7

■ **BUDDY LEWIS** Lewis, John Kelly b: 8/10/16, Gastonia, N.C. BL/TR, 6′1″, 175 lbs. Deb: 9/16/35

YEAR	TM/L	G	AB	R	H	2B	3B	HR	RBI	BB	SO	AVG	OBP	SLG	OPS	OPS+	BR+	SB	CS	SBR	FA	FR	G/POS	TPR
1935	Was-A	8	28	0	3	0	0	0	2	0	5	.107	.107	.107	214	-46	-6	0	0	0	.941	-0	/3-6	-0.6
1936	Was-A	143	601	100	175	21	13	6	67	47	46	.291	.347	.399	746	89	-12	6	6	-1	.933	5	*3-139	-0.2
1937	Was-A	156	668	107	210	32	6	10	79	52	44	.314	.367	.425	792	104	3	11	5	1	.938	-19	*3-156	-0.9
1938	Was-A★	151	656	122	194	35	9	12	91	58	35	.296	.354	.431	785	103	1	17	9	1	.912	-0	*3-151	0.7
1939	Was-A	140	536	87	171	23	**16**	10	75	72	27	.319	.402	.478	879	134	29	10	9	-1	.933	14	*3-134	4.2
1940	Was-A	148	600	101	190	38	10	6	63	74	36	.317	.393	.443	836	124	23	15	10	-0	.960	-1	*O-112(0-0-112),3-36	1.6
1941	Was-A	149	569	97	169	29	11	9	72	82	30	.297	.386	.434	820	122	20	10	7	-0	.972	3	O-96(0-0-96),3-49	1.8
1945	Was-A	69	258	42	86	14	7	2	37	37	15	.333	.423	.465	888	172	25	1	2	-0	.981	4	O-69(0-0-69)	2.5
1946	Was-A	150	582	82	170	28	13	7	45	59	26	.292	.359	.421	780	125	19	5	3	0	.970	4	*O-145(8-1-137)	1.8
1947	Was-A★	140	506	67	132	15	4	6	48	51	27	.261	.330	.342	672	89	-7	6	6	-1	.968	1	*O-130(0-0-130)	-1.2
1949	Was-A	95	257	25	63	14	4	3	28	41	12	.245	.355	.366	721	93	-2	2	2	-0	.979	-0	O-67(0-0-67)	-0.5
Total	11	1349	5261	830	1563	249	93	71	607	573	303	.297	.368	.420	789	112	92	83	59	-2	.927	11	3-671,O-619(8-1-611)	9.2

■ **JOHNNY LEWIS** Lewis, Johnny Joe b: 8/10/39, Greenville, Ala. BL/TR, 6′1″, 189 lbs. Deb: 4/14/64 C

YEAR	TM/L	G	AB	R	H	2B	3B	HR	RBI	BB	SO	AVG	OBP	SLG	OPS	OPS+	BR+	SB	CS	SBR	FA	FR	G/POS	TPR
1964	StL-N	40	94	10	22	2	2	2	7	13	23	.234	.327	.362	689	86	-1	2	2	-0	.966	-1	O-36(2-0-34)	-0.4
1965	NY-N	148	477	64	117	15	3	15	45	59	117	.245	.332	.384	716	105	4	4	7	-2	.975	1	*O-142(0-48-101)	-0.5
1966	NY-N	65	166	21	32	6	1	5	20	21	43	.193	.283	.331	615	72	-6	2	0	0	.988	-3	O-49(11-8-31)	-1.2
1967	NY-N	13	34	2	4	1	0	0	2	2	11	.118	.167	.147	314	-10	-5	0	0	0	1.000	-0	O-10(2-0-9)	-0.6
Total	4	266	771	97	175	24	6	22	74	95	194	.227	.314	.359	673	90	-9	8	9	-1	.977	-3	O-237(15-56-175)	-2.7

■ **MARK LEWIS** Lewis, Mark David b: 11/30/69, Hamilton, Ohio BR/TR, 6′1″, 190 lbs. Deb: 4/26/91

YEAR	TM/L	G	AB	R	H	2B	3B	HR	RBI	BB	SO	AVG	OBP	SLG	OPS	OPS+	BR+	SB	CS	SBR	FA	FR	G/POS	TPR
1991	Cle-A	84	314	29	83	15	1	0	30	15	45	.264	.298	.318	616	70	-13	2	2	-0	.966	-14	2-50,S-36	-2.4
1992	Cle-A	122	413	44	109	21	0	5	30	25	69	.264	.311	.351	662	87	-8	4	5	-1	.954	-9	*S-121/3-1	-1.0
1993	Cle-A	14	52	6	13	2	0	1	5	0	7	.250	.250	.346	596	59	-3	3	0	1	.964	-3	S-13	-0.5
1994	Cle-A	20	73	6	15	5	0	1	8	2	13	.205	.227	.315	542	38	-7	1	0	0	.902	-7	S-13/3-6,2-1	-1.2
1995	*Cin-N	81	171	25	58	13	1	3	30	21	33	.339	.411	.480	891	135	9	0	3	-1	.968	2	3-72/2-2,S-2	1.0
1996	Det-A	145	545	69	147	30	3	11	55	42	109	.270	.328	.396	724	82	-15	6	1	1	.987	-7	*2-144/D-1	-1.3
1997	*SF-N	118	341	50	91	14	6	10	42	23	62	.267	.321	.431	752	97	-2	3	2	-0	.945	-12	3-69,2-29/D-1	-1.3
1998	Phi-N	142	518	52	129	21	2	9	54	48	111	.249	.316	.349	666	74	-19	3	3	-0	.978	16	*2-140	0.3
1999	Cin-N	88	173	18	44	16	0	6	28	7	24	.254	.283	.451	734	80	-6	0	0	0	.938	-9	3-52/2-2	-1.4
2000	Cin-N	11	19	1	2	1	0	0	3	1	3	.105	.150	.158	308	-21	-4	0	0	0	.909	0	/3-5	-0.3
	Bal-A	71	163	19	44	17	0	2	21	12	31	.270	.324	.411	735	87	-3	7	2	1	.857	5	3-29,2-21,S-14,/D-4	0.3
Total	10	896	2782	319	735	155	13	48	306	196	507	.264	.316	.381	697	83	-71	29	18	0	.977	-40	2-389,3-234,S-199,/D	-7.8

■ **PHIL LEWIS** Lewis, Philip b: 10/8/1884, Pittsburgh, Pa. d: 8/8/59, Port Wentworth, Ga. BR/TR, 6′, 195 lbs. Deb: 4/14/05

YEAR	TM/L	G	AB	R	H	2B	3B	HR	RBI	BB	SO	AVG	OBP	SLG	OPS	OPS+	BR+	SB	CS	SBR	FA	FR	G/POS	TPR
1905	Bro-N	118	433	32	110	9	2	3	33	16		.254	.282	.305	587	81	-11	16			.904	-6	*S-118	-1.4
1906	Bro-N	136	452	40	110	8	4	0	37	43		.243	.309	.279	588	90	-4	14			.922	-22	*S-135	-2.5
1907	Bro-N	136	475	52	118	11	1	0	30	23		.248	.286	.276	562	83	-10	16			.938	-20	*S-136	-3.0
1908	Bro-N	118	415	22	91	5	6	1	30	13		.219	.243	.267	510	66	-17	9			.943	-7	*S-116	-2.4
Total	4	508	1775	146	429	33	13	4	130	95		.242	.281	.282	563	80	-43	55			.926	-55	S-505	-9.3

■ **BILL LEWIS** Lewis, William Henry "Buddy" b: 10/15/04, Ripley, Tenn. d: 10/24/77, Memphis, Tenn. BR/TR, 5′9″, 165 lbs. Deb: 6/3/33

YEAR	TM/L	G	AB	R	H	2B	3B	HR	RBI	BB	SO	AVG	OBP	SLG	OPS	OPS+	BR+	SB	CS	SBR	FA	FR	G/POS	TPR
1933	StL-N	15	35	8	14	1	0	1	8	2	3	.400	.432	.514	947	161	3	0			1.000	1	/C-8	0.4
1935	Bos-N	6	4	1	0	0	0	0	0	1	1	.000	.200	.000	200	-45	-1	0			.000	0	/C-1	-0.1
1936	Bos-N	29	62	11	19	2	0	0	3	12	7	.306	.419	.339	758	113	2	0			.967	-4	C-21	-0.1
Total	3	50	101	20	33	3	0	1	11	15	11	.327	.414	.386	800	124	4	0			.981	-3	/C-30	0.2

■ **JIM LEYRITZ** Leyritz, James Joseph b: 12/27/63, Lakewood, Ohio BR/TR, 6′, 195 lbs. Deb: 6/8/90 Career OF: (25-LF 0-CF 30-RF)

YEAR	TM/L	G	AB	R	H	2B	3B	HR	RBI	BB	SO	AVG	OBP	SLG	OPS	OPS+	BR+	SB	CS	SBR	FA	FR	G/POS	TPR
1990	NY-A	92	303	28	78	13	1	5	25	27	51	.257	.332	.356	689	92	-3	2	3	-1	.929	-19	3-69,O-14L,C-11	-2.3
1991	NY-A	32	77	8	14	3	0	0	4	13	15	.182	.300	.221	521	46	-5	0	1	-0	.909	-8	3-18/C-5,1-3,D-1	-1.3
1992	NY-A	63	144	17	37	6	0	7	26	14	22	.257	.348	.444	792	121	4	0	1	-0	.990	3	D-31,C-18/1-2,3O2	0.7
1993	NY-A	95	259	43	80	14	0	14	53	37	59	.309	.411	.525	936	155	21	0	0	0	.993	-6	1-29,O-28R,D-21,C	1.1
1994	NY-A	75	249	47	66	12	0	17	58	35	61	.265	.369	.518	887	130	11	0	0	0	1.000	-3	C-37,D-25,1-10	0.8
1995	*NY-A	77	264	37	71	12	0	7	37	37	73	.269	.375	.394	769	102	2	1	1	-0	.993	-3	C-46,1-18,D-15	0.0
1996	*NY-A	88	265	23	70	10	0	7	40	30	68	.264	.359	.381	740	87	-4	2	0	0	.995	-4	C-55,3-13,D-12,/1O2	-0.5
1997	Ana-A	84	294	47	81	7	0	11	50	37	56	.276	.362	.412	774	102	1	1	1	-0	1.000	-1	C-58,1-15,D-13	0.2
	Tex-A	37	85	11	24	4	0	0	14	23	22	.282	.450	.329	780	102	2	1	0	0	.984	-1	C-11/1-9,D-9	0.1
	Yr	121	379	58	105	11	0	11	64	60	78	.277	.384	.393	777	102	3	2	1	0	.998	-2	C-69,1-24,D-22	0.3
1998	Bos-A	52	129	17	37	6	0	8	24	21	34	.287	.395	.519	914	132	7	0	0	0	1.000	1	D-39/C-1,1-1	0.5
	*SD-N	62	143	17	38	10	0	4	18	21	40	.266	.386	.420	806	121	5	0	0	0	.987	-3	C-24,1-20/3-1,O-1L	0.2
1999	SD-N	50	134	17	32	5	0	8	21	15	37	.239	.333	.455	789	105	1	0	0	0	.994	4	C-24,1-19/3-1	0.4
	*NY-A	31	66	8	15	4	1	0	5	13	17	.227	.354	.318	673	74	-2	0	0	0	.986	1	D-14/1-9,C-1,3-1	-0.2
2000	NY-A	24	55	2	12	0	0	1	4	7	14	.218	.317	.273	590	52	-4	0	0	0	1.000	0	D-15/C-2,1-1	-0.4
	LA-N	41	60	3	12	1	0	1	8	7	12	.200	.294	.267	561	45	-5	0	0	0	1.000	-2	/1-8,O-6(5-0-1),C-3	-0.8
Total	11	903	2527	325	667	107	2	90	387	337	581	.264	.365	.415	780	106	31	7	7	-1	.995	-42	C-308,D-195,13/O2	-1.5

■ **CARLOS LEZCANO** Lezcano, Carlos Manuel (Rubio) b: 9/30/55, Arecibo, P.R. BR/TR, 6′2″, 185 lbs. Deb: 4/10/80

YEAR	TM/L	G	AB	R	H	2B	3B	HR	RBI	BB	SO	AVG	OBP	SLG	OPS	OPS+	BR+	SB	CS	SBR	FA	FR	G/POS	TPR
1980	Chi-N	42	88	15	18	4	1	3	12	11	29	.205	.300	.375	675	81	-2	1	2	-0	.948	-4	O-39(0-39-0)	-0.7
1981	Chi-N	7	14	1	1	0	0	0	2	0	4	.071	.071	.071	143	-57	-3	0	0	0	1.000	-1	/O-5(1-0-4)	-0.4
Total	2	49	102	16	19	4	1	3	14	11	33	.186	.272	.333	605	64	-5	1	2	-0	.952	-4	/O-44(1-39-4)	-1.1

■ **SIXTO LEZCANO** Lezcano, Sixto Joaquin (Curras) b: 11/28/53, Arecibo, P.R. BR/TR, 5′11″, 175 lbs. Deb: 9/10/74 Career OF: (126-LF 21-CF 1058-RF)

YEAR	TM/L	G	AB	R	H	2B	3B	HR	RBI	BB	SO	AVG	OBP	SLG	OPS	OPS+	BR+	SB	CS	SBR	FA	FR	G/POS	TPR
1974	Mil-A	15	54	5	13	2	0	2	9	4	9	.241	.293	.389	682	95	-0	1	1	-0	.972	2	O-15(0-0-15)	0.1
1975	Mil-A	134	429	55	106	19	3	11	43	46	93	.247	.326	.382	708	99	-1	5	5	-1	.977	-3	*O-129(0-2-128)/D-2	-1.1
1976	Mil-A	145	513	53	146	19	5	7	56	51	112	.285	.352	.382	734	117	11	14	10	-0	.973	8	*O-142(64-17-66)/D-3	1.2
1977	Mil-A	109	400	50	109	21	4	21	49	52	78	.273	.359	.503	862	132	18	6	5	-0	.988	13	*O-108(0-0-108)	2.4
1978	Mil-A	132	442	62	129	21	4	15	61	64	83	.292	.383	.459	842	135	22	3	3	-0	.979	10	*O-127(0-0-127)/D-3	2.5
1979	Mil-A	138	473	84	152	29	3	28	101	77	74	.321	.420	.573	992	165	45	4	3	-0	.986	4	*O-135(0-0-135)/D-1	3.9
1980	Mil-A	112	411	51	94	19	3	18	55	39	75	.229	.300	.421	721	98	-2	1	1	-0	.983	6	*O-108(0-0-108)/D-4	-0.2
1981	StL-N	72	214	26	57	8	2	5	28	40	40	.266	.382	.393	774	117	6	0	1	-0	.973	-4	O-65(32-0-34)	-0.1
1982	SD-N	138	470	73	136	26	6	16	84	78	69	.289	.393	.472	865	149	33	2	1	0	.990	16	*O-134(0-0-134)	4.3
1983	SD-N	97	317	41	74	11	2	8	49	47	66	.233	.334	.356	691	95	-2	0	0	0	.968	5	O-91(0-0-91)	-0.1
	*Phi-N	18	39	8	11	1	0	0	7	5	9	.282	.364	.308	671	89	-0	1	0	0	1.000	-1	O-15(1-2-13)	-0.1
	Yr	115	356	49	85	12	2	8	56	52	75	.239	.337	.351	689	94	-2	1	0	0	.971	5	*O-106(1-2-104)	-0.2
1984	Phi-N	109	256	36	71	6	2	14	40	38	43	.277	.371	.480	851	135	12	0	1	-0	.981	-1	O-87(4-0-83)	0.8
1985	Pit-N	72	116	16	24	2	0	3	9	35	17	.207	.395	.302	696	98	2	0	0	0	.967	-2	O-40(25-0-16)	-0.2
Total	12	1291	4134	560	1122	184	34	148	591	576	768	.271	.363	.440	803	125	143	37	31	-3	.980	52	*O-1196R/D-13	13.4

YEAR	TM/L	G	AB	R	H	2B	3B	HR	RBI	BB	SO	AVG	OBP	SLG	OPS	OPS+	BR+	SB	CS	SBR	FA	FR	G/POS	TPR
■ **STEVE LIBBY** Libby, Stephen Augustus b: 12/8/1853, Scarborough, Me. d: 3/31/35, Milford, Conn. 6'1.5", 168 lbs. Deb: 5/10/1879																								
1879	Buf-N	1	2	0	0	0	0	0	0	0	1	.000	.000	.000	0	-98	-0				1.000	0	/1-1	0.0
■ **AL LIBKE** Libke, Albert Walter b: 9/12/18, Tacoma, Wash. BL/TR, 6'4", 215 lbs. Deb: 4/19/45 Career OF: (27-LF 0-CF 197-RF)																								
1945	Cin-N	130	449	41	127	23	5	4	53	34	62	.283	.336	.383	719	102	0	6			.963	2	*O-108R/P-4,1-2	-0.5
1946	Cin-N	124	431	32	109	22	1	5	42	43	50	.253	.322	.343	665	92	-5	0			.972	-5	*O-115(0-0-115)/P-1	-1.4
Total	2	254	880	73	236	45	6	9	95	77	112	.268	.329	.364	693	97	-5	6			.967	-3	O-223R/P-5,1-2	-1.9
■ **FRANKIE LIBRAN** Libran, Francisco (Rosas) b: 5/6/48, Mayaguez, P.R. BR/TR, 6', 168 lbs. Deb: 9/3/69																								
1969	SD-N	10	10	1	1	1	0	0	1	1	2	.100	.182	.200	382	7	-1	0	0	0	1.000	1	/S-9	0.0
■ **JOHN LICKERT** Lickert, John Wilbur b: 4/4/60, Pittsburgh, Pa. BR/TR, 5'11", 175 lbs. Deb: 9/19/81																								
1981	Bos-A	1	0	0	0	0	0	0	0	0	0	—	—	—	—	—	0	0	0	0	1.000	-0	/C-1	0.0
■ **DAVE LIDDELL** Liddell, David Alexander (b: b: 6/15/66, Los Angeles, Cal. BR/TR, 6', 190 lbs. Deb: 6/3/90																								
1990	NY-N	1	1	1	1	0	0	0	0	0	0	1.000	1.000	1.000	2000	453	0	0	0	0	1.000	-0	/C-1	0.0
■ **MIKE LIEBERTHAL** Lieberthal, Michael Scott b: 1/18/72, Glendale, Cal. BR/TR, 6', 170 lbs. Deb: 6/30/94																								
1994	Phi-N	24	79	6	21	3	1	1	5	3	5	.266	.301	.367	668	71	-3	0	0	0	.969	-3	C-22	-0.5
1995	Phi-N	16	47	1	12	2	0	0	4	5	5	.255	.327	.298	625	66	-2	0	0	0	.991	3	C-14	0.1
1996	Phi-N	50	166	21	42	8	0	7	23	10	30	.253	.303	.428	731	89	-3	0	0	0	.990	0	C-43	0.0
1997	Phi-N	134	455	59	112	27	1	20	77	44	76	.246	.318	.442	760	97	-4	3	4	-1	.988	-10	*C-129/D-1	-0.6
1998	Phi-N	86	313	39	80	15	3	8	45	17	44	.256	.309	.399	708	83	-8	2	1	0	.988	-1	C-83	-0.4
1999	Phi-N★	145	510	84	153	33	1	31	96	44	86	.300	.368	.551	919	125	18	0	0	0	**.997**	-5	*C-143	2.1
2000	Phi-N★	108	389	55	108	30	0	15	71	40	53	.278	.354	.470	824	104	2	2	0	0	.993	-11	*C-106	-0.1
Total	7	563	1959	265	528	118	6	82	321	163	299	.270	.335	.461	797	101	0	7	5	-0	.991	-27	C-540/D-1	0.6
■ **JEFF LIEFER** Liefer, Jeffrey David b: 8/17/74, Fontana, Cal. BL/TR, 6'3", 195 lbs. Deb: 4/7/99 Career OF: (14-LF 0-CF 8-RF)																								
1999	Chi-A	45	113	8	28	7	1	0	14	8	28	.248	.298	.327	625	59	-7	2	0	0	1.000	2	O-17(14-0-3),1-15/D-9	-0.6
2000	Chi-A	5	11	0	2	0	0	0	0	0	4	.182	.182	.182	364	-7	-2	0	0	0	1.000	-2	/O-5(0-0-5),1-1	-0.3
Total	2	50	124	8	30	7	1	0	14	8	32	.242	.288	.315	602	53	-9	2	0	0	1.000	0	/O-22L,1-16,D-9	-0.9
■ **FRED LIESE** Liese, Frederick Richard b: 10/7/1885, Wisconsin d: 6/30/67, Los Angeles, Cal. BL/TL, 5'8", 150 lbs. Deb: 4/14/10																								
1910	Bos-N	5	4	0	0	0	0	0	0	1	2	.000	.200	.000	200	-39	-1	0			.000	0	H	-0.1
■ **GENE LILLARD** Lillard, Robert Eugene b: 11/12/13, Santa Barbara, Cal d: 4/12/91, Goleta, Cal. BR/TR, 5'10.5", 178 lbs. Deb: 5/8/36 F																								
1936	Chi-N	19	34	6	7	1	0	0	2	3	8	.206	.270	.235	506	36	-3	0			.947	-1	/S-4,3-3	-0.3
1939	Chi-N	23	10	3	1	0	0	0	0	6	3	.100	.438	.100	538	51	-0	0			1.000	0	P-20	0.0
1940	StL-N	2	0	0	0	0	0	0	0	0	0	—	—	—	—	—	0	0			1.000	0	/P-2	0.0
Total	3	44	44	9	8	1	0	0	2	9	11	.182	.321	.205	525	43	-3	0			1.000	-1	/P-22,S-4,3-3	-0.3
■ **BILL LILLARD** Lillard, William Beverly b: 1/10/18, Goleta, Cal. BR/TR, 5'10", 170 lbs. Deb: 9/11/39 F																								
1939	Phi-A	7	19	4	6	1	0	0	1	3	1	.316	.409	.368	778	102	0	0	0	0	.974	2	/S-7	0.3
1940	Phi-A	73	206	26	49	8	2	1	21	28	28	.238	.332	.311	643	69	-9	0	1	-0	.921	-18	S-69/2-1	-2.2
Total	2	80	225	30	55	9	2	1	22	31	29	.244	.339	.316	654	72	-9	0	1	-0	.927	-16	/S-76,2-1	-1.9
■ **JIM LILLIE** Lillie, James J. "Grasshopper" (b: James J. Lilly) b: 7/27/1861, New Haven, Conn. d: 11/9/1890, Kansas City, Mo. Deb: 5/17/1883 Career OF: (147-LF 38-CF 204-RF)																								
1883	Buf-N	50	201	25	47	7	3	1	29	1	31	.234	.238	.313	551	64	-9				.835	-7	O-47C/P-3,C-2,S32	-1.4
1884	Buf-N	114	471	68	105	12	5	3	53	5	71	.223	.231	.289	520	60	-22				.852	16	*O-114(0-0-114)/P-2	-0.6
1885	Buf-N	112	430	49	107	13	3	2	30	6	39	.249	.259	.307	566	80	-11				.862	0	*O-112R/S-3,1-1	-1.1
1886	KC-N	114	416	37	73	9	0	0	22	11	80	.175	.197	.197	394	19	-40	13			.884	11	*O-114(114-0-0)/P-1	-3.0
Total	4	390	1518	179	332	41	11	6	134	23	221	.219	.230	.272	502	54	-82	13			.863	21	O-387R/P-6,S-4,C123	-6.1
■ **BOB LILLIS** Lillis, Robert Perry b: 6/2/30, Altadena, Cal. BR/TR, 5'11", 160 lbs. Deb: 8/30/58 MC																								
1958	LA-N	20	69	10	27	3	1	1	5	4	2	.391	.432	.507	940	143	4	1	2	-0	.964	-3	S-19	0.2
1959	LA-N	30	48	7	11	2	0	0	2	3	4	.229	.275	.271	545	43	-4	0	0	0	.919	8	S-20	0.5
1960	LA-N	48	60	6	16	4	0	0	6	2	6	.267	.290	.333	624	66	-3	2	0	0	.982	15	S-23,3-14/2-1	1.3
1961	LA-N	19	9	0	1	0	0	0	1	1	1	.111	.200	.111	311	-13	-1	0	0	0	1.000	1	3-12/2-1,S-1	0.0
	StL-N	86	230	24	50	4	0	0	21	7	13	.217	.247	.235	482	26	-24	3	3	-0	.928	2	S-56,2-24	-1.7
	Yr	105	239	24	51	4	0	0	22	8	14	.213	.245	.230	475	25	-25	3	3	-0	.924	3	S-57,2-25,3-12	-1.7
1962	Hou-N	129	457	38	114	12	4	1	30	28	23	.249	.293	.300	593	64	-23	7	3	0	.972	9	S-99,2-33/3-9	-0.4
1963	Hou-N	147	469	31	93	13	1	1	19	15	35	.198	.230	.237	466	37	-39	3	4	-1	.957	-5	*S-124,2-19/3-6	-3.7
1964	Hou-N	109	332	31	89	11	2	0	17	11	10	.268	.292	.313	605	75	-12	4	9	-2	.995	1	2-52,S-43,3-12	-0.7
1965	Hou-N	124	408	34	90	12	1	0	20	20	10	.221	.267	.255	522	51	-26	2	2	-0	.968	-12	*S-104/3-9,2-6	-3.2
1966	Hou-N	68	164	14	38	6	0	0	11	7	4	.232	.263	.268	531	52	-11	1	1	-0	.951	-9	2-35,S-18/3-6	-1.8
1967	Hou-N	37	82	3	20	1	0	0	5	1	8	.244	.253	.256	509	48	-6	0	1	-0	.947	3	S-23/2-3,3-2	-0.1
Total	10	817	2328	198	549	68	9	3	137	99	116	.236	.271	.277	548	54	-143	23	25	-4	.959	8	S-530,2-174/3-70	-9.6
■ **LOU LIMMER** Limmer, Louis b: 3/10/25, New York, N.Y. BL/TL, 6'2", 190 lbs. Deb: 4/22/51																								
1951	Phi-A	94	214	25	34	9	1	5	30	28	40	.159	.256	.280	537	44	-17	1	0	0	.988	2	1-58	-1.7
1954	Phi-A	115	316	41	73	10	3	14	32	35	37	.231	.308	.415	722	96	-3	2	3	-1	.988	2	1-79	-0.6
Total	2	209	530	66	107	19	4	19	62	63	77	.202	.287	.360	647	75	-20	3	3	-0	.988	4	1-137	-2.3
■ **RUFINO LINARES** Linares, Rufino (b: Rufino De La Cruz (Linares)) b: 2/28/51, San Pedro De Macoris, D.R. d: 5/16/98, San Pedro De Macoris, D.R. BR/TR, 6', 170 lbs. Deb: 4/10/81																								
1981	Atl-N	78	253	27	67	9	2	5	25	9	28	.265	.290	.375	666	85	-6	8	4	0	.963	3	O-60(60-0-0)	-0.5
1982	Atl-N	77	191	28	57	7	1	2	17	7	29	.298	.327	.377	704	92	-2	5	2	0	1.000	0	O-53(51-0-4)	-0.4
1984	Atl-N	34	58	4	12	3	0	1	10	6	12	.207	.281	.310	592	62	-3	0	0	0	.958	1	O-13(12-0-1)	-0.3
1985	Cal-A	18	43	7	11	2	0	3	11	2	5	.256	.289	.512	801	114	1	2	0	0	1.000	-1	D-14/O-2(0-0-2)	0.0
Total	4	207	545	66	147	21	3	11	63	24	74	.270	.302	.380	682	88	-10	15	6	1	.977	4	O-128(123-0-7)/D-14	-1.2
■ **CARL LIND** Lind, Henry Carl "Hooks" b: 9/19/03, New Orleans, La. d: 8/4/46, New York, N.Y. BR/TR, 6', 160 lbs. Deb: 9/14/27																								
1927	Cle-A	12	37	2	5	0	0	0	1	5	7	.135	.256	.135	391	4	-5	1	0	0	.969	2	2-11/S-1	-0.3
1928	Cle-A	154	650	102	191	42	4	1	54	36	48	.294	.331	.375	706	84	-15	8	5	0	.960	4	*2-154	-0.7
1929	Cle-A	66	225	19	54	8	1	0	13	13	17	.240	.282	.284	566	44	-19	0	2	-1	.957	16	2-64/3-1	-0.1
1930	Cle-A	24	69	8	17	3	0	0	6	3	7	.246	.278	.290	568	43	-6	0	1	-0	.940	11	S-22/2-2	0.6
Total	4	256	981	131	267	53	5	1	74	57	79	.272	.313	.339	652	69	-45	9	8	-1	.960	33	2-231/S-23,3-1	-0.5
■ **JACK LIND** Lind, Jackson Hugh b: 6/8/46, Denver, Col. BB/TR, 6', 170 lbs. Deb: 9/10/74 C																								
1974	Mil-A	9	17	4	4	2	0	0	1	3	2	.235	.350	.353	703	103	0	0	0	0	1.000	-0	/S-5,2-4	0.1
1975	Mil-A	17	20	1	1	0	0	0	0	2	12	.050	.136	.050	186	-45	-4	1	0	0	.919	5	/S-9,3-6,1-1	0.2
Total	2	26	37	5	5	2	0	0	1	5	14	.135	.238	.189	427	23	-4	1	0	0	.943	5	/S-14,3-6,2-4,1-1	0.3
■ **JOSE LIND** Lind, Jose (Salgado) "Chico" b: 5/1/64, Toa Baja, P.R. BR/TR, 5'11", 175 lbs. Deb: 8/28/87																								
1987	Pit-N	35	143	21	46	8	4	0	11	8	12	.322	.358	.434	791	108	1	2	1	0	.995	6	2-35	1.0
1988	Pit-N	154	611	82	160	24	4	2	49	42	75	.262	.309	.324	633	83	-13	15	4	2	.987	3	*2-153	-0.5
1989	Pit-N	153	578	52	134	21	3	2	48	39	64	.232	.283	.289	572	66	-26	15	1	3	.976	-14	*2-151	-3.5
1990	*Pit-N	152	514	46	134	28	5	1	48	35	52	.261	.309	.340	650	82	-13	8	0	2	.991	17	*2-152	1.0
1991	*Pit-N	150	502	53	133	16	6	3	54	30	56	.265	.309	.339	648	83	-11	7	4	0	.989	23	*2-149	1.6
1992	*Pit-N	135	468	38	110	14	1	0	39	26	29	.235	.277	.269	546	56	-27	3	1	0	**.992**	12	*2-134	-1.2
1993	KC-A	136	431	33	107	13	2	0	37	13	36	.248	.274	.288	561	48	-31	3	2	-0	**.994**	-4	*2-136	-2.8
1994	KC-A	85	290	34	78	16	2	1	31	16	34	.269	.307	.348	655	66	-15	9	5	0	.988	2	2-84/D-1	-0.8
1995	KC-A	29	97	4	26	3	0	0	6	3	8	.268	.290	.299	589	53	-7	0	1	-0	.992	-2	2-29	-0.7

YEAR	TM/L	G	AB	R	H	2B	3B	HR	RBI	BB	SO	AVG	OBP	SLG	OPS	OPS+	BR+	SB	CS	SBR	FA	FR	G/POS	TPR
	Cal-A	15	43	5	7	2	0	0	1	3	4	.163	.217	.209	427	12	-6	0	0	0	1.000	4	2-15	-0.1
	Yr	44	140	9	33	5	0	0	7	6	12	.236	.267	.271	539	40	-12	0	1	-0	.995	1	2-44	-0.8
Total	9	1044	3677	368	935	145	27	9	324	215	370	.254	.297	.316	613	70	-147	62	19	7	.988	46	*2-1038/D-1	-6.0
■ EM LINDBECK	Lindbeck, Emert Desmond b: 8/27/35, Kewanee, Ill. BL/TR, 6', 185 lbs. Deb: 4/22/60																							
1960	Det-A	2	1	0	0	0	0	0	0	1	0	.000	.500	.000	500	46	0	0	0	0	.000	0	H	0.0
■ JOHNNY LINDELL	Lindell, John Harlan b: 8/30/16, Greeley, Colo. d: 8/27/85, Newport Beach, Cal. BR/TR, 6'4.5", 217 lbs. Deb: 4/18/41 Career OF: (282-LF 293-CF 126-RF)																							
1941	NY-A	1	1	0	0	0	0	0	0	0	0	.000	.000	.000	0	-99	-0	0	0	0	.000	0	H	0.0
1942	NY-A	27	24	1	6	1	0	0	4	0	5	.250	.250	.292	542	53	-2	0	0	0	.923	-0	P-23	0.0
1943	*NY-A☆	122	441	53	108	17	**12**	4	51	51	55	.245	.329	.365	694	102	1	2	5	-1	.966	-2	*O-122(3-55-66)	-0.8
1944	NY-A	149	594	91	178	33	**16**	18	103	44	56	.300	.351	.500	851	137	25	5	4	-0	.986	9	*O-149(2-148-0)	3.1
1945	NY-A	41	159	26	45	6	3	1	20	17	10	.283	.363	.377	740	110	2	2	1	0	.982	0	O-41(0-41-0)	0.1
1946	NY-A	102	332	41	86	10	5	10	40	32	47	.259	.328	.410	738	104	1	4	1	1	.982	-0	O-74(5-31-39),1-14	-0.2
1947	*NY-A	127	476	66	131	18	7	11	67	32	70	.275	.322	.412	734	104	0	1	2	-0	.978	7	*O-118(102-10-11)	-0.1
1948	NY-A	88	309	58	98	17	2	13	55	35	50	.317	.387	.511	898	139	16	0	0	0	.994	2	O-79(72-1-7)	1.2
1949	*NY-A	78	211	33	51	10	0	6	27	35	27	.242	.350	.374	724	92	-3	3	0	1	.983	-6	O-65(63-3-1)	-1.1
1950	NY-A	7	21	2	4	0	0	0	2	4	2	.190	.320	.190	510	34	-2	0	0	0	.857	-2	/O-6(6-0-0)	-0.4
	StL-N	36	113	16	21	5	2	5	16	15	24	.186	.287	.398	685	74	-5	0			.984	-2	O-33(29-4-0)	-0.9
1953	Pit-N	58	91	11	26	6	1	4	15	16	15	.286	.404	.505	909	136	5	0	0	0	.962	2	P-27/1-2	0.0
	Phi-N	11	18	3	7	1	0	0	2	6	2	.389	.542	.444	986	162	2	0	0	0	1.000	-1	/P-5,O-2(0-0-2)	0.0
	Yr	69	109	14	33	7	1	4	17	22	17	.303	.429	.495	924	141	8	0	0	0	.964	1	P-32/1-2,O-2(0-0-2)	0.0
1954	Phi-N	7	5	0	1	0	0	0	2	2	3	.200	.429	.200	629	70	-0	0	0	0	.000	0	H	0.0
Total	12	854	2795	401	762	124	48	72	404	289	366	.273	.344	.429	773	113	43	17	13		.980	7	O-689C/P-55,1-16	0.9
■ JIM LINDEMAN	Lindeman, James William b: 1/10/62, Evanston, Ill. BR/TR, 6'1", 200 lbs. Deb: 9/3/86 Career OF: (48-LF 6-CF 90-RF)																							
1986	StL-N	19	55	7	14	1	0	1	6	2	10	.255	.281	.327	608	68	-3	1	1	-0	.992	-1	1-17/3-1,O-1(1-0-0)	-0.5
1987	*StL-N	75	207	20	43	13	0	8	28	11	56	.208	.258	.386	644	67	-11	3	1	0	.976	-1	O-49(1-0-48),1-20	-1.4
1988	StL-N	17	43	3	9	1	0	2	7	2	9	.209	.244	.372	617	74	-2	0	0	0	.941	-2	O-12(4-0-8)/1-3	-0.4
1989	StL-N	73	45	8	5	1	0	0	2	3	18	.111	.167	.133	300	-13	-7	0	0	0	.989	0	1-42/O-5(3-0-2)	-0.7
1990	Det-A	12	32	5	7	1	0	2	8	2	13	.219	.265	.438	702	92	-1	0	0	0	1.000	-1	D-10/1-1,O-1(0-0-1)	-0.2
1991	Phi-N	65	95	13	32	5	0	0	12	13	14	.337	.417	.389	806	129	4	0	1	-0	1.000	-5	O-30(14-6-10)/1-1	-0.2
1992	Phi-N	29	39	6	10	1	0	1	6	3	11	.256	.310	.359	668	89	-1	0	0	0	1.000	-3	/O-9(4-0-7)	-0.4
1993	Hou-N	9	23	2	8	3	0	0	0	0	7	.348	.348	.478	826	123	1	0	0	0	1.000	1	/1-9	0.1
1994	NY-N	52	137	18	37	8	1	7	20	6	35	.270	.306	.496	802	106	0	0	0	0	.948	-3	O-33(21-0-14)/1-4	-0.4
Total	9	351	676	82	165	34	1	21	89	42	173	.244	.292	.391	683	83	-17	4	3	-0	.970	-14	O-140R/1-97,D-10,3	-4.1
■ BOB LINDEMANN	Lindemann, John Frederick Mann b: 6/5/1881, Philadelphia, Pa. d: 12/19/51, Williamsport, Pa. BB/TR, 6', 175 lbs. Deb: 8/28/01																							
1901	Phi-A	3	9	0	1	0	0	0	0	0		.111	.111	.111	222	-37	-2	0			.600	-0	/O-3(0-0-3)	-0.2
■ WALT LINDEN	Linden, Walter Charles b: 3/27/24, Chicago, Ill. BR/TR, 6'1", 190 lbs. Deb: 4/30/50																							
1950	Bos-N	3	5	0	2	1	0	0	0	1	0	.400	.500	.600	1100	201	1	0			1.000	-1	/C-3	0.0
■ CHRIS LINDSAY	Lindsay, Christian Haller "Pinky" or "The Crab" b: 7/24/1878, Beaver County, Pa. d: 1/25/41, Cleveland, Ohio BR/TR, 6', 190 lbs. Deb: 7/6/05																							
1905	Det-A	88	329	38	88	14	1	0	31	18		.267	.315	.316	631	100	-0	10			.978	-0	1-88	-0.2
1906	Det-A	141	499	59	112	16	2	0	33	45		.224	.293	.265	557	73	-15	18			.977	-8	*1-122,2-17/3-1	-2.7
Total	2	229	828	97	200	30	3	0	64	63		.242	.301	.285	586	83	-15	28			.978	-8	1-210/2-17,3-1	-2.9
■ BILL LINDSAY	Lindsay, William Gibbons b: 2/24/1881, Madison, N.C. d: 7/14/63, Greensboro, N.C. BL/TR, 5'10.5", 165 lbs. Deb: 6/21/11																							
1911	Cle-A	19	66	6	16	2	0	0	5	1		.242	.265	.273	537	49	-5	2			.883	2	3-15/2-1	-0.2
■ DOUG LINDSEY	Lindsey, Michael Douglas b: 9/22/67, Austin, Tex. BR/TR, 6'2", 200 lbs. Deb: 10/6/91																							
1991	Phi-N	1	3	0	0	0	0	0	0	0	3	.000	.000	.000	0	-99	-1	0	0	0	1.000	0	/C-1	-0.1
1993	Phi-N	2	2	0	1	0	0	0	0	0	1	.500	.500	.500	1000	171	0	0	0	0	1.000	-0	/C-2	0.0
	Chi-A	2	1	0	0	0	0	0	0	0	0	.000	.000	.000	0	-99	-0	0	0	0	1.000	0	/C-2	0.0
Total	2	5	6	0	1	0	0	0	0	0	4	.167	.167	.167	333	-8	-1	0	0	0	1.000	1	/C-5	-0.1
■ ROD LINDSEY	Lindsey, Rodney Lee b: 1/28/76, Opelika, Ala. BR/TR, 5'8", 175 lbs. Deb: 9/2/2000																							
2000	Det-A	11	3	6	1	1	0	0	0	0	1	.333	.500	.667	1167	198	1	2	1	0	1.000	-3	/O-7(2-4-2)	-0.2
■ BILL LINDSEY	Lindsey, William Donald b: 4/12/60, Staten Island, N.Y. BR/TR, 6'3", 195 lbs. Deb: 7/18/87																							
1987	Chi-A	9	16	2	3	0	0	0	1	0	3	.188	.188	.188	375	-0	-2	0	0	0	1.000	2	/C-9	0.0
■ CHUCK LINDSTROM	Lindstrom, Charles William b: 9/7/36, Chicago, Ill. BR/TR, 5'11", 175 lbs. Deb: 9/28/58 F																							
1958	Chi-A	1	1	1	1	0	1	0	1	1	0	1.000	1.000	3.000	4000	975	1	0	0	0	1.000	-0	/C-1	0.1
■ FREDDIE LINDSTROM	Lindstrom, Frederick Charles (b: Frederick Anthony Lindstrom) b: 11/21/05, Chicago, Ill. d: 10/4/81, Chicago, Ill. BR/TR, 5'11", 170 lbs. Deb: 4/15/24 FH Career OF: (187-LF 291-CF 74-RF)																							
1924	*NY-N	52	79	19	20	3	1	0	4	6	10	.253	.314	.316	630	71	-3	3	1	0	.911	7	2-23,3-11	0.5
1925	NY-N	104	356	43	102	15	12	4	33	22	20	.287	.332	.430	761	97	-3	5	9	-2	.957	-1	3-96/2-1,S-1	0.0
1926	NY-N	140	543	90	164	19	9	9	76	39	21	.302	.351	.420	771	108	5	11			.962	-3	*3-138/O-1(0-0-1)	1.1
1927	NY-N	138	562	107	172	36	8	7	58	40	40	.306	.354	.436	790	111	8	10			.968	1	3-87,O-51(51-0-0)	1.1
1928	NY-N	153	646	99	**231**	39	9	14	107	25	21	.358	.383	.511	894	131	27	15			**.958**	15	*3-153	5.0
1929	NY-N	130	549	99	175	23	6	15	91	30	28	.319	.354	.464	819	101	-0	10			.966	7	*3-128	1.3
1930	NY-N	148	609	127	231	39	7	22	106	48	33	.379	.425	.575	999	142	41	15			.953	6	*3-148	4.9
1931	NY-N	78	303	38	91	12	6	5	36	26	12	.300	.356	.429	785	113	5	5			.975	-7	O-73(0-0-73)/2-4	-0.6
1932	NY-N	144	595	83	161	26	5	15	92	27	28	.271	.303	.407	710	91	-9	6			.982	0	*O-128(0-128-0),3-15	-1.2
1933	Pit-N	138	538	70	167	39	10	5	55	33	22	.310	.350	.448	798	127	18	1			.988	11	*O-130(20-111-0)	2.6
1934	Pit-N	97	383	59	111	24	4	4	49	23	21	.290	.333	.405	738	94	-3	1			.990	1	O-92(92-0-0)	-0.7
1935	*Chi-N	90	342	49	94	22	4	3	62	10	13	.275	.297	.389	686	82	-9	1			.979	-2	O-50(0-50-0),3-33	-1.1
1936	Bro-N	26	106	12	28	4	0	0	10	5	7	.264	.297	.302	599	61	-6	1			.982	1	O-26(24-2-0)	-0.6
Total	13	1438	5611	895	1747	301	81	103	779	334	276	.311	.351	.449	800	110	71	84	10		.959	37	3-809,O-551C/2-28,S	12.3
■ CARL LINHART	Linhart, Carl James b: 12/14/29, Zborov, Czech. BL/TR, 5'11", 184 lbs. Deb: 8/2/52																							
1952	Det-A	3	2	0	0	0	0	0	0	0	0	.000	.000	.000	0	-99	-1	0	0	0	.000	0	H	-0.1
■ COLE LINIAK	Liniak, Cole Edward b: 8/23/76, Encinitas, Cal. BR/TR, 6'1", 180 lbs. Deb: 9/3/99																							
1999	Chi-N	12	29	3	7	2	0	0	2	1	4	.241	.267	.310	577	46	-2	0	1	-0	1.000	-2	3-10	-0.4
2000	Chi-N	3	3	0	0	0	0	0	0	0	2	.000	.000	.000	0	-99	-1	0	0	0	.000	0	/H	-0.1
Total	2	15	32	3	7	2	0	0	2	1	6	.219	.242	.281	524	32	-3	0	1	-0	1.000	-2	/3-10	-0.5
■ BOB LINTON	Linton, Claud Clarence b: 4/18/03, Emerson, Ark. d: 4/3/80, Destin, Fla. BL/TR, 6', 185 lbs. Deb: 4/26/29																							
1929	Pit-N	17	18	0	2	0	0	0	1	1	2	.111	.158	.111	269	-31	-4	0			1.000	0	/C-8	-0.3
■ LARRY LINTZ	Lintz, Larry b: 10/10/49, Martinez, Cal. BB/TR, 5'9", 150 lbs. Deb: 7/14/73																							
1973	Mon-N	52	116	20	29	1	0	0	3	17	18	.250	.351	.259	609	69	-4	12	4	1	.945	2	2-34,S-15	0.2
1974	Mon-N	113	319	60	76	10	1	0	20	44	50	.238	.334	.276	610	68	-12	50	7	9	.961	-13	2-67,S-31/3-1	-0.9
1975	Mon-N	46	132	18	26	0	0	0	3	23	18	.197	.316	.197	513	43	-9	17	9	1	.970	-6	2-39/S-2	-1.3
	StL-N	27	18	6	5	1	0	0	1	3	2	.278	.381	.333	714	96	0	4	0	1	.889	9	/2-6,S-6	1.0
	Yr	73	150	24	31	1	0	0	4	26	20	.207	.324	.213	537	49	-9	21	9	1	.963	3	2-45/S-8	-0.3
1976	Oak-A	68	1	21	0	0	0	0	0	2	0	.000	.667	.000	667	111	0	31	11	3	1.000	-0	D-19/2-5,O-3(1-0-2)	0.3
1977	Oak-A	41	30	11	4	1	0	0	0	8	13	.133	.333	.167	500	42	-2	13	5	1	1.000	11	2-28/S-2,3-1,D-5	1.0

YEAR	TM/L	G	AB	R	H	2B	3B	HR	RBI	BB	SO	AVG	OBP	SLG	OPS	OPS+	BR+	SB	CS	SBR	FA	FR	G/POS	TPR
1978	Cle-A	3	0	1	0	0	0	0	0	0	0	—	—	—	—	—	0	1	2	-0	.000	0	R	-0.1
Total	6	350	616	137	140	13	1	0	27	97	101	.227	.336	.252	588	63	-27	128	38	15	.962	3	2-179/S-56,D-24,O3	0.2
■ **PHIL LINZ**	Linz, Philip Francis b: 6/4/39, Baltimore, Md. BR/TR, 6'1", 180 lbs. Deb: 4/13/62																							
1962	NY-A	71	129	28	37	8	0	1	14	6	17	.287	.319	.372	691	88	-2	6	2	1	.937	-3	S-21/3-8,2-5,O-2R	-0.3
1963	*NY-A	72	186	22	50	9	0	2	12	15	18	.269	.330	.349	680	91	-2	1	6	-2	.963	1	S-22,3-13,O-12C,/2	-0.1
1964	*NY-A	112	368	63	92	21	3	5	25	43	61	.250	.332	.364	696	92	-3	3	4	-1	.952	11	S-55,3-41/2-5,O-3C	1.2
1965	NY-A	99	285	37	59	12	1	2	16	30	33	.207	.283	.277	560	60	-15	2	1	0	.954	11	S-71/3-4,O-4R,2-1	0.2
1966	Phi-N	40	70	4	14	3	0	0	6	2	14	.200	.222	.243	465	29	-7	0	0	0	.971	1	3-14/S-6,2-3	-0.6
1967	Phi-N	23	18	4	4	2	0	1	5	2	1	.222	.300	.500	800	124	0	0	0	0	.833	-1	/S-7,3-1	-0.1
	NY-N	24	58	8	12	2	0	0	1	4	10	.207	.270	.241	511	48	-4	0	0	0	.964	-2	2-11/S-8,3-1,O-1L	-0.5
	Yr	47	76	12	16	4	0	1	6	6	11	.211	.277	.303	580	66	-3	0	0	0	.963	-4	S-15,2-11/3-2,O-1L	-0.6
1968	NY-N	78	258	19	54	7	0	0	17	10	41	.209	.244	.236	481	45	-17	1	0	0	.968	-12	2-71	-2.7
Total	7	519	1372	185	322	64	4	11	96	112	195	.235	.296	.311	607	72	-49	13	13	-2	.952	6	S-190,2-102/3-82,O	-2.9
■ **JOHNNY LIPON**	Lipon, John Joseph "Skids" b: 11/10/22, Martins Ferry, O. d: 8/17/98, Houston, Tex. BR/TR, 6', 175 lbs. Deb: 8/16/42 MC																							
1942	Det-A	34	131	5	25	2	0	0	9	7	7	.191	.232	.206	438	22	-13	1	3	-1	.945	7	S-34	-0.5
1946	Det-A	14	20	4	6	0	0	0	1	5	3	.300	.440	.300	740	103	0	0	0	0	.933	3	/S-8,3-1	0.4
1948	Det-A	121	458	65	133	18	8	5	52	68	22	.290	.384	.397	782	105	5	4	4	-1	.970	-12	*S-117/2-1,3-1	0.0
1949	Det-A	127	439	57	110	14	6	3	59	75	24	.251	.362	.330	693	84	-8	2	4	-1	.965	4	*S-120	0.1
1950	Det-A	147	601	104	176	27	6	2	63	81	26	.293	.378	.368	745	89	-8	9	6	-0	.958	9	*S-147	0.9
1951	Det-A	129	487	56	129	15	1	0	38	49	27	.265	.335	.300	634	72	-18	7	6	-1	.949	-13	*S-125	-2.3
1952	Det-A	39	136	17	30	4	2	0	12	16	6	.221	.303	.279	582	62	-7	3	1	0	.978	-3	S-39	-0.7
	Bos-A	79	234	25	48	8	1	0	18	32	20	.205	.301	.248	549	50	-15	1	1	-0	.982	14	S-69/3-7	0.3
	Yr	118	370	42	78	12	3	0	30	48	26	.211	.301	.259	561	54	-22	4	2	0	**.981**	12	*S-108/3-7	-0.4
1953	Bos-A	60	145	18	31	7	0	0	13	14	16	.214	.283	.262	545	46	-11	1	0	0	.951	4	S-58	-0.3
	StL-A	7	9	0	2	0	0	0	1	0	1	.222	.222	.222	444	20	-1	0	0	0	1.000	-1	/3-6,2-1	-0.2
	Yr	67	154	18	33	7	0	0	14	14	17	.214	.280	.260	540	44	-12	1	0	0	.951	3	S-58/3-6,2-1	-0.5
1954	Cin-N	1	1	0	0	0	0	0	0	0	0	.000	.000	.000	0	-97	-0	0	0	0	.000	0	H	0.0
Total	9	758	2661	351	690	95	24	10	266	347	152	.259	.346	.324	671	77	-76	28	25	-3	.961	13	S-717/3-15,2-2	-2.3
■ **NIG LIPSCOMB**	Lipscomb, Gerard b: 2/24/11, Rutherfordton, N.C d: 2/27/78, Huntersville, N.C. BR/TR, 6', 175 lbs. Deb: 4/23/37																							
1937	StL-A	36	96	11	31	9	1	0	8	11	10	.323	.398	.438	836	110	2	0	0	0	.963	2	2-27/P-3,3-1	0.5
■ **BOB LIPSKI**	Lipski, Robert Peter b: 7/7/38, Scranton, Pa. BL/TR, 6'1", 180 lbs. Deb: 4/28/63																							
1963	Cle-A	2	1	0	0	0	0	0	0	0	1	.000	.000	.000	0	-99	-0	0	0	0	1.000	0	/C-2	0.0
■ **NELSON LIRIANO**	Liriano, Nelson Arturo (Bonilla) b: 6/3/64, Puerto Plata, D.R. BB/TR, 5'10", 172 lbs. Deb: 8/25/87																							
1987	Tor-A	37	158	29	38	6	2	2	10	16	22	.241	.310	.342	652	71	-6	13	2	2	.995	3	2-37	0.0
1988	Tor-A	99	276	36	73	6	2	3	23	11	40	.264	.298	.333	631	76	-9	12	5	1	.961	-13	2-80,D-11/3-1	-2.0
1989	*Tor-A	132	418	51	110	26	3	5	53	43	51	.263	.335	.376	710	102	1	16	7	1	.980	-18	*2-122/D-5	-1.3
1990	Tor-A	50	170	16	36	7	2	1	15	16	20	.212	.283	.294	578	61	-9	3	5	-1	.983	-12	2-49	-2.2
	Min-A	53	185	30	47	5	7	0	13	22	24	.254	.333	.357	690	87	-3	5	2	0	.968	-15	2-50/S-1,D-2	-1.7
	Yr	103	355	46	83	12	9	1	28	38	44	.234	.310	.327	636	75	-11	8	7	-1	.975	-28	2-99/D-2,S-1	-3.9
1991	KC-A	10	22	5	9	0	0	0	1	0	2	.409	.409	.409	818	127	1	0	1	-0	1.000	1	2-10	0.1
1993	Col-N	48	151	28	46	6	3	2	15	18	22	.305	.379	.424	803	98	0	6	4	-0	.975	-13	S-35,2-16/3-1	-1.0
1994	Col-N	87	255	39	65	17	5	3	31	42	44	.255	.360	.396	756	83	-5	0	2	-1	.973	-5	2-79/S-3,3-2	-0.7
1995	Pit-N	107	259	29	74	12	1	5	38	24	34	.286	.351	.398	749	95	-1	2	2	-0	.981	-18	2-67/3-5,S-1	-1.7
1996	Pit-N	112	217	23	58	14	2	3	30	14	22	.267	.312	.392	703	82	-6	2	0	0	.984	-6	2-36/3-9,S-5	-1.0
1997	LA-N	76	88	10	20	6	0	1	11	6	12	.227	.277	.330	606	63	-5	0	0	0	.949	-4	2-17/1-2,3-1,S-1	-0.8
1998	Col-N	12	17	0	0	0	0	0	0	0	7	.000	.000	.000	0	-82	-4	0	0	0	1.000	-1	/2-3,S-1	-0.5
Total	11	823	2216	296	576	105	27	25	240	212	300	.260	.326	.366	692	84	-47	59	30	2	.976	-103	2-566/S-47,3-19,D1	-12.8
■ **JOE LIS**	Lis, Joseph Anthony b: 8/15/46, Somerville, N.J. BR/TR, 6', 195 lbs. Deb: 9/5/70 Career OF: (53-LF 0-CF 6-RF)																							
1970	Phi-N	13	37	1	7	2	0	1	4	5	11	.189	.286	.324	610	65	-2	0	0	0	.947	0	/O-9(9-0-0)	-0.2
1971	Phi-N	59	123	16	26	6	0	6	10	16	43	.211	.312	.407	719	102	0	0	1	-0	.978	-3	O-35(35-0-0)	-0.5
1972	Phi-N	62	140	13	34	6	0	6	18	30	34	.243	.380	.414	794	122	5	0	1	-0	.996	1	1-30,O-14(8-0-6)	0.3
1973	Min-A	103	253	37	62	11	1	9	25	28	66	.245	.327	.403	731	101	0	0	1	-0	.987	2	1-96/D-1	-0.4
1974	Min-A	24	41	5	8	0	0	0	3	5	12	.195	.298	.195	493	43	-3	0	0	0	.992	0	1-18	-0.4
	Cle-A	57	109	15	22	3	0	6	16	14	30	.202	.293	.394	687	97	-1	1	0	0	1.000	-0	1-31/3-9,O-1L,D-9	-0.2
	Yr	81	150	20	30	3	0	6	19	19	42	.200	.294	.340	634	82	-4	1	0	0	.997	-0	1-49/3-9,D-9,O-1L	-0.6
1975	Cle-A	9	13	4	4	2	0	2	8	3	3	.308	.471	.923	1394	286	3	0	0	0	1.000	-0	/1-8,D-1	0.3
1976	Cle-A	20	51	4	16	1	0	2	7	8	8	.314	.407	.451	858	153	4	0	0	0	1.000	-0	1-17/D-1	0.2
1977	Sea-A	9	13	1	3	0	0	0	1	1	2	.231	.286	.231	516	43	-1	0	0	0	1.000	-1	/1-4,C-1	-0.2
Total	8	356	780	96	182	31	1	32	92	110	209	.233	.334	.399	733	105	6	1	3	-1	.992	-1	1-204/O-59L,D-12,3C	-1.1
■ **RICK LISI**	Lisi, Riccardo Patrick Emilio b: 3/17/56, Halifax, N.S., Can. BR/TR, 6', 175 lbs. Deb: 5/9/81																							
1981	Tex-A	9	16	6	5	0	0	0	1	4	0	.313	.450	.313	763	130	1	0	1	-0	1.000	-2	/O-8(0-2-6)	-0.1
■ **PAT LISTACH**	Listach, Patrick Alan b: 9/12/67, Natchitoches, La. BB/TR, 5'9", 170 lbs. Deb: 4/8/92 Career OF: (4-LF 87-CF 2-RF)																							
1992	Mil-A	149	579	93	168	19	6	1	47	55	124	.290	.353	.349	702	99	1	54	18	6	.966	-7	*S-148/2-1,O-1(0-1-0)	1.1
1993	Mil-A	98	356	50	87	15	1	3	30	37	70	.244	.321	.317	638	73	-13	18	9	1	.975	-16	S-95/O-6(0-6-0)	-2.0
1994	Mil-A	16	54	8	16	3	0	0	2	3	8	.296	.333	.352	685	74	-2	2	1	0	.958	-0	S-16	-0.1
1995	Mil-A	101	334	35	73	8	2	0	25	25	61	.219	.277	.254	531	37	-30	13	3	2	1.000	-1	2-59,S-36,O-11C,/3	-2.3
1996	Mil-A	87	317	51	76	16	2	1	33	36	51	.240	.319	.312	632	58	-20	25	5	4	.982	-0	O-68(2-66-0),2-12/S-7	-1.4
1997	Hou-N	52	132	13	24	2	2	0	6	11	24	.182	.250	.227	477	27	-14	4	2	0	.951	-8	S-31/O-6(1-4-1)	-2.0
Total	6	503	1772	250	444	63	13	5	143	167	338	.251	.318	.309	627	68	-78	116	38	12	.967	-33	S-333/O-92C,2-72,3	-6.7
■ **PETE LISTER**	Lister, Morris Elmer b: 7/21/1881, Savanna, Ill. d: 3/27/47, St.Petersburg, Fla BR/TR, Deb: 9/14/07																							
1907	Cle-A	22	65	5	18	2	0	0	4	3		.277	.319	.308	627	99	-0	2			.974	-1	1-22	-0.2
■ **SCOTT LITTLE**	Little, Dennis Scott b: 1/19/63, E.St.Louis, Ill. BR/TR, 6', 198 lbs. Deb: 7/27/89																							
1989	Pit-N	3	4	0	1	0	0	0	0	0	1	.250	.250	.250	500	45	-0	0	0	0	1.000	1	/O-1(0-0-1)	0.1
■ **HARRY LITTLE**	Little, Harry A. b: St.Louis, Mo. TR, Deb: 7/16/1877																							
1877	StL-N	3	12	2	2	0	0	0	0	1	6	.167	.231	.167	397	29	-1				1.000	-0	/O-3(0-3-0)	-0.1
	Lou-N	1	3	0	0	0	0	0	0	1	1	.000	.250	.000	250	-13	-0				.857	0	/2-1	0.0
	Yr	4	15	2	2	0	0	0	0	2	7	.133	.235	.133	369	19	-1				1.000	0	/O-3(0-3-0),2-1	-0.1
■ **MARK LITTLE**	Little, Mark Travis b: 7/11/72, Edwardsville, Ill. BR/TR, 6', 195 lbs. Deb: 9/12/98																							
1998	StL-N	7	12	0	1	0	0	0	0	2	5	.083	.214	.083	298	-18	-2	1	0	0	1.000	-0	/O-7(3-0-4)	-0.2
■ **BRYAN LITTLE**	Little, Richard Bryan "Twig" b: 10/8/59, Houston, Tex. BB/TR, 5'10", 160 lbs. Deb: 7/29/82 C																							
1982	Mon-N	29	42	6	9	0	0	0	3	4	6	.214	.283	.214	497	40	-3	2	1	0	1.000	-2	2-16,S-10	-0.5
1983	Mon-N	106	350	48	91	15	3	1	36	50	22	.260	.356	.329	684	91	-2	4	5	-1	.968	-32	S-66,2-51	-2.8
1984	Mon-N	85	266	31	65	11	1	0	9	34	19	.244	.332	.293	625	81	-6	2	3	-1	.982	-22	2-77/S-2	-2.5
1985	Chi-A	73	188	35	47	9	1	2	27	26	21	.250	.350	.340	691	87	-3	0	1	-0	.989	-6	2-68/3-2,S-1	-0.6
1986	Chi-A	20	35	3	6	1	0	0	2	4	4	.171	.256	.200	456	25	-4	0	0	0	1.000	0	2-12/S-7,3-1	-0.3
	NY-A	14	41	3	8	1	0	0	0	2	7	.195	.233	.220	452	24	-4	0	0	0	.975	5	2-14	0.2
	Yr	34	76	6	14	2	0	0	2	6	11	.184	.244	.211	454	25	-8	0	0	0	.983	6	2-26/S-7,3-1	-0.1
Total	5	327	922	126	226	37	5	3	77	120	79	.245	.336	.306	642	80	-22	8	10	-2	.987	-56	2-238/S-86,3-3	-6.5

YEAR	TM/L	G	AB	R	H	2B	3B	HR	RBI	BB	SO	AVG	OBP	SLG	OPS	OPS+	BR+	SB	CS	SBR	FA	FR	G/POS	TPR
■ **JACK LITTLE**	Little, William Arthur b: 3/12/1891, Mart, Tex. d: 7/27/61, Dallas, Tex. BR/TR, 5'11", 175 lbs. Deb: 7/2/12																							
1912	NY-A	3	12	2	3	0	0	0	0	1		.250	.357	.250	607	70	-0	2			1.000	0	/O-3(0-3-0)	0.0
■ **DENNIS LITTLEJOHN**	Littlejohn, Dennis Gerald b: 10/4/54, Santa Monica, Cal. BR/TR, 6'2", 200 lbs. Deb: 7/9/78																							
1978	SF-N	2	0	0	0	0	0	0	0	0	0	—	—	—	—	—	0	0	0	0	.000	0	/C-2	0.0
1979	SF-N	63	193	15	38	6	1	1	13	21	46	.197	.276	.254	530	49	-14	0	0	0	.986	5	C-63	-0.6
1980	SF-N	13	29	2	7	1	0	0	2	7	7	.241	.389	.276	665	91	0	0	0	0	.983	2	C-10	0.2
Total	3	78	222	17	45	7	1	1	15	28	53	.203	.292	.257	549	55	-13	0	0	0	.985	7	/C-75	-0.4
■ **LARRY LITTLETON**	Littleton, Larry Marvin b: 4/3/54, Charlotte, N.C. BR/TR, 6'1", 185 lbs. Deb: 4/12/81																							
1981	Cle-A	26	23	2	0	0	0	0	1	3	6	.000	.115	.000	115	-65	-5	0	0	0	1.000	-10	O-24(19-6-1)	-1.6
■ **GREG LITTON**	Litton, Jon Gregory b: 7/13/64, New Orleans, La. BR/TR, 6', 190 lbs. Deb: 5/2/89 Career OF: (42-LF 0-CF 50-RF)																							
1989	*SF-N	71	143	12	36	5	3	4	17	7	29	.252	.291	.413	704	102	-0	0	2	-1	.953	-5	3-34,2-15/S-9,OC	-0.6
1990	SF-N	93	204	17	50	9	1	1	24	11	45	.245	.287	.314	601	68	-9	1	0	0	.985	-11	O-56R,2-18/S-7,3-5	-2.2
1991	SF-N	59	127	13	23	7	1	1	15	11	25	.181	.252	.276	527	50	-9	0	2	-1	.989	-2	1-15,2-15,3-11,/SOCP	-1.2
1992	SF-N	68	140	9	32	5	0	4	15	11	33	.229	.285	.350	635	84	-3	0	1	-0	.992	-3	2-31,3-10/1-8,SO	-0.6
1993	Sea-A	72	174	25	52	17	0	3	25	18	30	.299	.368	.448	816	116	4	0	1	-0	1.000	1	O-22L,2-17,1-13,D/3S	0.3
1994	Bos-A	11	21	2	2	0	0	0	1	0	5	.095	.095	.095	190	-48	-5	0	0	0	1.000	2	/2-4,1-3,3-2,D-1	-0.3
Total	6	374	809	78	195	43	5	13	97	58	167	.241	.295	.355	650	81	-22	1	6	-2	.997	-18	2-100/O-91R,31SDCP	-4.6
■ **JACK LITTRELL**	Littrell, Jack Napier b: 1/22/29, Louisville, Ky. BR/TR, 6', 179 lbs. Deb: 4/19/52																							
1952	Phi-A	4	2	0	0	0	0	0	0	1	2	.000	.333	.000	333	-2	-0	0	0	0	1.000	0	/S-2,3-1	0.0
1954	Phi-A	9	30	7	9	2	0	1	3	6	3	.300	.417	.467	883	141	2	1	0	0	.976	-1	/S-9	0.2
1955	KC-A	37	70	7	14	0	1	0	1	4	12	.200	.243	.229	472	27	-7	0	0	0	.947	0	S-22/1-6,2-4	-0.6
1957	Chi-N	61	153	8	29	4	2	1	13	9	43	.190	.235	.261	496	34	-14	0	0	0	.944	1	S-47/2-6,3-5	-1.0
Total	4	111	255	22	52	6	3	2	17	20	60	.204	.262	.275	536	45	-20	1	0	0	.949	0	/S-80,2-10,1-6,3-6	-1.4
■ **DANNY LITWHILER**	Litwhiler, Daniel Webster b: 8/31/16, Ringtown, Pa. BR/TR, 5'10.5", 198 lbs. Deb: 4/25/40 C																							
1940	Phi-N	36	142	10	49	2	2	5	17	3	13	.345	.363	.493	856	139	7	1			.986	1	O-34(2-3-31)	0.6
1941	Phi-N	151	590	72	180	29	6	18	66	39	43	.305	.350	.466	816	134	23	1			.964	17	*O-150(148-0-2)	3.2
1942	Phi-N★	151	591	59	160	25	9	9	56	27	42	.271	.310	.389	700	109	4	2			**1.000**	-2	*O-151(130-0-24)	-0.7
1943	Phi-N	36	139	23	36	6	0	5	17	11	14	.259	.313	.410	723	113	2	1			.989	5	O-34(34-0-0)	0.5
	*StL-N	80	258	40	72	14	3	7	31	19	31	.279	.333	.438	771	117	5	1			1.000	1	O-70(70-0-0)	0.2
	Yr	116	397	63	108	20	3	12	48	30	45	.272	.326	.428	755	115	6	2			.996	6	*O-104(104-0-0)	0.7
1944	*StL-N	140	492	53	130	25	5	15	82	37	56	.264	.328	.427	755	109	5	2			.974	-1	*O-136(136-0-0)	-0.3
1946	StL-N	6	5	0	0	0	0	0	0	1	1	.000	.167	.000	167	-49	-1	0			.000	0	H	-0.1
	Bos-N	79	247	29	72	12	2	8	38	19	23	.291	.347	.453	800	125	7	1			.985	-3	O-65(65-0-0)/3-2	-0.1
	Yr	85	252	29	72	12	2	8	38	20	24	.286	.343	.444	788	121	6	1			.985	-3	O-65(65-0-0)/3-2	-0.2
1947	Bos-N	91	226	38	59	5	2	7	31	25	43	.261	.337	.394	731	96	-2	1			.976	-6	O-66(64-0-1)	-1.1
1948	Bos-N	13	33	0	9	2	0	0	6	4	2	.273	.385	.333	718	97	0	0			1.000	2	/O-8(8-0-0)	0.1
	Cin-N	106	338	51	93	19	2	14	44	48	41	.275	.365	.467	833	128	13	1			.988	2	O-83(5-1-77),3-15	1.3
	Yr	119	371	51	102	21	2	14	50	52	43	.275	.367	.456	823	125	13	1			.990	4	O-91(13-1-77),3-15	1.4
1949	Cin-N	102	292	35	85	18	1	11	48	44	42	.291	.384	.473	857	127	12	0			.987	-5	O-82(11-1-71)/3-3	0.4
1950	Cin-N	54	112	15	29	4	0	6	12	20	21	.259	.371	.455	827	116	3	0			.958	-3	O-29(8-0-21)	-0.1
1951	Cin-N	12	29	3	8	1	0	2	3	2	5	.276	.323	.517	840	120	1	0	0	0	.933	-1	/O-7(0-0-7)	0.0
Total	11	1057	3494	428	982	162	32	107	451	299	377	.281	.342	.438	780	119	78	11	0		.982	9	O-915(681-5-234)/3-20	3.9
■ **PADDY LIVINGSTON**	Livingston, Patrick Joseph b: 1/14/1880, Cleveland, Ohio d: 9/19/77, Cleveland, Ohio BR/TR, 5'8", 197 lbs. Deb: 9/2/01 C																							
1901	Cle-A	1	2	0	0	0	0	0	0	0		.000	.333	.000	333	-2	-0	0			1.000	-1	/C-1	-0.1
1906	Cin-N	50	139	8	22	1	4	0	8	12		.158	.259	.223	483	48	-8	0			.960	3	C-47	-0.1
1909	Phi-A	64	175	15	41	6	4	0	15	15		.234	.323	.314	638	99	0	4			.969	9	C-64	1.7
1910	Phi-A	37	120	11	25	4	3	0	9	6		.208	.264	.292	555	75	-4	2			.968	4	C-37	0.4
1911	Phi-A	27	71	9	17	4	0	0	8	7		.239	.316	.296	612	72	-3	1			.977	5	C-26	0.4
1912	Cle-A	20	47	5	11	2	1	0	3	1		.234	.280	.319	599	69	-2	0			.976	0	C-14	-0.1
1917	StL-N	7	20	0	4	0	0	0	2	0	1	.200	.200	.200	400	23	-2	2			1.000	1	/C-6	-0.1
Total	7	206	574	48	120	17	12	0	45	41	1	.209	.287	.280	568	73	-18	9			.969	21	C-195	2.1
■ **MICKEY LIVINGSTON**	Livingston, Thompson Orville b: 11/15/14, Newberry, S.C. d: 4/3/83, Newberry, S.C. BR/TR, 6'1.5", 185 lbs. Deb: 9/17/38																							
1938	Was-A	2	4	0	3	2	0	0	1	0	1	.750	.750	1.250	2000	421	2	0	0	0	.667	-1	/C-2	0.1
1941	Phi-N	95	207	16	42	6	1	0	18	20	38	.203	.276	.242	518	49	-14	2			.974	-1	C-71/1-1	-1.1
1942	Phi-N	89	239	20	49	6	1	2	22	25	20	.205	.283	.264	547	64	-11	0			.987	-6	C-78/1-6	-1.4
1943	Phi-N	84	265	25	66	9	2	3	18	19	18	.249	.304	.332	636	87	-5	1			.988	-2	C-84/1-2	-0.2
	Chi-N	36	111	11	29	5	1	4	16	12	8	.261	.333	.432	766	122	3	1			1.000	-1	C-31/1-4	0.4
	Yr	120	376	36	95	14	3	7	34	31	26	.253	.313	.362	675	98	-2	2			**.991**	-3	*C-115/1-6	0.2
1945	*Chi-N	71	224	19	57	4	2	2	23	19	6	.254	.324	.317	641	80	-6	2			.990	-1	C-68/1-1	-0.2
1946	Chi-N	66	176	14	45	14	0	2	20	20	19	.256	.338	.369	708	103	1	0			.981	2	C-56	0.5
1947	Chi-N	19	33	2	7	2	0	0	3	1	5	.212	.235	.273	508	36	-3	0			1.000	-0	/C-7	-0.3
	NY-N	5	6	0	1	0	0	0	0	1	2	.167	.286	.167	452	23	-1	0			.800	0	/C-1	0.0
	Yr	24	39	2	8	2	0	0	3	2	7	.205	.244	.256	500	34	-4	0			.970	-0	/C-8	-0.3
1948	NY-N	45	99	9	21	4	1	2	12	21	11	.212	.350	.333	683	85	-1	1			.980	-1	C-42	0.0
1949	NY-N	19	57	6	17	2	0	4	12	2	8	.298	.333	.544	877	132	2	0			.985	-1	C-19	0.2
	Bos-N	28	64	6	15	2	1	0	6	3	5	.234	.290	.297	587	61	-4	0			.977	1	C-22	-0.2
	Yr	47	121	12	32	4	1	4	18	5	13	.264	.310	.413	723	95	-1	0			.980	-1	C-41	0.0
1951	Bro-N	2	5	0	2	0	0	0	2	1	0	.400	.500	.400	900	142	0	0	0	0	1.000	-0	/C-2	0.0
Total	10	561	1490	128	354	56	9	19	153	144	141	.238	.310	.326	636	82	-36	7	0		.984	-11	C-483/1-14	-2.2
■ **SCOTT LIVINGSTONE**	Livingstone, Scott Louis b: 7/15/65, Dallas, Tex. BL/TR, 6', 198 lbs. Deb: 7/19/91 Career OF: (0-LF 0-CF 1-RF)																							
1991	Det-A	44	127	19	37	5	0	2	11	10	25	.291	.343	.378	721	98	-0	2	1	0	.980	1	3-43	0.0
1992	Det-A	117	354	43	100	21	0	4	46	21	36	.282	.323	.376	698	95	-3	1	3	-1	.962	-6	*3-112	-1.0
1993	Det-A	98	304	39	89	10	2	2	39	19	32	.293	.334	.359	693	87	-6	1	3	-1	.955	-3	3-62,D-32	-1.1
1994	Det-A	15	23	0	5	1	0	0	1	1	4	.217	.250	.261	511	32	-2	0	0	0	1.000	0	/1-5,3-1,D-5	-0.2
	SD-N	57	180	11	49	12	1	2	10	6	22	.272	.296	.383	679	78	-6	2	2	-0	.942	-1	3-50	-0.7
1995	SD-N	99	196	26	66	15	0	5	32	15	22	.337	.384	.490	874	133	9	2	1	0	.991	-2	1-43,3-13/2-4	0.4
1996	*SD-N	102	172	20	51	4	1	2	20	9	22	.297	.331	.366	698	89	-3	0	1	-0	.993	0	1-22,3-16	-0.4
1997	SD-N	23	26	1	4	1	0	0	3	2	1	.154	.214	.192	407	8	-4	0	0	0	.750	2	/3-3,1-2,2-1	-0.2
	StL-N	42	41	3	7	1	0	0	3	1	10	.171	.190	.195	386	1	-6	1	0	0	1.000	-0	/3-2,O-1(0-0-1),D-1	-0.6
	Yr	65	67	4	11	2	0	0	6	3	11	.164	.200	.194	394	4	-9	1	0	0	.778	1	/3-5,1-2,2-1,O-1R,D	-0.8
1998	Mon-N	76	110	1	23	6	0	0	12	5	15	.209	.243	.264	507	34	-11	1	1	-0	.938	-1	3-17/1-3,D-5	-1.1
Total	8	673	1533	163	431	76	4	17	177	89	189	.281	.321	.369	690	86	-31	10	12	-2	.958	-9	3-319/1-75,D-43,2O	-4.9
■ **ABEL LIZOTTE**	Lizotte, Abel b: 4/13/1870, Lewiston, Me. d: 12/4/26, Wilkes-Barre, Pa. 5'8", 174 lbs. Deb: 9/17/1896																							
1896	Pit-N	7	29	3	3	0	0	0	3	2	2	.103	.161	.103	265	-31	-5	1			.952	1	/1-7	-0.4
■ **WINSTON LLENAS**	Llenas, Winston Enriquillo (Davila) b: 9/23/43, Santiago, D.R. BR/TR, 5'10", 165 lbs. Deb: 8/15/68 C Career OF: (40-LF 0-CF 8-RF)																							
1968	Cal-A	16	39	5	5	1	0	0	1	2	5	.128	.190	.154	344	6	-4	0	0	0	.800	-3	/3-9	-0.9
1969	Cal-A	34	47	4	8	2	0	0	0	2	10	.170	.204	.213	417	18	-5	0	0	0	.929	-2	/3-9	-0.8
1972	Cal-A	44	64	3	17	3	0	0	7	3	8	.266	.299	.313	611	87	-1	0	0	0	.950	-1	3-10/2-2,O-2(2-0-0)	-0.3
1973	Cal-A	78	130	16	35	1	0	1	25	10	16	.269	.326	.300	626	84	-3	0	0	0	1.000	-4	2-20,3-11/O-4L,D-4	-0.6
1974	Cal-A	72	138	16	36	6	0	2	17	11	19	.261	.315	.348	663	96	-1	0	0	0	1.000	-8	O-32L,2-15,D-10,/3	-1.0

YEAR	TM/L	G	AB	R	H	2B	3B	HR	RBI	BB	SO	AVG	OBP	SLG	OPS	OPS+	BR+	SB	CS	SBR	FA	FR	G/POS	TPR
1975	Cal-A	56	113	6	21	4	0	0	11	10	11	.186	.252	.221	473	37	-9	0	1	-0	1.000	4	2-12,O-10L/1-6,3D	-0.6
Total	6	300	531	50	122	17	0	3	61	38	69	.230	.284	.279	562	66	-23	0	1	-0	1.000	-13	/2-49,O-48L,3-44,D1	-4.2
■ MIKE LOAN	Loan, William Joseph b: 9/27/1894, Philadelphia, Pa. d: 11/21/66, Springfield, Pa. BR/TR, 5'11", 185 lbs. Deb: 9/18/12																							
1912	Phi-N	1	2	1	1	0	0	0	0	0	0	.500	.500	.500	1000	163	0	0			1.000	-1	/C-1	0.0
■ BOB LOANE	Loane, Robert Kenneth b: 8/5/14, Berkeley, Cal. BR/TR, 6', 190 lbs. Deb: 7/29/39																							
1939	Was-A	3	9	2	0	0	0	0	1	4	4	.000	.308	.000	308	-16	-1	0	0	0	.909	2	/O-3(0-3-0)	0.0
1940	Bos-N	13	22	4	5	3	0	0	1	2	5	.227	.292	.364	655	84	-1	2			1.000	0	O-10(2-8-0)	0.0
Total	2	16	31	6	5	3	0	0	2	6	9	.161	.297	.258	555	54	-2	2	0		.969	2	/O-13(2-11-0)	0.0
■ FRANK LOBERT	Lobert, Frank John b: 11/26/1883, Williamsport, Pa. d: 5/29/32, Pittsburgh, Pa. BR/TR, 6', 180 lbs. Deb: 6/6/14 F																							
1914	Bal-F	11	30	3	6	0	1	0	2	0	0	.200	.200	.267	467	26	-4	0			.870	-2	/3-7,2-1	-0.5
■ HANS LOBERT	Lobert, John Bernard "Honus" b: 10/18/1881, Wilmington, Del. d: 9/14/68, Philadelphia, Pa. BR/TR, 5'9", 170 lbs. Deb: 9/21/03 FMC Career OF: (21-LF 2-CF 0-RF)																							
1903	Pit-N	5	13	1	1	1	0	0	0	1		.077	.143	.154	297	-15	-2	1			.778	-1	/3-3,2-1,S-1	-0.3
1905	Chi-N	14	46	7	9	2	0	0	1	3		.196	.260	.239	499	47	-3	4			.918	0	3-13/O-1(0-1-0)	-0.3
1906	Cin-N	79	268	39	83	5	5	0	19	19		.310	.366	.366	732	123	7	20			.959	-11	3-35,S-31,2-10,/O-1C	-0.2
1907	Cin-N	148	537	61	132	9	12	1	41	37		.246	.299	.313	612	88	-8	30			.941	-18	*S-142/3-5	-2.4
1908	Cin-N	155	570	71	167	17	18	4	63	46		.293	.348	.407	755	145	27	47			.921	-26	3-99,S-35,O-21L	0.5
1909	Cin-N	122	425	50	90	13	5	4	52	48		.212	.304	.294	598	86	-6	30			.921	-14	*3-122	-1.8
1910	Cin-N	93	314	43	97	6	6	3	40	30	9	.309	.369	.395	764	128	11	41			.932	-2	3-90	1.2
1911	Phi-N	147	541	94	154	20	9	9	72	66	31	.285	.368	.405	772	115	11	40			.954	-17	*3-147	-0.2
1912	Phi-N	65	257	37	84	12	5	2	33	19	13	.327	.373	.436	809	113	4	13			.976	-13	3-64	-0.7
1913	Phi-N	150	573	98	172	28	11	7	55	42	34	.300	.353	.424	777	117	11	41			**.974**	-15	*3-145/S-3,2-1	0.0
1914	Phi-N	135	505	83	139	24	5	1	52	49	32	.275	.343	.349	691	99	0	31			**.943**	-26	*3-133/S-2	-2.4
1915	NY-N	106	386	46	97	18	4	0	38	25	24	.251	.304	.319	622	94	-3	14	15	-2	.950	-6	*3-103	-1.0
1916	NY-N	48	76	6	17	3	2	0	11	5	8	.224	.272	.316	587	84	-2	2			.961	2	3-20	0.1
1917	NY-N	50	52	4	10	1	0	1	5	5	5	.192	.276	.269	545	70	-2	2			.906	2	3-21	0.0
Total	14	1317	4563	640	1252	159	82	32	482	395	156	.274	.337	.366	703	109	47	316	15		.944	-143	3-1000,S-214/O-23L,2	-7.5
■ HARRY LOCHHEAD	Lochhead, Robert Henry b: 3/29/1876, Stockton, Cal. d: 8/22/09, Stockton, Cal. BR/TR, 5'11", 172 lbs. Deb: 4/16/1899																							
1899	Cle-N	148	541	52	129	7	1	1	43	21		.238	.280	.261	540	52	-35	23			.909	2	*S-146/2-1,P-1	-2.3
1901	Det-A	1	4	2	2	0	0	0	0	0		.500	.600	.500	1100	198	1	0			.857	-0	/S-1	0.0
	Phi-A	9	34	3	3	0	0	0	2	3		.088	.162	.088	250	-28	-6	0			.757	-8	/S-9	-1.3
	Yr	10	38	5	5	0	0	0	2	3		.132	.214	.132	346	-3	-5	0			.773	-9	S-10	-1.3
Total	2	158	579	57	134	7	1	1	45	24		.231	.275	.252	527	48	-40	23			.903	-7	S-156/P-1,2-1	-3.6
■ DON LOCK	Lock, Don Wilson b: 7/27/36, Wichita, Kan. BR/TR, 6'2", 202 lbs. Deb: 7/17/62																							
1962	Was-A	71	225	30	57	6	2	12	37	30	63	.253	.341	.458	799	114	4	4	5	-1	.973	3	O-67(67-1-0)	0.3
1963	Was-A	149	531	71	134	20	1	27	82	70	151	.252	.342	.446	788	119	14	7	3	0	.980	15	*O-146(10-135-9)	2.5
1964	Was-A	152	512	73	127	17	4	28	80	79	137	.248	.350	.461	811	124	17	4	2	0	.987	13	*O-149(0-135-25)	2.6
1965	Was-A	143	418	52	90	15	1	16	39	57	115	.215	.317	.371	687	96	-2	1	3	-1	.969	2	*O-136(0-136-0)	-0.4
1966	Was-A	138	386	52	90	13	1	16	48	57	126	.233	.335	.396	731	110	6	2	6	-2	.977	7	*O-129(0-126-4)	0.8
1967	Phi-N	112	313	46	79	13	1	14	51	43	98	.252	.352	.435	786	123	10	9	5	0	.973	-2	O-97(1-96-1)	0.6
1968	Phi-N	99	248	27	52	7	2	8	34	26	64	.210	.285	.351	635	90	-3	3	4	-1	.955	-5	O-78(8-46-27)	-1.3
1969	Phi-N	4	4	0	0	0	0	0	0	0	1	.000	.000	.000	0	-99	-1	0	0	0	.000	-0	/O-1(1-0-0)	-0.1
	Bos-A	53	58	8	13	1	0	1	2	11	21	.224	.348	.293	641	77	-1	0	1	-0	1.000	-6	O-28(15-9-4)/1-4	-0.9
Total	8	921	2695	359	642	92	12	122	373	373	776	.238	.334	.417	751	111	43	30	29	-4	.976	27	O-831(102-684-70)/1-4	4.1
■ MARSHALL LOCKE	Locke, Marshall Pinkney Wilder b: 3/12/1857, Ashland, Ohio d: 3/6/40, Ashland, Ohio Deb: 7/5/1884																							
1884	Ind-a	7	29	5	7	0	1	0	5	0		.241	.241	.310	552	81	-1				.800	-1	/O-7(0-3-4)	-0.2
■ KEITH LOCKHART	Lockhart, Keith Virgil b: 11/10/64, Whittier, Cal. BL/TR, 5'10", 170 lbs. Deb: 4/5/94																							
1994	SD-N	27	43	4	9	0	0	2	6	4	10	.209	.292	.349	641	68	-2	1	0	0	1.000	-1	3-13/2-5,S-1,O-1R	-0.3
1995	KC-A	94	274	41	88	19	3	6	33	14	21	.321	.363	.478	841	115	6	8	1	1	.974	-8	2-61,3-17,D-14	0.1
1996	KC-A	138	433	49	118	33	3	7	55	30	40	.273	.323	.411	734	84	-11	11	6	0	.975	2	2-84,3-55/D-1	-0.5
1997	*Atl-N	96	147	25	41	5	3	6	32	14	17	.279	.346	.476	822	110	2	0	0	0	.983	-6	2-20,3-11/D-4	-0.3
1998	*Atl-N	109	366	50	94	21	0	9	37	29	37	.257	.313	.388	701	83	-9	2	2	-0	.984	-4	2-97/3-1,D-2	-0.9
1999	*Atl-N	108	161	20	42	3	1	1	21	19	21	.261	.343	.311	653	67	-8	3	1	0	1.000	1	2-25,3-10/D-4	-0.5
2000	*Atl-N	113	275	32	73	12	3	2	32	29	31	.265	.336	.353	688	75	-10	4	1	1	.979	11	2-74,3-18	0.4
Total	7	685	1699	221	465	93	13	33	216	139	177	.274	.332	.402	734	87	-33	29	11	3	.980	-5	2-366,3-125/D-25,OS	-2.0
■ GENE LOCKLEAR	Locklear, Gene b: 7/19/49, Lumberton, N.C. BL/TR, 5'10", 165 lbs. Deb: 4/5/73																							
1973	Cin-N	29	26	6	5	0	0	0	0	2	5	.192	.276	.192	468	34	-2	0	0	0	1.000	-1	/O-5(1-0-4)	-0.4
	SD-N	67	154	20	37	6	1	3	25	21	22	.240	.331	.351	682	97	-0	9	4	1	.952	2	O-37(37-0-0)	0.0
	Yr	96	180	26	42	6	1	3	25	23	27	.233	.324	.328	651	87	-3	9	4	1	.954	1	O-42(38-0-4)	-0.4
1974	SD-N	39	74	7	20	3	2	1	3	4	12	.270	.308	.405	713	103	-0	0	1	-0	1.000	1	O-12(8-0-4)	-0.1
1975	SD-N	100	237	31	76	11	1	5	27	22	26	.321	.381	.439	820	135	11	4	2	0	.970	-1	O-51(50-0-2)	0.8
1976	SD-N	43	67	9	15	3	0	0	8	4	15	.224	.268	.269	536	57	-4	0	0	0	.952	-1	O-11(11-0-0)	-0.5
	NY-A	13	32	2	7	1	0	0	1	2	7	.219	.265	.250	515	52	-2	0	0	0	1.000	-1	/O-3(3-0-0),D-6	-0.3
1977	NY-A	1	5	1	3	0	0	0	2	0	0	.600	.600	.600	1200	231	1	0	0	0	.667	-0	/O-1(1-0-0)	0.1
Total	5	292	595	76	163	24	4	9	66	55	87	.274	.337	.373	711	105	3	13	7	0	.962	-0	O-120(111-0-10)/D-6	-0.4
■ STU LOCKLIN	Locklin, Stuart Carlton b: 7/22/28, Appleton, Wis. BL/TL, 6'1.5", 190 lbs. Deb: 6/23/55																							
1955	Cle-A	16	18	4	3	1	0	0	0	3	4	.167	.286	.222	508	37	-2	0	0	0	1.000	-3	/O-7(0-4-3)	-0.4
1956	Cle-A	9	6	0	1	0	0	0	0	0	1	.167	.167	.167	333	-12	-1	0	0	0	1.000	-0	/O-1(0-0-1)	-0.1
Total	2	25	24	4	4	1	0	0	0	3	5	.167	.259	.208	468	26	-3	0	0	0	1.000	-3	/O-8(0-4-4)	-0.5
■ WHITEY LOCKMAN	Lockman, Carroll Walter b: 7/25/26, Lowell, N.C. BL/TR, 6'1", 175 lbs. Deb: 7/5/45 MC Career OF: (556-LF 163-CF 47-RF)																							
1945	NY-N	32	129	16	44	9	0	3	18	13	10	.341	.410	.481	890	145	8	1			.961	-4	O-32(0-32-0)	0.3
1947	NY-N	2	2	0	1	0	0	0	1	0	0	.500	.500	.500	1000	165	0	0			.000	0	H	0.0
1948	NY-N	146	584	117	167	24	10	18	59	68	63	.286	.361	.454	815	119	15	8			.987	7	*O-144(53-91-0)	1.5
1949	NY-N	151	617	97	186	32	7	11	65	62	31	.301	.368	.429	798	113	12	12			.973	4	*O-151(151-0-0)	0.5
1950	NY-N	129	532	72	157	28	5	6	52	42	29	.295	.349	.400	749	96	-3	1			.978	9	*O-128(123-6-0)	-0.3
1951	*NY-N	153	614	85	173	27	7	12	73	50	32	.282	.339	.407	746	99	-1	4	5	-1	.986	4	*1-119,O-34(34-0-0)	-0.5
1952	NY-N★	154	606	99	176	17	4	13	58	67	52	.290	.363	.396	759	110	9	2	4	-1	.992	2	*1-154	0.5
1953	NY-N	150	607	85	179	22	4	9	61	52	36	.295	.351	.389	739	91	-7	3	4	-1	.989	7	*1-120,O-30(0-3-28)	-0.9
1954	*NY-N	148	570	73	143	17	3	16	60	59	31	.251	.321	.375	697	80	-17	2	2	-0	.987	-8	*1-145/O-2(1-1-0)	-3.3
1955	NY-N	147	576	76	157	19	0	15	49	39	34	.273	.322	.384	706	86	-12	3	3	-0	.983	-4	O-81(79-2-1),1-68	-2.4
1956	NY-N	48	169	13	46	7	1	1	10	16	17	.272	.335	.343	678	83	-4	0	2	-1	.960	-1	O-39(38-1-1)/1-7	-0.8
	StL-N	70	193	14	48	0	2	0	10	18	8	.249	.313	.269	582	59	-11	2	2	-0	.955	-8	O-57(32-23-8)/1-2	-2.2
	Yr	118	362	27	94	7	3	1	20	34	25	.260	.323	.304	627	70	-14	2	4	-1	.957	-8	O-96(70-24-9)/1-9	-3.0
1957	NY-N	133	456	51	113	9	4	7	30	39	19	.248	.310	.331	641	73	-17	5	5	-1	.991	-6	*1-102,O-27(22-3-4)	-3.2
1958	SF-N	92	122	15	29	5	0	2	7	13	8	.238	.311	.328	639	71	-5	0	0	0	1.000	-11	O-25(23-0-4),2-15/1-7	-1.6
1959	Bal-A	38	69	7	15	1	1	0	2	8	4	.217	.299	.261	560	56	-4	0	0	0	.992	-4	1-22/2-5,O-1(0-0-1)	-0.8
	Cin-N	52	84	10	22	5	1	0	7	4	6	.262	.295	.345	641	68	-4	0	0	0	.971	0	1-20/2-6,3-1,O-1C	-0.4
1960	Cin-N	21	10	6	2	0	0	1	1	2	3	.200	.385	.500	885	138	1	0	0	0	1.000	0	/1-5	0.1
Total	15	1666	5940	836	1658	222	49	114	563	552	383	.279	.342	.391	733	95	-40	43	27		.989	-9	1-771,O-752L/2-26,3	-13.5

YEAR	TM/L	G	AB	R	H	2B	3B	HR	RBI	BB	SO	AVG	OBP	SLG	OPS	OPS+	BR+	SB	CS	SBR	FA	FR	G/POS	TPR
■ SKIP LOCKWOOD	Lockwood, Claude Edward b: 8/17/46, Boston, Mass. BR/TR, 6', 190 lbs. Deb: 4/23/65																							
1965	KC-A	42	33	4	4	0	0	0	0	7	11	.121	.293	.121	414	23	-3	0	0	0	1.000	2	/3-7	-0.1
1969	Sea-A	6	7	0	0	0	0	0	0	0	2	.000	.000	.000	0	-99	-2	0	0	0	1.000	0	/P-6	0.0
1970	Mil-A	27	53	2	12	1	0	1	2	1	11	.226	.241	.302	543	48	-4	0	0	0	.970	-1	P-27	0.0
1971	Mil-A	36	62	2	5	1	0	1	4	5	20	.081	.149	.145	294	-17	-10	0	0	0	**1.000**	-3	P-33	0.0
1972	Mil-A	31	53	3	7	0	0	0	0	3	12	.132	.193	.132	325	-2	-7	0	1	-0	.958	-3	P-29	0.0
1973	Mil-A	37	0	0	0	0	0	0	0	0	0	—	—	—	—	—	0	0	0	0	.944	0	P-37	0.0
1974	Cal-A	37	0	0	0	0	0	0	0	0	0	—	—	—	—	—	0	0	0	0	1.000	-0	P-37	0.0
1975	NY-N	24	6	0	1	0	0	0	1	0	0	.167	.167	.167	333	-8	-1	0	0	0	.800	-1	P-24	0.0
1976	NY-N	56	18	2	6	1	0	0	2	2	3	.333	.400	.389	789	132	1	0	1	-0	.867	-0	P-56	0.0
1977	NY-N	63	15	1	3	0	0	0	1	0	1	.200	.200	.200	400	8	-2	0	0	0	.875	-2	P-63	0.0
1978	NY-N	57	11	1	2	1	0	1	1	0	5	.182	.182	.545	727	100	-0	0	0	0	.900	-2	P-57	0.0
1979	NY-N	28	2	0	0	0	0	0	0	0	1	.000	.000	.000	0	-99	-1	0	0	0	.800	-1	P-27	0.0
1980	Bos-A	24	0	0	0	0	0	0	0	0	0	—	—	—	—	—	0	0	0	0	1.000	-1	P-24	0.0
Total	13	468	260	15	40	4	0	3	11	18	66	.154	.214	.204	418	19	-28	0	2	-1	.947	-11	P-420/3-7	-0.1
■ MILO LOCKWOOD	Lockwood, Milo Hathaway b: 4/7/1858, Solon, Ohio d: 10/9/1897, Economy, Pa. 5'10", 160 lbs. Deb: 4/17/1884																							
1884	Was-U	20	67	9	14	1	0	0		8		.209	.293	.224	517	61	-5				.773	2	O-11(1-7-3),P-11/3-3	-0.2
■ DARIO LODIGIANI	Lodigiani, Dario Antonio b: 6/6/16, San Francisco, Cal BR/TR, 5'8", 150 lbs. Deb: 4/18/38 C																							
1938	Phi-A	93	325	36	91	15	1	6	44	34	25	.280	.361	.388	748	90	-5	3	0	1	.953	-6	2-80,3-13	-0.4
1939	Phi-A	121	393	46	102	22	4	6	44	42	18	.260	.337	.382	719	85	-9	2	0	0	.944	2	3-89,2-28	-0.2
1940	Phi-A	1	1	0	0	0	0	0	0	0	0	.000	.000	.000	0	-99	-0	0	0	0	.000	0	H	0.0
1941	Chi-A	87	322	39	77	19	2	4	40	31	19	.239	.316	.348	663	76	-11	0	4	-1	.962	6	3-86	-0.3
1942	Chi-A	59	168	9	47	7	0	0	15	18	10	.280	.353	.321	674	92	-1	3	4	-1	.944	6	3-43/2-7	0.6
1946	Chi-A	44	155	12	38	8	0	0	13	16	14	.245	.324	.297	620	77	-4	4	0	1	.935	-5	3-44	-0.9
Total	6	405	1364	142	355	71	7	16	156	141	86	.260	.338	.358	696	84	-31	12	8	-0	.947	3	3-275,2-115	-1.2
■ PAUL LoDUCA	LoDuca, Paul Anthony b: 4/12/72, Brooklyn, N.Y. BR/TR, 5'10", 193 lbs. Deb: 6/21/98																							
1998	LA-N	6	14	2	4	1	0	0	1	0	1	.286	.286	.357	643	72	-1	0	0	0	1.000	-1	/C-4	-0.1
1999	LA-N	36	95	11	22	1	0	3	11	10	9	.232	.318	.337	655	70	-4	1	2	-0	.990	3	C-34	0.0
2000	LA-N	34	65	6	16	2	0	2	8	6	8	.246	.310	.369	679	74	-3	0	2	-1	.992	7	C-20/O-8(7-0-2),3-1	0.4
Total	3	76	174	19	42	4	0	5	20	16	18	.241	.313	.351	663	72	-8	1	4	-1	.991	9	/C-58,O-8(7-0-2),3-1	0.3
■ GEORGE LOEPP	Loepp, George Herbert b: 9/11/01, Detroit, Mich. d: 9/4/67, Los Angeles, Cal. BR/TR, 5'11", 170 lbs. Deb: 8/29/28																							
1928	Bos-A	15	51	6	9	3	1	0	3	5	12	.176	.250	.275	525	38	-5	0	0	0	.949	-0	O-14(1-10-6)	-0.6
1930	Was-A	50	134	23	37	7	1	0	14	20	9	.276	.382	.343	725	85	-2	0	4	-1	.958	-5	O-48(12-34-3)	-1.0
Total	2	65	185	29	46	10	2	0	17	25	21	.249	.347	.324	672	73	-7	0	4	-1	.956	-6	/O-62(13-44-9)	-1.6
■ KENNY LOFTON	Lofton, Kenneth b: 5/31/67, E.Chicago, Ind. BL/TL, 6', 180 lbs. Deb: 9/14/91																							
1991	Hou-N	20	74	9	15	1	0	0	0	5	19	.203	.253	.216	469	35	-6	2	1	0	.977	0	O-20(0-20-0)	-0.7
1992	Cle-A	148	576	96	164	15	8	5	42	68	54	.285	.362	.365	727	106	6	**66**	12	**10**	.982	17	*O-143(0-143-0)	3.2
1993	Cle-A	148	569	116	185	28	8	1	42	81	83	.325	.410	.408	818	121	21	**70**	14	**11**	.979	13	*O-146(0-146-0)	4.4
1994	Cle-A★	112	459	105	**160**	32	9	12	57	52	56	.349	.417	.536	953	143	30	**60**	12	**9**	.993	8	*O-112(0-112-0)	4.4
1995	*Cle-A★	118	481	93	149	22	**13**	7	53	40	49	.310	.364	.453	817	110	7	**54**	15	7	.970	1	*O-114(0-114-0)/D-2	1.5
1996	*Cle-A★	154	662	132	210	35	4	14	67	61	82	.317	.375	.446	820	107	8	**75**	17	**11**	.975	10	*O-152(0-152-0)	2.7
1997	*Atl-N†	122	493	90	164	20	6	5	48	64	83	.333	.411	.428	839	118	16	27	20	-1	.983	11	*O-122(0-122-0)	2.6
1998	*Cle-A★	154	600	101	169	31	6	12	64	87	80	.282	.374	.413	788	101	3	54	10	8	.978	5	*O-154(0-154-0)	1.7
1999	*Cle-A★	120	465	110	140	28	6	7	39	79	84	.301	.409	.432	841	110	10	25	6	3	.989	3	*O-119(0-119-0)/D-1	1.6
2000	Cle-A	137	543	107	151	23	5	15	73	79	72	.278	.374	.422	796	98	0	30	7	4	.989	10	*O-135(0-135-0)/D-1	1.4
Total	10	1233	4922	959	1507	235	65	78	485	616	662	.306	.386	.428	813	111	95	463	114	62	.982	76	*O-1217(0-1217-0)/D-4	22.8
■ DICK LOFTUS	Loftus, Richard Joseph b: 3/7/01, Concord, Mass. d: 1/21/72, Concord, Mass. BL/TR, 6', 155 lbs. Deb: 4/20/24																							
1924	Bro-N	46	81	18	22	6	0	0	8	7	2	.272	.330	.346	675	84	-2	1	0	0	1.000	-3	O-29(6-14-9)/1-1	-0.6
1925	Bro-N	51	131	16	31	6	0	0	13	5	5	.237	.275	.282	558	44	-11	2	0	0	.977	1	O-38(3-0-35)	-1.2
Total	2	97	212	34	53	12	0	0	21	12	7	.250	.296	.307	603	59	-13	3	0	1	.985	-3	/O-67(9-14-44),1-1	-1.8
■ TOM LOFTUS	Loftus, Thomas Joseph b: 11/15/1856, St.Louis, Mo. d: 4/16/10, Dubuque, Iowa BR, 168 lbs. Deb: 8/17/1877 M																							
1877	StL-N	3	11	2	2	0	0	0	0	0	1	.182	.182	.182	364	16	-1				.778	2	/O-3(1-0-2)	0.1
1883	StL-a	6	22	1	4	0	0	0		2		.182	.250	.182	432	39	-1				.882	0	/O-6(0-6-0)	-0.1
Total	2	9	33	3	6	0	0	0	0	2	1	.182	.229	.182	410	32	-2				.846	2	/O-9(1-6-2)	0.0
■ JOHNNY LOGAN	Logan, John "Yatcha" b: 3/23/27, Endicott, N.Y. BR/TR, 5'11", 175 lbs. Deb: 4/17/51																							
1951	Bos-N	62	169	14	37	7	1	0	16	18	13	.219	.298	.272	570	59	-10	0	0	0	.958	4	S-58	-0.2
1952	Bos-N	117	456	56	129	21	3	4	42	31	33	.283	.334	.368	702	98	-2	1	2	-0	**.972**	18	*S-117	2.4
1953	Mil-N	150	611	100	167	27	8	11	73	41	33	.273	.326	.398	724	93	-7	2	2	-0	**.975**	21	*S-150	2.5
1954	Mil-N	154	560	66	154	17	7	8	66	51	51	.275	.342	.373	715	92	-6	2	0	0	**.969**	14	*S-154	2.1
1955	Mil-N★	154	595	95	177	**37**	5	13	83	58	58	.297	.364	.442	806	118	16	3	3	-0	.963	8	*S-154	3.6
1956	Mil-N	148	545	69	153	27	5	15	46	46	49	.281	.342	.431	773	113	9	3	0	1	.968	3	*S-148	2.6
1957	*Mil-N☆	129	494	59	135	19	7	10	49	31	49	.273	.321	.401	722	100	-1	5	0	1	.960	24	*S-129	3.5
1958	*Mil-N★	145	530	54	120	20	0	11	53	40	57	.226	.287	.326	613	68	-26	1	2	-0	.959	10	*S-144	-0.4
1959	Mil-N☆	138	470	59	137	17	0	13	50	57	45	.291	.372	.411	782	118	13	1	3	-1	.975	-3	*S-138	2.1
1960	Mil-N	136	482	52	118	14	4	7	42	43	40	.245	.309	.334	643	82	-12	1	1	-0	.956	2	*S-136	0.1
1961	Mil-N	18	19	0	2	1	0	0	1	1	3	.105	.150	.158	308	-19	-3	0	0	0	1.000	-0	/S-2	-0.4
	Pit-N	27	52	5	12	4	0	0	5	4	8	.231	.286	.308	593	57	-3	0	0	0	1.000	0	/3-7,S-6	-0.2
	Yr	45	71	5	14	5	0	0	6	5	11	.197	.250	.268	518	38	-6	0	0	0	.964	0	/S-8,3-7	-0.6
1962	Pit-N	44	80	7	24	3	0	1	12	7	6	.300	.356	.375	731	96	-0	0	0	0	.980	2	3-19	0.1
1963	Pit-N	81	181	15	42	2	1	0	9	23	27	.232	.325	.254	579	69	-6	0	0	0	.920	2	S-44/3-4	-0.1
Total	13	1503	5244	651	1407	216	41	93	547	451	472	.268	.331	.378	710	95	-38	19	13	-0	.965	105	*S-1380/3-30	17.7
■ PETE LOHMAN	Lohman, George F. b: 10/21/1864, Washington Co., Minn. d: 11/21/28, Los Angeles, Cal. Deb: 5/11/1891																							
1891	Was-a	32	109	18	21	1	4	1	11	16	17	.193	.302	.303	604	76	-3	1			.914	-3	C-21/O-8R,3-4,S2	-0.4
■ HOWARD LOHR	Lohr, Howard Sylvester b: 6/3/1892, Philadelphia, Pa. d: 6/9/77, Philadelphia, Pa. BR/TR, 6', 165 lbs. Deb: 6/17/14																							
1914	Cin-N	18	47	6	10	1	1	0	7	0	8	.213	.213	.277	489	44	-3	2			.926	-3	O-17(0-17-1)	-0.8
1916	Cle-A	3	7	0	1	0	0	0	1	0	1	.143	.143	.143	286	-13	-1	1			1.000	-1	/O-3(0-0-3)	-0.2
Total	2	21	54	6	11	1	1	0	8	0	9	.204	.204	.259	463	36	-4	3			.933	-4	/O-20(0-17-4)	-1.0
■ JACK LOHRKE	Lohrke, Jack Wayne "Lucky" b: 2/25/24, Los Angeles, Cal. BR/TR, 6', 180 lbs. Deb: 4/18/47																							
1947	NY-N	112	329	44	79	12	4	11	35	46	29	.240	.337	.401	738	95	-3	3			.939	-2	*3-111	-0.5
1948	NY-N	97	280	35	70	15	1	5	31	30	30	.250	.323	.364	687	85	-6	3			.898	-2	3-50,2-36	-0.6
1949	NY-N	55	180	32	48	11	4	5	22	16	12	.267	.333	.456	789	110	2	3			.969	4	2-23,3-19,S-15	0.8
1950	NY-N	30	43	4	8	0	0	0	4	4	8	.186	.255	.186	441	18	-5	0			.958	0	3-16/2-1	-0.5
1951	*NY-N	23	40	3	8	0	0	1	3	10	2	.200	.360	.275	635	73	-1	0	0	0	.943	-1	3-17/S-1	-0.2
1952	Phi-N	25	29	4	6	0	0	0	1	4	3	.207	.303	.207	510	44	-2	0	0	0	1.000	1	/S-5,3-3,2-1	-0.1
1953	Phi-N	12	13	3	2	0	0	0	0	1	2	.154	.214	.154	368	-2	-2	0	0	0	.750	1	/2-2,S-2,3-1	-0.1
Total	7	354	914	125	221	38	9	22	96	111	86	.242	.327	.375	702	87	-17	9	0		.928	2	3-217/2-63,S-23	-1.2
■ ALBERTO LOIS	Lois, Alberto (b: Alberto Louis (Pie)) b: 5/6/56, Hato Mayor, D.R. BR/TR, 5'9", 175 lbs. Deb: 9/8/78																							
1978	Pit-N	3	4	0	1	0	1	0	0	0	1	.250	.250	.750	1000	163	0	0	0	0	1.000	-0	/O-2(2-1-0)	0.0
1979	Pit-N	11	0	6	0	0	0	0	0	0	0	—	—	—	—	—	0	1	1	-0	.000	0	/R	0.0
Total	2	14	4	6	1	0	1	0	0	0	1	.250	.250	.750	1000	163	0	1	1	-0	1.000	-0	/O-2(2-1-0)	0.0

YEAR	TM/L	G	AB	R	H	2B	3B	HR	RBI	BB	SO	AVG	OBP	SLG	OPS	OPS+	BR+	SB	CS	SBR	FA	FR	G/POS	TPR
■ **RON LOLICH**	Lolich, Ronald John b: 9/19/46, Portland, Ore. BR/TR, 6′1″, 185 lbs. Deb: 7/18/71																							
1971	Chi-A	2	8	0	1	1	0	0	0	0	2	.125	.125	.250	375	4	-1	0	0	0	1.000	-1	/O-2(0-0-2)	-0.2
1972	Cle-A	24	80	4	15	1	0	2	8	4	20	.188	.226	.275	501	47	-5	0	0	0	1.000	-1	O-22(4-0-19)	-0.8
1973	Cle-A	61	140	16	32	7	0	2	15	7	27	.229	.265	.321	587	63	-7	0	2	-1	.909	-4	O-32(5-0-27),D-12	-1.4
Total	3	87	228	20	48	9	0	4	23	11	49	.211	.247	.303	549	56	-13	0	2	-1	.953	-5	/O-56(9-0-48),D-12	-2.4
■ **SHERM LOLLAR**	Lollar, John Sherman b: 8/23/24, Durham, Ark. d: 9/24/77, Springfield, Mo. BR/TR, 6′1″, 185 lbs. Deb: 4/20/46 C																							
1946	Cle-A	28	62	7	15	6	0	1	9	5	9	.242	.299	.387	686	97	-1	0	1	-0	.990	-3	C-24	-0.3
1947	*NY-A	11	32	4	7	0	1	1	6	1	5	.219	.242	.375	617	71	-1	0	1	-0	1.000	1	/C-9	-0.1
1948	NY-A	22	38	0	8	0	0	0	4	1	6	.211	.231	.211	441	18	-4	0	0	0	.976	1	C-10	-0.3
1949	StL-A	109	284	28	74	9	1	8	49	32	22	.261	.340	.384	723	88	-6	0	1	-0	.988	-3	C-93	-0.5
1950	StL-A☆	126	396	55	111	22	3	13	65	64	25	.280	.391	.449	841	110	7	2	0	0	.981	-5	*C-109	0.8
1951	StL-A	98	310	44	78	21	0	8	44	43	26	.252	.350	.397	747	99	-0	1	0	0	**.995**	-2	C-85/3-1	0.2
1952	Chi-A	132	375	35	90	15	0	13	50	54	34	.240	.354	.384	738	104	3	1	0	0	.989	-2	*C-120	0.8
1953	Chi-A	113	334	46	96	19	0	8	54	47	29	.287	.388	.416	804	114	8	1	0	0	**.994**	-2	*C-107/1-1	1.1
1954	Chi-A☆	107	316	31	77	13	0	7	34	37	28	.244	.336	.351	687	85	-6	0	1	-0	.993	-3	C-93	-0.5
1955	Chi-A☆	138	426	67	111	13	1	16	61	68	34	.261	.375	.408	783	108	6	2	2	-0	.995	10	*C-136	2.2
1956	Chi-A★	136	450	55	132	28	2	11	75	53	34	.293	.387	.438	825	116	12	2	0	0	**.993**	4	*C-132	2.1
1957	Chi-A	101	351	33	90	11	2	11	70	35	24	.256	.346	.393	739	101	1	2	0	0	.998	-2	C-96	0.5
1958	Chi-A☆	127	421	53	115	16	0	20	84	57	37	.273	.370	.454	824	128	17	2	1	0	.987	2	*C-116	2.5
1959	*Chi-A★	140	505	63	134	22	3	22	84	55	49	.265	.348	.451	799	119	13	4	3	-0	.993	10	*C-122,1-24	2.8
1960	Chi-A★	129	421	43	106	23	0	7	46	42	39	.252	.331	.356	688	87	-7	2	0	0	**.995**	-2	*C-123	-0.3
1961	Chi-A	116	337	38	95	10	1	7	41	37	22	.282	.363	.380	743	100	1	0	0	0	**.998**	-10	*C-107	-0.4
1962	Chi-A	84	220	17	59	12	0	2	26	32	23	.268	.369	.350	719	95	-0	1	0	0	.991	-8	C-66	-0.5
1963	Chi-A	35	73	4	17	4	0	0	6	8	7	.233	.317	.288	605	72	-2	0	0	0	.981	-2	C-23/1-2	-0.4
Total	18	1752	5351	623	1415	244	14	155	808	671	453	.264	.359	.402	761	104	40	20	10	1	.992	-16	*C-1571/1-27,3-1	9.7
■ **DOUG LOMAN**	Loman, Douglas Edward b: 5/9/58, Bakersfield, Cal. BL/TL, 5′11″, 185 lbs. Deb: 9/3/84																							
1984	Mil-A	23	76	13	21	4	0	2	12	15	7	.276	.402	.408	810	130	4	0	2	-1	.967	3	O-23(21-0-4)	0.5
1985	Mil-A	24	66	10	14	3	2	0	7	1	12	.212	.224	.318	542	47	-5	0	0	0	1.000	1	O-20(0-8-15)	-0.4
Total	2	47	142	23	35	7	2	2	19	16	19	.246	.327	.366	693	93	-1	0	2	-1	.981	4	/O-43(21-8-19)	0.1
■ **STEVE LOMASNEY**	Lomasney, Steven James b: 8/29/77, Melrose, Mass. BR/TR, 6′, 185 lbs. Deb: 10/3/99																							
1999	Bos-A	1	2	0	0	0	0	0	0	0	2	.000	.000	.000	0	-97	-1	0	0	0	1.000	2	/C-1	0.1
■ **GEORGE LOMBARD**	Lombard, George Paul b: 9/14/75, Atlanta, Ga. BL/TR, 6′, 208 lbs. Deb: 9/4/98																							
1998	Atl-N	6	6	2	2	0	0	1	1	0	1	.333	.333	.833	1167	194	1	1	0	0	1.000	-0	/O-2(0-0-2)	0.1
1999	Atl-N	6	6	1	2	0	0	0	0	1	2	.333	.429	.333	762	96	0	2	0	0	1.000	-1	/O-4(2-0-2)	0.0
2000	Atl-N	27	39	8	4	0	0	0	2	1	14	.103	.146	.103	249	-36	-8	4	0	1	1.000	-2	O-15(5-0-11)	-0.9
Total	3	39	51	11	8	0	0	1	3	2	17	.157	.204	.216	419	7	-7	7	0	2	1.000	-3	/O-21(7-0-15)	-0.8
■ **ERNIE LOMBARDI**	Lombardi, Ernesto Natali "Schnozz" or "Bocci" b: 4/6/08, Oakland, Cal. d: 9/26/77, Santa Cruz, Cal. BR/TR, 6′3″, 230 lbs. Deb: 4/15/31 H																							
1931	Bro-N	73	182	20	54	7	1	4	23	12	12	.297	.340	.412	752	102	0	1			.984	3	C-50	0.6
1932	Cin-N	118	413	43	125	22	9	11	68	41	19	.303	.371	.479	851	131	18	0			.963	-11	*C-110	1.4
1933	Cin-N	107	350	30	99	21	1	4	47	16	17	.283	.322	.383	704	102	0	2			.972	-16	C-95	-0.9
1934	Cin-N	132	417	42	127	19	4	9	62	16	22	.305	.335	.434	769	107	3	0			.989	-3	*C-111	0.6
1935	Cin-N	120	332	36	114	23	3	12	64	16	6	.343	.379	.539	918	148	21	0			.983	-6	C-82	2.0
1936	Cin-N☆	121	387	42	129	23	2	12	68	19	16	.333	.375	.496	871	142	21	1			.962	-13	*C-105	1.4
1937	Cin-N☆	120	368	41	123	22	1	9	59	14	17	.334	.362	.473	835	132	15	1			.973	-18	C-90	0.2
1938	Cin-N★	129	489	60	167	30	1	19	95	40	14	**.342**	.391	.524	915	154	34	0			.985	-3	*C-123	3.9
1939	*Cin-N★	130	450	43	129	26	2	20	85	35	19	.287	.342	.487	829	120	11	0			.984	4	*C-120	2.1
1940	*Cin-N★	109	376	50	120	22	0	14	74	31	14	.319	.382	.489	871	137	19	0			.989	-4	*C-101	2.1
1941	Cin-N	117	398	33	105	12	1	10	60	36	14	.264	.325	.374	699	96	-2	1			.983	-1	*C-116	0.3
1942	Bos-N★	105	309	32	102	14	0	11	46	37	12	**.330**	.403	.482	886	162	24	1			.980	-16	C-85	1.4
1943	NY-N★	104	295	19	90	7	0	10	51	16	11	.305	.347	.431	778	123	8	1			.971	-14	C-73	-0.1
1944	NY-N	117	373	37	95	13	0	10	58	33	25	.255	.317	.370	687	93	-4	0			.968	-15	*C-100	-1.3
1945	NY-N†	115	368	46	113	7	1	19	70	43	11	.307	.387	.486	873	140	20	0			.983	2	C-96	2.7
1946	NY-N	88	238	19	69	4	1	12	39	18	24	.290	.347	.466	814	129	8	0			.978	1	C-63	1.3
1947	NY-N	48	110	8	31	5	0	4	21	7	9	.282	.325	.436	761	100	-0	0			.980	-3	C-24	-0.2
Total	17	1853	5855	601	1792	277	27	190	990	430	262	.306	.358	.460	818	126	195	8			.979	-113	*C-1544	17.5
■ **PHIL LOMBARDI**	Lombardi, Phillip Arden b: 2/20/63, Abilene, Tex. BR/TR, 6′2″, 200 lbs. Deb: 4/26/86																							
1986	NY-A	20	36	6	10	3	0	2	6	4	7	.278	.366	.528	894	141	2	0	0	0	.867	-1	/O-8(8-0-0),C-3	0.1
1987	NY-A	5	8	0	1	0	0	0	0	0	2	.125	.125	.125	250	-34	-2	0	0	0	1.000	-0	/C-3	-0.2
1989	NY-N	18	48	4	11	1	0	1	3	5	8	.229	.302	.313	614	80	-1	0	0	0	.980	-1	C-16/1-1	-0.2
Total	3	43	92	10	22	4	0	3	9	9	17	.239	.314	.380	694	95	-1	0	0	0	.975	-2	/C-22,O-8(8-0-0),1-1	-0.3
■ **STEVE LOMBARDOZZI**	Lombardozzi, Stephen Paul b: 4/26/60, Malden, Mass. BR/TR, 6′, 175 lbs. Deb: 7/12/85																							
1985	Min-A	28	54	10	20	4	1	0	6	6	6	.370	.433	.481	915	142	3	3	2	-0	.982	11	2-26	1.5
1986	Min-A	156	453	53	103	20	5	8	33	52	76	.227	.308	.347	655	76	-15	3	1	0	**.991**	-3	*2-155	-1.0
1987	*Min-A	136	432	51	103	19	3	8	38	33	66	.238	.299	.352	650	69	-19	5	1	1	.977	-1	*2-133	-1.2
1988	Min-A	103	287	34	60	15	2	3	27	35	48	.209	.299	.307	606	68	-12	2	5	-1	.986	-7	2-90,S-12/3-5	-1.8
1989	Hou-N	21	37	5	8	3	1	1	3	4	9	.216	.293	.432	725	109	0	0	0	0	.922	0	2-18/3-1	0.1
1990	Hou-N	2	1	0	0	0	0	0	0	1	1	.000	.500	.000	500	52	0	0	0	0	.000	0	/H	0.0
Total	6	446	1264	153	294	61	12	20	107	131	206	.233	.308	.347	655	76	-42	13	9	-0	.983	1	2-422/S-12,3-6	-2.4
■ **WALTER LONERGAN**	Lonergan, Walter E. b: 9/22/1885, Boston, Mass. d: 1/23/58, Lexington, Mass. BR/TR, 5′7″, 156 lbs. Deb: 8/17/11																							
1911	Bos-A	10	26	2	7	0	0	0	1	1		.269	.296	.269	566	59	-1	1			.935	-1	/2-7,S-1,3-1	-0.2
■ **LONG**	Long Deb: 8/29/1888																							
1888	Lou-a	1	2	0	0	0	0	0	0	1		.000	.333	.000	333	11	-0	0			.000	-0	/O-1(0-0-1)	0.0
■ **DAN LONG**	Long, Daniel W. b: 8/27/1867, Boston, Mass. d: 4/30/29, Sausalito, Cal. Deb: 8/27/1890																							
1890	Bal-a	21	77	19	12	0	0	0	2	14		.156	.301	.156	457	33	-6	16			.939	-1	O-21(0-21-0)	-0.6
■ **HERMAN LONG**	Long, Herman C. "Germany" or "Flying Dutchman" b: 4/13/1866, Chicago, Ill. d: 9/17/09, Denver, Colo. BL/TR, 5′8.5″, 160 lbs. Deb: 4/17/1889 Career OF: (18-LF 1-CF 0-RF)																							
1889	KC-a	136	574	137	158	32	6	3	60	64	63	.275	.358	.368	726	101	0	89			.874	32	*S-128/2-8,O-1(1-0-0)	3.1
1890	Bos-N	101	431	95	108	15	3	8	52	40	34	.251	.320	.355	675	90	-7	49			.898	11	*S-101	0.6
1891	Bos-N	139	577	129	163	21	12	9	75	80	51	.282	.377	.407	785	115	10	60			.902	15	*S-139	2.6
1892	*Bos-N	151	646	115	181	33	6	6	78	44	36	.280	.334	.378	712	105	1	57			.889	14	*S-141,O-12L/3-1	2.0
1893	Bos-N	128	552	**149**	159	22	6	6	58	73	32	.288	.376	.382	758	94	-5	38			.883	16	*S-123/2-5	1.5
1894	Bos-N	104	475	136	154	28	11	12	79	35	17	.324	.375	.505	881	102	-2	24			.885	3	*S-98/O-5(5-0-0),2-3	0.5
1895	Bos-N	125	540	109	170	23	10	9	75	31	13	.315	.355	.444	800	98	-5	36			.892	-5	*S-123/2-2	-0.3
1896	Bos-N	120	502	106	173	26	8	6	101	26	16	.345	.383	.464	847	116	9	38			.897	10	*S-120	2.2
1897	*Bos-N	107	450	89	145	32	7	3	69	23		.322	.358	.444	802	105	1	22			.905	-3	*S-107/O-1(1-0-0)	0.3
1898	Bos-N	144	589	99	156	21	10	6	99	39		.265	.311	.365	676	89	-11	20			.923	1	*S-142/2-2	-0.2
1899	Bos-N	145	578	91	153	30	8	6	100	45		.265	.321	.375	697	83	-16	20			.929	-10	*S-143/1-2	-1.7
1900	Bos-N	125	486	80	127	19	4	**12**	66	44		.261	.325	.391	716	86	-11	26			.937	-6	*S-125	-1.0
1901	Bos-N	138	518	54	112	14	6	3	68	25		.216	.254	.284	537	51	-33	20			**.946**	-3	*S-138	-3.1
1902	Bos-N	120	437	40	101	11	0	2	44	31		.231	.284	.270	554	70	-15	24			**.946**	23	*S-107,2-13	1.2
1903	NY-A	22	80	6	15	3	0	0	8	2		.188	.207	.225	432	28	-7	3			.889	-5	S-22	-1.2

YEAR	TM/L	G	AB	R	H	2B	3B	HR	RBI	BB	SO	AVG	OBP	SLG	OPS	OPS+	BR+	SB	CS	SBR	FA	FR	G/POS	TPR
	Det-A	69	239	21	53	12	0	0	23	10		.222	.256	.272	528	60	-12	11			.879	0	S-38,2-31	-1.0
	Yr	91	319	27	68	15	0	0	31	12		.213	.244	.260	504	52	-19	14			.883	-4	S-60,2-31	-2.2
1904	Phi-N	1	4	0	1	0	0	0	0	0		.250	.250	.250	500	56	-0	0			.889	1	/2-1	0.1
Total	16	1875	7678	1456	2129	342	97	91	1055	612	262	.277	.335	.383	718	93	-102	537			.906	95	*S-1795/2-65,O13	5.6

■ JIMMIE LONG Long, James Albert b: 6/29/1898, Ft.Dodge, Iowa d: 9/14/70, Ft.Dodge, Iowa BR/TR, 5′11″, 160 lbs. Deb: 9/12/22

YEAR	TM/L	G	AB	R	H	2B	3B	HR	RBI	BB	SO	AVG	OBP	SLG	OPS	OPS+	BR+	SB	CS	SBR	FA	FR	G/POS	TPR
1922	Chi-A	3	3	0	0	0	0	0	0	1	0	.000	.250	.000	250	-30	-1	0	0	0	1.000	-1	/C-2	-0.1

■ JIM LONG Long, James M. b: 11/15/1862, Louisville, Ky. d: 12/12/32, Louisville, Ky. 5′10″, 160 lbs. Deb: 8/9/1891

YEAR	TM/L	G	AB	R	H	2B	3B	HR	RBI	BB	SO	AVG	OBP	SLG	OPS	OPS+	BR+	SB	CS	SBR	FA	FR	G/POS	TPR
1891	Lou-a	6	25	5	6	0	0	0	4	3	6	.240	.367	.240	607	75	-0	1			.857	1	/O-6(4-2-0)	0.0
1893	Bal-N	55	226	31	48	8	1	2	25	16	27	.212	.276	.283	560	48	-18	23			.893	-1	O-55(55-0-0)	-2.0
Total	2	61	251	36	54	8	1	2	29	19	33	.215	.286	.279	565	51	-18	24			.890	-0	/O-61(59-2-0)	-2.0

■ JEOFF LONG Long, Jeoffrey Keith b: 10/9/41, Covington, Ky. BR/TR, 6′1″, 200 lbs. Deb: 7/31/63

YEAR	TM/L	G	AB	R	H	2B	3B	HR	RBI	BB	SO	AVG	OBP	SLG	OPS	OPS+	BR+	SB	CS	SBR	FA	FR	G/POS	TPR
1963	StL-N	5	5	0	1	0	0	0	0	0	1	.200	.200	.200	400	14	-1	0	0	0	.000	0	H	-0.1
1964	StL-N	28	43	5	10	1	0	1	4	6	18	.233	.340	.326	666	81	-1	0	0	0	.833	-2	/O-4(0-0-4),1-3	-0.3
	Chi-A	23	35	0	5	0	0	0	5	4	15	.143	.231	.143	374	7	-4	0	0	0	1.000	-1	/1-5,O-5(5-0-0)	-0.6
Total	2	56	83	5	16	1	0	1	9	10	34	.193	.287	.241	528	48	-6	0	0	0	.750	-2	/O-9(5-0-4),1-8	-1.0

■ DALE LONG Long, Richard Dale b: 2/6/26, Springfield, Mo. d: 1/27/91, Palm Coast, Fla. BL/TL, 6′4″, 210 lbs. Deb: 4/21/51 C

YEAR	TM/L	G	AB	R	H	2B	3B	HR	RBI	BB	SO	AVG	OBP	SLG	OPS	OPS+	BR+	SB	CS	SBR	FA	FR	G/POS	TPR
1951	Pit-N	10	12	1	2	0	0	1	1	0	3	.167	.167	.417	583	50	-1	0	0	0	1.000	-0	/1-1	-0.1
	StL-A	34	105	11	25	5	1	2	11	10	22	.238	.310	.362	672	79	-3	0	0	0	.988	-1	1-28/O-1(1-0-0)	-0.5
1955	Pit-N	131	419	59	122	19	**13**	16	79	48	72	.291	.365	.513	879	132	19	0	1	-0	.988	6	*1-119	1.7
1956	Pit-N★	148	517	64	136	20	7	27	91	54	85	.263	.333	.485	818	119	13	1	0	0	.982	-3	*1-138	0.2
1957	Pit-N	7	22	0	4	1	0	0	5	4	10	.182	.308	.227	535	48	-2	0	0	0	1.000	0	/1-7	-0.2
	Chi-N	123	397	55	121	19	0	21	62	52	63	.305	.387	.511	898	141	23	1	1	-0	.995	-1	*1-104	1.6
	Yr	130	419	55	125	20	0	21	67	56	73	.298	.382	.496	879	136	22	1	1	-0	.995	-1	*1-111	1.4
1958	Chi-N	142	480	68	130	26	4	20	75	66	64	.271	.361	.467	828	119	13	2	0	0	.992	-2	*1-137/C-2	0.5
1959	Chi-N	110	296	34	70	10	3	14	37	31	53	.236	.309	.432	741	96	-3	0	0	0	.985	-2	1-85	-0.9
1960	SF-N	37	54	4	9	0	0	3	6	7	7	.167	.262	.333	596	66	-3	0	0	0	1.000	0	1-10	-0.3
	*NY-A	26	41	6	15	3	1	3	10	5	6	.366	.435	.707	1142	216	6	0	0	0	.988	-1	1-11	0.6
1961	Was-A	123	377	52	94	20	4	17	49	39	41	.249	.321	.459	780	107	3	0	0	0	.983	-5	1-95	-0.8
1962	Was-A	67	191	17	46	8	0	4	24	18	22	.241	.310	.346	655	77	-6	5	1	1	.996	-0	1-51	-0.9
	*NY-A	41	94	12	28	4	0	4	17	18	9	.298	.411	.468	879	140	6	1	0	0	.992	1	1-31	0.6
	Yr	108	285	29	74	12	0	8	41	36	31	.260	.345	.386	731	98	-0	6	1	1	.995	1	1-82	-0.3
1963	NY-A	14	15	1	3	0	0	0	0	1	3	.200	.250	.200	450	28	-1	0	0	0	.917	-1	/1-2	-0.2
Total	10	1013	3020	384	805	135	33	132	467	353	460	.267	.345	.464	809	116	65	10	3	1	.988	-7	1-819/C-2,O-1(1-0-0)	1.3

■ RYAN LONG Long, Ryan Marcus b: 2/3/73, Houston, Tex. BR/TR, 6′2″, 215 lbs. Deb: 7/16/97

YEAR	TM/L	G	AB	R	H	2B	3B	HR	RBI	BB	SO	AVG	OBP	SLG	OPS	OPS+	BR+	SB	CS	SBR	FA	FR	G/POS	TPR
1997	KC-A	6	9	2	2	0	0	0	2	0	3	.222	.300	.222	522	38	-1	0	0	0	1.000	-1	/O-5(1-0-4),D-1	-0.1

■ TERRENCE LONG Long, Terrence Deon b: 2/29/76, Montgomery, Ala. BL/TL, 6′1″, 190 lbs. Deb: 4/14/99

YEAR	TM/L	G	AB	R	H	2B	3B	HR	RBI	BB	SO	AVG	OBP	SLG	OPS	OPS+	BR+	SB	CS	SBR	FA	FR	G/POS	TPR
1999	NY-N	3	3	0	0	0	0	0	0	0	2	.000	.000	.000	0	-99	-1	0	0	0	.000	0	-0,-0	-0.1
2000	*Oak-A	138	584	104	168	34	4	18	80	43	77	.288	.338	.452	790	100	-1	5	0	1	.971	-3	*O-137(0-137-0)	-0.1
Total	2	141	587	104	168	34	4	18	80	43	79	.286	.336	.450	786	99	-2	5	0	1	.971	-3	O-137(0-137-0)	-0.2

■ TOM LONG Long, Thomas Augustus b: 6/1/1890, Mitchum, Ala. d: 6/15/72, Mobile, Ala. BR/TR, 5′10.5″, 165 lbs. Deb: 9/11/11

YEAR	TM/L	G	AB	R	H	2B	3B	HR	RBI	BB	SO	AVG	OBP	SLG	OPS	OPS+	BR+	SB	CS	SBR	FA	FR	G/POS	TPR
1911	Was-A	14	48	1	11	3	0	0	5	1		.229	.245	.292	537	50	-3	4			.875	-2	O-13(4-0-9)	-0.6
1912	Was-A	1	1	0	0	0	0	0	0	0		.000	.000	.000	0	-99	-0	0			.000	0	H	0.0
1915	StL-N	140	507	61	149	21	**25**	2	61	31	50	.294	.339	.446	785	137	20	19	15	-1	.927	-4	*O-136(2-51-87)	0.8
1916	StL-N	119	403	37	118	11	10	1	33	10	43	.293	.312	.377	689	112	4	21	14	-0	.945	-8	*O-106(3-12-94)	-1.1
1917	StL-N	144	530	49	123	12	14	3	41	37	44	.232	.285	.325	609	89	-8	21			.919	-19	*O-137(30-0-104)	-3.9
Total	5	418	1489	148	401	47	49	6	140	79	137	.269	.309	.379	688	110	13	65	29		.928	-33	O-392(39-63-294)	-4.8

■ TONY LONGMIRE Longmire, Anthony Eugene b: 8/12/68, Vallejo, Cal. BL/TR, 6′1″, 197 lbs. Deb: 9/3/93

YEAR	TM/L	G	AB	R	H	2B	3B	HR	RBI	BB	SO	AVG	OBP	SLG	OPS	OPS+	BR+	SB	CS	SBR	FA	FR	G/POS	TPR
1993	*Phi-N	11	13	1	3	0	0	0	1	0	1	.231	.231	.231	462	24	-1	0	0	0	1.000	0	/O-2(2-0-0)	-0.1
1994	Phi-N	69	139	10	33	11	0	0	17	10	27	.237	.293	.317	610	58	-9	2	1	0	.941	-2	O-32(13-0-21)	-1.2
1995	Phi-N	59	104	21	37	7	0	3	19	11	19	.356	.422	.510	932	143	7	1	1	-0	1.000	0	O-23(19-2-2)	0.6
Total	3	139	256	32	73	18	0	3	37	21	47	.285	.344	.391	735	91	-3	3	2	-0	.967	-2	/O-57(34-2-23)	-0.7

■ JOE LONNETT Lonnett, Joseph Paul b: 2/7/27, Beaver Falls, Pa. BR/TR, 5′10″, 180 lbs. Deb: 4/22/56 C

YEAR	TM/L	G	AB	R	H	2B	3B	HR	RBI	BB	SO	AVG	OBP	SLG	OPS	OPS+	BR+	SB	CS	SBR	FA	FR	G/POS	TPR
1956	Phi-N	16	22	2	4	0	0	0	0	2	7	.182	.250	.182	432	19	-2	0	0	0	1.000	0	/C-7	-0.2
1957	Phi-N	67	160	12	27	5	0	5	15	22	39	.169	.273	.294	567	54	-10	0	0	0	.997	5	C-65	-0.3
1958	Phi-N	17	50	0	7	2	0	0	2	2	11	.140	.173	.180	353	-6	-8	0	0	0	.988	2	C-15	-0.5
1959	Phi-N	43	93	8	16	1	0	1	10	14	17	.172	.287	.215	502	36	-8	0	1	-0	.983	-6	C-43	-1.3
Total	4	143	325	22	54	8	0	6	27	40	74	.166	.262	.246	508	37	-29	0	1	-0	.992	1	C-130	-2.3

■ BRUCE LOOK Look, Bruce Michael b: 6/9/43, Lansing, Mich. BL/TR, 5′11″, 183 lbs. Deb: 4/17/68 F

YEAR	TM/L	G	AB	R	H	2B	3B	HR	RBI	BB	SO	AVG	OBP	SLG	OPS	OPS+	BR+	SB	CS	SBR	FA	FR	G/POS	TPR
1968	Min-A	59	118	7	29	4	0	0	9	20	24	.246	.355	.280	635	90	-0	0	1	-0	.996	2	C-41	0.3

■ DEAN LOOK Look, Dean Zachary b: 7/23/37, Lansing, Mich. BR/TR, 5′11″, 185 lbs. Deb: 9/22/61 F

YEAR	TM/L	G	AB	R	H	2B	3B	HR	RBI	BB	SO	AVG	OBP	SLG	OPS	OPS+	BR+	SB	CS	SBR	FA	FR	G/POS	TPR
1961	Chi-A	3	6	0	0	0	0	0	0	0	1	.000	.000	.000	0	-99	-2	0	0	0	1.000	-0	/O-1(1-0-0)	-0.2

■ STAN LOPATA Lopata, Stanley Edward "Stash" b: 9/12/25, Delray, Mich. BR/TR, 6′2″, 210 lbs. Deb: 9/19/48

YEAR	TM/L	G	AB	R	H	2B	3B	HR	RBI	BB	SO	AVG	OBP	SLG	OPS	OPS+	BR+	SB	CS	SBR	FA	FR	G/POS	TPR
1948	Phi-N	6	15	2	2	1	0	0	2	0	4	.133	.133	.200	333	-11	-2	0			1.000	0	/C-4	-0.2
1949	Phi-N	83	240	31	65	9	2	8	27	21	44	.271	.330	.425	755	104	1	1			.973	-3	C-58	0.1
1950	*Phi-N	58	129	10	27	2	2	1	11	22	25	.209	.325	.279	604	61	-7	1			.974	1	C-51	-0.4
1951	Phi-N	3	5	0	0	0	0	0	0	0	0	.000	.000	.000	0	-99	-1	0	0	0	1.000	0	/C-1	-0.1
1952	Phi-N	57	179	25	49	9	1	4	27	36	33	.274	.395	.402	798	123	7	1	1	-0	.987	6	C-55	1.7
1953	Phi-N	81	234	34	56	12	3	8	31	28	39	.239	.321	.419	739	91	-3	3	1	0	.987	4	C-80	0.5
1954	Phi-N	86	259	42	75	14	5	14	42	33	37	.290	.372	.544	916	136	13	1	3	-1	.989	9	C-75/1-1	2.3
1955	Phi-N★	99	303	49	82	9	3	22	58	58	62	.271	.391	.538	929	146	21	4	1	1	.995	4	C-66,1-24	2.7
1956	Phi-N☆	146	535	96	143	33	7	32	95	75	93	.267	.358	.535	893	138	29	5	2	0	.982	-18	*C-102,1-39	1.5
1957	Phi-N	116	388	50	92	18	2	18	67	56	81	.237	.335	.433	768	108	4	2	2	-0	.988	-9	*C-108	0.1
1958	Phi-N	86	258	36	64	9	0	9	33	60	63	.248	.394	.388	781	109	6	0	1	-0	.987	-9	C-80	0.1
1959	Mil-N	25	48	0	5	0	0	0	4	3	13	.104	.157	.104	261	-31	-9	0	0	0	1.000	-3	C-11/1-2	-1.2
1960	Mil-N	7	8	0	1	0	0	0	0	1	3	.125	.222	.125	347	-2	-1	0	0	0	.944	1	/C-4	0.0
Total	13	853	2601	375	661	116	25	116	397	393	497	.254	.354	.452	805	115	57	18	11		.986	-15	C-695/1-66	7.1

■ DAVEY LOPES Lopes, David Earl b: 5/3/45, E.Providence, R.I. BR/TR, 5′9″, 170 lbs. Deb: 9/22/72 MC Career OF: (86-LF 98-CF 66-RF)

YEAR	TM/L	G	AB	R	H	2B	3B	HR	RBI	BB	SO	AVG	OBP	SLG	OPS	OPS+	BR+	SB	CS	SBR	FA	FR	G/POS	TPR
1972	LA-N	11	42	6	9	4	0	0	1	7	6	.214	.327	.310	636	84	-1	4	0	1	.964	-2	2-11	-0.2
1973	LA-N	142	535	77	147	13	5	6	37	62	77	.275	.355	.351	707	101	2	36	16	2	.984	-13	*2-135/O-5R,S-2,3-1	0.0
1974	*LA-N	145	530	95	141	26	3	10	35	66	71	.266	.352	.383	735	110	8	59	18	7	.965	-22	*2-143	0.2
1975	LA-N	155	618	108	162	24	6	8	41	91	93	.262	.359	.359	718	104	6	**77**	12	**13**	.979	-23	*2-137,O-24C,S-14	0.5
1976	LA-N	117	427	72	103	17	7	4	20	56	49	.241	.335	.342	677	94	-2	**63**	10	**10**	.964	-20	*2-100,O-19(0-19-0)	-0.6
1977	*LA-N	134	502	85	142	19	5	11	53	73	69	.283	.376	.406	782	110	10	47	12	6	.979	8	*2-130	3.1
1978	*LA-N★	151	587	93	163	25	4	17	58	71	70	.278	.356	.421	776	117	13	45	4	**9**	.974	3	*2-147/O-2(0-2-0)	3.5
1979	LA-N★	153	582	109	154	20	6	28	73	97	88	.265	.373	.464	837	129	25	44	4	8	.981	-34	*2-152	0.8
1980	LA-N★	141	553	79	139	15	3	10	49	58	71	.251	.324	.344	667	88	-8	23	7	3	.980	-16	*2-140	-1.4
1981	*LA-N★	58	214	35	44	2	0	5	17	22	35	.206	.289	.285	574	66	-10	20	2	4	.993	-4	2-55	-0.7
1982	Oak-A	128	450	58	109	19	3	11	42	40	51	.242	.305	.371	677	89	-7	28	12	2	.977	-19	*2-125/O-6(0-6-0)	-1.8
1983	Oak-A	147	494	64	137	13	4	17	67	51	61	.277	.347	.423	770	118	12	22	4	3	.983	-38	*2-123,D-12/O-7R,3	-1.6

YEAR	TM/L	G	AB	R	H	2B	3B	HR	RBI	BB	SO	AVG	OBP	SLG	OPS	OPS+	BR+	SB	CS	SBR	FA	FR	G/POS	TPR
1984	Oak-A	72	230	32	59	11	1	9	36	31	36	.257	.347	.430	778	122	7	12	0	3	.965	-8	O-42R,2-17/3-5,D-9	0.1
	*Chi-N	16	17	5	4	1	0	0	0	6	5	.235	.435	.294	729	99	0	3	0	1	1.000	-2	/O-9(2-1-6),2-2	-0.1
1985	Chi-N	99	275	52	78	11	0	11	44	46	37	.284	.386	.444	830	118	8	47	4	9	.991	-12	O-79L/3-4,2-1	0.3
1986	Chi-N	59	157	38	47	8	2	6	22	31	16	.299	.421	.490	911	140	10	17	6	2	.902	-4	3-32,O-22(21-0-2)	0.6
	*Hou-N	37	98	11	23	2	1	1	13	12	9	.235	.318	.306	624	75	-3	8	2	1	1.000	5	O-19(9-10-1)/3-5	0.2
	Yr	96	255	49	70	10	3	7	35	43	25	.275	.383	.420	803	117	7	25	8	3	1.000	1	O-41(30-10-3),3-37	0.8
1987	Hou-N	47	43	4	10	2	0	1	6	13	8	.233	.411	.349	760	108	1	2	1	0	.857	-1	/O-5(5-0-0)	0.0
Total	16	1812	6354	1023	1671	232	50	155	614	833	852	.263	.351	.388	740	107	71	557	114	83	.977	-201	*2-1418,O-239C/3DS	2.9
■ **AL LOPEZ**	Lopez, Alfonso Ramon b: 8/20/08, Tampa, Fla. BR/TR, 5'11", 165 lbs. Deb: 9/27/28 MH																							
1928	Bro-N	3	12	0	0	0	0	0	0	0	0	.000	.000	.000	0	-99	-4	0			1.000	-2	/C-3	-0.5
1930	Bro-N	128	421	60	130	20	4	6	57	33	35	.309	.362	.418	780	89	-7	3			.983	5	*C-126	0.5
1931	Bro-N	111	360	38	97	13	4	0	40	28	33	.269	.324	.328	652	76	-12	1			.977	-8	*C-105	-1.3
1932	Bro-N	126	404	44	111	18	6	1	43	34	35	.275	.331	.356	687	87	-7	3			.976	-2	*C-125	-0.2
1933	Bro-N	126	372	39	112	11	4	3	41	21	39	.301	.338	.376	715	108	4	10			.991	18	*C-124/2-1	3.0
1934	Bro-N★	140	439	58	120	23	2	7	54	49	44	.273	.349	.383	732	101	1	2			.982	-7	*C-137/2-2,3-2	0.2
1935	Bro-N	128	379	50	95	12	4	3	39	35	36	.251	.316	.327	643	75	-13	2			.980	6	*C-126	0.0
1936	Bos-N	128	426	46	103	12	5	7	50	41	41	.242	.311	.343	654	81	-11	1			.975	10	*C-127/1-1	0.6
1937	Bos-N	105	334	31	68	11	1	3	38	35	57	.204	.281	.269	551	55	-21	3			.984	8	*C-102	-0.6
1938	Bos-N	71	236	19	63	6	1	1	14	11	24	.267	.305	.314	619	78	-7	5			.989	3	C-71	0.0
1939	Bos-N	131	412	32	104	22	1	8	49	40	45	.252	.319	.369	688	91	-6	1			.986	3	*C-129	0.4
1940	Bos-N	36	119	20	35	3	1	2	17	6	8	.294	.328	.387	715	102	0	1			.987	2	C-36	0.4
	Pit-N	59	174	15	45	6	2	1	24	13	13	.259	.310	.333	643	78	-5	5			.992	4	C-59	0.2
	Yr	95	293	35	80	9	3	3	41	19	21	.273	.317	.355	672	87	-5	6			**.990**	6	C-95	0.6
1941	Pit-N★	114	317	33	84	9	1	5	43	31	23	.265	.330	.347	677	91	-3	0			.980	-0	*C-114	0.3
1942	Pit-N	103	289	17	74	8	2	1	26	34	17	.256	.338	.308	646	88	-3	0			**.995**	6	C-99	0.8
1943	Pit-N	118	372	40	98	9	4	1	39	44	25	.263	.341	.317	659	88	-5	2			**.991**	8	*C-116/3-1	1.1
1944	Pit-N	115	331	27	76	12	1	1	34	34	24	.230	.303	.281	584	62	-16	4			**.984**	4	*C-115	-0.6
1945	Pit-N	91	243	22	53	8	0	0	18	35	12	.218	.317	.251	568	57	-13	1			.992	8	C-91	0.0
1946	Pit-N	56	150	13	46	2	0	1	12	23	14	.307	.399	.340	739	108	3	1			.985	1	C-56	0.7
1947	Cle-A	61	126	9	33	1	0	0	14	9	13	.262	.311	.270	581	64	-6	1	1	-0	1.000	0	C-57	-0.4
Total	19	1950	5916	613	1547	206	43	51	652	556	538	.261	.326	.337	663	83	-131	46	1		.985	66	*C-1918/3-3,2-3,1-1	4.6
■ **ART LOPEZ**	Lopez, Arturo (Rodriguez) b: 6/8/37, Mayaguez, P.R. BL/TL, 5'9", 170 lbs. Deb: 4/12/65																							
1965	NY-A	38	49	5	7	0	0	0	0	1	6	.143	.160	.143	303	-13	-7	0	0	0	.958	-2	O-16(3-0-14)	-1.0
■ **CARLOS LOPEZ**	Lopez, Carlos Antonio (Morales) b: 9/27/50, Mazatlan, Mexico BR/TR, 6', 190 lbs. Deb: 9/17/76																							
1976	Cal-A	9	10	1	0	0	0	0	0	2	3	.000	.167	.000	167	-52	-2	2	0	0	1.000	-1	/O-4(1-0-4),D-1	-0.3
1977	Sea-A	99	297	39	84	18	1	8	34	14	61	.283	.322	.431	753	104	1	16	4	2	.972	3	O-90(0-7-87)/D-2	0.2
1978	Bal-A	129	193	21	46	6	0	4	20	9	34	.238	.276	.332	607	75	-7	5	7	-1	.988	-25	*O-114(0-41-91)/D-1	-3.6
Total	3	237	500	61	130	24	1	12	54	25	98	.260	.301	.384	685	90	-8	23	11	1	.979	-23	O-208(1-48-182)/D-4	-3.7
■ **HECTOR LOPEZ**	Lopez, Hector Headley (Swainson) b: 7/9/29, Colon; Panama BR/TR, 5'11", 182 lbs. Deb: 5/12/55 Career OF: (477-LF 21-CF 172-RF)																							
1955	KC-A	128	483	50	140	15	2	15	68	33	58	.290	.339	.422	761	103	0	1	4	-1	.936	15	3-93,2-36	1.7
1956	KC-A	151	561	91	153	27	3	18	69	63	73	.273	.349	.428	777	104	2	4	5	-1	.940	1	*3-121,O-20C/2-8,S	0.2
1957	KC-A	121	391	51	115	19	4	11	35	41	66	.294	.361	.448	809	118	9	1	6	-2	.937	4	*3-111/2-4,O-3(2-0-1)	1.2
1958	KC-A	151	564	84	147	28	4	17	73	49	61	.261	.322	.415	737	99	-1	2	2	-0	.974	6	2-96,3-55/S-1,O-1L	1.2
1959	KC-A	35	135	22	38	10	3	6	24	8	23	.281	.326	.533	860	129	5	1	0	0	.933	-12	2-33	-0.4
	NY-A	112	406	60	115	16	2	16	69	28	54	.283	.339	.451	789	119	9	3	1	0	.926	-5	3-76,O-35(35-0-0)	0.2
	Yr	147	541	82	153	26	5	22	93	36	77	.283	.336	.471	807	122	14	4	1	1	.926	-17	3-76,O-35L,2-33	-0.2
1960	*NY-A	131	408	66	116	14	6	9	42	46	64	.284	.362	.414	777	116	10	1	1	-0	.976	-0	*O-106L/2-5,3-1	0.3
1961	*NY-A	93	243	27	54	7	2	3	22	24	38	.222	.295	.305	599	64	-13	1	0	0	.977	1	O-72(65-0-9)	-1.5
1962	*NY-A	106	335	45	92	19	1	6	48	33	53	.275	.340	.391	731	99	-0	0	1	-0	.984	3	O-84(64-0-21)/2-1,3-1	-0.2
1963	*NY-A	130	433	54	108	13	4	14	52	35	71	.249	.306	.395	700	95	-3	1	2	-0	.957	-3	*O-124(104-0-21)/2-1	-1.4
1964	*NY-A	127	285	34	74	9	3	10	34	24	54	.260	.319	.418	737	101	0	1	1	-0	.971	-13	*O-103(80-1-31)/3-1	-1.8
1965	NY-A	111	283	25	74	12	2	7	39	26	61	.261	.326	.392	718	104	1	0	0	0	.942	-8	O-75(20-0-55)/1-2	-1.2
1966	NY-A	54	117	14	25	4	1	4	16	8	20	.214	.270	.368	637	84	-3	0	0	0	.936	-2	O-29(13-0-17)	-0.7
Total	12	1450	4644	623	1251	193	37	136	591	418	696	.269	.333	.415	747	104	17	16	23	-5	.967	-13	O-652L,3-459,2/S1	-2.4
■ **JAVY LOPEZ**	Lopez, Javier (Torres) b: 11/5/70, Ponce, P.R. BR/TR, 6'3", 185 lbs. Deb: 9/18/92																							
1992	*Atl-N	9	16	3	6	2	0	0	2	0	1	.375	.375	.500	875	137	1	0	0	0	1.000	1	/C-9	0.2
1993	Atl-N	8	16	1	6	1	1	1	2	0	2	.375	.412	.750	1162	201	2	0	0	0	.975	2	/C-7	0.4
1994	Atl-N	80	277	27	68	9	0	13	35	17	61	.245	.301	.419	720	83	-7	0	2	-1	.995	2	C-75	-0.1
1995	*Atl-N	100	333	37	105	11	4	14	51	14	57	.315	.347	.498	845	116	7	0	1	-0	.988	2	C-93	1.3
1996	*Atl-N	138	489	56	138	19	1	23	69	28	84	.282	.325	.466	791	100	-1	1	6	-2	.994	19	*C-135	2.3
1997	*Atl-N★	123	414	52	122	28	1	23	68	40	82	.295	.364	.534	898	129	16	1	1	-0	.993	-3	*C-117	2.0
1998	*Atl-N★	133	489	73	139	21	1	34	106	30	85	.284	.333	.540	873	125	15	5	3	0	**.995**	10	*C-128/D-1	3.3
1999	Atl-N	65	246	34	78	18	1	11	45	20	41	.317	.375	.533	908	126	9	0	3	-1	.991	-5	C-60/D-4	0.7
2000	*Atl-N	134	481	60	138	21	1	24	89	35	80	.287	.340	.484	825	106	3	0	0	0	.993	-8	*C-132	0.3
Total	9	790	2761	343	800	130	10	143	467	184	493	.290	.341	.499	840	113	45	7	16	-4	.993	20	C-756/D-5	10.4
■ **LUIS LOPEZ**	Lopez, Luis Antonio b: 9/1/64, Brooklyn, N.Y. BR/TR, 6'1", 190 lbs. Deb: 9/14/90																							
1990	LA-N	6	6	0	0	0	0	0	0	0	2	.000	.000	.000	0	-99	-2	0	0	0	1.000	-0	/1-1	-0.2
1991	Cle-A	35	82	7	18	4	1	0	7	4	7	.220	.264	.293	557	54	-5	0	0	0	1.000	-2	C-12,1-10/3-1,OD	-0.8
Total	2	41	88	7	18	4	1	0	7	4	9	.205	.247	.273	520	43	-7	0	0	0	.977	-2	/C-12,1-11,D-6,O3	-1.0
■ **LUIS LOPEZ**	Lopez, Luis Manuel (Santos) b: 9/4/70, Cidra, P.R. BB/TR, 5'11", 175 lbs. Deb: 9/7/93																							
1993	SD-N	17	43	1	5	1	0	0	1	0	8	.116	.116	.140	256	-31	-8	0	0	0	.983	3	2-15	-0.5
1994	SD-N	77	235	29	65	16	1	2	20	15	39	.277	.328	.379	707	86	-5	3	2	-0	.941	2	S-43,2-29/3-5	0.1
1996	*SD-N	63	139	10	25	3	0	2	11	9	35	.180	.235	.245	480	28	-15	0	0	0	.981	-3	S-35,2-22/3-2	-1.5
1997	NY-N	78	178	19	48	12	1	1	19	12	42	.270	.330	.365	695	85	-4	2	4	-1	.966	7	S-45,2-20/3-4	0.5
1998	NY-N	117	266	37	67	13	2	2	22	20	60	.252	.314	.338	652	73	-10	2	2	-0	.975	-16	2-50,S-39,3-11,/O-9L	-2.3
1999	NY-N	68	104	11	22	4	0	2	13	12	33	.212	.311	.308	619	59	-6	1	1	-0	.971	-2	S-33,2-16/3-9	-0.7
2000	Mil-N	78	201	24	53	14	0	6	27	9	35	.264	.312	.423	735	85	-5	1	2	-0	.959	5	S-45,2-22/3-6	0.3
Total	7	498	1166	131	285	63	4	15	113	77	252	.244	.302	.344	646	69	-53	9	11	-2	.957	-4	S-240,2-174/3-37,O	-4.1
■ **MENDY LOPEZ**	Lopez, Mendy (Aude) b: 10/15/74, Pimentel, D.R. BR/TR, 6'2", 190 lbs. Deb: 6/3/98																							
1998	KC-A	74	206	18	50	10	2	1	15	12	40	.243	.288	.325	613	58	-13	5	2	0	.955	18	S-72/3-2	1.0
1999	KC-A	7	20	2	8	0	1	0	3	0	5	.400	.429	.500	929	133	1	0	0	0	1.000	-3	/2-6,S-1	-0.1
2000	Fla-N	4	3	0	0	0	0	0	0	1	1	.000	.250	.000	250	-31	-1	0	0	0	.000	0	/H	-0.1
Total	3	85	229	20	58	10	3	1	18	13	46	.253	.299	.336	635	63	-12	5	2	0	.955	15	/S-73,2-6,3-2	0.8
■ **BRIS LORD**	Lord, Bristol Robotham "The Human Eyeball" b: 9/21/1883, Upland, Pa. d: 11/13/64, Prince Frederick, Md. BR/TR, 5'9", 185 lbs. Deb: 4/21/05 Career OF: (320-LF 192-CF 202-RF)																							
1905	*Phi-A	66	238	38	57	14	0	0	13	14		.239	.285	.298	583	83	-5	3			.963	1	O-61(4-38-19)	-0.8
1906	Phi-A	118	434	50	101	13	7	1	44	27		.233	.281	.302	583	80	-10	12			.941	-2	*O-115(5-103-7)	-2.0
1907	Phi-A	57	170	12	31	3	0	1	11	14		.182	.249	.218	466	48	-10	2			.951	-1	O-53(10-40-4)/P-1	-1.5
1909	Cle-A	69	249	26	67	7	3	1	25	8		.269	.295	.333	628	94	-2	10			.992	6	O-67(48-3-16)	0.0
1910	Cle-A	58	210	23	46	8	7	0	17	12		.219	.268	.324	592	84	-5	4			.958	4	O-56(24-0-32)	-0.4
	*Phi-A	70	279	54	78	13	11	1	20	23		.280	.337	.416	752	137	11	6			.980	4	O-70(64-4-2)	1.2
	Yr	128	489	77	124	21	18	1	37	35		.254	.307	.376	684	114	6	10			.972	8	*O-126(88-4-34)	0.8

YEAR	TM/L	G	AB	R	H	2B	3B	HR	RBI	BB	SO	AVG	OBP	SLG	OPS	OPS+	BR+	SB	CS	SBR	FA	FR	G/POS	TPR
1911	*Phi-A	134	574	92	178	37	11	3	55	35		.310	.355	.429	784	120	14	15			.963	8	*O-132(122-1-9)	1.5
1912	Phi-A	97	378	63	90	12	9	0	25	34		.238	.309	.317	627	82	-9	15			.942	-0	O-97(18-0-78)	-1.4
1913	Bos-N	73	235	22	59	12	1	6	26	8	22	.251	.276	.387	663	86	-5	7			.914	-10	O-62(25-3-35)	-1.9
Total	8	742	2767	380	707	119	49	13	236	175	22	.256	.304	.348	652	95	-22	74			.957	8	O-713L/P-1	-5.3
■ HARRY LORD Lord, Harry Donald b: 3/8/1882, Porter, Me. d: 8/9/48, Westbrook, Maine BL/TR, 5'10.5", 165 lbs. Deb: 9/25/07 M Career OF: (33-LF 4-CF 10-RF)																								
1907	Bos-A	10	38	4	6	1	0	0	3	1		.158	.179	.184	364	16	-4	1			.919	0	3-10	-0.3
1908	Bos-A	145	560	61	145	15	6	2	37	22		.259	.297	.318	614	97	-3	23			.902	-10	*3-144	-1.0
1909	Bos-A	136	534	89	168	12	7	0	31	20		.315	.349	.363	712	122	12	36			.929	-7	*3-134	1.0
1910	Bos-A	77	288	25	72	5	5	1	32	14		.250	.294	.313	607	88	-5	17			.927	-5	3-70/S-1	-0.9
	Chi-A	44	165	26	49	6	3	0	10	14		.297	.352	.370	722	132	6	17			.952	-11	3-44	-0.4
	Yr	121	453	51	121	11	8	1	42	28		.267	.315	.333	649	103	1	34			.935	-16	*3-114/S-1	-1.3
1911	Chi-A	141	561	103	180	18	18	3	61	32		.321	.364	.433	797	126	18	43			.941	-17	*3-138	0.5
1912	Chi-A	151	570	81	152	19	12	5	54	52		.267	.333	.368	702	104	2	28			.895	-27	*3-106,O-45(32-4-9)	-2.4
1913	Chi-A	150	547	62	144	18	12	1	42	45	39	.263	.327	.346	673	98	-2	24			.924	-31	*3-150	-3.2
1914	Chi-A	21	69	8	13	1	1	1	3	5	3	.188	.243	.275	519	57	-4	2	2	-0	.933	-6	3-19/O-1(1-0-0)	-1.1
1915	Buf-F	97	359	50	97	12	6	1	21	21	15	.270	.311	.345	656	83	-14	15			.946	-14	3-92/O-1(0-0-1),M	-2.8
Total	9	972	3691	509	1026	107	70	14	294	226	57	.278	.326	.356	682	104	7	206	2		.924	-127	3-907/O-47L,S-1	-10.6
■ CARLTON LORD Lord, William Carlton b: 1/7/1900, Philadelphia, Pa. d: 8/15/47, Chester, Pa. BR/TR, 5'11", 170 lbs. Deb: 7/12/23																								
1923	Phi-N	17	47	3	11	2	0	0	2	2	3	.234	.265	.277	542	39	-4	0	1	-0	.833	-1	3-14	-0.4
■ MARK LORETTA Loretta, Mark David b: 8/14/71, Santa Monica, Cal. BR/TR, 6', 175 lbs. Deb: 9/4/95 Career OF: (1-LF 0-CF 0-RF)																								
1995	Mil-A	19	50	13	13	3	0	1	3	4	7	.260	.327	.380	707	79	-2	1	1	-0	.979	-1	S-13/2-4,D-1	-0.1
1996	Mil-A	73	154	20	43	3	0	1	13	14	15	.279	.339	.318	657	65	-8	2	1	0	.989	7	2-28,3-23,S-21	0.1
1997	Mil-A	132	418	56	120	17	5	5	47	47	60	.287	.362	.388	749	95	-2	5	5	-1	.980	10	2-63,S-44,1-19,3/D	1.0
1998	Mil-N	140	434	55	137	29	0	6	54	42	47	.316	.385	.424	809	112	9	9	6	-0	.992	5	1-70,S-56,3-22,2/O	1.3
1999	Mil-N	153	587	93	170	34	5	5	67	52	59	.290	.357	.390	748	90	-8	4	1	1	.986	-16	S-74,1-66,2-17,3-14	-2.1
2000	Mil-N	91	352	49	99	21	1	7	40	37	38	.281	.351	.406	758	92	-4	0	3	-1	.995	-11	S-90/2-1	-0.8
Total	6	608	1995	286	582	107	11	25	224	196	226	.292	.361	.394	755	94	-14	21	17	-1	.985	-7	S-298,1-155,2/3DO	-0.6
■ SCOTT LOUCKS Loucks, Scott Gregory b: 11/11/56, Anchorage, Alaska BR/TR, 6', 178 lbs. Deb: 9/1/80																								
1980	Hou-N	8	3	4	1	0	0	0	0	0	2	.333	.333	.333	667	94	-0	0	0	0	1.000	-2	/O-4(0-2-2)	-0.2
1981	Hou-N	10	7	2	4	0	0	0	0	1	3	.571	.625	.571	1196	254	2	1	0	0	1.000	-2	/O-5(0-5-0)	0.0
1982	Hou-N	44	49	6	11	2	0	0	3	3	17	.224	.269	.265	535	54	-3	4	1	1	.978	-7	O-37(0-37-0)	-1.0
1983	Hou-N	7	14	2	3	0	0	0	0	1	4	.214	.267	.214	481	37	-1	2	2	-0	1.000	0	/O-6(1-5-0)	-0.1
1985	Pit-N	4	7	1	2	2	0	0	1	2	2	.286	.444	.571	1016	184	1	0	0	0	1.000	-1	/O-4(3-0-1)	0.0
Total	5	73	80	15	21	4	0	0	4	7	28	.262	.322	.313	634	83	-2	7	3	0	.985	-10	/O-56(4-49-3)	-1.3
■ BALDY LOUDEN Louden, William P. b: 8/27/1885, Piedmont, W.Va. d: 12/8/35, Piedmont, W.Va. BR/TR, 5'11", 175 lbs. Deb: 9/13/07																								
1907	NY-A	4	9	4	1	0	0	0	0	2		.111	.273	.111	384	21	-1	1			.750	1	/3-3	0.0
1912	Det-A	122	403	57	97	12	4	1	36	58		.241	.352	.298	649	89	-3	28			.951	23	2-87,3-26/S-5	2.2
1913	Det-A	76	191	28	46	4	5	0	23	24	22	.241	.344	.314	658	94	-1	6			.906	0	2-30,3-26/S-6,O-5R	0.1
1914	Buf-F	126	431	73	135	11	4	6	63	52	41	.313	.391	.399	790	113	3	35			.931	-18	*S-115	-0.6
1915	Buf-F	141	469	67	132	18	5	4	48	64	45	.281	.372	.367	739	106	-1	30			.978	14	2-88,S-27,3-19	1.8
1916	Cin-N	134	439	38	96	16	4	1	32	54	54	.219	.313	.280	593	85	-6	12			**.968**	17	*2-108,S-23	1.6
Total	6	603	1942	267	507	61	22	12	202	254	162	.261	.355	.334	689	98	-7	112			.961	37	2-313,S-176/3-74,O	5.1
■ CHARLIE LOUDENSLAGER Loudenslager, Charles Edward b: 5/21/1881, Baltimore, Md. d: 10/31/33, Baltimore, Md. TR, 5'9", 186 lbs. Deb: 4/15/04																								
1904	Bro-N	1	2	0	0	0	0	0	0	0		.000	.000	.000	0	-99	-0	0			1.000	-1	/2-1	-0.1
■ BILL LOUGHLIN Loughlin, William H. b: Baltimore, Md. Deb: 5/9/1883																								
1883	Bal-a	1	5	0	2	0	0	0		0		.400	.400	.400	800	154	0				.000	-0	/O-1(0-0-1)	0.0
■ LOUGHRAN Loughran b: New York, N.Y. Deb: 6/6/1884																								
1884	NY-N	9	29	4	3	1	1	0	3	7	11	.103	.278	.207	485	54	-1				.857	-3	/C-9,O-1(0-0-1)	-0.3
■ TOM LOVELACE Lovelace, Thomas Rivers b: 10/19/1897, Wolfe City, Tex. d: 7/12/79, Dallas, Tex. BR/TR, 5'11", 170 lbs. Deb: 9/23/22																								
1922	Pit-N	1	1	0	0	0	0	0	0	0	0	.000	.000	.000	0	-99	-0	0	0	0	.000	0	H	0.0
■ LEN LOVETT Lovett, Leonard Walker b: 7/17/1852, Lancaster Co., Pa d: 11/18/22, Newark, Del. BR/TR, Deb: 8/4/1873																								
1873	Res-n	1	5	1	2	0	0	0	1	0	0	.400	.400	.400	800	150	0	0	0	0	.500	-0	/P-1	0.0
1875	Cen-n	6	21	2	5	1	0	0	2	1	5	.238	.273	.286	558	103	0	0	0	0	.700	-1	/O-6(1-0-5)	0.0
Total	2 n	7	26	3	7	1	0	0	3	1	5	.269	.296	.308	604	113	1	0	0	0	.700	-1	/O-6(1-0-5),P-1	0.0
■ MEM LOVETT Lovett, Merritt Marwood b: 6/15/12, Chicago, Ill. d: 9/19/95, Downers Grove, Ill. BR/TR, 5'9.5", 165 lbs. Deb: 9/4/33																								
1933	Chi-A	1	1	0	0	0	0	0	0	0	0	.000	.000	.000	0	-99	-0	0	0	0	.000	0	H	0.0
■ JAY LOVIGLIO Loviglio, John Paul b: 5/30/56, Freeport, N.Y. BR/TR, 5'9", 160 lbs. Deb: 9/2/80																								
1980	Phi-N	16	5	7	0	0	0	0	0	1	0	.000	.167	.000	167	-47	-1	1	2	-0	1.000	1	/2-1	0.0
1981	Chi-A	14	15	5	4	0	0	0	2	1	1	.267	.313	.267	579	70	-1	2	2	-0	.786	3	/3-4,2-3,D-2	0.2
1982	Chi-A	15	31	5	6	0	0	0	2	1	4	.194	.219	.194	412	14	-4	2	1	0	.964	4	2-13/D-2	0.1
1983	Chi-N	1	1	0	0	0	0	0	0	0	1	.000	.000	.000	0	-95	-0	0	0	0	.000	0	/H	0.0
Total	4	46	52	17	10	0	0	0	4	3	6	.192	.236	.192	429	21	-5	5	5	-1	.971	9	/2-17,D-4,3-4	0.3
■ JOE LOVITTO Lovitto, Joseph b: 1/6/51, San Pedro, Cal. BB/TR, 6', 185 lbs. Deb: 4/15/72 Career OF: (26-LF 209-CF 26-RF)																								
1972	Tex-A	117	330	23	74	9	1	1	19	37	54	.224	.306	.267	573	75	-9	13	11	-1	.976	4	*O-103(8-77-23)	-1.2
1973	Tex-A	26	44	3	6	1	0	0	0	5	7	.136	.224	.159	384	10	-5	1	0	0	.898	1	3-20/O-3(0-2-1)	-0.4
1974	Tex-A	113	283	27	63	9	3	2	26	25	36	.223	.286	.297	583	69	-11	6	8	-1	.972	-12	*O-107(0-105-2)/1-5	-2.9
1975	Tex-A	50	106	17	22	3	0	1	8	13	16	.208	.294	.264	558	59	-5	2	2	-0	.985	-6	O-38C/1-2,C-1,D-2	-1.3
Total	4	306	763	70	165	22	4	4	53	80	113	.216	.292	.271	564	67	-31	22	21	-3	.975	-14	O-251C/3-20,1-7,DC	-5.8
■ TOREY LOVULLO Lovullo, Salvatore Anthony b: 7/25/65, Santa Monica, Cal. BB/TR, 6', 180 lbs. Deb: 9/10/88 Career OF: (1-LF 0-CF 2-RF)																								
1988	Det-A	12	21	2	8	1	1	1	2	1	2	.381	.409	.667	1076	204	3	0	0	0	1.000	-0	/2-9,3-3	0.3
1989	Det-A	29	87	8	10	2	0	1	4	14	20	.115	.238	.172	410	18	-9	0	0	0	1.000	-3	1-18,3-11	-1.4
1991	NY-A	22	51	0	9	2	0	0	2	5	7	.176	.250	.216	466	30	-5	0	0	0	.940	0	3-22	-0.5
1993	Cal-A	116	367	42	92	20	0	6	30	36	49	.251	.319	.354	674	78	-11	7	6	-1	.981	-24	2-91,3-14/S-9,O1	-3.1
1994	Sea-A	36	72	9	16	5	0	2	7	9	13	.222	.309	.375	684	74	-3	1	0	0	1.000	3	2-20/3-5,D-2	0.1
1996	Oak-A	65	82	15	18	4	0	3	9	11	17	.220	.326	.378	704	79	-3	1	2	-0	1.000	2	1-42,3-11/2-2,SOD	-0.2
1998	Cle-A	6	19	1	4	1	0	0	1	1	2	.211	.250	.263	513	33	-2	0	0	0	.947	-1	/2-5,3-1	-0.3
1999	Phi-N	17	38	3	8	0	0	2	5	3	11	.211	.268	.368	637	57	-3	0	0	0	1.000	0	/1-6,2-6	-0.2
Total	8	303	737	80	165	35	1	15	60	80	121	.224	.302	.335	638	69	-33	9	8	-1	.984	-23	2-133/1-67,3-67,SDO	-5.3
■ FLETCHER LOW Low, Fletcher b: 4/7/1893, Essex, Mass. d: 6/6/73, Hanover, N.H. BR/TR, 5'10.5", 175 lbs. Deb: 10/7/15																								
1915	Bos-N	1	4	1	1	0	1	0	1	0	0	.250	.250	.750	1000	207	0	0			1.000	-0	/3-1	0.0
■ CHARLIE LOWE Lowe, Charles b: Baltimore, Md. Deb: 9/28/1872																								
1872	Atl-n	7	31	1	5	0	0	0	3	0	2	.161	.161	.161	323	-0	-4	0	0	0	.820	-1	/2-7	-0.4
■ DICK LOWE Lowe, Richard Alvern b: 1/28/1854, Evansville, Wis. d: 6/28/22, Janesville, Wis. Deb: 6/26/1884																								
1884	Det-N	1	3	0	1	0	0	0	0	0	1	.333	.333	.333	667	117	0				.125	-3	/C-1	-0.2

■ BOBBY LOWE Lowe, Robert Lincoln "Link" b: 7/10/1868, Pittsburgh, Pa. d: 12/8/51, Detroit, Mich. BR/TR, 5'10", 150 lbs. Deb: 4/19/1890 M Career OF: (173-LF 56-CF 11-RF)

YEAR	TM/L	G	AB	R	H	2B	3B	HR	RBI	BB	SO	AVG	OBP	SLG	OPS	OPS+	BR+	SB	CS	SBR	FA	FR	G/POS	TPR
1890	Bos-N	52	207	35	58	13	2	2	21	26	32	.280	.366	.391	757	112	3	15			.951	-9	S-24,O-15C,3-12	-0.5
1891	Bos-N	125	497	92	129	19	5	6	74	53	54	.260	.342	.354	696	92	-6	43			.927	-6	*O-107L,2-17/S-2,3P	-1.3
1892	*Bos-N	124	475	79	115	16	7	3	57	37	47	.242	.308	.324	632	83	-11	36			.928	14	O-90L,3-14,S-13,2	-0.3
1893	Bos-N	126	526	130	157	19	5	14	89	55	29	.298	.369	.433	803	105	1	22			.936	1	*2-121/S-5	0.6
1894	Bos-N	133	613	158	212	34	11	17	115	50	25	.346	.401	.520	921	112	8	23			.927	-6	*2-130/S-2,3-1	0.7
1895	Bos-N	100	417	102	124	12	7	7	62	40	16	.297	.370	.410	780	94	-5	24			.954	18	*2-100	1.4
1896	Bos-N	73	306	59	98	11	4	2	48	20	12	.320	.370	.402	772	98	-2	15			.965	25	2-73	2.2
1897	*Bos-N	123	499	87	154	24	8	5	106	32		.309	.355	.419	774	98	-3	16			.952	-4	*2-123	-0.2
1898	Bos-N	147	559	65	152	11	7	4	94	29		.272	.311	.338	649	82	-15	12			.958	16	*2-145/S-2	0.8
1899	Bos-N	152	559	81	152	5	9	4	88	35		.272	.316	.335	650	72	-23	17			.954	3	*2-148/S-4	-1.2
1900	Bos-N	127	474	65	132	11	5	3	71	26		.278	.323	.342	665	74	-18	15			.951	-7	*2-127	-1.7
1901	Bos-N	129	491	47	125	11	1	3	47	17		.255	.284	.299	583	63	-23	22			.912	-5	*3-111,2-18	-2.5
1902	Chi-N	121	480	44	119	13	3	0	35	12		.248	.274	.287	561	75	-15	17			.956	29	*2-119/3-2	1.6
1903	Chi-N	32	105	14	28	5	3	0	15	4		.267	.319	.371	690	99	-0	5			.948	4	2-22/1-6,3-1	0.4
1904	Pit-N	1	1	0	0	0	0	0	0	0		.000	.000	.000	0	-97	-0	0			.000	0	H	-0.0
	Det-A	140	506	47	105	14	6	0	40	17		.208	.236	.259	495	58	-24	15			.964	-0	*2-140,M	-2.7
1905	Det-A	58	181	17	35	7	2	0	9	13		.193	.255	.254	509	61	-8	3			.980	-3	O-24L,3-22/2-6,S1	-1.2
1906	Det-A	41	145	11	30	3	0	1	12	4		.207	.233	.248	482	49	-9	3			.915	8	S-19,2-17/3-5	0.0
1907	Det-A	17	37	2	9	2	0	0	5	4		.243	.317	.297	614	93	-0	0			.870	-4	3-10/O-4(2-1-1),S-2	-0.5
Total	18	1821	7078	1135	1934	230	85	71	988	474	215	.273	.325	.360	685	86	-151	303			.951	73	*2-1316,O-240L,3/S1P	-4.4

■ MIKE LOWELL Lowell, Michael Averett b: 2/24/74, San Juan, P.R. BR/TR, 6'4", 195 lbs. Deb: 9/13/98

YEAR	TM/L	G	AB	R	H	2B	3B	HR	RBI	BB	SO	AVG	OBP	SLG	OPS	OPS+	BR+	SB	CS	SBR	FA	FR	G/POS	TPR
1998	NY-A	8	15	1	4	0	0	0	0	0	1	.267	.267	.267	533	41	-1	0	0	0	1.000	-0	/3-7	-0.2
1999	Fla-N	97	308	32	78	15	0	12	47	26	69	.253	.322	.419	740	91	-5	0	0	0	.981	-5	3-83	-0.9
2000	Fla-N	140	508	73	137	38	0	22	91	54	75	.270	.350	.474	825	111	8	4	0	1	.968	5	*3-136	1.4
Total	3	245	831	106	219	53	0	34	138	80	145	.264	.338	.450	788	102	1	4	0	1	.973	-1	3-226	0.3

■ JOHN LOWENSTEIN Lowenstein, John Lee b: 1/27/47, Wolf Point, Mont. BL/TR, 6', 175 lbs. Deb: 9/2/70 Career OF: (687-LF 49-CF 201-RF)

YEAR	TM/L	G	AB	R	H	2B	3B	HR	RBI	BB	SO	AVG	OBP	SLG	OPS	OPS+	BR+	SB	CS	SBR	FA	FR	G/POS	TPR
1970	Cle-A	17	43	5	11	3	1	1	6	1	9	.256	.273	.442	715	89	-1	1	0	0	1.000	4	2-10/3-2,O-2L,S-1	0.3
1971	Cle-A	58	140	15	26	5	0	4	9	16	28	.186	.269	.307	576	58	-8	1	5	-2	.986	-6	2-29,O-18(7-5-8)/S-3	-1.5
1972	Cle-A	68	151	16	32	8	1	6	21	20	43	.212	.304	.397	701	104	1	2	4	-1	1.000	-2	O-58(27-3-29)/1-2	-0.5
1973	Cle-A	98	305	42	89	16	1	6	40	23	41	.292	.341	.410	751	109	3	5	3	0	.931	-10	O-51R,2-25/3-8,1D	-0.7
1974	Cle-A	140	508	65	123	14	2	8	48	53	85	.242	.316	.325	641	85	-9	36	17	2	.986	-1	*O-100L,3-28,1-12,/2	-1.5
1975	Cle-A	91	265	37	64	5	1	12	33	28	28	.242	.314	.404	718	102	0	15	10	-0	.983	-5	O-36L,D-31/3-8,2-2	-0.8
1976	Cle-A	93	229	33	47	8	2	2	14	25	35	.205	.283	.284	567	67	-9	11	8	-0	.972	-5	O-61R,D-11/1-9	-1.9
1977	Cle-A	81	149	24	36	6	1	4	12	21	29	.242	.335	.376	711	97	-0	1	8	-3	1.000	-3	O-39L,D-19/1-1	-0.8
1978	Tex-A	77	176	28	39	8	3	5	21	37	29	.222	.363	.386	749	110	4	16	3	2	.926	-9	3-25,D-21,O-16L	-0.5
1979	*Bal-A	97	197	33	50	8	2	11	34	30	37	.254	.355	.482	837	128	8	16	4	2	.992	-8	O-72L/1-1,3-1,D-3	0.0
1980	Bal-A	104	196	38	61	8	0	4	27	32	29	.311	.408	.413	821	127	9	7	3	0	.992	-11	O-91(88-0-3)/D-3	-0.4
1981	Bal-A	83	189	19	47	7	0	6	20	22	32	.249	.330	.381	711	105	1	7	6	-1	.990	-12	O-73(67-0-10)/D-4	-1.4
1982	Bal-A	122	322	69	103	15	2	24	66	54	59	.320	.419	.602	1022	177	35	7	6	-1	**1.000**	-7	*O-111(110-0-2)	2.3
1983	*Bal-A	122	310	52	87	13	2	15	60	49	55	.281	.381	.481	861	138	17	2	1	0	.982	-11	*O-107L/2-1,D-1	0.2
1984	Bal-A	105	270	34	64	13	0	8	28	33	54	.237	.322	.374	696	94	-2	1	0	0	.971	-8	O-67(68-0-0),D-22/1-2	-1.3
1985	Bal-A	12	26	0	2	0	0	0	2	2	3	.077	.143	.077	220	-39	-5	0	0	0	1.000	-0	/O-4(4-0-0),D-6	-0.5
Total	16	1368	3476	510	881	137	18	116	441	446	596	.253	.340	.403	743	108	44	128	78	1	.984	-96	O-906L,D-125/321S	-9.0

■ TERRELL LOWERY Lowery, Quenton Terrell b: 10/25/70, Oakland, Cal. BR/TR, 6'3", 180 lbs. Deb: 9/13/97

YEAR	TM/L	G	AB	R	H	2B	3B	HR	RBI	BB	SO	AVG	OBP	SLG	OPS	OPS+	BR+	SB	CS	SBR	FA	FR	G/POS	TPR
1997	Chi-N	9	14	2	4	0	0	0	0	3	3	.286	.412	.286	697	85	-0	1	0	0	1.000	1	/O-6(5-2-0)	0.1
1998	Chi-N	24	15	2	3	1	0	0	1	3	7	.200	.333	.267	600	58	-1	0	0	0	.929	-7	O-22(2-20-0)	-0.8
1999	TB-A	66	185	25	48	15	1	2	17	19	53	.259	.332	.384	715	81	-5	0	2	-1	.971	-7	O-60(29-36-1)	-1.3
2000	SF-N	24	34	13	15	4	0	1	5	7	8	.441	.548	.647	1195	215	7	1	0	0	.917	-6	O-20(13-0-8)/D-1	0.1
Total	4	123	248	42	70	20	1	3	23	32	71	.282	.369	.407	776	98	1	2	2	-0	.964	-19	O-108(49-58-9)/D-1	-1.9

■ PEANUTS LOWREY Lowrey, Harry Lee b: 8/27/18, Culver City, Cal. d: 7/2/86, Inglewood, Cal. BR/TR, 5'8.5", 170 lbs. Deb: 4/14/42 C Career OF: (548-LF 387-CF 62-RF)

YEAR	TM/L	G	AB	R	H	2B	3B	HR	RBI	BB	SO	AVG	OBP	SLG	OPS	OPS+	BR+	SB	CS	SBR	FA	FR	G/POS	TPR
1942	Chi-N	27	58	4	11	0	0	1	4	4	4	.190	.242	.241	483	43	-4	0			.978	-1	O-19(7-15-0)	-0.6
1943	Chi-N	130	480	59	140	25	12	1	63	35	24	.292	.340	.400	740	115	8	13			.982	14	*O-113C,S-16/2-3	2.0
1945	*Chi-N	143	523	72	148	22	7	7	89	48	27	.283	.343	.392	735	106	4	11			.987	4	*O-138(125-14-0)/S-2	0.0
1946	Chi-N★	144	540	75	139	24	5	4	54	56	22	.257	.328	.343	671	92	-6	10			.979	8	*O-126(73-60-0),3-20	-0.4
1947	Chi-N	115	448	56	126	17	5	5	37	38	26	.281	.339	.375	714	93	-5	2			.945	9	3-91,O-25(18-6-1)/2-6	0.3
1948	Chi-N	129	435	47	128	12	3	2	54	34	31	.294	.347	.349	696	93	-4	2			.983	-1	*O-103L/3-9,2-2,S-1	-1.1
1949	Chi-N	38	111	18	30	5	0	2	10	9	8	.270	.325	.369	694	88	-2	3			.966	-4	O-31(28-3-1)/3-1	-0.8
	Cin-N	89	309	48	85	16	2	2	25	37	11	.275	.354	.359	714	91	-3	1			.995	8	O-78(77-1-0)	-0.1
	Yr	127	420	66	115	21	2	4	35	46	19	.274	.347	.362	709	90	-5	4			.989	4	*O-109(105-4-1)/3-1	-0.9
1950	Cin-N	91	264	34	60	14	0	1	11	36	7	.227	.320	.292	612	62	-14	0			.987	1	O-72(66-2-6)/2-1	-1.7
	StL-N	17	56	10	15	0	0	1	4	6	1	.268	.349	.321	671	74	-2	0			1.000	1	/2-6,3-5,O-4(3-1-0)	0.0
	Yr	108	320	44	75	14	0	2	15	42	8	.234	.325	.297	622	64	-16	0			.982	2	O-76(69-3-6)/2-7,3-5	-1.7
1951	StL-N	114	370	52	112	19	5	5	40	35	12	.303	.366	.422	788	111	6	0	1	-0	.983	-1	O-85C,3-11/2-3	0.2
1952	StL-N	132	374	48	107	18	2	1	48	34	13	.286	.352	.353	705	96	-1	3	2	-0	.978	-9	*O-106(63-35-6)/3-6	-1.6
1953	StL-N	104	182	26	49	9	2	5	27	15	21	.269	.325	.423	748	93	-2	1	0	0	1.000	-10	O-38R,2-10/3-1	-1.2
1954	StL-N	74	61	6	7	1	2	0	5	9	9	.115	.229	.197	425	12	-8	0	0	0	1.000	-5	O-12(3-1-9)	-1.3
1955	Phi-N	54	106	9	20	4	0	0	8	7	10	.189	.239	.226	465	25	-11	2	0	0	.973	-6	O-28(6-9-14)/2-2,1-1	-1.8
Total	13	1401	4317	564	1177	186	45	37	479	403	226	.273	.336	.362	699	92	-45	48	3		.983	9	O-978L,3-144/2-33,S1	-8.1

■ DWIGHT LOWRY Lowry, Dwight (b: Dwight Lowery) b: 10/23/57, Lumberton, N.C. d: 7/10/97, Jamestown, N.Y. BL/TR, 6'3", 210 lbs. Deb: 4/3/84

YEAR	TM/L	G	AB	R	H	2B	3B	HR	RBI	BB	SO	AVG	OBP	SLG	OPS	OPS+	BR+	SB	CS	SBR	FA	FR	G/POS	TPR
1984	Det-A	32	45	8	11	2	0	2	7	3	11	.244	.292	.422	714	95	-0	0	0	0	1.000	5	C-31	0.5
1986	Det-A	56	150	21	46	4	0	3	18	17	19	.307	.392	.393	785	115	4	0	0	0	.992	-1	C-55/1-1,O-1(0-0-1)	0.5
1987	Det-A	13	25	0	5	2	0	0	1	0	6	.200	.200	.280	480	27	-3	0	0	0	1.000	1	C-12/1-1	-0.2
1988	Min-A	7	7	0	0	0	0	0	0	0	2	.000	.000	.000	0	-97	-2	0	0	0	1.000	2	/C-5	0.0
Total	4	108	227	29	62	8	0	5	26	20	38	.273	.343	.374	717	96	-1	0	0	0	.995	7	C-103/1-2,O-1(0-0-1)	0.8

■ JOHN LOWRY Lowry, John D. b: Baltimore, Md. Deb: 6/12/1875

YEAR	TM/L	G	AB	R	H	2B	3B	HR	RBI	BB	SO	AVG	OBP	SLG	OPS	OPS+	BR+	SB	CS	SBR	FA	FR	G/POS	TPR
1875	Was-n	6	22	2	3	0	0	0	0	1	0	.136	.174	.136	310	10	-2	0	1	-0	.727	-1	/O-6(0-6-0)	-0.3

■ WILLIE LOZADO Lozado, William b: 5/12/59, New York, N.Y. BR/TR, 6', 166 lbs. Deb: 7/16/84

YEAR	TM/L	G	AB	R	H	2B	3B	HR	RBI	BB	SO	AVG	OBP	SLG	OPS	OPS+	BR+	SB	CS	SBR	FA	FR	G/POS	TPR
1984	Mil-A	43	107	15	29	8	2	1	20	12	23	.271	.345	.411	756	113	2	0	3	-1	.925	-1	3-36/S-6,2-1,D-1	0.0

■ STEVE LUBRATICH Lubratich, Steven George b: 5/1/55, Oakland, Cal. BR/TR, 6', 170 lbs. Deb: 9/27/81

YEAR	TM/L	G	AB	R	H	2B	3B	HR	RBI	BB	SO	AVG	OBP	SLG	OPS	OPS+	BR+	SB	CS	SBR	FA	FR	G/POS	TPR
1981	Cal-A	7	21	2	3	1	0	0	1	0	2	.143	.143	.190	333	-5	-3	1	0	0	1.000	2	/3-6	-0.1
1983	Cal-A	57	156	12	34	9	0	0	7	4	17	.218	.237	.276	513	41	-13	0	1	-0	.949	16	S-23,3-22,2-14	0.5
Total	2	64	177	14	37	10	0	0	8	4	19	.209	.227	.266	492	36	-15	1	1	-0	.988	18	/3-28,S-23,2-14	0.4

■ HAL LUBY Luby, Hugh Max b: 6/13/13, Blackfoot, Idaho d: 5/4/86, Eugene, Ore. BR/TR, 5'10", 185 lbs. Deb: 9/10/36

YEAR	TM/L	G	AB	R	H	2B	3B	HR	RBI	BB	SO	AVG	OBP	SLG	OPS	OPS+	BR+	SB	CS	SBR	FA	FR	G/POS	TPR
1936	Phi-A	9	38	3	7	1	0	0	3	0	7	.184	.205	.211	416	3	-6	2	0	0	.880	-4	/2-9	-0.8
1944	NY-N	111	323	30	82	10	2	2	35	52	15	.254	.364	.316	680	93	-1	2			.943	16	3-65,2-45/1-1	1.9
Total	2	120	361	33	89	11	2	2	38	52	22	.247	.349	.305	654	83	-7	4	0		.954	12	/3-65,2-54,1-1	1.1

■ JOHNNY LUCADELLO Lucadello, John b: 2/22/19, Thurber, Tex. BB/TR, 5'11", 160 lbs. Deb: 9/24/38 Career OF: (1-LF 0-CF 0-RF)

YEAR	TM/L	G	AB	R	H	2B	3B	HR	RBI	BB	SO	AVG	OBP	SLG	OPS	OPS+	BR+	SB	CS	SBR	FA	FR	G/POS	TPR
1938	StL-A	7	20	1	3	1	0	0	0	0	0	.150	.150	.200	350	-13	-4	0	0	0	.909	-1	/3-6	-0.4
1939	StL-A	9	30	0	7	2	0	0	4	2	4	.233	.281	.300	581	48	-2	0	0	0	.912	-4	/2-7	-0.6
1940	StL-A	17	63	15	20	4	2	2	10	6	4	.317	.394	.540	934	137	3	1	0	0	.968	0	2-16	0.5

YEAR	TM/L	G	AB	R	H	2B	3B	HR	RBI	BB	SO	AVG	OBP	SLG	OPS	OPS+	BR+	SB	CS	SBR	FA	FR	G/POS	TPR
1941	StL-A	107	351	58	98	22	4	2	31	48	23	.279	.366	.382	748	95	-2	5	2	0	.962	-16	2-70,S-12/3-6,O-1L	-1.1
1946	StL-A	87	210	21	52	7	1	1	15	36	20	.248	.358	.305	662	82	-4	0	1	-0	.942	-7	3-37,2-19	-1.0
1947	NY-A	12	12	0	1	0	0	0	0	1	5	.083	.154	.083	237	-33	-2	0	0	0	1.000	-2	/2-5	-0.4
Total	6	239	686	95	181	36	7	5	60	93	56	.264	.353	.359	712	88	-10	6	3	0	.965	-29	2-117/3-49,S-12,O-1L	-3.0
■ RED LUCAS	Lucas, Charles Frederick "The Nashville Narcissus" b: 4/28/02, Columbia, Tenn. d: 7/9/86, Nashville, Tenn. BL/TR, 5'9.5", 170 lbs. Deb: 4/19/23 Career OF: (1-LF 0-CF 0-RF)																							
1923	NY-N	3	2	0	0	0	0	0	0	0	1	.000	.000	.000	0	-99	-1	0	0	0	1.000	1	/P-3	0.0
1924	Bos-N	33	33	5	11	1	0	0	5	1	4	.333	.353	.364	717	96	-0	0	0	0	1.000	1	P-27/3-2	0.0
1925	Bos-N	6	20	1	3	0	0	0	2	2	4	.150	.227	.150	377	-2	-3	0	0	0	.968	0	/2-6	-0.3
1926	Cin-N	66	76	15	23	4	4	0	14	10	13	.303	.384	.461	844	130	3	0			1.000	-1	P-39/2-1	0.0
1927	Cin-N	80	150	14	47	5	2	0	28	12	10	.313	.368	.373	741	102	1	0			.983	-6	P-37/2-5,S-3,O-1L	-0.4
1928	Cin-N	39	73	8	23	2	1	0	7	4	6	.315	.351	.370	721	90	-1	0			**1.000**	-0	P-27	0.0
1929	Cin-N	76	140	15	41	6	0	0	13	13	15	.293	.353	.336	689	75	-5	1			.949	0	P-32	0.0
1930	Cin-N	80	113	18	38	4	1	2	19	17	4	.336	.423	.442	866	115	4	0			**1.000**	-3	P-33	0.0
1931	Cin-N	97	153	15	43	4	0	0	17	12	9	.281	.333	.307	641	78	-4	0			.984	1	P-29	0.0
1932	Cin-N	76	150	13	43	11	2	0	19	10	9	.287	.335	.387	722	97	-1	0			.973	-0	P-31	0.0
1933	Cin-N	75	122	14	35	6	1	1	15	12	6	.287	.356	.377	733	111	2	0			**1.000**	0	P-29	0.0
1934	Pit-N	68	105	11	23	5	1	0	8	6	16	.219	.261	.286	547	45	-8	1			.939	-3	P-29	0.0
1935	Pit-N	47	66	6	21	6	0	0	10	7	11	.318	.392	.409	801	112	1	0			.968	-1	P-20	0.0
1936	Pit-N	69	108	11	26	4	1	0	14	8	17	.241	.293	.296	589	58	-6	0			.976	-1	P-27	0.0
1937	Pit-N	59	82	8	22	3	0	0	17	7	6	.268	.326	.305	631	72	-3	0			1.000	-2	P-20	0.0
1938	Pit-N	33	46	1	5	0	0	0	2	3	2	.109	.163	.109	272	-24	-8	0			1.000	-1	P-13	0.0
Total	16	907	1439	155	404	61	13	3	190	124	133	.281	.340	.347	687	84	-29	2	0		.981	-14	P-396/2-12,S-3,3O	-0.7
■ FRED LUCAS	Lucas, Frederick Warrington "Fritz" b: 1/19/03, Vineland, N.J. d: 3/11/87, Cambridge, Md. BR/TR, 5'10", 165 lbs. Deb: 7/15/35																							
1935	Phi-N	20	34	1	9	0	0	0	2	3	6	.265	.324	.265	589	55	-2	0			.944	-2	O-10(4-3-3)	-0.4
■ JOHNNY LUCAS	Lucas, John Charles "Buster" b: 2/10/03, Glen Carbon, Ill. d: 10/31/70, Maryville, Ill. BR/TL, 5'10", 186 lbs. Deb: 4/15/31																							
1931	Bos-A	3	2	0	0	0	0	0	0	0	1	.000	.000	.000	0	-99	-1	0	0	0	.000	-1	/O-2(1-1-0)	-0.2
1932	Bos-A	1	1	0	0	0	0	0	0	0	0	.000	.000	.000	0	-99	-0	0	0	0	.000	0	H	0.0
Total	2	4	3	0	0	0	0	0	0	0	1	.000	.000	.000	0	-99	-1	0	0	0	—	-1	/O-2(1-1-0)	-0.2
■ FRANK LUCE	Luce, Frank Edward b: 12/6/1896, Spencer, Ohio d: 2/3/42, Milwaukee, Wis. BL/TR, 5'11", 180 lbs. Deb: 9/17/23																							
1923	Pit-N	9	12	2	6	0	0	0	3	2	2	.500	.571	.500	1071	181	2	2	1	0	1.000	-2	/O-5(3-1-1)	0.0
■ JOE LUCEY	Lucey, Joseph Earl "Scootch" b: 3/27/1897, Holyoke, Mass. d: 7/30/80, Holyoke, Mass. BR/TR, 6', 168 lbs. Deb: 7/6/20																							
1920	NY-A	3	3	0	0	0	0	0	0	0	0	.000	.000	.000	0	-97	-1	0	0	0	1.000	0	/2-1,S-1	0.0
1925	Bos-A	10	15	0	2	0	0	0	0	0	4	.133	.133	.133	267	-32	-3	0	0	0	.889	-1	/P-7,S-3	-0.3
Total	2	13	18	0	2	0	0	0	0	0	4	.111	.111	.111	222	-43	-4	0	0	0	.778	-0	/P-7,S-4,2-1	-0.3
■ FRED LUDERUS	Luderus, Frederick William b: 9/12/1885, Milwaukee, Wis. d: 1/5/61, Three Lakes, Wis. BL/TR, 5'11.5", 185 lbs. Deb: 9/23/09																							
1909	Chi-N	11	37	8	11	1	1	1	9	3		.297	.366	.459	825	152	2	0			.950	-2	1-11	0.0
1910	Chi-N	24	54	5	11	1	1	0	3	4	3	.204	.259	.259	518	52	-3	0			.975	-0	1-17	-0.4
	Phi-N	21	68	10	20	5	2	0	14	9	5	.294	.385	.426	811	132	3	2			.985	1	1-19	0.3
	Yr	45	122	15	31	6	3	0	17	13	8	.254	.331	.352	683	98	-0	2			.981	0	1-36	-0.1
1911	Phi-N	146	551	69	166	24	11	16	99	40	76	.301	.353	.472	825	128	18	6			.985	-2	*1-146	1.2
1912	Phi-N	148	572	77	147	31	5	10	69	44	65	.257	.318	.381	699	85	-13	8			.990	10	*1-146	-0.7
1913	Phi-N	155	588	67	154	32	7	18	86	34	51	.262	.304	.432	736	105	1	5			.984	1	*1-155	-0.2
1914	Phi-N	121	443	55	110	16	5	12	55	33	31	.248	.308	.388	696	100	-1	2			.975	1	*1-121	-0.3
1915	*Phi-N	141	499	55	157	36	7	7	62	42	36	.315	.376	.457	833	150	29	9	7	-0	.993	10	*1-141	3.9
1916	Phi-N	146	508	52	143	26	3	5	53	41	32	.281	.341	.374	715	115	10	8			.982	-2	*1-146	0.5
1917	Phi-N	154	522	57	136	24	4	5	72	65	35	.261	.349	.351	700	110	8	5			.991	5	*1-154	1.0
1918	Phi-N	125	468	54	135	23	2	5	67	42	33	.288	.351	.378	729	115	9	4			.988	7	*1-125	1.4
1919	Phi-N	138	509	60	149	30	6	5	49	54	48	.293	.365	.405	770	123	15	6			.985	10	*1-138	2.3
1920	Phi-N	16	32	1	5	2	0	0	4	3	6	.156	.229	.219	447	28	-3	0	1	-0	.983	0	/1-7	-0.4
Total	12	1346	4851	570	1344	251	54	84	642	414	421	.277	.340	.403	743	113	73	55	8		.986	39	*1-1326	8.6
■ BILL LUDWIG	Ludwig, William Lawrence b: 5/27/1882, Louisville, Ky. d: 9/5/47, Louisville, Ky. BR/TR, Deb: 4/16/08																							
1908	StL-N	66	187	15	34	2	2	0	8	16		.182	.246	.214	460	50	-10	3			.952	-3	C-62	-0.9
■ ROY LUEBBE	Luebbe, Roy John b: 9/17/1900, Parkersburg, Iowa d: 8/21/85, Papillion, Neb. BB/TR, 6', 175 lbs. Deb: 8/22/25																							
1925	NY-A	8	15	1	0	0	0	0	3	2	6	.000	.118	.000	118	-69	-4	0	0	0	1.000	1	/C-8	-0.2
■ HENRY LUFF	Luff, Henry T. b: 9/14/1856, Philadelphia, Pa. d: 10/11/16, Philadelphia, Pa. 5'11", 175 lbs. Deb: 4/21/1875 Career OF: (14-LF 3-CF 4-RF)																							
1875	NH-n	38	166	15	45	10	3	2	18	0	5	.271	.271	.404	675	150	9	3	3	-0	.689	-4	3-30,P-10/O-4R,S-1	0.2
1882	Det-N	3	11	1	3	2	0	0	1	0	0	.273	.273	.455	727	129	0				.667	-1	/2-3,O-1(0-1-0)	-0.1
	Cin-a	28	120	16	28	2	2	0	6	2		.233	.246	.283	529	74	-3				.922	-2	1-27/O-1(0-0-1)	-0.7
1883	Lou-a	6	23	1	4	0	0	0	2	0		.174	.174	.174	348	13	-2				.868	-1	/1-4,O-2(0-1-1)	-0.3
1884	Phi-U	26	111	9	30	4	2	0		4		.270	.296	.342	638	100	-3				.733	-3	O-12L/1-6,3-5,2-3	-0.6
	KC-U	5	19	0	1	0	0	0		1		.053	.100	.053	153	-60	-4				.444	-4	/3-4,O-4(3-1-1)	-0.8
	Yr	31	130	9	31	4	2	0		5		.238	.267	.300	567	78	-7				.706	-7	O-16L/3-9,1-6,2-3	-1.4
Total	3	68	284	27	66	8	4	0	9	7	0	.232	.251	.289	540	73	-13				.911	-12	/1-37,O-20L,3-9,2-6	-2.5
■ JULIO LUGO	Lugo, Julio Cesar b: 11/16/75, Barahona, D.R. BR/TR, 6', 165 lbs. Deb: 4/15/2000																							
2000	Hou-N	116	420	78	119	22	5	10	40	37	93	.283	.347	.431	778	90	-6	22	9	2	.951	-15	S-60,2-45/O-6(3-1-2)	-1.2
■ ROB LUKACHYK	Lukachyk, Robert James b: 7/24/68, Jersey City, N.J. BL/TR, 6', 185 lbs. Deb: 7/5/96																							
1996	Mon-N	2	2	0	0	0	0	0	0	0	1	.000	.000	.000	0	-98	-1	0	0	0	.000	0	/H	-0.1
■ MATT LUKE	Luke, Matthew Clifford b: 2/26/71, Long Beach, Cal. BL/TL, 6'5", 220 lbs. Deb: 4/3/96																							
1996	NY-A	1	0	1	0	0	0	0	0	0	0	—	—	—	—	—	0	0	0	0	.000	0	/R	0.0
1998	LA-N	33	77	10	22	7	0	3	11	3	18	.286	.313	.494	806	115	1	0	0	0	.958	3	O-15(13-0-2),1-12	0.3
	Cle-A	2	2	0	0	0	0	0	0	0	0	.000	.000	.000	0	-97	-1	0	0	0	.000	0	/H	-0.1
	LA-N	69	160	24	34	5	1	9	23	14	42	.213	.280	.425	705	87	-4	2	1	0	1.000	3	O-48(36-0-12)/1-6	-0.3
1999	Ana-A	18	30	4	9	0	0	3	6	2	10	.300	.344	.600	944	135	1	0	0	0	1.000	0	/O-6(2-0-4),1-4	0.1
Total	3	123	269	39	65	12	1	15	40	19	70	.242	.294	.461	755	99	-2	2	1	0	.991	5	/O-69(51-0-18),1-22	0.0
■ EDDIE LUKON	Lukon, Edward Paul "Mongoose" b: 8/5/20, Burgettstown, Pa. d: 11/7/96, Canonsburg, Pa. BL/TL, 5'10", 168 lbs. Deb: 8/6/41																							
1941	Cin-N	23	86	6	23	3	0	0	3	6	6	.267	.315	.302	618	74	-3	1			.980	2	O-22(0-0-22)	-0.2
1945	Cin-N	2	8	1	1	0	0	0	0	0	1	.125	.125	.125	250	-31	-1	0			1.000	0	/O-2(0-2-0)	-0.2
1946	Cin-N	102	312	31	78	8	8	12	34	26	29	.250	.310	.442	752	116	4	3			.985	2	O-83(72-0-11)	0.1
1947	Cin-N	86	200	26	41	6	1	11	33	28	36	.205	.306	.410	716	89	-4	0			1.000	-2	O-55(33-0-25)	-0.8
Total	4	213	606	64	143	17	9	23	70	60	72	.236	.307	.408	714	99	-4	4			.989	3	O-162(105-2-58)	-1.1
■ MIKE LUM	Lum, Michael Ken-Wai b: 10/27/45, Honolulu, Hawaii BL/TL, 6', 180 lbs. Deb: 9/12/67 C Career OF: (359-LF 171-CF 315-RF)																							
1967	Atl-N	9	26	1	6	0	0	0	1	1	4	.231	.259	.231	490	42	-2	0	1	-0	.944	1	/O-6(0-6-0)	-0.1
1968	Atl-N	122	232	22	52	7	3	3	21	14	35	.224	.280	.319	599	79	-6	3	5	-1	.976	-9	O-95(74-7-21)	-2.3
1969	*Atl-N	121	168	20	45	8	0	1	22	16	18	.268	.332	.333	665	86	-3	0	0	0	.992	-8	O-89(56-16-21)	-1.3
1970	Atl-N	123	291	25	74	17	2	7	28	17	43	.254	.307	.399	705	83	-8	3	2	-0	.988	-3	O-98(36-33-35)	-1.4
1971	Atl-N	145	454	56	122	14	1	13	55	47	43	.269	.344	.390	734	101	1	0	3	-1	.990	9	*O-125(10-17-104)/1-1	0.4
1972	Atl-N	123	369	40	84	14	2	9	38	50	52	.228	.325	.350	674	84	-7	1	4	-1	.976	4	*O-109(30-20-62)/1-2	-0.9
1973	Atl-N	138	513	74	151	26	6	16	82	41	89	.294	.354	.462	816	116	10	2	5	-1	.991	-3	1-84,O-64(48-2-14)	-0.3

YEAR	TM/L	G	AB	R	H	2B	3B	HR	RBI	BB	SO	AVG	OBP	SLG	OPS	OPS+	BR+	SB	CS	SBR	FA	FR	G/POS	TPR
1974	Atl-N	106	361	50	84	11	2	11	50	45	49	.233	.321	.366	687	88	-6	0	2	-1	.994	-5	1-60,O-50(14-9-25)	-1.9
1975	Atl-N	124	364	32	83	8	2	8	36	39	38	.228	.303	.327	630	72	-14	2	4	-1	.992	-1	1-60,O-38(1-32-5)	-2.3
1976	*Cin-N	84	136	15	31	5	1	3	20	22	24	.228	.340	.346	685	93	-1	0	1	-0	1.000	-6	O-38(33-2-5)	-1.0
1977	Cin-N	81	125	14	20	1	0	5	16	9	33	.160	.222	.288	510	35	-12	2	0	0	1.000	-3	O-24(12-1-11)/1-8	-1.5
1978	Cin-N	86	146	15	39	7	1	6	23	22	18	.267	.363	.452	815	126	5	0	0	0	.987	-1	O-43(10-26-9)/1-7	0.4
1979	Atl-N	111	217	27	54	6	0	6	27	18	34	.249	.306	.359	666	75	-7	0	2	-1	.998	2	1-51/O-3(3-0-0)	-0.9
1980	Atl-N	93	83	7	17	3	0	0	5	18	19	.205	.347	.241	587	65	-3	0	0	0	1.000	-3	O-19(19-0-0),1-10	-0.7
1981	Atl-N	10	11	1	1	0	0	0	0	2	2	.091	.231	.091	322	-6	-1	0	0	0	1.000	0	/O-1(1-0-0)	-0.1
	Chi-N	41	58	5	14	1	0	2	7	5	5	.241	.313	.362	675	87	-1	0	0	0	.923	-4	O-14(12-0-3)/1-1	-0.6
	Yr	51	69	6	15	1	0	2	7	7	7	.217	.299	.319	618	72	-2	0	0	0	.938	-4	O-15(13-0-3)/1-1	-0.7
Total	15	1517	3554	404	877	128	20	90	431	366	506	.247	.322	.370	692	89	-53	13	29	-7	.986	-29	O-816L,1-284	-14.5
■ HARRY LUMLEY	Lumley, Harry G "Judge" b: 9/29/1880, Forest City, Pa. d: 5/22/38, Binghamton, N.Y. BL/TL, 5'10", 183 lbs. Deb: 4/14/04 M																							
1904	Bro-N	150	577	79	161	23	**18**	**9**	78	41		.279	.331	.428	759	137	23	30			.955	4	*O-150(0-0-150)	2.1
1905	Bro-N	130	505	50	148	19	10	7	47	36		.293	.340	.412	752	134	19	22			.912	-1	*O-129(0-0-129)	1.3
1906	Bro-N	133	484	72	157	23	12	9	61	48		.324	.386	**.477**	864	**184**	**45**	35			.949	1	*O-131(0-0-131)	4.4
1907	Bro-N	127	454	47	121	23	11	9	66	31		.267	.316	.425	741	144	19	18			.959	-4	*O-118(0-0-118)	1.2
1908	Bro-N	127	440	36	95	13	12	4	39	29		.216	.266	.327	593	93	-5	4			.955	-5	*O-116(0-0-116)	-1.9
1909	Bro-N	55	172	13	43	8	3	0	14	16		.250	.314	.331	645	104	1	1			.948	2	O-52(0-0-52),M	0.0
1910	Bro-N	8	21	3	3	0	0	0	0	3	6	.143	.280	.143	423	25	-2	0			.833	-1	/O-4(0-0-4)	-0.3
Total	7	730	2653	300	728	109	66	38	305	204	6	.274	.328	.408	737	135	100	110			.946	-5	O-700(0-0-700)	6.8
■ JERRY LUMPE	Lumpe, Jerry Dean b: 6/2/33, Lincoln, Mo. BL/TR, 6'2", 185 lbs. Deb: 4/17/56 C																							
1956	NY-A	20	62	12	16	3	0	0	4	5	11	.258	.313	.306	620	66	-3	1	1	-0	.916	3	S-17/3-1	0.1
1957	*NY-A	40	103	15	35	6	2	0	11	9	13	.340	.393	.437	830	128	4	2	2	-0	.956	-2	3-30/S-6	0.2
1958	*NY-A	81	232	34	59	8	4	3	32	23	21	.254	.324	.362	686	92	-3	1	2	-0	.943	4	3-65/S-5	0.1
1959	NY-A	18	45	2	10	0	0	0	2	6	7	.222	.314	.222	536	52	-3	0	0	0	1.000	2	3-12/S-4,2-1	0.0
	KC-A	108	403	47	98	11	5	3	28	41	32	.243	.313	.318	631	72	-15	2	1	0	.986	-10	2-61,S-56/3-4	-1.6
	Yr	126	448	49	108	11	5	3	30	47	39	.241	.313	.308	621	70	-17	2	1	0	.987	-8	2-62,S-60,3-16	-1.6
1960	KC-A	146	574	69	156	19	3	8	53	48	49	.272	.328	.357	685	85	-12	1	1	-0	.982	-7	*2-134,S-15	-0.9
1961	KC-A	148	569	81	167	29	9	3	54	48	39	.293	.351	.392	742	96	-2	1	0	0	.979	16	*2-147	2.6
1962	KC-A	156	641	89	193	34	10	10	83	44	38	.301	.346	.432	778	103	2	0	2	-1	.986	-4	*2-156/S-2	1.2
1963	KC-A	157	595	75	161	26	7	5	59	58	44	.271	.335	.363	698	91	-6	3	2	-0	.988	2	*2-155	1.0
1964	Det-A☆	158	624	75	160	21	6	6	46	50	61	.256	.314	.338	652	80	-16	2	1	0	.983	-21	*2-158	-2.5
1965	Det-A	145	502	72	129	15	3	4	39	56	34	.257	.335	.323	658	87	-7	7	0	2	.985	-18	*2-139	-1.3
1966	Det-A	113	385	30	89	14	3	1	26	24	44	.231	.276	.291	567	62	-19	0	3	-1	.991	-6	2-95	-1.9
1967	Det-A	81	177	19	41	4	0	4	17	16	18	.232	.295	.322	617	80	-4	0	0	0	.963	-3	2-54/3-6	-0.5
Total	12	1371	4912	620	1314	190	52	47	454	428	411	.268	.327	.356	683	87	-84	20	15	-1	.984	-44	*2-1100,3-118,S-105	-3.5
■ FERNANDO LUNAR	Lunar, Fernando Jose b: 5/25/77, Cantanura, Venez. BR/TR, 6'1", 195 lbs. Deb: 5/8/2000																							
2000	Atl-N	22	54	5	10	1	0	0	5	3	15	.185	.267	.204	470	21	-6	0	2	-1	.993	8	C-22	0.1
	Bal-A	9	16	0	2	0	0	0	1	0	4	.125	.176	.125	301	-22	-3	0	0	0	1.000	3	/C-9	0.0
Total	1	31	70	5	12	1	0	0	6	3	19	.171	.247	.186	432	12	-9	0	2	-1	.995	10	/C-31	0.1
■ DON LUND	Lund, Donald Andrew b: 5/18/23, Detroit, Mich. BR/TR, 6', 200 lbs. Deb: 7/3/45 C																							
1945	Bro-N	4	3	0	0	0	0	0	0	1	1	.000	.250	.000	250	-27	-0	0			.000	0	H	0.0
1947	Bro-N	11	20	5	6	2	0	2	5	3	7	.300	.391	.700	1091	178	2	0			1.000	-0	/O-5(5-0-0)	0.2
1948	Bro-N	27	69	9	13	4	0	1	5	5	16	.188	.243	.290	533	42	-6	1			.977	-2	O-25(17-0-8)	-0.9
	StL-A	63	161	21	40	7	4	3	25	10	17	.248	.305	.398	702	84	-5	0	0	0	1.000	-4	O-45(21-0-25)	-1.1
1949	Det-A	2	2	0	0	0	0	0	0	0	1	.000	.000	.000	0	-99	-1	0	0	0	.000	0	H	-0.1
1952	Det-A	8	23	1	7	0	0	0	1	3	3	.304	.385	.304	689	93	-0	0	1	-0	1.000	0	/O-7(0-0-7)	-0.1
1953	Det-A	131	421	51	108	21	4	9	47	39	65	.257	.323	.390	712	93	-5	3	3	-0	.980	1	*O-123(37-29-69)	-1.0
1954	Det-A	35	54	4	7	2	0	0	3	4	3	.130	.190	.167	356	-2	-8	1	0	0	.971	-8	O-31(19-3-11)	-1.7
Total	7	281	753	91	181	36	8	15	86	65	113	.240	.305	.369	674	81	-22	5	4		.983	-12	O-236(99-32-120)	-4.7
■ GORDY LUND	Lund, Gordon Thomas b: 2/23/41, Iron Mountain, Mich BR/TR, 5'11", 170 lbs. Deb: 8/1/67																							
1967	Cle-A	3	8	1	2	1	0	0	0	0	2	.250	.250	.375	625	82	-0	0	0	0	.667	-2	/S-2	-0.2
1969	Sea-A	20	38	4	10	0	0	0	1	5	7	.263	.349	.263	612	75	-1	1	1	-0	.927	-1	S-17/2-1,3-1	0.0
Total	2	23	46	5	12	1	0	0	1	5	9	.261	.333	.283	616	76	-1	1	1	-0	.902	-2	/S-19,3-1,2-1	-0.2
■ TOM LUNDSTEDT	Lundstedt, Thomas Robert b: 4/10/49, Davenport, Iowa BB/TR, 6'4", 195 lbs. Deb: 8/31/73																							
1973	Chi-N	4	5	0	0	0	0	0	0	0	1	.000	.000	.000	0	-93	-1	0	0	0	1.000	1	/C-4	-0.1
1974	Chi-N	22	32	1	3	0	0	0	0	5	7	.094	.216	.094	310	-11	-5	0	0	0	.987	2	C-22	-0.3
1975	Min-A	18	28	2	3	0	0	0	1	4	5	.107	.219	.107	326	-5	-4	0	0	0	1.000	1	C-14/D-2	-0.2
Total	3	44	65	3	6	0	0	0	1	9	13	.092	.203	.092	295	-15	-10	0	0	0	.993	4	/C-40,D-2	-0.6
■ HARRY LUNTE	Lunte, Harry August b: 9/15/1892, St.Louis, Mo. d: 7/27/65, St.Louis, Mo. BR/TR, 5'11.5", 165 lbs. Deb: 5/19/19																							
1919	Cle-A	26	77	2	15	2	0	0	2	1	7	.195	.215	.221	436	21	-8	0			.935	-2	S-24	-0.9
1920	*Cle-A	23	71	6	14	0	0	0	7	5	6	.197	.250	.197	447	19	-8	0	1	-0	.979	3	S-21/2-2	-0.4
Total	2	49	148	8	29	2	0	0	9	6	13	.196	.232	.209	442	20	-16	0	1		.955	1	/S-45,2-2	-1.3
■ TONY LUPIEN	Lupien, Ulysses John b: 4/23/17, Chelmsford, Mass. BL/TL, 5'10.5", 185 lbs. Deb: 9/12/40																							
1940	Bos-A	10	19	5	9	3	2	0	4	1	1	.474	.500	.842	1342	232	4	0	0	0	1.000	-0	/1-8	0.3
1942	Bos-A	128	463	63	130	25	7	3	70	50	20	.281	.351	.384	735	103	2	10	12	-2	.992	-7	*1-121	-1.8
1943	Bos-A	154	608	65	155	21	9	4	47	54	23	.255	.317	.339	656	90	-8	16	9		.993	4	*1-153	-1.3
1944	Phi-N	153	597	82	169	23	9	5	52	56	29	.283	.347	.377	723	107	6	18			.992	1	*1-151	-0.1
1945	Phi-N	15	54	1	17	1	0	0	3	6	0	.315	.383	.333	717	103	1	2			1.000	3	1-15	0.3
1948	Chi-A	154	617	69	152	19	3	6	54	74	38	.246	.327	.316	643	74	-23	11	7	-0	.993	-4	*1-154	-3.2
Total	6	614	2358	285	632	92	30	18	230	241	111	.268	.337	.355	692	94	-19	57	28		.993	-4	1-602	-5.8
■ AL LUPLOW	Luplow, Alvin David b: 3/13/39, Saginaw, Mich. BL/TR, 5'11", 180 lbs. Deb: 9/16/61																							
1961	Cle-A	5	18	0	1	0	0	0	0	2	6	.056	.150	.056	206	-44	-4	0	0	0	1.000	2	/O-5(1-0-4)	-0.3
1962	Cle-A	97	318	54	88	15	3	14	45	36	44	.277	.361	.475	836	127	12	1	0	0	.960	-3	O-86(70-0-24)	0.4
1963	Cle-A	100	295	34	69	6	2	7	27	33	62	.234	.317	.339	656	85	-6	4	4	-1	.994	3	O-85(14-0-73)	-0.9
1964	Cle-A	19	18	1	2	0	0	0	1	1	8	.111	.158	.111	269	-24	-3	0	0	0	1.000	-1	/O-5(0-1-4)	-0.4
1965	Cle-A	53	45	3	6	2	0	1	4	3	14	.133	.188	.244	432	22	-5	0	1	-0	1.000	-2	/O-6(2-1-3)	-0.7
1966	NY-N	111	334	31	84	9	1	7	31	38	46	.251	.332	.347	679	91	-3	2	6	-2	.987	-12	*O-101(16-24-71)	-2.3
1967	NY-N	41	112	11	23	1	0	3	9	8	19	.205	.264	.295	559	61	-6	0	0	0	.966	-4	O-33(6-16-16)	-1.2
	Pit-N	55	103	13	19	1	0	1	8	6	14	.184	.236	.223	460	32	-9	1	0	0	.961	3	O-25(15-2-8)	-0.8
	Yr	96	215	24	42	2	0	4	17	14	33	.195	.251	.260	512	47	-15	1	0	0	.963	-1	O-58(21-18-24)	-2.0
Total	7	481	1243	147	292	34	6	33	125	127	213	.235	.312	.352	664	85	-23	8	11	-2	.977	-14	O-346(124-44-203)	-6.2
■ SCOTT LUSADER	Lusader, Scott Edward b: 9/30/64, Chicago, Ill. BL/TL, 5'10", 165 lbs. Deb: 9/1/87																							
1987	Det-A	23	47	8	15	3	1	1	8	5	7	.319	.385	.489	874	135	2	1	0	0	.967	-5	O-22(6-3-16)/D-1	-0.3
1988	Det-A	16	16	3	1	0	0	1	3	1	4	.063	.118	.250	368	-0	-2	0	0	0	1.000	-1	/O-4(2-2-2),D-6	-0.4
1989	Det-A	40	103	15	26	4	0	1	8	9	21	.252	.313	.320	633	81	-3	3	0	1	.933	-6	O-33(4-8-24)/D-1	-0.9
1990	Det-A	45	87	13	21	2	0	2	16	12	8	.241	.333	.333	667	86	-1	0	0	0	.982	-7	O-42(12-5-27)/D-2	-1.0
1991	NY-A	11	7	2	1	0	0	0	1	1	3	.143	.250	.143	393	12	-1	0	1	-0	1.000	-1	/O-4(1-3-0),D-1	-0.2
Total	5	135	260	41	64	9	1	5	36	28	43	.246	.319	.346	666	86	-4	4	1	1	.961	-20	O-105(25-21-69)/D-11	-2.8
■ ERNIE LUSH	Lush, Ernest Benjamin b: 10/31/1884, Bridgeport, Conn. d: 2/26/37, Detroit, Mich. BR/TL, Deb: 7/20/10 F																							
1910	StL-N	1	4	0	0	0	0	0	0	1	1	.000	.200	.000	200	-42	-1	0			1.000	-0	/O-1(0-1-0)	-0.1

YEAR	TM/L	G	AB	R	H	2B	3B	HR	RBI	BB	SO	AVG	OBP	SLG	OPS	OPS+	BR+	SB	CS	SBR	FA	FR	G/POS	TPR
■ **JOHNNY LUSH**	Lush, John Charles b: 10/8/1885, Williamsport, Pa. d: 11/18/46, Beverly Hills, Cal BL/TL, 5'9.5", 165 lbs. Deb: 4/22/04 Career OF: (0-LF 14-CF 58-RF)																							
1904	Phi-N	106	369	39	102	22	3	2	42	27		.276	.336	.369	704	122	9	12			.950	-10	1-62,O-33(0-0-33)/P-7	-0.4
1905	Phi-N	6	16	3	5	0	0	0	1	1		.313	.389	.313	701	114	0	0			.667	-1	/O-3(0-2-1),P-2	-0.1
1906	Phi-N	76	212	28	56	7	1	0	15	14		.264	.310	.307	616	92	-2	6			.907	5	P-37,O-22(0-6-16)/1-2	0.0
1907	Phi-N	17	40	5	8	1	1	0	5	1		.200	.220	.275	495	56	-2	1			1.000	0	/P-8,O-4(0-3-1)	-0.2
	StL-N	27	82	6	23	2	3	0	5	5		.280	.322	.378	700	123	2	4			.917	-3	P-20/O-7(0-3-4)	-0.3
	Yr	44	122	11	31	3	4	0	10	6		.254	.289	.344	633	101	-0	5			.941	-3	P-28,O-11(0-6-5)	-0.5
1908	StL-N	45	89	7	15	2	0	0	2	7		.169	.229	.191	420	36	-6	1			.926	0	P-38	0.0
1909	StL-N	45	92	11	22	5	0	0	14	6		.239	.293	.293	586	87	-1	2			.945	-1	P-34/O-3(0-0-3)	-0.1
1910	StL-N	47	93	8	21	1	3	0	10	8	11	.226	.287	.301	588	74	-3	2			.928	-2	P-36	0.0
Total	7	369	993	107	252	40	11	2	94	69	11	.254	.307	.322	630	98	-4	28			.926	-12	P-182/O-72R,1-64	-1.1
■ **BILLY LUSH**	Lush, William Lucas b: 11/10/1873, Bridgeport, Conn. d: 8/28/51, Hawthorne, N.Y. BB/TR, 5'7", 165 lbs. Deb: 9/3/1895 F Career OF: (238-LF 138-CF 86-RF)																							
1895	Was-N	5	18	2	6	0	0	0	2	2	1	.333	.400	.333	733	92	-0	0			.692	-1	/O-5(4-0-1)	-0.1
1896	Was-N	97	352	74	87	9	11	4	45	66	49	.247	.369	.369	738	95	-1	28			.885	-2	*O-91(10-14-68)/2-3	-0.7
1897	Was-N	3	12	1	0	0	0	0	0	2		.000	.143	.000	143	-61	-3	0			1.000	1	/O-3(0-0-3)	-0.2
1901	Bos-N	7	27	2	5	1	1	0	3	3		.185	.267	.296	563	58	-1	0			.960	3	/O-7(0-7-0)	0.1
1902	Bos-N	120	413	68	92	8	1	2	19	76		.223	.346	.262	608	87	-2	30			.952	11	*O-116(10-104-2)/3-1	0.3
1903	Det-A	119	423	71	116	18	14	1	33	70		.274	.379	.390	769	135	21	14			.968	12	*O-101L,3-12/2-3,S	2.8
1904	Cle-A	138	477	76	123	13	8	1	50	72		.258	.359	.325	684	118	13	12			.959	3	*O-138(125-13-0)	0.9
Total	7	489	1722	294	429	49	35	8	152	291	50	.249	.360	.332	692	107	27	84			.943	25	O-461L/3-13,2-6,S-3	3.1
■ **CHARLIE LUSKEY**	Luskey, Charles Melton b: 4/6/1876, Washington, D.C. d: 12/20/62, Bethesda, Md. BR/TR, 5'7", 165 lbs. Deb: 9/12/01																							
1901	Was-A	11	41	8	8	3	1	0	3	2		.195	.233	.317	550	52	-3	0			.818	-1	/O-8(8-0-0),C-3	-0.4
■ **LUKE LUTENBERG**	Lutenberg, Charles William b: 10/4/1864, Quincy, Ill. d: 12/24/38, Quincy, Ill. BR/TR, 6'2", 225 lbs. Deb: 7/7/1894																							
1894	Lou-N	70	255	43	49	10	4	0	23	23	21	.192	.282	.263	545	34	-27	4			.977	1	1-68/2-2	-2.0
■ **LYLE LUTTRELL**	Luttrell, Lyle Kenneth b: 2/22/30, Bloomington, Ill. d: 7/11/84, Chattanooga, Tenn BR/TR, 6', 180 lbs. Deb: 5/15/56																							
1956	Was-A	38	122	17	23	5	3	2	9	8	19	.189	.256	.328	584	53	-9	5	1	1	.939	-7	S-37	-1.1
1957	Was-A	19	45	4	9	4	0	0	5	3	8	.200	.250	.289	539	47	-3	0	0	0	.927	-5	S-17	-0.8
Total	2	57	167	21	32	9	3	2	14	11	27	.192	.254	.317	572	52	-12	5	1	1	.936	-12	/S-54	-1.9
■ **RED LUTZ**	Lutz, Louis William b: 12/17/1898, Cincinnati, Ohio d: 2/22/84, Cincinnati, Ohio BR/TR, 5'10", 170 lbs. Deb: 5/31/22																							
1922	Cin-N	1	1	0	1	1	0	0	0	0	0	1.000	1.000	2.000	3000	669	1	0	0	0	.000	0	/C-1	0.1
■ **JOE LUTZ**	Lutz, Rollin Joseph b: 2/18/25, Keokuk, Iowa BL/TL, 6', 195 lbs. Deb: 4/17/51 C																							
1951	StL-A	14	36	7	6	0	1	0	2	6	9	.167	.286	.222	508	38	-3	0	0	0	1.000	-1	1-11	-0.4
■ **RUBE LUTZKE**	Lutzke, Walter John b: 11/17/1897, Milwaukee, Wis. d: 3/6/38, Granville, Wis. BR/TR, 5'11", 175 lbs. Deb: 4/18/23																							
1923	Cle-A	143	511	71	131	20	6	3	65	59	57	.256	.338	.337	675	78	-16	9	6	-0	.939	17	*3-141/S-2	1.0
1924	Cle-A	106	341	37	83	18	3	0	42	38	46	.243	.328	.314	642	65	-17	4	0	1	.947	19	*3-103/2-3	0.9
1925	Cle-A	81	238	31	52	9	0	1	16	26	29	.218	.295	.269	564	44	-20	2	4	-1	.936	-0	3-69,2-10	-1.7
1926	Cle-A	142	475	42	124	28	6	0	59	34	35	.261	.313	.345	658	71	-21	6	3	0	.960	-1	*3-142	-1.2
1927	Cle-A	100	311	35	78	12	3	0	41	22	29	.251	.307	.309	615	60	-19	2	1	0	.938	6	3-98	-0.6
Total	5	572	1876	216	468	87	18	4	223	179	196	.249	.319	.321	641	66	-93	23	14	0	.945	42	3-553/2-13,S-2	-1.6
■ **KEITH LUULOA**	Luuloa, Keith H. M. b: 12/24/74, Honolulu, Hawaii BR/TR, 6', 185 lbs. Deb: 5/17/2000																							
2000	Ana-A	6	18	3	6	0	0	0	0	1	1	.333	.368	.333	702	79	-0	0	0	0	.833	-1	/S-4,2-3	-0.1
■ **GREG LUZINSKI**	Luzinski, Gregory Michael b: 11/22/50, Chicago, Ill. BR/TR, 6'1", 225 lbs. Deb: 9/9/70 C Career OF: (1221-LF 0-CF 1-RF)																							
1970	Phi-N	8	12	0	2	0	0	0	0	3	5	.167	.333	.167	500	39	-1	0	1	-0	1.000	1	/1-3	-0.1
1971	Phi-N	28	100	13	30	8	0	3	15	12	32	.300	.386	.470	856	141	6	2	0	0	.996	6	1-28	1.1
1972	Phi-N	150	563	66	158	33	5	18	68	42	114	.281	.334	.453	787	119	12	0	4	-1	.960	1	*O-145(145-0-1)/1-2	0.3
1973	Phi-N	161	610	76	174	26	4	29	97	51	135	.285	.347	.484	831	125	19	3	3	-0	**.993**	-2	*O-159(159-0-0)	0.7
1974	Phi-N	85	302	29	82	14	1	7	48	29	76	.272	.335	.394	729	99	-0	3	0	1	.981	7	O-82(82-0-0)	0.2
1975	Phi-N★	161	596	85	179	35	3	34	**120**	89	151	.300	.398	.540	939	152	43	3	6	-1	.966	-7	*O-159(159-0-0)	2.6
1976	*Phi-N★	149	533	74	162	28	1	21	95	50	107	.304	.375	.478	854	137	26	1	2	-0	.964	-8	*O-144(144-0-0)	0.9
1977	*Phi-N★	149	554	99	171	35	3	39	130	80	140	.309	.399	.594	993	155	43	3	2	-0	.964	-5	*O-148(148-0-0)	3.2
1978	*Phi-N★	155	540	85	143	32	2	35	101	100	135	.265	.390	.526	916	152	40	8	7	-1	.984	-7	*O-154(154-0-0)	2.7
1979	Phi-N	137	452	47	114	23	1	18	81	56	103	.252	.347	.427	774	107	5	3	3	-0	.946	-15	*O-125(125-0-0)	-1.6
1980	*Phi-N	106	368	44	84	19	1	19	56	60	100	.228	.346	.440	786	112	6	3	0	1	.993	-12	*O-105(105-0-0)	-1.0
1981	Chi-A	104	378	55	100	15	1	21	62	58	80	.265	.367	.476	843	144	22	0	0	0	.000	0	*D-103	2.0
1982	Chi-A	159	583	87	170	37	1	18	102	89	120	.292	.391	.451	842	130	27	1	1	-0	.000	0	*D-156	2.2
1983	*Chi-A	144	502	73	128	26	1	32	95	70	117	.255	.358	.502	860	129	20	2	1	0	1.000	0	*D-139/1-2	1.6
1984	Chi-A	125	412	47	98	13	0	13	58	56	80	.238	.333	.364	697	89	-5	5	1	1	.000	0	*D-114	-0.8
Total	15	1821	6505	880	1795	344	24	307	1128	845	1495	.276	.366	.478	844	129	263	37	31	-3	.972	-40	*O-1221L,D-512/1-35	14.0
■ **MITCH LYDEN**	Lyden, Mitchell Scott b: 12/14/64, Portland, Ore. BR/TR, 6'3", 225 lbs. Deb: 6/16/93																							
1993	Fla-N	6	10	2	3	0	0	1	1	0	3	.300	.300	.600	900	127	0	0	0	0	1.000	-1	/C-2	-0.1
■ **SCOTT LYDY**	Lydy, Donald Scott b: 10/26/68, Mesa, Ariz. BR/TR, 6'5", 195 lbs. Deb: 5/18/93																							
1993	Oak-A	41	102	11	23	5	0	2	7	8	39	.225	.288	.333	622	71	-4	2	0	0	.958	-2	O-38(17-5-16)/D-2	-0.7
■ **JERRY LYNCH**	Lynch, Gerald Thomas b: 7/17/30, Bay City, Mich. BL/TR, 6'1", 189 lbs. Deb: 4/15/54																							
1954	Pit-N	98	284	27	68	4	5	8	36	20	43	.239	.292	.373	665	73	-12	2	2	-0	.965	-4	O-83(46-4-36)	-2.1
1955	Pit-N	88	282	43	80	18	6	5	28	22	33	.284	.336	.443	779	106	2	2	2	-0	.950	-2	O-71(40-0-32)/C-2	-0.4
1956	Pit-N	19	19	1	3	0	1	0	0	1	4	.158	.200	.263	463	24	-2	0	0	0	1.000	0	/O-1(1-0-0)	-0.2
1957	Cin-N	67	124	11	32	4	1	4	13	6	18	.258	.292	.403	696	79	-4	0	0	0	1.000	-2	O-24(1-0-22)/C-2	-0.6
1958	Cin-N	122	420	58	131	20	5	16	68	18	54	.312	.340	.498	838	112	6	1	4	-1	.970	-7	*O-101(1-0-101)	-0.5
1959	Cin-N	117	379	49	102	16	3	17	58	29	50	.269	.323	.462	784	103	1	2	0	0	.979	2	O-98(97-0-1)	-0.3
1960	Cin-N	102	159	23	46	8	2	6	27	16	25	.289	.358	.478	836	124	5	0	0	0	.913	-4	O-32(31-0-1)	0.0
1961	*Cin-N	96	181	33	57	13	2	13	50	27	25	.315	.407	.624	1031	166	17	2	2	-0	.948	-4	O-44(42-0-2)	1.0
1962	Cin-N	114	288	41	81	15	4	12	57	24	38	.281	.339	.486	825	115	5	3	3	-0	.970	-0	O-73(70-0-3)	0.1
1963	Cin-N	22	32	5	8	3	0	2	9	1	5	.250	.294	.531	825	129	1	0	0	0	1.000	-1	/O-7(4-0-3)	-0.1
	Pit-N	88	237	26	63	6	3	10	36	22	28	.266	.331	.443	774	120	6	0	1	-0	.960	-6	O-64(64-0-0)	-0.4
	Yr	110	269	31	71	9	3	12	45	23	33	.264	.327	.454	780	121	7	0	1	-0	.962	-7	O-71(68-0-3)	-0.5
1964	Pit-N	114	297	35	81	14	2	16	66	26	57	.273	.333	.495	828	130	11	0	1	-0	.983	-13	O-78(77-0-1)	-0.6
1965	Pit-N	73	121	7	34	1	0	5	16	8	26	.281	.331	.413	744	108	1	0	2	-1	.903	-3	O-26(23-0-3)	-0.4
1966	Pit-N	64	56	5	12	1	0	1	6	4	10	.214	.267	.286	552	54	-3	0	0	0	1.000	-0	/O-4(4-0-0)	-0.4
Total	13	1184	2879	364	798	123	34	115	470	224	416	.277	.331	.463	795	110	35	12	17	-3	.964	-46	O-706(501-4-205)/C-4	-4.9
■ **HENRY LYNCH**	Lynch, Henry W. b: 4/8/1866, Worcester, Mass. d: 11/23/25, Worcester, Mass. BB, 5'7", 143 lbs. Deb: 9/21/1893																							
1893	Chi-N	4	14	0	3	2	0	0	2	1	1	.214	.267	.357	624	66	-1	0			.833	-1	/O-4(0-0-4)	-0.2
■ **DANNY LYNCH**	Lynch, Matt Dan "Dummy" b: 2/7/26, Dallas, Tex. d: 6/30/78, Plano, Tex. BR/TR, 5'11", 174 lbs. Deb: 9/14/48																							
1948	Chi-N	7	7	3	2	0	0	1	1	1	1	.286	.375	.714	1089	197	1	0			1.000	0	/2-1	0.1
■ **MIKE LYNCH**	Lynch, Michael Joseph b: 9/10/1875, St.Paul, Minn. d: 4/1/47, Jennings Lodge, Ore TR, 5'10", 155 lbs. Deb: 4/24/02																							
1902	Chi-N	7	28	4	4	0	0	0	0	2		.143	.200	.143	343	6	-3	0			.929	-1	/O-7(0-7-0)	-0.4
■ **TOM LYNCH**	Lynch, Thomas James b: 4/3/1860, Bennington, Vt. d: 3/28/55, Cohoes, N.Y. BL/TR, 5'10.5", 170 lbs. Deb: 8/18/1884 U Career OF: (18-LF 10-CF 0-RF)																							
1884	Wil-U	16	58	6	16	3	1	0		5		.276	.333	.362	695	108	-1				.846	-3	/C-8,O-8(8-0-0),1-1	-0.3

YEAR	TM/L	G	AB	R	H	2B	3B	HR	RBI	BB	SO	AVG	OBP	SLG	OPS	OPS+	BR+	SB	CS	SBR	FA	FR	G/POS	TPR
	Phi-N	13	48	7	15	4	2	0	3	4	5	.313	.365	.479	845	171	4				.860	-2	/C-7,O-7(1-6-0)	0.3
1885	Phi-N	13	53	7	10	3	0	0	1	10	3	.189	.317	.245	563	86	-0				.838	3	O-13(9-4-0)	0.2
Total	2	42	159	20	41	10	3	0	4	19	8	.258	.337	.358	696	119	3				.887	-2	/O-28L,C-15,1-1	0.2
■ WALT LYNCH Lynch, Walter Edward "Jabber" b: 4/15/1897, Buffalo, N.Y. d: 12/21/76, Daytona Beach, Fla TR, 6', 176 lbs. Deb: 7/8/22																								
1922	Bos-A	3	2	1	1	0	0	0	0	0	0	.500	.500	.500	1000	163	0	0	0	0	1.000	0	/C-3	0.0
■ BYRD LYNN Lynn, Byrd "Birdie" b: 3/13/1889, Unionville, Ill. d: 2/5/40, Napa, Cal. BR/TR, 5'11", 165 lbs. Deb: 4/16/16																								
1916	Chi-A	31	40	4	9	1	0	0	3	4	7	.225	.311	.250	561	68	-1	2			.952	8	C-13	0.8
1917	*Chi-A	35	72	7	16	2	0	0	5	7	11	.222	.300	.250	550	67	-3	1			.959	-2	C-29	-0.3
1918	Chi-A	5	8	0	2	0	0	0	0	2	1	.250	.400	.250	650	95	0	0			1.000	-1	/C-4	-0.1
1919	*Chi-A	29	66	4	15	4	0	0	4	4	9	.227	.271	.288	559	57	-4	0			.982	1	C-28	-0.2
1920	Chi-A	16	25	0	8	2	1	0	3	1	3	.320	.346	.480	826	117	0	0	0	0	1.000	-1	C-14	0.0
Total	5	116	211	15	50	9	1	0	15	18	31	.237	.303	.289	592	72	-7	3	0		.969	5	/C-88	0.2
■ FRED LYNN Lynn, Fredric Michael b: 2/3/52, Chicago, Ill. BL/TL, 6'1", 190 lbs. Deb: 9/5/74 Career OF: (135-LF 1584-CF 144-RF)																								
1974	Bos-A	15	43	5	18	2	2	2	10	6	6	.419	.500	.698	1198	226	7	0	0	0	1.000	-0	O-12(6-4-2)/D-1	0.6
1975	*Bos-A★	145	528	**103**	175	**47**	7	21	105	62	90	.331	.405	**.566**	**971**	158	40	10	5	0	.983	13	*O-144(0-144-0)	5.0
1976	Bos-A★	132	507	76	159	32	8	10	65	48	67	.314	.374	.467	842	130	19	14	9	-0	.984	14	*O-128(0-127-1)/D-5	3.0
1977	Bos-A★	129	497	81	129	29	5	18	76	51	63	.260	.332	.447	779	98	-1	2	3	-1	.994	8	*O-125(0-125-0)/D-1	0.5
1978	Bos-A★	150	541	75	161	33	3	22	82	75	50	.298	.384	.492	876	131	23	3	6	-1	.984	8	*O-149(0-149-0)	2.9
1979	Bos-A★	147	531	116	177	42	1	39	122	82	79	**.333**	.426	**.637**	**1063**	**173**	**55**	2	2	-0	.987	7	*O-143(0-143-0)/D-1	**5.7**
1980	Bos-A★	110	415	67	125	32	3	12	61	58	39	.301	.387	.480	866	129	18	12	0	3	.994	9	*O-110(0-110-0)	2.8
1981	Cal-A★	76	256	28	56	8	1	5	31	38	42	.219	.327	.316	643	86	-4	1	2	-0	.978	1	O-69(0-69-0)	-0.4
1982	*Cal-A★	138	472	89	141	38	1	21	86	58	72	.299	.379	.517	896	143	28	7	8	-1	.991	-3	*O-133(0-133-0)	2.3
1983	Cal-A★	117	437	56	119	20	3	22	74	55	83	.272	.356	.483	839	130	18	2	2	-0	.993	-2	*O-113(0-113-0)/D-2	1.5
1984	Cal-A	142	517	84	140	28	4	23	79	77	97	.271	.367	.474	841	132	23	2	2	-0	.982	-10	*O-140(0-62-112)	0.8
1985	Bal-A	124	448	59	118	12	1	23	68	53	100	.263	.343	.449	791	118	11	7	3	0	.994	2	*O-123(0-123-0)	1.2
1986	Bal-A	112	397	67	114	13	1	23	67	53	59	.287	.374	.499	873	137	21	2	2	-0	.984	-4	*O-107(0-107-0)/D-1	1.5
1987	Bal-A	111	396	49	100	24	0	23	60	39	72	.253	.321	.487	808	113	6	3	7	-2	.991	-3	*O-101(0-102-0)/D-8	0.1
1988	Bal-A	87	301	37	76	13	1	18	37	28	66	.252	.316	.482	798	123	8	2	2	-0	.991	0	O-83(0-64-21)/D-2	0.7
	Det-A	27	90	9	20	1	0	7	19	5	16	.222	.271	.467	738	106	0	0	0	0	1.000	0	O-22(19-3-0)/D-3	0.0
	Yr	114	391	46	96	14	1	25	56	33	82	.246	.306	.478	784	120	8	2	2	-0	.992	1	*O-105(19-67-21)/D-5	0.7
1989	Det-A	117	353	44	85	11	1	11	46	47	71	.241	.332	.371	703	100	1	1	1	-0	.992	-1	O-68(68-0-0),D-46	-0.4
1990	SD-N	90	196	18	47	3	1	6	23	22	44	.240	.320	.357	677	85	-4	2	0	0	1.000	-4	O-55(42-6-8)	-0.9
Total	17	1969	6925	1063	1960	388	43	306	1111	857	1116	.283	.364	.484	848	129	269	72	54	-3	.988	35	*O-1825C/D-70	26.9
■ JERRY LYNN Lynn, Jerome Edward b: 4/14/16, Scranton, Pa. d: 9/25/72, Scranton, Pa. BR/TR, 5'10", 164 lbs. Deb: 9/19/37																								
1937	Was-A	1	3	0	2	1	0	0	0	0	0	.667	.667	1.000	1667	329	1	0	0	0	1.000	1	/2-1	0.2
■ RUSS LYON Lyon, Russell Mayo b: 6/26/13, Ball Ground, Ga. d: 12/24/75, Charleston, S.C. BR/TR, 6'1", 230 lbs. Deb: 4/21/44																								
1944	Cle-A	7	11	1	2	0	0	0	0	1	1	.182	.250	.182	432	25	-1	0	0	0	.909	0	/C-3	-0.1
■ BARRY LYONS Lyons, Barry Stephen b: 6/3/60, Biloxi, Miss. BR/TR, 6'1", 202 lbs. Deb: 4/19/86																								
1986	NY-N	6	9	1	0	0	0	0	2	1	2	.000	.100	.000	100	-72	-2	0	0	0	.941	0	/C-3	-0.2
1987	NY-N	53	130	15	33	4	1	4	24	8	24	.254	.307	.392	699	88	-3	0	0	0	.984	0	C-49	-0.1
1988	NY-N	50	91	5	21	7	1	0	11	3	12	.231	.255	.330	585	70	-4	0	0	0	.979	-2	C-32/1-1	-0.5
1989	NY-N	79	235	15	58	13	0	3	27	11	28	.247	.286	.340	627	82	-6	0	1	-0	.980	1	C-76	-0.1
1990	NY-N	24	80	8	19	0	0	2	7	2	9	.237	.265	.313	578	58	-5	0	0	0	.980	3	C-23	0.0
	LA-N	3	5	1	1	0	0	1	2	0	1	.200	.200	.800	1000	166	0	0	0	0	1.000	-1	/C-2	0.0
	Yr	27	85	9	20	0	0	3	9	2	10	.235	.261	.341	603	65	-4	0	0	0	.980	3	C-25	0.0
1991	LA-N	9	9	0	0	0	0	0	0	0	2	.000	.000	.000	0	-99	-2	0	0	0	1.000	1	/C-6	-0.1
	Cal-A	2	5	0	1	0	0	0	0	0	0	.200	.200	.200	400	11	-1	0	0	0	1.000	0	/1-2	-0.1
1995	Chi-A	27	64	8	17	2	0	5	16	4	14	.266	.309	.531	840	119	1	0	0	0	.987	3	C-16/1-4,D-6	0.4
Total	7	253	628	53	150	26	2	15	89	29	92	.239	.278	.358	636	78	-20	0	1	-0	.981	6	C-207/1-7,D-6	-0.7
■ DENNY LYONS Lyons, Dennis Patrick Aloysius b: 3/12/1866, Cincinnati, Ohio d: 1/2/29, W.Covington, Ky. BR/TR, 5'10", 185 lbs. Deb: 9/18/1885																								
1885	Pro-N	4	16	3	2	1	0	0	1	0	3	.125	.125	.188	313	-0	-2				.824	-0	/3-4	-0.2
1886	Phi-a	32	123	22	26	3	1	0	11	8		.211	.281	.252	534	67	-5	7			.807	-7	3-32	-0.9
1887	Phi-a	137	617	128	256	43	14	6	102	47		.415	.421	.523	943	162	47	73			.866	-6	*3-137	3.5
1888	Phi-a	111	456	93	135	22	5	6	83	41		.296	.363	.406	769	147	25	39			.878	-13	*3-111	1.2
1889	Phi-a	131	510	135	168	36	4	9	82	79	44	.329	.426	.469	895	157	41	10			.860	9	*3-130/1-1	4.3
1890	Phi-a	88	339	79	120	29	5	7	73	57		.354	**.461**	**.531**	**992**	**193**	42	21			.909	9	3-88	4.5
1891	StL-a	120	451	124	142	24	3	11	84	88	58	.315	.445	.455	900	137	23	9			.871	-6	*3-120	1.6
1892	NY-N	108	389	71	100	16	7	8	51	59	37	.257	.359	.396	755	130	15	11			.871	-5	*3-108	1.1
1893	Pit-N	131	490	103	150	19	16	3	105	97	29	.306	.430	.429	858	131	27	19			.918	5	*3-131	2.8
1894	Pit-N	72	257	52	82	14	4	4	51	43	13	.319	.424	.451	876	112	7	14			.897	9	3-72	1.3
1895	StL-N	34	132	24	39	6	0	2	25	15	7	.295	.380	.386	766	99	0	3			.889	-5	3-34	-0.3
1896	Pit-N	118	436	77	134	25	6	4	71	67	25	.307	.406	.420	825	123	17	13			.893	-15	*3-116	0.4
1897	Pit-N	37	131	22	27	6	4	2	17	22		.206	.346	.359	705	90	-1	5			.989	-1	1-35/3-2	-0.2
Total	13	1123	4347	933	1381	244	69	62	756	623	216	.318	.407	.442	850	138	237	224			.882	-25	*3-1085/1-36	19.1
■ ED LYONS Lyons, Edward Hoyte "Mouse" b: 5/12/23, Winston-Salem, N.C BR/TR, 5'9", 165 lbs. Deb: 9/15/47 C																								
1947	Was-A	7	26	2	4	0	0	0	0	2	2	.154	.214	.154	368	3	-3	0	0	0	1.000	4	/2-7	0.1
■ HARRY LYONS Lyons, Harry Pratt b: 3/25/1866, Chester, Pa. d: 6/29/12, Mauricetown, N.J. BR/TR, 5'10.5", 157 lbs. Deb: 8/29/1887 Career OF: (142-LF 245-CF 17-RF)																								
1887	Phi-N	1	5	0	1	0	0	0	0	1	0	.200	.200	.000	200	-38	-1	0			.500	-0	/O-1(1-0-0)	-0.1
	*StL-a	2	8	2	1	0	0	0	1	0		.125	.125	.125	250	-27	-1	2			1.000	1	/2-1,O-1(0-0-1)	0.0
1888	*StL-a	123	499	66	97	10	5	4	63	20		.194	.230	.259	488	51	-30	36			.891	6	*O-122C/3-2,S-1,2-1	-2.5
1889	NY-N	5	20	1	2	0	1	0	2	2	0	.100	.182	.200	382	7	-3	0			1.000	-1	/O-5(0-1-4)	-0.3
1890	Roc-a	133	584	83	152	11	11	3	58	27		.260	.294	.332	626	91	-8	47			.920	11	*O-132L/3-2,C-1,P-1	-0.1
1892	NY-N	96	411	67	98	5	2	0	53	33	29	.238	.297	.260	557	70	-14	25			.910	3	O-96(10-86-0)	-1.7
1893	NY-N	47	187	27	51	5	2	0	21	14	6	.273	.323	.321	644	71	-8	10			.917	2	O-47(1-46-0)	-0.7
Total	6	407	1714	246	402	31	21	7	198	97	35	.235	.277	.289	566	69	-65	120			.908	21	O-404C/3-4,2-2,PCS	-5.4
■ PAT LYONS Lyons, Patrick Jerry b: 3/1860, Canada d: 1/20/14, Springfield, Ohio TR, Deb: 7/21/1890																								
1890	Cle-N	11	38	2	2	1	0	0	1	4	4	.053	.143	.079	222	-36	-7	0			.839	-5	2-11	-1.1
■ STEVE LYONS Lyons, Stephen John b: 6/3/60, Tacoma, Wash. BL/TR, 6'3", 195 lbs. Deb: 4/15/85 Career OF: (59-LF 237-CF 43-RF)																								
1985	Bos-A	133	371	52	98	14	3	5	30	32	64	.264	.324	.358	683	83	-8	12	9	-1	.973	-8	*O-114C/3-1,S-1,D-5	-1.7
1986	Bos-A	59	124	20	31	7	2	1	14	12	23	.250	.316	.363	679	84	-3	2	3	-1	.972	-5	O-55(0-55-0)	-0.9
	Chi-A	42	123	10	25	2	1	0	6	7	24	.203	.252	.236	488	33	-11	2	3	-1	.987	1	O-35L/3-3,1-1,D-1	-1.2
	Yr	101	247	30	56	9	3	1	20	19	47	.227	.285	.300	584	58	-14	4	6	-1	.978	-4	O-90C/3-3,1-1,D-1	-2.1
1987	Chi-A	76	193	26	54	11	1	1	19	12	37	.280	.322	.363	685	79	-6	3	1	0	.971	11	3-51,O-15C/2-1,D-6	0.4
1988	Chi-A	146	472	59	127	28	3	5	45	32	59	.269	.317	.373	690	93	-5	1	2	-0	.927	10	*3-128,O-14C/2-4,C1	0.5
1989	Chi-A	140	443	51	117	21	3	2	50	35	68	.264	.319	.339	658	88	-7	9	6	-0	.982	-8	2-70,1-40,3-28,O/SCD	-1.6
1990	Chi-A	94	146	22	28	6	1	1	11	10	41	.192	.248	.267	516	45	-11	1	0	0	.991	-1	1-61,2-15/O-7C,3SDP	-1.3
1991	Bos-A	87	212	15	51	10	1	4	17	11	35	.241	.278	.354	632	70	-9	10	3	1	1.000	0	O-45C,2-16,3/1SDP	-0.8
1992	Atl-N	11	14	0	1	0	1	0	1	0	4	.071	.071	.214	286	-21	-2	0	0	0	1.000	-2	/O-6(2-0-4),2-2	-0.4
	Mon-N	16	13	2	3	0	0	0	1	1	3	.231	.286	.231	516	48	-1	1	2	-0	1.000	-2	/O-8(7-1-0),1-1	-0.3
	Yr	27	27	2	4	0	1	0	2	1	7	.148	.179	.222	401	13	-3	1	2	-0	1.000	-3	O-14(9-1-4)/2-2,1-1	-0.7
	Bos-A	21	28	3	7	0	1	0	2	2	1	.250	.300	.321	621	69	-1	0	1	-0	1.000	-0	/1-8,O-5R,2-1,D-2	-0.2

YEAR	TM/L	G	AB	R	H	2B	3B	HR	RBI	BB	SO	AVG	OBP	SLG	OPS	OPS+	BR+	SB	CS	SBR	FA	FR	G/POS	TPR
1993	Bos-A	28	23	4	3	1	0	0	0	2	5	.130	.200	.174	374	1	-3	1	2	-0	1.000	-1	O-10C/2-9,C-1,13D	-0.4
Total	9	853	2162	264	545	100	17	19	196	156	364	.252	.304	.340	644	77	-67	42	32	-2	.979	-4	O-334C,3-229,21/DSCP	-7.9
■ TERRY LYONS	Lyons, Terence Hilbert b: 12/14/08, New Holland, Ohio d: 9/9/59, Dayton, Ohio BR/TR, 6'0.5", 165 lbs. Deb: 4/19/29																							
1929	Phi-N	1	0	0	0	0	0	0	0	0	0	—	—	—	—	—	0	0			.000	0	/1-1	0.0
■ TED LYONS	Lyons, Theodore Amar b: 12/28/1900, Lake Charles, La. d: 7/25/86, Sulphur, La. BB/TR, 5'11", 200 lbs. Deb: 7/2/23 MCH																							
1923	Chi-A	9	5	0	1	0	0	0	1	1	3	.200	.333	.200	533	43	-0	0	0	0	1.000	1	/P-9	0.0
1924	Chi-A	41	77	10	17	0	1	0	6	5	13	.221	.277	.247	524	37	-7	0	0	0	.902	-3	P-41	0.0
1925	Chi-A	43	97	6	18	3	0	0	7	3	13	.186	.218	.216	434	11	-13	0	0	0	.957	2	P-43	0.0
1926	Chi-A	41	104	7	22	1	1	0	3	1	10	.212	.219	.240	459	20	-12	0	0	0	.955	4	P-39	0.0
1927	Chi-A	41	110	16	28	6	2	1	9	6	17	.255	.293	.373	666	74	-5	0	0	0	.979	0	P-39	0.0
1928	Chi-A	49	91	10	23	2	0	0	8	1	9	.253	.261	.275	536	41	-8	0	0	0	.920	2	P-39	0.0
1929	Chi-A	40	91	7	20	4	0	0	11	9	13	.220	.290	.264	554	44	-8	0	0	0	.946	2	P-37/O-1(0-0-1)	0.0
1930	Chi-A	57	122	20	38	6	3	1	15	2	18	.311	.323	.434	757	93	-2	0	0	0	.938	3	P-42	0.0
1931	Chi-A	42	33	6	5	0	0	0	3	2	1	.152	.200	.152	352	-7	-5	0	0	0	.957	-1	P-22	0.0
1932	Chi-A	49	73	11	19	2	1	1	10	4	10	.260	.308	.356	664	76	-3	0	0	0	.964	-1	P-33	0.0
1933	Chi-A	51	91	11	26	2	1	1	11	4	6	.286	.316	.363	678	83	-2	0	1	-0	.983	0	P-36	0.0
1934	Chi-A	50	97	9	20	4	0	1	16	3	19	.206	.245	.278	523	34	-10	0	0	0	.939	2	P-30	0.0
1935	Chi-A	29	82	5	18	4	0	0	6	3	4	.220	.256	.268	524	35	-8	0	0	0	**1.000**	-1	P-23	0.0
1936	Chi-A	26	70	2	11	0	0	0	5	5	12	.157	.213	.157	370	-7	-12	0	0	0	**1.000**	1	P-26	0.0
1937	Chi-A	23	57	6	12	0	0	0	3	9	14	.211	.318	.211	529	36	-5	0	0	0	**1.000**	0	P-22	0.0
1938	Chi-A	24	72	9	14	2	0	0	4	2	9	.194	.216	.222	438	10	-10	0	0	0	.982	2	P-23	0.0
1939	Chi-A☆	21	61	5	18	3	0	0	8	5	7	.295	.348	.344	693	76	-2	0	0	0	.912	-1	P-21	0.0
1940	Chi-A	22	75	4	18	4	0	0	7	2	7	.240	.260	.293	553	43	-6	0	0	0	.923	-2	P-22	0.0
1941	Chi-A	22	74	8	20	2	0	0	6	2	6	.270	.289	.297	587	56	-5	0	0	0	.981	1	P-22	0.0
1942	Chi-A	20	67	10	16	4	0	0	10	3	7	.239	.282	.299	580	65	-3	0	0	0	.980	1	P-20	0.0
1946	Chi-A	5	14	0	0	0	0	0	0	1	3	.000	.067	.000	67	-83	-3	0	0	0	1.000	0	/P-5,M	0.0
Total	21	705	1563	162	364	49	9	5	149	73	201	.233	.270	.285	556	44	-130	0	1	-0	.958	11	P-594/O-1(0-0-1)	0.0
■ BILL LYONS	Lyons, William Allen b: 4/26/58, Alton, Ill. BR/TR, 6'1", 175 lbs. Deb: 7/20/83																							
1983	StL-N	42	60	3	10	1	1	0	3	1	11	.167	.180	.217	397	10	-7	3	2	-0	.985	2	2-23/3-8,S-2	-0.5
1984	StL-N	46	73	13	16	3	0	0	3	9	13	.219	.305	.260	565	62	-3	3	1	0	.991	14	2-25,S-11/3-3	1.2
Total	2	88	133	16	26	4	1	0	6	10	24	.195	.252	.241	492	39	-11	6	3	0	.989	16	/2-48,S-13,3-11	0.7
■ DAD LYTLE	Lytle, Edward Benson "Pop" b: 3/10/1862, Racine, Wis. d: 12/21/50, Long Beach, Cal. BR/TR, 5'11", 160 lbs. Deb: 8/11/1890																							
1890	Chi-N	1	4	1	0	0	0	0	0	0	1	.000	.000	.000	0	-96	-1	0			1.000	1	/O-1(0-0-1)	0.0
	Pit-N	15	55	2	8	1	0	0	0	8	9	.145	.254	.164	418	25	-5	0			.837	-6	/2-8,O-7(0-4-3)	-1.0
	Yr	16	59	3	8	1	0	0	0	8	10	.136	.239	.153	391	16	-6	0			.824	-5	/O-8(0-4-4),2-8	-1.0
■ JIM LYTTLE	Lyttle, James Lawrence b: 5/20/46, Hamilton, Ohio BL/TR, 6', 186 lbs. Deb: 5/17/69																							
1969	NY-A	28	83	7	15	4	0	0	4	4	19	.181	.218	.229	447	26	-8	1	2	-0	.983	1	O-28(0-28-0)	-0.9
1970	NY-A	87	126	20	39	7	1	3	14	10	26	.310	.360	.452	813	129	5	3	6	-1	.989	-9	O-70(2-4-64)	-0.8
1971	NY-A	49	86	7	17	5	0	1	7	8	18	.198	.274	.291	564	64	-4	0	2	-1	1.000	-3	O-29(3-6-20)	-0.9
1972	Chi-A	44	82	8	19	5	2	0	5	1	28	.232	.241	.341	582	70	-3	0	1	-0	1.000	-2	O-21(0-16-5)	-0.7
1973	Mon-N	49	116	12	30	5	1	4	19	9	14	.259	.312	.422	734	98	-1	0	2	-1	.974	2	O-36(29-7-0)	0.0
1974	Mon-N	25	9	1	3	0	0	0	2	1	3	.333	.400	.333	733	101	0	0	0	0	1.000	-6	O-18(14-5-0)	-0.6
1975	Mon-N	44	55	7	15	4	0	0	6	13	6	.273	.412	.345	757	107	1	0	1	-0	1.000	-3	O-16(5-8-3)	-0.3
1976	Mon-N	42	85	6	23	4	1	1	8	7	13	.271	.326	.376	703	95	-1	0	0	0	.977	-3	O-29(12-0-20)	-0.5
	LA-N	23	68	3	15	3	0	0	5	8	12	.221	.303	.265	567	63	-3	0	1	-0	1.000	4	O-18(1-17-1)	0.0
	Yr	65	153	9	38	7	1	1	13	15	25	.248	.315	.327	642	81	-4	0	1	-0	.990	2	O-47(13-17-21)	-0.5
Total	8	391	710	71	176	37	5	9	70	61	139	.248	.308	.352	660	86	-14	4	15	-4	.988	-18	O-265(66-91-113)	-4.7
■ KEVIN MAAS	Maas, Kevin Christian b: 1/20/65, Castro Valley, Cal. BL/TL, 6'3", 209 lbs. Deb: 6/29/90																							
1990	NY-A	79	254	42	64	9	0	21	41	43	76	.252	.367	.535	902	149	17	1	2	-0	.983	-3	1-57,D-18	0.9
1991	NY-A	148	500	69	110	14	1	23	63	83	128	.220	.336	.390	726	100	1	5	1	1	.983	-1	*D-109,1-36	-0.6
1992	NY-A	98	286	35	71	12	0	11	35	25	63	.248	.309	.406	714	99	-1	3	1	0	.986	-3	D-62,1-22	-0.7
1993	NY-A	59	151	20	31	4	0	9	25	24	32	.205	.318	.411	729	97	-1	1	1	-0	.984	-1	D-31,1-17	-0.5
1995	Min-A	22	57	5	11	4	0	1	5	7	11	.193	.281	.316	597	55	-4	0	0	0	.936	-2	D-12/1-8	-0.6
Total	5	406	1248	171	287	43	1	65	169	182	310	.230	.332	.422	754	107	12	10	5	0	.982	-10	D-232,1-140	-1.5
■ JOHN MABRY	Mabry, John Steven b: 10/17/70, Wilmington, Del. BL/TR, 6'4", 195 lbs. Deb: 4/23/94 Career OF: (78-LF 8-CF 233-RF)																							
1994	StL-N	6	23	2	7	3	0	0	3	2	4	.304	.360	.435	795	108	0	0	0	0	1.000	1	/O-6(0-0-6)	0.1
1995	StL-N	129	388	35	119	21	1	5	41	24	45	.307	.350	.405	755	99	-1	0	3	-1	.994	2	1-73,O-39(11-0-29)	-0.7
1996	*StL-N	151	543	63	161	30	2	13	74	37	84	.297	.345	.431	776	104	3	3	2	-0	.994	-11	*1-146,O-14(1-0-13)	-2.1
1997	StL-N	116	388	40	110	19	0	5	36	39	77	.284	.353	.371	725	91	-4	0	1	-0	1.000	-6	O-78(4-6-71),1-49/3-1	-1.7
1998	StL-N	142	377	41	94	22	0	9	46	30	76	.249	.306	.379	686	80	-12	0	2	-1	.971	-10	O-80L,3-38,1-16	-2.5
1999	Sea-A	87	262	34	64	14	0	9	33	20	60	.244	.298	.401	699	78	-9	2	1	0	.989	0	O-43R,3-24,1-20,/D	-1.1
2000	Sea-A	48	103	18	25	5	0	1	7	10	31	.243	.322	.320	642	65	-5	0	1	-0	.862	-6	3-22,O-19R/1-3,PD	-1.2
	SD-N	48	123	17	28	8	0	7	25	5	38	.228	.258	.463	721	82	-4	0	0	0	.980	-2	O-32(2-0-30)/1-2	-0.8
Total	7	727	2207	250	608	122	3	49	265	167	415	.275	.330	.400	730	91	-33	5	10	-2	.989	-33	O-311R,1-309/3-85,DP	-10.0
■ HARVEY MacDONALD	Mac Donald, Harvey Forsyth b: 5/18/1898, New York, N.Y. d: 10/4/65, Manoa, Pa. BL/TL, 5'11", 170 lbs. Deb: 6/12/28																							
1928	Phi-N	13	16	0	4	0	0	0	2	2	3	.250	.333	.250	583	53	-1	0			1.000	-0	/O-2(0-0-2)	-0.1
■ MACEY	Macey b: Columbus, Ohio Deb: 10/2/1890																							
1890	Phi-a	1	1	0	0	0	0	0	0	0		.000	.000	.000	0	-99	-0	0			1.000	-1	/C-1	-0.1
■ MIKE MACFARLANE	Macfarlane, Michael Andrew b: 4/12/64, Stockton, Cal. BR/TR, 6'1", 205 lbs. Deb: 7/23/87																							
1987	KC-A	8	19	0	4	1	0	0	3	2	2	.211	.286	.263	549	46	-1	0	0	0	1.000	-1	/C-8	-0.2
1988	KC-A	70	211	25	56	15	0	4	26	21	37	.265	.335	.393	728	102	1	0	0	0	.994	-15	C-68	-1.0
1989	KC-A	69	157	13	35	6	0	2	19	7	27	.223	.265	.299	564	59	-9	0	0	0	.996	2	C-59/D-4	-0.4
1990	KC-A	124	400	37	102	24	4	6	58	25	69	.255	.310	.380	690	94	-4	1	0	0	.991	-19	*C-112/D-5	-1.7
1991	KC-A	84	267	34	74	18	2	13	41	17	52	.277	.334	.506	840	128	9	1	0	0	.993	-12	C-69/D-4	0.2
1992	KC-A	129	402	51	94	28	3	17	48	30	89	.234	.311	.445	756	107	2	1	5	-2	.993	-1	*C-104,D-13	0.5
1993	KC-A	117	388	55	106	27	0	20	67	40	83	.273	.365	.497	862	122	12	2	5	-1	.985	4	*C-114	2.0
1994	KC-A	92	314	53	80	17	3	14	47	35	71	.255	.362	.462	824	106	3	1	0	0	.993	4	C-81/D-8	1.1
1995	*Bos-A	115	364	45	82	18	1	15	51	38	78	.225	.322	.404	726	85	-9	2	1	0	.993	-3	*C-111/D-3	-0.5
1996	KC-A	112	379	58	104	24	2	19	54	31	57	.274	.341	.499	839	109	4	3	3	-0	.993	-10	C-99/D-9	0.0
1997	KC-A	82	257	34	61	14	2	8	35	24	47	.237	.317	.401	718	84	-6	0	2	-1	.991	-13	C-81	-1.5
1998	KC-A	3	11	1	1	0	0	0	0	0	2	.091	.091	.091	182	-51	-2	0	0	0	1.000	-0	/C-3	-0.3
	Oak-A	78	207	28	52	12	0	7	34	12	34	.251	.305	.411	716	86	-5	1	0	0	.989	-2	C-70	-0.3
	Yr	81	218	29	53	12	0	7	34	12	36	.243	.295	.394	689	79	-7	1	0	0	.990	-3	C-73	-0.6
1999	Oak-A	81	226	24	55	17	0	4	31	13	52	.243	.287	.372	659	69	-11	0	0	0	.997	-3	C-79/D-1	-0.9
Total	13	1164	3602	458	906	221	17	129	514	295	700	.252	.325	.430	755	98	-16	12	16	-3	.992	-71	*C-1058/D-47	-3.0
■ ED MacGAMWELL	Mac Gamwell, Edward M. b: 1/10/1879, Buffalo, N.Y. d: 5/26/24, Albany, N.Y. BL/TL, Deb: 4/14/05																							
1905	Bro-N	4	16	0	4	0	0	0	0	1		.250	.294	.250	544	68	-1	0			.951	-1	/1-4	-0.1
■ KEN MACHA	Macha, Kenneth Edward b: 9/29/50, Monroeville, Pa. BR/TR, 6'2", 217 lbs. Deb: 9/14/74 FC Career OF: (3-LF 0-CF 4-RF)																							
1974	Pit-N	5	5	1	3	1	0	0	1	0	0	.600	.600	.800	1400	300	1	0	0	0	1.000	-0	/C-1	0.1
1977	Pit-N	35	95	2	26	4	0	0	11	6	17	.274	.317	.316	633	68	-4	1	1	-0	.964	-5	3-17,1-11/O-4(3-0-1)	-1.0

YEAR	TM/L	G	AB	R	H	2B	3B	HR	RBI	BB	SO	AVG	OBP	SLG	OPS	OPS+	BR+	SB	CS	SBR	FA	FR	G/POS	TPR
1978	Pit-N	29	52	5	11	1	1	0	5	12	10	.212	.359	.269	629	75	-1	2	0	0	.970	-3	3-21	-0.5
1979	Mon-N	25	36	8	10	3	1	0	4	2	9	.278	.333	.417	750	104	0	0	0	0	1.000	1	3-13/1-2,O-2R,C-1	0.1
1980	Mon-N	49	107	10	31	5	1	1	8	11	17	.290	.361	.383	745	108	1	0	2	-1	.910	-5	3-33/1-2,C-1,O-1R	-0.5
1981	Tor-A	37	85	4	17	2	0	0	6	8	15	.200	.269	.224	492	41	-6	1	1	-0	.892	-1	3-19,1-16/C-1,D-2	-0.9
Total	6	180	380	30	98	16	3	1	35	39	68	.258	.330	.324	654	80	-9	4	4	-1	.938	-13	3-103/1-31,O-7R,CD	-2.7

■ MIKE MACHA

Macha, Michael William b: 2/17/54, Victoria, Tex. BR/TR, 5'11", 180 lbs. Deb: 4/20/79 F

YEAR	TM/L	G	AB	R	H	2B	3B	HR	RBI	BB	SO	AVG	OBP	SLG	OPS	OPS+	BR+	SB	CS	SBR	FA	FR	G/POS	TPR
1979	Atl-N	6	13	2	2	0	0	0	1	1	5	.154	.214	.154	368	2	-2	0	0	0	.769	0	/3-3	-0.1
1980	Tor-A	5	8	0	0	0	0	0	0	0	1	.000	.000	.000	0	-96	-2	0	0	0	.778	1	/3-2,C-1	-0.2
Total	2	11	21	2	2	0	0	0	1	1	6	.095	.136	.095	232	-33	-4	0	0	0	.773	1	/3-5,C-1	-0.3

■ ROBERT MACHADO

Machado, Robert Alexis b: 6/3/73, Caracas, Venez. BR/TR, 6'1", 205 lbs. Deb: 7/24/96

YEAR	TM/L	G	AB	R	H	2B	3B	HR	RBI	BB	SO	AVG	OBP	SLG	OPS	OPS+	BR+	SB	CS	SBR	FA	FR	G/POS	TPR
1996	Chi-A	4	6	1	4	1	0	0	2	0	0	.667	.667	.833	1500	290	2	0	0	0	1.000	-1	/C-4	0.1
1997	Chi-A	10	15	1	3	0	1	0	2	1	6	.200	.250	.333	583	53	-1	0	0	0	1.000	2	C-10	0.1
1998	Chi-A	34	111	14	23	6	0	3	15	7	22	.207	.254	.342	597	55	-8	0	0	0	.981	-3	C-34	-0.8
1999	Mon-N	17	22	3	4	1	0	0	0	2	6	.182	.250	.227	477	23	-3	0	0	0	1.000	-1	C-17	-0.3
2000	Sea-A	8	14	2	3	0	0	1	1	1	4	.214	.267	.429	695	74	-1	0	0	0	1.000	3	/C-8	0.2
Total	5	73	168	21	37	8	1	4	20	11	38	.220	.268	.351	619	60	-10	0	0	0	.988	-0	/C-73	-0.7

■ DAVE MACHEMER

Machemer, David Ritchie b: 5/24/51, St.Joseph, Mo. BR/TR, 5'11.5", 180 lbs. Deb: 6/21/78

YEAR	TM/L	G	AB	R	H	2B	3B	HR	RBI	BB	SO	AVG	OBP	SLG	OPS	OPS+	BR+	SB	CS	SBR	FA	FR	G/POS	TPR
1978	Cal-A	10	22	6	6	1	0	1	2	2	1	.273	.333	.455	788	124	1	0	1	-0	1.000	-2	/2-5,3-3,S-1	-0.2
1979	Det-A	19	26	8	5	1	0	0	2	3	2	.192	.276	.231	507	37	-2	0	3	-1	.972	5	2-11/O-1(1-0-0),D-1	0.1
Total	2	29	48	14	11	2	0	1	4	5	3	.229	.302	.333	635	74	-2	0	4	-1	.978	2	/2-16,3-3,D-1,OS	-0.1

■ JOSE MACIAS

Macias, Jose Prado (Salazar) b: 1/25/74, Panama City, Pan. BB/TR, 5'10", 173 lbs. Deb: 5/12/99 Career OF: (0-LF 1-CF 2-RF)

YEAR	TM/L	G	AB	R	H	2B	3B	HR	RBI	BB	SO	AVG	OBP	SLG	OPS	OPS+	BR+	SB	CS	SBR	FA	FR	G/POS	TPR
1999	Det-A	5	4	2	1	0	0	1	2	0	1	.250	.250	1.000	1250	200	1	0	0	0	1.000	3	/2-1	0.3
2000	Det-A	73	173	25	44	3	5	2	24	18	24	.254	.328	.364	692	77	-6	2	0	0	.976	0	2-39,3-26/O-3R,SD	-0.3
Total	2	78	177	27	45	3	5	3	26	18	25	.254	.327	.379	705	80	-5	2	0	0	.978	3	/2-40,3-26,O-3R,DS	0.0

■ CONNIE MACK

Mack, Cornelius Alexander "The Tall Tactician" (b: Cornelius Alexander McGillicuddy)
b: 12/22/1862, E.Brookfield, Mass d: 2/8/56, Philadelphia, Pa. BR/TR, 6'1", 150 lbs. Deb: 9/11/1886 FMH Career OF: (6-LF 3-CF 46-RF)

YEAR	TM/L	G	AB	R	H	2B	3B	HR	RBI	BB	SO	AVG	OBP	SLG	OPS	OPS+	BR+	SB	CS	SBR	FA	FR	G/POS	TPR
1886	Was-N	10	36	4	13	2	1	0	5	0	2	.361	.361	.472	833	161	2	0			.957	9	C-10	1.1
1887	Was-N	82	322	35	71	6	1	0	20	8	17	.220	.228	.226	454	28	-30	26			.906	3	C-76/O-5(2-2-1),2-2	-1.7
1888	Was-N	85	300	49	56	5	6	3	29	17	18	.187	.249	.273	523	70	-9	31			.916	5	C-79/O-4L,S-1,1-1	0.3
1889	Was-N	98	386	51	113	16	1	0	42	15	12	.293	.333	.339	672	94	-3	26			.891	5	C-45,O-34R,1-22	0.3
1890	Buf-P	123	503	95	134	15	12	0	53	47	13	.266	.353	.344	697	94	-1	16			.925	-11	*C-112/O-9(0-1-8),1-5	-0.2
1891	Pit-N	75	280	43	60	10	0	0	29	19	11	.214	.286	.250	536	58	-14	4			.926	9	C-72/1-3	0.0
1892	Pit-N	97	346	39	84	9	4	1	31	21	22	.243	.298	.301	598	81	-8	11			**.951**	24	C-92/O-3(1-0-2),1-1	2.1
1893	Pit-N	37	133	22	38	3	1	0	15	10	9	.286	.358	.323	681	83	-3	4			.941	6	C-37	0.5
1894	Pit-N	70	231	33	57	7	1	1	21	21	14	.247	.320	.299	619	50	-19	8			.948	6	C-70,M	-0.5
1895	Pit-N	14	49	12	15	2	0	0	4	7	1	.306	.404	.347	750	100	1	1			.962	-2	C-12/1-1,M	0.0
1896	Pit-N	33	120	9	26	4	1	0	16	5	8	.217	.248	.267	515	37	-11	0			.974	1	1-28/C-5,M	-0.9
Total	11	724	2706	392	667	79	28	5	265	170	127	.246	.305	.300	604	72	-95	127			.927	54	C-610/1-61,O-55R,2S	1.0

■ DENNY MACK

Mack, Dennis Joseph (b: Dennis Joseph McGee) b: 1851, Easton, Pa.
d: 4/10/1888, Wilkes-Barre, Pa. BR/TR, 5'7", 164 lbs. Deb: 5/6/1871 MU NA OF: (2-LF 1-CF 3-RF) Career OF: (2-LF 4-CF 1-RF)

YEAR	TM/L	G	AB	R	H	2B	3B	HR	RBI	BB	SO	AVG	OBP	SLG	OPS	OPS+	BR+	SB	CS	SBR	FA	FR	G/POS	TPR
1871	Rok-n	25	122	34	30	7	1	0	17	8	7	.246	.292	.320	612	79	-2	12	0	3	.936	0	*1-24/P-3,S-1,O-1L	0.1
1872	Ath-n	47	205	68	59	9	1	0	34	**23**	9	.288	.360	.341	701	116	5	9	5	0	.948	-3	1-26,S-21	0.2
1873	Phi-n	48	205	55	60	5	0	0	20	15	9	.293	.341	.317	658	93	-2	6	2	1	.936	2	*1-42/O-4R,S-3,2-1	0.1
1874	Phi-n	56	246	48	51	8	4	0	22	2	3	.207	.214	.272	486	53	-13	4	0	1	.900	-4	*1-56	-1.2
1876	StL-N	48	191	32	39	5	0	1	7	11	5	.204	.262	.261	523	79	-3				.886	-8	S-41/2-5,O-2(1-1-0)	-0.8
1880	Buf-N	17	59	5	12	0	0	0	3	5	7	.203	.266	.203	469	60	-2				.940	-1	S-16/2-1	-0.3
1882	Lou-a	72	264	41	48	3	1	0		16		.182	.229	.201	429	49	-13				.898	-3	S-49,2-24/O-5C,M	-1.2
1883	Pit-a	60	224	26	44	5	3	0		13		.196	.241	.246	486	59	-9				.844	4	S-38,1-25/2-1	-0.5
Total	4 n	176	778	205	200	29	6	0	93	48	28	.257	.300	.310	610	85	-12	31	7	4	.926	-4	1-148/S-25,O-5R,P2	-0.8
Total	4	197	738	104	143	13	4	1	10	45	12	.194	.244	.230	473	60	-27				.886	-8	S-144/2-31,1-25,O-7C	-2.8

■ EARLE MACK

Mack, Earle Thaddeus (b: Earle Thaddeus McGillicuddy)
b: 2/1/1890, Spencer, Mass. d: 2/4/67, Upper Darby Township, Pa. BL/TR, 5'8", 140 lbs. Deb: 10/5/10 FMC

YEAR	TM/L	G	AB	R	H	2B	3B	HR	RBI	BB	SO	AVG	OBP	SLG	OPS	OPS+	BR+	SB	CS	SBR	FA	FR	G/POS	TPR
1910	Phi-A	1	4	0	2	0	1	0	0	0		.500	.500	1.000	1500	372	1	0			1.000	-1	/C-1	0.1
1911	Phi-A	2	4	0	0	0	0	0	0	0		.000	.000	.000	0	-99	-1	0			.000	0	/3-2	-0.1
1914	Phi-A	2	8	0	0	0	0	0	1	0	0	.000	.000	.000	0	-99	-2	1			1.000	0	/1-2	-0.2
Total	3	5	16	0	2	0	1	0	1	0	0	.125	.125	.250	375	11	-2	1			1.000	-1	/1-2,3-2,C-1	-0.2

■ JOE MACK

Mack, Joseph John (b: Joseph John Maciarz) b: 1/4/12, Chicago, Ill. d: 12/19/98, Atlanta, Ga. BB/TL, 5'11.5", 185 lbs. Deb: 4/17/45

YEAR	TM/L	G	AB	R	H	2B	3B	HR	RBI	BB	SO	AVG	OBP	SLG	OPS	OPS+	BR+	SB	CS	SBR	FA	FR	G/POS	TPR
1945	Bos-N	66	260	30	60	13	1	3	44	34	39	.231	.320	.323	643	79	-7	1			.991	0	1-65	-1.0

■ REDDY MACK

Mack, Joseph (b: Joseph McNamara) b: 5/2/1866, Ireland d: 12/30/16, Newport, Ky. 5'8", 182 lbs. Deb: 9/16/1885

YEAR	TM/L	G	AB	R	H	2B	3B	HR	RBI	BB	SO	AVG	OBP	SLG	OPS	OPS+	BR+	SB	CS	SBR	FA	FR	G/POS	TPR
1885	Lou-a	11	41	7	10	1	0	0	5	2		.244	.295	.268	564	79	-1				.885	0	2-11	0.0
1886	Lou-a	137	483	82	118	23	11	1	56	68		.244	.342	.344	686	109	5	13			.900	6	*2-137	1.4
1887	Lou-a	128	561	117	230	23	8	1	69	83		.410	.415	.395	811	124	19	22			.912	5	*2-128	2.4
1888	Lou-a	112	446	77	97	13	5	3	34	52		.217	.320	.289	609	98	2	18			.907	4	*2-112	0.9
1889	Bal-a	136	519	84	125	24	7	1	87	60	69	.241	.329	.320	649	84	-11	23			.897	-11	*2-135/O-1(0-1-0)	-1.4
1890	Bal-a	26	95	14	27	3	5	0	11	10		.284	.370	.421	791	127	3	7			.932	1	2-26	0.4
Total	6	550	2145	381	607	87	36	6	262	275	69	.283	.352	.340	692	104	18	83			.905	5	2-549/O-1(0-1-0)	3.7

■ QUINN MACK

Mack, Quinn David b: 9/11/65, Los Angeles, Cal. BL/TL, 5'10", 185 lbs. Deb: 6/16/94 F

YEAR	TM/L	G	AB	R	H	2B	3B	HR	RBI	BB	SO	AVG	OBP	SLG	OPS	OPS+	BR+	SB	CS	SBR	FA	FR	G/POS	TPR
1994	Sea-A	5	21	1	5	3	0	0	2	1	3	.238	.273	.381	654	65	-1	2	0	0	1.000	-0	/O-4(3-1-0),D-1	-0.1

■ RAY MACK

Mack, Raymond James (b: Raymond James Mlckovsky) b: 8/31/16, Cleveland, Ohio d: 5/7/69, Bucyrus, Ohio BR/TR, 6', 200 lbs. Deb: 9/9/38

YEAR	TM/L	G	AB	R	H	2B	3B	HR	RBI	BB	SO	AVG	OBP	SLG	OPS	OPS+	BR+	SB	CS	SBR	FA	FR	G/POS	TPR
1938	Cle-A	2	6	2	2	0	1	0	2	0	1	.333	.333	.667	1000	147	0	0	0	0	1.000	2	/2-2	0.2
1939	Cle-A	36	112	12	17	4	1	1	6	12	19	.152	.240	.232	472	22	-14	0	2	-1	.976	2	2-34/3-1	-0.9
1940	Cle-A★	146	530	60	150	21	5	12	69	51	77	.283	.346	.409	755	98	-2	4	2	0	.965	-9	*2-146	-0.1
1941	Cle-A	145	500	54	114	22	4	9	44	54	69	.228	.303	.342	645	74	-20	8	4	0	.970	-5	*2-145	-1.5
1942	Cle-A	143	481	43	108	14	6	2	45	41	51	.225	.288	.291	579	67	-22	9	3	1	.969	-4	*2-143	-1.6
1943	Cle-A	153	545	56	120	25	2	7	62	47	61	.220	.285	.312	596	79	-16	8	3	1	.967	-2	*2-153	-1.0
1944	Cle-A	83	284	24	66	15	3	0	29	28	45	.232	.301	.306	608	77	-9	4	1	1	.951	10	2-83	0.7
1946	Cle-A	61	171	13	35	6	2	1	9	23	27	.205	.299	.281	580	67	-7	2	2	-0	.970	1	2-61	-0.4
1947	NY-A	1	0	0	0	0	0	0	0	0	0	—	—	—	—	—	0	0	0	0	.000	0	R	0.0
	Chi-N	21	78	9	17	6	0	2	12	5	15	.218	.274	.372	646	73	-3	0			.965	7	2-21	0.5
Total	9	791	2707	273	629	113	24	34	278	261	365	.232	.301	.330	631	76	-92	35	17		.966	3	2-788/3-1	-4.1

■ SHANE MACK

Mack, Shane Lee b: 12/7/63, Los Angeles, Cal. BR/TR, 6', 190 lbs. Deb: 5/25/87 F Career OF: (393-LF 358-CF 149-RF)

YEAR	TM/L	G	AB	R	H	2B	3B	HR	RBI	BB	SO	AVG	OBP	SLG	OPS	OPS+	BR+	SB	CS	SBR	FA	FR	G/POS	TPR
1987	SD-N	105	238	28	57	11	3	4	25	18	47	.239	.301	.361	663	77	-8	4	6	-1	.982	-8	O-91(0-90-2)	-1.8
1988	SD-N	56	119	13	29	3	0	0	12	14	21	.244	.338	.269	607	78	-3	5	1	1	.983	-3	O-55(9-46-6)	-0.6
1990	Min-A	125	313	50	102	10	4	8	44	29	69	.326	.392	.460	852	129	13	13	4	1	.988	1	*O-109(23-43-51)/D-4	1.3
1991	*Min-A	143	442	79	137	27	8	18	74	34	79	.310	.367	.529	897	139	22	13	9	-0	.977	-9	*O-140(48-36-81)/D-1	1.0
1992	Min-A	156	600	101	189	31	6	16	75	64	106	.315	.395	.467	861	136	30	26	14	1	.988	1	*O-155(150-9-4)	2.7
1993	Min-A	128	503	66	139	30	4	10	61	41	76	.276	.336	.412	747	99	-1	15	5	2	.986	14	*O-128(64-67-2)	1.3
1994	Min-A	81	303	55	101	21	2	15	61	32	51	.333	.408	.564	972	147	22	4	1	1	.990	1	O-75(66-24-0)/D-4	1.9
1997	Bos-A	60	130	13	41	7	0	3	17	9	24	.315	.373	.438	812	109	2	2	1	0	1.000	-7	O-45(3-43-0)/D-5	-0.5
1998	Oak-A	3	2	1	0	0	0	0	0	0	0	.000	.000	.000	0	-99	-1	0	0	0	.000	0	/H	-0.1

YEAR	TM/L	G	AB	R	H	2B	3B	HR	RBI	BB	SO	AVG	OBP	SLG	OPS	OPS+	BR+	SB	CS	SBR	FA	FR	G/POS	TPR
	KC-A	66	207	30	58	15	1	6	29	15	36	.280	.346	.449	796	102	1	8	2	1	.982	-2	O-32(30-0-3),D-21	-0.2
	Yr	69	209	31	58	15	1	6	29	15	36	.278	.343	.445	788	101	0	8	2	1	.982	-2	O-32(30-0-3),D-21	-0.3
Total	9	923	2857	436	853	155	28	80	398	256	509	.299	.367	.456	823	120	77	90	43	5	.985	-12	O-830L/D-35	5.0
■ PETE MACKANIN	Mackanin, Peter b: 8/1/51, Chicago, Ill. BR/TR, 6′2″, 190 lbs. Deb: 7/3/73 C Career OF: (4-LF 0-CF 1-RF)																							
1973	Tex-A	44	90	3	9	2	0	0	2	4	26	.100	.147	.122	270	-24	-15	0	0	0	.947	2	S-33,3-10	-1.1
1974	Tex-A	2	6	0	1	0	1	0	0	0	2	.167	.167	.500	667	88	-0	0	0	0	1.000	2	/S-2	0.2
1975	Mon-N	130	448	59	101	19	6	12	44	31	99	.225	.279	.375	654	77	-16	11	5	1	.966	18	*2-127/S-1,3-1	1.2
1976	Mon-N	114	380	36	85	15	2	8	33	15	66	.224	.257	.337	594	65	-18	6	2	1	.965	-2	*2-100/3-8,S-3,O-1L	-1.5
1977	Mon-N	55	85	9	19	2	2	1	6	4	17	.224	.258	.329	588	58	-5	3	1	0	1.000	3	/2-9,S-8,3-5,O-4L	-0.1
1978	Phi-N	5	8	0	2	0	0	0	1	0	4	.250	.250	.250	500	40	-1	0	0	0	1.000	0	/1-1,3-1	-0.1
1979	Phi-N	13	9	2	1	0	0	1	2	1	2	.111	.200	.444	644	69	-0	0	0	0	1.000	3	/2-2,S-2,3-2	0.2
1980	Min-A	108	319	31	85	18	0	4	35	14	34	.266	.297	.361	658	74	-12	6	2	1	.968	16	2-71,S-30/1-4,3D	1.0
1981	Min-A	77	225	21	52	7	1	4	18	7	40	.231	.258	.324	582	63	-11	1	2	-0	.980	-5	2-31,S-28,1-10,/3D	-1.4
Total	9	548	1570	161	355	63	12	30	141	76	290	.226	.265	.339	603	65	-78	27	12	2	.968	36	2-340,S-107/3-34,1DO	-1.6
■ ERIC MacKENZIE	Mac Kenzie, Eric Hugh b: 8/29/32, Glendon, Alberta, Can. BL/TR, 6′, 185 lbs. Deb: 4/23/55																							
1955	KC-A	1	1	0	0	0	0	0	0	0	0	.000	.000	.000	0	-99	-0	0	0	0	.000	0	/C-1	0.0
■ GORDON MacKENZIE	Mac Kenzie, Henry Gordon b: 7/9/37, St.Petersburg, Fla BR/TR, 5′11″, 175 lbs. Deb: 8/13/61 C																							
1961	KC-A	11	24	1	3	0	0	0	1	1	6	.125	.160	.125	285	-22	-4	0	0	0	1.000	-0	/C-7	-0.4
■ FELIX MACKIEWICZ	Mackiewicz, Felix Thaddeus b: 11/20/17, Chicago, Ill. d: 12/20/93, Olivette, Mo. BR/TR, 6′2″, 195 lbs. Deb: 9/7/41																							
1941	Phi-A	5	14	3	4	0	1	0	0	1	0	.286	.333	.429	762	103	0	0	0	0	1.000	-1	/O-3(0-1-2)	-0.1
1942	Phi-A	6	14	3	3	2	0	0	2	0	4	.214	.214	.357	571	59	-1	0	0	0	1.000	0	/O-3(0-2-1)	-0.1
1943	Phi-A	9	16	1	1	0	0	0	0	2	8	.063	.167	.063	229	-32	-3	0	0	0	1.000	0	/O-3(0-2-1)	-0.3
1945	Cle-A	120	359	42	98	14	7	2	37	44	41	.273	.356	.368	723	115	7	5	5	-1	.987	5	*O-112(0-112-0)	1.0
1946	Cle-A	78	258	35	67	15	4	0	16	16	32	.260	.305	.349	654	88	-5	5	1	1	.983	-2	O-72(0-71-1)	-0.8
1947	Cle-A	2	5	0	0	0	0	0	0	0	2	.000	.000	.000	0	-99	-1	0	0	0	1.000	-0	/O-2(0-2-0)	-0.2
	Was-A	3	6	1	1	1	0	0	0	0	1	.167	.167	.333	500	38	-1	0	0	0	1.000	-1	/O-3(0-3-0)	-0.2
	Yr	5	11	1	1	1	0	0	0	0	3	.091	.091	.182	273	-26	-2	0	0	0	1.000	-1	/O-5(0-5-0)	-0.4
Total	6	223	672	85	174	32	12	2	55	63	88	.259	.325	.351	676	97	-3	10	6	0	.986	2	O-198(0-193-5)	-0.7
■ STEVE MACKO	Macko, Steven Joseph b: 9/6/54, Burlington, Iowa d: 11/15/81, Arlington, Tex. BL/TR, 5′10″, 160 lbs. Deb: 8/18/79																							
1979	Chi-N	19	40	2	9	1	0	0	3	4	8	.225	.295	.250	545	46	-3	0	0	0	1.000	4	2-10/3-4	0.2
1980	Chi-N	6	20	2	6	2	0	0	2	0	3	.300	.300	.400	700	87	-0	0	0	0	1.000	1	/S-3,3-2,2-1	0.1
Total	2	25	60	4	15	3	0	0	5	4	11	.250	.297	.300	597	59	-3	0	0	0	1.000	6	/2-11,3-6,S-3	0.3
■ LONNIE MACLIN	Maclin, Lonnie Lee b: 2/17/67, Clayton, Mo. BL/TL, 5′11″, 185 lbs. Deb: 9/7/93																							
1993	StL-N	12	13	2	1	0	0	0	1	0	5	.077	.077	.077	154	-60	-3	1	0	0	1.000	-2	/O-5(5-0-0)	-0.4
■ MAX MACON	Macon, Max Cullen b: 10/14/15, Pensacola, Fla. d: 8/5/89, Jupiter, Fla. BL/TL, 6′3″, 175 lbs. Deb: 4/21/38 Career OF: (21-LF 2-CF 1-RF)																							
1938	StL-N	46	36	5	11	0	0	0	3	2	4	.306	.342	.306	648	75	-1	0			.946	0	P-38/O-1(0-0-1)	0.0
1940	Bro-N	2	1	0	1	0	0	0	0	0	0	1.000	1.000	1.000	2000	427	0	0			.000	-0	/P-2	0.0
1942	Bro-N	26	43	4	12	2	1	0	1	2	4	.279	.311	.372	683	98	-0	1			.960	-0	P-14	0.0
1943	Bro-N	45	55	7	9	0	0	0	6	0	1	.164	.164	.164	327	-5	-7	1			1.000	0	P-25/1-3	-0.2
1944	Bos-N	106	366	38	100	15	3	3	36	12	23	.273	.296	.355	651	79	-11	7			.977	-2	1-72,O-22(21-2-0)/P-1	-1.8
1947	Bos-N	1	1	0	0	0	0	0	0	0	0	.000	.000	.000	0	-99	-0	0			1.000	0	/P-1	0.0
Total	6	226	502	54	133	17	4	3	46	16	32	.265	.288	.333	620	72	-19	9			.965	-2	/P-81,1-75,O-23L	-2.0
■ WADDY MacPHEE	Mac Phee, Walter Scott b: 12/23/1899, Brooklyn, N.Y. d: 1/20/80, Charlotte, N.C. BR/TR, 5′8″, 140 lbs. Deb: 9/27/22																							
1922	NY-N	2	7	2	2	0	1	0	0	1	0	.286	.375	.571	946	140	0	0	0	0	.889	1	/3-2	0.1
■ JIMMY MACULLAR	Macullar, James F. "Little Mac" b: 1/16/1855, Boston, Mass. d: 4/8/24, Baltimore, Md. BR/TL, 5′6″, 155 lbs. Deb: 5/5/1879 MU Career OF: (3-LF 112-CF 9-RF)																							
1879	Syr-N	64	246	24	52	9	0	0	13	3	27	.211	.221	.248	469	61	-9				.864	1	S-37,O-26C/2-4,3M	-0.7
1882	Cin-a	79	299	44	70	6	6	0	22	14		.234	.268	.294	563	85	-5				.922	-0	*O-79(0-79-0)	-0.7
1883	Cin-a	14	48	4	8	2	0	0	4	4		.167	.231	.208	439	40	-3				.900	-4	O-14(2-6-7)/S-1	-0.6
1884	Bal-a	107	360	73	73	16	6	4		36		.203	.290	.314	603	93	-2				.866	1	*S-107	0.2
1885	Bal-a	100	320	52	61	7	6	3	26	49		.191	.306	.278	584	87	-3				.877	0	*S-98/O-2(0-0-2),P-1	0.1
1886	Bal-a	85	268	49	55	7	1	0	26	49		.205	.332	.239	571	82	-2	23			.852	-10	S-82/O-2L,2-1,P-1	-0.8
Total	6	449	1541	246	319	47	19	7	91	155	27	.207	.285	.276	561	83	-24	23			.865	-11	S-325,O-123C/2-5,P3	-2.5
■ GENE MADDEN	Madden, Eugene b: 6/5/1890, Elm Grove, W.Va. d: 4/6/49, Utica, N.Y. BL/TR, 5′10″, 155 lbs. Deb: 4/20/16																							
1916	Pit-N	1	1	0	0	0	0	0	0	0	0	.000	.000	.000	0	-99	-0	0			.000	0	H	0.0
■ FRANK MADDEN	Madden, Francis A. "Red" b: 10/17/1892, Pittsburgh, Pa. d: 4/30/52, Pittsburgh, Pa. Deb: 7/4/14																							
1914	Pit-F	2	2	0	1	0	0	0	1	0	0	.500	.500	.500	1000	174	0	0			.000	0	/C-1	0.0
■ BUNNY MADDEN	Madden, Thomas Francis b: 9/14/1882, Boston, Mass. d: 1/20/54, Cambridge, Mass. BR/TR, 5′10″, 190 lbs. Deb: 6/3/09																							
1909	Bos-A	10	17	0	4	0	0	0	1	0		.235	.235	.235	471	48	-1	0			.941	1	/C-7	0.1
1910	Bos-A	14	35	4	13	3	0	0	4	3		.371	.436	.457	893	175	3	0			.938	-3	C-12	0.1
1911	Bos-A	4	15	2	3	0	0	0	2	2		.200	.294	.200	494	39	-1	0			1.000	-2	/C-4	-0.3
	Phi-N	28	76	4	21	1	1	0	4	0	13	.276	.276	.316	592	65	-4	0			.924	3	C-22	0.1
Total	3	56	143	10	41	4	1	0	11	5	13	.287	.315	.329	644	87	-3	0			.935	-1	/C-45	-0.0
■ TOMMY MADDEN	Madden, Thomas Joseph b: 7/31/1883, Philadelphia, Pa. d: 7/26/30, Philadelphia, Pa. BL/TL, 5′11″, 160 lbs. Deb: 9/10/06																							
1906	Bos-N	4	15	1	4	0	0	0	0	1		.267	.313	.267	579	83	-0	0			1.000	-0	/O-4(4-0-0)	-0.1
1910	NY-A	1	1	0	0	0	0	0	0	0		.000	.000	.000	0	-95	-0	0			.000	-0	H	-0.1
Total	2	5	16	1	4	0	0	0	0	1		.250	.294	.250	544	71	-1	0			1.000	-1	/O-4(5-0-0)	-0.2
■ CLARENCE MADDERN	Maddern, Clarence James b: 9/26/21, Bisbee, Ariz. d: 8/9/86, Tucson, Ariz. BR/TR, 6′1″, 185 lbs. Deb: 9/19/46																							
1946	Chi-N	3	3	0	0	0	0	0	0	0	0	.000	.250	.000	250	-27	-0	0			1.000	-0	/O-2(2-0-0)	-0.1
1948	Chi-N	80	214	16	54	12	1	4	27	10	25	.252	.301	.374	675	85	-5	0			.981	-2	O-55(48-0-10)	-1.1
1949	Chi-N	10	9	1	3	0	0	1	2	2	0	.333	.455	.667	1121	202	1	0			1.000	0	/1-1	0.2
1951	Cle-A	11	12	0	2	0	0	0	0	0	1	.167	.167	.167	333	-10	-2	0	0	0	.667	-0	/O-1(1-0-0)	-0.2
Total	4	104	238	17	59	12	1	5	29	12	26	.248	.301	.370	671	84	-6	0	0		.973	-2	/O-58(51-0-10),1-1	-1.2
■ ELLIOTT MADDOX	Maddox, Elliott b: 12/21/47, East Orange, N.J. BR/TR, 5′11″, 181 lbs. Deb: 4/7/70 Career OF: (77-LF 472-CF 189-RF)																							
1970	Det-A	109	258	30	64	13	4	3	24	30	42	.248	.333	.364	698	92	-3	2	3	-1	.919	0	3-40,O-37L,S-19,/2	-0.4
1971	Was-A	128	258	38	56	8	2	1	18	51	42	.217	.346	.275	621	83	-4	10	4	1	.990	-3	*O-103(12-84-10),3-12	-0.9
1972	Tex-A	98	294	40	74	7	2	0	10	49	53	.252	.362	.289	651	100	2	20	10	1	.990	4	O-94(11-70-14)	0.4
1973	Tex-A	100	172	24	41	1	0	1	17	29	28	.238	.358	.262	619	80	-3	5	4	-0	.981	-7	O-89C/3-7,D-1	-1.3
1974	NY-A	137	466	75	141	26	2	3	45	69	48	.303	.397	.386	783	128	20	6	5	-0	.986	9	*O-135C/2-2,3-1	2.5
1975	NY-A	55	218	36	67	10	3	1	23	21	24	.307	.386	.394	781	123	8	9	3	1	1.000	8	O-55(0-55-0)/2-1	1.5
1976	*NY-A	18	46	4	10	2	0	0	3	4	3	.217	.280	.261	541	60	-2	0	1	-0	1.000	-1	O-13(0-6-7)/D-2	-0.4
1977	Bal-A	49	107	14	28	7	0	2	9	13	9	.262	.363	.383	746	110	2	2	2	-0	.990	-4	O-45(1-44-0)/3-1	-0.3
1978	NY-N	119	389	43	100	18	2	2	39	71	38	.257	.374	.329	704	102	4	2	11	-3	.988	-3	O-79R,3-43/1-1	-0.6
1979	NY-N	86	224	21	60	13	0	1	12	20	27	.268	.336	.339	675	88	-3	3	2	-0	.985	-1	O-65(2-26-40),3-11	-0.7
1980	NY-N	130	411	35	101	16	1	4	34	52	44	.246	.339	.319	658	87	-6	1	9	-3	.956	-3	*3-115/O-4(0-3-1),1-2	-1.4
Total	11	1029	2843	360	742	121	16	18	234	409	358	.261	.361	.334	694	100	16	60	54	-6	.989	-1	O-719C,3-230/S21D	-1.6

YEAR	TM/L	G	AB	R	H	2B	3B	HR	RBI	BB	SO	AVG	OBP	SLG	OPS	OPS+	BR+	SB	CS	SBR	FA	FR	G/POS	TPR
■ GARRY MADDOX	Maddox, Garry Lee b: 9/1/49, Cincinnati, Ohio BR/TR, 6'3", 184 lbs. Deb: 4/25/72																							
1972	SF-N	125	458	62	122	26	7	12	58	14	97	.266	.294	.432	726	103	-1	13	6	1	.979	4	*O-121(20-96-6)	0.0
1973	SF-N	144	587	81	187	30	10	11	76	24	73	.319	.352	.460	812	118	13	24	10	2	.969	8	*O-140(0-140-0)	2.0
1974	SF-N	135	538	74	153	31	3	8	50	29	64	.284	.325	.398	722	97	-3	21	9	1	.986	7	*O-131(0-131-0)	0.2
1975	SF-N	17	52	4	7	1	0	1	4	6	3	.135	.237	.212	449	24	-5	1	1	-0	1.000	3	O-13(0-13-0)	-0.3
	Phi-N	99	374	50	109	25	8	4	46	36	54	.291	.361	.433	795	115	8	24	3	4	.983	18	O-97(0-97-0)	2.8
	Yr	116	426	54	116	26	8	5	50	42	57	.272	.346	.406	752	104	2	25	4	4	.985	21	*O-110(0-110-0)	2.5
1976	*Phi-N	146	531	75	175	37	6	6	68	42	59	.330	.383	.456	839	133	23	29	12	2	.989	24	*O-144(0-144-0)	4.8
1977	*Phi-N	139	571	85	167	27	10	14	74	24	58	.292	.326	.448	774	101	-1	22	6	3	.977	14	*O-138(0-138-0)	1.5
1978	*Phi-N	155	598	62	172	34	3	11	68	39	89	.288	.333	.410	743	106	3	33	7	5	.983	21	*O-154(0-154-0)	2.9
1979	Phi-N	148	548	70	154	28	6	13	61	17	71	.281	.308	.425	733	95	-5	26	13	1	.996	**27**	*O-140(0-140-0)	2.2
1980	*Phi-N	143	549	59	142	31	3	11	73	18	52	.259	.282	.386	668	80	-16	25	5	4	.976	14	*O-143(0-143-0)	0.1
1981	*Phi-N	94	323	37	85	7	1	5	40	17	42	.263	.302	.337	640	78	-10	9	4	1	.977	9	O-94(0-93-0)	-0.1
1982	Phi-N	119	412	39	117	27	2	8	61	12	32	.284	.304	.417	722	98	-3	7	5	-0	**.992**	7	*O-111(0-111-0)	0.4
1983	*Phi-N	97	324	27	89	14	2	4	32	17	31	.275	.313	.367	680	89	-5	7	6	-1	.977	-0	O-95(0-95-0)	-0.7
1984	Phi-N	77	241	29	68	11	0	5	19	13	29	.282	.319	.390	709	97	-1	3	2	-0	1.000	0	O-69(0-69-0)	-0.2
1985	Phi-N	105	218	22	52	8	1	4	23	13	26	.239	.284	.339	624	72	-8	4	2	0	.980	-12	O-94(0-93-0)	-2.2
1986	Phi-N	6	7	1	3	0	0	0	1	2	1	.429	.556	.429	984	169	1	0	1	-0	1.000	-1	/O-3(0-3-0)	-0.1
Total	15	1749	6331	777	1802	337	62	117	754	323	781	.285	.323	.413	736	100	-10	248	92	22	.983	142	*O-1687(20-1660-6)	13.3
■ JERRY MADDOX	Maddox, Jerry Glenn b: 7/28/53, Whittier, Cal. BR/TR, 6'2", 200 lbs. Deb: 6/3/78																							
1978	Atl-N	7	14	1	3	0	0	0	1	1	2	.214	.267	.214	481	32	-1	0	0	0	.909	-0	/3-5	-0.2
■ ART MADISON	Madison, Arthur b: 1/14/1871, Clarksburg, Mass. d: 1/27/33, N.Adams, Mass. BR/TR, 5'9", 165 lbs. Deb: 9/9/1895																							
1895	Phi-N	11	34	6	12	3	0	0	8	1	1	.353	.371	.441	813	109	0	4			.955	-1	/S-6,2-3,3-2	0.0
1899	Pit-N	42	118	20	32	2	4	0	19	11		.271	.338	.356	694	91	-1	1			.953	-5	2-19,S-15/3-2	-0.4
Total	2	53	152	26	44	5	4	0	27	12	1	.289	.345	.375	720	95	-1	5			.926	-6	/2-22,S-21,3-4	-0.4
■ SCOTTI MADISON	Madison, Charles Scott b: 9/12/59, Pensacola, Fla. BB/TR, 5'11", 195 lbs. Deb: 7/6/85 Career OF: (2-LF 0-CF 1-RF)																							
1985	Det-A	6	11	0	0	0	0	0	1	2	0	.000	.154	.000	154	-54	-2	0	0	0	1.000	-0	/C-1,D-3	-0.2
1986	Det-A	2	7	0	0	0	0	0	1	0	3	.000	.000	.000	0	-99	-2	0	0	0	.667	-1	/3-1,D-1	-0.3
1987	KC-A	7	15	4	4	3	0	0	0	1	5	.267	.313	.467	779	100	-0	0	0	0	1.000	-1	/1-4,C-3	-0.1
1988	KC-A	16	35	4	6	2	0	0	2	4	5	.171	.256	.229	485	37	-3	1	0	0	1.000	-2	/C-4,O-3L,1-2,D-4	-0.4
1989	Cin-N	40	98	13	17	7	0	1	7	8	9	.173	.243	.276	519	46	-7	0	1	-0	1.000	2	3-26	-0.5
Total	5	71	166	21	27	12	0	1	11	15	22	.163	.236	.253	489	37	-14	1	1	-0	.985	-1	/3-27,D-8,C-8,1O	-1.5
■ ED MADJESKI	Madjeski, Edward William (b: Edward William Majewski) b: 7/20/08, Far Rockaway, N.Y d: 11/11/94, Montgomery, Ohio BR/TR, 5'11", 178 lbs. Deb: 5/2/32																							
1932	Phi-A	17	35	4	8	0	0	0	3	3	6	.229	.289	.229	518	35	-3	0	0	0	1.000	2	/C-8	-0.1
1933	Phi-A	51	142	17	40	4	0	0	17	4	21	.282	.301	.310	611	62	-8	0	0	0	.958	-4	C-41	-0.9
1934	Phi-A	8	8	1	3	1	0	0	2	0	1	.375	.375	.500	875	129	0	0	0	0	.000	-1	/C-1	0.0
	Chi-A	85	281	36	62	14	2	5	32	14	31	.221	.260	.338	598	52	-21	2	0	0	.973	2	C-79	-1.3
	Yr	93	289	37	65	15	2	5	34	14	32	.225	.263	.343	606	54	-21	2	0	0	.971	2	C-80	-1.3
1937	NY-N	5	15	0	3	0	0	0	2	0	2	.200	.200	.200	400	9	-2	0			1.000	-2	/C-5	-0.4
Total	4	166	481	58	116	19	2	5	56	21	61	.241	.274	.320	595	53	-34	2	0		.970	-2	C-134	-2.7
■ BILL MADLOCK	Madlock, Bill b: 1/2/51, Memphis, Tenn. BR/TR, 5'11", 185 lbs. Deb: 9/7/73 C																							
1973	Tex-A	21	77	16	27	5	3	1	5	7	9	.351	.412	.532	944	171	7	3	2	-0	.918	-6	3-21	0.1
1974	Chi-N	128	453	65	142	21	5	9	54	42	39	.313	.378	.442	820	124	14	11	7	-0	.946	-12	*3-121	0.2
1975	Chi-N★	130	514	77	182	29	7	7	64	42	34	**.354**	.406	.479	885	139	27	9	7	-0	.943	-11	*3-128	1.6
1976	Chi-N	142	514	68	174	36	1	15	84	56	27	**.339**	.415	.500	915	146	32	15	11	-1	.961	-20	*3-136	1.2
1977	SF-N	140	533	70	161	28	1	12	46	43	33	.302	.361	.426	787	111	8	13	10	-1	.949	-17	*3-126/2-6	-1.2
1978	SF-N	122	447	76	138	26	3	15	44	48	39	.309	.380	.481	861	145	26	16	5	2	.974	-24	*2-114/1-3	1.1
1979	SF-N	69	249	37	65	9	2	7	41	18	19	.261	.311	.398	708	99	-1	11	3	1	.976	-14	2-63/1-5	-1.1
	*Pit-N	85	311	48	102	17	3	7	44	34	22	.328	.396	.469	865	129	13	21	8	2	.969	-6	3-85	0.8
	Yr	154	560	85	167	26	5	14	85	52	41	.298	.359	.438	796	117	13	32	11	3	.969	-20	3-85,2-63/1-5	-0.3
1980	Pit-N	137	494	62	137	22	4	10	53	45	33	.277	.343	.399	741	105	3	16	10	0	.955	-17	*3-127,1-12	-1.7
1981	Pit-N★	82	279	35	95	23	1	6	45	34	17	**.341**	.418	.495	912	153	20	18	6	2	.956	-4	3-78	1.8
1982	Pit-N	154	568	92	181	33	3	19	95	48	39	.319	.376	.488	863	136	27	18	6	2	.952	-6	*3-146/1-3	2.1
1983	Pit-N★	130	473	68	153	21	0	12	68	49	24	**.323**	.389	.444	833	127	18	3	4	-1	.958	-14	*3-126	0.2
1984	Pit-N	103	403	38	102	16	0	4	44	26	29	.253	.300	.323	623	75	-14	3	1	0	.942	-8	3-98/1-1	-2.5
1985	Pit-N	110	399	49	100	23	1	10	41	39	42	.251	.325	.388	714	100	-0	3	3	-0	.940	-16	3-98,1-12	-1.9
	*LA-N	34	114	20	41	4	0	2	15	10	11	.360	.425	.447	873	149	8	7	1	1	.948	3	3-32	1.2
	Yr	144	513	69	141	27	1	12	56	49	53	.275	.347	.402	749	110	7	10	4	1	.943	-13	*3-130,1-12	-0.7
1986	LA-N	111	379	38	106	17	0	10	60	30	43	.280	.341	.404	744	112	6	3	3	-0	.910	-8	*3-101/1-2	-0.5
1987	LA-N	21	61	5	11	1	0	3	7	6	5	.180	.265	.344	609	61	-4	0	0	0	.912	-4	3-16/1-1	-0.8
	*Det-A	87	326	56	91	17	0	14	50	28	45	.279	.354	.460	815	119	9	4	3	-0	.989	-2	D-64,1-22/3-1	0.3
Total	15	1806	6594	920	2008	348	34	163	860	605	510	.305	.369	.442	811	123	201	174	90	7	.948	-185	*3-1440,2-183/D-64,1	0.9
■ SAL MADRID	Madrid, Salvador b: 6/9/20, ElPaso, Tex. d: 2/24/77, Ft.Wayne, Ind. BR/TR, 5'9", 165 lbs. Deb: 9/17/47																							
1947	Chi-N	8	24	0	3	1	0	0	1	1	6	.125	.160	.167	327	-14	-4	0			.956	4	/S-8	0.0
■ DAVE MAGADAN	Magadan, David Joseph b: 9/30/62, Tampa, Fla. BL/TR, 6'3", 200 lbs. Deb: 9/7/86																							
1986	NY-N	10	18	3	8	0	0	0	3	3	1	.444	.524	.444	968	175	2	0	0	0	1.000	1	/1-9	0.3
1987	NY-N	85	192	21	61	13	1	3	24	22	22	.318	.388	.443	831	126	8	0	0	0	.981	3	3-50,1-13	0.9
1988	*NY-N	112	314	39	87	15	0	1	35	60	39	.277	.396	.334	731	117	11	0	1	-0	.988	-1	1-71,3-48	0.6
1989	NY-N	127	374	47	107	22	3	4	41	49	37	.286	.370	.393	763	124	13	1	0	0	.991	3	1-87,3-28	1.1
1990	NY-N	144	451	74	148	28	6	6	72	74	55	.328	**.425**	.457	882	143	30	2	1	0	**.998**	3	*1-113,3-19	2.6
1991	NY-N	124	418	58	108	23	0	4	51	83	50	.258	.384	.342	726	106	8	1	1	-0	.996	2	*1-122	0.1
1992	NY-N	99	321	33	91	9	1	3	28	56	44	.283	.390	.346	736	111	8	1	0	0	.941	-13	3-93/1-2	-0.5
1993	Fla-N	66	227	22	65	12	0	4	29	44	30	.286	.404	.392	796	108	5	0	1	-0	.961	1	3-63/1-2	0.6
	Sea-A	71	228	27	59	11	0	1	21	36	33	.259	.360	.320	680	83	-4	2	0	0	.991	-1	1-41,3-27/D-2	-0.8
1994	Fla-N	74	211	30	58	7	0	1	17	39	25	.275	.390	.322	713	86	-2	0	0	0	.958	-5	3-48,1-16	-0.8
1995	Hou-N	127	348	44	109	24	0	2	51	71	56	.313	.430	.399	829	129	19	2	1	0	.922	-7	*3-100,1-11	1.2
1996	Chi-N	78	169	23	43	10	0	3	17	29	23	.254	.364	.367	731	91	-1	0	2	-1	.963	-7	3-51,1-10	-0.9
1997	Oak-A	128	271	38	82	10	1	4	30	50	40	.303	.415	.391	806	114	8	1	0	0	.940	0	3-49,1-30,D-25	0.6
1998	Oak-A	35	109	12	35	8	0	1	13	13	12	.321	.393	.422	815	115	3	0	1	-0	.918	2	3-30/1-7	0.4
1999	SD-N	116	248	20	68	12	1	2	30	45	36	.274	.386	.355	741	97	1	1	3	-1	.969	-3	3-52,1-42	-0.5
2000	SD-N	95	132	13	36	7	0	2	21	32	23	.273	.415	.371	786	107	3	0	0	0	.952	-1	3-29/1-8,S-2,D-2	0.2
Total	15	1491	4031	504	1165	211	13	41	483	706	526	.289	.396	.378	775	113	110	11	11	-1	.951	-22	3-687,1-584/D-29,S	5.1
■ EVER MAGALLANES	Magallanes, Everado (Espinoza) b: 11/6/65, Chihuahua, Mexico BL/TR, 5'10", 165 lbs. Deb: 5/17/91																							
1991	Cle-A	3	2	0	0	0	0	0	0	1	1	.000	.333	.000	333	1	-0	0	0	0	1.000	-1	/S-2	-0.1
■ LEE MAGEE	Magee, Leo Christopher (b: Leopold Christopher Hoernschemeyer) b: 6/4/1889, Cincinnati, Ohio d: 3/14/66, Columbus, Ohio BB/TR, 5'11", 165 lbs. Deb: 7/4/11 M Career OF: (230-LF 285-CF 8-RF)																							
1911	StL-N	26	69	9	18	1	1	0	8	8	8	.261	.338	.304	642	82	-1	4			.975	-2	2-18/S-3	-0.3
1912	StL-N	128	458	60	133	13	8	0	40	39	29	.290	.347	.354	701	94	-3	16			.956	7	O-85L,2-23/1-6,S-1	0.0
1913	StL-N	137	531	54	142	13	7	2	31	34	30	.267	.314	.330	643	85	-11	23			.982	13	*O-108L,2-22/1-6,S	-0.2
1914	StL-N	142	529	59	150	23	4	2	40	42	24	.284	.337	.353	691	107	4	36			.970	5	*O-102C,1-39/2-6	0.1
1915	Bro-F	121	452	87	146	19	10	4	49	22	19	.323	.356	.436	792	123	6	34			.937	-1	*2-115/1-2,M	0.7

YEAR	TM/L	G	AB	R	H	2B	3B	HR	RBI	BB	SO	AVG	OBP	SLG	OPS	OPS+	BR+	SB	CS	SBR	FA	FR	G/POS	TPR
1916	NY-A	131	510	57	131	18	4	3	45	50	31	.257	.324	.325	650	93	-4	29	25	-2	.975	4	*O-128(21-107-0)/2-2	-1.2
1917	NY-A	51	173	17	38	4	1	0	8	13	18	.220	.278	.254	532	62	-8	3			.938	-8	O-50(2-48-0)	-2.2
	StL-A	36	112	11	19	1	0	0	4	6	6	.170	.212	.179	390	20	-11	3			.971	6	3-20/2-6,1-5,O-1R	-0.5
	Yr	87	285	28	57	5	1	0	12	19	24	.200	.252	.225	477	46	-18	6			.938	-2	O-51C,3-20/2-6,1-5	-2.7
1918	Cin-N	119	459	61	133	22	13	0	28	28	19	.290	.331	.394	725	123	11	19			.956	9	*2-114/3-3	2.5
1919	Bro-N	45	181	16	43	7	2	0	7	5	8	.238	.262	.298	560	67	-8	5			.938	-1	2-36/3-9	-0.9
	Chi-N	79	267	36	78	12	4	1	17	18	16	.292	.339	.378	717	115	5	14			.978	-6	O-45C,S-13,3-10,/2	-0.3
	Yr	124	448	52	121	19	6	1	24	23	24	.270	.309	.346	655	95	-3	19			.978	-7	O-45C,2-43,3-19,S	-1.2
Total	9	1015	3741	467	1031	133	54	12	277	265	208	.276	.325	.350	675	98	-20	186	25		.969	27	O-519C,2-349/1-58,3S	-2.3

■ SHERRY MAGEE Magee, Sherwood Robert b: 8/6/1884, Clarendon, Pa. d: 3/13/29, Philadelphia, Pa. BR/TR, 5'11", 179 lbs. Deb: 6/29/04 U Career OF: (1601-LF 140-CF 125-RF)

YEAR	TM/L	G	AB	R	H	2B	3B	HR	RBI	BB	SO	AVG	OBP	SLG	OPS	OPS+	BR+	SB	CS	SBR	FA	FR	G/POS	TPR
1904	Phi-N	95	364	51	101	15	12	3	57	14		.277	.308	.409	717	125	9	11			.921	5	O-94(19-1-74)/1-1	0.9
1905	Phi-N	155	603	100	180	24	17	5	98	44		.299	.354	.420	774	135	25	48			.963	10	*O-155(155-0-0)	2.7
1906	Phi-N	154	563	77	159	36	8	6	67	52		.282	.348	.407	755	135	22	55			.982	11	*O-154(154-0-0)	2.6
1907	Phi-N	140	503	75	165	28	12	4	**85**	53		.328	.396	.455	852	169	40	46			.978	7	*O-139(139-0-0)	4.3
1908	Phi-N	143	508	79	144	30	16	2	57	49		.283	.359	.417	776	143	25	40			.970	2	*O-142(142-0-0)	2.1
1909	Phi-N	143	522	60	141	33	14	2	66	43		.270	.339	.398	737	128	16	38			.970	-6	*O-143(143-0-0)	0.1
1910	Phi-N	154	519	**110**	172	39	17	6	**123**	94	36	**.331**	**.445**	**.507**	**952**	**172**	**51**	49			.974	-13	*O-154(126-23-5)	3.1
1911	Phi-N	121	445	79	128	32	5	15	94	49	33	.288	.366	.483	849	135	19	22			**.981**	3	*O-120(120-0-1)	1.7
1912	Phi-N	132	464	79	142	25	9	6	66	55	54	.306	.388	.438	825	118	12	30			.963	-11	*O-124(124-0-0)/1-6	-0.5
1913	Phi-N	138	470	92	144	36	6	11	70	38	36	.306	.369	.479	848	136	21	23			.968	-10	*O-123(106-8-9)/1-4	0.5
1914	Phi-N	146	544	96	**171**	**39**	11	15	**103**	55	42	.314	.380	**.509**	890	154	34	25			.940	9	O-67L,S-39,1-32,/2	4.5
1915	Bos-N	156	571	72	160	34	12	2	87	54	39	.280	.350	.392	742	130	21	15	12	-1	.981	15	*O-135(34-102-0),1-21	2.9
1916	Bos-N	122	419	44	101	17	5	3	54	44	52	.241	.322	.327	649	104	3	10			.978	-5	*O-120L/1-2,S-1	-0.9
1917	Bos-N	72	246	24	63	8	4	1	29	13	23	.256	.302	.333	635	100	-0	7			.954	2	O-65(63-0-2)/1-2	-0.2
	Cin-N	45	137	17	44	8	4	0	23	16	7	.321	.400	.438	838	164	11	4			.989	4	O-41(29-0-12)/1-2	1.4
	Yr	117	383	41	107	16	8	1	52	29	30	.279	.338	.371	709	124	11	11			.967	6	*O-106(92-0-14)/1-4	1.2
1918	Cin-N	115	400	46	119	15	13	2	**76**	37	18	.298	.370	.415	785	142	20	14			.981	-2	1-66,O-38(34-2-1)/2-6	1.6
1919	*Cin-N	56	163	11	35	6	1	0	21	26	19	.215	.337	.264	601	84	-2	4			.990	-3	O-47(44-1-2)/2-1,3-1	-0.8
Total	16	2087	7441	1112	2169	425	166	83	1176	736	359	.291	.364	.427	790	137	325	441	12		.970	16	*O-1861L,1-136/S23	26.0

■ WENDELL MAGEE Magee, Wendell Errol b: 8/3/72, Hattiesburg, Miss. BR/TR, 6', 225 lbs. Deb: 8/16/96

YEAR	TM/L	G	AB	R	H	2B	3B	HR	RBI	BB	SO	AVG	OBP	SLG	OPS	OPS+	BR+	SB	CS	SBR	FA	FR	G/POS	TPR
1996	Phi-N	38	142	9	29	7	0	2	14	9	33	.204	.252	.296	547	43	-12	0	0	0	.978	3	O-37(6-18-18)	-1.0
1997	Phi-N	38	115	7	23	4	0	1	9	9	20	.200	.258	.261	519	36	-11	1	4	-1	.960	5	O-38(0-38-0)	-0.7
1998	Phi-N	20	75	9	22	6	1	1	11	7	11	.293	.354	.440	794	106	1	0	0	0	.941	0	O-19(19-0-0)	0.0
1999	Phi-N	12	14	4	5	1	0	2	5	1	4	.357	.400	.857	1257	201	2	0	0	0	1.000	-1	/O-4(1-2-1)	0.1
2000	Det-A	91	186	31	51	4	2	7	31	10	28	.274	.311	.430	741	88	-4	1	0	0	1.000	-13	O-76(18-5-56)/D-6	-1.7
Total	5	199	532	60	130	22	3	13	70	36	96	.244	.292	.370	663	71	-24	2	4	-1	.975	-5	O-174(44-63-75)/D-6	-3.3

■ HARL MAGGERT Maggert, Harl Vestin b: 2/13/1883, Cromwell, Ind. d: 1/7/63, Fresno, Cal. BL/TR, 5'8", 155 lbs. Deb: 9/4/07 F

YEAR	TM/L	G	AB	R	H	2B	3B	HR	RBI	BB	SO	AVG	OBP	SLG	OPS	OPS+	BR+	SB	CS	SBR	FA	FR	G/POS	TPR
1907	Pit-N	3	6	1	0	0	0	0	0	2		.000	.250	.000	250	-21	-1	1			1.000	0	/O-2(2-0-0)	-0.1
1912	Phi-A	74	242	39	62	8	6	1	13	36		.256	.357	.351	708	107	3	10			.939	-6	O-61(39-17-5)	-0.6
Total	2	77	248	40	62	8	6	1	13	38		.250	.354	.343	697	104	2	11			.942	-6	/O-63(41-17-5)	-0.7

■ HARL MAGGERT Maggert, Harl Warren b: 5/4/14, Los Angeles, Cal. d: 7/10/86, Citrus Heights, Cal. BR/TR, 6', 190 lbs. Deb: 4/19/38 F

YEAR	TM/L	G	AB	R	H	2B	3B	HR	RBI	BB	SO	AVG	OBP	SLG	OPS	OPS+	BR+	SB	CS	SBR	FA	FR	G/POS	TPR
1938	Bos-N	66	89	12	25	3	0	3	19	10	20	.281	.354	.416	769	123	3	0			.944	-0	O-10(8-0-2)/3-8	0.2

■ STUBBY MAGNER Magner, Edmund Burke b: 2/20/1888, Kalamazoo, Mich. d: 9/6/56, Chillicothe, Ohio BR/TR, 5'3", 135 lbs. Deb: 7/12/11

YEAR	TM/L	G	AB	R	H	2B	3B	HR	RBI	BB	SO	AVG	OBP	SLG	OPS	OPS+	BR+	SB	CS	SBR	FA	FR	G/POS	TPR
1911	NY-A	13	33	3	7	0	0	0	4	4		.212	.297	.212	509	40	-3	1			.970	-0	/S-6,2-5	-0.2

■ JOHN MAGNER Magner, John T. b: 1855, St.Louis, Mo. Deb: 7/14/1879 U

YEAR	TM/L	G	AB	R	H	2B	3B	HR	RBI	BB	SO	AVG	OBP	SLG	OPS	OPS+	BR+	SB	CS	SBR	FA	FR	G/POS	TPR
1879	Cin-N	1	4	0	0	0	0	0	1	0	1	.000	.000	.000	0	-99	-1				.500	-0	/O-1(0-1-0)	-0.1

■ GEORGE MAGOON Magoon, George Henry "Maggie" or "Topsy" b: 3/27/1875, St.Albans, Maine d: 12/6/43, Rochester, N.H. BR/TR, 5'10", 160 lbs. Deb: 6/29/1898

YEAR	TM/L	G	AB	R	H	2B	3B	HR	RBI	BB	SO	AVG	OBP	SLG	OPS	OPS+	BR+	SB	CS	SBR	FA	FR	G/POS	TPR
1898	Bro-N	93	343	35	77	7	0	1	39	30		.224	.293	.254	546	57	-19	7			.925	13	S-93	0.0
1899	Bal-N	62	207	26	53	8	3	0	31	26		.256	.353	.324	677	82	-5	7			.923	5	S-62	0.4
	Chi-N	59	189	24	43	5	1	0	21	24		.228	.333	.265	598	67	-7	5			.896	6	S-59	0.2
	Yr	121	396	50	96	13	4	0	52	50		.242	.344	.295	639	75	-12	12			.909	12	*S-121	0.6
1901	Cin-N	127	460	47	116	16	7	1	53	52		.252	.331	.324	655	97	-0	15			.919	-20	*S-112,2-15	-1.6
1902	Cin-N	45	162	29	44	9	2	0	23	13		.272	.344	.352	696	105	1	7			.930	4	2-41/S-3	0.6
1903	Cin-N	42	139	6	30	6	0	0	9	19		.216	.314	.259	573	58	-7	2			.971	5	2-32/3-9	-0.2
	Chi-A	94	334	32	76	11	3	0	25	30		.228	.303	.278	581	79	-7	4			.936	-21	2-94	-2.9
Total	5	522	1834	199	439	62	16	2	201	194		.239	.321	.294	615	78	-45	47			.916	-8	S-329,2-182/3-9	-3.5

■ TOM MAGRANN Magrann, Thomas Joseph b: 12/9/63, Hollywood, Fla. BR/TR, 6'3", 177 lbs. Deb: 9/7/89

YEAR	TM/L	G	AB	R	H	2B	3B	HR	RBI	BB	SO	AVG	OBP	SLG	OPS	OPS+	BR+	SB	CS	SBR	FA	FR	G/POS	TPR
1989	Cle-A	9	10	0	0	0	0	0	0	0	4	.000	.000	.000	0	-98	-3	0	0	0	1.000	3	/C-9	0.1

■ FREDDIE MAGUIRE Maguire, Frederick Edward b: 5/10/1899, Roxbury, Mass. d: 11/3/61, Boston, Mass. BR/TR, 5'11", 155 lbs. Deb: 9/22/22

YEAR	TM/L	G	AB	R	H	2B	3B	HR	RBI	BB	SO	AVG	OBP	SLG	OPS	OPS+	BR+	SB	CS	SBR	FA	FR	G/POS	TPR
1922	NY-N	5	12	4	4	0	0	0	1	0	1	.333	.333	.333	667	72	-0	1	0	0	.944	2	/2-3	0.1
1923	*NY-N	41	30	11	6	1	0	0	2	2	4	.200	.250	.233	483	29	-3	1	0	0	.881	12	2-16/3-1	0.9
1928	Chi-N	140	574	67	160	24	7	1	41	25	38	.279	.312	.350	662	74	-22	6			.976	**51**	*2-138	3.1
1929	Bos-N	138	496	54	125	26	8	0	41	19	40	.252	.284	.337	620	55	-36	8			.971	8	*2-138/S-1	-2.2
1930	Bos-N	146	516	54	138	21	5	0	52	20	22	.267	.297	.328	625	53	-40	4			.969	-4	*2-146	-3.5
1931	Bos-N	148	492	36	112	18	2	0	26	16	26	.228	.259	.272	532	45	-39	3			**.976**	9	*2-148	-2.0
Total	6	618	2120	226	545	90	22	1	163	82	131	.257	.289	.322	611	57	-140	23	0		.971	77	2-589/S-1,3-1	-3.6

■ JACK MAGUIRE Maguire, Jack b: 2/5/25, St.Louis, Mo. BR/TR, 5'11", 165 lbs. Deb: 4/18/50 Career OF: (30-LF 0-CF 13-RF)

YEAR	TM/L	G	AB	R	H	2B	3B	HR	RBI	BB	SO	AVG	OBP	SLG	OPS	OPS+	BR+	SB	CS	SBR	FA	FR	G/POS	TPR
1950	NY-N	29	40	3	7	2	0	0	3	3	13	.175	.233	.225	458	21	-5	0			1.000	1	/O-9(4-0-5),1-2	-0.4
1951	NY-N	16	20	6	8	1	1	1	4	2	2	.400	.455	.700	1155	204	3	0	0	0	1.000	-0	/O-8(0-0-8)	0.2
	Pit-N	8	5	1	0	0	0	0	0	1	0	.000	.167	.000	167	-50	-1	0	0	0	1.000	1	/2-1,3-1	0.0
	Yr	24	25	7	8	1	1	1	4	3	2	.320	.393	.560	953	151	2	0	0	0	1.000	0	/O-8(0-0-8),2-1,3-1	0.2
	StL-A	41	127	15	31	2	1	1	14	12	21	.244	.309	.299	609	63	-6	1	0	0	.969	-0	O-26(26-0-0)/3-5,2-2	-0.8
Total	2	94	192	25	46	5	2	2	21	18	36	.240	.305	.318	622	66	-9	1	0		.979	2	/O-43L,3-6,2-3,1-2	-1.0

■ JIM MAHADY Mahady, James Bernard b: 4/22/01, Cortland, N.Y. d: 8/9/36, Cortland, N.Y. BR/TR, 5'11", 170 lbs. Deb: 10/2/21

YEAR	TM/L	G	AB	R	H	2B	3B	HR	RBI	BB	SO	AVG	OBP	SLG	OPS	OPS+	BR+	SB	CS	SBR	FA	FR	G/POS	TPR
1921	NY-N	1	0	0	0	0	0	0	0	0	0	—	—	—	—	—	0	0	0	0	1.000	0	/2-1	0.0

■ ART MAHAN Mahan, Arthur Leo b: 6/8/13, Somerville, Mass. BL/TL, 5'11", 178 lbs. Deb: 4/30/40

YEAR	TM/L	G	AB	R	H	2B	3B	HR	RBI	BB	SO	AVG	OBP	SLG	OPS	OPS+	BR+	SB	CS	SBR	FA	FR	G/POS	TPR
1940	Phi-N	146	544	55	133	24	5	2	39	40	37	.244	.297	.318	615	73	-21	4			.992	4	*1-145/P-1	-3.0

■ FRANK MAHAR Mahar, Frank Edward b: 12/4/1878, Natick, Mass. d: 12/5/61, Somerville, Mass. TR, 5'10.5", Deb: 8/29/02

YEAR	TM/L	G	AB	R	H	2B	3B	HR	RBI	BB	SO	AVG	OBP	SLG	OPS	OPS+	BR+	SB	CS	SBR	FA	FR	G/POS	TPR
1902	Phi-N	1	1	0	0	0	0	0	0	0		.000	.000	.000	0	-99	-0	0			.000	0	H	0.0

■ BILLY MAHARG Maharg, William Joseph b: 3/19/1881, Philadelphia, Pa. d: 11/20/53, Philadelphia, Pa. BR/TR, 5'4.5", 155 lbs. Deb: 5/18/12

YEAR	TM/L	G	AB	R	H	2B	3B	HR	RBI	BB	SO	AVG	OBP	SLG	OPS	OPS+	BR+	SB	CS	SBR	FA	FR	G/POS	TPR
1912	Det-A	1	1	0	0	0	0	0	0	0		.000	.000	.000	0	-99	-0	0			1.000	1	/3-1	0.0
1916	Phi-N	1	1	0	0	0	0	0	0	0	0	.000	.000	.000	0	-97	-0	0			.000	-0	/O-1(0-0-1)	-0.1
Total	2	2	2	0	0	0	0	0	0	0	0	.000	.000	.000	0	-99	-0	0			—	0	/O-1(0-0-1),3-1	-0.1

■ RON MAHAY Mahay, Ronald Matthew b: 6/28/71, Crestwood, Ill. BL/TL, 6'2", 185 lbs. Deb: 5/21/95

YEAR	TM/L	G	AB	R	H	2B	3B	HR	RBI	BB	SO	AVG	OBP	SLG	OPS	OPS+	BR+	SB	CS	SBR	FA	FR	G/POS	TPR
1995	Bos-A	5	20	3	4	2	0	1	3	1	6	.200	.273	.450	723	81	-1	0	0	0	1.000	-1	/O-5(0-5-0)	-0.1
1997	Bos-A	28	0	0	0	0	0	0	0	0	0	—	—	—	—	—	0	0	0	0	1.000	-0	P-28	0.0
1998	Bos-A	29	0	0	0	0	0	0	0	0	0	—	—	—	—	—	0	0	0	0	.750	-1	P-29	0.0

YEAR	TM/L	G	AB	R	H	2B	3B	HR	RBI	BB	SO	AVG	OBP	SLG	OPS	OPS+	BR+	SB	CS	SBR	FA	FR	G/POS	TPR
1999	Oak-A	6	0	0	0	0	0	0	0	0	0	—	—	—	—	—	0	0	0	0	1.000	-0	/P-6	0.0
2000	Oak-A	5	0	0	0	0	0	0	0	0	0	—	—	—	—	—	0	0	0	0	1.000	-0	/P-5	0.0
	Fla-N	18	4	0	2	1	0	0	0	0	1	.500	.500	.750	1250	221	1	0	0	0	1.000	0	P-18	0.0
Total	5	91	24	3	6	3	0	1	3	1	7	.250	.308	.500	808	103	0	0	0	0	.941	-2	/P-86,O-5(0-5-0)	-0.1
■ TOM MAHER Maher, Thomas Francis b: 7/6/1870, Philadelphia, Pa. d: 8/25/29, Philadelphia, Pa. Deb: 4/24/02																								
1902	Phi-N	1	0	0	0	0	0	0	0	0		—	—	—	—	—	0	0			.000	0	R	0.0
■ GREG MAHLBERG Mahlberg, Gregory John b: 8/8/52, Milwaukee, Wis. BR/TR, 5'10", 180 lbs. Deb: 9/24/78																								
1978	Tex-A	1	1	0	0	0	0	0	0	0	0	.000	.000	.000	0	-99	-0	0	0	0	1.000	0	/C-1	0.0
1979	Tex-A	7	17	2	2	0	0	1	1	2	4	.118	.211	.294	505	35	-2	0	0	0	1.000	-2	/C-7	-0.3
Total	2	8	18	2	2	0	0	1	1	2	4	.111	.200	.278	478	28	-2	0	0	0	1.000	-2	/C-8	-0.3
■ DAN MAHONEY Mahoney, Daniel J. b: 3/20/1864, Springfield, Mass. d: 2/1/04, Springfield, Mass. BR/TR, 5'9.5", 165 lbs. Deb: 8/20/1892																								
1892	Cin-N	5	21	1	4	0	1	0	1	1	4	.190	.227	.286	513	56	-1	0			.943	2	/C-5	0.1
1895	Was-N	6	12	2	2	0	0	0	1	0	0	.167	.167	.167	333	-14	-2	0			1.000	-1	/C-2,1-1	-0.2
Total	2	11	33	3	6	0	1	0	2	1	4	.182	.206	.242	448	28	-3	0			.949	1	/C-7,1-1	-0.1
■ DANNY MAHONEY Mahoney, Daniel Joseph b: 9/6/1888, Haverhill, Mass. d: 9/28/60, Utica, N.Y. BR/TR, 5'6.5", 145 lbs. Deb: 5/15/11																								
1911	Cin-N	1	0	0	0	0	0	0	0	0	0	—	—	—	—	—	0	0			.000	0	R	0.0
■ MIKE MAHONEY Mahoney, George W. "Big Mike" b: 12/5/1873, Boston, Mass. d: 1/3/40, Boston, Mass. BR, 6'4", 220 lbs. Deb: 5/18/1897																								
1897	Bos-N	2	2	1	1	0	0	0	1	0		.500	.500	.500	1000	155	0	0			1.000	0	/C-1,P-1	0.0
1898	StL-N	2	7	0	0	0	0	0	0	0		.000	.000	.000	0	-98	-2	0			.920	-0	/1-2	-0.2
Total	2	4	9	1	1	0	0	0	1	0		.111	.111	.111	222	-36	-2	0			.920	-0	/1-2,P-1,C-1	-0.2
■ JIM MAHONEY Mahoney, James Thomas "Moe" b: 5/26/34, Englewood, N.J. BR/TR, 6', 175 lbs. Deb: 7/28/59 C																								
1959	Bos-A	31	23	10	3	0	0	1	4	3	7	.130	.231	.261	492	33	-2	0	0	0	.940	10	S-30	0.9
1961	Was-A	43	108	10	26	0	1	0	6	5	23	.241	.274	.259	534	44	-8	1	2	-0	.968	12	S-31/2-2	0.5
1962	Cle-A	41	74	12	18	4	0	3	5	3	14	.243	.273	.419	692	86	-2	0	0	0	.964	8	S-23/2-8,3-1	0.8
1965	Hou-N	5	5	0	1	0	0	0	0	0	3	.200	.200	.200	400	14	-1	0	0	0	1.000	0	/S-5	0.0
Total	4	120	210	32	48	4	1	4	15	11	47	.229	.267	.314	581	57	-13	1	2	-0	.962	31	/S-89,2-10,3-1	2.2
■ MIKE MAHONEY Mahoney, Michael John b: 12/5/72, Des Moines, Iowa BR/TR, 6'1", 200 lbs. Deb: 9/8/2000																								
2000	Chi-N	4	7	1	2	1	0	0	1	1	0	.286	.444	.429	873	125	0	0	0	0	1.000	-2	/C-4	-0.1
■ BOB MAIER Maier, Robert Phillip b: 9/5/15, Dunellen, N.J. d: 8/4/93, S.Plainfield, N.J. BR/TR, 5'8", 180 lbs. Deb: 4/17/45																								
1945	*Det-A	132	486	58	128	25	7	1	34	38	32	.263	.317	.350	667	88	-8	7	11	-2	.936	-13	*3-124/O-5(5-0-0)	-2.4
■ EMIL MAILHO Mailho, Emil Pierre "Lefty" b: 12/16/09, Berkeley, Cal. BL/TL, 5'10", 165 lbs. Deb: 4/14/36																								
1936	Phi-A	21	18	5	1	0	0	0	0	5	3	.056	.261	.056	316	-18	-3	0	0	0	1.000	-0	/O-1(1-0-0)	-0.3
■ CHARLIE MAISEL Maisel, Charles Louis b: 4/21/1894, Catonsville, Md. d: 8/25/53, Baltimore, Md. BR/TR, 6', Deb: 10/2/15																								
1915	Bal-F	1	4	0	0	0	0	0	0	0	0	.000	.000	.000	0	-97	-1	0			1.000	0	/C-1	-0.1
■ FRITZ MAISEL Maisel, Frederick Charles "Flash" b: 12/23/1889, Catonsville, Md. d: 4/22/67, Baltimore, Md. BR/TR, 5'7.5", 170 lbs. Deb: 8/11/13 F Career OF: (0-LF 26-CF 1-RF)																								
1913	NY-A	51	187	33	48	4	3	0	12	34	20	.257	.371	.310	681	99	1	25			.950	-5	3-51	-0.2
1914	NY-A	150	548	78	131	23	9	2	47	76	69	.239	.334	.325	659	98	0	**74**	17	**10**	.928	-18	*3-148	-0.4
1915	NY-A	135	530	77	149	16	6	4	46	48	35	.281	.342	.357	699	109	5	51	12	7	.940	-9	*3-134	0.7
1916	NY-A	53	158	18	36	5	0	0	7	20	18	.228	.318	.259	578	72	-5	4			.980	-5	O-26(0-26-0),3-11/2-4	-1.3
1917	NY-A	113	404	46	80	4	4	0	20	36	18	.198	.267	.228	495	51	-23	29			.967	-1	*2-100/3-7	-2.6
1918	StL-A	90	284	43	66	4	2	0	16	46	17	.232	.341	.261	602	84	-3	11			.949	-4	3-79/O-1(0-0-1)	-0.6
Total	6	592	2111	295	510	56	24	6	148	260	177	.242	.327	.299	626	88	-25	194	29		.938	-44	3-430,2-104/O-27C	-4.4
■ GEORGE MAISEL Maisel, George John b: 3/12/1892, Catonsville, Md. d: 11/20/68, Baltimore, Md. BR/TR, 5'10.5", 180 lbs. Deb: 5/1/13 F																								
1913	StL-A	11	18	2	3	2	0	0	1	1	7	.167	.211	.278	488	44	-1	0			.833	-2	/O-5(2-3-0)	-0.4
1916	Det-A	8	5	2	0	0	0	0	0	0	2	.000	.000	.000	0	-97	-1	0			.857	2	/3-3	0.1
1921	Chi-N	111	393	54	122	7	2	0	43	11	13	.310	.334	.338	673	78	-12	17	7	1	.978	0	*O-108(0-107-1)	-1.4
1922	Chi-N	38	84	9	16	1	1	0	6	8	2	.190	.261	.226	487	26	-9	1	3	-1	1.000	-2	O-26(2-13-11)	-1.3
Total	4	168	500	67	141	10	3	0	50	20	24	.282	.314	.314	628	66	-23	18	10		.979	-2	O-139(4-123-12)/3-3	-3.0
■ HANK MAJESKI Majeski, Henry "Heeney" b: 12/13/16, Staten Island, N.Y d: 8/9/91, Staten Island, N.Y. BR/TR, 5'9", 180 lbs. Deb: 5/17/39 Career OF: (1-LF 0-CF 0-RF)																								
1939	Bos-N	106	367	35	100	16	1	7	54	18	30	.272	.310	.379	689	91	-6	2			.945	12	3-99	0.9
1940	Bos-N	3	3	0	0	0	0	0	0	0	0	.000	.000	.000	0	-99	-1	0			.000	0	H	-0.1
1941	Bos-N	19	55	5	8	5	0	0	3	1	13	.145	.161	.236	397	11	-7	0			.911	1	3-11	-0.6
1946	NY-A	8	12	1	1	0	1	0	0	0	3	.083	.083	.250	333	-9	-2	0	0	0	.750	-1	/3-2	-0.3
	Phi-A	78	264	25	66	14	3	1	25	26	13	.250	.320	.337	657	84	-6	3	2	-0	.967	8	3-72	0.2
	Yr	86	276	26	67	14	4	1	25	26	16	.243	.310	.333	644	80	-7	3	2	-0	.964	7	3-74	-0.1
1947	Phi-A	141	479	54	134	26	5	8	72	53	31	.280	.358	.405	763	110	6	1	0	0	**.988**	7	*3-134/S-4,2-1	1.4
1948	Phi-A	148	590	88	183	41	4	12	120	48	43	.310	.368	.454	822	118	13	2	1	0	**.975**	1	*3-142/S-8	1.4
1949	Phi-A	114	448	62	124	26	5	9	67	29	23	.277	.326	.417	744	99	-3	0	1	-0	.957	-4	*3-113	-0.8
1950	Chi-A	122	414	47	128	18	2	6	46	42	34	.309	.377	.406	783	103	2	1	4	-1	.970	10	*3-112	1.0
1951	Chi-A	12	35	4	9	4	0	0	6	1	0	.257	.278	.371	649	76	-1	0	0	0	.950	-0	/3-9	-0.1
	Phi-A	89	323	41	92	19	4	5	42	35	24	.285	.358	.415	773	106	3	1	2	-0	.974	14	3-88	1.5
	Yr	101	358	45	101	23	4	5	48	36	24	.282	.351	.411	762	104	2	1	2	-0	.972	14	3-97	1.4
1952	Phi-A	34	117	14	30	2	2	2	20	19	10	.256	.365	.359	724	96	-0	0	1	-0	.976	4	3-34	0.4
	Cle-A	36	54	7	16	2	0	0	9	7	7	.296	.377	.333	710	106	1	0	0	0	.913	-0	3-11/2-3	0.1
	Yr	70	171	21	46	4	2	2	29	26	17	.269	.369	.351	720	101	1	0	1	-0	.966	4	3-45/2-3	0.5
1953	Cle-A	50	50	6	15	1	0	2	12	3	8	.300	.352	.440	792	116	1	0	0	0	1.000	-2	2-10/3-7,O-1(1-0-0)	-0.1
1954	*Cle-A	57	121	10	34	4	0	3	17	7	14	.281	.320	.388	709	92	-2	0	0	0	.990	4	2-25,3-10	0.4
1955	Cle-A	36	48	3	9	2	0	2	6	8	3	.188	.328	.354	682	80	-1	0	0	0	1.000	-2	/3-9,2-4	-0.3
	Bal-A	16	41	2	7	1	0	0	2	2	4	.171	.209	.195	404	10	-5	0	0	0	1.000	-3	/3-8,2-5	-0.8
	Yr	52	89	5	16	3	0	2	8	10	7	.180	.277	.281	558	50	-6	0	0	0	1.000	-5	3-17/2-9	-1.1
Total	13	1069	3421	404	956	181	27	57	501	299	260	.279	.342	.398	740	100	-8	10	11		.968	49	3-861/2-48,S-12,O-1L	4.2
■ MIKE MAKSUDIAN Maksudian, Michael Bryant b: 5/28/66, Belleville, Ill. BL/TR, 5'11", 220 lbs. Deb: 9/2/92																								
1992	Tor-A	3	3	0	0	0	0	0	0	0	0	.000	.000	.000	0	-96	-1	0	0	0	.000	0	/1-1	-0.1
1993	Min-A	5	12	2	2	1	0	0	2	4	2	.167	.375	.250	625	71	-0	0	0	0	1.000	1	/1-4,3-1	0.0
1994	Chi-N	26	26	6	7	2	0	0	4	10	4	.269	.472	.346	818	120	2	0	1	-0	1.000	-0	/1-3,C-2,3-2	0.1
Total	3	34	41	8	9	3	0	0	6	14	6	.220	.418	.293	711	92	1	0	1	-0	1.000	1	/1-8,3-3,C-2	0.0
■ JOSE MALAVE Malave, Jose Francisco b: 5/31/71, Cumana, Venez. BR/TR, 6'2", 212 lbs. Deb: 5/23/96																								
1996	Bos-A	41	102	12	24	3	0	4	17	2	25	.235	.257	.382	639	58	-7	0	0	0	.978	-6	O-38(8-0-30)	-1.3
1997	Bos-A	4	4	0	0	0	0	0	0	0	2	.000	.000	.000	0	-98	-1	0	0	0	1.000	-1	/O-4(4-0-0)	-0.2
Total	2	45	106	12	24	3	0	4	17	2	27	.226	.248	.368	616	52	-8	0	0	0	.979	-7	/O-42(12-0-30)	-1.5
■ CHARLIE MALAY Malay, Charles Francis b: 6/13/1879, Brooklyn, N.Y. d: 9/18/49, Brooklyn, N.Y. BB/TR, 5'11.5", 175 lbs. Deb: 4/24/05 F																								
1905	Bro-N	102	349	33	88	7	2	1	31	22		.252	.300	.292	593	83	-7	13			.932	-9	2-75,O-25(1-23-1)/S-1	-1.8
■ JOE MALAY Malay, Joseph Charles b: 10/25/05, Brooklyn, N.Y. d: 3/19/89, Bridgeport, Conn. BL/TL, 6', 175 lbs. Deb: 9/7/33 F																								
1933	NY-N	8	24	0	3	0	0	0	2	0	0	.125	.125	.125	250	-29	-4	0			1.000	2	/1-8	-0.3

YEAR	TM/L	G	AB	R	H	2B	3B	HR	RBI	BB	SO	AVG	OBP	SLG	OPS	OPS+	BR+	SB	CS	SBR	FA	FR	G/POS	TPR
1935	NY-N	1	1	0	1	0	0	0	0	0	0	1.000	1.000	1.000	2000	447	0	0			.000	0	H	0.0
Total	2	9	25	0	4	0	0	0	2	0	0	.160	.160	.160	320	-9	-3	0			1.000	2	/1-8	-0.3
■ CANDY MALDONADO	Maldonado, Candido (Guadarrama) b: 9/5/60, Humacao, P.R. BR/TR, 6', 190 lbs. Deb: 9/7/81 Career OF: (489-LF 97-CF 688-RF)																							
1981	LA-N	11	12	0	1	0	0	0	0	0	5	.083	.083	.083	167	-55	-2	0	0	0	1.000	-2	/O-9(4-0-5)	-0.5
1982	LA-N	6	4	0	0	0	0	0	0	1	2	.000	.200	.000	200	-41	-1	0	0	0	1.000	-1	/O-3(3-0-1)	-0.1
1983	*LA-N	42	62	5	12	1	1	1	6	5	14	.194	.254	.290	544	51	-4	0	0	0	1.000	-8	O-33(12-3-19)	-1.3
1984	LA-N	116	254	25	68	14	0	5	28	19	29	.268	.321	.382	703	98	-1	0	3	-1	.955	-16	*O-102(7-31-67)/3-4	-2.2
1985	*LA-N	121	213	20	48	7	1	5	19	19	40	.225	.289	.338	627	77	-7	1	1	-0	.984	-22	*O-113(44-57-24)	-3.3
1986	SF-N	133	405	49	102	31	3	18	85	20	77	.252	.292	.477	769	114	5	4	4	-1	.983	-4	*O-101(47-6-62)/3-1	-0.4
1987	*SF-N	118	442	69	129	28	4	20	85	34	78	.292	.351	.509	860	131	18	8	8	-1	.973	-6	*O-116(4-0-115)	0.5
1988	SF-N	142	499	53	127	23	1	12	68	37	89	.255	.315	.377	692	102	1	6	5	-0	.962	-3	*O-139(0-0-139)	-0.7
1989	*SF-N	129	345	39	75	23	0	9	41	37	69	.217	.299	.362	661	91	-5	4	1	1	.974	-6	*O-116(0-0-116)	-1.4
1990	Cle-A	155	590	76	161	32	2	22	95	49	134	.273	.334	.446	780	117	12	3	5	-1	.993	7	*O-134(104-0-41),D-20	1.3
1991	Mil-A	34	111	11	23	6	0	5	20	13	23	.207	.290	.396	687	90	-2	1	0	0	.976	-2	O-24(12-0-13)	-0.5
	*Tor-A	52	177	26	49	9	0	7	28	23	53	.277	.379	.446	825	123	6	3	0	1	.990	0	O-52(52-0-1)/D-9	0.6
	Yr	86	288	37	72	15	0	12	48	36	76	.250	.345	.427	773	111	5	4	0	1	.986	-2	O-76(64-0-14)/D-9	0.1
1992	*Tor-A	137	489	64	133	25	4	20	66	59	112	.272	.359	.462	821	123	15	2	2	-0	.978	5	*O-132(129-0-4)/D-4	1.6
1993	Chi-N	70	140	8	26	5	0	3	15	13	40	.186	.260	.286	545	47	-11	0	0	0	.914	-5	O-41(29-0-14)	-1.7
	Cle-A	28	81	11	20	2	0	5	20	11	18	.247	.337	.457	794	112	1	0	1	-0	.976	-3	O-26(2-0-25)/D-2	-0.3
1994	Cle-A	42	92	14	18	5	1	5	12	19	31	.196	.333	.435	768	96	-1	1	1	-0	1.000	-1	D-25/O-5(5-0-0)	-0.3
1995	Tor-A	61	160	22	43	13	0	7	25	25	45	.269	.374	.481	856	121	5	1	1	-0	.988	-8	O-58(26-0-38)/D-1	-0.4
	Tex-A	13	30	6	7	3	0	2	5	7	5	.233	.378	.533	912	131	1	0	1	-0	1.000	-0	O-11(9-0-4)	0.0
	Yr	74	190	28	50	16	0	9	30	32	50	.263	.375	.489	864	123	7	1	2	-0	.990	-8	O-69(35-0-42)/D-1	-0.4
Total	15	1410	4106	498	1042	227	17	146	618	391	864	.254	.325	.424	749	107	31	34	33	-4	.977	-74	*O-1215R/D-61,3-5	-9.1
■ JIM MALER	Maler, James Michael b: 8/16/58, New York, N.Y. BR/TR, 6'4", 230 lbs. Deb: 9/3/81																							
1981	Sea-A	12	23	1	8	1	0	0	2	2	1	.348	.423	.391	814	131	1	1	0	0	1.000	-0	/1-5,D-2	0.1
1982	Sea-A	64	221	18	50	8	3	4	26	12	35	.226	.275	.344	619	67	-10	0	0	0	.991	3	1-57/D-5	-1.1
1983	Sea-A	26	66	5	12	1	0	1	3	5	11	.182	.260	.242	503	38	-6	0	3	-1	1.000	0	1-19/D-5	-0.8
Total	3	102	310	24	70	10	3	5	31	19	47	.226	.284	.326	609	65	-15	1	3	-1	.994	3	/1-81,D-12	-1.8
■ TONY MALINOSKY	Malinosky, Anthony Francis b: 10/5/09, Collinsville, Ill. BR/TR, 5'10.5", 165 lbs. Deb: 4/26/37																							
1937	Bro-N	35	79	7	18	2	0	0	3	9	11	.228	.307	.253	560	53	-5	0			.833	-9	3-13,S-11	-1.4
■ BOBBY MALKMUS	Malkmus, Robert Edward b: 7/4/31, Newark, N.J. BR/TR, 5'9", 180 lbs. Deb: 6/1/57																							
1957	Mil-N	13	22	6	2	0	1	0	0	3	3	.091	.200	.182	382	4	-3	0	0	0	.972	4	/2-7	0.1
1958	Was-A	41	70	5	13	2	1	0	3	4	15	.186	.230	.243	473	31	-7	0	0	0	.964	8	2-26/3-2,S-1	0.2
1959	Was-A	6	0	0	0	0	0	0	0	0	0	—	—	—	—	—	0	0	0	0	.000	0	R	0.0
1960	Phi-N	79	133	16	28	4	1	1	12	11	28	.211	.271	.278	549	51	-9	2	2	-0	1.000	7	S-29,2-23,3-12	-0.1
1961	Phi-N	121	342	39	79	8	2	7	31	20	43	.231	.277	.327	605	61	-20	1	3	-1	.988	16	2-58,S-34,3-25	0.3
1962	Phi-N	8	5	3	1	1	0	0	0	0	1	.200	.200	.400	600	58	-0	0	0	0	1.000	2	/S-1	0.2
Total	6	268	572	69	123	15	5	8	46	38	90	.215	.266	.301	567	53	-39	3	5	-1	.982	36	2-114/S-65,3-39	0.7
■ JERRY MALLETT	Mallett, Gerald Gordon b: 9/18/35, Bonne Terre, Mo. BR/TR, 6'5", 208 lbs. Deb: 9/19/59																							
1959	Bos-A	4	15	1	4	0	0	0	1	1	3	.267	.313	.267	579	58	-1	0	0	0	1.000	3	/O-4(0-4-0)	0.2
■ LES MALLON	Mallon, Leslie Clyde b: 11/21/05, Sweetwater, Tex. d: 4/17/91, Granbury, Tex. BR/TR, 5'8", 160 lbs. Deb: 4/14/31 Career OF: (0-LF 0-CF 1-RF)																							
1931	Phi-N	122	375	41	116	19	2	1	45	29	40	.309	.359	.379	738	91	-4	0			.956	6	2-97/1-5,S-3,3-3	0.8
1932	Phi-N	103	347	44	90	16	0	5	31	28	28	.259	.318	.349	667	71	-14	1			.955	-31	2-88/3-5	-3.9
1934	Bos-N	42	166	23	49	6	1	0	18	15	12	.295	.354	.343	697	95	-1	0			.967	-4	2-42	-0.2
1935	Bos-N	116	412	48	113	24	2	2	25	28	37	.274	.322	.357	679	89	-6	3			.975	-14	2-73,3-36/O-1(0-0-1)	-1.4
Total	4	383	1300	156	368	65	5	8	119	100	117	.283	.336	.359	695	85	-24	4			.962	-43	2-300/3-44,1-5,SO	-4.7
■ BEN MALLONEE	Mallonee, Howard Bennett "Lefty" b: 3/31/1894, Baltimore, Md. d: 2/19/78, Baltimore, Md. BL/TL, 5'6", 150 lbs. Deb: 9/14/21																							
1921	Phi-A	7	25	2	6	1	0	0	4	1	2	.240	.269	.280	549	40	-2	1	0	0	1.000	0	/O-6(0-6-0)	-0.2
■ JULE MALLONEE	Mallonee, Julius Norris b: 4/4/1900, Charlotte, N.C. d: 12/26/34, Charlotte, N.C. BL/TR, 6'2", 180 lbs. Deb: 8/4/25																							
1925	Chi-A	2	3	1	0	0	0	0	0	1	0	.000	.250	.000	250	-34	-1	0	0	0	1.000	-0	/O-1(0-1-0)	-0.1
■ JIM MALLORY	Mallory, James Baugh "Sunny Jim" b: 9/1/18, Lawrenceville, Va. BR/TR, 6'1", 170 lbs. Deb: 9/8/40																							
1940	Was-A	4	12	2	2	0	0	0	0	1	1	.167	.231	.167	397	5	-2	0	0	0	1.000	1	/O-3(1-1-1)	-0.1
1945	StL-N	13	43	3	10	2	0	0	5	0	2	.233	.233	.279	512	41	-4	0			.923	-2	O-11(8-3-2)	-0.6
	NY-N	37	94	10	28	1	0	0	9	6	7	.298	.340	.309	649	80	-2	1			.979	-0	O-21(8-9-4)	-0.4
	Yr	50	137	13	38	3	0	0	14	6	9	.277	.308	.299	607	68	-6	1			.959	-2	O-32(16-12-6)	-1.0
Total	2	54	149	15	40	3	0	0	14	7	10	.268	.301	.289	590	63	-8	1	0		.964	-1	/O-35(17-13-7)	-1.1
■ SHELDON MALLORY	Mallory, Sheldon b: 7/16/53, Argo, Ill. BL/TL, 6'2", 175 lbs. Deb: 4/10/77																							
1977	Oak-A	64	126	19	27	4	1	0	5	11	18	.214	.293	.262	555	53	-8	12	5	1	.977	-3	O-45(9-17-21)/1-4,D-7	-1.1
■ MARTY MALLOY	Malloy, Marty Thomas b: 4/6/72, Gainesville, Fla. BL/TR, 5'10", 160 lbs. Deb: 9/6/98																							
1998	*Atl-N	11	28	3	5	1	0	1	1	2	2	.179	.233	.321	555	44	-2	0	0	0	1.000	2	2-10	0.0
■ HARRY MALMBERG	Malmberg, Harry William "Swede" b: 7/31/26, Fairfield, Ala. d: 10/29/76, San Francisco, Cal BR/TR, 6'1", 170 lbs. Deb: 4/12/55 C																							
1955	Det-A	67	208	25	45	5	2	0	19	29	19	.216	.312	.260	572	56	-12	0	1	-0	.985	6	2-65	-0.2
■ EDDIE MALONE	Malone, Edward Russell b: 6/16/20, Chicago, Ill. BR/TR, 5'10", 175 lbs. Deb: 7/17/49																							
1949	Chi-A	55	170	17	46	7	2	1	16	29	19	.271	.377	.353	730	97	0	2	1	0	.990	-3	C-51	-0.1
1950	Chi-A	31	71	2	16	2	0	0	10	10	8	.225	.321	.254	575	50	-5	0	0	0	1.000	2	C-21	-0.2
Total	2	86	241	19	62	9	2	1	26	39	27	.257	.361	.324	684	83	-5	2	1	0	.993	-2	/C-72	-0.3
■ FERGY MALONE	Malone, Ferguson G. b: 1842, Ireland d: 1/1/05, Seattle, Wash. BR/TL, 5'8", 156 lbs. Deb: 6/3/1871 MU NA OF: (0-LF 2-CF 0-RF)																							
1871	Ath-n	27	134	33	46	7	1	1	33	9	4	.343	.385	.433	817	136	7	9	3	1	.856	9	*C-27	1.1
1872	Ath-n	41	213	46	60	5	3	0	39	4	5	.282	.295	.333	628	92	-2	3	0	1	**.884**	4	C-24,1-17	0.2
1873	Phi-n	53	259	59	75	11	2	0	43	14	7	.290	.326	.347	673	97	-1	2	1	0	.898	5	*C-53/S-1,M	0.2
1874	Chi-n	47	223	33	56	5	0	0	28	4	0	.251	.264	.274	538	72	-7	2	1	0	.820	4	*C-47,M	-0.2
1875	Phi-n	29	123	15	28	2	1	0	10	1	2	.228	.234	.260	494	69	-4	1	0	0	.919	-3	1-22/C-6,O-2(0-2-0)	-0.5
1876	Phi-N	22	96	14	22	2	0	0	6	0	1	.229	.229	.250	479	60	-4				.777	-2	C-20/O-3(0-0-3),S-1	-0.5
1884	Phi-U	1	4	0	1	0	0	0		0		.250	.250	.250	500	56	-0				.818	-1	/C-1,M	-0.1
Total	5 n	197	952	186	265	30	7	1	153	32	18	.278	.302	.328	630	93	-7	17	5	2	.856	19	C-157/1-39,O-2C,S-1	0.8
Total	2	23	100	14	23	2	0	0	6	0	1	.230	.230	.250	480	60	-4				.780	-3	/C-21,O-3(0-0-3),S-1	-0.6
■ LEW MALONE	Malone, Lewis Aloysius b: 3/13/1897, Baltimore, Md. d: 2/17/72, Brooklyn, N.Y. BR/TR, 5'11", 175 lbs. Deb: 5/31/15 Career OF: (0-LF 0-CF 4-RF)																							
1915	Phi-A	76	201	17	41	4	4	1	17	21	40	.204	.283	.279	561	70	-8	7	1	1	.919	-4	2-43,3-12/O-4R,S-2	-1.0
1916	Phi-A	5	4	1	0	0	0	0	0	1	2	.000	.200	.000	200	-42	-1	0			1.000	-0	/S-1	-0.1
1917	Bro-N	1	0	1	0	0	0	0	0	0	0	—	—	—	—	—	0	0			.000	0	R	0.0
1919	Bro-N	51	162	9	33	7	3	0	11	6	18	.204	.232	.284	516	54	-9	1			.934	-6	3-47/2-2,S-2	-1.6
Total	4	133	367	28	74	11	7	1	28	28	60	.202	.260	.278	538	62	-18	8	1		.910	-11	/3-59,2-45,S-5,O-4R	-2.7
■ JOHN MALONEY	Maloney, John Deb: 9/15/1876																							
1876	NY-N	2	7	1	2	0	1	0	2	0	1	.286	.286	.571	857	206	1				.800	-0	/O-2(0-2-0)	0.0
1877	Har-N	1	4	0	1	0	0	0	0	0	0	.250	.250	.250	500	65	-0				.250	-1	/O-1(0-1-0)	-0.1
Total	2	3	11	1	3	0	1	0	2	0	1	.273	.273	.455	727	152	1				.556	-1	/O-3(0-3-0)	-0.1

YEAR	TM/L	G	AB	R	H	2B	3B	HR	RBI	BB	SO	AVG	OBP	SLG	OPS	OPS+	BR+	SB	CS	SBR	FA	FR	G/POS	TPR
■ PAT MALONEY Maloney, Patrick William b: 1/19/1888, Grosvenor Dale, Conn. d: 6/27/79, Pawtucket, R.I. BR/TR, 6', 150 lbs. Deb: 6/19/12																								
1912	NY-A	25	79	9	17	1	0	0	4	6		.215	.279	.228	507	43	-6	3			.926	2	O-20(0-20-0)	-0.5
■ BILLY MALONEY Maloney, William Alphonse b: 6/5/1878, Lewiston, Me. d: 9/2/60, Breckenridge, Tex. BL/TR, 5'10", 177 lbs. Deb: 5/2/01 Career OF: (16-LF 414-CF 163-RF)																								
1901	Mil-A	86	290	42	85	3	4	0	22	7		.293	.328	.331	659	87	-5	11			.952	9	C-72/O-8(0-8-0)	1.0
1902	StL-A	30	112	8	23	3	0	0	11	6		.205	.258	.232	490	37	-9	0			.906	-4	O-23(1-0-22)/C-7	-1.3
	Cin-N	27	89	13	22	4	0	1	7	2		.247	.272	.326	598	77	-3	8			.848	-3	O-18(10-6-2)/C-7	-0.6
1905	Chi-N	145	558	78	145	17	14	2	56	43		.260	.325	.351	676	98	-2	**59**			.954	3	*O-145(0-12-134)	-0.6
1906	Bro-N	151	566	71	125	15	7	0	32	49		.221	.286	.272	558	80	-13	38			.966	11	*O-151(0-149-2)	-1.0
1907	Bro-N	144	502	51	115	7	10	0	32	31		.229	.287	.283	570	86	-9	25			.967	5	*O-144(0-144-0)	-1.2
1908	Bro-N	113	359	31	70	5	7	3	17	24		.195	.255	.273	528	71	-12	14			.947	4	*O-107(5-95-3)/C-4	-1.4
Total	6	696	2476	294	585	54	42	6	177	162		.236	.294	.299	593	83	-52	155			.954	26	O-596C/C-90	-5.1
■ FRANK MALZONE Malzone, Frank James b: 2/28/30, Bronx, N.Y. BR/TR, 5'10", 180 lbs. Deb: 9/17/55																								
1955	Bos-A	6	20	2	7	1	0	0	1	1	3	.350	.381	.400	781	101	0	0	0	0	1.000	2	/3-4	0.2
1956	Bos-A	27	103	15	17	3	1	2	11	9	8	.165	.232	.272	504	29	-11	1	0	0	.931	1	3-26	-1.0
1957	Bos-A★	153	634	82	185	31	5	15	103	31	41	.292	.326	.427	753	98	-3	2	1	0	**.954**	14	*3-153	1.2
1958	Bos-A★	155	627	76	185	30	2	15	87	33	53	.295	.334	.421	755	100	-1	1	3	-1	.950	17	*3-155	1.5
1959	Bos-A★	154	604	90	169	34	2	19	92	42	58	.280	.328	.437	765	103	1	6	0	1	.953	8	*3-154	1.0
1960	Bos-A★	152	595	60	161	30	2	14	79	36	42	.271	.317	.398	715	89	-10	2	3	-1	.948	8	*3-151	-0.4
1961	Bos-A	151	590	74	157	21	4	14	87	44	49	.266	.318	.386	705	85	-13	1	3	-1	.950	-5	*3-149	-2.0
1962	Bos-A	156	619	74	175	20	3	21	95	35	43	.283	.321	.426	748	96	-5	0	1	-0	.967	5	*3-156	-0.1
1963	Bos-A★	151	580	66	169	25	2	15	71	31	45	.291	.331	.419	750	105	3	0	2	-1	.964	4	*3-148	0.6
1964	Bos-A☆	148	537	62	142	19	0	13	56	37	43	.264	.314	.372	687	86	-10	0	0	0	.959	-0	*3-143	-1.1
1965	Bos-A	106	364	40	87	20	0	3	34	28	38	.239	.295	.319	614	70	-14	1	1	-0	.969	-3	3-96	-1.9
1966	Cal-A	82	155	6	32	5	0	2	12	10	11	.206	.255	.277	532	54	-9	0	0	0	.925	-1	3-35	-1.2
Total	12	1441	5428	647	1486	239	21	133	728	337	434	.274	.318	.399	717	91	-70	14	14	-2	.955	47	*3-1370	-3.2
■ GUS MANCUSO Mancuso, August Rodney "Blackie" b: 12/5/05, Galveston, Tex. d: 10/26/84, Houston, Tex. BR/TR, 5'10", 185 lbs. Deb: 4/30/28 FC																								
1928	StL-N	11	38	2	7	0	1	0	3	0	5	.184	.184	.237	421	9	-5	0			.984	4	C-11	0.0
1930	*StL-N	76	227	39	83	17	2	7	59	18	16	.366	.415	.551	965	127	10	1			.969	1	C-61	1.3
1931	*StL-N	67	187	13	49	16	1	1	23	18	13	.262	.327	.374	701	85	-4	2			.972	6	C-56	0.6
1932	StL-N	103	310	25	88	23	1	5	43	30	15	.284	.347	.413	760	100	1	0			.977	8	C-82	1.3
1933	*NY-N	144	481	39	127	17	2	6	56	48	21	.264	.331	.345	676	95	-2	0			.972	2	*C-142	0.9
1934	NY-N	122	383	32	94	14	0	7	46	27	19	.245	.295	.337	632	70	-16	0			.977	6	*C-122	-0.3
1935	NY-N★	128	447	33	133	18	2	5	56	30	16	.298	.342	.380	722	95	-3	1			.972	-5	*C-126	0.0
1936	*NY-N	139	519	55	156	21	3	9	63	39	28	.301	.351	.405	755	104	3	0			.977	5	*C-138	1.6
1937	*NY-N★	86	287	30	80	17	1	4	39	17	20	.279	.319	.387	706	90	-4	1			.982	16	C-81	1.6
1938	NY-N	52	158	19	55	8	0	2	15	17	13	.348	.411	.437	848	132	8	0			.977	4	C-44	1.4
1939	Chi-N	80	251	17	58	10	0	2	17	24	19	.231	.298	.295	593	59	-14	0			.981	5	C-76	-0.5
1940	Bro-N	60	144	16	33	8	0	0	16	13	7	.229	.293	.285	578	56	-8	0			.982	7	C-56	0.1
1941	StL-N	106	328	25	75	13	1	2	37	37	19	.229	.309	.293	601	66	-14	0			.989	11	*C-105	0.2
1942	StL-N	5	13	0	1	0	0	0	1	0	0	.077	.077	.077	154	-51	-2	0			.917	-1	/C-3	-0.4
	NY-N	39	109	4	21	1	1	0	8	14	7	.193	.285	.220	505	48	-7	1			.982	3	C-38	-0.2
	Yr	44	122	4	22	1	1	0	9	14	7	.180	.265	.205	470	38	-9	1			.977	1	C-41	-0.6
1943	NY-N	94	252	11	50	5	0	2	20	28	16	.198	.284	.242	526	52	-15	0			.974	-0	C-77	-1.2
1944	NY-N	78	195	15	49	4	1	1	25	30	20	.251	.351	.297	649	84	-3	0			.976	5	C-72	0.5
1945	Phi-N	70	176	11	35	5	0	0	16	28	10	.199	.309	.227	536	52	-10	2			.988	1	C-70	-0.6
Total	17	1460	4505	386	1194	197	16	53	543	418	264	.265	.328	.351	679	85	-88	8			.977	75	*C-1360	6.3
■ FRANK MANCUSO Mancuso, Frank Octavius b: 5/23/18, Houston, Tex. BR/TR, 6', 195 lbs. Deb: 4/18/44 F																								
1944	*StL-A	88	244	19	50	11	0	1	24	20	32	.205	.271	.262	533	50	-16	1	0	0	.953	-6	C-87	-1.8
1945	StL-A	119	365	39	98	13	3	1	38	46	44	.268	.354	.329	682	94	-1	0	2	-1	.989	-6	*C-115	-0.1
1946	StL-A	87	262	22	63	8	3	3	23	30	31	.240	.323	.328	651	78	-7	1	0	0	.973	-18	C-85	-2.1
1947	Was-A	43	131	5	30	5	1	0	13	5	11	.229	.257	.282	540	51	-9	0	0	0	.958	-4	C-35	-1.1
Total	4	337	1002	85	241	37	7	5	98	101	118	.241	.314	.306	620	74	-33	2	2	-0	.972	-34	C-322	-5.1
■ CARL MANDA Manda, Carl Alan b: 11/16/1888, Little River, Kan. d: 3/9/83, Artesia, N.Mex. BR/TR, 5'10", 170 lbs. Deb: 9/11/14																								
1914	Chi-A	9	15	2	4	0	0	0	1	3	3	.267	.389	.267	656	99	0	1			.971	4	/2-7	0.5
■ JIM MANGAN Mangan, James Daniel b: 9/24/29, San Francisco, Cal. BR/TR, 5'10", 190 lbs. Deb: 4/16/52																								
1952	Pit-N	11	13	1	2	0	0	0	2	1	3	.154	.214	.154	368	4	-2	0	0	0	.833	-1	/C-4	-0.2
1954	Pit-N	14	26	2	5	0	0	0	2	4	9	.192	.300	.192	492	32	-2	0	0	0	1.000	0	/C-7	-0.2
1956	NY-N	20	20	2	2	0	0	0	1	4	6	.100	.250	.100	350	-1	-3	0	0	0	1.000	0	C-15	-0.2
Total	3	45	59	5	9	0	0	0	5	9	18	.153	.265	.153	417	15	-7	0	0	0	.985	-0	/C-26	-0.6
■ ANGEL MANGUAL Mangual, Angel Luis (Guilbe) b: 3/19/47, Juana Diaz, P.R. BR/TR, 5'10", 180 lbs. Deb: 9/15/69 F Career OF: (82-LF 130-CF 133-RF)																								
1969	Pit-N	6	4	1	1	1	0	0	0	0	0	.250	.250	.500	750	108	0	0	0	0	.000	-1	/O-3(2-0-1)	-0.1
1971	*Oak-A	94	287	32	82	8	1	4	30	17	27	.286	.326	.362	688	97	-2	1	4	-1	.988	-2	O-81(17-57-9)	-0.8
1972	*Oak-A	91	272	19	67	13	2	5	32	14	48	.246	.286	.364	650	97	-2	0	1	-0	.971	3	O-74(2-22-52)	-0.3
1973	*Oak-A	74	192	20	43	4	1	3	13	8	34	.224	.259	.302	561	61	-10	1	1	-0	.947	-5	O-50R,D-14/1-2,2-1	-1.9
1974	*Oak-A	115	365	37	85	14	4	9	43	17	59	.233	.267	.367	634	87	-8	3	0	1	.961	-7	O-74R,D-37/3-1	-1.9
1975	Oak-A	62	109	13	24	3	0	1	6	3	18	.220	.241	.275	516	47	-8	0	1	-0	.978	-9	O-39(21-6-14),D-15	-1.9
1976	Oak-A	8	12	0	2	1	0	0	1	0	1	.167	.167	.250	417	22	-1	0	1	-0	1.000	-2	/O-7(0-0-7)	-0.4
Total	7	450	1241	122	304	44	8	22	125	59	187	.245	.280	.346	627	83	-31	5	8	-2	.969	-23	O-328R/D-66,1-2,32	-7.3
■ PEPE MANGUAL Mangual, Jose Manuel (Guilbe) b: 5/23/52, Ponce, P.R. BR/TR, 5'10", 165 lbs. Deb: 9/6/72 F																								
1972	Mon-N	8	11	2	3	0	0	0	0	1	5	.273	.333	.273	606	73	-0	0	1	-0	1.000	-1	/O-3(2-0-1)	-0.2
1973	Mon-N	33	62	9	11	2	1	3	7	6	18	.177	.250	.387	637	71	-3	2	4	-1	.966	-3	O-22(20-1-1)	-0.8
1974	Mon-N	23	61	10	19	3	0	0	4	5	15	.311	.364	.361	724	98	-0	5	0	1	1.000	-6	O-22(18-2-8)	-0.7
1975	Mon-N	140	514	84	126	16	2	9	45	74	115	.245	.345	.337	681	86	-8	33	11	3	.972	-4	*O-138(1-135-2)	-1.3
1976	Mon-N	66	215	34	56	9	1	3	16	50	49	.260	.404	.353	758	112	6	17	7	1	.968	-1	O-62(34-36-1)	0.4
	NY-N	41	102	15	19	5	2	1	9	10	32	.186	.259	.304	563	63	-5	7	3	0	.985	-2	O-38(12-22-5)	-0.9
	Yr	107	317	49	75	14	3	4	25	60	81	.237	.361	.338	699	99	2	24	10	2	.973	-3	*O-100(46-58-6)	-0.5
1977	NY-N	8	7	1	1	0	0	0	2	1	4	.143	.250	.143	393	9	-1	0	0	0	.833	-1	/O-4(2-2-0)	-0.2
Total	6	319	972	155	235	35	6	16	83	147	238	.242	.345	.340	684	89	-11	64	26	5	.972	-18	O-289(89-198-18)	-3.7
■ GEORGE MANGUS Mangus, George Graham b: 5/22/1890, Red Creek, N.Y. d: 8/10/33, Rutland, Mass. BL/TR, 5'11.5", 165 lbs. Deb: 8/20/12																								
1912	Phi-N	10	25	2	5	3	0	0	3	1	6	.200	.231	.320	551	47	-2	0			.750	-1	/O-5(5-0-0)	-0.4
■ CLYDE MANION Manion, Clyde Jennings "Pete" b: 10/30/1896, Jefferson City, Mo d: 9/4/67, Detroit, Mich. BR/TR, 5'11", 175 lbs. Deb: 5/5/20																								
1920	Det-A	32	80	4	22	4	1	0	8	4	7	.275	.318	.350	668	79	-3	0	0	0	.940	-2	C-30	-0.2
1921	Det-A	12	10	0	2	0	0	0	2	2	2	.200	.385	.200	585	53	-1	0	0	0	1.000	1	/C-3	0.0
1922	Det-A	42	69	9	19	4	1	0	12	4	6	.275	.315	.362	677	79	-2	0	1	-0	.932	-2	C-22/1-1	-0.4
1923	Det-A	23	22	0	3	0	0	0	2	2	2	.136	.208	.136	345	-8	-3	0	0	0	.857	-0	/C-3,1-1	-0.4
1924	Det-A	14	13	1	3	0	0	0	2	1	1	.231	.286	.231	516	35	-1	0	0	0	.750	-1	/C-3,1-1	-0.2
1926	Det-A	75	176	15	35	4	0	0	14	24	16	.199	.295	.222	517	36	-16	1	1	-0	.972	-0	C-74	-1.2
1927	Det-A	1	0	0	0	0	0	0	0	1	0	—	1.000	—	1000	174	0	0	0	0	.000	0	H	0.0
1928	StL-A	76	243	25	55	5	1	2	31	15	18	.226	.274	.280	554	44	-20	3	0	1	.980	12	C-71	-0.3
1929	StL-A	35	111	16	27	2	0	0	11	15	3	.243	.333	.261	595	53	-7	1	0	0	.976	5	C-34	0.0
1930	StL-A	57	148	12	32	1	0	1	11	24	17	.216	.326	.243	569	45	-12	0	1	-0	.985	11	C-56	0.2

YEAR	TM/L	G	AB	R	H	2B	3B	HR	RBI	BB	SO	AVG	OBP	SLG	OPS	OPS+	BR+	SB	CS	SBR	FA	FR	G/POS	TPR
1932	Cin-N	49	135	7	28	4	0	0	12	14	16	.207	.282	.237	519	43	-11	0			.970	4	C-47	-0.4
1933	Cin-N	36	84	3	14	1	0	0	3	8	7	.167	.239	.179	418	21	-8	0			.981	4	C-34	-0.3
1934	Cin-N	25	54	4	10	0	0	0	4	4	7	.185	.241	.185	427	16	-6	0			1.000	3	C-24	-0.3
Total	13	477	1145	96	250	25	3	3	112	118	102	.218	.293	.253	546	45	-90	5	3		.973	33	C-401/1-3	-3.5

■ PHIL MANKOWSKI

Mankowski, Philip Anthony b: 1/9/53, Buffalo, N.Y. BL/TR, 6', 180 lbs. Deb: 8/30/76

YEAR	TM/L	G	AB	R	H	2B	3B	HR	RBI	BB	SO	AVG	OBP	SLG	OPS	OPS+	BR+	SB	CS	SBR	FA	FR	G/POS	TPR
1976	Det-A	24	85	9	23	2	1	1	4	4	8	.271	.303	.353	656	88	-1	0	0	0	.971	2	3-23	0.1
1977	Det-A	94	286	21	79	7	3	3	27	16	41	.276	.319	.353	672	79	-8	1	2	-0	.964	13	3-85/2-1	0.3
1978	Det-A	88	222	28	61	8	0	4	20	22	28	.275	.346	.365	710	97	-0	2	3	-1	.972	-1	3-80/D-1	-0.3
1979	Det-A	42	99	11	22	4	0	0	8	10	16	.222	.294	.263	556	50	-7	0	0	0	.963	-0	3-36/D-1	-0.7
1980	NY-N	8	12	1	2	1	0	0	1	2	4	.167	.286	.250	536	52	-1	0	0	0	.571	-1	/3-3	-0.2
1982	NY-N	13	35	2	8	1	0	0	4	1	6	.229	.250	.257	507	42	-3	0	1	-0	.957	-1	3-13	-0.4
Total	6	269	739	72	195	23	4	8	64	55	103	.264	.318	.338	657	79	-20	3	6	-1	.962	13	3-240/D-2,2-1	-1.2

■ CHARLIE MANLOVE

Manlove, Charles Henry Weeks "Chick" b: 10/8/1862, Philadelphia, Pa. d: 2/12/52, Altoona, Pa. BR/TR, 5'9", 165 lbs. Deb: 5/31/1884

YEAR	TM/L	G	AB	R	H	2B	3B	HR	RBI	BB	SO	AVG	OBP	SLG	OPS	OPS+	BR+	SB	CS	SBR	FA	FR	G/POS	TPR
1884	Alt-U	2	7	1	3	0	0	0		0		.429	.429	.429	857	158	0				1.000	-1	/C-1,O-1(0-1-0)	-0.1
	NY-N	3	10	0	0	0	0	0	0	0	4	.000	.000	.000	0	-98	-2				.833	-1	/C-3,O-1(0-0-1)	-0.3
Total	1	5	17	1	3	0	0	0	0	0	4	.176	.176	.176	353	9	-2				.880	-2	/C-4,O-2(0-1-1)	-0.4

■ GARTH MANN

Mann, Ben Garth "Red" b: 11/16/15, Brandon, Tex. d: 9/11/80, Italy, Tex. BR/TR, 6', 155 lbs. Deb: 5/14/44

YEAR	TM/L	G	AB	R	H	2B	3B	HR	RBI	BB	SO	AVG	OBP	SLG	OPS	OPS+	BR+	SB	CS	SBR	FA	FR	G/POS	TPR
1944	Chi-N	1	0	1	0	0	0	0	0	0	0	—	—	—	—	—	0	0			.000	0	R	0.0

■ FRED MANN

Mann, Fred J. b: 4/1/1858, Sutton, Vt. d: 4/6/16, Springfield, Mass. BL/TR, 5'10.5", 178 lbs. Deb: 5/1/1882 Career OF: (39-LF 444-CF 28-RF)

YEAR	TM/L	G	AB	R	H	2B	3B	HR	RBI	BB	SO	AVG	OBP	SLG	OPS	OPS+	BR+	SB	CS	SBR	FA	FR	G/POS	TPR
1882	Wor-N	19	77	12	18	5	0	0	7	2	15	.234	.253	.299	552	74	-2				.703	-6	3-18/1-1	-0.8
	Phi-a	29	121	13	28	7	4	0		4		.231	.256	.355	611	93	-1				.798	-10	3-29	-1.1
1883	Col-a	96	394	61	98	18	13	1		18		.249	.282	.368	650	117	9				.854	-3	*O-82C/1-9,3-6,S-1	0.2
1884	Col-a	99	366	70	101	12	18	7		25		.276	.341	.464	805	174	31				.857	-6	*O-97(0-97-0)/2-2	2.0
1885	Pit-a	99	391	60	99	17	6	0	41	31		.253	.318	.327	645	106	4				.908	-8	*O-97(0-97-0)/3-3	-0.7
1886	Pit-a	116	440	85	110	16	14	2	60	45		.250	.335	.364	698	119	11	26			.878	-3	*O-116(0-115-1)	0.3
1887	Cle-a	64	282	45	103	15	7	2	41	23		.365	.385	.444	829	135	13	25			.879	1	O-64(37-0-27)	1.0
	Phi-a	55	244	42	78	14	6	0	32	15		.320	.336	.389	725	102	0	16			.916	-4	O-55(0-55-0)	-0.5
	Yr	119	526	87	181	29	13	2	73	38		.344	.362	.418	780	119	13	41			.896	-3	*O-119(37-55-27)	0.5
Total	6	577	2315	388	635	104	68	12	181	163	15	.274	.323	.383	707	121	64	67			.881	-39	O-511C/3-56,1-10,2S	0.4

■ JOHNNY MANN

Mann, John Leo b: 2/4/1898, Fontanet, Ind. d: 3/31/77, Terre Haute, Ind. BR/TR, 5'11", 160 lbs. Deb: 4/18/28

YEAR	TM/L	G	AB	R	H	2B	3B	HR	RBI	BB	SO	AVG	OBP	SLG	OPS	OPS+	BR+	SB	CS	SBR	FA	FR	G/POS	TPR
1928	Chi-A	6	6	0	2	0	0	0	1	1	0	.333	.429	.333	762	104	0	0	0	0	1.000	0	/3-2	0.0

■ KELLY MANN

Mann, Kelly John b: 8/17/67, Santa Monica, Cal. BR/TR, 6'3", 215 lbs. Deb: 9/4/89

YEAR	TM/L	G	AB	R	H	2B	3B	HR	RBI	BB	SO	AVG	OBP	SLG	OPS	OPS+	BR+	SB	CS	SBR	FA	FR	G/POS	TPR
1989	Atl-N	7	24	1	5	2	0	0	1	0	6	.208	.240	.292	532	50	-2	0	0	0	1.000	2	/C-7	0.1
1990	Atl-N	11	28	2	4	1	0	1	2	0	6	.143	.143	.286	429	14	-3	0	0	0	1.000	-1	C-10	-0.4
Total	2	18	52	3	9	3	0	1	3	0	12	.173	.189	.288	477	30	-5	0	0	0	1.000	1	/C-17	-0.3

■ LES MANN

Mann, Leslie "Major" b: 11/18/1893, Lincoln, Neb. d: 1/14/62, Pasadena, Cal. BR/TR, 5'9", 172 lbs. Deb: 4/30/13 Career OF: (708-LF 414-CF 277-RF)

YEAR	TM/L	G	AB	R	H	2B	3B	HR	RBI	BB	SO	AVG	OBP	SLG	OPS	OPS+	BR+	SB	CS	SBR	FA	FR	G/POS	TPR
1913	Bos-N	120	407	54	103	24	7	3	51	18	73	.253	.291	.369	660	86	-9	7			.960	-2	*O-120(12-103-6)	-1.9
1914	*Bos-N	126	389	44	96	16	11	4	40	24	50	.247	.292	.375	668	99	-2	9			.952	13	*O-123(5-104-14)	0.4
1915	Chi-F	135	470	74	144	12	**19**	4	58	36	40	.306	.357	.438	795	131	10	18			.969	5	*O-130(94-7-33)/S-1	1.0
1916	Chi-N	127	415	46	113	13	9	2	29	19	31	.272	.307	.361	669	95	-3	11	7	-0	.972	-8	*O-115(74-20-26)	-1.8
1917	Chi-N	117	444	63	121	19	10	1	44	27	46	.273	.316	.367	683	101	0	14			.953	0	*O-116(106-11-2)	-0.6
1918	*Chi-N	129	489	69	141	27	7	2	55	38	45	.288	.342	.384	727	118	10	21			.961	-3	*O-129(129-0-0)	0.2
1919	Chi-N	80	299	31	68	8	8	1	22	11	29	.227	.257	.318	575	72	-11	12			.982	2	O-78(78-0-0)	-1.5
	Bos-N	40	145	15	41	6	4	3	20	9	14	.283	.329	.441	770	136	6	7			.929	3	O-40(40-0-0)	0.7
	Yr	120	444	46	109	14	12	4	42	20	43	.245	.281	.358	639	92	-6	19			.962	4	*O-118(118-0-0)	-0.8
1920	Bos-N	115	424	48	117	7	8	3	32	38	42	.276	.341	.351	693	104	3	7	7	-1	.980	3	*O-110(102-0-8)	-0.1
1921	StL-N	97	256	57	84	12	7	7	30	23	28	.328	.390	.512	902	140	14	5	5	-1	.969	0	O-79(1-66-12)	1.1
1922	StL-N	84	147	42	51	14	1	2	20	16	12	.347	.415	.497	911	141	9	0	1	-0	.978	-11	O-57(10-47-0)	-0.4
1923	StL-N	38	89	20	33	5	2	5	11	9	5	.371	.434	.640	1075	184	11	0	0	0	.979	-3	O-26(5-6-16)	0.6
	Cin-N	8	1	1	0	0	0	0	0	0	0	.000	.000	.000	0	-99	-0	0	0	0	.000	0	H	0.0
	Yr	46	90	21	33	5	2	5	11	9	5	.367	.430	.633	1063	181	10	0	0	0	.979	-3	O-26(5-6-16)	0.6
1924	Bos-N	32	102	13	28	7	4	0	10	8	10	.275	.333	.422	755	105	1	1	0	0	1.000	2	O-28(7-0-21)	0.1
1925	Bos-N	60	184	27	63	11	4	2	20	5	11	.342	.373	.478	851	127	7	6	1	1	.992	-2	O-57(5-11-41)	0.3
1926	Bos-N	50	129	23	39	8	2	1	20	9	9	.302	.348	.419	766	116	3	5			.966	-6	O-46(17-17-16)	-0.6
1927	Bos-N	29	66	8	17	3	1	0	6	8	3	.258	.338	.333	671	87	-1	2			.955	-2	O-24(5-3-17)	-0.5
	NY-N	29	67	13	22	4	1	2	10	8	7	.328	.400	.507	907	142	4	2			1.000	-4	O-22(15-5-2)	-0.1
	Yr	58	133	21	39	7	2	2	16	16	10	.293	.369	.421	790	116	3	4			.973	-6	O-46(20-8-19)	-0.6
1928	NY-N	82	193	29	51	7	1	2	25	18	9	.264	.330	.342	672	76	-7	2			.952	-19	O-68(3-14-63)	-2.9
Total	16	1498	4716	677	1332	203	106	44	503	324	464	.282	.332	.398	731	109	45	129	21		.966	-32	*O-1368L/S-1	-6.0

■ JIM MANNING

Manning, James H. b: 1/31/1862, Fall River, Mass. d: 10/22/29, Edinburg, Tex. BB/TR, 5'7", 157 lbs. Deb: 5/16/1884 M Career OF: (118-LF 135-CF 8-RF)

YEAR	TM/L	G	AB	R	H	2B	3B	HR	RBI	BB	SO	AVG	OBP	SLG	OPS	OPS+	BR+	SB	CS	SBR	FA	FR	G/POS	TPR
1884	Bos-N	89	345	52	83	8	6	2	35	19	47	.241	.280	.316	596	88	-5				.878	1	O-73C/S-9,2-9,3-3	-0.5
1885	Bos-N	84	306	34	63	8	9	2	27	19	36	.206	.252	.310	563	84	-5				.898	9	*O-83(12-63-8)/S-1	0.2
	Det-N	20	78	15	21	4	0	1	9	4	10	.269	.305	.359	664	114	1				.802	-6	S-20	-0.4
	Yr	104	384	49	84	12	9	3	36	23	46	.219	.263	.320	583	90	-4				.898	3	O-83(12-63-8),S-21	-0.2
1886	Det-N	26	97	14	18	2	3	0	7	6	10	.186	.233	.268	501	51	-6	7			.947	-1	O-26(26-0-0)/S-1	-0.7
1887	Det-N	13	57	5	15	1	0	0	3	5	4	.263	.276	.212	487	36	-4	3			.867	-4	O-10(10-0-0)/S-3	-0.8
1889	KC-a	132	506	68	103	16	7	3	68	54	61	.204	.297	.281	577	61	-26	58			.927	-10	O-69L,2-63/S-1,3-1	-3.1
Total	5	364	1389	188	303	39	25	8	149	107	168	.218	.278	.297	575	73	-45	68			.903	-11	O-261C/2-72,S-35,3	-5.3

■ JACK MANNING

Manning, John E. b: 12/20/1853, Braintree, Mass.
d: 8/15/29, Boston, Mass. BR/TR, 5'8.5", 158 lbs. Deb: 4/23/1873 M NA OF: (2-LF 2-CF 67-RF) Career OF: (2-LF 16-CF 605-RF)

YEAR	TM/L	G	AB	R	H	2B	3B	HR	RBI	BB	SO	AVG	OBP	SLG	OPS	OPS+	BR+	SB	CS	SBR	FA	FR	G/POS	TPR
1873	Bos-n	32	159	29	43	6	1	0	22	1	11	.270	.275	.321	596	71	-7	1	0	0	.940	1	1-29/O-5(2-0-3)	-0.3
1874	Bal-n	42	174	32	61	8	2	0	18	2	2	.351	.358	.420	777	149	9	0	0	0	.839	-2	P-22,2-22/S-4,13	0.1
	Har-n	1	5	1	1	0	0	0	0	0	0	.200	.200	.200	400	27	-0	0	0	0	.167	-2	/3-1	-0.2
	Yr	43	179	33	62	8	2	0	18	2	2	.346	.354	.413	767	146	9	0	0	0	.793	-4	P-22,2-22/S-4,31	-0.1
1875	Bos-n	77	348	71	94	11	3	1	46	2	9	.270	.274	.328	602	104	1	5	5	-1	.802	-1	*O-65R,P-27/1-3,3-1	0.2
1876	Bos-N	70	295	52	76	13	0	2	25	7	5	.258	.281	.330	611	101	0				.777	-5	*O-56R,P-34/S-1,2-1	-0.5
1877	Cin-N	57	252	47	80	16	7	0	36	5	6	.317	.331	.437	767	157	17				.742	-13	S-26,1-17,O-12C,P/2M	0.2
1878	Bos-N	60	248	41	63	10	1	0	23	10	16	.254	.283	.302	585	86	-4				.753	-13	*O-59(0-3-56)/P-3	-1.7
1880	Cin-N	48	190	20	41	6	3	2	17	7	15	.216	.244	.311	554	87	-2				.798	-3	O-47(0-2-47)/1-1	-0.5
1881	Buf-N	1	1	0	0	0	0	0	0	0	0	.000	.000	.000	0	-99	-0				1.000	0	/O-1(1-0-0)	0.0
1883	Phi-N	98	420	60	112	31	5	0	37	20	37	.267	.300	.364	664	110	7				.853	10	*O-98(0-0-98)	1.4
1884	Phi-N	104	424	71	115	29	4	5	52	40	67	.271	.334	.394	728	134	18				.847	-1	*O-104(0-0-104)	1.4
1885	Phi-N	107	445	61	114	24	4	3	40	37	27	.256	.313	.348	662	116	9				.896	-6	*O-107(0-0-107)	0.2
1886	Bal-a	137	556	78	124	18	7	1	45	50		.223	.291	.286	577	83	-10	24			.887	-10	*O-137(0-0-137)	-1.8
Total	3 n	152	686	133	199	25	6	1	86	5	22	.290	.295	.348	644	106	3	6	5	-0	.785	-4	/O-70R,P-49,1-33,2S3	-0.2
Total	9	682	2831	430	725	147	31	13	275	176	173	.256	.301	.345	646	108	35	24			.844	-40	O-621R/P-47,S-27,12	-1.3

■ RICK MANNING

Manning, Richard Eugene b: 9/2/54, Niagara Falls, N.Y. BL/TR, 6'1", 180 lbs. Deb: 5/23/75 Career OF: (90-LF 1317-CF 118-RF)

YEAR	TM/L	G	AB	R	H	2B	3B	HR	RBI	BB	SO	AVG	OBP	SLG	OPS	OPS+	BR+	SB	CS	SBR	FA	FR	G/POS	TPR
1975	Cle-A	120	480	69	137	16	5	3	35	44	62	.285	.348	.358	706	100	1	19	11	0	.974	13	*O-118(28-69-32)/D-1	1.0
1976	Cle-A	138	552	73	161	24	7	6	43	41	75	.292	.341	.393	734	116	10	16	10	0	.987	8	*O-136(0-136-0)	1.6
1977	Cle-A	68	252	33	57	7	3	5	18	21	35	.226	.286	.337	623	71	-10	9	5	0	.990	5	O-68(0-68-0)	-0.6
1978	Cle-A	148	566	65	149	27	3	3	50	38	62	.263	.311	.337	648	83	-13	12	12	-2	.995	5	*O-144(0-144-0)	-1.1
1979	Cle-A	144	560	67	145	12	2	3	51	55	48	.259	.326	.304	630	71	-21	30	8	4	.986	15	*O-141(0-141-0)/D-1	-0.4

YEAR	TM/L	G	AB	R	H	2B	3B	HR	RBI	BB	SO	AVG	OBP	SLG	OPS	OPS+	BR+	SB	CS	SBR	FA	FR	G/POS	TPR
1980	Cle-A	140	471	55	110	17	4	3	52	63	66	.234	.326	.306	632	74	-15	12	6	1	.990	8	*O-139(0-139-0)	-0.8
1981	Cle-A	103	360	47	88	15	3	4	33	40	57	.244	.320	.336	656	90	-4	25	3	4	.987	13	*O-103(0-103-0)	1.4
1982	Cle-A	152	562	71	152	18	2	8	44	54	60	.270	.334	.352	687	89	-7	12	8	-0	.978	6	*O-152(0-152-0)	-0.3
1983	Cle-A	50	194	20	54	6	0	1	10	12	22	.278	.320	.325	645	75	-6	7	3	0	.987	3	O-50(0-50-0)	-0.3
	Mil-A	108	375	40	86	14	4	3	33	26	40	.229	.281	.312	593	68	-17	11	2	2	.991	6	*O-108(0-108-0)	-1.0
	Yr	158	569	60	140	20	4	4	43	38	62	.246	.294	.316	611	71	-23	18	5	2	.990	9	*O-158(0-158-0)	-1.3
1984	Mil-A	119	341	53	85	10	5	7	31	34	32	.249	.319	.370	689	94	-3	5	7	-1	.987	-14	*O-114(0-113-0)/D-1	-1.9
1985	Mil-A	79	216	19	47	9	1	2	18	14	19	.218	.265	.296	562	54	-14	1	0	0	.976	-6	O-74(1-57-17)/D-2	-2.0
1986	Mil-A	89	205	31	52	7	3	8	27	17	20	.254	.314	.434	748	98	-1	5	3	0	.988	-5	O-83(40-29-18)/D-5	-0.7
1987	Mil-A	97	114	21	26	7	1	0	13	12	18	.228	.302	.307	609	60	-6	4	0	1	.958	-19	O-78(21-8-51)/D-2	-2.4
Total	13	1555	5248	664	1349	189	43	56	458	471	616	.257	.319	.341	661	84	-107	168	78	10	.985	40	*O-1508C/D-12	-7.5

■ TIM MANNING

Manning, Timothy Edward b: 12/3/1853, Henley-On-Thames, England d: 6/11/34, Oak Park, Ill. BR/TR, 5'10", 170 lbs. Deb: 5/1/1882

YEAR	TM/L	G	AB	R	H	2B	3B	HR	RBI	BB	SO	AVG	OBP	SLG	OPS	OPS+	BR+	SB	CS	SBR	FA	FR	G/POS	TPR
1882	Pro-N	21	76	7	8	0	0	0	8	5	13	.105	.160	.105	266	-13	-9				.787	-10	S-17/C-4	-1.8
1883	Bal-a	35	121	23	26	5	0	0		14		.215	.296	.256	552	77	-3				.913	3	2-35	0.2
1884	Bal-a	91	341	49	70	14	5	2		26		.205	.275	.293	569	82	-6				.907	-2	*2-91	-0.5
1885	Bal-a	43	157	17	32	8	1	0	16	10		.204	.265	.268	532	70	-5				.919	3	2-41/3-3	-0.1
	Pro-N	10	35	3	2	1	0	0	0	1	11	.057	.083	.086	169	-47	-5				.854	-3	S-10	-0.8
Total	4	200	730	99	138	28	6	2	24	56	24	.189	.256	.252	508	63	-29				.911	-9	2-167/S-27,C-4,3-3	-3.0

■ DON MANNO

Manno, Donald D. b: 5/4/15, Williamsport, Pa. d: 3/11/95, Williamsport, Pa. BR/TR, 6'1", 190 lbs. Deb: 9/22/40

YEAR	TM/L	G	AB	R	H	2B	3B	HR	RBI	BB	SO	AVG	OBP	SLG	OPS	OPS+	BR+	SB	CS	SBR	FA	FR	G/POS	TPR
1940	Bos-N	3	7	1	2	0	0	1	4	0	2	.286	.286	.714	1000	177	1	0			1.000	0	/O-2(0-0-2)	0.1
1941	Bos-N	22	30	2	5	1	0	0	4	3	7	.167	.242	.200	442	27	-3	0			1.000	-1	/O-5(5-0-0),3-3,1-1	-0.5
Total	2	25	37	3	7	1	0	1	8	3	9	.189	.250	.297	547	56	-2	0			1.000	-1	/O-7(5-0-2),3-3,1-1	-0.4

■ FRED MANRIQUE

Manrique, Fred Eloy (Reyes) b: 11/5/61, Edo Bolivar, Venez. BR/TR, 6'1", 175 lbs. Deb: 8/23/81

YEAR	TM/L	G	AB	R	H	2B	3B	HR	RBI	BB	SO	AVG	OBP	SLG	OPS	OPS+	BR+	SB	CS	SBR	FA	FR	G/POS	TPR
1981	Tor-A	14	28	1	4	0	0	0	1	0	12	.143	.172	.143	315	-8	-4	0	1	-0	.949	3	S-11/3-2,D-1	-0.1
1984	Tor-A	10	9	0	3	0	0	0	1	0	1	.333	.333	.333	667	82	-0	0	0	0	.938	3	/2-9,D-1	0.3
1985	Mon-N	9	13	5	4	1	1	1	1	1	3	.308	.357	.769	1126	219	2	0	0	0	1.000	2	/2-2,S-2,3-1	0.4
1986	StL-N	13	17	2	3	0	0	1	1	1	1	.176	.222	.353	575	57	-1	1	0	0	1.000	-2	/3-4,2-1	-0.3
1987	Chi-A	115	298	30	77	13	3	4	29	19	69	.258	.305	.362	667	74	-11	5	3	0	.984	19	2-92,S-23/D-5	1.2
1988	Chi-A	140	345	43	81	10	6	5	37	21	54	.235	.285	.342	627	75	-12	6	5	-0	.985	12	*2-129,S-12/D-1	0.3
1989	Chi-A	65	187	23	56	13	1	2	30	8	30	.299	.335	.412	747	112	3	0	4	-1	.961	-5	2-57/S-2,3-1,D-1	-0.3
	Tex-A	54	191	23	55	12	0	2	22	9	33	.288	.320	.382	702	96	-1	4	1	1	.963	-11	S-37,2-17/3-6	-0.9
	Yr	119	378	46	111	25	1	4	52	17	63	.294	.327	.397	724	104	1	4	5	-1	.952	-16	2-74,S-39/3-7,D-1	-1.2
1990	Min-A	69	228	22	54	10	0	5	29	4	35	.237	.256	.346	603	63	-12	2	0	0	.974	-10	2-67/D-1	-2.0
1991	Oak-A	9	21	2	3	0	0	0	0	2	1	.143	.217	.143	360	2	-3	0	0	0	.955	-0	/S-7,2-2	-0.3
Total	9	498	1337	151	340	59	11	20	151	65	239	.254	.293	.360	653	79	-40	18	14	-1	.976	11	2-376/S-94,3-14,D	-1.7

■ JOHN MANSELL

Mansell, John b: 1861, Auburn, N.Y. d: 2/20/25, Romulus, N.Y. BL, 5'10", 168 lbs. Deb: 5/9/1882 F

YEAR	TM/L	G	AB	R	H	2B	3B	HR	RBI	BB	SO	AVG	OBP	SLG	OPS	OPS+	BR+	SB	CS	SBR	FA	FR	G/POS	TPR
1882	Phi-a	31	126	17	30	3	1	0	17	4		.238	.262	.278	539	73	-4				.791	-4	O-31(0-31-0)	-0.8

■ MIKE MANSELL

Mansell, Michael R. b: 1/15/1858, Auburn, N.Y. d: 12/4/02, Auburn, N.Y. BL, 5'11", 175 lbs. Deb: 5/1/1879 F

YEAR	TM/L	G	AB	R	H	2B	3B	HR	RBI	BB	SO	AVG	OBP	SLG	OPS	OPS+	BR+	SB	CS	SBR	FA	FR	G/POS	TPR
1879	Syr-N	67	242	24	52	4	2	1	13	5	45	.215	.231	.260	491	69	-7				.881	15	*O-67(67-0-0)	0.4
1880	Cin-N	53	187	22	36	6	2	2	12	4	37	.193	.209	.278	487	64	-7				.865	12	O-53(53-0-0)	0.2
1882	Pit-a	79	347	59	96	**18**	**16**	2		7		.277	.291	.438	729	150	18				.829	3	*O-79(79-0-0)	1.7
1883	Pit-a	96	412	90	106	12	13	3		25		.257	.300	.371	671	120	10				.883	4	*O-96(96-0-0)	1.0
1884	Pit-a	27	100	15	14	0	3	1		7		.140	.204	.230	434	42	-6				.796	-2	O-27(24-0-3)	-0.8
	Phi-a	20	70	6	14	1	1	0		5		.200	.253	.243	496	59	-3				.762	-1	O-20(16-4-0)	-0.4
	Ric-a	29	113	21	34	2	5	0		8		.301	.363	.407	770	153	7				.763	-5	O-29(0-2-27)	0.1
	Yr	76	283	42	62	3	9	1		20		.219	.280	.304	584	90	-3				.775	-7	O-76(40-6-30)	-1.1
Total	5	371	1471	237	352	43	42	9	25	61	82	.239	.271	.344	615	106	12				.854	27	O-371(335-6-30)	2.2

■ TOM MANSELL

Mansell, Thomas E. "Brick" b: 1/1/1855, Auburn, N.Y. d: 10/6/34, Auburn, N.Y. BL/TR, 5'8", 160 lbs. Deb: 5/1/1879 F

YEAR	TM/L	G	AB	R	H	2B	3B	HR	RBI	BB	SO	AVG	OBP	SLG	OPS	OPS+	BR+	SB	CS	SBR	FA	FR	G/POS	TPR
1879	Tro-N	40	177	29	43	6	0	0	11	3	9	.243	.256	.277	532	81	-3				.742	-6	O-40(38-2-0)	-1.1
	Syr-N	1	4	0	1	0	0	0	0	0	0	.250	.250	.250	500	74	-0				1.000	-0	/O-1(0-0-1)	0.0
	Yr	41	181	29	44	6	0	0	11	3	9	.243	.255	.276	532	81	-3				.747	-6	O-41(38-2-1)	-1.1
1883	Det-N	34	131	22	29	4	1	0	10	8	13	.221	.266	.267	533	66	-5				.758	-2	O-34(0-0-34)/P-1	-0.6
	StL-a	28	112	23	45	8	1	0	24	7		.402	.437	.491	928	188	11				.786	-6	O-28(25-2-1)	0.4
1884	Cin-a	65	266	49	66	4	6	0	23	15		.248	.301	.308	609	94	-2				.752	-11	O-65(41-25-1)	-1.3
	Col-a	23	77	9	15	1	3	0	6	6		.195	.262	.286	548	85	-1				.667	-4	O-23(23-0-0)	-0.5
	Yr	88	343	58	81	5	9	0	29	21		.236	.292	.303	595	93	-2				.739	-15	O-88(64-25-1)	-1.8
Total	3	191	767	132	199	23	11	0	74	39	22	.259	.300	.318	619	100	0				.751	-28	O-191(127-29-37)/P-1	-3.1

■ FELIX MANTILLA

Mantilla, Felix (Lamela) b: 7/29/34, Isabela, P.R. BR/TR, 6', 160 lbs. Deb: 6/21/56 Career OF: (74-LF 76-CF 10-RF)

YEAR	TM/L	G	AB	R	H	2B	3B	HR	RBI	BB	SO	AVG	OBP	SLG	OPS	OPS+	BR+	SB	CS	SBR	FA	FR	G/POS	TPR
1956	Mil-N	35	53	9	15	1	1	0	3	1	8	.283	.309	.340	649	79	-2	0	1	-0	1.000	9	S-15/3-3	0.8
1957	*Mil-N	71	182	28	43	9	1	4	21	14	34	.236	.298	.363	661	82	-5	2	0	0	.931	6	S-35,2-13/3-7,O-1C	0.5
1958	*Mil-N	85	226	37	50	5	1	7	19	20	20	.221	.285	.345	630	72	-10	2	0	0	.987	-6	O-43C,2-21/S-5,3-2	-1.6
1959	Mil-N	103	251	26	54	5	0	3	19	16	31	.215	.268	.271	539	48	-19	6	1	1	.970	4	2-60,S-23/3-9,O-7C	-1.0
1960	Mil-N	63	148	21	38	7	0	3	11	7	16	.257	.295	.365	660	86	-3	3	1	0	.956	-12	2-26,S-25/O-8(3-5-0)	-1.3
1961	Mil-N	45	93	13	20	3	0	1	5	10	16	.215	.298	.280	578	58	-5	1	1	-0	.933	-4	S-19,2-10,O-10C,/3	-0.9
1962	NY-N	141	466	54	128	17	4	11	59	37	51	.275	.335	.399	734	94	-4	3	1	0	.948	-7	3-95,S-25,2-14	-0.9
1963	Bos-A	66	178	27	56	8	0	6	15	20	14	.315	.384	.461	845	131	8	2	1	0	.965	-5	S-27,O-11(0-11-0)/2-5	0.5
1964	Bos-A	133	425	69	123	20	1	30	64	41	46	.289	.357	.553	910	142	23	0	1	-0	.984	-6	O-48L,2-45/3-7,S-6	2.0
1965	Bos-A★	150	534	60	147	17	2	18	92	79	84	.275	.377	.416	793	118	15	7	3	0	.976	-22	*2-123,O-27L/1-2	0.3
1966	Hou-N	77	151	16	33	5	0	6	22	11	32	.219	.280	.371	651	85	-3	1	0	0	.990	-2	1-14,3-14/2-9,O-1L	-0.5
Total	11	969	2707	360	707	97	10	89	330	256	352	.261	.331	.403	734	100	-5	27	10	2	.977	-44	2-326,S-180,O3/1	-2.1

■ MICKEY MANTLE

Mantle, Mickey Charles "The Commerce Comet" b: 10/20/31, Spavinaw, Okla.
d: 8/13/95, Dallas, Tex. BB/TR, 5'11", 198 lbs. Deb: 4/17/51 CH Career OF: (129-LF 1745-CF 146-RF)

YEAR	TM/L	G	AB	R	H	2B	3B	HR	RBI	BB	SO	AVG	OBP	SLG	OPS	OPS+	BR+	SB	CS	SBR	FA	FR	G/POS	TPR
1951	*NY-A	96	341	61	91	11	5	13	65	43	74	.267	.349	.443	792	117	7	8	7	-1	.959	-6	O-86(0-3-85)	-0.2
1952	*NY-A☆	142	549	94	171	37	7	23	87	75	111	.311	.394	.530	**924**	166	**47**	4	1	1	.968	3	*O-141(0-121-20)/3-1	4.8
1953	*NY-A★	127	461	105	136	24	3	21	92	79	90	.295	.398	.497	895	145	31	8	4	0	.982	1	*O-121(0-116-4)/S-1	2.6
1954	NY-A★	146	543	**129**	163	17	12	27	102	102	107	.300	.411	.525	936	160	47	5	2	0	.975	-1	*O-144C/S-4,2-1	4.0
1955	*NY-A★	147	517	121	158	25	**11**	**37**	99	**113**	97	.306	**.433**	**.611**	**1044**	**181**	**61**	8	1	1	.995	8	*O-145(0-145-0)/S-2	**6.2**
1956	*NY-A★	150	533	**132**	188	22	5	**52**	**130**	112	99	**.353**	.467	**.705**	**1172**	**213**	**89**	10	1	2	.990	8	*O-144(0-144-0)	**8.7**
1957	*NY-A★	144	474	**121**	173	28	6	34	94	**146**	75	.365	.515	.665	1179	223	**91**	16	3	2	.979	0	*O-139(0-139-0)	**8.7**
1958	*NY-A★	150	519	**127**	158	21	1	**42**	97	**129**	120	.304	.445	.592	1036	**189**	**69**	18	3	3	.977	-0	*O-150(0-150-0)	**6.5**
1959	NY-A★	144	541	104	154	23	4	31	75	93	126	.285	.392	.514	905	**152**	40	21	3	4	**.995**	8	*O-143(0-143-0)	**4.5**
1960	*NY-A★	153	527	**119**	145	17	6	**40**	94	111	125	.275	.402	.558	**960**	**166**	**51**	14	3	2	.991	-1	*O-150(0-150-0)	**4.5**
1961	*NY-A★	153	514	**132**	163	16	6	54	128	**126**	112	.317	.452	**.687**	1138	**210**	**85**	12	1	2	.983	4	*O-150(0-150-0)	**8.3**
1962	*NY-A★	123	377	96	121	15	1	30	89	**122**	78	.321	**.488**	**.605**	**1093**	**198**	**61**	9	0	2	.978	-6	*O-117(0-94-23)	**5.2**
1963	*NY-A†	65	172	40	54	8	0	15	35	40	32	.314	.443	.622	1065	197	24	2	1	0	.990	-2	O-52(0-52-0)	2.1
1964	*NY-A★	143	465	92	141	25	2	35	111	99	102	.303	**.426**	.591	**1017**	**177**	**51**	6	3	0	.978	-13	*O-132(17-102-13)	3.5
1965	NY-A†	122	361	44	92	12	1	19	46	73	76	.255	.380	.452	832	136	19	4	1	1	.966	-4	*O-108(108-0-0)	1.0
1966	NY-A	108	333	40	96	12	1	23	56	57	76	.288	.392	.538	930	171	31	1	1	-0	1.000	-7	O-97(4-93-0)	2.3
1967	NY-A★	144	440	63	108	17	0	22	55	107	113	.245	.394	.434	828	150	32	1	1	-0	.993	0	*1-131	2.7
1968	NY-A★	144	435	57	103	14	1	18	54	106	97	.237	.387	.398	785	143	28	6	2	1	.988	-3	*1-131	2.0
Total	18	2401	8102	1677	2415	344	72	536	1509	1733	1710	.298	.423	.557	979	173	865	153	38	20	.982	-9	*O-2019C,1-262/S23	77.4

YEAR	TM/L	G	AB	R	H	2B	3B	HR	RBI	BB	SO	AVG	OBP	SLG	OPS	OPS+	BR+	SB	CS	SBR	FA	FR	G/POS	TPR
■ **JEFF MANTO** Manto, Jeffrey Paul b: 8/23/64, Bristol, Pa. BR/TR, 6'3", 210 lbs. Deb: 6/7/90 Career OF: (4-LF 0-CF 0-RF)																								
1990	Cle-A	30	76	12	17	5	1	2	14	21	18	.224	.392	.395	786	121	3	0	1	-0	.990	1	1-25/3-5	0.3
1991	Cle-A	47	128	15	27	7	0	2	13	14	22	.211	.308	.313	621	72	-5	2	0	0	.929	1	3-32,1-14/C-5,O-1L	-0.3
1993	Phi-N	8	18	0	1	0	0	0	0	0	3	.056	.105	.056	161	-56	-4	0	0	0	1.000	-0	/3-6,S-1	-0.4
1995	Bal-A	89	254	31	65	9	0	17	38	24	69	.256	.325	.492	817	107	2	0	3	-1	.959	-2	3-69,D-13/1-4	-0.1
1996	Bos-A	10	30	5	8	3	1	2	4	3	6	.267	.353	.633	986	140	2	0	0	0	.963	4	/2-4,S-4	0.5
	Sea-A	21	54	7	10	3	0	1	4	9	12	.185	.302	.296	598	52	-4	0	1	-0	.971	0	3-16/O-1(1-0-0),D-2	-0.4
	Bos-A	12	18	3	2	0	0	0	2	5	6	.111	.304	.111	415	11	-2	0	0	0	.960	4	3-10/1-1	0.1
	Yr	43	102	15	20	6	1	3	10	17	24	.196	.317	.363	679	70	-5	0	1	-0	.967	8	3-26/2-4,S-4,DO1	0.2
1997	Cle-A	16	30	3	8	3	0	2	7	1	10	.267	.290	.567	857	113	0	0	0	0	1.000	-1	/3-7,1-6,O-1(1-0-0)	-0.1
1998	Cle-A	7	14	3	1	0	0	0	1	1	5	.071	.133	.071	205	-43	-3	0	0	0	1.000	-1	/1-4,3-2,2-1	-0.4
	Det-A	16	30	6	8	2	0	1	3	3	11	.267	.353	.433	786	102	0	1	0	0	.977	-2	1-10/O-1(1-0-0),D-6	-0.1
	Cle-A	8	23	5	7	1	0	2	5	1	5	.304	.333	.609	942	134	1	0	1	-0	1.000	0	/3-6,1-3	0.1
	Yr	31	67	14	16	3	0	3	9	5	21	.239	.301	.418	719	83	-2	1	1	-0	.979	-2	1-17/3-8,D-6,2-1,O	-0.4
1999	Cle-A	12	25	5	5	0	0	1	2	11	11	.200	.444	.320	764	95	0	0	0	0	1.000	1	3-10/1-1	0.1
	NY-A	6	8	0	1	0	0	0	0	2	4	.125	.300	.125	425	14	-1	0	0	0	1.000	-0	/1-3,3-1	-0.1
	Yr	18	33	5	6	0	0	1	2	13	15	.182	.413	.273	686	78	-0	0	0	0	1.000	1	3-11/1-4	0.0
2000	Col-N	7	5	2	4	2	0	1	4	2	0	.800	.857	1.800	2657	428	3	0	0	0	1.000	0	/1-1,3-1	0.3
Total	9	289	713	97	164	35	2	31	97	97	182	.230	.330	.415	745	94	-8	3	6	-1	.960	6	3-165/1-72,D-21,2SCO	-0.5
■ **CHARLIE MANUEL** Manuel, Charles Fuqua b: 1/4/44, Northfork, W.Va. BL/TR, 6'4", 200 lbs. Deb: 4/8/69 MC																								
1969	*Min-A	83	164	14	34	6	0	2	24	28	33	.207	.323	.280	603	69	-6	1	0	0	.967	-6	O-46(41-1-4)	-1.4
1970	*Min-A	59	64	4	12	0	0	1	7	6	17	.188	.268	.234	502	39	-5	0	0	0	1.000	-3	O-11(9-0-2)	-0.8
1971	Min-A	18	16	1	2	1	0	0	1	1	8	.125	.176	.188	364	3	-2	0	0	0	.000	-0	/O-1(0-0-1)	-0.3
1972	Min-A	63	122	6	25	5	0	1	8	4	16	.205	.236	.270	507	48	-8	0	0	0	.977	-1	O-28(20-0-9)	-1.1
1974	LA-N	4	3	0	1	0	0	0	1	1	0	.333	.500	.333	833	142	0	0	0	0	.000	0	H	0.0
1975	LA-N	15	15	0	2	0	0	0	2	0	3	.133	.133	.133	267	-27	-3	0	0	0	.000	0	H	-0.3
Total	6	242	384	25	76	12	0	4	43	40	77	.198	.277	.260	537	52	-24	1	0	0	.973	-9	/O-86(70-1-16)	-3.9
■ **JERRY MANUEL** Manuel, Jerry b: 12/23/53, Hahira, Ga. BB/TR (BR 1981-82), 6', 165 lbs. Deb: 9/18/75 MC																								
1975	Det-A	6	18	0	1	0	0	0	0	0	4	.056	.056	.056	111	-66	-4	0	0	0	.944	3	/2-6	-0.1
1976	Det-A	54	43	4	6	1	0	0	2	3	9	.140	.213	.163	376	11	-5	1	0	0	.921	10	2-47/S-4,D-1	0.7
1980	Mon-N	7	6	0	0	0	0	0	0	0	2	.000	.000	.000	0	-99	-2	0	0	0	.941	3	/S-7	0.1
1981	*Mon-N	27	55	10	11	5	0	3	10	6	11	.200	.279	.455	733	104	-0	0	0	0	.987	-0	2-23/S-2	0.0
1982	SD-N	2	5	0	1	0	1	0	1	1	0	.200	.333	.600	933	165	0	0	0	0	1.000	-1	/2-1,S-1,3-1	-0.1
Total	5	96	127	14	19	6	1	3	13	10	26	.150	.217	.283	501	42	-10	1	0	0	.949	14	/2-77,S-14,3-1,D-1	0.6
■ **FRANK MANUSH** Manush, Frank Benjamin b: 9/18/1883, Tuscumbia, Ala. d: 1/5/65, Laguna Beach, Cal. BR/TR, 5'10.5", 175 lbs. Deb: 8/31/08 F																								
1908	Phi-A	23	77	6	12	2	1	0	0	2		.156	.188	.208	395	27	-6	2			.933	-5	3-20/2-2	-1.2
■ **HEINIE MANUSH** Manush, Henry Emmett b: 7/20/01, Tuscumbia, Ala. d: 5/12/71, Sarasota, Fla. BL/TL, 6'1", 200 lbs. Deb: 4/20/23 FCH Career OF: (1379-LF 309-CF 159-RF)																								
1923	Det-A	109	308	59	103	20	5	4	54	20	21	.334	.406	.471	877	133	15	3	5	-1	.953	-5	O-79(72-0-7)	0.3
1924	Det-A	120	422	83	122	24	8	9	68	27	30	.289	.355	.448	803	108	3	14	5	1	.979	-6	*O-106(99-1-6)/1-1	-0.9
1925	Det-A	99	278	46	84	14	3	5	47	24	21	.302	.362	.428	790	101	0	8	3	1	.982	-5	O-73(13-56-5)	-0.7
1926	Det-A	136	498	95	188	35	8	14	86	31	28	**.378**	.421	.564	985	153	37	11	5	1	.967	-4	*O-120(11-104-5)	2.7
1927	Det-A	151	593	102	177	31	18	6	90	47	29	.298	.354	.442	796	104	2	12	8	-0	.971	-3	*O-149(3-147-0)	-0.7
1928	StL-A	154	638	104	**241**	**47**	20	13	108	39	14	.378	.414	.575	989	153	46	17	5	2	.992	2	*O-154(154-0-0)	3.6
1929	StL-A	142	574	85	204	**45**	10	6	81	43	24	.355	.401	.500	901	126	22	9	8	-1	.987	-2	*O-141(141-0-0)	0.7
1930	StL-A	49	198	26	65	16	4	2	29	5	7	.328	.345	.480	825	103	0	3	1	0	.990	2	O-48(48-0-0)	-0.1
	Was-A	88	356	74	129	33	8	7	65	26	17	.362	.406	.559	965	141	22	4	3	-0	.988	-2	O-86(86-0-0)	1.2
	Yr	137	554	100	194	49	12	9	94	31	24	.350	.385	.531	915	128	22	7	4	0	.989	1	*O-134(134-0-0)	1.1
1931	Was-A	146	616	110	189	41	11	6	70	36	27	.307	.351	.438	789	106	4	3	3	-0	.977	-11	*O-143(143-0-0)	-1.4
1932	Was-A	149	625	121	214	41	14	14	116	36	29	.342	.383	.520	903	133	29	7	2	1	.988	-0	*O-146(146-0-0)	1.9
1933	*Was-A	153	658	115	**221**	32	**17**	5	95	36	18	.336	.372	.459	831	120	18	6	4	-0	.982	-2	*O-150(150-0-0)	0.7
1934	Was-A★	137	556	88	194	42	11	11	89	36	23	.349	.392	.523	915	140	30	7	3	0	.980	-0	*O-131(130-1-0)	2.1
1935	Was-A	119	479	68	131	26	9	4	56	35	17	.273	.328	.390	719	88	-10	2	0	0	.985	3	*O-111(111-0-0)	-1.2
1936	Bos-A	82	313	43	91	15	5	0	45	17	11	.291	.329	.371	700	69	-16	1	3	-1	.966	-8	O-72(72-0-0)	-2.6
1937	Bro-N	132	466	57	155	25	7	4	73	40	24	.333	.389	.442	831	123	16	6			.970	-12	*O-123(0-0-123)	-0.3
1938	Bro-N	17	51	9	12	3	1	0	6	5	4	.235	.304	.333	637	73	-2	1			1.000	1	O-12(0-0-12)	-0.1
	Pit-N	15	13	2	4	1	1	0	4	2	0	.308	.400	.538	938	155	1	0			.000	0	H	0.1
	Yr	32	64	11	16	4	2	0	10	7	4	.250	.324	.375	699	90	-1	1			1.000	1	O-12(0-0-12)	0.0
1939	Pit-N	10	12	0	0	0	0	0	1	1	1	.000	.077	.000	77	-79	-3	0			1.000	-0	/O-1(0-0-1)	-0.3
Total	17	2008	7654	1287	2524	491	160	110	1183	506	345	.330	.377	.479	856	121	214	114	58		.979	-50	*O-1845L/1-1	5.0
■ **KIRT MANWARING** Manwaring, Kirt Dean b: 7/15/65, Elmira, N.Y. BR/TR, 5'11", 190 lbs. Deb: 9/15/87																								
1987	SF-N	6	7	0	1	0	0	0	0	0	1	.143	.250	.143	393	8	-1	0	0	0	.909	-1	/C-6	-0.2
1988	SF-N	40	116	12	29	7	0	1	15	2	21	.250	.281	.336	617	80	-3	0	1	-0	.979	-2	C-40	-0.4
1989	*SF-N	85	200	14	42	4	2	0	18	11	28	.210	.265	.250	515	49	-13	2	1	0	.982	-0	C-81	-1.0
1990	SF-N	8	13	0	2	0	1	0	1	0	3	.154	.154	.308	462	25	-1	0	0	0	1.000	2	/C-8	0.1
1991	SF-N	67	178	16	40	9	0	0	19	9	22	.225	.274	.275	549	57	-10	1	1	-0	.988	1	C-67	-0.6
1992	SF-N	109	349	24	85	10	5	4	26	29	42	.244	.311	.335	646	88	-6	2	1	0	.994	1	*C-108	0.1
1993	SF-N	130	432	48	119	15	1	5	49	41	76	.275	.347	.350	696	90	-5	1	3	-1	**.998**	-0	*C-130	0.2
1994	SF-N	97	316	30	79	17	1	1	29	25	50	.250	.311	.320	631	68	-15	1	1	-0	.993	5	C-97	-0.4
1995	SF-N	118	379	21	95	15	2	4	36	27	72	.251	.317	.332	650	74	-14	1	0	0	.990	-12	*C-118	-1.9
1996	SF-N	49	145	9	34	6	0	1	14	16	24	.234	.323	.297	620	67	-6	0	1	-0	.993	1	C-49	-0.3
	Hou-N	37	82	5	18	3	0	0	4	3	16	.220	.264	.256	520	41	-7	0	0	0	.995	5	C-37	0.0
	Yr	86	227	14	52	9	0	1	18	19	40	.229	.303	.282	585	59	-13	0	1	-0	.994	6	C-86	-0.3
1997	Col-N	104	337	22	76	6	4	1	27	30	78	.226	.293	.276	569	41	-28	1	5	-2	.994	-11	*C-100	-3.5
1998	Col-N	110	291	30	72	12	3	2	26	38	49	.247	.340	.330	670	64	-14	1	5	-2	.988	5	*C-108	-0.6
1999	Col-N	48	137	17	41	7	1	2	14	12	23	.299	.377	.409	785	78	-4	0	0	0	.981	-2	C-44/D-1	-0.4
Total	13	1008	2982	248	733	111	20	21	278	243	505	.246	.313	.318	631	68	-128	10	19	-4	.991	-9	C-993/D-1	-8.9
■ **CLIFF MAPES** Mapes, Clifford Franklin b: 3/13/22, Sutherland, Neb. d: 12/5/96, Pryor, Okla. BL/TR, 6'3", 205 lbs. Deb: 4/20/48																								
1948	NY-A	53	88	19	22	11	1	1	12	6	13	.250	.298	.432	730	94	-2	1	1	-0	.958	1	O-21(9-6-6)	-0.1
1949	*NY-A	111	304	56	75	13	3	7	38	58	50	.247	.369	.378	747	98	0	6	0	1	.976	3	*O-108(4-58-49)	0.1
1950	*NY-A	108	356	60	88	14	6	12	61	47	61	.247	.338	.421	760	96	-3	1	6	-2	.950	-7	*O-102(4-21-80)	-1.5
1951	NY-A	45	51	6	11	3	1	2	8	4	14	.216	.273	.431	704	92	-1	0	0	0	1.000	-9	O-34(2-3-29)	-1.0
	StL-A	56	201	32	55	7	2	7	30	26	33	.274	.360	.433	792	110	3	0	1	-0	.983	-1	O-53(15-12-31)	-0.1
	Yr	101	252	38	66	10	3	9	38	30	47	.262	.343	.433	775	109	2	0	1	-0	.986	-10	O-87(17-15-60)	-1.1
1952	Det-A	86	193	26	38	7	0	9	23	27	42	.197	.295	.373	669	84	-5	0	1	-0	.967	-10	O-63(5-18-43)	-1.7
Total	5	459	1193	199	289	55	13	38	172	168	213	.242	.338	.406	743	97	-8	8	9	-1	.969	-23	O-381(39-118-238)	-4.3
■ **HOWARD MAPLE** Maple, Howard Albert "Mape" b: 7/20/03, Adrian, Mo. d: 11/9/70, Portland, Ore. BL/TR, 5'7", 175 lbs. Deb: 5/19/32																								
1932	Was-A	44	41	6	10	0	1	0	7	7	7	.244	.367	.293	660	74	-1	0	0	0	1.000	-3	C-41	-0.3
■ **GEORGE MAPPES** Mappes, George Richard "Dick" b: 12/25/1865, St.Louis, Mo. d: 2/20/34, St.Louis, Mo. Deb: 9/23/1885																								
1885	Bal-a	6	19	2	4	0	1	0	0	1		.211	.250	.316	566	79	-0				.875	-2	/2-6	-0.2
1886	StL-N	6	14	1	2	0	0	0	0	1	5	.143	.200	.143	343	6	-1	0			1.000	-1	/C-3,3-2,2-1	-0.2
Total	2	12	33	3	6	0	1	0	0	2	5	.182	.229	.242	471	48	-2	0			.848	-3	/2-7,C-3,3-2	-0.4

YEAR	TM/L	G	AB	R	H	2B	3B	HR	RBI	BB	SO	AVG	OBP	SLG	OPS	OPS+	BR+	SB	CS	SBR	FA	FR	G/POS	TPR
■ RABBIT MARANVILLE Maranville, Walter James Vincent b: 11/11/1891, Springfield, Mass. d: 1/5/54, New York, N.Y. BR/TR, 5'5", 155 lbs. Deb: 9/10/12 MH																								
1912	Bos-N	26	86	8	18	2	0	0	8	9	14	.209	.292	.233	524	44	-6	1			.929	6	S-26	0.1
1913	Bos-N	143	571	68	141	13	8	2	48	68	62	.247	.330	.308	638	81	-12	25			.949	15	*S-143	1.3
1914	*Bos-N	156	586	74	144	23	6	4	78	45	56	.246	.306	.326	632	88	-9	28			.938	**52**	*S-156	**5.7**
1915	Bos-N	149	509	51	124	23	6	2	43	45	65	.244	.308	.324	632	96	-3	18	12	-0	.941	19	*S-149	2.9
1916	Bos-N	155	604	79	142	16	13	4	38	50	69	.235	.296	.325	620	94	-4	32	15	2	**.947**	22	*S-155	3.3
1917	Bos-N	142	561	69	146	19	13	3	43	40	47	.260	.312	.357	668	111	6	27			.947	14	*S-142	3.4
1918	Bos-N	11	38	3	12	0	1	0	3	4	0	.316	.381	.368	749	134	2	0			.932	2	S-11	0.4
1919	Bos-N	131	480	44	128	18	10	5	43	36	23	.267	.319	.377	696	113	7	12			.941	**29**	*S-131	**4.9**
1920	Bos-N	134	493	48	131	19	15	1	43	28	24	.266	.305	.371	676	98	-3	14	11	-1	.948	14	*S-133	2.1
1921	Pit-N	153	612	90	180	25	12	1	70	47	38	.294	.347	.379	727	90	-8	25	12	1	.962	-11	*S-153	0.0
1922	Pit-N	155	672	115	198	26	15	0	63	61	43	.295	.355	.378	733	88	-11	24	13	1	.961	7	*S-138,2-18	1.2
1923	Pit-N	141	581	78	161	19	9	1	41	42	34	.277	.327	.346	673	76	-20	14	11	-1	**.965**	12	*S-141	0.7
1924	Pit-N	152	594	62	158	33	20	2	71	35	53	.266	.307	.399	706	86	-13	18	14	-1	**.973**	5	*2-152	-0.5
1925	Chi-N	75	266	37	62	10	3	0	23	29	20	.233	.308	.293	602	54	-18	6	5	-0	.955	4	S-74,M	-0.6
1926	Bro-N	78	234	32	55	8	5	0	24	26	24	.235	.312	.312	624	69	-10	7			.948	10	S-60,2-18	0.6
1927	StL-N	9	29	0	7	1	0	0	0	2	2	.241	.290	.276	566	51	-2	0			.962	3	/S-9	0.2
1928	*StL-N	112	366	40	88	14	10	1	34	36	27	.240	.310	.342	652	69	-17	3			.969	-5	*S-112/2-2	-1.0
1929	Bos-N	146	560	87	159	26	10	0	55	47	33	.284	.344	.366	710	79	-18	13			.961	20	*S-145/2-1	1.6
1930	Bos-N	142	558	85	157	26	8	2	43	48	23	.281	.344	.367	711	75	-22	9			**.965**	-13	*S-138/3-4	-1.7
1931	Bos-N	145	562	69	146	22	5	0	33	56	34	.260	.329	.317	646	77	-17	9			.949	-24	*S-137,2-11	-3.0
1932	Bos-N	149	571	67	134	20	4	0	37	46	28	.235	.295	.284	579	59	-32	4			**.975**	6	*2-149	-1.7
1933	Bos-N	143	478	46	104	15	4	0	38	36	34	.218	.274	.266	539	59	-25	2			.971	-27	*2-142	-4.6
1935	Bos-N	23	67	3	10	2	0	0	5	3	3	.149	.186	.179	365	-2	-10	0			.963	-5	2-20	-1.3
Total	23	2670	10078	1255	2605	380	177	28	884	839	756	.258	.318	.340	658	82	-245	291	93		.952	154	*S-2153,2-513/3-4	14.0
■ JOHNNY MARCUM Marcum, John Alfred "Footsie" b: 9/9/09, Campbellsburg, Ky. d: 9/10/84, Louisville, Ky. BL/TR, 5'11", 197 lbs. Deb: 9/7/33																								
1933	Phi-A	5	12	2	2	0	0	0	0	2	1	.167	.286	.167	452	22	-1	0	0	0	1.000	0	/P-5	0.0
1934	Phi-A	58	112	10	30	4	0	1	13	3	5	.268	.287	.330	617	61	-7	0	1	-0	.949	-0	P-37	0.0
1935	Phi-A	64	119	13	37	2	1	2	17	9	5	.311	.359	.395	754	96	-1	0	0	0	.896	-3	P-39	0.0
1936	Bos-A	48	88	6	18	3	0	2	7	3	5	.205	.231	.307	538	30	-10	0	0	0	.950	0	P-31	0.0
1937	Bos-A	51	86	12	23	8	0	0	13	7	4	.267	.323	.360	683	69	-4	0	0	0	.981	1	P-37	0.0
1938	Bos-A	19	37	3	5	0	0	0	3	6	9	.135	.256	.135	391	1	-6	0	0	0	1.000	-1	P-15	0.0
1939	StL-A	16	22	3	10	1	0	0	5	1	2	.455	.478	.500	978	147	2	0	0	0	1.000	-0	P-12	0.0
	Chi-A	38	57	7	16	0	0	0	12	5	1	.281	.339	.281	619	58	-3	0	0	0	.941	-1	P-19	0.0
	Yr	54	79	10	26	1	0	0	17	6	3	.329	.376	.342	718	83	-2	0	0	0	.962	-1	P-31	0.0
Total	7	299	533	56	141	18	1	5	70	36	32	.265	.311	.330	641	62	-30	0	1	-0	.953	-4	P-195	0.0
■ RED MARION Marion, John Wyeth b: 3/14/14, Richburg, S.C. d: 3/13/75, San Jose, Cal. BR/TR, 6'2", 175 lbs. Deb: 9/16/35 F																								
1935	Was-A	4	11	1	2	1	0	1	1	0	2	.182	.182	.545	727	85	-0	0	0	0	.833	-0	/O-3(1-1-1)	-0.1
1943	Was-A	14	17	2	3	0	0	0	1	3	1	.176	.300	.176	476	42	-1	0	0	0	1.000	-1	/O-4(4-0-0)	-0.2
Total	2	18	28	3	5	1	0	1	2	3	3	.179	.258	.321	579	63	-2	0	0	0	.923	-1	/O-7(5-1-1)	-0.3
■ MARTY MARION Marion, Martin Whiteford "Slats" or "The Octopus" b: 12/1/17, Richburg, S.C. BR/TR, 6'2", 170 lbs. Deb: 4/16/40 FMC																								
1940	StL-N	125	435	44	121	18	1	3	46	21	34	.278	.311	.345	656	76	-14	9			.949	-6	*S-125	-1.2
1941	StL-N	155	547	50	138	22	3	3	58	42	48	.252	.308	.320	628	72	-20	8			.954	7	*S-155	-0.2
1942	*StL-N	147	485	66	134	**38**	5	0	54	48	50	.276	.343	.375	718	102	2	8			.960	7	*S-147	2.1
1943	*StL-N★	129	418	38	117	15	3	1	52	32	37	.280	.334	.337	671	90	-5	1			.970	25	*S-128	3.1
1944	*StL-N★	144	506	50	135	26	2	6	63	43	50	.267	.324	.362	686	91	-6	1			**.972**	5	*S-144	1.0
1945	StL-N†	123	430	63	119	27	5	1	59	39	39	.277	.340	.370	709	95	-3	2			.967	-2	*S-122	0.5
1946	*StL-N★	146	498	51	116	29	4	3	46	59	53	.233	.318	.325	643	79	-13	1			.973	**19**	*S-145	1.6
1947	StL-N★	149	540	57	147	19	6	4	74	49	58	.272	.334	.352	686	79	-16	3			**.981**	**20**	*S-141	1.3
1948	StL-N†	144	567	70	143	26	4	4	43	37	54	.252	.298	.333	631	67	-26	1			**.974**	9	*S-142	-0.8
1949	StL-N☆	134	515	61	140	31	2	5	70	37	42	.272	.323	.369	692	81	-14	0			.976	17	*S-134	1.1
1950	StL-N★	106	372	36	92	10	2	4	40	44	55	.247	.327	.317	644	67	-17	1			.978	-1	*S-101	-1.2
1952	StL-A	67	186	16	46	11	0	2	19	19	17	.247	.320	.339	659	81	-5	0	2	-1	.980	-7	S-63,M	-0.9
1953	StL-A	3	7	0	0	0	0	0	0	0	0	.000	.000	.000	0	-98	-2	0	0	0	1.000	-1	/3-2,M	-0.4
Total	13	1572	5506	602	1448	272	37	36	624	470	537	.263	.323	.345	668	81	-139	35	2		.969	92	*S-1547/3-2	6.0
■ ROGER MARIS Maris, Roger Eugene (b: Roger Eugene Maras) b: 9/10/34, Hibbing, Minn. d: 12/14/85, Houston, Tex. BL/TR, 6', 204 lbs. Deb: 4/16/57																								
1957	Cle-A	116	358	61	84	9	5	14	51	60	79	.235	.346	.405	751	106	3	8	4	0	.975	5	*O-112(26-87-8)	0.4
1958	Cle-A	51	182	26	41	5	1	9	27	17	33	.225	.291	.412	704	94	-2	4	2	0	.967	5	O-47(0-27-23)	0.0
	KC-A	99	401	61	99	14	3	19	53	28	52	.247	.299	.439	738	99	-2	0	0	0	.975	-4	O-99(0-21-90)	-1.0
	Yr	150	583	87	140	19	4	28	80	45	85	.240	.297	.431	727	97	-4	4	2	0	.972	1	*O-146(0-48-113)	-1.0
1959	KC-A★	122	433	69	118	21	7	16	72	58	53	.273	.362	.464	827	123	14	2	1	0	.975	6	*O-117(0-6-113)	1.6
1960	*NY-A★	136	499	98	141	18	7	39	**112**	70	65	.283	.374	**.581**	955	164	43	2	2	-0	.985	3	*O-131(0-7-128)	4.0
1961	*NY-A★	161	590	**132**	159	16	4	**61**	**142**	94	67	.269	.376	.620	997	170	57	0	0	0	.968	-11	*O-160(0-11-156)	3.4
1962	*NY-A★	157	590	92	151	34	1	33	100	87	78	.256	.357	.485	842	128	23	1	0	0	.991	-4	*O-154(0-64-103)	1.1
1963	*NY-A	90	312	53	84	14	1	23	53	35	40	.269	.347	.542	888	146	18	1	0	0	.988	2	O-86(0-1-86)	1.5
1964	*NY-A	141	513	86	144	12	2	26	71	62	78	.281	.365	.464	829	127	19	3	0	1	.996	-0	*O-137(0-32-105)	1.2
1965	NY-A	46	155	22	37	7	0	8	27	29	29	.239	.359	.439	797	126	6	0	0	0	.971	-2	O-43(0-0-43)	0.1
1966	NY-A	119	348	37	81	9	2	13	43	36	60	.233	.310	.382	692	101	0	0	0	0	.993	-7	O-95(0-1-94)	-1.4
1967	*StL-N	125	410	64	107	18	7	9	55	52	61	.261	.350	.405	755	117	10	0	0	0	.991	2	*O-118(0-2-118)	0.4
1968	*StL-N	100	310	25	79	18	2	5	45	24	38	.255	.310	.374	685	106	2	0	0	0	.983	3	O-84(0-0-84)	-0.1
Total	12	1463	5101	826	1325	195	42	275	851	652	733	.260	.348	.476	824	128	191	21	9	1	.982	-3	*O-1383(26-259-1151)	11.2
■ GENE MARKLAND Markland, Cleneth Eugene "Mousey" b: 12/26/19, Detroit, Mich. d: 6/15/99, Barefoot Bay, Fla. BR/TR, 5'10", 160 lbs. Deb: 4/25/50																								
1950	Phi-A	5	8	2	1	0	0	0	0	3	0	.125	.364	.125	489	30	-1	0	0	0	1.000	0	/2-5	0.0
■ HARRY MARNIE Marnie, Harry Sylvester b: 7/6/18, Philadelphia, Pa. BR/TR, 6'1", 178 lbs. Deb: 9/15/40																								
1940	Phi-N	11	34	4	6	0	0	0	4	4	2	.176	.263	.176	440	24	-3	0			.984	6	2-11	0.3
1941	Phi-N	61	158	12	38	3	3	0	11	13	25	.241	.298	.297	596	71	-6	0			.990	5	2-39,S-16/3-3	0.1
1942	Phi-N	24	30	3	5	0	0	0	0	1	2	.167	.194	.167	360	6	-4	1			.971	8	2-11/S-7,3-1	0.5
Total	3	96	222	19	49	3	3	0	15	18	29	.221	.279	.261	540	55	-13	1			.987	19	/2-61,S-23,3-4	0.9
■ FRED MAROLEWSKI Marolewski, Fred Daniel "Fritz" b: 10/6/28, Chicago, Ill. BR/TR, 6'2.5", 205 lbs. Deb: 9/19/53																								
1953	StL-N	1	0	0	0	0	0	0	0	0	0	—	—	—	—	—	0	0	0	0	.000	0	/1-1	0.0
■ OLLIE MARQUARDT Marquardt, Albert Ludwig b: 9/22/02, Toledo, Ohio d: 2/7/68, Port Clinton, Ohio BR/TR, 5'9", 156 lbs. Deb: 4/14/31																								
1931	Bos-A	17	39	4	7	1	0	0	2	3	4	.179	.238	.205	443	18	-5	0	1	-0	.946	-3	2-13/S-1,3-1	-0.7
■ GONZALO MARQUEZ Marquez, Gonzalo Enrique (Moya) b: 3/31/46, Carupano, Venez. d: 12/20/84, Valencia, Venez. BL/TL, 5'11", 180 lbs. Deb: 8/11/72 Career OF: (0-LF 0-CF 1-RF)																								
1972	*Oak-A	23	21	2	8	0	0	0	4	3	4	.381	.480	.381	861	167	2	1	1	-0	.929	-0	/1-2	0.2
1973	Oak-A	23	25	1	6	1	0	0	2	0	4	.240	.240	.280	520	49	-2	0	0	0	.000	-1	/2-2,1-1,O-1R,D-1	-0.3
	Chi-N	19	58	5	13	2	0	1	4	3	4	.224	.274	.310	585	57	-3	0	0	0	.994	2	1-18	-0.2
1974	Chi-N	11	11	1	0	0	0	0	0	1	2	.000	.083	.000	83	-72	-3	0	0	0	1.000	-0	/1-1	-0.3
Total	3	76	115	9	27	3	0	1	10	7	14	.235	.290	.287	577	62	-6	1	1	-0	.989	1	/1-22,2-2,D-1,O-1R	-0.6
■ LUIS MARQUEZ Marquez, Luis Angel (Sanchez) "Canena" b: 10/28/25, Aguadilla, P.R. d: 3/1/88, Aguadilla, P.R. BR/TR, 5'10.5", 174 lbs. Deb: 4/18/51																								
1951	Bos-N	68	122	19	24	5	1	0	11	10	20	.197	.274	.254	528	46	-9	4	4	-1	1.000	-2	O-43(21-23-3)	-1.4

YEAR	TM/L	G	AB	R	H	2B	3B	HR	RBI	BB	SO	AVG	OBP	SLG	OPS	OPS+	BR+	SB	CS	SBR	FA	FR	G/POS	TPR
1954	Chi-N	17	12	2	1	0	0	0	0	2	4	.083	.214	.083	298	-19	-2	3	0	1	1.000	-4	O-14(4-10-0)	-0.6
	Pit-N	14	9	3	1	0	0	0	0	4	0	.111	.385	.111	496	37	-1	0	0	0	1.000	-1	/O-4(1-1-2)	-0.2
	Yr	31	21	5	2	0	0	0	0	6	4	.095	.296	.095	392	7	-3	3	0	1	1.000	-5	O-18(5-11-2)	-0.8
Total	2	99	143	24	26	5	1	0	11	16	24	.182	.278	.231	509	40	-12	7	4	0	1.000	-7	/O-61(26-34-5)	-2.2
■ BOB MARQUIS Marquis, Robert Rudolph b: 12/23/24, Oklahoma City, Okla. BL/TL, 6′1″, 170 lbs. Deb: 4/17/53																								
1953	Cin-N	40	44	9	12	1	1	2	3	4	11	.273	.333	.477	811	107	0	0	0	0	.905	-2	O-10(2-8-0)	-0.2
■ ROGER MARQUIS Marquis, Roger Julian "Noonie" b: 4/5/37, Holyoke, Mass. BL/TL, 6′, 190 lbs. Deb: 9/25/55																								
1955	Bal-A	1	1	0	0	0	0	0	0	0	0	.000	.000	.000	0	-99	-0	0	0	0	.000	-0	/O-1(0-0-1)	-0.1
■ LEFTY MARR Marr, Charles W. b: 9/19/1862, Cincinnati, Ohio d: 1/11/12, New Britain, Conn. BL/TL, Deb: 10/3/1886 Career OF: (0-LF 9-CF 197-RF)																								
1886	Cin-a	8	29	2	8	1	1	0	2	1		.276	.323	.379	702	116	0	1			.696	-1	/O-8(0-8-0)	-0.1
1889	Col-a	139	546	110	167	26	**15**	1	75	87	32	.306	.407	.414	821	141	35	29			.856	12	3-66,O-47R,S-26,/1C	4.0
1890	Cin-N	130	527	91	157	17	12	1	73	46	29	.298	.361	.381	742	117	11	44			.930	-11	O-64(0-0-64),3-63/S-3	0.0
1891	Cin-N	72	286	32	74	9	7	0	32	25	15	.259	.323	.339	662	92	-3	16			.835	-10	O-72(0-0-72)	-1.2
	Cin-a	14	57	9	11	1	0	0	4	7	4	.193	.281	.211	492	38	-5	2			.923	-1	O-14(0-0-14)	-0.5
Total	4	363	1445	244	417	54	35	2	186	166	80	.289	.368	.379	746	118	38	92			.853	-10	O-205R,3-129/S-29,1C	2.2
■ ELI MARRERO Marrero, Elieser b: 11/17/73, Havana, Cuba BR/TR, 6′1″, 180 lbs. Deb: 9/3/97																								
1997	StL-N	17	45	4	11	2	0	2	7	2	13	.244	.277	.422	699	81	-1	4	0	1	.969	1	C-17	0.1
1998	StL-N	83	254	28	62	18	1	4	20	28	42	.244	.319	.370	689	81	-7	6	2	1	.991	-2	C-73/1-2	-0.4
1999	StL-N	114	317	32	61	13	1	6	34	18	56	.192	.238	.297	535	34	-33	11	2	2	.987	-0	C-96,1-20	-2.6
2000	*StL-N	53	102	21	23	3	1	5	17	9	16	.225	.307	.422	729	81	-3	5	0	1	1.000	6	C-38/1-7	0.5
Total	4	267	718	85	157	36	3	17	78	57	127	.219	.280	.348	628	60	-44	26	4	4	.989	4	C-224/1-29	-2.4
■ ORESTE MARRERO Marrero, Oreste Vilato (Vazquez) b: 10/31/69, Bayamon, P.R. BL/TL, 6′, 195 lbs. Deb: 8/12/93																								
1993	Mon-N	32	81	10	17	5	1	1	4	14	16	.210	.326	.333	660	74	-3	1	3	-1	.991	-0	1-32	-0.6
1996	LA-N	10	8	2	3	1	0	0	1	1	3	.375	.444	.500	944	161	1	0	0	0	1.000	-0	/1-1	0.1
Total	2	42	89	12	20	6	1	1	5	15	19	.225	.337	.348	685	81	-2	1	3	-1	.991	-1	/1-33	-0.5
■ WILLIAM MARRIOTT Marriott, William Earl b: 4/18/1893, Pratt, Kan. d: 8/11/69, Berkeley, Cal. BL/TR, 6′, 170 lbs. Deb: 9/6/17 Career OF: (3-LF 0-CF 0-RF)																								
1917	Chi-N	3	6	0	0	0	0	0	0	0	1	.000	.000	.000	0	-93	-1	0			.667	-0	/O-1(1-0-0)	-0.2
1920	Chi-N	14	43	7	12	4	2	0	5	6	5	.279	.367	.465	832	135	2	1	1	-0	.892	-4	2-14	-0.2
1921	Chi-N	30	38	3	12	1	1	0	7	4	1	.316	.381	.395	776	105	0	0	1	-0	.826	-1	/2-6,S-1,3-1,O-1L	-0.1
1925	Bos-N	103	370	37	99	9	1	1	40	28	26	.268	.322	.305	628	67	-18	3	8	-2	.928	3	3-89/O-1(1-0-0)	-1.0
1926	Bro-N	109	360	39	96	13	9	3	42	17	20	.267	.303	.378	681	84	-9	12			.927	-8	*3-104	-1.1
1927	Bro-N	6	9	0	1	0	1	0	1	2	2	.111	.273	.333	606	61	-1	0			.889	1	/3-2	0.0
Total	6	265	826	86	220	27	14	4	95	57	55	.266	.317	.347	664	78	-26	16	10		.925	-9	3-196/2-20,O-3L,S-1	-2.6
■ ARMANDO MARSANS Marsans, Armando b: 10/3/1887, Matanzas, Cuba d: 9/3/60, Havana, Cuba BR/TR, 5′10″, 157 lbs. Deb: 7/4/11 Career OF: (51-LF 459-CF 71-RF)																								
1911	Cin-N	58	138	17	36	2	2	0	11	15	11	.261	.346	.304	651	86	-2	11			.968	-5	O-34(5-16-13)/1-1,3-1	-0.9
1912	Cin-N	110	416	59	132	19	7	1	38	20	17	.317	.353	.404	757	110	5	35			.975	-3	O-98(7-82-13)/1-6	-0.5
1913	Cin-N	118	435	49	129	7	6	0	38	17	25	.297	.327	.340	668	91	-5	37			.963	-5	O-94C,1-22/3-2,S-1	-1.7
1914	Cin-N	36	124	16	37	3	0	0	22	14	6	.298	.374	.323	697	105	1	13			.916	1	O-36(36-0-0)	0.1
	StL-F	9	40	5	14	0	2	0	2	3	0	.350	.395	.450	845	123	1	4			.927	0	/2-7,S-2	0.1
1915	StL-F	36	124	16	22	3	0	0	6	14	5	.177	.261	.202	462	29	-13	5			.975	3	O-35(0-35-0)	-1.4
1916	StL-A	151	528	51	134	12	1	1	60	57	41	.254	.333	.286	619	91	-4	46	26	1	.977	5	*O-150(0-150-0)	-0.9
1917	StL-A	75	257	31	59	12	0	0	20	20	6	.230	.285	.276	561	74	-8	11			.963	-4	O-67(0-67-0)/3-5,2-1	-1.9
	NY-A	25	88	10	20	4	0	0	15	8	3	.227	.292	.273	564	72	-3	6			.974	3	O-25(0-25-0)	-0.2
	Yr	100	345	41	79	16	0	0	35	28	9	.229	.287	.275	562	73	-11	17			.967	-1	O-92(0-92-0)/3-5,2-1	-2.1
1918	NY-A	37	123	13	29	5	1	0	9	5	3	.236	.266	.293	558	67	-5	3			.943	-6	O-36(0-28-8)	-1.5
Total	8	655	2273	267	612	67	19	2	221	173	117	.269	.325	.318	643	88	-35	171	26		.967	-11	O-575C/1-29,2-8,3S	-8.8
■ FRED MARSH Marsh, Fred Francis b: 1/5/24, Valley Falls, Kan. BR/TR, 5′10″, 180 lbs. Deb: 4/19/49 Career OF: (2-LF 0-CF 1-RF)																								
1949	Cle-A	1	0	0	0	0	0	0	0	0	0	—	—	—	—	—	0	0	0	0	.000	0	R	0.0
1951	StL-A	130	445	44	108	21	4	4	43	36	56	.243	.299	.335	634	69	-20	4	4	-1	.928	3	*3-117/S-3,2-2	-1.7
1952	StL-A	11	24	3	5	1	0	0	1	5	4	.208	.345	.250	595	65	-1	0	1	-0	.963	2	/2-9,S-3	0.1
	Was-A	9	24	1	1	0	0	0	1	1	4	.042	.080	.042	122	-68	-5	0	0	0	1.000	-2	/2-5,O-2(2-0-0)	-0.8
	StL-A	76	223	25	64	8	1	2	26	22	29	.287	.351	.359	710	95	-1	3	2	-0	.945	-15	S-57,3-21	-1.4
	Yr	96	271	29	70	9	1	2	28	28	37	.258	.328	.321	649	79	-7	3	3	-0	.945	-15	S-60,3-21,2-14,/O-2L	-2.1
1953	Chi-A	67	95	22	19	1	0	2	2	13	26	.200	.303	.274	576	55	-6	0	3	-1	.940	7	3-32,S-17/1-5,2-2	0.0
1954	Chi-A	62	98	21	30	5	2	0	4	9	16	.306	.364	.398	762	105	1	4	2	0	.975	18	3-36/S-3,1-2,O-1R	1.9
1955	Bal-A	89	303	30	66	7	1	2	19	35	33	.218	.301	.267	568	58	-18	1	2	-0	.983	-15	2-76,3-18,S-16	-2.8
1956	Bal-A	20	24	2	3	0	0	0	0	4	3	.125	.250	.125	375	2	-3	1	0	0	.929	0	/S-8,3-8,2-5	-0.2
Total	7	465	1236	148	296	43	8	10	96	125	171	.239	.310	.311	622	69	-54	13	14	-2	.928	-2	3-232,S-107/2-99,1O	-4.9
■ TOM MARSH Marsh, Thomas Owen b: 12/27/65, Toledo, Ohio BR/TR, 6′2″, 180 lbs. Deb: 6/5/92																								
1992	Phi-N	42	125	7	25	3	2	2	16	2	23	.200	.219	.304	523	47	-9	0	1	-0	.971	-1	O-35(25-0-12)	-1.3
1994	Phi-N	8	18	3	5	1	1	0	3	1	1	.278	.316	.444	760	93	-0	0	0	0	.889	-1	/O-7(3-0-4)	-0.2
1995	Phi-N	43	109	13	32	3	1	3	15	4	25	.294	.319	.422	741	93	-1	0	1	-0	.939	-0	O-29(24-4-1)	-0.2
Total	3	93	252	23	62	7	4	5	34	7	49	.246	.269	.365	634	71	-11	0	2	-1	.952	-3	/O-71(52-4-17)	-1.7
■ CHARLIE MARSHALL Marshall, Charles Anthony (b: Charles Anthony Marczlewicz) b: 8/28/19, Wilmington, Del. BR/TR, 5′10.5″, 178 lbs. Deb: 6/14/41																								
1941	StL-N	1	0	0	0	0	0	0	0	0	0	—	—	—	—	—	0	0			1.000	-0	/C-1	0.0
■ DAVE MARSHALL Marshall, David Lewis b: 1/14/43, Artesia, Cal. BL/TR, 6′1″, 190 lbs. Deb: 9/7/67																								
1967	SF-N	1	0	0	0	0	0	0	0	0	0	—	—	—	—	—	0	0	0	0	.000	0	R	0.0
1968	SF-N	76	174	17	46	5	1	1	16	20	37	.264	.344	.322	665	101	1	2	1	0	.924	-6	O-50(24-0-28)	-0.9
1969	SF-N	110	267	32	62	7	1	2	33	40	68	.232	.343	.288	631	80	-6	1	8	-3	.956	-10	O-87(79-0-17)	-2.4
1970	NY-N	92	189	21	46	10	1	6	29	17	43	.243	.306	.402	708	88	-4	4	1	1	.973	-1	O-43(12-0-33)	-0.6
1971	NY-N	100	214	28	51	9	1	3	21	26	54	.238	.326	.332	658	88	-3	3	1	0	.989	-4	O-64(25-0-39)	-1.0
1972	NY-N	72	156	21	39	5	0	4	11	22	28	.250	.346	.359	705	103	1	3	3	-0	.972	-3	O-42(1-4-38)	-0.4
1973	SD-N	39	49	4	14	5	0	0	4	8	9	.286	.397	.388	784	128	2	0	1	-0	1.000	-1	/O-8(0-0-8)	0.1
Total	7	490	1049	123	258	41	4	16	114	133	239	.246	.336	.338	675	92	-8	13	15	-2	.966	-24	O-294(141-4-163)	-5.2
■ DOC MARSHALL Marshall, Edward Harbert "Eddie" b: 6/4/06, New Albany, Miss. d: 9/1/99, Lake San Marcos, Cal. BR/TR, 5′11″, 150 lbs. Deb: 9/28/29																								
1929	NY-N	5	15	6	6	2	0	0	2	1	0	.400	.438	.533	971	140	1	0			1.000	-2	/2-5	-0.1
1930	NY-N	78	223	33	69	5	3	0	21	13	9	.309	.350	.359	709	73	-9	0			.947	-3	S-45,2-17/3-5	-0.7
1931	NY-N	68	194	15	39	6	2	0	10	8	8	.201	.233	.253	485	31	-19	1			.956	4	2-47,S-11/3-3	-1.2
1932	NY-N	68	226	18	56	8	1	0	28	6	11	.248	.270	.292	562	52	-15	1			.922	-3	S-63	-1.3
Total	4	219	658	72	170	21	6	0	61	28	28	.258	.291	.309	599	56	-42	2			.931	-4	S-119/2-69,3-8	-3.3
■ JOE MARSHALL Marshall, Joseph Hanley "Home Run Joe" b: 2/19/1876, Audubon, Minn. d: 9/11/31, Santa Monica, Cal BR/TR, 5′8″, 170 lbs. Deb: 9/7/03 Career OF: (2-LF 1-CF 23-RF)																								
1903	Pit-N	10	23	2	6	1	2	0	2	0		.261	.261	.478	739	106	-0	0			1.000	-4	/S-3,O-3(2-1-0),2-1	-0.4
1906	StL-N	33	95	2	15	1	2	0	7	6		.158	.216	.211	426	34	-7	0			.903	-1	O-23(0-0-23)/1-4	-1.1
Total	2	43	118	4	21	2	4	0	9	6		.178	.224	.263	487	50	-7	0			.903	-5	/O-26R,1-4,S-3,2-1	-1.5
■ KEITH MARSHALL Marshall, Keith Alan b: 7/2/51, San Francisco, Cal. BR/TR, 6′2″, 175 lbs. Deb: 4/7/73																								
1973	KC-A	8	9	0	2	1	0	0	3	1	4	.222	.300	.333	633	73	-0	0	0	0	1.000	-3	/O-8(5-2-2)	-0.3

YEAR	TM/L	G	AB	R	H	2B	3B	HR	RBI	BB	SO	AVG	OBP	SLG	OPS	OPS+	BR+	SB	CS	SBR	FA	FR	G/POS	TPR
■ MIKE MARSHALL	Marshall, Michael Allen b: 1/12/60, Libertyville, Ill. BR/TR, 6'5", 220 lbs. Deb: 9/7/81 Career OF: (123-LF 0-CF 657-RF)																							
1981	*LA-N	14	25	2	5	3	0	0	1	1	4	.200	.259	.320	579	66	-1	0	0	0	1.000	-1	/1-3,3-3,O-2(1-0-1)	-0.2
1982	LA-N	49	95	10	23	3	0	5	9	13	23	.242	.339	.432	771	117	2	2	0	0	1.000	-4	O-19(3-0-16),1-13	-0.3
1983	*LA-N	140	465	47	132	17	1	17	65	43	127	.284	.351	.434	785	117	10	7	3	0	.976	-7	*O-109(0-0-109),1-33	-0.4
1984	LA-N☆	134	495	68	127	27	0	21	65	40	93	.257	.316	.438	754	111	6	4	3	-0	.981	4	*O-118(116-0-4),1-15	0.4
1985	*LA-N	135	518	72	152	27	2	28	95	37	137	.293	.344	.515	860	141	26	3	10	-3	.991	-0	*O-125(1-0-124)/1-7	1.6
1986	LA-N	103	330	47	77	11	0	19	53	27	90	.233	.299	.439	739	109	2	4	4	-1	.963	-2	O-97(1-0-97)	-0.5
1987	LA-N	104	402	45	118	19	0	16	72	18	79	.294	.330	.460	790	109	4	0	5	-2	.987	-6	*O-102(0-0-102)	-0.9
1988	*LA-N	144	542	63	150	27	2	20	82	24	93	.277	.316	.445	761	120	11	4	1	1	.966	-1	O-90(0-0-90),1-53	0.5
1989	LA-N	105	377	41	98	21	1	11	42	33	78	.260	.328	.408	736	111	5	2	5	-1	.978	-2	*O-102(0-0-102)	-0.1
1990	NY-N	53	163	24	39	8	1	6	27	7	40	.239	.283	.411	694	89	-3	0	2	-1	.993	-1	1-42/O-1(0-0-1)	-0.7
	*Bos-A	30	112	10	32	6	1	4	12	4	26	.286	.316	.464	781	111	1	0	0	0	1.000	1	D-14/1-8,O-8(0-0-8)	0.1
1991	Bos-A	22	62	4	18	4	0	1	7	0	19	.290	.290	.403	694	86	-1	0	0	0	.979	-3	/1-5,O-4(1-0-3),D-7	-0.4
	Cal-A	2	7	0	0	0	0	0	0	0	1	.000	.000	.000	0	-99	-2	0	0	0	1.000	0	/1-1,D-1	-0.2
	Yr	24	69	4	18	4	0	1	7	0	20	.261	.261	.362	623	67	-3	0	0	0	.984	-2	/D-8,1-6,O-4(1-0-3)	-0.6
Total	11	1035	3593	433	971	173	8	148	530	247	810	.270	.324	.446	770	115	60	26	33	-6	.978	-21	O-777R,1-180/D-22,3	-1.1
■ MAX MARSHALL	Marshall, Milo May b: 9/18/13, Shenandoah, Iowa d: 9/16/93, Salem, Ore. BL/TR, 6'1", 180 lbs. Deb: 5/10/42																							
1942	Cin-N	131	530	49	135	17	6	7	43	34	38	.255	.301	.349	650	90	-8	4			.976	-10	*O-129(43-11-79)	-2.8
1943	Cin-N	132	508	55	120	11	8	4	39	34	52	.236	.287	.313	600	74	-18	8			.981	-5	*O-129(0-0-129)	-3.4
1944	Cin-N	66	229	36	56	13	2	4	23	21	10	.245	.308	.371	679	94	-2	3			.965	2	O-59(1-0-58)	-0.5
Total	3	329	1267	140	311	41	16	15	105	89	100	.245	.297	.339	635	84	-28	15			.975	-14	O-317(44-11-266)	-6.7
■ JIM MARSHALL	Marshall, Rufus James b: 5/25/31, Danville, Ill. BL/TL, 6'1", 190 lbs. Deb: 4/15/58 MC																							
1958	Bal-A	85	191	17	41	4	3	5	19	18	30	.215	.282	.346	628	76	-7	3	2	-0	1.000	-5	1-52/O-8(3-0-5)	-1.5
	Chi-N	26	81	12	22	2	0	5	11	12	13	.272	.372	.481	854	126	3	1	0	0	.992	-4	1-15,O-11(0-0-11)	-0.1
1959	Chi-N	108	294	39	74	10	1	11	40	33	39	.252	.327	.405	732	95	-2	0	1	-0	.997	1	1-72/O-8(7-0-3)	-0.7
1960	SF-N	75	118	19	28	2	2	2	13	17	24	.237	.333	.339	672	90	-1	0	1	-0	.968	-3	1-28/O-6(6-0-0)	-0.7
1961	SF-N	44	36	5	8	0	0	1	7	3	8	.222	.282	.306	588	58	-2	0	0	0	1.000	-0	/1-4,O-2(1-0-1)	-0.2
1962	NY-N	17	32	6	11	1	0	3	4	3	6	.344	.400	.656	1056	175	3	0	0	0	1.000	-0	/1-5,O-1(0-0-1)	0.3
	Pit-N	55	100	13	22	5	1	2	12	15	19	.220	.322	.350	672	80	-3	1	0	0	1.000	1	1-26	-0.3
	Yr	72	132	19	33	6	1	5	16	18	25	.250	.340	.424	764	103	1	1	0	0	1.000	1	1-31/O-1(0-0-1)	0.0
Total	5	410	852	111	206	24	7	29	106	101	139	.242	.323	.388	711	93	-9	5	4	-0	.994	-10	1-202/O-36(17-0-21)	-3.2
■ WILLARD MARSHALL	Marshall, Willard Warren b: 2/8/21, Richmond, Va. BL/TR, 6'1", 205 lbs. Deb: 4/14/42																							
1942	NY-N★	116	401	41	103	9	2	11	59	26	20	.257	.307	.372	679	98	-2	1			.975	-0	*O-107(67-46-1)	-0.8
1946	NY-N	131	510	63	144	18	3	13	48	33	29	.282	.327	.406	733	107	3	3			.978	2	*O-125(51-59-15)	-0.2
1947	NY-N★	155	587	102	171	19	6	36	107	67	30	.291	.366	.528	894	134	26	3			.972	12	*O-155(0-0-155)	3.2
1948	NY-N	143	537	72	146	21	8	14	86	64	34	.272	.350	.419	769	107	5	2			.983	4	*O-142(0-0-142)	0.4
1949	NY-N★	141	499	81	153	19	3	12	70	78	20	.307	.401	.429	830	123	19	4			.974	6	*O-138(2-0-136)	2.0
1950	Bos-N	105	298	38	70	10	2	5	40	36	5	.235	.319	.332	652	77	-10	1			.958	1	O-85(14-9-64)	-1.2
1951	Bos-N	136	469	65	132	24	7	11	62	48	18	.281	.351	.433	784	118	11	0	3	-1	**1.000**	-8	*O-136(0-0-136)	-0.2
1952	Bos-N	21	66	5	15	4	1	2	11	4	4	.227	.271	.409	681	89	-1	0	0	0	.938	1	O-16(0-0-16)	-0.1
	Cin-N	107	397	52	106	23	1	8	46	37	21	.267	.333	.390	723	100	-0	0	1	-0	.985	2	*O-105(0-0-105)	-0.2
	Yr	128	463	57	121	27	2	10	57	41	25	.261	.324	.393	717	99	-1	0	1	-0	.979	3	*O-121(0-0-121)	-0.3
1953	Cin-N	122	357	51	95	14	6	17	62	41	28	.266	.342	.482	824	111	5	0	0	0	.995	6	O-95(0-0-95)	0.8
1954	Chi-A	47	71	7	18	2	0	1	7	11	9	.254	.354	.324	678	84	-1	0	0	0	.960	-7	O-29(7-0-22)	-0.9
1955	Chi-A	22	41	6	7	0	0	0	6	13	1	.171	.370	.171	541	48	-2	0	0	0	.957	-1	O-12(4-0-8)	-0.4
Total	11	1246	4233	583	1160	163	39	130	604	458	219	.274	.347	.423	770	109	52	14	4		.979	20	*O-1145(145-114-895)	2.4
■ BILL MARSHALL	Marshall, William Henry b: 2/14/11, Dorchester, Mass. d: 5/5/77, Sacramento, Cal. BR/TR, 5'8.5", 156 lbs. Deb: 6/20/31																							
1931	Bos-A	1	0	1	0	0	0	0	0	0	0	—	—	—	—	—	0	0	0	0	.000	0	R	0.0
1934	Cin-N	6	8	0	1	0	0	0	0	0	2	.125	.125	.125	250	-34	-1	0			.875	1	/2-2	-0.1
Total	2	7	8	1	1	0	0	0	0	0	2	.125	.125	.125	250	-34	-1	0	0		.875	1	/2-2	-0.1
■ DOC MARSHALL	Marshall, William Riddle b: 9/22/1875, Butler, Pa. d: 12/11/59, Clinton, Ill. BR/TR, 6', 185 lbs. Deb: 4/15/04 Career OF: (3-LF 4-CF 17-RF)																							
1904	Phi-N	8	20	1	2	0	0	0	1	0		.100	.100	.100	200	-40	-3	0			.944	2	/C-7	-0.1
	NY-N	1	0	0	0	0	0	0	0	0		—	—	—	—	—	0	0			.000	0	/C-1	0.0
	Bos-N	13	43	3	9	0	1	0	2	2		.209	.244	.256	500	56	-2	2			.955	1	C-10/O-1(1-0-0)	0.0
	NY-N	10	17	3	6	1	0	0	2	1		.353	.389	.412	801	141	1	0			.955	2	/C-2,O-2(1-0-1),2-1	0.3
	Yr	32	80	7	17	1	1	0	5	3		.213	.241	.250	491	52	-5	2			.952	5	C-20/O-3(2-0-1),2-1	0.2
1906	NY-N	38	102	8	17	3	2	0	7	7		.167	.234	.235	470	45	-7	7			1.000	-2	O-16(1-3-13),C-13/1-2	-0.9
	StL-N	39	123	6	34	4	1	0	10	6		.276	.315	.325	641	104	0	1			.961	9	C-38	1.4
	Yr	77	225	14	51	7	3	0	17	13		.227	.278	.284	562	76	-7	8			.969	7	C-51,O-16(1-3-13)/1-2	0.5
1907	StL-N	84	268	19	54	8	2	2	18	12		.201	.246	.269	515	64	-12	2			.952	5	C-83	0.2
1908	StL-N	6	14	0	1	0	0	0	1	0		.071	.071	.071	143	-57	-2	0			1.000	2	/C-6	0.0
	Chi-N	12	20	4	6	0	1	0	3	0		.300	.300	.400	700	118	0	0			1.000	5	/C-4,O-3(0-1-2)	0.5
	Yr	18	34	4	7	0	1	0	4	0		.206	.206	.265	471	49	-2	0			1.000	7	C-10/O-3(0-1-2)	0.5
1909	Bro-N	50	149	7	30	7	1	0	10	6		.201	.232	.262	494	55	-8	3			.968	-5	C-49/O-1(0-0-1)	-1.0
Total	5	261	756	51	159	23	8	2	54	34		.210	.251	.270	521	64	-34	15			.961	19	C-213/O-23R,1-2,2-1	0.4
■ DOC MARTEL	Martel, Leon Alphonse "Marty" b: 1/29/1883, Weymouth, Mass. d: 10/11/47, Washington, D.C. BR/TR, 6', 185 lbs. Deb: 7/6/09																							
1909	Phi-N	24	41	1	11	3	1	0	7	4		.268	.333	.390	724	123	1	0			.974	4	C-12	0.7
1910	Bos-N	10	31	0	4	0	0	0	1	2	3	.129	.182	.129	311	-9	-4	0			.980	-0	1-10	-0.5
Total	2	34	72	1	15	3	1	0	8	6	3	.208	.269	.278	547	64	-3	0			.974	4	/C-12,1-10	0.2
■ AL MARTIN	Martin, Albert (a.k.a. Albert May In 1872) Deb: 5/7/1872																							
1872	Eck-n	4	18	2	5	0	0	0	2	0	0	.278	.278	.278	556	84	-0	0	0	0	.636	-3	/2-4	-0.3
1874	Atl-n	7	29	1	4	0	0	0	1	0	1	.138	.138	.138	276	-13	-3	0	0	0	.646	-2	/2-6,O-1(1-0-0)	-0.4
1875	Atl-n	6	26	1	3	0	0	0	1	0	0	.115	.115	.115	231	-22	-3	0	0	0	.909	-1	/O-6(0-6-0)	-0.3
Total	3 n	17	73	4	12	0	0	0	4	0	1	.164	.164	.164	329	9	-6	0	0	0	.643	-6	/2-10,O-7(1-6-0)	-1.0
■ AL MARTIN	Martin, Albert Lee b: 11/24/67, West Covina, Cal. BL/TL, 6'2", 210 lbs. Deb: 7/28/92																							
1992	Pit-N	12	12	1	2	0	1	0	2	0	5	.167	.167	.333	500	39	-1	0	0	0	1.000	-2	/O-7(7-0-0)	-0.3
1993	Pit-N	143	480	85	135	26	8	18	64	42	122	.281	.340	.481	822	117	11	16	9	0	.975	-10	*O-136(81-63-6)	-0.1
1994	Pit-N	82	276	48	79	12	4	9	33	34	56	.286	.369	.457	825	112	5	15	6	1	.979	2	O-77(67-13-0)	0.7
1995	Pit-N	124	439	70	124	25	3	13	41	44	92	.282	.351	.442	792	105	3	20	11	1	.977	-3	*O-121(95-42-0)	-0.1
1996	Pit-N	155	630	101	189	40	1	18	72	54	116	.300	.357	.452	810	109	8	38	12	4	.965	-14	*O-152(142-26-0)	-0.6
1997	Pit-N	113	423	64	123	24	7	13	59	45	83	.291	.363	.473	836	115	9	23	7	3	.957	-8	*O-110(110-0-0)	0.0
1998	Pit-N	125	440	57	105	15	2	12	47	32	91	.239	.298	.364	661	72	-18	20	3	3	.985	6	*O-114(114-0-0)/D-2	-1.3
1999	Pit-N	143	541	97	150	36	8	24	63	49	119	.277	.338	.506	845	110	6	20	3	3	.952	-7	*O-133(133-0-0)	-0.2
2000	SD-N	93	346	62	106	13	6	11	27	28	54	.306	.362	.474	836	116	8	6	8	-1	.950	-3	O-89(89-0-0)	0.0
	*Sea-A	42	134	19	31	2	4	4	9	8	31	.231	.285	.396	680	72	-6	4	1	1	.963	2	O-35(20-7-9)/D-2	-0.4
Total	9	1032	3721	604	1044	193	44	122	417	336	769	.281	.343	.454	798	105	25	162	60	15	.968	-38	O-974(858-151-15)/D-4	-2.3
■ BILLY MARTIN	Martin, Alfred Manuel b: 5/16/28, Berkeley, Cal. d: 12/25/89, Johnson City, N.Y. BR/TR, 5'11.5", 165 lbs. Deb: 4/18/50 MC																							
1950	NY-A	34	36	10	9	1	0	1	8	3	3	.250	.308	.361	669	73	-2	0	0	0	.976	-1	2-22/3-1	-0.2
1951	*NY-A	51	58	10	15	1	2	0	2	4	9	.259	.328	.345	673	85	-1	0	1	-0	.988	16	2-23/S-6,3-2,O-1C	1.5
1952	*NY-A	109	363	32	97	13	3	3	33	22	31	.267	.323	.344	668	91	-5	3	6	-1	.984	18	*2-107	1.8
1953	*NY-A	149	587	72	151	24	6	15	75	43	56	.257	.314	.395	710	94	-7	6	7	-1	.985	-1	*2-146,S-18	0.2
1955	*NY-A	20	70	8	21	2	0	1	9	7	9	.300	.364	.371	735	100	0	1	2	-0	.977	1	2-17/S-3	0.2

YEAR	TM/L	G	AB	R	H	2B	3B	HR	RBI	BB	SO	AVG	OBP	SLG	OPS	OPS+	BR+	SB	CS	SBR	FA	FR	G/POS	TPR
1956	*NY-A★	121	458	76	121	24	5	9	49	30	56	.264	.314	.397	711	90	-9	7	3	0	.980	-14	*2-105,3-16	-1.5
1957	NY-A	43	145	12	35	5	2	1	12	3	14	.241	.262	.324	586	60	-8	2	1	0	.947	-3	2-26,3-13	-1.0
	KC-A	73	265	33	68	9	3	9	27	12	20	.257	.296	.415	712	91	-4	7	1	1	.987	-20	2-52,3-20/S-2	-2.0
	Yr	116	410	45	103	14	5	10	39	15	34	.251	.284	.383	667	80	-12	9	2	1	.973	-23	2-78,3-33/S-2	-3.0
1958	Det-A	131	498	56	127	19	1	7	42	16	62	.255	.282	.339	622	65	-24	5	3	0	.958	-18	S-88,3-41	-3.5
1959	Cle-A	73	242	37	63	7	0	9	24	8	18	.260	.292	.401	693	92	-4	0	2	-1	.997	-11	2-67/3-4	-1.1
1960	Cin-N	103	317	34	78	17	1	3	16	27	34	.246	.305	.334	640	74	-11	0	1	-0	.975	-13	2-97	-1.9
1961	Mil-N	6	6	1	0	0	0	0	0	0	1	.000	.000	.000	0	-99	-2	0	0	0	.000	0	H	-0.2
	Min-A	108	374	44	92	15	5	6	36	13	42	.246	.277	.361	638	65	-19	3	2	-0	.963	-15	*2-105/S-1	-2.6
Total	11	1021	3419	425	877	137	28	64	333	188	355	.257	.301	.369	671	81	-95	34	29	-3	.980	-61	2-767,S-118/3-97,O	-10.3
■ **PHONNEY MARTIN**	Martin, Alphonse Case b: 8/4/1845, New York, N.Y. d: 5/24/33, Hollis, N.Y. 5′7″, 148 lbs. Deb: 4/26/1872 M																							
1872	Tro-n	25	117	27	36	2	1	0	14	0	1	.308	.308	.342	650	98	-0	0	0	0	.780	-1	O-25(0-0-25)/P-8	0.0
	Eck-n	18	78	13	12	0	0	0	9	1	2	.154	.165	.154	318	-2	-8	3	1	0	.806	1	P-10/O-9(0-0-9),M	-0.1
	Yr	43	195	40	48	2	1	0	23	1	3	.246	.250	.267	517	62	-7	3	1	0	.776	-0	O-34(0-0-34),P-18	-0.1
1873	Mut-n	31	140	12	31	1	0	0	14	0	4	.221	.221	.229	450	34	-11	0	1	-0	.680	-7	O-30(0-0-30)/P-6	-1.0
Total	2 n	74	335	52	79	3	1	0	37	1	7	.236	.238	.251	489	50	-19	3	2	-0	.747	-7	/O-64(0-0-64),P-24	-1.1
■ **BABE MARTIN**	Martin, Boris Michael (b: Boris Michael Martinovich) b: 3/28/20, Seattle, Wash. BR/TR, 5′11.5″, 194 lbs. Deb: 9/25/44																							
1944	StL-A	2	4	0	3	1	0	0	1	0	0	.750	.750	1.000	1750	376	1	0	0	0	1.000	-0	/O-1(1-0-0)	0.1
1945	StL-A	54	185	13	37	5	2	2	16	11	24	.200	.245	.281	526	50	-12	0	1	-0	.992	6	O-48(43-0-6)/1-6	-1.0
1946	StL-A	3	9	0	2	0	0	0	1	1	2	.222	.300	.222	522	45	-1	0	0	0	1.000	1	/C-2	0.0
1948	Bos-A	4	4	0	2	0	0	0	0	0	1	.500	.500	.500	1000	158	0	0	0	0	.000	0	/C-1	0.0
1949	Bos-A	2	2	0	0	0	0	0	0	0	0	.000	.000	.000	0	-93	-1	0	0	0	.000	0	/C-1	-0.1
1953	StL-A	4	2	0	0	0	0	0	0	1	0	.000	.333	.000	333	-4	-0	0	0	0	.000	0	/C-1	0.0
Total	6	69	206	13	44	6	2	2	18	13	27	.214	.260	.291	552	56	-12	0	1	-0	.992	6	/O-49(44-0-6),1-6,C-5	-1.0
■ **FRANK MARTIN**	Martin, Frank b: 2/28/1879, Chicago, Ill. d: 9/30/24, Chicago, Ill. Deb: 6/30/1897																							
1897	Lou-N	2	8	1	2	0	0	0	0	0		.250	.250	.250	500	33	-1	0			.813	0	/2-2	0.0
1898	Chi-N	1	4	0	0	0	0	0	0	0		.000	.000	.000	0	-99	-1	0			1.000	0	/2-1	-0.1
1899	NY-N	17	54	5	14	2	0	0	1	2		.259	.298	.296	595	66	-3	0			.824	2	3-17	0.0
Total	3	20	66	6	16	2	0	0	1	2		.242	.275	.273	548	52	-4	0			.870	3	/3-17,2-3	-0.1
■ **HERSH MARTIN**	Martin, Hershel Ray b: 9/19/09, Birmingham, Ala. d: 11/17/80, Cuba, Mo. BB/TR, 6′2″, 190 lbs. Deb: 4/23/37																							
1937	Phi-N	141	579	102	164	35	7	8	49	69	66	.283	.362	.409	771	101	2	11			.978	5	*O-139(3-136-0)	0.3
1938	Phi-N☆	120	466	58	139	36	6	3	39	34	48	.298	.347	.421	768	113	8	8			.965	1	*O-116(0-115-2)	0.6
1939	Phi-N	111	393	59	111	28	5	1	22	42	27	.282	.355	.387	741	102	2	4			.976	11	O-95(9-73-13)	0.9
1940	Phi-N	33	83	10	21	6	1	0	5	9	9	.253	.326	.349	675	90	-1	1			.979	-0	O-23(0-19-4)	-0.2
1944	NY-A	85	328	49	99	12	4	9	47	34	26	.302	.371	.445	816	128	12	5	2	0	.964	3	O-80(78-2-0)	1.1
1945	NY-A	117	408	53	109	18	6	7	53	65	31	.267	.368	.392	760	115	9	4	1	1	.984	3	*O-102(97-3-2)	0.7
Total	6	607	2257	331	643	135	29	28	215	253	207	.285	.359	.408	766	109	31	33	3		.974	22	O-555(187-348-21)	3.4
■ **JERRY MARTIN**	Martin, Jerry Lindsey b: 5/11/49, Columbia, S.C. BR/TR, 6′1″, 195 lbs. Deb: 9/7/74 F Career OF: (215-LF 411-CF 337-RF)																							
1974	Phi-N	13	14	2	3	1	0	0	1	1	5	.214	.267	.286	552	52	-1	0	0	0	1.000	-3	O-11(6-3-2)	-0.5
1975	Phi-N	57	113	15	24	7	1	2	11	11	16	.212	.288	.345	633	72	-4	2	2	-0	.979	-3	O-49(8-41-0)	-0.9
1976	*Phi-N	130	121	30	30	7	0	2	15	7	28	.248	.289	.355	644	80	-3	3	2	-0	.975	-30	*O-110(73-23-15)/1-1	-3.7
1977	*Phi-N	116	215	34	56	16	3	6	28	18	42	.260	.329	.447	776	101	0	6	4	-0	.984	-19	*O-106(45-18-51)/1-1	-2.2
1978	*Phi-N	128	266	40	72	13	4	9	36	28	65	.271	.342	.451	794	119	6	9	5	0	.987	-15	*O-112(48-22-55)	-1.2
1979	Chi-N	150	534	74	145	34	3	19	73	38	85	.272	.323	.453	777	100	-1	2	4	-1	.981	-2	*O-144(0-140-4)	-0.5
1980	Chi-N	141	494	57	112	22	2	23	73	38	107	.227	.285	.419	704	88	-10	8	3	1	.978	-12	*O-129(5-103-42)	-2.5
1981	SF-N	72	241	23	58	5	3	4	25	21	52	.241	.309	.336	646	85	-5	6	2	1	.993	-4	O-64(10-58-0)	-1.0
1982	KC-A	147	519	52	138	22	1	15	65	38	138	.266	.318	.399	717	95	-4	1	1	-0	.980	4	*O-142(11-3-134)/D-3	-0.7
1983	KC-A	13	44	4	14	2	0	2	13	1	7	.318	.333	.500	833	125	1	1	0	0	.957	-2	O-13(0-0-13)	-0.1
1984	NY-N	51	91	6	14	1	0	3	5	6	29	.154	.206	.264	470	32	-9	0	0	0	1.000	-1	O-30(9-0-21)/1-3	-1.1
Total	11	1018	2652	337	666	130	17	85	345	207	574	.251	.309	.409	718	93	-28	38	23	0	.982	-87	O-910C/1-5,D-3	-14.4
■ **JACK MARTIN**	Martin, John Christopher b: 4/19/1887, Plainfield, N.J. d: 7/4/80, Plainfield, N.J. BR/TR, 5′9″, 159 lbs. Deb: 4/25/12																							
1912	NY-A	71	231	30	52	6	1	0	17	37		.225	.347	.260	606	70	-7	14			.898	3	S-65/3-4,2-1	0.0
1914	Bos-N	33	85	10	18	2	0	0	5	6	7	.212	.264	.235	499	49	-5	0			.949	0	3-26/1-1,2-1	-0.5
	Phi-N	83	292	26	74	5	3	0	21	27	29	.253	.319	.291	610	77	-8	6			.930	-3	S-83	-0.5
	Yr	116	377	36	92	7	3	0	26	33	36	.244	.307	.279	585	71	-13	6			.930	-3	S-83,3-26/1-1,2-1	-1.0
Total	2	187	608	66	144	13	4	0	43	70	36	.237	.323	.271	594	71	-20	20			.915	-0	S-148/3-30,2-2,1-1	-1.0
■ **PEPPER MARTIN**	Martin, Johnny Leonard Roosevelt "The Wild Horse Of The Osage" b: 2/29/04, Temple, Okla. d: 3/5/65, McAlester, Okla. BR/TR, 5′8″, 170 lbs. Deb: 4/16/28 C Career OF: (31-LF 314-CF 273-RF)																							
1928	*StL-N	39	13	11	4	0	0	0	0	1	2	.308	.400	.308	708	86	-0	2			1.000	-2	/O-4(0-0-4)	-0.2
1930	StL-N	6	1	5	0	0	0	0	0	0	0	.000	.000	.000	0	-97	-0	0			.000	0	H	0.0
1931	*StL-N	123	413	68	124	32	8	7	75	30	40	.300	.351	.467	818	114	7	16			.967	0	*O-110(0-110-0)	0.5
1932	StL-N	85	323	47	77	19	6	4	34	30	31	.238	.305	.372	677	79	-10	9			.976	-1	O-69(5-64-0),3-15	-1.2
1933	StL-N★	145	599	**122**	189	36	12	8	57	67	46	.316	.387	.456	843	133	27	**26**			.943	-3	*3-145	3.1
1934	*StL-N★	110	454	76	131	25	11	5	49	32	41	.289	.337	.425	762	96	-3	**23**			.936	-5	*3-107/P-1	-0.3
1935	StL-N★	135	539	121	161	41	6	9	54	33	58	.299	.341	.447	789	106	4	20			.904	-14	*3-114,O-16(1-5-10)	-0.7
1936	StL-N	143	572	121	177	36	11	11	76	58	66	.309	.373	.469	842	126	20	**23**			.976	-10	*O-127R,3-15/P-1	0.3
1937	StL-N☆	98	339	60	103	27	8	5	38	33	50	.304	.366	.475	841	124	11	9			.973	11	O-82(0-40-42)/3-5	1.8
1938	StL-N	91	269	34	79	18	2	2	38	18	34	.294	.340	.398	738	97	-1	4			.986	-3	O-62(1-38-23)/3-4	-0.6
1939	StL-N	88	281	48	86	17	7	3	37	30	35	.306	.375	.448	823	113	6	6			.975	-4	O-51(8-37-8),3-22	0.1
1940	StL-N	86	228	28	72	15	4	3	39	22	24	.316	.378	.456	835	122	7	6			.974	-3	O-63(16-10-40)/3-2	0.2
1944	StL-N	40	86	15	24	4	0	2	4	15	11	.279	.386	.395	781	118	3	2			.980	-4	O-29(0-7-22)	-0.3
Total	13	1189	4117	756	1227	270	75	59	501	369	438	.298	.358	.443	801	112	71	146			.973	-36	O-613C,3-429/P-2	2.7
■ **J. C. MARTIN**	Martin, Joseph Clifton b: 12/13/36, Axton, Va. BL/TR, 6′2″, 200 lbs. Deb: 9/10/59 C Career OF: (1-LF 0-CF 0-RF)																							
1959	Chi-A	3	4	0	1	0	0	0	1	0	1	.250	.250	.250	500	38	-0	0	0	0	.667	-0	/3-2	0.0
1960	Chi-A	7	20	0	2	1	0	0	2	0	6	.100	.100	.150	250	-34	-4	0	0	0	1.000	-0	/3-5,1-1	-0.4
1961	Chi-A	110	274	26	63	8	3	5	32	21	31	.230	.290	.336	625	68	-13	1	2	-0	.988	9	1-60,3-36	-0.6
1962	Chi-A	18	26	0	2	0	0	0	2	0	3	.077	.077	.077	154	-59	-6	0	0	0	1.000	-1	/C-6,1-1,3-1	-0.6
1963	Chi-A	105	259	25	53	11	1	5	28	26	35	.205	.280	.313	592	67	-11	0	0	0	.983	14	C-98/1-3,3-1	0.7
1964	Chi-A	122	294	23	58	10	1	4	22	16	30	.197	.244	.279	523	46	-22	0	0	0	.986	8	*C-120	-1.0
1965	Chi-A	119	230	21	60	12	0	2	21	24	29	.261	.336	.339	675	98	-0	2	1	0	.982	1	*C-112/1-4,3-2	0.4
1966	Chi-A	67	157	13	40	5	3	2	20	14	24	.255	.320	.363	683	103	0	0	0	0	.982	-1	C-63	0.2
1967	Chi-A	101	252	22	59	12	1	4	22	30	41	.234	.318	.337	655	97	-1	4	4	-1	.987	3	C-96/1-1	0.6
1968	NY-N	78	244	20	55	9	2	3	31	21	31	.225	.300	.316	616	84	-4	0	0	0	.994	-3	C-53,1-14	-0.7
1969	*NY-N	66	177	12	37	5	1	4	21	12	32	.209	.259	.316	576	59	-10	0	0	0	.996	-6	C-48/1-2	-1.5
1970	Chi-N	40	77	11	12	1	0	1	4	20	11	.156	.337	.208	545	44	-5	0	0	0	.983	2	C-36/1-3	-0.3
1971	Chi-N	47	125	13	33	5	0	2	17	12	16	.264	.338	.352	690	84	-2	1	1	-0	.996	2	C-43/O-1(1-0-0)	0.2
1972	Chi-N	25	50	3	12	3	0	0	7	5	9	.240	.309	.300	609	67	-2	1	0	0	.970	-3	C-17	-0.4
Total	14	908	2189	189	487	82	12	32	230	201	299	.222	.293	.315	608	72	-80	9	8	-1	.987	26	C-692/1-89,3-47,O-1L	-3.4
■ **MIKE MARTIN**	Martin, Joseph Michael b: 12/3/58, Portland, Ore. BL/TR, 6′2″, 193 lbs. Deb: 8/15/86																							
1986	Chi-N	8	13	1	1	1	0	0	0	2	4	.077	.200	.154	354	-1	-2	0	0	0	1.000	0	/C-8	-0.2
■ **JOE MARTIN**	Martin, Joseph Samuel "Silent Joe" b: 1/1/1876, Hollidaysburg, Pa. d: 5/25/64, Altoona, Pa. BL/TR, 5′9.5″, 155 lbs. Deb: 4/28/03																							
1903	Was-A	35	119	11	27	4	5	0	7	5		.227	.258	.345	603	78	-3	2			.892	-5	2-15,3-13/O-7(1-0-6)	-0.8

YEAR	TM/L	G	AB	R	H	2B	3B	HR	RBI	BB	SO	AVG	OBP	SLG	OPS	OPS+	BR+	SB	CS	SBR	FA	FR	G/POS	TPR
	StL-A	44	173	18	37	6	4	0	7	6		.214	.249	.295	543	64	-8	0			.983	-3	O-38(4-0-34)/2-6,3-1	-1.3
	Yr	79	292	29	64	10	9	0	14	11		.219	.252	.315	568	70	-11	2			.959	-8	O-45R,2-21,3-14	-2.1
■ NORBERTO MARTIN	Martin, Norberto Edonal (McDonald) b: 12/10/66, San Pedro De Macoris, D.R. BR/TR, 5'10", 164 lbs. Deb: 9/20/93 Career OF: (12-LF 0-CF 7-RF)																							
1993	Chi-A	8	14	3	5	0	0	0	2	1	1	.357	.400	.357	757	108	0	0	0	0	.957	3	/2-5,D-1	0.3
1994	Chi-A	45	131	19	36	7	1	1	16	9	16	.275	.321	.366	688	78	-4	4	2	0	.982	-6	2-28/S-6,3-5,O-2L,D	-0.8
1995	Chi-A	72	160	17	43	7	4	2	17	3	25	.269	.287	.400	687	80	-5	5	0	1	.950	-3	2-17,O-12R,D-10,/3S	-0.6
1996	Chi-A	70	140	30	49	7	0	1	14	6	17	.350	.377	.421	798	107	2	10	2	2	.943	10	S-24,D-22,2-10,/3-3	1.2
1997	Chi-A	71	213	24	64	7	1	2	27	6	31	.300	.320	.371	691	83	-6	1	4	-1	.960	-12	S-28,3-17/2-9,D-6	-1.6
1998	Ana-A	79	195	20	42	2	0	1	13	6	29	.215	.239	.241	480	25	-21	3	1	0	.982	10	2-54,D-10/3-5,OS	-0.9
1999	Tor-A	9	27	3	6	2	0	0	0	4	4	.222	.364	.296	660	70	-1	0	0	0	.974	1	/2-8,S-1	0.0
Total	7	354	880	116	245	32	6	7	89	35	123	.278	.308	.352	661	72	-36	23	9	2	.976	3	2-131/S-68,D-50,3O	-2.4
■ STU MARTIN	Martin, Stuart McGuire b: 11/17/13, Rich Square, N.C. d: 1/11/97, Severn, N.C. BL/TR, 6', 155 lbs. Deb: 4/14/36																							
1936	StL-N☆	92	332	63	99	21	4	6	41	29	27	.298	.356	.440	796	114	6	17			.949	-13	2-83/S-3	-0.2
1937	StL-N	90	223	34	58	6	1	1	17	32	18	.260	.353	.309	662	80	-5	3			.946	-6	2-48/1-9,S-1	-0.9
1938	StL-N	114	417	54	116	26	2	1	27	30	28	.278	.328	.357	685	84	-9	4			.967	-10	2-99	-1.2
1939	StL-N	120	425	60	114	26	7	3	30	33	40	.268	.325	.384	709	85	-9	4			**.977**	-3	*2-107/1-1	-0.6
1940	StL-N	112	369	45	88	12	6	4	32	33	35	.238	.301	.336	637	71	-14	4			.972	-25	3-73,2-33	-3.7
1941	Pit-N	88	233	37	71	13	2	0	19	10	17	.305	.341	.378	719	103	1	2			.972	-4	2-53/3-2,1-1	0.0
1942	Pit-N	42	120	16	27	4	2	1	12	8	10	.225	.273	.317	590	71	-5	1			.979	-11	2-30/1-1,S-1	-1.5
1943	Chi-N	64	118	13	26	4	0	0	5	15	10	.220	.308	.254	563	64	-5	1			.980	1	2-22/3-8,1-2	-0.3
Total	8	722	2237	322	599	112	24	16	183	190	185	.268	.327	.361	688	86	-41	36			.966	-71	2-475/3-83,1-14,S-5	-8.4
■ GENE MARTIN	Martin, Thomas Eugene b: 1/12/47, Americus, Ga. BL/TR, 6'0.5", 190 lbs. Deb: 7/28/68																							
1968	Was-A	9	11	1	4	1	0	1	1	0	1	.364	.364	.727	1091	232	2	0	0	0	.000	-1	/O-2(2-0-0)	0.1
■ JOE MARTIN	Martin, William Joseph "Smokey Joe" b: 8/28/11, Seymour, Mo. d: 9/28/60, Buffalo, N.Y. BR/TR, 5'11.5", 181 lbs. Deb: 4/27/36																							
1936	NY-N	7	15	0	4	1	0	0	2	0	4	.267	.313	.333	646	75	-1	0			1.000	1	/3-7	0.0
1938	Chi-A	1	0	0	0	0	0	0	0	0	0	—	—	—	—	—	—	0	0	0	.000	0	R	0.0
Total	2	8	15	0	4	1	0	0	2	0	4	.267	.313	.333	646	75	-1	0	0		1.000	1	/3-7	0.0
■ BILLY MARTIN	Martin, William Lloyd b: 2/13/1894, Washington, D.C. d: 9/14/49, Arlington, Va. BR/TR, 5'8.5", 170 lbs. Deb: 10/6/14																							
1914	Bos-N	1	3	0	0	0	0	0	0	0	0	.000	.000	.000	0	-99	-1	0			.500	-1	/S-1	-0.2
■ SANDY MARTINEZ	Martinez, Angel Sandy (Martinez) b: 10/3/72, Villa Mella, D.R. BL/TR, 6'2", 200 lbs. Deb: 6/24/95																							
1995	Tor-A	62	191	12	46	12	0	2	25	7	45	.241	.271	.335	606	57	-12	0	0	0	.986	-3	C-61	-1.1
1996	Tor-A	76	229	17	52	9	3	3	18	16	58	.227	.289	.332	621	57	-15	0	0	0	.993	5	C-75	-0.6
1997	Tor-A	3	2	1	0	0	0	0	0	1	1	.000	.333	.000	333	-3	-0	0	0	0	.933	2	/C-3	0.1
1998	*Chi-N	45	87	7	23	9	1	0	7	13	21	.264	.366	.391	757	96	-0	1	0	0	.985	0	C-33	0.2
1999	Chi-N	17	30	1	5	0	0	1	1	0	11	.167	.167	.267	433	7	-4	0	0	0	.959	-0	C-12	-0.4
2000	Fla-N	10	18	1	4	2	0	0	0	0	8	.222	.222	.333	556	40	-2	0	0	0	1.000	2	/C-9	0.1
Total	6	213	557	39	130	32	4	6	51	37	144	.233	.288	.338	626	60	-34	1	0	0	.987	7	C-193	-1.7
■ CARLOS MARTINEZ	Martinez, Carlos Alberto Escobar (b: Carlos Alberto Escobar (Martinez)) b: 8/11/64, LaGuaira, Venez. BR/TR, 6'5", 175 lbs. Deb: 9/2/88																							
1988	Chi-A	17	55	5	9	1	0	0	0	0	12	.164	.164	.182	345	-3	-7	1	0	0	.909	3	3-15/D-2	-0.5
1989	Chi-A	109	350	44	105	22	0	5	32	21	57	.300	.341	.406	747	112	5	4	1	1	.912	-6	3-68,1-34,O-10L,/D	-0.2
1990	Chi-A	92	272	18	61	6	5	4	24	10	40	.224	.252	.327	579	62	-15	0	4	-1	.988	-5	1-82/O-1(1-0-0),D-3	-2.7
1991	Cle-A	72	257	22	73	14	0	5	30	10	43	.284	.316	.397	713	95	-2	3	2	-0	.968	-4	D-41,1-31	-1.0
1992	Cle-A	69	228	23	60	9	1	5	35	7	21	.263	.288	.377	665	87	-5	1	2	-0	.996	-5	1-37,3-28/D-4	-1.3
1993	Cle-A	80	262	26	64	10	0	5	31	20	29	.244	.298	.340	638	71	-11	1	1	-0	.934	-9	3-35,1-22,D-19	-2.2
1995	Cal-A	26	61	7	11	1	0	1	9	6	7	.180	.265	.246	511	34	-6	0	0	0	.968	2	3-16/1-4,D-2	-0.4
Total	7	465	1485	145	383	63	6	25	161	74	209	.258	.295	.359	654	81	-41	10	10	-1	.986	-25	1-210,3-162/D-72,O	-8.3
■ CARMELO MARTINEZ	Martinez, Carmelo (Salgado) b: 7/28/60, Dorado, P.R. BR/TR, 6'2", 220 lbs. Deb: 8/22/83 Career OF: (588-LF 0-CF 12-RF)																							
1983	Chi-N	29	89	8	23	3	0	6	16	4	19	.258	.290	.494	785	108	0	0	0	0	.992	-0	1-26/3-1,O-1(1-0-0)	-0.1
1984	*SD-N	149	488	64	122	28	2	13	66	68	82	.250	.346	.395	742	108	6	1	3	-1	.976	21	*O-142(142-0-0)/1-2	2.1
1985	SD-N	150	514	64	130	28	1	21	72	87	82	.253	.364	.434	798	124	18	0	4	-1	.978	13	*O-150(150-0-0)/1-3	2.4
1986	SD-N	113	244	28	58	10	0	9	25	35	46	.238	.336	.389	725	101	1	1	1	-0	.978	-0	O-60(59-0-0),1-26/3-1	-0.2
1987	SD-N	139	447	59	122	21	2	15	70	70	82	.273	.375	.430	805	117	12	5	5	-1	.968	-3	O-78(78-0-0),1-65	0.2
1988	SD-N	121	365	48	86	12	0	18	65	35	57	.236	.303	.416	719	106	2	1	1	-0	.993	10	O-64(55-0-11),1-41	0.8
1989	SD-N	111	267	23	59	12	2	6	39	32	54	.221	.304	.348	653	86	-5	0	0	0	.982	1	O-65(65-0-0),1-32	-0.7
1990	Phi-N	71	198	23	48	8	0	8	31	29	37	.242	.339	.404	743	104	1	2	1	0	.994	-2	1-43,O-20(20-0-1)	-0.4
	*Pit-N	12	19	3	4	1	0	2	4	1	5	.211	.250	.579	829	126	0	0	0	0	1.000	0	/1-5,O-2(2-0-0)	0.1
	Yr	83	217	26	52	9	0	10	35	30	42	.240	.332	.419	751	106	2	2	1	0	.995	-2	1-48,O-22(22-0-1)	-0.3
1991	Pit-N	11	16	1	4	0	0	0	0	1	2	.250	.294	.250	544	55	-1	0	0	0	.945	-1	/1-8	-0.2
	KC-A	44	121	17	25	6	0	4	17	27	25	.207	.351	.355	707	96	-0	0	1	-0	.991	4	1-43/D-1	0.1
	Cin-N	53	138	12	32	5	0	6	19	15	37	.232	.307	.399	706	93	-1	0	0	0	.985	0	1-25,O-16(16-0-0)	-0.3
Total	9	1003	2906	350	713	134	7	108	424	404	528	.245	.340	.408	747	108	35	10	16	-3	.980	41	O-598L,1-319/3-2,D	3.8
■ TINO MARTINEZ	Martinez, Constantino b: 12/7/67, Tampa, Fla. BL/TR, 6'2", 210 lbs. Deb: 8/20/90																							
1990	Sea-A	24	68	4	15	4	0	0	5	9	9	.221	.312	.279	591	66	-3	0	0	0	1.000	0	1-23	-0.4
1991	Sea-A	36	112	11	23	2	0	4	9	11	24	.205	.276	.330	607	67	-5	0	0	0	.993	2	1-29/D-5	-0.5
1992	Sea-A	136	460	53	118	19	2	16	66	42	77	.257	.321	.411	732	103	1	2	1	0	.995	1	1-78,D-47	-0.5
1993	Sea-A	109	408	48	108	25	1	17	60	45	56	.265	.345	.456	801	112	6	0	3	-1	.997	-3	*1-103/D-6	-0.8
1994	Sea-A	97	329	42	86	21	0	20	61	29	52	.261	.323	.508	831	108	2	1	2	-0	.997	-2	1-82/D-8	-0.7
1995	*Sea-A★	141	519	92	152	35	3	31	111	62	91	.293	.373	.551	924	135	26	0	0	0	.993	4	*1-139/D-1	1.5
1996	*NY-A	155	595	82	174	28	0	25	117	68	85	.292	.367	.466	832	109	8	2	1	0	**.996**	-4	*1-151/D-3	-0.9
1997	*NY-A★	158	594	96	176	31	2	44	141	75	75	.296	.378	.577	955	146	39	3	1	0	.994	5	*1-150/D-9	2.8
1998	*NY-A	142	531	92	149	33	1	28	123	61	83	.281	.361	.505	866	127	21	2	1	0	.992	-1	*1-142	0.6
1999	*NY-A	159	589	95	155	27	2	28	105	69	86	.263	.343	.458	802	103	2	3	4	-1	.995	8	*1-158	-0.5
2000	*NY-A	155	569	69	147	37	4	16	91	52	74	.258	.329	.422	751	90	-10	4	1	1	.994	-0	*1-154	-2.1
Total	11	1312	4774	684	1303	262	15	229	889	523	712	.273	.349	.478	827	113	88	17	14	-1	.995	9	*1-1209/D-79	-1.5
■ DAVE MARTINEZ	Martinez, David b: 9/26/64, New York, N.Y. BL/TL, 5'10", 175 lbs. Deb: 6/15/86 Career OF: (117-LF 857-CF 703-RF)																							
1986	Chi-N	53	108	13	15	1	1	1	7	6	22	.139	.191	.194	386	6	-14	4	2	0	.988	-4	O-46(9-39-1)	-1.8
1987	Chi-N	142	459	70	134	18	8	8	36	57	96	.292	.373	.418	791	105	5	16	8	1	.980	1	*O-139(14-134-3)	0.5
1988	Chi-N	75	256	27	65	10	1	4	34	21	46	.254	.315	.348	663	86	-4	7	3	0	.970	-1	O-72(0-70-2)	-0.6
	Mon-N	63	191	24	49	3	5	2	12	17	48	.257	.317	.356	673	89	-3	16	6	1	.992	-5	O-60(1-44-22)	-0.7
	Yr	138	447	51	114	13	6	6	46	38	94	.255	.316	.351	667	87	-7	23	9	2	.979	-5	*O-132(1-114-24)	-1.3
1989	Mon-N	126	361	41	99	16	7	3	27	27	57	.274	.325	.382	707	100	-0	23	4	4	.967	-18	*O-118(0-104-38)	-1.7
1990	Mon-N	118	391	60	109	13	5	11	39	24	48	.279	.322	.422	744	107	3	13	11	-1	.989	-3	*O-108(0-103-22)/P-1	-0.2
1991	Mon-N	124	396	47	117	18	5	7	42	20	54	.295	.334	.419	753	112	5	16	7	1	.982	-1	*O-112(36-34-54)	0.4
1992	Cin-N	135	393	47	100	20	5	3	31	42	54	.254	.326	.354	680	90	-5	12	8	-0	.991	-4	*O-111(3-105-6),1-21	-1.2
1993	SF-N	91	241	28	58	12	1	5	27	27	39	.241	.317	.361	678	84	-6	6	3	0	.993	-5	O-73(3-43-34)	-1.1
1994	SF-N	97	235	23	58	9	3	4	27	21	22	.247	.314	.362	676	79	-7	3	4	-1	1.000	-5	O-58(3-3-53),1-25	-1.7
1995	Chi-A	119	303	49	93	16	4	5	37	32	41	.307	.375	.436	811	115	7	8	2	1	.976	-10	O-59R,1-47/P-1,D-5	-0.6
1996	Chi-A	146	440	85	140	20	8	10	53	52	52	.318	.394	.468	862	123	17	15	7	1	.988	-17	*O-121(3-73-73),1-23	-0.2
1997	Chi-A	145	504	78	144	16	6	12	55	55	69	.286	.359	.413	772	105	5	12	6	1	.996	-4	*O-105R,1-52/D-1	-0.5
1998	TB-A	90	309	31	79	11	0	3	20	35	52	.256	.335	.320	656	70	-13	8	7	-1	.994	3	O-86(0-2-85)/1-1,D-1	-1.4
1999	TB-A	143	514	79	146	25	5	6	66	60	76	.284	.364	.387	752	91	-5	13	6	1	.985	-7	*O-140(2-52-93)	-1.5

YEAR	TM/L	G	AB	R	H	2B	3B	HR	RBI	BB	SO	AVG	OBP	SLG	OPS	OPS+	BR+	SB	CS	SBR	FA	FR	G/POS	TPR
2000	TB-A	29	104	12	27	4	2	1	12	10	17	.260	.325	.365	690	75	-4	1	4	-1	1.000	2	O-28(0-0-28)	-0.4
	Chi-N	18	54	5	10	1	1	0	1	2	8	.185	.214	.241	455	15	-7	1	0	0	1.000	-1	O-10(9-1-0)/1-9	-0.8
	Tex-A	38	119	14	32	4	1	2	12	14	20	.269	.351	.370	720	80	-3	2	1	0	1.000	4	O-35(0-0-35)	-0.1
	Tor-A	47	180	29	56	10	1	2	22	24	28	.311	.395	.411	806	103	2	4	2	0	.982	7	O-47(0-0-47)/1-4	0.6
	Yr	114	403	55	115	18	4	5	46	48	65	.285	.364	.387	751	94	-6	7	7	-1	.992	13	O-110(0-0-110)/1-4	0.1
Total	15	1799	5558	762	1531	227	69	89	560	546	849	.275	.343	.389	732	95	-27	180	91	8	.986	-65	*O-1528C,1-182/D-7,P	-13.0

■ DOMINGO MARTINEZ

Martinez, Domingo Emilio (La Fontaine) b: 8/4/67, Santo Domingo, D.R. BR/TR, 6'2", 215 lbs. Deb: 9/11/92

YEAR	TM/L	G	AB	R	H	2B	3B	HR	RBI	BB	SO	AVG	OBP	SLG	OPS	OPS+	BR+	SB	CS	SBR	FA	FR	G/POS	TPR
1992	Tor-A	7	8	2	5	0	0	1	3	0	1	.625	.625	1.000	1625	333	2	0	0	0	1.000	-1	/1-7	0.2
1993	Tor-A	8	14	2	4	0	0	1	3	1	7	.286	.333	.500	833	120	0	0	0	0	1.000	1	/1-7,3-1	0.1
Total	2	15	22	4	9	0	0	2	6	1	8	.409	.435	.682	1117	196	3	0	0	0	1.000	0	/1-14,3-1	0.3

■ EDGAR MARTINEZ

Martinez, Edgar b: 1/2/63, New York, N.Y. BR/TR, 5'11", 175 lbs. Deb: 9/12/87

YEAR	TM/L	G	AB	R	H	2B	3B	HR	RBI	BB	SO	AVG	OBP	SLG	OPS	OPS+	BR+	SB	CS	SBR	FA	FR	G/POS	TPR
1987	Sea-A	13	43	6	16	5	2	0	5	2	5	.372	.413	.581	994	152	3	0	0	0	1.000	1	3-12/D-1	0.4
1988	Sea-A	14	32	0	9	4	0	0	5	4	7	.281	.361	.406	767	110	0	0	0	0	.929	-4	3-13	-0.4
1989	Sea-A	65	171	20	41	5	0	2	20	17	26	.240	.319	.304	623	74	-5	2	1	0	.949	-6	3-61	-1.2
1990	Sea-A	144	487	71	147	27	2	11	49	74	62	.302	.399	.433	833	131	23	1	4	-1	.928	-1	*3-143/D-2	2.1
1991	Sea-A	150	544	98	167	35	1	14	52	84	72	.307	.407	.452	859	137	31	0	3	-1	.962	3	*3-144/D-2	3.3
1992	Sea-A★	135	528	100	181	**46**	3	18	73	54	61	**.343**	.408	.544	951	164	44	14	4	2	.943	1	*3-103,D-28/1-2	4.6
1993	Sea-A	42	135	20	32	7	0	4	13	28	19	.237	.368	.378	746	100	1	0	0	0	.889	-4	D-24,3-16	-0.4
1994	Sea-A	89	326	47	93	23	1	13	51	53	42	.285	.390	.482	872	121	11	6	2	1	.950	6	3-64,D-23	1.5
1995	*Sea-A★	145	511	**121**	182	**52**	0	29	113	116	87	**.356**	**.482**	.628	**1110**	**184**	**70**	4	3	-0	.800	-1	*D-138/3-4,1-3	5.5
1996	Sea-A★	139	499	121	163	52	2	26	103	123	84	.327	.467	.595	1062	166	57	3	3	-0	.967	-1	*D-134/1-4,3-2	4.3
1997	*Sea-A★	155	542	104	179	35	1	28	108	119	86	.330	.460	.554	1013	164	59	2	4	-1	.986	-1	*D-144/1-7,3-1	4.5
1998	Sea-A	154	556	86	179	46	1	29	102	106	96	.322	**.433**	.565	998	157	50	1	1	-0	1.000	2	*D-147/1-4	4.0
1999	Sea-A	142	502	86	169	35	1	24	86	97	99	.337	**.450**	.554	1003	158	49	7	2	1	1.000	-0	*D-143/1-5	3.7
2000	*Sea-A★	153	556	100	180	31	0	37	**145**	96	95	.324	.428	.579	1007	156	50	3	0	1	1.000	-0	*D-146/1-2	3.8
Total	14	1540	5432	980	1738	403	14	235	925	973	841	.320	.429	.529	958	151	444	43	27	0	.946	-7	D-932,3-563/1-27	35.7

■ FELIX MARTINEZ

Martinez, Felix (Mata) b: 5/18/74, Nagua, D.R. BB/TR, 6', 168 lbs. Deb: 9/3/97

YEAR	TM/L	G	AB	R	H	2B	3B	HR	RBI	BB	SO	AVG	OBP	SLG	OPS	OPS+	BR+	SB	CS	SBR	FA	FR	G/POS	TPR
1997	KC-A	16	31	3	7	1	1	0	3	6	8	.226	.351	.323	674	76	-1	0	0	0	.975	2	S-12/D-2	0.2
1998	KC-A	34	85	7	11	1	1	0	5	5	21	.129	.187	.165	352	-7	-13	3	1	0	.956	2	S-32/2-2	-0.9
1999	KC-A	6	7	1	1	0	0	0	0	0	0	.143	.143	.143	286	-26	-1	0	0	0	.000	-1	/S-2,2-1	-0.2
2000	TB-A	106	299	42	64	11	4	2	17	32	68	.214	.307	.298	604	54	-21	9	3	1	.976	40	*S-106	2.6
Total	4	162	422	53	83	13	6	2	25	43	97	.197	.285	.270	555	43	-36	12	4	1	.972	44	S-152/2-3,D-2	1.7

■ TONY MARTINEZ

Martinez, Gabriel Antonio (Diaz) b: 3/18/40, Perico, Cuba d: 8/24/91, Miami, Fla. BR/TR, 5'10", 165 lbs. Deb: 4/9/63

YEAR	TM/L	G	AB	R	H	2B	3B	HR	RBI	BB	SO	AVG	OBP	SLG	OPS	OPS+	BR+	SB	CS	SBR	FA	FR	G/POS	TPR
1963	Cle-A	43	141	10	22	4	0	0	8	5	18	.156	.185	.184	369	4	-18	1	1	-0	.961	-6	S-41	-2.3
1964	Cle-A	9	14	1	3	1	0	0	2	0	2	.214	.214	.286	500	38	-1	0	1	-0	1.000	4	/2-4,S-1	0.3
1965	Cle-A	4	3	0	0	0	0	0	0	0	0	.000	.000	.000	0	-99	-1	0	0	0	.000	0	H	-0.1
1966	Cle-A	17	17	2	5	0	0	0	0	1	6	.294	.333	.294	627	82	-0	1	1	-0	.833	1	/S-5,2-4	0.1
Total	4	73	175	13	30	5	0	0	10	6	26	.171	.199	.200	399	13	-20	2	3	-1	.958	-1	/S-47,2-8	-2.0

■ GREG MARTINEZ

Martinez, Gregory Alfred b: 1/27/72, Las Vegas, Nev. BB/TR, 5'10", 168 lbs. Deb: 3/31/98

YEAR	TM/L	G	AB	R	H	2B	3B	HR	RBI	BB	SO	AVG	OBP	SLG	OPS	OPS+	BR+	SB	CS	SBR	FA	FR	G/POS	TPR
1998	Mil-N	13	3	2	0	0	0	0	0	1	2	.000	.250	.000	250	-27	-1	2	0	0	.000	-2	/O-6(6-0-0)	-0.2

■ BUCK MARTINEZ

Martinez, John Albert b: 11/7/48, Redding, Cal. BR/TR, 5'10", 190 lbs. Deb: 6/18/69 Career OF: (0-LF 0-CF 1-RF)

YEAR	TM/L	G	AB	R	H	2B	3B	HR	RBI	BB	SO	AVG	OBP	SLG	OPS	OPS+	BR+	SB	CS	SBR	FA	FR	G/POS	TPR
1969	KC-A	72	205	14	47	6	1	4	23	8	25	.229	.258	.327	585	62	-11	0	0	0	.972	-1	C-55/O-1(0-0-1)	-1.0
1970	KC-A	6	9	1	1	0	0	0	0	2	1	.111	.273	.111	384	10	-1	0	0	0	.958	2	/C-5	0.1
1971	KC-A	22	46	3	7	2	0	0	1	5	9	.152	.235	.196	431	23	-5	0	1	-0	.968	2	C-21	-0.2
1973	KC-A	14	32	2	8	1	0	1	6	4	5	.250	.333	.375	708	92	-0	0	0	0	.966	-1	C-14	0.0
1974	KC-A	43	107	10	23	3	1	1	8	14	19	.215	.317	.290	607	71	-4	0	1	-0	.977	1	C-38	-0.2
1975	KC-A	80	226	15	51	9	2	3	23	21	28	.226	.294	.323	617	72	-8	1	0	0	.980	-0	C-79	-0.5
1976	*KC-A	95	267	24	61	13	3	5	34	16	45	.228	.272	.356	628	82	-7	0	0	0	.991	5	C-94	0.2
1977	KC-A	29	80	3	18	4	0	1	9	3	12	.225	.253	.313	566	53	-5	0	1	-0	.993	3	C-28	-0.2
1978	Mil-A	89	256	26	56	10	1	1	20	14	42	.219	.259	.277	537	51	-17	1	1	-0	.978	-3	C-89	-1.7
1979	Mil-A	69	196	17	53	8	0	4	26	8	25	.270	.299	.372	671	80	-6	0	1	-0	.967	-2	C-68/P-1	-0.6
1980	Mil-A	76	219	16	49	9	0	3	17	12	33	.224	.267	.306	573	58	-13	1	0	0	.985	11	C-76	0.1
1981	Tor-A	45	128	13	29	8	1	4	21	11	16	.227	.293	.398	691	92	-2	1	0	0	.991	2	C-45	0.2
1982	Tor-A	96	260	26	63	17	0	10	37	24	34	.242	.306	.423	729	90	-4	1	1	-0	.988	6	C-93	0.5
1983	Tor-A	88	221	27	56	14	0	10	33	29	39	.253	.340	.452	792	109	3	0	1	-0	.989	-3	C-85	0.3
1984	Tor-A	102	232	24	51	13	1	5	37	29	49	.220	.312	.349	661	80	-6	0	3	-1	.995	-4	C-98/D-1	-0.8
1985	Tor-A	42	99	11	16	3	0	4	14	10	12	.162	.245	.313	559	50	-7	0	0	0	.988	4	C-42	-0.2
1986	Tor-A	81	160	13	29	8	0	2	12	20	25	.181	.272	.269	541	47	-12	0	0	0	.994	-1	C-78/D-1	-1.1
Total	17	1049	2743	245	618	128	10	58	321	230	419	.225	.287	.343	630	73	-104	5	10	-2	.984	19	*C-1008/D-2,P-1,O-1R	-5.1

■ JOSE MARTINEZ

Martinez, Jose (Azcuiz) b: 7/26/42, Cardenas, Cuba BR/TR, 5'10", 190 lbs. Deb: 6/18/69 C Career OF: (2-LF 0-CF 0-RF)

YEAR	TM/L	G	AB	R	H	2B	3B	HR	RBI	BB	SO	AVG	OBP	SLG	OPS	OPS+	BR+	SB	CS	SBR	FA	FR	G/POS	TPR
1969	Pit-N	77	168	20	45	6	0	1	16	9	32	.268	.309	.321	630	78	-5	1	3	-1	.975	10	2-42,S-20/3-5,O-2L	0.7
1970	Pit-N	19	20	1	1	0	0	0	0	1	5	.050	.095	.050	145	-61	-5	0	0	0	1.000	3	/3-7,2-4,S-1	-0.1
Total	2	96	188	21	46	6	0	1	16	10	37	.245	.286	.293	579	63	-9	1	3	-1	.966	13	/2-46,S-21,3-12,O-2L	0.6

■ MANNY MARTINEZ

Martinez, Manuel (De Jesus) b: 10/3/70, San Pedro De Macoris, D.R. BR/TR, 6'2", 169 lbs. Deb: 6/14/96

YEAR	TM/L	G	AB	R	H	2B	3B	HR	RBI	BB	SO	AVG	OBP	SLG	OPS	OPS+	BR+	SB	CS	SBR	FA	FR	G/POS	TPR
1996	Sea-A	9	17	3	4	2	1	0	3	3	5	.235	.350	.471	821	105	0	2	0	0	1.000	0	/O-8(2-4-3)	0.0
	Phi-N	13	36	2	8	0	2	0	0	1	11	.222	.263	.333	596	55	-2	2	1	0	.955	0	O-11(1-1-10)	-0.3
1998	Pit-N	73	180	21	45	11	2	6	24	9	44	.250	.293	.433	727	87	-4	0	3	-1	.989	-8	O-62(26-37-3)	-1.3
1999	Mon-N	137	331	48	81	12	7	2	26	17	51	.245	.282	.341	623	58	-22	19	6	2	.968	-4	*O-126(0-126-1)	-2.1
Total	3	232	564	74	138	25	12	8	53	30	111	.245	.286	.374	661	69	-28	23	10	2	.974	-12	O-207(29-168-17)	-3.7

■ MARTY MARTINEZ

Martinez, Orlando (Oliva) b: 8/23/41, Havana, Cuba BB/TR (BR 1962), 6'1", 175 lbs. Deb: 5/2/62 MC Career OF: (21-LF 0-CF 0-RF)

YEAR	TM/L	G	AB	R	H	2B	3B	HR	RBI	BB	SO	AVG	OBP	SLG	OPS	OPS+	BR+	SB	CS	SBR	FA	FR	G/POS	TPR
1962	Min-A	37	18	13	3	0	1	0	3	3	4	.167	.286	.278	563	51	-1	0	0	0	.920	8	S-11/3-1	0.7
1967	Atl-N	44	73	14	21	2	1	0	5	11	11	.288	.388	.342	731	112	2	0	1	-0	.920	4	S-25/2-9,C-3,3-2,1	0.8
1968	Atl-N	113	356	34	82	5	3	0	12	29	28	.230	.292	.261	553	67	-14	6	6	-1	.955	-5	S-54,3-37,2-16,C-14	-1.5
1969	Hou-N	78	198	14	61	5	4	0	15	10	21	.308	.341	.374	715	102	0	0	0	0	1.000	-9	O-21L,S-17,3-15,/CP2	-0.8
1970	Hou-N	75	150	12	33	3	0	0	12	9	22	.220	.264	.240	504	38	-13	0	0	0	.990	-6	S-29,3-10/C-6,2-4	-1.6
1971	Hou-N	32	62	4	16	3	1	0	4	3	6	.258	.292	.339	631	80	-2	1	0	0	.968	1	/2-9,S-7,1-4,3-3	0.0
1972	StL-N	9	7	0	3	0	0	0	2	0	1	.429	.429	.429	857	146	0	0	0	0	1.000	0	/S-3,2-2,3-1	0.1
	Oak-A	22	40	3	5	0	0	0	1	3	6	.125	.186	.125	311	-7	-5	0	0	0	.944	3	2-17/S-6,3-1	-0.1
	Tex-A	26	41	3	6	1	1	0	3	2	8	.146	.186	.220	406	21	-4	0	1	-0	.944	-2	/S-5,3-4,2-1	-0.6
	Yr	48	81	6	11	1	1	0	4	5	14	.136	.186	.173	359	8	-9	0	1	-0	.946	2	2-18,S-11/3-5	-0.7
Total	7	436	945	97	230	19	11	0	57	70	107	.243	.298	.287	584	70	-37	7	8	-1	.950	-5	S-157/3-74,2-59,CO1P	-3.0

■ PABLO MARTINEZ

Martinez, Pablo Made (Valera) b: 6/29/69, Sabana Grande, D.R. BB/TR, 5'10", 155 lbs. Deb: 7/20/96

YEAR	TM/L	G	AB	R	H	2B	3B	HR	RBI	BB	SO	AVG	OBP	SLG	OPS	OPS+	BR+	SB	CS	SBR	FA	FR	G/POS	TPR
1996	Atl-N	4	2	1	1	0	0	0	0	0	0	.500	.500	.500	1000	156	0	0	1	-0	1.000	1	/S-1	0.0

■ RAMON MARTINEZ

Martinez, Ramon E. b: 10/10/72, Philadelphia, Pa. BR/TR, 6'1", 170 lbs. Deb: 6/20/98

YEAR	TM/L	G	AB	R	H	2B	3B	HR	RBI	BB	SO	AVG	OBP	SLG	OPS	OPS+	BR+	SB	CS	SBR	FA	FR	G/POS	TPR
1998	SF-N	19	19	4	6	1	0	0	0	4	2	.316	.435	.368	803	121	1	0	0	0	1.000	5	2-14	0.6
1999	SF-N	61	144	21	38	6	0	5	19	14	17	.264	.329	.410	739	92	-2	1	2	-0	.992	7	2-27,S-12,3-11,/D-1	0.6
2000	*SF-N	88	189	30	57	13	2	6	25	15	22	.302	.356	.487	843	118	5	3	2	-0	.991	-6	S-44,2-32/1-2,3-2	0.2
Total	3	168	352	55	101	20	2	11	44	33	41	.287	.350	.449	799	108	4	4	4	-1	.996	6	/2-73,S-56,3-13,1D	1.4

■ CHITO MARTINEZ

Martinez, Reyenaldo Ignacio b: 12/19/65, Belize City, British Honduras (Belize) BL/TL, 5'10", 180 lbs. Deb: 7/5/91 Career OF: (1-LF 0-CF 110-RF)

YEAR	TM/L	G	AB	R	H	2B	3B	HR	RBI	BB	SO	AVG	OBP	SLG	OPS	OPS+	BR+	SB	CS	SBR	FA	FR	G/POS	TPR
1991	Bal-A	67	216	32	58	12	1	13	33	11	51	.269	.304	.514	818	127	6	1	1	-0	.982	2	O-54(1-0-53)/1-1,D-4	0.7

YEAR	TM/L	G	AB	R	H	2B	3B	HR	RBI	BB	SO	AVG	OBP	SLG	OPS	OPS+	BR+	SB	CS	SBR	FA	FR	G/POS	TPR
1992	Bal-A	83	198	26	53	10	1	5	25	31	47	.268	.372	.404	776	114	5	0	1	-0	.973	1	O-52(0-0-52)/D-4	0.4
1993	Bal-A	8	15	0	0	0	0	0	0	4	4	.000	.211	.000	211	-37	-3	0	0	0	1.000	-2	/O-5(0-0-5),D-2	-0.5
Total	3	158	429	58	111	22	2	18	58	46	102	.259	.333	.445	779	115	8	1	2	-0	.978	2	O-111R/D-10,1-1	0.6
■ HECTOR MARTINEZ Martinez, Rodolfo Hector (Santos) b: 5/11/39, Las Villas, Cuba BR/TR, 5'10", 160 lbs. Deb: 9/30/62																								
1962	KC-A	1	1	0	0	0	0	0	0	0	1	.000	.000	.000	0	-96	-0	0	0	0	.000	0	H	0.0
1963	KC-A	6	14	2	4	0	0	1	3	1	3	.286	.375	.500	875	135	1	0	1	-0	1.000	0	/O-3(0-3-0)	0.0
Total	2	7	15	2	4	0	0	1	3	1	4	.267	.353	.467	820	120	0	0	1	-0	1.000	0	/O-3(0-3-0)	0.0
■ TED MARTINEZ Martinez, Teodoro Noel (Encarnacion) b: 12/10/47, Barahona, D.R. BR/TR (BB 1973 (part)), 6', 165 lbs. Deb: 7/18/70																								
1970	NY-N	4	16	0	1	0	0	0	0	0	3	.063	.063	.063	125	-66	-4	0	0	0	1.000	1	/2-4,S-1	-0.3
1971	NY-N	38	125	16	36	5	2	1	10	4	22	.288	.326	.384	710	102	0	6	0	1	.976	-7	S-23,2-13/3-3,O-1L	-0.3
1972	NY-N	103	330	22	74	5	5	1	19	12	49	.224	.254	.279	532	52	-21	7	4	0	.994	1	2-47,S-42,O-15L,/3	-1.5
1973	*NY-N	92	263	34	67	11	0	1	14	13	38	.255	.295	.308	603	68	-11	3	5	-1	.941	-4	S-44,O-21C,3-14,/2	-1.3
1974	NY-N	116	334	32	73	15	7	2	43	14	40	.219	.250	.323	573	61	-19	3	2	-0	.952	14	S-75,3-12,2-11,O-10C	0.2
1975	StL-N	16	21	1	4	2	0	0	2	0	2	.190	.190	.286	476	30	-2	0	0	0	1.000	-1	/O-7R,2-2,S-1,3-1	-0.4
	*Oak-A	86	87	7	15	0	0	0	3	2	9	.172	.200	.172	372	6	-11	1	1	-0	.955	4	S-45,2-31,3-14	-0.5
1977	LA-N	67	137	21	41	6	1	1	10	2	20	.299	.309	.380	689	84	-3	3	4	-1	.992	14	2-27,S-13,3-12	1.2
1978	LA-N	54	55	13	14	1	0	1	5	4	14	.255	.317	.327	644	80	-1	3	2	-0	.912	10	S-17,3-16,2-10	1.0
1979	LA-N	81	112	19	30	5	1	0	2	4	16	.268	.293	.330	623	71	-5	3	2	-0	.769	-0	3-23,S-21,2-18	-0.4
Total	9	657	1480	165	355	50	16	7	108	55	213	.240	.271	.309	580	62	-77	29	20	-1	.956	31	S-282,2-168/3-97,O	-2.3
■ JOE MARTY Marty, Joseph Anton b: 9/1/13, Sacramento, Cal. d: 10/4/84, Sacramento, Cal. BR/TR, 6', 182 lbs. Deb: 4/22/37																								
1937	Chi-N	88	290	41	84	17	2	5	44	28	30	.290	.356	.414	770	104	2	3			.976	-2	O-84(1-83-0)	-0.2
1938	*Chi-N	76	235	32	57	8	3	7	35	18	26	.243	.305	.391	696	88	-4	0			.987	-4	O-68(0-64-6)	-1.0
1939	Chi-N	23	76	6	10	1	0	2	10	4	13	.132	.175	.224	399	6	-10	2			.933	-2	O-21(1-1-19)	-1.4
	Phi-N	91	299	32	76	12	6	9	44	24	27	.254	.310	.425	734	98	-2	1			.974	3	O-79(6-56-18)/P-1	-0.2
	Yr	114	375	38	86	13	6	11	54	28	40	.229	.283	.384	667	79	-13	3			.968	1	*O-100(7-57-37)/P-1	-1.6
1940	Phi-N	123	455	52	123	21	8	13	50	17	50	.270	.298	.437	735	105	0	2			.974	2	*O-118(0-115-3)	0.0
1941	Phi-N	137	477	60	128	19	3	8	39	51	41	.268	.344	.371	715	105	4	6			.964	-6	*O-132(0-131-1)	-0.6
Total	5	538	1832	223	478	78	22	44	222	142	187	.261	.318	.400	717	97	-11	14			.972	-9	O-502(8-450-47)/P-1	-3.4
■ BOB MARTYN Martyn, Robert Gordon b: 8/15/30, Weiser, Idaho BL/TR, 6', 176 lbs. Deb: 6/18/57																								
1957	KC-A	58	131	10	35	2	4	1	12	11	20	.267	.324	.366	690	87	-2	1	3	-1	.976	-3	O-49(13-9-28)	-0.8
1958	KC-A	95	226	25	59	10	7	2	23	26	36	.261	.337	.394	731	99	-0	1	4	-1	.967	-5	O-63(27-1-45)	-0.9
1959	KC-A	1	1	0	0	0	0	0	0	0	0	.000	.000	.000	0	-98	-0	0	0	0	.000	0	R	0.0
Total	3	154	358	35	94	12	11	3	35	37	56	.263	.332	.383	714	94	-3	2	7	-2	.970	-8	O-112(40-10-73)	-1.7
■ GARY MARTZ Martz, Gary Arthur b: 1/10/51, Spokane, Wash. BR/TR, 6'4", 210 lbs. Deb: 7/8/75																								
1975	KC-A	1	1	0	0	0	0	0	0	0	0	.000	.000	.000	0	-97	-0	0	0	0	1.000	-0	/O-1(1-0-0)	-0.1
■ JOHN MARZANO Marzano, John Robert b: 2/14/63, Philadelphia, Pa. BR/TR, 5'11", 197 lbs. Deb: 7/31/87																								
1987	Bos-A	52	168	20	41	11	0	5	24	7	41	.244	.287	.399	685	77	-6	0	1	-0	.986	1	C-52	-0.3
1988	Bos-A	10	29	3	4	1	0	0	1	1	3	.138	.167	.172	339	-5	-4	0	0	0	1.000	5	C-10	0.2
1989	Bos-A	7	18	5	8	3	0	1	3	0	2	.444	.444	.778	1222	224	3	0	0	0	1.000	-0	/C-7	0.3
1990	Bos-A	32	83	8	20	4	0	0	6	5	10	.241	.284	.289	573	58	-5	0	1	-0	1.000	4	C-32	0.1
1991	Bos-A	49	114	10	30	8	0	0	9	1	16	.263	.276	.333	609	64	-6	0	0	0	.985	-2	C-48	-0.6
1992	Bos-A	19	50	4	4	2	1	0	1	2	12	.080	.132	.160	292	-17	-8	0	0	0	.968	0	C-18/D-1	-0.7
1995	Tex-A	2	6	1	2	0	0	0	0	0	0	.333	.333	.333	667	72	-0	0	0	0	1.000	-0	/C-2	0.0
1996	Sea-A	41	106	8	26	6	0	0	6	7	15	.245	.316	.302	618	57	-7	0	0	0	.986	0	C-39	-0.5
1997	Sea-A	39	87	7	25	3	0	1	10	7	15	.287	.340	.356	697	83	-2	0	0	0	.976	4	C-37/D-1	0.3
1998	Sea-A	50	133	13	31	7	1	4	12	9	24	.233	.325	.391	715	85	-3	0	0	0	.997	8	C-48/D-1	0.7
Total	10	301	794	79	191	45	2	11	72	39	138	.241	.291	.344	635	67	-37	0	2	-1	.988	20	C-293/D-3	-0.5
■ CLYDE MASHORE Mashore, Clyde Wayne b: 5/29/45, Concord, Cal. BR/TR, 5'11", 184 lbs. Deb: 7/11/69 Career OF: (87-LF 48-CF 52-RF)																								
1969	Cin-N	2	1	1	0	0	0	0	0	0	0	.000	.000	.000	0	-95	-0	0	0	0	.000	0	H	0.0
1970	Mon-N	13	25	2	4	0	0	1	3	4	11	.160	.276	.280	556	49	-2	0	0	0	1.000	-2	O-10(2-8-0)	-0.4
1971	Mon-N	66	114	20	22	5	0	1	7	10	22	.193	.258	.263	521	48	-8	1	0	0	.967	-11	O-47(19-29-5)/3-1	-2.1
1972	Mon-N	93	176	23	40	7	1	3	23	14	41	.227	.284	.330	614	73	-6	6	1	1	.988	-13	O-74(23-8-46)	-2.2
1973	Mon-N	67	103	12	21	3	0	3	14	15	28	.204	.305	.320	625	71	-4	4	3	-0	.958	-3	O-44(43-3-1)/2-1	-0.9
Total	5	241	419	58	87	15	1	8	47	43	102	.208	.281	.305	587	64	-20	11	4	1	.974	-28	O-175L/2-1,3-1	-5.6
■ DAMON MASHORE Mashore, Damon Wayne b: 10/31/69, Ponce, P.R. BR/TR, 5'11", 195 lbs. Deb: 6/5/96																								
1996	Oak-A	50	105	20	28	7	1	3	12	16	31	.267	.369	.438	807	105	1	4	0	1	.985	-11	O-48(35-7-15)	-0.9
1997	Oak-A	92	279	55	69	10	2	3	18	50	82	.247	.371	.330	701	86	-3	5	4	-0	.991	-0	O-89(28-71-6)	-0.4
1998	Ana-A	43	98	13	23	6	0	2	11	9	22	.235	.318	.357	675	75	-4	1	0	0	1.000	-4	O-35(1-7-28)/D-7	-0.8
Total	3	185	482	88	120	23	3	8	41	75	135	.249	.360	.359	719	88	-6	10	4	1	.991	-15	O-172(64-85-49)/D-7	-2.1
■ PHIL MASI Masi, Philip Samuel b: 1/6/16, Chicago, Ill. d: 3/29/90, Mt.Prospect, Ill. BR/TR, 5'10", 180 lbs. Deb: 4/23/39 Career OF: (1-LF 0-CF 4-RF)																								
1939	Bos-N	46	114	14	29	7	2	1	14	9	15	.254	.315	.377	692	92	-2	0			.960	-3	C-42	-0.2
1940	Bos-N	63	138	11	27	4	1	1	14	14	14	.196	.270	.261	531	50	-9	0			.966	-1	C-52	-0.8
1941	Bos-N	87	180	17	40	8	2	3	18	16	13	.222	.286	.339	625	79	-6	4			.978	-7	C-83	-0.9
1942	Bos-N	57	87	14	19	3	1	0	9	12	4	.218	.313	.276	589	74	-3	2			.961	2	C-39/O-4(1-0-4)	0.0
1943	Bos-N	80	238	27	65	9	1	2	28	27	20	.273	.347	.345	692	102	1	7			.991	-6	C-73	-0.1
1944	Bos-N	89	251	33	69	13	5	3	23	31	20	.275	.355	.402	757	108	3	4			.977	-0	C-63,1-12/3-2	0.6
1945	Bos-N†	114	371	55	101	25	4	7	46	42	32	.272	.348	.418	766	112	5	9			.980	1	C-95/1-7	1.1
1946	Bos-N★	133	397	52	106	17	5	3	62	55	41	.267	.358	.358	715	102	2	5			.981	-5	*C-124	0.4
1947	Bos-N★	126	411	54	125	22	4	9	50	47	27	.304	.377	.443	820	120	12	7			**.989**	-6	*C-123	1.2
1948	*Bos-N★	113	376	43	95	19	0	5	44	35	26	.253	.318	.343	661	80	-10	2			.988	1	*C-109	-0.4
1949	Bos-N	37	105	13	22	2	0	0	6	14	10	.210	.303	.229	531	47	-7	1			.993	-2	C-37	-0.7
	Pit-N	48	135	16	37	6	1	2	13	17	16	.274	.355	.378	733	94	-1	1			.994	-2	C-44/1-2	0.0
	Yr	85	240	29	59	8	1	2	19	31	26	.246	.332	.313	645	74	-8	2			**.994**	-3	C-81/1-2	-0.7
1950	Chi-A	122	377	38	105	17	2	7	55	49	36	.279	.366	.390	756	96	-2	2	1	0	**.996**	-1	*C-114	0.3
1951	Chi-A	84	225	24	61	11	2	4	28	32	27	.271	.367	.391	758	107	3	1	0	0	.979	-0	C-78	0.6
1952	Chi-A	30	63	9	16	1	1	0	7	10	10	.254	.356	.302	658	84	-1	0	0	0	.956	0	C-25	0.0
Total	14	1229	3468	420	917	164	31	47	417	410	311	.264	.344	.370	714	97	-14	45	1		.983	-27	*C-1101/1-21,O-4R,3	1.1
■ HARRY MASKREY Maskrey, Harry H. b: 12/21/1861, Mercer, Pa. d: 8/17/30, Mercer, Pa. Deb: 9/21/1882 F																								
1882	Lou-a	1	4	0	0	0	0	0		0		.000	.000	.000	0	-99	-1				.000	-1	/O-1(0-1-0)	-0.1
■ LEECH MASKREY Maskrey, Samuel Leech b: 2/11/1854, Mercer, Pa. d: 4/1/22, Mercer, Pa. BR/TR, 5'8", 150 lbs. Deb: 5/2/1882 F Career OF: (328-LF 48-CF 43-RF)																								
1882	Lou-a	76	288	30	65	14	2	0		9		.226	.249	.288	537	85	-4				.902	-0	*O-76(75-0-1)/2-1	-0.5
1883	Lou-a	96	361	50	73	13	8	1		10		.202	.224	.291	515	70	-11				.914	9	*O-96(45-41-14)/S-1	-0.4
1884	Lou-a	105	412	48	103	13	4	0	36	17		.250	.281	.301	582	94	-2				.896	2	*O-103L/3-3,S-1	-0.2
1885	Lou-a	109	423	54	97	8	11	1	46	19		.229	.269	.307	576	82	-9				.899	-3	*O-108(108-0-0)/3-3	-1.3
1886	Lou-a	5	19	1	3	1	0	0	2	1		.158	.200	.211	411	27	-2	0			.800	-1	/O-5(3-0-2)	-0.3
	Cin-a	27	98	7	19	3	1	0	10	5		.194	.240	.245	485	51	-6	4			.926	1	O-26(0-7-19)/3-2	-0.4
	Yr	32	117	8	22	4	1	0	12	6		.188	.234	.239	473	47	-7	4			.915	-0	O-31(3-7-21)/3-2	-0.7
Total	5	418	1601	190	360	52	26	2	94	61		.225	.256	.294	550	80	-32	4			.904	7	O-414L/3-8,S-2,2-1	-3.1
■ CHARLIE MASON Mason, Charles E. b: 6/25/1853, New Orleans, La. d: 10/21/36, Philadelphia, Pa. BR/TR, 175 lbs. Deb: 4/26/1875 M																								
1875	Cen-n	12	47	5	11	0	0	0	3	0	1	.234	.234	.234	468	69	-1	0	0	0	.719	0	O-10(3-0-7)/1-2,C-1	0.0

YEAR	TM/L	G	AB	R	H	2B	3B	HR	RBI	BB	SO	AVG	OBP	SLG	OPS	OPS+	BR+	SB	CS	SBR	FA	FR	G/POS	TPR
	Was-n	8	33	2	3	0	0	0	1	0	3	.091	.091	.091	182	-38	-4	0	0	0	.909	2	/O-8(8-0-0),P-1	-0.2
	Yr	20	80	7	14	0	0	0	4	0	4	.175	.175	.175	350	23	-6	0	0	0	.796	2	O-18L/1-2,C-1,P-1	-0.2
1883	Phi-a	1	2	0	1	0	0	0	1	0		.500	.500	.500	1000	204	0				.000	-0	/O-1(0-0-1)	0.0
■ **DON MASON**	Mason, Donald Stetson b: 12/20/44, Boston, Mass. BL/TR, 5'11", 160 lbs. Deb: 4/14/66																							
1966	SF-N	42	25	8	3	0	0	1	1	0	2	.120	.120	.240	360	-3	-3	0	1	-0	.905	5	/2-9	0.2
1967	SF-N	4	3	0	0	0	0	0	0	0	0	.000	.000	.000	0	-99	-1	0	0	0	1.000	1	/2-2	0.0
1968	SF-N	10	19	3	3	0	0	0	1	1	4	.158	.200	.158	358	9	-2	1	1	-0	1.000	-1	/2-5,S-4,3-2	-0.4
1969	SF-N	104	250	43	57	4	2	0	13	36	29	.228	.325	.260	585	67	-10	1	5	-2	.956	10	2-51,3-21/S-7	0.1
1970	SF-N	46	36	4	5	0	0	0	1	5	7	.139	.244	.139	383	5	-5	0	0	0	.950	2	2-14	-0.3
1971	SD-N	113	344	43	73	12	1	2	11	27	35	.212	.270	.270	540	57	-20	6	4	-0	.965	-12	2-90/3-3	-2.8
1972	SD-N	9	11	1	2	0	0	0	0	1	1	.182	.250	.182	432	26	-1	0	0	0	.692	-0	/2-3	-0.1
1973	SD-N	8	8	0	0	0	0	0	0	0	2	.000	.000	.000	0	-99	-2	0	0	0	.750	1	/2-1	-0.2
Total	8	336	696	102	143	16	3	3	27	70	80	.205	.278	.250	528	52	-44	8	11	-2	.955	5	2-175/3-26,S-11	-3.5
■ **JIM MASON**	Mason, James Percy b: 8/14/50, Mobile, Ala. BL/TR, 6'2", 190 lbs. Deb: 9/26/71																							
1971	Was-A	3	9	0	3	0	0	0	0	1	3	.333	.400	.333	733	116	0	0	0	0	.955	2	/S-3	0.3
1972	Tex-A	46	147	10	29	3	0	0	10	9	39	.197	.248	.218	466	41	-11	0	0	0	.948	-6	S-32,3-10	-1.5
1973	Tex-A	92	238	23	49	7	2	3	19	23	48	.206	.276	.290	566	62	-12	0	1	-0	.947	9	S-74,2-19/3-1	0.4
1974	NY-A	152	440	41	110	18	6	5	37	35	87	.250	.305	.352	658	90	-6	1	2	-0	.964	-4	*S-152	0.6
1975	NY-A	94	223	17	34	3	2	2	16	22	49	.152	.229	.211	439	25	-22	0	2	-1	.955	-10	S-93/2-1	-2.4
1976	*NY-A	93	217	17	39	7	1	1	14	9	37	.180	.212	.235	447	31	-19	0	0	0	.966	7	S-93	-0.4
1977	Tor-A	22	79	10	13	3	0	0	2	7	10	.165	.233	.203	435	20	-9	1	1	-0	.971	-5	S-22	-1.1
	Tex-A	36	55	9	12	3	0	1	7	6	10	.218	.295	.327	622	69	-2	0	0	0	.976	7	S-32/3-1,D-1	0.6
	Yr	58	134	19	25	6	0	1	9	13	20	.187	.259	.254	512	40	-11	1	1	-0	.973	3	S-54/3-1,D-1	-0.5
1978	Tex-A	55	105	10	20	4	0	0	3	5	17	.190	.227	.229	456	28	-10	0	0	0	.938	1	S-42,3-11/2-1,D-1	-0.7
1979	Mon-N	40	71	3	13	5	1	0	6	7	16	.183	.256	.282	538	47	-5	0	2	-1	.966	0	S-33/3-6	-0.4
Total	9	633	1584	140	322	53	12	12	114	124	316	.203	.262	.275	536	54	-96	2	8	-2	.959	2	S-576/3-29,2-21,D-2	-4.6
■ **GORDON MASSA**	Massa, Gordon Richard "Moose" or "Duke" b: 9/2/35, Cincinnati, Ohio BL/TR, 6'3", 210 lbs. Deb: 9/24/57																							
1957	Chi-N	6	15	2	7	1	0	0	3	4	3	.467	.579	.533	1112	205	3	0	0	0	1.000	-3	/C-6	0.0
1958	Chi-N	2	2	0	0	0	0	0	0	0	2	.000	.000	.000	0	-99	-1	0	0	0	.000	0	H	-0.1
Total	2	8	17	2	7	1	0	0	3	4	5	.412	.524	.471	994	172	2	0	0	0	1.000	-3	/C-6	-0.1
■ **ROY MASSEY**	Massey, Roy Hardee "Red" b: 10/9/1890, Sevierville, Tenn. d: 6/23/54, Atlanta, Ga. BL/TR, 5'11", 170 lbs. Deb: 4/16/18																							
1918	Bos-N	66	203	20	59	6	2	0	18	23	20	.291	.363	.340	703	120	6	1			.954	-3	O-45C/3-2,1-1,S-1	0.0
■ **BILL MASSEY**	Massey, William Harry "Big Bill" b: 1/1871, Philadelphia, Pa. d: 10/9/40, Manila, Philippines BR/TR, 5'11", 168 lbs. Deb: 9/18/1894																							
1894	Cin-N	13	53	7	15	3	0	0	5	3	2	.283	.321	.340	661	57	-4	0			.991	-1	1-10/2-2,3-1	-0.4
■ **MIKE MASSEY**	Massey, William Herbert b: 9/28/1893, Galveston, Tex. d: 10/17/71, Shreveport, La. BB/TR, 6', 195 lbs. Deb: 4/12/17																							
1917	Bos-N	31	91	12	18	0	0	0	2	15	15	.198	.318	.198	516	63	-3	2			.900	-8	2-25	-1.2
■ **DAN MASTELLER**	Masteller, Dan Patrick b: 3/17/68, Toledo, Ohio BL/TL, 6', 185 lbs. Deb: 6/23/95																							
1995	Min-A	71	198	21	47	12	0	3	21	18	19	.237	.304	.343	648	68	-9	1	2	-0	.994	-4	1-48,O-22(6-0-16)/D-8	-1.8
■ **VICTOR MATA**	Mata, Victor Jose (Abreu) b: 6/17/61, Santiago, D.R. BR/TR, 6'1", 165 lbs. Deb: 7/22/84																							
1984	NY-A	30	70	8	23	5	0	1	6	0	12	.329	.338	.443	781	119	2	1	1	-0	.942	-6	O-28(2-21-8)	-0.5
1985	NY-A	6	7	1	1	0	0	0	0	0	0	.143	.143	.143	286	-22	-1	0	0	0	1.000	-2	/O-3(1-1-2)	-0.3
Total	2	36	77	9	24	5	0	1	6	0	12	.312	.321	.416	736	106	0	1	1	-0	.943	-7	/O-31(3-22-10)	-0.8
■ **TOM MATCHICK**	Matchick, John Thomas b: 9/7/43, Hazleton, Pa. BL/TR, 6', 175 lbs. Deb: 9/2/67																							
1967	Det-A	8	6	1	1	0	0	0	0	0	2	.167	.167	.167	333	-1	-1	0	0	0	1.000	0	/S-1	-0.1
1968	*Det-A	80	227	18	46	6	2	3	14	10	46	.203	.249	.286	535	60	-11	0	2	-1	.950	-14	S-59,2-13/1-6	-2.4
1969	Det-A	94	298	25	72	11	2	0	32	15	51	.242	.278	.292	570	57	-17	3	0	1	.972	-7	2-47,3-27/S-6,1-2	-2.1
1970	Bos-A	10	14	2	1	0	0	0	0	2	2	.071	.188	.071	259	-24	-2	0	1	-0	1.000	-1	/3-2,2-1,S-1	-0.4
	KC-A	55	158	11	31	3	2	0	11	5	23	.196	.226	.241	466	29	-15	0	0	0	.985	13	S-43,2-10/3-1	0.2
	Yr	65	172	13	32	3	2	0	11	7	25	.186	.222	.227	449	24	-18	0	1	-0	.985	12	S-44,2-11/3-3	-0.2
1971	Mil-A	42	114	6	25	1	0	1	7	7	23	.219	.264	.254	519	48	-8	3	2	-0	.979	1	3-41/2-1	-0.7
1972	Bal-A	3	9	0	2	0	0	0	0	0	1	.222	.222	.222	444	32	-1	0	1	-0	.857	-1	/3-3	-0.2
Total	6	292	826	63	178	21	6	4	64	39	148	.215	.255	.270	525	49	-55	6	6	-1	.967	-8	S-110/3-74,2-72,1-8	-5.7
■ **RUBEN MATEO**	Mateo, Ruben Amaury b: 2/10/78, San Cristobal, D.R. BR/TR, 6', 170 lbs. Deb: 6/12/99																							
1999	Tex-A	32	122	16	29	9	1	5	18	4	28	.238	.268	.451	719	75	-5	3	0	1	1.000	-1	O-31(0-31-0)	-0.4
2000	Tex-A	52	206	32	60	11	0	7	19	10	34	.291	.339	.447	786	94	-2	6	0	1	.980	5	O-52(0-52-0)	0.4
Total	2	84	328	48	89	20	1	12	37	14	62	.271	.313	.448	761	87	-7	9	0	2	.986	4	/O-83(0-83-0)	0.0
■ **MIKE MATHENY**	Matheny, Michael Scott b: 9/22/70, Columbus, Ohio BR/TR, 6'3", 205 lbs. Deb: 4/7/94																							
1994	Mil-A	28	53	3	12	3	0	1	2	3	13	.226	.293	.340	633	60	-3	0	1	-0	.989	3	C-27	0.0
1995	Mil-A	80	166	13	41	9	1	0	21	12	28	.247	.306	.313	619	58	-10	2	1	0	.986	4	C-80	-0.3
1996	Mil-A	106	313	31	64	15	2	8	46	14	80	.204	.245	.342	587	45	-27	3	2	-0	.985	-2	*C-104/D-1	-2.2
1997	Mil-A	123	320	29	78	16	1	4	32	17	68	.244	.297	.338	634	64	-17	0	1	-0	.993	18	*C-121/1-2	0.7
1998	Mil-N	108	320	24	76	13	0	6	27	11	63	.237	.278	.334	612	60	-19	1	0	0	.987	-7	*C-107	-2.0
1999	Tor-A	57	163	16	35	6	0	3	17	12	37	.215	.273	.307	579	47	-13	0	0	0	.995	18	C-57	0.7
2000	StL-N	128	417	43	109	22	1	6	47	32	96	.261	.320	.362	682	72	-18	0	0	0	.994	6	*C-124/1-8	-0.5
Total	7	630	1752	159	415	84	5	28	192	101	385	.237	.288	.338	627	59	-108	6	5	-0	.991	40	C-620/1-10,D-1	-3.6
■ **JOE MATHES**	Mathes, Joseph John b: 7/28/1891, Milwaukee, Wis. d: 12/21/78, St.Louis, Mo. BB/TR, 6'0.5", 180 lbs. Deb: 9/19/12																							
1912	Phi-A	4	14	0	2	0	0	0	0	0		.143	.200	.143	343	-2	-2	0			.889	-1	/3-4	-0.3
1914	StL-F	26	85	10	25	3	0	0	6	9	11	.294	.362	.329	691	85	-3	1			.938	-4	2-23	-0.7
1916	Bos-N	2	0	0	0	0	0	0	0	0	0	—	—	—	—	—	0	0			.000	-1	/2-2	-0.1
Total	3	32	99	10	27	3	0	0	6	9	11	.273	.339	.303	642	74	-4	1			.921	-6	/2-25,3-4	-1.1
■ **EDDIE MATHEWS**	Mathews, Edwin Lee b: 10/13/31, Texarkana, Tex. BL/TR, 6'1", 200 lbs. Deb: 4/15/52 MCH Career OF: (52-LF 0-CF 0-RF)																							
1952	Bos-N	145	528	80	128	23	5	25	58	59	115	.242	.320	.447	767	114	8	6	4	-0	.957	-10	*3-142	-0.2
1953	Mil-N★	157	579	110	175	31	8	**47**	135	99	83	.302	.406	.627	1033	**175**	**64**	1	3	-1	.939	3	*3-157	**6.2**
1954	Mil-N	138	476	96	138	21	4	40	103	113	61	.290	.428	.603	1031	**177**	57	10	3	1	.966	-2	*3-127,O-10(10-0-0)	5.4
1955	Mil-N★	141	499	108	144	23	5	41	101	**109**	98	.289	.417	.601	1018	175	56	3	4	-1	.952	-4	*3-137	5.0
1956	Mil-N☆	151	552	103	150	21	2	37	95	91	86	.272	.376	.518	894	146	37	6	0	1	.944	-12	*3-150	2.5
1957	*Mil-N☆	148	572	109	167	28	9	32	94	90	79	.292	.388	.540	928	157	47	3	1	0	.964	-2	*3-147	4.5
1958	*Mil-N☆	149	546	97	137	18	1	31	77	85	85	.251	.354	.458	812	123	18	5	0	1	.955	5	*3-149	2.4
1959	Mil-N★	148	594	118	182	16	8	**46**	114	80	71	.306	.391	.593	984	172	60	2	0	1	.961	3	*3-148	6.2
1960	Mil-N★	153	548	108	152	19	7	39	124	111	113	.277	.401	.551	952	**170**	**56**	7	3	0	.950	-13	*3-153	4.3
1961	Mil-N★	152	572	103	175	23	6	32	91	**93**	95	.306	.405	.535	940	156	48	12	7	0	.961	-6	*3-151	4.1
1962	Mil-N★	152	536	106	142	25	6	29	90	**101**	90	.265	.383	.496	880	138	31	4	2	0	.964	2	*3-140/1-7	3.1
1963	Mil-N	158	547	82	144	27	4	23	84	**124**	119	.263	**.400**	.453	854	147	39	3	4	-1	**.968**	15	*3-121,O-42(42-0-0)	5.3
1964	Mil-N	141	502	83	117	19	1	23	74	85	100	.233	.345	.412	758	112	9	2	2	-0	.962	2	*3-128/1-7	1.0
1965	Mil-N	156	546	77	137	23	0	32	95	73	110	.251	.342	.469	811	125	18	1	0	0	.956	9	*3-153	2.8
1966	Atl-N	134	452	72	113	21	4	16	53	63	82	.250	.342	.420	762	109	6	1	1	-0	.946	-2	*3-127	0.3
1967	Hou-N	101	328	39	78	13	2	10	38	48	65	.238	.337	.381	718	109	4	2	4	-1	.987	-4	1-79,3-24	-0.6
	Det-A	36	108	14	25	3	0	6	19	15	23	.231	.336	.426	762	121	3	0	0	0	.933	-2	3-21,1-13	0.0

YEAR	TM/L	G	AB	R	H	2B	3B	HR	RBI	BB	SO	AVG	OBP	SLG	OPS	OPS+	BR+	SB	CS	SBR	FA	FR	G/POS	TPR
1968	*Det-A	31	52	4	11	0	0	3	8	5	12	.212	.281	.385	665	97	-0	0	0	0	.974	-1	/1-6,3-6	-0.1
Total	17	2391	8537	1509	2315	354	72	512	1453	1444	1487	.271	.378	.509	888	145	562	68	39	1	.956	-20	*3-2181,1-112/O-52L	52.2
■ NELSON MATHEWS	Mathews, Nelson Elmer b: 7/21/41, Columbia, Ill. BR/TR, 6′4″, 195 lbs. Deb: 9/9/60 F																							
1960	Chi-N	3	8	1	2	0	0	0	0	0	2	.250	.250	.250	500	38	-1	0	0	0	1.000	0	/O-2(0-0-2)	-0.1
1961	Chi-N	3	9	0	1	0	0	0	0	0	2	.111	.111	.111	222	-40	-2	0	0	0	1.000	0	/O-2(0-2-0)	-0.2
1962	Chi-N	15	49	5	15	2	0	2	13	5	4	.306	.393	.469	862	126	2	3	3	-0	.962	-2	O-14(0-14-0)	-0.1
1963	Chi-N	61	155	12	24	3	2	4	10	16	48	.155	.234	.277	511	44	-11	3	4	-1	.979	-2	O-46(0-46-0)	-1.7
1964	KC-A	157	573	58	137	27	5	14	60	43	143	.239	.293	.377	670	82	-14	2	3	-1	.968	9	*O-154(0-154-0)	-1.1
1965	KC-A	67	184	17	39	7	7	2	15	24	49	.212	.303	.359	662	89	-3	0	2	-1	.981	-2	O-57(25-26-8)	-0.8
Total	6	306	978	93	218	39	14	22	98	88	248	.223	.289	.359	648	78	-29	8	12	-2	.972	4	O-275(25-242-10)	-4.0
■ BOBBY MATHEWS	Mathews, Robert T. b: 11/21/1851, Baltimore, Md. d: 4/17/1898, Baltimore, Md. BR/TR, 5′5.5″, 140 lbs. Deb: 5/4/1871 U NA OF: (2-LF 0-CF 13-RF) Career OF: (3-LF 11-CF 52-RF)																							
1871	Kek-n	19	89	15	24	3	1	0	10	2	0	.270	.286	.326	612	74	-3	2	1	0	.840	-0	P-19	0.0
1872	Bal-n	50	223	36	50	1	0	0	21	3	2	.224	.235	.229	463	41	-16	1	1	-0	.780	-3	*P-49/O-8(0-0-8),3-3	-0.3
1873	Mut-n	52	223	40	43	3	3	0	13	10	3	.193	.227	.233	461	37	-16	1	1	-0	.759	-3	*P-52/O-5(0-0-5)	-0.1
1874	Mut-n	65	298	46	72	6	1	0	30	3	4	.242	.249	.268	518	64	-12	2	0	0	.774	-2	*P-65/3-1,O-1(1-0-0)	-0.1
1875	Mut-n	70	264	23	48	6	2	0	15	2	5	.182	.188	.220	408	39	-16	1	2	-0	.838	-6	*P-70/O-1(1-0-0)	0.0
1876	NY-N	56	221	19	40	4	1	0	9	3	2	.181	.195	.211	406	40	-12				.810	-3	*P-56/O-1(0-0-1)	0.0
1877	Cin-N	15	59	5	10	0	0	0	0	1	2	.169	.183	.169	353	13	-5				.862	-3	P-15/O-1(1-0-0),S-1	-0.2
1879	Pro-N	43	173	25	35	2	0	1	10	7	12	.202	.233	.231	465	55	-8				.956	-5	P-27,O-21(0-0-21)/3-5	-0.8
1881	Pro-N	16	57	6	11	1	0	0	4	5	6	.193	.258	.211	469	50	-3				.810	-3	P-14/O-5(0-0-5)	-0.2
	Bos-N	19	71	2	12	2	0	0	4	0	5	.169	.169	.197	366	15	-7				.818	-4	O-18(1-9-9)/P-5	-0.9
	Yr	35	128	8	23	3	0	0	8	5	11	.180	.211	.203	414	32	-10				.811	-7	O-23(1-9-14),P-19	-1.1
1882	Bos-N	45	169	17	38	6	0	0	13	8	18	.225	.260	.260	520	67	-6				.867	-10	P-34,O-13(0-0-13)/S-1	-0.6
1883	Phi-a	45	167	15	31	2	0	0	11	5		.186	.209	.198	407	29	-13				.874	-2	P-44/O-3(1-1-1)	-0.1
1884	Phi-a	49	184	26	34	5	1	0		7		.185	.215	.223	437	40	-12				.775	-1	P-49/O-1(0-1-0)	0.1
1885	Phi-a	48	179	22	30	3	0	0	12	10		.168	.212	.184	396	24	-15				.881	-0	P-48/O-1(0-0-1)	0.0
1886	Phi-a	24	88	16	21	3	0	0	10	3		.239	.264	.273	536	67	-3	1			.843	-0	P-24/O-1(0-0-1)	-0.1
1887	Phi-a	7	29	5	9	0	0	0	0	4		.310	.310	.200	510	44	-2	0			.889	0	/P-7	0.0
Total	5 n	256	1097	160	237	19	7	0	89	20	14	.216	.230	.246	476	49	-64	7	5	-0	.797	-15	P-255/O-15R,3-4	-0.5
Total	10	367	1397	158	271	28	2	1	73	53	45	.194	.222	.217	439	42	-86	1			.845	-30	P-323/O-65R,3-5,S-2	-2.8
■ JIMMY MATHISON	Mathison, James Michael Ignatius b: 11/11/1878, Baltimore, Md. d: 7/4/11, Baltimore, Md. TR, Deb: 8/29/02																							
1902	Bal-A	29	91	12	24	2	1	0	7	9		.264	.368	.308	676	85	-1	2			.889	-3	3-28/S-1	-0.3
■ JOHN MATIAS	Matias, John Roy b: 8/15/44, Honolulu, Hawaii BL/TL, 5′11″, 170 lbs. Deb: 4/7/70																							
1970	Chi-A	58	117	7	22	2	0	2	6	3	22	.188	.215	.256	471	28	-11	1	0	0	.941	-4	O-22(5-0-17),1-18	-1.8
■ FRANCISCO MATOS	Matos, Francisco Aguirre (Mancebo) b: 7/23/69, Santo Domingo, D.R. BR/TR, 6′1″, 160 lbs. Deb: 7/17/94																							
1994	Oak-A	14	28	1	7	1	0	0	2	1	2	.250	.276	.286	562	49	-2	1	0	0	.925	1	2-12/D-2	-0.1
■ LUIS MATOS	Matos, Luis D. b: 10/30/78, Bayamon, P.R. BR/TR, 6′, 180 lbs. Deb: 6/19/2000																							
2000	Bal-A	72	182	21	41	6	3	1	17	12	30	.225	.284	.308	592	52	-14	13	4	1	.988	4	O-69(1-44-25)/D-3	-0.8
■ PASCUAL MATOS	Matos, Pascual (Cuevas) b: 12/23/74, Barahona, D.R. BR/TR, 6′2″, 180 lbs. Deb: 5/11/99																							
1999	Atl-N	6	8	0	1	0	0	0	2	0	1	.125	.125	.125	250	-37	-2	0	0	0	1.000	0	/C-5	-0.1
■ C. V. MATTESON	Matteson, Clifford Virgil b: 11/1861, Ohio d: 12/18/31, Seville, Ohio Deb: 6/13/1884																							
1884	StL-U	1	4	0	0	0	0	0		0		.000	.000	.000	0	-97	-1				.000	-1	/O-1(0-1-0),P-1	-0.1
■ GARY MATTHEWS	Matthews, Gary Nathaniel Jr. b: 8/25/74, San Francisco, Cal. BB/TR, 6′3″, 200 lbs. Deb: 6/4/99 F																							
1999	SD-N	23	36	4	8	0	0	0	7	9	9	.222	.378	.222	600	62	-2	2	0	0	1.000	-2	O-17(6-2-10)	-0.4
2000	Chi-N	80	158	24	30	1	2	4	14	15	28	.190	.264	.297	562	43	-14	3	0	1	.978	-7	O-61(46-21-1)	-2.0
Total	2	103	194	28	38	1	2	4	21	24	37	.196	.288	.284	571	47	-16	5	0	1	.982	-9	/O-78(52-23-11)	-2.4
■ GARY MATTHEWS	Matthews, Gary Nathaniel Sr. b: 7/5/50, San Fernando, Cal. BR/TR, 6′3″, 190 lbs. Deb: 9/6/72 FC Career OF: (1446-LF 0-CF 431-RF)																							
1972	SF-N	20	62	11	18	1	1	4	14	7	13	.290	.362	.532	895	149	4	0	1	-0	.971	-1	O-19(10-0-9)	0.2
1973	SF-N	148	540	74	162	22	10	12	58	58	83	.300	.369	.444	813	119	15	17	5	2	.983	6	*O-145(144-0-1)	1.5
1974	SF-N	154	561	87	161	27	6	16	82	70	69	.287	.369	.442	811	120	16	11	9	-1	.970	5	*O-151(150-0-1)	1.1
1975	SF-N	116	425	67	119	22	3	12	58	65	53	.280	.378	.431	809	119	12	13	4	1	.967	8	*O-113(113-0-0)	1.6
1976	SF-N	156	587	79	164	28	4	20	84	75	94	.279	.362	.443	805	124	19	12	5	1	.975	-3	*O-156(156-0-0)	0.8
1977	Atl-N	148	555	89	157	25	5	17	64	67	90	.283	.362	.438	800	101	2	22	8	2	.965	8	*O-145(145-0-0)	0.6
1978	Atl-N	129	474	75	135	20	5	18	62	61	92	.285	.369	.462	831	118	12	8	7	-1	.969	2	*O-127(1-0-127)	0.7
1979	Atl-N★	156	631	97	192	34	5	27	90	60	75	.304	.365	.502	867	125	21	18	6	2	.974	1	*O-156(0-0-156)	1.6
1980	Atl-N	155	571	79	159	17	3	19	75	42	93	.278	.328	.419	746	104	2	11	3	1	.960	-3	*O-143(6-0-137)	-0.8
1981	*Phi-N	101	359	62	108	21	3	9	67	59	42	.301	.404	.451	855	136	19	15	2	3	.963	1	*O-100(100-0-0)	2.0
1982	Phi-N	162	616	89	173	31	1	19	83	66	87	.281	.352	.427	779	114	12	21	4	3	.966	3	*O-162(162-0-0)	1.2
1983	*Phi-N	132	446	66	115	18	2	10	50	69	81	.258	.357	.374	732	104	4	13	9	-0	.974	-1	*O-122(122-0-0)	-0.3
1984	*Chi-N	147	491	101	143	21	2	14	82	**103**	97	.291	**.417**	.428	845	126	22	17	8	1	.955	-4	*O-145(145-0-0)	1.4
1985	Chi-N	97	298	45	70	12	0	13	40	59	64	.235	.365	.406	771	104	3	2	0	0	.977	-2	O-85(85-0-0)	-0.2
1986	Chi-N	123	370	49	96	16	1	21	46	60	59	.259	.363	.478	841	121	11	3	2	-0	.940	-8	*O-105(105-0-0)	-0.1
1987	Chi-N	44	42	3	11	3	0	0	8	4	11	.262	.326	.333	659	72	-2	0	0	0	1.000	-0	/O-2(2-0-0)	-0.2
	Sea-A	45	119	10	28	1	0	3	15	15	22	.235	.321	.319	640	67	-5	0	1	-0	.000	0	D-39	-0.7
Total	16	2033	7147	1083	2011	319	51	234	978	940	1125	.281	.367	.439	805	116	168	183	74	14	.968	12	*O-1876L/D-39	10.4
■ BOB MATTHEWS	Matthews, Robert b: Camden, N.J. Deb: 9/25/1891																							
1891	Phi-a	1	3	1	1	0	0	0	0	0	1	.333	.600	.333	933	167	1	0			.000	-0	/O-1(0-0-1)	0.0
■ WID MATTHEWS	Matthews, Wid Curry "Matty" b: 10/20/1896, Raleigh, Ill d: 10/5/65, Hollywood, Cal. BL/TL, 5′8.5″, 155 lbs. Deb: 4/18/23																							
1923	Phi-A	129	485	52	133	11	6	1	25	50	27	.274	.343	.328	671	76	-16	16	16	-2	.947	-8	*O-127(2-125-0)	-3.1
1924	Was-A	53	169	25	51	10	4	0	13	11	4	.302	.355	.408	763	100	-0	3	8	-2	.985	5	O-44(1-43-0)	0.1
1925	Was-A	10	9	2	4	0	0	0	1	0	1	.444	.444	.444	889	129	0	0	0	0	1.000	-0	/O-1(0-1-0)	0.0
Total	3	192	663	79	188	21	10	1	39	61	32	.284	.348	.350	697	83	-16	19	24	-4	.957	-4	O-172(3-169-0)	-3.0
■ STEVE MATTHIAS	Matthias, Stephen J. b: 1860, Mitchellville, Md. BR/TR, 5′8″, 160 lbs. Deb: 4/20/1884																							
1884	CP-U	37	142	24	39	7	1	0		5		.275	.299	.338	637	93	-5				.840	2	S-36/O-2(0-2-0)	-0.2
■ BOBBY MATTICK	Mattick, Robert James b: 12/5/15, Sioux City, Iowa BR/TR, 5′11″, 178 lbs. Deb: 5/5/38 FM																							
1938	Chi-N	1	1	0	1	0	0	0	1	0	0	1.000	1.000	1.000	2000	439	0	0			.000	0	/S-1	0.0
1939	Chi-N	51	178	16	51	12	1	0	23	6	19	.287	.314	.365	679	80	-5	1			.927	7	S-48	0.5
1940	Chi-N	128	441	30	96	15	0	0	33	19	33	.218	.250	.252	502	39	-36	5			.946	10	*S-126/3-1	-1.8
1941	Cin-N	20	60	8	11	3	0	0	7	8	7	.183	.279	.233	513	45	-4	1			.982	-2	S-12/3-5,2-1	-0.5
1942	Cin-N	6	10	0	2	1	0	0	0	0	1	.200	.200	.300	500	45	-1	0			1.000	1	/S-3	0.1
Total	5	206	690	54	161	31	1	0	64	33	60	.233	.269	.281	550	52	-46	7			.943	17	S-190/3-6,2-1	-1.7
■ WALLY MATTICK	Mattick, Walter Joseph "Chink" b: 3/12/1887, St.Louis, Mo. d: 11/5/68, Los Altos, Cal. BR/TR, 5′10″, 180 lbs. Deb: 4/11/12 F																							
1912	Chi-A	90	285	45	74	7	9	1	35	27		.260	.334	.358	692	101	0	15			.982	-3	O-79(2-66-10)	-0.8
1913	Chi-A	71	207	15	39	8	1	0	11	18	16	.188	.253	.237	490	44	-15	3			.977	2	O-64(7-56-0)	-1.9
1918	StL-N	8	14	0	2	0	0	0	1	2	3	.143	.333	.143	476	49	-1	0			1.000	0	/O-3(0-0-3)	0.0
Total	3	169	506	60	115	15	10	1	47	47	19	.227	.302	.302	604	77	-15	18			.980	-1	O-146(9-122-13)	-2.7

YEAR	TM/L	G	AB	R	H	2B	3B	HR	RBI	BB	SO	AVG	OBP	SLG	OPS	OPS+	BR+	SB	CS	SBR	FA	FR	G/POS	TPR
■ MIKE MATTIMORE	Mattimore, Michael Joseph b: 1859, Renovo, Pa. d: 4/28/31, Butte, Mont. BL/TL, 5'8.5", 160 lbs. Deb: 5/3/1887 Career OF: (23-LF 10-CF 32-RF)																							
1887	NY-N	8	32	5	8	1	0	0	4	0	6	.250	.250	.281	531	50	-2	1			.889	-1	/P-7,O-2(0-2-0)	0.0
1888	Phi-a	41	142	22	38	6	5	0	12	12		.268	.333	.380	714	129	5	16			.915	5	P-26,O-16(1-1-15)	0.3
1889	Phi-a	23	73	10	17	1	2	1	8	9	7	.233	.333	.342	676	94	-0	6			.944	-3	O-12(3-5-4)/1-7,P-5	-0.3
	KC-a	19	75	6	12	1	1	0	5	3	16	.160	.192	.200	392	11	-9	0			.844	-2	O-19(19-1-0)/P-1	-0.9
	Yr	42	148	16	29	2	3	1	13	12	23	.196	.265	.270	536	52	-10	6			.873	-5	O-31(22-6-4)/1-7,P-6	-1.2
1890	Bro-a	33	129	14	17	1	1	0	7	16		.132	.238	.155	393	17	-13	11			.887	-6	P-19,O-14(0-1-13)	-0.9
Total	4	124	451	57	92	10	9	1	36	40	29	.204	.278	.273	550	64	-20	34			.853	-7	/O-63R,P-58,1-7	-1.8
■ DON MATTINGLY	Mattingly, Donald Arthur b: 4/20/61, Evansville, Ind. BL/TL, 6', 175 lbs. Deb: 9/8/82 Career OF: (33-LF 2-CF 47-RF)																							
1982	NY-A	7	12	0	2	0	0	0	1	0	1	.167	.167	.167	333	-8	-2	0	0	0	1.000	1	/O-6(5-0-1),1-1	-0.1
1983	NY-A	91	279	34	79	15	4	4	32	21	31	.283	.336	.409	744	108	3	0	0	0	.974	-10	O-48R,1-42/2-1	-1.2
1984	NY-A★	153	603	91	**207**	**44**	2	23	110	41	33	**.343**	.386	.537	923	**159**	46	1	1	-0	**.996**	13	*1-133,O-19(13-1-6)	4.9
1985	NY-A★	159	652	107	211	**48**	3	35	**145**	56	41	.324	.379	.567	946	159	51	2	2	-0	**.995**	-11	*1-159	2.9
1986	NY-A★	162	677	117	**238**	**53**	2	31	113	53	35	.352	.399	**.573**	**973**	**163**	**57**	0	0	0	**.996**	-7	*1-160/3-3,D-1	3.9
1987	NY-A★	141	569	93	186	38	2	30	115	51	38	.327	.383	.559	942	147	38	1	4	-1	**.996**	-4	*1-140/D-1	2.2
1988	NY-A★	144	599	94	186	37	0	18	88	41	29	.311	.358	.462	820	129	22	1	0	0	.993	-4	*1-143/O-1(1-0-0),D-1	0.8
1989	NY-A★	158	631	79	191	37	2	23	113	51	30	.303	.356	.477	833	134	27	3	0	1	.995	-5	*1-145,D-17/O-1R	1.2
1990	NY-A	102	394	40	101	16	0	5	42	28	20	.256	.311	.335	646	80	-10	1	0	0	.997	6	1-89,D-13/O-1(1-0-0)	-1.1
1991	NY-A	152	587	64	169	35	0	9	68	46	42	.288	.344	.394	737	103	3	2	0	0	.996	-4	*1-127,D-22	-1.0
1992	NY-A	157	640	89	184	40	0	14	86	39	43	.287	.329	.416	745	108	5	3	0	1	**.997**	7	*1-143,D-15	0.2
1993	NY-A	134	530	78	154	27	2	17	86	61	42	.291	.366	.445	811	121	16	0	0	0	**.998**	-2	*1-130/D-5	0.2
1994	NY-A	97	372	62	113	20	1	6	51	60	24	.304	.400	.411	812	114	11	0	0	0	**.998**	3	1-97	0.4
1995	*NY-A	128	458	59	132	32	2	7	49	40	35	.288	.347	.413	759	98	-2	0	2	-1	.994	-1	*1-125/D-1	-1.4
Total	14	1785	7003	1007	2153	442	20	222	1099	588	444	.307	.363	.471	834	128	265	14	9	-0	.996	-19	*1-1634/D-76,O32	11.9
■ RALPH MATTIS	Mattis, Ralph "Matty" b: 8/24/1890, Roxborough, Pa. d: 9/13/60, Williamsport, Pa. BR/TR, 5'11", 172 lbs. Deb: 4/22/14																							
1914	Pit-F	36	85	14	21	4	1	0	8	9	11	.247	.326	.318	644	77	-4	2			.938	2	O-24(12-0-12)	-0.4
■ CLOY MATTOX	Mattox, Cloy Mitchell "Monk" b: 11/24/02, Leesville, Va. d: 8/3/85, Danville, Va. BL/TR, 5'8", 168 lbs. Deb: 9/1/29 F																							
1929	Phi-A	3	6	0	1	0	0	0	0	1	1	.167	.286	.167	452	19	-1	0	0	0	.875	-0	/C-3	-0.1
■ JIM MATTOX	Mattox, James Powell b: 12/17/1896, Leesville, Va. d: 10/12/73, Myrtle Beach, S.C. BL/TR, 5'9.5", 168 lbs. Deb: 4/30/22 F																							
1922	Pit-N	29	51	11	15	1	1	0	3	1	3	.294	.308	.353	661	69	-2	0	0	0	.984	1	C-21	0.0
1923	Pit-N	22	32	4	6	1	1	0	1	0	5	.188	.235	.281	517	35	-3	0	0	0	.960	1	/C-8	-0.2
Total	2	51	83	15	21	2	2	0	4	1	8	.253	.279	.325	604	56	-5	0	0	0	.978	2	/C-29	-0.2
■ LEN MATUSZEK	Matuszek, Leonard James b: 9/27/54, Toledo, Ohio BL/TR, 6'2", 195 lbs. Deb: 9/3/81 Career OF: (53-LF 0-CF 2-RF)																							
1981	Phi-N	13	11	1	3	1	0	0	1	3	1	.273	.429	.364	792	121	1	0	1	-0	1.000	2	/1-1,3-1	0.2
1982	Phi-N	25	39	1	3	1	0	0	3	1	10	.077	.122	.103	225	-36	-7	0	1	-0	.750	-2	/3-8,1-3	-1.0
1983	Phi-N	28	80	12	22	6	1	4	16	4	14	.275	.310	.525	835	129	2	0	1	-0	1.000	-1	1-21	0.0
1984	Phi-N	101	262	40	65	17	1	12	43	39	54	.248	.354	.458	812	125	9	4	3	-0	.990	4	1-81/O-1(1-0-0)	0.9
1985	Tor-A	62	151	23	32	6	2	2	15	11	24	.212	.265	.318	583	57	-9	2	1	0	1.000	0	D-54/1-5	-1.0
	*LA-N	43	63	10	14	2	1	3	13	8	14	.222	.319	.429	748	111	1	0	1	-0	1.000	-1	O-17(17-0-0),1-10/3-1	-0.2
1986	LA-N	91	199	26	52	7	0	9	28	21	47	.261	.335	.432	767	118	4	2	2	-0	1.000	-4	O-37(35-0-2),1-31	-0.2
1987	LA-N	16	15	0	1	0	0	0	0	1	4	.067	.125	.067	192	-49	-3	0	0	0	1.000	0	/1-3	-0.3
Total	7	379	820	113	192	40	5	30	119	88	168	.234	.314	.405	719	99	-2	8	10	-2	.990	-2	1-155/O-55L,D-54,3	-1.6
■ GENE MAUCH	Mauch, Gene William "Skip" b: 11/18/25, Salina, Kan. BR/TR, 5'10", 165 lbs. Deb: 4/18/44 M																							
1944	Bro-N	5	15	2	2	1	0	0	2	2	3	.133	.235	.200	435	24	-2	0			1.000	-2	/S-5	-0.3
1947	Pit-N	16	30	8	9	0	0	0	1	7	6	.300	.432	.300	732	95	0	0			.963	-2	/2-6,S-4	-0.1
1948	Bro-N	12	13	1	2	0	0	0	0	1	4	.154	.214	.154	368	1	-2	0			.950	1	/2-7,S-1	0.0
	Chi-N	53	138	18	28	3	2	1	7	26	10	.203	.329	.275	605	68	-5	1			.925	-6	2-26,S-19	-0.9
	Yr	65	151	19	30	3	2	1	7	27	14	.199	.320	.265	585	62	-7	1			.929	-5	2-33,S-20	-0.9
1949	Chi-N	72	150	15	37	6	2	1	7	21	15	.247	.339	.333	673	83	-3	3			.971	12	2-25,S-19/3-7	1.0
1950	Bos-N	48	121	17	28	5	0	1	15	14	9	.231	.316	.298	614	67	-6	1			.968	-1	2-28/3-7,S-5	-0.5
1951	Bos-N	19	20	5	2	0	0	0	1	7	4	.100	.333	.100	433	24	-2	0	0	0	1.000	-0	S-10/3-3,2-2	-0.2
1952	StL-N	7	3	0	0	0	0	0	0	1	2	.000	.250	.000	250	-25	-0	0	0	0	.500	0	/S-2	-0.1
1956	Bos-A	7	25	4	8	0	0	0	1	3	3	.320	.393	.320	713	80	-1	0	0	0	.935	-2	/2-6	-0.2
1957	Bos-A	65	222	23	60	10	3	2	28	22	26	.270	.339	.369	708	88	-3	1	0	0	.962	-10	2-58	-0.9
Total	9	304	737	93	176	25	7	5	62	104	82	.239	.335	.312	647	75	-23	6	0		.958	-10	2-158/S-65,3-17	-2.2
■ AL MAUL	Maul, Albert Joseph "Smiling Al" b: 10/9/1865, Philadelphia, Pa. d: 5/3/58, Philadelphia, Pa. BR/TR, 6', 175 lbs. Deb: 6/20/1884 Career OF: (84-LF 21-CF 80-RF)																							
1884	Phi-U	1	4	0	0	0	0	0		0		.000	.000	.000	0	-99	-1				1.000	-0	/P-1	0.0
1887	Phi-N	16	71	15	32	2	2	1	4	15	10	.451	.451	.464	915	146	4	5			.897	2	/O-8(6-2-0),P-7,1-2	0.3
1888	Pit-N	74	259	21	54	9	4	0	31	21	45	.208	.276	.274	550	82	-4	9			.975	-1	1-38,O-34(0-3-31)/P-3	-0.8
1889	Pit-N	68	257	37	71	6	6	4	44	29	41	.276	.356	.393	749	121	8	18			.946	11	O-64(39-0-25)/P-6	1.4
1890	Pit-P	45	162	31	42	6	2	0	21	22	12	.259	.348	.321	669	86	-2	5			.904	4	P-30,O-15(11-3-1)/S-1	-0.1
1891	Pit-N	47	149	15	28	2	4	0	14	20	28	.188	.284	.255	539	59	-7	4			.877	-2	O-40(20-12-8)/P-8	-0.9
1893	Was-N	44	134	10	34	8	4	0	12	33	14	.254	.405	.373	778	110	4	1			.889	1	P-37/O-7(5-0-2)	0.1
1894	Was-N	41	124	23	30	3	3	2	20	14	11	.242	.352	.363	715	75	-5	1			.877	3	P-28,O-12(1-0-11)	-0.1
1895	Was-N	22	72	9	18	5	2	0	16	6	7	.250	.308	.375	683	76	-3	0			.933	1	P-16/O-4(2-0-2)	-0.1
1896	Was-N	8	28	6	8	1	1	0	5	3	2	.286	.355	.393	748	97	-0	0			.923	-1	/P-8	0.0
1897	Was-N	1	1	0	0	0	0	0	0	0		.000	.000	.000	0	-99	-0	0			1.000	0	/P-1	0.0
	Bal-N	2	3	0	1	0	0	0	0	0		.333	.333	.333	667	76	-0	0			1.000	-0	/P-2	0.0
	Yr	3	4	0	1	0	0	0	0	0		.250	.250	.250	500	32	-0	0			1.000	-0	/P-3	0.0
1898	Bal-N	29	93	21	19	3	2	0	10	16		.204	.333	.280	613	75	-2	1			.978	-5	P-28/O-1(0-1-0)	0.0
1899	Bro-N	4	11	2	3	0	0	0	0	1		.273	.333	.273	606	65	-0	0			.900	0	/P-4	0.0
1900	Phi-N	5	15	2	3	0	0	0	1	2		.200	.294	.200	494	38	-1	0			.917	0	/P-5	0.0
1901	NY-N	3	8	1	3	0	0	0	1	0		.375	.375	.375	750	122	0	0			1.000	0	/P-3	0.0
Total	15	410	1391	193	346	45	30	7	179	182	170	.249	.336	.332	668	91	-11	44			.910	13	P-187,O-185L/1-40,S	-0.2
■ MARK MAULDIN	Mauldin, Marshall Reese b: 11/5/14, Atlanta, Ga. d: 9/2/90, Union City, Ga. BR/TR, 5'11", 170 lbs. Deb: 9/10/34																							
1934	Chi-A	10	38	3	10	2	0	1	3	0	3	.263	.263	.395	658	66	-2	0	0	0	.906	-0	3-10	-0.2
■ ROB MAURER	Maurer, Robert John b: 1/7/67, Evansville, Ind. BL/TL, 6'3", 210 lbs. Deb: 9/8/91																							
1991	Tex-A	13	16	0	1	1	0	0	2	2	6	.063	.211	.125	336	-5	-2	0	0	0	1.000	1	/1-4,D-2	-0.1
1992	Tex-A	8	9	1	2	0	0	0	1	1	2	.222	.300	.222	522	50	-1	0	0	0	1.000	0	/1-3,D-1	0.0
Total	2	21	25	1	3	1	0	0	3	3	8	.120	.241	.160	401	14	-3	0	0	0	1.000	1	/1-7,D-3	-0.1
■ CARMEN MAURO	Mauro, Carmen Louis b: 11/10/26, St.Paul, Minn. BL/TR, 6', 167 lbs. Deb: 10/1/48																							
1948	Chi-N	3	5	2	1	0	0	1	1	2	0	.200	.429	.800	1229	235	1	0			1.000	1	/O-2(0-1-1)	0.1
1950	Chi-N	62	185	19	42	4	3	1	10	13	31	.227	.285	.297	582	54	-12	3			.946	-3	O-49(18-1-30)	-1.8
1951	Chi-N	13	29	3	5	1	0	0	3	2	6	.172	.250	.207	457	24	-3	0	0	0	.900	1	/O-6(0-5-1)	-0.3
1953	Bro-N	8	9	1	0	0	0	0	0	0	4	.000	.000	.000	0	-98	-3	0	0	0	1.000	-0	/O-1(0-0-1)	-0.3
	Was-A	17	23	1	4	0	1	0	2	1	3	.174	.208	.261	469	27	-2	0	0	0	1.000	-0	/O-6(3-3-0)	-0.3
	Phi-A	64	165	14	44	4	4	0	17	19	21	.267	.342	.339	682	81	-4	3	4	-1	.969	-1	O-49(4-38-7)/3-1	-0.7
	Yr	81	188	15	48	4	5	0	19	20	24	.255	.327	.330	657	76	-6	3	4	-1	.971	-1	O-55(7-41-7)/3-1	-1.0
Total	4	167	416	40	96	9	8	2	33	37	65	.231	.298	.305	604	61	-23	6	4		.958	-4	O-113(25-48-40)/3-1	-3.3

YEAR	TM/L	G	AB	R	H	2B	3B	HR	RBI	BB	SO	AVG	OBP	SLG	OPS	OPS+	BR+	SB	CS	SBR	FA	FR	G/POS	TPR
■ BOB MAVIS Mavis, Robert Henry b: 4/8/18, Milwaukee, Wis. BL/TR, 5'7", 160 lbs. Deb: 9/17/49																								
1949	Det-A	1	0	0	0	0	0	0	0	0	0	—	—	—	—	—	0	0	0	0	.000	0	R	0.0
■ DAL MAXVILL Maxvill, Charles Dallan b: 2/18/39, Granite City, Ill. BR/TR, 5'11", 160 lbs. Deb: 6/10/62 C																								
1962	StL-N	79	189	20	42	3	1	1	18	17	39	.222	.290	.265	554	46	-14	1	2	-0	.962	-2	S-76/3-1	-1.1
1963	StL-N	53	51	12	12	2	0	0	3	6	11	.235	.316	.275	590	66	-2	0	0	0	.974	7	S-24/2-9,3-3	0.6
1964	*StL-N	37	26	4	6	0	0	0	4	0	7	.231	.231	.231	462	28	-2	1	0	0	.972	6	2-15,S-13/3-1,O-1R	0.4
1965	StL-N	68	89	10	12	2	2	0	10	7	15	.135	.206	.202	408	14	-10	0	0	0	.993	13	2-49,S-12	0.5
1966	StL-N	134	394	25	96	14	3	0	24	37	61	.244	.312	.294	606	69	-15	3	0	1	.967	24	*S-128/2-5,O-1(1-0-0)	2.0
1967	*StL-N	152	476	37	108	14	4	1	41	48	66	.227	.299	.279	578	67	-19	0	2	-1	.974	3	*S-148/2-7	-0.5
1968	*StL-N	151	459	51	116	8	5	1	24	52	71	.253	.330	.298	629	91	-3	0	2	-1	.969	-9	*S-151	-0.1
1969	StL-N	132	372	27	65	10	2	2	32	44	52	.175	.264	.228	492	39	-30	1	1	-0	.969	21	*S-131	0.6
1970	StL-N	152	399	35	80	5	2	0	28	51	56	.201	.291	.223	514	39	-33	0	0	0	**.982**	**38**	*S-136,2-22	1.9
1971	StL-N	142	356	31	80	10	1	0	24	43	45	.225	.310	.258	568	60	-17	1	2	-0	.979	**29**	*S-140	2.6
1972	StL-N	105	276	22	61	6	1	1	23	31	47	.221	.300	.261	561	61	-13	0	1	-0	.980	9	S-95,2-11	0.5
	*Oak-A	27	36	2	9	1	0	0	1	1	11	.250	.270	.278	548	67	-2	0	1	-0	.983	4	2-24/S-4	0.3
1973	Oak-A	29	19	0	4	0	0	0	1	1	3	.211	.250	.211	461	33	-2	0	0	0	.966	4	S-18,2-11/3-1	0.2
	Pit-N	74	217	19	41	4	3	0	17	22	40	.189	.264	.235	499	40	-17	0	0	0	.971	4	S-74	-0.6
1974	Pit-N	8	22	3	4	0	0	0	0	2	4	.182	.250	.182	432	23	-2	0	0	0	.946	1	/S-8	-0.1
	*Oak-A	60	52	3	10	0	0	0	2	8	10	.192	.300	.192	492	47	-3	0	0	0	1.000	9	2-30,S-29/3-1	0.8
1975	Oak-A	20	10	1	2	0	0	0	0	0	0	.200	.200	.200	400	14	-1	0	0	0	.955	2	S-20/2-2	0.2
Total	14	1423	3443	302	748	79	24	6	252	370	538	.217	.295	.259	554	57	-187	7	11	-2	.973	160	*S-1207,2-185/3-7,O	8.2
■ CHARLIE MAXWELL Maxwell, Charles Richard "Smokey" b: 4/8/27, Lawton, Mich. BL/TL, 5'11", 185 lbs. Deb: 9/20/50																								
1950	Bos-A	3	8	1	0	0	0	0	0	1	3	.000	.111	.000	111	-63	-2	0	0	0	1.000	1	/O-2(0-0-1)	-0.1
1951	Bos-A	49	80	8	15	1	0	3	12	9	18	.188	.270	.313	582	52	-6	0	1	-0	.926	-1	O-13(5-0-8)	-0.7
1952	Bos-A	8	15	0	1	1	0	0	0	3	11	.067	.222	.133	356	0	-2	0	0	0	.966	2	/1-3,O-3(0-1-2)	-0.1
1954	Bos-A	74	104	9	26	4	1	0	5	12	21	.250	.328	.308	635	67	-4	3	0	1	1.000	-7	O-27(21-3-6)	-1.2
1955	Bal-A	4	4	0	0	0	0	0	0	0	1	.000	.000	.000	0	-99	-1	0	0	0	.000	0	H	-0.1
	Det-A	55	109	19	29	7	1	7	18	8	20	.266	.328	.541	869	134	4	0	0	0	.967	2	O-26(22-0-4)/1-2	0.5
	Yr	59	113	19	29	7	1	7	18	8	21	.257	.317	.522	839	126	3	0	0	0	.967	2	O-26(22-0-4)/1-2	0.4
1956	Det-A☆	141	500	96	163	14	3	28	87	79	74	.326	.420	.534	954	150	37	1	1	-0	.987	13	*O-136(134-0-2)	4.0
1957	Det-A★	138	492	75	136	23	3	24	82	76	84	.276	.379	.482	860	130	21	3	2	-0	**.997**	14	*O-137(137-0-3)	2.8
1958	Det-A	131	397	56	108	14	4	13	65	64	54	.272	.373	.426	799	111	8	6	1	1	.986	-1	*O-114(113-0-3),1-14	0.1
1959	Det-A	145	518	81	130	12	2	31	95	81	91	.251	.359	.461	820	117	13	0	2	-1	.986	10	*O-136(136-0-0)	1.4
1960	Det-A	134	482	70	114	16	5	24	81	58	75	.237	.326	.440	766	102	1	5	0	1	**.996**	8	*O-120(120-0-0)	0.2
1961	Det-A	79	131	11	30	4	2	5	18	20	24	.229	.336	.405	740	94	-1	0	0	0	.965	2	O-25(22-0-4)	-0.1
1962	Det-A	30	67	5	13	2	0	1	9	8	10	.194	.280	.269	549	47	-5	0	0	0	.966	-1	O-15(0-0-15)/1-1	-0.7
	Chi-A	69	206	30	61	8	3	9	43	34	32	.296	.396	.495	891	139	12	0	0	0	.990	0	O-56(49-0-7)/1-6	0.8
	Yr	99	273	35	74	10	3	10	52	42	42	.271	.368	.440	808	115	7	0	0	0	.985	-1	O-71(49-0-22)/1-7	0.1
1963	Chi-A	71	130	17	30	4	2	3	17	31	27	.231	.379	.362	740	111	3	0	0	0	1.000	-4	O-24(24-0-0),1-17	-0.2
1964	Chi-A	2	2	0	0	0	0	0	0	0	0	.000	.000	.000	0	-99	-1	0	0	0	.000	0	H	-0.1
Total	14	1133	3245	478	856	110	26	148	532	484	545	.264	.363	.451	814	116	78	18	7	2	.988	37	O-834(783-4-55)/1-43	6.5
■ JASON MAXWELL Maxwell, Jason Ramond b: 3/26/72, Lewisburg, Tenn. BR/TR, 6', 185 lbs. Deb: 9/1/98 Career OF: (0-LF 1-CF 1-RF)																								
1998	Chi-N	7	3	2	1	0	0	1	2	0	2	.333	.333	1.333	1667	301	1	0	0	0	1.000	0	/2-1	0.1
2000	Min-A	64	111	14	27	6	0	1	11	9	32	.243	.306	.324	630	57	-7	2	1	0	.967	12	2-30,3-19/S-5,OD	0.6
Total	2	71	114	16	28	6	0	2	13	9	34	.246	.306	.351	657	63	-6	2	1	0	.968	13	/2-31,3-19,D-7,SO	0.7
■ CARLOS MAY May, Carlos b: 5/17/48, Birmingham, Ala. BL/TR, 6', 215 lbs. Deb: 9/6/68 F Career OF: (653-LF 0-CF 26-RF)																								
1968	Chi-A	17	67	4	12	1	0	0	1	3	15	.179	.214	.194	408	24	-6	0	0	0	.960	-2	O-17(15-0-2)	-1.0
1969	Chi-A★	100	367	62	103	18	2	18	62	58	66	.281	.387	.488	875	137	19	1	4	-1	.982	-1	*O-100(80-0-22)	1.1
1970	Chi-A	150	555	83	158	28	4	12	68	79	96	.285	.377	.414	791	114	12	12	5	1	.991	1	*O-141(141-0-0)/1-7	0.6
1971	Chi-A	141	500	64	147	21	7	7	70	62	61	.294	.379	.406	785	119	14	16	7	1	.986	-5	*1-130/O-9(9-0-0)	0.0
1972	Chi-A☆	148	523	83	161	26	3	12	68	79	70	.308	.408	.438	845	149	35	23	14	0	.983	-1	*O-145(145-0-0)/1-5	2.9
1973	Chi-A	149	553	62	148	20	0	20	96	53	73	.268	.337	.412	749	106	4	8	6	-0	.992	1	D-75,O-70(70-0-0)/1-2	-0.1
1974	Chi-A	149	551	66	137	19	2	8	58	46	76	.249	.308	.334	642	82	-12	8	9	-1	.988	6	*O-129(129-0-0),D-13	-1.7
1975	Chi-A	128	454	55	123	19	2	8	53	67	46	.271	.375	.374	750	111	9	12	7	0	.989	1	1-63,O-46L,D-19	0.2
1976	Chi-A	20	63	7	11	2	0	0	3	9	5	.175	.278	.206	484	43	-4	4	0	1	1.000	-1	D-10/O-9(9-0-0)	-0.6
	*NY-A	87	288	38	80	11	2	3	40	34	32	.278	.364	.361	725	114	6	1	1	-0	.950	0	D-71/O-7(7-0-0),1-1	0.4
	Yr	107	351	45	91	13	2	3	43	43	37	.259	.348	.333	682	101	2	5	1	1	.891	-1	D-81,O-16(16-0-0)/1-1	-0.2
1977	NY-A	65	181	21	41	7	1	2	16	17	24	.227	.296	.309	606	66	-8	0	0	0	1.000	-1	D-53/O-4(2-0-2)	-1.1
	Cal-A	11	18	0	6	0	0	0	1	5	1	.333	.478	.333	812	131	1	0	0	0	1.000	0	/1-3,D-1	0.1
	Yr	76	199	21	47	7	1	2	17	22	25	.236	.315	.312	627	73	-7	0	0	0	1.000	-1	D-54/O-4(2-0-2),1-3	-1.0
Total	10	1165	4120	545	1127	172	23	90	536	512	565	.274	.360	.392	752	111	71	85	53	0	.984	-1	O-677L,D-242,1-211	0.8
■ DAVE MAY May, David La France b: 12/23/43, New Castle, Del. BL/TR, 5'10.5", 186 lbs. Deb: 7/28/67 F Career OF: (88-LF 542-CF 411-RF)																								
1967	Bal-A	36	85	12	20	1	1	1	7	6	13	.235	.286	.306	592	75	-3	0	0	0	.969	-0	O-19(1-0-18)	-0.5
1968	Bal-A	84	152	15	29	6	3	0	7	19	27	.191	.285	.270	555	69	-5	3	3	-0	.984	-11	O-61(1-16-47)	-2.2
1969	*Bal-A	78	120	8	29	6	0	3	10	9	23	.242	.305	.367	672	86	-2	2	1	0	.940	-4	O-40(0-0-40)	-0.8
1970	Bal-A	25	31	6	6	0	1	1	6	4	4	.194	.286	.355	641	75	-1	0	0	0	1.000	-2	/O-9(0-0-9)	-0.4
	Mil-A	100	342	36	82	8	1	7	31	44	56	.240	.330	.330	660	82	-8	8	6	-0	.989	8	O-99(0-99-1)	-0.2
	Yr	125	373	42	88	8	2	8	37	48	60	.236	.326	.332	659	81	-9	8	6	-0	.989	6	*O-108(0-99-10)	-0.6
1971	Mil-A	144	501	74	139	20	3	16	65	50	59	.277	.347	.425	772	119	12	15	9	0	.975	10	*O-142(2-94-48)	1.9
1972	Mil-A	143	500	49	119	20	2	9	45	47	56	.238	.307	.340	647	94	-4	11	13	-2	.985	15	*O-138(0-138-0)	0.6
1973	Mil-A★	156	624	96	189	23	4	25	93	44	78	.303	.354	.473	826	134	26	6	7	-1	.979	3	*O-152(0-152-0)/D-2	2.4
1974	Mil-A	135	477	56	108	15	1	10	42	28	73	.226	.274	.325	599	72	-18	4	3	-0	.989	-3	*O-121(5-17-108)/D-8	-2.8
1975	Atl-N	82	203	28	56	8	0	12	40	25	27	.276	.361	.493	853	130	8	1	1	-0	.964	-1	O-53(13-17-24)	0.5
1976	Atl-N	105	214	27	46	5	3	3	23	26	31	.215	.303	.308	611	69	-8	5	1	1	.972	0	O-60(41-0-19)	-1.1
1977	Tex-A	120	340	46	82	14	1	7	42	32	43	.241	.314	.350	664	80	-9	4	3	-0	.969	-4	*O-111(21-2-92)/D-5	-1.8
1978	Mil-A	39	77	9	15	4	0	2	11	9	10	.195	.295	.325	620	74	-3	0	0	0	.944	0	O-16(4-7-5)/D-8	-0.3
	Pit-N	5	4	0	0	0	0	0	0	1	1	.000	.200	.000	200	-38	-1	0	0	0	.000	0	H	-0.1
Total	12	1252	3670	462	920	130	20	96	422	344	501	.251	.320	.375	695	97	-16	60	47	-3	.978	10	*O-1021C/D-23	-4.8
■ DERRICK MAY May, Derrick Brant b: 7/14/68, Rochester, N.Y. BL/TR, 6'4", 225 lbs. Deb: 9/6/90 F Career OF: (537-LF 0-CF 83-RF)																								
1990	Chi-N	17	61	8	15	3	0	1	11	2	7	.246	.270	.344	614	63	-3	1	0	0	.972	0	O-17(17-0-0)	-0.3
1991	Chi-N	15	22	4	5	2	0	1	3	2	1	.227	.292	.455	746	102	-0	0	0	0	1.000	0	/O-7(7-0-0)	0.0
1992	Chi-N	124	351	33	96	11	0	8	45	14	40	.274	.307	.373	680	89	-5	5	3	0	.969	-11	*O-108(98-0-14)	-2.0
1993	Chi-N	128	465	62	137	25	2	10	77	31	41	.295	.340	.422	762	104	2	10	3	1	.970	1	*O-122(121-0-2)	0.0
1994	Chi-N	100	345	43	98	19	2	8	51	30	34	.284	.341	.420	762	99	-1	3	2	-0	.994	2	O-92(92-0-0)	-0.1
1995	Mil-A	32	113	15	28	3	1	1	9	5	18	.248	.286	.319	604	54	-8	0	1	-0	.971	-0	O-32(32-0-0)	-0.9
	Hou-N	78	206	29	62	15	1	8	41	19	24	.301	.363	.500	863	134	10	5	0	1	.974	-5	O-55(43-0-12)/1-1	0.4
1996	Hou-N	109	259	24	65	12	3	5	33	30	33	.251	.333	.378	712	95	-2	2	2	-0	.970	4	O-71(70-0-3)	0.0
1997	Phi-N	83	149	8	34	5	1	1	13	8	26	.228	.268	.295	563	47	-12	4	1	1	.961	-3	O-56(7-0-49)	-1.6
1998	Mon-N	85	180	13	43	8	0	5	15	11	24	.239	.283	.367	649	70	-8	0	0	0	.984	-2	O-48(48-0-0)/D-2	-1.1
1999	Bal-A	26	49	5	13	0	0	4	12	4	6	.265	.321	.510	831	112	1	0	0	0	1.000	0	/O-5(2-0-3),D-9	0.1
Total	10	797	2200	244	596	103	10	52	310	156	254	.271	.321	.398	719	92	-26	30	12	2	.975	-12	O-613L/D-11,1-1	-5.5
■ JERRY MAY May, Jerry Lee b: 12/14/43, Staunton, Va. d: 6/30/96, Swoope, Va. BR/TR, 6'2.5", 195 lbs. Deb: 9/19/64																								
1964	Pit-N	11	31	1	8	0	0	0	3	3	9	.258	.324	.258	582	66	-1	0	0	0	.988	4	C-11	0.3
1965	Pit-N	4	2	0	1	0	0	0	1	0	0	.500	.500	.500	1000	182	0	0	0	0	1.000	-0	/C-4	0.0

YEAR	TM/L	G	AB	R	H	2B	3B	HR	RBI	BB	SO	AVG	OBP	SLG	OPS	OPS+	BR+	SB	CS	SBR	FA	FR	G/POS	TPR
1966	Pit-N	42	52	6	13	4	0	1	2	2	15	.250	.291	.385	676	86	-1	0	1	-0	.984	8	C-41	0.7
1967	Pit-N	110	325	23	88	13	2	3	22	36	55	.271	.349	.351	700	100	1	0	0	0	.993	-0	*C-110	0.6
1968	Pit-N	137	416	26	91	15	2	1	33	41	80	.219	.293	.272	565	72	-14	0	0	0	.988	4	*C-135	-0.3
1969	Pit-N	62	190	21	44	8	0	7	23	9	53	.232	.274	.384	658	84	-5	1	1	-0	.994	-5	C-52	-0.8
1970	Pit-N	51	139	13	29	4	2	1	16	21	25	.209	.317	.288	605	65	-7	0	0	0	.994	13	C-45	0.8
1971	KC-A	71	218	16	55	13	2	1	24	27	37	.252	.335	.344	679	93	-1	0	0	0	.997	0	C-71	0.2
1972	KC-A	53	116	10	22	5	1	1	4	14	13	.190	.277	.276	553	65	-5	0	0	0	.979	-1	C-41	-0.5
1973	KC-A	11	30	4	4	1	1	0	2	3	5	.133	.235	.233	469	30	-3	0	0	0	.940	-2	C-11	-0.4
	NY-N	4	8	0	2	0	0	0	0	1	1	.250	.333	.250	583	65	-0	0	0	0	1.000	-1	/C-4	-0.1
Total	10	556	1527	120	357	63	10	15	130	157	293	.234	.310	.318	627	81	-35	1	2	-0	.990	21	C-525	0.5
■ LEE MAY	May, Lee Andrew b: 3/23/43, Birmingham, Ala. BR/TR, 6'3", 205 lbs. Deb: 9/1/65 FC Career OF: (48-LF 0-CF 40-RF)																							
1965	Cin-N	5	4	1	0	0	0	0	0	0	1	.000	.000	.000	0	-94	-1	0	0	0	.000	0	H	-0.1
1966	Cin-N	25	75	14	25	5	1	2	10	0	14	.333	.333	.507	840	119	2	0	1	-0	.972	-1	1-16	0.0
1967	Cin-N	127	438	54	116	29	2	12	57	19	80	.265	.310	.422	733	97	-2	4	8	-2	.994	2	1-81,O-48(32-0-16)	-1.0
1968	Cin-N	146	559	78	162	32	1	22	80	34	100	.290	.337	.469	806	132	20	4	7	-2	.996	0	*1-122,O-33(11-0-22)	1.2
1969	Cin-N★	158	607	85	169	32	3	38	110	45	142	.278	.334	.529	863	132	23	5	4	-0	.993	-1	*1-156/O-7(5-0-2)	1.0
1970	*Cin-N	153	605	78	153	34	2	34	94	38	125	.253	.299	.484	784	106	1	1	1	-0	.993	0	*1-153	-1.1
1971	Cin-N★	147	553	85	154	17	3	39	98	42	135	.278	.334	.532	866	145	29	3	0	1	.994	-7	*1-143	1.3
1972	Hou-N★	148	592	87	168	31	2	29	98	52	145	.284	.344	.490	834	137	27	3	1	0	.996	-3	*1-146	1.3
1973	Hou-N	148	545	65	147	24	3	28	105	34	122	.270	.315	.479	794	117	10	1	1	-0	.993	-3	*1-144	-0.5
1974	Hou-N	152	556	59	149	26	0	24	85	17	97	.268	.298	.444	743	110	3	1	0	0	.994	1	*1-145	-0.6
1975	Bal-A	146	580	67	152	28	3	20	99	36	91	.262	.311	.424	735	113	7	1	2	-0	.993	3	*1-144/D-2	-0.2
1976	Bal-A	148	530	61	137	17	4	25	**109**	41	104	.258	.315	.447	763	130	17	4	1	1	.996	0	1-94,D-52	1.0
1977	Bal-A	150	585	75	148	16	2	27	99	38	119	.253	.299	.426	724	101	-1	2	2	-0	.995	-7	*1-110,D-39	-1.6
1978	Bal-A	148	556	56	137	16	1	25	80	31	110	.246	.287	.414	701	101	-2	5	2	0	.973	-0	*D-140/1-4	-0.7
1979	*Bal-A	124	456	59	116	15	0	19	69	28	100	.254	.299	.412	711	93	-6	3	4	-1	.913	-1	*D-117/1-2	-1.1
1980	Bal-A	78	222	20	54	10	2	7	31	15	53	.243	.291	.401	692	88	-4	2	0	0	1.000	-0	D-58/1-7	-0.6
1981	*KC-A	26	55	3	16	3	0	0	8	3	14	.291	.328	.345	673	95	-0	0	1	-0	1.000	-1	/1-8,D-4	-0.2
1982	KC-A	42	91	12	28	5	2	3	12	14	18	.308	.400	.505	905	147	6	0	0	0	.989	-2	1-32/D-2	0.3
Total	18	2071	7609	959	2031	340	31	354	1244	487	1570	.267	.315	.459	774	116	129	39	35	-4	.994	-19	*1-1507,D-414/O-88L	-1.6
■ PINKY MAY	May, Merrill Glend b: 1/18/11, Laconia, Ind. d: 9/4/2000, Corydon, Ind. BR/TR, 5'11.5", 165 lbs. Deb: 4/21/39 F																							
1939	Phi-N	135	464	49	133	27	3	2	62	41	20	.287	.346	.371	717	95	-3	4			**.956**	8	*3-132	1.0
1940	Phi-N★	136	501	59	147	24	2	1	48	58	33	.293	.371	.355	727	105	6	2			.954	13	*3-135/S-1	2.3
1941	Phi-N	142	490	46	131	17	4	0	39	55	30	.267	.344	.318	662	91	-5	2			**.972**	**25**	*3-140	2.6
1942	Phi-N	115	345	25	82	15	0	0	18	51	17	.238	.338	.281	619	86	-4	3			.963	17	*3-107	1.8
1943	Phi-N	137	415	31	117	19	2	1	48	56	21	.282	.369	.345	713	111	8	2			**.963**	11	*3-132	2.2
Total	5	665	2215	210	610	102	11	4	215	261	121	.275	.354	.337	691	98	3	13			.962	74	3-646/S-1	9.9
■ MILT MAY	May, Milton Scott b: 8/1/50, Gary, Ind. BL/TR, 6', 190 lbs. Deb: 9/8/70 FC																							
1970	Pit-N	5	4	1	2	1	0	0	2	0	0	.500	.600	.750	1350	265	1	0	0	0	.000	0	H	0.1
1971	*Pit-N	49	126	15	35	1	0	6	25	9	16	.278	.326	.429	754	113	2	0	0	0	1.000	3	C-31	0.6
1972	*Pit-N	57	139	12	39	10	0	0	14	10	13	.281	.329	.353	681	96	-1	0	0	0	.985	5	C-33	0.5
1973	Pit-N	101	283	29	76	8	1	7	31	34	26	.269	.351	.378	729	105	2	0	1	-0	.973	-6	C-79	-0.1
1974	Hou-N	127	405	47	117	17	4	7	54	39	33	.289	.353	.402	755	116	8	0	1	-0	**.993**	2	*C-116	1.5
1975	Hou-N	111	386	29	93	15	1	4	52	26	41	.241	.289	.316	605	73	-15	1	2	-0	.986	1	*C-102	-1.0
1976	Det-A	6	25	2	7	1	0	0	1	0	1	.280	.280	.320	600	73	-1	0	0	0	1.000	1	/C-6	0.0
1977	Det-A	115	397	32	99	9	3	12	46	26	31	.249	.296	.378	673	78	-13	0	0	0	.986	7	*C-111	-0.1
1978	Det-A	105	352	24	88	9	0	10	37	27	26	.250	.307	.361	668	85	-7	0	0	0	.979	1	C-94	-0.2
1979	Det-A	6	11	1	3	2	0	0	3	1	1	.273	.333	.455	788	107	0	0	0	0	1.000	1	/C-5	0.1
	Chi-A	65	202	23	51	13	0	7	28	14	27	.252	.307	.421	728	94	-2	0	0	0	.981	1	C-65	0.2
	Yr	71	213	24	54	15	0	7	31	15	28	.254	.309	.423	731	95	-2	0	0	0	.982	2	C-70	0.3
1980	SF-N	111	358	27	93	16	2	6	50	25	40	.260	.310	.366	676	90	-5	0	1	-0	.986	-4	*C-103	-0.6
1981	SF-N	97	316	20	98	17	0	2	33	34	29	.310	.377	.383	760	118	8	1	4	-1	.989	-1	C-93	1.1
1982	SF-N	114	395	29	104	19	0	9	39	28	38	.263	.312	.380	692	93	-4	0	1	-0	.987	-1	*C-110	-0.1
1983	SF-N	66	186	18	46	6	0	6	20	21	23	.247	.324	.376	700	96	-1	2	2	-0	.981	-2	C-56	-0.1
	Pit-N	7	12	0	3	0	0	0	0	1	1	.250	.308	.250	558	55	-1	0	0	0	1.000	2	/C-4	0.1
	Yr	73	198	18	49	6	0	6	20	22	24	.247	.323	.369	691	94	-2	2	2	-0	.983	0	C-60	0.0
1984	Pit-N	50	96	4	17	3	0	1	8	10	15	.177	.255	.240	494	40	-8	0	1	-0	.993	5	C-26	-0.3
Total	15	1192	3693	313	971	147	11	77	443	305	361	.263	.321	.371	692	93	-36	4	13	-4	.986	14	*C-1034	1.7
■ JOHN MAYBERRY	Mayberry, John Claiborn b: 2/18/49, Detroit, Mich. BL/TL, 6'3", 220 lbs. Deb: 9/10/68 C																							
1968	Hou-N	4	9	0	0	0	0	0	0	0	2	.000	.100	.000	100	-69	-2	0	0	0	1.000	-0	/1-2	-0.3
1969	Hou-N	5	4	0	0	0	0	0	0	1	1	.000	.200	.000	200	-41	-1	0	0	0	.000	0	H	-0.1
1970	Hou-N	50	148	23	32	3	2	5	14	21	33	.216	.322	.365	687	87	-3	1	1	-0	.995	3	1-45	-0.3
1971	Hou-N	46	137	16	25	0	1	7	14	13	32	.182	.263	.350	614	74	-5	0	0	0	.997	-3	1-37	-1.1
1972	KC-A	149	503	65	150	24	3	25	100	78	74	.298	.396	.507	903	168	43	0	2	-1	**.995**	-0	*1-146	3.5
1973	KC-A★	152	510	87	142	20	2	26	100	**122**	79	.278	**.420**	.478	898	141	33	3	0	1	.994	-5	*1-149/D-1	1.7
1974	KC-A★	126	427	63	100	13	1	22	69	77	72	.234	.359	.424	783	118	11	4	2	0	.990	-2	*1-106,D-16	0.1
1975	KC-A	156	554	95	161	38	1	34	106	**119**	73	.291	.419	.547	966	**167**	**53**	5	3	0	.988	3	*1-131,D-27	4.5
1976	*KC-A	161	594	76	138	22	2	13	95	82	73	.232	.327	.342	669	95	-2	3	2	-0	.996	-3	*1-160/D-2	-1.9
1977	*KC-A	153	543	73	125	22	1	23	82	83	86	.230	.340	.401	741	100	1	1	3	-1	**.995**	-6	*1-145/D-8	-1.4
1978	Tor-A	152	515	51	129	15	2	22	70	60	57	.250	.333	.416	749	107	5	1	2	-0	.993	-14	*1-139/D-7	-1.9
1979	Tor-A	137	464	61	127	22	1	21	74	69	60	.274	.374	.461	835	122	16	1	1	-0	.995	-8	*1-135	-0.1
1980	Tor-A	149	501	62	124	19	2	30	82	77	80	.248	.351	.473	824	118	13	0	0	0	.994	-4	*1-136/D-8	0.0
1981	Tor-A	94	290	34	72	6	1	17	43	44	45	.248	.363	.452	814	125	10	1	1	-0	.993	-6	1-80,D-10	-0.1
1982	Tor-A	17	33	7	9	0	0	2	3	7	5	.273	.415	.455	869	127	2	0	0	0	1.000	-1	D-13/1-4	0.0
	NY-A	69	215	20	45	7	0	8	27	28	38	.209	.315	.353	668	84	-4	0	0	0	.996	-4	1-63/D-4	-1.1
	Yr	86	248	27	54	7	0	10	30	35	43	.218	.329	.367	696	90	-3	0	0	0	.996	-4	1-67,D-17	-1.1
Total	15	1620	5447	733	1379	211	19	255	879	881	810	.253	.363	.439	802	122	171	20	17	-2	.994	-49	*1-1478/D-96	1.5
■ LEE MAYE	Maye, Arthur Lee b: 12/11/34, Tuscaloosa, Ala. BL/TR, 6'2", 190 lbs. Deb: 7/17/59 Career OF: (554-LF 259-CF 298-RF)																							
1959	Mil-N	51	140	17	42	5	1	4	16	7	26	.300	.338	.436	774	114	2	2	2	-0	.976	1	O-44(24-0-21)	0.1
1960	Mil-N	41	83	14	25	6	0	0	2	7	21	.301	.363	.373	736	110	1	5	0	1	.968	-1	O-19(15-0-4)	0.1
1961	Mil-N	110	373	68	101	11	5	14	41	36	50	.271	.340	.440	779	112	6	10	1	2	.972	-2	O-96(26-0-72)	-0.1
1962	Mil-N	99	349	40	85	10	0	10	41	25	58	.244	.296	.358	654	77	-12	9	3	1	.977	1	O-94(38-60-2)	-1.4
1963	Mil-N	124	442	67	120	22	7	11	34	36	52	.271	.331	.428	758	118	10	14	2	2	.983	-8	*O-111(70-73-3)	-0.1
1964	Mil-N	153	588	96	179	**44**	5	10	74	34	54	.304	.347	.447	794	121	16	5	10	-2	.961	-1	*O-135(54-92-0)/3-5	0.7
1965	Mil-N	15	53	8	16	2	0	2	7	2	6	.302	.339	.453	792	120	1	0	0	0	.962	1	O-13(4-9-0)	0.2
	Hou-N	108	415	38	104	17	7	3	36	20	37	.251	.287	.347	634	83	-10	1	5	-2	.953	3	*O-103(92-11-3)	-1.6
	Yr	123	468	46	120	19	7	5	43	22	43	.256	.293	.359	652	88	-9	1	5	-2	.954	4	*O-116(96-20-3)	-1.4
1966	Hou-N	115	358	38	103	12	4	9	36	20	26	.288	.325	.419	744	113	5	4	3	-0	.949	-1	O-97(97-0-0)	-0.1
1967	Cle-A	115	297	43	77	20	4	9	27	26	47	.259	.321	.444	765	123	8	3	3	-0	.981	-10	O-77(23-10-54)/2-1	-0.7
1968	Cle-A	109	299	20	84	13	2	4	26	15	24	.281	.317	.378	695	112	3	0	0	0	.984	1	O-80(71-0-10)/1-1	0.0
1969	Cle-A	43	108	9	27	5	0	1	15	8	15	.250	.308	.324	632	74	-4	1	0	0	.982	1	O-28(26-0-2)	-0.5
	Was-A	71	238	41	69	9	3	9	26	20	25	.290	.345	.466	811	132	9	1	3	-1	.944	-6	O-65(6-4-56)	-0.1
	Yr	114	346	50	96	14	3	10	41	28	40	.277	.333	.422	755	112	5	2	3	-1	.957	-5	O-93(32-4-58)	-0.6
1970	Was-A	96	255	28	67	12	1	7	30	21	32	.263	.321	.400	721	103	0	4	2	0	1.000	-8	O-68(6-0-63)/3-1	-1.1
	Chi-A	6	6	0	1	0	0	0	1	0	1	.167	.167	.167	333	-8	-1	0	0	0	.000	0	H	-0.1

YEAR	TM/L	G	AB	R	H	2B	3B	HR	RBI	BB	SO	AVG	OBP	SLG	OPS	OPS+	BR+	SB	CS	SBR	FA	FR	G/POS	TPR
	Yr	102	261	28	68	12	1	7	31	21	33	.261	.318	.395	713	100	-1	4	2	0	1.000	-8	O-68(6-0-63)/3-1	-1.2
1971	Chi-A	32	44	6	9	2	0	1	7	5	7	.205	.286	.318	604	69	-2	0	0	0	1.000	-1	O-10(2-0-8)	-0.3
Total	13	1288	4048	533	1109	190	39	94	419	282	481	.274	.324	.410	734	108	33	59	34	1	.970	-31	*O-1040L/3-6,1-1,2	-5.0
■ **ED MAYER**	Mayer, Edward H. b: 8/16/1866, Marshall, Ill. d: 5/18/13, Chicago, Ill. 5'8.5", 155 lbs. Deb: 4/19/1890 Career OF: (4-LF 28-CF 1-RF)																							
1890	Phi-N	117	484	49	117	25	5	1	70	22	36	.242	.286	.320	606	75	-17	20			.878	-4	*3-114/O-4(0-4-0)	-1.7
1891	Phi-N	68	268	24	50	2	4	0	31	14	29	.187	.238	.224	462	34	-23	7			.895	-6	3-31,O-29C/S-7,2-1	-2.6
Total	2	185	752	73	167	27	9	1	101	36	65	.222	.269	.286	555	60	-40	27			.882	-10	3-145/O-33C,S-7,2-1	-4.3
■ **SAM MAYER**	Mayer, Samuel Frankel (b: Samuel Frankel Erskine) b: 2/28/1893, Atlanta, Ga. d: 7/1/62, Atlanta, Ga. BR/TL, 5'10", 164 lbs. Deb: 9/14/15 F																							
1915	Was-A	11	29	5	7	0	0	1	4	4	2	.241	.333	.345	678	101	0	1	2	-0	1.000	0	/O-9(1-0-8),P-1,1-1	-0.1
■ **WALLY MAYER**	Mayer, Walter A. b: 7/8/1890, Cincinnati, Ohio d: 11/18/51, Minnetonka, Minn. BR/TR, 5'11", 168 lbs. Deb: 9/28/11																							
1911	Chi-A	1	3	0	0	0	0	0	0	2		.000	.400	.000	400	16	-0	0			.900	-1	/C-1	-0.1
1912	Chi-A	9	9	1	0	0	0	0	0	1		.000	.100	.000	100	-73	-2	0			1.000	-0	/C-6	-0.2
1914	Chi-A	40	85	7	14	3	1	0	5	14	23	.165	.290	.224	514	55	-4	1	1	-0	.968	5	C-33/3-1	0.3
1915	Chi-A	22	54	3	12	3	1	0	5	5	8	.222	.288	.315	603	78	-2	0	2	-1	.990	-1	C-20	-0.2
1917	Bos-A	4	12	2	2	0	0	0	0	5	2	.167	.412	.167	578	78	0	0			.964	2	/C-4	0.2
1918	Bos-A	26	49	7	11	4	0	0	5	7	7	.224	.321	.306	628	91	-0	0			.964	-1	C-23	0.0
1919	StL-A	30	62	2	14	4	1	0	5	8	11	.226	.314	.323	637	77	-2	0			.959	6	C-25	0.5
Total	7	132	274	22	53	14	3	0	20	42	51	.193	.303	.266	569	68	-10	1	3		.969	10	C-112/3-1	0.5
■ **PADDY MAYES**	Mayes, Adair Bushyhead b: 3/17/1885, Locust Grove, Okla. d: 5/28/62, Fayetteville, Ark. BL/TR, 5'11", 160 lbs. Deb: 6/11/11																							
1911	Phi-N	5	5	1	0	0	0	0	0	1	2	.000	.286	.000	286	-17	-1	0			1.000	-0	/O-2	-0.1
■ **BUSTER MAYNARD**	Maynard, James Walter b: 3/25/13, Henderson, N.C. d: 9/7/77, Durham, N.C. BR/TR, 5'11", 170 lbs. Deb: 9/17/40 Career OF: (32-LF 91-CF 23-RF)																							
1940	NY-N	7	29	6	8	2	2	1	2	2	6	.276	.323	.586	909	145	2	0			.929	-1	/O-7(0-3-4)	0.0
1942	NY-N	89	190	17	47	4	1	4	32	19	19	.247	.319	.342	661	93	-2	3			.982	-0	O-58(7-48-4),3-10/2-1	-0.3
1943	NY-N	121	393	43	81	8	2	9	32	24	27	.206	.252	.305	557	60	-21	3			.965	-6	O-74(25-39-13),3-22	-3.3
1946	NY-N	7	4	2	0	0	0	0	0	1	1	.000	.200	.000	200	-41	-1	0			.750	-1	/O-3(0-1-2)	-0.2
Total	4	224	616	68	136	14	5	14	66	46	53	.221	.276	.328	604	74	-22	6			.967	-8	O-142C/3-32,2-1	-3.8
■ **CHICK MAYNARD**	Maynard, Le Roy Evans b: 11/2/1896, Turners Falls, Mass. d: 1/31/57, Bangor, Maine BL/TR, 5'9", 150 lbs. Deb: 6/27/22																							
1922	Bos-A	12	24	1	3	0	0	0	0	3	2	.125	.222	.125	347	-8	-4	0	1	-0	.872	-2	S-12	-0.6
■ **BRENT MAYNE**	Mayne, Brent Danem b: 4/19/68, Loma Linda, Cal. BL/TR, 6'1", 190 lbs. Deb: 9/18/90																							
1990	KC-A	5	13	2	3	0	0	0	1	3	3	.231	.375	.231	606	74	-0	0	1	-0	.970	1	/C-5	0.0
1991	KC-A	85	231	22	58	8	0	3	31	23	42	.251	.319	.325	644	78	-7	2	4	-1	.987	4	C-80/D-1	0.1
1992	KC-A	82	213	16	48	10	0	0	18	11	26	.225	.263	.272	536	49	-14	0	4	-1	.990	2	C-62/3-8,D-1	-1.1
1993	KC-A	71	205	22	52	9	1	2	22	18	31	.254	.317	.337	654	72	-8	3	2	-0	.995	6	C-68/D-1	0.2
1994	KC-A	46	144	19	37	5	1	2	20	14	27	.257	.323	.347	670	70	-6	1	0	0	.996	6	C-42/D-3	0.2
1995	KC-A	110	307	23	77	18	1	1	27	25	41	.251	.313	.326	639	66	-15	0	1	-0	.995	11	*C-103	0.1
1996	NY-N	70	99	9	26	6	0	1	6	12	22	.263	.342	.354	696	88	-1	0	1	-0	1.000	-4	C-21	-0.5
1997	Oak-A	85	256	29	74	12	0	6	22	18	33	.289	.345	.406	752	97	-1	1	0	0	.996	-11	C-83	-0.7
1998	SF-N	94	275	26	75	15	0	3	32	37	47	.273	.361	.360	721	96	-0	2	1	0	.991	-7	C-88	-0.3
1999	SF-N	117	322	39	97	32	0	2	39	43	65	.301	.392	.419	811	114	8	2	2	-0	.995	-4	*C-105	0.9
2000	Col-N	117	335	36	101	21	0	6	64	47	48	.301	.389	.418	807	81	-8	1	3	-1	.990	-2	*C-105/P-1	-0.5
Total	11	882	2400	243	648	136	3	26	282	251	385	.270	.343	.362	705	82	-54	12	19	-4	.993	3	C-762/3-8,D-6,P-1	-1.6
■ **EDDIE MAYO**	Mayo, Edward Joseph "Hotshot" (b: Edward Joseph Mayoski) b: 4/15/10, Holyoke, Mass. BL/TR, 5'11", 178 lbs. Deb: 5/22/36 C																							
1936	*NY-N	46	141	11	28	4	1	1	8	11	12	.199	.257	.262	519	40	-12	0			.981	5	3-40	-0.6
1937	Bos-N	65	172	19	39	6	1	1	18	15	20	.227	.293	.291	583	65	-8	1			.956	-4	3-50	-1.1
1938	Bos-N	8	14	2	3	0	0	1	4	1	0	.214	.267	.429	695	98	-0	0			.923	2	/3-6,S-2	0.2
1943	Phi-A	128	471	49	103	10	1	0	28	34	32	.219	.278	.244	523	54	-27	2	0	0	**.976**	-3	*3-123	-3.1
1944	Det-A	154	607	76	151	18	3	5	63	57	23	.249	.317	.313	630	76	-18	9	13	-3	.978	**29**	*2-143,S-11	1.8
1945	*Det-A†	134	501	71	143	24	3	10	54	47	29	.285	.347	.405	752	111	6	7	7	-1	**.980**	18	*2-124	3.1
1946	Det-A	51	202	21	51	9	2	0	22	14	12	.252	.301	.317	618	68	-8	6	2	1	.965	-11	2-49	-1.7
1947	Det-A	142	535	66	149	28	4	6	48	48	28	.279	.338	.379	717	96	-3	3	7	-2	.983	-23	*2-142	-2.1
1948	Det-A	106	370	35	92	20	1	2	42	30	19	.249	.310	.324	634	67	-18	1	9	-3	.975	-10	2-86,3-10	-2.5
Total	9	834	3013	350	759	119	16	26	287	257	175	.252	.313	.328	641	78	-88	29	38		.978	3	2-544,3-229/S-13	-6.0
■ **JACKIE MAYO**	Mayo, John Lewis b: 7/26/25, Litchfield, Ill. BL/TR, 6'1", 190 lbs. Deb: 9/19/48																							
1948	Phi-N	12	35	7	8	2	1	0	3	7	7	.229	.386	.343	729	101	0	1			1.000	1	O-11(11-0-0)	0.1
1949	Phi-N	45	39	3	5	0	0	0	2	4	5	.128	.209	.128	338	-8	-6	0			.889	-7	O-25(0-1-24)	-1.3
1950	*Phi-N	18	36	1	8	3	0	0	3	2	5	.222	.263	.306	569	50	-3	0			.958	-3	O-15(15-0-0)	-0.6
1951	Phi-N	9	7	1	1	0	0	0	0	0	0	.143	.143	.143	286	-23	-1	0	0	0	1.000	-2	/O-5(5-0-0)	-0.3
1952	Phi-N	50	119	13	29	5	0	1	4	12	17	.244	.313	.311	624	74	-4	1	3	-1	1.000	4	O-27(24-1-2)/1-6	-0.3
1953	Phi-N	5	4	0	0	0	0	0	0	0	1	.000	.000	.000	0	-99	-1	0	0	0	.000	-0	/O-1(0-0-1)	-0.2
Total	6	139	240	25	51	10	1	1	12	25	35	.213	.292	.275	567	56	-14	2	3		.972	-7	/O-84(55-2-27),1-6	-2.6
■ **WILLIE MAYS**	Mays, Willie Howard "Say Hey" b: 5/6/31, Westfield, Ala. BR/TR, 5'11", 180 lbs. Deb: 5/25/51 CH Career OF: (10-LF 2827-CF 21-RF)																							
1951	*NY-N	121	464	59	127	22	5	20	68	57	60	.274	.356	.472	828	120	12	7	4	0	.976	11	*O-121(0-121-0)	2.0
1952	NY-N	34	127	17	30	2	4	4	23	16	17	.236	.326	.409	736	102	0	4	1	1	.991	8	O-34(0-34-0)	0.8
1954	*NY-N★	151	565	119	195	33	**13**	41	110	66	57	**.345**	.415	**.667**	**1083**	176	**61**	8	5	0	.985	16	*O-151(0-151-0)	**6.7**
1955	NY-N★	152	580	123	185	18	**13**	**51**	127	79	60	.319	.404	**.659**	**1063**	**176**	**62**	24	4	**4**	.982	**20**	*O-152(0-152-0)	**7.6**
1956	NY-N★	152	578	101	171	27	8	36	84	68	65	.296	.371	.557	928	146	37	**40**	10	**5**	.979	12	*O-152(0-152-0)	4.7
1957	NY-N★	152	585	112	195	26	**20**	35	97	76	62	.333	.411	**.626**	1037	**174**	**61**	**38**	19	2	.980	11	*O-150(0-150-0)	**6.6**
1958	SF-N★	152	600	**121**	208	33	11	29	96	78	56	.347	.423	.583	**1006**	**167**	**58**	**31**	6	**5**	.980	17	*O-151(0-151-0)	**7.2**
1959	SF-N★	151	575	125	180	43	5	34	104	65	58	.313	.385	.583	967	157	45	**27**	4	**5**	.984	7	*O-147(2-146-0)	4.9
1960	SF-N★	153	595	107	**190**	29	12	29	103	61	70	.319	.386	.555	941	164	51	25	10	2	.981	14	*O-152(0-152-0)	**6.0**
1961	SF-N★	154	572	**129**	176	32	3	40	123	81	77	.308	.395	.584	979	162	51	18	9	1	.980	10	*O-153(0-153-0)	5.5
1962	*SF-N★	162	621	130	189	36	5	**49**	141	78	85	.304	.385	.615	1001	167	56	18	2	3	.991	14	*O-161(0-161-0)	**6.7**
1963	SF-N★	157	596	115	187	32	7	38	103	66	83	.314	.384	.582	966	176	57	8	3	1	.981	13	*O-157(0-157-0)/S-1	**7.0**
1964	SF-N★	157	578	121	171	21	9	**47**	111	82	72	.296	.384	**.607**	**992**	**171**	**54**	19	5	2	.984	14	*O-155C/1-1,S-1,3-1	**6.7**
1965	SF-N★	157	558	118	177	21	3	**52**	112	76	71	.317	**.399**	**.645**	**1044**	**184**	**61**	9	4	1	.983	16	*O-151(1-147-5)	**7.5**
1966	SF-N★	152	552	99	159	29	4	37	103	70	81	.288	.370	.556	926	149	36	5	1	1	.982	12	*O-150(1-145-5)	4.5
1967	SF-N★	141	486	83	128	22	2	22	70	51	92	.263	.336	.453	788	125	15	6	0	1	.976	-2	*O-134(0-134-0)	1.2
1968	SF-N★	148	498	84	144	20	5	23	79	67	81	.289	.376	.488	864	158	36	12	6	1	.978	0	*O-142(0-142-0)/1-1	3.7
1969	SF-N★	117	403	64	114	17	3	13	58	49	71	.283	.365	.437	802	126	14	6	2	1	.976	-7	*O-108(0-106-2)/1-1	0.5
1970	SF-N★	139	478	94	139	15	2	28	83	79	90	.291	.395	.506	901	141	29	5	0	1	.975	2	*O-129(0-129-0)/1-5	2.8
1971	*SF-N★	136	417	82	113	24	5	18	61	**112**	123	.271	**.429**	.482	911	160	39	23	3	4	.970	-2	O-84(0-84-0),1-48	3.7
1972	SF-N	19	49	8	9	2	0	0	3	17	5	.184	.394	.224	618	79	-0	3	0	1	1.000	-1	O-14(0-14-0)	-0.1
	NY-N★	69	195	27	52	9	1	8	19	43	43	.267	.402	.446	848	144	13	1	5	-2	.974	0	O-49(1-48-0),1-11	1.1
	Yr	88	244	35	61	11	1	8	22	60	48	.250	.400	.402	802	131	13	4	5	-1	.979	-1	O-63(1-62-0),1-11	1.0
1973	*NY-N★	66	209	24	44	10	0	6	25	27	47	.211	.304	.344	648	81	-6	1	0	0	.991	-5	O-45(5-43-9),1-17	-1.4
Total	22	2992	10881	2062	3283	523	140	660	1903	1464	1526	.302	.387	.557	944	157	845	338	103	38	.981	180	*O-2842C/1-84,S-2,3	95.9
■ **BILL MAZEROSKI**	Mazeroski, William Stanley "Maz" b: 9/5/36, Wheeling, W.Va. BR/TR, 5'11.5", 183 lbs. Deb: 7/7/56 C																							
1956	Pit-N	81	255	30	62	8	1	3	14	18	24	.243	.293	.318	611	66	-12	0	0	0	.981	11	2-81	0.5
1957	Pit-N	148	526	59	149	27	7	8	54	27	49	.283	.319	.407	726	96	-4	3	3	-0	.978	4	*2-144	1.1
1958	Pit-N★	152	567	69	156	24	6	19	68	25	71	.275	.309	.439	748	98	-4	1	1	-0	.980	19	*2-152	2.6
1959	Pit-N★	135	493	50	119	15	6	7	59	29	54	.241	.285	.339	624	66	-24	1	3	-1	.981	-9	*2-133	-2.4

YEAR	TM/L	G	AB	R	H	2B	3B	HR	RBI	BB	SO	AVG	OBP	SLG	OPS	OPS+	BR+	SB	CS	SBR	FA	FR	G/POS	TPR
1960	*Pit-N★	151	538	58	147	21	5	11	64	40	50	.273	.325	.392	717	95	-4	4	0	1	**.989**	**25**	*2-151	3.4
1961	Pit-N	152	558	71	148	21	2	13	59	26	55	.265	.302	.380	681	79	-17	2	1	0	.975	**31**	*2-152	2.6
1962	Pit-N★	159	572	55	155	24	9	14	81	37	47	.271	.318	.418	735	95	-5	0	3	-1	.985	**41**	*2-159	4.8
1963	Pit-N†	142	534	43	131	22	3	8	52	32	46	.245	.288	.343	631	80	-14	2	0	0	.984	**57**	*2-138	5.9
1964	Pit-N☆	162	601	66	161	22	8	10	64	29	52	.268	.302	.381	683	91	-8	1	1	-0	.975	**34**	*2-162	4.1
1965	Pit-N	130	494	52	134	17	1	6	54	18	34	.271	.300	.346	646	81	-13	2	1	0	**.988**	26	*2-127	2.5
1966	Pit-N	162	621	56	163	22	7	16	82	31	62	.262	.299	.398	696	91	-8	4	3	-0	**.992**	**41**	*2-162	4.8
1967	Pit-N★	163	639	62	167	25	3	9	77	30	55	.261	.294	.352	647	84	-14	1	2	-0	.981	17	*2-163	1.7
1968	Pit-N	143	506	36	127	18	2	3	42	38	38	.251	.306	.312	618	87	-8	3	4	-1	.981	**26**	*2-142	3.3
1969	Pit-N	67	227	13	52	7	1	3	25	22	16	.229	.303	.308	611	73	-8	1	1	-0	.988	14	2-65	1.0
1970	*Pit-N	112	367	29	84	14	0	7	39	27	40	.229	.285	.324	610	64	-19	2	0	0	.987	24	*2-102	1.2
1971	*Pit-N	70	193	17	49	3	1	1	16	15	8	.254	.308	.295	603	72	-7	0	0	0	.986	-1	2-46/3-7	-0.6
1972	*Pit-N	34	64	3	12	4	0	0	3	3	5	.188	.224	.250	474	35	-6	0	0	0	.986	3	2-15/3-3	-0.2
Total	17	2163	7755	769	2016	294	62	138	853	447	706	.260	.302	.367	669	84	-175	27	23	-2	.983	362	*2-2094/3-10	36.3

■ MEL MAZZERA

Mazzera, Melvin Leonard "Mike" b: 1/31/14, Stockton, Cal. d: 12/19/97, Stockton, Cal. BL/TL, 5'11", 180 lbs. Deb: 9/9/35

YEAR	TM/L	G	AB	R	H	2B	3B	HR	RBI	BB	SO	AVG	OBP	SLG	OPS	OPS+	BR+	SB	CS	SBR	FA	FR	G/POS	TPR
1935	StL-A	12	30	4	7	2	0	1	2	4	9	.233	.324	.400	724	82	-1	0	0	0	.950	-1	O-10(4-3-3)	-0.2
1937	StL-A	7	7	1	2	2	0	0	0	0	2	.286	.286	.571	857	110	0	0	0	0	.000	0	H	0.0
1938	StL-A	86	204	33	57	8	2	6	29	12	25	.279	.329	.426	755	88	-5	1	1	-0	.976	-1	O-47(25-8-14)	-0.7
1939	StL-A	33	110	21	33	5	2	3	22	10	20	.300	.364	.464	827	108	1	0	0	0	.983	0	O-25(18-0-7)	0.0
1940	Phi-N	69	156	16	37	5	4	0	13	19	15	.237	.320	.321	641	80	-4	1			.985	-4	O-42(26-2-16),1-11	-1.0
Total	5	207	507	75	136	22	8	10	66	45	71	.268	.333	.402	735	90	-8	2	1		.978	-6	O-124(73-13-40)/1-11	-1.9

■ LEE MAZZILLI

Mazzilli, Lee Louis b: 3/25/55, New York, N.Y. BB/TR, 6'1", 185 lbs. Deb: 9/7/76 C Career OF: (201-LF 647-CF 30-RF)

YEAR	TM/L	G	AB	R	H	2B	3B	HR	RBI	BB	SO	AVG	OBP	SLG	OPS	OPS+	BR+	SB	CS	SBR	FA	FR	G/POS	TPR
1976	NY-N	24	77	9	15	2	0	2	7	14	10	.195	.326	.299	625	83	-1	5	4	-0	.983	2	O-23(2-21-0)	0.0
1977	NY-N	159	537	66	134	24	3	6	46	72	72	.250	.342	.339	680	87	-8	22	15	-0	.992	11	*O-156(0-156-0)	0.2
1978	NY-N	148	542	78	148	28	5	16	61	69	82	.273	.356	.432	788	124	17	20	13	-0	.987	14	*O-144(0-144-0)	3.1
1979	NY-N★	158	597	78	181	34	4	15	79	93	74	.303	.397	.449	846	135	32	34	12	3	.989	8	*O-143(0-143-0),1-15	4.2
1980	NY-N	152	578	82	162	31	4	16	76	82	92	.280	.373	.431	803	127	23	41	15	4	.983	1	1-92,O-66(0-66-0)	2.3
1981	NY-N	95	324	36	74	14	5	6	34	46	53	.228	.328	.358	686	96	-1	17	7	1	.970	-0	O-89(51-40-0)	-0.3
1982	Tex-A	58	195	23	47	8	0	4	17	28	26	.241	.339	.344	683	93	-1	11	6	0	.945	-3	O-26(11-15-2),D-24	-0.5
	NY-A	37	128	20	34	2	0	6	17	15	15	.266	.347	.422	769	112	2	2	3	-1	.995	-3	1-23/O-2(2-0-0),D-9	-0.3
	Yr	95	323	43	81	10	0	10	34	43	41	.251	.342	.375	717	100	1	13	9	-0	.949	-6	D-33,O-28C,1-23	-0.8
1983	Pit-N	109	246	37	59	9	0	5	24	49	43	.240	.370	.337	708	95	0	15	5	2	.985	0	O-57(5-53-0)/1-7	0.1
1984	Pit-N	111	266	37	63	11	1	4	21	40	42	.237	.339	.331	670	89	-3	8	1	1	.989	-7	O-74(74-0-0)/1-5	-1.2
1985	Pit-N	92	117	20	33	8	0	1	9	29	17	.282	.425	.376	801	127	6	4	1	1	.986	-1	1-19/O-5(3-3-0)	0.4
1986	Pit-N	61	93	18	21	2	1	1	8	26	25	.226	.395	.301	696	93	1	3	3	-0	1.000	-3	O-18(16-3-0)/1-7	-0.4
	*NY-N	39	58	10	16	3	0	2	7	12	11	.276	.417	.431	848	138	4	1	1	-0	1.000	-1	O-10(8-0-2)/1-8	0.2
	Yr	100	151	28	37	5	1	3	15	38	36	.245	.403	.351	754	109	4	4	4	-1	1.000	-4	O-28(24-3-2),1-15	-0.2
1987	NY-N	88	124	26	38	8	1	3	24	21	14	.306	.407	.460	867	136	7	5	3	0	1.000	-6	O-25(12-2-13),1-13	0.0
1988	*NY-N	68	116	9	17	2	0	0	12	12	16	.147	.233	.164	396	16	-12	4	1	1	1.000	-4	O-18(13-0-6),1-16	-1.9
1989	NY-N	48	60	10	11	2	0	2	7	17	19	.183	.364	.317	680	101	1	3	0	1	.889	-4	O-10(4-1-5)/1-8	-0.3
	*Tor-A	28	66	12	15	3	0	4	11	17	16	.227	.400	.455	855	143	5	2	0	0	.944	-1	D-19/1-2,O-2(0-0-2)	0.4
Total	14	1475	4124	571	1068	191	24	93	460	642	627	.259	.361	.385	746	109	71	197	90	12	.986	4	O-868C,1-215/D-52	6.0

■ JIMMY McALEER

McAleer, James Robert "Loafer" b: 7/10/1864, Youngstown, Ohio d: 4/29/31, Youngstown, Ohio BR/TR, 6', 175 lbs. Deb: 4/24/1889 M Career OF: (128-LF 887-CF 2-RF)

YEAR	TM/L	G	AB	R	H	2B	3B	HR	RBI	BB	SO	AVG	OBP	SLG	OPS	OPS+	BR+	SB	CS	SBR	FA	FR	G/POS	TPR
1889	Cle-N	110	447	66	105	6	6	0	35	30	49	.235	.289	.275	564	59	-24	37			.955	9	*O-110(0-110-0)	-1.6
1890	Cle-P	86	341	58	91	8	7	1	42	37	33	.267	.340	.340	681	89	-4	21			.940	11	O-86(0-86-0)	0.3
1891	Cle-N	136	565	97	135	16	11	1	61	49	47	.239	.305	.312	617	77	-18	51			.924	5	*O-136(124-13-0)	-1.4
1892	*Cle-N	149	571	92	136	26	7	4	70	63	54	.238	.318	.329	647	92	-6	40			.948	12	*O-149(0-149-0)	-0.4
1893	Cle-N	91	350	63	83	5	1	2	41	35	21	.237	.314	.274	588	54	-24	32			.928	4	*O-91(2-89-0)	-2.1
1894	Cle-N	64	253	36	73	15	1	2	40	13	17	.289	.331	.379	710	68	-14	14			.953	3	O-64(0-64-0)	-1.1
1895	*Cle-N	132	532	85	144	17	3	0	68	38	37	.271	.326	.314	640	62	-31	32			.934	2	*O-132(0-132-0)	-3.0
1896	*Cle-N	116	455	70	131	16	4	1	54	47	32	.288	.361	.347	708	82	-11	24			.958	7	*O-116(0-116-0)	-1.0
1897	Cle-N	24	91	6	20	2	0	0	10	7		.220	.283	.242	525	37	-8	4			.947	-1	O-24(1-23-0)	-0.9
1898	Cle-N	106	366	47	87	3	0	0	48	46		.238	.331	.246	577	67	-13	7			.965	3	*O-104(1-102-1)/2-2	-1.6
1901	Cle-A	3	7	0	1	0	0	0	0	0		.143	.143	.143	286	-22	-1	0			1.000	-1	/O-2(0-2-0),P-1,3-1,M	-0.2
1902	StL-A	2	3	0	2	0	0	0	0	0		.667	.667	.667	1333	274	1	0			.000	-1	/O-2(0-1-1),M	0.0
1907	StL-A	2	0	0	0	0	0	0	0	0		—	—	—			0	0			.000	0	RM	0.0
Total	13	1021	3981	620	1008	114	40	11	469	365	290	.253	.322	.310	632	72	-153	262			.944	53	*O-1016C/2-2,3-1,P	-13.0

■ JACK McALEESE

McAleese, John James b: 1877, Sharon, Pa. d: 11/15/50, New York, N.Y. BR/TR, 5'8", Deb: 8/10/01 Career OF: (27-LF 32-CF 20-RF)

YEAR	TM/L	G	AB	R	H	2B	3B	HR	RBI	BB	SO	AVG	OBP	SLG	OPS	OPS+	BR+	SB	CS	SBR	FA	FR	G/POS	TPR
1901	Chi-A	1	1	0	0	0	0	0	0	0		.000	.000	.000	0	-99	-0	0			1.000	0	/P-1	0.0
1909	StL-A	85	267	33	57	7	0	0	12	32		.213	.318	.240	558	82	-3	18			.910	-3	O-79(27-32-20)/3-2	-1.2
Total	2	86	268	33	57	7	0	0	12	32		.213	.317	.239	556	82	-4	18			.910	-3	/O-79C,3-2,P-1	-1.2

■ BILL McALLESTER

McAllester, William Lusk b: 12/29/1889, Chattanooga, Tenn. d: 3/3/70, Chattanooga, Tenn. BR/TR, 6', 175 lbs. Deb: 5/2/13

YEAR	TM/L	G	AB	R	H	2B	3B	HR	RBI	BB	SO	AVG	OBP	SLG	OPS	OPS+	BR+	SB	CS	SBR	FA	FR	G/POS	TPR
1913	StL-A	49	85	3	13	4	0	0	6	11	12	.153	.250	.200	450	33	-7	2			.908	-4	C-39	-0.9

■ SPORT McALLISTER

McAllister, Lewis William b: 7/23/1874, Austin, Miss. d: 7/17/62, Wyandotte, Mich. BB/TR, 5'11", 180 lbs. Deb: 8/7/1896 Career OF: (17-LF 13-CF 128-RF)

YEAR	TM/L	G	AB	R	H	2B	3B	HR	RBI	BB	SO	AVG	OBP	SLG	OPS	OPS+	BR+	SB	CS	SBR	FA	FR	G/POS	TPR
1896	Cle-N	8	27	2	6	2	0	0	1	0	2	.222	.250	.296	546	41	-2	1			.500	-6	/O-4(0-3-9),C-2,P-1	-0.8
1897	Cle-N	43	137	23	30	5	1	0	11	12		.219	.287	.270	557	45	-11	3			.894	-6	O-28R/S-4,P-4,1C2	-1.6
1898	Cle-N	17	57	8	13	3	1	0	9	5		.228	.290	.316	606	75	-2	0			.941	1	/P-9,O-8(0-4-4)	0.0
1899	Cle-N	113	418	29	99	6	8	1	31	19		.237	.273	.297	570	61	-23	5			.943	-15	O-79R,C-17/3-7,1SP2	-3.6
1901	Det-A	90	306	45	92	9	4	3	57	15		.301	.344	.386	729	97	-1	17			.898	-19	C-35,1-28,O-11R,3/S	-1.6
1902	Det-A	21	67	8	14	1	0	1	8	2		.209	.243	.269	512	41	-5	0			1.000	-0	/1-5,S-5,2-3,C3O	-0.5
	Bal-A	3	11	0	1	0	0	0	1	1		.091	.167	.091	258	-26	-2	0			.923	-0	/2-2,1-1	-0.2
	Det-A	45	162	11	34	4	2	0	24	3		.210	.229	.259	488	34	-14	1			.991	-1	1-21,O-11R/C-7,3S	-1.5
	Yr	69	240	19	49	5	2	1	33	6		.204	.230	.254	484	33	-22	1			.992	-1	1-27,O-12R/C-9,S32D	-2.2
1903	Det-A	78	265	31	69	8	2	0	22	10		.260	.297	.306	603	84	-5	5			.888	-7	S-46,C-18/O-5R,31	-1.0
Total	7	418	1450	157	358	38	18	5	164	67	2	.247	.287	.308	595	67	-67	32			.914	-55	O-147R/C-83,1S3P2	-10.8

■ JIM McANANY

McAnany, James b: 9/4/36, Los Angeles, Cal. BR/TR, 5'10", 196 lbs. Deb: 9/19/58

YEAR	TM/L	G	AB	R	H	2B	3B	HR	RBI	BB	SO	AVG	OBP	SLG	OPS	OPS+	BR+	SB	CS	SBR	FA	FR	G/POS	TPR
1958	Chi-A	5	13	0	0	0	0	0	0	0	5	.000	.000	.000	0	-99	-4	0	0	0	1.000	1	/O-3(0-0-3)	-0.3
1959	*Chi-A	67	210	22	58	9	3	0	27	19	26	.276	.339	.348	687	90	-3	2	1	0	.966	-1	O-67(4-2-63)	-0.5
1960	Chi-A	3	2	0	0	0	0	0	0	0	2	.000	.000	.000	0	-99	-1	0	0	0	.000	0	H	-0.1
1961	Chi-N	11	10	1	3	1	0	0	0	1	3	.300	.364	.400	764	101	0	0	0	0	.000	-0	/O-1(0-0-1)	0.0
1962	Chi-N	7	6	0	0	0	0	0	0	1	2	.000	.143	.000	143	-56	-1	0	0	0	.000	0	H	-0.1
Total	5	93	241	23	61	10	3	0	27	21	38	.253	.316	.320	635	75	-8	2	1	0	.968	-1	/O-71(4-2-67)	-1.0

■ BUB McATEE

McAtee, Michael James "Butch" b: 3/1845, Troy, N.Y. d: 10/18/1876, Troy, N.Y. TR, 5'9", 160 lbs. Deb: 5/8/1871

YEAR	TM/L	G	AB	R	H	2B	3B	HR	RBI	BB	SO	AVG	OBP	SLG	OPS	OPS+	BR+	SB	CS	SBR	FA	FR	G/POS	TPR
1871	Chi-n	26	135	34	37	8	2	0	10	5	2	.274	.300	.363	663	81	-5	5	3	0	.943	1	*1-26	-0.2
1872	Tro-n	25	129	30	28	3	1	0	15	1	2	.217	.223	.256	479	46	-8	0	2	-1	.948	1	1-25	-0.5
Total	2 n	51	264	64	65	11	3	0	25	6	4	.246	.263	.311	574	65	-13	5	5	-1	.945	2	/1-51	-0.7

■ IKE McAULEY

McAuley, James Earl b: 8/19/1891, Wichita, Kan. d: 4/6/28, Des Moines, Iowa BR/TR, 5'9.5", 150 lbs. Deb: 9/10/14

YEAR	TM/L	G	AB	R	H	2B	3B	HR	RBI	BB	SO	AVG	OBP	SLG	OPS	OPS+	BR+	SB	CS	SBR	FA	FR	G/POS	TPR
1914	Pit-N	15	24	3	3	0	0	0	0	0	8	.125	.125	.125	250	-27	-4	0			.900	1	/S-5,3-3,2-2	-0.3
1915	Pit-N	5	15	0	2	1	0	0	0	0	6	.133	.133	.200	333	0	-2	0			.917	-3	/S-5	-0.5
1916	Pit-N	4	8	1	2	0	0	0	1	0	1	.250	.250	.250	500	53	-0	0			.938	1	/S-4	0.0
1917	StL-N	3	7	0	2	0	0	0	1	0	1	.286	.286	.286	571	78	-0	0			.833	-2	/S-3	-0.3

YEAR	TM/L	G	AB	R	H	2B	3B	HR	RBI	BB	SO	AVG	OBP	SLG	OPS	OPS+	BR+	SB	CS	SBR	FA	FR	G/POS	TPR
1925	Chi-N	37	125	10	35	7	2	0	11	11	12	.280	.343	.368	711	80	-4	1	0	0	.949	-8	S-37	-0.7
Total	5	64	179	14	44	8	2	0	13	11	28	.246	.293	.313	606	62	-10	1	0		.940	-12	/S-54,3-3,2-2	-1.8
■ GENE McAULIFFE	McAuliffe, Eugene Leo b: 2/28/1872, Randolph, Mass. d: 4/29/53, Randolph, Mass. BR/TR, 6'1", 180 lbs. Deb: 8/17/04																							
1904	Bos-N	1	2	0	1	0	0	0	0	0		.500	.500	.500	1000	217	0	0			.667	-1	/C-1	0.0
■ DICK McAULIFFE	McAuliffe, Richard John b: 11/29/39, Hartford, Conn. BL/TR, 5'11", 176 lbs. Deb: 9/17/60																							
1960	Det-A	8	27	2	7	0	1	0	1	2	6	.259	.310	.333	644	72	-1	0	0	0	.884	1	/S-7	0.1
1961	Det-A	80	285	36	73	12	4	6	33	24	39	.256	.323	.389	712	87	-5	2	3	-1	.933	-29	S-55,3-22	-3.0
1962	Det-A	139	471	50	124	20	5	12	63	64	76	.263	.351	.403	755	99	0	4	2	0	.965	-21	2-70,3-49,S-16	-1.4
1963	Det-A	150	568	77	149	18	6	13	61	64	75	.262	.337	.384	721	98	-0	11	5	1	.963	-24	*S-133,2-15	-1.2
1964	Det-A	162	557	85	134	18	7	24	66	77	96	.241	.336	.427	763	109	7	8	5	0	.958	-8	*S-160	1.4
1965	Det-A★	113	404	61	105	13	6	15	54	49	62	.260	.343	.433	776	118	10	6	9	-2	.956	-15	*S-112	0.2
1966	Det-A★	124	430	83	118	16	8	23	56	66	80	.274	.375	.509	884	148	28	5	7	-1	.964	-11	*S-105,3-15	2.6
1967	Det-A★	153	557	92	133	16	7	22	65	105	118	.239	.366	.411	777	126	21	6	5	-0	.965	-14	*2-145,S-43	2.2
1968	*Det-A	151	570	**95**	142	24	10	16	56	82	99	.249	.346	.411	756	125	18	8	7	-1	.986	-20	*2-148/S-5	1.2
1969	Det-A	74	271	49	71	10	5	11	33	47	41	.262	.371	.458	829	125	10	2	5	-1	.976	-0	2-72	1.4
1970	Det-A	146	530	73	124	21	1	12	50	101	62	.234	.360	.345	705	95	-0	5	6	-1	.975	-6	*2-127,S-15,3-12	0.3
1971	Det-A	128	477	67	99	16	6	18	57	53	67	.208	.293	.379	673	86	-10	4	1	1	.987	7	*2-123/S-7	0.7
1972	*Det-A	122	408	47	98	16	3	8	30	59	59	.240	.339	.353	692	103	3	0	0	0	.975	-7	*2-116/S-3,3-1	0.3
1973	Det-A	106	343	39	94	18	1	12	47	49	52	.274	.366	.437	804	118	9	0	4	-1	.986	5	*2-102/S-2,D-1	1.9
1974	Bos-A	100	272	32	57	13	1	5	24	39	40	.210	.311	.320	631	76	-8	2	0	0	.971	-8	2-53,3-40/S-3,D-3	-1.3
1975	Bos-A	7	15	0	2	0	0	0	1	1	2	.133	.188	.133	321	-7	-2	0	0	0	.769	-2	/3-7	-0.4
Total	16	1763	6185	888	1530	231	71	197	697	882	974	.247	.344	.403	748	108	79	63	59	-7	.977	-150	2-971,S-666,3-146,/D	5.0
■ GEORGE McAVOY	McAvoy, George Robert b: 3/12/1884, E.Liverpool, Ohio Deb: 7/17/14																							
1914	Phi-N	1	1	0	0	0	0	0	0	0	0	.000	.000	.000	0	-94	-0	0			.000	0	H	0.0
■ WICKEY McAVOY	McAvoy, James Eugene b: 10/22/1894, Rochester, N.Y. d: 7/6/73, Rochester, N.Y. BR/TR, 5'11", 172 lbs. Deb: 9/29/13 Career OF: (0-LF 0-CF 1-RF)																							
1913	Phi-A	4	9	0	1	0	0	0	0	0	4	.111	.200	.111	311	-9	-1	0			1.000	1	/C-4	0.0
1914	Phi-A	8	16	1	2	0	1	0	0	0	4	.125	.125	.250	375	13	-2	0			.971	1	/C-8	-0.1
1915	Phi-A	68	184	12	35	7	2	0	6	11	32	.190	.236	.250	486	47	-13	0	2	-1	.931	5	C-64	-0.5
1917	Phi-A	10	24	1	6	1	0	1	4	0	3	.250	.250	.417	667	105	-0	0			.955	3	/C-8	0.4
1918	Phi-A	83	271	14	66	5	3	0	32	13	23	.244	.283	.284	567	70	-10	5			.960	5	C-74/P-1,1-1,O-1R	0.2
1919	Phi-A	62	170	10	24	5	2	0	11	14	21	.141	.207	.194	401	13	-20	1			.973	-3	C-57	-1.9
Total	6	235	674	38	134	18	8	1	53	38	87	.199	.245	.254	498	47	-46	6	2		.954	13	C-215/O-1R,1-1,P-1	-1.9
■ ALGIE McBRIDE	McBride, Algernon Griggs b: 5/23/1869, Washington, D.C. d: 1/10/56, Georgetown, Ohio BL/TL, 5'9", 152 lbs. Deb: 5/12/1896																							
1896	Chi-N	9	29	2	7	1	1	1	7	7	3	.241	.389	.448	837	116	1	0			.917	0	/O-9(9-0-0)	0.0
1898	Cin-N	120	486	94	147	14	12	2	43	51		.302	.383	.393	776	114	10	16			.959	7	*O-120(4-115-1)	0.8
1899	Cin-N	64	251	57	87	12	5	1	23	30		.347	.431	.446	877	138	15	5			.950	-2	O-64(5-45-14)	0.7
1900	Cin-N	112	436	59	120	15	8	4	59	25		.275	.320	.374	694	94	-5	12			.915	-9	*O-110(14-10-86)	-1.9
1901	Cin-N	30	123	19	29	7	0	2	18	7		.236	.282	.341	624	86	-2	0			.968	-2	O-28(11-19-0)	-0.6
	NY-N	68	264	27	74	11	0	2	29	12		.280	.317	.345	661	95	-2	3			.948	-4	O-65(0-0-65)	-0.8
	Yr	98	387	46	103	18	0	4	47	19		.266	.306	.344	649	92	-4	3			.956	-6	O-93(11-19-65)	-1.4
Total	5	403	1589	258	464	60	26	12	179	132	3	.292	.356	.385	741	108	16	36			.946	-10	O-396(43-189-166)	-1.8
■ BAKE McBRIDE	McBride, Arnold Ray b: 2/3/49, Fulton, Mo. BL/TR, 6'2", 190 lbs. Deb: 7/26/73																							
1973	StL-N	40	63	8	19	3	0	0	5	4	10	.302	.362	.349	712	98	0	0	1	-0	.976	1	O-17(1-16-0)	0.0
1974	StL-N	150	559	81	173	19	5	6	56	43	57	.309	.372	.394	766	115	12	30	11	3	.990	14	*O-144(0-144-0)	2.6
1975	StL-N	116	413	70	124	10	9	5	36	34	52	.300	.355	.404	759	107	4	26	8	3	.990	7	*O-107(0-107-0)	1.1
1976	StL-N☆	72	272	40	91	13	4	3	24	18	28	.335	.389	.445	833	135	12	10	5	0	.981	9	O-66(0-66-0)	2.1
1977	StL-N	43	122	21	32	5	1	4	20	7	19	.262	.302	.418	720	93	-2	9	3	1	1.000	-5	O-33(0-33-0)	-0.6
	*Phi-N	85	280	55	95	20	5	11	41	25	25	.339	.399	.564	964	149	19	27	4	5	.986	1	O-73(0-21-54)	2.1
	Yr	128	402	76	127	25	6	15	61	32	44	.316	.371	.520	891	133	18	36	7	5	.990	-4	*O-106(0-54-54)	1.5
1978	*Phi-N	122	472	68	127	20	4	10	49	28	68	.269	.317	.392	709	96	-3	28	3	5	**.996**	5	*O-119(0-1-118)	0.0
1979	Phi-N	151	582	82	163	16	12	12	60	41	77	.280	.332	.411	742	98	-2	25	14	1	.989	15	*O-147(0-0-147)	0.6
1980	*Phi-N	137	554	68	171	33	10	9	87	26	58	.309	.345	.453	798	115	10	13	10	-1	.990	6	*O-133(0-1-133)	0.9
1981	*Phi-N	58	221	26	60	17	1	2	21	11	25	.271	.306	.385	691	91	-3	5	0	1	.987	-4	O-56(0-0-56)	-1.0
1982	Cle-A	27	85	8	31	3	3	0	13	2	12	.365	.379	.471	850	132	4	2	2	-0	1.000	-2	O-22(0-0-22)	0.0
1983	Cle-A	70	230	21	67	8	1	1	18	9	26	.291	.321	.348	669	81	-6	8	2	1	.977	0	O-46(0-0-46),D-15	-0.8
Total	11	1071	3853	548	1153	167	55	63	430	248	457	.299	.348	.420	768	109	45	183	63	18	.989	46	O-963(1-389-576)/D-15	7.0
■ GEORGE McBRIDE	McBride, George Florian b: 11/20/1880, Milwaukee, Wis. d: 7/2/73, Milwaukee, Wis. BR/TR, 5'11", 170 lbs. Deb: 9/12/01 MC																							
1901	Mil-A	3	12	0	2	0	0	0	0	1		.167	.231	.167	397	12	-1	0			1.000	-1	/S-3	-0.2
1905	Pit-N	27	87	9	19	4	0	0	7	6		.218	.277	.264	541	60	-4	2			.902	-4	3-17/S-8	-0.8
	StL-N	81	281	22	61	1	2	2	34	14		.217	.264	.256	520	57	-15	10			.938	-2	S-80/1-1	-1.5
	Yr	108	368	31	80	5	2	2	41	20		.217	.267	.258	525	58	-19	12			.935	-6	S-88,3-17/1-1	-2.3
1906	StL-N	90	313	24	53	8	2	0	13	17		.169	.215	.208	422	33	-25	5			.944	9	S-90	-1.4
1908	Was-A	155	518	47	120	10	6	0	34	41		.232	.292	.274	566	92	-4	12			.948	32	*S-155	3.7
1909	Was-A	156	504	38	118	16	0	0	34	36		.234	.294	.266	560	81	-10	17			**.935**	11	*S-156	0.6
1910	Was-A	154	514	54	118	19	4	1	55	61		.230	.321	.288	609	95	-1	11			.939	27	*S-154	3.4
1911	Was-A	154	557	58	131	11	4	0	59	52		.235	.312	.269	581	64	-26	15			.941	24	*S-154	0.9
1912	Was-A	152	521	56	118	13	7	1	52	38		.226	.288	.284	572	63	-25	17			**.941**	**31**	*S-152	1.6
1913	Was-A	150	499	52	107	18	7	1	52	43	46	.214	.286	.285	571	66	-22	12			**.960**	12	*S-150	0.0
1914	Was-A	156	503	49	102	12	4	0	24	43	70	.203	.274	.243	516	53	-28	12	14	-2	**.958**	12	*S-156	-0.9
1915	Was-A	146	476	54	97	8	6	1	30	29	60	.204	.251	.252	503	50	-31	10	5	0	**.968**	9	*S-146	-1.2
1916	Was-A	139	466	36	106	15	4	1	36	23	58	.227	.271	.283	555	67	-20	8			.957	13	*S-139	0.3
1917	Was-A	50	141	6	27	3	0	0	9	10	17	.191	.265	.213	477	46	-9	1			.943	-1	S-41/3-6,2-2	-0.8
1918	Was-A	18	53	2	7	0	0	0	1	0	11	.132	.132	.132	264	-21	-8	1			.986	2	S-14/2-2	-0.6
1919	Was-A	15	40	3	8	1	1	0	4	3	6	.200	.256	.275	531	49	-3	0			.932	1	S-15	-0.1
1920	Was-A	13	41	6	9	1	0	0	3	2	3	.220	.256	.244	500	34	-4	0	0	0	.966	-3	S-13	-0.6
Total	16	1659	5526	516	1203	140	47	7	447	419	271	.218	.281	.264	544	65	-235	133	19		.948	170	*S-1626/3-23,2-4,1	2.4
■ JOHN McBRIDE	McBride, John F. Deb: 10/12/1890																							
1890	Phi-a	1	2	0	0	0	0	0	0	0		.000	.000	.000	0	-99	-0	0			1.000	1	/O-1(0-1-0)	0.0
■ TOM McBRIDE	McBride, Thomas Raymond b: 11/2/14, Bonham, Tex. BR/TR, 6', 190 lbs. Deb: 4/23/43 Career OF: (116-LF 91-CF 115-RF)																							
1943	Bos-A	26	96	11	23	3	1	0	7	7	3	.240	.291	.292	583	70	-4	2	0	0	.984	0	O-24(0-21-3)	-0.4
1944	Bos-A	71	216	29	53	7	3	0	24	8	13	.245	.276	.306	581	67	-10	4	0	1	.992	-1	O-57(23-14-22)/1-5	-1.3
1945	Bos-A	100	344	38	105	11	7	1	47	26	17	.305	.354	.387	741	112	5	2	2	-0	.984	-0	O-81(15-50-22),1-11	0.1
1946	*Bos-A	61	153	21	46	5	2	0	19	9	6	.301	.340	.359	699	90	-2	0	1	-0	1.000	-7	O-43(10-2-32)	-1.1
1947	Bos-A	2	5	0	1	0	0	0	0	0	0	.200	.200	.200	400	11	-1	0	0	0	1.000	1	/O-1(0-0-1)	0.0
	Was-A	56	166	19	45	4	2	0	15	15	9	.271	.331	.319	651	84	-4	3	1	0	.972	-4	O-51(43-4-5)/3-1	-1.1
	Yr	58	171	19	46	4	2	0	15	15	9	.269	.328	.316	644	81	-4	3	1	0	.973	-3	O-52(43-4-6)/3-1	-1.1
1948	Was-A	92	206	22	53	9	1	1	29	28	15	.257	.346	.325	671	81	-5	2	2	-0	.983	2	O-55(25-0-30)	-0.6
Total	6	408	1186	140	326	39	16	2	141	93	63	.275	.328	.340	668	88	-20	13	6	1	.985	-9	O-312L/1-16,3-1	-4.4
■ SWAT McCABE	McCabe, James Arthur b: 11/20/1881, Towanda, Pa. d: 12/9/44, Bristol, Conn. BL/TR, 5'10", Deb: 9/23/09																							
1909	Cin-N	3	11	2	6	1	0	0	0	0		.545	.545	.636	1182	269	2	1			.625	-1	/O-3(0-3-0)	0.1
1910	Cin-N	13	35	3	9	1	0	0	5	1	2	.257	.297	.286	583	73	-1	0			1.000	1	/O-9(0-0-9)	-0.1
Total	2	16	46	5	15	2	0	0	5	1	2	.326	.354	.370	724	118	1	1			.875	-1	/O-12(0-3-9)	0.0

YEAR	TM/L	G	AB	R	H	2B	3B	HR	RBI	BB	SO	AVG	OBP	SLG	OPS	OPS+	BR+	SB	CS	SBR	FA	FR	G/POS	TPR
■ JOE McCABE	McCabe, Joseph Robert b: 8/27/38, Indianapolis, Ind. BR/TR, 6', 190 lbs. Deb: 4/18/64																							
1964	Min-A	14	19	1	3	0	0	0	2	0	8	.158	.158	.158	316	-12	-3	0	0	0	1.000	0	C-12	-0.2
1965	Was-A	14	27	1	5	0	0	1	5	4	13	.185	.290	.296	587	68	-1	1	0	0	.972	-3	C-11	-0.3
Total	2	28	46	2	8	0	0	1	7	4	21	.174	.240	.239	479	36	-4	1	0	0	.986	-2	/C-23	-0.5
■ BILL McCABE	McCabe, William Francis b: 10/28/1892, Chicago, Ill. d: 9/2/66, Chicago, Ill. BB/TR (BL 1918), 5'9.5", 180 lbs. Deb: 4/16/18 Career OF: (7-LF 1-CF 21-RF)																							
1918	*Chi-N	29	45	9	8	0	1	0	5	4	7	.178	.245	.222	467	42	-3	2			.939	5	2-13/O-4(1-0-2)	0.2
1919	Chi-N	33	84	8	13	3	1	0	5	9	15	.155	.253	.214	467	41	-6	3			.950	-1	O-20(0-1-19)/S-4,3-1	-0.9
1920	Chi-N	3	2	1	1	0	0	0	0	0	0	.500	.500	.500	1000	184	0	0	0	0	.000	0	H	0.0
	*Bro-N	41	68	10	10	0	0	0	3	2	6	.147	.171	.147	318	-8	-9	1	2	-0	.882	4	S-13/O-6L,2-4,3-3	-0.6
	Yr	44	70	11	11	0	0	0	3	2	6	.157	.181	.157	338	-2	-9	1	2	-0	.882	4	S-13/O-6L,2-4,3-3	-0.6
Total	3	106	199	28	32	3	2	0	13	15	28	.161	.227	.196	423	26	-18	6	2		.943	8	/O-30R,S-17,2-17,3	-1.3
■ HARRY McCAFFERY	McCaffery, Harry Charles b: 11/25/1858, St.Louis, Mo. d: 4/19/28, St.Louis, Mo. BR/TR, 5'10.5", 185 lbs. Deb: 6/15/1882 U Career OF: (5-LF 5-CF 18-RF)																							
1882	Lou-a	1	4	1	1	0	0	0		0		.250	.250	.250	500	73	-0				1.000	-1	/2-1	-0.1
	StL-a	38	153	23	42	8	6	0		3		.275	.288	.405	694	127	4				.891	4	O-23R/2-8,3-7,1-1	0.7
	Yr	39	157	24	43	8	6	0		3		.274	.287	.401	689	125	4				.891	3	O-23R/2-9,3-7,1-1	0.6
1883	StL-a	5	18	0	1	0	0	0	1	1		.056	.105	.056	161	-44	-3				.889	1	/O-5(0-5-0)	-0.2
1885	Cin-a	1	5	0	0	0	0	0	0	0		.000	.000	.000	0	-98	-1				.000	-0	/P-1	0.0
Total	3	45	180	24	44	8	6	0	1	4		.244	.261	.356	616	101	-0				.891	4	/O-28R,2-9,3-7,P1	0.4
■ SPARROW McCAFFREY	McCaffrey, Charles P. b: 1868, Philadelphia, Pa. d: 4/29/1894, Philadelphia, Pa. 120 lbs. Deb: 8/13/1889																							
1889	Col-a	2	1	1	1	0	0	0	0	1	0	1.000	1.000	1.000	2000	495	1	0			.000	0	/C-2	0.1
■ BRIAN McCALL	McCall, Brian Allen "Bam" b: 1/25/43, Kentfield, Cal. BL/TL, 5'10", 170 lbs. Deb: 9/18/62																							
1962	Chi-A	4	8	2	3	0	0	2	3	0	2	.375	.375	1.125	1500	287	2	0	0	0	1.000	0	/O-1(0-1-0)	0.2
1963	Chi-A	3	7	1	0	0	0	0	0	1	2	.000	.125	.000	125	-62	-2	0	0	0	1.000	-0	/O-2(0-0-2)	-0.2
Total	2	7	15	3	3	0	0	2	3	1	4	.200	.250	.600	850	126	0	0	0	0	1.000	0	/O-3(0-1-2)	0.0
■ JACK McCANDLESS	McCandless, Scott Cook b: 5/5/1891, Pittsburgh, Pa. d: 8/17/61, Pittsburgh, Pa. BL/TR, 6', 170 lbs. Deb: 9/10/14																							
1914	Bal-F	11	31	5	8	0	1	0	1	3	0	.258	.343	.323	665	79	-1	0			1.000	-0	/O-8(0-1-7)	-0.2
1915	Bal-F	117	406	47	87	6	7	5	34	41	99	.214	.296	.300	596	66	-24	9			.945	3	*O-105(23-58-25)	-3.0
Total	2	128	437	52	95	6	8	5	35	44	99	.217	.299	.302	601	67	-26	9			.948	3	O-113(23-59-32)	-3.2
■ EMMETT McCANN	McCann, Robert Emmett b: 3/4/02, Philadelphia, Pa. d: 4/15/37, Philadelphia, Pa. BR/TR, 5'11", 150 lbs. Deb: 4/19/20																							
1920	Phi-A	13	34	4	9	1	1	0	3	3	1	.265	.342	.353	695	84	-1	0	1	-0	.907	-0	S-11	-0.1
1921	Phi-A	52	157	15	35	5	0	0	15	4	6	.223	.242	.255	497	27	-17	2	1	0	.949	-0	S-32/3-9,2-2,1-1	-1.3
1926	Bos-A	6	3	0	0	0	0	0	0	1	1	.000	.250	.000	250	-32	-1	0	0	0	1.000	-0	/S-1,3-1	-0.1
Total	3	71	194	19	44	6	1	0	18	8	8	.227	.261	.268	529	36	-19	2	2	-0	.939	-1	/S-44,3-10,2-2,1-1	-1.5
■ ROGER McCARDELL	McCardell, Roger Morton b: 8/29/32, Gorsuch Mills, Md. d: 11/13/96, Perry Point, Md. BR/TR, 6', 200 lbs. Deb: 5/8/59																							
1959	SF-N	4	4	0	0	0	0	0	0	0	0	.000	.000	.000	0	-99	-1	0	0	0	1.000	0	/C-3	-0.1
■ BILL McCARREN	McCarren, William Joseph b: 11/4/1895, Fortenia, Pa. d: 9/11/83, Denver, Colo. BR/TR, 5'11.5", 170 lbs. Deb: 5/4/23																							
1923	Bro-N	69	216	28	53	10	1	3	27	22	39	.245	.326	.343	669	79	-6	0	1	-0	.927	-2	3-66/O-1(0-0-1)	-0.5
■ ALEX McCARTHY	McCarthy, Alexander George b: 5/12/1888, Chicago, Ill. d: 3/12/78, Salisbury, Md. BR/TR, 5'9", 150 lbs. Deb: 10/7/10 Career OF: (1-LF 0-CF 0-RF)																							
1910	Pit-N	3	12	1	1	0	1	0	0	0	2	.083	.083	.250	333	-3	-2	0			.875	0	/S-3	-0.2
1911	Pit-N	50	150	18	36	5	1	2	31	14	24	.240	.305	.327	632	74	-6	4			.981	-1	S-33,2-11/3-1,O-1L	-0.4
1912	Pit-N	111	401	53	111	12	4	1	41	30	26	.277	.332	.334	666	84	-9	8			.962	3	*2-105/3-4	-0.4
1913	Pit-N	31	74	7	15	5	0	0	10	7	7	.203	.298	.270	568	66	-3	1			.902	-2	S-12,3-12/2-6	-0.5
1914	Pit-N	57	173	14	26	0	1	1	14	6	17	.150	.192	.179	371	11	-19	2			.975	11	3-36,2-10/S-6	-0.7
1915	Pit-N	21	49	3	10	0	1	0	3	5	10	.204	.291	.245	536	64	-2	1	2	-0	.950	1	/2-9,S-5,3-4,1-1	-0.2
	Chi-N	23	72	4	19	3	0	1	6	5	7	.264	.329	.347	676	105	0	2	3	-1	.972	11	2-12,3-12/S-1	1.2
	Yr	44	121	7	29	3	1	1	9	10	17	.240	.313	.306	619	88	-1	3	5	-1	.964	12	2-21,3-16/S-6,1-1	1.0
1916	Chi-N	37	107	10	26	2	3	0	6	11	7	.243	.341	.318	659	93	-0	1			.931	-2	2-34/S-3	-0.2
	Pit-N	50	146	11	29	3	0	0	3	15	10	.199	.282	.219	501	54	-7	3			.955	-5	S-39/2-7,3-5	-1.1
	Yr	87	253	21	55	5	3	0	9	26	17	.217	.308	.261	569	72	-7	4			.951	-7	S-42,2-41/3-5	-1.3
1917	Pit-N	49	151	15	33	4	0	0	8	11	13	.219	.276	.245	521	58	-7	1			.964	7	3-26,2-13/S-9	0.1
Total	8	432	1335	136	306	34	11	5	122	104	123	.229	.295	.282	577	67	-54	23	5		.957	22	2-207,S-111,3/1O	-2.4
■ JERRY McCARTHY	McCarthy, Jerome Francis b: 5/23/23, Brooklyn, N.Y. d: 10/3/65, Oceanside, N.Y. BL/TL, 6'1", 205 lbs. Deb: 6/19/48																							
1948	StL-A	2	3	0	1	0	0	0	0	0	0	.333	.333	.333	667	76	-0	0	0	0	.600	-1	/1-2	-0.1
■ JACK McCARTHY	McCarthy, John Arthur b: 3/26/1869, Gilbertville, Mass d: 9/11/31, Chicago, Ill. BL/TL, 5'9", 155 lbs. Deb: 8/3/1893 Career OF: (844-LF 121-CF 83-RF)																							
1893	Cin-N	49	195	28	55	8	3	0	22	22	7	.282	.355	.354	709	86	-4	6			.887	-1	O-47(10-1-37)/1-2	-0.6
1894	Cin-N	40	167	29	45	9	1	0	21	17	6	.269	.348	.335	683	63	-10	3			.895	2	O-25(5-0-20),1-15	-0.7
1898	Pit-N	137	537	75	155	13	12	4	78	34		.289	.336	.380	716	107	4	7			.935	4	*O-137(137-0-0)	-0.5
1899	Pit-N	139	565	109	173	22	17	4	69	39		.306	.355	.427	782	114	9	28			.962	-5	*O-139(133-6-0)	-0.7
1900	Chi-N	124	503	68	148	16	7	0	48	24		.294	.329	.354	683	92	-6	22			.944	-1	*O-123(96-1-26)	-1.5
1901	Cle-A	86	343	60	110	14	7	0	32	30		.321	.382	.402	784	123	12	9			.949	-1	O-86(85-1-0)	0.5
1902	Cle-A	95	359	45	102	31	5	0	41	24		.284	.329	.398	727	105	2	12			.944	-5	O-95(95-0-0)	-0.8
1903	Cle-A	108	415	47	110	20	8	0	43	19		.265	.299	.352	651	96	-2	15			.964	-3	*O-108(108-0-0)	-1.2
	Chi-N	24	101	11	28	5	0	0	14	4		.277	.305	.327	631	82	-3	8			.947	-3	O-24(24-0-0)	-0.7
1904	Chi-N	115	432	36	114	14	2	0	51	23		.264	.307	.306	613	89	-6	14			.961	-5	*O-115(25-90-0)	-1.7
1905	Chi-N	59	170	16	47	4	3	0	14	10		.276	.320	.335	656	92	-2	8			.986	2	O-37(18-19-0)/1-6	-0.2
1906	Bro-N	91	322	23	98	13	1	0	35	20		.304	.347	.351	698	128	10	9			.924	2	O-86(83-3-0)	0.7
1907	Bro-N	25	91	4	20	2	0	0	8	2		.220	.237	.242	478	54	-5	4			1.000	-4	O-25(25-0-0)	-1.2
Total	12	1092	4200	551	1205	171	66	8	476	268	13	.287	.333	.365	698	101	-1	145			.946	-16	*O-1047L/1-23	-8.6
■ JOHNNY McCARTHY	McCarthy, John Joseph b: 1/7/10, Chicago, Ill. d: 9/13/73, Mundelein, Ill. BL/TL, 6'1.5", 185 lbs. Deb: 9/2/34																							
1934	Bro-N	17	39	7	7	2	0	1	5	2	2	.179	.220	.308	527	42	-3	0			.961	1	1-13	-0.3
1935	Bro-N	22	48	9	12	1	1	0	4	2	9	.250	.280	.313	593	60	-3	1			.982	-3	1-19	-0.6
1936	NY-N	4	16	1	7	0	0	1	2	0	1	.438	.438	.625	1063	185	2	1			.981	1	/1-4	0.3
1937	*NY-N	114	420	53	117	19	3	10	65	24	37	.279	.322	.410	732	96	-3	2			.987	2	*1-110	-1.1
1938	NY-N	134	470	55	128	13	4	8	59	39	28	.272	.329	.368	697	91	-6	3			.993	-3	*1-125	-2.1
1939	NY-N	50	80	12	21	6	1	1	11	3	8	.262	.298	.400	698	85	-2	0			1.000	-4	1-12/O-4(0-1-3),P-1	-0.7
1940	NY-N	51	67	6	16	4	0	0	5	2	8	.239	.261	.299	559	53	-4	0			1.000	1	/1-6	-0.4
1941	NY-N	14	40	1	13	3	0	0	12	3	0	.325	.372	.400	772	115	1	0			.987	0	/1-8,O-1(1-0-0)	0.0
1943	Bos-N	78	313	32	95	24	6	2	33	10	19	.304	.327	.438	765	122	7	1			.996	1	1-78	0.3
1946	Bos-N	2	7	0	1	0	0	0	1	2	0	.143	.333	.143	476	37	-0	0			1.000	-1	/1-2	-0.1
1948	NY-N	56	57	6	15	0	1	2	12	3	2	.263	.300	.404	704	88	-1	0			.966	-0	/1-6	-0.2
Total	11	542	1557	182	432	72	16	25	209	90	114	.277	.319	.392	712	95	-14	8			.990	-5	1-383/O-5(1-1-3),P-1	-4.9
■ JOE McCARTHY	McCarthy, Joseph N. b: 12/25/1881, Syracuse, N.Y. d: 1/12/37, Syracuse, N.Y. BR/TR, Deb: 9/27/05																							
1905	NY-A	1	2	0	0	0	0	0	0	0		.000	.000	.000	0	-90	-0	0			1.000	0	/C-1	0.0
1906	StL-N	15	37	3	9	2	0	0	2	2		.243	.282	.297	579	84	-1	0			.984	-0	C-15	0.0
Total	2	16	39	3	9	2	0	0	2	2		.231	.268	.282	550	74	-1	0			.985	-0	/C-16	0.0

YEAR	TM/L	G	AB	R	H	2B	3B	HR	RBI	BB	SO	AVG	OBP	SLG	OPS	OPS+	BR+	SB	CS	SBR	FA	FR	G/POS	TPR
■ TOMMY McCARTHY	McCarthy, Thomas Francis Michael b: 7/24/1863, Boston, Mass. d: 8/5/22, Boston, Mass. BR/TR, 5'7", 170 lbs. Deb: 7/10/1884 MH Career OF: (515-LF 31-CF 647-RF)																							
1884	Bos-U	53	209	37	45	2	2	0		6		.215	.237	.244	481	47	-19				.794	-2	O-48(41-2-7)/P-7	-1.9
1885	Bos-N	40	148	16	27	2	0	0	11	5	25	.182	.209	.196	405	33	-11				.865	3	O-40(39-0-1)	-0.8
1886	Phi-N	8	27	6	5	2	1	0	3	2	3	.185	.241	.333	575	73	-1	1			.818	-1	/O-8(0-0-8),P-1	-0.2
1887	Phi-N	18	72	7	15	4	0	0	6	2	5	.208	.219	.243	462	27	-7	15			.818	-9	/O-8L,2-5,S-3,3-2	-1.4
1888	*StL-a	131	511	107	140	20	3	1	68	38		.274	.328	.331	659	100	-1	93			.932	30	*O-131(0-12-119)/P-2	2.5
1889	StL-a	140	604	136	176	24	7	2	63	46	26	.291	.348	.364	712	91	-10	57			.893	14	*O-140R/2-2,P-1	0.2
1890	StL-a	133	548	137	192	28	9	6	69	66		.350	.430	.467	898	144	29	**83**			.893	7	*O-102R,3-32/2-1,M	3.1
1891	StL-a	134	570	124	176	20	6	8	92	49	19	.309	.374	.407	781	107	2	37			.898	2	*O-112R,2-14,S/3P	0.3
1892	*Bos-N	152	603	119	146	19	5	4	63	93	29	.242	.347	.310	657	91	-5	53			.883	2	*O-152(0-1-151)	-1.0
1893	Bos-N	116	462	107	160	28	6	5	111	64	10	.346	.429	.465	894	128	18	46			.902	3	*O-108L/2-7,S-3	1.0
1894	Bos-N	127	539	118	188	21	8	13	126	59	17	.349	.419	.490	909	110	8	43			.904	11	*O-127L/S-2,2-1,P-1	0.6
1895	Bos-N	117	452	90	131	13	2	2	73	72	12	.290	.391	.341	732	83	-10	18			.885	-10	*O-109(109-0-0)/2-9	-2.4
1896	Bro-N	104	377	62	94	8	4	3	47	34	17	.249	.316	.316	632	71	-15	22			.920	-2	*O-103(102-0-1)	-2.3
Total	13	1273	5122	1066	1495	191	53	44	732	536	163	.292	.364	.375	740	99	-23	468			.897	49	*O-1188R/2-39,3SP	-2.3
■ BILL McCARTHY	McCarthy, William John b: 2/14/1886, Boston, Mass. d: 2/4/28, Washington, D.C. TR, Deb: 6/5/05																							
1905	Bos-N	1	3	0	0	0	0	0	0	0		.000	.000	.000	0	-99	-1	0			.667	-0	/C-1	-0.1
1907	Cin-N	3	8	1	1	0	0	0	0	0		.125	.125	.125	250	-21	-1	0			1.000	-1	/C-3	-0.2
Total	2	4	11	1	1	0	0	0	0	0		.091	.091	.091	182	-43	-2	0			.842	-1	/C-4	-0.3
■ FRANK McCARTON	McCarton, Francis b: 10/6/1854, Middletown, Conn. d: 6/17/07, New York, N.Y. Deb: 4/26/1872																							
1872	Man-n	19	85	17	28	4	1	0	10	1	3	.329	.337	.400	737	133	4	0	0	0	.791	-2	O-19(0-18-1)	0.1
■ DAVID McCARTY	McCarty, David Andrew b: 11/23/69, Houston, Tex. BR/TL, 6'5", 215 lbs. Deb: 5/17/93 Career OF: (61-LF 2-CF 71-RF)																							
1993	Min-A	98	350	36	75	15	2	2	21	19	80	.214	.257	.286	542	45	-27	2	6	-2	.959	5	O-67L,1-36/D-2	-2.9
1994	Min-A	44	131	21	34	8	2	1	12	7	32	.260	.322	.374	696	79	-4	2	1	0	.981	1	1-32,O-14(9-0-5)	-0.6
1995	Min-A	25	55	10	12	3	1	0	4	4	18	.218	.283	.309	592	54	-4	0	1	-0	.993	-2	1-18/O-5(2-0-4)	-0.7
	SF-N	12	20	1	5	1	0	0	2	2	4	.250	.318	.300	618	66	-1	1	0	0	.833	-1	/O-4(0-0-4),1-2	-0.2
1996	SF-N	91	175	16	38	3	0	6	24	18	43	.217	.297	.337	635	70	-8	2	1	0	.990	-4	1-51,O-20(5-0-15)	-1.5
1998	Sea-A	8	18	1	5	0	0	1	2	5	4	.278	.435	.444	879	130	1	1	0	0	1.000	-1	/O-5(0-0-5),1-2	0.0
2000	KC-A	103	270	34	75	14	2	12	53	22	68	.278	.332	.478	810	101	-0	0	0	0	.992	11	1-63,O-11L/S-1,D-7	0.5
Total	6	381	1019	119	244	44	7	22	118	77	249	.239	.299	.361	660	72	-43	8	9	-1	.990	8	1-204,O-126R/D-9,S	-5.4
■ LEW McCARTY	McCarty, George Lewis b: 11/17/1888, Milton, Pa. d: 6/9/30, Reading, Pa. BR/TR, 5'11.5", 192 lbs. Deb: 8/30/13																							
1913	Bro-N	9	26	1	6	0	0	0	2	2	2	.231	.286	.231	516	47	-2	0			1.000	0	/C-9	-0.1
1914	Bro-N	90	284	20	72	14	2	1	30	14	22	.254	.293	.327	621	83	-7	1			.970	1	C-84	0.1
1915	Bro-N	84	276	19	66	9	4	0	19	7	23	.239	.261	.301	561	68	-11	7	4	0	.969	-8	C-81	-1.4
1916	Bro-N	55	150	17	47	6	1	0	13	14	16	.313	.383	.367	750	127	5	4			.985	-4	C-27,1-17	0.4
	NY-N	25	68	6	27	3	4	0	9	7	9	.397	.453	.559	1012	222	10	0			.993	0	C-24	1.3
	Yr	80	218	23	74	9	5	0	22	21	25	.339	.405	.427	832	155	15	4			.989	-3	C-51,1-17	1.7
1917	*NY-N	56	162	15	40	3	2	2	19	14	6	.247	.311	.327	638	99	-0	1			.979	-3	C-54	0.1
1918	NY-N	86	257	16	69	7	3	0	24	17	13	.268	.321	.319	640	97	-1	3			.975	-7	C-75	-0.1
1919	NY-N	85	210	17	59	5	4	2	21	18	15	.281	.341	.371	712	115	4	2			.970	-8	C-59	0.1
1920	NY-N	36	38	2	5	0	0	0	0	4	2	.132	.214	.132	346	1	-5	2	0	0	1.000	2	/C-5	-0.2
	StL-N	5	7	0	2	0	0	0	0	5	0	.286	.583	.286	869	160	1	0	0	0	1.000	-1	/C-3	0.1
	Yr	41	45	2	7	0	0	0	0	9	2	.156	.296	.156	452	33	-3	2	0	0	1.000	1	/C-8	-0.1
1921	StL-N	1	1	0	0	0	0	0	0	0	1	.000	.000	.000	0	-99	-0	0	0	0	.000	0	H	0.0
Total	9	532	1479	113	393	47	20	5	137	102	109	.266	.318	.335	653	97	-5	20	4		.975	-28	C-421/1-17	0.3
■ TIM McCARVER	McCarver, James Timothy b: 10/16/41, Memphis, Tenn. BL/TR, 6'1", 195 lbs. Deb: 9/10/59 Career OF: (15-LF 0-CF 1-RF)																							
1959	StL-N	8	24	3	4	1	0	0	0	2	1	.167	.231	.208	439	17	-3	0	0	0	.971	-2	/C-6	-0.5
1960	StL-N	10	10	3	2	0	0	0	0	0	2	.200	.200	.200	400	9	-1	0	0	0	1.000	-0	/C-5	-0.1
1961	StL-N	22	67	5	16	2	1	1	6	0	5	.239	.239	.343	582	47	-5	0	0	0	.969	-2	C-20	-0.6
1963	StL-N	127	405	39	117	12	7	4	51	27	43	.289	.336	.383	719	97	-1	5	2	0	.994	-0	*C-126	0.5
1964	*StL-N	143	465	53	134	19	3	9	52	40	44	.288	.346	.400	746	101	1	2	0	0	.987	-9	*C-137	-0.1
1965	StL-N	113	409	48	113	17	2	11	48	31	26	.276	.329	.408	737	97	-1	5	1	1	**.995**	-4	*C-111	0.1
1966	StL-N★	150	543	50	149	19	**13**	12	68	36	38	.274	.322	.424	745	105	3	9	6	-0	.992	-4	*C-148	0.7
1967	*StL-N★	138	471	68	139	26	3	14	69	54	32	.295	.374	.452	826	137	23	8	8	-1	**.997**	4	*C-130	3.5
1968	*StL-N	128	434	35	110	15	6	5	48	26	31	.253	.297	.350	647	95	-3	4	3	-0	.986	3	*C-109	0.6
1969	StL-N	138	515	46	134	27	3	7	51	49	26	.260	.327	.365	692	93	-5	4	9	-2	.986	9	*C-136	0.9
1970	Phi-N	44	164	16	47	11	1	4	14	14	10	.287	.346	.439	785	112	2	2	2	-0	.991	0	C-44	0.5
1971	Phi-N	134	474	51	132	20	5	8	46	43	26	.278	.340	.392	732	107	4	5	3	0	.985	-8	*C-125	0.3
1972	Phi-N	45	152	14	36	8	0	2	14	17	15	.237	.322	.329	651	83	-3	1	2	-0	.989	-3	C-40	-0.5
	Mon-N	77	239	19	60	5	1	5	20	19	14	.251	.309	.343	652	84	-5	4	4	-1	.990	1	C-45,O-14(14-0-1)/3-6	-0.4
	Yr	122	391	33	96	13	1	7	34	36	29	.246	.314	.338	652	83	-8	5	6	-1	.990	-3	C-85,O-14(14-0-1)/3-6	-0.9
1973	StL-N	130	331	30	88	16	4	3	49	38	31	.266	.345	.366	711	97	-1	2	0	0	.986	-6	1-77,C-11	-1.2
1974	StL-N	74	106	13	23	0	1	0	11	22	6	.217	.366	.236	602	72	-3	0	1	-0	.969	-1	C-21/1-6	-0.3
	Bos-A	11	28	3	7	1	0	0	1	4	1	.250	.344	.286	629	77	-1	1	0	0	1.000	1	/C-8,D-2	0.1
1975	Bos-A	12	21	1	8	2	1	0	3	1	3	.381	.409	.571	981	161	2	0	0	0	.957	-0	/C-7,1-1	0.2
	Phi-N	47	59	6	15	2	0	1	7	14	7	.254	.397	.339	736	102	1	0	0	0	.984	1	C-10/1-1	0.3
1976	*Phi-N	90	155	26	43	11	2	3	29	35	14	.277	.414	.432	846	136	9	2	1	0	1.000	5	C-41/1-2	1.7
1977	*Phi-N	93	169	28	54	13	2	6	30	28	11	.320	.422	.527	949	146	12	3	5	-1	.988	2	C-42/1-3	1.4
1978	*Phi-N	90	146	18	36	9	1	1	14	28	24	.247	.375	.342	717	101	1	2	2	-0	.995	2	C-34,1-11	0.4
1979	Phi-N	79	137	13	33	5	1	1	12	19	12	.241	.338	.314	651	76	-4	2	0	0	.989	3	C-31/O-1(1-0-0)	0.0
1980	Phi-N	6	5	2	1	1	0	0	2	1	0	.200	.333	.400	733	98	-0	0	0	0	1.000	-0	/1-2	0.0
Total	21	1909	5529	590	1501	242	57	97	645	548	422	.271	.340	.388	729	102	24	61	49	-4	.990	-9	*C-1387,1-103/O3D	7.5
■ AL McCAULEY	McCauley, Allen A. b: 3/4/1863, Indianapolis, Ind. d: 8/24/17, Wayne Twnshp., Ind BL/TL, 6', 180 lbs. Deb: 6/21/1884																							
1884	Ind-a	17	53	7	10	0	1	0	5	12		.189	.358	.226	585	97	1				1.000	0	P-10/1-5,O-3(0-0-3)	-0.2
1890	Phi-N	112	418	63	102	25	7	1	42	57	38	.244	.346	.344	690	99	0	8			.973	-6	*1-116	-1.5
1891	Was-a	59	206	36	58	5	8	1	31	30	13	.282	.378	.398	776	128	8	9			.969	-2	1-59	0.1
Total	3	188	677	106	170	30	16	2	78	99	51	.251	.357	.352	708	107	9	17			.971	-7	1-180/P-10,O-3(0-0-3)	-1.6
■ JIM McCAULEY	McCauley, James Adelbert b: 3/24/1863, Stanley, N.Y. d: 9/14/30, Canandaigua, N.Y. BL/TR, 6', 180 lbs. Deb: 9/17/1884																							
1884	StL-a	1	2	0	0	0	0	0		0		.000	.000	.000	0	-97	-0				.818	1	/C-1	0.1
1885	Buf-N	24	84	4	15	2	1	0	7	11	12	.179	.274	.226	500	61	-3				.936	-1	C-21/O-4(0-4-0)	-0.2
	Chi-N	3	6	1	1	0	0	0	0	2	3	.167	.375	.167	542	70	-0				.800	-3	/C-2,O-2(0-0-2)	-0.3
	Yr	27	90	5	16	2	1	0	7	13	15	.178	.282	.222	504	62	-3				.927	-3	C-23/O-6(0-4-2)	-0.5
1886	Bro-a	11	30	5	7	1	0	0	3	11		.233	.439	.267	706	122	2	2			.846	-1	C-11	0.1
Total	3	39	122	10	23	3	1	0	10	24	15	.189	.322	.230	551	76	-2	2			.893	-3	/C-35,O-6(0-4-2)	-0.3
■ PAT McCAULEY	McCauley, Patrick M. b: 6/10/1870, Ware, Mass. d: 1/23/17, Newark, N.J. TR, 5'10.5", 156 lbs. Deb: 9/5/1893																							
1893	StL-N	5	16	0	1	0	0	0	0	0	1	.063	.063	.063	125	-67	-4	0			.808	1	/C-5	-0.2
1896	Was-N	26	84	14	21	3	0	3	11	7	8	.250	.315	.393	708	86	-2	3			.917	0	C-24/O-1(0-1-0)	0.0
1903	NY-A	6	19	0	1	0	0	0	1	0		.053	.053	.053	105	-64	-4	0			.920	-2	/C-6	-0.6
Total	3	37	119	14	23	3	0	3	12	7	9	.193	.244	.294	538	44	-10	3			.900	-2	/C-35,O-1(0-1-0)	-0.8
■ BILL McCAULEY	McCauley, William H. b: 12/20/1869, Washington, D.C. d: 1/27/26, Washington, D.C. Deb: 8/31/1895																							
1895	Was-N	1	2	0	0	0	0	0	0	0	0	.000	.000	.000	0	-99	-1	0			.714	0	/S-1	0.0

YEAR	TM/L	G	AB	R	H	2B	3B	HR	RBI	BB	SO	AVG	OBP	SLG	OPS	OPS+	BR+	SB	CS	SBR	FA	FR	G/POS	TPR
■ HARRY McCHESNEY	McChesney, Harry Vincent "Pud" b: 6/1/1880, Pittsburgh, Pa. d: 8/11/60, Pittsburgh, Pa. BR/TR, 5'9", 165 lbs. Deb: 9/17/04																							
1904	Chi-N	22	88	9	23	6	2	0	11	4		.261	.293	.375	668	106	0	2			.967	-2	O-22(0-1-21)	-0.3
■ SCOTT McCLAIN	McClain, Scott Michael b: 5/19/72, Simi Valley, Cal. BR/TR, 6'3", 209 lbs. Deb: 5/14/98																							
1998	TB-A	9	20	2	2	0	0	0	0	2	6	.100	.217	.100	317	-13	-3	0	0	0	.966	0	/1-5,3-3	-0.3
■ PETE McCLANAHAN	McClanahan, Robert Hugh b: 10/24/06, Coldspring, Tex. d: 10/28/87, Mont Belvieu, Tex. BR/TR, 5'9", 170 lbs. Deb: 4/24/31																							
1931	Pit-N	7	4	2	2	0	0	0	0	2	0	.500	.667	.500	1167	220	1	0			.000	0	H	0.1
■ HARVEY McCLELLAN	McClellan, Harvey McDowell "Little Mac" b: 12/22/1894, Cynthiana, Ky. d: 11/6/25, Cynthiana, Ky. BR/TR, 5'9.5", 143 lbs. Deb: 5/31/19																							
1919	Chi-A	7	12	2	4	0	0	0	1	1	1	.333	.385	.333	718	102	0	0			1.000	1	/3-3,S-2	0.1
1920	Chi-A	10	18	4	6	1	1	0	5	4	1	.333	.455	.500	955	153	2	2	0	0	.917	-3	/S-4,3-2	-0.1
1921	Chi-A	63	196	20	35	4	1	1	14	14	18	.179	.237	.224	461	18	-24	2	3	-1	.968	18	2-21,S-15,O-15R,/3	-0.6
1922	Chi-A	91	301	28	68	17	3	2	28	16	32	.226	.272	.322	594	55	-21	3	2	-0	.971	-5	3-71/S-8,2-2,O-1C	-2.0
1923	Chi-A	141	550	67	129	29	3	1	41	27	44	.235	.270	.304	574	52	-40	14	11	-1	.958	-18	*S-139/2-2	-4.3
1924	Chi-A	32	85	9	15	3	0	0	9	6	7	.176	.239	.212	451	17	-11	2	0	0	.938	3	S-21/2-7,3-1,O-1R	-0.5
Total	6	344	1162	130	257	54	8	4	98	68	103	.221	.267	.292	559	46	-94	23	16		.952	-4	S-189/3-82,2-32,O	-7.4
■ BILL McCLELLAN	McClellan, William Henry b: 3/22/1856, Chicago, Ill. d: 7/3/29, Chicago, Ill. BL/TL, 5'5.5", 156 lbs. Deb: 5/20/1878																							
1878	Chi-N	48	205	26	46	6	1	0	29	2	13	.224	.232	.263	495	59	-9				.866	-9	*2-42/S-5,O-1(0-0-1)	-1.5
1881	Pro-N	68	259	30	43	3	1	0	16	15	21	.166	.212	.185	397	26	-21				.855	-8	S-50,O-17(0-1-16)/2-1	-2.5
1883	Phi-N	80	326	42	75	21	4	1	33	19	18	.230	.272	.328	601	89	-2				.849	5	*S-78/O-2(0-2-0),3-1	0.4
1884	Phi-N	111	450	71	116	13	2	3	33	28	43	.258	.301	.316	617	99	1				.852	-12	*S-111/O-1(0-1-0)	-0.7
1885	Bro-a	112	464	85	124	22	7	0	46	28		.267	.317	.345	662	108	5				.837	-5	3-57,2-55	0.3
1886	Bro-a	141	595	131	152	33	9	1	68	56		.255	.322	.346	668	108	5	43			.907	-7	*2-141	0.3
1887	Bro-a	136	628	109	224	24	6	1	53	80		.357	.363	.334	697	94	-2	70			.879	-23	*2-136	-1.6
1888	Bro-a	74	278	33	57	7	3	0	21	40		.205	.307	.252	559	80	-4	13			.905	-7	2-56,O-18(0-1-17)	-0.9
	Cle-a	22	72	6	16	0	0	0	5	6		.222	.282	.222	504	64	-3	6			.875	-4	O-15(0-0-15)/2-5,S-2	-0.6
	Yr	96	350	39	73	7	3	0	26	46		.209	.302	.246	548	77	-7	19			.897	-11	2-61,O-33(0-1-32)/S-2	-1.5
Total	8	792	3277	533	853	129	33	6	304	274	95	.260	.305	.308	613	89	-31	132			.893	-68	2-436,S-246/3-58,O	-6.8
■ LLOYD McCLENDON	McClendon, Lloyd Glenn b: 1/11/59, Gary, Ind. BR/TR, 5'11", 195 lbs. Deb: 4/6/87 C Career OF: (138-LF 0-CF 130-RF)																							
1987	Cin-N	45	72	8	15	5	0	2	13	4	15	.208	.250	.361	611	57	-5	1	0	0	.981	-2	C-12/1-5,3-1,O-1L	-0.6
1988	Cin-N	72	137	9	30	4	0	3	14	15	22	.219	.305	.314	619	75	-4	4	0	1	1.000	-3	C-23,O-17L,1-12,/3	-0.7
1989	*Chi-N	92	259	47	74	12	1	12	40	37	31	.286	.377	.479	856	133	12	6	4	-0	.962	-7	O-45L,1-28/3-6,C-5	0.2
1990	Chi-N	49	107	5	17	3	0	1	10	14	21	.159	.256	.215	471	29	-10	1	0	0	.980	1	O-23(23-0-0)/C-8,1-8	-1.0
	Pit-N	4	3	1	1	0	0	1	2	0	1	.333	.333	1.333	1667	349	1	0	0	0	.000	-0	/O-1(1-0-0)	0.1
	Yr	53	110	6	18	3	0	2	12	14	22	.164	.258	.245	504	37	-9	1	0	0	.980	1	O-24(24-0-0)/C-8,1-8	-0.9
1991	*Pit-N	85	163	24	47	7	0	7	24	18	23	.288	.366	.460	826	133	7	2	1	0	.966	-7	O-32R,1-22/C-2	-0.2
1992	*Pit-N	84	190	26	48	8	1	3	20	28	24	.253	.355	.353	707	102	1	1	3	-1	.964	-7	O-60(10-0-50),1-18	-0.9
1993	Pit-N	88	181	21	40	11	1	2	19	23	17	.221	.309	.326	635	70	-7	0	3	-1	.967	-9	O-61(21-0-47)/1-6	-2.0
1994	Pit-N	51	92	9	22	4	0	4	12	4	11	.239	.278	.413	691	76	-4	0	1	-0	.967	-2	O-20(12-0-9)/1-2	-0.6
Total	8	570	1204	150	294	54	3	35	154	143	165	.244	.328	.381	710	94	-9	15	12	-1	.966	-36	O-260L,1-101/C-50,3	-5.7
■ JEFF McCLESKEY	McCleskey, Jefferson Lamar b: 11/6/1891, Americus, Ga. d: 5/11/71, Americus, Ga. BL/TR, 5'11", 160 lbs. Deb: 9/8/13																							
1913	Bos-N	2	3	0	0	0	0	0	0	1	0	.000	.250	.000	250	-25	-0	0			.750	-0	/3-2	-0.1
■ McCLOSKEY	McCloskey b: Brooklyn, N.Y. Deb: 5/25/1875																							
1875	Was-n	11	40	1	7	0	0	0	4	1	2	.175	.195	.175	370	31	-3	0	1	-0	.673	-7	C-11	-0.9
■ BILL McCLOSKEY	McCloskey, William George b: 5/1854, Pennsylvania 5'8", 155 lbs. Deb: 8/18/1884																							
1884	Wil-U	9	30	0	3	0	0	0		0		.100	.100	.100	200	-38	-6				.588	1	/O-5(3-3-0),C-5	-0.4
■ HAL McCLURE	McClure, Harold Murray "Mac" b: 8/8/1859, Lewisburg, Pa. d: 3/1/19, Lewisburg, Pa. BR/TR, 6', 165 lbs. Deb: 5/10/1882																							
1882	Bos-N	2	6	1	2	0	0	0	0	0	1	.333	.333	.333	667	115	0				.750	-0	/O-2(0-0-2)	0.0
■ LARRY McCLURE	McClure, Lawrence Ledwith b: 10/3/1885, Wayne, W.Va. d: 8/31/49, Huntington, W.Va. BR/TR, 5'6.5", 130 lbs. Deb: 7/26/10																							
1910	NY-A	1	1	0	0	0	0	0	0	0		.000	.000	.000	0	-95	-0	0			.000	0	/O-1	0.0
■ AMBY McCONNELL	McConnell, Ambrose Moses b: 4/29/1883, N.Pownal, Vt. d: 5/20/42, Utica, N.Y. BL/TR, 5'7", 150 lbs. Deb: 4/17/08																							
1908	Bos-A	140	502	77	140	10	6	2	43	38		.279	.343	.335	678	117	10	31			.939	-19	*2-126/S-3	-0.9
1909	Bos-A	121	453	61	108	7	8	0	36	34		.238	.300	.289	589	84	-8	26			.954	15	*2-121	0.9
1910	Bos-A	11	35	6	6	0	0	0	1	5		.171	.310	.171	481	50	-2	4			.959	-1	2-10	-0.3
	Chi-A	33	120	13	33	2	3	0	5	7		.275	.320	.342	662	112	1	4			.952	-1	2-32	0.1
	Yr	44	155	19	39	2	3	0	6	12		.252	.318	.303	621	97	-0	8			.954	-2	2-42	-0.2
1911	Chi-A	104	396	45	111	11	5	1	34	23		.280	.331	.341	672	90	-5	7			**.973**	-7	*2-103	-1.0
Total	4	409	1506	202	398	30	22	3	119	107		.264	.324	.319	644	98	-3	72			.954	-13	2-392/S-3	-1.2
■ GEORGE McCONNELL	McConnell, George Neely "Slats" b: 9/16/1877, Shelbyville, Tenn d: 5/10/64, Chattanooga, Tenn. BR/TR, 6'3", 190 lbs. Deb: 4/13/09																							
1909	NY-A	13	43	4	9	0	1	0	5	1		.209	.227	.256	483	52	-2	1			.964	2	1-11/P-2	-0.2
1912	NY-A	42	91	11	27	4	2	0	8	4		.297	.333	.385	718	99	-0	0			.913	5	P-23/1-2	0.0
1913	NY-A	39	67	4	12	2	0	0	2	0	11	.179	.179	.209	388	13	-7	0			.965	5	P-35/1-1	0.0
1914	Chi-N	1	2	0	0	0	0	0	0	0	1	.000	.000	.000	0	-99	-0	0			1.000	0	/P-1	0.0
1915	Chi-F	53	125	14	31	6	2	1	18	0	16	.248	.254	.352	606	74	-7	2			.974	3	P-44	0.0
1916	Chi-N	28	57	2	9	0	0	0	0	2	4	.158	.200	.158	358	10	-6	0			.952	2	P-28	0.0
Total	6	176	385	35	88	12	5	1	33	7	32	.229	.248	.294	542	57	-24	3			.953	16	P-133/1-14	-0.2
■ SAM McCONNELL	McConnell, Samuel Faulkner b: 6/8/1895, Philadelphia, Pa. d: 6/27/81, Phoenixville, Pa. BL/TR, 5'6.5", 150 lbs. Deb: 4/19/15																							
1915	Phi-A	6	11	1	2	1	0	0	0	1	3	.182	.250	.273	523	58	-1	0			.842	2	/3-5	0.1
■ DON McCORMACK	McCormack, Donald Ross b: 9/18/55, Omak, Wash. BR/TR, 6'3", 205 lbs. Deb: 9/30/80																							
1980	Phi-N	2	1	0	1	0	0	0	0	0	0	1.000	1.000	1.000	2000	436	0	0	0	0	1.000	1	/C-2	0.1
1981	Phi-N	3	4	0	1	0	0	0	0	0	1	.250	.250	.250	500	40	-0	0	0	0	1.000	0	/C-3	0.0
Total	2	5	5	0	2	0	0	0	0	0	1	.400	.400	.400	800	121	0	0	0	0	1.000	1	/C-5	0.1
■ FRANK McCORMICK	McCormick, Frank Andrew "Buck" b: 6/9/11, New York, N.Y. d: 11/21/82, Manhasset, N.Y. BR/TR, 6'4", 205 lbs. Deb: 9/11/34 C Career OF: (0-LF 0-CF 1-RF)																							
1934	Cin-N	12	16	1	5	2	1	0	5	0	1	.313	.313	.563	875	132	1	0			.941	-1	/1-2	0.0
1937	Cin-N	24	83	5	27	5	0	0	9	2	4	.325	.341	.386	727	102	0	1			1.000	1	1-20/2-4,O-1(0-0-1)	-0.1
1938	Cin-N★	151	640	89	**209**	40	4	5	106	18	17	.327	.348	.425	773	115	11	1			.995	-3	*1-151	-0.7
1939	*Cin-N★	156	630	99	**209**	41	4	18	**128**	40	16	.332	.374	.495	869	131	26	1			**.996**	2	*1-156	1.2
1940	*Cin-N★	155	618	93	**191**	**44**	3	19	127	52	26	.309	.367	.482	850	131	25	2			**.995**	1	*1-155	1.1
1941	Cin-N★	154	603	77	162	31	5	17	97	40	13	.269	.318	.421	740	107	3	2			**.995**	1	*1-154	-1.1
1942	Cin-N★	145	564	58	156	24	0	13	89	45	18	.277	.332	.388	721	111	6	1			.993	6	*1-144	-0.2
1943	Cin-N†	126	472	56	143	28	0	8	59	29	15	.303	.345	.413	758	120	10	2			.995	3	*1-120	0.8
1944	Cin-N☆	153	581	85	177	37	3	20	102	57	17	.305	.371	.482	853	144	33	7			.992	12	*1-153	3.7
1945	Cin-N†	152	580	68	160	33	0	10	81	56	22	.276	.345	.384	729	105	4	6			.994	5	*1-151	0.1
1946	Phi-N★	135	504	46	143	20	2	11	66	36	21	.284	.333	.397	730	110	5	2			**.999**	4	*1-134	0.4
1947	Phi-N	15	40	7	9	2	0	1	8	3	2	.225	.279	.350	629	69	-2	0			.989	-1	1-12	-0.3
	Bos-N	81	212	24	75	18	2	2	43	11	8	.354	.386	.486	871	133	9	2			.996	-1	1-46	0.7
	Yr	96	252	31	84	20	2	3	51	14	10	.333	.368	.464	833	123	8	2			.995	-2	1-58	0.4

YEAR	TM/L	G	AB	R	H	2B	3B	HR	RBI	BB	SO	AVG	OBP	SLG	OPS	OPS+	BR+	SB	CS	SBR	FA	FR	G/POS	TPR
1948	*Bos-N	75	180	14	45	9	2	4	34	10	9	.250	.289	.389	678	84	-5	0			.987	3	1-50	-0.4
Total	13	1534	5723	722	1711	334	26	128	954	399	189	.299	.348	.434	781	118	125	27			.995	31	*1-1448/2-4,O-1R	5.2

■ MOOSE McCORMICK McCormick, Harry Elwood b: 2/28/1881, Philadelphia, Pa. d: 7/9/62, Lewisburg, Pa. BL/TL, 5'11", 180 lbs. Deb: 4/14/04

YEAR	TM/L	G	AB	R	H	2B	3B	HR	RBI	BB	SO	AVG	OBP	SLG	OPS	OPS+	BR+	SB	CS	SBR	FA	FR	G/POS	TPR
1904	NY-N	59	203	28	54	9	5	1	26	13		.266	.323	.374	697	110	2	13			.916	-5	O-55(2-52-1)	-0.5
	Pit-N	66	238	25	69	10	6	2	23	13		.290	.332	.408	740	124	6	6			.940	-6	O-66(18-0-48)	-0.3
	Yr	125	441	53	123	19	11	3	49	26		.279	.328	.392	720	118	8	19			.928	-11	*O-121(20-52-49)	-0.8
1908	Phi-N	11	22	0	2	0	0	0	2	2		.091	.167	.091	258	-17	-3	0			1.000	-0	/O-5(5-0-0)	-0.4
	NY-N	73	252	31	76	16	3	0	32	4		.302	.315	.389	704	119	4	6			.901	-11	O-65(59-0-12)	-1.2
	Yr	84	274	31	78	16	3	0	34	6		.285	.302	.365	667	108	1	6			.910	-11	O-70(64-0-12)	-1.6
1909	NY-N	110	413	68	120	21	8	3	27	49		.291	.373	.402	775	138	19	4			.924	-14	*O-110(87-0-23)	-0.1
1912	*NY-N	42	39	4	13	4	1	0	8	6	9	.333	.422	.487	909	144	2	1			.667	-3	/O-6(1-1-4),1-1	0.0
1913	*NY-N	57	80	9	22	2	3	0	15	5	13	.275	.318	.375	693	97	-1	0			.909	-2	O-15(0-2-13)	-0.3
Total	5	418	1247	165	356	62	26	6	133	92	22	.285	.340	.391	732	122	30	30			.920	-40	O-322(172-55-101)/1-1	-2.8

■ JIM McCORMICK McCormick, James Ambrose b: 11/2/1868, Spencer, Mass. d: 2/1/48, Saco, Maine BR/TR, 6'1", 160 lbs. Deb: 9/10/1892

YEAR	TM/L	G	AB	R	H	2B	3B	HR	RBI	BB	SO	AVG	OBP	SLG	OPS	OPS+	BR+	SB	CS	SBR	FA	FR	G/POS	TPR
1892	StL-N	3	11	0	0	0	0	0	0	1	5	.000	.083	.000	83	-78	-2	0			1.000	-0	/2-2,3-1	-0.2

■ JERRY McCORMICK McCormick, John b: Philadelphia, Pa. d: 9/19/05, Philadelphia, Pa. Deb: 5/1/1883 Career OF: (5-LF 0-CF 1-RF)

YEAR	TM/L	G	AB	R	H	2B	3B	HR	RBI	BB	SO	AVG	OBP	SLG	OPS	OPS+	BR+	SB	CS	SBR	FA	FR	G/POS	TPR
1883	Bal-a	93	389	40	102	16	6	0		2		.262	.266	.334	600	89	-6				.799	0	*3-93	-0.3
1884	Phi-U	67	295	41	84	12	2	0		4		.285	.294	.339	633	99	-9				.811	14	3-54/2-5,O-5L,SP	0.5
	Was-U	42	157	23	34	8	2	0		1		.217	.222	.293	515	57	-13				.792	-6	3-38/S-4	-1.6
	Yr	109	452	64	118	20	4	0		5		.261	.269	.323	592	84	-22				**.806**	8	3-92/S-7,2-5,O-5L,P	-1.1
Total	2	202	841	104	220	36	10	0		7		.262	.268	.328	596	86	-27				.802	8	3-185/S-7,O-5L,2P	-1.4

■ MIKE McCORMICK McCormick, Michael J. "Kid" or "Dude" b: 5/1883, Scotland d: 11/18/53, Jersey City, N.J. BR/TR, 5'3", 155 lbs. Deb: 4/14/04

YEAR	TM/L	G	AB	R	H	2B	3B	HR	RBI	BB	SO	AVG	OBP	SLG	OPS	OPS+	BR+	SB	CS	SBR	FA	FR	G/POS	TPR
1904	Bro-N	105	347	28	64	5	4	0	27	43		.184	.278	.222	500	56	-16	22			**.914**	-3	*3-104/2-1	-1.8

■ MIKE McCORMICK McCormick, Myron Winthrop b: 5/6/17, Angels Camp, Cal. d: 4/14/76, Ventura, Cal. BR/TR, 6', 200 lbs. Deb: 4/16/40

YEAR	TM/L	G	AB	R	H	2B	3B	HR	RBI	BB	SO	AVG	OBP	SLG	OPS	OPS+	BR+	SB	CS	SBR	FA	FR	G/POS	TPR
1940	*Cin-N	110	417	48	125	20	0	1	30	13	36	.300	.326	.355	681	87	-8	8			.986	8	*O-107(51-50-6)	-0.5
1941	Cin-N	110	369	52	106	17	3	4	31	30	24	.287	.341	.382	723	103	1	4			.976	7	*O-101(82-19-0)	0.4
1942	Cin-N	40	135	18	32	2	3	1	11	13	7	.237	.304	.319	623	82	-3	0			.990	1	O-38(13-26-0)	-0.4
1943	Cin-N	4	15	0	2	0	0	0	0	2	0	.133	.235	.133	369	8	-2	0			.909	-0	/O-4(0-4-0)	-0.3
1946	Cin-N	23	74	10	16	2	0	0	5	8	4	.216	.293	.243	536	55	-4	0			1.000	-1	O-21(0-21-0)	-0.4
	Bos-N	59	164	23	43	6	2	1	16	11	7	.262	.309	.341	650	83	-4	0			.973	-2	O-48(10-33-5)	-0.8
	Yr	82	238	33	59	8	2	1	21	19	11	.248	.304	.311	614	75	-8	0			.982	-1	O-69(10-54-5)	-1.2
1947	Bos-N	92	284	42	81	13	7	3	36	20	21	.285	.332	.412	744	99	-1	1			.981	-12	O-79(26-62-1)	-1.5
1948	*Bos-N	115	343	45	104	22	7	1	39	32	34	.303	.363	.417	780	112	6	1			.975	-11	*O-100(56-34-20)	-1.0
1949	*Bro-N	55	139	17	29	5	1	2	14	14	12	.209	.281	.302	583	54	-9	1			1.000	-6	O-49(38-7-5)	-1.7
1950	NY-N	4	4	0	0	0	0	0	0	0	2	.000	.000	.000	0	-99	-1	0			.000	0	H	-0.1
	Chi-A	55	138	16	32	4	3	0	10	16	6	.232	.312	.304	616	60	-8	0	1	-0	.982	-1	O-44(2-42-0)	-1.0
1951	Was-A	81	243	31	70	9	3	1	23	29	20	.288	.364	.362	726	98	0	1	2	-0	.966	1	O-62(24-12-28)	-0.2
Total	10	748	2325	302	640	100	29	14	215	188	173	.275	.330	.361	692	90	-33	16	3		.980	-14	O-653(302-310-65)	-7.5

■ BARRY McCORMICK McCormick, William J. b: 12/25/1874, Maysville, Ky. d: 1/28/56, Cincinnati, Ohio TR, 5'9", Deb: 9/25/1895 U

YEAR	TM/L	G	AB	R	H	2B	3B	HR	RBI	BB	SO	AVG	OBP	SLG	OPS	OPS+	BR+	SB	CS	SBR	FA	FR	G/POS	TPR
1895	Lou-N	3	12	2	3	0	1	0	0	0	0	.250	.250	.417	667	75	-1	1			1.000	-2	/S-2,2-1	-0.2
1896	Chi-N	45	168	22	37	3	1	1	23	14	30	.220	.280	.268	548	43	-14	9			.835	-5	3-35/S-6,2-3,O-1R	-1.6
1897	Chi-N	101	419	87	112	8	10	2	55	33		.267	.324	.348	672	75	-16	44			.851	-2	3-56,S-46/2-1	-1.3
1898	Chi-N	137	530	76	131	15	9	2	78	47		.247	.314	.321	635	82	-12	15			.888	4	*3-136/S-1,2-1	-0.6
1899	Chi-N	102	376	48	97	15	2	2	52	25		.258	.311	.324	636	76	-12	14			.941	5	2-99/S-3	-0.2
1900	Chi-N	110	379	35	83	13	5	3	48	38		.219	.292	.303	595	67	-17	8			.907	-9	S-84,3-21/2-5	-1.9
1901	Chi-N	115	427	45	100	15	6	1	32	31		.234	.288	.304	592	75	-14	12			.911	0	*S-112/3-3	-1.0
1902	StL-A	139	504	55	124	14	4	3	51	37		.246	.304	.308	612	71	-19	10			.905	-11	*3-132/S-7,O-1(0-1-0)	-2.6
1903	StL-A	61	207	13	45	6	1	1	16	18		.217	.283	.271	554	69	-7	5			.969	-4	2-28,3-28/S-4	-1.1
	Was-A	63	219	14	47	10	2	0	23	10		.215	.255	.279	534	59	-11	3			.960	8	2-63	-0.2
	Yr	124	426	27	92	16	3	1	39	28		.216	.269	.275	544	64	-18	8			.962	4	2-91,3-28/S-4	-1.3
1904	Was-A	113	404	36	88	11	1	0	39	27		.218	.274	.250	524	67	-14	9			.938	-1	*2-113	-1.6
Total	10	989	3645	433	867	110	42	15	417	280	30	.238	.297	.303	600	71	-138	130			.885	-17	3-411,2-314,S-265,/O	-12.3

■ BARNEY McCOSKY McCosky, William Barney b: 4/11/17, Coal Run, Pa. d: 9/6/96, Venice, Fla. BL/TR, 6'1", 184 lbs. Deb: 4/18/39

YEAR	TM/L	G	AB	R	H	2B	3B	HR	RBI	BB	SO	AVG	OBP	SLG	OPS	OPS+	BR+	SB	CS	SBR	FA	FR	G/POS	TPR
1939	Det-A	147	611	120	190	33	14	4	58	70	45	.311	.384	.430	814	100	1	20	4	3	.986	9	*O-145(0-145-0)	0.9
1940	*Det-A	143	589	123	**200**	39	**19**	4	57	67	41	.340	.408	.491	899	120	19	13	9	-0	.983	-1	*O-141(0-141-0)	1.3
1941	Det-A	127	494	80	160	25	8	3	55	61	33	.324	.401	.425	827	108	8	8	3	1	.985	5	*O-122(21-101-0)	0.9
1942	Det-A	154	600	75	176	28	11	7	50	68	37	.293	.365	.412	777	109	8	11	5	1	.981	3	*O-154(145-7-2)	0.3
1946	Det-A	25	91	11	18	5	0	1	11	17	9	.198	.324	.286	610	67	-4	0	0	0	.966	-1	O-24(0-24-0)	-0.5
	Phi-A	92	308	33	109	17	4	1	34	43	13	.354	.433	.445	878	146	21	2	2	-0	.981	-4	O-85(0-85-0)	1.6
	Yr	117	399	44	127	22	4	2	45	60	22	.318	.407	.409	816	127	17	2	2	-0	.978	-4	*O-109(0-109-0)	1.1
1947	Phi-A	137	546	77	179	22	7	1	52	57	29	.328	.395	.399	795	119	16	1	4	-1	.983	4	*O-136(114-23-0)	1.0
1948	Phi-A	135	515	95	168	21	5	0	46	68	22	.326	.405	.386	791	111	11	1	3	-1	.990	-3	*O-134(134-0-0)	-0.3
1950	Phi-A	66	179	19	43	10	1	0	11	22	12	.240	.323	.307	631	63	-10	0	0	0	.987	-5	O-42(42-0-0)	-1.7
1951	Phi-A	12	27	4	8	2	0	1	1	3	4	.296	.367	.481	848	125	1	0	0	0	1.000	-1	/O-7(5-0-2)	0.0
	Cin-N	25	50	2	16	2	1	1	11	4	2	.320	.370	.460	830	120	1	0	0	0	1.000	-3	O-11(4-7-1)	-0.2
	Cle-A	31	61	8	13	3	0	0	2	8	5	.213	.304	.262	567	57	-4	1	0	0	1.000	-1	O-16(1-2-13)	-0.5
1952	Cle-A	54	80	14	17	4	1	1	6	8	5	.213	.284	.325	609	74	-3	1	1	-0	.944	-5	O-19(11-0-9)	-1.0
1953	Cle-A	22	21	3	4	3	0	0	3	1	4	.190	.227	.333	561	51	-2	0	0	0	.000	0	H	-0.2
Total	11	1170	4172	664	1301	214	71	24	397	497	261	.312	.386	.414	801	109	64	58	31	2	.984	-1	*O-1036(477-535-27)	1.6

■ WILLIE McCOVEY McCovey, Willie Lee "Stretch" b: 1/10/38, Mobile, Ala. BL/TL, 6'4", 210 lbs. Deb: 7/30/59 H Career OF: (257-LF 0-CF 19-RF)

YEAR	TM/L	G	AB	R	H	2B	3B	HR	RBI	BB	SO	AVG	OBP	SLG	OPS	OPS+	BR+	SB	CS	SBR	FA	FR	G/POS	TPR
1959	SF-N	52	192	32	68	9	5	13	38	22	35	.354	.431	.656	1087	189	24	2	0	0	.989	-2	1-51	2.0
1960	SF-N	101	260	37	62	15	3	13	51	45	53	.238	.351	.469	820	130	11	1	1	-0	.985	-3	1-71	0.4
1961	SF-N	106	328	59	89	12	3	18	50	37	60	.271	.354	.491	845	126	12	1	2	-0	.985	-2	1-84	0.5
1962	*SF-N	91	229	41	67	6	1	20	54	29	35	.293	.372	.590	962	156	17	3	3	-0	.976	-2	O-57(45-0-12),1-17	1.1
1963	SF-N★	152	564	103	158	19	5	**44**	102	50	119	.280	.350	.566	916	161	42	1	1	-0	.942	3	*O-135(134-0-2),1-23	3.9
1964	SF-N	130	364	55	80	14	1	18	54	61	73	.220	.340	.412	752	108	5	2	1	0	.935	-6	O-83(78-0-5),1-26	-0.7
1965	SF-N	160	540	93	149	17	4	39	92	88	118	.276	.383	.539	922	152	39	0	4	-1	.991	-3	*1-156	2.7
1966	SF-N★	150	502	85	148	26	6	36	96	76	100	.295	.394	.586	979	163	44	2	1	0	.984	-3	*1-145	3.4
1967	SF-N	135	456	73	126	17	4	31	91	71	110	.276	.381	.535	916	162	37	3	3	-0	.989	1	*1-127	3.2
1968	SF-N★	148	523	81	153	16	4	**36**	**105**	72	71	.293	.383	**.545**	**928**	**176**	**49**	4	2	0	.985	3	*1-146	4.8
1969	SF-N★	149	491	101	157	26	2	**45**	**126**	121	66	.320	**.458**	**.656**	**1114**	**212**	**79**	0	0	0	.992	-6	*1-148	6.3
1970	SF-N★	152	495	98	143	39	2	39	126	**137**	75	.289	.446	**.612**	**1058**	**183**	**64**	0	0	0	.989	13	*1-146	**6.3**
1971	*SF-N★	105	329	45	91	13	0	18	70	64	57	.277	.401	.480	881	151	24	0	2	-1	.983	-2	1-95	1.6
1972	SF-N	81	263	30	56	8	0	14	35	38	45	.213	.317	.403	720	102	1	0	0	0	.986	-5	1-74	-1.1
1973	SF-N	130	383	52	102	14	3	29	75	105	78	.266	.425	.546	971	161	36	1	0	0	.988	1	*1-117	2.8
1974	SD-N	128	344	53	87	19	1	22	63	96	76	.253	.417	.506	923	164	34	1	0	0	.987	-6	*1-104	2.1
1975	SD-N	122	413	43	104	17	0	23	68	57	80	.252	.347	.460	807	130	16	1	0	0	.986	-1	*1-115	0.7
1976	SD-N	71	202	20	41	9	0	7	36	21	39	.203	.281	.351	633	86	-5	0	0	0	.991	5	1-51	-0.4
	Oak-A	11	24	0	5	0	0	0	0	3	4	.208	.296	.208	505	57	-1	0	0	0	.000	0	/D-9	-0.2
1977	SF-N	141	478	54	134	21	0	28	86	67	106	.280	.369	.500	869	131	21	3	0	1	.989	-7	*1-136	0.7
1978	SF-N	108	351	32	80	19	2	12	64	36	57	.228	.300	.396	696	97	-3	1	0	0	.987	-4	1-97	-1.2
1979	SF-N	117	353	34	88	9	0	15	57	36	70	.249	.321	.402	723	103	1	0	2	-1	.987	-1	1-89	-0.7

YEAR	TM/L	G	AB	R	H	2B	3B	HR	RBI	BB	SO	AVG	OBP	SLG	OPS	OPS+	BR+	SB	CS	SBR	FA	FR	G/POS	TPR
1980	SF-N	48	113	8	23	8	0	1	16	13	23	.204	.291	.301	592	67	-5	0	0	0	.992	-2	1-27	-0.9
Total	22	2588	8197	1229	2211	353	46	521	1555	1345	1550	.270	.377	.515	892	148	541	26	22	-2	.987	-30	*1-2045,O-275L/D-9	37.3
■ **ART McCOY** McCoy, Arthur Gray b: 7/1864, Danville, Pa. d: 3/22/04, Danville, Pa. 168 lbs. Deb: 7/8/1889																								
1889	Was-N	2	6	0	0	0	0	0	0	2	1	.000	.250	.000	250	-29	-1	0			.889	-2	/2-2	-0.2
■ **BENNY McCOY** McCoy, Benjamin Jenison b: 11/9/15, Jenison, Mich. BL/TR, 5'9", 170 lbs. Deb: 9/14/38																								
1938	Det-A	7	15	2	3	1	0	0	0	1	2	.200	.250	.267	517	28	-2	0	0	0	.963	2	/2-6,3-1	0.1
1939	Det-A	55	192	38	58	13	6	1	33	29	26	.302	.394	.448	842	107	2	3	1	0	.958	-2	2-34,S-16	0.4
1940	Phi-A	134	490	56	126	26	5	7	62	65	44	.257	.345	.373	719	88	-8	2	2	-0	.951	-16	*2-130/3-1	-1.5
1941	Phi-A	141	517	86	140	12	7	8	61	95	50	.271	.384	.368	751	102	5	3	3	-0	.963	-13	*2-135	0.0
Total	4	337	1214	182	327	52	18	16	156	190	122	.269	.369	.381	750	97	-2	8	6	-0	.957	-28	2-305/S-16,3-2	-1.0
■ **QUINTON McCRACKEN** McCracken, Quinton Antoine b: 3/16/70, Wilmington, N.C. BB/TR, 5'8", 170 lbs. Deb: 9/17/95																								
1995	Col-N	3	1	0	0	0	0	0	0	0	1	.000	.000	.000	0	-78	-0	0	0	0	.000	-0	/O-1(0-1-0)	-0.1
1996	Col-N	124	283	50	82	13	6	3	40	32	62	.290	.364	.410	774	84	-6	17	6	2	.957	-15	O-93(8-85-4)	-1.8
1997	Col-N	147	325	69	95	11	1	3	36	42	62	.292	.375	.360	735	76	-10	28	11	2	.980	-16	*O-132(0-132-0)	-2.2
1998	TB-A	155	614	77	179	38	7	7	59	41	107	.292	.339	.410	749	92	-7	19	10	1	.992	9	*O-153(58-103-0)	0.1
1999	TB-A	40	148	20	37	6	1	1	18	14	23	.250	.319	.324	643	64	-8	6	5	-0	.988	-3	O-40(26-20-0)	-1.1
2000	TB-A	15	31	5	.4	0	0	0	2	6	4	.129	.270	.129	399	6	-4	0	1	-0	1.000	-1	O-11(9-3-0)	-0.6
Total	6	484	1402	221	397	68	15	14	155	135	259	.283	.349	.383	732	81	-35	70	33	4	.983	-27	O-430(101-344-4)	-5.7
■ **TOM McCRAW** McCraw, Tommy Lee b: 11/21/40, Malvern, Ark. BL/TL, 6', 183 lbs. Deb: 6/4/63 C Career OF: (241-LF 90-CF 125-RF)																								
1963	Chi-A	102	280	38	71	11	3	6	33	21	46	.254	.313	.379	691	94	-2	15	4	2	.993	-1	1-97	-0.6
1964	Chi-A	125	368	47	96	11	5	6	36	32	65	.261	.327	.367	694	95	-2	15	7	1	.992	-7	1-84,O-36(32-2-3)	-1.5
1965	Chi-A	133	273	38	65	12	1	5	21	25	48	.238	.309	.344	653	91	-3	12	7	0	.993	-8	1-72,O-64(37-31-3)	-1.5
1966	Chi-A	151	389	49	89	16	4	5	48	29	40	.229	.291	.329	620	83	-9	20	11	1	.990	-2	*1-121,O-41(29-0-16)	-1.8
1967	Chi-A	125	453	55	107	18	3	11	45	33	55	.236	.290	.362	652	95	-4	24	10	2	.991	11	*1-123/O-6(1-4-1)	0.2
1968	Chi-A	136	477	51	112	16	12	9	44	36	58	.235	.295	.375	671	101	-0	20	5	3	.986	2	*1-135	-0.4
1969	Chi-A	93	240	21	62	12	2	2	25	21	24	.258	.326	.350	676	85	-5	1	3	-1	.989	-10	1-44,O-41(11-16-17)	-2.0
1970	Chi-A	129	332	39	73	11	2	6	31	21	50	.220	.275	.319	594	61	-18	12	3	2	.987	-3	1-59,O-49(21-12-18)	-2.6
1971	Was-A	122	207	33	44	6	4	7	25	19	38	.213	.294	.382	676	96	-2	3	3	-0	.958	-9	O-60(26-1-37),1-30	-1.5
1972	Cle-A	129	391	43	101	13	5	7	33	41	47	.258	.335	.371	706	106	4	12	10	-1	1.000	-1	O-84(42-22-24),1-38	-0.5
1973	Cal-A	99	264	25	70	7	0	3	24	30	42	.265	.345	.326	670	97	-0	3	2	-0	1.000	2	O-34(32-1-1),1-25/D-8	-0.2
1974	Cal-A	56	119	21	34	8	0	3	17	12	13	.286	.351	.429	780	131	5	2	1	0	1.000	2	1-29,O-12(7-0-5)/D-3	0.5
	Cle-A	45	112	17	34	8	0	3	17	5	11	.304	.339	.455	794	128	4	0	1	-0	.990	2	1-38/O-1(0-1-0)	0.3
	Yr	101	231	38	68	16	0	6	34	17	24	.294	.345	.442	787	130	8	2	2	-0	.994	4	1-67,O-13(7-1-5)/D-3	0.8
1975	Cle-A	23	51	7	14	1	1	2	5	7	7	.275	.362	.451	813	129	2	4	1	1	1.000	-2	1-16/O-3(3-0-0)	0.0
Total	13	1468	3956	484	972	150	42	75	404	332	544	.246	.311	.362	672	94	-32	143	68	8	.991	-22	1-911,O-431L/D-11	-11.6
■ **RODNEY McCRAY** McCray, Rodney Duncan b: 9/13/63, Detroit, Mich. BR/TR, 5'10", 175 lbs. Deb: 4/30/90																								
1990	Chi-A	32	6	8	0	0	0	0	0	1	4	.000	.143	.000	143	-58	-1	6	0	1	1.000	-5	O-13(3-7-4)/D-7	-0.5
1991	Chi-A	17	7	2	2	0	0	0	0	0	2	.286	.286	.286	571	60	-0	1	1	-0	1.000	-2	/O-8(4-2-2),D-6	-0.2
1992	NY-N	18	1	3	1	0	0	0	1	0	0	1.000	1.000	1.000	2000	475	0	2	0	0	1.000	-4	O-13(1-1-11)	-0.3
Total	3	67	14	13	3	0	0	0	1	1	6	.214	.267	.214	481	36	-1	9	1	2	1.000	-10	/O-34(8-10-17),D-13	-1.0
■ **FRANK McCREA** McCrea, Francis William b: 9/6/1896, Jersey City, N.J. d: 2/25/81, Dover, N.J. BR/TR, 5'9", 155 lbs. Deb: 9/26/25																								
1925	Cle-A	1	5	1	1	0	0	0	0	0	0	.200	.200	.200	400	2	-1	0	0	0	1.000	-1	/C-1	-0.1
■ **WALT McCREDIE** McCredie, Walter Henry b: 11/29/1876, Manchester, Iowa d: 7/29/34, Portland, Ore. BL/TR, 6'2", 195 lbs. Deb: 4/20/03																								
1903	Bro-N	56	213	40	69	5	0	0	20	24		.324	.397	.347	745	116	6	10			.925	-4	O-56(0-0-56)	-0.1
■ **TOM McCREERY** McCreery, Thomas Livingston b: 10/19/1874, Beaver, Pa. d: 7/3/41, Beaver, Pa. BB/TR, 5'11", 180 lbs. Deb: 6/8/1895 Career OF: (39-LF 203-CF 390-RF)																								
1895	Lou-N	31	108	18	35	3	1	0	10	8	15	.324	.376	.370	746	99	0	3			.875	-6	O-18R/P-8,S-4,31	-0.6
1896	Lou-N	115	441	87	155	23	**21**	7	65	42	58	.351	.409	.546	956	157	35	26			.916	1	*O-111R/2-1,P-1	2.5
1897	Lou-N	91	344	55	96	5	6	4	40	40		.279	.354	.363	718	93	-3	13			.859	-5	*O-91(1-1-89)	-1.1
	NY-N	49	177	36	53	8	5	1	28	22		.299	.380	.418	798	114	4	15			.900	-2	O-45(0-0-45)/2-3	0.0
	Yr	140	521	91	149	13	11	5	68	62		.286	.363	.382	745	100	1	28			.871	-7	*O-136(1-1-134)/2-3	-1.1
1898	NY-N	35	121	15	24	4	3	1	17	19		.198	.307	.306	613	78	-3	3			.820	-5	O-35(1-0-35)	-1.0
	Pit-N	53	190	33	59	5	7	2	20	26		.311	.394	.442	836	142	11	3			.934	-1	O-51(0-46-5)	0.6
	Yr	88	311	48	83	9	10	3	37	45		.267	.360	.389	749	117	8	6			.901	-6	O-86(1-46-40)	-0.4
1899	Pit-N	119	460	77	149	21	9	3	65	47		.324	.390	.428	818	125	16	11			.911	-7	O-98C/S-9,2-7	0.3
1900	Pit-N	43	132	20	29	4	3	1	13	16		.220	.304	.318	622	71	-5	2			.887	2	O-35(17-1-17)/P-1	-0.5
1901	Bro-N	91	335	47	97	11	14	3	53	32		.290	.355	.433	788	124	10	13			.947	4	O-82(4-78-0)/1-4,S-2	1.0
1902	Bro-N	112	430	49	105	8	4	4	57	29		.244	.295	.309	604	86	-8	16			.979	-1	*1-108/O-4(1-0-3)	-1.1
1903	Bro-N	40	141	13	37	5	2	0	10	20		.262	.354	.326	680	97	0	5			.892	-2	O-38(0-2-36)	-0.3
	Bos-N	23	83	15	18	2	1	1	10	9		.217	.293	.301	595	72	-3	6			.900	0	O-23(0-23-0)	-0.4
	Yr	63	224	28	55	7	3	1	20	29		.246	.332	.317	649	88	-3	11			.896	-2	O-61(0-25-36)	-0.7
Total	9	802	2962	465	857	99	76	27	388	310	73	.289	.359	.401	760	113	55	116			.906	-22	O-631R,1-113/S2P3	-0.6
■ **FRANK McCUE** McCue, Frank Aloysius b: 10/4/1898, Chicago, Ill. d: 7/5/53, Chicago, Ill. BB/TR, 5'9", 150 lbs. Deb: 9/15/22																								
1922	Phi-A	2	5	0	0	0	0	0	0	0	0	.000	.000	.000	0	-97	-1	0	0	0	.000	0	/3-2	-0.1
■ **CLYDE McCULLOUGH** McCullough, Clyde Edward b: 3/4/17, Nashville, Tenn. d: 9/18/82, San Francisco, Cal. BR/TR, 5'11.5", 180 lbs. Deb: 4/28/40 C																								
1940	Chi-N	9	26	4	4	1	0	0	1	5	5	.154	.290	.192	483	36	-2	0			1.000	3	/C-7	0.1
1941	Chi-N	125	418	41	95	9	2	9	53	34	67	.227	.289	.323	612	75	-15	5			.982	-8	*C-119	-1.6
1942	Chi-N	109	337	39	95	22	1	5	31	25	47	.282	.331	.398	729	117	6	7			.980	-1	C-97	1.2
1943	Chi-N	87	266	20	63	5	2	2	23	24	33	.237	.302	.293	596	73	-9	6			.977	-16	C-81	-2.2
1946	Chi-N	95	307	38	88	18	5	4	34	22	39	.287	.338	.417	755	116	5	2			.991	-2	C-89	0.8
1947	Chi-N	86	234	25	59	12	4	3	30	20	20	.252	.314	.376	690	86	-5	1			.984	7	C-64	0.5
1948	Chi-N☆	69	172	10	36	4	2	1	7	15	25	.209	.273	.273	546	50	-12	0			.973	5	C-51	-0.5
1949	Pit-N	91	241	30	57	9	3	4	21	24	30	.237	.316	.349	665	76	-8	1			.985	8	C-90	0.4
1950	Pit-N	103	279	28	71	16	4	6	34	31	35	.254	.340	.405	745	92	-3	3			.985	-8	*C-100	-0.6
1951	Pit-N	92	259	26	77	9	2	8	39	27	31	.297	.366	.440	806	113	5	2	0	0	.988	10	C-87	1.9
1952	Pit-N	66	172	10	40	5	1	1	15	10	18	.233	.283	.291	573	58	-10	0	1	-0	.981	7	C-61/1-1	-0.1
1953	Chi-N☆	77	229	21	59	3	2	6	23	15	23	.258	.303	.367	670	72	-10	0	0	0	.987	-3	C-73	-0.9
1954	Chi-N	31	81	9	21	7	0	3	17	5	5	.259	.310	.457	767	96	-1	0	0	0	.981	-2	C-26/3-3	-0.1
1955	Chi-N	44	81	7	16	0	0	0	10	8	15	.198	.278	.198	475	29	-8	0	0	0	.989	7	C-37	0.0
1956	Chi-N	14	19	0	4	1	0	0	1	0	5	.211	.211	.263	474	27	-2	0	0	0	1.000	1	/C-7	-0.1
Total	15	1098	3121	308	785	121	28	52	339	265	398	.252	.314	.358	672	85	-68	27	1		.984	7	C-989/3-3,1-1	-1.2
■ **HARRY McCURDY** McCurdy, Harry Henry "Hank" b: 9/15/1899, Stevens Point, Wis. d: 7/21/72, Houston, Tex. BL/TR, 5'11", 187 lbs. Deb: 7/4/22																								
1922	StL-N	13	27	3	8	2	2	0	5	1	1	.296	.321	.519	840	119	1	0	0	0	.967	-1	/C-9,1-2	0.0
1923	StL-N	67	185	17	49	11	2	0	15	11	11	.265	.306	.346	652	73	-7	3	1	0	.969	-7	C-58	-1.0
1926	Chi-A	44	86	16	28	7	2	1	11	6	10	.326	.370	.488	858	127	3	0	1	-0	.974	-4	C-25/1-8	0.0
1927	Chi-A	86	262	34	75	19	3	1	27	32	24	.286	.366	.393	759	99	0	6	4	-0	.972	-3	C-82	0.2
1928	Chi-A	49	103	12	27	10	0	2	13	8	15	.262	.315	.417	733	92	-2	1	3	-1	.964	-4	C-34	-0.4
1930	Phi-N	80	148	23	49	6	2	1	25	15	12	.331	.393	.419	812	90	-2	0			.966	-5	C-41	-0.5
1931	Phi-N	66	150	21	43	9	0	1	25	23	16	.287	.382	.367	748	95	-0	2			.968	-1	C-45	0.1
1932	Phi-N	62	136	13	32	6	1	1	14	17	13	.235	.325	.316	641	65	-6	0			.974	-1	C-42	-0.5
1933	Phi-N	73	54	9	15	1	0	2	12	16	6	.278	.451	.407	858	130	3	0			.000	0	/C-2	0.3

YEAR	TM/L	G	AB	R	H	2B	3B	HR	RBI	BB	SO	AVG	OBP	SLG	OPS	OPS+	BR+	SB	CS	SBR	FA	FR	G/POS	TPR
1934	Cin-N	3	6	0	0	0	0	0	1	0	0	.000	.000	.000	0	-99	-2	0			1.000	1	/1-1	-0.1
Total	10	543	1157	148	326	71	12	9	148	129	108	.282	.355	.387	743	92	-12	12	9		.970	-24	C-338/1-11	-1.9
■ TERRY McDANIEL McDaniel, Terrence Keith b: 12/6/66, Kansas City, Mo. BR/TR, 5'9", 205 lbs. Deb: 8/31/91																								
1991	NY-N	23	29	3	6	1	0	0	2	1	11	.207	.233	.241	475	34	-3	2	0	0	1.000	-3	O-14(7-5-4)	-0.5
■ RAY McDAVID McDavid, Ray Darnell b: 7/20/71, San Diego, Cal. BL/TR, 6'3", 190 lbs. Deb: 7/15/94																								
1994	SD-N	9	28	2	7	1	0	0	2	1	8	.250	.276	.286	562	48	-2	1	0	0	1.000	-0	/O-7(4-2-1)	-0.2
1995	SD-N	11	17	2	3	0	0	0	0	2	6	.176	.263	.176	440	19	-2	1	1	-0	1.000	-2	/O-7(0-7-0)	-0.4
Total	2	20	45	4	10	1	0	0	2	3	14	.222	.271	.244	515	37	-4	2	1	0	1.000	-2	/O-14(4-9-1)	-0.6
■ RED McDERMOTT McDermott, Frank A. b: 11/12/1889, Philadelphia, Pa. d: 9/11/64, Philadelphia, Pa. BR/TR, 5'6", 150 lbs. Deb: 8/6/12																								
1912	Det-A	5	15	2	4	1	0	0	0	0		.267	.313	.333	646	87	-0	1			1.000	-0	/O-5(5-0-0)	-0.1
■ JOE McDERMOTT McDermott, Joseph Deb: 5/4/1871																								
1871	Kek-n	2	8	3	2	0	0	0	1	1	1	.250	.333	.250	583	70	-0	1	0	0	.500	-0	/O-2(0-2-0)	0.0
1872	Eck-n	7	32	3	9	3	0	0	3	1	2	.281	.303	.375	678	126	2	0	0	0	.643	0	/P-7	0.0
Total	2 n	9	40	6	11	3	0	0	4	2	3	.275	.310	.350	660	112	1	1	0	0	.643	-0	/P-7,O-2(0-2-0)	0.0
■ MICKEY McDERMOTT McDermott, Maurice Joseph "Maury" b: 8/29/28, Poughkeepsie, N.Y. BL/TL, 6'2", 170 lbs. Deb: 4/24/48 C																								
1948	Bos-A	7	8	2	3	1	0	0	0	0	0	.375	.375	.500	875	125	0	0	0	0	1.000	1	/P-7	0.0
1949	Bos-A	12	33	3	7	3	0	0	6	3	6	.212	.278	.303	581	50	-2	0	0	0	.941	-0	P-12	0.0
1950	Bos-A	39	44	11	16	5	0	0	12	9	3	.364	.472	.477	949	131	3	0	0	0	.938	1	P-38	0.0
1951	Bos-A	43	66	8	18	1	1	1	6	3	14	.273	.314	.364	678	76	-2	0	1	-0	.950	1	P-34	0.0
1952	Bos-A	36	62	10	14	1	1	1	7	4	11	.226	.273	.323	595	60	-3	0	0	0	.944	-0	P-30	0.0
1953	Bos-A	45	93	9	28	8	0	1	13	2	13	.301	.316	.419	735	92	-1	0	1	-0	.957	1	P-32	0.0
1954	Was-A	54	95	7	19	3	0	0	4	7	12	.200	.255	.232	486	36	-8	0	0	0	.955	1	P-30	0.0
1955	Was-A	70	95	10	25	4	0	1	10	6	16	.263	.314	.337	651	79	-3	1	0	0	.943	0	P-31	0.0
1956	*NY-A	46	52	4	11	0	0	1	4	8	13	.212	.317	.269	586	58	-3	0	0	0	1.000	-0	P-23	0.0
1957	KC-A	58	49	6	12	1	0	4	7	9	16	.245	.362	.510	872	133	2	0	0	0	.960	1	P-29/1-2	0.0
1958	Det-A	4	3	0	1	0	0	0	1	0	2	.333	.333	.333	667	78	-0	0	0	0	.000	-0	/P-2	0.0
1961	StL-N	22	14	1	1	1	0	0	3	0	4	.071	.071	.143	214	-41	-3	0	0	0	1.000	-0	P-19	0.0
	KC-A	7	5	0	1	1	0	0	1	1	2	.200	.333	.400	733	93	-0	0	0	0	.500	-0	/P-4	0.0
Total	12	443	619	71	156	29	2	9	74	52	112	.252	.312	.349	661	76	-22	1	2	-0	.951	4	P-291/1-2	0.0
■ TERRY McDERMOTT McDermott, Terrence Michael b: 3/20/51, Rockville Cen., N.Y BR/TR, 6'3", 205 lbs. Deb: 9/12/72																								
1972	LA-N	9	23	2	3	0	0	0	0	2	8	.130	.200	.130	330	-5	-3	0	0	0	1.000	-1	/1-7	-0.4
■ SANDY McDERMOTT McDermott, Thomas Nathaniel b: 3/15/1856, Zanesville, Ohio d: 11/23/22, Mansfield, Ohio Deb: 6/18/1885																								
1885	Bal-a	1	0	0	0	0	0	0	0	0		—	—	—	—	—	0				.000	0	/2-1	0.0
■ McDONALD McDonald Deb: 5/18/1872																								
1872	Eck-n	1	4	0	0	0	0	0	0	0	0	.000	.000	.000	0	-99	-1	0	0	0	.333	-1	/S-1	-0.2
■ TEX McDONALD McDonald, Charles E. (b: Charles C. Crabtree) b: 1/31/1891, Farmersville, Tex. d: 3/31/43, Houston, Tex. BL/TR, 5'10", 160 lbs. Deb: 4/11/12 Career OF: (14-LF 1-CF 141-RF)																								
1912	Cin-N	61	140	16	36	3	4	1	15	13	24	.257	.329	.357	686	90	-2	5			.915	-9	S-42	-0.8
1913	Cin-N	11	10	1	3	0	0	0	2	0	1	.300	.300	.300	600	72	-0	0			.000	0	/S-1	0.0
	Bos-N	62	145	24	52	4	4	0	18	15	17	.359	.422	.441	864	144	9	4			.869	-1	3-31/2-6,O-1(0-0-1)	0.9
	Yr	73	155	25	55	4	4	0	20	15	18	.355	.415	.432	847	140	8	4			.869	-1	3-31/2-6,S-1,O-1R	0.9
1914	Pit-F	67	223	27	71	16	7	3	29	13	23	.318	.361	.493	855	132	6	9			.925	-3	O-29(0-0-29),2-27/S-5	0.2
	Buf-F	69	250	32	74	13	6	3	32	20	26	.296	.353	.432	785	111	-0	11			.953	-3	O-61(2-1-58),2-10	-0.6
	Yr	136	473	59	145	29	13	6	61	33	49	.307	.357	.461	818	121	5	20			.943	-6	O-90(2-1-87),2-37/S-5	-0.4
1915	Buf-F	87	251	31	68	9	6	6	39	27	34	.271	.346	.426	773	114	1	5			.924	-7	O-65(12-0-53)	-1.0
Total	4	357	1019	131	304	45	27	13	135	88	125	.298	.359	.434	793	118	13	34			.936	-22	O-156R/S-48,2-43,3	-1.3
■ JACK McDONALD McDonald, Daniel b: 1847, Brooklyn, N.Y. d: 11/23/1880, Brooklyn, N.Y. 5'11", 154 lbs. Deb: 5/2/1872																								
1872	Atl-n	15	62	9	16	3	1	0	4	0	1	.258	.258	.339	597	70	-3	0	0	0	.720	-2	O-15(1-0-14)	-0.3
■ DAVE McDONALD McDonald, David Bruce b: 5/20/43, New Albany, Ind. BL/TR, 6'3", 215 lbs. Deb: 9/15/69																								
1969	NY-A	9	23	0	5	1	0	0	2	2	5	.217	.280	.261	541	54	-1	0	1	-0	.960	-1	/1-7	-0.3
1971	Mon-N	24	39	3	4	2	0	1	4	4	14	.103	.186	.231	417	17	-4	0	0	0	.983	-1	/1-8,O-1(1-0-0)	-0.6
Total	2	33	62	3	9	3	0	1	6	6	19	.145	.221	.242	463	31	-6	0	1	-0	.972	-1	/1-15,O-1(1-0-0)	-0.9
■ ED McDONALD McDonald, Edward C. b: 10/28/1886, Albany, N.Y. d: 3/11/46, Albany, N.Y. BR/TR, 6', 180 lbs. Deb: 8/5/11																								
1911	Bos-N	54	175	28	36	7	3	1	21	40	39	.206	.359	.297	657	78	-4	11			.955	-6	3-53/S-1	-0.8
1912	Bos-N	121	459	70	119	23	6	2	34	70	91	.259	.363	.349	712	94	-2	22			.940	0	*3-118	0.1
1913	Chi-N	1	0	0	0	0	0	0	0	0	0	—	—	—	—	—	0	0			.000	0	R	0.0
Total	3	176	634	98	155	30	9	3	55	110	130	.244	.362	.334	697	89	-6	33			.945	-6	3-171/S-1	-0.7
■ JIM McDONALD McDonald, James b: Philadelphia, Pa. BR/TR, 6', 180 lbs. Deb: 6/2/02																								
1902	NY-N	2	9	0	3	0	0	0	1	0		.333	.333	.333	667	107	0	0			1.000	-0	/O-2(0-0-2)	0.0
■ JIM McDONALD McDonald, James A. b: 8/6/1860, San Francisco, Cal. d: 9/14/14, San Francisco, Cal. Deb: 6/20/1884 Career OF: (1-LF 13-CF 3-RF)																								
1884	Was-U	2	6	0	1	0	0	0		0		.167	.167	.167	333	1	-1				.700	-1	/C-1,O-1(0-0-1)	-0.2
	Pit-a	38	145	11	23	3	0	0		2		.159	.170	.179	349	14	-13				.795	-6	3-22,O-15(1-12-2)/2-1	-1.8
1885	Buf-N	5	14	0	0	0	0	0	0	0	4	.000	.000	.000	0	-97	-3				.875	2	/S-4,O-1(0-1-0)	-0.1
Total	2	45	165	11	24	3	0	0	0	2	4	.145	.156	.164	319	4	-17				.848	-6	/3-22,O-17C,S-4,2C	-2.1
■ JASON McDONALD McDonald, Jason Adam b: 3/20/72, Modesto, Cal. BB/TR, 5'8", 175 lbs. Deb: 6/5/97 Career OF: (70-LF 155-CF 64-RF)																								
1997	Oak-A	78	236	47	62	11	4	4	14	36	49	.263	.363	.394	757	99	1	13	8	0	.961	-10	O-74(17-66-0)	-0.9
1998	Oak-A	70	175	25	44	9	0	1	16	27	33	.251	.361	.320	681	81	-4	10	4	1	.956	-3	O-60(11-33-25)	-0.6
1999	Oak-A	100	187	26	39	2	1	3	8	25	48	.209	.312	.278	590	54	-12	6	3	0	.993	-13	O-89C/2-1,D-5	-2.4
2000	Tex-A	38	94	15	22	5	0	3	13	17	25	.234	.357	.383	740	85	-2	4	4	-1	.988	4	O-32(11-3-26)	0.0
Total	4	286	692	113	167	27	5	11	51	105	155	.241	.348	.342	690	81	-18	33	19	1	.973	-22	O-255C/D-5,2-1	-3.9
■ JOHN McDONALD McDonald, John Joseph b: 9/24/74, New London, Conn. BR/TR, 5'11", 175 lbs. Deb: 7/4/99																								
1999	Cle-A	18	21	2	7	0	0	0	0	0	3	.333	.333	.333	667	68	-1	0	1	-0	1.000	5	/2-7,S-6	0.4
2000	Cle-A	9	9	0	4	0	0	0	0	0	1	.444	.444	.444	889	123	0	0	0	0	1.000	1	/S-7,2-2	0.2
Total	2	27	30	2	11	0	0	0	0	0	4	.367	.367	.367	733	84	-1	0	1	-0	.950	7	/S-13,2-9	0.6
■ JOE McDONALD McDonald, Malcolm Joseph b: 4/9/1888, Texas d: 5/30/63, Baytown, Tex. BR/TR, 5'11", 175 lbs. Deb: 9/6/10																								
1910	StL-A	10	32	4	5	0	0	0	1	1		.156	.182	.156	338	6	-3	0			.821	-3	3-10	-0.7
■ KEITH McDONALD McDonald, William Keith b: 2/8/73, Yokosuka, Japan BR/TR, 6'2", 215 lbs. Deb: 7/4/2000																								
2000	StL-N	6	7	3	3	0	0	3	5	2	1	.429	.556	1.714	2270	441	4	0	0	0	1.000	0	/C-4	0.3
■ JIM McDONNELL McDonnell, James William "Mack" b: 8/15/22, Gagetown, Mich. d: 4/24/93, Detroit, Mich. BL/TR, 5'11", 165 lbs. Deb: 9/23/43																								
1943	Cle-A	2	1	1	0	0	0	0	0	2	1	.000	.667	.000	667	108	0	0	0	0	1.000	-0	/C-1	0.0
1944	Cle-A	20	43	5	10	0	0	0	4	4	3	.233	.298	.233	530	55	-2	0	0	0	.900	-2	C-13	-0.4
1945	Cle-A	28	51	3	10	2	0	0	8	2	4	.196	.226	.235	462	36	-4	0	0	0	.980	8	C-23	0.5
Total	3	50	95	9	20	2	0	0	12	8	8	.211	.272	.232	503	48	-6	0	0	0	.953	6	/C-37	0.1

YEAR	TM/L	G	AB	R	H	2B	3B	HR	RBI	BB	SO	AVG	OBP	SLG	OPS	OPS+	BR+	SB	CS	SBR	FA	FR	G/POS	TPR
■ **ED McDONOUGH**	McDonough, Edward Sebastian b: 9/11/1886, Elgin, Ill. d: 9/2/26, Elgin, Ill. BR/TR, 6', 160 lbs. Deb: 8/3/09																							
1909	Phi-N	1	1	0	0	0	0	0	0	0		.000	.000	.000	0	-99	-0	0			1.000	0	/C-1	0.0
1910	Phi-N	5	9	1	1	0	0	0	0	0	1	.111	.111	.111	222	-34	-2	0			1.000	-1	/C-4	-0.2
Total	2	6	10	1	1	0	0	0	0	0	1	.100	.100	.100	200	-40	-2	0			1.000	-1	/C-5	-0.2
■ **GIL McDOUGALD**	McDougald, Gilbert James b: 5/19/28, San Francisco, Cal BR/TR, 6'1", 180 lbs. Deb: 4/20/51																							
1951	*NY-A	131	402	72	123	23	4	14	63	56	54	.306	.396	.488	884	143	25	14	5	1	.949	-16	3-82,2-55	1.3
1952	*NY-A★	152	555	65	146	16	5	11	78	57	73	.263	.336	.369	705	102	1	6	5	-0	.968	12	*3-117,2-38	1.5
1953	*NY-A	141	541	82	154	27	7	10	83	60	65	.285	.361	.416	777	113	10	3	4	-1	.953	6	*3-136,2-26	1.5
1954	NY-A	126	394	66	102	22	2	12	48	62	64	.259	.367	.416	783	118	11	3	4	-1	.989	1	2-92,3-35	1.8
1955	*NY-A	141	533	79	152	10	8	13	53	65	77	.285	.365	.407	772	109	7	6	4	-0	**.985**	19	*2-126,3-17	3.5
1956	*NY-A☆	120	438	79	136	13	3	13	56	68	59	.311	.407	.443	850	128	20	3	8	-2	.970	3	S-92,2-31/3-5	3.0
1957	*NY-A★	141	539	87	156	25	**9**	13	62	59	71	.289	.364	.442	805	121	16	2	5	-1	.976	15	*S-121,2-21/3-7	4.2
1958	*NY-A★	138	503	69	126	19	1	14	65	59	75	.250	.333	.376	708	98	-1	6	2	1	.977	-3	*2-115,S-19	0.7
1959	NY-A★	127	434	44	109	16	8	4	34	35	40	.251	.311	.353	664	85	-9	0	3	-1	.989	8	2-53,S-52,3-25	0.5
1960	*NY-A	119	337	54	87	16	4	8	34	38	45	.258	.339	.401	739	105	2	2	4	-1	.945	-3	3-84,2-42	0.0
Total	10	1336	4676	697	1291	187	51	112	576	559	623	.276	.358	.410	768	112	82	45	44	-6	.984	42	2-599,3-508,S-284	18.0
■ **ODDIBE McDOWELL**	McDowell, Oddibe b: 8/25/62, Hollywood, Fla. BL/TL, 5'9", 165 lbs. Deb: 5/19/85																							
1985	Tex-A	111	406	63	97	14	5	18	42	36	85	.239	.306	.431	737	98	-2	25	7	3	.993	10	*O-103(0-103-0)/D-4	1.0
1986	Tex-A	154	572	105	152	24	7	18	49	65	112	.266	.342	.427	768	105	4	33	15	2	.991	3	*O-148(0-147-0)/D-1	0.8
1987	Tex-A	128	407	65	98	26	4	14	52	51	99	.241	.325	.428	753	97	-2	24	2	5	.989	-2	*O-125(0-126-0)	0.0
1988	Tex-A	120	437	55	108	19	5	6	37	41	89	.247	.315	.355	669	85	-9	33	10	4	.989	-3	*O-113(0-113-0)/D-3	-0.9
1989	Cle-A	69	239	33	53	5	2	3	22	25	36	.222	.298	.297	595	67	-10	12	5	1	.992	2	O-64(63-1-0)/D-2	-1.0
	Atl-N	76	280	56	85	18	4	7	24	27	37	.304	.365	.471	836	134	12	15	10	-0	.978	5	O-68(0-68-0)	1.7
1990	Atl-N	113	305	47	74	14	0	7	25	21	53	.243	.296	.357	653	74	-11	13	2	2	.971	-6	O-72(12-60-1)	-1.6
1994	Tex-A	59	183	34	48	5	1	1	15	28	39	.262	.360	.317	677	77	-5	14	2	2	.983	-4	O-53(0-31-27)/D-2	-0.7
Total	7	830	2829	458	715	125	28	74	266	294	550	.253	.325	.395	720	94	-22	169	53	19	.987	5	O-746(75-649-28)/D-12	-0.7
■ **PRYOR McELVEEN**	McElveen, Pryor Mynatt "Humpty" b: 11/5/1881, Atlanta, Ga. d: 10/27/51, Pleasant Hill, Tenn. BR/TR, 5'10", 168 lbs. Deb: 4/26/09																							
1909	Bro-N	81	258	22	51	8	1	3	25	14		.198	.242	.271	513	61	-13	6			.938	-5	3-37,O-13R,S-10,/12	-1.9
1910	Bro-N	74	213	19	48	8	3	1	26	22	47	.225	.307	.305	612	81	-5	6			.943	-5	3-54/S-6,2-3,C-1	-0.9
1911	Bro-N	16	31	1	6	0	0	0	5	0	3	.194	.194	.194	387	9	-4	0			.929	-1	/2-5,S-1	-0.5
Total	3	171	502	42	105	16	4	4	56	36	50	.209	.268	.281	548	67	-21	12			.941	-11	/3-91,S-17,2-13,O1C	-3.3
■ **LEE McELWEE**	McElwee, Leland Stanford b: 5/23/1894, LaMesa, Cal. d: 2/8/57, Union, Maine BR/TR, 5'10.5", 160 lbs. Deb: 7/3/16																							
1916	Phi-A	54	155	9	41	3	0	0	10	8	17	.265	.301	.284	584	79	-4	0			.883	-2	3-30/O-9R,2-3,1S	-0.6
■ **FRANK McELYEA**	McElyea, Frank b: 8/4/18, Hawthorne Twsp., Ill. d: 4/19/87, Evansville, Ind. BR/TR, 6'6", 221 lbs. Deb: 9/10/42																							
1942	Bos-N	7	4	2	0	0	0	0	0	0	0	.000	.000	.000	0	-99	-1	0			1.000	-0	/O-1(1-0-0)	-0.1
■ **JOE McEWING**	McEwing, Joseph Earl b: 10/19/72, Bristol, Pa. BR/TR, 5'10", 170 lbs. Deb: 9/2/98 Career OF: (76-LF 35-CF 26-RF)																							
1998	StL-N	10	20	5	4	1	0	0	1	1	3	.200	.273	.250	523	39	-2	0	1	-0	1.000	-1	/2-6,O-3(1-1-1)	-0.3
1999	StL-N	152	513	65	141	28	4	9	44	41	87	.275	.336	.398	733	84	-12	7	4	0	.980	0	2-96,O-66L/3-6,1S	-0.9
2000	*NY-N	87	153	20	34	14	1	2	19	5	29	.222	.252	.366	618	55	-11	3	1	0	1.000	-11	O-52L,3-19,2-16,/S	-2.0
Total	3	249	686	90	179	43	5	11	64	47	119	.261	.316	.386	702	77	-25	10	6	0	.994	-11	O-121L,2-118/3-25,S1	-3.2
■ **GUY McFADDEN**	McFadden, Guy G. b: 9/3/1872, Topeka, Kan. d: 3/10/11, Topeka, Kan. Deb: 8/24/1895																							
1895	StL-N	4	14	1	3	0	0	0	2	0	2	.214	.214	.214	429	11	-2	0			.968	-1	/1-4	-0.2
■ **LEON McFADDEN**	McFadden, Leon b: 4/26/44, Little Rock, Ark. BR/TR, 6'2", 195 lbs. Deb: 9/6/68																							
1968	Hou-N	16	47	2	13	1	0	0	1	6	10	.277	.358	.298	656	101	0	1	0	0	.968	-1	S-16	0.1
1969	Hou-N	44	74	3	13	2	0	0	3	4	9	.176	.218	.203	421	19	-8	1	2	-0	.944	-3	O-17(4-0-13)/S-8	-1.2
1970	Hou-N	2	0	0	0	0	0	0	0	0	0	—	—	—	—	—	0	0	0	0	.000	0	R	0.0
Total	3	62	121	5	26	3	0	0	4	10	19	.215	.275	.240	514	50	-8	2	2	-0	.966	-4	/S-24,O-17(4-0-13)	-1.1
■ **ALEX McFARLAN**	McFarlan, Alexander Shepherd b: 11/11/1866, Kentucky d: 3/2/39, Pewee Valley, Ky. Deb: 6/19/1892 F																							
1892	Lou-N	14	42	2	7	0	0	0	1	8	11	.167	.300	.167	467	46	-2	1			.773	-3	O-12(0-0-12)/2-2	-0.5
■ **CHRIS McFARLAND**	McFarland, Christopher b: 8/17/1861, Fall River, Mass. d: 5/24/18, New Bedford, Mass. 5'9", 170 lbs. Deb: 4/19/1884																							
1884	Bal-U	3	14	2	3	1	0	0		0		.214	.214	.286	500	46	-1				.571	-1	/O-3(0-3-0),P-1	-0.2
■ **ED McFARLAND**	McFarland, Edward William b: 8/3/1874, Cleveland, Ohio d: 11/28/59, Cleveland, Ohio BR/TR, 5'10", 180 lbs. Deb: 7/7/1893 Career OF: (3-LF 5-CF 2-RF)																							
1893	Cle-N	8	22	5	9	2	1	0	6	1	2	.409	.458	.591	1049	168	2	0			1.000	-4	/O-5(0-5-0),3-2,C-1	-0.1
1896	StL-N	83	290	48	70	13	4	3	36	15	17	.241	.281	.345	626	67	-15	7			.961	8	C-80/O-2(0-0-2)	0.1
1897	StL-N	31	107	14	35	5	2	1	17	8		.327	.374	.439	813	117	2	2			.965	2	C-23/1-3,O-3L,2-1	0.5
	Phi-N	38	130	18	29	3	5	1	16	14		.223	.308	.346	654	75	-5	2			.951	-2	C-37	-0.3
	Yr	69	237	32	64	8	7	2	33	22		.270	.337	.388	725	93	-3	4			.957	0	C-60/1-3,O-3L,2-1	0.2
1898	Phi-N	121	429	65	121	21	5	3	71	44		.282	.352	.375	727	113	8	4			.960	-1	*C-121	1.6
1899	Phi-N	96	324	59	108	22	9	2	57	36		.333	.403	.475	879	146	21	9			.968	13	C-94	3.8
1900	Phi-N	94	344	50	105	14	8	0	38	29		.305	.364	.392	757	110	5	9			**.963**	-3	C-93/3-1	1.0
1901	Phi-N	74	295	33	84	14	2	1	32	18		.285	.326	.356	682	96	-2	11			.970	2	C-74	0.7
1902	Chi-A	75	246	29	56	9	2	1	25	19		.228	.291	.293	584	65	-11	8			.967	2	C-69/1-1	-0.2
1903	Chi-A	61	201	15	42	7	2	1	19	14		.209	.264	.279	542	66	-8	3			.968	-0	C-56/1-1	-0.3
1904	Chi-A	50	160	22	44	11	3	0	20	17		.275	.348	.381	730	136	7	2			.975	-11	C-49	0.1
1905	Chi-A	80	250	24	70	13	4	0	31	23		.280	.345	.364	709	130	9	5			.973	6	C-70	2.4
1906	*Chi-A	12	23	0	4	1	0	0	3	3		.174	.269	.217	487	54	-1	0			.973	-1	/C-7	-0.1
1907	Chi-A	52	138	11	39	9	1	0	8	12		.283	.340	.362	702	128	4	3			.972	-2	C-43	0.7
1908	Bos-A	19	48	5	10	2	1	0	4	1		.208	.224	.292	516	66	-0	0			.978	4	C-13	0.3
Total	14	894	3007	398	826	146	49	13	383	254	19	.275	.335	.369	704	104	13	65			.967	15	C-830/O-10C,1-5,32	10.2
■ **HERM McFARLAND**	McFarland, Hermas Walter b: 3/11/1870, Des Moines, Iowa d: 9/21/35, Richmond, Va. BL/TR, 5'6", 150 lbs. Deb: 4/21/1896																							
1896	Lou-N	30	110	11	21	4	1	1	12	9	14	.191	.252	.273	525	40	-10	4			.833	-3	O-28(3-18-9)/C-1	-1.3
1898	Cin-N	19	64	10	18	1	3	0	11	7		.281	.361	.391	752	108	1	3			.968	-2	O-17(13-3-1)	-0.3
1901	Chi-A	132	473	83	130	21	9	4	59	75		.275	.384	.383	767	116	14	33			.946	5	*O-132(132-0-0)	1.0
1902	Chi-A	7	27	5	5	0	0	0	4	2		.185	.241	.185	427	20	-3	1			1.000	-0	/O-7(2-0-5)	-0.3
	Bal-A	61	242	54	78	19	6	3	36	36		.322	.418	.488	906	144	16	10			.965	6	O-61(0-61-0)	1.8
	Yr	68	269	59	83	19	6	3	40	38		.309	.402	.457	859	133	13	11			.967	6	O-68(2-61-5)	1.5
1903	NY-A	103	362	41	88	16	9	5	45	46		.243	.333	.378	712	106	4	13			.939	-3	*O-103(39-58-7)	-0.5
Total	5	352	1278	204	340	61	28	13	167	175	14	.266	.362	.388	750	110	21	64			.941	2	O-348(189-140-22)/C-1	0.4
■ **HOWIE McFARLAND**	McFarland, Howard Alexander b: 3/7/10, ElReno, Okla. d: 4/7/93, Wichita, Kan. BR/TR, 6', 175 lbs. Deb: 7/16/45																							
1945	Was-A	6	11	0	1	0	0	0	2	0	3	.091	.091	.091	182	-52	-2	0	0	0	1.000	-0	/O-3(1-0-2)	-0.3
■ **ORLANDO McFARLANE**	McFarlane, Orlando Dejesus (Quesada) b: 6/28/38, Oriente, Cuba BR/TR, 6', 180 lbs. Deb: 4/23/62																							
1962	Pit-N	8	23	0	2	0	0	0	1	1	4	.087	.125	.087	212	-42	-5	0	0	0	1.000	2	/C-8	-0.2
1964	Pit-N	37	78	5	19	5	0	0	1	4	27	.244	.280	.308	588	66	-4	0	0	0	.983	-6	C-35/O-1(0-0-1)	-0.9
1966	Det-A	49	138	16	35	7	0	5	13	9	46	.254	.304	.413	717	102	0	0	0	0	.991	-2	C-33	0.0
1967	Cal-A	12	22	0	5	0	0	0	3	1	7	.227	.261	.227	488	47	-1	0	0	0	.935	-1	/C-6	-0.2
1968	Cal-A	18	31	1	9	0	0	0	2	5	9	.290	.389	.290	679	112	1	0	0	0	.977	-0	/C-9	0.1
Total	5	124	292	22	70	12	0	5	20	20	93	.240	.291	.332	623	78	-9	0	0	0	.985	-8	/C-91,O-1(0-0-1)	-1.2

■ **PATSY McGAFFIGAN** McGaffigan, Mark Andrew b: 9/12/1888, Carlyle, Ill. d: 12/22/40, Carlyle, Ill. BR/TR, 5'8", 140 lbs. Deb: 4/16/17

YEAR	TM/L	G	AB	R	H	2B	3B	HR	RBI	BB	SO	AVG	OBP	SLG	OPS	OPS+	BR+	SB	CS	SBR	FA	FR	G/POS	TPR
1917	Phi-N	19	60	5	10	1	0	0	6	0	7	.167	.167	.183	350	7	-7	1			.920	-1	S-17/O-1(0-0-1)	-0.7
1918	Phi-N	54	192	17	39	3	2	1	8	16	23	.203	.268	.255	523	56	-10	3			.948	-12	2-53/S-1	-2.4
Total	2	73	252	22	49	4	2	1	14	16	30	.194	.245	.238	483	45	-16	4			.923	-12	/2-53,S-18,O-1(0-0-1)	-3.1

■ **EDDIE McGAH** McGah, Edward Joseph b: 9/30/21, Oakland, Cal. BR/TR, 6', 183 lbs. Deb: 4/26/46

YEAR	TM/L	G	AB	R	H	2B	3B	HR	RBI	BB	SO	AVG	OBP	SLG	OPS	OPS+	BR+	SB	CS	SBR	FA	FR	G/POS	TPR
1946	Bos-A	15	37	2	8	1	1	0	1	7	7	.216	.341	.297	638	75	-1	0	0	0	.981	-2	C-14	-0.3
1947	Bos-A	9	14	1	0	0	0	0	2	3	0	.000	.176	.000	176	-45	-3	0	0	0	.964	2	/C-7	-0.1
Total	2	24	51	3	8	1	1	0	3	10	7	.157	.295	.216	511	41	-4	0	0	0	.975	-0	/C-21	-0.4

■ **AMBROSE McGANN** McGann, Ambrose b: 1875, Baltimore, Md. 170 lbs. Deb: 5/2/1895

YEAR	TM/L	G	AB	R	H	2B	3B	HR	RBI	BB	SO	AVG	OBP	SLG	OPS	OPS+	BR+	SB	CS	SBR	FA	FR	G/POS	TPR
1895	Lou-N	20	73	9	21	5	2	0	9	8	6	.288	.358	.411	769	105	1	6			.852	-2	/S-8,3-6,O-5(0-0-5)	-0.1

■ **DAN McGANN** McGann, Dennis Lawrence "Cap" b: 7/15/1871, Shelbyville, Ky. d: 12/13/10, Louisville, Ky. BB/TR, 6', 190 lbs. Deb: 8/8/1896

YEAR	TM/L	G	AB	R	H	2B	3B	HR	RBI	BB	SO	AVG	OBP	SLG	OPS	OPS+	BR+	SB	CS	SBR	FA	FR	G/POS	TPR
1896	Bos-N	43	171	25	55	6	7	2	30	12	10	.322	.383	.474	857	118	4	2			.905	-17	2-43	-0.9
1898	Bal-N	145	535	99	161	18	8	5	106	53		.301	.404	.393	796	126	22	33			.983	2	*1-145	2.1
1899	Bro-N	63	214	49	52	11	4	2	32	21		.243	.362	.360	722	96	-0	16			.985	2	1-61	0.1
	Was-N	76	280	65	96	9	8	5	58	14		.343	.410	.486	896	147	18	11			.990	2	1-76	1.8
	Yr	139	494	114	148	20	12	7	90	35		.300	.389	.431	820	124	18	27			**.988**	4	*1-137	1.9
1900	StL-N	121	444	79	132	10	9	4	58	32		.297	.376	.387	763	112	8	26			**.990**	-1	*1-121/2-1	0.6
1901	StL-N	103	423	73	115	15	9	6	56	16		.272	.333	.392	726	116	8	17			.984	-3	*1-103	0.3
1902	Bal-A	68	250	40	79	10	8	0	42	19		.316	.378	.420	798	116	6	17			.987	3	1-68	0.7
	NY-N	61	227	25	68	5	7	0	21	12		.300	.356	.383	740	129	8	12			.981	2	1-61	0.9
1903	NY-N	129	482	75	130	21	6	3	50	32		.270	.331	.357	688	92	-5	36			**.988**	-0	*1-129	-0.8
1904	NY-N	141	517	81	148	22	6	6	71	36		.286	.354	.387	741	123	14	42			**.991**	3	*1-141	1.6
1905	*NY-N	136	491	88	147	23	14	5	75	55		.299	.391	.434	825	143	27	22			**.991**	5	*1-136	3.0
1906	NY-N	134	451	62	107	14	8	0	37	60		.237	.344	.304	647	100	2	30			**.995**	3	*1-133	0.4
1907	NY-N	81	262	29	78	9	1	2	36	29		.298	.383	.363	745	129	10	9			.994	5	1-81	1.5
1908	Bos-N	135	475	52	114	8	5	2	55	38		.240	.321	.291	612	97	0	9			.988	5	*1-121/2-9	0.3
Total	12	1436	5222	842	1482	181	100	42	727	429	10	.284	.364	.381	745	117	122	282			.989	10	*1-1376/2-53	11.6

■ **CHIPPY McGARR** McGarr, James B. b: 5/10/1863, Worcester, Mass. d: 6/6/04, Worcester, Mass. BR/TR, 5'7", 168 lbs. Deb: 7/11/1884 U

YEAR	TM/L	G	AB	R	H	2B	3B	HR	RBI	BB	SO	AVG	OBP	SLG	OPS	OPS+	BR+	SB	CS	SBR	FA	FR	G/POS	TPR
1884	CP-U	19	70	10	11	2	0	0		0		.157	.157	.186	343	4	-10				.905	-6	2-13/O-6(5-0-1)	-1.4
1886	Phi-a	71	267	41	71	9	3	2	31	9		.266	.295	.345	640	99	-1	17			.850	1	S-71	0.1
1887	Phi-a	137	559	93	181	23	6	1	63	23		.324	.326	.366	692	93	-6	84			.875	-1	*S-137	-0.2
1888	StL-a	34	132	17	31	1	0	0	13	6		.235	.268	.242	511	58	-7	25			.895	-3	2-33/S-1	-0.7
1889	KC-a	25	108	22	31	3	0	0	16	6	11	.287	.330	.315	645	79	-3	12			.857	-2	3-11/O-6R,2-5,S-3	-0.4
	Bal-a	3	7	1	1	0	0	0	0	1	1	.143	.250	.143	393	13	-1	0			.583	-2	/S-3	-0.2
	Yr	28	115	23	32	3	0	0	16	7	12	.278	.325	.304	630	76	-4	12			.857	-4	3-11/O-6R,S-6,2-5	-0.6
1890	Bos-N	121	487	68	115	12	7	1	51	34	38	.236	.291	.296	587	66	-23	39			**.933**	-2	*3-115/S-5,O-1(0-0-1)	-2.0
1893	Cle-N	63	249	38	77	12	0	0	28	20	15	.309	.363	.357	720	87	-5	24			.886	0	3-63	-0.3
1894	Cle-N	128	523	94	144	24	6	2	74	28	29	.275	.316	.356	672	59	-36	31			.902	-7	*3-128	-3.2
1895	*Cle-N	113	422	86	114	14	2	2	59	35	33	.270	.328	.327	655	65	-23	19			.872	-4	*3-109/2-4	-2.0
1896	*Cle-N	113	455	68	122	16	4	1	53	22	30	.268	.302	.327	629	62	-26	16			.924	-7	*3-113/C-1	-2.7
Total	10	827	3279	538	898	116	28	9	388	184	157	.274	.311	.330	641	71	-141	267			.903	-31	3-539,S-220/2-55,OC	-13.0

■ **JIM McGARR** McGarr, James Vincent "Reds" b: 11/9/1888, Philadelphia, Pa. d: 7/21/81, Miami, Fla. BR/TR, 5'9.5", 170 lbs. Deb: 5/18/12

YEAR	TM/L	G	AB	R	H	2B	3B	HR	RBI	BB	SO	AVG	OBP	SLG	OPS	OPS+	BR+	SB	CS	SBR	FA	FR	G/POS	TPR
1912	Det-A	1	4	0	0	0	0	0	0	0	0	.000	.000	.000	0	-99	-1	0			.800	-0	/2-1	-0.2

■ **DAN McGARVEY** McGarvey, Daniel Francis b: 12/2/1887, Philadelphia, Pa. d: 3/7/47, Philadelphia, Pa. Deb: 5/18/12

YEAR	TM/L	G	AB	R	H	2B	3B	HR	RBI	BB	SO	AVG	OBP	SLG	OPS	OPS+	BR+	SB	CS	SBR	FA	FR	G/POS	TPR
1912	Det-A	1	3	0	0	0	0	0	0	0	1	.000	.400	.000	400	18	-0	0			.667	0	/O-1	0.0

■ **JACK McGEACHY** McGeachy, John Charles b: 5/23/1864, Clinton, Mass.
d: 4/5/30, Cambridge, Mass. BR/TR, 5'8", 165 lbs. Deb: 6/17/1886 Career OF: (72-LF 201-CF 331-RF)

YEAR	TM/L	G	AB	R	H	2B	3B	HR	RBI	BB	SO	AVG	OBP	SLG	OPS	OPS+	BR+	SB	CS	SBR	FA	FR	G/POS	TPR
1886	Det-N	6	27	3	9	0	1	0	4	0	3	.333	.333	.407	741	121	1	2			.875	-1	/O-6(6-0-0)	0.0
	StL-N	59	226	31	46	12	3	2	24	1	37	.204	.207	.310	517	59	-11	8			.880	2	O-55(0-55-0)/2-2,3-2	-1.0
	Yr	65	253	34	55	12	4	2	28	1	40	.217	.220	.320	541	66	-10	10			.880	1	O-61(6-55-0)/2-2,3-2	-1.0
1887	Ind-N	99	410	49	114	17	3	1	56	5	16	.278	.280	.333	613	72	-15	27			.894	7	*O-98(0-97-2)/3-1,P-1	-1.0
1888	Ind-N	118	452	45	99	15	2	0	30	5	21	.219	.231	.261	492	56	-23	49			.932	5	*O-117R/S-1,P-1	-1.9
1889	Ind-N	131	532	83	142	32	1	2	63	9	39	.267	.282	.342	624	73	-22	37			.918	9	*O-131(0-0-131)/P-3	-1.2
1890	Bro-P	104	443	84	108	24	4	1	65	19	12	.244	.278	.323	601	57	-30	21			.906	-1	*O-104(22-31-52)	-2.6
1891	Phi-a	50	201	24	46	4	3	2	13	6	12	.229	.255	.308	563	61	-11	9			.920	2	O-50(4-12-34)	-0.9
	Bos-a	41	178	26	45	2	1	1	21	12	8	.253	.304	.292	596	72	-7	11			.910	-4	O-41(38-0-3)	-1.0
	Yr	91	379	50	91	6	4	3	34	18	20	.240	.278	.301	579	66	-18	20			.916	-2	O-91(42-12-37)	-1.9
Total	6	608	2469	345	609	106	18	9	276	57	148	.247	.265	.314	579	65	-118	164			.909	18	O-602R/P-5,3-3,2S	-9.6

■ **MIKE McGEARY** McGeary, Michael Henry b: 1851, Philadelphia, Pa. BR/TR, 5'7", 138 lbs. Deb: 5/9/1871 M NA OF: (0-LF 1-CF 7-RF) Career OF: (0-LF 1-CF 2-RF)

YEAR	TM/L	G	AB	R	H	2B	3B	HR	RBI	BB	SO	AVG	OBP	SLG	OPS	OPS+	BR+	SB	CS	SBR	FA	FR	G/POS	TPR
1871	Tro-n	29	148	42	39	4	0	0	12	6	0	.264	.292	.291	583	67	-6	**20**	4	3	**.897**	-2	*C-26/S-3	-0.3
1872	Ath-n	47	225	68	81	9	2	0	35	2	1	.360	.366	.418	783	140	10	13	8	0	.867	7	C-23,S-23/O-1(0-0-1)	1.1
1873	Ath-n	52	275	63	83	8	1	0	31	1	1	.302	.304	.338	643	84	-7	3	6	-1	.805	-5	*S-44,C-13/3-1	-1.0
1874	Ath-n	54	271	61	87	10	2	0	22	1	2	.321	.324	.373	696	113	2	10	2	2	.837	7	C-28,S-26/O-4(0-0-4)	0.8
1875	Phi-n	68	310	71	90	6	2	0	37	1	1	.290	.293	.323	615	109	2	19	4	3	.743	4	3-27,2-23,S-18,/OM	0.5
1876	StL-N	61	278	48	72	3	0	0	30	2	1	.259	.266	.272	538	84	-4				.889	5	*2-56/C-5,O-1C,3-1	0.3
1877	StL-N	57	258	35	65	3	2	0	20	2	16	.252	.258	.279	537	73	-7				.883	7	2-39,3-19	0.2
1879	Pro-N	85	374	62	103	7	2	0	35	5	13	.275	.285	.305	590	96	-2				.884	1	*2-73,3-12	0.3
1880	Pro-N	18	59	5	8	0	0	0	1	0	6	.136	.136	.136	271	-8	-6				.887	3	3-17/2-2,S-1,M	-0.3
	Cle-N	31	111	14	28	2	1	0	6	4	3	.252	.278	.288	567	94	-1				.887	-4	3-29/O-2(0-0-2)	-0.4
	Yr	49	170	19	36	2	1	0	7	4	9	.212	.230	.235	465	60	-7				.887	-1	3-46/2-2,O-2R,S-1	-0.7
1881	Cle-N	11	41	1	9	0	0	0	5	0	6	.220	.220	.220	439	41	-3				.724	-7	3-11,M	-0.9
1882	Det-N	34	133	14	19	4	1	0	2	2	20	.143	.156	.188	344	10	-13				.928	8	S-33/2-3	-0.3
Total	5 n	250	1229	305	380	37	7	0	137	11	5	.309	.315	.351	666	104	1	65	24	6	.808	11	S-114/C-90,3-28,2O	1.1
Total	6	297	1254	179	304	19	6	0	99	15	55	.242	.252	.268	519	72	-35				.885	13	2-173/3-89,S-34,CO	-1.1

■ **DAN McGEE** McGee, Daniel Aloysius b: 9/29/11, New York, N.Y. d: 12/4/91, Lakehurst, N.J. BR/TR, 5'8.5", 152 lbs. Deb: 7/14/34

YEAR	TM/L	G	AB	R	H	2B	3B	HR	RBI	BB	SO	AVG	OBP	SLG	OPS	OPS+	BR+	SB	CS	SBR	FA	FR	G/POS	TPR
1934	Bos-N	7	22	2	3	0	0	0	1	3	6	.136	.240	.136	376	4	-3	0			.951	3	/S-7	0.0

■ **FRANK McGEE** McGee, Francis De Sales b: 4/28/1899, Columbus, Ohio d: 1/30/34, Columbus, Ohio BR/TR, 5'11.5", 175 lbs. Deb: 9/19/25

YEAR	TM/L	G	AB	R	H	2B	3B	HR	RBI	BB	SO	AVG	OBP	SLG	OPS	OPS+	BR+	SB	CS	SBR	FA	FR	G/POS	TPR
1925	Was-A	2	3	0	0	0	0	0	0	0	1	.000	.000	.000	0	-99	-1	0	0	0	1.000	0	/1-2	-0.1

■ **PAT McGEE** McGee, Patrick b: Philadelphia, Pa. d: 6/21/1889, New York, N.Y. Deb: 9/24/1874 Career OF: (6-LF 47-CF 0-RF)

YEAR	TM/L	G	AB	R	H	2B	3B	HR	RBI	BB	SO	AVG	OBP	SLG	OPS	OPS+	BR+	SB	CS	SBR	FA	FR	G/POS	TPR
1874	Atl-n	16	65	4	11	1	0	0	6	0	3	.169	.169	.185	354	15	-5	0	0	0	.795	-1	O-15(6-9-0)/S-2,2-1	-0.5
1875	Mut-n	25	95	4	17	2	0	0	9	0	10	.179	.179	.200	379	30	-7	0	0	0	.848	-2	O-25(0-25-0)	-0.7
	Atl-n	18	65	3	10	3	1	0	5	1	4	.154	.167	.231	397	42	-3	0	0	0	.912	6	O-13(0-13-0)/2-6,3-1	0.2
	Yr	43	160	7	27	5	1	0	14	1	14	.169	.174	.213	386	34	-10	0	0	0	.875	4	O-38(0-38-0)/2-6,3-1	-0.5
Total	2 n	59	225	11	38	6	1	0	20	1	17	.169	.173	.204	377	29	-15	0	0	0	.849	3	/O-53C,2-7,S-2,3-1	-1.0

■ **WILLIE McGEE** McGee, Willie Dean b: 11/2/58, San Francisco, Cal. BB/TR, 6'1", 175 lbs. Deb: 5/10/82 Career OF: (146-LF 1351-CF 535-RF)

YEAR	TM/L	G	AB	R	H	2B	3B	HR	RBI	BB	SO	AVG	OBP	SLG	OPS	OPS+	BR+	SB	CS	SBR	FA	FR	G/POS	TPR
1982	*StL-N	123	422	43	125	12	8	4	56	12	58	.296	.319	.391	710	97	-3	24	12	1	.958	-9	*O-117(1-116-0)	-1.2
1983	StL-N★	147	601	75	172	22	8	5	75	26	98	.286	.316	.374	690	90	-9	39	8	6	.987	8	*O-145(0-145-0)	0.4
1984	StL-N	145	571	82	166	19	11	6	50	29	80	.291	.326	.394	720	104	2	43	10	6	.985	11	*O-141(0-141-0)	1.8
1985	*StL-N★	152	612	114	**216**	26	**18**	10	82	34	86	**.353**	.387	.503	890	148	38	56	16	7	.978	13	*O-149(3-146-0)	5.7
1986	StL-N	124	497	65	127	22	7	7	48	37	82	.256	.308	.370	679	87	-10	19	16	-1	**.991**	15	*O-121(0-122-0)	0.3

YEAR	TM/L	G	AB	R	H	2B	3B	HR	RBI	BB	SO	AVG	OBP	SLG	OPS	OPS+	BR+	SB	CS	SBR	FA	FR	G/POS	TPR
1987	*StL-N★	153	620	76	177	37	11	11	105	24	90	.285	.314	.434	748	94	-7	16	4	2	.981	8	*O-152(0-152-0)/S-1	0.2
1988	StL-N★	137	562	73	164	24	6	3	50	32	84	.292	.331	.372	703	100	0	41	6	7	.975	10	*O-135(0-135-0)	1.7
1989	StL-N	58	199	23	47	10	2	3	17	10	34	.236	.276	.352	628	76	-7	8	6	-0	.976	2	O-47(0-47-0)	-0.6
1990	StL-N	125	501	76	168	32	5	3	62	38	86	**.335**	.383	.437	820	125	17	28	9	3	.957	16	*O-124(0-118-6)	3.5
	*Oak-A	29	113	23	31	3	2	0	15	10	18	.274	.333	.336	670	91	-1	3	0	1	.986	1	O-28(0-28-0)/D-1	0.0
1991	SF-N	131	497	67	155	30	3	4	43	34	74	.312	.358	.408	767	119	12	17	9	1	.978	-2	*O-128(0-89-48)	0.9
1992	SF-N	138	474	56	141	20	2	1	36	29	88	.297	.339	.354	694	102	1	13	4	1	.976	3	*O-119(0-31-90)	0.3
1993	SF-N	130	475	53	143	28	1	4	46	38	67	.301	.354	.389	744	102	2	10	9	-1	.979	0	*O-126(0-0-126)	-0.5
1994	SF-N	45	156	19	44	3	0	5	23	15	24	.282	.345	.397	742	97	-1	3	0	1	.988	0	O-42(0-0-42)	-0.2
1995	*Bos-A	67	200	32	57	11	3	2	15	9	41	.285	.316	.400	716	82	-6	5	2	0	.973	-7	O-64(3-27-47)	-1.3
1996	*StL-N	123	309	52	95	15	2	5	41	18	60	.307	.350	.417	767	102	1	5	2	0	.962	-4	O-83(35-11-42)/1-6	-0.6
1997	StL-N	122	300	29	90	19	4	3	38	22	59	.300	.348	.420	768	101	0	8	2	1	.981	-9	O-81(18-18-53)/D-3	-0.9
1998	StL-N	120	269	27	68	10	1	3	34	14	49	.253	.290	.331	621	63	-14	7	2	1	.938	-13	O-88(56-6-38)/1-1,D-3	-2.9
1999	StL-N	132	271	25	68	7	0	0	20	17	60	.251	.295	.277	572	46	-22	7	4	0	.972	-15	O-89(30-19-43)/1-3	-3.8
Total	18	2201	7649	1010	2254	350	94	79	856	448	1238	.295	.335	.396	731	100	-6	352	121	35	.976	28	*O-1979C/1-10,D-7,S	2.8

■ DAN McGEEHAN

McGeehan, Daniel De Sales b: 6/7/1885, Jeddo, Pa. d: 7/12/55, Hazleton, Pa. BR/TR, 5'6", 135 lbs. Deb: 4/22/11 F

YEAR	TM/L	G	AB	R	H	2B	3B	HR	RBI	BB	SO	AVG	OBP	SLG	OPS	OPS+	BR+	SB	CS	SBR	FA	FR	G/POS	TPR
1911	StL-N	3	9	0	2	0	0	0	1	0	1	.222	.222	.222	444	25	-1	0			.818	-1	/2-3	-0.2

■ ED McGHEE

McGhee, Warren Edward b: 9/29/24, Perry, Ark. d: 2/13/86, Memphis, Tenn. BR/TR, 5'11", 170 lbs. Deb: 9/20/50

YEAR	TM/L	G	AB	R	H	2B	3B	HR	RBI	BB	SO	AVG	OBP	SLG	OPS	OPS+	BR+	SB	CS	SBR	FA	FR	G/POS	TPR
1950	Chi-A	3	6	0	1	0	1	0	0	0	1	.167	.167	.500	667	67	-0	0	0	0	1.000	-0	/O-1(0-0-1)	-0.1
1953	Phi-A	104	358	36	94	11	4	1	29	32	43	.263	.328	.324	652	74	-12	4	3	-0	.982	7	O-99(1-97-1)	-1.0
1954	Phi-A	21	53	5	11	2	0	2	9	4	8	.208	.263	.358	622	69	-3	0	1	-0	.933	1	O-13(2-11-0)	-0.3
	Chi-A	42	75	12	17	1	0	0	5	12	8	.227	.333	.240	573	57	-4	5	0	1	.982	-3	O-34(5-18-11)	-0.7
	Yr	63	128	17	28	3	0	2	14	16	16	.219	.306	.289	595	62	-6	5	1	1	.960	-3	O-47(7-29-11)	-1.0
1955	Chi-A	26	13	6	1	0	0	0	0	6	1	.077	.368	.077	445	24	-1	2	1	0	.923	-6	O-17(5-12-0)	-0.7
Total	4	196	505	59	124	14	5	3	43	54	61	.246	.322	.311	633	70	-20	11	5	1	.975	-2	O-164(13-138-13)	-2.8

■ BILL McGHEE

McGhee, William Mac "Fibber" b: 9/5/05, Shawmut, Ala. d: 3/10/84, Decatur, Ga. BL/TL, 5'10.5", 185 lbs. Deb: 7/5/44

YEAR	TM/L	G	AB	R	H	2B	3B	HR	RBI	BB	SO	AVG	OBP	SLG	OPS	OPS+	BR+	SB	CS	SBR	FA	FR	G/POS	TPR
1944	Phi-A	77	287	27	83	12	0	1	19	21	20	.289	.338	.341	679	96	-2	2	1	0	.989	-0	1-75	-0.6
1945	Phi-A	93	250	24	63	6	1	0	19	24	16	.252	.320	.284	604	76	-7	3	2	-0	.989	-5	O-48(40-0-9)/1-8	-1.6
Total	2	170	537	51	146	18	1	1	38	45	36	.272	.329	.315	644	87	-9	5	3	0	.990	-5	/1-83,O-48(40-0-9)	-2.2

■ BILL McGILVRAY

McGilvray, William Alexander "Big Bill" b: 4/29/1883, Portland, Ore. d: 5/23/52, Denver, Colo. BL/TL, 6', 160 lbs. Deb: 4/17/08

YEAR	TM/L	G	AB	R	H	2B	3B	HR	RBI	BB	SO	AVG	OBP	SLG	OPS	OPS+	BR+	SB	CS	SBR	FA	FR	G/POS	TPR
1908	Cin-N	2	2	0	0	0	0	0	0	0	0	.000	.000	.000	0	-99	-0	0			.000	0	H	-0.1

■ TIM McGINLEY

McGinley, Timothy S. b: Philadelphia, Pa. d: 11/2/1899, Oakland, Cal. 5'9.5", 155 lbs. Deb: 4/30/1875

YEAR	TM/L	G	AB	R	H	2B	3B	HR	RBI	BB	SO	AVG	OBP	SLG	OPS	OPS+	BR+	SB	CS	SBR	FA	FR	G/POS	TPR
1875	Cen-n	13	52	5	12	0	1	0	5	0	4	.231	.231	.269	500	80	-1	0	0	0	.646	-7	C-12/O-2(0-0-2)	-0.6
	NH-n	32	131	13	36	3	1	0	10	0	7	.275	.275	.313	588	119	3	1	1	-0	.807	-5	C-32,3-2	-0.1
	Yr	45	183	18	48	3	2	0	15	0	11	.262	.262	.301	563	107	3	1	1	-0	.762	-11	C-44/O-2(0-0-2),3-2	-0.7
1876	Bos-N	9	40	5	6	0	0	0	2	0	1	.150	.150	.150	300	0	-4				.600	-3	/O-6(0-6-0),C-3	-0.7

■ FRANK McGINN

McGinn, Frank J. b: 1869, Cincinnati, Ohio d: 11/19/1897, Cincinnati, Ohio Deb: 6/9/1890

YEAR	TM/L	G	AB	R	H	2B	3B	HR	RBI	BB	SO	AVG	OBP	SLG	OPS	OPS+	BR+	SB	CS	SBR	FA	FR	G/POS	TPR
1890	Pit-N	1	4	0	0	0	0	0	0	0	2	.000	.000	.000	0	-99	-1	0			1.000	-0	/O-1(0-1-0)	-0.1

■ RUSS McGINNIS

McGinnis, Russell Brent b: 6/18/63, Coffeyville, Kan. BR/TR, 6'3", 225 lbs. Deb: 6/3/92 Career OF: (1-LF 0-CF 0-RF)

YEAR	TM/L	G	AB	R	H	2B	3B	HR	RBI	BB	SO	AVG	OBP	SLG	OPS	OPS+	BR+	SB	CS	SBR	FA	FR	G/POS	TPR
1992	Tex-A	14	33	2	8	4	0	0	4	3	7	.242	.306	.364	669	90	-0	0	0	0	1.000	-3	C-10/1-2,3-2	-0.4
1995	KC-A	3	5	1	0	0	0	0	0	1	1	.000	.167	.000	167	-51	-1	0	0	0	1.000	-1	/1-1,3-1,O-1(1-0-0)	-0.2
Total	2	17	38	3	8	4	0	0	4	4	8	.211	.286	.316	602	69	-2	0	0	0	1.000	-4	/C-10,3-3,1-3,O-1L	-0.6

■ JOHN McGLONE

McGlone, John T. b: 1864, Brooklyn, N.Y. d: 11/24/27, Brooklyn, N.Y. TR, 5'10", 165 lbs. Deb: 10/7/1886

YEAR	TM/L	G	AB	R	H	2B	3B	HR	RBI	BB	SO	AVG	OBP	SLG	OPS	OPS+	BR+	SB	CS	SBR	FA	FR	G/POS	TPR
1886	Was-N	4	15	2	1	0	0	0	1	0	3	.067	.067	.067	133	-63	-3	0			.846	-1	/3-4	-0.4
1887	Cle-a	21	86	14	27	2	1	0	10	7		.314	.337	.304	641	82	-1	15			.854	1	3-21	0.0
1888	Cle-a	55	203	22	37	1	3	1	22	16		.182	.249	.232	480	56	-9	26			.787	-6	3-48/O-7(0-7-0)	-1.4
Total	3	80	304	38	65	3	4	1	33	23	3	.214	.265	.242	507	58	-14	41			.810	-7	/3-73,O-7(0-7-0)	-1.8

■ ART McGOVERN

McGovern, Arthur John b: 2/27/1882, St.John, N.B., Can. d: 11/14/15, Thornton, R.I. BR/TR, 5'10", 160 lbs. Deb: 4/21/05

YEAR	TM/L	G	AB	R	H	2B	3B	HR	RBI	BB	SO	AVG	OBP	SLG	OPS	OPS+	BR+	SB	CS	SBR	FA	FR	G/POS	TPR
1905	Bos-A	15	44	1	5	1	0	0	1	4		.114	.204	.136	340	9	-4	0			.951	-4	C-15	-0.8

■ BEAUTY McGOWAN

McGowan, Frank Bernard b: 11/8/01, Branford, Conn. d: 5/6/82, Hamden, Conn. BL/TR, 5'11", 190 lbs. Deb: 4/12/22

YEAR	TM/L	G	AB	R	H	2B	3B	HR	RBI	BB	SO	AVG	OBP	SLG	OPS	OPS+	BR+	SB	CS	SBR	FA	FR	G/POS	TPR
1922	Phi-A	99	300	36	69	10	5	1	20	40	46	.230	.323	.307	629	63	-16	6	5	-0	.965	9	O-82(0-56-28)	-1.2
1923	Phi-A	95	287	41	73	9	1	1	19	36	25	.254	.340	.303	643	69	-12	4	3	-0	.971	-0	O-79(26-17-36)	-1.7
1928	StL-A	47	168	35	61	13	4	2	18	16	15	.363	.425	.524	949	143	11	2	1	0	.962	-1	O-47(0-11-37)	0.6
1929	StL-A	125	441	62	112	26	6	2	51	61	34	.254	.346	.354	700	78	-14	5	2	0	.975	7	*O-117(0-34-84)	-1.4
1937	Bos-N	9	12	0	1	0	0	0	0	1	2	.083	.154	.083	237	-37	-2	0			1.000	-1	/O-2(0-0-2)	-0.3
Total	5	375	1208	174	316	58	16	6	108	154	122	.262	.347	.351	698	80	-33	17	11		.970	13	O-327(26-118-187)	-4.0

■ JOHN McGRAW

McGraw, John Joseph "Mugsy" or "Little Napoleon"
b: 4/7/1873, Truxton, N.Y. d: 2/25/34, New Rochelle, N.Y. BL/TR, 5'7", 155 lbs. Deb: 8/26/1891 MH Career OF: (21-LF 9-CF 30-RF)

YEAR	TM/L	G	AB	R	H	2B	3B	HR	RBI	BB	SO	AVG	OBP	SLG	OPS	OPS+	BR+	SB	CS	SBR	FA	FR	G/POS	TPR
1891	Bal-a	33	115	17	31	3	5	0	14	12	17	.270	.359	.383	741	111	2	4			.811	-15	S-21/O-9(0-0-9),2-3	-1.1
1892	Bal-N	79	286	41	77	13	2	1	26	32	21	.269	.355	.339	694	107	3	15			.897	1	O-34R,2-34/S-8,3-3	0.4
1893	Bal-N	127	480	123	154	9	10	5	64	101	11	.321	.454	.412	866	129	27	38			.894	-23	*S-117,O-11(10-0-1)	0.8
1894	*Bal-N	124	512	156	174	18	14	1	92	91	12	.340	.451	.436	887	110	13	78			.892	-2	*3-118/2-6	1.0
1895	*Bal-N	96	388	110	143	13	6	2	48	60	9	.369	.459	.448	908	131	21	61			.878	9	*3-95/2-1	2.6
1896	*Bal-N	23	77	20	25	2	2	0	14	11	4	.325	.422	.403	825	116	2	13			.833	-2	3-18/1-1	0.1
1897	*Bal-N	106	391	90	127	15	3	0	48	99		.325	**.471**	.379	849	126	24	44			.886	-13	*3-105	1.1
1898	Bal-N	143	515	**143**	176	8	10	0	53	**112**		.342	.475	.396	871	148	43	43			.900	-12	*3-137/O-3(0-3-0)	3.1
1899	Bal-N	117	399	**140**	156	13	3	1	33	**124**		.391	**.547**	.446	994	165	50	73			.945	2	*3-117,M	4.9
1900	StL-N	99	334	84	115	10	4	2	33	85		.344	**.505**	.416	921	157	37	29			.909	-9	*3-99	2.6
1901	Bal-A	73	232	71	81	14	9	0	28	61		.349	.508	.487	995	169	28	24			.890	-20	3-69,M	0.9
1902	Bal-A	20	63	14	18	3	2	1	3	17		.286	.451	.444	896	143	5	5			.864	-8	3-19,M	-0.2
	NY-N	35	107	13	25	0	0	0	5	26		.234	.401	.234	635	97	2	7			.926	-3	S-34,M	0.1
1903	NY-N	12	11	2	3	0	0	0	1	1		.273	.467	.273	739	108	0	1			.000	-2	/2-2,O-2L,S-1,3M	-0.2
1904	NY-N	5	12	0	4	0	0	0	0	3		.333	.467	.333	800	142	1	0			.947	3	/2-2,S-2,M	0.4
1905	NY-N	3	0	0	0	0	0	0	0	0		—	—	—	—	—	0	1			.000	-0	/O-1(1-0-0),M	0.0
1906	NY-N	4	2	0	0	0	0	0	0	1		.000	.333	.000	333	4	-0	0			.000	0	/3-1,M	0.0
Total	16	1099	3924	1024	1309	121	70	13	462	836	74	.334	.466	.410	876	135	259	436			.898	-93	3-782,S-183/O-60R,21	16.5

■ FRED McGRIFF

McGriff, Frederick Stanley b: 10/31/63, Tampa, Fla. BL/TL, 6'3", 215 lbs. Deb: 5/17/86

YEAR	TM/L	G	AB	R	H	2B	3B	HR	RBI	BB	SO	AVG	OBP	SLG	OPS	OPS+	BR+	SB	CS	SBR	FA	FR	G/POS	TPR
1986	Tor-A	3	5	1	1	0	0	0	0	0	2	.200	.200	.200	400	9	-1	0	0	0	1.000	-0	/1-1,D-2	-0.1
1987	Tor-A	107	295	58	73	16	0	20	43	60	104	.247	.376	.505	881	128	13	3	2	-0	.983	-1	D-90,1-14	0.8
1988	Tor-A	154	536	100	151	35	4	34	82	79	149	.282	.378	.552	930	156	40	6	1	1	**.997**	-5	*1-153	2.5
1989	*Tor-A	161	551	98	148	27	3	**36**	92	119	132	.269	.402	.525	**927**	**162**	**49**	7	4	0	.989	-1	*1-159/D-2	3.7
1990	Tor-A	153	557	91	167	21	1	35	88	94	108	.300	.403	.530	932	156	43	5	3	0	.996	9	*1-147/D-6	4.2
1991	SD-N	153	528	84	147	19	1	31	106	105	135	.278	.400	.494	894	146	35	4	1	1	.990	-11	*1-153	1.4
1992	SD-N★	152	531	79	152	30	4	**35**	104	96	108	.286	.396	.556	952	164	46	8	6	-0	.991	-1	*1-151	3.6
1993	SD-N	83	302	52	83	11	1	18	46	42	55	.275	.365	.497	862	126	11	4	3	-0	.983	-6	1-83	-0.3
	*Atl-N	68	255	59	79	18	1	19	55	34	51	.310	.393	.612	1005	163	22	1	0	0	.992	-1	1-66	1.5
	Yr	151	557	111	162	29	2	37	101	76	106	.291	.378	.549	927	143	33	5	3	0	.987	-7	*1-149	1.2
1994	Atl-N★	113	424	81	135	25	1	34	94	50	76	.318	.392	.623	1014	156	34	7	3	0	.994	-5	*1-112	1.8
1995	*Atl-N★	144	528	85	148	27	1	27	93	65	99	.280	.365	.489	853	119	14	3	6	-1	.996	0	*1-144	0.0
1996	*Atl-N★	159	617	81	182	37	1	28	107	68	116	.295	.367	.494	861	118	16	7	3	0	.992	5	*1-158	0.6

YEAR	TM/L	G	AB	R	H	2B	3B	HR	RBI	BB	SO	AVG	OBP	SLG	OPS	OPS+	BR+	SB	CS	SBR	FA	FR	G/POS	TPR
1997	*Atl-N	152	564	77	156	25	1	22	97	68	112	.277	.358	.441	800	106	5	5	0	1	.990	-4	*1-149	-1.1
1998	TB-A	151	564	73	160	33	0	19	81	79	118	.284	.374	.443	817	109	9	7	2	1	.995	-4	*1-135,D-14	-0.7
1999	TB-A	144	529	75	164	30	1	32	104	86	107	.310	.407	.552	959	140	33	1	0	0	.989	6	*1-125,D-18	2.4
2000	TB-A★	158	566	82	157	18	0	27	106	91	120	.277	.377	.452	830	109	10	2	0	0	.993	-4	*1-144,D-10	-0.8
Total	15	2055	7352	1176	2103	372	20	417	1298	1136	1592	.286	.384	.512	896	135	382	70	34	4	.992	-23	*1-1894,D-142	19.5
■ TERRY McGRIFF McGriff, Terence Roy b: 9/23/63, Fort Pierce, Fla. BR/TR, 6'2", 195 lbs. Deb: 7/11/87																								
1987	Cin-N	34	89	6	20	3	0	2	11	8	17	.225	.289	.326	615	60	-5	0	0	0	.983	4	C-33	0.0
1988	Cin-N	35	96	9	19	3	0	1	4	12	31	.198	.287	.260	547	56	-5	1	0	0	.990	3	C-32	0.0
1989	Cin-N	6	11	1	3	0	0	0	2	2	3	.273	.385	.273	657	88	-0	0	0	0	.929	1	/C-6	0.1
1990	Cin-N	2	4	0	0	0	0	0	0	0	1	.000	.000	.000	0	-96	-1	0	0	0	1.000	1	/C-1	0.0
	Hou-N	4	5	0	0	0	0	0	0	0	0	.000	.000	.000	0	-99	-1	0	0	0	.900	0	/C-4	-0.1
	Yr	6	9	0	0	0	0	0	0	0	1	.000	.000	.000	0	-99	-2	0	0	0	.938	1	/C-5	-0.1
1993	Fla-N	3	7	0	0	0	0	0	0	1	2	.000	.125	.000	125	-60	-2	0	0	0	1.000	-0	/C-3	-0.2
1994	StL-N	42	114	10	25	6	0	0	13	13	11	.219	.310	.272	582	55	-7	0	0	0	.991	3	C-39	-0.2
Total	6	126	326	26	67	12	0	3	30	36	65	.206	.288	.270	558	51	-22	1	0	0	.985	11	C-118	-0.4
■ MARK McGRILLIS McGrillis, Mark A. b: 10/22/1872, Philadelphia, Pa. d: 5/16/35, Philadelphia, Pa. Deb: 9/17/1892																								
1892	StL-N	1	3	0	0	0	0	0	0	0	1	.000	.000	.000	0	-99	-1	0			1.000	-0	/3-1	-0.1
■ JOE McGUCKIN McGuckin, Joseph W. b: 3/13/1862, Paterson, N.J. d: 12/31/03, Yonkers, N.Y. 5'8.5", 160 lbs. Deb: 8/27/1890																								
1890	Bal-a	11	37	2	4	0	0	0	2	6		.108	.250	.108	358	6	-4	3			.962	3	O-11(0-0-11)	-0.1
■ JOHN McGUINNESS McGuinness, John James b: 1857, Ireland d: 12/19/16, Binghamton, N.Y. 5'10.5", 150 lbs. Deb: 5/6/1876																								
1876	NY-N	1	4	0	0	0	0	0	0	0	0	.000	.000	.000	0	-99	-1				.500	-2	/2-1,C-1	-0.2
1879	Syr-N	12	51	7	15	1	1	0	4	0	6	.294	.294	.353	647	126	2				.928	-1	1-12	0.0
1884	Phi-U	53	220	25	52	8	1	0		5		.236	.253	.282	535	67	-15				.959	-0	1-48/2-5,S-1	-1.7
Total	3	66	275	32	67	9	2	0	4	5	6	.244	.257	.291	548	75	-14				.954	-2	/1-60,2-6,S-1,C-1	-1.9
■ JIM McGUIRE McGuire, James A. b: 2/4/1875, Dunkirk, N.Y. d: 1/26/17, Buffalo, N.Y. TR, Deb: 9/10/01																								
1901	Cle-A	18	69	4	16	2	0	0	3	0		.232	.232	.261	493	38	-6	0			.913	1	S-18	-0.4
■ DEACON McGUIRE McGuire, James Thomas b: 11/18/1863, Youngstown, Ohio d: 10/31/36, Duck Lake, Mich. BR/TR, 6'1", 185 lbs. Deb: 6/21/1884 MC Career OF: (6-LF 4-CF 23-RF)																								
1884	Tol-a	45	151	12	28	7	0	1		5		.185	.217	.252	468	50	-8				.906	-8	C-41/O-4(1-3-0),S-3	-1.2
1885	Det-N	34	121	11	23	4	2	0	9	5	23	.190	.222	.256	478	54	-6				.920	14	C-31/O-3(3-0-0)	1.0
1886	Phi-N	50	167	25	33	7	1	2	18	19	25	.198	.280	.287	567	72	-5	2			.899	-6	C-49/O-1(0-0-1)	-0.6
1887	Phi-N	41	161	22	57	6	6	2	23	11	8	.354	.362	.467	829	122	4	3			.884	-1	C-41	0.6
1888	Phi-N	12	51	7	17	4	2	0	11	4	9	.333	.382	.490	872	168	4	0			.800	-5	C-10/3-2	-0.1
	Det-N	3	13	0	0	0	0	0	0	0	4	.000	.000	.000	0	-99	-3	0			.810	-2	/C-3	-0.5
	Yr	15	64	7	17	4	2	0	11	4	13	.266	.309	.391	699	117	1	0			.802	-7	C-13/3-2	-0.6
	Cle-a	26	94	15	24	1	3	1	13	7		.255	.333	.362	695	126	3	2			.891	-1	C-17/1-6,O-3(0-0-3)	0.2
1890	Roc-a	87	331	46	99	16	4	4	53	21		.299	.356	.408	763	135	14	8			.938	8	C-71,1-15/O-3L,P-1	2.4
1891	Was-a	114	413	55	125	22	10	3	66	43	34	.303	.382	.426	808	137	21	10			.911	-12	*C-98,O-18R/3-3,1-1	1.5
1892	Was-N	97	315	46	73	14	4	4	43	61	49	.232	.360	.340	699	115	8	7			.936	-1	C-89/1-8,O-1(0-0-1)	1.4
1893	Was-N	63	237	29	61	14	3	1	26	26	12	.257	.338	.354	693	86	-5	3			.889	-5	C-50,1-12	-0.5
1894	Was-N	104	425	67	130	18	6	6	78	33	19	.306	.366	.419	784	92	-6	11			.918	-1	*C-104	0.2
1895	Was-N	133	538	89	181	30	8	10	97	40	18	.336	.388	.478	865	124	18	17			.937	12	*C-133/S-1	3.4
1896	Was-N	108	389	60	125	25	3	2	70	30	14	.321	.379	.416	795	110	5	12			.936	-1	*C-98/1-1	1.2
1897	Was-N	93	327	51	112	17	7	4	53	21		.343	.386	.474	860	127	12	9			.947	8	C-73/1-6	2.2
1898	Was-N	131	489	59	131	18	3	1	57	24		.268	.310	.323	633	82	-12	10			.967	4	C-93,1-37,M	0.0
1899	Was-N	59	199	25	54	3	1	1	12	16		.271	.335	.312	646	79	-5	3			.973	-4	C-56/1-1	-0.4
	Bro-N	46	157	22	50	12	4	0	23	12		.318	.385	.446	831	125	5	4			.971	2	C-46	1.0
	Yr	105	356	47	104	15	5	1	35	28		.292	.357	.371	728	99	-0	7			.972	-2	*C-102/1-1	0.6
1900	*Bro-N	71	241	20	69	15	2	0	34	19		.286	.348	.365	714	91	-3	2			.952	-6	C-69	-0.3
1901	Bro-N	85	301	28	89	16	4	0	40	18		.296	.342	.375	717	105	2	4			.960	-4	C-81/1-3	0.5
1902	Det-A	73	229	27	52	14	1	2	23	24		.227	.300	.323	624	71	-9	0			.952	-5	C-70	-0.6
1903	Det-A	72	248	15	62	12	1	0	21	19		.250	.306	.306	612	87	-4	3			.960	-6	C-69/1-1	-0.2
1904	NY-A	101	322	17	67	12	2	0	20	27		.208	.276	.258	533	66	-12	2			.970	13	C-97/1-1	1.2
1905	NY-A	72	228	9	50	7	2	0	33	18		.219	.291	.268	558	69	-7	3			.975	-6	C-71	-0.7
1906	NY-A	51	144	11	43	5	0	0	14	12		.299	.365	.333	698	108	2	3			.966	-1	C-49/1-1	0.5
1907	NY-A	1	1	0	0	0	0	0	0	0		.000	.000	.000	0	-93	-0	0			1.000	1	/C-1	0.0
	Bos-A	6	4	1	3	0	0	1	1	0		.750	.750	1.500	2250	620	2	0			.000	0	HM	0.2
	Yr	7	5	1	3	0	0	1	1	0		.600	.600	1.200	1800	470	2	0			1.000	1	/C-1	0.2
1908	Bos-A	1	1	0	0	0	0	0	0	0		.000	.000	.000	0	-97	-0	0			.000	0	HM	0.0
	Cle-A	1	4	0	1	1	0	0	2	0		.250	.250	.500	750	142	0	0			1.000	-0	/1-1	0.0
	Yr	2	5	0	1	1	0	0	2	0		.200	.200	.400	600	93	-0	0			1.000	-0	/1-1	0.0
1910	Cle-A	1	3	0	1	0	0	0	0	0		.333	.500	.333	833	159	0	0			1.000	-1	/C-1,M	-0.1
1912	Det-A	1	2	1	1	0	0	0	0	0		.500	.500	.500	1000	192	0	0			.714	0	/C-1	0.1
Total	26	1782	6306	770	1761	300	79	45	840	515	215	.279	.341	.372	713	101	15	118			.938	-14	*C-1612/1-94,O3SP	12.4
■ MICKEY McGUIRE McGuire, M C Adolphus b: 1/18/41, Dayton, Ohio BR/TR, 5'10", 170 lbs. Deb: 9/7/62																								
1962	Bal-A	6	4	0	0	0	0	0	0	0	0	.000	.000	.000	0	-99	-1	0	0	0	1.000	-0	/S-5	-0.1
1967	Bal-A	10	17	2	4	0	0	0	2	0	2	.235	.235	.235	471	40	-1	0	0	0	1.000	-2	/2-4	-0.4
Total	2	16	21	2	4	0	0	0	2	0	2	.190	.190	.190	381	11	-2	0	0	0	1.000	-3	/S-5,2-4	-0.5
■ RYAN McGUIRE McGuire, Ryan Byron b: 11/23/71, Bellflower, Cal. BL/TL, 6'2", 210 lbs. Deb: 6/5/97 Career OF: (70-LF 10-CF 38-RF)																								
1997	Mon-N	84	199	22	51	15	2	3	17	19	34	.256	.321	.397	718	87	-4	1	4	-1	.960	1	O-44R,1-30/D-3	-0.7
1998	Mon-N	130	210	17	39	9	0	1	10	32	55	.186	.293	.243	536	44	-17	0	0	0	.980	-7	1-78,O-46(33-7-8)	-2.8
1999	Mon-N	88	140	17	31	7	2	2	18	27	33	.221	.347	.343	690	78	-4	1	1	-0	.997	4	1-58,O-23(16-1-7)	-0.3
2000	NY-N	1	2	0	0	0	0	0	0	1	0	.000	.333	.000	333	-6	-0	0	0	0	1.000	0	/O-1(0-0-1)	0.0
Total	4	303	551	56	121	31	4	6	45	79	122	.220	.317	.323	641	68	-25	2	5	-1	.991	-2	1-166,O-114L/D-3	-3.8
■ BILL McGUIRE McGuire, William Patrick b: 2/14/64, Omaha, Neb. BR/TR, 6'3", 205 lbs. Deb: 8/2/88																								
1988	Sea-A	9	16	1	3	0	0	0	2	3	2	.188	.316	.188	503	43	-1	0	0	0	1.000	-0	/C-9	-0.1
1989	Sea-A	14	28	2	5	0	0	1	4	2	6	.179	.233	.286	519	44	-2	0	0	0	1.000	4	C-14	0.3
Total	2	23	44	3	8	0	0	1	6	5	8	.182	.265	.250	515	44	-3	0	0	0	1.000	4	/C-23	0.2
■ BILL McGUNNIGLE McGunnigle, William Henry "Gunner" b: 1/1/1855, Boston, Mass. d: 3/9/1899, Brockton, Mass. BR/TR, 5'9", 155 lbs. Deb: 5/2/1879 M																								
1879	Buf-N	47	171	22	30	0	1	0	5	5	24	.175	.199	.187	386	27	-13				.918	1	O-34(0-0-34),P-14	-0.8
1880	Buf-N	7	22	0	4	0	0	0	1	0	4	.182	.182	.182	364	23	-2				1.000	-2	/P-5,O-3(1-1-1)	-0.2
	Wor-N	1	4	0	0	0	0	0	0	0	2	.000	.000	.000	0	-92	-1				1.000	-1	/O-1(1-0-1)	-0.2
	Yr	8	26	0	4	0	0	0	1	0	6	.154	.154	.154	308	5	-3				1.000	-2	/P-5,O-4(2-1-2)	-0.4
1882	Cle-N	1	5	2	1	0	0	0	0	0	1	.200	.200	.200	400	30	-0				.000	-1	/O-1(0-1-0)	-0.1
Total	3	56	202	24	35	0	1	0	6	5	31	.173	.193	.183	376	25	-16				.900	-1	/O-39(2-2-36),P-19	-1.3
■ MARK McGWIRE McGwire, Mark David b: 10/1/63, Pomona, Cal. BR/TR, 6'5", 225 lbs. Deb: 8/22/86																								
1986	Oak-A	18	53	10	10	1	0	3	9	4	18	.189	.259	.377	636	76	-2	0	1	-0	.833	-3	3-16	-0.5
1987	Oak-A★	151	557	97	161	28	4	**49**	118	71	131	.289	.374	**.618**	992	168	53	1	1	-0	.992	-7	*1-145/3-8,O-3(0-0-3)	3.5
1988	*Oak-A★	155	550	87	143	22	1	32	99	76	117	.260	.354	.478	832	135	26	0	0	0	.993	-8	*1-154/O-1(0-0-1)	0.8
1989	*Oak-A★	143	490	74	113	17	0	33	95	83	94	.231	.345	.467	813	132	21	1	1	-0	.995	7	*1-141/D-2	1.8
1990	*Oak-A★	156	523	87	123	16	0	39	108	**110**	116	.235	.375	.489	864	146	35	2	1	0	.997	-5	*1-154/D-2	1.9

YEAR	TM/L	G	AB	R	H	2B	3B	HR	RBI	BB	SO	AVG	OBP	SLG	OPS	OPS+	BR+	SB	CS	SBR	FA	FR	G/POS	TPR
1991	Oak-A†	154	483	62	97	22	0	22	75	93	116	.201	.333	.383	716	103	4	2	1	0	.997	2	*1-152	-0.5
1992	*Oak-A★	139	467	87	125	22	0	42	104	90	105	.268	.391	**.585**	976	**180**	51	0	1	-0	.995	-10	*1-139	3.1
1993	Oak-A	27	84	16	28	6	0	9	24	21	19	.333	.472	.726	1198	231	16	0	1	-0	1.000	-1	1-25	1.2
1994	Oak-A	47	135	26	34	3	0	9	25	37	40	.252	.413	.474	887	140	10	0	0	0	.988	-2	1-40/D-5	0.4
1995	Oak-A†	104	317	75	87	13	0	39	90	88	77	.274	.447	.685	1132	200	51	1	1	-0	.986	-1	1-91,D-10	3.8
1996	Oak-A★	130	423	104	132	21	0	**52**	113	116	112	.312	**.468**	**.730**	**1199**	**201**	70	0	0	0	.990	-5	*1-109,D-18	4.9
1997	Oak-A★	105	366	48	104	24	0	34	81	58	98	.284	.388	.628	1016	162	33	1	0	0	.994	-1	*1-101	2.2
	StL-N	51	174	38	44	3	0	24	42	43	61	.253	.414	.684	1098	183	22	2	0	0	.998	-1	1-50	1.6
1998	StL-N★	155	509	130	152	21	0	**70**	147	**162**	155	.299	**.473**	**.752**	**1225**	**218**	**95**	1	0	0	.992	-6	*1-151	7.2
1999	StL-N★	153	521	118	145	21	1	**65**	**147**	133	141	.278	.427	.697	1124	**177**	63	0	0	0	.990	-4	*1-151	4.3
2000	*StL-N†	89	236	60	72	8	0	32	73	76	78	.305	.486	.746	1232	204	42	1	0	0	.998	-7	1-70	2.7
Total	15	1777	5888	1119	1570	248	6	554	1350	1261	1478	.267	.402	.593	995	168	590	12	8	-0	.993	-51	*1-1673/D-37,3-24,O	38.4
■ **JIM McHALE**	McHale, James Bernard "J.B." b: 12/17/1875, Miners Mills, Pa. d: 6/17/59, Los Angeles, Cal. BR/TR, 5′11″, 165 lbs. Deb: 4/14/08																							
1908	Bos-A	21	67	9	15	2	2	0	7	4		.224	.278	.313	591	90	-1	4			.970	-2	O-19(1-18-0)	-0.4
■ **JOHN McHALE**	McHale, John Joseph b: 9/21/21, Detroit, Mich. BL/TR, 6′, 200 lbs. Deb: 5/28/43																							
1943	Det-A	4	3	0	0	0	0	0	0	1	1	.000	.250	.000	250	-23	-0	0	0	0	.000	0	H	0.0
1944	Det-A	1	1	0	0	0	0	0	0	0	0	.000	.000	.000	0	-95	-0	0	0	0	.000	0	H	0.0
1945	*Det-A	19	14	0	2	0	0	0	1	1	4	.143	.250	.143	393	14	-1	0	0	0	1.000	0	/1-3	-0.1
1947	Det-A	39	95	10	20	1	0	3	11	7	24	.211	.265	.316	580	59	-5	1	1	-0	.995	-1	1-25	-0.7
1948	Det-A	1	1	0	0	0	0	0	0	0	0	.000	.000	.000	0	-97	-0	0	0	0	.000	0	H	0.0
Total	5	64	114	10	22	1	0	3	12	9	29	.193	.258	.281	539	49	-8	1	1	-0	.995	-1	/1-28	-0.8
■ **BOB McHALE**	McHale, Robert Emmet "Rabbit" b: 2/25/1872, Michigan Bluff, Cal. d: 6/9/52, Sacramento, Cal. Deb: 5/9/1898																							
1898	Was-N	11	33	5	6	2	0	0	7	1		.182	.270	.242	513	47	-2	1			.900	-1	/O-9(0-9-0),S-1,1-1	-0.4
■ **AUSTIN McHENRY**	McHenry, Austin Bush "Mac" b: 9/22/1895, Wrightsville, O. d: 11/27/22, Jefferson Twsp., Ohio BR/TR, 5′11″, 152 lbs. Deb: 6/22/18																							
1918	StL-N	80	272	32	71	12	6	1	29	21	24	.261	.319	.360	679	111	3	8			.952	2	O-80(80-0-0)	0.1
1919	StL-N	110	371	41	106	19	11	1	47	19	57	.286	.322	.404	727	125	10	7			.985	1	*O-103(73-26-7)	0.6
1920	StL-N	137	504	66	142	19	11	10	65	25	73	.282	.316	.423	738	115	7	8	11	-2	.952	2	*O-133(89-52-0)	0.1
1921	StL-N	152	574	92	201	37	8	17	102	38	48	.350	.393	.531	924	145	36	10	20	-5	.965	7	*O-152(146-0-6)	2.6
1922	StL-N	64	238	31	72	18	3	5	43	14	27	.303	.344	.466	810	112	3	2	2	-0	.935	7	O-61(61-0-0)	0.5
Total	5	543	1959	262	592	105	39	34	286	117	229	.302	.343	.448	791	126	59	35	33		.960	18	O-529(449-78-13)	3.9
■ **VANCE McHENRY**	McHenry, Vance Loren b: 7/10/56, Chico, Cal. BR/TR, 5′9″, 165 lbs. Deb: 8/13/81																							
1981	Sea-A	15	18	3	4	0	0	0	2	1	1	.222	.263	.222	485	39	-1	0	0	0	.893	0	S-13/D-1	-0.1
1982	Sea-A	3	1	0	0	0	0	0	0	0	0	.000	.000	.000	0	-97	-0	0	0	0	.500	-0	/S-1,D-1	-0.1
Total	2	18	19	3	4	0	0	0	2	1	1	.211	.250	.211	461	32	-2	0	0	0	.867	-0	/S-14,D-2	-0.2
■ **IRISH McILVEEN**	McIlveen, Henry Cooke b: 7/27/1880, Belfast, Ireland d: 10/18/60, Lorain, Ohio BL/TL, 5′11.5″, 180 lbs. Deb: 7/10/06																							
1906	Pit-N	5	5	1	2	0	0	0	0	0		.400	.400	.400	800	143	0	0			1.000	0	/P-2	0.0
1908	NY-A	44	169	17	36	3	3	0	8	14		.213	.277	.266	543	76	-4	6			.949	0	O-44(13-1-30)	-0.7
1909	NY-A	4	3	0	0	0	0	0	0	1		.000	.250	.000	250	-20	-0	0			.000	0	H	0.0
Total	3	53	177	18	38	3	3	0	8	15		.215	.280	.266	545	76	-4	6			.949	0	/O-44(13-1-30),P-2	-0.7
■ **STUFFY McINNIS**	McInnis, John Phalen "Jack" b: 9/19/1890, Gloucester, Mass. d: 2/16/60, Ipswich, Mass. BR/TR, 5′9.5″, 162 lbs. Deb: 4/12/09 M Career OF: (1-LF 0-CF 0-RF)																							
1909	Phi-A	19	46	4	11	0	0	1	4	2		.239	.286	.304	590	85	-1	0			.886	4	S-14	0.4
1910	Phi-A	38	73	10	22	2	4	0	12	7		.301	.363	.438	801	152	4	3			.927	-5	S-17/2-5,3-4,O-1L	0.0
1911	*Phi-A	126	468	76	150	20	10	3	77	25		.321	.361	.425	787	121	12	23			.982	-15	1-97,S-24	-0.4
1912	Phi-A	153	568	83	186	25	13	3	101	49		.327	.384	.433	817	138	28	27			.984	3	*1-153	2.7
1913	*Phi-A	148	543	79	176	30	4	4	90	45	31	.324	.382	.416	798	137	25	16			**.992**	-2	*1-148	2.0
1914	*Phi-A	149	576	74	181	12	8	1	95	19	27	.314	.341	.368	709	118	10	25	19	-1	**.995**	0	*1-149	0.5
1915	Phi-A	119	456	44	143	14	4	0	49	14	17	.314	.337	.362	699	113	5	8	8	-1	.989	5	*1-119	0.6
1916	Phi-A	140	512	42	151	25	3	1	60	25	19	.295	.331	.361	693	114	6	7			.992	7	*1-140	1.0
1917	Phi-A	150	567	50	172	19	4	0	44	33	19	.303	.342	.351	693	113	7	18			.993	2	*1-150	0.5
1918	*Bos-A	117	423	40	115	11	5	0	56	19	10	.272	.306	.322	628	91	-6	10			**.992**	4	1-94,3-23	-0.4
1919	Bos-A	120	440	32	134	12	5	1	58	23	11	.305	.341	.361	702	103	1	8			.995	3	*1-118	0.0
1920	Bos-A	148	559	50	166	21	3	2	71	18	19	.297	.321	.356	677	83	-15	6	11	-3	**.996**	-1	*1-148	-2.2
1921	Bos-A	152	584	72	179	31	10	0	76	21	9	.307	.335	.394	729	88	-12	2	4	-1	**.999**	4	*1-152	-1.8
1922	Cle-A	142	537	58	164	28	7	1	78	15	5	.305	.325	.389	715	85	-13	1	5	-2	**.997**	-5	*1-140	-2.8
1923	Bos-N	154	607	70	191	23	9	2	95	26	12	.315	.343	.392	735	97	-3	7	8	-1	.991	4	*1-154	-1.0
1924	Bos-N	146	581	57	169	23	7	1	59	15	6	.291	.311	.360	671	83	-15	9	3	1	.994	7	*1-146	-1.7
1925	*Pit-N	59	155	19	57	10	4	0	24	17	1	.368	.437	.484	921	126	7	1	1	-0	.993	1	1-46	0.5
1926	Pit-N	47	127	12	38	6	1	0	13	7	3	.299	.336	.362	698	83	-3	1			.988	-1	1-40	-0.6
1927	Phi-N	1	0	0	0	0	0	0	0	0	0	—	—	—	—	—	0	0			1.000	-0	/1-1,M	0.0
Total	19	2128	7822	872	2405	312	101	20	1062	380	189	.307	.343	.381	723	106	37	172	59		.993	17	*1-1995/S-55,3-27,2O	-2.7
■ **TIM McINTOSH**	McIntosh, Timothy Allen b: 3/21/65, Minneapolis, Minn. BR/TR, 5′11″, 195 lbs. Deb: 9/3/90 Career OF: (15-LF 0-CF 7-RF)																							
1990	Mil-A	5	5	1	1	0	0	1	1	0	2	.200	.200	.800	1000	168	0	0	0	0	.875	-0	/C-4	0.0
1991	Mil-A	7	11	2	4	1	0	1	1	0	4	.364	.364	.727	1091	199	1	0	0	0	.000	-2	/O-4(4-0-0),1-1,D-2	0.0
1992	Mil-A	35	77	7	14	3	0	0	6	3	9	.182	.232	.221	452	28	-7	1	3	-1	.983	1	C-14,O-10L/1-7,D-3	-0.8
1993	Mil-A	1	0	0	0	0	0	0	0	0	0	—	—	—	—	—	0	0	0	0	.000	0	/C-1	0.0
	Mon-N	20	21	2	2	1	0	0	2	0	7	.095	.095	.143	238	-36	-4	0	0	0	1.000	-3	/O-7(2-0-6),C-5	-0.7
1996	NY-A	3	3	0	0	0	0	0	0	0	0	.000	.000	.000	0	-99	-1	0	0	0	.000	-0	/C-1,1-1,3-1	-0.1
Total	5	71	117	12	21	5	0	2	10	3	22	.179	.213	.274	487	34	-11	1	3	-1	.973	-4	/C-25,O-21L,1-9,D3	-1.6
■ **MATTY McINTYRE**	McIntyre, Matthew W. b: 6/12/1880, Stonington, Conn. d: 4/2/20, Detroit, Mich. BL/TL, 5′11″, 175 lbs. Deb: 7/3/01																							
1901	Phi-A	82	308	38	85	12	4	0	46	30		.276	.346	.341	687	87	-5	11			.921	-3	O-82(82-0-0)	-1.1
1904	Det-A	152	578	74	146	11	10	2	46	44		.253	.310	.317	627	101	2	11			.959	12	*O-152(151-0-1)	0.5
1905	Det-A	131	495	59	130	21	5	0	30	48		.263	.330	.325	656	107	5	9			.968	17	*O-131(131-0-0)	1.5
1906	Det-A	133	493	63	128	19	11	0	39	56		.260	.338	.343	680	110	7	29			.982	12	*O-133(132-1-0)	1.2
1907	Det-A	20	81	6	23	1	1	0	9	7		.284	.341	.321	662	107	1	3			1.000	3	O-20(20-0-0)	0.2
1908	*Det-A	151	569	**105**	168	24	13	0	28	83		.295	.392	.383	775	146	32	20			**.977**	16	*O-151(151-0-0)	4.4
1909	*Det-A	125	476	65	116	18	9	1	34	54		.244	.325	.326	650	101	1	13			.975	-0	*O-122(119-3-0)	-0.6
1910	Det-A	83	305	40	72	15	5	0	25	39		.236	.323	.318	641	94	-1	4			.946	4	O-77(58-17-2)	-0.2
1911	Chi-A	146	569	102	184	19	11	1	52	64		.323	.397	.401	797	127	22	17			.948	-2	*O-146(0-31-115)	1.2
1912	Chi-A	49	84	10	14	0	0	0	10	14		.167	.300	.167	467	36	-6	3			1.000	-1	O-25(12-1-10)	-0.8
Total	10	1072	3958	562	1066	140	69	4	319	439		.269	.346	.343	689	110	58	120			.964	56	*O-1039(856-53-128)	6.3
■ **OTTO McIVOR**	McIvor, Edward Otto b: 7/26/1884, Greenville, Tex. d: 5/4/54, Dallas, Tex. BB/TL, 5′11.5″, 175 lbs. Deb: 4/18/11																							
1911	StL-N	30	62	11	14	2	1	1	9	9	14	.226	.333	.339	672	91	-1	0			.926	-3	O-17(3-6-8)	-0.5
■ **DAVE McKAY**	McKay, David Lawrence b: 3/14/50, Vancouver, B.C., Can BB/TR (BR 1975-76, 77 (part)), 6′1″, 195 lbs. Deb: 8/22/75 C																							
1975	Min-A	33	125	8	32	4	1	2	16	6	14	.256	.295	.352	647	81	-3	1	1	-0	.923	2	3-33	-0.2
1976	Min-A	45	138	8	28	2	0	0	8	9	27	.203	.272	.217	489	43	-9	1	2	-0	.911	-1	3-41/S-2,D-1	-1.2
1977	Tor-A	95	274	18	54	4	3	3	22	7	51	.197	.223	.266	489	32	-26	2	1	0	.968	7	2-40,3-32,S-20,/D-2	-1.6
1978	Tor-A	145	504	59	120	20	8	7	45	20	91	.238	.269	.351	620	71	-20	4	4	-1	.984	-7	*2-140/S-3,3-2,D-1	-2.0
1979	Tor-A	47	156	19	34	9	0	0	12	7	19	.218	.256	.276	532	43	-12	1	1	-0	.974	6	2-46/3-2	-0.4
1980	Oak-A	123	295	29	72	16	1	1	29	10	57	.244	.283	.315	598	68	-13	1	1	-0	.977	-6	2-62,3-54,S-10	-1.6
1981	*Oak-A	79	224	25	59	11	1	4	21	16	43	.263	.318	.375	693	104	1	4	1	1	.926	-4	3-43,2-38/S-7	-0.1

YEAR	TM/L	G	AB	R	H	2B	3B	HR	RBI	BB	SO	AVG	OBP	SLG	OPS	OPS+	BR+	SB	CS	SBR	FA	FR	G/POS	TPR
1982	Oak-A	78	212	25	42	4	1	4	17	11	35	.198	.238	.283	521	44	-16	6	1	1	.968	-3	2-59,3-16/S-3	-1.7
Total	8	645	1928	191	441	70	15	21	170	86	337	.229	.268	.313	581	62	-100	20	12	0	.976	-6	2-385,3-223/S-45,D	-8.8
■ ED McKEAN	McKean, Edwin John "Mack" b: 6/6/1864, Grafton, Ohio d: 8/16/19, Cleveland, Ohio BR/TR, 5'9", 160 lbs. Deb: 4/16/1887 Career OF: (47-LF 4-CF 1-RF)																							
1887	Cle-a	132	599	97	214	16	13	2	54	60		.357	.358	.375	733	108	7	76			.847	-8	*S-123/2-8,O-4(4-0-0)	0.3
1888	Cle-a	131	548	94	164	21	15	6	68	28		.299	.340	.425	765	149	29	52			.909	3	S-78,O-48L/2-9,3-1	3.0
1889	Cle-N	123	500	88	159	22	8	5	75	42	25	.318	.375	.424	799	126	17	35			.907	6	*S-122/2-1	2.3
1890	Cle-N	136	530	95	157	15	14	7	61	87	25	.296	.401	.417	818	141	31	23			.903	-18	*S-134/2-3	1.6
1891	Cle-N	141	603	115	170	13	12	6	69	64	19	.282	.352	.373	725	107	5	14			.887	-12	*S-141	-0.3
1892	*Cle-N	129	531	76	139	14	10	0	93	49	29	.262	.325	.326	651	93	-5	19			.862	-45	*S-129	-4.0
1893	Cle-N	125	545	103	169	29	24	4	133	50	14	.310	.372	.473	846	117	10	16			.902	-4	*S-125	1.0
1894	Cle-N	130	554	116	198	30	15	8	128	49	12	.357	.412	.509	921	116	13	33			.905	-21	*S-130	-0.1
1895	*Cle-N	132	569	131	194	32	17	8	119	46	26	.341	.397	.499	896	123	17	13			.907	-18	*S-132	0.5
1896	*Cle-N	133	571	100	193	29	12	7	112	45	9	.338	.388	.468	856	118	13	13			.915	-33	*S-133	-1.1
1897	Cle-N	125	523	83	143	21	14	2	78	40		.273	.330	.379	708	82	-15	15			.920	-30	*S-125	-3.3
1898	Cle-N	151	604	89	172	23	1	9	94	56		.285	.346	.371	717	107	5	11			.932	-36	*S-151	-2.1
1899	StL-N	67	277	40	72	7	3	3	40	20		.260	.310	.339	649	76	-10	4			.886	-17	S-42,1-15,2-10	-2.2
Total	13	1655	6954	1227	2144	272	158	67	1124	636	159	.308	.365	.417	781	114	118	324			.900	-232	*S-1565/O-52L,213	-4.4
■ BILL McKECHNIE	McKechnie, William Boyd "Deacon" b: 8/7/1886, Wilkinsburg, Pa. d: 10/29/65, Bradenton, Fla. BB/TR, 5'10", 160 lbs. Deb: 9/8/07 MCH Career OF: (0-LF 1-CF 1-RF)																							
1907	Pit-N	3	8	0	1	0	0	0	0	0		.125	.125	.125	250	-21	-1	0			1.000	-1	/3-2,2-1	-0.2
1910	Pit-N	71	212	23	46	1	2	0	12	11	23	.217	.256	.241	496	42	-16	4			.971	8	2-36,S-14/3-8,1-4	-0.7
1911	Pit-N	104	321	40	73	8	7	2	37	28	18	.227	.293	.315	608	68	-15	9			.975	-0	1-57,2-17,S-12,/3-6	-1.5
1912	Pit-N	24	73	8	18	0	1	0	4	4	5	.247	.286	.274	560	54	-5	2			.978	2	3-13/S-4,2-3,1-2	-0.2
1913	Bos-N	1	4	1	0	0	0	0	0	0	1	.000	.200	.000	200	-39	-1	0			1.000	0	/O-1(0-1-0)	-0.1
	NY-A	45	112	7	15	0	0	0	8	8	17	.134	.198	.134	332	-2	-14	2			.950	5	2-28/S-7,3-2	-0.9
1914	Ind-F	149	570	107	173	24	6	2	38	53	36	.304	.368	.377	745	93	-12	47			.939	23	*3-149	1.6
1915	New-F	127	451	49	113	22	5	1	43	41	31	.251	.316	.328	644	86	-16	28			.956	2	*3-117/O-1(0-0-1),M	-1.2
1916	NY-N	71	260	22	64	9	1	0	17	7	20	.246	.269	.288	557	75	-8	7			.940	-3	3-71	-1.1
	Cin-N	37	130	4	36	3	0	0	10	3	12	.277	.293	.300	593	84	-3	4			.960	-4	3-35	-0.7
	Yr	108	390	26	100	12	1	0	27	10	32	.256	.277	.292	569	78	-11	11			.947	-8	*3-106	-1.8
1917	Cin-N	48	134	11	34	3	1	0	15	7	7	.254	.296	.291	587	84	-3	5			.943	-7	2-26,S-13/3-4	-1.0
1918	Pit-N	126	435	34	111	13	9	2	43	24	22	.255	.297	.340	637	91	-5	12			.966	-1	*3-126	-0.3
1920	Pit-N	40	133	13	29	3	1	1	13	4	7	.218	.241	.278	519	47	-9	7	4	0	.943	-1	3-20,S-10/2-6,1-1	-1.0
Total	11	846	2843	319	713	86	33	8	240	190	199	.251	.301	.313	614	76	-106	127	4		.952	22	3-553,2-117/1-64,SO	-7.3
■ FRANK McKEE	McKee, Frank b: Philadelphia, Pa. Deb: 6/11/1884																							
1884	Was-U	4	17	2	3	0	0	0		1		.176	.222	.176	399	23	-2				.200	-2	/O-3(0-0-3),3-2,C-1	-0.3
■ RED McKEE	McKee, Raymond Ellis b: 7/20/1890, Shawnee, Ohio d: 8/5/72, Saginaw, Mich. BL/TR, 5'11", 180 lbs. Deb: 4/19/13																							
1913	Det-A	68	187	18	53	3	4	1	20	21	21	.283	.359	.358	717	112	3	7			.950	-5	C-62	0.3
1914	Det-A	34	64	7	12	1	1	0	8	14	16	.188	.342	.234	576	71	-2	1	2	-0	.964	-6	C-27	-0.7
1915	Det-A	55	106	10	29	5	0	1	17	13	16	.274	.353	.349	702	105	1	1			.954	-6	C-35	-0.3
1916	Det-A	32	76	3	16	1	2	0	4	6	11	.211	.268	.276	545	61	-4	0			.955	-5	C-26	-0.7
Total	4	189	433	38	110	10	7	2	49	54	64	.254	.339	.323	663	95	-1	9	2		.954	-22	C-150	-1.4
■ WALT McKEEL	McKeel, Walt Thomas b: 1/17/72, Wilson, N.C. BR/TR, 6'2", 200 lbs. Deb: 9/14/96																							
1996	Bos-A	1	0	0	0	0	0	0	0	0	0	—	—	—	—	—	0	0	0	0	.000	0	/C-1	0.0
1997	Bos-A	5	3	0	0	0	0	0	0	0	1	.000	.000	.000	0	-98	-1	0	0	0	1.000	0	/C-4,1-1	-0.1
Total	2	6	3	0	0	0	0	0	0	0	1	.000	.000	.000	0	-98	-1	0	0	0	1.000	0	/C-5,1-1	-0.1
■ JIM McKEEVER	McKeever, James b: 4/19/1861, St.John, N.B., Can. d: 8/19/1897, Boston, Mass. 5'10", 170 lbs. Deb: 4/17/1884																							
1884	Bos-U	16	66	13	9	0	0	0		0		.136	.136	.136	273	-17	-11				.869	-6	C-12/O-4(0-0-4)	-1.4
■ JOHN McKELVEY	McKelvey, John Wellington b: 8/27/1847, Rochester, N.Y. d: 5/31/44, Rochester, N.Y. BR/TR, 5'7.5", 175 lbs. Deb: 4/21/1875																							
1875	NH-n	43	188	26	43	3	1	0	10	5	8	.229	.249	.255	504	86	-1	3	1	0	.656	-8	O-39(0-4-35)/3-5	-0.5
■ RUSS McKELVY	McKelvy, Russell Errett b: 9/8/1854, Swissvale, Pa. d: 10/19/15, Omaha, Neb. BR/TR, Deb: 5/1/1878																							
1878	Ind-N	63	253	33	57	4	3	2	36	5	38	.225	.240	.289	529	84	-3				.846	6	*O-62(0-62-0)/P-4	0.0
1882	Pit-a	1	4	0	0	0	0	0		0		.000	.000	.000	0	-99	-1				.000	-0	/O-1(0-0-1)	-0.1
Total	2	64	257	33	57	4	3	2	36	5	38	.222	.237	.284	521	81	-4				.846	5	/O-63(0-62-1),P-4	-0.1
■ ED McKENNA	McKenna, Edward J. b: St.Louis, Mo. Deb: 7/29/1874																							
1874	Phi-n	1	4	0	0	0	0	0	0	0	1	.000	.000	.000	0	-97	-1	0	0	0	1.000	0	/1-1	-0.1
1877	StL-N	1	5	0	1	0	0	0	0	0	1	.200	.200	.200	400	28	-0				1.000	-0	/O-1(0-1-0)	-0.1
1884	Was-U	32	117	19	22	1	0	0		4		.188	.215	.197	411	26	-14				.876	-14	C-23,O-10(0-2-8)/3-7	-2.3
Total	2	33	122	19	23	1	0	0	0	4	1	.189	.214	.197	411	26	-14				.556	-14	/C-23,O-11(0-3-8),3-7	-2.4
■ DAVE McKEOUGH	McKeough, David J. b: 12/1/1863, Utica, N.Y. d: 7/11/01, Utica, N.Y. 5'7", 158 lbs. Deb: 4/22/1890																							
1890	Roc-a	62	218	38	49	5	0	0	20	29		.225	.316	.248	563	72	-6	14			.929	-4	C-47,S-13/2-2,3-1	-0.5
1891	Phi-a	15	54	4	14	1	1	0	3	8	6	.259	.355	.315	670	92	-0	0			.854	-4	C-14/S-1	-0.3
Total	2	77	272	42	63	6	1	0	23	37	6	.232	.324	.261	585	76	-7	14			.912	-9	/C-61,S-14,2-2,3-1	-0.8
■ RICH McKINNEY	McKinney, Charles Richard b: 11/22/46, Piqua, Ohio BR/TR, 5'11", 185 lbs. Deb: 6/26/70																							
1970	Chi-A	43	119	12	20	5	0	4	17	11	25	.168	.244	.311	555	50	-8	3	2	-0	.931	2	3-23,S-11	-0.5
1971	Chi-A	114	369	35	100	11	2	8	46	35	37	.271	.337	.377	714	99	-0	0	0	0	.968	-9	2-67,O-25(0-0-25)/3-5	-0.7
1972	NY-A	37	121	10	26	2	0	1	7	7	13	.215	.258	.256	514	55	-7	1	0	0	.917	-3	3-33	-1.1
1973	Oak-A	48	65	9	16	3	0	1	7	7	4	.246	.319	.338	658	90	-1	0	0	0	.900	-1	3-17/2-7,O-3L,D-6	-0.1
1974	Oak-A	5	7	0	1	0	0	0	0	0	0	.143	.143	.143	286	-19	-1	0	0	0	1.000	-2	/2-3	-0.4
1975	Oak-A	8	7	0	1	0	0	0	2	1	2	.143	.250	.143	393	14	-1	0	0	0	1.000	-0	/1-1,D-2	-0.1
1977	Oak-A	86	198	13	35	7	0	6	21	16	43	.177	.238	.303	541	47	-15	0	1	-0	.978	-4	1-32,D-18/3-7,O2	-2.2
Total	7	341	886	79	199	28	2	20	100	77	124	.225	.289	.328	617	73	-33	4	3	-0	.911	-17	/3-85,2-80,1-33,ODS	-5.1
■ BOB McKINNEY	McKinney, Robert Francis b: 10/4/1875, McSherrystown, Pa. d: 8/19/46, Hanover, Pa. BR/TR, 5'7", 165 lbs. Deb: 7/23/01																							
1901	Phi-A	2	2	0	0	0	0	0	0	0		.000	.000	.000	0	-96	-1	0			.000	-1	/2-1,3-1	-0.2
■ ALEX McKINNON	McKinnon, Alexander J. b: 8/14/1856, Boston, Mass. d: 7/24/1887, Charlestown, Mass BR, 5'11.5", 170 lbs. Deb: 5/1/1884 M																							
1884	NY-N	116	470	66	128	21	13	3	73	8	62	.272	.285	.391	676	108	3				.955	-2	*1-116	-0.9
1885	StL-N	100	411	42	121	21	6	1	44	8	31	.294	.308	.382	690	130	13				**.978**	0	*1-100,M	0.4
1886	StL-N	122	491	75	148	24	7	8	72	21	23	.301	.330	.428	758	138	22	10			.963	-6	*1-119/O-3(0-3-0)	0.5
1887	Pit-N	48	208	26	76	16	4	1	30	8	9	.365	.365	.475	840	140	11	6			.977	3	1-48	0.8
Total	4	386	1580	209	473	82	30	13	219	45	125	.299	.315	.411	726	127	48	16			.967	-5	1-383/O-3(0-3-0)	0.8
■ JIM McKNIGHT	McKnight, James Arthur b: 6/1/36, Bee Branch, Ark. d: 2/24/94, Van Buren County, Ark. BR/TR, 6'1", 185 lbs. Deb: 9/22/60 F																							
1960	Chi-N	3	6	0	2	0	0	0	1	0	1	.333	.333	.333	667	84	-0	0	0	0	.667	-2	/2-1,O-1(0-0-1)	-0.2
1962	Chi-N	60	85	6	19	0	1	0	5	2	13	.224	.241	.247	488	30	-8	0	0	0	.955	3	/3-9,O-5(0-0-5),2-2	-0.6
Total	2	63	91	6	21	0	1	0	6	2	14	.231	.247	.253	500	34	-8	0	0	0	.875	1	/3-9,O-6(0-0-6),2-3	-0.8
■ JEFF McKNIGHT	McKnight, Jefferson Alan b: 2/18/63, Conway, Ark. BB/TR, 6', 188 lbs. Deb: 6/6/89 F																							
1989	NY-N	6	12	2	3	0	0	0	0	2	1	.250	.357	.250	607	80	-0	0	0	0	1.000	-3	/2-4,1-1,3-1,S-1	-0.3
1990	Bal-A	29	75	11	15	2	0	1	4	5	17	.200	.259	.267	526	49	-5	0	0	0	1.000	-3	1-15/O-8L,2-5,SD	-0.9
1991	Bal-A	16	41	2	7	1	0	0	2	2	7	.171	.209	.195	404	13	-5	1	0	0	1.000	-0	/O-7(6-0-1),1-2,D-4	-0.5

YEAR	TM/L	G	AB	R	H	2B	3B	HR	RBI	BB	SO	AVG	OBP	SLG	OPS	OPS+	BR+	SB	CS	SBR	FA	FR	G/POS	TPR
1992	NY-N	31	85	10	23	3	1	2	13	2	8	.271	.287	.400	687	94	-1	0	1	-0	.980	-3	2-14/1-9,3-3,S-3,O	-0.4
1993	NY-N	105	164	19	42	3	1	2	13	13	31	.256	.315	.323	638	72	-6	0	0	0	.943	-7	S-29,2-15,1-10,/3C	-1.2
1994	NY-N	31	27	1	4	1	0	0	2	4	12	.148	.258	.185	443	18	-3	0	0	0	1.000	-0	/1-2	-0.3
Total	6	218	404	45	94	10	2	5	34	28	76	.233	.286	.304	590	63	-21	1	1	-0	.996	-16	/1-39,2-38,S-34,O3DC	-3.6
■ ED McLANE	McLane, Edward Cameron b: 8/20/1881, Weston, Mass. d: 8/21/75, Baltimore, Md. 5'10", 179 lbs. Deb: 10/6/07																							
1907	Bro-N	1	2	0	0	0	0	0	0	0		.000	.333	.000	333	5	-0	0			.333	-1	/O-1(0-0-1)	-0.1
■ ART McLARNEY	McLarney, Arthur James b: 12/20/08, Ft.Worden, Wash. d: 12/20/84, Seattle, Wash. BB/TR, 6', 168 lbs. Deb: 8/23/32																							
1932	NY-N	9	23	2	3	1	0	0	3	1	3	.130	.167	.174	341	-8	-4	0			1.000	-1	/S-7	-0.5
■ POLLY McLARRY	McLarry, Howard Zell b: 3/25/1891, Leonard, Tex. d: 11/4/71, Bonham, Tex. BL/TR, 6', 185 lbs. Deb: 9/2/12																							
1912	Chi-A	2	2	0	0	0	0	0	0	0		.000	.000	.000	0	-99	-1	0			.000	0	H	-0.1
1915	Chi-N	68	127	16	25	3	0	1	12	14	20	.197	.277	.244	521	58	-6	2	2	-0	.957	3	2-21,1-18	-0.4
Total	2	70	129	16	25	3	0	1	12	14	20	.194	.273	.240	513	56	-7	2	2		.957	3	/2-21,1-18	-0.5
■ BARNEY McLAUGHLIN	McLaughlin, Bernard b: 1857, Ireland d: 2/13/21, Lowell, Mass. BR/TR, Deb: 8/2/1884 F Career OF: (4-LF 3-CF 17-RF)																							
1884	KC-U	42	162	15	37	7	3	0		9		.228	.269	.309	578	86	-7				.762	-4	O-24R,2-12/P-7,S-2	-0.9
1887	Phi-N	50	216	26	56	8	3	1	26	11	27	.259	.263	.302	565	53	-13	2			.879	-11	2-50	-2.0
1890	Syr-a	86	329	43	87	8	1	2	40	47		.264	.360	.313	673	110	7	13			.902	-12	S-86	-0.2
Total	3	178	707	84	180	23	7	3	66	67	27	.255	.312	.309	621	86	-13	15			.900	-27	/S-88,2-62,O-24R,P	-3.1
■ FRANK McLAUGHLIN	McLaughlin, Francis Edward b: 6/19/1856, Lowell, Mass. d: 4/5/17, Lowell, Mass. BR/TR, 5'9", 160 lbs. Deb: 8/9/1882 F Career OF: (2-LF 10-CF 4-RF)																							
1882	Wor-N	15	55	7	12	0	2	1	4	0	11	.218	.218	.345	564	76	-2				.760	-3	S-14/O-1(0-1-0)	-0.4
1883	Pit-a	29	114	15	25	2	0	1		6		.219	.258	.263	521	71	-3				.802	-1	S-25/O-4C,2-2,P-2	-0.3
1884	Cin-U	16	67	10	16	4	1	2		2		.239	.261	.418	679	95	-3				.740	-7	S-16	-0.8
	CP-U	15	67	11	16	4	1	0		1		.239	.250	.328	578	74	-4				.888	6	2-14/S-1,O-1(0-0-1)	0.2
	KC-U	32	123	17	28	11	0	1		9		.228	.280	.341	622	101	-3				.847	-9	2-10,O-10C/3-9,SP	-1.0
	Yr	63	257	38	60	19	2	3		12		.233	.268	.358	626	92	-10				.873	-10	2-24,S-22,O-11C,/3P	-1.6
Total	3	107	426	60	97	21	4	5	4	18	11	.228	.259	.331	590	85	-15				.769	-15	/S-61,2-26,O-16C,3P	-2.3
■ JAMES McLAUGHLIN	McLaughlin, James b: San Francisco, Cal. Deb: 5/3/1884																							
1884	Was-U	10	37	3	7	3	0	0		0		.189	.189	.270	459	39	-4				.696	-3	/S-9,3-1	-0.6
■ KID McLAUGHLIN	McLaughlin, James Anson "Sunshine" b: 4/12/1888, Randolph, N.Y. d: 11/13/34, Allegany, N.Y. BL/TR, 5'8.5", 158 lbs. Deb: 6/30/14																							
1914	Cin-N	3	2	1	0	0	0	0	0	0	0	.000	.000	.000	0	-97	-0	0			1.000	-1	/O-2(0-2-0)	-0.1
■ JIM McLAUGHLIN	McLaughlin, James Robert b: 1/3/02, St.Louis, Mo. d: 12/18/68, Mount Vernon, Ill. BR/TR, 5'8.5", 168 lbs. Deb: 4/18/32																							
1932	StL-A	1	1	0	0	0	0	0	1	0	0	.000	.000	.000	0	-95	-0	0	0	0	.000	0	/3-1	0.0
■ TOM McLAUGHLIN	McLaughlin, Thomas b: 3/28/1860, Louisville, Ky. d: 7/21/21, Louisville, Ky. TR, Deb: 7/17/1883 Career OF: (9-LF 9-CF 1-RF)																							
1883	Lou-a	42	146	16	28	1	2	0		5		.192	.219	.226	445	47	-8				.844	4	S-19,O-17C/1-5,32	-0.4
1884	Lou-a	98	335	41	67	11	6	0	21	22		.200	.262	.269	530	77	-7				.892	18	*S-94/3-4,2-1	1.3
1885	Lou-a	112	411	49	87	13	9	2	41	15		.212	.245	.302	546	72	-13				.883	1	*2-93,S-19	-0.7
1886	NY-a	74	250	27	34	3	1	0	16	26		.136	.220	.156	376	19	-22	13			.886	7	S-63,2-10/O-1(1-0-0)	-1.1
1891	Was-a	14	41	9	11	0	1	0	3	7	6	.268	.400	.317	717	111	1	3			.871	-0	S-14	0.1
Total	5	340	1183	142	227	28	19	2	81	75	6	.192	.247	.253	500	61	-49	16			.886	30	S-209,2-106/O-18L,31	-0.8
■ RALPH McLAURIN	McLaurin, Ralph Edgar b: 5/23/1885, Kissimmee, Fla. d: 2/11/43, McColl, S.C. Deb: 9/5/08																							
1908	StL-N	8	22	2	5	0	0	0	0	0		.227	.227	.227	455	47	-1	0			.875	-0	/O-6(6-0-0)	-0.2
■ LARRY McLEAN	McLean, John Bannerman b: 7/18/1881, Fredericton, N.B., Canada d: 3/24/21, Boston, Mass. BR/TR, 6'5", 228 lbs. Deb: 4/26/01																							
1901	Bos-A	9	19	4	4	1	0	0	2	0		.211	.211	.263	474	31	-2	1			1.000	0	/1-5	-0.1
1903	Chi-N	1	4	0	0	0	0	0	1	1		.000	.200	.000	200	-42	-1	0			.889	-0	/C-1	-0.1
1904	StL-N	27	84	5	14	2	1	0	4	4		.167	.205	.214	419	31	-7	1			.954	-2	C-24	-0.7
1906	Cin-N	12	35	3	7	2	0	0	2	4		.200	.282	.257	539	65	-1	0			.954	-1	C-12	-0.2
1907	Cin-N	113	374	35	108	9	9	0	54	13		.289	.313	.361	674	107	1	4			.975	-3	C-89,1-13	0.8
1908	Cin-N	99	309	24	67	9	4	1	28	15		.217	.258	.282	539	74	-10	2			.963	-6	C-69,1-19	-1.0
1909	Cin-N	95	324	26	83	12	2	2	36	21		.256	.307	.324	632	97	-2	1			.978	-6	C-95	0.2
1910	Cin-N	127	423	27	126	14	7	2	71	26	23	.298	.340	.378	718	114	6	4			.983	-4	*C-119	1.4
1911	Cin-N	107	328	24	94	7	2	0	34	20	18	.287	.330	.320	650	85	-7	1			.968	8	C-98	0.9
1912	Cin-N	102	333	17	81	15	1	1	27	18	15	.243	.284	.303	587	63	-18	1			.973	-2	C-98	-1.1
1913	StL-N	48	152	7	41	9	0	0	12	6	9	.270	.297	.329	626	80	-4	0			.981	-8	C-42	-0.9
	*NY-N	30	75	3	24	4	0	0	9	4	4	.320	.354	.373	728	107	1	1			.953	-4	C-28	-0.1
	Yr	78	227	10	65	13	0	0	21	10	13	.286	.316	.344	660	89	-4	1			.970	-12	C-70	-1.0
1914	NY-N	79	154	8	40	6	0	0	14	4	9	.260	.283	.299	582	76	-5	4			.973	-4	C-74	-0.5
1915	NY-N	13	33	0	5	0	0	0	4	0	1	.152	.152	.152	303	-9	-4	0			.985	2	C-12	-0.2
Total	13	862	2647	183	694	90	26	6	298	136	79	.262	.301	.323	623	86	-52	20			.973	-29	C-761/1-37	-1.6
■ MARK McLEMORE	McLemore, Mark Tremell b: 10/4/64, San Diego, Cal. BB/TR, 5'11", 195 lbs. Deb: 9/13/86 Career OF: (88-LF 1-CF 144-RF)																							
1986	Cal-A	5	4	0	0	0	0	0	0	1	2	.000	.200	.000	200	-40	-1	0	1	-0	1.000	4	/2-2	0.2
1987	Cal-A	138	433	61	102	13	3	3	41	48	72	.236	.312	.300	612	66	-20	25	8	3	.974	-5	*2-132/S-6,D-3	-1.5
1988	Cal-A	77	233	38	56	11	2	2	16	25	28	.240	.314	.330	644	83	-5	13	7	0	.979	7	2-63/3-5,D-1	0.4
1989	Cal-A	32	103	12	25	3	1	0	14	7	19	.243	.297	.291	589	68	-4	6	1	1	.966	3	2-27/D-1	0.0
1990	Cal-A	20	48	4	7	2	0	0	2	4	9	.146	.212	.188	399	13	-6	1	0	0	1.000	-1	/2-8,S-8,D-1	-0.6
	Cle-A	8	12	2	2	0	0	0	0	0	6	.167	.167	.167	333	-7	-2	0	0	0	1.000	3	/3-4,2-3,D-1	0.1
	Yr	28	60	6	9	2	0	0	2	4	15	.150	.203	.183	386	9	-7	1	0	0	1.000	2	2-11/S-8,3-4,D-2	-0.5
1991	Hou-N	21	61	6	9	1	0	0	2	6	13	.148	.224	.164	388	11	-7	0	1	-0	.975	1	2-19	-0.6
1992	Bal-A	101	228	40	56	7	2	0	27	21	26	.246	.309	.294	603	68	-9	11	5	1	.978	9	2-70,D-17	0.1
1993	Bal-A	148	581	81	165	27	5	4	72	64	92	.284	.356	.368	724	91	-6	21	15	-1	.987	12	*O-124R,2-25/3-4,D	-0.1
1994	Bal-A	104	343	44	88	11	1	3	29	51	50	.257	.354	.321	675	72	-13	20	5	3	.981	-3	2-96/O-7(0-0-7),D-1	-0.8
1995	Tex-A	129	467	73	122	20	5	5	41	59	71	.261	.348	.358	705	82	-11	21	11	1	.986	-1	O-73(69-0-5),2-66/D-2	-1.0
1996	*Tex-A	147	517	84	150	23	4	5	46	87	69	.290	.392	.379	771	92	-3	27	10	2	.985	20	*2-147/O-1(0-0-1)	2.4
1997	Tex-A	89	349	47	91	17	2	1	25	40	54	.261	.340	.330	670	72	-13	7	5	-0	.980	-6	2-89/O-1(1-0-0)	-1.5
1998	*Tex-A	126	461	79	114	15	1	5	53	89	64	.247	.371	.317	688	78	-11	12	4	1	.975	-7	*2-122/D-2	-1.0
1999	*Tex-A	144	566	105	155	20	7	6	45	83	79	.274	.367	.366	732	84	-11	16	8	1	.983	5	*2-135,O-11(4-0-7)	0.0
2000	*Sea-A	138	481	72	118	23	1	3	46	81	78	.245	.355	.316	671	74	-17	30	14	2	.987	-4	*2-129,O-14(14-1-0)	-1.2
Total	15	1427	4887	748	1260	193	34	37	459	666	732	.258	.348	.334	682	78	-140	210	95	13	.981	34	*2-1133,O-231R/DS3	-5.1
■ RALPH McLEOD	McLeod, Ralph Alton b: 10/19/16, N.Quincy, Mass. BL/TL, 6', 170 lbs. Deb: 9/14/38																							
1938	Bos-N	6	7	1	2	1	0	0	0	0	2	.286	.286	.429	714	105	-0	0			1.000	-0	/O-1(1-0-0)	0.0
■ JIM McLEOD	McLeod, Soule James b: 9/12/08, Jones, La. d: 8/3/81, Little Rock, Ark. BR/TR, 6', 187 lbs. Deb: 5/22/30																							
1930	Was-A	18	34	3	9	1	0	0	1	1	5	.265	.306	.294	600	53	-2	1	1	-0	1.000	-1	3-10/S-7	-0.2
1932	Was-A	7	0	1	0	0	0	0	0	1	0	—	1.000	—	1000	183	0	0	0	0	1.000	0	/S-1	0.1
1933	Phi-N	67	232	20	45	6	1	0	15	12	25	.194	.237	.228	465	30	-21	1			.914	-6	3-67/S-1	-2.6
Total	3	92	266	24	54	7	1	0	16	14	30	.203	.248	.237	485	33	-23	2	1		.922	-6	/3-77,S-9	-2.7
■ JACK McMAHON	McMahon, John Henry b: 10/15/1869, Waterbury, Conn. d: 12/30/1894, Bridgeport, Conn. BR/TL, 5'10", 165 lbs. Deb: 8/8/1892																							
1892	NY-N	40	147	21	33	5	7	1	24	10	9	.224	.278	.374	653	98	-1	3			.973	-2	1-36/C-5	-0.3
1893	NY-N	11	30	5	10	2	1	0	4	2	0	.333	.375	.467	842	123	1	0			.891	-1	C-11	0.1
Total	2	51	177	26	43	7	8	1	28	12	9	.243	.295	.390	685	103	-0	3			.900	-3	/1-36,C-16	-0.2

■ **FRANK McMANUS** McManus, Francis E. b: 9/21/1875, Lawrence, Mass. d: 9/1/23, Syracuse, N.Y. TR, 5'7", 150 lbs. Deb: 9/14/1899

YEAR	TM/L	G	AB	R	H	2B	3B	HR	RBI	BB	SO	AVG	OBP	SLG	OPS	OPS+	BR+	SB	CS	SBR	FA	FR	G/POS	TPR
1899	Was-N	7	21	3	8	1	0	0	2	2		.381	.435	.429	863	139	1	3			.931	0	/C-7	0.2
1903	Bro-N	2	7	0	0	0	0	0	0	0		.000	.000	.000	0	-99	-2	0			.929	1	/C-2	-0.1
1904	Det-A	1	0	0	0	0	0	0	0	0		—	—	—	—	—	0	0			.000	0	/C-1	0.0
	NY-A	4	7	0	0	0	0	0	0	0		.000	.000	.000	0	-96	-2	0			.900	-1	/C-4	-0.3
	Yr	5	7	0	0	0	0	0	0	0		.000	.000	.000	0	-97	-2	0			.900	-1	/C-5	-0.3
Total	3	14	35	3	8	1	0	0	2	2		.229	.270	.257	527	50	-2	3			.925	-0	/C-14	-0.2

■ **JIM McMANUS** McManus, James Michael b: 7/20/36, Brookline, Mass. BL/TL, 6'4", 215 lbs. Deb: 9/21/60

YEAR	TM/L	G	AB	R	H	2B	3B	HR	RBI	BB	SO	AVG	OBP	SLG	OPS	OPS+	BR+	SB	CS	SBR	FA	FR	G/POS	TPR
1960	KC-A	5	13	3	4	0	0	1	2	1	2	.308	.357	.538	896	138	1	0	0	0	1.000	-0	/1-3	0.0

■ **MARTY McMANUS** McManus, Martin Joseph b: 3/14/1900, Chicago, Ill. d: 2/18/66, St.Louis, Mo. BR/TR, 5'10.5", 160 lbs. Deb: 9/26/20 M Career OF: (0-LF 0-CF 1-RF)

YEAR	TM/L	G	AB	R	H	2B	3B	HR	RBI	BB	SO	AVG	OBP	SLG	OPS	OPS+	BR+	SB	CS	SBR	FA	FR	G/POS	TPR
1920	StL-A	1	3	0	1	0	1	0	1	0	0	.333	.333	1.000	1333	237	0	0	0	0	.667	-0	/3-1	0.0
1921	StL-A	121	412	49	107	19	8	3	64	27	30	.260	.308	.367	675	68	-21	5	3	0	.952	-11	2-96,3-13/1-9,S-2	-2.7
1922	StL-A	154	606	88	189	34	11	11	109	38	41	.312	.358	.459	817	108	6	9	6	-0	.964	3	*2-153/1-1	1.2
1923	StL-A	154	582	86	180	35	10	15	94	49	50	.309	.367	.481	848	116	11	14	10	-0	.960	-1	*2-133,1-20	1.1
1924	StL-A	123	442	71	147	23	5	5	80	55	40	.333	.409	.441	850	112	9	13	9	-0	.972	7	*2-119	1.8
1925	StL-A	154	587	108	169	**44**	8	13	90	73	69	.288	.371	.457	828	104	3	5	11	-3	.967	4	*2-154/O-1(0-0-1)	0.7
1926	StL-A	149	549	102	156	30	10	9	68	55	62	.284	.350	.424	775	97	-4	5	7	-1	.958	15	3-84,2-61/1-4	1.6
1927	Det-A	108	369	60	99	19	7	9	69	34	38	.268	.332	.431	763	95	-4	8	7	-1	.960	-2	S-39,2-35,3-22,/1-6	0.0
1928	Det-A	139	500	78	144	37	5	8	73	51	32	.288	.355	.430	785	104	2	11	13	-2	.955	0	3-92,1-45/S-2	0.4
1929	Det-A	154	599	99	168	32	8	18	90	60	52	.280	.347	.451	798	103	2	16	11	-0	.972	8	*3-150/S-8	1.8
1930	Det-A	132	484	74	155	40	4	9	89	59	28	.320	.396	.475	872	118	14	**23**	8	2	**.966**	6	*3-130/S-3,1-1	2.7
1931	Det-A	107	362	39	98	17	3	3	53	49	22	.271	.361	.359	720	87	-6	7	3	0	.950	13	3-79,2-21/1-1	1.1
	Bos-A	17	62	8	18	4	0	1	9	8	1	.290	.371	.403	775	110	1	1	1	-0	1.000	8	3-11/2-7	0.9
	Yr	124	424	47	116	21	3	4	62	57	23	.274	.362	.366	728	90	-5	8	4	0	.956	21	3-90,2-28/1-1	2.0
1932	Bos-A	93	302	39	71	19	4	5	24	36	30	.235	.317	.374	691	80	-9	1	2	-0	.969	6	2-49,3-30/S-2,1M	0.0
1933	Bos-A	106	366	51	104	30	4	3	36	49	21	.284	.369	.413	781	108	5	3	0	1	.957	-5	3-76,2-26/1-4,M	0.4
1934	Bos-N	119	435	56	120	18	0	8	47	32	42	.276	.330	.372	702	95	-3	5			.964	-5	2-73,3-37	-0.3
Total	15	1831	6660	1008	1926	401	88	120	996	675	558	.289	.357	.430	787	101	6	126	91		.965	44	2-927,3-725/1-92,SO	10.7

■ **JIMMY McMATH** McMath, Jimmy Lee b: 8/10/49, Tuscaloosa, Ala. BL/TL, 6'1.5", 195 lbs. Deb: 9/7/68

YEAR	TM/L	G	AB	R	H	2B	3B	HR	RBI	BB	SO	AVG	OBP	SLG	OPS	OPS+	BR+	SB	CS	SBR	FA	FR	G/POS	TPR
1968	Chi-N	6	14	0	2	0	0	0	2	0	6	.143	.143	.143	286	-13	-2	0	0	0	1.000	0	/O-3(3-0-0)	-0.2

■ **GEORGE McMILLAN** McMillan, George A. "Reddy" b: Evansville, Ind. 5'8", 175 lbs. Deb: 8/11/1890

YEAR	TM/L	G	AB	R	H	2B	3B	HR	RBI	BB	SO	AVG	OBP	SLG	OPS	OPS+	BR+	SB	CS	SBR	FA	FR	G/POS	TPR
1890	NY-N	10	35	4	5	0	0	0	1	7	4	.143	.286	.143	429	26	-3	1			.800	-1	O-10(1-0-9)	-0.4

■ **NORM McMILLAN** McMillan, Norman Alexis "Bub" b: 10/5/1895, Latta, S.C. d: 9/28/69, Marion, S.C. BR/TR, 6', 175 lbs. Deb: 4/12/22

YEAR	TM/L	G	AB	R	H	2B	3B	HR	RBI	BB	SO	AVG	OBP	SLG	OPS	OPS+	BR+	SB	CS	SBR	FA	FR	G/POS	TPR
1922	*NY-A	33	78	7	20	1	2	0	11	6	10	.256	.310	.321	630	63	-4	4	1	1	.921	-8	O-26(0-15-12)/3-5	-1.2
1923	Bos-A	131	459	37	116	24	5	0	42	28	44	.253	.299	.327	625	64	-25	13	5	1	.942	13	3-67,2-34,S-28	-0.3
1924	StL-A	76	201	25	56	12	2	0	27	12	17	.279	.332	.358	690	73	-8	6	4	-0	.966	-3	2-37,3-19/S-7,1-2	-0.9
1928	Chi-N	49	123	11	27	2	2	1	12	13	19	.220	.299	.293	592	56	-8	0			.977	-1	2-19,3-18	-0.7
1929	*Chi-N	124	495	77	134	35	5	5	55	36	43	.271	.324	.392	716	76	-19	13			.944	6	*3-120	-0.5
Total	5	413	1356	157	353	74	16	6	147	95	133	.260	.313	.352	665	69	-64	36	10		.944	7	3-229/2-90,S-35,O1	-3.6

■ **ROY McMILLAN** McMillan, Roy David b: 7/17/29, Bonham, Tex. d: 11/2/97, Bonham, Tex. BR/TR, 5'11", 170 lbs. Deb: 4/17/51 MC

YEAR	TM/L	G	AB	R	H	2B	3B	HR	RBI	BB	SO	AVG	OBP	SLG	OPS	OPS+	BR+	SB	CS	SBR	FA	FR	G/POS	TPR
1951	Cin-N	85	199	21	42	4	0	1	8	17	26	.211	.273	.246	519	40	-17	0	0	0	.963	5	S-54,3-12/2-1	-0.9
1952	Cin-N	154	540	60	132	32	2	7	57	45	81	.244	.306	.350	656	82	-14	4	5	-1	.971	11	*S-154	0.6
1953	Cin-N	155	557	51	130	15	4	5	43	43	52	.233	.290	.302	591	54	-37	2	4	-1	.972	14	*S-155	-1.1
1954	Cin-N	154	588	86	147	21	2	4	42	47	54	.250	.311	.313	624	61	-33	4	2	0	.959	6	*S-154	-1.4
1955	Cin-N	151	470	50	126	21	2	1	37	66	33	.268	.366	.328	694	81	-10	4	4	-1	.969	17	*S-150	1.9
1956	Cin-N★	150	479	51	126	16	7	3	62	76	54	.263	.370	.344	714	88	-5	4	3	-0	**.975**	**30**	*S-150	3.8
1957	Cin-N★	151	448	50	122	25	5	1	55	66	44	.272	.373	.357	730	91	-3	5	1	1	**.977**	-8	*S-151	0.2
1958	Cin-N	145	393	48	90	18	3	1	25	47	33	.229	.313	.298	611	60	-22	5	2	0	**.980**	4	*S-145	-0.6
1959	Cin-N	79	246	38	65	14	2	9	24	27	27	.264	.347	.447	794	106	2	0	2	-1	.974	-7	S-73	0.1
1960	Cin-N	124	399	42	94	12	2	10	42	35	40	.236	.304	.351	655	77	-12	2	0	0	.964	-13	*S-116,2-10	-1.6
1961	Mil-N	154	505	42	111	16	0	7	48	61	86	.220	.309	.293	602	65	-25	2	4	-1	**.975**	-0	*S-154	-1.2
1962	Mil-N	137	468	66	115	13	0	12	41	60	53	.246	.338	.350	688	87	-7	2	2	-0	.972	1	*S-135	0.5
1963	Mil-N	100	320	35	80	10	1	4	29	17	25	.250	.292	.325	617	78	-9	1	5	-2	.979	7	S-94	0.5
1964	Mil-N	8	13	1	4	0	0	0	2	0	2	.308	.308	.308	615	73	-0	1	0	0	.933	-1	/S-8	-0.1
	NY-N	113	379	30	80	8	2	1	25	14	16	.211	.247	.251	498	42	-29	3	1	0	.976	-1	*S-111	-2.1
	Yr	121	392	31	84	8	2	1	27	14	18	.214	.249	.253	501	43	-30	4	1	1	.975	-2	*S-119	-2.2
1965	NY-N	157	528	44	128	19	2	1	42	24	60	.242	.281	.292	572	64	-25	1	0	0	.964	-4	*S-153	-1.8
1966	NY-N	76	220	24	47	9	1	1	12	20	25	.214	.285	.277	562	59	-12	1	1	-0	.975	6	S-71	-0.2
Total	16	2093	6752	739	1639	253	35	68	594	665	711	.243	.316	.321	637	72	-258	41	36	-4	.972	66	*S-2028/3-12,2-11	-3.4

■ **TOM McMILLAN** McMillan, Thomas Erwin b: 9/13/51, Richmond, Va. BR/TR, 5'9", 165 lbs. Deb: 9/17/77

YEAR	TM/L	G	AB	R	H	2B	3B	HR	RBI	BB	SO	AVG	OBP	SLG	OPS	OPS+	BR+	SB	CS	SBR	FA	FR	G/POS	TPR
1977	Sea-A	2	5	0	0	0	0	0	0	0	0	.000	.000	.000	0	-99	-1	0	0	0	1.000	-0	/S-2	-0.2

■ **TOMMY McMILLAN** McMillan, Thomas Law "Rebel" b: 4/18/1888, Pittston, Pa. d: 7/15/66, Orlando, Fla. BR/TR, 5'5", 130 lbs. Deb: 8/19/08 Career OF: (0-LF 14-CF 0-RF)

YEAR	TM/L	G	AB	R	H	2B	3B	HR	RBI	BB	SO	AVG	OBP	SLG	OPS	OPS+	BR+	SB	CS	SBR	FA	FR	G/POS	TPR
1908	Bro-N	43	147	9	35	3	0	0	3	9		.238	.296	.259	554	80	-3	5			.873	-5	S-29,O-14(0-14-0)	-0.9
1909	Bro-N	108	373	18	79	15	1	0	24	20		.212	.254	.257	511	61	-18	11			.914	-10	*S-105/2-2,3-1	-2.8
1910	Bro-N	23	74	2	13	1	0	0	2	6	10	.176	.237	.189	427	26	-7	4			.898	-1	S-23	-0.8
	Cin-N	82	248	20	46	0	3	0	13	31	23	.185	.281	.210	491	46	-16	7			.927	10	S-82	-0.4
	Yr	105	322	22	59	1	3	0	15	37	33	.183	.271	.205	476	41	-23	11			.921	8	*S-105	-1.2
1912	NY-A	41	149	24	34	2	0	0	12	15		.228	.303	.242	545	53	-9	18			.948	-8	S-41	-1.4
Total	4	297	991	73	207	21	4	0	54	81	33	.209	.273	.238	512	56	-53	45			.917	-15	S-280/O-14C,2-2,3-1	-6.3

■ **BILLY McMILLON** McMillon, William Edward b: 11/17/71, Otero, N.Mex. BL/TL, 5'11", 172 lbs. Deb: 7/26/96

YEAR	TM/L	G	AB	R	H	2B	3B	HR	RBI	BB	SO	AVG	OBP	SLG	OPS	OPS+	BR+	SB	CS	SBR	FA	FR	G/POS	TPR
1996	Fla-N	28	51	4	11	0	0	0	4	5	14	.216	.286	.216	501	36	-5	0	0	0	1.000	-2	O-15(15-0-0)	-0.7
1997	Fla-N	13	18	0	2	1	0	0	1	0	7	.111	.111	.167	278	-30	-3	0	0	0	1.000	0	/O-2(0-0-2)	-0.3
	Phi-N	24	72	10	21	4	1	2	13	6	17	.292	.346	.458	804	109	1	2	1	0	.957	3	O-21(19-0-2)	0.3
	Yr	37	90	10	23	5	1	2	14	6	24	.256	.302	.400	702	83	-2	2	1	0	.957	3	O-23(19-0-4)	0.0
2000	Det-A	46	123	20	37	7	1	4	24	19	19	.301	.399	.472	870	123	5	1	0	0	.964	-1	D-24,O-15(3-0-13)	0.2
Total	3	111	264	34	71	12	2	6	42	30	57	.269	.346	.398	743	93	-2	3	1	0	.968	-0	/O-53(37-0-17),D-24	-0.5

■ **HUGH McMULLEN** McMullen, Hugh Raphael b: 12/16/01, LaCygne, Kan. d: 5/23/86, Whittier, Cal. BB/TR, 6'1", 180 lbs. Deb: 9/19/25

YEAR	TM/L	G	AB	R	H	2B	3B	HR	RBI	BB	SO	AVG	OBP	SLG	OPS	OPS+	BR+	SB	CS	SBR	FA	FR	G/POS	TPR
1925	NY-N	5	15	1	2	1	0	0	0	0	3	.133	.133	.200	333	-17	-3	0	0	0	1.000	-2	/C-5	-0.4
1926	NY-N	57	91	5	17	2	0	0	6	2	18	.187	.204	.209	413	11	-11	1			.942	-0	C-56	-0.9
1928	Was-A	1	1	0	0	0	0	0	0	0	1	.000	.000	.000	0	-99	-0	0	0	0	.000	0	H	0.0
1929	Cin-N	1	1	0	0	0	0	0	0	0	0	.000	.000	.000	0	-99	-0	0			1.000	0	/C-1	0.0
Total	4	64	108	6	19	3	0	0	6	2	22	.176	.191	.204	395	5	-15	1	0		.947	-2	/C-62	-1.3

■ **KEN McMULLEN** McMullen, Kenneth Lee b: 6/1/42, Oxnard, Cal. BR/TR, 6'3", 195 lbs. Deb: 9/17/62 Career OF: (12-LF 0-CF 8-RF)

YEAR	TM/L	G	AB	R	H	2B	3B	HR	RBI	BB	SO	AVG	OBP	SLG	OPS	OPS+	BR+	SB	CS	SBR	FA	FR	G/POS	TPR
1962	LA-N	6	11	0	3	0	0	0	0	0	3	.273	.273	.273	545	50	-1	0	0	0	1.000	-0	/O-2(2-0-0)	-0.1
1963	LA-N	79	233	16	55	9	0	5	28	20	46	.236	.299	.339	638	89	-3	1	2	-0	.933	6	3-71/2-1,O-1(1-0-0)	0.2
1964	LA-N	24	67	3	14	0	0	1	2	3	7	.209	.243	.254	497	43	-5	0	1	-0	.991	-3	1-13/3-4,O-3(1-0-2)	-1.0
1965	Was-A	150	555	75	146	18	6	18	54	47	90	.263	.325	.414	739	110	7	2	0	0	.954	6	*3-142/O-8(3-0-5),1-1	1.2
1966	Was-A	147	524	48	122	19	4	13	54	44	89	.233	.292	.359	651	87	-9	3	1	0	.951	-1	*3-141/1-8,O-1(0-0-1)	-1.2
1967	Was-A	146	563	73	138	22	2	16	67	46	84	.245	.303	.377	680	104	1	5	3	0	.965	12	*3-145	1.5
1968	Was-A	151	557	66	138	11	2	20	62	63	66	.248	.327	.382	710	118	12	1	3	-1	.962	5	*3-145,S-11	1.8

YEAR	TM/L	G	AB	R	H	2B	3B	HR	RBI	BB	SO	AVG	OBP	SLG	OPS	OPS+	BR+	SB	CS	SBR	FA	FR	G/POS	TPR
1969	Was-A	158	562	83	153	25	2	19	87	70	103	.272	.354	.425	779	123	17	4	5	-1	.976	19	*3-154	3.5
1970	Was-A	15	59	5	12	2	0	0	3	5	10	.203	.266	.237	503	42	-5	0	0	0	.971	6	3-15	0.1
	Cal-A	124	422	50	98	9	3	14	61	59	81	.232	.331	.367	698	96	-2	1	0	0	.959	9	*3-122	0.7
	Yr	139	481	55	110	11	3	14	64	64	91	.229	.323	.351	674	89	-7	1	0	0	.960	15	*3-137	0.8
1971	Cal-A	160	593	63	148	19	2	21	68	53	74	.250	.314	.395	709	107	4	1	1	-0	.966	-1	*3-158	0.2
1972	Cal-A	137	472	36	127	18	1	9	34	48	59	.269	.337	.369	705	116	9	1	2	-0	.970	2	*3-137	1.2
1973	LA-N	42	85	6	21	5	0	5	18	6	13	.247	.297	.482	779	118	1	0	0	0	.922	5	3-24	0.6
1974	*LA-N	44	60	5	15	1	0	3	12	2	12	.250	.274	.417	691	95	-1	0	0	0	1.000	-1	/3-7,2-3	-0.1
1975	LA-N	39	46	4	11	1	1	2	14	7	12	.239	.340	.435	774	119	1	0	0	0	1.000	1	3-11/1-3	0.2
1976	Oak-A	98	186	20	41	6	2	5	23	22	33	.220	.306	.355	661	97	-1	1	1	-0	.952	-1	3-35,1-26,D-23,/O2	-0.5
1977	Mil-A	63	136	15	31	7	1	5	19	15	33	.228	.305	.404	709	91	-2	0	0	0	.978	2	D-29,1-11/3-7	-0.2
Total	16	1583	5131	568	1273	172	26	156	606	510	815	.248	.318	.383	701	105	24	20	19	-2	.961	66	*3-1318/1-62,DOS2	8.1

■ FRED McMULLIN

McMullin, Frederick William b: 10/13/1891, Scammon, Kan. d: 11/21/52, Los Angeles, Cal. BR/TR, 5'11", 170 lbs. Deb: 8/27/14

YEAR	TM/L	G	AB	R	H	2B	3B	HR	RBI	BB	SO	AVG	OBP	SLG	OPS	OPS+	BR+	SB	CS	SBR	FA	FR	G/POS	TPR
1914	Det-A	1	1	0	0	0	0	0	0	0	0	.000	.000	.000	0	-97	-0	0			.667	0	/S-1	0.0
1916	Chi-A	68	187	8	48	3	0	0	10	19	30	.257	.332	.273	604	81	-4	9			.950	-4	3-63/S-2,2-1	-0.7
1917	*Chi-A	59	194	35	46	2	1	0	12	27	17	.237	.339	.258	597	81	-3	9			.932	-13	3-52/S-2	-1.7
1918	Chi-A	70	235	32	65	7	0	1	16	25	26	.277	.356	.319	675	103	2	7			.941	-2	3-69/2-1	0.2
1919	*Chi-A	60	170	31	50	8	4	0	19	11	18	.294	.355	.388	743	108	2	4			.931	-0	3-46/2-5	0.3
1920	Chi-A	46	127	14	25	1	4	0	13	9	13	.197	.255	.268	523	39	-11	1	1	-0	.962	-5	3-29/2-3,S-1	-1.5
Total	6	304	914	120	234	21	9	1	70	91	105	.256	.333	.302	635	85	-15	30	1		.942	-24	3-259/2-10,S-6	-3.4

■ JOHN McMULLIN

McMullin, John F. "Lefty" b: 1848, Philadelphia, Pa. d: 4/11/1881, Philadelphia, Pa. BR/TL, 5'9", 160 lbs. Deb: 5/9/1871 Career OF: (119-LF 84-CF 12-RF)

YEAR	TM/L	G	AB	R	H	2B	3B	HR	RBI	BB	SO	AVG	OBP	SLG	OPS	OPS+	BR+	SB	CS	SBR	FA	FR	G/POS	TPR
1871	Tro-n	29	136	38	38	0	5	0	32	8	6	.279	.319	.353	672	92	-1	11	1	2	.871	0	*P-29/S-1	0.0
1872	Mut-n	54	237	48	61	6	1	0	25	11	6	.257	.290	.291	581	85	-2	8	2	1	.871	6	*O-53(41-1-11)/P-3	0.5
1873	Ath-n	52	227	54	62	7	1	0	29	8	4	.273	.298	.313	611	76	-8	9	1	2	.828	-4	*O-51(51-0-0)/P-1	-0.6
1874	Ath-n	55	260	61	90	10	2	2	32	8	13	.346	.366	.423	789	140	10	4	3	-0	.771	-4	*O-55(5-51-1)	0.4
1875	Phi-n	54	222	33	57	9	4	2	19	5	12	.257	.273	.360	633	114	3	6	10	-2	.835	-1	*O-54(22-32-0)/P-4	0.1
Total	5 n	244	1082	234	308	32	13	4	137	40	41	.285	.310	.349	660	103	1	38	17	2	.829	-3	*O-213L/P-37,S-1	0.4

■ CARL McNABB

McNabb, Carl Mac "Skinny" b: 1/25/17, Stevenson, Ala. BR/TR, 5'9", 155 lbs. Deb: 4/20/45

YEAR	TM/L	G	AB	R	H	2B	3B	HR	RBI	BB	SO	AVG	OBP	SLG	OPS	OPS+	BR+	SB	CS	SBR	FA	FR	G/POS	TPR
1945	Det-A	1	1	0	0	0	0	0	0	0	1	.000	.000	.000	0	-94	-0	0	0	0	.000	0	H	0.0

■ ERIC McNAIR

McNair, Donald Eric "Boob" b: 4/12/09, Meridian, Miss. d: 3/11/49, Meridian, Miss. BR/TR, 5'8.5", 160 lbs. Deb: 9/20/29 Career OF: (0-LF 0-CF 1-RF)

YEAR	TM/L	G	AB	R	H	2B	3B	HR	RBI	BB	SO	AVG	OBP	SLG	OPS	OPS+	BR+	SB	CS	SBR	FA	FR	G/POS	TPR
1929	Phi-A	4	8	2	4	1	0	0	3	0	0	.500	.500	.625	1125	181	1	1	0	0	1.000	-0	/S-4	0.1
1930	*Phi-A	78	237	27	63	12	2	0	34	9	19	.266	.296	.333	629	57	-16	5	2	0	.915	-7	S-31,3-29/2-5,O-1R	-1.6
1931	*Phi-A	79	280	41	76	10	1	5	33	11	19	.271	.306	.368	674	72	-12	1	4	-1	.915	-6	3-47,2-16,S-13	-1.5
1932	Phi-A	135	554	87	158	**47**	3	18	95	28	29	.285	.323	.478	801	101	-2	8	4	0	.953	-7	*S-133	0.1
1933	Phi-A	89	310	57	81	15	4	7	48	15	32	.261	.302	.403	705	84	-8	2	1	0	.966	-2	S-46,2-27	-0.5
1934	Phi-A	151	599	80	168	20	4	17	82	35	42	.280	.321	.412	734	91	-10	7	8	-1	.951	4	*S-151	0.3
1935	Phi-A	137	526	55	142	22	2	4	57	35	33	.270	.319	.342	661	72	-22	3	7	-2	.955	-21	*S-121,3-11/1-2	-3.4
1936	Bos-A	128	494	68	141	36	2	4	74	27	34	.285	.329	.391	720	73	-22	3	3	-0	.966	-12	S-84,2-35,3-11	-2.3
1937	Bos-A	126	455	60	133	29	4	12	76	30	33	.292	.340	.453	793	94	-5	10	7	-0	.969	-6	*2-106/S-9,3-4,1-1	-0.4
1938	Bos-A	46	96	9	15	1	1	0	7	3	6	.156	.182	.188	369	-7	-16	0	1	-0	.870	3	S-15,2-14/3-3	-1.1
1939	Chi-A	129	479	62	155	18	5	7	82	38	41	.324	.375	.426	800	102	1	17	9	1	.937	4	*3-103,2-19/S-9	1.0
1940	Chi-A	66	251	26	57	13	1	7	31	12	26	.227	.265	.371	636	62	-15	1	7	-2	.958	-17	2-65/3-1	-2.9
1941	Det-A	23	59	5	11	1	0	0	3	4	4	.186	.250	.203	453	19	-7	0	0	0	.970	-2	3-11/S-3	-0.8
1942	Det-A	26	68	5	11	2	0	1	4	3	5	.162	.197	.235	432	20	-7	0	1	-0	.881	-8	S-21	-1.5
	Phi-A	34	103	8	25	2	0	0	4	11	5	.243	.316	.262	578	64	-5	1	0	0	.952	-6	S-29/2-1	-0.9
	Yr	60	171	13	36	4	0	1	8	14	10	.211	.270	.251	522	46	-12	1	1	-0	.927	-13	S-50/2-1	-2.4
Total	14	1251	4519	592	1240	229	29	82	633	261	328	.274	.318	.392	710	80	-145	59	54	-6	.949	-83	S-669,2-288,3/1O	-15.4

■ MIKE McNALLY

McNally, Michael Joseph "Minooka Mike" b: 9/9/1892, Minooka, Pa.
d: 5/29/65, Bethlehem, Pa. BR/TR, 5'11", 150 lbs. Deb: 4/21/15 Career OF: (0-LF 1-CF 0-RF)

YEAR	TM/L	G	AB	R	H	2B	3B	HR	RBI	BB	SO	AVG	OBP	SLG	OPS	OPS+	BR+	SB	CS	SBR	FA	FR	G/POS	TPR
1915	Bos-A	23	53	7	8	0	1	0	0	3	7	.151	.196	.189	385	16	-6	0	2	-1	.891	1	3-18/2-5	-0.6
1916	*Bos-A	87	135	28	23	0	0	0	9	10	19	.170	.228	.170	398	20	-13	9			.964	7	2-35,3-14/S-7,O-1C	-0.6
1917	Bos-A	42	50	9	15	1	0	0	2	6	3	.300	.375	.320	695	113	1	3			.935	6	3-14/S-9,2-6	0.8
1919	Bos-A	33	42	10	11	4	0	0	6	1	2	.262	.279	.357	636	83	-1	4			.950	9	S-11,3-11/2-3	0.8
1920	Bos-A	93	312	42	80	5	1	0	23	31	24	.256	.326	.279	604	64	-15	13	10	-1	.930	-9	2-76/S-8,1-6	-2.3
1921	*NY-A	71	215	36	56	4	2	1	24	14	15	.260	.306	.312	617	57	-14	5	6	-1	.974	18	3-49,2-16	0.5
1922	*NY-A	52	143	20	36	2	2	0	18	16	14	.252	.331	.294	625	63	-7	3	0	1	.983	-0	3-34/2-9,S-4,1-1	-0.4
1923	NY-A	30	38	5	8	0	0	0	1	3	4	.211	.268	.211	479	27	-4	2	0	0	1.000	0	S-13/3-7,2-5	-0.3
1924	NY-A	49	69	11	17	0	0	0	2	7	5	.246	.316	.246	562	46	-5	1	1	-0	.985	10	2-25,3-13/S-6	0.5
1925	Was-A	12	21	1	3	0	0	0	0	1	4	.143	.182	.143	325	-17	-4	0	0	0	1.000	1	/3-7,S-2,2-1	-0.3
Total	10	492	1078	169	257	16	6	1	85	92	97	.238	.299	.267	567	54	-68	40	19		.946	41	2-181,3-167/S-60,1O	-1.9

■ GEORGE McNAMARA

McNamara, George Francis b: 1/11/01, Chicago, Ill. d: 6/12/90, Hinsdale, Ill. BL/TR, 6', 175 lbs. Deb: 9/28/22

YEAR	TM/L	G	AB	R	H	2B	3B	HR	RBI	BB	SO	AVG	OBP	SLG	OPS	OPS+	BR+	SB	CS	SBR	FA	FR	G/POS	TPR
1922	Was-A	3	11	3	3	0	0	0	1	1	2	.273	.333	.273	606	63	-1	0	0	0	1.000	-1	/O-3(0-0-3)	-0.1

■ JIM McNAMARA

McNamara, James Patrick b: 6/10/65, Nashua, N.H. BL/TR, 6'4", 210 lbs. Deb: 4/9/92

YEAR	TM/L	G	AB	R	H	2B	3B	HR	RBI	BB	SO	AVG	OBP	SLG	OPS	OPS+	BR+	SB	CS	SBR	FA	FR	G/POS	TPR
1992	SF-N	30	74	6	16	1	0	1	9	6	25	.216	.275	.270	545	58	-4	0	0	0	.993	-0	C-30	-0.3
1993	SF-N	4	7	0	1	0	0	0	1	0	1	.143	.143	.143	286	-24	-1	0	0	0	1.000	-0	/C-4	-0.1
Total	2	34	81	6	17	1	0	1	10	6	26	.210	.264	.259	524	51	-5	0	0	0	.993	-0	/C-34	-0.4

■ DINNY McNAMARA

McNamara, John Raymond b: 9/16/05, Lexington, Mass. d: 12/20/63, Arlington, Mass. BL/TR, 5'9", 165 lbs. Deb: 7/2/27

YEAR	TM/L	G	AB	R	H	2B	3B	HR	RBI	BB	SO	AVG	OBP	SLG	OPS	OPS+	BR+	SB	CS	SBR	FA	FR	G/POS	TPR
1927	Bos-N	11	9	3	0	0	0	0	0	0	3	.000	.000	.000	0	-99	-3	0			1.000	0	/O-3(0-3-0)	-0.2
1928	Bos-N	9	4	2	1	0	0	0	0	0	1	.250	.250	.250	500	33	-0	0			1.000	-0	/O-3(0-1-2)	-0.1
Total	2	20	13	5	1	0	0	0	0	0	4	.077	.077	.077	154	-63	-3	0			1.000	-0	/O-6(0-4-2)	-0.3

■ BOB McNAMARA

McNamara, Robert Maxey b: 9/19/16, Denver, Colo. BR/TR, 5'10", 170 lbs. Deb: 5/27/39

YEAR	TM/L	G	AB	R	H	2B	3B	HR	RBI	BB	SO	AVG	OBP	SLG	OPS	OPS+	BR+	SB	CS	SBR	FA	FR	G/POS	TPR
1939	Phi-A	9	9	0	2	1	0	0	3	1	1	.222	.300	.333	633	63	-1	0	0	0	1.000	0	/3-5,S-2,1-1,2-1	0.0

■ TOM McNAMARA

McNamara, Thomas Henry b: 11/5/1895, Roxbury, Mass. d: 5/5/74, Danvers, Mass. BR/TR, 6'2", 200 lbs. Deb: 6/25/22

YEAR	TM/L	G	AB	R	H	2B	3B	HR	RBI	BB	SO	AVG	OBP	SLG	OPS	OPS+	BR+	SB	CS	SBR	FA	FR	G/POS	TPR
1922	Pit-N	1	1	0	0	0	0	0	0	0	0	.000	.000	.000	0	-99	-0	0	0	0	.000	0	H	0.0

■ RUSTY McNEALY

McNealy, Robert Lee b: 8/12/58, Sacramento, Cal. BL/TL, 5'8", 160 lbs. Deb: 9/4/83

YEAR	TM/L	G	AB	R	H	2B	3B	HR	RBI	BB	SO	AVG	OBP	SLG	OPS	OPS+	BR+	SB	CS	SBR	FA	FR	G/POS	TPR
1983	Oak-A	15	4	5	0	0	0	0	0	0	0	.000	.000	.000	0	-99	-1	0	1	-0	1.000	-2	/O-5(1-4-1),D-7	-0.3

■ EARL McNEELY

McNeely, George Earl b: 5/12/1898, Sacramento, Cal. d: 7/16/71, Sacramento, Cal. BR/TR, 5'9", 155 lbs. Deb: 8/9/24 C Career OF: (105-LF 281-CF 196-RF)

YEAR	TM/L	G	AB	R	H	2B	3B	HR	RBI	BB	SO	AVG	OBP	SLG	OPS	OPS+	BR+	SB	CS	SBR	FA	FR	G/POS	TPR
1924	*Was-A	43	179	31	59	5	6	0	15	5	21	.330	.355	.425	779	104	0	3	1	0	.973	-2	O-42(0-42-2)	-0.3
1925	*Was-A	122	385	76	110	14	2	3	37	48	54	.286	.378	.356	734	89	-5	15	16	-2	.975	-2	*O-112(7-103-2)/1-1	-1.3
1926	Was-A	124	442	84	134	20	12	0	48	44	28	.303	.373	.403	775	105	4	18	6	2	.969	0	*O-118(65-52-2)	-0.1
1927	Was-A	73	185	40	51	10	4	0	16	11	13	.276	.320	.373	693	80	-6	11	4	1	.977	-7	O-47(3-32-14)/1-4	-1.3
1928	StL-A	127	496	66	117	27	7	0	44	37	39	.236	.299	.319	618	61	-29	8	6	-0	.984	7	*O-120(2-1-118)	-3.1
1929	StL-A	69	230	27	56	8	1	1	18	7	13	.243	.272	.300	572	45	-19	2	1	0	.980	-2	O-62(18-2-42)	-2.9
1930	StL-A	76	235	33	64	19	1	0	20	22	14	.272	.340	.362	701	75	-9	8	3	1	.939	-7	O-38(8-26-4),1-27	-1.6
1931	StL-A	49	102	12	23	4	0	0	15	9	5	.225	.288	.265	553	45	-8	4	4	-1	.969	-5	O-37(2-23-12)/1-1	-1.4
Total	8	683	2254	369	614	107	33	4	213	183	187	.272	.335	.354	689	78	-71	69	41	1	.974	-21	O-576C/1-33	-12.0

■ JEFF McNEELY

McNeely, Jeffrey Lavern b: 10/18/69, Monroe, N.C. BR/TR, 6'2", 190 lbs. Deb: 9/5/93

YEAR	TM/L	G	AB	R	H	2B	3B	HR	RBI	BB	SO	AVG	OBP	SLG	OPS	OPS+	BR+	SB	CS	SBR	FA	FR	G/POS	TPR
1993	Bos-A	21	37	10	11	1	1	0	1	7	9	.297	.409	.378	787	106	1	6	0	1	.917	-3	O-13(0-13-0)/D-3	0.0

YEAR	TM/L	G	AB	R	H	2B	3B	HR	RBI	BB	SO	AVG	OBP	SLG	OPS	OPS+	BR+	SB	CS	SBR	FA	FR	G/POS	TPR
■ **NORM McNEIL**	McNeil, Norman Francis b: 10/22/1892, Chicago, Ill. d: 4/11/42, Buffalo, N.Y. BR/TR, 5'11", 180 lbs. Deb: 6/21/19																							
1919	Bos-A	5	9	0	3	0	0	0	1	1	0	.333	.400	.333	733	113	0	0			.818	-2	/C-5	-0.1
■ **JERRY McNERTNEY**	McNertney, Gerald Edward b: 8/7/36, Boone, Iowa BR/TR, 6'1", 195 lbs. Deb: 4/16/64 C																							
1964	Chi-A	73	186	16	40	5	0	3	23	19	24	.215	.298	.290	588	66	-8	0	0	0	.987	8	C-69	0.2
1966	Chi-A	44	59	3	13	0	0	0	1	7	6	.220	.303	.220	523	57	-3	1	1	-0	.969	5	C-37	0.3
1967	Chi-A	56	123	8	28	6	0	3	13	6	14	.228	.275	.350	624	87	-2	0	0	0	.996	13	C-52	1.4
1968	Chi-A	74	169	18	37	4	1	3	18	18	29	.219	.302	.308	609	84	-3	0	0	0	.985	14	C-64/1-1	1.5
1969	Sea-A	128	410	39	99	18	1	8	55	29	63	.241	.292	.349	640	80	-12	1	0	0	.988	2	*C-122	-0.5
1970	Mil-A	111	296	27	72	11	1	6	22	22	33	.243	.304	.348	652	79	-9	1	4	-1	.984	-9	C-94,1-13	-1.6
1971	StL-N	56	128	15	37	4	2	4	22	12	14	.289	.350	.445	795	119	3	0	0	0	.985	-3	C-36	0.2
1972	StL-N	39	48	3	10	3	1	0	9	6	16	.208	.296	.313	609	74	-2	0	0	0	.982	2	C-10	0.0
1973	Pit-N	9	4	0	1	0	0	0	0	0	0	.250	.250	.250	500	40	-0	0	0	0	1.000	1	/C-9	0.1
Total	9	590	1423	129	337	51	6	27	163	119	199	.237	.301	.338	639	81	-36	3	5	-1	.987	33	C-493/1-14	1.6
■ **PAT McNULTY**	McNulty, Patrick Howard b: 2/27/1899, Cleveland, Ohio d: 5/4/63, Hollywood, Cal. BL/TR, 5'11", 160 lbs. Deb: 9/5/22																							
1922	Cle-A	22	59	10	16	2	1	0	5	9	5	.271	.368	.339	707	85	-1	4	1	1	.956	-3	O-22(1-19-2)	-0.5
1924	Cle-A	101	291	46	78	13	5	0	26	33	22	.268	.347	.347	694	78	-9	10	7	-0	.961	-4	O-75(11-20-44)	-1.7
1925	Cle-A	118	373	70	117	18	2	6	43	47	23	.314	.392	.421	813	105	4	7	7	-1	.965	-2	*O-111(3-29-81)	-0.5
1926	Cle-A	48	56	3	14	2	1	0	6	5	9	.250	.311	.321	633	65	-3	0	1	-0	.909	-2	/O-9(2-5-2)	-0.5
1927	Cle-A	19	41	3	13	1	0	0	4	4	3	.317	.378	.341	719	87	-1	1	2	-0	.906	-1	O-12(1-11-0)	-0.2
Total	5	308	820	132	238	36	9	6	84	98	62	.290	.368	.378	746	91	-10	22	18	-1	.957	-11	O-229(18-84-129)	-3.4
■ **BILL McNULTY**	McNulty, William Francis b: 8/29/46, Sacramento, Cal. BR/TR, 6'4", 205 lbs. Deb: 7/9/69																							
1969	Oak-A	5	17	0	0	0	0	0	0	0	10	.000	.000	.000	0	-99	-5	0	0	0	1.000	1	/O-5(5-0-0)	-0.4
1972	Oak-A	4	10	0	1	0	0	0	0	2	1	.100	.250	.100	350	7	-1	0	0	0	.800	-2	/3-3	-0.3
Total	2	9	27	0	1	0	0	0	0	2	11	.037	.103	.037	140	-61	-6	0	0	0	1.000	-0	/O-5(5-0-0),3-3	-0.7
■ **BID McPHEE**	McPhee, John Alexander b: 11/1/1859, Massena, N.Y. d: 1/3/43, San Diego, Cal. BR/TR, 5'8", 152 lbs. Deb: 5/2/1882 MH Career OF: (0-LF 1-CF 3-RF)																							
1882	Cin-a	78	311	43	71	8	7	1	31	11		.228	.255	.309	563	84	-6				**.920**	-1	*2-78	-0.4
1883	Cin-a	96	367	61	90	10	10	2	42	18		.245	.281	.343	624	95	-3				**.928**	3	*2-96	0.3
1884	Cin-a	112	450	107	125	8	7	5	64	27		.278	.327	.360	687	118	9				.924	16	*2-112	2.6
1885	Cin-a	110	431	78	114	12	4	0	46	19		.265	.306	.311	617	94	-3				**.936**	6	*2-110	0.6
1886	Cin-a	140	560	139	150	23	12	**8**	70	59		.268	.343	.395	738	127	17	40			**.939**	31	*2-140	4.5
1887	Cin-a	129	595	137	211	20	**19**	2	87	55		.355	.360	.407	767	111	8	95			.924	26	*2-129	3.1
1888	Cin-a	111	458	88	110	12	10	4	51	43		.240	.312	.336	648	102	1	54			**.940**	31	*2-111	3.3
1889	Cin-a	135	540	109	145	25	7	5	57	60	29	.269	.346	.369	715	100	-0	63			**.946**	**41**	*2-135/3-1	3.8
1890	Cin-N	132	528	125	135	16	22	3	39	82	26	.256	.362	.386	748	119	14	55			.942	30	*2-132	4.3
1891	Cin-N	138	562	107	144	14	16	6	38	74	35	.256	.345	.370	715	107	6	33			**.954**	23	*2-138	3.0
1892	Cin-N	144	573	111	157	19	12	4	60	84	48	.274	.373	.370	743	127	22	44			.948	25	*2-144	4.9
1893	Cin-N	127	491	101	138	17	11	3	68	94	20	.281	.401	.379	779	105	7	25			.954	**34**	*2-127	3.8
1894	Cin-N	128	483	113	151	21	10	5	93	91	23	.313	.428	.429	856	103	5	33			.945	34	*2-128	3.4
1895	Cin-N	115	432	107	129	24	12	1	75	73	30	.299	.409	.417	826	109	8	30			.955	15	*2-115	2.2
1896	Cin-N	117	433	81	132	18	7	1	87	51	18	.305	.391	.386	776	98	0	48			**.978**	6	*2-117	0.9
1897	Cin-N	81	282	45	85	13	7	1	39	35		.301	.386	.408	794	103	1	9			.966	12	2-81	1.5
1898	Cin-N	133	486	72	121	26	9	1	60	66		.249	.341	.346	687	91	-6	21			.956	-12	*2-130/O-3(0-0-3)	-1.1
1899	Cin-N	112	376	60	105	17	7	1	65	41		.279	.361	.370	731	99	-0	18			.954	-1	*2-106/O-1(0-1-0)	0.3
Total	18	2138	8358	1684	2313	303	189	53	1072	983	229	.277	.355	.373	728	106	78	568			.944	318	*2-2129/O-4R,3-1	41.0
■ **MART McQUAID**	McQuaid, Mortimer Martin b: 6/28/1861, Chicago, Ill. d: 3/5/28, Chicago, Ill. Deb: 8/15/1891																							
1891	StL-a	4	11	1	4	2	0	0	1	0	1	.364	.364	.545	909	139	0	1			1.000	-1	/2-3,O-1(1-0-0)	0.0
1898	Was-N	1	4	0	0	0	0	0	0	0	0	.000	.000	.000	0	-99	-1	0			.333	-1	/O-1(1-0-0)	-0.2
Total	2	5	15	1	4	2	0	0	1	0	1	.267	.267	.400	667	82	-1	1			.333	-1	/2-3,O-2(2-0-0)	-0.2
■ **JERRY McQUAIG**	McQuaig, Gerald Joseph b: 1/31/12, Douglas, Ga. BR/TR, 5'11", 183 lbs. Deb: 8/25/34																							
1934	Phi-A	7	16	2	1	0	0	0	1	2	4	.063	.167	.063	229	-40	-3	0	0	0	.889	-1	/O-6(5-0-1)	-0.5
■ **MOX McQUERY**	McQuery, William Thomas b: 6/28/1861, Garrard Co., Ky. d: 6/12/1900, Cincinnati, Ohio 6'4", Deb: 8/20/1884																							
1884	Cin-U	35	132	31	37	5	0	2		8		.280	.321	.364	685	99	-4				.978	1	1-35	-0.5
1885	Det-N	70	278	34	76	15	4	3	30	8	29	.273	.294	.388	682	119	5				.882	-12	1-70	-1.2
1886	KC-N	122	449	62	111	27	4	4	38	36	44	.247	.303	.352	655	93	-5	4			.969	1	*1-122	-1.4
1890	Syr-a	122	461	64	142	17	6	2	55	53		.308	.383	.384	767	141	26	26			.972	-1	*1-122	1.2
1891	Was-a	68	261	40	63	9	4	2	37	18	19	.241	.305	.330	635	86	-5	3			.977	1	1-68	-0.9
Total	5	417	1581	231	429	73	18	13	160	123	92	.271	.327	.365	692	110	17	33			.956	-10	1-417	-2.8
■ **GLENN McQUILLEN**	McQuillen, Glenn Richard "Red" b: 4/19/15, Strasburg, Va. d: 6/8/89, Gardenville, Md. BR/TR, 6', 198 lbs. Deb: 6/16/38																							
1938	StL-A	43	116	14	33	4	0	0	13	4	12	.284	.308	.319	627	57	-8	0	1	-0	.971	-0	O-30(30-0-0)	-0.9
1941	StL-A	7	21	4	7	2	1	0	3	1	2	.333	.364	.524	887	128	1	0	1	-0	.933	-0	/O-6(3-0-3)	0.0
1942	StL-A	100	339	40	96	15	12	3	47	10	17	.283	.306	.425	730	103	-1	1	1	-0	.969	-5	O-77(68-0-9)	-1.1
1946	StL-A	59	166	24	40	3	3	1	12	19	18	.241	.319	.313	632	73	-6	0	2	-1	.977	-2	O-48(44-0-5)	-1.1
1947	StL-A	1	1	0	0	0	0	0	0	0	0	.000	.000	.000	0	-98	-0	0	0	0	.000	0	H	0.0
Total	5	210	643	82	176	24	16	4	75	34	49	.274	.311	.379	691	87	-14	1	5	-2	.970	-7	O-161(145-0-17)	-3.1
■ **GEORGE McQUINN**	McQuinn, George Hartley b: 5/29/10, Arlington, Va. d: 12/24/78, Alexandria, Va. BL/TL, 5'11", 165 lbs. Deb: 4/14/36																							
1936	Cin-N	38	134	5	27	3	4	0	13	10	22	.201	.262	.284	546	50	-10	0			.992	1	1-38	-1.2
1938	StL-A	148	602	100	195	42	7	12	82	58	49	.324	.384	.477	861	115	13	4	5	-1	.992	-0	*1-148	-0.2
1939	StL-A☆	154	617	101	195	37	13	20	94	65	42	.316	.383	.515	898	125	22	6	5	-0	.993	10	*1-154	1.5
1940	StL-A☆	151	594	78	166	39	10	16	84	57	58	.279	.343	.460	802	104	2	3	3	-0	**.992**	10	*1-150	-0.2
1941	StL-A	130	495	93	147	28	4	18	80	74	30	.297	.388	.479	867	124	18	5	4	-0	**.995**	8	*1-125	1.4
1942	StL-A☆	145	554	86	145	32	5	12	78	60	77	.262	.335	.403	737	105	3	1	1	-0	.991	1	*1-144	-1.0
1943	StL-A	125	449	53	109	19	2	12	74	56	65	.243	.327	.374	701	103	1	4	3	-0	.992	2	*1-122	-0.3
1944	*StL-A★	146	516	83	129	26	3	11	72	85	74	.250	.357	.376	733	103	4	4	3	-0	**.994**	-5	*1-146	-0.9
1945	StL-A†	139	483	69	134	31	3	7	61	65	51	.277	.364	.398	762	115	10	1	1	-0	.991	4	*1-136	0.8
1946	Phi-A	136	484	47	109	23	6	3	35	64	62	.225	.317	.316	633	78	-14	4	2	0	.988	3	*1-134	-1.6
1947	*NY-A★	144	517	84	157	24	3	13	80	78	66	.304	.395	.437	832	132	24	0	2	-1	.994	-2	*1-142	1.8
1948	NY-A★	94	302	33	75	11	4	11	41	40	38	.248	.336	.421	757	102	-0	0	2	-1	.993	-1	1-90	-0.5
Total	12	1550	5747	832	1588	315	64	135	794	712	634	.276	.357	.424	781	109	74	32	31		.992	31	*1-1529	-0.4
■ **BRIAN McRAE**	McRae, Brian Wesley b: 8/27/67, Bradenton, Fla. BB/TR, 6', 185 lbs. Deb: 8/7/90 F Career OF: (0-LF 1307-CF 4-RF)																							
1990	KC-A	46	168	21	48	8	3	2	23	9	29	.286	.322	.405	727	104	0	4	3	-0	1.000	4	O-45(0-45-0)	0.4
1991	KC-A	152	629	86	164	28	9	8	64	24	99	.261	.290	.372	662	81	-17	20	11	1	.993	8	*O-150(0-150-0)	-1.0
1992	KC-A	149	533	63	119	23	5	4	52	42	88	.223	.287	.308	595	65	-25	18	5	2	.993	10	*O-148(0-148-0)	-1.4
1993	KC-A	153	627	78	177	28	9	12	69	37	105	.282	.326	.413	739	92	-8	23	14	0	.983	5	*O-153(0-153-0)	-0.1
1994	KC-A	114	436	71	119	22	6	4	40	54	67	.273	.361	.378	739	87	-7	28	8	3	.988	-6	*O-110(0-110-4)/D-4	-0.8
1995	Chi-N	137	580	92	167	38	7	12	48	47	92	.288	.349	.440	788	108	6	27	8	3	.991	10	*O-137(0-137-0)	2.1
1996	Chi-N	157	624	111	172	32	5	17	66	73	84	.276	.362	.425	787	104	5	37	9	5	.986	1	*O-155(0-155-0)	1.2
1997	Chi-N	108	417	63	100	27	5	6	28	52	62	.240	.330	.372	702	81	-11	14	6	1	.996	7	*O-107(0-107-0)	-0.2
	NY-N	45	145	23	36	5	2	5	15	13	22	.248	.319	.414	733	93	-2	3	4	-1	.957	-5	O-41(0-41-0)	-0.7
	Yr	153	562	86	136	32	7	11	43	65	84	.242	.327	.383	710	84	-13	17	10	0	.987	2	*O-148(0-148-0)	-0.9
1998	NY-N	159	552	79	146	36	5	21	79	80	90	.264	.363	.462	825	117	14	20	11	1	.987	-2	*O-154(0-154-0)	1.4
1999	NY-N	96	298	35	66	12	1	8	36	39	57	.221	.322	.349	671	72	-13	2	6	-2	.994	-7	O-87(0-87-0)	-2.0

YEAR	TM/L	G	AB	R	H	2B	3B	HR	RBI	BB	SO	AVG	OBP	SLG	OPS	OPS+	BR+	SB	CS	SBR	FA	FR	G/POS	TPR
	Col-N	7	23	1	6	2	0	1	1	2	7	.261	.370	.478	849	89	-0	0	0	0	1.000	-0	/O-7(0-7-0)	-0.1
	Yr	103	321	36	72	14	1	9	37	41	64	.224	.325	.358	683	73	-13	2	6	-2	.994	-8	O-94(0-94-0)	-2.1
	Tor-A	31	82	11	16	3	1	3	11	16	22	.195	.340	.366	706	79	-2	0	1	-0	1.000	0	D-15,O-13(0-13-0)	-0.3
Total	10	1354	5114	734	1336	264	58	103	532	488	824	.261	.332	.396	728	92	-59	196	86	13	.990	23	*O-1307C/D-19	-1.5

■ HAL McRAE

McRae, Harold Abraham b: 7/10/45, Avon Park, Fla. BR/TR, 5′11″, 180 lbs. Deb: 7/11/68 FMC Career OF: (360-LF 33-CF 94-RF)

YEAR	TM/L	G	AB	R	H	2B	3B	HR	RBI	BB	SO	AVG	OBP	SLG	OPS	OPS+	BR+	SB	CS	SBR	FA	FR	G/POS	TPR
1968	Cin-N	17	51	1	10	1	0	0	2	4	14	.196	.255	.216	470	40	-4	1	1	-0	.926	-4	2-16	-0.7
1970	*Cin-N	70	165	18	41	6	1	8	23	15	23	.248	.315	.442	757	100	-1	0	2	-1	.981	-5	O-46(46-0-1)/3-6,2-1	-0.9
1971	Cin-N	99	337	39	89	24	2	9	34	11	35	.264	.291	.427	719	103	-0	3	2	-0	.966	-1	O-91(66-28-0)	-0.6
1972	*Cin-N	61	97	9	27	4	0	5	26	2	10	.278	.307	.474	781	126	3	0	0	0	.867	-6	O-12(0-3-9),3-11	-0.4
1973	KC-A	106	338	36	79	18	3	9	50	34	38	.234	.315	.385	699	89	-5	2	2	-0	.963	-4	O-64(3-0-63),D-37/3-2	-1.3
1974	KC-A	148	539	71	167	36	4	15	88	54	68	.310	.378	.475	853	136	25	11	8	-0	.950	2	D-90,O-56L/3-1	2.2
1975	KC-A★	126	480	58	147	38	6	5	71	47	47	.306	.373	.442	815	126	17	11	8	-0	.986	-1	*O-114L,D-12/3-1	0.8
1976	*KC-A★	149	527	75	175	34	5	8	73	64	43	.332	**.412**	.461	**873**	154	**38**	22	12	1	.970	-0	*D-117,O-31(31-0-0)	3.5
1977	*KC-A	162	641	104	191	**54**	11	21	92	59	43	.298	.369	.515	884	137	32	18	14	-1	.958	4	*D-115,O-47(47-0-0)	2.9
1978	*KC-A	156	623	90	170	39	5	16	72	51	62	.273	.334	.429	762	110	7	17	8	1	1.000	0	*D-153/O-3(3-0-0)	0.4
1979	KC-A	101	393	55	113	32	4	10	74	38	46	.288	.356	.466	822	117	9	5	4	-0	.000	0	*D-100	0.6
1980	*KC-A	124	489	73	145	39	5	14	83	29	56	.297	.346	.483	829	123	14	10	2	2	1.000	-1	*D-110/O-9(9-0-0)	1.2
1981	*KC-A	101	389	38	106	23	2	7	36	34	33	.272	.334	.396	730	111	5	3	4	-1	.909	0	D-97/O-4(2-0-2)	0.1
1982	KC-A★	159	613	91	189	**46**	8	27	**133**	55	61	.308	.370	.542	912	146	38	4	4	-1	.500	-0	*D-158/O-1(1-0-0)	3.2
1983	KC-A	157	589	84	183	41	6	12	82	50	68	.311	.374	.462	836	128	23	2	3	-1	.000	0	*D-156	1.8
1984	*KC-A	106	317	30	96	13	4	3	42	34	47	.303	.372	.397	770	112	6	0	3	-1	.000	0	D-94	0.2
1985	*KC-A	112	320	41	83	19	0	14	70	44	45	.259	.351	.450	801	117	8	0	1	-0	.000	0	*D-106	0.4
1986	KC-A	112	278	22	70	14	0	7	37	18	39	.252	.300	.378	677	81	-8	0	0	0	.000	0	D-75	-1.0
1987	KC-A	18	32	5	10	3	0	1	9	5	1	.313	.405	.500	905	135	2	0	0	0	.000	0	/D-7	0.1
Total	19	2084	7218	940	2091	484	66	191	1097	648	779	.290	.355	.454	809	122	211	109	78	-3	.966	-16	*D-1427,O-478L/3-21,2	12.5

■ McREMER

McRemer Deb: 6/20/1884

YEAR	TM/L	G	AB	R	H	2B	3B	HR	RBI	BB	SO	AVG	OBP	SLG	OPS	OPS+	BR+	SB	CS	SBR	FA	FR	G/POS	TPR
1884	Was-U	1	3	0	0	0	0	0		0		.000	.000	.000	0	-99	-1				1.000	0	/O-1(0-0-1)	-0.1

■ KEVIN McREYNOLDS

McReynolds, Walter Kevin b: 10/16/59, Little Rock, Ark. BR/TR, 6′1″, 210 lbs. Deb: 6/2/83 Career OF: (1067-LF 468-CF 27-RF)

YEAR	TM/L	G	AB	R	H	2B	3B	HR	RBI	BB	SO	AVG	OBP	SLG	OPS	OPS+	BR+	SB	CS	SBR	FA	FR	G/POS	TPR
1983	SD-N	39	140	15	31	3	1	4	14	12	29	.221	.283	.343	626	75	-5	2	1	0	.989	0	O-38(3-32-10)	-0.6
1984	*SD-N	147	525	68	146	26	6	20	75	34	69	.278	.322	.465	787	119	11	3	6	-1	.991	18	*O-143(0-143-0)	2.8
1985	SD-N	152	564	61	132	24	4	15	75	43	81	.234	.292	.371	662	85	-12	4	0	1	.993	23	*O-150(0-150-0)	1.1
1986	SD-N	158	560	89	161	31	6	26	96	66	83	.287	.364	.504	867	140	29	8	6	-0	.977	-14	*O-154(108-109-3)	1.2
1987	NY-N	151	590	86	163	32	5	29	95	39	70	.276	.322	.495	817	119	13	14	1	3	.987	9	*O-150(150-0-0)	1.8
1988	*NY-N	147	552	82	159	30	2	27	99	38	56	.288	.338	.496	835	144	28	21	0	5	.985	10	*O-147(147-1-0)	4.1
1989	NY-N	148	545	74	148	25	3	22	85	46	74	.272	.329	.450	779	127	17	15	7	1	.969	15	*O-145(145-0-0)	3.0
1990	NY-N	147	521	75	140	23	1	24	82	71	61	.269	.358	.455	812	122	16	9	2	1	.988	5	*O-144(144-0-0)	1.9
1991	NY-N	143	522	65	135	32	1	16	74	49	46	.259	.325	.416	740	108	4	6	6	-1	.993	2	*O-141(125-33-2)	0.2
1992	KC-A	109	373	45	92	25	0	13	49	67	48	.247	.361	.418	780	115	9	7	1	1	.986	-3	*O-106(94-0-12)/D-1	0.4
1993	KC-A	110	351	44	86	22	4	11	42	37	56	.245	.319	.425	743	92	-4	2	2	-0	.990	0	*O-104(104-0-0)/D-1	-0.7
1994	NY-N	51	180	23	46	11	2	4	21	20	34	.256	.330	.406	736	91	-2	2	0	0	1.000	2	O-47(47-0-0)	-0.1
Total	12	1502	5423	727	1439	284	35	211	807	522	707	.265	.331	.447	779	116	103	93	32	9	.987	68	*O-1469L/D-2	15.1

■ PETE McSHANNIC

McShannic, Peter Robert b: 3/20/1864, Pittsburgh, Pa. d: 11/30/46, Toledo, Ohio BB/TR, 5′7″, 190 lbs. Deb: 9/15/1888

YEAR	TM/L	G	AB	R	H	2B	3B	HR	RBI	BB	SO	AVG	OBP	SLG	OPS	OPS+	BR+	SB	CS	SBR	FA	FR	G/POS	TPR
1888	Pit-N	26	98	5	19	1	0	0	5	1	9	.194	.218	.204	422	38	-7	3			.907	-0	3-26	-0.6

■ TRICK McSORLEY

McSorley, John Bernard b: 12/6/1852, St.Louis, Mo. d: 2/9/36, St.Louis, Mo. BR/TR, 5′4″, 142 lbs. Deb: 5/6/1875 Career OF: (5-LF 0-CF 0-RF)

YEAR	TM/L	G	AB	R	H	2B	3B	HR	RBI	BB	SO	AVG	OBP	SLG	OPS	OPS+	BR+	SB	CS	SBR	FA	FR	G/POS	TPR
1875	RS-n	15	52	4	11	0	0	0	2	0	3	.212	.212	.212	423	53	-2	3	0	1	.745	1	/3-9,O-7(6-1-0)	-0.1
1884	Tol-a	21	68	12	17	1	0	0		3		.250	.282	.265	546	77	-2				.974	1	1-16/O-5L,3-1,P-1	-0.2
1885	StL-N	2	6	2	3	1	0	0	1	2	1	.500	.625	.667	1292	340	2				.400	-2	/3-2	0.0
1886	StL-a	5	20	1	3	3	0	0	0	0		.150	.150	.300	450	38	-2	0			.765	-3	/S-5	-0.4
Total	3	28	94	15	23	5	0	0	1	5	1	.245	.283	.298	581	85	-1	0	0		.400	-4	/1-16,S-5,O-5L,3P	-0.6

■ PAUL McSWEENEY

McSweeney, Paul A. b: 4/3/1867, St.Louis, Mo. d: 8/12/51, St.Louis, Mo. Deb: 9/20/1891

YEAR	TM/L	G	AB	R	H	2B	3B	HR	RBI	BB	SO	AVG	OBP	SLG	OPS	OPS+	BR+	SB	CS	SBR	FA	FR	G/POS	TPR
1891	StL-a	3	12	2	3	1	0	0	2	0	0	.250	.308	.333	641	73	-1	1			.643	-2	/2-3,3-1	-0.2

■ JIM McTAMANY

McTamany, James Edward b: 7/1/1863, Philadelphia, Pa. d: 4/16/16, Lenni, Pa. BR/TR, 5′8″, 190 lbs. Deb: 8/15/1885

YEAR	TM/L	G	AB	R	H	2B	3B	HR	RBI	BB	SO	AVG	OBP	SLG	OPS	OPS+	BR+	SB	CS	SBR	FA	FR	G/POS	TPR
1885	Bro-a	35	131	21	36	7	2	1	13	9		.275	.321	.382	703	121	3				.896	-5	O-35(35-0-0)	-0.3
1886	Bro-a	111	418	86	106	23	10	2	56	54		.254	.353	.371	724	126	14	18			.893	14	*O-111(0-107-4)	2.1
1887	Bro-a	134	596	123	210	22	10	1	68	76		.352	.365	.344	709	97	1	66			.918	8	*O-134(0-134-0)	0.3
1888	KC-a	130	516	94	127	12	10	4	41	67		.246	.345	.331	677	110	7	55			.913	6	*O-130(0-80-50)	0.9
1889	Col-a	139	529	113	146	21	7	4	52	116	66	.276	.407	.365	772	127	27	40			.902	-5	*O-139(0-139-0)	1.4
1890	Col-a	125	466	**140**	120	27	7	1	48	**112**		.258	.405	.352	757	132	28	43			.940	2	*O-125(0-125-0)	2.2
1891	Col-a	81	304	59	76	17	9	3	35	58	48	.250	.374	.395	768	127	13	20			.929	-2	O-81(0-81-0)	0.6
	Phi-a	58	218	57	49	6	3	3	21	43	44	.225	.365	.321	686	96	1	13			.901	0	O-58(0-57-1)	-0.1
	Yr	139	522	116	125	23	12	6	56	101	92	.239	.370	.364	734	114	13	33			.917	-2	*O-139(0-138-1)	0.5
Total	7	813	3178	693	870	135	58	19	334	535	158	.274	.373	.355	728	117	93	255			.913	16	O-813(35-723-55)	7.1

■ BILL McTIGUE

McTigue, William Patrick "Rebel" b: 1/3/1891, Nashville, Tenn. d: 5/8/20, Nashville, Tenn. BL/TL, 6′1.5″, 175 lbs. Deb: 5/2/11

YEAR	TM/L	G	AB	R	H	2B	3B	HR	RBI	BB	SO	AVG	OBP	SLG	OPS	OPS+	BR+	SB	CS	SBR	FA	FR	G/POS	TPR
1911	Bos-N	14	12	1	1	1	0	0	0	0	5	.083	.083	.167	250	-28	-2	0			.875	-1	P-14	0.0
1912	Bos-N	10	13	2	1	0	0	0	1	1	5	.077	.143	.077	220	-38	-2	0			1.000	1	P-10	0.0
1913	Bos-N	1	0	0	0	0	0	0	0	0	0	—	—	—	—	—		0			.000	0	R	0.0
1916	Det-A	3	1	0	0	0	0	0	0	0	0	.000	.000	.000	0	-97	-0	0			1.000	0	/P-3	0.0
Total	4	28	26	3	2	1	0	0	1	1	10	.077	.111	.115	226	-36	-5	0			.957	0	/P-27	0.0

■ CAL McVEY

McVey, Calvin Alexander b: 8/30/1850, Montrose, Iowa
d: 8/20/26, San Francisco, Cal BR/TR, 5′9″, 170 lbs. Deb: 5/5/1871 M NA OF: (4-LF 32-CF 66-RF) Career OF: (1-LF 1-CF 6-RF)

YEAR	TM/L	G	AB	R	H	2B	3B	HR	RBI	BB	SO	AVG	OBP	SLG	OPS	OPS+	BR+	SB	CS	SBR	FA	FR	G/POS	TPR
1871	Bos-n	29	153	43	**66**	9	5	0	43	1	2	.431	.435	.556	991	177	14	6	0	1	.873	1	*C-29/O-5(0-0-5),3-1	1.1
1872	Bos-n	46	237	56	76	10	2	0	41	1	1	.321	.324	.380	703	110	1	6	1	1	.869	4	*C-40,O-11(2-0-9)/3-1	0.5
1873	Bal-n	38	192	49	73	4	5	2	34	3	2	.380	.390	.484	874	159	13	1	0	0	.907	-1	C-25/O-6C,S-5,213M	0.9
1874	Bos-n	70	343	**91**	**123**	21	6	3	**71**	1	3	.359	.360	.481	842	159	20	5	0	1	.710	-2	*O-57(0-8-49),C-23	1.7
1875	Bos-n	82	389	89	138	**36**	9	3	**87**	1	5	.355	.356	**.517**	**873**	193	34	7	0	2	.949	6	*1-55,O-23C,C-16,/P	3.5
1876	Chi-N	63	310	62	107	15	0	1	53	2	4	.345	.352	.406	757	136	9				.959	4	*1-55,P-11/C-6,O3	0.8
1877	Chi-N	60	266	58	98	9	7	0	36	8	11	.368	.387	.455	842	147	13				.859	-13	*C-40,3-17,P-17,/21	0.0
1878	Cin-N	61	271	43	83	10	4	2	28	5	10	.306	.319	.395	714	147	14				.814	-10	*3-61/C-3,M	0.5
1879	Cin-N	81	354	64	105	18	6	0	55	8	13	.297	.312	.381	694	134	13				.946	-7	*1-72/O-7R,P-3,3CM	0.3
Total	5 n	265	1314	328	476	80	27	8	276	7	13	.362	.366	.482	848	161	82	25	1	5	.876	8	C-133,O-102R/1S23P	7.7
Total	4	265	1201	227	393	52	17	3	172	23	38	.327	.340	.407	747	140	49				.951	-26	1-128/3-80,C-50,PO2	1.6

■ GEORGE McVEY

McVey, George W. b: 9/16/1865, Port Jervis, N.Y. d: 5/3/1896, Quincy, Ill. BR/TR, 6′1″, 185 lbs. Deb: 9/19/1885

YEAR	TM/L	G	AB	R	H	2B	3B	HR	RBI	BB	SO	AVG	OBP	SLG	OPS	OPS+	BR+	SB	CS	SBR	FA	FR	G/POS	TPR
1885	Bro-a	6	21	2	3	0	0	0	1	2		.143	.217	.143	360	15	-2				.967	-0	/1-3,C-3	-0.2

■ BILL McWILLIAMS

McWilliams, William Henry b: 11/28/10, Dubuque, Iowa d: 1/21/97, Garland, Tex. BR/TR, 6′, 185 lbs. Deb: 7/8/31

YEAR	TM/L	G	AB	R	H	2B	3B	HR	RBI	BB	SO	AVG	OBP	SLG	OPS	OPS+	BR+	SB	CS	SBR	FA	FR	G/POS	TPR
1931	Bos-A	2	2	0	0	0	0	0	0	0	1	.000	.000	.000	0	-99	-1	0	0	0	.000	0	H	-0.1

■ BOB MEACHAM

Meacham, Robert Andrew b: 8/25/60, Los Angeles, Cal. BB/TR (BR 1987-88), 6′1″, 180 lbs. Deb: 6/30/83

YEAR	TM/L	G	AB	R	H	2B	3B	HR	RBI	BB	SO	AVG	OBP	SLG	OPS	OPS+	BR+	SB	CS	SBR	FA	FR	G/POS	TPR
1983	NY-A	22	51	5	12	2	0	0	4	4	10	.235	.304	.275	578	63	-2	8	0	2	.929	9	S-18/3-4	0.9
1984	NY-A	99	360	62	91	13	4	2	25	32	70	.253	.319	.328	647	83	-8	9	5	0	.955	-12	S-96/2-2	-0.9
1985	NY-A	156	481	70	105	16	2	1	47	54	102	.218	.304	.266	570	59	-26	25	7	3	.963	-17	*S-155	-2.3
1986	NY-A	56	161	19	36	7	1	0	10	17	39	.224	.309	.280	589	62	-8	3	6	-1	.948	-5	S-56	-0.8

YEAR	TM/L	G	AB	R	H	2B	3B	HR	RBI	BB	SO	AVG	OBP	SLG	OPS	OPS+	BR+	SB	CS	SBR	FA	FR	G/POS	TPR
1987	NY-A	77	203	28	55	11	1	5	21	19	33	.271	.351	.409	760	102	1	6	5	-0	.961	-1	S-56,2-25/D-1	0.5
1988	NY-A	47	115	18	25	9	0	0	7	14	22	.217	.313	.296	609	72	-4	7	1	1	.959	-7	S-24,2-21/3-5	-0.9
Total	6	457	1371	202	324	58	8	8	114	140	276	.236	.316	.308	624	73	-47	58	24	4	.957	-32	S-405/2-48,3-9,D-1	-3.5
■ CHARLIE MEAD Mead, Charles Richard b: 4/9/21, Vermilion, Alberta, Canada BL/TR, 6'1.5", 185 lbs. Deb: 8/28/43																								
1943	NY-N	37	146	9	40	6	1	1	13	10	15	.274	.321	.349	670	93	-2	3			.976	1	O-37(0-3-34)	-0.4
1944	NY-N	39	78	5	14	1	0	1	8	5	7	.179	.229	.231	460	30	-7	0			.981	2	O-23(13-3-7)	-0.7
1945	NY-N	11	37	4	10	1	0	1	6	5	2	.270	.357	.378	736	103	0	0			.962	1	O-11(0-1-11)	0.1
Total	3	87	261	18	64	8	1	3	27	20	24	.245	.299	.318	617	75	-9	3			.975	4	/O-71(13-7-52)	-1.0
■ LOUIE MEADOWS Meadows, Michael Ray b: 4/29/61, Maysville, N.C. BL/TL, 5'11", 190 lbs. Deb: 7/3/86																								
1986	Hou-N	6	6	1	2	0	0	0	0	0	0	.333	.333	.333	667	87	-0	1	0	0	.000	-0	/O-1(0-0-1)	0.0
1988	Hou-N	35	42	5	8	0	1	2	3	6	8	.190	.292	.381	673	95	-0	4	2	0	1.000	0	O-10(7-1-3)	0.0
1989	Hou-N	31	51	5	9	0	0	3	10	1	14	.176	.192	.353	545	55	-3	1	2	-0	1.000	-4	O-14(12-0-4)/1-1	-0.9
1990	Hou-N	15	14	3	2	0	0	0	0	2	4	.143	.250	.143	393	11	-2	0	0	0	1.000	-2	/O-9(7-0-2)	-0.4
	Phi-N	15	14	1	1	0	0	0	0	1	2	.071	.133	.071	205	-42	-3	0	0	0	1.000	-2	/O-4(3-2-0)	-0.5
	Yr	30	28	4	3	0	0	0	0	3	6	.107	.194	.107	301	-15	-4	0	0	0	1.000	-4	O-13(10-2-2)	-0.9
Total	4	102	127	15	22	0	1	5	13	10	28	.173	.234	.307	541	54	-8	6	4	-0	1.000	-9	/O-38(29-3-10),1-1	-1.8
■ PAT MEANEY Meaney, Patrick J. b: 7/1871, Philadelphia, Pa. d: 10/20/22, Philadelphia, Pa. BR/TR, Deb: 5/18/12																								
1912	Det-A	1	2	0	0	0	0	0	0	1		.000	.500	.000	500	48	0	0			.833	-0	/S-1	0.0
■ CHARLIE MEARA Meara, Charles Edward "Goggy" b: 4/16/1891, New York, N.Y. d: 2/8/62, Bronx, N.Y. BL/TR, 5'10", 160 lbs. Deb: 6/1/14																								
1914	NY-A	4	7	2	2	0	0	0	1	2	2	.286	.444	.286	730	120	0	0	1	-0	1.000	-1	/O-3(0-2-2)	-0.1
■ PAT MEARES Meares, Patrick James b: 9/6/68, Salina, Kan. BR/TR, 6', 188 lbs. Deb: 5/5/93																								
1993	Min-A	111	346	33	87	14	3	0	33	7	52	.251	.268	.309	578	55	-22	4	5	-1	.961	-1	*S-111	-1.5
1994	Min-A	80	229	29	61	12	1	2	24	14	50	.266	.314	.354	668	72	-10	5	1	1	.963	2	S-79	-0.1
1995	Min-A	116	390	57	105	19	4	12	49	15	68	.269	.315	.431	746	91	-6	10	4	1	.965	-9	*S-114/O-3(0-2-1)	-0.4
1996	Min-A	152	517	66	138	26	7	8	67	17	90	.267	.302	.391	693	72	-23	9	4	1	.965	-30	*S-150/O-1(0-1-0)	-3.7
1997	Min-A	134	439	63	121	23	3	10	60	18	86	.276	.328	.410	738	90	-7	7	7	-1	.969	13	*S-134	1.6
1998	Min-A	149	543	56	141	26	3	9	70	24	86	.260	.298	.368	667	71	-23	7	4	0	.966	-16	*S-149	-2.5
1999	Pit-N	21	91	15	28	4	0	0	7	9	20	.308	.382	.352	734	88	-1	0	0	0	.939	1	S-21	0.2
2000	Pit-N	132	462	55	111	22	2	13	47	36	91	.240	.306	.381	687	73	-20	1	0	0	.967	25	*S-126	1.5
Total	8	895	3017	374	792	146	23	54	357	140	543	.263	.307	.380	687	76	-112	43	25	1	.965	-14	S-884/O-4(0-3-1)	-4.9
■ RAY MEDEIROS Medeiros, Ray Antone "Pep" b: 5/9/26, Oakland, Cal. BR/TR, 5'10", 163 lbs. Deb: 4/25/45																								
1945	Cin-N	1	0	0	0	0	0	0	0	0	0	—	—	—	—	—	0	0			.000	0	R	0.0
■ LUIS MEDINA Medina, Luis Main b: 3/26/63, Santa Monica, Cal. BR/TL, 6'4", 200 lbs. Deb: 9/2/88																								
1988	Cle-A	16	51	10	13	0	0	6	8	2	18	.255	.309	.608	917	146	3	0	0	0	1.000	-0	1-16	0.2
1989	Cle-A	30	83	8	17	1	0	4	8	6	35	.205	.258	.361	620	72	-3	0	1	-0	.500	-1	D-25/O-3(1-0-2),1-1	-0.6
1991	Cle-A	5	16	0	1	0	0	0	0	1	7	.063	.118	.063	180	-48	-3	0	0	0	.000	0	/D-5	-0.4
Total	3	51	150	18	31	1	0	10	16	9	60	.207	.261	.413	674	85	-4	0	1	-0	1.000	-2	/D-30,1-17,O-3(1-0-2)	-0.8
■ JOE MEDWICK Medwick, Joseph Michael "Ducky" or "Muscles" b: 11/24/11, Carteret, N.J. d: 3/21/75, St.Petersburg, Fla BR/TR, 5'10", 187 lbs. Deb: 9/2/32 H Career OF: (1790-LF 19-CF 43-RF)																								
1932	StL-N	26	106	13	37	12	1	2	12	2	10	.349	.367	.538	905	136	5	3			.970	0	O-26(7-19-0)	0.4
1933	StL-N	148	595	92	182	40	10	18	98	26	56	.306	.337	.497	835	129	20	5			.980	8	*O-147(147-0-0)	2.1
1934	*StL-N★	149	620	110	198	40	**18**	18	106	21	83	.319	.343	.529	872	122	17	3			.960	4	*O-149(144-0-5)	1.2
1935	StL-N★	154	634	132	224	46	13	23	126	30	59	.353	.386	.576	962	149	41	4			.965	3	*O-154(154-0-0)	3.4
1936	StL-N★	155	636	115	**223**	**64**	13	18	**138**	34	33	.351	.387	.577	964	157	47	3			.985	14	*O-155(155-0-0)	5.1
1937	StL-N★	156	633	**111**	**237**	**56**	10	**31**	**154**	41	50	**.374**	.414	**.641**	**1056**	**179**	**66**	4			**.988**	4	*O-156(156-0-0)	5.9
1938	StL-N★	146	590	100	190	**47**	8	21	**122**	42	41	.322	.369	.536	905	138	29	0			.974	8	*O-144(144-0-0)	2.9
1939	StL-N★	150	606	98	201	48	8	14	117	45	44	.332	.380	.507	886	128	23	6			.976	5	*O-149(149-0-0)	1.9
1940	StL-N	37	158	21	48	12	0	3	20	6	8	.304	.329	.437	766	104	0	0			.988	-0	O-37(37-0-0)	-0.2
	Bro-N★	106	423	62	127	18	12	14	66	26	28	.300	.345	.499	844	123	12	2			.980	5	*O-103(103-0-0)	1.1
	Yr	143	581	83	175	30	12	17	86	32	36	.301	.341	.482	823	118	12	2			.982	5	*O-140(140-0-0)	0.9
1941	*Bro-N★	133	538	100	171	33	10	18	88	38	35	.318	.364	.517	881	140	26	2			.983	1	*O-131(130-0-1)	2.0
1942	Bro-N★	142	553	69	166	37	4	4	96	32	25	.300	.338	.403	742	115	9	2			.990	-3	*O-140(140-0-0)	-0.2
1943	Bro-N	48	173	13	47	10	0	0	25	10	8	.272	.315	.329	645	86	-3	1			.971	-5	O-42(42-0-0)	-1.2
	NY-N	78	324	41	91	20	3	5	45	9	14	.281	.300	.407	708	103	-1	0			.988	5	O-74(74-0-0)/1-3	-0.1
	Yr	126	497	54	138	30	3	5	70	19	22	.278	.306	.380	686	97	-4	1			.983	-0	*O-116(116-0-0)/1-3	-1.3
1944	NY-N★	128	490	64	165	24	3	7	85	38	24	.337	.386	.441	826	133	21	2			.993	8	*O-122(122-0-0)	2.2
1945	NY-N	26	92	14	28	4	0	3	11	2	2	.304	.319	.446	765	110	1	2			.979	-1	O-23(23-0-0)	-0.2
	Bos-N	66	218	17	62	13	0	0	26	12	12	.284	.325	.344	669	85	-4	3			1.000	1	O-38(38-0-0),1-15	-0.7
	Yr	92	310	31	90	17	0	3	37	14	14	.290	.323	.374	697	93	-4	5			.992	-0	O-61(61-0-0),1-15	-0.9
1946	Bro-N	41	77	7	24	4	0	2	18	6	5	.312	.369	.442	811	128	3	0			1.000	-3	O-18(18-0-0)/1-1	-0.1
1947	StL-N	75	150	19	46	12	0	4	28	16	12	.307	.373	.467	840	117	4	0			1.000	-5	O-43(7-0-36)	-0.3
1948	StL-N	20	19	0	4	0	0	0	2	1	2	.211	.250	.211	461	24	-2	0			.000	-0	/O-1(0-0-1)	-0.2
Total	17	1984	7635	1198	2471	540	113	205	1383	437	551	.324	.362	.505	867	133	312	42			.980	49	*O-1852L/1-19	25.0
■ TOMMY MEE Mee, Thomas William "Judge" b: 3/18/1890, Chicago, Ill. d: 5/16/81, Chicago, Ill. BR/TR, 5'8", 165 lbs. Deb: 6/14/10																								
1910	StL-A	8	19	1	3	2	0	0	1	0		.158	.158	.263	421	34	-2	0			.828	-1	/S-6,2-1,3-1	-0.3
■ DAD MEEK Meek, Frank J. b: 3/14/1867, St.Louis, Mo. d: 12/22/22, St.Louis, Mo. Deb: 5/10/1889																								
1889	StL-a	2	2	2	1	0	0	0	1	0	0	.500	.500	.500	1000	164	0	1			.667	0	/C-2	0.0
1890	StL-a	4	16	3	5	0	0	0	1	0		.313	.313	.313	625	74	-1	1			.913	3	/C-4	0.2
Total	2	6	18	5	6	0	0	0	2	0	0	.333	.333	.333	667	84	-0	2			.898	3	/C-6	0.2
■ SAMMY MEEKS Meeks, Samuel Mack b: 4/23/23, Anderson, S.C. BR/TR, 5'9", 160 lbs. Deb: 4/29/48																								
1948	Was-A	24	33	4	4	1	0	0	2	1	12	.121	.147	.152	299	-21	-6	0	0	0	.939	-0	S-10/2-1	-0.6
1949	Cin-N	16	36	10	11	2	0	2	6	2	6	.306	.342	.528	870	128	1	1			1.000	6	/2-8,S-3	0.7
1950	Cin-N	39	95	7	27	5	0	1	8	6	14	.284	.327	.368	695	82	-2	1			.951	-4	S-29/3-2	-0.5
1951	Cin-N	23	35	4	8	0	0	0	2	0	4	.229	.229	.229	457	23	-4	1	0	0	.929	-1	/3-4,S-1	-0.5
Total	4	102	199	25	50	8	0	3	18	9	36	.251	.284	.337	620	64	-11	3	0		.953	0	/S-43,2-9,3-6	-0.9
■ DUTCH MEIER Meier, Arthur Ernst b: 3/30/1879, St.Louis, Mo. d: 3/23/48, Chicago, Ill. BR/TR, 5'10", 175 lbs. Deb: 5/12/06																								
1906	Pit-N	82	273	32	70	11	4	0	16	13		.256	.298	.326	624	90	-4	4			.975	-12	O-52(29-6-18),S-17	-2.0
■ DAVE MEIER Meier, David Keith b: 8/8/59, Helena, Mont. BR/TR, 6', 185 lbs. Deb: 4/3/84 Career OF: (102-LF 3-CF 16-RF)																								
1984	Min-A	59	147	18	35	8	1	0	13	6	9	.238	.273	.306	579	57	-8	0	1	-0	.978	-4	O-50(41-0-10)/3-1,D-4	-1.5
1985	Min-A	71	104	15	27	6	0	1	8	18	12	.260	.374	.346	720	93	-0	0	6	-2	.987	-9	O-63(55-3-4)/D-3	-1.3
1987	Tex-A	13	21	4	6	1	0	0	0	0	4	.286	.286	.333	619	63	-1	0	0	0	.917	-1	/O-8(6-0-2)	-0.2
1988	Chi-N	2	5	0	2	0	0	0	1	0	1	.400	.400	.400	800	125	0	0	0	0	1.000	-1	/3-1	-0.1
Total	4	145	277	37	70	15	1	1	22	24	26	.253	.317	.325	642	73	-10	0	7	-2	.978	-15	O-121L/D-7,3-2	-3.1
■ WALT MEINERT Meinert, Walter Henry b: 12/11/1890, New York, N.Y. d: 11/9/58, Decatur, Ill. BL/TL, 5'7.5", 150 lbs. Deb: 9/6/13																								
1913	StL-A	4	8	1	3	0	0	0	0	1	3	.375	.444	.375	819	144	1	1			1.000	-0	/O-2(0-0-2)	0.0
■ FRANK MEINKE Meinke, Frank Louis b: 10/18/1863, Chicago, Ill. d: 11/8/31, Chicago, Ill. BR, 5'10.5", 172 lbs. Deb: 5/1/1884 F Career OF: (2-LF 0-CF 4-RF)																								
1884	Det-N	92	341	28	56	5	7	6	24	6	89	.164	.179	.273	451	42	-22				.839	-3	S-51,P-35/O-4R,32	-1.2

YEAR	TM/L	G	AB	R	H	2B	3B	HR	RBI	BB	SO	AVG	OBP	SLG	OPS	OPS+	BR+	SB	CS	SBR	FA	FR	G/POS	TPR
1885	Det-N	1	3	0	0	0	0	0	0	0	1	.000	.000	.000	0	-99	-1				1.000	-0	/O-1(1-0-0),P-1	0.0
Total	2	93	344	28	56	5	7	6	24	6	90	.163	.177	.270	447	41	-22				1.000	-3	/S-51,P-36,O-5R,23	-1.2
■ BOB MEINKE Meinke, Robert Bernard b: 6/25/1887, Chicago, Ill. d: 12/29/52, Chicago, Ill. BR/TR, 5'10", 135 lbs. Deb: 8/22/10 F																								
1910	Cin-N	2	1	0	0	0	0	0	0	1	0	.000	.500	.000	500	51	0	0			1.000	1	/S-2	0.1
■ GEORGE MEISTER Meister, George B. b: 6/5/1864, Dorzbach, Germany d: 8/24/08, Pittsburgh, Pa. Deb: 8/15/1884																								
1884	Tol-a	34	119	9	23	6	0	0		3		.193	.244	.244	488	58	-5				.817	-10	3-34	-1.3
■ JOHN MEISTER Meister, John F. b: 5/10/1863, Allentown, Pa. d: 1/17/23, Philadelphia, Pa. 5'8", 175 lbs. Deb: 8/24/1886 Career OF: (0-LF 22-CF 0-RF)																								
1886	NY-a	45	186	35	44	7	3	2	21	4		.237	.253	.339	591	89	-3	1			.906	-8	2-45	-0.8
1887	NY-a	39	173	24	51	6	2	1	21	16		.295	.303	.306	609	73	-5	9			.930	-9	O-22C,2-14/3-3,S-1	-1.2
Total	2	84	359	59	95	13	5	3	42	20		.265	.277	.324	600	81	-8	10			.905	-17	/2-59,O-22C,3-3,S-1	-2.0
■ KARL MEISTER Meister, Karl Daniel "Dutch" b: 5/15/1891, Marietta, Ohio d: 8/15/67, Marietta, Ohio BR/TR, 6', 178 lbs. Deb: 8/10/13																								
1913	Cin-N	4	7	1	2	1	0	0	2	0	4	.286	.286	.429	714	103	-0	0			.667	-2	/O-4(1-3-0)	-0.2
■ MOXIE MEIXELL Meixell, Merton Merrill b: 10/18/1887, Lake Crystal, Minn d: 8/17/82, Los Angeles, Cal. BL/TR, 5'10", 168 lbs. Deb: 7/7/12																								
1912	Cle-A	3	2	0	1	0	0	0	0	0		.500	.500	.500	1000	181	0	0			.000	0	/O-1	0.0
■ MIGUEL MEJIA Mejia, Miguel b: 3/25/75, San Pedro De Macoris, D.R. BR/TR, 6'1", 155 lbs. Deb: 4/4/96																								
1996	*StL-N	45	23	10	2	0	0	0	0	0	10	.087	.087	.087	174	-54	-5	6	3	0	.933	-6	O-21(5-11-6)	-1.1
■ ROBERTO MEJIA Mejia, Roberto Antonio (Diaz) b: 4/14/72, Hato Mayor, D.R. BR/TR, 5'11", 160 lbs. Deb: 7/15/93																								
1993	Col-N	65	229	31	53	14	5	5	20	13	63	.231	.276	.402	677	68	-11	4	1	1	.963	7	2-65	-0.1
1994	Col-N	38	116	11	28	8	1	4	14	15	33	.241	.328	.431	759	82	-3	3	1	0	.959	-3	2-34	-0.3
1995	Col-N	23	52	5	8	1	0	1	4	0	17	.154	.170	.231	401	3	-7	0	1	-0	.971	1	2-16	-0.6
1997	StL-N	7	14	0	1	1	0	0	2	0	5	.071	.071	.143	214	-46	-3	0	0	0	.900	-2	/2-3,O-1(1-0-1)	-0.5
Total	4	133	411	47	90	24	6	10	40	28	118	.219	.272	.380	652	60	-24	7	3	0	.961	3	2-118/O-1(1-0-1)	-1.5
■ ROMAN MEJIAS Mejias, Roman (Gomez) b: 8/9/30, Abreus, Las Villas, Cuba BR/TR, 6', 175 lbs. Deb: 4/13/55																								
1955	Pit-N	71	167	14	36	8	1	3	21	9	13	.216	.256	.329	585	55	-11	1	3	-1	.926	-0	O-44(30-1-14)	-1.4
1957	Pit-N	58	142	12	39	7	4	2	15	6	13	.275	.309	.423	731	97	-1	2	2	-0	1.000	-2	O-42(7-7-29)	-0.4
1958	Pit-N	76	157	17	42	3	2	5	19	2	27	.268	.281	.408	689	82	-5	2	0	0	.973	-1	O-57(41-10-8)	-0.7
1959	Pit-N	96	276	28	65	6	1	7	28	21	48	.236	.301	.341	642	71	-11	1	2	-0	.970	-0	O-85(15-21-52)	-1.5
1960	Pit-N	3	1	1	0	0	0	0	0	0	1	.000	.000	.000	0	-99	-0	0	0	0	.000	0	H	0.0
1961	Pit-N	4	1	1	0	0	0	0	0	0	1	.000	.000	.000	0	-99	-0	0	0	0	1.000	-1	/O-2(2-0-0)	-0.1
1962	Hou-N	146	566	82	162	12	3	24	76	30	83	.286	.329	.445	774	114	9	12	4	1	.946	-4	*O-142(1-1-141)	-0.4
1963	Bos-A	111	357	43	81	18	0	11	39	14	36	.227	.262	.370	632	72	-14	4	1	1	.973	2	O-86(7-65-15)	-1.5
1964	Bos-A	62	101	14	24	3	1	2	4	7	16	.238	.294	.347	640	74	-4	0	0	0	.962	-3	O-37(14-13-11)	-0.8
Total	9	627	1768	212	449	57	12	54	202	89	238	.254	.296	.391	688	86	-37	22	12	1	.963	-8	O-495(117-118-270)	-6.8
■ SAM MEJIAS Mejias, Samuel Elias b: 5/9/52, Santiago, D.R. BR/TR, 6', 170 lbs. Deb: 9/6/76 C																								
1976	StL-N	18	21	1	3	1	0	0	0	2	2	.143	.217	.190	408	16	-2	2	0	0	1.000	-3	O-17(3-1-13)	-0.5
1977	Mon-N	74	101	14	23	4	1	3	8	2	17	.228	.243	.376	619	65	-5	1	0	0	.966	-12	O-56(4-21-31)	-1.9
1978	Mon-N	67	56	9	13	1	0	0	6	2	5	.232	.259	.250	509	43	-4	0	0	0	.949	-14	O-52(24-4-25)/P-1	-2.0
1979	Chi-N	31	11	4	2	0	0	0	0	2	5	.182	.308	.182	490	34	-1	0	0	0	.875	-8	O-23(15-5-3)	-0.9
	Cin-N	7	2	1	1	0	0	0	0	0	0	.500	.500	.500	1000	173	0	0	0	0	1.000	-2	/O-5(0-5-0)	-0.2
	Yr	38	13	5	3	0	0	0	0	2	5	.231	.333	.231	564	53	-1	0	0	0	.889	-10	O-28(15-10-3)	-1.1
1980	Cin-N	71	108	16	30	5	1	1	10	6	13	.278	.322	.370	692	93	-1	4	2	0	.989	-13	O-67(8-50-17)	-1.6
1981	Cin-N	66	49	6	14	2	0	0	7	2	9	.286	.314	.327	640	80	-1	1	0	0	.972	-16	O-58(0-16-42)	-1.9
Total	6	334	348	51	86	13	2	4	31	16	51	.247	.282	.330	613	69	-15	8	2	1	.973	-68	O-278(54-102-131)/P-1	-9.0
■ DUTCH MELE Mele, Albert Ernest b: 1/11/15, New York, N.Y. d: 2/12/75, Hollywood, Fla. BL/TL, 6'0.5", 195 lbs. Deb: 9/14/37																								
1937	Cin-N	6	14	1	2	1	0	0	1	1	1	.143	.200	.214	414	13	-2	0			1.000	-2	/O-5(2-0-3)	-0.4
■ SAM MELE Mele, Sabath Anthony b: 1/21/23, Astoria, N.Y. BR/TR, 6'1", 187 lbs. Deb: 4/15/47 MC Career OF: (90-LF 101-CF 674-RF)																								
1947	Bos-A	123	453	71	137	14	8	12	73	37	35	.302	.356	.448	805	114	8	0	3	-1	.992	-3	*O-116(3-29-87)/1-1	0.1
1948	Bos-A	66	180	25	42	12	1	2	25	13	21	.233	.292	.344	637	66	-9	1	1	-0	.971	-4	O-55(3-0-52)	-1.5
1949	Bos-A	18	46	1	9	1	1	0	7	7	14	.196	.302	.261	563	46	-4	2	0	0	.955	-0	O-11(0-0-11)	-0.4
	Was-A	78	264	21	64	12	2	3	25	17	34	.242	.288	.337	625	67	-14	2	1	0	.966	-8	O-63(1-24-44),1-11	-2.4
	Yr	96	310	22	73	13	3	3	32	24	48	.235	.290	.326	616	63	-18	4	1	1	.964	-9	O-74(1-24-55),1-11	-2.8
1950	Was-A	126	435	57	119	21	6	12	86	51	40	.274	.351	.432	783	105	2	2	0	0	.990	-5	O-99(6-26-72),1-16	-0.6
1951	Was-A	143	558	58	153	**36**	7	5	94	32	31	.274	.315	.391	705	92	-9	2	3	-1	.993	3	*O-124(2-17-107),1-15	-1.1
1952	Was-A	9	28	2	12	3	0	2	10	1	2	.429	.448	.750	1198	237	5	0	0	0	.917	-1	/O-7(0-1-6)	0.4
	Chi-A	123	423	46	105	18	2	14	59	48	40	.248	.328	.400	727	101	-0	1	2	-0	1.000	-6	*O-112(0-0-112)/1-3	-1.1
	Yr	132	451	48	117	21	2	16	69	49	42	.259	.335	.421	756	109	4	1	2	-0	.994	-7	*O-119(0-1-118)/1-3	-0.7
1953	Chi-A	140	481	64	132	26	8	12	82	58	47	.274	.353	.437	789	109	6	3	1	0	.996	-8	*O-138(0-4-138)/1-2	-0.7
1954	Bal-A	72	230	17	55	9	4	5	32	18	26	.239	.294	.378	673	90	-4	1	0	0	.962	-4	O-62(40-0-24)	-1.2
	Bos-A	42	132	22	42	6	0	7	23	12	12	.318	.384	.523	906	132	6	0	1	-0	.994	-4	1-22,O-13(3-0-13)	0.0
	Yr	114	362	39	97	15	4	12	55	30	38	.268	.327	.431	758	107	2	1	1	-0	.961	-8	O-75(43-0-37),1-22	-1.2
1955	Bos-A	14	31	1	4	2	0	0	1	0	7	.129	.129	.194	323	-13	-5	1	0	0	1.000	2	/O-7(6-0-1)	-0.3
	Cin-N	35	62	4	13	1	0	2	7	5	13	.210	.279	.323	602	56	-4	0	1	-0	.960	-1	O-13(12-0-1)/1-1	-0.6
1956	Cle-A	57	114	17	29	7	0	4	20	12	20	.254	.325	.421	746	94	-1	0	1	-0	.969	-0	O-20(14-0-6)/1-8	-0.3
Total	10	1046	3437	406	916	168	39	80	544	311	342	.267	.329	.408	737	97	-25	15	14	-2	.985	-39	O-840R/1-79	-9.7
■ FRANCISCO MELENDEZ Melendez, Francisco Javier (Villegas) b: 1/25/64, Rio Piedras, P.R. BL/TL, 6', 190 lbs. Deb: 8/26/84																								
1984	Phi-N	21	23	0	3	0	0	0	2	1	5	.130	.167	.130	297	-15	-3	0	0	0	1.000	1	1-10	-0.3
1986	Phi-N	9	8	0	2	0	0	0	0	0	2	.250	.250	.250	500	37	-1	0	0	0	1.000	-0	/1-2	-0.1
1987	SF-N	12	16	2	5	0	0	1	1	0	3	.313	.313	.500	813	117	0	0	0	0	1.000	-1	/1-5	0.0
1988	SF-N	23	26	1	5	0	0	0	3	3	2	.192	.276	.192	468	38	-2	0	0	0	1.000	-1	/1-6,O-1(1-0-0)	-0.4
1989	Bal-A	9	11	1	3	0	0	0	3	1	2	.273	.333	.273	606	75	-0	0	0	0	1.000	0	/1-5	0.0
Total	5	74	84	4	18	0	0	1	9	5	14	.214	.258	.250	508	43	-6	0	0	0	1.000	-1	/1-28,O-1(1-0-0)	-0.8
■ LUIS MELENDEZ Melendez, Luis Antonio (Santana) b: 8/11/49, Aibonito, P.R. BR/TR, 6', 165 lbs. Deb: 9/7/70																								
1970	StL-N	21	70	11	21	1	0	0	8	2	12	.300	.319	.314	634	69	-3	3	0	1	1.000	1	O-18(0-5-13)	-0.3
1971	StL-N	88	173	25	39	3	1	0	11	24	29	.225	.320	.254	574	62	-8	2	0	0	.959	-10	O-66(4-20-45)	-2.0
1972	StL-N	118	332	32	79	11	3	5	28	25	34	.238	.293	.334	628	79	-10	5	4	-0	.959	-6	*O-105(4-69-40)	-2.1
1973	StL-N	121	341	35	91	18	1	2	35	27	50	.267	.321	.343	664	84	-7	2	7	-2	.990	2	O-95(2-65-30)	-1.1
1974	StL-N	83	124	15	27	4	3	0	8	11	9	.218	.287	.298	585	64	-6	2	2	-0	.977	-8	O-46(23-22-10)/S-1	-1.6
1975	StL-N	110	291	33	77	8	5	2	27	16	25	.265	.303	.347	650	77	-9	3	2	-0	.983	-6	O-89(36-49-7)	-1.9
1976	StL-N	20	24	0	3	0	0	0	0	0	3	.125	.125	.125	250	-29	-4	0	0	0	1.000	-1	/O-8(4-4-0)	-0.5
	SD-N	72	119	15	29	5	0	0	5	3	12	.244	.262	.286	548	60	-7	1	1	-0	.988	-12	O-60(24-29-10)	-2.1
	Yr	92	143	15	32	5	0	0	5	3	15	.224	.240	.259	498	44	-11	1	1	-0	.990	-13	O-68(28-33-10)	-2.6
1977	SD-N	8	3	1	0	0	0	0	0	1	1	.000	.250	.000	250	-29	-1	0	0	0	1.000	-1	/O-2(0-2-0)	-0.1
Total	8	641	1477	167	366	50	13	9	122	109	175	.248	.300	.318	618	73	-54	18	16	-2	.977	-40	O-489(97-265-155)/S-1	-11.7
■ ADAM MELHUSE Melhuse, Adam Michael b: 3/27/72, Santa Clara, Cal. BB/TR, 6'2", 185 lbs. Deb: 6/16/2000																								
2000	LA-N	1	1	0	0	0	0	0	0	0	1	.000	.000	.000	0	-99	-0	0	0	0	.000	0	/H	0.0
	Col-N	23	23	3	4	0	1	0	4	3	5	.174	.269	.261	530	27	-3	0	0	0	1.000	-1	/1-3,C-1,O-1(0-0-1)	-0.3
	Yr	24	24	3	4	0	1	0	4	3	6	.167	.259	.250	509	23	-3	0	0	0	1.000	-1	/1-3,C-1,O-1(0-0-1)	-0.3

YEAR	TM/L	G	AB	R	H	2B	3B	HR	RBI	BB	SO	AVG	OBP	SLG	OPS	OPS+	BR+	SB	CS	SBR	FA	FR	G/POS	TPR
■ **SKI MELILLO** Melillo, Oscar Donald "Spinach" b: 8/4/1899, Chicago, Ill. d: 11/14/63, Chicago, Ill. BR/TR, 5'8", 150 lbs. Deb: 4/18/26 MC																								
1926	StL-A	99	385	54	98	18	5	1	30	32	31	.255	.315	.335	650	66	-19	6	7	-1	.965	8	2-88,3-11	-0.9
1927	StL-A	107	356	45	80	18	2	0	26	25	28	.225	.276	.287	562	45	-30	3	6	-1	.935	-2	*2-101	-2.9
1928	StL-A	51	132	9	25	2	0	0	9	9	11	.189	.241	.205	446	18	-16	2	1	0	.961	4	2-28,3-19	-1.0
1929	StL-A	141	494	57	146	17	10	5	67	29	30	.296	.337	.401	738	86	-11	11	6	0	.973	23	*2-141	1.5
1930	StL-A	149	574	62	147	30	10	5	59	23	44	.256	.287	.369	656	63	-34	15	9	0	.979	**27**	*2-148	-0.2
1931	StL-A	151	617	88	189	34	11	2	75	37	29	.306	.346	.407	752	94	-6	7	11	-2	.968	**33**	*2-151	3.2
1932	StL-A	154	612	71	148	19	11	3	66	36	42	.242	.286	.324	610	54	-42	6	6	-1	.981	11	*2-153	-2.1
1933	StL-A	132	496	50	145	23	6	3	79	29	18	.292	.333	.381	714	83	-12	12	10	-1	**.991**	**23**	*2-130	1.7
1934	StL-A	144	552	54	133	19	3	2	55	28	27	.241	.279	.297	576	45	-45	4	6	-1	**.981**	18	*2-141	-1.8
1935	StL-A	19	62	8	13	3	0	0	5	8	4	.210	.300	.258	558	43	-5	0	0	0	.970	0	2-18	-0.4
	Bos-A	106	400	45	104	13	2	1	39	38	22	.260	.327	.310	637	61	-22	3	2	-0	.973	18	*2-105	0.3
	Yr	125	462	53	117	16	2	1	44	46	26	.253	.324	.303	627	59	-27	3	2	-0	.973	19	*2-123	-0.1
1936	Bos-A	98	327	39	74	12	4	0	32	28	16	.226	.287	.287	575	40	-31	0	0	0	.980	-8	2-93	-3.0
1937	Bos-A	26	56	8	14	2	0	0	6	5	4	.250	.311	.286	597	50	-4	0	1	-0	.939	-3	2-19/S-2,3-2	-0.7
Total	12	1377	5063	590	1316	210	64	22	548	327	306	.260	.306	.340	646	64	-277	69	65	-8	.973	151	*2-1316/3-32,S-2	-6.3
■ **JOE MELLANA** Mellana, Joseph Peter b: 3/11/05, Oakland, Cal. d: 11/1/69, Larkspur, Cal. BR/TR, 5'10", 180 lbs. Deb: 9/21/27																								
1927	Phi-A	4	7	1	2	0	0	0	2	0	1	.286	.286	.286	571	46	-1	0	0	0	.889	2	/3-2	0.1
■ **BILL MELLOR** Mellor, William Harpin b: 6/6/1874, Camden, N.J. d: 11/5/40, Bridgeton, R.I. BR/TR, 6', 190 lbs. Deb: 7/28/02																								
1902	Bal-A	10	36	4	13	3	0	0	5	3		.361	.410	.444	855	131	2	1			.978	-1	1-10	0.0
■ **JUAN MELO** Melo, Juan Esteban b: 5/11/76, Bani, D.R. BB/TR, 6'3", 206 lbs. Deb: 9/2/2000																								
2000	SF-N	11	13	0	1	0	0	0	1	0	5	.077	.077	.077	154	-66	-3	0	0	0	1.000	-1	/2-6	-0.4
■ **PAUL MELOAN** Meloan, Paul B. "Molly" b: 8/23/1888, Paynesville, Mo. d: 2/11/50, Taft, Cal. BR/TL, 5'10.5", 175 lbs. Deb: 8/2/10																								
1910	Chi-A	65	222	23	54	6	6	0	23	17		.243	.314	.324	639	104	1	4			.948	3	O-65(0-0-65)	0.2
1911	Chi-A	1	3	0	1	0	0	0	1	0		.333	.333	.333	667	89	-0	0			.000	-1	/O-1(0-0-1)	-0.1
	StL-A	64	206	30	54	11	2	3	14	15		.262	.318	.379	697	98	-1	7			.904	-6	O-54(1-0-53)	-1.0
	Yr	65	209	30	55	11	2	3	15	15		.263	.319	.378	697	98	-1	7			.893	-6	O-55(1-0-54)	-1.1
Total	2	130	431	53	109	17	8	3	38	32		.253	.316	.350	667	101	-0	11			.923	-3	O-120(1-0-119)	-0.9
■ **DAVE MELTON** Melton, David Olin b: 10/3/28, Pampa, Tex. BR/TR, 6', 185 lbs. Deb: 4/17/56																								
1956	KC-A	3	3	0	1	0	0	0	0	0	0	.333	.333	.333	667	76	-0	0	0	0	1.000	-1	/O-3(3-0-0)	-0.1
1958	KC-A	9	6	0	0	0	0	0	0	0	5	.000	.000	.000	0	-98	-2	0	0	0	1.000	-0	/O-2(2-0-0)	-0.2
Total	2	12	9	0	1	0	0	0	0	0	5	.111	.111	.111	222	-39	-2	0	0	0	1.000	-1	/O-5(5-0-0)	-0.3
■ **BILL MELTON** Melton, William Edwin b: 7/7/45, Gulfport, Miss. BR/TR, 6'2", 200 lbs. Deb: 5/4/68 Career OF: (3-LF 0-CF 79-RF)																								
1968	Chi-A	34	109	5	29	8	0	2	16	10	32	.266	.328	.394	722	117	2	1	1	-0	.968	3	3-33	0.6
1969	Chi-A	157	556	67	142	26	2	23	87	56	106	.255	.329	.433	762	106	4	1	2	-0	.952	7	*3-148,O-11(3-0-8)	1.0
1970	Chi-A	141	514	74	135	15	1	33	96	56	107	.263	.345	.488	834	123	15	2	4	-1	1.000	9	O-71(0-0-71),3-70	1.9
1971	Chi-A☆	150	543	72	146	18	2	**33**	86	61	87	.269	.354	.492	846	133	23	3	3	-0	.968	27	*3-148	5.2
1972	Chi-A	57	208	22	51	5	0	7	30	23	31	.245	.320	.370	691	103	1	1	1	-0	.935	3	3-56	0.4
1973	Chi-A	152	560	83	155	29	1	20	87	75	66	.277	.364	.439	803	121	17	4	4	-1	.953	14	*3-151/D-1	3.0
1974	Chi-A	136	495	63	120	17	0	21	63	59	60	.242	.329	.404	733	107	5	3	2	-0	.939	-3	*3-123,D-11	0.0
1975	Chi-A	149	512	62	123	16	0	15	70	78	106	.240	.349	.359	709	99	2	5	4	-0	.945	1	*3-138,D-11	0.1
1976	Cal-A	118	341	31	71	17	3	6	42	44	53	.208	.302	.328	631	90	-4	2	0	0	.992	-3	D-51,1-30,3-21	-1.1
1977	Cle-A	50	133	17	32	11	0	0	14	17	21	.241	.336	.323	659	83	-3	1	3	-1	1.000	1	1-15,D-14,3-13	-0.4
Total	10	1144	3971	496	1004	162	9	160	591	479	669	.253	.340	.419	759	112	61	23	24	-3	.949	57	3-901/D-88,O-82R,1	10.7
■ **MITCH MELUSKEY** Meluskey, Mitchell Wade b: 9/18/73, Yakima, Wash. BB/TR, 6', 185 lbs. Deb: 8/30/98																								
1998	Hou-N	8	8	1	2	1	0	0	0	1	4	.250	.333	.375	708	88	-0	0	0	0	1.000	0	/C-3	0.0
1999	Hou-N	10	33	4	7	1	0	1	3	5	6	.212	.316	.333	649	65	-2	1	0	0	1.000	-0	C-10	-0.1
2000	Hou-N	117	337	47	101	21	0	14	69	55	74	.300	.404	.487	891	117	10	1	0	0	.982	-12	*C-103/3-1	0.4
Total	3	135	378	52	110	23	0	15	72	61	84	.291	.395	.471	866	112	9	2	0	0	.984	-12	C-116/3-1	0.3
■ **BOB MELVIN** Melvin, Robert Paul b: 10/28/61, Palo Alto, Cal. BR/TR, 6'4", 205 lbs. Deb: 5/25/85 C																								
1985	Det-A	41	82	10	18	4	1	0	4	3	21	.220	.247	.293	540	47	-6	0	0	0	.989	8	C-41	0.3
1986	SF-N	89	268	24	60	14	2	5	25	15	69	.224	.265	.347	612	71	-12	3	2	-0	.988	7	C-84/3-1	-0.1
1987	*SF-N	84	246	31	49	8	0	11	31	17	44	.199	.251	.366	617	64	-14	0	4	-1	.998	4	C-78/1-1	-0.8
1988	SF-N	92	273	23	64	13	1	8	27	13	46	.234	.269	.377	647	87	-6	0	2	-1	.984	-8	C-89/1-1	-1.0
1989	Bal-A	85	278	22	67	10	1	1	32	15	53	.241	.280	.295	575	64	-13	1	4	-1	.991	-9	C-75/D-9	-2.0
1990	Bal-A	93	301	30	73	14	1	5	37	11	53	.243	.269	.346	615	73	-12	0	1	-0	.997	1	C-76,D-10/1-1	-0.8
1991	Bal-A	79	228	11	57	10	0	1	23	11	46	.250	.285	.307	592	66	-11	0	0	0	.998	6	C-72/D-4	-0.1
1992	KC-A	32	70	5	22	5	0	0	6	5	13	.314	.360	.386	746	106	1	0	0	0	1.000	-0	C-21/1-3	0.1
1993	Bos-A	77	176	13	39	7	0	3	23	7	44	.222	.255	.313	568	49	-13	0	0	0	.994	-8	C-76/1-1	-1.7
1994	NY-A	9	14	2	4	0	0	1	3	0	3	.286	.286	.500	786	101	-0	0	0	0	1.000	-1	/C-4,1-4,D-1	-0.1
	Chi-A	11	19	3	3	0	0	0	1	1	4	.158	.200	.158	358	-6	-3	0	0	0	1.000	2	C-11	-0.1
	Yr	20	33	5	7	0	0	1	4	1	7	.212	.235	.303	538	39	-3	0	0	0	1.000	1	C-15/1-4,D-1	-0.2
Total	10	692	1955	174	456	85	6	35	212	98	396	.233	.270	.337	607	69	-88	4	13	-4	.993	2	C-627/D-24,1-11,3-1	-6.3
■ **CARLOS MENDOZA** Mendoza, Carlos Ramon b: 11/4/74, Bolivar, Venez. BL/TL, 5'11", 160 lbs. Deb: 9/3/97																								
1997	NY-N	15	12	6	3	0	0	0	1	4	2	.250	.500	.250	750	108	1	0	0	0	1.000	-1	/O-3(2-3-0)	0.0
2000	Col-N	13	10	0	1	0	0	0	0	1	4	.100	.182	.100	282	-21	-2	0	1	-0	.000	-1	/O-3(3-0-0)	-0.3
Total	2	28	22	6	4	0	0	0	1	5	6	.182	.379	.182	561	47	-1	0	1	-0	.833	-2	/O-6(5-3-0)	-0.3
■ **MINNIE MENDOZA** Mendoza, Cristobal Rigoberto (Carreras) b: 11/16/33, Ceiba Del Agua, Cuba BR/TR, 6', 180 lbs. Deb: 4/9/70 C																								
1970	Min-A	16	16	2	3	0	0	0	2	0	1	.188	.188	.188	375	4	-2	0	0	0	1.000	0	/3-5,2-4	-0.2
■ **MARIO MENDOZA** Mendoza, Mario (Aizpuru) b: 12/26/50, Chihuahua, Mex. BR/TR, 5'11", 187 lbs. Deb: 4/26/74																								
1974	*Pit-N	91	163	10	36	1	2	0	15	8	35	.221	.262	.252	513	46	-12	1	1	-0	.964	5	S-87	-0.1
1975	Pit-N	56	50	8	9	1	0	0	2	3	17	.180	.226	.200	426	19	-5	0	0	0	.952	8	S-53/3-1	0.4
1976	Pit-N	50	92	6	17	5	0	0	12	4	15	.185	.219	.239	458	30	-9	0	1	-0	.967	12	S-45/3-2,2-1	0.6
1977	Pit-N	70	81	5	16	3	0	0	4	3	10	.198	.226	.235	461	23	-9	0	0	0	.928	12	S-45,3-19/P-1	0.5
1978	Pit-N	57	55	5	12	1	0	1	3	2	9	.218	.283	.291	574	58	-3	3	1	0	.980	9	2-21,3-18,S-14	0.8
1979	Sea-A	148	373	26	74	10	3	1	29	9	62	.198	.219	.249	469	26	-39	3	0	1	.968	28	*S-148	0.1
1980	Sea-A	114	277	27	68	6	3	2	14	16	42	.245	.287	.310	597	63	-14	3	4	-1	.959	12	*S-114	0.6
1981	Tex-A	88	229	18	53	6	1	0	22	7	25	.231	.257	.266	524	54	-14	2	1	0	.970	3	S-88	-0.2
1982	Tex-A	12	17	1	2	0	0	0	0	0	4	.118	.118	.118	235	-37	-3	0	0	0	.882	2	S-12	-0.1
Total	9	686	1337	106	287	33	9	4	101	52	219	.215	.247	.262	509	41	-107	12	8	-0	.961	91	S-606/3-40,2-22,P-1	2.6
■ **MIKE MENDOZA** Mendoza, Michael Joseph b: 11/26/55, Inglewood, Cal. BR/TR, 6'5", 215 lbs. Deb: 9/7/79																								
1979	Hou-N	2	0	0	0	0	0	0	0	0	0	—	—	—	—	—	0	0	0	0	.000	0	/P-1	0.0
■ **FRANK MENECHINO** Menechino, Frank b: 1/7/71, Staten Island, N.Y. BR/TR, 5'9", 175 lbs. Deb: 9/7/99																								
1999	Oak-A	9	9	0	2	0	0	0	0	0	4	.222	.222	.222	444	15	-1	0	0	0	1.000	2	/S-5,3-1	0.1
2000	*Oak-A	66	145	31	37	9	1	6	26	20	45	.255	.349	.455	805	104	1	1	4	-1	.973	16	2-51/S-5,3-4,P-1,D	1.6
Total	2	75	154	31	39	9	1	6	26	20	49	.253	.343	.442	784	99	-0	1	4	-1	1.000	18	/2-51,S-10,3-5,DP	1.7
■ **JOCK MENEFEE** Menefee, John b: 1/15/1868, Rowlesburg, W.Va. d: 3/11/53, Belle Vernon, Pa. BR/TR, 6', 165 lbs. Deb: 8/17/1892 Career OF: (7-LF 3-CF 44-RF)																								
1892	Pit-N	2	3	0	0	0	0	0	0	0	0	.000	.000	.000	0	-99	-1	0			1.000	0	/O-1(0-0-1),P-1	-0.1

YEAR	TM/L	G	AB	R	H	2B	3B	HR	RBI	BB	SO	AVG	OBP	SLG	OPS	OPS+	BR+	SB	CS	SBR	FA	FR	G/POS	TPR
1893	Lou-N	22	73	10	20	2	1	0	12	13	5	.274	.391	.329	720	100	1	2			.913	3	P-15/O-7(1-2-4)	0.1
1894	Lou-N	29	79	7	13	1	0	0	4	8	7	.165	.250	.177	427	5	-12	2			.940	2	P-28/2-1	0.0
	Pit-N	13	47	6	12	1	2	0	7	3	3	.255	.300	.362	662	59	-3	2			.909	2	P-13	0.0
	Yr	42	126	13	25	2	2	0	11	11	10	.198	.268	.246	514	26	-15	4			.928	5	P-41/2-1	0.0
1895	Pit-N	2	0	0	0	0	0	0	0	0	0	—	—	—	—	—	0	0			.667	0	/P-2	0.0
1898	NY-N	1	5	0	0	0	0	0	0	0		.000	.000	.000	0	-99	-1	0			.750	0	/P-1	0.0
1900	Chi-N	17	46	5	5	0	0	0	4	2		.109	.180	.109	289	-20	-7	0			.889	-2	P-16	0.0
1901	Chi-N	48	152	19	39	5	3	0	13	8		.257	.327	.329	656	94	-1	4			.913	-2	O-24R,P-21/1-2,2-1	-0.3
1902	Chi-N	65	216	24	50	4	1	0	15	15		.231	.303	.259	562	76	-5	4			.952	-4	O-23R,P-22,1-18,/32	-0.8
1903	Chi-N	22	64	3	13	3	0	0	2	3		.203	.239	.250	489	40	-5	0			.896	3	P-20/1-2	-0.1
Total	9	221	685	74	152	16	7	0	57	52	15	.222	.295	.266	561	60	-35	14			.918	3	P-139/O-55R,1-22,23	-1.2

■ DENIS MENKE

Menke, Denis John b: 7/21/40, Bancroft, Iowa BR/TR, 6', 190 lbs. Deb: 4/14/62 C Career OF: (3-LF 0-CF 2-RF)

YEAR	TM/L	G	AB	R	H	2B	3B	HR	RBI	BB	SO	AVG	OBP	SLG	OPS	OPS+	BR+	SB	CS	SBR	FA	FR	G/POS	TPR
1962	Mil-N	50	146	12	28	3	1	2	16	16	38	.192	.280	.267	548	49	-10	0	1	-0	.980	5	2-20,3-15/S-9,1O	-0.4
1963	Mil-N	146	518	58	121	16	4	11	50	37	106	.234	.292	.344	636	83	-11	6	7	-1	.976	12	S-82,3-51,2-22,/1O	0.9
1964	Mil-N	151	505	79	143	29	5	20	65	68	77	.283	.373	.479	852	137	26	4	2	0	.964	2	*S-141,2-15/3-6	4.3
1965	Mil-N	71	181	16	44	13	1	4	18	18	28	.243	.315	.392	707	97	-1	1	3	-1	.967	-7	S-54/1-8,3-4	-0.5
1966	Atl-N	138	454	55	114	20	4	15	60	71	87	.251	.360	.412	772	112	9	0	7	-2	.955	-22	*S-106,3-39/1-7	-0.7
1967	Atl-N	129	418	37	95	14	3	7	39	65	62	.227	.335	.325	661	91	-3	5	7	-1	.965	-23	*S-124/3-3	-1.8
1968	Hou-N	150	542	56	135	23	6	6	56	64	81	.249	.335	.347	682	107	6	5	8	-2	.982	-17	*2-119,S-35/1-5,3-4	0.0
1969	Hou-N★	154	553	72	149	25	5	10	90	87	87	.269	.373	.387	760	115	14	2	7	-2	.956	-9	*S-131,2-23/1-9,3-1	2.0
1970	Hou-N★	154	562	82	171	26	6	13	92	82	80	.304	.398	.441	839	130	26	6	5	-0	.954	-16	*S-133,2-21/1-5,3O	2.7
1971	Hou-N	146	475	57	117	26	3	1	43	59	68	.246	.332	.320	652	88	-6	4	5	-1	.997	-3	*1-101,3-32,S-17,/2	-1.7
1972	*Cin-N	140	447	41	104	19	2	9	50	58	76	.233	.327	.345	672	97	-1	0	1	-0	.955	1	*3-130,1-11	-0.2
1973	*Cin-N	139	241	38	46	10	0	3	26	69	53	.191	.375	.270	645	86	-1	1	1	-0	.966	16	*3-123/S-7,2-5,1-1	1.6
1974	Hou-N	30	29	2	3	1	0	0	1	4	10	.103	.212	.138	350	-1	-4	0	0	0	1.000	3	1-12/3-7,2-3,S-2	-0.1
Total	13	1598	5071	605	1270	225	40	101	606	698	853	.250	.346	.370	717	104	45	34	54	-11	.961	-58	S-841,3-420,21/O	6.1

■ MIKE MENOSKY

Menosky, Michael William "Leaping Mike" b: 10/16/1894, Glen Campbell, Pa. d: 4/11/83, Detroit, Mich. BL/TR, 5'10", 163 lbs. Deb: 4/18/14

YEAR	TM/L	G	AB	R	H	2B	3B	HR	RBI	BB	SO	AVG	OBP	SLG	OPS	OPS+	BR+	SB	CS	SBR	FA	FR	G/POS	TPR
1914	Pit-F	68	140	26	37	4	1	2	9	16	30	.264	.352	.350	702	92	-3	5			.942	-3	O-41(6-3-32)	-0.8
1915	Pit-F	17	21	3	2	0	0	0	1	2	0	.095	.208	.095	304	-13	-3	2			.917	-2	/O-9(6-1-2)	-0.6
1916	Was-A	11	37	5	6	1	1	0	3	1	10	.162	.184	.243	427	29	-3	1			.952	1	/O-9(1-8-0)	-0.3
1917	Was-A	114	322	46	83	12	10	1	34	45	55	.258	.359	.366	726	123	10	22			.982	8	O-94(93-0-1)	1.5
1919	Was-A	116	342	62	98	15	3	6	39	44	46	.287	.379	.401	780	120	10	13			.979	0	*O-103(87-15-1)	0.6
1920	Bos-A	141	532	80	158	24	9	3	64	65	52	.297	.383	.393	776	111	10	23	19	-2	.961	-3	*O-141(141-0-0)	0.0
1921	Bos-A	133	477	77	143	18	5	3	45	60	45	.300	.388	.377	766	99	2	12	6	1	.970	-4	*O-133(133-0-0)	-1.2
1922	Bos-A	126	406	61	115	16	5	3	32	40	33	.283	.355	.369	724	90	-5	9	5	0	.977	6	*O-103(74-4-26)	-0.7
1923	Bos-A	84	188	22	43	8	4	0	25	22	19	.229	.310	.314	623	64	-10	3	6	-1	.920	3	O-49(28-18-3)	-1.1
Total	9	810	2465	382	685	98	38	18	252	295	290	.278	.364	.370	735	100	7	90	36		.967	7	O-682(569-49-65)	-2.6

■ ED MENSOR

Mensor, Edward "The Midget" b: 11/7/1886, Woodville, Ore. d: 4/20/70, Salem, Ore. BB/TR, 5'6", 145 lbs. Deb: 7/15/12 Career OF: (5-LF 46-CF 24-RF)

YEAR	TM/L	G	AB	R	H	2B	3B	HR	RBI	BB	SO	AVG	OBP	SLG	OPS	OPS+	BR+	SB	CS	SBR	FA	FR	G/POS	TPR
1912	Pit-N	39	99	19	26	3	2	0	1	23	12	.263	.402	.333	735	104	2	10			.955	-2	O-32(0-20-12)	-0.2
1913	Pit-N	44	56	9	10	1	0	0	1	8	13	.179	.292	.196	489	43	-4	2			.971	-1	O-18(1-16-1)/2-1,S-1	-0.5
1914	Pit-N	44	89	15	18	2	1	1	6	22	13	.202	.372	.281	653	99	1	2			.969	2	O-25(4-10-11)	0.2
Total	3	127	244	43	54	6	3	1	8	53	38	.221	.367	.283	649	89	-1	14			.964	-2	/O-75C,S-1,2-1	-0.5

■ TED MENZE

Menze, Theodore Charles b: 11/4/1897, St.Louis, Mo. d: 12/23/69, St.Louis, Mo. BR/TR, 5'9", 172 lbs. Deb: 4/23/18

YEAR	TM/L	G	AB	R	H	2B	3B	HR	RBI	BB	SO	AVG	OBP	SLG	OPS	OPS+	BR+	SB	CS	SBR	FA	FR	G/POS	TPR
1918	StL-N	1	3	0	0	0	0	0	0	0	2	.000	.000	.000	0	-99	-1	0			1.000	-0	/O-1(1-0-0)	-0.1

■ RUDY MEOLI

Meoli, Rudolph Bartholomew b: 5/1/51, Troy, N.Y. BL/TR, 5'9", 165 lbs. Deb: 9/9/71

YEAR	TM/L	G	AB	R	H	2B	3B	HR	RBI	BB	SO	AVG	OBP	SLG	OPS	OPS+	BR+	SB	CS	SBR	FA	FR	G/POS	TPR
1971	Cal-A	7	3	0	0	0	0	0	0	0	1	.000	.000	.000	0	-99	-1	0	0	0	.000	0	H	-0.1
1973	Cal-A	120	305	36	68	12	1	2	23	31	38	.223	.295	.289	583	70	-12	2	4	-1	.933	-2	S-95,3-13/2-8	-0.5
1974	Cal-A	36	90	9	22	2	0	0	3	8	10	.244	.306	.267	573	70	-3	2	4	-1	.946	2	3-20/S-8,1-1,2-1	-0.2
1975	Cal-A	70	126	12	27	2	1	0	6	15	20	.214	.298	.246	544	59	-6	3	0	1	.976	0	S-28,3-15,2-11,/D-3	-0.3
1978	Chi-N	47	29	10	3	0	1	0	2	6	4	.103	.257	.172	430	20	-3	1	0	0	.900	6	/2-6,3-5	0.4
1979	Phi-N	30	73	2	13	4	1	0	6	9	15	.178	.268	.260	529	43	-6	2	0	0	.984	3	S-16,2-15/3-1	0.0
Total	6	310	626	69	133	20	4	2	40	69	88	.212	.291	.267	557	61	-31	10	8	-1	.944	10	S-147/3-54,2-41,D1	-0.7

■ ORLANDO MERCADO

Mercado, Orlando (Rodriguez) b: 11/7/61, Arecibo, P.R. BR/TR, 6', 195 lbs. Deb: 9/13/82

YEAR	TM/L	G	AB	R	H	2B	3B	HR	RBI	BB	SO	AVG	OBP	SLG	OPS	OPS+	BR+	SB	CS	SBR	FA	FR	G/POS	TPR
1982	Sea-A	9	17	1	2	0	0	1	6	0	5	.118	.118	.294	412	8	-2	0	0	0	1.000	1	/C-8,D-1	-0.1
1983	Sea-A	66	178	10	35	11	2	1	16	14	27	.197	.259	.298	557	51	-12	2	2	-0	.995	4	C-65	-0.6
1984	Sea-A	30	78	5	17	3	1	0	5	4	12	.218	.265	.282	547	52	-5	1	0	0	.992	-6	C-29	-1.0
1986	Tex-A	46	102	7	24	1	1	1	7	6	13	.235	.284	.294	579	56	-6	0	1	-0	.996	16	C-45	1.0
1987	Det-A	10	22	2	3	0	0	0	1	2	0	.136	.208	.136	345	-6	-3	0	0	0	.980	3	C-10	0.0
	LA-N	7	5	1	3	1	0	0	1	1	1	.600	.667	.800	1467	294	2	0	0	0	1.000	0	/C-7	0.2
1988	Oak-A	16	24	3	3	0	0	1	1	3	8	.125	.222	.250	472	33	-2	0	0	0	.959	1	C-16	-0.1
1989	Min-A	19	38	1	4	0	0	0	1	4	4	.105	.190	.105	296	-14	-6	1	0	0	1.000	4	C-19	-0.1
1990	NY-N	42	90	10	19	1	0	3	7	8	11	.211	.290	.322	612	68	-4	0	0	0	.991	2	C-40	-0.1
	Mon-N	8	8	0	2	0	0	0	0	0	1	.250	.250	.250	500	39	-1	0	0	0	1.000	3	/C-8	0.2
	Yr	50	98	10	21	1	0	3	7	8	12	.214	.287	.316	603	66	-5	0	0	0	.992	4	C-48	0.1
Total	8	253	562	40	112	17	4	7	45	42	82	.199	.261	.281	542	48	-40	4	3	-0	.993	27	C-247/D-1	-0.6

■ ORLANDO MERCED

Merced, Orlando Luis (Villanueva) b: 11/2/66, Hato Rey, P.R. BB/TR, 5'11", 170 lbs. Deb: 6/27/90 Career OF: (52-LF 0-CF 531-RF)

YEAR	TM/L	G	AB	R	H	2B	3B	HR	RBI	BB	SO	AVG	OBP	SLG	OPS	OPS+	BR+	SB	CS	SBR	FA	FR	G/POS	TPR
1990	Pit-N	25	24	3	5	1	0	0	0	1	9	.208	.240	.250	490	36	-2	0	0	0	.000	-0	/C-1,O-1(0-0-1)	-0.3
1991	*Pit-N	120	411	83	113	17	2	10	50	64	81	.275	.374	.399	773	119	12	8	4	0	.988	-8	*1-105/O-7(0-0-7)	-0.2
1992	*Pit-N	134	405	50	100	28	5	6	60	52	63	.247	.336	.385	721	105	3	5	4	-0	.995	0	*1-114,O-17(0-0-17)	-0.5
1993	Pit-N	137	447	68	140	26	4	8	70	77	64	.313	.415	.443	858	130	23	3	3	-0	.965	3	*O-109(0-0-109),1-42	1.7
1994	Pit-N	108	386	48	105	21	3	9	51	42	58	.272	.345	.412	757	95	-2	4	1	1	.981	-9	O-68(0-0-68),1-55	-1.8
1995	Pit-N	132	487	75	146	29	4	15	83	52	74	.300	.369	.468	837	117	12	7	2	1	.976	1	*O-107(4-0-104),1-35	0.6
1996	Pit-N	120	453	69	130	24	1	17	80	51	74	.287	.359	.457	816	110	7	8	4	0	.988	15	*O-115(0-0-115)/1-1	1.6
1997	Tor-A	98	368	45	98	23	2	9	40	47	62	.266	.354	.413	767	99	0	7	3	0	.985	8	O-96(0-0-96)/1-1,D-1	0.3
1998	Min-A	63	204	22	59	12	0	5	33	17	29	.289	.347	.422	768	97	-1	1	4	-1	.982	-1	1-38,O-13(0-0-13)/D-8	-0.6
	Bos-A	9	9	0	0	0	0	0	2	2	3	.000	.182	.000	182	-46	-2	0	0	0	1.000	0	/O-1(0-0-1),D-1	-0.2
	Yr	72	213	22	59	12	0	5	35	19	32	.277	.339	.404	743	91	-3	1	4	-1	.982	-1	1-38,O-14(0-0-14)/D-9	-0.8
	Chi-N	12	10	2	3	0	0	1	5	1	2	.300	.364	.600	964	143	1	0	0	0	1.000	-1	/O-4(4-0-0)	0.0
1999	Mon-N	93	194	25	52	12	1	8	26	26	27	.268	.355	.464	818	108	2	2	1	0	.962	-0	O-44(44-0-0)/1-7,D-2	0.0
Total	10	1051	3398	490	951	193	22	88	500	432	546	.280	.363	.427	790	110	53	45	26	1	.979	10	O-582R,1-398/D-12,C	0.6

■ HENRY MERCEDES

Mercedes, Henry Felipe (Perez) b: 7/23/69, Santo Domingo, D.R. BR/TR, 6'1", 210 lbs. Deb: 4/22/92

YEAR	TM/L	G	AB	R	H	2B	3B	HR	RBI	BB	SO	AVG	OBP	SLG	OPS	OPS+	BR+	SB	CS	SBR	FA	FR	G/POS	TPR
1992	Oak-A	9	5	1	4	0	1	0	1	0	1	.800	.800	1.200	2000	479	2	0	0	0	.875	-0	/C-9	0.2
1993	Oak-A	20	47	5	10	2	0	0	3	2	15	.213	.260	.255	515	42	-4	1	1	-0	.987	-0	C-18/D-1	-0.3
1995	KC-A	23	43	7	11	2	0	0	9	8	13	.256	.385	.302	687	81	-1	0	0	0	.986	-3	C-22	-0.3
1996	KC-A	4	4	1	1	0	0	0	0	0	1	.250	.250	.250	500	27	-0	0	0	0	1.000	-1	/C-4	-0.1
1997	Tex-A	23	47	4	10	4	0	0	4	6	25	.213	.302	.298	600	54	-3	0	0	0	.988	0	C-23	-0.2
Total	5	79	146	18	36	8	1	0	17	16	55	.247	.329	.315	644	71	-6	1	1	-0	.983	-4	/C-76,D-1	-0.7

■ LUIS MERCEDES

Mercedes, Luis Roberto (Santana) b: 2/15/68, San Pedro De Macoris, D.R. BR/TR, 6', 180 lbs. Deb: 9/8/91

YEAR	TM/L	G	AB	R	H	2B	3B	HR	RBI	BB	SO	AVG	OBP	SLG	OPS	OPS+	BR+	SB	CS	SBR	FA	FR	G/POS	TPR
1991	Bal-A	19	54	10	11	2	0	0	2	4	9	.204	.259	.241	499	41	-4	0	0	0	1.000	-2	O-15(13-0-3)/D-1	-0.7
1992	Bal-A	23	50	7	7	2	0	0	4	8	9	.140	.271	.180	451	28	-5	0	1	-0	.956	2	O-16(1-2-13)/D-7	-0.3
1993	Bal-A	10	24	1	7	2	0	0	0	5	4	.292	.414	.375	789	109	1	1	1	-0	1.000	-0	/O-8(0-0-8),D-2	0.0

YEAR	TM/L	G	AB	R	H	2B	3B	HR	RBI	BB	SO	AVG	OBP	SLG	OPS	OPS+	BR+	SB	CS	SBR	FA	FR	G/POS	TPR
	SF-N	18	25	1	4	0	1	0	3	1	3	.160	.250	.240	490	33	-2	0	1	-0	1.000	-1	/O-5(1-3-1)	-0.4
Total	3	70	153	19	29	6	1	0	9	18	25	.190	.287	.242	529	47	-11	1	3	-1	.976	-2	/O-44(15-5-25),D-10	-1.4
■ WIN MERCER Mercer, George Barclay b: 6/20/1874, Chester, W.Va. d: 1/12/03, San Francisco, Cal BR/TR, 5'7", 140 lbs. Deb: 4/21/1894 Career OF: (21-LF 24-CF 31-RF)																								
1894	Was-N	53	165	29	48	5	2	2	29	9	20	.291	.328	.382	709	73	-8	9			.944	2	P-50/O-4(0-0-4)	-0.1
1895	Was-N	64	201	26	51	9	1	1	26	12	33	.254	.306	.323	629	63	-11	7			.874	-7	P-44/S-7,O-6R,32	-0.7
1896	Was-N	49	156	23	38	1	1	1	14	9	18	.244	.302	.282	584	54	-10	9			.856	1	P-46/O-1(0-0-1)	0.0
1897	Was-N	50	139	23	44	2	5	0	19	6		.317	.354	.403	757	100	-0	7			.858	-1	P-47	0.0
1898	Was-N	80	249	38	80	3	5	2	25	18		.321	.369	.398	767	120	6	14			.863	-9	P-33,S-23,O-19C,/32	-0.4
1899	Was-N	108	375	73	112	6	7	1	35	32		.299	.360	.360	720	99	0	16			.846	-14	3-62,P-23,O-16L,/S1	-1.6
1900	NY-N	76	248	32	73	4	0	0	27	26		.294	.366	.310	676	92	-1	15			.931	-2	P-33,3-19,O-14R,/S2	-0.3
1901	Was-A	51	140	26	42	7	2	0	16	23		.300	.402	.379	781	119	5	10			.944	-2	P-24,O-16C/1-7,S3	-0.1
1902	Det-A	35	100	8	18	2	0	0	6	6		.180	.226	.200	426	19	-11	1			.935	4	P-35	0.0
Total	9	566	1773	278	506	39	23	7	197	141	71	.285	.344	.345	689	87	-30	88			.903	-29	P-335/3-90,O-76R,S12	-3.2
■ JOHN MERCER Mercer, John Locke b: 6/22/1892, Taylortown, La. d: 12/22/82, Shreveport, La. BL/TL, 5'10.5", 155 lbs. Deb: 6/25/12																								
1912	StL-N	1	1	0	0	0	0	0	0	0	0	.000	.000	.000	0	-99	-0	0			.500	-0	/1-1	-0.1
■ ANDY MERCHANT Merchant, James Anderson b: 8/30/50, Mobile, Ala. BL/TR, 5'11", 185 lbs. Deb: 9/28/75																								
1975	Bos-A	1	4	1	2	0	0	0	0	1	0	.500	.600	.500	1100	197	1	0	0	0	1.000	-1	/C-1	0.0
1976	Bos-A	2	2	0	0	0	0	0	0	0	2	.000	.000	.000	0	-89	-0	0	0	0	1.000	-0	/C-1	-0.1
Total	2	3	6	1	2	0	0	0	0	1	2	.333	.429	.333	762	109	0	0	0	0	1.000	-1	/C-2	-0.1
■ ART MEREWETHER Merewether, Arthur Francis "Merry" b: 7/7/02, E.Providence, R.I. d: 2/2/97, Bayside, N.Y. BR/TR, 5'9.5", 155 lbs. Deb: 7/10/22																								
1922	Pit-N	1	1	0	0	0	0	0	0	0	0	.000	.000	.000	0	-99	-0	0	0	0	.000	0	H	0.0
■ FRED MERKLE Merkle, Frederick Charles (b: Carl Frederick Rudolf Merkle) b: 12/20/1888, Watertown, Wis. d: 3/2/56, Daytona Beach, Fla. BR/TR, 6'1", 190 lbs. Deb: 9/21/07 C Career OF: (11-LF 29-CF 8-RF)																								
1907	NY-N	15	47	0	12	1	0	0	5	1		.255	.271	.277	547	69	-2	0			.949	-1	1-15	-0.4
1908	NY-N	38	41	6	11	2	1	1	7	4		.268	.333	.439	772	140	2	0			1.000	-2	1-11/O-5R,2-1,3-1	-0.1
1909	NY-N	79	236	15	45	9	1	0	20	16		.191	.245	.237	482	49	-14	8			.976	-3	1-70/2-1	-2.1
1910	NY-N	144	506	75	148	35	14	4	70	44	59	.292	.353	.441	793	131	18	23			.981	1	*1-144	1.7
1911	*NY-N	149	541	80	153	24	10	12	84	43	60	.283	.342	.431	773	112	7	49			.985	15	*1-148	1.8
1912	*NY-N	129	479	82	148	22	6	11	84	42	70	.309	.374	.449	823	121	13	37			.980	-1	*1-129	0.8
1913	*NY-N	153	563	78	147	30	12	3	69	41	60	.261	.315	.373	688	95	-5	35			.986	-4	*1-153	-1.3
1914	NY-N	146	512	71	132	25	7	7	63	52	80	.258	.327	.375	702	112	7	23			.990	3	*1-146	0.7
1915	NY-N	140	505	52	151	25	3	4	62	36	39	.299	.348	.384	732	129	17	20	15	-1	.989	-1	*1-110,O-30(0-27-5)	1.1
1916	NY-N	112	401	45	95	19	3	7	44	33	46	.237	.308	.352	659	108	3	17			.984	0	*1-112	0.1
	*Bro-N	23	69	6	16	1	0	0	2	7	4	.232	.312	.246	558	70	-2	2			.992	-1	1-15/O-4(3-1-0)	-0.4
	Yr	135	470	51	111	20	3	7	46	40	50	.236	.308	.336	644	102	1	19			.985	-1	*1-127/O-4(3-1-0)	-0.3
1917	Bro-N	2	8	1	1	1	0	0	0	0	1	.125	.125	.250	375	13	-1	0			1.000	0	/1-2	-0.1
	Chi-N	146	549	65	146	30	9	3	57	42	60	.266	.323	.370	692	104	3	13			.983	-3	*1-140/O-6(5-1-0)	-0.5
	Yr	148	557	66	147	31	9	3	57	42	61	.264	.320	.368	688	103	2	13			.983	-3	*1-142/O-6(5-1-0)	-0.6
1918	*Chi-N	129	482	55	143	25	5	3	65	35	36	.297	.349	.388	737	122	12	21			.990	1	*1-129	1.1
1919	Chi-N	133	498	52	133	20	6	3	62	33	35	.267	.315	.349	665	99	-1	20			.985	-10	*1-132/2-1	-1.6
1920	Chi-N	92	330	33	94	20	4	3	38	24	32	.285	.335	.397	732	108	3	3	5	-1	.985	-0	1-85/O-1(1-0-0)	0.0
1925	NY-A	7	13	4	5	1	0	0	1	1	1	.385	.429	.462	890	128	1	1	0	0	1.000	-0	/1-5	0.0
1926	NY-A	1	2	0	0	0	0	0	0	0	0	.000	.000	.000	0	-99	-1	0	0	0	1.000	-0	/1-1	-0.1
Total	16	1638	5782	720	1580	290	81	61	733	454	583	.273	.331	.383	714	109	59	272	20		.985	-6	*1-1547/O-46C,2-3,3	0.7
■ LOU MERLONI Merloni, Louis William b: 4/6/71, Framingham, Mass. BR/TR, 5'10", 188 lbs. Deb: 5/10/98 Career OF: (1-LF 0-CF 0-RF)																								
1998	Bos-A	39	96	10	27	6	0	1	15	7	20	.281	.343	.375	718	85	-2	1	0	0	.974	-3	2-32/3-5,S-1	-0.3
1999	*Bos-A	43	126	18	32	7	0	1	13	8	16	.254	.309	.333	642	62	-7	0	0	0	.956	6	S-24/3-9,2-8,1OD	0.0
2000	Bos-A	40	128	10	41	11	2	0	18	4	22	.320	.346	.438	783	93	-1	1	0	0	.928	-2	3-40	-0.3
Total	3	122	350	38	100	24	2	2	46	19	58	.286	.332	.383	714	80	-11	2	0	0	.912	1	/3-54,2-40,S-25,DO1	-0.6
■ ED MERRILL Merrill, Edward Mason b: 5/1860, Maysville, Ky. d: 8/18/24, Chicago, Ill. 5'11", 176 lbs. Deb: 5/5/1882																								
1882	Lou-a	1	0	0	0	0	0	0		0		—	—	—	—	—	0				.000	-0	/O-1(0-1-0)	0.0
	Wor-N	2	8	0	1	0	0	0	4	0	1	.125	.125	.125	250	-19	-1				.714	-1	/3-2	-0.1
1884	Ind-a	55	196	14	35	3	1	0		6		.179	.207	.204	411	35	-13				.900	-4	2-55	-1.4
Total	2	58	204	14	36	3	1	0	4	6	1	.176	.204	.201	405	33	-14				.900	-5	/2-55,3-2,O-1(0-1-0)	-1.5
■ LLOYD MERRIMAN Merriman, Lloyd Archer "Citation" b: 8/2/24, Clovis, Cal. BL/TL, 6', 195 lbs. Deb: 4/24/49																								
1949	Cin-N	103	287	35	66	12	5	4	26	21	36	.230	.285	.348	633	68	-14	2			.969	-1	O-86(0-86-0)	-1.6
1950	Cin-N	92	298	44	77	15	3	2	31	30	23	.258	.330	.349	679	79	-9	6			.989	-4	O-84(2-81-1)	-1.5
1951	Cin-N	114	359	34	87	23	2	5	36	31	34	.242	.303	.359	662	76	-12	8	4	0	.997	9	*O-102(31-76-0)	-0.7
1954	Cin-N	73	112	12	30	8	1	0	16	23	10	.268	.406	.357	763	98	1	3	0	1	.981	-1	O-25(9-0-16)	0.0
1955	Chi-A	1	1	0	0	0	0	0	0	0	0	.000	.000	.000	0	-97	-0	0	0	0	.000	0	H	0.0
	Chi-N	72	145	15	31	6	1	1	8	21	21	.214	.313	.290	603	62	-8	1	0	0	.977	-6	O-47(8-36-3)	-1.5
Total	5	455	1202	140	291	64	12	12	117	126	124	.242	.317	.345	662	75	-42	20	4		.985	-2	O-344(50-279-20)	-5.3
■ GEORGE MERRITT Merritt, George Washington b: 4/14/1880, Paterson, N.J. d: 2/21/38, Memphis, Tenn. TR, 6', 160 lbs. Deb: 9/6/01																								
1901	Pit-N	4	11	2	3	0	1	0	0	0		.273	.385	.455	839	139	1	0			1.000	-0	/P-3	0.0
1902	Pit-N	2	9	2	3	1	0	0	2	0		.333	.333	.444	778	135	0	0			1.000	1	/O-2(2-0-0)	0.1
1903	Pit-N	9	27	4	4	0	1	0	3	2		.148	.233	.222	456	29	-3	1			.889	-2	/O-7(1-0-6),P-1	-0.4
Total	3	15	47	8	10	1	2	0	5	2		.213	.288	.319	608	74	-2	1			.929	-1	/O-9(3-0-6),P-4	-0.3
■ HERM MERRITT Merritt, Herman G. b: 11/12/1900, Independence, Kan. d: 5/26/27, Kansas City, Mo. BR/TR, Deb: 8/24/21																								
1921	Det-A	20	46	3	17	1	2	0	6	1	5	.370	.396	.478	874	123	2	1	0	0	.882	-6	S-17	-0.3
■ JOHN MERRITT Merritt, John Howard b: 10/12/1894, Tupelo, Miss. d: 11/3/55, Tupelo, Miss. BR/TL, 5'11", 170 lbs. Deb: 9/27/13																								
1913	NY-N	1	0	0	0	0	0	0	0	0	0	—	—	—	—	—	0	0			.000	-0	/O-1(0-0-1)	0.0
■ BILL MERRITT Merritt, William Henry b: 7/30/1870, Lowell, Mass. d: 11/17/37, Lowell, Mass. BR/TR, 5'7", 160 lbs. Deb: 8/8/1891																								
1891	Chi-N	11	42	4	9	1	0	0	4	2	2	.214	.250	.238	488	42	-3	0			.955	-3	C-11/1-1	-0.5
1892	Lou-N	46	168	22	33	4	2	1	13	11	15	.196	.246	.262	508	58	-9	3			.940	-3	C-46	-0.7
1893	Bos-N	39	141	30	49	6	3	3	26	13	13	.348	.403	.496	899	128	5	3			.945	-4	C-37/O-2(2-0-0)	0.3
1894	Bos-N	10	26	3	6	1	0	0	6	8	0	.231	.412	.269	681	62	-1	0			.881	1	/C-8,O-1(0-1-0)	0.0
	Pit-N	36	109	18	30	1	2	1	18	15	7	.275	.363	.349	712	73	-5	2			.952	-1	C-28/1-4,O-2(2-0-0)	-0.2
	Cin-N	30	117	17	38	6	1	1	22	10	3	.325	.388	.419	806	91	-2	4			.956	-2	C-25/3-3,1-1,O-1R	-0.1
	Yr	76	252	38	74	8	3	2	46	33	10	.294	.380	.373	753	80	-7	6			.942	-2	C-61/1-5,O-4L,3-3	-0.3
1895	Cin-N	22	79	9	14	2	0	0	12	6	5	.177	.235	.203	438	13	-10	2			.955	-1	C-20/2-1	-0.8
	Pit-N	67	239	32	68	5	1	0	27	18	16	.285	.340	.314	654	73	-9	2			.935	-2	C-63/1-2	-0.4
	Yr	89	318	41	82	7	1	0	39	24	21	.258	.314	.286	600	57	-20	4			.939	-3	C-83/1-2,2-1	-1.2
1896	Pit-N	77	282	26	82	8	2	1	42	18	10	.291	.336	.344	680	83	-7	3			.941	2	C-62/3-5,2-3,1-3,S	0.1
1897	Pit-N	62	209	21	55	6	1	1	26	9		.263	.297	.316	613	64	-11	2			.946	-4	C-53/1-7	-0.9
1899	Bos-N	1	2	0	0	0	0	0	0	0		.000	.333	.000	333	-5	-0	0			1.000	0	/C-1	0.0
Total	8	401	1414	182	384	40	12	8	196	110	71	.272	.327	.334	661	75	-51	21			.942	-18	C-354/1-18,3-8,O2S	-3.2
■ JACK MERSON Merson, John Warren b: 1/17/22, Elkridge, Md. d: 4/28/2000, Elkridge, Md. BR/TR, 5'11", 175 lbs. Deb: 9/14/51																								
1951	Pit-N	13	50	6	18	2	2	1	14	1	7	.360	.373	.540	913	138	2	0	0	0	.987	2	2-13	0.5
1952	Pit-N	111	398	41	98	20	2	5	38	22	38	.246	.287	.344	632	72	-15	1	1	-0	.978	-6	2-81,3-27	-1.8

YEAR	TM/L	G	AB	R	H	2B	3B	HR	RBI	BB	SO	AVG	OBP	SLG	OPS	OPS+	BR+	SB	CS	SBR	FA	FR	G/POS	TPR
1953	Bos-A	1	4	0	0	0	0	0	0	0	0	.000	.000	.000	0	-95	-1	0	0	0	.875	0	/2-1	-0.1
Total	3	125	452	47	116	22	4	6	52	23	45	.257	.294	.363	657	78	-14	1	1	-0	.978	-3	/2-95,3-27	-1.4

■ SAM MERTES

Mertes, Samuel Blair "Sandow" b: 8/6/1872, San Francisco, Cal. d: 3/11/45, San Francisco, Cal BR/TR, 6', 225 lbs. Deb: 6/30/1896 Career OF: (687-LF 182-CF 110-RF)

YEAR	TM/L	G	AB	R	H	2B	3B	HR	RBI	BB	SO	AVG	OBP	SLG	OPS	OPS+	BR+	SB	CS	SBR	FA	FR	G/POS	TPR
1896	Phi-N	37	143	20	34	4	4	0	14	8	10	.238	.288	.322	609	61	-8	19			.907	-1	O-35(1-33-1)/S-1,2-1	-1.0
1898	Chi-N	83	269	45	80	4	8	1	47	34		.297	.388	.383	771	121	9	27			.880	2	O-60R,S-14/2-4,1-2	0.8
1899	Chi-N	117	426	83	127	13	16	9	81	33		.298	.349	.467	816	126	13	45			.923	-1	*O-108C/1-3,S-1	0.5
1900	Chi-N	127	481	72	142	25	4	7	60	42		.295	.356	.407	763	114	9	38			.923	-5	O-88C,1-33/S-7	-0.1
1901	Chi-A	137	545	94	151	16	17	5	98	52		.277	.347	.396	743	108	7	46			.940	-6	*2-132/O-5(5-0-0)	0.1
1902	Chi-A	129	497	60	140	23	7	1	79	37		.282	.334	.362	696	97	-2	46			.922	6	*O-120L/S-5,C-2,P123	-0.2
1903	NY-N	138	517	100	145	**32**	14	7	**104**	61		.280	.360	.437	797	122	14	45			**.973**	8	*O-137L/C-1,1-1	1.4
1904	NY-N	148	532	83	147	28	11	4	78	54		.276	.346	.393	739	123	14	47			.956	-1	*O-147(130-17-0)/S-1	0.5
1905	*NY-N	150	551	81	154	27	17	5	108	56		.279	.351	.417	769	126	17	52			.960	-11	*O-150(149-2-0)	-0.3
1906	NY-N	71	253	37	60	9	6	1	33	29		.237	.323	.332	655	102	1	21			.970	1	O-71(71-0-1)	-0.2
	StL-N	53	191	20	47	7	4	0	19	16		.246	.304	.325	629	100	-0	10			.890	-6	O-53(53-0-0)	-1.1
	Yr	124	444	57	107	16	10	1	52	45		.241	.315	.329	644	101	1	31			.938	-5	*O-124(124-0-1)	-1.3
Total	10	1190	4405	695	1227	188	108	40	721	422	10	.279	.346	.398	744	113	74	396			.938	-14	O-974L,2-138/1SC3P	0.4

■ LENNIE MERULLO

Merullo, Leonard Richard b: 5/5/17, Boston, Mass. BR/TR, 5'11", 168 lbs. Deb: 9/12/41 F

YEAR	TM/L	G	AB	R	H	2B	3B	HR	RBI	BB	SO	AVG	OBP	SLG	OPS	OPS+	BR+	SB	CS	SBR	FA	FR	G/POS	TPR
1941	Chi-N	7	17	3	6	1	0	0	1	2	0	.353	.421	.412	833	140	1	1			.968	2	/S-7	0.3
1942	Chi-N	143	515	53	132	23	3	2	37	35	45	.256	.310	.324	634	89	-8	14			.946	-1	*S-143	0.2
1943	Chi-N	129	453	37	115	18	3	1	25	26	42	.254	.297	.313	611	78	-14	7			.940	-12	*S-125	-1.7
1944	Chi-N	66	193	20	41	8	1	1	16	16	18	.212	.276	.280	556	57	-11	3			.937	2	S-56/1-1	-0.5
1945	*Chi-N	121	394	40	94	18	0	2	37	31	30	.239	.297	.299	597	68	-17	7			.948	-4	*S-118	-1.3
1946	Chi-N	65	126	14	19	8	0	0	7	11	13	.151	.219	.214	433	24	-13	2			.946	18	S-44	0.7
1947	Chi-N	108	373	24	90	16	1	0	29	15	26	.241	.274	.290	564	52	-26	4			.949	7	*S-108	-1.3
Total	7	639	2071	191	497	92	8	6	152	136	174	.240	.291	.301	591	69	-88	38			.945	11	S-601/1-1	-3.6

■ MATT MERULLO

Merullo, Matthew Bates b: 8/4/65, Winchester, Mass. BL/TR, 6'2", 200 lbs. Deb: 4/12/89 F

YEAR	TM/L	G	AB	R	H	2B	3B	HR	RBI	BB	SO	AVG	OBP	SLG	OPS	OPS+	BR+	SB	CS	SBR	FA	FR	G/POS	TPR
1989	Chi-A	31	81	5	18	1	0	1	8	6	14	.222	.276	.272	547	56	-5	0	1	-0	.973	-4	C-27/D-1	-0.8
1991	Chi-A	80	140	8	32	1	0	5	21	9	18	.229	.275	.343	618	72	-6	0	0	0	.989	-1	C-27,1-16/D-6	-0.6
1992	Chi-A	24	50	3	9	1	1	0	3	1	8	.180	.212	.240	452	27	-5	0	0	0	.971	-1	C-16/D-1	-0.5
1993	Chi-A	8	20	1	1	0	0	0	0	0	1	.050	.050	.050	100	-75	-5	0	0	0	.000	0	/D-6	-0.5
1994	Cle-A	4	10	1	1	0	0	0	0	2	1	.100	.250	.100	350	-5	-2	0	0	0	.957	-0	/C-4	-0.2
1995	Min-A	76	195	19	55	14	1	1	27	14	27	.282	.340	.379	719	87	-4	0	1	-0	.987	-8	C-46,D-13/1-2	-1.0
Total	6	223	496	37	116	17	2	7	59	32	69	.234	.286	.319	604	64	-25	0	2	-1	.981	-14	C-120/D-27,1-18	-3.6

■ STEVE MESNER

Mesner, Stephan Mathias b: 1/13/18, Los Angeles, Cal. d: 4/6/81, San Diego, Cal. BR/TR, 5'9", 178 lbs. Deb: 9/23/38

YEAR	TM/L	G	AB	R	H	2B	3B	HR	RBI	BB	SO	AVG	OBP	SLG	OPS	OPS+	BR+	SB	CS	SBR	FA	FR	G/POS	TPR
1938	Chi-N	2	4	2	1	0	0	0	0	1	1	.250	.400	.250	650	80	-0	0			.667	-1	/S-1	-0.1
1939	Chi-N	17	43	7	12	4	0	0	6	3	4	.279	.340	.372	713	90	-1	0			.927	1	S-12/2-1,3-1	0.1
1941	StL-N	24	69	8	10	1	0	0	10	5	6	.145	.203	.159	362	3	-9	0			.958	5	3-22	-0.3
1943	Cin-N	137	504	53	137	26	1	0	52	26	20	.272	.309	.327	636	85	-11	6			.944	1	*3-130	-0.9
1944	Cin-N	121	414	31	100	17	4	1	47	34	20	.242	.301	.309	610	75	-14	1			.951	-7	*3-120	-2.1
1945	Cin-N	150	540	52	137	19	1	1	52	52	18	.254	.322	.298	620	74	-18	4			.971	12	*3-148/2-3	-0.4
Total	6	451	1574	153	397	67	6	2	167	121	69	.252	.308	.306	614	75	-52	11			.956	10	3-421/S-13,2-4	-3.7

■ BOBBY MESSENGER

Messenger, Charles Walter b: 3/19/1884, Bangor, Me. d: 7/10/51, Bath, Maine BB/TR, 5'10.5", 165 lbs. Deb: 8/30/09

YEAR	TM/L	G	AB	R	H	2B	3B	HR	RBI	BB	SO	AVG	OBP	SLG	OPS	OPS+	BR+	SB	CS	SBR	FA	FR	G/POS	TPR
1909	Chi-A	31	112	18	19	1	1	0	0	13		.170	.268	.196	464	49	-6	7			.950	-2	O-31(0-0-31)	-1.0
1910	Chi-A	9	26	7	6	0	1	0	4	4		.231	.375	.308	683	119	1	3			.846	-0	/O-8(8-0-0)	0.0
1911	Chi-A	13	17	4	2	0	1	0	0	3		.118	.250	.235	485	37	-1	0			.875	-1	/O-4(4-0-0)	-0.2
1914	StL-A	1	2	0	0	0	0	0	0	0	0	.000	.000	.000	0	-99	-0	0			.000	-0	/O-1(0-0-1)	-0.1
Total	4	54	157	29	27	1	3	0	4	20	0	.172	.282	.217	498	57	-7	10			.918	-3	/O-44(12-0-32)	-1.3

■ TOM MESSITT

Messitt, Thomas John b: 7/27/1874, Frankford, Pa. d: 9/22/34, Chicago, Ill. 5'9", 177 lbs. Deb: 9/14/1899

YEAR	TM/L	G	AB	R	H	2B	3B	HR	RBI	BB	SO	AVG	OBP	SLG	OPS	OPS+	BR+	SB	CS	SBR	FA	FR	G/POS	TPR
1899	Lou-N	3	11	0	1	0	0	0	0	0		.091	.091	.091	182	-50	-2	0			1.000	1	/C-3	-0.1

■ AL METCALF

Metcalf, Alfred Tristram b: 12/31/1852, Brooklyn, N.Y. d: 9/2/14, Brooklyn, N.Y. Deb: 5/27/1875

YEAR	TM/L	G	AB	R	H	2B	3B	HR	RBI	BB	SO	AVG	OBP	SLG	OPS	OPS+	BR+	SB	CS	SBR	FA	FR	G/POS	TPR
1875	Mut-n	8	32	2	7	0	0	0	1	0	3	.219	.219	.219	438	50	-2	2	0	0	.667	-2	/3-5,O-2(0-0-2),S-1	-0.2

■ MIKE METCALFE

Metcalfe, Michael Henry b: 1/2/73, Quantico, Va. BR/TR, 5'10", 175 lbs. Deb: 9/18/98

YEAR	TM/L	G	AB	R	H	2B	3B	HR	RBI	BB	SO	AVG	OBP	SLG	OPS	OPS+	BR+	SB	CS	SBR	FA	FR	G/POS	TPR
1998	LA-N	4	1	0	0	0	0	0	0	0	1	.000	.000	.000	0	-99	-0	2	0	0	.000	0	/2-1	0.0
2000	LA-N	4	12	0	1	0	0	0	0	1	2	.083	.154	.083	237	-40	-3	0	0	0	1.000	-1	/O-4(3-1-0),2-1	-0.4
Total	2	8	13	0	1	0	0	0	0	1	3	.077	.143	.077	220	-44	-3	2	0	0	1.000	-1	/O-4(3-1-0),2-2	-0.4

■ SCAT METHA

Metha, Frank Joseph b: 12/13/13, Los Angeles, Cal. d: 3/2/75, Fountain Valley, Cal. BR/TR, 5'11", 165 lbs. Deb: 4/22/40

YEAR	TM/L	G	AB	R	H	2B	3B	HR	RBI	BB	SO	AVG	OBP	SLG	OPS	OPS+	BR+	SB	CS	SBR	FA	FR	G/POS	TPR
1940	Det-A	26	37	6	9	0	1	0	3	2	8	.243	.282	.297	579	46	-3	0	1	-0	.960	4	2-10/3-6	0.1

■ BUD METHENY

Metheny, Arthur Beauregard b: 6/1/15, St.Louis, Mo. BL/TL, 5'11", 190 lbs. Deb: 4/27/43

YEAR	TM/L	G	AB	R	H	2B	3B	HR	RBI	BB	SO	AVG	OBP	SLG	OPS	OPS+	BR+	SB	CS	SBR	FA	FR	G/POS	TPR
1943	*NY-A	103	360	51	94	18	2	9	36	39	34	.261	.333	.397	731	113	5	2	3	-1	.963	-12	O-91(0-0-91)	-1.4
1944	NY-A	137	518	72	124	16	1	14	67	56	57	.239	.316	.355	671	89	-8	5	5	-1	.956	-8	*O-132(11-0-121)	-2.7
1945	NY-A	133	509	64	126	18	2	8	53	54	31	.248	.325	.338	662	88	-7	5	2	0	.984	-6	*O-128(0-0-128)	-2.4
1946	NY-A	3	3	0	0	0	0	0	0	0	0	.000	.000	.000	0	-99	-1	0	0	0	.000	0	H	-0.1
Total	4	376	1390	187	344	52	5	31	156	149	122	.247	.323	.359	682	94	-11	12	10	-1	.968	-26	O-351(11-0-340)	-6.6

■ CATFISH METKOVICH

Metkovich, George Michael b: 10/8/20, Angels Camp, Cal. d: 5/17/95, Costa Mesa, Cal. BL/TL, 6'1", 185 lbs. Deb: 7/16/43 Career OF: (33-LF 465-CF 158-RF)

YEAR	TM/L	G	AB	R	H	2B	3B	HR	RBI	BB	SO	AVG	OBP	SLG	OPS	OPS+	BR+	SB	CS	SBR	FA	FR	G/POS	TPR
1943	Bos-A	78	321	34	79	14	4	5	27	19	38	.246	.294	.361	656	90	-5	1	3	-1	.955	-3	O-76(0-54-25)/1-2	-1.3
1944	Bos-A	134	549	94	152	28	8	9	59	31	57	.277	.319	.406	725	108	3	13	4	1	.962	5	O-82(0-81-3),1-50	0.4
1945	Bos-A	138	539	65	140	26	3	5	62	51	70	.260	.331	.347	677	94	-4	19	6	2	.985	-4	1-97,O-42(0-29-14)	-1.3
1946	*Bos-A	86	281	42	69	15	2	4	25	36	39	.246	.333	.356	689	88	-4	8	3	1	.948	-11	O-81(6-2-73)	-1.8
1947	Cle-A	126	473	68	120	22	7	5	40	32	51	.254	.302	.362	664	86	-10	5	3	0	.989	1	*O-119(0-119-2)/1-1	-1.3
1949	Chi-A	93	338	50	80	9	4	5	45	41	24	.237	.321	.331	652	75	-13	5	4	-0	.968	-7	O-87(9-79-1)	-2.2
1951	Pit-N	120	423	51	124	21	3	3	40	28	23	.293	.338	.378	717	90	-6	3	2	-0	.994	1	O-69(3-66-0),1-37	-0.8
1952	Pit-N	125	373	41	101	18	3	7	41	32	29	.271	.335	.391	726	98	-1	5	2	0	.988	-7	1-72,O-33(5-21-8)	-1.1
1953	Pit-N	26	41	5	6	0	1	1	7	6	3	.146	.255	.268	524	37	-4	0	0	0	1.000	-1	/1-5,O-4(0-3-1)	-0.5
	Chi-N	61	124	19	29	9	0	2	12	16	10	.234	.326	.355	681	76	-4	2	1	0	1.000	-5	O-38(10-11-18)/1-7	-1.0
	Yr	87	165	24	35	9	1	3	19	22	13	.212	.309	.333	642	66	-8	2	1	0	1.000	-6	O-42(10-14-19),1-12	-1.5
1954	Mil-N	68	123	7	34	5	1	1	15	15	15	.276	.360	.358	717	94	-1	0	0	0	1.000	1	1-18,O-13(0-0-13)	-0.1
Total	10	1055	3585	476	934	167	36	47	373	307	359	.261	.323	.367	689	91	-49	61	28	4	.976	-28	O-644C,1-289	-11.0

■ CHARLIE METRO

Metro, Charles (b: Charles Moreskonich) b: 4/28/19, Nanty Glo, Pa. BR/TR, 5'11.5", 178 lbs. Deb: 5/4/43 MC Career OF: (72-LF 22-CF 10-RF)

YEAR	TM/L	G	AB	R	H	2B	3B	HR	RBI	BB	SO	AVG	OBP	SLG	OPS	OPS+	BR+	SB	CS	SBR	FA	FR	G/POS	TPR
1943	Det-A	44	40	12	8	0	0	0	2	3	6	.200	.256	.200	456	32	-3	1	1	-0	.966	-2	O-14(1-11-2)	-0.6
1944	Det-A	38	78	8	15	0	1	0	5	3	10	.192	.222	.218	440	25	-8	1	0	0	1.000	-2	O-20(9-10-2)	-1.0
	Phi-A	24	40	4	4	0	0	0	1	7	6	.100	.234	.100	334	-3	-5	0	0	0	1.000	-1	O-11(9-0-2)/3-5,2-2	-0.7
	Yr	62	118	12	19	0	1	0	6	10	16	.161	.227	.178	405	16	-13	1	0	0	1.000	-2	O-31(18-10-4)/3-5,2-2	-1.7
1945	Phi-A	65	200	18	42	10	1	3	15	23	33	.210	.291	.315	606	76	-6	1	1	-0	.972	-5	O-57(53-1-4)	-1.5
Total	3	171	358	42	69	10	2	3	23	36	55	.193	.266	.257	523	51	-22	3	2	-0	.980	-9	O-102L/3-5,2-2	-3.8

■ LENNY METZ

Metz, Leonard Raymond b: 7/6/1899, Louisville, Colo. d: 2/24/53, Denver, Colo. BR/TR, 5'10.5", 170 lbs. Deb: 9/11/23

YEAR	TM/L	G	AB	R	H	2B	3B	HR	RBI	BB	SO	AVG	OBP	SLG	OPS	OPS+	BR+	SB	CS	SBR	FA	FR	G/POS	TPR
1923	Phi-N	12	37	4	8	0	0	0	3	4	3	.216	.310	.216	526	37	-3	0	0	0	.969	1	/2-6,S-6	-0.2
1924	Phi-N	7	7	1	2	0	0	0	1	1	0	.286	.375	.286	661	71	-0	0	0	0	.846	0	/S-6	0.0

YEAR	TM/L	G	AB	R	H	2B	3B	HR	RBI	BB	SO	AVG	OBP	SLG	OPS	OPS+	BR+	SB	CS	SBR	FA	FR	G/POS	TPR
1925	Phi-N	11	14	1	0	0	0	0	0	0	2	.000	.000	.000	0	-92	-4	0	0	0	1.000	2	/S-9,2-2	-0.2
Total	3	30	58	6	10	0	0	0	4	5	5	.172	.250	.172	422	11	-7	0	0	0	.951	3	/S-21,2-8	-0.4
■ **ROGER METZGER** Metzger, Roger Henry b: 10/10/47, Fredericksburg, Tex BB/TR (BL 1970, 80), 6', 165 lbs. Deb: 6/16/70																								
1970	Chi-N	1	2	0	0	0	0	0	0	0	0	.000	.000	.000	0	-89	-1	0	0	0	.833	1	/S-1	0.1
1971	Hou-N	150	562	64	132	14	**11**	0	26	44	50	.235	.295	.299	594	70	-22	15	6	1	.977	-5	*S-148	-0.8
1972	Hou-N	153	641	84	142	12	3	2	38	60	71	.222	.289	.259	548	58	-34	23	9	2	.971	5	*S-153	-1.0
1973	Hou-N	154	580	67	145	11	**14**	1	35	39	70	.250	.301	.322	623	73	-21	10	4	1	**.982**	-19	*S-149	-2.2
1974	Hou-N	143	572	66	145	18	10	0	30	37	73	.253	.299	.320	619	76	-19	9	7	-0	.976	-11	*S-143	-1.3
1975	Hou-N	127	450	54	102	7	9	2	26	41	39	.227	.291	.296	587	68	-20	4	5	-1	.977	11	*S-126	0.5
1976	Hou-N	152	481	37	101	13	8	0	29	52	63	.210	.287	.270	557	65	-22	1	1	-0	**.986**	-3	*S-150/2-2	-0.8
1977	Hou-N	97	269	24	50	9	6	0	16	32	24	.186	.272	.264	536	49	-20	2	0	0	.973	-4	S-96/2-1	-1.5
1978	Hou-N	45	123	11	27	4	1	0	6	12	9	.220	.289	.268	557	61	-6	0	0	0	.964	-4	S-42/2-1	-0.7
	SF-N	75	235	17	61	6	1	0	17	12	17	.260	.296	.294	589	68	-10	8	1	1	.974	-12	S-74	-1.5
	Yr	120	358	28	88	10	2	0	23	24	26	.246	.293	.285	578	66	-17	8	1	1	.970	-16	*S-116/2-1	-2.2
1979	SF-N	94	259	24	65	7	8	0	31	23	31	.251	.312	.340	652	83	-6	11	3	1	.956	2	S-78,2-10/3-1	0.5
1980	SF-N	28	27	5	2	0	0	0	0	3	2	.074	.167	.074	241	-31	-5	0	0	0	.971	3	S-13/2-1	-0.2
Total	11	1219	4201	453	972	101	71	5	254	355	449	.231	.293	.293	585	67	-186	83	36	6	.976	-36	*S-1173/2-15,3-1	-8.9
■ **WILLIAM METZIG** Metzig, William Andrew b: 12/4/18, Ft.Dodge, Iowa BR/TR, 6'1", 180 lbs. Deb: 9/19/44																								
1944	Chi-A	5	16	1	2	0	0	0	1	1	4	.125	.176	.125	301	-13	-2	0	0	0	1.000	2	/2-5	0.0
■ **ALEX METZLER** Metzler, Alexander b: 1/4/03, Fresno, Cal. d: 11/30/73, Fresno, Cal. BL/TR, 5'9", 167 lbs. Deb: 9/16/25																								
1925	Chi-N	9	38	2	7	2	0	0	2	3	7	.184	.244	.237	481	23	-4	0	0	0	1.000	2	/O-9(0-9-0)	-0.3
1926	Phi-A	20	67	8	16	3	0	0	12	7	5	.239	.311	.284	594	53	-5	1	0	0	1.000	2	O-17(15-1-1)	-0.4
1927	Chi-A	134	543	87	173	29	11	3	61	61	39	.319	.396	.429	826	117	15	15	11	-1	.965	16	*O-134(0-133-4)	2.3
1928	Chi-A	139	464	71	141	18	14	3	55	77	30	.304	.410	.422	832	121	17	16	8	1	.968	-4	*O-134(50-43-46)	0.5
1929	Chi-A	146	568	80	156	23	13	2	49	80	45	.275	.367	.371	739	92	-5	9	5	0	.960	1	*O-142(132-10-0)	-1.4
1930	Chi-A	56	79	12	14	4	0	0	5	11	6	.177	.278	.228	506	31	-8	0	2	-1	.969	-5	O-27(21-1-5)	-1.4
	StL-A	56	209	30	54	6	3	1	23	21	12	.258	.326	.330	656	65	-11	5	1	1	.951	-5	O-56(1-36-19)	-1.7
	Yr	112	288	42	68	10	3	1	28	32	18	.236	.313	.302	615	57	-19	5	3	0	.955	-10	O-83(22-37-24)	-3.1
Total	6	560	1968	290	561	85	41	9	207	260	144	.285	.374	.384	757	97	-0	46	27	1	.965	6	O-519(219-233-75)	-2.4
■ **HENSLEY MEULENS** Meulens, Hensley Filemon Acasio "Bam-Bam" b: 6/23/67, Willemstad, Curacao BR/TR, 6'3", 212 lbs. Deb: 8/23/89 Career OF: (118-LF 0-CF 18-RF)																								
1989	NY-A	8	28	2	5	0	0	0	1	2	8	.179	.233	.179	412	18	-3	0	1	-0	.875	2	/3-8	-0.1
1990	NY-A	23	83	12	20	7	0	3	10	9	25	.241	.337	.434	771	113	1	1	0	0	.963	3	O-23(23-0-0)	0.4
1991	NY-A	96	288	37	64	8	1	6	29	18	97	.222	.277	.319	597	64	-14	3	0	1	.967	2	O-73L,D-13/1-7	-1.4
1992	NY-A	2	5	1	3	0	0	1	1	1	0	.600	.667	1.200	1867	416	2	0	0	0	1.000	0	/3-2	0.2
1993	NY-A	30	53	8	9	1	1	2	5	8	19	.170	.279	.340	618	67	-3	0	1	-0	1.000	-4	O-24(22-0-1)/1-3,3-1	-0.8
1997	Mon-N	16	24	6	7	1	0	2	6	4	10	.292	.393	.583	976	152	2	0	1	-0	1.000	-2	/O-8(8-0-0),1-3	-0.1
1998	Ari-N	7	15	1	1	0	0	1	1	0	6	.067	.067	.267	333	-18	-3	0	0	0	1.000	-1	/O-4(4-0-4)	-0.4
Total	7	182	496	67	109	17	2	15	53	42	165	.220	.290	.353	643	76	-17	4	3	-0	.972	-0	O-132L/1-13,D-13,3	-2.2
■ **IRISH MEUSEL** Meusel, Emil Frederick b: 6/9/1893, Oakland, Cal. d: 3/1/63, Long Beach, Cal. BR/TR, 5'11.5", 178 lbs. Deb: 10/1/14 FC Career OF: (1008-LF 61-CF 158-RF)																								
1914	Was-A	1	2	0	0	0	0	0	0	0	0	.000	.000	.000	0	-96	-0	0			1.000	-0	/O-1(1-0-0)	-0.1
1918	Phi-N	124	473	48	132	25	6	4	62	30	21	.279	.323	.383	706	108	4	18			.972	8	*O-120(71-45-0)/2-4	0.6
1919	Phi-N	135	521	65	159	26	7	5	59	15	13	.305	.327	.411	738	113	7	24			.968	-2	*O-128(59-15-54)	-0.1
1920	Phi-N	138	518	75	160	27	8	14	69	32	27	.309	.349	.473	822	129	17	17	11	-0	.929	-5	*O-129(99-0-43)/1-3	0.7
1921	Phi-N	84	343	59	121	21	7	12	51	18	17	.353	.385	.560	945	136	17	8	4	0	.929	2	O-84(38-1-46)	1.2
	*NY-N	62	243	37	80	12	6	2	36	15	12	.329	.373	.453	826	117	6	5	9	-2	.971	-1	O-62(62-0-1)	-0.2
	Yr	146	586	96	201	33	13	14	87	33	29	.343	.380	.515	895	129	23	13	13	-2	.947	1	*O-146(100-1-47)	1.0
1922	*NY-N	154	617	100	204	28	17	16	132	35	33	.331	.369	.509	877	123	19	12	10	-1	.980	-8	*O-154(154-0-0)	-0.3
1923	*NY-N	146	595	102	177	22	14	19	**125**	38	16	.297	.341	.477	818	115	10	8	8	-1	.949	-8	*O-145(145-0-0)	-1.0
1924	*NY-N	139	549	75	170	26	9	6	102	33	18	.310	.351	.423	774	109	7	11	7	-0	.967	-7	*O-138(138-0-0)	-1.1
1925	NY-N	135	516	82	169	35	8	21	111	26	19	.328	.363	.548	912	135	24	5	4	-0	.959	0	*O-126(118-0-8)	1.3
1926	NY-N	129	449	51	131	25	10	6	65	16	18	.292	.322	.432	754	103	-0	5			.958	-5	*O-112(112-0-0)	-1.4
1927	Bro-N	42	74	7	18	3	1	1	7	11	5	.243	.341	.351	693	85	-1	0			1.000	-0	O-17(11-0-6)	-0.3
Total	11	1289	4900	701	1521	250	93	106	819	269	199	.310	.348	.464	813	118	108	113	53		.959	-25	*O-1216L/2-4,1-3	-0.7
■ **BOB MEUSEL** Meusel, Robert William "Long Bob" b: 7/19/1896, San Jose, Cal. d: 11/28/77, Downey, Cal. BR/TR, 6'3", 190 lbs. Deb: 4/14/20 F Career OF: (694-LF 43-CF 571-RF)																								
1920	NY-A	119	460	75	151	40	7	11	83	20	72	.328	.359	.517	876	126	14	4	4	-1	.947	-10	O-64R,3-45/1-2	0.1
1921	*NY-A	149	598	104	190	40	16	24	135	34	88	.318	.356	.559	915	128	20	17	6	2	.934	5	*O-147(10-0-137)	1.4
1922	*NY-A	121	473	61	151	26	11	16	84	40	58	.319	.376	.522	898	129	19	13	8	0	.950	0	*O-121(47-1-74)	0.9
1923	*NY-A	132	460	59	144	29	10	9	91	31	52	.313	.359	.478	837	117	9	13	15	-2	.953	-7	*O-121(78-0-43)	-0.9
1924	NY-A	143	579	93	188	40	11	12	120	32	43	.325	.365	.494	859	120	14	26	14	1	.951	-7	*O-143(93-2-49)/3-2	-0.3
1925	NY-A	156	624	101	181	34	12	**33**	**138**	54	55	.290	.348	.542	889	125	18	13	14	-2	.985	-9	*O-131(86-0-46),3-27	-0.2
1926	*NY-A	108	413	73	130	22	3	12	81	37	32	.315	.373	.470	842	121	11	16	17	-2	.960	-6	*O-107(68-1-38)	-0.5
1927	*NY-A	135	516	75	174	47	9	8	103	45	58	.337	.393	.510	902	137	27	24	10	2	.950	-4	*O-131(83-0-48)	1.4
1928	*NY-A	131	518	77	154	45	5	11	113	39	56	.297	.349	.467	816	116	10	6	9	-2	.975	4	*O-131(87-0-44)	0.2
1929	NY-A	100	391	46	102	15	3	10	57	17	42	.261	.292	.391	683	79	-14	1	5	-2	.968	3	O-96(56-0-40)	-1.9
1930	Cin-N	113	443	62	128	30	8	10	62	26	63	.289	.330	.460	790	93	-7	9			.962	-4	*O-112(70-39-4)	-1.6
Total	11	1407	5475	826	1693	368	95	156	1067	375	619	.309	.356	.497	852	119	122	142	102		.958	-35	*O-1304L/3-74,1-2	-1.4
■ **BENNY MEYER** Meyer, Bernhard "Earache" b: 1/1/1888, Hematite, Mo. d: 2/6/74, Festus, Mo. BR/TR, 5'9", 170 lbs. Deb: 4/9/13 C Career OF: (87-LF 19-CF 174-RF)																								
1913	Bro-N	38	87	12	17	0	1	1	10	10	14	.195	.278	.253	531	51	-5	8			.943	-2	O-26(2-17-7)/C-1	-0.9
1914	Bal-F	143	500	76	152	18	10	5	40	71	53	.304	.395	.410	805	116	6	23			.916	-11	*O-132(12-2-118)/S-4	-1.1
1915	Bal-F	35	120	20	29	2	0	0	5	37	13	.242	.424	.258	682	91	-0	6			.931	-3	O-34(0-0-34)	-0.6
	Buf-F	93	333	37	77	8	6	1	29	40	37	.231	.316	.300	616	72	-17	9			.947	-6	O-88(73-0-15)	-2.9
	Yr	128	453	57	106	10	6	1	34	77	50	.234	.348	.289	637	78	-17	15			.943	-10	*O-122(73-0-49)	-3.5
1925	Phi-N	1	1	1	1	1	0	0	0	0	0	1.000	1.000	2.000	3000	594	1	0	0	0	.000	0	/2-1	0.1
Total	4	310	1041	146	276	29	17	7	84	158	117	.265	.365	.346	711	95	-15	46	0		.931	-22	O-280R/S-4,2-1,C-1	-5.4
■ **DAN MEYER** Meyer, Daniel Thomas b: 8/3/52, Hamilton, Ohio BL/TR, 5'11", 180 lbs. Deb: 9/14/74 Career OF: (315-LF 1-CF 11-RF)																								
1974	Det-A	13	50	5	10	1	1	3	7	1	1	.200	.231	.440	671	86	-1	1	0	0	.967	1	O-12(12-0-0)	-0.1
1975	Det-A	122	470	56	111	17	3	8	47	26	25	.236	.279	.336	615	70	-19	8	3	1	.950	-0	O-74(74-0-0),1-46	-2.8
1976	Det-A	105	294	37	74	8	4	2	16	17	22	.252	.293	.327	619	78	-8	10	0	2	.988	-4	O-47(47-0-0),1-19/D-1	-1.5
1977	Sea-A	159	582	75	159	24	4	22	90	43	51	.273	.324	.442	766	107	5	11	8	-0	.992	1	*1-159	-0.5
1978	Sea-A	123	444	38	101	18	1	8	56	24	39	.227	.267	.327	594	66	-21	7	3	0	.989	-2	*1-121/O-2(2-0-0),D-1	-3.0
1979	Sea-A	144	525	72	146	21	7	20	74	29	35	.278	.321	.459	780	106	3	11	7	-0	.936	-14	*3-101,O-31L,1-15	-1.4
1980	Sea-A	146	531	56	146	25	6	11	71	31	42	.275	.316	.407	723	96	-4	8	4	0	.961	-10	*O-123L/3-5,1-4,D-7	-1.9
1981	Sea-A	83	252	26	66	10	1	3	22	10	16	.262	.293	.345	638	80	-7	4	3	-0	.961	-2	3-49,O-14L/1-3,D-3	-1.0
1982	Oak-A	120	383	28	92	17	3	8	59	18	33	.240	.274	.363	637	77	-13	1	1	-0	.990	-3	1-58,D-38,O-11(4-0-8)	-2.2
1983	Oak-A	69	169	15	32	9	0	1	13	19	11	.189	.271	.260	532	50	-11	0	0	0	.987	-6	1-41,D-12,O-11L,/3	-2.0
1984	Oak-A	20	22	1	7	3	1	0	4	0	2	.318	.318	.545	864	143	1	0	0	0	.944	0	/1-3,D-1	0.1
1985	Oak-A	14	12	2	0	0	0	0	0	1	0	.000	.077	.000	77	-83	-3	0	0	0	.000	-0	/3-1,O-1(0-0-1),D-1	-0.4
Total	12	1118	3734	411	944	153	31	86	459	219	277	.253	.296	.379	675	86	-80	61	29	3	.991	-38	1-469,O-326L,3-157,/D	-16.7
■ **GEORGE MEYER** Meyer, George Francis b: 8/3/09, Chicago, Ill. d: 1/3/92, Hoffman Estates, Ill. BR/TR, 5'9", 160 lbs. Deb: 9/3/38																								
1938	Chi-A	24	81	10	24	2	2	0	9	11	17	.296	.387	.370	757	89	-1	3	1	0	.967	6	2-24	0.6

■ DUTCH MEYER
Meyer, Lambert Dalton b: 10/6/15, Waco, Tex. BR/TR, 5′10.5″, 181 lbs. Deb: 6/23/37

YEAR	TM/L	G	AB	R	H	2B	3B	HR	RBI	BB	SO	AVG	OBP	SLG	OPS	OPS+	BR+	SB	CS	SBR	FA	FR	G/POS	TPR
1937	Chi-N	1	0	0	0	0	0	0	0	0	0	—	—	—	—	—	0	0			.000	0	R	0.0
1940	Det-A	23	58	12	15	3	0	0	6	4	10	.259	.317	.310	628	58	-4	2	0	0	.960	0	2-21	-0.2
1941	Det-A	46	153	12	29	9	1	1	14	8	13	.190	.230	.281	511	31	-15	1	1	-0	.972	6	2-40	-0.7
1942	Det-A	14	52	5	17	3	0	2	9	4	4	.327	.386	.500	886	137	2	0	1	-0	.989	6	2-14	0.9
1945	Cle-A	130	524	71	153	29	8	7	48	40	32	.292	.342	.418	760	125	15	2	4	-1	.978	-32	*2-130	-1.2
1946	Cle-A	72	207	13	48	5	3	0	16	26	16	.232	.321	.285	606	75	-6	0	1	-0	.977	-13	2-64	-1.8
Total	6	286	994	113	262	49	12	10	93	82	75	.264	.322	.367	689	94	-8	5	7		.977	-32	2-269	-3.0

■ LEO MEYER
Meyer, Leo b: 3/29/1888, Iowa d: 9/2/68, Smyrna, Del. TR, Deb: 9/27/09

YEAR	TM/L	G	AB	R	H	2B	3B	HR	RBI	BB	SO	AVG	OBP	SLG	OPS	OPS+	BR+	SB	CS	SBR	FA	FR	G/POS	TPR
1909	Bro-N	7	23	1	3	0	0	0	0	2		.130	.200	.130	330	3	-3	0			.882	2	/S-7	-0.1

■ SCOTT MEYER
Meyer, Scott William b: 8/19/57, Evergreen Park, Ill BR/TR, 6′1″, 195 lbs. Deb: 9/10/78

YEAR	TM/L	G	AB	R	H	2B	3B	HR	RBI	BB	SO	AVG	OBP	SLG	OPS	OPS+	BR+	SB	CS	SBR	FA	FR	G/POS	TPR
1978	Oak-A	8	9	1	1	1	0	0	0	0	4	.111	.111	.222	333	-9	-1	0	0	0	1.000	-1	/C-7	-0.2

■ JOEY MEYER
Meyer, Tanner Joe b: 5/10/62, Honolulu, Hawaii BR/TR, 6′3″, 260 lbs. Deb: 4/4/88

YEAR	TM/L	G	AB	R	H	2B	3B	HR	RBI	BB	SO	AVG	OBP	SLG	OPS	OPS+	BR+	SB	CS	SBR	FA	FR	G/POS	TPR
1988	Mil-A	103	327	22	86	18	0	11	45	23	88	.263	.313	.419	732	102	0	0	1	-0	.986	-0	D-66,1-33	-0.4
1989	Mil-A	53	147	13	33	6	0	7	29	12	36	.224	.283	.408	691	93	-2	1	0	0	.982	-1	D-31,1-18	-0.4
Total	2	156	474	35	119	24	0	18	74	35	124	.251	.304	.416	720	100	-2	1	1	-0	.984	-1	/D-97,1-51	-0.8

■ BILLY MEYER
Meyer, William Adam b: 1/14/1892, Knoxville, Tenn. d: 3/31/57, Knoxville, Tenn. BR/TR, 5′9.5″, 170 lbs. Deb: 9/6/13 M

YEAR	TM/L	G	AB	R	H	2B	3B	HR	RBI	BB	SO	AVG	OBP	SLG	OPS	OPS+	BR+	SB	CS	SBR	FA	FR	G/POS	TPR
1913	Chi-A	1	1	0	1	0	0	0	0	0	0	1.000	1.000	1.000	2000	490	0	0			.857	1	/C-1	0.1
1916	Phi-A	50	138	6	32	2	2	1	12	8	11	.232	.274	.297	571	75	-5	3			.961	7	C-48	0.7
1917	Phi-A	62	162	9	38	5	1	0	9	7	14	.235	.271	.278	548	68	-7	0			.962	9	C-55	0.8
Total	3	113	301	15	71	7	3	1	21	15	25	.236	.274	.289	563	73	-11	3			.960	18	C-104	1.6

■ LEVI MEYERLE
Meyerle, Levi Samuel "Long Levi" b: 7/1845, Philadelphia, Pa. d: 11/4/21, Philadelphia, Pa. BR/TR, 6′1″, 177 lbs. Deb: 5/20/1871 NA OF: (2-LF 0-CF 29-RF)

YEAR	TM/L	G	AB	R	H	2B	3B	HR	RBI	BB	SO	AVG	OBP	SLG	OPS	OPS+	BR+	SB	CS	SBR	FA	FR	G/POS	TPR
1871	Ath-n	26	130	45	64	9	3	**4**	40	2	1	**.492**	**.500**	**.700**	**1200**	**243**	**23**	4	0	1	.646	-8	*3-26/P-1	0.9
1872	Ath-n	27	146	31	48	10	5	1	31	0	1	.329	.329	.486	815	147	7	0	0	0	.773	5	O-26(0-0-26)/3-1	0.9
1873	Phi-n	48	238	53	83	14	4	3	58	2	0	.349	.354	.479	833	140	10	5	0	1	.743	-6	*3-48/S-1	0.3
1874	Chi-n	53	254	65	100	19	1	1	45	3	4	**.394**	**.401**	.488	**889**	**182**	**22**	3	1	0	.833	-15	2-31,3-14/S-5,O-5R	0.4
1875	Phi-n	68	301	55	95	14	8	1	54	0	2	.316	.316	.425	741	149	13	7	2	1	.859	-10	2-36,3-20,1-16	0.2
1876	Phi-N	55	259	46	87	12	8	0	34	3	2	.336	.347	.449	797	165	17				.791	-3	*3-49/O-3R,2-3,P-2	1.3
1877	Cin-N	27	107	11	35	7	2	0	15	0	4	.327	.327	.430	757	154	7				.822	1	S-18,2-12/O-1(0-1-0)	0.7
1884	Phi-U	3	11	0	1	1	0	0		0		.091	.091	.182	273	-21	-2				.789	-1	/1-2,O-1(0-0-1)	-0.3
Total	5 n	222	1069	249	390	66	21	10	228	7	8	.365	.369	.494	863	166	76	19	3	3	.704	-35	3-109/2-67,O-31R,1SP	2.7
Total	3	85	377	57	123	20	10	0	49	3	6	.326	.334	.436	770	156	21				.891	-4	/3-49,S-18,2-15,O1P	1.7

■ CHAD MEYERS
Meyers, Chad William b: 8/8/75, Omaha, Neb. BR/TR, 6′, 190 lbs. Deb: 8/6/99 Career OF: (4-LF 10-CF 0-RF)

YEAR	TM/L	G	AB	R	H	2B	3B	HR	RBI	BB	SO	AVG	OBP	SLG	OPS	OPS+	BR+	SB	CS	SBR	FA	FR	G/POS	TPR
1999	Chi-N	43	142	17	33	9	0	0	4	9	27	.232	.292	.296	588	50	-11	4	2	0	.983	-2	2-32,O-14(4-10-0)	-1.1
2000	Chi-N	36	52	8	9	2	0	0	5	3	11	.173	.232	.212	444	13	-7	1	0	0	1.000	-0	/2-8,3-8	-0.6
Total	2	79	194	25	42	11	0	0	9	12	38	.216	.276	.273	549	40	-18	5	2	0	.986	-2	/2-40,O-14C,3-8	-1.7

■ HENRY MEYERS
Meyers, Henry L. b: 1860, Philadelphia, Pa. d: 6/28/1898, Harrisburg, Pa. Deb: 8/30/1890

YEAR	TM/L	G	AB	R	H	2B	3B	HR	RBI	BB	SO	AVG	OBP	SLG	OPS	OPS+	BR+	SB	CS	SBR	FA	FR	G/POS	TPR
1890	Phi-a	5	19	2	3	0	0	0	1	1		.158	.238	.158	396	17	-2	2			.684	-3	/3-5	-0.4

■ CHIEF MEYERS
Meyers, John Tortes b: 7/29/1880, Riverside, Cal. d: 7/25/71, San Bernardino, Cal. BR/TR, 5′11″, 194 lbs. Deb: 4/16/09

YEAR	TM/L	G	AB	R	H	2B	3B	HR	RBI	BB	SO	AVG	OBP	SLG	OPS	OPS+	BR+	SB	CS	SBR	FA	FR	G/POS	TPR
1909	NY-N	90	220	15	61	10	5	1	30	22		.277	.359	.382	741	128	7	3			.963	2	C-64	1.7
1910	NY-N	127	365	25	104	18	0	1	62	40	18	.285	.362	.342	704	106	4	5			.969	5	*C-117	2.0
1911	*NY-N	133	391	48	130	18	9	1	61	25	33	.332	.392	.432	824	126	14	7			.979	-3	*C-128	2.1
1912	*NY-N	126	371	60	133	16	5	6	54	47	20	.358	.441	.477	918	147	26	8			.973	-10	*C-122	2.5
1913	*NY-N	120	378	37	118	18	5	3	47	37	22	.312	.387	.410	797	127	14	7			.967	1	*C-116	2.6
1914	NY-N	134	381	33	109	13	5	1	55	34	25	.286	.357	.354	711	116	8	4			.970	-12	*C-126	0.6
1915	NY-N	110	289	24	67	10	5	1	26	26	18	.232	.311	.311	622	94	-2	4	4	-1	**.986**	-5	C-96	0.0
1916	*Bro-N	80	239	21	59	10	3	0	21	26	15	.247	.336	.314	650	97	0	2			.984	7	C-74	1.6
1917	Bro-N	47	132	8	28	3	0	0	3	13	7	.212	.283	.235	518	58	-6	4			.974	-6	C-44	-1.0
	Bos-N	25	68	5	17	4	4	0	4	4	4	.250	.311	.426	737	133	2	0			1.000	7	C-24	1.3
	Yr	72	200	13	45	7	4	0	7	17	11	.225	.292	.300	592	82	-4	4			.984	1	C-68	0.3
Total	9	992	2834	276	826	120	41	14	363	274	162	.291	.367	.378	744	117	68	44	4		.974	-14	C-911	13.4

■ LOU MEYERS
Meyers, Lewis Henry "Crazy Horse" b: 12/9/1859, Cincinnati, Ohio d: 11/30/20, Cincinnati, Ohio BR/TR, 5′11″, 165 lbs. Deb: 5/10/1884

YEAR	TM/L	G	AB	R	H	2B	3B	HR	RBI	BB	SO	AVG	OBP	SLG	OPS	OPS+	BR+	SB	CS	SBR	FA	FR	G/POS	TPR
1884	Cin-U	2	3	1	0	0	0	0		1		.000	.250	.000	250	-17	-1				.667	-2	/C-2,O-1(0-0-1)	-0.2

■ MICKEY MICELOTTA
Micelotta, Robert Peter b: 10/20/28, Corona, N.Y. BR/TR, 5′11″, 185 lbs. Deb: 4/20/54

YEAR	TM/L	G	AB	R	H	2B	3B	HR	RBI	BB	SO	AVG	OBP	SLG	OPS	OPS+	BR+	SB	CS	SBR	FA	FR	G/POS	TPR
1954	Phi-N	13	3	2	0	0	0	0	0	1	1	.000	.250	.000	250	-28	-1	0	0	0	1.000	0	/S-1	0.0
1955	Phi-N	4	4	0	0	0	0	0	0	0	0	.000	.000	.000	0	-99	-1	0	0	0	1.000	0	/S-2	-0.1
Total	2	17	7	2	0	0	0	0	0	1	1	.000	.125	.000	125	-64	-2	0	0	0	1.000	1	/S-3	-0.1

■ GENE MICHAEL
Michael, Eugene Richard "Stick" b: 6/2/38, Kent, Ohio BB/TR, 6′2″, 183 lbs. Deb: 7/15/66 MC

YEAR	TM/L	G	AB	R	H	2B	3B	HR	RBI	BB	SO	AVG	OBP	SLG	OPS	OPS+	BR+	SB	CS	SBR	FA	FR	G/POS	TPR
1966	Pit-N	30	33	9	5	2	1	0	2	0	7	.152	.152	.273	424	15	-4	0	0	0	.903	5	/S-8,2-2,3-1	0.2
1967	LA-N	98	223	20	45	3	1	0	7	11	30	.202	.246	.224	470	39	-18	1	3	-1	.950	5	S-83	-0.9
1968	NY-A	61	116	8	23	3	0	1	8	2	23	.198	.218	.250	468	43	-8	3	2	-0	.939	-1	S-43/P-1	-0.7
1969	NY-A	119	412	41	112	24	4	2	31	43	56	.272	.342	.364	706	101	1	7	4	0	.968	-1	*S-118	1.5
1970	NY-A	134	435	42	93	10	1	2	38	50	93	.214	.295	.255	550	56	-25	3	1	0	.957	2	*S-123/3-4,2-3	-0.9
1971	NY-A	139	456	36	102	15	0	3	35	48	64	.224	.302	.276	578	69	-18	3	3	-0	.973	17	*S-136	1.5
1972	NY-A	126	391	29	91	7	4	1	32	32	45	.233	.292	.279	571	73	-13	4	2	0	.969	24	*S-121	2.8
1973	NY-A	129	418	30	94	11	1	3	47	26	51	.225	.270	.278	548	56	-24	1	3	-1	.965	5	*S-129	-0.5
1974	NY-A	81	177	19	46	9	0	0	13	14	24	.260	.314	.311	625	82	-4	0	0	0	.970	5	2-45,S-39/3-2	0.5
1975	Det-A	56	145	15	31	2	0	3	13	8	28	.214	.255	.290	545	51	-9	0	0	0	.938	-4	S-44/2-7,3-4	-0.9
Total	10	973	2806	249	642	86	12	15	226	234	421	.229	.290	.284	574	66	-123	22	18	-1	.962	55	S-844/2-57,3-11,P-1	2.6

■ CASS MICHAELS
Michaels, Casimir Eugene (Played In 1943 Under Real Name Of Casimir Eugene Kwietniewski)
b: 3/4/26, Detroit, Mich. d: 11/12/82, Grosse Pointe, Mich. BR/TR, 5′11″, 175 lbs. Deb: 8/19/43

YEAR	TM/L	G	AB	R	H	2B	3B	HR	RBI	BB	SO	AVG	OBP	SLG	OPS	OPS+	BR+	SB	CS	SBR	FA	FR	G/POS	TPR
1943	Chi-A	2	7	0	0	0	0	0	0	0	0	.000	.000	.000	0	-99	-2	0	0	0	1.000	-1	/3-2	-0.4
1944	Chi-A	27	68	4	12	4	1	0	5	2	5	.176	.200	.265	465	33	-6	0	0	0	.930	6	S-21/3-3	0.1
1945	Chi-A	129	445	47	109	8	5	2	54	37	28	.245	.307	.299	606	78	-12	8	7	-1	.936	10	*S-126/2-1	0.7
1946	Chi-A	91	291	37	75	8	0	1	22	29	36	.258	.333	.296	629	80	-7	9	3	1	.957	3	2-66,3-13/S-6	0.0
1947	Chi-A	110	355	31	97	15	4	3	34	39	28	.273	.350	.363	714	102	1	10	5	0	.982	11	2-60,3-44/S-2	1.6
1948	Chi-A	145	484	47	120	12	6	5	56	69	42	.248	.344	.329	673	82	-11	8	2	1	.957	13	S-85,2-55/O-1(0-1-0)	1.1
1949	Chi-A★	154	561	73	173	27	9	6	83	101	50	.308	.417	.421	837	126	25	5	7	-1	.976	12	*2-154	4.2
1950	Chi-A	36	138	21	43	6	3	4	19	13	8	.312	.375	.486	861	122	4	0	0	0	.964	-6	2-35	0.0
	Was-A★	106	388	48	97	8	4	4	47	55	39	.250	.345	.322	667	75	-14	2	3	-1	.975	8	*2-104	-0.1
	Yr	142	526	69	140	14	7	8	66	68	47	.266	.352	.365	717	88	-9	2	3	-1	.972	2	*2-139	-0.1
1951	Was-A	138	485	59	125	20	4	4	45	61	41	.258	.342	.340	682	86	-8	1	1	-0	.964	-23	*2-128	-2.5
1952	Was-A	22	86	10	20	4	1	1	7	7	15	.233	.290	.337	628	77	-3	0	0	0	.977	1	2-22	-0.1
	StL-A	55	166	21	44	8	2	3	25	23	16	.265	.354	.392	746	104	1	1	0	0	.916	-0	3-42/2-8	0.2
	Phi-A	55	200	22	50	4	5	1	18	23	11	.250	.330	.335	665	80	-5	3	0	1	.993	-13	2-55	-1.5
	Yr	132	452	53	114	16	8	5	50	53	42	.252	.332	.356	688	89	-7	4	0	1	.989	-13	2-85,3-42	-1.4
1953	Phi-A	117	411	53	103	10	0	12	42	51	56	.251	.335	.363	697	85	-8	7	0	**2**	.970	-11	*2-110	-0.9
1954	Chi-A	101	282	35	74	13	2	7	44	56	31	.262	.392	.397	789	113	7	10	4	1	.958	-4	3-91/2-2	0.4
Total	12	1288	4367	508	1142	147	46	53	501	566	406	.262	.349	.353	702	92	-38	64	32	3	.973	3	2-800,S-240,3-195,/O	2.8

YEAR	TM/L	G	AB	R	H	2B	3B	HR	RBI	BB	SO	AVG	OBP	SLG	OPS	OPS+	BR+	SB	CS	SBR	FA	FR	G/POS	TPR
■ **RALPH MICHAELS** Michaels, Ralph Joseph b: 5/3/02, Etna, Pa. d: 8/5/88, Monroeville, Pa. BR/TR, 5'10.5", 178 lbs. Deb: 4/16/24																								
1924	Chi-N	8	11	0	4	0	0	0	2	0	1	.364	.364	.364	727	95	-0	0	0	0	.929	1	/S-4	0.1
1925	Chi-N	22	50	10	14	1	0	0	6	6	9	.280	.357	.300	657	69	-2	1	0	0	.975	3	3-15/1-1,2-1,S-1	0.2
1926	Chi-N	2	0	1	0	0	0	0	0	0	0	—	—	—	—	—	0	0			.000	0	H	0.0
Total	3	32	61	11	18	1	0	0	8	6	10	.295	.358	.311	670	73	-2	1	0		.933	3	/3-15,S-5,2-1,1-1	0.3
■ **ED MICKELSON** Mickelson, Edward Allen b: 9/9/26, Ottawa, Ill. BR/TR, 6'3", 205 lbs. Deb: 9/18/50																								
1950	StL-N	5	10	1	1	0	0	0	0	2	3	.100	.250	.100	350	-4	-1	0			1.000	1	/1-4	-0.1
1953	StL-A	7	15	1	2	1	0	0	2	2	6	.133	.235	.200	435	18	-2	0	0	0	1.000	0	/1-3	-0.2
1957	Chi-N	6	12	0	0	0	0	0	1	0	4	.000	.000	.000	0	-99	-3	0	0	0	1.000	1	/1-2	-0.3
Total	3	18	37	2	3	1	0	0	3	4	13	.081	.171	.108	279	-23	-7	0	0		1.000	2	/1-9	-0.6
■ **EZRA MIDKIFF** Midkiff, Ezra Millington "Salt Rock" b: 11/13/1882, Salt Rock, W.Va. d: 3/20/57, Huntington, W.Va. BL/TR, 5'10", 180 lbs. Deb: 10/5/09																								
1909	Cin-N	1	2	0	0	0	0	0	0	0		.000	.000	.000	0	-99	-0	0			.000	-1	/3-1	-0.1
1912	NY-A	21	86	9	21	1	0	0	9	7		.244	.301	.256	557	56	-5	4			.901	2	3-21	-0.3
1913	NY-A	83	284	22	56	9	1	0	14	12	33	.197	.232	.236	468	37	-23	9			.957	18	3-76/S-4,2-2	-0.4
Total	3	105	372	31	77	10	1	0	23	19	33	.207	.247	.239	487	41	-28	13			.942	18	/3-98,S-4,2-2	-0.8
■ **DOUG MIENTKIEWICZ** Mientkiewicz, Douglas Andrew b: 6/19/74, Toledo, Ohio BL/TR, 6'2", 195 lbs. Deb: 9/18/98																								
1998	Min-A	8	25	1	5	1	0	0	2	4	3	.200	.310	.240	550	45	-2	1	1	-0	1.000	-1	/1-8	-0.3
1999	Min-A	118	327	34	75	21	3	2	32	43	51	.229	.326	.330	656	66	-16	1	1	-0	**.997**	-2	*1-110	-2.5
2000	Min-A	3	14	0	6	0	0	0	4	0	0	.429	.429	.429	857	112	0	0	0	0	1.000	-1	/1-3	-0.1
Total	3	129	366	35	86	22	3	2	38	47	54	.235	.329	.328	656	66	-18	2	2	-0	.997	-3	1-121	-2.9
■ **ED MIERKOWICZ** Mierkowicz, Edward Frank "Butch" or "Mouse" b: 3/6/24, Wyandotte, Mich. BR/TR, 6'4", 205 lbs. Deb: 8/31/45																								
1945	*Det-A	10	15	0	2	2	0	0	2	1	3	.133	.188	.267	454	29	-1	0	0	0	1.000	-1	/O-6(6-0-0)	-0.3
1947	Det-A	21	42	6	8	1	0	1	1	1	12	.190	.209	.286	495	36	-4	1	0	0	.947	-1	O-10(10-0-0)	-0.6
1948	Det-A	3	5	0	1	0	0	0	1	2	2	.200	.429	.200	629	69	-0	0	0	0	1.000	0	/O-1(1-0-0)	0.0
1950	StL-N	1	1	0	0	0	0	0	0	0	1	.000	.000	.000	0	-95	-0	0			.000	0	H	0.0
Total	4	35	63	6	11	3	0	1	4	4	18	.175	.224	.270	494	36	-6	1	0		.968	-2	/O-17(17-0-0)	-0.9
■ **MATT MIESKE** Mieske, Matthew Todd b: 2/13/68, Midland, Mich. BR/TR, 6', 192 lbs. Deb: 5/3/93																								
1993	Mil-A	23	58	9	14	0	0	3	7	4	14	.241	.290	.397	687	84	-2	0	2	-1	.936	-2	O-22(1-9-12)	-0.4
1994	Mil-A	84	259	39	67	13	1	10	38	21	62	.259	.322	.432	754	88	-5	3	5	-1	.976	-3	O-80(6-0-80)/D-1	-1.2
1995	Mil-A	117	267	42	67	13	1	12	48	27	45	.251	.329	.442	771	93	-3	2	4	-1	.979	-3	*O-108(0-0-108)/D-2	-1.0
1996	Mil-A	127	374	46	104	24	3	14	64	26	76	.278	.328	.471	799	95	-4	1	5	-2	.996	1	*O-122(9-10-108)	-0.8
1997	Mil-A	84	253	39	63	15	3	5	21	19	50	.249	.301	.391	693	78	-8	1	0	0	.962	-4	O-74(26-0-52)/D-5	-1.4
1998	Chi-N	77	97	16	29	7	0	1	12	11	17	.299	.376	.402	778	101	1	0	0	0	.974	-14	O-62(50-3-12)	-1.4
1999	Sea-A	24	41	11	15	0	0	4	7	2	9	.366	.395	.659	1054	166	4	0	0	0	1.000	-4	O-20(6-3-13)/D-1	0.0
	*Hou-N	54	109	13	31	5	0	5	22	6	22	.284	.322	.468	790	98	-1	0	0	0	1.000	-1	O-37(30-0-7)	-0.3
2000	Hou-N	62	81	7	14	1	2	1	5	7	17	.173	.247	.272	519	29	-9	0	0	0	.933	-4	O-18(14-0-4)	-1.2
	Ari-N	11	8	3	2	0	0	1	2	1	1	.250	.333	.625	958	134	0	0	0	0	1.000	0	/O-1(0-0-1)	0.0
	Yr	73	89	10	16	1	2	2	7	8	18	.180	.255	.303	558	38	-9	0	0	0	.941	-4	O-19(14-0-5)	-1.2
Total	8	663	1547	225	406	78	10	56	226	124	313	.262	.322	.434	756	90	-27	7	16	-4	.979	-33	O-544(142-25-397)/D-9	-7.7
■ **LARRY MIGGINS** Miggins, Lawrence Edward "Irish" b: 8/20/25, Bronx, N.Y. BR/TR, 6'4", 198 lbs. Deb: 10/3/48																								
1948	StL-N	1	1	1	0	0	0	0	0	0	0	.000	.000	.000	0	-95	-0	0			.000	0	H	0.0
1952	StL-N	42	96	7	22	5	1	2	10	3	19	.229	.253	.365	617	69	-4	0	1	-0	.967	-4	O-25(23-0-2)/1-1	-1.1
Total	2	43	97	8	22	5	1	2	10	3	19	.227	.250	.361	611	67	-5	0	1		.967	-4	/O-25(23-0-2),1-1	-1.1
■ **JOHN MIHALIC** Mihalic, John Michael b: 11/13/11, Cleveland, Ohio d: 4/24/87, Ft.Oglethorpe, Ga. BR/TR, 5'11", 172 lbs. Deb: 9/18/35																								
1935	Was-A	6	22	4	5	3	0	0	6	2	3	.227	.292	.364	655	71	-1	1	0	0	.966	-1	/S-6	-0.1
1936	Was-A	25	88	15	21	2	1	0	8	14	14	.239	.343	.284	627	60	-5	2	1	0	.972	1	2-25	-0.2
1937	Was-A	38	107	13	27	5	2	0	8	17	9	.252	.355	.336	691	79	-3	2	1	0	.981	4	2-28/S-3	0.3
Total	3	69	217	32	53	10	3	0	22	33	26	.244	.344	.318	662	70	-9	5	2	0	.977	4	/2-53,S-9	0.0
■ **EDDIE MIKSIS** Miksis, Edward Thomas b: 9/11/26, Burlington, N.J. BR/TR, 6'0.5", 185 lbs. Deb: 6/17/44 Career OF: (34-LF 106-CF 88-RF)																								
1944	Bro-N	26	91	12	20	2	0	0	11	6	11	.220	.268	.242	510	45	-7	4			.896	-4	3-15,S-10	-1.0
1946	Bro-N	23	48	3	7	0	0	0	5	3	3	.146	.212	.146	357	2	-6	0			.970	0	3-13/2-1	-0.7
1947	*Bro-N	45	86	18	23	1	0	4	10	9	8	.267	.337	.419	755	96	-1	0			1.000	3	2-13,O-11L/3-5,S-2	0.2
1948	Bro-N	86	221	28	47	7	1	2	16	19	27	.213	.278	.281	559	50	-15	5			.967	4	2-54,3-22/S-5	-1.0
1949	*Bro-N	50	113	17	25	5	0	1	6	7	8	.221	.267	.292	559	48	-8	3			.978	6	3-29/S-4,2-3,1-1	-0.3
1950	Bro-N	51	76	13	19	2	1	2	10	5	10	.250	.296	.382	678	75	-3	3			.964	5	2-15,S-15/3-7	0.3
1951	Bro-N	19	10	6	2	1	0	0	0	1	2	.200	.333	.300	633	70	-0	0	0	0	1.000	2	/3-6,2-1	0.2
	Chi-N	102	421	48	112	13	3	4	35	33	36	.266	.319	.340	659	76	-14	11	5	1	.969	3	*2-102	-0.5
	Yr	121	431	54	114	14	3	4	35	34	38	.265	.320	.339	658	76	-14	11	5	1	.969	5	*2-103/3-6	-0.3
1952	Chi-N	93	383	44	89	20	1	2	19	20	32	.232	.272	.305	578	59	-21	4	4	-1	.950	-13	2-54,S-40	-3.1
1953	Chi-N	142	577	61	145	17	6	8	39	33	59	.251	.293	.343	636	64	-31	13	4	1	.954	-13	2-92,S-53	-3.0
1954	Chi-N	38	99	9	20	3	0	2	3	3	9	.202	.225	.293	518	33	-10	1	0	0	.961	4	2-21/3-2,O-1(1-0-0)	-0.4
1955	Chi-N	131	481	52	113	14	2	9	41	32	55	.235	.283	.328	611	62	-27	3	6	-1	**.989**	5	*O-111(0-76-41),3-18	-2.8
1956	Chi-N	114	356	54	85	10	3	9	27	32	40	.239	.303	.360	663	79	-11	4	2	0	.975	-3	3-48,O-33C,2-19,/S	-1.4
1957	StL-N	49	38	3	8	0	0	1	2	7	7	.211	.333	.289	623	68	-2	0	0	0	1.000	-11	O-31(11-3-18)	-1.3
	Bal-A	1	1	0	0	0	0	0	0	0	0	.000	.000	.000	0	-99	-0	0	0	0	.000	0	H	0.0
1958	Bal-A	3	2	0	0	0	0	0	0	0	1	.000	.000	.000	0	-99	-1	0	0	0	.000	0	/S-1	-0.1
	Cin-N	69	50	15	7	0	0	0	4	5	5	.140	.218	.140	358	-2	-7	1	1	-0	1.000	-4	O-32R,3-14/2-7,S1	-1.1
Total	14	1042	3053	383	722	95	17	44	228	215	313	.236	.288	.322	610	62	-164	52	22		.962	-17	2-382,O-219C,3S/1	-16.0
■ **HORACE MILAN** Milan, Horace Robert b: 4/7/1894, Linden, Tenn. d: 6/29/55, Texarkana, Ark. BR/TR, 5'9", 175 lbs. Deb: 8/29/15 F																								
1915	Was-A	11	27	6	11	1	1	0	7	8	7	.407	.543	.519	1061	214	5	2			1.000	-3	O-10(2-4-4)	0.2
1917	Was-A	31	73	8	21	3	1	0	9	4	9	.288	.342	.356	698	114	1	4			.932	-4	O-23(23-0-0)	-0.4
Total	2	42	100	14	32	4	2	0	16	12	16	.320	.404	.400	804	144	6	6			.944	-6	/O-33(25-4-4)	-0.2
■ **CLYDE MILAN** Milan, Jesse Clyde "Deerfoot" b: 3/25/1887, Linden, Tenn. d: 3/3/53, Orlando, Fla. BL/TR, 5'9", 168 lbs. Deb: 8/19/07 FMC																								
1907	Was-A	48	183	22	51	3	3	0	9	8		.279	.323	.328	651	117	3	8			.929	4	O-47(0-30-17)	0.5
1908	Was-A	130	485	55	116	10	12	1	32	38		.239	.304	.315	619	110	6	29			.959	9	*O-122(0-122-0)	1.0
1909	Was-A	130	400	36	80	12	4	1	15	31		.200	.268	.257	525	69	-14	10			.972	5	*O-120(29-89-2)	-1.7
1910	Was-A	142	531	89	148	17	6	0	16	71		.279	.379	.333	713	129	22	44			.946	11	*O-142(0-142-0)	2.9
1911	Was-A	154	616	109	194	24	8	3	35	74		.315	.395	.394	789	123	21	58			.957	11	*O-154(0-154-0)	2.1
1912	Was-A	154	601	105	184	19	11	1	79	63		.306	.377	.379	756	116	13	**88**			.935	8	*O-154(0-154-0)	1.1
1913	Was-A	154	579	92	174	18	9	3	54	58	25	.301	.367	.378	745	116	12	**75**			.932	-7	*O-154(0-154-0)	-0.7
1914	Was-A	115	437	63	129	19	11	1	39	32	26	.295	.346	.396	742	118	8	38	21	1	.949	-4	*O-113(1-112-0)	-0.2
1915	Was-A	153	573	83	165	13	7	2	66	53	32	.288	.353	.346	699	107	5	40	19	2	.946	-0	*O-151(0-151-0)	-0.4
1916	Was-A	150	565	58	154	14	3	1	45	56	31	.273	.343	.313	657	98	-0	34	21	0	.961	17	*O-149(0-149-0)	0.7
1917	Was-A	155	579	60	170	15	4	0	48	58	26	.294	.364	.333	697	114	11	20			.962	-5	*O-153(0-153-0)	-0.5
1918	Was-A	128	503	56	146	18	5	0	56	36	14	.290	.344	.346	690	110	5	26			.972	2	*O-124(0-124-0)	-0.1
1919	Was-A	88	321	43	92	12	6	0	37	40	16	.287	.371	.361	732	107	4	11			.953	-3	O-86(0-86-0)	-0.5
1920	Was-A	126	506	70	163	22	5	3	41	28	12	.322	.364	.403	767	106	4	10	12	-2	.971	8	*O-123(115-0-8)	0.4
1921	Was-A	113	406	55	117	19	11	1	40	37	13	.288	.351	.397	747	95	-3	4	5	-1	.931	2	O-99(34-15-52)	-0.9
1922	Was-A	42	74	8	17	5	0	0	5	2	2	.230	.250	.297	547	44	-6	0	0	0	1.000	1	O-12(3-0-9),M	-0.6
Total	16	1982	7359	1004	2100	240	105	17	617	685	197	.285	.353	.353	706	109	93	495	78		.953	58	*O-1903(182-1635-88)	3.1

YEAR	TM/L	G	AB	R	H	2B	3B	HR	RBI	BB	SO	AVG	OBP	SLG	OPS	OPS+	BR+	SB	CS	SBR	FA	FR	G/POS	TPR
■ LARRY MILBOURNE	Milbourne, Lawrence William b: 2/14/51, Port Norris, N.J. BB/TR, 6′, 165 lbs. Deb: 4/6/74 Career OF: (4-LF 0-CF 0-RF)																							
1974	Hou-N	112	136	31	38	2	1	0	9	10	14	.279	.329	.309	638	83	-3	6	2	1	.974	17	2-87/S-8,O-4(4-0-0)	1.7
1975	Hou-N	73	151	17	32	1	2	1	9	6	14	.212	.247	.265	512	45	-12	1	2	-0	.968	10	2-43,S-22	0.1
1976	Hou-N	59	145	22	36	4	0	0	7	14	10	.248	.319	.276	595	77	-4	6	1	1	.965	-1	2-32	-0.2
1977	Sea-A	86	242	24	53	10	0	2	21	6	20	.219	.244	.285	529	44	-19	3	1	0	.982	4	2-41,S-40/3-1,D-1	-1.0
1978	Sea-A	93	234	31	53	6	2	2	20	9	6	.226	.255	.295	550	55	-14	5	7	-1	.989	16	3-32,S-23,2-15,D-10	0.1
1979	Sea-A	123	356	40	99	13	4	2	26	19	20	.278	.315	.354	669	79	-11	5	3	0	.981	-17	S-65,2-49,3-11	-2.1
1980	Sea-A	106	258	31	68	6	6	0	26	19	13	.264	.317	.333	650	78	-8	7	6	-1	.976	0	2-38,S-34/3-6,D-8	-0.3
1981	*NY-A	61	163	24	51	7	2	1	12	9	14	.313	.353	.399	751	118	4	2	0	0	.955	-7	S-39,2-14/3-3,D-3	-0.1
1982	NY-A	14	27	2	4	1	0	0	0	1	4	.148	.179	.185	364	0	-4	0	1	-0	.917	1	/S-9,2-3,3-3	-0.3
	Min-A	29	98	9	23	1	1	0	1	7	8	.235	.286	.265	551	51	-6	1	1	-0	.981	-10	2-26	-1.6
	Cle-A	82	291	29	80	11	4	2	25	12	20	.275	.308	.361	669	83	-7	2	5	-1	.981	-6	2-63,S-21/3-9,D-1	-1.0
	Yr	125	416	40	107	13	5	2	26	20	32	.257	.295	.327	621	70	-17	3	7	-2	.979	-15	2-92,S-30,3-12,/D-1	-2.9
1983	Phi-N	41	66	3	16	0	1	0	4	4	7	.242	.286	.273	558	56	-4	2	1	0	.963	1	2-27/S-8,3-3	-0.2
	NY-A	31	70	5	14	4	0	0	2	5	10	.200	.263	.257	520	46	-5	1	1	-0	1.000	3	2-19/S-6,3-4	-0.1
1984	Sea-A	79	211	22	56	5	1	1	22	12	16	.265	.305	.313	618	72	-8	0	2	-1	.900	-9	3-40,2-14/S-5,D-6	-1.8
Total	11	989	2448	290	623	71	24	11	184	133	176	.254	.295	.317	612	70	-101	41	33	-3	.974	1	2-471,S-280,3/DO	-6.6
■ DON MILES	Miles, Donald Ray b: 3/13/36, Indianapolis, Ind. BL/TR, 6′1″, 210 lbs. Deb: 9/9/58																							
1958	LA-N	8	22	2	4	0	0	0	0	0	6	.182	.217	.182	399	7	-3	0	0	0	1.000	2	/O-5(5-0-0)	-0.2
■ DEE MILES	Miles, Wilson Daniel b: 2/15/09, Kellerman, Ala. d: 11/2/76, Birmingham, Ala. BL/TR, 6′, 175 lbs. Deb: 7/7/35																							
1935	Was-A	60	215	28	57	5	2	0	29	7	13	.265	.291	.307	598	57	-14	6	4	-0	.970	2	O-45(0-0-45)	-1.4
1936	Was-A	25	59	8	14	1	2	0	7	1	5	.237	.250	.322	572	43	-6	0	1	-0	.958	0	O-10(1-0-9)	-0.6
1939	Phi-A	106	320	49	96	17	6	1	37	15	17	.300	.331	.400	731	88	-7	3	4	-1	.968	-7	O-77(1-20-57)	-1.7
1940	Phi-A	88	236	26	71	9	6	1	23	8	18	.301	.327	.403	729	90	-4	1	1	-0	.945	-1	O-50(15-18-18)	-0.7
1941	Phi-A	80	170	14	53	7	1	0	15	4	8	.312	.331	.365	696	86	-4	0	1	-0	1.000	0	O-35(25-2-8)	-0.6
1942	Phi-A	99	346	41	94	12	5	0	22	12	10	.272	.300	.335	635	79	-11	5	3	0	.984	-3	O-81(9-46-28)	-1.7
1943	Bos-A	45	121	9	26	2	2	0	10	3	3	.215	.234	.264	498	45	-9	0	2	-1	.968	-1	O-25(1-24-0)	-1.2
Total	7	503	1467	175	411	53	24	2	143	50	74	.280	.306	.353	659	76	-53	15	16	-2	.971	-10	O-323(52-110-165)	-7.9
■ MIKE MILEY	Miley, Michael Wilfred b: 3/30/53, Yazoo City, Miss. d: 1/6/77, Baton Rouge, La. BB/TR (BR 1975 (part)), 6′1″, 185 lbs. Deb: 7/6/75																							
1975	Cal-A	70	224	17	39	3	2	4	26	16	54	.174	.232	.259	491	42	-18	0	1	-0	.939	-9	S-70	-1.9
1976	Cal-A	14	38	4	7	2	0	0	4	4	8	.184	.262	.237	499	50	-2	1	0	0	.981	-2	S-14	-0.2
Total	2	84	262	21	46	5	2	4	30	20	62	.176	.237	.256	492	43	-20	1	1	-0	.945	-11	/S-84	-2.1
■ FELIX MILLAN	Millan, Felix Bernardo (Martinez) b: 8/21/43, Yabucoa, P.R. BR/TR, 5′11″, 172 lbs. Deb: 6/2/66																							
1966	Atl-N	37	91	20	25	6	0	0	5	2	6	.275	.290	.341	631	74	-3	3	1	0	.973	-2	2-25/S-1,3-1	-0.3
1967	Atl-N	41	136	13	32	3	3	2	6	4	10	.235	.268	.346	613	75	-5	0	3	-1	.972	3	2-41	0.1
1968	Atl-N	149	570	49	165	22	2	1	33	22	26	.289	.323	.340	663	99	-1	6	6	-1	.980	3	*2-145	1.6
1969	*Atl-N★	162	652	98	174	23	5	6	57	34	35	.267	.311	.345	656	83	-15	14	3	2	**.980**	-16	*2-162	-1.9
1970	Atl-N†	142	590	100	183	25	5	2	37	35	23	.310	.354	.380	734	91	-7	16	5	2	.979	-19	*2-142	-1.4
1971	Atl-N★	143	577	65	167	20	8	2	45	37	22	.289	.335	.362	698	92	-6	11	7	-0	.982	6	*2-141	1.0
1972	Atl-N	125	498	46	128	19	3	1	38	23	28	.257	.294	.313	607	66	-21	6	4	-0	.987	-16	*2-120	-3.2
1973	*NY-N	153	638	82	185	23	4	3	37	35	22	.290	.333	.353	686	91	-7	2	2	-0	.989	-4	*2-153	-0.1
1974	NY-N	136	518	50	139	15	2	1	33	31	14	.268	.320	.311	630	78	-15	5	1	1	.979	-20	*2-134	-2.6
1975	NY-N	162	676	81	191	37	2	1	56	36	28	.283	.330	.348	678	92	-8	1	6	-2	.972	-25	*2-162	-2.4
1976	NY-N	139	531	55	150	25	2	1	35	41	19	.282	.342	.343	685	101	1	2	4	-1	.977	-24	*2-136	-1.6
1977	NY-N	91	314	40	78	11	2	2	21	18	9	.248	.296	.315	611	67	-15	1	1	-0	.977	-16	2-89	-2.7
Total	12	1480	5791	699	1617	229	38	22	403	318	242	.279	.324	.343	667	87	-101	67	43	-0	.980	-129	*2-1450/3-1,S-1	-13.5
■ KEVIN MILLAR	Millar, Kevin Charles b: 9/24/71, Los Angeles, Cal. BR/TR, 6′1″, 195 lbs. Deb: 4/11/98 Career OF: (18-LF 0-CF 1-RF)																							
1998	Fla-N	2	2	1	1	0	0	0	0	1	0	.500	.667	.500	1167	224	1	0	0	0	.833	1	/3-2	0.1
1999	Fla-N	105	351	48	100	17	4	9	67	40	64	.285	.369	.433	802	108	5	1	0	0	.995	-2	1-94/3-1,O-1(1-0-0)	-0.5
2000	Fla-N	123	259	36	67	14	3	14	42	36	47	.259	.366	.498	864	122	9	0	0	0	.989	4	1-34,O-18L,3-13,/D	0.9
Total	3	230	612	85	168	31	7	23	109	77	111	.275	.369	.461	830	114	14	1	0	0	.993	3	1-128/O-19L,3-16,D	0.5
■ FRANK MILLARD	Millard, Frank E. b: 7/4/1865, E.St.Louis, Ill. d: 7/4/1892, Galveston, Tex. Deb: 5/4/1890																							
1890	StL-a	1	1	0	0	0	0	0	0	1		.000	.500	.000	500	42	0	0			.625	1	/2-1	0.0
■ DUSTY MILLER	Miller, Charles Bradley b: 9/10/1868, Oil City, Pa. d: 9/3/45, Memphis, Tenn. BL/TR, 5′11.5″, 170 lbs. Deb: 9/23/1889																							
1889	Bal-a	11	40	4	6	1	1	0	6	2	11	.150	.209	.225	434	23	-4	3			.636	-7	/S-8,O-3(2-1-0)	-1.0
1890	StL-a	26	96	17	21	5	3	1	10	8		.219	.279	.365	643	78	-4	4			.872	3	O-24(9-15-0)/S-3	-0.1
1895	Cin-N	132	529	103	177	31	16	10	112	33	34	.335	.378	.510	888	123	14	43			.937	11	*O-132(0-11-121)	1.5
1896	Cin-N	125	504	91	162	38	12	4	93	33	30	.321	.368	.468	836	112	6	76			.902	-2	*O-125(1-0-124)	-0.2
1897	Cin-N	119	440	83	139	27	1	4	70	48		.316	.393	.409	802	105	4	29			.929	2	*O-119(0-0-119)	0.0
1898	Cin-N	152	586	99	175	24	12	3	90	38		.299	.351	.396	747	106	3	32			.929	8	*O-152(0-0-152)	0.4
1899	Cin-N	81	327	45	83	12	6	0	37	9		.254	.280	.327	607	65	-17	18			.927	6	O-81(1-2-79)	-1.3
	StL-N	10	39	3	8	1	0	0	3	3		.205	.279	.231	510	39	-3	1			.875	-1	O-10(0-10-0)	-0.4
	Yr	91	366	48	91	13	6	0	40	12		.249	.280	.317	597	62	-20	19			.921	6	O-91(1-12-79)	-1.7
Total	7	656	2561	445	771	139	51	22	421	174	75	.301	.353	.421	774	103	-0	206			.923	20	O-646(13-39-595)/S-11	-1.1
■ BRUCE MILLER	Miller, Charles Bruce b: 3/4/47, Fort Wayne, Ind. BR/TR, 6′1″, 185 lbs. Deb: 8/4/73																							
1973	SF-N	12	21	1	3	0	0	0	2	2	3	.143	.217	.143	360	2	-3	0	0	0	.900	1	/3-4,2-3,S-1	-0.2
1974	SF-N	73	198	19	55	7	1	0	16	11	15	.278	.319	.323	642	76	-6	1	1	-0	.938	13	3-41,S-13/2-9	0.8
1975	SF-N	99	309	22	74	6	3	1	31	15	26	.239	.277	.288	565	55	-19	0	1	-0	.949	10	3-68,2-21/S-6	-0.9
1976	SF-N	12	25	1	4	1	0	0	2	2	5	.160	.222	.200	422	20	-3	0	0	0	.920	-1	/2-8,3-2	-0.4
Total	4	196	553	43	136	14	4	1	51	30	49	.246	.287	.291	578	59	-30	1	2	-0	.944	22	3-115/2-41,S-20	-0.7
■ CHARLIE MILLER	Miller, Charles Elmer b: 1/4/1892, Warrensburg, Mo. d: 4/23/72, Warrensburg, Mo. TR, Deb: 9/18/12																							
1912	StL-A	1	2	0	0	0	0	0	0	0		.000	.000	.000	0	-99	-1	0			1.000	-0	/S-1	-0.1
■ CHARLIE MILLER	Miller, Charles Hess b: 12/30/1877, Conestoga, Pa. d: 1/13/51, Millersville, Pa. BR/TR, 6′, 190 lbs. Deb: 10/2/15																							
1915	Bal-F	1	1	0	0	0	0	0	0	0	0	.000	.000	.000	0	-97	-0	0			.000	0	H	0.0
■ CHUCK MILLER	Miller, Charles Marion b: 9/18/1889, Woodville, Ohio d: 6/16/61, Houston, Tex. BL/TL, 5′8.5″, 155 lbs. Deb: 9/19/13																							
1913	StL-N	4	12	0	2	0	0	0	1	0	2	.167	.167	.167	333	-5	-2	0			1.000	-1	/O-3(2-0-1)	-0.3
1914	StL-N	36	36	4	7	1	0	0	2	3	9	.194	.256	.222	479	43	-2	2			1.000	-3	O-14(6-5-2)	-0.6
Total	2	40	48	4	9	1	0	0	3	3	11	.188	.235	.208	444	31	-4	2			1.000	-4	/O-17(8-5-3)	-0.9
■ DUSTY MILLER	Miller, Dakin Evans b: 9/3/1876, Malvern, Iowa d: 4/19/50, Stockton, Cal. BL/TR, 5′10″, 175 lbs. Deb: 4/17/02																							
1902	Chi-N	51	187	17	46	4	1	0	13	7		.246	.299	.278	577	80	-4	10			.955	1	O-51(46-1-4)	-0.6
■ DAMIAN MILLER	Miller, Damian Donald b: 10/13/69, LaCrosse, Wis. BR/TR, 6′3″, 202 lbs. Deb: 8/10/97																							
1997	Min-A	25	66	5	18	1	0	2	13	2	12	.273	.294	.379	673	73	-3	0	0	0	1.000	-1	C-20/D-3	-0.3
1998	Ari-N	57	168	17	48	14	2	3	14	11	43	.286	.337	.446	783	104	1	1	0	0	.986	2	C-46/O-2R,1-1,D-2	0.5
1999	Ari-N	86	296	35	80	19	0	11	47	19	78	.270	.319	.446	765	90	-5	0	0	0	.991	17	C-86	1.6
2000	Ari-N	100	324	43	89	24	0	10	44	36	74	.275	.349	.441	790	97	-2	2	2	-0	.992	-3	C-97/1-2,S-1	0.1
Total	4	268	854	100	235	58	2	26	118	68	207	.275	.332	.439	771	94	-9	3	2	-0	.991	15	C-249/D-5,1-3,OS	1.9
■ DARRELL MILLER	Miller, Darrell Keith b: 2/26/58, Washington, D.C. BR/TR, 6′2″, 200 lbs. Deb: 8/14/84 Career OF: (34-LF 8-CF 54-RF)																							
1984	Cal-A	17	41	5	7	0	0	0	1	4	9	.171	.244	.171	415	17	-5	0	0	0	.990	-1	1-16/O-1(1-0-0)	-0.6

YEAR	TM/L	G	AB	R	H	2B	3B	HR	RBI	BB	SO	AVG	OBP	SLG	OPS	OPS+	BR+	SB	CS	SBR	FA	FR	G/POS	TPR
1985	Cal-A	51	48	8	18	2	1	2	7	1	10	.375	.400	.583	983	166	4	0	1	-0	.952	-11	O-45R/C-1,3-1,D-4	-0.7
1986	Cal-A	33	57	6	13	2	1	0	4	4	8	.228	.279	.298	577	58	-3	0	0	0	1.000	-10	O-23(11-3-9),C-10/D-2	-1.4
1987	Cal-A	53	108	14	26	5	0	4	16	9	13	.241	.311	.398	709	89	-2	1	0	0	.984	-6	C-33,O-18L/3-1,D-1	-0.7
1988	Cal-A	70	140	21	31	4	1	2	7	9	29	.221	.292	.307	599	70	-6	2	1	0	.987	3	C-53/O-8(7-2-0),D-1	-0.1
Total	5	224	394	54	95	13	3	8	35	27	69	.241	.303	.350	653	80	-11	3	2	-0	.987	-25	/C-97,O-95R,1-16,D3	-3.5

■ BING MILLER Miller, Edmund John b: 8/30/1894, Vinton, Iowa d: 5/7/66, Philadelphia, Pa. BR/TR, 6', 185 lbs. Deb: 4/16/21 FC Career OF: (380-LF 242-CF 997-RF)

YEAR	TM/L	G	AB	R	H	2B	3B	HR	RBI	BB	SO	AVG	OBP	SLG	OPS	OPS+	BR+	SB	CS	SBR	FA	FR	G/POS	TPR
1921	Was-A	114	420	57	121	28	8	9	71	25	50	.288	.334	.457	791	105	1	3	4	-1	.945	2	*O-109(92-3-14)	-0.6
1922	Phi-A	143	535	90	179	29	12	21	90	24	42	.335	.371	.551	922	134	24	10	10	-1	.977	5	*O-139(15-90-36)	1.8
1923	Phi-A	123	458	68	137	25	4	12	64	27	34	.299	.344	.450	793	106	2	9	3	1	.978	-1	*O-119(104-0-15)	-0.7
1924	Phi-A	113	398	62	136	22	4	6	62	12	24	.342	.376	.462	839	114	7	11	5	1	.973	-2	O-94(10-9-75)/1-7	-0.1
1925	Phi-A	124	474	78	151	29	10	10	81	19	14	.319	.355	.485	841	105	1	11	6	0	.975	-10	*O-115(22-0-96),1-12	-1.7
1926	Phi-A	38	110	13	32	6	2	2	13	11	6	.291	.355	.436	792	100	-0	4	1	1	1.000	-5	O-34(10-0-26)/1-1	-0.7
	StL-A	94	353	60	117	27	5	4	50	22	12	.331	.382	.470	852	116	8	7	9	-2	.939	4	O-94(26-16-54)	0.3
	Yr	132	463	73	149	33	7	6	63	33	18	.322	.376	.462	838	112	7	11	10	-1	.950	-1	*O-128(36-16-80)/1-1	-0.4
1927	StL-A	143	492	83	160	32	7	5	75	30	26	.325	.375	.449	824	109	6	8	7	-1	.970	4	*O-126(37-61-29)	0.2
1928	Phi-A	139	510	76	168	34	7	8	85	27	24	.329	.372	.471	843	117	12	10	6	0	.968	0	*O-133(28-43-66)	0.3
1929	*Phi-A	147	556	84	184	32	16	8	93	40	25	.331	.380	.489	869	118	14	24	9	2	.970	6	*O-145(9-4-133)	1.0
1930	*Phi-A	154	585	89	177	38	7	9	100	47	22	.303	.357	.438	795	96	-4	13	13	-2	.976	5	*O-154(0-13-142)	-1.1
1931	*Phi-A	137	534	75	150	43	5	8	77	36	16	.281	.338	.425	763	94	-6	5	3	0	.987	6	*O-137(0-0-137)	-0.8
1932	Phi-A	95	305	40	90	17	4	7	58	20	11	.295	.343	.446	788	99	-1	7	3	0	.979	1	O-84(5-0-79)	-0.4
1933	Phi-A	67	120	22	33	7	1	2	17	12	7	.275	.346	.400	746	96	-1	4	2	0	1.000	-6	O-30(10-3-18)/1-6	-0.8
1934	Phi-A	81	177	22	43	10	2	1	22	16	14	.243	.309	.339	648	70	-8	1	0	0	1.000	-3	O-46(4-0-42)	-1.3
1935	Bos-A	78	138	18	42	8	1	3	26	10	8	.304	.356	.442	798	99	-1	0	1	-0	.962	-2	O-29(1-0-28)	-0.4
1936	Bos-A	30	47	9	14	2	1	1	6	5	5	.298	.377	.447	824	97	-0	0	0	0	1.000	-3	O-13(7-0-7)	-0.3
Total	16	1820	6212	946	1934	389	96	116	990	383	340	.311	.359	.461	820	108	54	127	82	-1	.971	2	*O-1601R/1-26	-5.3

■ EDDIE MILLER Miller, Edward Lee b: 6/29/57, San Pablo, Cal. BB/TR, 5'9", 175 lbs. Deb: 9/5/77

YEAR	TM/L	G	AB	R	H	2B	3B	HR	RBI	BB	SO	AVG	OBP	SLG	OPS	OPS+	BR+	SB	CS	SBR	FA	FR	G/POS	TPR
1977	Tex-A	17	6	7	2	0	0	0	1	1	1	.333	.429	.333	762	110	0	3	1	0	1.000	-0	/O-2(0-2-0),D-3	0.0
1978	Atl-N	6	21	5	3	1	0	0	2	2	4	.143	.250	.190	440	22	-2	3	0	1	1.000	-1	/O-5(2-3-0)	-0.3
1979	Atl-N	27	113	12	35	1	0	0	5	5	24	.310	.350	.319	669	78	-3	15	2	3	.988	3	O-27(1-27-0)	0.2
1980	Atl-N	11	19	3	3	0	0	0	0	0	5	.158	.158	.158	316	-11	-3	1	2	-0	1.000	-3	/O-9(1-8-0)	-0.7
1981	Atl-N	50	134	29	31	3	1	0	7	7	29	.231	.285	.269	553	56	-8	23	5	3	.985	-1	O-36(28-2-7)	-0.8
1982	Det-A	14	25	3	1	0	0	0	0	4	4	.040	.250	.040	290	-14	-4	0	3	-1	1.000	-0	/O-8(0-3-5),D-1	-0.6
1984	SD-N	13	14	4	4	0	1	1	2	0	4	.286	.286	.643	929	155	1	4	0	1	1.000	-1	/O-8(0-4-4)	0.1
Total	7	138	332	63	79	5	2	1	17	19	71	.238	.297	.274	571	57	-18	49	13	6	.989	-4	/O-95(32-49-16),D-4	-2.1

■ EDDIE MILLER Miller, Edward Robert "Eppie" b: 11/26/16, Pittsburgh, Pa. d: 7/31/97, Lake Worth, Fla. BR/TR, 5'9", 180 lbs. Deb: 9/9/36

YEAR	TM/L	G	AB	R	H	2B	3B	HR	RBI	BB	SO	AVG	OBP	SLG	OPS	OPS+	BR+	SB	CS	SBR	FA	FR	G/POS	TPR
1936	Cin-N	5	10	0	1	0	0	0	0	1	1	.100	.182	.100	282	-24	-2	0			.938	-0	/S-4,2-1	-0.2
1937	Cin-N	36	60	3	9	3	1	0	5	3	8	.150	.190	.233	424	15	-7	0			.926	7	S-30/3-4	0.1
1939	Bos-N	77	296	32	79	12	2	4	31	16	21	.267	.315	.361	677	88	-6	4			.970	12	S-77	1.2
1940	Bos-N★	151	569	78	157	33	3	14	79	41	43	.276	.330	.418	748	111	7	8			**.970**	15	*S-151	3.3
1941	Bos-N★	154	585	54	140	27	3	6	68	35	72	.239	.288	.326	614	76	-20	8			**.966**	12	*S-154	0.4
1942	Bos-N★	142	534	47	130	28	2	6	47	22	42	.243	.279	.337	616	81	-15	11			**.983**	4	*S-142	0.0
1943	Cin-N★	154	576	49	129	26	4	2	71	33	43	.224	.271	.293	564	64	-28	8			**.979**	**27**	*S-154	1.2
1944	Cin-N†	155	536	48	112	21	5	4	55	41	41	.209	.269	.289	558	59	-30	9			.971	12	*S-155	-0.5
1945	Cin-N	115	421	46	100	27	2	13	49	18	38	.238	.275	.404	679	89	-9	4			**.975**	5	*S-115	0.5
1946	Cin-N†	91	299	30	58	10	0	6	36	25	34	.194	.258	.288	546	57	-18	5			.970	24	S-88	1.1
1947	Cin-N†	151	545	69	146	**38**	4	19	87	49	40	.268	.333	.457	790	109	5	5			.972	-5	*S-151	0.9
1948	Phi-N	130	468	45	115	20	1	14	61	19	40	.246	.281	.382	664	79	-15	1			.966	-14	*S-122	-2.2
1949	Phi-N	85	266	21	55	10	1	6	29	29	21	.207	.294	.320	614	66	-13	1			.986	-10	2-82/S-1	-1.9
1950	StL-N	64	172	17	39	8	0	3	22	19	21	.227	.307	.326	633	64	-9	0			.980	14	S-51/2-1	0.7
Total	14	1510	5337	539	1270	263	28	97	640	351	465	.238	.290	.352	643	80	-159	64			.972	102	*S-1395/2-84,3-4	4.6

■ ED MILLER Miller, Edwin J. "Big Ed" b: 11/24/1888, Annville, Pa. d: 4/17/80, S.Lebanon Twsp, Pa BR/TR, 6', 180 lbs. Deb: 6/29/12 Career OF: (1-LF 0-CF 8-RF)

YEAR	TM/L	G	AB	R	H	2B	3B	HR	RBI	BB	SO	AVG	OBP	SLG	OPS	OPS+	BR+	SB	CS	SBR	FA	FR	G/POS	TPR
1912	StL-A	13	46	4	9	1	0	0	5	2		.196	.245	.217	462	34	-4	1			.951	-4	/1-8,S-5	-0.8
1914	StL-A	41	58	8	8	0	1	0	4	4	13	.138	.219	.172	391	18	-6	1	3	-1	.981	-2	/1-8,2-5,O-5R,3-2	-0.9
1918	Cle-A	32	96	9	22	4	3	0	3	12	10	.229	.321	.333	654	89	-1	2			.977	1	1-22/O-4(1-0-3)	-0.1
Total	3	86	200	21	39	5	4	0	12	18	23	.195	.275	.260	535	58	-11	4	3		.972	-5	/1-38,O-9R,2-5,S3	-1.8

■ ELMER MILLER Miller, Elmer b: 7/28/1890, Sandusky, Ohio d: 11/28/44, Beloit, Wis. BR/TR, 6', 175 lbs. Deb: 4/26/12

YEAR	TM/L	G	AB	R	H	2B	3B	HR	RBI	BB	SO	AVG	OBP	SLG	OPS	OPS+	BR+	SB	CS	SBR	FA	FR	G/POS	TPR
1912	StL-N	12	37	5	7	1	0	0	3	4	9	.189	.268	.216	485	34	-3	1			1.000	0	O-11(4-3-4)	-0.4
1915	NY-A	26	83	4	12	1	0	0	3	4	14	.145	.193	.157	350	5	-10	0			.955	-4	O-26(0-20-6)	-1.7
1916	NY-A	43	152	12	34	3	2	1	18	11	18	.224	.280	.289	570	70	-6	8			.969	5	O-42(18-9-15)	-0.4
1917	NY-A	114	379	43	95	11	3	3	35	40	44	.251	.336	.319	656	99	1	11			.961	-6	*O-112(33-53-26)	-1.3
1918	NY-A	67	202	18	49	9	2	1	22	19	17	.243	.317	.322	639	91	-2	2			.947	4	O-62(3-53-6)	-0.2
1921	*NY-A	56	242	41	72	9	8	4	36	19	16	.298	.356	.450	806	102	0	2	2	-0	.947	3	O-56(0-56-0)	0.1
1922	NY-A	51	172	31	46	7	2	3	18	11	12	.267	.311	.384	695	79	-6	2	3	-1	.982	-2	O-51(7-41-3)	-1.0
	Bos-A	44	147	16	28	2	3	4	16	5	10	.190	.222	.327	549	42	-13	3	1	0	.957	-0	O-35(2-33-0)	-1.5
	Yr	95	319	47	74	9	5	7	34	16	22	.232	.271	.357	628	62	-19	5	4	-0	.970	-2	O-86(9-74-3)	-2.5
Total	7	413	1414	170	343	43	20	16	151	113	140	.243	.307	.335	642	80	-40	29	6		.960	-0	O-395(67-268-60)	-6.4

■ ELMER MILLER Miller, Elmer Joseph "Lefty" b: 4/17/03, Detroit, Mich. d: 1/8/87, Corona, Cal. BL/TL, 5'11", 189 lbs. Deb: 6/21/29

YEAR	TM/L	G	AB	R	H	2B	3B	HR	RBI	BB	SO	AVG	OBP	SLG	OPS	OPS+	BR+	SB	CS	SBR	FA	FR	G/POS	TPR
1929	Phi-N	31	38	3	9	1	0	1	4	1	5	.237	.256	.342	599	44	-3	0			.750	2	/P-8,O-4(0-0-4)	-0.1

■ KOHLY MILLER Miller, Frank A. b: 1/1874, Cumru Township, Pa. d: 3/29/51, Reading, Pa. Deb: 9/16/1892

YEAR	TM/L	G	AB	R	H	2B	3B	HR	RBI	BB	SO	AVG	OBP	SLG	OPS	OPS+	BR+	SB	CS	SBR	FA	FR	G/POS	TPR
1892	Was-N	1	3	0	0	0	0	0	0	0	1	.000	.000	.000	0	-99	-1	0			.400	-1	/S-1	-0.2
	StL-N	1	4	0	0	0	0	0	0	0	0	.000	.000	.000	0	-99	-1	0			.500	-1	/3-1	-0.2
	Yr	2	7	0	0	0	0	0	0	0	1	.000	.000	.000	0	-99	-2	0			.400	-2	/S-1,3-1	-0.4
1897	Phi-N	3	11	2	2	0	0	0	1	2		.182	.308	.182	490	32	-1	0			.857	-2	/2-3	-0.3
Total	2	5	18	2	2	0	0	0	1	2	1	.111	.200	.111	311	-13	-3	0			.857	-5	/2-3,3-1,S-1	-0.7

■ GEORGE MILLER Miller, George C. b: 2/19/1853, Newport, Ky. d: 7/24/29, Norwood, Ohio BR/TR, 5'5", 160 lbs. Deb: 9/6/1877

YEAR	TM/L	G	AB	R	H	2B	3B	HR	RBI	BB	SO	AVG	OBP	SLG	OPS	OPS+	BR+	SB	CS	SBR	FA	FR	G/POS	TPR
1877	Cin-N	11	37	4	6	1	0	0	3	5	2	.162	.262	.189	451	50	-2				.918	0	C-11	-0.1
1884	Cin-a	6	20	6	5	1	1	0	3	1		.250	.318	.400	718	127	1				.975	2	/C-6	0.3
Total	2	17	57	10	11	2	1	0	6	6	2	.193	.281	.263	544	79	-1				.938	2	/C-17	0.2

■ DOGGIE MILLER Miller, George Frederick "Foghorn" or "Calliope" b: 8/15/1864, Brooklyn, N.Y. d: 4/6/09, Brooklyn, N.Y. BR/TR, 5'6", 145 lbs. Deb: 5/1/1884 M Career OF: (146-LF 68-CF 96-RF)

YEAR	TM/L	G	AB	R	H	2B	3B	HR	RBI	BB	SO	AVG	OBP	SLG	OPS	OPS+	BR+	SB	CS	SBR	FA	FR	G/POS	TPR
1884	Pit-a	89	347	46	78	10	2	0		13		.225	.257	.265	522	71	-10				.798	-5	O-49L,C-36/3-3,2-1	-1.3
1885	Pit-a	42	166	19	27	3	1	0	13	4		.163	.182	.193	375	19	-15				.893	-5	C-33/O-6L,S-2,3-2	-1.5
1886	Pit-a	83	317	70	80	15	1	2	36	43		.252	.343	.325	668	110	5	35			.918	-22	C-61,O-23L/2-1	-1.0
1887	Pit-N	87	377	58	118	17	4	1	34	35	13	.313	.317	.325	641	83	-6	33			.928	-22	C-73,O-14(2-11-1)/3-1	-1.9
1888	Pit-N	103	404	50	112	17	5	0	36	18	16	.277	.319	.344	663	121	10	27			.908	-15	C-68,O-32(25-5-2)/3-4	0.0
1889	Pit-N	104	422	77	113	25	3	6	56	31	11	.268	.321	.384	705	107	4	16			.889	-5	C-76,O-27(6-5-16)/3-3	0.4
1890	Pit-N	138	549	85	150	24	3	4	66	68	11	.273	.357	.350	707	120	18	32			.850	1	3-88,O-25R,S-13,C/2	1.9
1891	Pit-N	135	548	80	156	19	6	4	57	59	26	.285	.357	.363	721	113	10	35			.938	-16	C-41,S-37,3-34,O/1	-0.1
1892	Pit-N	149	623	103	158	15	12	2	59	69	14	.254	.335	.326	661	99	1	28			.906	-11	O-76C,C-63,S-19,/3	-0.8
1893	Pit-N	41	154	23	28	6	1	0	17	17	8	.182	.284	.234	518	39	-13	3			.916	-0	C-40	-0.8
1894	StL-N	127	481	93	163	9	11	8	86	58	9	.339	.414	.453	868	109	9	17			.832	-14	3-52,C-41,2-18,1/OSM	0.0
1895	StL-N	122	494	81	144	15	4	5	74	25	12	.291	.333	.368	702	82	-14	18			.829	-22	3-46,C-47,O-21R,/S1	-2.6

YEAR	TM/L	G	AB	R	H	2B	3B	HR	RBI	BB	SO	AVG	OBP	SLG	OPS	OPS+	BR+	SB	CS	SBR	FA	FR	G/POS	TPR
1896	Lou-N	98	324	54	89	17	4	1	33	27	9	.275	.334	.361	695	87	-6	16			.922	-16	C-48,2-25/O-8R,31S	-1.5
Total	13	1318	5206	839	1416	192	57	33	567	467	129	.272	.333	.345	678	97	-8	260			.918	-152	C-637,O-309L,3/S21	-9.2

■ **HUGHIE MILLER** Miller, Hugh Stanley "Cotton" b: 12/28/1887, St.Louis, Mo. d: 12/24/45, Jefferson Barracks, Mo. BR/TR, 6'1.5", 175 lbs. Deb: 6/18/11

YEAR	TM/L	G	AB	R	H	2B	3B	HR	RBI	BB	SO	AVG	OBP	SLG	OPS	OPS+	BR+	SB	CS	SBR	FA	FR	G/POS	TPR
1911	Phi-N	1	0	0	0	0	0	0	0	0	0	—	—	—		—	0	0			.000	0	R	0.0
1914	StL-F	132	490	51	109	20	5	0	46	27	57	.222	.264	.284	548	47	-44	4			.990	0	*1-130	-5.0
1915	StL-F	7	6	0	3	1	0	0	3	0	0	.500	.500	.667	1167	216	1	0			1.000	-0	/1-6	0.1
Total	3	140	496	51	112	21	5	0	49	27	57	.226	.267	.288	555	49	-43	4			.990	-0	1-136	-4.9

■ **JAKE MILLER** Miller, Jacob George (b: Jacob George Munzing) b: 12/1/1895, Baltimore, Md. d: 8/24/74, Towson, Md. BR/TR, 5'10", 170 lbs. Deb: 7/16/22

YEAR	TM/L	G	AB	R	H	2B	3B	HR	RBI	BB	SO	AVG	OBP	SLG	OPS	OPS+	BR+	SB	CS	SBR	FA	FR	G/POS	TPR
1922	Pit-N	3	11	0	1	0	0	0	0	2	0	.091	.231	.091	322	-14	-2	1	0	0	.889	0	/O-3(0-0-3)	-0.2

■ **HACK MILLER** Miller, James Eldridge b: 2/13/13, Celeste, Tex. d: 11/21/66, Dallas, Tex. BR/TR, 5'11.5", 215 lbs. Deb: 4/18/44

YEAR	TM/L	G	AB	R	H	2B	3B	HR	RBI	BB	SO	AVG	OBP	SLG	OPS	OPS+	BR+	SB	CS	SBR	FA	FR	G/POS	TPR
1944	Det-A	5	5	1	1	0	0	1	3	1	1	.200	.333	.800	1133	207	1	0	0	0	1.000	0	/C-5	0.1
1945	Det-A	2	4	0	3	0	0	0	1	0	0	.750	.750	.750	1500	315	1	0	0	0	1.000	-0	/C-2	0.1
Total	2	7	9	1	4	0	0	1	4	1	1	.444	.500	.778	1278	250	2	0	0	0	1.000	-0	/C-7	0.2

■ **JIM MILLER** Miller, James McCurdy "Rabbit" b: 10/2/1880, Pittsburgh, Pa. d: 2/7/37, Pittsburgh, Pa. BR/TR, 5'8", 165 lbs. Deb: 9/9/01

YEAR	TM/L	G	AB	R	H	2B	3B	HR	RBI	BB	SO	AVG	OBP	SLG	OPS	OPS+	BR+	SB	CS	SBR	FA	FR	G/POS	TPR
1901	NY-N	18	58	3	8	0	0	0	3	6		.138	.219	.138	357	5	-7	1			.936	-2	2-18	-0.9

■ **JOHN MILLER** Miller, John Allen b: 3/14/44, Alhambra, Cal. BR/TR, 5'11", 195 lbs. Deb: 9/11/66 Career OF: (9-LF 0-CF 0-RF)

YEAR	TM/L	G	AB	R	H	2B	3B	HR	RBI	BB	SO	AVG	OBP	SLG	OPS	OPS+	BR+	SB	CS	SBR	FA	FR	G/POS	TPR
1966	NY-A	6	23	1	2	0	0	1	2	0	9	.087	.087	.217	304	-16	-3	0	0	0	1.000	-1	/1-3,O-3(3-0-0)	-0.5
1969	LA-N	26	38	3	8	1	0	1	1	2	9	.211	.250	.316	566	62	-2	0	0	0	1.000	-2	/O-6L,1-5,3-2,2-1	-0.5
Total	2	32	61	4	10	1	0	2	3	2	18	.164	.190	.279	469	33	-6	0	0	0	1.000	-3	/O-9L,1-8,3-2,2-1	-1.0

■ **DOTS MILLER** Miller, John Barney b: 9/9/1886, Kearny, N.J. d: 9/5/23, Saranac Lake, N.Y. BR/TR, 5'11.5", 170 lbs. Deb: 4/16/09 Career OF: (0-LF 1-CF 0-RF)

YEAR	TM/L	G	AB	R	H	2B	3B	HR	RBI	BB	SO	AVG	OBP	SLG	OPS	OPS+	BR+	SB	CS	SBR	FA	FR	G/POS	TPR
1909	*Pit-N	151	560	71	156	31	13	3	87	39		.279	.329	.396	725	115	8	14			**.953**	-11	*2-150	-0.2
1910	Pit-N	120	444	45	101	13	10	1	48	33	41	.227	.284	.309	592	69	-19	11			.946	-19	*2-119/1-1,S-1	-3.9
1911	Pit-N	137	470	82	126	17	8	6	78	51	48	.268	.348	.377	725	99	-1	17			.943	-6	*2-129	-0.5
1912	Pit-N	148	567	74	156	33	12	4	87	37	45	.275	.324	.397	721	98	-4	18			.985	1	*1-147	-0.7
1913	Pit-N	154	580	75	158	24	20	7	90	37	52	.272	.317	.419	736	114	8	20			.985	-4	*1-150/S-3	0.0
1914	StL-N	155	573	67	166	27	10	4	88	34	52	.290	.339	.393	732	119	12	16			.993	0	1-91,S-60/2-5	1.5
1915	StL-N	150	553	73	146	17	10	2	72	43	48	.264	.324	.342	666	101	1	27	19	-1	.991	4	1-94,2-55/3-9,S-3	0.3
1916	StL-N	143	505	47	120	22	7	1	46	40	49	.238	.300	.315	615	89	-6	18			.993	2	1-93,2-38,S-21,/3-1	-0.5
1917	StL-N	148	544	61	135	15	9	2	45	33	52	.248	.295	.320	615	91	-6	14			.960	19	2-92,1-46,S-11	1.5
1919	StL-N	101	346	38	80	10	4	1	24	13	23	.231	.265	.292	557	72	-13	6			.981	2	1-68,2-28	-1.4
1920	Phi-N	98	343	41	87	12	2	1	27	16	17	.254	.289	.309	598	68	-14	13	6	1	.948	-9	2-59,3-17,S-12,/1O	-2.2
1921	Phi-N	84	320	37	95	11	3	0	23	15	27	.297	.330	.350	680	74	-11	3	5	-1	.940	1	3-41,1-38/2-6	-1.1
Total	12	1589	5805	711	1526	232	108	32	715	391	454	.263	.314	.357	671	95	-45	177	30		.988	-21	1-737,2-681,S/3O	-7.2

■ **JOE MILLER** Miller, Joseph A. b: 2/17/1861, Baltimore, Md. d: 4/23/28, Wheeling, W.Va. BR, 5'9.5", 165 lbs. Deb: 5/1/1884

YEAR	TM/L	G	AB	R	H	2B	3B	HR	RBI	BB	SO	AVG	OBP	SLG	OPS	OPS+	BR+	SB	CS	SBR	FA	FR	G/POS	TPR
1884	Tol-a	105	423	46	101	12	8	1		26		.239	.284	.312	597	91	-4				.864	1	*S-105	0.0
1885	Lou-a	98	339	44	62	9	5	0	24	28		.183	.249	.239	488	55	-17				.891	3	*S-79,3-11/2-8	-1.0
Total	2	203	762	90	163	21	13	1	24	54		.214	.269	.280	548	75	-21				.876	4	S-184/3-11,2-8	-1.0

■ **JOE MILLER** Miller, Joseph Wick b: 7/24/1850, Germany d: 8/30/1891, White Bear Lake, Minn. 5'10.5", 169 lbs. Deb: 6/26/1872

YEAR	TM/L	G	AB	R	H	2B	3B	HR	RBI	BB	SO	AVG	OBP	SLG	OPS	OPS+	BR+	SB	CS	SBR	FA	FR	G/POS	TPR
1872	Nat-n	1	4	0	1	0	0	0	0	0	0	.250	.250	.250	500	46	-0	0	0	0	.923	-0	/1-1	0.0
1875	Wes-n	13	50	4	6	1	0	0	0	0	3	.120	.120	.140	260	-9	-5	0	0	0	.870	4	2-13	-0.2
	Chi-n	15	54	1	8	0	0	0	1	0	7	.148	.148	.148	296	3	-5	0	0	0	.788	-3	2-14/O-1(1-0-1)	-0.8
	Yr	28	104	5	14	1	0	0	1	0	10	.135	.135	.144	279	-3	-10	0	0	0	.832	1	2-27/O-1(1-0-1)	-1.0
Total	2 n	29	108	5	15	1	0	0	1	0	10	.139	.139	.148	287	-1	-11	0	0	0	.870	1	/2-27,O-1(1-0-1),1-1	-1.0

■ **KEITH MILLER** Miller, Keith Alan b: 6/12/63, Midland, Mich. BR/TR, 5'11", 185 lbs. Deb: 6/16/87 Career OF: (49-LF 65-CF 28-RF)

YEAR	TM/L	G	AB	R	H	2B	3B	HR	RBI	BB	SO	AVG	OBP	SLG	OPS	OPS+	BR+	SB	CS	SBR	FA	FR	G/POS	TPR
1987	NY-N	25	51	14	19	2	2	0	1	2	6	.373	.407	.490	898	144	3	8	1	1	.967	2	2-16	0.7
1988	NY-N	40	70	9	15	1	1	1	5	6	10	.214	.276	.300	576	69	-3	0	5	-2	.946	-7	2-16/S-8,3-6,O-1R	-1.2
1989	NY-N	57	143	15	33	7	0	1	7	5	27	.231	.262	.301	562	63	-7	6	0	1	.967	-4	2-23,O-14C/S-8,3-2	-0.9
1990	NY-N	88	233	42	60	8	0	1	12	23	46	.258	.329	.305	634	76	-7	16	3	2	.980	5	O-61(7-53-5),2-11/S-4	0.0
1991	NY-N	98	275	41	77	22	1	4	23	23	44	.280	.347	.411	757	113	5	14	4	2	.972	0	2-60,O-28R/3-2,S-2	0.8
1992	KC-A	106	416	57	118	24	4	4	38	31	46	.284	.354	.389	743	105	3	16	6	1	.971	-20	2-93,O-16(16-0-0)/D-1	-1.3
1993	KC-A	37	108	9	18	3	0	0	3	8	19	.167	.231	.194	425	15	-13	3	1	0	.889	-6	3-21/O-4L,2-3,D-6	-1.8
1994	KC-A	5	15	1	2	0	0	0	0	0	3	.133	.133	.133	267	-30	-3	0	0	0	1.000	1	/O-4(4-0-0),3-2	-0.2
1995	KC-A	9	15	2	5	0	0	1	3	2	4	.333	.412	.533	945	142	1	0	0	0	1.000	-0	/O-4(4-0-1),D-4	0.1
Total	9	465	1326	190	347	67	8	12	92	100	205	.262	.325	.351	676	88	-20	63	20	7	.969	-28	2-222,O-132C/3-33,SD	-3.8

■ **ED MILLER** Miller, L. Edward b: Tecumseh, Mich. Deb: 7/18/1884

YEAR	TM/L	G	AB	R	H	2B	3B	HR	RBI	BB	SO	AVG	OBP	SLG	OPS	OPS+	BR+	SB	CS	SBR	FA	FR	G/POS	TPR
1884	Tol-a	8	24	2	6	0	0	0	1	1		.250	.280	.250	530	72	-1				.615	-1	/O-8(6-1-2)	-0.1

■ **HACK MILLER** Miller, Laurence H. b: 1/1/1894, New York, N.Y. d: 9/16/71, Oakland, Cal. BR/TR, 5'9", 195 lbs. Deb: 9/22/16

YEAR	TM/L	G	AB	R	H	2B	3B	HR	RBI	BB	SO	AVG	OBP	SLG	OPS	OPS+	BR+	SB	CS	SBR	FA	FR	G/POS	TPR
1916	Bro-N	3	3	0	1	0	1	0	1	1	1	.333	.500	1.000	1500	345	1	0			1.000	-1	/O-3(0-2-1)	0.0
1918	*Bos-A	12	29	2	8	2	0	0	4	0	4	.276	.276	.345	621	89	-1	0			1.000	-3	O-10(9-1-0)	-0.4
1922	Chi-N	122	466	61	164	28	5	12	78	26	39	.352	.389	.511	899	128	18	3	3	-0	.959	-3	*O-116(115-0-2)	0.6
1923	Chi-N	135	485	74	146	24	2	20	88	27	39	.301	.343	.482	825	116	9	6	5	-0	.978	6	*O-129(129-0-0)	0.3
1924	Chi-N	53	131	17	44	8	1	4	25	8	11	.336	.379	.504	882	133	6	1	0	0	.948	-4	O-32(32-0-0)	-0.1
1925	Chi-N	24	86	10	24	3	2	2	9	2	9	.279	.303	.430	734	84	-2	0	1	-0	.878	-3	O-21(21-0-0)	-0.7
Total	6	349	1200	164	387	65	11	38	205	64	103	.322	.361	.490	851	120	31	10	9		.962	-8	O-311(306-3-3)	-0.3

■ **LEMMIE MILLER** Miller, Lemmie Earl b: 6/2/60, Dallas, Tex. BR/TR, 6'1", 190 lbs. Deb: 5/22/84

YEAR	TM/L	G	AB	R	H	2B	3B	HR	RBI	BB	SO	AVG	OBP	SLG	OPS	OPS+	BR+	SB	CS	SBR	FA	FR	G/POS	TPR
1984	LA-N	8	12	1	2	0	0	0	0	1	2	.167	.231	.167	397	13	-1	0	0	0	1.000	-1	/O-5(4-0-1)	-0.3

■ **OTTO MILLER** Miller, Lowell Otto "Moonie" b: 6/1/1889, Minden, Neb. d: 3/29/62, Brooklyn, N.Y. BR/TR, 6', 196 lbs. Deb: 7/16/10 C

YEAR	TM/L	G	AB	R	H	2B	3B	HR	RBI	BB	SO	AVG	OBP	SLG	OPS	OPS+	BR+	SB	CS	SBR	FA	FR	G/POS	TPR
1910	Bro-N	31	66	5	11	3	0	0	2	2	19	.167	.203	.212	415	22	-7	1			.987	9	C-28	0.4
1911	Bro-N	25	62	7	13	2	2	0	8	0	4	.210	.210	.306	516	46	-5	2			.927	-3	C-22	-0.7
1912	Bro-N	98	316	35	88	18	1	1	31	18	50	.278	.325	.351	677	88	-5	11			.975	13	C-94	1.5
1913	Bro-N	104	320	26	87	11	7	0	26	10	31	.272	.294	.350	644	81	-9	7			.971	14	*C-103/1-1	1.4
1914	Bro-N	54	169	17	39	6	1	0	9	7	20	.231	.261	.278	539	59	-9	0			.964	0	C-50/1-1	-0.5
1915	Bro-N	84	254	20	57	4	6	0	25	6	28	.224	.245	.287	533	60	-13	3			.981	8	C-83	0.2
1916	*Bro-N	73	216	16	55	9	2	1	17	7	29	.255	.281	.329	610	85	-4	6			.968	4	C-69	0.6
1917	Bro-N	92	274	19	63	5	4	1	17	14	29	.230	.272	.288	561	70	-10	5			.979	1	C-91	-0.1
1918	Bro-N	75	228	8	44	6	1	0	8	9	20	.193	.230	.228	458	40	-16	1			.972	4	C-62/1-1	-0.8
1919	Bro-N	51	164	18	37	5	0	0	5	7	14	.226	.257	.256	513	53	-9	2			.966	2	C-51	-0.3
1920	*Bro-N	90	301	16	87	9	2	0	33	9	18	.289	.312	.332	644	82	-7	0	5	-2	**.986**	-2	C-89	-0.4
1921	Bro-N	91	286	22	67	8	6	1	27	9	26	.234	.260	.315	575	50	-21	2	1	0	.972	9	C-91	-0.6
1922	Bro-N	59	180	20	47	11	1	1	23	6	13	.261	.285	.350	635	63	-10	0	0	0	.968	3	C-57	-0.3
Total	13	927	2836	229	695	97	33	5	231	104	301	.245	.275	.308	583	67	-125	40	6		.973	62	C-890/1-3	0.4

■ **KEITH MILLER** Miller, Neal Keith b: 3/7/63, Dallas, Tex. BB/TR, 5'11", 175 lbs. Deb: 4/23/88

YEAR	TM/L	G	AB	R	H	2B	3B	HR	RBI	BB	SO	AVG	OBP	SLG	OPS	OPS+	BR+	SB	CS	SBR	FA	FR	G/POS	TPR
1988	Phi-N	47	48	4	8	3	0	0	6	5	13	.167	.245	.229	474	36	-4	0	0	0	1.000	-3	/O-4(2-1-1),3-3,S-1	-0.8
1989	Phi-N	8	10	0	3	1	0	0	0	0	3	.300	.300	.400	700	98	-0	0	0	0	1.000	-1	/O-2(0-2-0)	-0.1
Total	2	55	58	4	11	4	0	0	6	5	16	.190	.254	.259	513	47	-4	0	0	0	1.000	-4	/O-6(2-3-1),3-3,S-1	-0.9

■ **NORM MILLER** Miller, Norman Calvin b: 2/5/46, Los Angeles, Cal. BL/TR, 5'11", 195 lbs. Deb: 9/11/65 Career OF: (82-LF 40-CF 266-RF)

YEAR	TM/L	G	AB	R	H	2B	3B	HR	RBI	BB	SO	AVG	OBP	SLG	OPS	OPS+	BR+	SB	CS	SBR	FA	FR	G/POS	TPR
1965	Hou-N	11	15	2	3	0	1	0	1	1	7	.200	.250	.333	583	67	-1	0	0	0	1.000	-0	/O-2(2-0-0)	-0.1
1966	Hou-N	11	34	1	5	0	0	1	3	2	8	.147	.194	.235	430	20	-4	0	0	0	1.000	0	/O-8(5-0-3),3-2	-0.4

YEAR	TM/L	G	AB	R	H	2B	3B	HR	RBI	BB	SO	AVG	OBP	SLG	OPS	OPS+	BR+	SB	CS	SBR	FA	FR	G/POS	TPR
1967	Hou-N	64	190	15	39	9	3	1	14	19	42	.205	.278	.300	578	68	-8	2	0	0	.967	1	O-53(53-0-0)	-1.0
1968	Hou-N	79	257	35	61	18	2	6	28	22	48	.237	.310	.393	703	112	3	6	5	-0	.971	-3	O-74(2-7-65)	-0.5
1969	Hou-N	119	409	58	108	21	4	4	50	47	77	.264	.350	.364	714	102	2	4	4	-1	.984	-1	*O-114(8-14-97)	-0.5
1970	Hou-N	90	226	29	54	9	0	4	29	41	33	.239	.358	.332	690	90	-2	3	1	0	.947	-5	O-72(4-3-68)/C-1	-0.9
1971	Hou-N	45	74	5	19	5	0	2	10	5	13	.257	.313	.405	718	105	0	0	0	0	1.000	-5	O-20(0-6-15)/C-1	-0.5
1972	Hou-N	67	107	18	26	4	0	4	13	13	23	.243	.331	.393	723	107	1	1	0	0	1.000	-4	O-29(6-10-13)	-0.4
1973	Hou-N	3	3	0	0	0	0	0	0	0	2	.000	.000	.000	0	-99	-1	0	0	0	.000	-0	/O-1(0-0-1)	-0.1
	Atl-N	9	8	2	3	1	0	1	6	3	3	.375	.545	.875	1420	267	2	0	0	0	.667	-0	/O-1(1-0-0)	0.2
	Yr	12	11	2	3	1	0	1	6	3	5	.273	.429	.636	1065	181	1	0	0	0	.667	-1	/O-2(1-0-1)	0.1
1974	Atl-N	42	41	1	7	1	0	1	5	7	9	.171	.292	.268	560	55	-2	0	0	0	1.000	-1	/O-4(1-0-4)	-0.3
Total	10	540	1364	166	325	68	10	24	159	160	265	.238	.325	.356	680	95	-8	16	10	0	.972	-18	O-378R/C-2,3-2	-4.5
■ ORLANDO MILLER	Miller, Orlando (Salmon) b: 1/13/69, Changuinola, Pan. BR/TR, 6'1", 180 lbs. Deb: 7/8/94																							
1994	Hou-N	16	40	3	13	0	1	2	9	2	12	.325	.386	.525	911	142	2	1	0	0	1.000	-1	S-11/2-3	0.2
1995	Hou-N	92	324	36	85	20	1	5	36	22	71	.262	.319	.377	696	89	-6	3	4	-1	.964	5	S-89	0.6
1996	Hou-N	139	468	43	120	26	2	15	58	14	116	.256	.293	.417	709	92	-8	3	7	-2	.958	-12	*S-117,3-29	-1.2
1997	Det-A	50	111	13	26	7	1	2	10	5	24	.234	.292	.369	661	72	-5	1	0	0	.979	-0	S-31,D-11/3-4,1-3	-0.4
Total	4	297	943	95	244	53	5	24	113	43	223	.259	.306	.402	708	90	-16	8	11	-2	.964	-9	S-248/3-33,D-11,12	-0.8
■ OTTO MILLER	Miller, Otis Louis b: 2/2/01, Belleville, Ill. d: 7/26/59, Belleville, Ill. BR/TR, 5'10.5", 168 lbs. Deb: 4/17/27																							
1927	StL-A	51	76	8	17	5	0	0	8	8	5	.224	.306	.289	595	53	-5	0	1	-0	.938	-4	S-35,3-11	-0.7
1930	Bos-A	112	370	49	106	22	5	0	40	26	21	.286	.333	.373	706	82	-10	2	4	-1	.948	-6	3-83,2-15	-1.0
1931	Bos-A	107	389	38	106	12	1	0	43	15	20	.272	.301	.308	610	64	-20	1	1	-0	.953	-1	3-75,2-25	-1.6
1932	Bos-A	2	2	0	0	0	0	0	0	0	0	.000	.000	.000	0	-99	-1	0	0	0	.000	0	H	-0.1
Total	4	272	837	95	229	39	6	0	91	49	46	.274	.315	.335	650	71	-36	3	6	-1	.949	-11	3-169/2-40,S-35	-3.4
■ RALPH MILLER	Miller, Ralph Joseph b: 2/29/1896, Ft.Wayne, Ind. d: 3/18/39, Ft.Wayne, Ind. BR/TR, 6', 190 lbs. Deb: 4/14/20 Career OF: (1-LF 0-CF 0-RF)																							
1920	Phi-N	97	338	28	74	14	1	0	28	11	32	.219	.246	.266	512	45	-24	3	4	-1	.940	0	3-91/1-3,S-2,O-1L	-2.4
1921	Phi-N	57	204	19	62	10	0	3	26	6	10	.304	.327	.397	724	84	-5	3	5	-1	.910	0	S-46,3-10	-0.1
1924	*Was-A	9	15	1	2	0	0	0	0	1	1	.133	.188	.133	321	-17	-3	0	0	0	.941	0	/2-3	-0.2
Total	3	163	557	48	138	24	1	3	54	18	43	.248	.274	.311	584	59	-31	6	9	-2	.927	1	3-101/S-48,2-3,1O	-2.7
■ RAY MILLER	Miller, Raymond Peter b: 2/12/1888, Pittsburgh, Pa. d: 4/7/27, Pittsburgh, Pa. BL/TL, 5'10", 168 lbs. Deb: 4/14/17																							
1917	Cle-A	19	21	1	4	1	0	0	2	8	3	.190	.414	.238	652	92	0	0			1.000	1	/1-4	0.2
	Pit-N	6	27	1	4	1	0	0	0	2	3	.148	.207	.185	392	20	-3	0			1.000	0	/1-6	-0.3
Total	1	25	48	2	8	2	0	0	2	10	6	.167	.310	.208	519	56	-2	0			1.000	2	/1-10	-0.1
■ RICK MILLER	Miller, Richard Alan b: 4/19/48, Grand Rapids, Mich. BL/TL, 6', 185 lbs. Deb: 9/4/71 Career OF: (118-LF 854-CF 297-RF)																							
1971	Bos-A	15	33	9	11	5	0	1	7	8	8	.333	.463	.576	1039	180	4	0	2	-1	.969	1	O-14(4-4-6)	0.4
1972	Bos-A	89	98	13	21	4	1	3	15	11	27	.214	.294	.367	661	91	-1	0	2	-1	.967	-11	O-75(24-47-4)	-1.6
1973	Bos-A	143	441	65	115	17	7	6	43	51	59	.261	.341	.372	713	95	-2	12	7	0	.978	-4	*O-137(15-71-61)	-1.1
1974	Bos-A	114	280	41	73	8	1	5	22	37	47	.261	.347	.350	697	94	-1	13	2	2	.989	2	*O-105(21-77-7)	0.0
1975	*Bos-A	77	108	21	21	2	1	0	15	21	20	.194	.326	.231	557	55	-6	3	2	-0	.981	-8	O-65(25-15-26)	-1.6
1976	Bos-A	105	269	40	76	15	3	0	27	34	47	.283	.363	.361	724	100	1	11	10	-1	.991	5	O-82(17-37-32)/D-4	0.2
1977	Bos-A	86	189	34	48	9	3	0	24	22	30	.254	.341	.333	674	76	-6	11	5	1	.992	-7	O-79(2-29-48)/D-1	-1.4
1978	Cal-A	132	475	66	125	25	4	1	37	54	70	.263	.343	.339	682	96	-1	3	13	-4	.989	15	*O-129(0-93-36)	0.8
1979	*Cal-A	120	427	60	125	15	5	2	28	50	69	.293	.368	.365	734	102	3	5	4	-0	.989	10	*O-117(0-117-0)/D-2	1.2
1980	Cal-A	129	412	52	113	14	3	2	38	48	71	.274	.351	.337	689	92	-3	7	3	0	.984	5	*O-118(0-98-24)	0.1
1981	Bos-A	97	316	38	92	17	2	2	33	28	36	.291	.351	.377	727	103	2	3	5	-1	.987	-3	O-95(0-95-0)	-0.3
1982	Bos-A	135	409	50	104	13	2	4	38	40	41	.254	.324	.325	649	75	-13	5	6	-1	.983	-6	*O-127(0-127-0)	-2.2
1983	Bos-A	104	262	41	75	10	2	2	21	28	30	.286	.357	.363	720	92	-2	3	3	-0	.993	0	O-66(6-22-40)/1-2,D-2	-0.5
1984	Bos-A	95	123	17	32	5	1	0	12	17	22	.260	.350	.317	667	82	-2	1	1	-0	.974	-7	O-31(0-21-10)/1-8	-1.0
1985	Bos-A	41	45	5	15	2	0	0	9	5	6	.333	.400	.378	778	110	1	1	0	0	1.000	-2	/O-8(4-1-3),D-4	-0.1
Total	15	1482	3887	552	1046	161	35	28	369	454	583	.269	.348	.350	698	92	-27	78	65	-6	.986	-10	*O-1248C/D-13,1-10	-7.1
■ ROD MILLER	Miller, Rodney Carter b: 1/16/40, Portland, Ore. BL/TR, 5'10", 160 lbs. Deb: 9/28/57																							
1957	Bro-N	1	1	0	0	0	0	0	0	0	1	.000	.000	.000	0	-91	-0	0	0	0	.000	0	H	0.0
■ DOC MILLER	Miller, Roy Oscar b: 2/4/1883, Chatham, Ontario, Canada d: 7/31/38, Jersey City, N.J. BL/TL, 5'10.5", 170 lbs. Deb: 5/4/10																							
1910	Chi-N	1	1	0	0	0	0	0	0	0	0	.000	.000	.000	0	-99	-0	0			.000	0	H	0.0
	Bos-N	130	482	48	138	27	4	3	55	33	52	.286	.333	.378	711	103	0	17			.951	-12	*O-130(6-0-127)	-1.9
	Yr	131	483	48	138	27	4	3	55	33	52	.286	.333	.377	710	102	-0	17			.951	-12	*O-130(6-0-127)	-1.9
1911	Bos-N	146	577	69	**192**	36	3	7	91	43	43	.333	.379	.442	821	120	14	32			.961	2	*O-146(0-3-143)	0.8
1912	Bos-N	51	201	26	47	8	1	2	24	14	17	.234	.287	.313	600	63	-11	6			.948	3	O-50(0-0-50)	-1.0
	Phi-N	67	177	24	51	12	5	0	21	9	13	.288	.323	.412	735	94	-2	3			.986	2	O-40(0-0-40)	-0.2
	Yr	118	378	50	98	20	6	2	45	23	30	.259	.303	.360	663	78	-13	9			.964	5	O-90(0-0-90)	-1.2
1913	Phi-N	69	87	9	30	6	0	0	11	6	6	.345	.400	.414	814	127	3	2			.800	-4	O-12(0-0-12)	-0.1
1914	Cin-N	93	192	8	49	7	2	0	33	16	18	.255	.313	.313	625	83	-4	4			.976	-4	O-47(23-3-23)	-1.1
Total	5	557	1717	184	507	96	15	12	235	121	149	.295	.343	.390	733	102	0	64			.958	-13	O-425(29-6-395)	-3.5
■ RUDY MILLER	Miller, Rudel Charles b: 7/12/1900, Kalamazoo, Mich. d: 1/22/94, Kalamazoo, Mich. BR/TR, 6'1", 180 lbs. Deb: 9/19/29																							
1929	Phi-A	2	4	1	1	0	0	0	1	3	0	.250	.571	.250	821	115	0	0	0	0	.750	-0	/3-2	0.0
■ TOM MILLER	Miller, Thomas P. "Reddy" b: 1850, Philadelphia, Pa. d: 5/29/1876, Philadelphia, Pa. Deb: 10/24/1874																							
1874	Ath-n	4	16	1	8	0	0	0	5	0	0	.500	.500	.500	1000	204	2	0	0	0	.793	0	/C-4,O-1(0-1-1)	0.1
1875	StL-n	56	214	18	35	2	0	0	12	1	8	.164	.167	.173	340	20	-15	2	0	0	.827	-3	*C-53/3-2	-1.5
Total	2 n	60	230	19	43	2	0	0	17	1	8	.187	.190	.196	386	37	-13	2	0	0	.824	-3	/C-57,3-2,O-1(0-1-1)	-1.4
■ TOM MILLER	Miller, Thomas Royall b: 7/5/1897, Powhatan Court House, Va. d: 8/13/80, Richmond, Va. BL/TR, 5'11", 180 lbs. Deb: 7/29/18																							
1918	Bos-N	2	2	0	0	0	0	0	0	0	0	.000	.000	.000	0	-99	-0	1			.000	0	H	-0.1
1919	Bos-N	7	6	2	2	0	0	0	0	0	1	.333	.333	.333	667	105	0	0			.000	0	H	0.0
Total	2	9	8	2	2	0	0	0	0	0	1	.250	.250	.250	500	53	-0	1				0	-0,-0	-0.1
■ WARD MILLER	Miller, Ward Taylor "Windy" or "Grump" b: 7/5/1884, Mt.Carroll, Ill. d: 9/4/58, Dixon, Ill. BL/TR, 5'11", 177 lbs. Deb: 4/14/09																							
1909	Pit-N	15	56	2	8	0	1	0	4	4		.143	.213	.179	392	20	-5	2			.967	-1	O-14(0-14-0)	-0.8
	Cin-N	43	113	17	35	3	1	0	4	6		.310	.345	.354	699	118	2	9			.981	-7	O-26(17-16-3)	-0.6
	Yr	58	169	19	43	3	2	0	8	10		.254	.300	.296	596	84	-3	11			.976	-8	O-40(17-30-3)	-1.4
1910	Cin-N	81	126	21	30	6	0	0	10	22	13	.238	.356	.286	641	92	-0	10			.944	2	O-26(0-11-15)	0.0
1912	Chi-N	86	241	45	74	11	4	0	22	26	18	.307	.377	.386	763	109	4	11			.943	-8	O-64(13-38-14)	-0.8
1913	Chi-N	80	203	23	48	5	7	1	16	34	33	.236	.349	.345	694	98	1	13			.980	3	O-63(47-11-5)	0.1
1914	StL-F	121	402	49	118	17	7	4	50	59	36	.294	.397	.400	798	112	3	18			.953	10	*O-111(74-31-6)	0.8
1915	StL-F	154	536	80	164	19	9	1	63	79	39	.306	.400	.381	781	114	7	33			.963	3	*O-154(154-0-0)	0.3
1916	StL-A	146	485	72	129	17	5	1	50	72	76	.266	.371	.328	699	116	13	25	21	-2	.943	-5	*O-136(3-0-133)	-0.2
1917	StL-A	43	82	13	17	1	1	1	2	16	15	.207	.350	.280	630	96	1	7			.966	-4	O-25(12-4-9)	-0.5
Total	8	769	2244	322	623	79	35	8	221	318	230	.278	.375	.355	729	108	24	128	21		.957	-8	O-619(320-125-185)	-1.7
■ WARREN MILLER	Miller, Warren Lemuel "Gitz" b: 7/14/1885, Philadelphia, Pa. d: 8/12/56, Philadelphia, Pa. BL/TL, 5'10", 160 lbs. Deb: 7/29/09																							
1909	Was-A	26	51	5	11	0	0	0	1	4		.216	.273	.216	488	57	-2	0			1.000	-1	O-15(1-10-4)	-0.5
1911	Was-A	21	34	3	5	0	0	0	0	0		.147	.147	.147	294	-18	-5	0			.778	-2	/O-9(1-0-8)	-0.7
Total	2	47	85	8	16	0	0	0	1	4		.188	.225	.188	413	25	-8	0			.931	-3	/O-24(2-10-12)	-1.2

YEAR	TM/L	G	AB	R	H	2B	3B	HR	RBI	BB	SO	AVG	OBP	SLG	OPS	OPS+	BR+	SB	CS	SBR	FA	FR	G/POS	TPR
■ BILL MILLER	Miller, William Alexander b: 5/23/1879, Bad Schwalbach, Germany d: 9/8/57, Ashtabula, Ohio BL/TL, 6'2", 170 lbs. Deb: 8/23/02																							
1902	Pit-N	1	5	0	1	0	0	0	2	0		.200	.200	.200	400	23	-0	0			.000	-0	/O-1(0-0-1)	-0.1
■ JOE MILLETTE	Millette, Joseph Anthony b: 8/12/66, Walnut Creek, Cal. BR/TR, 6'1", 180 lbs. Deb: 7/16/92																							
1992	Phi-N	33	78	5	16	0	0	0	2	5	10	.205	.271	.205	476	37	-6	1	0	0	.974	10	S-26/3-3,2-1	0.6
1993	Phi-N	10	10	3	2	0	0	0	2	1	2	.200	.273	.200	473	29	-1	0	0	0	1.000	3	/S-7,3-3	0.3
Total	2	43	88	8	18	0	0	0	4	6	12	.205	.271	.205	475	36	-7	1	0	0	.978	13	/S-33,3-6,2-1	0.9
■ RALPH MILLIARD	Milliard, Ralph Gregory b: 12/30/73, Willemstad, Curacao BR/TR, 5'11", 170 lbs. Deb: 5/12/96																							
1996	Fla-N	24	62	7	10	2	0	0	1	14	16	.161	.316	.194	509	40	-5	2	0	0	.955	5	2-24	0.1
1997	Fla-N	8	30	2	6	0	0	0	2	3	3	.200	.314	.200	514	40	-2	1	1	-0	1.000	4	/2-8	0.1
1998	NY-N	10	1	3	0	0	0	0	0	0	1	.000	.000	.000	0	-99	-0	0	0	0	.833	1	/2-5,S-1	0.1
Total	3	42	93	12	16	2	0	0	3	17	20	.172	.313	.194	506	38	-8	3	1	0	.963	10	/2-37,S-1	0.3
■ WALLY MILLIES	Millies, Walter Louis b: 10/18/06, Chicago, Ill. d: 2/28/95, Oak Lawn, Ill. BR/TR, 5'10.5", 170 lbs. Deb: 9/23/34																							
1934	Bro-N	2	7	0	0	0	0	0	0	0	0	.000	.000	.000	0	-99	-2	0			1.000	1	/C-2	-0.1
1936	Was-A	74	215	26	67	10	2	0	25	11	8	.312	.345	.377	722	83	-6	1	0	0	.968	1	C-72	-0.1
1937	Was-A	59	179	21	40	7	1	0	28	9	15	.223	.261	.274	534	36	-18	1	0	0	.971	2	C-56	-1.2
1939	Phi-N	84	205	12	48	3	0	0	12	9	5	.234	.270	.249	519	41	-17	0			.964	-7	C-84	-2.0
1940	Phi-N	26	43	1	3	0	0	0	0	4	4	.070	.149	.070	219	-39	-8	0			.958	2	C-24	-0.6
1941	Phi-N	1	2	0	0	0	0	0	0	0	0	.000	.000	.000	0	-99	-1	0			.800	0	/C-1	0.0
Total	6	246	651	60	158	20	3	0	65	33	32	.243	.280	.283	563	47	-51	2	0		.966	-2	C-239	-4.0
■ JOCKO MILLIGAN	Milligan, John b: 8/8/1861, Philadelphia, Pa. d: 8/29/23, Philadelphia, Pa. BR/TR, 6', 192 lbs. Deb: 5/1/1884 Career OF: (0-LF 6-CF 3-RF)																							
1884	Phi-a	66	268	39	77	20	3	3		8		.287	.308	.418	726	126	6				**.939**	13	C-65/O-1(0-1-0)	2.3
1885	Phi-a	67	265	35	71	15	4	2	39	7		.268	.289	.377	667	103	-0				.935	11	C-61/1-6,O-2(0-0-2)	1.4
1886	Phi-a	75	301	52	76	17	3	5	45	21		.252	.301	.379	680	111	3	18			.919	5	C-40,1-29/O-5C,3-2	0.7
1887	Phi-a	95	398	54	135	27	4	2	50	21		.339	.344	.411	755	110	4	8			.966	3	1-50,C-47/O-1(0-1-0)	0.6
1888	*StL-a	63	219	19	55	6	2	5	37	17		.251	.311	.365	676	105	0	3			.941	8	C-58/1-5	1.1
1889	StL-a	72	273	53	100	30	2	12	76	16	19	.366	.408	.623	1030	170	21	2			.933	14	C-66/1-9	3.4
1890	Phi-P	62	234	38	69	9	3	3	57	19	19	.295	.363	.397	760	101	-0	2			.893	4	C-59/1-3	0.7
1891	Phi-a	118	455	75	138	**35**	12	11	106	56	51	.303	.397	.505	903	158	33	2			.939	0	C-87,1-32	3.2
1892	Was-N	88	323	40	89	20	9	4	43	26	24	.276	.335	.430	766	135	12	2			.947	5	C-59,1-28	2.1
1893	Bal-N	24	102	19	25	5	2	1	19	5	7	.245	.294	.363	656	73	-5	2			.981	1	1-22/C-1	-0.3
	NY-N	42	147	16	34	5	6	1	25	14	14	.231	.302	.367	670	77	-6	2			.934	14	C-42	1.0
	Yr	66	249	35	59	10	8	2	44	19	21	.237	.299	.365	664	76	-10	4			.932	15	C-43,1-22	0.7
Total	10	772	2985	440	869	189	50	49	497	210	134	.291	.341	.433	774	123	69	41			.930	78	C-585,1-184/O-9C,3	16.2
■ RANDY MILLIGAN	Milligan, Randy Andre b: 11/27/61, San Diego, Cal. BR/TR, 6'1", 228 lbs. Deb: 9/12/87 Career OF: (19-LF 0-CF 0-RF)																							
1987	NY-N	3	1	0	0	0	0	0	0	1	1	.000	.500	.000	500	49	0	0	0	0	.000	0	/H	0.0
1988	Pit-N	40	82	10	18	5	0	3	8	20	24	.220	.379	.390	769	123	3	1	2	-0	.987	-1	1-25/O-2(1-0-0)	0.0
1989	Bal-A	124	365	56	98	23	5	12	45	74	75	.268	.396	.458	853	144	24	9	5	0	.995	2	*1-117/D-1	1.9
1990	Bal-A	109	362	64	96	20	1	20	60	88	68	.265	.412	.492	903	157	31	6	3	0	.990	5	1-98/D-9	3.0
1991	Bal-A	141	483	57	127	17	2	16	70	84	108	.263	.374	.406	780	121	16	0	5	-2	.990	3	*1-106,D-25/O-9L	0.8
1992	Bal-A	137	462	71	111	21	1	11	53	106	81	.240	.386	.361	748	108	10	0	1	-0	.994	-6	*1-129/D-6	-0.6
1993	Cin-N	83	234	30	64	11	1	6	29	46	49	.274	.395	.406	801	115	7	0	2	-1	.994	5	1-61/O-9(9-0-0)	0.6
	Cle-A	19	47	7	20	7	0	0	7	14	4	.426	.557	.574	1132	206	8	0	0	0	1.000	-1	1-18/D-1	0.6
1994	Mon-N	47	82	10	19	2	0	2	12	14	21	.232	.344	.329	673	76	-3	0	0	0	.978	2	1-33	-0.3
Total	8	703	2118	305	553	106	10	70	284	447	431	.261	.393	.420	813	127	98	16	18	-3	.992	9	1-587/D-42,O-20L	6.0
■ JACK MILLS	Mills, Abbott Paige b: 10/23/1889, S.Williamstown, Mass. d: 6/3/73, Washington, D.C. BL/TR, 6', 165 lbs. Deb: 7/1/11																							
1911	Cle-A	13	17	5	5	0	0	0	1	1		.294	.368	.294	663	85	-0	1			1.000	2	/3-7	0.1
■ CHARLIE MILLS	Mills, Charles b: 9/1844, Brooklyn, N.Y. d: 4/10/1874, Brooklyn, N.Y. 6', Deb: 5/18/1871 U																							
1871	Mut-n	32	146	27	36	4	3	0	22	1	0	.247	.252	.315	567	68	-4	2	0	0	.866	-2	*C-29/O-4(0-0-4),3-1	-0.4
1872	Mut-n	6	31	6	4	0	0	0	2	0	0	.129	.129	.129	258	-22	-4	0	0	0	.667	-1	/O-4(0-0-4),C-3	-0.4
Total	2 n	38	177	33	40	4	3	0	24	1	0	.226	.230	.282	513	53	-8	2	0	0	.854	-3	/C-32,O-8(0-0-8),3-1	-0.8
■ BUSTER MILLS	Mills, Colonel Buster "Bus" b: 9/16/08, Ranger, Tex. d: 12/1/91, Arlington, Tex. BR/TR, 5'11.5", 195 lbs. Deb: 4/18/34 MC																							
1934	StL-N	29	72	7	17	4	1	1	8	4	11	.236	.295	.361	656	70	-3	0			1.000	-0	O-18(0-17-1)	-0.4
1935	Bro-N	17	56	12	12	2	1	1	7	5	11	.214	.323	.339	662	80	-1	0			.971	-2	O-17(11-6-0)	-0.4
1937	Bos-A	123	505	85	149	25	8	7	58	46	41	.295	.361	.418	779	92	-6	11	8	-0	.946	-5	*O-120(107-10-5)	-1.6
1938	StL-A	123	466	66	133	24	4	3	46	43	46	.285	.350	.373	723	81	-13	7	8	-1	.964	3	*O-113(106-6-1)	-1.6
1940	NY-A	34	63	10	25	3	3	1	15	7	5	.397	.457	.587	1044	176	7	0	0	0	1.000	-2	O-14(12-0-2)	0.4
1942	Cle-A	80	195	19	54	4	2	1	26	23	18	.277	.353	.333	687	99	0	5	4	-0	.973	2	O-53(13-37-3)	0.0
1946	Cle-A	9	22	1	6	0	0	0	3	3	5	.273	.360	.273	633	84	-0	0	1	-0	1.000	-0	/O-6(6-0-0)	-0.2
Total	7	415	1379	200	396	62	19	14	163	131	137	.287	.355	.390	746	91	-17	23	21		.964	-5	O-341(255-76-12)	-3.8
■ EVERETT MILLS	Mills, Everett b: 1/20/1845, Newark, N.J. d: 6/22/08, Newark, N.J. 6'1", 174 lbs. Deb: 5/5/1871 M																							
1871	Oly-n	32	157	38	43	6	4	1	24	3	1	.274	.287	.382	670	95	-0	2	3	-1	.967	3	*1-32	0.2
1872	Bal-n	55	266	55	79	14	2	0	34	3	2	.297	.305	.365	669	100	-1	0	2	-1	.931	2	*1-55,M	0.1
1873	Bal-n	54	263	64	87	19	**9**	0	57	2	1	.331	.336	.471	807	138	12	1	0	0	**.949**	2	*1-53/O-1(0-1-0)	1.0
1874	Har-n	53	244	39	69	6	1	0	19	4	2	.283	.294	.316	610	91	-3	1	1	-0	.920	-2	*1-53	-0.3
1875	Har-n	80	342	59	89	8	4	1	48	0	3	.260	.260	.316	576	94	-3	6	4	-0	.945	2	*1-80	0.0
1876	Har-N	63	255	28	66	8	1	0	23	1	3	.259	.263	.299	562	80	-6				.939	-2	*1-63	-1.0
Total	5 n	274	1272	255	367	53	20	2	182	12	9	.289	.295	.366	662	104	4	10	10	-1	.941	6	1-273/O-1(0-1-0)	1.0
■ FRANK MILLS	Mills, Frank Le Moyne b: 5/13/1895, Knoxville, Ohio d: 8/31/83, Youngstown, Ohio BL/TR, 6', 180 lbs. Deb: 9/22/14																							
1914	Cle-A	4	8	0	1	0	0	0	0	1	2	.125	.222	.125	347	4	-1	0			.900	-1	/C-2	-0.2
■ BRAD MILLS	Mills, James Bradley b: 1/19/57, Exeter, Cal. BL/TR, 6', 195 lbs. Deb: 6/8/80 C																							
1980	Mon-N	21	60	1	18	1	0	0	8	5	6	.300	.354	.317	671	88	-1	0	1	-0	.977	-1	3-18	-0.3
1981	*Mon-N	17	21	3	5	1	0	0	1	2	1	.238	.304	.286	590	67	-1	0	0	0	1.000	0	/3-7,2-2	-0.1
1982	Mon-N	54	67	6	15	3	0	1	2	5	11	.224	.278	.313	591	64	-3	0	0	0	.867	-3	3-13	-0.7
1983	Mon-N	14	20	1	5	0	0	0	1	2	3	.250	.318	.250	568	60	-1	0	0	0	1.000	-1	/3-3,1-1	-0.2
Total	4	106	168	11	43	5	0	1	12	14	21	.256	.313	.304	617	73	-6	0	1	-0	.959	-5	/3-41,2-2,1-1	-1.3
■ RUPERT MILLS	Mills, Rupert Frank b: 10/12/1892, Newark, N.J. d: 7/20/29, Lake Hopatcong, N.J. BR/TR, 6'2", 185 lbs. Deb: 6/23/15																							
1915	New-F	41	134	12	27	5	1	0	16	6	21	.201	.241	.254	495	42	-13	6			.976	0	1-37	-1.5
■ BILL MILLS	Mills, William Henry b: 11/2/20, Boston, Mass. BR/TR, 5'10", 175 lbs. Deb: 5/19/44																							
1944	Phi-A	5	4	0	1	0	0	0	0	1	1	.250	.400	.250	650	89	0	0	0	0	.000	0	/C-1	0.0
■ PETE MILNE	Milne, William James b: 4/10/25, Mobile, Ala. d: 4/11/99, Mobile, Ala. BL/TR, 6'1", 180 lbs. Deb: 9/15/48																							
1948	NY-N	12	27	0	6	0	1	0	2	1	6	.222	.250	.296	546	47	-2	0			.867	-2	/O-9(2-5-2)	-0.5
1949	NY-N	31	29	5	7	1	0	1	6	3	6	.241	.313	.379	692	85	-1	0			1.000	-0	/O-1(1-0-0)	-0.1
1950	NY-N	4	4	1	1	0	1	0	1	0	1	.250	.250	.750	1000	151	0	0			.000	0	H	0.0
Total	3	47	60	6	14	1	2	1	9	4	13	.233	.281	.367	648	73	-2	0			.882	-2	/O-10(3-5-2)	-0.6
■ BRIAN MILNER	Milner, Brian Tate b: 11/17/59, Fort Worth, Tex. BR/TR, 6'2", 200 lbs. Deb: 6/23/78																							
1978	Tor-A	2	9	3	4	0	1	0	2	0	1	.444	.444	.667	1111	204	1	0	0	0	.800	-3	/C-2	-0.1

YEAR	TM/L	G	AB	R	H	2B	3B	HR	RBI	BB	SO	AVG	OBP	SLG	OPS	OPS+	BR+	SB	CS	SBR	FA	FR	G/POS	TPR
■ **EDDIE MILNER**	Milner, Eddie James b: 5/21/55, Columbus, Ohio BL/TL, 5'11", 173 lbs. Deb: 9/2/80																							
1980	Cin-N	6	3	1	0	0	0	0	0	0	0	.000	.000	.000	0	-99	-1	0	0	0	.000	0	/H	-0.1
1981	Cin-N	8	5	0	1	1	0	0	1	1	1	.200	.333	.400	733	106	0	0	0	0	1.000	-1	/O-4(2-0-2)	-0.1
1982	Cin-N	113	407	61	109	23	5	4	31	41	40	.268	.338	.378	716	98	-1	18	12	-0	.987	-3	*O-107(65-30-37)	-0.8
1983	Cin-N	146	502	77	131	23	6	9	33	68	60	.261	.350	.384	735	100	1	41	12	5	.990	20	*O-139(0-138-1)	2.5
1984	Cin-N	117	336	44	78	8	4	7	29	51	50	.232	.337	.342	679	87	-4	21	13	0	.983	10	*O-108(0-108-0)	0.5
1985	Cin-N	145	453	82	115	19	7	3	33	61	31	.254	.344	.347	690	89	-5	35	13	3	.983	15	*O-135(0-135-0)	1.3
1986	Cin-N	145	424	70	110	22	6	15	47	36	56	.259	.317	.446	763	104	1	18	11	0	.990	7	*O-127(0-127-0)	0.7
1987	*SF-N	101	214	38	54	14	0	4	19	24	33	.252	.328	.374	702	90	-3	10	9	-1	.993	-9	O-84(0-84-0)	-1.4
1988	Cin-N	23	51	3	9	1	0	0	2	4	9	.176	.236	.196	432	24	-5	2	2	-0	.968	-0	O-15(2-11-2)	-0.6
Total	9	804	2395	376	607	111	28	42	195	286	280	.253	.335	.376	710	94	-17	145	72	7	.987	38	O-719(69-633-42)	2.0
■ **JOHN MILNER**	Milner, John David "The Hammer" b: 12/28/49, Atlanta, Ga. d: 1/4/2000, East Point, Ga. BL/TL, 6', 185 lbs. Deb: 9/15/71																							
1971	NY-N	9	18	1	3	1	0	0	1	0	3	.167	.167	.222	389	9	-2	0	0	0	1.000	1	/O-3(3-0-0)	-0.1
1972	NY-N	117	362	52	86	12	2	17	38	51	74	.238	.340	.423	762	118	9	2	1	0	.965	3	O-91(88-0-3),1-10	0.7
1973	*NY-N	129	451	69	108	12	3	23	72	62	84	.239	.333	.432	765	112	7	1	1	-0	.989	-7	1-95,O-29(29-0-0)	-0.9
1974	NY-N	137	507	70	128	19	0	20	63	66	77	.252	.339	.408	747	110	6	10	2	2	.994	-1	*1-133	-0.4
1975	NY-N	91	220	24	42	11	0	7	29	33	22	.191	.302	.336	638	81	-6	1	1	-0	.985	6	O-31(29-2-0),1-29	-0.4
1976	NY-N	127	443	56	120	25	4	15	78	65	53	.271	.364	.447	811	137	22	0	7	-2	.985	4	*O-112(112-0-0),1-12	1.7
1977	NY-N	131	388	43	99	20	3	12	57	61	55	.255	.356	.415	771	111	7	6	2	1	.994	-1	1-87,O-22(21-0-1)	0.1
1978	Pit-N	108	295	39	80	17	0	6	38	34	25	.271	.347	.390	736	101	1	5	0	1	1.000	-2	O-69(68-0-1),1-28	-0.4
1979	*Pit-N	128	326	52	90	9	4	16	60	53	37	.276	.379	.475	854	126	13	3	5	-1	.958	-2	O-64(64-0-0),1-48	0.5
1980	Pit-N	114	238	31	58	6	0	8	34	52	29	.244	.379	.370	749	108	5	2	2	-0	.991	-5	1-70,O-11(10-0-1)	-0.4
1981	Pit-N	34	59	6	14	1	0	2	9	5	3	.237	.297	.356	653	82	-1	0	0	0	.980	-2	/1-8,O-8(8-0-0)	-0.5
	*Mon-N	31	76	6	18	5	0	3	9	12	6	.237	.341	.421	762	114	1	0	1	-0	.978	1	1-21	0.1
	Yr	65	135	12	32	6	0	5	18	17	9	.237	.322	.393	715	100	-0	0	1	-0	.979	-2	1-29/O-8(8-0-0)	-0.4
1982	Mon-N	26	28	1	3	0	0	0	2	4	2	.107	.219	.107	326	-6	-4	0	0	0	1.000	0	/1-5	-0.4
	Pit-N	33	25	5	6	2	0	2	8	6	3	.240	.406	.560	966	163	2	1	0	0	1.000	-0	/1-1	0.3
	Yr	59	53	6	9	2	0	2	10	10	5	.170	.313	.321	633	76	-2	1	0	0	1.000	0	/1-6	-0.1
Total	12	1215	3436	455	855	140	16	131	498	504	473	.249	.347	.413	760	112	60	31	22	-1	.991	-4	1-547,O-440(432-2-6)	-0.1
■ **MIKE MILOSEVICH**	Milosevich, Michael "Mollie" b: 1/13/15, Zeigler, Ill. d: 2/3/66, E.Chicago, Ind. BR/TR, 5'10.5", 172 lbs. Deb: 4/30/44																							
1944	NY-A	94	312	27	77	11	4	0	32	30	37	.247	.313	.308	621	75	-10	1	2	-0	.954	7	S-91	0.4
1945	NY-A	30	69	5	15	2	0	0	7	6	6	.217	.289	.246	536	54	-4	0	0	0	.957	1	S-22/2-1	-0.2
Total	2	124	381	32	92	13	4	0	39	36	43	.241	.309	.297	605	71	-14	1	2	-0	.954	8	S-113/2-1	0.2
■ **DON MINCHER**	Mincher, Donald Ray b: 6/24/38, Huntsville, Ala. BL/TR, 6'3", 213 lbs. Deb: 4/18/60																							
1960	Was-A	27	79	10	19	4	1	2	5	11	11	.241	.333	.392	726	96	-0	0	1	-0	.977	-4	1-20	-0.6
1961	Min-A	35	101	18	19	5	1	5	11	22	11	.188	.333	.406	739	91	-1	0	1	-0	.969	-2	1-29	-0.5
1962	Min-A	86	121	20	29	1	1	9	29	34	24	.240	.406	.488	894	134	7	0	0	0	.978	-1	1-25	0.4
1963	Min-A	82	225	41	58	8	0	17	42	30	51	.258	.353	.520	873	138	11	0	0	0	.983	-5	1-60	0.3
1964	Min-A	120	287	45	68	12	4	23	56	27	51	.237	.303	.547	850	130	10	0	0	0	.992	-0	1-76	0.6
1965	*Min-A	128	346	43	87	17	3	22	65	49	73	.251	.348	.509	856	134	15	1	3	-1	.992	-5	1-99/O-1(1-0-0)	0.4
1966	Min-A	139	431	53	108	30	0	14	62	58	68	.251	.342	.418	760	110	6	3	2	-0	.992	3	*1-130	0.3
1967	Cal-A★	147	487	81	133	23	3	25	76	69	69	.273	.368	.487	855	157	35	0	3	-1	.994	-2	*1-142/O-1(0-0-1)	2.5
1968	Cal-A	120	399	35	94	12	1	13	48	43	65	.236	.316	.368	685	111	5	0	2	-1	.991	-3	*1-113	-0.6
1969	Sea-A★	140	427	53	105	14	0	25	78	78	69	.246	.369	.454	823	131	19	10	11	-2	.995	8	*1-122	1.6
1970	Oak-A	140	463	62	114	18	0	27	74	56	71	.246	.331	.460	791	120	12	5	4	-0	.990	2	*1-137	0.3
1971	Oak-A	28	92	9	22	6	1	2	8	20	14	.239	.375	.391	766	120	3	1	1	-0	.996	3	1-27	0.4
	Was-A	100	323	35	94	15	1	10	45	53	52	.291	.394	.437	831	143	20	2	1	0	.990	3	1-88	1.8
	Yr	128	415	44	116	21	2	12	53	73	66	.280	.390	.427	816	138	23	3	2	-0	.991	6	*1-115	2.2
1972	Tex-A	61	191	23	45	10	0	6	39	46	23	.236	.389	.382	771	136	11	2	1	0	.994	6	1-59	1.4
	*Oak-A	47	54	2	8	1	0	0	5	10	16	.148	.281	.167	448	37	-4	0	2	-1	.988	-1	1-11	-0.6
	Yr	108	245	25	53	11	0	6	44	56	39	.216	.366	.335	701	115	7	2	3	-1	.993	5	1-70	0.8
Total	13	1400	4026	530	1003	176	16	200	643	606	668	.249	.351	.450	801	127	149	24	32	-6	.990	2	*1-1138/O-2(1-0-1)	7.7
■ **ED MINCHER**	Mincher, Edward John b: 1851, Baltimore, Md. Deb: 5/4/1871																							
1871	Kek-n	9	36	4	8	0	0	0	5	0	0	.222	.222	.222	444	28	-3	1	0	0	.852	-0	/O-9(9-0-0)	-0.2
1872	Nat-n	11	53	5	6	0	0	0	4	0	1	.113	.113	.113	226	-26	-8	0	0	0	.837	2	O-11(11-0-0)	-0.4
Total	2 n	20	89	9	14	0	0	0	9	0	1	.157	.157	.157	315	-5	-12	1	0	0	.842	2	/O-20(20-0-0)	-0.6
■ **DAN MINNEHAN**	Minnehan, Daniel Joseph b: 11/28/1865, Troy, N.Y. d: 8/8/29, Troy, N.Y. BR/TR, 5'10", 145 lbs. Deb: 9/20/1895																							
1895	Lou-N	8	34	6	13	0	0	0	6	1	1	.382	.400	.382	782	109	1	0			.920	-0	/3-7,O-2(0-2-0)	0.0
■ **DAMON MINOR**	Minor, Damon Reed b: 1/5/74, Canton, Ohio BL/TL, 6'7", 230 lbs. Deb: 9/2/2000 F																							
2000	SF-N	10	9	3	4	0	0	3	6	2	1	.444	.545	1.444	1990	407	4	0	0	0	1.000	-0	/1-4	0.3
■ **RYAN MINOR**	Minor, Ryan Dale b: 1/5/74, Canton, Ohio BR/TR, 6'7", 225 lbs. Deb: 9/13/98 F																							
1998	Bal-A	9	14	3	6	1	0	0	1	0	3	.429	.429	.500	929	143	1	0	0	0	.833	0	/3-6,1-3,D-1	0.1
1999	Bal-A	46	124	13	24	7	0	3	10	8	43	.194	.242	.323	565	44	-11	1	0	0	.963	10	3-45/1-1	0.0
2000	Bal-A	32	84	4	11	1	0	0	3	3	20	.131	.170	.143	313	-20	-15	0	0	0	.926	1	3-26/1-5	-1.4
Total	3	87	222	20	41	9	0	3	14	11	66	.185	.226	.266	492	26	-25	1	0	0	.947	11	/3-77,1-9,D-1	-1.3
■ **MINNIE MINOSO**	Minoso, Saturnino Orestes Armas (Arrieta) (b: Saturnino Orestes Arrieta (Armas)) b: 11/29/22, Havana, Cuba BR/TR, 5'10", 175 lbs. Deb: 4/19/49 C Career OF: (1512-LF 83-CF 87-RF)																							
1949	Cle-A	9	16	2	3	0	0	1	1	2	2	.188	.350	.375	725	94	-0	0	1	-0	1.000	-1	/O-7(0-0-7)	-0.2
1951	Cle-A	8	14	3	6	2	0	0	2	1	1	.429	.529	.571	1101	209	2	0	0	0	.952	-0	/1-7	0.2
	Chi-A★	138	516	109	167	32	14	10	74	71	41	.324	.419	.498	917	150	38	31	10	3	.961	-12	O-82L,3-68/S-1	2.5
	Yr	146	530	112	173	34	**14**	10	76	72	42	.326	.422	.500	922	152	41	**31**	10	**3**	.961	-12	O-82L,3-68/1-7,S-1	2.7
1952	Chi-A★	147	569	96	160	24	9	13	61	71	46	.281	.375	.424	798	121	17	**22**	16	-1	.979	4	*O-143L/3-9,S-1	1.3
1953	Chi-A★	151	556	104	174	24	8	15	104	74	43	.313	.410	.466	875	132	28	**25**	16	-0	.967	6	*O-147(145-0-2),3-10	2.4
1954	Chi-A★	153	568	119	182	29	**18**	19	116	77	46	.320	.416	**.535**	951	154	43	18	11	0	.978	13	*O-146(120-16-13)/3-9	4.9
1955	Chi-A	139	517	79	149	26	7	10	70	76	43	.288	.390	.424	813	115	13	19	8	1	.971	12	*O-138(135-2-7)/3-2	1.8
1956	Chi-A	151	545	106	172	29	**11**	21	88	86	40	.316	.430	.525	954	149	42	12	6	1	.974	3	*O-148L/3-8,1-1	3.5
1957	Chi-A★	153	568	96	176	**36**	5	12	103	79	54	.310	.413	.454	867	136	32	18	15	-1	.984	6	*O-152(152-0-0)/3-1	2.8
1958	Cle-A	149	556	94	168	25	2	24	80	59	53	.302	.384	.484	868	141	32	14	14	-2	.975	13	*O-147(147-0-0)/3-1	3.5
1959	Cle-A★	148	570	92	172	32	0	21	92	54	46	.302	.379	.468	848	136	29	8	10	-2	.985	16	*O-148(148-0-0)	3.4
1960	Chi-A★	154	591	89	**184**	32	4	20	105	52	63	.311	.380	.481	860	132	27	17	13	-1	.980	5	*O-154(152-0-5)	2.1
1961	Chi-A	152	540	91	151	28	3	14	82	67	46	.280	.376	.420	796	114	13	9	4	1	.956	3	*O-147(147-0-0)	0.8
1962	StL-N	39	97	14	19	5	0	1	10	7	17	.196	.271	.278	549	44	-8	4	0	1	.972	-1	O-27(27-0-0)	-0.9
1963	Was-A	109	315	38	72	12	2	4	30	33	38	.229	.317	.317	635	79	-8	8	6	-0	.955	-5	O-74(74-0-0)/3-8	-1.9
1964	Chi-A	30	31	4	7	0	0	1	5	5	3	.226	.351	.323	674	91	-0	0	0	0	1.000	0	/O-5(4-0-1)	0.0
1976	Chi-A	3	8	0	1	0	0	0	0	0	2	.125	.125	.125	250	-27	-1	0	0	0	.000	0	/D-3	-0.1
1980	Chi-A	2	2	0	0	0	0	0	0	0	0	.000	.000	.000	0	-99	-1	0	0	0	.000	0	/H	-0.1
Total	17	1835	6579	1136	1963	336	83	186	1023	814	584	.298	.391	.459	851	130	298	205	130	-0	.974	62	*O-1665L,3-116/1DS	26.0
■ **DOUG MIRABELLI**	Mirabelli, Douglas Anthony b: 10/18/70, Kingman, Ariz. BR/TR, 6'1", 205 lbs. Deb: 8/27/96																							
1996	SF-N	9	18	2	4	1	0	0	1	3	4	.222	.333	.278	611	66	-1	0	0	0	1.000	-1	/C-8	-0.1
1997	SF-N	6	7	0	1	0	0	0	0	1	3	.143	.250	.143	393	6	-1	0	0	0	1.000	0	/C-6	-0.1
1998	SF-N	10	17	2	4	2	0	1	4	2	6	.235	.316	.529	845	124	0	0	0	0	.974	1	C-10	0.2
1999	SF-N	33	87	10	22	6	0	1	10	9	25	.253	.330	.356	686	79	-3	0	0	0	1.000	-2	C-30	-0.3

YEAR	TM/L	G	AB	R	H	2B	3B	HR	RBI	BB	SO	AVG	OBP	SLG	OPS	OPS+	BR+	SB	CS	SBR	FA	FR	G/POS	TPR
2000	*SF-N	82	230	23	53	10	2	6	28	36	57	.230	.340	.370	709	85	-5	1	0	0	.985	-7	C-80	-0.7
Total	5	140	359	37	84	19	2	8	43	51	95	.234	.334	.365	699	83	-9	1	0	0	.989	-9	C-134	-1.0

■ WILLY MIRANDA Miranda, Guillermo (Perez) b: 5/24/26, Velasco, Cuba d: 9/7/96, Baltimore, Md. BB/TR, 5'9.5", 150 lbs. Deb: 5/6/51

YEAR	TM/L	G	AB	R	H	2B	3B	HR	RBI	BB	SO	AVG	OBP	SLG	OPS	OPS+	BR+	SB	CS	SBR	FA	FR	G/POS	TPR
1951	Was-A	7	9	2	4	0	0	0	0	0	0	.444	.444	.444	889	143	1	0	0	0	.818	-0	/S-2,1-1	0.0
1952	Chi-A	12	8	1	2	1	0	0	0	3	0	.250	.455	.375	830	131	1	0	0	0	1.000	4	/S-4,3-4,2-1	0.5
	StL-A	7	11	2	1	0	1	0	1	3	1	.091	.286	.273	558	54	-1	0	0	0	.900	-1	/S-7	-0.1
	Chi-A	58	142	13	31	3	1	0	7	10	14	.218	.275	.254	528	47	-10	1	0	0	.975	11	S-50/2-1,3-1	0.3
	Yr	77	161	16	34	4	2	0	8	16	15	.211	.287	.261	547	52	-10	1	0	0	.970	14	S-61/3-5,2-2	0.7
1953	StL-A	17	6	2	1	0	0	0	0	1	1	.167	.286	.167	452	24	-1	1	1	-0	.933	3	/S-8,3-6	0.3
	NY-A	48	58	12	13	0	0	1	5	5	10	.224	.286	.276	562	54	-4	1	1	-0	.984	17	S-45	1.4
	Yr	65	64	14	14	0	0	1	5	6	11	.219	.286	.266	551	51	-4	2	2	-0	.979	20	S-53/3-6	1.7
1954	NY-A	92	116	12	29	4	2	1	12	10	10	.250	.310	.345	654	82	-3	0	3	-1	.948	16	S-88/2-4,3-1	1.6
1955	Bal-A	153	487	42	124	12	6	1	38	42	58	.255	.315	.310	625	74	-18	4	3	-0	.958	19	*S-153/2-1	1.3
1956	Bal-A	148	461	38	100	16	4	2	34	46	73	.217	.288	.282	570	55	-30	3	6	-1	.962	2	*S-147	-1.8
1957	Bal-A	115	314	29	61	3	0	0	20	24	42	.194	.251	.204	455	28	-31	2	1	0	.966	-3	*S-115	-2.7
1958	Bal-A	102	214	15	43	6	0	1	8	14	25	.201	.250	.243	493	38	-18	1	1	-0	.962	-2	*S-102	-1.4
1959	Bal-A	65	88	8	14	5	0	0	7	7	16	.159	.221	.216	437	21	-10	0	0	0	.974	22	S-47,3-11/2-5	1.4
Total	9	824	1914	176	423	50	14	6	132	165	250	.221	.284	.271	555	54	-125	13	16	-3	.962	88	S-768/3-23,2-12,1-1	0.8

■ JOHN MISSE Misse, John Beverly b: 5/30/1885, Highland, Kan. d: 3/18/70, St.Joseph, Mo. BR/TR, 5'8", 150 lbs. Deb: 5/26/14

YEAR	TM/L	G	AB	R	H	2B	3B	HR	RBI	BB	SO	AVG	OBP	SLG	OPS	OPS+	BR+	SB	CS	SBR	FA	FR	G/POS	TPR
1914	StL-F	99	306	28	60	8	1	0	22	36	52	.196	.281	.229	509	38	-31	3			.948	14	2-50,S-48/3-2	-1.4

■ CLARENCE MITCHELL Mitchell, Clarence Elmer b: 2/22/1891, Franklin, Neb. d: 11/6/63, Grand Island, Neb. BL/TL, 5'11.5", 190 lbs. Deb: 6/2/11 C Career OF: (12-LF 0-CF 8-RF)

YEAR	TM/L	G	AB	R	H	2B	3B	HR	RBI	BB	SO	AVG	OBP	SLG	OPS	OPS+	BR+	SB	CS	SBR	FA	FR	G/POS	TPR
1911	Det-A	5	4	2	2	0	0	0	0	1		.500	.600	.500	1100	198	1	0			1.000	-1	/P-5	0.0
1916	Cin-N	56	117	11	28	2	1	0	11	4	6	.239	.264	.274	538	67	-5	1			.985	-2	P-29/1-9,O-3(5-0-0)	-0.5
1917	Cin-N	47	90	13	25	3	0	0	5	5	5	.278	.316	.311	627	97	-0	0			.982	-0	P-32/1-6,O-5(5-0-0)	-0.1
1918	Bro-N	10	24	2	6	1	1	0	2	0	3	.250	.250	.375	625	90	-0	0			.750	-2	/O-6(0-0-6),1-2,P-1	-0.4
1919	Bro-N	34	49	7	18	1	0	1	2	4	4	.367	.415	.449	864	156	3	0			.976	1	P-23	0.0
1920	*Bro-N	55	107	9	25	2	2	0	11	8	9	.234	.287	.290	577	64	-5	1	0	0	1.000	1	P-19,1-11/O-4(2-0-2)	-0.4
1921	Bro-N	46	91	11	24	5	0	0	12	5	7	.264	.316	.319	635	66	-4	3	1	0	.945	3	P-37/1-4	-0.1
1922	Bro-N	56	155	21	45	6	3	3	28	19	6	.290	.371	.426	797	106	2	3	1	0	.992	3	1-42/P-5	0.1
1923	Phi-N	53	78	10	21	3	2	1	9	4	11	.269	.305	.397	702	75	-3	0	0	0	.880	-3	P-29	0.0
1924	Phi-N	69	102	7	26	3	0	0	13	2	7	.255	.276	.284	561	45	-8	0	0	0	**1.000**	3	P-30	0.0
1925	Phi-N	52	92	7	18	2	0	0	13	5	9	.196	.237	.217	455	16	-12	1	0	0	**1.000**	4	P-32/1-2	0.0
1926	Phi-N	39	78	8	19	4	0	0	6	5	5	.244	.289	.295	584	55	-5	2	0	0	.986	4	P-28/1-4	0.0
1927	Phi-N	18	42	5	10	2	0	1	6	2	1	.238	.273	.357	630	67	-2	0			.963	1	P-13	0.0
1928	Phi-N	5	4	0	1	0	0	0	0	0	0	.250	.250	.250	500	30	-0	0			1.000	0	/P-3	0.0
	*StL-N	19	56	0	7	1	0	0	1	0	3	.125	.125	.143	268	-30	-11	0			.982	2	P-19	0.0
	Yr	24	60	0	8	1	0	0	1	0	3	.133	.133	.150	283	-26	-11	0			.983	3	P-22	0.0
1929	StL-N	26	66	9	18	3	1	0	9	4	6	.273	.314	.348	663	63	-4	1			.974	-1	P-25	0.0
1930	StL-N	1	2	0	1	0	0	0	0	0	0	.500	.500	.500	1000	138	0	0			.000	-0	/P-1	0.0
	NY-N	24	47	9	12	1	0	0	1	1	5	.255	.271	.277	547	33	-5	0			1.000	2	P-24	0.0
	Yr	25	49	9	13	1	0	0	1	1	5	.265	.280	.286	566	38	-5	0			1.000	2	P-25	0.0
1931	NY-N	27	73	5	16	2	0	1	4	2	4	.219	.240	.288	528	42	-6	0			.885	-2	P-27	0.0
1932	NY-N	8	10	2	2	0	0	0	0	1	1	.200	.273	.200	473	30	-1	0			.833	-1	/P-8	0.0
Total	18	650	1287	138	324	41	10	7	133	72	92	.252	.293	.315	609	64	-65	9	1		.972	14	P-390/1-80,O-18L	-1.4

■ FRED MITCHELL Mitchell, Frederick Francis (b: Frederick Francis Yapp) b: 6/5/1878, Cambridge, Mass. d: 10/13/70, Newton, Mass. BR/TR, 5'9.5", 185 lbs. Deb: 4/27/01 MC Career OF: (1-LF 2-CF 0-RF)

YEAR	TM/L	G	AB	R	H	2B	3B	HR	RBI	BB	SO	AVG	OBP	SLG	OPS	OPS+	BR+	SB	CS	SBR	FA	FR	G/POS	TPR
1901	Bos-A	20	44	5	7	0	2	0	4	2		.159	.196	.250	446	23	-5	0			.875	-0	P-17/2-2,S-1	-0.1
1902	Bos-A	1	1	0	0	0	0	0	0	0		.000	.000	.000	0	-97	-0	0			.667	0	/P-1	0.0
	Phi-A	20	48	7	9	1	1	0	3	1		.188	.204	.250	454	24	-5	1			.942	2	P-18/O-1(0-1-0)	-0.1
	Yr	21	49	7	9	1	1	0	3	1		.184	.200	.245	445	22	-5	1			.927	2	P-19/O-1(0-1-0)	-0.1
1903	Phi-N	29	95	11	19	4	0	0	10	0		.200	.200	.242	442	27	-9	0			.857	-3	P-28	0.0
1904	Phi-N	25	82	9	17	3	1	0	3	5		.207	.253	.268	521	63	-4	1			.981	3	P-13/1-9,3-2,O-1C	-0.2
	Bro-N	8	24	3	7	1	1	0	6	1		.292	.346	.417	763	139	1	0			.906	1	/P-8	0.0
	Yr	33	106	12	24	4	2	0	9	6		.226	.274	.302	576	80	-3	1			.952	4	P-21/1-9,3-2,O-1C	-0.2
1905	Bro-N	27	79	4	15	0	0	0	8	4		.190	.238	.190	428	30	-7	0			.881	-2	P-12/1-7,3-4,S-1,O	-0.6
1910	NY-A	68	196	16	45	7	2	0	18	9		.230	.274	.286	560	71	-7	6			.968	-15	C-62	-1.8
1913	Bos-N	4	3	0	1	0	0	0	0	0	2	.333	.333	.333	667	89	-0	0			.000	0	H	0.0
Total	7	202	572	55	120	16	7	0	52	22	2	.210	.245	.262	508	52	-35	8			.904	-14	/P-97,C-62,1-16,3OS2	-2.8

■ JOHNNY MITCHELL Mitchell, John Franklin b: 8/9/1894, Detroit, Mich. d: 11/4/65, Birmingham, Mich. BB/TR, 5'8", 155 lbs. Deb: 5/21/21

YEAR	TM/L	G	AB	R	H	2B	3B	HR	RBI	BB	SO	AVG	OBP	SLG	OPS	OPS+	BR+	SB	CS	SBR	FA	FR	G/POS	TPR
1921	NY-A	13	42	4	11	1	0	0	2	4	4	.262	.326	.286	612	56	-3	1	0	0	.958	-6	/S-7,2-5	-0.7
1922	NY-A	4	4	1	0	0	0	0	0	0	1	.000	.000	.000	0	-98	-1	0	0	0	1.000	-1	/S-4	-0.2
	Bos-A	59	203	20	51	4	1	1	8	16	17	.251	.318	.296	614	61	-11	1	2	-0	.962	-5	S-58	-1.0
	Yr	63	207	21	51	4	1	1	8	16	18	.246	.313	.290	603	58	-12	1	2	-0	.963	-6	S-62	-1.2
1923	Bos-A	92	347	40	78	15	4	0	19	34	18	.225	.296	.291	587	55	-23	7	11	-2	.961	-0	S-87/2-5	-1.6
1924	Bro-N	64	243	42	64	10	0	1	16	37	22	.263	.361	.317	678	86	-3	3	1	0	.951	-1	S-64	0.4
1925	Bro-N	97	336	45	84	8	3	0	18	28	19	.250	.308	.292	599	55	-22	2	0	0	.947	-4	S-90	-1.5
Total	5	329	1175	152	288	38	8	2	63	119	81	.245	.317	.296	613	62	-63	14	14	-2	.955	-17	S-310/2-10	-4.6

■ KEITH MITCHELL Mitchell, Keith Alexander b: 8/6/69, San Diego, Cal. BR/TR, 5'10", 180 lbs. Deb: 7/23/91

YEAR	TM/L	G	AB	R	H	2B	3B	HR	RBI	BB	SO	AVG	OBP	SLG	OPS	OPS+	BR+	SB	CS	SBR	FA	FR	G/POS	TPR
1991	*Atl-N	48	66	11	21	0	0	2	5	8	12	.318	.392	.409	801	118	2	3	1	0	.970	-7	O-34(24-1-10)	-0.5
1994	Sea-A	46	128	21	29	2	0	5	15	18	22	.227	.327	.359	686	75	-5	0	0	0	.980	-7	O-38(27-3-11)/D-6	-1.2
1996	Cin-N	11	15	2	4	1	0	1	3	1	3	.267	.313	.533	846	117	0	0	0	0	.875	-1	O-5(2-1-2)	0.0
1998	Bos-A	23	33	4	9	2	0	0	6	7	5	.273	.400	.333	733	92	-0	1	0	0	1.000	-3	D-12,O-10(4-0-6)	-0.3
Total	4	128	242	38	63	5	0	8	29	34	42	.260	.354	.380	734	91	-2	4	1	1	.969	-17	/O-87(57-5-29),D-18	-2.0

■ KEVIN MITCHELL Mitchell, Kevin Darnell b: 1/13/62, San Diego, Cal. BR/TR, 5'11", 210 lbs. Deb: 9/4/84 Career OF: (756-LF 6-CF 53-RF)

YEAR	TM/L	G	AB	R	H	2B	3B	HR	RBI	BB	SO	AVG	OBP	SLG	OPS	OPS+	BR+	SB	CS	SBR	FA	FR	G/POS	TPR
1984	NY-N	7	14	0	3	0	0	0	1	0	3	.214	.214	.214	429	21	-1	0	1	-0	.833	-1	/3-5	-0.3
1986	*NY-N	108	328	51	91	22	2	12	43	33	61	.277	.345	.466	812	125	11	3	3	-0	.983	-11	O-68L,S-24/3-7,1-2	-0.1
1987	SD-N	62	196	19	48	7	1	7	26	20	38	.245	.315	.398	713	91	-3	0	0	0	.945	4	3-51/O-3(3-0-0)	0.0
	*SF-N	69	268	49	82	13	1	15	44	28	50	.306	.376	.530	906	144	16	9	6	-0	.962	-5	3-68/O-3(2-0-1),S-1	1.0
	Yr	131	464	68	130	20	2	22	70	48	88	.280	.350	.474	824	121	13	9	6	-0	.954	-2	*3-119/O-6(5-0-1),S-1	1.0
1988	SF-N	148	505	60	127	25	7	19	80	48	85	.251	.323	.442	764	123	13	5	5	-1	.943	-5	*3-102,O-40(40-0-0)	0.7
1989	*SF-N★	154	543	100	158	34	6	**47**	**125**	87	115	.291	.392	**.635**	**1027**	**194**	**66**	3	4	-1	.978	7	*O-147(147-0-0)/3-2	**7.0**
1990	SF-N★	140	524	90	152	24	2	35	93	58	87	.290	.363	.544	907	151	35	4	7	-2	.971	7	*O-138(138-0-0)	3.7
1991	SF-N	113	371	52	95	13	1	27	69	43	57	.256	.341	.515	856	142	20	2	3	-1	.970	3	*O-100(100-0-0)/1-1	1.9
1992	Sea-A	99	360	48	103	24	0	9	67	35	46	.286	.354	.428	782	117	8	0	2	-1	1.000	-0	O-69(69-0-0),D-26	0.5
1993	Cin-N	93	323	56	110	21	3	19	64	25	48	.341	.390	.601	990	160	26	1	0	0	.957	1	O-87(85-0-2)	2.5
1994	Cin-N	95	310	57	101	18	1	30	77	59	62	.326	.438	.681	1119	188	41	2	0	0	.972	4	O-89(89-0-0)/1-1	4.1
1996	Bos-A	27	92	9	28	4	0	2	13	11	14	.304	.385	.413	798	100	0	0	0	0	.935	-3	O-21(1-0-21)/D-4	-0.4
	Cin-N	37	114	18	37	11	0	6	26	26	16	.325	.450	.579	1029	168	12	0	0	0	.978	-2	O-31(31-0-0)/1-3	0.9
1997	Cle-A	20	59	7	9	1	0	4	11	9	11	.153	.275	.373	648	65	-3	1	0	0	.000	-1	D-16/O-1(1-0-0)	-0.4
1998	Oak-A	51	127	14	29	7	1	2	21	9	26	.228	.279	.346	626	63	-7	0	0	0	1.000	-2	D-23,O-10(10-0-0)/1-2	-1.0
Total	13	1223	4134	630	1173	224	25	234	760	491	719	.284	.363	.520	883	143	235	30	31	-4	.971	-5	O-807L,3-235/D-69,S1	20.1

■ DALE MITCHELL
Mitchell, Loren Dale b: 8/23/21, Colony, Okla. d: 1/5/87, Tulsa, Okla. BL/TL, 6'1", 195 lbs. Deb: 9/15/46

YEAR	TM/L	G	AB	R	H	2B	3B	HR	RBI	BB	SO	AVG	OBP	SLG	OPS	OPS+	BR+	SB	CS	SBR	FA	FR	G/POS	TPR
1946	Cle-A	11	44	7	19	3	0	0	5	1	2	.432	.444	.500	944	175	4	1	0	0	1.000	-0	O-11(0-11-0)	0.4
1947	Cle-A	123	493	69	156	16	10	1	34	23	14	.316	.347	.396	742	109	4	2	5	-1	.977	-9	*O-115(83-42-1)	-1.4
1948	*Cle-A	141	608	82	204	30	8	4	56	45	17	.336	.383	.431	814	119	16	13	18	-3	**.991**	4	*O-140(140-1-0)	0.5
1949	Cle-A★	149	640	81	**203**	16	**23**	3	56	43	11	.317	.360	.428	788	110	7	10	3	1	**.994**	3	*O-149(149-0-0)	0.0
1950	Cle-A	130	506	81	156	27	5	3	49	67	21	.308	.390	.399	789	106	6	3	7	-2	.972	-11	*O-127(127-0-0)	-1.6
1951	Cle-A	134	510	83	148	21	7	11	62	53	16	.290	.358	.424	782	117	12	7	7	-1	.992	-6	*O-124(124-0-0)	-0.5
1952	Cle-A★	134	511	61	165	26	3	5	58	52	9	.323	.387	.415	801	132	22	6	6	-1	.992	-5	*O-128(128-0-0)	0.7
1953	Cle-A	134	500	76	150	26	4	13	60	42	20	.300	.354	.446	800	118	11	3	1	0	.970	-6	*O-125(125-0-0)	-0.2
1954	*Cle-A	53	60	6	17	1	0	1	6	9	1	.283	.377	.350	727	98	0	0	0	0	.889	-1	/O-6(6-0-0),1-1	-0.1
1955	Cle-A	61	58	4	15	2	1	0	10	4	3	.259	.306	.328	634	68	-3	0	0	0	1.000	-1	/1-8,O-3(3-0-0)	-0.4
1956	Cle-A	38	30	2	4	0	0	0	6	7	2	.133	.297	.133	431	17	-3	0	0	0	.000	-0	/O-1(1-0-0)	-0.4
	*Bro-N	19	24	3	7	1	0	0	1	0	3	.292	.292	.333	625	63	-1	0	0	0	1.000	-0	/O-2(2-0-0)	-0.2
Total	11	1127	3984	555	1244	169	61	41	403	346	119	.312	.368	.416	784	114	75	45	47	-7	.985	-32	O-931(888-54-1)/1-9	-3.2

■ MIKE MITCHELL
Mitchell, Michael Francis b: 12/12/1879, Springfield, Ohio d: 7/16/61, Phoenix, Ariz. BR/TR, 6'1", 185 lbs. Deb: 4/11/07 Career OF: (126-LF 76-CF 905-RF)

YEAR	TM/L	G	AB	R	H	2B	3B	HR	RBI	BB	SO	AVG	OBP	SLG	OPS	OPS+	BR+	SB	CS	SBR	FA	FR	G/POS	TPR
1907	Cin-N	148	558	64	163	17	12	3	47	37		.292	.339	.382	721	121	12	17			.962	22	*O-146(3-0-144)/1-2	3.1
1908	Cin-N	119	406	41	90	9	6	1	37	46		.222	.304	.281	585	89	-4	18			.959	1	*O-118(3-0-115)/1-1	-1.0
1909	Cin-N	145	523	83	162	17	**17**	4	86	57		.310	.378	.430	808	152	31	37			.962	6	*O-145(0-0-144)/1-1	3.3
1910	Cin-N	156	583	79	167	16	**18**	5	88	59	56	.286	.356	.401	757	126	19	35			.958	-3	*O-149(0-22-127)/1-7	0.9
1911	Cin-N	142	529	74	154	22	22	2	84	44	34	.291	.348	.427	775	121	13	35			.971	11	*O-140(1-0-139)	1.6
1912	Cin-N	147	552	60	156	14	13	4	78	41	43	.283	.333	.377	710	97	-3	23			.947	-1	*O-144(0-0-144)	-1.1
1913	Chi-N	82	279	37	73	11	6	4	35	32	33	.262	.340	.387	727	107	3	15			.941	4	O-82(72-0-10)	0.3
	Pit-N	54	199	25	54	8	2	1	16	14	15	.271	.319	.347	666	94	-2	8			.946	7	O-54(0-54-0)	0.2
	Yr	136	478	62	127	19	8	5	51	46	48	.266	.331	.370	702	102	1	23			.943	11	*O-136(72-54-10)	0.5
1914	Pit-N	76	273	31	64	11	5	2	23	16	16	.234	.279	.333	613	86	-6	5			.984	9	O-76(0-0-76)	-0.1
	Was-A	55	193	20	55	5	3	1	20	22	19	.285	.361	.358	719	112	3	9	7	-0	.957	4	O-53(47-0-6)	0.5
Total	8	1124	4095	514	1138	130	104	27	514	368	216	.278	.340	.380	720	114	65	202	7		.959	60	*O-1107R/1-11	7.7

■ BOBBY MITCHELL
Mitchell, Robert McKasha b: 2/6/1856, Cincinnati, Ohio d: 5/1/33, Springfield, Ohio BL/TL, 5'5", 135 lbs. Deb: 9/6/1877 Career OF: (0-LF 10-CF 4-RF)

YEAR	TM/L	G	AB	R	H	2B	3B	HR	RBI	BB	SO	AVG	OBP	SLG	OPS	OPS+	BR+	SB	CS	SBR	FA	FR	G/POS	TPR
1877	Cin-N	13	49	5	10	3	0	0	5	1	2	.204	.220	.265	485	59	-2				.920	-1	P-12/O-2(0-1-1)	-0.1
1878	Cin-N	13	49	4	12	0	0	0	8	1	4	.245	.260	.245	505	74	-1				.944	0	/P-9,S-2,O-1(0-1-1)	0.0
1879	Cle-N	30	109	11	16	2	2	0	6	0	14	.147	.147	.202	349	14	-10				.714	-6	P-23/O-9(0-8-1)	-0.5
1882	StL-a	1	4	0	0	0	0	0		0		.000	.000	.000	0	-96	-1				.000	-1	/O-1(0-0-1),P-1	-0.1
Total	4	57	211	20	38	5	2	0	19	2	20	.180	.188	.223	411	35	-14				.811	-7	/P-45,O-13C,S-2	-0.7

■ BOBBY MITCHELL
Mitchell, Robert Van b: 4/7/55, Salt Lake City, Utah BL/TL, 5'10", 170 lbs. Deb: 9/1/80

YEAR	TM/L	G	AB	R	H	2B	3B	HR	RBI	BB	SO	AVG	OBP	SLG	OPS	OPS+	BR+	SB	CS	SBR	FA	FR	G/POS	TPR
1980	LA-N	9	3	1	1	0	0	0	0	1	0	.333	.500	.333	833	139	0	0	0	0	1.000	-3	/O-8(0-7-1)	-0.3
1981	LA-N	10	8	0	1	0	0	0	0	1	4	.125	.222	.125	347	1	-1	0	0	0	1.000	-3	/O-7(1-6-1)	-0.4
1982	Min-A	124	454	48	113	11	6	2	28	54	53	.249	.331	.313	644	76	-13	8	9	-1	.997	14	*O-121(5-115-6)	-0.3
1983	Min-A	59	152	26	35	4	2	1	15	28	21	.230	.354	.303	656	80	-3	1	1	-0	.990	-3	O-44(1-43-0)	-0.7
Total	4	202	617	75	150	15	8	3	43	84	78	.243	.337	.308	645	76	-17	9	10	-2	.996	5	O-180(7-171-8)	-1.7

■ BOBBY MITCHELL
Mitchell, Robert Vance b: 10/22/43, Norristown, Pa. BR/TR, 6'4", 190 lbs. Deb: 7/5/70

YEAR	TM/L	G	AB	R	H	2B	3B	HR	RBI	BB	SO	AVG	OBP	SLG	OPS	OPS+	BR+	SB	CS	SBR	FA	FR	G/POS	TPR
1970	NY-A	10	22	1	5	2	0	0	4	2	3	.227	.320	.318	638	81	-1	0	2	-1	1.000	1	/O-7(0-2-5)	0.0
1971	Mil-A	35	55	7	10	1	1	2	6	6	18	.182	.262	.345	608	72	-2	0	2	-1	.974	1	O-19(2-7-10)	-0.3
1973	Mil-A	47	130	12	29	6	0	5	20	5	32	.223	.252	.385	636	79	-4	4	1	1	.960	-4	O-20(10-0-10),D-19	-0.9
1974	Mil-A	88	173	27	42	6	2	5	20	18	46	.243	.318	.387	705	103	0	7	6	-1	.969	-5	D-53,O-26(10-2-14)	-0.7
1975	Mil-A	93	229	39	57	14	3	9	41	25	69	.249	.323	.454	777	117	4	3	4	-1	.992	-4	O-72(72-0-0),D-11	-0.4
Total	5	273	609	86	143	29	6	21	91	56	168	.235	.301	.406	707	100	-2	14	15	-2	.984	-11	O-144(94-11-39)/D-83	-2.3

■ RALPH MITTERLING
Mitterling, Ralph "Sarge" b: 4/19/1890, Freeburg, Pa. d: 1/22/56, Pittsburgh, Pa. BR/TR, 5'10", 165 lbs. Deb: 7/7/16

YEAR	TM/L	G	AB	R	H	2B	3B	HR	RBI	BB	SO	AVG	OBP	SLG	OPS	OPS+	BR+	SB	CS	SBR	FA	FR	G/POS	TPR
1916	Phi-A	13	39	1	6	0	0	0	2	3	6	.154	.214	.154	368	11	-4	0			.944	-2	O-12(1-11-0)	-0.8

■ GEORGE MITTERWALD
Mitterwald, George Eugene b: 6/7/45, Berkeley, Cal. BR/TR, 6'2", 206 lbs. Deb: 9/15/66 C Career OF: (1-LF 0-CF 0-RF)

YEAR	TM/L	G	AB	R	H	2B	3B	HR	RBI	BB	SO	AVG	OBP	SLG	OPS	OPS+	BR+	SB	CS	SBR	FA	FR	G/POS	TPR
1966	Min-A	3	5	1	1	0	0	0	0	0	0	.200	.200	.200	400	14	-1	0	0	0	1.000	1	/C-3	0.0
1968	Min-A	11	34	1	7	1	0	0	1	3	8	.206	.270	.235	506	52	-2	0	0	0	.961	0	C-10	-0.1
1969	*Min-A	69	187	18	48	8	0	5	13	17	47	.257	.329	.380	708	96	-1	0	1	-0	.987	11	C-63/O-1(1-0-0)	1.2
1970	*Min-A	117	369	36	82	12	2	15	46	34	84	.222	.291	.388	679	84	-9	3	5	-1	.996	24	*C-117	2.0
1971	Min-A	125	388	38	97	13	1	13	44	39	104	.250	.319	.389	708	97	-2	3	3	-0	.986	-10	*C-120	-0.7
1972	Min-A	64	163	12	30	4	1	1	8	9	37	.184	.227	.239	466	37	-13	0	1	-0	.984	6	C-61	-0.5
1973	Min-A	125	432	50	112	15	0	16	64	39	111	.259	.328	.405	733	101	0	3	1	0	.992	-1	*C-122/D-3	0.5
1974	Chi-N	78	215	17	54	7	0	7	28	18	42	.251	.315	.381	696	90	-3	1	3	-1	.974	-4	C-68	-0.5
1975	Chi-N	84	200	19	44	4	3	5	26	19	42	.220	.288	.345	633	72	-8	0	0	0	.976	-1	C-59,1-10	-0.7
1976	Chi-N	101	303	19	65	7	0	5	28	16	63	.215	.254	.287	541	49	-20	1	2	-0	.981	0	C-64,1-25	-2.0
1977	Chi-N	110	349	40	83	22	0	9	43	28	69	.238	.296	.378	675	72	-14	3	1	0	.989	12	*C-109/1-1	0.3
Total	11	887	2645	251	623	93	7	76	301	222	607	.236	.298	.362	660	80	-72	14	17	-3	.987	40	C-796/1-36,D-3,O-1L	-0.5

■ JOHNNY MIZE
Mize, John Robert "The Big Cat" b: 1/7/13, Demorest, Ga. d: 6/2/93, Demorest, Ga. BL/TR, 6'2", 215 lbs. Deb: 4/16/36 CH

YEAR	TM/L	G	AB	R	H	2B	3B	HR	RBI	BB	SO	AVG	OBP	SLG	OPS	OPS+	BR+	SB	CS	SBR	FA	FR	G/POS	TPR
1936	StL-N	126	414	76	136	30	8	19	93	50	32	.329	.402	.577	979	162	35	1			.994	1	1-97/O-8(0-0-8)	2.5
1937	StL-N★	145	560	103	204	40	7	25	113	56	57	.364	.427	.595	1021	171	55	2			.988	-13	*1-144	2.8
1938	StL-N	149	531	85	179	34	**16**	27	102	74	47	.337	.422	**.614**	**1036**	172	52	0			.989	-2	*1-140	3.7
1939	StL-N★	153	564	104	197	44	14	**28**	108	92	49	**.349**	.444	**.626**	**1070**	**174**	**60**	0			.987	-4	*1-152	**4.1**
1940	StL-N★	155	579	111	182	31	13	**43**	**137**	82	49	.314	.404	**.636**	**1039**	**173**	**56**	7			.990	-7	*1-153	3.5
1941	StL-N★	126	473	67	150	**39**	8	16	100	70	45	.317	.406	.535	941	153	34	4			.994	3	*1-122	2.6
1942	NY-N★	142	541	97	165	25	7	26	**110**	60	39	.305	.380	**.521**	901	161	40	3			**.995**	-3	*1-138	2.6
1946	NY-N★	101	377	70	127	18	3	22	70	62	26	.337	.437	.576	1013	185	43	3			.989	5	*1-101	4.6
1947	NY-N★	154	586	**137**	177	26	2	**51**	**138**	74	42	.302	.384	.614	998	160	48	2			**.996**	9	*1-154	4.9
1948	NY-N★	152	560	110	162	26	4	**40**	125	94	37	.289	.395	.564	959	156	44	4			.991	4	*1-152	4.2
1949	NY-N★	106	388	59	102	15	0	18	62	50	19	.263	.351	.441	792	111	6	1			.994	2	*1-101	0.4
	*NY-A	13	23	4	6	1	0	1	2	4	2	.261	.393	.435	828	119	1	0	0	0	.980	-0	/1-6	0.0
1950	*NY-A	90	274	43	76	12	0	25	72	29	24	.277	.351	.595	946	143	14	0	1	-0	.996	-3	1-72	0.8
1951	*NY-A	113	332	37	86	14	1	10	49	36	24	.259	.339	.398	736	102	1	1	0	0	.994	-4	1-93	-0.6
1952	*NY-A	78	137	9	36	9	0	4	29	11	15	.263	.327	.416	743	112	2	0	0	0	.987	1	1-27	0.2
1953	*NY-A★	81	104	6	26	3	0	4	27	12	17	.250	.339	.394	733	101	0	0	0	0	1.000	-0	1-15	-0.1
Total	15	1884	6443	1118	2011	367	83	359	1337	856	524	.312	.397	.562	959	157	491	28	1		.992	-14	*1-1667/O-8(0-0-8)	36.2

■ JOHN MIZEROCK
Mizerock, John Joseph b: 12/8/60, Punxsutawney, Pa. BL/TR, 5'11", 190 lbs. Deb: 4/12/83

YEAR	TM/L	G	AB	R	H	2B	3B	HR	RBI	BB	SO	AVG	OBP	SLG	OPS	OPS+	BR+	SB	CS	SBR	FA	FR	G/POS	TPR
1983	Hou-N	33	85	8	13	4	1	1	10	12	15	.153	.265	.259	524	49	-6	0	0	0	.967	1	C-33	-0.4
1985	Hou-N	15	38	6	9	4	0	0	6	2	8	.237	.293	.342	635	79	-1	0	0	0	.966	3	C-15	0.3
1986	Hou-N	44	81	9	15	1	1	1	6	24	16	.185	.377	.259	637	81	-1	0	0	0	.987	4	C-42	0.4
1989	Atl-N	11	27	1	6	0	0	0	2	0	3	.222	.222	.222	444	27	-3	0	0	0	1.000	1	C-11	-0.2
Total	4	103	231	24	43	9	2	2	24	38	42	.186	.309	.268	577	64	-10	0	0	0	.979	8	C-101	0.1

■ BILL MIZEUR
Mizeur, William Francis "Bad Bill" b: 6/22/1897, Nokomis, Ill. d: 8/27/76, Decatur, Ill. BL/TR, 6', 180 lbs. Deb: 9/30/23

YEAR	TM/L	G	AB	R	H	2B	3B	HR	RBI	BB	SO	AVG	OBP	SLG	OPS	OPS+	BR+	SB	CS	SBR	FA	FR	G/POS	TPR
1923	StL-A	1	1	0	0	0	0	0	0	0	0	.000	.000	.000		-95	-0	0	0	0	.000	0	H	0.0
1924	StL-A	1	1	0	0	0	0	0	0	0	0	.000	.000	.000		-94	-0	0	0	0	.000	0	H	0.0
Total	2	2	2	0	0	0	0	0	0	0	0	.000	.000	.000	0	-94	-1	0	0	0		0	-0,-0	0.0

■ DAVE MOATES
Moates, David Allan b: 1/30/48, Great Lakes, Ill. BL/TL, 5'9", 163 lbs. Deb: 9/21/74

YEAR	TM/L	G	AB	R	H	2B	3B	HR	RBI	BB	SO	AVG	OBP	SLG	OPS	OPS+	BR+	SB	CS	SBR	FA	FR	G/POS	TPR
1974	Tex-A	1	0	0	0	0	0	0	0	0	0	—	—	—	—	—	0	0	0	0	.000	0	R	0.0

YEAR	TM/L	G	AB	R	H	2B	3B	HR	RBI	BB	SO	AVG	OBP	SLG	OPS	OPS+	BR+	SB	CS	SBR	FA	FR	G/POS	TPR
1975	Tex-A	54	175	21	48	9	0	3	14	13	15	.274	.324	.377	702	99	-1	9	2	1	.984	1	O-51(1-49-1)/D-1	0.1
1976	Tex-A	85	137	21	33	7	1	0	13	11	18	.241	.297	.307	604	75	-4	6	3	0	.991	-10	O-66(8-37-25)/D-7	-1.6
Total	3	140	312	42	81	16	1	3	27	24	33	.260	.313	.346	659	88	-5	15	5	2	.987	-9	O-117(9-86-26)/D-8	-1.5

■ CHAD MOELLER
Moeller, Chad Edward b: 2/18/75, Upland, Cal. BR/TR, 6'3", 207 lbs. Deb: 6/20/2000

YEAR	TM/L	G	AB	R	H	2B	3B	HR	RBI	BB	SO	AVG	OBP	SLG	OPS	OPS+	BR+	SB	CS	SBR	FA	FR	G/POS	TPR
2000	Min-A	48	128	13	27	3	1	1	9	9	33	.211	.263	.273	536	34	-13	1	0	0	.979	2	C-48	-0.8

■ DANNY MOELLER
Moeller, Daniel Edward b: 3/23/1885, DeWitt, Iowa d: 4/14/51, Florence, Ala. BB/TR, 5'11", 165 lbs. Deb: 9/24/07

YEAR	TM/L	G	AB	R	H	2B	3B	HR	RBI	BB	SO	AVG	OBP	SLG	OPS	OPS+	BR+	SB	CS	SBR	FA	FR	G/POS	TPR
1907	Pit-N	11	42	4	12	1	1	0	3	4		.286	.348	.357	705	119	1	2			.800	-2	O-11(0-0-11)	-0.2
1908	Pit-N	36	109	14	21	3	1	0	9	9		.193	.254	.239	493	57	-5	4			.950	-5	O-27(3-1-23)	-1.3
1912	Was-A	132	519	90	143	26	10	6	46	52		.276	.346	.399	745	112	7	30			.944	10	*O-132(31-0-101)	1.0
1913	Was-A	153	589	88	139	15	10	5	42	72	103	.236	.322	.321	643	86	-9	62			.926	6	*O-153(16-0-137)	-1.2
1914	Was-A	151	571	83	143	19	10	1	45	71	89	.250	.341	.324	665	96	-1	26	25	-3	.930	-1	*O-150(1-1-149)	-1.5
1915	Was-A	118	438	65	99	11	10	2	23	59	63	.226	.319	.311	630	87	-7	32	10	4	.952	-3	*O-116(21-0-95)	-1.3
1916	Was-A	78	240	30	59	8	1	1	23	30	35	.246	.335	.300	635	92	-2	13			.963	2	O-63(23-0-40)	-0.4
	Cle-A	25	30	5	2	0	0	0	1	5	6	.067	.200	.067	267	-19	-4	2			1.000	-2	/O-8(3-2-3),2-1	-0.7
	Yr	103	270	35	61	8	1	1	24	35	41	.226	.319	.274	593	78	-6	15			.966	-1	O-71(26-2-43)/2-1	-1.1
Total	7	704	2538	379	618	83	43	15	192	302	296	.243	.328	.328	656	93	-20	171	35		.938	5	O-660(98-4-559)/2-1	-5.6

■ JOE MOFFETT
Moffett, Joseph W. b: 6/1859, Wheeling, W.Va. 6', 179 lbs. Deb: 5/6/1884 F

YEAR	TM/L	G	AB	R	H	2B	3B	HR	RBI	BB	SO	AVG	OBP	SLG	OPS	OPS+	BR+	SB	CS	SBR	FA	FR	G/POS	TPR
1884	Tol-a	56	204	17	41	5	3	0		2		.201	.209	.255	464	49	-12				.957	-5	1-38,3-11/2-4,O-3C	-1.9

■ SAM MOFFETT
Moffett, Samuel R. b: 3/14/1857, Wheeling, W.Va. d: 5/5/07, Butte, Mont. BR/TR, 6', 175 lbs. Deb: 5/15/1884 F Career OF: (14-LF 6-CF 31-RF)

YEAR	TM/L	G	AB	R	H	2B	3B	HR	RBI	BB	SO	AVG	OBP	SLG	OPS	OPS+	BR+	SB	CS	SBR	FA	FR	G/POS	TPR
1884	Cle-N	67	256	26	47	12	2	0	15	8	56	.184	.208	.246	454	41	-17				.827	6	O-42R,P-24/1-2,32	-0.7
1887	Ind-N	11	42	6	6	1	0	0	1	1	6	.143	.143	.146	289	-20	-7	2			.857	-3	/P-6,O-5(1-2-3)	-0.4
1888	Ind-N	10	35	6	4	0	0	0	0	5	4	.114	.225	.114	339	11	-3	0			.750	-3	/P-7,O-3(0-3-0)	-0.2
Total	3	88	333	38	57	13	2	0	16	14	66	.171	.202	.220	422	30	-27	2			.821	1	/O-50R,P-37,1-2,23	-1.3

■ JOHN MOHARDT
Mohardt, John Henry b: 1/21/1898, Pittsburgh, Pa. d: 11/24/61, LaJolla, Cal. BR/TR, 5'10", 165 lbs. Deb: 4/15/22

YEAR	TM/L	G	AB	R	H	2B	3B	HR	RBI	BB	SO	AVG	OBP	SLG	OPS	OPS+	BR+	SB	CS	SBR	FA	FR	G/POS	TPR
1922	Det-A	5	1	2	1	0	0	0	0	1	0	1.000	1.000	1.000	2000	436	1	0	1	-0	1.000	-1	/O-3(1-1-1)	-0.1

■ KID MOHLER
Mohler, Ernest Follette b: 12/13/1874, Oneida, Ill. d: 11/4/61, San Francisco, Cal. BR/TL, 5'4.5", 145 lbs. Deb: 9/29/1894

YEAR	TM/L	G	AB	R	H	2B	3B	HR	RBI	BB	SO	AVG	OBP	SLG	OPS	OPS+	BR+	SB	CS	SBR	FA	FR	G/POS	TPR
1894	Was-N	3	9	0	1	0	0	0	0	2	4	.111	.273	.111	384	-5	-2	0			.952	2	/2-3	0.0

■ JOHNNY MOKAN
Mokan, John Leo b: 9/23/1895, Buffalo, N.Y. d: 2/10/85, Buffalo, N.Y. BR/TR, 5'7", 165 lbs. Deb: 4/15/21

YEAR	TM/L	G	AB	R	H	2B	3B	HR	RBI	BB	SO	AVG	OBP	SLG	OPS	OPS+	BR+	SB	CS	SBR	FA	FR	G/POS	TPR
1921	Pit-N	19	52	7	14	3	2	0	9	5	3	.269	.333	.404	737	92	-1	0	0	0	.946	0	O-15(6-0-7)	-0.1
1922	Pit-N	31	89	9	23	3	1	0	8	9	3	.258	.327	.315	641	65	-4	0	1	-0	.903	-4	O-23(3-0-20)	-1.0
	Phi-N	47	151	20	38	7	1	3	27	16	25	.252	.327	.371	698	73	-6	1	0	0	.905	-6	O-37(36-2-3)/3-2	-1.4
	Yr	78	240	29	61	10	2	3	35	25	28	.254	.327	.350	677	70	-10	1	1	-0	.905	-10	O-60(39-2-23)/3-2	-2.4
1923	Phi-N	113	400	76	125	23	3	10	48	53	31	.313	.401	.460	861	113	9	6	11	-3	.969	7	*O-105(84-21-2)/3-1	0.6
1924	Phi-N	96	366	50	95	15	1	7	44	30	27	.260	.321	.363	684	74	-13	7	5	-0	.986	-0	O-94(93-2-0)	-2.1
1925	Phi-N	75	209	30	69	11	2	6	42	27	9	.330	.417	.488	905	120	7	3	5	-1	.984	-12	O-68(36-32-2)	-0.9
1926	Phi-N	127	456	68	138	23	5	6	62	41	31	.303	.365	.414	780	104	3	4			.967	-8	*O-123(67-0-67)	-1.5
1927	Phi-N	74	213	22	61	13	2	0	33	25	21	.286	.361	.366	728	94	-1	5			.962	-9	O-63(27-9-28)	-1.4
Total	7	582	1936	282	563	98	17	32	273	206	150	.291	.364	.409	773	97	-6	26	22		.966	-32	O-528(352-66-129)/3-3	-7.8

■ FENTON MOLE
Mole, Fenton Le Roy "Muscles" b: 6/14/25, San Leandro, Cal. BL/TL, 6'1.5", 200 lbs. Deb: 9/1/49

YEAR	TM/L	G	AB	R	H	2B	3B	HR	RBI	BB	SO	AVG	OBP	SLG	OPS	OPS+	BR+	SB	CS	SBR	FA	FR	G/POS	TPR
1949	NY-A	10	27	2	5	2	1	0	2	3	5	.185	.267	.333	600	58	-2	0	0	0	1.000	1	/1-8	-0.1

■ BEN MOLINA
Molina, Benjamin Jose b: 7/20/74, Rio Piedras, P.R. BR/TR, 5'11", 200 lbs. Deb: 9/21/98

YEAR	TM/L	G	AB	R	H	2B	3B	HR	RBI	BB	SO	AVG	OBP	SLG	OPS	OPS+	BR+	SB	CS	SBR	FA	FR	G/POS	TPR
1998	Ana-A	2	1	0	0	0	0	0	0	0	0	.000	.000	.000	0	-99	-0	0	0	0	1.000	-0	/C-2	0.0
1999	Ana-A	31	101	8	26	5	0	1	10	6	6	.257	.312	.337	649	66	-5	0	1	-0	.991	7	C-30	0.3
2000	Ana-A	130	473	59	133	20	2	14	71	23	33	.281	.323	.421	743	86	-11	1	0	0	.991	2	*C-127/D-2	0.0
Total	3	163	575	67	159	25	2	15	81	29	39	.277	.320	.405	725	82	-16	1	1	-0	.991	9	C-159/D-2	0.3

■ IZZY MOLINA
Molina, Islay b: 6/3/71, New York, N.Y. BR/TR, 6', 200 lbs. Deb: 8/15/96

YEAR	TM/L	G	AB	R	H	2B	3B	HR	RBI	BB	SO	AVG	OBP	SLG	OPS	OPS+	BR+	SB	CS	SBR	FA	FR	G/POS	TPR
1996	Oak-A	14	25	0	5	2	0	0	1	1	3	.200	.231	.280	511	29	-3	0	0	0	1.000	0	C-12/D-1	-0.2
1997	Oak-A	48	111	6	22	3	1	3	7	3	17	.198	.219	.324	544	40	-10	0	0	0	.992	5	C-48	-0.3
1998	Oak-A	6	2	1	1	0	0	0	0	0	0	.500	.500	.500	1000	165	0	0	0	0	1.000	2	/C-5	0.2
Total	3	68	138	7	28	5	1	3	8	4	20	.203	.225	.319	544	40	-13	0	0	0	.993	7	/C-65,D-1	-0.3

■ JOSE MOLINA
Molina, Jose Benjamin (Matta) b: 6/3/75, Baymon, P.R. BR/TR, 6'1", 195 lbs. Deb: 9/6/99

YEAR	TM/L	G	AB	R	H	2B	3B	HR	RBI	BB	SO	AVG	OBP	SLG	OPS	OPS+	BR+	SB	CS	SBR	FA	FR	G/POS	TPR
1999	Chi-N	10	19	3	5	1	0	0	1	2	4	.263	.333	.316	649	67	-1	0	0	0	1.000	3	C-10	0.2

■ BOB MOLINARO
Molinaro, Robert Joseph b: 5/21/50, Newark, N.J. BL/TR, 6', 190 lbs. Deb: 9/18/75

YEAR	TM/L	G	AB	R	H	2B	3B	HR	RBI	BB	SO	AVG	OBP	SLG	OPS	OPS+	BR+	SB	CS	SBR	FA	FR	G/POS	TPR
1975	Det-A	6	19	2	5	0	1	0	1	1	0	.263	.300	.368	668	84	-0	0	0	0	1.000	-0	/O-6(0-0-6)	-0.1
1977	Det-A	4	4	0	1	1	0	0	0	0	2	.250	.250	.500	750	94	-0	0	0	0	.000	0	H	0.0
	Chi-A	1	2	0	1	0	0	0	0	0	1	.500	.500	.500	1000	174	0	1	0	0	1.000	-0	/O-1(0-0-1)	0.0
	Yr	5	6	0	2	1	0	0	0	0	3	.333	.333	.500	833	119	0	1	0	0	1.000	-0	/O-1(0-0-1)	0.0
1978	Chi-A	105	286	39	75	5	5	6	27	19	12	.262	.315	.378	693	93	-3	22	6	3	1.000	-7	O-62(12-1-50),D-32	-1.1
1979	Bal-A	8	6	0	0	0	0	0	0	1	3	.000	.143	.000	143	-60	-1	1	0	0	1.000	-1	/O-5(5-0-0)	-0.2
1980	Chi-A	119	344	48	100	16	4	5	36	26	29	.291	.353	.404	757	107	4	18	7	2	.957	-2	O-49(49-0-0),D-47	0.0
1981	Chi-A	47	42	7	11	1	1	1	9	8	1	.262	.392	.405	797	133	2	1	0	0	1.000	-0	/O-2(1-0-1),D-4	0.2
1982	Chi-N	65	66	6	13	1	0	1	12	6	5	.197	.264	.258	521	45	-5	1	1	-0	1.000	-1	/O-4(4-0-0)	-0.7
	Phi-N	19	14	0	4	0	0	0	2	3	1	.286	.412	.286	697	96	0	1	0	0	.000	0	H	0.0
	Yr	84	80	6	17	1	0	1	14	9	6	.213	.292	.262	555	55	-5	2	1	0	1.000	-1	/O-4(4-0-0)	-0.7
1983	Phi-N	19	18	1	2	1	0	1	3	0	2	.111	.111	.333	444	19	-2	0	0	0	.000	0	H	-0.3
	Det-A	8	2	3	0	0	0	0	0	1	1	.000	.333	.000	333	1	-0	1	1	-0	.000	0	/D-1	0.0
Total	8	401	803	106	212	25	11	14	90	65	57	.264	.328	.375	702	95	-6	46	15	5	.980	-12	O-129(71-1-58)/D-84	-2.2

■ PAUL MOLITOR
Molitor, Paul Leo b: 8/22/56, St.Paul, Minn. BR/TR, 6', 185 lbs. Deb: 4/7/78 C Career OF: (4-LF 43-CF 4-RF)

YEAR	TM/L	G	AB	R	H	2B	3B	HR	RBI	BB	SO	AVG	OBP	SLG	OPS	OPS+	BR+	SB	CS	SBR	FA	FR	G/POS	TPR
1978	Mil-A	125	521	73	142	26	4	6	45	19	54	.273	.303	.372	676	89	-9	30	12	2	.976	-5	2-91,S-31/3-1,D-2	-0.3
1979	Mil-A	140	584	88	188	27	16	9	62	48	48	.322	.375	.469	845	126	21	33	13	3	.979	1	*2-122,S-10/D-8	3.2
1980	Mil-A†	111	450	81	137	29	2	9	37	48	48	.304	.375	.438	813	126	17	34	7	5	.971	-2	2-91,S-12/3-1,D-7	2.6
1981	*Mil-A	64	251	45	67	11	0	2	19	25	29	.267	.341	.335	675	100	1	10	6	0	.976	2	O-46(0-43-4),D-16	0.1
1982	*Mil-A	160	666	**136**	201	26	8	19	71	69	93	.302	.368	.450	819	132	29	41	9	6	.942	-1	*3-150/S-4,D-6	3.2
1983	Mil-A	152	608	95	164	28	6	15	47	59	74	.270	.336	.410	746	113	10	41	8	6	.966	2	*3-146/D-2	1.6
1984	Mil-A	13	46	3	10	1	0	0	6	2	8	.217	.250	.239	489	38	-4	1	0	0	.933	4	/3-7,D-4	0.0
1985	Mil-A★	140	576	93	171	28	3	10	48	54	80	.297	.358	.408	766	110	8	21	7	2	.953	-2	*3-135/D-4	0.6
1986	Mil-A	105	437	62	123	24	6	9	55	40	81	.281	.342	.426	767	104	2	20	5	3	.944	2	3-91,D-10/O-4(4-0-0)	0.5
1987	Mil-A	118	465	**114**	164	**41**	5	16	75	69	67	.353	.438	.566	1004	159	42	45	10	6	.947	-10	D-58,3-41,2-19	3.4
1988	Mil-A★	154	609	115	190	34	6	13	60	71	54	.312	.386	.452	837	132	28	41	10	6	.941	-8	*3-105,D-49/2-1	2.4
1989	Mil-A	155	615	84	194	35	4	11	56	64	67	.315	.384	.439	823	133	28	27	11	2	.950	4	*3-112,D-28,2-16	3.3
1990	Mil-A	103	418	64	119	27	6	12	45	37	51	.285	.344	.464	808	125	13	18	3	3	.988	-1	2-60,1-37/3-2,D-4	1.3
1991	Mil-A★	158	665	**133**	**216**	32	**13**	17	75	77	62	.325	.400	.489	888	148	45	19	8	1	.986	-1	*D-112,1-46	3.7
1992	Mil-A★	158	609	89	195	36	7	12	89	73	66	.320	.396	.461	857	142	36	31	6	5	.996	-4	*D-108,1-48	3.0
1993	*Tor-A★	160	636	121	**211**	37	5	22	111	77	71	.332	.406	.509	916	144	40	22	4	3	.985	-1	*D-137,1-23	3.1
1994	Tor-A★	115	454	86	155	30	4	14	75	55	48	.341	.414	.518	931	138	27	20	0	4	1.000	0	*D-110/1-5	2.2
1995	Tor-A	130	525	63	142	31	2	15	60	61	57	.270	.352	.423	775	101	1	12	0	3	.000	0	*D-129	-0.3
1996	Min-A	161	660	99	**225**	41	8	9	113	56	72	.341	.395	.468	863	115	17	18	6	2	.993	1	*D-143,1-17	0.8
1997	Min-A	135	538	63	164	32	4	10	89	45	73	.305	.358	.435	793	104	4	11	4	1	.991	-1	*D-122,1-12	-0.4

YEAR	TM/L	G	AB	R	H	2B	3B	HR	RBI	BB	SO	AVG	OBP	SLG	OPS	OPS+	BR+	SB	CS	SBR	FA	FR	G/POS	TPR
1998	Min-A	126	502	75	141	29	5	4	69	45	41	.281	.341	.382	724	87	-9	9	2	1	1.000	0	*D-115/1-9	-1.4
Total	21	2683	10835	1782	3319	605	114	234	1307	1094	1244	.306	.372	.448	820	122	347	504	131	65	.950	-21	*D-1174,3-791,21/SO	32.6

■ FRED MOLLENKAMP

Mollenkamp, Frederick Henry b: 3/15/1890, Cincinnati, Ohio d: 11/1/48, Cincinnati, Ohio Deb: 8/29/14

YEAR	TM/L	G	AB	R	H	2B	3B	HR	RBI	BB	SO	AVG	OBP	SLG	OPS	OPS+	BR+	SB	CS	SBR	FA	FR	G/POS	TPR
1914	Phi-N	3	8	0	1	0	0	0	0	2	0	.125	.300	.125	425	26	-1	0			1.000	2	/1-3	0.1

■ FRITZ MOLLWITZ

Mollwitz, Frederick August b: 6/16/1890, Coburg, Germany d: 10/3/67, Bradenton, Fla. BR/TR, 6'2", 170 lbs. Deb: 9/26/13

YEAR	TM/L	G	AB	R	H	2B	3B	HR	RBI	BB	SO	AVG	OBP	SLG	OPS	OPS+	BR+	SB	CS	SBR	FA	FR	G/POS	TPR
1913	Chi-N	2	7	1	3	0	0	0	0	0	0	.429	.429	.429	857	145	0	0			1.000	-0	/1-2	0.0
1914	Chi-N	13	20	0	3	0	0	0	1	0	3	.150	.150	.150	300	-11	-3	1			.962	-1	/1-4,O-1(0-0-1)	-0.4
	Cin-N	32	111	12	18	2	0	0	5	3	9	.162	.198	.180	378	12	-12	2			.991	1	1-32	-1.3
	Yr	45	131	12	21	2	0	0	6	3	12	.160	.191	.176	367	9	-15	3			.989	0	1-36/O-1(0-0-1)	-1.7
1915	Cin-N	153	525	36	136	21	3	1	51	15	49	.259	.281	.316	597	79	-14	19	11	0	**.996**	0	*1-153	-2.0
1916	Cin-N	65	183	12	41	4	4	0	16	5	12	.224	.245	.290	534	65	-8	6			.981	-1	1-54	-1.1
	Chi-N	33	71	1	19	2	0	0	11	7	6	.268	.333	.296	629	85	-1	4			.976	-1	1-19/O-6(4-0-2)	-0.3
	Yr	98	254	13	60	6	4	0	27	12	18	.236	.271	.291	562	71	-9	10			.980	-2	1-73/O-6(4-0-2)	-1.4
1917	Pit-N	36	140	15	36	4	1	0	12	8	8	.257	.297	.300	597	81	-3	4			.994	-1	1-36/2-1	-0.6
1918	Pit-N	119	432	43	116	12	7	0	45	23	24	.269	.305	.329	634	90	-5	23			.990	-0	*1-119	-1.0
1919	Pit-N	56	168	11	29	2	4	0	12	15	18	.173	.249	.232	481	43	-11	9			.994	-3	1-53/O-1(0-0-1)	-1.8
	StL-N	25	83	7	19	3	0	0	5	7	3	.229	.289	.265	554	71	-3	2			.994	1	1-25	-0.3
	Yr	81	251	18	48	5	4	0	17	22	21	.191	.262	.243	505	52	-14	11			.994	-3	1-78/O-1(0-0-1)	-2.1
Total	7	534	1740	138	420	50	19	1	158	83	132	.241	.278	.294	572	72	-60	70	11		.991	-6	1-497/O-8(4-0-4),2-1	-8.8

■ BLAS MONACO

Monaco, Blas b: 11/16/15, San Antonio, Tex. d: 2/10/2000, San Antonio, Tex. BB/TR, 5'11", 170 lbs. Deb: 8/18/37

YEAR	TM/L	G	AB	R	H	2B	3B	HR	RBI	BB	SO	AVG	OBP	SLG	OPS	OPS+	BR+	SB	CS	SBR	FA	FR	G/POS	TPR
1937	Cle-A	5	7	0	2	0	1	0	2	0	2	.286	.375	.571	946	134	0	0	0	0	1.000	0	/2-3	0.1
1946	Cle-A	12	6	2	0	0	0	0	0	1	1	.000	.143	.000	143	-62	-1	0	0	0	.000	0	H	-0.1
Total	2	17	13	2	2	0	1	0	2	1	3	.154	.267	.308	574	53	-1	0	0	0	1.000	0	/2-3	0.0

■ SHANE MONAHAN

Monahan, Shane Hartland b: 8/12/74, Syosset, N.Y. BL/TR, 6', 195 lbs. Deb: 7/9/98

YEAR	TM/L	G	AB	R	H	2B	3B	HR	RBI	BB	SO	AVG	OBP	SLG	OPS	OPS+	BR+	SB	CS	SBR	FA	FR	G/POS	TPR
1998	Sea-A	62	211	17	51	8	1	4	28	8	53	.242	.269	.346	615	59	-13	1	2	-0	.992	1	O-62(61-3-2)	-1.4
1999	Sea-A	16	15	3	2	0	0	0	0	0	6	.133	.133	.133	267	-32	-3	0	0	0	1.000	-3	/O-9(7-0-3),D-3	-0.5
Total	2	78	226	20	53	8	1	4	28	8	59	.235	.261	.332	593	53	-16	1	2	-0	.992	-2	/O-71(68-3-5),D-3	-1.9

■ FREDDIE MONCEWICZ

Moncewicz, Frederick Alfred b: 9/1/03, Brockton, Mass. d: 4/23/69, Brockton, Mass. BR/TR, 5'8.5", 175 lbs. Deb: 6/19/28

YEAR	TM/L	G	AB	R	H	2B	3B	HR	RBI	BB	SO	AVG	OBP	SLG	OPS	OPS+	BR+	SB	CS	SBR	FA	FR	G/POS	TPR
1928	Bos-A	3	1	0	0	0	0	0	0	0	1	.000	.000	.000	0	-99	-0	0	0	0	1.000	0	/S-2	0.0

■ ALEX MONCHAK

Monchak, Alex b: 12/22/19, Bayonne, N.J. BR/TR, 6', 180 lbs. Deb: 6/22/40 C

YEAR	TM/L	G	AB	R	H	2B	3B	HR	RBI	BB	SO	AVG	OBP	SLG	OPS	OPS+	BR+	SB	CS	SBR	FA	FR	G/POS	TPR
1940	Phi-N	19	14	1	2	0	0	0	0	0	6	.143	.143	.143	286	-22	-2	1			.833	0	/S-9,2-1	-0.2

■ RICK MONDAY

Monday, Robert James b: 11/20/45, Batesville, Ark. BL/TL, 6'3", 200 lbs. Deb: 9/3/66 Career OF: (60-LF 1490-CF 170-RF)

YEAR	TM/L	G	AB	R	H	2B	3B	HR	RBI	BB	SO	AVG	OBP	SLG	OPS	OPS+	BR+	SB	CS	SBR	FA	FR	G/POS	TPR
1966	KC-A	17	41	4	4	1	1	0	2	6	16	.098	.213	.171	383	12	-5	1	1	-0	.964	-1	O-15(0-15-0)	-0.7
1967	KC-A	124	406	52	102	14	6	14	58	42	107	.251	.324	.419	743	122	11	3	6	-1	.972	15	*O-113(3-110-0)	2.3
1968	Oak-A★	148	482	56	132	24	7	8	49	72	143	.274	.373	.402	775	142	26	14	6	1	.978	-0	*O-144(0-144-0)	2.6
1969	Oak-A	122	399	57	108	17	4	12	54	72	100	.271	.389	.424	812	133	20	12	3	2	.964	-2	*O-119(0-119-0)	1.8
1970	Oak-A	112	376	63	109	19	7	10	37	58	99	.290	.388	.457	845	137	20	17	11	-0	.981	1	*O-109(0-109-0)	1.9
1971	*Oak-A	116	355	53	87	9	3	18	56	49	93	.245	.337	.439	776	121	9	6	9	-2	.984	-0	*O-111(0-111-0)	0.5
1972	Chi-N	138	434	68	108	22	5	11	42	78	102	.249	.365	.399	763	105	5	12	9	-1	**.996**	-6	*O-134(0-132-2)	-0.5
1973	Chi-N	149	554	93	148	24	5	26	56	92	124	.267	.372	.469	842	123	18	5	12	-3	.973	1	*O-148(0-148-0)	1.3
1974	Chi-N	142	538	84	158	19	7	20	58	70	94	.294	.377	.467	844	130	22	7	9	-2	.984	2	*O-139(0-139-0)	1.9
1975	Chi-N	136	491	89	131	29	4	17	60	83	95	.267	.374	.446	820	121	16	8	3	1	.973	1	*O-131(0-131-0)	1.4
1976	Chi-N	137	534	107	145	20	5	32	77	60	125	.272	.347	.507	855	129	19	5	9	-2	.993	7	*O-103(5-99-0),1-32	2.0
1977	*LA-N	118	392	47	90	13	1	15	48	60	109	.230	.332	.383	715	91	-4	1	4	-1	.991	-11	*O-115(0-114-1)/1-3	-1.8
1978	*LA-N★	119	342	54	87	14	1	19	57	49	100	.254	.349	.468	817	127	12	2	4	-1	.995	-11	*O-103(11-80-30)/1-1	-0.2
1979	LA-N	12	33	2	10	0	0	0	2	5	6	.303	.395	.303	698	94	0	0	0	0	.964	-0	O-10(0-8-3)	0.0
1980	LA-N	96	194	35	52	7	1	10	25	28	49	.268	.363	.469	832	133	9	2	2	-0	.969	-7	O-50(1-31-25)	0.0
1981	*LA-N	66	130	24	41	1	2	11	25	24	42	.315	.426	.608	1033	198	17	1	2	-0	.962	-6	O-41(6-0-37)	1.0
1982	LA-N	104	210	37	54	6	4	11	42	39	51	.257	.376	.481	857	142	12	2	1	0	.943	-7	O-57(18-0-40)/1-4	0.3
1983	*LA-N	99	178	21	44	7	1	6	20	29	42	.247	.353	.399	752	108	3	0	0	0	.969	-4	O-44(14-0-31)/1-4	-0.4
1984	LA-N	31	47	4	9	2	0	1	7	8	16	.191	.309	.298	607	72	-2	0	0	0	.987	-1	1-10/O-2(2-0-1)	-0.4
Total	19	1986	6136	950	1619	248	64	241	775	924	1513	.264	.362	.443	805	124	209	98	91	-10	.979	-29	*O-1688C/1-54	13.0

■ RAUL MONDESI

Mondesi, Raul Ramon (Avelino) b: 3/12/71, San Cristobal, D.R. BR/TR, 5'11", 202 lbs. Deb: 7/19/93

YEAR	TM/L	G	AB	R	H	2B	3B	HR	RBI	BB	SO	AVG	OBP	SLG	OPS	OPS+	BR+	SB	CS	SBR	FA	FR	G/POS	TPR
1993	LA-N	42	86	13	25	3	1	4	10	4	16	.291	.322	.488	811	120	2	4	1	1	.951	-5	O-40(20-6-17)	-0.3
1994	LA-N	112	434	63	133	27	8	16	56	16	78	.306	.334	.516	850	126	14	11	8	-0	.965	2	*O-112(0-15-109)	1.0
1995	*LA-N★	139	536	91	153	23	6	26	88	33	96	.285	.332	.496	828	126	17	27	4	5	.980	14	*O-138(0-24-114)	2.9
1996	*LA-N	157	634	98	188	40	7	24	88	32	122	.297	.335	.495	831	125	20	14	7	1	.967	16	*O-157(0-0-157)	2.7
1997	LA-N	159	616	95	191	42	5	30	87	44	105	.310	.362	.541	902	143	36	32	15	2	.989	17	*O-159(0-0-159)	4.5
1998	LA-N	148	580	85	162	26	5	30	90	30	112	.279	.318	.497	815	117	11	16	10	0	.980	0	*O-148(0-94-54)	0.9
1999	LA-N	159	601	98	152	29	5	33	99	71	134	.253	.335	.483	817	110	7	36	9	5	.982	6	*O-158(0-1-158)	0.9
2000	Tor-A	96	388	78	105	22	2	24	67	32	73	.271	.331	.523	854	110	4	22	6	3	.967	6	O-96(0-0-96)	0.7
Total	8	1012	3875	621	1109	212	39	187	585	262	736	.286	.336	.506	841	123	111	162	60	15	.976	56	*O-1008(20-140-864)	13.3

■ DON MONEY

Money, Donald Wayne "Brooks" b: 6/7/47, Washington, D.C. BR/TR, 6'1", 190 lbs. Deb: 4/10/68 Career OF: (63-LF 0-CF 0-RF)

YEAR	TM/L	G	AB	R	H	2B	3B	HR	RBI	BB	SO	AVG	OBP	SLG	OPS	OPS+	BR+	SB	CS	SBR	FA	FR	G/POS	TPR
1968	Phi-N	4	13	1	3	2	0	0	2	2	4	.231	.333	.385	718	115	0	0	1	-0	1.000	-1	/S-4	-0.1
1969	Phi-N	127	450	41	103	22	2	6	42	43	83	.229	.298	.327	624	77	-14	1	3	-1	.969	17	*S-126	1.8
1970	Phi-N	120	447	66	132	25	4	14	66	43	68	.295	.366	.463	829	124	15	4	7	-2	.961	11	*3-119/S-2	2.4
1971	Phi-N	121	439	40	98	22	8	7	38	31	80	.223	.279	.358	637	79	-13	4	1	1	.953	5	3-68,O-40L,2-20	-0.9
1972	Phi-N	152	536	54	119	16	2	15	52	41	92	.222	.280	.343	623	74	-19	5	7	-1	**.978**	20	*3-151/S-2	-0.1
1973	Mil-A	145	556	75	158	28	2	11	61	53	53	.284	.350	.401	751	113	10	22	5	3	**.971**	-23	*3-124,S-21	-0.9
1974	Mil-A☆	159	629	85	178	32	3	15	65	62	80	.283	.349	.415	764	120	16	19	6	2	**.989**	-10	*3-157/2-1,D-1	0.8
1975	Mil-A	109	405	58	112	16	1	15	43	31	51	.277	.333	.432	765	114	7	7	9	-2	.951	-21	3-99/S-7	-1.6
1976	Mil-A★	117	439	51	117	18	4	12	62	47	50	.267	.337	.408	745	120	11	6	5	-0	.958	-4	*3-103,D-10/S-1	0.6
1977	Mil-A†	152	570	86	159	28	3	25	83	57	70	.279	.352	.470	822	122	17	8	5	0	.981	-3	*2-116,O-23L,3-15,/D	1.9
1978	Mil-A★	137	518	88	152	30	2	14	54	48	70	.293	.361	.440	801	124	16	3	0	1	.994	-2	1-61,2-36,3-25,D/S	1.3
1979	Mil-A	92	350	52	83	20	1	6	38	40	47	.237	.319	.351	670	81	-9	1	0	0	1.000	-2	D-33,3-26,1-19,2-16	-1.2
1980	Mil-A	86	289	39	74	17	1	17	46	40	36	.256	.348	.498	847	133	13	0	0	0	.940	0	3-55,1-14,D-14,/2-2	1.1
1981	*Mil-A	60	185	17	40	7	0	2	14	19	27	.216	.293	.286	579	71	-7	0	0	0	.977	-5	3-56/1-1,D-2	-1.3
1982	*Mil-A	96	275	40	78	14	3	16	55	32	38	.284	.360	.531	891	150	18	0	2	-1	.923	5	D-66,3-16,1-11,/2-1	2.0
1983	Mil-A	43	114	5	17	5	0	1	8	11	17	.149	.224	.219	443	24	-12	0	0	0	.980	4	D-28,3-11/1-2	-0.9
Total	16	1720	6215	798	1623	302	36	176	729	600	866	.261	.330	.406	736	106	49	80	51	-0	.968	-7	*3-1025,2-192,DS1/O	4.9

■ FRANK MONROE

Monroe, Frank W. b: Hamilton, Ohio Deb: 7/18/1884

YEAR	TM/L	G	AB	R	H	2B	3B	HR	RBI	BB	SO	AVG	OBP	SLG	OPS	OPS+	BR+	SB	CS	SBR	FA	FR	G/POS	TPR
1884	Ind-a	2	8	1	0	0	0	0			0	.000	.000	.000	0	-99	-2				1.000	-1	/O-1(0-0-1),C-1	-0.3

■ JOHN MONROE

Monroe, John Allen b: 8/24/1898, Farmersville, Tex. d: 6/19/56, Conroe, Tex. BL/TR, 5'10", 160 lbs. Deb: 4/16/21

YEAR	TM/L	G	AB	R	H	2B	3B	HR	RBI	BB	SO	AVG	OBP	SLG	OPS	OPS+	BR+	SB	CS	SBR	FA	FR	G/POS	TPR
1921	NY-N	19	21	4	3	0	0	1	3	3	6	.143	.280	.286	566	50	-2	0	0	0	.846	2	/2-8,S-1	0.0
	Phi-N	41	133	13	38	4	2	1	8	11	9	.286	.345	.368	713	82	-3	2	2	-0	.938	5	2-28/3-9	0.3
	Yr	60	154	17	41	4	2	2	11	14	15	.266	.335	.357	692	79	-4	2	2	-0	.920	7	2-36/3-9,S-1	0.3

■ ED MONTAGUE

Montague, Edward Francis b: 7/24/05, San Francisco, Cal. d: 6/17/88, Daly City, Cal. BR/TR, 5'10", 165 lbs. Deb: 5/14/28

YEAR	TM/L	G	AB	R	H	2B	3B	HR	RBI	BB	SO	AVG	OBP	SLG	OPS	OPS+	BR+	SB	CS	SBR	FA	FR	G/POS	TPR
1928	Cle-A	32	51	12	12	0	1	0	3	6	7	.235	.339	.275	613	62	-3	0	0	0	.914	5	S-15/3-9	0.4
1930	Cle-A	58	179	37	47	5	2	1	16	37	38	.263	.392	.330	721	82	-3	1	5	-2	.917	-15	S-46,3-13	-1.3
1931	Cle-A	64	193	27	55	8	3	1	26	21	22	.285	.358	.373	731	87	-3	3	4	-1	.924	16	S-64	1.5

YEAR	TM/L	G	AB	R	H	2B	3B	HR	RBI	BB	SO	AVG	OBP	SLG	OPS	OPS+	BR+	SB	CS	SBR	FA	FR	G/POS	TPR
1932	Cle-A	66	192	29	47	5	1	0	24	21	24	.245	.326	.281	607	55	-12	3	3	-0	.891	-13	S-57,3-11	-2.1
Total	4	220	615	105	161	18	7	2	69	85	91	.262	.357	.324	681	74	-21	7	12	-3	.912	-7	S-182/3-33	-1.5
■ WILLIE MONTANEZ	Montanez, Guillermo (Naranjo) b: 4/1/48, Catano, P.R. BL/TL, 6′1″, 193 lbs. Deb: 4/12/66 Career OF: (2-LF 267-CF 85-RF)																							
1966	Cal-A	8	2	2	0	0	0	0	0	0	2	.000	.000	.000	0	-99	-1	1	0	0	1.000	0	/1-2	0.0
1970	Phi-N	18	25	3	6	0	0	0	3	1	4	.240	.269	.240	509	39	-2	0	0	0	1.000	-1	O-10(1-0-9)/1-5	-0.3
1971	Phi-N	158	599	78	153	27	6	30	99	67	105	.255	.333	.471	804	126	19	4	7	-2	.972	5	*O-158(0-137-24)/1-9	1.8
1972	Phi-N	147	531	60	131	**39**	3	13	64	58	108	.247	.322	.405	727	103	2	1	3	-1	.985	14	*O-130(0-130-0),1-14	1.1
1973	Phi-N	146	552	69	145	16	5	11	65	46	80	.263	.326	.370	696	90	-7	2	6	-2	.994	-6	1-99,O-51(0-0-51)	-2.6
1974	Phi-N	143	527	55	160	33	1	7	79	32	57	.304	.347	.410	757	107	4	3	6	-1	.992	-1	*1-137/O-1(0-0-1)	-1.0
1975	Phi-N	21	84	9	24	8	0	2	16	4	12	.286	.318	.452	771	108	0	1	0	0	.990	2	1-21	0.1
	SF-N	135	518	52	158	26	2	8	85	45	50	.305	.365	.409	774	110	7	5	3	0	.994	-1	*1-134	-0.5
	Yr	156	602	61	182	34	2	10	101	49	62	.302	.359	.415	774	110	8	6	3	0	.993	0	*1-155	-0.4
1976	SF-N	60	230	22	71	15	2	2	20	15	15	.309	.354	.417	771	115	4	2	1	0	.989	4	1-58	0.4
	Atl-N	103	420	52	135	14	0	9	64	21	32	.321	.354	.419	773	112	6	0	4	-1	.986	-6	*1-103	-1.0
	Yr	163	650	74	206	29	2	11	84	36	47	.317	.354	.418	772	113	10	2	5	-1	.987	-1	*1-161	-0.6
1977	Atl-N★	136	544	70	156	31	1	20	68	35	60	.287	.330	.458	788	97	-2	1	1	-0	.992	-4	*1-134	-1.6
1978	NY-N	159	609	66	156	32	0	17	96	60	92	.256	.324	.392	716	103	1	9	4	1	.995	3	*1-158	-0.6
1979	NY-N	109	410	36	96	19	0	5	47	25	48	.234	.280	.317	597	65	-21	0	1	-0	.989	3	*1-108	-2.6
	Tex-A	38	144	19	46	6	0	8	24	8	14	.319	.359	.528	887	137	7	0	1	-0	.995	1	1-19,D-17	0.6
1980	SD-N	128	481	39	132	12	4	6	63	36	52	.274	.329	.353	682	96	-3	3	4	-1	.994	1	*1-124	-1.1
	Mon-N	14	19	1	4	0	0	0	1	3	3	.211	.318	.211	529	50	-1	0	1	-0	1.000	0	/1-4	-0.2
	Yr	142	500	40	136	12	4	6	64	39	55	.272	.328	.348	676	94	-4	3	5	-1	.994	1	*1-128	-1.3
1981	Mon-N	26	62	6	11	0	1	0	5	4	9	.177	.227	.210	437	24	-6	0	0	0	.992	1	1-16	-0.6
	Pit-N	29	38	2	10	0	0	1	1	1	2	.263	.282	.342	624	74	-1	0	0	0	1.000	-1	1-11	-0.3
	Yr	55	100	8	21	0	1	1	6	5	11	.210	.248	.260	508	43	-7	0	0	0	.995	0	1-27	-0.9
1982	Pit-N	36	32	4	9	1	0	0	1	3	3	.281	.343	.313	655	82	-1	0	0	0	1.000	0	/1-2,O-2(1-0-0)	-0.1
	Phi-N	18	16	0	1	0	0	0	1	1	3	.063	.118	.063	180	-47	-3	0	0	0	1.000	1	/1-6	-0.3
	Yr	54	48	4	10	1	0	0	2	4	6	.208	.269	.229	498	40	-4	0	0	0	1.000	1	/1-8,O-2(1-0-0)	-0.4
Total	14	1632	5843	645	1604	279	25	139	802	465	751	.275	.331	.402	733	101	2	32	42	-8	.992	15	*1-1164,O-352C/D-17	-8.8
■ RENE MONTEAGUDO	Monteagudo, Rene (Miranda) b: 3/12/16, Havana, Cuba d: 9/14/73, Hialeah, Fla. BL/TL, 5′7″, 165 lbs. Deb: 9/6/38 F																							
1938	Was-A	5	6	0	3	0	0	0	1	0	0	.500	.500	.500	1000	162	1	0	0	0	1.000	-1	/P-5	0.0
1940	Was-A	27	33	4	6	1	1	0	1	1	4	.182	.206	.273	479	24	-4	0	0	0	.941	-1	P-27	0.0
1944	Was-A	10	38	2	11	2	0	0	4	0	1	.289	.289	.342	632	84	-1	0	0	0	.929	-1	/O-9(0-0-9)	-0.3
1945	Phi-N	114	193	26	58	6	0	0	15	28	7	.301	.389	.332	721	104	3	2			.918	-1	O-35(12-0-23),P-14	0.0
Total	4	156	270	32	78	9	1	0	21	29	12	.289	.358	.330	687	94	-2	2	0		.889	-4	/P-46,O-44(12-0-32)	-0.3
■ FELIPE MONTEMAYOR	Montemayor, Felipe Angel "Monty" b: 2/7/30, Monterrey, Mexico BL/TL, 6′2″, 185 lbs. Deb: 4/14/53																							
1953	Pit-N	28	55	5	6	4	0	0	2	4	13	.109	.210	.182	391	3	-8	0	0	0	1.000	1	O-12(1-11-0)	-0.8
1955	Pit-N	36	95	10	20	1	3	2	8	18	24	.211	.342	.347	689	85	-2	1	0	0	.957	-5	O-28(6-14-9)	-0.8
Total	2	64	150	15	26	5	3	2	10	22	37	.173	.295	.287	582	55	-10	1	0	0	.974	-5	/O-40(7-25-9)	-1.6
■ AL MONTGOMERY	Montgomery, Alvin Atlas b: 7/3/20, Loving, N.Mex. d: 4/26/42, Waverly, Va. BR/TR, 5′10.5″, 185 lbs. Deb: 6/20/41																							
1941	Bos-N	42	52	4	10	1	0	0	4	9	8	.192	.323	.212	534	55	-3	0			.976	-6	C-30	-0.8
■ RAY MONTGOMERY	Montgomery, Raymond James b: 8/8/69, Bronxville, N.Y. BR/TR, 6′3″, 195 lbs. Deb: 7/3/96																							
1996	Hou-N	12	14	4	3	1	0	1	4	1	5	.214	.267	.500	767	105	-0	0	0	0	1.000	-2	/O-6(5-1-2)	-0.2
1997	Hou-N	29	68	8	16	4	1	0	4	5	18	.235	.288	.324	611	62	-4	0	0	0	1.000	-0	O-18(2-2-15)	-0.5
1998	Hou-N	6	5	2	2	0	0	0	0	0	0	.400	.400	.400	800	114	0	0	0	0	1.000	-1	/O-2(1-0-1)	0.0
Total	3	47	87	14	21	5	1	1	8	6	23	.241	.290	.356	647	72	-4	0	0	0	1.000	-3	/O-26(8-3-18)	-0.7
■ BOB MONTGOMERY	Montgomery, Robert Edward b: 4/16/44, Nashville, Tenn. BR/TR, 6′1″, 203 lbs. Deb: 9/6/70																							
1970	Bos-A	22	78	8	14	2	0	1	4	6	20	.179	.247	.244	491	33	-7	0	0	0	.981	0	C-22	-0.6
1971	Bos-A	67	205	19	49	11	2	2	24	16	43	.239	.304	.341	645	77	-6	1	0	0	.989	-3	C-66	-0.6
1972	Bos-A	24	77	7	22	1	0	2	7	3	17	.286	.313	.377	689	99	-0	0	0	0	.985	-2	C-22	-0.2
1973	Bos-A	34	128	18	41	6	2	7	25	7	36	.320	.356	.563	918	146	7	0	0	0	.974	1	C-33	0.9
1974	Bos-A	88	254	26	64	10	0	4	38	13	50	.252	.291	.339	630	75	-8	3	0	1	.977	-6	C-79/D-5	-1.1
1975	*Bos-A	62	195	16	44	10	1	2	26	4	37	.226	.245	.318	563	53	-12	1	1	-0	.987	-5	C-53/1-6,D-3	-1.6
1976	Bos-A	31	93	10	23	3	1	3	13	5	20	.247	.286	.398	684	88	-2	0	1	-0	.983	-1	C-30/D-1	-0.2
1977	Bos-A	17	40	6	12	2	0	2	7	4	9	.300	.378	.500	878	123	1	0	0	0	.982	-0	C-15	0.1
1978	Bos-A	10	29	2	7	1	1	0	5	2	12	.241	.290	.345	635	70	-1	0	0	0	.976	0	C-10	0.0
1979	Bos-A	32	86	13	30	4	1	0	7	4	24	.349	.378	.419	796	109	1	1	0	0	.984	-4	C-31	-0.2
Total	10	387	1185	125	306	50	8	23	156	64	268	.258	.300	.372	672	83	-27	6	2	1	.983	-19	C-361/D-9,1-6	-3.5
■ CHARLIE MONTOYO	Montoyo, Jose Carlos (Diaz) b: 10/17/65, Florida, P.R. BR/TR, 5′10″, 170 lbs. Deb: 9/7/93																							
1993	Mon-N	4	5	1	2	1	0	0	3	0	0	.400	.400	.600	1000	157	0	0	0	0	.000	0	/2-3	0.0
■ AL MONTREUIL	Montreuil, Allan Arthur b: 8/23/43, New Orleans, La. BR/TR, 5′5″, 158 lbs. Deb: 9/1/72																							
1972	Chi-N	5	11	0	1	0	0	0	0	1	4	.091	.167	.091	258	-23	-2	0	0	0	1.000	0	/2-5	-0.2
■ DAN MONZON	Monzon, Daniel Francisco b: 5/17/46, Bronx, N.Y. d: 1/21/96, Santo Domingo, D.R. BR/TR, 5′10″, 182 lbs. Deb: 4/25/72 Career OF: (2-LF 0-CF 0-RF)																							
1972	Min-A	55	55	13	15	1	0	0	5	8	12	.273	.365	.291	656	92	-0	1	0	0	.977	9	2-13/3-5,S-3,O-1L	1.1
1973	Min-A	39	76	10	17	1	1	0	4	11	9	.224	.330	.263	593	66	-3	1	0	0	.968	9	2-17,3-14/O-1(1-0-0)	0.7
Total	2	94	131	23	32	2	1	0	9	19	21	.244	.344	.275	619	77	-3	2	0	0	.971	18	/2-30,3-19,S-3,O-2L	1.8
■ JOE MOOCK	Moock, Joseph Geoffrey b: 3/12/44, Plaquemine, La. BL/TR, 6′1″, 180 lbs. Deb: 9/1/67																							
1967	NY-N	13	40	2	9	2	0	0	5	0	7	.225	.225	.275	500	43	-3	0	0	0	.917	2	3-12	-0.2
■ GEORGE MOOLIC	Moolic, George Henry "Prunes" b: 3/12/1865, Lawrence, Mass. d: 2/19/15, Methuen, Mass. BR/TR, 5′7″, 145 lbs. Deb: 5/1/1886																							
1886	Chi-N	16	56	9	8	3	0	0	2	2	17	.143	.172	.196	369	10	-6	0			.945	3	C-15/O-2(0-0-2)	-0.2
■ WALLY MOON	Moon, Wallace Wade b: 4/3/30, Bay, Ark. BL/TR, 6′, 175 lbs. Deb: 4/13/54 C Career OF: (621-LF 212-CF 394-RF)																							
1954	StL-N	151	635	106	193	29	9	12	76	71	73	.304	.375	.435	809	109	10	18	10	0	.978	2	*O-148(10-139-0)	0.4
1955	StL-N	152	593	86	175	24	8	19	76	47	65	.295	.350	.459	809	113	10	11	11	-1	.975	-9	*O-100(34-44-28),1-51	-0.8
1956	StL-N	149	540	86	161	22	11	16	68	80	50	.298	.390	.469	858	129	24	12	9	-1	.988	0	O-97(0-1-96),1-52	1.8
1957	StL-N★	142	516	86	152	28	5	24	73	62	57	.295	.371	.508	879	131	23	5	6	-1	.966	-9	*O-133(89-13-48)	0.6
1958	StL-N	108	290	36	69	10	3	7	38	47	30	.238	.344	.366	710	85	-5	2	3	-1	.984	-8	O-82(31-8-54)	-1.8
1959	*LA-N★	145	543	93	164	26	**11**	19	74	81	64	.302	.396	.495	891	126	22	15	6	1	.983	-4	*O-143(128-4-29)/1-1	1.2
1960	LA-N	138	469	74	140	21	6	13	69	67	53	.299	.387	.452	839	121	15	6	10	-2	.986	4	*O-127(115-0-18)	1.1
1961	LA-N	134	463	79	152	25	3	17	88	89	79	.328	**.438**	.505	943	137	29	7	5	-0	.970	-9	*O-133(126-0-19)	1.2
1962	LA-N	95	244	36	59	9	1	4	31	30	33	.242	.327	.336	663	84	-5	5	2	0	.981	-2	O-36(24-0-12),1-32	-1.1
1963	LA-N	122	343	41	90	13	2	8	48	45	43	.262	.350	.382	732	119	9	5	5	-1	.962	-13	O-96(48-3-60)	-1.1
1964	LA-N	68	118	8	26	2	1	2	9	12	22	.220	.292	.305	597	74	-4	1	1	-0	1.000	-1	O-23(6-0-17)	-0.7
1965	*LA-N	53	89	6	18	3	0	1	11	13	22	.202	.304	.270	574	67	-4	2	0	0	1.000	-2	O-23(10-0-13)	-0.7
Total	12	1457	4843	737	1399	212	60	142	661	644	591	.289	.374	.445	819	117	124	89	68	-4	.978	-50	*O-1141L,1-136	0.1
■ AL MOORE	Moore, Albert James b: 8/4/02, Brooklyn, N.Y. d: 11/29/74, AtSea N.Y.To P.R BR/TR, 5′10″, 174 lbs. Deb: 9/27/25																							
1925	NY-N	2	8	0	1	0	0	0	0	1	2	.125	.222	.125	347	-9	-1	0	1	-0	1.000	-0	/O-2(2-0-0)	-0.2
1926	NY-N	28	81	12	18	4	0	0	10	5	7	.222	.267	.272	539	46	-6	2			.966	3	O-20(5-16-0)	-0.4
Total	2	30	89	12	19	4	0	0	10	6	9	.213	.263	.258	522	41	-7	2	1		.968	3	/O-22(7-16-0)	-0.6

■ JUNIOR MOORE Moore, Alvin Earl b: 1/25/53, Waskom, Tex. BR/TR, 5'11", 185 lbs. Deb: 8/2/76 Career OF: (61-LF 0-CF 12-RF)

YEAR	TM/L	G	AB	R	H	2B	3B	HR	RBI	BB	SO	AVG	OBP	SLG	OPS	OPS+	BR+	SB	CS	SBR	FA	FR	G/POS	TPR
1976	Atl-N	20	26	1	7	1	0	0	2	4	4	.269	.387	.308	695	93	0	0	0	0	.929	1	/3-6,2-1,O-1(1-0-0)	0.1
1977	Atl-N	112	361	41	94	9	3	5	34	33	29	.260	.324	.343	668	71	-14	4	5	-1	.942	-4	*3-104/2-1	-2.1
1978	Chi-A	24	65	8	19	0	1	0	4	6	7	.292	.352	.323	675	90	-1	1	1	-0	.857	-0	D-12/3-6,O-5(5-0-0)	-0.2
1979	Chi-A	88	201	24	53	6	2	1	23	12	20	.264	.305	.328	634	71	-8	0	2	-1	.966	-9	O-61L,D-10/2-2	-1.9
1980	Chi-A	45	121	9	31	4	1	1	10	7	11	.256	.297	.331	627	72	-5	0	2	-1	.929	-2	3-34/O-3L,1-1,D-2	-0.8
Total	5	289	774	83	204	20	7	7	73	62	71	.264	.320	.335	654	73	-28	5	10	-2	.936	-14	3-150/O-70L,D-24,21	-4.9

■ ANSE MOORE Moore, Anselm Winn b: 9/22/17, Delhi, La. d: 10/29/93, Pearl, Miss. BL/TR, 6'1", 190 lbs. Deb: 4/17/46

YEAR	TM/L	G	AB	R	H	2B	3B	HR	RBI	BB	SO	AVG	OBP	SLG	OPS	OPS+	BR+	SB	CS	SBR	FA	FR	G/POS	TPR
1946	Det-A	51	134	16	28	4	0	1	8	12	9	.209	.279	.261	540	48	-9	1	1	-0	.971	1	O-32(17-0-15)	-1.1

■ ARCHIE MOORE Moore, Archie Francis b: 8/30/41, Upper Darby, Pa. BL/TL, 6'2", 190 lbs. Deb: 4/20/64

YEAR	TM/L	G	AB	R	H	2B	3B	HR	RBI	BB	SO	AVG	OBP	SLG	OPS	OPS+	BR+	SB	CS	SBR	FA	FR	G/POS	TPR
1964	NY-A	31	23	4	4	2	0	0	1	2	9	.174	.240	.261	501	39	-2	0	0	0	1.000	-2	/O-8(0-5-3),1-7	-0.4
1965	NY-A	9	17	1	7	2	0	1	4	4	4	.412	.524	.706	1230	248	4	0	0	0	.889	-0	/O-5(1-0-5)	0.3
Total	2	40	40	5	11	4	0	1	5	6	13	.275	.370	.450	820	128	2	0	0	0	.929	-2	/O-13(1-5-8),1-7	-0.1

■ CHARLEY MOORE Moore, Charles Wesley b: 12/1/1884, Jackson Co., Ind. d: 7/29/70, Portland, Ore. BR/TR, 5'10", 160 lbs. Deb: 4/16/12

YEAR	TM/L	G	AB	R	H	2B	3B	HR	RBI	BB	SO	AVG	OBP	SLG	OPS	OPS+	BR+	SB	CS	SBR	FA	FR	G/POS	TPR
1912	Chi-N	5	9	2	2	0	1	0	2	0	1	.222	.222	.444	667	80	-0	0			.800	1	/S-2,2-1,3-1	0.0

■ CHARLIE MOORE Moore, Charles William b: 6/21/53, Birmingham, Ala. BR/TR, 5'11", 180 lbs. Deb: 9/8/73 Career OF: (49-LF 8-CF 341-RF)

YEAR	TM/L	G	AB	R	H	2B	3B	HR	RBI	BB	SO	AVG	OBP	SLG	OPS	OPS+	BR+	SB	CS	SBR	FA	FR	G/POS	TPR
1973	Mil-A	8	27	0	5	0	1	0	3	2	4	.185	.241	.259	501	42	-2	0	0	0	.981	3	/C-8	0.1
1974	Mil-A	72	204	17	50	10	4	0	19	21	34	.245	.316	.333	649	87	-3	3	4	-1	.985	3	C-61/D-6	0.1
1975	Mil-A	73	241	26	70	20	1	1	29	17	31	.290	.337	.394	731	106	1	1	5	-2	.960	-6	C-47,O-22(16-0-6)/D-1	-0.5
1976	Mil-A	87	241	33	46	7	4	3	16	43	45	.191	.316	.290	606	80	-5	1	2	-0	.969	-3	C-49,O-28L/3-1,D-2	-0.8
1977	Mil-A	138	375	42	93	15	6	5	45	31	39	.248	.307	.360	667	81	-10	1	7	-2	.980	-7	*C-137	-1.3
1978	Mil-A	96	268	30	72	7	1	5	31	12	24	.269	.300	.358	658	84	-6	4	2	0	.983	-2	C-95	-0.4
1979	Mil-A	111	337	45	101	16	2	5	38	29	32	.300	.357	.404	761	105	3	8	5	0	.979	9	*C-106	1.6
1980	Mil-A	111	320	42	93	13	2	2	30	24	28	.291	.340	.363	703	96	-2	10	5	0	.989	-15	*C-105	-1.2
1981	*Mil-A	48	156	16	47	8	3	1	9	12	13	.301	.351	.410	761	125	5	1	4	-1	.970	-0	C-34/O-8(3-0-5),D-6	0.5
1982	*Mil-A	133	456	53	116	22	4	6	45	29	49	.254	.300	.360	660	86	-10	2	10	-3	.988	5	*O-115R,C-20/2-1	-1.2
1983	Mil-A	151	529	65	150	27	6	2	49	55	42	.284	.355	.369	724	108	7	11	4	1	.978	0	*O-150R/C-7,D-1	0.0
1984	Mil-A	70	188	13	44	7	1	2	17	10	26	.234	.276	.314	590	66	-9	0	4	-1	.984	-3	O-61(0-7-56)/C-7	-1.6
1985	Mil-A	105	349	35	81	13	4	0	31	27	53	.232	.289	.292	581	60	-19	4	0	1	.977	5	*C-102/O-3(0-0-3)	-0.9
1986	Mil-A	80	235	24	61	12	3	3	39	21	38	.260	.320	.374	695	86	-5	5	5	-1	.992	13	C-72/O-4R,2-1,D-2	1.0
1987	Tor-A	51	107	15	23	10	1	1	7	13	12	.215	.306	.355	661	73	-4	0	0	0	.984	6	C-44/O-5(2-0-3)	0.3
Total	15	1334	4033	456	1052	187	43	36	408	346	470	.261	.321	.355	676	89	-58	51	57	-9	.980	9	C-894,O-396R/D-18,23	-4.3

■ DEE MOORE Moore, D C b: 4/6/14, Hedley, Tex. d: 7/2/97, Williston, N.Dak. BR/TR, 5'11", 190 lbs. Deb: 9/12/36 Career OF: (6-LF 0-CF 0-RF)

YEAR	TM/L	G	AB	R	H	2B	3B	HR	RBI	BB	SO	AVG	OBP	SLG	OPS	OPS+	BR+	SB	CS	SBR	FA	FR	G/POS	TPR
1936	Cin-N	6	10	4	4	2	1	0	1	0	3	.400	.400	.800	1200	230	2	0			1.000	-0	/P-2,C-1	0.0
1937	Cin-N	7	13	2	1	0	0	0	0	1	2	.077	.200	.077	277	-23	-2	0			.931	2	/C-6	0.0
1943	Bro-N	37	79	8	20	3	0	0	12	11	8	.253	.344	.291	636	84	-1	1			.982	-6	C-15/3-9	-0.7
	Phi-N	37	113	13	27	4	1	1	8	15	8	.239	.328	.319	647	91	-1	0			.960	-0	C-21/O-6L,3-5,1-1	-0.1
	Yr	74	192	21	47	7	1	1	20	26	16	.245	.335	.307	642	88	-2	1			.968	-7	C-36,3-14/O-6L,1-1	-0.8
1946	Phi-N	11	13	2	1	0	0	0	1	7	3	.077	.400	.077	477	41	-0	0			1.000	0	/C-6,1-2	0.0
Total	4	98	228	29	53	9	2	1	22	34	24	.232	.335	.303	637	85	-3	1			.962	-5	/C-49,3-14,O-6L,1P	-0.8

■ GENE MOORE Moore, Eugene Jr. "Rowdy" b: 8/26/09, Lancaster, Tex. d: 3/12/78, Jackson, Miss. BL/TL, 5'11", 175 lbs. Deb: 9/19/31 F

YEAR	TM/L	G	AB	R	H	2B	3B	HR	RBI	BB	SO	AVG	OBP	SLG	OPS	OPS+	BR+	SB	CS	SBR	FA	FR	G/POS	TPR
1931	Cin-N	4	14	2	2	1	0	0	1	0	0	.143	.143	.214	357	-6	-2	0			1.000	0	/O-3(3-0-0)	-0.2
1933	StL-N	11	38	6	15	3	2	0	8	4	10	.395	.452	.579	1031	183	4	1			.967	0	O-10(0-10-0)	0.4
1934	StL-N	9	18	2	5	1	0	0	1	2	2	.278	.350	.333	683	79	-0	0			.923	1	/O-3(0-3-0)	0.0
1935	StL-N	3	3	0	0	0	0	0	0	0	1	.000	.000	.000	0	-96	-1	0			.000	0	H	-0.1
1936	Bos-N	151	637	91	185	38	12	13	67	40	80	.290	.335	.449	784	117	13	6			.977	15	*O-151(0-0-151)	1.8
1937	Bos-N☆	148	561	88	159	29	10	16	70	61	73	.283	.358	.456	814	132	24	11			.978	14	*O-148(0-0-148)	2.8
1938	Bos-N	54	180	27	49	8	3	3	19	16	20	.272	.338	.400	738	114	3	1			.981	1	O-47(0-0-47)	0.1
1939	Bro-N	107	306	45	69	13	6	3	39	40	50	.225	.315	.337	652	73	-12	4			.961	-6	O-86(2-1-83)/1-1	-2.3
1940	Bro-N	10	26	3	7	2	0	0	2	1	3	.269	.296	.346	642	72	-1	0			1.000	-1	/O-6(0-0-6)	-0.2
	Bos-N	103	363	46	106	24	1	5	39	25	32	.292	.338	.405	743	110	4	2			.986	6	O-94(0-1-94)	0.5
	Yr	113	389	49	113	26	1	5	41	26	35	.290	.335	.401	736	107	3	2			.986	5	*O-100(0-1-100)	0.3
1941	Bos-N	129	397	42	108	17	8	5	43	45	37	.272	.349	.393	742	114	7	5			.968	4	*O-110(1-28-84)	0.6
1942	Was-A	1	2	0	0	0	0	0	0	0	1	.000	.000	.000	0	-99	-1	0	0	0	.000	-1	/O-1(0-1-0)	-0.1
1943	Was-A	92	254	41	68	14	3	2	39	19	29	.268	.321	.370	691	106	1	0	2	-1	.985	0	O-57(24-1-32)/1-1	-0.3
1944	*StL-A	110	390	56	93	13	6	6	58	24	37	.238	.284	.349	633	76	-13	0	5	-2	.968	2	O-98(0-0-98)/1-1	-2.1
1945	StL-A	110	354	48	92	16	2	5	50	40	26	.260	.337	.359	695	97	-1	1	3	-1	.970	-3	*O-100(1-0-99)	-1.2
Total	14	1042	3543	497	958	179	53	58	436	317	401	.270	.333	.400	733	105	26	31	10		.975	32	O-914(31-45-842)/1-3	-0.3

■ FERDIE MOORE Moore, Ferdinand Depage b: 2/21/1896, Camden, N.J. d: 5/6/47, Atlantic City, N.J. Deb: 10/2/14

YEAR	TM/L	G	AB	R	H	2B	3B	HR	RBI	BB	SO	AVG	OBP	SLG	OPS	OPS+	BR+	SB	CS	SBR	FA	FR	G/POS	TPR
1914	Phi-A	2	4	1	2	0	0	0	1	0	2	.500	.500	.500	1000	209	0	0			.895	-1	/1-2	0.0

■ GARY MOORE Moore, Gary Douglas b: 2/24/45, Tulsa, Okla. BR/TL, 5'10", 175 lbs. Deb: 5/3/70

YEAR	TM/L	G	AB	R	H	2B	3B	HR	RBI	BB	SO	AVG	OBP	SLG	OPS	OPS+	BR+	SB	CS	SBR	FA	FR	G/POS	TPR
1970	LA-N	7	16	2	3	0	2	0	0	0	1	.188	.188	.438	625	65	-1	1	0	0	1.000	-1	/O-5(0-0-5),1-1	-0.2

■ EDDIE MOORE Moore, Graham Edward b: 1/18/1899, Barlow, Ky. d: 2/10/76, Ft.Myers, Fla. BR/TR, 5'7", 165 lbs. Deb: 9/25/23 Career OF: (69-LF 18-CF 58-RF)

YEAR	TM/L	G	AB	R	H	2B	3B	HR	RBI	BB	SO	AVG	OBP	SLG	OPS	OPS+	BR+	SB	CS	SBR	FA	FR	G/POS	TPR
1923	Pit-N	6	26	6	7	1	0	0	1	2	3	.269	.321	.308	629	65	-1	1	0	0	.923	-5	/S-6	-0.5
1924	Pit-N	72	209	47	75	8	4	2	13	27	12	.359	.437	.464	901	139	13	6	7	-1	.988	4	O-35(1-0-34),3-13/2-4	1.3
1925	*Pit-N	142	547	106	163	29	8	6	77	73	26	.298	.383	.413	796	97	-1	19	7	2	.952	-6	*2-122,O-15R/3-3	-0.3
1926	Pit-N	43	132	19	30	8	1	0	19	12	6	.227	.292	.303	595	57	-8	3			.911	-11	2-24/3-9,S-1	-1.8
	Bos-N	54	184	17	49	3	2	0	15	16	12	.266	.325	.304	629	77	-6	6			.973	-3	2-39,S-14/3-1	-0.6
	Yr	97	316	36	79	11	3	0	34	28	18	.250	.311	.304	615	68	-14	9			.950	-14	2-63,S-15,3-10	-2.4
1927	Bos-N	112	411	53	124	14	4	1	32	39	17	.302	.364	.363	726	103	3	5			.947	-3	3-52,2-39,O-16C,/S	0.3
1928	Bos-N	68	215	27	51	9	0	2	18	19	12	.237	.299	.307	606	62	-12	7			.958	6	O-54(54-0-0)/2-1	-1.0
1929	Bro-N	111	402	48	119	18	6	0	48	44	16	.296	.370	.371	740	86	-8	3			.955	-18	2-74,S-36/O-2R,3-1	-1.8
1930	Bro-N	76	196	24	55	13	1	1	20	21	7	.281	.356	.372	729	77	-7	1			.991	3	2-23,O-23L,S-17,/3	-0.3
1932	NY-N	37	87	9	23	3	0	1	6	9	6	.264	.340	.333	674	84	-2	1			.930	3	S-21/3-6,2-5	0.3
1934	Cle-A	27	65	4	10	2	0	0	8	10	4	.154	.267	.185	451	18	-8	0	0	0	.932	1	2-18/3-3,S-2	-0.6
Total	10	748	2474	360	706	108	26	13	257	272	121	.285	.359	.366	725	89	-35	52	14		.956	-30	2-349,O-145L/S-98,3	-5.0

■ HARRY MOORE Moore, Henry S. Deb: 4/17/1884

YEAR	TM/L	G	AB	R	H	2B	3B	HR	RBI	BB	SO	AVG	OBP	SLG	OPS	OPS+	BR+	SB	CS	SBR	FA	FR	G/POS	TPR
1884	Was-U	111	461	77	155	23	5	1		19		.336	.363	.414	777	139	10				.820	-9	*O-105(102-2-1)/S-8	-0.1

■ JACKIE MOORE Moore, Jackie Spencer b: 2/19/39, Jay, Fla. BR/TR, 6', 180 lbs. Deb: 4/18/65 MC

YEAR	TM/L	G	AB	R	H	2B	3B	HR	RBI	BB	SO	AVG	OBP	SLG	OPS	OPS+	BR+	SB	CS	SBR	FA	FR	G/POS	TPR
1965	Det-A	21	53	2	5	0	0	0	2	6	12	.094	.186	.094	281	-17	-8	0	0	0	.985	4	C-20	-0.4

■ JIMMY MOORE Moore, James William b: 4/24/03, Paris, Tenn. d: 3/7/86, Memphis, Tenn. BR/TR, 6'0.5", 187 lbs. Deb: 4/17/30

YEAR	TM/L	G	AB	R	H	2B	3B	HR	RBI	BB	SO	AVG	OBP	SLG	OPS	OPS+	BR+	SB	CS	SBR	FA	FR	G/POS	TPR
1930	Chi-A	16	39	4	8	2	0	0	2	6	3	.205	.326	.256	582	52	-3	0	0	0	.900	0	O-11(11-0-0)	-0.3
	*Phi-A	15	50	10	19	3	0	2	12	2	4	.380	.404	.560	964	136	3	1	1	-0	.958	-0	O-13(8-1-4)	0.1
	Yr	31	89	14	27	5	0	2	14	8	7	.303	.367	.427	794	100	0	1	1	-0	.932	-0	O-24(19-1-4)	-0.2
1931	*Phi-A	49	143	18	32	5	1	2	21	11	13	.224	.284	.315	599	54	-10	0	1	-0	.973	0	O-36(24-2-10)	-1.1
Total	2	80	232	32	59	10	1	4	35	19	20	.254	.316	.358	674	71	-10	1	2	-0	.958	0	/O-60(43-3-14)	-1.3

■ JERRIE MOORE Moore, Jeremiah S. b: Detroit, Mich. d: 9/26/1890, Wayne, Mich. BL, 5'11", 170 lbs. Deb: 4/17/1884

YEAR	TM/L	G	AB	R	H	2B	3B	HR	RBI	BB	SO	AVG	OBP	SLG	OPS	OPS+	BR+	SB	CS	SBR	FA	FR	G/POS	TPR
1884	Alt-U	20	80	10	25	3	1	1		0		.313	.313	.412	725	116	-1				.800	-8	C-12/O-9(1-2-6)	-0.7
	Cle-N	9	30	1	6	0	0	0	10	0	5	.200	.200	.200	400	25	-3				.887	-1	/C-9	-0.3

YEAR	TM/L	G	AB	R	H	2B	3B	HR	RBI	BB	SO	AVG	OBP	SLG	OPS	OPS+	BR+	SB	CS	SBR	FA	FR	G/POS	TPR
1885	Det-N	6	23	2	4	1	0	0	0	1	3	.174	.208	.217	426	38	-2				.800	-3	/C-6	-0.4
Total	2	35	133	13	35	4	1	1	10	1	8	.263	.269	.331	599	83	-5				.830	-12	/C-27,O-9(1-2-6)	-1.4

■ JOHNNY MOORE

Moore, John Francis b: 3/23/02, Waterville, Conn. d: 4/4/91, Bradenton, Fla. BL/TR, 5'10.5", 175 lbs. Deb: 9/15/28

YEAR	TM/L	G	AB	R	H	2B	3B	HR	RBI	BB	SO	AVG	OBP	SLG	OPS	OPS+	BR+	SB	CS	SBR	FA	FR	G/POS	TPR
1928	Chi-N	4	4	0	0	0	0	0	0	0	0	.000	.000	.000	0	-99	-1	0			.000	0	H	-0.1
1929	Chi-N	37	63	13	18	1	0	2	8	4	6	.286	.338	.397	735	81	-2	0			.971	-0	O-15(10-4-1)	-0.3
1931	Chi-N	39	104	19	25	3	1	2	16	7	5	.240	.288	.346	634	69	-5	1			.964	1	O-22(12-9-1)	-0.5
1932	*Chi-N	119	443	59	135	24	5	13	64	22	38	.305	.342	.470	811	117	9	4			.983	1	*O-109(4-91-14)	0.7
1933	Cin-N	135	514	60	135	19	5	1	44	29	16	.263	.306	.325	631	81	-12	4			.974	5	*O-132(75-57-0)	-1.4
1934	Cin-N	16	42	5	8	1	1	0	5	3	2	.190	.244	.262	506	36	-4	0			1.000	-0	O-10(0-0-10)	-0.5
	Phi-N	116	458	68	157	34	6	11	93	40	18	.343	.397	.515	912	125	17	7			.981	7	*O-115(10-0-108)	1.6
	Yr	132	500	73	165	35	7	11	98	43	20	.330	.384	.494	878	120	14	7			.983	6	*O-125(10-0-118)	1.1
1935	Phi-N	153	600	84	194	33	3	19	93	45	50	.323	.375	.483	859	117	15	4			.973	-10	*O-150(2-0-148)	-0.4
1936	Phi-N	124	472	85	155	24	3	16	68	26	22	.328	.365	.494	858	117	11	1			.948	-8	*O-112(78-0-35)	-0.4
1937	Phi-N	96	307	46	98	16	2	9	59	18	18	.319	.357	.472	829	114	5	2			.943	-3	O-72(30-2-42)	-0.1
1945	Chi-N	7	6	0	1	0	0	0	2	1	1	.167	.286	.167	452	28	-1	0			.000	0	H	-0.1
Total	10	846	3013	439	926	155	26	73	452	195	176	.307	.352	.449	801	109	32	23			.970	-7	O-737(221-163-359)	-1.5

■ JO-JO MOORE

Moore, Joseph Gregg "The Gause Ghost" b: 12/25/08, Gause, Tex. BL/TR, 5'11", 155 lbs. Deb: 9/17/30

YEAR	TM/L	G	AB	R	H	2B	3B	HR	RBI	BB	SO	AVG	OBP	SLG	OPS	OPS+	BR+	SB	CS	SBR	FA	FR	G/POS	TPR
1930	NY-N	3	5	1	1	0	0	0	0	0	1	.200	.200	.200	400	-3	-1	0			1.000	-0	/O-1(0-1-0)	-0.1
1931	NY-N	4	8	0	2	1	0	0	3	0	1	.250	.250	.375	625	68	-0	1			1.000	-0	/O-1(1-0-0)	-0.1
1932	NY-N	86	361	53	110	15	2	2	27	20	18	.305	.341	.374	715	94	-3	4			.982	-4	O-86(85-1-0)	-1.1
1933	*NY-N	132	524	56	153	16	5	0	42	21	27	.292	.323	.342	665	91	-6	4			.966	3	*O-132(111-21-0)	-1.0
1934	NY-N†	139	580	106	192	37	4	15	61	31	23	.331	.370	.486	856	130	24	5			.954	-10	*O-131(112-20-0)	0.7
1935	NY-N★	155	681	108	201	28	9	15	71	53	24	.295	.353	.429	782	111	10	5			.972	2	*O-155(155-0-0)	0.4
1936	*NY-N☆	152	649	110	205	29	9	7	63	37	27	.316	.358	.421	779	110	9	2			.981	8	*O-149(149-0-0)	0.8
1937	*NY-N★	142	580	89	180	37	10	6	57	46	37	.310	.364	.440	804	116	13	7			.975	-7	*O-140(140-0-0)	-0.2
1938	NY-N☆	125	506	76	153	23	6	11	56	22	27	.302	.335	.437	772	110	5	2			.978	-5	*O-114(114-0-0)	-0.6
1939	NY-N	138	562	80	151	23	2	10	47	45	17	.269	.324	.370	694	85	-12	5			.986	3	*O-136(136-0-0)	-1.7
1940	NY-N★	138	543	83	150	33	4	6	46	43	30	.276	.337	.385	722	98	-1	7			.982	-1	*O-133(133-0-0)	-1.0
1941	NY-N	121	428	47	117	16	2	7	40	30	15	.273	.322	.369	692	93	-5	4			.972	-4	*O-116(112-4-0)	-1.5
Total	12	1335	5427	809	1615	258	53	79	513	348	247	.298	.344	.408	752	105	33	46			.975	-14	*O-1294(1248-47-0)	-5.4

■ KELVIN MOORE

Moore, Kelvin Orlando b: 9/26/57, Leroy, Ala. BR/TR, 6'1", 195 lbs. Deb: 8/28/81

YEAR	TM/L	G	AB	R	H	2B	3B	HR	RBI	BB	SO	AVG	OBP	SLG	OPS	OPS+	BR+	SB	CS	SBR	FA	FR	G/POS	TPR
1981	*Oak-A	14	47	5	12	0	1	1	3	5	15	.255	.327	.362	689	103	0	1	0	0	1.000	-1	1-13	-0.1
1982	Oak-A	21	67	6	15	1	1	2	6	3	23	.224	.257	.358	615	70	-3	0	1	-0	.971	-2	1-20	-0.6
1983	Oak-A	41	124	12	26	4	0	5	16	10	39	.210	.274	.363	637	78	-4	2	4	-1	.994	-3	1-40	-1.0
Total	3	76	238	23	53	5	2	8	25	18	77	.223	.280	.361	642	81	-7	3	5	-1	.989	-5	/1-73	-1.7

■ KERWIN MOORE

Moore, Kerwin Lamar b: 10/29/70, Detroit, Mich. BB/TR, 6'1", 190 lbs. Deb: 8/30/96

YEAR	TM/L	G	AB	R	H	2B	3B	HR	RBI	BB	SO	AVG	OBP	SLG	OPS	OPS+	BR+	SB	CS	SBR	FA	FR	G/POS	TPR
1996	Oak-A	22	16	4	1	1	0	0	0	2	6	.063	.167	.125	292	-25	-3	1	0	0	1.000	-5	O-18(0-18-0)/D-2	-0.8

■ MOLLY MOORE

Moore, Maurice Deb: 6/30/1875

YEAR	TM/L	G	AB	R	H	2B	3B	HR	RBI	BB	SO	AVG	OBP	SLG	OPS	OPS+	BR+	SB	CS	SBR	FA	FR	G/POS	TPR
1875	Atl-n	21	86	5	19	4	0	0	5	0	4	.221	.221	.267	488	79	-1	0	1	-0	.747	-5	S-14/1-8,O-2R,C23	-0.5

■ RANDY MOORE

Moore, Randolph Edward b: 6/21/06, Naples, Tex. d: 6/12/92, Mt.Pleasant, Tex. BL/TR, 6', 185 lbs. Deb: 4/12/27 Career OF: (66-LF 13-CF 339-RF)

YEAR	TM/L	G	AB	R	H	2B	3B	HR	RBI	BB	SO	AVG	OBP	SLG	OPS	OPS+	BR+	SB	CS	SBR	FA	FR	G/POS	TPR
1927	Chi-A	6	15	0	0	0	0	0	0	0	2	.000	.000	.000	0	-99	-4	0	0	0	1.000	1	/O-4(0-0-4)	-0.4
1928	Chi-A	24	61	6	13	4	1	0	5	3	5	.213	.250	.311	561	47	-5	0	1	-0	.946	0	O-16(2-0-14)	-0.6
1930	Bos-N	83	191	24	55	9	0	2	34	10	13	.288	.323	.366	690	69	-10	3			.986	-2	O-34(11-12-11),3-13	-1.1
1931	Bos-N	83	192	19	50	8	1	3	34	13	3	.260	.311	.359	670	83	-5	1			.952	0	O-29L,3-22/2-1	-0.6
1932	Bos-N	107	351	41	103	21	2	3	43	15	11	.293	.322	.390	713	94	-3	1			.987	-7	O-41R,3-31,1-22,/C	-1.4
1933	Bos-N	135	497	64	150	23	7	8	70	40	16	.302	.356	.425	781	133	21	3			.979	-0	*O-122(12-0-110),1-10	1.3
1934	Bos-N	123	422	55	120	21	2	7	64	40	16	.284	.346	.393	740	105	3	2			.965	-2	O-72(16-0-56),1-37	-0.6
1935	Bos-N	125	407	42	112	20	4	4	42	26	16	.275	.319	.373	692	93	-5	1			.950	0	O-78(7-0-71),1-21	-1.1
1936	Bro-N	42	88	4	21	3	0	0	14	8	1	.239	.302	.273	575	55	-5	0			.964	-4	O-21(0-0-21)	-1.0
1937	Bro-N	13	22	3	3	1	0	0	2	3	2	.136	.240	.182	422	16	-3	0			.889	0	C-10	-0.2
	StL-N	8	7	0	0	0	0	0	0	0	0	.000	.000	.000	0	-98	-2	0			.000	-0	/O-1(1-0-0)	-0.2
	Yr	21	29	3	3	1	0	0	2	3	2	.103	.188	.138	325	-10	-4	0			.889	-0	C-10/O-1(1-0-0)	-0.4
Total	10	749	2253	258	627	110	17	27	308	158	85	.278	.326	.378	705	95	-18	11	1		.969	-15	O-418R/1-90,3-66,C2	-5.9

■ BOBBY MOORE

Moore, Robert Vincent b: 10/27/65, Cincinnati, Ohio BR/TR, 5'9", 165 lbs. Deb: 9/5/91

YEAR	TM/L	G	AB	R	H	2B	3B	HR	RBI	BB	SO	AVG	OBP	SLG	OPS	OPS+	BR+	SB	CS	SBR	FA	FR	G/POS	TPR
1991	KC-A	18	14	3	5	1	0	0	0	1	2	.357	.400	.429	829	129	1	3	2	-0	1.000	-4	O-13(9-5-0)	-0.3

■ TERRY MOORE

Moore, Terry Bluford b: 5/27/12, Vernon, Ala. d: 3/29/95, Collinsville, Ill. BR/TR, 5'11", 195 lbs. Deb: 4/16/35 MC Career OF: (0-LF 1189-CF 1-RF)

YEAR	TM/L	G	AB	R	H	2B	3B	HR	RBI	BB	SO	AVG	OBP	SLG	OPS	OPS+	BR+	SB	CS	SBR	FA	FR	G/POS	TPR
1935	StL-N	119	456	63	131	34	3	6	53	15	40	.287	.314	.414	729	90	-7	13			.984	14	*O-117(0-117-0)	0.4
1936	StL-N	143	590	85	156	39	4	5	47	37	52	.264	.309	.369	678	82	-16	9			.977	22	*O-133(0-133-0)	0.3
1937	StL-N	115	461	76	123	17	3	5	43	32	41	.267	.317	.349	666	79	-13	13			.988	14	*O-106(0-106-0)	-0.2
1938	StL-N	94	312	49	85	21	3	4	21	46	19	.272	.366	.397	763	104	3	9			.987	9	O-75(0-75-0)/3-6	1.0
1939	StL-N★	130	417	65	123	25	2	17	77	43	38	.295	.362	.487	849	119	11	6			**.994**	11	*O-121(0-121-0)/P-1	1.8
1940	StL-N★	136	537	92	163	33	4	17	64	42	44	.304	.356	.475	831	121	14	18			.987	17	*O-133(0-133-0)	2.8
1941	StL-N★	122	493	86	145	26	4	6	68	52	31	.294	.364	.400	763	108	6	3			.984	7	*O-121(0-121-1)	1.0
1942	*StL-N★	130	489	80	141	26	3	6	49	56	26	.288	.364	.391	754	112	9	10			.986	-3	*O-126(0-126-0)/3-1	0.3
1946	*StL-N	91	278	32	73	14	1	3	28	18	26	.263	.312	.353	665	85	-6	0			.982	1	O-66(0-66-0)	-0.7
1947	StL-N	127	460	61	130	17	1	7	45	38	39	.283	.339	.370	708	84	-10	1			.983	1	*O-120(0-120-0)	-1.2
1948	StL-N	91	207	30	48	11	0	4	18	27	12	.232	.321	.343	664	75	-7	0			.993	-10	O-71(0-71-0)	-1.8
Total	11	1298	4700	719	1318	263	28	80	513	406	368	.280	.340	.399	739	98	-17	82			.985	83	*O-1189C/3-7,P-1	3.7

■ SCRAPPY MOORE

Moore, William Allen b: 12/16/1892, St.Louis, Mo. d: 10/13/64, Little Rock, Ark. BR/TR, 5'8", 153 lbs. Deb: 6/21/17

YEAR	TM/L	G	AB	R	H	2B	3B	HR	RBI	BB	SO	AVG	OBP	SLG	OPS	OPS+	BR+	SB	CS	SBR	FA	FR	G/POS	TPR
1917	StL-A	4	8	1	1	0	0	0	0	1	0	.125	.222	.125	347	6	-1	0			.750	0	/3-2	-0.1

■ BILL MOORE

Moore, William Henry "Willie" b: 12/12/03, Kansas City, Mo. d: 5/24/72, Kansas City, Mo. BL/TR, 5'11", 170 lbs. Deb: 9/7/26

YEAR	TM/L	G	AB	R	H	2B	3B	HR	RBI	BB	SO	AVG	OBP	SLG	OPS	OPS+	BR+	SB	CS	SBR	FA	FR	G/POS	TPR
1926	Bos-A	5	18	2	3	0	0	0	0	0	2	.167	.167	.167	333	-13	-3	0	0	0	1.000	0	/C-5	-0.2
1927	Bos-A	44	69	7	15	2	0	0	4	13	8	.217	.341	.246	588	56	-4	0	0	0	.938	2	C-42	-0.1
Total	2	49	87	9	18	2	0	0	4	13	10	.207	.310	.230	540	43	-7	0	0	0	.946	2	/C-47	-0.3

■ BILL MOORE

Moore, William Ross b: 10/10/60, Los Angeles, Cal. BR/TL, 6'1", 185 lbs. Deb: 7/19/86

YEAR	TM/L	G	AB	R	H	2B	3B	HR	RBI	BB	SO	AVG	OBP	SLG	OPS	OPS+	BR+	SB	CS	SBR	FA	FR	G/POS	TPR
1986	Mon-N	6	12	0	2	0	0	0	0	0	4	.167	.167	.167	333	-8	-2	0	0	0	1.000	-1	/1-3,O-1(0-0-1)	-0.3

■ ANDRES MORA

Mora, Andres (Ibarra) b: 5/25/55, Rio Bravo, Mex. BR/TR, 6', 180 lbs. Deb: 4/13/76 Career OF: (158-LF 0-CF 3-RF)

YEAR	TM/L	G	AB	R	H	2B	3B	HR	RBI	BB	SO	AVG	OBP	SLG	OPS	OPS+	BR+	SB	CS	SBR	FA	FR	G/POS	TPR
1976	Bal-A	73	220	18	48	11	0	6	25	13	49	.218	.262	.350	612	83	-6	1	0	0	.951	-2	D-34,O-31(30-0-2)	-1.0
1977	Bal-A	77	233	32	57	8	2	13	44	5	53	.245	.264	.464	727	100	-2	0	0	0	1.000	-9	O-57(57-0-0)/3-1,D-5	-1.3
1978	Bal-A	76	229	21	49	8	0	8	14	13	47	.214	.259	.354	613	75	-8	0	1	-0	.978	1	O-69(69-0-0)/D-1	-1.1
1980	Cle-A	9	18	0	2	0	0	0	0	0	0	.111	.111	.111	222	-39	-3	0	0	0	1.000	0	/O-3(2-0-1)	-0.4
Total	4	235	700	71	156	27	2	27	83	31	149	.223	.258	.383	641	83	-19	1	1	-0	.978	-10	O-160L/D-40,3-1	-3.8

■ MELVIN MORA

Mora, Melvin b: 2/2/72, Agua Negra, Venez. BR/TR, 5'10", 160 lbs. Deb: 5/30/99 Career OF: (40-LF 27-CF 11-RF)

YEAR	TM/L	G	AB	R	H	2B	3B	HR	RBI	BB	SO	AVG	OBP	SLG	OPS	OPS+	BR+	SB	CS	SBR	FA	FR	G/POS	TPR
1999	*NY-N	66	31	6	5	0	0	0	1	4	7	.161	.278	.161	439	15	-4	2	1	0	1.000	-11	O-45L/2-4,3-3,S-1	-1.4
2000	NY-N	79	215	35	56	13	2	6	30	18	48	.260	.323	.423	747	90	-4	7	3	0	.958	-8	S-44,O-28C/2-4,3-4	-0.8
	Bal-A	53	199	25	58	9	3	2	17	17	32	.291	.359	.397	756	94	-1	5	8	-2	.952	1	S-52/2-1	0.2
Total	2	198	445	66	119	22	5	8	48	39	87	.267	.336	.393	729	87	-9	14	12	-1	.955	-18	/S-97,O-73L,2-9,3-7	-2.0

■ JOSE MORALES
Morales, Jose Manuel (Hernandez) b: 12/30/44, Frederiksted, V.I. BR/TR, 6′, 195 lbs. Deb: 8/13/73 C Career OF: (7-LF 0-CF 0-RF)

YEAR	TM/L	G	AB	R	H	2B	3B	HR	RBI	BB	SO	AVG	OBP	SLG	OPS	OPS+	BR+	SB	CS	SBR	FA	FR	G/POS	TPR
1973	Oak-A	6	14	0	4	1	0	0	1	1	5	.286	.333	.357	690	100	-0	0	1	-0	.000	0	/D-3	0.0
	Mon-N	5	5	0	2	0	0	0	0	0	0	.400	.400	.400	800	118	0	0	0	0	.000	0	H	0.0
1974	Mon-N	25	26	3	7	4	0	1	5	1	7	.269	.296	.538	835	123	1	0	0	0	.800	-1	/C-2	0.0
1975	Mon-N	93	163	18	49	6	1	2	24	14	21	.301	.356	.387	742	102	0	0	2	-1	.983	4	1-27/O-6(6-0-0),C-5	0.2
1976	Mon-N	104	158	12	50	11	0	4	37	3	20	.316	.337	.462	799	120	3	0	0	0	.977	1	1-21,C-12	0.4
1977	Mon-N	65	74	3	15	4	1	1	9	5	12	.203	.253	.324	577	55	-5	0	0	0	1.000	-2	/C-8,1-8	-0.7
1978	Min-A	101	242	22	76	13	1	2	38	20	35	.314	.369	.401	770	114	5	0	1	-0	.000	0	D-77/C-1,1-1,O-1L	0.2
1979	Min-A	92	191	21	51	5	1	2	27	14	27	.267	.324	.335	659	75	-6	0	0	0	1.000	-0	D-77/1-1	-0.9
1980	Min-A	97	241	36	73	17	2	8	36	22	19	.303	.364	.490	853	123	7	0	0	0	1.000	-1	D-86/C-2,1-2	0.4
1981	Bal-A	38	86	6	21	3	0	2	14	3	13	.244	.270	.349	619	77	-3	0	0	0	1.000	-0	D-22/1-3	-0.4
1982	Bal-A	3	3	0	0	0	0	0	0	0	2	.000	.000	.000	0	-99	-1	0	0	0	.000	0	/H	-0.1
	LA-N	35	30	1	9	1	0	1	8	4	8	.300	.382	.433	816	131	1	0	0	0	.000	0	H	0.0
1983	*LA-N	47	53	4	15	3	0	3	8	1	11	.283	.296	.509	806	120	1	0	0	0	.951	-0	/1-4	0.1
1984	LA-N	22	19	0	3	0	0	0	0	1	2	.158	.200	.158	358	2	-2	0	0	0	.000	0	H	-0.3
Total	12	733	1305	126	375	68	6	26	207	89	182	.287	.336	.408	744	102	2	0	4	-1	.981	2	D-265/1-67,C-30,O-7L	-1.1

■ JERRY MORALES
Morales, Julio Ruben (Torres) b: 2/18/49, Yabucao, P.R. BR/TR, 5′10″, 175 lbs. Deb: 9/5/69 Career OF: (261-LF 505-CF 560-RF)

YEAR	TM/L	G	AB	R	H	2B	3B	HR	RBI	BB	SO	AVG	OBP	SLG	OPS	OPS+	BR+	SB	CS	SBR	FA	FR	G/POS	TPR
1969	SD-N	19	41	5	8	2	0	1	6	5	7	.195	.283	.317	600	71	-2	0	2	-1	1.000	-1	O-19(10-9-1)	-0.4
1970	SD-N	28	58	6	9	0	1	1	4	3	11	.155	.197	.241	438	17	-7	0	0	0	.926	-5	O-26(23-0-4)	-1.3
1971	SD-N	12	17	1	2	0	0	0	1	2	2	.118	.211	.118	328	-5	-2	1	0	0	1.000	-1	/O-7(4-1-2)	-0.4
1972	SD-N	115	347	38	83	15	7	4	18	35	54	.239	.309	.357	666	96	-3	4	6	-1	.987	4	O-96(34-56-12)/3-4	-0.4
1973	SD-N	122	388	47	109	23	2	9	34	27	55	.281	.328	.420	748	115	6	6	5	-0	.991	1	*O-100(31-50-27)	0.3
1974	Chi-N	151	534	70	146	21	7	15	82	46	63	.273	.333	.423	757	106	3	2	12	-4	.975	-7	*O-143(83-32-41)	-1.4
1975	Chi-N	153	578	62	156	21	0	12	91	50	65	.270	.333	.369	702	91	-7	3	7	-2	.979	0	*O-151(0-20-136)	-1.7
1976	Chi-N	140	537	66	147	17	0	16	67	41	49	.274	.325	.395	720	95	-4	3	8	-2	.983	3	*O-136(3-8-131)	-1.0
1977	Chi-N★	136	490	56	142	34	5	11	69	43	75	.290	.350	.447	796	101	1	0	3	-1	.985	-7	*O-128(6-125-3)	-0.9
1978	StL-N	130	457	44	109	19	8	4	46	33	44	.239	.291	.341	633	77	-15	4	4	-1	.977	-0	*O-126(0-34-94)	-2.2
1979	Det-A	129	440	50	93	23	1	14	56	30	56	.211	.265	.364	628	65	-22	10	4	1	.986	-9	*O-119(18-20-88)/D-7	-3.5
1980	NY-N	94	193	19	49	7	1	3	30	13	31	.254	.304	.347	651	84	-4	2	3	-1	.973	-7	O-63(3-55-6)	-1.3
1981	Chi-N	84	245	27	70	6	2	1	25	22	29	.286	.347	.339	686	91	-2	1	1	-0	.986	-6	O-72(17-49-8)	-1.0
1982	Chi-N	65	116	14	33	2	2	4	30	9	7	.284	.336	.440	776	112	2	1	2	-0	1.000	-5	O-41(12-36-4)	-0.5
1983	Chi-N	63	87	11	17	9	0	0	11	7	19	.195	.255	.299	554	51	-6	0	0	0	1.000	-6	O-29(17-10-3)	-1.3
Total	15	1441	4528	516	1173	199	36	95	570	366	567	.259	.316	.382	698	91	-62	37	57	-12	.983	-44	*O-1256R/D-7,3-4	-17.0

■ RICH MORALES
Morales, Richard Angelo b: 9/20/43, San Francisco, Cal. BR/TR, 5′11″, 170 lbs. Deb: 8/8/67 C Career OF: (0-LF 0-CF 1-RF)

YEAR	TM/L	G	AB	R	H	2B	3B	HR	RBI	BB	SO	AVG	OBP	SLG	OPS	OPS+	BR+	SB	CS	SBR	FA	FR	G/POS	TPR
1967	Chi-A	8	10	0	0	0	0	0	0	0	2	.000	.000	.000	0	-99	-2	0	0	0	.944	2	/S-7	-0.1
1968	Chi-A	10	29	2	5	0	0	0	0	2	5	.172	.226	.172	398	22	-3	0	0	0	.966	2	/S-7,2-5	0.0
1969	Chi-A	55	121	12	26	0	1	0	6	7	18	.215	.269	.231	501	39	-10	1	0	0	.976	10	2-38,S-13/3-1	0.3
1970	Chi-A	62	112	6	18	2	0	1	2	9	16	.161	.230	.205	435	20	-12	1	0	0	.967	6	S-24,3-20,2-12	-0.4
1971	Chi-A	84	185	19	45	8	0	2	14	22	26	.243	.336	.319	655	84	-3	2	3	-1	.976	-1	S-57,3-18/2-3,O-1R	0.0
1972	Chi-A	110	287	24	59	7	1	2	20	19	49	.206	.262	.258	520	54	-16	2	3	-1	.968	-1	S-86,2-16,3-14	-1.0
1973	Chi-A	7	4	1	0	0	0	0	1	1	1	.000	.200	.000	200	-38	-1	0	0	0	1.000	1	/3-5,2-2	0.0
	SD-N	90	244	9	40	6	1	0	16	27	36	.164	.247	.197	444	27	-24	0	1	-0	.988	22	2-79,S-10	0.3
1974	SD-N	54	61	8	12	3	0	1	5	8	6	.197	.290	.295	585	67	-3	1	0	0	.933	7	S-29,2-18/3-6,1-1	0.6
Total	8	480	1053	81	205	26	3	6	64	95	159	.195	.268	.242	510	46	-74	7	7	-1	.970	47	S-233,2-173/3-64,1O	-0.3

■ WILLIE MORALES
Morales, William Anthony b: 9/7/72, Tucson, Ariz. BR/TR, 5′10″, 182 lbs. Deb: 4/9/2000

YEAR	TM/L	G	AB	R	H	2B	3B	HR	RBI	BB	SO	AVG	OBP	SLG	OPS	OPS+	BR+	SB	CS	SBR	FA	FR	G/POS	TPR
2000	Bal-A	3	11	1	3	1	0	0	0	0	3	.273	.273	.364	636	61	-1	0	0	0	1.000	1	/C-3	0.1

■ CHARLIE MORAN
Moran, Charles Barthell "Uncle Charlie" b: 2/22/1878, Nashville, Tenn. d: 6/14/49, Horse Cave, Ky. BR/TR, 5′8″, 180 lbs. Deb: 9/9/03 U

YEAR	TM/L	G	AB	R	H	2B	3B	HR	RBI	BB	SO	AVG	OBP	SLG	OPS	OPS+	BR+	SB	CS	SBR	FA	FR	G/POS	TPR
1903	StL-N	4	14	2	6	0	0	0	1	0		.429	.429	.429	857	149	1	1			1.000	-1	/P-3,S-1	0.0
1908	StL-N	21	63	2	11	1	2	0	2	0		.175	.175	.254	429	38	-5	0			.903	-3	C-16	-0.7
Total	2	25	77	4	17	1	2	0	3	0		.221	.221	.286	506	61	-4	1			.903	-4	/C-16,P-3,S-1	-0.7

■ CHARLES MORAN
Moran, Charles Vincent b: 3/26/1879, Washington, D.C. d: 4/11/34, Washington, D.C. TR, Deb: 4/29/03 Career OF: (0-LF 0-CF 1-RF)

YEAR	TM/L	G	AB	R	H	2B	3B	HR	RBI	BB	SO	AVG	OBP	SLG	OPS	OPS+	BR+	SB	CS	SBR	FA	FR	G/POS	TPR
1903	Was-A	98	373	41	84	14	5	1	24	33		.225	.297	.298	594	77	-10	8			**.943**	5	S-96/2-2	-0.1
1904	Was-A	62	243	27	54	10	0	0	7	23		.222	.289	.263	553	77	-6	7			.919	-13	S-61/3-1	-1.9
	StL-A	82	272	15	47	3	1	0	14	25		.173	.242	.191	434	40	-18	2			.937	-3	3-81/O-1(0-0-1)	-2.0
	Yr	144	515	42	101	13	1	0	21	48		.196	.265	.225	490	58	-23	9			.938	-16	3-82,S-61/O-1(0-0-1)	-3.9
1905	StL-A	27	82	6	16	1	0	0	5	10		.195	.290	.207	498	62	-3	3			.954	-4	2-20/3-5	-0.7
Total	3	269	970	89	201	28	6	1	50	91		.207	.279	.252	531	66	-36	20			.935	-15	S-157/3-87,2-22,O-1R	-4.7

■ HERBIE MORAN
Moran, John Herbert b: 2/16/1884, Costello, Pa. d: 9/21/54, Clarkson, N.Y. BL/TR, 5′5″, 150 lbs. Deb: 4/16/08

YEAR	TM/L	G	AB	R	H	2B	3B	HR	RBI	BB	SO	AVG	OBP	SLG	OPS	OPS+	BR+	SB	CS	SBR	FA	FR	G/POS	TPR
1908	Phi-A	19	59	4	9	0	0	0	4	6		.153	.242	.153	395	27	-4	1			.952	1	O-19(0-10-9)	-0.5
	Bos-N	8	29	3	8	0	0	0	2	2		.276	.364	.276	639	106	0	1			1.000	2	/O-8(8-0-0)	0.3
1909	Bos-N	8	31	8	7	1	0	0	0	5		.226	.333	.258	591	80	-1	0			1.000	-1	/O-8(8-0-0)	-0.2
1910	Bos-N	20	67	11	8	0	0	0	3	13	14	.119	.280	.119	400	17	-6	6			.958	4	O-20(11-0-9)	-0.4
1912	Bro-N	130	508	77	140	18	10	1	40	69	38	.276	.368	.356	724	102	4	28			.961	8	*O-129(2-73-55)	0.3
1913	Bro-N	132	515	71	137	15	5	0	26	45	29	.266	.333	.315	648	83	-10	21			.950	2	*O-129(3-6-121)	-1.5
1914	Cin-N	107	395	43	93	10	5	1	35	41	29	.235	.312	.294	606	78	-10	26			.954	-5	*O-107(1-24-82)	-2.3
	*Bos-N	41	154	24	41	3	1	0	4	17	11	.266	.347	.299	646	93	-1	4			.940	-8	O-41(0-17-30)	-1.2
	Yr	148	549	67	134	13	6	1	39	58	40	.244	.322	.295	617	82	-11	30			.950	-13	*O-148(1-41-112)	-3.5
1915	Bos-N	130	419	59	84	13	5	0	21	66	41	.200	.320	.255	576	79	-8	16	10	0	.964	-6	*O-123(15-12-101)	-2.2
Total	7	595	2177	300	527	60	26	2	135	264	162	.242	.332	.296	629	83	-35	103	10		.957	-2	O-584(48-142-407)	-7.7

■ PAT MORAN
Moran, Patrick Joseph b: 2/7/1876, Fitchburg, Mass. d: 3/7/24, Orlando, Fla. BR/TR, 5′10″, 180 lbs. Deb: 5/15/01 M

YEAR	TM/L	G	AB	R	H	2B	3B	HR	RBI	BB	SO	AVG	OBP	SLG	OPS	OPS+	BR+	SB	CS	SBR	FA	FR	G/POS	TPR
1901	Bos-N	52	180	12	38	5	1	2	18	3		.211	.228	.283	512	44	-13	3			.973	-5	C-28,1-13/3-4,SO2	-1.6
1902	Bos-N	80	251	22	60	5	5	1	24	17		.239	.303	.311	614	89	-3	6			**.982**	1	C-71/1-3,O-1(0-0-1)	0.5
1903	Bos-N	109	389	40	102	25	5	7	54	29		.262	.331	.406	737	114	6	8			.967	19	*C-107/1-1	3.4
1904	Bos-N	113	398	26	90	11	3	4	34	18		.226	.267	.299	566	77	-11	10			.957	4	C-72,3-39/1-2	0.1
1905	Bos-N	85	267	22	64	11	5	2	22	8		.240	.270	.341	611	83	-7	3			**.986**	13	C-78	1.4
1906	*Chi-N	70	226	22	57	13	1	0	35	7		.252	.281	.319	599	82	-5	6			.979	3	C-61	0.4
1907	*Chi-N	65	198	8	45	5	1	1	19	10		.227	.271	.278	549	68	-8	5			.973	0	C-59	-0.2
1908	Chi-N	50	150	12	39	5	1	0	12	13		.260	.323	.307	630	97	-0	6			.968	1	C-45	0.6
1909	Chi-N	77	246	18	54	11	1	1	23	16		.220	.278	.285	563	73	-8	2			.984	1	C-74	0.1
1910	Phi-N	68	199	13	47	7	1	0	11	17	16	.236	.306	.281	587	69	-8	6			.989	0	C-56	-0.2
1911	Phi-N	34	103	2	19	3	0	0	8	3	13	.184	.208	.214	421	18	-11	0			.984	-1	C-32	-1.0
1912	Phi-N	13	26	1	3	1	0	0	1	1	7	.115	.148	.154	302	-16	-4	0			.955	-2	C-13	-0.5
1913	Phi-N	1	1	0	0	0	0	0	0	0	0	.000	.000	.000	0	-96	-0	0			.000	0	H	0.0
1914	Phi-N	1	0	0	0	0	0	0	1	0	0	—	—	—		—	0	0			.000	0	/C-1	0.0
Total	14	818	2634	198	618	102	24	18	262	142	36	.235	.283	.312	595	78	-73	55			.976	34	C-697/3-43,1-19,OS2	3.0

■ AL MORAN
Moran, Richard Alan b: 12/5/38, Detroit, Mich. BR/TR, 6′1.5″, 190 lbs. Deb: 4/9/63

YEAR	TM/L	G	AB	R	H	2B	3B	HR	RBI	BB	SO	AVG	OBP	SLG	OPS	OPS+	BR+	SB	CS	SBR	FA	FR	G/POS	TPR
1963	NY-N	119	331	26	64	5	2	1	23	36	60	.193	.274	.230	504	46	-22	3	7	-2	.951	6	*S-116/3-1	-0.9
1964	NY-N	16	22	2	5	0	0	0	4	2	2	.227	.292	.227	519	50	-1	0	0	0	.957	4	S-15/3-1	0.3
Total	2	135	353	28	69	5	2	1	27	38	62	.195	.276	.229	505	46	-23	3	7	-2	.951	10	S-131/3-2	-0.6

■ ROY MORAN
Moran, Roy Ellis "Deedle" b: 9/17/1884, Vincennes, Ind. d: 7/18/66, Atlanta, Ga. BR/TR, 5′8″, 155 lbs. Deb: 9/3/12

YEAR	TM/L	G	AB	R	H	2B	3B	HR	RBI	BB	SO	AVG	OBP	SLG	OPS	OPS+	BR+	SB	CS	SBR	FA	FR	G/POS	TPR
1912	Was-A	7	13	1	2	0	0	0	0	8		.154	.476	.154	630	82	1	3			.889	-0	/O-6(5-0-0)	0.0

■ BILL MORAN Moran, William L. b: 10/10/1869, Joliet, Ill. d: 4/8/16, Joliet, Ill. 175 lbs. Deb: 5/7/1892

YEAR	TM/L	G	AB	R	H	2B	3B	HR	RBI	BB	SO	AVG	OBP	SLG	OPS	OPS+	BR+	SB	CS	SBR	FA	FR	G/POS	TPR
1892	StL-N	24	81	2	11	1	0	0	5	2	12	.136	.157	.148	305	-8	-11	0			.891	-4	C-22/O-2(2-0-0)	-1.2
1895	Chi-N	15	55	8	9	2	1	1	9	3	2	.164	.220	.291	511	29	-6	2			.827	-2	C-15	-0.5
Total	2	39	136	10	20	3	1	1	14	5	14	.147	.183	.206	389	10	-17	2			.866	-6	/C-37,O-2(2-0-0)	-1.7

■ BILLY MORAN Moran, William Nelson b: 11/27/33, Montgomery, Ala. BR/TR, 5'11", 185 lbs. Deb: 4/15/58

YEAR	TM/L	G	AB	R	H	2B	3B	HR	RBI	BB	SO	AVG	OBP	SLG	OPS	OPS+	BR+	SB	CS	SBR	FA	FR	G/POS	TPR
1958	Cle-A	115	257	26	58	11	0	1	18	13	23	.226	.263	.280	543	51	-17	3	2	-0	.960	13	2-74,S-38	0.1
1959	Cle-A	11	17	1	5	0	0	0	2	0	1	.294	.294	.294	588	64	-1	0	0	0	1.000	-1	/2-6,S-5	-0.1
1961	LA-A	54	173	17	45	7	1	2	22	17	16	.260	.330	.347	677	73	-6	0	0	0	.966	-5	2-51/S-2	-0.7
1962	LA-A★	160	659	90	186	25	3	17	74	39	80	.282	.326	.407	733	99	-2	5	1	1	.986	19	*2-160	3.1
1963	LA-A	153	597	67	164	29	5	7	65	31	57	.275	.314	.375	689	98	-3	1	1	-0	.973	15	*2-151	2.6
1964	LA-A	50	198	26	53	10	1	0	11	13	20	.268	.316	.328	644	88	-3	1	3	-1	.929	-7	3-47/2-3,S-1	-1.2
	Cle-A	69	151	14	31	6	0	1	10	18	16	.205	.294	.265	559	57	-8	0	1	-0	.972	3	3-42,2-15/1-2	-0.5
	Yr	119	349	40	84	16	1	1	21	31	36	.241	.306	.301	607	73	-12	1	4	-1	.947	-4	3-89,2-18/1-2,S-1	-1.7
1965	Cle-A	22	24	1	3	0	0	0	0	2	5	.125	.222	.125	347	1	-3	0	0	0	1.000	1	/2-7,S-1	-0.2
Total	7	634	2076	242	545	88	10	28	202	133	218	.263	.310	.355	665	85	-44	10	8	-1	.976	39	2-467/3-89,S-47,1-2	3.1

■ MICKEY MORANDINI Morandini, Michael Robert b: 4/22/66, Kittanning, Pa. BL/TR, 5'11", 171 lbs. Deb: 9/1/90

YEAR	TM/L	G	AB	R	H	2B	3B	HR	RBI	BB	SO	AVG	OBP	SLG	OPS	OPS+	BR+	SB	CS	SBR	FA	FR	G/POS	TPR
1990	Phi-N	25	79	9	19	4	0	1	3	6	19	.241	.294	.329	623	71	-3	3	0	1	.990	1	2-25	-0.1
1991	Phi-N	98	325	38	81	11	4	1	20	29	45	.249	.315	.317	632	79	-9	13	2	2	.986	8	2-97	0.4
1992	Phi-N	127	422	47	112	8	8	3	30	25	64	.265	.306	.344	650	84	-9	8	3	1	.991	11	*2-124/S-3	0.6
1993	*Phi-N	120	425	57	105	19	9	3	33	34	73	.247	.310	.355	666	79	-13	13	2	2	.990	-1	*2-111	-0.6
1994	Phi-N	87	274	40	80	16	5	2	26	34	33	.292	.378	.409	787	103	2	10	5	0	.985	4	2-79	1.0
1995	Phi-N★	127	494	65	140	34	7	6	49	42	80	.283	.350	.417	767	101	1	9	6	-0	.989	-1	*2-122	0.6
1996	Phi-N	140	539	64	135	24	6	3	32	49	87	.250	.323	.334	657	73	-20	26	5	4	.982	-9	*2-137	-1.8
1997	Phi-N	150	553	83	163	40	2	1	39	62	91	.295	.374	.380	754	98	1	16	13	-1	.990	-15	*2-146/S-1	-0.8
1998	*Chi-N	154	582	93	172	20	4	8	53	72	84	.296	.382	.385	766	99	2	13	1	3	**.993**	-17	*2-152	-0.5
1999	Chi-N	144	456	60	110	18	5	4	37	48	61	.241	.322	.329	651	66	-23	6	6	-1	.991	-3	*2-132	-2.0
2000	Phi-N	91	302	31	76	13	3	0	22	29	54	.252	.325	.315	640	62	-17	5	2	0	.987	-5	2-85	-1.7
	Tor-A	35	107	10	29	2	1	0	7	7	23	.271	.316	.308	624	58	-7	1	0	0	.993	6	2-35	0.1
Total	11	1298	4558	597	1222	209	54	32	351	437	714	.268	.340	.359	698	84	-95	123	45	11	.989	-20	*2-1245/S-4	-4.8

■ MIKE MORDECAI Mordecai, Michael Howard b: 12/13/67, Birmingham, Ala. BR/TR, 5'11", 175 lbs. Deb: 5/8/94 Career OF: (0-LF 1-CF 1-RF)

YEAR	TM/L	G	AB	R	H	2B	3B	HR	RBI	BB	SO	AVG	OBP	SLG	OPS	OPS+	BR+	SB	CS	SBR	FA	FR	G/POS	TPR
1994	Atl-N	4	4	1	1	0	0	1	3	1	0	.250	.400	1.000	1400	244	1	0	0	0	1.000	-0	/S-4	0.1
1995	*Atl-N	69	75	10	21	6	0	3	11	9	16	.280	.357	.480	837	115	2	0	0	0	1.000	-2	2-21/1-9,3-6,S-6,O	0.0
1996	*Atl-N	66	108	12	26	5	0	2	8	9	24	.241	.299	.343	642	65	-5	1	0	0	.985	-1	2-20,3-10/S-6,1-1	-0.6
1997	Atl-N	61	81	8	14	2	1	0	3	6	16	.173	.230	.222	452	19	-10	0	1	-0	1.000	-2	3-19/2-4,S-4,1OD	-1.2
1998	Mon-N	73	119	12	24	4	2	3	10	9	20	.202	.258	.345	602	58	-8	1	0	0	.953	-2	S-30,2-21,3-11,/1-1	-0.7
1999	Mon-N	109	226	29	53	10	2	5	25	20	31	.235	.300	.363	662	68	-11	2	5	-1	.962	0	2-38,S-38,3-32,/1-1	-0.9
2000	Mon-N	86	169	20	48	16	0	4	16	12	34	.284	.335	.450	785	95	-2	2	2	-0	.937	-2	3-58,S-10/2-9,1-3	-0.3
Total	7	468	782	92	187	43	5	18	76	66	141	.239	.300	.376	676	72	-33	6	8	-1	.957	-9	3-136,2-113/S-98,1OD	-3.6

■ RAY MOREHART Morehart, Raymond Anderson b: 12/2/1899, Terrell, Tex. d: 1/13/89, Dallas, Tex. BL/TR, 5'9", 157 lbs. Deb: 8/9/24

YEAR	TM/L	G	AB	R	H	2B	3B	HR	RBI	BB	SO	AVG	OBP	SLG	OPS	OPS+	BR+	SB	CS	SBR	FA	FR	G/POS	TPR
1924	Chi-A	31	100	10	20	4	2	0	8	17	7	.200	.316	.280	596	56	-6	3	1	0	.873	-12	S-27/2-2	-1.4
1926	Chi-A	73	192	27	61	10	3	0	21	11	15	.318	.358	.401	759	101	0	3	11	-3	.950	-5	2-48	-0.7
1927	NY-A	73	195	45	50	7	2	1	20	29	18	.256	.353	.328	681	80	-5	4	4	-1	.945	4	2-53	-0.1
Total	3	177	487	82	131	21	7	1	49	57	40	.269	.347	.347	694	83	-11	10	16	-3	.946	-13	2-103/S-27	-2.2

■ DANNY MOREJON Morejon, Daniel (Torres) b: 7/21/30, Havana, Cuba BR/TR, 6'1", 175 lbs. Deb: 7/11/58

YEAR	TM/L	G	AB	R	H	2B	3B	HR	RBI	BB	SO	AVG	OBP	SLG	OPS	OPS+	BR+	SB	CS	SBR	FA	FR	G/POS	TPR
1958	Cin-N	12	26	4	5	0	0	0	1	9	2	.192	.400	.192	592	60	-1	1	0	0	1.000	-2	O-11(2-6-3)	-0.4

■ KEITH MORELAND Moreland, Bobby Keith b: 5/2/54, Dallas, Tex. BR/TR, 6', 200 lbs. Deb: 10/1/78 Career OF: (119-LF 44-CF 560-RF)

YEAR	TM/L	G	AB	R	H	2B	3B	HR	RBI	BB	SO	AVG	OBP	SLG	OPS	OPS+	BR+	SB	CS	SBR	FA	FR	G/POS	TPR
1978	Phi-N	1	2	0	0	0	0	0	0	0	0	.000	.000	.000	0	-99	-1	0	0	0	1.000	0	/C-1	0.0
1979	Phi-N	14	48	3	18	3	2	0	8	3	5	.375	.412	.521	933	148	3	0	0	0	1.000	-0	C-13	0.3
1980	*Phi-N	62	159	13	50	8	0	4	29	8	14	.314	.347	.440	788	112	2	3	1	0	.967	-1	C-39/3-4,O-2(0-0-2)	0.3
1981	*Phi-N	61	196	16	50	7	0	6	37	15	13	.255	.311	.383	694	92	-2	1	2	-0	.982	-7	C-50/3-7,1-2,O-2R	-0.9
1982	Chi-N	138	476	50	124	17	2	15	68	46	71	.261	.330	.399	729	100	0	0	6	-2	.989	-21	O-86L,C-44/3-2	-2.6
1983	Chi-N	154	533	76	161	30	3	16	70	68	73	.302	.384	.460	844	127	21	0	3	-1	.976	-6	*O-151(0-0-151)/C-3	0.7
1984	*Chi-N	140	495	59	138	17	3	16	80	34	71	.279	.329	.422	751	101	-0	1	4	-1	.976	-7	*O-103R,1-29/3-8,C	-1.6
1985	Chi-N	161	587	74	180	30	3	14	106	68	58	.307	.380	.440	819	116	14	12	3	2	.976	-9	*O-148R,1-12,3-11,/C	-0.1
1986	Chi-N	156	586	72	159	30	0	12	79	53	48	.271	.332	.384	716	90	-8	3	6	-1	.980	-9	*O-121R,3-24,C-13,1	-2.6
1987	Chi-N	153	563	63	150	29	1	27	88	39	66	.266	.314	.465	779	99	-2	3	3	-0	.934	4	*3-150/1-1	-0.1
1988	SD-N	143	511	40	131	23	0	5	64	40	51	.256	.310	.331	641	86	-9	2	3	-1	.994	-3	1-73,O-64(64-0-0)/3-2	-2.1
1989	Det-A	90	318	34	95	16	0	5	35	27	33	.299	.357	.396	754	115	6	3	2	-0	1.000	-6	D-51,1-31,3-12,/C-1	-0.4
	Bal-A	33	107	11	23	4	0	1	10	4	12	.215	.243	.280	524	49	-7	0	0	0	.000	0	D-29	-0.9
	Yr	123	425	45	118	20	0	6	45	31	45	.278	.330	.367	697	99	-1	3	2	-0	1.000	-6	D-80,1-31,3-12,/C-1	-1.3
Total	12	1306	4581	511	1279	214	14	121	674	405	515	.279	.339	.411	751	103	17	28	33	-5	.979	-65	O-677R,3-220,C1/D	-10.0

■ HARRY MORELOCK Morelock, A. Harry b: 11/1869, Philadelphia, Pa. Deb: 8/21/1891

YEAR	TM/L	G	AB	R	H	2B	3B	HR	RBI	BB	SO	AVG	OBP	SLG	OPS	OPS+	BR+	SB	CS	SBR	FA	FR	G/POS	TPR
1891	Phi-N	4	14	1	1	0	0	0	0	3	3	.071	.235	.071	307	-9	-2	0			.824	-4	/S-4	-0.5
1892	Phi-N	1	3	0	0	0	0	0	0	1	0	.000	.250	.000	250	-23	-0	0			.600	-1	/3-1	-0.1
Total	2	5	17	1	1	0	0	0	0	4	3	.059	.238	.059	297	-11	-2	0			.824	-4	/S-4,3-1	-0.6

■ JOSE MORENO Moreno, Jose De Los Santos (b: Jose De Los Santos Mauricio (Moreno))
b: 11/1/57, Santo Domingo, D.R. BB/TR, 6', 175 lbs. Deb: 5/24/80 Career OF: (4-LF 0-CF 5-RF)

YEAR	TM/L	G	AB	R	H	2B	3B	HR	RBI	BB	SO	AVG	OBP	SLG	OPS	OPS+	BR+	SB	CS	SBR	FA	FR	G/POS	TPR
1980	NY-N	37	46	6	9	2	1	2	9	3	12	.196	.245	.413	658	83	-1	1	0	0	.917	0	/2-4,3-4	-0.1
1981	SD-N	34	48	5	11	2	0	0	6	1	8	.229	.245	.271	516	50	-3	4	1	1	1.000	-0	/O-9(4-0-5),2-1	-0.3
1982	Cal-A	11	3	3	0	0	0	0	0	2	0	.000	.400	.000	400	21	-0	0	2	-1	1.000	1	/2-2,D-1	0.0
Total	3	82	97	14	20	4	1	2	15	6	20	.206	.252	.330	582	66	-5	5	3	0	.947	1	/O-9R,2-7,3-4,D-1	-0.4

■ OMAR MORENO Moreno, Omar Renan (Quintero) b: 10/24/52, Puerto Armuelles, Panama BL/TL, 6'2", 180 lbs. Deb: 9/6/75 Career OF: (22-LF 1221-CF 83-RF)

YEAR	TM/L	G	AB	R	H	2B	3B	HR	RBI	BB	SO	AVG	OBP	SLG	OPS	OPS+	BR+	SB	CS	SBR	FA	FR	G/POS	TPR
1975	Pit-N	6	6	1	1	0	0	0	0	1	1	.167	.286	.167	452	28	-1	1	0	0	.000	-1	/O-1(1-0-0)	-0.1
1976	Pit-N	48	122	24	33	4	1	2	12	16	24	.270	.360	.369	729	106	1	15	5	2	.960	-1	O-42(0-41-0)	0.1
1977	Pit-N	150	492	69	118	19	9	7	34	38	102	.240	.296	.358	653	72	-20	53	16	6	.977	8	*O-147(0-147-0)	-0.6
1978	Pit-N	155	515	95	121	15	7	2	33	81	104	.235	.342	.303	645	78	-12	**71**	22	8	.984	17	*O-152(0-152-0)	1.2
1979	*Pit-N	162	695	110	196	21	12	8	69	51	104	.282	.334	.381	715	90	-9	**77**	21	**10**	.975	23	*O-162(0-162-0)	2.3
1980	Pit-N	162	676	87	168	20	**13**	2	36	57	101	.249	.309	.325	634	76	-21	96	33	10	.990	27	*O-162(0-162-0)	1.5
1981	Pit-N	103	434	62	120	18	8	1	35	26	76	.276	.322	.362	684	91	-5	39	14	4	.997	10	*O-103(0-103-0)	0.8
1982	Pit-N	158	645	82	158	18	9	3	44	44	121	.245	.294	.315	609	68	-27	60	26	4	.983	13	*O-157(0-157-0)	-1.2
1983	Hou-N	97	405	48	98	12	11	0	25	22	72	.242	.283	.326	609	73	-16	30	13	2	.977	9	O-97(0-97-0)	-0.6
	NY-A	48	152	17	38	9	1	1	17	8	31	.250	.287	.342	630	75	-5	7	3	0	.992	-0	O-48(0-48-0)	-0.5
1984	NY-A	117	355	37	92	12	6	4	38	18	48	.259	.297	.361	657	84	-8	20	11	1	.985	3	*O-108(0-108-0)/D-1	-0.6
1985	NY-A	34	66	12	13	4	1	1	4	1	16	.197	.209	.333	542	47	-5	1	1	-0	1.000	0	O-26(3-19-4)/D-1	-0.5
	KC-A	24	70	9	17	1	3	2	12	3	8	.243	.284	.429	712	91	-1	0	1	-0	1.000	-3	O-21(0-13-8)	-0.5
	Yr	58	136	21	30	5	4	3	16	4	24	.221	.248	.382	631	70	-6	1	2	-0	1.000	-3	O-47(3-32-12)/D-1	-1.0
1986	Atl-N	118	359	46	84	18	6	4	27	21	77	.234	.276	.351	627	68	-16	17	16	-2	.970	-3	O-97(18-12-71)	-2.6
Total	12	1382	4992	699	1257	171	87	37	386	387	885	.252	.308	.343	651	79	-145	487	182	43	.982	103	*O-1323C/D-2	-1.3

■ CHET MORGAN Morgan, Chester Collins "Chick" b: 6/6/10, Cleveland, Miss. d: 9/20/91, Pasadena, Tex. BL/TR, 5'9", 160 lbs. Deb: 4/19/35

YEAR	TM/L	G	AB	R	H	2B	3B	HR	RBI	BB	SO	AVG	OBP	SLG	OPS	OPS+	BR+	SB	CS	SBR	FA	FR	G/POS	TPR
1935	Det-A	14	23	2	4	1	0	0	1	5	0	.174	.321	.217	539	43	-2	0	0	0	.909	-0	/O-4(4-0-0)	-0.2

YEAR	TM/L	G	AB	R	H	2B	3B	HR	RBI	BB	SO	AVG	OBP	SLG	OPS	OPS+	BR+	SB	CS	SBR	FA	FR	G/POS	TPR
1938	Det-A	74	306	50	87	6	1	0	27	20	12	.284	.330	.310	641	58	-19	5	6	-1	.980	0	O-74(6-68-0)	-2.0
Total	2	88	329	52	91	7	1	0	28	25	12	.277	.330	.304	634	57	-21	5	6	-1	.977	0	/O-78(10-68-0)	-2.2
■ **ED MORGAN** Morgan, Edward Carre b: 5/22/04, Cairo, Ill. d: 4/9/80, New Orleans, La. BR/TR, 6'0.5", 180 lbs. Deb: 4/11/28 Career OF: (1-LF 18-CF 102-RF)																								
1928	Cle-A	76	265	42	83	24	6	4	54	21	17	.313	.366	.494	860	123	8	5	5	-1	.968	1	1-36,O-21C,3-14	0.6
1929	Cle-A	93	318	60	101	19	10	3	37	37	24	.318	.392	.469	861	116	8	4	3	-0	.908	-11	O-80(0-0-80)	-0.9
1930	Cle-A	150	584	122	204	47	11	26	136	62	66	.349	.413	.601	1014	148	41	8	4	0	.987	-3	*1-129,O-19(0-0-19)	2.6
1931	Cle-A	131	462	87	162	33	4	11	86	83	46	.351	.451	.511	961	144	33	4	5	-1	.984	2	*1-117/3-3	2.2
1932	Cle-A	144	532	96	156	32	7	4	68	94	44	.293	.402	.402	804	102	5	7	6	-1	.985	-8	*1-142/3-1	-1.5
1933	Cle-A	39	121	10	32	3	3	1	13	7	9	.264	.305	.364	668	73	-5	1	1	-0	.997	2	1-32/O-1(1-0-0)	-0.5
1934	Bos-A	138	528	95	141	28	4	3	79	81	46	.267	.367	.352	719	80	-13	7	1	1	.988	-7	*1-137	-3.1
Total	7	771	2810	512	879	186	45	52	473	385	252	.313	.398	.467	864	117	78	36	25	-1	.986	-23	1-593,O-121R/3-18	-0.6
■ **EDDIE MORGAN** Morgan, Edwin Willis "Pepper" b: 11/19/14, Brady Lake, Ohio d: 6/27/82, Lakewood, Ohio BL/TL, 5'10", 160 lbs. Deb: 4/14/36																								
1936	StL-N	8	18	4	5	0	0	1	3	2	4	.278	.350	.444	794	113	0	0			.889	-0	/O-4(0-0-4)	0.0
1937	Bro-N	31	48	4	9	3	0	0	5	9	7	.188	.316	.250	566	55	-3	0			.984	-3	/1-7,O-7(1-1-5)	-0.6
Total	2	39	66	8	14	3	0	1	8	11	11	.212	.325	.303	628	70	-2	0			.842	-3	/O-11(1-1-9),1-7	-0.6
■ **BILL MORGAN** Morgan, Henry William b: 10/1857, Washington, D.C. Deb: 5/4/1875 Career OF: (0-LF 2-CF 25-RF)																								
1875	RS-n	19	69	11	18	4	0	0	1	5	4	.261	.311	.319	630	132	3	2	1	0	.824	-5	O-10(3-7-0)/P-7,3-7	-0.2
1878	Mil-N	14	56	2	11	0	0	0	5	3	9	.196	.237	.196	434	41	-3				.769	-6	O-13(0-1-12)/3-3,2-1	-0.9
1882	Pit-a	17	66	10	17	2	1	0		4		.258	.300	.318	618	114	1				.688	-8	O-11(0-0-11)/C-7	-0.5
1884	Ric-a	6	20	0	2	0	0	0		1		.100	.143	.100	243	-20	-3				.850	-2	/C-3,O-2(0-0-2),2-1	-0.4
	Bal-U	2	9	1	2	0	0	0		1		.222	.300	.222	522	55	-1				.909	0	/C-1,2-1,O-1(0-1-0)	-0.1
Total	3	39	151	13	32	2	1	0	5	9	9	.212	.256	.238	495	64	-6				.743	-16	/O-27R,C-11,2-3,3-3	-1.9
■ **RED MORGAN** Morgan, James Edward b: 10/6/1883, Neola, Iowa d: 3/25/81, New York, N.Y. TR, Deb: 6/20/06																								
1906	Bos-A	88	307	20	66	6	3	1	21	16		.215	.270	.264	534	67	-11	7			.866	-13	3-88	-2.5
■ **JOE MORGAN** Morgan, Joe Leonard b: 9/19/43, Bonham, Tex. BL/TR, 5'7", 160 lbs. Deb: 9/21/63 H Career OF: (14-LF 2-CF 0-RF)																								
1963	Hou-N	8	25	5	6	0	1	0	3	5	5	.240	.367	.320	687	106	0	1	0	0	.909	-3	/2-7	-0.2
1964	Hou-N	10	37	4	7	0	0	0	0	6	7	.189	.302	.189	492	44	-2	0	1	-0	.949	-0	2-10	-0.2
1965	Hou-N	157	601	100	163	22	12	14	40	**97**	77	.271	.375	.418	793	132	29	20	9	1	.969	-2	*2-157	4.3
1966	Hou-N†	122	425	60	121	14	8	5	42	89	43	.285	.412	.391	803	134	25	11	8	-0	.965	-16	*2-117	1.9
1967	Hou-N	133	494	73	136	27	11	6	42	81	51	.275	.380	.411	790	131	22	29	5	5	.979	-5	*2-130/O-1(1-0-0)	3.6
1968	Hou-N	10	20	6	5	0	1	0	0	7	4	.250	.444	.350	794	144	2	3	0	1	.882	-4	/2-5,O-1(1-0-0)	-0.2
1969	Hou-N	147	535	94	126	18	5	15	43	110	74	.236	.367	.372	739	110	11	49	14	6	.972	-4	*2-132,O-14(12-2-0)	2.2
1970	Hou-N★	144	548	102	147	28	9	8	52	102	55	.268	.384	.396	780	114	15	42	13	5	.979	11	*2-142	3.9
1971	Hou-N	160	583	87	149	27	**11**	13	56	88	52	.256	.354	.407	761	118	15	40	8	6	.986	-3	*2-157	3.1
1972	*Cin-N★	149	552	**122**	161	23	4	16	73	**115**	44	.292	**.419**	.435	854	152	44	58	17	7	**.990**	-7	*2-149	5.6
1973	*Cin-N★	157	576	116	167	35	2	26	82	111	61	.290	.408	.493	901	157	48	67	15	**9**	.990	-8	*2-154	**6.1**
1974	Cin-N★	149	512	107	150	31	3	22	67	120	69	.293	**.430**	.494	924	160	47	58	12	9	.982	-13	*2-142	5.3
1975	*Cin-N★	146	498	107	163	27	6	17	94	**132**	52	.327	**.471**	.508	**979**	**169**	**55**	67	10	11	**.986**	-7	*2-142	**7.0**
1976	*Cin-N★	141	472	113	151	30	5	27	111	114	41	.320	**.453**	**.576**	**1029**	**186**	**58**	60	9	10	.981	-23	*2-133	5.6
1977	Cin-N★	153	521	113	150	21	6	22	78	117	58	.288	.420	.478	898	138	33	49	10	7	**.993**	-18	*2-151	3.1
1978	Cin-N★	132	441	68	104	27	0	13	75	79	40	.236	.354	.385	740	107	6	19	5	2	.980	-31	*2-124	-1.7
1979	*Cin-N★	127	436	70	109	26	1	9	32	93	45	.250	.383	.376	759	107	8	28	6	4	.980	-13	*2-121	0.6
1980	*Hou-N	141	461	66	112	17	5	11	49	**93**	47	.243	.370	.373	743	117	14	24	6	3	.988	-12	*2-130	1.2
1981	SF-N	90	308	47	74	16	1	8	31	66	37	.240	.374	.377	751	116	9	14	5	1	.991	-11	2-87	0.4
1982	SF-N	134	463	68	134	19	4	14	61	85	60	.289	.402	.438	840	135	25	24	4	4	.989	-6	*2-120/3-3	3.1
1983	*Phi-N	123	404	72	93	20	1	16	59	89	54	.230	.374	.403	778	117	12	18	2	3	.971	-2	*2-117	2.1
1984	Oak-A	116	365	50	89	21	0	6	43	66	39	.244	.361	.351	712	105	5	8	3	1	.977	-31	*2-100/D-5	-2.0
Total	22	2649	9277	1650	2517	449	96	268	1133	1865	1015	.271	.395	.427	823	133	480	689	162	95	.981	-206	*2-2527/O-16L,D-5,3	54.8
■ **JOE MORGAN** Morgan, Joseph Michael b: 11/19/30, Walpole, Mass. BL/TR, 5'10", 170 lbs. Deb: 4/14/59 MC																								
1959	Mil-N	13	23	2	5	1	0	0	1	2	4	.217	.280	.261	541	49	-2	0	0	0	.913	-2	/2-7	-0.3
	KC-A	20	21	2	4	0	1	0	3	3	7	.190	.292	.286	577	58	-1	0	0	0	1.000	-1	/3-2	-0.2
1960	Phi-N	26	83	5	11	2	2	0	2	6	11	.133	.191	.205	396	8	-11	0	0	0	.971	1	3-24	-1.0
	Cle-A	22	47	6	14	2	0	2	4	6	4	.298	.377	.468	845	131	2	0	0	0	.889	-2	3-12/O-2(0-0-2)	0.0
1961	Cle-A	4	10	0	2	0	0	0	0	1	3	.200	.273	.200	473	29	-1	0	0	0	1.000	0	/O-2(0-2-0)	-0.1
1964	StL-N	3	3	0	0	0	0	0	0	0	2	.000	.000	.000	0	-92	-1	0	0	0	.000	0	H	-0.1
Total	4	88	187	15	36	5	3	2	10	18	31	.193	.263	.283	547	49	-13	0	0	0	.944	-3	/3-38,2-7,O-4(0-2-2)	-1.7
■ **KEVIN MORGAN** Morgan, Kevin Lee b: 3/3/70, Lafayette, La. BR/TR, 6'1", 170 lbs. Deb: 6/15/97																								
1997	NY-N	1	1	0	0	0	0	0	0	0	0	.000	.000	.000	0	-99	-0	0	0	0	1.000	0	/3-1	0.0
■ **RAY MORGAN** Morgan, Raymond Caryll b: 6/14/1889, Baltimore, Md. d: 2/15/40, Baltimore, Md. BR/TR, 5'8.5", 155 lbs. Deb: 8/7/11 Career OF: (0-LF 0-CF 2-RF)																								
1911	Was-A	25	89	11	19	2	0	0	5	4		.213	.247	.236	483	36	-8	2			.900	-3	3-25	-1.0
1912	Was-A	81	273	40	65	10	7	1	30	29		.238	.318	.337	655	87	-5	11			.939	-7	2-76/S-4,3-1	-1.0
1913	Was-A	138	481	58	131	19	8	0	57	68	63	.272	.369	.345	714	107	7	19			.950	-6	*2-134/S-4	0.4
1914	Was-A	147	491	50	126	22	8	1	49	62	34	.257	.352	.340	692	104	4	24	17	-1	.948	-9	*2-146	-0.4
1915	Was-A	62	193	21	45	5	4	0	21	30	15	.233	.342	.301	643	91	-1	6	5	-0	.965	-4	2-57/S-2,3-2	-0.5
1916	Was-A	99	315	41	84	12	4	1	29	59	29	.267	.398	.340	738	123	13	14			.957	-17	2-82/S-9,1-3,3-1	-0.2
1917	Was-A	101	338	32	90	9	1	1	33	40	29	.266	.346	.308	653	101	1	7			.961	-8	2-95/3-3	-0.5
1918	Was-A	88	300	25	70	11	1	0	30	28	14	.233	.311	.277	588	79	-7	4			.959	-5	2-80/O-2(0-0-2)	-1.2
Total	8	741	2480	278	630	90	33	4	254	320	184	.254	.348	.322	670	98	4	87	22		.953	-58	2-670/3-32,S-19,1O	-4.4
■ **BOBBY MORGAN** Morgan, Robert Morris b: 6/29/26, Oklahoma City, Okla. BR/TR, 5'9", 175 lbs. Deb: 4/18/50																								
1950	Bro-N	67	199	38	45	10	3	7	21	32	43	.226	.342	.412	754	95	-1	0			.969	6	3-52,S-10	0.5
1952	*Bro-N	67	191	36	45	8	0	7	16	46	35	.236	.392	.387	779	115	6	2	2	-0	.968	3	3-60/2-5,S-4	0.9
1953	*Bro-N	69	196	35	51	6	2	7	33	33	47	.260	.370	.418	788	103	1	2	2	-0	.920	-2	3-36,S-21	0.1
1954	Phi-N	135	455	58	119	25	2	14	50	70	68	.262	.360	.418	778	102	2	3	1	0	.954	-22	*S-129/3-8,2-5	-0.9
1955	Phi-N	136	483	61	112	20	2	10	49	73	72	.232	.333	.344	676	81	-12	6	4	-0	.980	-13	2-88,S-41/3-6,1-1	-1.5
1956	Phi-N	8	25	1	5	0	0	0	1	6	4	.200	.355	.200	555	56	-1	0	0	0	.857	1	/3-5,2-3	-0.1
	StL-N	61	113	14	22	7	0	3	20	15	24	.195	.289	.336	625	67	-5	0	2	-1	.980	1	2-13,3-11/S-6	-0.4
	Yr	69	138	15	27	7	0	3	21	21	28	.196	.302	.312	613	65	-7	0	2	-1	.877	1	3-16,2-16/S-6	-0.5
1957	Phi-N	2	0	0	0	0	0	0	0	0	0	—	—	—	—	—	0	0	0	0	1.000	0	/2-1	0.0
	Chi-N	125	425	43	88	20	2	5	27	52	87	.207	.295	.299	594	61	-23	5	0	1	.976	8	*2-116,3-12	-0.6
	Yr	127	425	43	88	20	2	5	27	52	87	.207	.295	.299	594	61	-23	5	0	1	.976	8	*2-117,3-12	-0.6
1958	Chi-N	1	1	0	0	0	0	0	0	0	1	.000	.000	.000	0	-99	-0	0	0	0	.000	0	H	0.0
Total	8	671	2088	286	487	96	11	53	217	327	381	.233	.339	.366	705	88	-33	18	11		.978	-18	2-231,S-211,3-190,/1	-2.0
■ **VERN MORGAN** Morgan, Vernon Thomas b: 8/8/28, Emporia, Va. d: 11/8/75, Minneapolis, Minn. BL/TR, 6'1", 190 lbs. Deb: 8/10/54 C																								
1954	Chi-N	24	64	3	15	2	0	0	2	1	10	.234	.246	.266	512	33	-6	0	0	0	.895	-4	3-15	-1.1
1955	Chi-N	7	7	1	1	0	0	0	1	3	4	.143	.400	.143	543	52	-0	0	0	0	.667	-1	/3-2	-0.1
Total	2	31	71	4	16	2	0	0	3	4	14	.225	.267	.254	520	36	-7	0	0	0	.864	-5	/3-17	-1.2
■ **BILL MORGAN** Morgan, William b: 1856, Brooklyn, N.Y. d: 9/9/08, New York, N.Y. Deb: 8/6/1883 Career OF: (18-LF 6-CF 14-RF)																								
1883	Pit-a	32	114	12	18	2	1	0		7		.158	.207	.193	400	31	-8				.825	-2	S-21/O-6C,C-5,2-2	-0.8
1884	Was-a	45	162	8	28	1	1	0		8		.173	.216	.191	408	39	-10				.781	-5	O-31L,C-12/2-2,S-2	-1.3
Total	2	77	276	20	46	3	2	0		15		.167	.212	.192	404	35	-18				.771	-6	/O-37L,S-23,C-17,2	-2.1

YEAR	TM/L	G	AB	R	H	2B	3B	HR	RBI	BB	SO	AVG	OBP	SLG	OPS	OPS+	BR+	SB	CS	SBR	FA	FR	G/POS	TPR
■ MOE MORHARDT	Morhardt, Meredith Goodwin b: 1/16/37, Manchester, Conn. BL/TL, 6'1", 185 lbs. Deb: 9/7/61																							
1961	Chi-N	7	18	3	5	0	0	0	1	3	5	.278	.381	.278	659	78	-0	0	0	0	.962	-1	/1-7	-0.2
1962	Chi-N	18	16	1	2	0	0	0	2	2	8	.125	.222	.125	347	-4	-2	0	0	0	.000	0	H	-0.2
Total	2	25	34	4	7	0	0	0	3	5	13	.206	.308	.206	514	39	-3	0	0	0	.962	-1	/1-7	-0.4
■ GENE MORIARITY	Moriarity, Eugene John b: 1/5/1865, Holyoke, Mass. BL/TL, 5'8", 130 lbs. Deb: 6/18/1884 Career OF: (49-LF 3-CF 12-RF)																							
1884	Bos-N	4	16	1	1	0	0	0	0	0	8	.063	.063	.063	125	-61	-3				.714	-1	/O-4(1-3-0)	-0.3
	Ind-a	10	37	4	8	0	2	0	4	0		.216	.216	.324	541	76	-1				.769	-1	/O-7(0-0-7),P-2,3-1	-0.2
1885	Det-N	11	39	1	1	1	0	0	0	0	10	.026	.026	.051	77	-75	-7				.905	2	/O-6R,3-4,S-1,P-1	-0.5
1892	StL-N	47	177	20	31	4	1	3	19	4	37	.175	.207	.260	466	43	-13	7			.820	2	O-47(47-0-0)	-1.4
Total	3	72	269	26	41	5	3	3	23	4	55	.152	.174	.227	401	24	-24	7			.822	2	/O-64L,3-5,P-3,S-1	-2.4
■ ED MORIARTY	Moriarty, Edward Jerome b: 10/12/12, Holyoke, Mass. d: 9/29/91, Holyoke, Mass. BR/TR, 5'10.5", 180 lbs. Deb: 6/21/35																							
1935	Bos-N	8	34	4	11	2	1	1	1	0	6	.324	.324	.529	853	136	1	0			.923	-4	/2-8	-0.2
1936	Bos-N	6	6	1	1	0	0	0	0	0	1	.167	.167	.167	333	-11	-1	0			.000	0	H	-0.1
Total	2	14	40	5	12	2	1	1	1	0	7	.300	.300	.475	775	114	0	0			.923	-4	/2-8	-0.3
■ GEORGE MORIARTY	Moriarty, George Joseph b: 6/7/1884, Chicago, Ill. d: 4/8/64, Miami, Fla. BR/TR, 6', 185 lbs. Deb: 9/27/03 FMU Career OF: (30-LF 9-CF 5-RF)																							
1903	Chi-N	1	5	1	0	0	0	0	0	0		.000	.000	.000	0	-99	-1	0			1.000	-0	/3-1	-0.2
1904	Chi-N	4	13	0	0	0	0	0	0	1		.000	.071	.000	71	-77	-3	0			.778	-0	/3-2,O-2(0-2-0)	-0.3
1906	NY-A	65	197	22	46	7	7	0	23	17		.234	.298	.340	638	90	-2	8			.912	1	3-39,O-15L/1-5,2-1	-0.1
1907	NY-A	126	437	51	121	16	5	0	43	25		.277	.320	.336	657	101	0	28			.899	-10	3-91,1-22/O-9C,2S	-0.9
1908	NY-A	101	348	25	82	12	1	0	27	11		.236	.269	.276	545	76	-9	22			.976	8	1-52,3-28,O-10L,/2	-0.2
1909	*Det-A	133	473	43	129	20	4	1	39	24		.273	.309	.338	648	100	-1	34			**.939**	2	*3-106,1-24	0.4
1910	Det-A	136	490	53	123	24	3	2	60	33		.251	.308	.324	632	92	-5	33			.927	-1	*3-134	-0.3
1911	Det-A	130	478	51	116	20	4	1	60	27		.243	.287	.308	595	63	-25	28			.929	-4	*3-129/1-1	-2.5
1912	Det-A	105	375	38	93	23	1	0	54	26		.248	.316	.315	630	83	-8	27			.987	-8	1-71,3-33	-1.7
1913	Det-A	104	347	29	83	5	2	0	30	24	25	.239	.302	.265	567	67	-14	33			.938	-3	3-94/O-7(7-0-0)	-1.6
1914	Det-A	132	465	56	118	19	5	1	40	39	27	.254	.318	.323	641	90	-6	34	15	2	.956	17	*3-126/1-3	1.8
1915	Det-A	31	38	2	8	1	0	0	0	5	7	.211	.318	.237	555	63	-2	1	1	-0	.875	-0	3-12/1-1,2-1,O-1C	-0.2
1916	Chi-A	7	5	1	1	0	0	0	0	2	0	.200	.429	.200	629	88	0	0			1.000	1	/1-1,3-1	0.1
Total	13	1075	3671	372	920	147	32	5	376	234	59	.251	.303	.312	616	84	-76	248	16		.931	3	3-796,1-180/O-44L,2S	-5.7
■ BILL MORIARTY	Moriarty, William Joseph b: 8/1883, Chicago, Ill. d: 12/25/16, Elgin, Ill. BR/TR, 6'2", 180 lbs. Deb: 4/29/09 F																							
1909	Cin-N	6	20	1	4	1	0	0	1	0		.200	.200	.250	450	40	-1	2			.944	0	/S-6	-0.1
■ BILL MORLEY	Morley, William M. (b: William Morley Jennings) b: 1/23/1890, Holland, Mich. d: 5/14/85, Lubbock, Tex. BR/TR, 5'11", 170 lbs. Deb: 9/8/13																							
1913	Was-A	2	3	0	0	0	0	0	0	0	0	.000	.000	.000	0	-98	-1	0			.000	0	/2-1	-0.1
■ RUSS MORMAN	Morman, Russell Lee b: 4/28/62, Independence, Mo. BR/TR, 6'4", 220 lbs. Deb: 8/3/86 Career OF: (28-LF 0-CF 12-RF)																							
1986	Chi-A	49	159	18	40	5	0	4	17	16	36	.252	.328	.358	686	84	-3	1	0	0	.989	-3	1-47	-0.9
1988	Chi-A	40	75	8	18	2	0	0	3	3	17	.240	.269	.267	536	51	-5	0	0	0	.981	-3	1-22,O-10(10-0-0)/D-3	-0.9
1989	Chi-A	37	58	5	13	2	0	0	8	6	16	.224	.297	.259	555	59	-3	1	0	0	.988	1	1-35/D-1	-0.3
1990	KC-A	12	37	5	10	4	2	1	3	3	3	.270	.325	.568	893	147	2	0	0	0	1.000	-0	/O-8(8-0-0),1-3,D-1	0.1
1991	KC-A	12	23	1	6	0	0	0	1	1	5	.261	.292	.261	553	54	-1	0	0	0	1.000	0	/1-8,O-2(2-0-0),D-1	-0.2
1994	Fla-N	13	33	2	7	0	1	1	2	2	9	.212	.278	.364	641	64	-2	0	0	0	.987	2	/1-8	-0.1
1995	Fla-N	34	72	9	20	2	1	3	7	3	12	.278	.316	.458	774	101	-0	0	0	0	.955	-2	O-18(6-0-12)/1-3	-0.3
1996	Fla-N	6	6	0	1	1	0	0	0	1	2	.167	.286	.333	619	65	-0	0	0	0	1.000	-0	/1-2	-0.1
1997	Fla-N	4	7	3	2	1	0	1	2	0	2	.286	.286	.857	1143	194	1	1	0	0	1.000	0	/O-2(2-0-0),1-1	0.1
Total	9	207	470	51	117	17	4	10	43	35	102	.249	.306	.366	672	82	-12	3	0	1	.989	-7	1-129/O-40L,D-6	-2.6
■ JEFF MORONKO	Moronko, Jeffrey Robert b: 8/17/59, Houston, Tex. BR/TR, 6'2", 190 lbs. Deb: 9/1/84 Career OF: (1-LF 0-CF 1-RF)																							
1984	Cle-A	7	19	1	3	1	0	0	3	3	5	.158	.273	.211	483	35	-2	0	0	0	.895	-0	/3-6,D-1	-0.2
1987	NY-A	7	11	0	1	0	0	0	0	0	2	.091	.167	.091	258	-29	-2	0	0	0	1.000	-0	/3-3,S-2,O-2(1-0-1)	-0.2
Total	2	14	30	1	4	1	0	0	3	3	7	.133	.235	.167	402	12	-4	0	0	0	.926	-0	/3-9,O-2L,S-2,D-1	-0.4
■ JOHN MORRILL	Morrill, John Francis "Honest John" b: 2/19/1855, Boston, Mass. d: 4/2/32, Brookline, Mass. BR/TR, 5'10.5", 155 lbs. Deb: 4/24/1876 M Career OF: (2-LF 12-CF 12-RF)																							
1876	Bos-N	66	281	38	73	5	2	0	26	3	5	.260	.270	.295	565	87	-4				.857	7	2-37,C-23/O-5C,1-3	0.4
1877	Bos-N	61	242	47	73	5	1	0	28	6	15	.302	.319	.331	649	101	0				.864	-9	3-30,1-18,O-11R,/2	-0.8
1878	Bos-N	60	233	26	56	5	1	0	23	5	16	.240	.256	.270	527	68	-8				.957	2	*1-59/O-1(0-1-0),3-1	-0.8
1879	Bos-N	84	348	56	98	18	5	0	49	14	32	.282	.309	.362	671	118	6				.878	3	3-51,1-33	0.8
1880	Bos-N	86	342	51	81	16	8	2	44	11	37	.237	.261	.348	609	108	3				.966	0	1-46,3-40/P-3	0.2
1881	Bos-N	81	311	47	90	19	3	1	39	12	30	.289	.316	.379	695	123	8				.969	9	*1-74/2-4,P-3,3-2	1.3
1882	Bos-N	83	349	73	101	19	11	2	54	18	29	.289	.324	.424	748	137	14				.964	-3	*1-76/S-3,2-2,O3PM	0.4
1883	Bos-N	97	404	83	129	33	16	6	68	15	68	.319	.344	.525	868	155	25				**.974**	-1	*1-81/O-7C,3-6,S2PM	1.5
1884	Bos-N	111	438	80	114	19	7	3	61	30	87	.260	.308	.356	664	109	5				.971	3	*1-91,2-17/P-7,3OM	0.0
1885	Bos-N	111	394	74	89	20	7	4	44	64	78	.226	.334	.343	677	124	14				.969	4	*1-92,2-17/3-2,M	0.9
1886	Bos-N	117	430	86	106	25	6	7	69	56	81	.247	.333	.381	715	121	13	9			.895	-3	S-55,1-42,2-20,/PM	0.8
1887	Bos-N	127	541	79	178	32	6	12	81	37	86	.329	.330	.438	769	112	7	19			.984	4	*1-127,M	-0.1
1888	Bos-N	135	486	60	96	18	7	4	39	55	68	.198	.282	.288	570	81	-9	21			.979	9	*1-133/2-2,M	-1.3
1889	Was-N	44	146	20	27	5	0	2	16	30	23	.185	.328	.260	588	70	-4	12			.980	-1	1-40/3-3,2-1,P-1,M	-0.8
1890	Bos-P	2	7	1	1	0	0	0	2	2	1	.143	.333	.143	476	28	-1	0			.750	-1	/S-1,1-1	-0.1
Total	15	1265	4952	821	1312	239	80	43	643	358	656	.265	.310	.367	677	111	69	61			.971	23	1-916,3-138,2/SOCP	2.4
■ DOYT MORRIS	Morris, Doyt Theodore b: 7/15/16, Stanley, N.C. d: 7/4/84, Gastonia, N.C. BR/TR, 6'4", 195 lbs. Deb: 6/6/37																							
1937	Phi-A	6	13	0	2	0	0	0	0	0	3	.154	.154	.154	308	-23	-2	0	0	0	1.000	-0	/O-3(2-1-0)	-0.2
■ E. MORRIS	Morris, E. b: Trenton, N.J. Deb: 9/11/1884																							
1884	Bal-U	1	3	0	0	0	0	0		0		.000	.000	.000	0	-91	-1				.500	-1	/O-1(0-0-1),P-1	-0.1
■ JOHN MORRIS	Morris, John Daniel b: 2/23/61, N.Bellmore, N.Y. BL/TL, 6'1", 185 lbs. Deb: 8/5/86																							
1986	StL-N	39	100	8	24	0	1	1	14	7	15	.240	.290	.290	580	61	-5	6	2	1	.986	-1	O-31(5-4-26)	-0.7
1987	*StL-N	101	157	22	41	6	4	3	23	11	22	.261	.314	.408	721	88	-3	5	2	0	.989	-15	O-74(2-8-68)	-1.9
1988	StL-N	20	38	3	11	2	1	0	3	1	7	.289	.308	.395	702	99	-0	0	0	0	.857	-5	O-16(11-3-2)	-0.6
1989	StL-N	96	117	8	28	4	1	2	14	4	22	.239	.264	.342	606	70	-5	1	0	0	1.000	-13	O-51(10-11-32)	-1.9
1990	StL-N	18	18	0	2	0	0	0	0	3	6	.111	.238	.111	349	-1	-2	0	0	0	1.000	-2	/O-6(0-1-5)	-0.4
1991	Phi-N	85	127	15	28	2	1	1	6	12	25	.220	.293	.276	568	61	-6	2	0	0	.974	-10	O-57(11-27-24)	-1.8
1992	Cal-A	43	57	4	11	1	0	1	3	4	11	.193	.258	.263	521	46	-4	1	0	0	1.000	-3	O-14(5-0-9)/D-6	-0.8
Total	7	402	614	60	145	15	8	8	63	42	108	.236	.288	.326	614	69	-26	15	4	2	.981	-49	O-249(44-54-166)/D-6	-8.1
■ WALTER MORRIS	Morris, John Walter b: 1/31/1880, Rockwall, Tex. d: 8/2/61, Dallas, Tex. BR/TR, 5'11", Deb: 8/31/08																							
1908	StL-N	23	73	1	13	1	1	0	2	0		.178	.178	.219	397	28	-6	1			.938	4	S-23	-0.2
■ P. MORRIS	Morris, P. b: Rockford, Ill. Deb: 5/14/1884																							
1884	Was-U	1	3	0	0	0	0	0		0		.000	.000	.000	0	-99	-1				.750	0	/S-1	-0.1
■ WARREN MORRIS	Morris, Warren Randall b: 1/11/74, Alexandria, La. BL/TR, 5'11", 190 lbs. Deb: 4/5/99																							
1999	Pit-N	147	511	65	147	20	3	15	73	59	88	.288	.364	.427	790	99	0	3	7	-2	.979	4	*2-144	0.8
2000	Pit-N	144	528	68	137	31	2	3	43	65	78	.259	.343	.343	686	75	-19	7	10	-2	.979	20	*2-134	0.5
Total	2	291	1039	133	284	51	5	18	116	124	166	.273	.353	.384	737	87	-19	10	17	-4	.979	23	2-278	1.3

YEAR	TM/L	G	AB	R	H	2B	3B	HR	RBI	BB	SO	AVG	OBP	SLG	OPS	OPS+	BR+	SB	CS	SBR	FA	FR	G/POS	TPR
■ HAL MORRIS	Morris, William Harold b: 4/9/65, Fort Rucker, Ala. BL/TL, 6'4", 215 lbs. Deb: 7/29/88 Career OF: (56-LF 0-CF 6-RF)																							
1988	NY-A	15	20	1	2	0	0	0	0	0	9	.100	.100	.100	200	-44	-4	0	0	0	1.000	-1	/O-4(3-0-2),D-1	-0.5
1989	NY-A	15	18	2	5	0	0	0	4	1	4	.278	.316	.278	594	69	-1	0	0	0	1.000	-2	/O-5(2-3-0),1-2,D-1	-0.2
1990	*Cin-N	107	309	50	105	22	3	7	36	21	32	.340	.384	.498	882	135	14	9	3	1	.995	-0	1-80/O-6(6-0-0)	1.0
1991	Cin-N	136	478	72	152	33	1	14	59	46	61	.318	.379	.479	858	135	22	10	4	1	.992	4	*1-128/O-1(1-0-0)	1.9
1992	Cin-N	115	395	41	107	21	3	6	53	45	53	.271	.348	.385	733	105	3	6	6	-1	**.999**	5	*1-109	0.0
1993	Cin-N	101	379	48	120	18	0	7	49	34	51	.317	.376	.420	795	112	7	2	2	-0	.994	3	1-98	0.1
1994	Cin-N	112	436	60	146	30	4	10	78	34	62	.335	.389	.491	880	129	19	6	2	1	.994	1	*1-112	1.0
1995	*Cin-N	101	359	53	100	25	2	11	51	29	58	.279	.334	.451	785	105	2	1	1	-0	.994	5	1-99	-0.2
1996	Cin-N	142	528	82	165	32	4	16	80	50	76	.313	.377	.479	857	123	18	7	5	-0	.993	-2	*1-140	0.3
1997	Cin-N	96	333	42	92	20	1	1	33	23	43	.276	.329	.351	680	77	-11	3	1	0	.990	-4	1-89	-2.3
1998	KC-A	127	472	50	146	27	2	1	40	32	52	.309	.354	.381	736	89	-7	1	0	0	.990	-5	1-46,O-39L,D-39	-1.8
1999	Cin-N	80	102	10	29	9	0	0	16	10	21	.284	.348	.373	721	80	-3	0	0	0	.991	-2	1-25/O-4(4-0-0),D-1	-0.5
2000	Cin-N	59	63	9	14	2	1	2	6	12	10	.222	.355	.381	736	83	-1	0	0	0	1.000	3	1-16/O-1(0-0-1),D-1	0.0
	Det-A	40	106	15	33	7	0	1	8	19	16	.311	.416	.406	822	113	3	0	0	0	.990	1	1-38/O-1(1-0-0)	0.1
Total	13	1246	3998	535	1216	246	21	76	513	356	548	.304	.364	.433	797	110	63	45	24	2	.994	7	1-982/O-61L,D-43	-1.1
■ JIM MORRISON	Morrison, James Forrest b: 9/23/52, Pensacola, Fla. BR/TR, 5'11", 182 lbs. Deb: 9/18/77 Career OF: (9-LF 0-CF 3-RF)																							
1977	Phi-N	5	7	3	3	0	0	0	1	1	1	.429	.500	.429	929	145	1	0	0	0	.875	1	/3-5	0.1
1978	*Phi-N	53	108	12	17	1	1	3	10	10	21	.157	.235	.269	504	40	-9	1	1	-0	.968	13	2-31/3-3,O-1(1-0-0)	0.6
1979	Chi-A	67	240	38	66	14	0	14	35	15	48	.275	.328	.508	837	122	6	11	3	1	.982	1	2-48,3-29	1.0
1980	Chi-A	162	604	66	171	40	0	15	57	36	74	.283	.332	.424	756	106	4	9	6	-0	.969	-3	*2-161/S-1,D-1	1.0
1981	Chi-A	90	290	27	68	8	1	10	34	10	29	.234	.265	.372	637	84	-7	3	2	-0	.956	8	3-87/2-1,D-1	-0.1
1982	Chi-A	51	166	17	37	7	3	7	19	13	15	.223	.279	.428	707	91	-3	0	1	-0	.914	-14	3-50/D-1	-1.8
	Pit-N	44	86	10	24	4	1	4	15	5	14	.279	.319	.488	807	119	2	2	0	0	.964	2	3-26/O-2L,2-1,S-1	0.4
1983	Pit-N	66	158	16	48	7	2	6	25	9	25	.304	.349	.487	836	126	5	2	6	-2	.973	3	2-28,3-26/S-7	0.8
1984	Pit-N	100	304	38	87	14	2	11	45	20	52	.286	.332	.454	786	119	7	0	1	-1	.938	0	3-61,2-26/S-2,1-1	0.7
1985	Pit-N	92	244	17	62	10	0	4	22	8	44	.254	.281	.344	625	75	-9	3	0	1	.961	1	3-59,2-15/O-1(1-0-0)	-0.8
1986	Pit-N	154	537	58	147	35	4	23	88	47	88	.274	.337	.482	819	120	13	9	8	-1	.946	-13	*3-151/2-1,S-1	-0.3
1987	Pit-N	96	348	41	92	22	1	9	46	27	57	.264	.319	.411	730	91	-5	8	5	0	.975	1	3-82,S-17/2-9	-0.4
	*Det-A	34	117	15	24	1	1	4	19	2	26	.205	.225	.333	558	47	-9	2	1	0	.962	3	3-16/2-3,S-3,O1D	-0.6
1988	Det-A	24	74	7	16	5	0	0	6	0	14	.216	.216	.284	500	40	-6	0	2	-1	1.000	-0	D-14/1-4,3-4,O-2L,S	-0.8
	Atl-N	51	92	6	14	2	0	2	13	10	13	.152	.235	.239	474	35	-8	0	1	-0	.933	0	3-20/O-4(4-0-0),P-3	-0.8
Total	12	1089	3375	371	876	170	16	112	435	213	521	.260	.308	.419	727	98	-18	50	37	-2	.949	2	3-619,2-324/SDO1P	-1.0
■ JON MORRISON	Morrison, Jonathan W. b: 1859, London, Ontario, Canada 5'9.5", 167 lbs. Deb: 8/1/1884																							
1884	Ind-a	44	182	26	48	6	8	1		7		.264	.306	.401	707	132	6				.784	3	O-44(0-44-0)	0.7
1887	NY-a	9	40	7	10	0	0	0	3	6		.250	.268	.118	386	10	-4	0			.600	-4	/O-9(0-9-0)	-0.7
Total	2	53	222	33	58	6	8	1	3	13		.261	.299	.356	656	110	3	0			.756	-1	/O-53(0-53-0)	0.0
■ TOM MORRISON	Morrison, Thomas J. b: 1875, St.Louis, Mo. 5'3", 145 lbs. Deb: 9/18/1895																							
1895	Lou-N	6	22	3	6	0	2	0	4	1	1	.273	.304	.455	759	100	-0	0			1.000	-3	/S-3,3-3	-0.2
1896	Lou-N	8	27	3	4	1	0	0	0	4	4	.148	.258	.185	443	19	-3	0			.864	-1	/3-5,O-2(0-0-2),S-1	-0.3
Total	2	14	49	6	10	1	2	0	4	5	5	.204	.278	.306	584	55	-3	0			.839	-3	/3-8,S-4,O-2(0-0-2)	-0.5
■ JACK MORRISSEY	Morrissey, John Albert "King" b: 5/2/1876, Lansing, Mich. d: 10/30/36, Lansing, Mich. BB/TR, 5'10", 160 lbs. Deb: 9/18/02																							
1902	Cin-N	12	39	5	11	1	1	0	3	4		.282	.349	.359	708	108	0	0			.941	-2	2-11/O-1(1-0-0)	-0.1
1903	Cin-N	29	89	14	22	1	0	0	9	14		.247	.350	.258	608	67	-3	3			.922	-10	2-17/O-8(6-2-0),S-2	-1.4
Total	2	41	128	19	33	2	1	0	12	18		.258	.349	.289	638	78	-3	3			.930	-12	/2-28,O-9(7-2-0),S-2	-1.5
■ JOHN MORRISSEY	Morrissey, John J. b: 12/30/1856, Janesville, Wis. d: 4/29/1884, Janesville, Wis. Deb: 5/2/1881 F																							
1881	Buf-N	12	47	3	10	2	0	0	3	0	3	.213	.213	.255	468	47	-3				.865	-2	3-12	-0.4
1882	Det-N	2	7	1	2	0	0	0	0	0	2	.286	.286	.286	571	84	-0				.714	-1	/3-2	-0.1
Total	2	14	54	4	12	2	0	0	3	0	5	.222	.222	.259	481	52	-3				.841	-3	/3-14	-0.5
■ JO-JO MORRISSEY	Morrissey, Joseph Anselm b: 1/16/04, Warren, R.I. d: 5/2/50, Worcester, Mass. BR/TR, 6'1.5", 178 lbs. Deb: 4/12/32																							
1932	Cin-N	89	269	15	65	10	1	0	13	14	15	.242	.282	.286	568	55	-17	2			.967	8	S-45,2-42,3-12,/O-1L	-0.4
1933	Cin-N	148	534	43	123	20	0	0	26	20	22	.230	.261	.268	529	52	-33	5			.964	-9	2-88,S-63,3-15	-3.5
1936	Chi-A	17	38	3	7	1	0	0	6	2	3	.184	.225	.211	436	8	-6	0	0	0	.895	0	/3-9,S-4,2-1	-0.4
Total	3	254	841	61	195	31	1	0	45	36	40	.232	.266	.271	537	51	-56	7	0		.971	-0	2-131,S-112/3-36,O	-4.3
■ TOM MORRISSEY	Morrissey, Thomas J. b: 1861, Janesville, Wis. d: 9/23/41, Janesville, Wis. 5'11", 180 lbs. Deb: 9/27/1884 F																							
1884	Mil-U	12	47	3	8	2	0	0		0		.170	.170	.213	383	28	-5				.710	-1	3-12	-0.6
■ BUD MORSE	Morse, Newell Obediah b: 9/4/04, Berkeley, Cal. d: 4/6/87, Sparks, Nev. BL/TR, 5'9", 150 lbs. Deb: 9/14/29																							
1929	Phi-A	8	27	1	2	0	0	0	0	0	2	.074	.074	.074	148	-60	-6	0	0	0	.975	2	/2-8	-0.4
■ HAP MORSE	Morse, Peter Raymond "Pete" b: 12/6/1886, St.Paul, Minn. d: 6/19/74, St.Paul, Minn. BR/TR, 5'8", 160 lbs. Deb: 4/18/11																							
1911	StL-N	4	8	0	0	0	0	0	0	1	2	.000	.111	.000	111	-70	-2	0			.750	-0	/S-2,O-1(1-0-0)	-0.2
■ CHARLIE MORTON	Morton, Charles Hazen b: 10/12/1854, Kingsville, Ohio d: 12/9/21, Massillon, Ohio BR/TR, 150 lbs. Deb: 5/2/1882 MU Career OF: (15-LF 27-CF 1-RF)																							
1882	Pit-a	25	103	12	29	0	3	0		5		.282	.315	.340	655	127	3				.816	1	O-25(0-25-0)/3-3,S-1	0.3
	StL-a	9	32	2	2	0	1	0		2		.063	.118	.125	243	-17	-4				.708	-4	/2-7,O-3(1-2-0)	-0.8
	Yr	34	135	14	31	0	4	0		7		.230	.268	.289	556	90	-1				.821	-3	O-28C/2-7,3-3,S-1	-0.5
1884	Tol-a	32	111	11	18	6	2	0		7		.162	.212	.252	464	49	-6				.861	-1	3-16,O-15L/P-3,2M	-0.5
1885	Det-N	22	79	9	14	1	2	0	3	5	10	.177	.226	.241	467	51	-4				.750	2	3-18/S-4,M	-0.2
Total	3	88	325	34	63	7	8	0	3	19	10	.194	.238	.265	503	66	-11				.841	-3	/O-43C,3-37,2-8,SP	-1.2
■ GUY MORTON	Morton, Guy Jr. "Moose" b: 11/4/30, Tuscaloosa, Ala. BR/TR, 6'2", 200 lbs. Deb: 9/17/54 F																							
1954	Bos-A	1	1	0	0	0	0	0	0	0	1	.000	.000	.000	0	-90	-0	0	0	0	.000	0	H	0.0
■ BUBBA MORTON	Morton, Wycliffe Nathaniel b: 12/13/31, Washington, D.C. BR/TR, 5'10.5", 180 lbs. Deb: 4/19/61 Career OF: (33-LF 38-CF 212-RF)																							
1961	Det-A	77	108	26	31	5	1	2	19	9	25	.287	.347	.407	755	98	-0	3	1	0	.952	-4	O-30(8-2-20)	-0.5
1962	Det-A	90	195	30	51	6	3	4	17	32	32	.262	.366	.385	750	99	1	1	1	-0	.991	-2	O-62(1-30-33)/1-3	-0.4
1963	Det-A	6	11	2	1	0	0	0	2	2	1	.091	.231	.091	322	-5	-2	0	0	0	.875	-0	/O-3(0-3-0)	-0.2
	Mil-N	15	28	1	5	0	0	0	4	2	3	.179	.258	.179	437	28	-2	0	0	0	1.000	-1	/O-9(6-3-0)	-0.4
1966	Cal-A	15	50	4	11	1	0	0	4	2	6	.220	.250	.240	490	43	-4	1	1	-0	1.000	0	O-14(0-0-14)	-0.5
1967	Cal-A	80	201	23	63	9	3	0	32	22	29	.313	.387	.388	775	135	9	0	3	-1	1.000	-6	O-61(9-0-55)	-0.1
1968	Cal-A	81	163	13	44	6	0	1	18	14	18	.270	.343	.325	668	107	2	2	1	0	.985	-4	O-50(3-0-47)/3-1	-0.6
1969	Cal-A	87	172	18	42	10	1	7	32	28	29	.244	.360	.436	796	128	7	0	0	0	1.000	-0	O-49(6-0-43)/1-1	0.5
Total	7	451	928	117	248	37	8	14	128	111	143	.267	.352	.370	722	106	10	7	7	-1	.988	-17	O-278R/1-4,3-1	-2.2
■ WALT MORYN	Moryn, Walter Joseph "Moose" b: 4/12/26, St.Paul, Minn. d: 7/21/96, Winfield, Ill. BL/TR, 6'2", 205 lbs. Deb: 6/29/54																							
1954	Bro-N	48	91	16	25	4	2	2	14	7	11	.275	.333	.429	762	94	-1	0	0	0	.881	-0	O-20(6-0-15)	-0.2
1955	Bro-N	11	19	3	5	1	0	1	3	5	4	.263	.417	.474	890	132	1	0	0	0	.833	-2	/O-7(1-0-6)	-0.1
1956	Chi-N	147	529	69	151	27	3	23	67	50	67	.285	.351	.478	829	122	16	4	2	0	.983	10	*O-141(1-0-140)	2.1
1957	Chi-N	149	568	76	164	33	0	19	88	50	90	.289	.349	.447	797	114	11	0	2	-1	.960	7	*O-147(0-0-147)	1.2
1958	Chi-N☆	143	512	77	135	26	7	26	77	62	83	.264	.352	.494	846	123	16	1	2	-0	.978	5	*O-141(141-0-0)	1.2
1959	Chi-N	117	381	41	89	14	1	14	48	44	66	.234	.318	.386	704	87	-7	0	0	0	.989	0	*O-104(97-1-9)	-1.3
1960	Chi-N	38	109	12	32	4	0	2	11	13	19	.294	.369	.385	754	108	2	2	1	0	.964	0	O-30(25-0-5)	0.0
	StL-N	75	200	24	49	4	3	11	35	17	38	.245	.304	.460	764	97	-1	0	0	0	.990	-3	O-62(29-0-39)	-0.7
	Yr	113	309	36	81	8	3	13	46	30	57	.262	.327	.434	761	101	0	2	1	0	.981	-3	O-92(54-0-44)	-0.7

YEAR	TM/L	G	AB	R	H	2B	3B	HR	RBI	BB	SO	AVG	OBP	SLG	OPS	OPS+	BR+	SB	CS	SBR	FA	FR	G/POS	TPR
1961	StL-N	17	32	0	4	2	0	0	2	1	5	.125	.152	.188	339	-10	-5	0	0	0	.889	-1	/O-7(3-0-4)	-0.7
	Pit-N	40	65	6	13	1	0	3	9	2	10	.200	.235	.354	589	53	-5	0	0	0	.950	1	O-11(6-0-5)	-0.4
	Yr	57	97	6	17	3	0	3	11	3	15	.175	.208	.299	507	31	-10	0	0	0	.931	-0	O-18(9-0-9)	-1.1
Total	8	785	2506	324	667	116	16	101	354	251	393	.266	.338	.446	784	108	27	7	7	-1	.972	17	O-670(309-1-370)	1.1

■ ROSS MOSCHITTO
Moschitto, Rosaire Allen b: 2/15/45, Fresno, Cal. BR/TR, 6'2", 175 lbs. Deb: 4/15/65

YEAR	TM/L	G	AB	R	H	2B	3B	HR	RBI	BB	SO	AVG	OBP	SLG	OPS	OPS+	BR+	SB	CS	SBR	FA	FR	G/POS	TPR
1965	NY-A	96	27	12	5	0	0	1	3	0	12	.185	.185	.296	481	35	-2	0	0	0	.941	-26	O-89(10-55-24)	-3.1
1967	NY-A	14	9	1	1	0	0	0	0	1	2	.111	.200	.111	311	-6	-1	0	0	0	1.000	-2	/O-8(2-4-2)	-0.4
Total	2	110	36	13	6	0	0	1	3	1	14	.167	.189	.250	439	25	-4	0	0	0	.944	-28	/O-97(12-59-26)	-3.5

■ LLOYD MOSEBY
Moseby, Lloyd Anthony b: 11/5/59, Portland, Ark. BL/TR, 6'3", 200 lbs. Deb: 5/24/80 C Career OF: (101-LF 1327-CF 113-RF)

YEAR	TM/L	G	AB	R	H	2B	3B	HR	RBI	BB	SO	AVG	OBP	SLG	OPS	OPS+	BR+	SB	CS	SBR	FA	FR	G/POS	TPR
1980	Tor-A	114	389	44	89	24	1	9	46	25	85	.229	.282	.365	647	73	-15	4	6	-1	.982	6	*O-104(12-6-86)/D-6	-1.6
1981	Tor-A	100	378	36	88	16	2	9	43	24	86	.233	.280	.357	638	78	-11	11	8	-0	.989	3	*O-100(0-80-21)	-1.1
1982	Tor-A	147	487	51	115	20	9	9	52	33	106	.236	.295	.370	665	74	-17	11	7	-0	.992	-1	*O-145(0-145-0)	-1.9
1983	Tor-A	151	539	104	170	31	7	18	81	51	85	.315	.380	.499	879	132	23	27	8	3	.983	10	*O-147(0-147-0)	3.5
1984	Tor-A	158	592	97	166	28	**15**	18	92	78	122	.280	.372	.470	841	126	23	39	9	5	.990	17	*O-156(0-156-0)	4.3
1985	*Tor-A	152	584	92	151	30	7	18	70	76	91	.259	.348	.426	774	108	7	37	15	3	.980	1	*O-152(0-152-0)	0.9
1986	Tor-A★	152	589	89	149	24	5	21	86	64	122	.253	.332	.418	750	100	0	32	11	3	.984	3	*O-147(0-147-0)/D-3	0.5
1987	Tor-A	155	592	106	167	27	4	26	96	70	124	.282	.360	.473	833	116	14	39	7	6	.980	-8	*O-153(0-153-0)/D-2	1.0
1988	Tor-A	128	472	77	113	17	7	10	42	70	93	.239	.345	.369	714	99	1	31	8	4	.984	-6	*O-125(11-117-6)/D-1	-0.2
1989	*Tor-A	135	502	72	111	25	3	11	43	56	101	.221	.307	.349	655	86	-9	24	7	3	.986	-3	*O-120(0-120-0),D-14	-1.1
1990	Det-A	122	431	64	107	16	5	14	51	48	77	.248	.331	.406	737	104	2	17	5	2	.983	8	*O-116(14-104-0)/D-4	1.1
1991	Det-A	74	260	37	68	15	1	6	35	21	43	.262	.324	.396	720	97	-1	8	1	1	.955	-1	O-64(64-0-0)/D-7	-0.3
Total	12	1588	5815	869	1494	273	66	169	737	616	1135	.257	.334	.414	748	102	17	280	92	29	.984	28	*O-1529C/D-37	5.1

■ ARNIE MOSER
Moser, Arnold Robert b: 8/9/15, Houston, Tex. BR/TR, 5'11", 165 lbs. Deb: 6/20/37

YEAR	TM/L	G	AB	R	H	2B	3B	HR	RBI	BB	SO	AVG	OBP	SLG	OPS	OPS+	BR+	SB	CS	SBR	FA	FR	G/POS	TPR
1937	Cin-N	5	5	0	0	0	0	0	0	0	2	.000	.000	.000	0	-99	-1	0			.000	0	H	-0.1

■ JERRY MOSES
Moses, Gerald Braheen b: 8/9/46, Yazoo City, Miss. BR/TR, 6'3", 210 lbs. Deb: 5/9/65 Career OF: (1-LF 0-CF 1-RF)

YEAR	TM/L	G	AB	R	H	2B	3B	HR	RBI	BB	SO	AVG	OBP	SLG	OPS	OPS+	BR+	SB	CS	SBR	FA	FR	G/POS	TPR
1965	Bos-A	4	4	1	1	0	0	1	1	0	2	.250	.250	1.000	1250	224	1	0	0	0	.000	0	H	0.1
1968	Bos-A	6	18	2	6	0	0	2	4	1	4	.333	.368	.667	1035	196	2	0	1	-0	.963	-3	/C-6	-0.1
1969	Bos-A	53	135	13	41	9	1	4	17	5	23	.304	.333	.474	807	117	3	0	1	-0	.981	-5	C-36	-0.2
1970	Bos-A☆	92	315	26	83	18	1	6	35	21	45	.263	.314	.384	698	85	-6	1	1	-0	.990	2	C-88/O-1(1-0-0)	-0.1
1971	Cal-A	69	181	12	41	8	2	4	15	10	34	.227	.267	.359	626	82	-5	0	0	0	.977	5	C-63/O-1(0-0-1)	0.2
1972	Cle-A	52	141	9	31	3	0	4	14	11	29	.220	.290	.326	617	81	-3	0	0	0	.982	1	C-39/1-3	-0.2
1973	NY-A	21	59	5	15	2	0	0	3	2	6	.254	.279	.288	567	62	-3	0	0	0	1.000	5	C-17/D-1	0.3
1974	Det-A	74	198	19	47	6	3	4	19	11	38	.237	.284	.359	643	81	-5	0	1	-0	.985	0	C-74	-0.3
1975	SD-N	13	19	1	3	2	0	0	1	2	3	.158	.238	.263	501	42	-2	0	0	0	.900	-1	/C-5	-0.2
	Chi-A	2	2	1	1	0	1	0	0	0	0	.500	.500	1.500	2000	441	1	0	0	0	1.000	-0	/1-1,D-1	0.1
Total	9	386	1072	89	269	48	8	25	109	63	184	.251	.297	.381	678	89	-19	1	4	-1	.984	3	C-328/1-4,D-2,O-2L	-0.4

■ JOHN MOSES
Moses, John William b: 8/9/57, Los Angeles, Cal. BB/TL, 5'10", 170 lbs. Deb: 8/23/82 C Career OF: (164-LF 334-CF 180-RF)

YEAR	TM/L	G	AB	R	H	2B	3B	HR	RBI	BB	SO	AVG	OBP	SLG	OPS	OPS+	BR+	SB	CS	SBR	FA	FR	G/POS	TPR
1982	Sea-A	22	44	7	14	5	1	1	3	4	5	.318	.375	.545	920	145	3	5	1	1	.947	-4	O-19(8-3-9)	-0.1
1983	Sea-A	93	130	19	27	4	1	0	6	12	20	.208	.280	.254	534	46	-9	11	5	1	.979	-9	O-71(34-31-7),D-10	-1.9
1984	Sea-A	19	35	3	12	1	1	0	2	2	5	.343	.395	.429	823	129	1	1	0	0	1.000	-4	O-19(7-14-0)/D-1	-0.3
1985	Sea-A	33	62	4	12	0	0	0	3	2	8	.194	.219	.194	412	14	-7	5	2	0	1.000	-7	O-29(1-28-0)	-1.4
1986	Sea-A	103	399	56	102	16	3	3	34	34	65	.256	.314	.333	647	76	-13	25	18	-1	.987	2	O-93(2-91-0)/1-7,D-4	-1.3
1987	Sea-A	116	390	58	96	16	4	3	38	29	49	.246	.303	.331	634	65	-20	23	15	-0	.987	-2	*O-100C/1-16,D-5	-2.2
1988	Min-A	105	206	33	65	10	3	2	12	15	21	.316	.368	.422	790	117	5	11	6	0	1.000	-14	O-82(29-20-43)/D-2	-1.1
1989	Min-A	129	242	33	68	12	3	1	31	19	23	.281	.336	.368	704	92	-2	14	7	1	.988	-24	*O-108R/1-2,P-1,D-3	-2.8
1990	Min-A	115	172	26	38	3	1	1	14	19	19	.221	.306	.267	573	58	-9	2	3	-1	1.000	-17	O-85R,D-10/1-6,P-2	-2.9
1991	Det-A	13	21	5	1	1	0	0	1	2	7	.048	.130	.095	226	-36	-4	4	0	1	1.000	-2	O-12(11-0-1)	-0.6
1992	Sea-A	21	22	3	3	1	0	0	1	5	4	.136	.296	.182	478	37	-2	0	0	0	1.000	-4	O-18(17-1-1)/D-1	-0.7
Total	11	769	1723	247	438	69	17	11	145	143	226	.254	.315	.333	648	75	-57	101	57	2	.990	-86	O-636C/D-36,1-31,P	-15.3

■ WALLY MOSES
Moses, Wallace b: 10/8/10, Uvalda, Ga. d: 10/10/90, Vidalia, Ga. BL/TL, 5'10", 160 lbs. Deb: 4/17/35 C

YEAR	TM/L	G	AB	R	H	2B	3B	HR	RBI	BB	SO	AVG	OBP	SLG	OPS	OPS+	BR+	SB	CS	SBR	FA	FR	G/POS	TPR
1935	Phi-A	85	345	60	112	21	3	5	35	25	18	.325	.375	.446	822	113	6	3	4	-1	.943	0	O-80(0-0-80)	0.1
1936	Phi-A	146	585	98	202	35	11	7	66	62	32	.345	.410	.479	888	121	20	12	6	1	.974	3	*O-144(0-136-9)	1.8
1937	Phi-A☆	154	649	113	208	48	13	25	86	54	38	.320	.374	.550	925	132	29	9	7	-0	.958	6	*O-154(0-0-154)	2.2
1938	Phi-A	142	589	86	181	29	8	8	49	58	31	.307	.369	.424	794	101	1	15	5	2	.966	5	*O-139(0-0-139)	-0.2
1939	Phi-A	115	437	68	134	28	7	3	33	44	23	.307	.370	.423	793	105	3	7	4	0	.965	-1	*O-103(0-5-100)	-0.3
1940	Phi-A	142	537	91	166	41	9	9	50	75	44	.309	.396	.469	865	126	22	6	4	-0	.974	4	*O-133(0-2-131)	1.7
1941	Phi-A	116	438	78	132	31	4	4	35	62	27	.301	.388	.418	806	116	12	3	3	-0	.975	9	*O-109(0-0-109)	1.3
1942	Chi-A	146	577	73	156	28	4	7	49	74	27	.270	.353	.369	722	106	5	16	10	0	.980	7	*O-145(3-14-130)	0.4
1943	Chi-A	150	599	82	147	22	**12**	3	48	55	47	.245	.310	.337	647	89	-9	56	14	7	.979	9	*O-148(0-23-125)	-0.2
1944	Chi-A	136	535	82	150	26	9	3	34	52	22	.280	.345	.379	725	108	6	21	7	2	.975	-2	*O-134(0-0-134)	-0.3
1945	Chi-A†	140	569	79	168	**35**	15	2	50	69	33	.295	.373	.420	793	134	25	11	5		.977	9	*O-139(0-0-139)	2.6
1946	Chi-A	56	168	20	46	9	1	4	16	17	20	.274	.344	.411	755	115	3	2	2	-0	1.000	-1	O-36(2-14-22)	0.1
	*Bos-A	48	175	23	36	11	3	2	17	14	15	.206	.268	.337	606	65	-9	2	4	-1	.979	0	O-44(0-2-43)	-1.1
	Yr	104	343	43	82	20	4	6	33	31	35	.239	.306	.373	679	88	-6	4	6	-1	.989	-0	O-80(2-16-65)	-1.0
1947	Bos-A	90	255	32	70	18	2	2	27	27	16	.275	.344	.384	728	95	-2	3	0	1	.974	-3	O-58(0-0-58)	-0.6
1948	Bos-A	78	189	26	49	12	1	2	29	21	19	.259	.340	.365	705	83	-5	5	0	1	.981	1	O-45(0-0-45)	-0.3
1949	Phi-A	110	308	49	85	19	3	1	25	51	19	.276	.381	.367	747	102	2	1	3	-1	.983	-3	O-92(1-1-91)	-0.4
1950	Phi-A	88	265	47	70	16	5	2	21	40	17	.264	.365	.385	750	94	-2	0	1	-0	.987	5	O-62(4-7-51)	0.0
1951	Phi-A	70	136	17	26	6	0	0	9	21	9	.191	.304	.235	539	46	-10	2	2	-0	.984	2	O-27(0-0-27)	-0.9
Total	17	2012	7356	1124	2138	435	110	89	679	821	457	.291	.364	.416	779	109	98	174	81	10	.973	51	*O-1792(10-204-1587)	5.9

■ DOC MOSKIMAN
Moskiman, William Bankhead b: 12/20/1879, Oakland, Cal. d: 1/11/53, San Leandro, Cal. BR/TR, 6', 170 lbs. Deb: 8/23/10

YEAR	TM/L	G	AB	R	H	2B	3B	HR	RBI	BB	SO	AVG	OBP	SLG	OPS	OPS+	BR+	SB	CS	SBR	FA	FR	G/POS	TPR
1910	Bos-A	5	9	1	1	0	0	0	1	2		.111	.273	.111	384	20	-1	0			1.000	0	/1-2,O-1(0-0-1)	0.0

■ JIM MOSOLF
Mosolf, James Frederick b: 8/21/05, Puyallup, Wash. d: 12/28/79, Dallas, Ore. BL/TR, 5'10", 186 lbs. Deb: 9/9/29

YEAR	TM/L	G	AB	R	H	2B	3B	HR	RBI	BB	SO	AVG	OBP	SLG	OPS	OPS+	BR+	SB	CS	SBR	FA	FR	G/POS	TPR
1929	Pit-N	8	13	3	6	1	1	0	2	1	1	.462	.500	.692	1192	188	2	0			1.000	0	/O-3(3-0-0)	0.2
1930	Pit-N	40	51	16	17	2	1	0	9	8	7	.333	.424	.412	835	103	1	0			.765	-3	O-12(1-1-9)/P-1	-0.3
1931	Pit-N	39	44	7	11	1	0	1	8	8	5	.250	.365	.341	706	92	-0	0			1.000	-1	/O-4(3-0-1)	-0.1
1933	Chi-N	31	82	13	22	5	1	0	9	5	8	.268	.326	.390	716	104	0	0			.964	1	O-22(19-3-0)	0.0
Total	4	118	190	39	56	9	3	2	28	22	21	.295	.374	.405	779	107	3	0			.929	-4	/O-41(26-4-10),P-1	-0.2

■ JULIO MOSQUERA
Mosquera, Julio Alberto (Cervantes) b: 1/29/72, Panama City, Panama BR/TR, 6', 165 lbs. Deb: 8/17/96

YEAR	TM/L	G	AB	R	H	2B	3B	HR	RBI	BB	SO	AVG	OBP	SLG	OPS	OPS+	BR+	SB	CS	SBR	FA	FR	G/POS	TPR
1996	Tor-A	8	22	2	5	2	0	0	2	0	3	.227	.261	.318	579	46	-2	0	1	-0	1.000	1	/C-8	0.0
1997	Tor-A	3	8	0	2	1	0	0	0	0	2	.250	.250	.375	625	60	-0	0	0	0	1.000	-1	/C-3	-0.1
Total	2	11	30	2	7	3	0	0	2	0	5	.233	.258	.333	591	49	-2	0	1	-0	1.000	1	/C-11	-0.1

■ CHARLIE MOSS
Moss, Charles Crosby b: 3/20/11, Meridian, Miss. d: 10/9/91, Meridian, Miss. BR/TR, 5'10", 160 lbs. Deb: 5/19/34

YEAR	TM/L	G	AB	R	H	2B	3B	HR	RBI	BB	SO	AVG	OBP	SLG	OPS	OPS+	BR+	SB	CS	SBR	FA	FR	G/POS	TPR
1934	Phi-A	10	10	3	2	0	0	0	1	0	0	.200	.200	.200	400	4	-1	0	0	0	1.000	-1	/C-6	-0.2
1935	Phi-A	4	3	1	1	0	0	0	1	1	0	.333	.500	.333	833	120	0	0	0	0	.000	0	/C-1	0.0
1936	Phi-A	33	44	2	11	1	1	0	10	6	5	.250	.340	.318	658	65	-2	1	0	0	.929	-2	C-19	-0.3
Total	3	47	57	6	14	1	1	0	12	7	5	.246	.328	.298	626	58	-4	1	0	0	.935	-2	/C-26	-0.5

■ HOWIE MOSS
Moss, Howard Glenn b: 10/17/19, Gastonia, N.C. d: 5/7/89, Baltimore, Md. BR/TR, 5'11.5", 185 lbs. Deb: 4/14/42

YEAR	TM/L	G	AB	R	H	2B	3B	HR	RBI	BB	SO	AVG	OBP	SLG	OPS	OPS+	BR+	SB	CS	SBR	FA	FR	G/POS	TPR
1942	NY-N	7	14	0	0	0	0	0	0	0	4	.000	.000	.000	0	-99	-3	0			1.000	0	/O-3(2-1-0)	-0.4
1946	Cin-N	7	26	1	5	0	0	0	1	0	4	.192	.222	.192	415	19	-3	0			1.000	0	/O-6(0-0-6)	-0.3

YEAR	TM/L	G	AB	R	H	2B	3B	HR	RBI	BB	SO	AVG	OBP	SLG	OPS	OPS+	BR+	SB	CS	SBR	FA	FR	G/POS	TPR
	Cle-A	8	32	2	2	0	0	0	0	3	9	.063	.143	.063	205	-44	-6	0	1	-0	.857	0	/3-8	-0.7
Total	2	22	72	3	7	0	0	0	1	3	17	.097	.145	.097	242	-32	-12	0	1		1.000	0	/O-9(2-1-6),3-8	-1.4

■ LES MOSS Moss, John Lester b: 5/14/25, Tulsa, Okla. BR/TR, 5'11", 205 lbs. Deb: 9/10/46 MC

YEAR	TM/L	G	AB	R	H	2B	3B	HR	RBI	BB	SO	AVG	OBP	SLG	OPS	OPS+	BR+	SB	CS	SBR	FA	FR	G/POS	TPR
1946	StL-A	12	35	4	13	3	0	0	5	3	5	.371	.436	.457	893	142	2	1	0	0	.968	1	C-12	0.4
1947	StL-A	96	274	17	43	5	2	6	27	35	48	.157	.255	.255	510	41	-22	0	0	0	.983	-5	C-96	-2.4
1948	StL-A	107	335	35	86	12	1	14	46	39	50	.257	.334	.424	758	98	-2	0	0	0	.988	-9	*C-103	-0.5
1949	StL-A	97	278	28	81	11	0	10	39	49	32	.291	.399	.439	838	117	8	0	1	-0	.970	-5	C-83	0.7
1950	StL-A	84	222	24	59	6	0	8	34	26	32	.266	.343	.401	744	87	-5	0	1	-0	.957	-1	C-60	-0.3
1951	StL-A	16	47	5	8	2	0	1	7	6	8	.170	.264	.277	541	45	-4	0	0	0	.967	-0	C-12	-0.3
	Bos-A	71	202	18	40	6	0	3	26	25	34	.198	.289	.272	562	48	-15	0	0	0	.984	-1	C-69	-1.2
	Yr	87	249	23	48	8	0	4	33	31	42	.193	.285	.273	558	47	-18	0	0	0	.981	-1	C-81	-1.5
1952	StL-A	52	118	11	29	3	0	3	12	15	13	.246	.331	.347	678	86	-2	0	1	-0	.957	-3	C-39	-0.4
1953	StL-A	78	239	21	66	14	1	2	28	18	31	.276	.329	.368	698	86	-5	0	1	-0	.978	-6	C-71	-0.8
1954	Bal-A	50	126	7	31	3	0	0	5	14	16	.246	.321	.270	591	68	-5	0	0	0	.972	-2	C-38	-0.6
1955	Bal-A	29	56	5	19	1	0	2	6	7	4	.339	.413	.464	877	146	4	0	1	-0	1.000	2	C-17	0.6
	Chi-A	32	59	5	15	2	0	2	7	6	10	.254	.333	.390	723	91	-1	0	0	0	.990	-0	C-32	0.0
	Yr	61	115	10	34	3	0	4	13	13	14	.296	.372	.426	798	116	3	0	1	-0	.994	2	C-49	0.6
1956	Chi-A	56	127	20	31	4	0	10	22	18	15	.244	.338	.512	850	120	3	0	0	0	.994	-6	C-49	-0.2
1957	Chi-A	42	115	10	31	3	0	2	12	20	18	.270	.378	.348	726	99	1	0	0	0	.980	-7	C-39	-0.5
1958	Chi-A	2	1	0	0	0	0	0	0	1	0	.000	.500	.000	500	51	0	0	0	0	.000	0	H	0.0
Total	13	824	2234	210	552	75	4	63	276	282	316	.247	.333	.369	702	86	-43	1	5	-2	.978	-42	C-720	-5.5

■ JOHNNY MOSTIL Mostil, John Anthony "Bananas" b: 6/1/1896, Chicago, Ill. d: 12/10/70, Midlothian, Ill. BR/TR, 5'8.5", 168 lbs. Deb: 6/20/18 Career OF: (20-LF 856-CF 32-RF)

YEAR	TM/L	G	AB	R	H	2B	3B	HR	RBI	BB	SO	AVG	OBP	SLG	OPS	OPS+	BR+	SB	CS	SBR	FA	FR	G/POS	TPR
1918	Chi-A	10	33	4	9	2	2	0	4	1	6	.273	.294	.455	749	125	1	1			.923	-2	/2-9	-0.1
1921	Chi-A	100	326	43	98	21	7	3	42	28	35	.301	.379	.436	814	109	5	10	12	-2	.946	0	O-91(1-90-0)/2-1	-0.1
1922	Chi-A	132	458	74	139	28	14	7	70	38	39	.303	.375	.472	846	120	13	14	10	-0	.966	5	*O-123(18-105-0)	1.1
1923	Chi-A	153	546	91	159	37	15	3	64	62	51	.291	.376	.430	806	113	11	41	16	**3**	.974	22	*O-143C/3-5,S-1	2.9
1924	Chi-A	118	385	75	125	22	5	4	49	45	41	.325	.401	.439	840	120	13	7	11	-2	.974	7	*O-102(1-90-12)	1.2
1925	Chi-A	153	605	**135**	181	36	16	2	50	**90**	52	.299	.400	.421	822	115	17	**43**	20	2	**.985**	7	*O-153(0-153-0)	1.8
1926	Chi-A	148	600	120	197	41	15	4	42	79	55	.328	.415	.467	882	135	33	**35**	14	**3**	.968	17	*O-147(0-147-0)	4.4
1927	Chi-A	13	16	3	2	0	0	0	1	0	1	.125	.176	.125	301	-21	-3	1	0		.857	-2	/O-6(0-6-0)	-0.4
1928	Chi-A	133	503	69	136	19	8	0	51	66	54	.270	.360	.340	699	86	-8	23	21	-2	.976	18	*O-131(0-120-11)	0.1
1929	Chi-A	12	35	4	8	3	0	0	3	6	2	.229	.341	.314	656	71	-1	1	1	-0	.963	-1	O-11(0-10-1)	-0.3
Total	10	972	3507	618	1054	209	82	23	376	415	336	.301	.386	.427	812	113	78	176	105		.971	72	O-907C/2-10,3-5,S-1	10.6

■ ANDY MOTA Mota, Andres Alberto (Matos) b: 3/4/66, Santo Domingo, D.R. BR/TR, 5'10", 180 lbs. Deb: 8/31/91 F

YEAR	TM/L	G	AB	R	H	2B	3B	HR	RBI	BB	SO	AVG	OBP	SLG	OPS	OPS+	BR+	SB	CS	SBR	FA	FR	G/POS	TPR
1991	Hou-N	27	90	4	17	2	0	1	6	1	17	.189	.198	.244	442	25	-9	2	0	0	.970	-3	2-27	-1.2

■ JOSE MOTA Mota, Jose Manuel (Matos) b: 3/16/65, Santo Domingo, D.R. BB/TR, 5'9", 155 lbs. Deb: 5/25/91 F

YEAR	TM/L	G	AB	R	H	2B	3B	HR	RBI	BB	SO	AVG	OBP	SLG	OPS	OPS+	BR+	SB	CS	SBR	FA	FR	G/POS	TPR
1991	SD-N	17	36	4	8	0	0	0	2	2	7	.222	.282	.222	504	42	-3	0	0	0	.962	0	2-13/S-3	-0.2
1995	KC-A	2	2	0	0	0	0	0	0	0	0	.000	.000	.000	0	-99	-1	0	0	0	1.000	0	/2-2	0.0
Total	2	19	38	4	8	0	0	0	2	2	7	.211	.268	.211	479	35	-3	0	0	0	.965	1	/2-15,S-3	-0.2

■ MANNY MOTA Mota, Manuel Rafael (Geronimo) b: 2/18/38, Santo Domingo, D.R. BR/TR, 5'11", 168 lbs. Deb: 4/16/62 FC Career OF: (725-LF 270-CF 118-RF)

YEAR	TM/L	G	AB	R	H	2B	3B	HR	RBI	BB	SO	AVG	OBP	SLG	OPS	OPS+	BR+	SB	CS	SBR	FA	FR	G/POS	TPR
1962	SF-N	47	74	9	13	1	0	0	9	7	8	.176	.256	.189	445	22	-8	3	2	-0	1.000	-2	O-27(22-2-4)/3-7,2-3	-1.0
1963	Pit-N	59	126	20	34	2	3	0	7	7	18	.270	.313	.333	647	86	-2	0	2	-1	.953	-5	O-37(35-2-2)/2-1	-1.0
1964	Pit-N	115	271	43	75	8	3	5	32	10	31	.277	.310	.384	694	94	-2	4	1	1	.961	-16	O-93(57-50-7)/C-1,2-1	-2.2
1965	Pit-N	121	294	47	82	7	6	4	29	22	32	.279	.333	.384	718	101	0	2	2	-0	.985	-14	O-95(35-60-15)	-1.8
1966	Pit-N	116	322	54	107	16	7	5	46	25	28	.332	.387	.472	860	137	17	7	7	-1	.994	-11	O-96(45-52-12)/3-4	0.1
1967	Pit-N	120	349	53	112	14	8	4	56	14	46	.321	.351	.441	792	125	10	3	2	-0	.988	-6	O-99(48-48-13)/3-2	0.1
1968	Pit-N	111	331	35	93	10	2	1	33	20	19	.281	.324	.332	656	99	-1	4	2	0	.981	-7	O-92L/2-1,3-1	-1.4
1969	Mon-N	31	89	6	28	1	1	0	0	6	11	.315	.358	.348	706	98	-0	1	3	-1	.907	-2	O-22(1-17-5)	-0.4
	LA-N	85	294	35	95	6	4	3	30	26	25	.323	.380	.401	781	128	11	5	4	-0	.969	0	O-80(75-4-10)	0.7
	Yr	116	383	41	123	7	5	3	30	32	36	.321	.375	.389	764	120	11	6	7	-1	.954	-2	*O-102(76-21-15)	0.3
1970	LA-N	124	417	63	127	12	6	3	37	47	37	.305	.379	.384	763	110	7	11	6	0	.973	-0	*O-111(109-1-4)/3-1	0.2
1971	LA-N	91	269	24	84	13	5	0	34	20	20	.312	.362	.398	760	122	8	4	3	-0	.965	-9	O-80(62-0-24)	-0.6
1972	LA-N	118	371	57	120	16	5	5	48	27	15	.323	.377	.434	811	133	16	4	4	-1	.993	-8	O-99(96-3-0)	0.2
1973	LA-N★	89	293	33	92	11	2	0	23	25	12	.314	.370	.365	735	109	4	1	3	-1	1.000	-6	O-74(74-0-0)	-0.8
1974	*LA-N	66	57	5	16	2	0	0	16	5	4	.281	.349	.316	665	91	-1	0	0	0	1.000	-1	/O-3(3-0-0)	-0.2
1975	LA-N	52	49	3	13	1	0	0	10	5	1	.265	.357	.286	643	84	-1	0	0	0	1.000	-0	/O-5(5-0-0)	-0.1
1976	LA-N	50	52	1	15	3	0	0	13	7	5	.288	.373	.346	719	107	1	0	0	0	1.000	1	/O-6(6-0-0)	0.1
1977	*LA-N	49	38	5	15	1	0	1	4	10	0	.395	.521	.500	1021	176	5	1	1	-0	1.000	-0	/O-1(1-0-0)	0.5
1978	*LA-N	37	33	2	10	1	0	0	6	3	4	.303	.361	.333	694	95	-0	0	0	0	.000	0	H	-0.1
1979	LA-N	47	42	1	15	0	0	0	3	3	4	.357	.400	.357	757	110	1	0	0	0	.000	-0	/O-1(1-0-0)	0.0
1980	LA-N	7	7	0	3	0	0	0	2	0	0	.429	.429	.429	857	143	0	0	0	0	.000	0	/H	0.0
1982	LA-N	1	1	0	0	0	0	0	0	0	0	.000	.000	.000	0	-99	-0	0	0	0	.000	0	/H	0.0
Total	20	1536	3779	496	1149	125	52	31	438	289	320	.304	.358	.389	747	112	66	50	42	-4	.979	-87	*O-1021L/3-15,2-6,C	-7.7

■ DARRYL MOTLEY Motley, Darryl De Wayne b: 1/21/60, Muskogee, Okla. BR/TR, 5'9", 196 lbs. Deb: 8/10/81

YEAR	TM/L	G	AB	R	H	2B	3B	HR	RBI	BB	SO	AVG	OBP	SLG	OPS	OPS+	BR+	SB	CS	SBR	FA	FR	G/POS	TPR
1981	KC-A	42	125	15	29	4	0	2	8	7	15	.232	.278	.312	590	70	-5	1	3	-1	.968	3	O-39(2-0-38)	-0.5
1983	KC-A	19	68	9	16	1	2	3	11	2	8	.235	.268	.441	709	91	-1	2	1	0	.978	1	O-18(3-2-15)/D-1	-0.1
1984	*KC-A	146	522	64	148	25	6	15	70	28	73	.284	.321	.441	762	108	4	10	12	-2	.984	-2	*O-138(105-3-45)	-0.6
1985	*KC-A	123	383	45	85	20	1	17	49	18	57	.222	.261	.413	673	81	-12	6	4	-0	.967	-8	*O-114(44-0-76)/D-7	-2.5
1986	KC-A	72	217	22	44	9	1	7	20	11	31	.203	.241	.350	591	57	-13	0	2	-1	.979	-8	O-66(3-1-62)/D-2	-2.4
	Atl-N	5	10	1	2	1	0	0	0	1	1	.200	.273	.300	573	55	-1	0	0	0	1.000	-0	/O-3(0-0-3)	-0.1
1987	Atl-N	6	8	0	0	0	0	0	1	0	1	.000	.000	.000	0	-95	-2	0	0	0	1.000	-0	/O-2(2-0-0)	-0.3
Total	6	413	1333	156	324	60	10	44	159	67	186	.243	.282	.402	684	86	-30	19	22	-4	.976	-15	O-380(159-6-239)/D-10	-6.5

■ BITSY MOTT Mott, Elisha Matthew b: 6/12/18, Arcadia, Fla. BR/TR, 5'8", 155 lbs. Deb: 4/17/45

YEAR	TM/L	G	AB	R	H	2B	3B	HR	RBI	BB	SO	AVG	OBP	SLG	OPS	OPS+	BR+	SB	CS	SBR	FA	FR	G/POS	TPR
1945	Phi-N	90	289	21	64	8	0	0	22	27	25	.221	.290	.249	539	52	-18	2			.944	13	S-63,2-27/3-7	0.0

■ CHAD MOTTOLA Mottola, Charles Edward b: 10/15/71, Augusta, Ga. BR/TR, 6'3", 220 lbs. Deb: 4/23/96

YEAR	TM/L	G	AB	R	H	2B	3B	HR	RBI	BB	SO	AVG	OBP	SLG	OPS	OPS+	BR+	SB	CS	SBR	FA	FR	G/POS	TPR
1996	Cin-N	35	79	10	17	3	0	3	6	6	16	.215	.271	.367	638	66	-4	2	2	-0	1.000	-2	O-31(0-1-30)	-0.7
2000	Tor-A	3	9	1	2	0	0	0	2	0	4	.222	.300	.222	522	35	-1	0	0	0	1.000	-0	/O-3(0-0-3)	-0.1
Total	2	38	88	11	19	3	0	3	8	6	20	.216	.274	.352	626	63	-5	2	2	-0	1.000	-2	/O-34(0-1-33)	-0.8

■ CURT MOTTON Motton, Curtell Howard b: 9/24/40, Darnell, La. BR/TR, 5'7.5", 175 lbs. Deb: 7/5/67 C

YEAR	TM/L	G	AB	R	H	2B	3B	HR	RBI	BB	SO	AVG	OBP	SLG	OPS	OPS+	BR+	SB	CS	SBR	FA	FR	G/POS	TPR
1967	Bal-A	27	65	5	13	2	0	2	9	5	14	.200	.278	.323	601	78	-2	0	1	-0	.973	1	O-18(18-0-1)	-0.3
1968	Bal-A	83	217	27	43	7	0	8	25	31	43	.198	.301	.341	642	94	-1	1	3	-1	.989	2	O-54(54-0-0)	-0.4
1969	*Bal-A	56	89	15	27	6	0	6	21	13	10	.303	.398	.573	971	167	8	3	1	0	1.000	-3	O-20(16-0-4)	0.5
1970	Bal-A	52	84	16	19	3	1	3	19	18	20	.226	.369	.393	762	109	2	1	2	-0	1.000	-1	O-21(20-0-2)	-0.1
1971	*Bal-A	38	53	13	10	1	0	4	8	10	12	.189	.317	.434	751	112	1	0	0	0	1.000	-2	O-16(12-0-5)	-0.2
1972	Mil-A	6	6	1	1	0	0	1	2	1	2	.167	.286	.667	952	181	1	0	0	0	.000	-1	/O-3(3-0-0)	-0.1
	Cal-A	42	39	6	6	1	0	0	1	5	12	.154	.250	.179	429	31	-3	0	0	0	1.000	-0	O-9(9-0-0)	-0.4
	Yr	48	45	7	7	1	0	1	3	6	14	.156	.255	.244	499	52	-3	0	0	0	1.000	-1	O-12(12-0-0)	-0.5
1973	Bal-A	5	6	2	2	0	0	1	4	1	1	.333	.429	.833	1262	250	1	0	0	0	.000	-0	/O-1(1-0-0),D-1	0.1
1974	*Bal-A	7	8	0	0	0	0	0	0	2	2	.000	.200	.000	200	-40	-1	0	0	0	1.000	-0	/O-2(0-0-2),D-1	-0.2
Total	8	316	567	85	121	20	1	25	89	86	116	.213	.322	.384	707	105	4	5	7	-1	.991	-5	O-144(133-0-14)/D-2	-1.1

YEAR	TM/L	G	AB	R	H	2B	3B	HR	RBI	BB	SO	AVG	OBP	SLG	OPS	OPS+	BR+	SB	CS	SBR	FA	FR	G/POS	TPR
■ FRANK MOTZ	Motz, Frank H. b: 10/1/1868, Freeburg, Pa. d: 3/18/44, Akron, Ohio 6', 160 lbs. Deb: 8/27/1890																							
1890	Phi-N	1	2	1	0	0	0	0	0	1	1	.000	.333	.000	333	-1	-0				1.000	0	/1-1	0.0
1893	Cin-N	43	156	16	40	7	1	2	25	19	10	.256	.352	.353	705	85	-3	3			.981	6	1-43	0.2
1894	Cin-N	18	69	8	14	4	0	0	12	9	1	.203	.304	.261	565	36	-7	2			.995	4	1-18	-0.3
Total	3	62	227	25	54	11	1	2	37	29	12	.238	.337	.322	659	68	-11	6			.985	10	/1-62	-0.1
■ ALLIE MOULTON	Moulton, Albert Theodore b: 1/16/1886, Medway, Mass. d: 7/10/68, Peabody, Mass. BR/TR, 5'6", 155 lbs. Deb: 9/25/11																							
1911	StL-A	4	15	4	1	0	0	0	1	4		.067	.263	.067	330	-6	-2	0			.938	-1	/2-4	-0.3
■ FRANK MOUNTAIN	Mountain, Frank Henry b: 5/17/1860, Ft.Edward, N.Y. d: 11/19/39, Schenectady, N.Y. BR/TR, 5'11", 185 lbs. Deb: 7/19/1880 Career OF: (18-LF 16-CF 2-RF)																							
1880	Tro-N	2	9	1	2	0	0	0	0	0	4	.222	.222	.222	444	49	-0				1.000	0	/P-2	0.0
1881	Det-N	7	25	0	4	1	1	0	4	2	8	.160	.222	.280	502	55	-1				.923	-1	/P-7	0.0
1882	Wor-N	5	16	1	1	0	0	0	1	0	5	.063	.063	.063	125	-58	-3				.889	-1	/P-5	0.0
	Phi-a	9	36	5	12	3	0	0		2		.333	.368	.417	785	147	2				.917	1	/P-8,O-1(0-0-1)	0.0
	Wor-N	20	70	8	19	2	2	2	5	3	18	.271	.301	.443	744	132	2				.870	-3	P-13/O-6C,1-2,S-1	-0.2
1883	Col-a	70	276	36	60	14	5	3		9		.217	.242	.337	579	92	-2				.848	2	P-59,O-12(8-4-0)	0.0
1884	Col-a	58	210	26	50	7	3	4		9		.238	.283	.357	640	117	5				.919	2	P-42,O-17(9-7-1)	0.0
1885	Pit-a	5	20	1	2	0	1	0	1	1		.100	.143	.200	343	8	-2				.846	0	/P-5	0.0
1886	Pit-a	18	55	6	8	1	1	0	2	13		.145	.319	.200	519	64	-2	3			.959	-0	1-16/P-2	-0.3
Total	7	194	717	84	158	28	13	9	13	39	35	.220	.265	.333	599	96	-1	3			.880	0	P-143/O-36L,1-18,S	-0.5
■ JAMES MOUTON	Mouton, James Raleigh b: 12/29/68, Denver, Colo. BR/TR, 5'9", 175 lbs. Deb: 4/4/94 Career OF: (194-LF 152-CF 169-RF)																							
1994	Hou-N	99	310	43	76	11	0	2	16	27	69	.245	.316	.300	616	65	-15	24	5	4	.982	-5	O-96(1-19-80)	-2.0
1995	Hou-N	104	298	42	78	18	2	4	27	25	59	.262	.327	.376	703	91	-4	25	8	3	1.000	-7	O-94(38-22-38)	-1.0
1996	Hou-N	122	300	40	79	15	1	3	34	38	55	.263	.346	.350	696	91	-3	21	9	1	.971	-4	*O-108(79-29-5)	-0.7
1997	Hou-N	86	180	24	38	9	1	3	23	18	30	.211	.290	.322	612	62	-10	9	7	-0	1.000	-7	O-61(9-39-14)	-1.7
1998	SD-N	55	63	8	12	2	1	0	7	7	11	.190	.271	.254	525	42	-5	4	3	-0	.969	-5	O-33(16-4-14)/D-1	-1.1
1999	Mon-N	95	122	18	32	5	1	2	13	18	31	.262	.366	.369	735	89	-1	6	2	1	.981	-11	O-56(32-16-11)/D-1	-1.2
2000	Mil-N	87	159	28	37	7	1	2	17	30	43	.233	.365	.327	692	78	-4	13	4	1	.989	-2	O-45(19-23-7)	-0.5
Total	7	648	1432	203	352	67	7	16	137	163	298	.246	.330	.336	666	78	-44	102	38	9	.985	-41	O-493L/D-2	-8.2
■ LYLE MOUTON	Mouton, Lyle Joseph b: 5/13/69, Lafayette, La. BR/TR, 6'4", 240 lbs. Deb: 6/7/95																							
1995	Chi-A	58	179	23	54	16	0	5	27	19	46	.302	.375	.475	850	125	7	1	0	0	.990	-0	O-53(29-0-30)/D-2	0.4
1996	Chi-A	87	214	25	63	8	1	7	39	22	50	.294	.366	.439	805	107	3	3	0	1	.970	-7	O-47(21-0-29),D-28	-0.6
1997	Chi-A	88	242	26	65	9	0	5	23	14	66	.269	.311	.368	679	80	-7	4	4	-1	.969	-4	O-67(16-0-55),D-11	-1.4
1998	Bal-A	18	39	5	12	2	0	2	7	4	8	.308	.372	.513	885	129	2	0	0	0	1.000	-3	O-16(6-0-12)/D-2	-0.1
1999	Mil-N	14	17	2	3	1	0	1	3	2	3	.176	.263	.412	675	68	-1	0	0	0	1.000	-1	/O-3(2-0-1)	-0.2
2000	Mil-N	42	97	14	27	7	1	2	16	10	29	.278	.352	.433	785	99	-0	1	0	0	.978	2	O-27(22-1-4)	0.1
Total	6	307	788	95	224	43	2	22	115	71	202	.284	.348	.428	776	102	2	9	4	1	.978	-13	O-213(96-1-131)/D-43	-1.8
■ RAY MOWE	Mowe, Raymond Benjamin b: 7/12/1889, Rochester, Ind. d: 8/14/68, Sarasota, Fla. BL/TR, 5'7.5", 160 lbs. Deb: 9/25/13																							
1913	Bro-N	5	9	0	1	0	0	0	0	0	1	.111	.200	.111	311	-10	-1	0			.941	1	/S-2	0.0
■ MIKE MOWREY	Mowrey, Harry Harlan b: 4/20/1884, Browns Mill, Pa. d: 3/20/47, Chambersburg, Pa. BR/TR, 5'10", 180 lbs. Deb: 9/24/05																							
1905	Cin-N	7	30	4	8	1	0	0	6	1		.267	.290	.300	590	69	-1	0			.759	-0	/3-7	-0.1
1906	Cin-N	21	53	3	17	3	0	0	6	5		.321	.379	.377	757	130	2	2			.930	4	3-15/2-1,S-1	0.6
1907	Cin-N	138	448	43	113	16	6	1	44	35		.252	.308	.321	629	93	-4	10			.929	-19	*3-127,S-11	-2.2
1908	Cin-N	77	227	17	50	9	1	0	23	12		.220	.266	.269	534	73	-7	5			.936	-7	3-56/S-3,O-3L,2-1	-1.5
1909	Cin-N	38	115	10	22	5	0	0	5	20		.191	.311	.235	546	70	-3	2			.947	1	3-22,S-13	-0.2
	StL-N	12	29	3	7	1	0	0	4	4		.241	.333	.276	609	95	0	1			.921	-1	/2-7,3-2	-0.1
	Yr	50	144	13	29	6	0	0	9	24		.201	.315	.243	559	75	-3	3			.948	-1	3-24,S-13/2-7	-0.3
1910	StL-N	143	489	69	138	24	6	2	70	67	38	.282	.375	.368	744	121	15	21			.927	12	*3-141	3.2
1911	StL-N	137	471	59	126	29	7	0	61	59	46	.268	.355	.359	714	103	3	15			.944	7	*3-134/S-1	1.3
1912	StL-N	114	408	59	104	13	8	2	50	46	29	.255	.335	.341	675	87	-7	19			.931	3	*3-108	-0.1
1913	StL-N	132	450	61	117	18	4	0	33	53	40	.260	.342	.318	660	90	-4	21			.953	16	*3-131	1.6
1914	Pit-N	79	284	24	72	7	5	1	25	22	20	.254	.316	.324	640	94	-2	8			.960	-2	3-78	-0.2
1915	Pit-F	151	521	56	146	26	6	1	49	66	39	.280	.367	.359	725	105	-2	40			**.959**	-19	*3-151	-1.8
1916	*Bro-N	144	495	57	121	22	6	0	60	50	60	.244	.320	.313	633	92	-3	16			**.965**	0	*3-144	0.1
1917	Bro-N	83	271	20	58	9	5	0	25	29	25	.214	.292	.284	576	75	-7	7			.952	-3	3-80/2-2	-0.9
Total	13	1276	4291	485	1099	183	54	7	461	469	297	.256	.334	.329	663	96	-21	167			.944	-10	*3-1196/S-29,2-11,O	-0.3
■ JOE MOWRY	Mowry, Joseph Aloysius b: 4/6/08, St.Louis, Mo. d: 2/9/94, St.Louis, Mo. BB/TR, 6', 198 lbs. Deb: 5/13/33																							
1933	Bos-N	86	249	25	55	8	5	0	20	15	22	.221	.273	.293	567	67	-11	1			.994	1	O-64(48-5-11)	-1.5
1934	Bos-N	25	79	9	17	3	0	1	4	3	13	.215	.244	.291	535	46	-6	0			.976	0	O-20(4-0-16)/2-1	-0.7
1935	Bos-N	81	136	17	36	8	1	1	13	11	13	.265	.324	.360	685	91	-2	0			.970	-7	O-45(30-2-13)	-1.0
Total	3	192	464	51	108	19	6	2	37	29	48	.233	.284	.313	596	71	-19	1			.985	-7	O-129(82-7-40)/2-1	-3.2
■ MIKE MOYNAHAN	Moynahan, Michael b: 1856, Chicago, Ill. d: 4/9/1899, Chicago, Ill. BL/TR, Deb: 8/20/1880 Career OF: (33-LF 0-CF 3-RF)																							
1880	Buf-N	27	100	12	33	5	1	0	14	6	9	.330	.368	.400	768	157	6				.862	-6	S-27	0.1
1881	Cle-N	33	135	12	31	5	1	0	8	3	14	.230	.246	.281	528	69	-4				.883	-2	O-32(32-0-0)/3-1	-0.8
	Det-N	1	4	1	1	0	0	0	0	0	1	.250	.250	.250	500	55	-0				.857	1	/3-1	0.0
	Yr	34	139	13	32	5	1	0	8	3	15	.230	.246	.281	527	69	-5				.883	-2	O-32(32-0-0)/3-2	-0.8
1883	Phi-a	95	400	90	124	18	10	1	67	31		.310	.360	.412	772	135	14				.833	0	*S-95	1.5
1884	Phi-a	1	4	0	0	0	0	0		0		.000	.000	.000	0	-94	-1				.000	-0	/O-1(0-0-1)	-0.1
	Cle-N	12	45	9	13	2	1	0	6	7	11	.289	.385	.378	762	136	2				.852	-0	/2-6,S-3,O-3(1-0-2)	0.2
Total	4	169	688	124	202	30	13	1	95	47	35	.294	.339	.379	718	125	17				.837	-9	S-125/O-36L,2-6,3-2	0.9
■ HEINIE MUELLER	Mueller, Clarence Francis b: 9/16/1899, Creve Coeur, Mo. d: 1/23/75, DeSoto, Mo. BL/TL, 5'8", 158 lbs. Deb: 9/25/20 Career OF: (83-LF 368-CF 109-RF)																							
1920	StL-N	4	22	0	7	1	0	0	1	2	4	.318	.375	.364	739	117	1	1	0	0	1.000	0	/O-4(1-0-4)	0.1
1921	StL-N	55	176	25	62	10	6	1	34	11	22	.352	.397	.494	891	137	9	2	4	-1	.976	-3	O-54(0-51-3)	0.4
1922	StL-N	61	159	20	43	7	2	3	26	14	18	.270	.329	.396	726	91	-3	2	1	0	.947	-3	O-44(10-34-0)	-0.7
1923	StL-N	78	265	39	91	16	9	5	41	18	16	.343	.392	.528	920	144	16	4	3	-0	.963	2	O-74(0-71-3)	1.4
1924	StL-N	92	296	39	78	12	6	2	37	19	16	.264	.312	.365	677	82	-8	8	7	-1	.962	-2	O-53(2-42-9),1-27	-1.5
1925	StL-N	78	243	33	76	16	4	1	26	17	11	.313	.365	.424	789	99	-0	0	3	-1	.955	-3	O-72(2-57-13)	-0.7
1926	StL-N	52	191	36	51	7	5	3	28	11	6	.267	.330	.403	733	93	-2	8			.950	-1	O-51(0-21-30)	-0.6
	NY-N	85	305	36	76	6	2	4	29	21	17	.249	.300	.321	621	68	-14	7			.950	5	O-82(10-38-35)	-1.4
	Yr	137	496	72	127	13	7	7	57	32	23	.256	.312	.353	664	78	-16	15			.950	4	*O-133(10-59-65)	-2.0
1927	NY-N	84	190	33	55	6	1	3	19	25	12	.289	.384	.379	763	105	2	2			.944	-7	O-56(49-5-2)/1-1	-0.8
1928	Bos-N	42	151	25	34	3	1	0	19	17	9	.225	.316	.258	574	54	-9	1			.985	6	O-41(4-37-0)	-0.5
1929	Bos-N	46	93	10	19	2	1	0	11	12	12	.204	.302	.247	549	39	-9	2			1.000	-4	O-24(4-11-10)	-1.3
1935	StL-A	16	27	0	5	1	0	0	1	1	4	.185	.214	.222	437	12	-4	0	0	0	.955	-1	/1-3,O-2(1-1-0)	-0.4
Total	11	693	2118	296	597	87	37	22	272	168	147	.282	.342	.389	731	94	-20	37	18		.960	-11	O-557C/1-31	-6.0
■ DON MUELLER	Mueller, Donald Frederick "Mandrake The Magician" b: 4/14/27, St.Louis, Mo. BL/TR, 6', 185 lbs. Deb: 8/2/48 F																							
1948	NY-N	36	81	12	29	4	1	1	9	0	3	.358	.358	.469	827	121	2	0			.973	-1	O-22(18-1-1)	0.0
1949	NY-N	51	56	5	13	4	0	0	1	5	6	.232	.295	.304	599	61	-3	0			1.000	-1	/O-6(2-0-4)	-0.4
1950	NY-N	132	525	60	153	15	6	7	84	10	26	.291	.309	.383	691	80	-16	1			.986	-5	*O-125(3-0-122)	-2.4
1951	NY-N	122	469	58	130	10	7	16	69	19	13	.277	.307	.431	737	95	-5	1	1	-0	.983	-2	*O-115(0-0-115)	-1.0
1952	NY-N	126	456	61	128	14	7	12	49	34	24	.281	.333	.421	754	107	4	2	1	0	.987	-1	*O-120(0-0-120)	-0.1
1953	NY-N	131	480	56	160	12	2	6	60	19	13	.333	.360	.404	764	97	-2	2	0	0	.972	-4	*O-122(11-0-111)	-1.0

YEAR	TM/L	G	AB	R	H	2B	3B	HR	RBI	BB	SO	AVG	OBP	SLG	OPS	OPS+	BR+	SB	CS	SBR	FA	FR	G/POS	TPR
1954	*NY-N★	153	619	90	**212**	35	8	4	71	22	17	.342	.367	.444	811	110	8	2	3	-1	.979	-0	*O-153(0-0-153)	0.1
1955	NY-N★	147	605	67	185	21	4	8	83	19	12	.306	.330	.393	724	91	-8	1	2	-0	.976	-11	*O-146(0-0-146)	-2.6
1956	NY-N	138	453	38	122	12	1	5	41	15	7	.269	.293	.333	626	68	-20	0	1	-0	.989	-9	*O-117(0-0-117)	-3.5
1957	NY-N	135	450	45	116	7	1	6	37	13	16	.258	.280	.318	598	60	-25	2	0	0	.989	-1	*O-115(0-0-115)	-3.0
1958	Chi-A	70	166	7	42	5	0	0	16	11	9	.253	.299	.283	583	62	-8	0	0	0	.968	-5	O-43(0-0-43)	-1.5
1959	Chi-A	4	4	0	2	0	0	0	0	0	0	.500	.500	.500	1000	178	0	0	0	0	.000	0	H	0.0
Total	12	1245	4364	499	1292	139	37	65	520	167	146	.296	.324	.390	713	89	-74	11	8		.982	-38	*O-1084(34-1-1047)	-15.4
■ HEINIE MUELLER	Mueller, Emmett Jerome b: 7/20/12, St.Louis, Mo. d: 10/3/86, Orlando, Fla. BB/TR, 5'6", 167 lbs. Deb: 4/19/38 Career OF: (33-LF 1-CF 35-RF)																							
1938	Phi-N	136	444	53	111	12	4	4	34	64	43	.250	.346	.322	668	87	-6	2			.967	-27	*2-111,3-21	-2.6
1939	Phi-N	115	341	46	95	19	4	9	43	33	34	.279	.342	.437	779	111	5	4			.964	-14	2-51,3-17,O-17R,/S	-0.6
1940	Phi-N	97	263	24	65	13	2	3	28	37	23	.247	.344	.346	690	95	-1	2			.966	-9	2-34,O-31L,3-13,/1	-0.9
1941	Phi-N	93	233	21	53	11	1	1	22	22	24	.227	.302	.296	598	72	-9	2			.980	-4	2-29,O-21R,3-19	-1.2
Total	4	441	1281	144	324	55	11	17	127	156	124	.253	.337	.353	690	93	-11	10			.968	-54	2-225/3-70,O-69R,1S	-5.3
■ RAY MUELLER	Mueller, Ray Coleman "Iron Man" b: 3/8/12, Pittsburg, Kan. d: 6/29/94, Lower Paxton Township, Pa. BR/TR, 5'9", 175 lbs. Deb: 5/11/35 C																							
1935	Bos-N	42	97	10	22	5	0	3	11	3	11	.227	.250	.371	621	70	-5	0			.978	-2	C-40	-0.5
1936	Bos-N	24	71	5	14	4	0	0	5	5	17	.197	.250	.254	504	38	-6	0			.986	-4	C-23	-0.8
1937	Bos-N	64	187	21	47	9	2	2	26	18	36	.251	.317	.353	670	90	-3	1			.995	2	C-57	0.3
1938	Bos-N	83	274	23	65	8	6	4	35	16	28	.237	.282	.354	636	82	-8	3			.993	-2	C-75	-0.6
1939	Pit-N	86	180	14	42	8	1	2	18	14	22	.233	.289	.322	611	65	-9	0			.971	-3	C-81	-0.9
1940	Pit-N	4	3	1	1	0	0	0	1	2	0	.333	.600	.333	933	165	1	0			1.000	1	/C-4	0.1
1943	Cin-N	141	427	50	111	19	4	8	52	56	42	.260	.347	.379	726	111	7	1			.988	20	*C-140	3.7
1944	Cin-N★	155	555	54	159	24	4	10	73	53	47	.286	.353	.398	751	115	11	4			.983	-5	*C-155	1.6
1946	Cin-N	114	378	35	96	18	4	8	48	27	37	.254	.309	.386	695	100	-2	0			**.994**	10	*C-100	1.4
1947	Cin-N	71	192	17	48	11	0	6	33	16	25	.250	.311	.401	712	88	-4	1			.984	-1	C-55	-0.2
1948	Cin-N	14	34	2	7	1	0	0	2	4	3	.206	.289	.235	525	45	-3	0			.982	1	C-10	-0.1
1949	Cin-N	32	106	7	29	4	0	1	13	5	13	.274	.319	.340	658	76	-4	1			1.000	-3	C-31	-0.5
	NY-N	56	170	17	38	2	2	5	23	13	14	.224	.279	.347	626	67	-8	1			.982	1	C-56	-0.5
	Yr	88	276	24	67	6	2	6	36	18	27	.243	.294	.344	638	70	-12	2			.988	-2	C-87	-1.0
1950	NY-N	4	11	0	1	1	0	0	0	0	2	.091	.091	.182	273	-30	-2	0			1.000	2	/C-4	0.0
	Pit-N	67	156	17	42	7	0	6	24	11	14	.269	.321	.429	751	92	-2	2			.996	2	C-63	0.2
	Yr	71	167	17	43	8	0	6	24	11	16	.257	.307	.413	720	85	-4	2			.996	4	C-67	0.2
1951	Bos-N	28	70	8	11	2	0	1	9	7	11	.157	.234	.229	462	27	-7	0	0	0	1.000	3	C-23	-0.3
Total	14	985	2911	281	733	123	23	56	373	250	322	.252	.314	.368	681	91	-43	14	0		.988	21	C-917	2.9
■ WALTER MUELLER	Mueller, Walter John b: 12/6/1894, Central, Mo. d: 8/16/71, St.Louis, Mo. BR/TR, 5'8", 160 lbs. Deb: 5/7/22 F																							
1922	Pit-N	32	122	21	33	5	1	2	18	5	7	.270	.305	.377	682	74	-5	1	0	0	.976	6	O-31(0-0-31)	-0.1
1923	Pit-N	40	111	11	34	4	4	0	20	4	6	.306	.336	.414	751	95	-1	2	2	-0	.941	1	O-26(19-0-7)	-0.2
1924	Pit-N	30	50	6	13	1	1	0	8	4	4	.260	.327	.320	647	73	-2	1	0	0	1.000	-1	O-15(8-5-2)	-0.3
1926	Pit-N	19	62	8	15	0	1	0	3	0	2	.242	.242	.274	516	37	-5	0			.969	0	O-15(14-0-1)	-0.6
Total	4	121	345	46	95	10	7	2	49	13	19	.275	.307	.362	670	74	-13	4	2		.966	7	/O-87(41-5-41)	-1.2
■ BILL MUELLER	Mueller, William Lawrence "Hawk" b: 11/9/20, Bay City, Mich. BR/TR, 6'1.5", 180 lbs. Deb: 8/29/42																							
1942	Chi-A	26	85	5	14	1	0	0	5	12	9	.165	.276	.176	452	29	-8	2	1	0	.978	7	O-26(0-23-3)	-0.1
1945	Chi-A	13	9	3	0	0	0	0	0	2	1	.000	.182	.000	182	-47	-2	1	0	0	.778	-3	/O-7(0-5-2)	-0.5
Total	2	39	94	8	14	1	0	0	5	14	10	.149	.266	.160	426	22	-9	3	1	0	.960	4	/O-33(0-28-5)	-0.6
■ BILL MUELLER	Mueller, William Richard b: 3/17/71, Maryland Heights, Mo. BB/TR, 5'11", 175 lbs. Deb: 4/18/96																							
1996	SF-N	55	200	31	66	15	1	0	19	24	26	.330	.404	.415	819	121	7	0	0	0	.966	-3	3-45/2-8	0.5
1997	*SF-N	128	390	51	114	26	3	7	44	48	71	.292	.374	.428	802	113	8	4	3	-0	.956	8	*3-122	1.7
1998	SF-N	145	534	93	157	27	0	9	59	79	83	.294	.386	.395	781	113	13	3	3	-0	.952	-0	*3-137,2-10	1.3
1999	SF-N	116	414	61	120	24	0	2	36	65	52	.290	.390	.362	752	99	3	4	2	0	.958	-9	*3-108/2-3	-0.5
2000	*SF-N	153	560	97	150	29	4	10	55	52	62	.268	.337	.387	724	88	-10	4	2	0	**.974**	-3	*3-145/2-2	-1.2
Total	5	597	2098	333	607	121	8	28	213	268	294	.289	.374	.395	768	104	21	15	10	-0	.961	-7	3-557/2-23	1.8
■ MIKE MULDOON	Muldoon, Michael D. b: 1858, Ireland 5'8", 165 lbs. Deb: 5/1/1882 Career OF: (21-LF 2-CF 3-RF)																							
1882	Cle-N	84	341	50	84	17	5	6	45	10	28	.246	.268	.378	646	108	3				.880	3	*3-61,O-23(21-2-0)	0.6
1883	Cle-N	98	378	54	86	22	3	0	29	10	39	.228	.247	.302	549	67	-15				.825	-9	*3-98/O-2(0-0-2)	-1.9
1884	Cle-N	110	422	46	101	16	6	2	38	18	67	.239	.270	.320	590	82	-9				.833	-7	*3-109/O-1(0-0-1),2-1	-1.2
1885	Bal-a	102	410	47	103	20	6	2	52	20		.251	.293	.344	637	102	1				.870	-3	*3-101/2-1	0.0
1886	Bal-a	101	381	57	76	13	8	0	23	34		.199	.269	.276	544	72	-12	12			.912	2	2-57,3-44	-0.6
Total	5	495	1932	254	450	88	28	10	187	92	134	.233	.270	.323	593	86	-31	12			.846	-14	3-413/2-59,O-26L	-3.1
■ TONY MULLANE	Mullane, Anthony John "Count" or "The Apollo Of The Box" b: 1/20/1859, Cork, Ireland d: 4/25/44, Chicago, Ill. BB/TR (BL 1882, TB 1882 (part1893 (PART)), 5'10.5", 165 lbs. Deb: 8/27/1881 Career OF: (57-LF 59-CF 39-RF)																							
1881	Det-N	5	19	0	5	0	0	0	1	0	0	.263	.263	.263	526	63	-1				.882	0	/P-5	0.0
1882	Lou-a	77	303	46	78	13	1	0		13		.257	.288	.307	595	107	3				.959	10	*P-55,1-13,O-12C,/2	-0.1
1883	StL-a	83	307	38	69	11	6	0	33	13		.225	.256	.300	556	74	-9				.851	2	P-53,O-30L/2-3,1-2	-0.3
1884	Tol-a	95	352	49	97	19	3	3		33		.276	.339	.372	712	127	11				.889	7	P-67,O-19L/1-7,3S2	0.0
1886	Cin-a	91	324	59	73	12	5	0	39	25		.225	.283	.293	576	78	-9	20			.899	-0	P-63,O-27C/1-4,3S2	-0.6
1887	Cin-a	56	215	35	60	6	3	3	23	16		.279	.292	.327	619	71	-8	20			.944	-2	P-48/O-9(7-2-0)	-0.2
1888	Cin-a	51	175	27	44	4	4	1	16	8		.251	.296	.337	633	97	-1	12			.888	-2	P-44/1-4,O-3R,2-2	-0.2
1889	Cin-a	63	196	53	58	16	4	0	29	27	21	.296	.387	.418	805	125	7	24			.920	-1	P-33,3-18,O-12C,/1	0.3
1890	Cin-N	81	286	41	79	9	8	0	34	39	30	.276	.375	.364	738	116	7	19			.941	-2	O-28R,P-25,3-21,S/1	0.3
1891	Cin-N	64	209	16	31	1	2	0	10	18	33	.148	.229	.172	402	17	-22	4			.958	-3	P-51,O-12(6-5-1)/3-4	-0.6
1892	Cin-N	39	118	14	20	3	1	0	9	9	8	.169	.246	.212	458	39	-9	4			.926	5	P-37/1-2	0.0
1893	Cin-N	16	52	11	15	0	0	1	6	5	3	.288	.383	.346	729	92	-0	1			.939	0	P-15/3-1	0.0
	Bal-N	38	114	15	26	2	1	0	14	5	14	.228	.261	.263	524	39	-10	5			.943	2	P-34/O-2(2-0-0),1-1	-0.1
	Yr	54	166	26	41	2	1	1	20	10	17	.247	.302	.289	591	56	-11	6			.942	2	P-49/O-2L,3-1,1-1	-0.1
1894	Bal-N	21	53	3	21	3	0	0	9	6	3	.396	.475	.453	928	119	2	2			.889	-1	P-21	0.0
	Cle-N	4	13	0	1	0	0	0	0	4	2	.077	.294	.077	371	-6	-2	1			.944	2	/P-4	0.0
	Yr	25	66	3	22	3	0	0	9	10	5	.333	.436	.379	815	94	-0	3			.911	1	P-25	0.0
Total	13	784	2736	407	677	99	38	8	223	221	114	.247	.307	.316	623	87	-41	112			.918	18	P-555,O-154C/31S2	-1.5
■ GREG MULLEAVY	Mulleavy, Gregory Thomas "Moe" b: 9/25/05, Detroit, Mich. d: 2/1/80, Arcadia, Cal. BR/TR, 5'9", 167 lbs. Deb: 7/4/30 C																							
1930	Chi-A	77	289	27	76	14	5	0	28	20	23	.263	.311	.346	657	69	-14	5	2	0	.918	-5	S-73	-1.0
1932	Chi-A	1	3	0	0	0	0	0	0	0	0	.000	.000	.000	0	-99	-1	0	0	0	1.000	0	/2-1	-0.1
1933	Bos-A	1	0	1	0	0	0	0	0	0	0	—	—	—	—	—	0	0	0	0	.000	0	R	0.0
Total	3	79	292	28	76	14	5	0	28	20	23	.260	.308	.342	650	67	-15	5	2	0	.918	-5	/S-73,2-1	-1.1
■ MULLEN	Mullen Deb: 8/17/1872																							
1872	Cle-n	1	4	1	0	0	0	0	0	0	0	.000	.000	.000	0	-99	-1	0	0	0	.400	-0	/O-1(0-0-1)	-0.1
■ CHARLIE MULLEN	Mullen, Charles George b: 3/15/1889, Seattle, Wash. d: 6/6/63, Seattle, Wash. BR/TR, 5'10.5", 155 lbs. Deb: 5/18/10																							
1910	Chi-A	41	123	15	24	2	1	0	13	4		.195	.220	.228	448	42	-8	4			.982	1	1-37/O-2(0-0-2)	-1.0
1911	Chi-A	20	59	7	12	2	1	0	5	5		.203	.266	.271	537	51	-4	1			.969	0	1-20	-0.4
1914	NY-A	93	323	33	84	8	0	0	44	33	55	.260	.332	.285	617	86	-5	11	17	-4	.994	3	1-93	-0.9
1915	NY-A	40	90	11	24	1	0	0	7	10	12	.267	.340	.278	618	85	-1	5	2	0	.982	1	1-27	-0.1
1916	NY-A	59	146	11	39	9	1	0	18	9	13	.267	.310	.342	652	94	-2	7			.943	-4	2-20,1-17/O-6(1-2-3)	-0.7
Total	5	253	741	77	183	22	3	0	87	61	80	.247	.306	.285	591	78	-20	28	19		.988	0	1-194/2-20,O-8(1-2-5)	-3.1

YEAR	TM/L	G	AB	R	H	2B	3B	HR	RBI	BB	SO	AVG	OBP	SLG	OPS	OPS+	BR+	SB	CS	SBR	FA	FR	G/POS	TPR
■ **MOON MULLEN**	Mullen, Ford Parker b: 2/9/17, Olympia, Wash. BL/TR, 5'9", 165 lbs. Deb: 4/18/44																							
1944	Phi-N	118	464	51	124	9	4	0	31	28	32	.267	.315	.304	618	77	-14	4			.963	-7	*2-114/3-1	-1.5
■ **JOHN MULLEN**	Mullen, John b: Philadelphia, Pa. BL/TL, Deb: 9/9/1876																							
1876	Phi-N	1	3	0	0	0	0	0	0	0	0	.000	.000	.000	0	-99	-1				.714	0	/C-1	0.0
■ **BILLY MULLEN**	Mullen, William John b: 1/23/1896, St.Louis, Mo. d: 5/4/71, St.Louis, Mo. BR/TR, 5'8", 160 lbs. Deb: 10/2/20																							
1920	StL-A	2	4	0	0	0	0	0	0	0	0	.000	.000	.000	0	-97	-1	0	0	0	1.000	-1	/2-1	-0.2
1921	StL-A	4	4	0	0	0	0	0	0	2	1	.000	.333	.000	333	-8	-1	0	0	0	1.000	0	/3-2	0.0
1923	Bro-N	4	11	1	3	0	0	0	0	0	0	.273	.273	.273	545	46	-1	0	0	0	.875	-0	/3-4	-0.1
1926	Det-A	11	13	2	1	0	0	0	0	5	1	.077	.333	.077	410	11	-1	1	0	0	.875	-0	/3-9	-0.1
1928	StL-A	15	18	2	7	1	0	0	2	3	4	.389	.476	.444	921	139	1	0	0	0	.867	1	/3-6	0.2
Total	5	36	50	5	11	1	0	0	2	10	6	.220	.350	.240	590	56	-3	1	0	0	.884	-1	/3-21,2-1	-0.2
■ **FREDDIE MULLER**	Muller, Frederick William b: 12/21/07, Newark, Cal. d: 10/20/76, Davis, Cal. BR/TR, 5'10", 170 lbs. Deb: 7/8/33																							
1933	Bos-A	15	48	6	9	1	1	0	3	5	5	.188	.264	.250	514	37	-4	1	0	0	.923	-4	2-14	-0.7
1934	Bos-A	2	1	1	0	0	0	0	0	1	0	.000	.500	.000	500	36	-0	0	0	0	.800	-0	/2-1,3-1	0.0
Total	2	17	49	7	9	1	1	0	3	6	5	.184	.273	.245	518	38	-4	1	0	0	.914	-5	/2-15,3-1	-0.7
■ **EDDIE MULLIGAN**	Mulligan, Edward Joseph b: 8/27/1894, St.Louis, Mo. d: 3/15/82, San Rafael, Cal. BR/TR, 5'9", 152 lbs. Deb: 9/23/15																							
1915	Chi-N	11	22	5	8	1	0	0	2	5	1	.364	.481	.409	891	170	2	2	2	-0	.907	3	S-10/3-1	0.6
1916	Chi-N	58	189	13	29	3	4	0	9	8	30	.153	.200	.212	412	24	-17	1			.888	3	S-58	-1.1
1921	Chi-A	151	609	82	153	21	12	1	45	32	53	.251	.293	.330	623	59	-38	13	18	-3	.955	-13	*3-151/S-1	-4.3
1922	Chi-A	103	372	39	87	14	8	0	31	22	32	.234	.278	.315	593	55	-26	7	7	-1	.971	4	3-84/S-7	-1.6
1928	Pit-N	27	43	4	10	2	0	0	1	3	4	.233	.283	.279	562	45	-3	0			.929	0	/3-6,2-4	-0.3
Total	5	350	1235	143	287	41	24	1	88	70	120	.232	.278	.307	585	54	-82	23	27		.961	-3	3-242/S-76,2-4	-6.7
■ **JOHN MULLIGAN**	Mulligan, John Deb: 6/14/1884																							
1884	Was-U	1	4	2	1	0	0	0		0		.250	.250	.250	500	54	-0				1.000	1	/3-1	0.1
■ **SEAN MULLIGAN**	Mulligan, Sean Patrick b: 4/25/70, Lynwood, Cal. BR/TR, 6'2", 205 lbs. Deb: 9/1/96																							
1996	SD-N	2	1	0	0	0	0	0	0	0	0	.000	.000	.000	0	-99	-0	0	0	0	.000	0	/H	0.0
■ **GEORGE MULLIN**	Mullin, George Joseph "Wabash George" b: 7/4/1880, Toledo, Ohio d: 1/7/44, Wabash, Ind. BR/TR, 5'11", 188 lbs. Deb: 5/4/02 Career OF: (2-LF 2-CF 8-RF)																							
1902	Det-A	40	120	20	39	4	3	0	11	8		.325	.367	.408	776	113	2	1			.921	1	P-35/O-4(0-1-3)	-0.1
1903	Det-A	46	126	11	35	9	1	1	12	2		.278	.295	.389	683	107	1	1			.936	5	P-41/O-1(1-0-0)	0.0
1904	Det-A	53	155	14	45	10	2	0	8	10		.290	.337	.381	718	131	5	1			.936	7	P-45/O-2(0-0-2)	-0.1
1905	Det-A	47	135	15	35	4	0	0	12	12		.259	.320	.289	609	93	-1	4			.962	7	P-44/O-1	0.0
1906	Det-A	50	142	13	32	6	4	0	6	4		.225	.247	.324	571	76	-4	2			.957	2	P-40/2-1,O-1(0-0-1)	-0.1
1907	*Det-A	70	157	16	34	5	3	0	13	12		.217	.276	.287	563	77	-4	2			.961	4	P-46/1-1	0.0
1908	*Det-A	55	125	13	32	2	2	1	8	7		.256	.306	.328	634	102	0	2			.961	3	P-39	0.0
1909	*Det-A	53	126	13	27	7	0	0	17	13		.214	.288	.270	558	73	-4	2			.973	0	P-40/O-2(0-0-2)	-0.1
1910	Det-A	50	129	15	33	6	2	1	11	8		.256	.299	.357	656	99	-1	1			.944	-0	P-38/O-2(1-1-0)	-0.1
1911	Det-A	40	98	4	28	7	2	0	5	10		.286	.352	.398	750	104	0	1			.941	-2	P-30	0.0
1912	Det-A	38	90	13	25	5	1	0	12	17		.278	.393	.356	748	118	3	0			.929	0	P-30	0.0
1913	Det-A	12	20	1	7	0	0	0	1	4	1	.350	.458	.350	808	139	1	0			.950	0	/P-7	0.0
	Was-A	12	21	4	4	0	0	0	0	2	5	.190	.292	.190	482	41	-1	1			.960	1	P-11	0.0
	Yr	24	41	5	11	0	0	0	1	6	6	.268	.375	.268	643	89	-0	1			.956	1	P-18	0.0
1914	Ind-F	43	77	11	24	5	3	0	21	11	15	.312	.404	.455	859	121	1	0			.915	-4	P-36	0.0
1915	New-F	6	10	0	1	0	0	0	0	2	0	.100	.250	.100	350	0	-1	0			1.000	-1	/P-5	0.0
Total	14	615	1531	163	401	70	23	3	137	122	21	.262	.319	.344	663	99	-2	18			.947	24	P-487/O-13R,1-1,2-1	-0.5
■ **HENRY MULLIN**	Mullin, Henry J. b: 4/1862, St.John, N.B., Canada d: 11/8/27, Beverly, Mass. BR, 5'9", 160 lbs. Deb: 6/4/1884																							
1884	Was-a	34	120	13	17	3	1	0		8		.142	.195	.183	379	27	-9				.869	-1	O-34(4-29-1)/3-1	-0.9
	Bos-U	2	8	1	0	0	0	0		0		.000	.000	.000	0	-99	-2				1.000	3	/O-2(0-2-0)	0.0
Total	1	36	128	14	17	3	1	0		8		.133	.184	.172	356	18	-11				.882	2	/O-36(4-31-1),3-1	-0.9
■ **JIM MULLIN**	Mullin, James Henry b: 10/16/1883, New York, N.Y. d: 1/24/25, Philadelphia, Pa. BR/TR, 5'10", 173 lbs. Deb: 6/1/04 Career OF: (1-LF 0-CF 0-RF)																							
1904	Phi-A	22	52	5	14	1	0	1	5	3		.269	.321	.346	668	106	0	2			.985	-5	/1-7,2-5,S-2,O-1L	-0.6
	Was-A	27	102	10	19	2	2	0	4	4		.186	.224	.245	469	49	-6	3			.981	6	2-27	0.0
	Phi-A	19	58	4	10	0	0	0	4	2		.172	.238	.172	411	29	-4	2			.984	-1	1-19	-0.6
	Yr	68	212	19	43	3	2	1	13	9		.203	.252	.250	502	58	-10	7			.965	-0	2-32,1-26/S-2,O-1L	-1.2
1905	Was-A	50	163	18	31	7	6	0	13	5		.190	.214	.307	521	67	-7	5			.928	-3	2-40/1-6	-1.1
Total	2	118	375	37	74	10	8	1	26	14		.197	.236	.275	511	62	-17	12			.946	-4	/2-72,1-32,S-2,O-1L	-2.3
■ **PAT MULLIN**	Mullin, Patrick Joseph b: 11/1/17, Trotter, Pa. d: 8/14/99, Brownsville, Pa. BL/TR, 6'2", 190 lbs. Deb: 9/18/40 C																							
1940	Det-A	4	4	0	0	0	0	0	0	0	0	.000	.000	.000	0	-91	-1	0	0	0	.000	-1	/O-1(0-1-0)	-0.2
1941	Det-A	54	220	42	76	11	5	5	23	18	18	.345	.400	.509	909	126	8	5	1	1	.944	-4	O-51(0-51-0)	0.3
1946	Det-A	93	276	34	68	13	4	3	35	25	36	.246	.311	.355	666	81	-7	3	5	-1	.949	-3	O-75(0-1-75)	-1.4
1947	Det-A☆	116	398	62	102	28	6	15	62	63	66	.256	.359	.470	829	126	13	3	8	-2	.988	8	*O-106(0-0-106)	1.6
1948	Det-A★	138	496	91	143	16	11	23	80	77	57	.288	.385	.504	889	132	22	1	2	-0	.972	0	*O-131(0-10-123)	1.6
1949	Det-A	104	310	55	83	8	6	12	59	42	29	.268	.357	.448	805	112	4	1	2	-0	.989	-4	O-79(61-18-3)	-0.5
1950	Det-A	69	142	16	31	5	0	6	23	20	23	.218	.315	.380	695	75	-6	1	4	-1	1.000	-1	O-32(21-0-13)	-0.9
1951	Det-A	110	295	41	83	11	6	12	51	40	38	.281	.367	.481	849	128	11	2	2	-0	.939	-9	O-83(76-4-6)	-0.4
1952	Det-A	97	255	29	64	13	5	7	35	31	30	.251	.332	.424	756	108	2	4	2	0	.979	2	O-65(60-2-5)	0.0
1953	Det-A	79	97	11	26	1	0	4	17	14	15	.268	.360	.402	762	107	1	0	1	-0	.944	-2	O-14(10-0-4)	-0.2
Total	10	864	2493	381	676	106	43	87	385	330	312	.271	.358	.453	811	115	47	20	27	-5	.970	-14	O-637(228-87-335)	-0.1
■ **RANCE MULLINIKS**	Mulliniks, Steven Rance b: 1/15/56, Tulare, Cal. BL/TR, 6', 170 lbs. Deb: 6/18/77																							
1977	Cal-A	78	271	36	73	13	2	3	21	23	36	.269	.329	.365	694	93	-3	1	1	-0	.963	2	S-77	0.7
1978	Cal-A	50	119	6	22	3	1	1	6	8	23	.185	.242	.252	494	41	-9	2	0	0	.953	2	S-47/D-2	-0.4
1979	Cal-A	22	68	7	10	0	0	1	8	4	14	.147	.205	.191	397	8	-9	0	0	0	.957	-7	S-22	-1.4
1980	KC-A	36	54	8	14	3	0	0	6	7	10	.259	.344	.315	659	81	-1	0	0	0	.981	2	S-18,2-14	0.2
1981	KC-A	24	44	6	10	3	0	0	5	2	7	.227	.261	.295	556	61	-2	0	1	-0	.900	3	2-10/S-7,3-5	0.1
1982	Tor-A	112	311	32	76	25	0	4	35	37	49	.244	.327	.363	690	82	-7	3	2	-0	.938	-16	*3-102,S-16	-2.4
1983	Tor-A	129	364	54	100	34	3	10	49	57	43	.275	.374	.467	841	122	12	0	2	-1	.971	-18	*3-116,S-15/2-2	-0.7
1984	Tor-A	125	343	41	111	21	5	3	42	33	44	.324	.385	.440	825	123	11	2	3	-1	**.968**	-13	*3-119/S-3,2-1	-0.4
1985	*Tor-A	129	366	55	108	26	1	10	57	55	54	.295	.387	.454	841	126	15	2	0	0	**.971**	-16	*3-119	-0.3
1986	Tor-A	117	348	50	90	22	0	11	45	43	60	.259	.342	.417	759	103	2	1	1	-0	**.975**	-1	*3-110/2-1,D-5	-0.1
1987	Tor-A	124	332	37	103	28	1	11	44	34	55	.310	.374	.500	874	127	13	1	1	-0	.927	-6	3-96,D-22/S-1	0.4
1988	Tor-A	119	337	49	101	21	1	12	48	56	57	.300	.399	.475	874	143	21	1	0	0	1.000	-0	*D-108/3-7	1.8
1989	*Tor-A	103	273	25	65	11	2	3	29	34	40	.238	.322	.326	648	85	-5	0	0	0	.985	1	D-73,3-29	-0.6
1990	Tor-A	57	97	11	28	4	0	2	16	22	19	.289	.420	.392	812	126	5	2	1	0	.949	-0	3-22,D-10/1-3	0.4
1991	*Tor-A	97	240	27	60	12	1	2	24	44	44	.250	.366	.333	700	92	-1	0	0	0	1.000	0	D-81/3-5	-0.4
1992	Tor-A	3	2	1	1	0	0	0	0	1	0	.500	.667	.500	1167	221	0	0	0	0	.000	0	/D-2	0.0
Total	16	1325	3569	445	972	226	17	73	435	460	555	.272	.357	.407	763	107	41	15	12	-1	.961	-68	3-730,D-303,S/21	-3.1
■ **FRAN MULLINS**	Mullins, Francis Joseph b: 5/14/57, Oakland, Cal. BR/TR, 6', 180 lbs. Deb: 9/1/80																							
1980	Chi-A	21	62	9	12	4	0	0	3	9	8	.194	.296	.258	554	53	-4	0	1	-0	.981	-2	3-21	-0.7
1984	SF-N	57	110	8	24	8	0	2	10	9	29	.218	.277	.345	623	77	-4	3	1	0	.969	9	S-28,3-28/2-4	0.8

YEAR	TM/L	G	AB	R	H	2B	3B	HR	RBI	BB	SO	AVG	OBP	SLG	OPS	OPS+	BR+	SB	CS	SBR	FA	FR	G/POS	TPR
1986	Cle-A	28	40	3	7	4	0	0	5	2	11	.175	.214	.275	489	33	-4	0	0	0	.953	8	2-13,S-11/1-1,D-1	0.5
Total	3	106	212	20	43	16	0	2	18	20	48	.203	.272	.307	578	61	-11	3	2	-0	.968	15	/3-49,S-39,2-17,D1	0.6
■ JOE MULVEY Mulvey, Joseph H. b: 10/27/1858, Providence, R.I. d: 8/21/28, Philadelphia, Pa. BR/TR, 5'11.5", 178 lbs. Deb: 5/31/1883																								
1883	Pro-N	4	16	1	2	1	0	0	2	0	1	.125	.125	.188	313	-6	-2				.692	-3	/S-4	-0.4
	Phi-N	3	12	2	6	1	0	0	3	0	1	.500	.500	.583	1083	250	2				.750	-1	/3-3	0.1
	Yr	7	28	3	8	2	0	0	5	0	2	.286	.286	.357	643	96	-0				.692	-3	/S-4,3-3	-0.3
1884	Phi-N	100	401	47	92	11	2	2	32	4	49	.229	.237	.282	519	66	-15				.834	11	*3-100	-0.2
1885	Phi-N	107	443	74	119	25	6	6	64	3	18	.269	.274	.393	666	116	6				.848	-7	*3-107	0.1
1886	Phi-N	107	430	71	115	16	10	2	53	15	31	.267	.292	.365	657	98	-2	27			.879	-19	*3-107/O-1(0-0-1)	-1.7
1887	Phi-N	111	495	93	157	21	6	2	78	21	14	.317	.321	.369	690	86	-10	43			.865	-15	*3-111	-2.0
1888	Phi-N	100	398	37	86	12	3	0	39	9	33	.216	.235	.261	497	55	-20	18			.891	-14	*3-100	-3.2
1889	Phi-N	129	544	77	157	21	9	6	77	23	25	.289	.319	.393	712	91	-10	23			.893	1	*3-129	-0.6
1890	Phi-P	120	519	96	149	26	16	5	87	27	36	.287	.326	.428	754	98	-5	20			.857	-16	*3-120	-1.5
1891	Phi-a	113	453	62	115	9	13	5	66	17	32	.254	.287	.364	651	86	-12	11			.894	3	*3-113	-0.6
1892	Phi-N	25	98	9	14	1	1	0	4	6	9	.143	.200	.173	373	13	-10	2			.883	3	3-25	-0.7
1893	Was-N	55	226	21	53	9	4	0	19	7	8	.235	.264	.310	574	54	-16	2			.874	5	3-55	-0.8
1895	Bro-N	13	49	8	15	4	1	0	8	2	0	.306	.333	.429	762	104	0	1			.917	2	3-13	0.2
Total	12	987	4084	598	1080	157	71	28	532	134	257	.264	.287	.355	642	84	-94	147			.871	-48	3-983/S-4,O-1(0-0-1)	-11.3
■ JERRY MUMPHREY Mumphrey, Jerry Wayne b: 9/9/52, Tyler, Tex. BB/TR, 6'2", 185 lbs. Deb: 9/10/74																								
1974	StL-N	5	2	2	0	0	0	0	0	0	0	.000	.000	.000	0	-99	-1	0	0	0	.000	-0	/O-1(1-0-0)	-0.1
1975	StL-N	11	16	2	6	2	0	0	1	4	3	.375	.500	.500	1000	172	2	0	0	0	1.000	1	/O-3(0-0-3)	0.2
1976	StL-N	112	384	51	99	15	5	1	26	37	53	.258	.325	.331	655	86	-7	22	6	3	.993	6	O-94(15-77-12)	-0.1
1977	StL-N	145	463	73	133	20	10	2	38	47	70	.287	.354	.387	741	100	1	22	15	-0	.971	-2	*O-133(49-67-34)	-0.5
1978	StL-N	125	367	41	96	13	4	2	37	30	40	.262	.319	.335	654	84	-8	14	10	-0	.995	-8	*O-116(48-30-48)	-2.1
1979	StL-N	124	339	53	100	10	3	3	32	26	39	.295	.345	.369	714	94	-2	8	11	-2	.984	-13	*O-114(83-19-20)	-2.2
1980	SD-N	160	564	61	168	24	3	4	59	49	90	.298	.354	.372	726	109	7	52	5	10	.974	8	*O-153(0-153-0)	2.5
1981	*NY-A	80	319	44	98	11	5	6	32	24	27	.307	.356	.429	785	127	11	14	9	-0	.966	7	O-79(0-79-0)	1.8
1982	NY-A	123	477	76	143	24	10	9	68	50	66	.300	.366	.449	815	124	16	11	3	1	.986	9	*O-123(0-123-0)	2.5
1983	NY-A	83	267	41	70	11	4	7	36	28	33	.262	.332	.412	744	107	3	2	3	-1	.983	7	O-83(0-83-0)	0.9
	Hou-N	44	143	17	48	10	2	1	17	22	23	.336	.428	.455	882	154	12	5	0	1	.990	0	O-43(0-43-0)	1.3
1984	Hou-N★	151	524	66	152	20	3	9	83	56	79	.290	.359	.391	750	119	14	15	7	1	.988	0	*O-137(0-137-0)	1.4
1985	Hou-N	130	444	52	123	25	2	8	61	37	57	.277	.333	.396	729	106	3	6	7	-1	.969	-0	*O-126(0-58-68)	-0.2
1986	Chi-N	111	309	37	94	11	2	5	32	26	45	.304	.358	.401	760	101	1	2	3	-1	.982	-16	O-92(39-65-21)	-1.8
1987	Chi-N	118	309	41	103	19	2	13	44	35	47	.333	.401	.534	935	140	18	1	1	-0	.992	-2	O-85(78-1-6)	1.2
1988	Chi-N	63	66	3	9	2	0	0	9	7	16	.136	.219	.167	386	12	-7	0	0	0	1.000	-1	/O-4(4-0-0)	-0.9
Total	15	1585	4993	660	1442	217	55	70	575	478	688	.289	.351	.396	748	109	62	174	80	10	.981	-3	*O-1386(317-935-212)	3.9
■ JOHN MUNCE Munce, John Lewis "Big John" b: 11/18/1857, Philadelphia, Pa. d: 3/15/17, Philadelphia, Pa. 5'8.5", 160 lbs. Deb: 8/19/1884																								
1884	Wil-U	7	21	1	4	0	0	0		1		.190	.227	.190	418	27	-2				.667	-1	/O-7(0-2-6)	-0.3
■ JAKE MUNCH Munch, Jacob Ferdinand b: 11/16/1890, Morton, Pa. d: 6/8/66, Lansdowne, Pa. BL/TL, 6'2.5", 170 lbs. Deb: 5/27/18																								
1918	Phi-A	22	30	3	8	0	1	0	0	0	5	.267	.267	.333	600	80	-1	0			.667	-2	/O-3(0-1-2),1-2	-0.3
■ GEORGE MUNDINGER Mundinger, George b: 11/20/1854, New Orleans, La. d: 10/12/10, Covington, La. BR/TR, 6'2", 200 lbs. Deb: 5/9/1884																								
1884	Ind-a	3	8	1	2	0	0	0	3	0		.250	.250	.250	500	65	-0				.750	-3	/C-3	-0.3
■ BILL MUNDY Mundy, William Edward b: 6/28/1889, Salineville, Ohio d: 9/23/58, Kalamazoo, Mich. BL/TL, 5'10", 154 lbs. Deb: 8/17/13																								
1913	Bos-A	16	47	4	12	0	0	0	4	4	12	.255	.314	.255	569	65	-2	0			.952	-2	1-14	-0.5
■ HORATIO MUNN Munn, Horatio Brinsmade b: 7/26/1851, Newark, N.J. d: 2/17/10, Brooklyn, N.Y. Deb: 9/6/1875																								
1875	Atl-n	1	4	0	0	0	0	0	0	0	0	.000	.000	.000	0	-99	-1	0	0	0	.833	-0	/2-1	-0.1
■ JOSE MUNOZ Munoz, Jose Luis b: 11/11/67, Chicago, Ill. BB/TR, 5'11", 165 lbs. Deb: 4/7/96																								
1996	Chi-A	17	27	7	7	0	0	0	1	4	1	.259	.355	.259	614	62	-1	0	0	0	.923	-2	/2-7,S-2,3-1,O-1L,D	-0.3
■ NOE MUNOZ Munoz, Noe b: 11/11/67, Escatepec, Mexico BR/TR, 6'2", 180 lbs. Deb: 4/30/95																								
1995	LA-N	2	1	0	0	0	0	0	0	0	0	.000	.000	.000	0	-99	-0	0	0	0	1.000	1	/C-2	0.0
■ PEDRO MUNOZ Munoz, Pedro Javier (Gonzalez) b: 9/19/68, Ponce, P.R. BR/TR, 5'10", 207 lbs. Deb: 9/1/90 Career OF: (127-LF 0-CF 273-RF)																								
1990	Min-A	22	85	13	23	4	1	0	5	2	16	.271	.287	.341	629	70	-3	3	0	1	.972	-1	O-21(3-0-19)/D-1	-0.5
1991	Min-A	51	138	15	39	7	1	7	26	9	31	.283	.331	.500	831	121	3	3	0	1	.989	0	O-44(10-0-39)/D-2	0.3
1992	Min-A	127	418	44	113	16	3	12	71	17	90	.270	.300	.409	710	94	-5	4	5	-1	.987	-1	*O-122(7-0-117)/D-3	-1.0
1993	Min-A	104	326	34	76	11	1	13	38	25	97	.233	.294	.393	686	82	-9	1	2	-0	.983	-6	*O-102(64-0-41)	-1.8
1994	Min-A	75	244	35	72	15	2	11	36	19	67	.295	.351	.508	859	118	6	0	0	0	.965	-4	O-58(42-0-19),D-12	-0.1
1995	Min-A	104	376	45	113	17	0	18	58	19	86	.301	.339	.489	829	112	5	0	3	-1	.926	-4	D-77,O-25(1-0-24)/1-3	-0.5
1996	Oak-A	34	121	17	31	5	0	6	18	9	31	.256	.308	.446	754	89	-2	0	0	0	1.000	-3	D-18,O-14(0-0-14)	-0.6
Total	7	517	1708	203	467	75	8	67	252	100	418	.273	.317	.444	762	100	-5	11	10	-1	.980	-19	O-386R,D-113/1-3	-4.2
■ RED MUNSON Munson, Clarence Hanford b: 7/31/1883, Cincinnati, Ohio d: 2/19/57, Mishawaka, Ind. TR, Deb: 8/28/05																								
1905	Phi-N	9	26	1	3	1	0	0	2	0		.115	.115	.154	269	-21	-4	0			.857	-1	/C-8	-0.4
■ ERIC MUNSON Munson, Eric Walter b: 10/3/77, San Diego, Cal. BL/TR, 6'3", 220 lbs. Deb: 7/18/2000																								
2000	Det-A	3	5	0	0	0	0	0	1	0	1	.000	.000	.000	0	-99	-2	0	0	0	.941	-1	/1-3	-0.2
■ JOE MUNSON Munson, Joseph Martin Napoleon (b: Joseph Martin Napoleon Carlson) b: 11/6/1899, Renovo, Pa. d: 2/24/91, Drexel Hill, Pa. BL/TR, 5'9", 184 lbs. Deb: 9/18/25																								
1925	Chi-N	9	35	5	13	3	1	0	3	3	1	.371	.436	.514	950	140	2	1	1	-0	1.000	-0	/O-9(0-0-9)	0.1
1926	Chi-N	33	101	17	26	2	2	3	15	8	4	.257	.318	.406	724	93	-1	0			.898	-2	O-28(16-0-12)	-0.6
Total	2	42	136	22	39	5	3	3	18	11	5	.287	.349	.434	783	105	1	1	1		.922	-2	/O-37(16-0-21)	-0.5
■ THURMAN MUNSON Munson, Thurman Lee b: 6/7/47, Akron, Ohio d: 8/2/79, Canton, Ohio BR/TR, 5'11", 191 lbs. Deb: 8/8/69 Career OF: (3-LF 0-CF 24-RF)																								
1969	NY-A	26	86	6	22	1	2	1	9	10	10	.256	.333	.349	682	94	-1	0	1	-0	.986	-1	C-25	0.0
1970	NY-A	132	453	59	137	25	4	6	53	57	56	.302	.389	.415	804	128	19	5	7	-1	.989	6	*C-125	3.1
1971	NY-A★	125	451	71	113	15	4	10	42	52	65	.251	.337	.368	705	106	4	6	5	-0	**.998**	-1	*C-117/O-1(0-0-1)	0.8
1972	NY-A	140	511	54	143	16	3	7	46	47	58	.280	.344	.364	708	115	9	6	7	-1	.977	-5	*C-132	1.1
1973	NY-A★	147	519	80	156	29	4	20	74	48	64	.301	.364	.487	852	143	28	4	6	-1	.984	2	*C-142/D-1	4.0
1974	NY-A★	144	517	64	135	19	2	13	60	44	66	.261	.320	.381	701	103	1	2	0	0	.974	2	*C-137/D-4	1.1
1975	NY-A★	157	597	83	190	24	3	12	102	45	52	.318	.372	.429	801	128	22	3	2	-0	.972	9	*C-130,D-22/1-2,O3	3.6
1976	*NY-A★	152	616	79	186	27	1	17	105	29	38	.302	.343	.432	774	127	19	14	11	-1	.981	-6	*C-121,D-21,O-11R	1.8
1977	*NY-A★	149	595	85	183	28	5	18	100	39	55	.308	.352	.462	814	121	16	5	6	-1	.984	-5	*C-136,D-10	1.6
1978	*NY-A†	154	617	73	183	27	1	6	71	35	70	.297	.337	.373	710	102	1	2	3	-1	.986	-0	*C-125,D-14,O-13R	0.5
1979	NY-A	97	382	42	110	18	3	3	39	32	37	.288	.343	.374	717	95	-2	1	2	-0	.978	-6	C-88/1-3,D-5	-0.4
Total	11	1423	5344	696	1558	229	32	113	701	438	571	.292	.350	.410	760	117	118	48	50	-7	.982	-1	*C-1278/D-77,O13	17.2
■ JOHN MUNYAN Munyan, John B. b: 11/14/1860, Chester, Pa. d: 2/18/45, Endicott, N.Y. Deb: 7/12/1887 Career OF: (14-LF 5-CF 14-RF)																								
1887	Cle-a	16	61	9	17	1	1	0	6	3		.279	.279	.293	572	61	-3	4			.762	-2	O-12(3-3-6)/C-3,3-2	-0.4
1890	Col-a	2	7	1	1	0	0	0	0	0		.143	.250	.143	393	17	-1	0			.667	0	/O-2(0-2-0)	-0.1
	StL-a	96	342	61	91	15	7	4	42	32		.266	.341	.386	727	100	-2	11			.939	-3	C-83/O-7L,2-5,3S	0.2
	Yr	98	349	62	92	15	7	4	42	32		.264	.339	.381	720	99	-3	11			.939	-3	C-83/O-9L,2-5,3S	0.1
1891	StL-a	60	176	41	41	4	3	0	19	41	39	.233	.389	.290	679	82	-3	13			.940	-8	C-43,O-12R/S-5,3-3	-0.7
Total	3	174	586	112	150	20	11	4	67	76	39	.256	.350	.345	695	90	-9	28			.937	-12	C-129/O-33L,3-8,S2	-1.0

YEAR	TM/L	G	AB	R	H	2B	3B	HR	RBI	BB	SO	AVG	OBP	SLG	OPS	OPS+	BR+	SB	CS	SBR	FA	FR	G/POS	TPR

■ BOBBY MURCER

Murcer, Bobby Ray b: 5/20/46, Oklahoma City, Okla BL/TR, 5'11", 180 lbs. Deb: 9/8/65 Career OF: (56-LF 789-CF 839-RF)

YEAR	TM/L	G	AB	R	H	2B	3B	HR	RBI	BB	SO	AVG	OBP	SLG	OPS	OPS+	BR+	SB	CS	SBR	FA	FR	G/POS	TPR
1965	NY-A	11	37	2	9	0	1	1	4	5	12	.243	.333	.378	712	102	0	0	0	0	.932	7	S-11	0.9
1966	NY-A	21	69	3	12	1	1	0	5	4	5	.174	.219	.217	437	27	-7	2	2	-0	.931	-4	S-18	-1.0
1969	NY-A	152	564	82	146	24	4	26	82	50	103	.259	.323	.454	776	120	12	7	5	-0	.964	-5	*O-118(0-27-99),3-31	0.1
1970	NY-A	159	581	95	146	23	3	23	78	87	100	.251	.351	.420	771	118	15	15	10	-0	.992	10	*O-155(0-155-0)	2.1
1971	NY-A★	146	529	94	175	25	6	25	94	91	60	.331	**.429**	.543	**972**	**185**	**61**	14	8	0	.985	-1	*O-143(0-143-0)	**6.0**
1972	NY-A★	153	585	**102**	171	30	7	33	96	63	67	.292	.363	.537	900	171	49	11	9	-1	.992	10	*O-151(0-151-0)	**6.0**
1973	NY-A★	160	616	83	187	29	2	22	95	50	67	.304	.359	.464	823	135	27	6	7	-1	.985	2	*O-160(0-160-0)	2.4
1974	NY-A★	156	606	69	166	25	4	10	88	57	59	.274	.338	.378	716	108	6	14	5	1	.978	0	*O-156(0-59-101)	0.1
1975	SF-N★	147	526	80	157	29	4	11	91	91	45	.298	.404	.432	835	127	22	9	5	0	.981	-8	*O-144(0-2-143)	0.7
1976	SF-N	147	533	73	138	20	2	23	90	84	78	.259	.364	.433	797	122	17	12	7	0	.961	-0	*O-146(0-0-146)	0.9
1977	Chi-N	154	554	90	147	18	3	27	89	80	77	.265	.361	.455	816	106	5	16	7	1	.980	-4	*O-150R/2-1,S-1	-0.6
1978	Chi-N	146	499	66	140	22	6	9	64	80	57	.281	.380	.403	783	106	7	14	5	1	.979	-17	*O-138(0-33-121)	-1.5
1979	Chi-N	58	190	22	49	4	1	7	22	36	20	.258	.379	.400	779	103	2	2	3	-1	1.000	3	O-54(0-0-54)	0.1
	NY-A	74	264	42	72	12	0	8	33	25	32	.273	.340	.409	749	103	1	1	1	-0	.983	-4	O-70(12-59-7)	-0.4
1980	*NY-A	100	297	41	80	9	1	13	57	34	28	.269	.348	.438	786	116	7	2	0	0	.955	-9	O-59(44-0-18),D-33	-0.5
1981	*NY-A	50	117	14	31	6	0	6	24	12	15	.265	.333	.470	803	131	4	0	0	0	.000	0	D-33	0.4
1982	NY-A	65	141	12	32	6	0	7	30	12	15	.227	.292	.418	711	94	-2	2	1	0	.000	0	D-47	-0.3
1983	NY-A	9	22	2	4	2	0	1	1	1	1	.182	.217	.409	626	71	-1	0	0	0	.000	0	/D-5	-0.1
Total	17	1908	6730	972	1862	285	45	252	1043	862	841	.277	.361	.445	806	124	226	127	75	2	.981	-19	*O-1644R,D-118/3S2	15.3

■ SIMMY MURCH

Murch, Simeon Augustus b: 11/21/1880, Castine, Me. d: 6/6/39, Exeter, N.H. BR/TR, 6'4", 220 lbs. Deb: 9/20/04

YEAR	TM/L	G	AB	R	H	2B	3B	HR	RBI	BB	SO	AVG	OBP	SLG	OPS	OPS+	BR+	SB	CS	SBR	FA	FR	G/POS	TPR
1904	StL-N	13	51	3	7	1	0	0	1	1		.137	.154	.157	311	-4	-6	0			.905	-3	/2-6,3-6,S-1	-0.9
1905	StL-N	4	9	0	1	0	0	0	0	0		.111	.111	.111	222	-35	-1	0			.750	-3	/2-2,S-1	-0.5
1908	Bro-N	6	11	1	2	1	0	0	0	1		.182	.250	.273	523	70	-0	0			.964	-1	/1-2	-0.1
Total	3	23	71	4	10	2	0	0	1	2		.141	.164	.169	333	3	-8	0			.880	-6	/2-8,3-6,1-2,S-2	-1.5

■ WILBUR MURDOCH

Murdoch, Wilbur Edwin b: 3/14/1875, Avon, N.Y. d: 10/29/41, Los Angeles, Cal. Deb: 8/29/08

YEAR	TM/L	G	AB	R	H	2B	3B	HR	RBI	BB	SO	AVG	OBP	SLG	OPS	OPS+	BR+	SB	CS	SBR	FA	FR	G/POS	TPR
1908	StL-N	27	62	5	16	3	0	0	5	3		.258	.292	.306	599	96	-0	4			.913	-5	O-16(13-5-0)	-0.7

■ TIM MURNANE

Murnane, Timothy Hayes b: 6/4/1852, Naugatuck, Conn. d: 2/7/17, Boston, Mass. BL/TR, 5'9.5", 172 lbs. Deb: 4/26/1872 M NA OF: (1-LF 49-CF 20-RF) Career OF: (3-LF 27-CF 20-RF)

YEAR	TM/L	G	AB	R	H	2B	3B	HR	RBI	BB	SO	AVG	OBP	SLG	OPS	OPS+	BR+	SB	CS	SBR	FA	FR	G/POS	TPR
1872	Man-n	23	113	29	41	1	0	0	13	0	1	.363	.363	.372	735	134	5	1	0	0	.881	-5	1-23	0.0
1873	Ath-n	41	176	53	39	3	0	1	10	8	13	.222	.255	.256	511	49	-12	7	2	1	.797	-4	O-30(0-24-6),1-10/2-6	-1.0
1874	Ath-n	21	82	11	17	2	0	0	11	1	3	.207	.217	.232	449	40	-6	1	0	-0	.857	-5	O-14(0-1-13)/2-6,1-3	-0.8
1875	Phi-n	69	313	71	85	5	0	1	30	7	7	.272	.287	.297	585	100	-1	**30**	9	3	.918	2	1-31,O-26C,2-15	0.3
1876	Bos-N	69	316	60	87	4	3	2	34	8	12	.275	.301	.334	635	109	3				.927	-4	*1-65/O-3(2-1-0),2-1	-0.3
1877	Bos-N	35	140	23	39	7	1	1	15	6	7	.279	.308	.364	673	107	1				.815	-1	O-30(0-25-5)/1-5	-0.1
1878	Pro-N	49	188	35	45	6	1	0	14	8	12	.239	.270	.282	552	82	-3				.940	1	*1-48/O-1(0-1-0)	-0.4
1884	Bos-U	76	311	55	73	5	2	0		22		.235	.285	.264	549	68	-20				.950	-5	1-63,O-16(1-0-15),M	-2.7
Total	4 n	154	684	164	182	11	0	2	64	16	24	.266	.283	.291	574	83	-13	38	12	4	.830	-13	/O-70C,1-67,2-27	-1.5
Total	4	229	955	173	244	22	7	3	63	44	31	.255	.291	.305	596	90	-20				.938	-8	1-181/O-50C,2-1	-3.5

■ MURPHY

Murphy Deb: 8/16/1884

YEAR	TM/L	G	AB	R	H	2B	3B	HR	RBI	BB	SO	AVG	OBP	SLG	OPS	OPS+	BR+	SB	CS	SBR	FA	FR	G/POS	TPR
1884	Bos-U	1	3	0	0	0	0	0		1		.000	.250	.000	250	-18	-1				.333	-3	/C-1,O-1(1-0-0)	-0.3

■ CLARENCE MURPHY

Murphy, Clarence Deb: 6/17/1886

YEAR	TM/L	G	AB	R	H	2B	3B	HR	RBI	BB	SO	AVG	OBP	SLG	OPS	OPS+	BR+	SB	CS	SBR	FA	FR	G/POS	TPR
1886	Lou-a	1	3	0	0	0	0	0	0	0		.000	.000	.000	0	-95	-1	0			1.000	0	/O-1(1-0-0)	-0.1

■ CONNIE MURPHY

Murphy, Cornelius David "Stone Face" b: 11/1/1870, Northfield, Mass. d: 12/14/45, New Bedford, Mass. BL/TR, 5'8", 155 lbs. Deb: 9/17/1893

YEAR	TM/L	G	AB	R	H	2B	3B	HR	RBI	BB	SO	AVG	OBP	SLG	OPS	OPS+	BR+	SB	CS	SBR	FA	FR	G/POS	TPR
1893	Cin-N	6	17	3	3	1	0	0	2	1	2	.176	.222	.235	458	21	-2	0			.917	-2	/C-4	-0.3
1894	Cin-N	1	4	0	0	0	0	0	0	1	1	.000	.200	.000	200	-47	-1	0			.500	-1	/C-1	-0.2
Total	2	7	21	3	3	1	0	0	2	2	3	.143	.217	.190	408	6	-3	0			.857	-3	/C-5	-0.5

■ DALE MURPHY

Murphy, Dale Bryan b: 3/12/56, Portland, Ore. BR/TR, 6'5", 215 lbs. Deb: 9/13/76 Career OF: (101-LF 1044-CF 747-RF)

YEAR	TM/L	G	AB	R	H	2B	3B	HR	RBI	BB	SO	AVG	OBP	SLG	OPS	OPS+	BR+	SB	CS	SBR	FA	FR	G/POS	TPR
1976	Atl-N	19	65	3	17	6	0	0	9	7	9	.262	.333	.354	687	89	-1	0	0	0	.974	-0	C-19	0.0
1977	Atl-N	18	76	5	24	8	1	2	14	0	8	.316	.316	.526	842	108	1	0	1	-0	.954	-2	C-18	-0.1
1978	Atl-N	151	530	66	120	14	3	23	79	42	145	.226	.287	.394	681	80	-15	11	7	-0	.984	4	*1-129,C-21	-2.0
1979	Atl-N	104	384	53	106	7	2	21	57	38	67	.276	.344	.469	813	111	6	6	1	1	.980	-9	1-76,C-27	-0.6
1980	Atl-N★	156	569	98	160	27	2	33	89	59	133	.281	.350	.510	859	133	24	9	6	-0	.985	11	*O-154(4-129-21)/1-1	3.3
1981	Atl-N	104	369	43	91	12	1	13	50	44	72	.247	.327	.390	717	100	0	14	5	1	.981	4	*O-103(0-102-1)/1-3	0.5
1982	*Atl-N★	162	598	113	168	23	2	36	**109**	93	134	.281	.380	.507	887	140	33	23	11	1	.979	-1	*O-162(65-118-8)	3.1
1983	Atl-N★	162	589	131	178	24	4	36	**121**	90	110	.302	.396	**.540**	**936**	146	38	30	4	5	.985	5	*O-160(28-136-2)	4.7
1984	Atl-N★	162	607	94	176	32	8	**36**	100	79	134	.290	.374	**.547**	920	145	36	19	7	2	.987	1	*O-160(0-160-0)	3.8
1985	Atl-N★	162	616	**118**	185	32	2	**37**	111	**90**	141	.300	.390	.539	929	148	41	10	3	1	.980	-5	*O-161(0-161-0)	3.7
1986	Atl-N★	160	614	89	163	29	7	29	83	75	141	.265	.347	.477	825	118	15	7	7	-1	.981	-4	*O-159(0-155-6)	0.9
1987	Atl-N★	159	566	115	167	27	1	44	105	115	136	.295	.420	.580	1000	154	47	16	6	1	.977	12	*O-159(0-0-159)	5.1
1988	Atl-N	156	592	77	134	35	4	24	77	74	125	.226	.314	.421	735	104	3	3	5	-1	.992	18	*O-156(0-0-156)	1.5
1989	Atl-N	154	574	60	131	16	0	20	84	65	142	.228	.309	.361	670	88	-8	3	2	-0	.985	4	*O-151(0-82-70)	-0.8
1990	Atl-N	97	349	38	81	14	0	17	55	41	84	.232	.315	.418	733	94	-3	9	2	1	.981	4	O-97(0-0-97)	-0.1
	Phi-N	57	214	22	57	9	1	7	28	20	46	.266	.329	.416	745	104	1	0	1	-0	.992	3	O-55(1-1-53)	0.1
	Yr	154	563	60	138	23	1	24	83	61	130	.245	.320	.417	737	97	-2	9	3	1	.985	7	*O-152(1-1-150)	0.0
1991	Phi-N	153	544	66	137	33	1	18	81	48	93	.252	.313	.415	728	104	2	1	0	0	.983	4	*O-147(0-0-147)	0.1
1992	Phi-N	18	62	5	10	1	0	2	7	1	13	.161	.175	.274	449	25	-6	0	0	0	.950	-3	O-16(1-0-16)	-1.1
1993	Col-N	26	42	1	6	1	0	0	7	5	15	.143	.234	.167	401	8	-5	0	0	0	1.000	-1	O-13(2-0-11)	-0.7
Total	18	2180	7960	1197	2111	350	39	398	1266	986	1748	.265	.348	.469	817	119	206	161	68	12	.983	45	*O-1853C,1-209/C-85	21.4

■ DANNY MURPHY

Murphy, Daniel Francis b: 8/11/1876, Philadelphia, Pa. d: 11/22/55, Jersey City, N.J. BR/TR, 5'9", 175 lbs. Deb: 9/17/00 C Career OF: (3-LF 12-CF 597-RF)

YEAR	TM/L	G	AB	R	H	2B	3B	HR	RBI	BB	SO	AVG	OBP	SLG	OPS	OPS+	BR+	SB	CS	SBR	FA	FR	G/POS	TPR
1900	NY-N	22	74	11	20	1	0	0	6	8		.270	.341	.284	625	77	-2	4			.888	-6	2-22	-0.6
1901	NY-N	5	20	0	4	0	0	0	0	0		.200	.238	.200	438	29	-2	0			.895	-3	/2-5	-0.5
1902	Phi-A	76	291	48	91	11	8	1	48	13		.313	.351	.416	766	107	2	12			.963	-12	2-76	-0.8
1903	Phi-A	133	513	66	140	31	11	1	60	13		.273	.295	.382	677	97	-3	17			.949	-13	*2-133	-1.5
1904	Phi-A	150	557	78	160	30	17	7	77	22		.287	.320	.440	760	132	18	22			.941	13	*2-150	3.6
1905	*Phi-A	151	537	71	149	34	4	6	71	42		.277	.339	.389	728	129	17	23			.955	-8	*2-151	1.1
1906	Phi-A	119	448	48	135	28	6	2	60	21		.301	.341	.404	745	129	14	17			.955	-11	*2-119	0.5
1907	Phi-A	124	469	51	127	23	3	2	57	30		.271	.317	.345	663	109	4	11			.965	14	*2-122	2.0
1908	Phi-A	142	525	51	139	28	7	4	66	32		.265	.309	.368	677	112	6	16			.963	10	O-84R,2-56/1-2	1.4
1909	Phi-A	149	541	61	152	28	14	5	69	35		.281	.332	.412	744	132	18	19			**.977**	-2	*O-149(0-0-149)	1.1
1910	*Phi-A	151	560	70	168	28	18	4	64	31		.300	.338	.436	774	143	24	18			.974	-2	*O-151(0-0-151)	1.8
1911	*Phi-A	141	508	104	167	27	11	6	66	50		.329	.398	.461	858	142	28	22			.961	6	*O-136(0-0-136)/2-4	2.7
1912	Phi-A	36	130	27	42	6	2	2	20	16		.323	.401	.446	848	147	8	8			.891	-6	O-36(0-0-36)	0.0
1913	Phi-A	40	59	3	19	5	1	0	6	4	8	.322	.365	.441	806	139	3	0			1.000	-2	/O-9(0-0-9)	0.0
1914	Bro-F	52	161	16	49	9	0	4	32	17	16	.304	.374	.435	809	121	2	4			.986	1	O-46(1-0-45)	0.1
1915	Bro-F	5	6	0	1	0	0	0	0	0	0	.167	.167	.167	333	-6	-1	0			1.000	-1	/2-1,O-1(0-0-1)	-0.2
Total	16	1496	5399	705	1563	289	102	44	702	335	24	.289	.336	.405	742	124	137	193			.953	-22	2-839,O-612R/1-2	10.7

■ DANNY MURPHY

Murphy, Daniel Francis b: 8/23/42, Beverly, Mass. BL/TR, 5'11", 185 lbs. Deb: 6/18/60

YEAR	TM/L	G	AB	R	H	2B	3B	HR	RBI	BB	SO	AVG	OBP	SLG	OPS	OPS+	BR+	SB	CS	SBR	FA	FR	G/POS	TPR
1960	Chi-N	31	75	7	9	2	0	1	6	4	13	.120	.175	.187	362	-1	-11	0	0	0	.976	-1	O-21(0-16-5)	-1.3
1961	Chi-N	4	13	3	5	0	0	2	3	1	5	.385	.429	.846	1275	225	2	0	0	0	1.000	0	/O-4(0-0-4)	0.2
1962	Chi-N	14	35	5	7	3	1	0	3	2	9	.200	.243	.343	586	53	-2	0	0	0	1.000	-3	/O-5(2-1-6)	-0.5

YEAR	TM/L	G	AB	R	H	2B	3B	HR	RBI	BB	SO	AVG	OBP	SLG	OPS	OPS+	BR+	SB	CS	SBR	FA	FR	G/POS	TPR
1969	Chi-A	17	1	0	0	0	0	0	0	2	0	.000	.667	.000	667	95	0	0	0	0	1.000	-0	P-17	0.0
1970	Chi-A	51	6	3	2	0	0	1	1	2	2	.333	.500	.833	1333	252	1	0	0	0	.933	-1	P-51	0.0
Total	5	117	130	18	23	5	1	4	13	11	29	.177	.246	.323	570	53	-9	0	0	0	.947	-4	/P-68,O-30(2-17-15)	-1.6
■ DANNY MURPHY Murphy, Daniel Joseph "Handsome Dan" b: 9/10/1864, Brooklyn, N.Y. d: 12/14/15, Brooklyn, N.Y. 156 lbs. Deb: 4/26/1892																								
1892	NY-N	8	26	2	3	0	0	0	0	5	4	.115	.258	.115	373	14	-2	0			.900	-2	/C-8	-0.3
■ DAVE MURPHY Murphy, David Francis "Dirty Dave" b: 5/4/1876, Adams, Mass. d: 4/8/40, Adams, Mass. TR, Deb: 8/28/05																								
1905	Bos-N	3	11	0	2	0	0	0	1	0		.182	.182	.182	364	9	-1	0			1.000	-2	/S-2,3-1	-0.4
■ DWAYNE MURPHY Murphy, Dwayne Keith b: 3/18/55, Merced, Cal. BL/TR, 6'1", 185 lbs. Deb: 4/8/78 C Career OF: (57-LF 1181-CF 46-RF)																								
1978	Oak-A	60	52	15	10	2	0	0	5	7	14	.192	.288	.231	519	50	-3	0	1	-0	1.000	-10	O-45(21-12-14)/D-5	-1.4
1979	Oak-A	121	388	57	99	10	4	11	40	84	80	.255	.389	.387	776	116	13	15	11	-1	.988	8	*O-118(2-115-3)	1.8
1980	Oak-A	159	573	86	157	18	2	13	68	102	96	.274	.386	.380	766	119	20	26	15	0	.990	24	*O-158(0-158-0)	4.2
1981	*Oak-A	107	390	58	98	10	3	15	60	73	91	.251	.372	.408	780	131	18	10	4	1	.985	12	*O-106(0-106-0)/D-1	3.1
1982	Oak-A	151	543	84	129	15	1	27	94	94	122	.238	.353	.418	771	116	14	26	8	3	.983	22	*O-147C/S-1,D-1	3.7
1983	Oak-A	130	471	55	107	17	2	17	75	62	105	.227	.317	.380	697	97	-2	7	5	-0	.979	10	*O-124(0-124-0)/D-7	0.6
1984	Oak-A	153	559	93	143	18	2	33	88	74	111	.256	.346	.472	818	133	25	4	5	-1	.988	21	*O-153(0-153-0)	4.3
1985	Oak-A	152	523	77	122	21	3	20	59	84	123	.233	.343	.400	742	111	9	4	5	-1	.989	9	*O-150(0-150-0)	1.5
1986	Oak-A	98	329	50	83	11	3	9	39	56	80	.252	.368	.386	754	114	9	3	1	0	.993	11	O-97(0-97-0)/D-1	1.9
1987	Oak-A	82	219	39	51	7	0	8	35	58	61	.233	.394	.374	768	113	7	4	4	-1	.984	0	O-79(0-79-0)/1-1,2-1	0.6
1988	Det-A	49	144	14	36	5	0	4	19	24	26	.250	.361	.368	729	109	3	1	1	-0	1.000	1	O-43(4-35-10)/D-3	0.3
1989	Phi-N	98	156	20	34	5	0	9	27	29	44	.218	.341	.423	764	117	4	0	1	-0	.986	-6	O-52(30-5-19)	-0.4
Total	12	1360	4347	648	1069	139	20	166	609	747	953	.246	.359	.402	761	116	116	100	61	1	.987	102	*O-1272C/D-18,2-1,1S	20.2
■ ED MURPHY Murphy, Edward Joseph b: 8/23/18, Joliet, Ill. d: 12/10/91, Joliet, Ill. BR/TR, 5'11", 190 lbs. Deb: 9/10/42																								
1942	Phi-N	13	28	2	7	2	0	0	4	2	4	.250	.300	.321	621	86	-1	0			1.000	-0	/1-8	-0.1
■ TONY MURPHY Murphy, Francis J. b: 1863, Brooklyn, N.Y. 5'6", 145 lbs. Deb: 10/15/1884																								
1884	NY-a	1	3	1	1	0	0	0		0		.333	.333	.333	667	121	0				1.000	-1	/C-1	-0.1
■ FRANK MURPHY Murphy, Francis Patrick b: 4/16/1875, N.Tarrytown, N.Y. d: 11/4/12, Central Islip, N.Y. TR, Deb: 7/2/01																								
1901	Bos-N	45	176	13	46	5	3	1	18	4		.261	.282	.341	623	73	-6	6			.939	4	O-45(45-0-0)	-0.5
	NY-N	35	130	10	21	3	0	0	8	6		.162	.199	.185	383	12	-14	2			.847	-10	2-23,O-12(12-0-0)	-2.5
	Yr	80	306	23	67	8	3	1	26	10		.219	.246	.275	521	49	-20	8			.940	-6	O-57(57-0-0),2-23	-3.0
■ DUMMY MURPHY Murphy, Herbert Courtland b: 12/18/1886, Olney, Ill. d: 8/10/62, Tallahassee, Fla. BR/TR, 5'10", 165 lbs. Deb: 4/14/14																								
1914	Phi-N	9	26	1	4	1	0	0	3	0	4	.154	.185	.192	377	12	-3	0			.864	3	/S-9	0.1
■ HOWARD MURPHY Murphy, Howard b: 1/1/1882, Birmingham, Ala. d: 10/5/26, Fort Worth, Tex. BL/TR, 5'8.5", 150 lbs. Deb: 8/4/09																								
1909	StL-N	25	60	3	12	0	0	0	3	4		.200	.250	.200	450	42	-4	1			.925	-2	O-19(0-19-0)	-0.7
■ EDDIE MURPHY Murphy, John Edward b: 10/2/1891, Hancock, N.Y. d: 2/21/69, Dunmore, Pa. BL/TR, 5'9", 155 lbs. Deb: 8/26/12 Career OF: (10-LF 0-CF 558-RF)																								
1912	Phi-A	33	142	24	45	4	1	0	6	11		.317	.370	.359	729	113	3	7			.947	0	O-33(0-0-33)	0.1
1913	*Phi-A	137	508	105	150	14	7	1	30	70	44	.295	.391	.356	747	122	17	21			.942	-12	*O-135(0-0-135)	-0.2
1914	*Phi-A	148	573	101	156	12	9	3	43	87	46	.272	.379	.340	720	121	19	36	32	-3	.941	-5	*O-148(0-0-148)	0.3
1915	Phi-A	68	260	37	60	3	4	0	17	29	15	.231	.315	.273	588	79	-6	13	3	2	.899	-5	O-58(0-0-58)/3-6	-1.3
	Chi-A	70	273	51	86	11	5	0	26	39	12	.315	.410	.392	802	136	14	20	12	0	.952	-1	O-70(3-0-67)	1.0
	Yr	138	533	88	146	14	9	0	43	68	27	.274	.365	.334	698	109	8	33	15	2	.933	-6	*O-128(3-0-125)/3-6	-0.3
1916	Chi-A	51	105	14	22	5	1	0	4	9	5	.210	.284	.276	561	68	-4	3			1.000	-3	O-24(0-0-24)/3-1	-0.9
1917	Chi-A	53	51	9	16	2	1	0	16	5	1	.314	.386	.392	778	135	2	4			1.000	-4	/O-9(1-0-8)	-0.2
1918	Chi-A	91	286	36	85	9	3	0	23	22	18	.297	.350	.350	699	110	3	6			.958	-10	O-63(1-0-62)/2-8	-1.1
1919	*Chi-A	30	35	8	17	4	0	0	5	7	0	.486	.571	.600	1171	228	7	0			.917	-0	/O-6(2-0-4)	0.6
1920	Chi-A	58	118	22	40	2	1	0	19	12	4	.339	.405	.373	777	107	2	1	3	-1	.886	1	O-19(0-0-19)/3-3	0.1
1921	Chi-A	6	5	1	1	0	0	0	0	0	0	.200	.200	.200	400	2	-1	0	0	0	.000	0	H	-0.1
1926	Pit-N	16	17	3	2	0	0	0	6	3	0	.118	.250	.118	368	2	-2	0			1.000	-0	/O-3(3-0-0)	-0.3
Total	11	761	2373	411	680	66	32	4	195	294	145	.287	.374	.346	720	114	54	111	50		.942	-39	O-568R/3-10,2-8	-2.0
■ JOHN MURPHY Murphy, John Patrick b: 1879, New Haven, Conn. d: 4/20/49, Andover, Mass. 5'7.5", 160 lbs. Deb: 9/10/02																								
1902	StL-N	1	3	1	2	1	0	0	1	1		.667	.750	1.000	1750	458	1	0			1.000	-1	/3-1	0.1
1903	Det-A	5	22	1	4	1	0	0	1	0		.182	.182	.227	409	23	-2	0			.852	-1	/S-5	-0.3
Total	2	6	25	2	6	2	0	0	2	1		.240	.269	.320	589	79	-1	0			.852	-2	/S-5,3-1	-0.2
■ LARRY MURPHY Murphy, Lawrence Patrick BL, Deb: 5/30/1891																								
1891	Was-a	101	400	73	106	15	3	1	35	63	27	.265	.372	.325	697	104	6	29			.874	-5	*O-101(69-3-30)	-0.1
■ LEO MURPHY Murphy, Leo Joseph "Red" b: 1/7/1889, Terre Haute, Ind. d: 8/12/60, Racine, Wis. BR/TR, 6'1", 179 lbs. Deb: 5/2/15																								
1915	Pit-N	31	41	4	4	0	0	0	4	4	12	.098	.178	.098	275	-16	-6	0			.932	-4	C-20	-0.9
■ MIKE MURPHY Murphy, Michael Jerome b: 8/19/1888, Forestville, Pa. d: 10/26/52, Johnson City, N.Y. BR/TR, 5'9", 170 lbs. Deb: 5/17/12																								
1912	StL-N	1	1	0	0	0	0	0	1	0	0	.000	.000	.000	0	-99	-0	0			.000	0	/C-1	0.0
1916	Phi-A	14	27	0	3	0	0	0	1	1	3	.111	.143	.111	254	-25	-4	0			.973	-3	C-12	-0.8
Total	2	15	28	0	3	0	0	0	2	1	3	.107	.138	.107	245	-28	-4	0			.973	-3	/C-13	-0.8
■ MORGAN MURPHY Murphy, Morgan Edward b: 2/14/1867, E.Providence, R.I. d: 10/3/38, Providence, R.I. BR/TR, 5'8", 160 lbs. Deb: 4/22/1890 Career OF: (1-LF 3-CF 1-RF)																								
1890	Bos-P	68	246	38	56	10	2	2	32	24	31	.228	.301	.309	610	59	-15	16			.903	4	C-67/S-2,O-1C,3-1	-0.5
1891	Bos-a	106	402	60	87	11	4	4	54	36	58	.216	.289	.294	582	68	-18	17			**.954**	11	*C-104/O-4(1-2-1)	0.2
1892	Cin-N	74	234	29	46	8	2	2	24	25	57	.197	.277	.274	550	67	-9	4			.955	0	C-74	-0.2
1893	Cin-N	57	200	25	47	5	1	1	19	14	35	.235	.295	.285	580	53	-14	1			.932	-5	C-56/1-1	-1.2
1894	Cin-N	76	261	42	70	9	0	1	37	26	36	.268	.337	.314	651	56	-19	6			.901	-4	C-75/S-1,3-1	-1.3
1895	Cin-N	25	82	15	22	2	0	0	16	11	8	.268	.355	.293	648	65	-4	6			.907	-3	C-25	-0.4
1896	StL-N	49	175	12	45	5	2	0	11	8	14	.257	.290	.309	598	60	-10	1			.926	-2	C-48	-0.6
1897	StL-N	63	211	13	36	2	0	0	12	6		.171	.197	.180	377	-0	-30	1			.946	-2	C-54/1-8	-2.4
1898	Pit-N	5	16	0	2	0	0	0	2	1		.125	.176	.125	301	-14	-2	0			.957	1	/C-5	-0.1
	Phi-N	25	86	6	17	3	0	0	11	6		.198	.258	.233	491	43	-6	0			.964	0	C-25	-0.4
	Yr	30	102	6	19	3	0	0	13	7		.186	.245	.216	461	34	-9	0			.963	1	C-30	-0.5
1900	Phi-N	11	36	2	10	0	1	0	3	0		.278	.278	.333	611	69	-2	0			.980	2	C-11	0.1
1901	Phi-A	9	28	5	6	1	0	0	6	0		.214	.214	.250	464	27	-3	1			.929	0	/C-8,1-1	-0.2
Total	11	568	1977	247	444	56	12	10	227	157	239	.225	.286	.280	567	53	-132	53			.936	3	C-552/1-10,O-5C,S3	-7.0
■ PAT MURPHY Murphy, Patrick J. b: 1/2/1857, Auburn, Mass. d: 5/16/27, Worcester, Mass. TR, 5'10", 160 lbs. Deb: 9/2/1887																								
1887	NY-N	17	58	4	14	2	0	0	4	2	4	.241	.241	.250	491	38	-5	1			.847	2	C-17	-0.2
1888	*NY-N	28	106	11	18	1	0	0	4	6	11	.170	.214	.179	394	27	-8	3			.913	3	C-28	-0.3
1889	NY-N	9	28	5	10	1	1	1	4	2	0	.357	.400	.571	971	170	2	0			.872	-2	/C-9	0.1
1890	NY-N	32	119	14	28	5	1	0	9	14	13	.235	.321	.294	615	79	-3	3			.905	-5	C-29/O-3(1-1-1),S-1	-0.5
Total	4	86	311	34	70	9	2	1	21	24	28	.225	.278	.272	550	64	-13	7			.895	-3	/C-83,O-3(1-1-1),S-1	-0.9
■ DICK MURPHY Murphy, Richard Lee b: 10/25/31, Cincinnati, Ohio BL/TL, 5'11", 170 lbs. Deb: 6/13/54																								
1954	Cin-N	6	1	1	0	0	0	0	0	0	1	.000	.000	.000	0	-97	-0	0	0	0	.000	0	H	0.0
■ BUZZ MURPHY Murphy, Robert R. b: 4/26/1895, Denver, Colo. d: 5/11/38, Denver, Colo. BL/TL, 5'8.5", 155 lbs. Deb: 7/14/18																								
1918	Bos-N	9	32	6	12	2	3	1	9	3	5	.375	.429	.719	1147	259	6	0			1.000	-2	/O-9(9-0-0)	0.4

YEAR	TM/L	G	AB	R	H	2B	3B	HR	RBI	BB	SO	AVG	OBP	SLG	OPS	OPS+	BR+	SB	CS	SBR	FA	FR	G/POS	TPR
1919	Was-A	79	252	19	66	7	4	0	28	19	32	.262	.326	.321	648	83	-5	5			.959	2	O-73(19-54-0)	-0.8
Total	2	88	284	25	78	9	7	1	37	22	37	.275	.338	.366	704	101	0	5			.961	0	/O-82(28-54-0)	-0.4

■ BILLY MURPHY

Murphy, William Eugene b: 5/7/44, Pineville, La. BR/TR, 6'1", 190 lbs. Deb: 4/15/66

YEAR	TM/L	G	AB	R	H	2B	3B	HR	RBI	BB	SO	AVG	OBP	SLG	OPS	OPS+	BR+	SB	CS	SBR	FA	FR	G/POS	TPR
1966	NY-N	84	135	15	31	4	1	3	13	7	34	.230	.273	.341	613	71	-5	1	2	-0	.955	-9	O-57(8-48-1)	-1.7

■ WILLIE MURPHY

Murphy, William H. "Gentle Willie" b: 3/23/1864, Springfield, Mass. BL, 5'11", 198 lbs. Deb: 5/1/1884

YEAR	TM/L	G	AB	R	H	2B	3B	HR	RBI	BB	SO	AVG	OBP	SLG	OPS	OPS+	BR+	SB	CS	SBR	FA	FR	G/POS	TPR
1884	Cle-N	42	168	18	38	3	3	1	9	1	23	.226	.231	.298	528	63	-7				.720	-5	O-42(34-3-5)	-1.2
	Was-a	5	21	3	10	0	0	0		1		.476	.542	.476	1018	266	4				.700	-0	/O-4(4-0-0),2-1	0.3
Total	1	47	189	21	48	3	3	1	9	2	23	.254	.269	.317	587	83	-3				.718	-5	/O-46(38-3-5),2-1	-0.9

■ YALE MURPHY

Murphy, William Henry "Tot" or "Midget" b: 11/11/1869, Southville, Mass.
d: 2/14/06, Southville, Mass. BL/TR, 5'3", 125 lbs. Deb: 4/19/1894 Career OF: (30-LF 2-CF 22-RF)

YEAR	TM/L	G	AB	R	H	2B	3B	HR	RBI	BB	SO	AVG	OBP	SLG	OPS	OPS+	BR+	SB	CS	SBR	FA	FR	G/POS	TPR
1894	*NY-N	75	283	65	77	6	2	0	28	52	23	.272	.385	.307	692	69	-12	28			.898	-12	S-49,O-21R/3-3,21	-1.7
1895	NY-N	51	184	35	37	6	2	0	16	27	13	.201	.303	.255	559	46	-14	7			.944	-4	O-33L/S-8,3-8,2-1	-1.7
1897	NY-N	5	8	1	0	0	0	0	1	2		.000	.200	.000	200	-46	-2	0			.800	-2	/S-3,2-2	-0.3
Total	3	131	475	101	114	12	4	0	45	81	36	.240	.351	.282	633	59	-28	35			.890	-18	/S-60,O-54L,3-11,21	-3.7

■ TONY MURRAY

Murray, Anthony Joseph b: 4/30/04, Chicago, Ill. d: 3/19/74, Chicago, Ill. BR/TR, 5'10.5", 154 lbs. Deb: 10/6/23

YEAR	TM/L	G	AB	R	H	2B	3B	HR	RBI	BB	SO	AVG	OBP	SLG	OPS	OPS+	BR+	SB	CS	SBR	FA	FR	G/POS	TPR
1923	Chi-N	2	4	0	1	0	0	0	0	0	0	.250	.400	.250	650	75	-0	0	0	0	1.000	-2	/O-2(1-2-1)	-0.2

■ CALVIN MURRAY

Murray, Calvin Duane b: 7/30/71, Dallas, Tex. BR/TR, 5'11", 190 lbs. Deb: 6/22/99

YEAR	TM/L	G	AB	R	H	2B	3B	HR	RBI	BB	SO	AVG	OBP	SLG	OPS	OPS+	BR+	SB	CS	SBR	FA	FR	G/POS	TPR
1999	SF-N	15	19	1	5	2	0	0	5	2	4	.263	.333	.368	702	83	-0	1	0	0	1.000	-3	/O-9(3-6-0)	-0.3
2000	*SF-N	108	194	35	47	12	1	2	22	29	33	.242	.350	.345	695	82	-5	9	3	1	.980	-20	*O-106(2-104-0)	-2.2
Total	2	123	213	36	52	14	1	2	27	31	37	.244	.348	.347	696	82	-5	10	3	1	.981	-22	O-115(5-110-0)	-2.5

■ EDDIE MURRAY

Murray, Eddie Clarence b: 2/24/56, Los Angeles, Cal. BB/TR, 6'2", 200 lbs. Deb: 4/7/77 FC

YEAR	TM/L	G	AB	R	H	2B	3B	HR	RBI	BB	SO	AVG	OBP	SLG	OPS	OPS+	BR+	SB	CS	SBR	FA	FR	G/POS	TPR
1977	Bal-A	160	611	81	173	29	2	27	88	48	104	.283	.336	.470	806	125	19	0	1	-0	.992	-4	*D-111,1-42/O-3L	0.8
1978	Bal-A☆	161	610	85	174	32	3	27	95	70	97	.285	.360	.480	840	143	34	6	5	-0	.997	1	*1-157/3-3,D-1	2.5
1979	*Bal-A	159	606	90	179	30	2	25	99	72	78	.295	.372	.475	847	132	27	10	2	2	.994	-1	*1-157/D-2	1.7
1980	Bal-A	158	621	100	186	36	2	32	116	54	71	.300	.357	.519	876	138	31	7	2	1	.994	-9	*1-154/D-1	1.2
1981	Bal-A★	99	378	57	111	21	2	**22**	**78**	40	43	.294	.363	.534	897	156	26	2	3	-1	**.999**	10	1-99	3.0
1982	Bal-A★	151	550	87	174	30	1	32	110	70	82	.316	.395	.549	944	157	43	7	2	1	**.997**	1	*1-149/D-2	3.5
1983	*Bal-A★	156	582	115	178	30	3	33	111	86	90	.306	.398	.538	936	**158**	**47**	5	1	1	.993	4	*1-153/D-2	4.1
1984	Bal-A★	162	588	97	180	26	3	29	110	**107**	87	.306	**.415**	.509	923	157	**50**	10	2	2	.992	8	*1-159/D-3	4.9
1985	Bal-A★	156	583	111	173	37	1	31	124	84	68	.297	.387	.523	910	151	42	5	2	0	.987	13	*1-154/D-2	4.3
1986	Bal-A☆	137	495	61	151	25	1	17	84	78	49	.305	.400	.463	862	136	27	3	0	1	.989	-3	*1-119,D-16	1.7
1987	Bal-A	160	618	89	171	28	3	30	91	73	80	.277	.353	.477	830	121	18	1	2	-0	.993	12	*1-156/D-4	1.9
1988	Bal-A	161	603	75	171	27	2	28	84	75	78	.284	.363	.474	837	136	29	5	2	0	.989	10	*1-103,D-58	3.0
1989	LA-N	160	594	66	147	29	1	20	88	87	85	.247	.346	.401	746	115	13	7	2	1	**.996**	13	*1-159/3-2	1.6
1990	LA-N	155	558	96	184	22	3	26	95	82	64	.330	.417	.520	936	160	48	8	5	0	.992	4	*1-150	4.2
1991	LA-N★	153	576	69	150	23	1	19	96	55	74	.260	.325	.403	728	106	4	10	3	1	.995	9	*1-149/3-1	0.3
1992	NY-N	156	551	64	144	37	2	16	93	66	74	.261	.340	.423	763	117	12	4	2	0	.991	-4	*1-154	-0.3
1993	NY-N	154	610	77	174	28	1	27	100	40	61	.285	.329	.467	796	112	8	2	2	-0	.988	-1	*1-154	-0.8
1994	Cle-A	108	433	57	110	21	1	17	76	31	53	.254	.304	.425	729	85	-11	8	4	0	.988	-2	D-82,1-26	-1.8
1995	*Cle-A	113	436	68	141	21	0	21	82	39	65	.323	.379	.516	895	128	18	5	1	1	.984	3	D-95,1-18	1.3
1996	Cle-A	88	336	33	88	9	1	12	45	34	45	.262	.330	.402	732	84	-8	3	0	1	1.000	0	D-87/1-1	-1.2
	*Bal-A	64	230	36	59	12	0	10	34	27	42	.257	.335	.439	774	94	-2	1	0	0	.000	0	D-62	-0.5
	Yr	152	566	69	147	21	1	22	79	61	87	.260	.332	.417	749	88	-11	4	0	1	1.000	0	*D-149/1-1	-1.7
1997	Ana-A	46	160	13	35	7	0	3	15	13	24	.219	.277	.319	596	55	-11	1	0	0	.000	0	D-45	-1.3
	LA-N	9	7	0	2	0	0	0	3	2	2	.286	.444	.286	730	104	0	0	0	0	.000	0	/H	0.0
Total	21	3026	11336	1627	3255	560	35	504	1917	1333	1516	.287	.363	.476	839	130	463	110	43	9	.993	63	*1-2413,D-573/3-6,O	34.1

■ ED MURRAY

Murray, Edward Francis b: 5/8/1895, Mystic, Conn. d: 11/8/70, Cheyenne, Wyoming BR/TR, 5'6", 145 lbs. Deb: 6/24/17

YEAR	TM/L	G	AB	R	H	2B	3B	HR	RBI	BB	SO	AVG	OBP	SLG	OPS	OPS+	BR+	SB	CS	SBR	FA	FR	G/POS	TPR
1917	StL-A	1	1	0	0	0	0	0	0	0	1	.000	.000	.000	0	-99	-0	0			.000	0	/S-1	0.0

■ GLENN MURRAY

Murray, Glenn Everett b: 11/23/70, Manning, S.C. BR/TR, 6'2", 225 lbs. Deb: 5/10/96

YEAR	TM/L	G	AB	R	H	2B	3B	HR	RBI	BB	SO	AVG	OBP	SLG	OPS	OPS+	BR+	SB	CS	SBR	FA	FR	G/POS	TPR
1996	Phi-N	38	97	8	19	3	0	2	6	7	36	.196	.250	.289	539	41	-8	1	1	-0	1.000	1	O-27(1-2-24)	-0.9

■ JIM MURRAY

Murray, James Oscar b: 1/16/1878, Galveston, Tex. d: 4/25/45, Galveston, Tex. BR/TL, 5'10", 180 lbs. Deb: 9/2/02

YEAR	TM/L	G	AB	R	H	2B	3B	HR	RBI	BB	SO	AVG	OBP	SLG	OPS	OPS+	BR+	SB	CS	SBR	FA	FR	G/POS	TPR
1902	Chi-N	12	47	3	8	0	0	0	1	2		.170	.204	.170	374	16	-5	0			1.000	-1	O-12(0-0-12)	-0.6
1911	StL-A	31	102	8	19	5	0	3	11	5		.186	.224	.324	548	54	-7	0			.935	-0	O-25(0-1-24)	-0.8
1914	Bos-N	39	112	10	26	4	2	0	12	6	24	.232	.277	.304	581	73	-4	2			.941	-8	O-32(18-1-13)	-1.4
Total	3	82	261	21	53	9	2	3	24	13	24	.203	.244	.287	531	56	-16	2			.949	-9	/O-69(18-2-49)	-2.8

■ MIAH MURRAY

Murray, Jeremiah J. b: 1/1/1865, Boston, Mass. d: 1/11/22, Boston, Mass. BR/TR, 5'11.5", 170 lbs. Deb: 5/17/1884 U

YEAR	TM/L	G	AB	R	H	2B	3B	HR	RBI	BB	SO	AVG	OBP	SLG	OPS	OPS+	BR+	SB	CS	SBR	FA	FR	G/POS	TPR
1884	Pro-N	8	27	1	5	0	0	0	1	1	8	.185	.214	.185	399	27	-2				.836	-4	/C-7,O-1(0-1-0),1-1	-0.6
1885	Lou-a	12	43	4	8	0	0	0	3	2		.186	.239	.186	425	36	-3				.863	1	C-12/1-2	-0.1
1888	Was-N	12	42	1	4	1	0	0	3	1	7	.095	.116	.119	235	-26	-6	0			.912	-0	C-10/1-2	-0.5
1891	Was-a	2	8	0	0	0	0	0	0	0	1	.000	.000	.000	0	-99	-2	0			1.000	3	/C-2	0.1
Total	4	34	120	6	17	1	0	0	7	4	16	.142	.176	.150	326	3	-13	0			.884	-1	/C-31,1-5,O-1(0-1-0)	-1.1

■ RED MURRAY

Murray, John Joseph b: 3/4/1884, Arnot, Pa. d: 12/4/58, Sayre, Pa. BR/TR, 5'10.5", 190 lbs. Deb: 6/16/06 Career OF: (318-LF 149-CF 718-RF)

YEAR	TM/L	G	AB	R	H	2B	3B	HR	RBI	BB	SO	AVG	OBP	SLG	OPS	OPS+	BR+	SB	CS	SBR	FA	FR	G/POS	TPR
1906	StL-N	46	144	18	37	9	7	1	16	9		.257	.305	.438	743	137	5	5			.962	-3	O-34(4-11-20)/C-7	0.2
1907	StL-N	132	485	46	127	10	10	7	46	24		.262	.301	.367	668	113	5	23			.935	5	*O-131(124-1-6)	0.2
1908	StL-N	154	593	64	167	19	15	7	62	37		.282	.332	.400	732	140	25	48			.914	-4	*O-154(0-89-67)	1.5
1909	NY-N	149	570	74	150	15	12	**7**	91	45		.263	.319	.368	688	112	6	48			.947	3	*O-149(29-0-120)	0.2
1910	NY-N	149	553	78	153	27	8	4	87	52	51	.277	.345	.376	721	110	7	57			.948	4	*O-148(24-0-124)	0.4
1911	*NY-N	140	488	70	142	27	15	3	78	43	37	.291	.354	.426	781	114	8	48			.954	-11	*O-131(50-2-83)	-0.9
1912	*NY-N	143	549	83	152	26	20	3	92	27	45	.277	.320	.413	734	97	-5	38			**.968**	2	*O-143(27-0-117)	-1.0
1913	*NY-N	147	520	70	139	21	3	2	59	34	28	.267	.320	.331	650	85	-10	35			.965	10	*O-147(32-1-116)	-0.8
1914	NY-N	86	139	19	31	6	3	0	23	9	7	.223	.270	.309	580	75	-5	11			1.000	-10	O-49(16-0-34)	-1.7
1915	NY-N	45	127	12	28	1	2	3	11	7	15	.220	.261	.331	592	83	-3	2	3	-1	.959	-1	O-34(1-30-3)	-0.7
	Chi-N	51	144	20	43	6	1	0	11	8	8	.299	.340	.354	694	110	2	6	5	-0	.966	1	O-40(7-11-25)/2-1	0.1
	Yr	96	271	32	71	7	3	3	22	15	23	.262	.303	.343	646	98	-1	8	8	-1	.963	1	O-74(8-41-28)/2-1	-0.6
1917	NY-N	22	22	1	1	1	0	0	3	4	3	.045	.192	.091	283	-12	-3	0			1.000	-3	O-11(4-4-3)/C-1	-0.7
Total	11	1264	4334	555	1170	168	96	37	579	299	194	.270	.323	.379	702	108	31	321	8		.950	-6	*O-1171R/C-8,2-1	-3.2

■ LARRY MURRAY

Murray, Larry b: 4/1/53, Chicago, Ill. BB/TR, 5'11", 179 lbs. Deb: 9/7/74 Career OF: (59-LF 56-CF 84-RF)

YEAR	TM/L	G	AB	R	H	2B	3B	HR	RBI	BB	SO	AVG	OBP	SLG	OPS	OPS+	BR+	SB	CS	SBR	FA	FR	G/POS	TPR
1974	NY-A	6	1	1	0	0	0	0	0	0	0	.000	.000	.000	0	-99	-0	0	1	-0	.000	-2	/O-3(1-1-2)	-0.3
1975	NY-A	6	1	1	0	0	0	0	0	0	0	.000	.000	.000	0	-99	-0	0	0	0	1.000	-2	/O-4(2-1-1)	-0.2
1976	NY-A	8	10	2	1	0	0	0	2	1	2	.100	.182	.100	282	-16	-1	2	0	0	1.000	-1	/O-7(0-6-1)	-0.2
1977	Oak-A	90	162	19	29	5	2	1	9	17	36	.179	.257	.253	510	40	-13	12	3	2	.992	-13	O-78C/S-1,D-3	-2.6
1978	Oak-A	11	12	1	1	0	0	0	0	3	2	.083	.267	.083	350	3	-1	0	0	0	1.000	-1	/O-6(5-0-1)	-0.3
1979	Oak-A	105	226	25	42	11	2	2	20	28	34	.186	.276	.279	554	53	-15	6	6	-1	.963	-1	O-90(24-12-57)/2-3	-1.9
Total	6	226	412	49	73	16	4	3	31	49	74	.177	.265	.257	522	44	-32	20	10	1	.975	-20	O-188R/2-3,D-3,S-1	-5.5

■ RAY MURRAY

Murray, Raymond Lee "Deacon" b: 10/12/17, Spring Hope, N.C. BR/TR, 6'3", 204 lbs. Deb: 4/25/48

YEAR	TM/L	G	AB	R	H	2B	3B	HR	RBI	BB	SO	AVG	OBP	SLG	OPS	OPS+	BR+	SB	CS	SBR	FA	FR	G/POS	TPR
1948	Cle-A	4	4	0	0	0	0	0	0	0	3	.000	.000	.000	0	-99	-1	0	0	0	.000	0	H	-0.1
1950	Cle-A	55	139	16	38	8	2	1	13	12	13	.273	.331	.381	712	85	-4	1	0	0	.972	-5	C-45	-0.6
1951	Cle-A	1	1	0	1	0	0	0	1	0	0	1.000	1.000	1.000	2000	468	1	0	0	0	1.000	1	/C-1	0.1
	Phi-A	40	122	10	26	6	0	0	13	14	8	.213	.294	.262	556	50	-8	0	0	0	.985	-3	C-39	-0.9

YEAR	TM/L	G	AB	R	H	2B	3B	HR	RBI	BB	SO	AVG	OBP	SLG	OPS	OPS+	BR+	SB	CS	SBR	FA	FR	G/POS	TPR
	Yr	41	123	10	27	6	0	0	14	14	8	.220	.299	.268	568	53	-8	0	0	0	.986	-2	C-40	-0.8
1952	Phi-A	44	136	14	28	5	0	1	10	9	13	.206	.255	.265	520	42	-11	0	0	0	.995	7	C-42	-0.1
1953	Phi-A	84	268	25	76	14	3	6	41	18	25	.284	.331	.425	756	99	-1	0	0	0	.989	4	C-78	0.6
1954	Bal-A	22	61	4	15	4	1	0	2	2	5	.246	.270	.344	614	73	-3	0	0	0	.989	1	C-21	-0.1
Total	6	250	731	69	184	37	6	8	80	55	67	.252	.305	.352	657	75	-27	1	0	0	.987	6	C-226	-1.1

■ RICH MURRAY Murray, Richard Dale b: 7/6/57, Los Angeles, Cal. BR/TR, 6'4", 195 lbs. Deb: 6/7/80 F

YEAR	TM/L	G	AB	R	H	2B	3B	HR	RBI	BB	SO	AVG	OBP	SLG	OPS	OPS+	BR+	SB	CS	SBR	FA	FR	G/POS	TPR
1980	SF-N	53	194	19	42	8	2	4	24	11	48	.216	.259	.340	599	67	-9	2	1	0	.987	0	1-53	-1.3
1983	SF-N	4	10	0	2	0	0	0	1	0	3	.200	.200	.200	400	11	-1	0	0	0	1.000	-0	/1-3	-0.2
Total	2	57	204	19	44	8	2	4	25	11	51	.216	.256	.333	589	65	-10	2	1	0	.988	0	/1-56	-1.5

■ BOBBY MURRAY Murray, Robert Hayes b: 7/4/1894, St.Albans, Vt. d: 1/4/79, Nashua, N.H. BL/TR, 5'7", 155 lbs. Deb: 9/24/23

YEAR	TM/L	G	AB	R	H	2B	3B	HR	RBI	BB	SO	AVG	OBP	SLG	OPS	OPS+	BR+	SB	CS	SBR	FA	FR	G/POS	TPR
1923	Was-A	10	37	2	7	1	0	0	2	1	4	.189	.211	.216	427	13	-5	1	0	0	1.000	2	3-10	-0.2

■ TOM MURRAY Murray, Thomas W. b: 1866, Savannah, Ga. BR, 5'7", 150 lbs. Deb: 6/20/1894

YEAR	TM/L	G	AB	R	H	2B	3B	HR	RBI	BB	SO	AVG	OBP	SLG	OPS	OPS+	BR+	SB	CS	SBR	FA	FR	G/POS	TPR
1894	Phi-N	1	2	0	0	0	0	0	0	0	2	.000	.000	.000	0	-99	-1	0			.833	0	/S-1	0.0

■ BILL MURRAY Murray, William Allenwood "Dasher" b: 9/6/1893, Vinalhaven, Me. d: 9/14/43, Boston, Mass. BB/TR, 5'11", 165 lbs. Deb: 6/27/17

YEAR	TM/L	G	AB	R	H	2B	3B	HR	RBI	BB	SO	AVG	OBP	SLG	OPS	OPS+	BR+	SB	CS	SBR	FA	FR	G/POS	TPR
1917	Was-A	8	21	2	3	0	1	0	4	2	2	.143	.217	.238	455	39	-2	1			.889	-2	/2-6,S-1	-0.4

■ IVAN MURRELL Murrell, Ivan Augustus (Peters) b: 4/24/45, Almirante, Panama BR/TR, 6'2", 196 lbs. Deb: 9/28/63 Career OF: (175-LF 112-CF 73-RF)

YEAR	TM/L	G	AB	R	H	2B	3B	HR	RBI	BB	SO	AVG	OBP	SLG	OPS	OPS+	BR+	SB	CS	SBR	FA	FR	G/POS	TPR
1963	Hou-N	2	5	1	1	0	0	0	0	0	2	.200	.200	.200	400	17	-1	0	0	0	1.000	-0	/O-2(0-2-0)	-0.1
1964	Hou-N	10	14	1	2	1	0	0	1	0	6	.143	.143	.214	357	-1	-2	0	0	0	1.000	-1	/O-5(4-0-1)	-0.4
1967	Hou-N	10	29	2	9	0	0	0	1	1	9	.310	.333	.310	644	88	-0	1	0	0	.846	-0	/O-6(5-0-1)	-0.1
1968	Hou-N	32	59	3	6	1	1	0	3	1	17	.102	.117	.153	269	-20	-9	0	0	0	.931	2	O-15(4-2-9)	-0.9
1969	SD-N	111	247	19	63	10	6	3	25	11	65	.255	.292	.381	673	91	-4	3	4	-1	.959	-3	O-72(23-41-14)/1-2	-1.1
1970	SD-N	125	347	43	85	9	3	12	35	17	93	.245	.288	.392	680	84	-10	9	7	-0	.970	3	*O-101(61-24-20)/1-1	-1.1
1971	SD-N	103	255	23	60	6	3	7	24	7	60	.235	.264	.365	629	82	-7	5	2	0	.978	0	O-72(55-16-2)	-1.1
1972	SD-N	5	7	0	1	0	0	0	1	0	3	.143	.143	.143	286	-20	-1	0	0	0	1.000	0	/O-1(0-0-1)	-0.1
1973	SD-N	93	210	23	48	13	1	9	21	2	52	.229	.236	.429	664	87	-5	2	0	0	.959	-1	O-37(10-18-12),1-24	-0.9
1974	Atl-N	73	133	11	33	1	1	2	12	5	35	.248	.275	.316	591	62	-7	0	0	0	.983	-1	O-32(13-9-13),1-13	-1.0
Total	10	564	1306	126	308	41	15	33	123	44	342	.236	.266	.366	632	77	-46	20	13	-0	.965	-2	O-343L/1-40	-6.8

■ DANNY MURTAUGH Murtaugh, Daniel Edward b: 10/8/17, Chester, Pa. d: 12/2/76, Chester, Pa. BR/TR, 5'9", 165 lbs. Deb: 7/6/41 MC

YEAR	TM/L	G	AB	R	H	2B	3B	HR	RBI	BB	SO	AVG	OBP	SLG	OPS	OPS+	BR+	SB	CS	SBR	FA	FR	G/POS	TPR
1941	Phi-N	85	347	34	76	8	1	0	11	26	31	.219	.275	.248	523	50	-23	**18**			.978	2	2-85/S-1	-1.6
1942	Phi-N	144	506	48	122	16	4	0	27	49	39	.241	.311	.289	599	80	-12	13			.939	6	S-60,3-53,2-32	0.2
1943	Phi-N	113	451	65	123	17	4	1	35	57	23	.273	.357	.335	692	104	4	4			.974	0	*2-113	1.2
1946	Phi-N	6	19	1	4	1	0	1	3	2	2	.211	.286	.421	707	102	-0	0			.958	-4	/2-6	-0.4
1947	Bos-N	3	8	0	1	0	0	0	0	1	2	.125	.222	.125	347	-6	-1	0			1.000	-0	/2-2,3-2	-0.1
1948	Pit-N	146	514	56	149	21	5	1	71	60	40	.290	.365	.356	721	94	-2	10			.979	1	*2-146	0.7
1949	Pit-N	75	236	16	48	7	2	2	24	29	17	.203	.291	.275	566	51	-16	2			.975	3	2-74	-0.9
1950	Pit-N	118	367	34	108	20	5	2	37	47	42	.294	.376	.392	768	99	1	2			.976	3	*2-108	1.0
1951	Pit-N	77	151	9	30	7	0	1	11	16	19	.199	.284	.265	549	47	-11	0	0	0	.970	-2	2-65/3-3	-1.1
Total	9	767	2599	263	661	97	21	8	219	287	215	.254	.331	.317	648	81	-61	49	0		.975	10	2-631/S-61,3-58	-1.0

■ TONY MUSER Muser, Anthony Joseph b: 8/1/47, Van Nuys, Cal. BL/TL, 6'2", 190 lbs. Deb: 9/14/69 MC Career OF: (15-LF 10-CF 1-RF)

YEAR	TM/L	G	AB	R	H	2B	3B	HR	RBI	BB	SO	AVG	OBP	SLG	OPS	OPS+	BR+	SB	CS	SBR	FA	FR	G/POS	TPR
1969	Bos-A	2	9	0	1	0	0	0	1	0	1	.111	.200	.111	311	-10	-1	0	0	0	1.000	1	/1-2	-0.1
1971	Chi-A	11	16	2	5	0	1	0	0	1	1	.313	.353	.438	790	119	0	0	0	0	.963	0	/1-4	0.1
1972	Chi-A	44	61	6	17	2	2	1	9	2	6	.279	.302	.426	728	113	1	1	1	-0	.986	-0	1-29/O-1(0-0-1)	-0.1
1973	Chi-A	109	309	38	88	14	3	4	30	33	36	.285	.354	.388	742	105	3	8	4	0	.992	-3	1-89,D-13/O-2(2-0-0)	-0.6
1974	Chi-A	103	206	16	60	5	1	1	18	6	22	.291	.315	.340	654	86	-4	1	4	-1	.998	-4	1-80,D-13	-1.3
1975	Chi-A	43	111	11	27	3	0	0	6	7	8	.243	.288	.270	558	58	-6	2	1	0	.993	2	1-41	-0.7
	Bal-A	80	82	11	26	3	0	0	11	8	9	.317	.378	.354	731	115	2	0	0	0	.996	1	1-62	0.2
	Yr	123	193	22	53	6	0	0	17	15	17	.275	.327	.306	633	83	-4	2	1	0	.994	3	*1-103	-0.5
1976	Bal-A	136	326	25	74	7	1	1	30	21	34	.227	.274	.264	538	62	-16	1	1	-0	.991	1	*1-109,O-12L,D-10	-2.3
1977	Bal-A	120	118	14	27	6	0	0	7	13	16	.229	.305	.280	585	65	-5	1	2	-0	.992	1	1-77,O-11(5-6-0)/D-1	-0.6
1978	Mil-A	15	30	0	4	1	1	0	5	3	5	.133	.212	.233	445	25	-3	0	0	0	.988	-0	1-12	-0.4
Total	9	663	1268	123	329	41	9	7	117	95	138	.259	.312	.323	634	82	-30	14	13	-1	.992	-1	1-505/D-37,O-26L	-5.8

■ STAN MUSIAL Musial, Stanley Frank "Stan The Man" b: 11/21/20, Donora, Pa. BL/TL, 6', 175 lbs. Deb: 9/17/41 H Career OF: (943-LF 325-CF 750-RF)

YEAR	TM/L	G	AB	R	H	2B	3B	HR	RBI	BB	SO	AVG	OBP	SLG	OPS	OPS+	BR+	SB	CS	SBR	FA	FR	G/POS	TPR
1941	StL-N	12	47	8	20	4	0	1	7	2	1	.426	.449	.574	1023	175	4	1			1.000	0	O-11(3-0-8)	0.4
1942	*StL-N	140	467	87	147	32	10	10	72	62	25	.315	.397	.490	888	148	29	6			.984	1	*O-135(133-2-2)	2.5
1943	*StL-N★	157	617	108	**220**	**48**	**20**	13	81	72	18	**.357**	**.425**	**.562**	**988**	**176**	**60**	9			.982	11	*O-155(34-10-117)	**6.3**
1944	*StL-N★	146	568	112	**197**	**51**	14	12	94	90	28	.347	**.440**	**.549**	**990**	**174**	**59**	7			.987	3	*O-146(1-38-124)	**5.4**
1946	*StL-N★	156	624	**124**	**228**	**50**	**20**	16	103	73	31	**.365**	.434	**.587**	**1021**	**180**	**65**	7			.989	-1	*1-114,O-42(42-0-0)	**5.9**
1947	StL-N★	149	587	113	183	30	13	19	95	80	24	.312	.398	.504	902	132	28	4			.994	-7	*1-149	1.6
1948	StL-N★	155	611	**135**	**230**	**46**	**18**	39	**131**	79	34	**.376**	**.450**	**.702**	**1152**	**196**	**81**	7			.981	-8	*O-155(41-64-76)/1-2	**6.6**
1949	StL-N★	157	612	128	**207**	**41**	**13**	36	123	107	38	.338	**.438**	.624	1062	174	65	3			**.991**	-19	*O-156(3-72-117)/1-1	4.1
1950	StL-N★	146	555	105	192	41	7	28	109	87	36	**.346**	.437	**.596**	**1034**	**161**	**51**	5			.964	-13	O-77(56-14-10),1-69	3.0
1951	StL-N★	152	578	**124**	205	30	**12**	32	108	98	40	**.355**	.449	.614	1063	**182**	**69**	4	5	-1	.974	4	O-91(84-10-1),1-60	6.2
1952	StL-N★	154	578	**105**	**194**	**42**	6	21	91	96	29	**.336**	.432	**.538**	**970**	**167**	**56**	7	7	-1	.987	-7	*O-129C,1-25/P-1	4.3
1953	StL-N★	157	593	127	200	**53**	9	30	113	**105**	32	.337	**.437**	.609	1046	169	63	3	4	-1	.984	-9	*O-157(141-9-26)	4.2
1954	StL-N★	153	591	**120**	195	**41**	9	35	126	103	39	.330	.433	.607	1040	166	60	1	7	-2	**.990**	-2	*O-152(8-0-147),1-10	4.8
1955	StL-N★	154	562	97	179	30	5	33	108	80	39	.319	.411	.566	977	156	47	5	4	-0	.992	1	*1-110,O-51(21-0-33)	3.9
1956	StL-N★	156	594	87	184	33	6	27	**109**	75	39	.310	.390	.522	912	142	36	2	0	0	.993	6	*1-103,O-53(3-0-51)	3.5
1957	StL-N★	134	502	82	176	38	3	29	102	66	34	**.351**	**.428**	.612	**1040**	172	52	1	1	-0	.992	2	*1-130	4.6
1958	StL-N★	135	472	64	159	35	2	17	62	72	26	.337	.426	.528	953	145	33	0	0	0	.989	8	*1-124	3.4
1959	StL-N★	115	341	37	87	13	2	14	44	60	25	.255	.367	.428	795	104	3	0	2	-1	.990	2	1-90/O-3(3-0-0)	0.0
1960	StL-N★	116	331	49	91	17	1	17	63	41	34	.275	.358	.486	845	118	9	1	1	-0	.990	-1	O-59(53-0-6),1-29	0.2
1961	StL-N★	123	372	46	107	22	4	15	70	52	35	.288	.376	.489	866	116	9	0	0	0	**.994**	0	*O-103(103-0-0)	0.4
1962	StL-N★	135	433	57	143	18	1	19	82	64	46	.330	.420	.508	928	135	23	3	0	1	.977	-3	*O-119(97-0-23)	1.4
1963	StL-N★	124	337	34	86	10	2	12	58	35	43	.255	.329	.404	732	100	2	2	0	0	.968	-7	O-96(96-0-0)	-1.2
Total	22	3026	10972	1949	3630	725	177	475	1951	1599	696	.331	.418	.559	977	157	902	78	31		.984	-38	*O-1890L,1-1016/P-1	71.5

■ DANNY MUSSER Musser, William Daniel b: 9/5/05, Zion, Pa. d: 3/2/2000, Upper Sandusky, O. BL/TR, 5'9.5", 160 lbs. Deb: 9/18/32

YEAR	TM/L	G	AB	R	H	2B	3B	HR	RBI	BB	SO	AVG	OBP	SLG	OPS	OPS+	BR+	SB	CS	SBR	FA	FR	G/POS	TPR
1932	Was-A	1	2	0	1	0	0	0	0	0	0	.500	.500	.500	1000	162	0	0	0	0	.000	0	/3-1	0.0

■ GEORGE MYATT Myatt, George Edward "Mercury", "Stud" or "Foghorn" b: 6/14/14, Denver, Colo. d: 9/14/2000, Orlando, Fla. BL/TR, 5'11", 167 lbs. Deb: 8/16/38 MC

YEAR	TM/L	G	AB	R	H	2B	3B	HR	RBI	BB	SO	AVG	OBP	SLG	OPS	OPS+	BR+	SB	CS	SBR	FA	FR	G/POS	TPR
1938	NY-N	43	170	27	52	2	1	3	10	14	13	.306	.362	.382	745	104	1	10			.919	7	S-24,3-19	1.1
1939	NY-N	22	53	7	10	2	0	0	3	3	6	.189	.271	.226	498	35	-5	2			.907	1	3-14	-0.4
1943	Was-A	42	53	11	13	3	0	0	3	13	7	.245	.394	.302	696	109	1	3	0	1	.930	-1	2-11/S-2,3-2	0.2
1944	Was-A	140	538	86	153	19	6	0	40	54	44	.284	.357	.342	699	105	5	26	10	2	.957	-22	*2-121,S-15/O-3R	-0.7
1945	Was-A	133	490	81	145	17	7	1	39	63	43	.296	.378	.365	744	127	19	30	11	3	.972	-19	2-94,O-32R/3-6,S-1	0.6
1946	Was-A	15	34	7	8	1	0	0	4	2	3	.235	.297	.265	562	61	-2	1	1	-0	.900	-2	/3-7,2-2	-0.4
1947	Was-A	12	7	1	0	0	0	0	0	4	4	.000	.364	.000	364	6	-1	0	0	0	1.000	0	/2-1	-0.1
Total	7	407	1345	220	381	44	14	4	99	156	120	.283	.362	.346	708	108	19	72	22		.962	-35	2-229/3-48,S-42,O	0.3

■ GLENN MYATT Myatt, Glenn Calvin b: 7/9/1897, Argenta, Ark. d: 8/9/69, Houston, Tex. BL/TR, 5'11", 165 lbs. Deb: 4/15/20

YEAR	TM/L	G	AB	R	H	2B	3B	HR	RBI	BB	SO	AVG	OBP	SLG	OPS	OPS+	BR+	SB	CS	SBR	FA	FR	G/POS	TPR
1920	Phi-A	70	196	14	49	8	3	0	18	12	22	.250	.293	.321	615	62	-11	1	3	-1	.900	-5	O-37(1-0-36),C-22	-1.7
1921	Phi-A	44	69	6	14	2	0	0	5	6	7	.203	.267	.232	499	28	-7	1	0	0	.939	2	C-27	-0.4
1923	Cle-A	92	220	36	63	7	6	3	40	16	18	.286	.338	.414	751	97	-2	0	2	-1	.934	-8	C-69	-0.6

YEAR	TM/L	G	AB	R	H	2B	3B	HR	RBI	BB	SO	AVG	OBP	SLG	OPS	OPS+	BR+	SB	CS	SBR	FA	FR	G/POS	TPR
1924	Cle-A	105	342	55	117	22	7	8	73	33	12	.342	.402	.518	919	134	16	6	1	1	.978	-15	C-95	0.8
1925	Cle-A	106	358	51	97	15	9	11	54	29	24	.271	.329	.455	784	97	-4	3	1	0	.973	-18	C-98/O-1(1-0-0)	-1.4
1926	Cle-A	56	117	14	29	5	2	0	13	13	13	.248	.323	.325	648	69	-5	1	0	0	1.000	-1	C-35	-0.4
1927	Cle-A	55	94	15	23	6	0	2	8	12	7	.245	.336	.372	709	83	-2	1	1	-0	.978	2	C-26	0.0
1928	Cle-A	58	125	9	36	7	2	1	15	13	13	.288	.355	.400	755	97	-0	0	2	-1	.967	-9	C-30	-0.8
1929	Cle-A	59	129	14	30	4	1	1	17	7	5	.233	.277	.302	580	47	-10	0	1	-0	.976	-1	C-41	-0.9
1930	Cle-A	86	265	30	78	23	2	2	37	18	17	.294	.342	.419	760	88	-5	2	3	-1	.977	-7	C-71	-0.7
1931	Cle-A	65	195	21	48	14	2	1	29	21	13	.246	.319	.354	673	73	-8	2	1	0	.991	-4	C-53	-0.8
1932	Cle-A	82	252	45	62	12	1	8	46	27	21	.246	.326	.397	723	81	-8	2	2	-0	.988	-8	C-65	-1.1
1933	Cle-A	40	77	10	18	4	0	0	7	15	8	.234	.372	.286	658	73	-2	0	1	-0	.965	-1	C-27	-0.2
1934	Cle-A	36	107	18	34	6	1	0	12	13	5	.318	.392	.393	784	101	1	1	0	0	.980	-1	C-34	0.2
1935	Cle-A	10	36	1	3	1	0	0	2	4	3	.083	.175	.111	286	-24	-7	0	0	0	1.000	-1	C-10	-0.7
	NY-N	13	18	2	4	0	1	1	6	0	3	.222	.222	.500	722	90	-0	0	0		1.000	-1	/C-4	-0.1
1936	Det-A	27	78	5	17	1	0	0	5	9	4	.218	.299	.231	530	32	-8	0	0	0	1.000	-2	C-27	-0.8
Total	16	1004	2678	346	722	137	37	38	387	248	195	.270	.334	.391	725	85	-63	20	18		.974	-78	C-734/O-38(2-0-36)	-9.6

■ BUDDY MYER

Myer, Charles Solomon b: 3/16/04, Ellisville, Miss. d: 10/31/74, Baton Rouge, La. BL/TR, 5′10.5″, 163 lbs. Deb: 9/26/25 Career OF: (12-LF 0-CF 1-RF)

YEAR	TM/L	G	AB	R	H	2B	3B	HR	RBI	BB	SO	AVG	OBP	SLG	OPS	OPS+	BR+	SB	CS	SBR	FA	FR	G/POS	TPR
1925	*Was-A	4	8	1	2	0	0	0	0	0	1	.250	.250	.250	500	28	-1	0	0	0	1.000	-2	/S-4	-0.3
1926	Was-A	132	434	66	132	18	6	1	62	45	19	.304	.370	.380	750	98	-0	10	11	-2	.928	-18	*S-118/3-8	-0.7
1927	Was-A	15	51	7	11	1	0	0	7	8	3	.216	.322	.235	557	47	-4	3	1	0	.933	-3	S-15	-0.4
	Bos-A	133	469	59	135	22	11	2	47	48	15	.288	.359	.394	753	97	-2	9	5	0	.940	7	*S-101,3-14,O-10L/2	1.6
	Yr	148	520	66	146	23	11	2	54	56	18	.281	.355	.379	734	92	-5	12	6	1	.939	4	*S-116,3-14,O-10L/2	1.2
1928	Bos-A	147	536	78	168	26	6	1	44	53	28	.313	.379	.390	769	104	5	**30**	16	1	.967	4	*3-144	1.8
1929	Was-A	141	563	80	169	29	10	3	82	63	33	.300	.373	.403	776	99	0	18	7	2	.958	-15	2-88,3-53	-0.7
1930	Was-A	138	541	97	164	18	8	2	61	58	31	.303	.373	.377	750	90	-6	14	11	-1	.965	-19	*2-134/O-2(1-0-1)	-2.0
1931	Was-A	139	591	114	173	33	11	4	56	58	42	.293	.360	.406	766	100	1	11	14	-2	**.984**	-17	*2-137	-0.9
1932	Was-A	143	577	120	161	38	16	5	52	69	33	.279	.360	.426	786	104	4	12	7	0	.975	-18	*2-139	-0.5
1933	*Was-A	131	530	95	160	29	15	4	61	60	29	.302	.374	.436	810	115	12	6	8	-1	.978	-1	*2-129	1.6
1934	Was-A	139	524	103	160	33	8	3	57	102	32	.305	.419	.416	835	121	21	6	6	-1	.975	-13	*2-135	1.6
1935	Was-A☆	151	616	115	215	36	11	5	100	96	40	**.349**	.440	.468	907	139	41	7	6	-1	.979	8	*2-151	5.3
1936	Was-A	51	156	31	42	5	2	0	15	42	11	.269	.427	.327	754	94	2	7	2	1	.985	3	2-43	0.8
1937	Was-A☆	125	430	54	126	16	10	1	65	78	41	.293	.407	.384	791	105	8	2	6	-2	.966	-17	*2-119/O-1(1-0-0)	-0.3
1938	Was-A	127	437	79	147	22	8	6	71	93	32	.336	.454	.465	918	140	33	9	5	0	**.982**	2	*2-121	3.8
1939	Was-A	83	258	33	78	10	3	1	32	40	18	.302	.396	.376	772	106	4	4	1	1	.968	-1	2-65	0.7
1940	Was-A	71	210	28	61	14	4	0	29	34	10	.290	.389	.395	785	111	5	6	3	0	.967	4	2-54	1.1
1941	Was-A	53	107	14	27	3	1	0	9	18	10	.252	.360	.299	659	80	-2	2	0	0	.982	-8	2-24	-0.8
Total	17	1923	7038	1174	2131	353	130	38	850	965	428	.303	.389	.406	795	108	121	156	109	-4	.974	-103	*2-1340,S-238,3/O	11.7

■ GEORGE MYERS

Myers, George D. b: 11/13/1860, Buffalo, N.Y. d: 12/14/26, Buffalo, N.Y. BR/TR, 5′8″, 170 lbs. Deb: 5/2/1884 Career OF: (27-LF 69-CF 14-RF)

YEAR	TM/L	G	AB	R	H	2B	3B	HR	RBI	BB	SO	AVG	OBP	SLG	OPS	OPS+	BR+	SB	CS	SBR	FA	FR	G/POS	TPR
1884	Buf-N	78	325	34	59	9	2	2	32	13	33	.182	.213	.240	453	41	-22				.837	-10	C-49,O-34(16-18-0)	-2.6
1885	Buf-N	89	326	40	67	7	2	0	19	23	40	.206	.258	.239	497	60	-14				.899	-6	C-69,O-23(0-21-1)	-1.5
1886	StL-N	79	295	26	56	7	3	0	27	18	42	.190	.236	.234	470	46	-18	6			.928	-13	C-72/O-6(0-5-1),3-1	-2.3
1887	Ind-N	69	257	25	73	8	1	1	20	22	7	.284	.298	.272	570	62	-11	26			.929	-13	C-50,O-15C/1-6,3-1	-1.8
1888	Ind-N	66	248	36	59	9	0	2	16	16	14	.238	.292	.298	591	87	-3	28			.929	-8	C-47,3-14,O-10R/1	-0.7
1889	Ind-N	43	149	22	29	3	0	0	12	17	13	.195	.294	.215	509	42	-11	12			.909	4	O-23(6-17-0),C-18/1-1	-0.6
Total	6	424	1600	183	343	43	8	5	126	109	149	.214	.260	.250	510	56	-80	72			.901	-46	C-305,O-111C/3-16,1	-9.5

■ GREG MYERS

Myers, Gregory Richard b: 4/14/66, Riverside, Cal. BL/TR, 6′2″, 205 lbs. Deb: 9/12/87

YEAR	TM/L	G	AB	R	H	2B	3B	HR	RBI	BB	SO	AVG	OBP	SLG	OPS	OPS+	BR+	SB	CS	SBR	FA	FR	G/POS	TPR
1987	Tor-A	7	9	1	1	0	0	0	0	0	3	.111	.111	.111	222	-40	-2	0	0	0	1.000	2	/C-7	0.0
1989	Tor-A	17	44	0	5	2	0	0	1	2	9	.114	.152	.159	311	-12	-7	0	1	-0	1.000	2	C-11/D-6	-0.4
1990	Tor-A	87	250	33	59	7	1	5	22	22	33	.236	.298	.332	630	75	-9	0	1	-0	.993	-0	C-87	-0.5
1991	Tor-A	107	309	25	81	22	0	8	36	21	45	.262	.309	.411	720	94	-3	0	0	0	.979	-4	*C-104	-0.2
1992	Tor-A	22	61	4	14	6	0	1	13	5	5	.230	.288	.377	665	81	-2	0	0	0	.991	0	C-18/D-1	0.0
	Cal-A	8	17	0	4	1	0	0	0	0	6	.235	.235	.294	529	47	-1	0	0	0	1.000	2	/C-8	0.1
	Yr	30	78	4	18	7	0	1	13	5	11	.231	.277	.359	636	74	-3	0	0	0	.993	2	C-26/D-1	0.1
1993	Cal-A	108	290	27	74	10	0	7	40	17	47	.255	.301	.362	663	75	-11	3	3	-0	.986	-8	C-97/D-2	-1.4
1994	Cal-A	45	126	10	31	6	0	2	8	10	27	.246	.301	.341	643	64	-7	0	2	-1	.991	-2	C-41/D-1	-0.6
1995	Cal-A	85	273	35	71	12	2	9	38	17	49	.260	.306	.418	723	87	-6	0	1	-0	.989	-4	C-61,D-16	-0.7
1996	Min-A	97	329	37	94	22	3	6	47	19	52	.286	.325	.426	750	86	-7	0	0	0	.985	-12	C-90	-1.3
1997	Min-A	62	165	24	44	11	1	5	28	16	29	.267	.331	.436	768	97	-1	0	0	0	.986	-1	C-38,D-10	-0.1
	Atl-N	9	9	0	1	0	0	0	1	1	3	.111	.200	.111	311	-16	-2	0	0	0	1.000	2	/C-2	0.0
1998	*SD-N	69	171	19	42	10	0	4	20	17	36	.246	.314	.374	688	87	-4	0	1	-0	.987	-4	C-52	-0.5
1999	SD-N	50	128	9	37	4	0	3	15	13	14	.289	.355	.391	745	96	-1	0	0	0	.986	-5	C-41	-0.4
	*Atl-N	34	72	10	16	2	0	2	9	13	16	.222	.341	.333	675	72	-3	0	0	0	.994	6	C-31	0.4
	Yr	84	200	19	53	6	0	5	24	26	30	.265	.350	.370	720	86	-4	0	0	0	.990	1	C-72	0.0
2000	Bal-A	43	125	9	28	6	0	3	12	8	29	.224	.271	.344	615	56	-9	0	0	0	1.000	1	C-28/D-8	-0.6
Total	13	850	2378	243	602	121	7	55	290	181	403	.253	.307	.379	686	80	-72	3	9	-2	.988	-26	C-716/D-44	-6.2

■ HENRY MYERS

Myers, Henry C. b: 5/1858, Philadelphia, Pa. d: 4/18/1895, Philadelphia, Pa. BR/TR, 5′9″, 159 lbs. Deb: 8/20/1881 M

YEAR	TM/L	G	AB	R	H	2B	3B	HR	RBI	BB	SO	AVG	OBP	SLG	OPS	OPS+	BR+	SB	CS	SBR	FA	FR	G/POS	TPR
1881	Pro-N	1	4	0	0	0	0	0	0	0	2	.000	.000	.000	0	-99	-1				1.000	-0	/S-1	-0.1
1882	Bal-a	69	294	43	53	3	0	0		12		.180	.212	.190	403	40	-17				.822	-7	*S-68/P-6,M	-1.9
1884	Wil-U	6	24	3	3	0	0	0		0		.125	.125	.125	250	-23	-4				.875	4	/S-5,2-1	0.0
Total	3	76	322	46	56	3	0	0	0	12	2	.174	.204	.183	387	32	-22				.826	-3	/S-74,P-6,2-1	-2.0

■ HY MYERS

Myers, Henry Harrison b: 4/27/1889, E.Liverpool, Ohio d: 5/1/65, Minerva, Ohio BR/TR, 5′9.5″, 175 lbs. Deb: 8/30/09 Career OF: (5-LF 1150-CF 28-RF)

YEAR	TM/L	G	AB	R	H	2B	3B	HR	RBI	BB	SO	AVG	OBP	SLG	OPS	OPS+	BR+	SB	CS	SBR	FA	FR	G/POS	TPR
1909	Bro-N	6	22	1	5	1	0	0	6	2		.227	.292	.273	564	78	-1	1			1.000	-1	/O-6(0-0-6)	-0.2
1911	Bro-N	13	43	2	7	1	0	0	0	2	3	.163	.200	.186	386	9	-5	1			.889	-2	O-13(0-12-1)	-0.8
1914	Bro-N	70	227	35	65	3	9	0	17	7	24	.286	.316	.379	695	104	0	2			.964	-6	O-60(4-45-12)	-1.0
1915	Bro-N	153	605	69	150	21	7	2	46	17	51	.248	.275	.316	591	77	-18	19	22	-4	.964	7	*O-153(0-153-0)	-2.8
1916	*Bro-N	113	412	54	108	12	14	3	36	21	35	.262	.308	.381	689	108	3	17			.969	1	*O-106(0-105-1)	-0.4
1917	Bro-N	120	471	37	126	15	10	1	41	18	25	.268	.294	.348	643	94	-4	5			.982	-3	O-66C,1-22,2-19,3	-1.3
1918	Bro-N	107	407	36	104	9	8	4	40	20	26	.256	.292	.346	638	95	-4	17			.975	13	*O-107(0-107-0)	0.2
1919	Bro-N	133	512	62	157	23	**14**	5	**73**	23	34	.307	.339	**.436**	774	129	16	13			.979	9	*O-131(0-131-0)	1.8
1920	*Bro-N	154	582	83	177	36	**22**	4	80	35	54	.304	.345	.462	807	126	18	9	13	-3	.978	4	*O-152(0-152-0)/3-2	1.0
1921	Bro-N	144	549	51	158	14	4	4	68	22	51	.288	.318	.350	667	74	-20	8	6	-0	.968	6	*O-124C,2-21/3-1	-1.9
1922	Bro-N	153	618	82	196	20	9	6	89	13	26	.317	.331	.408	739	90	-10	9	10	-2	.974	6	*O-152(0-152-0)/2-1	-1.2
1923	StL-N	96	330	29	99	18	2	2	48	12	19	.300	.330	.385	715	90	-5	5	3	0	.977	6	O-87(0-87-0)	-0.2
1924	StL-N	43	124	12	26	5	1	1	15	3	10	.210	.228	.290	519	39	-11	1	2	-0	.945	-3	O-22(1-17-4),3-12/2-3	-1.5
1925	StL-N	1	1	0	0	0	0	0	0	0	0	.000	.000	.000	0	-98	-0	0	0	0	.000	0	H	0.0
	Cin-N	3	6	1	1	1	0	0	0	0	0	.167	.167	.333	500	25	-1	0	0	0	1.000	-1	/O-3(0-3-0)	-0.1
	StL-N	1	1	1	1	0	0	0	0	0	0	1.000	1.000	1.000	2000	403	0	0	0	0	.000	0	H	0.0
	Yr	5	8	2	2	1	0	0	0	0	0	.250	.250	.375	625	58	-1	0	0	0	1.000	-1	/O-3(0-3-0)	-0.1
Total	14	1310	4910	555	1380	179	100	32	559	195	358	.281	.312	.378	690	95	-42	107	56		.972	39	*O-1182C/2-44,3-30,1	-8.4

■ BERT MYERS

Myers, James Albert b: 4/8/1874, Frederick, Md. d: 10/12/15, Washington, D.C. BR/TR, 5′10″, Deb: 4/25/1896

YEAR	TM/L	G	AB	R	H	2B	3B	HR	RBI	BB	SO	AVG	OBP	SLG	OPS	OPS+	BR+	SB	CS	SBR	FA	FR	G/POS	TPR
1896	StL-N	122	454	47	116	12	8	0	37	40	32	.256	.320	.317	637	71	-18	8			.867	-9	*3-121/S-1	-2.2
1898	Was-N	31	110	14	29	1	4	0	13	13		.264	.341	.345	687	97	-0	2			.835	-3	3-31	-0.2
1900	Phi-N	7	28	5	5	1	0	0	2	3		.179	.258	.214	472	31	-3	1			.909	2	/3-7	-0.1
Total	3	160	592	66	150	14	12	0	52	56	32	.253	.321	.318	639	74	-21	11			.863	-10	3-159/S-1	-2.5

YEAR	TM/L	G	AB	R	H	2B	3B	HR	RBI	BB	SO	AVG	OBP	SLG	OPS	OPS+	BR+	SB	CS	SBR	FA	FR	G/POS	TPR
■ AL MYERS	Myers, James Albert "Cod" b: 10/22/1863, Danville, Ill. d: 12/24/27, Marshall, Ill. BR/TR, 5'8.5", 165 lbs. Deb: 9/27/1884																							
1884	Mil-U	12	46	6	15	6	0	0		0		.326	.326	.457	783	249	7				.848	2	2-12	0.8
1885	Phi-N	93	357	25	73	13	2	1	28	11	41	.204	.228	.261	489	59	-16				.884	-18	*2-93	-2.9
1886	KC-N	118	473	69	131	22	9	4	51	22	42	.277	.309	.387	696	104	1	3			.913	2	*2-118	0.6
1887	Was-N	105	402	45	124	9	5	2	36	40	26	.308	.312	.301	613	75	-10	18			.909	-5	2-78,S-27	-1.0
1888	Was-N	132	502	46	104	12	7	2	46	37	46	.207	.270	.271	541	77	-11	20			.918	-25	*2-132	-3.1
1889	Was-N	46	176	24	46	3	0	0	20	22	7	.261	.347	.278	625	81	-3	10			.942	3	2-46	0.2
	Phi-N	75	305	52	82	14	2	0	28	36	9	.269	.354	.328	681	84	-6	8			.853	-8	2-75	-1.0
	Yr	121	481	76	128	17	2	0	48	58	16	.266	.351	.310	661	83	-9	18			.886	-4	*2-121	-0.8
1890	Phi-N	117	487	95	135	29	7	2	81	57	46	.277	.365	.378	742	114	9	44			.948	14	*2-117	2.4
1891	Phi-N	135	514	67	118	27	2	2	69	69	46	.230	.331	.302	633	83	-10	8			.937	-10	*2-135	-1.3
Total	8	833	3262	429	828	135	34	13	359	294	263	.254	.314	.320	634	88	-41	111			.914	-43	2-806/S-27	-5.3
■ LYNN MYERS	Myers, Lynnwood Lincoln b: 2/23/14, Enola, Pa. d: 1/19/2000, Harrisburg, Pa. BR/TR, 5'6.5", 145 lbs. Deb: 7/13/38 F																							
1938	StL-N	70	227	18	55	10	2	1	19	9	25	.242	.271	.317	588	58	-13	9			.944	-1	S-69	-1.0
1939	StL-N	74	117	24	28	6	1	0	10	12	23	.239	.310	.308	618	63	-6	1			.897	5	S-36,3-13/2-5	0.1
Total	2	144	344	42	83	16	3	1	29	21	48	.241	.285	.314	599	60	-19	10			.930	4	S-105/3-13,2-5	-0.9
■ HAP MYERS	Myers, Ralph Edward b: 4/8/1888, San Francisco, Cal. d: 6/30/67, San Francisco, Cal. BR/TR, 6'3", 175 lbs. Deb: 4/16/10																							
1910	Bos-A	3	6	0	2	0	0	0	0	0		.333	.333	.333	667	106	0	0			1.000	0	/O-2(0-0-2)	0.0
1911	StL-A	11	37	4	11	1	0	0	1	1		.297	.316	.324	640	82	-1	0			.976	-2	1-11	-0.3
	Bos-A	13	38	3	14	2	0	0	0	4		.368	.429	.421	850	139	2	4			.947	-1	1-12	0.1
	Yr	24	75	7	25	3	0	0	1	5		.333	.375	.373	748	111	1	4			.963	-3	1-23	-0.2
1913	Bos-N	140	524	74	143	20	1	2	50	38	48	.273	.333	.326	659	87	-8	57			.987	5	*1-135	-0.7
1914	Bro-F	92	305	61	67	10	5	1	29	44	43	.220	.322	.295	617	69	-17	43			.989	1	1-88	-1.9
1915	Bro-F	118	341	61	98	9	1	1	36	32	39	.287	.352	.328	680	93	-7	28			.990	1	*1-107	-0.9
Total	5	377	1251	203	335	42	7	4	116	119	130	.268	.338	.322	660	85	-31	132			.987	4	1-353/O-2(0-0-2)	-3.7
■ RICHIE MYERS	Myers, Richard b: 4/7/30, Sacramento, Cal. BR/TR, 5'6", 150 lbs. Deb: 4/21/56																							
1956	Chi-N	4	1	1	0	0	0	0	0	0	0	.000	.000	.000	0	-99	-0	0	0	0	.000	0	H	0.0
■ ROD MYERS	Myers, Roderick Demond b: 1/14/73, Conroe, Tex. BL/TL, 6', 190 lbs. Deb: 6/21/96																							
1996	KC-A	22	63	9	18	7	0	1	11	7	16	.286	.357	.444	802	101	0	3	2	-0	1.000	-3	O-19(4-15-1)	-0.3
1997	KC-A	31	101	14	26	7	0	2	9	17	22	.257	.370	.386	756	95	-0	4	0	1	.982	-2	O-26(12-9-10)	-0.2
Total	2	53	164	23	44	14	0	3	20	24	38	.268	.365	.409	774	98	-0	7	2	1	.989	-5	/O-45(16-24-11)	-0.5
■ BILLY MYERS	Myers, William Harrison b: 8/14/10, Enola, Pa. d: 4/10/95, Carlisle, Pa. BR/TR, 5'8", 168 lbs. Deb: 4/16/35 F																							
1935	Cin-N	117	445	60	119	15	10	5	36	29	81	.267	.315	.380	695	89	-8	10			.939	3	*S-112	0.4
1936	Cin-N	98	323	45	87	9	6	6	27	28	56	.269	.328	.390	718	99	-1	6			.938	8	S-98	1.4
1937	Cin-N	124	335	35	84	13	3	7	43	44	57	.251	.339	.370	710	97	-1	0			.948	4	*S-121/2-6	1.2
1938	Cin-N	134	442	57	112	18	6	12	47	41	80	.253	.317	.403	719	99	-1	2			.939	2	*S-123,2-11	1.0
1939	*Cin-N	151	509	79	143	18	6	9	56	71	90	.281	.369	.393	762	104	5	4			.951	6	*S-151	2.2
1940	*Cin-N	90	282	33	57	14	2	5	30	30	56	.202	.283	.319	603	65	-14	0			.961	-5	S-88	-1.2
1941	Chi-N	24	63	10	14	1	0	1	4	7	25	.222	.310	.286	596	71	-2	1			.939	4	S-19/2-1	0.3
Total	7	738	2399	319	616	88	33	45	243	250	445	.257	.328	.377	706	93	-22	23			.946	23	S-712/2-18	5.3
■ XAVIER NADY	Nady, Xavier Clifford b: 11/14/78, Salina, Kan. BR/TR, 6'4", 220 lbs. Deb: 9/30/2000																							
2000	SD-N	1	1	1	1	0	0	0	0	0	0	1.000	1.000	1.000	2000	434	1	0	0	0	.000	0	/H	0.0
■ TIM NAEHRING	Naehring, Timothy James b: 2/1/67, Cincinnati, Ohio BR/TR, 6'2", 205 lbs. Deb: 7/15/90 Career OF: (1-LF 0-CF 0-RF)																							
1990	Bos-A	24	85	10	23	6	0	2	12	8	15	.271	.333	.412	745	102	0	0	0	0	.918	-1	S-19/3-5,2-1	0.0
1991	Bos-A	20	55	1	6	1	0	0	3	6	15	.109	.197	.127	324	-8	-8	0	0	0	.956	-1	S-17/3-2,2-1	-0.8
1992	Bos-A	72	186	12	43	8	0	3	14	18	31	.231	.309	.323	632	72	-7	0	0	0	.992	16	S-30,2-23,3-10,/OD	1.1
1993	Bos-A	39	127	14	42	10	0	1	17	10	26	.331	.380	.433	813	111	2	1	0	0	.973	-4	2-15,D-10/3-9,S-4	-0.1
1994	Bos-A	80	297	41	82	18	1	7	42	30	56	.276	.350	.414	765	92	-3	1	3	-1	.981	-1	2-49,3-11/1-8,SD	-0.2
1995	*Bos-A	126	433	61	133	27	2	10	57	77	66	.307	.416	.448	864	121	17	0	2	-1	.954	7	*3-124/D-1	2.2
1996	Bos-A	116	430	77	124	16	0	17	65	49	63	.288	.366	.444	811	102	2	2	1	0	.963	1	*3-116/2-1	0.3
1997	Bos-A	70	259	38	74	18	1	9	40	38	40	.286	.379	.467	846	117	7	1	1	-0	.981	-7	3-68/D-1	0.0
Total	8	547	1872	254	527	104	4	49	250	236	312	.282	.367	.420	787	102	10	5	7	-1	.962	9	3-345/2-90,S-78,D1O	2.5
■ BILL NAGEL	Nagel, William Taylor b: 8/19/15, Memphis, Tenn. d: 10/8/81, Freehold, N.J. BR/TR, 6'1", 190 lbs. Deb: 4/20/39																							
1939	Phi-A	105	341	39	86	19	4	12	39	25	86	.252	.307	.437	744	90	-7	2	1	0	.944	-15	2-56,3-43/P-1	-1.6
1941	Phi-N	17	56	2	8	1	1	0	6	3	14	.143	.186	.196	383	8	-7	0			.935	3	2-12/O-2(2-0-0),3-1	-0.3
1945	Chi-A	67	220	21	46	10	3	3	27	15	41	.209	.263	.323	585	71	-9	3	1	0	.984	-3	1-57/3-1	-1.6
Total	3	189	617	62	140	30	8	15	72	43	141	.227	.281	.374	655	77	-23	5	2		.942	-15	/2-68,1-57,3-45,OP	-3.5
■ LOU NAGELSEN	Nagelsen, Louis Marcellus (b: Louis Marcellus Nageleisen) b: 6/29/1887, Piqua, Ohio d: 10/21/65, Fort Wayne, Ind. BR/TR, 6'2", 180 lbs. Deb: 9/10/12																							
1912	Cle-A	2	3	0	0	0	0	0	0	0		.000	.000	.000	0	-97	-1	0			1.000	-1	/C-2	-0.2
■ RUSS NAGELSON	Nagelson, Russell Charles b: 9/19/44, Cincinnati, Ohio BL/TR, 6', 205 lbs. Deb: 9/11/68																							
1968	Cle-A	5	3	0	1	0	0	0	0	2	2	.333	.600	.333	933	192	1	0	0	0	.000	0	H	0.1
1969	Cle-A	12	17	1	6	0	0	0	0	3	3	.353	.450	.353	803	123	1	0	0	0	1.000	-1	/O-3(1-0-2),1-1	0.0
1970	Cle-A	17	24	3	3	1	0	1	2	3	9	.125	.222	.292	514	39	-2	0	0	0	1.000	-0	/O-4(1-0-3)	-0.3
	Det-A	28	32	5	6	0	0	0	2	5	6	.188	.297	.188	485	36	-3	0	0	0	1.000	-1	/O-4(3-0-2),1-1	-0.4
	Yr	45	56	8	9	1	0	1	4	8	15	.161	.266	.232	498	38	-5	0	0	0	1.000	-2	/O-8(4-0-5),1-1	-0.7
Total	3	62	76	9	16	1	0	1	4	13	20	.211	.326	.263	589	64	-3	0	0	0	1.000	-2	/O-11(5-0-7),1-2	-0.6
■ TOM NAGLE	Nagle, Thomas Edward b: 10/30/1865, Milwaukee, Wis. d: 3/9/46, Milwaukee, Wis. BR/TR, 5'10", 150 lbs. Deb: 4/22/1890																							
1890	Chi-N	38	144	21	39	5	1	1	11	7	24	.271	.318	.340	658	88	-3	4			.939	-7	C-33/O-6(0-0-6)	-0.6
1891	Chi-N	8	25	3	3	0	0	0	1	1	3	.120	.154	.120	274	-20	-4	0			.906	-3	/C-7,O-1(1-0-0)	-0.6
Total	2	46	169	24	42	5	1	1	12	8	27	.249	.294	.308	602	73	-6	4			.935	-11	/C-40,O-7(1-0-6)	-1.2
■ BILL NAHORODNY	Nahorodny, William Gerard b: 8/31/53, Hamtramck, Mich. BR/TR, 6'2", 200 lbs. Deb: 9/27/76																							
1976	Phi-N	3	5	0	1	1	0	0	0	0	0	.200	.200	.400	600	65	-0	0	0	0	1.000	0	/C-2	0.0
1977	Chi-A	7	23	3	6	1	0	1	4	2	3	.261	.320	.435	755	104	0	0	0	0	1.000	-1	/C-7	0.0
1978	Chi-A	107	347	29	82	11	2	8	35	23	52	.236	.288	.349	636	77	-11	1	0	0	.980	-3	*C-104/1-4,D-1	-1.0
1979	Chi-A	65	179	20	46	10	0	6	29	18	23	.257	.325	.413	738	98	-1	0	1	-0	.973	-0	C-60/D-3	0.1
1980	Atl-N	59	157	14	38	12	0	5	18	8	21	.242	.287	.414	701	91	-2	0	2	-1	.990	-7	C-54/1-1	-0.9
1981	Atl-N	14	13	0	3	1	0	0	2	1	3	.231	.286	.308	593	67	-1	0	0	0	1.000	0	/C-3,1-1	-0.1
1982	Cle-A	39	94	6	21	5	1	4	18	2	9	.223	.240	.426	665	79	-3	0	0	0	1.000	-3	C-35	-0.6
1983	Det-A	2	1	0	0	0	0	0	0	1	0	.000	.500	.000	500	53	0	0	0	0	.000	0	/H	0.0
1984	Sea-A	12	25	2	6	0	0	1	3	1	7	.240	.321	.360	681	89	-0	0	1	-0	.976	-3	C-10/1-1	-0.3
Total	9	308	844	74	203	41	3	25	109	56	118	.241	.292	.385	678	85	-18	1	4	-1	.983	-17	C-275/1-7,D-4	-2.8
■ FRANK NALEWAY	Naleway, Frank "Chick" b: 7/5/02, Chicago, Ill. d: 1/28/49, Chicago, Ill. BR/TR, 5'9.5", 165 lbs. Deb: 9/16/24																							
1924	Chi-A	1	2	0	0	0	0	0	0	1	0	.000	.333	.000	333	-10	-0	0	0	0	.750	-1	/S-1	-0.1
■ DOC NANCE	Nance, William G. "Kid" (b: Willie G. Cooper) b: 8/2/1876, Ft.Worth, Tex. d: 5/28/58, Fort Worth, Tex. BR/TR, 5'7", 165 lbs. Deb: 8/19/1897																							
1897	Lou-N	35	120	25	29	5	3	3	17	20		.242	.355	.408	763	105	1	3			.986	4	O-35(0-7-28)	0.2
1898	Lou-N	22	76	13	24	5	0	1	16	12		.316	.416	.421	837	142	5	2			.946	2	O-22(0-0-22)	0.5

YEAR	TM/L	G	AB	R	H	2B	3B	HR	RBI	BB	SO	AVG	OBP	SLG	OPS	OPS+	BR+	SB	CS	SBR	FA	FR	G/POS	TPR
1901	Det-A	132	461	72	129	24	5	3	66	51		.280	.355	.373	728	98	-1	9			.932	1	*O-132(130-0-2)	-0.7
Total	3	189	657	110	182	34	8	7	99	83		.277	.362	.385	747	104	5	14			.943	6	O-189(130-7-52)	0.0
■ **AL NAPLES**	Naples, Aloysius Francis b: 8/29/27, St.George, N.Y. BR/TR, 5'9", 168 lbs. Deb: 6/25/49																							
1949	StL-A	2	7	0	1	1	0	0	0	0	1	.143	.143	.286	429	12	-1	0	0	0	.875	-1	/S-2	-0.2
■ **DANNY NAPOLEON**	Napoleon, Daniel b: 1/11/42, Claysburg, Pa. BR/TR, 5'11", 190 lbs. Deb: 4/14/65																							
1965	NY-N	68	97	5	14	1	1	0	7	8	23	.144	.224	.175	400	15	-11	0	0	0	.941	1	O-15(14-0-1)/3-7	-1.1
1966	NY-N	12	33	2	7	2	0	0	0	1	10	.212	.235	.273	508	42	-3	0	1	-0	.929	-0	O-10(10-0-0)	-0.4
Total	2	80	130	7	21	3	1	0	7	9	33	.162	.227	.200	427	22	-13	0	1	-0	.938	1	/O-25(24-0-1),3-7	-1.5
■ **HAL NARAGON**	Naragon, Harold Richard b: 10/1/28, Zanesville, Ohio BL/TR, 6', 175 lbs. Deb: 9/23/51 C																							
1951	Cle-A	3	8	0	2	0	0	0	0	1	0	.250	.400	.250	650	83	-0	0	0	0	.929	0	/C-2	0.0
1954	*Cle-A	46	101	10	24	2	2	0	12	9	12	.238	.300	.297	597	63	-5	0	0	0	1.000	-2	C-45	-0.5
1955	Cle-A	57	127	12	41	9	2	1	14	15	8	.323	.394	.449	843	122	4	1	0	0	.991	-4	C-52	0.3
1956	Cle-A	53	122	11	35	3	1	3	18	13	9	.287	.360	.402	762	99	-0	0	0	0	.988	-12	C-48	-1.0
1957	Cle-A	57	121	12	31	1	1	0	8	12	9	.256	.328	.281	609	69	-5	0	0	0	.990	-2	C-39	-0.5
1958	Cle-A	9	9	2	3	0	1	0	0	0	0	.333	.333	.556	889	144	0	0	0	0	.000	0	H	0.0
1959	Cle-A	14	36	6	10	4	1	0	5	3	2	.278	.350	.444	794	121	1	0	0	0	1.000	-1	C-10	0.0
	Was-A	71	195	12	47	3	2	0	11	8	9	.241	.275	.277	551	52	-13	0	1	-0	.993	-2	C-54	-1.2
	Yr	85	231	18	57	7	3	0	16	11	11	.247	.287	.303	590	63	-12	0	1	-0	.994	-3	C-64	-1.2
1960	Was-A	33	92	7	19	2	0	0	5	8	4	.207	.277	.228	505	39	-8	0	0	0	.978	-2	C-29	-0.9
1961	Min-A	57	139	10	42	2	1	2	11	4	8	.302	.326	.374	700	82	-4	0	0	0	.994	-5	C-36	-0.7
1962	Min-A	24	35	1	8	1	0	0	3	3	1	.229	.289	.257	547	47	-3	0	0	0	1.000	0	/C-9	-0.2
Total	10	424	985	83	262	27	11	6	87	76	62	.266	.323	.334	657	77	-31	1	1	-0	.991	-29	C-324	-4.7
■ **BILL NARLESKI**	Narleski, William Edward "Cap" b: 6/9/1899, Perth Amboy, N.J. d: 6/20/64, Laurel Springs, N.J. BR/TR, 5'9", 160 lbs. Deb: 4/18/29 F																							
1929	Bos-A	96	260	30	72	16	1	0	25	21	22	.277	.333	.346	679	77	-9	4	4	-1	.957	-17	S-51,2-29/3-7	-1.9
1930	Bos-A	39	98	11	23	9	0	0	7	7	5	.235	.306	.327	632	63	-6	0	0	0	.915	-8	S-19,3-14/2-5	-1.1
Total	2	135	358	41	95	25	1	0	32	28	27	.265	.326	.341	666	73	-14	4	4	-1	.949	-25	/S-70,2-34,3-21	-3.0
■ **JERRY NARRON**	Narron, Jerry Austin b: 1/15/56, Goldsboro, N.C. BL/TR, 6'3", 205 lbs. Deb: 4/13/79 C																							
1979	NY-A	61	123	17	21	3	1	4	18	9	26	.171	.227	.309	536	44	-10	0	0	0	.973	-4	C-56/D-1	-1.3
1980	Sea-A	48	107	7	21	3	0	4	18	13	18	.196	.283	.336	620	68	-5	0	0	0	.992	-10	C-39/D-1	-1.3
1981	Sea-A	76	203	13	45	5	0	3	17	16	35	.222	.285	.291	576	64	-9	0	0	0	.996	-14	C-65	-2.2
1983	Cal-A	10	22	1	3	0	0	1	4	1	3	.136	.174	.273	447	21	-2	0	0	0	.895	-1	/C-6,D-1	-0.3
1984	Cal-A	69	150	9	37	5	0	3	17	8	12	.247	.289	.340	629	74	-5	0	0	0	.994	-8	C-46/1-7	-1.2
1985	Cal-A	67	132	12	29	4	0	5	14	11	17	.220	.280	.364	643	75	-5	0	0	0	1.000	2	C-45/1-1,D-7	-0.1
1986	*Cal-A	57	95	5	21	3	1	1	8	9	14	.221	.295	.305	601	65	-5	0	0	0	.988	1	C-51/D-2	-0.2
1987	Sea-A	4	8	0	0	0	0	0	0	0	2	.000	.000	.000	0	-95	-2	0	0	0	1.000	-0	/C-3	-0.2
Total	8	392	840	64	177	23	2	21	96	67	127	.211	.272	.318	590	62	-44	0	0	0	.989	-33	C-311/D-12,1-8	-6.8
■ **SAM NARRON**	Narron, Samuel b: 8/25/13, Middlesex, N.C. d: 12/31/96, Middlesex, N.C. BR/TR, 5'10", 180 lbs. Deb: 9/15/35 C																							
1935	StL-N	4	7	0	3	0	0	0	0	0	0	.429	.429	.429	857	126	0	0			1.000	-0	/C-1	0.0
1942	StL-N	10	10	0	4	0	0	0	1	0	0	.400	.400	.400	800	125	0	0			1.000	-0	/C-2	0.0
1943	*StL-N	10	11	0	1	0	0	0	0	1	2	.091	.167	.091	258	-24	-2	0			1.000	1	/C-3	-0.1
Total	3	24	28	0	8	0	0	0	1	1	2	.286	.310	.286	596	67	-1	0			1.000	1	/C-6	-0.1
■ **COTTON NASH**	Nash, Charles Francis b: 7/24/42, Jersey City, N.J. BR/TR, 6'6", 220 lbs. Deb: 9/1/67																							
1967	Chi-A	3	3	1	0	0	0	0	0	1	0	.000	.250	.000	250	-21	-0	0	0	0	.833	-1	/1-3	-0.1
1969	Min-A	6	9	0	2	0	0	0	0	1	2	.222	.300	.222	522	47	-1	0	0	0	1.000	1	/1-6,O-1(1-0-0)	0.0
1970	Min-A	4	4	1	1	0	0	0	2	1	1	.250	.400	.250	650	82	-0	0	1	-0	1.000	-0	/1-2	-0.1
Total	3	13	16	2	3	0	0	0	2	3	3	.188	.316	.188	503	45	-1	0	1	-0	.965	0	/1-11,O-1(1-0-0)	-0.2
■ **KEN NASH**	Nash, Kenneth Leland (Played One Game In 1912 under name of Costello) b: 7/14/1888, Weymouth, Mass. d: 2/16/77, Epsom, N.H. BB/TR, 5'8", 140 lbs. Deb: 7/4/12																							
1912	Cle-A	11	23	2	4	0	0	0	0	3		.174	.269	.174	443	27	-2	0			.826	-3	/S-8	-0.5
1914	StL-N	24	51	4	14	3	1	0	6	6	10	.275	.351	.373	723	116	1	0			.875	-6	3-10/2-6,S-3	-0.6
Total	2	35	74	6	18	3	1	0	6	9	10	.243	.325	.311	636	87	-1	0			.760	-10	/S-11,3-10,2-6	-1.1
■ **BILLY NASH**	Nash, William Mitchell b: 6/24/1865, Richmond, Va. d: 11/15/29, E.Orange, N.J. BR/TR, 5'8.5", 167 lbs. Deb: 8/5/1884 MU																							
1884	Ric-a	45	166	31	33	8	8	1		12		.199	.281	.361	643	109	2				.828	7	3-45	0.9
1885	Bos-N	26	94	9	24	4	0	0	11	2	9	.255	.271	.298	569	87	-1				.864	-4	3-19/2-8	-0.4
1886	Bos-N	109	417	61	117	11	8	1	45	24	28	.281	.320	.353	672	108	5	16			.863	-5	*3-90,S-17/O-2(1-1-0)	0.2
1887	Bos-N	121	535	100	200	24	12	6	94	60	30	.374	.376	.434	810	124	17	43			.884	9	*3-117/O-5(4-0-1)	2.3
1888	Bos-N	135	526	71	149	18	15	4	75	50	46	.283	.350	.397	747	136	22	20			**.913**	26	*3-105,2-31	**4.8**
1889	Bos-N	128	481	84	132	20	2	3	76	79	44	.274	.379	.343	722	97	-0	26			.905	12	*3-128/P-1	1.2
1890	Bos-P	129	488	103	130	28	6	5	90	88	43	.266	.383	.379	762	97	-1	26			.866	18	*3-129/P-1	1.5
1891	Bos-N	140	537	92	148	24	9	5	95	74	50	.276	.369	.382	750	106	4	28			.900	-12	*3-140	-0.5
1892	*Bos-N	135	526	94	137	25	5	4	95	59	42	.260	.338	.350	688	99	-1	31			**.898**	24	*3-135/O-1(1-0-0)	2.3
1893	Bos-N	128	485	115	141	27	6	10	123	85	29	.291	.399	.433	832	112	8	30			**.923**	3	*3-128	1.1
1894	Bos-N	132	512	132	148	23	6	8	87	91	23	.289	.399	.404	804	87	-10	20			**.933**	6	*3-132	-0.2
1895	Bos-N	133	513	97	149	24	6	10	110	74	19	.290	.383	.419	802	99	-1	18			.881	-6	*3-133	-0.4
1896	Phi-N	65	227	29	56	9	1	3	30	34	21	.247	.355	.335	690	83	-4	3			.911	7	3-65,M	0.3
1897	Phi-N	104	337	45	87	20	2	0	39	60		.258	.373	.329	703	89	-3	4			.919	-8	3-79,S-19/2-4	-0.7
1898	Phi-N	20	70	9	17	2	1	0	9	11		.243	.346	.300	646	89	-1	0			.958	-1	3-20	-0.1
Total	15	1550	5914	1072	1668	267	87	60	979	803	384	.282	.366	.381	747	103	34	265			.897	77	*3-1465/2-43,S-36,OP	12.3
■ **ROB NATAL**	Natal, Robert Marcel b: 11/13/65, Long Beach, Cal. BR/TR, 5'11", 190 lbs. Deb: 7/18/92																							
1992	Mon-N	5	6	0	0	0	0	0	0	1	1	.000	.143	.000	143	-57	-1	0	0	0	.909	-0	/C-4	-0.2
1993	Fla-N	41	117	3	25	4	1	1	6	6	22	.214	.276	.291	566	49	-8	1	0	0	1.000	3	C-38	-0.4
1994	Fla-N	10	29	2	8	2	0	0	2	5	5	.276	.382	.345	727	89	-0	1	0	0	.983	3	/C-8	0.3
1995	Fla-N	16	43	2	10	2	1	2	6	1	9	.233	.250	.465	715	83	-1	0	0	0	.988	-1	C-13	-0.1
1996	Fla-N	44	90	4	12	1	1	0	2	15	31	.133	.257	.167	424	15	-11	0	1	-0	.976	0	C-43	-0.9
1997	Fla-N	4	4	2	2	1	0	1	3	2	0	.500	.667	1.500	2167	468	2	0	0	0	1.000	0	/C-4	0.3
Total	6	120	289	13	57	10	3	4	19	30	68	.197	.282	.294	576	52	-20	2	1	0	.986	5	C-110	-1.0
■ **PETE NATON**	Naton, Peter Alphonsus b: 9/9/31, Flushing, N.Y. BR/TR, 6'1", 200 lbs. Deb: 6/16/53																							
1953	Pit-N	6	12	2	2	0	0	0	1	2	1	.167	.286	.167	452	22	-1	0	0	0	1.000	-1	/C-4	-0.2
■ **SANDY NAVA**	Nava, Vincent P. (b: Irwin Sandy) b: 4/12/1850, San Francisco, Cal d: 6/15/06, Baltimore, Md. 5'6", 155 lbs. Deb: 5/5/1882 Career OF: (1-LF 0-CF 2-RF)																							
1882	Pro-N	28	97	15	20	2	0	0	7	1	13	.206	.214	.227	441	42	-6				.867	-7	C-27/O-1(0-0-1)	-1.0
1883	Pro-N	29	100	18	24	4	2	0	16	3	17	.240	.262	.320	582	74	-3				.813	-4	C-27/O-2(1-0-1)	-0.5
1884	Pro-N	34	116	10	11	0	0	0	6	11	35	.095	.173	.095	268	-13	-15				.887	1	C-27/S-6,2-1	-1.0
1885	Bal-a	8	27	2	5	1	0	0	4	1		.185	.214	.222	437	39	-2				.825	-5	/C-8	-0.6
1886	Bal-a	2	5	0	1	0	0	0	0	0		.200	.200	.200	400	26	-0	1			.500	-1	/S-1,C-1	-0.1
Total	5	101	345	45	61	7	2	0	33	16	65	.177	.213	.209	422	33	-26	1			.857	-16	/C-90,S-7,O-3R,2-1	-3.2
■ **TITO NAVARRO**	Navarro, Norberto (Rodriguez) b: 9/12/70, Rio Piedras, P.R. BB/TR, 5'10", 165 lbs. Deb: 9/6/93																							
1993	NY-N	12	17	1	1	0	0	0	1	0	4	.059	.059	.059	118	-69	-4	0	0	0	1.000	1	/S-2	-0.3
■ **EARL NAYLOR**	Naylor, Earl Eugene b: 5/19/19, Kansas City, Mo. d: 1/16/90, Winter Haven, Fla. BR/TR, 6', 190 lbs. Deb: 4/15/42																							
1942	Phi-N	76	168	9	33	4	1	0	14	11	18	.196	.246	.232	478	42	-12	1			.984	-5	O-34(2-22-11),P-20	-1.8

YEAR	TM/L	G	AB	R	H	2B	3B	HR	RBI	BB	SO	AVG	OBP	SLG	OPS	OPS+	BR+	SB	CS	SBR	FA	FR	G/POS	TPR
1943	Phi-N	33	120	12	21	2	0	3	14	12	16	.175	.256	.267	522	53	-7	1			.964	6	O-33(0-33-0)	-0.2
1946	Bro-N	3	2	1	0	0	0	0	0	0	1	.000	.000	.000	0	-99	-1	0			.000	0	H	-0.1
Total	3	112	290	22	54	6	1	3	28	23	35	.186	.248	.245	493	46	-20	2			.971	1	/O-67(2-55-11),P-20	-2.1

■ JACK NEAGLE

Neagle, John Henry b: 1/2/1858, Syracuse, N.Y. d: 9/20/04, Syracuse, N.Y. BR/TR, 5'6", 155 lbs. Deb: 7/8/1879

YEAR	TM/L	G	AB	R	H	2B	3B	HR	RBI	BB	SO	AVG	OBP	SLG	OPS	OPS+	BR+	SB	CS	SBR	FA	FR	G/POS	TPR
1879	Cin-N	3	12	1	2	0	0	0	2	0	0	.167	.167	.167	333	11	-1				.000	-1	/O-2(0-1-1),P-2	-0.1
1883	Phi-N	18	73	6	12	1	0	0	4	1	9	.164	.176	.178	354	9	-7				.840	-2	O-12(11-1-0)/P-8	-0.5
	Bal-a	9	35	3	10	4	0	0		2		.286	.324	.400	724	128	1				.769	-3	/P-6,O-5(1-0-4)	-0.2
	Pit-a	27	101	14	19	0	1	0		5		.188	.226	.208	434	43	-6				.839	-3	P-16,O-15(0-8-7)	-0.5
	Yr	36	136	17	29	4	1	0		7		.213	.252	.257	509	66	-5				.818	-6	P-22,O-20(1-8-11)	-0.7
1884	Pit-a	43	148	13	22	6	0	0		6		.149	.187	.189	376	23	-12				.760	-5	P-38/O-6(2-2-2)	-0.4
Total	3	100	369	37	65	11	1	0	6	14	9	.176	.208	.211	420	36	-26				.785	-14	/P-70,O-40(14-12-14)	-1.7

■ CHARLIE NEAL

Neal, Charles Lenard b: 1/30/31, Longview, Tex. d: 11/18/96, Dallas, Tex. BR/TR, 5'10", 165 lbs. Deb: 4/17/56

YEAR	TM/L	G	AB	R	H	2B	3B	HR	RBI	BB	SO	AVG	OBP	SLG	OPS	OPS+	BR+	SB	CS	SBR	FA	FR	G/POS	TPR
1956	*Bro-N	62	136	22	39	5	1	2	14	14	19	.287	.353	.382	736	91	-1	2	2	-0	.972	2	2-51/S-1	0.3
1957	Bro-N	128	448	62	121	13	7	12	62	53	83	.270	.358	.411	768	96	-1	11	4	1	.949	-3	*S-100,3-23/2-3	0.6
1958	LA-N	140	473	87	120	9	6	22	65	61	91	.254	.345	.438	783	102	2	7	6	-1	.976	12	*2-132/S-9	2.3
1959	*LA-N★	151	616	103	177	30	**11**	19	83	43	86	.287	.338	.464	802	103	3	17	6	2	**.989**	20	*2-151/S-1	3.5
1960	LA-N★	139	477	60	122	23	2	8	40	48	75	.256	.325	.363	688	83	-11	5	5	-1	.977	-16	*2-136/S-3	-1.8
1961	LA-N	108	341	40	80	6	1	10	48	30	49	.235	.298	.346	644	65	-17	3	2	-0	.976	2	*2-104	-0.7
1962	NY-N	136	508	59	132	14	9	11	58	56	90	.260	.333	.388	721	91	-6	2	8	-2	.970	-8	2-85,S-39,3-12	-0.6
1963	NY-N	72	253	26	57	12	1	3	18	27	49	.225	.302	.316	619	77	-7	1	2	-0	.961	0	3-66/S-8	-0.8
	Cin-N	34	64	2	10	1	0	0	3	5	15	.156	.217	.172	389	13	-7	0	1	-0	.927	-2	3-19/2-1,S-1	-1.1
	Yr	106	317	28	67	13	1	3	21	32	64	.211	.286	.287	573	64	-14	1	3	-1	.955	-2	3-85/S-9,2-1	-1.9
Total	8	970	3316	461	858	113	38	87	391	337	557	.259	.331	.394	725	90	-45	48	36	-2	.978	7	2-663,S-162,3-120	1.7

■ OFFA NEAL

Neal, Theophilus Fountain b: 6/5/1876, Benton, Ill. d: 4/11/50, Mt.Vernon, Ill. BL/TR, 6', 185 lbs. Deb: 9/30/05

YEAR	TM/L	G	AB	R	H	2B	3B	HR	RBI	BB	SO	AVG	OBP	SLG	OPS	OPS+	BR+	SB	CS	SBR	FA	FR	G/POS	TPR
1905	NY-N	4	13	0	0	0	0	0	0	0		.000	.000	.000	0	-98	-3	0			1.000	-1	/3-3,2-1	-0.4

■ GREASY NEALE

Neale, Alfred Earle b: 11/5/1891, Parkersburg, W.Va. d: 11/2/73, Lake Worth, Fla. BL/TR (BB 1916-18 (partS)), 6', 170 lbs. Deb: 4/12/16 C

YEAR	TM/L	G	AB	R	H	2B	3B	HR	RBI	BB	SO	AVG	OBP	SLG	OPS	OPS+	BR+	SB	CS	SBR	FA	FR	G/POS	TPR
1916	Cin-N	138	530	53	139	13	5	0	20	19	79	.262	.295	.306	601	87	-9	17			.973	11	*O-133(79-55-2)	-0.6
1917	Cin-N	121	385	40	113	14	9	3	33	24	36	.294	.343	.400	743	133	14	25			.979	-5	*O-119(79-27-13)	0.4
1918	Cin-N	107	371	57	100	11	11	1	32	24	38	.270	.324	.367	691	112	5	23			**.981**	10	*O-102(78-12-12)	1.1
1919	*Cin-N	139	500	57	121	10	12	1	54	47	51	.242	.316	.316	632	93	-3	28			.959	2	*O-138(24-5-109)	-1.0
1920	Cin-N	150	530	55	135	10	7	3	46	45	48	.255	.322	.317	639	85	-9	29	12	2	.987	14	*O-150(0-3-148)	-0.1
1921	Phi-N	22	57	7	12	1	0	0	1	14	9	.211	.366	.228	594	56	-3	3	4	-1	.842	-5	O-16(0-0-16)	-1.0
	Cin-N	63	241	39	58	10	5	0	12	22	16	.241	.307	.324	630	70	-10	9	6	-0	.964	1	O-60(1-8-53)	-1.4
	Yr	85	298	46	70	11	5	0	13	36	25	.235	.319	.305	625	67	-13	12	10	-1	.950	-4	O-76(1-8-69)	-2.4
1922	Cin-N	25	43	11	10	2	1	0	2	6	3	.233	.353	.326	679	77	-1	5	2	0	.864	-4	O-16(5-0-11)	-0.5
1924	Cin-N	3	4	0	0	0	0	0	0	0	1	.000	.000	.000	0	-99	-1	0	0	0	1.000	-0	/O-2(2-0-0)	-0.2
Total	8	768	2661	319	688	71	50	8	200	201	281	.259	.319	.332	651	94	-18	139	24		.972	24	O-736(268-110-364)	-3.3

■ JOE NEALE

Neale, Joseph Hunt b: 5/7/1866, Wadsworth, Ohio d: 12/30/13, Akron, Ohio BR/TR, 5'8", 153 lbs. Deb: 6/21/1886

YEAR	TM/L	G	AB	R	H	2B	3B	HR	RBI	BB	SO	AVG	OBP	SLG	OPS	OPS+	BR+	SB	CS	SBR	FA	FR	G/POS	TPR
1886	Lou-a	2	5	0	0	0	0	0	0	0		.000	.000	.000	0	-95	-1	0			1.000	0	/O-2(1-0-1),P-1	-0.1
1887	Lou-a	5	22	3	4	0	0	0	1	3		.182	.182	.053	234	-32	-3	1			.833	0	/P-5	0.0
1890	StL-a	11	30	4	2	0	0	0	1	3		.067	.152	.067	218	-31	-5	0			1.000	-2	P-10/O-1(1-0-0)	0.0
1891	StL-a	15	51	6	6	0	1	1	8	3	11	.118	.167	.216	382	8	-7	1			.933	2	P-15	0.0
Total	4	33	108	13	12	0	1	1	10	9	11	.111	.158	.133	291	-14	-16	2			.930	0	/P-31,O-3(2-0-1)	-0.1

■ JIM NEALON

Nealon, James Joseph b: 12/15/1884, Sacramento, Cal. d: 4/2/10, San Francisco, Cal. BR/TR, 6'1.5", Deb: 4/12/06

YEAR	TM/L	G	AB	R	H	2B	3B	HR	RBI	BB	SO	AVG	OBP	SLG	OPS	OPS+	BR+	SB	CS	SBR	FA	FR	G/POS	TPR
1906	Pit-N	154	556	82	142	21	12	3	**83**	53		.255	.327	.353	679	107	4	15			.987	1	*1-154	0.3
1907	Pit-N	105	381	29	98	10	8	0	47	23		.257	.301	.325	627	95	-3	11			.978	0	*1-104	-0.6
Total	2	259	937	111	240	31	20	3	130	76		.256	.317	.342	658	102	1	26			.983	1	1-258	-0.3

■ TOM NEEDHAM

Needham, Thomas Joseph "Deerfoot" b: 5/17/1879, Steubenville, Ohio d: 12/13/26, Steubenville, Ohio BR/TR, 5'10", 180 lbs. Deb: 5/12/04

YEAR	TM/L	G	AB	R	H	2B	3B	HR	RBI	BB	SO	AVG	OBP	SLG	OPS	OPS+	BR+	SB	CS	SBR	FA	FR	G/POS	TPR
1904	Bos-N	84	269	18	70	12	3	4	19	11		.260	.292	.372	664	108	1	3			.945	4	C-77/O-1(0-1-0)	1.3
1905	Bos-N	83	271	21	59	6	1	2	17	24		.218	.293	.269	563	70	-10	3			.949	-8	C-77/O-3(0-3-0),1-2	-1.1
1906	Bos-N	83	285	11	54	8	2	1	12	13		.189	.230	.242	472	49	-18	3			.962	-7	C-76/2-5,1-2,3-1,O	-2.0
1907	Bos-N	86	260	19	51	6	2	1	19	18		.196	.264	.246	510	60	-12	4			.967	-11	C-78/1-1	-1.7
1908	NY-N	54	91	8	19	3	0	0	11	12		.209	.339	.242	581	82	-1	0			.975	7	C-47	1.0
1909	Chi-N	13	28	3	4	0	0	0	0	0		.143	.143	.143	286	-11	-4	0			.980	1	/C-7	-0.2
1910	*Chi-N	31	76	9	14	3	1	0	10	10	10	.184	.287	.250	537	57	-4	1			.982	3	C-27/1-1	0.2
1911	Chi-N	27	62	4	12	2	0	0	5	9	14	.194	.315	.226	541	52	-4	2			.984	6	C-23	0.4
1912	Chi-N	33	90	12	16	5	0	0	10	7	13	.178	.260	.233	493	36	-8	3			.994	-1	C-32	-0.6
1913	Chi-N	20	42	5	10	4	1	0	11	4	8	.238	.304	.381	685	95	-0	0			.962	4	C-14/1-1	0.5
1914	Chi-N	9	17	3	2	1	0	0	3	1	4	.118	.167	.176	343	2	-2	1			.943	1	/C-7	0.0
Total	11	523	1491	113	311	50	10	8	117	109	49	.209	.274	.272	546	66	-60	20			.963	-1	C-465/1-7,2-5,O3	-2.2

■ TROY NEEL

Neel, Troy Lee b: 9/14/65, Freeport, Tex. BL/TR, 6'4", 210 lbs. Deb: 5/30/92

YEAR	TM/L	G	AB	R	H	2B	3B	HR	RBI	BB	SO	AVG	OBP	SLG	OPS	OPS+	BR+	SB	CS	SBR	FA	FR	G/POS	TPR
1992	Oak-A	24	53	8	14	3	0	3	9	5	15	.264	.339	.491	830	137	2	0	1	-0	.846	-2	/O-9(9-0-0),1-2,D-9	0.0
1993	Oak-A	123	427	59	124	21	0	19	63	49	101	.290	.369	.473	842	132	19	3	5	-1	.981	-0	D-85,1-34	1.0
1994	Oak-A	83	278	43	74	13	0	15	48	38	61	.266	.358	.475	833	123	10	2	3	-1	.994	-0	1-45,D-35	0.3
Total	3	230	758	110	212	37	0	37	120	92	177	.280	.363	.475	838	129	31	5	9	-2	.986	-3	D-129/1-81,O-9(9-0-0)	1.3

■ CAL NEEMAN

Neeman, Calvin Amandus b: 2/18/29, Valmeyer, Ill. BR/TR, 6'1", 192 lbs. Deb: 4/16/57

YEAR	TM/L	G	AB	R	H	2B	3B	HR	RBI	BB	SO	AVG	OBP	SLG	OPS	OPS+	BR+	SB	CS	SBR	FA	FR	G/POS	TPR
1957	Chi-N	122	415	37	107	17	1	10	39	22	87	.258	.300	.376	676	81	-11	0	0	0	.990	1	*C-118	-0.5
1958	Chi-N	76	201	30	52	7	0	12	29	21	41	.259	.338	.473	810	113	3	0	0	0	.992	1	C-71	0.7
1959	Chi-N	44	105	7	17	2	0	3	9	11	23	.162	.241	.267	508	36	-10	0	0	0	.994	-1	C-38	-1.0
1960	Chi-N	9	13	0	2	1	0	0	0	0	5	.154	.154	.231	385	4	-2	0	0	0	1.000	4	/C-9	0.2
	Phi-N	59	160	13	29	6	2	4	13	16	42	.181	.264	.319	583	59	-9	0	0	0	.979	5	C-52	-0.3
	Yr	68	173	13	31	7	2	4	13	16	47	.179	.257	.312	569	55	-11	0	0	0	.982	8	C-61	-0.1
1961	Phi-N	19	31	0	7	1	0	0	2	4	8	.226	.314	.258	572	55	-2	1	0	0	.986	2	C-19	0.1
1962	Pit-N	24	50	5	9	1	1	1	5	3	10	.180	.226	.300	526	40	-4	0	0	0	.983	8	C-24	0.4
1963	Cle-A	9	9	0	0	0	0	0	0	1	5	.000	.100	.000	100	-70	-2	0	0	0	1.000	3	/C-9	0.1
	Was-A	14	18	1	1	0	0	0	0	1	0	.056	.105	.056	161	-54	-4	0	0	0	.970	2	C-12	-0.2
	Yr	23	27	1	1	0	0	0	0	2	5	.037	.103	.037	140	-59	-6	0	0	0	.985	5	C-21	-0.1
Total	7	376	1002	93	224	35	4	30	97	79	221	.224	.286	.356	642	72	-41	1	0	0	.988	24	C-352	-0.5

■ DOUG NEFF

Neff, Douglas Williams b: 10/8/1891, Harrisonburg, Va. d: 5/23/32, Cape Charles, Va. BR/TR, 5'9", 141 lbs. Deb: 6/26/14

YEAR	TM/L	G	AB	R	H	2B	3B	HR	RBI	BB	SO	AVG	OBP	SLG	OPS	OPS+	BR+	SB	CS	SBR	FA	FR	G/POS	TPR
1914	Was-A	3	2	0	0	0	0	0	0	0	0	.000	.000	.000	0	-96	-0	0			.889	2	/S-3	0.1
1915	Was-A	30	60	1	10	1	0	0	4	4	6	.167	.219	.183	402	20	-6	1	2	-0	.867	-4	3-12,2-10/S-7	-1.0
Total	2	33	62	1	10	1	0	0	4	4	6	.161	.212	.177	390	16	-6	1	2		.900	-2	/3-12,2-10,S-10	-0.9

■ CY NEIGHBORS

Neighbors, Flemon Cecil b: 9/23/1880, Fayetteville, Mo. d: 5/20/64, Tacoma, Wash. BR, 5'10", 178 lbs. Deb: 4/29/08

YEAR	TM/L	G	AB	R	H	2B	3B	HR	RBI	BB	SO	AVG	OBP	SLG	OPS	OPS+	BR+	SB	CS	SBR	FA	FR	G/POS	TPR
1908	Pit-N	1	0	0	0	0	0	0	0	0		—	—	—	—	—	0	0			.000	-1	/O-1(1-0-0)	-0.1

■ BOB NEIGHBORS

Neighbors, Robert Otis b: 11/9/17, Talihina, Okla. d: 8/8/52, North Korea (Mia) BR/TR, 5'11", 165 lbs. Deb: 9/16/39

YEAR	TM/L	G	AB	R	H	2B	3B	HR	RBI	BB	SO	AVG	OBP	SLG	OPS	OPS+	BR+	SB	CS	SBR	FA	FR	G/POS	TPR
1939	StL-A	7	11	3	2	0	0	1	1	0	1	.182	.182	.455	636	56	-1	0	0	0	.917	-0	/S-5	-0.1

■ MIKE NEILL

Neill, Michael Robert b: 4/27/70, Martinsville, Va. BL/TL, 6'2", 190 lbs. Deb: 7/27/98

YEAR	TM/L	G	AB	R	H	2B	3B	HR	RBI	BB	SO	AVG	OBP	SLG	OPS	OPS+	BR+	SB	CS	SBR	FA	FR	G/POS	TPR
1998	Oak-A	6	15	2	4	1	0	0	0	2	4	.267	.353	.333	686	82	-0	0	0	0	1.000	0	/O-6(4-2-0)	0.0

YEAR	TM/L	G	AB	R	H	2B	3B	HR	RBI	BB	SO	AVG	OBP	SLG	OPS	OPS+	BR+	SB	CS	SBR	FA	FR	G/POS	TPR
■ TOMMY NEILL	Neill, Thomas White b: 11/7/19, Hartselle, Ala. d: 9/22/80, Houston, Tex. BL/TR, 6'2", 200 lbs. Deb: 9/10/46																							
1946	Bos-N	13	45	8	12	2	0	0	7	2	1	.267	.298	.311	609	72	-2	0			1.000	-1	O-13(13-0-0)	-0.4
1947	Bos-N	7	10	1	2	0	1	0	0	1	2	.200	.333	.400	733	96	-0	0			1.000	-1	/O-2(1-0-1)	-0.1
Total	2	20	55	9	14	2	1	0	7	3	3	.255	.305	.327	632	77	-2	0			1.000	-2	/O-15(14-0-1)	-0.5
■ BERNIE NEIS	Neis, Bernard Edmund b: 9/26/1895, Bloomington, Ill. d: 11/29/72, Inverness, Fla. BB/TR (BR 1920-21), 5'7", 160 lbs. Deb: 4/14/20																							
1920	*Bro-N	95	249	38	63	11	2	2	22	26	35	.253	.329	.337	666	89	-3	9	9	-1	.957	-2	O-83(11-7-65)	-1.0
1921	Bro-N	102	230	34	59	5	4	4	34	25	41	.257	.332	.365	697	81	-6	9	7	-0	.946	-6	O-77(11-24-45)/2-1	-1.6
1922	Bro-N	61	70	15	16	4	1	1	9	13	8	.229	.349	.357	707	83	-1	3	2	-0	.897	-5	O-27(7-3-17)	-0.7
1923	Bro-N	126	445	78	122	17	4	5	37	36	38	.274	.330	.364	694	85	-9	8	8	-1	.941	6	*O-111(13-87-11)	-1.0
1924	Bro-N	80	211	43	64	8	3	4	26	27	17	.303	.385	.427	811	121	7	4	2	0	.937	-4	O-62(19-22-22)	-0.1
1925	Bos-N	106	355	47	101	20	2	5	45	38	19	.285	.354	.394	748	100	0	8	10	-2	.970	11	O-87(9-76-2)	0.4
1926	Bos-N	30	93	16	20	5	2	0	8	8	10	.215	.277	.312	589	64	-5	4			.925	2	O-23(15-8-0)	-0.5
1927	Cle-A	32	96	17	29	9	0	4	18	18	9	.302	.412	.521	933	140	6	0	1	-0	.978	5	O-29(5-24-0)	0.8
	Chi-A	45	76	9	22	5	0	0	11	10	9	.289	.372	.355	727	92	-1	1	0	0	.927	-3	O-21(6-9-7)	-0.4
	Yr	77	172	26	51	14	0	4	29	28	18	.297	.395	.448	843	120	6	1	1	-0	.962	2	O-50(11-33-7)	0.4
Total	8	677	1825	297	496	84	18	25	210	201	186	.272	.346	.379	724	94	-12	46	39		.950	3	O-520(96-260-169)/2-1	-4.1
■ ERNIE NEITZKE	Neitzke, Ernest Fredrich b: 11/13/1894, Toledo, Ohio d: 4/27/77, Sylvania, Ohio BR/TR, 5'10", 180 lbs. Deb: 6/2/21																							
1921	Bos-A	11	25	3	6	0	0	0	2	4	4	.240	.345	.240	585	53	-2	0	0	0	.875	-1	/O-8(4-1-3),P-2	-0.3
■ DAVE NELSON	Nelson, David Earl b: 6/20/44, Fort Sill, Okla. BR/TR (BB 1968 (part)), 5'10", 160 lbs. Deb: 4/11/68 C																							
1968	Cle-A	88	189	26	44	4	5	0	19	17	35	.233	.300	.307	606	85	-3	23	7	3	.987	-2	2-59,S-14	0.3
1969	Cle-A	52	123	11	25	0	0	0	6	9	26	.203	.263	.203	466	31	-11	4	3	-0	.966	4	2-33/O-2(1-0-1)	-0.5
1970	Was-A	47	107	5	17	1	0	0	4	7	24	.159	.211	.168	379	6	-14	2	2	0	.986	1	2-33	-1.1
1971	Was-A	85	329	47	92	11	3	5	33	23	29	.280	.329	.377	706	105	2	17	8	1	.938	-13	3-84/2-1	-1.2
1972	Tex-A	145	499	68	113	16	3	2	28	67	81	.226	.324	.283	607	85	-7	51	17	5	.945	-12	*3-119,O-15(5-10-0)	-1.7
1973	Tex-A★	142	576	71	165	24	4	7	48	34	78	.286	.326	.378	705	102	1	43	16	4	.984	-12	*2-140	0.2
1974	Tex-A	121	474	71	112	13	1	3	42	34	72	.236	.293	.287	580	69	-19	25	13	1	.969	1	*2-120/D-1	-0.9
1975	Tex-A	28	80	9	17	1	0	2	10	8	10	.213	.292	.300	592	68	-3	6	0	1	.959	1	2-23/D-1	-0.4
1976	*KC-A	78	153	24	36	4	2	1	17	14	26	.235	.299	.307	607	77	-4	15	5	2	.975	2	2-46,D-22/1-3	0.0
1977	KC-A	27	48	8	9	3	1	0	4	7	11	.188	.291	.292	583	59	-3	1	3	-1	.926	-2	2-11/D-7	-0.5
Total	10	813	2578	340	630	77	19	20	211	220	392	.244	.307	.312	619	81	-62	187	73	16	.976	-31	2-466,3-203/D-31,OS1	-5.4
■ ROCKY NELSON	Nelson, Glenn Richard b: 11/18/24, Portsmouth, Ohio BL/TL, 5'11", 178 lbs. Deb: 4/27/49																							
1949	StL-N	82	244	28	54	8	4	4	32	11	12	.221	.258	.336	594	55	-16	1			1.000	-4	1-70	-2.2
1950	StL-N	76	235	27	58	10	4	1	20	26	9	.247	.324	.336	661	71	-10	4			.992	3	1-70	-0.8
1951	StL-N	9	18	3	4	1	0	0	1	1	0	.222	.263	.278	541	45	-1	0	0	0	1.000	-1	/1-4,O-1(1-0-0)	-0.3
	Pit-N	71	195	29	52	7	4	1	14	10	7	.267	.302	.359	661	75	-7	1	1	-0	.990	1	1-32,O-12(12-0-0)	-0.9
	Yr	80	213	32	56	8	4	1	15	11	7	.263	.299	.352	651	73	-8	1	1	-0	.991	-0	1-36,O-13(13-0-0)	-1.2
	Chi-A	6	5	0	0	0	0	0	0	1	0	.000	.167	.000	167	-53	-1	0	0	0	.000	0	H	-0.1
1952	*Bro-N	37	39	6	10	1	0	0	3	7	4	.256	.370	.282	652	82	-1	0	0	0	1.000	-1	/1-5	-0.2
1954	Cle-A	4	4	0	0	0	0	0	0	0	1	.000	.000	.000	0	-98	-1	0	0	0	1.000	-0	/1-2	-0.1
1956	Bro-N	31	96	7	20	2	0	4	15	4	10	.208	.240	.354	594	53	-6	0	0	0	.991	2	1-25	-0.7
	StL-N	38	56	6	13	5	0	3	8	6	6	.232	.306	.482	789	108	0	0	0	0	1.000	1	1-14/O-8(8-0-0)	0.0
	Yr	69	152	13	33	7	0	7	23	10	16	.217	.265	.401	667	73	-6	0	0	0	.993	2	1-39/O-8(8-0-0)	-0.7
1959	Pit-N	98	175	31	51	11	0	6	32	23	19	.291	.383	.457	840	124	6	0	0	0	.994	-4	1-56/O-2(1-0-1)	0.1
1960	*Pit-N	93	200	34	60	11	1	7	35	24	15	.300	.389	.470	859	133	10	1	2	-0	.996	1	1-73	0.7
1961	Pit-N	75	127	15	25	5	1	5	13	17	11	.197	.301	.370	671	77	-4	0	0	0	.996	-1	1-35	-0.7
Total	9	620	1394	186	347	61	14	31	173	130	94	.249	.318	.379	698	84	-31	7	3		.995	-3	1-386/O-23(22-0-1)	-5.2
■ JAMIE NELSON	Nelson, James Victor b: 9/5/59, Clinton, Okla. BR/TR, 5'11", 180 lbs. Deb: 7/21/83																							
1983	Sea-A	40	96	9	21	3	0	1	5	13	12	.219	.312	.281	593	62	-5	4	2	0	.978	3	C-39	0.0
■ CANDY NELSON	Nelson, John W b: 3/14/1849, Brooklyn, N.Y. d: 9/4/10, Brooklyn, N.Y. BL/TR, 5'6", 145 lbs. Deb: 6/11/1872 NA OF: (1-LF 12-CF 6-RF) Career OF: (4-LF 29-CF 48-RF)																							
1872	Tro-n	4	20	2	7	0	0	0	4	0	2	.350	.350	.350	700	114	0	0	0	0	1.000	-1	/O-3(0-3-0),S-1	0.0
	Eck-n	18	76	12	19	2	0	0	8	2	2	.250	.269	.276	546	80	-0	1	0	0	.818	1	/2-9,O-8(0-8-0),3-3	0.1
	Yr	22	96	14	26	2	0	0	12	2	4	.271	.286	.292	577	89	0	1	0	0	.813	1	O-11C/2-9,3-3,S-1	0.1
1873	Mut-n	36	168	28	55	4	1	0	22	1	2	.327	.331	.363	694	107	1	2	0	0	.869	-8	2-27/O-6R,3-5,C1	-0.5
1874	Mut-n	65	297	55	73	7	5	0	31	**9**	5	.246	.268	.303	571	80	-7	6	0	1	.824	-18	*2-51,S-14/O-1(0-1-0)	-2.1
1875	Mut-n	70	276	28	55	7	1	0	23	9	0	.199	.225	.232	456	56	-12	4	2	0	.855	-0	2-49,3-23/S-2,O-1L	-1.4
1878	Ind-N	19	84	12	11	1	0	0	5	5	11	.131	.180	.143	323	8	-7				.841	-6	S-19	-1.3
1879	Tro-N	28	106	17	28	7	1	0	10	8	4	.264	.316	.349	665	127	4				.834	4	S-24/O-4(4-0-0)	0.7
1881	Wor-N	24	103	13	29	1	0	1	15	5	6	.282	.315	.320	635	95	-1				.898	2	S-24	0.3
1883	NY-a	97	417	75	127	19	6	0		31		.305	.353	.379	732	130	14				.875	-5	*S-97	1.0
1884	*NY-a	111	432	114	110	15	3	1		**74**		.255	.375	.310	685	129	20				.879	-16	*S-110/2-1	0.6
1885	NY-a	107	420	98	107	12	4	1	30	**61**		.255	.353	.310	663	120	15				.892	13	*S-107/3-1	2.8
1886	NY-a	109	413	89	93	7	2	0	23	64		.225	.332	.252	584	88	-1	14			.855	-8	S-73,O-36(0-28-8)	-0.7
1887	NY-a	68	305	61	111	5	1	0	24	48		.364	.380	.272	653	87	0	29			.895	10	O-37(0-1-36),S-32/2-1	0.9
	NY-N	1	2	0	0	0	0	0	0	0	1	.000	.000	.000	0	-99	-1	0			.000	0	/3-1	0.0
1890	Bro-a	60	223	44	56	3	2	0	12	35		.251	.365	.283	648	94	1	12			.866	-8	S-57/O-4(0-0-4)	-0.5
Total	4 n	193	837	125	209	20	7	0	88	21	11	.250	.268	.290	558	79	-18	13	2	2	.844	-25	2-136/3-31,O-19C,S1C	-3.9
Total	9	624	2505	523	672	70	19	3	119	331	22	.268	.349	.302	650	107	43	55			.875	-14	S-543/O-81R,3-2,2-2	3.8
■ LYNN NELSON	Nelson, Lynn Bernard "Line Drive" b: 2/24/05, Sheldon, N.Dak. d: 2/15/55, Kansas City, Mo. BL/TR, 5'10.5", 170 lbs. Deb: 4/18/30																							
1930	Chi-N	37	18	0	4	1	1	0	2	0	1	.222	.222	.389	611	44	-2	0			.966	1	P-37	0.0
1933	Chi-N	29	21	5	5	1	1	0	1	1	3	.238	.273	.381	654	85	-0	0			1.000	1	P-24	0.0
1934	Chi-N	2	0	0	0	0	0	0	0	0	0	—	—	—	—	—	0	0			.000	-0	/P-2	0.0
1937	Phi-A	74	113	18	40	6	2	4	29	6	13	.354	.387	.549	935	135	6	1	0	0	1.000	-0	P-30/O-6(6-0-0)	0.2
1938	Phi-A	67	112	12	31	0	0	0	15	7	12	.277	.319	.277	596	52	-8	0	0	0	.952	-0	P-32	0.0
1939	Phi-A	40	80	3	15	2	0	0	5	2	13	.188	.217	.213	429	10	-11	0	1	-0	.950	-1	P-35	0.0
1940	Det-A	19	23	4	8	0	0	1	3	0	6	.348	.348	.478	826	102	0	0	0	0	1.000	0	/P-6	0.0
Total	7	268	367	42	103	10	4	5	55	16	48	.281	.313	.371	683	74	-16	1	1		.967	1	P-166/O-6(6-0-0)	0.2
■ RAY NELSON	Nelson, Raymond "Kell" (b: Raymond Nelson Kellogg) b: 8/4/1875, Holyoke, Mass. d: 1/8/61, Mt.Vernon, N.Y. BR/TR, 5'9", 150 lbs. Deb: 5/6/01																							
1901	NY-N	39	130	12	26	2	0	0	7	10		.200	.262	.215	478	41	-9	3			.885	-3	2-39	-1.2
■ RICKY NELSON	Nelson, Ricky Lee b: 5/8/59, Eloy, Ariz. BL/TR, 6', 200 lbs. Deb: 5/17/83																							
1983	Sea-A	98	291	32	74	13	3	5	36	17	50	.254	.295	.371	667	79	-9	7	4	0	.971	-8	O-91(46-1-50)/D-1	-2.0
1984	Sea-A	9	15	2	3	0	0	1	2	2	4	.200	.294	.400	694	91	-0	0	0	0	1.000	-0	/O-2(0-0-2),D-3	-0.1
1985	Sea-A	6	2	2	0	0	0	0	0	0	1	.000	.000	.000	0	-99	-1	0	0	0	1.000	-1	/O-3(0-0-3)	-0.2
1986	Sea-A	10	12	2	2	0	0	0	1	0	4	.167	.167	.167	333	-9	-2	1	0	0	.667	-0	/O-1(0-1-0),D-5	-0.2
Total	4	123	320	38	79	13	3	6	39	19	59	.247	.289	.363	652	75	-11	8	4	0	.965	-9	/O-97(46-2-55),D-9	-2.5
■ ROB NELSON	Nelson, Robert Augustus b: 5/17/64, Pasadena, Cal. BL/TL, 6'4", 215 lbs. Deb: 9/9/86																							
1986	Oak-A	5	9	1	2	1	0	0	0	1	4	.222	.300	.333	633	78	-0	0	0	0	.800	0	/1-2,D-1	0.0
1987	Oak-A	7	24	1	4	1	0	0	0	0	12	.167	.167	.208	375	-2	-3	0	0	0	.968	3	/1-7	-0.1
	SD-N	10	11	0	1	0	0	0	1	1	8	.091	.167	.091	258	-31	-2	0	0	0	1.000	-0	/1-2	-0.2
1988	SD-N	7	21	4	4	0	0	1	3	2	9	.190	.261	.333	594	71	-1	0	0	0	.981	1	/1-5	-0.1
1989	SD-N	42	82	6	16	0	1	3	7	20	29	.195	.353	.329	682	96	0	1	3	-1	.991	3	1-31	0.2

YEAR	TM/L	G	AB	R	H	2B	3B	HR	RBI	BB	SO	AVG	OBP	SLG	OPS	OPS+	BR+	SB	CS	SBR	FA	FR	G/POS	TPR
1990	SD-N	5	5	0	0	0	0	0	0	0	4	.000	.000	.000	0	-99	-1	0	0	0	.000	0	/H	-0.2
Total	5	76	152	12	27	2	1	4	11	24	66	.178	.290	.283	573	62	-8	1	3	-1	.983	6	/1-47,D-1	-0.4
■ **TEX NELSON**	Nelson, Robert Sydney "Babe" b: 8/7/36, Dallas, Tex. BL/TL, 6'3", 220 lbs. Deb: 6/22/55																							
1955	Bal-A	25	31	4	6	0	0	0	1	7	13	.194	.342	.194	536	50	-2	0	0	0	.889	0	/O-6(6-0-0),1-2	-0.2
1956	Bal-A	39	68	5	14	2	0	0	5	7	22	.206	.280	.235	515	40	-6	0	0	0	.939	-3	O-24(9-0-16)	-0.9
1957	Bal-A	15	23	2	5	0	2	0	5	1	5	.217	.280	.391	671	87	-1	0	0	0	1.000	-2	/O-8(2-0-6)	-0.3
Total	3	79	122	11	25	2	2	0	11	15	40	.205	.297	.254	551	52	-8	0	0	0	.938	-5	/O-38(17-0-22),1-2	-1.4
■ **TOMMY NELSON**	Nelson, Tom Cousineau b: 5/1/17, Chicago, Ill. d: 9/24/73, San Diego, Cal. BR/TR, 5'11.5", 180 lbs. Deb: 4/17/45																							
1945	Bos-N	40	121	6	20	2	0	0	6	4	13	.165	.192	.182	374	4	-16	1			.910	-3	3-20,2-12	-1.8
■ **DICK NEN**	Nen, Richard Le Roy b: 9/24/39, South Gate, Cal. BL/TL, 6'2", 205 lbs. Deb: 9/18/63 F																							
1963	LA-N	7	8	2	1	0	0	1	1	3	3	.125	.364	.500	864	157	1	0	0	0	1.000	-1	/1-5	0.0
1965	Was-A	69	246	18	64	7	1	6	31	19	47	.260	.316	.370	686	96	-2	1	2	-0	.993	8	1-65	0.2
1966	Was-A	94	235	20	50	8	0	6	30	28	46	.213	.297	.323	620	79	-6	0	2	-1	.990	-2	1-76	-1.4
1967	Was-A	110	238	21	52	7	1	6	29	21	39	.218	.282	.332	614	84	-5	0	1	-0	.995	1	1-65/O-1(1-0-0)	-0.9
1968	Chi-N	81	94	8	17	1	1	2	16	6	17	.181	.230	.277	507	48	-6	0	0	0	.987	-1	1-52	-0.9
1970	Was-A	6	5	1	1	0	0	0	0	0	0	.200	.200	.200	400	11	-1	0	0	0	1.000	0	/1-1	0.0
Total	6	367	826	70	185	23	3	21	107	77	152	.224	.291	.335	626	82	-19	1	5	-2	.992	7	1-264/O-1(1-0-0)	-3.0
■ **JACK NESS**	Ness, John Charles b: 11/11/1884, Chicago, Ill. d: 12/4/57, DeLand, Fla. BR/TR, 6'2", 165 lbs. Deb: 5/9/11																							
1911	Det-A	12	39	6	6	0	0	0	2	2		.154	.195	.154	349	-2	-5	0			.977	1	1-12	-0.5
1916	Chi-A	75	258	32	69	7	5	1	34	9	32	.267	.310	.345	655	96	-2	4			.979	-5	1-69	-1.0
Total	2	87	297	38	75	7	5	1	36	11	32	.253	.295	.320	615	82	-8	4			.978	-4	/1-81	-1.5
■ **GRAIG NETTLES**	Nettles, Graig b: 8/20/44, San Diego, Cal. BL/TR, 6', 186 lbs. Deb: 9/6/67 FC Career OF: (58-LF 2-CF 13-RF)																							
1967	Min-A	3	3	0	1	1	0	0	0	0	0	.333	.333	.667	1000	175	0	0	0	0	.000	0	H	0.0
1968	Min-A	22	76	13	17	2	1	5	8	7	20	.224	.298	.474	771	125	2	0	0	0	.968	1	O-16(2-1-13)/3-5,1-3	0.2
1969	*Min-A	96	225	27	50	9	2	7	26	32	47	.222	.322	.373	695	92	-2	1	2	-0	.987	-5	O-54(53-1-0),3-21	-1.1
1970	Cle-A	157	549	81	129	13	1	26	62	81	77	.235	.336	.404	741	99	-0	3	1	0	**.967**	28	*3-154/O-3(3-0-0)	2.8
1971	Cle-A	158	598	78	156	18	1	28	86	82	56	.261	.353	.435	788	112	10	7	4	0	.973	**42**	*3-158	5.5
1972	Cle-A	150	557	65	141	28	0	17	70	57	50	.253	.327	.395	722	110	7	2	3	-1	.956	5	*3-150	1.2
1973	NY-A	160	552	65	129	18	0	22	81	78	76	.234	.336	.386	722	107	6	0	0	0	.953	26	*3-157/D-2	3.1
1974	NY-A	155	566	74	139	21	1	22	75	59	75	.246	.320	.403	723	109	6	1	0	0	.961	16	*3-154/S-1	2.2
1975	NY-A★	157	581	71	155	24	4	21	91	51	88	.267	.328	.430	758	115	10	1	3	-1	.964	11	*3-157	2.0
1976	*NY-A	158	583	88	148	29	2	**32**	93	62	94	.254	.330	.475	805	135	24	11	6	0	.965	17	*3-158/S-1	**4.2**
1977	*NY-A★	158	589	99	150	23	4	37	107	68	79	.255	.335	.496	831	124	18	2	5	-1	.974	-3	*3-156/D-1	1.2
1978	*NY-A★	159	587	81	162	23	2	27	93	59	69	.276	.348	.460	808	128	21	1	1	-0	.975	-6	*3-159/S-2	1.3
1979	*NY-A★	145	521	71	132	15	1	20	73	59	53	.253	.329	.401	730	98	-2	1	2	-0	.966	9	*3-144	0.5
1980	*NY-A★	89	324	52	79	14	0	16	45	42	42	.244	.332	.435	768	110	4	0	0	0	.960	-3	3-88/S-1	0.0
1981	*NY-A	103	349	46	85	7	1	15	46	47	49	.244	.335	.398	733	112	6	0	2	-1	.972	8	3-97/D-4	1.2
1982	NY-A	122	405	47	94	11	2	18	55	51	49	.232	.319	.402	722	98	-1	1	5	-2	.934	8	*3-113/D-3	0.3
1983	NY-A	129	462	56	123	17	3	20	75	51	65	.266	.343	.446	789	120	12	0	1	-0	.956	1	*3-126/D-1	1.0
1984	*SD-N	124	395	56	90	11	1	20	65	58	55	.228	.334	.413	747	109	5	0	0	0	.936	-10	*3-119	-0.7
1985	SD-N★	137	440	66	115	23	1	15	61	72	59	.261	.365	.420	786	121	14	0	0	0	.959	-9	*3-130	0.3
1986	SD-N	126	354	36	77	9	0	16	55	41	62	.218	.302	.379	681	88	-6	0	1	-0	.941	-2	*3-114	-1.1
1987	Atl-N	112	177	16	37	8	1	5	33	22	25	.209	.296	.350	647	67	-8	1	0	0	.951	-0	3-40/1-6	-0.9
1988	Mon-N	80	93	5	16	4	0	1	14	9	19	.172	.245	.247	492	40	-7	0	0	0	.818	-2	3-12/1-5	-1.0
Total	22	2700	8986	1193	2225	328	28	390	1314	1088	1209	.248	.332	.421	753	110	118	32	36	-6	.961	132	*3-2412/O-73L,1DS	22.2
■ **JIM NETTLES**	Nettles, James William b: 3/2/47, San Diego, Cal. BL/TL, 6', 186 lbs. Deb: 9/7/70 F																							
1970	Min-A	13	20	3	5	0	0	0	0	1	5	.250	.286	.250	536	48	-1	0	1	-0	1.000	-2	O-11(5-1-5)	-0.5
1971	Min-A	70	168	17	42	5	1	6	24	19	24	.250	.326	.399	725	101	0	3	2	-0	.986	2	O-62(2-57-3)	0.1
1972	Min-A	102	235	28	48	5	2	4	15	32	52	.204	.302	.294	596	74	-7	4	3	-0	.982	-1	O-78(12-58-8)/1-1	-1.1
1974	Det-A	43	141	20	32	5	1	6	17	15	26	.227	.306	.404	710	99	-0	3	4	-1	1.000	-1	O-41(8-4-30)	-0.4
1979	KC-A	11	23	0	2	0	0	0	1	3	2	.087	.192	.087	279	-21	-4	0	0	0	1.000	0	/O-8(7-0-1),1-1	-0.4
1981	Oak-A	1	0	0	0	0	0	0	0	0	0	—	—	—	—	—	0	0	0	0	.000	-0	/O-1(0-0-1)	0.0
Total	6	240	587	68	129	15	4	16	57	70	109	.220	.305	.341	646	83	-12	10	10	-1	.988	-3	O-201(34-120-48)/1-2	-2.3
■ **MORRIS NETTLES**	Nettles, Morris b: 1/26/52, Los Angeles, Cal. BL/TL, 6'1", 170 lbs. Deb: 4/26/74																							
1974	Cal-A	56	175	27	48	4	0	0	8	16	38	.274	.335	.297	632	88	-2	20	11	1	.990	-6	O-54(3-37-14)	-1.0
1975	Cal-A	112	294	50	68	11	0	0	23	26	57	.231	.296	.269	565	65	-13	22	15	-0	.974	-2	O-90(39-38-17)/D-9	-1.9
Total	2	168	469	77	116	15	0	0	31	42	95	.247	.311	.279	590	74	-15	42	26	0	.980	-8	O-144(42-75-31)/D-9	-2.9
■ **MILO NETZEL**	Netzel, Miles A. b: 5/12/1886, Eldred, Pa. d: 3/18/38, Oxnard, Cal. BL/TL, Deb: 9/16/09																							
1909	Cle-A	10	37	2	7	1	0	0	3	3		.189	.250	.216	466	46	-2	1			.800	-3	/3-6,O-2(2-0-0)	-0.7
■ **OTTO NEU**	Neu, Otto Adam b: 9/24/1894, Springfield, Ohio d: 9/19/32, Kenton, Ohio BR/TR, 5'11", 170 lbs. Deb: 7/10/17																							
1917	StL-A	1	0	0	0	0	0	0	0	0	0	—	—	—	—	—	0	0			.000	0	/S-1	0.0
■ **JOHNNY NEUN**	Neun, John Henry b: 10/28/1900, Baltimore, Md. d: 3/28/90, Baltimore, Md. BB/TL, 5'10.5", 175 lbs. Deb: 4/14/25 MC																							
1925	Det-A	60	75	15	20	3	3	0	4	9	12	.267	.345	.387	732	87	-2	2	3	-1	.990	-1	1-13	-0.3
1926	Det-A	97	242	47	72	14	4	0	15	27	26	.298	.370	.388	759	97	-1	4	7	-2	.993	-3	1-49	-0.8
1927	Det-A	79	204	38	66	9	4	0	27	35	13	.324	.427	.407	834	116	7	22	7	2	.980	-3	1-53	0.3
1928	Det-A	36	108	15	23	3	1	0	5	7	10	.213	.261	.259	520	36	-10	2	2	-0	.975	-0	1-25	-1.2
1930	Bos-N	81	212	39	69	12	2	2	23	21	18	.325	.389	.429	818	101	1	9			.991	0	1-55	-0.2
1931	Bos-N	79	104	17	23	1	3	0	11	11	14	.221	.302	.288	590	62	-5	2			.994	-0	1-36	-0.7
Total	6	432	945	171	273	42	17	2	85	110	93	.289	.366	.376	742	91	-10	41	19		.987	-7	1-231	-2.9
■ **ALEXANDER NEVIN**	Nevin, Alexander Brown b: 10/3/1850, Allegheny City, Pa. d: 10/10/21, Pensacola, Fla. Deb: 6/17/1873																							
1873	Res-n	13	53	7	11	1	2	0	2	0	3	.208	.208	.302	509	54	-3	0	0	0	.579	-8	3-12/O-1(0-0-1)	-0.8
■ **PHIL NEVIN**	Nevin, Phillip Joseph b: 1/19/71, Fullerton, Cal. BR/TR, 6'2", 180 lbs. Deb: 6/11/95 Career OF: (81-LF 0-CF 9-RF)																							
1995	Hou-N	18	60	4	7	1	0	0	1	7	13	.117	.221	.133	354	-4	-9	1	0	0	.933	1	3-16	-0.8
	Det-A	29	96	9	21	3	1	2	12	11	27	.219	.318	.333	652	70	-4	0	0	0	.963	-0	O-27(27-0-0)/D-2	-0.5
1996	Det-A	38	120	15	35	5	0	8	19	8	39	.292	.341	.533	874	117	3	1	0	0	.943	5	3-24/O-9L,C-4,D-1	0.7
1997	Det-A	93	251	32	59	16	1	9	35	25	68	.235	.307	.414	721	87	-5	0	1	-0	.986	-0	O-40L,D-30,3-17,/1C	-0.8
1998	Ana-A	75	237	27	54	8	1	8	27	17	67	.228	.293	.371	665	71	-10	0	0	0	.989	-7	C-69/1-2,D-3	-1.3
1999	SD-N	128	383	52	103	27	0	24	85	51	82	.269	.356	.527	884	130	16	1	0	0	.982	1	3-67,C-31,O-13R,1/D	1.7
2000	SD-N	143	538	87	163	34	1	31	107	59	121	.303	.376	.543	919	136	29	2	0	0	.929	-8	*3-142	2.1
Total	6	524	1685	226	442	94	4	82	286	178	417	.262	.338	.469	807	108	19	5	1	1	.946	-9	3-266,C-105/O-89L,D1	1.1
■ **DON NEWCOMBE**	Newcombe, Donald "Newk" b: 6/14/26, Madison, N.J. BL/TR, 6'4", 225 lbs. Deb: 5/20/49																							
1949	*Bro-N★	39	96	8	22	4	0	0	10	5	16	.229	.267	.271	538	43	-8	0			**1.000**	1	P-38	0.0
1950	Bro-N★	40	97	8	24	3	1	1	8	10	19	.247	.318	.330	648	69	-4	0			.969	-0	P-40	0.0
1951	Bro-N★	40	103	11	23	3	1	0	8	8	9	.223	.286	.272	558	50	-7	0	0	0	.958	1	P-40	0.0
1954	Bro-N	31	47	6	15	1	0	0	4	4	6	.319	.373	.340	713	85	-1	0	0	0	.931	-1	P-29	0.0
1955	*Bro-N★	57	117	18	42	9	1	7	23	6	18	.359	.395	.632	1028	163	10	1	0	0	.907	-2	P-34	0.0
1956	*Bro-N	52	111	13	26	6	0	2	16	12	18	.234	.315	.342	657	71	-4	1	0	0	.985	0	P-38	0.0
1957	Bro-N	34	74	8	17	2	0	1	7	11	11	.230	.329	.297	627	64	-3	0	1	-0	.964	1	P-28	0.0
1958	LA-N	11	12	2	5	0	0	0	0	2	2	.417	.500	.417	917	141	1	0	0	0	1.000	0	P-11	0.0

YEAR	TM/L	G	AB	R	H	2B	3B	HR	RBI	BB	SO	AVG	OBP	SLG	OPS	OPS+	BR+	SB	CS	SBR	FA	FR	G/POS	TPR
	Cin-N	39	60	9	21	1	0	1	9	8	10	.350	.426	.417	843	118	2	0	0	0	1.000	-2	P-20	0.0
	Yr	50	72	11	26	1	0	1	9	10	12	.361	.439	.417	856	122	3	0	0	0	**1.000**	-2	P-31	0.0
1959	Cin-N	61	105	10	32	2	0	3	21	17	23	.305	.402	.410	811	113	3	0	0	0	.978	-1	P-30	0.0
1960	Cin-N	24	36	0	5	1	0	0	1	3	8	.139	.205	.167	372	3	-5	0	0	0	.895	-1	P-16	0.0
	Cle-A	24	20	1	6	1	0	0	1	1	7	.300	.333	.350	683	88	-0	0	0	0	.889	-1	P-20	0.0
Total	10	452	878	94	238	33	3	15	108	87	147	.271	.339	.367	706	85	-17	2	1		.963	-6	P-344	0.0
■ **JOHN NEWELL**	Newell, John A. b: 1/14/1868, Wilmington, Del. d: 1/28/19, Wilmington, Del. BR/TL, Deb: 7/22/1891																							
1891	Pit-N	5	18	1	2	0	0	0	2	0	0	.111	.158	.111	269	-22	-3	0			.846	-2	/3-5	-0.4
■ **T. E. NEWELL**	Newell, T. E. b: St.Louis, Mo. Deb: 8/8/1877																							
1877	StL-N	1	3	0	0	0	0	0	0	0	0	.000	.000	.000	0	-99	-1				.833	0	/S-1	0.0
■ **MARC NEWFIELD**	Newfield, Marc Alexander b: 10/19/72, Sacramento, Cal. BR/TR, 6'4", 205 lbs. Deb: 7/6/93 Career OF: (212-LF 0-CF 24-RF)																							
1993	Sea-A	22	66	5	15	3	0	1	7	2	8	.227	.261	.318	579	54	-4	0	1	-0	.000	-2	D-15/O-5(5-0-0)	-0.7
1994	Sea-A	12	38	3	7	1	0	1	4	2	4	.184	.225	.289	514	31	-4	0	0	0	1.000	-1	/O-3(3-0-0),D-9	-0.5
1995	Sea-A	24	85	7	16	3	0	3	14	3	16	.188	.225	.329	554	42	-8	0	0	0	1.000	-0	O-24(23-0-1)	-0.8
	SD-N	21	55	6	17	5	1	1	7	2	8	.309	.333	.491	824	118	1	0	0	0	1.000	-0	O-19(19-0-0)	0.0
1996	SD-N	84	191	27	48	11	0	5	26	16	44	.251	.316	.387	703	89	-3	1	1	-0	.970	-7	O-51(30-0-23)/1-2	-1.2
	Mil-A	49	179	21	55	15	0	7	31	11	26	.307	.361	.508	869	112	3	0	1	-0	.990	1	O-49(49-0-0)	0.2
1997	Mil-A	50	157	14	36	8	0	1	18	14	27	.229	.301	.299	600	57	-10	0	0	0	.977	-3	O-28(28-0-0),D-18	-1.4
1998	Mil-N	93	186	15	44	7	0	3	25	19	29	.237	.311	.323	633	67	-9	0	1	-0	.962	-2	O-55(55-0-0)/D-1	-1.2
Total	6	355	957	98	238	53	1	22	132	69	162	.249	.307	.375	682	77	-33	1	4	-1	.981	-14	O-234L/D-43,1-2	-5.6
■ **DAVID NEWHAN**	Newhan, David Matthew b: 9/7/73, Fullerton, Cal. BL/TR, 5'10", 180 lbs. Deb: 6/4/99 Career OF: (0-LF 0-CF 5-RF)																							
1999	SD-N	32	43	7	6	1	0	2	6	1	11	.140	.159	.302	461	14	-6	2	1	0	.970	8	2-19/1-1,3-1	0.3
2000	SD-N	14	20	5	3	1	0	1	2	6	7	.150	.346	.350	696	81	-0	0	0	0	1.000	-2	/2-3,O-5(0-0-5),3-2	-0.3
	Phi-N	10	17	3	3	0	0	0	0	2	6	.176	.263	.176	440	14	-2	0	0	0	1.000	4	/2-5	0.1
	Yr	24	37	8	6	1	0	1	2	8	13	.162	.311	.270	581	50	-3	0	0	0	1.000	1	/2-8,O-5(0-0-5),3-2	-0.2
Total	2	56	80	15	12	2	0	3	8	9	24	.150	.236	.287	523	33	-9	2	1	0	.979	10	/2-27,O-5R,3-3,1-1	0.1
■ **AL NEWMAN**	Newman, Albert Dwayne b: 6/30/60, Kansas City, Mo. BB/TR, 5'9", 183 lbs. Deb: 6/14/85 Career OF: (11-LF 1-CF 0-RF)																							
1985	Mon-N	25	29	7	5	1	0	0	1	3	4	.172	.250	.207	457	31	-3	2	1	0	1.000	10	2-15/S-2	0.8
1986	Mon-N	95	185	23	37	3	0	1	8	21	20	.200	.282	.232	514	44	-14	11	11	-1	.967	9	2-59,S-22	-0.4
1987	*Min-A	110	307	44	68	15	5	0	29	34	27	.221	.299	.303	602	58	-18	15	11	-1	.982	-11	S-55,2-47,3-12,/OD	-2.2
1988	Min-A	105	260	35	58	7	0	0	19	29	34	.223	.301	.250	551	54	-15	12	3	2	.966	-4	3-60,S-28,2-23,/D-2	-1.6
1989	Min-A	141	446	62	113	18	2	0	38	59	46	.253	.343	.303	646	78	-11	25	12	1	.980	-22	2-84,3-37,S-31,/OD	-2.8
1990	Min-A	144	388	43	94	14	0	0	30	33	34	.242	.305	.278	583	60	-20	13	6	1	.993	-2	2-89,S-48,3-28,/O-3L	-1.7
1991	*Min-A	118	246	25	47	5	0	0	19	23	21	.191	.263	.211	474	31	-22	4	5	-1	.987	-1	S-55,2-35,3-35,/1OD	-2.1
1992	Tex-A	116	246	25	54	5	0	0	12	34	26	.220	.317	.240	557	60	-12	9	6	-0	.983	12	2-72,3-28,S-20,/OD	0.2
Total	8	854	2107	264	476	68	7	1	156	236	212	.226	.306	.266	572	58	-114	91	55	1	.984	-10	2-424,S-261,3/DO1	-9.8
■ **CHARLIE NEWMAN**	Newman, Charles "Decker" b: 11/5/1868, Juda, Wis. d: 11/23/47, San Diego, Cal. BR/TR, Deb: 7/11/1892																							
1892	NY-N	3	12	1	4	0	0	0	1	2	0	.333	.429	.333	762	133	1	3			.750	-0	/O-3(3-0-0)	0.0
	Chi-N	16	61	4	10	0	0	0	2	1	6	.164	.177	.164	341	3	-7	2			.950	-3	O-16(16-0-0)	-1.1
	Yr	19	73	5	14	0	0	0	3	3	6	.192	.224	.192	415	26	-7	5			.917	-3	O-19(19-0-0)	-1.1
■ **JEFF NEWMAN**	Newman, Jeffrey Lynn b: 9/11/48, Fort Worth, Tex. BR/TR, 6'2", 218 lbs. Deb: 6/30/76 MC																							
1976	Oak-A	43	77	5	15	4	0	0	4	4	12	.195	.235	.247	481	43	-6	0	0	0	.981	6	C-43	0.2
1977	Oak-A	94	162	17	36	9	0	4	15	4	24	.222	.246	.352	597	61	-9	2	0	0	.970	10	C-94/P-1	0.3
1978	Oak-A	105	268	25	64	7	1	9	32	18	40	.239	.289	.373	662	90	-5	0	3	-1	.969	-5	C-61,1-36/D-2	-1.1
1979	Oak-A☆	143	516	53	119	17	2	22	71	27	88	.231	.270	.399	669	82	-15	2	1	0	.977	-1	C-81,1-46/3-7,D-7	-1.5
1980	Oak-A	127	438	37	102	19	1	15	56	25	81	.233	.276	.384	659	85	-11	3	4	-1	.982	-9	1-60,C-55/3-2,2D	-2.2
1981	*Oak-A	68	216	17	50	12	0	3	15	9	28	.231	.262	.329	591	73	-8	0	2	-1	.995	2	C-37,1-30	-0.7
1982	Oak-A	72	251	19	50	11	0	6	30	14	49	.199	.242	.315	556	54	-17	0	1	-0	.989	-1	C-67/1-3,3-1,D-1	-1.5
1983	Bos-A	59	132	11	25	4	0	3	7	10	31	.189	.257	.288	545	46	-10	0	1	-0	.990	2	C-51/D-6	-0.7
1984	Bos-A	24	63	5	14	2	0	1	3	5	16	.222	.279	.302	581	58	-4	0	0	0	.992	2	C-24	-0.1
Total	9	735	2123	189	475	85	4	63	233	116	369	.224	.266	.357	622	73	-83	7	12	-3	.981	7	C-513,1-175/D-25,32P	-7.3
■ **PATRICK NEWNAM**	Newnam, Patrick Henry b: 12/10/1880, Hempstead, Tex. d: 6/20/38, San Antonio, Tex. BL/TR, 6', 180 lbs. Deb: 5/29/10																							
1910	StL-A	103	384	45	83	3	8	2	26	29		.216	.275	.281	556	79	-10	16			.972	-4	*1-103	-1.8
1911	StL-A	20	62	11	12	4	0	0	5	12		.194	.351	.258	609	74	-1	4			.986	1	1-20	-0.1
Total	2	123	446	56	95	7	8	2	31	41		.213	.287	.278	565	78	-11	20			.974	-3	1-123	-1.9
■ **SKEETER NEWSOME**	Newsome, Lamar Ashby b: 10/18/10, Phenix City, Ala. d: 8/31/89, Columbus, Ga. BR/TR, 5'9", 170 lbs. Deb: 4/19/35																							
1935	Phi-A	59	145	18	30	7	1	1	10	5	9	.207	.233	.290	523	35	-14	2	1	0	.956	8	S-24,2-13/3-4,O-1R	-0.4
1936	Phi-A	127	471	41	106	15	2	0	46	25	27	.225	.266	.265	531	32	-51	13	4	1	.957	7	*S-123/2-2,3-1,O-1L	-3.0
1937	Phi-A	122	438	53	111	22	1	1	30	37	22	.253	.312	.315	627	59	-27	11	5	1	.954	7	*S-122	-1.0
1938	Phi-A	17	48	7	13	4	0	0	7	1	4	.271	.286	.354	640	61	-3	1	1	-0	.971	1	S-15	-0.1
1939	Phi-A	99	248	22	55	9	1	0	17	19	12	.222	.277	.266	543	40	-22	5	7	-1	.950	1	S-93/2-2	-1.6
1941	Bos-A	93	227	28	51	6	0	2	17	22	11	.225	.296	.278	574	51	-16	10	4	1	.958	15	S-69,2-23	0.4
1942	Bos-A	29	95	7	26	6	0	0	9	9	5	.274	.337	.337	673	87	-2	2	1	0	.925	3	3-12,2-10/S-7	0.2
1943	Bos-A	114	449	48	119	21	2	1	22	21	21	.265	.301	.327	628	82	-11	5	6	-1	.962	14	S-98,3-15	1.1
1944	Bos-A	136	472	41	114	26	3	0	41	33	21	.242	.291	.309	600	72	-17	4	3	-0	.963	11	*S-126/2-8,3-1	0.4
1945	Bos-A	125	438	45	127	30	1	1	48	20	15	.290	.322	.370	692	98	-2	6	3	0	.963	22	2-82,S-33,3-11	2.8
1946	Phi-N	112	375	35	87	10	2	1	23	30	23	.232	.289	.277	566	63	-18	4			.955	-12	*S-107/2-3,3-2	-2.6
1947	Phi-N	95	310	36	71	8	2	2	22	24	24	.229	.284	.287	572	54	-21	4			.969	2	S-85/2-6,3-3	-1.4
Total	12	1128	3716	381	910	164	15	9	292	246	194	.245	.293	.304	597	62	-205	67	35		.959	78	S-902,2-149/3-49,O	-5.2
■ **WARREN NEWSON**	Newson, Warren Dale b: 7/3/64, Newnan, Ga. BL/TL, 5'7", 202 lbs. Deb: 5/29/91																							
1991	Chi-A	71	132	20	39	5	0	4	25	28	34	.295	.419	.424	843	137	8	2	2	-0	.962	-10	O-50(16-1-34)/D-3	-0.3
1992	Chi-A	63	136	19	30	3	0	1	11	37	38	.221	.387	.265	652	87	-0	3	0	1	1.000	-4	O-50(17-0-33)/D-4	-0.5
1993	*Chi-A	26	40	9	12	0	0	2	6	9	12	.300	.429	.450	879	139	3	0	0	0	1.000	-1	D-10/O-5(2-0-3)	0.1
1994	Chi-A	63	102	16	26	5	0	2	7	14	23	.255	.345	.363	708	84	-2	1	0	0	.979	-4	O-34(9-0-26)/D-3	-0.7
1995	Chi-A	51	85	19	20	0	2	3	9	23	27	.235	.404	.388	792	112	3	1	1	-0	.978	-1	O-24(12-0-14)/D-7	0.1
	*Sea-A	33	72	15	21	2	0	2	6	16	18	.292	.420	.403	823	114	2	1	0	0	.971	-2	O-23(18-2-4)	0.0
	Yr	84	157	34	41	2	2	5	15	39	45	.261	.411	.395	806	114	5	2	1	0	.975	-3	O-47(30-2-18)/D-7	0.1
1996	*Tex-A	91	235	34	60	14	1	10	31	37	82	.255	.357	.451	808	97	-1	3	0	1	.992	2	O-66(8-0-58)/D-9	-0.1
1997	Tex-A	81	169	23	36	10	1	10	23	31	53	.213	.335	.462	797	100	-0	3	0	1	.949	-8	O-58(20-0-44)/D-9	-0.9
1998	Tex-A	10	21	1	4	1	0	0	2	1	5	.190	.227	.238	465	20	-2	0	0	0	1.000	-1	/O-6(6-0-0),D-3	-0.4
Total	8	489	992	156	248	40	4	34	120	196	292	.250	.374	.401	775	103	10	14	3	2	.978	-29	O-316(108-3-216)/D-48	-2.7
■ **GUS NIARHOS**	Niarhos, Constantine Gregory b: 12/6/20, Birmingham, Ala. BR/TR, 6', 165 lbs. Deb: 6/9/46 C																							
1946	NY-A	37	40	11	9	1	1	0	2	11	2	.225	.392	.300	692	94	0	1	0	0	.989	6	C-29	0.7
1948	NY-A	83	228	41	61	12	2	0	19	52	15	.268	.404	.338	741	99	3	1	3	-1	.990	11	C-82	1.6
1949	*NY-A	32	43	7	12	2	1	0	6	13	8	.279	.456	.372	828	120	2	0	0	0	1.000	4	C-30	0.7
1950	NY-A	1	0	0	0	0	0	0	0	0	0	—	—	—	—	—	0	0	0	0	.000	0	R	0.0
	Chi-A	41	105	17	34	4	0	0	16	14	6	.324	.408	.362	770	101	1	0	0	0	.978	8	C-36	1.0
	Yr	42	105	17	34	4	0	0	16	14	6	.324	.408	.362	770	101	1	0	0	0	.978	8	C-36	1.0
1951	Chi-A	66	168	27	43	6	0	1	10	47	9	.256	.419	.310	728	101	4	4	3	-0	.985	4	C-59	1.0
1952	Bos-A	29	58	4	6	0	0	0	4	12	9	.103	.268	.103	371	6	-7	0	0	0	.992	6	C-25	0.0
1953	Bos-A	16	35	6	7	1	1	0	2	4	4	.200	.300	.286	586	56	-2	0	1	-0	.985	4	C-16	0.2

YEAR	TM/L	G	AB	R	H	2B	3B	HR	RBI	BB	SO	AVG	OBP	SLG	OPS	OPS+	BR+	SB	CS	SBR	FA	FR	G/POS	TPR
1954	Phi-N	3	5	0	1	0	0	0	0	0	1	.200	.200	.200	400	5	-1	0	0	0	1.000	1	/C-3	0.0
1955	Phi-N	7	9	1	1	0	0	0	0	0	2	.111	.111	.111	222	-42	-2	0	0	0	1.000	1	/C-7	-0.1
Total	9	315	691	114	174	26	5	1	59	153	56	.252	.390	.308	699	89	-2	6	7	-1	.988	45	C-287	5.1

■ SAM NICHOL Nichol, Samuel Anderson b: 4/20/1869, County Antrim, Ireland d: 4/19/37, Steubenville, Ohio BR/TR, 5'10", 178 lbs. Deb: 10/5/1888

YEAR	TM/L	G	AB	R	H	2B	3B	HR	RBI	BB	SO	AVG	OBP	SLG	OPS	OPS+	BR+	SB	CS	SBR	FA	FR	G/POS	TPR
1888	Pit-N	8	22	3	1	0	0	0	0	2	2	.045	.125	.045	170	-47	-4	0			.952	0	/O-8(0-8-0)	-0.3
1890	Col-a	14	56	7	9	0	0	0	4	2		.161	.190	.161	350	4	-7	3			.903	3	O-14(14-0-0)	-0.4
Total	2	22	78	10	10	0	0	0	4	4	2	.128	.171	.128	299	-10	-10	3			.923	3	/O-22(14-8-0)	-0.7

■ DON NICHOLAS Nicholas, Donald Leigh b: 10/30/30, Phoenix, Ariz. BL/TR, 5'7", 150 lbs. Deb: 4/16/52

YEAR	TM/L	G	AB	R	H	2B	3B	HR	RBI	BB	SO	AVG	OBP	SLG	OPS	OPS+	BR+	SB	CS	SBR	FA	FR	G/POS	TPR
1952	Chi-A	3	2	0	0	0	0	0	0	0	0	.000	.000	.000	0	-99	-1	0	0	0	.000	0	H	-0.1
1954	Chi-A	7	0	3	0	0	0	0	0	1	0	—	1.000	—	1000	185	0	0	1	-0	.000	0	H	0.0
Total	2	10	2	3	0	0	0	0	0	1	0	.000	.333	.000	333	-2	-0	0	1	-0		0	-0,-0	-0.1

■ SIMON NICHOLLS Nicholls, Simon Burdette b: 7/18/1882, Germantown, Md. d: 3/12/11, Baltimore, Md. BL/TR, 5'11.5", 165 lbs. Deb: 9/18/03

YEAR	TM/L	G	AB	R	H	2B	3B	HR	RBI	BB	SO	AVG	OBP	SLG	OPS	OPS+	BR+	SB	CS	SBR	FA	FR	G/POS	TPR
1903	Det-A	2	8	0	3	0	0	0	0	0		.375	.375	.375	750	129	0	0			.600	-2	/S-2	-0.2
1906	Phi-A	12	44	1	8	1	0	0	1	3		.182	.234	.205	439	36	-3	0			.965	-2	S-12	-0.6
1907	Phi-A	124	460	75	139	12	2	0	23	24		.302	.338	.337	675	113	6	13			.930	-20	S-82,2-28,3-13	-1.2
1908	Phi-A	150	550	58	119	17	3	4	31	35		.216	.265	.280	545	72	-17	14			.913	-20	*S-120,2-23/3-7	-3.8
1909	Phi-A	21	71	10	15	2	1	0	3	3		.211	.243	.268	511	60	-3	0			.889	0	S-14/3-5,1-1	-0.3
1910	Cle-A	3	0	0	0	0	0	0	0	0		—	—	—	—	—	0	0			.000	-1	/S-3	-0.1
Total	6	312	1133	144	284	32	6	4	58	65		.251	.292	.300	593	86	-17	27			.917	-46	S-233/2-51,3-25,1-1	-6.2

■ AL NICHOLS Nichols, Albert H. b: Brooklyn, N.Y. 5'11", 180 lbs. Deb: 4/24/1875

YEAR	TM/L	G	AB	R	H	2B	3B	HR	RBI	BB	SO	AVG	OBP	SLG	OPS	OPS+	BR+	SB	CS	SBR	FA	FR	G/POS	TPR
1875	Atl-n	32	131	4	20	2	0	0	9	0	6	.153	.153	.168	321	13	-10	0	0	0	.785	9	3-32	-0.2
1876	NY-N	57	214	20	38	4	0	0	9	2	3	.178	.187	.198	385	33	-13				.779	5	*3-57	-0.5
1877	Lou-N	6	19	1	4	0	1	0	0	0	2	.211	.211	.316	526	54	-1				.706	4	/2-3,S-1,3-1,1-1	0.3
Total	2	63	233	21	42	4	1	0	9	2	5	.180	.189	.208	397	35	-14				.785	9	/3-58,2-3,1-1,S-1	-0.2

■ ART NICHOLS Nichols, Arthur Francis (b: Arthur Francis Meikle)
b: 7/14/1871, Manchester, N.H. d: 8/9/45, Willimantic, Conn. BR/TR, 5'10", 175 lbs. Deb: 9/16/1898 Career OF: (7-LF 30-CF 14-RF)

YEAR	TM/L	G	AB	R	H	2B	3B	HR	RBI	BB	SO	AVG	OBP	SLG	OPS	OPS+	BR+	SB	CS	SBR	FA	FR	G/POS	TPR
1898	Chi-N	14	42	7	12	1	0	0	6	4		.286	.388	.310	697	101	0	6			.968	1	C-14	0.2
1899	Chi-N	17	47	5	12	2	0	1	11	0		.255	.286	.362	647	79	-2	3			.931	-1	C-15	-0.2
1900	Chi-N	8	25	1	5	0	0	0	0	3		.200	.286	.200	486	36	-2	1			.938	-1	/C-7	-0.2
1901	StL-N	93	308	50	75	11	3	1	33	10		.244	.290	.308	598	77	-9	14			.960	-4	C-47,O-40(0-29-11)	-0.9
1902	StL-N	73	251	36	67	12	0	1	31	21		.267	.333	.327	660	108	3	18			.984	-7	1-56,C-11/O-4(0-1-3)	-0.4
1903	StL-N	36	120	13	23	2	0	0	9	12		.192	.281	.208	490	42	-9	9			.972	-5	1-25/O-7(7-0-0),C-2	-1.4
Total	6	241	793	112	194	28	3	3	90	50		.245	.308	.299	606	81	-18	51			.952	-17	/C-96,1-81,O-51C	-2.9

■ CARL NICHOLS Nichols, Carl Edward b: 10/14/62, Los Angeles, Cal. BR/TR, 6', 208 lbs. Deb: 9/14/86

YEAR	TM/L	G	AB	R	H	2B	3B	HR	RBI	BB	SO	AVG	OBP	SLG	OPS	OPS+	BR+	SB	CS	SBR	FA	FR	G/POS	TPR
1986	Bal-A	5	5	0	0	0	0	0	0	1	4	.000	.167	.000	167	-51	-1	0	0	0	1.000	-0	/C-5	-0.1
1987	Bal-A	13	21	4	8	1	0	0	3	1	4	.381	.409	.429	838	126	1	0	0	0	1.000	1	C-13	0.2
1988	Bal-A	18	47	2	9	1	0	0	1	3	10	.191	.240	.213	453	29	-4	0	0	0	.987	6	C-13/O-3(0-0-3)	0.2
1989	Hou-N	8	13	0	1	0	0	0	2	0	3	.077	.077	.077	154	-58	-3	0	0	0	1.000	-0	/C-6	-0.3
1990	Hou-N	32	49	7	10	3	0	0	11	8	11	.204	.328	.265	593	67	-2	0	0	0	.986	3	C-15/1-3,O-1(1-0-0)	0.1
1991	Hou-N	20	51	3	10	3	0	0	1	5	17	.196	.268	.255	523	51	-3	0	0	0	.971	3	C-17	0.1
Total	6	96	186	16	38	8	0	0	18	18	49	.204	.278	.247	525	49	-13	0	0	0	.985	12	/C-69,O-4(1-0-3),1-3	0.2

■ ROY NICHOLS Nichols, Roy b: 3/3/21, Little Rock, Ark. BR/TR, 5'11", 155 lbs. Deb: 5/6/44

YEAR	TM/L	G	AB	R	H	2B	3B	HR	RBI	BB	SO	AVG	OBP	SLG	OPS	OPS+	BR+	SB	CS	SBR	FA	FR	G/POS	TPR
1944	NY-N	11	9	3	2	1	0	0	0	2	2	.222	.364	.333	697	97	0	0			1.000	2	/2-1,3-1	0.2

■ REID NICHOLS Nichols, Thomas Reid b: 8/5/58, Ocala, Fla. BR/TR, 5'11", 165 lbs. Deb: 9/16/80 Career OF: (124-LF 247-CF 62-RF)

YEAR	TM/L	G	AB	R	H	2B	3B	HR	RBI	BB	SO	AVG	OBP	SLG	OPS	OPS+	BR+	SB	CS	SBR	FA	FR	G/POS	TPR
1980	Bos-A	12	36	5	8	0	1	0	3	3	8	.222	.282	.278	560	51	-2	0	1	-0	.962	0	/O-9(0-9-0),D-1	-0.2
1981	Bos-A	39	48	13	9	0	1	0	3	2	6	.188	.220	.229	449	28	-4	0	1	-0	1.000	-4	O-27(1-25-1)/3-1,D-7	-1.0
1982	Bos-A	92	245	35	74	16	1	7	33	14	28	.302	.342	.461	804	112	4	5	3	0	.989	-2	O-82(30-57-2)/D-4	0.0
1983	Bos-A	100	274	35	78	22	1	6	22	26	36	.285	.353	.438	791	108	3	7	5	-0	.994	2	O-72C,D-18/S-1	0.3
1984	Bos-A	74	124	14	28	5	1	1	14	12	18	.226	.309	.306	616	68	-5	2	1	0	.988	-4	O-48(17-26-4)/D-1	-1.0
1985	Bos-A	21	32	3	6	1	0	1	3	2	4	.188	.257	.313	570	53	-2	1	0	0	.933	-2	O-10(2-7-1)/2-3,D-4	-0.4
	Chi-A	51	118	20	35	7	1	1	15	15	13	.297	.376	.398	774	108	2	5	5	-1	1.000	-12	O-48(25-27-8)/D-1	-1.1
	Yr	72	150	23	41	8	1	2	18	17	17	.273	.351	.380	731	96	-0	6	5	-0	.988	-14	O-58(27-34-9)/D-5,2-3	-1.5
1986	Chi-A	74	136	9	31	4	0	2	18	11	23	.228	.286	.301	587	58	-8	5	4	-0	.989	-4	O-53L/2-2,D-3	-1.3
1987	Mon-N	77	147	22	39	8	2	4	20	14	13	.265	.333	.429	762	97	-1	2	1	0	.990	-4	O-59(7-50-5)/3-3	-0.5
Total	8	540	1160	156	308	63	8	22	131	99	149	.266	.328	.391	719	91	-14	27	21	-1	.990	-29	O-408C/D-39,2-5,3S	-5.2

■ DAVE NICHOLSON Nicholson, David Lawrence b: 8/29/39, St.Louis, Mo. BR/TR, 6'2", 215 lbs. Deb: 5/24/60

YEAR	TM/L	G	AB	R	H	2B	3B	HR	RBI	BB	SO	AVG	OBP	SLG	OPS	OPS+	BR+	SB	CS	SBR	FA	FR	G/POS	TPR
1960	Bal-A	54	113	17	21	1	1	5	11	20	55	.186	.308	.345	653	77	-4	0	2	-1	.982	-5	O-44(34-0-11)	-1.1
1962	Bal-A	97	173	25	30	4	1	9	15	27	76	.173	.289	.364	653	79	-5	3	4	-1	.983	-7	O-80(34-20-27)	-1.6
1963	Chi-A	126	449	53	103	11	4	22	70	63	175	.229	.324	.419	743	108	5	2	1	0	.970	2	*O-123(123-0-0)	0.0
1964	Chi-A	97	294	40	60	6	1	13	39	52	126	.204	.330	.364	693	95	-1	0	2	-1	.972	-2	O-92(91-0-1)	-0.9
1965	Chi-A	54	85	11	13	2	1	2	12	9	40	.153	.234	.271	505	46	-6	0	0	0	1.000	-9	O-36(25-12-1)	-1.7
1966	Hou-N	100	280	36	69	8	4	10	31	46	92	.246	.359	.411	769	122	9	1	1	-0	.968	2	O-90(13-5-73)	0.6
1967	Atl-N	10	25	2	5	0	0	0	1	2	9	.200	.259	.200	459	34	-2	0	0	0	1.000	-0	/O-7(7-1-0)	-0.3
Total	7	538	1419	184	301	32	12	61	179	219	573	.212	.320	.381	701	97	-4	6	10	-2	.974	-19	O-472(327-38-113)	-5.0

■ FRED NICHOLSON Nicholson, Fred "Shoemaker" b: 9/1/1894, Honey Grove, Tex. d: 1/23/72, Kilgore, Tex. BR/TR, 5'10.5", 173 lbs. Deb: 4/11/17 Career OF: (119-LF 19-CF 65-RF)

YEAR	TM/L	G	AB	R	H	2B	3B	HR	RBI	BB	SO	AVG	OBP	SLG	OPS	OPS+	BR+	SB	CS	SBR	FA	FR	G/POS	TPR
1917	Det-A	13	14	4	4	1	0	0	1	1	2	.286	.333	.357	690	111	0	0			1.000	-1	/O-3(1-0-2)	-0.1
1919	Pit-N	30	66	8	18	2	2	1	6	6	11	.273	.333	.409	742	118	1	2			.939	-1	O-17(13-1-3)/1-1	0.0
1920	Pit-N	99	247	33	89	16	7	4	30	18	31	.360	.404	.530	934	162	19	9	6	-0	.957	2	O-58(28-18-13)	1.9
1921	Bos-N	83	245	36	80	11	7	5	41	17	29	.327	.370	.490	860	133	11	5	4	-0	.983	-7	O-59(57-0-3)/1-4,2-2	0.0
1922	Bos-N	78	222	31	56	4	5	2	29	23	24	.252	.336	.342	678	79	-7	5	7	-1	.915	-4	O-63(20-0-44)	-1.6
Total	5	303	794	112	247	34	21	12	107	65	97	.311	.367	.452	819	124	25	21	17		.950	-11	O-200L/1-5,2-2	0.2

■ KEVIN NICHOLSON Nicholson, Kevin Ronald b: 3/29/76, Vancouver, B.C., Can. BB/TR, 5'10", 190 lbs. Deb: 6/23/2000

YEAR	TM/L	G	AB	R	H	2B	3B	HR	RBI	BB	SO	AVG	OBP	SLG	OPS	OPS+	BR+	SB	CS	SBR	FA	FR	G/POS	TPR
2000	SD-N	37	97	7	21	6	1	1	8	4	31	.216	.255	.330	585	49	-8	1	0	0	.983	5	S-30/2-4	0.0

■ OVID NICHOLSON Nicholson, Ovid Edward b: 12/30/1888, Salem, Ind. d: 3/24/68, Salem, Ind. BL/TR, 5'9.5", 155 lbs. Deb: 9/17/12

YEAR	TM/L	G	AB	R	H	2B	3B	HR	RBI	BB	SO	AVG	OBP	SLG	OPS	OPS+	BR+	SB	CS	SBR	FA	FR	G/POS	TPR
1912	Pit-N	6	11	2	5	0	0	0	3	1	2	.455	.500	.455	955	164	1	0			1.000	-1	/O-4(4-0-0)	0.0

■ PARSON NICHOLSON Nicholson, Thomas C. "Deacon" b: 4/14/1863, Blaine, Ohio d: 2/28/17, Bellaire, Ohio 5'6", 190 lbs. Deb: 9/14/1888

YEAR	TM/L	G	AB	R	H	2B	3B	HR	RBI	BB	SO	AVG	OBP	SLG	OPS	OPS+	BR+	SB	CS	SBR	FA	FR	G/POS	TPR
1888	Det-N	24	85	11	22	2	3	1	9	2	7	.259	.284	.388	672	113	1	6			.935	-2	2-24	0.0
1890	Tol-a	134	523	78	140	16	11	4	72	42		.268	.333	.363	696	102	-0	46			.929	-8	*2-134/C-1	-0.3
1895	Was-N	10	38	7	7	2	1	0	5	7	4	.184	.311	.289	601	56	-2	6			.797	-2	S-10	-0.3
Total	3	168	646	96	169	20	15	5	86	51	11	.262	.325	.362	688	100	-2	58			.930	-12	2-158/S-10,C-1	-0.6

■ BILL NICHOLSON Nicholson, William Beck "Swish" b: 12/11/14, Chestertown, Md. d: 3/8/96, Chestertown, Md. BL/TR, 6', 205 lbs. Deb: 6/13/36

YEAR	TM/L	G	AB	R	H	2B	3B	HR	RBI	BB	SO	AVG	OBP	SLG	OPS	OPS+	BR+	SB	CS	SBR	FA	FR	G/POS	TPR
1936	Phi-A	11	12	2	0	0	0	0	0	0	5	.000	.000	.000	0	-99	-4	0	0	0	1.000	-0	/O-1(0-0-1)	-0.4
1939	Chi-N	58	220	37	65	12	5	5	38	20	29	.295	.354	.464	818	116	5	0			.955	1	O-58(0-0-58)	0.2
1940	Chi-N★	135	491	78	146	27	7	25	98	50	67	.297	.366	.534	899	148	31	2			.950	-2	*O-123(43-0-81)	2.1
1941	Chi-N★	147	532	74	135	26	1	26	98	82	91	.254	.357	.453	810	132	22	1			.971	6	*O-143(3-0-140)	2.0
1942	Chi-N	152	588	83	173	22	11	21	78	76	80	.294	.382	.476	859	156	42	8			.986	11	*O-151(0-0-151)	**4.6**
1943	Chi-N★	154	608	95	188	30	9	**29**	**128**	71	86	.309	.386	.531	917	166	50	4			.978	6	*O-154(0-0-154)	4.7
1944	Chi-N★	156	582	**116**	167	35	8	**33**	**122**	93	71	.287	.391	.545	935	162	48	3			.979	2	*O-156(0-0-156)	4.0

YEAR	TM/L	G	AB	R	H	2B	3B	HR	RBI	BB	SO	AVG	OBP	SLG	OPS	OPS+	BR+	SB	CS	SBR	FA	FR	G/POS	TPR
1945	*Chi-N†	151	559	82	136	28	4	13	88	92	73	.243	.356	.377	734	106	7	4			.990	1	*O-151(0-0-151)	-0.3
1946	Chi-N	105	296	36	65	13	2	8	41	44	44	.220	.325	.358	683	95	-2	1			.973	2	O-80(0-0-80)	-0.2
1947	Chi-N	148	487	69	119	28	1	26	75	87	83	.244	.364	.466	831	124	17	1			**.990**	-1	*O-140(0-0-140)	1.2
1948	Chi-N	143	494	68	129	24	5	19	67	81	60	.261	.371	.445	816	125	18	2			.980	-3	*O-136(0-0-136)	1.1
1949	Phi-N	98	299	42	70	8	3	11	40	45	53	.234	.344	.391	735	99	0	1			.995	3	O-91(0-0-92)	0.0
1950	Phi-N	41	58	3	13	2	1	3	10	8	16	.224	.318	.448	766	101	-0	0			.952	-2	O-15(0-0-15)	-0.3
1951	Phi-N	85	170	23	41	9	2	8	30	25	24	.241	.342	.459	801	115	3	0	1	-0	.987	-3	O-41(0-0-41)	-0.1
1952	Phi-N	55	88	17	24	3	0	6	19	14	26	.273	.390	.511	902	150	6	0	0	0	1.000	-2	O-19(0-0-19)	0.4
1953	Phi-N	38	62	12	13	5	1	2	16	12	20	.210	.338	.419	757	97	-0	0	0	0	1.000	-2	O-12(0-0-12)	-0.3
Total	16	1677	5546	837	1484	272	60	235	948	800	828	.268	.365	.465	830	133	243	27	1		.979	17	*O-1471(46-0-1427)	18.7
■ **GEORGE NICOL**	Nicol, George Edward b: 10/17/1870, Barry, Ill. d: 8/10/24, Milwaukee, Wis. TL, 5'7", 155 lbs. Deb: 9/23/1890																							
1890	StL-a	3	7	4	2	1	0	0	1	4		.286	.545	.429	974	164	1	0			1.000	-0	/P-3	0.0
1891	Chi-N	3	6	0	2	0	1	0	3	0	1	.333	.333	.667	1000	189	1	0			.000	-1	/P-3	0.0
1894	Pit-N	9	22	8	9	1	0	0	3	0	1	.409	.409	.455	864	109	0	0			.800	-1	/P-9	0.0
	Lou-N	28	112	12	38	6	4	0	19	2	4	.339	.362	.464	826	105	1	4			.791	-5	O-26(0-0-26)/P-2	-0.4
	Yr	37	134	20	47	7	4	0	22	2	5	.351	.370	.463	832	105	1	4			.791	-6	O-26(0-0-26),P-11	-0.4
Total	3	43	147	24	51	8	5	0	26	6	6	.347	.381	.469	850	112	2	4			.692	-7	/O-26(0-0-26),P-17	-0.4
■ **HUGH NICOL**	Nicol, Hugh b: 1/1/1858, Campsie, Scotland d: 6/27/21, Lafayette, Ind. BR/TR, 5'4", 145 lbs. Deb: 5/3/1881 M Career OF: (3-LF 20-CF 802-RF)																							
1881	Chi-N	26	108	13	22	2	0	0	7	4	12	.204	.232	.222	454	42	-7				.932	3	O-26(2-12-12)/S-1	-0.4
1882	Chi-N	47	186	19	37	9	1	1	16	7	29	.199	.228	.274	502	58	-9				.887	10	O-47(0-0-47)/S-8	0.1
1883	StL-a	94	368	73	105	13	3	0	39	18		.285	.319	.337	656	105	1				.916	12	*O-84(1-1-84),2-11	1.2
1884	StL-a	110	442	79	116	14	5	0		22		.262	.302	.317	619	99	-1				.873	23	*O-87R,2-23/S-1,3-1	2.0
1885	*StL-a	112	425	59	88	11	1	0	45	34		.207	.271	.238	508	59	-20				.888	13	*O-111(0-0-111)/3-1	-0.6
1886	StL-a	67	253	44	52	6	3	0	19	26		.206	.280	.253	533	64	-11	38			.942	-4	O-57(0-1-56)/S-8,2-4	-1.3
1887	Cin-a	125	561	122	188	18	2	1	34	86		.335	.341	.267	608	69	-17	**138**			.918	-3	*O-125(0-6-119)	-1.7
1888	Cin-a	135	548	112	131	10	2	1	35	67		.239	.330	.270	600	88	-5	103			.957	-3	*O-125R,2-12/S-1	-0.8
1889	Cin-a	122	474	82	121	7	8	2	58	54	35	.255	.338	.316	654	84	-9	80			.918	1	*O-115R/2-7,3-3	-0.7
1890	Cin-N	50	186	28	39	1	4	0	19	19	12	.210	.283	.258	541	58	-10	24			.921	-6	O-46(0-0-46)/S-3,2-1	-1.4
Total	10	888	3551	631	899	91	29	5	272	337	88	.253	.307	.282	589	78	-87	383			.912	49	O-823R/2-58,S-22,3	-3.6
■ **STEVE NICOSIA**	Nicosia, Steven Richard b: 8/6/55, Paterson, N.J. BR/TR, 5'10", 185 lbs. Deb: 7/8/78																							
1978	Pit-N	3	5	0	0	0	0	0	0	1	0	.000	.167	.000	167	-48	-1	0	0	0	1.000	1	/C-1	0.0
1979	*Pit-N	70	191	22	55	16	0	4	13	23	17	.288	.364	.435	799	112	3	0	2	-1	.991	4	C-65	0.9
1980	Pit-N	60	176	16	38	8	0	1	22	19	16	.216	.296	.278	574	60	-9	0	1	-0	.984	-1	C-58	-0.8
1981	Pit-N	54	169	21	39	10	1	2	18	13	10	.231	.286	.337	623	74	-6	3	1	0	.982	1	C-52	-0.3
1982	Pit-N	39	100	6	28	3	0	1	7	11	13	.280	.351	.340	691	91	-1	0	1	-0	.990	3	C-35/O-3(3-0-0)	0.3
1983	Pit-N	21	46	4	6	2	0	1	1	1	7	.130	.149	.239	388	6	-6	0	0	0	.988	-1	C-15	-0.7
	SF-N	15	33	4	11	0	0	0	6	3	2	.333	.389	.333	722	105	0	0	0	0	.984	2	/C-9	0.3
	Yr	36	79	8	17	2	0	1	7	4	9	.215	.253	.278	531	47	-6	0	0	0	.986	1	C-24	-0.4
1984	SF-N	48	132	9	40	11	2	2	19	8	14	.303	.343	.462	805	129	4	1	1	-0	.985	-5	C-41	0.0
1985	Mon-N	42	71	4	12	2	0	0	1	7	11	.169	.244	.197	441	26	-7	1	0	0	.988	-5	C-23/1-2	-1.2
	Tor-A	6	15	0	4	0	0	0	1	0	0	.267	.267	.267	533	46	-1	0	0	0	1.000	1	/C-6	0.0
Total	8	358	938	86	233	52	3	11	88	86	90	.248	.312	.345	658	82	-23	5	6	-1	.987	-1	C-305/O-3(3-0-0),1-2	-1.5
■ **CHARLIE NIEBERGALL**	Niebergall, Charles Arthur "Nig" b: 5/23/1899, New York, N.Y. d: 8/29/82, Holiday, Fla. BR/TR, 5'10", 160 lbs. Deb: 6/17/21																							
1921	StL-N	5	6	1	1	0	0	0	0	0	0	.167	.167	.167	333	-12	-1	0	0	0	1.000	-1	/C-3	-0.1
1923	StL-N	9	28	2	3	1	0	0	1	2	2	.107	.167	.143	310	-18	-5	0	0	0	1.000	-0	/C-7	-0.4
1924	StL-N	40	58	6	17	6	0	0	7	3	9	.293	.339	.397	735	98	-0	0	0	0	.951	1	C-34	0.2
Total	3	54	92	9	21	7	0	0	8	5	11	.228	.276	.304	580	55	-6	0	0	0	.966	1	/C-44	-0.3
■ **AL NIEHAUS**	Niehaus, Albert Bernard b: 6/1/1899, Cincinnati, Ohio d: 10/14/31, Cincinnati, Ohio BR/TR, 5'11", 175 lbs. Deb: 4/22/25																							
1925	Pit-N	17	64	7	14	8	0	0	7	1	5	.219	.242	.344	586	45	-5	0	0	0	.962	-1	1-15	-0.8
	Cin-N	51	147	16	44	10	2	0	14	13	10	.299	.360	.395	755	95	-1	1	4	-1	.988	2	1-45	-0.2
	Yr	68	211	23	58	18	2	0	21	14	15	.275	.326	.379	705	80	-7	1	4	-1	.981	1	1-60	-1.0
■ **BERT NIEHOFF**	Niehoff, John Albert b: 5/13/1884, Louisville, Colo. d: 12/8/74, Inglewood, Cal. BR/TR, 5'10.5", 170 lbs. Deb: 10/4/13 C																							
1913	Cin-N	2	8	0	0	0	0	0	0	0	2	.000	.000	.000	0	-99	-2	0			.917	2	/3-2	0.0
1914	Cin-N	142	484	46	117	16	9	4	49	38	77	.242	.298	.337	635	86	-9	20			.924	7	*3-134/2-3	0.2
1915	*Phi-N	148	529	61	126	27	2	2	49	30	63	.238	.280	.308	588	77	-15	21	11	1	.946	-7	*2-148	-2.1
1916	Phi-N	146	548	65	133	**42**	4	4	61	37	57	.243	.292	.356	648	95	-4	20	14	-1	.936	-2	*2-144/3-2	-0.4
1917	Phi-N	114	361	30	92	17	4	2	42	23	29	.255	.303	.341	644	93	-3	8			.945	18	2-96/1-7,3-6	1.9
1918	StL-N	22	84	5	15	2	0	0	5	3	10	.179	.207	.202	409	26	-7	2			.975	2	2-22	-0.6
	NY-N	7	23	3	6	0	0	0	1	0	4	.261	.261	.261	522	60	-1	0			.871	-2	/2-7	-0.4
	Yr	29	107	8	21	2	0	0	6	3	14	.196	.218	.215	433	33	-9	2			.954	-1	2-29	-1.0
Total	6	581	2037	210	489	104	19	12	207	131	242	.240	.288	.327	615	84	-42	71	25		.943	18	2-420,3-144/1-7	-1.4
■ **MILT NIELSEN**	Nielsen, Milton Robert b: 2/8/25, Tyler, Minn. BL/TL, 5'11", 190 lbs. Deb: 9/27/49																							
1949	Cle-A	3	9	1	1	0	0	0	0	2	4	.111	.273	.111	384	4	-1	0	0	0	1.000	-0	/O-3(0-3-0)	-0.2
1951	Cle-A	16	6	1	0	0	0	0	0	1	1	.000	.143	.000	143	-63	-1	0	0	0	.000	0	H	-0.1
Total	2	19	15	2	1	0	0	0	0	3	5	.067	.222	.067	289	-22	-3	0	0	0	1.000	-0	/O-3(0-3-0)	-0.3
■ **BUTCH NIEMAN**	Nieman, Elmer Le Roy b: 2/8/18, Herkimer, Kan. d: 11/2/93, Topeka, Kan. BL/TL, 6'2", 195 lbs. Deb: 5/2/43																							
1943	Bos-N	101	335	39	84	15	8	7	46	39	39	.251	.331	.406	737	114	5	4			.963	1	O-93(77-0-16)	0.1
1944	Bos-N	134	468	65	124	16	6	16	65	47	47	.265	.332	.427	759	108	4	5			.975	-2	*O-126(86-0-46)	-0.5
1945	Bos-N	97	247	43	61	15	0	14	56	43	33	.247	.361	.478	839	131	10	11			.932	0	O-57(43-0-14)	0.7
Total	3	332	1050	147	269	46	14	37	167	129	119	.256	.339	.432	771	116	20	20			.961	-0	O-276(206-0-76)	0.3
■ **BOB NIEMAN**	Nieman, Robert Charles b: 1/26/27, Cincinnati, Ohio d: 3/10/85, Corona, Cal. BR/TR, 5'11", 195 lbs. Deb: 9/14/51																							
1951	StL-A	12	43	6	16	3	1	2	8	3	5	.372	.413	.628	1041	174	4	0	0	0	.962	0	O-11(11-0-0)	0.3
1952	StL-A	131	478	66	138	22	2	18	74	46	73	.289	.352	.456	808	120	12	0	4	-1	.976	1	*O-125(32-0-94)	0.6
1953	Det-A	142	508	72	143	32	5	15	69	57	57	.281	.354	.453	807	118	12	0	3	-1	.979	3	*O-135(74-0-64)	0.7
1954	Det-A	91	251	24	66	14	1	8	35	22	32	.263	.322	.422	745	105	1	0	2	-1	.984	-2	O-62(62-0-0)	-0.6
1955	Chi-A	99	272	36	77	11	2	11	53	36	37	.283	.371	.460	831	119	7	1	0	0	.976	-7	O-78(29-0-52)	-0.2
1956	Chi-A	14	40	3	12	1	0	2	4	4	4	.300	.364	.475	839	118	1	0	1	-0	1.000	1	O-10(0-0-10)	0.1
	Bal-A	114	388	60	125	20	6	12	64	86	59	.322	.445	.497	943	161	39	1	5	-2	.980	7	*O-114(114-0-0)	3.6
	Yr	128	428	63	137	21	6	14	68	90	63	.320	.438	.495	934	156	39	1	6	-2	.982	7	*O-124(114-0-10)	3.7
1957	Bal-A	129	445	61	123	17	6	13	70	63	86	.276	.369	.429	798	125	16	4	4	-1	.980	5	*O-120(116-0-4)	1.4
1958	Bal-A	105	366	56	119	20	2	16	60	44	57	.325	.398	.522	919	159	30	2	8	-2	.961	-7	*O-100(100-0-0)	1.4
1959	Bal-A	118	360	49	105	18	2	21	60	42	55	.292	.369	.528	897	146	22	1	2	-0	.973	-0	O-97(97-0-0)	1.6
1960	StL-N	81	188	19	54	13	5	4	31	24	31	.287	.374	.473	847	120	6	0	1	-0	.940	-8	O-55(53-0-2)	-0.6
1961	StL-N	6	17	0	8	1	0	0	2	0	2	.471	.471	.529	1000	150	1	0	0	0	1.000	-1	/O-4(4-0-0)	0.0
	Cle-A	39	65	2	23	6	0	2	10	7	4	.354	.417	.538	955	157	5	1	0	0	.960	0	O-12(7-0-5)	0.5
1962	Cle-A	2	1	0	0	0	0	0	1	0	1	.000	.000	.000	0	-99	-0	0	0	0	.000	0	H	0.0
	*SF-N	30	30	1	9	2	0	1	3	1	9	.300	.323	.467	789	111	0	0	0	0	1.000	-1	/O-3(3-0-0)	0.0
Total	12	1113	3452	455	1018	180	32	125	544	435	512	.295	.375	.474	849	132	155	10	30	-8	.975	-8	O-926(702-0-231)	8.8
■ **AL NIEMIEC**	Niemiec, Alfred Joseph b: 5/18/11, Meriden, Conn. d: 10/29/95, Kirkland, Wash. BR/TR, 5'11", 158 lbs. Deb: 9/19/34																							
1934	Bos-A	9	32	2	7	0	0	0	3	3	4	.219	.286	.219	504	30	-3	0	0	0	1.000	4	/2-9	0.1
1936	Phi-A	69	203	22	40	3	2	1	20	26	16	.197	.291	.246	538	35	-21	2	2	-0	.972	10	2-52/S-5	-0.6
Total	2	78	235	24	47	3	2	1	23	29	20	.200	.291	.243	533	34	-24	2	2	-0	.976	15	/2-61,S-5	-0.5

YEAR	TM/L	G	AB	R	H	2B	3B	HR	RBI	BB	SO	AVG	OBP	SLG	OPS	OPS+	BR+	SB	CS	SBR	FA	FR	G/POS	TPR
■ **TOM NIETO**	Nieto, Thomas Andrew b: 10/27/60, Downey, Cal. BR/TR, 6'1", 205 lbs. Deb: 5/10/84																							
1984	StL-N	33	86	7	24	4	0	3	12	5	18	.279	.319	.430	749	112	1	0	0	0	.994	4	C-32	0.6
1985	*StL-N	95	253	15	57	10	2	0	34	26	37	.225	.305	.281	586	65	-11	0	2	-1	.990	-4	C-95	-1.3
1986	Mon-N	30	65	5	13	3	1	1	7	6	21	.200	.278	.323	601	66	-3	0	1	-0	.978	-3	C-30	-0.6
1987	Min-A	41	105	7	21	7	1	1	12	8	24	.200	.276	.314	590	54	-7	0	0	0	.996	2	C-40/D-1	-0.4
1988	Min-A	24	60	1	4	0	0	0	0	1	17	.067	.097	.067	163	-52	-12	0	0	0	.991	3	C-24	-0.9
1989	Phi-N	11	20	1	3	0	0	0	0	6	7	.150	.370	.150	520	54	-1	0	0	0	1.000	3	C-11	0.3
1990	Phi-N	17	30	1	5	0	0	0	4	3	11	.167	.265	.167	431	21	-3	0	0	0	.984	2	C-17	0.0
Total	7	251	619	37	127	24	4	5	69	55	135	.205	.281	.281	562	56	-36	0	3	-1	.991	7	C-249/D-1	-2.3
■ **JOSE NIEVES**	Nieves, Jose Miguel (Pinto) b: 6/16/75, Guacara, Venez. BR/TR, 6'1", 180 lbs. Deb: 8/7/98																							
1998	Chi-N	2	1	0	0	0	0	0	0	0	0	.000	.000	.000	0	-97	-0	0	0	0	.000	-0	/S-1	-0.1
1999	Chi-N	54	181	16	45	9	1	2	18	8	25	.249	.295	.343	638	62	-11	0	2	-1	.935	4	S-52	-0.3
2000	Chi-N	82	198	17	42	6	3	5	24	11	43	.212	.254	.348	602	51	-16	1	1	-0	.949	-2	3-39,S-24/2-7	-1.5
Total	3	138	380	33	87	15	4	7	42	19	68	.229	.273	.345	618	56	-27	1	3	-1	.945	2	/S-77,3-39,2-7	-1.9
■ **MELVIN NIEVES**	Nieves, Melvin Ramos b: 12/28/71, San Juan, P.R. BB/TR, 6'2", 210 lbs. Deb: 9/1/92 Career OF: (91-LF 8-CF 242-RF)																							
1992	Atl-N	12	19	0	4	1	0	0	1	2	7	.211	.286	.263	549	53	-1	0	0	0	.727	-1	/O-6(3-0-3)	-0.3
1993	SD-N	19	47	4	9	0	0	2	3	3	21	.191	.255	.319	574	52	-3	0	0	0	.931	-1	O-15(0-0-15)	-0.5
1994	SD-N	10	19	2	5	1	0	1	4	3	10	.263	.364	.474	837	120	1	0	0	0	1.000	1	/O-6(2-0-4)	0.1
1995	SD-N	98	234	32	48	6	1	14	38	19	88	.205	.279	.419	698	84	-7	2	3	-1	.990	-6	O-79(62-6-15)/1-2	-1.4
1996	Det-A	120	431	71	106	23	4	24	60	44	158	.246	.324	.485	809	101	-1	1	2	-0	.943	4	*O-105(21-0-84),D-11	-0.3
1997	Det-A	116	359	46	82	18	1	20	64	39	157	.228	.313	.451	764	97	-3	1	7	-2	.979	-2	O-99(0-2-99),D-10	-1.2
1998	Cin-N	83	119	8	30	4	0	2	17	26	42	.252	.386	.336	722	91	-0	0	0	0	1.000	-2	O-25(3-0-22)/D-3	-0.3
Total	7	458	1228	163	284	53	6	63	187	136	483	.231	.316	.438	755	94	-14	4	12	-3	.962	-7	O-335R/D-24,1-2	-3.9
■ **TOM NILAND**	Niland, Thomas James "Honest Tom" b: 4/14/1870, Brookfield, Mass. d: 4/30/50, Lynn, Mass. BR/TR, 5'11", 160 lbs. Deb: 4/19/1896																							
1896	StL-N	18	68	3	12	0	1	0	3	5	4	.176	.243	.206	449	20	-8	0			.913	-4	O-13(6-0-7)/S-5	-1.1
■ **HARRY NILES**	Niles, Herbert Clyde b: 9/10/1880, Buchanan, Mich. d: 4/18/53, Sturgis, Mich. BR/TR, 5'8", 175 lbs. Deb: 4/24/06 Career OF: (95-LF 19-CF 184-RF)																							
1906	StL-A	142	541	71	124	14	4	2	31	46		.229	.297	.281	578	85	-9	30			.967	9	*O-108(0-6-102),3-34	-0.4
1907	StL-A	120	492	65	142	9	5	2	35	28		.289	.331	.339	670	114	7	19			.949	-5	*2-116/O-1(0-0-1)	0.4
1908	NY-A	95	361	43	90	14	6	4	24	25		.249	.305	.355	660	113	5	18			.928	-24	2-85/O-7(1-1-5)	-2.2
	Bos-A	18	33	4	8	0	0	1	3	6		.242	.375	.333	708	127	1	3			1.000	-1	/2-8,S-2	0.1
	Yr	113	394	47	98	14	6	5	27	31		.249	.312	.353	664	114	6	21			.934	-24	2-93/O-7(1-1-5),S-2	-2.1
1909	Bos-A	145	546	65	134	12	5	1	38	39		.245	.311	.291	602	88	-6	27			.952	-0	*O-117L,3-13/S-9,2	-1.4
1910	Bos-A	18	57	6	12	3	0	1	3	4		.211	.262	.316	578	79	-2	1			.920	-0	O-15(4-0-11)	-0.3
	Cle-A	70	240	25	51	6	4	1	18	15		.213	.267	.283	551	72	-8	9			.975	-4	O-50(13-0-37)/S-7,3-5	-1.6
	Yr	88	297	31	63	9	4	2	21	19		.212	.266	.290	556	73	-10	10			.962	-4	O-65(17-0-48)/S-7,3-5	-1.9
Total	5	608	2270	279	561	58	24	12	152	163		.247	.306	.310	616	95	-12	107			.960	-25	O-298R,2-214/3-52,S	-5.4
■ **BILL NILES**	Niles, William E. b: 1/11/1867, Covington, Ky. d: 7/3/36, Springfield, Ohio 160 lbs. Deb: 5/13/1895																							
1895	Pit-N	11	37	2	8	0	0	0	0	5	2	.216	.310	.216	526	39	-3	2			.930	1	3-10/2-1	-0.2
■ **RABBIT NILL**	Nill, George Charles b: 7/14/1881, Ft.Wayne, Ind. d: 5/24/62, Fort Wayne, Ind. BR/TR, 5'7", 160 lbs. Deb: 9/27/04																							
1904	Was-A	15	48	4	8	0	1	0	3	5		.167	.273	.208	481	54	-2	0			.878	-4	2-15	-0.7
1905	Was-A	103	319	46	58	7	3	3	31	33		.182	.269	.251	520	68	-11	12			.897	-2	3-52,2-33/S-6	-1.3
1906	Was-A	89	315	37	74	8	2	0	15	47		.235	.340	.273	613	97	2	16			.882	5	S-31,2-25,3-15,O-15C	0.8
1907	Was-A	66	215	21	47	7	3	0	25	15		.219	.282	.279	561	86	-3	6			.962	-2	2-39,O-18(17-0-1)/3-1	-0.6
	Cle-A	12	43	5	12	1	0	0	2	3		.279	.326	.302	628	100	0	2			.815	-4	/3-7,S-4	-0.4
	Yr	78	258	26	59	8	3	0	27	18		.229	.289	.283	572	88	-3	8			.962	-5	2-39,O-18L/3-8,S-4	-1.0
1908	Cle-A	11	23	3	5	0	0	0	1	0		.217	.217	.217	435	41	-2	0			.833	0	/S-6,O-3(2-0-2),2-1	-0.1
Total	5	296	963	116	204	23	9	3	77	103		.212	.297	.264	561	82	-16	36			.943	-6	2-113/3-75,S-47,O	-2.3
■ **DAVE NILSSON**	Nilsson, David Wayne b: 12/14/69, Brisbane, Queensland, Australia BL/TR, 6'3", 215 lbs. Deb: 5/18/92 Career OF: (80-LF 0-CF 105-RF)																							
1992	Mil-A	51	164	15	38	8	0	4	25	17	18	.232	.304	.354	658	85	-3	2	2	-0	.992	0	C-46/1-3,D-2	-0.1
1993	Mil-A	100	296	35	76	10	2	7	40	37	36	.257	.339	.375	714	93	-2	3	6	-1	.981	-9	C-91/1-4,D-4	-0.8
1994	Mil-A	109	397	51	109	28	3	12	69	34	61	.275	.332	.451	783	95	-4	1	0	0	.994	-5	C-60,D-43/1-5	-0.7
1995	Mil-A	81	263	41	73	12	1	12	53	24	41	.278	.343	.468	810	103	0	2	0	0	.981	-2	O-58R,D-14/1-7,C-2	-0.4
1996	Mil-A	123	453	81	150	33	2	17	84	57	68	.331	.409	.525	935	129	21	2	3	-1	.965	-2	O-61R,D-40,1-24,/C	1.0
1997	Mil-A	156	554	71	154	33	0	20	81	65	88	.278	.356	.446	802	107	6	2	3	-1	.991	-7	1-74,D-59,O-22L	-1.2
1998	Mil-N	102	309	39	83	14	1	12	56	33	48	.269	.341	.437	778	103	1	2	2	-0	.984	-10	1-49,O-37(37-0-3)/C-7	-1.3
1999	Mil-N★	115	343	56	106	19	1	21	62	53	64	.309	.405	.554	958	141	22	1	2	-0	.991	-15	*C-101/D-1	1.2
Total	8	837	2779	389	789	157	10	105	470	320	424	.284	.360	.461	821	110	41	15	18	-3	.988	-49	C-309,O-178R,1-1661,D	-2.3
■ **AL NIXON**	Nixon, Albert Richard "Humpty Dumpty" b: 4/11/1886, Atlantic City, N.J d: 11/9/60, Opelousas, La. BR/TL, 5'7.5", 164 lbs. Deb: 9/4/15																							
1915	Bro-N	14	26	3	6	1	0	0	2	2	4	.231	.286	.269	555	67	-1	1	1	-0	1.000	-2	O-14(8-1-1)	-0.3
1916	Bro-N	1	2	0	2	0	0	0	0	0	0	1.000	1.000	1.000	2000	501	1	0			.000	-0	/O-1(1-0-0)	0.1
1918	Bro-N	6	11	1	5	0	0	0	0	0	0	.455	.455	.455	909	178	1	0			1.000	-0	/O-4(2-0-1)	0.1
1921	Bos-N	55	138	25	33	6	3	1	9	7	11	.239	.281	.348	629	69	-6	3	2	-0	.980	-2	O-43(22-10-13)	-1.1
1922	Bos-N	86	318	35	84	14	4	2	22	9	19	.264	.284	.352	637	66	-17	6	6	-1	.975	1	O-79(48-22-11)	-2.1
1923	Bos-N	88	321	53	88	12	4	0	19	24	14	.274	.334	.336	671	81	-8	2	3	-1	.987	9	O-80(14-62-4)	-0.4
1926	Phi-N	93	311	38	91	18	2	4	41	13	20	.293	.323	.402	725	90	-5	5			.977	-2	O-88(0-88-0)	-1.1
1927	Phi-N	54	154	18	48	7	0	0	18	5	5	.312	.333	.357	690	84	-4	1			.969	-0	O-44(0-43-1)	-0.6
1928	Phi-N	25	64	7	15	2	0	0	7	6	4	.234	.300	.266	566	47	-5	1			1.000	-0	O-20(10-0-10)	-0.6
Total	9	422	1345	180	372	60	13	7	118	66	77	.277	.314	.356	670	78	-44	19	12		.980	2	O-373(105-226-41)	-6.0
■ **TROT NIXON**	Nixon, Christopher Trotman b: 4/11/74, Durham, N.C. BL/TL, 6'1", 195 lbs. Deb: 9/21/96																							
1996	Bos-A	2	4	2	2	1	0	0	0	0	1	.500	.500	.750	1250	206	1	1	0	0	1.000	-0	/O-2(0-0-2)	0.1
1998	*Bos-A	13	27	3	7	1	0	0	0	1	3	.259	.286	.296	582	51	-2	0	0	0	1.000	0	/O-7(1-0-6),D-2	-0.2
1999	*Bos-A	124	381	67	103	22	5	15	52	53	75	.270	.364	.472	836	108	5	3	1	0	.968	-5	*O-121(0-0-121)	-0.6
2000	Bos-A	123	427	66	118	27	8	12	60	63	85	.276	.372	.461	833	105	4	8	1	1	.991	3	*O-118(0-6-115)/D-1	0.2
Total	4	262	839	138	230	51	13	27	112	117	164	.274	.366	.462	829	105	7	12	2	2	.981	-2	O-248(1-6-244)/D-3	-0.5
■ **OTIS NIXON**	Nixon, Otis Junior b: 1/9/59, Columbus Co., N.C. BB/TR, 6'2", 180 lbs. Deb: 9/9/83 F Career OF: (357-LF 1136-CF 72-RF)																							
1983	NY-A	13	14	2	2	0	0	0	0	1	5	.143	.200	.143	343	-4	-2	2	0	0	.938	-1	/O-9(0-4-5)	-0.2
1984	Cle-A	49	91	16	14	0	0	0	1	8	11	.154	.222	.154	376	6	-11	12	6	1	1.000	-2	O-46(43-4-0)	-1.4
1985	Cle-A	104	162	34	38	4	0	3	9	8	27	.235	.271	.315	585	60	-9	20	11	1	.971	-7	O-80(53-26-0),D-11	-1.7
1986	Cle-A	105	95	33	25	4	1	0	8	13	12	.263	.352	.326	678	88	-1	23	6	3	.969	-23	O-95(84-14-0)/D-5	-2.2
1987	Cle-A	19	17	2	1	0	0	0	1	3	4	.059	.200	.059	259	-26	-3	2	3	-1	1.000	-4	O-17(11-7-0)/D-2	-0.7
1988	Mon-N	90	271	47	66	8	2	0	15	28	42	.244	.314	.288	602	71	-9	46	13	6	.994	-2	O-82(25-61-0)	-0.8
1989	Mon-N	126	258	41	56	7	2	0	21	33	36	.217	.306	.260	566	62	-12	37	12	4	.988	-15	O-98(13-92-1)	-2.5
1990	Mon-N	119	231	46	58	6	2	1	20	28	33	.251	.332	.307	639	80	-6	50	13	6	.994	-9	O-88(21-71-0)/S-1	-0.9
1991	Atl-N	124	401	81	119	10	1	0	26	47	40	.297	.373	.327	700	93	-1	72	21	8	.987	1	*O-115(55-17-48)	0.5
1992	*Atl-N	120	456	79	134	14	2	2	22	39	54	.294	.349	.346	696	92	-3	41	18	3	.991	13	*O-111(2-102-16)	1.1
1993	*Atl-N	134	461	77	124	12	3	1	24	61	63	.269	.354	.315	669	80	-11	47	13	6	.990	8	*O-116(0-115-2)	0.5
1994	Bos-A	103	398	60	109	15	1	0	25	55	65	.274	.362	.317	679	74	-14	42	10	6	.989	2	*O-103(0-103-0)	-0.5
1995	Tex-A	139	589	87	174	21	2	0	45	58	85	.295	.359	.338	696	81	-15	50	21	4	.989	5	*O-138(0-138-0)	-0.4
1996	Tor-A	125	496	87	142	15	1	1	29	71	68	.286	.377	.327	703	80	-12	54	13	7	.994	12	*O-125(0-125-0)	0.8
1997	Tor-A	103	401	54	105	12	1	1	26	52	54	.262	.347	.304	651	71	-15	47	10	7	.996	4	*O-102(0-102-0)/D-1	-0.3
	LA-N	42	175	30	48	6	2	1	18	13	24	.274	.324	.349	673	83	-5	12	2	2	.990	3	O-42(0-42-0)	0.1

YEAR	TM/L	G	AB	R	H	2B	3B	HR	RBI	BB	SO	AVG	OBP	SLG	OPS	OPS+	BR+	SB	CS	SBR	FA	FR	G/POS	TPR
1998	Min-A	110	448	71	133	6	6	1	20	44	56	.297	.362	.344	706	84	-9	37	7	6	.989	3	*O-108(0-108-0)	0.1
1999	*Atl-N	84	151	31	31	2	1	0	8	23	15	.205	.310	.232	542	40	-13	26	7	3	.981	-10	O-52(50-5-0)	-2.0
Total	17	1709	5115	878	1379	142	27	11	318	585	694	.270	.345	.314	660	77	-151	620	186	71	.989	-21	*O-1527C/D-19,S-1	-10.5
■ DONELL NIXON	Nixon, Robert Donell b: 12/31/61, Evergreen, N.C. BR/TR, 6'1", 185 lbs. Deb: 4/7/87 F																							
1987	Sea-A	46	132	17	33	4	0	3	12	13	28	.250	.327	.348	675	75	-4	21	7	2	1.000	0	O-32(1-32-0)/D-6	-0.2
1988	SF-N	59	78	15	27	3	0	0	6	10	12	.346	.420	.385	805	138	4	11	8	-0	.983	-8	O-46(32-15-0)	-0.5
1989	*SF-N	95	166	23	44	2	0	1	15	11	30	.265	.311	.295	606	76	-5	10	3	1	.967	-14	O-64(15-29-26)	-2.0
1990	Bal-A	8	20	1	5	2	0	0	2	1	7	.250	.286	.350	636	79	-1	5	0	1	1.000	-1	/O-4(4-0-0),D-3	0.0
Total	4	208	396	56	109	11	0	4	35	35	77	.275	.337	.333	671	88	-6	47	18	4	.983	-23	O-146(52-76-26)/D-9	-2.7
■ RUSS NIXON	Nixon, Russell Eugene b: 2/19/35, Cleves, Ohio BL/TR, 6'1", 200 lbs. Deb: 4/20/57 MC																							
1957	Cle-A	62	185	15	52	7	1	2	18	12	12	.281	.325	.362	687	88	-3	0	1	-0	.984	-6	C-57	-0.7
1958	Cle-A	113	376	42	113	17	4	9	46	13	38	.301	.324	.439	763	111	4	0	3	-1	.991	-10	*C-101	-0.2
1959	Cle-A	82	258	23	62	10	3	1	29	15	28	.240	.282	.314	596	66	-12	0	0	0	.985	-7	C-74	-1.6
1960	Cle-A	25	82	6	20	5	0	1	6	6	6	.244	.311	.341	653	79	-2	0	1	-0	.993	-0	C-25	-0.2
	Bos-A	80	272	24	81	17	3	5	33	13	23	.298	.330	.438	767	102	0	0	1	-0	.987	-17	C-74	-1.4
	Yr	105	354	30	101	22	3	6	39	19	29	.285	.325	.415	741	97	-2	0	2	-1	.989	-17	C-99	-1.6
1961	Bos-A	87	242	24	70	12	2	1	19	13	19	.289	.331	.368	699	84	-5	0	1	-0	.975	-3	C-66	-0.5
1962	Bos-A	65	151	11	42	7	2	1	19	8	14	.278	.314	.371	685	81	-4	0	0	0	1.000	-2	C-38	-0.4
1963	Bos-A	98	287	27	77	18	1	5	30	22	32	.268	.329	.390	719	98	-1	0	0	0	.992	-10	C-76	-0.7
1964	Bos-A	81	163	10	38	7	0	1	20	14	29	.233	.302	.294	596	64	-8	0	0	0	.990	-4	C-45	-1.0
1965	Bos-A	59	137	11	37	5	1	0	11	6	23	.270	.301	.321	622	72	-5	0	0	0	.981	-6	C-38	-1.0
1966	Min-A	51	96	5	25	2	1	0	7	7	13	.260	.317	.302	619	74	-3	0	0	0	.986	-4	C-32	-0.6
1967	Min-A	74	170	16	40	6	1	1	22	18	29	.235	.309	.300	609	74	-5	0	0	0	.994	-12	C-69	-1.6
1968	Bos-A	29	85	1	13	2	0	0	6	7	13	.153	.217	.176	394	19	-8	0	0	0	.994	-5	C-27	-1.4
Total	12	906	2504	215	670	115	19	27	266	154	279	.268	.313	.361	674	84	-53	0	7	-2	.988	-85	C-722	-11.3
■ RAY NOBLE	Noble, Rafael Miguel (Magee) b: 3/15/19, Central Hatillo, Cuba d: 5/9/98, Brooklyn, N.Y. BR/TR, 5'11", 210 lbs. Deb: 4/18/51																							
1951	*NY-N	55	141	16	33	6	0	5	26	6	26	.234	.265	.383	648	72	-6	0	0	0	.974	-5	C-41	-0.9
1952	NY-N	6	5	0	0	0	0	0	0	0	1	.000	.000	.000	0	-99	-1	0	0	0	1.000	0	/C-5	-0.1
1953	NY-N	46	97	15	20	0	1	4	14	19	14	.206	.353	.351	703	83	-2	1	0	0	.982	-1	C-41	-0.1
Total	3	107	243	31	53	6	1	9	40	25	41	.218	.299	.362	661	74	-9	1	0	0	.979	-5	/C-87	-1.1
■ JUNIOR NOBOA	Noboa, Milciades Arturo (Diaz) b: 11/10/64, Azua, D.R. BR/TR, 5'10", 160 lbs. Deb: 8/22/84																							
1984	Cle-A	23	11	3	4	0	0	0	0	0	2	.364	.364	.364	727	100	-0	1	0	0	1.000	4	2-19/D-1	0.4
1987	Cle-A	39	80	7	18	2	1	0	7	3	6	.225	.253	.275	528	40	-7	1	0	0	.983	4	2-21/S-8,3-5,D-1	-0.2
1988	Cal-A	21	16	4	1	0	0	0	0	0	1	.063	.063	.063	125	-67	-3	0	0	0	.967	9	/2-9,S-3,3-2	0.5
1989	Mon-N	21	44	3	10	0	0	0	1	1	3	.227	.244	.227	472	35	-4	0	0	0	1.000	7	2-13/S-4,3-1	0.4
1990	Mon-N	81	158	15	42	7	2	0	14	7	14	.266	.301	.335	637	78	-5	4	1	1	1.000	-17	2-31/O-9R,3-8,SP	-2.2
1991	Mon-N	67	95	5	23	3	0	1	2	1	8	.242	.250	.305	555	56	-6	2	3	-1	1.000	-3	/O-7R,2-6,3-2,S1	-0.9
1992	NY-N	46	47	7	7	0	0	0	3	3	8	.149	.216	.149	365	5	-6	0	0	0	.977	6	2-16/3-3,S-2	0.0
1994	Oak-A	17	40	3	13	1	1	0	6	2	5	.325	.357	.400	757	104	0	1	0	0	.943	1	2-14/S-1	0.2
	Pit-N	2	2	0	0	0	0	0	0	0	0	.000	.000	.000	0	-99	-1	0	0	0	1.000	0	/S-1	-0.1
Total	8	317	493	47	118	13	4	1	33	17	47	.239	.268	.288	556	54	-31	9	4	1	.981	10	2-129/S-28,3-21,OD1P	-1.9
■ PAUL NOCE	Noce, Paul David b: 12/16/59, San Francisco, Cal. BR/TR, 5'10", 175 lbs. Deb: 6/1/87																							
1987	Chi-N	70	180	17	41	9	2	3	14	6	49	.228	.261	.350	611	58	-11	5	3	0	.983	19	2-36,S-35/3-2	1.1
1990	Cin-N	1	1	0	1	0	0	0	0	0	0	1.000	1.000	1.000	2000	434	0	0	0	0	.000	0	/H	0.0
Total	2	71	181	17	42	9	2	3	14	6	49	.232	.265	.354	618	60	-11	5	3	0	.983	19	/2-36,S-35,3-2	1.1
■ GEORGE NOFTSKER	Noftsker, George Washington b: 8/24/1859, Shippensburg, Pa. d: 5/8/31, Shippensburg, Pa. BR/TR, 5'8", 135 lbs. Deb: 4/17/1884																							
1884	Alt-U	7	25	0	1	0	0	0		0		.040	.040	.040	80	-75	-6				.818	1	/O-5(0-1-4),C-3	-0.4
■ MATT NOKES	Nokes, Matthew Dodge b: 10/31/63, San Diego, Cal. BL/TR, 6'1", 185 lbs. Deb: 9/3/85 Career OF: (3-LF 0-CF 3-RF)																							
1985	SF-N	19	53	3	11	2	0	2	5	1	9	.208	.236	.358	595	67	-3	0	0	0	.977	-1	C-14	-0.3
1986	Det-A	7	24	2	8	1	0	1	2	1	1	.333	.360	.500	860	132	1	0	0	0	1.000	2	/C-7	0.3
1987	*Det-A★	135	461	69	133	14	2	32	87	35	70	.289	.347	.536	882	135	22	2	1	0	.992	-9	*C-109,D-19/O-3L,3	1.6
1988	Det-A	122	382	53	96	18	0	16	53	34	58	.251	.314	.424	738	109	4	0	1	-0	.989	-3	*C-110/D-4	0.7
1989	Det-A	87	268	15	67	10	0	9	39	17	37	.250	.300	.388	688	95	-3	1	0	0	.978	-6	C-51,D-33	-0.7
1990	Det-A	44	111	12	30	5	1	3	8	4	14	.270	.308	.414	722	99	-0	0	0	0	.984	-3	D-24,C-19	-0.3
	NY-A	92	240	21	57	4	0	8	32	20	33	.237	.307	.354	661	84	-5	2	2	-0	.995	-7	C-46,D-30/O-2(0-0-2)	-1.2
	Yr	136	351	33	87	9	1	11	40	24	47	.248	.307	.373	680	89	-6	2	2	-0	.993	-10	C-65,D-54/O-2(0-0-2)	-1.5
1991	NY-A	135	456	52	122	20	0	24	77	25	49	.268	.313	.469	782	113	6	3	2	-0	.992	-14	*C-130/D-3	0.0
1992	NY-A	121	384	42	86	9	1	22	59	37	62	.224	.297	.424	722	101	-1	0	1	-0	.993	-11	*C-111	-0.6
1993	NY-A	76	217	25	54	8	0	10	35	16	31	.249	.306	.424	730	97	-2	0	0	0	.992	-5	C-56,D-11	-0.4
1994	NY-A	28	79	11	23	3	0	7	19	5	16	.291	.333	.595	928	138	4	0	0	0	.975	0	C-17/1-4,D-5	0.4
1995	Bal-A	26	49	4	6	1	0	2	6	4	11	.122	.189	.265	454	16	-6	0	0	0	.989	3	C-16/D-2	-0.2
	Col-N	10	11	1	2	1	0	0	0	1	4	.182	.250	.273	523	29	-1	0	0	0	.909	-0	/C-3	-0.1
Total	11	902	2735	310	695	96	4	136	422	200	395	.254	.311	.441	752	106	15	8	7	-1	.990	-53	C-689,D-131/O-5L,13	-0.8
■ JOE NOLAN	Nolan, Joseph William b: 5/12/51, St.Louis, Mo. BL/TR, 6', 190 lbs. Deb: 9/21/72																							
1972	NY-N	4	10	0	0	0	0	0	0	1	3	.000	.091	.000	91	-74	-2	0	0	0	.938	-1	/C-3	-0.3
1975	Atl-N	4	4	0	1	0	0	0	0	1	0	.250	.400	.250	650	80	-0	0	0	0	1.000	-0	/C-1	0.0
1977	Atl-N	62	82	13	23	3	0	3	9	13	12	.280	.379	.427	806	103	1	1	0	0	1.000	-1	C-19	0.1
1978	Atl-N	95	213	22	49	7	3	4	22	34	28	.230	.339	.347	686	83	-4	3	2	-0	.979	-6	C-61	-0.8
1979	Atl-N	89	230	28	57	9	3	4	21	27	28	.248	.335	.365	700	85	-4	1	3	-1	.983	-7	C-74	-1.0
1980	Atl-N	17	22	2	6	1	0	0	2	2	4	.273	.333	.318	652	80	-1	0	0	0	1.000	1	/C-6	0.1
	Cin-N	53	154	14	48	7	0	3	24	13	8	.312	.365	.416	781	117	4	0	0	0	.982	1	C-51	0.7
	Yr	70	176	16	54	8	0	3	26	15	12	.307	.361	.403	765	112	3	0	0	0	.983	2	C-57	0.8
1981	Cin-N	81	236	25	73	18	1	1	26	24	19	.309	.375	.407	782	120	7	1	2	-0	**.995**	-11	C-81	-0.2
1982	Bal-A	77	219	24	51	7	1	6	35	16	35	.233	.285	.356	641	75	-8	1	1	-0	.978	-3	C-72	-0.8
1983	*Bal-A	73	184	25	51	11	1	5	24	16	31	.277	.342	.429	771	113	3	0	0	0	.980	-10	C-65	-0.5
1984	Bal-A	35	62	2	18	1	1	1	9	12	10	.290	.405	.387	793	123	3	0	0	0	.962	-1	D-11/C-6	0.2
1985	Bal-A	31	38	1	5	2	0	0	6	5	5	.132	.233	.184	417	16	-4	0	0	0	1.000	1	/C-5,D-4	-0.4
Total	11	621	1454	156	382	66	10	27	178	164	183	.263	.340	.378	718	95	-7	7	8	-1	.984	-37	C-444/D-15	-2.9
■ RED NONNENKAMP	Nonnenkamp, Leo William b: 7/7/10, St.Louis, Mo. BL/TL, 5'11", 165 lbs. Deb: 9/6/33																							
1933	Pit-N	1	1	0	0	0	0	0	0	0	1	.000	.000	.000	0	-99	-0	0			.000	0	H	0.0
1938	Bos-A	87	180	37	51	4	1	0	18	21	13	.283	.358	.317	675	67	-8	6	1	1	.968	2	O-39(5-5-29)/1-5	-0.7
1939	Bos-A	58	75	12	18	2	1	0	5	12	6	.240	.345	.293	638	62	-4	0	1	-0	.962	-3	O-15(7-4-4)	-0.7
1940	Bos-A	9	7	0	0	0	0	0	1	0	4	.000	.125	.000	125	-62	-2	0	0	0	.000	0	H	-0.2
Total	4	155	263	49	69	6	2	0	24	33	24	.262	.347	.300	647	62	-14	6	2		.966	-1	/O-54(12-9-33),1-5	-1.6
■ PETE NOONAN	Noonan, Peter John b: 11/24/1881, W.Stockbridge, Mass. d: 2/11/65, Great Barrington, Mass. BR/TR, 6', 180 lbs. Deb: 6/20/04																							
1904	Phi-A	39	114	13	23	3	1	2	13	1		.202	.209	.298	507	56	-6	1			.969	-4	C-22,1-10	-0.9
1906	Chi-N	5	3	0	1	0	0	0	0	0		.333	.333	.333	667	102	-0	0			1.000	0	/1-1	0.0
	StL-N	44	125	8	21	1	3	1	9	11		.168	.235	.248	483	53	-7	1			.957	3	C-23,1-16	-0.2
	Yr	49	128	8	22	1	3	1	9	11		.172	.237	.250	487	54	-7	1			.957	3	C-23,1-17	-0.2
1907	StL-N	74	237	19	53	7	3	1	16	9		.224	.252	.291	543	73	-9	3			.951	3	C-70	0.1
Total	3	162	479	40	98	11	7	4	38	21		.205	.238	.282	520	64	-21	5			.955	2	C-115/1-27	-1.0

YEAR	TM/L	G	AB	R	H	2B	3B	HR	RBI	BB	SO	AVG	OBP	SLG	OPS	OPS+	BR+	SB	CS	SBR	FA	FR	G/POS	TPR
■ TIM NORDBROOK	Nordbrook, Timothy Charles b: 7/7/49, Baltimore, Md. BR/TR, 6'1", 180 lbs. Deb: 9/13/74																							
1974	Bal-A	6	15	4	4	0	0	0	1	2	2	.267	.353	.267	620	83	-0	1	0	0	1.000	1	/S-5,2-1	0.2
1975	Bal-A	40	34	6	4	1	0	0	0	7	7	.118	.268	.147	415	21	-3	0	0	0	.970	5	S-37/2-3	0.4
1976	Bal-A	27	22	4	5	0	0	0	0	3	5	.227	.320	.227	547	66	-1	0	0	0	1.000	3	2-14,S-12	0.3
	Cal-A	5	8	1	0	0	0	0	0	1	3	.000	.111	.000	111	-70	-2	1	0	0	.941	2	/S-4,2-1,D-1	0.0
	Yr	32	30	5	5	0	0	0	0	4	8	.167	.265	.167	431	30	-3	1	0	0	.978	5	S-16,2-15/D-1	0.3
1977	Chi-A	15	20	2	5	0	0	0	1	7	4	.250	.444	.250	694	95	0	1	0	0	.850	-2	S-11/3-1,D-2	0.0
	Tor-A	24	63	9	11	0	1	0	1	4	11	.175	.224	.206	430	18	-7	1	0	0	.989	1	S-24	-0.4
	Yr	39	83	11	16	0	1	0	2	11	15	.193	.287	.217	504	39	-7	2	0	0	.947	-1	S-35/D-2,3-1	-0.4
1978	Tor-A	7	0	1	0	0	0	0	0	0	0	—	1.000	—	1000	200	0	0	0	0	1.000	2	/S-7	0.2
	Mil-A	2	5	0	0	0	0	0	0	1	1	.000	.167	.000	167	-49	-1	0	0	0	.909	0	/S-2	0.0
	Yr	9	5	1	0	0	0	0	0	1	1	.000	.286	.000	286	-13	-1	0	0	0	.941	2	/S-9	0.2
1979	Mil-A	2	2	0	1	0	0	0	0	0	0	.500	.500	.500	1000	171	0	0	0	0	1.000	-1	/S-2	0.0
Total	6	128	169	27	30	1	1	0	3	25	33	.178	.287	.195	482	38	-13	4	0	1	.961	12	S-104/2-19,D-3,3-1	0.7
■ WAYNE NORDHAGEN	Nordhagen, Wayne Oren b: 7/4/48, Thief River Falls, Minn. BR/TR, 6'2", 205 lbs. Deb: 7/16/76 Career OF: (125-LF 3-CF 139-RF)																							
1976	Chi-A	22	53	6	10	2	0	0	5	4	12	.189	.246	.226	472	39	-4	0	0	0	1.000	0	O-10(0-0-10)/C-5,D-6	-0.4
1977	Chi-A	52	124	16	39	7	3	4	22	2	12	.315	.325	.516	842	125	4	1	0	0	.944	-10	O-46(12-2-34)/C-3,D-2	-0.7
1978	Chi-A	68	206	28	62	16	0	5	35	5	18	.301	.318	.451	769	113	3	0	1	-0	.941	-8	O-36L,D-16,C-12	-0.8
1979	Chi-A	78	193	20	54	15	0	7	25	13	22	.280	.325	.466	792	111	2	0	0	0	1.000	-0	D-47,O-12R/C-5,P-2	0.0
1980	Chi-A	123	415	45	115	22	4	15	59	10	45	.277	.296	.458	754	104	0	0	1	-0	.969	-5	O-74(45-0-33),D-32	-0.9
1981	Chi-A	65	208	19	64	8	1	6	33	10	25	.308	.342	.442	785	127	7	0	1	-0	.947	-7	O-60(25-1-36)	-0.3
1982	Tor-A	44	115	8	32	3	0	1	14	9	13	.278	.331	.330	661	75	-4	0	2	-1	1.000	-1	D-32,O-10(10-0-1)	-0.6
	Pit-N	1	4	0	2	0	0	0	2	0	1	.500	.500	.500	1000	175	0	0	0	0	1.000	0	/O-1(1-0-0)	0.0
	Tor-A	28	70	4	18	3	0	0	6	1	9	.257	.268	.300	568	51	-5	0	0	0	.000	0	D-28	-0.6
1983	Chi-N	21	35	1	5	1	0	1	4	0	5	.143	.167	.257	424	15	-4	0	0	0	1.000	-1	/O-7(7-0-0)	-0.6
Total	8	502	1423	147	401	77	8	39	205	54	162	.282	.309	.429	739	101	-1	1	5	-2	.962	-31	O-256R,D-163/C-25,P	-4.9
■ LOU NORDYKE	Nordyke, Louis Ellis b: 8/7/1876, Brighton, Iowa d: 9/27/45, Los Angeles, Cal. BL/TR, 6', 185 lbs. Deb: 4/18/06																							
1906	StL-A	25	53	4	13	1	0	0	7	10		.245	.365	.264	629	102	1	3			.942	-3	1-12	-0.2
■ IRV NOREN	Noren, Irving Arnold b: 11/29/24, Jamestown, N.Y. BL/TL, 6', 190 lbs. Deb: 4/18/50 C Career OF: (293-LF 374-CF 163-RF)																							
1950	Was-A	138	542	80	160	27	10	14	98	67	77	.295	.375	.459	834	118	14	5	2	0	.984	16	*O-121(0-121-0),1-17	2.5
1951	Was-A	129	509	82	142	33	5	8	86	51	35	.279	.345	.411	755	105	3	10	7	-0	.978	21	*O-126(0-126-0)	2.0
1952	Was-A	12	49	4	12	3	1	0	2	6	3	.245	.327	.347	674	91	-1	1	0	0	1.000	3	O-12(0-12-0)	0.2
	*NY-A	93	272	36	64	13	2	5	21	26	34	.235	.316	.353	669	91	-4	4	2	0	1.000	-7	O-60(18-18-25),1-19	-1.4
	Yr	105	321	40	76	16	3	5	23	32	37	.237	.318	.352	670	91	-4	5	2	0	1.000	-4	O-72(18-30-25),1-19	-1.2
1953	*NY-A	109	345	55	92	12	6	6	46	42	39	.267	.350	.388	738	103	2	3	3	-0	.991	-1	O-96(21-44-38)	-0.4
1954	NY-A★	125	426	70	136	21	6	12	66	43	38	.319	.383	.481	864	140	23	4	6	-1	.980	-1	*O-116(55-23-49)/1-1	1.6
1955	*NY-A	132	371	49	94	19	1	8	59	43	33	.253	.336	.375	710	92	-4	5	2	0	.980	-0	*O-126(117-10-3)	-1.0
1956	NY-A	29	37	4	8	1	0	0	6	12	7	.216	.408	.243	651	78	-0	0	0	0	.875	-2	O-10(4-0-6)/1-1	-0.3
1957	KC-A	81	160	8	34	8	0	2	16	11	19	.213	.267	.300	567	54	-10	0	0	0	.990	-2	1-25/O-6(0-0-6)	-1.4
	StL-N	17	30	3	11	4	1	1	10	4	6	.367	.441	.667	1108	189	4	0	1	-0	1.000	-2	/O-8(1-0-7)	0.1
1958	StL-N	117	178	24	47	9	1	4	22	13	21	.264	.328	.393	721	87	-3	0	1	-0	.974	-17	O-77(59-14-10)	-2.3
1959	StL-N	8	8	0	1	1	0	0	0	0	2	.125	.125	.250	375	-3	-1	0	0	0	.000	-1	/O-2(2-0-0),1-1	-0.2
	Chi-N	65	156	27	50	6	2	4	19	13	24	.321	.384	.462	845	125	6	2	0	0	1.000	3	O-40(16-6-18)/1-1	0.8
	Yr	73	164	27	51	7	2	4	19	13	26	.311	.372	.451	823	118	4	2	0	0	1.000	2	O-42(18-6-18)/1-2	0.6
1960	Chi-N	12	11	0	1	0	0	0	1	3	4	.091	.286	.091	377	9	-1	0	0	0	.833	-1	/1-1,O-1(0-0-1)	-0.2
	LA-N	26	25	1	5	0	0	1	1	1	8	.200	.231	.320	551	46	-2	0	0	0	.000	0	H	-0.2
	Yr	38	36	1	6	0	0	1	2	4	12	.167	.250	.250	500	36	-3	0	0	0	1.000	-1	/1-1,O-1(0-0-1)	-0.4
Total	11	1093	3119	443	857	157	35	65	453	335	350	.275	.349	.410	759	106	24	34	24	-1	.984	10	O-801C/1-66	-0.2
■ DAN NORMAN	Norman, Daniel Edmund b: 1/11/55, Los Angeles, Cal. BR/TR (BB 1908 (part)), 6'2", 195 lbs. Deb: 9/27/77																							
1977	NY-N	7	16	2	4	1	0	0	0	4	2	.250	.400	.313	713	99	0	0	0	0	1.000	-1	/O-6(0-1-6)	-0.1
1978	NY-N	19	64	7	17	0	1	4	10	2	14	.266	.288	.484	772	116	1	1	0	0	1.000	-1	O-18(1-0-18)	0.0
1979	NY-N	44	110	9	27	3	1	3	11	10	26	.245	.314	.373	687	90	-2	2	0	0	.967	-0	O-33(8-0-25)	-0.3
1980	NY-N	69	92	5	17	1	1	2	9	6	14	.185	.235	.283	517	45	-7	5	0	1	1.000	-3	O-19(9-0-10)	-1.0
1982	Mon-N	53	66	6	14	3	0	2	7	7	20	.212	.288	.348	636	76	-2	0	1	-0	.969	-6	O-31(17-6-8)	-0.9
Total	5	192	348	29	79	8	3	11	37	29	76	.227	.288	.362	650	81	-10	8	1	1	.981	-11	O-107(35-7-67)	-2.3
■ BILL NORMAN	Norman, Henry Willis Patrick b: 7/16/10, St.Louis, Mo. d: 4/21/62, Milwaukee, Wis. BR/TR, 6'2", 190 lbs. Deb: 8/8/31 MC																							
1931	Chi-A	24	55	7	10	2	0	0	6	4	10	.182	.237	.218	455	22	-6	0	1	-0	.933	-1	O-17(3-14-0)	-0.8
1932	Chi-A	13	48	6	11	3	1	0	2	2	3	.229	.260	.333	593	56	-3	0	0	0	.917	-2	O-13(1-11-1)	-0.5
Total	2	37	103	13	21	5	1	0	8	6	13	.204	.248	.272	520	38	-10	0	1	-0	.928	-3	/O-30(4-25-1)	-1.3
■ LES NORMAN	Norman, Leslie Eugene b: 2/25/69, Warren, Mich. BR/TR, 6'1", 185 lbs. Deb: 5/29/95																							
1995	KC-A	24	40	6	9	0	1	0	4	6	6	.225	.326	.275	601	58	-2	0	1	-0	.958	-2	O-17(4-5-8)/D-5	-0.5
1996	KC-A	54	49	9	6	0	0	0	0	6	14	.122	.232	.122	355	-7	-8	1	1	-0	1.000	-7	O-38(15-3-20)/D-7	-1.4
Total	2	78	89	15	15	0	1	0	4	12	20	.169	.275	.191	466	22	-10	1	2	-0	.986	-9	/O-55(19-8-28),D-12	-1.9
■ NELSON NORMAN	Norman, Nelson Augusto b: 5/23/58, San Pedro De Macoris, D.R. BB/TR (BR 1978, 1979 (part)), 6'2", 160 lbs. Deb: 5/20/78																							
1978	Tex-A	23	34	1	9	2	0	0	1	0	5	.265	.265	.324	588	64	-2	0	0	0	.984	10	S-18/3-6	0.9
1979	Tex-A	147	343	36	76	9	3	0	21	19	41	.222	.262	.265	528	43	-27	4	1	1	.952	-16	*S-142/2-1	-3.1
1980	Tex-A	17	32	4	7	0	0	0	1	1	1	.219	.242	.219	461	28	-3	0	1	-0	.943	7	S-17	0.4
1981	Tex-A	7	13	1	3	1	0	0	2	1	2	.231	.286	.308	593	75	-0	0	0	0	.963	3	/S-5	0.3
1982	Pit-N	3	3	0	0	0	0	0	0	0	0	.000	.000	.000	0	-97	-1	0	0	0	.000	-1	/2-2,S-1	-0.2
1987	Mon-N	1	4	0	0	0	0	0	0	0	1	.000	.000	.000	0	-97	-1	0	0	0	.667	-1	/S-1	-0.2
Total	6	198	429	42	95	12	3	0	25	21	50	.221	.258	.263	521	42	-34	4	2	0	.954	2	S-184/3-6,2-3	-1.9
■ JIM NORRIS	Norris, James Francis b: 12/20/48, Brooklyn, N.Y. BL/TL, 5'10", 175 lbs. Deb: 4/7/77 Career OF: (83-LF 121-CF 185-RF)																							
1977	Cle-A	133	440	59	119	23	6	2	37	64	57	.270	.363	.364	727	102	3	26	17	-0	.982	12	*O-124(3-74-49)/1-3	1.2
1978	Cle-A	113	315	41	89	14	5	2	27	42	20	.283	.367	.378	745	111	6	12	7	0	.988	0	O-78R,D-15/1-6	0.3
1979	Cle-A	124	353	50	87	15	6	3	30	44	35	.246	.330	.348	678	83	-8	15	10	-0	.982	0	O-93(47-23-28),D-13	-1.1
1980	Tex-A	119	174	23	43	5	0	0	16	23	16	.247	.335	.276	611	72	-6	6	3	0	1.000	-18	O-82R,1-10/D-1	-2.6
Total	4	489	1282	173	338	57	17	7	110	173	128	.264	.351	.351	702	95	-4	59	37	0	.985	-5	O-377R/D-29,1-19	-2.2
■ LEO NORRIS	Norris, Leo John b: 5/17/08, Bay St.Louis, Miss d: 2/13/87, Zachary, La. BR/TR, 5'11", 165 lbs. Deb: 4/14/36																							
1936	Phi-N	154	581	64	154	27	4	11	76	39	79	.265	.315	.382	697	79	-18	4			.936	-8	*S-121,2-38	-1.4
1937	Phi-N	116	381	45	98	24	3	9	36	21	53	.257	.296	.407	703	82	-10	3			.949	-12	2-74,3-24,S-20	-1.7
Total	2	270	962	109	252	51	7	20	112	60	132	.262	.307	.392	699	80	-28	7			.940	-21	S-141,2-112/3-24	-3.1
■ BILLY NORTH	North, William Alex b: 5/15/48, Seattle, Wash. BB/TR (BR 1971), 5'11", 185 lbs. Deb: 9/3/71 Career OF: (16-LF 1023-CF 29-RF)																							
1971	Chi-N	8	16	3	6	0	0	0	0	4	6	.375	.524	.375	899	138	1	1	1	-0	1.000	-2	/O-6(1-0-5)	-0.1
1972	Chi-N	66	127	22	23	2	3	0	4	13	33	.181	.262	.244	507	40	-10	6	0	1	.955	-8	O-48(9-26-15)	-1.9
1973	Oak-A	146	554	98	158	10	5	5	34	78	89	.285	.376	.348	725	111	12	53	20	5	.980	24	*O-138(0-136-2)/D-6	3.6
1974	*Oak-A	149	543	79	141	20	5	4	33	69	86	.260	.348	.337	685	105	6	**54**	26	3	.991	18	*O-138(0-138-0)/D-8	2.4
1975	*Oak-A	140	524	74	143	17	5	1	43	81	80	.273	.374	.330	705	103	6	30	12	2	.975	20	*O-138(4-134-0)/D-1	2.4
1976	Oak-A	154	590	91	163	20	5	2	31	73	95	.276	.358	.337	695	109	9	**75**	29	6	.978	6	*O-144(0-137-7)/D-8	1.9
1977	Oak-A	56	184	32	48	3	3	1	9	32	25	.261	.376	.326	702	95	0	17	13	-1	.983	-4	O-52(0-52-0)/D-1	-0.5
1978	Oak-A	24	52	5	11	4	0	0	5	9	13	.212	.349	.288	638	86	-1	3	2	-0	1.000	-2	O-17(0-17-0)	-0.3
	*LA-N	110	304	54	71	10	0	0	10	65	48	.234	.372	.266	638	81	-4	27	8	3	.975	-2	*O-103(1-102-0)	-0.4

YEAR	TM/L	G	AB	R	H	2B	3B	HR	RBI	BB	SO	AVG	OBP	SLG	OPS	OPS+	BR+	SB	CS	SBR	FA	FR	G/POS	TPR
1979	SF-N	142	460	87	119	15	4	5	30	96	84	.259	.388	.341	729	108	10	58	24	4	.987	3	*O-130(0-130-0)	1.6
1980	SF-N	128	415	73	104	12	1	1	19	81	78	.251	.374	.292	666	90	-1	45	19	3	.982	10	*O-115(1-114-0)	1.1
1981	SF-N	46	131	22	29	7	0	1	12	26	28	.221	.354	.298	652	88	-1	26	8	3	.966	-2	O-37(0-37-0)	-0.1
Total	11	1169	3900	640	1016	120	31	20	230	627	665	.261	.366	.323	689	99	28	395	162	30	.981	61	*O-1066C/D-24	9.7

■ HUB NORTHEN Northen, Hubbard Elwin b: 8/16/1885, Atlanta, Tex. d: 10/1/47, Shreveport, La. BL/TL, 5′8″, 175 lbs. Deb: 9/10/10

YEAR	TM/L	G	AB	R	H	2B	3B	HR	RBI	BB	SO	AVG	OBP	SLG	OPS	OPS+	BR+	SB	CS	SBR	FA	FR	G/POS	TPR
1910	StL-A	26	96	6	19	1	0	0	16	5		.198	.238	.208	446	42	-6	2			.926	-2	O-26(0-26-0)	-1.1
1911	Cin-N	1	0	0	0	0	0	0	0	0	0	—	—	—	—	—	0	0			.000	0	H	0.0
	Bro-N	19	76	16	24	2	2	0	1	14	9	.316	.429	.395	823	137	5	4			.911	2	O-19(0-19-0)	0.5
	Yr	20	76	16	24	2	2	0	1	14	9	.316	.429	.395	823	137	5	4			.911	2	O-19(0-19-0)	0.5
1912	Bro-N	118	412	54	116	26	6	3	46	41	46	.282	.352	.396	748	109	5	8			.950	-7	*O-102(10-43-49)	-0.9
Total	3	164	584	76	159	29	8	3	63	60	55	.272	.345	.365	710	103	3	14			.939	-7	O-147(10-88-49)	-1.5

■ RON NORTHEY Northey, Ronald James b: 4/26/20, Mahanoy City, Pa. d: 4/16/71, Pittsburgh, Pa. BL/TR, 5′10″, 195 lbs. Deb: 4/14/42 FC

YEAR	TM/L	G	AB	R	H	2B	3B	HR	RBI	BB	SO	AVG	OBP	SLG	OPS	OPS+	BR+	SB	CS	SBR	FA	FR	G/POS	TPR
1942	Phi-N	127	402	31	101	13	2	5	31	28	33	.251	.300	.331	631	89	-7	2			.952	1	*O-109(0-0-109)	-1.3
1943	Phi-N	147	586	72	163	31	5	16	68	51	52	.278	.339	.430	769	127	18	2			.978	3	*O-145(0-0-145)	1.2
1944	Phi-N	152	570	72	164	35	9	22	104	67	51	.288	.367	.496	863	146	34	1			.981	4	*O-151(0-0-151)	2.8
1946	Phi-N	128	438	55	109	24	6	16	62	39	59	.249	.313	.441	754	116	6	1			.971	-6	*O-111(0-0-111)	-0.4
1947	Phi-N	13	47	7	12	3	0	0	3	6	3	.255	.340	.319	659	79	-1	1			1.000	-1	O-13(0-0-13)	-0.3
	StL-N	110	311	52	91	19	3	15	63	48	29	.293	.391	.518	908	133	15	0			.949	-12	O-94(15-0-79)/3-2	0.1
	Yr	123	358	59	103	22	3	15	66	54	32	.288	.384	.492	876	127	14	1			.955	-13	*O-107(15-0-92)/3-2	-0.2
1948	StL-N	96	246	40	79	10	1	13	64	38	25	.321	.420	.528	949	147	17	0			.989	-10	O-67(0-0-67)	0.5
1949	StL-N	90	265	28	69	18	2	7	50	31	15	.260	.338	.423	760	98	-1	0			.980	-11	O-73(0-0-73)	-1.3
1950	Cin-N	27	77	11	20	5	0	5	9	15	6	.260	.380	.519	900	134	4	0			.955	-5	O-24(0-0-24)	-0.2
	Chi-N	53	114	11	32	9	0	4	20	10	9	.281	.339	.465	804	110	1	0			.976	-1	O-27(0-0-27)	0.0
	Yr	80	191	22	52	14	0	9	29	25	15	.272	.356	.487	843	120	5	0			.969	-6	O-51(0-0-51)	-0.2
1952	Chi-N	1	1	0	0	0	0	0	0	0	0	.000	.000	.000	0	-99	-0	0	0	0	.000	0	H	0.0
1955	Chi-A	14	14	1	5	2	0	1	4	3	3	.357	.471	.714	1185	209	2	0	0	0	1.000	-1	/O-2(0-0-2)	0.2
1956	Chi-A	53	48	4	17	2	0	3	23	8	1	.354	.446	.583	1030	168	5	0	0	0	1.000	-1	/O-4(3-0-3)	0.4
1957	Chi-A	40	27	0	5	1	0	0	7	11	5	.185	.421	.222	643	80	0	0	0	0	.000	0	H	0.0
	Phi-N	33	26	1	7	0	0	1	5	6	6	.269	.406	.385	791	118	1	0	0	0	.000	0	H	0.1
Total	12	1084	3172	385	874	172	28	108	513	361	297	.276	.352	.450	802	124	94	7	0		.972	-38	O-820(18-0-804)/3-2	1.8

■ SCOTT NORTHEY Northey, Scott Richard b: 10/15/46, Philadelphia, Pa. BR/TR, 6′, 175 lbs. Deb: 9/2/69 F

YEAR	TM/L	G	AB	R	H	2B	3B	HR	RBI	BB	SO	AVG	OBP	SLG	OPS	OPS+	BR+	SB	CS	SBR	FA	FR	G/POS	TPR
1969	KC-A	20	61	11	16	2	2	1	7	7	19	.262	.338	.410	748	108	1	6	3	0	.973	-0	O-18(0-18-0)	0.0

■ JIM NORTHRUP Northrup, James Thomas b: 11/24/39, Breckenridge, Mich. BL/TR, 6′3″, 190 lbs. Deb: 9/30/64 Career OF: (310-LF 466-CF 708-RF)

YEAR	TM/L	G	AB	R	H	2B	3B	HR	RBI	BB	SO	AVG	OBP	SLG	OPS	OPS+	BR+	SB	CS	SBR	FA	FR	G/POS	TPR
1964	Det-A	5	12	1	1	1	0	0	0	0	3	.083	.083	.167	250	-32	-2	1	0	0	1.000	-1	/O-2(0-2-1)	-0.3
1965	Det-A	80	219	20	45	12	3	2	16	12	50	.205	.253	.315	568	60	-12	1	1	-0	.976	-4	O-54(10-6-38)	-2.0
1966	Det-A	123	419	53	111	24	6	16	58	33	52	.265	.325	.465	790	121	11	4	7	-2	.980	10	*O-113(3-11-106)	1.2
1967	Det-A	144	495	63	134	18	6	10	61	43	83	.271	.333	.392	725	110	6	7	1	1	.972	-20	*O-143(65-94-39)	-2.0
1968	*Det-A	154	580	76	153	29	7	21	90	50	87	.264	.326	.447	773	129	19	4	5	-1	.979	8	*O-151(12-47-103)	1.9
1969	Det-A	148	543	79	160	31	5	25	66	52	83	.295	.360	.508	868	135	24	4	2	0	.985	4	*O-143(29-89-49)	2.3
1970	Det-A	139	504	71	132	21	3	24	80	58	68	.262	.346	.458	805	119	13	3	6	-1	.993	3	*O-136(34-39-78)	0.8
1971	Det-A	136	459	72	124	27	2	16	71	60	43	.270	.357	.442	799	121	13	7	4	0	.981	-20	*O-108(42-68-39),1-32	-1.5
1972	*Det-A	134	426	40	111	15	2	8	42	38	47	.261	.324	.362	686	101	0	4	7	-2	.978	-16	*O-127(50-42-72)/1-2	-2.6
1973	Det-A	119	404	55	124	14	7	12	44	38	41	.307	.368	.465	833	125	13	4	4	-1	.982	-9	*O-116(51-10-78)	-0.2
1974	Det-A	97	376	41	89	12	1	11	42	36	46	.237	.303	.362	665	88	-6	0	0	0	.973	3	O-97(0-2-97)	-0.9
	Mon-N	21	54	3	13	1	0	2	8	5	9	.241	.305	.370	675	84	-1	0	0	0	1.000	-2	O-13(7-0-6)	-0.5
	Bal-A	8	7	2	4	0	0	1	3	2	1	.571	.667	1.000	1667	386	3	0	0	0	1.000	-1	/O-6(4-0-2),D-1	0.2
1975	Bal-A	84	194	27	53	13	0	5	29	22	22	.273	.353	.418	771	125	6	0	1	-0	.979	-12	O-58(3-56-0)/D-3	-0.7
Total	12	1392	4692	603	1254	218	42	153	610	449	635	.267	.335	.429	765	115	86	39	38	-5	.981	-57	*O-1267R/1-34,D-4	-4.3

■ FRANK NORTON Norton, Frank Prescott Deb: 5/5/1871

YEAR	TM/L	G	AB	R	H	2B	3B	HR	RBI	BB	SO	AVG	OBP	SLG	OPS	OPS+	BR+	SB	CS	SBR	FA	FR	G/POS	TPR
1871	Oly-n	1	1	0	0	0	0	0	0	0	1	.000	.000	.000	0	-99	-0	0	0	0	.000	-1	/3-1,O-1(0-0-1)	-0.1

■ GREG NORTON Norton, Gregory Blakemoor b: 7/6/72, San Leandro, Cal. BB/TR, 6′1″, 190 lbs. Deb: 8/18/96

YEAR	TM/L	G	AB	R	H	2B	3B	HR	RBI	BB	SO	AVG	OBP	SLG	OPS	OPS+	BR+	SB	CS	SBR	FA	FR	G/POS	TPR
1996	Chi-A	11	23	4	5	0	0	2	3	4	6	.217	.333	.478	812	107	0	0	1	-0	.778	-2	/S-6,3-2,D-2	-0.2
1997	Chi-A	18	34	5	9	2	2	0	1	2	8	.265	.306	.441	747	96	-0	0	0	0	.864	0	3-11/D-2	0.0
1998	Chi-A	105	299	38	71	17	2	9	36	26	77	.237	.303	.398	701	83	-8	3	3	-0	.994	-7	1-79,3-11/2-1,D-2	-2.1
1999	Chi-A	132	436	62	111	26	0	16	50	69	93	.255	.359	.424	783	99	-0	4	4	-1	.922	-4	*3-120,1-26/D-1	-0.5
2000	Chi-A	71	201	25	49	6	1	6	28	26	47	.244	.336	.373	709	79	-6	1	0	0	.926	-6	3-47,1-17/D-3	-1.2
Total	5	337	993	134	245	51	5	33	118	127	231	.247	.336	.408	744	90	-15	8	8	-1	.921	-19	3-191,1-122/D-10,S2	-4.0

■ WILLIE NORWOOD Norwood, Willie b: 11/7/50, Greene County, Ala. BR/TR, 6′, 185 lbs. Deb: 4/21/77

YEAR	TM/L	G	AB	R	H	2B	3B	HR	RBI	BB	SO	AVG	OBP	SLG	OPS	OPS+	BR+	SB	CS	SBR	FA	FR	G/POS	TPR
1977	Min-A	39	83	15	19	3	0	3	9	6	17	.229	.281	.373	654	78	-3	6	1	1	.952	-4	O-28(3-20-8)/D-5	-0.6
1978	Min-A	125	428	56	109	22	3	8	46	28	64	.255	.305	.376	681	89	-7	25	10	2	.944	-2	*O-115(101-14-4)/D-6	-1.2
1979	Min-A	96	270	32	67	13	3	6	30	20	51	.248	.300	.385	685	80	-8	9	5	0	.974	-4	O-71(0-44-28),D-14	-1.4
1980	Min-A	34	73	6	12	2	0	1	8	3	13	.164	.197	.233	430	16	-8	1	1	-0	1.000	-1	O-17(0-5-17)/D-9	-1.1
Total	4	294	854	109	207	40	6	18	93	57	145	.242	.292	.367	659	79	-26	41	17	3	.959	-12	O-231(104-83-57)/D-34	-4.3

■ JOE NOSSEK Nossek, Joseph Rudolph b: 11/8/40, Cleveland, Ohio BR/TR, 6′, 178 lbs. Deb: 4/18/64 C

YEAR	TM/L	G	AB	R	H	2B	3B	HR	RBI	BB	SO	AVG	OBP	SLG	OPS	OPS+	BR+	SB	CS	SBR	FA	FR	G/POS	TPR
1964	Min-A	7	1	1	0	0	0	0	0	0	0	.000	.000	.000	0	-99	-0	0	0	0	.000	-1	/O-2(1-1-0)	-0.1
1965	*Min-A	87	170	19	37	9	0	2	16	7	22	.218	.253	.306	559	55	-10	2	0	0	.970	-6	O-48(2-46-2)/3-9	-1.8
1966	Min-A	4	0	0	0	0	0	0	0	0	0	—	—	—	—	—	0	0	0	0	.000	-1	/O-2(0-2-0)	-0.1
	KC-A	87	230	13	60	10	3	1	27	8	21	.261	.286	.343	629	83	-6	4	2	0	.983	3	O-78(12-65-3)/3-1	-0.5
	Yr	91	230	13	60	10	3	1	27	8	21	.261	.286	.343	629	82	-6	4	2	0	.983	2	O-80(12-67-3)/3-1	-0.6
1967	KC-A	87	166	12	34	6	1	0	10	4	26	.205	.224	.253	477	42	-12	2	0	0	.982	-3	O-63(35-32-0)	-1.9
1969	Oak-A	13	6	0	0	0	0	0	0	0	0	.000	.000	.000	0	-99	-2	0	0	0	1.000	-4	O-12(9-3-0)	-0.6
	StL-N	9	5	2	1	0	0	0	0	0	3	.200	.200	.200	400	12	-1	0	0	0	1.000	0	/O-1(0-1-0)	-0.1
1970	StL-N	1	1	0	0	0	0	0	0	0	0	.000	.000	.000	0	-98	-0	0	0	0	.000	0	H	0.0
Total	6	295	579	47	132	25	4	3	53	19	72	.228	.254	.301	554	60	-31	8	2	1	.980	-11	O-206(59-150-5)/3-10	-5.1

■ LOU NOVIKOFF Novikoff, Louis Alexander "The Mad Russian" b: 10/12/15, Glendale, Ariz. d: 9/30/70, South Gate, Cal. BR/TR, 5′10″, 185 lbs. Deb: 4/15/41

YEAR	TM/L	G	AB	R	H	2B	3B	HR	RBI	BB	SO	AVG	OBP	SLG	OPS	OPS+	BR+	SB	CS	SBR	FA	FR	G/POS	TPR
1941	Chi-N	62	203	22	49	8	0	5	24	11	15	.241	.284	.355	638	82	-6	0			1.000	-4	O-54(51-0-3)	-1.3
1942	Chi-N	128	483	48	145	25	5	7	64	24	28	.300	.337	.416	753	125	13	3			.964	-2	*O-120(120-0-0)	0.4
1943	Chi-N	78	233	22	65	7	3	0	28	18	15	.279	.333	.335	668	95	-2	0			.980	-8	O-61(60-1-0)	-1.4
1944	Chi-N	71	139	15	39	4	2	3	19	10	11	.281	.329	.403	732	106	1	1			.976	-5	O-29(28-1-0)	-0.6
1946	Phi-N	17	23	0	7	1	0	0	3	1	2	.304	.333	.348	681	96	-0	0			1.000	0	/O-3(3-0-0)	0.0
Total	5	356	1081	107	305	45	10	15	138	64	71	.282	.325	.384	709	107	6	4			.976	-19	O-267(262-2-3)	-2.9

■ RUBE NOVOTNEY Novotney, Ralph Joseph b: 8/5/24, Streator, Ill. d: 7/16/87, Redondo Beach, Cal. BR/TR, 6′, 187 lbs. Deb: 4/29/49

YEAR	TM/L	G	AB	R	H	2B	3B	HR	RBI	BB	SO	AVG	OBP	SLG	OPS	OPS+	BR+	SB	CS	SBR	FA	FR	G/POS	TPR
1949	Chi-N	22	67	4	18	2	1	0	6	3	11	.269	.300	.328	628	70	-3	0			.958	0	C-20	-0.2

■ LES NUNAMAKER Nunamaker, Leslie Grant b: 1/25/1889, Aurora, Neb. d: 11/14/38, Hastings, Neb. BR/TR, 6′2″, 190 lbs. Deb: 4/28/11

YEAR	TM/L	G	AB	R	H	2B	3B	HR	RBI	BB	SO	AVG	OBP	SLG	OPS	OPS+	BR+	SB	CS	SBR	FA	FR	G/POS	TPR
1911	Bos-A	62	183	18	47	4	3	0	19	12		.257	.303	.311	614	72	-7	1			.972	6	C-59	0.3
1912	Bos-A	35	103	15	26	5	2	0	6	6		.252	.313	.340	652	82	-3	2			.971	-3	C-35	-0.3
1913	Bos-A	29	65	9	14	5	2	0	9	8	8	.215	.311	.354	665	92	-1	2			.977	3	C-27	0.5
1914	Bos-A	5	5	0	1	0	0	0	0	1	0	.200	.333	.200	533	61	-0	0			1.000	0	/C-3,1-1	0.0
	NY-A	87	257	19	68	10	3	2	29	22	34	.265	.327	.350	678	104	1	11	9	-1	.971	4	C-70/1-5	1.2
	Yr	92	262	19	69	10	3	2	29	23	34	.263	.328	.347	675	103	1	11	9	-1	.971	5	C-73/1-6	1.2
1915	NY-A	87	249	24	56	6	3	0	17	23	24	.225	.293	.273	566	70	-9	3	2	-0	.964	-4	C-77/1-2	-0.8

YEAR	TM/L	G	AB	R	H	2B	3B	HR	RBI	BB	SO	AVG	OBP	SLG	OPS	OPS+	BR+	SB	CS	SBR	FA	FR	G/POS	TPR
1916	NY-A	91	260	25	77	14	7	0	28	34	21	.296	.380	.404	784	133	11	4			.983	-6	C-79	1.2
1917	NY-A	104	310	22	81	9	2	0	33	21	25	.261	.310	.303	613	86	-5	5			.976	-4	C-91	-0.2
1918	StL-A	85	274	22	71	9	2	0	22	28	16	.259	.339	.307	645	98	-0	6			.979	0	C-81/1-1,O-1(0-0-1)	0.8
1919	Cle-A	26	56	6	14	1	1	0	7	2	6	.250	.276	.304	579	59	-3	0			.927	-4	C-16	-0.7
1920	*Cle-A	34	54	10	18	3	3	0	14	4	5	.333	.379	.500	879	128	2	1	0	0	.963	1	C-17/1-6	0.4
1921	Cle-A	46	131	16	47	7	2	0	25	11	8	.359	.408	.443	851	115	3	1	1	-0	.970	4	C-46	0.9
1922	Cle-A	25	43	8	13	2	0	0	7	4	3	.302	.362	.349	711	85	-1	0	0	0	.936	-2	C-13	-0.2
Total	12	716	1990	194	533	75	30	2	216	176	150	.268	.332	.339	670	95	-12	36	12		.972	-5	C-614/1-15,O-1(0-0-1)	3.1

■ ABRAHAM NUNEZ Nunez, Abraham Orlando (Adames) b: 3/16/76, Santo Domingo, D.R. BB/TR, 5′11″, 160 lbs. Deb: 8/27/97

YEAR	TM/L	G	AB	R	H	2B	3B	HR	RBI	BB	SO	AVG	OBP	SLG	OPS	OPS+	BR+	SB	CS	SBR	FA	FR	G/POS	TPR
1997	Pit-N	19	40	3	9	2	2	0	6	3	10	.225	.295	.375	670	73	-2	1	0	0	1.000	1	S-12/2-9	0.1
1998	Pit-N	24	52	6	10	2	0	1	2	12	14	.192	.344	.288	632	68	-2	4	2	0	.930	4	S-23	0.4
1999	Pit-N	90	259	25	57	8	0	0	17	28	54	.220	.299	.251	550	41	-23	9	1	2	.953	9	S-65,2-14	-0.7
2000	Pit-N	40	91	10	20	1	0	1	8	8	14	.220	.283	.264	547	40	-8	0	0	0	.978	5	S-21/2-6	-0.2
Total	4	173	442	44	96	13	2	2	33	51	92	.217	.301	.269	570	47	-35	14	3	2	.956	19	S-121/2-29	-0.4

■ JON NUNNALLY Nunnally, Jonathan Keith b: 11/9/71, Pelham, N.C. BL/TR, 5′10″, 190 lbs. Deb: 4/26/95

YEAR	TM/L	G	AB	R	H	2B	3B	HR	RBI	BB	SO	AVG	OBP	SLG	OPS	OPS+	BR+	SB	CS	SBR	FA	FR	G/POS	TPR
1995	KC-A	119	303	51	74	15	6	14	42	51	86	.244	.357	.472	829	112	5	6	4	-0	.971	-4	*O-107(16-7-92)/D-4	-0.3
1996	KC-A	35	90	16	19	5	1	5	17	13	25	.211	.311	.456	766	91	-2	0	0	0	.968	-1	O-29(7-0-24)/D-4	-0.4
1997	KC-A	13	29	8	7	0	1	1	4	5	7	.241	.353	.414	767	97	-0	0	0	0	1.000	-1	/O-9(1-0-8)	-0.2
	Cin-N	65	201	38	64	12	3	13	35	26	51	.318	.402	.602	1004	157	16	7	3	0	.984	-2	O-60(14-46-11)	1.5
1998	Cin-N	74	174	29	36	9	0	7	20	34	38	.207	.340	.379	719	88	-3	3	4	-1	.956	-4	O-70(6-24-53)	-0.9
1999	Bos-A	10	14	4	4	1	0	0	1	0	6	.286	.286	.357	643	61	-1	0	0	0	.000	-1	/O-2(1-0-1),D-3	-0.2
2000	NY-N	48	74	16	14	5	1	2	6	17	26	.189	.341	.365	706	81	-2	3	1	0	.977	-4	O-34(25-11-4)	-0.6
Total	6	364	885	162	218	47	12	42	125	146	239	.246	.356	.469	825	111	15	19	12	-0	.971	-17	O-311(70-88-193)/D-11	-1.1

■ TALMADGE NUNNARI Nunnari, Talmadge Raphael b: 4/9/75, Pensacola, Fla. BL/TL, 6′1″, 205 lbs. Deb: 9/7/2000

YEAR	TM/L	G	AB	R	H	2B	3B	HR	RBI	BB	SO	AVG	OBP	SLG	OPS	OPS+	BR+	SB	CS	SBR	FA	FR	G/POS	TPR
2000	Mon-N	18	5	2	1	0	0	0	1	6	2	.200	.636	.200	836	124	1	0	0	0	1.000	0	1-14	0.1

■ EMORY NUSZ Nusz, Emory Moberly b: 4/2/1866, Frederick, Md. d: 8/3/1893, Point Of Rocks, Md. Deb: 4/26/1884

YEAR	TM/L	G	AB	R	H	2B	3B	HR	RBI	BB	SO	AVG	OBP	SLG	OPS	OPS+	BR+	SB	CS	SBR	FA	FR	G/POS	TPR
1884	Was-U	1	4	1	0	0	0	0		0		.000	.000	.000	0	-99	-1				.500	-0	/O-1(1-0-0)	-0.1

■ DIZZY NUTTER Nutter, Everett Clarence b: 8/27/1893, Roseville, Ohio d: 7/25/58, Battle Creek, Mich. BL/TR, 5′9″, 160 lbs. Deb: 9/7/19

YEAR	TM/L	G	AB	R	H	2B	3B	HR	RBI	BB	SO	AVG	OBP	SLG	OPS	OPS+	BR+	SB	CS	SBR	FA	FR	G/POS	TPR
1919	Bos-N	18	52	4	11	0	0	0	3	4	5	.212	.268	.212	479	47	-3	1			1.000	2	O-12(0-12-0)	-0.3

■ CHARLIE NYCE Nyce, Charles Reiff (b: Charles Reiff Nice) b: 7/1/1870, Philadelphia, Pa. d: 5/9/08, Philadelphia, Pa. 5′8″, 160 lbs. Deb: 5/28/1895

YEAR	TM/L	G	AB	R	H	2B	3B	HR	RBI	BB	SO	AVG	OBP	SLG	OPS	OPS+	BR+	SB	CS	SBR	FA	FR	G/POS	TPR
1895	Bos-N	9	35	7	8	5	0	2	9	4	2	.229	.325	.543	868	113	0	0			.889	-1	/S-9	0.0

■ CHRIS NYMAN Nyman, Christopher Curtis b: 6/6/55, Pomona, Cal. BR/TR, 6′4″, 200 lbs. Deb: 7/28/82 F

YEAR	TM/L	G	AB	R	H	2B	3B	HR	RBI	BB	SO	AVG	OBP	SLG	OPS	OPS+	BR+	SB	CS	SBR	FA	FR	G/POS	TPR
1982	Chi-A	28	65	6	16	1	0	0	2	3	9	.246	.279	.262	541	50	-4	3	2	-0	.994	0	1-24/O-2(1-0-1)	-0.5
1983	Chi-A	21	28	12	8	0	0	2	4	4	7	.286	.394	.500	894	139	2	2	2	-0	1.000	1	1-10,D-10	0.2
Total	2	49	93	18	24	1	0	2	6	7	16	.258	.317	.333	650	78	-3	5	4	-0	.996	1	/1-34,D-10,O-2(1-0-1)	-0.3

■ NYLS NYMAN Nyman, Nyls Wallace Rex b: 3/7/54, Detroit, Mich. BL/TR, 6′, 170 lbs. Deb: 9/6/74 F

YEAR	TM/L	G	AB	R	H	2B	3B	HR	RBI	BB	SO	AVG	OBP	SLG	OPS	OPS+	BR+	SB	CS	SBR	FA	FR	G/POS	TPR
1974	Chi-A	5	14	5	9	2	1	0	4	0	1	.643	.667	.929	1595	347	4	1	0	0	1.000	1	/O-3(3-0-0)	0.5
1975	Chi-A	106	327	36	74	6	3	2	28	11	34	.226	.256	.281	537	51	-21	10	4	1	.958	-4	O-94(62-26-8)/D-4	-3.0
1976	Chi-A	8	15	2	2	1	0	0	1	0	3	.133	.133	.200	333	-3	-2	1	0	0	1.000	-1	/O-7(6-1-0)	-0.3
1977	Chi-A	1	1	0	0	0	0	0	0	0	0	.000	.000	.000	0	-99	-0	0	0	0	.000	0	H	0.0
Total	4	120	357	43	85	9	4	2	33	11	38	.238	.267	.303	569	60	-19	12	4	1	.962	-4	O-104(71-27-8)/D-4	-2.8

■ REBEL OAKES Oakes, Ennis Telfair b: 12/17/1883, Arizona, La. d: 3/1/48, Lisbon, La. BL/TR, 5′8″, 170 lbs. Deb: 4/14/09 M

YEAR	TM/L	G	AB	R	H	2B	3B	HR	RBI	BB	SO	AVG	OBP	SLG	OPS	OPS+	BR+	SB	CS	SBR	FA	FR	G/POS	TPR
1909	Cin-N	120	415	55	112	10	5	3	31	40		.270	.341	.340	681	112	6	23			.979	-2	*O-113(4-99-10)	-0.1
1910	StL-N	131	468	50	118	14	6	0	43	38	38	.252	.315	.308	623	85	-9	18			.939	-7	*O-127(3-118-6)	-2.3
1911	StL-N	154	551	69	145	13	6	2	59	41	35	.263	.320	.319	639	81	-14	25			.961	11	*O-151(1-150-0)	-1.4
1912	StL-N	136	495	57	139	19	5	3	58	31	24	.281	.328	.358	686	90	-8	26			.947	-2	*O-136(0-136-0)	-1.9
1913	StL-N	147	539	60	158	14	5	0	49	43	32	.293	.350	.338	687	98	-0	22			.968	-2	*O-145(0-145-0)	-1.4
1914	Pit-F	145	571	82	178	18	10	7	75	35	22	.312	.359	.415	774	111	-0	28			.960	6	*O-145(0-145-0),M	-0.4
1915	Pit-F	153	580	55	161	24	5	0	82	37	19	.278	.323	.336	659	86	-19	21			.973	-3	*O-153(0-152-1),M	-3.7
Total	7	986	3619	428	1011	112	42	15	397	265	170	.279	.334	.346	680	95	-44	163			.961	1	O-970(8-945-17)	-11.2

■ PRINCE OANA Oana, Henry Kauhane b: 1/22/08, Waipahu, Hawaii d: 6/19/76, Austin, Tex. BR/TR, 6′2″, 193 lbs. Deb: 4/22/34

YEAR	TM/L	G	AB	R	H	2B	3B	HR	RBI	BB	SO	AVG	OBP	SLG	OPS	OPS+	BR+	SB	CS	SBR	FA	FR	G/POS	TPR
1934	Phi-N	6	21	3	5	1	0	0	3	0	1	.238	.238	.286	524	35	-2	0			1.000	1	/O-4(4-0-0)	-0.1
1943	Det-A	20	26	5	10	2	1	1	7	1	2	.385	.407	.654	1061	193	3	0	0	0	.750	-0	P-10	0.0
1945	Det-A	4	5	0	1	0	0	0	0	0	0	.200	.200	.200	400	15	-1	0	0	0	1.000	-0	/P-3	0.0
Total	3	30	52	8	16	3	1	1	10	1	3	.308	.321	.462	782	108	0	0	0		.778	0	/P-13,O-4(4-0-0)	-0.1

■ JOHNNY OATES Oates, Johnny Lane b: 1/21/46, Sylva, N.C. BL/TR, 5′11″, 188 lbs. Deb: 9/17/70 MC

YEAR	TM/L	G	AB	R	H	2B	3B	HR	RBI	BB	SO	AVG	OBP	SLG	OPS	OPS+	BR+	SB	CS	SBR	FA	FR	G/POS	TPR
1970	Bal-A	5	18	2	5	0	1	0	2	2	0	.278	.350	.389	739	102	0	0	0	0	.939	1	/C-4	0.1
1972	Bal-A	85	253	20	66	12	1	4	21	28	31	.261	.335	.364	698	105	2	5	7	-1	**.995**	-3	C-82	0.1
1973	Atl-N	93	322	27	80	6	0	4	27	22	31	.248	.299	.304	603	63	-16	1	4	-1	.981	-6	C-86	-2.0
1974	Atl-N	100	291	22	65	10	0	1	21	23	24	.223	.280	.268	548	52	-19	2	3	-1	.992	12	C-91	-0.4
1975	Atl-N	8	18	0	4	1	0	0	0	1	4	.222	.263	.278	541	48	-1	0	0	0	1.000	-0	/C-6	-0.2
	Phi-N	90	269	28	77	14	0	1	25	33	29	.286	.364	.349	714	95	-1	1	0	0	.990	2	C-82	0.5
	Yr	98	287	28	81	15	0	1	25	34	33	.282	.358	.345	703	92	-2	1	0	0	.990	1	C-88	0.3
1976	*Phi-N	37	99	10	25	2	0	0	8	8	12	.253	.308	.273	581	64	-4	0	1	-0	.994	2	C-33	-0.2
1977	*LA-N	60	156	18	42	4	0	3	11	11	11	.269	.317	.353	670	80	-4	1	0	0	.987	5	C-56	0.2
1978	*LA-N	40	75	5	23	1	0	0	6	5	3	.307	.350	.320	670	89	-1	0	1	-0	.956	-2	C-24	-0.2
1979	LA-N	26	46	4	6	2	0	0	2	4	1	.130	.200	.174	374	3	-6	0	1	-0	.975	3	C-20	-0.3
1980	NY-A	39	64	6	12	3	0	1	3	2	3	.188	.224	.281	505	38	-6	1	2	-0	.991	3	C-39	-0.3
1981	NY-A	10	26	4	5	1	0	0	0	2	0	.192	.250	.231	481	40	-2	0	0	0	.963	1	C-10	-0.1
Total	11	593	1637	146	410	56	2	14	126	141	149	.250	.311	.313	623	73	-58	11	19	-4	.987	16	C-533	-2.8

■ SHERMAN OBANDO Obando, Sherman Omar (Gainor) b: 1/23/70, Bocas Del Toro, Pan. BR/TR, 6′4″, 215 lbs. Deb: 4/10/93

YEAR	TM/L	G	AB	R	H	2B	3B	HR	RBI	BB	SO	AVG	OBP	SLG	OPS	OPS+	BR+	SB	CS	SBR	FA	FR	G/POS	TPR
1993	Bal-A	31	92	8	25	2	0	3	15	4	26	.272	.309	.391	701	83	-2	0	0	0	.929	-1	D-21/O-8(1-0-7)	-0.5
1995	Bal-A	16	38	0	10	1	0	0	3	2	12	.263	.300	.289	589	53	-3	1	0	0	.923	-0	/O-7(0-0-7),D-7	-0.3
1996	Mon-N	89	178	30	44	9	0	8	22	22	48	.247	.333	.433	766	98	-1	2	0	0	.962	-1	O-47(0-0-47)	-0.4
1997	Mon-N	41	47	3	6	1	0	2	9	6	14	.128	.241	.277	517	35	-5	0	0	0	1.000	-3	O-15(1-0-14)/D-2	-0.8
Total	4	177	355	41	85	13	0	13	49	34	100	.239	.311	.386	697	81	-10	3	0	1	.957	-6	/O-77(2-0-75),D-30	-2.0

■ HENRY OBERBECK Oberbeck, Henry A. b: 5/17/1858, Missouri d: 8/26/21, St.Louis, Mo. Deb: 5/7/1883 Career OF: (7-LF 4-CF 28-RF)

YEAR	TM/L	G	AB	R	H	2B	3B	HR	RBI	BB	SO	AVG	OBP	SLG	OPS	OPS+	BR+	SB	CS	SBR	FA	FR	G/POS	TPR
1883	Pit-a	2	9	1	2	1	0	0		0		.222	.222	.333	556	80	-0				1.000	0	/1-2	0.0
	StL-a	4	14	0	0	0	0	0		0		.000	.000	.000	0	-95	-3				.833	1	/O-4(3-1-0)	-0.2
	Yr	6	23	1	2	1	0	0		0		.087	.087	.130	217	-30	-3				.833	1	/O-4(3-1-0),1-2	-0.2
1884	Bal-U	33	125	19	23	4	0	0		3		.184	.203	.216	419	25	-15				.878	2	O-28(1-0-27)/3-8,P-2	-1.1
	KC-U	27	90	7	17	3	0	0		7		.189	.247	.222	470	50	-8				.823	7	3-15/O-7L,P-6,1-3	0.0
	Yr	60	215	26	40	7	0	0		10		.186	.222	.219	441	34	-23				.908	9	O-35R,3-23/P-8,1-3	-1.1
Total	2	66	238	27	42	8	0	0		10		.176	.210	.210	420	28	-26				.901	9	/O-39R,3-23,P-8,1-5	-1.3

■ KEN OBERKFELL Oberkfell, Kenneth Ray b: 5/4/56, Highland, Ill. BL/TR, 6′, 210 lbs. Deb: 8/22/77

YEAR	TM/L	G	AB	R	H	2B	3B	HR	RBI	BB	SO	AVG	OBP	SLG	OPS	OPS+	BR+	SB	CS	SBR	FA	FR	G/POS	TPR
1977	StL-N	9	9	0	1	0	0	0	1	0	3	.111	.111	.111	222	-41	-2	0	0	0	1.000	-1	/2-6	-0.2
1978	StL-N	24	50	7	6	1	0	0	0	3	1	.120	.170	.140	310	-13	-8	0	0	0	.987	3	2-17/3-4	-0.4
1979	StL-N	135	369	53	111	19	5	1	35	57	35	.301	.400	.388	788	115	10	4	1	1	**.985**	-4	*2-117,3-17/S-2	1.2

YEAR	TM/L	G	AB	R	H	2B	3B	HR	RBI	BB	SO	AVG	OBP	SLG	OPS	OPS+	BR+	SB	CS	SBR	FA	FR	G/POS	TPR
1980	StL-N	116	422	58	128	27	6	3	46	51	23	.303	.380	.417	797	118	12	4	4	-1	.989	-8	*2-101,3-16	0.9
1981	StL-N	102	376	43	110	12	6	2	45	37	28	.293	.356	.372	728	104	3	13	5	1	.956	11	*3-102/S-1	1.4
1982	*StL-N	137	470	55	136	22	5	2	34	40	31	.289	.346	.370	717	99	0	11	9	-1	**.972**	11	*3-135/2-1	0.9
1983	StL-N	151	488	62	143	26	5	3	38	61	27	.293	.373	.385	758	110	9	12	6	1	**.960**	3	*3-127,2-32/S-1	1.3
1984	StL-N	50	152	17	47	11	1	0	11	16	10	.309	.379	.395	773	121	5	1	2	-0	.967	4	3-46/2-2,S-1	0.8
	Atl-N	50	172	21	40	8	1	1	10	15	17	.233	.294	.308	602	65	-8	1	3	-1	.964	-5	3-45/2-4	-1.6
	Yr	100	324	38	87	19	2	1	21	31	27	.269	.334	.349	683	90	-4	2	5	-1	.966	-1	3-91/2-6,S-1	-0.8
1985	Atl-N	134	412	30	112	19	4	3	35	51	38	.272	.360	.359	720	96	-0	1	2	-0	.963	-1	*3-117,2-16	-0.3
1986	Atl-N	151	503	62	136	24	3	5	48	83	40	.270	.376	.360	736	98	2	7	4	0	.976	9	*3-130,2-41	1.2
1987	Atl-N	135	508	59	142	29	2	3	48	48	29	.280	.344	.362	706	83	-11	3	3	-0	.979	-4	*3-126,2-11	-1.7
1988	Atl-N	120	422	42	117	20	4	3	40	32	28	.277	.331	.365	696	95	-2	4	5	-1	.951	-7	*3-113/2-1	-1.1
	Pit-N	20	54	7	12	2	0	0	2	5	6	.222	.288	.259	547	59	-3	0	0	0	1.000	-4	2-11/S-3,3-2,1-1	-0.7
	Yr	140	476	49	129	22	4	3	42	37	34	.271	.326	.353	679	91	-5	4	5	-1	.952	-10	*3-115,2-12/S-3,1-1	-1.8
1989	Pit-N	14	40	2	5	1	0	0	2	2	2	.125	.167	.150	317	-9	-6	0	0	0	.988	-1	/1-9,2-3	-0.7
	*SF-N	83	116	17	37	5	1	2	15	8	8	.319	.373	.431	804	133	5	0	1	-0	.971	-4	3-38/1-7,2-7	0.0
	Yr	97	156	19	42	6	1	2	17	10	10	.269	.321	.359	680	97	-1	0	1	-0	.971	-5	3-38,1-16,2-10	-0.7
1990	Hou-N	77	150	10	31	6	1	1	12	15	17	.207	.283	.280	563	57	-9	1	1	-0	.935	-2	3-24,1-11,2-11	-1.2
1991	Hou-N	53	70	7	16	4	0	0	14	14	8	.229	.357	.286	643	88	-0	0	0	0	1.000	0	1-13/3-4	-0.1
1992	Cal-A	41	91	6	24	1	0	0	10	8	5	.264	.323	.275	598	69	-4	0	1	-0	.986	-7	2-21/1-2,D-5	-1.1
Total	16	1602	4874	558	1354	237	44	29	446	546	356	.278	.353	.362	716	97	-6	62	47	-3	.965	-5	*3-1046,2-402/1SD	-1.4
■ MIKE O'BERRY O'Berry, Preston Michael b: 4/20/54, Birmingham, Ala. BR/TR, 6'2", 195 lbs. Deb: 4/8/79																								
1979	Bos-A	43	59	8	10	1	0	1	4	5	16	.169	.246	.237	483	29	-6	0	0	0	.957	0	C-43	-0.5
1980	Chi-N	19	48	7	10	1	0	0	5	5	13	.208	.283	.229	512	41	-4	0	0	0	.982	4	C-19	0.1
1981	Cin-N	55	111	6	20	3	1	1	5	14	19	.180	.272	.252	524	49	-7	0	0	0	.983	3	C-55	-0.3
1982	Cin-N	21	45	5	10	2	0	0	3	10	13	.222	.364	.267	630	77	-1	0	0	0	.990	-1	C-21	-0.1
1983	Cal-A	26	60	7	10	1	0	1	5	3	11	.167	.206	.233	440	21	-7	0	0	0	1.000	-1	C-26	-0.6
1984	NY-A	13	32	3	8	2	0	0	5	2	2	.250	.294	.313	607	71	-1	0	0	0	1.000	1	C-12/3-1	0.0
1985	Mon-N	20	21	2	4	0	0	0	0	4	3	.190	.320	.190	510	49	-1	0	0	0	1.000	3	C-20	0.3
Total	7	197	376	38	72	10	1	3	27	43	77	.191	.276	.247	524	46	-27	1	0	0	.984	10	C-196/3-1	-1.1
■ JIM OBRADOVICH Obradovich, James Thomas b: 9/13/49, Fort Campbell, Ky. BL/TL, 6'2", 200 lbs. Deb: 9/12/78																								
1978	Hou-N	10	17	3	3	0	1	0	2	1	3	.176	.222	.294	516	47	-1	0	0	0	1.000	-0	/1-3	-0.2
■ CHARLIE O'BRIEN O'Brien, Charles Hugh b: 5/1/60, Tulsa, Okla. BR/TR, 6'2", 190 lbs. Deb: 6/2/85																								
1985	Oak-A	16	11	3	3	1	0	0	1	3	3	.273	.429	.364	792	129	1	0	0	0	.958	-0	C-16	0.1
1987	Mil-A	10	35	2	7	3	1	0	0	4	4	.200	.282	.343	625	63	-2	0	1	-0	1.000	6	C-10	0.4
1988	Mil-A	40	118	12	26	6	0	2	9	5	16	.220	.252	.322	574	59	-7	0	1	-0	.991	12	C-40	0.7
1989	Mil-A	62	188	22	44	10	0	6	35	21	11	.234	.339	.383	722	104	2	0	0	0	.986	7	C-62	1.2
1990	Mil-A	46	145	11	27	7	2	0	11	11	26	.186	.253	.262	515	45	-11	0	0	0	.992	5	C-46	-0.3
	NY-N	28	68	6	11	3	0	0	9	10	8	.162	.278	.206	484	36	-6	0	0	0	.986	9	C-28	0.5
1991	NY-N	69	168	16	31	6	0	2	14	17	25	.185	.275	.256	531	51	-11	0	2	-1	.991	19	C-67	1.1
1992	NY-N	68	156	15	33	12	0	2	13	16	18	.212	.289	.327	616	75	-5	0	1	-0	.979	5	C-64	0.2
1993	NY-N	67	188	15	48	11	0	4	23	14	14	.255	.314	.378	691	85	-4	1	1	-0	.986	11	C-65	1.0
1994	Atl-N	51	152	24	37	11	0	8	28	15	24	.243	.324	.474	797	102	0	0	0	0	.991	3	C-48	0.5
1995	*Atl-N	67	198	18	45	7	0	9	23	29	40	.227	.343	.399	742	92	-2	0	1	-0	.992	4	C-64	0.5
1996	Tor-A	109	324	33	77	17	0	13	44	29	68	.238	.332	.410	743	87	-7	0	1	-0	.995	3	*C-105	0.1
1997	Tor-A	69	225	22	49	15	1	4	27	22	45	.218	.318	.347	664	73	-9	0	2	-1	.995	19	C-69	1.3
1998	Chi-A	57	164	12	43	9	0	4	18	9	31	.262	.309	.390	699	82	-4	0	0	0	.988	1	C-57	0.0
	Ana-A	5	11	1	2	0	0	0	0	1	2	.182	.250	.182	432	15	-1	0	0	0	1.000	0	/C-5	-0.1
	Yr	62	175	13	45	9	0	4	18	10	33	.257	.305	.377	682	78	-6	0	0	0	.989	1	C-62	-0.1
1999	Ana-A	27	62	3	6	0	0	1	4	1	12	.097	.138	.145	284	-28	-12	0	0	0	.993	9	C-27	-0.2
2000	Mon-N	9	19	1	4	1	0	1	2	2	7	.211	.286	.421	707	75	-1	0	0	0	1.000	-2	/C-9	-0.3
Total	15	800	2232	216	493	119	4	56	261	209	354	.221	.305	.353	658	75	-79	1	10	-3	.990	109	C-782	6.7
■ EDDIE O'BRIEN O'Brien, Edward Joseph b: 12/11/30, S.Amboy, N.J. BR/TR, 5'9", 165 lbs. Deb: 4/25/53 FC Career OF: (6-LF 57-CF 0-RF)																								
1953	Pit-N	89	261	21	62	5	3	0	14	17	30	.238	.289	.280	569	50	-19	6	1	1	.935	-14	S-81	-2.5
1955	Pit-N	75	236	26	55	3	1	0	8	18	13	.233	.290	.254	544	47	-18	4	5	-1	.993	1	O-56(1-56-0)/3-7,S-4	-2.0
1956	Pit-N	63	53	17	14	2	0	0	3	2	2	.264	.291	.302	593	61	-3	1	1	-0	.978	9	S-23/O-6L,3-4,2P	0.8
1957	Pit-N	3	4	0	0	0	0	0	0	0	0	.000	.000	.000	0	-99	-1	0	0	0	1.000	0	/P-3	0.0
1958	Pit-N	1	0	0	0	0	0	0	0	0	0	—	—	—	—	—	0	0	0	0	.000	-0	/P-1	0.0
Total	5	231	554	64	131	10	4	0	25	37	45	.236	.288	.269	557	48	-41	11	7	-0	.942	-4	S-108/O-62C,3-11,P2	-3.7
■ DINK O'BRIEN O'Brien, Frank Aloysius b: 9/13/1894, San Francisco, Cal. d: 11/4/71, Monterey Park, Cal. BR/TR, 5'8", 160 lbs. Deb: 4/26/23																								
1923	Phi-N	15	21	3	7	2	0	0	0	2	1	.333	.391	.429	820	104	0	0	0	0	.909	0	/C-9	0.1
■ GEORGE O'BRIEN O'Brien, George Joseph b: 11/4/1889, Cleveland, Ohio d: 3/24/66, Columbus, Ohio BR/TR, 6', 185 lbs. Deb: 8/16/15																								
1915	StL-A	3	9	1	2	0	0	0	0	1	2	.222	.300	.222	522	59	-0	0			.933	-1	/C-3	-0.1
■ JERRY O'BRIEN O'Brien, Jeremiah b: 2/2/1864, New York d: 7/4/11, Binghamton, N.Y. Deb: 7/30/1887																								
1887	Was-N	1	4	0	0	0	0	0	0	0	2	.000	.000	.000	0	-99	-1	0			.714	-0	/2-1	-0.1
■ JOHN O'BRIEN O'Brien, John E. b: 10/22/1851, Columbus, Ohio d: 12/31/14, Fall River, Mass. TR, 5'11.5", 187 lbs. Deb: 4/19/1884																								
1884	Bal-U	18	77	7	19	1	1	0		2		.247	.266	.286	552	61	-6				.865	0	O-18(3-14-1)	-0.5
■ JOHN O'BRIEN O'Brien, John J. "Chewing Gum" b: 7/14/1870, St.John, N.B., Can d: 5/13/13, Lewiston, Maine BL/TR, 175 lbs. Deb: 4/22/1891																								
1891	Bro-N	43	167	22	41	4	2	0	26	12	17	.246	.308	.293	601	76	-5	4			.854	-22	2-43	-2.3
1893	Chi-N	4	14	3	5	0	1	0	1	2	2	.357	.471	.500	971	160	1	0			.900	-2	/2-4	0.0
1895	Lou-N	128	539	82	138	10	4	1	50	45	20	.256	.325	.295	620	65	-26	15			.938	3	*2-125/1-3	-1.4
1896	Lou-N	49	186	24	63	9	1	2	24	13	7	.339	.385	.430	815	119	5	4			.919	-1	2-49	0.5
	Was-N	73	270	38	72	6	3	4	33	27	12	.267	.344	.356	700	85	-6	4			.952	3	2-73	0.0
	Yr	122	456	62	135	15	4	6	57	40	19	.296	.361	.386	747	98	-1	8			.938	2	*2-122	0.5
1897	Was-N	86	320	37	78	12	2	3	45	19		.244	.309	.322	630	67	-16	6			.942	4	2-86	-0.7
1899	Bal-N	39	135	14	26	4	0	1	17	15		.193	.283	.244	527	43	-11	4			.966	7	2-39	-0.2
	Pit-N	79	279	26	63	2	4	1	33	21		.226	.285	.272	557	53	-18	8			.946	3	2-79	-1.1
	Yr	118	414	40	89	6	4	2	50	36		.215	.284	.263	547	50	-28	12			.953	9	*2-118	-1.3
Total	6	501	1910	246	486	47	17	12	229	154	58	.254	.322	.316	637	72	-74	45			.936	-6	2-498/1-3	-5.2
■ JACK O'BRIEN O'Brien, John Joseph b: 2/5/1873, Watervliet, N.Y. d: 6/10/33, Watervliet, N.Y. BL/TR, 6'1", 165 lbs. Deb: 4/14/1899 Career OF: (165-LF 68-CF 62-RF)																								
1899	Was-N	127	468	68	132	11	5	6	51	31		.282	.331	.365	696	92	-6	17			.926	4	*O-121(121-0-0)/3-4	-1.1
1901	Was-A	11	45	5	8	0	0	0	5	3		.178	.245	.178	423	19	-5	2			.929	-0	O-11(11-0-0)	-0.5
	Cle-A	92	375	54	106	14	5	0	39	22		.283	.329	.347	676	91	-4	13			.941	-3	O-92(31-0-61)/3-1	-1.0
	Yr	103	420	59	114	14	5	0	44	25		.271	.320	.329	649	83	-9	15			.939	-3	*O-103(42-0-61)/3-1	-1.5
1903	*Bos-A	96	338	44	71	14	4	3	38	21		.210	.262	.302	564	65	-14	10			.958	-6	O-71C,3-11/2-4,S-1	-2.5
Total	3	326	1226	171	317	39	14	9	133	77		.259	.308	.335	643	82	-29	42			.937	-5	O-295L/3-16,2-4,S-1	-5.1
■ JACK O'BRIEN O'Brien, John K. (b: John K. Bryne) b: 6/12/1860, Philadelphia, Pa. d: 11/20/10, Philadelphia, Pa. BR/TR, 5'10", 184 lbs. Deb: 5/2/1882 Career OF: (5-LF 36-CF 31-RF)																								
1882	Phi-a	62	241	44	73	13	3	3	37	13		.303	.339	.419	768	138	8				**.925**	11	C-45,O-18R/3-1,1-1	2.1
1883	Phi-a	94	390	74	113	14	10	0	70	25		.290	.333	.377	709	117	6				.876	-1	C-58,O-25C,3-19,/S	0.8
1884	Phi-a	36	138	25	39	6	1	1		9		.283	.340	.362	702	121	3				.930	-0	C-30/O-5(0-5-0),1-1	0.5
1885	Phi-a	62	225	35	60	9	1	2	30	20		.267	.340	.342	682	109	3				.903	-8	C-43/S-9,1-7,O-3R,3	-0.2

YEAR	TM/L	G	AB	R	H	2B	3B	HR	RBI	BB	SO	AVG	OBP	SLG	OPS	OPS+	BR+	SB	CS	SBR	FA	FR	G/POS	TPR
1886	Phi-a	105	423	65	107	25	7	0	56	38		.253	.325	.345	670	109	4	23			.918	-15	C-36,3-27,1-24,S/2O	-0.7
1887	Bro-a	30	129	18	34	4	1	1	17	6		.264	.264	.301	564	56	-8	8			.839	-8	C-25/O-4(1-0-3),2-1	-1.1
1888	Bal-a	57	196	25	44	11	5	0	18	17		.224	.300	.332	631	105	1	14			.925	-15	C-37,O-13(4-0-9)/1-7	-1.0
1890	Phi-a	109	433	80	113	24	14	4	80	52		.261	.356	.409	765	126	14	31			.976	4	*1-109/O-1(0-0-1),C-1	0.7
Total	8	555	2175	366	583	106	42	11	308	180		.268	.331	.369	700	114	32	76			.903	-31	C-275,1-149/O3S2	1.1
■ JOHNNY O'BRIEN	O'Brien, John Thomas b: 12/11/30, S.Amboy, N.J. BR/TR, 5'9", 170 lbs. Deb: 4/19/53 F																							
1953	Pit-N	89	279	28	69	13	2	2	22	21	36	.247	.309	.330	639	67	-13	1	1	-0	.982	1	2-77/S-1	-0.7
1955	Pit-N	84	278	22	83	15	2	1	25	20	19	.299	.348	.378	726	94	-2	1	1	-0	.969	5	2-78	0.8
1956	Pit-N	73	104	13	18	1	0	0	3	5	7	.173	.211	.183	394	7	-13	0	0	0	.959	5	2-53/P-8,S-1	-0.5
1957	Pit-N	34	35	7	11	2	1	0	1	1	4	.314	.368	.429	797	117	1	0	0	0	.857	-2	P-16/S-8,2-2	-0.1
1958	Pit-N	3	1	1	0	0	0	0	0	0	1	.000	.000	.000	0	-99	-0	0	0	0	.000	0	H	0.0
	StL-N	12	2	3	0	0	0	0	0	1	0	.000	.333	.000	333	-2	-0	0	0	0	1.000	0	/S-5,P-1,2-1	0.0
	Yr	15	3	4	0	0	0	0	0	1	1	.000	.250	.000	250	-26	-1	0	0	0	1.000	0	/S-5,P-1,2-1	0.0
1959	Mil-N	44	116	16	23	4	0	1	8	11	15	.198	.273	.259	532	47	-9	0	0	0	.987	-3	2-37	-0.9
Total	6	339	815	90	204	35	5	4	59	59	82	.250	.307	.320	628	68	-38	2	2	-0	.974	6	2-248/P-25,S-15	-1.4
■ PETE O'BRIEN	O'Brien, Peter J. b: 6/17/1877, Binghamton, N.Y. d: 1/31/17, Jersey City, N.J. BL/TR, 5'7", 170 lbs. Deb: 9/21/01																							
1901	Cin-N	16	54	1	11	1	0	1	3	2		.204	.232	.278	510	51	-3	0			.889	-2	2-15	-0.6
1906	StL-A	151	524	44	122	9	4	2	57	42		.233	.293	.277	570	82	-10	25			.933	-41	*2-120,3-20,S-11	-5.5
1907	Cle-A	43	145	9	33	5	2	0	6	7		.228	.263	.290	553	76	-4	1			.949	-11	2-15,3-12,S-12	-1.6
	Was-A	39	134	6	25	3	1	0	12	12		.187	.259	.224	482	59	-6	4			.912	4	3-26,S-13/2-1	-0.1
	Yr	82	279	15	58	8	3	0	18	19		.208	.261	.258	519	68	-10	5			.911	-7	3-38,S-25,2-16	-1.7
Total	3	249	857	60	191	18	7	3	78	63		.223	.279	.271	550	76	-24	30			.930	-50	2-151/3-58,S-36	-7.8
■ PETE O'BRIEN	O'Brien, Peter James b: 6/16/1867, Chicago, Ill. d: 6/30/37, York Township, Du Page County, Ill. BR/TR, 5'9.5", 165 lbs. Deb: 4/29/1890																							
1890	Chi-N	27	106	15	30	7	0	3	16	5	10	.283	.315	.434	749	113	1	4			.929	-2	2-27	0.0
■ PETE O'BRIEN	O'Brien, Peter Michael b: 2/9/58, Santa Monica, Cal. BL/TL, 6'1", 198 lbs. Deb: 9/3/82 Career OF: (40-LF 0-CF 21-RF)																							
1982	Tex-A	20	67	13	16	4	1	4	13	6	8	.239	.301	.507	809	124	2	1	0	0	1.000	-0	O-11(11-0-0)/1-3,D-4	0.1
1983	Tex-A	154	524	53	124	24	5	8	53	58	62	.237	.314	.347	661	83	-11	5	4	-0	.993	13	*1-133,O-27R/D-1	-0.8
1984	Tex-A	142	520	57	149	26	2	18	80	53	50	.287	.353	.448	801	116	11	3	5	-1	.992	1	*1-141/O-1(0-0-1)	0.2
1985	Tex-A	159	573	69	153	34	3	22	92	69	53	.267	.347	.452	799	115	12	5	10	-2	.995	-6	*1-159	-0.6
1986	Tex-A	156	551	86	160	23	3	23	90	87	66	.290	.387	.468	855	128	24	4	4	-1	.992	2	*1-155	1.5
1987	Tex-A	159	569	84	163	26	1	23	88	59	61	.286	.354	.457	810	113	10	0	4	-1	.992	16	*1-158/O-2(0-0-2),D-1	1.5
1988	Tex-A	156	547	57	149	24	1	16	71	72	73	.272	.357	.408	765	111	9	1	4	-1	.995	13	*1-155/D-1	1.0
1989	Cle-A	155	554	75	144	24	1	12	55	83	48	.260	.358	.372	730	104	6	3	1	0	.994	3	*1-154/D-1	-0.2
1990	Sea-A	108	366	32	82	18	0	5	27	44	33	.224	.311	.314	625	74	-12	0	0	0	.995	4	1-97/O-6(6-0-0),D-6	-1.5
1991	Sea-A	152	560	58	139	29	3	17	88	44	61	.248	.304	.402	706	93	-6	0	1	-0	**.997**	1	*1-132,D-18,O-13L	-1.5
1992	Sea-A	134	396	40	88	15	1	14	52	40	27	.222	.294	.371	665	85	-9	2	1	0	.996	2	1-81,D-36	-1.3
1993	Sea-A	72	210	30	54	7	0	7	27	26	21	.257	.339	.390	729	94	-2	0	0	0	.988	0	D-52/1-9,O-1(1-0-0)	-0.5
Total	12	1567	5437	654	1421	254	21	169	736	641	563	.261	.340	.409	749	104	34	24	34	-7	.994	49	*1-1377,D-120/O-61L	-2.1
■ RAY O'BRIEN	O'Brien, Raymond Joseph b: 10/31/1892, St.Louis, Mo. d: 3/31/42, St.Louis, Mo. BL/TL, 5'9", 175 lbs. Deb: 6/27/16																							
1916	Pit-N	16	57	5	12	3	2	0	3	1	14	.211	.224	.333	557	69	-2	0			.864	-1	O-14(7-0-7)	-0.4
■ SYD O'BRIEN	O'Brien, Sydney Lloyd b: 12/18/44, Compton, Cal. BR/TR, 6'1", 185 lbs. Deb: 4/15/69 Career OF: (0-LF 0-CF 1-RF)																							
1969	Bos-A	100	263	47	64	10	5	9	29	15	37	.243	.287	.422	709	91	-4	2	3	-1	.939	-1	3-53,S-15,2-12	-0.5
1970	Chi-A	121	441	48	109	13	2	8	44	22	62	.247	.286	.340	626	69	-19	3	3	-0	.938	-6	3-68,2-43/S-5	-2.4
1971	Cal-A	90	251	25	50	8	1	5	21	15	33	.199	.247	.299	546	58	-15	0	2	-1	.961	-1	S-52/2-7,3-6,1-1,O	-1.2
1972	Cal-A	36	39	10	7	2	0	1	1	6	10	.179	.289	.308	597	82	-1	0	0	0	.889	1	/3-8,S-4,2-3,1-1	0.0
	Mil-A	31	58	5	12	2	0	1	5	2	13	.207	.233	.293	526	57	-3	0	1	-0	.852	-1	/3-9,2-7	-0.5
	Yr	67	97	15	19	4	0	2	6	8	23	.196	.257	.299	556	68	-4	0	1	-0	.861	0	3-17,2-10/S-4,1-1	-0.5
Total	4	378	1052	135	242	35	8	24	100	60	155	.230	.274	.347	621	72	-42	5	9	-2	.934	-8	3-144/S-76,2-72,1O	-4.6
■ TOMMY O'BRIEN	O'Brien, Thomas Edward "Obie" b: 12/19/18, Anniston, Ala. d: 11/5/78, Anniston, Ala. BR/TR, 5'11", 195 lbs. Deb: 4/24/43																							
1943	Pit-N	89	232	35	72	12	7	2	26	15	24	.310	.352	.448	801	126	7	0			.964	-6	O-48(17-0-31)/3-9	-0.2
1944	Pit-N	85	156	27	39	6	2	3	20	21	12	.250	.343	.372	714	97	-0	1			.965	-9	O-48(15-0-33)/3-1	-1.2
1945	Pit-N	58	161	23	54	6	5	0	18	9	13	.335	.374	.435	809	120	4	0			.961	-6	O-45(12-0-33)	-0.4
1949	Bos-A	49	125	24	28	5	0	3	10	21	12	.224	.336	.336	672	73	-5	1	0	0	.984	-2	O-32(0-8-25)	-0.8
1950	Bos-A	9	31	0	4	1	0	0	3	3	5	.129	.206	.161	367	-5	-5	0	0	0	1.000	-1	/O-9(3-4-2)	-0.6
	Was-A	3	9	1	1	0	0	0	1	1	0	.111	.200	.111	311	-20	-2	0	0	0	1.000	1	/O-3(2-0-1)	-0.1
	Yr	12	40	1	5	1	0	0	4	4	5	.125	.205	.150	355	-8	-7	0	0	0	1.000	-0	O-12(5-4-3)	-0.7
Total	5	293	714	110	198	30	14	8	78	70	66	.277	.344	.392	736	100	-1	2	0		.970	-24	O-185(49-12-125)/3-10	-3.3
■ TOM O'BRIEN	O'Brien, Thomas H. b: 6/22/1860, Salem, Mass. d: 4/21/21, Worcester, Mass. BR/TR, 6'1", 185 lbs. Deb: 6/14/1882 Career OF: (19-LF 13-CF 3-RF)																							
1882	Wor-N	22	89	9	18	1	1	0	7	1	10	.202	.211	.236	447	42	-6				.789	-2	O-20(16-4-0)/2-2,3-1	-0.8
1883	Bal-a	33	138	16	37	6	4	0		5		.268	.294	.370	663	109	1				.825	-4	2-29/O-4(0-4-0)	-0.2
1884	Bos-U	103	449	80	118	31	8	4		12		.263	.282	.394	676	105	-11				.853	1	*2-99/O-3L,1-2,C-1	-0.6
1885	Bal-a	8	33	4	7	3	0	0	5	2		.212	.257	.303	560	78	-1				.932	1	/1-6,2-2	0.0
1887	NY-a	31	131	13	27	3	2	0	18	2		.206	.212	.248	460	29	-12	10			.963	-2	1-20/O-8C,3-2,2P	-1.3
1890	Roc-a	73	273	36	52	6	5	0	31	30		.190	.273	.249	522	58	-14	6			.971	-4	1-68/2-8	-2.1
Total	6	270	1113	158	259	50	20	4	61	52	10	.233	.267	.323	590	79	-43	16			.846	-10	2-142/1-96,O-35L,3PC	-5.0
■ TOM O'BRIEN	O'Brien, Thomas J. b: 2/20/1873, Verona, Pa. d: 2/4/01, Phoenix, Ariz. Deb: 5/10/1897 Career OF: (169-LF 61-CF 32-RF)																							
1897	*Bal-N	50	147	25	37	6	0	0	32	20		.252	.349	.293	642	70	-6	7			.968	0	1-25,O-24(13-1-10)	-0.6
1898	Bal-N	18	60	9	13	0	0	0	14	10		.217	.338	.217	555	59	-3	0			.833	0	O-16(0-0-16)	-0.3
	Pit-N	107	413	53	107	10	8	1	45	25		.259	.318	.329	648	87	-7	13			.924	-3	O-69C,1-21/3-8,2S	-1.3
	Yr	125	473	62	120	10	8	1	59	35		.254	.321	.315	636	84	-10	13			.911	-3	O-85C,1-21/3-8,2S	-1.6
1899	NY-N	151	577	101	171	22	10	6	77	44		.296	.350	.400	751	109	7	23			.933	-2	*O-128L,3-21/S-2,21	-0.6
1900	*Pit-N	102	376	61	109	22	6	3	61	21		.290	.349	.404	753	107	3	12			.961	-11	1-65,O-25L/2-4,S-2	-0.9
Total	4	428	1573	249	437	60	24	10	229	120		.278	.341	.366	707	97	-5	55			.928	-15	O-262L,1-112/3-29,2S	-3.7
■ DARBY O'BRIEN	O'Brien, William D. b: 9/1/1863, Peoria, Ill. d: 6/15/1893, Peoria, Ill. BR/TR, 6'1", 186 lbs. Deb: 4/16/1887 Career OF: (655-LF 46-CF 4-RF)																							
1887	NY-a	127	562	97	197	30	13	5	73	40		.351	.355	.437	792	126	18	49			.913	6	*O-121L,1-10/S-2,3P	1.6
1888	Bro-a	136	532	105	149	27	6	2	65	30		.280	.327	.365	692	122	12	55			.932	2	*O-136(136-0-0)	1.0
1889	*Bro-a	136	567	146	170	30	11	5	80	61	76	.300	.384	.418	802	128	22	91			.906	-7	*O-136(136-0-0)	1.0
1890	*Bro-N	85	350	78	110	28	6	2	63	32	43	.314	.378	.446	824	139	17	38			.960	4	O-85(44-42-0)	1.6
1891	Bro-N	103	395	79	100	18	6	5	57	39	53	.253	.331	.367	698	104	2	31			.951	2	*O-103(103-0-0)	0.1
1892	Bro-N	122	490	72	119	14	5	1	56	29	52	.243	.289	.298	587	81	-12	57			.956	4	*O-122(115-3-4)	-1.8
Total	6	709	2896	577	845	147	47	20	394	231	224	.292	.344	.387	732	117	58	321			.934	11	O-703L/1-10,S-2,P3	3.5
■ BILLY O'BRIEN	O'Brien, William Smith b: 3/14/1860, Albany, N.Y. d: 5/26/11, Kansas City, Mo. BR/TR, 6', 185 lbs. Deb: 9/27/1884 Career OF: (1-LF 3-CF 0-RF)																							
1884	StP-U	8	30	1	7	3	0	0		0		.233	.233	.333	567	129	0				.840	1	/3-8,P-2	0.1
	KC-U	4	17	2	4	0	0	0		0		.235	.235	.235	471	49	-2				.714	1	/3-3,1-1	-0.1
	Yr	12	47	3	11	3	0	0		0		.234	.234	.298	532	92	-2				.795	2	3-11/P-2,1-1	0.0
1887	Was-N	113	474	71	147	16	12	**19**	73	21	17	.310	.317	.492	810	128	16	11			.974	-3	*1-104/O-4C,3-4,2-2	0.2
1888	Was-N	133	528	42	119	15	2	9	66	9	70	.225	.238	.313	551	79	-13	10			.975	-4	*1-132/3-1	-2.9
1889	Was-N	2	8	1	0	0	0	0	0	1	1	.000	.111	.000	111	-72	-2	0			1.000	-0	/1-2	-0.2
1890	Bro-a	96	388	47	108	25	8	4	67	28		.278	.332	.415	747	124	10	5			.973	-2	*1-96	-0.1
Total	5	356	1445	164	385	59	22	32	206	59	88	.266	.289	.395	684	108	9	26			.974	-8	1-335/3-16,O-4C,2P	-3.0

■ ALEX OCHOA Ochoa, Alex b: 3/29/72, Miami Lakes, Fla. BR/TR, 6', 185 lbs. Deb: 9/18/95

YEAR	TM/L	G	AB	R	H	2B	3B	HR	RBI	BB	SO	AVG	OBP	SLG	OPS	OPS+	BR+	SB	CS	SBR	FA	FR	G/POS	TPR
1995	NY-N	11	37	7	11	1	0	0	0	2	10	.297	.333	.324	658	77	-1	1	0	0	1.000	1	O-10(0-0-10)	-0.1
1996	NY-N	82	282	37	83	19	3	4	33	17	30	.294	.339	.426	764	105	1	4	3	-0	.966	3	O-76(0-0-76)	0.1
1997	NY-N	113	238	31	58	14	1	3	22	18	32	.244	.302	.349	651	72	-10	3	4	-1	.982	-9	O-88(0-4-84)/D-1	-2.2
1998	Min-A	94	249	35	64	14	2	2	25	10	35	.257	.288	.353	642	65	-13	6	3	0	.969	-4	O-74(21-4-52)/D-3	-1.8
1999	Mil-N	119	277	47	83	16	3	8	40	45	43	.300	.407	.466	872	121	11	6	4	-0	.979	-5	O-85(50-9-31)/D-1	0.3
2000	Cin-N	118	244	50	77	21	3	13	58	24	27	.316	.384	.586	970	135	13	9	4	1	.977	-14	O-95(74-3-37)	-0.3
Total	6	537	1327	207	376	85	12	30	178	116	177	.283	.347	.433	780	101	1	29	18	0	.975	-28	O-428(145-20-290)/D-5	-4.0

■ WHITEY OCK Ock, Harold David b: 3/17/12, Brooklyn, N.Y. d: 3/18/75, Mt.Kisco, N.Y. BR/TR, 5'11", 180 lbs. Deb: 9/29/35

YEAR	TM/L	G	AB	R	H	2B	3B	HR	RBI	BB	SO	AVG	OBP	SLG	OPS	OPS+	BR+	SB	CS	SBR	FA	FR	G/POS	TPR
1935	Bro-N	1	3	0	0	0	0	0	0	1	2	.000	.250	.000	250	-27	-1	0			1.000	-0	/C-1	-0.1

■ DANNY O'CONNELL O'Connell, Daniel Francis b: 1/21/27, Paterson, N.J. d: 10/2/69, Clifton, N.J. BR/TR, 6', 180 lbs. Deb: 7/14/50 C

YEAR	TM/L	G	AB	R	H	2B	3B	HR	RBI	BB	SO	AVG	OBP	SLG	OPS	OPS+	BR+	SB	CS	SBR	FA	FR	G/POS	TPR
1950	Pit-N	79	315	39	92	16	1	8	32	24	33	.292	.342	.425	768	97	-1	7			.977	17	S-65,3-12	1.9
1953	Pit-N	149	588	88	173	26	8	7	55	57	42	.294	.361	.401	762	99	0	3	4	-1	.958	7	*3-104,2-47	0.9
1954	Mil-N	146	541	61	151	28	4	2	37	38	46	.279	.329	.357	685	84	-13	2	2	-0	.979	9	*2-103,3-35/1-8,S-1	0.3
1955	Mil-N	124	453	47	102	15	4	6	40	28	43	.225	.278	.316	593	60	-27	2	2	-0	.981	16	*2-114/3-7,S-1	-0.3
1956	Mil-N	139	498	71	119	17	9	2	42	76	42	.239	.344	.321	666	86	-8	3	3	-0	.985	-6	*2-138/3-4,S-1	-0.4
1957	Mil-N	48	183	29	43	9	1	1	8	19	20	.235	.314	.311	625	74	-6	1	0	0	.982	7	2-48	0.4
	NY-N	95	364	57	97	18	3	7	28	33	30	.266	.331	.390	721	93	-3	8	3	1	.980	6	2-68,3-30	0.8
	Yr	143	547	86	140	27	4	8	36	52	50	.256	.325	.364	689	87	-10	9	3	1	.981	12	*2-116,3-30	1.2
1958	SF-N	107	306	44	71	12	2	3	23	51	35	.232	.342	.314	655	77	-9	2	1	0	.986	3	*2-104/3-3	0.1
1959	SF-N	34	58	6	11	3	0	0	0	5	15	.190	.254	.241	495	34	-5	0	1	-0	.927	7	3-26/2-8	0.2
1961	Was-A	138	493	61	128	30	1	1	37	77	62	.260	.363	.331	694	88	-5	15	5	2	.939	1	3-73,2-61	0.2
1962	Was-A	84	236	24	62	7	2	2	18	23	28	.263	.328	.335	663	80	-6	5	1	1	.961	-1	3-41,2-22	-0.6
Total	10	1143	4035	527	1049	181	35	39	320	431	396	.260	.335	.351	686	84	-85	48	22		.980	66	2-713,3-335/S-68,1	3.5

■ JIMMY O'CONNELL O'Connell, James Joseph b: 2/11/01, Sacramento, Cal. d: 11/11/76, Bakersfield, Cal. BL/TR, 5'10.5", 175 lbs. Deb: 4/17/23 Career OF: (1-LF 79-CF 14-RF)

YEAR	TM/L	G	AB	R	H	2B	3B	HR	RBI	BB	SO	AVG	OBP	SLG	OPS	OPS+	BR+	SB	CS	SBR	FA	FR	G/POS	TPR
1923	*NY-N	87	252	42	63	9	2	6	39	34	32	.250	.351	.373	724	92	-2	7	3	0	.980	-8	O-64(0-64-0)/1-8	-1.2
1924	NY-N	52	104	24	33	4	2	2	18	11	16	.317	.388	.452	840	128	4	2	1	0	.952	-7	O-29(1-15-14)/2-1	-0.4
Total	2	139	356	66	96	13	4	8	57	45	48	.270	.361	.396	757	102	2	9	4	1	.974	-15	/O-93C,1-8,2-1	-1.6

■ JOHN O'CONNELL O'Connell, John Charles b: 6/13/04, Verona, Pa. d: 10/17/92, Canton, Ohio BR/TR, 6', 170 lbs. Deb: 8/16/28

YEAR	TM/L	G	AB	R	H	2B	3B	HR	RBI	BB	SO	AVG	OBP	SLG	OPS	OPS+	BR+	SB	CS	SBR	FA	FR	G/POS	TPR
1928	Pit-N	1	1	0	0	0	0	0	0	0	0	.000	.000	.000	0	-96	-0	0			1.000	1	/C-1	0.0
1929	Pit-N	2	7	1	1	1	0	0	0	1	1	.143	.250	.286	536	32	-1	0			1.000	-0	/C-2	-0.1
Total	2	3	8	1	1	1	0	0	0	1	1	.125	.222	.250	472	17	-1	0			1.000	0	/C-3	-0.1

■ JOHN O'CONNELL O'Connell, John Joseph d: 5/14/08, Derry, N.H. 5'9.5", 170 lbs. Deb: 8/22/1891 Career OF: (0-LF 0-CF 2-RF)

YEAR	TM/L	G	AB	R	H	2B	3B	HR	RBI	BB	SO	AVG	OBP	SLG	OPS	OPS+	BR+	SB	CS	SBR	FA	FR	G/POS	TPR
1891	Bal-a	8	29	2	5	1	0	0	7	3	6	.172	.250	.207	457	31	-3	2			.938	-3	/S-3,2-3,O-2(0-0-2)	-0.5
1902	Det-A	8	22	1	4	0	0	0	0	3		.182	.280	.182	462	29	-2	0			.919	1	/2-6,1-2	-0.1
Total	2	16	51	3	9	1	0	0	7	6	6	.176	.263	.196	459	30	-5	2			.885	-2	/2-9,S-3,1-2,O-2R	-0.6

■ PAT O'CONNELL O'Connell, Patrick b: 1862, Brooklyn, N.Y. d: 5/5/1892, Brooklyn, N.Y. Deb: 4/17/1890

YEAR	TM/L	G	AB	R	H	2B	3B	HR	RBI	BB	SO	AVG	OBP	SLG	OPS	OPS+	BR+	SB	CS	SBR	FA	FR	G/POS	TPR
1890	Bro-a	11	40	7	9	2	1	0	3	7		.225	.340	.325	665	100	0	3			.830	-1	3-10/1-1	-0.1

■ PAT O'CONNELL O'Connell, Patrick H. b: 6/10/1861, Bangor, Me. d: 1/24/43, Lewiston, Maine BR/TR, 5'10", 175 lbs. Deb: 7/22/1886

YEAR	TM/L	G	AB	R	H	2B	3B	HR	RBI	BB	SO	AVG	OBP	SLG	OPS	OPS+	BR+	SB	CS	SBR	FA	FR	G/POS	TPR
1886	Bal-a	42	166	20	30	3	2	0	8	11		.181	.236	.223	459	45	-10	10			.782	-4	O-41(0-41-0)/1-1,P-1	-1.4

■ DAN O'CONNOR O'Connor, Daniel Cornelius b: 8/1868, Guelph, Ont., Canada d: 3/3/42, Guelph, Ont., Canada BL/TR, 6'2", 185 lbs. Deb: 6/3/1890

YEAR	TM/L	G	AB	R	H	2B	3B	HR	RBI	BB	SO	AVG	OBP	SLG	OPS	OPS+	BR+	SB	CS	SBR	FA	FR	G/POS	TPR
1890	Lou-a	6	26	3	12	1	1	0	5	1		.462	.481	.577	1058	217	4	5			1.000	-1	/1-6	0.2

■ JOHNNY O'CONNOR O'Connor, John Charles "Bucky" b: 12/1/1891, Cahirciveen, Ire. d: 5/30/82, Bonner Springs, Kan. BR/TR, 5'9", Deb: 9/16/16

YEAR	TM/L	G	AB	R	H	2B	3B	HR	RBI	BB	SO	AVG	OBP	SLG	OPS	OPS+	BR+	SB	CS	SBR	FA	FR	G/POS	TPR
1916	Chi-N	1	0	0	0	0	0	0	0	0	0	—	—	—	—	—	0	0			.000	0	/C-1	0.0

■ JACK O'CONNOR O'Connor, John Joseph "Rowdy Jack" or "Peach Pie" b: 6/2/1869, St.Louis, Mo. d: 11/14/37, St.Louis, Mo. BR/TR, 5'10", 170 lbs. Deb: 4/20/1887 M Career OF: (42-LF 113-CF 217-RF)

YEAR	TM/L	G	AB	R	H	2B	3B	HR	RBI	BB	SO	AVG	OBP	SLG	OPS	OPS+	BR+	SB	CS	SBR	FA	FR	G/POS	TPR
1887	Cin-a	12	42	4	6	0	0	0	1	2		.143	.143	.100	243	-31	-7	3			.947	3	/O-7(7-0-0),C-5	-0.3
1888	Cin-a	36	137	14	28	3	1	1	17	6		.204	.243	.263	506	59	-7	12			.795	-0	O-34(11-21-2)/C-2	-0.7
1889	Col-a	107	398	69	107	17	7	4	60	33	37	.269	.331	.377	708	107	4	26			**.955**	-1	C-84,O-19R/2-4,1-3	0.8
1890	Col-a	121	457	89	148	14	10	2	66	38		.324	.377	.411	788	142	24	29			**.962**	10	*C-106/O-9C,S-8,23	3.7
1891	Col-a	56	229	28	61	12	3	0	37	11	14	.266	.300	.345	645	90	-4	10			.878	3	O-40(7-0-33),C-21	0.0
1892	*Cle-N	140	572	71	142	22	5	1	58	25	48	.248	.282	.309	592	76	-19	17			.935	9	*O-106(6-0-100),C-34	-1.2
1893	Cle-N	96	384	72	110	23	1	4	75	29	12	.286	.341	.383	724	87	-9	29			.949	-2	C-56,O-44(2-27-15)	-0.6
1894	Cle-N	86	330	67	104	23	7	2	51	15	7	.315	.345	.445	790	86	-9	15			.942	7	C-45,O-33(1-27-5)/1-7	-0.1
1895	Cle-N	90	343	52	100	14	10	0	58	31	22	.292	.355	.391	746	87	-7	11			.927	-4	C-48,1-41/3-1	-0.6
1896	*Cle-N	68	256	41	76	11	1	1	43	15	12	.297	.343	.359	702	81	-8	15			.966	-7	C-37,1-17,O-12(0-3-9)	-1.0
1897	Cle-N	103	397	49	115	21	4	2	69	26		.290	.338	.378	716	84	-10	20			.941	-12	O-52C,1-36,C-13	-2.1
1898	Cle-N	131	478	50	119	17	4	1	56	26		.249	.291	.308	598	72	-18	8			.983	3	1-69,C-48,O-15R	-1.1
1899	StL-N	84	289	33	73	5	6	0	43	15		.253	.299	.311	610	66	-14	7			.943	2	C-57,1-26	-0.6
1900	StL-N	10	32	4	7	0	0	0	6	2		.219	.306	.219	524	46	-2	0			.957	-1	C-10	-0.2
	*Pit-N	43	147	15	35	4	1	0	19	3		.238	.263	.279	542	49	-10	5			.944	-9	C-40/1-2	-1.5
	Yr	53	179	19	42	4	1	0	25	5		.235	.271	.268	539	49	-13	5			.947	-10	C-50/1-2	-1.7
1901	Pit-N	61	202	16	39	7	3	0	22	10		.193	.238	.257	496	42	-15	2			.978	-1	C-59	-1.0
1902	Pit-N	49	170	13	50	1	2	1	28	3		.294	.306	.341	648	96	-1	2			.979	-3	C-42/1-6,O-1(0-0-1)	0.0
1903	NY-A	64	212	13	43	4	1	0	12	8		.203	.235	.231	466	38	-16	4			.988	1	C-63/1-1	-1.0
1904	StL-A	14	47	4	10	1	0	0	2	2		.213	.245	.234	479	55	-2	0			.943	-4	C-14	-0.6
1906	StL-A	55	174	8	33	0	0	0	11	2		.190	.199	.190	389	23	-15	4			.990	10	C-51	-0.1
1907	StL-A	25	89	2	14	2	0	0	4	0		.157	.176	.180	356	13	-9	0			.991	-2	C-25	-1.0
1910	StL-A	1	0	0	0	0	0	0	0	0		—	—	—	—	—	0	0			1.000	-0	/C-1,M	0.0
Total	21	1452	5385	714	1420	201	66	19	738	302	152	.264	.307	.336	643	79	-155	219			.962	0	C-861,O-372R,1/S23	-9.2

■ PADDY O'CONNOR O'Connor, Patrick Francis b: 8/4/1879, County Kerry, Ireland d: 8/17/50, Springfield, Mass. BR/TR, 5'8", 168 lbs. Deb: 4/17/08 C

YEAR	TM/L	G	AB	R	H	2B	3B	HR	RBI	BB	SO	AVG	OBP	SLG	OPS	OPS+	BR+	SB	CS	SBR	FA	FR	G/POS	TPR
1908	Pit-N	12	16	1	3	0	0	0	2	0		.188	.188	.188	375	20	-1	0			.889	-2	/C-4	-0.3
1909	*Pit-N	9	16	1	5	1	0	0	3	0		.313	.313	.375	688	104	-0	0			.700	-2	/C-3,3-1	-0.2
1910	Pit-N	6	4	0	1	0	0	0	0	1	1	.250	.400	.250	650	85	-0	0			1.000	-0	/C-1	0.0
1914	StL-N	10	9	0	0	0	0	0	0	2	2	.000	.250	.000	250	-24	-1	0			1.000	-0	/C-7	-0.2
1915	Pit-F	70	219	15	50	10	1	0	16	14	30	.228	.278	.283	561	58	-16	4			.987	4	C-66	-0.6
1918	NY-A	1	3	0	1	0	0	0	0	0	1	.333	.333	.333	667	99	-0	0			1.000	-0	/C-1	0.0
Total	6	108	267	17	60	11	1	0	21	17	34	.225	.276	.273	550	57	-18	4			.979	-0	/C-82,3-1	-1.3

■ KEN O'DEA O'Dea, James Kenneth b: 3/16/13, Lima, N.Y. d: 12/17/85, Lima, N.Y. BL/TR, 6', 180 lbs. Deb: 4/21/35

YEAR	TM/L	G	AB	R	H	2B	3B	HR	RBI	BB	SO	AVG	OBP	SLG	OPS	OPS+	BR+	SB	CS	SBR	FA	FR	G/POS	TPR
1935	*Chi-N	76	202	30	52	13	2	6	38	26	18	.257	.345	.431	776	106	2	0			.964	-2	C-63	0.3
1936	Chi-N	80	189	36	58	10	3	2	38	38	18	.307	.423	.423	846	126	9	0			.979	-3	C-55	0.9
1937	Chi-N	83	219	31	66	7	5	4	32	24	26	.301	.370	.434	804	113	4	1			.985	-6	C-64	0.1
1938	*Chi-N	86	247	22	65	12	1	3	33	12	18	.263	.297	.356	654	77	-8	1			.970	4	C-71	0.0
1939	NY-N	52	97	7	17	1	0	3	11	10	16	.175	.252	.278	531	42	-8	0			.947	-2	C-30	-0.9
1940	NY-N	48	96	9	23	4	1	0	12	16	15	.240	.348	.302	650	80	-2	0			.992	2	C-31	0.2
1941	NY-N	59	89	13	19	5	1	3	17	8	20	.213	.278	.393	672	86	-2	0			1.000	1	C-14	0.0
1942	*StL-N	58	192	22	45	7	1	5	32	17	23	.234	.297	.359	656	85	-4	0			.979	10	C-49	1.0
1943	*StL-N	71	203	15	57	11	2	3	25	19	25	.281	.345	.399	744	110	2	0			.989	6	C-56	1.2
1944	*StL-N	85	265	35	66	11	2	6	37	37	29	.249	.343	.374	717	100	1	1			.994	7	C-69	1.2

YEAR	TM/L	G	AB	R	H	2B	3B	HR	RBI	BB	SO	AVG	OBP	SLG	OPS	OPS+	BR+	SB	CS	SBR	FA	FR	G/POS	TPR
1945	StL-N†	100	307	36	78	18	2	4	43	50	31	.254	.359	.365	723	99	1	0			**.995**	3	C-91	0.9
1946	StL-N	22	57	2	7	2	0	1	3	8	8	.123	.231	.211	441	25	-6	0			.991	5	C-22	0.0
	Bos-N	12	32	4	7	0	0	0	2	8	4	.219	.375	.219	594	70	-1	0			1.000	-1	C-12	-0.1
	Yr	34	89	6	14	2	0	1	5	16	12	.157	.286	.213	499	41	-7	0			.994	4	C-34	-0.1
Total	12	832	2195	262	560	101	20	40	323	273	251	.255	.338	.374	712	95	-12	3			.983	26	C-627	4.8

■ PAUL O'DEA O'Dea, Paul "Lefty" b: 7/3/20, Cleveland, Ohio d: 12/11/78, Cleveland, Ohio BL/TL, 6', 200 lbs. Deb: 4/19/44 Career OF: (36-LF 0-CF 58-RF)

YEAR	TM/L	G	AB	R	H	2B	3B	HR	RBI	BB	SO	AVG	OBP	SLG	OPS	OPS+	BR+	SB	CS	SBR	FA	FR	G/POS	TPR
1944	Cle-A	76	173	25	55	9	0	0	13	23	21	.318	.401	.370	771	126	7	2	2	-0	.949	-5	O-41(36-0-5)/P-3,1-3	0.0
1945	Cle-A	87	221	21	52	2	2	1	21	20	26	.235	.299	.276	575	70	-8	3	0	1	.992	2	O-53(0-0-53)/P-1	-1.0
Total	2	163	394	46	107	11	2	1	34	43	47	.272	.345	.317	662	95	-1	5	2	0	.975	-2	/O-94R,P-4,1-3	-1.0

■ HEINIE ODOM Odom, Herman Boyd b: 10/13/1900, Rusk, Tex. d: 8/31/70, Rusk, Tex. BB/TR, 6', 170 lbs. Deb: 4/22/25

YEAR	TM/L	G	AB	R	H	2B	3B	HR	RBI	BB	SO	AVG	OBP	SLG	OPS	OPS+	BR+	SB	CS	SBR	FA	FR	G/POS	TPR
1925	NY-A	1	1	0	1	0	0	0	0	0	0	1.000	1.000	1.000	2000	416	0	0	0	0	1.000	0	/3-1	0.1

■ BLUE MOON ODOM Odom, Johnny Lee b: 5/29/45, Macon, Ga. BR/TR, 6', 185 lbs. Deb: 9/5/64

YEAR	TM/L	G	AB	R	H	2B	3B	HR	RBI	BB	SO	AVG	OBP	SLG	OPS	OPS+	BR+	SB	CS	SBR	FA	FR	G/POS	TPR
1964	KC-A	5	5	1	0	0	0	0	0	1	4	.000	.167	.000	167	-47	-1	0	0	0	.800	0	/P-5	0.0
1965	KC-A	1	0	0	0	0	0	0	0	0	0	—	—	—	—	—	0	0	0	0	1.000	0	/P-1	0.0
1966	KC-A	17	31	1	3	0	0	0	2	3	16	.097	.176	.097	273	-20	-5	0	0	0	.970	2	P-14	0.0
1967	KC-A	33	28	4	8	1	0	0	0	1	14	.286	.310	.321	632	90	-0	0	1	-0	.897	0	P-29	0.0
1968	Oak-A★	42	78	14	17	2	0	1	2	6	29	.218	.282	.282	564	75	-2	0	0	0	.964	1	P-32	0.0
1969	Oak-A★	43	79	15	21	2	1	5	16	2	24	.266	.293	.506	799	125	2	0	0	0	.937	1	P-32	0.0
1970	Oak-A	37	54	8	13	2	0	3	7	3	18	.241	.281	.444	725	100	-0	1	0	0	.929	2	P-29	0.0
1971	Oak-A	37	50	8	8	0	1	1	1	2	24	.160	.192	.260	452	28	-5	0	0	0	.850	-1	P-25	0.0
1972	*Oak-A	59	66	16	8	1	0	2	2	1	29	.121	.134	.227	362	7	-8	4	2	0	.873	0	P-31	0.0
1973	*Oak-A	51	1	5	0	0	0	0	0	0	0	.000	.000	.000	0	-99	-0	1	2	-0	.875	-1	P-30	0.0
1974	*Oak-A	43	0	3	0	0	0	0	0	0	0	—	—	—	—	—	0	0	0	0	.821	1	P-34	0.0
1975	Oak-A	8	0	1	0	0	0	0	0	0	0	—	—	—	—	—	0	0	0	0	.750	0	/P-7	0.0
	Cle-A	3	0	0	0	0	0	0	0	0	0	—	—	—	—	—	0	0	0	0	1.000	-0	/P-3	0.0
	Yr	11	0	1	0	0	0	0	0	0	0	—	—	—	—	—	0	0	0	0	.800	-0	P-10	0.0
	Atl-N	15	13	0	1	1	0	0	1	0	5	.077	.077	.154	231	-36	-2	0	0	0	.944	0	P-15	0.0
1976	Chi-A	8	0	0	0	0	0	0	0	0	0	—	—	—	—	—	0	0	0	0	.600	-1	/P-8	0.0
Total	13	402	405	76	79	9	2	12	31	19	163	.195	.235	.316	551	60	-22	6	5	-0	.904	5	P-295	0.0

■ HARRY O'DONNELL O'Donnell, Harry Herman "Butch" b: 4/2/1894, Philadelphia, Pa. d: 1/31/58, Philadelphia, Pa. BR/TR, 5'8", 175 lbs. Deb: 4/30/27

YEAR	TM/L	G	AB	R	H	2B	3B	HR	RBI	BB	SO	AVG	OBP	SLG	OPS	OPS+	BR+	SB	CS	SBR	FA	FR	G/POS	TPR
1927	Phi-N	16	16	1	1	0	0	0	2	2	2	.063	.167	.063	229	-36	-3	0			1.000	1	C-12	-0.2

■ JOHN O'DONNELL O'Donnell, John b: Littlestown, Pa. Deb: 7/16/1884

YEAR	TM/L	G	AB	R	H	2B	3B	HR	RBI	BB	SO	AVG	OBP	SLG	OPS	OPS+	BR+	SB	CS	SBR	FA	FR	G/POS	TPR
1884	Phi-U	1	4	0	1	0	0	0		0		.250	.250	.250	500	56	-0				.545	-2	/C-1	-0.2

■ LEFTY O'DOUL O'Doul, Francis Joseph b: 3/4/1897, San Francisco, Cal. d: 12/7/69, San Francisco, Cal. BL/TL, 6', 180 lbs. Deb: 4/29/19

YEAR	TM/L	G	AB	R	H	2B	3B	HR	RBI	BB	SO	AVG	OBP	SLG	OPS	OPS+	BR+	SB	CS	SBR	FA	FR	G/POS	TPR
1919	NY-A	19	16	2	4	0	0	0	1	1	2	.250	.294	.250	544	53	-1	1			.500	-1	/P-3,O-1(0-0-1)	-0.1
1920	NY-A	13	12	2	2	1	0	0	1	1	1	.167	.231	.250	481	26	-1	0	0	0	.000	-1	/P-2,O-1(0-1-0)	-0.1
1922	NY-A	8	9	0	3	1	0	0	4	0	2	.333	.333	.444	778	99	-0	0	0	0	1.000	-0	/P-6	0.0
1923	Bos-A	36	35	2	5	0	0	0	4	2	3	.143	.189	.143	332	-12	-6	0	0	0	.958	1	P-23/O-1(0-0-1)	-0.1
1928	NY-N	114	354	67	113	19	4	8	46	30	8	.319	.372	.463	836	117	8	9			.962	-12	O-94(94-0-0)	-1.0
1929	Phi-N	154	638	152	**254**	35	6	32	122	76	19	**.398**	**.465**	.622	1087	157	58	2			.971	5	*O-154(139-0-15)	4.5
1930	Phi-N	140	528	122	202	37	7	22	97	63	21	.383	.453	.604	1057	142	38	3			.953	-5	*O-131(131-0-0)	2.0
1931	Bro-N	134	512	85	172	32	11	7	75	48	16	.336	.396	.482	879	136	26	5			.954	-1	*O-132(132-0-0)	1.8
1932	Bro-N	148	595	120	219	32	8	21	90	50	20	**.368**	.423	.555	978	164	54	11			.979	-5	*O-148(148-0-0)	4.0
1933	Bro-N	43	159	14	40	5	1	5	21	15	6	.252	.320	.390	710	106	1	2			.947	-3	O-41(41-0-0)	-0.4
	*NY-N★	78	229	31	70	9	1	9	35	29	17	.306	.388	.472	860	147	15	1			.974	-6	O-63(32-0-31)	0.6
	Yr	121	388	45	110	14	2	14	56	44	23	.284	.361	.438	799	130	16	3			.962	-8	*O-104(73-0-31)	0.2
1934	NY-N	83	177	27	56	4	3	9	46	18	7	.316	.383	.525	908	144	11	2			.968	-5	O-38(27-0-11)	0.3
Total	11	970	3264	624	1140	175	41	113	542	333	122	.349	.413	.532	945	142	203	36	0		.964	-33	O-804(744-1-59)/P-34	11.5

■ FRED ODWELL Odwell, Frederick William "Fritz" b: 9/25/1872, Downsville, N.Y. d: 8/19/48, Downsville, N.Y. BL/TR, 5'9.5", 160 lbs. Deb: 4/16/04

YEAR	TM/L	G	AB	R	H	2B	3B	HR	RBI	BB	SO	AVG	OBP	SLG	OPS	OPS+	BR+	SB	CS	SBR	FA	FR	G/POS	TPR
1904	Cin-N	129	468	75	133	22	10	1	58	26		.284	.333	.380	713	110	5	30			.956	14	*O-126(107-14-5)/2-1	1.3
1905	Cin-N	130	468	79	113	10	9	**9**	65	26		.241	.293	.359	652	85	-10	21			.967	4	*O-126(56-4-66)	-1.3
1906	Cin-N	58	202	20	45	5	4	0	21	15		.223	.286	.287	573	76	-6	11			.963	3	O-57(0-0-57)	-0.6
1907	Cin-N	94	274	24	74	5	7	0	24	22		.270	.336	.339	675	107	2	10			.975	5	O-84(77-0-8)/2-1	0.3
Total	4	411	1412	198	365	42	30	10	168	89		.258	.313	.352	665	96	-9	72			.964	26	O-393(240-18-136)/2-2	-0.3

■ CHUCK OERTEL Oertel, Charles Frank "Ducky" or "Snuffy" b: 3/12/31, Coffeyville, Kan. BL/TR, 5'8", 165 lbs. Deb: 9/1/58

YEAR	TM/L	G	AB	R	H	2B	3B	HR	RBI	BB	SO	AVG	OBP	SLG	OPS	OPS+	BR+	SB	CS	SBR	FA	FR	G/POS	TPR
1958	Bal-A	14	12	4	2	0	0	1	1	1	1	.167	.231	.417	647	78	-0	0	0	0	1.000	-1	/O-2(2-0-1)	-0.1

■ RON OESTER Oester, Ronald John b: 5/5/56, Cincinnati, Ohio BB/TR, 6'2", 190 lbs. Deb: 9/10/78 C

YEAR	TM/L	G	AB	R	H	2B	3B	HR	RBI	BB	SO	AVG	OBP	SLG	OPS	OPS+	BR+	SB	CS	SBR	FA	FR	G/POS	TPR
1978	Cin-N	6	8	1	3	0	0	0	1	0	2	.375	.375	.375	750	110	0	0	0	0	1.000	1	/S-6	0.1
1979	Cin-N	6	3	0	0	0	0	0	0	0	1	.000	.000	.000	0	-99	-1	0	0	0	1.000	1	/S-2	0.0
1980	Cin-N	100	303	40	84	16	2	2	20	26	44	.277	.336	.363	699	95	-2	6	2	1	.980	-14	2-79,S-17/3-3	-1.1
1981	Cin-N	105	354	45	96	16	7	5	42	42	49	.271	.348	.398	747	110	5	2	5	-1	.980	5	*2-103/S-9	1.5
1982	Cin-N	151	549	63	143	19	4	9	47	35	82	.260	.305	.359	664	83	-13	5	6	-1	.972	4	*2-118,S-29,3-13	-0.2
1983	Cin-N	157	549	63	145	23	5	11	58	49	106	.264	.326	.384	710	93	-6	2	2	-0	.977	-25	*2-154	-2.3
1984	Cin-N	150	553	54	134	26	3	3	38	41	97	.242	.296	.316	612	69	-22	7	2	1	.980	-16	*2-147/S-1	-3.1
1985	Cin-N	152	526	59	155	26	3	1	34	51	65	.295	.357	.361	718	97	-1	5	0	1	.989	5	*2-149	1.4
1986	Cin-N	153	523	52	135	23	2	8	44	52	84	.258	.326	.356	682	84	-11	9	2	1	.978	18	*2-151	1.7
1987	Cin-N	69	237	28	60	9	6	2	23	22	51	.253	.317	.367	684	77	-8	2	3	-1	.974	6	2-69	0.1
1988	Cin-N	54	150	20	42	7	0	0	10	9	24	.280	.321	.327	647	83	-3	0	2	-1	.995	2	2-49/S-5	0.0
1989	Cin-N	109	305	23	75	15	0	1	14	32	47	.246	.318	.305	622	76	-9	1	0	0	.985	8	*2-102/S-2	0.2
1990	*Cin-N	64	154	10	46	10	1	0	13	10	29	.299	.341	.377	718	93	-1	1	2	-0	.982	-8	2-50/3-3	-0.9
Total	13	1276	4214	458	1118	190	33	42	344	369	681	.265	.325	.356	681	87	-71	40	26	-0	.980	-14	*2-1171/S-71,3-19	-2.6

■ BOB O'FARRELL O'Farrell, Robert Arthur b: 10/19/1896, Waukegan, Ill. d: 2/20/88, Waukegan, Ill. BR/TR, 5'9.5", 180 lbs. Deb: 9/5/15 M

YEAR	TM/L	G	AB	R	H	2B	3B	HR	RBI	BB	SO	AVG	OBP	SLG	OPS	OPS+	BR+	SB	CS	SBR	FA	FR	G/POS	TPR
1915	Chi-N	2	3	0	1	0	0	0	0	0	0	.333	.333	.333	667	102	-0	0			.667	-1	/C-2	-0.1
1916	Chi-N	1	0	0	0	0	0	0	0	0	0	—	—	—	—	—	0	0			.000	0	/C-1	0.0
1917	Chi-N	3	8	1	3	2	0	0	1	1	0	.375	.444	.625	1069	209	1	1			1.000	-1	/C-3	0.0
1918	*Chi-N	52	113	9	32	7	3	1	14	10	15	.283	.347	.425	772	132	4	0			.974	-6	C-45	0.1
1919	Chi-N	49	125	11	27	4	2	0	9	7	10	.216	.258	.280	538	61	-6	2			.965	-4	C-38	-0.7
1920	Chi-N	94	270	29	67	11	4	3	19	34	23	.248	.332	.352	684	95	-1	1	0	0	.956	-6	C-86	0.0
1921	Chi-N	96	260	32	65	12	7	4	32	18	14	.250	.299	.396	695	82	-7	2	0	0	.967	-5	C-90	-0.7
1922	Chi-N	128	392	68	127	18	8	4	60	79	34	.324	.439	.441	880	125	19	5	3	0	.977	16	*C-125	4.0
1923	Chi-N	131	452	73	144	25	4	12	84	67	38	.319	.408	.471	879	131	22	10	3	1	.976	1	*C-124	3.2
1924	Chi-N	71	183	25	44	6	2	3	28	30	13	.240	.347	.344	692	85	-3	2	0	0	.984	-2	C-57	-0.1
1925	Chi-N	17	22	2	4	0	1	0	3	2	5	.182	.250	.273	523	33	-2	0	0	0	1.000	-1	/C-3	-0.3
	StL-N	94	317	37	88	13	2	3	32	46	26	.278	.373	.360	732	86	-5	0	1	-0	.975	-5	C-92	-0.3
	Yr	111	339	39	92	13	3	3	35	48	31	.271	.365	.354	719	83	-7	0	1	-0	.975	-6	C-95	-0.6
1926	*StL-N	147	492	63	144	30	9	7	68	61	44	.293	.371	.433	804	111	9	1			.983	10	*C-146	2.7
1927	StL-N	61	178	19	47	10	1	0	18	23	22	.264	.348	.331	680	80	-4	3			.979	-0	C-53,M	-0.1
1928	StL-N	16	52	6	11	1	0	0	4	13	9	.212	.369	.231	600	59	-2	2			.985	0	C-14	-0.1
	NY-N	75	133	23	26	6	0	2	20	34	16	.195	.359	.286	645	70	-5	2			.988	-1	C-63	-0.2
	Yr	91	185	29	37	7	0	2	24	47	25	.200	.362	.270	632	67	-7	4			.987	-1	C-77	-0.3
1929	NY-N	91	248	35	76	14	3	4	42	28	30	.306	.384	.435	819	103	2	3			.979	-5	C-84	0.2
1930	NY-N	94	249	37	75	16	4	4	54	31	21	.301	.381	.446	827	101	1	1			.973	0	C-69	0.5

YEAR	TM/L	G	AB	R	H	2B	3B	HR	RBI	BB	SO	AVG	OBP	SLG	OPS	OPS+	BR+	SB	CS	SBR	FA	FR	G/POS	TPR
1931	NY-N	85	174	11	39	8	3	1	19	21	23	.224	.311	.322	633	72	-7	0			.980	1	C-80	-0.3
1932	NY-N	50	67	7	16	3	0	0	8	11	10	.239	.354	.284	638	76	-2	0			.969	2	C-41	0.1
1933	StL-N	55	163	16	39	4	2	2	20	15	25	.239	.303	.325	629	76	-5	0			.970	-5	C-50	-0.8
1934	Cin-N	44	123	10	30	8	3	1	9	11	19	.244	.306	.382	688	85	-3	0			.993	-0	C-42,M	-0.1
	Chi-N	22	67	3	15	3	0	0	5	3	11	.224	.257	.269	526	42	-6	0			1.000	2	C-22	-0.2
	Yr	66	190	13	45	11	3	1	14	14	30	.237	.289	.342	631	70	-8	0			.996	2	C-64	-0.3
1935	StL-N	14	10	0	0	0	0	0	0	2	0	.000	.167	.000	167	-49	-2	0			1.000	1	/C-8	-0.1
Total	21	1492	4101	517	1120	201	58	51	549	547	408	.273	.360	.388	748	97	-2	35	7		.976	-9	*C-1338	6.7
■ JOSE OFFERMAN	Offerman, Jose Antonio (Dono) b: 11/8/68, San Pedro De Macoris, D.R. BB/TR, 6', 165 lbs. Deb: 8/19/90 Career OF: (0-LF 1-CF 0-RF)																							
1990	LA-N	29	58	7	9	0	0	1	7	4	14	.155	.210	.207	417	15	-7	1	0	0	.946	-2	S-27	-0.7
1991	LA-N	52	113	10	22	2	0	0	3	25	32	.195	.345	.212	558	62	-4	3	2	-0	.945	2	S-50	0.0
1992	LA-N	149	534	67	139	20	8	1	30	57	98	.260	.332	.333	665	90	-6	23	16	-1	.935	-18	*S-149	-1.4
1993	LA-N	158	590	77	159	21	6	1	62	71	75	.269	.350	.331	680	88	-7	30	13	2	.950	-7	*S-158	0.1
1994	LA-N	72	243	27	51	8	4	1	25	38	38	.210	.317	.288	605	63	-12	2	1	0	.967	-4	S-72	-1.0
1995	*LA-N★	119	429	69	123	14	6	4	33	69	67	.287	.389	.375	765	113	11	2	7	-2	.932	-10	*S-115	0.9
1996	KC-A	151	561	85	170	33	8	5	47	74	98	.303	.385	.417	802	103	5	24	10	2	.994	-1	1-96,2-38,S-36,/O-1C	0.2
1997	KC-A	106	424	59	126	23	6	2	39	41	64	.297	.359	.394	753	94	-3	9	10	-2	.981	-20	*2-101/D-1	-1.8
1998	KC-A	158	607	102	191	28	**13**	7	66	89	96	.315	.407	.438	845	117	19	45	12	6	.974	1	*2-152/D-6	3.1
1999	*Bos-A★	149	586	107	172	37	**11**	8	69	96	79	.294	.395	.435	830	108	10	18	12	-0	.975	-29	*2-128,D-18/1-8	-1.3
2000	Bos-A	116	451	73	115	14	3	9	41	70	70	.255	.356	.359	716	79	-13	0	8	-3	.981	-5	2-80,1-39/D-9	-1.9
Total	11	1259	4596	683	1277	200	65	39	422	634	731	.278	.367	.375	742	96	-8	157	91	3	.943	-92	S-607,2-499,1/DO	-3.8
■ ROWLAND OFFICE	Office, Rowland Johnie b: 10/25/52, Sacramento, Cal. BL/TL, 6', 170 lbs. Deb: 8/5/72																							
1972	Atl-N	2	5	1	2	0	0	0	0	1	2	.400	.500	.400	900	145	0	0	0	0	1.000	0	/O-1(0-1-0)	0.0
1974	Atl-N	131	248	20	61	16	1	3	31	16	30	.246	.292	.355	647	77	-8	5	3	0	.994	-25	*O-119(1-118-0)	-3.6
1975	Atl-N	126	355	30	103	14	1	3	30	23	41	.290	.339	.361	699	91	-4	2	2	-0	.967	-6	*O-107(1-106-0)	-1.4
1976	Atl-N	99	359	51	101	17	1	4	34	37	49	.281	.352	.368	719	98	-0	2	8	-2	.986	-3	O-92(0-92-0)	-0.8
1977	Atl-N	124	428	42	103	13	1	5	39	23	58	.241	.284	.311	595	53	-28	2	4	-1	.988	7	*O-104(1-103-0)/1-1	-2.3
1978	Atl-N	146	404	40	101	13	1	9	40	22	52	.250	.299	.354	653	73	-14	8	6	-0	.990	-3	*O-136(0-138-0)	-2.0
1979	Atl-N	124	277	35	69	14	2	2	37	27	33	.249	.320	.336	656	74	-9	5	4	-0	.988	-13	O-97(0-97-0)	-2.4
1980	Mon-N	116	292	36	78	13	4	6	30	36	39	.267	.348	.401	748	108	4	3	3	-0	.987	-11	O-97(3-27-68)	-1.1
1981	Mon-N	26	40	4	7	0	0	0	0	4	6	.175	.250	.175	425	22	-4	0	0	0	.938	-3	O-15(0-3-12)	-0.9
1982	Mon-N	3	3	0	1	1	0	0	0	0	1	.333	.333	.667	1000	170	0	0	0	0	1.000	0	/O-1(1-0-0)	0.0
1983	NY-A	2	2	0	0	0	0	0	1	0	0	.000	.000	.000	0	-99	-1	0	0	0	1.000	0	/O-2(0-2-0)	-0.1
Total	11	899	2413	259	626	101	11	32	242	189	311	.259	.317	.350	668	79	-64	27	30	-5	.985	-57	O-771(7-687-80)/1-1	-14.6
■ JIM OGLESBY	Oglesby, James Dorn b: 8/10/05, Schofield, Mo. d: 9/1/55, Tulsa, Okla. BL/TL, 6', 190 lbs. Deb: 4/14/36																							
1936	Phi-A	3	11	0	2	0	0	0	2	2	0	.182	.308	.182	490	24	-1	0	0	0	1.000	0	/1-3	-0.1
■ BEN OGLIVIE	Oglivie, Benjamin Ambrosio (Palmer) b: 2/11/49, Colon, Panama BL/TL, 6'2", 170 lbs. Deb: 9/4/71 Career OF: (1098-LF 15-CF 357-RF)																							
1971	Bos-A	14	38	2	10	3	0	0	4	0	5	.263	.263	.342	605	66	-2	0	0	0	.958	1	O-11(10-0-1)	-0.1
1972	Bos-A	94	253	27	61	10	2	8	30	18	61	.241	.294	.391	685	97	-1	1	1	-0	.981	-1	O-65(32-0-33)	-0.7
1973	Bos-A	58	147	16	32	9	1	2	9	9	32	.218	.272	.333	605	66	-7	1	1	-0	.983	0	O-32(4-0-28),D-13	-0.9
1974	Det-A	92	252	28	68	11	3	4	29	34	38	.270	.357	.385	742	109	4	12	3	2	.947	-5	O-63(61-0-2),1-10/D-4	-0.4
1975	Det-A	100	332	45	95	14	1	9	36	16	62	.286	.323	.416	739	103	0	11	8	-0	.975	6	O-86(76-0-10)/1-5,D-2	0.1
1976	Det-A	115	305	36	87	12	3	15	47	11	44	.285	.317	.492	808	129	9	9	4	1	.986	1	O-64R/1-9,D-1	0.8
1977	Det-A	132	450	63	118	24	2	21	61	40	80	.262	.327	.464	791	107	4	9	9	-1	.976	7	*O-118(0-0-118)/D-2	0.3
1978	Mil-A	128	469	71	142	29	4	18	72	52	69	.303	.372	.497	869	142	26	11	7	-0	.980	1	O-89L,D-27,1-11	2.1
1979	Mil-A	139	514	88	145	30	4	29	81	48	56	.282	.346	.525	871	131	21	12	5	1	.985	-0	*O-120L,D-13/1-9	1.4
1980	Mil-A★	156	592	94	180	26	2	**41**	118	54	71	.304	.367	.563	930	156	43	11	9	-1	.978	21	*O-152(150-1-2)/D-4	5.5
1981	*Mil-A	107	400	53	97	15	2	14	72	37	49	.243	.316	.395	711	109	4	2	2	-0	.982	-3	*O-101(99-2-0)/D-6	-0.4
1982	*Mil-A★	159	602	92	147	22	1	34	102	70	81	.244	.327	.453	780	119	15	3	5	-1	.982	13	*O-159(159-0-0)	1.9
1983	Mil-A★	125	411	49	115	19	3	13	66	60	64	.280	.377	.436	812	133	20	4	6	-1	.985	6	*O-113(113-0-0)/D-8	2.0
1984	Mil-A	131	461	49	121	16	2	12	60	44	56	.262	.328	.384	712	100	0	0	6	-2	.970	-4	*O-125(113-0-23)/D-1	-1.1
1985	Mil-A	101	341	40	99	17	2	10	61	37	51	.290	.363	.440	803	119	9	0	2	-1	.965	-3	O-91(48-0-54)/D-4	0.1
1986	Mil-A	103	346	31	98	20	1	5	53	30	33	.283	.340	.390	731	95	-2	1	2	-0	.991	4	O-50(50-0-2),D-42	-0.2
Total	16	1754	5913	784	1615	277	33	235	901	560	852	.273	.340	.450	790	119	143	87	70	-5	.978	44	*O-1439L,D-127/1-44	10.4
■ BRUCE OGRODOWSKI	Ogrodowski, Ambrose Francis "Brusie" b: 2/17/12, Hoytville, Pa. d: 3/5/56, San Francisco, Cal. BR/TR, 5'11", 175 lbs. Deb: 4/14/36																							
1936	StL-N	94	237	28	54	15	1	1	20	10	20	.228	.259	.312	571	53	-16	0			.989	4	C-85	-0.8
1937	StL-N	90	279	37	65	10	3	3	31	11	17	.233	.267	.323	590	58	-17	2			.984	2	C-87	-0.9
Total	2	184	516	65	119	25	4	4	51	21	37	.231	.263	.318	581	56	-32	2			.986	6	C-172	-1.7
■ HAL O'HAGEN	O'Hagen, Harry P. b: 9/30/1873, Washington, D.C. d: 1/14/13, Newark, N.J. 6', 173 lbs. Deb: 9/24/1892																							
1892	Was-N	1	4	1	1	0	0	0	0	0	2	.250	.250	.250	500	53	-0	0			1.000	1	/C-1	0.0
1902	Chi-N	33	115	11	22	1	3	0	10	11		.191	.262	.252	514	60	-5	9			.983	4	1-33	-0.2
	NY-N	4	11	0	1	0	0	0	0	0		.091	.091	.091	182	-44	-2	0			1.000	-0	/O-4(0-3-1)	-0.3
	Cle-A	3	13	2	5	2	0	0	1	0		.385	.385	.538	923	160	1	2			1.000	1	/1-3	0.1
	NY-N	22	73	5	11	2	1	0	8	2		.151	.195	.205	400	24	-7	3			.973	-0	1-18/O-4(0-0-4)	-0.8
	Yr	59	199	16	34	3	4	0	18	13		.171	.229	.226	455	52	-14	12			.980	4	1-51/O-8(0-3-5)	-1.3
Total	2	63	216	19	40	5	4	0	19	13	2	.185	.238	.245	483	49	-13	14			.981	4	/1-54,O-8(0-3-5),C-1	-1.2
■ GREG O'HALLORAN	O'Halloran, Gregory Joseph b: 5/21/68, Toronto, Ont., Can. BL/TR, 6'2", 205 lbs. Deb: 5/16/94																							
1994	Fla-N	12	11	1	2	0	0	0	1	0	1	.182	.182	.182	364	-5	-2	0	0	0	1.000	0	/C-1	-0.1
■ KID O'HARA	O'Hara, James Francis b: 12/19/1875, Wilkes-Barre, Pa. d: 12/1/54, Canton, Ohio BB/TR, 5'7.5", 152 lbs. Deb: 9/15/04																							
1904	Bos-N	8	29	3	6	0	0	0	0	4		.207	.303	.207	510	60	-1	1			.923	0	/O-8(0-0-8)	-0.1
■ TOM O'HARA	O'Hara, Thomas F. b: 7/13/1885, Waverly, N.Y. d: 6/8/54, Denver, Colo. Deb: 9/19/06																							
1906	StL-N	14	53	8	16	1	0	0	0	3		.302	.339	.321	660	110	1	3			.889	-2	O-14(14-0-0)	-0.2
1907	StL-N	48	173	11	41	2	1	0	5	12		.237	.286	.260	547	74	-5	1			.943	-1	O-47(24-0-23)	-1.0
Total	2	62	226	19	57	3	1	0	5	15		.252	.299	.274	573	82	-5	4			.930	-3	O-61(38-0-23)	-1.2
■ BILL O'HARA	O'Hara, William Alexander b: 8/14/1883, Toronto, Ont., Can. d: 6/13/31, Jersey City, N.J. BL/TR, 5'10", Deb: 4/15/09 Career OF: (11-LF 93-CF 11-RF)																							
1909	NY-N	115	360	48	85	9	3	1	30	41		.236	.318	.286	604	86	-5	31			.978	2	*O-111(11-89-11)	-0.9
1910	StL-N	9	20	1	3	0	0	0	2	1	3	.150	.190	.150	340	-0	-3	0			1.000	-0	/O-4(0-4-0),P-1,1-1	-0.3
Total	2	124	380	49	88	9	3	1	32	42	3	.232	.311	.279	590	82	-7	31			.979	2	O-115C/1-1,P-1	-1.2
■ AUGIE OJEDA	Ojeda, Octavio Augie b: 12/20/74, Los Angeles, Cal. BB/TR, 5'9", 165 lbs. Deb: 6/4/2000																							
2000	Chi-N	28	77	10	17	3	1	2	8	10	9	.221	.310	.364	674	71	-4	0	1	-0	.989	3	S-25/2-4	0.1
■ LEN OKRIE	Okrie, Leonard Joseph b: 7/16/23, Detroit, Mich. BR/TR, 6', 185 lbs. Deb: 6/16/48 FC																							
1948	Was-A	19	42	1	10	0	1	0	1	1	7	.238	.256	.286	542	45	-3	0	0	0	.981	2	C-17	-0.1
1950	Was-A	17	27	1	6	0	0	0	2	6	7	.222	.382	.222	605	61	-1	0	0	0	1.000	1	C-17	0.0
1951	Was-A	5	8	1	1	1	0	0	0	2	1	.125	.300	.250	550	51	-1	0	0	0	.850	1	/C-5	0.0
1952	Bos-A	1	1	0	0	0	0	0	0	0	1	.000	.000	.000	0	-93	-0	0	0	0	1.000	0	/C-1	0.0
Total	4	42	78	3	17	1	1	0	3	9	16	.218	.307	.256	563	51	-5	0	0	0	.965	4	/C-40	-0.1
■ JIM OLANDER	Olander, James Bentley b: 2/21/63, Tucson, Ariz. BR/TR, 6'1", 185 lbs. Deb: 9/20/91																							
1991	Mil-A	12	9	2	0	0	0	0	0	2	5	.000	.182	.000	182	-46	-2	0	0	0	1.000	-2	/O-9(2-5-1),D-2	-0.4

■ **DAVE OLDFIELD** Oldfield, David b: 12/18/1864, Philadelphia, Pa. d: 8/28/39, Philadelphia, Pa. BB/TL, 5'7", 175 lbs. Deb: 6/28/1883

YEAR	TM/L	G	AB	R	H	2B	3B	HR	RBI	BB	SO	AVG	OBP	SLG	OPS	OPS+	BR+	SB	CS	SBR	FA	FR	G/POS	TPR
1883	Bal-a	1	4	0	0	0	0	0		0		.000	.000	.000	0	-97	-1				.667	-1	/C-1	-0.2
1885	Bro-a	10	25	2	8	1	0	0	2	3		.320	.414	.360	774	145	2				.873	1	/C-9,O-2(0-1-1)	0.3
1886	Bro-a	14	55	7	13	1	0	0	5	2		.236	.263	.255	518	62	-2	1			.833	-3	C-13/S-1,O-1(0-0-1)	-0.4
	Was-N	21	71	2	10	2	0	0	2	5	15	.141	.197	.169	366	13	-7	0			.899	-3	C-12/O-9(0-3-6)	-0.9
Total	3	46	155	11	31	4	0	0	9	10	15	.200	.253	.226	479	50	-9	1			.857	-7	/C-35,O-12(0-4-8),S-1	-1.2

■ **JOHN OLDHAM** Oldham, John Hardin b: 11/6/32, Salinas, Cal. BR/TL, 6'3", 198 lbs. Deb: 9/2/56

YEAR	TM/L	G	AB	R	H	2B	3B	HR	RBI	BB	SO	AVG	OBP	SLG	OPS	OPS+	BR+	SB	CS	SBR	FA	FR	G/POS	TPR
1956	Cin-N	1	0	0	0	0	0	0	0	0	0	—	—	—	—	—	0	0	0	0	.000	0	R	0.0

■ **BOB OLDIS** Oldis, Robert Carl b: 1/5/28, Preston, Iowa BR/TR, 6'1", 185 lbs. Deb: 4/28/53 C

YEAR	TM/L	G	AB	R	H	2B	3B	HR	RBI	BB	SO	AVG	OBP	SLG	OPS	OPS+	BR+	SB	CS	SBR	FA	FR	G/POS	TPR
1953	Was-A	7	16	0	4	0	0	0	3	1	2	.250	.294	.250	544	49	-1	0	0	0	1.000	2	/C-7	0.1
1954	Was-A	11	24	1	8	1	0	0	0	1	3	.333	.360	.375	735	107	0	0	0	0	.941	-1	/C-8,3-2	0.0
1955	Was-A	6	6	1	0	0	0	0	0	1	0	.000	.143	.000	143	-62	-1	0	0	0	1.000	0	/C-6	-0.1
1960	*Pit-N	22	20	1	4	1	0	0	1	1	2	.200	.238	.250	488	34	-2	0	0	0	1.000	3	C-22	0.1
1961	Pit-N	4	5	0	0	0	0	0	0	0	0	.000	.000	.000	0	-99	-1	0	0	0	1.000	3	/C-4	0.1
1962	Phi-N	38	80	9	21	1	0	1	10	13	10	.262	.366	.313	678	87	-1	0	1	-0	.987	1	C-30	0.1
1963	Phi-N	47	85	8	19	3	0	0	8	3	5	.224	.250	.259	509	47	-6	0	0	0	.979	5	C-43	0.0
Total	7	135	236	20	56	6	0	1	22	20	22	.237	.297	.275	572	60	-12	0	1	-0	.983	12	C-120/3-2	0.3

■ **RUBE OLDRING** Oldring, Reuben Henry b: 5/30/1884, New York, N.Y. d: 9/9/61, Bridgeton, N.J. BR/TR, 5'10", 186 lbs. Deb: 10/2/05 Career OF: (455-LF 626-CF 48-RF)

YEAR	TM/L	G	AB	R	H	2B	3B	HR	RBI	BB	SO	AVG	OBP	SLG	OPS	OPS+	BR+	SB	CS	SBR	FA	FR	G/POS	TPR
1905	NY-A	8	30	2	9	0	1	1	6	2		.300	.344	.467	810	140	1	4			.967	5	/S-8	0.7
1906	Phi-A	59	174	15	42	10	1	0	19	2		.241	.263	.310	573	77	-5	7			.897	2	3-49/S-3,2-2,1-1	-0.2
1907	Phi-A	117	441	48	126	27	8	1	40	7		.286	.305	.390	695	118	7	29			.974	-9	*O-117(0-116-1)	-0.9
1908	Phi-A	116	434	38	96	14	2	1	39	18		.221	.267	.270	536	70	-15	13			.941	3	*O-116(21-95-0)	-2.1
1909	Phi-A	90	326	39	75	13	8	1	28	20		.230	.287	.328	615	92	-3	17			.963	-1	O-89(32-56-1)/1-1	-1.0
1910	Phi-A	134	546	79	168	27	14	4	57	23		.308	.340	.430	771	143	23	17			**.978**	-1	*O-134(1-130-3)	1.7
1911	*Phi-A	121	495	84	147	11	14	3	59	21		.297	.332	.394	726	104	1	21			**.979**	-9	*O-119(0-119-0)	-1.6
1912	Phi-A	99	395	61	119	14	5	1	24	10		.301	.324	.370	693	102	-1	17			.974	-3	O-98(11-86-0)	-1.0
1913	*Phi-A	137	538	101	152	27	9	5	71	34	37	.283	.328	.394	722	113	7	40			.968	-7	*O-131(131-0-0)/S-5	-0.6
1914	*Phi-A	119	466	68	129	21	7	3	49	18	35	.277	.308	.371	679	108	2	14	16	-3	.965	-6	*O-117(105-11-1)	-1.3
1915	Phi-A	107	408	49	101	23	3	6	42	22	21	.248	.293	.363	655	100	-3	11	6	0	.982	5	O-96(88-8-0)/3-8	-0.2
1916	Phi-A	40	146	10	36	8	3	0	14	9	9	.247	.290	.342	633	95	-2	1			.897	-2	O-40(40-0-0)	-0.6
	NY-A	43	158	17	37	8	0	1	12	12	13	.234	.288	.304	592	76	-5	6			.957	-3	O-43(0-2-41)	-1.2
	Yr	83	304	27	73	16	3	1	26	21	22	.240	.289	.322	612	85	-7	7			.926	-5	O-83(40-2-41)	-1.8
1918	Phi-A	49	133	5	31	2	1	0	11	8	10	.233	.282	.263	545	64	-6	0			.949	-8	O-30(26-3-1)/2-2,3-2	-1.7
Total	13	1239	4690	616	1268	205	76	27	471	206	125	.270	.307	.364	671	103	1	197	22		.966	-35	*O-1130C/3-59,S21	-10.0

■ **CHARLEY O'LEARY** O'Leary, Charles Timothy b: 10/15/1882, Chicago, Ill. d: 1/6/41, Chicago, Ill. BR/TR, 5'7", 165 lbs. Deb: 4/14/04 C

YEAR	TM/L	G	AB	R	H	2B	3B	HR	RBI	BB	SO	AVG	OBP	SLG	OPS	OPS+	BR+	SB	CS	SBR	FA	FR	G/POS	TPR
1904	Det-A	135	456	39	97	10	3	1	16	21		.213	.254	.254	508	63	-19	9			.933	6	*S-135	-1.0
1905	Det-A	148	512	47	109	13	1	0	33	29		.213	.259	.242	501	59	-24	13			.933	-8	*S-148	-2.9
1906	Det-A	128	443	34	97	13	2	2	34	17		.219	.253	.271	524	62	-20	8			.926	-8	*S-127	-2.6
1907	*Det-A	139	465	61	112	19	1	0	34	32		.241	.298	.286	584	83	-8	11			.943	-5	*S-138	-0.9
1908	*Det-A	65	211	21	53	9	3	0	17	9		.251	.295	.322	617	96	-1	4			.920	-12	S-64/2-1	-1.3
1909	*Det-A	76	261	29	53	10	0	0	13	6		.203	.224	.241	465	45	-17	9			.922	-4	3-54,2-15/S-4,O-2L	-2.2
1910	Det-A	65	211	23	51	7	1	0	9	9		.242	.276	.284	560	71	-8	7			.935	1	2-38,S-18/3-6	-0.6
1911	Det-A	74	256	29	68	8	2	0	25	21		.266	.336	.313	648	77	-7	10			.966	4	2-67/3-6	-0.2
1912	Det-A	3	10	1	2	0	0	0	1	0		.200	.200	.200	400	15	-1	0			1.000	2	/2-3	0.1
1913	StL-N	121	406	32	88	15	5	0	31	20	34	.217	.260	.278	539	55	-24	3			.951	-8	*S-103,2-15	-2.7
1934	StL-A	1	1	1	1	0	0	0	0	0	0	1.000	1.000	1.000	2000	385	0	0	0	0	.000	0	H	0.0
Total	11	955	3232	317	731	104	18	3	213	164	34	.226	.270	.272	543	67	-129	74	0		.935	-32	S-737,2-139/3-66,O	-14.3

■ **DAN O'LEARY** O'Leary, Daniel "Hustling Dan" b: 10/22/1856, Detroit, Mich. d: 6/24/22, Chicago, Ill. BL, 5'10", 165 lbs. Deb: 9/3/1879 M

YEAR	TM/L	G	AB	R	H	2B	3B	HR	RBI	BB	SO	AVG	OBP	SLG	OPS	OPS+	BR+	SB	CS	SBR	FA	FR	G/POS	TPR
1879	Pro-N	2	7	1	3	0	0	0	2	0	0	.429	.429	.429	857	187	1				.000	-1	/O-2(0-0-2)	0.0
1880	Bos-N	3	12	1	3	2	0	0	1	0	3	.250	.250	.417	667	126	0				1.000	-1	/O-3(0-0-3)	-0.1
1881	Det-N	2	8	0	0	0	0	0	0	0	2	.000	.000	.000	0	-96	-2				.714	-1	/O-2(0-2-0)	-0.2
1882	Wor-N	6	22	2	4	1	0	0	2	5	5	.182	.333	.227	561	82	0				.800	-2	/O-6(0-6-0)	-0.2
1884	Cin-U	32	132	14	34	0	2	1		5		.258	.285	.311	595	74	-8				.862	2	O-32(22-10-0),M	-0.6
Total	5	45	181	18	44	3	2	1	5	10	10	.243	.283	.298	581	75	-9				.843	-2	/O-45(22-18-5)	-1.1

■ **TROY O'LEARY** O'Leary, Troy Franklin b: 8/4/69, Compton, Cal. BL/TL, 6', 196 lbs. Deb: 5/9/93

YEAR	TM/L	G	AB	R	H	2B	3B	HR	RBI	BB	SO	AVG	OBP	SLG	OPS	OPS+	BR+	SB	CS	SBR	FA	FR	G/POS	TPR
1993	Mil-A	19	41	3	12	3	0	0	3	5	9	.293	.370	.366	735	100	0	0	0	0	1.000	-1	O-19(15-0-5)	-0.2
1994	Mil-A	27	66	9	18	1	1	2	7	5	12	.273	.333	.409	742	86	-1	1	1	-0	1.000	-1	O-21(13-0-10)/D-1	-0.3
1995	Bos-A	112	399	60	123	31	6	10	49	29	64	.308	.357	.491	848	114	7	5	3	0	.976	-5	*O-105(16-13-91)/D-3	-0.1
1996	Bos-A	149	497	68	129	28	5	15	81	47	80	.260	.328	.427	755	87	-10	3	2	-0	.971	-26	*O-146(66-17-110)	-3.9
1997	Bos-A	146	499	65	154	32	4	15	80	39	70	.309	.361	.479	840	115	10	0	5	-2	.979	-1	*O-142(24-0-119)/D-1	0.1
1998	*Bos-A	156	611	95	165	36	8	23	83	36	108	.270	.316	.468	784	98	-3	2	2	-0	.990	7	*O-155(155-0-0)	-0.2
1999	*Bos-A	157	596	84	167	36	4	28	103	56	91	.280	.346	.495	841	108	6	1	2	-0	.993	5	*O-157(157-0-2)	0.5
2000	Bos-A	138	513	68	134	30	4	13	70	44	76	.261	.322	.411	733	81	-16	0	2	-1	.988	1	*O-137(137-0-0)	-1.8
Total	8	904	3222	452	902	197	32	106	476	261	510	.280	.338	.460	797	100	-7	12	17	-3	.985	-22	O-882(583-30-337)/D-5	-5.9

■ **JOHN OLERUD** Olerud, John Garrett b: 8/5/68, Seattle, Wash. BL/TL, 6'5", 220 lbs. Deb: 9/3/89

YEAR	TM/L	G	AB	R	H	2B	3B	HR	RBI	BB	SO	AVG	OBP	SLG	OPS	OPS+	BR+	SB	CS	SBR	FA	FR	G/POS	TPR
1989	Tor-A	6	8	2	3	0	0	0	0	0	1	.375	.375	.375	750	114	0	0	0	0	1.000	0	/1-5,D-1	0.0
1990	Tor-A	111	358	43	95	15	1	14	48	57	75	.265	.368	.430	798	120	11	0	2	-1	.986	-1	D-90,1-18	0.5
1991	*Tor-A	139	454	64	116	30	1	17	68	68	84	.256	.360	.438	798	115	10	0	2	-1	.996	-4	*1-135/D-1	-0.4
1992	*Tor-A	138	458	68	130	28	0	16	66	70	61	.284	.380	.450	830	126	17	1	0	0	.994	-2	*1-133/D-1	0.6
1993	*Tor-A★	158	551	109	200	**54**	2	24	107	114	65	**.363**	**.478**	.599	**1077**	**186**	**74**	0	2	-1	.992	1	*1-137,D-20	5.7
1994	Tor-A	108	384	47	114	29	2	12	67	61	53	.297	.397	.477	874	124	15	1	2	-0	.993	2	*1-104/D-3	0.6
1995	Tor-A	135	492	72	143	32	0	8	54	84	54	.291	.398	.404	803	110	11	0	0	0	.997	-2	*1-133	-0.4
1996	Tor-A	125	398	59	109	25	0	18	61	60	37	.274	.382	.472	855	115	10	1	0	0	.998	-1	*1-101,D-15	0.0
1997	NY-N	154	524	90	154	34	1	22	102	85	67	.294	.405	.489	894	138	32	0	0	0	.995	5	*1-146	2.2
1998	NY-N	160	557	91	197	36	4	22	93	96	73	.354	.452	.551	1003	165	57	2	2	-0	.996	3	*1-157	4.4
1999	*NY-N	162	581	107	173	39	0	19	96	125	66	.298	.431	.463	894	130	34	3	0	1	.994	3	*1-160	2.2
2000	*Sea-A	159	565	84	161	45	0	14	103	102	96	.285	.398	.439	837	115	16	0	2	-1	**.996**	14	*1-158	1.4
Total	12	1555	5330	836	1595	367	11	186	865	922	732	.299	.409	.477	886	133	288	8	12	-2	.995	19	*1-1387,D-131	16.8

■ **FRANK OLIN** Olin, Franklin Walter b: 1/9/1860, Woodford, Vt. d: 5/21/51, St.Louis, Mo. BL, Deb: 7/4/1884 Career OF: (28-LF 7-CF 3-RF)

YEAR	TM/L	G	AB	R	H	2B	3B	HR	RBI	BB	SO	AVG	OBP	SLG	OPS	OPS+	BR+	SB	CS	SBR	FA	FR	G/POS	TPR
1884	Was-a	21	83	12	32	4	1	0		7		.386	.433	.458	891	216	11				.775	-7	2-12,O-11(1-7-3)	0.4
	Was-U	1	4	0	0	0	0	0		0		.000	.000	.000	0	-99	-1				.000	-0	/O-1(1-0-0)	-0.1
	Tol-a	26	86	16	22	0	1	1		5		.256	.304	.314	618	99	-0				.875	0	O-26(26-0-0)	0.0
1885	Det-N	1	4	1	2	0	0	0	0	0	0	.500	.500	.500	1000	224	1				.667	-0	/3-1	0.0
Total	2	49	177	29	56	4	2	1	0	12	0	.316	.363	.379	742	148	10				.849	-7	/O-38L,2-12,3-1	0.3

■ **JOSE OLIVA** Oliva, Jose (Galvez) b: 3/3/71, San Pedro De Macoris, D.R. d: 12/22/97, San Cristobal, D.R. BR/TR, 6'3", 215 lbs. Deb: 7/1/94

YEAR	TM/L	G	AB	R	H	2B	3B	HR	RBI	BB	SO	AVG	OBP	SLG	OPS	OPS+	BR+	SB	CS	SBR	FA	FR	G/POS	TPR
1994	Atl-N	19	59	9	17	5	0	6	11	7	10	.288	.364	.678	1042	160	5	0	1	-0	.932	2	3-16	0.6
1995	Atl-N	48	109	7	17	4	0	5	12	7	22	.156	.207	.330	537	38	-10	0	0	0	.902	-1	3-25/1-1	-1.1
	StL-N	22	74	8	9	1	0	2	8	5	24	.122	.198	.216	414	9	-10	0	0	0	.977	-2	3-18/1-2	-1.3
	Yr	70	183	15	26	5	0	7	20	12	46	.142	.203	.284	487	26	-20	0	0	0	.933	-3	3-43/1-3	-2.4
Total	2	89	242	24	43	10	0	13	31	19	56	.178	.243	.380	624	60	-15	0	1	-0	.932	-2	/3-59,1-3	-1.8

YEAR	TM/L	G	AB	R	H	2B	3B	HR	RBI	BB	SO	AVG	OBP	SLG	OPS	OPS+	BR+	SB	CS	SBR	FA	FR	G/POS	TPR
■ TONY OLIVA	Oliva, Pedro (Lopez) b: 7/20/40, Pinar Del Rio, Cuba BL/TR, 6′2″, 190 lbs. Deb: 9/9/62 C Career OF: (10-LF 39-CF 1139-RF)																							
1962	Min-A	9	9	3	4	1	0	0	3	3	2	.444	.583	.556	1139	201	2	0	0	0	1.000	-0	/O-2(0-0-2)	0.1
1963	Min-A	7	7	0	3	0	0	0	1	0	2	.429	.429	.429	857	138	0	0	0	0	.000	0	H	0.0
1964	Min-A★	161	672	**109**	**217**	**43**	9	32	94	34	68	**.323**	.361	.557	918	150	42	12	6	1	.981	5	*O-159(2-9-154)	3.8
1965	*Min-A★	149	576	107	**185**	40	5	16	98	55	64	**.321**	.384	.491	876	141	31	19	9	1	.964	7	*O-147(0-8-143)	3.0
1966	Min-A★	159	622	99	**191**	32	7	25	87	42	72	.307	.356	.502	857	135	27	13	7	0	.972	14	*O-159(0-19-140)	3.3
1967	Min-A★	146	557	76	161	**34**	6	17	83	44	61	.289	.350	.463	813	128	19	11	3	1	.987	12	*O-146(0-0-146)	2.4
1968	Min-A★	128	470	54	136	24	5	18	68	45	61	.289	.360	.477	837	145	25	10	9	-1	.983	8	*O-126(0-0-126)	2.6
1969	*Min-A†	153	637	97	**197**	**39**	4	24	101	45	66	.309	.358	.496	854	134	26	10	13	-2	.982	13	*O-152(0-0-152)	3.0
1970	*Min-A★	157	628	96	**204**	**36**	7	23	107	38	67	.325	.366	.514	881	138	30	5	4	-0	.968	21	*O-157(0-3-154)	4.3
1971	Min-A†	126	487	73	164	30	3	22	81	25	44	**.337**	.372	**.546**	918	152	31	4	1	1	.969	-1	*O-121(0-0-121)	2.6
1972	Min-A	10	28	1	9	1	0	0	1	2	5	.321	.367	.357	724	111	0	0	0	0	.857	-3	/O-9(8-0-1)	-0.3
1973	Min-A	146	571	63	166	20	0	16	92	45	44	.291	.347	.410	757	108	6	2	1	0	.000	0	*D-142	0.2
1974	Min-A	127	459	43	131	16	2	13	57	27	31	.285	.328	.414	742	109	4	0	1	-0	.000	0	*D-112	0.1
1975	Min-A	131	455	46	123	10	0	13	58	41	45	.270	.348	.378	726	104	3	0	1	-0	.000	0	*D-120	-0.1
1976	Min-A	67	123	3	26	3	0	1	16	2	13	.211	.236	.260	496	44	-9	0	0	0	.000	0	D-32	-1.0
Total	15	1676	6301	870	1917	329	48	220	947	448	645	.304	.356	.476	832	130	239	86	55	-0	.975	76	*O-1178R,D-406	24.0
■ ED OLIVARES	Olivares, Edward (Balzac) b: 11/5/38, Mayaguez, P.R. BR/TR, 5′11″, 180 lbs. Deb: 9/16/60 F																							
1960	StL-N	3	5	0	0	0	0	0	0	0	3	.000	.000	.000	0	-92	-1	0	0	0	.500	-0	/3-1	-0.2
1961	StL-N	21	30	2	5	0	0	0	1	0	4	.167	.167	.167	333	-10	-5	1	0	0	1.000	-2	O-10(5-0-5)	-0.7
Total	2	24	35	2	5	0	0	0	1	0	7	.143	.143	.143	286	-21	-6	1	0	0	1.000	-3	/O-10(5-0-5),3-1	-0.9
■ AL OLIVER	Oliver, Albert b: 10/14/46, Portsmouth, Ohio BL/TL, 6′, 195 lbs. Deb: 9/23/68 Career OF: (481-LF 835-CF 80-RF)																							
1968	Pit-N	4	8	1	1	0	0	0	0	0	4	.125	.125	.125	250	-25	-1	0	0	0	1.000	0	/O-1(0-0-1)	-0.1
1969	Pit-N	129	463	55	132	19	2	17	70	21	38	.285	.334	.445	779	119	10	8	5	0	.991	-1	*1-106,O-21(13-0-8)	0.0
1970	*Pit-N	151	551	63	149	33	5	12	83	35	35	.270	.330	.414	744	100	-1	1	1	-0	.986	1	O-80(28-0-54),1-77	-1.0
1971	*Pit-N	143	529	69	149	31	7	14	64	27	72	.282	.323	.446	769	116	9	4	3	-0	.981	8	*O-116(0-116-0),1-25	1.3
1972	*Pit-N★	140	565	88	176	27	4	12	89	34	44	.312	.356	.437	793	127	19	2	4	-1	.985	1	*O-138(0-138-0)/1-3	1.5
1973	Pit-N	158	654	90	191	38	7	20	99	22	52	.292	.320	.463	783	118	12	6	0	1	.964	-2	*O-109(0-109-0),1-50	0.4
1974	*Pit-N	147	617	96	198	38	12	11	85	33	58	.321	.360	.475	835	137	28	10	1	2	.986	7	O-98(0-98-0),1-49	3.1
1975	*Pit-N★	155	628	90	176	39	8	18	84	25	73	.280	.313	.454	767	112	6	4	2	0	.987	2	*O-153(0-153-0)/1-4	0.4
1976	Pit-N★	121	443	62	143	22	5	12	61	26	29	.323	.367	.476	843	137	20	6	2	1	.984	7	*O-106(0-106-0)/1-3	2.6
1977	Pit-N	154	568	75	175	29	6	19	82	40	38	.308	.358	.481	838	119	15	13	16	-3	.981	0	*O-148(128-36-0)	0.7
1978	Tex-A	133	525	65	170	35	5	14	89	31	41	.324	.364	.490	853	138	24	8	9	-1	.987	6	*O-107(100-8-0),D-26	2.4
1979	Tex-A	136	492	69	159	28	4	12	76	34	34	.323	.372	.470	841	127	18	4	5	-1	.975	0	*O-119(49-71-0),D-10	1.4
1980	Tex-A★	163	656	96	209	43	3	19	117	39	47	.319	.361	.480	842	132	27	5	7	-1	.973	4	*O-157L/1-1,D-4	2.3
1981	Tex-A★	102	421	53	130	29	1	4	55	24	28	.309	.349	.411	760	125	12	3	0	1	1.000	-0	*D-101/1-1	1.0
1982	Mon-N★	160	617	90	**204**	**43**	2	22	**109**	61	59	**.331**	.394	.514	908	149	41	5	2	0	.986	-9	*1-159	2.3
1983	Mon-N★	157	614	70	184	**38**	3	8	84	44	44	.300	.348	.410	759	110	8	1	3	-1	.990	2	*1-153/O-1(0-0-1)	0.0
1984	SF-N	91	339	27	101	19	2	0	34	20	27	.298	.339	.366	705	101	0	2	2	-0	.985	-1	1-82	-0.6
	Phi-N	28	93	9	29	7	0	0	14	7	9	.312	.360	.387	747	108	1	1	2	-0	.987	-3	1-19/O-5(5-0-0)	-0.4
	Yr	119	432	36	130	26	2	0	48	27	36	.301	.343	.370	714	103	1	3	4	-1	.985	-4	*1-101/O-5(5-0-0)	-1.0
1985	LA-N	35	79	1	20	5	0	0	8	5	11	.253	.298	.316	614	74	-3	1	0	0	.882	-2	O-17(17-0-0)	-0.6
	*Tor-A	61	187	20	47	6	1	5	23	7	13	.251	.282	.374	656	76	-6	0	0	0	1.000	-0	D-59/1-1	-0.8
Total	18	2368	9049	1189	2743	529	77	219	1326	535	756	.303	.348	.451	799	122	239	84	64	-4	.980	19	*O-1376C,1-733,D-200	15.9
■ DAVE OLIVER	Oliver, David Jacob b: 4/7/51, Stockton, Cal. BL/TR, 5′11″, 175 lbs. Deb: 9/25/77 C																							
1977	Cle-A	7	22	2	7	0	1	0	3	4	0	.318	.444	.409	854	139	2	0	0	0	.949	1	/2-7	0.2
■ GENE OLIVER	Oliver, Eugene George b: 3/22/35, Moline, Ill. BR/TR, 6′2″, 225 lbs. Deb: 6/6/59 Career OF: (87-LF 0-CF 6-RF)																							
1959	StL-N	68	172	14	42	9	0	6	28	7	41	.244	.274	.401	675	72	-7	3	2	-0	.955	-5	O-42(41-0-3)/C-9,1-5	-1.5
1961	StL-N	22	52	8	14	2	0	4	9	6	10	.269	.367	.538	905	124	2	0	0	0	1.000	2	C-15/O-1(1-0-0)	0.4
1962	StL-N	122	345	42	89	19	1	14	45	50	59	.258	.354	.441	794	102	1	5	2	0	.991	-4	C-98/O-8(6-0-2),1-3	0.2
1963	StL-N	39	102	10	23	4	0	6	18	13	19	.225	.313	.441	754	105	1	0	0	0	.981	1	C-35	0.4
	Mil-N	95	296	34	74	12	2	11	47	27	59	.250	.323	.416	739	112	5	4	4	-1	.985	-14	1-55,O-35(35-0-0)/C-2	-1.6
	Yr	134	398	44	97	16	2	17	65	40	78	.244	.321	.422	743	110	5	4	4	-1	.985	-13	1-55,C-37,O-35L	-1.2
1964	Mil-N	93	279	45	77	15	1	13	49	17	41	.276	.320	.477	797	120	7	3	7	-2	.982	-6	1-76/C-1	-0.5
1965	Mil-N	122	392	56	106	20	0	21	58	36	61	.270	.336	.482	819	127	13	5	4	-0	.976	1	C-64,1-52/O-1(1-0-0)	1.5
1966	Atl-N	76	191	19	37	9	1	8	24	16	43	.194	.256	.377	633	72	-8	2	0	0	.990	11	C-48/1-5,O-2(2-0-0)	0.6
1967	Atl-N	17	51	8	10	2	0	3	6	6	8	.196	.281	.412	692	97	-0	0	0	0	.968	2	C-14	0.2
	Phi-N	85	263	29	59	16	0	7	34	29	56	.224	.304	.365	669	90	-4	2	2	-0	.987	-12	C-79/1-2	-1.3
	Yr	102	314	37	69	18	0	10	40	35	64	.220	.300	.373	673	91	-4	2	2	-0	.984	-10	C-93/1-2	-1.1
1968	Bos-A	16	35	2	5	0	0	0	1	4	12	.143	.250	.143	393	20	-3	0	0	0	.984	-2	C-10/O-1(0-0-1)	-0.5
	Chi-N	8	11	1	4	0	0	0	1	3	2	.364	.500	.364	864	152	1	0	0	0	1.000	0	/1-2,C-1,O-1(1-0-0)	0.1
1969	Chi-N	23	27	0	6	3	0	0	0	1	9	.222	.276	.333	609	62	-1	0	0	0	1.000	2	/C-6	0.1
Total	10	786	2216	268	546	111	5	93	320	215	420	.246	.317	.427	744	103	6	24	21	-2	.985	-24	C-382,1-200/O-91L	-1.9
■ JOE OLIVER	Oliver, Joseph Melton b: 7/24/65, Memphis, Tenn. BR/TR, 6′3″, 210 lbs. Deb: 7/15/89																							
1989	Cin-N	49	151	13	41	8	0	3	23	6	28	.272	.304	.384	688	92	-2	0	0	0	.986	-1	C-47	0.0
1990	*Cin-N	121	364	34	84	23	0	8	52	37	75	.231	.305	.360	665	79	-10	1	1	-0	**.992**	2	*C-118	-0.2
1991	Cin-N	94	269	21	58	11	0	11	41	18	53	.216	.265	.379	644	76	-9	0	0	0	.980	-1	C-90	-0.6
1992	Cin-N	143	485	42	131	25	1	10	57	35	75	.270	.321	.388	708	97	-2	2	3	-1	.992	-1	*C-141/1-1	0.5
1993	Cin-N	139	482	40	115	28	0	14	75	27	91	.239	.280	.384	664	76	-18	0	0	0	.992	-9	*C-133,1-12/O-1R	-2.0
1994	Cin-N	6	19	1	4	0	0	1	5	2	3	.211	.286	.368	654	70	-1	0	0	0	.980	2	/C-6	0.1
1995	Mil-A	97	337	43	92	20	0	12	51	27	66	.273	.332	.439	772	93	-4	2	4	-1	.982	-6	C-91/1-2,D-6	-0.5
1996	Cin-N	106	289	31	70	12	1	11	46	28	54	.242	.313	.405	718	87	-6	2	0	0	.992	10	C-97/1-3,O-3(2-0-1)	0.9
1997	Cin-N	111	349	28	90	13	0	14	43	25	58	.258	.317	.415	732	89	-6	1	3	-1	.990	-0	*C-106/1-4	-0.2
1998	Det-A	50	155	8	35	8	0	4	22	7	33	.226	.259	.355	614	57	-10	0	1	-0	.982	-3	C-48/1-2	-1.0
	Sea-A	29	85	12	19	3	0	2	10	10	15	.224	.305	.329	635	65	-4	1	0	0	.984	-4	C-29	-0.6
	Yr	79	240	20	54	11	0	6	32	17	48	.225	.276	.346	622	60	-14	1	1	-0	.983	-7	C-77/1-2	-1.6
1999	Pit-N	45	134	10	27	8	0	1	13	10	33	.201	.257	.284	541	37	-13	2	0	0	.993	3	C-44	-0.7
2000	*Sea-A	69	200	33	53	13	1	10	35	14	38	.265	.313	.490	803	102	-0	2	1	0	.995	1	C-66/1-1,D-1	0.3
Total	12	1059	3319	316	819	172	3	101	473	246	622	.247	.302	.392	693	83	-87	13	13	-2	.989	-9	*C-1016/1-25,D-7,O	-4.0
■ NATE OLIVER	Oliver, Nathaniel "Peewee" b: 12/13/40, St.Petersburg, Fla. BR/TR, 5′10″, 160 lbs. Deb: 4/9/63 Career OF: (1-LF 0-CF 0-RF)																							
1963	LA-N	65	163	23	39	2	3	1	9	13	25	.239	.299	.307	606	80	-4	3	4	-1	.961	5	2-57/S-2	0.4
1964	LA-N	99	321	28	78	9	0	0	21	31	57	.243	.310	.271	581	70	-12	7	4	0	.967	-10	2-98/S-1	-1.5
1965	LA-N	8	1	3	1	0	0	0	0	0	0	1.000	1.000	1.000	2000	498	1	1	0	0	1.000	1	/2-2	0.2
1966	*LA-N	80	119	17	23	2	0	0	3	13	17	.193	.278	.210	488	41	-9	3	3	-0	.977	11	2-68/S-2,3-1	0.5
1967	LA-N	77	232	18	55	6	2	0	7	13	50	.237	.283	.280	564	67	-10	3	2	-0	.973	-8	2-39,S-32/O-1(1-0-0)	-1.5
1968	SF-N	36	73	3	13	2	0	0	1	1	13	.178	.189	.205	395	18	-7	0	1	-0	.950	1	2-14,S-13/3-1	-0.6
1969	NY-A	1	1	0	0	0	0	0	0	0	0	.000	.000	.000	0	-99	-0	0	0	0	.000	0	H	0.0
	Chi-N	44	44	15	7	3	0	1	4	1	10	.159	.196	.295	491	32	-4	0	1	-0	1.000	11	2-13	0.7
Total	7	410	954	107	216	24	5	2	45	72	172	.226	.284	.268	553	62	-46	17	15	-2	.969	10	2-291/S-50,3-2,O-1L	-1.8
■ BOB OLIVER	Oliver, Robert Lee b: 2/8/43, Shreveport, La. BR/TR, 6′2″, 215 lbs. Deb: 9/10/65 F Career OF: (15-LF 48-CF 165-RF)																							
1965	Pit-N	3	2	1	0	0	0	0	0	0	0	.000	.000	.000	0	-99	-1	0	0	0	1.000	-0	/O-3(3-0-0)	-0.1
1969	KC-A	118	394	43	100	8	4	13	43	21	74	.254	.295	.393	688	91	-6	5	5	-1	.977	5	O-98C,1-12/3-8	-0.7
1970	KC-A	160	612	83	159	24	6	27	99	42	126	.260	.311	.451	761	108	4	3	3	-0	.993	-8	*1-115,3-46	-1.4
1971	KC-A	128	373	35	91	12	2	8	52	14	88	.244	.281	.351	632	79	-12	0	0	0	.988	-0	1-68,O-48(1-0-47)/3-2	-2.0

YEAR	TM/L	G	AB	R	H	2B	3B	HR	RBI	BB	SO	AVG	OBP	SLG	OPS	OPS+	BR+	SB	CS	SBR	FA	FR	G/POS	TPR
1972	KC-A	16	63	7	17	2	1	1	6	2	12	.270	.292	.381	673	100	-0	1	0	0	.979	3	O-16(0-0-16)	0.3
	Cal-A	134	509	47	137	20	4	19	70	27	97	.269	.310	.436	746	127	14	4	3	-0	.994	-6	*1-127/O-8(1-0-7)	-0.3
	Yr	150	572	54	154	22	5	20	76	29	109	.269	.308	.430	738	124	14	5	3	0	.994	-3	*1-127,O-24(1-0-23)	0.0
1973	Cal-A	151	544	51	144	24	1	18	89	33	100	.265	.313	.412	724	111	6	1	1	-0	.952	-1	3-49,O-47R,1-32,D	-0.1
1974	Cal-A	110	359	22	89	9	1	8	55	16	51	.248	.282	.345	627	84	-8	2	1	0	.985	-12	1-57,3-46/O-4R,D-1	-2.6
	Bal-A	9	20	1	3	2	0	0	4	0	5	.150	.150	.250	400	14	-2	1	1	-0	.974	1	/1-4,D-1	-0.2
	Yr	119	379	23	92	11	1	8	59	16	56	.243	.275	.340	616	81	-11	3	2	-0	.984	-11	1-61,3-46/O-4R,D-2	-2.8
1975	NY-A	18	38	3	5	1	0	0	1	1	9	.132	.154	.158	312	-12	-6	0	0	0	1.000	-0	/1-8,3-1,D-3	-0.7
Total	8	847	2914	293	745	102	19	94	419	156	562	.256	.298	.400	698	100	-12	17	14	-1	.991	-19	1-423,O-224R,3-152,/D	-7.8
■ **TOM OLIVER** Oliver, Thomas Noble "Rebel" b: 1/15/03, Montgomery, Ala. d: 2/26/88, Montgomery, Ala. BR/TR, 6', 168 lbs. Deb: 4/14/30 C																								
1930	Bos-A	154	646	86	189	34	2	0	46	42	25	.293	.339	.351	690	78	-20	6	6	-1	.982	15	*O-154(0-154-0)	-1.2
1931	Bos-A	148	586	52	162	35	5	0	70	25	17	.276	.307	.353	660	77	-20	4	6	-1	**.993**	13	*O-148(0-148-0)	-1.2
1932	Bos-A	122	455	39	120	23	3	0	37	25	12	.264	.305	.327	632	66	-23	1	6	-2	.983	8	*O-116(0-116-0)	-1.9
1933	Bos-A	90	244	25	63	9	1	0	23	13	7	.258	.296	.303	599	60	-14	1	1	-0	.985	-1	O-86(0-86-0)	-1.6
Total	4	514	1931	202	534	101	11	0	176	105	61	.277	.316	.340	656	73	-78	12	19	-4	.986	35	O-504(0-504-0)	-5.9
■ **LUIS OLMO** Olmo, Luis Francisco (Rodriguez) (b: Luis Francisco Rodriquez (Olmo)) b: 8/11/19, Arecibo, P.R. BR/TR, 5'11.5", 190 lbs. Deb: 7/23/43 Career OF: (149-LF 154-CF 30-RF)																								
1943	Bro-N	57	238	39	72	6	4	4	37	8	20	.303	.325	.412	737	112	2	3			.957	-2	O-57(1-54-2)	-0.1
1944	Bro-N	136	520	65	134	20	5	9	85	17	37	.258	.284	.367	651	84	-13	10			.971	-8	O-64C,2-42,3-31	-2.2
1945	Bro-N	141	556	62	174	27	**13**	10	110	36	33	.313	.356	.462	818	127	18	15			.971	-9	*O-106L,3-31/2-1	0.3
1949	*Bro-N	38	105	15	32	4	1	1	14	5	11	.305	.336	.390	727	91	-1	2			.950	-4	O-34(17-16-1)	-0.7
1950	Bos-N	69	154	23	35	7	1	5	22	18	23	.227	.308	.383	691	86	-3	3			.974	-9	O-55(18-11-24)/3-1	-1.4
1951	Bos-N	21	56	4	11	1	1	0	4	4	4	.196	.250	.250	500	38	-5	0	1	-0	1.000	-3	O-16(10-6-2)	-0.9
Total	6	462	1629	208	458	65	25	29	272	88	128	.281	.319	.405	724	102	-3	33	1		.968	-34	O-332C/3-63,2-43	-5.0
■ **BARNEY OLSEN** Olsen, Bernard Charles b: 9/11/19, Everett, Mass. d: 3/30/77, Everett, Mass. BR/TR, 5'11", 179 lbs. Deb: 4/17/41																								
1941	Chi-N	24	73	13	21	6	1	1	4	4	11	.288	.325	.438	763	118	1	0			.947	1	O-23(0-23-0)	0.2
■ **GREG OLSON** Olson, Gregory William b: 9/6/60, Marshall, Minn. BR/TR, 6', 200 lbs. Deb: 6/27/89																								
1989	Min-A	3	2	0	1	0	0	0	0	0	0	.500	.500	.500	1000	171	0	0	0	0	1.000	0	/C-3	0.0
1990	Atl-N★	100	298	36	78	12	1	7	36	30	51	.262	.333	.379	713	90	-4	1	1	-0	.987	-7	C-97/3-1	-0.5
1991	*Atl-N	133	411	46	99	25	0	6	44	44	48	.241	.319	.345	664	82	-9	1	1	-0	.995	3	*C-127	0.0
1992	Atl-N	95	302	27	72	14	2	3	27	34	31	.238	.318	.328	645	78	-8	2	1	0	.998	7	C-94	0.5
1993	*Atl-N	83	262	23	59	10	0	4	24	29	27	.225	.305	.309	614	64	-13	1	0	0	.988	-2	C-81	-1.0
Total	5	414	1275	132	309	61	3	20	131	137	157	.242	.319	.342	661	79	-33	5	3	0	.992	2	C-402/3-1	-1.0
■ **IVY OLSON** Olson, Ivan Massie b: 10/14/1885, Kansas City, Mo. d: 9/1/65, Inglewood, Cal. BR/TR, 5'10.5", 175 lbs. Deb: 4/12/11 C Career OF: (8-LF 0-CF 2-RF)																								
1911	Cle-A	140	545	89	142	20	8	1	50	34		.261	.311	.332	643	79	-16	20			.909	-17	*S-139/3-1	-2.3
1912	Cle-A	125	467	68	118	13	1	0	33	21		.253	.291	.285	575	63	-23	16			.917	6	S-56,3-36,2-21,/O-3L	-1.2
1913	Cle-A	104	370	47	92	13	3	0	32	22	28	.249	.296	.300	596	72	-13	7			.953	4	3-73,1-21/2-1	-0.9
1914	Cle-A	89	310	22	75	6	2	1	20	13	24	.242	.275	.284	559	65	-14	15	9	0	.942	12	S-31,2-23,3-19,/O1	0.1
1915	Cin-N	63	207	18	48	5	4	0	14	12	13	.232	.274	.295	569	71	-7	10	6	0	.938	13	2-39,3-15/1-7	0.7
	Bro-N	18	26	2	2	0	1	0	3	1	0	.077	.111	.154	265	-20	-4	0			.909	-1	/S-7,2-1,3-1,O-1R	-0.5
	Yr	81	233	20	50	5	5	0	17	13	13	.215	.256	.279	535	61	-11	10	6	0	.938	12	2-40,3-16/1-7,SO	0.2
1916	*Bro-N	108	351	29	89	13	4	1	38	21	27	.254	.298	.322	620	88	-5	14			.920	-12	*S-103/2-3,1-1	-1.2
1917	Bro-N	139	580	64	156	18	5	2	38	14	34	.269	.291	.328	619	87	-10	6			.941	-6	*S-133/3-6	-0.7
1918	Bro-N	126	506	63	121	16	4	1	17	27	18	.239	.286	.292	578	77	-14	21			.918	-25	*S-126	-3.5
1919	Bro-N	140	590	73	**164**	14	9	1	38	30	12	.278	.316	.337	654	94	-4	26			.947	-2	*S-140	0.4
1920	*Bro-N	143	637	71	162	13	11	1	46	20	19	.254	.278	.314	592	68	-27	4	7	-2	.935	-7	*S-125,2-21	-2.9
1921	Bro-N	151	652	88	174	22	10	3	35	28	26	.267	.301	.345	646	68	-30	4	9	-2	.943	5	*S-133,2-20	-1.2
1922	Bro-N	136	551	63	150	26	6	1	47	25	10	.272	.306	.347	653	69	-26	8	5	0	.960	-6	2-85,S-51	-2.3
1923	Bro-N	82	292	33	76	11	1	1	35	14	10	.260	.296	.315	611	63	-16	5	0	1	.974	5	2-72/3-4,1-2,S-2	-0.7
1924	Bro-N	10	27	0	6	1	0	0	0	3	1	.222	.300	.259	559	53	-2	0	0	0	.941	-2	/S-8,2-2	-0.3
Total	14	1574	6111	730	1575	191	69	13	446	285	222	.258	.295	.318	613	74	-212	156	36		.932	-34	*S-1054,2-288,3/1O	-16.5
■ **KARL OLSON** Olson, Karl Arthur "Ole" b: 7/6/30, Kentfield, Cal. BR/TR, 6'3", 205 lbs. Deb: 6/30/51																								
1951	Bos-A	5	10	0	1	0	0	0	0	0	3	.100	.100	.100	200	-42	-2	0	0	0	1.000	-1	/O-5(2-0-3)	-0.3
1953	Bos-A	25	57	5	7	2	0	1	6	1	9	.123	.138	.211	348	-7	-9	0	0	0	.970	-4	O-24(23-2-0)	-1.4
1954	Bos-A	101	227	25	59	12	2	1	20	12	23	.260	.297	.344	641	68	-10	2	1	0	.957	-8	O-78(29-36-16)	-2.1
1955	Bos-A	26	48	7	12	1	2	0	1	1	10	.250	.265	.354	619	60	-3	0	0	0	1.000	-5	O-21(11-8-5)	-0.8
1956	Was-A	106	313	34	77	10	2	4	22	28	41	.246	.310	.329	639	69	-14	1	1	-0	.990	-10	*O-101(16-84-3)	-2.8
1957	Was-A	8	12	2	2	0	0	0	0	1	2	.167	.231	.167	397	10	-1	0	0	0	1.000	-1	/O-6(2-4-0)	-0.2
	Det-A	8	14	1	2	0	0	0	1	0	6	.143	.143	.143	286	-21	-2	0	0	0	1.000	-1	/O-5(4-1-0)	-0.4
	Yr	16	26	3	4	0	0	0	1	1	8	.154	.185	.154	339	-6	-4	0	0	0	1.000	-2	O-11(6-5-0)	-0.6
Total	6	279	681	74	160	25	6	6	50	43	94	.235	.281	.316	597	57	-42	3	2	-0	.979	-28	O-240(87-135-27)	-8.0
■ **MARV OLSON** Olson, Marvin Clement "Sparky" b: 5/28/07, Gayville, S.Dak. d: 2/5/98, Tyndall, S.Dak. BR/TR, 5'7", 160 lbs. Deb: 9/13/31																								
1931	Bos-A	15	53	8	10	1	0	0	5	9	3	.189	.306	.208	514	40	-4	0	0	0	.963	3	2-15	0.0
1932	Bos-A	115	403	58	100	14	6	0	25	61	26	.248	.347	.313	660	74	-13	1	5	-2	.955	-15	*2-106/3-1	-2.2
1933	Bos-A	3	1	1	0	0	0	0	0	0	1	.000	.000	.000	0	-99	-0	0	0	0	.000	0	/2-1	0.0
Total	3	133	457	67	110	15	6	0	30	70	30	.241	.342	.300	641	70	-18	1	5	-2	.956	-12	2-122/3-1	-2.2
■ **TOM O'MALLEY** O'Malley, Thomas Patrick b: 12/25/60, Orange, N.J. BL/TR, 6', 190 lbs. Deb: 5/8/82																								
1982	SF-N	92	291	26	80	12	4	2	27	33	39	.275	.351	.364	715	100	1	0	3	-1	.965	0	3-83/2-1,S-1	-0.1
1983	SF-N	135	410	40	106	16	1	5	45	52	47	.259	.348	.339	687	94	-2	2	4	-1	.940	1	*3-117	-0.4
1984	SF-N	13	25	2	3	0	0	0	0	2	2	.120	.185	.120	305	-13	-4	0	0	0	1.000	-0	/3-7	-0.5
	Chi-A	12	16	0	2	0	0	0	3	0	5	.125	.125	.125	250	-29	-3	0	0	0	1.000	-2	/3-6	-0.5
1985	Bal-A	8	14	1	1	0	0	1	2	0	2	.071	.071	.286	357	-8	-2	0	0	0	.833	-1	/3-3	-0.3
1986	Bal-A	56	181	19	46	9	0	1	18	17	21	.254	.318	.320	639	76	-6	0	1	-0	.938	-1	3-55	-0.8
1987	Tex-A	45	117	10	32	8	0	1	12	15	9	.274	.356	.368	724	92	-1	0	0	0	.962	-4	3-40/2-1	-0.6
1988	Mon-N	14	27	3	7	0	0	0	2	3	4	.259	.333	.259	593	69	-1	0	0	0	.905	1	/3-7	0.0
1989	NY-N	9	11	2	6	2	0	0	8	0	2	.545	.545	.727	1273	274	2	0	0	0	1.000	-0	/3-3	0.2
1990	NY-N	82	121	14	27	7	0	3	14	11	20	.223	.288	.355	643	76	-4	0	0	0	.983	2	3-38/1-3	-0.2
Total	9	466	1213	117	310	54	5	13	131	133	151	.256	.332	.340	672	87	-19	2	8	-2	.951	-5	3-359/1-3,2-2,S-1	-3.2
■ **OLLIE O'MARA** O'Mara, Oliver Edward b: 3/8/1891, St.Louis, Mo. d: 10/24/89, Reno, Nev. BR/TR, 5'9", 155 lbs. Deb: 9/8/12																								
1912	Det-A	1	4	0	0	0	0	0	0	0		.000	.000	.000	0	-99	-1	0			.857	0	/S-1	-0.1
1914	Bro-N	67	247	41	65	10	2	1	7	16	26	.263	.316	.332	648	91	-3	14			.918	-12	S-63	-1.2
1915	Bro-N	149	577	77	141	26	3	0	31	51	40	.244	.308	.300	608	83	-11	11	12	-2	.906	-34	*S-149	-4.1
1916	*Bro-N	72	193	18	39	5	2	0	15	12	20	.202	.249	.249	497	52	-11	10			.898	-5	S-51	-1.5
1918	Bro-N	121	450	29	96	8	1	1	24	7	18	.213	.242	.242	484	48	-28	11			.951	-2	*3-121	-3.0
1919	Bro-N	2	7	1	0	0	0	0	0	0	0	.000	.000	.000	0	-98	-2	0			.875	-0	/3-2	-0.2
Total	6	412	1478	166	341	49	8	2	77	86	104	.231	.280	.279	559	69	-56	46	12		.907	-53	S-264,3-123	-10.1
■ **TOM O'MEARA** O'Meara, Thomas Edward b: 12/12/1872, Chicago, Ill. d: 2/16/02, Fort Wayne, Ind. Deb: 9/29/1895																								
1895	Cle-N	1	1	1	0	0	0	0	0	1	0	.000	.500	.000	500	34	-0	0			.500	-0	/C-1	0.0
1896	Cle-N	12	33	5	5	0	0	0	0	5	7	.152	.263	.152	415	10	-4	0			.914	-1	/C-9,1-1	-0.4
Total	2	13	34	6	5	0	0	0	0	6	7	.147	.275	.147	422	12	-4	0			.892	-1	/C-10,1-1	-0.4

YEAR TM/L	G	AB	R	H	2B	3B	HR	RBI	BB	SO	AVG	OBP	SLG	OPS	OPS+	BR+	SB	CS	SBR	FA	FR	G/POS	TPR
■ O'NEAL O'Neal Deb: 10/23/1874																							
1874 Har-n	1	3	0	0	0	0	0	0	0	1	.000	.000	.000	0	-95	-1	0	0	0	.667	1	/O-1(0-0-1)	0.0
■ DENNY O'NEIL O'Neil, Dennis b: 11/22/1866, Holyoke, Mass. d: 11/15/22, Rushville, Ind. BL/TL, 6'2.5", 200 lbs. Deb: 6/18/1893																							
1893 StL-N	7	25	3	3	0	0	0	2	4	0	.120	.241	.120	361	-3	-4	3			.986	-1	/1-7	-0.4
■ MICKEY O'NEIL O'Neil, George Michael b: 4/12/1900, St.Louis, Mo. d: 4/8/64, St.Louis, Mo. BR/TR, 5'10", 185 lbs. Deb: 9/12/19 C																							
1919 Bos-N	11	28	3	6	0	0	0	1	1	7	.214	.241	.214	456	39	-2	0			.981	3	C-11	0.2
1920 Bos-N	112	304	19	86	5	4	0	28	21	20	.283	.339	.326	665	96	-1	4	4	-1	.962	8	*C-105/2-1	1.5
1921 Bos-N	98	277	26	69	9	4	2	29	23	21	.249	.307	.332	639	73	-11	2	2	-0	.968	8	C-95	0.2
1922 Bos-N	83	251	18	56	5	2	0	26	14	11	.223	.267	.259	526	38	-23	1	0	0	.978	0	C-79	-1.7
1923 Bos-N	96	306	29	65	7	4	0	20	17	14	.212	.258	.261	520	39	-27	3	2	-0	.973	14	C-95	-0.7
1924 Bos-N	106	362	32	89	4	1	0	22	14	27	.246	.276	.262	538	47	-27	4	3	-0	.985	1	*C-106	-1.9
1925 Bos-N	70	222	29	57	6	5	2	30	21	16	.257	.327	.356	682	81	-6	1	2	-0	.972	-8	C-69	-1.0
1926 Bro-N	75	201	19	42	5	3	0	20	23	8	.209	.293	.264	557	52	-13	3			.965	-3	C-74	-1.2
1927 Was-A	5	6	0	0	0	0	0	0	0	1	.000	.000	.000	0	-99	-2	0	0	0	1.000	-0	/C-4	-0.2
NY-N	16	38	2	5	0	0	0	3	5	2	.132	.233	.132	364	-0	-5	0			.969	3	C-16	-0.1
Total 9	672	1995	177	475	41	23	4	179	139	127	.238	.292	.288	579	58	-118	18	13		.972	26	C-654/2-1	-4.9
■ JOHN O'NEIL O'Neil, John Francis b: 4/19/20, Shelbiana, Ky. BR/TR, 5'9", 155 lbs. Deb: 4/16/46																							
1946 Phi-N	46	94	12	25	3	0	0	9	5	12	.266	.303	.298	601	73	-3	0			.940	4	S-32	0.2
■ FRED O'NEILL O'Neill, Frederick James "Tip" b: 1865, London, Ontario, Canada d: 3/7/1892, London, Ont., Can. 5'7", 142 lbs. Deb: 5/3/1887																							
1887 NY-a	6	27	4	9	1	1	0	3	1		.333	.357	.423	780	122	1	3			.800	-1	/O-6(0-1-5)	-0.1
■ HARRY O'NEILL O'Neill, Harry Mink b: 5/8/17, Philadelphia, Pa. d: 3/6/45, Iwo Jima, Marianas Islands BR/TR, 6'3", 205 lbs. Deb: 7/23/39																							
1939 Phi-A	1	0	0	0	0	0	0	0	0	0	—	—	—	—	—	0	0	0	0	.000	0	/C-1	0.0
■ TIP O'NEILL O'Neill, James Edward b: 5/25/1858, Woodstock, Ont., Canada d: 12/31/15, Montreal, Que., Can BR/TR, 6'1.5", 167 lbs. Deb: 5/5/1883 Career OF: (1010-LF 6-CF 6-RF)																							
1883 NY-N	23	76	8	15	3	0	0	5	3	15	.197	.228	.237	465	42	-5				.917	-2	P-19/O-7(0-1-6)	-0.2
1884 StL-a	78	297	49	82	13	11	3	54	12		.276	.309	.424	733	132	9				.811	-6	O-64(59-5-0),P-17/1-1	0.0
1885 *StL-a	52	206	44	72	7	4	3	38	13		.350	.399	.466	865	165	15				.881	-1	O-52(52-0-0)	1.1
1886 *StL-a	138	579	106	190	28	14	3	**107**	47		.328	.385	.440	826	151	33	9			.927	8	*O-138(138-0-0)	3.2
1887 *StL-a	124	567	**167**	**275**	**52**	**19**	**14**	**123**	50		**.485**	**.490**	**.691**	**1180**	**205**	**69**	30			.895	-6	*O-124(124-0-0)	**4.7**
1888 *StL-a	130	529	96	**177**	24	10	5	98	44		**.335**	.390	.446	836	151	28	26			.937	-1	*O-130(130-0-0)	2.2
1889 StL-a	134	534	123	179	33	8	9	110	72	37	.335	.419	.478	897	137	24	28			.936	-2	*O-134(134-0-0)	1.6
1890 Chi-P	137	577	112	174	20	16	3	75	65	36	.302	.377	.407	784	105	4	29			.926	-12	*O-137(137-0-0)	-1.0
1891 StL-a	127	514	111	166	28	4	10	95	61	33	.323	.404	.451	855	126	15	25			.935	-12	*O-127(127-0-0)	-0.1
1892 Cin-N	109	419	63	105	14	6	2	52	53	25	.251	.339	.327	666	103	3	14			.922	-3	*O-109(109-0-0)	-1.0
Total 10	1052	4298	879	1435	222	92	52	757	420	146	.334	.392	.458	851	140	194	161			.917	-38	*O-1022L/P-36,1-1	10.5
■ JIM O'NEILL O'Neill, James Leo b: 2/23/1893, Minooka, Pa. d: 9/5/76, Chambersburg, Pa. BR/TR, 5'10.5", 165 lbs. Deb: 4/15/20 F Career OF: (0-LF 0-CF 1-RF)																							
1920 Was-A	86	294	27	85	17	7	1	40	13	30	.289	.324	.405	728	95	-3	7	3	0	.943	-5	S-80/2-2	-0.3
1923 Was-A	23	33	6	9	1	0	0	3	1	3	.273	.294	.303	597	60	-2	0	0	0	.946	3	/2-8,3-4,S-1,O-1R	0.1
Total 2	109	327	33	94	18	7	1	43	14	33	.287	.321	.394	715	91	-5	7	3	0	.943	-3	/S-81,2-10,3-4,O-1R	-0.2
■ JOHN O'NEILL O'Neill, John J. b: New York, N.Y. TR, Deb: 9/6/1899																							
1899 NY-N	2	7	0	0	0	0	0	0	0		.000	.000	.000	0	-99	-2	0			.929	1	/C-2	-0.1
1902 NY-N	2	8	0	0	0	0	0	0	0		.000	.000	.000	0	-99	-2	0			.933	1	/C-2	-0.1
Total 2	4	15	0	0	0	0	0	0	0		.000	.000	.000	0	-99	-4	0			.931	2	/C-4	-0.2
■ JACK O'NEILL O'Neill, John Joseph b: 1/10/1873, Maam, Ireland d: 6/29/35, Minooka, Pa. BR/TR, 5'10", 165 lbs. Deb: 4/21/02 F																							
1902 StL-N	63	192	13	27	1	1	0	12	13		.141	.214	.156	371	15	-19	2			.973	1	C-59	-1.3
1903 StL-N	75	246	23	58	9	1	0	27	13		.236	.288	.280	568	64	-11	11			.972	16	C-74	1.1
1904 Chi-N	51	168	8	36	5	0	1	19	6		.214	.258	.262	520	61	-8	1			.981	5	C-49	0.2
1905 Chi-N	53	172	16	34	4	2	0	12	8		.198	.277	.244	522	54	-9	6			.974	7	C-50	0.2
1906 Bos-N	61	167	14	30	5	1	0	4	12		.180	.243	.222	465	46	-10	0			.971	12	C-48/1-2,O-1(0-0-1)	0.7
Total 5	303	945	74	185	24	5	1	74	52		.196	.258	.235	493	49	-58	20			.974	40	C-280/1-2,O-1(0-0-1)	0.9
■ MIKE O'NEILL O'Neill, Michael Joyce (a.k.a. Michael Joyce In 1901) b: 9/7/1877, Maam, Ireland d: 8/12/59, Scranton, Pa. BL/TL, 5'11", 185 lbs. Deb: 9/20/01 F																							
1901 StL-N	6	15	3	6	0	0	0	2	3		.400	.526	.400	926	179	2	0			.875	-1	/P-5	0.0
1902 StL-N	51	135	21	43	5	3	2	15	2		.319	.333	.444	778	146	6	3			.920	0	P-36/O-3(3-0-0)	0.0
1903 StL-N	41	110	12	25	2	2	0	6	8		.227	.303	.282	585	69	-4	3			.882	-1	P-19,O-13(13-0-0)	-0.3
1904 StL-N	30	91	9	21	7	2	0	16	5		.231	.286	.352	637	101	-0	0			.910	1	P-25/O-3(3-0-0)	0.0
1907 Cin-N	9	29	5	2	0	2	0	2	2		.069	.129	.207	336	5	-3	1			.864	-0	/O-9(9-0-0)	-0.5
Total 5	137	380	50	97	14	9	2	41	20		.255	.306	.355	662	102	0	4			.907	-1	/P-85,O-28(28-0-0)	-0.8
■ PAUL O'NEILL O'Neill, Paul Andrew b: 2/25/63, Columbus, Ohio BL/TL, 6'4", 215 lbs. Deb: 9/3/85 Career OF: (99-LF 23-CF 1718-RF)																							
1985 Cin-N	5	12	1	4	1	0	0	1	0	2	.333	.333	.417	750	103	0	0	0	0	1.000	1	/O-2(2-0-0)	0.1
1986 Cin-N	3	2	0	0	0	0	0	0	1	1	.000	.333	.000	333	-0	0	0	0	0	.000	0	/H	0.0
1987 Cin-N	84	160	24	41	14	1	7	28	18	29	.256	.331	.488	819	109	2	2	1	0	.949	-3	O-42R/1-2,P-1	-0.3
1988 Cin-N	145	485	58	122	25	3	16	73	38	65	.252	.309	.414	723	102	0	8	6	-0	.984	1	*O-118(0-8-114),1-21	-0.5
1989 Cin-N	117	428	49	118	24	2	15	74	46	64	.276	.349	.446	795	122	12	20	5	3	.983	4	*O-115(0-4-115)	1.6
1990 *Cin-N	145	503	59	136	28	0	16	78	53	103	.270	.342	.421	764	104	3	13	11	-1	.993	6	*O-141(0-1-141)	0.5
1991 Cin-N★	152	532	71	136	36	0	28	91	73	107	.256	.347	.481	828	126	18	12	7	0	.994	13	*O-150(0-0-150)	2.7
1992 Cin-N	148	496	59	122	19	1	14	66	77	85	.246	.350	.373	723	102	3	6	3	0	**.997**	15	*O-143(0-0-143)	1.5
1993 NY-A	141	498	71	155	34	1	20	75	44	69	.311	.369	.504	874	137	25	2	4	-1	.992	-11	*O-138(46-0-103)/D-2	0.6
1994 NY-A★	103	368	68	132	25	1	21	83	72	56	**.359**	.464	.603	1067	179	47	5	4	-0	.995	2	O-99(12-0-90)/D-4	3.9
1995 *NY-A★	127	460	82	138	30	4	22	96	71	76	.300	.395	.526	921	138	27	1	2	-0	.987	-4	*O-121(25-0-107)/D-4	1.5
1996 *NY-A	150	546	89	165	35	1	19	91	102	76	.302	.416	.474	890	124	24	0	1	-0	**1.000**	8	*O-146R/1-1,D-3	2.2
1997 *NY-A★	149	553	89	179	42	0	21	117	75	92	.324	.404	.514	918	139	33	10	7	-0	.984	5	*O-146R/1-2,D-2	2.8
1998 *NY-A★	152	602	95	191	40	2	24	116	57	103	.317	.378	.510	888	133	29	15	1	3	.987	6	*O-150(0-0-150)/D-1	2.7
1999 *NY-A	153	597	70	170	39	4	19	110	66	89	.285	.358	.459	817	108	7	11	9	-1	.974	5	*O-151(0-0-151)	0.2
2000 *NY-A	142	566	79	160	26	0	18	100	51	90	.283	.342	.424	766	94	-5	14	9	-0	.993	8	*O-140(0-0-140)/D-2	-0.4
Total 16	1916	6808	964	1969	418	20	260	1199	844	1107	.289	.369	.471	840	122	224	119	70	2	.989	55	*O-1802R/1-26,D-18,P	19.1
■ PEACHES O'NEILL O'Neill, Philip Bernard b: 8/30/1879, Anderson, Ind. d: 8/2/55, Anderson, Ind. BR/TR, 5'11", 165 lbs. Deb: 4/16/04																							
1904 Cin-N	8	15	0	4	0	0	0	1	1		.267	.313	.267	579	73	-0	0			.900	-3	/C-5,1-1	-0.4
■ STEVE O'NEILL O'Neill, Stephen Francis b: 7/6/1891, Minooka, Pa. d: 1/26/62, Cleveland, Ohio BR/TR, 5'10", 165 lbs. Deb: 9/18/11 FMC																							
1911 Cle-A	9	27	1	4	1	0	0	1	4		.148	.281	.185	466	31	-2	2			.986	4	/C-9	0.2
1912 Cle-A	69	215	17	49	4	0	0	14	12		.228	.272	.247	518	47	-15	2			.961	9	C-68	0.0
1913 Cle-A	80	234	19	69	13	3	0	29	10	24	.295	.329	.376	705	103	0	5			.973	3	C-80	1.0
1914 Cle-A	87	269	28	68	12	2	0	20	15	35	.253	.292	.312	605	79	-8	1	3	-1	.956	0	C-82/1-1	-0.1
1915 Cle-A	121	386	32	91	14	2	2	34	26	41	.236	.293	.298	590	75	-13	2	3	-1	.968	5	*C-115	0.2
1916 Cle-A	130	378	30	89	23	0	0	29	24	33	.235	.288	.296	584	71	-14	2			.971	5	*C-128	0.1
1917 Cle-A	129	370	21	68	10	2	0	29	41	55	.184	.272	.222	494	47	-22	2			.980	1	*C-127	-1.2
1918 Cle-A	114	359	34	87	8	7	1	35	48	22	.242	.343	.312	655	89	-3	5			**.983**	1	*C-113	0.9
1919 Cle-A	125	398	46	115	35	7	2	47	48	21	.289	.373	.427	800	117	10	4			.977	-7	*C-123	1.4
1920 *Cle-A	149	489	63	157	39	5	3	55	69	39	.321	.408	.440	848	121	17	3	5	-1	.976	-5	*C-148	2.3

YEAR	TM/L	G	AB	R	H	2B	3B	HR	RBI	BB	SO	AVG	OBP	SLG	OPS	OPS+	BR+	SB	CS	SBR	FA	FR	G/POS	TPR
1921	Cle-A	106	335	39	108	22	1	1	50	57	22	.322	.424	.403	827	110	8	0	1	-0	.982	3	*C-105	1.7
1922	Cle-A	133	392	33	122	27	4	2	65	73	25	.311	.423	.416	839	118	15	2	2	-0	.974	-14	*C-130	0.8
1923	Cle-A	113	330	31	82	12	0	0	50	64	34	.248	.374	.285	659	75	-9	0	4	-1	.968	-12	*C-111	-1.4
1924	Bos-A	106	307	29	73	15	1	0	38	63	23	.238	.371	.293	664	73	-10	0	2	-1	.970	0	C-92	-0.4
1925	NY-A	35	91	7	26	5	0	1	13	10	3	.286	.363	.374	736	89	-1	0	0	0	.946	3	C-31	0.3
1927	StL-A	74	191	14	44	7	0	1	22	20	6	.230	.303	.283	586	51	-14	0	3	-1	.983	1	C-60	-1.0
1928	StL-A	10	24	4	7	1	0	0	6	8	0	.292	.485	.333	818	115	1	0	0	0	.958	-4	C-10	-0.2
Total	17	1590	4795	448	1259	248	34	13	537	592	383	.263	.349	.337	685	88	-60	30	23		.972	-6	*C-1532/1-1	4.6

■ BILL O'NEILL O'Neill, William John b: 1/22/1880, St.John, N.B., Can. d: 7/20/20, Woodhaven, N.Y. BB/TR, 5'11", 175 lbs. Deb: 5/7/04 Career OF: (22-LF 87-CF 87-RF)

YEAR	TM/L	G	AB	R	H	2B	3B	HR	RBI	BB	SO	AVG	OBP	SLG	OPS	OPS+	BR+	SB	CS	SBR	FA	FR	G/POS	TPR
1904	Bos-A	17	51	7	10	1	0	0	5	2		.196	.226	.216	442	38	-4	0			.933	-2	/O-9(8-1-0),S-2	-0.7
	Was-A	95	365	33	89	10	1	1	16	22		.244	.294	.285	579	85	-6	22			.893	-12	O-93(14-79-0)/2-3	-2.6
	Yr	112	416	40	99	11	1	1	21	24		.238	.286	.276	562	79	-10	22			.896	-14	*O-102C/2-3,S-2	-3.3
1906	*Chi-A	94	330	37	82	4	1	1	21	22		.248	.301	.276	577	83	-6	19			.949	-6	O-93(0-7-87)	-1.8
Total	2	206	746	77	181	15	2	2	42	46		.243	.293	.276	569	81	-15	41			.919	-20	O-195C/2-3,S-2	-5.1

■ RALPH ONIS Onis, Manuel Dominguez "Curly" b: 10/24/08, Tampa, Fla. d: 1/4/95, Tampa, Fla. BR/TR, 5'9", 180 lbs. Deb: 4/27/35

YEAR	TM/L	G	AB	R	H	2B	3B	HR	RBI	BB	SO	AVG	OBP	SLG	OPS	OPS+	BR+	SB	CS	SBR	FA	FR	G/POS	TPR
1935	Bro-N	1	1	0	1	0	0	0	0	0	0	1.000	1.000	1.000	2000	449	0	0			.500	-0	/C-1	0.0

■ EDDIE ONSLOW Onslow, Edward Joseph b: 2/17/1893, Meadville, Pa. d: 5/8/81, Dennison, Ohio BL/TL, 6', 170 lbs. Deb: 8/7/12 F

YEAR	TM/L	G	AB	R	H	2B	3B	HR	RBI	BB	SO	AVG	OBP	SLG	OPS	OPS+	BR+	SB	CS	SBR	FA	FR	G/POS	TPR
1912	Det-A	36	128	11	29	1	2	1	13	3		.227	.250	.289	539	56	-8	3			.972	-3	1-35	-1.2
1913	Det-A	17	55	7	14	1	0	0	8	5	9	.255	.328	.273	601	77	-1	1			.990	-1	1-17	-0.3
1918	Cle-A	2	6	0	1	0	0	0	0	0	1	.167	.167	.167	333	1	-1	0			.000	-1	/O-1(1-0-0)	-0.2
1927	Was-A	9	18	1	4	1	0	0	1	1	0	.222	.263	.278	541	41	-2	0	0	0	1.000	0	/1-5	-0.2
Total	4	64	207	19	48	3	2	1	22	9	10	.232	.271	.280	551	59	-12	4	0		.979	-5	/1-57,O-1(1-0-0)	-1.9

■ JACK ONSLOW Onslow, John James b: 10/13/1888, Scottdale, Pa. d: 12/22/60, Concord, Mass. BR/TR, 5'11", 180 lbs. Deb: 5/2/12 FMC

YEAR	TM/L	G	AB	R	H	2B	3B	HR	RBI	BB	SO	AVG	OBP	SLG	OPS	OPS+	BR+	SB	CS	SBR	FA	FR	G/POS	TPR
1912	Det-A	36	69	7	11	1	0	0	4	10		.159	.284	.174	458	33	-6	1			.948	1	C-35/O-1	-0.3
1917	NY-N	9	8	1	2	1	0	0	0	0	1	.250	.333	.375	708	121	0	0			.929	-0	/C-9	0.0
Total	2	45	77	8	13	2	0	0	4	10	1	.169	.289	.195	484	41	-5	1			.947	0	/C-44,O-1	-0.3

■ STEVE ONTIVEROS Ontiveros, Steven Robert b: 10/26/51, Bakersfield, Cal. BB/TR, 6', 185 lbs. Deb: 8/5/73 Career OF: (7-LF 3-CF 11-RF)

YEAR	TM/L	G	AB	R	H	2B	3B	HR	RBI	BB	SO	AVG	OBP	SLG	OPS	OPS+	BR+	SB	CS	SBR	FA	FR	G/POS	TPR
1973	SF-N	24	33	3	8	0	0	1	5	4	7	.242	.324	.333	658	79	-1	0	0	0	1.000	1	/1-5,O-1(0-0-1)	0.0
1974	SF-N	120	343	45	91	15	1	4	33	57	41	.265	.375	.350	725	99	2	0	0	0	.929	-6	3-75,1-19/O-2(1-0-1)	-0.6
1975	SF-N	108	325	21	94	16	0	3	31	55	44	.289	.395	.366	761	108	6	2	0	0	.923	-2	3-89/O-8(2-0-7),1-4	0.4
1976	SF-N	59	74	8	13	3	0	0	5	6	11	.176	.247	.216	463	31	-7	0	0	0	1.000	-5	/3-7,O-7(4-3-2),1-4	-1.3
1977	Chi-N	156	546	54	163	32	3	10	68	81	69	.299	.392	.423	815	107	8	3	3	-0	.955	-2	*3-155	0.4
1978	Chi-N	82	276	34	67	14	4	1	22	34	33	.243	.326	.333	659	75	-8	0	2	-1	.965	10	3-77/1-1	-0.1
1979	Chi-N	152	519	58	148	28	2	4	57	58	68	.285	.365	.370	735	92	-3	0	1	-0	.941	-4	*3-142/1-1	-1.1
1980	Chi-N	31	77	7	16	3	0	1	3	14	17	.208	.330	.286	615	68	-3	0	0	0	.929	-1	3-24	-0.4
Total	8	732	2193	230	600	111	10	24	224	309	290	.274	.367	.366	734	94	-6	5	6	-1	.944	-9	3-569/1-34,O-18R	-2.7

■ JOSE OQUENDO Oquendo, Jose Manuel (Contreras) b: 7/4/63, Rio Piedras, P.R. BB/TR (BR 1983 (part)), 5'10", 160 lbs. Deb: 5/2/83 C Career OF: (11-LF 7-CF 47-RF)

YEAR	TM/L	G	AB	R	H	2B	3B	HR	RBI	BB	SO	AVG	OBP	SLG	OPS	OPS+	BR+	SB	CS	SBR	FA	FR	G/POS	TPR
1983	NY-N	120	328	29	70	7	0	1	17	19	60	.213	.261	.244	505	41	-26	8	9	-1	.960	6	*S-116	-1.2
1984	NY-N	81	189	23	42	5	0	0	10	15	26	.222	.286	.249	535	52	-12	10	1	2	.972	2	S-67	-0.3
1986	StL-N	76	138	20	41	4	1	0	13	15	20	.297	.366	.341	707	97	-0	2	3	-1	.956	-6	S-29,2-21/3-1,O-1L	-0.4
1987	*StL-N	116	248	43	71	9	0	1	24	54	29	.286	.414	.335	749	99	3	4	4	-1	1.000	3	O-46R,2-32,S-23,/31P	0.6
1988	StL-N	148	451	36	125	10	1	7	46	52	40	.277	.352	.350	702	101	2	4	6	-1	.997	8	2-69,3-47,S-17,1O/PC	1.2
1989	StL-N	163	556	59	162	28	7	1	48	79	59	.291	.380	.372	752	112	12	3	5	-1	**.994**	20	*2-156/S-7,1-1	3.8
1990	StL-N	156	469	38	118	17	5	1	37	74	46	.252	.354	.316	669	85	-7	1	1	-0	**.996**	-1	*2-150/S-4	-0.4
1991	StL-N	127	366	37	88	11	4	1	26	67	48	.240	.359	.301	660	87	-3	1	2	-0	.988	15	*2-118,S-22/1-3,P-1	1.6
1992	StL-N	14	35	3	9	3	1	0	3	5	3	.257	.350	.400	750	115	1	0	0	0	1.000	0	/2-9,S-5	0.1
1993	StL-N	46	73	7	15	0	0	0	4	12	8	.205	.318	.205	523	44	-5	0	0	0	.988	14	S-22,2-16	1.0
1994	StL-N	55	129	13	34	2	2	0	9	21	16	.264	.367	.310	677	80	-3	1	1	-0	.945	-5	S-28,2-16	-0.6
1995	StL-N	88	220	31	46	8	3	2	17	35	21	.209	.318	.300	618	64	-11	1	1	-0	.981	6	2-62,S-24/3-2,O-1R	-0.1
Total	12	1190	3202	339	821	104	24	14	254	448	376	.256	.349	.317	666	85	-49	35	33	-4	.992	63	2-649,S-364/O31PC	5.3

■ TOM ORAN Oran, Thomas b: 1845, d: 9/22/1886, St.Louis, Mo. Deb: 5/4/1875

YEAR	TM/L	G	AB	R	H	2B	3B	HR	RBI	BB	SO	AVG	OBP	SLG	OPS	OPS+	BR+	SB	CS	SBR	FA	FR	G/POS	TPR
1875	RS-n	19	81	7	15	3	1	0	10	1	1	.185	.195	.247	442	58	-3	3	2	-0	.633	-4	O-19(0-2-17)/S-1	-0.5

■ ERNIE ORAVETZ Oravetz, Ernest Eugene b: 1/24/32, Johnstown, Pa. BB/TL, 5'4", 145 lbs. Deb: 4/11/55

YEAR	TM/L	G	AB	R	H	2B	3B	HR	RBI	BB	SO	AVG	OBP	SLG	OPS	OPS+	BR+	SB	CS	SBR	FA	FR	G/POS	TPR
1955	Was-A	100	263	24	71	5	1	0	25	26	19	.270	.338	.297	635	76	-8	1	2	-0	.967	-3	O-57(0-17-42)	-1.4
1956	Was-A	88	137	20	34	3	2	0	11	27	20	.248	.372	.299	671	79	-3	1	0	0	.946	-2	O-31(20-3-9)	-0.6
Total	2	188	400	44	105	8	3	0	36	53	39	.262	.350	.298	648	77	-11	2	2	-0	.961	-5	/O-88(20-20-51)	-2.0

■ LUIS ORDAZ Ordaz, Luis Javier b: 8/12/75, Maracaibo, Venez. BR/TR, 5'11", 170 lbs. Deb: 9/3/97

YEAR	TM/L	G	AB	R	H	2B	3B	HR	RBI	BB	SO	AVG	OBP	SLG	OPS	OPS+	BR+	SB	CS	SBR	FA	FR	G/POS	TPR
1997	StL-N	12	22	3	6	1	0	0	1	1	2	.273	.304	.318	623	64	-1	3	0	1	.964	1	S-11	0.1
1998	StL-N	57	153	9	31	5	0	0	8	12	18	.203	.261	.235	496	32	-15	2	0	0	.945	13	S-54/3-2,2-1	0.2
1999	StL-N	10	9	3	1	0	0	0	2	1	2	.111	.200	.111	311	-18	-2	1	0	0	.786	1	/S-8,2-1,3-1	-0.1
2000	KC-A	65	104	17	23	2	0	0	11	5	10	.221	.264	.240	504	29	-11	4	2	0	.986	-3	S-38,2-22	-1.1
Total	4	144	288	32	61	8	0	0	22	19	32	.212	.263	.240	503	31	-29	10	2	2	.949	11	S-111/2-24,3-3	-0.9

■ TONY ORDENANA Ordenana, Antonio (Rodriguez) "Mosquito" b: 10/30/18, Guanabacoa, Havana, Cuba d: 9/29/88, Miami, Fla. BR/TR, 5'9", 158 lbs. Deb: 10/3/43

YEAR	TM/L	G	AB	R	H	2B	3B	HR	RBI	BB	SO	AVG	OBP	SLG	OPS	OPS+	BR+	SB	CS	SBR	FA	FR	G/POS	TPR
1943	Pit-N	1	4	0	2	0	0	0	3	0	0	.500	.500	.500	1000	183	0	0			1.000	1	/S-1	0.1

■ MAGGLIO ORDONEZ Ordonez, Maggio (Delgado) b: 1/28/74, Caracas, Venez. BR/TR, 5'11", 170 lbs. Deb: 8/29/97

YEAR	TM/L	G	AB	R	H	2B	3B	HR	RBI	BB	SO	AVG	OBP	SLG	OPS	OPS+	BR+	SB	CS	SBR	FA	FR	G/POS	TPR
1997	Chi-A	21	69	12	22	6	0	4	11	2	8	.319	.338	.580	918	139	3	1	2	-0	1.000	2	O-19(0-0-19)	0.3
1998	Chi-A	145	535	70	151	25	2	14	65	28	53	.282	.329	.415	744	94	-5	9	7	-0	.985	3	*O-145(0-22-136)	-0.9
1999	Chi-A★	157	624	100	188	34	3	30	117	47	64	.301	.351	.510	861	116	13	13	6	1	.991	12	*O-153(0-0-153)/D-2	1.6
2000	*Chi-A★	153	588	102	185	34	3	32	126	60	64	.315	.380	.546	926	129	26	18	4	3	.983	5	*O-152(0-0-152)	2.3
Total	4	476	1816	284	546	99	8	80	319	137	189	.301	.354	.496	850	115	37	41	19	2	.987	22	O-469(0-22-460)/D-2	3.3

■ REY ORDONEZ Ordonez, Reynaldo b: 1/11/71, Havana, Cuba BR/TR, 5'9", 160 lbs. Deb: 4/1/96

YEAR	TM/L	G	AB	R	H	2B	3B	HR	RBI	BB	SO	AVG	OBP	SLG	OPS	OPS+	BR+	SB	CS	SBR	FA	FR	G/POS	TPR
1996	NY-N	151	502	51	129	12	4	1	30	22	53	.257	.290	.303	592	59	-30	1	3	-1	.962	2	*S-150	-1.5
1997	NY-N	120	356	35	77	5	3	1	33	18	36	.216	.256	.256	512	36	-33	11	5	1	**.983**	16	*S-118	-0.8
1998	NY-N	153	505	46	124	20	2	1	42	23	60	.246	.280	.299	579	53	-34	3	6	-1	.975	12	*S-151	-1.2
1999	*NY-N	154	520	49	134	24	2	1	60	49	59	.258	.323	.317	640	65	-27	8	4	0	**.994**	6	*S-154	-0.7
2000	NY-N	45	133	10	25	5	0	0	9	17	16	.188	.280	.226	506	31	-14	0	0	0	.965	-5	S-44	-1.5
Total	5	623	2016	191	489	66	11	4	174	129	224	.243	.289	.292	582	53	-139	23	18	-1	.977	30	S-617	-5.7

■ JOE ORENGO Orengo, Joseph Charles b: 11/29/14, San Francisco, Cal d: 7/24/88, San Francisco, Cal. BR/TR, 6', 185 lbs. Deb: 4/18/39

YEAR	TM/L	G	AB	R	H	2B	3B	HR	RBI	BB	SO	AVG	OBP	SLG	OPS	OPS+	BR+	SB	CS	SBR	FA	FR	G/POS	TPR
1939	StL-N	7	3	0	0	0	0	0	0	0	1	.000	.000	.000	0	-94	-1	0			.667	-0	/S-7	-0.1
1940	StL-N	129	415	58	119	23	4	7	56	65	90	.287	.383	.412	795	113	9	9			.952	5	2-77,3-34,S-19	2.1
1941	NY-N	77	252	23	54	11	2	4	25	28	49	.214	.298	.321	619	73	-9	1			.958	18	3-59/S-9,2-6	1.2
1943	NY-N	83	266	28	58	8	2	6	29	36	46	.218	.311	.331	642	85	-5	1			.992	4	1-82	-0.5
	Bro-N	7	15	1	3	2	0	0	1	4	2	.200	.368	.333	702	103	0	0			1.000	-0	/3-6	0.0
	Yr	90	281	29	61	10	2	6	30	40	48	.217	.315	.331	646	86	-5	1			.992	4	1-82/3-6	-0.5
1944	Det-A	46	154	14	31	10	0	0	10	20	29	.201	.297	.266	563	58	-8	1	1	-0	.903	6	S-29,3-11/1-5,2-2	0.0
1945	Chi-A	17	15	5	1	0	0	0	1	3	2	.067	.222	.067	289	-15	-2	0	0	0	.923	1	/3-7,2-1	-0.1
Total	6	366	1120	129	266	54	8	17	122	156	219	.237	.332	.346	678	88	-15	12	1		.957	34	3-117/1-87,2-86,S	2.6

YEAR	TM/L	G	AB	R	H	2B	3B	HR	RBI	BB	SO	AVG	OBP	SLG	OPS	OPS+	BR+	SB	CS	SBR	FA	FR	G/POS	TPR
■ KEVIN ORIE	Orie, Kevin Leonard b: 9/1/72, West Chester, Pa. BR/TR, 6'4", 210 lbs. Deb: 4/1/97																							
1997	Chi-N	114	364	40	100	23	5	8	44	39	57	.275	.353	.431	784	102	1	2	2	-0	.971	11	*3-112/S-3	1.2
1998	Chi-N	64	204	24	37	14	0	2	21	18	35	.181	.258	.279	537	40	-18	1	1	-0	.966	-1	3-57	-1.9
	Fla-N	48	175	23	46	8	1	6	17	14	24	.263	.335	.423	758	103	1	1	0	0	.939	6	3-48	0.7
	Yr	112	379	47	83	22	1	8	38	32	59	.219	.294	.346	639	67	-18	2	1	0	.952	6	*3-105	-1.2
1999	Fla-N	77	240	26	61	16	0	6	29	22	43	.254	.325	.396	720	86	-6	1	0	0	.961	1	3-64/1-1	-0.4
Total	3	303	983	113	244	61	6	22	111	93	159	.248	.323	.390	713	85	-22	5	3	0	.961	17	3-281/S-3,1-1	-0.4
■ GEORGE ORME	Orme, George William b: 9/16/1891, Lebanon, Ind. d: 3/16/62, Indianapolis, Ind. BR/TR, 5'10", 160 lbs. Deb: 9/14/20																							
1920	Bos-A	4	6	4	2	0	0	0	1	3	0	.333	.556	.333	889	146	1	0	0	0	1.000	0	/O-3(0-1-2)	0.1
■ JESS ORNDORFF	Orndorff, Jesse Walworth Thayer b: 1/15/1881, Chicago, Ill. d: 9/28/60, Cardiff-By-The- Sea, Cal. BB/TR, 6', 168 lbs. Deb: 4/18/07																							
1907	Bos-N	5	17	0	2	0	0	0	0	0		.118	.118	.118	235	-26	-2	0			.900	-2	/C-5	-0.5
■ FRANK O'ROURKE	O'Rourke, James Francis "Blackie" b: 11/28/1894, Hamilton, Ont., Can d: 5/14/86, Chatham, N.J. BR/TR, 5'10.5", 165 lbs. Deb: 6/12/12 Career OF: (0-LF 1-CF 2-RF)																							
1912	Bos-N	61	196	11	24	3	1	0	16	11	50	.122	.177	.148	325	-10	-30	1			.915	-6	S-59/3-1	-3.2
1917	Bro-N	64	198	18	47	7	1	0	15	14	25	.237	.294	.283	577	75	-5	11			.954	7	3-58	0.4
1918	Bro-N	4	12	0	2	0	0	0	2	1	3	.167	.231	.167	397	22	-1	0			.857	1	/2-2,O-1	0.0
1920	Was-A	14	54	8	16	1	0	0	5	2	5	.296	.321	.315	636	71	-2	2	1	0	.952	4	S-13/3-1	0.3
1921	Was-A	123	444	51	104	17	8	3	54	26	56	.234	.287	.329	616	60	-28	6	7	-1	.922	-7	*S-122	-2.2
1922	Bos-A	67	216	28	57	14	3	1	17	20	28	.264	.335	.370	705	84	-5	6	6	-1	.909	-12	S-49,3-20	-1.1
1924	Det-A	47	181	28	50	11	2	0	19	12	19	.276	.332	.359	691	79	-6	7	4	0	.970	11	2-40/S-7	0.7
1925	Det-A	124	482	88	141	40	7	5	57	32	37	.293	.350	.436	786	100	-2	5	8	-2	**.971**	15	*2-118/3-6	1.4
1926	Det-A	111	363	43	88	16	1	1	41	35	33	.242	.321	.300	621	62	-20	8	6	-0	.936	10	3-60,2-41,S-10	-0.5
1927	StL-A	140	538	85	144	25	3	1	39	64	43	.268	.358	.331	689	77	-16	18	8	1	.955	11	*3-121,2-16/1-3	0.4
1928	StL-A	99	391	54	103	24	3	1	62	21	19	.263	.303	.348	650	68	-18	10	2	2	.954	-9	3-96/S-2	-2.0
1929	StL-A	154	585	81	147	23	9	2	62	41	28	.251	.306	.332	637	62	-34	14	7	1	.943	-18	*3-151/2-3,S-2	-3.9
1930	StL-A	115	400	52	107	15	4	1	41	35	30	.268	.326	.333	659	65	-21	11	9	-1	.950	10	3-84,S-23/1-3	-0.3
1931	StL-A	8	9	0	2	0	0	0	0	0	1	.222	.222	.222	444	17	-1	1	1	-0	1.000	1	/S-2,1-1	-0.1
Total	14	1131	4069	547	1032	196	42	15	430	314	377	.254	.315	.333	649	68	-189	100	59		.949	17	3-598,S-289,2/1O	-10.1
■ JIM O'ROURKE	O'Rourke, James Henry, "Orator Jim" b: 9/1/1850, Bridgeport, Conn. d: 1/8/19, Bridgeport, Conn. BR/TR, 5'8", 185 lbs. Deb: 4/26/1872 FMUH NA OF: (0-LF 44-CF 23-RF) Career OF: (770-LF 419-CF 195-RF)																							
1872	Man-n	23	101	25	31	4	1	0	12	2	0	.307	.320	.366	687	117	3	1	0	0	.727	-5	S-15/C-9,3-2,1-1	-0.2
1873	Bos-n	57	280	79	98	19	3	1	48	14	1	.350	.381	.450	831	135	10	4	2	0	.916	1	1-32,O-22(0-0-22)/C-9	0.9
1874	Bos-n	70	331	82	104	15	8	**5**	61	4	5	.314	.322	.453	776	138	12	11	2	2	.943	1	*1-70	1.3
1875	Bos-n	75	358	97	106	13	7	**6**	72	9	6	.296	.313	.422	735	148	16	17	5	2	.800	-5	O-45C,3-27/1-6,C-1	1.1
1876	Bos-N	70	327	61	102	17	3	2	43	15	17	.312	.358	.420	778	156	18				.856	-3	*O-68(9-60-0)/1-2,C-1	1.1
1877	Bos-N	61	265	**68**	96	14	4	0	23	**20**	9	.362	**.407**	.445	852	162	19				.846	-0	*O-60(23-35-3)/1-1	1.4
1878	Bos-N	60	255	44	71	17	7	1	29	5	21	.278	.292	.412	704	120	4				.860	4	*O-57(0-57-0)/1-2,C-2	0.5
1879	Pro-N	81	362	69	126	19	9	1	46	13	10	.348	**.371**	.459	829	174	28				.785	-9	*O-56R,1-20/C-5,3-3	1.7
1880	Bos-N	86	363	71	100	20	11	**6**	45	21	8	.275	.315	.441	756	158	22				.907	-3	O-37R,1-19,S-17,3/C	1.8
1881	Buf-N	83	348	71	105	21	7	0	30	27	18	.302	.352	.402	754	139	16				.821	-20	*3-56,O-18L/C-8,S1M	-0.2
1882	Buf-N	84	370	62	104	15	6	2	37	13	13	.281	.305	.370	676	114	5				.866	-0	*O-81C/S-2,C-2,3M	0.2
1883	Buf-N	94	436	102	143	29	8	1	38	15	13	.328	.350	.438	788	135	17				.866	-12	O-61L,C-33/3-8,SPM	0.6
1884	Buf-N	108	467	119	**162**	33	7	5	63	35	17	**.347**	.392	.480	872	167	35				.894	-9	*O-86L,1-18,C/P3M	2.0
1885	NY-N	112	477	119	143	21	**16**	5	42	40	21	.300	.354	.442	796	158	31				.940	-16	*O-112(0-112-0)/C-8	1.1
1886	NY-N	105	440	106	136	26	6	1	34	39	21	.309	.365	.402	768	132	17	14			.926	8	O-63(1-62-0),C-47/1-2	2.4
1887	NY-N	103	433	73	149	15	13	3	88	36	11	.344	.352	.411	762	116	10	46			.890	-9	C-40,3-38,O-28L,/2	0.4
1888	*NY-N	107	409	50	112	16	6	4	50	24	30	.274	.319	.372	690	121	10	25			.960	-1	O-87L,C-15/1-4,3-2	0.7
1889	*NY-N	128	502	89	161	36	7	3	81	40	34	.321	.372	.438	810	126	16	33			.893	-8	*O-128(128-0-0)/C-1	0.4
1890	NY-P	111	478	112	172	37	5	9	115	33	20	.360	.410	.515	925	135	20	23			.930	5	*O-111(10-1-100)	1.9
1891	NY-N	136	555	92	164	28	7	5	95	26	29	.295	.334	.398	732	118	11	19			.906	-1	*O-126(126-1-0),C-14	0.7
1892	NY-N	115	448	62	136	28	5	0	56	30	30	.304	.354	.388	742	126	14	16			.913	-10	*O-111L/C-4,1-1	-0.6
1893	Was-N	129	547	75	157	22	5	2	95	49	26	.287	.354	.356	711	92	-6	15			.927	5	O-87L,1-33/C-9,M	-0.7
1904	NY-N	1	4	1	1	0	0	0	0	0		.250	.250	.250	500	52	-0	0			.800	-1	/C-1	-0.1
Total	4 n	225	1070	283	339	51	19	12	193	29	12	.317	.335	.434	768	138	41	33	9	4	.933	-8	1-109/O-67C,3-29,CS	3.1
Total	19	1774	7486	1446	2340	414	132	50	1010	481	348	.313	.355	.421	776	133	288	191			.898	-80	*O-1377L,C-209,31/SP2	15.3
■ CHARLIE O'ROURKE	O'Rourke, James Patrick b: 6/22/37, Walla Walla, Wash. BR/TR, 6'2", 195 lbs. Deb: 6/16/59																							
1959	StL-N	2	2	0	0	0	0	0	0	0	0	.000	.000	.000	0	-94	-1	0	0	0	.000	0	H	-0.1
■ QUEENIE O'ROURKE	O'Rourke, James Stephen b: 12/26/1883, Bridgeport, Conn. d: 12/22/55, Sparrows Point, Md BR/TR, 5'7", 150 lbs. Deb: 8/15/08 F																							
1908	NY-A	34	108	5	25	1	0	0	3	4		.231	.259	.241	500	62	-5	4			1.000	-6	O-14L,S-11/2-4,3-3	-1.3
■ JOHN O'ROURKE	O'Rourke, John b: 8/23/1849, Bridgeport, Conn. d: 6/23/11, Boston, Mass. BL/TL, 6', 190 lbs. Deb: 5/1/1879 F																							
1879	Bos-N	72	317	69	108	17	11	6	**62**	8	32	.341	.357	**.521**	**877**	181	26				.882	2	*O-71(0-70-1)	2.3
1880	Bos-N	81	313	30	86	22	8	3	36	18	32	.275	.314	.425	739	153	17				.871	5	*O-81(3-78-1)	1.8
1883	NY-a	77	315	49	85	19	5	2		21		.270	.315	.381	696	118	6				.856	-3	*O-76(0-76-0)/1-1	0.0
Total	3	230	945	148	279	58	24	11	98	47	64	.295	.329	.442	771	150	50				.871	4	O-228(3-224-2)/1-1	4.1
■ JOE O'ROURKE	O'Rourke, Joseph Leo Jr. b: 10/28/04, Philadelphia, Pa. d: 6/27/90, Philadelphia, Pa. BL/TR, 5'7", 145 lbs. Deb: 4/19/29 F																							
1929	Phi-N	3	3	0	0	0	0	0	0	0	1	.000	.000	.000	0	-94	-1	0			.000	0	H	-0.1
■ PATSY O'ROURKE	O'Rourke, Joseph Leo Sr. b: 4/13/1881, Philadelphia, Pa. d: 4/18/56, Philadelphia, Pa. BR/TR, 5'7", 160 lbs. Deb: 4/16/08 F																							
1908	StL-N	53	164	8	32	4	2	0	16	14		.195	.263	.244	506	65	-6	2			.860	-7	S-53	-1.4
■ TOM O'ROURKE	O'Rourke, Thomas Joseph b: 10/1865, New York, N.Y. d: 7/19/29, New York, N.Y. TR, 5'9", 158 lbs. Deb: 5/11/1887 Career OF: (0-LF 0-CF 2-RF)																							
1887	Bos-N	22	85	12	19	3	0	0	10	7	6	.224	.233	.192	425	19	-8	4			.777	-5	C-21/O-1(0-0-1),3-1	-1.0
1888	Bos-N	20	74	3	13	0	0	0	4	1	9	.176	.187	.176	362	16	-7	2			.881	1	C-20/O-1(0-0-1)	-0.4
1890	NY-N	2	7	1	0	0	0	0	0	1	0	.000	.125	.000	125	-63	-1	0			.864	1	/C-2	0.0
	Syr-a	41	153	16	33	8	0	0	12	12		.216	.277	.268	545	68	-6	2			.907	-12	C-40/1-1	-1.3
Total	3	85	319	32	65	11	0	0	26	21	15	.204	.242	.221	463	39	-23	8			.867	-15	/C-83,O-2R,1-1,3-1	-2.7
■ TIM O'ROURKE	O'Rourke, Timothy Patrick "Voiceless Tim" b: 5/18/1864, Chicago, Ill. d: 4/20/38, Seattle, Wash. BL/TR, 5'10", 170 lbs. Deb: 5/27/1890 Career OF: (32-LF 1-CF 40-RF)																							
1890	Syr-a	87	332	48	94	13	6	1	46	36		.283	.360	.367	728	128	13	22			.866	-11	3-87	0.4
1891	Col-a	34	136	22	38	1	3	0	12	15	7	.279	.359	.331	690	104	1	9			.879	0	3-34	0.2
1892	Bal-N	63	239	40	74	8	4	0	35	24	19	.310	.373	.377	749	123	7	12			.869	-14	S-58/O-4(2-1-1),3-1	-0.4
1893	Bal-N	31	135	22	49	4	1	0	19	12	4	.363	.423	.407	830	119	4	5			.980	-4	O-25(25-0-0)/3-5,S-1	-0.2
	Lou-N	92	352	80	99	8	4	0	53	77	15	.281	.421	.327	748	108	12	22			.865	-21	S-60,O-26(4-0-22)/3-6	-0.5
	Yr	123	487	102	148	12	5	0	72	89	19	.304	.422	.349	771	112	16	27			.861	-25	S-61,O-51L,3-11	-0.7
1894	Lou-N	55	220	46	61	3	3	0	27	23	9	.277	.351	.318	669	67	-11	9			.977	-1	1-30,O-18R/S-3,32	-0.9
	StL-N	18	71	10	20	4	1	0	10	8	3	.282	.354	.366	721	74	-3	2			.861	-2	3-18	-0.4
	Was-N	7	25	4	5	2	1	0	2	2	1	.200	.259	.360	619	49	-2	0			.909	1	/2-4,S-3	-0.1
	Yr	80	316	60	86	9	5	0	39	33	13	.272	.345	.332	677	67	-16	11			.977	-2	1-30,3-21,O-18R,/S2	-1.4
Total	5	387	1510	272	440	43	23	1	204	197	58	.291	.380	.352	732	105	22	81			.861	-51	3-154,S-125/O-73R,12	-1.9
■ DAVE ORR	Orr, David L. b: 9/29/1859, New York, N.Y. d: 6/2/15, Richmond Hill, N.Y. BR/TR, 5'11", 250 lbs. Deb: 5/17/1883 M																							
1883	NY-a	1	4	1	1	1	0	0		0		.250	.250	.500	750	130	0				1.000	0	/1-1	0.0
	NY-N	1	3	0	0	0	0	0	0	0	1	.000	.000	.000	0	-99	-1				1.000	0	/O-1(1-0-0)	-0.1

YEAR	TM/L	G	AB	R	H	2B	3B	HR	RBI	BB	SO	AVG	OBP	SLG	OPS	OPS+	BR+	SB	CS	SBR	FA	FR	G/POS	TPR
	NY-a	12	46	5	15	3	3	2	11	0		.326	.326	.652	978	198	5				.938	-2	1-12	0.2
1884	*NY-a	110	458	82	**162**	32	13	9	112	5		**.354**	.362	.539	901	**195**	**45**				.960	-5	*1-110/O-3(0-0-3)	2.7
1885	NY-a	107	444	76	152	29	**21**	6	77	8		.342	.358	**.543**	901	**197**	47				.966	-3	*1-107/P-3	3.0
1886	NY-a	136	571	93	**193**	25	**31**	7	91	17		.338	.363	**.527**	**890**	**186**	**52**	16			**.981**	-0	*1-136	3.4
1887	NY-a	84	367	63	149	25	10	2	66	22		.406	.408	.516	924	164	29	17			.969	-1	1-81/O-3(0-3-0),M	1.6
1888	Bro-a	99	394	57	120	20	5	1	59	7		.305	.330	.388	718	130	12	11			.979	4	*1-99	0.6
1889	Col-a	134	560	70	183	31	12	4	87	9	38	.327	.340	.446	786	129	18	12			.983	9	*1-134	1.3
1890	Bro-P	107	464	89	172	32	13	6	124	30	11	.371	.414	.534	948	144	26	10			.972	-5	*1-107	0.9
Total	8	791	3311	536	1147	198	108	37	627	98	50	.346	.366	.502	867	162	233	66			.973	-3	1-787/O-7(1-3-3),P-3	13.6

■ BILLY ORR

Orr, William John b: 4/22/1891, San Francisco, Cal d: 3/10/67, St.Helena, Cal. BR/TR, 5′11″, 168 lbs. Deb: 5/3/13

YEAR	TM/L	G	AB	R	H	2B	3B	HR	RBI	BB	SO	AVG	OBP	SLG	OPS	OPS+	BR+	SB	CS	SBR	FA	FR	G/POS	TPR
1913	Phi-A	30	67	6	13	1	1	0	7	4	10	.194	.239	.239	478	41	-5	1			.967	-2	S-16/1-3,3-3,2-2	-0.6
1914	Phi-A	10	24	3	4	1	1	0	1	2	5	.167	.231	.292	522	59	-1	1	1	-0	.810	-4	/S-6,3-1	-0.6
Total	2	40	91	9	17	2	2	0	8	6	15	.187	.287	.253	490	46	-6	2	1		.927	-6	/S-22,3-4,1-3,2-2	-1.2

■ ERNIE ORSATTI

Orsatti, Ernest Ralph b: 9/8/02, Los Angeles, Cal. d: 9/4/68, Canoga Park, Cal. BL/TL, 5′7.5″, 154 lbs. Deb: 9/4/27 Career OF: (93-LF 281-CF 156-RF)

YEAR	TM/L	G	AB	R	H	2B	3B	HR	RBI	BB	SO	AVG	OBP	SLG	OPS	OPS+	BR+	SB	CS	SBR	FA	FR	G/POS	TPR
1927	StL-N	27	92	15	29	7	3	0	12	11	12	.315	.388	.457	845	122	3	2			.922	-1	O-26(0-6-20)	0.0
1928	*StL-N	27	69	10	21	6	0	3	15	10	11	.304	.400	.522	922	137	4	0			1.000	-2	O-17(2-0-15)/1-5	0.1
1929	StL-N	113	346	64	115	21	7	3	39	33	43	.332	.394	.460	853	110	6	7			.974	4	O-77(9-2-67),1-10	0.3
1930	*StL-N	48	131	24	42	8	4	1	15	12	18	.321	.382	.466	848	100	0	1			.985	4	1-22,O-11(0-0-11)	0.1
1931	*StL-N	70	158	27	46	16	6	0	19	14	16	.291	.349	.468	817	113	3	1			.988	-5	O-45(30-6-9)/1-1	-0.4
1932	StL-N	101	375	44	126	27	6	2	44	18	29	.336	.368	.456	824	117	9	5			.976	-9	O-96(40-55-1)/1-1	-0.4
1933	StL-N	120	436	55	130	21	6	0	38	33	33	.298	.348	.374	721	101	1	14			.986	2	*O-107(6-96-5)/1-3	-0.1
1934	*StL-N	105	337	39	101	14	4	0	31	27	31	.300	.353	.365	718	87	-5	6			.986	-2	O-90(0-90-0)	-0.9
1935	StL-N	90	221	28	53	9	3	1	24	18	25	.240	.297	.321	618	64	-11	10			.975	-5	O-60(6-26-28)	-1.8
Total	9	701	2165	306	663	129	39	10	237	176	218	.306	.360	.416	776	102	9	46			.979	-14	O-529C/1-42	-3.1

■ JOHN ORSINO

Orsino, John Joseph "Horse" b: 4/22/38, Teaneck, N.J. BR/TR, 6′3″, 215 lbs. Deb: 7/14/61

YEAR	TM/L	G	AB	R	H	2B	3B	HR	RBI	BB	SO	AVG	OBP	SLG	OPS	OPS+	BR+	SB	CS	SBR	FA	FR	G/POS	TPR
1961	SF-N	25	83	5	23	3	2	4	12	3	13	.277	.310	.506	816	116	1	0	0	0	.959	-3	C-25	0.0
1962	*SF-N	18	48	4	13	2	0	0	4	5	11	.271	.340	.313	652	78	-1	0	0	0	.963	-2	C-16	-0.2
1963	Bal-A	116	379	53	103	18	1	19	56	38	53	.272	.352	.475	827	134	17	2	3	-1	.990	-7	*C-109/1-3	1.6
1964	Bal-A	81	248	21	55	10	0	8	23	23	55	.222	.293	.359	652	81	-7	0	0	0	.976	1	C-66/1-5	-0.3
1965	Bal-A	77	232	30	54	10	2	9	28	23	51	.233	.315	.409	725	102	1	1	0	0	.987	-8	C-62/1-5	-0.4
1966	Was-A	14	23	1	4	1	0	0	0	0	7	.174	.174	.217	391	12	-3	0	0	0	1.000	-0	/1-5,C-2	-0.3
1967	Was-A	1	1	0	0	0	0	0	0	0	1	.000	.000	.000	0	-99	-0	0	0	0	.000	0	H	0.0
Total	7	332	1014	114	252	44	5	40	123	92	191	.249	.321	.420	742	106	8	3	3	-0	.982	-18	C-280/1-18	0.4

■ JOE ORSULAK

Orsulak, Joseph Michael b: 5/31/62, Glen Ridge, N.J. BL/TL, 6′1″, 196 lbs. Deb: 9/1/83 Career OF: (449-LF 216-CF 669-RF)

YEAR	TM/L	G	AB	R	H	2B	3B	HR	RBI	BB	SO	AVG	OBP	SLG	OPS	OPS+	BR+	SB	CS	SBR	FA	FR	G/POS	TPR
1983	Pit-N	7	11	0	2	0	0	0	1	0	2	.182	.182	.182	364	1	-1	0	1	-0	1.000	0	/O-4(0-4-0)	-0.2
1984	Pit-N	32	67	12	17	1	2	0	3	1	7	.254	.275	.328	604	69	-3	3	1	0	1.000	-1	O-25(7-12-5)	-0.5
1985	Pit-N	121	397	54	119	14	6	0	21	26	27	.300	.344	.365	710	100	-0	24	11	1	.976	-0	*O-115(41-72-16)	-0.2
1986	Pit-N	138	401	60	100	19	6	2	19	28	38	.249	.300	.342	642	75	-14	24	11	1	.981	-5	*O-120(9-46-73)	-2.2
1988	Bal-A	125	379	48	109	21	3	8	27	23	30	.288	.333	.422	755	113	6	9	8	-1	.979	-6	*O-117(36-14-76)	-0.4
1989	Bal-A	123	390	59	111	22	5	7	55	41	35	.285	.356	.421	776	122	11	5	3	0	.985	7	*O-109(20-0-91)/D-5	1.5
1990	Bal-A	124	413	49	111	14	3	11	57	46	48	.269	.343	.397	741	110	6	6	8	-1	.989	11	*O-109(30-0-80)/D-5	1.2
1991	Bal-A	143	486	57	135	22	1	5	43	28	45	.278	.322	.358	680	92	-6	6	2	1	.997	10	*O-132(85-1-68)/D-2	0.1
1992	Bal-A	117	391	45	113	18	3	4	39	28	34	.289	.343	.381	724	100	0	5	4	-0	.983	4	*O-110(14-0-98)/D-1	0.1
1993	NY-N	134	409	59	116	15	4	8	35	28	25	.284	.333	.399	731	96	-3	5	4	-0	.978	-6	*O-114(66-40-23)/1-4	-1.2
1994	NY-N	96	292	39	76	3	0	8	42	16	21	.260	.305	.353	658	72	-12	4	2	0	.979	-8	O-90(18-13-63)/1-6	-2.4
1995	NY-N	108	290	41	82	19	2	1	37	19	35	.283	.329	.372	701	87	-5	1	3	-1	.965	-8	O-86(56-0-31)/1-1	-1.7
1996	Fla-N	120	217	23	48	6	1	2	19	16	38	.221	.275	.286	560	50	-16	1	1	-0	.956	-3	O-59(30-14-19)/1-2	-2.0
1997	Mon-N	106	150	13	34	12	1	1	7	18	17	.227	.310	.340	650	70	-7	0	1	-0	1.000	-12	O-63L,1-15/D-1	-2.1
Total	14	1494	4293	559	1173	186	37	57	405	318	402	.273	.327	.374	700	93	-44	93	60	-1	.982	-18	*O-1253R/1-28,D-14	-10.0

■ JORGE ORTA

Orta, Jorge (Nunez) b: 11/26/50, Mazatlan, Mexico BL/TR, 5′10″, 175 lbs. Deb: 4/15/72 Career OF: (96-LF 3-CF 246-RF)

YEAR	TM/L	G	AB	R	H	2B	3B	HR	RBI	BB	SO	AVG	OBP	SLG	OPS	OPS+	BR+	SB	CS	SBR	FA	FR	G/POS	TPR
1972	Chi-A	51	124	20	25	3	1	3	11	6	37	.202	.244	.315	559	64	-6	3	3	-0	.958	-0	S-18,2-14/3-9	-0.4
1973	Chi-A	128	425	46	113	9	10	6	40	37	87	.266	.326	.376	703	94	-3	8	8	-1	.969	-27	*2-122/S-1	-2.4
1974	Chi-A	139	525	73	166	31	2	10	67	40	88	.316	.368	.440	808	128	19	9	5	0	.971	-13	*2-123,D-10/S-3	1.5
1975	Chi-A†	140	542	64	165	26	10	11	83	48	67	.304	.365	.450	816	128	19	16	9	0	.978	-12	*2-135/D-2	1.7
1976	Chi-A	158	636	74	174	29	8	14	72	38	77	.274	.320	.410	730	112	8	24	8	2	.971	2	O-77L,3-49,D-31	0.6
1977	Chi-A	144	564	71	159	27	8	11	84	46	49	.282	.338	.417	755	105	3	4	4	-1	.970	-47	*2-139	-3.7
1978	Chi-A	117	420	45	115	19	2	13	53	42	39	.274	.345	.421	767	114	8	1	2	-0	.984	-22	*2-114/D-2	-0.9
1979	Chi-A	113	325	49	85	18	3	11	46	44	33	.262	.351	.437	788	111	5	1	5	-2	.978	-11	D-62,2-41	-0.7
1980	Cle-A☆	129	481	78	140	18	3	10	64	71	44	.291	.384	.403	788	116	13	6	5	-0	.982	13	*O-120(0-2-118)/D-7	1.9
1981	Cle-A	88	338	50	92	14	3	5	34	21	43	.272	.317	.376	692	100	-0	4	3	-0	.994	4	O-86(0-1-86)	-0.1
1982	LA-N	86	115	13	25	5	0	2	8	12	13	.217	.297	.313	610	73	-4	0	1	-0	.947	1	O-17(1-0-16)	-0.4
1983	Tor-A	103	245	30	58	6	3	10	38	19	29	.237	.292	.408	700	85	-5	1	2	-0	1.000	-3	D-70,O-17(5-0-12)	-1.1
1984	*KC-A	122	403	50	120	23	7	9	50	28	39	.298	.346	.457	803	119	10	0	1	-0	.980	-3	D-83,O-26L/2-1	0.3
1985	*KC-A	110	300	32	80	21	1	4	45	22	28	.267	.321	.383	704	92	-4	2	1	0	.000	0	D-85	-0.6
1986	KC-A	106	336	35	93	14	2	9	46	23	34	.277	.323	.411	734	96	-2	0	3	-1	.000	0	D-87	-0.6
1987	KC-A	21	50	3	9	4	0	2	4	3	8	.180	.226	.380	606	55	-3	0	0	0	.000	0	D-12	-0.4
Total	16	1755	5829	733	1619	267	63	130	745	500	715	.278	.338	.412	750	108	57	79	60	-4	.974	-118	2-689,D-451,O/3S	-5.3

■ FRANK ORTENZIO

Ortenzio, Frank Joseph b: 2/24/51, Fresno, Cal. BR/TR, 6′2″, 215 lbs. Deb: 9/9/73

YEAR	TM/L	G	AB	R	H	2B	3B	HR	RBI	BB	SO	AVG	OBP	SLG	OPS	OPS+	BR+	SB	CS	SBR	FA	FR	G/POS	TPR
1973	KC-A	9	25	1	7	2	0	1	6	2	6	.280	.333	.480	813	118	1	0	0	0	.983	1	/1-7,D-1	0.1

■ AL ORTH

Orth, Albert Lewis "Smiling Al" or "The Curveless Wonder" b: 9/5/1872, Tipton, Ind. d: 10/8/48, Lynchburg, Va. BL/TR, 6′, 200 lbs. Deb: 8/15/1895 U Career OF: (20-LF 21-CF 14-RF)

YEAR	TM/L	G	AB	R	H	2B	3B	HR	RBI	BB	SO	AVG	OBP	SLG	OPS	OPS+	BR+	SB	CS	SBR	FA	FR	G/POS	TPR
1895	Phi-N	11	45	8	16	4	0	1	13	1	6	.356	.370	.511	881	125	1	0			.842	-1	P-11	0.0
1896	Phi-N	25	82	12	21	3	3	1	13	3	11	.256	.282	.402	685	80	-3	2			.901	1	P-25	0.0
1897	Phi-N	53	152	26	50	7	4	1	17	3		.329	.342	.447	789	110	1	5			.929	0	P-36/O-6(3-3-0)	0.0
1898	Phi-N	39	123	17	36	6	4	1	14	3		.293	.310	.431	740	117	2	1			.959	1	P-32/O-1(0-0-1)	0.1
1899	Phi-N	22	62	5	13	3	1	1	5	1		.210	.222	.339	561	55	-4	2			.793	-4	P-21/O-1(1-0-0)	0.0
1900	Phi-N	39	129	6	40	4	1	1	21	2		.310	.326	.380	706	95	-1	2			.943	1	P-33/O-3(0-3-0)	0.0
1901	Phi-N	41	128	14	36	6	0	1	15	3		.281	.303	.352	655	88	-2	3			.945	1	P-35/O-4(0-4-0)	-0.1
1902	Was-A	56	175	20	38	3	2	2	10	9		.217	.255	.291	547	51	-12	2			.923	-0	P-38,O-13R/1-1,S-1	-0.4
1903	Was-A	55	162	19	49	9	7	0	11	4		.302	.323	.444	768	126	4	3			.920	-2	P-36/S-7,O-4L,1-2	-0.1
1904	Was-A	31	102	7	22	3	1	0	11	1		.216	.238	.265	503	60	-5	2			.816	-2	O-18(12-6-0),P-10	-0.8
	NY-A	24	64	6	19	1	1	0	7	0		.297	.308	.344	651	101	-0	2			.968	1	P-20/O-2(0-1-1)	0.0
	Yr	55	166	13	41	4	2	0	18	1		.247	.265	.295	560	76	-5	4			.969	-2	P-30,O-20(12-7-1)	-0.8
1905	NY-A	55	131	13	24	3	1	1	8	4		.183	.213	.244	458	40	-9	2			.940	-0	P-40/1-1,O-1(0-0-1)	-0.1
1906	NY-A	47	135	12	37	2	2	1	17	6		.274	.305	.341	646	93	-1	2			.934	0	P-45/O-1(0-0-1)	0.1
1907	NY-A	44	105	11	34	6	0	1	13	4		.324	.355	.410	764	133	4	1			.920	2	P-36/O-1(1-0-0)	0.0
1908	NY-A	38	69	4	20	1	2	0	4	2		.290	.310	.362	672	117	1	0			.980	-1	P-21	0.0
1909	NY-A	22	34	3	9	0	1	0	5	5		.265	.359	.324	683	115	1	1			1.000	-2	/2-6,P-1	-0.1
Total	15	602	1698	183	464	61	30	12	184	51	17	.273	.298	.366	663	91	-24	30			.932	-5	P-440/O-55C,S-8,21	-1.4

■ JUNIOR ORTIZ

Ortiz, Adalberto Colon b: 10/24/59, Humacao, P.R. BR/TR, 5′11″, 176 lbs. Deb: 9/20/82

YEAR	TM/L	G	AB	R	H	2B	3B	HR	RBI	BB	SO	AVG	OBP	SLG	OPS	OPS+	BR+	SB	CS	SBR	FA	FR	G/POS	TPR
1982	Pit-N	7	15	1	3	1	0	0	0	1	3	.200	.250	.267	517	43	-1	0	0	0	1.000	1	/C-7	0.0
1983	Pit-N	5	8	1	1	0	0	0	0	1	0	.125	.222	.125	347	-1	-1	0	0	0	1.000	0	/C-4	-0.1
	NY-N	68	185	10	47	5	0	0	12	3	34	.254	.270	.281	551	53	-12	1	0	0	.965	1	C-67	-0.9

YEAR	TM/L	G	AB	R	H	2B	3B	HR	RBI	BB	SO	AVG	OBP	SLG	OPS	OPS+	BR+	SB	CS	SBR	FA	FR	G/POS	TPR
	Yr	73	193	11	48	5	0	0	12	4	34	.249	.268	.275	542	51	-13	1	0	0	.967	1	C-71	-1.0
1984	NY-N	40	91	6	18	3	0	0	11	5	15	.198	.240	.231	470	33	-8	1	0	0	.980	-4	C-32	-1.1
1985	Pit-N	23	72	4	21	2	0	1	5	3	17	.292	.320	.361	681	91	-1	1	0	0	.985	1	C-23	0.1
1986	Pit-N	49	110	11	37	6	0	0	14	9	13	.336	.387	.391	777	112	2	0	1	-0	.983	-1	C-36	0.2
1987	Pit-N	75	192	16	52	8	1	1	22	15	23	.271	.324	.339	662	75	-7	0	2	-1	.975	-0	C-72	-0.5
1988	Pit-N	49	118	8	33	6	0	2	18	9	9	.280	.341	.381	722	109	1	1	4	-1	.983	-2	C-40	0.0
1989	Pit-N	91	230	16	50	6	1	1	22	20	20	.217	.286	.265	551	61	-12	2	2	-0	.995	-10	C-84	-1.9
1990	Min-A	71	170	18	57	7	1	0	18	12	16	.335	.386	.388	774	110	3	0	4	-1	1.000	2	C-68/D-3	0.6
1991	*Min-A	61	134	9	28	5	1	0	11	15	12	.209	.293	.261	555	52	-8	0	1	-0	.995	-0	C-60	-0.7
1992	Cle-A	86	244	20	61	7	0	0	24	12	23	.250	.296	.279	575	63	-12	1	3	-1	.989	-1	C-86	-1.0
1993	Cle-A	95	249	19	55	13	0	0	20	11	26	.221	.268	.273	541	46	-19	1	0	0	.990	11	C-95	-0.3
1994	Tex-A	29	76	3	21	2	0	0	9	5	11	.276	.329	.303	632	65	-4	0	1	-0	.992	-1	C-28	-0.4
Total	13	749	1894	142	484	71	4	5	186	121	222	.256	.306	.305	612	69	-78	8	18	-5	.986	-4	C-702/D-3	-6.0
■ DAVID ORTIZ	Ortiz, David Americo (Arias) b: 11/18/75, Santo Domingo, D.R. BL/TL, 6'4", 230 lbs. Deb: 9/2/97																							
1997	Min-A	15	49	10	16	3	0	1	6	2	19	.327	.353	.449	802	106	0	0	0	0	.989	1	1-11/D-1	0.0
1998	Min-A	86	278	47	77	20	0	9	46	39	72	.277	.376	.446	822	111	5	1	0	0	.989	0	1-70,D-10	-0.1
1999	Min-A	10	20	1	0	0	0	0	0	5	12	.000	.200	.000	200	-41	-4	0	0	0	1.000	-0	/1-1,D-5	-0.4
2000	Min-A	130	415	59	117	36	1	10	63	57	81	.282	.369	.446	814	100	0	1	0	0	.996	-1	D-88,1-27	-0.7
Total	4	241	762	117	210	59	1	20	115	103	184	.276	.366	.434	800	100	2	2	0	0	.991	-0	1-109,D-104	-1.2
■ HECTOR ORTIZ	Ortiz, Hector (Montanez) b: 10/14/69, Rio Piedras, P.R. BR/TR, 6', 205 lbs. Deb: 9/14/98																							
1998	KC-A	4	4	1	0	0	0	0	0	0	0	.000	.000	.000	0	-97	-1	0	0	0	1.000	-1	/C-3,1-1	-0.2
2000	KC-A	26	88	15	34	6	0	0	5	8	8	.386	.443	.455	898	127	4	0	0	0	.993	-2	C-26	0.4
Total	2	30	92	16	34	6	0	0	5	8	8	.370	.426	.435	861	118	3	0	0	0	.993	-2	/C-29,1-1	0.2
■ JAVIER ORTIZ	Ortiz, Javier Victor b: 1/22/63, Boston, Mass. BR/TR, 6'4", 220 lbs. Deb: 6/15/90																							
1990	Hou-N	30	77	7	21	5	1	1	10	12	11	.273	.371	.403	773	116	2	1	1	-0	.978	-3	O-25(20-1-9)	-0.2
1991	Hou-N	47	83	7	23	4	1	1	5	14	14	.277	.381	.386	767	123	3	0	0	0	1.000	-3	O-24(15-0-11)	0.0
Total	2	77	160	14	44	9	2	2	15	26	25	.275	.376	.394	770	120	5	1	1	-0	.987	-6	/O-49(35-1-20)	-0.2
■ JOSE ORTIZ	Ortiz, Jose Daniel (Santos) b: 6/13/77, Santo Domingo, D.R. BR/TR, 5'9", 160 lbs. Deb: 9/15/2000																							
2000	Oak-A	7	11	4	2	0	0	0	1	2	3	.182	.308	.182	490	29	-1	0	0	0	.857	-1	/2-3,D-4	-0.1
■ JOSE ORTIZ	Ortiz, Jose Luis (Irizarry) b: 6/25/47, Ponce, P.R. BR/TR, 5'9.5", 155 lbs. Deb: 9/4/69																							
1969	Chi-A	16	11	0	3	1	0	0	2	1	0	.273	.333	.364	697	90	-0	0	0	0	1.000	-2	/O-8(2-5-2)	-0.2
1970	Chi-A	15	24	4	8	1	0	0	1	2	2	.333	.407	.375	782	113	1	1	0	0	1.000	1	/O-8(1-5-2)	0.2
1971	Chi-N	36	88	10	26	7	1	0	3	4	10	.295	.347	.398	745	96	-0	2	2	-0	1.000	-2	O-30(0-29-1)	-0.3
Total	3	67	123	14	37	9	1	0	6	7	12	.301	.358	.390	748	99	0	3	2	-0	1.000	-3	/O-46(3-39-5)	-0.3
■ LUIS ORTIZ	Ortiz, Luis Alberto (Galarza) b: 5/25/70, Santo Domingo, D.R. BR/TR, 6', 190 lbs. Deb: 8/31/93																							
1993	Bos-A	9	12	0	3	0	0	0	1	0	2	.250	.250	.250	500	33	-1	0	0	0	1.000	1	/3-5,D-3	-0.1
1994	Bos-A	7	18	3	3	2	0	0	6	1	5	.167	.211	.278	488	23	-2	0	0	0	.000	0	/D-6	-0.2
1995	Tex-A	41	108	10	25	5	2	1	18	6	18	.231	.272	.343	615	57	-7	0	1	-0	.867	-5	3-35/D-3	-1.1
1996	Tex-A	3	7	1	2	0	1	1	1	0	1	.286	.286	1.000	1286	196	1	0	0	0	.000	0	/D-1	0.1
Total	4	60	145	14	33	7	3	2	26	7	26	.228	.263	.359	622	58	-9	0	1	-0	.875	-4	/3-40,D-13	-1.3
■ ROBERTO ORTIZ	Ortiz, Roberto Gonzalo (Nunez) b: 6/30/15, Camaguey, Cuba d: 9/15/71, Miami, Fla. BR/TR, 6'4", 200 lbs. Deb: 9/6/41 F																							
1941	Was-A	22	79	10	26	1	2	1	17	3	10	.329	.354	.430	784	112	1	0	1	-0	.860	-2	O-21(0-0-21)	-0.2
1942	Was-A	20	42	4	7	1	3	1	4	5	11	.167	.271	.405	676	89	-1	0	0	0	.941	-1	/O-9(1-0-8)	-0.2
1943	Was-A	1	4	0	1	0	0	0	0	0	0	.250	.250	.250	500	48	-0	0	1	-0	1.000	0	/O-1(0-0-1)	-0.1
1944	Was-A	85	316	36	80	11	4	5	35	19	47	.253	.312	.361	673	96	-2	4	1	1	.949	-3	O-80(10-0-71)	-1.1
1949	Was-A	40	129	12	36	3	0	1	11	9	12	.279	.326	.326	652	74	-5	0	0	0	.946	-1	O-32(4-0-28)	-0.7
1950	Was-A	39	75	4	17	2	1	0	8	7	12	.227	.301	.280	581	52	-5	0	0	0	1.000	-3	O-19(0-0-19)	-0.8
	Phi-A	6	14	1	1	0	0	0	3	0	3	.071	.071	.071	143	-65	-3	0	0	0	1.000	-1	/O-3(1-0-3)	-0.4
	Yr	45	89	5	18	2	1	0	11	7	15	.202	.268	.247	515	34	-9	0	0	0	1.000	-3	O-22(1-0-22)	-1.2
Total	6	213	659	67	168	18	10	8	78	43	95	.255	.310	.349	659	84	-16	4	3	-0	.942	-10	O-165(16-0-151)	-3.5
■ JOHN ORTON	Orton, John Andrew b: 12/8/65, Santa Cruz, Cal. BR/TR, 6'1", 192 lbs. Deb: 8/20/89																							
1989	Cal-A	16	39	4	7	1	0	0	4	2	17	.179	.220	.205	425	21	-4	0	0	0	.988	5	C-16	0.1
1990	Cal-A	31	84	8	16	5	0	1	6	5	31	.190	.244	.286	530	49	-6	0	1	-0	.987	1	C-31	-0.4
1991	Cal-A	29	69	7	14	4	0	0	3	10	17	.203	.313	.261	573	60	-3	0	1	-0	.994	9	C-28/D-1	0.6
1992	Cal-A	43	114	11	25	3	0	2	12	7	32	.219	.276	.298	575	61	-6	1	1	-0	.981	8	C-43	0.4
1993	Cal-A	37	95	5	18	5	0	1	4	7	24	.189	.252	.274	526	40	-8	1	2	-0	.980	5	C-35/O-1(1-0-0)	-0.2
Total	5	156	401	35	80	18	0	4	29	31	121	.200	.265	.274	540	49	-28	2	5	-1	.985	28	C-153/O-1(1-0-0),D-1	0.5
■ OSSIE ORWOLL	Orwoll, Oswald Christian b: 11/17/1900, Portland, Ore. d: 5/8/67, Decorah, Iowa BL/TL, 6', 174 lbs. Deb: 4/13/28																							
1928	Phi-A	64	170	28	52	13	2	0	22	16	24	.306	.366	.406	771	100	0	3	1	0	.983	-1	1-34,P-27	-0.2
1929	Phi-A	30	51	6	13	2	1	0	6	2	11	.255	.283	.333	616	56	-3	0	0	0	1.000	-2	P-12/O-9(1-8-0)	-0.4
Total	2	94	221	34	65	15	3	0	28	18	35	.294	.347	.389	736	90	-3	3	1	0	.970	-3	/P-39,1-34,O-9(1-8-0)	-0.6
■ FRED OSBORN	Osborn, Wilfred Pearl "Ossie" b: 11/28/1883, Nevada, Ohio d: 9/2/54, Upper Sandusky, O. BL/TR, 5'9", 178 lbs. Deb: 6/8/07																							
1907	Phi-N	56	163	22	45	2	3	0	9	3		.276	.298	.325	623	97	-1	4			1.000	-4	O-36(8-26-1)/1-1	-0.8
1908	Phi-N	152	555	62	148	19	12	2	44	30		.267	.305	.355	660	107	3	16			.969	2	*O-152(0-146-6)	-0.3
1909	Phi-N	58	189	14	35	4	1	0	19	12		.185	.238	.217	455	41	-13	6			.979	10	O-54(0-54-0)	-0.7
Total	3	266	907	98	228	25	16	2	72	45		.251	.290	.321	611	91	-12	26			.975	8	O-242(8-226-7)/1-1	-1.8
■ FRED OSBORNE	Osborne, Frederick W. b: Hampton, Iowa TL, Deb: 7/14/1890																							
1890	Pit-N	41	168	24	40	8	3	1	14	6	18	.238	.269	.339	608	87	-3	0			.828	1	O-35(28-1-6)/P-8	-0.2
■ BOBO OSBORNE	Osborne, Lawrence Sidney b: 10/12/35, Chattahoochee, Ga. BL/TR, 6'1", 205 lbs. Deb: 6/27/57 F Career OF: (0-LF 0-CF 6-RF)																							
1957	Det-A	11	27	4	4	1	0	0	1	3	7	.148	.233	.185	419	15	-3	0	0	0	1.000	-1	/O-5(0-0-5),1-4	-0.4
1958	Det-A	2	2	0	0	0	0	0	0	0	0	.000	.000	.000	0	-93	-1	0	0	0	.000	0	H	-0.1
1959	Det-A	86	209	27	40	7	1	3	21	16	41	.191	.256	.278	533	44	-16	1	0	0	.983	-1	1-56/O-1(0-0-1)	-2.0
1961	Det-A	71	93	8	20	7	0	2	13	20	15	.215	.354	.355	709	88	-1	1	0	0	.957	-2	/3-8,1-11	-0.4
1962	Det-A	64	74	12	17	1	0	0	7	16	25	.230	.374	.243	617	68	-2	0	0	0	.857	-2	3-13/1-7,C-1	-0.4
1963	Was-A	125	358	42	76	14	1	12	44	49	83	.212	.312	.358	670	87	-6	0	0	0	.988	-3	1-81,3-16	-1.5
Total	6	359	763	93	157	30	2	17	86	104	171	.206	.306	.317	623	71	-29	2	0	0	.987	-9	1-159/3-37,O-6R,C-1	-4.8
■ KEITH OSIK	Osik, Keith Richard b: 10/22/68, Port Jefferson, N.Y. BR/TR, 6', 185 lbs. Deb: 4/5/96 Career OF: (2-LF 0-CF 0-RF)																							
1996	Pit-N	48	140	18	41	14	1	1	14	14	22	.293	.361	.429	790	105	1	1	0	0	.977	-3	C-41/3-2,O-2(2-0-0)	0.1
1997	Pit-N	49	105	10	27	9	1	0	7	9	21	.257	.322	.362	684	77	-3	0	1	-0	.989	-3	C-32/2-4,1-1,3-1	-0.5
1998	Pit-N	39	98	8	21	4	0	0	7	13	16	.214	.319	.255	574	53	-6	1	2	-0	1.000	6	C-26/3-7	0.1
1999	Pit-N	66	167	12	31	3	1	2	13	11	30	.186	.240	.251	492	25	-19	0	0	0	.997	0	C-50/P-1	-1.6
2000	Pit-N	46	123	11	36	6	1	4	22	14	11	.293	.387	.455	843	113	3	3	0	1	.992	-3	C-26,3-12/1-5,PD	0.2
Total	5	248	633	59	156	36	4	7	63	61	100	.246	.322	.349	672	73	-25	5	3	0	.990	-2	C-175/3-22,1-6,2POD	-1.7
■ HARRY OSTDIEK	Ostdiek, Henry Girard b: 4/12/1881, Ottumwa, Iowa d: 5/6/56, Minneapolis, Minn. BR/TR, 5'11", 185 lbs. Deb: 9/10/04																							
1904	Cle-A	7	18	1	3	0	1	0	3	3		.167	.318	.278	596	90	-0	1			.946	-0	/C-7	0.0
1908	Bos-A	1	3	0	0	0	0	0	0	0		.000	.000	.000	0	-97	-1	0			.889	0	/C-1	0.0
Total	2	8	21	1	3	0	1	0	3	3		.143	.280	.238	518	65	-1	1			.935	0	/C-8	0.0

YEAR	TM/L	G	AB	R	H	2B	3B	HR	RBI	BB	SO	AVG	OBP	SLG	OPS	OPS+	BR+	SB	CS	SBR	FA	FR	G/POS	TPR
■ CHAMP OSTEEN	Osteen, James Champlin b: 2/24/1877, Hendersonville, N.C. d: 12/14/62, Greenville, S.C. BL/TR, 5'8", 150 lbs. Deb: 9/18/03																							
1903	Was-A	10	40	4	8	0	2	0	4	2		.200	.256	.300	556	65	-2	0			.938	1	S-10	-0.1
1904	NY-A	28	107	15	21	1	4	2	9	1		.196	.218	.336	555	71	-4	0			.930	-2	3-17/S-8,1-4	-0.6
1908	StL-N	29	112	2	22	4	0	0	11	0		.196	.204	.232	436	41	-8	0			.847	-6	S-17,3-12	-1.6
1909	StL-N	16	45	6	9	1	0	0	7	7		.200	.308	.222	530	69	-1	1			.879	-6	S-16	-0.8
Total	4	83	304	27	60	6	6	2	31	10		.197	.233	.276	509	60	-15	1			.890	-13	/S-51,3-29,1-4	-3.1
■ RED OSTERGARD	Ostergard, Roy Lund b: 5/16/1896, Denmark, Wis. d: 1/13/77, Hemet, Cal. BR/TR, 5'10.5", 175 lbs. Deb: 6/14/21																							
1921	Chi-A	12	11	2	4	0	0	0	0	0	2	.364	.364	.364	727	87	-0	0	0	0	.000	0	H	0.0
■ CHARLIE OSTERHOUT	Osterhout, Charles H. b: 1856, Syracuse, N.Y. d: 5/21/33, Syracuse, N.Y. TR, Deb: 6/23/1879																							
1879	Syr-N	2	8	0	0	0	0	0	0	0	0	.000	.000	.000	0	-99	-2				1.000	-0	/O-1(0-1-0),C-1	-0.2
■ BRIAN OSTROSSER	Ostrosser, Brian Leonard b: 6/17/49, Hamilton, Ont., Can BL/TR, 6', 175 lbs. Deb: 8/5/73																							
1973	NY-N	4	5	0	0	0	0	0	0	0	2	.000	.000	.000	0	-99	-1	0	0	0	1.000	-0	/S-4	-0.2
■ JOHNNY OSTROWSKI	Ostrowski, John Thaddeus b: 10/17/17, Chicago, Ill. d: 11/13/92, Chicago, Ill. BR/TR, 5'10.5", 170 lbs. Deb: 9/24/43 Career OF: (87-LF 9-CF 15-RF)																							
1943	Chi-N	10	29	2	6	0	1	0	3	3	8	.207	.303	.276	579	69	-1	0			1.000	-2	/O-5(5-0-0),3-4	-0.4
1944	Chi-N	8	13	2	2	1	0	0	2	1	4	.154	.214	.231	445	25	-1	0			.500	-1	/O-2(2-0-0)	-0.2
1945	Chi-N	7	10	4	3	2	0	0	1	0	0	.300	.300	.500	800	123	0	0			.750	-1	/3-4	-0.1
1946	Chi-N	64	160	20	34	4	2	3	12	20	31	.213	.300	.319	619	77	-5	1			.934	1	3-50/2-1	-0.4
1948	Bos-A	1	1	0	0	0	0	0	0	0	1	.000	.000	.000	0	-95	-0	0	0	0	.000	0	H	0.0
1949	Chi-A	49	158	19	42	9	4	5	31	15	41	.266	.333	.468	802	115	2	4	3	-0	.944	-4	O-41(40-0-3)/3-8	-0.4
1950	Chi-A	21	45	9	10	1	1	2	2	9	8	.222	.364	.422	786	104	0	0	0	0	1.000	-1	O-14(6-1-8)	-0.1
	Was-A	55	141	16	32	2	1	4	23	20	31	.227	.327	.340	668	75	-5	2	0	0	.947	-0	O-45(34-7-4)	-0.7
	Chi-A	1	4	1	2	1	0	0	0	0	1	.500	.500	.750	1250	223	1	0	0	0	1.000	-0	/O-1(0-1-0)	0.0
	Yr	77	190	26	44	4	2	6	25	29	40	.232	.339	.368	708	85	-4	2	0	0	.958	-2	O-60(40-9-12)	-0.8
Total	7	216	561	73	131	20	9	14	74	68	125	.234	.321	.376	697	89	-10	7	3		.950	-9	O-108L/3-66,2-1	-2.3
■ WILLIS OTANEZ	Otanez, Willis Alexander b: 4/19/73, Las Vega Baja, D.R. BR/TR, 6'1", 200 lbs. Deb: 8/25/98 Career OF: (0-LF 0-CF 2-RF)																							
1998	Bal-A	3	5	0	1	0	0	0	0	0	2	.200	.200	.200	400	5	-1	0	0	0	1.000	-1	/O-2(0-0-2)	-0.1
1999	Bal-A	29	80	7	17	3	0	2	11	6	16	.213	.276	.325	601	55	-6	0	0	0	.917	-1	3-22/1-5,D-3	-0.6
	Tor-A	42	127	21	32	8	0	5	13	9	30	.252	.307	.433	740	85	-3	0	0	0	.953	-2	3-24,1-13/D-4	-0.6
	Yr	71	207	28	49	11	0	7	24	15	46	.237	.295	.391	686	73	-9	0	0	0	.934	-3	3-46,1-18/D-7	-1.2
Total	2	74	212	28	50	11	0	7	24	15	48	.236	.293	.387	679	72	-10	0	0	0	.917	-4	/3-46,1-18,D-7,O-2R	-1.3
■ REGGIE OTERO	Otero, Regino Jose (Gomez) b: 9/7/15, Havana, Cuba d: 10/21/88, Hialeah, Fla. BL/TR, 6', 165 lbs. Deb: 9/2/45 C																							
1945	Chi-N	14	23	1	9	0	0	0	5	2	2	.391	.440	.391	831	135	1	0			.967	0	/1-8	0.1
■ RICKY OTERO	Otero, Ricardo (Figueroa) b: 4/15/72, Vega Baja, P.R. BB/TR, 5'7", 150 lbs. Deb: 4/26/95																							
1995	NY-N	35	51	5	7	2	0	0	1	3	10	.137	.185	.176	362	-4	-8	2	1	0	1.000	-2	O-23(15-9-0)	-1.0
1996	Phi-N	104	411	54	112	11	7	2	32	34	30	.273	.331	.348	679	79	-12	16	10	0	.985	13	*O-100(0-100-0)	0.2
1997	Phi-N	50	151	20	38	6	2	0	3	19	15	.252	.339	.318	657	73	-5	0	3	-1	1.000	6	O-42(1-40-1)	0.0
Total	3	189	613	79	157	19	9	2	36	56	55	.256	.321	.326	648	71	-25	18	14	-1	.990	16	O-165(16-149-1)	-0.8
■ AMOS OTIS	Otis, Amos Joseph b: 4/26/47, Mobile, Ala. BR/TR, 5'11", 166 lbs. Deb: 9/6/67 C Career OF: (63-LF 1825-CF 46-RF)																							
1967	NY-N	19	59	6	13	2	0	0	1	5	13	.220	.292	.254	547	59	-3	0	4	-1	1.000	-2	O-16(2-14-3)/3-1	-0.8
1969	NY-N	48	93	6	14	3	1	0	4	6	27	.151	.202	.204	406	14	-11	1	0	0	1.000	-2	O-35(16-18-1)/3-3	-1.5
1970	KC-A★	159	620	91	176	**36**	9	11	58	68	67	.284	.356	.424	780	114	12	33	2	**7**	.990	14	*O-159(0-159-0)	2.9
1971	KC-A★	147	555	80	167	26	4	15	79	40	74	.301	.350	.443	793	125	16	**52**	8	**9**	.990	20	*O-144(0-144-0)	4.3
1972	KC-A†	143	540	75	158	28	2	11	54	50	59	.293	.356	.413	769	129	19	28	12	2	.992	10	*O-137(0-137-0)	3.0
1973	KC-A★	148	583	89	175	21	4	26	93	63	47	.300	.369	.484	853	129	22	13	9	-0	.986	3	*O-135(0-135-0),D-14	2.1
1974	KC-A	146	552	87	157	31	9	12	73	58	67	.284	.355	.438	793	120	14	18	5	2	.986	10	*O-143(0-143-0)/D-2	2.3
1975	KC-A	132	470	87	116	26	6	9	46	66	48	.247	.344	.385	730	103	3	39	11	5	.988	3	*O-130(0-130-0)	0.7
1976	*KC-A★	153	592	93	165	**40**	2	18	86	55	100	.279	.345	.444	789	129	21	26	7	3	.992	-5	*O-152(0-152-0)	1.6
1977	*KC-A	142	478	85	120	20	8	17	78	71	88	.251	.348	.433	781	110	8	23	7	3	.991	1	*O-140(0-140-0)	1.0
1978	*KC-A	141	486	74	145	30	7	22	96	66	54	.298	.387	.525	911	150	33	32	8	4	**.995**	10	*O-136(0-136-0)/D-1	4.6
1979	KC-A	151	577	100	170	28	2	18	90	68	92	.295	.372	.444	816	117	15	30	5	5	**.992**	5	*O-146(0-146-0)/D-4	2.2
1980	*KC-A	107	394	56	99	16	3	10	53	39	70	.251	.323	.383	707	92	-4	16	1	3	.988	7	*O-105(0-105-0)	0.4
1981	*KC-A	99	372	49	100	22	3	9	57	31	59	.269	.328	.417	745	114	6	16	7	1	.993	11	O-97(13-86-1)/D-1	1.7
1982	KC-A	125	475	73	136	25	3	11	88	37	65	.286	.340	.421	762	108	5	9	5	0	.997	-1	*O-125(0-125-0)	0.3
1983	KC-A	98	356	35	93	16	3	4	41	27	63	.261	.313	.357	670	84	-8	5	2	0	.996	3	O-96(0-55-41)/D-1	-0.7
1984	Pit-N	40	97	6	16	4	0	0	10	7	15	.165	.221	.206	427	21	-10	0	0	0	.964	2	O-32(32-0-0)	-1.0
Total	17	1998	7299	1092	2020	374	66	193	1007	757	1008	.277	.347	.425	773	114	137	341	93	42	.991	87	*O-1928C/D-23,3-4	23.1
■ BILL OTIS	Otis, Paul Franklin b: 12/24/1889, Scituate, Mass. d: 12/15/90, Duluth, Minn. BL/TR, 5'10.5", 150 lbs. Deb: 7/4/12																							
1912	NY-A	4	17	1	1	0	0	0	2	3		.059	.200	.059	259	-24	-3	0			.917	1	/O-4(0-4-0)	-0.3
■ MEL OTT	Ott, Melvin Thomas "Master Melvin" b: 3/2/09, Gretna, La. d: 11/21/58, New Orleans, La. BL/TR, 5'9", 170 lbs. Deb: 4/27/26 MH Career OF: (29-LF 128-CF 2167-RF)																							
1926	NY-N	35	60	7	23	2	0	0	4	1	9	.383	.393	.417	810	120	2	1			.913	1	O-10(10-0-0)	0.2
1927	NY-N	82	163	23	46	7	3	1	19	13	9	.282	.335	.380	716	91	-2	2			.982	-7	O-32(13-21-0)	-1.0
1928	NY-N	124	435	69	140	26	4	18	77	52	36	.322	.397	.524	921	138	24	3			.970	-3	*O-115R/2-5,3-1	1.3
1929	NY-N	150	545	138	179	37	2	42	151	**113**	38	.328	.449	.635	1084	166	59	6			.973	9	*O-149(0-0-149)/2-1	5.0
1930	NY-N	148	521	122	182	34	5	25	119	103	35	.349	**.458**	.578	1036	152	48	9			.969	6	*O-146(0-0-146)	3.7
1931	NY-N	138	497	104	145	23	8	29	115	**80**	44	.292	.392	.545	937	**153**	38	10			.981	8	*O-137(0-71-66)	3.9
1932	NY-N	154	566	119	180	30	8	**38**	123	**100**	39	.318	**.424**	.601	1025	**175**	**63**	6			.984	2	*O-154(0-0-154)	**5.4**
1933	*NY-N	152	580	98	164	36	1	23	103	**75**	48	.283	.367	.467	834	139	30	1			.983	-14	*O-152(0-19-143)	0.8
1934	NY-N★	153	582	119	190	29	10	**35**	**135**	85	43	.326	.415	.591	1006	**170**	**59**	0			.974	-9	*O-153(0-16-137)	3.9
1935	NY-N★	152	593	113	191	33	6	31	114	82	58	.322	.407	.555	962	159	50	7			**.990**	6	*O-137(0-0-137),3-15	4.6
1936	*NY-N★	150	534	120	175	28	6	**33**	135	111	41	.328	.448	**.588**	**1036**	**179**	**64**	6			.985	-3	*O-148(0-0-148)	4.9
1937	*NY-N★	151	545	99	160	28	2	**31**	95	**102**	69	.294	.408	.523	931	149	40	7			.939	0	3-60,O-91(0-0-91)	3.6
1938	NY-N★	150	527	**116**	164	23	6	**36**	116	118	47	.311	**.442**	.583	1024	**178**	**61**	2			.957	1	*3-113,O-37(0-0-37)	6.3
1939	NY-N★	125	396	85	122	23	2	27	80	100	50	.308	**.449**	.581	1030	173	45	2			.973	-5	O-96(0-0-96),3-20	3.4
1940	NY-N★	151	536	89	155	27	3	19	79	100	50	.289	.407	.457	864	137	31	6			.982	2	*O-111(0-0-111),3-42	2.8
1941	NY-N★	148	525	89	150	29	0	27	90	100	68	.286	.403	.495	898	149	37	5			.968	5	*O-145(1-0-144)	3.3
1942	NY-N★	152	549	**118**	162	21	0	**30**	93	**109**	61	.295	.415	.497	**912**	**165**	**49**	6			.990	-1	*O-152(0-0-152),M	4.0
1943	NY-N★	125	380	65	89	12	2	18	47	95	48	.234	.391	.418	810	133	20	7			.975	1	*O-111(0-0-111)/3-1,M	1.4
1944	NY-N★	120	399	91	115	16	4	26	82	90	47	.288	.423	.544	967	171	41	2			.986	-4	*O-103(0-0-103)/3-4,M	3.1
1945	NY-N†	135	451	73	139	23	0	21	79	71	41	.308	.411	.499	910	150	32	1			.983	-4	*O-118(0-0-118),M	2.1
1946	NY-N	31	68	2	5	1	0	1	4	8	15	.074	.171	.132	303	-13	-10	0			1.000	-1	O-16(0-0-16),M	-1.2
1947	NY-N	4	4	0	0	0	0	0	0	0	0	.000	.000	.000	0	-99	-1	0			.000	0	HM	-0.1
Total	22	2730	9456	1859	2876	488	72	511	1860	1708	896	.304	.414	.533	947	155	777	89			.980	-10	*O-2313R,3-256/2-6	61.4
■ ED OTT	Ott, Nathan Edward b: 7/11/51, Muncy, Pa. BL/TR, 5'10", 198 lbs. Deb: 6/10/74 C																							
1974	Pit-N	7	5	1	0	0	0	0	0	0	1	.000	.000	.000	0	-99	-1	0	0	0	1.000	-1	/O-2(0-0-2)	-0.2
1975	Pit-N	5	5	0	1	0	0	0	0	0	0	.200	.200	.200	400	11	-1	0	0	0	1.000	-0	/C-2	-0.1
1976	Pit-N	27	39	2	12	2	0	0	5	3	5	.308	.357	.359	716	103	0	0	0	0	1.000	-1	/C-8	0.0
1977	Pit-N	104	311	40	82	14	3	7	38	32	41	.264	.336	.395	732	93	-3	7	7	-1	.982	-5	C-90	-0.5
1978	Pit-N	112	379	49	102	18	4	9	38	27	56	.269	.318	.409	727	97	-2	4	1	1	.975	-9	C-97/O-4(4-0-0)	-0.6
1979	*Pit-N	117	403	49	110	20	2	7	51	26	62	.273	.317	.385	702	86	-8	0	1	-0	.994	-3	*C-116	-0.6
1980	Pit-N	120	392	35	102	14	0	8	41	33	47	.260	.318	.357	675	87	-7	1	6	-2	.983	-4	*C-117/O-3(3-0-0)	-0.8

YEAR	TM/L	G	AB	R	H	2B	3B	HR	RBI	BB	SO	AVG	OBP	SLG	OPS	OPS+	BR+	SB	CS	SBR	FA	FR	G/POS	TPR
1981	Cal-A	75	258	20	56	8	1	2	22	17	42	.217	.268	.279	547	58	-14	2	1	0	.979	1	C-72	-1.1
Total	8	567	1792	196	465	76	10	33	195	138	254	.259	.314	.368	682	86	-35	14	16	-3	.983	-21	C-502/O-9(7-0-2)	-3.9
■ BILLY OTT Ott, William Joseph b: 11/23/40, New York, N.Y. BB/TR, 6'1", 180 lbs. Deb: 9/4/62																								
1962	Chi-N	12	28	3	4	0	0	1	2	2	10	.143	.200	.250	450	19	-3	0	0	0	1.000	-0	/O-7(0-0-7)	-0.4
1964	Chi-N	20	39	4	7	3	0	0	1	3	10	.179	.238	.256	495	38	-3	0	1	-0	1.000	-2	O-10(0-0-10)	-0.6
Total	2	32	67	7	11	3	0	1	3	5	20	.164	.222	.254	476	30	-6	0	1	-0	1.000	-2	/O-17(0-0-17)	-1.0
■ JOE OTTEN Otten, Joseph G. b: Murphysboro, Ill. TR, Deb: 7/5/1895																								
1895	StL-N	26	87	8	21	0	0	0	8	5	8	.241	.283	.241	524	36	-8	2			.947	-4	C-24/O-2(1-1-0)	-0.8
■ BILLY OTTERSON Otterson, William John b: 5/4/1862, Pittsburgh, Pa. d: 9/21/40, Pittsburgh, Pa. BR/TR, 5'7", 124 lbs. Deb: 9/4/1887																								
1887	Bro-a	30	108	16	28	4	1	2	15	8		.259	.259	.320	579	60	-6	8			.859	1	S-30	-0.3
■ PHIL OUELLETTE Ouellette, Philip Roland b: 11/10/61, Salem, Ore. BB/TR, 6', 190 lbs. Deb: 9/10/86																								
1986	SF-N	10	23	1	4	0	0	0	0	3	3	.174	.269	.174	443	26	-2	0	0	0	1.000	0	/C-9	-0.2
■ JOHNNY OULLIBER Oulliber, John Andrew b: 2/24/11, New Orleans, La. d: 12/26/80, New Orleans, La. BR/TR, 5'11", 165 lbs. Deb: 7/25/33																								
1933	Cle-A	22	75	9	20	1	0	0	3	4	5	.267	.313	.280	593	55	-5	0	0	0	1.000	-3	O-18(12-0-6)	-0.9
■ CHINK OUTEN Outen, William Austin b: 6/17/05, Mt.Holly, N.C. d: 9/11/61, Durham, N.C. BL/TR, 6', 200 lbs. Deb: 4/16/33																								
1933	Bro-N	93	153	20	38	10	0	4	17	20	15	.248	.335	.392	727	112	3	1			.982	-13	C-56	-0.9
■ JIMMY OUTLAW Outlaw, James Paulus b: 1/20/13, Orme, Tenn. BR/TR, 5'8", 168 lbs. Deb: 4/20/37 Career OF: (229-LF 61-CF 104-RF)																								
1937	Cin-N	49	165	18	45	7	3	0	11	3	31	.273	.290	.352	641	77	-6	2			.914	4	3-41	0.0
1938	Cin-N	4	0	1	0	0	0	0	0	0	0	—	—	—	—		0	0			.000	0	R	0.0
1939	Bos-N	65	133	15	35	2	0	0	5	10	14	.263	.315	.278	593	65	-6	1			.964	-3	O-39(15-22-2)/3-2	-1.1
1943	Det-A	20	67	8	18	1	0	1	6	8	4	.269	.347	.328	675	91	-1	0	0	0	1.000	0	O-16(4-3-9)	-0.1
1944	Det-A	139	535	69	146	20	6	3	57	41	40	.273	.327	.350	677	88	-8	7	8	-1	.964	-3	*O-137(71-6-60)	-2.2
1945	*Det-A	132	446	56	121	16	5	0	34	45	33	.271	.338	.330	668	88	-6	6	7	-1	.967	-4	*O-105(82-17-8),3-21	-1.7
1946	Det-A	92	299	36	78	14	2	2	31	29	24	.261	.328	.341	669	82	-7	5	4	-0	1.000	-8	O-43(26-10-9),3-38	-1.8
1947	Det-A	70	127	20	29	7	1	0	15	21	14	.228	.338	.299	637	76	-4	3	1	0	.983	-7	O-37(21-3-13)/3-9	-1.2
1948	Det-A	74	198	33	56	12	0	0	25	31	15	.283	.383	.343	726	91	-1	0	1	-0	.920	1	3-47,O-13(10-0-3)	-0.1
1949	Det-A	5	4	1	1	0	0	0	0	0	1	.250	.250	.250	500	32	-0	0	0	0	.000	0	H	0.0
Total	10	650	1974	257	529	79	17	6	184	188	176	.268	.333	.334	668	85	-38	24	21		.972	-19	O-390L,3-158	-8.2
■ MICKEY OWEN Owen, Arnold Malcolm b: 4/4/16, Nixa, Mo. BR/TR, 5'10", 190 lbs. Deb: 5/2/37 C																								
1937	StL-N	80	234	17	54	4	2	0	20	15	13	.231	.277	.265	542	47	-17	1			.974	-3	C-78	-1.6
1938	StL-N	122	397	45	106	25	2	4	36	32	14	.267	.325	.370	695	86	-8	2			.980	1	*C-116	0.0
1939	StL-N	131	344	32	89	18	2	3	35	43	28	.259	.344	.349	693	82	-8	6			.982	4	*C-126	0.3
1940	StL-N	117	307	27	81	16	2	0	27	34	13	.264	.341	.329	670	81	-7	4			.980	3	*C-113	0.1
1941	*Bro-N★	128	386	32	89	15	2	1	44	34	14	.231	.296	.288	584	62	-19	1			.995	6	*C-128	-0.6
1942	Bro-N★	133	421	53	109	16	3	0	44	44	17	.259	.330	.311	642	87	-6	10			.987	5	*C-133	0.7
1943	Bro-N☆	106	365	31	95	11	2	0	54	25	15	.260	.309	.301	611	77	-11	4			.987	-6	*C-100/3-3,S-1	-1.1
1944	Bro-N☆	130	461	43	126	20	3	1	42	36	17	.273	.326	.336	662	88	-7	4			.979	-11	*C-125/2-1	-1.1
1945	Bro-N	24	84	5	24	9	0	0	11	10	2	.286	.368	.393	761	113	2	0			.963	-3	C-24	0.0
1949	Chi-N	62	198	15	54	9	3	2	18	12	13	.273	.318	.379	696	88	-4	1			.969	-1	C-59	-0.2
1950	Chi-N	86	259	22	63	11	0	2	21	13	16	.243	.282	.309	591	56	-17	2			.978	3	C-86	-1.0
1951	Chi-N	58	125	10	23	6	0	0	15	19	13	.184	.292	.232	524	42	-10	0	0	0	.969	8	C-57	0.0
1954	Bos-A	32	68	6	16	3	0	1	11	9	6	.235	.325	.324	648	70	-3	0	1	-0	.989	-2	C-30	-0.4
Total	13	1209	3649	338	929	163	21	14	378	326	181	.255	.318	.322	640	76	-113	36	1		.982	3	*C-1175/3-3,2-1,S-1	-4.9
■ DAVE OWEN Owen, Dave b: 4/25/58, Cleburne, Tex. BB/TR, 6'2", 170 lbs. Deb: 9/6/83 F																								
1983	Chi-N	16	22	1	2	0	1	0	2	2	7	.091	.167	.182	348	-3	-3	1	0	0	1.000	4	S-14/3-3	0.1
1984	Chi-N	47	93	8	18	2	2	1	10	8	15	.194	.272	.290	562	53	-6	1	2	-0	.969	1	S-35/3-6,2-4	-0.3
1985	Chi-N	22	19	6	7	0	0	0	4	1	5	.368	.400	.368	768	105	0	1	1	-0	.917	2	/S-7,3-7,2-4	0.2
1988	KC-A	7	5	0	0	0	0	0	0	0	3	.000	.000	.000	0	-99	-1	0	0	0	.941	4	/S-7	0.3
Total	4	92	139	15	27	2	3	1	16	11	30	.194	.263	.273	537	47	-10	3	3	-0	.969	10	/S-63,3-16,2-8	0.3
■ LARRY OWEN Owen, Lawrence Thomas b: 5/31/55, Cleveland, Ohio BR/TR, 5'11", 185 lbs. Deb: 8/14/81																								
1981	Atl-N	13	16	0	0	0	0	0	0	1	4	.000	.059	.000	59	-80	-4	0	0	0	.964	2	C-10	-0.2
1982	Atl-N	2	3	1	1	1	0	0	0	0	1	.333	.333	.667	1000	167	0	0	0	0	1.000	-0	/C-2	0.0
1983	Atl-N	17	17	0	2	0	0	0	1	0	2	.118	.118	.118	235	-32	-3	0	1	-0	.970	1	C-16	-0.2
1985	Atl-N	26	71	7	17	3	0	2	12	8	17	.239	.316	.366	683	85	-1	0	0	0	.966	3	C-25	0.2
1987	KC-A	76	164	17	31	6	0	5	14	16	51	.189	.261	.317	578	51	-12	0	0	0	.983	19	C-75	0.9
1988	KC-A	37	81	5	17	1	0	1	3	9	23	.210	.304	.259	564	59	-4	0	0	0	.989	5	C-37	0.3
Total	6	171	352	30	68	11	0	8	30	34	98	.193	.268	.293	561	51	-24	0	1	-0	.980	29	C-165	1.0
■ MARV OWEN Owen, Marvin James "Freck" b: 3/22/06, Agnew, Cal. d: 6/22/91, Mountain View, Cal. BR/TR, 6'1", 175 lbs. Deb: 4/16/31																								
1931	Det-A	105	377	35	84	11	6	3	39	29	38	.223	.282	.308	590	53	-26	2	2	-0	.937	1	S-37,3-37,1-27,/2-4	-2.2
1933	Det-A	138	550	77	144	24	9	2	65	44	56	.262	.321	.349	670	76	-19	2	2	-0	.944	-11	*3-136	-2.4
1934	*Det-A	154	565	79	179	34	9	8	96	59	37	.317	.385	.451	837	115	13	3	3	-0	.956	-7	*3-154	1.0
1935	*Det-A	134	483	52	127	24	5	2	71	43	37	.263	.326	.346	672	76	-17	1	4	-1	.958	-10	*3-131	-2.2
1936	Det-A	154	583	72	172	20	4	9	105	53	41	.295	.361	.389	750	85	-13	9	6	-0	.952	-4	*3-153/1-2	-1.0
1937	Det-A	107	396	48	114	22	5	1	45	41	24	.288	.358	.376	734	83	-10	3	4	-1	**.970**	0	*3-106	-0.6
1938	Chi-A	141	577	84	162	23	6	6	55	45	31	.281	.337	.373	710	76	-22	6	4	-0	.948	0	*3-140	-1.5
1939	Chi-A	58	194	22	46	9	0	0	15	16	15	.237	.302	.284	585	49	-15	4	5	-1	.953	-2	3-55	-1.5
1940	Bos-A	20	57	4	12	0	0	0	6	8	4	.211	.308	.211	518	36	-5	0	0	0	.962	2	/3-9,1-8	-0.4
Total	9	1011	3782	473	1040	167	44	31	497	338	283	.275	.339	.367	706	80	-114	30	30	-4	.953	-30	3-921/1-37,S-37,2-4	-10.8
■ SPIKE OWEN Owen, Spike Dee b: 4/19/61, Cleburne, Tex. BB/TR, 5'10", 170 lbs. Deb: 6/25/83 F																								
1983	Sea-A	80	306	36	60	11	3	2	21	24	44	.196	.259	.271	530	44	-23	10	6	0	.970	-0	S-80	-1.5
1984	Sea-A	152	530	67	130	18	8	3	43	46	63	.245	.309	.326	636	77	-16	16	8	1	.977	16	*S-151	1.7
1985	Sea-A	118	352	41	91	10	6	6	37	34	27	.259	.324	.372	696	89	-5	11	5	1	.975	**30**	*S-117	3.6
1986	Sea-A	112	402	46	99	22	6	0	35	34	42	.246	.307	.331	637	73	-15	1	3	-1	.972	34	*S-112	2.9
	*Bos-A	42	126	21	23	2	1	1	10	17	9	.183	.285	.238	523	44	-10	3	1	0	.976	-2	S-42	-0.7
	Yr	154	528	67	122	24	7	1	45	51	51	.231	.301	.309	610	66	-24	4	4	-1	.973	**32**	*S-154	2.2
1987	Bos-A	132	437	50	113	17	7	2	48	53	43	.259	.340	.343	683	80	-11	11	8	-0	.975	-14	*S-130	-1.2
1988	*Bos-A	89	257	40	64	14	1	5	18	27	27	.249	.325	.370	695	90	-3	0	1	-0	.967	-1	S-76/D-7	0.1
1989	Mon-N	142	437	52	102	17	4	6	41	76	44	.233	.351	.332	683	95	-0	3	2	-0	**.979**	11	*S-142	2.2
1990	Mon-N	149	453	55	106	24	5	5	35	70	60	.234	.337	.342	679	91	-4	8	6	-0	**.989**	-12	*S-148	-0.7
1991	Mon-N	139	424	39	108	22	8	3	26	42	61	.255	.323	.366	689	95	-3	2	6	-2	.986	8	*S-133	1.3
1992	Mon-N	122	386	52	104	16	3	7	40	50	30	.269	.353	.381	734	109	5	9	4	1	.982	-10	*S-116	0.5
1993	NY-A	103	334	41	78	16	2	2	20	29	30	.234	.295	.311	606	65	-16	3	2	-0	.968	10	S-96/D-2	0.1
1994	Cal-A	82	268	30	83	17	2	3	37	49	17	.310	.418	.422	840	116	9	2	8	-2	.956	0	3-70/S-5,1-4,2-1,D	0.6
1995	Cal-A	82	218	17	50	9	3	1	28	18	22	.229	.288	.312	600	57	-14	3	2	-0	.945	-18	3-29,S-25,2-16	-2.8
Total	13	1544	4930	587	1211	215	59	46	439	569	519	.246	.326	.341	667	83	-107	82	62	-4	.977	51	*S-1373/3-99,2-17,D1	6.1
■ JAYHAWK OWENS Owens, Claude Jayhawk b: 2/10/69, Cincinnati, Ohio BR/TR, 6'1", 200 lbs. Deb: 6/6/93																								
1993	Col-N	33	86	12	18	5	0	3	6	6	30	.209	.277	.372	649	62	-5	1	0	0	.957	1	C-32	-0.2
1994	Col-N	6	12	4	3	0	1	0	1	3	3	.250	.400	.417	817	97	0	0	0	0	1.000	1	/C-6	0.1
1995	*Col-N	18	45	7	11	2	0	4	12	2	15	.244	.292	.556	847	91	-1	0	0	0	.988	2	C-16	0.2

YEAR	TM/L	G	AB	R	H	2B	3B	HR	RBI	BB	SO	AVG	OBP	SLG	OPS	OPS+	BR+	SB	CS	SBR	FA	FR	G/POS	TPR
1996	Col-N	73	180	31	43	9	1	4	17	27	56	.239	.341	.367	708	70	-7	4	1	1	.974	-4	C-68	-0.7
Total	4	130	323	54	75	16	2	11	36	38	104	.232	.321	.396	717	72	-13	5	1	1	.973	0	C-122	-0.6
■ ERIC OWENS Owens, Eric Blake b: 2/3/71, Danville, Va. BR/TR, 6'1", 185 lbs. Deb: 6/6/95 Career OF: (205-LF 94-CF 98-RF)																								
1995	Cin-N	2	2	0	2	0	0	0	1	0	0	1.000	1.000	1.000	2000	432	1	0	0	0	.000	0	/3-2	0.1
1996	Cin-N	88	205	26	41	6	0	0	9	23	38	.200	.284	.229	513	37	-18	16	2	3	.986	-5	O-52(52-0-0)/2-6,3-5	-2.1
1997	Cin-N	27	57	8	15	0	0	0	3	4	11	.263	.311	.263	575	52	-4	3	2	-0	.938	-4	O-18(9-8-1)/2-2	-0.8
1998	Mil-N	34	40	5	5	2	0	1	4	2	6	.125	.167	.250	417	8	-5	0	0	0	1.000	-4	O-16(10-5-2)/2-4	-1.0
1999	SD-N	149	440	55	117	22	3	9	61	38	50	.266	.328	.391	719	88	-9	33	7	5	.990	-16	*O-116L,1-12/3-4,2	-2.2
2000	SD-N	145	583	87	171	19	7	6	51	45	63	.293	.348	.381	729	89	-9	29	14	1	**1.000**	1	*O-144(65-34-68)/2-1	-1.1
Total	6	445	1327	181	351	49	10	16	129	112	168	.265	.326	.353	678	77	-44	81	25	9	.994	-29	O-346L/2-14,1-12,3	-7.1
■ FRANK OWENS Owens, Frank Walter "Yip" b: 1/26/1886, Toronto, Ont., Can. d: 7/2/58, Minneapolis, Minn. BR/TR, 6', 170 lbs. Deb: 9/11/05																								
1905	Bos-A	1	2	0	0	0	0	0	0	0		.000	.000	.000	0	-99	-0	0			1.000	-0	/C-1	-0.1
1909	Chi-A	64	174	12	35	4	1	0	17	8		.201	.245	.236	480	54	-9	3			.959	-6	C-57	-1.1
1914	Bro-F	58	184	15	51	7	3	2	20	9	16	.277	.314	.380	695	89	-6	2			.967	-14	C-58	-1.7
1915	Bal-F	99	334	32	84	14	7	3	28	17	34	.251	.290	.362	652	80	-15	4			.976	2	C-99	-0.5
Total	4	222	694	59	170	25	11	5	65	34	50	.245	.284	.334	618	77	-30	9			.969	-19	C-215	-3.4
■ JACK OWENS Owens, Furman Lee b: 5/6/08, Converse, S.C. d: 11/14/58, Greenville, S.C. BR/TR, 6'1", 186 lbs. Deb: 9/21/35																								
1935	Phi-A	2	8	0	2	0	0	0	1	0	1	.250	.250	.250	500	30	-1	0	0	0	.900	-0	/C-2	-0.1
■ RED OWENS Owens, Thomas Llewellyn b: 11/1/1874, Pottsville, Pa. d: 8/20/52, Harrisburg, Pa. BR/TR, Deb: 7/28/1899																								
1899	Phi-N	8	21	0	1	0	0	0	1	2		.048	.130	.048	178	-52	-4	0			.914	-1	/2-8	-0.5
1905	Bro-N	43	168	14	36	6	2	1	20	6		.214	.241	.292	533	63	-8	1			.929	4	2-43	-0.4
Total	2	51	189	14	37	6	2	1	21	8		.196	.228	.265	493	49	-13	1			.927	3	/2-51	-0.9
■ HENRY OXLEY Oxley, Henry Havelock b: 1/4/1858, Covehead, P.E.I., Canada d: 10/12/45, Somerville, Mass. 5'11", 163 lbs. Deb: 7/30/1884																								
1884	NY-N	2	4	0	0	0	0	0	0	1	2	.000	.200	.000	200	-31	-1				.900	1	/C-2	0.0
	NY-a	1	3	0	0	0	0	0		0		.000	.000	.000	0	-99	-1				.889	0	/C-1	0.0
Total	1	3	7	0	0	0	0	0	0	1	2	.000	.125	.000	125	-56	-1				.895	1	/C-3	0.0
■ ANDY OYLER Oyler, Andrew Paul "Pepper" b: 5/5/1880, Newville, Pa. d: 10/24/70, E.Pennsboro Twsp., Pa. BR/TR, 5'6.5", 138 lbs. Deb: 5/8/02																								
1902	Bal-A	27	77	9	17	1	0	1	6	8		.221	.318	.273	591	62	-4	3			.947	-8	3-20/O-3C,S-2,2-1	-1.1
■ RAY OYLER Oyler, Raymond Francis b: 8/4/38, Indianapolis, Ind. d: 1/26/81, Seattle, Wash. BR/TR, 5'11", 165 lbs. Deb: 4/18/65																								
1965	Det-A	82	194	22	36	6	0	5	13	21	61	.186	.265	.294	559	58	-11	1	0	0	.955	6	S-57,2-11/1-1,3-1	0.0
1966	Det-A	71	210	16	36	8	3	1	9	23	62	.171	.263	.252	515	48	-14	0	0	0	.965	15	S-69	0.6
1967	Det-A	148	367	33	76	14	2	1	29	37	91	.207	.283	.264	548	61	-17	0	2	-1	.964	15	*S-146	0.8
1968	*Det-A	111	215	13	29	6	1	1	12	20	59	.135	.215	.186	401	22	-20	0	2	-1	.977	9	*S-111	-0.6
1969	Sea-A	106	255	24	42	5	0	7	22	31	80	.165	.260	.267	527	48	-18	1	2	-0	.965	9	*S-106	0.0
1970	Cal-A	24	24	2	2	0	0	0	1	3	6	.083	.185	.083	269	-24	-4	0	0	0	1.000	-1	S-13/3-2	-0.5
Total	6	542	1265	110	221	39	6	15	86	135	359	.175	.259	.251	510	48	-84	2	6	-2	.966	52	S-502/2-11,3-3,1-1	0.3
■ PABLO OZUNA Ozuna, Pablo Jose b: 8/25/78, Santo Domingo, D.R. BR/TR, 6', 160 lbs. Deb: 4/23/2000																								
2000	Fla-N	14	24	2	8	1	0	0	0	0	2	.333	.333	.375	708	83	-1	1	0	0	.967	1	/2-7	0.1
■ CHARLIE PABOR Pabor, Charles Henry b: 9/24/1846, New York, N.Y. d: 4/23/13, New Haven, Conn. BL/TL, 5'8", 155 lbs. Deb: 5/4/1871 M																								
1871	Cle-n	29	142	24	42	2	4	0	18	1	3	.296	.301	.366	667	96	0	1	0	0	.773	-5	*O-28(28-0-0)/P-7,M	-0.3
1872	Cle-n	21	92	12	19	0	0	0	7	0	0	.207	.207	.207	413	29	-7	0	0	0	.863	-0	O-20(19-0-1)/P-2	-0.4
1873	Atl-n	55	228	36	82	8	3	0	42	6	3	.360	.376	.421	797	153	17	2	0	0	.807	-4	*O-55(55-0-0)	1.1
1874	Phi-n	17	77	11	17	0	1	0	1	0	0	.221	.221	.247	468	48	-4	0	1	-0	.553	-1	O-17(2-3-13)	-0.4
1875	Atl-n	42	153	14	36	2	2	0	11	1	1	.235	.240	.275	515	90	-0	0	0	0	.803	1	O-42(42-0-0)/P-1,M	0.2
	NH-n	6	23	4	8	0	2	0	2	0	1	.348	.348	.522	870	227	3	0	0	0	.818	-1	/O-6(6-0-0),M	0.2
	Yr	48	176	18	44	2	4	0	13	1	2	.250	.254	.307	561	108	3	0	0	0	.804	-0	O-48(48-0-0)/P-1	0.4
Total	5 n	170	715	101	204	12	12	0	81	8	8	.285	.293	.336	629	102	9	3	1	0	.787	-11	O-168(152-3-14)/P-10	0.4
■ ED PABST Pabst, Edward D. A. b: 1868, St.Louis, Mo. d: 6/19/40, St.Louis, Mo. 5'11", 170 lbs. Deb: 9/26/1890																								
1890	Phi-a	8	25	7	10	2	0	0	3	5		.400	.500	.480	980	190	3	3			.963	4	/O-8(8-0-0)	0.6
	StL-a	4	14	1	2	0	1	0	0	0		.143	.143	.286	429	23	-1	0			1.000	1	/O-4(4-0-0)	0.0
	Yr	12	39	8	12	2	1	0	3	5		.308	.386	.410	797	129	1	3			.972	5	O-12(12-0-0)	0.6
■ JIM PACIOREK Paciorek, James Joseph b: 6/7/60, Detroit, Mich. BR/TR, 6'3", 203 lbs. Deb: 4/9/87 F																								
1987	Mil-A	48	101	16	23	5	0	2	10	12	20	.228	.310	.337	646	69	-4	1	0	0	.980	-4	1-21,3-15/O-5L,D-2	-0.9
■ JOHN PACIOREK Paciorek, John Francis b: 2/11/45, Detroit, Mich. BR/TR, 6'2", 200 lbs. Deb: 9/29/63 F																								
1963	Hou-N	1	3	4	3	0	0	0	3	2	0	1.000	1.000	1.000	2000	509	2	0	0	0	1.000	0	/O-1(0-0-1)	0.2
■ TOM PACIOREK Paciorek, Thomas Marian b: 11/2/46, Detroit, Mich. BR/TR, 6'4", 215 lbs. Deb: 9/12/70 F Career OF: (476-LF 73-CF 281-RF)																								
1970	LA-N	8	9	2	2	1	0	0	0	0	3	.222	.300	.333	633	73	-0	0	0	0	1.000	-1	/O-3(1-0-2)	-0.1
1971	LA-N	2	2	0	1	0	0	0	1	0	0	.500	.500	.500	1000	196	0	0	0	0	1.000	-0	/O-1(1-0-0)	0.0
1972	LA-N	11	47	4	12	4	0	1	6	1	7	.255	.271	.404	675	92	-1	1	0	0	.979	1	/1-6,O-6(1-0-5)	-0.1
1973	LA-N	96	195	26	51	8	0	5	18	11	35	.262	.304	.379	684	92	-3	3	3	-0	.979	-15	O-77(36-22-25)/1-4	-2.2
1974	*LA-N	85	175	23	42	8	6	1	24	10	32	.240	.285	.371	656	86	-4	1	3	-1	.944	-16	O-77(44-23-15)/1-1	-2.5
1975	LA-N	62	145	14	28	8	0	1	5	11	29	.193	.250	.269	519	46	-11	4	3	-0	.972	-9	O-54(30-2-25)	-2.4
1976	Atl-N	111	324	39	94	10	4	4	36	19	57	.290	.335	.383	718	97	-1	2	3	-1	.983	-12	O-84R,1-12/3-1	-2.0
1977	Atl-N	72	155	20	37	8	0	3	15	6	46	.239	.267	.348	615	57	-9	1	0	0	.984	-2	1-32/O-9(4-2-3),3-1	-1.3
1978	Atl-N	5	9	2	3	0	0	0	0	0	1	.333	.333	.333	667	78	-0	0	0	0	1.000	-0	/1-2	-0.1
	Sea-A	70	251	32	75	20	3	4	30	15	39	.299	.338	.450	789	121	6	2	2	-0	.980	-3	O-54(53-4-0),D-12/1-3	0.0
1979	Sea-A	103	310	38	89	23	4	6	42	28	62	.287	.356	.445	801	113	5	6	4	-0	1.000	-2	O-75(47-0-29),1-15	-0.1
1980	Sea-A	126	418	44	114	19	1	15	59	17	67	.273	.303	.431	733	98	-3	3	2	-0	1.000	-3	O-60R,1-36,D-23	-1.1
1981	Sea-A★	104	405	50	132	28	2	14	66	35	50	.326	.385	.509	894	150	25	13	10	-1	.974	6	*O-103(84-12-14)	2.7
1982	Chi-A	104	382	49	119	27	4	11	55	24	53	.312	.366	.490	856	133	17	3	3	-0	.993	-1	*1-102/O-6(6-0-0)	0.9
1983	*Chi-A	115	420	65	129	32	3	9	63	25	58	.307	.350	.462	812	117	9	6	1	1	1.000	-10	1-67,O-55L/D-2	-0.6
1984	Chi-A	111	363	35	93	21	2	4	29	25	69	.256	.311	.358	669	81	-9	6	0	1	.993	-13	1-67,O-41(25-0-17)	-2.6
1985	Chi-A	46	122	14	30	2	0	0	9	8	22	.246	.298	.262	560	53	-8	2	0	0	.970	-2	O-23(21-0-2),D-12/1-6	-1.0
	NY-N	46	116	14	33	3	1	1	11	6	14	.284	.325	.353	679	92	-1	1	0	0	1.000	-5	O-29(6-0-24)/1-8	-0.8
1986	Tex-A	88	213	17	61	7	0	4	22	3	41	.286	.306	.376	682	82	-5	1	3	-1	.967	-1	O-25L,1-23,3-21,/SD	-0.9
1987	Tex-A	27	60	6	17	3	0	3	12	1	19	.283	.306	.483	790	105	0	0	1	-0	1.000	-0	1-12,O-12(8-0-5)/D-3	-0.1
Total	18	1392	4121	494	1162	232	30	86	503	245	704	.282	.328	.415	744	102	7	55	38	-1	.979	-89	O-794L,1-396/D-61,3S	-14.3
■ FRANKIE PACK Pack, Frank b: 4/10/28, Morristown, Tenn. d: 1/26/2000, Hendersonville, N.C. BL/TR, 6', 190 lbs. Deb: 6/5/49																								
1949	StL-A	1	1	0	0	0	0	0	0	0	1	.000	.000	.000	0	-96	-0	0	0	0	.000	0	H	0.0
■ DICK PADDEN Padden, Richard Joseph "Brains" b: 9/17/1870, Martins Ferry, O. d: 10/31/22, Martins Ferry, O. BR/TR, 5'10", 165 lbs. Deb: 7/15/1896																								
1896	Pit-N	61	219	33	53	4	8	2	24	14	9	.242	.294	.361	654	75	-9	8			.931	-12	2-61	-1.5
1897	Pit-N	134	517	84	146	16	10	2	58	38		.282	.350	.364	714	92	-5	18			.941	2	*2-134	0.3
1898	Pit-N	128	463	61	119	7	6	2	43	35		.257	.335	.311	646	87	-6	11			.947	-2	*2-128	-0.3
1899	Was-N	134	451	66	125	20	7	2	61	24		.277	.337	.366	703	94	-4	27			.913	8	S-85,2-48	1.0
1901	StL-N	123	489	71	125	17	7	2	62	31		.256	.315	.331	646	92	-5	26			.950	1	*2-115/S-8	-0.3
1902	StL-A	117	413	54	109	26	3	1	40	30		.264	.327	.349	676	89	-6	11			**.967**	18	*2-117	1.2
1903	StL-A	29	94	7	19	3	0	0	6	9		.202	.306	.234	540	65	-3	5			.955	6	2-29	0.3
1904	StL-A	132	453	42	108	19	4	0	36	40		.238	.325	.298	623	104	4	23			.959	-9	*2-132	-0.4

YEAR	TM/L	G	AB	R	H	2B	3B	HR	RBI	BB	SO	AVG	OBP	SLG	OPS	OPS+	BR+	SB	CS	SBR	FA	FR	G/POS	TPR
1905	StL-A	16	58	5	10	1	1	0	4	3		.172	.213	.224	437	41	-4	3			.950	0	2-16	-0.4
Total	9	874	3157	423	814	113	46	11	334	224	9	.258	.326	.333	660	90	-38	132			.950	11	2-780/S-93	-0.1

■ TOM PADDEN

Padden, Thomas Francis b: 10/6/08, Manchester, N.H. d: 6/10/73, Manchester, N.H. BR/TR, 5′11.5″, 170 lbs. Deb: 5/29/32

YEAR	TM/L	G	AB	R	H	2B	3B	HR	RBI	BB	SO	AVG	OBP	SLG	OPS	OPS+	BR+	SB	CS	SBR	FA	FR	G/POS	TPR
1932	Pit-N	47	118	13	31	6	1	0	10	9	7	.263	.315	.331	645	75	-4	0			.985	-1	C-43	-0.2
1933	Pit-N	30	90	5	19	2	0	0	8	2	6	.211	.237	.233	470	35	-8	0			.984	6	C-27	0.0
1934	Pit-N	82	237	27	76	12	2	0	22	30	23	.321	.399	.388	787	109	5	3			.978	-5	C-76	0.4
1935	Pit-N	97	302	35	82	9	1	1	30	48	26	.272	.371	.318	689	84	-4	1			.966	14	C-94	1.4
1936	Pit-N	88	281	22	70	9	2	1	31	22	41	.249	.304	.306	610	63	-14	0			.976	2	C-87	-0.7
1937	Pit-N	35	98	14	28	2	0	0	8	13	11	.286	.369	.306	675	85	-1	1			.983	6	C-34	0.7
1943	Phi-N	17	41	5	12	0	0	0	1	2	6	.293	.341	.293	634	87	-1	0			1.000	4	C-16	0.4
	Was-A	3	3	1	0	0	0	0	0	1	1	.000	.250	.000	250	-25	-0	0	0	0	1.000	0	/C-2	0.0
Total	7	399	1170	122	318	40	6	2	110	127	121	.272	.345	.321	666	80	-28	5	0		.977	27	C-379	2.0

■ DEL PADDOCK

Paddock, Delmar Harold b: 6/8/1887, Volga, S.Dak. d: 2/6/52, Remer, Minn BL/TR, 5′9″, 165 lbs. Deb: 4/14/12

YEAR	TM/L	G	AB	R	H	2B	3B	HR	RBI	BB	SO	AVG	OBP	SLG	OPS	OPS+	BR+	SB	CS	SBR	FA	FR	G/POS	TPR
1912	Chi-A	1	1	0	0	0	0	0	0	0		.000	.000	.000	0	-99	-0	0			.000	0	H	0.0
	NY-A	46	156	26	45	5	3	1	14	23		.288	.393	.378	772	114	4	9			.894	-7	3-41/2-2,O-1(0-0-1)	-0.2
	Yr	47	157	26	45	5	3	1	14	23		.287	.391	.376	767	113	4	9			.894	-7	3-41/2-2,O-1(0-0-1)	-0.2

■ DON PADGETT

Padgett, Don Wilson b: 12/5/11, Caroleen, N.C. d: 12/9/80, High Point, N.C. BL/TR, 6′, 190 lbs. Deb: 4/23/37 Career OF: (62-LF 11-CF 168-RF)

YEAR	TM/L	G	AB	R	H	2B	3B	HR	RBI	BB	SO	AVG	OBP	SLG	OPS	OPS+	BR+	SB	CS	SBR	FA	FR	G/POS	TPR
1937	StL-N	123	446	62	140	22	6	10	74	30	43	.314	.357	.457	815	117	10	4			.955	3	*O-109(0-6-102)	0.6
1938	StL-N	110	388	59	105	26	5	8	65	18	28	.271	.303	.425	728	93	-5	0			.962	5	O-71(3-5-63),1-16/C-6	-0.6
1939	StL-N	92	233	38	93	15	3	5	53	18	11	.399	.444	.554	998	157	19	1			.978	-3	C-61/1-6	1.9
1940	StL-N	93	240	24	58	15	1	6	41	26	14	.242	.321	.387	708	89	-3	1			.962	-8	C-72/1-2	-0.8
1941	StL-N	107	324	39	80	18	0	5	44	21	16	.247	.293	.349	642	75	-11	0			.959	-9	O-62(59-0-3),C-18/1-2	-2.4
1946	Bro-N	19	30	2	5	1	0	1	9	4	4	.167	.265	.300	565	59	-2	0			1.000	-1	C-10	-0.3
	Bos-N	44	98	6	25	3	0	2	21	5	7	.255	.291	.347	638	80	-3	0			.939	-6	C-26	-0.8
	Yr	63	128	8	30	4	0	3	30	9	11	.234	.285	.336	621	75	-5	0			.954	-7	C-36	-1.1
1947	Phi-N	75	158	14	50	8	1	0	24	16	5	.316	.383	.380	763	107	2	0			.962	-7	C-39	-0.3
1948	Phi-N	36	74	3	17	3	0	0	7	3	2	.230	.260	.270	530	44	-6	0			.957	-4	C-19	-0.9
Total	8	699	1991	247	573	111	16	37	338	141	130	.288	.336	.415	752	101	1	6			.962	-32	C-251,O-242R/1-26	-3.6

■ ERNIE PADGETT

Padgett, Ernest Kitchen "Red" b: 3/1/1899, Philadelphia, Pa. d: 4/15/57, E.Orange, N.J. BR/TR, 5′8″, 155 lbs. Deb: 10/3/23

YEAR	TM/L	G	AB	R	H	2B	3B	HR	RBI	BB	SO	AVG	OBP	SLG	OPS	OPS+	BR+	SB	CS	SBR	FA	FR	G/POS	TPR
1923	Bos-N	4	11	3	2	0	0	0	0	2	0	.182	.308	.182	490	33	-1	0	0	0	.947	2	/S-2,2-1	0.1
1924	Bos-N	138	502	42	128	25	9	1	46	37	56	.255	.310	.347	657	79	-15	4	9	-2	.967	-11	*3-113,2-29	-2.1
1925	Bos-N	86	256	31	78	9	7	0	29	14	14	.305	.341	.395	735	96	-2	3	5	-1	.964	-20	2-47,S-18/3-7	-1.9
1926	Cle-A	36	62	7	13	0	1	0	6	8	3	.210	.300	.242	542	42	-5	1	0	0	.930	2	3-29/S-2	-0.2
1927	Cle-A	7	7	1	2	0	0	0	0	0	2	.286	.286	.286	571	48	-1	0	0	0	1.000	-0	/2-4	-0.1
Total	5	271	838	84	223	34	17	1	81	61	75	.266	.318	.351	669	80	-24	8	14	-3	.957	-27	3-149/2-81,S-22	-4.2

■ DENNIS PAEPKE

Paepke, Dennis Ray b: 4/17/45, Long Beach, Cal. BR/TR, 6′, 202 lbs. Deb: 6/2/69

YEAR	TM/L	G	AB	R	H	2B	3B	HR	RBI	BB	SO	AVG	OBP	SLG	OPS	OPS+	BR+	SB	CS	SBR	FA	FR	G/POS	TPR
1969	KC-A	12	27	2	3	1	0	0	0	2	3	.111	.172	.148	321	-10	-4	0	0	0	1.000	3	/C-8	-0.1
1971	KC-A	60	152	11	31	6	0	2	14	8	29	.204	.244	.283	527	49	-10	0	0	0	.994	-3	C-32,O-17(1-0-16)	-1.4
1972	KC-A	2	6	0	0	0	0	0	0	1	2	.000	.143	.000	143	-55	-1	0	0	0	.842	1	/C-2	0.0
1974	KC-A	6	12	0	2	0	0	0	0	1	2	.167	.231	.167	397	15	-1	0	1	-0	1.000	-1	/C-4,O-1(0-0-1)	-0.2
Total	4	80	197	13	36	7	0	2	14	12	36	.183	.230	.249	478	36	-17	0	1	-0	.984	-1	/C-46,O-18(1-0-17)	-1.7

■ ANDY PAFKO

Pafko, Andrew "Handy Andy" or "Pruschka" b: 2/25/21, Boyceville, Wis. BR/TR, 6′, 190 lbs. Deb: 9/24/43 C Career OF: (362-LF 803-CF 443-RF)

YEAR	TM/L	G	AB	R	H	2B	3B	HR	RBI	BB	SO	AVG	OBP	SLG	OPS	OPS+	BR+	SB	CS	SBR	FA	FR	G/POS	TPR
1943	Chi-N	13	58	7	22	3	0	0	10	2	5	.379	.400	.431	831	142	3	1			1.000	-2	O-13(0-13-0)	0.0
1944	Chi-N	128	469	47	126	16	2	6	62	28	23	.269	.315	.350	665	87	-8	2			.983	15	*O-123(0-123-1)	0.3
1945	*Chi-N†	144	534	64	159	24	12	12	110	45	36	.298	.361	.455	816	129	19	5			**.995**	3	*O-140(0-140-0)	1.8
1946	Chi-N	65	234	18	66	6	4	3	39	27	15	.282	.366	.380	746	114	5	4			.978	11	O-64(0-64-0)	1.4
1947	Chi-N★	129	513	68	155	25	7	13	66	31	39	.302	.346	.454	800	115	9	4			.985	7	*O-127(0-127-0)	1.3
1948	Chi-N★	142	548	82	171	30	2	26	101	50	50	.312	.375	.516	891	145	32	3			.938	13	*3-139	4.4
1949	Chi-N★	144	519	79	146	29	2	18	69	63	33	.281	.369	.449	818	121	16	4			.987	-7	O-98(1-89-9),3-49	0.7
1950	Chi-N★	146	514	95	156	24	8	36	92	69	32	.304	.397	.591	989	158	43	4			.978	-1	*O-144(0-138-6)	3.7
1951	Chi-N	49	178	26	47	5	3	12	35	17	10	.264	.342	.528	870	128	6	1	1	-0	.992	2	O-48(0-48-0)	0.7
	Bro-N	84	277	42	69	11	0	18	58	35	27	.249	.350	.484	834	120	7	1	4	-1	.993	-2	O-76(70-9-0)	-0.1
	Yr	133	455	68	116	16	3	30	93	52	37	.255	.347	.501	848	123	14	2	5	-1	.993	0	*O-124(70-57-0)	0.6
1952	*Bro-N	150	551	76	158	17	5	19	85	64	48	.287	.366	.439	805	121	16	4	3	-0	.988	-7	*O-139L,3-13	0.0
1953	Mil-N	140	516	70	153	23	4	17	72	37	33	.297	.347	.455	803	114	10	2	1	0	.976	-4	*O-139(0-0-139)	0.1
1954	Mil-N	138	510	61	146	22	4	14	69	37	36	.286	.339	.427	767	105	3	1	2	-0	.969	-4	*O-138(0-7-131)	-0.6
1955	Mil-N	86	252	29	67	3	5	5	34	7	23	.266	.297	.377	674	81	-7	1	2	-0	.980	-8	O-58(1-7-52),3-12	-1.8
1956	Mil-N	45	93	15	24	5	0	2	9	10	13	.258	.330	.376	706	95	-1	0	0	0	.978	-5	O-37(33-0-5)	-0.7
1957	*Mil-N	83	220	31	61	6	1	8	27	10	22	.277	.312	.423	734	102	-0	1	0	0	.982	-6	O-69(32-1-36)	-0.9
1958	*Mil-N	95	164	17	39	7	1	3	23	15	17	.238	.309	.348	657	80	-5	0	0	0	1.000	-14	O-93(80-3-17)	-2.2
1959	Mil-N	71	142	17	31	8	2	1	15	14	15	.218	.293	.324	617	70	-6	0	0	0	.978	-12	O-64(40-22-9)	-2.0
Total	17	1852	6292	844	1796	264	62	213	976	561	477	.285	.351	.449	800	118	142	38	13		.984	-21	*O-1570C,3-213	6.1

■ JOSE PAGAN

Pagan, Jose Antonio (Rodriguez) b: 5/5/35, Barceloneta, P.R. BR/TR, 5′9″, 165 lbs. Deb: 8/4/59 C Career OF: (83-LF 0-CF 10-RF)

YEAR	TM/L	G	AB	R	H	2B	3B	HR	RBI	BB	SO	AVG	OBP	SLG	OPS	OPS+	BR+	SB	CS	SBR	FA	FR	G/POS	TPR
1959	SF-N	31	46	7	8	1	0	0	1	2	8	.174	.208	.196	404	9	-6	1	0	0	.900	3	3-18/S-5,2-3	-0.2
1960	SF-N	18	49	8	14	2	2	0	2	1	6	.286	.300	.408	708	97	-0	2	2	-0	.917	-8	S-11/3-1	-0.8
1961	SF-N	134	434	38	110	15	2	5	46	31	45	.253	.306	.332	638	72	-17	8	5	0	.964	-19	*S-132/O-4(3-0-2)	-2.5
1962	*SF-N	164	580	73	150	25	6	7	57	47	77	.259	.315	.359	674	82	-15	13	9	-0	**.973**	-25	*S-164	-2.6
1963	SF-N	148	483	46	113	12	1	6	39	26	67	.234	.279	.300	579	67	-20	10	7	-0	.970	-18	*S-143/2-1,O-1(1-0-0)	-2.9
1964	SF-N	134	367	33	82	10	1	1	28	35	66	.223	.293	.264	557	57	-20	5	4	-0	.958	-18	*S-132/O-8(6-0-2)	-3.1
1965	SF-N	26	83	10	17	4	0	0	5	8	9	.205	.275	.253	528	48	-6	1	0	0	.941	-5	S-26	-0.9
	Pit-N	42	38	6	9	1	0	0	1	1	7	.237	.275	.263	538	52	-2	1	0	0	.923	8	3-15/S-7	0.6
	Yr	68	121	16	26	5	0	0	6	9	16	.215	.275	.256	531	50	-8	2	0	0	.923	3	S-33,3-15	-0.3
1966	Pit-N	109	368	44	97	15	6	4	54	13	38	.264	.296	.370	666	84	-8	0	2	-1	.949	3	3-83,S-18/2-3,O-3L	-0.6
1967	Pit-N	81	211	17	61	6	2	1	19	10	28	.289	.330	.351	681	95	-1	1	1	-0	.938	10	3-25,O-23L,S-16,/2C	0.9
1968	Pit-N	80	163	24	36	7	1	4	21	11	32	.221	.282	.350	632	90	-2	2	3	-1	.924	-5	3-30,O-19L/S-8,21	-0.9
1969	Pit-N	108	274	29	78	11	4	9	42	17	46	.285	.329	.453	781	119	6	1	0	0	.954	-4	3-44,O-23(21-0-2)/2-1	0.1
1970	*Pit-N	95	230	21	61	14	1	7	29	20	24	.265	.324	.426	750	101	-0	1	1	-0	.957	-3	3-53/O-4R,1-1,2-1	-0.3
1971	*Pit-N	57	158	16	38	1	0	5	15	16	25	.241	.314	.342	656	86	-3	0	0	0	.980	-2	3-41/O-3(3-0-0),1-2	-0.5
1972	Pit-N	53	127	11	32	9	0	3	8	5	17	.252	.286	.394	679	93	-2	0	0	0	.899	-8	3-32/O-2(2-0-0)	-1.1
1973	Phi-N	46	78	4	16	5	0	0	5	1	15	.205	.215	.269	484	33	-7	0	1	-0	.958	-1	3-16/1-5,O-2L,2-1	-0.9
Total	15	1326	3689	387	922	138	26	52	372	244	510	.250	.300	.344	644	79	-105	46	35	-2	.963	-91	S-662,3-358/O21C	-15.7

■ MIKE PAGE

Page, Michael Randy b: 7/12/40, Woodruff, S.C. BL/TR, 6′2.5″, 210 lbs. Deb: 6/30/68

YEAR	TM/L	G	AB	R	H	2B	3B	HR	RBI	BB	SO	AVG	OBP	SLG	OPS	OPS+	BR+	SB	CS	SBR	FA	FR	G/POS	TPR
1968	Atl-N	20	28	1	5	0	0	0	1	1	9	.179	.207	.179	385	16	-3	0	0	0	1.000	-1	/O-6(1-0-5)	-0.5

■ MITCHELL PAGE

Page, Mitchell Otis b: 10/15/51, Los Angeles, Cal. BL/TR, 6′2″, 205 lbs. Deb: 4/9/77

YEAR	TM/L	G	AB	R	H	2B	3B	HR	RBI	BB	SO	AVG	OBP	SLG	OPS	OPS+	BR+	SB	CS	SBR	FA	FR	G/POS	TPR
1977	Oak-A	145	501	85	154	28	8	21	75	78	95	.307	.407	.521	928	153	39	42	5	**7**	.954	7	*O-133(131-0-5)/D-8	4.6
1978	Oak-A	147	516	62	147	25	7	17	70	53	95	.285	.356	.459	815	135	23	23	19	-2	.973	-1	*O-114(112-0-2),D-33	1.5
1979	Oak-A	133	478	51	118	11	2	9	42	52	93	.247	.325	.335	659	83	-11	17	16	-2	1.000	-0	*D-126/O-4(4-0-0)	-1.7
1980	Oak-A	110	348	58	85	10	4	17	51	35	87	.244	.315	.443	758	113	5	14	7	1	.000	0	*D-101	0.3
1981	Oak-A	34	92	9	13	1	0	4	13	7	29	.141	.202	.283	485	40	-7	2	1	0	.000	0	D-29	-0.9
1982	Oak-A	31	78	14	20	5	0	4	7	7	24	.256	.333	.474	808	124	2	3	4	-1	.000	0	D-24	0.1
1983	Oak-A	57	79	16	19	3	0	0	1	10	22	.241	.341	.278	619	77	-2	3	3	-0	1.000	-2	D-34,O-10(7-0-3)	-0.6

YEAR	TM/L	G	AB	R	H	2B	3B	HR	RBI	BB	SO	AVG	OBP	SLG	OPS	OPS+	BR+	SB	CS	SBR	FA	FR	G/POS	TPR
1984	Pit-N	16	12	2	4	1	0	0	0	3	4	.333	.467	.417	883	150	1	0	0	0	.000	0	H	0.1
Total	8	673	2104	297	560	84	21	72	259	245	449	.266	.348	.429	776	118	51	104	55	4	.963	3	D-355,O-261(254-0-10)	3.4
■ KARL PAGEL Pagel, Karl Douglas b: 3/29/55, Madison, Wis. BL/TL, 6′2″, 190 lbs. Deb: 9/21/78																								
1978	Chi-N	2	2	0	0	0	0	0	0	0	2	.000	.000	.000	0	-89	-0	0	0	0	.000	0	H	-0.1
1979	Chi-N	1	1	0	0	0	0	0	0	0	1	.000	.000	.000	0	-91	-0	0	0	0	.000	0	/H	0.0
1981	Cle-A	14	15	3	4	0	2	1	4	4	1	.267	.421	.733	1154	230	3	0	0	0	1.000	2	/1-6,D-1	0.4
1982	Cle-A	23	18	3	3	0	0	0	2	7	11	.167	.400	.167	567	63	-0	0	0	0	.970	0	1-10/D-1	-0.1
1983	Cle-A	8	20	1	6	0	0	0	1	0	5	.300	.300	.300	600	63	-1	0	0	0	.000	-1	/O-1(1-0-0),D-5	-0.2
Total	5	48	56	7	13	0	2	1	7	11	20	.232	.358	.357	715	99	0	0	0	0	.985	1	/1-16,D-7,O-1(1-0-0)	0.0
■ JIM PAGLIARONI Pagliaroni, James Vincent "Pag" b: 12/8/37, Dearborn, Mich. BR/TR, 6′4″, 210 lbs. Deb: 8/13/55																								
1955	Bos-A	1	0	0	0	0	0	0	1	0	0	—	—	—	—	—	-0	0	0	0	.000	0	/C-1	0.0
1960	Bos-A	28	62	7	19	5	2	2	9	13	11	.306	.434	.548	983	158	6	0	0	0	.990	-3	C-18	0.3
1961	Bos-A	120	376	50	91	17	0	16	58	55	74	.242	.345	.415	760	100	0	1	1	-0	.984	-4	*C-108	0.2
1962	Bos-A	90	260	39	67	14	0	11	37	36	55	.258	.359	.438	797	110	4	2	1	0	.987	-3	C-73	0.5
1963	Pit-N	92	252	27	58	5	0	11	26	36	57	.230	.331	.381	712	104	2	0	0	0	.988	4	C-85	1.1
1964	Pit-N	97	302	33	89	12	3	10	36	41	56	.295	.383	.454	836	135	15	1	0	0	.992	1	C-96	2.1
1965	Pit-N	134	403	42	108	15	0	17	65	41	84	.268	.340	.432	772	115	8	0	0	0	.994	-4	*C-131	1.0
1966	Pit-N	123	374	37	88	20	0	11	49	50	71	.235	.332	.377	709	96	-1	0	5	-2	**.997**	-14	*C-118	-1.2
1967	Pit-N	44	100	4	20	1	1	0	9	16	26	.200	.316	.230	546	59	-5	0	0	0	.984	-0	C-38	-0.4
1968	Oak-A	66	199	19	49	4	0	6	20	24	42	.246	.333	.357	690	115	4	0	0	0	.997	-9	C-63	-0.2
1969	Oak-A	14	27	1	4	1	0	1	2	5	2	.148	.303	.296	599	71	-1	0	0	0	.981	2	/C-7	0.1
	Sea-A	40	110	10	29	4	1	5	14	13	16	.264	.341	.455	796	123	3	0	0	0	.988	-6	C-29/1-2,O-1(0-0-1)	-0.2
	Yr	54	137	11	33	5	1	6	16	18	18	.241	.333	.423	757	113	2	0	0	0	.987	-4	C-36/1-2,O-1(0-0-1)	-0.1
Total	11	849	2465	269	622	98	7	90	326	330	494	.252	.346	.407	754	109	35	4	7	-2	.991	-36	C-767/1-2,O-1(0-0-1)	3.3
■ MIKE PAGLIARULO Pagliarulo, Michael Timothy b: 3/15/60, Medford, Mass. BL/TR (BB 1985 (1 GAME)), 6′2″, 195 lbs. Deb: 7/7/84																								
1984	NY-A	67	201	24	48	15	3	7	34	15	46	.239	.292	.448	739	105	1	0	0	0	.955	6	3-67	0.6
1985	NY-A	138	380	55	91	16	2	19	62	45	86	.239	.326	.442	768	111	5	0	0	0	.951	-17	*3-134	-1.4
1986	NY-A	149	504	71	120	24	3	28	71	54	120	.238	.317	.464	781	111	6	4	1	1	.953	6	*3-143/S-2	1.0
1987	NY-A	150	522	76	122	26	3	32	87	53	111	.234	.307	.479	786	105	2	1	3	-1	.959	4	*3-147/1-1	0.3
1988	NY-A	125	444	46	96	20	1	15	67	37	104	.216	.280	.367	647	80	-13	1	0	0	.943	-0	*3-124	-1.3
1989	NY-A	74	223	19	44	10	0	4	16	19	43	.197	.266	.296	562	59	-12	1	1	-0	.936	-4	3-69/D-1	-1.7
	SD-N	50	148	12	29	7	0	3	14	18	39	.196	.287	.304	591	69	-6	2	0	0	.936	0	3-49	-0.6
1990	SD-N	128	398	29	101	23	2	7	38	39	66	.254	.325	.374	699	91	-5	1	3	-1	.955	2	*3-116	-0.4
1991	*Min-A	121	365	38	102	20	0	6	36	21	55	.279	.324	.384	707	91	-5	1	2	-0	.965	12	*3-118/2-1	0.7
1992	Min-A	42	105	10	21	4	0	0	9	1	17	.200	.215	.238	453	26	-10	1	0	0	.962	3	3-37/D-1	-0.7
1993	Min-A	83	253	31	74	16	4	3	23	18	34	.292	.351	.423	774	107	2	6	6	-1	.984	0	3-79	0.2
	Bal-A	33	117	24	38	9	0	6	21	8	15	.325	.373	.556	929	140	6	0	0	0	.937	-1	3-28/1-4	0.5
	Yr	116	370	55	112	25	4	9	44	26	49	.303	.358	.465	823	118	9	6	6	-1	.969	-1	*3-107/1-4	0.7
1995	Tex-A	86	241	27	56	16	0	4	27	15	49	.232	.280	.349	629	61	-14	0	0	0	.963	5	3-68,1-11	-0.9
Total	11	1246	3901	462	942	206	18	134	505	343	785	.241	.308	.407	714	93	-42	18	16	-2	.955	15	*3-1179/1-16,D-2,S2	-3.7
■ TOM PAGNOZZI Pagnozzi, Thomas Alan b: 7/30/62, Tucson, Ariz. BR/TR, 6′1″, 190 lbs. Deb: 4/12/87																								
1987	*StL-N	27	48	8	9	1	0	2	9	4	13	.188	.250	.333	583	52	-3	1	0	0	1.000	-4	C-25/1-1	-0.6
1988	StL-N	81	195	17	55	9	0	0	15	11	32	.282	.320	.328	649	86	-4	0	0	0	.971	-2	C-28,1-28/3-5	-0.6
1989	StL-N	52	80	3	12	2	0	0	3	6	19	.150	.218	.175	393	13	-9	0	0	0	.982	-3	C-38/1-2,3-1	-1.2
1990	StL-N	69	220	20	61	15	0	2	23	14	37	.277	.323	.373	696	91	-3	1	1	-0	.989	10	C-63/1-2	1.0
1991	StL-N	140	459	38	121	24	5	2	57	36	63	.264	.323	.351	673	89	-7	9	13	-3	.991	-7	*C-139/1-3	-0.9
1992	StL-N★	139	485	33	121	26	3	7	44	28	64	.249	.292	.359	651	86	-10	2	5	-1	**.999**	-16	*C-138	-2.1
1993	StL-N	92	330	31	85	15	1	7	41	19	30	.258	.300	.373	673	80	-10	1	0	0	.991	-12	C-92	-1.6
1994	StL-N	70	243	21	66	12	1	7	40	21	39	.272	.330	.416	745	94	-2	0	0	0	**.998**	-7	C-70/1-1	-0.5
1995	StL-N	62	219	17	47	14	1	2	15	11	31	.215	.255	.315	570	50	-16	0	1	-0	.995	-2	C-61	-1.5
1996	*StL-N	119	407	48	110	23	0	13	55	24	78	.270	.314	.423	737	93	-5	4	1	1	.990	-1	*C-116/1-1	0.1
1997	StL-N	25	50	4	11	3	0	1	8	1	7	.220	.235	.340	575	49	-4	0	0	0	1.000	-5	C-13/1-2,3-1	-0.8
1998	StL-N	51	160	7	35	9	0	1	10	14	37	.219	.282	.294	575	52	-11	0	0	0	.982	-5	C-44	-1.3
Total	12	927	2896	247	733	153	11	44	320	189	450	.253	.301	.359	660	80	-84	18	21	-3	.992	-54	C-827/1-40,3-7	-10.0
■ REY PALACIOS Palacios, Robert Rey b: 11/8/62, Brooklyn, N.Y. BR/TR, 5′10″, 190 lbs. Deb: 9/8/88 Career OF: (0-LF 0-CF 2-RF)																								
1988	KC-A	5	11	2	1	0	0	0	0	0	4	.091	.091	.091	182	-48	-2	0	0	0	1.000	1	/C-3,3-1,D-1	-0.1
1989	KC-A	55	47	12	8	2	0	1	8	2	14	.170	.220	.277	497	39	-4	0	1	-0	.958	4	3-21,1-18,C-13,/OD	-0.1
1990	KC-A	41	56	8	13	3	0	2	9	5	24	.232	.295	.393	688	92	-1	2	2	-0	.992	4	C-27/1-7,3-3,O-1R	0.4
Total	3	101	114	22	22	5	0	3	17	7	42	.193	.246	.316	562	57	-7	2	3	-1	.994	9	/C-43,1-25,3-25,DO	0.2
■ ERV PALICA Palica, Ervin Martin (b: Ervin Martin Pavliecivich) b: 2/9/28, Lomita, Cal. d: 5/29/82, Huntington Beach, Cal. BR/TR, 6′1.5″, 180 lbs. Deb: 4/21/45																								
1945	Bro-N	2	0	0	0	0	0	0	0	0	0	—	—	—	—	—	0	0			.000	0	R	0.0
1947	Bro-N	3	0	0	0	0	0	0	0	0	0	—	—	—	—	—	0	0			.000	-0	/P-3	0.0
1948	Bro-N	45	39	6	5	1	1	0	3	4	12	.128	.209	.205	414	12	-5	0			1.000	-1	P-41	0.0
1949	*Bro-N	49	19	2	3	1	0	0	2	2	6	.158	.238	.211	449	20	-2	0			.875	-0	P-49	0.0
1950	Bro-N	48	68	4	15	4	0	1	8	0	8	.221	.221	.324	544	40	-6	2			.889	-4	P-43	0.0
1951	Bro-N	20	13	1	2	0	0	0	0	2	5	.154	.267	.154	421	16	-1	0	0	0	1.000	1	P-19	0.0
1953	Bro-N	4	1	0	1	0	0	0	0	0	0	1.000	1.000	1.000	2000	414	0	0	0	0	1.000	0	/P-4	0.0
1954	Bro-N	28	16	2	4	1	0	0	1	1	4	.250	.294	.313	607	56	-1	0	0	0	.875	-2	P-25	0.0
1955	Bal-A	33	55	3	13	1	0	0	3	4	18	.236	.288	.255	543	50	-4	0	0	0	.905	-1	P-33	0.0
1956	Bal-A	30	32	4	5	0	0	0	0	0	10	.156	.156	.156	313	-19	-6	0	0	0	.917	-0	P-29	0.0
Total	10	262	243	22	48	8	1	1	17	13	63	.198	.238	.251	489	31	-24	2	0		.921	-7	P-246	0.0
■ ORLANDO PALMEIRO Palmeiro, Orlando b: 1/19/69, Hoboken, N.J. BL/TL, 5′11″, 155 lbs. Deb: 7/1/95																								
1995	Cal-A	15	20	3	7	0	0	0	1	1	1	.350	.381	.350	731	93	-0	0	0	0	1.000	-2	/O-7(3-4-0),D-1	-0.2
1996	Cal-A	50	87	6	25	6	1	0	6	8	13	.287	.361	.379	740	87	-1	0	1	-0	1.000	-8	O-31(7-17-8)/D-4	-0.9
1997	Ana-A	74	134	19	29	2	2	0	8	17	11	.216	.309	.261	570	51	-9	2	2	-0	.975	-9	O-52(4-45-4),D-11	-1.8
1998	Ana-A	75	165	28	53	7	2	0	21	20	11	.321	.395	.388	782	104	2	5	4	-0	1.000	-4	O-54(46-6-4)/D-3	-0.3
1999	Ana-A	109	317	46	88	12	1	1	23	39	30	.278	.367	.331	699	81	-8	5	5	-1	.994	-5	O-92(60-1-35),D-12	-1.6
2000	Ana-A	108	243	38	73	20	2	0	25	38	20	.300	.399	.399	798	103	3	4	1	1	.984	-3	O-72(40-2-31),D-19	-0.3
Total	6	431	966	140	275	47	8	1	84	123	86	.285	.372	.353	725	87	-14	16	13	-1	.990	-31	O-308(160-75-82)/D-50	-5.1
■ RAFAEL PALMEIRO Palmeiro, Rafael (Corrales) b: 9/24/64, Havana, Cuba BL/TL, 6′, 188 lbs. Deb: 9/8/86 Career OF: (208-LF 2-CF 8-RF)																								
1986	Chi-N	22	73	9	18	4	0	3	12	4	6	.247	.295	.425	720	89	-1	1	1	-0	.900	-0	O-20(19-0-3)	-0.2
1987	Chi-N	84	221	32	61	15	1	14	30	20	26	.276	.339	.543	882	124	7	2	2	-0	1.000	-4	O-45(44-0-2),1-18	0.0
1988	Chi-N★	152	580	75	178	41	5	8	53	38	34	.307	.353	.436	789	120	14	12	2	2	.983	4	*O-147(145-2-3)/1-5	1.6
1989	Tex-A	156	559	76	154	23	4	8	64	63	48	.275	.355	.374	729	104	4	4	3	-0	.991	10	*1-147/D-6	0.4
1990	Tex-A	154	598	72	**191**	35	6	14	89	40	59	.319	.365	.468	833	131	24	3	3	-0	.995	-1	*1-146/D-6	1.2
1991	Tex-A★	159	631	115	203	**49**	3	26	88	68	72	.322	.393	.532	925	156	48	4	3	-0	.992	-4	*1-157/D-2	3.2
1992	Tex-A	159	608	84	163	27	4	22	85	72	83	.268	.355	.434	789	124	20	2	3	-1	.995	14	*1-156/D-2	2.3
1993	Tex-A	160	597	**124**	176	40	2	37	105	73	85	.295	.376	.554	931	153	43	22	3	4	.997	16	*1-160	4.5
1994	Bal-A	111	436	82	139	32	0	23	76	54	63	.319	.396	.550	947	134	22	7	3	0	.996	-2	*1-111	0.9
1995	Bal-A	143	554	89	172	30	2	39	104	62	65	.310	.383	.583	966	145	35	3	1	0	.997	9	*1-142	2.8
1996	*Bal-A	162	626	110	181	40	2	39	142	95	96	.289	.385	.546	932	133	32	8	0	2	.995	5	*1-159/D-3	2.1
1997	*Bal-A	158	614	95	156	24	2	38	110	67	109	.254	.332	.485	818	113	10	5	2	0	.993	5	*1-155/D-3	0.1

YEAR	TM/L	G	AB	R	H	2B	3B	HR	RBI	BB	SO	AVG	OBP	SLG	OPS	OPS+	BR+	SB	CS	SBR	FA	FR	G/POS	TPR
1998	Bal-A★	162	619	98	183	36	1	43	121	79	91	.296	.382	.565	947	144	40	11	7	-0	.994	8	*1-159/D-3	3.0
1999	*Tex-A★	158	565	96	183	30	1	47	148	97	69	.324	.426	.630	1056	157	50	2	4	-1	.996	-1	*D-135,1-28	3.4
2000	Tex-A	158	565	102	163	29	3	39	120	103	77	.288	.401	.558	958	135	31	2	1	0	.995	-5	*1-108,D-46	1.2
Total	15	2098	7846	1259	2321	455	36	400	1347	935	983	.296	.375	.516	891	134	380	88	38	6	.994	53	*1-1651,O-212L,D-206	26.5

■ DEAN PALMER

Palmer, Dean William b: 12/27/68, Tallahassee, Fla. BR/TR, 6'2", 195 lbs. Deb: 9/1/89 Career OF: (30-LF 0-CF 0-RF)

YEAR	TM/L	G	AB	R	H	2B	3B	HR	RBI	BB	SO	AVG	OBP	SLG	OPS	OPS+	BR+	SB	CS	SBR	FA	FR	G/POS	TPR
1989	Tex-A	16	19	0	2	2	0	0	1	0	12	.105	.105	.211	316	-13	-3	0	0	0	.667	-0	/3-6,S-1,O-1L,D-6	-0.3
1991	Tex-A	81	268	38	50	9	2	15	37	32	98	.187	.281	.403	684	88	-5	0	2	-1	.944	-10	3-50,O-29(29-0-0)/D-5	-1.7
1992	Tex-A	152	541	74	124	25	0	26	72	62	154	.229	.313	.420	733	107	4	10	4	1	.945	-10	*3-150	-0.5
1993	Tex-A	148	519	88	127	31	2	33	96	53	154	.245	.324	.503	827	123	15	11	10	-1	.922	-12	*3-148/S-1	0.2
1994	Tex-A	93	342	50	84	14	2	19	59	26	89	.246	.303	.465	768	94	-4	3	4	-1	.912	-2	3-91	-0.5
1995	Tex-A	36	119	30	40	6	0	9	24	21	21	.336	.451	.613	1065	170	13	1	1	-0	.948	1	3-36	1.3
1996	*Tex-A	154	582	98	163	26	2	38	107	59	145	.280	.351	.527	879	112	9	2	0	0	.953	-24	*3-154/D-1	-1.2
1997	Tex-A	94	355	47	87	21	0	14	55	26	84	.245	.298	.423	721	81	-11	1	0	0	.959	-8	3-93	-1.7
	KC-A	49	187	23	52	10	1	9	31	15	50	.278	.338	.487	825	109	2	1	2	-0	.924	-7	3-48/D-1	-0.5
	Yr	143	542	70	139	31	1	23	86	41	134	.256	.312	.445	757	91	-9	2	2	-0	.948	-16	*3-141/D-1	-2.2
1998	KC-A★	152	572	84	159	27	2	34	119	48	134	.278	.340	.510	851	114	10	8	2	1	.921	-21	*3-129,D-22	-1.0
1999	Det-A	150	560	92	147	25	2	38	100	57	153	.262	.341	.518	859	116	12	3	3	-0	.945	-9	*3-141/D-9	0.3
2000	Det-A	145	524	73	134	22	2	29	102	66	146	.256	.343	.471	815	107	5	4	2	0	.914	-22	*3-115,1-20,D-14	-1.7
Total	11	1270	4588	697	1169	218	15	264	803	465	1240	.255	.330	.481	811	109	47	44	30	-1	.935	-125	*3-1161/D-58,O1S	-7.3

■ EDDIE PALMER

Palmer, Edwin Henry "Baldy" b: 6/1/1893, Petty, Tex. d: 1/9/83, Marlow, Okla. BR/TR, 5'9.5", 175 lbs. Deb: 9/6/17

YEAR	TM/L	G	AB	R	H	2B	3B	HR	RBI	BB	SO	AVG	OBP	SLG	OPS	OPS+	BR+	SB	CS	SBR	FA	FR	G/POS	TPR
1917	Phi-A	16	52	7	11	1	0	0	5	7	7	.212	.305	.231	536	65	-2	1			.898	0	3-13/S-1	-0.2

■ JOE PALMISANO

Palmisano, Joseph b: 11/19/02, West Point, Ga. d: 11/5/71, Albuquerque, N.Mex. BR/TR, 5'8", 160 lbs. Deb: 5/31/31

YEAR	TM/L	G	AB	R	H	2B	3B	HR	RBI	BB	SO	AVG	OBP	SLG	OPS	OPS+	BR+	SB	CS	SBR	FA	FR	G/POS	TPR
1931	Phi-A	19	44	5	10	2	0	0	4	6	3	.227	.320	.273	593	54	-3	0	0	0	.960	-2	C-16/2-1	-0.3

■ STAN PALYS

Palys, Stanley Francis b: 5/1/30, Blakely, Pa. BR/TR, 6'2", 190 lbs. Deb: 9/20/53

YEAR	TM/L	G	AB	R	H	2B	3B	HR	RBI	BB	SO	AVG	OBP	SLG	OPS	OPS+	BR+	SB	CS	SBR	FA	FR	G/POS	TPR
1953	Phi-N	2	2	0	0	0	0	0	0	1	0	.000	.333	.000	333	-4	-0	0	0	0	.000	-0	/O-1(0-0-1)	-0.1
1954	Phi-N	2	4	0	1	0	0	0	0	1	1	.250	.400	.250	650	74	-0	0	0	0	1.000	0	/O-1(0-0-1)	0.0
1955	Phi-N	15	52	8	15	3	0	1	8	6	5	.288	.362	.404	766	105	0	1	0	0	1.000	-0	O-15(3-4-8)	0.0
	Cin-N	79	222	29	51	14	0	7	30	12	35	.230	.272	.387	660	69	-10	1	1	-0	.992	2	O-55(55-0-0)/1-1	-1.2
	Yr	94	274	37	66	17	0	8	38	18	40	.241	.290	.391	681	75	-10	2	1	0	.993	2	O-70(58-4-8)/1-1	-1.2
1956	Cin-N	40	53	5	12	0	0	2	5	6	13	.226	.305	.340	645	69	-2	0	0	0	.929	-2	O-10(7-0-4)	-0.5
Total	4	138	333	42	79	17	0	10	43	26	54	.237	.294	.378	673	74	-13	2	1	0	.988	-1	/O-82(65-4-14),1-1	-1.8

■ JIM PANKOVITS

Pankovits, James Franklin b: 8/6/55, Pennington Gap, Va. BR/TR, 5'10", 195 lbs. Deb: 5/27/84 Career OF: (28-LF 0-CF 20-RF)

YEAR	TM/L	G	AB	R	H	2B	3B	HR	RBI	BB	SO	AVG	OBP	SLG	OPS	OPS+	BR+	SB	CS	SBR	FA	FR	G/POS	TPR
1984	Hou-N	53	81	6	23	7	0	1	14	2	20	.284	.301	.407	709	105	0	2	1	0	.925	-5	2-15/S-4/O-3(3-0-0)	-0.4
1985	Hou-N	75	172	24	42	3	0	4	14	17	29	.244	.316	.331	647	84	-4	1	0	0	.983	0	O-33R,2-21/S-1,3-1	-0.4
1986	*Hou-N	70	113	12	32	6	1	1	7	11	25	.283	.347	.381	727	103	1	1	1	-0	.969	3	2-26/O-5(5-0-0),C-1	0.5
1987	Hou-N	50	61	7	14	2	0	1	8	6	13	.230	.299	.311	610	64	-3	2	0	0	1.000	5	/2-9,O-6(6-0-0),3-4	0.2
1988	Hou-N	68	140	13	31	7	1	2	12	8	28	.221	.273	.329	602	75	-5	2	1	0	.939	-2	2-31,3-11/1-2	-0.7
1990	Bos-A	2	0	0	0	0	0	0	0	0	0	—	—	—	—	—	0	0	0	0	.000	0	/2-2	0.0
Total	6	318	567	62	142	25	2	9	55	44	115	.250	.308	.349	657	86	-11	8	3	1	.961	1	2-104/O-47L,3-16,S1C	-0.8

■ KEN PAPE

Pape, Kenneth Wayne b: 10/1/51, San Antonio, Tex. BR/TR, 5'11", 195 lbs. Deb: 5/17/76

YEAR	TM/L	G	AB	R	H	2B	3B	HR	RBI	BB	SO	AVG	OBP	SLG	OPS	OPS+	BR+	SB	CS	SBR	FA	FR	G/POS	TPR
1976	Tex-A	21	23	7	5	1	0	1	4	3	2	.217	.357	.391	748	117	1	0	1	-0	.968	4	/S-6,3-4,2-1,D-3	0.5

■ STAN PAPI

Papi, Stanley Gerard b: 2/4/51, Fresno, Cal. BR/TR, 6', 178 lbs. Deb: 4/11/74 Career OF: (1-LF 0-CF 0-RF)

YEAR	TM/L	G	AB	R	H	2B	3B	HR	RBI	BB	SO	AVG	OBP	SLG	OPS	OPS+	BR+	SB	CS	SBR	FA	FR	G/POS	TPR
1974	StL-N	8	4	0	1	0	0	0	1	0	0	.250	.250	.250	500	40	-0	0	0	0	1.000	1	/S-7,2-1	0.0
1977	Mon-N	13	43	5	10	2	1	0	4	1	9	.233	.250	.326	576	55	-3	1	0	0	.952	-5	3-10/S-2,2-1	-0.8
1978	Mon-N	67	152	15	35	11	0	0	11	10	28	.230	.287	.303	589	65	-7	0	0	0	.976	-3	S-22,3-15/2-5	-0.9
1979	Bos-A	50	117	9	22	8	0	1	6	5	20	.188	.221	.282	503	33	-11	0	0	0	.982	13	2-26,S-21/D-1	0.4
1980	Bos-A	1	0	0	0	0	0	0	0	0	0	—	—	—	—	—	0	0	0	0	.000	0	/3-1	0.0
	Det-A	46	114	12	27	3	4	3	17	5	24	.237	.269	.412	681	82	-3	0	0	0	.973	-2	2-31,3-11/S-5,/1-1	-0.4
	Yr	47	114	12	27	3	4	3	17	5	24	.237	.269	.412	681	82	-3	0	0	0	.973	-2	2-31,3-12/S-5,1-1	-0.4
1981	Det-A	40	93	8	19	2	1	3	12	3	18	.204	.229	.344	573	61	-5	1	0	0	.941	-1	3-32/1-1,2-1,O-1L,D	-0.7
Total	6	225	523	49	114	26	6	7	51	24	99	.218	.255	.331	586	60	-30	2	0	0	.931	3	/3-69,2-65,S-57,D1O	-2.4

■ ERIK PAPPAS

Pappas, Erik Daniel b: 4/25/66, Chicago, Ill. BR/TR, 6', 190 lbs. Deb: 4/19/91 Career OF: (1-LF 0-CF 15-RF)

YEAR	TM/L	G	AB	R	H	2B	3B	HR	RBI	BB	SO	AVG	OBP	SLG	OPS	OPS+	BR+	SB	CS	SBR	FA	FR	G/POS	TPR
1991	Chi-N	7	17	1	3	0	0	0	2	1	5	.176	.222	.176	399	13	-2	0	0	0	1.000	1	/C-6	0.0
1993	StL-N	82	228	25	63	12	0	1	28	35	35	.276	.373	.342	715	95	-0	1	3	-1	.982	5	C-63,O-16(1-0-15)/1-2	0.6
1994	StL-N	15	44	8	4	1	0	0	5	10	13	.091	.273	.114	386	6	-6	0	0	0	.955	-4	C-15	-1.0
Total	3	104	289	34	70	13	0	1	35	46	53	.242	.348	.298	646	76	-8	1	3	-1	.978	2	/C-84,O-16R,1-2	-0.4

■ CRAIG PAQUETTE

Paquette, Craig Harold b: 3/28/69, Long Beach, Cal. BR/TR, 6', 190 lbs. Deb: 6/1/93 Career OF: (92-LF 0-CF 43-RF)

YEAR	TM/L	G	AB	R	H	2B	3B	HR	RBI	BB	SO	AVG	OBP	SLG	OPS	OPS+	BR+	SB	CS	SBR	FA	FR	G/POS	TPR
1993	Oak-A	105	393	35	86	20	4	12	46	14	108	.219	.246	.382	627	70	-19	4	2	0	.950	-9	*3-104/O-1(1-0-0),D-1	-2.7
1994	Oak-A	14	49	0	7	2	0	0	0	0	14	.143	.143	.184	327	-18	-9	1	0	0	1.000	1	3-14	-0.7
1995	Oak-A	105	283	42	64	13	1	13	49	12	88	.226	.260	.417	677	77	-11	5	2	0	.935	-12	3-75,O-20L/S-8,1-3	-2.1
1996	KC-A	118	429	61	111	15	1	22	67	23	101	.259	.300	.452	752	87	-10	5	3	0	.891	-11	3-51,O-47L,1-19,S/D	-2.1
1997	KC-A	77	252	26	58	15	1	8	33	10	57	.230	.265	.393	658	67	-13	2	2	-0	.935	2	3-72/O-4(4-0-0)	-1.1
1998	NY-N	7	19	3	5	2	0	0	0	0	6	.263	.263	.368	632	65	-1	1	0	0	1.000	-1	/3-4,1-2,O-1(1-0-0)	-0.2
1999	StL-N	48	157	21	45	6	0	10	37	6	38	.287	.313	.516	829	104	0	1	0	0	.955	-0	O-27R,3-10/2-7,1-6	-0.1
2000	*StL-N	134	384	47	94	24	2	15	61	27	83	.245	.298	.435	733	82	-12	4	3	-0	.942	-6	3-86,O-31L,1-28,2	-1.9
Total	8	608	1966	235	470	97	9	80	293	92	495	.239	.276	.420	695	78	-75	23	12	1	.941	-38	3-416,O-131L/12SD	-10.9

■ AL PARDO

Pardo, Alberto Judas b: 9/8/62, Oviedo, Spain BB/TR, 6'2", 187 lbs. Deb: 7/3/85

YEAR	TM/L	G	AB	R	H	2B	3B	HR	RBI	BB	SO	AVG	OBP	SLG	OPS	OPS+	BR+	SB	CS	SBR	FA	FR	G/POS	TPR
1985	Bal-A	34	75	3	10	1	0	0	1	3	15	.133	.167	.147	313	-14	-12	0	0	0	.979	3	C-29	-0.7
1986	Bal-A	16	51	3	7	1	0	1	3	0	14	.137	.137	.216	353	-6	-7	0	0	0	.987	-2	C-14/D-1	-0.9
1988	Phi-N	2	2	0	0	0	0	0	0	0	2	.000	.000	.000	0	-98	-0	0	0	0	1.000	-0	/C-2	-0.1
1989	Phi-N	1	1	0	0	0	0	0	0	0	0	.000	.000	.000	0	-99	-0	0	0	0	1.000	0	/C-1	0.0
Total	4	53	129	6	17	2	0	1	4	3	31	.132	.152	.171	322	-12	-20	0	0	0	.982	1	/C-46,D-1	-1.7

■ JOHNNY PAREDES

Paredes, Johnny Alfonso (Isambert) b: 9/2/62, Maracaibo, Venez. BR/TR, 5'11", 165 lbs. Deb: 4/29/88 Career OF: (0-LF 0-CF 1-RF)

YEAR	TM/L	G	AB	R	H	2B	3B	HR	RBI	BB	SO	AVG	OBP	SLG	OPS	OPS+	BR+	SB	CS	SBR	FA	FR	G/POS	TPR
1988	Mon-N	35	91	6	17	2	0	1	10	9	17	.187	.282	.242	523	49	-6	5	2	0	.976	0	2-28/O-1(0-0-1)	-0.5
1990	Det-A	6	8	2	1	0	0	0	0	1	0	.125	.222	.125	347	-0	-1	0	0	0	.917	1	/2-4	0.0
	Mon-N	3	6	0	2	1	0	0	1	1	0	.333	.429	.500	929	161	1	0	0	0	.889	1	/2-2	0.1
1991	Det-A	16	18	4	6	0	0	0	0	0	1	.333	.333	.333	667	84	-0	1	1	-0	.958	4	/2-7,3-1,S-1,D-2	0.3
Total	3	60	123	12	26	3	0	1	11	11	18	.211	.292	.260	552	56	-7	6	3	0	.965	6	/2-41,D-2,S-1,3O	-0.1

■ FREDDY PARENT

Parent, Frederick Alfred b: 11/25/1875, Biddeford, Me. d: 11/2/72, Sanford, Maine BR/TR, 5'7", 154 lbs. Deb: 7/14/1899 Career OF: (34-LF 102-CF 12-RF)

YEAR	TM/L	G	AB	R	H	2B	3B	HR	RBI	BB	SO	AVG	OBP	SLG	OPS	OPS+	BR+	SB	CS	SBR	FA	FR	G/POS	TPR
1899	StL-N	2	8	0	1	0	0	0	1	0		.125	.125	.125	250	-31	-1	0			.889	-1	/2-2	-0.2
1901	Bos-A	138	517	87	158	23	9	4	59	41		.306	.367	.408	775	117	12	16			.918	-0	*S-138	1.5
1902	Bos-A	138	567	91	156	31	8	3	62	24		.275	.309	.374	683	86	-12	16			.932	4	*S-138	-0.4
1903	*Bos-A	139	560	83	170	31	17	4	80	13		.304	.326	.441	767	122	13	24			.930	9	*S-139	2.7
1904	Bos-A	155	591	85	172	22	9	6	77	28		.291	.330	.389	719	120	13	20			.929	-8	*S-155	1.1
1905	Bos-A	153	602	55	141	16	5	0	33	47		.234	.296	.277	574	81	-12	25			.920	-11	*S-153	-1.9
1906	Bos-A	149	600	67	141	14	10	1	49	31		.235	.277	.297	574	80	-15	16			.933	-7	*S-143/2-6	-1.8
1907	Bos-A	114	409	51	113	19	5	1	26	22		.276	.321	.355	676	116	7	12			.978	-2	O-47L,S-43/3-7,2-5	0.5
1908	Chi-A	119	391	28	81	7	5	0	35	50		.207	.300	.251	551	81	-6	9			.930	5	*S-118	0.3
1909	Chi-A	136	472	61	123	10	5	0	30	46		.261	.335	.303	638	106	5	32			.929	17	S-98,O-38(7-30-1)/2-1	2.5
1910	Chi-A	81	258	23	46	6	1	1	16	29		.178	.266	.221	487	55	-13	14			.970	-2	O-62C,2-11/S-4,3-1	-2.0

YEAR	TM/L	G	AB	R	H	2B	3B	HR	RBI	BB	SO	AVG	OBP	SLG	OPS	OPS+	BR+	SB	CS	SBR	FA	FR	G/POS	TPR
1911	Chi-A	3	9	2	4	1	0	0	3	2		.444	.545	.556	1101	214	2	0			1.000	1	/2-3	0.2
Total	12	1327	4984	633	1306	180	74	20	471	333		.262	.315	.340	655	99	-7	184			.927	5	*S-1129,O-147C/2-28,3	2.5

■ MARK PARENT

Parent, Mark Alan b: 9/16/61, Ashland, Ore. BR/TR, 6'5", 225 lbs. Deb: 9/20/86

YEAR	TM/L	G	AB	R	H	2B	3B	HR	RBI	BB	SO	AVG	OBP	SLG	OPS	OPS+	BR+	SB	CS	SBR	FA	FR	G/POS	TPR
1986	SD-N	8	14	1	2	0	0	0	0	1	3	.143	.200	.143	343	-4	-2	0	0	0	.889	-1	/C-3	-0.3
1987	SD-N	12	25	0	2	0	0	0	2	0	9	.080	.080	.080	160	-60	-6	0	0	0	1.000	0	C-10	-0.5
1988	SD-N	41	118	9	23	3	0	6	15	6	23	.195	.234	.373	607	73	-5	0	0	0	.986	5	C-36	0.3
1989	SD-N	52	141	12	27	4	0	7	21	8	34	.191	.235	.369	604	70	-6	1	0	0	1.000	6	C-41/1-1	0.2
1990	SD-N	65	189	13	42	11	0	3	16	16	29	.222	.283	.328	611	67	-9	1	0	0	.992	8	C-60	0.3
1991	Tex-A	3	1	0	0	0	0	0	0	0	1	.000	.000	.000	0	-99	-0	0	0	0	1.000	1	/C-3	0.0
1992	Bal-A	17	34	4	8	1	0	2	4	3	7	.235	.316	.441	757	107	0	0	0	0	.988	4	C-16	0.5
1993	Bal-A	22	54	7	14	2	0	4	12	3	14	.259	.298	.519	817	110	0	0	0	0	.989	-1	C-21/D-1	0.0
1994	Chi-N	44	99	8	26	4	0	3	16	13	24	.263	.354	.394	748	96	-0	0	1	-0	.976	4	C-37	0.5
1995	Pit-N	69	233	25	54	9	0	15	33	23	62	.232	.301	.464	764	96	-2	0	0	0	.990	-10	C-67	-0.8
	Chi-N	12	32	5	8	2	0	3	5	3	7	.250	.314	.594	908	135	1	0	0	0	1.000	2	C-10	0.4
	Yr	81	265	30	62	11	0	18	38	26	69	.234	.302	.479	782	101	-1	0	0	0	.992	-8	C-77	-0.4
1996	Det-A	38	104	13	25	6	0	7	17	3	27	.240	.262	.500	762	87	-3	0	0	0	.994	-4	C-33/1-1	-0.4
	*Bal-A	18	33	4	6	1	0	2	6	2	10	.182	.229	.394	623	54	-3	0	0	0	.987	2	C-18	0.0
	Yr	56	137	17	31	7	0	9	23	5	37	.226	.254	.474	728	79	-5	0	0	0	.992	-2	C-51/1-1	-0.4
1997	Phi-N	39	113	4	17	3	0	0	8	7	39	.150	.200	.177	377	-0	-17	0	1	-0	.996	-0	C-38	-1.5
1998	Phi-N	34	113	7	25	4	0	1	13	10	30	.221	.285	.283	568	49	-8	1	1	-0	.987	-3	C-34	-1.0
Total	13	474	1303	112	279	50	0	53	168	98	319	.214	.270	.375	645	71	-58	3	3	-0	.990	14	C-427/1-2,D-1	-2.3

■ KELLY PARIS

Paris, Kelly Jay b: 10/17/57, Encino, Cal. BR/TR, 6', 180 lbs. Deb: 9/1/82

YEAR	TM/L	G	AB	R	H	2B	3B	HR	RBI	BB	SO	AVG	OBP	SLG	OPS	OPS+	BR+	SB	CS	SBR	FA	FR	G/POS	TPR
1982	StL-N	12	29	1	3	0	0	0	1	0	7	.103	.103	.103	207	-42	-5	0	0	0	.867	2	/3-5,S-4	-0.3
1983	Cin-N	56	120	13	30	6	0	0	7	15	22	.250	.338	.300	638	75	-3	8	2	1	1.000	-2	3-16,2-10/S-7,1-3	-0.4
1985	Bal-A	5	9	0	0	0	0	0	0	0	1	.000	.000	.000	0	-99	-2	0	0	0	.857	-0	/2-2,D-2	-0.3
1986	Bal-A	5	10	0	2	0	0	0	0	0	3	.200	.200	.200	400	9	-1	0	1	-0	.857	1	/3-3,D-2	-0.1
1988	Chi-A	14	44	6	11	0	0	3	6	0	6	.250	.250	.455	705	93	-1	0	0	0	1.000	-0	/1-9,3-4,D-1	-0.1
Total	5	92	212	20	46	6	0	3	14	15	39	.217	.272	.288	560	54	-13	8	3	1	.944	1	/3-28,1-12,2-12,SD	-1.2

■ TONY PARISSE

Parisse, Louis Peter b: 6/25/11, Philadelphia, Pa. d: 6/2/56, Philadelphia, Pa. BR/TR, 5'10", 165 lbs. Deb: 9/22/43

YEAR	TM/L	G	AB	R	H	2B	3B	HR	RBI	BB	SO	AVG	OBP	SLG	OPS	OPS+	BR+	SB	CS	SBR	FA	FR	G/POS	TPR
1943	Phi-A	6	17	0	3	0	0	0	1	2	2	.176	.263	.176	440	30	-1	0	0	0	1.000	0	/C-5	-0.1
1944	Phi-A	4	4	0	0	0	0	0	0	0	1	.000	.000	.000	0	-99	-1	0	0	0	.500	-1	/C-2	-0.2
Total	2	10	21	0	3	0	0	0	1	2	3	.143	.217	.143	360	6	-2	0	0	0	.960	-0	/C-7	-0.3

■ ACE PARKER

Parker, Clarence McKay b: 5/17/12, Portsmouth, Va. BR/TR, 6', 180 lbs. Deb: 4/24/37 Career OF: (2-LF 3-CF 0-RF)

YEAR	TM/L	G	AB	R	H	2B	3B	HR	RBI	BB	SO	AVG	OBP	SLG	OPS	OPS+	BR+	SB	CS	SBR	FA	FR	G/POS	TPR
1937	Phi-A	38	94	8	11	0	1	2	13	4	17	.117	.153	.202	355	-11	-17	0	0	0	.905	-5	S-19/2-9,O-5(2-3-0)	-1.9
1938	Phi-A	56	113	12	26	5	0	0	12	10	16	.230	.293	.274	567	44	-10	1	2	-0	.972	-5	S-26/2-9,3-9	-1.2
Total	2	94	207	20	37	5	1	2	25	14	33	.179	.231	.242	472	19	-26	1	2	-0	.934	-10	/S-45,2-18,3-9,O-5C	-3.1

■ PAT PARKER

Parker, Clarence Perkins b: 5/22/1893, Somerville, Mass. d: 3/21/67, Claremont, N.H. BR/TR, 5'7", 160 lbs. Deb: 8/10/15

YEAR	TM/L	G	AB	R	H	2B	3B	HR	RBI	BB	SO	AVG	OBP	SLG	OPS	OPS+	BR+	SB	CS	SBR	FA	FR	G/POS	TPR
1915	StL-A	3	6	0	1	0	0	0	1	0	3	.167	.167	.167	333	-0	-1	0	1	-0	1.000	-0	/O-2(0-0-2)	-0.1

■ DAVE PARKER

Parker, David Gene b: 6/9/51, Grenada, Miss. BL/TR, 6'5", 230 lbs. Deb: 7/12/73 C Career OF: (49-LF 30-CF 1791-RF)

YEAR	TM/L	G	AB	R	H	2B	3B	HR	RBI	BB	SO	AVG	OBP	SLG	OPS	OPS+	BR+	SB	CS	SBR	FA	FR	G/POS	TPR
1973	Pit-N	54	139	17	40	9	1	4	14	2	27	.288	.308	.453	761	111	1	1	1	-0	.964	0	O-39(4-16-19)	0.0
1974	*Pit-N	73	220	27	62	10	3	4	29	10	53	.282	.322	.409	731	107	1	3	3	-0	.964	1	O-49(11-14-27)/1-6	-0.1
1975	*Pit-N	148	558	75	172	35	10	25	101	38	89	.308	.358	**.541**	899	148	33	8	6	-0	.972	11	*O-141(0-0-141)	3.6
1976	Pit-N	138	537	82	168	28	10	13	90	30	80	.313	.351	.475	826	132	20	19	7	2	.956	7	*O-134(0-0-134)	2.3
1977	Pit-N★	159	637	107	**215**	**44**	8	21	88	58	107	**.338**	.399	.531	929	143	39	17	19	-3	.965	33	*O-158(0-0-158)/2-1	5.9
1978	Pit-N	148	581	102	194	32	12	30	117	57	92	**.334**	.395	**.585**	**981**	163	**48**	20	7	2	.960	8	*O-147(0-0-147)	**5.1**
1979	*Pit-N★	158	622	109	193	45	7	25	94	67	101	.310	.385	.526	911	140	34	20	4	3	.960	9	*O-158(0-0-158)	3.8
1980	Pit-N★	139	518	71	153	31	1	17	79	25	69	.295	.330	.458	788	116	9	10	7	-0	.965	4	*O-130(0-0-130)	0.6
1981	Pit-N★	67	240	29	62	14	3	9	48	9	25	.258	.291	.454	745	106	0	6	2	1	.941	-2	O-60(0-0-60)	-0.5
1982	Pit-N	73	244	41	66	19	3	6	29	22	45	.270	.333	.447	780	113	4	7	5	-0	.957	-1	O-63(0-0-63)	-0.1
1983	Pit-N	144	552	68	154	29	4	12	69	28	89	.279	.314	.411	725	97	-4	12	9	-1	.973	7	*O-142(0-0-142)	-0.5
1984	Cin-N	156	607	73	173	28	0	16	94	41	89	.285	.331	.410	741	103	1	11	10	-1	.974	5	*O-151(0-0-151)	-0.3
1985	Cin-N★	160	635	88	198	**42**	4	34	**125**	52	80	.312	.367	.551	918	146	37	5	13	-3	.972	13	*O-159(0-0-159)	3.9
1986	Cin-N★	162	637	89	174	31	3	31	116	56	126	.273	.333	.477	810	116	12	1	6	-2	.970	-2	*O-159(0-0-159)	-0.1
1987	Cin-N	153	589	77	149	28	0	26	97	44	104	.253	.314	.433	747	91	-8	7	3	0	.967	8	*O-142(0-0-142)/1-9	-0.8
1988	*Oak-A	101	377	43	97	18	1	12	55	32	70	.257	.315	.406	721	104	1	0	1	-0	.953	-0	D-61,O-34(34-0-0)/1-1	-0.2
1989	*Oak-A	144	553	56	146	27	0	22	97	38	91	.264	.313	.432	745	112	7	0	0	0	1.000	0	*D-140/O-1(0-0-1)	0.2
1990	Mil-A☆	157	610	71	176	30	3	21	92	41	102	.289	.337	.451	788	119	14	4	7	-2	.960	-1	*D-153/1-3	0.6
1991	Cal-A	119	466	45	108	22	2	11	56	29	91	.232	.281	.358	639	76	-16	3	2	-0	.000	0	*D-119	-2.0
	Tor-A	13	36	2	12	4	0	0	3	4	7	.333	.400	.444	844	128	1	0	1	-0	.000	0	D-11	0.1
	Yr	132	502	47	120	26	2	11	59	33	98	.239	.290	.365	655	80	-15	3	3	-0	.000	0	*D-130	-1.9
Total	19	2466	9358	1272	2712	526	75	339	1493	683	1537	.290	.342	.471	813	121	235	154	113	-6	.965	98	*O-1867R,D-484/1-19,2	21.5

■ DIXIE PARKER

Parker, Douglas Woolley b: 4/24/1895, Forest Home, Ala. d: 5/15/72, Tuscaloosa, Ala. BL/TR, 5'11", 160 lbs. Deb: 7/28/23

YEAR	TM/L	G	AB	R	H	2B	3B	HR	RBI	BB	SO	AVG	OBP	SLG	OPS	OPS+	BR+	SB	CS	SBR	FA	FR	G/POS	TPR
1923	Phi-N	4	5	0	1	0	0	0	1	0	1	.200	.200	.200	400	5	-1	0	0	0	.500	-1	/C-2	-0.1

■ SALTY PARKER

Parker, Francis James b: 7/8/13, E.St.Louis, Ill. d: 7/27/92, Houston, Tex. BR/TR, 6', 173 lbs. Deb: 8/13/36 MC

YEAR	TM/L	G	AB	R	H	2B	3B	HR	RBI	BB	SO	AVG	OBP	SLG	OPS	OPS+	BR+	SB	CS	SBR	FA	FR	G/POS	TPR
1936	Det-A	11	25	6	7	2	0	0	4	2	3	.280	.333	.360	693	71	-1	0	2	-1	.906	3	/S-7,1-2	0.2

■ WES PARKER

Parker, Maurice Wesley b: 11/13/39, Evanston, Ill. BB/TL, 6'1", 180 lbs. Deb: 4/19/64 Career OF: (34-LF 51-CF 76-RF)

YEAR	TM/L	G	AB	R	H	2B	3B	HR	RBI	BB	SO	AVG	OBP	SLG	OPS	OPS+	BR+	SB	CS	SBR	FA	FR	G/POS	TPR
1964	LA-N	124	214	29	55	7	1	3	10	14	45	.257	.306	.341	647	88	-3	5	4	-0	.971	-10	O-69(9-15-49),1-31	-1.8
1965	*LA-N	154	542	80	129	24	7	8	51	75	95	.238	.336	.352	688	101	2	13	7	0	**.997**	-1	*1-154/O-1(0-1-0)	-0.8
1966	*LA-N	156	475	67	120	17	5	12	51	69	83	.253	.353	.385	739	114	11	7	3	0	.992	1	*1-140,O-14(2-7-5)	0.4
1967	LA-N	139	413	56	102	16	5	5	31	65	83	.247	.359	.346	705	112	9	10	5	0	**.996**	5	*1-112,O-18(0-18-0)	0.9
1968	LA-N	135	468	42	112	22	2	3	27	49	87	.239	.314	.314	628	96	-2	4	6	-1	**.999**	1	*1-114,O-28(22-6-1)	-1.1
1969	LA-N	132	471	76	131	23	4	13	68	56	46	.278	.357	.427	784	128	17	4	1	1	.995	0	*1-128/O-2(0-1-1)	0.9
1970	LA-N	161	614	84	196	**47**	4	10	111	79	70	.319	.397	.458	854	134	31	8	2	1	**.996**	4	*1-161	2.3
1971	LA-N	157	533	69	146	24	1	6	62	63	63	.274	.352	.356	708	107	6	6	1	1	.996	3	*1-148,O-18(1-0-18)	-0.1
1972	LA-N	130	427	45	119	14	3	4	59	62	43	.279	.371	.354	725	110	8	3	5	-1	**.997**	1	*1-120/O-5(0-3-2)	-0.2
Total	9	1288	4157	548	1110	194	32	64	470	532	615	.267	.353	.375	729	112	80	60	34	1	.996	4	*1-1108,O-155R	0.5

■ RICK PARKER

Parker, Richard Alan b: 3/20/63, Kansas City, Mo. BR/TR, 6', 185 lbs. Deb: 5/4/90 Career OF: (44-LF 24-CF 28-RF)

YEAR	TM/L	G	AB	R	H	2B	3B	HR	RBI	BB	SO	AVG	OBP	SLG	OPS	OPS+	BR+	SB	CS	SBR	FA	FR	G/POS	TPR
1990	SF-N	54	107	19	26	5	0	2	14	10	15	.243	.314	.346	659	84	-2	6	1	1	.978	-10	O-35R/2-2,3-1,S-1	-1.2
1991	SF-N	13	14	0	1	0	0	0	1	1	5	.071	.133	.071	205	-42	-3	0	0	0	1.000	-1	/O-4(4-1-0)	-0.4
1993	Hou-N	45	45	11	15	3	0	0	4	3	8	.333	.375	.400	775	112	1	1	2	-0	1.000	-5	O-16(3-13-1)/2-1,S-1	-0.4
1994	NY-N	8	16	1	1	0	0	0	0	0	2	.063	.063	.063	125	-68	-4	0	0	0	1.000	0	/O-6(4-1-3)	-0.4
1995	LA-N	27	29	3	8	0	0	0	4	2	4	.276	.323	.276	598	66	-1	1	1	-0	1.000	-2	O-21(19-1-1)/3-2,S-2	-0.4
1996	LA-N	16	14	2	4	1	0	0	1	0	2	.286	.333	.357	690	89	-0	1	0	0	1.000	-1	/O-4(1-3-0)	-0.1
Total	6	163	225	36	55	9	0	2	24	16	36	.244	.300	.311	612	69	-10	9	4	1	.990	-19	/O-86L,S-4,3-3,2-3	-2.9

■ BILLY PARKER

Parker, William David b: 1/14/47, Hayneville, Ala. BR/TR, 5'8", 168 lbs. Deb: 9/9/71 Career OF: (5-LF 0-CF 0-RF)

YEAR	TM/L	G	AB	R	H	2B	3B	HR	RBI	BB	SO	AVG	OBP	SLG	OPS	OPS+	BR+	SB	CS	SBR	FA	FR	G/POS	TPR
1971	Cal-A	20	70	4	16	0	1	1	6	2	20	.229	.250	.300	550	59	-4	1	1	-0	.958	-1	2-20	-0.4
1972	Cal-A	36	80	11	17	2	0	2	8	9	17	.213	.292	.313	605	85	-2	0	2	-1	.951	-0	3-21/2-9,O-5L,S-1	-0.3
1973	Cal-A	38	102	14	23	2	1	0	7	8	23	.225	.288	.265	553	61	-5	0	1	-0	.959	-3	2-32/S-3,D-1	-0.7
Total	3	94	252	29	56	4	2	3	21	19	60	.222	.279	.290	569	68	-11	1	4	-1	.963	-5	/2-61,3-21,O-5L,SD	-1.4

■ FRANK PARKINSON Parkinson, Frank Joseph "Parky" b: 3/23/1895, Dickson City, Pa. d: 7/4/60, Trenton, N.J. BR/TR, 5'11", 175 lbs. Deb: 4/13/21

YEAR	TM/L	G	AB	R	H	2B	3B	HR	RBI	BB	SO	AVG	OBP	SLG	OPS	OPS+	BR+	SB	CS	SBR	FA	FR	G/POS	TPR
1921	Phi-N	108	391	36	99	20	2	5	32	13	81	.253	.277	.353	630	61	-22	3	4	-1	.931	9	*S-105/3-1	-0.2
1922	Phi-N	141	545	86	150	18	6	15	70	55	93	.275	.344	.413	757	86	-12	3	4	-1	.963	**31**	*2-139	2.1
1923	Phi-N	67	219	21	53	12	0	3	28	13	31	.242	.288	.338	625	58	-13	0	4	-1	.950	3	2-37,S-15,3-11	-0.9
1924	Phi-N	62	156	14	33	7	0	1	19	14	28	.212	.281	.276	556	44	-12	3	1	0	.952	7	3-28,S-21,2-10	-0.1
Total	4	378	1311	157	335	57	8	24	149	95	233	.256	.308	.366	674	69	-59	9	13	-3	.962	50	2-186,S-141/3-40	0.9

■ ART PARKS Parks, Artie William b: 11/1/11, Paris, Ark. d: 12/6/89, Little Rock, Ark. BL/TR, 5'9", 170 lbs. Deb: 9/25/37

YEAR	TM/L	G	AB	R	H	2B	3B	HR	RBI	BB	SO	AVG	OBP	SLG	OPS	OPS+	BR+	SB	CS	SBR	FA	FR	G/POS	TPR
1937	Bro-N	7	16	2	5	2	0	0	0	2	2	.313	.389	.438	826	122	1	0			1.000	0	/O-4(4-0-0)	0.0
1939	Bro-N	71	239	27	65	13	2	1	19	28	14	.272	.348	.356	704	86	-4	2			.977	-4	O-65(32-0-34)	-1.2
Total	2	78	255	29	70	15	2	1	19	30	16	.275	.351	.361	712	89	-3	2			.978	-4	/O-69(36-0-34)	-1.2

■ DEREK PARKS Parks, Derek Gavin b: 9/29/68, Covina, Cal. BR/TR, 6', 205 lbs. Deb: 9/11/92

YEAR	TM/L	G	AB	R	H	2B	3B	HR	RBI	BB	SO	AVG	OBP	SLG	OPS	OPS+	BR+	SB	CS	SBR	FA	FR	G/POS	TPR
1992	Min-A	7	6	1	2	0	0	0	0	1	1	.333	.500	.333	833	133	0	0	0	0	1.000	1	/C-7	0.2
1993	Min-A	7	20	3	4	0	0	0	1	1	2	.200	.238	.200	438	19	-2	0	0	0	.970	-0	/C-7	-0.2
1994	Min-A	31	89	6	17	6	0	1	9	4	20	.191	.242	.292	534	37	-9	0	1	-0	.993	-3	C-31	-1.0
Total	3	45	115	10	23	6	0	1	10	6	23	.200	.258	.278	536	40	-10	0	1	-0	.989	-2	/C-45	-1.0

■ BILL PARKS Parks, William Robert b: 6/4/1849, Easton, Pa. d: 10/10/11, Easton, Pa. BR/TR, 5'8", 150 lbs. Deb: 4/26/1875 M

YEAR	TM/L	G	AB	R	H	2B	3B	HR	RBI	BB	SO	AVG	OBP	SLG	OPS	OPS+	BR+	SB	CS	SBR	FA	FR	G/POS	TPR
1875	Was-n	27	111	13	20	0	0	0	6	1	1	.180	.188	.180	368	29	-7	1	1	-0	.836	3	O-17(16-1-0),P-14,M	0.0
	Phi-n	2	6	0	1	0	0	0	0	0	1	.167	.167	.167	333	16	-0	0	0	0	.500	-1	/P-2,O-2(2-0-0)	0.0
	Yr	29	117	13	21	0	0	0	6	1	2	.179	.186	.179	366	29	-8	1	1	-0	.833	3	O-19(18-1-0),P-16	0.0
1876	Bos-N	1	4	0	0	0	0	0	0	0	0	.000	.000	.000	0	-98	-1				.750	-0	/O-1(1-0-0)	-0.1

■ SAM PARRILLA Parrilla, Samuel (Monge) b: 6/12/43, Santurce, P.R. d: 2/9/94, Brooklyn, N.Y. BR/TR, 5'11", 185 lbs. Deb: 4/11/70

YEAR	TM/L	G	AB	R	H	2B	3B	HR	RBI	BB	SO	AVG	OBP	SLG	OPS	OPS+	BR+	SB	CS	SBR	FA	FR	G/POS	TPR
1970	Phi-N	11	16	0	2	1	0	0	0	1	4	.125	.176	.188	364	-3	-2	0	0	0	1.000	0	/O-3(3-0-0)	-0.3

■ LANCE PARRISH Parrish, Lance Michael b: 6/15/56, Clairton, Pa. BR/TR, 6'3", 220 lbs. Deb: 9/5/77 C

YEAR	TM/L	G	AB	R	H	2B	3B	HR	RBI	BB	SO	AVG	OBP	SLG	OPS	OPS+	BR+	SB	CS	SBR	FA	FR	G/POS	TPR
1977	Det-A	12	46	10	9	2	0	3	7	5	12	.196	.275	.435	709	85	-1	0	0	0	1.000	2	C-12	0.2
1978	Det-A	85	288	37	63	11	3	14	41	11	71	.219	.255	.424	679	85	-7	0	0	0	.987	5	C-79	0.1
1979	Det-A	143	493	65	136	26	3	19	65	49	105	.276	.344	.456	800	110	7	6	7	-1	.989	5	*C-142	1.6
1980	Det-A★	144	553	79	158	34	6	24	82	31	109	.286	.327	.499	826	120	13	6	4	-0	.990	-5	*C-121,D-16/1-5,O-5R	1.3
1981	Det-A	96	348	39	85	18	2	10	46	34	52	.244	.312	.394	705	98	-1	2	3	-1	.993	-2	C-90/D-5	0.0
1982	Det-A★	133	486	75	138	19	2	32	87	40	99	.284	.340	.529	868	134	21	3	4	-1	.989	9	*C-132/O-1(1-0-0)	3.4
1983	Det-A★	155	605	80	163	42	3	27	114	44	106	.269	.320	.483	803	120	15	1	3	-1	.995	0	*C-131,D-27	1.9
1984	*Det-A★	147	578	75	137	16	2	33	98	41	120	.237	.290	.443	733	100	-2	2	3	-1	.991	1	*C-127,D-22	0.3
1985	Det-A†	140	549	64	150	27	1	28	98	41	90	.273	.326	.479	805	118	12	2	6	-2	.993	-6	*C-120,D-22	0.9
1986	Det-A★	91	327	53	84	6	1	22	62	38	83	.257	.343	.483	826	122	10	0	0	0	.989	2	C-85/D-6	1.5
1987	Phi-N	130	466	42	114	21	0	17	67	47	104	.245	.315	.399	714	85	-10	0	1	-0	.989	-3	*C-127	-0.8
1988	Phi-N★	123	424	44	91	17	2	15	60	47	93	.215	.296	.370	666	88	-7	0	0	0	.988	-4	*C-117/1-1	-0.4
1989	Cal-A	124	433	48	103	12	1	17	50	42	104	.238	.308	.388	696	97	-3	1	1	-0	.993	-2	*C-122/D-2	0.2
1990	Cal-A★	133	470	54	126	14	0	24	70	46	107	.268	.340	.451	791	122	13	2	2	-0	.993	10	*C-131/1-4,D-1	3.1
1991	Cal-A	119	402	38	87	12	0	19	51	35	117	.216	.287	.388	675	85	-9	0	1	-0	.997	0	*C-111/1-3,D-5	-0.3
1992	Cal-A	24	83	7	19	2	0	4	11	5	22	.229	.273	.398	670	85	-2	0	0	0	.975	-5	C-22/D-2	-0.6
	Sea-A	69	192	19	45	11	1	8	21	19	48	.234	.307	.427	734	103	0	1	1	-0	.995	-4	C-34,1-16,D-14	-0.3
	Yr	93	275	26	64	13	1	12	32	24	70	.233	.297	.418	715	98	-2	1	1	-0	.987	-9	C-56,D-16,1-16	-0.9
1993	Cle-A	10	20	2	4	1	0	1	2	4	5	.200	.333	.400	733	97	-0	1	0	0	.950	4	C-10	0.4
1994	Pit-N	40	126	10	34	5	0	3	16	18	28	.270	.366	.381	746	94	-1	1	1	-0	.988	-2	C-38/1-1	-0.1
1995	Tor-A	70	178	15	36	9	0	4	22	15	52	.202	.268	.320	588	53	-13	0	0	0	1.000	9	C-67/D-1	0.0
Total	19	1988	7067	856	1782	305	27	324	1070	612	1527	.252	.315	.440	756	105	34	28	37	-7	.991	15	*C-1818,D-123/1-30,O	12.4

■ LARRY PARRISH Parrish, Larry Alton b: 11/10/53, Winter Haven, Fla. BR/TR, 6'3", 215 lbs. Deb: 9/6/74 MC Career OF: (3-LF 0-CF 405-RF)

YEAR	TM/L	G	AB	R	H	2B	3B	HR	RBI	BB	SO	AVG	OBP	SLG	OPS	OPS+	BR+	SB	CS	SBR	FA	FR	G/POS	TPR
1974	Mon-N	25	69	9	14	5	0	0	4	6	19	.203	.286	.275	561	54	-4	0	0	0	.986	8	3-24	0.3
1975	Mon-N	145	532	50	146	32	5	10	65	28	74	.274	.316	.410	725	96	-4	4	5	-1	.919	-3	*3-143/2-1,S-1	-1.0
1976	Mon-N	154	543	65	126	28	5	11	61	41	91	.232	.288	.363	651	81	-15	2	6	-2	.945	5	*3-153	-1.4
1977	Mon-N	123	402	50	99	19	2	11	46	37	71	.246	.316	.386	702	90	-6	2	4	-1	.936	-9	*3-115	-1.8
1978	Mon-N	144	520	68	144	39	4	15	70	32	103	.277	.321	.454	775	116	9	2	3	-1	.947	-5	*3-139	0.1
1979	Mon-N★	153	544	83	167	39	2	30	82	41	101	.307	.358	.551	909	146	32	5	1	1	.947	-9	*3-153	2.1
1980	Mon-N	126	452	55	115	27	3	15	72	36	80	.254	.315	.427	742	105	2	2	6	-2	.949	-8	*3-124	-1.0
1981	*Mon-N	97	349	41	85	19	3	8	44	28	73	.244	.300	.384	684	92	-5	0	0	0	.935	-17	3-95	-2.5
1982	Tex-A	128	440	59	116	15	0	17	62	30	84	.264	.316	.414	730	104	1	5	2	0	.962	-7	*O-124R/3-3,D-2	-1.2
1983	Tex-A	145	555	76	151	26	4	26	88	46	91	.272	.331	.474	805	121	14	0	0	0	.962	-5	*O-132(0-0-132),D-13	0.2
1984	Tex-A	156	613	72	175	42	1	22	101	42	116	.285	.337	.465	802	116	12	2	4	-1	.982	4	O-81R,D-63,3-12	0.9
1985	Tex-A	94	346	44	86	11	1	17	51	33	77	.249	.316	.434	749	101	0	0	2	-1	.991	-3	O-69(0-0-69),D-22/3-2	-0.8
1986	Tex-A	129	464	67	128	22	1	28	94	52	114	.276	.351	.509	860	127	17	3	1	0	.935	-5	D-98,3-30	0.9
1987	Tex-A★	152	557	79	149	22	1	32	100	49	154	.268	.330	.483	813	112	8	3	1	0	.918	-9	*D-122,3-28/O-1L	-0.4
1988	Tex-A	68	248	22	47	9	1	7	26	20	79	.190	.256	.319	574	58	-14	0	0	0	.000	0	D-67	-1.7
	*Bos-A	52	158	10	41	5	0	7	26	8	32	.259	.299	.424	723	96	-1	0	1	-0	.988	3	1-36,D-14	-0.1
	Yr	120	406	32	88	14	1	14	52	28	111	.217	.272	.360	632	73	-15	0	1	-0	.988	3	D-81,1-36	-1.8
Total	15	1891	6792	850	1789	360	33	256	992	529	1359	.263	.321	.439	760	106	45	30	36	-6	.941	-62	*3-1021,O-407R,D/1S2	-7.4

■ TOM PARROTT Parrott, Thomas William "Tacky Tom" b: 4/10/1868, Portland, Ore.
d: 1/1/32, Dundee, Ore. BR/TR, 5'10.5", 170 lbs. Deb: 6/18/1893 F Career OF: (15-LF 88-CF 28-RF)

YEAR	TM/L	G	AB	R	H	2B	3B	HR	RBI	BB	SO	AVG	OBP	SLG	OPS	OPS+	BR+	SB	CS	SBR	FA	FR	G/POS	TPR
1893	Chi-N	7	27	4	7	1	0	0	3	1	2	.259	.286	.296	582	56	-2	0			.800	-1	/P-4,3-2,2-1	-0.1
	Cin-N	24	68	5	13	1	1	1	9	1	9	.191	.203	.279	482	27	-8	0			.915	1	P-22/O-1(1-0-0)	-0.1
	Yr	31	95	9	20	2	1	1	12	2	11	.211	.227	.284	511	35	-9	0			.906	-0	P-26/3-2,2-1,O-1L	-0.2
1894	Cin-N	68	229	51	74	12	6	4	40	17	10	.323	.372	.480	853	100	-1	4			.929	5	P-41,O-13L,1-12,/S32	0.1
1895	Cin-N	64	201	35	69	13	7	3	41	11	8	.343	.377	.522	900	125	6	10			.922	1	P-41,1-14/O-9(1-8-0)	0.0
1896	StL-N	118	474	62	138	13	12	7	70	11	24	.291	.307	.414	721	93	-8	12			.951	13	*O-108C/P-7,1-6	-0.1
Total	4	281	999	157	301	40	26	15	163	41	53	.301	.329	.438	768	96	-12	26			.940	19	O-131C,P-115/132S	-0.2

■ JIGGS PARROTT Parrott, Walter Edward b: 7/14/1871, Portland, Ore. d: 4/16/1898, Phoenix, Ariz. 5'11", 160 lbs. Deb: 7/11/1892 F Career OF: (1-LF 0-CF 4-RF)

YEAR	TM/L	G	AB	R	H	2B	3B	HR	RBI	BB	SO	AVG	OBP	SLG	OPS	OPS+	BR+	SB	CS	SBR	FA	FR	G/POS	TPR
1892	Chi-N	78	333	38	67	8	5	2	22	8	30	.201	.222	.273	495	49	-22	7			.891	-2	3-78	-2.2
1893	Chi-N	110	455	54	111	10	9	1	65	13	25	.244	.267	.312	579	54	-32	25			.904	9	*3-99/2-7,O-4(0-0-4)	-1.7
1894	Chi-N	126	525	82	130	17	9	3	65	16	35	.248	.274	.331	605	43	-52	30			.932	-2	*2-125/3-1	-3.8
1895	Chi-N	3	4	0	1	0	0	0	0	0	0	.250	.250	.250	500	27	-0	0			.000	-2	/O-1(1-0-0),S-1,1-1	-0.2
Total	4	317	1317	174	309	35	23	6	152	37	90	.235	.258	.310	568	48	-106	62			.899	3	3-178,2-132/O-5R,1S	-7.9

■ CASEY PARSONS Parsons, Casey Robert b: 4/14/54, Wenatchee, Wash. BL/TR, 6'1", 180 lbs. Deb: 5/31/81

YEAR	TM/L	G	AB	R	H	2B	3B	HR	RBI	BB	SO	AVG	OBP	SLG	OPS	OPS+	BR+	SB	CS	SBR	FA	FR	G/POS	TPR
1981	Sea-A	36	22	6	5	1	0	1	5	1	4	.227	.320	.409	729	105	0	0	0	0	1.000	-5	O-24(3-2-19)/1-1	-0.5
1983	Chi-A	8	5	1	1	0	0	0	0	2	1	.200	.429	.200	629	77	-0	0	0	0	1.000	-1	/O-3(0-1-2),D-2	-0.1
1984	Chi-A	1	1	0	0	0	0	0	0	0	1	.000	.000	.000	0	-96	-0	0	0	0	.000	0	/H	0.0
1987	Cle-A	18	25	2	4	0	0	1	5	0	5	.160	.160	.280	440	13	-3	0	0	0	1.000	-1	/O-2(0-1-1),1-1,D-5	-0.4
Total	4	63	53	9	10	1	0	2	10	3	11	.189	.259	.321	579	57	-3	0	0	0	1.000	-6	/O-29(3-4-22),D-7,1-2	-1.0

■ DIXIE PARSONS Parsons, Edward Dixon b: 5/12/16, Talladega, Ala. d: 10/31/91, Longview, Tex. BR/TR, 6'2", 180 lbs. Deb: 8/16/39

YEAR	TM/L	G	AB	R	H	2B	3B	HR	RBI	BB	SO	AVG	OBP	SLG	OPS	OPS+	BR+	SB	CS	SBR	FA	FR	G/POS	TPR
1939	Det-A	5	1	0	0	0	0	0	0	1	1	.000	.500	.000	500	36	-0	0	0	0	1.000	0	/C-4	0.0
1942	Det-A	63	188	8	37	4	0	2	11	13	22	.197	.249	.250	499	37	-16	1	0	0	.981	10	C-62	-0.2
1943	Det-A	40	106	2	15	3	0	0	4	6	16	.142	.188	.170	357	4	-13	0	0	0	.975	5	C-40	-0.6
Total	3	108	295	10	52	7	0	2	15	20	39	.176	.229	.220	449	26	-28	1	0	0	.979	15	C-106	-0.8

YEAR	TM/L	G	AB	R	H	2B	3B	HR	RBI	BB	SO	AVG	OBP	SLG	OPS	OPS+	BR+	SB	CS	SBR	FA	FR	G/POS	TPR
■ JOHN PARSONS	Parsons, John S. b: Napoleon, Ohio 5'6", 138 lbs. Deb: 10/15/1884																							
1884	Cin-a	1	3	0	0	0	0	0	0	0	0	.000	.000	.000	0	-95	-1				1.000	-1	/O-1(0-0-2)	-0.1
■ ROY PARTEE	Partee, Roy Robert b: 9/7/17, Los Angeles, Cal. BR/TR, 5'10", 180 lbs. Deb: 4/23/43																							
1943	Bos-A	96	299	30	84	14	2	0	31	39	33	.281	.368	.341	709	106	4	0	0	0	.983	-6	C-91	0.4
1944	Bos-A	89	280	18	68	12	0	2	41	37	29	.243	.333	.307	640	85	-5	0	1	-0	.989	-6	C-85	-0.6
1946	*Bos-A	40	111	13	35	5	2	0	9	13	14	.315	.387	.396	783	113	2	0	0	0	.974	-6	C-38	-0.2
1947	Bos-A	60	169	14	39	2	0	0	16	18	23	.231	.305	.243	547	50	-11	0	0	0	.975	-1	C-54	-0.9
1948	StL-A	82	231	14	47	8	1	0	17	25	21	.203	.284	.247	531	41	-19	2	2	-0	.982	1	C-76	-1.5
Total	5	367	1090	89	273	41	5	2	114	132	120	.250	.334	.303	636	78	-29	2	3	-1	.982	-18	C-344	-2.8
■ STEVE PARTENHEIMER	Partenheimer, Harold Philip b: 8/30/1891, Greenfield, Mass. d: 6/16/71, Mansfield, Ohio BR/TR, 5'8.5", 145 lbs. Deb: 6/18/13 F																							
1913	Det-A	1	2	0	0	0	0	0	0	0	0	.000	.333	.000	333	-1	-0	0			.750	0	/3-1	0.0
■ JAY PARTRIDGE	Partridge, James Bugg b: 11/15/02, Mountville, Ga. d: 1/14/74, Nashville, Tenn. BL/TR, 5'11", 160 lbs. Deb: 4/12/27																							
1927	Bro-N	146	572	72	149	17	6	7	40	20	36	.260	.289	.348	637	70	-26	9			.938	-16	*2-140	-3.7
1928	Bro-N	37	73	18	18	0	1	0	12	13	6	.247	.368	.274	642	71	-2	2			.908	-5	2-18/3-2	-0.7
Total	2	183	645	90	167	17	7	7	52	33	42	.259	.299	.340	639	70	-28	11			.935	-20	2-158/3-2	-4.4
■ BEN PASCHAL	Paschal, Benjamin Edwin b: 10/13/1895, Enterprise, Ala. d: 11/10/74, Charlotte, N.C. BR/TR, 5'11", 185 lbs. Deb: 8/16/15																							
1915	Cle-A	9	9	0	1	0	0	0	0	0	3	.111	.111	.111	222	-33	-1	0			.000	0	H	-0.2
1920	Bos-A	9	28	5	10	0	0	0	5	5	2	.357	.455	.357	812	122	1	1	0	0	1.000	-0	/O-7(0-0-7)	0.1
1924	NY-A	4	12	2	3	1	0	0	3	1	0	.250	.308	.333	641	65	-1	0	0	0	1.000	-0	/O-4(0-4-0)	-0.1
1925	NY-A	89	247	49	89	16	5	12	56	22	29	.360	.417	.611	1028	161	22	14	9	-0	.953	-4	O-66(16-14-36)	1.2
1926	*NY-A	96	258	46	74	12	3	7	32	26	35	.287	.354	.438	792	108	2	7	6	-1	.935	-3	O-74(12-17-47)	-0.6
1927	NY-A	50	82	16	26	9	2	2	16	4	10	.317	.349	.549	898	134	3	0	2	-1	.976	-5	O-27(11-4-12)	-0.3
1928	*NY-A	65	79	12	25	6	1	1	15	8	11	.316	.379	.456	835	122	3	1	0	0	1.000	-6	O-25(16-1-8)	-0.4
1929	NY-A	42	72	13	15	3	0	2	11	6	3	.208	.269	.333	603	58	-5	1	1	-0	.951	-1	O-20(12-4-4)	-0.7
Total	8	364	787	143	243	47	11	24	138	72	93	.309	.369	.488	857	123	24	24	18		.953	-19	O-223(67-44-114)	-1.0
■ JOHNNY PASEK	Pasek, John Paul b: 6/25/05, Niagara Falls, N.Y. d: 3/13/76, Niagara Falls, N.Y BR/TR, 5'10", 175 lbs. Deb: 7/28/33																							
1933	Det-A	28	61	6	15	4	0	0	4	7	7	.246	.324	.311	635	68	-3	2	0	0	.989	-1	C-28	-0.2
1934	Chi-A	4	9	1	3	0	0	0	0	1	1	.333	.400	.333	733	88	-0	0	0	0	1.000	0	/C-4	0.0
Total	2	32	70	7	18	4	0	0	4	8	8	.257	.333	.314	648	70	-3	2	0	0	.990	-1	/C-32	-0.2
■ DODE PASKERT	Paskert, George Henry b: 8/28/1881, Cleveland, Ohio d: 2/12/59, Cleveland, Ohio BR/TR, 5'11", 165 lbs. Deb: 9/21/07 Career OF: (146-LF 1461-CF 35-RF)																							
1907	Cin-N	16	50	10	14	4	0	1	8	2		.280	.333	.420	753	130	2	2			.973	1	O-16(0-16-0)	0.2
1908	Cin-N	118	395	40	96	14	4	1	36	27		.243	.298	.306	604	96	-2	25			.953	5	*O-116(77-34-5)	-0.4
1909	Cin-N	104	322	49	81	7	4	0	33	34		.252	.327	.298	625	95	-1	23			.968	0	O-82(36-46-1)/1-6	-0.6
1910	Cin-N	144	506	63	152	21	5	2	46	70	60	.300	.389	.374	762	128	21	51			.957	14	*O-139(6-126-8)/1-2	2.9
1911	Phi-N	153	560	96	153	18	5	4	47	70	70	.273	.358	.345	703	96	-2	28			.979	8	*O-153(2-146-7)	-0.5
1912	Phi-N	145	540	102	170	37	5	2	43	91	67	.315	.420	.413	833	120	19	36			.967	5	*O-141C/2-2,3-1	1.4
1913	Phi-N	124	454	83	119	21	9	4	29	65	69	.262	.358	.374	733	105	4	12			.972	18	*O-120(1-119-0)	1.4
1914	Phi-N	132	451	59	119	25	6	3	44	56	68	.264	.349	.366	715	106	4	23			.958	12	*O-128(0-128-0)/S-4	0.8
1915	*Phi-N	109	328	51	80	17	4	3	39	35	38	.244	.319	.348	666	100	0	9	6	-0	.970	-2	O-92(19-74-1)/1-5	-0.9
1916	Phi-N	149	555	82	155	30	7	8	46	54	76	.279	.346	.402	748	125	17	22	21	-3	.983	1	*O-146(2-145-0)/S-1	0.6
1917	Phi-N	141	546	78	137	27	11	4	43	62	63	.251	.331	.363	693	108	6	19			**.984**	-2	*O-138(0-138-0)	-0.7
1918	*Chi-N	127	461	69	132	24	3	3	59	53	49	.286	.362	.371	733	121	13	20			.980	-3	*O-121(0-121-0)/3-6	0.2
1919	Chi-N	88	270	21	53	11	3	2	29	28	33	.196	.274	.281	556	67	-11	7			.969	-6	O-80(3-76-3)	-2.5
1920	Chi-N	139	487	57	136	22	10	5	71	64	58	.279	.366	.396	763	117	12	16	14	-1	.956	1	*O-137(0-136-1)	0.3
1921	Cin-N	27	92	8	16	1	1	0	4	4	8	.174	.208	.207	415	11	-12	0	2	-1	.984	1	O-24(0-15-9)	-1.3
Total	15	1716	6017	868	1613	279	77	42	577	715	659	.268	.350	.361	711	108	71	293	43		.969	52	*O-1633C/1-13,3-7,S2	0.9
■ KEVIN PASLEY	Pasley, Kevin Patrick b: 7/22/53, Bronx, N.Y. BR/TR, 6', 185 lbs. Deb: 10/2/74																							
1974	LA-N	1	0	0	0	0	0	0	0	0	0	—	—	—	—	—	0	0	0	0	1.000	-0	/C-1	0.0
1976	LA-N	23	52	4	12	2	0	0	2	3	7	.231	.273	.269	542	55	-3	0	0	0	.971	5	C-23	0.2
1977	LA-N	2	3	0	1	0	0	0	0	0	0	.333	.333	.333	667	80	-0	0	0	0	1.000	1	/C-2	0.0
	Sea-A	4	13	1	5	0	0	0	2	1	2	.385	.429	.385	813	125	1	0	0	0	1.000	-2	/C-4	-0.1
1978	Sea-A	25	54	3	13	5	0	1	5	2	4	.241	.268	.389	657	83	-1	0	0	0	1.000	-0	C-25	-0.1
Total	4	55	122	8	31	7	0	1	9	6	13	.254	.289	.336	625	76	-4	0	0	0	.986	3	/C-55	0.0
■ DAN PASQUA	Pasqua, Daniel Anthony b: 10/17/61, Yonkers, N.Y. BL/TL, 6', 203 lbs. Deb: 5/30/85 Career OF: (322-LF 0-CF 289-RF)																							
1985	NY-A	60	148	17	31	3	1	9	25	16	38	.209	.291	.426	717	96	-1	0	0	0	1.000	1	O-37(31-0-6),D-14	-0.2
1986	NY-A	102	280	44	82	17	0	16	45	47	78	.293	.400	.525	925	151	21	2	0	0	.987	-2	O-81(71-0-12)/1-5,D-3	1.6
1987	NY-A	113	318	42	74	7	1	17	42	40	99	.233	.320	.421	742	96	-2	0	2	-1	.985	-2	O-74L,D-20,1-12	-0.9
1988	Chi-A	129	422	48	96	16	2	20	50	46	100	.227	.308	.417	725	101	0	1	0	0	**.996**	7	*O-112L/1-7,D-2	0.4
1989	Chi-A	73	246	26	61	9	1	11	47	25	58	.248	.320	.427	747	111	3	1	2	-0	.993	2	O-66(52-0-20)/D-5	0.2
1990	Chi-A	112	325	43	89	27	3	13	58	37	66	.274	.352	.495	847	137	16	1	1	-0	.962	0	D-57,O-43(21-0-22)	1.3
1991	Chi-A	134	417	71	108	22	5	18	66	62	86	.259	.359	.465	824	129	17	0	2	-1	.991	-8	1-83,O-59(9-0-51)/D-8	0.3
1992	Chi-A	93	265	26	56	16	1	6	33	36	57	.211	.308	.347	655	84	-5	0	1	-0	.963	-2	O-81(0-0-81)/1-5,D-1	-1.1
1993	*Chi-A	78	176	22	36	10	1	5	20	26	51	.205	.307	.358	665	80	-5	2	2	-0	.984	-3	O-37R,1-32/D-6	-1.1
1994	Chi-A	11	23	2	5	2	0	2	4	0	9	.217	.217	.565	783	95	-0	0	0	0	.867	-1	/O-5(1-0-5),1-3	-0.1
Total	10	905	2620	341	638	129	15	117	390	335	642	.244	.333	.438	771	112	42	7	10	-2	.984	-8	O-595L,1-147,D-116	0.4
■ MIKE PASQUELLA	Pasquella, Michael John "Toney" (b: Michael John Pasquariello) b: 11/7/1898, Philadelphia, Pa. d: 4/5/65, Bridgeport, Conn. BR/TR, 5'11", 167 lbs. Deb: 7/9/19																							
1919	Phi-N	1	1	1	1	0	0	0	0	0	0	1.000	1.000	1.000	2000	469	0	0			.000	0	/1-1	0.0
	StL-N	1	1	0	0	0	0	0	0	0	1	.000	.000	.000	0	-99	-0	0			.000	0	H	0.0
	Yr	2	2	1	1	0	0	0	0	0	1	.500	.500	.500	1000	200	0	0			.000	0	/1-1	0.0
■ CLIFF PASTORNICKY	Pastornicky, Clifford Scott b: 11/18/58, Seattle, Wash. BR/TR, 5'10", 170 lbs. Deb: 6/14/83																							
1983	KC-A	10	32	4	4	0	0	2	5	0	3	.125	.125	.313	438	16	-4	0	0	0	.929	-0	3-10	-0.4
■ BOB PATE	Pate, Robert Wayne b: 12/3/53, Los Angeles, Cal. BR/TR, 6'3.5", 200 lbs. Deb: 6/2/80																							
1980	Mon-N	23	39	3	10	2	0	0	5	3	6	.256	.310	.308	617	73	-1	0	1	-0	1.000	-4	O-18(2-0-16)	-0.6
1981	Mon-N	8	6	0	2	0	0	0	0	1	0	.333	.429	.333	762	117	0	0	0	0	1.000	-2	/O-5(1-2-2)	-0.2
Total	2	31	45	3	12	2	0	0	5	4	6	.267	.327	.311	638	79	-1	0	1	-0	1.000	-5	/O-23(3-2-18)	-0.8
■ FREDDIE PATEK	Patek, Frederick Joseph "The Flea" b: 10/9/44, Seguin, Tex. BR/TR, 5'5", 148 lbs. Deb: 6/3/68																							
1968	Pit-N	61	208	31	53	4	2	2	18	12	37	.255	.302	.322	624	89	-3	18	7	2	.976	-1	S-52/O-5(2-0-3),3-1	0.1
1969	Pit-N	147	460	48	110	9	1	5	32	53	86	.239	.319	.296	615	75	-14	15	8	1	.954	-2	*S-146	0.1
1970	*Pit-N	84	237	42	58	10	5	1	19	29	46	.245	.327	.342	669	81	-6	8	2	1	.971	11	S-65	1.3
1971	KC-A	147	591	86	158	21	**11**	6	36	44	80	.267	.323	.371	694	97	-3	49	14	6	.968	10	*S-147	3.2
1972	KC-A†	136	518	59	110	25	4	0	32	47	64	.212	.282	.276	558	67	-21	33	7	5	.971	**30**	*S-136	3.4
1973	KC-A	135	501	82	117	19	5	5	45	54	63	.234	.312	.321	633	73	-17	36	14	3	.966	**35**	*S-135	3.7
1974	KC-A	149	537	72	121	18	6	3	38	77	69	.225	.326	.298	624	76	-14	33	15	2	.967	4	*S-149	0.9
1975	KC-A	136	483	58	110	14	5	5	45	42	65	.228	.292	.308	601	68	-20	32	7	5	.959	-7	*S-136/D-1	-0.6
1976	*KC-A★	144	432	58	104	19	3	1	43	50	63	.241	.322	.306	628	84	-8	51	15	6	.962	-6	*S-143/D-1	1.0
1977	*KC-A	154	497	72	130	26	6	5	60	41	84	.262	.324	.368	692	88	-8	**53**	13	7	.958	-19	*S-154	-0.4
1978	*KC-A★	138	440	54	109	23	1	2	46	42	56	.248	.315	.318	633	76	-13	38	11	5	.949	-25	*S-137	-2.0
1979	KC-A	106	306	30	77	17	0	1	37	16	42	.252	.295	.317	612	64	-15	11	12	-2	.955	-29	*S-104	-3.5
1980	Cal-A	86	273	41	72	10	5	5	34	15	26	.264	.304	.392	696	92	-4	7	6	-1	.953	-18	S-81	-1.5

YEAR	TM/L	G	AB	R	H	2B	3B	HR	RBI	BB	SO	AVG	OBP	SLG	OPS	OPS+	BR+	SB	CS	SBR	FA	FR	G/POS	TPR
1981	Cal-A	27	47	3	11	1	1	0	5	1	6	.234	.250	.298	548	57	-3	1	0	0	.983	2	2-16/3-7,S-3	0.0
Total	14	1650	5530	736	1340	216	55	41	490	523	787	.242	.311	.324	635	79	-150	385	131	39	.962	-15	*S-1588/2-16,3-8,OD	5.7
■ BOB PATRICK	Patrick, Robert Lee b: 10/27/17, Ft.Smith, Ark. d: 10/6/99, Ft.Smith, Ark. BR/TR, 6'2", 190 lbs. Deb: 9/20/41																							
1941	Det-A	5	7	2	2	0	0	0	0	0	1	.286	.286	.286	571	47	-1	0	0	0	.750	-1	/O-3(3-0-0)	-0.2
1942	Det-A	4	8	1	2	1	0	1	3	1	0	.250	.333	.750	1083	185	1	0	0	0	1.000	-0	/O-3(0-0-3)	0.0
Total	2	9	15	3	4	1	0	1	3	1	1	.267	.313	.533	846	118	0	0	0	0	.889	-1	/O-6(3-0-3)	-0.2
■ HARRY PATTEE	Pattee, Harry Ernest b: 1/17/1882, Charlestown, Mass. d: 7/17/71, Lynchburg, Va. BL/TR, 5'8", 149 lbs. Deb: 4/14/08																							
1908	Bro-N	80	264	19	57	5	2	0	9	25		.216	.286	.250	536	74	-7	24			.964	12	2-74	0.7
■ DAN PATTERSON	Patterson, Daniel Thomas b: 1846, New York, N.Y. TL, 5'9", 143 lbs. Deb: 5/18/1871 Career OF: (12-LF 9-CF 29-RF)																							
1871	Mut-n	32	151	31	31	2	0	0	13	1	0	.205	.211	.219	429	26	-12	2	1	0	.824	-2	*O-31(9-0-22)/2-2	-0.8
1872	Eck-n	12	47	5	9	2	0	0	4	0	1	.191	.191	.234	426	35	-3	0	0	0	.882	2	O-11(2-9-0)/1-1	0.0
1874	Mut-n	1	5	1	2	0	0	0	2	0	0	.400	.400	.400	800	153	0	0	0	0	1.000	-0	/1-1,O-1(1-0-0)	0.0
1875	Atl-n	12	45	4	9	0	0	0	4	0	0	.200	.200	.200	400	45	-2	1	0	0	.636	-6	/2-7,O-7(0-0-7)	-0.7
Total	4 n	57	248	41	51	4	0	0	23	1	1	.206	.209	.222	431	33	-17	3	1	0	.833	-7	/O-50R,2-9,1-2	-1.5
■ COREY PATTERSON	Patterson, Donald Corey b: 8/13/79, Atlanta, Ga. BL/TR, 5'10", 175 lbs. Deb: 9/19/2000																							
2000	Chi-N	11	42	9	7	1	0	2	2	3	14	.167	.239	.333	572	43	-4	1	1	-0	.963	-0	O-11(0-11-0)	-0.4
■ HAM PATTERSON	Patterson, Hamilton b: 10/13/1877, Belleville, Ill. d: 11/25/45, E.St.Louis, Ill. BR/TR, 6'2", 185 lbs. Deb: 5/18/09 F																							
1909	StL-A	17	49	2	10	1	0	0	5	0		.204	.204	.224	429	38	-4	1			1.000	-1	/1-6,O-6(6-0-0)	-0.6
	Chi-A	1	3	2	0	0	0	0	0	1		.000	.250	.000	250	-21	-0	0			1.000	1	/1-1	0.0
	Yr	18	52	4	10	1	0	0	5	1		.192	.208	.212	419	35	-4	1			1.000	-0	/1-7,O-6(6-0-0)	-0.6
■ HANK PATTERSON	Patterson, Henry Joseph Colquit b: 7/17/07, San Francisco, Cal. d: 9/30/70, Panorama City, Cal. BR/TR, 5'11.5", 170 lbs. Deb: 9/5/32																							
1932	Bos-A	1	1	0	0	0	0	0	0	0	0	.000	.000	.000	0	-99	-0	0	0	0	.000	0	/C-1	0.0
■ JOHN PATTERSON	Patterson, John Allen b: 2/11/67, Key West, Fla. BB/TR, 5'9", 160 lbs. Deb: 4/6/92																							
1992	SF-N	32	103	10	19	1	1	0	4	5	24	.184	.229	.214	443	28	-10	5	1	1	.960	6	2-22/O-5(0-5-0)	-0.3
1993	SF-N	16	16	1	3	0	0	1	2	0	5	.188	.188	.375	563	48	-1	0	1	-0	.000	0	H	-0.3
1994	SF-N	85	240	36	57	10	1	3	32	16	43	.237	.315	.325	640	70	-10	13	3	2	.979	-9	2-63	-1.5
1995	SF-N	95	205	27	42	5	3	1	14	14	41	.205	.294	.273	568	52	-14	4	2	0	.983	-6	2-53	-1.7
Total	4	228	564	74	121	16	5	5	52	35	113	.215	.289	.287	576	56	-35	22	7	2	.977	-9	2-138/O-5(0-5-0)	-3.8
■ CLAIRE PATTERSON	Patterson, Lorenzo Claire b: 10/5/1887, Arkansas City, Kan. d: 3/28/13, Mojave, Cal. BL/TR, 6' ", 180 lbs. Deb: 9/5/09																							
1909	Cin-N	4	8	0	1	0	0	0	1	0		.125	.125	.125	250	-23	-1	0			1.000	-0	/O-2(2-0-0)	-0.2
■ MIKE PATTERSON	Patterson, Michael Lee b: 1/26/58, Santa Monica, Cal. BL/TR, 5'10", 170 lbs. Deb: 4/15/81																							
1981	Oak-A	12	23	4	8	1	1	0	1	2	5	.348	.400	.478	878	160	2	0	1	-0	1.000	-1	/O-5(2-0-3),D-2	0.1
	NY-A	4	9	2	2	0	2	0	0	0	0	.222	.222	.667	889	150	0	0	0	0	1.000	-1	/O-4(3-0-1)	0.0
	Yr	16	32	6	10	1	3	0	1	2	5	.313	.353	.531	884	158	2	0	1	-0	1.000	-1	/O-9(5-0-4),D-2	0.1
1982	NY-A	11	16	3	3	1	0	1	1	2	6	.188	.278	.438	715	94	-0	1	0	0	1.000	-3	/O-9(2-7-0),D-1	-0.3
Total	2	27	48	9	13	2	3	1	2	4	11	.271	.327	.500	827	135	2	1	1	-0	1.000	-5	/O-18(7-7-4),D-3	-0.2
■ PAT PATTERSON	Patterson, William Jennings Bryan b: 1/29/01, Belleville, Ill. d: 10/1/77, St.Louis, Mo. BR/TR, 6', 175 lbs. Deb: 4/14/21 F																							
1921	NY-N	23	35	5	14	0	0	1	5	2	5	.400	.432	.486	918	142	2	0	1	-0	.970	4	3-14/S-7	0.6
■ GEORGE PATTISON	Pattison, George Deb: 4/24/1884																							
1884	Phi-U	2	7	0	1	0	0	0		0		.143	.143	.143	286	-14	-1				.500	-0	/O-2(1-0-1)	-0.1
■ GENE PATTON	Patton, Gene Tunney b: 7/8/26, Coatesville, Pa. BL/TR, 5'10", 165 lbs. Deb: 6/17/44																							
1944	Bos-N	1	0	0	0	0	0	0	0	0	0	—	—	—	—	—	0	0			.000	0	R	0.0
■ BILL PATTON	Patton, George William b: 10/12/12, Cornwall, Pa. d: 3/15/86, Philadelphia, Pa. BR/TR, 6'2", 180 lbs. Deb: 6/29/35																							
1935	Phi-A	9	10	1	3	1	0	0	2	2	3	.300	.417	.400	817	113	0	0	0	0	1.000	0	/C-3	0.1
■ TOM PATTON	Patton, Thomas Allen b: 9/5/35, Honey Brook, Pa. BR/TR, 5'9.5", 185 lbs. Deb: 4/30/57																							
1957	Bal-A	1	2	0	0	0	0	0	0	0	0	.000	.000	.000	0	-99	-1	0	0	0	1.000	1	/C-1	0.1
■ JOSH PAUL	Paul, Joshua William b: 5/19/75, Evanston, Ill. BR/TR, 6'1", 185 lbs. Deb: 9/7/99																							
1999	Chi-A	6	18	2	4	1	0	0	1	0	4	.222	.222	.278	500	26	-2	0	0	0	1.000	2	/C-6	0.0
2000	*Chi-A	36	71	15	20	3	2	1	8	5	17	.282	.338	.423	760	90	-1	1	0	0	.974	3	C-34/O-1(1-0-0)	0.3
Total	2	42	89	17	24	4	2	1	9	5	21	.270	.316	.393	709	78	-3	1	0	0	.979	5	/C-40,O-1(1-0-0)	0.3
■ LOU PAUL	Paul, Louis BR/TR, Deb: 9/5/1876																							
1876	Phi-N	3	12	2	2	1	0	0	0	0	0	.167	.167	.250	417	37	-1				.643	-2	/C-3	-0.3
■ CARLOS PAULA	Paula, Carlos (Conill) b: 11/28/27, Havana, Cuba d: 4/25/83, Miami, Fla. BR/TR, 6'3", 195 lbs. Deb: 9/6/54																							
1954	Was-A	9	24	2	4	1	0	0	2	2	4	.167	.231	.208	439	22	-3	0	0	0	1.000	1	/O-6(6-0-0)	-0.2
1955	Was-A	115	351	34	105	20	7	6	45	17	43	.299	.335	.447	782	115	5	2	3	-1	.941	-2	O-85(6-0-80)	-0.1
1956	Was-A	33	82	8	15	2	1	3	13	8	15	.183	.256	.341	597	56	-6	0	2	-1	.974	-1	O-20(9-0-11)	-0.8
Total	3	157	457	44	124	23	8	9	60	27	62	.271	.315	.416	731	99	-3	2	5	-1	.950	-2	O-111(21-0-91)	-1.1
■ GENE PAULETTE	Paulette, Eugene Edward b: 5/26/1891, Centralia, Ill. d: 2/8/66, Little Rock, Ark. BR/TR, 6', 150 lbs. Deb: 6/16/11																							
1911	NY-N	10	12	1	2	0	0	0	1	0	1	.167	.167	.167	333	-6	-2	0			.938	-1	/1-7,S-1,3-1	-0.3
1916	StL-A	5	4	1	2	0	0	0	0	1	1	.500	.600	.500	1100	242	1	0			.000	0	H	0.1
1917	StL-A	12	22	3	4	0	0	0	0	3	3	.182	.280	.182	462	43	-1	0			.982	0	/1-5,2-3,3-1	-0.1
	StL-N	95	332	32	88	21	7	0	34	16	16	.265	.303	.370	673	109	2	9			.993	-1	1-93	-0.2
1918	StL-N	125	461	33	126	15	3	0	52	27	16	.273	.316	.319	635	97	-2	11			.983	5	1-97,S-12/2-7,O3P	0.2
1919	StL-N	43	144	11	31	6	0	0	11	9	6	.215	.261	.257	518	60	-7	4			.990	2	1-35/S-3	-0.7
	Phi-N	67	243	20	63	8	3	1	31	19	10	.259	.316	.329	645	88	-3	10			.957	0	2-58,O-10(0-2-7)/1-1	-0.3
	Yr	110	387	31	94	14	3	1	42	28	16	.243	.296	.302	598	78	-10	14			.957	2	2-58,1-36,O-10R,/S	-1.0
1920	Phi-N	143	562	59	162	16	6	1	36	33	16	.288	.332	.343	676	90	-7	9	8	-1	.988	6	*1-139/S-2	-0.5
Total	6	500	1780	160	478	66	19	2	165	108	69	.269	.314	.330	644	92	-19	43	8		.988	11	1-377/2-68,S-18,O3P	-1.8
■ SI PAUXTIS	Pauxtis, Simon Francis b: 7/20/1885, Pittston, Pa. d: 3/13/61, Philadelphia, Pa. BR/TR, 6' ", 175 lbs. Deb: 9/18/09																							
1909	Cin-N	4	8	2	1	0	0	0	0	0		.125	.222	.125	347	8	-1	0			1.000	-1	/C-4	-0.2
■ DON PAVLETICH	Pavletich, Donald Stephen b: 7/13/38, Milwaukee, Wis. BR/TR, 5'11", 209 lbs. Deb: 4/20/57																							
1957	Cin-N	1	1	0	0	0	0	0	0	0	0	.000	.000	.000	0	-93	-0	0	0	0	.000	0	H	0.0
1959	Cin-N	1	0	1	0	0	0	0	0	0	0	—	—	—	—	—	0	0	0	0	.000	0	R	0.0
1962	Cin-N	34	63	7	14	3	0	1	7	8	18	.222	.310	.317	627	67	-3	0	0	0	1.000	1	1-25/C-2	-0.3
1963	Cin-N	71	183	18	38	11	0	5	18	17	12	.208	.275	.350	625	76	-6	0	0	0	.991	-3	1-57,C-13	-1.2
1964	Cin-N	34	91	12	22	4	0	5	11	10	17	.242	.317	.451	767	109	1	0	0	0	.983	-3	C-27/1-1	-0.1
1965	Cin-N	68	191	25	61	11	1	8	32	23	27	.319	.395	.513	908	144	11	1	1	-0	.986	-2	C-54/1-9	1.1
1966	Cin-N	83	235	29	69	13	2	12	38	18	37	.294	.346	.519	866	126	8	1	0	0	.975	-10	C-55,1-10	0.0
1967	Cin-N	74	231	25	55	14	3	6	34	21	38	.238	.313	.403	715	93	-2	2	1	0	.986	-5	C-66/1-6,3-1	-0.4
1968	Cin-N	46	98	11	28	3	1	2	11	8	23	.286	.352	.398	750	117	2	0	0	0	1.000	-0	1-22/C-5	0.1
1969	Chi-A	78	188	26	46	12	0	6	33	28	45	.245	.343	.404	747	103	1	0	0	0	.974	-6	C-51,1-13	-0.4
1970	Bos-A	32	65	4	9	1	1	0	6	10	15	.138	.253	.185	438	21	-7	1	0	0	1.000	1	1-16,C-10	-0.7
1971	Bos-A	14	27	5	7	1	0	1	3	5	5	.259	.375	.407	782	113	1	0	0	0	.973	-2	/C-8	-0.1
Total	12	536	1373	163	349	73	8	46	193	148	237	.254	.330	.420	750	103	7	5	2	0	.983	-31	C-291,1-159/3-1	-2.0

YEAR	TM/L	G	AB	R	H	2B	3B	HR	RBI	BB	SO	AVG	OBP	SLG	OPS	OPS+	BR+	SB	CS	SBR	FA	FR	G/POS	TPR
■ TED PAWELEK Pawelek, Theodore John "Porky" b: 8/15/19, Chicago Heights, Ill. d: 2/12/64, Chicago Heights, Ill. BL/TR, 5'10.5", 202 lbs. Deb: 9/13/46																								
1946	Chi-N	4	4	0	1	1	0	0	0	0	0	.250	.250	.500	750	112	0	0			.000	-0	/C-1	0.0
■ STAN PAWLOSKI Pawloski, Stanley Walter b: 9/6/31, Wanamie, Pa. BR/TR, 6'1", 175 lbs. Deb: 9/24/55																								
1955	Cle-A	2	8	0	1	0	0	0	0	0	2	.125	.125	.125	250	-31	-1	0	0	0	1.000	1	/2-2	0.0
■ FRED PAYNE Payne, Frederick Thomas b: 9/2/1880, Camden, N.Y. d: 1/16/54, Camden, N.Y. BR/TR, 5'10", 162 lbs. Deb: 4/21/06																								
1906	Det-A	72	222	23	60	5	5	0	20	13		.270	.316	.338	654	102	0	4			.966	-1	C-47,O-17(1-12-4)	0.4
1907	*Det-A	53	169	17	28	2	2	0	14	7		.166	.221	.201	422	34	-12	4			.981	3	C-46/O-5(3-1-1)	-0.6
1908	Det-A	20	45	3	3	0	0	0	2	3		.067	.176	.067	243	-20	-6	1			.954	-3	C-17/O-1(0-0-1)	-0.9
1909	Chi-A	32	82	8	20	2	0	0	12	5		.244	.295	.268	564	82	-2	0			.987	-2	C-27/O-3(0-0-3)	-0.1
1910	Chi-A	91	252	17	56	5	4	0	19	11		.222	.260	.274	534	70	-9	6			.974	-5	C-78/O-2(0-0-2)	-0.7
1911	Chi-A	66	133	14	27	2	1	1	19	8		.203	.259	.256	514	45	-10	6			.963	-4	C-56	-1.0
Total	6	334	903	82	194	16	12	1	86	47		.215	.265	.262	528	64	-39	21			.972	-11	C-271/O-28(4-13-11)	-2.9
■ GEORGE PAYNTER Paynter, George Washington (b: George Washington Paner) b: 7/6/1871, Cincinnati, Ohio d: 10/1/50, Cincinnati, Ohio BR/TR, 5'9", 125 lbs. Deb: 8/12/1894																								
1894	StL-N	1	4	0	0	0	0	0	0	1	0	.000	.200	.000	200	-48	-1	1			1.000	1	/O-1(0-1-0)	0.0
■ JAY PAYTON Payton, Jason Lee b: 11/22/72, Zanesville, Ohio BR/TR, 5'10", 185 lbs. Deb: 9/1/98																								
1998	NY-N	15	22	2	7	1	0	0	0	1	4	.318	.348	.364	711	89	-0	0	0	0	1.000	-1	O-10(8-0-1)	-0.1
1999	NY-N	13	8	1	2	1	0	0	1	0	2	.250	.333	.375	708	81	-0	1	2	-0	1.000	-2	/O-6(5-2-0)	-0.3
2000	*NY-N	149	488	63	142	23	1	17	62	30	60	.291	.336	.447	783	99	-2	5	11	-3	.981	0	*O-146(4-143-0)	-0.3
Total	3	177	518	66	151	25	1	17	63	31	66	.292	.336	.442	778	98	-2	6	13	-3	.982	-3	O-162(17-145-1)	-0.7
■ JOHNNY PEACOCK Peacock, John Gaston b: 1/10/10, Fremont, N.C. d: 10/17/81, Wilson, N.C. BL/TR, 5'11", 165 lbs. Deb: 9/23/37 Career OF: (1-LF 0-CF 0-RF)																								
1937	Bos-A	9	32	3	10	2	1	0	6	1	0	.313	.333	.438	771	89	-1	0	0	0	.980	1	/C-9	0.1
1938	Bos-A	72	195	29	59	7	1	1	39	17	4	.303	.358	.364	723	78	-6	4	1	1	.984	-9	C-57/1-1,O-1(1-0-0)	-1.1
1939	Bos-A	92	274	33	76	11	4	0	36	29	11	.277	.347	.347	693	75	-10	1	1	-0	.972	-8	C-84	-1.2
1940	Bos-A	63	131	20	37	4	1	0	13	23	10	.282	.390	.328	718	85	-2	1	1	-0	.994	-6	C-48	-0.6
1941	Bos-A	79	261	28	74	20	1	0	27	21	3	.284	.339	.368	707	85	-2	2	1	0	.988	-4	C-70	-0.5
1942	Bos-A	88	286	17	76	7	3	0	25	21	11	.266	.316	.311	627	74	-10	1	1	-0	.988	-6	C-82	-1.2
1943	Bos-A	48	114	7	23	3	1	0	7	10	9	.202	.266	.246	512	49	-7	1	1	-0	.972	-1	C-32	-0.7
1944	Bos-A	4	4	0	0	0	0	0	0	0	0	.000	.000	.000	0	-99	-1	0	0	0	1.000	0	/C-2	-0.1
	Phi-N	83	253	21	57	9	3	0	21	31	15	.225	.310	.285	594	70	-9	1			.990	1	C-73/2-1	-0.4
1945	Phi-N	33	74	6	15	6	0	0	6	6	0	.203	.262	.284	546	53	-5	1			.969	-5	C-23	-0.9
	Bro-N	48	110	11	28	5	1	0	14	24	10	.255	.388	.318	706	98	1	2			.975	1	C-38	0.3
	Yr	81	184	17	43	11	1	0	20	30	10	.234	.341	.304	645	82	-4	3			.973	-5	C-61	-0.6
Total	9	619	1734	175	455	74	16	1	194	183	73	.262	.333	.325	658	76	-55	14	6		.983	-37	C-518/2-1,O-1L,1-1	-6.3
■ ELIAS PEAK Peak, Elias b: 5/23/1859, Philadelphia, Pa. d: 12/17/16, Philadelphia, Pa. Deb: 4/19/1884																								
1884	Bos-U	1	3	2	2	0	0	0		1		.667	.750	.667	1417	338	1				1.000	-0	/O-1(0-0-1)	0.1
	Phi-U	54	215	35	42	6	4	0		7		.195	.221	.260	481	49	-20				.825	-6	2-47/O-5(4-0-1),S-2	-2.2
	Yr	55	218	37	44	6	4	0		8		.202	.230	.266	496	54	-19				.825	-6	2-47/O-6(4-0-2),S-2	-2.1
■ HARRY PEARCE Pearce, Harry James b: 7/12/1889, Philadelphia, Pa. d: 1/8/42, Philadelphia, Pa. BR/TR, 5'9", 158 lbs. Deb: 10/2/17																								
1917	Phi-N	7	16	2	4	3	0	0	2	0	4	.250	.294	.438	732	118	0	0			.967	5	/S-4	0.6
1918	Phi-N	60	164	16	40	3	2	0	18	9	31	.244	.295	.287	582	73	-5	5			.944	5	2-46/S-2,1-1,3-1	0.1
1919	Phi-N	68	244	24	44	3	3	0	9	8	27	.180	.209	.217	427	26	-21	6			.948	-1	2-43,S-23/3-2	-2.3
Total	3	135	424	42	88	9	5	0	29	17	62	.208	.247	.252	499	48	-26	11			.946	9	/2-89,S-29,3-3,1-1	-1.6
■ DICKEY PEARCE Pearce, Richard J. b: 2/29/1836, Brooklyn, N.Y. d: 10/12/08, Wareham, Mass. BR/TR, 5'3.5", 161 lbs. Deb: 5/18/1871 MU NA OF: (1-LF 0-CF 1-RF)																								
1871	Mut-n	33	163	31	44	5	0	0	20	4	1	.270	.287	.301	588	76	-3	0	0	0	.793	-7	*S-33	-0.7
1872	Mut-n	44	206	32	40	1	1	1	23	4	1	.194	.210	.223	433	35	-14	1	1	-0	**.839**	-0	*S-42/O-2(1-0-1),M	-1.1
1873	Atl-n	55	262	42	72	5	0	1	26	8	2	.275	.296	.305	602	88	-0	2	0	0	.780	5	*S-55/1-1,2-1	0.2
1874	Atl-n	56	255	48	75	1	0	0	26	6	1	.294	.310	.298	608	109	5	1	0	0	**.845**	9	*S-56/3-2,2-1	1.0
1875	StL-n	70	311	51	77	6	3	0	29	7	7	.248	.264	.286	550	100	2	8	3	1	.830	13	*S-70/P-2,M	1.2
1876	StL-N	25	105	12	21	1	0	0	10	3	5	.200	.229	.216	444	51	-5				.902	5	S-23/O-1(1-0-0),2-1	0.1
1877	StL-N	8	29	1	5	0	0	0	4	1	4	.172	.200	.172	372	19	-2				.950	3	/S-8	0.0
Total	5 n	258	1197	204	308	18	4	2	124	29	12	.257	.275	.284	559	84	-10	12	4	1	.818	19	S-256/P-2,3-2,2O1	0.6
Total	2	33	134	13	26	1	0	0	14	4	9	.194	.222	.206	428	44	-7				.914	7	/S-31,2-1,O-1(1-0-0)	0.1
■ DUCKY PEARCE Pearce, William C. b: 3/17/1885, Corning, Ohio d: 5/22/33, Brownstown, Ind. BR/TR, 6'1", 185 lbs. Deb: 7/1/08																								
1908	Cin-N	2	2	0	0	0	0	0	0	0	0	.000	.000	.000	0	-99	-0	0			1.000	1	/C-2	0.1
1909	Cin-N	2	2	0	0	0	0	0	0	0	0	.000	.000	.000	0	-99	-0	0			1.000	-0	/C-2	-0.1
Total	2	4	4	0	0	0	0	0	0	0	0	.000	.000	.000	0	-99	-1	0			1.000	1	/C-4	0.0
■ ALBIE PEARSON Pearson, Albert Gregory b: 9/12/34, Alhambra, Cal. BL/TL, 5'5", 141 lbs. Deb: 4/14/58																								
1958	Was-A	146	530	63	146	25	5	3	33	64	31	.275	.356	.358	714	99	1	7	8	-1	.980	6	*O-141(0-136-6)	-0.1
1959	Was-A	25	80	9	15	1	0	0	2	14	3	.188	.309	.200	509	43	-6	1	1	-0	.974	-2	O-21(0-11-10)	-0.9
	Bal-A	80	138	22	32	4	2	0	6	13	5	.232	.298	.290	588	64	-7	4	0	1	.987	-7	O-50(22-16-16)	-1.4
	Yr	105	218	31	47	5	2	0	8	27	8	.216	.302	.257	559	56	-13	5	1	1	.983	-9	O-71(22-27-26)	-2.3
1960	Bal-A	48	82	17	20	2	0	1	6	17	5	.244	.374	.305	679	87	-1	4	0	1	.975	-5	O-32(11-7-15)	-0.6
1961	LA-A	144	427	92	123	21	3	7	41	96	40	.288	.422	.400	823	109	10	11	3	1	.956	-1	*O-113(1-46-76)	0.4
1962	LA-A	160	614	**115**	160	29	6	5	42	95	36	.261	.361	.352	712	96	-1	15	6	1	.989	9	*O-160(0-143-17)	0.4
1963	LA-A★	154	578	92	176	26	5	6	47	92	37	.304	.403	.398	801	133	30	17	10	-0	.983	7	*O-148(2-135-15)	3.3
1964	LA-A	107	265	34	59	5	1	2	16	35	22	.223	.316	.272	587	72	-9	6	4	-0	.978	-3	O-66(10-52-7)	-1.5
1965	Cal-A	122	360	41	100	17	2	4	21	51	17	.278	.370	.369	740	114	8	12	1	2	.988	-4	*O-101(7-12-87)	0.1
1966	Cal-A	2	3	0	0	0	0	0	0	0	1	.000	.000	.000	0	-99	-1	0	0	0	.000	-0	/O-1(1-0-0)	-0.1
Total	9	988	3077	485	831	130	24	28	214	477	195	.270	.370	.355	725	102	25	77	33	5	.980	1	O-833(54-558-249)	-0.4
■ CHARLIE PECHOUS Pechous, Charles Edward b: 10/5/1896, Chicago, Ill. d: 9/13/80, Kenosha, Wis. BR/TR, 6', 170 lbs. Deb: 9/14/15																								
1915	Chi-F	18	51	4	9	3	0	0	4	4	15	.176	.236	.235	472	35	-5	1			.938	-1	3-18	-0.6
1916	Chi-N	22	69	5	10	1	1	0	4	3	21	.145	.181	.188	369	12	-7	1			.940	8	3-22	0.2
1917	Chi-N	13	41	2	10	0	0	0	1	2	9	.244	.295	.244	539	61	-2	1			1.000	-2	/3-7,S-5	-0.4
Total	3	53	161	11	29	4	1	0	9	9	45	.180	.228	.217	445	32	-14	3			.947	6	/3-47,S-5	-0.8
■ HAL PECK Peck, Harold Arthur b: 4/20/17, Big Bend, Wis. d: 4/13/95, Milwaukee, Wis. BL/TL, 5'11", 175 lbs. Deb: 5/13/43																								
1943	Bro-N	1	1	0	0	0	0	0	0	0	0	.000	.000	.000	0	-99	-0	0			.000	0	H	0.0
1944	Phi-A	2	8	0	2	0	0	0	1	0	2	.250	.250	.250	500	44	-1	0	2	-1	1.000	-0	/O-2(0-0-2)	-0.2
1945	Phi-A	112	449	51	124	22	9	5	39	37	28	.276	.331	.399	730	112	5	5	3	0	.943	-9	*O-110(0-0-110)	-1.2
1946	Phi-A	48	150	14	37	8	2	2	11	16	14	.247	.319	.367	686	92	-2	1	2	-0	.981	-3	O-35(0-0-35)	-0.7
1947	Cle-A	114	392	58	115	18	2	8	44	27	31	.293	.342	.411	753	112	5	3	3	-0	.983	-7	O-97(3-0-95)	-0.6
1948	*Cle-A	45	63	12	18	3	0	0	8	4	8	.286	.328	.333	662	78	-2	1	0	0	1.000	-2	/O-9(1-0-9)	-0.4
1949	Cle-A	33	29	1	9	1	0	0	9	3	3	.310	.375	.345	720	93	-0	0	0	0	1.000	-1	/O-2(0-0-2)	-0.1
Total	7	355	1092	136	305	52	13	15	112	87	86	.279	.334	.392	726	106	5	10	10		.965	-21	O-255(4-0-253)	-3.2
■ ROGER PECKINPAUGH Peckinpaugh, Roger Thorpe b: 2/5/1891, Wooster, Ohio d: 11/17/77, Cleveland, Ohio BR/TR, 5'10.5", 165 lbs. Deb: 9/15/10 M																								
1910	Cle-A	15	45	1	9	0	0	0	6	1		.200	.234	.200	434	36	-3	3			.906	-6	S-14	-1.0
1912	Cle-A	70	236	18	50	4	1	1	22	16		.212	.262	.250	512	45	-17	11			.924	-2	S-68	-1.5
1913	Cle-A	1	0	1	0	0	0	0	0	0	0	—	—	—	—	—	0	0			.000	0	H	0.0
	NY-A	95	340	35	91	10	7	1	32	24	47	.268	.316	.347	663	94	-4	19			.931	-5	S-93	-0.3

YEAR	TM/L	G	AB	R	H	2B	3B	HR	RBI	BB	SO	AVG	OBP	SLG	OPS	OPS+	BR+	SB	CS	SBR	FA	FR	G/POS	TPR
	Yr	96	340	36	91	10	7	1	32	24	47	.268	.316	.347	663	94	-4	19			.931	-5	S-93	-0.3
1914	NY-A	157	570	55	127	14	6	3	51	51	73	.223	.288	.284	572	72	-20	38	17	2	.956	3	*S-157,M	-0.3
1915	NY-A	142	540	67	119	18	7	5	44	49	72	.220	.289	.307	596	79	-16	19	12	-0	.942	11	*S-142	0.5
1916	NY-A	145	552	65	141	22	8	4	58	62	50	.255	.332	.346	678	101	1	18			.946	1	*S-145	1.3
1917	NY-A	148	543	63	141	24	7	0	41	64	46	.260	.340	.330	670	103	3	17			.934	10	*S-148	2.6
1918	NY-A	122	446	59	103	15	3	0	43	43	41	.231	.303	.278	581	74	-14	12			.961	**25**	*S-122	2.2
1919	NY-A	122	453	89	138	20	2	7	33	59	37	.305	.390	.404	794	122	15	10			.943	28	*S-121	5.2
1920	NY-A	139	534	109	144	26	6	8	54	72	47	.270	.356	.386	742	93	-4	8	12	-2	.962	3	*S-137	0.6
1921	*NY-A	149	577	128	166	25	7	8	71	84	44	.288	.380	.397	777	96	-1	2	2	-0	.948	-5	*S-149	1.0
1922	Was-A	147	520	62	132	14	4	2	48	55	36	.254	.329	.308	636	70	-22	11	6	0	.951	20	*S-147	1.5
1923	Was-A	154	568	73	150	18	4	2	62	64	30	.264	.340	.320	660	78	-16	10	8	-1	.948	**23**	*S-154	2.2
1924	*Was-A	155	523	72	142	20	5	2	73	72	45	.272	.360	.340	700	84	-11	9	6	-0	.963	9	*S-155	1.4
1925	*Was-A	126	422	67	124	16	4	4	64	49	23	.294	.367	.379	746	91	-5	13	4	1	.952	-16	*S-124/1-1	-0.5
1926	Was-A	57	147	19	35	4	1	1	14	28	12	.238	.360	.299	659	75	-4	3	0	1	.960	-1	S-46/1-1	0.0
1927	Chi-A	68	217	23	64	6	3	0	23	21	6	.295	.360	.350	710	87	-4	2	3	-1	.964	-1	S-60	0.1
Total	17	2012	7233	1006	1876	256	75	48	739	814	609	.259	.336	.335	672	87	-121	205	70		.949	98	*S-1982/1-2	15.0

■ BILL PECOTA Pecota, William Joseph b: 2/16/60, Redwood City, Cal. BR/TR, 6'2", 190 lbs. Deb: 9/19/86 Career OF: (13-LF 2-CF 19-RF)

YEAR	TM/L	G	AB	R	H	2B	3B	HR	RBI	BB	SO	AVG	OBP	SLG	OPS	OPS+	BR+	SB	CS	SBR	FA	FR	G/POS	TPR
1986	KC-A	12	29	3	6	2	0	0	2	3	3	.207	.303	.276	579	58	-2	0	2	-1	.974	6	3-12/S-2,D-4	0.3
1987	KC-A	66	156	22	43	5	1	3	14	15	25	.276	.343	.378	721	89	-2	5	0	1	.977	7	S-36,3-17,2-15,/D-1	0.9
1988	KC-A	90	178	25	37	3	3	1	15	18	34	.208	.288	.275	563	58	-10	7	2	1	.976	11	S-41,3-21,1-11,/OD2C	0.4
1989	KC-A	65	83	21	17	4	2	3	5	7	9	.205	.275	.410	684	91	-1	5	0	1	.988	4	S-29,O-15R,2-12,/31D	0.5
1990	KC-A	87	240	43	58	15	2	5	20	33	39	.242	.336	.383	719	102	1	8	5	0	.986	6	2-50,S-21,3-11,/O1D	1.0
1991	KC-A	125	398	53	114	23	2	6	45	41	45	.286	.356	.399	756	108	5	16	7	1	.983	-13	*3-102,2-34/S-9,1DOP	-0.6
1992	NY-N	117	269	28	61	13	0	2	26	25	40	.227	.295	.297	592	69	-11	9	3	1	.926	10	3-48,S-39,2-38,/P1	0.3
1993	*Atl-N	72	62	17	20	2	1	0	5	2	5	.323	.344	.387	731	94	-1	1	1	-0	1.000	1	3-23/2-4,O-1(0-0-1)	0.1
1994	Atl-N	64	112	11	24	5	0	2	16	16	16	.214	.313	.313	625	62	-6	1	0	0	.974	7	3-31/2-1,O-1(1-0-0)	0.2
Total	9	698	1527	223	380	72	11	22	148	160	216	.249	.324	.354	677	87	-26	52	20	4	.968	39	3-272,S-177,2/O1DPC	3.1

■ LES PEDEN Peden, Leslie Earl "Gooch" b: 9/17/23, Azle, Tex. BR/TR, 6'1.5", 212 lbs. Deb: 4/17/53 C

YEAR	TM/L	G	AB	R	H	2B	3B	HR	RBI	BB	SO	AVG	OBP	SLG	OPS	OPS+	BR+	SB	CS	SBR	FA	FR	G/POS	TPR
1953	Was-A	9	28	4	7	1	0	1	1	4	3	.250	.344	.393	737	101	0	0	0	0	1.000	-1	/C-8	0.0

■ STU PEDERSON Pederson, Stuart Russell b: 1/28/60, Palo Alto, Cal. BL/TL, 6', 185 lbs. Deb: 9/8/85

YEAR	TM/L	G	AB	R	H	2B	3B	HR	RBI	BB	SO	AVG	OBP	SLG	OPS	OPS+	BR+	SB	CS	SBR	FA	FR	G/POS	TPR
1985	LA-N	8	4	1	0	0	0	0	1	0	2	.000	.000	.000	0	-99	-1	0	0	0	1.000	-1	/O-5(3-0-2)	-0.3

■ JORGE PEDRE Pedre, Jorge Enrique b: 10/12/66, Culver City, Cal. BR/TR, 5'11", 210 lbs. Deb: 9/7/91

YEAR	TM/L	G	AB	R	H	2B	3B	HR	RBI	BB	SO	AVG	OBP	SLG	OPS	OPS+	BR+	SB	CS	SBR	FA	FR	G/POS	TPR
1991	KC-A	10	19	2	5	1	1	0	3	3	5	.263	.364	.421	785	116	0	0	0	0	.971	-0	/C-9,1-1	0.1
1992	Chi-N	4	4	0	0	0	0	0	0	0	1	.000	.000	.000	0	-98	-1	0	0	0	1.000	-1	/C-4	-0.2
Total	2	14	23	2	5	1	1	0	3	3	6	.217	.308	.348	656	81	-1	0	0	0	.973	-1	/C-13,1-1	-0.1

■ AL PEDRIQUE Pedrique, Alfredo Jose (Garcia) b: 8/11/60, Aragua, Venez. BR/TR, 6' ", 155 lbs. Deb: 4/14/87

YEAR	TM/L	G	AB	R	H	2B	3B	HR	RBI	BB	SO	AVG	OBP	SLG	OPS	OPS+	BR+	SB	CS	SBR	FA	FR	G/POS	TPR
1987	NY-N	5	6	1	0	0	0	0	0	1	2	.000	.143	.000	143	-61	-1	0	0	0	1.000	1	/S-4,2-1	0.0
	Pit-N	88	246	23	74	10	1	1	27	18	27	.301	.356	.362	718	90	-3	5	4	-0	.968	-12	S-76/3-3,2-2	-0.7
	Yr	93	252	24	74	10	1	1	27	19	29	.294	.350	.353	704	87	-4	5	4	-0	.969	-10	S-80/2-3,3-3	-0.7
1988	Pit-N	50	128	7	23	5	0	0	4	8	17	.180	.234	.219	452	31	-11	0	0	0	.974	2	S-46/3-5	-0.7
1989	Det-A	31	69	1	14	3	0	0	5	2	15	.203	.225	.246	472	34	-6	0	0	0	.960	8	3-12,S-12/2-8	0.2
Total	3	174	449	32	111	18	1	1	36	29	61	.247	.299	.298	597	64	-22	5	4	-0	.971	-1	S-138/3-20,2-11	-1.2

■ CHICK PEDROES Pedroes, Charles P. b: 10/27/1869, Chicago, Ill. d: 8/6/27, Chicago, Ill. Deb: 8/21/02

YEAR	TM/L	G	AB	R	H	2B	3B	HR	RBI	BB	SO	AVG	OBP	SLG	OPS	OPS+	BR+	SB	CS	SBR	FA	FR	G/POS	TPR
1902	Chi-N	2	6	0	0	0	0	0	0	0		.000	.000	.000	0	-99	-1	0			1.000	-0	/O-2(0-0-2)	-0.2

■ HOMER PEEL Peel, Homer Hefner b: 10/10/02, Port Sullivan, Tex d: 4/8/97, Shreveport, La. BR/TR, 5'9.5", 170 lbs. Deb: 9/13/27

YEAR	TM/L	G	AB	R	H	2B	3B	HR	RBI	BB	SO	AVG	OBP	SLG	OPS	OPS+	BR+	SB	CS	SBR	FA	FR	G/POS	TPR
1927	StL-N	2	2	0	0	0	0	0	0	0	1	.000	.000	.000	0	-97	-1	0			.000	-1	/O-1(0-0-1)	-0.1
1929	Phi-N	53	156	16	42	12	1	0	19	12	7	.269	.329	.359	688	66	-8	1			.990	-2	O-39(1-36-2)/1-1	-1.1
1930	StL-N	26	73	9	12	2	0	0	10	3	4	.164	.197	.192	389	-5	-12	0			.968	-4	O-21(6-0-15)	-1.6
1933	*NY-N	84	148	16	38	1	1	1	12	14	10	.257	.325	.297	622	80	-3	0			.962	-12	O-45(35-9-1)	-1.8
1934	NY-N	21	41	7	8	0	0	1	3	1	2	.195	.214	.268	483	29	-4	0			.929	-3	O-10(0-8-2)	-0.7
Total	5	186	420	48	100	15	2	2	44	30	24	.238	.294	.298	591	53	-29	1			.974	-22	O-116(42-53-21)/1-1	-5.3

■ JACK PEERSON Peerson, Jack Chiles b: 8/28/10, Brunswick, Ga. d: 10/23/66, Ft.Walton Beach, Fla. BR/TR, 5'11", 175 lbs. Deb: 9/7/35

YEAR	TM/L	G	AB	R	H	2B	3B	HR	RBI	BB	SO	AVG	OBP	SLG	OPS	OPS+	BR+	SB	CS	SBR	FA	FR	G/POS	TPR
1935	Phi-A	10	19	3	6	1	0	0	1	1	1	.316	.350	.368	718	87	-0	0	0	0	.952	0	/S-4	0.0
1936	Phi-A	8	34	7	11	1	1	0	5	0	3	.324	.324	.412	735	82	-1	0	1	-0	.942	4	/S-7,2-1	0.2
Total	2	18	53	10	17	2	1	0	6	1	4	.321	.333	.396	730	84	-1	0	1	-0	.945	4	/S-11,2-1	0.2

■ CHARLIE PEETE Peete, Charles "Mule" b: 2/22/29, Franklin, Va. d: 11/27/56, Caracas, Venez. BL/TR, 5'9.5", 190 lbs. Deb: 7/17/56

YEAR	TM/L	G	AB	R	H	2B	3B	HR	RBI	BB	SO	AVG	OBP	SLG	OPS	OPS+	BR+	SB	CS	SBR	FA	FR	G/POS	TPR
1956	StL-N	23	52	3	10	2	2	0	6	6	10	.192	.288	.308	596	60	-3	0	2	-1	1.000	-1	O-21(0-21-0)	-0.6

■ MONTE PEFFER Peffer, Monte (b: Montague Pfeiffer) b: 10/8/1891, New York, N.Y. d: 9/27/41, New York, N.Y. BR/TR, 5'4.5", 147 lbs. Deb: 9/29/13

YEAR	TM/L	G	AB	R	H	2B	3B	HR	RBI	BB	SO	AVG	OBP	SLG	OPS	OPS+	BR+	SB	CS	SBR	FA	FR	G/POS	TPR
1913	Phi-A	1	3	0	0	0	0	0	0	0	1	.000	.250	.000	250	-26	-0	0			.800	-0	/S-1	-0.1

■ JULIO PEGUERO Peguero, Julio Cesar b: 9/7/68, San Isidro, D.R. BB/TR, 6', 160 lbs. Deb: 4/8/92

YEAR	TM/L	G	AB	R	H	2B	3B	HR	RBI	BB	SO	AVG	OBP	SLG	OPS	OPS+	BR+	SB	CS	SBR	FA	FR	G/POS	TPR
1992	Phi-N	14	9	3	2	0	0	0	0	3	3	.222	.417	.222	639	86	0	0	0	0	1.000	-5	O-14(0-9-5)	-0.5

■ STEVE PEGUES Pegues, Steven Antone b: 5/21/68, Pontotoc, Miss. BR/TR, 6'2", 190 lbs. Deb: 7/6/94

YEAR	TM/L	G	AB	R	H	2B	3B	HR	RBI	BB	SO	AVG	OBP	SLG	OPS	OPS+	BR+	SB	CS	SBR	FA	FR	G/POS	TPR
1994	Cin-N	11	10	1	3	0	0	0	0	1	3	.300	.364	.300	664	76	-0	0	0	0	.833	-1	/O-4(3-0-1)	-0.1
	Pit-N	7	26	1	10	2	0	0	2	1	2	.385	.407	.462	869	124	1	1	0	0	1.000	-1	/O-7(5-2-0)	0.0
	Yr	18	36	2	13	2	0	0	2	2	5	.361	.395	.417	811	112	1	1	0	0	.929	-2	O-11(8-2-1)	-0.1
1995	Pit-N	82	171	17	42	8	0	6	16	4	36	.246	.267	.398	665	71	-8	1	2	-0	.954	-5	O-53(31-4-25)	-1.4
Total	2	100	207	19	55	10	0	6	18	6	41	.266	.290	.401	691	78	-7	2	2	-0	.950	-7	/O-64(39-6-26)	-1.5

■ HEINIE PEITZ Peitz, Henry Clement b: 11/28/1870, St.Louis, Mo. d: 10/23/43, Cincinnati, Ohio BR/TR, 5'11", 165 lbs. Deb: 10/15/1892 FC Career OF: (4-LF 0-CF 7-RF)

YEAR	TM/L	G	AB	R	H	2B	3B	HR	RBI	BB	SO	AVG	OBP	SLG	OPS	OPS+	BR+	SB	CS	SBR	FA	FR	G/POS	TPR
1892	StL-N	1	3	0	0	0	0	0	0	0	0	.000	.000	.000	0	-99	-1	0			1.000	-0	/C-1	-0.1
1893	StL-N	96	362	53	92	12	9	1	45	54	20	.254	.353	.345	698	86	-7	12			.948	9	C-74,S-11,O-10R,/1	0.7
1894	StL-N	99	338	52	89	19	9	3	49	43	21	.263	.348	.399	748	80	-12	14			.897	4	3-47,C-39,1-14,/P-1	-0.3
1895	StL-N	90	334	44	95	14	12	2	65	29	20	.284	.345	.416	761	97	-2	9			.937	1	C-71,1-11,3-10	0.5
1896	Cin-N	68	211	33	63	12	5	2	34	30	15	.299	.386	.431	817	108	2	7			.968	1	C-67	0.8
1897	Cin-N	77	266	35	78	11	7	1	44	18		.293	.340	.398	739	89	-5	3			**.979**	7	C-71/P-2	0.7
1898	Cin-N	105	330	49	90	15	5	1	43	35		.273	.348	.358	705	96	-2	9			.945	-3	*C-101	0.4
1899	Cin-N	94	293	45	79	13	2	1	43	45		.270	.371	.338	708	93	-1	11			.977	0	C-92/P-1	0.6
1900	Cin-N	91	294	34	75	14	1	2	34	20		.255	.318	.330	648	81	-8	5			.958	6	C-80/1-8	0.5
1901	Cin-N	82	269	24	82	13	5	1	24	23		.305	.364	.401	765	130	11	3			.982	2	C-49,2-21/3-6,1-2	1.8
1902	Cin-N	112	387	54	122	22	5	1	60	24		.315	.369	.406	775	127	12	7			.919	-2	2-48,C-47/1-6,3-6	1.6
1903	Cin-N	105	358	45	93	15	3	0	42	37		.260	.331	.318	649	77	-11	7			.970	-2	C-78,1-11/3-9,2-4	-0.4
1904	Cin-N	84	272	32	66	13	2	1	30	14		.243	.282	.316	598	78	-8	1			.975	4	C-64,1-18/3-1	0.3
1905	Pit-N	88	278	18	62	10	0	0	27	24		.223	.289	.259	548	62	-12	2			.965	-11	C-87/2-1	-1.6
1906	Pit-N	40	125	13	30	8	0	0	20	13		.240	.321	.304	625	91	-1	1			.979	0	C-38	0.3
1913	StL-N	3	4	1	1	0	1	0	0	0	0	.250	.250	.750	1000	182	0	0			.625	-2	/C-2,O-1(0-0-1)	-0.1
Total	16	1235	4124	532	1117	191	66	16	560	409	76	.271	.342	.361	702	92	-44	91			.963	15	C-961/3-79,1-75,2OSP	5.7

■ JOE PEITZ Peitz, Joseph b: 11/8/1869, St.Louis, Mo. d: 12/4/19, St.Louis, Mo. Deb: 7/5/1894 F

YEAR	TM/L	G	AB	R	H	2B	3B	HR	RBI	BB	SO	AVG	OBP	SLG	OPS	OPS+	BR+	SB	CS	SBR	FA	FR	G/POS	TPR
1894	StL-N	7	26	10	11	2	3	0	3	6	1	.423	.531	.731	1262	202	5	2			.818	1	/O-7(0-0-7)	0.4

YEAR	TM/L	G	AB	R	H	2B	3B	HR	RBI	BB	SO	AVG	OBP	SLG	OPS	OPS+	BR+	SB	CS	SBR	FA	FR	G/POS	TPR
■ EDDIE PELLAGRINI	Pellagrini, Edward Charles b: 3/13/18, Boston, Mass. BR/TR, 5′9″, 165 lbs. Deb: 4/22/46																							
1946	Bos-A	22	71	7	15	3	1	2	4	3	18	.211	.253	.366	620	68	-3	1	0	0	.891	-0	3-14/S-9	-0.3
1947	Bos-A	74	231	29	47	8	1	4	19	23	35	.203	.281	.299	580	57	-14	2	2	-0	.926	-6	3-42,S-26	-2.0
1948	StL-A	105	290	31	69	8	3	2	27	34	40	.238	.320	.307	627	65	-14	1	2	-0	.964	**24**	S-98	1.4
1949	StL-A	79	235	26	56	8	1	2	15	14	24	.238	.284	.306	590	54	-16	2	1	0	.961	7	S-76	-0.5
1951	Phi-N	86	197	31	46	4	5	5	30	23	25	.234	.326	.381	707	91	-3	5	1	1	.990	-17	2-53/S-8,3-6	-1.6
1952	Cin-N	46	100	15	17	2	0	1	3	8	18	.170	.231	.220	451	26	-10	1	0	0	.983	10	2-22/1-8,S-1,3-1	0.1
1953	Pit-N	78	174	16	44	3	2	4	19	14	20	.253	.309	.362	671	75	-7	1	1	-0	.972	-2	2-31,3-12/S-3	-0.7
1954	Pit-N	73	125	12	27	6	0	0	16	9	21	.216	.290	.264	554	46	-10	0	0	0	.968	2	3-31/2-7,S-1	-0.8
Total	8	563	1423	167	321	42	13	20	133	128	201	.226	.295	.316	611	62	-76	13	7	0	.956	16	S-222,2-113,3-106,/1	-4.4
■ LOUIS PELOUZE	Pelouze, Louis Henri b: 9/10/1863, Fort Monroe, Va. d: 1/9/39, New York, N.Y. BL/TL, 6′, 175 lbs. Deb: 7/24/1886																							
1886	StL-N	1	3	0	0	0	0	0	0	0	2	.000	.000	.000	0	-99	-1	0			1.000	0	/O-1(0-1-0)	0.0
■ DAN PELTIER	Peltier, Daniel Edward b: 6/30/68, Clifton Park, N.Y. BL/TL, 6′1″, 200 lbs. Deb: 6/26/92																							
1992	Tex-A	12	24	1	4	0	0	0	2	0	3	.167	.167	.167	333	-7	-3	0	0	0	.857	-3	O-10(1-0-9)	-0.7
1993	Tex-A	65	160	23	43	7	1	1	17	20	27	.269	.354	.344	697	92	-1	0	4	-1	.950	-7	O-55(2-0-54)/1-5	-1.1
1996	SF-N	31	59	3	15	2	0	0	9	7	9	.254	.333	.288	621	68	-2	0	0	0	1.000	-1	1-13/O-1(1-0-0)	-0.5
Total	3	108	243	27	62	9	1	1	28	27	39	.255	.332	.313	645	77	-7	0	4	-1	.943	-11	/O-66(4-0-63),1-18	-2.3
■ JOHN PELTZ	Peltz, John b: 4/23/1861, New Orleans, La. d: 2/27/06, New Orleans, La. BR/TR, Deb: 5/1/1884																							
1884	Ind-a	106	393	40	86	13	17	3		7		.219	.236	.361	598	95	-3				.818	4	*O-106(106-0-0)	-0.1
1888	Bal-a	1	4	1	1	0	0	0	0	0		.250	.250	.250	500	62	-0	1			.500	-0	/O-1(1-0-0)	-0.1
1890	Bro-a	98	384	55	87	9	6	1	33	32		.227	.289	.289	579	73	-13	10			.904	3	*O-98(0-98-0)	-1.2
	Syr-a	5	17	2	3	1	1	0	2	3		.176	.300	.353	653	103	0	0			.857	0	/O-5(0-5-0)	0.0
	Tol-a	20	73	8	18	2	2	0	13	3		.247	.286	.329	614	79	-2	7			.886	-2	O-20(0-20-0)	-0.4
	Yr	123	474	65	108	12	9	1	48	38		.228	.289	.297	587	75	-16	17			.900	1	*O-123(0-123-0)	-1.6
Total	3	230	871	106	195	25	26	4	48	45		.224	.266	.326	592	84	-18	18			.865	5	O-230(107-123-0)	-1.8
■ BROCK PEMBERTON	Pemberton, Brock b: 11/5/53, Tulsa, Okla. BB/TL, 6′3″, 190 lbs. Deb: 9/10/74																							
1974	NY-N	11	22	0	4	0	0	0	1	0	3	.182	.182	.182	364	2	-3	0	1	-0	1.000	1	/1-4	-0.3
1975	NY-N	2	2	0	0	0	0	0	0	0	1	.000	.000	.000	0	-99	-1	0	0	0	.000	0	H	-0.1
Total	2	13	24	0	4	0	0	0	1	0	4	.167	.167	.167	333	-7	-3	0	1	-0	1.000	1	/1-4	-0.4
■ RUDY PEMBERTON	Pemberton, Rudy Hector (Perez) b: 12/17/69, San Pedro De Macoris, D.R. BR/TR, 6′1″, 185 lbs. Deb: 4/26/95																							
1995	Det-A	12	30	3	9	3	1	0	3	1	5	.300	.344	.467	810	109	0	0	0	0	1.000	-0	/O-8(6-0-2),D-3	0.0
1996	Bos-A	13	41	11	21	8	0	1	10	2	4	.512	.556	.780	1336	228	8	3	1	0	1.000	-3	O-13(1-0-12)	0.4
1997	Bos-A	27	63	8	15	2	0	2	10	4	13	.238	.314	.365	679	75	-2	0	0	0	.949	-1	O-23(0-0-23)	-0.4
Total	3	52	134	22	45	13	1	3	23	7	22	.336	.395	.515	909	131	6	3	1	0	.968	-5	/O-44(7-0-37),D-3	0.0
■ BERT PENA	Pena, Adalberto (Rivera) b: 7/11/59, Santurce, P.R. BR/TR, 5′11″, 165 lbs. Deb: 9/14/81																							
1981	Hou-N	4	2	0	1	0	0	0	0	0	0	.500	.500	.500	1000	194	0	0	0	0	1.000	0	/S-3	0.0
1983	Hou-N	4	8	0	1	0	0	0	0	2	2	.125	.300	.125	425	23	-1	0	0	0	1.000	-1	/S-4	-0.2
1984	Hou-N	24	39	3	8	1	0	1	4	3	8	.205	.262	.308	570	64	-2	0	0	0	.956	6	S-21	0.5
1985	Hou-N	20	29	7	8	2	0	0	4	1	6	.276	.300	.345	645	82	-1	0	0	0	1.000	-1	/3-7,S-6,2-2	-0.1
1986	Hou-N	15	29	3	6	1	0	0	2	5	5	.207	.324	.241	565	60	-1	1	0	0	.907	1	S-10/3-2,2-1	0.1
1987	Hou-N	21	46	5	7	0	0	0	0	2	7	.152	.204	.152	356	-4	-7	0	0	0	.982	-1	S-19/3-1	-0.7
Total	6	88	153	18	31	4	0	1	10	13	28	.203	.269	.248	518	45	-11	1	0	0	.953	3	/S-63,3-10,2-3	-0.4
■ ANGEL PENA	Pena, Angel Maria b: 2/16/75, San Pedro De Macoris, D.R. BR/TR, 5′10″, 225 lbs. Deb: 9/8/98																							
1998	LA-N	6	13	1	3	0	0	0	0	0	6	.231	.231	.231	462	23	-1	0	0	0	1.000	1	/C-4	0.0
1999	LA-N	43	120	14	25	6	0	4	21	12	24	.208	.280	.358	639	64	-7	0	1	-0	.989	5	C-43	-0.1
Total	2	49	133	15	28	6	0	4	21	12	30	.211	.276	.346	622	60	-9	0	1	-0	.990	6	/C-47	-0.1
■ TONY PENA	Pena, Antonio Francisco (Padilla) b: 6/4/57, Monte Cristi, D.R. BR/TR, 6′, 181 lbs. Deb: 9/1/80 F Career OF: (0-LF 0-CF 3-RF)																							
1980	Pit-N	8	21	1	9	1	1	0	1	0	4	.429	.429	.571	1000	174	2	0	1	-0	.952	2	/C-6	0.3
1981	Pit-N	66	210	16	63	9	1	2	17	8	23	.300	.329	.381	710	98	-1	1	2	-0	.985	2	C-64	0.3
1982	Pit-N★	138	497	53	147	28	4	11	63	17	57	.296	.324	.435	759	107	3	2	5	-1	.982	-7	*C-137	0.1
1983	Pit-N	151	542	51	163	22	3	15	70	31	73	.301	.339	.435	774	110	6	6	7	-1	.992	-0	*C-149	1.2
1984	Pit-N★	147	546	77	156	27	2	15	78	36	79	.286	.334	.425	759	112	8	12	8	-0	.991	13	*C-146	2.8
1985	Pit-N★	147	546	53	136	27	2	10	59	29	67	.249	.287	.361	648	81	-15	12	8	-0	.988	9	*C-146/1-1	0.0
1986	Pit-N★	144	510	56	147	26	2	10	52	53	69	.288	.356	.406	762	107	6	9	10	-2	.981	5	*C-139/1-4	1.5
1987	*StL-N	116	384	40	82	13	4	5	44	36	54	.214	.283	.307	590	55	-25	6	1	1	.988	-1	*C-112/1-4,O-2(0-0-2)	-2.0
1988	StL-N	149	505	55	133	23	1	10	51	33	60	.263	.310	.372	682	94	-4	6	2	1	**.994**	6	*C-142/1-3	1.1
1989	StL-N★	141	424	36	110	17	2	4	37	35	33	.259	.319	.337	656	85	-8	5	3	0	**.997**	11	*C-134/O-1(0-0-1)	1.1
1990	*Bos-A	143	491	62	129	19	1	7	56	43	71	.263	.323	.348	672	84	-10	8	6	-0	.995	11	*C-142/1-1	0.9
1991	Bos-A	141	464	45	107	23	2	5	48	37	53	.231	.293	.321	614	66	-21	8	3	1	.995	9	*C-140	-0.4
1992	Bos-A	133	410	39	99	21	1	1	38	24	61	.241	.285	.305	590	61	-21	3	2	-0	.993	11	*C-132	-0.2
1993	Bos-A	126	304	20	55	11	0	4	19	25	46	.181	.248	.257	504	34	-29	1	3	-1	.995	22	*C-125/D-1	-0.1
1994	Cle-A	40	112	18	33	8	1	2	10	9	11	.295	.347	.438	785	100	-0	0	1	-0	.996	5	C-40	0.6
1995	*Cle-A	91	263	25	69	15	0	5	28	14	44	.262	.302	.376	679	74	-10	1	0	0	.987	10	C-91	0.5
1996	*Cle-A	67	174	14	34	4	0	1	27	15	25	.195	.259	.236	495	26	-20	0	1	-0	.992	7	C-67	-0.9
1997	Chi-A	31	67	4	11	1	0	0	8	8	13	.164	.253	.179	432	16	-8	0	0	0	1.000	3	C-30/3-1	-0.4
	*Hou-N	9	19	2	4	3	0	0	2	2	3	.211	.286	.368	654	72	-1	0	0	0	1.000	4	/C-8	0.3
Total	18	1988	6489	667	1687	298	27	107	708	455	846	.260	.311	.364	674	84	-148	80	63	-4	.991	122	*C-1950/1-13,O-3R,3D	6.7
■ ELVIS PENA	Pena, Elvis (Mendez) b: 9/15/76, San Pedro De Macoris, D.R. BB/TR, 5′11″, 164 lbs. Deb: 9/2/2000																							
2000	Col-N	10	9	1	3	1	0	0	1	1	1	.333	.400	.444	844	88	-0	1	0	0	1.000	-1	/S-3,2-1	0.0
■ GERONIMO PENA	Pena, Geronimo (Martinez) b: 3/29/67, Distrito Nacional, D.R. BB/TR, 6′1″, 195 lbs. Deb: 9/5/90																							
1990	StL-N	18	45	5	11	2	0	0	2	4	14	.244	.320	.289	609	69	-2	1	1	-0	.982	-1	2-11	-0.3
1991	StL-N	104	185	38	45	8	3	5	17	18	45	.243	.327	.400	727	103	1	15	5	2	.976	-3	2-83/O-4(4-0-0)	0.1
1992	StL-N	62	203	31	62	12	1	7	31	24	37	.305	.392	.478	870	150	14	13	8	0	.984	8	2-57	2.5
1993	StL-N	74	254	34	65	19	2	5	30	25	71	.256	.332	.406	738	98	-1	13	5	1	.966	-1	2-64	0.3
1994	StL-N	83	213	33	54	13	1	11	34	24	54	.254	.346	.479	825	114	4	9	1	2	.990	5	2-59/3-1	1.3
1995	StL-N	32	101	20	27	6	1	1	8	16	30	.267	.373	.376	749	98	0	3	2	-0	.976	-2	2-25	-0.1
1996	Cle-A	5	9	1	1	0	0	1	2	1	4	.111	.200	.444	644	57	-1	0	0	0	.000	0	/3-3,2-1	-0.1
Total	7	378	1010	162	265	60	8	30	124	112	255	.262	.349	.427	776	111	16	54	22	4	.978	7	2-300/3-4,O-4(4-0-0)	3.7
■ ROBERTO PENA	Pena, Roberto Cesar "Baby" (b: Roberto Cesar Zapata (Pena)) b: 4/17/37, Santo Domingo, D.R. d: 7/23/82, Santiago, D.R. BR/TR, 5′8″, 175 lbs. Deb: 4/12/65																							
1965	Chi-N	51	170	17	37	5	1	2	12	16	19	.218	.293	.294	587	64	-8	1	2	-0	.930	-10	S-50	-1.5
1966	Chi-N	6	17	0	3	2	0	0	1	0	4	.176	.176	.294	471	28	-2	0	0	0	.957	0	/S-5	-0.1
1968	Phi-N	138	500	56	130	13	2	1	38	34	63	.260	.310	.300	610	84	-9	3	5	-1	.954	6	*S-133	0.8
1969	SD-N	139	472	44	118	16	3	4	30	21	63	.250	.286	.322	608	73	-18	0	3	-1	.977	-23	S-65,2-33,3-27,1-12	-3.6
1970	Oak-A	19	58	4	15	1	0	0	3	3	4	.259	.295	.276	571	61	-3	1	1	-0	.961	-1	S-12/3-5	-0.3
	Mil-A	121	416	36	99	19	1	3	42	25	45	.238	.284	.310	595	63	-21	3	5	-1	.981	-16	S-99,2-15/1-7	-2.7
	Yr	140	474	40	114	20	1	3	45	28	49	.241	.286	.306	592	63	-24	4	6	-1	**.979**	-17	*S-111,2-15/1-7,3-5	-3.0
1971	Mil-A	113	274	17	65	9	3	3	28	15	37	.237	.279	.325	604	71	-11	2	1	0	.996	-5	1-50,3-37,S-23,/2-1	-1.7
Total	6	587	1907	174	467	65	10	13	154	114	235	.245	.291	.310	601	72	-72	10	17	-4	.962	-49	S-387/1-69,3-69,2	-9.1

YEAR	TM/L	G	AB	R	H	2B	3B	HR	RBI	BB	SO	AVG	OBP	SLG	OPS	OPS+	BR+	SB	CS	SBR	FA	FR	G/POS	TPR
■ ELMER PENCE	Pence, Elmer Clair b: 8/17/1900, Valley Springs, Cal. d: 9/17/68, San Francisco, Cal. BR/TR, 6', 185 lbs. Deb: 8/23/22																							
1922	Chi-A	1	0	0	0	0	0	0	0	0	0	—	—	—	—	—	0	0	0	0	1.000	-0	/O-1(0-0-1)	0.0
■ JIM PENDLETON	Pendleton, James Edward b: 1/7/24, St.Charles, Mo. d: 3/20/96, Houston, Tex. BR/TR, 6', 185 lbs. Deb: 4/17/53 Career OF: (189-LF 42-CF 63-RF)																							
1953	Mil-N	120	251	48	75	12	4	7	27	7	36	.299	.323	.462	785	108	2	6	5	-0	.961	-13	*O-105(75-15-25)/S-7	-1.4
1954	Mil-N	71	173	20	38	3	1	1	16	4	21	.220	.237	.266	503	33	-17	2	1	0	.950	-4	O-50(23-18-11)	-2.3
1955	Mil-N	8	10	0	0	0	0	0	0	0	2	.000	.000	.000	0	-99	-3	0	0	0	1.000	-0	/S-1,3-1,O-1(0-1-0)	-0.3
1956	Mil-N	14	11	0	0	0	0	0	0	1	3	.000	.083	.000	83	-80	-3	0	0	0	1.000	-0	/S-3,3-2,1-1,2-1	-0.3
1957	Pit-N	46	59	9	18	1	1	0	9	9	14	.305	.406	.356	762	110	1	0	0	0	.917	-3	/O-9(2-1-6),3-2,S-1	-0.2
1958	Pit-N	3	3	0	1	0	0	0	0	0	0	.333	.333	.333	667	79	-0	0	0	0	.000	0	H	0.0
1959	Cin-N	65	113	13	29	2	0	3	9	8	18	.257	.311	.354	665	75	-4	3	0	1	.971	0	O-24(24-0-0),3-16/S-3	-0.4
1962	Hou-N	117	321	30	79	12	2	8	36	14	57	.246	.282	.371	653	79	-10	0	0	0	.963	-6	O-90L/1-8,3-3,S-2	-2.1
Total	8	444	941	120	240	30	8	19	97	43	151	.255	.292	.365	656	76	-34	11	6	0	.959	-26	O-279L/3-24,S-17,12	-7.0
■ TERRY PENDLETON	Pendleton, Terry Lee b: 7/16/60, Los Angeles, Cal. BB/TR, 5'9", 180 lbs. Deb: 7/18/84 Career OF: (0-LF 0-CF 1-RF)																							
1984	StL-N	67	262	37	85	16	3	1	33	16	32	.324	.363	.420	783	123	7	20	5	3	.943	9	3-66	1.9
1985	*StL-N	149	559	56	134	16	3	5	69	37	75	.240	.287	.306	593	66	-25	17	12	-0	.965	23	*3-149	-0.6
1986	StL-N	159	578	56	138	26	5	1	59	34	59	.239	.282	.306	588	63	-30	24	6	3	.962	24	*3-156/O-1(0-0-1)	-0.5
1987	*StL-N	159	583	82	167	29	4	12	96	70	74	.286	.365	.412	777	103	4	19	12	-0	.949	16	*3-158	1.7
1988	StL-N	110	391	44	99	20	2	6	53	21	51	.253	.295	.361	655	86	-7	3	3	-0	.963	11	*3-101	0.4
1989	StL-N	162	613	83	162	28	5	13	74	44	81	.264	.314	.390	703	97	-3	9	5	0	**.971**	**30**	*3-161	2.9
1990	StL-N	121	447	46	103	20	2	6	58	30	58	.230	.280	.324	605	66	-21	7	5	-0	.947	7	*3-117	-1.5
1991	*Atl-N	153	586	94	**187**	34	8	22	86	43	70	**.319**	.367	.517	884	138	28	10	2	2	.950	**28**	*3-148	5.9
1992	*Atl-N★	160	640	98	**199**	39	1	21	105	37	67	.311	.349	.473	822	123	18	5	2	0	.960	13	*3-158	3.4
1993	*Atl-N	161	633	81	172	33	1	17	84	36	97	.272	.314	.408	722	91	-10	5	1	1	.959	12	*3-161	0.4
1994	Atl-N	77	309	25	78	18	3	7	30	12	57	.252	.280	.398	678	73	-13	2	0	0	.950	6	3-77	-0.6
1995	Fla-N	133	513	70	149	32	1	14	78	38	84	.290	.342	.439	780	104	2	1	2	-0	.952	0	*3-129	0.3
1996	Fla-N	111	406	30	102	20	1	7	58	26	75	.251	.301	.357	658	75	-15	0	2	-1	.961	7	*3-108	-0.8
	*Atl-N	42	162	21	33	6	0	4	17	15	36	.204	.271	.315	586	51	-12	2	1	0	.939	1	3-41	-1.0
	Yr	153	568	51	135	26	1	11	75	41	111	.238	.292	.345	638	68	-27	2	3	-1	.955	9	*3-149	-1.8
1997	Cin-N	50	113	11	28	9	0	1	17	12	14	.248	.320	.354	674	75	-4	2	1	0	.942	-6	3-32	-0.9
1998	KC-A	79	237	17	61	10	0	3	29	15	49	.257	.302	.338	639	64	-12	1	0	0	.957	-1	D-40,3-23	-1.4
Total	15	1893	7032	851	1897	356	39	140	946	486	979	.270	.318	.391	710	92	-93	127	59	7	.957	181	*3-1785/D-40,O-1R	9.6
■ SHANNON PENN	Penn, Shannon Dion b: 9/11/69, Cincinnati, Ohio BB/TR, 5'10", 160 lbs. Deb: 4/28/95																							
1995	Det-A	3	9	0	3	0	0	0	0	1	2	.333	.400	.333	733	94	-0	0	0	0	.864	2	/2-3	0.2
1996	Det-A	6	14	0	1	0	0	0	1	0	3	.071	.071	.071	143	-64	-3	0	0	0	.000	-0	/O-1(1-0-0),D-4	-0.4
Total	2	9	23	0	4	0	0	0	1	1	5	.174	.208	.174	382	-1	-3	0	0	0	.864	1	/D-4,2-3,O-1(1-0-0)	-0.2
■ WILL PENNYFEATHER	Pennyfeather, William Nathaniel b: 5/25/68, Perth Amboy, N.J. BR/TR, 6'2", 195 lbs. Deb: 6/27/92																							
1992	Pit-N	15	9	2	2	0	0	0	0	0	0	.222	.222	.222	444	26	-1	0	0	0	1.000	-4	O-10(1-6-5)	-0.5
1993	Pit-N	21	34	4	7	1	0	0	2	0	6	.206	.206	.235	441	18	-4	0	1	-0	1.000	-5	O-17(1-15-2)	-0.9
1994	Pit-N	4	3	0	0	0	0	0	0	0	0	.000	.000	.000	0	-99	-1	0	0	0	.000	-0	/O-1(1-0-0)	-0.1
Total	3	40	46	6	9	1	0	0	2	0	6	.196	.196	.217	413	11	-6	0	1	-0	1.000	-9	/O-28(3-21-7)	-1.5
■ JIMMY PEOPLES	Peoples, James Elsworth b: 10/8/1863, Big Beaver, Mich. d: 8/29/20, Detroit, Mich. TR, 5'8", 200 lbs. Deb: 5/29/1884 U Career OF: (5-LF 6-CF 24-RF)																							
1884	Cin-a	69	267	28	45	2	2	1	16	6		.169	.187	.202	389	26	-22				.829	0	S-47,C-14,O-10R,/31	-1.8
1885	Cin-a	7	22	1	4	0	0	0	1	1		.182	.217	.182	399	27	-2				.826	-1	/C-5,P-2,O-1(0-0-1)	-0.2
	Bro-a	41	151	21	30	4	1	1	15	5		.199	.229	.258	488	53	-8				.895	-2	C-37/S-2,1-1,3-1,O	-0.7
	Yr	48	173	22	34	4	1	1	16	6		.197	.228	.249	476	50	-10				.889	-4	C-42/P-2,O-2C,S13	-0.9
1886	Bro-a	93	340	43	74	7	3	3	38	20		.218	.261	.282	543	70	-12	20			.879	19	C-76,S-14/O-8L,3-1	1.1
1887	Bro-a	73	284	36	84	14	2	1	38	16		.296	.306	.332	638	77	-9	22			.853	-6	C-57/O-8R,S-4,12	-0.8
1888	Bro-a	32	103	15	20	5	3	0	17	8		.194	.259	.301	560	79	-2	10			.904	10	C-25/S-5,O-2(0-0-2)	0.9
1889	Col-a	29	100	13	23	6	2	1	16	6	8	.230	.274	.360	634	84	-2	3			.922	-4	C-22/O-5R,2-2,S-1	-0.4
Total	6	344	1267	157	280	38	13	7	141	62	8	.221	.252	.279	531	61	-58	55			.886	15	C-236/S-73,O123P	-1.9
■ JOE PEPITONE	Pepitone, Joseph Anthony "Pepi" b: 10/9/40, Brooklyn, N.Y. BL/TL, 6'2", 200 lbs. Deb: 4/10/62 C Career OF: (36-LF 386-CF 83-RF)																							
1962	NY-A	63	138	14	33	3	2	7	17	3	21	.239	.255	.442	697	86	-4	1	1	-0	1.000	-9	O-32(14-7-13),1-16	-1.4
1963	*NY-A★	157	580	79	157	16	3	27	89	23	63	.271	.307	.448	755	109	5	3	5	-1	.995	4	*1-143,O-16(0-7-9)	-0.1
1964	*NY-A★	160	613	71	154	12	3	28	100	24	63	.251	.283	.418	700	90	-10	2	1	0	.988	-6	*1-155,O-30(0-28-3)	-2.6
1965	NY-A★	143	531	51	131	18	3	18	62	43	59	.247	.306	.394	699	98	-2	4	2	0	**.997**	-3	*1-115,O-41(2-3-36)	-1.5
1966	NY-A	152	585	85	149	21	4	31	83	29	58	.255	.292	.463	755	118	10	4	3	-0	**.995**	1	*1-119,O-55(0-49-9)	0.3
1967	NY-A	133	501	45	126	18	3	13	64	34	62	.251	.303	.377	680	104	1	1	3	-1	.976	6	*O-123(0-123-0)/1-6	0.2
1968	NY-A	108	380	41	93	9	3	15	56	37	45	.245	.313	.403	716	119	8	8	2	1	.980	-6	O-92(4-88-0),1-12	0.0
1969	NY-A	135	513	49	124	16	3	27	70	30	42	.242	.285	.442	727	105	-0	8	6	-0	**.995**	-6	*1-132	-1.8
1970	Hou-N	75	279	44	70	9	5	14	35	18	28	.251	.299	.470	768	107	1	5	2	0	.995	-1	1-50,O-28(15-3-13)	-0.4
	Chi-N	56	213	38	57	9	2	12	44	15	15	.268	.316	.498	813	102	-0	0	2	-1	.992	2	O-56(0-56-0),1-13	-0.1
	Yr	131	492	82	127	18	7	26	79	33	43	.258	.306	.482	788	105	1	5	4	-0	.989	1	O-84(15-59-13),1-63	-0.5
1971	Chi-N	115	427	50	131	19	4	16	61	24	41	.307	.349	.482	832	117	9	1	2	-0	.990	-3	1-95,O-23(1-22-0)	-0.3
1972	Chi-N	66	214	23	56	5	0	8	21	13	22	.262	.313	.397	710	91	-3	1	2	-0	.997	-0	1-66	-0.8
1973	Chi-N	31	112	16	30	3	0	3	18	8	6	.268	.322	.375	697	86	-2	3	1	0	.985	0	1-28	-0.4
	Atl-N	3	11	0	4	0	0	0	1	1	1	.364	.417	.364	780	110	0	0	0	0	.963	-1	/1-3	-0.1
	Yr	34	123	16	34	3	0	3	19	9	7	.276	.331	.374	705	88	-2	3	1	0	.983	-1	1-31	-0.5
Total	12	1397	5097	606	1315	158	35	219	721	302	526	.258	.303	.432	735	105	14	41	32	-2	.993	-21	1-953,O-496C	-9.0
■ HENRY PEPLOSKI	Peploski, Henry Stephen "Pep" b: 9/15/05, Garlin, Poland d: 1/28/82, Dover, N.J. BL/TR, 5'9", 155 lbs. Deb: 9/19/29 F																							
1929	Bos-N	6	10	1	2	0	0	0	1	1	3	.200	.273	.200	473	20	-1	0			1.000	-0	/3-2	-0.1
■ PEPPER PEPLOSKI	Peploski, Joseph Aloysius b: 9/12/1891, Brooklyn, N.Y. d: 7/13/72, New York, N.Y. BR/TR, 5'8", 155 lbs. Deb: 6/24/13 F																							
1913	Det-A	2	4	1	2	0	0	0	0	0	0	.500	.500	.500	1000	196	0	0			1.000	-1	/3-2	0.0
■ DON PEPPER	Pepper, Donald Hoyte b: 10/8/43, Saratoga Sprgs., N.Y BL/TR, 6'4.5", 215 lbs. Deb: 9/10/66																							
1966	Det-A	4	3	0	0	0	0	0	0	0	1	.000	.000	.000	0	-98	-1	0	0	0	1.000	-0	/1-1	-0.1
■ RAY PEPPER	Pepper, Raymond Watson b: 8/5/05, Decatur, Ala. d: 3/24/96, Belle Mina, Ala. BR/TR, 6'2", 195 lbs. Deb: 4/15/32																							
1932	StL-N	21	57	3	14	2	1	0	7	5	13	.246	.306	.316	622	66	-3	1			.971	-0	O-17(16-0-1)	-0.4
1933	StL-N	3	9	2	2	0	0	1	2	0	1	.222	.222	.556	778	110	0	0			1.000	-0	/O-2(2-0-0)	0.0
1934	StL-A	148	564	71	168	24	6	7	101	29	67	.298	.333	.399	732	81	-16	1	4	-1	.963	5	*O-136(101-37-1)	-1.8
1935	StL-A	92	261	20	66	15	3	4	37	20	32	.253	.306	.379	685	73	-11	0	2	-1	.982	-3	O-57(27-4-26)	-1.7
1936	StL-A	75	124	13	35	5	0	2	23	5	23	.282	.310	.371	681	66	-7	0	2	-1	.941	-2	O-18(2-5-11)	-1.0
Total	5	339	1015	109	285	46	10	14	170	59	136	.281	.321	.387	708	77	-37	2	8		.967	-1	O-230(148-46-39)	-4.9
■ JACK PERCONTE	Perconte, John Patrick b: 8/31/54, Joliet, Ill. BL/TR, 5'10", 160 lbs. Deb: 9/13/80																							
1980	LA-N	14	17	2	4	0	0	0	2	2	1	.235	.316	.235	551	57	-1	3	0	1	1.000	3	/2-9	0.3
1981	LA-N	8	9	2	2	0	1	0	1	2	2	.222	.364	.444	808	133	0	1	1	-0	1.000	5	/2-2	0.5
1982	Cle-A	93	219	27	52	4	4	0	15	22	25	.237	.307	.292	599	66	-10	9	3	1	.976	8	2-82/D-2	0.3
1983	Cle-A	14	26	1	7	1	0	0	0	5	2	.269	.387	.308	695	91	-0	3	1	0	.950	8	2-13	0.8
1984	Sea-A	155	612	93	180	24	4	0	31	57	47	.294	.359	.346	705	97	-0	29	6	4	.981	0	*2-150	1.3
1985	Sea-A	125	485	60	128	17	7	2	23	50	36	.264	.336	.340	677	85	-9	31	2	6	.986	0	*2-125	0.5
1986	Chi-A	24	73	6	16	1	0	0	4	11	10	.219	.321	.233	554	52	-4	2	0	0	.990	-7	2-24	-0.9
Total	7	433	1441	191	389	47	16	2	76	149	123	.270	.342	.329	671	86	-23	78	13	13	.982	18	2-405/D-2	2.8

YEAR	TM/L	G	AB	R	H	2B	3B	HR	RBI	BB	SO	AVG	OBP	SLG	OPS	OPS+	BR+	SB	CS	SBR	FA	FR	G/POS	TPR
■ TONY PEREZ	Perez, Atanasio (Rigal) b: 5/14/42, Ciego De Avila, Cuba BR/TR, 6'2", 205 lbs. Deb: 7/26/64 FMCH																							
1964	Cin-N	12	25	1	2	1	0	0	1	3	9	.080	.179	.120	299	-14	-4	0	0	0	.981	-1	/1-6	-0.6
1965	Cin-N	104	281	40	73	14	4	12	47	21	67	.260	.316	.466	782	110	3	0	2	-1	.989	-2	1-93	-0.4
1966	Cin-N	99	257	25	68	10	4	4	39	14	44	.265	.308	.381	689	83	-6	1	0	0	.989	-5	1-75	-1.5
1967	Cin-N★	156	600	78	174	28	7	26	102	33	102	.290	.331	.490	821	119	13	0	3	-1	.963	-22	*3-139,1-18/2-1	-1.2
1968	Cin-N★	160	625	93	176	25	7	18	92	51	92	.282	.342	.430	772	123	17	3	2	-0	.952	5	*3-160	2.5
1969	Cin-N★	160	629	103	185	31	2	37	122	63	131	.294	.360	.526	886	138	31	4	2	0	.937	1	*3-160	3.2
1970	*Cin-N★	158	587	107	186	28	6	40	129	83	134	.317	.405	.589	994	162	52	8	3	1	.923	-7	*3-153/1-8	4.4
1971	Cin-N	158	609	72	164	22	3	25	91	51	120	.269	.327	.438	765	117	12	4	1	1	.959	7	*3-148,1-44	1.8
1972	*Cin-N	136	515	64	146	33	7	21	90	55	121	.283	.353	.497	850	148	30	4	2	0	.993	-5	*1-136	1.5
1973	*Cin-N	151	564	73	177	33	3	27	101	74	117	.314	.396	.527	923	162	47	3	1	0	.991	-4	*1-151	3.3
1974	Cin-N★	158	596	81	158	28	2	28	101	61	112	.265	.335	.460	795	123	16	1	3	-1	**.996**	-6	*1-157	-0.3
1975	*Cin-N★	137	511	74	144	28	3	20	109	54	101	.282	.354	.466	820	124	15	1	2	-0	.993	-5	*1-132	0.0
1976	*Cin-N★	139	527	77	137	32	6	19	91	50	88	.260	.330	.452	782	117	11	10	5	0	.996	-4	*1-136	-0.3
1977	Mon-N	154	559	71	158	32	6	19	91	63	111	.283	.357	.463	821	122	17	4	3	-0	.992	9	*1-148	1.6
1978	Mon-N	148	544	63	158	38	3	14	78	38	104	.290	.339	.449	788	120	13	2	0	0	.991	-1	*1-145	0.4
1979	Mon-N	132	489	58	132	29	4	13	73	38	82	.270	.326	.425	752	104	2	2	1	0	.991	-6	*1-129	-1.3
1980	Bos-A	151	585	73	161	31	3	25	105	41	93	.275	.324	.467	790	108	5	1	0	0	.993	-1	*1-137,D-13	-0.5
1981	Bos-A	84	306	35	77	11	3	9	39	27	66	.252	.312	.395	708	97	-2	0	0	0	.993	0	1-56,D-23	-0.6
1982	Bos-A	69	196	18	51	14	2	6	31	19	48	.260	.326	.444	769	103	1	0	1	-0	.857	0	D-46/1-2	-0.1
1983	*Phi-N	91	253	18	61	11	2	6	43	28	57	.241	.319	.372	691	92	-3	1	0	0	.998	1	1-69	-0.5
1984	Cin-N	71	137	9	33	6	1	2	15	11	21	.241	.297	.343	640	76	-4	0	0	0	.990	-2	1-31	-0.8
1985	Cin-N	72	183	25	60	8	0	6	33	22	22	.328	.400	.470	870	136	9	0	2	-1	.995	-2	1-50	0.4
1986	Cin-N	77	200	14	51	12	1	2	29	25	25	.255	.338	.355	693	87	-3	0	0	0	.984	-3	1-55	-0.9
Total	23	2777	9778	1272	2732	505	79	379	1652	925	1867	.279	.344	.463	808	122	272	49	33	-1	.992	-54	*1-1778,3-760/D-82,2	10.1
■ DANNY PEREZ	Perez, Daniel b: 2/26/71, ElPaso, Tex. BR/TR, 5'10", 188 lbs. Deb: 6/30/96																							
1996	Mil-A	4	4	0	0	0	0	0	0	0	0	.000	.000	.000	0	-96	-1	0	0	0	1.000	-0	/O-3(2-1-0)	-0.1
■ EDUARDO PEREZ	Perez, Eduardo Atanasio b: 9/11/69, Cincinnati, Ohio BR/TR, 6'4", 215 lbs. Deb: 7/27/93 F Career OF: (22-LF 0-CF 1-RF)																							
1993	Cal-A	52	180	16	45	6	2	4	30	9	39	.250	.293	.372	665	75	-7	5	4	-0	.962	10	3-45/D-3	0.4
1994	Cal-A	38	129	10	27	7	0	5	16	12	29	.209	.277	.380	656	66	-7	3	0	1	.997	-3	1-38	-1.2
1995	Cal-A	29	71	9	12	4	1	1	7	12	9	.169	.306	.296	602	58	-4	0	2	-1	.883	1	3-23/D-1	-0.4
1996	Cin-N	18	36	8	8	0	0	3	5	5	9	.222	.317	.472	789	104	0	0	0	0	1.000	2	/1-8,3-3	0.1
1997	Cin-N	106	297	44	75	18	0	16	52	29	76	.253	.323	.475	798	104	1	5	1	1	.996	-5	1-67,O-12L/3-8,D-1	-0.9
1998	Cin-N	84	172	20	41	4	0	4	30	21	45	.238	.328	.331	660	73	-6	0	1	-0	.985	7	1-51/3-1,O-1(1-0-0)	-0.3
1999	StL-N	21	32	6	11	2	0	1	9	7	6	.344	.462	.500	962	143	3	0	0	0	1.000	1	/O-6(6-0-0),1-5	0.3
2000	StL-N	35	91	9	27	4	0	3	10	5	19	.297	.354	.440	793	98	-0	1	0	0	1.000	1	1-24/O-4(4-0-0),3-2	-0.1
Total	8	383	1008	122	246	45	3	37	159	100	232	.244	.319	.405	724	87	-21	14	8	0	.994	13	1-193/3-82,O-23L,D	-2.1
■ EDDIE PEREZ	Perez, Eduardo Rafael b: 5/4/68, Ciudad Ojeda, Venez. BR/TR, 6'1", 175 lbs. Deb: 9/10/95																							
1995	Atl-N	7	13	1	4	1	0	1	4	0	2	.308	.308	.615	923	132	0	0	0	0	1.000	3	/C-5,1-1	0.3
1996	*Atl-N	68	156	19	40	9	1	4	17	8	19	.256	.297	.404	701	78	-5	0	0	0	.993	-0	C-54/1-7	-0.3
1997	*Atl-N	73	191	20	41	5	0	6	18	10	35	.215	.261	.335	596	54	-13	0	1	-0	.988	10	C-64/1-6	-0.1
1998	*Atl-N	61	149	18	50	12	0	6	32	15	28	.336	.404	.537	941	145	10	1	1	-0	.997	9	C-45/1-8,D-1	1.9
1999	*Atl-N	104	309	30	77	17	0	7	30	17	40	.249	.301	.372	673	69	-15	0	1	-0	.993	14	C-98/1-2	0.3
2000	Atl-N	7	22	0	4	1	0	0	3	0	2	.182	.182	.227	409	2	-3	0	0	0	.976	0	/C-7	-0.3
Total	6	320	840	88	216	45	1	24	104	50	126	.257	.307	.399	706	80	-27	1	3	-1	.992	35	C-273/1-24,D-1	1.8
■ MARTY PEREZ	Perez, Martin Roman b: 2/28/46, Visalia, Cal. BR/TR, 5'11", 160 lbs. Deb: 9/9/69																							
1969	Cal-A	13	13	3	3	0	0	0	0	2	1	.231	.333	.231	564	63	-1	0	0	0	1.000	6	/S-7,2-2,3-2	0.6
1970	Cal-A	3	3	0	0	0	0	0	1	0	0	.000	.000	.000	0	-99	-1	0	0	0	.833	1	/S-2	0.0
1971	Atl-N	130	410	28	93	15	3	4	32	25	44	.227	.273	.307	580	60	-21	1	2	-0	.955	-14	*S-126/2-1	-2.4
1972	Atl-N	141	479	33	109	13	1	1	28	30	55	.228	.277	.265	542	50	-30	0	3	-1	.957	-34	*S-141	-5.3
1973	Atl-N	141	501	66	125	15	5	8	57	49	66	.250	.319	.347	666	79	-14	2	3	-1	.962	-9	*S-139	-0.8
1974	Atl-N	127	447	51	116	20	5	2	34	35	51	.260	.315	.340	655	80	-12	2	0	0	.985	-9	*2-102,S-14/3-6	-1.3
1975	Atl-N	120	461	50	127	14	2	2	34	37	44	.275	.329	.328	657	80	-12	2	2	-0	.985	-8	*2-116/S-7	-1.3
1976	Atl-N	31	96	12	24	4	0	1	6	8	9	.250	.308	.323	631	74	-3	0	0	0	.976	-2	2-18,S-17/3-2	-0.3
	SF-N	93	332	37	86	13	1	2	26	30	28	.259	.320	.322	643	80	-8	3	4	-1	.979	7	2-89/S-5	0.5
	Yr	124	428	49	110	17	1	3	32	38	37	.257	.318	.322	640	79	-11	3	4	-1	.978	5	*2-107,S-22/3-2	0.2
1977	NY-A	1	4	0	2	0	0	0	0	0	1	.500	.500	.500	1000	175	0	0	0	0	1.000	1	/3-1	0.0
	Oak-A	115	373	32	86	14	5	2	23	29	65	.231	.291	.311	602	65	-18	1	3	-1	.974	0	*2-105,3-12/S-4	-1.3
	Yr	116	377	32	88	14	5	2	23	29	66	.233	.293	.313	606	66	-17	1	3	-1	.974	1	*2-105,3-13/S-4	-1.2
1978	Oak-A	16	12	1	0	0	0	0	0	0	5	.000	.000	.000	0	-99	-3	0	0	0	1.000	2	3-11/S-3,2-1	-0.1
Total	10	931	3131	313	771	108	22	22	241	245	369	.246	.303	.316	619	70	-123	11	17	-4	.958	-59	S-465,2-434/3-34	-11.6
■ NEIFI PEREZ	Perez, Neifi Neftali (Diaz) b: 2/2/75, Villa Mella, D.R. BB/TR, 6', 175 lbs. Deb: 8/31/96																							
1996	Col-N	17	45	4	7	2	0	0	3	0	8	.156	.156	.200	356	-6	-7	2	2	-0	.972	-0	S-14/2-4	-0.6
1997	Col-N	83	313	46	91	13	10	5	31	21	43	.291	.337	.444	781	83	-7	4	3	-0	.975	32	S-45,2-41/3-2	2.9
1998	Col-N	162	647	80	177	25	9	9	59	38	70	.274	.315	.382	697	67	-29	5	6	-1	.975	26	*S-162/C-1	0.9
1999	Col-N	157	690	108	193	27	**11**	12	70	28	54	.280	.309	.403	712	62	-39	13	5	1	.981	28	*S-157	0.4
2000	Col-N	162	651	92	187	39	11	10	71	30	63	.287	.319	.427	746	67	-31	3	6	-1	.978	**39**	*S-162	1.8
Total	5	581	2346	330	655	106	41	36	234	117	238	.279	.314	.405	720	66	-114	27	22	-2	.978	125	S-540/2-45,3-2,C-1	5.4
■ ROBERT PEREZ	Perez, Robert Alexander (Jimenez) b: 6/4/69, Bolivar, Venez. BR/TR, 6'3", 205 lbs. Deb: 7/20/94																							
1994	Tor-A	4	8	0	1	0	0	0	0	0	1	.125	.125	.125	250	-35	-2	0	0	0	1.000	-0	/O-4(2-0-2)	-0.2
1995	Tor-A	17	48	2	9	2	0	1	3	0	5	.188	.188	.292	479	22	-6	0	0	0	1.000	-0	O-15(5-0-11)	-0.6
1996	Tor-A	86	202	30	66	10	0	2	21	8	17	.327	.355	.406	761	92	-2	3	0	1	.983	-9	O-79(59-0-25)/D-2	-1.1
1997	Tor-A	37	78	4	15	4	1	2	6	0	16	.192	.192	.346	538	36	-7	0	0	0	1.000	-3	O-25(17-0-9)/D-7	-1.1
1998	Sea-A	17	35	3	6	1	0	2	6	0	5	.171	.171	.371	543	36	-3	0	0	0	1.000	-2	O-17(2-0-15)	-0.6
	Mon-N	52	106	9	25	1	0	1	8	2	23	.236	.257	.274	530	40	-9	0	0	0	.852	-4	O-29(29-0-0)	-1.4
Total	5	213	477	48	122	18	1	8	44	10	67	.256	.274	.348	622	59	-29	3	0	1	.975	-18	O-169(114-0-62)/D-9	-5.0
■ SANTIAGO PEREZ	Perez, Santiago Alberto b: 12/30/75, Santo Domingo, D.R. BB/TR, 6'2", 150 lbs. Deb: 6/3/2000																							
2000	Mil-N	24	52	8	9	2	0	0	2	8	9	.173	.295	.212	507	32	-5	4	0	1	.917	1	S-20	-0.2
■ TIMO PEREZ	Perez, Timoniel b: 4/8/77, Bani, D.R. BL/TL, 5'9", 167 lbs. Deb: 9/1/2000																							
2000	*NY-N	24	49	11	14	4	1	1	3	3	5	.286	.340	.469	809	105	0	1	1	-0	.970	-2	O-19(8-7-8)	-0.2
■ TOMAS PEREZ	Perez, Tomas Orlando b: 12/29/73, Barquisimeto, Venez BB/TR, 5'11", 165 lbs. Deb: 5/3/95																							
1995	Tor-A	41	98	12	24	3	1	1	8	7	18	.245	.295	.327	622	62	-6	0	1	-0	.954	1	S-31/2-7,3-1	-0.3
1996	Tor-A	91	295	24	74	13	4	1	19	25	29	.251	.312	.332	644	63	-16	1	2	-0	.970	12	2-75,3-11/S-5	-0.1
1997	Tor-A	40	123	9	24	3	2	0	9	11	28	.195	.267	.252	519	36	-11	1	1	-0	.993	9	S-32/2-8	0.0
1998	Tor-A	6	9	1	1	0	0	0	0	1	3	.111	.200	.111	311	-16	-2	0	0	0	1.000	-0	/S-4,2-1	-0.2
2000	Phi-N	45	140	17	31	7	1	1	13	11	30	.221	.278	.307	585	47	-12	1	1	-0	.976	-5	S-44	-1.3
Total	5	223	665	63	154	26	8	3	49	55	108	.232	.292	.308	601	53	-46	3	5	-1	.973	16	S-116/2-91,3-12	-1.9
■ TONY PEREZCHICA	Perezchica, Antonio Llamas (Gonzales) b: 4/20/66, Mexicali, Mex. BR/TR, 5'11", 165 lbs. Deb: 9/7/88																							
1988	SF-N	7	8	1	1	0	0	0	1	2	1	.125	.300	.125	425	27	-1	0	0	0	1.000	-1	/2-6	-0.2
1990	SF-N	4	3	1	1	0	0	0	0	1	2	.333	.500	.333	833	139	0	0	0	0	1.000	-2	/2-2,S-2	-0.1
1991	SF-N	23	48	2	11	4	1	0	3	2	12	.229	.260	.354	614	73	-2	0	1	-0	.947	-3	S-13/2-6	-0.5

YEAR	TM/L	G	AB	R	H	2B	3B	HR	RBI	BB	SO	AVG	OBP	SLG	OPS	OPS+	BR+	SB	CS	SBR	FA	FR	G/POS	TPR
	Cle-A	17	22	4	8	2	0	0	0	3	5	.364	.440	.455	895	147	2	0	0	0	1.000	-1	/S-6,3-3,2-2,D-1	0.1
1992	Cle-A	18	20	2	2	1	0	0	1	2	6	.100	.182	.150	332	-6	-3	0	0	0	.875	-1	/3-9,2-4,S-4,D-1	-0.4
Total	4	69	101	10	23	7	1	0	5	10	26	.228	.297	.317	614	74	-4	0	1	-0	.944	-8	/S-25,2-20,3-12,D-2	-1.1

■ BRODERICK PERKINS

Perkins, Broderick Phillip b: 11/23/54, Pittsburg, Cal. BL/TL, 5'10", 180 lbs. Deb: 7/7/78 Career OF: (10-LF 0-CF 31-RF)

YEAR	TM/L	G	AB	R	H	2B	3B	HR	RBI	BB	SO	AVG	OBP	SLG	OPS	OPS+	BR+	SB	CS	SBR	FA	FR	G/POS	TPR
1978	SD-N	62	217	14	52	14	1	2	33	5	29	.240	.257	.341	598	71	-9	4	0	1	.993	3	1-59	-0.9
1979	SD-N	57	87	8	23	0	0	0	8	8	12	.264	.326	.264	591	67	-4	0	0	0	.982	-1	1-28	-0.5
1980	SD-N	43	100	18	37	9	0	2	14	11	10	.370	.432	.520	952	175	10	2	1	0	.988	-4	1-20,O-10(0-0-10)	0.5
1981	SD-N	92	254	27	71	18	3	2	40	14	16	.280	.317	.398	715	110	2	0	4	-1	.997	-3	1-80/O-3(1-0-2)	-0.6
1982	SD-N	125	347	32	94	10	4	2	34	26	20	.271	.327	.340	667	92	-4	2	1	0	.994	-1	1-98,O-11(4-0-7)	-1.0
1983	Cle-A	79	184	23	50	10	0	0	24	9	19	.272	.306	.326	632	71	-7	1	5	-2	.991	0	1-19,O-17R,D-16	-1.0
1984	Cle-A	58	66	5	13	1	0	0	4	7	10	.197	.284	.212	496	39	-5	0	0	0	1.000	-0	D-10/1-2	-0.6
Total	7	516	1255	127	340	62	8	8	157	80	116	.271	.317	.352	669	90	-17	9	11	-2	.993	-4	1-306/O-41R,D-26	-4.1

■ CY PERKINS

Perkins, Ralph Foster b: 2/27/1896, Gloucester, Mass. d: 10/2/63, Philadelphia, Pa. BR/TR, 5'10.5", 158 lbs. Deb: 9/25/15 MC

YEAR	TM/L	G	AB	R	H	2B	3B	HR	RBI	BB	SO	AVG	OBP	SLG	OPS	OPS+	BR+	SB	CS	SBR	FA	FR	G/POS	TPR
1915	Phi-A	7	20	2	4	1	0	0	0	3	3	.200	.304	.250	554	68	-1	0			.920	1	/C-6	0.0
1917	Phi-A	6	18	1	3	0	0	0	2	2	1	.167	.250	.167	417	28	-1	0			.978	4	/C-6	0.3
1918	Phi-A	68	218	9	41	4	1	1	14	8	15	.188	.217	.229	446	34	-18	1			.990	12	C-60	-0.1
1919	Phi-A	101	305	22	77	12	7	2	29	27	22	.252	.313	.357	671	87	-6	2			.971	7	C-87/S-8	1.0
1920	Phi-A	148	492	40	128	24	6	5	52	28	35	.260	.303	.364	667	75	-19	5	6	-1	.979	**23**	*C-146/2-1	1.4
1921	Phi-A	141	538	58	155	31	4	12	73	32	32	.288	.329	.428	757	91	-9	5	9	-2	.971	5	*C-141	0.3
1922	Phi-A	148	505	58	135	20	6	6	69	40	30	.267	.322	.366	689	77	-17	1	7	-2	.984	-4	*C-141	-1.4
1923	Phi-A	143	500	53	135	34	5	2	65	65	30	.270	.356	.370	726	90	-6	1	3	-1	.971	-7	*C-137	-0.5
1924	Phi-A	128	392	31	95	19	4	0	32	31	20	.242	.304	.311	616	58	-25	3	4	-1	.983	-0	*C-128	-1.6
1925	Phi-A	65	140	21	43	10	0	1	18	26	6	.307	.426	.400	826	104	2	0	0	0	.980	11	C-58/3-1	1.5
1926	Phi-A	63	148	14	43	6	0	0	19	18	7	.291	.371	.331	702	80	-4	0	2	-1	.984	9	C-55	0.7
1927	Phi-A	59	137	11	35	7	2	1	15	12	8	.255	.315	.358	673	70	-6	0	2	-1	.979	1	C-54/1-1	-0.3
1928	Phi-A	19	29	1	5	0	0	0	1	1	1	.172	.200	.172	372	-1	-4	0	1	-0	.982	4	C-19	-0.1
1929	Phi-A	38	76	4	16	4	0	0	9	5	4	.211	.259	.263	522	34	-8	0	0	0	.990	2	C-38	-0.4
1930	Phi-A	20	38	1	6	2	0	0	4	2	3	.158	.200	.211	411	4	-6	0	0	0	.964	0	C-19/1-1	-0.4
1931	NY-A	16	47	3	12	1	0	0	7	1	4	.255	.286	.277	562	51	-3	0	0	0	1.000	-5	C-16	-0.7
1934	Det-A	1	1	0	0	0	0	0	0	0	0	.000	.000	.000	0	-99	-0	0	0	0	.000	0	H	0.0
Total	17	1171	3604	329	933	175	35	30	409	301	221	.259	.319	.352	670	75	-131	18	34		.978	62	*C-1111/S-8,1-2,32	-0.3

■ SAM PERLOZZO

Perlozzo, Samuel Benedict b: 3/4/51, Cumberland, Md. BR/TR, 5'9", 170 lbs. Deb: 9/13/77 C

YEAR	TM/L	G	AB	R	H	2B	3B	HR	RBI	BB	SO	AVG	OBP	SLG	OPS	OPS+	BR+	SB	CS	SBR	FA	FR	G/POS	TPR
1977	Min-A	10	24	6	7	0	2	0	0	2	3	.292	.346	.458	804	119	1	0	0	0	1.000	-3	2-10/3-1	-0.2
1979	SD-N	2	2	0	0	0	0	0	0	1	0	.000	.333	.000	333	-1	-0	0	0	0	.500	-1	/2-2	-0.2
Total	2	12	26	6	7	0	2	0	0	3	3	.269	.345	.423	768	110	0	0	0	0	.967	-5	/2-12,3-1	-0.4

■ JOHN PERRIN

Perrin, John Stephenson b: 2/4/1898, Escanaba, Mich. d: 6/24/69, Detroit, Mich. BL/TR, 5'9", 160 lbs. Deb: 7/11/21

YEAR	TM/L	G	AB	R	H	2B	3B	HR	RBI	BB	SO	AVG	OBP	SLG	OPS	OPS+	BR+	SB	CS	SBR	FA	FR	G/POS	TPR
1921	Bos-A	4	13	3	3	0	0	0	1	0	3	.231	.231	.231	462	19	-2	0	0	0	1.000	-2	/O-4(0-0-4)	-0.3

■ NIG PERRINE

Perrine, John Grover b: 1/14/1885, Clinton, Wis. d: 8/13/48, Kansas City, Mo. BR/TR, 5'9", 160 lbs. Deb: 4/11/07

YEAR	TM/L	G	AB	R	H	2B	3B	HR	RBI	BB	SO	AVG	OBP	SLG	OPS	OPS+	BR+	SB	CS	SBR	FA	FR	G/POS	TPR
1907	Was-A	44	146	13	25	4	1	0	15	13		.171	.253	.212	465	53	-7	10			.946	-3	2-24,S-18/3-2	-1.1

■ GEORGE PERRING

Perring, George Wilson b: 8/13/1884, Sharon, Wis. d: 8/20/60, Beloit, Wis. BR/TR (BB 1909 (1 GAME)), 6', 190 lbs. Deb: 4/25/08

YEAR	TM/L	G	AB	R	H	2B	3B	HR	RBI	BB	SO	AVG	OBP	SLG	OPS	OPS+	BR+	SB	CS	SBR	FA	FR	G/POS	TPR
1908	Cle-A	89	310	23	67	8	5	0	19	16		.216	.255	.274	529	72	-10	8			.928	-6	S-48,3-41	-1.5
1909	Cle-A	88	283	26	63	10	9	0	20	19		.223	.283	.322	605	87	-4	6			.932	6	3-67,S-11/2-4	0.4
1910	Cle-A	39	122	14	27	6	3	0	8	3		.221	.240	.320	560	74	-4	3			.931	2	3-33/1-4	-0.2
1914	KC-F	144	496	68	138	28	10	2	69	59	39	.278	.355	.387	742	106	-3	7			.934	9	*3-101,1-41/P-1,S-1	0.8
1915	KC-F	153	553	67	143	23	7	7	67	55	30	.259	.327	.363	690	98	-11	10			.958	15	*3-102,1-31,2-31,/S	0.7
Total	5	513	1764	198	438	75	34	9	183	152	69	.248	.310	.345	655	93	-33	34			.939	26	3-344/1-76,S-61,2P	0.2

■ BOYD PERRY

Perry, Boyd Glenn b: 3/21/14, Snow Camp, N.C. d: 6/29/90, Burlington, N.C. BR/TR, 5'10", 158 lbs. Deb: 5/23/41

YEAR	TM/L	G	AB	R	H	2B	3B	HR	RBI	BB	SO	AVG	OBP	SLG	OPS	OPS+	BR+	SB	CS	SBR	FA	FR	G/POS	TPR
1941	Det-A	36	83	9	15	5	0	0	11	10	9	.181	.269	.241	510	32	-8	1	0	0	.974	-0	S-25,2-11	-0.6

■ CHAN PERRY

Perry, Chan Everett b: 9/13/72, Live Oak, Fla. BR/TR, 6'2", 200 lbs. Deb: 8/3/2000

YEAR	TM/L	G	AB	R	H	2B	3B	HR	RBI	BB	SO	AVG	OBP	SLG	OPS	OPS+	BR+	SB	CS	SBR	FA	FR	G/POS	TPR
2000	Cle-A	13	14	1	1	0	0	0	0	0	5	.071	.071	.071	143	-62	-3	0	0	0	1.000	-2	/O-7(1-0-6),1-1,D-4	-0.5

■ CLAY PERRY

Perry, Clayton Shields b: 12/18/1881, Clayton, Wis. d: 1/13/54, Rice Lake, Wis. BR/TR, 5'10.5", 175 lbs. Deb: 9/2/08

YEAR	TM/L	G	AB	R	H	2B	3B	HR	RBI	BB	SO	AVG	OBP	SLG	OPS	OPS+	BR+	SB	CS	SBR	FA	FR	G/POS	TPR
1908	Det-A	7	17	0	2	0	0	0	0	0		.118	.167	.118	284	-7	-2	0			.850	0	/3-7	-0.2

■ GERALD PERRY

Perry, Gerald June b: 10/30/60, Savannah, Ga. BL/TR, 6', 190 lbs. Deb: 8/11/83 C Career OF: (87-LF 0-CF 3-RF)

YEAR	TM/L	G	AB	R	H	2B	3B	HR	RBI	BB	SO	AVG	OBP	SLG	OPS	OPS+	BR+	SB	CS	SBR	FA	FR	G/POS	TPR
1983	Atl-N	27	39	5	14	2	0	1	6	5	4	.359	.432	.487	919	144	2	0	1	-0	.982	-2	/1-7,O-1(1-0-0)	-0.1
1984	Atl-N	122	347	52	92	12	2	7	47	61	38	.265	.378	.372	750	104	4	15	12	-1	.988	-8	1-64,O-53(53-0-0)	-1.0
1985	Atl-N	110	238	22	51	5	0	3	13	23	28	.214	.284	.273	557	53	-14	9	5	0	.985	-0	1-55/O-1(1-0-0)	-1.9
1986	Atl-N	29	70	6	19	2	0	2	11	8	4	.271	.346	.386	732	96	-0	0	1	-0	.889	-5	O-21(21-0-1)/1-1	-0.7
1987	Atl-N	142	533	77	144	35	2	12	74	48	63	.270	.332	.411	742	91	-7	42	16	4	.990	-10	*1-136/O-7(7-0-0)	-2.2
1988	Atl-N★	141	547	61	164	29	1	8	74	36	49	.300	.344	.400	745	108	5	29	14	1	.988	1	*1-141	-0.3
1989	Atl-N	72	266	24	67	11	0	4	21	32	28	.252	.339	.338	677	92	-2	10	6	0	.987	1	1-72	-0.6
1990	KC-A	133	465	57	118	22	2	8	57	39	56	.254	.316	.361	677	90	-6	17	4	2	.986	2	D-68,1-51	-0.7
1991	StL-N	109	242	29	58	8	4	6	36	22	34	.240	.303	.380	683	90	-3	15	8	1	.989	-4	1-61/O-5(4-0-1)	-1.1
1992	StL-N	87	143	13	34	8	0	1	18	15	23	.238	.314	.315	629	81	-3	3	6	-1	.987	-4	1-29	-1.1
1993	StL-N	96	98	21	33	5	0	4	16	18	23	.337	.440	.510	950	157	9	1	1	-0	.976	-1	1-15/O-1(0-0-1)	0.6
1994	StL-N	60	77	12	25	7	0	3	18	15	12	.325	.435	.532	967	153	7	1	1	-0	.990	-2	1-13	0.4
1995	StL-N	65	79	4	13	4	0	0	5	6	12	.165	.224	.215	439	16	-10	0	0	0	1.000	-1	1-11	-1.1
Total	13	1193	3144	383	832	150	11	59	396	328	374	.265	.336	.376	712	95	-19	142	75	5	.988	-32	1-656/O-89L,D-68	-9.8

■ HERB PERRY

Perry, Herbert Edward b: 9/15/69, Live Oak, Fla. BR/TR, 6'2", 210 lbs. Deb: 5/3/94 Career OF: (6-LF 0-CF 0-RF)

YEAR	TM/L	G	AB	R	H	2B	3B	HR	RBI	BB	SO	AVG	OBP	SLG	OPS	OPS+	BR+	SB	CS	SBR	FA	FR	G/POS	TPR
1994	Cle-A	4	9	1	1	0	0	0	1	3	1	.111	.385	.111	496	36	-1	0	0	0	1.000	1	/1-2,3-2	0.0
1995	*Cle-A	52	162	23	51	13	1	3	23	13	28	.315	.380	.463	843	116	4	1	3	-1	1.000	0	1-45/3-1,D-6	0.0
1996	Cle-A	7	12	1	1	1	0	0	0	1	2	.083	.154	.167	321	-19	-2	1	0	0	1.000	-0	/1-5,3-1	-0.2
1999	TB-A	66	209	29	53	10	1	6	32	16	42	.254	.336	.397	733	85	-5	0	0	0	.955	7	3-42,1-14,D-10,/O-6L	0.1
2000	TB-A	7	28	2	6	1	0	0	1	2	7	.214	.267	.250	517	32	-3	0	0	0	.938	-1	/3-7,1-1	-0.4
	*Chi-A	109	383	69	118	29	1	12	61	22	68	.308	.360	.483	843	110	5	4	1	1	.969	11	*3-104/1-3,D-3	1.5
	Yr	116	411	71	124	30	1	12	62	24	75	.302	.354	.467	821	104	2	4	1	1	.967	10	*3-111/1-4,D-3	1.1
Total	5	245	803	125	230	54	3	21	118	57	148	.286	.352	.440	791	99	-1	6	4	-0	.963	17	3-157/1-70,D-19,O-6L	1.0

■ BOB PERRY

Perry, Melvin Gray b: 9/14/34, New Bern, N.C. BR/TR, 6'2", 180 lbs. Deb: 5/17/63

YEAR	TM/L	G	AB	R	H	2B	3B	HR	RBI	BB	SO	AVG	OBP	SLG	OPS	OPS+	BR+	SB	CS	SBR	FA	FR	G/POS	TPR
1963	LA-A	61	166	16	42	9	0	3	14	9	31	.253	.303	.361	665	91	-2	1	1	-0	.946	-7	O-55(7-23-26)	-1.2
1964	LA-A	70	221	19	61	8	1	3	16	14	52	.276	.319	.362	681	99	-1	1	1	-0	.975	-4	O-62(0-62-1)	-0.8
Total	2	131	387	35	103	17	1	6	30	23	83	.266	.312	.362	674	95	-3	2	2	-0	.962	-11	O-117(7-85-27)	-2.0

■ HANK PERRY

Perry, William Henry "Socks" b: 7/28/1886, Howell, Mich. d: 7/18/56, Pontiac, Mich. BL/TR, 5'11", 190 lbs. Deb: 4/12/12

YEAR	TM/L	G	AB	R	H	2B	3B	HR	RBI	BB	SO	AVG	OBP	SLG	OPS	OPS+	BR+	SB	CS	SBR	FA	FR	G/POS	TPR
1912	Det-A	13	36	3	6	1	0	0	0	3		.167	.231	.194	425	23	-4	0			1.000	2	/O-7(0-7-0)	-0.2

■ JOHNNY PESKY

Pesky, John Michael (b: John Michael Paveskovich) b: 9/27/19, Portland, Ore. BL/TR, 5'9", 168 lbs. Deb: 4/14/42 MC

YEAR	TM/L	G	AB	R	H	2B	3B	HR	RBI	BB	SO	AVG	OBP	SLG	OPS	OPS+	BR+	SB	CS	SBR	FA	FR	G/POS	TPR
1942	Bos-A	147	620	105	**205**	29	9	2	51	42	36	.331	.375	.416	791	118	14	12	7	0	.955	18	*S-147	4.4
1946	*Bos-A★	153	621	115	**208**	43	4	2	55	65	29	.335	.401	.427	827	124	22	9	8	-1	.969	12	*S-153	4.4
1947	Bos-A	155	638	106	**207**	27	8	0	39	72	22	.324	.393	.392	785	110	11	12	9	-1	.976	-11	*S-133,3-22	0.8
1948	Bos-A	143	565	124	159	26	6	3	55	99	32	.281	.394	.365	759	98	2	3	5	-1	.951	6	*3-141	0.6
1949	Bos-A	148	604	111	185	27	7	2	69	100	19	.306	.408	.384	792	103	7	8	4	0	.970	21	*3-148	2.7

YEAR	TM/L	G	AB	R	H	2B	3B	HR	RBI	BB	SO	AVG	OBP	SLG	OPS	OPS+	BR+	SB	CS	SBR	FA	FR	G/POS	TPR
1950	Bos-A	127	490	112	153	22	6	1	49	104	31	.312	.437	.388	825	103	8	2	1	0	.974	22	*3-116/S-8	2.7
1951	Bos-A	131	480	93	150	20	6	3	41	84	15	.313	.417	.398	815	110	11	2	2	-0	.961	9	*S-106,3-11/2-5	2.6
1952	Bos-A	25	67	10	10	2	0	0	2	15	5	.149	.313	.179	492	36	-5	0	3	-1	.917	-6	3-19/S-2	-1.3
	Det-A	69	177	26	45	4	0	1	9	41	11	.254	.394	.294	688	93	1	1	2	-0	.952	-6	S-41,2-22/3-3	-0.2
	Yr	94	244	36	55	6	0	1	11	56	16	.225	.372	.262	634	77	-5	1	5	-2	.953	-11	S-43,3-22,2-22	-1.5
1953	Det-A	103	308	43	90	22	1	2	24	27	10	.292	.353	.390	743	102	1	3	7	-2	.991	-14	2-73	-0.9
1954	Det-A	20	17	5	3	0	0	1	1	3	1	.176	.300	.353	653	80	-1	0	0	0	.000	0	H	-0.1
	Was-A	49	158	17	40	4	3	0	9	10	7	.253	.298	.316	614	72	-6	1	1	-0	.979	-8	2-37/S-1	-1.2
	Yr	69	175	22	43	4	3	1	10	13	8	.246	.298	.320	618	72	-7	1	1	-0	.979	-8	2-37/S-1	-1.3
Total	10	1270	4745	867	1455	226	50	17	404	662	218	.307	.394	.386	780	106	64	53	49	-5	.964	43	S-591,3-460,2-137	14.5
■ ROBERTO PETAGINE	Petagine, Roberto Antonio (Guerra) b: 6/7/71, Nueva Esparta, Venez. BL/TL, 6'1", 170 lbs. Deb: 4/4/94																							
1994	Hou-N	8	7	0	0	0	0	0	0	1	3	.000	.125	.000	125	-67	-2	0	0	0	1.000	-0	/1-2	-0.2
1995	SD-N	89	124	15	29	8	0	3	17	26	41	.234	.367	.371	738	99	1	0	0	0	.996	1	1-51/O-2(1-0-1)	-0.1
1996	NY-N	50	99	10	23	3	0	4	17	9	27	.232	.315	.384	699	87	-2	0	2	-1	.996	2	1-40	-0.3
1997	NY-N	12	15	2	1	0	0	0	2	3	6	.067	.222	.067	289	-21	-3	0	0	0	1.000	0	/1-6,O-1(1-0-0)	-0.2
1998	Cin-N	34	62	14	16	2	1	3	7	16	11	.258	.410	.468	878	129	3	1	0	0	1.000	-1	1-15,O-15(1-0-15)	0.1
Total	5	193	307	41	69	13	1	10	43	55	88	.225	.348	.371	719	92	-3	1	2	-0	.997	3	1-114/O-18(3-0-16)	-0.7
■ BILL PETERMAN	Peterman, William David b: 3/20/21, Philadelphia, Pa. d: 3/13/99, Philadelphia, Pa. BR/TR, 6'2", 185 lbs. Deb: 4/26/42																							
1942	Phi-N	1	1	0	1	0	0	0	0	0	0	1.000	1.000	1.000	2000	512	1	0			.000	0	/C-1	0.1
■ JOHN PETERS	Peters, John Paul b: 4/8/1850, Louisiana, Mo. d: 1/4/24, St.Louis, Mo. BR/TR, 5'7", 180 lbs. Deb: 5/23/1874 Career OF: (0-LF 0-CF 1-RF)																							
1874	Chi-n	55	239	39	69	10	0	1	25	2	11	.289	.295	.343	638	103	1	2	2	-0	.799	3	S-36,2-19	0.1
1875	Chi-n	69	297	40	85	16	2	0	34	0	3	.286	.286	.354	640	120	5	12	6	1	.871	10	*S-65/2-6	1.2
1876	Chi-N	66	319	70	111	14	2	1	47	3	2	.348	.357	.418	775	141	11				**.932**	-1	*S-66/P-1	1.1
1877	Chi-N	60	265	45	84	10	3	0	41	1	7	.317	.320	.377	697	106	1				.883	19	*S-60	1.9
1878	Mil-N	55	246	33	76	6	1	0	22	5	8	.309	.323	.341	664	111	2				.853	5	2-34,S-22	0.9
1879	Chi-N	83	379	45	93	13	2	1	31	1	19	.245	.247	.298	546	74	-11				.837	-8	*S-83	-1.5
1880	Pro-N	86	359	30	82	5	0	0	24	5	15	.228	.239	.242	481	66	-12				**.900**	-1	*S-86	-0.9
1881	Buf-N	54	229	21	49	8	1	0	25	3	12	.214	.224	.258	482	52	-12				.869	7	S-53/O-1(0-0-1)	-0.3
1882	Pit-a	78	333	46	96	10	1	0		4		.288	.297	.324	621	115	5				.883	6	*S-77/2-1	1.2
1883	Pit-a	8	28	3	3	0	0	0		0		.107	.107	.107	214	-32	-4				.818	3	/S-8	-0.1
1884	Pit-a	1	4	0	0	0	0	0		0		.000	.000	.000	0	-99	-1				.667	-1	/S-1	-0.2
Total	2 n	124	536	79	154	26	2	1	59	2	14	.287	.290	.349	639	112	6	14	8	0	.846	14	S-101/2-25	1.3
Total	9	491	2162	293	594	66	10	2	190	22	63	.275	.282	.318	600	94	-21				.881	28	S-456/2-35,O-1R,P-1	2.1
■ JOHN PETERS	Peters, John William "Big Pete" or "Shotgun" b: 7/14/1893, Kansas City, Kan. d: 2/21/32, Kansas City, Mo. BR/TR, 6', 192 lbs. Deb: 5/1/15																							
1915	Det-A	1	3	0	0	0	0	0	0	0	1	.000	.000	.000	0	-95	-1	0			1.000	1	/C-1	0.1
1918	Cle-A	1	1	0	0	0	0	0	0	1	1	.000	.500	.000	500	46	0	0			.500	-1	/C-1	-0.1
1921	Phi-N	55	155	7	45	4	0	3	23	6	13	.290	.329	.374	703	79	-4	1	0	0	.933	-13	C-44	-1.4
1922	Phi-N	55	143	15	35	9	1	4	24	9	18	.245	.308	.406	713	75	-6	0	1	-0	.953	-5	C-39	-0.8
Total	4	112	302	22	80	13	1	7	47	16	33	.265	.317	.384	701	76	-11	1	1		.934	-18	/C-85	-2.2
■ RICK PETERS	Peters, Richard Devin b: 11/21/55, Lynwood, Cal. BB/TR, 5'9", 170 lbs. Deb: 9/8/79 Career OF: (39-LF 167-CF 22-RF)																							
1979	Det-A	12	19	3	5	0	0	0	2	5	3	.263	.417	.263	680	85	-0	0	0	0	.000	-1	/3-3,2-2,O-1L,D-3	-0.1
1980	Det-A	133	477	79	139	19	7	2	42	54	48	.291	.371	.373	744	102	3	13	7	0	.977	0	*O-109(8-97-5),D-11	0.2
1981	Det-A	63	207	26	53	7	3	0	15	29	28	.256	.353	.319	672	91	-1	1	6	-2	.991	3	O-38(5-33-0),D-19	-0.1
1983	Oak-A	55	178	20	51	7	0	0	20	12	21	.287	.335	.326	661	88	-3	4	9	-2	.986	5	O-47(6-30-16)/D-8	-0.2
1986	Oak-A	44	38	7	7	1	0	0	1	7	7	.184	.311	.211	522	49	-2	2	2	-0	1.000	-5	O-27(19-7-1)/2-1	-0.8
Total	5	307	919	135	255	34	10	2	80	107	107	.277	.358	.343	701	95	-3	20	24	-4	.983	1	O-222C/D-41,2-3,3-3	-1.0
■ RUSTY PETERS	Peters, Russell Dixon b: 12/14/14, Roanoke, Va. BR/TR, 5'11", 170 lbs. Deb: 4/14/36 Career OF: (4-LF 0-CF 0-RF)																							
1936	Phi-A	45	119	12	26	3	2	3	16	4	28	.218	.244	.353	597	47	-11	1	1	-0	.898	1	S-25,3-10/O-2L,2-1	-0.8
1937	Phi-A	116	339	39	88	17	6	3	43	41	59	.260	.339	.372	711	80	-10	4	4	-1	.966	-13	2-70,3-31,S-13	-1.7
1938	Phi-A	2	7	0	0	0	0	0	0	0	1	.000	.000	.000	0	-99	-2	0	0	0	.714	-2	/S-2	-0.4
1940	Cle-A	30	71	5	17	3	2	0	7	4	14	.239	.280	.338	618	61	-4	1	0	0	.922	-0	/2-9,S-6,3-6,1-1	-0.3
1941	Cle-A	29	63	6	13	2	0	0	2	7	10	.206	.286	.238	524	42	-5	0	1	-0	.891	2	S-11/3-9,2-3	-0.3
1942	Cle-A	34	58	6	13	5	1	0	2	2	14	.224	.250	.345	595	70	-3	0	0	0	.944	2	S-24/2-1,3-1	0.0
1943	Cle-A	79	215	22	47	6	2	1	19	18	29	.219	.282	.279	561	69	-9	1	1	-0	.913	-6	3-46,S-14/2-6,O-2L	-1.5
1944	Cle-A	88	282	23	63	13	3	1	24	15	35	.223	.268	.301	569	65	-14	2	1	0	.976	-3	2-63,S-13/3-8	-1.4
1946	Cle-A	9	21	0	6	0	0	0	2	1	1	.286	.318	.286	604	74	-1	0	1	-0	1.000	0	/S-7	-0.1
1947	StL-A	39	47	10	16	4	0	0	2	6	8	.340	.415	.426	841	131	2	0	0	0	.955	7	2-13/S-2	1.0
Total	10	471	1222	123	289	53	16	8	117	98	199	.236	.295	.326	620	69	-56	9	9	-1	.966	-13	2-166,S-117,3/O1	-5.5
■ CHRIS PETERSEN	Petersen, Christopher Ronald b: 11/6/70, Boston, Mass. BR/TR, 5'11", 180 lbs. Deb: 5/25/99																							
1999	Col-N	7	13	1	2	0	0	0	2	2	3	.154	.267	.154	421	8	-2	0	0	0	.955	4	/2-6,S-1	0.2
■ BUDDY PETERSON	Peterson, Carl Francis b: 4/23/25, Portland, Ore. BR/TR, 5'9.5", 170 lbs. Deb: 9/14/55																							
1955	Chi-A	6	21	7	6	1	0	0	2	3	2	.286	.400	.333	733	96	0	0	0	0	.962	-1	/S-6	0.0
1957	Bal-A	7	17	1	3	2	0	0	0	2	2	.176	.263	.294	557	55	-1	0	0	0	.963	-1	/S-7	-0.2
Total	2	13	38	8	9	3	0	0	2	5	4	.237	.341	.316	657	80	-1	0	0	0	.962	-2	/S-13	-0.2
■ CAP PETERSON	Peterson, Charles Andrew b: 8/15/42, Tacoma, Wash. d: 5/16/80, Tacoma, Wash. BR/TR, 6'2", 195 lbs. Deb: 9/12/62 Career OF: (142-LF 0-CF 139-RF)																							
1962	SF-N	4	6	1	1	0	0	0	0	1	4	.167	.286	.167	452	25	-1	0	0	0	1.000	-1	/S-2	-0.1
1963	SF-N	22	54	7	14	2	0	1	2	2	13	.259	.286	.352	638	83	-1	0	0	0	.917	-7	/2-8,3-5,O-3L,S-1	-0.8
1964	SF-N	66	74	8	15	1	1	1	8	3	20	.203	.234	.284	518	44	-5	0	0	0	1.000	-3	O-10L/1-2,2-1,3-1	-0.9
1965	SF-N	63	105	14	26	7	0	3	15	10	16	.248	.313	.400	713	97	-1	0	0	0	1.000	-4	O-27(23-0-4)	-0.6
1966	SF-N	89	190	13	45	6	1	2	19	11	32	.237	.282	.311	593	63	-9	2	0	0	1.000	-3	O-51(50-0-1)/1-2	-1.5
1967	Was-A	122	405	35	97	17	2	8	46	32	61	.240	.300	.351	651	95	-3	0	3	-1	.970	0	*O-101(18-0-88)	-1.1
1968	Was-A	94	226	20	46	8	1	3	18	18	31	.204	.265	.288	553	70	-8	2	1	0	1.000	-1	O-53(14-0-39)	-1.5
1969	Cle-A	76	110	8	25	3	0	1	14	24	18	.227	.370	.282	652	82	-1	0	0	0	.977	-2	O-30(25-0-5)/3-4	-0.5
Total	8	536	1170	106	269	44	5	19	122	101	195	.230	.294	.325	619	80	-30	4	4	-1	.983	-18	O-275L/3-10,2-9,1S	-7.0
■ HARDY PETERSON	Peterson, Harding William b: 10/17/29, Perth Amboy, N.J. BR/TR, 6', 205 lbs. Deb: 5/5/55																							
1955	Pit-N	32	81	7	20	6	0	1	10	7	7	.247	.315	.358	673	79	-2	0	0	0	.965	6	C-31	0.4
1957	Pit-N	30	73	10	22	2	1	2	11	9	10	.301	.378	.438	816	122	2	0	1	-0	.985	2	C-30	0.5
1958	Pit-N	2	6	0	2	0	0	0	0	1	0	.333	.429	.333	762	108	0	0	0	0	1.000	-0	/C-2	0.0
1959	Pit-N	2	1	0	0	0	0	0	0	0	0	.000	.000	.000	0	-99	-0	0	0	0	1.000	1	/C-2	0.0
Total	4	66	161	17	44	8	1	3	21	17	17	.273	.346	.391	738	99	-0	0	1	-0	.976	7	/C-65	0.9
■ BOB PETERSON	Peterson, Robert A. b: 7/16/1884, Philadelphia, Pa. d: 11/27/62, Evesham Township, N.J. BR/TR, 6'1", 160 lbs. Deb: 4/18/06 Career OF: (1-LF 0-CF 0-RF)																							
1906	Bos-A	39	118	10	24	1	1	1	9	11		.203	.277	.254	531	67	-4	1			.899	-7	C-30/2-3,1-2,O-1L	-0.9
1907	Bos-A	4	13	1	1	0	0	0	0	0		.077	.077	.077	154	-51	-2	0			1.000	0	/C-4	-0.2
Total	2	43	131	11	25	1	1	1	9	11		.191	.259	.237	495	56	-6	1			.910	-7	/C-34,2-3,1-2,O-1L	-1.1
■ TED PETOSKEY	Petoskey, Frederick Lee b: 1/5/11, St.Charles, Mich. d: 11/30/96, Elgin, S.C. BR/TR, 5'11.5", 183 lbs. Deb: 9/9/34																							
1934	Cin-N	6	7	0	0	0	0	0	1	0	5	.000	.000	.000	0	-99	-2	0			1.000	1	/O-2(0-2-0)	-0.1
1935	Cin-N	4	5	0	2	0	0	0	0	0	1	.400	.400	.400	800	119	0	1			1.000	-1	/O-2(1-1-0)	-0.1
Total	2	10	12	0	2	0	0	0	1	0	6	.167	.167	.167	333	-11	-2	1			1.000	0	/O-4(1-3-0)	-0.2

■ GENO PETRALLI

Petralli, Eugene James b: 9/25/59, Sacramento, Cal. BL/TR (BB 1982-86, 87 (part)), 6'2", 185 lbs. Deb: 9/4/82 Career OF: (1-LF 0-CF 2-RF)

YEAR	TM/L	G	AB	R	H	2B	3B	HR	RBI	BB	SO	AVG	OBP	SLG	OPS	OPS+	BR+	SB	CS	SBR	FA	FR	G/POS	TPR
1982	Tor-A	16	44	3	16	2	0	0	1	4	6	.364	.417	.409	826	117	1	0	0	0	.981	-2	C-12/3-3	0.0
1983	Tor-A	6	4	0	0	0	0	0	0	1	1	.000	.200	.000	200	-37	-1	0	0	0	1.000	0	/C-5,D-1	0.0
1984	Tor-A	3	3	0	0	0	0	0	0	0	0	.000	.000	.000	0	-97	-1	0	0	0	1.000	0	/C-1,D-1	0.0
1985	Tex-A	42	100	7	27	2	0	0	11	8	12	.270	.330	.290	620	71	-4	1	0	0	.990	2	C-41	-0.1
1986	Tex-A	69	137	17	35	9	3	2	18	5	14	.255	.282	.409	690	83	-4	3	0	1	.988	-8	C-41,3-15/2-2,D-2	-0.9
1987	Tex-A	101	202	28	61	11	2	7	31	27	29	.302	.390	.480	870	129	9	0	2	-1	.995	-0	C-63,3-17/1-5,2OD	1.0
1988	Tex-A	129	351	35	99	14	2	7	36	41	52	.282	.360	.393	754	108	5	0	1	-0	.981	-1	C-85,D-23/3-9,12	0.8
1989	Tex-A	70	184	18	56	7	0	4	23	17	24	.304	.369	.408	777	117	4	0	0	0	.989	-12	C-49,D-16	-0.6
1990	Tex-A	133	325	28	83	13	1	0	21	50	49	.255	.360	.302	661	87	-4	0	2	-1	.991	-4	*C-118/3-7,2-3	-0.2
1991	Tex-A	87	199	21	54	8	1	2	20	21	25	.271	.341	.352	693	94	-1	2	1	0	.972	-10	C-66/3-7,D-5	-0.8
1992	Tex-A	94	192	11	38	12	0	1	18	20	34	.198	.274	.276	550	56	-11	0	0	0	.990	3	C-54,D-14/3-4,2-2	-0.6
1993	Tex-A	59	133	16	32	5	0	1	13	22	17	.241	.348	.301	649	79	-3	2	0	0	.990	-7	C-39/2-1,3-1,D-2	-0.7
Total	12	809	1874	184	501	83	9	24	192	216	263	.267	.346	.360	706	95	-8	8	6	-0	.987	-37	C-574/D-66,3-63,21O	-2.1

■ BEN PETRICK

Petrick, Benjamin Wayne b: 4/7/77, Salem, Ore. BR/TR, 6', 195 lbs. Deb: 9/1/99

YEAR	TM/L	G	AB	R	H	2B	3B	HR	RBI	BB	SO	AVG	OBP	SLG	OPS	OPS+	BR+	SB	CS	SBR	FA	FR	G/POS	TPR
1999	Col-N	19	62	13	20	3	0	4	12	10	13	.323	.417	.565	981	114	2	1	0	0	.982	-6	C-19	-0.3
2000	Col-N	52	146	32	47	10	1	3	20	20	33	.322	.411	.466	876	94	-1	1	2	-0	.985	-2	C-48	0.0
Total	2	71	208	45	67	13	1	7	32	30	46	.322	.412	.495	908	100	1	2	2	-0	.984	-8	/C-67	-0.3

■ RICO PETROCELLI

Petrocelli, Americo Peter b: 6/27/43, Brooklyn, N.Y. BR/TR, 6', 185 lbs. Deb: 9/21/63

YEAR	TM/L	G	AB	R	H	2B	3B	HR	RBI	BB	SO	AVG	OBP	SLG	OPS	OPS+	BR+	SB	CS	SBR	FA	FR	G/POS	TPR
1963	Bos-A	1	4	0	1	1	0	0	1	0	1	.250	.250	.500	750	101	-0	0	0	0	.833	-0	/S-1	0.0
1965	Bos-A	103	323	38	75	15	2	13	33	36	71	.232	.311	.412	723	98	-1	0	2	-1	.958	10	S-93	1.7
1966	Bos-A	139	522	58	124	20	1	18	59	41	99	.238	.297	.383	680	85	-10	1	1	-0	.954	1	*S-127/3-5	0.2
1967	*Bos-A★	142	491	53	127	24	2	17	66	49	93	.259	.332	.420	752	112	7	2	4	-1	.970	3	*S-141	2.3
1968	Bos-A	123	406	41	95	17	2	12	46	31	73	.234	.295	.374	669	95	-3	0	1	-0	**.978**	11	*S-117/1-1	2.0
1969	Bos-A★	154	535	92	159	32	2	40	97	98	68	.297	.407	.589	996	167	49	3	5	-1	**.981**	5	*S-153/3-1	**7.2**
1970	Bos-A	157	583	82	152	31	3	29	103	67	82	.261	.339	.473	812	114	10	1	1	-0	.970	-10	*S-141,3-18	1.8
1971	Bos-A	158	553	82	139	24	4	28	89	91	108	.251	.359	.461	820	122	17	2	0	0	**.976**	-1	*3-156	1.7
1972	Bos-A	147	521	62	125	15	2	15	75	78	91	.240	.341	.363	704	104	4	0	1	-0	.970	-1	*3-146	0.2
1973	Bos-A	100	356	44	87	13	1	13	45	47	64	.244	.334	.396	730	99	-0	0	0	0	.980	5	3-99	0.4
1974	Bos-A	129	454	53	121	23	1	15	76	48	74	.267	.339	.421	760	110	6	1	0	0	.962	-19	*3-116/D-9	-1.4
1975	*Bos-A	115	402	31	96	15	1	7	59	41	66	.239	.314	.333	647	76	-12	0	2	-1	.960	-18	*3-113/D-1	-3.3
1976	Bos-A	85	240	17	51	7	1	3	24	34	36	.213	.310	.287	598	67	-9	0	5	-2	.967	-4	3-73/2-5,1-1,S-1,D	-1.6
Total	13	1553	5390	653	1352	237	22	210	773	661	926	.251	.336	.420	755	108	58	10	22	-6	.969	-18	S-774,3-727/D-14,21	11.2

■ PAT PETTEE

Pettee, Patrick E. b: 1/10/1863, Natick, Mass. d: 10/9/34, Natick, Mass. BR/TR, 5'10", 170 lbs. Deb: 4/8/1891

YEAR	TM/L	G	AB	R	H	2B	3B	HR	RBI	BB	SO	AVG	OBP	SLG	OPS	OPS+	BR+	SB	CS	SBR	FA	FR	G/POS	TPR
1891	Lou-a	2	5	1	0	0	0	0	0	3	1	.000	.375	.000	375	9	-0	1			.818	-1	/2-2	-0.1

■ NED PETTIGREW

Pettigrew, Jim Ned b: 8/25/1881, Honey Grove, Tex. d: 8/20/52, Duncan, Okla. BR/TR, 5'11", 175 lbs. Deb: 4/23/14

YEAR	TM/L	G	AB	R	H	2B	3B	HR	RBI	BB	SO	AVG	OBP	SLG	OPS	OPS+	BR+	SB	CS	SBR	FA	FR	G/POS	TPR
1914	Buf-F	2	2	0	0	0	0	0	0	0	0	.000	.000	.000	0	-98	-1	0			.000	0	H	-0.1

■ JOE PETTINI

Pettini, Joseph Paul b: 1/26/55, Wheeling, W.Va. BR/TR, 5'9", 165 lbs. Deb: 7/10/80

YEAR	TM/L	G	AB	R	H	2B	3B	HR	RBI	BB	SO	AVG	OBP	SLG	OPS	OPS+	BR+	SB	CS	SBR	FA	FR	G/POS	TPR
1980	SF-N	63	190	19	44	3	1	1	9	17	33	.232	.295	.274	568	61	-10	5	2	0	.955	-13	S-42,3-18/2-8	-1.9
1981	SF-N	35	29	3	2	1	0	0	2	4	5	.069	.182	.103	285	-18	-4	1	0	0	.920	4	2-12,S-12/3-9	0.0
1982	SF-N	29	39	5	8	1	0	0	2	3	4	.205	.262	.231	493	39	-3	0	1	-0	.934	-1	S-26/3-1	-0.3
1983	SF-N	61	86	11	16	0	1	0	7	9	11	.186	.263	.209	472	33	-8	4	1	1	.949	11	S-26,2-14,3-12	0.6
Total	4	188	344	38	70	5	2	1	20	33	53	.203	.273	.238	512	45	-25	10	4	1	.943	2	S-106/3-40,2-34	-1.6

■ GARY PETTIS

Pettis, Gary George b: 4/3/58, Oakland, Cal. BB/TR, 6'1", 165 lbs. Deb: 9/13/82

YEAR	TM/L	G	AB	R	H	2B	3B	HR	RBI	BB	SO	AVG	OBP	SLG	OPS	OPS+	BR+	SB	CS	SBR	FA	FR	G/POS	TPR
1982	Cal-A	10	5	5	1	0	0	1	1	0	2	.200	.200	.800	1000	159	0	0	0	0	1.000	-2	/O-8(1-6-1)	-0.2
1983	Cal-A	22	85	19	25	2	3	3	6	7	15	.294	.348	.494	842	130	3	8	3	1	.982	2	O-21(0-20-1)	0.6
1984	Cal-A	140	397	63	90	11	6	2	29	60	115	.227	.333	.300	632	77	-10	48	17	5	.983	1	*O-134(0-135-0)	-0.6
1985	Cal-A	125	443	67	114	10	8	1	32	62	125	.257	.349	.323	671	86	-7	56	9	9	.990	17	*O-122(0-122-0)	1.8
1986	*Cal-A	154	539	93	139	23	4	5	58	69	132	.258	.342	.343	685	88	-7	50	13	6	.985	21	*O-153(0-153-0)/D-1	1.8
1987	Cal-A	133	394	49	82	13	2	1	17	52	124	.208	.302	.259	561	53	-26	24	5	4	.980	6	*O-131(0-131-0)	-1.7
1988	Det-A	129	458	65	96	14	4	3	36	47	85	.210	.285	.277	562	60	-24	44	10	6	.987	10	*O-126(0-126-0)/D-2	-0.8
1989	Det-A	119	444	77	114	8	6	1	18	84	106	.257	.375	.309	684	97	3	43	15	4	.988	5	*O-119(0-119-0)	1.0
1990	Tex-A	136	423	66	101	16	8	3	31	57	118	.239	.335	.336	670	88	-6	38	15	3	.993	4	*O-128(0-128-0)/D-2	0.1
1991	Tex-A	137	282	37	61	7	5	0	19	54	91	.216	.342	.277	619	75	-8	29	13	2	.977	-11	*O-126(0-126-0)/D-3	-1.7
1992	SD-N	30	30	0	6	1	0	0	0	2	11	.200	.250	.233	483	37	-2	1	0	0	.952	-3	O-14(0-13-1)	-0.6
	Det-A	48	129	27	26	4	3	1	12	27	34	.202	.340	.302	642	81	-2	13	4	1	.993	5	O-46(0-46-0)	0.3
Total	11	1183	3629	568	855	109	49	21	259	521	958	.236	.333	.310	643	80	-86	354	104	41	.986	54	*O-1128(1-1125-3)/D-8	-0.0

■ BOB PETTIT

Pettit, Robert Henry b: 7/19/1861, Williamstown, Mass. d: 11/1/10, Derby, Conn. BL/TR, 5'9", 160 lbs. Deb: 9/3/1887 Career OF: (3-LF 4-CF 76-RF)

YEAR	TM/L	G	AB	R	H	2B	3B	HR	RBI	BB	SO	AVG	OBP	SLG	OPS	OPS+	BR+	SB	CS	SBR	FA	FR	G/POS	TPR
1887	Chi-N	32	146	29	44	3	3	2	12	8	15	.301	.301	.370	671	76	-5	16			.894	-1	O-32(0-0-32)/C-1,P-1	-0.6
1888	Chi-N	43	169	23	43	1	4	4	23	7	9	.254	.288	.379	667	104	0	7			.931	-4	O-43(0-2-42)	-0.4
1891	Mil-a	21	80	10	14	4	0	1	5	7	7	.175	.267	.262	529	43	-7	2			.932	-6	/2-9,O-7(3-2-2),3-6	-1.1
Total	3	96	395	62	101	8	7	7	40	22	31	.256	.288	.351	640	79	-12	25			.919	-11	/O-82R,2-9,3-6,PC	-2.1

■ MARTY PEVEY

Pevey, Marty Ashley b: 12/25/62, Savannah, Ga. BL/TR, 6'1", 185 lbs. Deb: 5/16/89 C

YEAR	TM/L	G	AB	R	H	2B	3B	HR	RBI	BB	SO	AVG	OBP	SLG	OPS	OPS+	BR+	SB	CS	SBR	FA	FR	G/POS	TPR
1989	Mon-N	13	41	2	9	1	1	0	3	0	8	.220	.220	.293	512	45	-3	0	0	0	.985	-2	C-11/O-1(0-0-1)	-0.5

■ LARRY PEZOLD

Pezold, Lorenz Johannes b: 6/22/1893, New Orleans, La. d: 10/22/57, Baton Rouge, La. BR/TR, 5'9.5", 175 lbs. Deb: 7/27/14

YEAR	TM/L	G	AB	R	H	2B	3B	HR	RBI	BB	SO	AVG	OBP	SLG	OPS	OPS+	BR+	SB	CS	SBR	FA	FR	G/POS	TPR
1914	Cle-A	23	71	4	16	0	1	0	5	9	6	.225	.313	.254	566	68	-3	2	3	-1	.827	-1	3-20/O-1(0-0-1)	-0.5

■ FRED PFEFFER

Pfeffer, Nathaniel Frederick "Fritz" or "Dandelion"
b: 3/17/1860, Louisville, Ky. d: 4/10/32, Chicago, Ill. BR/TR, 5'10.5", 184 lbs. Deb: 5/1/1882 M Career OF: (0-LF 2-CF 1-RF)

YEAR	TM/L	G	AB	R	H	2B	3B	HR	RBI	BB	SO	AVG	OBP	SLG	OPS	OPS+	BR+	SB	CS	SBR	FA	FR	G/POS	TPR
1882	Tro-N	85	330	26	72	7	4	1	43	1	24	.218	.221	.273	493	60	-14				.857	11	*S-83/2-2	-0.1
1883	Chi-N	96	371	41	87	22	7	1	45	8	50	.235	.251	.340	590	71	-14				.887	17	*2-79,S-18/3-1,1-1	0.6
1884	Chi-N	112	467	105	135	10	10	25	101	25	47	.289	.325	.514	839	148	23				.903	**46**	*2-112/P-1	**6.3**
1885	*Chi-N	112	469	90	113	12	7	5	73	26	47	.241	.281	.328	609	85	-10				.893	25	*2-109/P-5,O-1(0-0-1)	1.9
1886	*Chi-N	118	474	88	125	17	8	7	95	36	46	.264	.316	.378	693	96	-4	30			.903	7	*2-118/1-1	0.7
1887	Chi-N	123	513	95	167	21	6	16	89	34	20	.326	.327	.447	774	100	-3	57			.917	25	*2-123/O-2(0-2-0)	2.2
1888	Chi-N	135	517	90	129	22	10	8	57	32	38	.250	.297	.377	674	106	2	64			.931	**38**	*2-135	4.4
1889	Chi-N	134	531	85	121	15	7	7	77	53	51	.228	.302	.322	624	71	-22	45			.943	19	*2-134	0.2
1890	Chi-P	124	499	86	128	21	8	5	80	44	23	.257	.319	.361	680	78	-18	27			.916	24	*2-124	0.9
1891	Chi-N	137	498	93	123	12	9	7	77	79	60	.247	.353	.349	703	105	5	40			.921	25	*2-137	3.1
1892	Lou-N	124	470	78	121	14	9	2	76	67	36	.257	.353	.338	691	119	14	27			.933	12	*2-116,1-10/P-1,M	2.8
1893	Lou-N	125	508	85	129	29	12	3	75	51	18	.254	.322	.376	698	92	-6	32			.939	6	*2-125	0.5
1894	Lou-N	105	414	70	128	12	15	5	61	30	14	.309	.357	.447	804	100	-1	32			.939	15	*2-91,S-15/P-1	1.5
1895	Lou-N	11	45	8	13	1	0	0	5	5	3	.289	.360	.311	671	79	-1	2			.742	-3	/S-5,2-3,1-3	-0.3
1896	NY-N	4	14	1	2	0	0	0	4	1	1	.143	.250	.143	393	5	-2	0			.760	-1	/2-4	-0.3
	Chi-N	94	360	45	88	16	7	2	52	23	20	.244	.294	.344	638	65	-20	22			.947	9	*2-94	-0.5
	Yr	98	374	46	90	16	7	2	56	24	21	.241	.292	.337	629	63	-21	22			.939	8	2-98	-0.8
1897	Chi-N	32	114	10	26	0	1	0	11	12		.228	.318	.246	563	48	-8	5			.883	-6	2-32	-1.1
Total	16	1671	6594	1096	1707	231	120	94	1021	527	498	.259	.312	.370	682	92	-78	383			.920	268	*2-1538,S-121/1PO3	22.8

■ BOBBY PFEIL

Pfeil, Robert Raymond b: 11/13/43, Passaic, N.J. BR/TR, 6'1", 180 lbs. Deb: 6/26/69 Career OF: (4-LF 0-CF 1-RF)

YEAR	TM/L	G	AB	R	H	2B	3B	HR	RBI	BB	SO	AVG	OBP	SLG	OPS	OPS+	BR+	SB	CS	SBR	FA	FR	G/POS	TPR
1969	NY-N	62	211	20	49	9	0	0	10	7	27	.232	.260	.275	535	49	-14	0	1	-0	.976	-4	3-49,2-11/O-2(2-0-0)	-2.0
1971	Phi-N	44	70	5	19	3	0	2	9	6	9	.271	.329	.400	729	106	0	1	1	-0	1.000	-2	3-15/C-4,O-3L,12S	-0.2
Total	2	106	281	25	68	12	0	2	19	13	36	.242	.278	.306	584	63	-14	1	2	-0	.980	-6	/3-64,2-12,O-5L,CS1	-2.2

■ GEORGE PFISTER

Pfister, George Edward b: 9/4/18, Bound Brook, N.J. d: 8/14/97, Somerset, N.J. BR/TR, 6', 200 lbs. Deb: 9/27/41 C

YEAR	TM/L	G	AB	R	H	2B	3B	HR	RBI	BB	SO	AVG	OBP	SLG	OPS	OPS+	BR+	SB	CS	SBR	FA	FR	G/POS	TPR
1941	Bro-N	1	2	0	0	0	0	0	0	0	0	.000	.000	.000	0	-96	-1	0			.000	0	/C-1	-0.1

■ MONTE PFYL

Pfyl, Meinhard Charles b: 5/11/1884, St.Louis, Mo. d: 10/18/45, San Francisco, Cal BL/TL, 6'3", 190 lbs. Deb: 7/30/07

YEAR	TM/L	G	AB	R	H	2B	3B	HR	RBI	BB	SO	AVG	OBP	SLG	OPS	OPS+	BR+	SB	CS	SBR	FA	FR	G/POS	TPR
1907	NY-N	1	0	0	0	0	0	0	0	0		—	—	—	—	—	-0	0			.000	0	/1-1	0.0

■ ART PHELAN

Phelan, Arthur Thomas "Dugan" b: 8/14/1887, Niantic, Ill. d: 12/27/64, Ft.Worth, Tex. BR/TR, 5'8", 160 lbs. Deb: 6/25/10 Career OF: (3-LF 0-CF 0-RF)

YEAR	TM/L	G	AB	R	H	2B	3B	HR	RBI	BB	SO	AVG	OBP	SLG	OPS	OPS+	BR+	SB	CS	SBR	FA	FR	G/POS	TPR
1910	Cin-N	23	42	7	9	0	0	0	4	7	6	.214	.327	.214	541	61	-2	5			1.000	-2	/3-8,2-5,O-3L,S-1	-0.4
1912	Cin-N	130	461	56	112	9	11	3	54	46	37	.243	.314	.330	644	79	-14	25			.924	-2	*3-127/2-3	-1.2
1913	Chi-N	91	261	41	65	11	6	2	35	29	26	.249	.331	.360	691	97	-1	8			.931	-8	2-46,3-38/S-1	-0.8
1914	Chi-N	25	46	5	13	2	1	0	3	4	3	.283	.340	.370	710	111	1	0			.905	-0	/3-7,2-3,S-2	0.1
1915	Chi-N	133	448	41	98	16	7	3	35	55	42	.219	.307	.306	613	86	-7	12	9	-1	.939	-2	*3-110,2-24	-0.6
Total	5	402	1258	150	297	38	25	8	131	141	114	.236	.317	.325	642	86	-22	50	9		.931	-14	3-290/2-81,S-4,O-3L	-2.9

■ DAN PHELAN

Phelan, Daniel T. b: 7/23/1864, Thomaston, Conn. d: 12/7/45, West Haven, Conn. Deb: 4/18/1890

YEAR	TM/L	G	AB	R	H	2B	3B	HR	RBI	BB	SO	AVG	OBP	SLG	OPS	OPS+	BR+	SB	CS	SBR	FA	FR	G/POS	TPR
1890	Lou-a	8	32	4	8	1	1	0	4	0		.250	.250	.344	594	77	-1	1			.975	0	/1-8	-0.2

■ DICK PHELAN

Phelan, James Dickson b: 12/10/1854, Towanda, Pa. d: 2/13/31, San Antonio, Tex. BR, Deb: 4/17/1884

YEAR	TM/L	G	AB	R	H	2B	3B	HR	RBI	BB	SO	AVG	OBP	SLG	OPS	OPS+	BR+	SB	CS	SBR	FA	FR	G/POS	TPR
1884	Bal-U	101	402	63	99	13	3	3		12		.246	.268	.316	584	69	-27				.872	-9	*2-100/3-5,O-1(0-1-0)	-2.8
1885	Buf-N	4	16	2	2	0	0	1	3	0	3	.125	.125	.313	438	37	-1				.808	-1	/2-4	-0.2
	StL-N	2	4	1	1	1	0	0	1	0	2	.250	.250	.500	750	147	0				1.000	-1	/3-2	0.0
	Yr	6	20	3	3	1	0	1	4	0	5	.150	.150	.350	500	58	-1				.808	-2	/2-4,3-2	-0.2
Total	2	107	422	66	102	14	3	4	4	12	5	.242	.263	.318	580	69	-28				.869	-10	2-104/3-7,O-1(0-1-0)	-3.0

■ NEALY PHELPS

Phelps, Cornelius Carman b: 11/19/1840, New York, N.Y. d: 2/12/1885, New York, N.Y. Deb: 7/1/1871

YEAR	TM/L	G	AB	R	H	2B	3B	HR	RBI	BB	SO	AVG	OBP	SLG	OPS	OPS+	BR+	SB	CS	SBR	FA	FR	G/POS	TPR
1871	Kek-n	1	3	0	0	0	0	0	0	1	0	.000	.250	.000	250	-20	-0	0	0	0	.889	-0	/1-1	0.0
1873	Mut-n	1	6	0	0	0	0	0	0	0	0	.000	.000	.000	0	-99	-1	0	0	0	1.000	-0	/1-1,O-1(0-0-1)	-0.1
1874	Mut-n	6	24	5	3	0	0	0	2	0	0	.125	.125	.125	250	-19	-3	0	0	0	.818	1	/O-6(0-0-6)	-0.1
1875	Mut-n	2	6	1	2	1	0	0	0	0	1	.333	.333	.500	833	176	0	0	0	0	1.000	1	/O-2(0-0-2)	0.1
1876	NY-N	1	3	0	0	0	0	0	0	0	1	.000	.000	.000	0	-99	-1				.667	-0	/O-1(0-1-0)	-0.1
	Phi-N	1	4	0	0	0	0	0	0	0	0	.000	.000	.000	0	-99	-1				.571	-1	/C-1	-0.2
	Yr	2	7	0	0	0	0	0	0	0	1	.000	.000	.000	0	-99	-1				.667	-2	/O-1(0-1-0),C-1	-0.3
Total	4 n	10	39	6	5	1	0	0	2	1	1	.128	.150	.154	304	-3	-5	0	0	0	.857	2	/O-9(0-0-9),1-2	-0.1

■ ED PHELPS

Phelps, Edward Jaykill "Yaller" b: 3/3/1879, Albany, N.Y. d: 1/31/42, E.Greenbush, N.Y. BR/TR, 5'11", 185 lbs. Deb: 9/3/02

YEAR	TM/L	G	AB	R	H	2B	3B	HR	RBI	BB	SO	AVG	OBP	SLG	OPS	OPS+	BR+	SB	CS	SBR	FA	FR	G/POS	TPR
1902	Pit-N	18	61	5	13	1	0	0	6	4		.213	.284	.230	513	57	-3	2			.968	-6	C-13/1-5	-0.8
1903	*Pit-N	81	273	32	77	7	3	2	31	17		.282	.338	.352	689	94	-2	2			.980	-8	C-76/1-3	-0.3
1904	Pit-N	94	302	29	73	5	3	0	28	15		.242	.289	.278	567	73	-9	2			.964	-11	C-91/1-1	-1.2
1905	Cin-N	44	156	18	36	5	3	0	18	12		.231	.306	.301	608	73	-5	4			.949	-6	C-44	-0.7
1906	Cin-N	12	40	3	11	0	2	1	5	3		.275	.326	.450	776	136	1	2			.987	-1	C-12	0.2
	Pit-N	43	118	9	28	3	1	0	12	9		.237	.302	.280	582	78	-3	1			.971	-3	C-40	-0.3
	Yr	55	158	12	39	3	3	1	17	12		.247	.308	.323	631	93	-1	3			.975	-4	C-52	-0.1
1907	Pit-N	43	113	11	24	1	0	0	12	9		.212	.282	.221	503	57	-5	1			.979	-3	C-35/1-1	-0.6
1908	Pit-N	34	64	3	15	2	2	0	11	2		.234	.269	.328	597	90	-1	0			.977	-0	C-20	0.0
1909	StL-N	104	306	43	76	13	1	0	22	39		.248	.350	.297	648	108	5	7			.954	-9	C-83	0.4
1910	StL-N	93	270	25	71	4	2	0	37	36	29	.263	.356	.293	649	93	-1	9			.976	-15	C-80	-0.9
1912	Bro-N	52	111	8	32	4	3	0	23	16	15	.288	.388	.378	766	114	3	1			.976	-4	C-32	0.1
1913	Bro-N	15	18	0	4	0	0	0	0	1	2	.222	.263	.222	485	38	-1	0			.875	-2	/C-4	-0.3
Total	11	633	1832	186	460	45	20	3	205	163	46	.251	.325	.302	627	88	-22	31			.968	-69	C-530/1-10	-4.4

■ BABE PHELPS

Phelps, Ernest Gordon "Blimp" b: 4/19/08, Odenton, Md. d: 12/10/92, Odenton, Md. BL/TR, 6'2", 225 lbs. Deb: 9/17/31

YEAR	TM/L	G	AB	R	H	2B	3B	HR	RBI	BB	SO	AVG	OBP	SLG	OPS	OPS+	BR+	SB	CS	SBR	FA	FR	G/POS	TPR
1931	Was-A	3	3	0	1	0	0	0	0	0	0	.333	.333	.333	667	75	-0	0	0	0	.000	0	H	0.0
1933	Chi-N	3	7	0	2	0	0	0	2	0	1	.286	.286	.286	571	64	-0	0			1.000	1	/C-2	0.0
1934	Chi-N	44	70	7	20	5	2	2	12	1	8	.286	.296	.500	796	111	1	0			.981	-2	C-18	-0.1
1935	Bro-N	47	121	17	44	7	2	5	22	9	10	.364	.408	.579	986	165	11	0			.957	-2	C-34	1.0
1936	Bro-N	115	319	36	117	23	2	5	57	27	18	.367	.421	.498	920	145	21	1			.977	-16	C-98/O-1(0-0-1)	1.0
1937	Bro-N	121	409	42	128	37	3	7	58	25	28	.313	.357	.469	826	121	11	2			.971	-7	*C-111	1.1
1938	Bro-N†	66	208	33	64	12	2	5	46	23	15	.308	.379	.457	836	126	8	2			.980	-4	C-55	0.7
1939	Bro-N★	98	323	33	92	21	2	6	42	24	24	.285	.336	.418	754	98	-1	0			.980	2	C-92	0.6
1940	Bro-N★	118	370	47	109	24	5	13	61	30	27	.295	.349	.492	841	122	10	2			.977	-9	C-99/1-1	0.7
1941	Bro-N	16	30	3	7	3	0	2	4	1	2	.233	.258	.533	791	114	0	0			.971	-1	C-11	0.0
1942	Pit-N	95	257	21	73	11	1	9	41	20	24	.284	.345	.440	785	126	8	2			.959	-3	C-72	1.0
Total	11	726	2117	239	657	143	19	54	345	160	157	.310	.362	.472	835	124	67	9	0		.974	-41	C-592/1-1,O-1(0-0-1)	6.0

■ JOSH PHELPS

Phelps, Joshua Lee b: 5/12/78, Anchorage, Alaska BR/TR, 6'3", 215 lbs. Deb: 6/13/2000

YEAR	TM/L	G	AB	R	H	2B	3B	HR	RBI	BB	SO	AVG	OBP	SLG	OPS	OPS+	BR+	SB	CS	SBR	FA	FR	G/POS	TPR
2000	Tor-A	1	1	0	0	0	0	0	0	0	1	.000	.000	.000	0	-99	-0	0	0	0	1.000	-0	/C-1	0.0

■ KEN PHELPS

Phelps, Kenneth Allen b: 8/6/54, Seattle, Wash. BL/TL, 6'1", 209 lbs. Deb: 9/20/80

YEAR	TM/L	G	AB	R	H	2B	3B	HR	RBI	BB	SO	AVG	OBP	SLG	OPS	OPS+	BR+	SB	CS	SBR	FA	FR	G/POS	TPR
1980	KC-A	3	4	0	0	0	0	0	0	0	2	.000	.000	.000	0	-99	-1	0	0	0	1.000	-0	/1-2	-0.1
1981	KC-A	21	22	1	3	0	1	0	1	1	13	.136	.174	.227	401	15	-2	0	0	0	1.000	0	/1-2,D-4	-0.2
1982	Mon-N	10	8	0	2	0	0	0	0	0	3	.250	.333	.250	583	64	-0	0	0	0	.000	0	H	-0.1
1983	Sea-A	50	127	10	30	4	1	7	16	13	25	.236	.307	.449	756	101	-0	0	0	0	1.000	2	1-22,D-19	0.0
1984	Sea-A	101	290	52	70	9	0	24	51	61	73	.241	.382	.521	903	149	21	3	3	-0	.987	-1	D-84/1-9	1.6
1985	Sea-A	61	116	18	24	3	0	9	24	24	33	.207	.343	.466	808	118	3	2	0	0	1.000	-0	D-25/1-8	0.2
1986	Sea-A	125	344	69	85	16	4	24	64	88	96	.247	.409	.526	935	151	28	2	3	-1	.983	-4	1-55,D-52	1.8
1987	Sea-A	120	332	68	86	13	1	27	68	80	75	.259	.414	.548	962	145	24	1	1	-0	1.000	-0	*D-114/1-1	1.9
1988	Sea-A	72	190	37	54	8	0	14	32	51	35	.284	.438	.547	985	167	19	1	0	0	.952	0	D-68/1-3	1.7
	NY-A	45	107	17	24	5	0	10	22	19	26	.224	.341	.551	893	147	6	0	0	0	.000	-0	D-24/1-1	0.6
	Yr	117	297	54	78	13	0	24	54	70	61	.263	.405	.549	954	160	26	1	0	0	.952	-0	D-92/1-4	2.3
1989	NY-A	86	185	26	46	3	0	7	29	27	47	.249	.344	.378	723	105	2	0	0	0	.980	-1	D-55/1-8	-0.2
	*Oak-A	11	9	0	1	1	0	0	0	4	0	.111	.385	.222	607	78	-0	0	0	0	.000	-0	/1-1,D-1	0.0
	Yr	97	194	26	47	4	0	7	29	31	47	.242	.347	.371	718	104	2	0	0	0	.980	-1	D-56/1-9	-0.2
1990	Oak-A	32	59	6	11	2	0	1	6	12	10	.186	.324	.271	595	71	-2	0	0	0	.964	0	D-15/1-5	-0.2
	Cle-A	24	61	4	7	0	0	0	0	10	11	.115	.239	.115	354	2	-8	1	0	0	1.000	0	1-14/D-6	-0.9
	Yr	56	120	10	18	2	0	1	6	22	21	.150	.282	.192	473	36	-10	1	0	0	.992	0	D-21,1-19	-1.1
Total	11	761	1854	308	443	64	7	123	313	390	449	.239	.377	.480	857	132	90	10	7	-0	.987	-4	D-467,1-131	6.1

■ DAVE PHILLEY

Philley, David Earl b: 5/16/20, Paris, Tex. BB/TR, 6', 188 lbs. Deb: 9/6/41 Career OF: (204-LF 590-CF 714-RF)

YEAR	TM/L	G	AB	R	H	2B	3B	HR	RBI	BB	SO	AVG	OBP	SLG	OPS	OPS+	BR+	SB	CS	SBR	FA	FR	G/POS	TPR
1941	Chi-A	7	9	4	2	1	0	0	0	3	3	.222	.417	.333	750	102	0	0	0	0	.000	-1	/O-2(2-0-0)	-0.1
1946	Chi-A	17	68	10	24	2	3	0	17	4	4	.353	.389	.471	859	145	4	5	0	1	.983	5	O-17(16-1-0)	0.9
1947	Chi-A	143	551	55	142	25	11	2	45	35	39	.258	.303	.354	657	85	-13	21	16	-1	.986	2	*O-133(39-95-0)/3-4	-1.8
1948	Chi-A	137	488	51	140	28	3	5	42	50	33	.287	.353	.387	740	100	-0	8	10	-2	.978	15	*O-128(6-123-0)	0.9
1949	Chi-A	146	598	84	171	20	8	0	44	54	51	.286	.347	.346	693	86	-12	13	4	1	.977	2	*O-145(0-3-143)	-1.3
1950	Chi-A	156	619	69	150	21	5	14	80	52	57	.242	.302	.360	662	71	-30	6	3	0	.980	1	*O-154(0-70-103)	-3.1
1951	Chi-A	7	25	0	6	2	0	0	2	2	3	.240	.296	.320	616	68	-1	0	0	0	.938	-0	/O-6(6-0-0)	-0.2
	Phi-A	125	468	71	123	18	7	7	59	63	38	.263	.354	.376	730	95	-2	9	6	-0	.978	2	*O-120(2-116-2)/3-2	-0.4
	Yr	132	493	71	129	20	7	7	61	65	41	.262	.351	.373	724	94	-3	9	6	-0	.976	2	*O-126(8-116-2)/3-2	-0.6
1952	Phi-A	151	586	80	154	25	4	7	71	59	35	.263	.334	.355	689	86	-10	11	4	1	.991	13	*O-149(0-149-0)/3-2	0.0
1953	Phi-A	157	620	80	188	30	9	9	59	51	35	.303	.358	.424	782	106	5	13	5	1	.981	-4	*O-157(0-31-129)/3-1	-0.4
1954	*Cle-A	133	452	48	102	13	3	12	60	57	48	.226	.312	.347	660	79	-13	2	4	-1	.984	-4	*O-129(1-0-129)	-2.3
1955	Cle-A	43	104	15	31	4	2	2	9	12	10	.298	.371	.433	803	111	2	0	2	-1	1.000	-3	O-34(2-0-32)	-0.3

YEAR	TM/L	G	AB	R	H	2B	3B	HR	RBI	BB	SO	AVG	OBP	SLG	OPS	OPS+	BR+	SB	CS	SBR	FA	FR	G/POS	TPR
	Bal-A	83	311	50	93	13	3	6	41	34	38	.299	.368	.418	786	119	8	1	2	-0	.970	-7	O-82(46-2-48)/3-2	-0.3
	Yr	126	415	65	124	17	5	8	50	46	48	.299	.369	.422	790	116	9	1	4	-1	.976	-9	*O-116(48-2-80)/3-2	-0.6
1956	Bal-A	32	117	13	24	4	2	1	17	18	13	.205	.311	.299	610	67	-6	3	1	0	.935	-4	O-31(23-0-16)/3-5	-1.1
	Chi-A	86	279	44	74	14	2	4	47	28	27	.265	.334	.373	707	85	-6	1	3	-1	.978	-9	1-51,O-30(17-0-19)	-1.9
	Yr	118	396	57	98	18	4	5	64	46	40	.247	.327	.351	678	80	-11	4	4	-1	.965	-13	O-61L,1-51/3-5	-3.0
1957	Chi-A	22	71	9	23	4	0	0	9	4	10	.324	.360	.380	740	102	0	1	1	-0	.975	1	O-17(0-0-17)/1-2	0.0
	Det-A	65	173	15	49	8	1	2	16	7	16	.283	.311	.376	687	85	-4	3	1	0	.996	1	1-27,O-12(4-0-8)/3-1	-0.5
	Yr	87	244	24	72	12	1	2	25	11	26	.295	.325	.377	703	90	-4	4	2	0	.965	2	O-29(4-0-25),1-29/3-1	-0.5
1958	Phi-N	91	207	30	64	11	4	3	31	15	20	.309	.359	.444	803	113	4	1	1	-0	1.000	-4	O-24(0-0-24),1-18	-0.2
1959	Phi-N	99	254	32	74	18	2	7	37	18	27	.291	.341	.461	801	109	3	0	0	0	1.000	1	O-34(0-0-34),1-24	0.1
1960	Phi-N	14	15	2	5	2	0	0	4	3	2	.333	.444	.467	911	149	1	0	0	0	.000	-2	/O-3(2-0-1),1-2	-0.1
	SF-N	39	61	5	10	0	0	1	7	6	14	.164	.239	.213	452	26	-6	0	0	0	.941	-1	O-10(10-0-0)/3-3	-0.8
	Yr	53	76	7	15	2	0	1	11	9	16	.197	.282	.263	546	53	-5	0	0	0	.941	-3	O-13(12-0-1)/3-3,1-2	-0.9
	Bal-A	14	34	6	9	2	1	1	5	4	5	.265	.342	.471	813	119	1	1	0	0	1.000	-0	/O-8(6-0-2),3-1	0.0
1961	Bal-A	99	144	13	36	9	2	1	23	10	20	.250	.299	.361	660	78	-5	2	0	0	1.000	-6	O-25(22-0-3)/1-1	-1.1
1962	Bos-A	38	42	3	6	2	0	0	4	5	3	.143	.250	.190	440	20	-5	0	0	0	1.000	-0	/O-4(0-0-4)	-0.5
Total	18	1904	6296	789	1700	276	72	84	729	594	551	.270	.335	.377	711	91	-84	101	63	0	.981	-0	*O-1454R,1-125/3-21	-14.5

■ ADOLFO PHILLIPS

Phillips, Adolfo Emilio (Lopez) b: 12/16/41, Bethania, Panama BR/TR, 6′, 177 lbs. Deb: 9/2/64

YEAR	TM/L	G	AB	R	H	2B	3B	HR	RBI	BB	SO	AVG	OBP	SLG	OPS	OPS+	BR+	SB	CS	SBR	FA	FR	G/POS	TPR
1964	Phi-N	13	13	4	3	0	0	0	0	3	3	.231	.375	.231	606	76	-0	0	0	0	1.000	-0	/O-4(3-2-1)	-0.1
1965	Phi-N	41	87	14	20	4	0	3	5	5	34	.230	.272	.379	651	83	-2	3	3	-0	1.000	-4	O-32(2-30-0)	-0.7
1966	Phi-N	2	3	1	0	0	0	0	0	0	0	.000	.000	.000	0	-99	-1	0	0	0	1.000	-0	/O-1(0-1-0)	-0.1
	Chi-N	116	416	68	109	29	1	16	36	43	135	.262	.348	.452	800	119	11	32	15	2	.978	12	*O-111(0-111-0)	2.2
	Yr	118	419	69	109	29	1	16	36	43	135	.260	.346	.449	795	118	10	32	15	2	.979	12	*O-112(0-112-0)	2.1
1967	Chi-N	144	448	66	120	20	7	17	70	80	93	.268	.386	.458	843	134	23	24	10	2	.981	15	*O-141(0-141-0)	3.8
1968	Chi-N	143	439	49	106	20	5	13	33	47	90	.241	.322	.399	720	108	5	9	7	-0	.979	6	*O-141(0-141-0)	0.8
1969	Chi-N	28	49	5	11	3	1	0	1	16	15	.224	.424	.327	751	100	1	1	3	-1	.956	-3	O-25(1-24-0)	-0.3
	Mon-N	58	199	25	43	4	4	4	7	19	62	.216	.288	.337	624	74	-7	6	5	-0	.981	-1	O-53(0-53-0)	-1.0
	Yr	86	248	30	54	7	5	4	8	35	77	.218	.319	.335	654	80	-6	7	8	-1	.973	-3	O-78(1-77-0)	-1.3
1970	Mon-N	92	214	36	51	6	3	6	21	36	51	.238	.353	.379	732	96	-0	7	1	1	.985	-6	O-75(6-71-0)	-0.7
1972	Cle-A	12	7	2	0	0	0	0	0	2	2	.000	.222	.000	222	-29	-1	0	0	0	1.000	-3	O-10(6-2-2)	-0.4
Total	8	649	1875	270	463	86	21	59	173	251	485	.247	.344	.410	754	110	28	82	44	3	.980	17	O-593(18-576-3)	3.5

■ J. R. PHILLIPS

Phillips, Charles Gene b: 4/29/70, West Covina, Cal. BL/TL, 6′1″, 185 lbs. Deb: 9/3/93

YEAR	TM/L	G	AB	R	H	2B	3B	HR	RBI	BB	SO	AVG	OBP	SLG	OPS	OPS+	BR+	SB	CS	SBR	FA	FR	G/POS	TPR
1993	SF-N	11	16	1	5	1	1	1	4	0	5	.313	.313	.688	1000	164	1	0	0	0	.971	0	/1-5	0.1
1994	SF-N	15	38	1	5	0	0	1	3	1	13	.132	.154	.211	364	-7	-6	1	0	0	.989	1	1-10	-0.5
1995	SF-N	92	231	27	45	9	0	9	28	19	69	.195	.256	.351	607	60	-14	1	1	-0	.993	-2	1-79/O-1(1-0-0)	-2.2
1996	SF-N	15	25	3	5	0	0	2	5	1	13	.200	.231	.440	671	75	-1	0	0	0	.981	-1	1-10	-0.2
	Phi-N	35	79	9	12	5	0	5	10	10	38	.152	.256	.405	661	70	-4	0	0	0	.957	3	O-15(0-0-15),1-11	-0.2
	Yr	50	104	12	17	5	0	7	15	11	51	.163	.250	.413	663	71	-5	0	0	0	.992	3	1-21,O-15(0-0-15)	-0.4
1997	Hou-N	13	15	2	2	0	0	1	4	0	7	.133	.133	.333	467	18	-2	0	0	0	1.000	-1	/1-3,O-3(0-0-3)	-0.3
1998	Hou-N	36	58	4	11	0	0	2	9	7	22	.190	.277	.293	570	51	-4	0	0	0	.962	-2	1-12/O-6(6-0-0)	-0.7
1999	Col-N	25	39	5	9	4	0	2	4	0	13	.231	.250	.487	737	63	-2	0	0	0	.933	2	/O-7(1-0-6),1-4	-0.1
Total	7	242	501	52	94	19	1	23	67	38	180	.188	.248	.367	615	59	-32	2	1	0	.989	1	1-134/O-32(8-0-24)	-4.1

■ DAMON PHILLIPS

Phillips, Damon Roswell "Dee" b: 6/8/19, Corsicana, Tex. BR/TR, 6′, 176 lbs. Deb: 7/19/42

YEAR	TM/L	G	AB	R	H	2B	3B	HR	RBI	BB	SO	AVG	OBP	SLG	OPS	OPS+	BR+	SB	CS	SBR	FA	FR	G/POS	TPR
1942	Cin-N	28	84	4	17	2	0	0	6	7	5	.202	.264	.226	490	44	-6	0			.964	7	S-27	0.3
1944	Bos-N	140	489	35	126	30	1	1	53	28	34	.258	.301	.329	630	74	-17	1			.932	-4	3-90,S-60	-1.6
1946	Bos-N	2	2	0	1	0	0	0	0	0	0	.500	.500	.500	1000	182	0	0			.000	0	H	0.0
Total	3	170	575	39	144	32	1	1	59	35	39	.250	.296	.315	611	70	-23	1			.956	3	/3-90,S-87	-1.3

■ EDDIE PHILLIPS

Phillips, Edward David b: 2/17/01, Worcester, Mass. d: 1/26/68, Buffalo, N.Y. BR/TR, 6′, 178 lbs. Deb: 5/4/24

YEAR	TM/L	G	AB	R	H	2B	3B	HR	RBI	BB	SO	AVG	OBP	SLG	OPS	OPS+	BR+	SB	CS	SBR	FA	FR	G/POS	TPR
1924	Bos-N	3	3	0	0	0	0	0	0	0	2	.000	.000	.000	0	-99	-1	0	0	0	1.000	0	/C-1	-0.1
1929	Det-A	68	221	24	52	13	1	2	21	20	16	.235	.302	.330	632	62	-13	0	1	-0	.967	-5	C-63	-1.3
1931	Pit-N	106	353	30	82	18	3	7	44	41	49	.232	.317	.360	677	82	-9	1			.986	-7	*C-103	-0.9
1932	NY-A	9	31	4	9	1	0	2	4	2	3	.290	.333	.516	849	123	1	1	0	0	1.000	1	/C-9	0.2
1934	Was-A	56	169	6	33	6	1	2	16	26	24	.195	.306	.278	584	54	-11	1	0	0	.984	-7	C-53	-1.4
1935	Cle-A	70	220	18	60	16	1	1	41	15	21	.273	.319	.368	687	76	-8	0	0	0	.980	-8	C-69	-1.2
Total	6	312	997	82	236	54	6	14	126	104	115	.237	.312	.345	657	72	-41	3	1		.980	-27	C-298	-4.7

■ EDDIE PHILLIPS

Phillips, Howard Edward b: 7/8/31, St.Louis, Mo. BB/TR, 6′1″, 180 lbs. Deb: 9/10/53

YEAR	TM/L	G	AB	R	H	2B	3B	HR	RBI	BB	SO	AVG	OBP	SLG	OPS	OPS+	BR+	SB	CS	SBR	FA	FR	G/POS	TPR
1953	StL-N	9	0	4	0	0	0	0	0	0	0	—	—	—	—	—	0	0	0	0	.000	0	R	0.0

■ JACK PHILLIPS

Phillips, Jack Dorn "Stretch" b: 9/6/21, Clarence, N.Y. BR/TR, 6′4″, 193 lbs. Deb: 8/22/47 Career OF: (1-LF 0-CF 0-RF)

YEAR	TM/L	G	AB	R	H	2B	3B	HR	RBI	BB	SO	AVG	OBP	SLG	OPS	OPS+	BR+	SB	CS	SBR	FA	FR	G/POS	TPR
1947	*NY-A	16	36	5	10	0	1	1	2	3	5	.278	.333	.417	750	109	0	0	0	0	.986	-2	1-10	-0.2
1948	NY-A	1	2	0	0	0	0	0	0	0	1	.000	.000	.000	0	-99	-1	0	0	0	.889	-0	/1-1	-0.1
1949	NY-A	45	91	16	28	4	1	1	10	12	9	.308	.388	.407	795	110	2	1	0	0	.977	-2	1-38	-0.1
	Pit-N	18	56	6	13	3	1	0	3	4	6	.232	.283	.321	605	60	-3	1			1.000	-0	1-16/3-1	-0.4
1950	Pit-N	69	208	25	61	7	6	5	34	20	17	.293	.355	.457	812	108	2	1			.986	2	1-54/3-3,P-1	0.2
1951	Pit-N	70	156	12	37	7	3	0	12	15	17	.237	.304	.321	625	66	-7	1	2	-0	.991	-1	1-53/3-4	-1.0
1952	Pit-N	1	1	0	0	0	0	0	0	0	0	.000	.000	.000	0	-97	-0	0	0	0	1.000	-0	/1-1	0.0
1955	Det-A	55	117	15	37	8	2	1	20	10	12	.316	.370	.444	815	121	3	0	0	0	.992	-1	1-35/3-3	0.0
1956	Det-A	67	224	31	66	13	2	1	20	21	19	.295	.355	.384	739	95	-2	1	1	-0	.981	-1	1-56/2-1,O-1(1-0-0)	-0.6
1957	Det-A	1	1	1	0	0	0	0	0	0	0	.000	.000	.000	0	-97	-0	0	0	0	.000	0	H	0.0
Total	9	343	892	111	252	42	16	9	101	85	86	.283	.345	.396	741	95	-6	5	3		.986	-6	1-264/3-11,O-1L,2P	-2.2

■ BUBBA PHILLIPS

Phillips, John Melvin b: 2/24/28, West Point, Miss. d: 6/22/93, Hattiesburg, Miss. BR/TR, 5′9″, 180 lbs. Deb: 4/30/55 Career OF: (111-LF 62-CF 46-RF)

YEAR	TM/L	G	AB	R	H	2B	3B	HR	RBI	BB	SO	AVG	OBP	SLG	OPS	OPS+	BR+	SB	CS	SBR	FA	FR	G/POS	TPR
1955	Det-A	95	184	18	43	4	0	3	23	14	20	.234	.295	.304	599	63	-10	2	1	0	.992	-1	O-65(61-2-4)/3-4	-1.3
1956	Chi-A	67	99	16	27	6	0	2	11	6	12	.273	.321	.394	715	87	-2	1	2	-0	1.000	-1	O-35(6-7-22)/3-2	-0.5
1957	Chi-A	121	393	38	106	13	3	7	42	28	32	.270	.323	.372	695	89	-6	5	3	0	.958	16	3-97,O-20(1-13-8)	0.8
1958	Chi-A	84	260	26	71	10	0	5	30	15	14	.273	.315	.369	684	89	-4	3	0	1	.954	7	3-47,O-37(19-15-4)	0.2
1959	*Chi-A	117	379	43	100	27	1	5	40	27	28	.264	.320	.380	699	92	-4	1	1	-0	.951	3	*3-100,O-23(8-14-1)	-0.3
1960	Cle-A	113	304	34	63	14	1	4	33	14	37	.207	.252	.299	551	50	-22	1	0	0	.953	-8	3-85,O-25(15-3-7)/S-1	-3.1
1961	Cle-A	143	546	64	144	23	1	18	72	29	61	.264	.307	.408	715	92	-8	1	0	0	.958	-18	*3-143	-2.7
1962	Cle-A	148	562	53	145	26	0	10	54	20	55	.258	.292	.358	650	76	-20	4	0	1	.977	-15	*3-145/O-3(0-3-0),2-1	-3.5
1963	Det-A	128	464	42	114	11	2	5	45	19	42	.246	.281	.310	592	63	-22	6	2	1	.961	1	*3-117/O-5(0-5-0)	-2.3
1964	Det-A	46	87	14	22	1	0	3	6	10	13	.253	.330	.368	698	92	-1	1	2	-0	.983	2	3-22/O-1(1-0-0)	0.0
Total	10	1062	3278	348	835	135	8	62	356	182	314	.255	.300	.358	658	79	-100	25	11	2	.960	-16	3-762,O-214L/2-1,S	-12.7

■ JACK PHILLIPS

Phillips, John Stephen b: 5/24/19, St.Louis, Mo. d: 6/16/58, St.Louis, Mo. BR/TR, 6′1″, 185 lbs. Deb: 7/13/45

YEAR	TM/L	G	AB	R	H	2B	3B	HR	RBI	BB	SO	AVG	OBP	SLG	OPS	OPS+	BR+	SB	CS	SBR	FA	FR	G/POS	TPR
1945	NY-N	2	2	1	1	0	0	0	0	0	0	.500	.500	.500	1000	176	0	0			1.000	-0	/P-1	0.0

■ TONY PHILLIPS

Phillips, Keith Anthony b: 4/25/59, Atlanta, Ga. BB/TR, 5′10″, 175 lbs. Deb: 5/10/82 Career OF: (566-LF 97-CF 169-RF)

YEAR	TM/L	G	AB	R	H	2B	3B	HR	RBI	BB	SO	AVG	OBP	SLG	OPS	OPS+	BR+	SB	CS	SBR	FA	FR	G/POS	TPR
1982	Oak-A	40	81	11	17	2	2	0	8	12	26	.210	.326	.284	610	73	-3	2	3	-1	.953	-5	S-39	-0.4
1983	Oak-A	148	412	54	102	12	3	4	35	48	70	.248	.329	.320	649	85	-7	16	5	2	.941	1	*S-101,2-63/3-4,D-1	0.6
1984	Oak-A	154	451	62	120	24	3	4	37	42	86	.266	.329	.359	688	97	-2	10	6	0	.941	-11	S-91,2-90/O-1(1-0-0)	-0.1
1985	Oak-A	42	161	23	45	12	2	4	17	13	34	.280	.333	.453	787	122	4	3	2	-0	.980	-0	3-31,2-24	0.4
1986	Oak-A	118	441	76	113	14	5	5	52	76	82	.256	.369	.345	714	103	6	15	10	-0	.976	1	2-88,3-30/O-4C,SD	1.0
1987	Oak-A	111	379	48	91	20	0	10	46	57	76	.240	.339	.372	711	95	-2	7	6	-1	.974	-3	2-87,3-11/S-9,OD	0.1
1988	*Oak-A	79	212	32	43	8	4	2	17	36	50	.203	.321	.307	628	80	-5	0	2	-1	.913	-20	3-32,O-31L,2-27,S/1D	-2.6
1989	*Oak-A	143	451	48	118	15	6	4	47	58	66	.262	.350	.348	698	101	2	3	8	-2	.985	-24	2-84,3-49,S-17,O/1	-2.2

YEAR	TM/L	G	AB	R	H	2B	3B	HR	RBI	BB	SO	AVG	OBP	SLG	OPS	OPS+	BR+	SB	CS	SBR	FA	FR	G/POS	TPR
1990	Det-A	152	573	97	144	23	5	8	55	99	85	.251	.365	.351	716	100	4	19	9	1	.931	6	*3-104,2-47,S-11,/OD	1.3
1991	Det-A	146	564	87	160	28	4	17	72	79	95	.284	.375	.438	813	122	19	10	5	0	.992	6	O-56L,3-46,2-36,DS	2.5
1992	Det-A	159	606	**114**	167	32	3	10	64	114	93	.276	.391	.388	779	118	20	12	10	-1	.968	4	O-69R,2-57,D-34,3/S	2.2
1993	Det-A	151	566	113	177	27	0	7	57	**132**	102	.313	.446	.398	843	130	33	16	11	-0	.969	-1	*O-108L,2-51/3-1,D	3.0
1994	Det-A	114	438	91	123	19	3	19	61	95	105	.281	.411	.468	879	126	20	13	5	1	.980	7	*O-104L,2-12/D-6	2.3
1995	Cal-A	139	525	119	137	21	1	27	61	113	135	.261	.395	.459	854	122	21	13	10	-1	.924	4	3-88,O-48(47-8-0)/D-2	2.2
1996	Chi-A	153	581	119	161	29	3	12	63	**125**	132	.277	.408	.399	808	111	16	13	8	0	.981	16	*O-150L/2-2,1-1	2.5
1997	Chi-A	36	129	23	40	6	0	2	9	29	29	.310	.440	.403	843	127	7	4	1	1	.972	2	O-28(0-0-28)/3-9	0.8
	Ana-A	105	405	73	107	28	2	6	48	73	89	.264	.379	.388	767	101	3	9	9	-1	.968	-15	2-43,O-35L,D-26,/3	-1.3
	Yr	141	534	96	147	34	2	8	57	102	118	.275	.394	.391	786	107	10	13	10	-1	.970	-13	O-63L,2-43,D-26,3	-0.5
1998	Tor-A	13	48	9	17	5	0	1	7	9	6	.354	.475	.521	995	158	5	0	0	0	.960	-1	O-13(11-0-4)	0.3
	NY-N	52	188	25	42	11	0	3	14	38	44	.223	.354	.330	684	83	-4	1	1	-0	.967	-2	O-51(43-0-15)	-0.7
1999	Oak-A	106	406	76	99	24	4	15	49	71	94	.244	.363	.433	797	107	5	11	3	1	.974	-28	2-66,O-62C/3-2,SD	-1.8
Total	18	2161	7617	1300	2023	360	50	160	819	1319	1499	.266	.377	.389	766	109	144	177	114	-1	.973	-63	O-786L,2-777,3SD/1	10.1
■ MARR PHILLIPS Phillips, Marr B. b: 6/16/1857, Pittsburgh, Pa. d: 4/1/28, Pittsburgh, Pa. BR, 5'6.5", 164 lbs. Deb: 5/1/1884																								
1884	Ind-a	97	413	41	111	18	8	0		5		.269	.279	.351	630	107	3				.862	14	*S-97	1.7
1885	Det-N	33	139	13	29	5	0	0	17	0	13	.209	.209	.245	453	46	-8				.881	3	S-33	-0.4
	Pit-a	4	15	1	4	0	0	0	2	2		.267	.353	.267	620	99	0				.875	-1	/S-4	-0.1
1890	Roc-a	64	257	18	53	8	0	0	34	16		.206	.261	.237	498	51	-16	10			.918	6	S-64	-0.7
Total	3	198	824	73	197	31	8	0	53	23	13	.239	.263	.296	559	79	-21	10			.884	21	S-198	0.5
■ MIKE PHILLIPS Phillips, Michael Dwaine b: 8/19/50, Beaumont, Tex. BL/TR, 6'1", 185 lbs. Deb: 4/15/73																								
1973	SF-N	63	104	18	25	3	4	1	9	6	17	.240	.288	.375	663	79	-3	0	3	-1	.931	-0	3-28,S-20/2-7	-0.3
1974	SF-N	100	283	19	62	6	1	2	20	14	37	.219	.258	.269	527	45	-21	4	5	-1	.909	4	3-34,2-30,S-23	-1.4
1975	SF-N	10	31	3	6	0	0	0	1	6	4	.194	.324	.194	518	44	-2	1	0	0	.969	4	/2-6,3-6	0.2
	NY-N	116	383	31	98	10	7	1	28	25	47	.256	.303	.326	630	78	-12	3	0	1	.944	1	*S-115/2-1	0.2
	Yr	126	414	34	104	10	7	1	29	31	51	.251	.305	.316	621	76	-14	4	0	1	.944	4	*S-115/2-7,3-6	0.4
1976	NY-N	87	262	30	67	4	6	4	29	25	29	.256	.321	.363	683	99	-1	2	2	-0	.955	-9	S-53,2-19,3-10	-0.4
1977	NY-N	38	86	5	18	2	1	1	3	2	15	.209	.244	.291	535	45	-7	0	1	-0	1.000	-5	S-24/3-9,2-4	-1.1
	StL-N	48	87	17	21	3	2	0	9	9	13	.241	.320	.322	641	74	-3	1	0	0	.971	5	2-31/S-5,3-5	0.4
	Yr	86	173	22	39	5	3	1	12	11	28	.225	.283	.306	590	60	-10	1	1	-0	.973	1	2-35,S-29,3-14	-0.7
1978	StL-N	76	164	14	44	8	1	1	28	13	25	.268	.330	.348	677	91	-2	0	0	0	.971	-1	2-55,S-10/3-1	0.0
1979	StL-N	44	97	10	22	3	1	1	6	10	9	.227	.306	.309	615	68	-4	0	0	0	.973	13	S-25,2-16/3-1	1.1
1980	StL-N	63	128	13	30	5	0	0	7	9	17	.234	.285	.273	558	55	-8	0	0	0	.971	13	S-37/2-9,3-8	0.8
1981	SD-N	14	29	1	6	0	1	0	0	0	3	.207	.207	.276	483	39	-2	1	0	0	.979	4	/2-9,S-1	0.2
	*Mon-N	34	55	5	12	2	0	0	4	5	15	.218	.283	.255	538	53	-3	0	1	-0	.974	0	S-26/2-6	-0.2
	Yr	48	84	6	18	2	1	0	4	5	18	.214	.258	.262	520	49	-6	1	1	-0	.974	4	S-27,2-15	0.0
1982	Mon-N	14	8	0	1	0	0	0	1	0	3	.125	.125	.125	250	-29	-1	0	0	0	1.000	3	2-10/S-2	0.1
1983	Mon-N	5	2	0	0	0	0	0	0	0	0	.000	.000	.000	0	-99	-1	0	0	0	.000	-1	/S-3,3-2	-0.2
Total	11	712	1719	166	412	46	24	11	145	124	234	.240	.294	.314	608	70	-70	12	12	-2	.956	29	S-344,2-203,3-104	-0.6
■ DICK PHILLIPS Phillips, Richard Eugene b: 11/24/31, Racine, Wis. d: 3/29/98, Burnaby, B.C., Canada BL/TR, 6', 180 lbs. Deb: 4/15/62 C																								
1962	SF-N	5	3	1	0	0	0	0	1	1	1	.000	.250	.000	250	-27	-1	0	0	0	1.000	-0	/1-1	-0.1
1963	Was-A	124	321	33	76	8	0	10	32	29	35	.237	.304	.355	659	84	-7	1	0	0	.994	4	1-68/2-5,3-4	-0.7
1964	Was-A	109	234	17	54	6	1	2	23	27	22	.231	.313	.291	604	70	-9	1	2	-0	.994	2	1-61/3-4	-1.2
1966	Was-A	25	37	3	6	0	0	0	4	2	5	.162	.225	.162	387	13	-4	0	0	0	1.000	-1	/1-5	-0.5
Total	4	263	595	54	136	14	1	12	60	59	63	.229	.302	.316	618	74	-20	2	2	-0	.995	5	1-135/3-8,2-5	-2.5
■ BILL PHILLIPS Phillips, William B. b: 1857, St.John, N.B., Canada d: 10/7/1900, Chicago, Ill. BR/TR, 202 lbs. Deb: 5/1/1879 Career OF: (0-LF 1-CF 1-RF)																								
1879	Cle-N	81	365	58	99	15	4	0	29	2	20	.271	.275	.334	609	101	0				.954	-5	*1-75,C-11/O-2(0-1-1)	-0.7
1880	Cle-N	85	334	41	85	14	10	1	36	6	29	.254	.268	.365	633	115	5				.963	2	*1-85	0.3
1881	Cle-N	85	357	51	97	18	10	1	44	5	19	.272	.282	.387	668	114	6				.966	-1	*1-85	0.1
1882	Cle-N	78	335	40	87	17	7	4	47	7	18	.260	.275	.388	663	114	5				.971	3	*1-78/C-1	0.1
1883	Cle-N	97	382	42	94	29	8	2	40	8	49	.246	.262	.380	641	93	-3				.967	-2	*1-97	-1.3
1884	Cle-N	111	464	58	128	25	12	3	46	18	80	.276	.303	.401	704	115	7				.959	-2	*1-111	-0.4
1885	Bro-a	99	391	65	118	16	11	3	63	27		.302	.364	.422	786	147	21				**.973**	0	*1-99	1.1
1886	Bro-a	141	585	68	160	26	15	0	72	33		.274	.313	.369	683	113	7	13			.978	-2	*1-141	-0.7
1887	Bro-a	132	578	82	187	34	11	2	101	45		.324	.330	.383	713	97	-3	16			**.982**	4	*1-132	-0.9
1888	KC-a	129	509	57	120	20	10	1	56	27		.236	.284	.320	604	88	-9	10			.980	3	*1-129	-1.6
Total	10	1038	4300	562	1175	214	98	17	534	178	215	.273	.299	.374	673	108	35	39			.971	1	*1-1032/C-12,O-2C	-4.0
■ BILL PHYLE Phyle, William Joseph b: 6/25/1875, Duluth, Minn. d: 8/6/53, Los Angeles, Cal. TR, Deb: 9/17/1898																								
1898	Chi-N	4	9	1	1	0	0	0	0	2		.111	.273	.111	384	11	-1	0			.800	-1	/P-3	0.0
1899	Chi-N	10	34	2	6	0	0	0	1	0		.176	.176	.176	353	-3	-5	0			.935	1	P-10	0.0
1901	NY-N	25	66	8	12	2	0	0	3	2		.182	.206	.212	418	22	-7	0			.903	1	P-24/S-1	0.0
1906	StL-N	22	73	6	13	3	1	0	4	5		.178	.231	.247	477	51	-4	2			.935	2	3-21	-0.2
Total	4	61	182	17	32	5	1	0	8	9		.176	.215	.214	429	28	-17	2			.907	3	/P-37,3-21,S-1	-0.2
■ ADAM PIATT Piatt, Adam David b: 2/8/76, Chicago, Ill. BR/TR, 6'2", 195 lbs. Deb: 4/24/2000																								
2000	*Oak-A	60	156	24	47	5	5	5	23	23	44	.301	.394	.494	888	126	7	0	1	-0	.950	-8	O-29R,3-13,D-13,/1	-0.4
■ MIKE PIAZZA Piazza, Michael Joseph b: 9/4/68, Norristown, Pa. BR/TR, 6'3", 197 lbs. Deb: 9/1/92																								
1992	LA-N	21	69	5	16	3	0	1	7	4	12	.232	.284	.319	603	71	-3	0	0	0	.990	-2	C-16	-0.4
1993	LA-N★	149	547	81	174	24	2	35	112	46	86	.318	.374	.561	935	155	41	3	4	-1	.989	5	*C-146/1-1	5.3
1994	LA-N★	107	405	64	129	18	0	24	92	33	65	.319	.371	.541	912	143	24	1	3	-1	.985	-12	*C-104	1.8
1995	*LA-N★	112	434	82	150	17	0	32	93	39	80	.346	.401	.606	1007	**177**	46	1	0	0	.990	-9	*C-112	4.3
1996	*LA-N★	148	547	87	184	16	0	36	105	81	93	.336	.423	.563	986	171	58	0	3	-1	.992	-5	*C-146	5.8
1997	LA-N★	152	556	104	201	32	1	40	124	69	77	.362	.435	.638	1073	**191**	**74**	5	1	1	.986	-4	*C-139/D-7	7.6
1998	LA-N	37	149	20	42	5	0	9	30	11	27	.282	.331	.497	828	121	4	0	0	0	.993	4	C-37	1.0
	Fla-N	5	18	1	5	0	1	0	5	0	0	.278	.278	.389	667	77	-1	0	0	0	.968	-0	/C-4	0.0
	NY-N★	109	394	67	137	33	0	23	76	47	53	.348	.420	.607	1026	168	39	1	0	0	.989	0	C-99/D-4	4.4
	Yr	151	561	88	184	38	1	32	111	58	80	.328	.393	.570	963	154	43	1	0	0	.990	4	*C-140/D-4	5.4
1999	*NY-N★	141	534	100	162	25	0	40	124	51	70	.303	.365	.575	940	137	28	2	2	-0	.989	-11	*C-137/D-1	2.4
2000	*NY-N†	136	482	90	156	26	0	38	113	58	69	.324	.400	.614	1014	157	41	4	2	0	**.997**	-8	*C-124/D-5	3.8
Total	9	1117	4135	701	1356	199	4	278	881	439	632	.328	.395	.580	974	159	352	17	15	-2	.990	-41	*C-1064/D-17,1-1	36.0
■ ROB PICCIOLO Picciolo, Robert Michael b: 2/4/53, Santa Monica, Cal. BR/TR, 6'2", 185 lbs. Deb: 4/9/77 C Career OF: (2-LF 0-CF 1-RF)																								
1977	Oak-A	148	419	35	84	12	3	2	22	9	55	.200	.219	.258	477	30	-41	1	4	-1	.966	7	*S-148	-2.2
1978	Oak-A	78	93	16	21	1	0	2	7	2	13	.226	.242	.301	543	55	-6	1	1	-0	.958	12	S-41,2-19,3-13	0.9
1979	Oak-A	115	348	37	88	16	2	2	27	3	45	.253	.261	.328	589	61	-20	2	1	0	.964	-3	*S-105/2-6,3-4,O-1L	-1.3
1980	Oak-A	95	271	32	65	9	2	5	18	2	63	.240	.245	.343	589	64	-14	1	1	-0	.977	-23	S-49,2-47/O-1(1-0-0)	-3.1
1981	*Oak-A	82	179	23	48	5	3	4	13	5	22	.268	.292	.397	689	102	-0	0	1	-0	.981	-15	S-82	-1.0
1982	Oak-A	18	49	3	11	1	0	0	3	1	10	.224	.240	.245	485	35	-4	1	0	0	.979	3	S-18	0.1
	Mil-A	22	21	7	6	1	0	0	1	1	4	.286	.318	.333	652	84	-0	0	0	0	1.000	2	2-11/S-6,D-1	0.1
	Yr	40	70	10	17	2	0	0	4	2	14	.243	.264	.271	535	50	-5	1	0	0	.973	5	S-24,2-11/D-1	0.2
1983	Mil-A	14	27	2	6	3	0	0	1	0	4	.222	.222	.333	556	55	-2	0	0	0	1.000	2	/S-7,2-2,3-2,1-1,D	0.1
1984	Cal-A	87	119	18	24	6	0	1	9	0	21	.202	.202	.277	479	31	-11	0	1	-0	.974	13	S-66,3-13/2-9,O-1R	0.5
1985	Oak-A	71	102	19	28	2	0	1	8	2	17	.275	.288	.324	612	73	-4	3	2	-0	.889	7	3-19,2-17,1-13,D/S	0.3
Total	9	730	1628	192	381	56	10	17	109	25	254	.234	.247	.312	559	55	-103	9	11	-2	.970	6	S-531,2-111/3-51,1DO	-5.6

YEAR	TM/L	G	AB	R	H	2B	3B	HR	RBI	BB	SO	AVG	OBP	SLG	OPS	OPS+	BR+	SB	CS	SBR	FA	FR	G/POS	TPR
■ NICK PICCIUTO Picciuto, Nicholas Thomas b: 8/27/21, Newark, N.J. d: 1/10/97, Winchester, Va. BR/TR, 5'8.5", 165 lbs. Deb: 5/11/45																								
1945	Phi-N	36	89	7	12	6	0	0	6	6	17	.135	.189	.202	392	9	-11	0			.839	-6	3-30/2-4	-1.7
■ VAL PICINICH Picinich, Valentine John b: 9/8/1896, New York, N.Y. d: 12/5/42, Nobleboro, Maine BR/TR, 5'9", 165 lbs. Deb: 7/25/16 C																								
1916	Phi-A	40	118	8	23	3	1	0	5	6	33	.195	.234	.237	471	44	-8	1			.967	-0	C-37	-0.6
1917	Phi-A	2	6	0	2	0	0	0	0	1	2	.333	.429	.333	762	135	0	0			.786	-1	/C-2	-0.1
1918	Was-A	47	148	13	34	3	3	0	12	9	25	.230	.274	.291	564	72	-6	0			.960	-2	C-46	-0.4
1919	Was-A	80	212	18	58	12	3	3	22	17	43	.274	.330	.401	731	106	1	6			.978	15	C-69	2.2
1920	Was-A	48	133	14	27	6	2	3	14	9	33	.203	.259	.346	605	61	-8	0	0	0	.978	9	C-45	0.4
1921	Was-A	45	141	10	39	9	0	0	12	16	21	.277	.354	.340	695	82	-3	0	3	-1	.966	3	C-45	0.2
1922	Was-A	76	210	16	48	12	2	0	19	23	33	.229	.311	.305	615	64	-11	1	0	0	.976	7	C-76	0.1
1923	Bos-A	87	268	33	74	21	1	2	31	46	32	.276	.386	.384	770	103	3	3	5	-1	.957	-2	C-81	0.5
1924	Bos-A	69	161	25	44	6	3	1	24	29	19	.273	.394	.366	760	97	0	5	1	1	.951	-4	C-52	0.0
1925	Bos-A	90	251	31	64	21	0	1	25	33	21	.255	.344	.351	694	77	-9	2	0	0	.968	-8	C-74/1-2	-1.1
1926	Cin-N	89	240	33	63	16	1	2	31	29	22	.262	.342	.363	705	92	-2	4			.967	-0	C-86	0.2
1927	Cin-N	65	173	16	44	8	3	0	12	24	15	.254	.345	.335	680	85	-3	3			.980	5	C-61	0.6
1928	Cin-N	96	324	29	98	15	1	7	35	20	25	.302	.343	.420	763	100	-1	1			.983	-3	C-93	0.3
1929	Bro-N	93	273	28	71	16	6	4	31	34	24	.260	.342	.407	749	86	-6	3			.979	-4	C-85	-0.4
1930	Bro-N	23	46	4	10	3	0	0	3	5	6	.217	.294	.283	577	41	-4	1			.944	-2	C-22	-0.5
1931	Bro-N	24	45	5	12	4	0	1	4	4	9	.267	.327	.422	749	100	-0	1			.967	1	C-15	0.1
1932	Bro-N	41	70	8	18	6	0	1	11	4	8	.257	.297	.386	683	84	-2	0			.985	-2	C-24	-0.3
1933	Bro-N	6	6	1	1	1	0	0	0	0	1	.167	.167	.333	500	42	-0	0			.889	0	/C-6	-0.0
	Pit-N	16	52	6	13	4	0	1	7	5	10	.250	.316	.385	700	99	-0	0			.982	-3	C-16	-0.2
	Yr	22	58	7	14	5	0	1	7	5	11	.241	.302	.379	681	95	-0	0			.969	-3	C-22	-0.2
Total	18	1037	2877	298	743	166	26	26	298	314	382	.258	.334	.361	695	86	-60	31	9		.970	11	C-935/1-2	1.0
■ CHARLIE PICK Pick, Charles Thomas b: 4/10/1888, Brookneal, Va. d: 6/26/54, Lynchburg, Va. BL/TR, 5'10", 160 lbs. Deb: 9/20/14 Career OF: (13-LF 4-CF 1-RF)																								
1914	Was-A	10	23	0	9	0	0	0	1	4	4	.391	.481	.391	873	157	2	1	2	-0	.833	-0	/O-7(6-0-1)	0.1
1915	Was-A	3	2	0	0	0	0	0	0	0	0	.000	.000	.000	0	-98	-0	0			.000	0	H	-0.1
1916	Phi-A	121	398	29	96	10	3	0	20	40	24	.241	.315	.281	597	83	-8	25	16	-0	.899	4	*3-108/O-8(5-3-0)	-0.1
1918	*Chi-N	29	89	13	29	4	1	0	12	14	4	.326	.417	.393	811	144	5	7			.964	-0	2-20/3-8	0.6
1919	Chi-N	75	269	27	65	8	6	0	18	14	12	.242	.292	.316	608	82	-6	17			.946	12	2-71/3-3	0.8
	Bos-N	34	114	12	29	1	1	1	7	7	5	.254	.325	.307	632	94	-0	4			.924	-2	2-21/3-5,O-3L,1-2	-0.2
	Yr	109	383	39	94	9	7	1	25	21	17	.245	.302	.313	615	86	-6	21			.942	10	2-92/3-8,O-3L,1-2	0.6
1920	Bos-N	95	383	34	105	16	6	2	28	23	11	.274	.320	.363	683	100	-0	10	16	-3	.952	0	2-94	-0.2
Total	6	367	1278	115	333	39	17	3	86	102	60	.261	.323	.325	648	95	-7	64	34		.949	14	2-206,3-124/O-18L,1	0.9
■ EDDIE PICK Pick, Edgar Everett b: 5/7/1899, Attleboro, Mass. d: 5/13/67, Santa Monica, Cal. BB/TR, 6', 185 lbs. Deb: 9/13/23																								
1923	Cin-N	9	8	2	3	0	0	0	2	3	3	.375	.545	.375	920	150	1	0	0	0	1.000	-1	/O-4(4-0-0)	-0.1
1924	Cin-N	3	2	0	0	0	0	0	0	0	1	.000	.000	.000	0	-99	-1	0	0	0	1.000	-0	/O-1(1-0-0)	-0.1
1927	Chi-N	54	181	23	31	5	2	2	15	20	26	.171	.254	.254	508	36	-16	0			.910	-6	3-49/2-1,O-1(0-0-1)	-1.9
Total	3	66	191	25	34	5	2	2	17	23	30	.178	.266	.257	523	40	-16	0	0		1.000	-8	/3-49,O-6(5-0-1),2-1	-2.1
■ CALVIN PICKERING Pickering, Calvin Elroy b: 9/29/76, St.Thomas, V.I. BL/TL, 6'5", 283 lbs. Deb: 9/12/98																								
1998	Bal-A	9	21	4	5	0	0	2	3	3	4	.238	.333	.524	857	120	1	1	0	0	.969	-1	/1-5,D-3	0.0
1999	Bal-A	23	40	4	5	1	0	1	5	11	16	.125	.314	.225	539	42	-3	0	0	0	.960	-1	/1-8,D-7	-0.4
Total	2	32	61	8	10	1	0	3	8	14	20	.164	.320	.328	648	69	-3	1	0	0	.963	-2	/1-13,D-10	-0.4
■ OLLIE PICKERING Pickering, Oliver Daniel b: 4/9/1870, Olney, Ill. d: 1/20/52, Vincennes, Ind. BL/TR, 5'10", 175 lbs. Deb: 8/9/1896 Career OF: (19-LF 612-CF 231-RF)																								
1896	Lou-N	45	165	28	50	6	4	1	22	12	11	.303	.350	.406	756	103	0	13			.901	3	O-45(3-44-0)	0.1
1897	Lou-N	64	249	34	62	5	2	1	21	26		.249	.325	.297	622	67	-11	20			.938	4	O-63(0-62-1)	-1.0
	Cle-N	46	182	33	64	5	2	1	22	11		.352	.392	.418	809	108	2	18			.950	-0	O-46(1-45-1)/2-1	-0.1
	Yr	110	431	67	126	10	4	2	43	37		.292	.352	.348	700	85	-9	38			.943	4	*O-109(1-107-2)/2-1	-1.1
1901	Cle-A	137	547	102	169	25	6	0	40	58		.309	.383	.377	760	116	15	36			.949	15	*O-137(2-110-25)	2.1
1902	Cle-A	69	293	46	75	5	2	3	26	19		.256	.306	.317	623	76	-9	22			.979	-2	O-64(3-57-4)/1-2	-1.4
1903	Phi-A	137	512	93	144	18	6	1	36	53		.281	.353	.346	699	105	5	40			.970	4	*O-135(0-134-1)	0.2
1904	Phi-A	124	455	56	103	10	3	0	30	45		.226	.299	.262	560	74	-12	17			.939	-0	*O-121(10-111-0)	-2.0
1907	StL-A	151	576	63	159	15	10	0	60	35		.276	.321	.337	658	110	6	15			.949	-11	*O-151(0-22-128)	-1.3
1908	Was-A	113	373	45	84	7	4	2	30	28		.225	.285	.282	566	92	-3	13			.940	-8	O-98(0-27-71)	-1.8
Total	8	886	3352	500	910	96	39	9	287	287	11	.271	.334	.331	665	97	-7	194			.949	4	O-860C/1-2,2-1	-5.2
■ URBANE PICKERING Pickering, Urbane Henry "Pick" b: 6/3/1899, Hoxie, Kan. d: 5/13/70, Modesto, Cal. BR/TR, 5'10", 180 lbs. Deb: 4/18/31																								
1931	Bos-A	103	341	48	86	13	4	9	52	33	53	.252	.318	.393	711	91	-5	3	4	-1	.967	-2	3-74,2-16	-0.4
1932	Bos-A	132	457	47	119	28	5	2	40	39	71	.260	.320	.357	677	77	-16	3	4	-1	.941	-7	*3-126/C-1	-1.8
Total	2	235	798	95	205	41	9	11	92	72	124	.257	.319	.372	691	83	-21	6	8	-1	.951	-9	3-200/2-16,C-1	-2.2
■ DAVE PICKETT Pickett, David T. b: 5/26/1874, Brookline, Mass. d: 4/22/50, Easton, Mass. 5'7.5", 170 lbs. Deb: 7/21/1898																								
1898	Bos-N	14	43	3	12	1	0	0	3	6		.279	.380	.302	682	91	-0	2			.955	-2	O-14(14-0-0)	-0.3
■ JOHN PICKETT Pickett, John Thomas b: 2/20/1866, Chicago, Ill. d: 7/4/22, Chicago, Ill. BR/TR, Deb: 6/6/1889 Career OF: (23-LF 4-CF 1-RF)																								
1889	KC-a	53	201	20	45	7	0	0	12	11	21	.224	.271	.259	530	48	-14	7			.900	-16	O-28L,3-14,2-11	-2.6
1890	Phi-P	100	407	82	114	7	9	4	64	40	17	.280	.347	.371	718	90	-6	12			.893	-22	*2-100	-1.9
1892	Bal-N	36	141	13	30	2	3	1	12	7	10	.213	.260	.291	551	65	-6	2			.915	-5	2-36	-0.9
Total	3	189	749	115	189	16	12	5	88	58	48	.252	.311	.326	637	75	-27	21			.900	-42	2-147/O-28L,3-14	-5.4
■ TY PICKUP Pickup, Clarence William b: 10/29/1897, Philadelphia, Pa. d: 8/2/74, Philadelphia, Pa. BR/TR, 6', 180 lbs. Deb: 4/30/18																								
1918	Phi-N	1	1	0	1	0	0	0	0	0	0	1.000	1.000	1.000	2000	478	0	0			1.000	-0	/O-1(0-0-1)	0.0
■ GRACIE PIERCE Pierce, Grayson S. b: New York, N.Y. d: 8/28/1894, New York, N.Y. BR/TR, Deb: 5/2/1882 U Career OF: (0-LF 23-CF 6-RF)																								
1882	Lou-a	9	33	3	10	1	0	0		1		.303	.324	.333	657	129	1				.864	1	/2-9	0.2
	Bal-a	41	151	8	30	2	1	0		3		.199	.214	.225	439	52	-7				.796	-10	2-38/O-3(0-0-3),S-1	-1.4
	Yr	50	184	11	40	3	1	0		4		.217	.234	.245	479	66	-6				.808	-9	2-47/O-3(0-0-3),S-1	-1.2
1883	Col-a	11	41	5	7	0	0	0		0		.171	.171	.171	341	11	-4				.744	-1	/2-6,O-5(0-4-1)	-0.4
	NY-N	18	62	3	5	0	1	0	2	1	9	.081	.095	.113	208	-37	-10				.850	-2	O-18(0-17-1)/2-1	-1.1
1884	NY-a	5	20	2	5	1	0	0		0		.250	.250	.300	550	81	-0				1.000	-5	/O-3(0-2-1),2-3	-0.5
Total	3	84	307	21	57	4	2	0	2	5	9	.186	.199	.212	410	36	-20				.795	-17	/2-57,O-29C,S-1	-3.2
■ JACK PIERCE Pierce, Lavern Jack b: 6/2/48, Laurel, Miss. BL/TR, 6', 210 lbs. Deb: 4/27/73																								
1973	Atl-N	11	20	0	1	0	0	0	0	1	8	.050	.095	.050	145	-55	-4	0	0	0	1.000	1	/1-6	-0.4
1974	Atl-N	6	9	1	1	0	0	0	0	1	0	.111	.200	.111	311	-11	-1	0	0	0	.958	0	/1-2	-0.1
1975	Det-A	53	170	19	40	6	1	8	22	20	40	.235	.323	.424	746	105	1	0	0	0	.971	-4	1-49	-0.8
Total	3	70	199	20	42	6	1	8	22	22	48	.211	.296	.372	668	83	-5	0	0	0	.973	-3	/1-57	-1.3
■ MAURY PIERCE Pierce, Maurice b: Baltimore, Md. Deb: 4/23/1884																								
1884	Was-U	2	7	0	1	0	0	0		0		.143	.143	.143	286	-14	-1				.778	0	/3-2	-0.1
■ ANDY PIERCY Piercy, Andrew J. b: 8/1856, San Jose, Cal. d: 12/27/32, San Jose, Cal. TR, Deb: 5/12/1881																								
1881	Chi-N	2	8	1	2	0	0	0	0	0	1	.250	.250	.250	500	55	-0				.750	-1	/3-1,2-1	-0.2
■ JUAN PIERRE Pierre, Juan D'Vaughn b: 8/14/77, Mobile, Ala. BL/TL, 6', 170 lbs. Deb: 8/7/2000																								
2000	Col-N	51	200	26	62	2	0	0	20	13	15	.310	.355	.320	675	57	-12	7	6	-1	.975	-0	O-50(0-50-0)	-1.2

■ JIM PIERSALL Piersall, James Anthony b: 11/14/29, Waterbury, Conn. BR/TR, 6', 175 lbs. Deb: 9/7/50 C Career OF: (113-LF 1214-CF 305-RF)

YEAR	TM/L	G	AB	R	H	2B	3B	HR	RBI	BB	SO	AVG	OBP	SLG	OPS	OPS+	BR+	SB	CS	SBR	FA	FR	G/POS	TPR
1950	Bos-A	6	7	4	2	0	0	0	0	4	0	.286	.545	.286	831	107	0	0	0	0	1.000	1	/O-2(0-2-0)	0.1
1952	Bos-A	56	161	28	43	8	0	1	16	28	26	.267	.379	.335	714	93	-0	3	3	-0	.928	-6	S-30,O-22(0-1-21)/3-1	-0.6
1953	Bos-A	151	585	76	159	21	9	3	52	41	52	.272	.329	.354	683	80	-16	11	10	-1	.987	16	*O-151(1-2-150)	-0.7
1954	Bos-A★	133	474	77	135	24	2	8	38	36	42	.285	.339	.395	734	90	-6	5	1	1	.985	0	*O-126(0-30-96)	-1.0
1955	Bos-A	149	515	68	146	25	5	13	62	67	52	.283	.368	.427	795	104	4	6	1	1	.993	13	*O-147(0-147-0)	1.1
1956	Bos-A★	155	601	91	176	**40**	6	14	87	58	48	.293	.356	.449	805	99	-1	7	7	-1	**.991**	**18**	*O-155(0-155-0)	0.8
1957	Bos-A	151	609	103	159	27	5	19	63	62	54	.261	.333	.415	749	98	-2	14	6	1	.990	13	*O-151(0-151-0)	0.5
1958	Bos-A	130	417	55	99	13	5	8	48	42	43	.237	.307	.350	657	75	-14	12	2	2	.985	9	*O-125(0-125-0)	-0.8
1959	Cle-A	100	317	42	78	13	2	4	30	25	31	.246	.305	.338	643	79	-9	6	3	0	.982	0	O-91(0-91-0)/3-1	-1.3
1960	Cle-A	138	486	70	137	12	4	18	66	24	38	.282	.316	.434	750	104	1	18	5	2	.992	10	*O-134(8-127-2)	0.7
1961	Cle-A	121	484	81	156	26	7	6	40	43	46	.322	.380	.442	822	122	16	8	2	1	**.991**	16	*O-120(0-120-0)	2.8
1962	Was-A	135	471	38	115	20	4	4	31	39	53	.244	.302	.329	631	70	-20	12	7	0	**.997**	7	*O-132(0-132-0)	-1.7
1963	Was-A	29	94	9	23	1	0	1	5	6	11	.245	.290	.287	577	63	-5	4	0	1	1.000	1	O-25(0-25-0)	-0.3
	NY-N	40	124	13	24	4	1	1	10	10	14	.194	.254	.266	520	49	-8	1	2	-0	1.000	-2	O-38(0-38-0)	-1.2
	LA-N	20	52	4	16	1	0	0	4	5	5	.308	.368	.327	695	103	0	0	1	-0	1.000	-2	O-18(1-12-5)	-0.3
1964	LA-A	87	255	28	80	11	0	2	13	16	32	.314	.354	.380	735	116	5	5	3	0	1.000	-6	O-72(48-32-0)	-0.4
1965	Cal-A	53	112	10	30	5	2	2	12	5	15	.268	.305	.402	707	101	-0	2	2	-0	.984	-4	O-41(29-10-4)	-0.6
1966	Cal-A	75	123	14	26	5	0	0	14	13	19	.211	.287	.252	539	58	-6	1	2	-0	.973	-10	O-63(25-14-27)	-2.1
1967	Cal-A	5	3	0	0	0	0	0	0	0	2	.000	.000	.000	0	-99	-1	0	0	0	1.000	-0	/O-1(1-0-0)	-0.1
Total	17	1734	5890	811	1604	256	52	104	591	524	583	.272	.334	.386	721	92	-63	115	57	5	.990	73	*O-1614C/S-30,3-2	-5.1

■ DAVE PIERSON Pierson, David P. b: 8/20/1855, Wilkes-Barre, Pa. d: 11/11/22, Newark, N.J. BR/TR, 5'7", 142 lbs. Deb: 4/25/1876 F

YEAR	TM/L	G	AB	R	H	2B	3B	HR	RBI	BB	SO	AVG	OBP	SLG	OPS	OPS+	BR+	SB	CS	SBR	FA	FR	G/POS	TPR
1876	Cin-N	57	234	33	55	4	1	0	13	1	9	.235	.239	.262	501	78	-3				.760	-2	C-31,O-30R/S-1,32P	-0.4

■ DICK PIERSON Pierson, Edmund Dana b: 10/24/1857, Wilkes-Barre, Pa. d: 7/20/22, Newark, N.J. TR, Deb: 6/23/1885 F

YEAR	TM/L	G	AB	R	H	2B	3B	HR	RBI	BB	SO	AVG	OBP	SLG	OPS	OPS+	BR+	SB	CS	SBR	FA	FR	G/POS	TPR
1885	NY-a	3	9	1	1	0	0	0	0	2		.111	.273	.111	384	27	-1				.682	-2	/2-3	-0.2

■ A.J. PIERZYNSKI Pierzynski, Anthony John b: 12/30/76, Bridgehampton, N.Y. BL/TR, 6'3", 218 lbs. Deb: 9/9/98

YEAR	TM/L	G	AB	R	H	2B	3B	HR	RBI	BB	SO	AVG	OBP	SLG	OPS	OPS+	BR+	SB	CS	SBR	FA	FR	G/POS	TPR
1998	Min-A	7	10	1	3	0	0	0	1	1	2	.300	.417	.300	717	89	-0	0	0	0	1.000	3	/C-6	0.3
1999	Min-A	9	22	3	6	2	0	0	3	1	4	.273	.333	.364	697	75	-1	0	0	0	1.000	-1	/C-9	-0.1
2000	Min-A	33	88	12	27	5	1	2	11	5	14	.307	.358	.455	812	99	-0	1	0	0	1.000	-1	C-32	0.0
Total	3	49	120	16	36	7	1	2	15	7	20	.300	.359	.425	784	94	-1	1	0	0	1.000	1	/C-47	0.2

■ TONY PIET Piet, Anthony Francis (b: Anthony Francis Pietruszka) b: 12/7/06, Berwick, Pa. d: 12/1/81, Hinsdale, Ill. BR/TR, 6', 175 lbs. Deb: 8/15/31 Career OF: (0-LF 0-CF 1-RF)

YEAR	TM/L	G	AB	R	H	2B	3B	HR	RBI	BB	SO	AVG	OBP	SLG	OPS	OPS+	BR+	SB	CS	SBR	FA	FR	G/POS	TPR
1931	Pit-N	44	167	22	50	12	4	0	24	13	24	.299	.354	.419	773	108	2	10			.987	-4	2-44/S-1	0.0
1932	Pit-N	154	574	66	162	25	8	7	85	46	56	.282	.343	.390	733	98	-1	19			.970	-28	*2-154	-1.8
1933	Pit-N	107	362	45	117	21	5	1	42	19	28	.323	.367	.417	784	124	11	12			.955	-5	2-97	1.3
1934	Cin-N	106	421	58	109	20	5	1	38	23	44	.259	.307	.337	644	74	-15	6			.934	-10	3-51,2-49	-2.0
1935	Cin-N	6	5	2	1	1	0	0	2	0	0	.200	.200	.400	600	59	-0	0			1.000	-0	/O-1(0-0-1)	-0.1
	Chi-A	77	292	47	87	17	5	3	27	33	27	.298	.375	.421	796	103	2	2	1	0	.975	4	2-59,3-17	0.9
1936	Chi-A	109	352	69	96	15	2	7	42	66	48	.273	.400	.386	787	92	-2	15	5	2	.966	6	2-68,3-32	0.9
1937	Chi-A	100	332	34	78	15	1	4	38	32	36	.235	.314	.322	636	61	-20	14	6	1	.939	2	3-86,2-13	-1.3
1938	Det-A	41	80	9	17	6	0	0	14	15	11	.213	.351	.287	638	58	-5	2	4	-1	.919	0	3-18/2-1	-0.5
Total	8	744	2585	352	717	132	30	23	312	247	274	.277	.350	.378	728	91	-29	80	16		.967	-37	2-485,3-204/O-1R,S	-2.6

■ SANDY PIEZ Piez, Charles William b: 10/13/1892, New York, N.Y. d: 12/29/30, Atlantic City, N.J. BR/TR, 5'10", 170 lbs. Deb: 4/17/14

YEAR	TM/L	G	AB	R	H	2B	3B	HR	RBI	BB	SO	AVG	OBP	SLG	OPS	OPS+	BR+	SB	CS	SBR	FA	FR	G/POS	TPR
1914	NY-N	37	8	9	3	0	1	0	3	0	1	.375	.375	.625	1000	202	1	4			1.000	-1	/O-5(2-2-1)	0.0

■ JOE PIGNATANO Pignatano, Joseph Benjamin b: 8/4/29, Brooklyn, N.Y. BR/TR, 5'10", 180 lbs. Deb: 4/28/57 C

YEAR	TM/L	G	AB	R	H	2B	3B	HR	RBI	BB	SO	AVG	OBP	SLG	OPS	OPS+	BR+	SB	CS	SBR	FA	FR	G/POS	TPR
1957	Bro-N	8	14	0	3	1	0	0	1	0	5	.214	.214	.286	500	30	-1	0	0	0	1.000	3	/C-6	0.2
1958	LA-N	63	142	18	31	4	0	9	17	16	26	.218	.306	.437	743	91	-2	4	1	1	1.000	10	C-57	1.0
1959	*LA-N	52	139	17	33	4	1	1	11	21	15	.237	.346	.302	648	69	-5	1	0	0	.997	7	C-49	0.4
1960	LA-N	58	90	11	21	4	0	2	9	15	17	.233	.343	.344	687	83	-2	1	1	-0	.984	15	C-40	1.5
1961	KC-A	92	243	31	59	10	3	4	22	36	42	.243	.350	.358	708	88	-3	2	2	-0	.979	1	C-83/3-2	0.1
1962	SF-N	7	5	2	1	0	0	0	0	4	0	.200	.556	.200	756	114	1	0	0	0	1.000	-1	/C-7	0.0
	NY-N	27	56	2	13	2	0	0	2	2	11	.232	.259	.268	526	41	-5	0	0	0	.991	4	C-25	0.0
	Yr	34	61	4	14	2	0	0	2	6	11	.230	.299	.262	561	51	-4	0	0	0	.992	4	C-32	0.0
Total	6	307	689	81	161	25	4	16	62	94	116	.234	.332	.351	684	80	-18	8	4	0	.990	39	C-267/3-2	3.2

■ JAY PIKE Pike, Jacob Emanuel b: Brooklyn, N.Y. BL/TL, Deb: 8/27/1877 F

YEAR	TM/L	G	AB	R	H	2B	3B	HR	RBI	BB	SO	AVG	OBP	SLG	OPS	OPS+	BR+	SB	CS	SBR	FA	FR	G/POS	TPR
1877	Har-N	1	4	0	1	0	0	0	0	0	0	.250	.250	.250	500	65	-0				.000	-1	/O-1(0-0-1)	-0.1

■ JESS PIKE Pike, Jess Willard b: 7/31/15, Dustin, Okla. d: 3/28/84, San Diego, Cal. BL/TR, 6'3", 175 lbs. Deb: 4/18/46

YEAR	TM/L	G	AB	R	H	2B	3B	HR	RBI	BB	SO	AVG	OBP	SLG	OPS	OPS+	BR+	SB	CS	SBR	FA	FR	G/POS	TPR
1946	NY-N	16	41	4	7	1	1	1	6	6	9	.171	.277	.317	594	68	-2	0			.929	-2	O-10(6-4)	-0.5

■ LIP PIKE Pike, Lipman Emanuel b: 5/25/1845, New York, N.Y. d: 10/10/1893, Brooklyn, N.Y. BL/TL, 5'8", 158 lbs. Deb: 5/9/1871 FM NA OF: (7-LF 98-CF 88-RF) Career OF: (0-LF 137-CF 0-RF)

YEAR	TM/L	G	AB	R	H	2B	3B	HR	RBI	BB	SO	AVG	OBP	SLG	OPS	OPS+	BR+	SB	CS	SBR	FA	FR	G/POS	TPR
1871	Tro-n	28	130	43	49	10	7	**4**	39	5	7	.377	.400	.654	1054	194	15	3	2	-0	.850	1	O-18R/2-7,1-4,M	1.0
1872	Bal-n	56	288	68	85	15	5	**7**	**61**	3	6	.295	.302	.455	757	124	6	8	1	1	.875	-13	O-25(6-5-16),2-24/3-9	-0.4
1873	Bal-n	56	286	71	90	14	8	**4**	50	7	4	.315	.331	.462	793	134	11	8	1	1	.704	-3	*O-56(0-2-54)/2-2	0.9
1874	Har-n	52	234	58	83	**22**	5	1	50	5	1	.355	.368	**.504**	872	168	16	4	1	1	.856	14	O-27C,S-20/2-7,3M	2.2
1875	StL-n	70	312	61	108	22	12	0	44	3	8	.346	.352	.494	846	**210**	**35**	25	10	2	.885	-2	*O-64C,2-10/3-2,S-1	2.9
1876	StL-N	63	290	55	91	19	10	1	50	8	9	.314	.341	.472	813	178	23				.896	-4	*O-62(0-62-0)/2-2	1.4
1877	Cin-N	58	262	45	78	12	4	**4**	23	9	7	.298	.321	.420	741	148	15				.802	-3	O-38C,2-22/S-2,M	1.0
1878	Cin-N	31	145	28	47	5	1	0	11	4	9	.324	.342	.372	715	149	8				.824	-4	O-31(0-31-0)	0.2
	Pro-N	5	22	4	5	0	1	0	4	1	1	.227	.261	.318	579	90	-0				.788	-3	/2-5	-0.3
	Yr	36	167	32	52	5	2	0	15	5	10	.311	.331	.365	697	140	8				.824	-7	O-31(0-31-0)/2-5	-0.1
1881	Wor-N	5	18	1	2	0	0	0	0	4	3	.111	.273	.111	384	24	-1				.647	-1	/O-5(0-5-0)	-0.3
1887	NY-a	1	4	0	0	0	0	0	0	0		.000	.000	.000	0	-99	-1	0			1.000	-0	/O-1(0-1-0)	-0.1
Total	5 n	262	1250	301	415	83	37	16	244	23	26	.332	.344	.496	840	161	84	48	15	5	.835	-3	O-190C/2-50,S-21,31	6.6
Total	5	163	741	133	223	36	16	5	88	26	29	.301	.328	.417	746	152	44	0			.833	-15	O-137C/2-29,S-2	1.9

■ AL PILARCIK Pilarcik, Alfred James b: 7/3/30, Whiting, Ind. BL/TL, 5'10", 180 lbs. Deb: 7/13/56

YEAR	TM/L	G	AB	R	H	2B	3B	HR	RBI	BB	SO	AVG	OBP	SLG	OPS	OPS+	BR+	SB	CS	SBR	FA	FR	G/POS	TPR
1956	KC-A	69	239	28	60	10	1	4	22	30	32	.251	.335	.351	686	81	-6	9	2	1	.976	3	O-67(0-64-3)	-0.5
1957	Bal-A	142	407	52	113	16	3	9	49	53	28	.278	.366	.398	764	116	10	14	7	1	.996	0	*O-126(2-54-79)	0.6
1958	Bal-A	141	379	40	92	21	0	1	24	42	37	.243	.322	.306	628	78	-11	7	3	0	.986	-14	*O-119(4-32-104)	-2.9
1959	Bal-A	130	273	37	77	12	1	3	16	30	25	.282	.355	.366	722	101	1	9	3	1	.978	-16	*O-106(3-8-102)	-1.6
1960	Bal-A	104	194	30	48	5	1	4	17	15	16	.247	.315	.345	660	79	-6	0	2	-1	1.000	-11	O-75(0-2-74)	-1.9
1961	KC-A	35	60	9	12	1	1	0	9	6	7	.200	.273	.250	523	40	-5	1	0	0	1.000	-1	O-21(0-2-19)	-0.7
	Chi-A	47	62	9	11	1	0	1	6	9	5	.177	.282	.242	524	42	-5	1	1	-0	.944	-0	O-17(2-14-1)	-0.6
	Yr	82	122	18	23	2	1	1	15	15	12	.189	.277	.246	523	41	-10	2	1	0	.971	-1	O-38(2-16-20)	-1.3
Total	6	668	1614	205	413	66	7	22	143	185	150	.256	.336	.346	683	89	-22	41	18	3	.986	-39	O-531(11-176-382)	-7.6

■ ANDY PILNEY Pilney, Antone James b: 1/19/13, Frontenac, Kan. d: 9/15/96, Kenner, La. BR/TR, 5'11", 174 lbs. Deb: 6/12/36

YEAR	TM/L	G	AB	R	H	2B	3B	HR	RBI	BB	SO	AVG	OBP	SLG	OPS	OPS+	BR+	SB	CS	SBR	FA	FR	G/POS	TPR
1936	Bos-N	3	2	0	0	0	0	0	0	0	1	.000	.000	.000	0	-99	-1	0			.000	0	H	-0.1

■ BABE PINELLI Pinelli, Ralph Arthur (b: Rinaldo Angelo Paolinelli) b: 10/18/1895, San Francisco, Cal d: 10/22/84, Daly City, Cal. BR/TR, 5'9", 165 lbs. Deb: 8/3/18 U

YEAR	TM/L	G	AB	R	H	2B	3B	HR	RBI	BB	SO	AVG	OBP	SLG	OPS	OPS+	BR+	SB	CS	SBR	FA	FR	G/POS	TPR
1918	Chi-A	24	78	7	18	1	1	1	7	7	8	.231	.302	.308	610	83	-2	3			.847	-7	3-24	-0.9
1920	Det-A	102	284	33	65	9	3	0	21	25	16	.229	.296	.282	578	55	-18	6	8	-1	.954	20	3-74,S-18/2-1	0.3

YEAR	TM/L	G	AB	R	H	2B	3B	HR	RBI	BB	SO	AVG	OBP	SLG	OPS	OPS+	BR+	SB	CS	SBR	FA	FR	G/POS	TPR
1922	Cin-N	156	547	77	167	19	7	1	72	48	37	.305	.368	.371	739	93	-4	17	22	-4	.945	21	*3-156	2.1
1923	Cin-N	117	423	44	117	14	5	0	51	27	29	.277	.320	.333	653	74	-16	10	14	-3	.938	9	*3-116	-0.2
1924	Cin-N	144	510	61	156	16	7	0	70	32	32	.306	.353	.365	718	94	-4	23	17	-1	.956	**27**	*3-143	3.1
1925	Cin-N	130	492	68	139	33	6	2	49	22	28	.283	.316	.386	702	80	-15	8	19	-5	.945	21	*3-109,S-17	0.9
1926	Cin-N	71	207	26	46	7	4	0	24	15	5	.222	.284	.295	579	58	-12	2			.978	1	3-40,S-27/2-3	-0.7
1927	Cin-N	30	76	11	15	2	0	1	4	6	7	.197	.265	.263	528	43	-6	2			.968	-1	3-15/S-9,2-5	-0.6
Total	8	774	2617	327	723	101	33	5	298	182	162	.276	.328	.346	674	79	-77	71	80		.947	91	3-677/S-71,2-9	4.0

■ LOU PINIELLA

Piniella, Louis Victor b: 8/28/43, Tampa, Fla. BR/TR, 6'2", 198 lbs. Deb: 9/4/64 MC Career OF: (1126-LF 6-CF 275-RF)

YEAR	TM/L	G	AB	R	H	2B	3B	HR	RBI	BB	SO	AVG	OBP	SLG	OPS	OPS+	BR+	SB	CS	SBR	FA	FR	G/POS	TPR
1964	Bal-A	4	1	0	0	0	0	0	0	0	0	.000	.000	.000	0	-99	-0	0	0	0	.000	0	H	0.0
1968	Cle-A	6	5	1	0	0	0	0	1	0	0	.000	.000	.000	0	-99	-1	0	0	0	1.000	-0	/O-2(2-0-0)	-0.2
1969	KC-A	135	493	43	139	21	6	11	68	33	56	.282	.331	.416	747	107	3	2	4	-1	.977	15	*O-129(126-3-0)	1.1
1970	KC-A	144	542	54	163	24	5	11	88	35	42	.301	.345	.424	770	111	7	3	6	-1	.984	4	*O-139(139-0-0)/1-1	0.2
1971	KC-A	126	448	43	125	21	5	3	51	21	43	.279	.314	.368	683	94	-5	5	3	0	.986	1	*O-115(115-0-0)	-1.2
1972	KC-A★	151	574	65	179	**33**	4	11	72	34	59	.312	.359	.441	800	138	25	7	2	1	.976	3	*O-150(150-0-0)	2.3
1973	KC-A	144	513	53	128	28	1	9	69	30	65	.250	.294	.361	654	77	-16	5	7	-1	.986	-5	*O-128(128-0-0)/D-9	-3.1
1974	NY-A	140	518	71	158	26	0	9	70	32	58	.305	.348	.407	755	119	12	1	8	-3	.989	11	*O-130L/1-1,D-6	1.4
1975	NY-A	74	199	7	39	4	1	0	22	16	22	.196	.266	.226	492	41	-15	0	0	0	.986	-3	O-46(15-0-31),D-12	-2.1
1976	*NY-A	100	327	36	92	16	6	3	38	18	34	.281	.323	.394	717	110	3	0	1	-0	.982	2	O-49(10-0-39),D-38	0.1
1977	*NY-A	103	339	47	112	19	3	12	45	20	31	.330	.369	.510	880	138	17	2	2	-0	.975	-4	O-51R,D-43/1-1	0.9
1978	*NY-A	130	472	67	148	34	5	6	69	34	36	.314	.362	.445	807	129	17	3	1	0	.969	2	*O-103(78-2-25),D-23	1.5
1979	NY-A	130	461	49	137	22	2	11	69	17	31	.297	.325	.425	750	103	1	3	2	-0	.982	3	*O-112(84-0-29),D-16	-0.2
1980	*NY-A	116	321	39	92	18	0	2	27	29	20	.287	.346	.361	707	96	-1	0	2	-1	.971	-7	*O-104(102-1-1)/D-7	-1.3
1981	*NY-A	60	159	16	44	9	0	5	18	13	9	.277	.331	.428	759	119	4	0	1	-0	.986	1	O-36(11-0-25),D-19	0.2
1982	NY-A	102	261	33	80	17	1	6	37	18	18	.307	.354	.448	802	120	7	0	1	-0	1.000	-1	D-55,O-40(13-0-27)	0.2
1983	NY-A	53	148	19	43	9	1	2	16	11	12	.291	.344	.405	749	109	2	0	1	-0	.959	-2	O-43(15-0-28)/D-1	-0.2
1984	NY-A	29	86	8	26	4	1	1	6	7	5	.302	.355	.407	762	115	2	0	0	0	1.000	1	O-24(15-0-9)/D-2	0.1
Total	18	1747	5867	651	1705	305	41	102	766	368	541	.291	.336	.409	745	109	61	32	41	-7	.981	21	*O-1401L,D-231/1-3	-0.3

■ ED PINKHAM

Pinkham, Edward b: 1849, Brooklyn, N.Y. TL, 5'7", 142 lbs. Deb: 5/8/1871

YEAR	TM/L	G	AB	R	H	2B	3B	HR	RBI	BB	SO	AVG	OBP	SLG	OPS	OPS+	BR+	SB	CS	SBR	FA	FR	G/POS	TPR
1871	Chi-n	24	95	27	25	5	5	1	17	**18**	3	.263	.381	.453	833	125	2	5	2	0	.754	9	3-18/O-8(0-0-8),P-3	0.8

■ GEORGE PINKNEY

Pinkney, George Burton b: 1/11/1862, Orange Prairie, Ill. d: 11/10/26, Peoria, Ill. BR/TR, 5'7", 160 lbs. Deb: 8/16/1884

YEAR	TM/L	G	AB	R	H	2B	3B	HR	RBI	BB	SO	AVG	OBP	SLG	OPS	OPS+	BR+	SB	CS	SBR	FA	FR	G/POS	TPR
1884	Cle-N	36	144	18	45	9	0	0	16	10	7	.313	.357	.375	732	126	4				.848	-8	2-25,S-11	-0.2
1885	Bro-a	110	447	77	124	16	5	0	42	27		.277	.328	.336	664	109	5				.904	-11	2-57,3-51/S-3	-0.2
1886	Bro-a	141	597	119	156	22	7	0	37	**70**		.261	.339	.322	660	106	6	32			.858	-16	*3-141/P-1	-0.6
1887	Bro-a	138	641	133	216	26	6	3	69	61		.337	.343	.348	691	92	-6	59			**.890**	13	*3-136/S-2	0.8
1888	Bro-a	143	575	**134**	156	18	8	4	52	66		.271	.358	.351	710	128	21	51			.898	-26	*3-143	-0.2
1889	*Bro-a	138	545	103	134	25	7	4	82	59	43	.246	.327	.339	667	90	-7	47			**.897**	-8	*3-138	-1.1
1890	*Bro-N	126	485	115	150	20	9	7	83	80	19	.309	.411	.431	842	145	30	47			.933	-15	*3-126	1.6
1891	Bro-N	135	501	80	137	19	6	2	71	67	32	.273	.367	.347	714	109	8	44			.904	-20	*3-130/S-5	-0.8
1892	StL-N	78	290	31	50	3	2	0	25	36	26	.172	.268	.197	465	43	-18	4			.888	-8	3-78	-2.4
1893	Lou-N	118	446	64	105	12	6	1	62	50	8	.235	.323	.296	619	71	-17	12			.923	-2	*3-118	-1.4
Total	10	1163	4671	874	1273	170	56	21	539	526	135	.273	.345	.338	683	103	27	296			.897	-99	*3-1061/2-82,S-21,P	-4.5

■ VADA PINSON

Pinson, Vada Edward b: 8/11/38, Memphis, Tenn. d: 10/21/95, Oakland, Cal. BL/TL, 5'11", 181 lbs. Deb: 4/15/58 C Career OF: (234-LF 1676-CF 549-RF)

YEAR	TM/L	G	AB	R	H	2B	3B	HR	RBI	BB	SO	AVG	OBP	SLG	OPS	OPS+	BR+	SB	CS	SBR	FA	FR	G/POS	TPR
1958	Cin-N	27	96	20	26	7	0	1	8	11	18	.271	.352	.375	727	88	-1	2	1	0	1.000	2	O-27(4-5-18)	0.0
1959	Cin-N★	154	648	**131**	205	**47**	9	20	84	55	98	.316	.371	.509	880	128	25	21	6	3	.984	20	*O-154(0-154-0)	4.0
1960	Cin-N★	154	652	107	187	**37**	12	20	61	47	96	.287	.339	.472	812	117	14	32	12	3	.981	9	*O-154(0-154-0)	2.0
1961	*Cin-N	154	607	101	**208**	34	8	16	87	39	63	.343	.383	.504	887	131	27	23	10	2	.976	19	*O-153(0-153-0)	4.2
1962	Cin-N	155	619	107	181	31	7	23	100	45	68	.292	.344	.477	821	114	11	26	8	3	.989	7	*O-152(0-152-0)	1.7
1963	Cin-N	162	652	96	**204**	37	**14**	22	106	36	80	.313	.350	.514	864	141	32	27	8	3	.979	9	*O-162(0-147-17)	4.1
1964	Cin-N	156	625	99	166	23	11	23	84	42	99	.266	.317	.448	765	109	6	8	2	1	.972	4	*O-156(0-156-0)	0.7
1965	Cin-N	159	669	97	204	34	10	22	94	43	81	.305	.353	.484	838	125	21	21	8	2	**.992**	15	*O-159(0-159-0)	3.4
1966	Cin-N	156	618	70	178	35	6	16	76	33	83	.288	.329	.442	771	103	2	18	10	0	.964	5	*O-154(0-139-24)	0.2
1967	Cin-N	158	650	90	187	28	**13**	18	66	26	86	.288	.318	.454	772	106	5	26	8	3	.986	5	*O-157(0-157-0)	0.8
1968	Cin-N	130	499	60	135	29	6	5	48	32	59	.271	.315	.383	697	102	1	17	11	-0	.978	-1	*O-123(1-120-3)	-0.4
1969	StL-N	132	495	58	126	22	6	10	70	35	63	.255	.308	.384	692	92	-6	4	4	-1	**.996**	1	*O-124(0-1-124)	-1.2
1970	Cle-A	148	574	74	164	28	6	24	82	28	69	.286	.322	.481	803	113	8	7	6	-1	.982	5	*O-141(15-14-120)/1-7	0.5
1971	Cle-A	146	566	60	149	23	4	11	35	21	58	.263	.297	.376	673	82	-14	25	6	3	.978	4	*O-141(9-100-39)/1-3	-1.3
1972	Cal-A	136	484	56	133	24	2	7	49	30	54	.275	.324	.376	700	114	7	17	6	2	.991	-5	*O-134(104-15-29)/1-1	-0.4
1973	Cal-A	124	466	56	121	14	6	8	57	20	55	.260	.290	.367	657	91	-7	5	5	-1	.965	-4	*O-120(75-32-25)	-1.9
1974	KC-A	115	406	46	112	18	2	6	41	21	45	.276	.315	.374	689	92	-4	21	5	3	.980	-5	*O-110R/1-1,D-2	-1.3
1975	KC-A	103	319	38	71	14	5	4	22	10	21	.223	.251	.335	586	63	-17	5	6	-1	.993	-3	O-82R/1-4,D-5	-2.5
Total	18	2469	9645	1366	2757	485	127	256	1170	574	1196	.286	.330	.442	772	110	110	305	122	24	.981	87	*O-2403C/1-16,D-7	12.6

■ WALLY PIPP

Pipp, Walter Clement b: 2/17/1893, Chicago, Ill. d: 1/11/65, Grand Rapids, Mich BL/TL, 6'1", 180 lbs. Deb: 6/29/13

YEAR	TM/L	G	AB	R	H	2B	3B	HR	RBI	BB	SO	AVG	OBP	SLG	OPS	OPS+	BR+	SB	CS	SBR	FA	FR	G/POS	TPR
1913	Det-A	12	31	3	5	0	3	0	5	2	6	.161	.235	.355	590	73	-1	0			.977	-1	1-10	-0.2
1915	NY-A	136	479	59	118	20	13	4	60	66	81	.246	.339	.367	706	112	7	18	7	2	**.992**	3	*1-134	0.8
1916	NY-A	151	545	70	143	20	14	**12**	93	54	82	.262	.331	.417	748	122	12	16			.992	6	*1-148	1.5
1917	NY-A	155	587	82	143	29	12	**9**	70	60	66	.244	.320	.380	700	112	7	11			.990	4	*1-155	0.8
1918	NY-A	91	349	48	106	15	9	2	44	22	34	.304	.345	.415	760	127	9	11			.988	0	1-91	0.8
1919	NY-A	138	523	74	144	23	10	7	50	39	42	.275	.330	.398	728	103	1	9			.991	1	*1-138	-0.2
1920	NY-A	153	610	109	171	30	14	11	76	48	54	.280	.339	.430	768	99	-3	4	10	-3	.991	0	*1-153	-0.9
1921	*NY-A	153	588	96	174	35	9	8	97	45	28	.296	.347	.427	774	94	-6	17	10	-1	.991	-4	*1-153	-1.9
1922	*NY-A	152	577	96	190	32	10	9	90	56	32	.329	.392	.466	859	120	18	7	12	-3	.993	-5	*1-152	0.0
1923	*NY-A	144	569	79	173	19	8	6	108	36	28	.304	.352	.397	749	95	-5	6	13	-3	.992	-4	*1-144	-2.0
1924	NY-A	153	589	88	174	30	**19**	9	114	51	36	.295	.352	.457	808	108	4	12	5	1	**.994**	2	*1-153	-0.3
1925	NY-A	62	178	19	41	6	3	3	24	13	12	.230	.286	.348	635	61	-11	3	3	-0	.991	4	1-47	-1.0
1926	Cin-N	155	574	72	167	22	15	6	99	49	26	.291	.352	.413	765	108	6	8			.992	2	*1-155	-0.2
1927	Cin-N	122	443	49	115	19	6	2	41	32	11	.260	.309	.343	653	77	-15	2			**.996**	0	*1-114	-2.2
1928	Cin-N	95	272	30	77	11	3	2	26	23	13	.283	.341	.368	709	87	-5	1			.989	1	1-72	-0.8
Total	15	1872	6914	974	1941	311	148	90	997	596	551	.281	.341	.408	749	104	18	125	60		.992	9	*1-1819	-5.8

■ JIM PIRIE

Pirie, James Moir b: 3/31/1853, Ontario, Canada d: 6/2/34, Dundas, Ont., Can. 5'8", 169 lbs. Deb: 9/25/1883

YEAR	TM/L	G	AB	R	H	2B	3B	HR	RBI	BB	SO	AVG	OBP	SLG	OPS	OPS+	BR+	SB	CS	SBR	FA	FR	G/POS	TPR
1883	Phi-N	5	19	1	3	0	0	0	0	0	2	.158	.158	.158	316	-4	-2				.577	-4	/S-5	-0.6

■ GREG PIRKL

Pirkl, Gregory Daniel b: 8/7/70, Long Beach, Cal. BR/TR, 6'5", 225 lbs. Deb: 8/13/93

YEAR	TM/L	G	AB	R	H	2B	3B	HR	RBI	BB	SO	AVG	OBP	SLG	OPS	OPS+	BR+	SB	CS	SBR	FA	FR	G/POS	TPR
1993	Sea-A	7	23	1	4	0	0	1	4	0	4	.174	.174	.304	478	25	-2	0	0	0	1.000	1	/1-5,D-2	-0.2
1994	Sea-A	19	53	7	14	3	0	6	11	1	12	.264	.291	.660	951	133	2	0	0	0	.983	-1	D-10/1-7	0.0
1995	Sea-A	10	17	2	4	0	0	0	0	1	7	.235	.278	.235	513	35	-2	0	0	0	1.000	1	/1-6,D-1	-0.1
1996	Sea-A	7	21	2	4	1	0	1	1	0	3	.190	.190	.381	571	40	-2	0	0	0	1.000	0	/1-2,D-3	-0.2
	Bos-A	2	2	0	0	0	0	0	0	0	1	.000	.000	.000		-98	-1	0	0	0	.000	0	/H	-0.1
	Yr	9	23	2	4	1	0	1	1	0	4	.174	.174	.348	522	27	-3	0	0	0	1.000	0	/D-3,1-2	-0.3
Total	4	45	116	12	26	4	0	8	16	2	27	.224	.244	.466	709	77	-5	0	0	0	.994	0	/1-20,D-16	-0.6

■ JIM PISONI

Pisoni, James Pete b: 8/14/29, St.Louis, Mo. BR/TR, 5'10", 169 lbs. Deb: 9/25/53

YEAR	TM/L	G	AB	R	H	2B	3B	HR	RBI	BB	SO	AVG	OBP	SLG	OPS	OPS+	BR+	SB	CS	SBR	FA	FR	G/POS	TPR
1953	StL-A	3	12	1	1	0	0	1	1	0	5	.083	.083	.333	417	8	-2	0	0	0	1.000	-0	/O-3(0-2-1)	-0.2
1956	KC-A	10	30	4	8	0	0	2	5	2	8	.267	.313	.467	779	103	-0	0	0	0	.966	4	/O-9(9-0-0)	0.4
1957	KC-A	44	97	14	23	2	2	3	12	10	17	.237	.321	.392	713	92	-1	0	0	0	.989	-3	O-44(0-44-1)	-0.5
1959	Mil-N	9	24	4	4	1	0	0	0	2	6	.167	.231	.208	439	20	-3	0	0	0	.941	-1	/O-9(2-8-0)	-0.4

YEAR	TM/L	G	AB	R	H	2B	3B	HR	RBI	BB	SO	AVG	OBP	SLG	OPS	OPS+	BR+	SB	CS	SBR	FA	FR	G/POS	TPR
	NY-A	17	17	2	3	0	1	0	1	1	9	.176	.222	.294	516	42	-1	0	0	0	1.000	-3	O-15(9-3-3)	-0.4
1960	NY-A	20	9	1	1	0	0	0	1	1	2	.111	.200	.111	311	-14	-1	0	0	0	.938	-5	O-18(12-6-0)	-0.7
Total	5	103	189	26	40	3	3	6	20	16	47	.212	.280	.354	635	71	-8	0	0	0	.978	-7	/O-98(32-63-5)	-1.8
■ ALEX PITKO	Pitko, Alexander "Spunk" b: 11/22/14, Burlington, N.J. BR/TR, 5'10", 180 lbs. Deb: 9/11/38																							
1938	Phi-N	7	19	2	6	1	0	0	2	3	3	.316	.409	.368	778	118	1	1			.889	-2	/O-7(0-0-7)	-0.1
1939	Was-A	4	8	0	1	0	0	0	1	1	3	.125	.222	.125	347	-10	-1	0	0	0	1.000	-1	/O-3(2-0-1)	-0.2
Total	2	11	27	2	7	1	0	0	3	4	6	.259	.355	.296	651	80	-1	1	0		.917	-3	/O-10(2-0-8)	-0.3
■ JAKE PITLER	Pitler, Jacob Albert b: 4/22/1894, New York, N.Y. d: 2/3/68, Binghamton, N.Y. BR/TR, 5'8", 150 lbs. Deb: 5/30/17 C																							
1917	Pit-N	109	382	39	89	8	5	0	23	30	24	.233	.297	.280	577	75	-10	6			**.966**	-12	*2-106/O-3(1-0-1)	-2.3
1918	Pit-N	2	1	1	0	0	0	0	0	1	0	.000	.500	.000	500	55	0	2			.667	0	/2-1	0.1
Total	2	111	383	40	89	8	5	0	23	31	24	.232	.298	.279	578	75	-10	8			.962	-11	2-107/O-3(1-0-1)	-2.2
■ CHRIS PITTARO	Pittaro, Christopher Francis b: 9/16/61, Trenton, N.J. BB/TR, 5'11", 170 lbs. Deb: 4/8/85																							
1985	Det-A	28	62	10	15	3	1	0	7	5	13	.242	.299	.323	621	71	-2	1	1	-0	.881	-1	3-22/2-4,D-1	-0.3
1986	Min-A	11	21	0	2	0	0	0	0	0	8	.095	.095	.095	190	-47	-4	0	0	0	.969	2	/2-8,S-4	-0.2
1987	Min-A	14	12	6	4	0	0	0	0	1	0	.333	.385	.333	718	90	-0	1	0	0	1.000	2	/2-8,D-2	0.2
Total	3	53	95	16	21	3	1	0	7	6	21	.221	.267	.274	541	48	-7	2	1	0	.968	4	/3-22,2-20,S-4,D-3	-0.3
■ PINKY PITTINGER	Pittinger, Clarke Alonzo b: 2/24/1899, Hudson, Mich. d: 11/4/77, Ft.Lauderdale, Fla. BR/TR, 5'10", 160 lbs. Deb: 4/15/21																							
1921	Bos-A	40	91	6	18	1	0	0	5	4	13	.198	.232	.209	440	13	-12	3	2	-0	.985	3	O-27L/3-3,S-2,2-1	-1.0
1922	Bos-A	66	186	16	48	3	0	0	7	9	10	.258	.299	.274	574	51	-13	2	5	-1	.920	5	3-33,S-29	-0.5
1923	Bos-A	60	177	15	38	5	0	0	15	5	10	.215	.236	.243	479	26	-19	3	1	0	.959	-11	2-42,S-10/3-3	-2.8
1925	Chi-N	59	173	21	54	7	2	0	15	12	7	.312	.364	.376	739	88	-3	5	4	-0	.940	4	S-24,3-24	0.4
1927	Cin-N	31	84	17	23	5	0	1	10	2	5	.274	.291	.369	660	78	-3	4			.963	3	2-20/S-9,3-2	0.1
1928	Cin-N	40	38	12	9	0	1	0	4	0	1	.237	.237	.289	526	37	-4	2			.892	8	S-12/2-4,3-4	0.5
1929	Cin-N	77	210	31	62	11	0	0	27	5	4	.295	.318	.348	666	68	-11	8			.956	2	S-50/3-8,2-4	-0.3
Total	7	373	959	118	252	32	3	1	83	37	50	.263	.294	.306	600	55	-64	27	12		.938	13	S-136/3-77,2-71,O	-3.6
■ JOE PITTMAN	Pittman, Joseph Wayne b: 1/1/54, Houston, Tex. BR/TR, 6'1", 180 lbs. Deb: 4/25/81 Career OF: (0-LF 0-CF 1-RF)																							
1981	*Hou-N	52	135	11	38	4	2	0	7	11	16	.281	.336	.341	676	97	-1	4	4	-1	.980	-9	2-35/3-4	-0.9
1982	Hou-N	15	10	0	2	1	0	0	0	0	2	.200	.200	.300	500	41	-1	0	0	0	1.000	0	/3-3,O-1(0-0-1)	-0.1
	SD-N	55	118	16	30	2	0	0	7	9	13	.254	.307	.271	578	66	-5	8	3	1	.964	-3	2-30,S-13	-0.5
	Yr	70	128	16	32	3	0	0	7	9	15	.250	.299	.273	573	65	-6	8	3	1	.964	-2	2-30,S-13/3-3,O-1R	-0.6
1984	SF-N	17	22	2	5	0	0	0	2	0	6	.227	.227	.227	455	29	-2	1	1	-0	.900	-2	/S-6,2-5,3-2	-0.4
Total	3	139	285	29	75	7	2	0	16	20	37	.263	.311	.302	613	77	-9	13	8	0	.974	-14	/2-70,S-19,3-9,O-1R	-1.9
■ GAYLEN PITTS	Pitts, Gaylen Richard b: 6/6/46, Wichita, Kan. BR/TR, 6'1", 175 lbs. Deb: 5/12/74 C																							
1974	Oak-A	18	41	4	10	3	0	0	3	5	4	.244	.326	.317	643	92	-0	0	0	0	.909	0	3-11/2-6,1-1	0.0
1975	Oak-A	10	3	1	1	1	0	0	1	0	0	.333	.333	.667	1000	181	0	0	0	0	.800	2	/3-6,S-2,2-1	0.2
Total	2	28	44	5	11	4	0	0	4	5	4	.250	.327	.341	667	98	-0	0	0	0	.895	2	/3-17,2-7,S-2,1-1	0.2
■ HERMAN PITZ	Pitz, Herman b: 7/18/1865, Brooklyn, N.Y. d: 9/3/24, Far Rockaway, N.Y. 5'6", 140 lbs. Deb: 4/18/1890																							
1890	Bro-a	61	189	26	26	0	0	0	6	45		.138	.312	.138	450	34	-13	25			.885	-7	C-34,3-16/O-9L,S2	-1.4
	Syr-a	29	95	17	21	0	0	0	3	13		.221	.321	.221	542	67	-3	14			.929	-5	C-27/S-1,O-1(0-1-0)	-0.5
	Yr	90	284	43	47	0	0	0	9	58		.165	.315	.165	481	44	-16	39			.906	-12	C-61,3-16,O-10L,/S2	-1.9
■ PHIL PLANTIER	Plantier, Phillip Alan b: 1/27/69, Manchester, N.H. BL/TR, 5'11", 195 lbs. Deb: 8/21/90																							
1990	Bos-A	14	15	1	2	1	0	0	3	4	6	.133	.350	.200	550	55	-1	0	0	0	.000	-0	/O-1(1-0-0),D-4	-0.1
1991	Bos-A	53	148	27	49	7	1	11	35	23	38	.331	.424	.615	1039	175	15	1	0	0	.976	-0	O-40(16-0-27)/D-5	1.4
1992	Bos-A	108	349	46	86	19	0	7	30	44	83	.246	.334	.361	695	89	-5	2	3	-1	.975	2	O-76(13-0-63),D-23	-0.6
1993	SD-N	138	462	67	111	20	1	34	100	61	124	.240	.338	.509	846	121	13	4	5	-1	.990	14	*O-134(134-0-0)	2.1
1994	SD-N	96	341	44	75	21	0	18	41	36	91	.220	.304	.440	744	93	-5	3	1	0	.988	6	O-91(91-0-0)	-0.1
1995	Hou-N	22	68	12	17	2	0	4	15	11	19	.250	.363	.456	818	123	2	0	0	0	.962	-3	O-20(8-0-12)	-0.1
	SD-N	54	148	21	38	4	0	5	19	17	29	.257	.333	.385	718	92	-2	1	1	-0	.958	4	O-39(39-0-0)	0.1
	Yr	76	216	33	55	6	0	9	34	28	48	.255	.343	.407	750	101	1	1	1	-0	.959	2	O-59(47-0-12)	0.0
1996	Oak-A	73	231	29	49	8	1	7	31	28	56	.212	.305	.346	652	66	-12	2	2	-0	.973	4	O-68(67-1-1)/D-1	-1.0
1997	SD-N	10	8	0	1	0	0	0	0	2	3	.125	.300	.125	425	18	-1	0	0	0	1.000	-1	/O-3(3-0-0)	-0.1
	StL-N	42	113	13	29	8	0	5	18	11	27	.257	.339	.460	799	108	1	0	3	-1	.981	-1	O-32(10-0-23)	-0.2
	Yr	52	121	13	30	8	0	5	18	13	30	.248	.336	.438	774	103	0	0	3	-1	.982	-2	O-35(13-0-23)	-0.3
Total	8	610	1883	260	457	90	3	91	292	237	476	.243	.335	.439	773	103	7	13	15	-2	.980	25	O-504(382-1-126)/D-33	1.4
■ DON PLARSKI	Plarski, Donald Joseph b: 11/9/29, Chicago, Ill. d: 12/29/81, St.Louis, Mo. BR/TR, 5'6", 160 lbs. Deb: 7/20/55																							
1955	KC-A	8	11	0	1	0	0	0	0	0	2	.091	.091	.091	182	-50	-2	1	0	0	1.000	-2	/O-6(0-6-0)	-0.4
■ ELMO PLASKETT	Plaskett, Elmo Alexander b: 6/27/38, Frederiksted, V.I. d: 11/2/98, Christiansted, V.I. BR/TR, 5'10", 195 lbs. Deb: 9/8/62																							
1962	Pit-N	7	14	2	4	0	0	1	3	1	3	.286	.333	.500	833	120	0	0	0	0	1.000	-1	/C-4	-0.1
1963	Pit-N	10	21	1	3	0	0	0	2	0	5	.143	.143	.143	286	-17	-3	0	0	0	1.000	-2	/C-5,3-1	-0.5
Total	2	17	35	3	7	0	0	1	5	1	8	.200	.222	.286	508	41	-3	0	0	0	1.000	-3	/C-9,3-1	-0.6
■ WHITEY PLATT	Platt, Mizell George b: 8/21/20, W.Palm Beach, Fla. d: 7/27/70, W.Palm Beach, Fla BR/TR, 6'2", 195 lbs. Deb: 9/16/42																							
1942	Chi-N	4	16	1	1	0	0	0	2	0	3	.063	.063	.063	125	-66	-3	0			1.000	0	/O-4(2-2-0)	-0.4
1943	Chi-N	20	41	2	7	3	0	0	2	1	7	.171	.190	.244	434	25	-4	0			.952	-3	O-14(7-7-0)	-0.9
1946	Chi-A	84	247	28	62	8	5	3	32	17	34	.251	.307	.360	667	89	-4	1	7	-2	.971	-3	O-61(25-23-14)	-1.3
1948	StL-A	123	454	57	123	22	10	7	82	39	51	.271	.331	.410	741	94	-6	1	4	-1	.948	-6	*O-114(114-0-0)	-2.1
1949	StL-A	102	244	29	63	8	2	3	29	24	27	.258	.325	.344	669	74	-10	0	1	-0	.986	0	O-59(59-0-0)/1-2	-1.3
Total	5	333	1002	117	256	41	17	13	147	81	122	.255	.314	.369	684	83	-27	2	12		.964	-12	O-252(207-32-14)/1-2	-6.0
■ AL PLATTE	Platte, Alfred Frederick Joseph b: 4/13/1890, Grand Rapids, Mich d: 8/29/76, Grand Rapids, Mich BL/TL, 5'7", 160 lbs. Deb: 9/1/13																							
1913	Det-A	9	18	1	2	1	0	0	0	1	1	.111	.158	.167	325	-5	-2	0			.800	-1	/O-5(5-0-0)	-0.4
■ RANCE PLESS	Pless, Rance b: 12/6/25, Greeneville, Tenn. BR/TR, 6', 145 lbs. Deb: 4/21/56																							
1956	KC-A	48	85	4	23	3	1	0	9	10	13	.271	.354	.329	684	81	-2	0	1	-0	1.000	2	1-15/3-5	-0.1
■ HERB PLEWS	Plews, Herbert Eugene b: 6/14/28, Helena, Mont. BL/TR, 5'11", 160 lbs. Deb: 4/18/56																							
1956	Was-A	91	256	24	69	10	7	1	25	26	40	.270	.339	.375	714	88	-4	1	2	-0	.947	-3	2-66/S-5,3-2	-0.4
1957	Was-A	104	329	51	89	19	4	1	26	28	39	.271	.331	.362	693	90	-4	0	3	-1	.979	-15	2-79,3-11/S-4	-1.5
1958	Was-A	111	380	46	98	12	6	2	29	17	45	.258	.291	.337	628	74	-14	2	3	-1	.976	-21	2-64,3-36	-3.2
1959	Was-A	27	40	4	9	0	0	0	2	3	5	.225	.279	.225	504	40	-3	0	1	-0	.971	1	/2-6	-0.2
	Bos-A	13	12	0	1	1	0	0	0	0	4	.083	.083	.167	250	-32	-2	0	0	0	.833	1	/2-2	-0.1
	Yr	40	52	4	10	1	0	0	2	3	9	.192	.236	.212	448	24	-5	0	1	-0	.951	2	/2-8	-0.3
Total	4	346	1017	125	266	42	17	4	82	74	133	.262	.314	.348	662	80	-28	3	9	-2	.967	-36	2-217/3-49,S-9	-5.4
■ WALTER PLOCK	Plock, Walter S. b: 7/2/1869, Philadelphia, Pa. d: 4/28/1900, Richmond, Va. 6'3", 180 lbs. Deb: 8/21/1891																							
1891	Phi-N	2	5	2	2	0	0	0	0	0	1	.400	.500	.400	900	159	0	0			.000	-1	/O-2(0-2-0)	-0.1
■ BILL PLUMMER	Plummer, William Francis b: 3/21/47, Oakland, Cal. BR/TR, 6'1", 200 lbs. Deb: 4/19/68 MC																							
1968	Chi-N	2	2	0	0	0	0	0	0	0	1	.000	.000	.000	0	-94	-0	0	0	0	1.000	0	/C-1	0.0
1970	Cin-N	4	8	0	1	0	0	0	0	0	2	.125	.222	.125	347	-4	-1	0	0	0	.857	-2	/C-4	-0.3
1971	Cin-N	10	19	0	0	0	0	0	0	0	4	.000	.000	.000	0	-99	-5	0	0	0	1.000	0	/C-4,3-2	-0.5
1972	Cin-N	38	102	8	19	4	0	2	9	4	20	.186	.217	.284	501	44	-8	0	0	0	.994	0	C-36/1-1,3-1	-0.7
1973	Cin-N	50	119	8	18	3	0	2	11	18	26	.151	.268	.227	495	41	-9	1	0	0	.994	-1	C-42/3-5	-0.9

YEAR	TM/L	G	AB	R	H	2B	3B	HR	RBI	BB	SO	AVG	OBP	SLG	OPS	OPS+	BR+	SB	CS	SBR	FA	FR	G/POS	TPR
1974	Cin-N	50	120	7	27	7	0	2	10	6	21	.225	.262	.333	595	67	-6	1	0	0	.974	5	C-49/3-1	0.1
1975	Cin-N	65	159	17	29	7	0	1	19	24	28	.182	.297	.245	543	51	-10	1	0	0	.990	-3	C-63	-1.1
1976	Cin-N	56	153	16	38	6	1	4	19	14	36	.248	.311	.379	690	93	-2	0	2	-1	.977	6	C-54	0.6
1977	Cin-N	51	117	10	16	5	0	1	7	17	34	.137	.246	.205	451	22	-13	1	1	-0	.986	-1	C-50	-1.3
1978	Sea-A	41	93	6	20	5	0	2	7	12	19	.215	.305	.333	638	80	-2	0	0	0	.978	-5	C-40	-0.7
Total	10	367	892	72	168	37	1	14	82	95	191	.188	.269	.279	549	53	-57	4	3	-0	.984	0	C-343/3-9,1-1	-4.8
■ BIFF POCOROBA	Pocoroba, Biff b: 7/25/53, Burbank, Cal. BB/TR (BL 1975 (part), 77 (PART), 80 (PART), 81-84), 5′10″, 180 lbs. Deb: 4/25/75																							
1975	Atl-N	67	188	15	48	7	1	1	22	20	11	.255	.327	.319	646	77	-5	0	0	0	.970	-4	C-62	-0.8
1976	Atl-N	54	174	16	42	7	0	0	14	19	12	.241	.316	.282	598	66	-7	1	0	0	.978	4	C-54	-0.1
1977	Atl-N	113	321	46	93	24	1	8	44	57	27	.290	.398	.445	844	113	8	3	4	-1	.989	2	*C-100	1.3
1978	Atl-N★	92	289	21	70	8	0	6	34	29	14	.242	.316	.332	648	73	-10	0	3	-1	.990	1	C-79	-0.7
1979	Atl-N	28	38	6	12	4	0	0	4	7	0	.316	.422	.421	843	122	2	1	1	-0	.933	0	/C-7	0.2
1980	Atl-N	70	83	7	22	4	0	2	8	11	11	.265	.351	.386	737	102	0	1	0	0	.934	-1	C-10	0.0
1981	Atl-N	57	122	4	22	4	0	0	8	12	15	.180	.265	.213	478	36	-10	0	0	0	.938	-5	3-21/C-9	-1.6
1982	*Atl-N	56	120	5	33	7	0	2	22	13	12	.275	.351	.383	734	101	0	0	0	0	.988	-4	C-36/3-2	-0.2
1983	Atl-N	55	120	11	32	6	0	2	16	12	7	.267	.333	.367	700	87	-2	0	0	0	.983	-3	C-34	-0.3
1984	Atl-N	4	2	1	0	0	0	0	0	2	0	.000	.500	.000	500	48	0	0	0	0	.000	0	/H	0.0
Total	10	596	1457	132	374	71	2	21	172	182	109	.257	.342	.351	693	86	-24	6	8	-1	.982	-9	C-391/3-23	-2.2
■ MIKE POEPPING	Poepping, Michael Harold b: 8/7/50, Little Falls, Minn. BR/TR, 6′6″, 230 lbs. Deb: 9/6/75																							
1975	Min-A	14	37	0	5	1	0	0	1	5	7	.135	.238	.162	400	15	-4	0	0	0	.950	-2	O-13(0-0-14)	-0.7
■ JIMMY POFAHL	Pofahl, James Willard b: 6/18/17, Faribault, Minn. d: 9/14/84, Owatonna, Minn. BR/TR, 5′11″, 185 lbs. Deb: 4/16/40																							
1940	Was-A	119	406	34	95	23	5	2	36	37	55	.234	.298	.330	628	67	-20	2	0	0	.952	-5	*S-112/2-4	-1.6
1941	Was-A	22	75	9	14	3	2	0	6	10	11	.187	.282	.280	562	52	-5	1	0	0	.934	-4	S-21	-0.7
1942	Was-A	84	283	22	59	7	2	0	28	29	30	.208	.282	.247	529	50	-18	4	3	-0	.956	1	S-49,2-15,3-14	-1.3
Total	3	225	764	65	168	33	9	2	70	76	96	.220	.290	.295	585	59	-44	7	3	0	.951	-8	S-182/2-19,3-14	-3.6
■ JOHN POFF	Poff, John William b: 10/23/52, Chillicothe, Ohio BL/TL, 6′2″, 190 lbs. Deb: 9/8/79																							
1979	Phi-N	12	19	2	2	1	0	0	1	1	4	.105	.150	.158	308	-15	-3	0	0	0	.875	-0	/O-4(4-0-0),1-1	-0.4
1980	Mil-A	19	68	7	17	1	2	1	7	3	7	.250	.282	.368	649	79	-2	0	0	0	1.000	-1	/O-7(0-0-7),1-3,D-7	-0.4
Total	2	31	87	9	19	2	2	1	8	4	11	.218	.253	.322	575	57	-5	0	0	0	.957	-1	/O-11(4-0-7),D-7,1-4	-0.8
■ AARON POINTER	Pointer, Aaron Elton "Hawk" b: 4/19/42, Little Rock, Ark. BR/TR, 6′2″, 185 lbs. Deb: 9/22/63																							
1963	Hou-N	2	5	0	1	0	0	0	0	0	1	.200	.200	.200	400	17	-1	0	0	0	1.000	-0	/O-1(0-0-1)	-0.1
1966	Hou-N	11	26	5	9	1	0	1	5	5	6	.346	.469	.500	969	182	3	1	1	-0	1.000	2	O-11(11-0-0)	0.4
1967	Hou-N	27	70	6	11	4	0	1	10	13	26	.157	.298	.257	555	62	-3	1	0	0	.951	1	O-22(22-0-0)	-0.3
Total	3	40	101	11	21	5	0	2	15	18	33	.208	.339	.317	656	91	-0	2	1	0	.966	3	/O-34(33-0-1)	0.0
■ PLACIDO POLANCO	Polanco, Placido Enrique b: 10/10/75, Santo Domingo, D.R. BR/TR, 5′10″, 168 lbs. Deb: 7/3/98																							
1998	StL-N	45	114	10	29	3	2	1	11	5	9	.254	.292	.342	634	67	-6	2	0	0	.952	11	S-28,2-14	0.7
1999	StL-N	88	220	24	61	9	3	1	19	15	24	.277	.323	.359	682	72	-9	1	3	-1	.979	-1	2-66/3-9,S-9	-0.8
2000	*StL-N	118	323	50	102	12	3	5	39	16	26	.316	.350	.418	768	93	-4	4	4	-1	.984	10	2-51,3-35,S-29,/1-1	0.9
Total	3	251	657	84	192	24	8	7	69	36	59	.292	.331	.385	716	81	-19	7	7	-1	.982	19	2-131/S-66,3-44,1-1	0.8
■ HUGH POLAND	Poland, Hugh Reid b: 1/19/13, Tompkinsville, Ky. d: 3/30/84, Guthrie, Ky. BL/TR, 5′11.5″, 185 lbs. Deb: 4/22/43																							
1943	NY-N	4	12	1	1	0	1	0	2	1	0	.083	.154	.250	404	16	-1	0			.889	-2	/C-4	-0.3
	Bos-N	44	141	5	27	7	0	0	13	4	11	.191	.214	.241	455	32	-13	0			.973	-2	C-38	-1.4
	Yr	48	153	6	28	7	1	0	15	5	11	.183	.209	.242	451	30	-14	0			.969	-4	C-42	-1.7
1944	Bos-N	8	23	1	3	1	0	0	2	0	1	.130	.130	.174	304	-14	-3	0			.939	1	/C-6	-0.2
1946	Bos-N	4	6	0	1	1	0	0	0	0	0	.167	.167	.333	500	40	-1	0			1.000	0	/C-2	0.0
1947	Phi-N	4	8	0	0	0	0	0	0	0	0	.000	.000	.000	0	-99	-2	0			1.000	1	/C-2	-0.2
	Cin-N	16	18	1	6	1	0	0	2	1	4	.333	.368	.389	757	102	0	0			.667	-1	/C-3	-0.1
	Yr	20	26	1	6	1	0	0	2	1	4	.231	.259	.269	528	41	-2	0			.867	-1	/C-5	-0.3
1948	Cin-N	3	3	0	1	0	0	0	0	0	0	.333	.333	.333	667	84	-0	0			.000	0	H	0.0
Total	5	83	211	8	39	10	1	0	19	6	16	.185	.207	.242	449	28	-20	0			.958	-4	/C-55	-2.2
■ KEVIN POLCOVICH	Polcovich, Kevin Michael b: 6/28/70, Auburn, N.Y. BR/TR, 5′9″, 170 lbs. Deb: 5/17/97																							
1997	Pit-N	84	245	37	67	16	1	4	21	21	45	.273	.353	.396	749	94	-2	2	2	-0	.969	20	S-80/2-2,3-1	2.4
1998	Pit-N	81	212	18	40	12	0	0	14	15	33	.189	.259	.245	504	33	-21	4	3	-0	.916	14	S-54,2-15/3-8	-0.2
Total	2	165	457	55	107	28	1	4	35	36	78	.234	.310	.326	636	66	-22	6	5	-0	.948	35	S-134/2-17,3-9	2.2
■ MARK POLHEMUS	Polhemus, Mark S. "Humpty Dumpty" b: 10/4/1862, Brooklyn, N.Y. d: 11/12/23, Lynn, Mass. 5′6.5″, 185 lbs. Deb: 7/13/1887																							
1887	Ind-N	20	77	6	20	1	0	0	8	2	9	.260	.260	.253	513	45	-5	4			.744	0	O-20(0-0-20)	-0.5
■ GUS POLIDOR	Polidor, Gustavo Adolfo (Gonzalez) b: 10/26/61, Caracas, Venezuela d: 4/28/95, Caracas, Venezuela BR/TR, 6′, 170 lbs. Deb: 9/7/85 Career OF: (0-LF 0-CF 1-RF)																							
1985	Cal-A	2	1	1	1	0	0	0	0	0	0	1.000	1.000	1.000	2000	452	0	0	0	0	1.000	0	/S-1,O-1(0-0-1)	0.0
1986	Cal-A	6	19	1	5	1	0	0	1	1	0	.263	.300	.316	616	69	-1	0	0	0	1.000	0	/2-4,S-1,3-1	-0.1
1987	Cal-A	63	137	12	36	3	0	2	15	2	15	.263	.279	.328	607	62	-7	0	0	0	.983	-6	S-46,3-11/2-3	-0.9
1988	Cal-A	54	81	4	12	3	0	0	4	3	11	.148	.179	.185	364	2	-11	0	0	0	.984	0	S-25,3-22/2-3,D-1	-1.0
1989	Mil-A	79	175	15	34	7	0	0	14	6	18	.194	.230	.234	464	31	-16	3	0	1	.923	3	3-30,2-29,S-21,/D-2	-1.1
1990	Mil-A	18	15	0	1	0	0	0	1	0	1	.067	.067	.067	133	-63	-3	0	0	0	1.000	2	3-14/2-2,S-2	-0.2
1993	Fla-N	7	6	0	1	1	0	0	0	0	2	.167	.167	.333	500	28	-1	0	0	0	.000	-0	/2-1,3-1	-0.1
Total	7	229	434	33	90	15	0	2	35	12	47	.207	.234	.256	490	35	-38	3	0	1	.970	-1	/S-96,3-79,2-42,DO	-3.4
■ NICK POLLY	Polly, Nicholas (b: Nicholas Joseph Polachanin) b: 4/18/17, Chicago, Ill. d: 1/17/93, Chicago, Ill. BR/TR, 5′11″, 190 lbs. Deb: 9/11/37																							
1937	Bro-N	10	18	2	4	0	0	0	2	0	1	.222	.222	.222	444	21	-2	0			.850	2	/3-7	0.0
1945	Bos-A	4	7	0	1	0	0	0	1	0	0	.143	.143	.143	286	-17	-1	0	0	0	1.000	-0	/3-2	-0.1
Total	2	14	25	2	5	0	0	0	3	0	1	.200	.200	.200	400	11	-3	0	0		.870	2	/3-9	-0.1
■ LUIS POLONIA	Polonia, Luis Andrew (Almonte) b: 10/12/64, Santiago, D.R. BL/TL, 5′8″, 152 lbs. Deb: 4/24/87 Career OF: (927-LF 87-CF 54-RF)																							
1987	Oak-A	125	435	78	125	16	10	4	49	32	64	.287	.336	.398	734	100	0	29	7	4	.979	-1	*O-104(35-69-8),D-18	0.0
1988	*Oak-A	84	288	51	84	11	4	2	27	21	40	.292	.340	.378	718	104	2	24	9	2	.988	1	O-76(76-0-1)/D-2	0.3
1989	Oak-A	59	206	31	59	6	4	1	17	9	15	.286	.316	.369	685	96	-2	13	4	1	.985	5	O-55(55-0-0)	0.3
	NY-A	66	227	39	71	11	2	2	29	16	29	.313	.363	.405	769	118	5	9	4	1	.982	4	O-53(53-0-0)/D-9	0.8
	Yr	125	433	70	130	17	6	3	46	25	44	.300	.341	.388	729	108	4	22	8	2	.984	8	*O-108(108-0-0)/D-9	1.1
1990	NY-A	11	22	2	7	0	0	0	3	0	1	.318	.318	.318	636	78	-1	1	0	0	.000	0	/D-4	-0.1
	Cal-A	109	381	50	128	7	9	2	32	25	42	.336	.378	.417	796	125	13	20	14	-1	.980	-5	O-85(73-13-0),D-11	0.4
	Yr	120	403	52	135	7	9	2	35	25	43	.335	.375	.412	787	122	12	21	14	-0	.980	-5	O-85(73-13-0),D-15	0.3
1991	Cal-A	150	604	92	179	28	8	2	50	52	74	.296	.353	.379	732	103	3	48	23	3	.981	1	*O-143(143-1-0)/D-4	0.2
1992	Cal-A	149	577	83	165	17	4	0	35	45	64	.286	.339	.329	668	87	-9	51	21	4	.980	2	O-99(99-0-0),D-47	-0.8
1993	Cal-A	152	576	75	156	17	6	1	32	48	53	.271	.329	.326	655	74	-20	55	24	4	.983	8	*O-141(141-0-0)/D-4	-1.1
1994	NY-A	95	350	62	109	21	6	1	36	37	36	.311	.384	.414	798	110	6	20	12	0	.976	2	O-84(84-0-0)/D-2	0.6
1995	NY-A	67	238	37	62	9	3	2	15	25	29	.261	.331	.349	680	78	-7	10	4	1	1.000	5	O-64(64-0-0)/D-1	-0.3
	*Atl-N	28	53	6	14	7	0	0	2	3	9	.264	.304	.396	700	80	-2	3	0	1	1.000	-4	O-15(11-4-1)	-0.5
1996	Bal-A	58	175	25	42	4	1	2	14	10	20	.240	.285	.309	594	50	-13	8	6	-0	.983	-2	O-34(32-0-2),D-18	-1.6
	*Atl-N	22	31	3	13	0	0	0	2	1	3	.419	.438	.419	857	121	1	1	1	-0	.800	-2	/O-7(7-0-0)	-0.1
1999	Det-A	87	333	46	108	21	8	10	32	16	32	.324	.359	.526	884	123	10	17	9	1	.986	-0	D-51,O-40(31-0-10)	0.6
2000	Det-A	80	267	37	73	10	5	6	25	22	25	.273	.331	.416	747	90	-4	8	5	0	1.000	-0	D-44,O-27(1-0-26)	-0.8
	*NY-A	37	77	11	22	4	0	1	5	7	7	.286	.345	.377	722	84	-2	4	2	0	.970	-5	O-28(22-0-6)/D-7	-0.6

YEAR	TM/L	G	AB	R	H	2B	3B	HR	RBI	BB	SO	AVG	OBP	SLG	OPS	OPS+	BR+	SB	CS	SBR	FA	FR	G/POS	TPR
	Yr	117	344	48	95	14	5	7	30	29	32	.276	.334	.407	741	89	-6	12	7	0	.987	-5	O-55(23-0-32),D-51	-1.4
Total	12	1379	4840	728	1417	189	70	36	405	369	543	.293	.345	.383	728	97	-18	321	145	20	.983	9	*O-1055L,D-222	-2.7
■ CARLOS PONCE Ponce, Carlos Antonio (Diaz) b: 2/7/59, Rio Piedras, P.R. BR/TR, 5'10", 170 lbs. Deb: 8/14/85																								
1985	Mil-A	21	62	4	10	2	0	1	5	1	9	.161	.175	.242	417	13	-7	0	0	0	1.000	-0	1-10/O-6(5-0-1),D-3	-0.9
■ RALPH POND Pond, Ralph Benjamin b: 5/4/1888, Eau Claire, Wis. d: 9/8/47, Cleveland, Ohio Deb: 6/8/10																								
1910	Bos-A	1	4	0	1	0	0	0	0	0		.250	.250	.250	500	55	-0	1			.000	-1	/O-1(0-1-0)	-0.1
■ HARLIN POOL Pool, Harold G "Samson" b: 3/12/08, Lakeport, Cal. d: 2/15/63, Rodeo, Cal. BL/TR, 5'10", 195 lbs. Deb: 5/30/34																								
1934	Cin-N	99	358	38	117	22	5	2	50	17	18	.327	.369	.433	802	117	8	3			.953	0	O-94(76-0-18)	0.3
1935	Cin-N	28	68	8	12	6	2	0	11	2	2	.176	.200	.324	524	39	-6	0			.962	-3	O-18(15-0-3)	-1.0
Total	2	127	426	46	129	28	7	2	61	19	20	.303	.343	.415	758	105	2	3			.954	-3	O-112(91-0-21)	-0.7
■ ED POOLE Poole, Edward I. b: 9/7/1874, Canton, Ohio d: 3/11/19, Malvern, Ohio BR/TR, 5'10", 175 lbs. Deb: 10/6/00 Career OF: (5-LF 8-CF 1-RF)																								
1900	Pit-N	2	4	1	2	0	1	1	3	0		.500	.500	1.750	2250	504	2	0			.500	-0	/O-1(1-0-0),P-1	0.0
1901	Pit-N	26	78	6	16	4	0	1	4	4		.205	.244	.295	539	54	-5	1			.933	-2	P-12,O-12C/2-1,3-1	-0.5
1902	Pit-N	1	4	0	1	0	0	0	0	0		.250	.250	.250	500	53	-0	0			.667	-0	/P-1	0.0
	Cin-N	17	61	7	7	2	0	0	1	0		.115	.115	.148	262	-17	-8	0			1.000	-1	P-16/O-1(0-1-0)	-0.1
	Yr	18	65	7	8	2	0	0	1	0		.123	.123	.154	277	-13	-9	0			**.976**	-1	P-17/O-1(0-1-0)	-0.1
1903	Cin-N	25	70	7	17	1	0	0	7	2		.243	.264	.257	521	44	-5	0			.929	2	P-25	0.0
1904	Bro-N	25	62	3	8	1	0	0	0	0		.129	.129	.145	274	-16	-8	0			.973	3	P-25	0.0
Total	5	96	279	24	51	8	1	2	15	6		.183	.200	.240	440	29	-25	1			.954	3	/P-80,O-14C,3-1,2-1	-0.6
■ JIM POOLE Poole, James Robert "Easy" b: 5/12/1895, Taylorsville, N.C. d: 1/2/75, Hickory, N.C. BL/TR, 6', 175 lbs. Deb: 4/14/25																								
1925	Phi-A	133	480	65	143	29	8	5	67	27	37	.298	.338	.423	761	86	-11	5	4	-0	.982	-7	*1-123	-2.5
1926	Phi-A	112	361	49	106	23	5	8	63	23	25	.294	.339	.452	791	99	-2	4	3	-0	.992	0	*1-101/O-1(0-0-1)	-0.8
1927	Phi-A	38	99	4	22	2	0	0	10	9	6	.222	.287	.242	529	36	-9	0	0	0	.993	0	1-31	-1.0
Total	3	283	940	118	271	54	13	13	140	59	68	.288	.333	.415	748	86	-22	9	7	-0	.987	-7	1-255/O-1(0-0-1)	-4.3
■ RAY POOLE Poole, Raymond Herman b: 1/16/20, Salisbury, N.C. BL/TR, 6', 180 lbs. Deb: 9/9/41																								
1941	Phi-A	2	2	0	0	0	0	0	0	0	1	.000	.000	.000	0	-99	-1	0	0	0	.000	0	H	-0.1
1947	Phi-A	13	13	1	3	0	0	0	1	1	4	.231	.286	.231	516	44	-1	0	0	0	.000	0	H	-0.1
Total	2	15	15	1	3	0	0	0	1	1	5	.200	.250	.200	450	25	-2	0	0	0		0	-0,-0	-0.2
■ TOM POORMAN Poorman, Thomas Iverson b: 10/14/1857, Lock Haven, Pa. d: 2/18/05, Lock Haven, Pa. BL/TR, 5'7", 135 lbs. Deb: 5/5/1880 Career OF: (0-LF 10-CF 476-RF)																								
1880	Buf-N	19	70	5	11	1	0	0	1	0	13	.157	.157	.171	329	11	-6				.879	-2	P-11,O-10(0-10-0)	-0.6
	Chi-N	7	25	3	5	1	2	0	0	0	2	.200	.200	.400	600	92	-0				.778	-2	/O-7(0-0-7),P-2	-0.1
	Yr	26	95	8	16	2	2	0	1	0	15	.168	.168	.232	400	33	-6				.750	-4	O-17(0-10-7),P-13	-0.7
1884	Tol-a	94	382	56	89	8	7	0		10		.233	.254	.291	545	75	-11				.845	4	*O-93(0-0-93)/P-1	-0.7
1885	Bos-N	56	227	44	54	5	3	3	25	7	32	.238	.261	.326	587	92	-2				.867	-2	O-56(0-0-56)	-0.4
1886	Bos-N	88	371	72	97	16	6	3	41	19	52	.261	.297	.361	659	103	1	31			.902	6	*O-88(0-0-88)	0.6
1887	Phi-a	135	620	140	190	18	**19**	4	61	35		.306	.317	.381	699	94	-6	88			.911	3	*O-135R/2-2,P-1	-0.4
1888	Phi-a	97	383	76	87	16	6	2	44	31		.227	.294	.316	609	96	-1	46			.898	-10	*O-97(0-0-97)	-1.1
Total	6	496	2078	396	533	65	43	12	172	102	99	.256	.285	.335	620	89	-26	165			.885	-4	O-486R/P-15,2-2	-2.7
■ DAVE POPE Pope, David b: 6/17/21, Talladega, Ala. d: 8/28/99, Cleveland, Ohio BL/TR, 5'10.5", 170 lbs. Deb: 7/1/52																								
1952	Cle-A	12	34	9	10	1	1	1	4	1	7	.294	.314	.471	785	124	1	0	0	0	1.000	-1	O-10(0-0-10)	-0.1
1954	*Cle-A	60	102	21	30	2	1	4	13	10	22	.294	.357	.451	808	118	2	2	1	0	1.000	-4	O-29(18-6-5)	-0.2
1955	Cle-A	35	104	17	31	5	0	6	22	12	31	.298	.376	.519	895	134	5	0	0	0	.954	-3	O-31(12-14-7)	0.1
	Bal-A	86	222	21	55	8	4	1	30	16	34	.248	.304	.333	638	77	-8	5	2	0	1.000	-8	O-73(19-37-31)	-1.9
	Yr	121	326	38	86	13	4	7	52	28	65	.264	.328	.393	720	97	-2	5	2	0	.986	-11	*O-104(31-51-38)	-1.8
1956	Bal-A	12	19	1	3	0	0	0	1	0	7	.158	.200	.158	358	-5	-3	0	0	0	1.000	-1	/O-4(2-0-3)	-0.4
	Cle-A	25	70	6	17	3	1	0	3	1	12	.243	.254	.314	568	48	-5	0	0	0	1.000	-1	O-18(4-12-2)	-0.7
	Yr	37	89	7	20	3	1	0	4	1	19	.225	.242	.281	523	38	-8	0	0	0	1.000	-2	O-22(6-12-5)	-1.1
Total	4	230	551	75	146	19	7	12	73	40	113	.265	.319	.390	710	92	-8	7	3	0	.990	-18	O-165(55-69-58)	-3.2
■ PAUL POPOVICH Popovich, Paul Edward b: 8/18/40, Flemington, W.Va. BB/TR (BR 1964, 66-67), 6', 175 lbs. Deb: 4/19/64																								
1964	Chi-N	1	1	0	1	0	0	0	0	0	0	1.000	1.000	1.000	2000	447	0	0	0	0	.000	0	H	0.0
1966	Chi-N	2	6	0	0	0	0	0	0	0	2	.000	.000	.000	0	-99	-2	0	0	0	.889	-1	/2-2	-0.3
1967	Chi-N	49	159	18	34	4	0	0	2	9	12	.214	.265	.239	504	43	-11	0	1	-0	.967	-4	S-31,2-17/3-2	-1.3
1968	LA-N	134	418	35	97	8	1	2	25	29	37	.232	.283	.270	554	72	-14	1	3	-1	.983	3	2-89,S-45/3-7	-0.2
1969	LA-N	28	50	5	10	0	0	0	4	1	4	.200	.216	.200	416	18	-5	0	0	0	.985	0	2-23/S-3	-0.4
	Chi-N	60	154	26	48	6	0	1	14	18	14	.312	.387	.370	757	100	1	0	1	-0	.974	-6	2-25/S-7,3-6,O-1C	-0.3
	Yr	88	204	31	58	6	0	1	18	19	18	.284	.348	.328	677	85	-3	0	1	-0	.978	-6	2-48,S-10/3-6,O-1C	-0.7
1970	Chi-N	78	186	22	47	5	1	4	20	18	18	.253	.325	.355	680	73	-7	0	1	-0	.990	-6	2-22,S-17,3-16	-1.0
1971	Chi-N	89	226	24	49	7	1	4	28	14	17	.217	.262	.310	572	54	-13	0	1	-0	.985	4	2-40,3-16/S-1	-0.8
1972	Chi-N	58	129	8	25	3	2	1	11	12	8	.194	.262	.271	534	47	-9	0	1	-0	.981	19	2-36/S-8,3-1	1.2
1973	Chi-N	99	280	24	66	6	3	2	24	18	27	.236	.284	.300	584	58	-16	3	2	-0	.981	26	2-84/S-9,3-1	1.5
1974	*Pit-N	59	83	9	18	2	1	0	5	5	10	.217	.261	.265	526	49	-6	0	0	0	.962	-1	2-12,S-10	-0.6
1975	Pit-N	25	40	5	8	1	0	0	1	3	2	.200	.273	.225	498	40	-3	0	0	0	1.000	-3	/2-8,S-8	-0.6
Total	11	682	1732	176	403	42	9	14	134	127	151	.233	.288	.292	580	62	-85	4	10	-3	.982	31	2-358,S-139/3-49,O	-2.8
■ GEORGE POPPLEIN Popplein, George J. b: 8/1840, Baltimore, Md. d: 3/31/01, Baltimore, Md. Deb: 7/11/1873																								
1873	Mar-n	1	4	0	0	0	0	0	0	0	0	.000	.000	.000	0	-99	-1	0	0	0	.500	-1	/S-1,O-1(0-1-0)	-0.2
■ TOM POQUETTE Poquette, Thomas Arthur b: 10/30/51, Eau Claire, Wis. BL/TR, 5'10", 175 lbs. Deb: 9/1/73 C																								
1973	KC-A	21	28	4	6	1	0	0	3	1	4	.214	.267	.250	517	43	-2	1	1	-0	.870	-4	O-20(0-2-18)	-0.7
1976	*KC-A	104	344	43	104	18	10	2	34	29	31	.302	.363	.430	794	131	13	6	5	-0	.979	-8	O-98(84-0-17)/D-2	0.0
1977	*KC-A	106	342	43	100	23	6	2	33	19	21	.292	.339	.412	751	103	1	1	4	-1	1.000	-2	O-96(72-1-28)	-0.6
1978	*KC-A	80	204	16	44	9	2	4	30	14	9	.216	.266	.338	604	67	-9	2	0	0	.955	4	O-63(48-1-17)/D-1	-0.8
1979	KC-A	21	26	1	5	0	0	0	3	1	4	.192	.222	.192	415	13	-3	0	0	0	1.000	-2	O-10(2-0-8)	-0.5
	Bos-A	63	154	14	51	9	0	2	23	8	7	.331	.376	.429	804	110	2	2	2	-0	.949	-7	O-43(3-30-11)/D-4	-0.5
	Yr	84	180	15	56	9	0	2	26	9	11	.311	.354	.394	749	97	-1	2	2	-0	.954	-9	O-53(5-30-19)/D-4	-1.0
1981	Bos-A	3	2	0	0	0	0	0	0	0	0	.000	.000	.000	0	-94	-0	0	0	0	.000	-1	/O-2(2-0-0)	-0.2
	Tex-A	30	64	2	10	1	0	0	7	5	1	.156	.229	.172	400	18	-7	0	1	-0	.963	-3	O-18(10-5-3)	-1.2
	Yr	33	66	2	10	1	0	0	7	5	1	.152	.222	.167	389	14	-7	0	1	-0	.963	-4	O-20(12-5-3)	-1.4
1982	KC-A	24	62	4	9	1	0	0	3	4	5	.145	.209	.161	370	3	-8	1	0	0	.957	-1	O-23(20-0-3)	-1.0
Total	7	452	1226	127	329	62	18	10	136	81	82	.268	.321	.373	694	92	-13	13	13	-2	.971	-24	O-373(241-39-105)/D-7	-5.5
■ DAN PORTER Porter, Daniel Edward b: 10/17/31, Decatur, Ill. BL/TL, 6', 164 lbs. Deb: 8/16/51																								
1951	Was-A	13	19	2	4	0	0	0	0	2	4	.211	.286	.211	496	36	-2	0	0	0	1.000	-0	/O-3(0-0-3)	-0.2
■ DARRELL PORTER Porter, Darrell Ray b: 1/17/52, Joplin, Mo. BL/TR, 6', 193 lbs. Deb: 9/2/71																								
1971	Mil-A	22	70	4	15	2	0	2	9	9	20	.214	.304	.329	632	80	-2	2	2	-0	.977	2	C-22	0.1
1972	Mil-A	18	56	2	7	1	0	1	2	5	21	.125	.210	.196	406	22	-5	0	0	0	.976	5	C-18	0.0
1973	Mil-A	117	350	50	89	19	2	16	67	57	85	.254	.365	.457	822	133	16	5	2	0	.977	-4	C-90,D-19	1.7
1974	Mil-A☆	131	432	59	104	15	4	12	56	50	88	.241	.326	.377	704	103	2	8	7	-1	.978	-3	*C-117/D-9	0.4
1975	Mil-A	130	409	66	95	12	5	18	60	89	77	.232	.376	.418	794	123	16	2	5	-1	.979	-2	*C-124/D-2	1.9
1976	Mil-A	119	389	43	81	14	1	5	32	51	61	.208	.302	.288	590	75	-12	2	0	0	.975	-5	*C-111/D-2	-1.2
1977	*KC-A	130	425	61	117	21	3	16	60	53	70	.275	.357	.452	809	118	11	1	0	0	.982	1	*C-125/D-1	1.7
1978	*KC-A★	150	520	77	138	27	6	18	78	75	75	.265	.360	.444	804	122	16	0	5	-2	.988	-6	*C-145/D-4	1.5

YEAR	TM/L	G	AB	R	H	2B	3B	HR	RBI	BB	SO	AVG	OBP	SLG	OPS	OPS+	BR+	SB	CS	SBR	FA	FR	G/POS	TPR
1979	KC-A★	157	533	101	155	23	10	20	112	**121**	65	.291	**.429**	.484	913	143	38	3	4	-1	.982	-2	*C-141,D-15	4.0
1980	*KC-A★	118	418	51	104	14	2	7	51	69	50	.249	.358	.342	700	92	-2	1	1	-0	.978	2	C-81,D-34	0.2
1981	StL-N	61	174	22	39	10	2	6	31	39	32	.224	.369	.408	777	117	5	1	2	-0	.979	-3	C-52	0.5
1982	*StL-N	120	373	46	86	18	5	12	48	66	66	.231	.349	.402	751	109	6	1	1	-0	.983	-5	*C-111	0.5
1983	StL-N	145	443	57	116	24	3	15	66	68	94	.262	.365	.431	796	120	13	1	3	-1	.989	-7	*C-133	1.1
1984	StL-N	127	422	56	98	16	3	11	68	60	79	.232	.335	.363	697	98	0	5	3	0	.984	-12	*C-122	-0.7
1985	*StL-N	84	240	30	53	12	2	10	36	41	48	.221	.337	.412	749	109	3	6	1	1	.990	-2	C-82	0.6
1986	Tex-A	68	155	21	41	6	0	12	29	22	51	.265	.360	.535	895	136	8	1	1	-0	.994	2	C-25,D-19	1.0
1987	Tex-A	85	130	19	31	3	0	7	21	30	43	.238	.389	.423	812	115	4	0	0	0	1.000	-0	D-35/C-7,1-5	0.3
Total	17	1782	5539	765	1369	237	48	188	826	905	1025	.247	.357	.409	766	113	117	39	37	-4	.982	-38	*C-1506,D-140/1-5	13.6
■ IRV PORTER	Porter, Irving Marble b: 5/17/1888, Lynn, Mass. d: 2/20/71, Lynn, Mass. BB/TR, 5'9", 155 lbs. Deb: 8/20/14																							
1914	Chi-A	1	4	1	1	0	0	0	0	0	1	.250	.250	.250	500	51	-0	0			1.000	-0	/O-1(0-0-1)	-0.1
■ JAY PORTER	Porter, J W "J W" b: 1/17/33, Shawnee, Okla. BR/TR, 6'2", 180 lbs. Deb: 7/30/52 Career OF: (14-LF 26-CF 22-RF)																							
1952	StL-A	33	104	12	26	4	1	0	7	10	10	.250	.316	.308	623	72	-4	4	0	1	.973	-1	O-29(3-26-0)/3-2	-0.5
1955	Det-A	24	55	6	13	2	0	0	3	8	15	.236	.333	.273	606	66	-2	0	0	0	1.000	-3	/1-6,C-4,O-4(4-0-0)	-0.6
1956	Det-A	14	21	0	2	0	0	0	3	0	8	.095	.095	.095	190	-49	-4	0	0	0	1.000	-1	/C-2,O-2(2-0-0)	-0.5
1957	Det-A	58	140	14	35	8	0	2	18	14	20	.250	.323	.350	673	82	-3	0	0	0	.953	-3	O-27(5-0-22),C-12/1-3	-0.7
1958	Cle-A	40	85	13	17	1	0	4	19	9	23	.200	.284	.353	637	76	-3	0	0	0	1.000	-3	C-20/1-4,3-1	-0.5
1959	Was-A	37	106	8	24	4	0	1	10	11	16	.226	.305	.292	598	65	-5	0	0	0	.993	-1	C-34/1-2	-0.5
	StL-N	23	33	5	7	3	0	1	2	1	4	.212	.257	.394	651	66	-2	0	0	0	1.000	0	C-19/1-1	-0.1
Total	6	229	544	58	124	22	1	8	62	53	96	.228	.301	.316	617	68	-24	4	0	1	.990	-12	/C-91,O-62C,1-16,3	-3.4
■ BO PORTER	Porter, Marquis Donnell b: 7/5/72, Newark, N.J. BR/TR, 6'2", 195 lbs. Deb: 5/9/99																							
1999	Chi-N	24	26	2	5	1	0	0	0	2	13	.192	.250	.231	481	23	-3	0	0	0	.941	-6	O-21(16-5-3)	-0.9
2000	*Oak-A	17	13	3	2	0	0	1	2	2	5	.154	.250	.357	607	53	-1	0	0	0	1.000	-4	O-16(1-2-14)	-0.5
Total	2	41	40	5	7	1	0	1	2	4	18	.175	.250	.275	525	33	-4	0	0	0	.967	-11	/O-37(17-7-17)	-1.4
■ MATTHEW PORTER	Porter, Matthew Sheldon b: Kansas City, Mo. Deb: 6/27/1884 M																							
1884	KC-U	3	12	1	1	1	0	0		0		.083	.083	.167	250	-30	-2				.750	1	/O-3(0-3-0),M	-0.1
■ DICK PORTER	Porter, Richard Twilley "Wiggles" or "Twitches" b: 12/30/01, Princess Anne, Md. d: 9/24/74, Philadelphia, Pa. BL/TR, 5'10", 170 lbs. Deb: 4/16/29																							
1929	Cle-A	71	192	26	63	16	5	1	24	17	14	.328	.386	.479	865	117	5	3	5	-1	.941	-5	O-28(4-0-24),2-20	-0.3
1930	Cle-A	119	480	100	168	43	8	4	57	55	31	.350	.420	.498	918	127	21	3	3	-0	.962	-4	*O-118(0-0-118)	0.6
1931	Cle-A	114	414	82	129	24	3	1	38	56	36	.312	.395	.391	786	102	3	6	9	-2	.970	-6	*O-109(0-0-109)/2-1	-1.1
1932	Cle-A	146	621	106	191	42	8	4	60	64	43	.308	.373	.420	793	99	-0	2	4	-1	.982	-11	*O-145(0-0-145)	-2.0
1933	Cle-A	132	499	73	133	19	6	0	41	51	42	.267	.335	.329	663	73	-19	4	4	-1	**.996**	-1	*O-124(7-0-119)	-2.7
1934	Cle-A	13	44	9	10	2	1	1	6	4	5	.227	.292	.386	678	73	-2	0	0	0	1.000	-1	O-10(0-0-10)	-0.4
	Bos-A	80	265	30	80	13	6	0	56	21	15	.302	.355	.396	752	87	-5	5	2	0	.940	-6	O-65(1-0-64)	-1.3
	Yr	93	309	39	90	15	7	1	62	25	20	.291	.346	.395	741	85	-7	5	2	0	.947	-7	O-75(1-0-74)	-1.7
Total	6	675	2515	426	774	159	37	11	282	268	186	.308	.376	.414	790	99	3	23	27	-4	.973	-35	O-599(12-0-589)/2-21	-7.2
■ BOB PORTER	Porter, Robert Lee b: 7/22/59, Yuma, Ariz. BL/TL, 5'10", 180 lbs. Deb: 5/13/81																							
1981	Atl-N	17	14	2	4	1	0	0	4	2	1	.286	.375	.357	732	106	0	0	0	0	.000	0	/H	0.0
1982	Atl-N	24	27	1	3	0	0	0	0	1	9	.111	.143	.111	254	-27	-5	0	0	0	1.000	-1	/O-4(4-0-0),1-1	-0.6
Total	2	41	41	3	7	1	0	0	4	3	10	.171	.227	.195	422	19	-4	0	0	0	1.000	-1	/O-4(4-0-0),1-1	-0.6
■ JORGE POSADA	Posada, Jorge Rafael (Villeta) b: 8/17/71, Santurce, P.R. BB/TR, 6'2", 190 lbs. Deb: 9/4/95																							
1995	*NY-A	1	0	0	0	0	0	0	0	0	0	—	—	—		—	0	0	0	0	1.000	-0	/C-1	0.0
1996	NY-A	8	14	1	1	0	0	0	0	1	6	.071	.133	.071	205	-46	-3	0	0	0	1.000	2	/C-4,D-3	-0.1
1997	*NY-A	60	188	29	47	12	0	6	25	30	33	.250	.362	.410	772	102	1	1	2	-0	.992	-7	C-60	-0.3
1998	*NY-A	111	358	56	96	23	0	17	63	47	92	.268	.353	.475	828	117	9	0	1	-0	.994	-5	C-99/1-1,D-6	0.9
1999	*NY-A	112	379	50	93	19	2	12	57	53	91	.245	.343	.401	744	90	-5	1	0	0	.993	-6	*C-109/1-1,D-1	-0.4
2000	*NY-A★	151	505	92	145	35	1	28	86	107	151	.287	.419	.527	946	140	35	2	2	-0	.993	-3	*C-142,1-12/D-4	3.6
Total	6	443	1444	228	382	89	3	63	231	238	373	.265	.374	.461	835	115	36	4	5	-1	.993	-19	C-415/1-14,D-14	3.7
■ LEO POSADA	Posada, Leopoldo Jesus (Hernandez) b: 4/15/36, Havana, Cuba BR/TR, 5'11", 175 lbs. Deb: 9/21/60																							
1960	KC-A	10	36	8	13	0	2	1	2	3	7	.361	.410	.556	966	158	3	1	0	0	1.000	-2	/O-9(4-0-8)	0.1
1961	KC-A	116	344	37	87	10	4	7	53	36	84	.253	.331	.366	697	85	-7	0	0	0	.973	-3	*O-102(69-20-29)	-1.5
1962	KC-A	29	46	6	9	1	1	0	3	7	14	.196	.302	.261	563	51	-3	0	0	0	1.000	-0	O-11(10-0-1)	-0.4
Total	3	155	426	51	109	11	7	8	58	46	105	.256	.334	.371	705	87	-8	1	0	0	.976	-5	O-122(83-20-38)	-1.8
■ SCOTT POSE	Pose, Scott Vernon b: 2/11/67, Davenport, Iowa BL/TR, 5'11", 165 lbs. Deb: 4/5/93																							
1993	Fla-N	15	41	0	8	2	0	0	3	2	4	.195	.233	.244	476	26	-4	0	2	-1	1.000	-3	O-10(6-8-0)	-0.9
1997	*NY-A	54	87	19	19	2	1	0	5	9	11	.218	.292	.264	556	47	-7	3	1	0	1.000	-9	O-45(28-3-17)/D-5	-1.5
1999	KC-A	86	137	27	39	3	0	0	12	21	22	.285	.380	.307	686	76	-4	6	2	1	.970	-3	O-25(18-1-6),D-20	-0.7
2000	KC-A	47	48	6	9	0	0	0	1	6	13	.188	.278	.188	465	21	-6	0	1	-0	1.000	-4	O-11(3-2-7)/D-4	-0.9
Total	4	202	313	52	75	7	1	0	21	38	50	.240	.322	.268	590	54	-20	9	6	-0	.990	-18	/O-91(55-14-30),D-29	-4.0
■ LEW POST	Post, Lewis G. b: 4/12/1875, Woodland, Mich. d: 8/21/44, Chicago, Ill. Deb: 9/21/02																							
1902	Det-A	3	12	2	1	0	0	0	2	0		.083	.083	.083	167	-53	-2	0			.800	-1	/O-3(0-0-3)	-0.3
■ SAM POST	Post, Samuel Gilbert b: 11/17/1896, Richmond, Va. d: 3/31/71, Portsmouth, Va. BL/TL, 6'1.5", 170 lbs. Deb: 4/22/22																							
1922	Bro-N	9	25	3	7	0	0	0	4	1	4	.280	.308	.280	588	53	-2	1	0	0	.982	-1	/1-8	-0.3
■ WALLY POST	Post, Walter Charles b: 7/9/29, St.Wendelin, Ohio d: 1/6/82, St.Henry, Ohio BR/TR, 6'1", 203 lbs. Deb: 9/18/49																							
1949	Cin-N	6	8	1	2	0	0	0	1	0	3	.250	.250	.250	500	34	-1	0			.750	-1	/O-3(1-1-1)	-0.2
1951	Cin-N	15	41	6	9	3	0	1	7	3	4	.220	.273	.366	639	69	-2	0	0	0	.963	1	/O-9(0-9-0)	-0.2
1952	Cin-N	19	58	5	9	1	0	2	7	4	20	.155	.222	.276	498	37	-5	0	0	0	1.000	2	O-16(15-1-0)	-0.5
1953	Cin-N	11	33	3	8	1	0	1	4	4	6	.242	.324	.364	688	78	-1	1	0	0	.960	1	O-11(0-4-7)	-0.1
1954	Cin-N	130	451	46	115	21	3	18	83	26	70	.255	.300	.435	735	86	-11	2	2	-0	.957	5	*O-116(0-1-115)	-1.0
1955	Cin-N	154	601	116	186	33	3	40	109	60	102	.309	.374	.574	948	139	32	7	4	0	.978	2	*O-154(0-0-154)	2.8
1956	Cin-N	143	539	94	134	25	3	36	83	37	124	.249	.302	.506	808	105	2	6	0	1	.969	12	*O-136(0-0-136)	1.1
1957	Cin-N	134	467	68	114	26	2	20	74	33	84	.244	.294	.437	731	87	-9	2	2	-0	.985	10	*O-124(1-0-123)	-0.4
1958	Phi-N	110	379	51	107	21	3	12	62	32	74	.282	.343	.449	792	109	4	0	2	-1	.952	8	O-91(2-0-90)	0.8
1959	Phi-N	132	468	62	119	17	6	22	94	36	101	.254	.312	.457	769	100	-1	0	0	0	.992	9	*O-120(2-0-118)	0.3
1960	Phi-N	34	84	11	24	6	1	2	12	9	24	.286	.355	.452	807	119	2	0	0	0	1.000	1	O-22(18-0-5)	0.2
	Cin-N	77	249	36	70	14	0	17	38	28	51	.281	.354	.542	896	139	13	0	2	-1	.985	4	O-67(44-0-23)	1.3
	Yr	111	333	47	94	20	1	19	50	37	75	.282	.354	.520	874	134	15	0	2	-1	.989	5	O-89(62-0-28)	1.5
1961	*Cin-N	99	282	44	83	16	3	20	57	22	61	.294	.348	.585	933	140	15	0	1	-0	.959	1	O-81(41-0-40)	1.1
1962	Cin-N	109	285	43	75	10	3	17	62	32	67	.263	.342	.498	840	118	7	1	0	0	.935	-4	O-90(88-0-2)	-0.1
1963	Cin-N	5	7	1	0	0	0	0	0	0	1	.000	.125	.000	125	-59	-1	0	0	0	1.000	0	/O-1(1-0-0)	-0.1
	Min-A	21	47	6	9	0	1	2	6	2	17	.191	.224	.362	586	60	-3	0	0	0	1.000	-2	O-12(2-0-10)	-0.6
1964	Cle-A	5	8	1	0	0	0	0	0	3	4	.000	.273	.000	273	-16	-1	0	0	0	.667	-1	/O-2(0-0-2)	-0.2
Total	15	1204	4007	594	1064	194	28	210	699	331	813	.266	.325	.485	810	109	40	19	13		.970	46	*O-1055(215-16-826)	4.2
■ MIKE POTTER	Potter, Michael Gary b: 5/16/51, Montebello, Cal. BR/TR, 6'1", 195 lbs. Deb: 9/6/76																							
1976	StL-N	9	16	0	0	0	0	0	0	1	6	.000	.059	.000	59	-82	-4	0	0	0	1.000	0	/O-4(4-0-0)	-0.4
1977	StL-N	5	7	0	0	0	0	0	0	0	2	.000	.000	.000	0	-99	-2	0	0	0	.000	-0	/O-1(0-0-1)	-0.2
Total	2	14	23	0	0	0	0	0	0	1	8	.000	.042	.000	42	-87	-6	0	0	0	1.000	-0	/O-5(4-0-1)	-0.6

YEAR	TM/L	G	AB	R	H	2B	3B	HR	RBI	BB	SO	AVG	OBP	SLG	OPS	OPS+	BR+	SB	CS	SBR	FA	FR	G/POS	TPR
■ **JOHN POTTS**	Potts, John Frederick "Fred" b: 2/6/1887, Tipp City, Ohio d: 9/5/62, Cleveland, Ohio BL/TR, 5'7", 165 lbs. Deb: 4/18/14																							
1914	KC-F	41	102	14	27	4	0	1	9	25	13	.265	.414	.333	747	110	1	7			.933	-4	O-31(1-5-25)	-0.4
■ **DAN POTTS**	Potts, Vivian b: 1/1869, Bristol, Pa. Deb: 10/3/1892																							
1892	Was-N	1	4	0	1	0	0	0	0	0	1	.250	.250	.250	500	53	-0	0			1.000	1	/C-1	0.0
■ **KEN POULSEN**	Poulsen, Ken Sterling b: 8/4/47, Van Nuys, Cal. BL/TR, 6'1", 190 lbs. Deb: 7/3/67																							
1967	Bos-A	5	5	0	1	1	0	0	0	0	2	.200	.200	.400	600	68	-0	0	0	0	.667	-1	/3-2,S-1	-0.1
■ **ALONZO POWELL**	Powell, Alonzo Sidney b: 12/12/64, San Francisco, Cal. BR/TR, 6'2", 190 lbs. Deb: 4/6/87 Career OF: (34-LF 6-CF 16-RF)																							
1987	Mon-N	14	41	3	8	3	0	0	4	5	17	.195	.283	.268	551	46	-3	0	0	0	1.000	-1	O-11(10-0-1)	-0.5
1991	Sea-A	57	111	16	24	6	1	3	12	11	24	.216	.293	.369	662	82	-3	0	2	-1	.960	-9	O-40(24-6-15)/1-7,D-7	-1.3
Total	2	71	152	19	32	9	1	3	16	16	41	.211	.290	.342	632	71	-6	0	2	-1	.968	-10	/O-51L,D-7,1-7	-1.8
■ **JAKE POWELL**	Powell, Alvin Jacob b: 7/15/08, Silver Spring, Md d: 11/4/48, Washington, D.C. BR/TR, 5'11.5", 180 lbs. Deb: 8/3/30 Career OF: (304-LF 258-CF 86-RF)																							
1930	Was-A	3	4	1	0	0	0	0	0	0	1	.000	.000	.000	0	-99	-1	0	0	0	1.000	-0	/O-2(1-0-1)	-0.1
1934	Was-A	9	35	6	10	2	0	0	1	4	2	.286	.359	.343	702	85	-1	1	1	-0	.955	1	/O-9(0-9-0)	0.0
1935	Was-A	139	551	88	172	26	10	6	98	37	37	.312	.360	.428	788	107	4	15	7	1	.976	0	*O-136(0-136-1)/2-2	0.2
1936	Was-A	53	210	40	62	11	5	1	30	18	21	.295	.357	.410	766	94	-2	10	4	1	.951	-7	O-53(0-53-0)	-0.9
	*NY-A	87	328	62	99	13	3	7	48	33	30	.302	.366	.424	789	98	-1	16	7	1	.976	1	O-84(42-42-0)	-0.3
	Yr	140	538	102	161	24	8	8	78	51	51	.299	.362	.418	780	96	-4	26	11	2	.967	-7	*O-137(42-95-0)	-1.2
1937	*NY-A	97	365	54	96	22	3	3	45	25	36	.263	.314	.364	678	70	-17	7	5	-0	.981	1	O-94(94-0-0)	-2.1
1938	*NY-A	45	164	27	42	12	1	2	20	15	20	.256	.326	.378	704	76	-6	3	1	0	.978	-3	O-43(37-1-6)	-1.0
1939	NY-A	31	86	12	21	4	1	1	9	3	8	.244	.270	.349	619	58	-6	1	2	-0	.983	0	O-23(19-2-3)	-0.6
1940	NY-A	12	27	3	5	0	0	0	2	1	4	.185	.214	.185	399	5	-4	0	0	0	1.000	0	/O-7(3-2-2)	-0.4
1943	Was-A	37	132	14	35	10	2	0	20	5	13	.265	.297	.371	668	99	-1	3	5	-1	.978	2	O-33(25-8-0)	-0.2
1944	Was-A	96	367	29	88	9	1	1	37	16	26	.240	.272	.278	549	60	-20	7	2	1	.980	0	O-90(58-0-32)/3-1	-2.6
1945	Was-A	31	98	4	19	2	0	0	3	8	8	.194	.255	.214	469	40	-8	1	1	-0	.950	-1	O-27(21-0-6)	-1.2
	Phi-N	48	173	13	40	5	0	1	14	8	13	.231	.265	.277	543	52	-11	1			.986	-4	O-44(4-5-35)	-1.8
Total	11	688	2540	353	689	116	26	22	327	173	219	.271	.320	.363	684	81	-74	65	35		.975	-9	O-645L/2-2,3-1	-11.0
■ **ABNER POWELL**	Powell, Charles Abner "Ab" b: 12/15/1860, Shenandoah, Pa. d: 8/7/53, New Orleans, La. BL/TR, 5'7", 160 lbs. Deb: 8/4/1884 Career OF: (8-LF 18-CF 21-RF)																							
1884	Was-U	48	191	36	54	10	5	0		3		.283	.294	.387	681	108	-4				.875	-2	O-30R,P-18/3-2,S2	-0.6
1886	Bal-a	11	39	4	7	2	1	0	7	1		.179	.200	.282	482	52	-2	4			.917	1	/P-7,O-4(3-0-1)	-0.2
	Cin-a	19	74	13	17	1	1	0	8	4		.230	.269	.270	540	67	-3	0			.760	0	O-13(5-6-2)/S-6,P-4	-0.2
	Yr	30	113	17	24	3	2	0	15	5		.212	.246	.274	520	62	-5	4			.735	0	O-17(8-6-3),P-11/S-6	-0.4
Total	2	78	304	53	78	13	7	0	15	8		.257	.276	.345	621	91	-9	4			.817	-1	/O-47R,P-29,S-7,32	-1.0
■ **HOSKEN POWELL**	Powell, Hosken b: 5/14/55, Selma, Ala. BL/TL, 6'1", 185 lbs. Deb: 4/5/78 Career OF: (33-LF 0-CF 480-RF)																							
1978	Min-A	121	381	55	94	20	2	3	31	45	31	.247	.326	.333	660	84	-7	11	5	1	.983	-1	*O-117(0-0-117)	-1.4
1979	Min-A	104	338	49	99	17	3	2	36	33	25	.293	.361	.379	740	96	-1	5	1	1	.977	-2	O-93(8-0-85)/D-5	-0.7
1980	Min-A	137	485	58	127	17	5	6	35	32	46	.262	.312	.355	666	76	-15	14	3	2	.968	7	*O-129(0-0-129)	-1.3
1981	Min-A	80	264	30	63	11	3	2	25	17	31	.239	.287	.326	613	71	-10	7	4	0	.970	2	O-64(12-0-52)/D-8	-1.2
1982	Tor-A	112	265	43	73	13	4	3	26	12	23	.275	.307	.389	696	82	-7	4	4	-1	.974	-9	O-75(8-0-68),D-19	-2.0
1983	Tor-A	40	83	6	14	0	0	1	7	5	8	.169	.216	.205	421	16	-9	2	0	0	.981	-4	O-33(5-0-29)/1-1,D-1	-1.4
Total	6	594	1816	241	470	78	17	17	160	144	164	.259	.316	.349	664	79	-49	43	17	4	.975	-8	O-511R/D-33,1-1	-8.0
■ **JIM POWELL**	Powell, James Edwin b: 8/30/1859, Richmond, Va. d: 11/20/29, Butte, Mont. 5'10", 170 lbs. Deb: 8/5/1884																							
1884	Ric-a	41	151	23	37	8	4	0		7		.245	.296	.351	647	112	2				.943	1	1-41	-0.1
■ **BOOG POWELL**	Powell, John Wesley b: 8/17/41, Lakeland, Fla. BL/TR, 6'4", 240 lbs. Deb: 9/26/61 Career OF: (431-LF 0-CF 1-RF)																							
1961	Bal-A	4	13	0	1	0	0	0	1	0	2	.077	.077	.077	154	-61	-3	0	0	0	1.000	-1	/O-3(3-0-0)	-0.4
1962	Bal-A	124	400	44	97	13	2	15	53	38	79	.243	.311	.398	709	95	-4	1	1	-0	.969	-7	*O-112(112-0-0)/1-1	-1.7
1963	Bal-A	140	491	67	130	22	2	25	82	49	87	.265	.331	.470	802	126	16	1	2	-0	.969	-8	*O-121(121-0-1),1-23	0.1
1964	Bal-A	134	424	74	123	17	0	39	99	76	91	.290	.400	**.606**	1007	176	44	0	0	0	.974	4	*O-124(124-0-0)/1-5	4.3
1965	Bal-A	144	472	54	117	20	2	17	72	71	93	.248	.351	.407	758	112	9	1	1	-0	.992	3	1-78,O-71(71-0-0)	0.4
1966	*Bal-A	140	491	78	141	18	0	34	109	67	125	.287	.374	.532	905	159	38	0	4	-1	.989	-7	*1-136	2.3
1967	Bal-A	125	415	53	97	14	1	13	55	55	94	.234	.326	.366	693	105	3	1	3	-1	.986	-4	*1-114	-0.9
1968	Bal-A★	154	550	60	137	21	1	22	85	73	97	.249	.340	.411	751	127	18	7	1	1	.990	-5	*1-149	0.6
1969	*Bal-A★	152	533	83	162	25	0	37	121	72	76	.304	.388	.559	947	161	42	1	1	-0	.995	-2	*1-144	3.0
1970	*Bal-A★	154	526	82	156	28	0	35	114	104	80	.297	.417	.549	967	163	48	1	1	-0	.992	-2	*1-145	3.5
1971	*Bal-A†	128	418	59	107	19	0	22	92	82	64	.256	.383	.459	842	139	24	1	0	0	.995	-3	*1-124	1.2
1972	Bal-A	140	465	53	117	20	1	21	81	65	92	.252	.348	.434	783	129	17	4	0	1	.988	-3	*1-133	0.6
1973	*Bal-A	114	370	52	98	13	1	11	54	85	64	.265	.402	.395	797	126	17	0	2	-1	.989	2	*1-111	1.0
1974	*Bal-A	110	344	37	91	13	1	12	45	52	58	.265	.361	.413	774	126	13	0	1	-0	.996	1	*1-102/D-1	0.6
1975	Cle-A	134	435	64	129	18	0	27	86	59	72	.297	.382	.524	906	154	31	1	3	-1	**.997**	-2	*1-121/D-5	1.9
1976	Cle-A	95	293	29	63	9	0	9	33	41	43	.215	.311	.338	649	91	-3	1	1	-0	.987	1	1-89	-1.0
1977	LA-N	50	41	0	10	0	0	0	5	12	9	.244	.415	.244	659	82	-0	0	0	0	.938	-1	/1-4	-0.1
Total	17	2042	6681	889	1776	270	11	339	1187	1001	1226	.266	.364	.462	826	134	311	20	21	-3	.991	-33	*1-1479,O-431L/D-6	15.4
■ **DANTE POWELL**	Powell, Le Jon Dante b: 8/25/73, Long Beach, Cal. BR/TR, 6'2", 185 lbs. Deb: 4/15/97																							
1997	*SF-N	27	39	8	12	1	0	1	3	4	11	.308	.372	.410	782	108	1	1	1	-0	1.000	-4	O-22(0-20-2)	-0.4
1998	SF-N	8	4	2	2	0	0	1	1	3	0	.500	.714	1.250	1964	429	2	0	0	0	1.000	-3	/O-8(0-8-0)	-0.1
1999	Ari-N	22	25	4	4	3	0	0	1	2	6	.160	.222	.280	502	26	-3	2	1	0	.929	-4	O-15(0-8-7)	-0.6
Total	3	57	68	14	18	4	0	2	5	9	17	.265	.351	.412	762	98	0	3	2	-0	.976	-11	/O-45(0-36-9)	-1.1
■ **MARTIN POWELL**	Powell, Martin J. b: 3/25/1856, Fitchburg, Mass. d: 2/5/1888, Fitchburg, Mass. BL/TL, 6', 170 lbs. Deb: 6/18/1881																							
1881	Det-N	55	219	47	74	9	4	1	38	15	9	.338	.380	.429	810	148	12				.947	-3	1-55/C-1	0.6
1882	Det-N	80	338	44	81	13	0	0	29	19	27	.240	.280	.278	558	80	-7				.940	-5	*1-80	-1.8
1883	Det-N	101	421	76	115	17	5	1	48	28	23	.273	.318	.344	663	106	5				.950	-3	*1-101	-0.6
1884	Cin-U	43	185	46	59	4	2	1		13		.319	.364	.378	742	116	-1				.940	-2	1-43	-0.7
1885	Phi-a	19	75	5	12	0	3	0	5	1		.160	.192	.240	432	34	-6				.973	-0	1-19	-0.7
Total	5	298	1238	218	341	43	14	3	120	76	59	.275	.318	.340	658	104	3				.947	-13	1-298/C-1	-3.2
■ **PAUL POWELL**	Powell, Paul Ray b: 3/19/48, San Angelo, Tex. BR/TR, 5'11", 185 lbs. Deb: 4/7/71																							
1971	Min-A	20	31	7	5	0	0	1	2	3	12	.161	.235	.258	493	38	-3	0	0	0	1.000	-2	O-15(0-15-0)	-0.5
1973	LA-N	2	1	0	0	0	0	0	0	0	1	.000	.000	.000	0	-99	-0	0	0	0	.000	-0	/O-1(1-0-0)	-0.1
1975	LA-N	8	10	2	2	1	0	0	0	1	2	.200	.273	.300	573	61	-1	0	0	0	.955	1	/C-7,O-1(1-0-0)	0.0
Total	3	30	42	9	7	1	0	1	2	4	15	.167	.239	.262	501	41	-3	0	0	0	1.000	-2	/O-17(2-15-0),C-7	-0.6
■ **RAY POWELL**	Powell, Raymond Reath "Rabbit" b: 11/20/1888, Siloam Springs, Ark. d: 10/16/62, Chillicothe, Mo. BL/TR, 5'9", 160 lbs. Deb: 4/16/13																							
1913	Det-A	2	0	0	0	0	0	0	0	0	0	—	—	—	—	—	0	0			.000	0	/O-1	0.0
1917	Bos-N	88	357	42	97	10	4	4	30	24	54	.272	.318	.356	673	113	5	12			.976	9	O-88(0-88-0)	0.8
1918	Bos-N	53	188	31	40	7	5	0	20	29	30	.213	.321	.303	624	95	-0	2			.949	-0	O-53(0-53-0)	-0.5
1919	Bos-N	123	470	51	111	12	12	2	33	41	79	.236	.303	.326	628	93	-4	16			.951	1	*O-122(0-1-120)	-1.1
1920	Bos-N	147	609	69	137	12	12	6	29	44	83	.225	.282	.314	595	74	-21	10	18	-4	.956	5	*O-147(0-147-1)	-3.3
1921	Bos-N	149	624	114	191	25	**18**	12	74	58	85	.306	.369	.462	830	125	22	6	17	-5	.954	3	*O-149(0-149-0)	1.4
1922	Bos-N	142	550	82	163	22	11	6	37	59	66	.296	.369	.409	778	105	5	3	12	-4	.980	12	*O-136(0-136-0)	0.7
1923	Bos-N	97	338	57	102	20	4	4	38	45	36	.302	.385	.420	806	117	10	1	6	-2	.941	-4	O-84(1-83-0)	0.1
1924	Bos-N	74	188	21	49	9	1	1	15	21	28	.261	.338	.335	673	85	-4	1	3	-1	.947	4	O-46(7-36-3)	-0.2
Total	9	875	3324	467	890	117	67	35	276	321	461	.268	.336	.375	711	102	12	51	56		.959	29	O-826(8-693-124)	-2.1

YEAR	TM/L	G	AB	R	H	2B	3B	HR	RBI	BB	SO	AVG	OBP	SLG	OPS	OPS+	BR+	SB	CS	SBR	FA	FR	G/POS	TPR
■ LEROY POWELL	Powell, Robert Leroy b: 10/17/33, Flint, Mich. BR/TR, 6'1", 190 lbs. Deb: 9/16/55																							
1955	Chi-A	1	0	0	0	0	0	0	0	0	0	—	—	—	—	—	0	0	0	0	.000	0	R	0.0
1957	Chi-A	1	0	1	0	0	0	0	0	0	0	—	—	—	—	—	0	0	0	0	.000	0	R	0.0
Total	2	2	0	1	0	0	0	0	0	0	0	—	—	—	—	—	0	0	0	0		0	-0,-0	0.0
■ TOM POWER	Power, Thomas E. b: San Francisco, Cal. d: 2/25/1898, San Francisco, Cal 5'11", 164 lbs. Deb: 8/27/1890																							
1890	Bal-a	38	125	11	26	3	1	0	6	13		.208	.293	.248	541	57	-7	6			.960	-4	1-26,2-12	-1.1
■ VIC POWER	Power, Victor Pellot (b: Victor Felipe Pellot (Pove)) b: 11/1/27, Arecibo, P.R. BR/TR, 5'11", 195 lbs. Deb: 4/13/54 Career OF: (41-LF 56-CF 18-RF)																							
1954	Phi-A	127	462	36	118	17	5	8	38	19	19	.255	.288	.366	654	78	-16	2	1	0	.985	10	*O-101C,1-21/S-1,3	-1.2
1955	KC-A★	147	596	91	190	34	10	19	76	35	27	.319	.357	.505	862	128	20	0	2	-1	.993	14	*1-144	2.5
1956	KC-A★	127	530	77	164	21	5	14	63	24	16	.309	.341	.447	788	106	3	2	2	-0	.993	8	1-76,2-47/O-7(7-0-0)	0.8
1957	KC-A	129	467	48	121	15	1	14	42	19	21	.259	.292	.385	678	82	-13	3	2	-0	**.998**	12	*1-113/O-6(0-0-6),2-4	-0.7
1958	KC-A	52	205	35	62	13	4	4	27	7	3	.302	.325	.463	789	112	3	1	1	-0	.992	6	1-50/2-1	0.6
	Cle-A	93	385	63	122	24	6	12	53	13	11	.317	.341	.504	845	133	15	2	1	0	.977	6	3-42,1-41,2-27,/SO	2.1
	Yr	145	590	98	184	37	**10**	16	80	20	14	.312	.336	.490	825	125	17	3	2	-0	.992	11	1-91,3-42,2-28,/SO	2.7
1959	Cle-A★	147	595	102	172	31	6	10	60	40	22	.289	.336	.412	748	108	6	9	13	-3	**.995**	10	*1-121,2-21/3-7	0.8
1960	Cle-A★	147	580	69	167	26	3	10	84	24	20	.288	.316	.395	711	94	-7	9	5	0	**.996**	21	*1-147/S-5,3-4	0.6
1961	Cle-A	147	563	64	151	34	4	5	63	38	16	.268	.316	.369	685	85	-13	4	3	-0	.994	18	*1-141/2-7	-0.3
1962	Min-A	144	611	80	177	28	2	16	63	22	35	.290	.318	.421	738	93	-7	7	1	1	.993	9	*1-142/2-2	-0.6
1963	Min-A	138	541	65	146	28	2	10	52	22	24	.270	.298	.384	683	88	-9	3	1	0	.992	-1	*1-124,2-18/3-5	-1.6
1964	Min-A	19	45	6	10	2	0	0	1	1	3	.222	.239	.267	506	40	-4	0	0	0	.990	1	1-12/2-1	-0.3
	LA-A	68	221	17	55	6	0	3	13	8	14	.249	.278	.317	595	72	-9	1	1	-0	1.000	2	1-48,3-28/2-5	-0.9
	Yr	87	266	23	65	8	0	3	14	9	17	.244	.272	.308	580	66	-13	1	1	-0	.998	4	1-60,3-28/2-6	-1.2
	Phi-N	18	48	1	10	4	0	0	3	2	3	.208	.240	.292	532	50	-3	0	0	0	.993	1	1-17	-0.3
1965	Cal-A	124	197	11	51	7	1	1	20	5	13	.259	.281	.320	601	72	-8	2	2	-0	.996	6	*1-107/2-6,3-2	-0.5
Total	12	1627	6046	765	1716	290	49	126	658	279	247	.284	.317	.411	728	97	-42	45	35	-2	.994	123	*1-1304,2-139,O/3S	1.0
■ MIKE POWERS	Powers, Ellis Foree b: 3/2/06, Toddspoint, Ky. d: 12/2/83, Louisville, Ky. BL/TL, 6'1", 185 lbs. Deb: 8/19/32																							
1932	Cle-A	14	33	4	6	4	0	0	5	2	2	.182	.229	.303	532	34	-3	0	0	0	.917	-2	/O-8(0-0-8)	-0.5
1933	Cle-A	24	47	6	13	2	1	0	2	6	6	.277	.358	.362	720	87	-1	2	1	0	.952	-2	O-11(4-0-8)	-0.3
Total	2	38	80	10	19	6	1	0	7	8	8	.237	.307	.338	644	65	-4	2	1	0	.939	-3	/O-19(4-0-16)	-0.8
■ JOHN POWERS	Powers, John Calvin b: 7/8/29, Birmingham, Ala. BL/TR, 6', 190 lbs. Deb: 9/24/55																							
1955	Pit-N	2	4	0	1	0	0	0	0	0	0	.250	.250	.250	500	34	-0	0	0	0	1.000	-0	/O-2(0-0-2)	0.0
1956	Pit-N	11	21	0	1	0	0	0	0	1	4	.048	.091	.048	139	-63	-5	0	0	0	1.000	-0	/O-5(4-0-1)	-0.5
1957	Pit-N	20	35	7	10	3	0	2	8	5	9	.286	.419	.543	961	161	3	0	0	0	1.000	0	/O-9(4-0-4)	0.3
1958	Pit-N	57	82	6	15	1	0	2	2	8	19	.183	.256	.268	524	40	-7	0	0	0	1.000	0	O-14(3-0-12)	-0.7
1959	Cin-N	43	43	8	11	2	1	2	4	3	13	.256	.319	.488	808	108	0	0	0	0	1.000	-1	/O-5(4-0-1)	-0.1
1960	Bal-A	10	18	3	2	0	0	0	0	3	1	.111	.238	.111	349	-2	-3	0	0	0	.833	-1	/O-4(0-0-4)	-0.3
	Cle-A	8	12	2	2	1	1	0	0	2	2	.167	.286	.417	702	90	-0	0	0	0	1.000	-1	/O-5(3-0-3)	-0.1
	Yr	18	30	5	4	1	1	0	0	5	3	.133	.257	.233	490	34	-3	0	0	0	.929	-1	/O-9(3-0-7)	-0.4
Total	6	151	215	26	42	7	2	6	14	22	48	.195	.282	.330	612	64	-11	0	0	0	.986	-2	/O-44(18-0-27)	-1.4
■ LES POWERS	Powers, Leslie Edwin b: 11/5/09, Seattle, Wash. d: 11/13/78, Santa Monica, Cal. BL/TL, 6', 175 lbs. Deb: 9/17/38																							
1938	NY-N	2	3	0	0	0	0	0	0	0	1	.000	.000	.000	0	-99	-1	0			.000	0	H	-0.1
1939	Phi-N	19	52	7	18	1	1	0	2	4	6	.346	.393	.404	797	118	1	0			.983	-2	1-13	-0.2
Total	2	21	55	7	18	1	1	0	2	4	7	.327	.373	.382	755	106	1	0			.983	-2	/1-13	-0.3
■ DOC POWERS	Powers, Michael Riley b: 9/22/1870, Pittsfield, Mass. d: 4/26/09, Philadelphia, Pa. BR/TR, Deb: 6/12/1898																							
1898	Lou-N	34	99	13	27	4	3	1	19	5		.273	.308	.404	712	105	0	1			.962	-3	C-22/1-6,O-1(1-0-0)	-0.1
1899	Lou-N	49	169	15	35	8	2	0	22	6		.207	.239	.278	517	42	-14	1			.942	-8	C-38/1-7	-1.7
	Was-N	14	38	3	10	2	0	0	3	1		.263	.282	.316	598	64	-2	0			.942	-0	C-12/1-1	-0.1
	Yr	63	207	18	45	10	2	0	25	7		.217	.247	.285	532	46	-16	1			.942	-8	C-50/1-8	-1.8
1901	Phi-A	116	431	53	108	26	5	1	47	18		.251	.292	.341	633	72	-17	10			.952	-5	*C-111/1-3	-1.0
1902	Phi-A	71	246	35	65	7	1	2	39	14		.264	.312	.325	637	74	-9	3			.950	5	C-68/1-3	0.2
1903	Phi-A	75	247	19	56	11	1	0	23	5		.227	.242	.279	521	54	-14	1			.982	-2	C-66/1-7	-1.0
1904	Phi-A	57	184	11	35	3	0	0	11	6		.190	.220	.207	426	33	-14	3			.965	-5	C-56/O-1(0-0-1)	-1.4
1905	*Phi-A	21	60	6	10	0	0	0	5	0		.167	.180	.167	347	10	-6	2			.928	3	C-21	-0.1
	NY-A	11	33	3	6	1	0	0	2	1		.182	.206	.212	418	29	-3	0			.975	-0	/1-7,C-4	-0.3
	*Phi-A	19	61	2	8	0	0	0	5	3		.131	.172	.131	303	-3	-7	2			.991	-5	C-19	-1.2
	Yr	51	154	11	24	1	0	0	12	4		.156	.182	.162	345	9	-16	4			.957	-2	C-44/1-7	-1.6
1906	Phi-A	58	185	5	29	1	0	0	7	1		.157	.170	.162	332	4	-20	2			.974	9	C-57/1-1	-0.6
1907	Phi-A	59	159	9	29	3	0	0	9	7		.182	.217	.201	418	33	-12	1			.983	14	C-59	0.7
1908	Phi-A	62	172	8	31	6	1	0	7	5		.180	.217	.227	443	41	-11	1			.967	7	C-60/1-2	0.2
1909	Phi-A	1	4	1	1	0	0	0	0	0		.250	.250	.250	500	57	-0	0			1.000	0	/C-1	0.0
Total	11	647	2088	183	450	72	13	4	199	72		.216	.248	.268	516	51	-129	27			.965	12	C-594/1-37,O-2(1-0-1)	-6.4
■ PHIL POWERS	Powers, Phillip B. "Grandmother" b: 7/26/1854, New York, N.Y. d: 12/22/14, New York, N.Y. BR/TR, 5'7", 166 lbs. Deb: 8/31/1878 U Career OF: (1-LF 3-CF 16-RF)																							
1878	Chi-N	8	31	2	5	1	1	0	2	1	5	.161	.188	.258	446	42	-2				.930	5	/C-8	0.3
1880	Bos-N	37	126	11	18	5	0	0	10	5	15	.143	.176	.183	358	22	-10				.851	-5	C-37/O-2(1-1-1)	-1.4
1881	Cle-N	5	15	1	1	0	0	0	0	1	2	.067	.125	.067	192	-40	-2				.955	-1	/C-4,3-1	-0.3
1882	Cin-a	16	60	4	13	1	1	0	5	3		.217	.254	.267	521	72	-2				.921	3	C-10/1-5,O-1(0-0-1)	0.1
1883	Cin-a	30	114	16	28	1	4	0	8	3		.246	.265	.325	590	84	-2				.893	-2	C-17,O-13(0-2-11)	-0.2
1884	Cin-a	34	130	10	18	1	0	0	8	5		.138	.170	.146	317	4	-13				.891	5	C-31/O-2(0-0-2),1-2	-0.6
1885	Cin-a	15	60	6	16	2	0	0	7	0		.267	.267	.300	567	77	-2				.833	-3	C-15	-0.3
	Bal-a	9	34	6	4	1	0	0	2	1		.118	.143	.147	290	-8	-4				.844	-4	/C-8,O-1(0-0-1)	-0.7
	Yr	24	94	12	20	3	0	0	9	1		.213	.221	.245	466	47	-6				.837	-7	C-23/O-1(0-0-1)	-1.0
Total	7	154	570	56	103	12	6	0	42	19	22	.181	.207	.223	430	40	-37				.877	-2	C-130/O-19R,1-7,3-1	-3.1
■ CARL POWIS	Powis, Carl Edgar "Jug" b: 1/11/28, Philadelphia, Pa. d: 5/10/99, Houston, Tex. BR/TR, 6', 185 lbs. Deb: 4/15/57																							
1957	Bal-A	15	41	4	8	3	1	0	2	7	9	.195	.327	.317	644	82	-1	2	0	0	.909	-1	O-13(0-0-13)	-0.2
■ ARQUIMEDEZ POZO	Pozo, Arquimedez (Ortiz) b: 8/24/73, Santo Domingo, D.R. BR/TR, 5'10", 160 lbs. Deb: 9/12/95																							
1995	Sea-A	1	1	0	0	0	0	0	0	0	0	.000	.000	.000	0	-99	-0	0	0	0	1.000	0	/2-1	0.0
1996	Bos-A	21	58	4	10	3	1	1	11	2	10	.172	.213	.310	523	30	-6	1	0	0	.930	3	2-10,3-10	-0.3
1997	Bos-A	4	15	0	4	1	0	0	3	0	5	.267	.267	.333	600	54	-1	0	0	0	.947	3	/3-4	0.2
Total	3	26	74	4	14	4	1	1	14	2	15	.189	.221	.311	532	33	-8	1	0	0	.952	6	/3-14,2-11	-0.1
■ JOHNNY PRAMESA	Pramesa, John Steven b: 8/28/25, Barton, Ohio d: 9/9/96, Los Angeles, Cal. BR/TR, 6'2", 210 lbs. Deb: 4/24/49																							
1949	Cin-N	17	25	2	6	1	0	1	2	3	5	.240	.321	.400	721	91	-0	0			.966	-1	C-13	-0.1
1950	Cin-N	74	228	14	70	10	1	5	30	19	15	.307	.363	.425	788	106	2	0			.981	0	C-73	0.6
1951	Cin-N	72	227	12	52	5	2	6	22	5	17	.229	.246	.348	594	57	-14	0	0	0	.968	-7	C-63	-1.8
1952	Chi-N	22	46	1	13	1	0	1	5	4	4	.283	.340	.370	710	96	-0	0	0	0	.958	2	C-17	0.2
Total	4	185	526	29	141	17	3	13	59	31	41	.268	.310	.386	696	84	-13	0	0		.973	-6	C-166	-1.1
■ DEL PRATT	Pratt, Derrill Burnham b: 1/10/1888, Walhalla, S.C. d: 9/30/77, Texas City, Tex. BR/TR, 5'11", 175 lbs. Deb: 4/11/12 Career OF: (3-LF 3-CF 8-RF)																							
1912	StL-A	152	570	76	172	26	15	5	69	36		.302	.348	.426	774	125	16	24			.943	14	*2-122,S-21/O-8R,3	3.3
1913	StL-A	155	592	60	175	31	13	2	87	40	57	.296	.341	.402	743	121	13	37			.951	5	*2-146/1-9	2.1
1914	StL-A	158	584	85	165	34	13	5	65	50	45	.283	.341	.411	752	131	19	37	28	-2	.944	-2	*2-152/O-5(2-0-3),S-1	2.0
1915	StL-A	159	602	61	175	31	11	3	78	26	43	.291	.323	.394	717	119	10	32	23	-1	.965	12	*2-158	2.4

YEAR	TM/L	G	AB	R	H	2B	3B	HR	RBI	BB	SO	AVG	OBP	SLG	OPS	OPS+	BR+	SB	CS	SBR	FA	FR	G/POS	TPR
1916	StL-A	158	596	64	159	35	12	5	**103**	54	56	.267	.331	.391	722	123	14	26	17	-0	.966	22	*2-158	4.2
1917	StL-A	123	450	40	111	22	8	1	53	33	36	.247	.301	.338	639	98	-2	18			.959	15	*2-119/1-2	1.6
1918	NY-A	126	477	65	131	19	7	2	55	35	26	.275	.327	.356	683	104	1	12			.969	12	*2-126	1.7
1919	NY-A	140	527	69	154	27	7	4	56	36	24	.292	.342	.393	735	105	3	22			.969	**28**	*2-140	3.4
1920	NY-A	154	574	84	180	37	8	4	97	50	24	.314	.372	.427	798	107	6	12	10	-1	.971	12	*2-154	1.9
1921	Bos-A	135	521	80	169	36	10	5	102	44	10	.324	.378	.461	839	116	12	8	10	-2	.961	-1	*2-134	1.2
1922	Bos-A	154	607	73	183	44	7	6	86	53	20	.301	.361	.427	788	106	5	7	10	-2	.966	-13	*2-154	-0.6
1923	Det-A	101	297	43	92	18	3	0	40	25	9	.310	.375	.391	766	104	2	6	1	1	.947	-10	2-60,1-17,3-12	-0.6
1924	Det-A	121	429	56	130	32	3	1	77	31	10	.303	.353	.399	751	95	-4	6	9	-2	.948	-2	2-65,1-51/3-4,O-1L	-0.9
Total	13	1836	6826	856	1996	392	117	43	968	513	360	.292	.345	.403	748	112	94	247	108		.960	91	*2-1688/1-79,S-22,3O	21.7

■ FRANK PRATT

Pratt, Francis Bruce “Truckhorse” b: 8/24/1897, Blocton, Ala. d: 3/8/74, Centreville, Ala. BL/TR, 5′9.5″, 155 lbs. Deb: 5/13/21

YEAR	TM/L	G	AB	R	H	2B	3B	HR	RBI	BB	SO	AVG	OBP	SLG	OPS	OPS+	BR+	SB	CS	SBR	FA	FR	G/POS	TPR
1921	Chi-A	1	1	0	0	0	0	0	0	0	0	.000	.000	.000	0	-99	-0	0	0	0	.000	0	H	0.0

■ LARRY PRATT

Pratt, Lester John b: 10/8/1886, Gibson City, Ill. d: 1/8/69, Peoria, Ill. BR/TR, 6′, 183 lbs. Deb: 9/19/14

YEAR	TM/L	G	AB	R	H	2B	3B	HR	RBI	BB	SO	AVG	OBP	SLG	OPS	OPS+	BR+	SB	CS	SBR	FA	FR	G/POS	TPR
1914	Bos-A	5	4	0	0	0	0	0	0	0	4	.000	.000	.000	0	-99	-1	0			.923	2	/C-5	0.1
1915	Bro-F	20	49	5	9	1	0	1	2	2	18	.184	.216	.265	481	35	-5	2			.949	-1	C-17	-0.5
	New-F	5	4	2	2	2	0	0	0	3	1	.500	.714	1.000	1714	403	2	2			1.000	-1	/C-3	0.2
	Yr	25	53	7	11	3	0	1	2	5	19	.208	.276	.321	597	69	-3	4			.953	-1	C-20	-0.3
Total	2	30	57	7	11	3	0	1	2	5	23	.193	.258	.298	556	58	-4	4			.949	0	/C-25	-0.2

■ TOM PRATT

Pratt, Thomas J. b: 1/26/1844, Chelsea, Mass. d: 9/28/08, Philadelphia, Pa. TL, 5′7.5″, 150 lbs. Deb: 10/18/1871 U

YEAR	TM/L	G	AB	R	H	2B	3B	HR	RBI	BB	SO	AVG	OBP	SLG	OPS	OPS+	BR+	SB	CS	SBR	FA	FR	G/POS	TPR
1871	Ath-n	1	6	2	2	0	0	0	1	0	0	.333	.333	.333	667	93	-0	0	0	0	.786	-1	/1-1	0.0

■ TODD PRATT

Pratt, Todd Alan b: 2/9/67, Bellevue, Neb. BR/TR, 6′3″, 225 lbs. Deb: 7/29/92 Career OF: (1-LF 0-CF 0-RF)

YEAR	TM/L	G	AB	R	H	2B	3B	HR	RBI	BB	SO	AVG	OBP	SLG	OPS	OPS+	BR+	SB	CS	SBR	FA	FR	G/POS	TPR
1992	Phi-N	16	46	6	13	1	0	2	10	4	12	.283	.340	.435	775	118	1	0	0	0	.972	-1	C-11	0.1
1993	*Phi-N	33	87	8	25	6	0	5	13	5	19	.287	.333	.529	862	128	3	0	0	0	.989	5	C-26	0.9
1994	Phi-N	28	102	10	20	6	1	2	9	12	29	.196	.281	.333	614	58	-6	0	1	-0	1.000	-1	C-28	-0.6
1995	Chi-N	25	60	3	8	2	0	0	4	6	21	.133	.212	.167	379	2	-9	0	0	0	.981	7	C-25	0.0
1997	NY-N	39	106	12	30	6	0	2	19	13	32	.283	.372	.396	768	105	1	0	1	-0	.990	5	C-36/D-1	0.8
1998	NY-N	41	69	9	19	9	1	2	18	2	20	.275	.296	.522	818	111	1	0	0	0	.973	-2	C-16/1-3	-0.1
1999	*NY-N	71	140	18	41	4	0	3	21	15	32	.293	.373	.386	759	96	-0	2	0	0	.996	6	C-52/1-1,O-1(1-0-0)	0.7
2000	*NY-N	80	160	33	44	6	0	8	25	22	31	.275	.380	.463	842	116	4	0	0	0	.997	4	C-71/D-1	1.1
Total	8	333	770	99	200	40	2	24	119	79	196	.260	.337	.410	748	95	-5	2	2	-0	.991	23	C-265/1-4,D-2,O-1L	2.9

■ MEL PREIBISCH

Preibisch, Melvin Adolphus “Primo” b: 11/23/14, Sealy, Tex. d: 4/12/80, Sealy, Tex. BR/TR, 5′11″, 185 lbs. Deb: 9/17/40

YEAR	TM/L	G	AB	R	H	2B	3B	HR	RBI	BB	SO	AVG	OBP	SLG	OPS	OPS+	BR+	SB	CS	SBR	FA	FR	G/POS	TPR
1940	Bos-N	11	40	3	9	2	0	0	5	2	4	.225	.262	.275	537	51	-3	0			1.000	1	O-11(0-11-0)	-0.2
1941	Bos-N	5	4	0	0	0	0	0	0	1	2	.000	.200	.000	200	-42	-1	0			1.000	-1	/O-2(1-1-1)	-0.2
Total	2	16	44	3	9	2	0	0	5	3	6	.205	.255	.250	505	42	-3	0			1.000	-0	/O-13(1-12-1)	-0.4

■ BOBBY PRESCOTT

Prescott, George Bertrand b: 3/27/31, Colon, Panama BR/TR, 5′11″, 180 lbs. Deb: 6/17/61

YEAR	TM/L	G	AB	R	H	2B	3B	HR	RBI	BB	SO	AVG	OBP	SLG	OPS	OPS+	BR+	SB	CS	SBR	FA	FR	G/POS	TPR
1961	KC-A	10	12	0	1	0	0	0	0	2	5	.083	.214	.083	298	-17	-2	0	0	0	.000	-1	/O-2(2-0-0)	-0.3

■ JIM PRESLEY

Presley, James Arthur b: 10/23/61, Pensacola, Fla. BR/TR, 6′1″, 200 lbs. Deb: 6/24/84 C

YEAR	TM/L	G	AB	R	H	2B	3B	HR	RBI	BB	SO	AVG	OBP	SLG	OPS	OPS+	BR+	SB	CS	SBR	FA	FR	G/POS	TPR
1984	Sea-A	70	251	27	57	12	1	10	36	6	63	.227	.248	.402	650	78	-9	1	1	-0	.958	-3	3-69/D-1	-1.3
1985	Sea-A	155	570	71	157	33	1	28	84	44	100	.275	.328	.484	813	118	13	2	2	-0	.961	7	*3-154	1.7
1986	Sea-A☆	155	616	83	163	33	4	27	107	32	172	.265	.305	.463	768	105	2	0	4	-1	.965	6	*3-155	0.4
1987	Sea-A	152	575	78	142	23	6	24	88	38	157	.247	.298	.433	731	86	-13	2	0	0	.953	11	*3-148/S-4,D-1	-0.3
1988	Sea-A	150	544	50	125	26	0	14	62	36	114	.230	.283	.355	637	74	-20	3	5	-1	.940	-13	*3-146/D-4	-3.4
1989	Sea-A	117	390	42	92	20	1	12	41	21	107	.236	.277	.385	661	82	-10	0	0	0	.924	-4	3-90,1-30/D-1	-1.6
1990	Atl-N	140	541	59	131	34	1	19	72	29	130	.242	.284	.414	699	85	-13	1	1	-0	.930	-3	*3-133,1-17	-1.7
1991	SD-N	20	59	3	8	0	0	1	5	4	16	.136	.203	.186	390	10	-7	0	1	-0	.923	-3	3-16	-1.1
Total	8	959	3546	413	875	181	14	135	495	210	859	.247	.292	.420	712	90	-57	9	14	-3	.949	-2	3-911/1-47,D-7,S-4	-7.3

■ WALT PRESTON

Preston, Walter B. b: 1870, Richmond, Va. d: 12/23/37, New Orleans, La. BL/TR, 6′, 175 lbs. Deb: 4/18/1895

YEAR	TM/L	G	AB	R	H	2B	3B	HR	RBI	BB	SO	AVG	OBP	SLG	OPS	OPS+	BR+	SB	CS	SBR	FA	FR	G/POS	TPR
1895	Lou-N	50	197	42	55	6	4	1	24	17	17	.279	.366	.365	732	95	-0	11			.893	-7	O-26(0-19-7),3-25	-0.7

■ JIM PRICE

Price, Jimmie William b: 10/13/41, Harrisburg, Pa. BR/TR, 6′, 195 lbs. Deb: 4/11/67

YEAR	TM/L	G	AB	R	H	2B	3B	HR	RBI	BB	SO	AVG	OBP	SLG	OPS	OPS+	BR+	SB	CS	SBR	FA	FR	G/POS	TPR
1967	Det-A	44	92	9	24	4	0	0	8	4	10	.261	.292	.304	596	74	-3	0	0	0	.974	0	C-24	-0.2
1968	*Det-A	64	132	12	23	4	0	3	13	13	14	.174	.253	.273	526	58	-7	0	0	0	.996	2	C-42	-0.4
1969	Det-A	72	192	21	45	8	0	9	28	18	20	.234	.300	.417	717	95	-2	0	0	0	.989	4	C-51	0.4
1970	Det-A	52	132	12	24	4	0	5	15	21	23	.182	.294	.326	620	70	-5	0	0	0	.979	-1	C-38	-0.5
1971	Det-A	29	54	4	13	2	0	1	7	6	3	.241	.328	.333	661	84	-1	0	0	0	.981	1	C-25	0.1
Total	5	261	602	58	129	22	0	18	71	62	70	.214	.290	.341	630	78	-18	0	0	0	.985	5	C-180	-0.6

■ JACKIE PRICE

Price, John Thomas Reid “Johnny” b: 11/13/12, Winborn, Miss. d: 10/2/67, San Francisco, Cal. BL/TR, 5′10.5″, 150 lbs. Deb: 8/18/46

YEAR	TM/L	G	AB	R	H	2B	3B	HR	RBI	BB	SO	AVG	OBP	SLG	OPS	OPS+	BR+	SB	CS	SBR	FA	FR	G/POS	TPR
1946	Cle-A	7	13	1	3	0	0	0	0	0	0	.231	.231	.231	462	31	-1	0	0	0	.947	2	/S-4	0.0

■ JOE PRICE

Price, Joseph Preston “Lumber” b: 4/10/1897, Milligan College, Tenn. d: 1/15/61, Washington, D.C. BR/TR, 6′1.5″, 187 lbs. Deb: 9/5/28

YEAR	TM/L	G	AB	R	H	2B	3B	HR	RBI	BB	SO	AVG	OBP	SLG	OPS	OPS+	BR+	SB	CS	SBR	FA	FR	G/POS	TPR
1928	NY-N	1	1	0	0	0	0	0	0	0	1	.000	.000	.000	0	-99	-0	0			.000	-1	/O-1(0-1-0)	-0.1

■ BOB PRICHARD

Prichard, Robert Alexander b: 10/21/17, Paris, Tex. d: 9/25/91, Abilene, Tex. BL/TL, 6′1″, 195 lbs. Deb: 6/14/39

YEAR	TM/L	G	AB	R	H	2B	3B	HR	RBI	BB	SO	AVG	OBP	SLG	OPS	OPS+	BR+	SB	CS	SBR	FA	FR	G/POS	TPR
1939	Was-A	26	85	8	20	5	0	0	8	19	16	.235	.375	.294	669	79	-2	0	2	-1	.992	-1	1-26	-0.5

■ JERRY PRIDDY

Priddy, Gerald Edward b: 11/9/19, Los Angeles, Cal. d: 3/3/80, N.Hollywood, Cal. BR/TR, 5′11.5″, 180 lbs. Deb: 4/17/41

YEAR	TM/L	G	AB	R	H	2B	3B	HR	RBI	BB	SO	AVG	OBP	SLG	OPS	OPS+	BR+	SB	CS	SBR	FA	FR	G/POS	TPR
1941	NY-A	56	174	18	37	7	0	1	26	18	16	.213	.290	.270	560	50	-13	4	2	0	.968	9	2-31,3-14,1-10	-0.2
1942	*NY-A	59	189	23	53	9	2	2	28	31	27	.280	.385	.381	766	118	6	0	1	-0	.944	5	3-35,1-11/2-8,S-3	1.2
1943	Was-A	149	560	68	152	31	3	4	62	67	76	.271	.350	.359	709	112	9	5	5	-1	.971	4	*2-134,S-15/3-1	2.2
1946	Was-A	138	511	54	130	22	8	6	58	57	73	.254	.332	.364	696	100	-0	9	3	1	.962	2	*2-138	1.0
1947	Was-A	147	505	42	108	20	3	3	49	62	79	.214	.301	.283	584	65	-24	7	6	-1	.980	-2	*2-146	-1.9
1948	StL-A	151	560	96	166	40	9	8	79	86	71	.296	.391	.443	834	118	16	6	5	-0	.968	24	*2-146	4.5
1949	StL-A	145	544	83	158	26	4	11	63	80	81	.290	.382	.414	796	106	6	5	3	0	.968	-3	*2-145	1.0
1950	Det-A	157	618	104	171	26	6	13	75	95	95	.277	.376	.401	777	96	-2	2	7	-2	.981	**31**	*2-157	3.3
1951	Det-A	154	584	73	152	22	6	8	57	69	73	.260	.338	.360	698	88	-9	4	3	-0	.980	10	*2-154/S-1	0.9
1952	Det-A	75	279	37	79	23	3	4	20	42	29	.283	.379	.430	809	124	10	1	8	-3	.968	-1	2-75	1.0
1953	Det-A	65	196	14	46	6	2	1	24	17	19	.235	.299	.301	600	63	-10	1	1	-0	.977	4	2-45,1-11/3-2	-0.4
Total	11	1296	4720	612	1252	232	46	61	541	624	639	.265	.353	.373	725	97	-13	44	44	-6	.973	82	*2-1179/3-52,1-32,S	12.6

■ CURTIS PRIDE

Pride, Curtis John b: 12/17/68, Washington, D.C. BL/TR, 6′, 205 lbs. Deb: 9/14/93

YEAR	TM/L	G	AB	R	H	2B	3B	HR	RBI	BB	SO	AVG	OBP	SLG	OPS	OPS+	BR+	SB	CS	SBR	FA	FR	G/POS	TPR
1993	Mon-N	10	9	3	4	1	1	1	5	0	3	.444	.444	1.111	1556	288	2	1	0	0	1.000	-0	/O-2(2-0-0)	0.2
1995	Mon-N	48	63	10	11	1	0	0	2	5	16	.175	.235	.190	426	13	-8	3	2	-0	.920	-4	O-24(24-1-0)	-1.2
1996	Det-A	95	267	52	80	17	5	10	31	31	63	.300	.372	.513	886	121	8	11	6	0	.967	-3	O-48(45-0-5),D-31	0.2
1997	Det-A	79	162	21	34	4	4	2	19	24	45	.210	.316	.321	636	67	-8	6	4	-0	.980	-6	O-35(34-0-3),D-23	-1.5
	Bos-A	2	2	1	1	0	0	1	1	0	1	.500	.500	2.000	2500	502	1	0	0	0	.000	0	/H	0.1
	Yr	81	164	22	35	4	4	3	20	24	46	.213	.317	.341	659	73	-6	6	4	-0	.980	-6	O-35(34-0-3),D-23	-1.4
1998	Atl-N	70	107	19	27	6	1	3	9	9	29	.252	.328	.411	739	93	-1	4	0	1	1.000	1	O-22(8-0-14)/D-2	0.0
2000	Bos-A	9	20	4	5	1	0	0	0	1	7	.250	.286	.300	586	47	-2	0	0	0	1.000	-1	/O-9(7-2-0),D-1	-0.2
Total	6	313	630	110	162	30	11	17	67	70	164	.257	.335	.421	756	93	-6	25	12	1	.973	-13	O-140(120-3-22)/D-57	-2.4

■ JOHNNY PRIEST

Priest, John Gooding b: 6/23/1886, St.Joseph, Mo. d: 11/4/79, Washington, D.C. BR/TR, 5′11″, 170 lbs. Deb: 5/30/11

YEAR	TM/L	G	AB	R	H	2B	3B	HR	RBI	BB	SO	AVG	OBP	SLG	OPS	OPS+	BR+	SB	CS	SBR	FA	FR	G/POS	TPR
1911	NY-A	8	21	2	3	0	0	0		2	2	.143	.250	.143	393	10	-2	3			.824	-3	/2-5,3-2	-0.6
1912	NY-A	2	2	1	1	0	0	0		1	0	.500	.500	.500	1000	176	0	0			.000	0	H	0.0
Total	2	10	23	3	4	0	0	0		3	2	.174	.269	.174	443	23	-2	3			.824	-3	/2-5,3-2	-0.6

YEAR	TM/L	G	AB	R	H	2B	3B	HR	RBI	BB	SO	AVG	OBP	SLG	OPS	OPS+	BR+	SB	CS	SBR	FA	FR	G/POS	TPR
■ TOM PRINCE	Prince, Thomas Albert b: 8/13/64, Kankakee, Ill. BR/TR, 5'11", 185 lbs. Deb: 9/22/87																							
1987	Pit-N	4	9	1	2	1	0	1	2	0	2	.222	.222	.667	889	123	0	0	0	0	1.000	1	/C-4	0.1
1988	Pit-N	29	74	3	13	2	0	0	6	4	15	.176	.218	.203	421	22	-7	0	0	0	.983	-2	C-28	-0.9
1989	Pit-N	21	52	1	7	4	0	0	5	6	12	.135	.224	.212	436	26	-5	1	1	-0	.960	-0	C-21	-0.5
1990	Pit-N	4	10	1	1	0	0	0	0	1	2	.100	.182	.100	282	-21	-2	0	1	-0	1.000	0	/C-3	-0.2
1991	Pit-N	26	34	4	9	3	0	1	2	7	3	.265	.405	.441	846	140	2	0	0	0	.984	1	C-19/1-1	0.4
1992	Pit-N	27	44	1	4	2	0	0	5	6	9	.091	.200	.136	336	-3	-6	1	1	-0	.977	3	C-19/3-1	-0.2
1993	Pit-N	66	179	14	35	14	0	2	24	13	38	.196	.276	.307	584	56	-11	1	1	-0	.984	-1	C-59	-0.9
1994	LA-N	3	6	2	2	0	0	0	1	1	3	.333	.429	.333	762	109	0	0	0	0	1.000	0	/C-3	0.0
1995	LA-N	18	40	3	8	2	1	1	4	4	10	.200	.273	.375	648	75	-2	0	0	0	.988	0	C-17	-0.1
1996	LA-N	40	64	6	19	6	0	1	11	6	15	.297	.375	.438	813	123	2	0	0	0	.994	9	C-35	1.2
1997	LA-N	47	100	17	22	5	0	3	14	5	15	.220	.278	.360	638	71	-5	0	0	0	.996	10	C-45	0.7
1998	LA-N	37	81	7	15	5	1	0	5	7	24	.185	.267	.272	538	45	-7	0	0	0	1.000	4	C-32	-0.1
1999	Phi-N	4	6	1	1	0	0	0	0	1	1	.167	.286	.167	452	18	-1	0	0	0	1.000	0	/C-4	0.0
2000	Phi-N	46	122	14	29	9	0	2	16	13	31	.238	.321	.361	682	71	-5	1	0	0	.996	3	C-46	0.0
Total	14	372	821	75	167	53	2	11	95	74	180	.203	.283	.313	596	61	-46	4	4	-1	.989	30	C-335/3-1,1-1	-0.5
■ WALTER PRINCE	Prince, Walter Farr b: 5/9/1861, Amherst, N.H. d: 3/2/38, Bristol, N.H. BL/TR, 5'9", 150 lbs. Deb: 8/7/1883																							
1883	Lou-a	4	11	1	2	0	0	0		0		.182	.182	.182	364	19	-1				.500	-2	/O-2(0-0-2),1-2,S-1	-0.3
1884	Det-N	7	21	0	3	0	0	0	1	3	4	.143	.250	.143	393	29	-2				.375	-3	/O-7(0-0-7)	-0.5
	Was-a	43	166	22	36	3	2	1		13		.217	.286	.277	563	95	1				.940	-6	1-43	-0.8
	Was-U	1	4	0	1	0	0	0		0		.250	.250	.250	500	54	-0				.818	-0	/1-1	-0.1
Total	2	55	202	23	42	3	2	1	1	16	4	.208	.276	.257	533	83	-2				.935	-11	/1-46,O-9(0-0-9),S-1	-1.7
■ BUDDY PRITCHARD	Pritchard, Harold William b: 1/25/36, South Gate, Cal. BR/TR, 6'1", 195 lbs. Deb: 4/21/57																							
1957	Pit-N	23	11	1	1	0	0	0	0	0	4	.091	.091	.091	182	-53	-2	0	0	0	.947	5	S-10/2-3	0.2
■ CHRIS PRITCHETT	Pritchett, Christopher Davis b: 1/31/70, Merced, Cal. BL/TR, 6'4", 185 lbs. Deb: 9/6/96																							
1996	Cal-A	5	13	1	2	0	0	0	1	0	3	.154	.154	.154	308	-22	-2	0	0	0	1.000	-0	/1-5	-0.3
1998	Ana-A	31	80	12	23	2	1	2	8	4	16	.287	.321	.412	734	89	-1	2	0	0	.995	4	1-29/D-1	0.1
1999	Ana-A	20	45	3	7	1	0	1	2	2	9	.156	.191	.244	436	10	-6	1	1	-0	.990	1	1-15/D-5	-0.6
2000	Phi-N	5	11	0	1	0	0	0	0	1	3	.091	.167	.091	258	-32	-2	0	0	0	1.000	1	/1-3	-0.1
Total	4	61	149	16	33	3	1	3	11	7	31	.221	.256	.315	572	46	-12	3	1	0	.995	5	/1-52,D-6	-0.9
■ GEORGE PROESER	Proeser, George "Yatz" b: 5/30/1864, Cincinnati, Ohio d: 10/13/41, New Burlington, O. BL/TL, 5'10", 190 lbs. Deb: 9/15/1888																							
1888	Cle-a	7	23	5	7	2	0	0	1	1		.304	.333	.391	725	136	1	0			.846	-1	/P-7	0.0
1890	Syr-a	13	53	11	13	1	1	1	6	10		.245	.365	.358	724	126	2	1			.895	-2	O-13(0-0-13)	0.0
Total	2	20	76	16	20	3	1	1	7	11		.263	.356	.368	725	129	3	1			.895	-3	/O-13(0-0-13),P-7	0.0
■ JAKE PROPST	Propst, William Jacob b: 3/10/1895, Kennedy, Ala. d: 2/24/67, Columbus, Miss. BL/TR, 5'10", 165 lbs. Deb: 8/7/23																							
1923	Was-A	1	1	0	0	0	0	0	0	0	0	.000	.000	.000	0	-99	-0	0	0	0	.000	0	H	0.0
■ DOC PROTHRO	Prothro, James Thompson b: 7/16/1893, Memphis, Tenn. d: 10/14/71, Memphis, Tenn. BR/TR, 5'10.5", 170 lbs. Deb: 9/26/20 M																							
1920	Was-A	6	13	2	5	0	0	0	2	0	4	.385	.385	.385	769	107	0	0	0	0	1.000	-1	/S-2,3-2	0.0
1923	Was-A	6	8	2	2	0	1	0	3	1	3	.250	.333	.500	833	124	0	0	0	0	1.000	3	/3-6	0.3
1924	Was-A	46	159	17	53	11	5	0	24	15	11	.333	.394	.465	860	125	6	4	4	-1	.915	-11	3-45	-0.3
1925	Bos-A	119	415	44	130	23	3	0	51	52	21	.313	.390	.383	773	97	-0	9	11	-2	.945	-6	*3-108/S-3	-0.1
1926	Cin-N	3	5	1	1	0	1	0	1	1	1	.200	.333	.600	933	151	0	0			1.000	-0	/3-2	0.0
Total	5	180	600	66	191	34	10	0	81	69	40	.318	.390	.408	798	105	6	13	15		.940	-14	3-163/S-5	-0.1
■ EARL PRUESS	Pruess, Earl Henry "Gibby" b: 4/2/1895, Chicago, Ill. d: 8/28/79, Branson, Mo. BR/TR, 5'10.5", 170 lbs. Deb: 9/15/20																							
1920	StL-A	1	0	1	0	0	0	0	0	1	0	—	1.000	—	1000	176	0	1	0	0	1.000	0	/O-1(0-0-1)	0.0
■ JIM PRUETT	Pruett, James Calvin b: 12/16/17, Nashville, Tenn. BR/TR, 5'10", 178 lbs. Deb: 9/26/44																							
1944	Phi-A	3	4	1	1	0	0	0	0	1	0	.250	.500	.250	750	119	0	0	0	0	1.000	1	/C-2	0.1
1945	Phi-A	6	9	1	2	0	0	0	0	1	2	.222	.300	.222	522	53	-1	0	1	-0	1.000	1	/C-4	0.0
Total	2	9	13	2	3	0	0	0	0	2	2	.231	.375	.231	606	77	-0	0	1	-0	1.000	1	/C-6	0.1
■ RON PRUITT	Pruitt, Ronald Ralph b: 10/21/51, Flint, Mich. BR/TR, 6', 185 lbs. Deb: 6/25/75 Career OF: (83-LF 6-CF 77-RF)																							
1975	Tex-A	14	17	2	3	0	0	0	0	1	3	.176	.222	.176	399	14	-2	0	0	0	1.000	-1	C-13/O-1(1-0-0)	-0.3
1976	Cle-A	47	86	7	23	1	1	0	5	16	8	.267	.382	.302	685	103	1	2	3	-1	1.000	2	O-26R/C-6,3-6,1D	0.2
1977	Cle-A	78	219	29	63	10	2	2	32	28	22	.288	.373	.379	752	109	4	2	3	-1	.972	-8	O-69R/C-4,3-1,D-4	-0.7
1978	Cle-A	71	187	17	44	6	1	6	17	16	20	.235	.296	.374	670	88	-3	2	1	0	.984	-6	C-48,O-16L/3-2,D-5	-0.9
1979	Cle-A	64	166	23	47	7	0	2	21	19	21	.283	.357	.361	718	94	-1	2	0	1	.957	-5	O-29L,D-14,C-11,/3	-0.7
1980	Cle-A	23	36	1	11	1	0	0	4	4	6	.306	.375	.333	708	95	-0	0	0	0	1.000	0	/O-6(0-1-5),3-2,D-2	0.0
	Chi-A	33	70	8	21	2	0	2	11	8	7	.300	.372	.414	786	116	2	0	0	0	1.000	-1	O-11L/C-5,3-3,1D	0.0
	Yr	56	106	9	32	3	0	2	15	12	13	.302	.373	.387	760	109	2	0	0	0	1.000	-1	O-17L/D-9,3-5,C1	0.0
1981	Cle-A	5	9	0	0	0	0	0	0	1	2	.000	.100	.000	100	-70	-2	0	0	0	1.000	-1	/O-3(2-0-1),C-1,D-1	-0.3
1982	SF-N	5	4	1	2	1	0	0	2	1	1	.500	.600	.750	1350	276	1	0	0	0	1.000	0	/C-1,O-1(0-0-1)	0.1
1983	SF-N	1	1	0	0	0	0	0	0	0	0	.000	.000	.000	0	-99	-0	0	0	0	.000	0	/H	0.0
Total	9	341	795	88	214	28	4	12	92	94	90	.269	.348	.360	708	97	-1	8	7	-1	.977	-20	O-162L/C-89,D-37,31	-2.6
■ GREG PRYOR	Pryor, Gregory Russell b: 10/2/49, Marietta, Ohio BR/TR, 6', 186 lbs. Deb: 6/4/76																							
1976	Tex-A	5	8	2	3	0	0	0	1	0	1	.375	.375	.375	750	118	0	0	0	0	1.000	0	/2-3,S-1,3-1	0.1
1978	Chi-A	82	222	27	58	11	0	2	15	11	18	.261	.299	.338	637	78	-7	3	1	0	.966	6	2-35,S-28,3-20	0.3
1979	Chi-A	143	476	60	131	23	3	3	34	35	41	.275	.327	.355	683	84	-10	3	4	-1	.961	-5	*S-119,2-25,3-22	-0.4
1980	Chi-A	122	338	32	81	18	4	1	29	12	35	.240	.270	.325	595	63	-18	2	2	-0	.975	22	S-76,3-41/2-5,D-1	1.1
1981	Chi-A	47	76	4	17	1	0	0	6	6	8	.224	.298	.237	534	57	-4	0	0	0	.931	4	3-27,S-13/2-5	0.0
1982	KC-A	73	152	23	41	10	1	2	12	10	20	.270	.315	.388	703	92	-2	2	0	0	.951	8	3-40,2-15,1-14,/S-7	0.6
1983	KC-A	68	115	9	25	4	0	1	14	7	8	.217	.262	.278	541	49	-8	0	0	0	.958	11	3-60/1-6,2-3	0.2
1984	*KC-A	123	270	32	71	11	1	4	25	12	28	.263	.302	.356	657	80	-7	0	3	-1	.970	17	*3-105,2-22/S-2,1D	0.8
1985	*KC-A	63	114	8	25	3	0	1	3	8	12	.219	.270	.272	542	49	-8	0	1	-0	.946	2	3-26,2-20,S-13,/1D	-0.5
1986	KC-A	63	112	7	19	4	0	0	7	3	14	.170	.191	.205	397	8	-14	1	1	-0	.935	6	3-35,S-17,2-12,/1-1	-0.8
Total	10	789	1883	204	471	85	9	14	146	104	185	.250	.293	.327	620	70	-78	11	12	-2	.952	71	3-377,S-276,2/1D	1.4
■ GEORGE PUCCINELLI	Puccinelli, George Lawrence "Pooch" or "Count" b: 6/22/07, San Francisco, Cal. d: 4/16/56, San Francisco, Cal BR/TR, 6'0.5", 190 lbs. Deb: 7/17/30																							
1930	*StL-N	11	16	5	9	1	0	3	8	0	1	.563	.563	1.188	1750	298	5	0			1.000	-1	/O-3(3-0-1)	0.3
1932	StL-N	31	108	17	30	8	0	3	11	12	13	.278	.350	.435	785	107	1	1			.942	2	O-30(24-0-6)	0.2
1934	StL-A	10	26	4	6	1	0	2	5	1	8	.231	.286	.500	786	92	-1	0	0	0	.941	1	/O-6(6-0-0)	0.0
1936	Phi-A	135	457	83	127	30	3	11	78	65	70	.278	.369	.429	798	98	-1	2	3	-1	.948	0	*O-117(1-0-116)	-0.8
Total	4	187	607	109	172	40	3	19	102	78	92	.283	.367	.453	820	105	4	3	3		.947	2	O-156(34-0-123)	-0.3
■ KIRBY PUCKETT	Puckett, Kirby b: 3/14/61, Chicago, Ill. BR/TR, 5'8", 210 lbs. Deb: 5/8/84 Career OF: (10-LF 1432-CF 276-RF)																							
1984	Min-A	128	557	63	165	12	5	0	31	16	69	.296	.321	.336	656	78	-16	14	7	1	.993	30	*O-128(0-128-0)	1.4
1985	Min-A	161	691	80	199	29	13	4	74	41	87	.288	.332	.385	716	90	-9	21	12	0	.984	21	*O-161(0-161-0)	1.1
1986	Min-A★	161	680	119	223	37	6	31	96	34	99	.328	.366	.537	903	138	34	20	12	0	.986	11	*O-160(0-160-0)	4.3
1987	*Min-A★	157	624	96	**207**	32	5	28	99	32	91	.332	.370	.534	904	131	27	12	7	0	.986	5	*O-147(0-147-0)/D-8	2.9
1988	Min-A★	158	657	109	**234**	42	5	24	121	23	83	.356	.380	.545	925	151	42	6	7	-1	.994	20	*O-158(0-158-0)	5.8
1989	Min-A★	159	635	75	**215**	45	4	9	85	41	59	**.339**	.381	.465	846	129	24	11	4	1	.991	18	*O-157(0-157-0)/D-2	4.2
1990	Min-A★	146	551	82	164	40	3	12	80	57	73	.298	.367	.446	813	119	14	5	4	-0	.989	8	*O-141C/2-1,3-1,SD	2.0
1991	*Min-A★	152	611	92	195	29	6	15	89	31	78	.319	.356	.460	816	118	14	11	5	1	.985	4	*O-152(0-144-19)	1.7

YEAR	TM/L	G	AB	R	H	2B	3B	HR	RBI	BB	SO	AVG	OBP	SLG	OPS	OPS+	BR+	SB	CS	SBR	FA	FR	G/POS	TPR
1992	Min-A★	160	639	104	**210**	38	4	19	110	44	97	.329	.377	.490	867	137	30	17	7	1	.993	6	*O-149C/2-2,3-2,SD	3.7
1993	Min-A★	156	622	89	184	39	3	22	89	47	93	.296	.352	.474	826	119	16	8	6	-0	.994	4	*O-139(1-95-47),D-17	1.6
1994	Min-A★	108	439	79	139	32	3	20	**112**	28	47	.317	.367	.540	907	130	18	6	3	0	.986	8	O-95(0-3-95),D-13	1.9
1995	Min-A★	137	538	83	169	39	0	23	99	56	89	.314	.382	.515	897	130	24	3	2	-0	.981	1	*O-109R,D-28/2-1,3S	1.7
Total	12	1783	7244	1071	2304	414	57	207	1085	450	965	.318	.363	.477	839	123	218	134	76	3	.989	137	*O-1696C/D-81,3-4,2S	32.3

■ JOHN PUHL

Puhl, John G. b: 1/10/1876, Brooklyn, N.Y. d: 8/24/1900, Bayonne, N.J. Deb: 10/13/1898

YEAR	TM/L	G	AB	R	H	2B	3B	HR	RBI	BB	SO	AVG	OBP	SLG	OPS	OPS+	BR+	SB	CS	SBR	FA	FR	G/POS	TPR
1898	NY-N	2	9	1	2	0	0	0	1	0		.222	.222	.222	444	28	-1	0			.667	-1	/3-2	-0.1
1899	NY-N	1	2	0	0	0	0	0	0	0		.000	.333	.000	333	-6	-0	0			.667	-0	/3-1	0.0
Total	2	3	11	1	2	0	0	0	1	0		.182	.250	.182	432	24	-1	0			.667	-1	/3-3	-0.1

■ TERRY PUHL

Puhl, Terry Stephen b: 7/8/56, Melville, Sask., Can BL/TR, 6'2", 200 lbs. Deb: 7/12/77 Career OF: (235-LF 343-CF 787-RF)

YEAR	TM/L	G	AB	R	H	2B	3B	HR	RBI	BB	SO	AVG	OBP	SLG	OPS	OPS+	BR+	SB	CS	SBR	FA	FR	G/POS	TPR
1977	Hou-N	60	229	40	69	13	5	0	10	30	31	.301	.385	.402	786	122	8	10	1	2	.992	3	O-59(48-11-1)	1.0
1978	Hou-N☆	149	585	87	169	25	6	3	35	48	46	.289	.347	.368	714	108	6	32	14	2	.992	15	*O-148(43-109-4)	2.1
1979	Hou-N	157	600	87	172	22	4	8	49	58	46	.287	.353	.377	730	105	5	30	22	-1	**1.000**	3	*O-152(6-109-40)	0.4
1980	*Hou-N	141	535	75	151	24	5	13	55	60	52	.282	.359	.419	778	126	19	27	11	2	.991	14	*O-135(4-30-107)	3.1
1981	*Hou-N	96	350	43	88	19	4	3	28	31	49	.251	.319	.354	674	96	-2	22	4	3	**1.000**	5	O-88(0-20-71)	0.2
1982	Hou-N	145	507	64	133	17	9	8	50	51	49	.262	.332	.379	711	106	4	17	9	1	.989	-6	*O-138(0-32-122)	-0.8
1983	Hou-N	137	465	66	136	25	7	8	44	36	48	.292	.346	.428	774	121	12	24	11	1	.991	-4	*O-124(0-13-118)	0.4
1984	Hou-N	132	449	66	135	19	7	9	55	59	45	.301	.383	.434	817	139	25	13	8	0	.986	-2	*O-126(8-0-123)	1.7
1985	Hou-N	57	194	34	55	14	3	2	23	18	23	.284	.347	.418	765	116	4	6	2	1	1.000	0	O-53(1-0-53)	0.2
1986	*Hou-N	81	172	17	42	10	0	3	14	15	24	.244	.305	.355	659	84	-4	3	2	-0	1.000	-4	O-47(5-0-42)	-1.1
1987	Hou-N	90	122	9	28	5	0	2	15	11	16	.230	.293	.320	613	65	-6	1	1	-0	.980	-6	O-40(28-5-9)	-1.3
1988	Hou-N	113	234	42	71	7	2	3	19	35	30	.303	.396	.389	785	131	11	22	4	3	.983	-7	O-78(48-1-33)	0.6
1989	Hou-N	121	354	41	96	25	4	0	27	45	39	.271	.355	.364	719	110	6	9	8	-1	1.000	-2	*O-103(37-11-64)/1-3	0.1
1990	Hou-N	37	41	5	12	1	0	0	8	5	7	.293	.383	.317	700	98	0	1	2	-0	1.000	-2	/O-8(6-2-0),1-1	-0.2
1991	KC-A	15	18	0	4	0	0	0	3	3	2	.222	.333	.222	556	57	-1	0	0	0	.000	-0	/O-1(1-0-0),D-2	-0.1
Total	15	1531	4855	676	1361	226	56	62	435	505	507	.280	.351	.388	740	113	86	217	99	13	.993	8	*O-1300R/1-4,D-2	6.3

■ RICH PUIG

Puig, Richard Gerald b: 3/16/53, Tampa, Fla. BL/TR, 5'10", 165 lbs. Deb: 9/13/74

YEAR	TM/L	G	AB	R	H	2B	3B	HR	RBI	BB	SO	AVG	OBP	SLG	OPS	OPS+	BR+	SB	CS	SBR	FA	FR	G/POS	TPR
1974	NY-N	4	10	0	0	0	0	0	0	1	2	.000	.091	.000	91	-74	-2	0	0	0	.923	-0	/2-3,3-1	-0.3

■ LUIS PUJOLS

Pujols, Luis Bienvenido (Toribio) b: 11/18/55, Santiago, D.R. BR/TR, 6'1", 195 lbs. Deb: 9/22/77 C

YEAR	TM/L	G	AB	R	H	2B	3B	HR	RBI	BB	SO	AVG	OBP	SLG	OPS	OPS+	BR+	SB	CS	SBR	FA	FR	G/POS	TPR
1977	Hou-N	6	15	0	1	0	0	0	0	0	5	.067	.067	.067	133	-70	-4	0	0	0	1.000	0	/C-6	-0.3
1978	Hou-N	56	153	11	20	8	1	1	11	12	45	.131	.199	.216	414	17	-18	0	0	0	.981	0	C-55/1-1	-1.7
1979	Hou-N	26	75	7	17	2	1	0	8	2	14	.227	.247	.280	527	46	-6	0	0	0	.993	1	C-26	-0.4
1980	*Hou-N	78	221	15	44	6	1	0	20	13	29	.199	.247	.235	482	38	-19	0	0	0	.990	-3	C-75/3-1	-2.0
1981	*Hou-N	40	117	5	28	3	1	1	14	10	17	.239	.299	.308	607	76	-4	1	0	0	.995	-1	C-39	-0.3
1982	Hou-N	65	176	8	35	6	2	4	15	10	40	.199	.242	.324	566	62	-10	0	3	-1	.991	5	C-64	-0.4
1983	Hou-N	40	87	4	17	2	0	0	12	5	14	.195	.239	.218	458	29	-8	0	0	0	.971	5	C-39	-0.3
1984	KC-A	4	5	0	1	0	0	0	1	0	0	.200	.200	.200	400	11	-1	0	0	0	1.000	0	/C-4	0.0
1985	Tex-A	1	1	0	1	0	0	0	0	0	0	1.000	1.000	1.000	2000	444	0	0	0	0	1.000	-0	/C-1	0.0
Total	9	316	850	50	164	27	6	6	81	52	164	.193	.241	.260	501	43	-67	1	3	-1	.987	7	C-309/3-1,1-1	-5.4

■ HARVEY PULLIAM

Pulliam, Harvey Jerome b: 10/20/67, San Francisco, Cal. BR/TR, 6', 205 lbs. Deb: 8/10/91

YEAR	TM/L	G	AB	R	H	2B	3B	HR	RBI	BB	SO	AVG	OBP	SLG	OPS	OPS+	BR+	SB	CS	SBR	FA	FR	G/POS	TPR
1991	KC-A	18	33	4	9	1	0	3	4	3	9	.273	.333	.576	909	146	2	0	0	0	.917	-2	O-15(11-0-5)	0.0
1992	KC-A	4	5	2	1	1	0	0	0	1	3	.200	.333	.400	733	102	0	0	0	0	1.000	0	/O-1(1-0-0),D-2	0.0
1993	KC-A	27	62	7	16	5	0	1	6	2	14	.258	.292	.387	679	76	-2	0	0	0	.971	-5	O-26(12-0-16)	-0.8
1995	Col-N	5	5	1	2	1	0	1	3	0	2	.400	.400	1.200	1600	234	1	0	0	0	.000	-0	/O-1(1-0-0)	0.1
1996	Col-N	10	15	2	2	0	0	0	0	2	6	.133	.235	.133	369	0	-2	0	0	0	1.000	-0	/O-3(3-0-0)	-0.2
1997	Col-N	59	67	15	19	3	0	3	9	5	15	.284	.333	.463	796	86	-1	0	1	-0	.962	-7	O-33(24-1-10)	-0.9
Total	6	123	187	31	49	11	0	8	22	13	49	.262	.313	.449	763	89	-3	0	1	-0	.956	-14	/O-79(52-1-31),D-2	-1.8

■ BLONDIE PURCELL

Purcell, William Aloysius b: Paterson, N.J. BR/TR, 5'9.5", 159 lbs. Deb: 5/1/1879 M Career OF: (480-LF 92-CF 430-RF)

YEAR	TM/L	G	AB	R	H	2B	3B	HR	RBI	BB	SO	AVG	OBP	SLG	OPS	OPS+	BR+	SB	CS	SBR	FA	FR	G/POS	TPR
1879	Syr-N	63	277	32	72	6	3	0	25	3	13	.260	.268	.303	571	99	1				.773	-13	O-47R,P-22/C-1	-1.0
	Cin-N	12	50	10	11	0	0	0	4	0	3	.220	.220	.220	440	48	-3				.750	1	O-10(0-7-3)/P-2	-0.2
	Yr	75	327	42	83	6	3	0	29	3	16	.254	.261	.291	551	91	-2				.767	-13	O-57R,P-24/C-1	-1.2
1880	Cin-N	77	325	48	95	13	6	1	24	5	13	.292	.303	.378	681	131	10				.814	-2	O-55(0-54-2),P-25/S-1	0.3
1881	Cle-N	20	80	3	14	2	1	0	4	5	8	.175	.224	.225	449	44	-5				.786	-2	O-20(7-13-0)	-0.7
	Buf-N	30	113	15	33	7	2	0	17	8	8	.292	.339	.389	728	130	4				.706	-6	O-25(25-0-0)/P-9	-0.4
	Yr	50	193	18	47	9	3	0	21	13	16	.244	.291	.321	613	95	-1				.748	-8	O-45(32-13-0)/P-9	-1.1
1882	Buf-N	84	380	79	105	18	6	2	40	14	27	.276	.302	.371	673	113	5				.820	-5	*O-82(78-5-0)/P-6	-0.3
1883	Phi-N	97	425	70	114	20	5	1	32	13	26	.268	.290	.346	636	101	2				.777	5	3-46,O-44L,P-11,M	0.5
1884	Phi-N	103	428	67	108	11	7	1	31	29	30	.252	.300	.318	618	99	1				.874	-0	*O-103(103-0-0)/P-1	-0.1
1885	Phi-a	66	304	71	90	15	5	0	22	16		.296	.337	.378	716	119	6				.858	-1	O-66(66-1-0)/P-1	0.2
	Bos-N	21	87	9	19	1	1	0	3	3	15	.218	.244	.253	497	63	-3				.840	-3	O-21(21-0-0)	-0.7
1886	Bal-a	26	85	17	19	0	1	0	8	17		.224	.365	.247	612	96	1	13			.867	-1	O-26(25-1-0)/S-1,P-1	0.0
1887	Bal-a	140	613	101	188	25	8	4	96	46		.307	.318	.344	662	90	-6	88			.925	-4	*O-140(0-0-140)/P-1	-0.9
1888	Bal-a	101	406	53	96	9	4	2	39	27		.236	.289	.293	582	89	-4	16			.906	-6	*O-100R/S-2,1-1	-1.1
	Phi-a	18	66	10	11	3	1	0	6	5		.167	.236	.242	479	54	-3	10			.903	0	O-17(0-0-17)/3-1	-0.3
	Yr	119	472	63	107	12	5	2	45	32		.227	.281	.286	568	84	-8	26			.905	-6	*O-117R/S-2,1-1,3-1	-1.4
1889	Phi-a	129	507	72	160	19	7	0	85	50	27	.316	.383	.381	763	119	14	22			.903	-10	*O-129(0-0-129)	0.3
1890	Phi-a	110	463	110	128	28	3	2	59	43		.276	.343	.363	706	109	4	48			.949	-1	*O-110(104-0-7)	0.0
Total	12	1097	4609	767	1263	177	60	13	495	284	170	.274	.314	.340	654	103	23	197			.869	-49	O-995L/P-79,3-47,S1C	-4.4

■ PID PURDY

Purdy, Everett Virgil b: 6/15/04, Beatrice, Neb. d: 1/16/51, Beatrice, Neb. BL/TR, 5'6", 150 lbs. Deb: 9/7/26

YEAR	TM/L	G	AB	R	H	2B	3B	HR	RBI	BB	SO	AVG	OBP	SLG	OPS	OPS+	BR+	SB	CS	SBR	FA	FR	G/POS	TPR
1926	Chi-A	11	33	5	6	2	1	0	6	2	1	.182	.229	.303	532	39	-3	0	1	-0	1.000	0	/O-9(0-0-9)	-0.4
1927	Cin-N	18	62	15	22	2	4	1	12	4	3	.355	.412	.565	976	164	5	0			.946	-3	O-16(0-16-0)	0.2
1928	Cin-N	70	223	32	69	11	1	0	25	23	13	.309	.377	.368	744	97	-0	1			.966	0	O-61(56-1-4)	-0.4
1929	Cin-N	82	181	22	49	7	5	1	16	19	8	.271	.350	.381	731	85	-4	2			.978	-1	O-42(34-0-8)	-0.7
Total	4	181	499	74	146	22	11	2	59	48	25	.293	.362	.393	754	97	-2	3	1		.969	-4	O-128(90-17-21)	-1.3

■ JESSE PURNELL

Purnell, Jesse Rhoades b: 5/11/1881, Glenside, Pa. d: 7/4/66, Philadelphia, Pa. BL/TR, 5'5.5", 140 lbs. Deb: 10/1/04

YEAR	TM/L	G	AB	R	H	2B	3B	HR	RBI	BB	SO	AVG	OBP	SLG	OPS	OPS+	BR+	SB	CS	SBR	FA	FR	G/POS	TPR
1904	Phi-N	7	19	2	2	0	0	0	1	4		.105	.292	.105	397	25	-1	1			.864	-1	/3-7	-0.2

■ BILLY PURTELL

Purtell, William Patrick b: 1/6/1886, Columbus, Ohio d: 3/17/62, Bradenton, Fla. BR/TR, 5'9", 170 lbs. Deb: 4/16/08 Career OF: (0-LF 1-CF 0-RF)

YEAR	TM/L	G	AB	R	H	2B	3B	HR	RBI	BB	SO	AVG	OBP	SLG	OPS	OPS+	BR+	SB	CS	SBR	FA	FR	G/POS	TPR
1908	Chi-A	26	69	3	9	2	0	0	3	2		.130	.155	.159	314	2	-7	2			.940	6	3-25	0.0
1909	Chi-A	103	361	34	93	9	3	0	40	19		.258	.302	.299	601	94	-3	14			.929	5	3-71,2-32	0.4
1910	Chi-A	102	368	21	82	5	3	1	36	21		.223	.272	.261	533	70	-13	5			.907	4	*3-102	-0.7
	Bos-A	49	168	15	35	1	2	1	15	18		.208	.289	.256	545	69	-6	2			.908	-5	3-41/S-8	-1.0
	Yr	151	536	36	117	6	5	2	51	39		.218	.278	.259	537	70	-19	7			.907	-1	*3-143/S-8	-1.7
1911	Bos-A	27	82	5	23	5	3	0	7	1		.280	.298	.415	712	99	-1	1			.867	-1	3-15/2-3,S-3,O-1C	-0.1
1914	Det-A	28	76	4	13	4	0	0	3	2	7	.171	.203	.224	426	27	-7	0	2	-1	.946	-1	3-16/S-2,2-1	-0.9
Total	5	335	1124	82	255	26	11	2	104	63	7	.227	.275	.275	550	73	-36	24	2		.915	9	3-270/2-36,S-13,O-1C	-2.3

■ ED PUTMAN

Putman, Eddy William b: 9/25/53, Los Angeles, Cal. BR/TR, 6'1", 190 lbs. Deb: 9/7/76

YEAR	TM/L	G	AB	R	H	2B	3B	HR	RBI	BB	SO	AVG	OBP	SLG	OPS	OPS+	BR+	SB	CS	SBR	FA	FR	G/POS	TPR
1976	Chi-N	5	7	0	3	0	0	0	0	0	0	.429	.429	.429	857	132	0	0	0	0	1.000	0	/C-3,1-1	0.0
1978	Chi-N	17	25	2	5	0	0	0	3	4	6	.200	.310	.200	510	40	-2	0	0	0	.950	-0	/3-8,1-3,C-2	-0.2
1979	Det-A	21	39	4	9	3	0	2	4	4	12	.231	.302	.462	764	99	-0	0	1	-0	1.000	1	C-16/1-5	0.1
Total	3	43	71	6	17	3	0	2	7	8	18	.239	.316	.366	683	81	-2	0	1	-0	1.000	1	/C-21,1-9,3-8	-0.1

YEAR	TM/L	G	AB	R	H	2B	3B	HR	RBI	BB	SO	AVG	OBP	SLG	OPS	OPS+	BR+	SB	CS	SBR	FA	FR	G/POS	TPR
■ PAT PUTNAM Putnam, Patrick Edward b: 12/3/53, Bethel, Vt. BL/TR, 6'1", 214 lbs. Deb: 9/2/77 Career OF: (17-LF 0-CF 1-RF)																								
1977	Tex-A	11	26	3	8	4	0	0	3	1	4	.308	.333	.462	795	113	0	0	1	-0	1.000	-1	/1-7,D-3	-0.1
1978	Tex-A	20	46	4	7	1	0	1	2	2	5	.152	.188	.239	427	19	-5	0	0	0	1.000	0	D-12/1-4	-0.6
1979	Tex-A	139	426	57	118	19	2	18	64	23	50	.277	.323	.458	781	109	4	1	6	-2	.994	0	1-96,D-32	-0.4
1980	Tex-A	147	410	42	108	16	2	13	55	36	49	.263	.323	.407	730	102	0	0	2	-1	.992	5	*1-137/3-1,D-1	-0.3
1981	Tex-A	95	297	33	79	17	2	8	35	17	38	.266	.306	.418	723	113	3	4	2	0	.993	3	1-94/O-3(3-0-1)	0.2
1982	Tex-A	43	122	14	28	8	0	2	9	10	18	.230	.293	.344	637	78	-4	0	2	-1	.990	1	1-39/3-1,O-1(1-0-0)	-0.6
1983	Sea-A	144	469	58	126	23	2	19	67	39	57	.269	.329	.448	777	107	4	2	1	0	.994	4	*1-125,D-11	0.0
1984	Sea-A	64	155	11	31	6	0	2	16	12	27	.200	.257	.277	535	49	-11	3	0	1	1.000	-1	D-30,O-13(13-0-0)/1-6	-1.3
	Min-A	14	38	1	3	1	0	0	4	4	12	.079	.167	.105	272	-22	-6	0	0	0	.000	0	D-11	-0.7
	Yr	78	193	12	34	7	0	2	20	16	39	.176	.239	.244	483	34	-17	3	0	1	1.000	-1	D-41,O-13(13-0-0)/1-6	-2.0
Total	8	677	1989	223	508	95	8	63	255	144	260	.255	.309	.406	715	96	-13	10	14	-3	.993	10	1-508,D-100/O-17L,3	-3.8
■ JIM PYBURN Pyburn, James Edward b: 11/1/32, Fairfield, Ala. BR/TR, 6', 190 lbs. Deb: 4/17/55 Career OF: (18-LF 77-CF 13-RF)																								
1955	Bal-A	39	98	5	20	2	2	0	7	8	24	.204	.271	.265	536	48	-7	1	1	-0	1.000	-5	3-33/O-1(0-0-1)	-1.2
1956	Bal-A	84	156	23	27	3	3	2	11	17	26	.173	.254	.269	524	41	-14	4	1	1	.975	-11	O-77(11-64-3)	-2.6
1957	Bal-A	35	40	8	9	0	0	1	2	9	6	.225	.367	.300	667	90	-0	1	0	0	1.000	-2	O-28(7-13-9)/C-1	-0.3
Total	3	158	294	36	56	5	5	3	20	34	56	.190	.277	.272	549	51	-21	6	2	1	.982	-18	O-106C/3-33,C-1	-4.1
■ EDDIE PYE Pye, Robert Edward b: 2/13/67, Columbia, Tenn. BR/TR, 5'10", 175 lbs. Deb: 6/3/94																								
1994	LA-N	7	10	2	1	0	0	0	0	1	4	.100	.182	.100	282	-26	-2	0	0	0	1.000	2	/2-3,S-3	0.1
1995	LA-N	7	8	0	0	0	0	0	0	0	4	.000	.000	.000	0	-99	-2	0	0	0	.000	0	/3-2	-0.2
Total	2	14	18	2	1	0	0	0	0	1	8	.056	.105	.056	161	-61	-4	0	0	0	1.000	2	/S-3,2-3,3-2	-0.1
■ FRANKIE PYTLAK Pytlak, Frank Anthony b: 7/30/08, Buffalo, N.Y. d: 5/8/77, Buffalo, N.Y. BR/TR, 5'7.5", 160 lbs. Deb: 4/22/32																								
1932	Cle-A	12	29	5	7	1	1	0	4	3	2	.241	.333	.345	678	71	-1	0	0	0	1.000	3	C-12	0.2
1933	Cle-A	80	248	36	77	10	6	2	33	17	10	.310	.355	.423	778	101	-0	3	4	-1	1.000	11	C-69	1.3
1934	Cle-A	91	289	46	75	12	4	0	35	36	11	.260	.352	.329	680	75	-10	11	2	2	.989	-10	C-88	-1.2
1935	Cle-A	55	149	14	44	6	1	1	12	11	4	.295	.348	.369	717	84	-3	3	2	-0	.984	-1	C-48	-0.1
1936	Cle-A	75	224	35	72	15	4	0	31	24	11	.321	.394	.424	819	101	1	5	2	0	.996	-6	C-58	-0.1
1937	Cle-A	125	397	60	125	15	6	1	44	52	15	.315	.404	.390	794	100	3	16	5	2	.986	10	*C-115	2.0
1938	Cle-A	113	364	46	112	14	7	1	43	36	15	.308	.376	.393	769	95	-2	9	5	-0	.987	-8	C-99	-0.3
1939	Cle-A	63	183	20	49	2	5	0	14	20	5	.268	.343	.333	676	76	-6	4	1	1	1.000	3	C-51	0.0
1940	Cle-A	62	149	16	21	2	1	0	16	17	5	.141	.234	.168	401	6	-21	0	1	-0	.996	7	C-58/O-1(0-0-1)	-1.1
1941	Bos-A	106	336	36	91	23	1	2	39	28	19	.271	.329	.363	692	81	-9	5	7	-1	.991	1	C-91	-0.4
1945	Bos-A	9	17	1	2	0	0	0	0	3	0	.118	.250	.118	368	8	-2	0	0	0	1.000	1	/C-6	-0.1
1946	Bos-A	4	14	1	2	0	0	0	1	0	0	.143	.143	.143	286	-19	-2	0	0	0	1.000	2	/C-4	0.0
Total	12	795	2399	316	677	100	36	7	272	247	97	.282	.355	.363	718	84	-53	56	29	2	.991	12	C-699/O-1(0-0-1)	0.2
■ TIM PYZNARSKI Pyznarski, Timothy Matthew b: 2/4/60, Chicago, Ill. BR/TR, 6'2", 195 lbs. Deb: 9/14/86																								
1986	SD-N	15	42	3	10	1	0	0	0	4	11	.238	.319	.262	581	63	-2	2	0	0	.977	-0	1-13	-0.3
■ JIM QUALLS Qualls, James Robert b: 10/9/46, Exeter, Cal. BB/TR, 5'10", 158 lbs. Deb: 4/10/69																								
1969	Chi-N	43	120	12	30	5	3	0	9	2	14	.250	.268	.342	610	62	-6	2	1	0	1.000	-3	O-35(0-35-0)/2-4	-1.1
1970	Mon-N	9	9	1	1	0	0	0	1	0	0	.111	.111	.111	222	-40	-2	0	0	0	1.000	-1	/2-2,O-2(2-0-0)	-0.3
1972	Chi-A	11	10	0	0	0	0	0	0	0	2	.000	.000	.000	0	-98	-2	0	0	0	1.000	0	/O-1(0-1-0)	-0.3
Total	3	63	139	13	31	5	3	0	10	2	16	.223	.239	.302	542	46	-10	2	1	0	1.000	-4	/O-38(2-36-0),2-6	-1.7
■ MEL QUEEN Queen, Melvin Douglas b: 3/26/42, Johnson City, N.Y. BL/TR, 6'1", 197 lbs. Deb: 4/13/64 FMC																								
1964	Cin-N	48	95	7	19	2	0	2	12	4	19	.200	.232	.284	517	43	-7	0	1	-0	.977	1	O-20(0-0-20)	-0.8
1965	Cin-N	5	3	0	0	0	0	0	0	0	1	.000	.000	.000	0	-94	-1	0	0	0	1.000	-0	/O-1(0-0-1)	-0.1
1966	Cin-N	56	55	4	7	1	0	0	5	10	12	.127	.262	.145	407	16	-6	0	0	0	1.000	-4	O-32(2-0-31)/P-7	-1.1
1967	Cin-N	49	81	6	17	4	0	0	5	4	10	.210	.247	.259	506	40	-6	2	0	0	.941	-2	P-31	0.0
1968	Cin-N	10	8	2	1	0	0	0	0	1	3	.125	.222	.125	347	6	-1	0	0	0	1.000	0	/P-5	0.0
1969	Cin-N	2	6	0	1	0	0	0	1	0	2	.167	.167	.167	333	-6	-1	0	0	0	1.000	-0	/P-2	0.0
1970	Cal-A	37	16	1	4	0	0	0	1	0	2	.250	.250	.250	500	40	-1	0	0	0	1.000	-1	P-34	0.0
1971	Cal-A	45	8	0	0	0	0	0	1	1	0	.000	.111	.000	111	-71	-2	0	0	0	.900	-1	P-44	0.0
1972	Cal-A	17	2	0	0	0	0	0	0	1	1	.000	.333	.000	333	5	-0	0	0	0	1.000	-0	P-17	0.0
Total	9	269	274	20	49	7	0	2	25	21	50	.179	.237	.226	464	30	-25	2	1	0	.951	-7	P-140/O-53(2-0-52)	-2.0
■ BILLY QUEEN Queen, William Eddleman "Doc" b: 11/28/28, Gastonia, N.C. BR/TR, 6'1", 185 lbs. Deb: 4/13/54																								
1954	Mil-N	3	2	0	0	0	0	0	0	0	2	.000	.000	.000	0	-99	-1	0	0	0	1.000	-0	/O-1(0-0-1)	-0.1
■ GEORGE QUELLICH Quellich, George William b: 2/10/06, Johnsville, Cal. d: 8/31/58, Johnsville, Cal. BR/TR, 6'1", 180 lbs. Deb: 8/1/31																								
1931	Det-A	13	54	6	12	5	0	1	11	3	4	.222	.263	.370	634	63	-3	1	0	0	1.000	1	O-13(13-0-0)	-0.2
■ JOE QUEST Quest, Joseph L. b: 11/16/1852, New Castle, Pa. d: 11/14/24, San Diego, Cal. BR/TR, 5'6", 150 lbs. Deb: 8/30/1871 U Career OF: (1-LF 0-CF 0-RF)																								
1871	Cle-n	3	13	1	3	1	0	0	2	1	0	.231	.286	.308	593	75	-0	0	0	0	.571	-2	/2-2,S-1	-0.2
1878	Ind-N	62	278	45	57	3	2	0	13	12	24	.205	.238	.230	468	63	-9				.876	2	*2-62	-0.4
1879	Chi-N	83	334	38	69	16	1	0	22	9	33	.207	.227	.260	488	57	-16				**.925**	14	*2-83	0.2
1880	Chi-N	82	300	37	71	12	1	0	27	8	16	.237	.256	.283	540	78	-7				.895	4	*2-80/S-2,3-1	0.0
1881	Chi-N	78	293	35	72	6	0	1	26	2	29	.246	.251	.276	527	63	-13				**.929**	6	*2-77/S-1	-0.3
1882	Chi-N	42	159	24	32	5	2	0	15	8	16	.201	.240	.258	497	57	-8				.879	-5	2-41/S-1	-1.0
1883	Det-N	37	137	22	32	8	2	0	15	10	18	.234	.286	.321	607	88	-1				.897	0	2-37	0.0
	StL-a	19	78	12	20	3	1	0	10	1		.256	.266	.321	586	83	-2				.890	-6	2-19	-0.6
1884	StL-a	81	310	46	64	9	5	0		19		.206	.257	.268	525	69	-10				.894	-9	*2-81	-1.5
	Pit-a	12	43	2	9	3	0	0		0		.209	.227	.279	506	65	-2				.938	0	/2-7,S-5	-0.1
	Yr	93	353	48	73	12	5	0		19		.207	.253	.269	522	69	-12				.898	-9	2-88/S-5	-1.6
1885	Det-N	55	200	24	39	8	2	0	21	14	25	.195	.248	.255	503	63	-8				.898	-1	2-39,S-15/O-1(1-0-0)	-0.7
1886	Phi-a	42	150	14	31	4	1	0	10	20		.207	.300	.247	547	71	-4	5			.847	2	S-41/2-2	-0.1
Total	9	593	2282	299	496	77	17	1	159	103	161	.217	.252	.267	519	67	-79	5	0		.902	6	2-528/S-65,O-1L,3-1	-4.5
■ HAL QUICK Quick, James Harold "Blondie" b: 10/4/17, Rome, Ga. d: 3/9/74, Swansea, Ill. BR/TR, 5'10.5", 163 lbs. Deb: 9/7/39																								
1939	Was-A	12	41	3	10	1	0	0	2	1	1	.244	.279	.268	547	44	-3	1	0	0	.927	1	S-10	-0.1
■ FRANK QUILICI Quilici, Francis Ralph "Guido" b: 5/11/39, Chicago, Ill. BR/TR, 6', 175 lbs. Deb: 7/18/65 MC																								
1965	*Min-A	56	149	16	31	5	1	0	7	15	33	.208	.280	.255	536	51	-9	1	1	-0	.990	3	2-52/S-4	-0.3
1967	*Min-A	23	19	2	2	1	0	0	0	3	4	.105	.227	.158	385	14	-2	0	0	0	1.000	1	2-13/3-8,S-1	-0.1
1968	Min-A	97	229	22	56	11	4	1	22	21	45	.245	.311	.341	651	93	-2	0	0	0	1.000	17	2-48,3-40/S-6,1-1	2.1
1969	Min-A	118	144	19	25	3	1	2	12	12	22	.174	.237	.250	487	36	-13	2	0	0	.935	24	3-84,2-36/S-1	1.4
1970	*Min-A	111	141	19	32	3	0	2	12	15	16	.227	.301	.291	592	63	-7	0	2	-1	.987	15	2-73,3-27/S-1	1.0
Total	5	405	682	78	146	23	6	5	53	66	120	.214	.284	.287	572	63	-32	3	3	-0	.993	60	2-222,3-159/S-13,1	4.1
■ LEE QUILLEN Quillen, Leon Abner b: 5/5/1882, North Branch, Minn. d: 5/14/65, St.Paul, Minn. BR/TR, 5'10", 165 lbs. Deb: 9/30/06																								
1906	Chi-A	4	9	1	3	0	0	0	0	0		.333	.333	.333	667	112	0	1			.600	-2	/S-3	-0.2
1907	Chi-A	49	151	17	29	5	0	0	14	10		.192	.256	.225	481	56	-7	8			.871	0	3-48	-0.7
Total	2	53	160	18	32	5	0	0	14	10		.200	.260	.231	491	59	-7	9			.871	-2	/3-48,S-3	-0.9
■ QUINLAN Quinlan Deb: 9/7/1874																								
1874	Phi-n	1	4	0	1	0	0	0	1	0	0	.250	.250	.250	500	59	-0	0	0	0	1.000	0	/S-1	0.0

YEAR	TM/L	G	AB	R	H	2B	3B	HR	RBI	BB	SO	AVG	OBP	SLG	OPS	OPS+	BR+	SB	CS	SBR	FA	FR	G/POS	TPR
■ FRANK QUINLAN Quinlan, Francis Patrick b: 3/9/1869, Marlborough, Mass. d: 5/4/04, Brockton, Mass. 5'9", 180 lbs. Deb: 10/5/1891																								
1891	Bos-a	2	5	0	0	0	0	0	0	0	2	.000	.000	.000	0	-99	-1	0			1.000	-1	/C-1,O-1(1-0-0)	-0.2
■ FINNERS QUINLAN Quinlan, Thomas Finners b: 10/21/1887, Scranton, Pa. d: 2/17/66, Scranton, Pa. BL/TL, 5'8", 154 lbs. Deb: 9/6/13																								
1913	StL-N	13	50	1	8	0	0	0	1	1	9	.160	.176	.160	336	-4	-7	0			.897	2	O-12(1-0-11)	-0.6
1915	Chi-A	42	114	11	22	3	0	0	7	4	11	.193	.270	.219	489	45	-8	3	4	-1	1.000	-2	O-32(9-10-13)	-1.2
Total	2	55	164	12	30	3	0	0	8	5	20	.183	.243	.201	444	31	-14	3	4		.961	0	/O-44(10-10-24)	-1.8
■ TOM QUINLAN Quinlan, Thomas Raymond b: 3/27/68, St.Paul, Minn. BR/TR, 6'3", 200 lbs. Deb: 9/4/90																								
1990	Tor-A	1	2	0	1	0	0	0	0	0	1	.500	.667	.500	1167	227	1	0	0	0	1.000	-0	/3-1	0.0
1992	Tor-A	13	15	2	1	1	0	0	2	2	9	.067	.176	.133	310	-12	-2	0	0	0	.909	-1	3-13	-0.3
1994	Phi-N	24	35	6	7	2	0	1	3	3	13	.200	.263	.343	606	55	-2	0	0	0	.966	2	3-20	-0.1
1996	Min-A	4	6	0	0	0	0	0	0	0	3	.000	.000	.000	0	-99	-2	0	0	0	.667	-1	/3-4	-0.2
Total	4	42	58	8	9	3	0	1	5	5	26	.155	.234	.259	493	30	-6	0	0	0	.932	0	/3-38	-0.6
■ FRANK QUINN Quinn, Frank J. b: 1876, Grand Rapids, Mich. d: 2/17/20, Camden, Ind. 5'8", Deb: 8/9/1899																								
1899	Chi-N	12	34	6	6	0	1	0	1	6		.176	.300	.235	535	49	-2	1			.909	-4	O-10(4-6-0)/2-1	-0.6
■ JOHN QUINN Quinn, John Edward "Pick" b: 9/12/1885, Framingham, Mass. d: 4/9/56, Marlboro, Mass. BR/TR, 5'11", 150 lbs. Deb: 10/9/11																								
1911	Phi-N	1	2	0	0	0	0	0	0	0	0	.000	.000	.000	0	-99	-1	0			1.000	-0	/C-1	-0.1
■ JOE QUINN Quinn, Joseph C. b: 8/1849, Chicago, Ill. d: 1/2/09, Chicago, Ill. 5'8.5", 148 lbs. Deb: 7/26/1871																								
1871	Kek-n	5	17	8	4	0	0	0	2	4	0	.235	.381	.235	616	81	-0	3	1	0	.964	2	/C-5	0.1
1877	Chi-N	4	14	1	1	0	0	0	0	1	0	.071	.133	.071	205	-30	-2				.667	0	/O-4(0-0-4)	-0.2
■ JOE QUINN Quinn, Joseph J. b: 12/25/1864, Sydney, Australia d: 11/12/40, St.Louis, Mo. BR/TR, 5'7", 158 lbs. Deb: 4/26/1884 M Career OF: (31-LF 66-CF 27-RF)																								
1884	StL-U	103	429	74	116	21	1	0		9		.270	.285	.324	609	81	-22				.945	-1	*1-100/O-3(1-0-2),S-1	-2.8
1885	StL-N	97	343	27	73	8	2	0	15	9	38	.213	.233	.248	481	59	-15				.875	-6	O-57L,3-31,1-11	-2.1
1886	StL-N	75	271	33	63	11	3	1	21	8	31	.232	.254	.306	561	75	-8	12			.895	-1	O-48C,2-15/1-7,3S	-1.0
1888	Bos-N	38	156	19	47	8	3	4	29	2	5	.301	.310	.468	778	143	7	12			.914	-7	2-38	0.1
1889	Bos-N	112	444	57	116	13	5	2	69	25	21	.261	.308	.327	635	73	-17	24			.860	-29	S-63,2-47/3-2	-3.7
1890	Bos-P	130	509	87	153	19	8	7	82	44	24	.301	.359	.411	769	99	-3	29			**.942**	15	*2-130	1.3
1891	Bos-N	124	508	70	122	8	10	3	63	28	28	.240	.288	.313	601	67	-24	24			.938	-23	*2-124	-3.8
1892	*Bos-N	143	532	63	116	14	1	1	59	35	40	.218	.275	.254	529	55	-30	17			**.951**	2	*2-143	-2.0
1893	StL-N	135	547	68	126	18	6	0	71	33	7	.230	.279	.285	564	50	-41	24			.942	-30	*2-135	-5.4
1894	StL-N	106	405	59	116	18	1	4	61	24	8	.286	.328	.365	693	67	-23	25			.952	21	*2-106	0.3
1895	StL-N	135	547	86	172	19	9	3	76	37	7	.314	.360	.399	759	97	-3	22			.945	-0	*2-135,M	0.2
1896	StL-N	48	191	19	40	6	1	1	17	9	5	.209	.252	.267	519	38	-17	8			.956	2	2-48	-1.1
	*Bal-N	24	82	22	27	1	1	0	5	6	1	.329	.375	.366	741	94	-1	6			.951	-3	/2-8,O-8R,3-5,S-1	-0.3
	Yr	72	273	41	67	7	2	1	22	15	6	.245	.290	.297	586	56	-18	14			.955	-1	2-56/O-8R,3-5,S-1	-1.4
1897	Bal-N	75	285	33	74	11	4	1	45	13		.260	.299	.337	636	68	-14	12			.946	9	3-37,S-21,2-11,/O1	-0.3
1898	Bal-N	12	32	5	8	1	0	0	5	1		.250	.273	.281	554	58	-2	0			.893	0	/3-8,2-1,O-1(1-0-0)	-0.1
	StL-N	103	375	35	94	10	5	0	36	24		.251	.301	.304	605	72	-14	13			.962	-1	2-62,S-41/O-1(0-0-1)	-0.9
	Yr	115	407	40	102	11	5	0	41	25		.251	.299	.302	601	71	-16	13			.960	-0	2-63,S-41/3-8,O-2L	-1.0
1899	Cle-N	147	615	73	176	24	6	0	72	21		.286	.312	.345	657	86	-13	22			**.962**	2	*2-147,M	-0.3
1900	StL-N	22	80	12	21	2	0	1	11	10		.262	.344	.325	669	86	-1	4			.933	-8	2-14/S-6,3-1	-0.8
	Cin-N	74	266	18	73	5	2	0	25	16		.274	.316	.308	624	74	-9	7			.950	-18	2-74	-2.2
	Yr	96	346	30	94	7	2	1	36	26		.272	.323	.312	635	77	-10	11			.947	-26	2-88/S-6,3-1	-3.0
1901	Was-A	66	266	33	67	11	2	2	34	11		.252	.287	.331	618	72	-10	7			.954	-14	2-66	-2.2
Total	17	1769	6883	893	1800	228	70	30	796	365	215	.262	.302	.328	631	74	-260	268			.946	-88	*2-1304,S-135,O1/3	-27.1
■ MARK QUINN Quinn, Mark David b: 5/21/74, LaMirada, Cal. BR/TR, 6'1", 175 lbs. Deb: 9/14/99																								
1999	KC-A	17	60	11	20	4	1	6	18	4	11	.333	.385	.733	1118	173	6	1	0	0	.964	-0	O-15(15-0-1)/D-1	0.5
2000	KC-A	135	500	76	147	33	2	20	78	35	91	.294	.344	.488	832	106	4	5	2	0	.988	4	O-81(78-1-4),D-48	0.3
Total	2	152	560	87	167	37	3	26	96	39	102	.298	.348	.514	863	113	10	6	2	1	.985	4	/O-96(93-1-5),D-49	0.8
■ PADDY QUINN Quinn, Paddy Deb: 5/4/1875																								
1875	Wes-n	11	43	4	14	1	0	0	5	0	1	.326	.326	.349	674	127	1	0	1	-0	.861	1	C-10/O-1(0-1-0)	0.1
	Har-n	5	13	1	3	0	0	0	1	1	3	.231	.286	.231	516	78	-0	0	1	-0	.833	-0	/C-3,O-3(0-1-2)	-0.1
	Chi-n	17	61	12	14	0	0	0	1	0	2	.230	.230	.230	459	59	-2	1	1	-0	.778	-5	C-11,O-10(0-9-1)	-0.7
	Yr	33	117	17	31	1	0	0	7	1	6	.265	.271	.274	545	87	-2	1	3	-1	.826	-5	C-24,O-14(0-11-3)	-0.7
■ PADDY QUINN Quinn, Patrick b: Boston, Mass. d: 3/1893, 5'8", 162 lbs. Deb: 9/9/1875																								
1875	Atl-n	2	8	2	1	0	0	0	0	0	0	.125	.125	.125	250	-15	-1	0	0	0	.800	-3	/O-2(0-1-1),S-1	-0.3
1881	Bos-N	1	4	0	0	0	0	0	0	0	0	.000	.000	.000	0	-99	-1				1.000	-0	/1-1	-0.1
	Wor-N	2	7	0	1	0	0	0	1	1	2	.143	.250	.143	393	25	-1				.714	-3	/C-2	-0.3
	Yr	3	11	0	1	0	0	0	1	1	2	.091	.167	.091	258	-16	-1				.714	-3	/C-2,1-1	-0.4
■ TOM QUINN Quinn, Thomas Oscar b: 4/25/1864, Annapolis, Md. d: 7/24/32, Pittsburgh, Pa. BR/TR, 5'8", 180 lbs. Deb: 9/2/1886																								
1886	Pit-a	3	11	1	0	0	0	0	0	0		.000	.000	.000	0	-99	-2	1			.929	-2	/C-3	-0.4
1889	Bal-a	55	194	18	34	2	1	1	15	19	22	.175	.252	.211	464	32	-17	6			.925	8	C-55	-0.4
1890	Pit-P	55	207	23	44	4	3	1	15	17	8	.213	.282	.275	557	54	-13	1			.888	-4	C-55	-1.0
Total	3	113	412	42	78	6	4	2	30	36	30	.189	.261	.238	499	40	-33	8			.910	2	C-113	-1.8
■ LUIS QUINONES Quinones, Luis Raul b: 4/28/62, Ponce, P.R. BB/TR, 5'11", 175 lbs. Deb: 5/27/83 Career OF: (0-LF 0-CF 4-RF)																								
1983	Oak-A	19	42	5	8	2	1	0	4	1	4	.190	.209	.286	495	37	-4	1	1	-0	1.000	1	/2-6,3-4,O-4R,SD	-0.3
1986	SF-N	71	106	13	19	1	3	0	11	3	17	.179	.209	.245	454	26	-11	3	1	0	.922	-7	S-33,3-31/2-8	-1.7
1987	Chi-N	49	101	12	22	6	0	0	8	10	16	.218	.288	.277	566	49	-7	0	0	0	.965	-7	S-28/2-4,3-1	-1.1
1988	Cin-N	23	52	4	12	3	0	1	11	2	11	.231	.259	.346	605	70	-2	1	1	-0	.974	1	S-10/2-4,3-4	0.0
1989	Cin-N	97	340	43	83	13	4	12	34	25	46	.244	.302	.412	713	99	-1	2	4	-1	.979	-5	2-53,3-50/S-5	-0.7
1990	*Cin-N	83	145	10	35	7	0	2	17	13	29	.241	.308	.331	639	73	-5	1	0	0	.981	9	3-22,2-13/S-9,1-1	0.5
1991	Cin-N	97	212	15	47	4	3	4	20	21	31	.222	.298	.325	623	72	-8	1	2	-0	.975	-4	2-33,3-19/S-5	-1.1
1992	Min-A	3	5	0	1	0	0	0	1	0	0	.200	.200	.200	400	12	-1	0	0	0	.714	-0	/3-1,S-1,D-1	-0.1
Total	8	442	1003	102	227	36	11	19	106	75	154	.226	.285	.341	626	72	-39	9	9	-1	.937	-11	3-132,2-121/S-94,DO1	-4.5
■ REY QUINONES Quinones, Rey Francisco (Santiago) b: 11/11/63, Rio Piedras, P.R. BR/TR, 5'11", 160 lbs. Deb: 5/17/86																								
1986	Bos-A	62	190	26	45	12	1	2	15	19	26	.237	.316	.342	658	79	-5	3	2	-0	.940	-8	S-62	-0.7
	Sea-A	36	122	6	23	4	0	0	7	5	31	.189	.220	.221	442	21	-13	1	1	-0	.945	1	S-36	-0.9
	Yr	98	312	32	68	16	1	2	22	24	57	.218	.280	.295	575	56	-19	4	3	-0	.942	-7	S-98	-1.6
1987	Sea-A	135	478	55	132	18	2	12	56	26	71	.276	.319	.397	716	84	-11	1	3	-1	.959	-10	*S-135	-0.7
1988	Sea-A	140	499	63	124	30	3	12	52	23	71	.248	.286	.393	678	84	-12	0	3	-1	.963	3	*S-135/D-4	0.0
1989	Sea-A	7	19	2	2	0	0	0	0	1	1	.105	.150	.105	255	-26	-3	0	0	0	.889	-2	/S-7	-0.5
	Pit-N	71	225	21	47	11	0	3	29	15	40	.209	.261	.298	559	62	-12	0	2	-1	.934	-11	S-69	-2.0
Total	4	451	1533	173	373	75	6	29	159	89	240	.243	.290	.357	646	74	-56	5	11	-3	.952	-27	S-444/D-4	-4.8
■ CARLOS QUINTANA Quintana, Carlos Narcis (Hernandez) b: 8/26/65, Estado Miranda, Venez. BR/TR, 6'2", 195 lbs. Deb: 9/16/88 Career OF: (6-LF 1-CF 85-RF)																								
1988	Bos-A	5	6	1	2	0	0	0	2	2	3	.333	.500	.333	833	133	0	0	0	0	1.000	-0	/O-3(0-0-3),D-1	0.0
1989	Bos-A	34	77	6	16	5	0	0	6	7	12	.208	.274	.273	547	51	-5	0	0	0	.926	-5	O-21(4-1-17)/1-1,D-7	-1.0
1990	*Bos-A	149	512	56	147	28	0	7	67	52	74	.287	.355	.383	738	102	2	1	2	-0	.987	15	*1-148/O-3(0-0-3)	0.6
1991	Bos-A	149	478	69	141	21	1	11	71	61	66	.295	.377	.412	789	113	10	1	0	0	.993	7	*1-138,O-13R/D-1	0.8
1993	Bos-A	101	303	31	74	5	0	1	19	31	52	.244	.318	.271	589	57	-18	1	0	0	.991	-1	1-53,O-51(1-0-50)	-2.4
Total	5	438	1376	163	380	59	1	19	165	153	207	.276	.351	.362	713	93	-10	3	2	-0	.990	15	1-340/O-91R,D-9	-2.0

■ MARSHALL QUINTON Quinton, Marshall J. b: Philadelphia, Pa. 5'11", 190 lbs. Deb: 8/7/1884 Career OF: (0-LF 0-CF 10-RF)

YEAR	TM/L	G	AB	R	H	2B	3B	HR	RBI	BB	SO	AVG	OBP	SLG	OPS	OPS+	BR+	SB	CS	SBR	FA	FR	G/POS	TPR
1884	Ric-a	26	94	12	22	5	0	0		0		.234	.242	.287	529	73	-3				.878	-9	C-14,O-10(0-0-10)/S-2	-1.0
1885	Phi-a	7	29	6	6	1	0	0	4	1		.207	.258	.241	499	55	-1				.869	-2	/C-7	-0.3
Total	2	33	123	18	28	6	0	0	4	1		.228	.246	.276	522	68	-4				.874	-11	/C-21,O-10R,S-2	-1.3

■ JAMIE QUIRK Quirk, James Patrick b: 10/22/54, Whittier, Cal. BL/TR, 6'4", 200 lbs. Deb: 9/4/75 C Career OF: (24-LF 0-CF 8-RF)

YEAR	TM/L	G	AB	R	H	2B	3B	HR	RBI	BB	SO	AVG	OBP	SLG	OPS	OPS+	BR+	SB	CS	SBR	FA	FR	G/POS	TPR
1975	KC-A	14	39	2	10	0	0	1	5	2	7	.256	.293	.333	626	75	-1	0	0	0	.909	0	O-10(10-0-0)/3-2,D-1	-0.2
1976	*KC-A	64	114	11	28	6	0	1	15	2	22	.246	.259	.325	583	70	-5	0	0	0	1.000	-1	D-19,S-12,3-11,/1-2	-0.6
1977	Mil-A	93	221	16	48	14	1	3	13	8	47	.217	.251	.330	581	57	-14	0	1	-0	.950	0	D-53,O-10(10-0-0)/3-8	-1.6
1978	KC-A	17	29	3	6	2	0	0	2	5	4	.207	.324	.276	599	68	-1	0	0	0	.926	2	3-10/S-2,D-1	0.1
1979	KC-A	51	79	8	24	6	1	1	11	5	13	.304	.353	.443	796	111	1	0	0	0	.944	-1	/C-9,S-5,3-3,D-9	0.1
1980	KC-A	62	163	13	45	5	0	5	21	7	24	.276	.310	.399	709	92	-2	3	2	-0	.929	-1	3-28,C-15/O-7R,1D	-0.3
1981	KC-A	46	100	8	25	7	0	0	10	6	17	.250	.299	.320	619	79	-3	0	2	-1	.985	-3	C-22/3-8,2-1,O-1R	-0.6
1982	KC-A	36	78	8	18	3	0	1	5	3	15	.231	.259	.308	567	55	-5	0	0	0	1.000	2	C-29/1-6,3-1,O-1L	-0.3
1983	StL-N	48	86	3	18	2	1	2	11	6	27	.209	.269	.326	594	64	-4	0	0	0	.929	-5	C-22/3-7,S-1	-0.9
1984	Chi-A	3	2	0	0	0	0	0	1	0	2	.000	.000	.000	0	-96	-1	0	0	0	1.000	0	/3-1	-0.1
	Cle-A	1	1	1	1	0	0	1	1	0	0	1.000	1.000	4.000	5000	1189	1	0	0	0	.000	0	/C-1	0.1
	Yr	4	3	1	1	0	0	1	2	0	2	.333	.333	1.333	1667	324	1	0	0	0	1.000	0	/3-1,C-1	0.0
1985	*KC-A	19	57	3	16	3	1	0	4	2	9	.281	.305	.368	674	83	-1	0	0	0	.986	-3	C-17/1-1	-0.3
1986	KC-A	80	219	24	47	10	0	8	26	17	41	.215	.274	.370	644	72	-9	0	1	-0	.989	11	C-41,3-24/1-6,O-1L	0.2
1987	KC-A	109	296	24	70	17	0	5	33	28	56	.236	.311	.345	656	72	-12	1	0	0	.986	-4	*C-108/S-1	-1.1
1988	KC-A	84	196	22	47	7	1	8	25	28	41	.240	.338	.408	746	107	2	1	5	-2	.982	14	C-79/1-1,3-1	1.8
1989	NY-A	13	24	0	2	0	0	0	0	3	5	.083	.185	.083	269	-22	-4	0	1	-0	1.000	1	/C-6,S-1,D-1	-0.3
	Oak-A	9	10	1	2	0	0	1	1	0	4	.200	.200	.500	700	95	-0	0	0	0	.500	-0	/3-3,C-2,1-1,O-1R	-0.1
	Bal-A	25	51	5	11	2	0	0	9	9	11	.216	.333	.255	588	70	-2	0	1	-0	1.000	5	C-24	0.4
	Yr	47	85	6	15	2	0	1	10	12	20	.176	.278	.235	514	47	-6	0	2	-1	1.000	6	C-32/3-3,S-1,D1O	0.0
1990	*Oak-A	56	121	12	34	5	1	3	26	14	34	.281	.360	.413	774	121	4	0	0	0	.977	-2	C-37/1-8,3-8,O-1R,D	0.4
1991	Oak-A	76	203	16	53	4	0	1	17	16	28	.261	.321	.296	617	76	-6	0	3	-1	.982	6	C-54/1-8,3-1,D-1	0.1
1992	*Oak-A	78	177	13	39	7	1	2	11	16	28	.220	.296	.305	601	72	-6	0	0	0	.973	5	C-59/1-9,3-2,D-1	0.1
Total	18	984	2266	193	544	100	7	43	247	177	435	.240	.300	.347	648	78	-67	5	16	-5	.982	28	C-525,3-118/D1OS2	-3.1

■ BRIAN RAABE Raabe, Brian Charles b: 11/5/67, New Ulm, Minn. BR/TR, 5'9", 177 lbs. Deb: 9/17/95

YEAR	TM/L	G	AB	R	H	2B	3B	HR	RBI	BB	SO	AVG	OBP	SLG	OPS	OPS+	BR+	SB	CS	SBR	FA	FR	G/POS	TPR
1995	Min-A	6	14	4	3	0	0	0	1	1	0	.214	.267	.214	481	27	-1	0	0	0	1.000	-1	/2-4,3-2	-0.2
1996	Min-A	7	9	0	2	0	0	0	1	0	1	.222	.222	.222	444	13	-1	0	0	0	.857	-1	/3-6,2-1	-0.1
1997	Sea-A	2	3	0	0	0	0	0	0	1	2	.000	.250	.000	250	-28	-1	0	0	0	1.000	-1	/3-2,2-1	-0.1
	Col-N	2	3	0	1	0	0	0	0	0	1	.333	.333	.333	667	61	-0	0	0	0	1.000	0	/2-1	0.0
Total	3	17	29	4	6	0	0	0	2	2	4	.207	.258	.207	465	21	-3	0	0	0	.889	-2	/3-10,2-7	-0.4

■ JOHN RABB Rabb, John Andrew b: 6/23/60, Los Angeles, Cal. BR/TR, 6'1", 180 lbs. Deb: 9/4/82 Career OF: (5-LF 0-CF 10-RF)

YEAR	TM/L	G	AB	R	H	2B	3B	HR	RBI	BB	SO	AVG	OBP	SLG	OPS	OPS+	BR+	SB	CS	SBR	FA	FR	G/POS	TPR
1982	SF-N	2	2	0	1	0	1	0	0	0	1	.500	.500	1.500	2000	441	1	0	0	0	1.000	-0	/O-1(1-0-0)	0.1
1983	SF-N	40	104	10	24	9	0	1	14	9	17	.231	.292	.346	638	79	-3	1	0	0	.973	4	C-31/O-2(0-0-2)	0.2
1984	SF-N	54	82	10	16	1	0	3	9	10	33	.195	.283	.317	600	71	-3	1	1	-0	.988	-2	1-13/O-8(3-0-6),C-6	-0.6
1985	Atl-N	3	2	0	0	0	0	0	0	0	1	.000	.000	.000	0	-94	-1	0	0	0	.000	-0	/O-1(1-0-0)	-0.1
1988	Sea-A	9	14	2	5	2	0	0	4	0	1	.357	.357	.500	857	131	1	0	0	0	1.000	0	/O-2(0-0-2),1-1,D-5	0.1
Total	5	108	204	22	46	12	1	4	27	19	53	.225	.291	.353	644	81	-6	2	1	0	.966	2	/C-37,1-14,O-14R,D	-0.3

■ JOE RABBITT Rabbitt, Joseph Patrick b: 1/16/1900, Frontenac, Kan. d: 12/5/69, Norwalk, Conn. BL/TR, 5'10", 165 lbs. Deb: 9/15/22

YEAR	TM/L	G	AB	R	H	2B	3B	HR	RBI	BB	SO	AVG	OBP	SLG	OPS	OPS+	BR+	SB	CS	SBR	FA	FR	G/POS	TPR
1922	Cle-A	2	3	1	1	0	0	0	0	0	0	.333	.333	.333	667	74	-0	0	0	0	.000	-1	/O-1(1-0-0)	-0.1

■ MARV RACKLEY Rackley, Marvin Eugene b: 7/25/21, Seneca, S.C. BL/TL, 5'10", 170 lbs. Deb: 4/15/47

YEAR	TM/L	G	AB	R	H	2B	3B	HR	RBI	BB	SO	AVG	OBP	SLG	OPS	OPS+	BR+	SB	CS	SBR	FA	FR	G/POS	TPR
1947	Bro-N	18	9	2	2	0	0	0	2	1	0	.222	.300	.222	522	39	-1	0			1.000	0	/O-2(0-1-1)	0.0
1948	Bro-N	88	281	55	92	13	5	0	15	19	25	.327	.370	.409	779	107	3	8			.949	-5	O-74(43-33-1)	-0.6
1949	*Bro-N	9	9	2	4	1	0	0	1	1	0	.444	.500	.556	1056	175	1	0			1.000	-0	/O-3(3-0-0)	0.1
	Pit-N	11	35	5	11	2	0	0	2	2	3	.314	.351	.371	723	92	-0	1			1.000	0	/O-8(8-0-0)	0.0
	*Bro-N	54	141	23	41	4	1	1	14	13	8	.291	.351	.355	705	86	-2	1			.986	-8	O-44(41-3-0)	-1.2
	Yr	74	185	30	56	7	1	1	17	16	11	.303	.358	.368	726	91	-2	2			.990	-8	O-55(44-11-0)	-1.1
1950	Cin-N	5	2	0	1	0	0	0	1	0	0	.500	.500	.500	1000	163	0	0			.000	0	H	0.0
Total	4	185	477	87	151	20	6	1	35	36	36	.317	.365	.390	754	100	1	10			.966	-13	O-131(87-45-2)	-1.7

■ CHARLEY RADBOURN Radbourn, Charles Gardner "Old Hoss" b: 12/11/1854, Rochester, N.Y. d: 2/5/1897, Bloomington, Ill. BR/TR (BB 1886 (part)), 5'9", 168 lbs. Deb: 5/5/1880 H Career OF: (15-LF 12-CF 93-RF)

YEAR	TM/L	G	AB	R	H	2B	3B	HR	RBI	BB	SO	AVG	OBP	SLG	OPS	OPS+	BR+	SB	CS	SBR	FA	FR	G/POS	TPR
1880	Buf-N	6	21	1	3	0	0	0	1	0	1	.143	.143	.143	286	-3	-2				.900	4	/O-3(0-0-3),2-3	0.2
1881	Pro-N	72	270	27	59	9	0	0	28	10	15	.219	.246	.252	498	58	-12				.906	-2	P-41,O-25R,S-13	-0.9
1882	Pro-N	83	326	30	78	11	0	1	32	12	22	.239	.266	.282	548	76	-8				.912	1	P-54,O-32(1-0-31)/S-1	-0.2
1883	Pro-N	89	381	59	108	11	3	3	48	14	16	.283	.309	.352	661	98	-1				.920	2	*P-76,O-20L/1-2	-0.3
1884	*Pro-N	87	361	48	83	7	1	1	37	26	42	.230	.282	.263	545	74	-10				.892	-6	*P-75/O-7R,1-5,S2	-0.3
1885	Pro-N	66	249	34	58	9	2	0	22	36	27	.233	.330	.285	615	103	3				.937	0	P-49,O-16(2-4-10)/2-2	-0.2
1886	Bos-N	66	253	30	60	5	1	2	22	17	36	.237	.285	.289	574	78	-6	5			.924	1	P-58/O-6(1-0-5)	-0.2
1887	Bos-N	51	193	25	58	2	2	1	24	18	21	.301	.308	.280	588	64	-8	6			.848	-4	P-50/O-2(0-0-2)	-0.1
1888	Bos-N	24	79	6	17	1	0	0	6	3	14	.215	.262	.228	490	56	-4	4			.895	-1	P-24	0.0
1889	Bos-N	35	122	17	23	1	0	1	13	9	19	.189	.256	.221	477	32	-11	3			.975	1	P-33/O-2(0-1-1),3-1	-0.1
1890	Bos-P	45	154	20	39	6	0	0	16	9	20	.253	.299	.292	591	55	-10	7			.935	0	P-41/O-4(0-0-4),1-1	-0.2
1891	Cin-N	29	96	11	17	2	2	0	10	4	11	.177	.225	.240	465	35	-8	1			.880	-3	P-26/O-2(1-1-0),3-1	-0.1
Total	12	653	2505	308	603	64	11	9	259	158	244	.241	.283	.281	564	72	-79	26			.913	-6	P-527,O-119R/S123	-2.4

■ JOHN RADCLIFF Radcliff, John Y. b: 6/29/1848, Philadelphia, Pa. d: 7/26/11, Ocean City, N.J. 5'6", 140 lbs. Deb: 5/20/1871 Career OF: (0-LF 1-CF 14-RF)

YEAR	TM/L	G	AB	R	H	2B	3B	HR	RBI	BB	SO	AVG	OBP	SLG	OPS	OPS+	BR+	SB	CS	SBR	FA	FR	G/POS	TPR
1871	Ath-n	28	145	47	44	7	5	0	22	6	1	.303	.331	.421	752	116	3	5	1	1	.804	3	*S-28	0.4
1872	Bal-n	56	297	70	86	13	4	1	44	0	2	.290	.290	.370	660	97	-3	3	3	-0	.771	-4	*S-50/3-6,2-1	-0.6
1873	Bal-n	45	245	59	70	7	0	0	33	3	2	.286	.294	.314	609	81	-5	0	0	0	.762	-1	3-24,S-23/2-1	-0.5
1874	Phi-n	23	103	20	25	7	0	1	14	2	0	.243	.257	.340	597	87	-2	1	1	-0	.800	-3	O-15R/2-4,S-3,31	-0.3
1875	Cen-n	5	23	2	4	0	0	0	0	1	0	.174	.208	.174	382	37	-1	0	0	0	.651	-1	/S-5	-0.2
Total	5 n	157	813	198	229	34	9	2	113	12	5	.282	.292	.353	645	93	-8	9	5	0	.764	-5	S-109/3-33,O-15R,21	-1.2

■ RIP RADCLIFF Radcliff, Raymond Allen b: 1/19/06, Kiowa, Okla. d: 5/23/62, Enid, Okla. BL/TL, 5'10", 170 lbs. Deb: 9/17/34

YEAR	TM/L	G	AB	R	H	2B	3B	HR	RBI	BB	SO	AVG	OBP	SLG	OPS	OPS+	BR+	SB	CS	SBR	FA	FR	G/POS	TPR
1934	Chi-A	14	56	7	15	2	1	0	5	0	2	.268	.268	.339	607	54	-4	1	0	0	.946	1	O-14(0-0-14)	-0.4
1935	Chi-A	146	623	95	178	28	8	10	68	53	21	.286	.336	.404	750	91	-9	4	4	-1	.968	-18	*O-142(142-0-0)	-3.3
1936	Chi-A★	138	618	120	207	31	7	8	82	44	12	.335	.381	.447	828	100	-0	6	3	0	.936	-17	*O-132(132-0-0)	-2.1
1937	Chi-A	144	584	105	190	38	10	4	79	53	25	.325	.383	.445	829	108	8	6	1	1	.966	-4	*O-139(139-0-0)	-0.3
1938	Chi-A	129	503	64	166	23	6	5	81	36	17	.330	.376	.429	805	99	-1	5	7	-1	.979	-1	O-99(99-0-0),1-23	-1.0
1939	Chi-A	113	397	49	105	25	2	2	53	26	21	.264	.313	.353	666	68	-19	6	4	-0	.970	-10	O-78(10-0-69),1-20	-3.4
1940	StL-A	150	584	83	**200**	33	9	7	81	47	20	.342	.392	.466	858	119	17	6	4	-0	.973	-6	*O-139(116-0-23)/1-4	0.2
1941	StL-A	19	71	12	20	2	2	2	14	10	1	.282	.370	.451	821	112	1	1	1	-0	1.000	-2	O-14(14-0-0)/1-3	-0.2
	Det-A	96	379	47	120	14	5	3	40	19	13	.317	.351	.404	755	90	-5	4	4	-0	.970	-5	O-87(85-0-2)	-1.6
	Yr	115	450	59	140	16	7	5	54	29	14	.311	.354	.411	765	94	-4	5	5	-1	.974	-8	*O-101(99-0-2)/1-3	-1.8
1942	Det-A	62	144	13	36	5	0	1	20	9	6	.250	.294	.306	600	64	-7	0	0	0	.978	-0	O-24(6-0-18)/1-4	-1.0
1943	Det-A	70	115	3	30	4	0	0	10	13	3	.261	.341	.296	637	81	-2	1	1	-0	1.000	-1	O-19(2-0-17)/1-1	-0.4
Total	10	1081	4074	598	1267	205	50	42	533	310	141	.311	.362	.417	779	96	-22	40	30	-2	.967	-62	O-887(745-0-143)/1-55	-13.5

■ DAVE RADER Rader, David Martin b: 12/26/48, Claremore, Okla. BL/TR, 5'11", 165 lbs. Deb: 9/5/71

YEAR	TM/L	G	AB	R	H	2B	3B	HR	RBI	BB	SO	AVG	OBP	SLG	OPS	OPS+	BR+	SB	CS	SBR	FA	FR	G/POS	TPR
1971	SF-N	3	4	0	0	0	0	0	0	0	0	.000	.000	.000	0	-99	-1	0	0	0	1.000	-0	/C-1	-0.1
1972	SF-N	133	459	44	119	14	1	6	41	29	31	.259	.308	.333	641	81	-12	1	2	-0	.985	-13	*C-127	-2.1

YEAR	TM/L	G	AB	R	H	2B	3B	HR	RBI	BB	SO	AVG	OBP	SLG	OPS	OPS+	BR+	SB	CS	SBR	FA	FR	G/POS	TPR
1973	SF-N	148	462	59	106	15	4	9	41	63	22	.229	.330	.338	667	82	-10	0	0	0	.991	-12	*C-148	-1.6
1974	SF-N	113	323	26	94	16	2	1	26	31	21	.291	.353	.362	715	96	-1	1	0	0	.984	-9	*C-109	-0.6
1975	SF-N	98	292	39	85	15	0	5	31	32	30	.291	.363	.394	757	106	3	1	0	0	.984	-3	C-94	0.4
1976	SF-N	88	255	25	67	15	0	1	22	27	21	.263	.333	.333	667	87	-4	2	0	0	.984	-9	C-81	-0.9
1977	StL-N	66	114	15	30	7	1	1	16	9	10	.263	.317	.368	685	85	-3	1	0	0	.976	4	C-38	0.3
1978	Chi-N	116	305	29	62	13	3	3	36	34	26	.203	.285	.295	580	56	-18	1	1	-0	.977	-13	*C-114	-2.8
1979	Phi-N	31	54	3	11	1	1	1	5	6	7	.204	.283	.315	598	61	-3	0	0	0	.932	-4	C-25	-0.6
1980	Bos-A	50	137	14	45	11	0	3	17	14	12	.328	.391	.474	865	129	6	1	1	-0	.981	3	C-34/D-9	0.9
Total	10	846	2405	254	619	107	12	30	235	245	180	.257	.329	.349	678	86	-42	8	4	0	.983	-56	C-771/D-9	-7.1
■ **DON RADER**	Rader, Donald Russell b: 9/5/1893, Wolcott, Ind. d: 6/26/83, Walla Walla, Wash BL/TR, 5'10", 164 lbs. Deb: 7/25/13																							
1913	Chi-A	4	3	1	1	1	0	0	0	0	0	.333	.333	.667	1000	193	0	0			.000	-1	/3-1,O-1(1-0-0)	0.0
1921	Phi-N	9	32	4	9	2	0	0	3	3	5	.281	.343	.344	687	76	-1	0	0	0	1.000	-6	/S-9	-0.6
Total	2	13	35	5	10	3	0	0	3	3	5	.286	.342	.371	714	84	-1	0	0		1.000	-6	/S-9,O-1(1-0-0),3-1	-0.6
■ **DOUG RADER**	Rader, Douglas Lee "Rojo" or "The Red Rooster" b: 7/30/44, Chicago, Ill. BR/TR, 6'3", 215 lbs. Deb: 7/31/67 MC Career OF: (0-LF 0-CF 1-RF)																							
1967	Hou-N	47	162	24	54	10	4	2	26	7	31	.333	.368	.481	850	146	9	0	3	-1	.972	-1	1-36/3-7	0.6
1968	Hou-N	98	333	42	89	16	4	6	43	31	51	.267	.332	.393	725	119	8	2	2	-0	.930	1	3-86/1-5	0.9
1969	Hou-N	155	569	62	140	25	3	11	83	62	103	.246	.327	.359	685	94	-4	1	5	-2	.945	14	*3-154/1-4	0.8
1970	Hou-N	156	576	90	145	25	3	25	87	57	102	.252	.323	.436	759	106	3	3	2	-0	**.966**	24	*3-154/1-1	2.5
1971	Hou-N	135	484	51	118	21	4	12	56	40	112	.244	.306	.378	684	95	-4	5	1	1	.946	2	*3-135	-0.3
1972	Hou-N	152	553	70	131	24	7	22	90	57	120	.237	.314	.425	739	110	6	5	5	-1	.958	18	*3-152	2.4
1973	Hou-N	154	574	79	146	26	0	21	89	46	97	.254	.313	.409	722	99	-2	4	3	-0	.945	-5	*3-152	-0.9
1974	Hou-N	152	533	61	137	27	3	17	78	60	131	.257	.337	.415	751	114	9	7	2	1	.965	5	*3-152	1.5
1975	Hou-N	129	448	41	100	23	2	12	48	42	101	.223	.297	.364	661	89	-8	5	4	-0	**.971**	8	*3-124/S-2	-0.1
1976	SD-N	139	471	45	121	22	4	9	55	55	102	.257	.338	.378	716	112	8	3	4	-1	.955	14	*3-137	2.1
1977	SD-N	52	170	19	46	8	3	5	27	33	40	.271	.392	.441	833	137	10	0	1	-0	.961	1	3-51	1.0
	Tor-A	96	313	47	75	18	2	13	40	38	65	.240	.328	.435	762	104	2	2	1	0	.966	1	3-45,D-34/1-7,O-1R	0.0
Total	11	1465	5186	631	1302	245	39	155	722	528	1055	.251	.325	.403	728	106	35	37	33	-3	.956	82	*3-1349/1-53,D-34,SO	10.5
■ **PAUL RADFORD**	Radford, Paul Revere "Shorty" b: 10/14/1861, Roxbury, Mass. d: 2/21/45, Boston, Mass. BR/TR, 5'6", 148 lbs. Deb: 5/1/1883 Career OF: (33-LF 153-CF 724-RF)																							
1883	Bos-N	72	258	46	53	6	3	0	14	9	26	.205	.232	.252	484	46	-16				.836	-5	*O-72(1-24-50)	-2.0
1884	*Pro-N	97	355	56	70	11	2	1	29	25	43	.197	.250	.248	498	58	-16				.882	5	*O-96(0-0-96)/P-2	-1.0
1885	Pro-N	105	371	55	90	12	5	0	32	33	43	.243	.304	.302	606	99	1				.852	1	*O-88R,S-16/P-3,2-1	0.1
1886	KC-N	122	493	78	113	17	5	0	20	58	48	.229	.310	.284	594	77	-13	39			.890	10	*O-92R,S-30/2-1	-0.3
1887	NY-a	128	592	127	235	15	5	4	45	**106**		.397	.403	.342	745	114	18	73			.833	-2	S-76,O-37R,2-18,/P	1.5
1888	Bro-a	90	308	48	67	9	3	2	29	35		.218	.305	.286	591	90	-2	33			.944	9	O-88(0-83-5)/2-2	0.4
1889	Cle-N	136	487	94	116	21	5	1	46	91	37	.238	.365	.308	673	91	-1	30			.942	-0	*O-136(0-2-136)/3-1	-0.3
1890	Cle-P	122	466	98	136	24	12	2	62	82	28	.292	.406	.408	814	128	25	25			.895	8	O-80R,S-36/3-7,2P	2.5
1891	Bos-a	133	456	102	118	11	5	0	65	96	36	.259	.393	.305	698	102	7	55			.906	20	*S-131/O-4(4-0-0),P-1	2.6
1892	Was-N	137	510	93	130	19	4	1	37	86	47	.255	.366	.314	679	109	10	35			.933	-7	O-62R,3-54,S-20,/2	0.2
1893	Was-N	124	464	87	106	18	3	2	34	104	42	.228	.378	.293	672	82	-6	32			.901	7	*O-123R/2-1,P-1	-0.4
1894	Was-N	95	325	61	78	13	5	0	49	65	23	.240	.378	.311	689	70	-13	24			.852	-0	S-47,2-25,O-24R	-0.8
Total	12	1361	5085	945	1312	176	57	13	462	790	373	.258	.351	.308	660	92	-8	346			.901	46	O-902R,S-356/3-62,2P	2.5
■ **RYAN RADMANOVICH**	Radmanovich, Ryan Ashley b: 8/9/71, Calgary, Alberta, Can. BL/TR, 6'2", 200 lbs. Deb: 4/13/98																							
1998	Sea-A	25	69	5	15	4	0	2	10	4	25	.217	.260	.362	623	60	-4	1	1	-0	1.000	-1	O-24(0-0-24)/1-1	-0.6
■ **JACK RADTKE**	Radtke, Jack William b: 4/14/13, Denver, Colo. BB/TR, 5'7", 160 lbs. Deb: 8/1/36																							
1936	Bro-N	33	31	8	3	0	0	0	2	4	9	.097	.200	.097	297	-18	-5	3			1.000	5	2-14/3-5,S-4	0.0
■ **JACK RAFTER**	Rafter, John Cornelius b: 2/20/1875, Troy, N.Y. d: 1/5/43, Troy, N.Y. BR/TR, 5'8", 165 lbs. Deb: 9/24/04																							
1904	Pit-N	1	3	0	0	0	0	0	0	0		.000	.000	.000	0	-97	-1	0			1.000	0	/C-1	-0.1
■ **TOM RAFTERY**	Raftery, Thomas Francis b: 10/5/1881, Boston, Mass. d: 12/31/54, Boston, Mass. BR/TR, 5'10.5", 175 lbs. Deb: 4/18/09																							
1909	Cle-A	8	32	6	7	2	1	0	0	4		.219	.306	.344	649	101	0	1			1.000	-1	/O-8(1-1-6)	-0.1
■ **TOM RAGLAND**	Ragland, Thomas b: 6/16/46, Talladega, Ala. BR/TR, 5'10", 155 lbs. Deb: 4/5/71																							
1971	Was-A	10	23	1	4	0	0	0	0	0	5	.174	.208	.174	382	10	-3	0	0	0	1.000	-1	2-10	-0.3
1972	Tex-A	25	58	3	10	2	0	0	2	5	11	.172	.238	.207	445	35	-5	0	1	-0	.982	-3	2-13/3-5,S-3	-0.8
1973	Cle-A	67	183	16	47	7	1	0	12	8	31	.257	.292	.306	598	67	-8	2	3	-1	.984	13	2-65/S-2	0.8
Total	3	102	264	20	61	9	1	0	14	13	47	.231	.272	.273	545	56	-15	2	4	-1	.985	10	/2-88,S-5,3-5	-0.3
■ **LARRY RAINES**	Raines, Lawrence Glenn Hope b: 3/9/30, St.Albans, W.Va. d: 1/28/78, Lansing, Mich. BR/TR, 5'10", 165 lbs. Deb: 4/16/57 Career OF: (8-LF 0-CF 0-RF)																							
1957	Cle-A	96	244	39	64	14	0	2	16	19	40	.262	.318	.344	662	82	-6	5	2	0	.922	-5	3-27,S-25,2-10,/O-8L	-1.0
1958	Cle-A	7	9	1	0	0	0	0	0	0	5	.000	.000	.000	0	-99	-2	0	1	-0	.933	4	/2-2	0.1
Total	2	103	253	40	64	14	0	2	16	19	45	.253	.308	.332	640	76	-9	5	3	0	.963	-2	/3-27,S-25,2-12,O-8L	-0.9
■ **TIM RAINES**	Raines, Timothy "Rock" b: 9/16/59, Sanford, Fla. BB/TR, 5'8", 178 lbs. Deb: 9/11/79 Career OF: (1929-LF 165-CF 1-RF)																							
1979	Mon-N	6	0	3	0	0	0	0	0	0	0	—	—	—	—	—	0	2	0	0	.000	0	/R	0.0
1980	Mon-N	15	20	5	1	0	0	0	0	6	3	.050	.269	.050	319	-6	-3	5	0	1	1.000	2	/2-7,O-1(1-0-0)	0.1
1981	*Mon-N★	88	313	61	95	13	7	5	37	45	31	.304	.394	.438	832	134	15	**71**	11	**12**	.976	2	O-81(81-0-0)/2-1	2.7
1982	Mon-N★	156	647	90	179	32	8	4	43	75	83	.277	.354	.369	723	101	2	**78**	16	**12**	.992	3	*O-120(120-0-0),2-36	1.4
1983	Mon-N★	156	615	**133**	183	32	8	11	71	97	70	.298	.395	.429	824	129	27	**90**	14	**15**	.988	16	*O-154(153-2-0)/2-7	5.3
1984	Mon-N★	160	622	106	192	**38**	9	8	60	87	69	.309	.395	.437	833	140	36	**75**	10	**13**	.988	10	*O-160(0-160-0)/2-2	5.8
1985	Mon-N★	150	575	115	184	30	13	11	41	81	60	.320	.407	.475	881	155	44	70	9	12	.993	10	*O-146(146-0-0)	6.1
1986	Mon-N★	151	580	91	194	35	10	9	62	78	60	**.334**	**.415**	.476	891	146	39	70	9	12	.979	11	*O-147(147-0-0)	**5.7**
1987	Mon-N★	139	530	**123**	175	34	8	18	68	90	52	.330	.431	.526	958	148	40	50	5	9	.987	16	*O-139(139-0-0)	5.7
1988	Mon-N	109	429	66	116	19	7	12	48	53	44	.270	.353	.431	785	119	11	33	7	5	.988	7	*O-108(108-0-0)	2.1
1989	Mon-N	145	517	76	148	29	6	9	60	93	48	.286	.398	.418	816	132	25	41	9	6	.996	3	*O-139(140-0-0)	3.1
1990	Mon-N	130	457	65	131	11	5	9	62	70	43	.287	.385	.392	777	119	14	49	16	5	.976	-1	*O-123(123-0-0)	1.5
1991	Chi-A	155	609	102	163	20	6	5	50	83	68	.268	.360	.345	705	98	2	51	15	6	.990	10	*O-133(134-1-0),D-19	1.3
1992	Chi-A	144	551	102	162	22	9	7	54	81	48	.294	.384	.405	789	123	19	45	6	8	.994	14	*O-129(129-1-0),D-14	3.7
1993	*Chi-A	115	415	75	127	16	4	16	54	64	35	.306	.402	.480	882	139	25	21	7	2	**1.000**	-1	*O-112(112-0-0)	2.2
1994	Chi-A	101	384	80	102	15	5	10	52	61	43	.266	.368	.409	777	102	2	13	0	3	.981	4	O-96(97-0-0)	0.5
1995	Chi-A	133	502	81	143	25	4	12	67	70	52	.285	.376	.422	798	112	11	13	2	2	.980	1	*O-107(107-0-1),D-22	0.8
1996	*NY-A	59	201	45	57	10	0	9	33	34	29	.284	.390	.468	857	116	6	10	1	2	.988	-1	O-50(50-0-0)/D-2	0.4
1997	*NY-A	74	271	56	87	20	2	4	38	41	34	.321	.410	.454	864	126	12	8	5	0	.988	-6	O-57(57-0-0),D-13	0.3
1998	*NY-A	109	321	53	93	13	1	5	47	55	49	.290	.398	.383	782	109	7	8	3	1	.985	-4	D-56,O-47(47-0-0)	0.0
1999	Oak-A	58	135	20	29	5	0	4	17	26	17	.215	.342	.341	682	78	-4	4	1	1	1.000	-4	O-38(38-1-0)/D-3	-0.8
Total	21	2353	8694	1548	2561	419	112	168	964	1290	938	.295	.388	.427	815	124	332	807	146	126	.988	92	*O-2087L,D-129/2-53	47.9
■ **JOHN RAINEY**	Rainey, John Paul b: 7/26/1864, Birmingham, Mich. d: 11/11/12, Detroit, Mich. BL/TR, 5'10", 164 lbs. Deb: 8/25/1887 Career OF: (0-LF 0-CF 28-RF)																							
1887	NY-N	17	63	6	22	3	0	0	12	5	6	.349	.349	.345	694	98	0	0			.818	-3	3-17	-0.2
1890	Buf-P	42	166	29	39	5	1	1	20	24	15	.235	.349	.295	644	79	-3	12			.870	0	O-28R/S-7,3-6,2-2	-0.2
Total	2	59	229	35	61	8	1	1	32	29	21	.266	.349	.308	657	84	-3	12			.827	-3	/O-28R,3-23,S-7,2-2	-0.4
■ **GARY RAJSICH**	Rajsich, Gary Louis b: 10/28/54, Youngstown, Ohio BL/TL, 6'2", 210 lbs. Deb: 4/9/82 F																							
1982	NY-N	80	162	17	42	8	3	2	12	17	40	.259	.333	.383	716	100	0	1	3	-1	1.000	-2	O-35(10-0-26)/1-2	-0.5
1983	NY-N	11	36	5	12	3	0	1	3	3	1	.333	.400	.500	900	149	2	0	0	0	1.000	-0	1-10	0.2
1984	StL-N	7	7	1	1	0	0	0	2	2	1	.143	.333	.143	476	39	-0	0	0	0	1.000	-0	/1-3	-0.1

YEAR	TM/L	G	AB	R	H	2B	3B	HR	RBI	BB	SO	AVG	OBP	SLG	OPS	OPS+	BR+	SB	CS	SBR	FA	FR	G/POS	TPR
1985	SF-N	51	91	5	15	6	0	0	10	17	22	.165	.296	.231	527	52	-5	0	1	-0	.990	-1	1-23	-0.9
Total	4	149	296	28	70	17	3	3	27	39	64	.236	.329	.345	674	90	-3	1	4	-1	.994	-4	/1-38,O-35(10-0-26)	-1.3

■ DOC RALSTON Ralston, Samuel Beryl b: 8/3/1885, Pierpont, Ohio d: 8/29/50, Lancaster, Pa. BR/TR, 6', 185 lbs. Deb: 9/8/10

YEAR	TM/L	G	AB	R	H	2B	3B	HR	RBI	BB	SO	AVG	OBP	SLG	OPS	OPS+	BR+	SB	CS	SBR	FA	FR	G/POS	TPR
1910	Was-A	21	73	4	15	1	0	0	3	3		.205	.256	.219	476	52	-4	2			.976	2	O-21(21-0-0)	-0.4

■ BOB RAMAZZOTTI Ramazzotti, Robert Louis b: 1/16/17, Elanora, Pa. d: 2/15/2000, Altoona, Pa. BR/TR, 5'8.5", 175 lbs. Deb: 4/20/46

YEAR	TM/L	G	AB	R	H	2B	3B	HR	RBI	BB	SO	AVG	OBP	SLG	OPS	OPS+	BR+	SB	CS	SBR	FA	FR	G/POS	TPR
1946	Bro-N	62	120	10	25	4	0	0	7	9	13	.208	.264	.242	505	43	-9	0			.939	5	3-30,2-16	-0.4
1948	Bro-N	4	3	0	0	0	0	0	0	0	1	.000	.000	.000	0	-97	-1	0			1.000	0	/3-2,2-1	-0.1
1949	Bro-N	5	13	1	2	0	0	1	3	0	3	.154	.154	.385	538	38	-1	0			.833	-1	/3-3	-0.2
	Chi-N	65	190	14	34	3	1	0	6	5	33	.179	.200	.205	405	9	-24	9			.972	6	3-36,S-12/2-4	-1.8
	Yr	70	203	15	36	3	1	1	9	5	36	.177	.197	.217	414	11	-26	9			.965	5	3-39,S-12/2-4	-2.0
1950	Chi-N	61	145	19	38	3	3	1	6	4	16	.262	.287	.345	631	66	-7	3			.961	-2	2-31,3-10/S-3	-0.8
1951	Chi-N	73	158	13	39	5	2	1	15	10	23	.247	.292	.323	614	64	-8	0	0	0	.950	13	S-51/2-6,3-1	0.7
1952	Chi-N	50	183	26	52	5	3	1	12	14	14	.284	.338	.361	699	93	-2	3	1	0	.979	-2	2-50	-0.1
1953	Chi-N	26	39	3	6	2	0	0	4	3	4	.154	.214	.205	419	10	-5	0	0	0	.911	-0	2-18	-0.5
Total	7	346	851	86	196	22	9	4	53	45	107	.230	.271	.291	562	52	-58	15	1		.966	18	2-126/3-82,S-66	-3.2

■ ALEX RAMIREZ Ramirez, Alexander Ramon b: 10/3/74, Caracas, Venez. BR/TR, 5'11", 180 lbs. Deb: 9/19/98 Career OF: (22-LF 2-CF 71-RF)

YEAR	TM/L	G	AB	R	H	2B	3B	HR	RBI	BB	SO	AVG	OBP	SLG	OPS	OPS+	BR+	SB	CS	SBR	FA	FR	G/POS	TPR
1998	Cle-A	3	8	1	1	0	0	0	0	0	3	.125	.125	.125	250	-34	-2	0	0	0	.833	-0	/O-3(2-0-1)	-0.2
1999	Cle-A	48	97	11	29	6	1	3	18	3	26	.299	.327	.474	801	97	-1	1	1	-0	.920	-7	O-29(5-1-23),D-14	-0.9
2000	Cle-A	41	112	13	32	5	1	5	12	5	17	.286	.316	.482	798	96	-1	1	0	0	.978	-3	O-31(15-1-16)/D-6	-0.4
	Pit-N	43	115	13	24	6	1	4	18	7	32	.209	.254	.383	637	58	-8	1	0	0	.949	-1	O-31(0-0-31)/1-1	-1.0
Total	3	135	332	38	86	17	3	12	48	15	78	.259	.293	.437	730	80	-11	3	1	0	.949	-11	/O-94R,D-20,1-1	-2.5

■ ARAMIS RAMIREZ Ramirez, Aramis (Nin) b: 6/25/78, Santo Domingo, D.R. BR/TR, 6'1", 190 lbs. Deb: 5/26/98

YEAR	TM/L	G	AB	R	H	2B	3B	HR	RBI	BB	SO	AVG	OBP	SLG	OPS	OPS+	BR+	SB	CS	SBR	FA	FR	G/POS	TPR
1998	Pit-N	72	251	23	59	9	1	6	24	18	72	.235	.297	.351	647	69	-12	0	1	-0	.941	-14	3-71	-2.5
1999	Pit-N	18	56	2	10	2	1	0	7	6	9	.179	.258	.250	508	29	-6	0	0	0	.930	0	3-17	-0.5
2000	Pit-N	73	254	19	65	15	2	6	35	10	36	.256	.297	.402	699	75	-10	0	0	0	.917	-4	3-72	-1.4
Total	3	163	561	44	134	26	4	12	66	34	117	.239	.293	.364	657	68	-28	0	1	-0	.928	-18	3-160	-4.4

■ JULIO RAMIREZ Ramirez, Julio Cesar (Figueroa) b: 8/10/77, San Juan De La Maguana, D.R. BR/TR, 5'11", 170 lbs. Deb: 9/10/99

YEAR	TM/L	G	AB	R	H	2B	3B	HR	RBI	BB	SO	AVG	OBP	SLG	OPS	OPS+	BR+	SB	CS	SBR	FA	FR	G/POS	TPR
1999	Fla-N	15	21	3	3	1	0	0	2	1	6	.143	.182	.190	372	-6	-3	0	1	-0	.950	-2	O-11(0-11-0)	-0.5

■ MANNY RAMIREZ Ramirez, Manuel Aristides (Onelcida) b: 5/30/72, Santo Domingo, D.R. BR/TR, 6', 190 lbs. Deb: 9/2/93

YEAR	TM/L	G	AB	R	H	2B	3B	HR	RBI	BB	SO	AVG	OBP	SLG	OPS	OPS+	BR+	SB	CS	SBR	FA	FR	G/POS	TPR
1993	Cle-A	22	53	5	9	1	0	2	5	2	8	.170	.200	.302	502	33	-5	0	0	0	1.000	0	D-20/O-1(0-0-1)	-0.6
1994	Cle-A	91	290	51	78	22	0	17	60	42	72	.269	.361	.521	882	124	10	4	2	0	.994	-1	O-84(0-0-84)/D-5	0.5
1995	*Cle-A★	137	484	85	149	26	1	31	107	75	112	.308	.406	.558	964	146	33	6	6	-1	.978	-4	*O-131(0-0-131)/D-5	2.0
1996	*Cle-A	152	550	94	170	45	3	33	112	85	104	.309	.404	.582	986	146	39	8	5	0	.970	8	*O-149(0-0-149)/D-3	3.6
1997	*Cle-A	150	561	99	184	40	0	26	88	79	115	.328	.417	.538	956	142	37	2	3	-1	.975	-0	*O-146(0-0-146)/D-4	2.6
1998	*Cle-A★	150	571	108	168	35	2	45	145	76	121	.294	.383	.599	982	145	37	5	3	0	.977	3	*O-148(0-0-148)/D-2	3.0
1999	*Cle-A★	147	522	131	174	34	3	44	**165**	96	131	.333	.448	**.663**	**1111**	**171**	**58**	2	4	-1	.975	-1	*O-146(0-0-145)/D-2	4.5
2000	Cle-A†	118	439	92	154	34	2	38	122	86	117	.351	.460	**.697**	**1157**	183	58	1	1	-0	.986	-2	O-93(0-0-93),D-25	4.4
Total	8	967	3470	665	1086	237	11	236	804	541	780	.313	.411	.592	1003	151	268	28	24	-2	.978	3	O-898(0-0-897)/D-66	20.0

■ MARIO RAMIREZ Ramirez, Mario (Torres) b: 9/12/57, Yauco, P.R. BR/TR, 5'9", 159 lbs. Deb: 4/25/80

YEAR	TM/L	G	AB	R	H	2B	3B	HR	RBI	BB	SO	AVG	OBP	SLG	OPS	OPS+	BR+	SB	CS	SBR	FA	FR	G/POS	TPR
1980	NY-N	18	24	2	5	0	0	0	0	1	7	.208	.240	.208	448	27	-2	0	0	0	1.000	3	/S-7/2-4,3-3	0.1
1981	SD-N	13	13	1	1	0	0	0	1	2	5	.077	.200	.077	277	-21	-2	0	0	0	1.000	4	/S-2,3-2	0.2
1982	SD-N	13	23	1	4	1	0	0	1	2	4	.174	.240	.217	457	30	-2	0	0	0	.963	2	/S-8,2-1,3-1	0.0
1983	SD-N	55	107	11	21	6	3	0	12	20	23	.196	.328	.308	637	80	-2	0	0	0	.985	-2	S-38/3-1	-0.2
1984	*SD-N	48	59	12	7	1	0	2	9	13	14	.119	.278	.237	515	46	-4	0	0	0	.971	-1	S-33/3-6,2-2	-0.3
1985	SD-N	37	60	6	17	0	0	2	5	3	11	.283	.317	.383	701	97	-0	0	0	0	.918	-5	S-27/2-7	-0.4
Total	6	184	286	33	55	8	3	4	28	41	64	.192	.296	.283	579	64	-13	0	0	0	.970	1	S-115/2-14,3-13	-0.6

■ MILT RAMIREZ Ramirez, Milton (Barboza) b: 4/2/50, Mayaguez, P.R. BR/TR, 5'9", 150 lbs. Deb: 4/11/70

YEAR	TM/L	G	AB	R	H	2B	3B	HR	RBI	BB	SO	AVG	OBP	SLG	OPS	OPS+	BR+	SB	CS	SBR	FA	FR	G/POS	TPR
1970	StL-N	62	79	8	15	2	1	0	3	8	9	.190	.264	.241	505	36	-7	0	1	-0	.923	10	S-59/3-1	0.5
1971	StL-N	4	11	2	3	0	0	0	0	2	1	.273	.385	.273	657	86	-0	0	0	0	.947	-1	/S-4	-0.1
1979	Oak-A	28	62	4	10	1	1	0	3	3	8	.161	.200	.210	410	11	-8	0	0	0	.923	-5	3-12,2-11/S-8	-1.2
Total	3	94	152	14	28	3	2	0	6	13	18	.184	.248	.230	479	30	-15	0	1	-0	.920	4	/S-71,3-13,2-11	-0.8

■ ORLANDO RAMIREZ Ramirez, Orlando (Leal) b: 12/18/51, Cartagena, Colombia BR/TR, 5'10", 175 lbs. Deb: 7/6/74

YEAR	TM/L	G	AB	R	H	2B	3B	HR	RBI	BB	SO	AVG	OBP	SLG	OPS	OPS+	BR+	SB	CS	SBR	FA	FR	G/POS	TPR
1974	Cal-A	31	86	4	14	0	0	0	7	6	23	.163	.217	.163	380	11	-10	2	1	0	.956	5	S-31	-0.1
1975	Cal-A	44	100	10	24	4	1	0	4	11	22	.240	.315	.300	615	80	-2	9	6	-0	.905	0	S-40	0.2
1976	Cal-A	30	70	3	14	1	0	0	5	6	11	.200	.263	.214	477	44	-5	3	2	-0	.966	4	S-30	0.2
1977	Cal-A	25	13	6	1	0	0	0	0	0	3	.077	.077	.077	154	-60	-3	1	0	0	1.000	8	/2-5,S-3,D-1	0.5
1979	Cal-A	13	12	1	0	0	0	0	0	1	6	.000	.143	.000	143	-60	-3	1	0	0	.844	4	S-10/D-1	0.2
Total	5	143	281	24	53	5	1	0	16	24	65	.189	.255	.214	468	37	-22	16	9	0	.931	22	S-114/2-5,D-2	1.0

■ RAFAEL RAMIREZ Ramirez, Rafael Emilio (Peguero) b: 2/18/58, San Pedro De Macoris, D.R. BR/TR, 6', 185 lbs. Deb: 8/4/80

YEAR	TM/L	G	AB	R	H	2B	3B	HR	RBI	BB	SO	AVG	OBP	SLG	OPS	OPS+	BR+	SB	CS	SBR	FA	FR	G/POS	TPR
1980	Atl-N	50	165	17	44	6	1	2	11	2	33	.267	.292	.352	644	76	-5	2	1	0	.949	-10	S-46	-1.1
1981	Atl-N	95	307	30	67	16	2	2	20	24	47	.218	.277	.303	580	63	-15	7	3	0	.942	-2	S-95	-0.7
1982	*Atl-N	157	609	74	169	24	4	10	52	36	49	.278	.321	.379	700	91	-7	27	14	1	.956	17	*S-157	2.8
1983	Atl-N	152	622	82	185	13	5	7	58	36	48	.297	.338	.368	706	89	-9	16	12	-1	.949	8	*S-152	1.6
1984	Atl-N☆	145	591	51	157	22	4	2	48	26	70	.266	.298	.327	624	70	-23	14	17	-3	.959	-3	*S-145	-1.5
1985	Atl-N	138	568	54	141	25	4	5	58	20	63	.248	.274	.333	607	65	-27	2	6	-2	.954	9	*S-133	-0.6
1986	Atl-N	134	496	57	119	21	1	8	33	21	60	.240	.275	.335	610	64	-25	19	8	1	.952	13	S-86,3-57/O-3(2-0-1)	-0.2
1987	Atl-N	56	179	22	47	12	0	1	21	8	16	.263	.302	.346	648	68	-8	6	3	0	.946	-6	S-38,3-12	-1.0
1988	Hou-N	155	566	51	156	30	5	6	59	18	61	.276	.302	.378	680	98	-4	3	2	-0	.965	-10	*S-154	-0.2
1989	Hou-N	151	537	46	132	20	2	6	54	29	64	.246	.284	.324	608	76	-18	3	1	0	.945	-41	*S-149	-5.2
1990	Hou-N	132	445	44	116	19	3	2	37	24	46	.261	.300	.330	630	75	-15	10	5	0	.953	-18	*S-129	-2.5
1991	Hou-N	101	233	17	55	10	0	1	20	13	40	.236	.276	.292	568	64	-12	3	3	-0	.953	-14	S-45,2-27/3-2	-2.4
1992	Hou-N	73	176	17	44	6	0	1	13	7	24	.250	.283	.301	584	68	-8	0	0	0	.961	-6	S-57/3-1	-1.1
Total	13	1539	5494	562	1432	224	31	53	484	264	621	.261	.297	.342	639	77	-175	112	75	-2	.953	-64	*S-1386/3-72,2-27,O	-12.1

■ DOMINGO RAMOS Ramos, Domingo Antonio (De Ramos) b: 3/29/58, Santiago, D.R. BR/TR, 5'10", 155 lbs. Deb: 9/8/78 Career OF: (1-LF 0-CF 0-RF)

YEAR	TM/L	G	AB	R	H	2B	3B	HR	RBI	BB	SO	AVG	OBP	SLG	OPS	OPS+	BR+	SB	CS	SBR	FA	FR	G/POS	TPR
1978	NY-A	1	0	0	0	0	0	0	0	0	0	—	—	—	—	—	0	0	0	0	.000	0	/S-1	0.0
1980	Tor-A	5	16	0	2	0	0	0	0	2	5	.125	.222	.125	347	-2	-2	0	0	0	1.000	-0	/2-2,S-2,D-1	-0.2
1982	Sea-A	8	26	3	4	2	0	0	1	3	2	.154	.241	.231	472	30	-3	0	0	0	.920	-5	/S-8	-0.8
1983	Sea-A	53	127	14	36	4	0	2	10	7	12	.283	.326	.362	688	86	-2	3	1	0	.948	8	S-28/2-8,3-8,D-2	0.8
1984	Sea-A	59	81	6	15	2	0	0	2	5	12	.185	.233	.210	442	24	-8	2	2	-0	.911	4	3-38,S-13/1-5,2-3	-0.4
1985	Sea-A	75	168	19	33	6	0	1	15	17	23	.196	.270	.250	520	43	-13	0	1	-0	.951	-8	S-36,2-20,1-14,/3-7	-1.7
1986	Sea-A	49	99	8	18	2	0	0	5	8	13	.182	.250	.202	452	25	-10	0	1	-0	.966	13	S-21,2-16/3-8,D-2	0.4
1987	Sea-A	42	103	9	32	6	0	2	11	3	12	.311	.336	.427	764	96	-1	0	1	-0	.953	7	S-25/3-7,2-6,D-2	0.7
1988	Cle-A	22	46	7	12	1	0	0	5	3	7	.261	.320	.283	603	68	-2	0	0	0	1.000	2	2-11/1-5,S-4,3-2	0.0
	Cal-A	10	15	3	2	0	0	0	0	0	0	.133	.133	.133	267	-26	-2	0	0	0	1.000	-0	/3-8,O-1(1-0-0)	-0.3
	Yr	32	61	10	14	1	0	0	5	3	7	.230	.277	.246	523	47	-4	0	0	0	1.000	2	2-11,3-10/1-5,SO	-0.3
1989	*Chi-N	85	179	18	47	6	2	1	19	17	23	.263	.333	.335	669	85	-3	1	1	-0	.959	3	S-42,3-30	0.2
1990	Chi-N	98	226	22	60	5	0	2	17	27	29	.265	.346	.314	661	77	-6	0	2	-1	.932	-15	3-66,S-21/2-1	-2.1
Total	11	507	1086	109	261	34	2	8	85	92	138	.240	.304	.297	601	64	-52	6	9	-2	.955	7	S-201,3-174/2-67,1DO	-3.4

■ CHUCHO RAMOS Ramos, Jesus Manuel (Garcia) b: 4/12/18, Maturin, Venez. d: 9/2/77, Caracas, Venez. BR/TL, 5'10.5", 167 lbs. Deb: 5/7/44

YEAR	TM/L	G	AB	R	H	2B	3B	HR	RBI	BB	SO	AVG	OBP	SLG	OPS	OPS+	BR+	SB	CS	SBR	FA	FR	G/POS	TPR
1944	Cin-N	4	10	1	5	1	0	0	0	0	0	.500	.500	.600	1100	217	1	0			1.000	-1	/O-3(1-0-3)	0.0

YEAR	TM/L	G	AB	R	H	2B	3B	HR	RBI	BB	SO	AVG	OBP	SLG	OPS	OPS+	BR+	SB	CS	SBR	FA	FR	G/POS	TPR
■ **JOHN RAMOS**	Ramos, John Joseph b: 8/6/65, Tampa, Fla. BR/TR, 6', 190 lbs. Deb: 9/18/91																							
1991	NY-A	10	26	4	8	1	0	0	3	1	3	.308	.333	.346	679	88	-0	0	0	0	1.000	0	/C-5,D-4	0.0
■ **KEN RAMOS**	Ramos, Kenneth Cecil b: 6/6/67, Sidney, Neb. BL/TL, 6'1", 185 lbs. Deb: 5/16/97																							
1997	Hou-N	14	12	0	0	0	0	0	1	2	0	.000	.143	.000	143	-61	-3	0	0	0	.000	-1	/O-2(1-0-1)	-0.4
■ **PEDRO RAMOS**	Ramos, Pedro (Guerra) "Pete" b: 4/28/35, Pinar Del Rio, Cuba BB/TR (BR 1955-59), 6', 185 lbs. Deb: 4/11/55																							
1955	Was-A	59	38	6	3	0	0	0	0	2	18	.079	.125	.079	204	-47	-8	0	1	-0	.964	-1	P-45	0.0
1956	Was-A	56	44	9	9	0	2	0	2	2	16	.205	.239	.295	535	40	-4	0	1	-0	1.000	-0	P-37	0.0
1957	Was-A	56	76	6	13	0	0	1	10	2	27	.171	.192	.211	403	10	-9	0	0	0	**1.000**	-0	P-43	0.0
1958	Was-A	53	88	9	21	1	0	0	10	0	33	.239	.239	.250	489	35	-8	0	0	0	.982	-1	P-43	0.0
1959	Was-A☆	45	75	7	11	1	1	1	2	4	38	.147	.190	.227	417	14	-9	1	0	0	**1.000**	-1	P-37	0.0
1960	Was-A	53	86	6	10	3	0	2	4	1	36	.116	.126	.221	347	-8	-13	0	0	0	**1.000**	0	P-43	0.0
1961	Min-A	53	93	8	16	1	0	3	11	3	42	.172	.206	.280	486	27	-10	0	0	0	.955	-3	P-42	0.0
1962	Cle-A	39	68	6	10	3	0	3	8	1	29	.147	.171	.324	495	31	-7	0	0	0	.962	0	P-37	0.0
1963	Cle-A	54	55	13	6	0	0	3	7	3	32	.109	.155	.273	428	17	-6	0	0	0	.963	-2	P-36	0.0
1964	Cle-A	44	39	6	7	0	0	2	2	2	22	.179	.220	.333	553	52	-3	0	0	0	.960	-1	P-36	0.0
	NY-A	13	5	0	0	0	0	0	0	0	2	.000	.000	.000	0	-98	-1	0	0	0	.000	-1	P-13	0.0
	Yr	57	44	6	7	0	0	2	2	2	24	.159	.196	.295	491	34	-4	0	0	0	.960	-2	P-49	0.0
1965	NY-A	65	12	0	1	0	0	0	0	0	8	.083	.083	.083	167	-53	-2	1	0	0	.895	-1	P-65	0.0
1966	NY-A	52	13	0	2	0	0	0	0	0	8	.154	.154	.154	308	-12	-2	0	0	0	.952	-0	P-52	0.0
1967	Phi-N	6	1	0	0	0	0	0	0	0	0	.000	.000	.000	0	-99	-0	0	0	0	1.000	1	/P-6	0.0
1969	Pit-N	5	1	0	0	0	0	0	0	0	1	.000	.000	.000	0	-99	-0	0	0	0	1.000	0	/P-5	0.0
	Cin-N	38	8	0	0	0	0	0	0	1	4	.000	.111	.000	111	-63	-2	0	0	0	1.000	-0	P-38	0.0
	Yr	43	9	0	0	0	0	0	0	1	5	.000	.100	.000	100	-67	-2	0	0	0	1.000	-0	P-43	0.0
1970	Was-A	5	1	0	0	0	0	0	0	1	0	.000	.500	.000	500	52	0	0	0	0	1.000	0	/P-4	0.0
Total	15	696	703	76	109	9	3	15	56	22	316	.155	.183	.240	423	14	-85	2	2	-0	.977	-9	P-582	0.0
■ **BOBBY RAMOS**	Ramos, Roberto b: 11/5/55, Havana, Cuba BR/TR, 5'11", 208 lbs. Deb: 9/26/78 C																							
1978	Mon-N	2	4	0	0	0	0	0	0	0	1	.000	.000	.000	0	-99	-1	0	0	0	1.000	0	/C-1	-0.1
1980	Mon-N	13	32	5	5	2	0	0	2	5	5	.156	.270	.219	489	38	-3	0	0	0	.964	0	C-12	-0.2
1981	Mon-N	26	41	4	8	1	0	1	3	3	5	.195	.250	.293	543	53	-3	0	0	0	.974	4	C-23	0.2
1982	NY-A	4	11	1	1	0	0	1	2	0	3	.091	.091	.364	455	18	-1	0	0	0	1.000	1	/C-4	0.0
1983	Mon-N	27	61	2	14	3	1	0	5	8	11	.230	.329	.311	640	79	-2	0	0	0	.984	4	C-25	0.4
1984	Mon-N	31	83	8	16	1	0	2	5	6	13	.193	.247	.277	524	49	-6	0	0	0	.982	7	C-31	0.2
Total	6	103	232	20	44	7	1	4	17	22	38	.190	.263	.280	543	53	-15	0	0	0	.980	15	/C-96	0.5
■ **FERNANDO RAMSEY**	Ramsey, Fernando David (Ramsey) b: 12/20/65, Rainbow, Panama BR/TR, 6'1", 175 lbs. Deb: 9/7/92																							
1992	Chi-N	18	25	0	3	0	0	0	2	0	6	.120	.120	.120	240	-31	-4	0	0	0	1.000	-4	O-15(0-15-0)	-1.0
■ **MIKE RAMSEY**	Ramsey, Michael James b: 7/8/60, Thomson, Ga. BB/TL, 6' ", 170 lbs. Deb: 4/6/87																							
1987	LA-N	48	125	18	29	4	2	0	12	10	32	.232	.289	.296	585	57	-8	2	4	-1	.973	-3	O-43(4-38-1)	-1.2
■ **MIKE RAMSEY**	Ramsey, Michael Jeffrey b: 3/29/54, Roanoke, Va. BB/TR, 6'1", 170 lbs. Deb: 9/4/78																							
1978	StL-N	12	5	4	1	0	0	0	0	0	1	.200	.200	.200	400	12	-1	0	0	0	.909	4	/S-4	0.3
1980	StL-N	59	126	11	33	8	1	0	8	3	17	.262	.279	.341	620	70	-5	0	0	0	.960	0	2-24,S-20/3-8	-0.3
1981	StL-N	47	124	19	32	3	0	0	9	8	16	.258	.303	.282	585	65	-5	4	0	1	.966	13	S-35/3-5,2-1,O-1L	1.1
1982	*StL-N	112	256	18	59	8	2	1	21	22	34	.230	.294	.289	583	63	-12	6	5	-0	.963	8	2-43,3-28,S-22,/O-2L	-0.1
1983	StL-N	97	175	25	46	4	3	1	16	12	23	.263	.314	.337	651	80	-5	4	2	0	.968	3	2-66,S-20/3-8,O-1L	0.1
1984	StL-N	21	15	1	1	1	0	0	0	1	3	.067	.125	.133	258	-28	-3	0	0	0	1.000	4	/2-7,S-7,3-1	0.2
	Mon-N	37	70	2	15	1	0	0	3	0	13	.214	.214	.229	443	26	-7	0	0	0	.975	1	S-26,2-12	-0.4
	Yr	58	85	3	16	2	0	0	3	1	16	.188	.198	.212	409	16	-10	0	0	0	.978	5	S-33,2-19/3-1	-0.2
1985	LA-N	9	15	1	2	1	0	0	0	2	4	.133	.235	.200	435	24	-2	0	0	0	.923	-0	/S-4,2-2	-0.1
Total	7	394	786	81	189	26	6	2	57	48	111	.240	.286	.296	582	63	-39	14	7	1	.964	33	2-155,S-138/3-50,O	0.8
■ **BILL RAMSEY**	Ramsey, William Thrace "Square Jaw" b: 10/20/20, Osceola, Ark. BR/TR, 6', 175 lbs. Deb: 4/19/45																							
1945	Bos-N	78	137	16	40	8	0	1	12	4	22	.292	.326	.372	699	93	-2	1			.963	-7	O-43(30-13-0)	-0.9
■ **DICK RAND**	Rand, Richard Hilton b: 3/7/31, South Gate, Cal. d: 1/22/96, Moreno Valley, Cal. BR/TR, 6'2", 185 lbs. Deb: 9/16/53																							
1953	StL-N	9	31	3	9	1	0	0	1	2	6	.290	.333	.323	656	72	-1	0	0	0	.984	3	/C-9	0.2
1955	StL-N	3	10	1	3	0	0	1	3	1	1	.300	.364	.600	964	150	1	0	1	-0	1.000	-2	/C-3	-0.1
1957	Pit-N	60	105	7	23	2	1	1	9	11	24	.219	.293	.286	579	58	-6	0	0	0	.973	0	C-57	-0.4
Total	3	72	146	11	35	3	1	2	13	14	31	.240	.306	.315	621	68	-7	0	1	-0	.977	2	/C-69	-0.3
■ **JOE RANDA**	Randa, Joseph Gregory b: 12/18/69, Milwaukee, Wis. BR/TR, 5'11", 190 lbs. Deb: 4/30/95																							
1995	KC-A	34	70	6	12	2	0	1	5	6	17	.171	.237	.243	480	25	-8	0	1	-0	.949	2	3-22/2-9,D-2	-0.6
1996	KC-A	110	337	36	102	24	1	6	47	26	47	.303	.354	.433	788	98	-1	13	4	1	.951	-4	3-92,2-15/1-7,D-1	-0.2
1997	Pit-N	126	443	58	134	27	9	7	60	41	64	.302	.369	.451	821	112	8	4	2	0	.937	20	*3-120,2-13	2.9
1998	Det-A	138	460	56	117	21	2	9	50	41	70	.254	.325	.367	692	79	-14	8	7	-1	.976	9	*3-118,2-20/1-1,D-1	-0.4
1999	KC-A	156	628	92	197	36	8	16	84	50	80	.314	.367	.473	840	110	9	5	4	-0	.952	10	*3-156	1.9
2000	KC-A	158	612	88	186	29	4	15	106	36	66	.304	.349	.438	787	96	-4	6	3	0	.957	4	*3-156/D-1	0.1
Total	6	722	2550	336	748	139	24	54	352	200	344	.293	.350	.430	780	98	-9	36	21	1	.954	40	3-664/2-57,1-8,D-5	3.7
■ **SAP RANDALL**	Randall, James Odell b: 8/19/60, Mobile, Ala. BB/TR, 5'11", 195 lbs. Deb: 8/2/88																							
1988	Chi-A	4	12	1	0	0	0	0	1	2	3	.000	.143	.000	143	-57	-3	0	0	0	1.000	0	/1-2,O-1(0-0-1),D-1	-0.3
■ **NEWT RANDALL**	Randall, Newton J. b: 2/3/1880, New Lowell, Ont., Canada d: 5/3/55, Duluth, Minn. BR/TR, 5'10", Deb: 4/18/07																							
1907	Chi-N	22	78	6	16	4	2	0	4	8		.205	.279	.308	587	79	-2	2			.904	1	O-21(1-1-21)	-0.2
	Bos-N	75	258	16	55	6	3	0	15	19		.213	.285	.260	545	71	-8	4			.920	-8	O-73(59-3-12)	-2.3
	Yr	97	336	22	71	10	5	0	19	27		.211	.284	.271	555	73	-10	6			.915	-7	O-94(60-4-33)	-2.5
■ **BOB RANDALL**	Randall, Robert Lee b: 6/10/48, Norton, Kan. BR/TR, 6'3", 180 lbs. Deb: 4/13/76 C																							
1976	Min-A	153	475	55	127	18	4	1	34	28	38	.267	.319	.328	647	88	-7	3	5	-1	.969	-4	*2-153	-0.3
1977	Min-A	103	306	36	73	13	2	0	22	15	25	.239	.290	.294	584	60	-17	1	4	-1	.985	10	*2-101/1-1,3-1,D-1	-0.3
1978	Min-A	119	330	36	89	11	3	0	21	24	22	.270	.331	.321	652	82	-7	5	3	0	.983	10	*2-116/3-2,D-1	0.9
1979	Min-A	80	199	25	49	7	0	0	14	15	17	.246	.299	.281	580	55	-12	2	2	-0	.983	7	2-71/3-7,S-1,O-1L	-0.3
1980	Min-A	5	15	2	3	1	0	0	0	1	0	.200	.250	.267	517	39	-1	0	0	0	.909	0	/3-4,2-1	-0.1
Total	5	460	1325	154	341	50	9	1	91	83	102	.257	.311	.311	622	74	-44	11	14	-2	.979	22	2-442/3-14,D-2,OS1	-0.1
■ **LEN RANDLE**	Randle, Leonard Shenoff b: 2/12/49, Long Beach, Cal. BB/TR (BR 1971), 5'10", 169 lbs. Deb: 6/16/71 Career OF: (62-LF 85-CF 6-RF)																							
1971	Was-A	75	215	27	47	11	0	2	13	24	56	.219	.300	.298	598	74	-7	1	1	-0	.967	5	2-66	0.2
1972	Tex-A	74	249	23	48	13	0	2	21	13	51	.193	.236	.269	505	52	-15	4	5	-1	.952	1	2-65/S-4,O-2(0-2-0)	-1.3
1973	Tex-A	10	29	3	6	1	1	1	1	0	2	.207	.207	.414	621	74	-1	0	2	-1	.964	-2	/2-5,O-2(0-2-0)	-0.4
1974	Tex-A	151	520	65	157	17	4	1	49	29	43	.302	.341	.356	697	103	2	26	17	-0	.935	1	3-89,2-40,O-21L,/SD	0.4
1975	Tex-A	156	601	85	166	24	7	4	57	57	80	.276	.343	.359	702	99	0	16	19	-3	.973	15	2-79,O-66C,3-17,/CSD	1.5
1976	Tex-A	142	539	53	121	11	6	1	51	46	63	.224	.288	.273	561	63	-24	30	15	1	.971	-4	*2-113,O-30L/3-2,D	-2.2
1977	NY-N	136	513	78	156	22	7	5	27	65	70	.304	.384	.404	788	117	14	33	21	-0	.961	-7	*3-110,2-20/O-6L,S	0.7
1978	NY-N	132	437	53	102	16	8	2	35	64	57	.233	.333	.320	653	86	-7	14	11	-1	.967	-7	*3-124/2-5	-1.7
1979	NY-A	20	39	2	7	0	0	0	3	3	2	.179	.238	.179	418	15	-5	0	0	0	1.000	-0	O-11(4-7-0)/D-2	-0.5
1980	Chi-N	130	489	67	135	19	6	5	39	50	55	.276	.344	.370	715	93	-4	19	13	-0	.929	-7	*3-111,2-17/O-6L	-1.2
1981	Sea-A	82	273	22	63	9	1	4	25	17	22	.231	.278	.315	593	68	-11	11	6	0	.986	7	3-59,2-21/O-5L,S-3	-0.4

YEAR	TM/L	G	AB	R	H	2B	3B	HR	RBI	BB	SO	AVG	OBP	SLG	OPS	OPS+	BR+	SB	CS	SBR	FA	FR	G/POS	TPR
1982	Sea-A	30	46	10	8	2	0	0	1	4	4	.174	.240	.217	457	26	-5	2	2	-0	.964	6	D-13/3-9,2-6	0.0
Total	12	1138	3950	488	1016	145	40	27	322	372	505	.257	.323	.335	658	87	-62	156	112	-5	.953	9	3-521,2-437,O/DSC	-4.9
■ **WILLIE RANDOLPH** Randolph, Willie Larry b: 7/6/54, Holly Hill, S.C. BR/TR, 5′11″, 166 lbs. Deb: 7/29/75 C																								
1975	*Pit-N	30	61	9	10	1	0	0	3	7	6	.164	.250	.180	430	21	-6	1	0	0	.962	4	2-14/3-1	-0.2
1976	*NY-A†	125	430	59	115	15	4	1	40	58	39	.267	.358	.328	686	103	4	37	12	4	.974	15	*2-124	3.3
1977	*NY-A★	147	551	91	151	28	11	4	40	64	53	.274	.351	.387	737	102	3	13	6	1	.980	6	*2-147	1.7
1978	NY-A	134	499	87	139	18	6	3	42	82	51	.279	.385	.357	741	112	12	36	7	5	.978	-8	*2-134	1.8
1979	NY-A	153	574	98	155	15	13	5	61	95	39	.270	.376	.368	744	104	7	33	12	3	.985	9	*2-153	2.7
1980	*NY-A★	138	513	99	151	23	7	7	46	**119**	45	.294	.429	.407	836	133	31	30	5	5	.976	-7	*2-138	3.6
1981	*NY-A★	93	357	59	83	14	3	2	24	57	24	.232	.338	.305	643	88	-4	14	5	1	.977	-2	2-93	0.1
1982	NY-A	144	553	85	155	21	4	3	36	75	35	.280	.369	.349	718	100	3	16	9	0	.981	-3	*2-142/D-1	0.9
1983	NY-A	104	420	73	117	21	1	2	38	53	32	.279	.361	.348	708	100	2	12	4	1	.979	3	*2-104	1.2
1984	NY-A	142	564	86	162	24	2	2	31	86	42	.287	.382	.348	729	108	10	10	6	0	.983	11	*2-142	2.9
1985	NY-A	143	497	75	137	21	2	5	40	85	39	.276	.386	.356	742	107	9	16	9	0	.985	-3	*2-143	1.4
1986	NY-A	141	492	76	136	15	2	5	50	94	49	.276	.396	.346	741	105	9	15	2	3	.972	-12	*2-139/D-1	0.7
1987	NY-A★	120	449	96	137	24	2	7	67	82	25	.305	.415	.414	829	122	19	11	1	2	.981	-2	*2-119/D-1	2.4
1988	NY-A	110	404	43	93	20	1	2	34	55	39	.230	.325	.300	625	77	-11	8	4	0	.988	8	*2-110	0.0
1989	LA-N★	145	549	62	155	18	0	2	36	71	51	.282	.369	.326	695	102	4	7	6	-1	.987	-1	*2-140	0.7
1990	LA-N	26	96	15	26	4	0	1	9	13	9	.271	.364	.344	707	98	0	1	0	0	.969	-2	2-26	-0.1
	*Oak-A	93	292	37	75	9	3	1	21	32	25	.257	.332	.318	651	86	-5	6	1	1	.982	-12	2-84/D-6	-1.4
1991	Mil-A	124	431	60	141	14	3	0	54	75	38	.327	.427	.374	800	127	20	4	2	0	.969	10	*2-121/D-2	3.3
1992	NY-N	90	286	29	72	11	1	2	15	40	34	.252	.352	.318	670	92	-1	1	3	-1	.977	-14	2-79	-1.5
Total	18	2202	8018	1239	2210	316	65	54	687	1243	675	.276	.375	.351	727	105	106	271	94	27	.980	0	*2-2152/D-11,3-1	23.5
■ **MERRITT RANEW** Ranew, Merritt Thomas b: 5/10/38, Albany, Ga. BL/TR, 5′10″, 180 lbs. Deb: 4/13/62 Career OF: (3-LF 0-CF 0-RF)																								
1962	Hou-N	71	218	26	51	6	8	4	24	14	43	.234	.289	.390	679	87	-5	2	2	-0	.980	-6	C-58	-0.8
1963	Chi-N	78	154	18	52	8	1	3	15	9	32	.338	.382	.461	843	134	7	1	0	0	.980	-5	C-37/1-9	0.4
1964	Chi-N	16	33	0	3	0	0	0	1	2	6	.091	.167	.091	258	-24	-5	0	0	0	1.000	2	/C-9	-0.3
	Mil-N	9	17	1	2	0	0	0	0	0	3	.118	.118	.118	235	-33	-3	0	1	-0	1.000	-1	/C-3	-0.4
	Yr	25	50	1	5	0	0	0	1	2	9	.100	.151	.100	251	-27	-8	0	1	-0	1.000	1	C-12	-0.7
1965	Cal-A	41	91	12	19	4	0	1	10	7	22	.209	.265	.286	551	58	-5	0	0	0	.988	-10	C-24	-1.5
1969	Sea-A	54	81	11	20	2	0	0	4	10	14	.247	.330	.272	601	71	-3	0	0	0	.969	-6	C-13/O-3(3-0-0),3-1	-0.9
Total	5	269	594	68	147	20	9	8	54	42	120	.247	.304	.352	656	83	-14	3	3	-0	.982	-25	C-144/1-9,O-3L,3-1	-3.5
■ **JEFF RANSOM** Ransom, Jeffrey Dean b: 11/11/60, Fresno, Cal. BR/TR, 5′11″, 185 lbs. Deb: 9/5/81																								
1981	SF-N	5	15	2	4	1	0	0	0	1	1	.267	.313	.333	646	85	-0	0	0	0	1.000	2	/C-5	0.2
1982	SF-N	15	44	5	7	0	0	0	3	6	7	.159	.260	.159	419	20	-5	0	0	0	.988	2	C-14	-0.3
1983	SF-N	6	20	3	4	0	0	1	3	4	7	.200	.333	.350	683	92	-0	0	0	0	.946	-2	/C-6	-0.1
Total	3	26	79	10	15	1	0	1	6	11	15	.190	.289	.241	529	50	-5	0	0	0	.980	2	/C-25	-0.2
■ **EARL RAPP** Rapp, Earl Wellington b: 5/20/21, Corunna, Mich. d: 2/13/92, Swedesboro, N.J. BL/TR, 6′2″, 185 lbs. Deb: 4/28/49																								
1949	Det-A	1	0	0	0	0	0	0	0	1	0	—	1.000	—	1000	175	0	0	0	0	.000	0	H	0.0
	Chi-A	19	54	3	14	1	1	0	11	5	6	.259	.322	.315	637	71	-2	1	1	-0	.974	2	O-13(11-0-2)	-0.1
	Yr	20	54	3	14	1	1	0	11	6	6	.259	.333	.315	648	74	-2	1	1	-0	.974	2	O-13(11-0-2)	-0.1
1951	NY-N	13	11	0	1	0	0	0	1	2	3	.091	.231	.091	322	-10	-2	0	0	0	.000	0	H	-0.2
	StL-A	26	98	14	32	5	3	2	14	11	11	.327	.394	.500	894	137	5	1	0	0	.979	0	O-25(0-0-25)	0.4
1952	StL-A	30	49	3	7	4	0	0	4	0	8	.143	.143	.224	367	1	-7	0	0	0	1.000	-1	/O-7(0-0-7)	-0.8
	Was-A	46	67	7	19	6	0	0	9	6	13	.284	.351	.373	724	105	0	0	0	0	.917	-2	O-10(0-0-10)	-0.2
	Yr	76	116	10	26	10	0	0	13	6	21	.224	.268	.310	579	61	-6	0	0	0	.958	-3	O-17(0-0-17)	-1.0
Total	3	135	279	27	73	16	4	2	39	25	41	.262	.325	.369	694	89	-5	2	1	0	.973	-0	/O-55(11-0-44)	-0.9
■ **GOLDIE RAPP** Rapp, Joseph Aloysius b: 2/6/1892, Cincinnati, Ohio d: 7/1/66, LaMesa, Cal. BB/TR, 5′10″, 165 lbs. Deb: 4/13/21																								
1921	NY-N	58	181	21	39	9	1	0	15	15	13	.215	.276	.276	552	46	-14	3	11	-3	.941	13	3-56	-0.1
	Phi-N	52	202	28	56	7	1	1	10	14	8	.277	.324	.337	661	70	-8	6	7	-1	.950	-2	3-50/2-1	-0.9
	Yr	110	383	49	95	16	2	1	25	29	21	.248	.301	.308	609	59	-22	9	18	-4	.945	10	*3-106/2-1	-1.0
1922	Phi-N	119	502	58	127	26	3	0	38	32	29	.253	.299	.317	616	54	-34	6	12	-3	.948	5	*3-117/S-2	-2.4
1923	Phi-N	47	179	27	47	5	0	1	10	14	14	.263	.320	.307	627	59	-10	1	1	-0	.947	-1	3-45	-0.8
Total	3	276	1064	134	269	47	5	2	73	75	64	.253	.303	.312	615	57	-67	16	31	-7	.947	14	3-268/S-2,2-1	-4.2
■ **BILL RARIDEN** Rariden, William Angel "Bedford Bill" b: 2/4/1888, Bedford, Ind. d: 8/28/42, Bedford, Ind. BR/TR, 5′10″, 168 lbs. Deb: 8/12/09																								
1909	Bos-N	13	42	1	6	1	0	0	1	4		.143	.217	.167	384	18	-4	1			.912	-3	C-13	-0.6
1910	Bos-N	49	137	15	31	5	1	1	14	12	22	.226	.293	.299	593	70	-5	1			.962	3	C-49	0.2
1911	Bos-N	70	246	22	56	9	0	0	21	21	18	.228	.288	.264	553	51	-16	3			.952	1	C-65/3-3,2-1	-0.9
1912	Bos-N	79	247	27	55	3	1	1	14	18	35	.223	.281	.255	536	46	-18	3			.964	-3	C-73	-1.5
1913	Bos-N	95	246	31	58	9	2	3	30	30	21	.236	.324	.325	649	84	-5	5			.976	-0	C-87	0.2
1914	Ind-F	131	396	44	93	15	5	0	47	61	43	.235	.337	.298	635	67	-22	12			.981	20	*C-130	1.0
1915	New-F	142	444	49	120	30	7	0	40	60	29	.270	.361	.369	730	112	2	8			.978	23	*C-142	3.9
1916	NY-N	120	351	23	78	9	3	1	29	55	32	.222	.333	.274	606	92	-1	4			.972	-9	*C-119	0.1
1917	*NY-N	101	266	20	72	10	1	0	25	42	17	.271	.372	.316	688	116	7	3			.971	-17	*C-100	-0.2
1918	NY-N	69	183	15	41	5	1	0	17	15	15	.224	.283	.262	545	68	-7	1			**.984**	-9	C-63	-1.2
1919	*Cin-N	74	218	16	47	6	3	1	24	17	19	.216	.275	.284	560	70	-8	4			.983	3	C-70	0.1
1920	Cin-N	39	101	9	25	3	0	0	10	5	0	.248	.283	.277	560	62	-5	2	0	0	.972	-0	C-37	-0.2
Total	12	982	2877	272	682	105	24	7	272	340	251	.237	.320	.298	618	78	-82	47	0		.973	9	C-948/3-3,2-1	0.9
■ **MORRIE RATH** Rath, Morris Charles b: 12/25/1886, Mobeetie, Tex. d: 11/18/45, Upper Darby, Pa. BL/TR, 5′8.5″, 160 lbs. Deb: 9/28/09 Career OF: (0-LF 0-CF 1-RF)																								
1909	Phi-A	7	26	4	7	1	0	0	3	2		.269	.387	.308	695	117	1	1			.846	2	/S-4,3-2	0.3
1910	Phi-A	18	26	3	4	0	0	0	1	5		.154	.290	.154	444	40	-2	0			.950	-2	3-11/2-3	-0.4
	Cle-A	24	67	5	13	3	0	0	0	10		.194	.299	.239	538	68	-2	2			.950	2	3-22/S-1	0.1
	Yr	42	93	8	17	3	0	0	1	15		.183	.296	.215	511	60	-4	2			.950	0	3-33/2-3,S-1	-0.3
1912	Chi-A	157	591	104	161	10	2	1	19	95		.272	.380	.301	681	98	5	30			**.963**	18	*2-157	2.6
1913	Chi-A	92	295	37	59	2	0	0	12	46	22	.200	.310	.207	517	52	-16	22			.962	-2	2-86	-1.7
1919	*Cin-N	138	537	77	142	13	1	1	29	64	24	.264	.343	.298	641	96	0	17			.974	13	*2-138	1.7
1920	Cin-N	129	506	61	135	7	4	2	28	36	24	.267	.319	.308	628	82	-11	10	11	-2	**.977**	-7	*2-126/3-1,O-1(0-0-1)	-1.9
Total	6	565	2048	291	521	36	7	4	92	258	70	.254	.342	.285	626	86	-25	82	11		.970	25	2-510/3-36,S-5,O-1R	0.7
■ **GENE RATLIFF** Ratliff, Kelly Eugene b: 9/28/45, Macon, Ga. BR/TR, 6′5″, 185 lbs. Deb: 5/15/65																								
1965	Hou-N	4	4	0	0	0	0	0	0	0	4	.000	.000	.000	0	-99	-1	0	0	0	.000	0	H	-0.1
■ **PAUL RATLIFF** Ratliff, Paul Hawthorne b: 1/23/44, San Diego, Cal. BL/TR, 6′2″, 190 lbs. Deb: 4/14/63																								
1963	Min-A	10	21	2	4	1	0	1	3	2	7	.190	.292	.381	673	85	-0	0	0	0	.976	2	/C-7	0.2
1970	*Min-A	69	149	19	40	7	2	5	22	15	51	.268	.363	.443	806	119	4	0	0	0	.980	-15	C-53	-1.0
1971	Min-A	21	44	3	7	1	0	2	6	4	17	.159	.229	.318	547	52	-3	0	0	0	1.000	1	C-15	-0.2
	Mil-A	23	41	3	7	1	0	3	7	5	21	.171	.277	.415	691	95	-0	0	0	0	.966	-1	C-13	-0.1
	Yr	44	85	6	14	2	0	5	13	9	38	.165	.253	.365	617	72	-3	0	0	0	.985	0	C-28	-0.3
1972	Mil-A	22	42	1	3	0	0	1	4	2	23	.071	.114	.143	256	-25	-6	0	0	0	1.000	-2	C-13	-1.0
Total	4	145	297	28	61	10	2	12	42	28	119	.205	.293	.374	667	86	-6	0	0	0	.983	-16	C-101	-2.1
■ **TOMMY RAUB** Raub, Thomas Jefferson b: 12/1/1870, Raubsville, Pa. d: 2/15/49, Phillipsburg, N.J. BR/TR, 5′10″, 155 lbs. Deb: 5/3/03 Career OF: (0-LF 0-CF 5-RF)																								
1903	Chi-N	36	84	6	19	3	2	0	7	5		.226	.278	.310	587	69	-4	3			.900	-4	C-12/1-6,O-5R,3-4	-0.7
1906	StL-N	24	78	9	22	2	4	0	2	4		.282	.325	.410	736	135	3	2			.957	-4	C-22	0.1
Total	2	60	162	15	41	5	6	0	9	9		.253	.301	.358	659	99	-1	5			.940	-8	/C-34,1-6,O-5R,3-4	-0.6

YEAR	TM/L	G	AB	R	H	2B	3B	HR	RBI	BB	SO	AVG	OBP	SLG	OPS	OPS+	BR+	SB	CS	SBR	FA	FR	G/POS	TPR
■ BOB RAUDMAN Raudman, Robert Joyce "Shorty" b: 3/14/42, Erie, Pa. BL/TL, 5'9.5", 185 lbs. Deb: 9/13/66																								
1966	Chi-N	8	29	1	7	2	0	0	2	1	4	.241	.267	.310	577	59	-2	0	0	0	.909	0	/O-8(8-0-0)	-0.2
1967	Chi-N	8	26	0	4	0	0	0	1	1	4	.154	.185	.154	339	-2	-3	0	0	0	.875	0	/O-8(0-0-8)	-0.4
Total	2	16	55	1	11	2	0	0	3	2	8	.200	.228	.236	464	30	-5	0	0	0	.889	0	/O-16(8-0-8)	-0.6
■ JOHNNY RAWLINGS Rawlings, John William "Red" b: 8/17/1892, Bloomfield, Iowa d: 10/16/72, Inglewood, Cal. BR/TR, 5'8", 158 lbs. Deb: 4/14/14 Career OF: (8-LF 1-CF 23-RF)																								
1914	Cin-N	33	60	9	13	1	0	0	8	6	8	.217	.288	.233	521	54	-3	1			.885	0	3-10/2-7,S-5	-0.3
	KC-F	61	193	19	41	3	0	0	15	22	25	.212	.296	.228	524	46	-17	6			.937	17	S-61	0.4
1915	KC-F	120	399	40	86	9	2	2	24	27	40	.216	.269	.263	532	52	-32	17			.926	-4	*S-120	-3.1
1917	Bos-N	122	371	37	95	9	4	2	31	38	32	.256	.337	.318	655	107	5	12			.977	11	2-96,S-17/3-1,O-1L	2.0
1918	Bos-N	111	410	32	85	7	3	0	21	30	31	.207	.265	.239	504	56	-21	10			.956	2	S-71,2-20,O-18R	-1.6
1919	Bos-N	77	275	30	70	8	2	1	16	16	20	.255	.298	.309	607	86	-5	10			.961	-12	2-58,O-10(7-1-5)/S-5	-1.8
1920	Bos-N	5	3	0	0	0	0	0	2	0	1	.000	.000	.000	0	-99	-1	0	0	0	1.000	-1	/2-1	-0.1
	Phi-N	98	384	39	90	19	2	3	30	22	25	.234	.278	.318	595	67	-16	9	6	-0	.970	-2	2-97	-1.8
	Yr	103	387	39	90	19	2	3	32	22	26	.233	.276	.315	591	67	-17	9	6	-0	.970	-2	2-98	-1.9
1921	Phi-N	60	254	20	74	14	2	1	16	8	12	.291	.318	.374	692	76	-8	5	5	-1	.954	5	2-60	-0.3
	*NY-N	86	307	40	82	8	1	1	30	18	19	.267	.316	.309	626	66	-14	4	4	-1	.970	-1	2-86/S-1	-1.4
	Yr	146	561	60	156	22	3	2	46	26	31	.278	.317	.339	656	71	-23	8	9	-1	.963	3	*2-146/S-1	-1.7
1922	NY-N	88	308	46	87	13	8	1	30	23	15	.282	.342	.386	729	87	-6	7	6	-1	.984	-4	2-77/3-5	-0.8
1923	Pit-N	119	461	53	131	18	4	1	45	25	29	.284	.322	.347	669	75	-17	9	0	2	.958	-9	*2-119	-1.9
1924	Pit-N	3	3	0	1	0	0	0	0	0	0	.333	.333	.333	667	78	-0	0	0	0	.000	0	H	0.0
1925	Pit-N	36	110	17	31	7	0	2	13	8	8	.282	.336	.400	736	82	-3	0	1	-0	.981	3	2-29	0.0
1926	Pit-N	61	181	27	42	6	0	0	20	14	10	.232	.287	.265	552	47	-13	3			.970	-3	2-59	-1.5
Total	12	1080	3719	409	928	122	28	14	303	257	275	.250	.303	.309	611	71	-153	92	22		.968	3	2-709,S-280/O-29R,3	-12.2
■ IRV RAY Ray, Irving Burton "Stubby" b: 1/22/1864, Harrington, Me. d: 2/21/48, Harrington, Me. BL/TR, 5'6", 165 lbs. Deb: 7/7/1888 Career OF: (0-LF 0-CF 70-RF)																								
1888	Bos-N	50	206	26	51	2	3	2	26	6	11	.248	.272	.316	588	85	-4	7			.879	-11	S-48/2-3	-1.3
1889	Bos-N	9	33	8	10	1	0	0	2	4	0	.303	.378	.333	712	94	-0	1			.875	-4	/S-5,3-4	-0.4
	Bal-a	26	106	20	36	4	1	0	17	7	6	.340	.397	.396	793	124	3	12			.784	-7	S-20/O-6(0-0-6)	-0.3
1890	Bal-a	38	139	28	50	6	2	1	20	15		.360	.433	.453	886	154	10	11			.894	-10	S-38	0.1
1891	Bal-a	103	418	72	116	17	5	0	58	54	18	.278	.366	.342	708	102	2	28			.885	-14	O-64(0-0-64),S-40	-1.0
Total	4	226	902	154	263	30	11	3	123	86	35	.292	.360	.359	720	109	11	59			.863	-46	S-151/O-70R,3-4,2-3	-2.9
■ JOHNNY RAY Ray, John Cornelius b: 3/1/57, Chouteau, Okla. BB/TR, 5'11", 185 lbs. Deb: 9/2/81 Career OF: (41-LF 0-CF 0-RF)																								
1981	Pit-N	31	102	10	25	11	0	0	6	6	9	.245	.287	.353	640	78	-3	0	0	0	.987	2	2-31	0.0
1982	Pit-N	162	647	79	182	30	7	7	63	36	34	.281	.320	.382	702	93	-7	16	7	1	.977	8	*2-162	1.2
1983	Pit-N	151	576	68	163	**38**	7	5	53	35	26	.283	.324	.399	723	97	-3	18	9	1	.983	17	*2-151	2.4
1984	Pit-N	155	555	75	173	**38**	6	6	67	37	31	.312	.358	.434	792	122	15	11	6	0	.984	-9	*2-149	1.5
1985	Pit-N	154	594	67	163	33	3	7	70	46	24	.274	.328	.375	703	97	-3	13	9	-0	.976	-15	*2-151	-1.0
1986	Pit-N	155	579	67	174	33	0	7	78	58	47	.301	.367	.394	761	107	7	6	9	-2	.993	5	*2-151	1.9
1987	Pit-N	123	472	48	129	19	3	5	54	41	36	.273	.331	.358	689	82	-12	4	2	0	.981	4	*2-119	-0.1
	Cal-A	30	127	16	44	11	0	0	15	3	10	.346	.362	.433	795	113	2	0	0	0	.986	-1	2-29/D-1	0.3
1988	Cal-A★	153	602	75	184	42	7	6	83	36	38	.306	.349	.429	777	120	15	4	1	1	.972	-7	*2-104,O-40L/D-6	1.6
1989	Cal-A	134	530	52	153	16	3	5	62	36	30	.289	.334	.358	692	97	-2	6	3	0	.984	4	*2-130	0.6
1990	Cal-A	105	404	47	112	23	0	5	43	19	44	.277	.310	.371	681	91	-5	2	3	-1	.987	12	*2-100/D-1	0.9
Total	10	1353	5188	604	1502	294	36	53	594	353	329	.290	.336	.391	727	101	4	80	49	0	.982	20	*2-1277/O-40L,D-8	8.7
■ LARRY RAY Ray, Larry Dale b: 3/11/58, Madison, Ind. BL/TR, 6'1", 195 lbs. Deb: 9/10/82																								
1982	Hou-N	5	6	0	1	0	0	0	1	0	4	.167	.167	.167	333	-7	-1	0	0	0	1.000	-0	/O-1(1-0-0)	-0.1
■ FLOYD RAYFORD Rayford, Floyd Kinnard b: 7/27/57, Memphis, Tenn. BR/TR, 5'10", 195 lbs. Deb: 4/17/80																								
1980	Bal-A	8	18	1	4	0	0	0	1	0	5	.222	.222	.222	444	22	-2	0	0	0	.900	0	/3-4,2-1,D-1	-0.2
1982	Bal-A	34	53	7	7	0	0	3	5	6	14	.132	.220	.302	522	42	-4	0	1	-0	.898	5	3-27/C-2,D-2	0.0
1983	StL-N	56	104	5	22	4	0	3	14	10	27	.212	.281	.337	617	70	-4	1	0	0	.883	-4	3-33	-0.9
1984	Bal-A	86	250	24	64	14	0	4	27	12	51	.256	.298	.360	658	83	-6	0	3	-1	.991	11	C-66,3-22/1-1	0.6
1985	Bal-A	105	359	55	110	21	1	18	48	10	69	.306	.325	.521	846	131	13	3	1	0	.972	-2	3-78,C-29/D-1	1.1
1986	Bal-A	81	210	15	37	4	0	8	19	15	50	.176	.231	.310	541	46	-16	0	0	0	.912	4	3-72,C-10/D-1	-1.2
1987	Bal-A	20	50	5	11	0	0	2	3	2	9	.220	.250	.340	590	56	-3	0	0	0	.980	6	C-17/3-1,D-1	0.3
Total	7	390	1044	112	255	43	1	38	117	55	225	.244	.284	.397	681	86	-23	4	5	-1	.931	21	3-237,C-124/D-6,12	-0.3
■ FRED RAYMER Raymer, Frederick Charles b: 11/12/1875, Leavenworth, Kan. d: 6/11/57, Los Angeles, Cal. BR/TR, 5'11", 185 lbs. Deb: 4/24/01 Career OF: (1-LF 0-CF 0-RF)																								
1901	Chi-N	120	463	41	108	14	2	0	43	11		.233	.257	.272	529	56	-26	18			.881	-17	3-82,S-29/1-5,2-3	-4.1
1904	Bos-N	114	419	28	88	12	3	1	27	13		.210	.236	.260	496	55	-23	17			**.958**	7	*2-114	-1.6
1905	Bos-N	137	498	26	105	14	2	0	31	8		.211	.232	.247	479	44	-35	15			.949	-18	*2-134/1-1,O-1(1-0-0)	-5.5
Total	3	371	1380	95	301	40	7	1	101	32		.218	.242	.259	501	51	-84	50			.954	-28	2-251/3-82,S-29,10	-11.2
■ HARRY RAYMOND Raymond, Harry H. "Jack" b: 2/20/1862, Utica, N.Y. d: 3/21/25, San Diego, Cal. 5'9", 179 lbs. Deb: 9/9/1888 Career OF: (1-LF 0-CF 1-RF)																								
1888	Lou-a	32	123	8	26	2	0	0	13	1		.211	.218	.228	445	44	-8	7			.884	-1	3-31/O-1(0-0-1)	-0.8
1889	Lou-a	130	515	58	123	12	9	0	47	19	45	.239	.270	.297	567	63	-26	19			.886	-1	*3-129/O-1(1-0-0),P-1	-2.1
1890	*Lou-a	123	521	91	135	7	4	2	51	22		.259	.293	.299	592	76	-17	18			.874	-2	*3-119/S-4	-1.5
1891	Lou-a	14	59	4	12	2	0	0	2	5	6	.203	.288	.237	525	51	-4	3			.898	5	S-14	0.2
1892	Pit-N	12	49	4	4	0	1	0	2	4	8	.082	.151	.122	273	-17	-7	1			.867	-2	3-12	-0.8
	Was-N	4	15	2	1	0	0	0	0	3	2	.067	.222	.067	289	-12	-2	1			.783	1	/3-4	-0.1
	Yr	16	64	6	5	0	1	0	2	7	10	.078	.169	.109	278	-16	-9	2			.838	-1	3-16	-0.9
Total	5	315	1282	167	301	23	14	2	115	54	61	.235	.270	.279	549	62	-63	49			.878	1	3-295/S-18,O-2L,P-1	-5.1
■ LOU RAYMOND Raymond, Louis Anthony (b: Louis Anthony Raymondjack) b: 12/11/1894, Buffalo, N.Y. d: 5/2/79, Rochester, N.Y. BR/TR, 5'10.5", 187 lbs. Deb: 5/2/19																								
1919	Phi-N	1	2	0	1	0	0	0	0	0	0	.500	.500	.500	1000	188	0	0			.000	0	/2-1	0.0
■ AL REACH Reach, Alfred James b: 5/25/1840, London, England d: 1/14/28, Atlantic City, N.J BL/TL, 5'6", 155 lbs. Deb: 5/20/1871 FM Career OF: (0-LF 4-CF 39-RF)																								
1871	Ath-n	26	133	43	47	7	6	0	34	5	6	.353	.377	.496	873	150	9	2	0	0	.844	-0	*2-26	0.4
1872	Ath-n	24	118	21	23	0	0	0	11	4	0	.195	.221	.195	416	29	-9	1	1	-0	.943	4	O-20(0-0-20)/1-4	-0.3
1873	Ath-n	13	73	13	16	5	1	0	9	0	0	.219	.219	.315	534	53	-5	2	0	0	.881	5	/2-9,O-7(0-4-3)	0.0
1874	Ath-n	14	55	8	7	2	0	0	2	0	4	.127	.127	.164	291	-7	-7	0	0	0	.732	4	O-14(0-0-14)	-0.1
1875	Ath-n	3	14	4	4	1	0	0	1	0	0	.286	.286	.357	643	110	0	2	1	0	1.000	-2	/O-2(0-0-2),2-1	-0.1
Total	5 n	80	393	89	97	15	7	0	57	9	10	.247	.264	.321	584	73	-12	7	2	1	.857	11	/O-43R,2-36,1-4	-0.1
■ BOB REACH Reach, Robert b: 8/28/1843, Williamsburg, N.Y. d: 5/19/22, Springfield, Mass. 5'5", 155 lbs. Deb: 4/23/1872 F																								
1872	Oly-n	2	8	1	2	0	0	0	0	0	0	.250	.250	.250	500	57	-0	0	0	0	.727	-1	/S-2	-0.1
1873	Was-n	1	5	1	1	0	0	0	0	0	0	.200	.200	.200	400	20	-0	0	0	0	.500	-1	/S-1	-0.1
Total	2 n	3	13	2	3	0	0	0	0	0	0	.231	.231	.231	462	42	-1	0	0	0	.632	-2	/S-3	-0.2
■ RANDY READY Ready, Randy Max b: 1/8/60, Fremont, Cal. BR/TR, 5'11", 180 lbs. Deb: 9/4/83 Career OF: (167-LF 0-CF 6-RF)																								
1983	Mil-A	12	37	8	15	3	2	1	6	6	3	.405	.488	.676	1164	234	7	0	1	-0	1.000	0	/3-4,D-6	0.6
1984	Mil-A	37	123	13	23	6	1	3	13	14	18	.187	.270	.325	595	66	-6	0	0	0	.946	3	3-36	-0.3
1985	Mil-A	48	181	29	48	9	5	1	21	14	23	.265	.321	.387	708	93	-2	0	0	0	.989	4	O-37L/3-7,2-3,D-2	0.0
1986	Mil-A	23	79	8	15	4	0	1	4	9	9	.190	.273	.278	551	49	-6	2	0	0	.950	-4	O-11L/2-7,3-3,D-1	-0.9
	SD-N	1	3	0	0	0	0	0	0	0	0	.000	.000	.000	0	-99	-1	0	0	0	.667	-0	/3-1	-0.1
1987	SD-N	124	350	69	108	26	6	12	54	67	44	.309	.424	.520	944	154	30	7	3	0	.912	2	3-52,2-51,O-16L	3.2
1988	SD-N	114	331	43	88	16	2	7	39	39	38	.266	.349	.390	738	114	6	6	2	1	.952	-10	3-57,2-26,O-16L	-0.2

YEAR	TM/L	G	AB	R	H	2B	3B	HR	RBI	BB	SO	AVG	OBP	SLG	OPS	OPS+	BR+	SB	CS	SBR	FA	FR	G/POS	TPR
1989	SD-N	28	67	4	17	2	1	0	5	11	6	.254	.359	.313	672	94	-0	0	0	0	.963	1	3-18/2-2,O-1(1-0-0)	0.1
	Phi-N	72	187	33	50	11	1	8	21	31	31	.267	.377	.465	843	140	10	4	3	-0	.962	-6	O-36(36-0-0),3-14/2-7	0.4
	Yr	100	254	37	67	13	2	8	26	42	37	.264	.372	.425	798	127	10	4	3	-0	.962	-4	O-37(37-0-0),3-32/2-9	0.5
1990	Phi-N	101	217	26	53	9	1	1	26	29	35	.244	.336	.309	645	79	-5	3	2	-0	1.000	-6	O-30(30-0-0),2-28	-1.2
1991	Phi-N	76	205	32	51	10	1	1	20	47	25	.249	.391	.322	713	104	4	2	1	0	.989	-7	2-66	-0.2
1992	*Oak-A	61	125	17	25	2	0	3	17	25	23	.200	.333	.288	621	80	-3	1	0	0	1.000	-3	O-24L,D-24/3-7,12	-0.7
1993	Mon-N	40	134	22	34	8	1	1	10	23	8	.254	.367	.351	718	89	-1	2	1	0	.968	3	2-28,1-13/3-3	0.2
1994	Phi-N	17	42	5	16	1	0	1	3	8	6	.381	.480	.476	956	147	3	0	1	-0	1.000	-3	2-11/3-1	0.1
1995	Phi-N	23	29	3	4	0	0	0	0	3	6	.138	.219	.138	357	-3	-4	0	1	-0	.967	-0	/1-3,2-1	-0.5
Total	13	777	2110	312	547	107	21	40	239	326	276	.259	.362	.387	748	108	34	27	15	1	.979	-27	2-234,3-203,O/D1	0.5
■ LEROY REAMS Reams, Leroy b: 8/11/43, Pine Bluff, Ark. BL/TR, 6'2", 175 lbs. Deb: 5/7/69																								
1969	Phi-N	1	1	0	0	0	0	0	0	0	1	.000	.000	.000	0	-99	-0	0	0	0	.000	0	H	0.0
■ PHIL REARDON Reardon, Philip Michael b: 10/3/1883, Brooklyn, N.Y. d: 9/28/20, Brooklyn, N.Y. BR/TR, Deb: 9/19/06																								
1906	Bro-N	5	14	0	1	0	0	0	0	0		.071	.133	.071	205	-39	-2	0			.917	1	/O-4(0-1-3)	-0.1
■ ART REBEL Rebel, Arthur Anthony b: 3/4/15, Cincinnati, Ohio BL/TL, 5'8", 180 lbs. Deb: 4/19/38																								
1938	Phi-N	7	9	2	2	0	0	0	1	1	1	.222	.300	.222	522	47	-1	0			1.000	-1	/O-3(0-1-2)	-0.2
1945	StL-N	26	72	12	25	4	0	0	5	6	4	.347	.397	.403	800	120	2	1			.976	2	O-18(0-0-18)	0.3
Total	2	33	81	14	27	4	0	0	6	7	5	.333	.386	.383	769	112	1	1			.978	1	/O-21(0-1-20)	0.1
■ JEFF REBOULET Reboulet, Jeffrey Allen b: 4/30/64, Dayton, Ohio BR/TR, 6', 169 lbs. Deb: 5/12/92 Career OF: (5-LF 3-CF 15-RF)																								
1992	Min-A	73	137	15	26	7	1	1	16	23	26	.190	.311	.277	588	64	-6	3	2	-0	.971	21	S-36,3-22,2-13,/OD	1.7
1993	Min-A	109	240	33	62	8	0	1	15	35	37	.258	.357	.304	662	79	-5	5	5	-1	.982	13	S-62,3-35,2-11,/OD	1.0
1994	Min-A	74	189	28	49	11	1	3	23	18	23	.259	.327	.376	703	81	-5	0	0	0	.963	-7	S-42,2-14,1-10,/3OD	-0.9
1995	Min-A	87	216	39	63	11	0	4	23	27	34	.292	.373	.398	771	101	1	1	2	-0	.993	10	S-39,3-22,1-17,2/C	1.1
1996	Min-A	107	234	20	52	9	0	0	23	25	34	.222	.300	.261	561	43	-20	4	2	0	.987	-5	S-37,3-36,2-22,1/OD	-2.2
1997	*Bal-A	99	228	26	54	9	0	4	27	23	44	.237	.310	.329	638	69	-10	3	0	1	.977	-3	2-63,S-22,3-12,/OD	-0.9
1998	Bal-A	79	126	20	31	6	0	1	8	19	34	.246	.354	.317	671	78	-3	0	1	-0	.974	3	2-28,S-28,3-23	0.2
1999	Bal-A	99	154	25	25	4	0	0	4	33	29	.162	.317	.188	506	35	-14	1	0	0	.987	23	3-56,2-36,S-10	0.9
2000	KC-A	66	182	29	44	7	0	0	14	23	32	.242	.327	.280	607	55	-12	3	1	0	.982	7	2-50,3-11/S-5,D-1	-0.2
Total	9	793	1706	235	406	72	2	14	153	226	293	.238	.331	.307	638	68	-76	20	13	-0	.976	60	S-281,2-252,3/1ODC	0.7
■ JOHN RECCIUS Reccius, John b: 10/29/1859, Louisville, Ky. d: 9/1/30, Louisville, Ky. 5'6.5", Deb: 5/2/1882 F																								
1882	Lou-a	74	266	46	63	12	3	1		23		.237	.298	.316	613	113	5				.857	-3	*O-65(0-55-11),P-13	0.1
1883	Lou-a	18	63	10	9	2	0	0	3	7		.143	.229	.175	403	34	-4				.833	-1	O-18(0-15-4)/P-1	-0.5
Total	2	92	329	56	72	14	3	1	3	30		.219	.284	.289	573	98	1				.851	-4	/O-83(0-70-15),P-14	-0.4
■ PHIL RECCIUS Reccius, Phillip b: 6/7/1862, Louisville, Ky. d: 2/15/03, Louisville, Ky. 5'9", 163 lbs. Deb: 9/25/1882 F Career OF: (4-LF 4-CF 13-RF)																								
1882	Lou-a	4	15	0	2	0	0	0		0		.133	.133	.133	267	-10	-2				.778	-0	/O-4(0-4-0)	-0.2
1883	Lou-a	1	3	1	1	1	0	0		0		.333	.333	.667	1000	231	0				1.000	-0	/O-1(0-0-1)	0.0
1884	Lou-a	73	263	23	63	9	2	3	21	5		.240	.267	.323	591	96	-1				.845	-2	3-51,P-18,S-10	-0.2
1885	Lou-a	102	402	57	97	8	10	1	38	13		.241	.267	.318	585	84	-8				.829	-2	*3-97/P-7	-0.7
1886	Lou-a	5	13	4	4	1	1	0	2	3		.308	.471	.538	1009	204	2	0			.889	1	/O-5(2-0-3),P-1	0.2
1887	Lou-a	11	45	9	17	2	0	0	4	8		.378	.391	.297	689	92	0	3			.926	2	O-10(2-0-8)/S-1	0.1
	Cle-a	62	253	23	71	6	3	0	29	24		.281	.295	.258	552	56	-12	9			.877	8	3-62/P-1	-0.3
	Yr	73	298	32	88	8	3	0	33	32		.295	.309	.263	572	62	-12	12			.877	10	3-62,O-10R/S-1,P-1	-0.2
1888	Lou-a	2	9	0	2	1	0	0	4	1		.222	.300	.333	633	105	0	0			.750	-2	/3-2	-0.1
1890	Roc-a	1	4	0	0	0	0	0	1	0		.000	.000	.000	0	-99	-1	0			.000	-0	/O-1(0-0-1)	-0.1
Total	8	261	1007	117	257	28	16	4	99	54		.255	.280	.305	585	81	-21	12			.848	5	3-212/P-27,O-21R,S	-1.3
■ JOHNNY REDER Reder, John Anthony b: 9/24/09, Lublin, Poland d: 4/12/90, Fall River, Mass. BR/TR, 6', 184 lbs. Deb: 4/16/32																								
1932	Bos-A	17	37	4	5	1	0	0	3	6	6	.135	.256	.162	418	11	-5	0	0	0	.990	0	1-10/3-1	-0.5
■ BUCK REDFERN Redfern, George Howard b: 4/7/02, Asheville, N.C. d: 9/8/64, Asheville, N.C. BR/TR, 5'11", 165 lbs. Deb: 4/11/28																								
1928	Chi-A	86	261	22	61	6	3	0	35	12	19	.234	.267	.280	547	44	-21	8	2	1	.953	6	2-45,S-33/3-1	-1.0
1929	Chi-A	21	46	0	6	0	0	0	3	3	3	.130	.184	.130	314	-18	-8	1	1	-0	.967	-5	2-11/3-5,S-4	-1.2
Total	2	107	307	22	67	6	3	0	38	15	22	.218	.255	.257	512	35	-29	9	3	1	.955	1	/2-56,S-37,3-6	-2.2
■ JOE REDFIELD Redfield, Joseph Randall b: 1/14/61, Doylestown, Pa. BR/TR, 6'2", 190 lbs. Deb: 6/4/88																								
1988	Cal-A	1	2	0	0	0	0	0	0	0	0	.000	.000	.000	0	-99	-1	0	0	0	1.000	0	/3-1	0.0
1991	Pit-N	11	18	1	2	0	0	0	0	4	1	.111	.273	.111	384	12	-2	0	1	-0	.917	-1	/3-9	-0.3
Total	2	12	20	1	2	0	0	0	0	4	1	.100	.250	.100	350	2	-3	0	1	-0	.923	-0	/3-10	-0.3
■ TIKE REDMAN Redman, Julian Jawonn b: 3/10/77, Tuscaloosa, Ala. BL/TL, 5'11", 166 lbs. Deb: 6/30/2000																								
2000	Pit-N	9	18	2	6	1	0	1	1	1	7	.333	.368	.556	924	130	1	1	0	0	1.000	1	/O-6(2-0-4)	0.2
■ GLENN REDMON Redmon, Glenn Vincent b: 1/11/48, Detroit, Mich. BR/TR, 5'11", 180 lbs. Deb: 9/8/74																								
1974	SF-N	7	17	0	4	3	0	0	4	1	3	.235	.278	.412	690	87	-0	0	0	0	.955	-1	/2-4	-0.1
■ BILLY REDMON Redmon, William T. b: Brooklyn, N.Y. BL/TL, Deb: 5/4/1875 Career OF: (0-LF 4-CF 3-RF)																								
1875	RS-n	19	82	12	16	2	0	0	1	2	7	.195	.214	.220	434	56	-3	3	0	1	.837	5	S-19/C-2	0.2
1877	Cin-N	3	12	1	3	1	0	0	3	1	1	.250	.308	.333	641	115	0				.833	2	/S-3	0.2
1878	Mil-N	48	187	16	43	8	0	0	21	8	13	.230	.262	.273	534	71	-6				.785	-17	S-39/O-7C,3-3,C-1	-2.1
Total	2	51	199	17	46	9	0	0	24	9	14	.231	.264	.276	541	73	-6				.791	-16	/S-42,O-7C,3-3,C-1	-1.9
■ HARRY REDMOND Redmond, Harry John b: 9/13/1887, Cleveland, Ohio d: 7/10/60, Cleveland, Ohio BR/TR, 5'8", 170 lbs. Deb: 9/7/09																								
1909	Bro-N	6	19	3	0	0	0	0	1	0		.000	.000	.000	0	-99	-4	0			.892	3	/2-5	-0.1
■ WAYNE REDMOND Redmond, Howard Wayne b: 11/25/45, Athens, Ala. BR/TR, 5'10", 165 lbs. Deb: 9/7/65																								
1965	Det-A	4	4	1	0	0	0	0	0	1	1	.000	.200	.000	200	-38	-1	0	0	0	1.000	-0	/O-2(1-1-0)	-0.1
1969	Det-A	5	3	0	0	0	0	0	0	0	2	.000	.000	.000	0	-96	-1	0	0	0	.000	0	H	-0.1
Total	2	9	7	1	0	0	0	0	0	1	3	.000	.125	.000	125	-60	-1	0	0	0	1.000	-0	/O-2(1-1-0)	-0.2
■ JACK REDMOND Redmond, John McKittrick "Red" (b: Jackson Mc Kittrick Redmond) b: 9/3/10, Florence, Ariz. d: 7/27/68, Garland, Tex. BL/TR, 5'11", 185 lbs. Deb: 4/22/35																								
1935	Was-A	22	34	8	6	1	0	1	7	3	1	.176	.243	.294	537	40	-3	0	0	0	.978	2	C-15	-0.1
■ MIKE REDMOND Redmond, Michael Patrick b: 5/5/71, Seattle, Wash. BR/TR, 6'1", 185 lbs. Deb: 5/31/98																								
1998	Fla-N	37	118	10	39	9	0	2	12	5	16	.331	.368	.458	826	122	4	0	0	0	.992	0	C-37	0.6
1999	Fla-N	84	242	22	73	9	0	1	27	26	34	.302	.381	.351	732	92	-2	0	0	0	.992	-0	C-82	0.3
2000	Fla-N	87	210	17	53	8	1	0	15	13	19	.252	.320	.300	620	61	-12	0	0	0	.996	8	C-85	-0.1
Total	3	208	570	49	165	26	1	3	54	44	69	.289	.356	.354	711	87	-10	0	0	0	.993	8	C-204	0.8
■ GARY REDUS Redus, Gary Eugene b: 11/1/56, Athens, Ala. BR/TR, 6'1", 185 lbs. Deb: 9/7/82 Career OF: (571-LF 132-CF 117-RF)																								
1982	Cin-N	20	83	12	18	3	2	1	7	5	21	.217	.261	.337	599	65	-4	11	2	2	.970	1	O-20(20-0-0)	-0.3
1983	Cin-N	125	453	90	112	20	9	17	51	71	111	.247	.353	.444	797	115	10	39	14	4	.972	9	*O-120(120-0-0)	1.8
1984	Cin-N	123	394	69	100	21	3	7	22	52	71	.254	.342	.376	718	97	-1	48	11	7	.967	-2	*O-114(93-24-1)	0.1
1985	Cin-N	101	246	51	62	14	4	6	28	44	52	.252	.368	.415	782	113	5	48	12	6	.986	-10	O-85(63-37-0)	0.0
1986	Phi-N	90	340	62	84	22	4	11	33	47	78	.247	.344	.432	776	109	4	25	7	3	.980	10	O-89(89-0-0)	1.4
1987	Chi-A	130	475	78	112	26	6	12	48	69	90	.236	.333	.392	724	89	-7	52	11	8	.979	4	*O-123(97-19-20)/D-4	-0.1
1988	Chi-A	77	262	42	69	10	4	6	34	33	52	.263	.350	.401	751	110	4	26	2	5	.987	1	O-68(54-16-2)/D-2	0.8

YEAR	TM/L	G	AB	R	H	2B	3B	HR	RBI	BB	SO	AVG	OBP	SLG	OPS	OPS+	BR+	SB	CS	SBR	FA	FR	G/POS	TPR
	Pit-N	30	71	12	14	2	0	2	4	15	19	.197	.345	.310	655	90	-0	5	2	0	.957	2	O-19(11-1-7)	0.2
1989	Pit-N	98	279	42	79	18	7	6	33	40	51	.283	.375	.462	837	143	16	25	6	3	.987	0	1-72,O-16(2-1-12)	1.5
1990	*Pit-N	96	227	32	56	15	3	6	23	33	38	.247	.347	.419	766	114	5	11	5	1	.988	-2	1-72/O-7(4-1-2)	-0.1
1991	*Pit-N	98	252	45	62	12	2	7	24	28	39	.246	.329	.393	721	104	1	17	3	3	.990	-11	1-47,O-33(11-12-11)	-1.2
1992	*Pit-N	76	176	26	45	7	3	3	12	17	25	.256	.321	.381	702	99	-0	11	4	1	1.000	-4	1-36,O-15(2-1-12)	-0.6
1993	Tex-A	77	222	28	64	12	4	6	31	23	35	.288	.355	.459	815	122	7	4	4	-1	.981	-8	O-61R/1-5,2-1,D-1	-0.4
1994	Tex-A	18	33	2	9	1	0	0	2	4	6	.273	.351	.303	654	71	-1	0	0	0	1.000	-2	/O-7(0-3-4),1-5	-0.3
Total	13	1159	3513	591	886	183	51	90	352	481	688	.252	.345	.410	755	107	39	322	83	42	.974	-12	O-777L,1-237/D-7,2	2.8
■ BOB REECE	Reece, Robert Scott b: 1/5/51, Sacramento, Cal. BR/TR, 6'1", 190 lbs. Deb: 4/22/78																							
1978	Mon-N	9	11	2	2	1	0	0	3	0	4	.182	.182	.273	455	26	-1	0	0	0	.947	1	/C-9	0.0
■ DARREN REED	Reed, Darren A. Douglas b: 10/16/65, Ojai, Cal. BR/TR, 6'1", 190 lbs. Deb: 5/1/90																							
1990	NY-N	26	39	5	8	4	1	1	2	3	11	.205	.262	.436	698	89	-1	1	0	0	.955	-1	O-14(2-7-6)	-0.2
1992	Mon-N	42	81	10	14	2	0	5	10	6	23	.173	.239	.383	621	74	-3	0	0	0	1.000	-3	O-29(8-0-21)	-0.7
	Min-A	14	33	2	6	2	0	0	4	2	11	.182	.229	.242	471	31	-3	0	0	0	1.000	-2	O-13(10-0-4)/D-1	-0.6
Total	2	82	153	17	28	8	1	6	16	11	45	.183	.242	.366	608	68	-7	1	0	0	.987	-6	/O-56(20-7-31),D-1	-1.5
■ HUGH REED	Reed, Hugh b: 1837, Chicago, Ill. d: 11/3/1883, Chicago, Ill. Deb: 8/26/1874																							
1874	Bal-n	1	4	0	0	0	0	0	0	0	0	.000	.000	.000	0	-99	-1	0	0	0	1.000	-0	/O-1(0-0-1)	-0.1
■ JEFF REED	Reed, Jeffrey Scott b: 11/12/62, Joliet, Ill. BL/TR, 6'2", 190 lbs. Deb: 4/5/84																							
1984	Min-A	18	21	3	3	3	0	0	1	2	6	.143	.217	.286	503	36	-2	0	0	0	.977	2	C-18	0.1
1985	Min-A	7	10	2	2	0	0	0	0	0	3	.200	.200	.200	400	9	-1	0	0	0	1.000	-0	/C-7	-0.1
1986	Min-A	68	165	13	39	6	1	2	9	16	19	.236	.308	.321	629	70	-7	1	0	0	.994	8	C-64	0.4
1987	Mon-N	75	207	15	44	11	0	1	21	12	20	.213	.259	.280	539	42	-17	0	1	-0	.970	-4	C-74	-1.9
1988	Mon-N	43	123	10	27	3	2	0	9	13	22	.220	.294	.276	571	62	-6	1	0	0	.995	2	C-39	-0.1
	Cin-N	49	142	10	33	6	0	1	7	15	19	.232	.306	.296	602	71	-5	0	0	0	.993	5	C-49	0.3
	Yr	92	265	20	60	9	2	1	16	28	41	.226	.300	.287	587	66	-11	1	0	0	.994	8	C-88	0.2
1989	Cin-N	102	287	16	64	11	0	3	23	34	46	.223	.310	.293	602	71	-10	0	0	0	.988	-5	C-99	-1.0
1990	*Cin-N	72	175	12	44	8	1	3	16	24	26	.251	.342	.360	702	89	-2	0	0	0	.987	2	C-70	0.3
1991	Cin-N	91	270	20	72	15	2	3	31	23	38	.267	.327	.370	697	92	-3	0	1	-0	.991	-2	C-89	0.0
1992	Cin-N	15	25	2	4	0	0	0	2	1	4	.160	.192	.160	352	1	-3	0	0	0	1.000	-0	/C-6	-0.3
1993	SF-N	66	119	10	31	3	0	6	12	16	22	.261	.348	.437	785	112	2	0	1	-0	1.000	3	C-37	0.7
1994	SF-N	50	103	11	18	3	0	1	7	11	21	.175	.254	.233	487	30	-11	0	0	0	.993	-4	C-33	-1.3
1995	SF-N	66	113	12	30	2	0	0	9	20	17	.265	.376	.283	659	79	-2	0	0	0	.995	3	C-42	0.3
1996	Col-N	116	341	34	97	20	1	8	37	43	65	.284	.368	.419	787	87	-6	2	2	-0	.982	-14	*C-111	-1.3
1997	Col-N	90	256	43	76	10	0	17	47	35	55	.297	.386	.535	921	112	5	2	1	0	.987	4	C-78	1.3
1998	Col-N	113	259	43	75	17	1	9	39	37	57	.290	.380	.467	848	100	1	0	0	0	.986	-3	C-99	0.2
1999	Col-N	46	106	11	27	5	0	2	11	17	24	.255	.363	.358	721	66	-5	0	1	-0	.983	-7	C-36	-1.0
	Chi-N	57	150	18	39	11	2	1	17	28	34	.260	.383	.380	763	96	0	1	1	-0	.987	-2	C-49/3-1,D-1	0.1
	Yr	103	256	29	66	16	2	3	28	45	58	.258	.375	.371	746	81	-6	1	2	-0	.985	-9	C-85/3-1,D-1	-0.9
2000	Chi-N	90	229	26	49	10	0	4	25	44	68	.214	.343	.310	653	68	-10	0	1	-0	.990	-5	C-71	-1.1
Total	17	1234	3101	311	774	144	10	61	323	391	566	.250	.336	.361	698	81	-82	7	9	-2	.988	-15	*C-1071/D-1,3-1	-4.4
■ JODY REED	Reed, Jody Eric b: 7/26/62, Tampa, Fla. BR/TR, 5'9", 165 lbs. Deb: 9/12/87 Career OF: (0-LF 0-CF 1-RF)																							
1987	Bos-A	9	30	4	9	1	1	0	8	4	0	.300	.382	.400	782	105	0	1	1	-0	1.000	5	/S-4,2-2,3-1	0.5
1988	*Bos-A	109	338	60	99	23	1	1	28	45	21	.293	.382	.376	758	109	6	1	3	-1	.971	3	S-94,2-11/3-4,D-1	1.5
1989	Bos-A	146	524	76	151	42	2	3	40	73	44	.288	.379	.393	772	111	10	4	5	-1	.967	1	S-77,2-70/3-4,OD	1.8
1990	*Bos-A	155	598	70	173	**45**	0	5	51	75	65	.289	.372	.390	762	108	9	4	4	-1	.990	-6	*2-119,S-50/D-1	0.9
1991	Bos-A	153	618	87	175	42	2	5	60	60	53	.283	.350	.382	732	98	-1	6	5	-0	.982	1	*2-152/S-6	0.4
1992	Bos-A	143	550	64	136	27	1	3	40	62	44	.247	.324	.316	640	75	-17	7	8	-1	.982	**24**	*2-142/D-1	0.9
1993	LA-N	132	445	48	123	21	2	2	31	38	40	.276	.335	.346	681	88	-7	1	3	-1	**.993**	19	*2-132	1.8
1994	Mil-A	108	399	48	108	22	0	2	37	57	34	.271	.365	.341	705	80	-10	5	4	-0	**.995**	11	*2-106	0.5
1995	SD-N	131	445	58	114	18	1	4	40	59	38	.256	.350	.328	678	83	-9	6	4	-0	.994	18	*2-130/S-5	1.5
1996	*SD-N	146	495	45	121	20	0	2	49	59	53	.244	.329	.297	626	71	-19	2	5	-1	.987	4	*2-145	-0.9
1997	Det-A	52	112	6	22	2	0	0	8	10	15	.196	.280	.214	494	32	-11	3	2	-0	.987	13	2-41/D-5	0.3
Total	11	1284	4554	566	1231	263	10	27	392	542	407	.270	.352	.350	702	90	-50	40	44	-7	.988	94	*2-1050,S-236/D-9,3O	9.2
■ JACK REED	Reed, John Burwell b: 2/2/33, Silver City, Miss. BR/TR, 6', 185 lbs. Deb: 4/23/61																							
1961	*NY-A	28	13	4	2	0	0	0	1	1	1	.154	.214	.154	368	0	-2	0	0	0	.933	-9	O-27(12-14-1)	-1.1
1962	NY-A	88	43	17	13	2	1	1	4	4	7	.302	.362	.465	827	125	1	2	1	0	.941	-23	O-75(20-39-16)	-2.2
1963	NY-A	106	73	18	15	3	1	0	1	9	14	.205	.293	.274	567	60	-4	5	1	1	1.000	-21	O-89(14-30-46)	-2.6
Total	3	222	129	39	30	5	2	1	6	14	22	.233	.308	.326	633	76	-4	7	2	1	.972	-53	O-191(46-83-63)	-5.9
■ MILT REED	Reed, Milton D. b: 7/4/1890, Atlanta, Ga. d: 7/27/38, Atlanta, Ga. BL/TR, 5'9.5", 150 lbs. Deb: 9/9/11																							
1911	StL-N	1	1	0	0	0	0	0	0	0	0	.000	.000	.000	0	-99	-0	0			.000	0	H	0.0
1913	Phi-N	13	24	4	6	1	0	0	0	1	5	.250	.280	.292	572	61	-1	1			.900	-4	/S-9,2-3	-0.5
1914	Phi-N	44	107	10	22	2	1	0	2	10	13	.206	.280	.243	523	52	-6	4			.887	-17	S-22,2-11/3-1	-2.5
1915	Bro-F	10	31	2	9	1	1	0	8	2	0	.290	.353	.387	740	109	-0	2			.864	-5	S-10	-0.5
Total	4	68	163	16	37	4	2	0	10	13	18	.227	.292	.276	568	63	-8	7			.880	-26	/S-41,2-14,3-1	-3.5
■ TED REED	Reed, Ralph Edwin b: 10/18/1890, Beaver, Pa. d: 2/16/59, Beaver, Pa. BR/TR, 5'11", 190 lbs. Deb: 9/10/15																							
1915	New-F	20	77	5	20	1	2	0	4	2	7	.260	.287	.325	612	76	-4	1			.863	-3	3-20	-0.7
■ BILLY REED	Reed, William Joseph b: 11/12/22, Shawano, Wis. BL/TR, 5'10.5", 175 lbs. Deb: 4/15/52																							
1952	Bos-N	15	52	4	13	0	0	0	0	0	5	.250	.264	.250	514	45	-4	0	0	0	.931	-7	2-14	-1.0
■ ICICLE REEDER	Reeder, James Edward b: 1865, Cincinnati, Ohio BR, 6', Deb: 6/24/1884																							
1884	Cin-a	3	14	0	2	0	0	0			0	.143	.143	.143	286	-6	-2				1.000	-0	/O-3(3-0-0)	-0.2
	Was-U	3	12	0	2	0	0	0			0	.167	.167	.167	333	1	-2				.500	-1	/O-3(0-1-2)	-0.3
Total	1	6	26	0	4	0	0	0			0	.154	.154	.154	308	-3	-3				.714	-1	/O-6(3-1-2)	-0.5
■ NICK REEDER	Reeder, Nicholas (b: Nicholas Herchenroeder) b: 3/22/1867, Louisville, Ky. d: 9/26/1894, Louisville, Ky. BR/TR, 5'9", 189 lbs. Deb: 4/11/1891																							
1891	Lou-a	1	2	0	0	0	0	0	0	0	1	.000	.000	.000	0	-99	-1	0			1.000	-0	/3-1	-0.1
■ RANDY REESE	Reese, Andrew Jackson b: 2/7/04, Tupelo, Miss. d: 1/10/66, Tupelo, Miss. BR/TR, 5'11", 180 lbs. Deb: 4/15/27 Career OF: (81-LF 26-CF 15-RF)																							
1927	NY-N	97	355	43	94	14	2	4	21	13	52	.265	.298	.349	648	73	-14	5			.912	-1	3-64,O-16(7-0-9)/1-1	-1.2
1928	NY-N	109	406	61	125	18	4	6	44	13	24	.308	.331	.416	747	94	-5	7			.941	-10	O-64L,2-26/1-6,S3	-1.7
1929	NY-N	58	209	36	55	11	3	0	21	15	19	.263	.316	.344	660	64	-12	8			.960	1	2-44/O-8(7-1-0),3-4	-0.9
1930	NY-N	67	172	26	47	4	2	4	25	10	12	.273	.313	.390	703	70	-9	1			.957	-3	O-32(8-23-2),3-10/1-1	-1.2
Total	4	331	1142	166	321	47	11	14	111	51	107	.281	.315	.378	694	78	-39	21			.954	-14	O-120L/3-84,2-70,1S	-5.0
■ POKEY REESE	Reese, Calvin b: 6/10/73, Columbia, S.C. BR/TR, 5'11", 180 lbs. Deb: 4/1/97																							
1997	Cin-N	128	397	48	87	15	0	4	26	31	82	.219	.284	.287	571	49	-29	25	7	3	.966	-2	*S-110/2-8,3-8	-2.0
1998	Cin-N	59	133	20	34	2	2	1	16	14	28	.256	.327	.323	650	71	-5	3	2	-0	.985	3	3-32,S-18/2-3	-0.1
1999	Cin-N	149	585	85	167	37	5	10	52	35	81	.285	.332	.417	749	86	-13	38	7	6	.991	-2	*2-146,S-16	-0.1
2000	Cin-N	135	518	76	132	20	6	12	46	45	86	.255	.322	.386	708	75	-20	29	3	5	.980	15	*2-133	0.7
Total	4	471	1633	229	420	74	13	27	140	125	277	.257	.317	.368	685	72	-68	95	19	14	.986	14	2-290,S-144/3-40	-1.5
■ PEE WEE REESE	Reese, Harold Henry b: 7/23/18, Ekron, Ky. d: 8/14/99, Louisville, Ky. BR/TR, 5'9", 175 lbs. Deb: 4/23/40 CH																							
1940	Bro-N	84	312	58	85	8	4	5	28	45	42	.272	.366	.372	738	98	1	15			.960	-14	S-83	-0.8

YEAR	TM/L	G	AB	R	H	2B	3B	HR	RBI	BB	SO	AVG	OBP	SLG	OPS	OPS+	BR+	SB	CS	SBR	FA	FR	G/POS	TPR
1941	*Bro-N	152	595	76	136	23	5	2	46	68	56	.229	.311	.294	605	68	-24	10			.946	8	*S-151	-0.5
1942	Bro-N★	151	564	87	144	24	5	3	53	82	55	.255	.350	.332	681	98	1	15			.959	17	*S-151	3.2
1946	Bro-N†	152	542	79	154	16	10	5	60	87	71	.284	.384	.378	762	116	14	10			.966	-4	*S-152	2.1
1947	*Bro-N★	142	476	81	135	24	4	12	73	**104**	67	.284	.414	.426	841	119	17	7			.966	-2	*S-142	2.4
1948	Bro-N★	151	566	96	155	31	4	9	75	79	63	.274	.363	.390	753	100	2	25			.962	10	*S-149	2.1
1949	*Bro-N★	155	617	**132**	172	27	3	16	73	116	59	.279	.396	.410	806	112	15	26			**.977**	2	*S-155	2.6
1950	Bro-N★	141	531	97	138	21	5	11	52	91	62	.260	.369	.380	750	96	-1	17			.963	2	*S-134/3-7	0.9
1951	Bro-N★	154	616	94	176	20	8	10	84	81	57	.286	.371	.393	763	103	5	20	14	-1	.953	-8	*S-154	0.6
1952	*Bro-N★	149	559	94	152	18	8	6	58	86	59	.272	.369	.365	734	103	5	**30**	5	**5**	.969	-11	*S-145	0.8
1953	*Bro-N★	140	524	108	142	25	7	13	61	82	61	.271	.374	.420	794	104	5	22	6	**3**	.966	-1	*S-135	1.8
1954	Bro-N☆	141	554	98	171	35	8	10	69	90	62	.309	.408	.455	863	121	20	8	5	0	.965	-4	*S-140	2.8
1955	*Bro-N	145	553	99	156	29	4	10	61	78	60	.282	.374	.403	777	103	5	8	7	-1	.965	-13	*S-142	0.3
1956	*Bro-N	147	572	85	147	19	2	9	46	56	69	.257	.324	.344	669	74	-19	13	4	1	.965	-9	*S-136,3-12	-1.6
1957	Bro-N	103	330	33	74	3	1	1	29	39	32	.224	.308	.248	557	47	-23	5	2	0	.943	10	3-75,S-23	-1.1
1958	LA-N	59	147	21	33	7	2	4	17	26	15	.224	.341	.381	722	88	-2	1	2	-0	.929	-8	S-22,3-21	-0.9
Total	16	2166	8058	1338	2170	330	80	126	885	1210	890	.269	.366	.377	743	98	21	232	45		.962	-25	*S-2014,3-115	14.7

■ JIMMIE REESE Reese, James Herman (b: James Herman Soloman) b: 10/1/01, New York, N.Y. d: 7/13/94, Santa Ana, Cal. BL/TR, 5′11.5″, 165 lbs. Deb: 4/19/30 C

YEAR	TM/L	G	AB	R	H	2B	3B	HR	RBI	BB	SO	AVG	OBP	SLG	OPS	OPS+	BR+	SB	CS	SBR	FA	FR	G/POS	TPR
1930	NY-A	77	188	44	65	14	2	3	18	11	8	.346	.382	.489	871	125	7	1	1	-0	.974	-9	2-48/3-5	-0.1
1931	NY-A	65	245	41	59	10	2	3	26	17	10	.241	.293	.335	627	68	-12	2	3	-1	.972	5	2-61	-0.4
1932	StL-N	90	309	38	82	15	0	2	26	20	19	.265	.314	.333	648	72	-12	4			.979	9	2-77	0.2
Total	3	232	742	123	206	39	4	8	70	48	37	.278	.324	.373	697	84	-17	7	4		.975	4	2-186/3-5	-0.3

■ RICH REESE Reese, Richard Benjamin b: 9/29/41, Leipsic, Ohio BL/TL, 6′3″, 200 lbs. Deb: 9/4/64

YEAR	TM/L	G	AB	R	H	2B	3B	HR	RBI	BB	SO	AVG	OBP	SLG	OPS	OPS+	BR+	SB	CS	SBR	FA	FR	G/POS	TPR
1964	Min-A	10	7	0	0	0	0	0	0	0	1	.000	.000	.000	0	-99	-2	0	0	0	1.000	0	/1-1	-0.2
1965	Min-A	14	7	0	2	1	0	0	0	2	2	.286	.444	.429	873	143	1	0	0	0	1.000	-0	/1-6,O-1(1-0-0)	0.0
1966	Min-A	3	2	0	0	0	0	0	0	1	2	.000	.333	.000	333	5	-0	0	0	0	.000	0	H	0.0
1967	Min-A	95	101	13	25	5	0	4	20	8	17	.248	.303	.416	719	102	0	0	0	0	.990	-1	1-36,O-10(10-0-0)	-0.2
1968	Min-A	126	332	40	86	15	2	4	28	18	36	.259	.303	.352	656	93	-3	3	1	0	.991	-2	1-87,O-15(15-0-0)	-1.0
1969	*Min-A	132	419	52	135	24	4	16	69	23	57	.322	.365	.513	878	140	21	1	5	-2	.993	-4	*1-117/O-5(5-0-0)	0.8
1970	*Min-A	153	501	63	131	15	5	10	56	48	70	.261	.335	.371	706	93	-4	5	4	-0	.992	-2	*1-146	-1.8
1971	Min-A	120	329	40	72	8	3	10	39	20	35	.219	.274	.353	627	74	-12	7	4	0	.994	-3	1-95/O-9(8-0-1)	-2.3
1972	Min-A	132	197	23	43	3	2	5	26	25	27	.218	.306	.330	636	85	-3	0	1	-0	.988	3	1-98,O-13(13-0-0)	-0.5
1973	Det-A	59	102	10	14	1	0	2	4	7	17	.137	.193	.206	399	11	-12	0	0	0	1.000	-3	1-37,O-21(21-0-1)	-1.8
	Min-A	22	23	7	4	1	1	1	3	6	6	.174	.345	.435	780	114	1	0	0	0	1.000	1	1-17	0.1
	Yr	81	125	17	18	2	1	3	7	13	23	.144	.225	.248	473	31	-12	0	0	0	1.000	-2	1-54,O-21(21-0-1)	-1.7
Total	10	866	2020	248	512	73	17	52	245	158	270	.253	.314	.384	698	95	-14	16	15	-2	.992	-10	1-640/O-74(73-0-2)	-6.9

■ BOBBY REEVES Reeves, Robert Edwin "Gunner" b: 6/24/04, Hill City, Tenn. d: 6/4/93, Chattanooga, Tenn. BR/TR, 5′11″, 170 lbs. Deb: 6/9/26 Career OF: (0-LF 0-CF 1-RF)

YEAR	TM/L	G	AB	R	H	2B	3B	HR	RBI	BB	SO	AVG	OBP	SLG	OPS	OPS+	BR+	SB	CS	SBR	FA	FR	G/POS	TPR
1926	Was-A	20	49	4	11	0	1	0	7	6	9	.224	.321	.265	587	56	-3	1	1	-0	.940	1	3-16/2-1,S-1	-0.1
1927	Was-A	112	380	37	97	11	5	1	39	21	53	.255	.296	.318	614	60	-23	3	1	0	.923	-7	S-96,3-12/2-2	-1.8
1928	Was-A	102	353	44	107	16	8	3	42	24	47	.303	.351	.419	770	102	1	4	8	-2	.908	-4	S-66,2-22/3-8,O-1R	0.3
1929	Bos-A	140	460	66	114	19	2	2	28	60	57	.248	.343	.311	654	71	-18	7	8	-1	.912	1	*3-131/2-2,S-2,1-1	-1.0
1930	Bos-A	92	272	41	59	7	4	2	18	50	36	.217	.345	.294	639	66	-12	6	2	1	.895	5	3-62,S-15,2-11	-0.2
1931	Bos-A	36	84	11	14	2	2	0	1	14	16	.167	.293	.238	531	43	-7	0	1	-0	.912	-8	2-29/P-1	-1.3
Total	6	502	1598	203	402	55	22	8	135	175	218	.252	.331	.329	660	73	-62	21	21	-3	.906	-11	3-229,S-180/2-67,P1O	-4.1

■ RUDY REGALADO Regalado, Rudolph Valentino b: 5/21/30, Los Angeles, Cal. BR/TR, 6′1″, 185 lbs. Deb: 4/13/54

YEAR	TM/L	G	AB	R	H	2B	3B	HR	RBI	BB	SO	AVG	OBP	SLG	OPS	OPS+	BR+	SB	CS	SBR	FA	FR	G/POS	TPR
1954	*Cle-A	65	180	21	45	5	0	2	24	19	16	.250	.335	.311	646	76	-5	0	2	-1	.967	-5	3-50/2-2	-1.2
1955	Cle-A	10	26	2	7	2	0	0	5	2	4	.269	.321	.346	668	77	-1	0	0	0	.955	2	/3-8,2-1	0.1
1956	Cle-A	16	47	4	11	1	0	0	2	4	1	.234	.308	.255	563	49	-3	0	0	0	.783	-7	3-14/1-1	-1.0
Total	3	91	253	27	63	8	0	2	31	25	21	.249	.329	.304	633	71	-9	0	2	-1	.944	-10	/3-72,2-3,1-1	-2.1

■ JOE REGAN Regan, Joseph Charles b: 7/12/1872, Seymour, Conn. d: 11/18/48, Hartford, Conn. BR/TR, 6′1″, Deb: 9/21/1898

YEAR	TM/L	G	AB	R	H	2B	3B	HR	RBI	BB	SO	AVG	OBP	SLG	OPS	OPS+	BR+	SB	CS	SBR	FA	FR	G/POS	TPR
1898	NY-N	2	5	1	1	0	0	0	2	0		.200	.200	.200	400	15	-1	0			1.000	-1	/O-2(0-0-2)	-0.1

■ BILL REGAN Regan, William Wright b: 1/23/1899, Pittsburgh, Pa. d: 6/11/68, Pittsburgh, Pa. BR/TR, 5′10″, 155 lbs. Deb: 6/2/26 Career OF: (0-LF 0-CF 1-RF)

YEAR	TM/L	G	AB	R	H	2B	3B	HR	RBI	BB	SO	AVG	OBP	SLG	OPS	OPS+	BR+	SB	CS	SBR	FA	FR	G/POS	TPR
1926	Bos-A	108	403	40	106	21	3	4	34	23	37	.263	.309	.360	669	77	-15	6	3	0	.965	17	*2-106	0.5
1927	Bos-A	129	468	43	128	37	10	2	66	26	51	.274	.315	.408	723	88	-10	10	10	-1	.960	3	*2-121	-0.5
1928	Bos-A	138	511	53	135	30	6	7	75	21	40	.264	.296	.387	683	80	-17	9	6	-0	.963	15	*2-137/O-1(0-0-1)	0.1
1929	Bos-A	104	371	38	107	27	7	1	54	22	38	.288	.328	.407	735	90	-6	7	5	-0	.962	-16	2-91,3-10/1-1	-1.9
1930	Bos-A	134	507	54	135	35	10	3	53	25	60	.266	.303	.393	696	78	-18	4	2	0	.963	-10	*2-127/3-2	-2.2
1931	Pit-N	28	104	8	21	8	0	1	10	5	19	.202	.239	.308	546	46	-8	2			.944	-0	2-28	-0.7
Total	6	641	2364	236	632	158	36	18	292	122	245	.267	.306	.387	694	81	-75	38	26		.962	8	2-610/3-12,1-1,O-1R	-4.7

■ TONY REGO Rego, Antone (b: Antone De Rego) b: 10/31/1897, Wailuku, Hawaii d: 1/6/78, Tulsa, Okla. BR/TR, 5′4″, 165 lbs. Deb: 6/21/24

YEAR	TM/L	G	AB	R	H	2B	3B	HR	RBI	BB	SO	AVG	OBP	SLG	OPS	OPS+	BR+	SB	CS	SBR	FA	FR	G/POS	TPR
1924	StL-A	24	59	5	13	1	0	0	5	1	3	.220	.233	.237	471	20	-7	0	0	0	.972	0	C-23	-0.6
1925	StL-A	20	32	5	13	2	1	0	3	3	2	.406	.472	.531	1003	147	2	0	0	0	.979	2	C-19	0.5
Total	2	44	91	10	26	3	1	0	8	4	5	.286	.323	.341	664	66	-5	0	0	0	.975	2	/C-42	-0.1

■ WALLY REHG Rehg, Walter Phillip b: 8/31/1888, Summerfield, Ill. d: 4/5/46, Burbank, Cal. BR/TR, 5′8″, 160 lbs. Deb: 4/14/12

YEAR	TM/L	G	AB	R	H	2B	3B	HR	RBI	BB	SO	AVG	OBP	SLG	OPS	OPS+	BR+	SB	CS	SBR	FA	FR	G/POS	TPR
1912	Pit-N	8	9	1	0	0	0	0	0	0	1	.000	.000	.000	0	-99	-2	0			1.000	-1	/O-2(0-1-1)	-0.3
1913	Bos-A	30	101	13	28	3	2	0	9	2	7	.277	.291	.347	638	84	-2	4			.943	-3	O-26(8-3-15)	-0.7
1914	Bos-A	88	151	14	33	4	2	0	11	18	11	.219	.306	.272	577	74	-5	5	8	-2	.980	-5	O-43(16-0-27)	-1.5
1915	Bos-A	5	5	2	1	0	0	0	0	0	1	.200	.200	.200	400	20	-1	1			1.000	-0	/O-1(0-0-1)	-0.1
1917	Bos-N	87	341	48	92	12	6	1	31	24	32	.270	.320	.349	669	111	4	13			.956	-5	O-86(0-0-86)	-0.6
1918	Bos-N	40	133	6	32	5	1	1	12	5	14	.241	.268	.316	584	81	-3	3			.988	2	O-38(30-1-7)	-0.3
1919	Cin-N	5	12	1	2	0	0	0	3	1	0	.167	.231	.167	397	21	-1	0			.875	0	/O-5(0-1-3)	-0.1
Total	7	263	752	85	188	24	11	2	66	50	66	.250	.299	.319	618	90	-10	26	8		.965	-12	O-201(54-6-140)	-3.6

■ FRANK REIBER Reiber, Frank Bernard "Tubby" b: 9/19/09, Huntington, W.Va. BR/TR, 5′8.5″, 169 lbs. Deb: 4/13/33

YEAR	TM/L	G	AB	R	H	2B	3B	HR	RBI	BB	SO	AVG	OBP	SLG	OPS	OPS+	BR+	SB	CS	SBR	FA	FR	G/POS	TPR
1933	Det-A	13	18	3	5	0	1	1	3	2	3	.278	.350	.556	906	134	1	0	0	0	.929	-2	/C-6	-0.1
1934	Det-A	3	1	0	0	0	0	0	0	2	0	.000	.667	.000	667	84	0	0	0	0	.000	0	H	0.0
1935	Det-A	8	11	3	3	0	0	0	1	3	3	.273	.429	.273	701	88	0	0	0	0	1.000	-1	/C-5	0.0
1936	Det-A	20	55	7	15	2	0	1	5	5	7	.273	.333	.364	697	72	-2	0	1	-0	.982	-4	C-17/O-1(0-0-1)	-0.5
Total	4	44	85	13	23	2	1	2	9	12	13	.271	.361	.388	749	89	-1	0	1	-0	.975	-6	/C-28,O-1(0-0-1)	-0.6

■ HERMAN REICH Reich, Herman Charles b: 11/23/17, Bell, Cal. BR/TL, 6′2″, 200 lbs. Deb: 5/3/49

YEAR	TM/L	G	AB	R	H	2B	3B	HR	RBI	BB	SO	AVG	OBP	SLG	OPS	OPS+	BR+	SB	CS	SBR	FA	FR	G/POS	TPR
1949	Was-A	2	2	0	0	0	0	0	0	0	1	.000	.000	.000	0	-99	-1	0	0	0	.000	0	H	-0.1
	Cle-A	1	2	0	1	0	0	0	0	1	0	.500	.667	.500	1167	215	1	0	0	0	.000	-0	/O-1(0-0-1)	0.0
	Yr	3	4	0	1	0	0	0	0	1	1	.250	.400	.250	650	75	-0	0	0	0	.000	-0	/O-1(0-0-1)	-0.1
	Chi-N	108	386	43	108	18	2	3	34	13	32	.280	.305	.360	665	80	-12	4			.989	14	1-85,O-16(0-0-16)	-0.1
Total	1	111	390	43	109	18	2	3	34	14	33	.279	.306	.359	665	80	-12	4	0		.969	14	/1-85,O-17(0-0-17)	-0.2

■ RICK REICHARDT Reichardt, Frederic Carl b: 3/16/43, Madison, Wis. BR/TR, 6′3″, 215 lbs. Deb: 9/1/64 Career OF: (713-LF 158-CF 39-RF)

YEAR	TM/L	G	AB	R	H	2B	3B	HR	RBI	BB	SO	AVG	OBP	SLG	OPS	OPS+	BR+	SB	CS	SBR	FA	FR	G/POS	TPR
1964	LA-A	11	37	0	6	0	0	0	0	1	12	.162	.184	.162	346	-3	-5	1	0	0	1.000	0	O-11(0-11-0)	-0.5
1965	Cal-A	20	75	8	20	4	0	1	6	5	12	.267	.321	.360	681	95	-0	4	1	1	.975	1	O-20(17-4-0)	0.0
1966	Cal-A	89	319	48	92	5	4	16	44	27	61	.288	.368	.480	847	145	19	8	4	0	.976	-1	O-87(77-20-0)	1.4
1967	Cal-A	146	498	56	132	14	2	17	69	35	90	.265	.322	.404	726	118	10	5	3	0	.974	10	*O-138(138-0-0)	1.4
1968	Cal-A	151	534	62	136	20	3	21	73	42	118	.255	.330	.421	751	131	19	8	7	-1	.989	9	*O-148(148-0-0)	2.2
1969	Cal-A	137	493	60	125	11	4	13	68	43	100	.254	.324	.371	695	99	-1	3	6	-1	.981	8	*O-136(136-0-0)/1-3	-0.3
1970	Cal-A	9	6	1	1	0	0	0	1	3	0	.167	.444	.167	611	78	0	0	0	0	1.000	-0	/O-1(0-0-1)	0.0

YEAR	TM/L	G	AB	R	H	2B	3B	HR	RBI	BB	SO	AVG	OBP	SLG	OPS	OPS+	BR+	SB	CS	SBR	FA	FR	G/POS	TPR
	Was-A	107	277	42	70	14	2	15	46	23	69	.253	.330	.480	810	127	9	2	4	-1	.985	-8	O-79(38-18-31)/3-1	-0.4
	Yr	116	283	43	71	14	2	15	47	26	69	.251	.333	.473	807	126	9	2	4	-1	.985	-8	O-80(38-18-32)/3-1	-0.4
1971	Chi-A	138	496	53	138	14	2	19	62	37	90	.278	.336	.429	765	112	7	5	10	-2	.981	-7	*O-128(117-15-0)/1-9	-1.1
1972	Chi-A	101	291	31	73	14	4	8	43	28	63	.251	.323	.409	732	114	5	2	2	-0	.981	-10	O-90(11-84-0)	-0.9
1973	Chi-A	46	153	15	42	8	1	3	16	8	29	.275	.315	.399	714	96	-1	2	3	-1	1.000	-2	O-37(30-6-1)/D-6	-0.6
	KC-A	41	127	15	28	5	2	3	17	11	28	.220	.283	.362	645	75	-5	0	1	-0	1.000	-1	D-31/O-7(1-0-6)	-0.7
	Yr	87	280	30	70	13	3	6	33	19	57	.250	.300	.382	682	86	-6	2	4	-1	1.000	-3	O-44(31-6-7),D-37	-1.3
1974	KC-A	1	1	0	1	0	0	0	0	0	0	1.000	1.000	1.000	2000	451	0	0	0	0	.000	0	H	0.0
Total	11	997	3307	391	864	109	24	116	445	263	672	.261	.328	.414	742	115	57	40	41	-6	.982	-2	O-882L/D-37,1-12,3	0.5

■ DICK REICHLE Reichle, Richard Wendell b: 11/23/1896, Lincoln, Ill. d: 6/13/67, Richmnond Heights, Mo. BL/TR, 6', 185 lbs. Deb: 9/19/22

YEAR	TM/L	G	AB	R	H	2B	3B	HR	RBI	BB	SO	AVG	OBP	SLG	OPS	OPS+	BR+	SB	CS	SBR	FA	FR	G/POS	TPR
1922	Bos-A	6	24	3	6	1	0	0	0	0	2	.250	.280	.292	572	50	-2	0	0	0	1.000	-0	/O-6(0-6-0)	-0.2
1923	Bos-A	122	361	40	93	17	3	1	39	22	34	.258	.315	.330	644	69	-16	3	6	-1	.976	-7	O-93(3-87-4)/1-2	-2.8
Total	2	128	385	43	99	18	3	1	39	22	36	.257	.313	.327	640	68	-18	3	6	-1	.977	-7	/O-99(3-93-4),1-2	-3.0

■ JESSIE REID Reid, Jessie Thomas b: 6/1/62, Honolulu, Hawaii BL/TL, 6'1", 200 lbs. Deb: 9/9/87

YEAR	TM/L	G	AB	R	H	2B	3B	HR	RBI	BB	SO	AVG	OBP	SLG	OPS	OPS+	BR+	SB	CS	SBR	FA	FR	G/POS	TPR
1987	SF-N	6	8	1	1	0	0	1	1	1	5	.125	.222	.500	722	89	-0	0	0	0	1.000	-1	/O-3(1-0-2)	-0.1
1988	SF-N	2	2	0	0	0	0	0	0	0	1	.000	.000	.000	0	-99	-1	0	0	0	.000	0	H	-0.1
Total	2	8	10	1	1	0	0	1	1	1	6	.100	.182	.400	582	54	-1	0	0	0	1.000	-1	/O-3(1-0-2)	-0.2

■ SCOTT REID Reid, Scott Donald b: 1/7/47, Chicago, Ill. BL/TR, 6'1", 195 lbs. Deb: 9/10/69

YEAR	TM/L	G	AB	R	H	2B	3B	HR	RBI	BB	SO	AVG	OBP	SLG	OPS	OPS+	BR+	SB	CS	SBR	FA	FR	G/POS	TPR
1969	Phi-N	13	19	5	4	0	0	0	0	7	5	.211	.423	.211	634	85	0	0	1	-0	1.000	-1	/O-5(2-4-0)	-0.1
1970	Phi-N	25	49	5	6	1	0	0	1	11	22	.122	.283	.143	426	18	-5	0	0	0	1.000	3	O-18(3-12-5)	-0.3
Total	2	38	68	10	10	1	0	0	1	18	27	.147	.326	.162	487	37	-5	0	1	-0	1.000	2	/O-23(5-16-5)	-0.4

■ BILLY REID Reid, William Alexander b: 5/17/1857, London, Ont., Can. d: 6/26/40, London, Ont., Can. BL/TR, 6', 170 lbs. Deb: 5/1/1883 Career OF: (17-LF 0-CF 0-RF)

YEAR	TM/L	G	AB	R	H	2B	3B	HR	RBI	BB	SO	AVG	OBP	SLG	OPS	OPS+	BR+	SB	CS	SBR	FA	FR	G/POS	TPR
1883	Bal-a	24	97	14	27	3	0	0		4		.278	.307	.309	616	96	-1				.842	-8	2-23/S-1	-0.7
1884	Pit-a	19	70	11	17	2	0	0		4		.243	.293	.271	565	86	-1				.724	-4	O-17(17-0-0)/3-1,2-1	-0.5
Total	2	43	167	25	44	5	0	0		8		.263	.301	.293	595	92	-1				.839	-12	/2-24,O-17L,3-1,S-1	-1.2

■ DUKE REILLEY Reilley, Alexander Aloysius "Midget" b: 8/25/1884, Chicago, Ill. d: 3/4/68, Indianapolis, Ind. BB/TR, 5'4.5", 148 lbs. Deb: 8/28/09

YEAR	TM/L	G	AB	R	H	2B	3B	HR	RBI	BB	SO	AVG	OBP	SLG	OPS	OPS+	BR+	SB	CS	SBR	FA	FR	G/POS	TPR
1909	Cle-A	20	62	10	13	0	0	0	0	4		.210	.258	.210	467	46	-4	5			.979	2	O-18(13-5-0)	-0.3

■ CHARLIE REILLEY Reilley, Charles E. b: 1856, Hartford, Conn. BR/TR, 5'10", 165 lbs. Deb: 5/1/1879 Career OF: (3-LF 15-CF 6-RF)

YEAR	TM/L	G	AB	R	H	2B	3B	HR	RBI	BB	SO	AVG	OBP	SLG	OPS	OPS+	BR+	SB	CS	SBR	FA	FR	G/POS	TPR
1879	Tro-N	62	236	17	54	5	1	0	19	1	20	.229	.232	.258	491	66	-8				.867	-16	C-49,1-11/O-2(1-0-1)	-2.2
1880	Cin-N	30	103	8	21	1	0	0	9	0	5	.204	.204	.214	417	42	-6				.759	-5	O-16(1-14-1),C-13/3-4	-1.1
1881	Det-N	19	70	8	12	2	0	0	3	0	10	.171	.171	.200	371	16	-7				.889	-4	C-10/O-4R,S-3,31	-0.9
	Wor-N	2	8	2	3	0	0	0	1	0	1	.375	.375	.375	750	129	0				1.000	-2	/C-2	-0.2
	Yr	21	78	10	15	2	0	0	4	0	11	.192	.192	.218	410	28	-6				.897	-6	C-12/O-4R,S-3,31	-1.1
1882	Pro-N	3	11	0	2	0	0	0	2	1	2	.182	.250	.182	432	41	-1				.714	-2	/C-3	-0.3
1884	Bos-U	3	11	1	0	0	0	0		1		.000	.083	.000	83	-74	-3				1.000	-1	/O-2(0-0-2),3-1	-0.3
Total	5	119	439	36	92	8	1	0	34	3	38	.210	.215	.232	447	48	-24				.867	-30	/C-77,O-24C,1-12,3S	-5.0

■ ARCH REILLY Reilly, Archer Edwin b: 8/17/1891, Alton, Ill. d: 11/29/63, Columbus, Ohio BR/TR, 5'10", 163 lbs. Deb: 6/1/17

YEAR	TM/L	G	AB	R	H	2B	3B	HR	RBI	BB	SO	AVG	OBP	SLG	OPS	OPS+	BR+	SB	CS	SBR	FA	FR	G/POS	TPR
1917	Pit-N	1	0	0	0	0	0	0	0	0	0	—	—	—	—	—	0	0			1.000	0	/3-1	0.0

■ BARNEY REILLY Reilly, Bernard Eugene b: 2/7/1885, Brockton, Mass. d: 11/15/34, St.Joseph, Mo. BR/TR, 6' ", 175 lbs. Deb: 7/2/09

YEAR	TM/L	G	AB	R	H	2B	3B	HR	RBI	BB	SO	AVG	OBP	SLG	OPS	OPS+	BR+	SB	CS	SBR	FA	FR	G/POS	TPR
1909	Chi-A	12	25	3	5	0	0	0	3	3		.200	.286	.200	486	56	-1	2			.962	4	2-11/O-1(0-0-1)	0.3

■ JOSH REILLY Reilly, Charles b: 1868, San Francisco, Cal. d: 6/13/38, San Francisco, Cal. Deb: 5/2/1896

YEAR	TM/L	G	AB	R	H	2B	3B	HR	RBI	BB	SO	AVG	OBP	SLG	OPS	OPS+	BR+	SB	CS	SBR	FA	FR	G/POS	TPR
1896	Chi-N	9	42	6	9	1	0	0	2	1	1	.214	.233	.238	471	23	-5	2			.857	-1	/2-8,S-1	-0.4

■ CHARLIE REILLY Reilly, Charles Thomas "Princeton Charlie" (b: Charles Thomas O'Reilly)
b: 2/15/1867, Princeton, N.J. d: 12/16/37, Los Angeles, Cal. BB/TR, 5'11", 190 lbs. Deb: 10/9/1889 Career OF: (11-LF 11-CF 4-RF)

YEAR	TM/L	G	AB	R	H	2B	3B	HR	RBI	BB	SO	AVG	OBP	SLG	OPS	OPS+	BR+	SB	CS	SBR	FA	FR	G/POS	TPR
1889	Col-a	6	23	5	11	1	0	3	6	2	2	.478	.538	.913	1452	326	7	9			.923	2	/3-6	0.7
1890	Col-a	137	530	75	141	23	3	4	77	35		.266	.319	.343	662	102	1	43			**.893**	28	*3-137	2.7
1891	Pit-N	114	415	43	91	8	5	3	44	29	58	.219	.277	.284	561	65	-19	20			.857	2	*3-99,S-11/O-4(1-3-0)	-1.4
1892	Phi-N	91	331	42	65	7	3	1	24	18	43	.196	.242	.245	487	47	-22	13			.905	10	3-70,O-15(5-8-2)/2-4	-1.0
1893	Phi-N	104	416	64	102	16	7	4	56	33	36	.245	.314	.346	661	76	-16	13			.895	-0	*3-104	-1.2
1894	Phi-N	40	136	21	40	1	2	0	19	16	10	.294	.381	.331	712	75	-5	9			.874	2	3-28/O-6L,2-4,S1	-0.2
1895	Phi-N	49	179	28	48	6	1	0	25	13	12	.268	.335	.313	648	67	-8	7			.900	-3	S-34,3-11/2-3,O-1R	-0.7
1897	Was-N	101	351	64	97	18	3	2	60	34		.276	.359	.362	720	91	-4	18			.905	18	*3-101	1.3
Total	8	642	2381	342	595	80	24	17	311	180	161	.250	.314	.325	639	80	-65	132			.890	59	3-556/S-46,O-26L,21	0.2

■ HAL REILLY Reilly, Harold John b: 4/1/1894, Oshkosh, Wis. d: 12/24/57, Chicago, Ill. BR/TR, 6', 180 lbs. Deb: 6/19/19

YEAR	TM/L	G	AB	R	H	2B	3B	HR	RBI	BB	SO	AVG	OBP	SLG	OPS	OPS+	BR+	SB	CS	SBR	FA	FR	G/POS	TPR
1919	Chi-N	1	3	0	0	0	0	0	0	0	1	.000	.000	.000	0	-99	-1	0			.000	-1	/O-1(1-0-0)	-0.1

■ JOHN REILLY Reilly, John Good "Long Jong" b: 10/5/1858, Cincinnati, Ohio d: 5/31/37, Cincinnati, Ohio BR/TR, 6'3", 178 lbs. Deb: 5/18/1880 Career OF: (27-LF 27-CF 24-RF)

YEAR	TM/L	G	AB	R	H	2B	3B	HR	RBI	BB	SO	AVG	OBP	SLG	OPS	OPS+	BR+	SB	CS	SBR	FA	FR	G/POS	TPR
1880	Cin-N	73	272	21	56	8	4	0	16	3	36	.206	.215	.265	479	62	-10				.947	-4	*1-72/O-3(0-0-3)	-1.7
1883	Cin-a	98	437	103	136	21	14	9	79	9		.311	.325	.485	810	149	21				.961	-1	*1-98/O-1(0-0-1)	1.0
1884	Cin-a	105	448	114	152	24	19	**11**	91	5		.339	.366	**.551**	**918**	186	40				.971	-2	*1-103/O-3(0-0-3),S-1	2.6
1885	Cin-a	111	482	92	143	18	11	5	60	11		.297	.322	.411	733	128	14				.963	-5	*1-107/O-7(0-2-5)	-0.1
1886	Cin-a	115	441	92	117	12	11	6	79	31		.265	.321	.383	704	116	7	19			.967	-1	*1-110/O-6(0-5-1)	-0.4
1887	Cin-a	134	573	106	192	35	14	10	96	22		.335	.352	.477	829	127	17	50			.980	-0	*1-127/O-9(1-6-2)	0.4
1888	Cin-a	127	527	112	169	28	14	**13**	**103**	17		.321	.363	**.501**	**864**	**167**	36	82			.977	-0	*1-117,O-10(0-2-8)	2.3
1889	Cin-a	111	427	84	111	24	13	5	66	34	37	.260	.340	.412	752	110	4	43			**.984**	-2	*1-109/O-2(1-1-0)	-0.6
1890	Cin-N	133	553	114	166	25	**26**	6	86	16	41	.300	.328	.472	800	133	18	29			.977	-3	*1-132/O-1(0-1-0)	0.2
1891	Cin-N	135	546	60	132	20	13	4	64	9	42	.242	.267	.348	615	78	-18	22			.982	-7	*1-100,O-36(25-10-1)	-3.2
Total	10	1142	4706	898	1374	215	139	69	740	157	156	.292	.325	.438	763	128	127	245			.972	-25	*1-1075/O-78L,S-1	0.5

■ JOE REILLY Reilly, Joseph J. b: 1861, New York, N.Y. 5'10", 140 lbs. Deb: 6/8/1885

YEAR	TM/L	G	AB	R	H	2B	3B	HR	RBI	BB	SO	AVG	OBP	SLG	OPS	OPS+	BR+	SB	CS	SBR	FA	FR	G/POS	TPR
1885	NY-a	10	40	6	7	3	0	0	3	2		.175	.214	.250	464	50	-2				.848	1	/2-8,3-2	0.0

■ TOM REILLY Reilly, Thomas Henry b: 8/3/1884, St.Louis, Mo. d: 10/18/18, New Orleans, La. BR/TR, 5'10", Deb: 7/27/08

YEAR	TM/L	G	AB	R	H	2B	3B	HR	RBI	BB	SO	AVG	OBP	SLG	OPS	OPS+	BR+	SB	CS	SBR	FA	FR	G/POS	TPR
1908	StL-N	29	81	5	14	1	0	1	3	2		.173	.193	.222	415	34	-6	4			.866	-6	S-29	-1.3
1909	StL-N	5	7	0	2	0	1	0	2	0		.286	.286	.571	857	176	0	0			1.000	0	/S-5	0.1
1914	Cle-A	1	1	0	0	0	0	0	0	0	0	.000	.000	.000	0	-96	-0	0			.000	0	H	0.0
Total	3	35	89	5	16	1	1	1	5	2	0	.180	.198	.247	445	44	-6	4			.875	-6	/S-34	-1.2

■ KEVIN REIMER Reimer, Kevin Michael b: 6/28/64, Macon, Ga. BL/TR, 6'2", 225 lbs. Deb: 9/13/88

YEAR	TM/L	G	AB	R	H	2B	3B	HR	RBI	BB	SO	AVG	OBP	SLG	OPS	OPS+	BR+	SB	CS	SBR	FA	FR	G/POS	TPR
1988	Tex-A	12	25	2	3	0	0	1	2	0	6	.120	.120	.240	360	-2	-3	0	0	0	.000	-0	/O-1(1-0-0),D-7	-0.4
1989	Tex-A	3	5	0	0	0	0	0	0	0	1	.000	.000	.000	0	-98	-1	0	0	0	.000	0	/D-1	-0.1
1990	Tex-A	64	100	5	26	9	1	2	15	10	22	.260	.333	.430	763	112	1	0	1	-0	.857	-2	D-21/O-9(5-0-5)	-0.2
1991	Tex-A	136	394	46	106	22	0	20	69	33	93	.269	.336	.477	814	125	12	0	3	-1	.948	-5	O-66(61-0-6),D-56	0.2
1992	Tex-A	148	494	56	132	32	2	16	58	42	103	.267	.337	.437	774	120	12	2	4	-1	.949	-3	*O-110(110-0-0),D-32	0.4
1993	Mil-A	125	437	53	109	22	1	13	60	30	72	.249	.305	.394	699	88	-9	5	4	-0	.962	-1	D-83,O-37(28-0-10)	-1.6
Total	6	488	1455	162	376	85	4	52	204	115	297	.258	.323	.430	752	108	12	7	12	-3	.948	-11	O-223(205-0-21),D-200	-1.7

■ MIKE REINBACH Reinbach, Michael Wayne b: 8/6/49, San Diego, Cal. BL/TR, 6'2", 195 lbs. Deb: 4/7/74

YEAR	TM/L	G	AB	R	H	2B	3B	HR	RBI	BB	SO	AVG	OBP	SLG	OPS	OPS+	BR+	SB	CS	SBR	FA	FR	G/POS	TPR
1974	Bal-A	12	20	2	5	1	0	0	2	2	5	.250	.318	.300	618	81	-0	0	0	0	1.000	-1	/O-3(1-0-2),D-3	-0.1

■ WALLY REINECKER Reinecker, Walter (b: Walter Joseph Smith) b: 4/21/1890, Pittsburgh, Pa. d: 4/18/57, Pittsburgh, Pa. BR/TR, 5'6", 150 lbs. Deb: 9/17/15

YEAR	TM/L	G	AB	R	H	2B	3B	HR	RBI	BB	SO	AVG	OBP	SLG	OPS	OPS+	BR+	SB	CS	SBR	FA	FR	G/POS	TPR
1915	Bal-F	3	8	0	1	0	0	0	0	0	0	.125	.222	.125	347	-1	-1	0			.571	-2	/3-3	-0.3

■ ART REINHOLZ Reinholz, Arthur August b: 1/27/03, Detroit, Mich. d: 12/29/80, New Port Richey, Fla. BR/TR, 5'10.5", 175 lbs. Deb: 9/27/28

YEAR	TM/L	G	AB	R	H	2B	3B	HR	RBI	BB	SO	AVG	OBP	SLG	OPS	OPS+	BR+	SB	CS	SBR	FA	FR	G/POS	TPR
1928	Cle-A	2	3	0	1	0	0	0	0	1	0	.333	.500	.333	833	122	0	0	0	0	.833	1	/3-2	0.1

■ CHARLIE REIPSCHLAGER Reipschlager, Charles W. b: 2/1854, d: 3/16/10, Atlantic City, N.J. BR/TR, 5'6.5", 160 lbs. Deb: 5/2/1883 Career OF: (8-LF 18-CF 5-RF)

YEAR	TM/L	G	AB	R	H	2B	3B	HR	RBI	BB	SO	AVG	OBP	SLG	OPS	OPS+	BR+	SB	CS	SBR	FA	FR	G/POS	TPR
1883	NY-a	37	145	8	27	4	2	0		4		.186	.208	.241	449	42	-9				.936	5	C-29/O-8(0-7-1)	-0.2
1884	*NY-a	59	233	21	56	13	2	0		1		.240	.250	.313	563	85	-4				.925	18	C-51/O-8(5-2-1)	1.6
1885	NY-a	72	268	29	65	11	1	0	21	9		.243	.270	.291	561	84	-4				.879	-8	C-59/O-6C,3-6,S2	-0.6
1886	NY-a	65	232	21	49	4	6	0	25	9		.211	.244	.280	524	67	-9	2			.880	-6	C-57/O-9(1-6-2)	-0.9
1887	Cle-a	63	242	20	60	8	3	0	17	11		.248	.251	.273	524	47	-16	7			.888	3	C-48,1-16	-0.9
Total	5	296	1120	99	257	40	14	0	63	34		.229	.248	.283	531	66	-43	9			.900	11	C-244/O-31C,1-16,32S	-1.0

■ BOBBY REIS Reis, Robert Joseph Thomas b: 1/2/09, Woodside, N.Y. d: 5/1/73, St.Paul, Minn. BR/TR, 6'1", 175 lbs. Deb: 9/19/31 Career OF: (19-LF 17-CF 15-RF)

YEAR	TM/L	G	AB	R	H	2B	3B	HR	RBI	BB	SO	AVG	OBP	SLG	OPS	OPS+	BR+	SB	CS	SBR	FA	FR	G/POS	TPR
1931	Bro-N	6	17	3	5	0	0	0	2	2	0	.294	.368	.294	663	81	-0	0			.933	-1	/3-6	-0.1
1932	Bro-N	1	4	0	1	0	0	0	0	0	1	.250	.250	.250	500	36	-0	0			.500	-1	/3-1	-0.1
1935	Bro-N	52	85	10	21	3	2	0	4	6	13	.247	.297	.329	626	70	-4	2			.950	2	O-21R,P-14/2-4,13	-0.2
1936	Bos-N	37	60	3	13	2	0	0	5	3	6	.217	.254	.250	504	39	-5	0			1.000	3	P-35/O-2(0-2-0)	-0.1
1937	Bos-N	45	86	10	21	5	0	0	6	13	12	.244	.343	.302	646	84	-1	2			1.000	-4	O-18(6-12-0)/P-4,1-4	-0.6
1938	Bos-N	34	49	6	9	0	0	0	4	1	3	.184	.200	.184	384	7	-6	1			1.000	-3	P-16,O-10L/S-3,C2	-0.7
Total	6	175	301	32	70	10	2	0	21	25	35	.233	.291	.279	570	59	-17	5			1.000	-2	/P-69,O-51L,3-8,12SC	-1.8

■ PETE REISER Reiser, Harold Patrick b: 3/17/19, St.Louis, Mo. d: 10/25/81, Palm Springs, Cal. BL/TR (BB 1940 (part),1948-52 (PARTS)), 5'10.5", 185 lbs. Deb: 7/23/40 C Career OF: (209-LF 413-CF 17-RF)

YEAR	TM/L	G	AB	R	H	2B	3B	HR	RBI	BB	SO	AVG	OBP	SLG	OPS	OPS+	BR+	SB	CS	SBR	FA	FR	G/POS	TPR
1940	Bro-N	58	225	34	66	11	4	3	20	15	33	.293	.338	.418	755	101	0	2			.960	-4	3-30,O-17(5-1-9)/S-5	-0.3
1941	*Bro-N★	137	536	**117**	184	**39**	**17**	14	76	46	71	**.343**	.406	**.558**	**964**	**163**	43	4			.981	12	*O-133(0-133-2)	**5.2**
1942	Bro-N★	125	480	89	149	33	5	10	64	48	45	.310	.375	.463	838	142	25	**20**			.969	-2	*O-125(0-125-0)	2.1
1946	Bro-N☆	122	423	75	117	21	5	11	73	55	58	.277	.361	.428	789	122	12	**34**			.978	7	O-97(69-28-0),3-15	1.4
1947	*Bro-N	110	388	68	120	23	2	5	46	68	41	.309	.415	.418	832	117	13	14			.988	-5	*O-108(51-62-0)	0.2
1948	Bro-N	64	127	17	30	8	2	1	19	29	21	.236	.382	.354	736	97	1	4			.981	-5	O-30(17-10-5)/3-4	-0.6
1949	Bos-N	84	221	32	60	8	3	8	40	33	42	.271	.369	.443	812	123	8	3			.980	-1	O-63(27-36-0)/3-4	0.4
1950	Bos-N	53	78	12	16	2	0	1	10	18	22	.205	.367	.269	637	75	-2	1			.979	-2	O-24(16-6-0)/3-1	-0.5
1951	Pit-N	74	140	22	38	9	3	2	13	27	20	.271	.389	.421	811	115	4	4	2	0	.982	-2	O-27(20-6-1)/3-5	0.1
1952	Cle-A	34	44	7	6	1	0	3	7	4	16	.136	.208	.364	572	61	-3	1	1	-0	1.000	-1	O-10(4-6-0)	-0.5
Total	10	861	2662	473	786	155	41	58	368	343	369	.295	.380	.450	829	127	101	87	3		.979	-1	O-634C/3-59,S-5	7.5

■ CHARLIE REISING Reising, Charles "Pop" b: 8/28/1861, Lanesville, Ind. d: 7/26/15, Louisville, Ky. Deb: 7/19/1884

YEAR	TM/L	G	AB	R	H	2B	3B	HR	RBI	BB	SO	AVG	OBP	SLG	OPS	OPS+	BR+	SB	CS	SBR	FA	FR	G/POS	TPR
1884	Ind-a	2	8	0	0	0	0	0		1		.000	.111	.000	111	-62	-1				.400	-1	/O-2(1-1-1)	-0.3

■ AL REISS Reiss, Albert Allen b: 1/8/09, Elizabeth, N.J. d: 5/13/89, Red Bank, N.J. BB/TR, 5'10.5", 165 lbs. Deb: 6/22/32

YEAR	TM/L	G	AB	R	H	2B	3B	HR	RBI	BB	SO	AVG	OBP	SLG	OPS	OPS+	BR+	SB	CS	SBR	FA	FR	G/POS	TPR
1932	Phi-A	9	5	0	1	0	0	0	1	1	1	.200	.333	.200	533	40	-0	0	0	0	1.000	0	/S-6	0.0

■ HEINIE REITZ Reitz, Henry P. b: 6/29/1867, Chicago, Ill. d: 11/10/14, Sacramento, Cal BL/TR, 5'7", 158 lbs. Deb: 4/27/1893

YEAR	TM/L	G	AB	R	H	2B	3B	HR	RBI	BB	SO	AVG	OBP	SLG	OPS	OPS+	BR+	SB	CS	SBR	FA	FR	G/POS	TPR
1893	Bal-N	130	490	90	140	17	13	1	76	65	32	.286	.377	.380	757	100	1	24			.939	-1	*2-130	0.5
1894	*Bal-N	108	446	86	135	22	**31**	2	105	42	24	.303	.372	.504	876	105	0	18			**.968**	27	*2-97,3-12	2.4
1895	Bal-N	71	245	45	72	15	5	0	29	18	11	.294	.350	.396	746	89	-4	15			.938	-5	2-48,3-18/S-1	-0.5
1896	*Bal-N	120	464	76	133	15	6	4	106	49	32	.287	.357	.371	728	91	-6	28			.952	-18	*2-118/S-3	-1.5
1897	*Bal-N	128	477	76	138	15	6	2	84	50		.289	.370	.358	728	93	-3	23			**.962**	22	*2-128	2.1
1898	Was-N	132	489	62	148	20	2	2	47	32		.303	.357	.364	721	107	4	11			**.959**	6	*2-132	1.5
1899	Pit-N	35	133	12	35	4	2	0	16	10		.263	.315	.323	638	75	-5	3			.976	3	2-35	0.0
Total	7	724	2744	447	801	108	65	11	463	266	99	.292	.363	.391	753	97	-12	122			.955	35	2-688/3-30,S-4	4.5

■ KEN REITZ Reitz, Kenneth John b: 6/24/51, San Francisco, Cal BR/TR, 6', 185 lbs. Deb: 9/5/72

YEAR	TM/L	G	AB	R	H	2B	3B	HR	RBI	BB	SO	AVG	OBP	SLG	OPS	OPS+	BR+	SB	CS	SBR	FA	FR	G/POS	TPR
1972	StL-N	21	78	5	28	4	0	0	10	2	4	.359	.375	.410	785	125	2	0	1	-0	.956	-4	3-20	-0.2
1973	StL-N	147	426	40	100	20	2	6	42	9	25	.235	.257	.333	591	63	-23	0	0	0	**.974**	-6	*3-135/S-1	-3.1
1974	StL-N	154	579	48	157	28	2	7	54	23	63	.271	.301	.363	664	86	-13	0	0	0	**.974**	-17	*3-151/S-2,2-1	-3.2
1975	StL-N	161	592	43	159	25	1	5	63	22	54	.269	.300	.340	640	75	-21	1	1	-0	.946	-21	*3-160	-4.5
1976	SF-N	155	577	40	154	21	1	5	66	24	48	.267	.297	.333	630	76	-18	5	4	-0	.959	2	*3-155/S-1	-1.9
1977	StL-N	157	587	58	153	36	1	17	79	19	74	.261	.292	.412	704	88	-12	2	6	-2	**.980**	-2	*3-157	-1.8
1978	StL-N	150	540	41	133	26	2	10	75	23	61	.246	.283	.357	641	79	-17	1	0	0	**.973**	1	*3-150	-1.9
1979	StL-N	159	605	42	162	41	2	8	73	25	85	.268	.301	.382	683	84	-14	1	0	0	.972	-13	*3-158	-3.0
1980	StL-N★	151	523	39	141	33	0	8	58	22	44	.270	.303	.379	682	86	-10	0	1	-0	**.979**	-4	*3-150	-1.8
1981	Chi-N	82	260	10	56	9	1	2	28	15	56	.215	.266	.281	547	53	-16	0	0	0	**.977**	5	3-81	-1.3
1982	Pit-N	7	10	0	0	0	0	0	0	1	4	.000	.091	.000	91	-70	-2	0	0	0	1.000	1	/3-4	-0.2
Total	11	1344	4777	366	1243	243	12	68	548	184	518	.260	.293	.359	651	79	-144	10	14	-3	.970	-58	*3-1321/S-4,2-1	-22.9

■ DESI RELAFORD Relaford, Desmond Lamont b: 9/16/73, Valdosta, Ga. BB/TR, 5'8", 155 lbs. Deb: 8/1/96

YEAR	TM/L	G	AB	R	H	2B	3B	HR	RBI	BB	SO	AVG	OBP	SLG	OPS	OPS+	BR+	SB	CS	SBR	FA	FR	G/POS	TPR
1996	Phi-N	15	40	2	7	2	0	0	1	3	9	.175	.233	.225	458	21	-5	1	0	0	.933	-1	/S-9,2-4	-0.5
1997	Phi-N	15	38	3	7	1	2	0	6	5	6	.184	.279	.316	595	55	-3	3	0	1	.977	-1	S-12	-0.2
1998	Phi-N	142	494	45	121	25	3	5	41	33	87	.245	.296	.338	634	65	-25	9	5	0	.960	-9	*S-137	-2.2
1999	Phi-N	65	211	31	51	11	2	1	26	19	34	.242	.322	.327	649	63	-12	4	3	-0	.952	7	S-63	0.0
2000	Phi-N	83	253	29	56	12	3	3	30	48	45	.221	.365	.328	693	76	-8	5	0	1	.930	-13	S-81	-1.3
	SD-N	45	157	26	32	2	0	2	16	27	26	.204	.332	.255	586	54	-10	8	0	2	.965	-5	S-45	-0.9
	Yr	128	410	55	88	14	3	5	46	75	71	.215	.352	.300	652	68	-18	13	0	3	.943	-18	*S-126	-2.2
Total	5	365	1193	136	274	53	10	11	120	135	207	.230	.319	.319	637	64	-62	30	8	4	.952	-22	S-347/2-4	-5.1

■ BUTCH REMENTER Rementer, Willis J. H. b: 3/14/1878, Philadelphia, Pa. d: 9/23/22, Philadelphia, Pa. BR/TR, 5'6.5", 180 lbs. Deb: 10/8/04

YEAR	TM/L	G	AB	R	H	2B	3B	HR	RBI	BB	SO	AVG	OBP	SLG	OPS	OPS+	BR+	SB	CS	SBR	FA	FR	G/POS	TPR
1904	Phi-N	1	2	0	0	0	0	0	0	0		.000	.000	.000	0	-99	-0	0			1.000	-0	/C-1	-0.1

■ JACK REMSEN Remsen, John Jay b: 4/1850, Brooklyn, N.Y. BR/TR, 5'11", 189 lbs. Deb: 5/2/1872

YEAR	TM/L	G	AB	R	H	2B	3B	HR	RBI	BB	SO	AVG	OBP	SLG	OPS	OPS+	BR+	SB	CS	SBR	FA	FR	G/POS	TPR
1872	Atl-n	37	164	25	40	4	5	0	13	2	6	.244	.253	.329	582	66	-9	1	2	-0	.792	2	*O-37(0-37-0)	-0.5
1873	Atl-n	50	207	29	61	4	6	1	29	2	2	.295	.301	.386	688	115	6	1	2	-0	.811	0	*O-50(0-50-0)	0.4
1874	Mut-n	64	284	52	65	9	3	2	38	0	5	.229	.229	.303	532	67	-11	6	0	1	.864	5	*O-63(8-57-0)/1-3	-0.3
1875	Har-n	86	358	70	96	10	4	0	34	5	4	.268	.278	.318	597	102	-0	6	3	0	.887	5	*O-86(0-81-5)	0.4
1876	Har-N	69	325	62	89	12	5	1	30	1	15	.274	.277	.352	629	100	-1				.887	8	*O-69(3-66-0)	0.3
1877	StL-N	33	123	14	32	3	4	0	13	4	3	.260	.283	.350	633	104	1				.906	2	O-33(0-33-0)	0.2
1878	Chi-N	56	224	32	52	11	1	1	19	**17**	33	.232	.286	.304	590	88	-3				**.944**	6	*O-56(0-56-0)	0.1
1879	Chi-N	42	152	14	33	4	2	0	8	2	23	.217	.227	.270	497	60	-7				.862	-2	O-31(5-26-0),1-11	-1.0
1881	Cle-N	48	172	14	30	4	3	0	13	9	31	.174	.215	.233	448	43	-11				.873	-1	O-48(0-48-0)	-1.3
1884	Phi-N	12	43	9	9	2	0	0	3	6	9	.209	.306	.256	562	83	-0				.952	0	O-12(0-12-0)	-0.1
	Bro-a	81	301	45	67	6	6	3		23		.223	.278	.312	590	91	-2				.914	4	*O-81(32-49-0)	-0.1
Total	4 n	237	1013	176	262	27	18	3	114	9	17	.259	.265	.330	595	88	-14	14	7	1	.845	12	O-236(8-225-5)/1-3	0.0
Total	6	341	1340	190	312	42	21	5	86	62	114	.233	.267	.307	574	84	-24				.900	17	O-330(40-290-0)/1-11	-1.9

■ JERRY REMY Remy, Gerald Peter b: 11/8/52, Fall River, Mass. BL/TR, 5'9", 165 lbs. Deb: 4/7/75 Career OF: (0-LF 0-CF 1-RF)

YEAR	TM/L	G	AB	R	H	2B	3B	HR	RBI	BB	SO	AVG	OBP	SLG	OPS	OPS+	BR+	SB	CS	SBR	FA	FR	G/POS	TPR
1975	Cal-A	147	569	82	147	17	5	1	46	45	55	.258	.313	.311	624	82	-13	34	21	0	.982	10	*2-147	0.7
1976	Cal-A	143	502	64	132	14	3	0	28	38	43	.263	.315	.303	618	87	-8	35	16	2	.977	15	*2-133/D-5	1.9
1977	Cal-A	154	575	74	145	19	10	4	44	59	59	.252	.324	.341	665	85	-11	41	17	3	.975	-12	*2-152/3-1	-1.2
1978	Bos-A☆	148	583	87	162	24	6	2	44	40	55	.278	.324	.350	674	81	-14	30	13	2	.983	2	*2-140/S-1,D-4	-0.2
1979	Bos-A	80	306	49	91	11	2	0	29	26	25	.297	.352	.346	699	85	-6	14	9	-0	.970	-21	2-76	-2.3
1980	Bos-A	63	230	24	72	7	2	0	9	10	14	.313	.342	.361	703	88	-4	14	6	1	.977	-3	2-60/O-1(0-0-1)	-0.3
1981	Bos-A	88	358	55	110	9	1	0	31	36	30	.307	.371	.338	709	99	1	9	2	1	.984	-7	2-87	0.0
1982	Bos-A	155	636	89	178	22	3	0	47	55	77	.280	.339	.324	663	79	-17	16	9	0	.982	-16	*2-154	-2.4
1983	Bos-A	146	592	73	163	16	5	0	43	40	35	.275	.321	.319	640	72	-22	11	3	1	.990	-31	*2-144	-4.3

YEAR	TM/L	G	AB	R	H	2B	3B	HR	RBI	BB	SO	AVG	OBP	SLG	OPS	OPS+	BR+	SB	CS	SBR	FA	FR	G/POS	TPR
1984	Bos-A	30	104	8	26	1	1	0	8	7	11	.250	.297	.279	576	58	-6	4	3	-0	.973	-3	2-24	-0.8
Total	10	1154	4455	605	1226	140	38	7	329	356	404	.275	.329	.328	658	82	-99	208	99	11	.981	-67	*2-1117/D-9,O-1R,S3	-8.9
■ RICK RENICK Renick, Warren Richard b: 3/16/44, London, Ohio BR/TR, 6', 190 lbs. Deb: 7/11/68 C Career OF: (59-LF 1-CF 4-RF)																								
1968	Min-A	42	97	16	21	5	2	3	13	9	42	.216	.283	.402	685	101	-0	0	0	0	.946	-0	S-40	0.3
1969	*Min-A	71	139	21	34	3	0	5	17	12	32	.245	.309	.374	683	88	-2	0	1	-0	.913	-8	3-30,O-10(8-0-2)/S-6	-1.1
1970	*Min-A	81	179	20	41	8	0	7	25	22	29	.229	.317	.391	708	93	-2	0	2	-1	.987	-3	3-30,O-25(25-1-0)/S-1	-0.7
1971	Min-A	27	45	4	10	2	0	1	8	5	14	.222	.314	.333	647	81	-1	0	0	0	.846	-3	/3-7,O-7(7-0-0)	-0.5
1972	Min-A	55	93	10	16	2	0	4	8	15	25	.172	.287	.323	610	77	-2	0	1	-0	1.000	-4	O-21L/1-6,3-4,S-1	-0.9
Total	5	276	553	71	122	20	2	20	71	63	142	.221	.304	.373	676	89	-8	0	4	-1	.940	-18	/3-71,O-63L,S-48,1	-2.9
■ BILL RENNA Renna, William Beneditto "Big Bill" b: 10/14/24, Hanford, Cal. BR/TR, 6'3", 218 lbs. Deb: 4/14/53																								
1953	NY-A	61	121	19	38	6	3	2	13	13	31	.314	.385	.463	848	133	6	0	1	-0	.983	-6	O-40(32-5-3)	-0.3
1954	Phi-A	123	422	52	98	15	4	13	53	41	60	.232	.305	.379	684	86	-9	1	3	-1	.972	6	*O-115(1-1-114)	-0.9
1955	KC-A	100	249	33	53	7	3	7	28	31	42	.213	.305	.349	654	75	-9	0	3	-1	.992	-6	O-79(8-0-72)	-1.9
1956	KC-A	33	48	12	13	3	0	2	5	3	10	.271	.314	.458	772	101	-0	1	0	0	.950	-6	O-25(22-0-3)	-0.6
1958	Bos-A	39	56	5	15	5	0	4	18	6	14	.268	.339	.571	910	136	3	0	0	0	1.000	-1	O-11(11-0-0)	0.1
1959	Bos-A	14	22	2	2	0	0	0	2	5	9	.091	.259	.091	350	0	-3	0	0	0	1.000	-2	/O-7(7-0-0)	-0.5
Total	6	370	918	123	219	36	10	28	119	99	166	.239	.317	.391	708	91	-14	2	7	-2	.979	-15	O-277(81-6-192)	-4.1
■ TONY RENSA Rensa, George Anthony "Pug" b: 9/29/01, Parsons, Pa. d: 1/4/87, Wilkes-Barre, Pa. BR/TR, 5'10", 180 lbs. Deb: 5/5/30																								
1930	Det-A	20	37	6	10	2	1	1	3	6	7	.270	.386	.459	846	111	1	1	0	0	.964	-1	C-18	0.0
	Phi-N	54	172	31	49	11	2	3	31	10	18	.285	.328	.424	752	75	-7	0			.932	-11	C-49	-1.4
1931	Phi-N	19	29	2	3	1	0	0	2	6	2	.103	.257	.138	395	8	-4	0			.958	2	C-17	-0.1
1933	NY-A	8	29	4	9	2	1	0	3	1	3	.310	.333	.448	782	112	0	0	1	-0	.977	-1	/C-8	-0.1
1937	Chi-A	26	57	10	17	5	1	0	5	8	6	.298	.385	.421	806	103	0	3	0	1	.975	1	C-23	0.3
1938	Chi-A	59	165	15	41	5	0	3	19	25	16	.248	.351	.333	684	71	-7	1	1	-0	.982	6	C-57	0.2
1939	Chi-A	14	25	3	5	0	0	0	2	1	2	.200	.231	.200	431	11	-3	0	0	0	.972	1	C-13	-0.2
Total	6	200	514	71	134	26	5	7	65	57	54	.261	.338	.372	710	74	-20	5	2		.965	-4	C-185	-1.3
■ EDGAR RENTERIA Renteria, Edgar Enrique b: 8/7/76, Barranquilla, Colombia BR/TR, 6'1", 172 lbs. Deb: 5/10/96																								
1996	Fla-N	106	431	68	133	18	3	5	31	33	68	.309	.361	.399	760	103	3	16	2	3	.979	12	*S-106	2.5
1997	*Fla-N	154	617	90	171	21	3	4	52	45	108	.277	.330	.340	671	80	-18	32	15	2	.975	-4	*S-153	-0.7
1998	Fla-N★	133	517	79	146	18	2	3	31	48	78	.282	.348	.342	690	87	-9	41	22	1	.966	-8	*S-129	-0.4
1999	StL-N	154	585	92	161	36	2	11	63	53	82	.275	.338	.400	738	85	-13	37	8	5	.959	-11	*S-151	-0.6
2000	*StL-N★	150	562	94	156	32	1	16	76	63	77	.278	.351	.423	775	94	-5	21	13	0	.958	-5	*S-149	0.2
Total	5	697	2712	423	767	125	11	39	253	242	413	.283	.344	.380	725	89	-42	147	60	11	.967	-15	S-688	1.0
■ RICH RENTERIA Renteria, Richard Avina b: 12/25/61, Harbor City, Cal. BR/TR, 5'9", 172 lbs. Deb: 9/14/86 Career OF: (3-LF 0-CF 0-RF)																								
1986	Pit-N	10	12	2	3	1	0	0	1	0	4	.250	.250	.333	583	58	-1	0	0	0	.600	0	/3-1	-0.1
1987	Sea-A	12	10	2	1	1	0	0	0	1	2	.100	.182	.200	382	1	-1	1	0	0	.833	1	/2-4,S-1,D-4	0.0
1988	Sea-A	31	88	6	18	9	0	0	6	2	8	.205	.222	.307	529	45	-7	1	3	-1	.958	4	D-12,S-11/3-5,2-4	-0.3
1993	Fla-N	103	263	27	67	9	2	2	30	21	31	.255	.315	.327	642	68	-11	0	2	-1	.989	-4	2-45,3-25/O-1(1-0-0)	-1.4
1994	Fla-N	28	49	5	11	0	0	2	4	1	4	.224	.269	.347	616	57	-3	0	1	-0	.929	-1	3-14/2-6,O-2(2-0-0)	-0.4
Total	5	184	422	42	100	20	2	4	41	25	49	.237	.286	.322	608	61	-23	2	6	-2	.986	1	/2-59,3-45,D-16,SO	-2.2
■ BOB REPASS Repass, Robert Willis b: 11/6/17, W.Pittston, Pa. BR/TR, 6'1", 185 lbs. Deb: 9/18/39																								
1939	StL-N	3	6	0	2	1	0	0	1	0	2	.333	.333	.500	833	114	0	0			1.000	0	/2-2	0.1
1942	Was-A	81	259	30	62	11	1	2	23	33	30	.239	.328	.313	640	81	-6	6	1	1	.973	-3	2-33,3-29,S-11	-0.4
Total	2	84	265	30	64	12	1	2	24	33	32	.242	.328	.317	645	82	-6	6	1		.973	-2	/2-35,3-29,S-11	-0.3
■ ROGER REPOZ Repoz, Roger Allen b: 8/3/40, Bellingham, Wash. BL/TL, 6'3", 195 lbs. Deb: 9/11/64 Career OF: (54-LF 357-CF 242-RF)																								
1964	NY-A	11	1	1	0	0	0	0	0	1	1	.000	.500	.000	500	52	0	0	0	0	1.000	-3	/O-9(0-0-9)	-0.3
1965	NY-A	79	218	34	48	7	4	12	28	25	57	.220	.300	.454	755	112	3	1	1	-0	.993	-2	O-69(0-65-7)	-0.2
1966	NY-A	37	43	4	15	4	1	0	9	4	8	.349	.404	.488	893	161	3	0	0	0	1.000	-10	O-30(0-28-5)	-0.8
	KC-A	101	319	40	69	10	3	11	34	44	80	.216	.315	.370	685	99	0	3	3	-0	.991	-3	O-52(8-41-3),1-45	-0.8
	Yr	138	362	44	84	14	4	11	43	48	88	.232	.325	.384	709	106	3	3	3	-0	.992	-13	O-82(8-69-8),1-45	-1.6
1967	KC-A	40	87	9	21	6	1	2	8	12	20	.241	.340	.402	742	122	3	4	2	0	1.000	1	O-31(16-9-6)	0.3
	Cal-A	74	176	25	44	9	1	5	20	19	37	.250	.323	.398	721	116	3	2	2	-0	.959	-3	O-63(6-54-4)	-0.1
	Yr	114	263	34	65	15	2	7	28	31	57	.247	.329	.399	728	118	6	6	4	-0	.972	-1	O-94(22-63-10)	0.2
1968	Cal-A	133	375	30	90	8	1	13	54	38	83	.240	.315	.371	686	111	5	8	7	-1	.987	-5	*O-114(0-71-52)	-0.6
1969	Cal-A	103	219	25	36	1	1	8	19	32	52	.164	.271	.288	559	59	-12	1	3	-1	.985	-5	O-48(13-22-16),1-31	-2.3
1970	Cal-A	137	407	50	97	17	6	18	47	45	90	.238	.319	.442	761	112	5	4	2	0	.995	-4	*O-110(6-42-68),1-18	-0.4
1971	Cal-A	113	297	39	59	11	1	13	41	60	69	.199	.335	.374	709	108	4	3	5	-1	1.000	-4	O-97(5-25-72),1-13	-0.6
1972	Cal-A	3	3	0	1	0	0	0	0	0	2	.333	.333	.333	667	105	0	0	0	0	.000	0	H	0.0
Total	9	831	2145	257	480	73	19	82	260	280	499	.224	.316	.390	706	106	14	26	25	-3	.989	-39	O-623C,1-107	-5.8
■ RIP REPULSKI Repulski, Eldon John b: 10/4/27, Sauk Rapids, Minn. d: 2/10/93, Waite Park, Minn. BR/TR, 6', 195 lbs. Deb: 4/14/53																								
1953	StL-N	153	567	75	156	25	4	15	66	33	71	.275	.325	.413	738	91	-8	3	6	-1	.987	-7	*O-153(0-153-0)	-2.3
1954	StL-N	152	619	99	175	39	5	19	79	43	75	.283	.333	.454	787	102	0	8	10	-2	.975	-5	*O-152(137-12-3)	-1.6
1955	StL-N	147	512	64	138	28	2	23	73	49	66	.270	.338	.467	805	111	7	5	7	-1	.974	-5	*O-141(110-1-32)	-0.7
1956	StL-N★	112	376	44	104	18	3	11	55	24	46	.277	.332	.428	760	102	1	2	2	-0	.974	-0	*O-100(99-1-1)	-0.6
1957	Phi-N	134	516	65	134	23	4	20	68	19	74	.260	.293	.436	729	95	-5	7	1	1	.968	3	*O-130(54-0-84)	-0.7
1958	Phi-N	85	238	33	58	9	4	13	40	15	47	.244	.300	.479	779	103	-0	0	0	0	.949	-2	O-56(35-0-21)	-0.5
1959	*LA-N	53	94	11	24	4	0	2	14	13	23	.255	.346	.362	707	83	-2	0	1	-0	1.000	-5	O-31(16-2-13)	-0.9
1960	LA-N	4	5	0	1	0	0	0	0	0	1	.200	.200	.200	400	9	-1	0	0	0	1.000	-1	/O-2(0-0-2)	-0.1
	Bos-A	73	136	14	33	6	1	3	20	10	25	.243	.295	.368	662	75	-5	0	0	0	1.000	-2	O-33(33-0-0)	-0.8
1961	Bos-A	15	25	2	7	1	0	0	1	1	5	.280	.308	.320	628	66	-1	0	2	-1	1.000	-1	/O-4(4-0-0)	-0.3
Total	9	928	3088	407	830	153	23	106	416	207	433	.269	.322	.436	758	98	-14	25	29	-5	.976	-24	O-802(488-169-156)	-8.5
■ LARRY RESSLER Ressler, Lawrence P. b: 8/10/1848, France d: 6/12/18, Reading, Pa. Deb: 4/26/1875																								
1875	Was-n	27	108	17	21	1	0	0	5	0	4	.194	.194	.204	398	40	-6	4	0	1	.831	6	O-20(0-3-17)/2-7	0.1
■ DINO RESTELLI Restelli, Dino Paul "Dingo" b: 9/23/24, St.Louis, Mo. BR/TR, 6'1.5", 191 lbs. Deb: 6/14/49																								
1949	Pit-N	72	232	41	58	11	0	12	40	35	26	.250	.358	.453	811	113	4	3			.961	5	O-61(0-47-14)/1-1	0.7
1951	Pit-N	21	38	1	7	1	0	1	3	2	4	.184	.225	.289	514	36	-3	0	0	0	.920	-1	O-11(8-4-0)	-0.5
Total	2	93	270	42	65	12	0	13	43	37	30	.241	.341	.430	770	103	1	3	0		.956	4	/O-72(8-51-14),1-1	0.2
■ MERV RETTENMUND Rettenmund, Mervin Weldon b: 6/6/43, Flint, Mich. BR/TR, 5'10", 195 lbs. Deb: 4/14/68 C Career OF: (228-LF 155-CF 436-RF)																								
1968	Bal-A	31	64	10	19	5	0	2	7	18	20	.297	.458	.469	927	181	8	1	1	-0	1.000	-5	O-23(4-13-13)	0.2
1969	*Bal-A	95	190	27	47	10	3	4	25	28	28	.247	.344	.395	739	105	2	6	1	1	.991	-10	O-78(45-18-21)	-1.0
1970	*Bal-A	106	338	60	109	17	2	18	58	38	59	.322	.396	.544	940	155	25	13	7	0	.976	-1	O-93(30-44-36)	2.1
1971	*Bal-A	141	491	81	156	23	4	11	75	87	60	.318	.424	.448	872	149	36	15	6	1	.977	-3	*O-134(46-40-72)	2.9
1972	Bal-A	102	301	40	70	10	2	6	21	41	37	.233	.325	.339	663	95	-1	6	4	-0	.989	-6	O-98(6-23-79)	-1.2
1973	*Bal-A	95	321	59	84	17	2	9	44	57	38	.262	.380	.411	791	124	12	11	2	2	.985	3	O-90(11-2-81)	1.3
1974	Cin-N	80	208	30	45	6	0	6	28	37	39	.216	.340	.332	672	90	-2	5	1	1	1.000	-5	O-69(0-9-60)	-1.0
1975	*Cin-N	93	188	24	45	6	1	2	19	35	22	.239	.359	.314	673	86	-2	5	0	1	1.000	-5	O-61(20-4-38)/3-1	-0.9
1976	SD-N	86	140	16	32	7	0	2	11	29	23	.229	.361	.321	682	103	2	4	1	1	.977	2	O-43(34-1-11)	0.3
1977	SD-N	107	126	23	36	6	1	4	17	33	28	.286	.438	.444	882	153	12	1	2	-0	1.000	-4	O-27(23-1-3)/3-1	0.6
1978	Cal-A	50	108	16	29	5	1	1	14	30	13	.269	.436	.361	797	131	7	0	3	-1	.968	-3	O-22(5-0-17),D-18	0.1
1979	*Cal-A	35	76	7	20	2	0	1	10	11	14	.263	.364	.329	693	91	-0	1	0	0	1.000	-3	D-17/O-9(4-0-5)	-0.3

YEAR	TM/L	G	AB	R	H	2B	3B	HR	RBI	BB	SO	AVG	OBP	SLG	OPS	OPS+	BR+	SB	CS	SBR	FA	FR	G/POS	TPR
1980	Cal-A	2	4	0	1	0	0	0	0	1	1	.250	.400	.250	650	84	-0	0	0	0	.000	0	/D-1	0.0
Total	13	1023	2555	393	693	114	16	66	329	445	382	.271	.383	.406	789	124	97	68	28	5	.985	-41	O-747R/D-36,3-2	3.1
■ KEN RETZER Retzer, Kenneth Leo b: 4/30/34, Wood River, Ill. BL/TR, 6', 185 lbs. Deb: 9/9/61																								
1961	Was-A	16	53	7	18	4	0	1	3	4	5	.340	.386	.472	858	130	2	1	0	0	.988	1	C-16	0.4
1962	Was-A	109	340	36	97	11	2	8	37	26	21	.285	.336	.400	736	98	-1	2	0	0	.985	0	C-99	0.4
1963	Was-A	95	265	21	64	10	0	5	31	17	20	.242	.292	.336	628	76	-9	2	0	0	.981	-11	C-81	-1.7
1964	Was-A	17	32	1	3	0	0	0	1	5	4	.094	.237	.094	331	-4	-4	0	0	0	.971	4	C-13	0.0
Total	4	237	690	65	182	25	2	14	72	52	50	.264	.318	.367	685	87	-12	5	0	1	.983	-6	C-209	-0.9
■ DAVE REVERING Revering, David Alvin b: 2/12/53, Roseville, Cal. BL/TR, 6'4", 210 lbs. Deb: 4/8/78																								
1978	Oak-A	152	521	49	141	21	3	16	46	26	55	.271	.305	.415	720	106	2	0	1	-0	.989	9	*1-138/D-3	0.3
1979	Oak-A	125	472	63	136	25	5	19	77	34	65	.288	.337	.483	820	125	15	1	4	-1	.986	2	*1-104,D-18	0.8
1980	Oak-A	106	376	48	109	21	5	15	62	32	37	.290	.346	.492	838	136	17	1	0	0	.989	3	1-95/D-5	1.5
1981	Oak-A	31	87	12	20	1	1	2	10	11	12	.230	.323	.333	657	94	-0	0	1	-0	.995	-1	1-29/D-2	-0.4
	*NY-A	45	119	8	28	4	1	2	7	11	20	.235	.300	.336	636	84	-2	0	1	-0	.994	3	1-44	-0.2
	Yr	76	206	20	48	5	2	4	17	22	32	.233	.310	.335	645	88	-3	0	2	-1	.994	2	1-73/D-2	-0.6
1982	NY-A	14	40	2	6	2	0	0	2	3	4	.150	.209	.200	409	13	-5	0	0	0	1.000	-2	1-13/D-1	-0.7
	Tor-A	55	135	15	29	6	0	5	18	22	30	.215	.325	.370	695	83	-3	0	3	-1	1.000	-0	D-49/1-4	-0.6
	Sea-A	29	82	8	17	3	1	3	12	9	17	.207	.286	.378	664	78	-3	0	0	0	.986	-1	1-27	-0.5
	Yr	98	257	25	52	11	1	8	32	34	51	.202	.296	.346	642	71	-10	0	3	-1	.992	-3	D-50,1-44	-1.8
Total	5	557	1832	205	486	83	16	62	234	148	240	.265	.321	.430	750	110	21	2	10	-3	.989	13	1-454/D-78	0.2
■ HENRY REVILLE Reville, Henry b: Baltimore, Md. Deb: 10/14/1874																								
1874	Bal-n	1	4	0	0	0	0	0	0	0	0	.000	.000	.000	0	-99	-1	0	0	0	1.000	1	/O-1(0-0-1)	0.0
■ WILLIAM REXTER Rexter, William H. b: Brooklyn, N.Y. Deb: 9/25/1875																								
1875	Atl-n	1	4	0	0	0	0	0	0	0	0	.000	.000	.000	0	-99	-1	0	0	0	1.000	-0	/O-1(0-0-1)	-0.1
■ GILBERTO REYES Reyes, Gilberto Rolando (Polanco) b: 12/10/63, Santo Domingo, D.R. BR/TR, 6'2", 203 lbs. Deb: 6/11/83																								
1983	LA-N	19	31	1	5	2	0	0	0	0	5	.161	.188	.226	413	14	-4	0	0	0	.944	2	C-19	-0.1
1984	LA-N	4	5	0	0	0	0	0	0	0	3	.000	.000	.000	0	-99	-1	0	0	0	1.000	-0	/C-2	-0.2
1985	LA-N	6	1	0	0	0	0	0	0	1	1	.000	.667	.000	667	105	0	0	0	0	1.000	2	/C-6	0.2
1987	LA-N	1	0	0	0	0	0	0	0	0	0	—	—	—	—	—	0	0	0	0	.000	-0	/C-1	0.0
1988	LA-N	5	9	1	1	0	0	0	0	0	3	.111	.111	.111	222	-37	-2	0	0	0	1.000	0	/C-5	-0.1
1989	Mon-N	4	5	0	1	0	0	0	1	0	1	.200	.200	.200	400	14	-1	0	0	0	1.000	1	/C-4	0.0
1991	Mon-N	83	207	11	45	9	0	0	13	19	51	.217	.286	.261	547	56	-12	2	4	-1	.975	14	C-80	0.5
Total	7	122	258	13	52	11	0	0	14	20	64	.202	.267	.244	511	45	-19	2	4	-1	.973	17	C-117	0.3
■ NAP REYES Reyes, Napoleon Aguilera b: 11/24/19, Santiago De Cuba, Cuba d: 9/15/95, Miami, Fla. BR/TR, 6'1", 205 lbs. Deb: 5/19/43 Career OF: (3-LF 0-CF 0-RF)																								
1943	NY-N	40	125	13	32	4	2	0	13	4	12	.256	.290	.320	610	76	-4	2			.994	-5	1-38/3-1	-1.2
1944	NY-N	116	374	38	108	16	5	8	53	15	24	.289	.325	.422	747	109	3	2			.990	2	1-63,3-37/O-3(3-0-0)	0.3
1945	NY-N	122	431	39	124	15	4	5	44	25	26	.288	.338	.376	714	97	-2	1			.961	-4	*3-115/1-5	-0.5
1950	NY-N	1	1	0	0	0	0	0	0	0	0	.000	.000	.000	0	-99	-0	0			.667	-0	/1-1	-0.1
Total	4	279	931	90	264	35	11	13	110	44	62	.284	.326	.387	713	99	-3	5			.960	-7	3-153,1-107/O-3L	-1.5
■ CARL REYNOLDS Reynolds, Carl Nettles b: 2/1/03, Larue, Tex. d: 5/29/78, Houston, Tex. BR/TR, 6', 194 lbs. Deb: 9/1/27																								
1927	Chi-A	14	42	5	9	3	0	1	7	5	7	.214	.313	.357	670	75	-2	1	2	-0	1.000	2	O-13(11-0-2)	-0.1
1928	Chi-A	84	291	51	94	21	11	2	36	17	13	.323	.371	.491	862	126	10	15	3	2	.979	-2	O-74(15-1-58)	0.5
1929	Chi-A	131	517	81	164	24	12	11	67	20	37	.317	.348	.474	821	111	6	19	9	1	.949	-2	*O-130(13-21-98)	-0.4
1930	Chi-A	138	563	103	202	25	18	22	104	20	39	.359	.388	.584	973	148	38	16	4	2	.975	10	*O-132(35-54-47)	3.7
1931	Chi-A	118	462	71	134	24	14	6	77	24	26	.290	.333	.442	775	108	4	17	6	2	.949	-4	*O-109(11-18-90)	-0.4
1932	Was-A	102	406	53	124	28	7	9	63	13	19	.305	.332	.475	807	108	3	8	4	0	.983	5	O-95(0-0-95)	0.2
1933	StL-A	135	475	81	136	26	14	8	71	49	25	.286	.357	.451	807	106	3	5	4	-0	.965	-2	*O-124(123-2-0)	-0.5
1934	Bos-A	113	413	61	125	26	9	4	86	27	28	.303	.350	.438	788	95	-4	5	3	0	.977	3	*O-100(2-66-33)	-0.4
1935	Bos-A	78	244	33	66	13	4	6	35	24	20	.270	.336	.430	766	91	-4	4	1	1	.975	6	O-64(3-1-60)	-0.1
1936	Was-A	89	293	41	81	18	2	4	41	21	22	.276	.329	.392	722	82	-9	8	4	0	.968	-0	O-72(0-4-69)	-1.2
1937	Chi-N	7	11	0	3	1	0	0	1	2	2	.273	.385	.364	748	100	0	0			.800	-0	/O-2(2-0-0)	0.0
1938	*Chi-N	125	497	59	150	28	10	3	67	22	32	.302	.335	.416	752	103	1	9			.983	-3	*O-125(63-83-4)	-0.7
1939	Chi-N	88	281	33	69	10	6	4	44	16	38	.246	.298	.367	665	76	-10	5			.972	2	O-72(3-51-18)	-1.1
Total	13	1222	4495	672	1357	247	107	80	699	260	308	.302	.346	.458	804	107	37	112	40		.970	15	*O-1112(281-301-574)	-0.5
■ CHARLIE REYNOLDS Reynolds, Charles Lawrence b: 5/1/1865, Williamsburg, Ind. d: 7/3/44, Denver, Colo. BR, 5'9", 175 lbs. Deb: 5/8/1889																								
1889	KC-a	1	4	1	1	0	0	0	1	0	1	.250	.250	.250	500	40	-0	0			1.000	-1	/C-1	-0.1
	Bro-a	12	42	5	9	1	1	0	3	1	6	.214	.233	.286	518	47	-3	2			.892	1	C-12	-0.1
	Yr	13	46	6	10	1	1	0	4	1	7	.217	.234	.283	517	46	-3	2			.893	-1	C-13	-0.2
■ DANNY REYNOLDS Reynolds, Daniel Vance "Squirrel" b: 11/27/19, Stony Point, N.C. BR/TR, 5'11", 158 lbs. Deb: 5/26/45																								
1945	Chi-A	29	72	6	12	2	1	0	4	3	8	.167	.200	.222	422	23	-7	1	2	-0	.947	2	S-14,2-11	-0.5
■ DON REYNOLDS Reynolds, Donald Edward b: 4/16/53, Arkadelphia, Ark. BR/TR, 5'8", 178 lbs. Deb: 4/7/78 F																								
1978	SD-N	57	87	8	22	2	0	0	10	15	14	.253	.363	.276	639	87	-1	1	0	0	.923	-4	O-25(22-0-3)	-0.6
1979	SD-N	30	45	6	10	1	2	0	6	7	6	.222	.327	.333	660	86	-1	0	1	-0	.950	-1	O-14(7-5-2)	-0.3
Total	2	87	132	14	32	3	2	0	16	22	20	.242	.351	.295	646	87	-1	1	1	-0	.935	-5	/O-39(29-5-5)	-0.9
■ CRAIG REYNOLDS Reynolds, Gordon Craig b: 12/27/52, Houston, Tex. BL/TR, 6'1", 175 lbs. Deb: 8/1/75 Career OF: (3-LF 0-CF 1-RF)																								
1975	*Pit-N	31	76	8	17	3	0	0	4	3	5	.224	.253	.263	516	44	-6	0	1	-0	.969	4	S-30	0.1
1976	Pit-N	7	4	1	1	0	0	1	1	0	0	.250	.250	1.000	1250	241	1	0	0	0	.889	2	/S-4,2-1	0.2
1977	Sea-A	135	420	41	104	12	3	4	28	15	23	.248	.279	.319	598	63	-22	6	6	-1	.955	8	*S-134	-0.1
1978	Sea-A☆	148	548	57	160	16	7	5	44	36	41	.292	.339	.374	713	101	1	9	6	-0	.960	4	*S-146	2.0
1979	Hou-N★	146	555	63	147	20	9	0	39	21	49	.265	.294	.333	627	75	-20	12	6	1	.965	-15	*S-143	-2.0
1980	*Hou-N	137	381	34	86	9	6	3	28	20	39	.226	.264	.304	569	63	-20	2	1	0	.969	12	*S-135	0.4
1981	*Hou-N	87	323	43	84	10	**12**	4	31	12	31	.260	.287	.402	689	99	-2	3	3	-0	.973	-5	S-85	0.2
1982	Hou-N	54	118	16	30	2	3	1	7	11	9	.254	.323	.347	671	95	-1	3	1	0	.958	2	S-35/3-7	0.5
1983	Hou-N	65	98	10	21	3	0	1	6	6	10	.214	.260	.276	535	52	-7	0	1	-0	.956	-4	2-26,3-15/S-8,O-1L	-1.0
1984	Hou-N	146	527	61	137	15	11	6	60	22	53	.260	.290	.364	654	89	-10	7	1	1	.965	18	*S-143/3-1	2.5
1985	Hou-N	107	379	43	103	18	8	4	32	12	30	.272	.294	.393	687	93	-5	4	4	-1	.977	10	*S-102/2-1	1.6
1986	*Hou-N	114	313	32	78	7	3	6	41	12	31	.249	.277	.348	625	73	-12	3	1	0	.978	-12	S-98/1-5,3-4,O-2L,P	-1.6
1987	Hou-N	135	374	35	95	17	3	4	28	30	44	.254	.309	.348	657	77	-13	5	1	1	.970	-12	*S-129/3-2	-1.2
1988	Hou-N	78	161	20	41	7	0	1	14	8	23	.255	.290	.317	607	77	-5	3	0	1	.970	-5	S-22,3-19,2-11,1-10	-0.8
1989	Hou-N	101	189	16	38	4	0	2	14	19	18	.201	.274	.254	528	54	-11	1	0	0	.979	8	2-29,S-26,3-10,/1PO	-0.1
Total	15	1491	4466	480	1142	143	65	42	377	227	406	.256	.293	.345	638	80	-132	58	32	2	.966	17	*S-1240/2-68,31OP	0.7
■ HAROLD REYNOLDS Reynolds, Harold Craig b: 11/26/60, Eugene, Ore. BB/TR, 5'11", 165 lbs. Deb: 9/2/83 F Career OF: (1-LF 0-CF 0-RF)																								
1983	Sea-A	20	59	8	12	4	1	0	1	2	9	.203	.230	.305	535	44	-5	0	2	-1	.975	-1	2-18	-0.6
1984	Sea-A	10	10	3	3	0	0	0	0	0	1	.300	.364	.300	664	87	-0	1	1	-0	1.000	4	/2-6	0.4
1985	Sea-A	67	104	15	15	3	1	0	6	17	14	.144	.264	.192	457	27	-10	3	2	-0	.960	19	2-61	1.0
1986	Sea-A	126	445	46	99	19	4	1	24	29	42	.222	.275	.290	565	53	-29	30	12	2	.977	29	*2-126	1.0
1987	Sea-A★	160	530	73	146	31	8	1	35	39	34	.275	.327	.370	697	80	-15	**60**	20	6	.977	19	*2-160	1.8
1988	Sea-A★	158	598	61	169	26	**11**	4	41	51	51	.283	.341	.383	724	98	-1	35	29	-2	.977	6	*2-158	0.7
1989	Sea-A	153	613	87	184	24	9	0	43	55	45	.300	.361	.369	729	103	4	25	18	-1	.980	**27**	*2-151/D-1	3.4
1990	Sea-A	160	642	100	162	36	5	5	55	81	52	.252	.339	.347	686	91	-6	31	16	1	.978	15	*2-160	1.5

YEAR	TM/L	G	AB	R	H	2B	3B	HR	RBI	BB	SO	AVG	OBP	SLG	OPS	OPS+	BR+	SB	CS	SBR	FA	FR	G/POS	TPR
1991	Sea-A	161	631	95	160	34	6	3	57	72	63	.254	.335	.341	675	87	-9	28	8	3	.978	5	*2-159/D-1	0.3
1992	Sea-A	140	458	55	113	23	3	3	33	45	41	.247	.318	.330	648	81	-11	15	12	-1	.982	2	*2-134/O-1(1-0-0),D-1	-0.6
1993	Bal-A	145	485	64	122	20	4	4	47	66	47	.252	.346	.334	680	80	-12	12	11	-1	.986	3	*2-141/D-1	-0.3
1994	Cal-A	74	207	33	48	10	1	0	11	23	18	.232	.312	.290	602	56	-13	10	7	-0	.996	-13	2-65/D-3	-2.2
Total	12	1374	4782	640	1233	230	53	21	353	480	417	.258	.329	.341	670	83	-107	250	138	7	.979	116	*2-1339/D-7,O-1L	6.4
■ R. J. REYNOLDS	Reynolds, Robert James b: 4/19/59, Sacramento, Cal. BB/TR, 6′, 190 lbs. Deb: 9/1/83																							
1983	LA-N	24	55	5	13	0	0	2	11	3	11	.236	.276	.345	621	72	-2	5	0	1	.931	-2	O-18(9-7-5)	-0.4
1984	LA-N	73	240	24	62	12	2	2	24	14	38	.258	.302	.350	652	84	-6	7	5	-0	.973	-7	O-63(25-19-34)	-1.6
1985	LA-N	73	207	22	55	10	4	0	25	13	31	.266	.312	.353	665	88	-3	6	3	0	.970	-2	O-54(31-5-24)	-0.8
	Pit-N	31	130	22	40	5	3	3	17	9	18	.308	.357	.462	819	129	5	12	2	2	.958	1	O-31(29-8-0)	0.7
	Yr	104	337	44	95	15	7	3	42	22	49	.282	.330	.395	724	104	1	18	5	2	.965	-1	O-85(60-13-24)	-0.1
1986	Pit-N	118	402	63	108	30	2	9	48	40	78	.269	.336	.420	757	105	2	16	9	0	.955	-15	*O-112(84-12-44)	-1.7
1987	Pit-N	117	335	47	87	24	1	7	51	34	80	.260	.328	.400	728	91	-4	14	1	3	.993	-6	O-99(29-0-72)	-1.2
1988	Pit-N	130	323	35	80	14	2	6	51	20	62	.248	.292	.359	651	87	-6	15	2	3	.974	-6	O-95(19-1-79)	-1.3
1989	Pit-N	125	363	45	98	16	2	6	48	34	66	.270	.334	.375	709	106	3	22	5	3	.990	-1	O-98(5-30-72)	0.3
1990	*Pit-N	95	215	25	62	10	1	0	19	23	35	.288	.357	.344	701	98	-0	12	2	2	.972	-6	O-59(13-24-26)	-0.5
Total	8	786	2270	288	605	121	17	35	294	190	419	.267	.325	.381	706	97	-12	109	29	14	.973	-44	O-629(244-106-356)	-6.5
■ RONN REYNOLDS	Reynolds, Ronn Dwayne b: 9/28/58, Wichita, Kan. BR/TR, 6′, 200 lbs. Deb: 9/29/82																							
1982	NY-N	2	4	0	0	0	0	0	0	1	1	.000	.200	.000	200	-40	-1	0	0	0	1.000	-1	/C-2	-0.2
1983	NY-N	24	66	4	13	1	0	0	2	8	12	.197	.284	.212	496	40	-5	0	0	0	.942	-1	C-24	-0.5
1985	NY-N	28	43	4	9	2	0	0	1	0	18	.209	.227	.256	483	36	-4	0	0	0	.990	6	C-25	0.3
1986	Phi-N	43	126	8	27	4	0	3	10	5	30	.214	.244	.317	562	52	-8	0	0	0	.991	1	C-42	-0.6
1987	Hou-N	38	102	5	17	4	0	1	7	3	29	.167	.190	.235	426	12	-13	0	1	-0	.975	4	C-38	-0.8
1990	SD-N	8	15	1	1	1	0	0	1	1	6	.067	.125	.133	258	-29	-3	0	0	0	1.000	1	/C-8	-0.2
Total	6	143	356	22	67	12	0	4	21	18	96	.188	.229	.256	485	32	-34	0	1	-0	.977	10	C-139	-2.0
■ TOMMIE REYNOLDS	Reynolds, Tommie D b: 8/15/41, Arizona, La. BR/TR (BB 1967 (part)), 6′2″, 190 lbs. Deb: 9/5/63 C Career OF: (276-LF 14-CF 92-RF)																							
1963	KC-A	8	19	1	1	1	0	0	0	1	7	.053	.143	.105	248	-28	-3	0	0	0	.800	-1	/O-5(5-0-0)	-0.5
1964	KC-A	31	94	11	19	1	0	2	9	10	22	.202	.292	.277	569	58	-5	0	0	0	.976	-0	O-25(25-0-0)/3-3	-0.7
1965	KC-A	90	270	34	64	11	3	1	22	36	41	.237	.327	.311	638	83	-5	9	2	1	.982	7	O-83(77-0-6)/3-1	-0.1
1967	NY-N	101	136	16	28	1	0	2	9	11	26	.206	.280	.257	537	56	-8	1	1	-0	.971	-13	O-72L/3-5,C-1	-2.5
1969	Oak-A	107	315	51	81	10	0	2	20	34	29	.257	.345	.308	652	87	-4	1	3	-1	.979	6	O-89(81-0-8)	-0.4
1970	Cal-A	59	120	11	30	3	1	1	6	6	10	.250	.291	.317	608	70	-5	1	1	-0	.969	0	O-32(4-1-28)/3-1	-0.6
1971	Cal-A	45	86	4	16	3	0	2	8	9	6	.186	.286	.291	576	68	-4	0	1	-0	.978	-2	O-26(6-0-23)/3-1	-0.7
1972	Mil-A	72	130	13	26	5	1	2	13	10	25	.200	.262	.300	562	68	-5	0	0	0	.961	-1	O-41(36-0-6)/1-1,3-1	-0.9
Total	8	513	1170	141	265	35	5	12	87	117	166	.226	.307	.296	603	73	-39	12	8	-0	.973	-4	O-373L/3-12,1-1,C-1	-6.4
■ BILL REYNOLDS	Reynolds, William Dee b: 8/14/1884, Eastland, Tex. d: 6/5/24, Carnegie, Okla. BR/TR, 6′, 185 lbs. Deb: 9/15/13																							
1913	NY-A	5	5	0	0	0	0	0	0	0	1	.000	.000	.000	0	-99	-1	0			.917	0	/C-5	-0.1
1914	NY-A	4	5	0	2	0	0	0	0	0	3	.400	.400	.400	800	141	0	0			1.000	0	/C-1	0.1
Total	2	9	10	0	2	0	0	0	0	0	4	.200	.200	.200	400	19	-1	0			.941	0	/C-6	0.0
■ BOBBY RHAWN	Rhawn, Robert John "Rocky" b: 2/13/19, Catawissa, Pa. d: 6/9/84, Danville, Pa. BR/TR, 5′8″, 180 lbs. Deb: 9/17/47																							
1947	NY-N	13	45	7	14	3	0	1	3	8	1	.311	.415	.444	860	128	2	0			.913	0	/2-8,3-5	0.2
1948	NY-N	36	44	11	12	2	1	1	8	8	6	.273	.385	.432	816	120	1	3			.872	1	S-14/3-7	0.2
1949	NY-N	14	29	8	5	0	0	0	2	7	2	.172	.333	.172	506	40	-2	1			.959	4	/2-8	0.2
	Pit-N	3	7	0	1	0	0	0	0	0	0	.143	.143	.143	286	-23	-1	0			.889	1	/3-2	0.0
	Yr	17	36	8	6	0	0	0	2	7	2	.167	.302	.167	469	29	-3	1			.959	4	/2-8,3-2	0.2
	Chi-A	24	73	12	15	4	1	0	5	12	8	.205	.318	.288	605	63	-4	0	1	-0	.959	3	3-19/S-3	-0.1
Total	3	90	198	38	47	9	2	2	18	35	17	.237	.352	.333	685	84	-4	4	1		.963	8	/3-33,S-17,2-16	0.5
■ CY RHEAM	Rheam, Kenneth Johnston b: 9/28/1893, Pittsburgh, Pa. d: 10/23/47, Pittsburgh, Pa. BR/TR, 6′ ″, 175 lbs. Deb: 5/20/14 Career OF: (13-LF 4-CF 6-RF)																							
1914	Pit-F	73	214	15	45	5	3	0	20	9	33	.210	.242	.262	504	38	-22	6			.976	-5	1-43,3-13,2-11,/O-1L	-2.9
1915	Pit-F	34	69	10	12	0	0	1	5	1	7	.174	.186	.217	403	13	-9	4			.959	0	O-22(12-4-6)/1-1	-1.1
Total	2	107	283	25	57	5	3	1	25	10	40	.201	.229	.251	480	32	-32	10			.976	-5	/1-44,O-23L,3-13,2	-4.0
■ BILLY RHIEL	Rhiel, William Joseph b: 8/16/1900, Youngstown, Ohio d: 8/16/46, Youngstown, Ohio BR/TR, 5′11″, 175 lbs. Deb: 4/20/29																							
1929	Bro-N	76	205	27	57	9	4	4	25	19	25	.278	.339	.420	759	89	-4	0			.979	1	2-47/3-7,S-2	-0.1
1930	Bos-N	20	47	3	8	4	0	0	4	2	5	.170	.204	.255	459	11	-7	0			.947	-4	3-13/2-2	-0.9
1932	Det-A	85	250	30	70	13	3	3	38	17	23	.280	.328	.392	720	82	-7	2	0	0	.956	-5	3-37,1-12/O-8L,2-1	-1.1
1933	Det-A	19	17	1	3	0	1	0	1	5	4	.176	.364	.294	658	75	-0	0	0	0	1.000	0	/O-1(1-0-0)	0.0
Total	4	200	519	61	138	26	8	7	68	43	57	.266	.323	.387	711	78	-18	2	0		.949	-8	/3-57,2-50,1-12,OS	-2.1
■ DUSTY RHODES	Rhodes, James Lamar b: 5/13/27, Mathews, Ala. BL/TR, 6′, 180 lbs. Deb: 7/15/52																							
1952	NY-N	67	176	34	44	8	1	10	36	23	33	.250	.340	.477	817	123	5	1	0	0	.917	-4	O-56(55-2-0)	-0.2
1953	NY-N	76	163	18	38	7	0	11	30	10	28	.233	.277	.479	756	91	-3	0	1	-0	.965	1	O-47(25-0-22)	-0.4
1954	*NY-N	82	164	31	56	7	3	15	50	18	25	.341	.410	.695	1105	181	19	1	0	0	.984	-3	O-37(33-2-1)	1.4
1955	NY-N	94	187	22	57	5	2	6	32	27	26	.305	.393	.449	842	122	7	1	1	-0	.986	-4	O-45(45-0-0)	0.0
1956	NY-N	111	244	20	53	10	3	8	33	30	41	.217	.303	.381	684	83	-6	0	0	0	.958	-5	O-68(64-0-5)	-1.5
1957	NY-N	92	190	20	39	5	1	4	19	18	34	.205	.278	.305	583	57	-12	0	0	0	1.000	-6	O-44(22-0-23)	-2.0
1959	SF-N	54	48	1	9	2	0	0	7	5	9	.188	.264	.229	493	34	-5	0	0	0	.000	0	H	-0.5
Total	7	576	1172	146	296	44	10	54	207	131	196	.253	.329	.445	775	104	5	3	2	-0	.963	-20	O-297(244-4-51)	-3.2
■ KARL RHODES	Rhodes, Karl Derrick "Tuffy" b: 8/21/68, Cincinnati, Ohio BL/TL, 5′11″, 170 lbs. Deb: 8/7/90																							
1990	Hou-N	38	86	12	21	6	1	1	3	13	12	.244	.343	.372	716	100	0	4	1	1	.955	-1	O-30(19-9-5)	-0.1
1991	Hou-N	44	136	7	29	3	1	1	12	14	26	.213	.291	.272	563	63	-7	2	2	-0	.958	3	O-44(0-0-44)	-0.5
1992	Hou-N	5	4	0	0	0	0	0	0	0	2	.000	.000	.000	0	-99	-1	0	0	0	.000	-1	/O-1(1-0-1)	-0.2
1993	Hou-N	5	2	0	0	0	0	0	0	0	0	.000	.000	.000	0	-99	-1	0	0	0	1.000	-1	/O-4(1-2-1)	-0.2
	Chi-N	15	52	12	15	2	1	3	7	11	9	.288	.413	.538	951	155	4	2	0	0	.970	-3	O-14(6-14-1)	0.2
	Yr	20	54	12	15	2	1	3	7	11	9	.278	.400	.519	919	147	4	2	0	0	.971	-4	O-18(7-16-2)	0.0
1994	Chi-N	95	269	39	63	17	0	8	19	33	64	.234	.320	.387	707	84	-6	6	4	-0	.967	-8	O-76(15-67-1)	-1.4
1995	Chi-N	13	16	2	2	0	0	0	2	0	4	.125	.125	.125	250	-34	-3	0	0	0	.889	-2	O-11(11-0-0)	-0.6
	Bos-A	10	25	2	2	1	0	0	1	3	4	.080	.179	.120	299	-20	-4	0	0	0	.947	-1	/O-9(0-9-0)	-0.5
Total	6	225	590	74	132	29	3	13	44	74	121	.224	.312	.349	661	79	-17	14	7	1	.960	-14	O-189(53-101-53)	-3.3
■ KEVIN RHOMBERG	Rhomberg, Kevin Jay b: 11/22/55, Dubuque, Iowa BR/TR, 6′, 175 lbs. Deb: 9/1/82 Career OF: (22-LF 1-CF 0-RF)																							
1982	Cle-A	16	18	3	6	0	0	1	1	2	4	.333	.400	.500	900	146	1	0	2	-1	.900	-0	/O-7(7-0-0),3-1,D-4	0.0
1983	Cle-A	12	21	2	10	0	0	0	2	2	4	.476	.522	.476	998	170	2	1	1	-0	1.000	-2	/O-9(8-1-0),D-1	0.0
1984	Cle-A	13	8	0	2	0	0	0	0	0	3	.250	.250	.250	500	38	-1	0	0	0	1.000	-2	/O-7L,1-1,2-1,D-1	-0.2
Total	3	41	47	5	18	0	0	1	3	4	11	.383	.431	.447	878	140	3	1	3	-1	.963	-4	/O-23L,D-6,2-1,13	-0.2
■ HAL RHYNE	Rhyne, Harold J. b: 3/30/1899, Paso Robles, Cal. d: 1/7/71, Orangevale, Cal. BR/TR, 5′8.5″, 163 lbs. Deb: 4/18/26																							
1926	Pit-N	109	366	46	92	14	3	2	39	35	21	.251	.327	.322	649	71	-14	1			.967	8	2-66,S-44/3-1	0.0
1927	*Pit-N	62	168	21	46	5	0	0	17	14	9	.274	.330	.304	633	66	-8	0			.963	-7	2-45,3-10/S-7	-1.2
1929	Bos-A	120	346	41	87	24	5	0	38	25	14	.251	.309	.350	659	71	-15	4	1	1	.935	-3	*S-113/3-1,O-1(0-0-1)	-0.6
1930	Bos-A	107	296	34	60	8	5	0	23	25	19	.203	.269	.264	533	37	-28	1	4	-1	.944	4	*S-107	-1.4
1931	Bos-A	147	565	75	154	34	3	0	51	57	41	.273	.341	.343	685	85	-11	3	3	-0	**.963**	17	*S-147	1.5
1932	Bos-A	71	207	26	47	12	5	0	14	23	14	.227	.310	.333	644	69	-10	3	2	-0	.966	-2	S-55/3-4,2-1	-0.7
1933	Chi-A	39	83	9	22	1	1	0	10	5	9	.265	.315	.301	616	67	-4	1	1	-0	.955	5	2-19,3-13/S-2	0.2
Total	7	655	2031	252	508	98	22	2	192	184	127	.250	.318	.323	641	69	-90	13	11		.950	23	S-475,2-131/3-29,O	-2.2

■ DEL RICE Rice, Delbert b: 10/27/22, Portsmouth, Ohio d: 1/26/83, Buena Park, Cal. BR/TR, 6'2", 190 lbs. Deb: 5/2/45 MC

YEAR	TM/L	G	AB	R	H	2B	3B	HR	RBI	BB	SO	AVG	OBP	SLG	OPS	OPS+	BR+	SB	CS	SBR	FA	FR	G/POS	TPR
1945	StL-N	83	253	27	66	17	3	1	28	16	33	.261	.313	.364	676	86	-5	0			.994	9	C-77	0.7
1946	*StL-N	55	139	10	38	8	1	1	12	8	16	.273	.313	.367	680	89	-2	0			.977	-0	C-53	0.0
1947	StL-N	97	261	28	57	7	3	12	44	36	40	.218	.315	.406	722	87	-6	1			.981	4	C-94	0.2
1948	StL-N	100	290	24	57	10	1	4	34	37	46	.197	.298	.279	578	54	-18	1			**.996**	8	C-99	-0.5
1949	StL-N	92	284	25	67	16	1	4	29	30	40	.236	.320	.342	661	74	-10	0			.992	-3	C-92	-0.8
1950	StL-N	130	414	39	101	20	3	9	54	43	65	.244	.323	.372	694	78	-13	0			.984	6	*C-130	0.0
1951	StL-N	122	374	34	94	13	1	9	47	34	26	.251	.319	.364	682	83	-9	0	0	0	.985	2	*C-120	-0.1
1952	StL-N	147	495	43	128	27	2	11	65	33	38	.259	.313	.388	701	93	-6	0	1	-0	.992	-4	*C-147	-0.3
1953	StL-N†	135	419	32	99	22	1	6	37	48	49	.236	.323	.337	660	72	-16	0	0	0	.988	-5	*C-135	-1.4
1954	StL-N	56	147	13	37	10	1	2	16	16	21	.252	.325	.374	699	81	-4	0	1	-0	.985	6	C-52	0.4
1955	StL-N	20	59	6	12	3	0	1	7	7	6	.203	.288	.305	593	58	-4	0	0	0	.964	-5	C-18	-0.8
	Mil-N	27	71	5	14	0	1	2	7	6	12	.197	.260	.310	570	53	-5	0	0	0	.981	1	C-22	-0.4
	Yr	47	130	11	26	3	1	3	14	13	18	.200	.273	.308	580	55	-8	0	0	0	.973	-5	C-40	-1.2
1956	Mil-N	71	188	15	40	9	1	3	17	18	34	.213	.282	.319	601	65	-10	0	0	0	.983	2	C-65	-0.5
1957	*Mil-N	54	144	15	33	1	1	9	20	17	37	.229	.311	.438	748	106	1	0	0	0	.992	6	C-48	0.9
1958	Mil-N	43	121	10	27	7	0	1	8	8	30	.223	.271	.306	577	57	-8	0	0	0	.995	-0	C-38	-0.7
1959	Mil-N	13	29	3	6	0	0	0	1	2	3	.207	.258	.207	465	28	-3	0	0	0	.956	-0	/C-9	-0.3
1960	Chi-N	18	52	2	12	3	0	0	4	2	7	.231	.259	.288	548	50	-4	0	0	0	.968	-2	C-18	-0.5
	StL-N	1	2	0	0	0	0	0	0	1	0	.000	.333	.000	333	1	-0	0	0	0	1.000	-0	/C-1	-0.1
	Yr	19	54	2	12	3	0	0	4	3	7	.222	.263	.278	541	49	-4	0	0	0	.970	-2	C-19	-0.6
	Bal-A	1	1	0	0	0	0	0	0	0	0	.000	.000	.000	0	-99	-0	0	0	0	1.000	-0	/C-1	0.0
1961	LA-A	44	83	11	20	4	0	4	11	20	19	.241	.388	.434	822	107	1	0	1	-0	.994	2	C-30	0.4
Total	17	1309	3826	342	908	177	20	79	441	382	522	.237	.312	.356	668	78	-121	2	3		.987	25	*C-1249	-3.8

■ SAM RICE Rice, Edgar Charles b: 2/20/1890, Morocco, Ind. d: 10/13/74, Rossmoor, Md. BL/TR, 5'9", 150 lbs. Deb: 8/7/15 H Career OF: (47-LF 601-CF 1657-RF)

YEAR	TM/L	G	AB	R	H	2B	3B	HR	RBI	BB	SO	AVG	OBP	SLG	OPS	OPS+	BR+	SB	CS	SBR	FA	FR	G/POS	TPR
1915	Was-A	4	8	0	3	0	0	0	0	0	1	.375	.375	.375	750	122	0	0			.889	0	/P-4	0.0
1916	Was-A	58	197	26	59	8	3	1	17	15	13	.299	.352	.386	738	123	5	4			.957	2	O-46(4-0-42)/P-5	0.5
1917	Was-A	155	586	77	177	25	7	0	69	50	41	.302	.360	.369	729	124	16	35			.960	8	*O-155(0-0-155)	1.8
1918	Was-A	7	23	3	8	1	0	0	3	2	0	.348	.400	.391	791	141	1	1			1.000	3	/O-6(0-0-6)	0.4
1919	Was-A	141	557	80	179	23	9	3	71	42	26	.321	.376	.411	787	122	16	26			.962	8	*O-141(0-0-141)	1.7
1920	Was-A	153	624	83	211	29	9	3	80	39	23	.338	.381	.428	809	117	15	**63**	30	**3**	.960	21	*O-153(0-153-0)	2.8
1921	Was-A	143	561	83	185	39	13	4	79	38	10	.330	.382	.467	849	121	17	26	12	2	.964	11	*O-141(0-137-4)	2.1
1922	Was-A	154	633	91	187	37	13	6	69	48	13	.295	.347	.423	770	105	3	20	9	1	.951	9	*O-154(0-154-0)	0.6
1923	Was-A	148	595	117	188	35	**18**	3	75	57	12	.316	.381	.450	832	125	21	20	8	2	.970	8	*O-147(0-0-147)	1.7
1924	*Was-A	154	646	106	**216**	39	14	1	76	46	24	.334	.382	.443	825	116	14	24	13	1	.967	4	*O-154(0-34-123)	0.7
1925	*Was-A	152	649	111	227	31	13	1	87	37	10	.350	.388	.442	831	113	12	26	11	2	.968	9	*O-152(0-29-133)	1.1
1926	Was-A	152	641	98	**216**	32	14	3	76	42	20	.337	.380	.445	824	117	15	24	23	-3	.961	7	*O-152(0-44-120)	0.8
1927	Was-A	142	603	98	179	33	14	2	65	36	11	.297	.336	.408	744	93	-7	19	6	2	.975	-0	*O-139(1-0-138)	-1.6
1928	Was-A	148	616	95	202	32	15	2	55	49	15	.328	.379	.438	818	115	14	16	3	**2**	.973	-8	*O-147(1-0-147)	-0.4
1929	Was-A	150	616	119	199	39	10	1	62	55	9	.323	.382	.424	806	106	7	16	8	1	.970	7	*O-147(0-0-147)	0.2
1930	Was-A	147	593	121	207	35	13	1	73	55	14	.349	.407	.457	864	118	18	13	8	0	.963	4	*O-145(0-15-133)	1.0
1931	Was-A	120	413	81	128	21	8	0	42	35	11	.310	.365	.400	765	100	1	6	5	-0	.970	1	*O-105(10-11-85)	-0.4
1932	Was-A	106	288	58	93	16	7	1	34	32	6	.323	.391	.438	828	116	7	7	4	0	.972	-3	O-69(10-14-48)	0.1
1933	*Was-A	73	85	19	25	4	3	1	12	2	7	.294	.326	.447	773	104	0	0	2	-1	1.000	-8	O-39(8-10-23)	-0.9
1934	Cle-A	97	335	48	98	19	1	1	33	28	9	.293	.351	.364	715	83	-8	5	1	1	.963	-7	O-78(13-0-65)	-1.7
Total	20	2404	9269	1514	2987	498	184	34	1078	708	275	.322	.374	.427	801	113	167	351	143		.965	75	*O-2270R/P-9	10.5

■ HAL RICE Rice, Harold Housten "Hoot" b: 2/11/24, Morganette, W.Va. d: 12/22/97, Bloomington, Ind. BL/TR, 6'1", 195 lbs. Deb: 9/25/48

YEAR	TM/L	G	AB	R	H	2B	3B	HR	RBI	BB	SO	AVG	OBP	SLG	OPS	OPS+	BR+	SB	CS	SBR	FA	FR	G/POS	TPR
1948	StL-N	8	31	3	10	1	2	0	3	2	4	.323	.364	.484	848	121	1	0			1.000	-1	/O-8(8-0-0)	0.0
1949	StL-N	40	46	3	9	2	1	1	9	3	7	.196	.245	.348	593	55	-3	0			1.000	-2	O-10(10-0-0)	-0.6
1950	StL-N	44	128	12	27	3	1	2	11	10	10	.211	.268	.297	565	46	-10	0			.972	-1	O-37(33-0-4)	-1.3
1951	StL-N	69	236	20	60	12	1	4	38	24	22	.254	.323	.364	687	84	-5	0	1	-0	.953	-3	O-63(48-0-16)	-1.2
1952	StL-N	98	295	37	85	14	5	7	45	16	26	.288	.325	.441	765	110	3	1	3	-1	.972	-5	O-81(77-4-5)	-0.9
1953	StL-N	8	8	0	2	0	0	0	0	0	3	.250	.250	.250	500	31	-1	0	0	0	.000	0	H	-0.1
	Pit-N	78	286	39	89	16	1	4	42	17	22	.311	.350	.416	766	99	-0	0	1	-0	.973	14	O-70(68-0-2)	0.8
	Yr	86	294	39	91	16	1	4	42	17	25	.310	.347	.412	759	97	-1	0	1	-0	.973	14	O-70(68-0-2)	0.7
1954	Pit-N	28	81	10	14	4	1	1	9	14	24	.173	.295	.284	579	52	-6	0	2	-1	1.000	3	O-24(24-0-2)	-0.5
	Chi-N	51	72	5	11	0	0	0	5	8	15	.153	.237	.153	390	4	-10	0	0	0	.897	-4	O-24(3-0-21)	-1.5
	Yr	79	153	15	25	4	1	1	14	22	39	.163	.269	.222	491	29	-16	0	2	-1	.966	-2	O-48(27-0-23)	-2.0
Total	7	424	1183	129	307	52	12	19	162	94	133	.260	.314	.372	686	82	-32	1	7		.969	0	O-317(271-4-50)	-5.3

■ HARRY RICE Rice, Harry Francis b: 11/22/01, Ware Station, Ill. d: 1/1/71, Portland, Ore. BL/TR, 5'9", 185 lbs. Deb: 4/18/23 Career OF: (28-LF 465-CF 421-RF)

YEAR	TM/L	G	AB	R	H	2B	3B	HR	RBI	BB	SO	AVG	OBP	SLG	OPS	OPS+	BR+	SB	CS	SBR	FA	FR	G/POS	TPR
1923	StL-A	4	3	0	0	0	0	0	0	0	0	.000	.000	.000	0	-95	-1	0	0	0	.000	0	H	-0.1
1924	StL-A	54	93	19	26	7	0	0	15	7	5	.280	.350	.355	704	77	-3	1	3	-1	.917	-0	3-15/2-4,1-2,S-2,O	-0.3
1925	StL-A	103	354	87	127	25	8	11	47	54	15	.359	.450	.568	1018	149	28	8	7	-1	.984	6	O-85R/1-3,C-1,23	2.4
1926	StL-A	148	578	86	181	27	10	9	59	63	40	.313	.384	.441	826	110	9	10	11	-2	.970	7	*O-133R/3-8,2-4,S-2	0.5
1927	StL-A	137	520	90	149	26	9	7	68	50	21	.287	.351	.412	763	94	-5	5	4	-0	.938	12	*O-130(0-44-87)/3-7	-0.2
1928	Det-A	131	510	87	154	21	12	6	81	44	27	.302	.360	.425	785	104	3	20	13	-0	.962	1	*O-129(0-129-0)/3-2	-0.2
1929	Det-A	130	536	97	163	33	7	6	69	61	23	.304	.379	.425	805	106	6	6	10	-2	.960	6	*O-127(0-127-0)/3-3	0.4
1930	Det-A	37	128	16	39	6	0	2	24	19	8	.305	.403	.398	801	102	1	0	3	-1	.944	-0	O-35(19-0-16)	-0.3
	NY-A	100	346	62	103	17	5	7	74	31	21	.298	.361	.436	797	106	3	3	3	-0	.969	8	O-87(4-83-0)/1-6,3-1	0.6
	Yr	137	474	78	142	23	5	9	98	50	29	.300	.372	.426	799	105	4	3	6	-1	.964	7	*O-122C/1-6,3-1	0.3
1931	Was-A	47	162	32	43	5	6	0	15	12	10	.265	.320	.370	690	81	-5	2	1	0	.968	-1	O-42(1-19-23)	-0.7
1933	Cin-N	143	510	44	133	19	6	0	54	35	24	.261	.316	.322	637	84	-10	4			**.991**	3	*O-141(0-10-131)/3-1	-1.7
Total	10	1034	3740	620	1118	186	63	48	506	376	194	.299	.368	.421	789	104	26	59	55		.966	39	O-911C/3-38,1-11,2SC	0.4

■ JIM RICE Rice, James Edward b: 3/8/53, Anderson, S.C. BR/TR, 6'2", 205 lbs. Deb: 8/19/74 C Career OF: (1504-LF 1-CF 43-RF)

YEAR	TM/L	G	AB	R	H	2B	3B	HR	RBI	BB	SO	AVG	OBP	SLG	OPS	OPS+	BR+	SB	CS	SBR	FA	FR	G/POS	TPR
1974	Bos-A	24	67	6	18	2	1	1	13	4	12	.269	.319	.373	693	92	-1	0	0	0	.800	-1	D-16/O-3(3-0-0)	-0.2
1975	Bos-A	144	564	92	174	29	4	22	102	36	122	.309	.354	.491	845	126	18	10	5	0	1.000	-1	O-90(90-0-0),D-54	1.1
1976	Bos-A	153	581	75	164	25	8	25	85	28	123	.282	.320	.482	802	118	11	8	5	0	.967	0	O-98(98-0-0),D-54	0.4
1977	Bos-A★	160	644	104	206	29	15	**39**	114	53	120	.320	.379	**.593**	972	143	37	5	4	-0	.956	1	*D-116,O-44(19-0-27)	3.1
1978	Bos-A★	163	677	121	**213**	25	**15**	**46**	**139**	58	126	.315	.373	**.600**	**973**	153	**45**	7	5	-0	.989	10	*O-114(101-1-15),D-49	4.9
1979	Bos-A★	158	619	117	201	39	6	39	130	57	97	.325	.385	.596	981	152	43	9	4	1	.984	2	*O-125(124-0-1),D-33	3.8
1980	Bos-A†	124	504	81	148	22	6	24	86	30	87	.294	.338	.504	842	121	13	8	3	1	.988	7	*O-109(109-0-0),D-15	1.5
1981	Bos-A	108	451	51	128	18	1	17	62	34	76	.284	.338	.441	779	116	9	2	2	-0	.988	5	*O-108(108-0-0)	0.9
1982	Bos-A	145	573	86	177	24	5	24	97	55	98	.309	.376	.494	870	129	23	0	1	-0	.969	-1	*O-145(145-0-0)	1.6
1983	Bos-A★	155	626	90	191	34	1	**39**	**126**	52	102	.305	.364	.550	914	137	31	0	2	-1	.984	17	*O-151(151-0-0)/D-4	4.0
1984	Bos-A★	159	657	98	184	25	7	28	122	44	102	.280	.326	.467	793	111	9	4	0	1	.989	12	*O-157(157-0-0)/D-2	1.5
1985	Bos-A★	140	546	85	159	20	3	27	103	51	75	.291	.354	.487	841	122	16	2	0	0	.964	0	*O-130(130-0-0)/D-7	1.1
1986	*Bos-A★	157	618	98	200	39	2	20	110	62	78	.324	.389	.490	879	137	32	0	1	-0	.977	17	*O-156(156-0-0)/D-1	4.1
1987	Bos-A	108	404	66	112	14	0	13	62	45	77	.277	.360	.408	768	100	1	1	1	-0	.977	4	O-94(94-0-0),D-12	0.0
1988	*Bos-A	135	485	57	128	18	3	15	72	48	89	.264	.334	.406	740	102	1	1	1	-0	.968	-2	*D-112,O-19(19-0-0)	-0.4
1989	Bos-A	56	209	22	49	10	2	3	28	13	39	.234	.283	.344	627	71	-8	1	0	0	.000	0	D-55	-1.0
Total	16	2089	8225	1249	2452	373	79	382	1451	670	1423	.298	.356	.502	858	127	280	58	34	1	.980	71	*O-1543L,D-530	26.4

■ LEN RICE Rice, Leonard Oliver b: 9/2/18, Lead, S.Dak. d: 6/13/92, Sonora, Cal. BR/TR, 6', 175 lbs. Deb: 4/26/44

YEAR	TM/L	G	AB	R	H	2B	3B	HR	RBI	BB	SO	AVG	OBP	SLG	OPS	OPS+	BR+	SB	CS	SBR	FA	FR	G/POS	TPR
1944	Cin-N	10	4	1	0	0	0	0	0	0	0	.000	.000	.000	0	-99	-1	0			1.000	1	/C-5	0.0
1945	Chi-N	32	99	10	23	3	0	0	7	5	8	.232	.269	.263	532	49	-7	2			.976	-1	C-29	-0.6
Total	2	42	103	11	23	3	0	0	7	5	8	.223	.259	.252	512	44	-8	2			.977	0	/C-34	-0.6

YEAR	TM/L	G	AB	R	H	2B	3B	HR	RBI	BB	SO	AVG	OBP	SLG	OPS	OPS+	BR+	SB	CS	SBR	FA	FR	G/POS	TPR
■ **BOB RICE**	Rice, Robert Turnbull b: 5/28/1899, Philadelphia, Pa. d: 2/20/86, Elizabethtown, Pa BR/TR, 5'10", 170 lbs. Deb: 9/1/26																							
1926	Phi-N	19	54	3	8	0	1	0	10	3	4	.148	.193	.185	378	2	-7	0			.864	1	3-15/2-2,S-2	-0.6
■ **CHRIS RICHARD**	Richard, Christopher Robert b: 6/7/74, San Diego, Cal. BL/TL, 6'2", 185 lbs. Deb: 7/17/2000																							
2000	StL-N	6	16	1	2	0	0	1	1	2	2	.125	.222	.313	535	33	-2	0	0	0	1.000	-0	/O-3(1-0-2),1-2	-0.2
	Bal-A	56	199	38	55	14	2	13	36	15	38	.276	.339	.563	902	127	7	7	5	-0	.989	-7	1-53/O-1(0-0-1),D-1	-0.4
Total	1	62	215	39	57	14	2	14	37	17	40	.265	.331	.544	875	120	5	7	5	-0	.989	-7	/1-55,O-4(1-0-3),D-1	-0.6
■ **LEE RICHARD**	Richard, Lee Edward "Bee Bee" b: 9/18/48, Lafayette, La. BR/TR (BB 1975), 5'11", 165 lbs. Deb: 4/7/71																							
1971	Chi-A	87	260	38	60	7	3	2	17	20	46	.231	.288	.304	592	66	-12	8	9	-1	.920	-0	S-68,O-16(0-16-0)	-0.7
1972	Chi-A	11	29	5	7	0	0	0	1	0	7	.241	.241	.241	483	43	-2	1	0	0	1.000	-0	/O-6(0-6-0),S-1	-0.2
1974	Chi-A	32	67	5	11	1	0	0	1	5	8	.164	.222	.179	401	16	-7	0	0	0	.821	3	3-12/S-6,2-3,O-1R,D	-0.4
1975	Chi-A	43	45	11	9	0	1	0	5	4	7	.200	.265	.244	510	44	-3	2	3	-1	1.000	6	3-12/S-9,2-5,D-5	0.3
1976	StL-N	66	91	12	16	4	2	0	5	4	9	.176	.211	.264	474	34	-8	1	0	0	.975	12	2-26,S-12/3-1	0.5
Total	5	239	492	71	103	12	6	2	29	33	77	.209	.260	.270	531	50	-32	12	12	-2	.923	20	/S-96,2-34,3-25,OD	-0.5
■ **GENE RICHARDS**	Richards, Eugene b: 9/29/53, Monticello, S.C. BL/TL, 6', 175 lbs. Deb: 4/6/77 Career OF: (634-LF 170-CF 23-RF)																							
1977	SD-N	146	525	79	152	16	11	5	32	60	80	.290	.365	.390	755	114	12	56	12	8	.963	1	*O-109(72-41-1),1-32	1.6
1978	SD-N	154	555	90	171	26	12	4	45	64	80	.308	.384	.420	803	135	27	37	17	2	.965	-12	*O-124(113-26-0),1-26	1.2
1979	SD-N	150	545	77	152	17	9	4	41	47	62	.279	.345	.365	710	100	0	24	8	2	.973	4	*O-132(20-102-10)	0.4
1980	SD-N	158	642	91	193	26	8	4	41	61	73	.301	.363	.385	748	116	14	61	16	8	.979	15	*O-156(156-0-1)	3.1
1981	SD-N	104	393	47	113	14	**12**	3	42	53	44	.288	.374	.407	781	131	17	20	8	2	.975	3	*O-102(101-0-0)	1.8
1982	SD-N	132	521	63	149	13	8	3	28	36	52	.286	.335	.359	693	99	-1	30	20	-0	.977	0	*O-103(103-0-0)/1-25	-0.8
1983	SD-N	95	233	37	64	11	3	3	22	17	17	.275	.327	.386	713	100	-0	14	5	1	.980	-1	O-54(54-0-0)	-0.2
1984	SF-N	87	135	18	34	4	0	0	4	18	28	.252	.340	.281	621	79	-3	5	3	0	.940	-1	O-26(15-1-11)	-0.5
Total	8	1026	3549	502	1028	127	63	26	255	356	436	.290	.358	.383	741	113	66	247	89	23	.972	10	O-806L/1-83	6.6
■ **FRED RICHARDS**	Richards, Fred Charles "Fuzzy" b: 11/3/27, Warren, Ohio BL/TL, 6'1.5", 185 lbs. Deb: 9/15/51																							
1951	Chi-N	10	27	1	8	2	0	0	4	2	3	.296	.345	.370	715	91	-0	0	0	0	1.000	1	/1-9	0.1
■ **PAUL RICHARDS**	Richards, Paul Rapier b: 11/21/08, Waxahachie, Tex. d: 5/4/86, Waxahachie, Tex. BR/TR, 6'1.5", 180 lbs. Deb: 4/17/32 M																							
1932	Bro-N	3	8	0	0	0	0	0	0	0	2	.000	.000	.000	0	-99	-2	0			1.000	4	/C-3	0.1
1933	NY-N	51	87	4	17	3	0	0	10	3	12	.195	.222	.230	452	30	-8	0			.989	1	C-36	-0.6
1934	NY-N	42	75	10	12	1	0	0	3	13	8	.160	.284	.173	457	26	-7	0			1.000	2	C-37	-0.4
1935	NY-N	7	4	0	1	0	0	0	0	2	1	.250	.500	.250	750	110	0	0			1.000	1	/C-4	0.2
	Phi-A	85	257	31	63	10	1	4	29	24	12	.245	.310	.339	648	68	-12	0	0	0	.977	-3	C-79	-1.1
1943	Det-A	100	313	32	69	7	1	5	33	38	35	.220	.307	.297	604	71	-11	1	0	0	**.986**	21	*C-100	1.8
1944	Det-A	95	300	24	71	13	0	3	37	35	30	.237	.318	.310	628	76	-9	8	3	1	.979	16	C-90	1.4
1945	*Det-A	83	234	26	60	12	1	3	32	19	31	.256	.315	.355	670	88	-4	4	0	1	**.995**	12	C-83	1.4
1946	Det-A	57	139	13	28	5	2	0	11	23	18	.201	.315	.266	581	60	-7	2	0	0	.997	15	C-54	1.2
Total	8	523	1417	140	321	51	5	15	155	157	149	.227	.305	.301	606	68	-60	15	3		.987	69	C-486	4.0
■ **RICHARDSON**	Richardson b: Boston, Mass. 5'4", 136 lbs. Deb: 7/10/1884																							
1884	CP-U	1	4	0	0	0	0	0				.000	.000	.000	0	-99	-1				.667	-1	/2-1	-0.2
■ **HARDY RICHARDSON**	Richardson, Abram Harding "Old True Blue" b: 4/21/1855, Clarksboro, N.J. d: 1/14/31, Utica, N.Y. BR/TR, 5'9.5", 170 lbs. Deb: 5/1/1879 Career OF: (375-LF 158-CF 11-RF)																							
1879	Buf-N	79	336	54	95	18	10	0	37	16	30	.283	.315	.396	711	130	10				.843	-6	*3-78/C-1	0.6
1880	Buf-N	83	343	48	89	18	8	0	17	14	37	.259	.289	.359	647	116	5				.848	-7	*3-81/C-5	0.1
1881	Buf-N	83	344	62	100	18	9	2	53	12	27	.291	.315	.413	727	129	11				.914	25	*O-79C/2-5,S-1,3-1	3.0
1882	Buf-N	83	354	61	96	20	8	2	57	11	33	.271	.293	.390	683	115	5				.898	16	*2-83	2.2
1883	Buf-N	92	399	73	124	34	7	1	56	22	20	.311	.347	.439	785	134	16				.903	19	*2-92	3.3
1884	Buf-N	102	439	85	132	27	9	6	60	22	41	.301	.334	.444	778	138	18				.897	8	2-71,O-24C/3-5,1-3	2.4
1885	Buf-N	96	426	90	136	19	11	6	44	20	22	.319	.350	.458	808	154	24				.905	13	2-50,O-48C/S-1,P-1	3.4
1886	Det-N	125	538	125	**189**	27	11	**11**	61	46	27	.351	.402	.504	906	169	44	42			.899	10	O-80L,2-42/P-4,S3	4.7
1887	*Det-N	120	574	131	209	25	18	8	94	31	40	.364	.366	.484	851	130	20	29			.941	17	2-64,O-59(58-1-0)	3.2
1888	Det-N	58	266	60	77	18	2	6	32	17	23	.289	.335	.440	774	145	13	13			.925	4	2-58	1.8
1889	Bos-N	132	536	122	163	33	10	6	79	48	44	.304	.367	.437	803	117	10	47			.924	13	2-86,O-46(46-0-0)	2.2
1890	Bos-P	130	555	126	181	26	14	13	**146**	52	46	.326	.384	.494	878	125	16	42			.950	2	*O-124L/S-6,1-1	1.2
1891	Bos-a	74	278	45	71	9	4	7	52	40	26	.255	.351	.392	743	114	5	16			.955	-0	O-60L/3-9,S-4,1-3	0.3
1892	Was-N	10	37	2	4	0	0	0	0	5	3	.108	.214	.108	322	-2	-4	2			.941	-0	/O-7(7-0-0),3-2,2-1	-0.5
	NY-N	64	248	36	53	11	5	2	34	21	26	.214	.278	.323	600	83	-6	14			.931	-1	2-33,O-17R/1-9,S-6	-0.5
	Yr	74	285	38	57	11	5	2	34	26	29	.200	.269	.295	564	72	-10	16			.933	-1	2-34,O-24L/1-9,S3	-1.0
Total	14	1331	5673	1120	1719	303	126	70	822	377	445	.303	.344	.435	779	130	188	205			.915	113	2-585,O-544L,3/S1CP	27.4
■ **NOLEN RICHARDSON**	Richardson, Clifford Nolen b: 1/18/03, Chattanooga, Tenn. d: 9/25/51, Athens, Ga. BR/TR, 6'1.5", 170 lbs. Deb: 4/16/29																							
1929	Det-A	13	21	2	4	0	0	0	2	2	1	.190	.261	.190	451	18	-3	1	1	-0	.839	-4	S-13	-0.6
1931	Det-A	38	148	13	40	9	2	0	16	6	3	.270	.299	.358	657	70	-7	2	1	0	.946	-2	3-38	-0.7
1932	Det-A	69	155	13	34	5	2	0	12	9	13	.219	.262	.277	540	38	-14	5	2	0	.986	11	3-65/S-4	-0.1
1935	NY-A	12	46	3	10	1	1	0	5	3	1	.217	.265	.283	548	44	-4	0	0	0	.922	-6	S-12	-0.9
1938	Cin-N	35	100	8	29	4	0	0	10	3	4	.290	.311	.330	641	78	-3	0			.966	-1	S-35	-0.2
1939	Cin-N	1	3	0	0	0	0	0	0	0	0	.000	.000	.000	0	-99	-1	0			1.000	1	/S-1	0.0
Total	6	168	473	39	117	19	5	0	45	23	22	.247	.282	.309	591	55	-31	8	4		.969	-2	3-103/S-65	-2.5
■ **DANNY RICHARDSON**	Richardson, Daniel b: 1/25/1863, Elmira, N.Y. d: 9/12/26, New York, N.Y. BR/TR, 5'8", 165 lbs. Deb: 5/22/1884 M Career OF: (41-LF 51-CF 51-RF)																							
1884	NY-N	74	277	36	70	8	1	1	27	16	17	.253	.294	.300	593	85	-5				.907	2	O-55(11-7-37),S-19	-0.3
1885	NY-N	49	198	26	52	9	3	0	25	10	14	.263	.298	.338	636	107	1				.950	-1	O-22R,3-21/P-9	0.2
1886	NY-N	68	237	43	55	9	1	1	27	17	21	.232	.283	.291	575	74	-7	12			.953	-0	O-64C/P-5,S-1,32	-0.9
1887	NY-N	122	486	79	161	19	10	3	62	36	25	.331	.337	.384	721	105	4	41			.928	15	*2-108,3-14/P-1	1.9
1888	*NY-N	135	561	82	127	16	7	8	61	15	35	.226	.248	.323	570	82	-12	35			**.942**	9	*2-135	0.2
1889	*NY-N	125	497	88	139	22	8	7	100	46	37	.280	.342	.398	740	106	3	32			.934	13	*2-125	1.8
1890	NY-P	123	528	102	135	12	9	4	80	37	19	.256	.307	.335	642	66	-29	37			.900	25	S-68,2-56	0.1
1891	NY-N	123	516	85	139	18	5	4	51	33	27	.269	.313	.347	660	96	-3	28			.952	**49**	*2-114/S-9	**4.4**
1892	Was-N	142	551	48	132	13	4	3	58	25	45	.240	.274	.294	568	74	-19	25			.931	**57**	S-93,2-49/3-1,M	4.2
1893	Bro-N	54	206	36	46	6	2	0	27	13	18	.223	.279	.272	551	49	-15	7			.949	-17	2-46/3-5,S-3	-2.5
1894	Lou-N	116	430	51	109	17	2	1	40	35	31	.253	.317	.309	626	55	-30	8			.916	3	*S-107,2-10	-1.7
Total	11	1131	4487	676	1165	149	52	32	558	283	289	.260	.301	.332	633	82	-112	225			.940	155	2-644,S-300,O/3P	7.4
■ **JEFF RICHARDSON**	Richardson, Jeffrey Scott b: 8/26/65, Grand Island, Neb. BR/TR, 6'2", 175 lbs. Deb: 7/14/89																							
1989	Cin-N	53	125	10	21	4	0	2	11	10	23	.168	.235	.248	483	37	-10	1	0	0	.969	-2	S-39/3-8	-1.0
1991	Pit-N	6	4	0	1	0	0	0	0	0	3	.250	.250	.250	500	42	-0	0	0	0	.000	-1	/3-3,S-2	-0.1
1993	Bos-A	15	24	3	5	2	0	0	2	1	3	.208	.240	.292	532	40	-2	0	0	0	1.000	6	/2-8,S-5,3-1,D-2	0.4
Total	3	74	153	13	27	6	0	2	13	11	29	.176	.236	.255	491	38	-13	1	0	0	.971	3	/S-46,3-12,2-8,D-2	-0.7
■ **KEN RICHARDSON**	Richardson, Kenneth Franklin b: 5/2/15, Orleans, Ind. d: 12/7/87, Woodland Hills, Cal BR/TR, 5'10.5", 187 lbs. Deb: 4/14/42 Career OF: (1-LF 0-CF 2-RF)																							
1942	Phi-A	6	15	1	1	0	0	0	0	2	0	.067	.176	.067	243	-30	-3	0	0	0	1.000	0	/O-3(1-0-2),1-1,3-1	-0.3
1946	Phi-N	6	20	1	3	1	0	0	2	0	2	.150	.150	.200	350	-1	-3	0			.939	-0	/2-6	-0.3
Total	2	12	35	2	4	1	0	0	2	2	2	.114	.162	.143	305	-14	-5	0	0		.939	-0	/2-6,O-3R,3-1,1-1	-0.6
■ **BOBBY RICHARDSON**	Richardson, Robert Clinton b: 8/19/35, Sumter, S.C. BR/TR, 5'9", 170 lbs. Deb: 8/5/55																							
1955	NY-A	11	26	2	4	0	0	0	3	2	0	.154	.214	.154	368	0	-4	1	1	-0	.864	-5	/2-6,S-4	-0.9
1956	NY-A	5	7	1	1	0	0	0	0	0	1	.143	.143	.143	286	-25	-1	0	0	0	1.000	2	/2-5	0.1

YEAR	TM/L	G	AB	R	H	2B	3B	HR	RBI	BB	SO	AVG	OBP	SLG	OPS	OPS+	BR+	SB	CS	SBR	FA	FR	G/POS	TPR
1957	*NY-A☆	97	305	36	78	11	1	0	19	9	26	.256	.277	.298	575	58	-18	1	3	-1	.979	5	2-93	-0.8
1958	*NY-A	73	182	18	45	6	2	0	14	8	5	.247	.279	.302	581	62	-10	1	3	-1	.973	8	2-51,3-13/S-2	0.1
1959	NY-A☆	134	469	53	141	18	6	2	33	26	20	.301	.337	.377	715	99	-1	5	5	-1	.970	2	*2-109,S-14,3-12	0.9
1960	*NY-A	150	460	45	116	12	3	1	26	35	19	.252	.305	.298	603	68	-21	6	6	-1	.973	-4	*2-141,3-11	-1.7
1961	*NY-A	162	662	80	173	17	5	3	49	30	23	.261	.295	.316	611	67	-32	9	7	-0	.978	-9	*2-161	-2.8
1962	*NY-A★	161	692	99	**209**	38	5	8	59	37	24	.302	.338	.406	744	103	1	11	9	-1	.982	-3	*2-161	1.2
1963	*NY-A★	151	630	72	167	20	6	3	48	25	22	.265	.295	.330	625	76	-21	15	1	3	.984	7	*2-150	0.2
1964	*NY-A★	159	679	90	181	25	4	4	50	28	36	.267	.296	.333	628	73	-25	11	2	2	.982	-14	*2-157/S-1	-2.4
1965	NY-A★	160	664	76	164	28	2	6	47	37	39	.247	.288	.322	610	74	-24	7	5	-0	.981	-3	*2-158	-1.4
1966	NY-A★	149	610	71	153	21	3	7	42	25	28	.251	.281	.330	611	78	-19	6	6	-1	.980	3	*2-147/3-2	-0.4
Total	12	1412	5386	643	1432	196	37	34	390	262	243	.266	.301	.335	636	77	-172	73	48	-1	.979	-11	*2-1339/3-38,S-21	-7.9

■ TOM RICHARDSON Richardson, Thomas Mitchell b: 8/7/1883, Louisville, Ill. d: 11/15/39, Onawa, Iowa BR/TR, 6′, 190 lbs. Deb: 8/2/17

YEAR	TM/L	G	AB	R	H	2B	3B	HR	RBI	BB	SO	AVG	OBP	SLG	OPS	OPS+	BR+	SB	CS	SBR	FA	FR	G/POS	TPR
1917	StL-A	1	1	0	0	0	0	0	0	0	0	.000	.000	.000	0	-99	-0	0			.000	0	H	0.0

■ BILL RICHARDSON Richardson, William Henry b: 9/24/1878, Salem, Ind. d: 11/6/49, Sullivan, Ind. BR/TR, 5′11″, 200 lbs. Deb: 9/20/01

YEAR	TM/L	G	AB	R	H	2B	3B	HR	RBI	BB	SO	AVG	OBP	SLG	OPS	OPS+	BR+	SB	CS	SBR	FA	FR	G/POS	TPR
1901	StL-N	15	52	7	11	2	0	2	7	6		.212	.293	.365	658	95	-0	1			.981	-1	1-15	-0.2

■ MIKE RICHARDT Richardt, Michael Anthony b: 5/24/58, Los Angeles, Cal. BR/TR, 6′, 170 lbs. Deb: 8/30/80

YEAR	TM/L	G	AB	R	H	2B	3B	HR	RBI	BB	SO	AVG	OBP	SLG	OPS	OPS+	BR+	SB	CS	SBR	FA	FR	G/POS	TPR
1980	Tex-A	22	71	2	16	2	0	0	8	1	7	.225	.236	.254	490	35	-6	0	0	0	.978	-1	2-20/D-1	-0.6
1982	Tex-A	119	402	34	97	10	0	3	43	23	42	.241	.284	.289	573	61	-22	9	1	2	.988	4	2-98,D-15/O-6(6-0-0)	-1.1
1983	Tex-A	22	83	9	13	2	1	1	7	2	11	.157	.176	.241	417	14	-10	2	1	0	.992	2	2-20	-0.7
1984	Tex-A	6	9	0	1	0	0	0	0	1	1	.111	.200	.111	311	-11	-1	0	1	-0	1.000	1	/2-4	-0.1
	Hou-N	16	15	1	4	1	0	0	2	0	1	.267	.267	.333	600	73	-1	0	0	0	.000	0	H	-0.1
Total	4	185	580	46	131	15	1	4	60	27	62	.226	.262	.276	537	50	-40	11	3	1	.988	6	2-142/D-16,O-6(6-0-0)	-2.6

■ LANCE RICHBOURG Richbourg, Lance Clayton b: 12/18/1897, DeFuniak Springs, Fla. d: 9/10/75, Crestview, Fla. BL/TR, 5′10.5″, 160 lbs. Deb: 7/4/21

YEAR	TM/L	G	AB	R	H	2B	3B	HR	RBI	BB	SO	AVG	OBP	SLG	OPS	OPS+	BR+	SB	CS	SBR	FA	FR	G/POS	TPR
1921	Phi-N	10	5	2	1	1	0	0	0	0	3	.200	.200	.400	600	51	-0	1	1	-0	1.000	2	/2-4	0.2
1924	Was-A	15	32	3	9	2	1	0	1	2	6	.281	.324	.406	730	90	-1	0	0	0	1.000	1	/O-7(0-0-7)	0.0
1927	Bos-N	115	450	57	139	12	9	2	34	22	30	.309	.342	.389	731	104	1	24			.953	-4	*O-110(0-3-107)	-1.2
1928	Bos-N	148	612	105	206	26	12	2	52	62	39	.337	.399	.428	828	123	22	11			.972	7	*O-148(0-0-148)	1.6
1929	Bos-N	139	557	76	170	24	13	3	56	42	26	.305	.355	.411	766	93	-6	7			.971	5	*O-134(2-0-132)	-1.1
1930	Bos-N	130	529	81	161	23	8	3	54	19	31	.304	.331	.395	726	77	-20	13			.971	-3	*O-128(0-0-128)	-3.0
1931	Bos-N	97	286	32	82	11	6	2	29	19	14	.287	.331	.388	719	96	-2	9			.981	-3	O-71(15-0-56)	-0.9
1932	Chi-N	44	148	22	38	2	2	1	21	8	4	.257	.295	.318	612	65	-7	0			.986	-1	O-33(1-3-29)	-1.0
Total	8	698	2619	378	806	101	51	13	247	174	153	.308	.352	.400	752	97	-13	65	1		.970	4	O-631(18-6-607)/2-4	-5.4

■ ROB RICHIE Richie, Robert Eugene b: 9/5/65, Reno, Nev. BL/TR, 6′2″, 190 lbs. Deb: 8/19/89

YEAR	TM/L	G	AB	R	H	2B	3B	HR	RBI	BB	SO	AVG	OBP	SLG	OPS	OPS+	BR+	SB	CS	SBR	FA	FR	G/POS	TPR
1989	Det-A	19	49	6	13	4	2	1	10	5	10	.265	.333	.490	823	132	2	0	1	-0	.917	-1	O-13(11-0-2)/D-4	0.0

■ DON RICHMOND Richmond, Donald Lester b: 10/27/19, Gillett, Pa. d: 5/24/81, Elmira, N.Y. BL/TR, 6′1″, 175 lbs. Deb: 9/16/41

YEAR	TM/L	G	AB	R	H	2B	3B	HR	RBI	BB	SO	AVG	OBP	SLG	OPS	OPS+	BR+	SB	CS	SBR	FA	FR	G/POS	TPR
1941	Phi-A	9	35	3	7	1	1	0	5	0	1	.200	.200	.286	486	28	-4	0	2	-1	.957	-2	/3-9	-0.6
1946	Phi-A	16	62	3	18	3	0	1	9	0	10	.290	.290	.387	677	89	-1	1	0	0	.940	-3	3-16	-0.4
1947	Phi-A	19	21	2	4	1	1	0	4	3	3	.190	.292	.333	625	72	-1	0	0	0	.500	-3	/3-4,2-1	-0.4
1951	StL-N	12	34	3	3	1	0	1	4	3	3	.088	.162	.206	368	-2	-5	0	1	-0	1.000	5	3-11	-0.1
Total	4	56	152	11	32	6	2	2	22	6	17	.211	.241	.316	556	51	-11	1	3	-1	.957	-4	/3-40,2-1	-1.5

■ LEE RICHMOND Richmond, J Lee b: 5/5/1857, Sheffield, Ohio d: 10/1/29, Toledo, Ohio TL, 5′10″, 155 lbs. Deb: 9/27/1879

YEAR	TM/L	G	AB	R	H	2B	3B	HR	RBI	BB	SO	AVG	OBP	SLG	OPS	OPS+	BR+	SB	CS	SBR	FA	FR	G/POS	TPR
1879	Bos-N	1	6	0	2	0	0	0	1	0	1	.333	.333	.333	667	118	0				1.000	0	/P-1	0.0
1880	Wor-N	77	309	44	70	8	4	0	34	9	32	.227	.248	.278	527	72	-9				.827	-13	*P-74,O-20(1-1-18)	-0.7
1881	Wor-N	61	252	31	63	5	1	0	28	10	10	.250	.279	.278	556	71	-8				.937	-1	P-53,O-11(0-2-9)	-0.4
1882	Wor-N	55	228	50	64	8	9	2	28	9	11	.281	.308	.421	729	128	7				.889	2	P-48,O-11(1-1-9)	0.0
1883	Pro-N	49	194	41	55	8	6	1	19	15	19	.284	.335	.402	737	120	5				.714	-10	O-41(33-3-5),P-12	-0.6
1886	Cin-a	8	29	3	8	0	0	0	3	3		.276	.344	.276	620	92	-0	0			.400	-4	/O-7(0-7-0),P-3	-0.3
Total	6	251	1018	169	262	29	20	3	113	46	73	.257	.289	.334	623	94	-7	0			.886	-26	P-191/O-90(35-14-41)	-2.0

■ JOHN RICHMOND Richmond, John H. b: 1854, Pennsylvania TR, 5′9″, 170 lbs. Deb: 4/22/1875 Career OF: (4-LF 122-CF 7-RF)

YEAR	TM/L	G	AB	R	H	2B	3B	HR	RBI	BB	SO	AVG	OBP	SLG	OPS	OPS+	BR+	SB	CS	SBR	FA	FR	G/POS	TPR
1875	Ath-n	29	125	29	25	2	0	0	12	1	4	.200	.206	.216	422	42	-8	1	0	0	.814	-2	2-17,O-11(2-3-6)/C-3	-0.9
1879	Syr-N	62	254	31	54	8	4	1	23	4	24	.213	.225	.287	512	76	-5				.874	-7	O-35(4-29-2),S-28/C-2	-1.2
1880	Bos-N	32	129	12	32	3	1	0	9	2	18	.248	.260	.287	546	88	-2				.844	-12	S-31/O-1(0-1-0)	-1.2
1881	Bos-N	27	98	13	27	2	2	1	12	6	7	.276	.317	.367	685	120	2				.969	-0	O-25(0-24-1)/S-2	0.1
1882	Cle-N	41	140	12	24	6	2	0	11	11	27	.171	.232	.243	475	54	-7				.917	3	O-41(0-41-0)	-0.5
	Phi-a	18	65	8	12	2	2	0	4	11		.185	.303	.277	580	87	-1				.892	0	O-18(0-17-1)	-0.1
1883	Col-a	92	385	63	109	7	8	0		25		.283	.327	.343	670	126	13				**.877**	26	*S-91/O-2(0-2-0)	**3.6**
1884	Col-a	105	398	57	100	13	7	3		35		.251	.317	.342	658	125	13				.866	-9	*S-105	0.7
1885	Pit-a	34	131	14	27	2	2	0	12	8		.206	.262	.252	514	64	-5				.849	-10	S-23,O-11(0-8-3)	-1.3
Total	7	411	1600	210	385	43	28	5	71	102	76	.241	.288	.312	600	101	10				.866	-10	S-280,O-133C/C-2	0.1

■ AL RICHTER Richter, Allen Gordon b: 2/7/27, Norfolk, Va. BR/TR, 5′11″, 165 lbs. Deb: 9/23/51

YEAR	TM/L	G	AB	R	H	2B	3B	HR	RBI	BB	SO	AVG	OBP	SLG	OPS	OPS+	BR+	SB	CS	SBR	FA	FR	G/POS	TPR
1951	Bos-A	5	11	1	1	0	0	0	0	3	0	.091	.286	.091	377	5	-1	0	0	0	1.000	2	/S-3	0.1
1953	Bos-A	1	0	0	0	0	0	0	0	0	0	—	—	—	—	—	0	0	0	0	1.000	0	/S-1	0.0
Total	2	6	11	1	1	0	0	0	0	3	0	.091	.286	.091	377	5	-1	0	0	0	1.000	3	/S-4	0.1

■ JOHN RICHTER Richter, John M. b: 2/8/1873, Louisville, Ky. d: 10/4/27, Louisville, Ky. 6′, 178 lbs. Deb: 10/6/1898

YEAR	TM/L	G	AB	R	H	2B	3B	HR	RBI	BB	SO	AVG	OBP	SLG	OPS	OPS+	BR+	SB	CS	SBR	FA	FR	G/POS	TPR
1898	Lou-N	3	13	1	2	0	0	0	0	0		.154	.154	.154	308	-12	-2	0			.929	0	/3-3	-0.1

■ JOE RICKERT Rickert, Joseph Francis "Diamond Joe" b: 12/12/1876, London, Ohio d: 10/15/43, Springfield, Ohio BR/TR, 5′10.5″, 165 lbs. Deb: 10/12/1898

YEAR	TM/L	G	AB	R	H	2B	3B	HR	RBI	BB	SO	AVG	OBP	SLG	OPS	OPS+	BR+	SB	CS	SBR	FA	FR	G/POS	TPR
1898	Pit-N	2	6	0	1	0	0	0	0	0		.167	.167	.167	333	-5	-1	0			1.000	1	/O-2(2-0-0)	0.0
1901	Bos-N	13	60	6	10	1	2	0	1	3		.167	.206	.250	456	29	-6	1			.974	2	O-13(13-0-0)	-0.4
Total	2	15	66	6	11	1	2	0	1	3		.167	.203	.242	445	27	-6	1			.979	3	/O-15(15-0-0)	-0.4

■ MARV RICKERT Rickert, Marvin August "Twitch" b: 1/8/21, Longbranch, Wash. d: 6/3/78, Oakville, Wash. BL/TR, 6′2″, 195 lbs. Deb: 9/10/42 Career OF: (164-LF 31-CF 110-RF)

YEAR	TM/L	G	AB	R	H	2B	3B	HR	RBI	BB	SO	AVG	OBP	SLG	OPS	OPS+	BR+	SB	CS	SBR	FA	FR	G/POS	TPR
1942	Chi-N	8	26	5	7	0	0	0	1	1	5	.269	.296	.269	566	69	-1	0			1.000	1	/O-6(0-6-0)	0.0
1946	Chi-N	111	392	44	103	18	3	7	47	28	54	.263	.314	.378	691	98	-3	3			.972	-6	*O-104(75-19-10)	-1.6
1947	Chi-N	71	137	7	20	0	0	2	15	15	17	.146	.230	.190	420	13	-17	0			.982	-1	O-30(18-3-9)/1-7	-2.0
1948	Cin-N	8	6	0	1	0	0	0	0	0	0	.167	.167	.167	333	-10	-1	0			.000	0	H	-0.1
	*Bos-N	3	13	1	3	0	1	0	2	0	1	.231	.286	.385	670	81	-0	0			1.000	1	/O-3(3-0-0)	0.1
	Yr	11	19	1	4	0	1	0	2	0	1	.211	.250	.316	566	54	-1	0			1.000	1	/O-3(3-0-0)	0.0
1949	Bos-N	100	277	44	81	18	3	6	49	23	38	.292	.347	.444	791	117	6	1			.981	-0	O-75(50-3-25),1-12	0.2
1950	Pit-N	17	20	0	3	0	0	0	4	0	4	.150	.150	.150	300	-20	-3	0			.000	-1	/O-3(0-0-3)	-0.5
	Chi-A	84	278	38	66	9	2	4	27	21	42	.237	.291	.327	618	60	-18	0	1	-0	.968	-6	O-78(18-0-63)/1-1	-2.6
Total	6	402	1149	139	284	45	9	19	145	88	161	.247	.302	.352	653	79	-38	4	1		.976	-12	O-299L/1-20	-6.5

■ DAVE RICKETTS Ricketts, David William b: 7/12/35, Pottstown, Pa. BB/TR, 6′2″, 195 lbs. Deb: 9/25/63 FC

YEAR	TM/L	G	AB	R	H	2B	3B	HR	RBI	BB	SO	AVG	OBP	SLG	OPS	OPS+	BR+	SB	CS	SBR	FA	FR	G/POS	TPR
1963	StL-N	3	8	0	2	0	0	0	0	0	2	.250	.250	.250	500	41	-1	0	0	0	1.000	-0	/C-3	-0.1
1965	StL-N	11	29	1	7	0	0	0	0	1	3	.241	.267	.241	508	40	-2	0	0	0	.977	-2	C-11	-0.4
1967	*StL-N	52	99	11	27	8	0	1	14	4	7	.273	.301	.384	685	96	-1	0	0	0	1.000	-0	C-21	0.0
1968	*StL-N	20	22	1	3	0	0	0	1	0	3	.136	.136	.136	273	-18	-3	0	0	0	1.000	-0	/C-1	-0.4
1969	StL-N	30	44	2	12	1	0	0	5	4	5	.273	.333	.295	629	77	-1	0	0	0	.983	1	/C-8	0.0
1970	Pit-N	14	11	0	2	0	0	0	0	1	3	.182	.250	.182	432	18	-1	0	0	0	.909	1	/C-7	-0.1
Total	6	130	213	15	53	9	0	1	20	10	23	.249	.283	.305	588	67	-9	0	0	0	.988	-1	/C-51	-1.0

YEAR	TM/L	G	AB	R	H	2B	3B	HR	RBI	BB	SO	AVG	OBP	SLG	OPS	OPS+	BR+	SB	CS	SBR	FA	FR	G/POS	TPR
■ BRANCH RICKEY Rickey, Wesley Branch "The Mahatma" b: 12/20/1881, Flat, Ohio d: 12/9/65, Columbia, Mo. BL/TR, 5'9", 175 lbs. Deb: 6/16/05 MH Career OF: (20-LF 1-CF 2-RF)																								
1905	StL-A	1	3	0	0	0	0	0	0	0		.000	.000	.000	0	-99	-1	0			1.000	-0	/C-1	-0.1
1906	StL-A	65	201	22	57	7	3	3	24	16		.284	.345	.393	738	137	8	4			.954	-8	C-55/O-1(0-0-1)	0.7
1907	NY-A	52	137	16	25	1	3	0	15	11		.182	.253	.234	487	51	-7	4			.846	-5	O-22(20-1-1),C-11/1-9	-1.4
1914	StL-A	2	2	0	0	0	0	0	0	0	1	.000	.000	.000	0	-99	-0	0			.000	0	HM	-0.1
Total	4	120	343	38	82	8	6	3	39	27	1	.239	.304	.324	628	97	-0	8			.940	-13	/C-67,O-23L,1-9	-0.9
■ CHRIS RICKLEY Rickley, Christian b: 10/7/1859, Philadelphia, Pa. d: 10/25/11, Philadelphia, Pa. 5'8", 160 lbs. Deb: 6/9/1884																								
1884	Phi-U	6	25	5	5	2	0	0		2		.200	.259	.280	539	68	-2				.757	0	/S-6	-0.1
■ JOHN RICKS Ricks, John Deb: 9/21/1891																								
1891	StL-a	5	18	3	3	0	0	0	0	0	2	.167	.167	.167	333	-4	-3	0			.810	-1	/3-5	-0.3
1894	StL-N	1	1	0	0	0	0	0	0	0	0	.000	.000	.000	0	-99	-0	0			.250	-1	/3-1	-0.1
Total	2	6	19	3	3	0	0	0	0	0	2	.158	.158	.158	316	-9	-3	0			.720	-2	/3-6	-0.4
■ FRED RICO Rico, Alfredo (Cruz) b: 7/4/44, Jerome, Ariz. BR/TR, 5'10", 180 lbs. Deb: 9/1/69																								
1969	KC-A	12	26	2	6	2	0	0	2	9	10	.231	.429	.308	736	108	1	0	1	-0	1.000	4	/O-9(0-2-7),3-1	0.4
■ ART RICO Rico, Arthur Raymond b: 7/23/1896, Roxbury, Mass. d: 1/3/19, Boston, Mass. BR/TR, 5'9.5", 185 lbs. Deb: 7/31/16																								
1916	Bos-N	4	4	0	0	0	0	0	0	0	0	.000	.000	.000	0	-99	-1	0			1.000	-0	/C-4	-0.1
1917	Bos-N	13	14	1	4	1	0	0	2	0	2	.286	.286	.357	643	102	-0	0			.950	-2	C-11/O-2(1-0-0)	-0.1
Total	2	17	18	1	4	1	0	0	2	0	2	.222	.222	.278	500	56	-1	0			.962	-2	/C-15,O-2(1-0-0)	-0.2
■ HARRY RICONDA Riconda, Henry Paul b: 3/17/1897, New York, N.Y. d: 11/15/58, Mahopac, N.Y. BR/TR, 5'10", 175 lbs. Deb: 4/19/23																								
1923	Phi-A	55	175	23	46	11	4	0	12	12	18	.263	.317	.371	689	80	-6	4	2	0	.911	4	3-47/S-2	0.1
1924	Phi-A	83	281	34	71	16	3	1	21	27	43	.253	.323	.342	664	71	-12	3	4	-1	.927	1	3-73/S-2	-0.7
1926	Bos-N	4	12	1	2	0	0	0	0	2	2	.167	.286	.167	452	27	-1	0			.818	-1	/3-4	-0.2
1928	Bro-N	92	281	22	63	15	4	3	35	20	28	.224	.285	.338	623	63	-16	6			.957	3	2-53,3-21,S-16	-0.9
1929	Pit-N	8	15	3	7	2	0	0	2	0	0	.467	.467	.600	1067	158	1	0			.840	-0	/S-4	0.1
1930	Cin-N	1	1	0	0	0	0	0	0	0	0	.000	.000	.000	0	-99	-0	0			.000	0	H	0.0
Total	6	243	765	83	189	44	11	4	70	61	91	.247	.309	.349	658	71	-34	13	6		.922	7	3-145/2-53,S-24	-1.6
■ JOHN RIDDLE Riddle, John H. b: 2/1864, Pennsylvania d: 5/5/21, Camden, N.J. BR/TR, Deb: 9/18/1889 Career OF: (9-LF 3-CF 2-RF)																								
1889	Was-N	11	37	3	8	3	0	0	3	2	8	.216	.256	.297	554	58	-2	0			.841	1	/C-9,O-2(0-0-2)	-0.1
1890	Phi-a	27	85	7	7	0	1	0	2	17		.082	.243	.106	349	3	-10	4			.914	-2	C-13,O-12L/2-2,3-1	-1.0
Total	2	38	122	10	15	3	1	0	5	19	8	.123	.246	.164	410	20	-12	4			.880	-2	/C-22,O-14L,2-2,3-1	-1.1
■ JOHNNY RIDDLE Riddle, John Ludy "Mutt" b: 10/3/05, Clinton, S.C. d: 12/15/98, Indianapolis, Ind. BR/TR, 5'11", 190 lbs. Deb: 4/17/30 FC																								
1930	Chi-A	25	58	7	14	3	1	0	4	3	6	.241	.290	.328	618	58	-4	0	0	0	1.000	-3	C-25	-0.5
1937	Was-A	8	26	2	7	0	0	0	3	0	2	.269	.296	.269	566	46	-2	0	0	0	.971	0	/C-8	-0.1
	Bos-N	2	3	0	0	0	0	0	0	1	0	.000	.250	.000	250	-29	-1	0			1.000	1	/C-2	0.0
1938	Bos-N	19	57	6	16	1	0	0	2	4	2	.281	.328	.298	626	81	-1	0			.951	4	C-19	0.4
1941	Cin-N	10	10	2	3	0	0	0	0	0	1	.300	.300	.300	600	69	-0	0			1.000	1	C-10	0.1
1944	Cin-N	1	0	0	0	0	0	0	0	0	0	—	—	—	—	—	0	0			.000	0	/C-1	0.0
1945	Cin-N	23	45	0	8	0	0	0	2	4	6	.178	.245	.178	423	19	-5	0			1.000	4	C-23	0.0
1948	Pit-N	10	15	1	3	0	0	0	0	1	2	.200	.250	.200	450	23	-2	0			1.000	0	C-10	-0.1
Total	7	98	214	18	51	4	1	0	11	13	19	.238	.288	.266	555	51	-15	0	0		.983	7	/C-98	-0.2
■ HANK RIEBE Riebe, Harvey Donald b: 10/10/21, Cleveland, Ohio BR/TR, 5'9.5", 175 lbs. Deb: 8/26/42																								
1942	Det-A	11	35	1	11	2	0	0	2	0	6	.314	.314	.371	686	85	-1	0	0	0	1.000	-1	C-11	-0.1
1947	Det-A	8	7	0	0	0	0	0	2	0	2	.000	.000	.000	0	-97	-2	0	0	0	1.000	-0	/C-3	-0.2
1948	Det-A	25	62	0	12	0	0	0	5	3	5	.194	.231	.194	424	13	-8	0	1	-0	1.000	0	C-24	-0.7
1949	Det-A	17	33	1	6	2	0	0	2	0	5	.182	.182	.242	424	12	-4	1	0	0	.960	-2	C-11	-0.6
Total	4	61	137	2	29	4	0	0	11	3	18	.212	.229	.241	469	26	-15	1	1	-0	.994	-3	/C-49	-1.6
■ NIKCO RIESGO Riesgo, Damon Nikco b: 1/11/67, Long Beach, Cal. BR/TR, 6'2", 185 lbs. Deb: 4/20/91																								
1991	Mon-N	4	7	1	1	0	0	0	0	3	1	.143	.400	.143	543	60	-0	0	0	0	.500	-0	/O-2(0-0-2)	0.0
■ JOE RIGGERT Riggert, Joseph Aloysius b: 12/11/1886, Janesville, Wis. d: 12/10/73, Kansas City, Mo. BR/TR, 5'9.5", 170 lbs. Deb: 5/12/11																								
1911	Bos-A	50	146	19	31	4	4	2	13	12		.212	.290	.336	626	75	-5	5			.929	-4	O-39(21-11-6)	-1.1
1914	Bro-N	27	83	6	16	1	3	2	6	4	20	.193	.230	.349	579	70	-4	2			.972	-1	O-20(1-0-20)	-0.6
	StL-N	34	89	9	19	5	2	0	8	5	14	.213	.255	.315	570	70	-4	4			.961	-3	O-30(9-19-2)	-0.9
	Yr	61	172	15	35	6	5	2	14	9	34	.203	.243	.331	574	70	-7	6			.966	-4	O-50(10-19-22)	-1.5
1919	Bos-N	63	240	34	68	8	5	4	17	25	30	.283	.356	.408	764	135	10	9			.950	2	O-61(0-61-0)	0.9
Total	3	174	558	68	134	18	14	8	44	46	64	.240	.305	.366	671	98	-2	20			.950	-6	O-150(31-91-28)	-1.7
■ ADAM RIGGS Riggs, Adam David b: 10/4/72, Steubenville, O. BR/TR, 6', 195 lbs. Deb: 8/7/97																								
1997	LA-N	9	20	3	4	1	0	0	1	4	3	.200	.333	.250	583	60	-1	1	0	0	1.000	0	/2-8	-0.1
■ LEW RIGGS Riggs, Lewis Sidney b: 4/22/10, Mebane, N.C. d: 8/12/75, Durham, N.C. BL/TR, 6', 175 lbs. Deb: 4/28/34																								
1934	StL-N	2	1	0	0	0	0	0	0	0	1	.000	.000	.000	0	-94	-0	0			.000	0	H	0.0
1935	Cin-N	142	532	73	148	26	8	5	46	43	32	.278	.334	.385	720	96	-3	8			.928	8	*3-135	0.9
1936	Cin-N★	141	538	69	138	20	12	6	57	38	33	.257	.314	.372	686	90	-9	5			.968	12	*3-140	0.8
1937	Cin-N	122	384	43	93	17	5	6	45	24	17	.242	.289	.359	648	79	-12	4			.941	20	*3-100/2-4,S-1	1.1
1938	Cin-N	142	531	53	134	21	13	2	55	40	28	.252	.311	.352	663	84	-12	3			.947	-1	*3-140	-0.8
1939	Cin-N	22	38	5	6	1	0	0	1	5	4	.158	.256	.184	440	20	-4	1			.957	-1	3-11	-0.5
1940	*Cin-N	41	72	8	21	7	1	1	9	2	4	.292	.311	.458	769	109	0	0			.943	2	3-11	0.3
1941	*Bro-N	77	197	27	60	13	4	5	36	16	12	.305	.357	.487	844	131	7	1			.932	-7	3-43/1-1,2-1	0.2
1942	Bro-N	70	180	20	50	5	0	3	22	13	9	.278	.333	.356	689	100	-0	0			.944	-6	3-46/1-1	-0.5
1946	Bro-N	1	4	0	0	0	0	0	0	0	0	.000	.000	.000	0	-99	-1	0			1.000	0	/3-1	-0.1
Total	10	760	2477	298	650	110	43	28	271	181	140	.262	.317	.375	692	91	-34	22			.945	27	3-627/2-5,1-2,S-1	1.4
■ TOPPER RIGNEY Rigney, Emory Elmo b: 1/7/1897, Groveton, Tex. d: 6/6/72, San Antonio, Tex. BR/TR, 5'9", 150 lbs. Deb: 4/12/22																								
1922	Det-A	155	536	68	161	17	7	2	63	68	44	.300	.380	.369	750	99	2	17	8	1	.938	-13	*S-155	0.6
1923	Det-A	129	470	63	148	24	11	1	74	55	35	.315	.389	.419	808	115	11	7	5	-0	.944	-16	*S-129	0.9
1924	Det-A	147	499	81	144	29	9	4	94	102	39	.289	.410	.407	817	113	14	11	11	-1	**.967**	10	*S-146	3.6
1925	Det-A	62	146	21	36	5	2	2	18	21	15	.247	.341	.349	691	77	-5	2	2	-0	.934	-14	S-51/3-4	-1.4
1926	Bos-A	148	525	71	142	32	6	4	53	108	31	.270	.395	.377	772	105	9	6	8	-1	**.969**	20	*S-146	4.1
1927	Bos-A	8	18	0	2	1	0	0	0	1	2	.111	.158	.167	325	-16	-3	0	0	0	1.000	-1	/3-4,S-1	-0.4
	Was-A	45	132	20	36	5	4	0	13	22	10	.273	.381	.371	752	97	0	1	2	-0	.929	-3	S-32/3-6	0.1
	Yr	53	150	20	38	6	4	0	13	23	12	.253	.356	.347	703	84	-3	1	2	-0	.932	-4	S-33,3-10	-0.3
Total	6	694	2326	324	669	113	39	13	315	377	176	.288	.388	.387	775	104	28	44	36	-3	.953	-18	S-660/3-14	7.5
■ BILL RIGNEY Rigney, William Joseph "Specs" or "The Cricket" b: 1/29/18, Alameda, Cal. BR/TR, 6'1", 178 lbs. Deb: 4/16/46 MC																								
1946	NY-N	110	360	38	85	9	1	3	31	36	29	.236	.307	.292	599	70	-14	9			.965	3	3-73,S-33	-1.0
1947	NY-N	130	531	84	142	24	3	17	59	51	54	.267	.337	.420	757	99	-1	7			.974	1	2-72,3-41,S-24	0.4
1948	NY-N★	113	424	72	112	17	3	10	43	47	54	.264	.342	.389	731	97	-2	4			.967	-11	*2-105/S-7	-0.7
1949	NY-N	122	389	53	108	19	6	6	47	47	38	.278	.356	.404	759	103	2	3			.928	-17	S-81,2-26,3-14	-0.8
1950	NY-N	56	83	8	15	2	0	0	8	8	13	.181	.253	.205	458	22	-9	0			.966	6	2-23,3-11	-0.3
1951	*NY-N	44	69	9	16	2	0	4	9	8	7	.232	.321	.435	755	100	-0	0	1	-0	.953	5	3-12/2-9	0.5
1952	NY-N	60	90	15	27	5	1	1	14	11	6	.300	.388	.411	799	121	3	2	3	-1	.889	-1	3-10/2-9,S-4,1-1	0.2

YEAR	TM/L	G	AB	R	H	2B	3B	HR	RBI	BB	SO	AVG	OBP	SLG	OPS	OPS+	BR+	SB	CS	SBR	FA	FR	G/POS	TPR
1953	NY-N	19	20	2	5	0	0	0	1	0	5	.250	.250	.250	500	30	-2	0	0	0	1.000	0	/3-2,2-1	-0.2
Total	8	654	1966	281	510	78	14	41	212	208	206	.259	.334	.376	710	91	-23	25	4		.971	-13	2-245,3-163,S-149,/1	-1.9
■ CULLEY RIKARD	Rikard, Culley b: 5/9/14, Oxford, Miss. d: 2/25/2000, Memphis, Tenn. BL/TR, 5′11″, 183 lbs. Deb: 9/20/41																							
1941	Pit-N	6	20	1	4	1	0	0	0	1	1	.200	.238	.250	488	38	-2	0			1.000	1	/O-5(3-3-0)	-0.1
1942	Pit-N	38	52	6	10	2	1	0	5	7	8	.192	.288	.269	557	62	-2	0			.958	-4	O-16(2-14-0)	-0.7
1947	Pit-N	109	324	57	93	16	4	4	32	50	39	.287	.384	.398	782	105	4	1			.978	-1	O-79(5-28-45)	0.0
Total	3	153	396	64	107	19	5	4	37	58	48	.270	.365	.374	739	97	-0	1			.978	-4	O-100(10-45-45)	-0.8
■ ERNEST RILES	Riles, Ernest b: 10/2/60, Cairo, Ga. BL/TR, 6′1″, 180 lbs. Deb: 5/14/85 Career OF: (2-LF 0-CF 3-RF)																							
1985	Mil-A	116	448	54	128	12	7	5	45	36	54	.286	.342	.377	719	97	-1	2	2	-0	.957	-19	*S-115/D-1	-0.8
1986	Mil-A	145	524	69	132	24	2	9	47	54	80	.252	.323	.357	680	82	-12	7	7	-1	.964	-30	*S-142	-2.8
1987	Mil-A	83	276	38	72	11	1	4	38	30	47	.261	.336	.351	687	80	-7	3	4	-1	.935	-6	3-65,S-21	-1.2
1988	Mil-A	41	127	7	32	6	1	1	9	7	26	.252	.291	.339	630	75	-4	2	2	-0	.958	1	3-28/S-9,D-5	-0.3
	SF-N	79	187	26	55	7	2	3	28	10	33	.294	.330	.401	731	114	3	1	2	-0	.975	8	3-30,2-17,S-16	1.2
1989	*SF-N	122	302	43	84	13	2	7	40	28	50	.278	.343	.404	747	116	6	0	6	-2	.962	-10	3-83,2-18/S-7,O-5R	-0.6
1990	SF-N	92	155	22	31	2	1	8	21	26	26	.200	.315	.381	696	94	-1	0	0	0	.986	-4	S-26,2-24,3-10	-0.4
1991	Oak-A	108	281	30	60	8	4	5	32	31	42	.214	.294	.324	618	75	-10	3	2	-0	.939	-10	3-69,S-20/2-7,1-5	-1.9
1992	Hou-N	39	61	5	16	1	0	1	4	2	11	.262	.286	.328	614	77	-2	1	0	0	1.000	-2	/S-6,3-5,1-4,2-2	-0.4
1993	Bos-A	94	143	15	27	8	0	5	20	20	40	.189	.297	.350	647	69	-6	1	3	-1	1.000	5	2-20,D-15,3-11,/1-1	-0.3
Total	9	919	2504	309	637	92	20	48	284	244	409	.254	.323	.365	687	89	-36	20	28	-5	.964	-67	S-362,3-301/2-88,D10	-7.5
■ JIM RILEY	Riley, James Joseph b: 11/10/1886, Buffalo, N.Y. d: 3/25/49, Buffalo, N.Y. BR/TR, 6′, 165 lbs. Deb: 8/2/10																							
1910	Bos-N	1	1	0	0	0	0	0	0	1	1	.000	.500	.000	500	46	0	0			.600	-0	/O-1(1-0-0)	0.0
■ JIM RILEY	Riley, James Norman b: 5/25/1895, Bayfield, N.B., Can d: 5/25/69, Seguin, Tex. BL/TR, 5′10.5″, 185 lbs. Deb: 7/3/21																							
1921	StL-A	4	11	0	0	0	0	0	0	1	3	.000	.083	.000	83	-73	-3	0	0	0	.818	-3	/2-4	-0.6
1923	Was-A	2	3	1	0	0	0	0	0	2	0	.000	.400	.000	400	12	-0	0	0	0	.882	-1	/1-2	-0.1
Total	2	6	14	1	0	0	0	0	0	3	3	.000	.176	.000	176	-50	-3	0	0	0	.818	-4	/2-4,1-2	-0.7
■ LEE RILEY	Riley, Leon Francis b: 8/20/06, Princeton, Neb. d: 9/13/70, Schenectady, N.Y. BL/TR, 6′1″, 185 lbs. Deb: 4/19/44																							
1944	Phi-N	4	12	1	1	1	0	0	1	0	0	.083	.083	.167	250	-32	-2	0			1.000	-1	/O-3(3-0-0)	-0.4
■ BILLY RILEY	Riley, William James "Pigtail Billy" b: 1855, Cincinnati, Ohio d: 11/9/1887, Cincinnati, Ohio BR/TR, 5′10″, 160 lbs. Deb: 5/5/1875																							
1875	Wes-n	8	33	4	5	1	0	0	1	1	1	.152	.176	.182	358	23	-3	0	0	0	.667	-0	/O-8(0-0-8)	-0.2
1879	Cle-N	43	161	14	23	2	0	0	9	2	26	.143	.153	.155	309	2	-16				.850	5	O-43(43-0-0)	-1.3
■ FRANK RINGO	Ringo, Frank C. b: 10/12/1860, Parkville, Mo. d: 4/12/1889, Kansas City, Mo. BR, 5′11″, 175 lbs. Deb: 5/1/1883 Career OF: (3-LF 11-CF 0-RF)																							
1883	Phi-N	60	221	24	42	10	1	0	12	6	34	.190	.211	.244	456	42	-14				.847	-9	C-39,O-11C/S-6,32	-1.7
1884	Phi-N	26	91	4	12	2	0	0	6	3	19	.132	.160	.154	313	-1	-10				.783	-16	C-26	-2.2
	Phi-a	2	6	0	0	0	0	0		0		.000	.000	.000	0	-94	-1				.762	1	/C-2	0.0
1885	Det-N	17	65	12	16	3	0	0	2	0	7	.246	.246	.292	538	73	-2				.852	2	/C-8,3-8,O-1(0-1-0)	0.1
	Pit-a	3	11	0	2	0	0	0	0	0		.182	.182	.182	364	15	-1				.941	3	/C-3	0.2
1886	Pit-a	15	56	3	12	2	2	0	5	1		.214	.228	.321	549	72	-2	0			.934	-0	/1-9,C-6	-0.2
	KC-N	16	56	6	13	7	0	0	7	5	10	.232	.295	.357	652	92	-1	0			.904	-6	C-13/O-2(0-2-0),3-1	-0.5
Total	4	139	506	49	97	24	3	0	32	15	70	.192	.215	.251	466	46	-31	0			.844	-24	/C-97,3-14,O-14C,1S2	-4.3
■ BOB RINKER	Rinker, Robert John b: 4/21/21, Audenried, Pa. BR/TR, 6′, 190 lbs. Deb: 9/6/50																							
1950	Phi-A	3	3	0	1	0	0	0	0	0	0	.333	.333	.333	667	72	-0	0	0	0	.000	0	/C-1	0.0
■ ARMANDO RIOS	Rios, Armando b: 9/13/71, Santurce, P.R. BL/TL, 5′9″, 180 lbs. Deb: 9/1/98																							
1998	SF-N	12	7	3	4	0	0	2	3	3	2	.571	.700	1.429	2129	469	4	0	0	0	1.000	-1	/O-5(2-1-2)	0.3
1999	SF-N	72	150	32	49	9	0	7	29	24	35	.327	.423	.527	950	149	12	7	4	0	.978	-1	O-53(14-2-39)	0.9
2000	*SF-N	115	233	38	62	15	5	10	50	31	43	.266	.352	.502	854	121	7	3	2	-0	.959	-6	O-93(19-0-76)/1-1	-0.2
Total	3	199	390	73	115	24	5	19	82	58	80	.295	.388	.528	916	138	23	10	6	0	.967	-8	O-151(35-3-117)/1-1	1.0
■ JUAN RIOS	Rios, Juan Onofre Velez (b: Juan Onofre Velez (Rios)) b: 6/14/42, Mayaguez, P.R. d: 8/28/95, Mayaguez, P.R. BR/TR, 6′3″, 185 lbs. Deb: 4/9/69																							
1969	KC-A	87	196	20	44	5	1	1	5	7	19	.224	.262	.276	538	50	-13	1	3	-1	.967	-16	2-46,S-32/3-4	-2.8
■ CAL RIPKEN	Ripken, Calvin Edwin Jr. b: 8/24/60, Havre De Grace, Md. BR/TR, 6′4″, 225 lbs. Deb: 8/10/81 F																							
1981	Bal-A	23	39	1	5	0	0	0	0	1	8	.128	.150	.128	278	-19	-6	0	0	0	.946	0	S-12/3-6	-0.6
1982	Bal-A	160	598	90	158	32	5	28	93	46	95	.264	.320	.475	795	115	11	3	3	-0	.972	-7	S-94,3-71	1.2
1983	*Bal-A★	162	663	**121**	**211**	**47**	2	27	102	58	97	.318	.373	.517	890	145	39	0	4	-1	.970	16	*S-162	**7.0**
1984	Bal-A★	162	641	103	195	37	7	27	86	71	89	.304	.375	.510	885	146	39	2	1	0	.971	**39**	*S-162	**9.3**
1985	Bal-A★	161	642	116	181	32	5	26	110	67	68	.282	.351	.469	820	125	22	2	3	-1	.967	7	*S-161	4.5
1986	Bal-A★	162	627	98	177	35	1	25	81	70	60	.282	.358	.461	819	123	20	4	2	0	.982	10	*S-162	4.6
1987	Bal-A★	162	624	97	157	28	3	27	98	81	77	.252	.339	.436	774	106	6	3	5	-1	.973	-4	*S-162	1.7
1988	Bal-A★	161	575	87	152	25	1	23	81	102	69	.264	.377	.431	808	129	26	2	2	-0	.973	-2	*S-161	3.6
1989	Bal-A★	162	646	80	166	30	0	21	93	57	72	.257	.320	.401	721	105	3	3	2	-0	.990	4	*S-162	2.0
1990	Bal-A★	161	600	78	150	28	4	21	84	82	66	.250	.345	.415	760	115	13	3	1	0	**.996**	-29	*S-161	-0.4
1991	Bal-A★	162	650	99	210	46	5	34	114	53	46	.323	.379	.566	945	164	54	6	1	1	**.986**	18	*S-162	**8.3**
1992	Bal-A★	162	637	73	160	29	1	14	72	64	50	.251	.326	.366	692	91	-7	4	3	-0	.984	-13	*S-162	-0.7
1993	Bal-A★	162	641	87	165	26	3	24	90	65	58	.257	.331	.420	751	96	-4	1	4	-1	.977	-5	*S-162	0.4
1994	Bal-A★	112	444	71	140	19	3	13	75	32	41	.315	.367	.459	826	106	4	1	0	0	**.985**	-13	*S-112	0.1
1995	Bal-A★	144	550	71	144	33	2	17	88	52	59	.262	.328	.422	750	92	-7	0	1	-0	**.989**	-1	*S-144	0.3
1996	*Bal-A★	163	640	94	178	40	1	26	102	59	78	.278	.343	.466	808	102	1	1	2	-0	.980	0	*S-158/3-6	1.3
1997	*Bal-A★	162	615	79	166	30	0	17	84	56	73	.270	.336	.402	737	94	-5	1	0	0	.949	6	*3-162/S-3	0.2
1998	Bal-A★	161	601	65	163	27	1	14	61	51	68	.271	.332	.389	722	88	-10	0	2	-1	**.979**	-3	*3-161	-1.2
1999	Bal-A★	86	332	51	113	27	0	18	57	13	31	.340	.371	.584	955	144	20	0	1	-0	.932	-11	3-85	0.9
2000	Bal-A†	83	309	43	79	16	0	15	56	23	37	.256	.313	.453	767	94	-4	0	0	0	.974	1	3-73,D-10	-0.3
Total	20	2873	11074	1604	3070	587	44	417	1627	1103	1242	.277	.346	.451	797	114	215	36	37	-5	.979	13	*S-2302,3-564/D-10	42.2
■ BILLY RIPKEN	Ripken, William Oliver b: 12/16/64, Havre De Grace, Md. BR/TR, 6′1″, 186 lbs. Deb: 7/11/87 F																							
1987	Bal-A	58	234	27	72	9	0	2	20	21	23	.308	.365	.372	737	99	0	4	1	1	.990	-3	2-58	0.1
1988	Bal-A	150	512	52	106	18	1	2	34	33	63	.207	.262	.258	520	47	-36	8	2	1	.984	2	*2-149/3-2,D-1	-2.9
1989	Bal-A	115	318	31	76	11	2	2	26	22	53	.239	.288	.305	593	69	-13	1	2	-0	.985	13	*2-114/D-1	0.2
1990	Bal-A	129	406	48	118	28	1	3	38	28	43	.291	.342	.387	729	107	4	5	2	0	.987	-9	*2-127	-0.1
1991	Bal-A	104	287	24	62	11	1	0	14	15	31	.216	.255	.261	516	45	-21	0	1	-0	.986	4	*2-103	-1.5
1992	Bal-A	111	330	35	76	15	0	4	36	18	26	.230	.276	.312	588	63	-17	2	3	-1	**.993**	0	*2-108/D-2	-1.5
1993	Tex-A	50	132	12	25	4	0	0	11	11	19	.189	.272	.220	492	35	-12	0	2	-1	.992	4	2-34,S-18/3-1	-0.6
1994	Tex-A	32	81	9	25	5	0	0	6	3	11	.309	.333	.370	704	81	-2	2	0	0	.970	2	3-18,2-12/S-2,1-1	0.0
1995	Cle-A	8	17	4	7	0	0	2	3	0	3	.412	.412	.765	1176	195	2	0	0	0	1.000	-3	/2-7,3-1	0.0
1996	Bal-A	57	135	19	31	8	0	2	12	9	18	.230	.283	.333	616	55	-9	0	0	0	.968	6	2-30,3-25/1-1	-0.3
1997	Tex-A	71	203	18	56	9	1	3	24	9	32	.276	.307	.374	681	73	-8	0	1	-0	.971	6	S-31,2-25,3-13,/1-9	0.0
1998	Det-A	27	74	8	20	3	0	0	5	5	10	.270	.325	.311	636	66	-4	3	2	-0	.926	-2	S-21/1-2,2-2,3-2,D	-0.3
Total	12	912	2729	287	674	121	6	20	229	174	332	.247	.296	.318	614	69	-116	25	16	-0	.987	20	2-769/S-72,3-62,1D	-6.9
■ JIMMY RIPPLE	Ripple, James Albert b: 10/14/09, Export, Pa. d: 7/16/59, Greensburg, Pa. BL/TR, 5′10″, 170 lbs. Deb: 4/20/36																							
1936	*NY-N	96	311	42	95	17	2	7	47	28	15	.305	.365	.441	805	117	7	1			.980	-0	O-76(0-75-1)	0.5
1937	*NY-N	121	426	70	135	23	3	5	66	29	20	.317	.362	.420	782	110	6	3			.980	-9	*O-111(0-54-57)	-0.8
1938	NY-N	134	501	68	131	21	3	10	60	49	21	.261	.333	.375	709	94	-4	2			.976	-3	*O-131(0-17-115)	-1.5
1939	NY-N	66	123	10	28	4	0	1	12	8	7	.228	.286	.285	570	53	-8	0			1.000	-2	O-23(9-4-10)	-1.1

YEAR	TM/L	G	AB	R	H	2B	3B	HR	RBI	BB	SO	AVG	OBP	SLG	OPS	OPS+	BR+	SB	CS	SBR	FA	FR	G/POS	TPR
	Bro-N	28	106	18	35	8	4	0	22	11	8	.330	.398	.481	879	131	5	0			1.000	-2	O-28(12-1-15)	0.1
	Yr	94	229	28	63	12	4	1	34	19	15	.275	.339	.376	714	90	-3	0			1.000	-3	O-51(21-5-25)	-1.0
1940	Bro-N	7	13	0	3	0	0	0	0	2	2	.231	.333	.231	564	55	-1	0			1.000	1	/O-3(1-0-2)	0.0
	*Cin-N	32	101	15	31	10	0	4	20	13	5	.307	.397	.525	921	151	7	1			1.000	-5	O-30(27-0-3)	0.1
	Yr	39	114	15	34	10	0	4	20	15	7	.298	.389	.491	881	139	6	1			1.000	-4	O-33(28-0-5)	0.1
1941	Cin-N	38	102	10	22	6	1	1	9	9	4	.216	.279	.324	603	69	-4	0			1.000	-2	O-25(7-0-18)	-0.9
1943	Phi-A	32	126	8	30	3	1	0	15	7	7	.238	.284	.278	561	65	-6	0	0	0	1.000	-4	O-31(10-0-21)	-1.3
Total	7	554	1809	241	510	92	14	28	251	156	89	.282	.343	.395	738	101	3	7	0		.984	-27	O-458(66-151-242)	-4.9

■ SWEDE RISBERG

Risberg, Charles August b: 10/13/1894, San Francisco, Cal d: 10/13/75, Red Bluff, Cal. BR/TR, 6′, 175 lbs. Deb: 4/11/17 Career OF: (0-LF 0-CF 3-RF)

YEAR	TM/L	G	AB	R	H	2B	3B	HR	RBI	BB	SO	AVG	OBP	SLG	OPS	OPS+	BR+	SB	CS	SBR	FA	FR	G/POS	TPR
1917	*Chi-A	149	474	59	96	20	8	1	45	59	65	.203	.297	.285	582	76	-13	16			.913	-39	*S-146	-4.8
1918	Chi-A	82	273	36	70	12	3	1	27	23	32	.256	.321	.333	654	97	-1	5			.944	-8	S-30,3-24,2-12,/1O	-0.8
1919	*Chi-A	119	414	48	106	19	6	2	38	35	38	.256	.317	.345	662	86	-8	19			.934	-13	S-97,1-22	-1.6
1920	Chi-A	126	458	53	122	21	10	2	65	31	45	.266	.316	.369	685	81	-14	12	10	-1	.934	-4	*S-124	-1.0
Total	4	476	1619	196	394	72	27	6	175	148	180	.243	.311	.332	644	83	-36	52	10		.928	-64	S-397/1-29,3-24,2O	-8.2

■ POP RISING

Rising, Percival Sumner b: 1/2/1872, Industry, Pa. d: 1/28/38, Rochester, Pa. Deb: 8/10/05

YEAR	TM/L	G	AB	R	H	2B	3B	HR	RBI	BB	SO	AVG	OBP	SLG	OPS	OPS+	BR+	SB	CS	SBR	FA	FR	G/POS	TPR
1905	Bos-A	11	29	2	3	1	1	0	2	2		.103	.161	.207	368	16	-3	0			1.000	0	/O-6(0-0-6),3-1	-0.3

■ CLAUDE RITCHEY

Ritchey, Claude Cassius "Little All Right" b: 10/5/1873, Emlenton, Pa. d: 11/8/51, Emlenton, Pa. BB/TR, 5′6.5″, 167 lbs. Deb: 4/22/1897 Career OF: (10-LF 1-CF 12-RF)

YEAR	TM/L	G	AB	R	H	2B	3B	HR	RBI	BB	SO	AVG	OBP	SLG	OPS	OPS+	BR+	SB	CS	SBR	FA	FR	G/POS	TPR
1897	Cin-N	101	337	58	95	12	4	0	41	42		.282	.370	.341	711	83	-7	11			.897	-16	S-70,O-22R/2-8	-1.8
1898	Lou-N	151	551	65	140	10	4	5	51	46		.254	.322	.314	636	84	-11	19			.919	-16	S-80,2-71	-1.9
1899	Lou-N	148	540	66	162	16	7	4	73	49		.300	.369	.378	747	105	5	21			.938	-4	*2-138,S-11	0.7
1900	*Pit-N	123	476	62	139	17	8	1	67	29		.292	.339	.368	707	94	-4	18			.952	7	*2-123	0.8
1901	Pit-N	140	540	66	160	20	4	1	74	47		.296	.358	.354	712	104	4	15			.941	2	*2-139/S-1	0.7
1902	Pit-N	115	405	54	112	13	1	2	55	53		.277	.370	.328	698	112	8	10			**.966**	6	*2-114/O-1(0-0-1)	1.5
1903	*Pit-N	138	506	66	145	28	10	0	59	55		.287	.360	.381	741	108	6	15			**.961**	19	*2-137	2.5
1904	Pit-N	156	544	79	143	22	12	0	51	59		.263	.338	.347	686	109	7	12			.958	-2	*2-156/S-2	0.6
1905	Pit-N	153	533	54	136	29	6	0	52	51		.255	.324	.332	656	93	-4	12			**.961**	-5	*2-153/S-2	-0.8
1906	Pit-N	152	484	46	130	21	5	1	62	68		.269	.369	.339	708	116	12	6			**.966**	1	*2-151	1.5
1907	Bos-N	144	499	45	127	17	4	2	51	50		.255	.329	.317	645	103	2	8			**.971**	14	*2-144	2.0
1908	Bos-N	121	421	44	115	10	3	2	36	50		.273	.361	.325	687	121	13	7			.967	16	*2-120	3.3
1909	Bos-N	30	87	4	15	1	0	0	3	8		.172	.242	.184	426	31	-7	1			.959	0	2-25	-0.7
Total	13	1672	5923	709	1619	216	68	18	675	607		.273	.348	.342	690	101	21	155			.957	22	*2-1479,S-166/O-23R	8.4

■ CHARLIE RITTER

Ritter, Charles J. Deb: 9/21/1885

YEAR	TM/L	G	AB	R	H	2B	3B	HR	RBI	BB	SO	AVG	OBP	SLG	OPS	OPS+	BR+	SB	CS	SBR	FA	FR	G/POS	TPR
1885	Buf-N	2	6	0	1	0	0	0	0	0	2	.167	.167	.167	333	8	-1				.813	0	/2-2	0.0

■ FLOYD RITTER

Ritter, Floyd Alexander b: 6/1/1870, Dorset, Ohio d: 2/7/43, Stevenson, Wash. BR/TR, 5′8″, 155 lbs. Deb: 6/4/1890

YEAR	TM/L	G	AB	R	H	2B	3B	HR	RBI	BB	SO	AVG	OBP	SLG	OPS	OPS+	BR+	SB	CS	SBR	FA	FR	G/POS	TPR
1890	Tol-a	1	3	0	0	0	0	0	0	0		.000	.000	.000	0	-97	-1	0			.778	0	/C-1	-0.1

■ LEW RITTER

Ritter, Lewis Elmer "Old Dog" b: 9/7/1875, Liverpool, Pa. d: 5/27/52, Harrisburg, Pa. BR/TR, 5′9″, 150 lbs. Deb: 9/10/02 Career OF: (6-LF 2-CF 8-RF)

YEAR	TM/L	G	AB	R	H	2B	3B	HR	RBI	BB	SO	AVG	OBP	SLG	OPS	OPS+	BR+	SB	CS	SBR	FA	FR	G/POS	TPR
1902	Bro-N	16	57	5	12	1	0	0	2	1		.211	.237	.228	465	43	-4	2			.973	3	C-16	0.1
1903	Bro-N	78	259	26	61	9	6	0	37	19		.236	.290	.317	607	75	-9	9			.940	-17	C-74/O-2(1-1-0)	-1.8
1904	Bro-N	72	214	23	53	4	1	0	19	20		.248	.318	.276	593	86	-3	17			.966	5	C-57/2-5,3-1	0.9
1905	Bro-N	92	311	32	68	10	5	1	28	15		.219	.255	.293	547	68	-13	16			.951	-14	C-84/O-4(0-1-3),3-2	-2.0
1906	Bro-N	73	226	22	47	1	3	0	15	16		.208	.263	.239	502	61	-10	6			.978	-8	C-53/O-9L,1-3,3-2	-1.5
1907	Bro-N	93	271	15	55	6	1	0	17	18		.203	.255	.232	488	57	-13	5			.969	-1	C-89	-0.7
1908	Bro-N	38	99	6	19	2	1	0	2	7		.192	.245	.232	478	55	-5	0			.961	-3	C-37	-0.6
Total	7	462	1437	129	315	33	17	1	120	96		.219	.271	.268	539	67	-57	55			.960	-36	C-410/O-15R,3-5,21	-5.6

■ WHITEY RITTERSON

Ritterson, Edward West b: 4/26/1855, Philadelphia, Pa. d: 7/28/17, Sellersville, Pa. BR/TR, 5′8″, Deb: 5/3/1876

YEAR	TM/L	G	AB	R	H	2B	3B	HR	RBI	BB	SO	AVG	OBP	SLG	OPS	OPS+	BR+	SB	CS	SBR	FA	FR	G/POS	TPR
1876	Phi-N	16	52	8	13	3	0	0	4	0	2	.250	.250	.308	558	86	-1				.671	-8	C-14/O-4(0-2-2),3-1	-0.7

■ JIM RITZ

Ritz, James L. b: 1874, Pittsburgh, Pa. d: 11/10/1896, Pittsburgh, Pa. Deb: 7/20/1894

YEAR	TM/L	G	AB	R	H	2B	3B	HR	RBI	BB	SO	AVG	OBP	SLG	OPS	OPS+	BR+	SB	CS	SBR	FA	FR	G/POS	TPR
1894	Pit-N	1	4	1	0	0	0	0	0	0	0	.000	.200	.000	200	-49	-1	1			.750	-0	/3-1	-0.1

■ LUIS RIVAS

Rivas, Luis Wilfredo b: 8/30/79, LaGuaira, Venez. BR/TR, 5′10″, 175 lbs. Deb: 9/16/2000

YEAR	TM/L	G	AB	R	H	2B	3B	HR	RBI	BB	SO	AVG	OBP	SLG	OPS	OPS+	BR+	SB	CS	SBR	FA	FR	G/POS	TPR
2000	Min-A	16	58	8	18	4	1	0	6	2	4	.310	.333	.414	747	83	-2	2	0	0	.983	-6	2-14/S-2	-0.6

■ GERMAN RIVERA

Rivera, German (Diaz) b: 7/6/60, Santurce, P.R. BR/TR, 6′2″, 195 lbs. Deb: 9/2/83

YEAR	TM/L	G	AB	R	H	2B	3B	HR	RBI	BB	SO	AVG	OBP	SLG	OPS	OPS+	BR+	SB	CS	SBR	FA	FR	G/POS	TPR
1983	LA-N	13	17	1	6	1	0	0	0	2	2	.353	.421	.412	833	132	1	0	1	-0	.929	2	/3-8	0.2
1984	LA-N	94	227	20	59	12	2	2	17	21	30	.260	.325	.357	682	92	-2	1	0	0	.937	16	3-90	1.3
1985	Hou-N	13	36	3	7	2	1	0	2	4	8	.194	.275	.306	581	64	-2	0	0	0	.941	3	3-11	0.1
Total	3	120	280	24	72	15	3	2	19	27	40	.257	.325	.354	678	91	-3	1	1	-0	.937	20	3-109	1.6

■ BOMBO RIVERA

Rivera, Jesus Manuel (Torres) b: 8/2/52, Ponce, P.R. BR/TR, 5′10″, 187 lbs. Deb: 4/17/75

YEAR	TM/L	G	AB	R	H	2B	3B	HR	RBI	BB	SO	AVG	OBP	SLG	OPS	OPS+	BR+	SB	CS	SBR	FA	FR	G/POS	TPR
1975	Mon-N	5	9	1	1	0	0	0	0	2	3	.111	.273	.111	384	9	-1	0	0	0	.889	-1	/O-5(4-0-2)	-0.2
1976	Mon-N	68	185	22	51	11	4	2	19	13	32	.276	.323	.411	734	103	0	1	0	0	.950	-0	O-56(44-0-15)	-0.2
1978	Min-A	101	251	35	68	8	2	3	23	35	47	.271	.365	.355	719	101	2	5	3	0	.982	-9	O-94(32-0-72)/D-1	-1.1
1979	Min-A	112	263	37	74	13	5	2	31	17	40	.281	.325	.392	717	89	-4	5	5	-1	.989	-4	*O-105(61-1-50)/D-2	-1.2
1980	Min-A	44	113	13	25	7	0	3	10	4	20	.221	.248	.363	611	61	-6	0	0	0	.922	-4	O-37(10-0-28)/D-1	-1.2
1982	KC-A	5	10	1	1	0	0	0	0	0	2	.100	.100	.100	200	-45	-2	0	0	0	1.000	-1	/O-3(2-0-1)	-0.3
Total	6	335	831	109	220	39	11	10	83	71	144	.265	.324	.374	698	90	-12	11	8	-0	.970	-19	O-300(153-1-168)/D-4	-4.2

■ LUIS RIVERA

Rivera, Luis Antonio (Pedraza) b: 1/3/64, Cidra, P.R. BR/TR, 5′9″, 170 lbs. Deb: 8/3/86 Career OF: (1-LF 0-CF 0-RF)

YEAR	TM/L	G	AB	R	H	2B	3B	HR	RBI	BB	SO	AVG	OBP	SLG	OPS	OPS+	BR+	SB	CS	SBR	FA	FR	G/POS	TPR
1986	Mon-N	55	166	20	34	11	1	0	13	17	33	.205	.286	.283	570	58	-9	1	1	-0	.953	-9	S-55	-1.4
1987	Mon-N	18	32	0	5	2	0	0	1	1	8	.156	.182	.219	401	5	-4	0	0	0	.923	2	S-15	-0.2
1988	Mon-N	123	371	35	83	17	3	4	30	24	69	.224	.273	.318	591	66	-16	3	4	-1	.962	-6	*S-116	-1.6
1989	Bos-A	93	323	35	83	17	1	5	29	20	60	.257	.302	.362	665	81	-8	2	3	-1	.958	-3	S-90/2-1,D-1	-0.6
1990	*Bos-A	118	346	38	78	20	0	7	45	25	58	.225	.280	.344	624	70	-14	4	3	-0	.965	11	*S-112/2-3,3-1	0.4
1991	Bos-A	129	414	64	107	22	3	8	40	35	86	.258	.321	.384	705	90	-6	4	4	-1	.959	3	*S-129	0.7
1992	Bos-A	102	288	17	62	11	1	0	29	26	56	.215	.287	.260	547	51	-18	4	3	-0	.966	14	S-93/2-1,3-1,O-1L,D	0.2
1993	Bos-A	62	130	13	27	8	1	1	7	11	36	.208	.275	.308	582	53	-9	1	2	-0	.969	12	2-27,S-27/3-2,D-7	0.5
1994	NY-N	32	43	11	12	2	1	3	5	4	14	.279	.367	.581	949	144	3	0	1	-0	.971	5	S-11/2-5	0.7
1997	Hou-N	7	13	2	3	0	1	0	3	1	6	.231	.286	.385	670	76	-0	0	0	0	.875	0	/S-6,2-1	0.0
1998	KC-A	42	89	14	22	4	0	0	7	7	17	.247	.302	.292	594	54	-6	1	1	-0	.961	6	S-30/2-6,3-6	0.2
Total	11	781	2215	249	516	114	12	28	209	171	443	.233	.292	.333	625	70	-89	20	22	-3	.961	35	S-684/2-44,3-10,DO	-1.1

■ JIM RIVERA

Rivera, Manuel Joseph "Jungle Jim" b: 7/22/22, New York, N.Y. BL/TL, 6′, 196 lbs. Deb: 4/15/52 Career OF: (98-LF 392-CF 594-RF)

YEAR	TM/L	G	AB	R	H	2B	3B	HR	RBI	BB	SO	AVG	OBP	SLG	OPS	OPS+	BR+	SB	CS	SBR	FA	FR	G/POS	TPR
1952	StL-A	97	336	45	86	13	6	4	30	29	59	.256	.319	.366	685	88	-6	8	7	-1	.976	9	O-88(8-81-0)	-0.1
	Chi-A	53	201	27	50	7	3	3	18	21	27	.249	.320	.358	678	88	-4	13	2	2	.988	4	O-53(0-53-0)	0.1
	Yr	150	537	72	136	20	9	7	48	50	86	.253	.319	.363	682	88	-9	21	9	1	.980	12	*O-141(8-134-0)	0.0
1953	Chi-A	156	567	79	147	26	**16**	11	78	53	70	.259	.329	.420	749	98	-3	22	15	-0	.976	-1	*O-156(0-153-3)	-1.2
1954	Chi-A	145	490	62	140	16	8	13	61	49	68	.286	.358	.431	788	111	7	18	10	0	.959	-17	*O-143(3-28-128)	-1.5
1955	Chi-A	147	454	71	120	24	4	10	52	62	59	.264	.354	.401	755	100	0	**25**	16	-0	.981	2	*O-143(2-50-115)	-0.3
1956	Chi-A	139	491	76	125	23	5	12	66	49	75	.255	.326	.395	721	88	-9	20	9	1	.976	1	*O-134(0-14-122)	-1.1
1957	Chi-A	125	402	51	103	21	6	14	52	40	80	.256	.328	.443	771	108	4	18	2	3	.974	-7	O-86(1-4-83),1-31	-0.5
1958	Chi-A	116	276	37	62	8	4	9	35	24	49	.225	.289	.380	669	84	-7	21	3	4	.994	-3	O-99(54-1-45)	-1.0
1959	*Chi-A	80	177	18	39	9	4	4	19	11	19	.220	.270	.384	654	78	-6	5	3	0	.976	-8	O-69(21-0-48)	-1.6
1960	Chi-A	48	17	17	5	0	0	1	1	3	3	.294	.400	.471	871	136	1	4	0	1	1.000	-6	O-24(9-1-14)	-0.5

YEAR	TM/L	G	AB	R	H	2B	3B	HR	RBI	BB	SO	AVG	OBP	SLG	OPS	OPS+	BR+	SB	CS	SBR	FA	FR	G/POS	TPR
1961	Chi-A	1	0	0	0	0	0	0	0	0	0	—	—	—	—	—	0	0	1	-0	.000	0	H	0.0
	KC-A	64	141	20	34	8	0	2	10	24	14	.241	.352	.340	692	84	-3	6	2	1	.981	-9	O-43(0-7-36)	-1.3
	Yr	65	141	20	34	8	0	2	10	24	14	.241	.352	.340	692	84	-2	6	3	0	.981	-9	O-43(0-7-36)	-1.3
Total	10	1171	3552	503	911	155	56	83	422	365	523	.256	.330	.402	731	96	-24	160	70	11	.977	-36	*O-1038R/1-31	-9.0

■ RUBEN RIVERA

Rivera, Ruben (Moreno) b: 11/14/73, Chorrera, Panama BR/TR, 6′3″, 200 lbs. Deb: 9/3/95

YEAR	TM/L	G	AB	R	H	2B	3B	HR	RBI	BB	SO	AVG	OBP	SLG	OPS	OPS+	BR+	SB	CS	SBR	FA	FR	G/POS	TPR
1995	NY-A	5	1	0	0	0	0	0	0	0	1	.000	.000	.000	0	-99	-0	0	0	0	1.000	-1	/O-4(4-0-0)	-0.1
1996	*NY-A	46	88	17	25	6	1	2	16	13	26	.284	.388	.443	832	110	2	6	2	1	1.000	-2	O-45(13-14-19)	0.0
1997	SD-N	17	20	2	5	1	0	0	1	2	9	.250	.318	.300	618	68	-1	2	1	0	1.000	-1	/O-7(2-4-4)	-0.2
1998	*SD-N	95	172	31	36	7	2	6	29	28	52	.209	.327	.378	705	92	-2	5	1	1	.973	-14	O-91(13-13-73)	-1.7
1999	SD-N	147	411	65	80	16	1	23	48	55	143	.195	.297	.406	704	82	-13	18	7	2	.976	5	*O-143(0-143-0)	-0.5
2000	SD-N	135	423	62	88	18	6	17	57	44	137	.208	.298	.400	697	79	-16	8	4	0	.984	6	*O-132(1-131-0)	-0.8
Total	6	445	1115	177	234	48	10	48	151	142	368	.210	.310	.400	710	84	-30	39	15	3	.981	-8	O-422(33-305-96)	-3.3

■ MICKEY RIVERS

Rivers, John Milton b: 10/31/48, Miami, Fla. BL/TL, 5′10″, 165 lbs. Deb: 8/4/70 Career OF: (78-LF 1145-CF 40-RF)

YEAR	TM/L	G	AB	R	H	2B	3B	HR	RBI	BB	SO	AVG	OBP	SLG	OPS	OPS+	BR+	SB	CS	SBR	FA	FR	G/POS	TPR
1970	Cal-A	17	25	6	8	2	0	0	3	3	5	.320	.414	.400	814	130	1	1	0	0	1.000	0	/O-5(0-0-5)	0.1
1971	Cal-A	79	268	31	71	12	2	1	12	19	38	.265	.316	.336	652	91	-4	13	1	3	.976	-3	O-76(4-61-18)	-0.7
1972	Cal-A	58	159	18	34	6	2	0	7	8	26	.214	.256	.277	533	62	-8	4	3	-0	.981	-1	O-48(6-38-7)	-1.2
1973	Cal-A	30	129	26	45	6	4	0	16	8	11	.349	.391	.457	849	150	8	8	3	1	.909	-4	O-29(0-29-0)	0.5
1974	Cal-A	118	466	69	133	19	**11**	3	31	39	47	.285	.342	.393	735	118	10	30	13	2	.994	10	*O-116(0-116-0)	2.0
1975	Cal-A	155	616	70	175	17	**13**	1	53	43	42	.284	.333	.359	692	103	2	**70**	14	**11**	.977	11	*O-152(27-125-0)/D-1	1.9
1976	*NY-A★	137	590	95	184	31	8	8	67	13	51	.312	.330	.432	762	123	14	43	7	7	.986	9	*O-136(0-136-0)	2.8
1977	*NY-A	138	565	79	184	18	5	12	69	18	45	.326	.351	.439	790	115	11	22	14	-0	.982	13	*O-136(0-136-0)/D-1	2.2
1978	*NY-A	141	559	78	148	25	8	11	48	29	51	.265	.305	.397	702	98	-3	25	5	4	.980	10	*O-138(0-138-0)	0.9
1979	NY-A	74	286	37	82	18	5	3	25	13	21	.287	.320	.416	736	99	-1	3	7	-2	.974	-6	O-69(0-69-0)/D-1	-0.9
	Tex-A	58	247	35	74	9	3	6	25	9	18	.300	.327	.433	760	104	1	7	2	1	.981	3	O-57(0-57-0)	0.4
	Yr	132	533	72	156	27	8	9	50	22	39	.293	.323	.424	747	101	-0	10	9	-1	.978	-3	*O-126(0-126-0)/D-1	-0.5
1980	Tex-A	147	630	96	210	32	6	7	60	20	34	.333	.355	.437	791	119	15	18	7	2	.978	10	*O-141(0-141-0)/D-4	2.4
1981	Tex-A	99	399	62	114	21	2	3	26	24	31	.286	.328	.371	699	107	3	9	5	0	.996	4	O-97(0-97-0)	0.7
1982	Tex-A	19	68	6	16	1	1	1	4	0	7	.235	.235	.324	559	54	-4	0	0	0	.000	0	D-16	-0.5
1983	Tex-A	96	309	37	88	17	0	1	20	11	21	.285	.312	.350	661	83	-7	9	4	1	.980	0	D-53,O-23(15-0-8)	-0.9
1984	Tex-A	102	313	40	94	13	1	4	33	9	23	.300	.320	.387	706	91	-4	5	5	-1	1.000	-0	D-48,O-30(26-2-2)	-0.7
Total	15	1468	5629	785	1660	247	71	61	499	266	471	.295	.329	.397	726	106	33	267	90	27	.982	57	*O-1253C,D-124	9.0

■ JOHNNY RIZZO

Rizzo, John Costa b: 7/30/12, Houston, Tex. d: 12/4/77, Houston, Tex. BR/TR, 6′, 190 lbs. Deb: 4/19/38

YEAR	TM/L	G	AB	R	H	2B	3B	HR	RBI	BB	SO	AVG	OBP	SLG	OPS	OPS+	BR+	SB	CS	SBR	FA	FR	G/POS	TPR
1938	Pit-N	143	555	97	167	31	9	23	111	54	61	.301	.368	.514	882	139	28	1			.951	-8	*O-140(140-0-0)	1.3
1939	Pit-N	94	330	49	86	23	3	6	55	42	27	.261	.349	.403	752	103	2	0			.974	-0	O-86(86-0-0)	-0.3
1940	Pit-N	9	28	1	5	1	0	0	2	5	5	.179	.324	.214	538	51	-2	0			.818	-2	/O-7(7-0-0)	-0.4
	Cin-N	31	110	17	31	6	0	4	17	14	14	.282	.363	.445	808	121	3	1			.974	5	O-30(30-0-0)	0.6
	Phi-N	103	367	53	107	12	2	20	53	37	31	.292	.358	.499	857	139	19	2			.968	6	O-91(56-23-15)/3-7	2.1
	Yr	143	505	71	143	19	2	24	72	56	50	.283	.357	.471	828	130	20	3			.964	9	*O-128(93-23-15)/3-7	2.3
1941	Phi-N	99	235	20	51	9	2	4	24	24	34	.217	.295	.323	618	77	-7	1			.968	0	O-62(3-8-53)/3-2	-1.0
1942	Bro-N	78	217	31	50	8	0	4	27	24	25	.230	.307	.323	630	83	-5	2			.977	-2	O-70(9-0-62)	-1.1
Total	5	557	1842	268	497	90	16	61	289	200	197	.270	.345	.435	781	116	38	7			.964	-1	O-486(331-31-130)/3-9	1.2

■ PHIL RIZZUTO

Rizzuto, Philip Francis "Scooter" (b: Fiero Francis Rizzuto) b: 9/25/17, Brooklyn, N.Y. BR/TR, 5′6″, 160 lbs. Deb: 4/14/41 H

YEAR	TM/L	G	AB	R	H	2B	3B	HR	RBI	BB	SO	AVG	OBP	SLG	OPS	OPS+	BR+	SB	CS	SBR	FA	FR	G/POS	TPR
1941	*NY-A	133	515	65	158	20	9	3	46	27	36	.307	.343	.398	741	97	-3	14	5	1	.957	16	*S-128	2.2
1942	*NY-A☆	144	553	79	157	24	7	4	68	44	40	.284	.343	.374	718	104	2	22	6	3	.962	**25**	*S-144	4.1
1946	NY-A	126	471	53	121	17	1	2	38	34	39	.257	.315	.310	625	74	-16	14	7	1	.961	13	*S-125	0.6
1947	*NY-A	153	549	78	150	26	9	2	60	57	31	.273	.350	.364	714	100	0	11	6	0	.969	16	*S-151	2.7
1948	NY-A	128	464	65	117	13	2	6	50	60	24	.252	.340	.328	668	79	-13	6	5	-0	.973	-11	*S-128	-1.6
1949	*NY-A	153	614	110	169	22	7	5	65	72	34	.275	.352	.358	711	88	-10	18	6	**2**	**.971**	3	*S-152	0.4
1950	*NY-A★	155	617	125	200	36	7	7	66	92	39	.324	.418	.439	857	123	25	12	8	-0	**.982**	9	*S-155	**4.0**
1951	*NY-A★	144	540	87	148	21	6	2	43	58	27	.274	.350	.346	696	92	-5	18	3	3	.968	6	*S-144	1.3
1952	*NY-A★	152	578	89	147	24	10	2	43	67	42	.254	.337	.341	678	95	-4	17	6	2	.976	19	*S-152	2.7
1953	*NY-A★	134	413	54	112	21	3	2	54	71	39	.271	.383	.351	734	103	5	4	3	-0	.963	-3	*S-133	1.3
1954	NY-A	127	307	47	60	11	0	2	15	41	23	.195	.292	.251	543	51	-20	3	2	-0	.968	-1	*S-126/2-1	-1.3
1955	*NY-A	81	143	19	37	4	1	1	9	22	18	.259	.369	.322	691	88	-1	7	1	1	.957	-9	S-79/2-1	-0.5
1956	NY-A	31	52	6	12	0	0	0	6	6	6	.231	.310	.231	541	46	-4	3	0	1	.934	3	S-30	0.2
Total	13	1661	5816	877	1588	239	62	38	563	651	398	.273	.351	.355	706	93	-44	149	58	12	.968	86	*S-1647/2-2	16.1

■ MEL ROACH

Roach, Melvin Earl b: 1/25/33, Richmond, Va. BR/TR, 6′1″, 190 lbs. Deb: 7/31/53 Career OF: (41-LF 0-CF 3-RF)

YEAR	TM/L	G	AB	R	H	2B	3B	HR	RBI	BB	SO	AVG	OBP	SLG	OPS	OPS+	BR+	SB	CS	SBR	FA	FR	G/POS	TPR
1953	Mil-N	5	2	1	0	0	0	0	0	0	1	.000	.000	.000	0	-99	-1	0	0	0	.000	0	/2-1	-0.1
1954	Mil-N	3	4	0	0	0	0	0	0	0	1	.000	.000	.000	0	-99	-1	0	0	0	1.000	-0	/1-1	-0.1
1957	Mil-N	7	6	1	1	0	0	0	0	0	3	.167	.167	.167	333	-11	-1	0	0	0	1.000	0	/2-5	-0.1
1958	Mil-N	44	136	14	42	7	0	3	10	6	15	.309	.338	.426	764	110	2	0	0	0	.993	-2	2-27/O-7(4-0-3),1-1	0.2
1959	Mil-N	19	31	1	3	0	0	0	0	2	4	.097	.152	.097	248	-35	-6	0	0	0	.880	1	/2-8,O-4(4-0-0),3-1	-0.5
1960	Mil-N	48	140	12	42	12	0	3	18	6	19	.300	.333	.450	783	121	3	0	0	0	.975	-8	O-21L,2-20/1-1,3-1	-0.4
1961	Mil-N	13	36	3	6	0	0	1	6	2	4	.167	.250	.250	500	35	-3	0	0	0	1.000	-2	/O-9(9-0-0),1-2	-0.6
	Chi-N	23	39	1	5	2	0	0	1	3	9	.128	.190	.179	370	-1	-6	1	0	0	.981	-1	/1-7,2-7	-0.7
	Yr	36	75	4	11	2	0	1	7	5	13	.147	.220	.213	433	16	-9	1	0	0	1.000	-3	/O-9(9-0-0),1-9,2-7	-1.3
1962	Phi-N	65	105	9	20	4	0	0	8	5	19	.190	.227	.229	456	23	-11	0	0	0	.951	-1	3-26/2-9,1-4,O-3L	-1.3
Total	8	227	499	42	119	25	0	7	43	24	75	.238	.278	.331	608	66	-24	1	0	0	.969	-12	/2-77,O-44L,3-28,1	-3.6

■ MIKE ROACH

Roach, Michael Stephen b: 12/23/1873, New York, N.Y. d: 11/12/16, New York, N.Y. Deb: 8/10/1899

YEAR	TM/L	G	AB	R	H	2B	3B	HR	RBI	BB	SO	AVG	OBP	SLG	OPS	OPS+	BR+	SB	CS	SBR	FA	FR	G/POS	TPR
1899	Was-N	24	78	7	17	1	0	0	7	3		.218	.265	.231	496	37	-7	3			.964	-5	C-20/1-3	-0.9

■ ROXEY ROACH

Roach, Wilbur Charles b: 11/28/1882, Anita, Pa. d: 12/26/47, Bay City, Mich. BR/TR, 5′11″, 160 lbs. Deb: 5/2/10

YEAR	TM/L	G	AB	R	H	2B	3B	HR	RBI	BB	SO	AVG	OBP	SLG	OPS	OPS+	BR+	SB	CS	SBR	FA	FR	G/POS	TPR
1910	NY-A	70	220	27	47	9	2	0	20	29		.214	.313	.273	586	79	-4	15			.913	-7	S-58/O-9(9-0-0)	-1.1
1911	NY-A	13	40	4	10	2	1	0	2	6		.250	.348	.350	698	89	-1	0			.891	-1	/S-8,2-5	-0.1
1912	Was-A	2	2	1	1	0	0	1	1	0		.500	.500	2.000	2500	600	1	0			.500	-1	/S-2	0.0
1915	Buf-F	92	346	35	93	20	3	2	31	17	34	.269	.303	.361	664	85	-13	11			.959	15	S-92	1.0
Total	4	177	608	67	151	31	6	3	54	52	34	.248	.311	.334	645	85	-17	26			.938	7	S-160/O-9(9-0-0),2-5	-0.2

■ MIKE ROARKE

Roarke, Michael Thomas b: 11/8/30, West Warwick, R.I. BR/TR, 6′2″, 195 lbs. Deb: 4/19/61 C

YEAR	TM/L	G	AB	R	H	2B	3B	HR	RBI	BB	SO	AVG	OBP	SLG	OPS	OPS+	BR+	SB	CS	SBR	FA	FR	G/POS	TPR
1961	Det-A	86	229	21	51	6	1	2	22	20	31	.223	.285	.284	569	51	-16	0	0	0	.988	4	C-85	-0.9
1962	Det-A	56	136	11	29	4	1	4	14	13	17	.213	.287	.346	632	67	-6	0	0	0	.982	6	C-53	0.1
1963	Det-A	23	44	5	14	0	0	0	1	2	3	.318	.362	.318	680	89	-0	0	0	0	.986	1	C-16	0.2
1964	Det-A	29	82	4	19	1	0	0	7	10	10	.232	.315	.244	559	57	-4	0	0	0	.994	3	C-27	0.0
Total	4	194	491	41	113	11	2	6	44	45	61	.230	.297	.297	595	60	-27	0	0	0	.987	14	C-181	-0.6

■ FRED ROAT

Roat, Frederick R. b: 11/10/1867, Oregon, Ill. d: 9/24/13, Oregon, Ill. TR, Deb: 5/10/1890 Career OF: (0-LF 0-CF 4-RF)

YEAR	TM/L	G	AB	R	H	2B	3B	HR	RBI	BB	SO	AVG	OBP	SLG	OPS	OPS+	BR+	SB	CS	SBR	FA	FR	G/POS	TPR
1890	Pit-N	57	215	18	48	2	0	2	17	16	22	.223	.286	.260	547	67	-8	7			.847	2	3-44/1-9,O-4(0-0-4)	-0.6
1892	Chi-N	8	31	4	6	0	1	0	2	2	3	.194	.242	.258	500	51	-2	2			.897	-3	/2-8	-0.4
Total	2	65	246	22	54	2	1	2	19	18	25	.220	.281	.260	541	65	-10	9			.847	-1	/3-44,1-9,2-8,O-4R	-1.0

■ TONY ROBELLO

Robello, Thomas Vardasco b: 2/9/13, San Leandro, Cal. d: 12/25/94, Fort Worth, Tex. BR/TR, 5′10.5″, 175 lbs. Deb: 8/13/33

YEAR	TM/L	G	AB	R	H	2B	3B	HR	RBI	BB	SO	AVG	OBP	SLG	OPS	OPS+	BR+	SB	CS	SBR	FA	FR	G/POS	TPR
1933	Cin-N	14	30	1	7	3	0	0	3	1	5	.233	.258	.333	591	69	-1	0			1.000	2	2-11/3-2	0.1
1934	Cin-N	2	2	0	0	0	0	0	0	0	1	.000	.000	.000	0	-99	-1	0			.000	0	H	-0.1
Total	2	16	32	1	7	3	0	0	3	1	6	.219	.242	.313	555	58	-2	0			1.000	2	/2-11,3-2	0.0

YEAR	TM/L	G	AB	R	H	2B	3B	HR	RBI	BB	SO	AVG	OBP	SLG	OPS	OPS+	BR+	SB	CS	SBR	FA	FR	G/POS	TPR
■ SKIPPY ROBERGE Roberge, Joseph Albert Armand b: 5/19/17, Lowell, Mass. d: 6/7/93, Lowell, Mass. BR/TR, 5'11", 185 lbs. Deb: 7/18/41																								
1941	Bos-N	55	167	12	36	6	0	0	15	9	18	.216	.256	.251	507	45	-12	0			.978	5	2-46/3-5,S-2	-0.5
1942	Bos-N	74	172	10	37	7	0	1	12	9	19	.215	.258	.273	531	57	-10	1			.977	8	2-29,3-27/S-6	0.1
1946	Bos-N	48	169	13	39	6	2	2	20	7	12	.231	.270	.325	595	68	-8	1			.973	2	3-48	-0.6
Total	3	177	508	35	112	19	2	3	47	25	49	.220	.261	.283	545	57	-30	2			.967	15	/3-80,2-75,S-8	-1.0
■ KEVIN ROBERSON Roberson, Kevin Lynn b: 1/29/68, Decatur, Ill. BB/TR, 6'4", 210 lbs. Deb: 7/15/93																								
1993	Chi-N	62	180	23	34	4	1	9	27	12	48	.189	.251	.372	624	65	-10	0	1	-0	.963	-6	O-51(14-0-42)	-1.9
1994	Chi-N	44	55	8	12	4	0	4	9	2	14	.218	.271	.509	780	99	-1	0	0	0	.800	-2	/O-9(0-0-9)	-0.3
1995	Chi-N	32	38	5	7	1	0	4	6	6	14	.184	.311	.526	837	118	1	0	1	-0	1.000	-2	O-11(10-0-1)	-0.2
1996	NY-N	27	36	8	8	1	0	3	9	7	17	.222	.364	.500	864	131	2	0	0	0	1.000	-2	O-10(1-0-9)	0.0
Total	4	165	309	44	61	10	1	20	51	27	93	.197	.277	.430	707	86	-8	0	2	-1	.955	-12	/O-81(25-0-61)	-2.4
■ RED ROBERTS Roberts, Charles Emory b: 8/8/18, Carrollton, Ga. d: 12/2/98, Atlanta, Ga. BR/TR, 6', 170 lbs. Deb: 9/3/43																								
1943	Was-A	9	23	1	6	1	0	1	3	4	2	.261	.370	.435	805	140	1	0	0	0	.778	-5	/S-6,3-1	-0.3
■ SKIPPER ROBERTS Roberts, Clarence Ashley b: 1/11/1888, Wardner, Idaho d: 12/24/63, Long Beach, Cal. BL/TR, 5'10.5", 175 lbs. Deb: 6/12/13																								
1913	StL-N	26	41	4	6	2	0	0	3	3	13	.146	.205	.195	400	15	-5	1			.859	-2	C-16	-0.6
1914	Pit-F	33	55	7	12	2	1	0	4	1	11	.218	.246	.291	537	46	-5	2			.941	-1	C-14	-0.6
	Chi-F	4	3	0	1	0	0	0	1	1	1	.333	.500	.333	833	138	0	0			.000	0	H	0.0
	Pit-F	19	39	5	10	2	1	1	4	1	8	.256	.293	.436	729	98	-1	1			.923	-4	/C-9,O-1(0-0-1)	-0.4
	Yr	56	97	12	23	4	2	1	9	3	20	.237	.275	.351	625	70	-6	3			.935	-5	C-23/O-1(0-0-1)	-1.0
Total	2	82	138	16	29	6	2	1	12	6	33	.210	.253	.304	558	54	-11	4			.906	-7	/C-39,O-1(0-0-1)	-1.6
■ CURT ROBERTS Roberts, Curtis Benjamin b: 8/16/29, Pineland, Tex. d: 11/14/69, Oakland, Cal. BR/TR, 5'8", 165 lbs. Deb: 4/13/54																								
1954	Pit-N	134	496	47	115	18	7	1	36	55	49	.232	.311	.302	613	62	-27	6	3	0	.969	2	*2-131	-1.5
1955	Pit-N	6	17	1	2	1	0	0	0	2	1	.118	.211	.176	387	4	-2	0	0	0	.913	-1	/2-6	-0.3
1956	Pit-N	31	62	6	11	5	2	0	4	5	12	.177	.239	.323	561	50	-5	1	0	0	.988	-2	2-27	-0.5
Total	3	171	575	54	128	24	9	1	40	62	62	.223	.300	.301	601	59	-34	7	3	0	.969	0	2-164	-2.3
■ DAVE ROBERTS Roberts, David Leonard b: 6/30/33, Panama City, Pan. BL/TL, 6', 172 lbs. Deb: 9/5/62																								
1962	Hou-N	16	53	3	13	3	0	1	10	8	8	.245	.355	.358	713	99	0	0	0	0	1.000	-1	O-12(6-0-6)/1-6	-0.2
1964	Hou-N	61	125	9	23	4	1	1	7	14	28	.184	.271	.256	527	52	-8	0	1	-0	.983	4	1-34/O-4(4-0-0)	-0.6
1966	Pit-N	14	16	3	2	1	0	0	0	0	7	.125	.125	.188	313	-15	-2	0	0	0	.950	0	/1-2	-0.2
Total	3	91	194	15	38	8	1	2	17	22	43	.196	.284	.278	563	60	-10	0	1	-0	.983	3	/1-42,O-16(10-0-6)	-1.0
■ DAVE ROBERTS Roberts, David Ray b: 5/31/72, Okinawa, Japan BL/TL, 5'10", 172 lbs. Deb: 8/7/99																								
1999	*Cle-A	41	143	26	34	4	0	2	12	9	16	.238	.283	.308	591	48	-11	11	3	1	1.000	-1	O-39(1-38-0)	-1.0
2000	Cle-A	19	10	1	2	0	0	0	0	2	2	.200	.333	.200	533	39	-1	1	1	-0	1.000	-5	O-17(12-5-1)	-0.6
Total	2	60	153	27	36	4	0	2	12	11	18	.235	.287	.301	587	48	-12	12	4	1	1.000	-7	/O-56(13-43-1)	-1.6
■ DAVE ROBERTS Roberts, David Wayne b: 2/17/51, Lebanon, Ore. BR/TR, 6'3", 215 lbs. Deb: 6/7/72 C Career OF: (3-LF 6-CF 10-RF)																								
1972	SD-N	100	418	38	102	17	0	5	33	18	64	.244	.275	.321	596	74	-16	7	2	1	.931	-6	3-84,2-20/S-3,C-1	-2.2
1973	SD-N	127	479	56	137	20	3	21	64	17	83	.286	.312	.472	784	124	12	11	2	2	.942	3	*3-111,2-12	1.7
1974	SD-N	113	318	26	53	10	1	5	18	32	69	.167	.247	.252	499	41	-25	2	0	0	.955	-4	*3-103/S-3,O-1(1-0-0)	-3.1
1975	SD-N	33	113	7	32	2	0	2	12	13	19	.283	.367	.354	721	107	2	3	1	0	.925	-4	3-30/2-5	-0.2
1977	SD-N	82	186	15	41	14	1	1	23	11	32	.220	.268	.323	590	64	-10	2	1	0	.982	-4	C-63/2-2,3-2,S-1	-1.2
1978	SD-N	54	97	7	21	4	1	1	7	12	25	.216	.309	.309	618	79	-3	0	0	0	.980	-1	C-41/1-8,O-2(1-1-0)	-0.3
1979	Tex-A	44	84	12	22	2	1	3	14	7	17	.262	.319	.417	735	98	-0	1	0	0	.980	2	C-14,O-11C/2-8,13D	0.2
1980	Tex-A	101	235	27	56	4	0	10	30	13	38	.238	.281	.383	664	83	-6	0	1	-0	.930	-21	3-37,S-33,C-22,/O12	-2.6
1981	*Hou-N	27	54	4	13	3	0	1	5	3	6	.241	.281	.352	633	83	-1	1	0	0	.958	0	1-10/3-7,2-3,C-1	-0.2
1982	Phi-N	28	33	2	6	1	0	0	2	2	8	.182	.229	.212	441	23	-3	0	1	-0	.818	1	3-11,C-10/2-7	-0.3
Total	10	709	2017	194	483	77	7	49	208	128	361	.239	.288	.357	645	83	-52	27	8	3	.939	-35	3-386,C-152/2S1OD	-8.2
■ BIP ROBERTS Roberts, Leon Joseph b: 10/27/63, Berkeley, Cal. BB/TR, 5'7", 165 lbs. Deb: 4/7/86 Career OF: (382-LF 72-CF 25-RF)																								
1986	SD-N	101	241	34	61	5	2	1	12	14	29	.253	.294	.303	597	66	-11	14	12	-1	.971	4	2-87	-0.5
1988	SD-N	5	9	1	3	0	0	0	0	1	2	.333	.400	.333	733	115	0	0	2	-1	.500	-1	/3-2,2-1	-0.1
1989	SD-N	117	329	81	99	15	8	3	25	49	45	.301	.393	.422	816	133	16	21	11	1	.976	-8	O-54L,3-37,S-14,/2	0.9
1990	SD-N	149	556	104	172	36	3	9	44	55	65	.309	.378	.433	811	122	17	46	12	6	.982	-1	O-75L,3-56,S-18,/2	2.3
1991	SD-N	117	424	66	119	13	3	3	32	37	71	.281	.344	.347	691	92	-4	26	11	2	.978	-7	2-68,O-46(19-29-0)	-0.8
1992	Cin-N★	147	532	92	172	34	6	4	45	62	54	.323	.396	.432	828	131	24	44	16	4	.993	-14	O-79L,2-42,3-36	1.4
1993	Cin-N	83	292	46	70	13	0	1	18	38	46	.240	.333	.295	628	70	-11	26	6	4	.984	-9	2-64,O-11L/3-3,S-1	-1.4
1994	SD-N	105	403	52	129	15	5	2	31	39	57	.320	.384	.397	781	107	6	21	7	2	.976	-15	2-90,O-20(16-5-0)	-0.3
1995	SD-N	73	296	40	90	14	0	2	25	17	36	.304	.346	.372	718	92	-3	20	2	4	.989	4	O-50(48-4-0),2-25/S-7	0.5
1996	KC-A	90	339	39	96	21	2	0	52	25	38	.283	.336	.357	693	76	-12	12	9	-1	.986	-6	2-63,D-16,O-11(8-2-1)	-1.5
1997	KC-A	97	346	44	107	17	2	1	36	21	53	.309	.351	.379	729	88	-5	15	3	2	.981	-4	O-84(82-2-0),3-10	-0.9
	*Cle-A	23	85	19	23	3	0	3	8	7	14	.271	.340	.412	752	92	-1	3	0	1	.932	-3	2-13,O-10(10-0-0)	-0.3
	Yr	120	431	63	130	20	2	4	44	28	67	.302	.348	.385	734	89	-6	18	3	3	.982	-6	O-94L,2-13,3-10	-1.2
1998	Det-A	34	113	17	28	6	0	0	9	16	14	.248	.351	.301	652	72	-4	6	1	1	1.000	-0	D-29/O-2(2-0-0),2-1	-0.5
	Oak-A	61	182	28	51	11	0	1	15	15	24	.280	.342	.357	699	84	-4	10	3	1	.970	-10	2-30,O-22(8-12-3)/3-3	-1.2
	Yr	95	295	45	79	17	0	1	24	31	38	.268	.345	.336	681	79	-8	16	4	2	.971	-11	2-31,D-29,O-24C,/3	-1.7
Total	12	1202	4147	663	1220	203	31	30	352	396	548	.294	.360	.380	740	100	7	264	95	25	.977	-70	2-501,O-464L,3/DS	-2.4
■ LEON ROBERTS Roberts, Leon Kauffman b: 1/22/51, Vicksburg, Mich. BR/TR, 6'3", 200 lbs. Deb: 9/3/74 C Career OF: (243-LF 29-CF 533-RF)																								
1974	Det-A	17	63	5	17	3	2	0	7	3	10	.270	.303	.381	684	92	-1	0	2	-1	.926	-3	O-17(0-1-16)	-0.5
1975	Det-A	129	447	51	115	17	5	10	38	36	94	.257	.318	.385	703	94	-4	3	7	-2	.982	8	*O-127(0-0-127)/D-1	-0.5
1976	Hou-N	87	235	31	68	11	2	7	33	19	43	.289	.350	.443	793	136	10	1	0	0	.980	-4	O-60(49-0-12)	0.4
1977	Hou-N	19	27	1	2	0	0	0	2	1	8	.074	.107	.074	181	-55	-6	0	0	0	1.000	-2	/O-9(4-0-6)	-0.8
1978	Sea-A	134	472	78	142	21	7	22	92	41	52	.301	.367	.515	881	146	28	6	3	0	.975	10	*O-128(0-0-128)/D-2	3.1
1979	Sea-A	140	450	61	122	24	6	15	54	56	64	.271	.354	.451	805	114	9	3	3	-0	.983	4	*O-136(67-0-69)/D-1	0.6
1980	Sea-A	119	374	48	94	18	3	10	33	43	59	.251	.330	.396	726	97	-1	8	4	0	.984	3	*O-104(20-20-70)/D-4	-0.2
1981	Tex-A	72	233	26	65	17	2	4	31	25	38	.279	.351	.421	772	128	9	3	4	-1	.992	-4	O-71(25-3-46)	0.0
1982	Tex-A	31	73	7	17	3	0	1	6	4	14	.233	.282	.315	597	67	-3	0	0	0	1.000	-5	O-28(11-2-17)/D-1	-0.9
	Tor-A	40	105	6	24	4	0	1	5	7	16	.229	.277	.295	572	52	-7	1	1	-0	1.000	-2	D-21,O-16(16-0-0)	-1.0
	Yr	71	178	13	41	7	0	2	11	11	30	.230	.279	.303	582	58	-10	1	1	-0	1.000	-7	O-44(27-2-17),D-22	-1.9
1983	KC-A	84	213	24	55	7	0	8	24	17	27	.258	.316	.404	720	96	-1	1	1	-0	.979	-6	O-76(41-3-35)/D-1	-1.0
1984	KC-A	29	45	4	10	1	1	0	3	4	3	.222	.300	.289	589	63	-2	0	0	0	1.000	-3	O-16(10-0-7)/P-1,D-3	-0.5
Total	11	901	2737	342	731	126	28	78	328	256	428	.267	.335	.419	754	108	30	26	25	-3	.982	-3	O-788R/D-34,P-1	-1.3
■ JIM ROBERTSON Robertson, Alfred James b: 1/29/28, Chicago, Ill. BR/TR, 5'9", 183 lbs. Deb: 4/15/54																								
1954	Phi-A	63	147	9	27	8	0	0	8	23	25	.184	.298	.238	536	48	-10	0	0	0	.974	-2	C-50	-1.0
1955	KC-A	6	8	1	2	0	0	0	0	1	2	.250	.333	.250	583	58	-0	0	0	0	1.000	0	/C-4	0.0
Total	2	69	155	10	29	8	0	0	8	24	27	.187	.300	.239	539	49	-10	0	0	0	.975	-2	/C-54	-1.0
■ ANDRE ROBERTSON Robertson, Andre Levett b: 10/2/57, Orange, Tex. BR/TR, 5'10", 160 lbs. Deb: 9/3/81																								
1981	*NY-A	10	19	1	5	1	0	0	0	0	3	.263	.263	.316	579	67	-1	1	1	-0	1.000	4	/S-8,2-3	0.3
1982	NY-A	44	118	16	26	5	0	2	9	8	19	.220	.270	.314	583	61	-6	0	0	0	.966	8	S-27,2-15/3-2	0.5
1983	NY-A	98	322	37	80	16	3	1	22	8	54	.248	.273	.326	599	67	-15	2	4	-1	.960	22	S-78,2-29	1.4
1984	NY-A	52	140	10	30	5	1	0	6	4	20	.214	.236	.264	500	40	-11	0	1	-0	.930	11	S-49/2-6	0.3
1985	NY-A	50	125	16	41	5	0	2	17	6	24	.328	.364	.416	780	116	3	1	2	-0	.867	-6	3-33,S-14/2-2	-0.3
Total	5	254	724	80	182	32	4	5	54	26	120	.251	.281	.327	609	69	-31	4	8	-2	.953	38	S-176/2-55,3-35	2.2

■ DARYL ROBERTSON Robertson, Daryl Berdene b: 1/5/36, Cripple Creek, Colo BR/TR, 6', 184 lbs. Deb: 5/4/62

YEAR	TM/L	G	AB	R	H	2B	3B	HR	RBI	BB	SO	AVG	OBP	SLG	OPS	OPS+	BR+	SB	CS	SBR	FA	FR	G/POS	TPR
1962	Chi-N	9	19	0	2	0	0	0	2	2	10	.105	.190	.105	296	-18	-3	0	0	0	1.000	-1	/S-6,3-1	-0.4

■ DAVE ROBERTSON Robertson, Davis Aydelotte b: 9/25/1889, Portsmouth, Va. d: 11/5/70, Virginia Beach, Va. BL/TL, 6', 186 lbs. Deb: 6/5/12

YEAR	TM/L	G	AB	R	H	2B	3B	HR	RBI	BB	SO	AVG	OBP	SLG	OPS	OPS+	BR+	SB	CS	SBR	FA	FR	G/POS	TPR
1912	NY-N	3	2	0	1	0	0	0	1	0	1	.500	.500	.500	1000	169	0	1			1.000	-1	/1-1,O-1(1-0-0)	0.0
1914	NY-N	82	256	25	68	12	3	2	32	10	26	.266	.299	.359	658	99	-2	9			.950	-2	O-71(15-0-56)	-0.8
1915	NY-N	141	544	72	160	17	10	3	58	22	52	.294	.326	.379	705	120	11	22	10	1	.956	-1	*O-138(16-0-123)	0.4
1916	NY-N	150	587	88	180	18	8	**12**	69	14	56	.307	.326	.426	752	137	22	21	17	-1	.960	5	*O-144(0-0-144)	2.0
1917	*NY-N	142	532	64	138	16	9	**12**	54	10	47	.259	.276	.391	667	107	1	17			.942	1	*O-140(0-1-140)	-0.7
1919	NY-N	1	0	0	0	0	0	0	0	0	0	—	—	—	—	—	0	0			.000	0	R	0.0
	Chi-N	27	96	8	20	2	0	1	10	1	10	.208	.224	.260	485	45	-6	3			.932	-2	O-25(1-24-0)	-1.2
	Yr	28	96	8	20	2	0	1	10	1	10	.208	.224	.260	485	45	-6	3			.932	-2	O-25(1-24-0)	-1.2
1920	Chi-N	134	500	68	150	29	11	10	75	40	44	.300	.353	.462	815	130	18	17	23	-4	.968	-9	*O-134(134-0-0)	-0.1
1921	Chi-N	22	36	7	8	3	0	0	14	1	3	.222	.243	.306	549	44	-3	0	2	-1	1.000	-2	/O-7(1-6-0)	-0.6
	Pit-N	60	230	29	74	18	3	6	48	12	16	.322	.361	.504	865	123	7	4	5	-1	.960	-4	O-58(2-1-55)	-0.2
	Yr	82	266	36	82	21	3	6	62	13	19	.308	.345	.477	823	113	4	4	7	-2	.962	-6	O-65(3-7-55)	-0.8
1922	NY-N	42	47	5	13	2	0	1	3	3	7	.277	.320	.383	703	80	-1	0	0	0	.909	-2	/O-8(1-6-1)	-0.3
Total	9	804	2830	366	812	117	44	47	364	113	262	.287	.318	.409	727	117	47	94	57		.955	-16	O-726(171-38-519)/1-1	-1.5

■ DON ROBERTSON Robertson, Donald Alexander b: 10/15/30, Harvey, Ill. BL/TL, 5'10", 180 lbs. Deb: 4/13/54

YEAR	TM/L	G	AB	R	H	2B	3B	HR	RBI	BB	SO	AVG	OBP	SLG	OPS	OPS+	BR+	SB	CS	SBR	FA	FR	G/POS	TPR
1954	Chi-N	14	6	2	0	0	0	0	0	0	2	.000	.000	.000	0	-99	-2	0	0	0	1.000	-2	/O-6(0-0-6)	-0.4

■ GENE ROBERTSON Robertson, Eugene Edward b: 12/25/1898, St.Louis, Mo. d: 10/21/81, Fallon, Nev. BL/TR, 5'7", 152 lbs. Deb: 7/4/19

YEAR	TM/L	G	AB	R	H	2B	3B	HR	RBI	BB	SO	AVG	OBP	SLG	OPS	OPS+	BR+	SB	CS	SBR	FA	FR	G/POS	TPR
1919	StL-A	5	7	1	1	0	0	0	0	1	2	.143	.250	.143	393	11	-1	0			.750	-2	/S-2	-0.2
1922	StL-A	18	27	2	8	2	1	0	1	1	1	.296	.321	.444	766	95	-0	1	0	0	.875	1	/3-7,S-6,2-1	0.1
1923	StL-A	78	251	36	62	10	1	0	17	21	7	.247	.310	.295	605	57	-16	4	2	0	.935	-14	3-74/2-1	-2.5
1924	StL-A	121	439	70	140	25	4	4	52	36	14	.319	.373	.421	795	99	-1	3	5	-1	.958	-11	*3-111/2-2	-0.6
1925	StL-A	154	582	97	158	26	5	14	76	81	30	.271	.364	.405	770	90	-8	10	7	-0	.939	-2	*3-154/S-1	-0.1
1926	StL-A	78	247	23	62	12	6	1	19	17	10	.251	.302	.360	662	69	-12	5	1	1	.924	-5	3-55,S-10/2-3	-1.1
1928	*NY-A	83	251	29	73	9	0	1	36	14	6	.291	.328	.339	667	78	-8	2	4	-1	.926	-8	3-70/2-3	-1.2
1929	NY-A	90	309	45	92	15	6	0	35	28	6	.298	.358	.385	743	98	-1	3	3	-0	.966	-11	3-77	-0.7
	Bos-N	8	28	1	8	0	0	0	6	1	0	.286	.310	.286	596	51	-2	1			.875	-2	/3-6,S-1	-0.3
1930	Bos-N	21	59	7	11	1	0	0	7	5	3	.186	.250	.203	453	12	-8	0			.949	-2	3-17	-0.9
Total	9	656	2200	311	615	100	23	20	249	205	79	.280	.344	.373	717	83	-57	29	22		.941	-56	3-571/S-20,2-10	-7.5

■ MIKE ROBERTSON Robertson, Michael Francis b: 10/9/70, Norwich, Conn. BL/TL, 6', 180 lbs. Deb: 9/6/96

YEAR	TM/L	G	AB	R	H	2B	3B	HR	RBI	BB	SO	AVG	OBP	SLG	OPS	OPS+	BR+	SB	CS	SBR	FA	FR	G/POS	TPR
1996	Chi-A	6	7	0	1	1	0	0	0	0	1	.143	.143	.286	429	5	-1	0	0	0	1.000	0	/1-2,D-2	-0.1
1997	Phi-N	22	38	3	8	2	1	0	4	0	6	.211	.268	.316	584	52	-3	1	0	0	1.000	-0	/1-5,O-5(4-0-1),D-1	-0.3
1998	Ari-N	11	13	0	2	0	0	0	0	0	2	.154	.154	.154	308	-19	-2	0	0	0	.000	0	/D-2	-0.2
Total	3	39	58	3	11	3	1	0	4	0	9	.190	.230	.276	505	31	-6	1	0	0	1.000	-0	/1-7,O-5(4-0-1),D-5	-0.6

■ BOB ROBERTSON Robertson, Robert Eugene b: 10/2/46, Frostburg, Md. BR/TR, 6'1", 210 lbs. Deb: 9/18/67 Career OF: (26-LF 0-CF 0-RF)

YEAR	TM/L	G	AB	R	H	2B	3B	HR	RBI	BB	SO	AVG	OBP	SLG	OPS	OPS+	BR+	SB	CS	SBR	FA	FR	G/POS	TPR
1967	Pit-N	9	35	4	6	0	0	2	4	3	12	.171	.237	.343	580	64	-2	0	0	0	.990	-0	/1-9	-0.3
1969	Pit-N	32	96	7	20	4	1	1	9	8	30	.208	.269	.302	571	61	-5	1	0	0	.996	1	1-26	-0.6
1970	*Pit-N	117	390	69	112	19	4	27	82	51	98	.287	.372	.564	937	150	27	4	1	1	.995	3	1-99/3-5,O-3(3-0-0)	2.2
1971	*Pit-N	131	469	65	127	18	2	26	72	60	101	.271	.358	.484	842	137	23	1	2	-0	.993	15	*1-126	2.9
1972	*Pit-N	115	306	25	59	11	0	12	41	41	84	.193	.294	.346	641	83	-7	1	1	-0	.993	9	1-89,O-23L,3-11	-0.4
1973	Pit-N	119	397	43	95	16	0	14	40	55	77	.239	.333	.385	719	101	1	0	4	-1	.995	5	*1-107	-0.4
1974	*Pit-N	91	236	25	54	11	0	16	48	33	48	.229	.323	.479	802	127	7	0	0	0	.991	-1	1-63	0.2
1975	*Pit-N	75	124	17	34	4	0	6	18	23	25	.274	.396	.452	848	136	7	0	0	0	.996	1	1-27	0.6
1976	Pit-N	61	129	10	28	5	1	2	25	16	23	.217	.303	.318	621	76	-4	0	1	-0	.996	-0	1-29	-0.7
1978	Sea-A	64	174	17	40	5	2	8	28	24	39	.230	.327	.420	746	109	2	0	0	0	1.000	-1	D-29,1-18	-0.1
1979	Tor-A	15	29	1	3	0	0	1	1	3	9	.103	.188	.207	394	6	-4	0	0	0	1.000	2	/1-9,D-4	-0.3
Total	11	829	2385	283	578	93	10	115	368	317	546	.242	.334	.434	769	115	45	7	9	-2	.994	34	1-602/D-33,O-26L,3	3.1

■ SHERRY ROBERTSON Robertson, Sherrard Alexander b: 1/1/19, Montreal, Que., Can. d: 10/23/70, Houghton, S.Dak. BL/TR, 6', 180 lbs. Deb: 9/8/40 C Career OF: (57-LF 1-CF 105-RF)

YEAR	TM/L	G	AB	R	H	2B	3B	HR	RBI	BB	SO	AVG	OBP	SLG	OPS	OPS+	BR+	SB	CS	SBR	FA	FR	G/POS	TPR
1940	Was-A	10	33	4	7	0	1	0	0	5	6	.212	.316	.273	589	58	-2	0	0	0	.940	1	S-10	0.0
1941	Was-A	1	3	0	0	0	0	0	0	0	3	.000	.000	.000	0	-99	-1	0	0	0	.750	0	/3-1	-0.1
1943	Was-A	59	120	22	26	4	1	3	14	17	19	.217	.319	.342	661	97	-0	0	2	-1	.897	-4	3-27/S-1	-0.5
1946	Was-A	74	230	30	46	6	3	6	19	30	42	.200	.292	.330	623	78	-7	6	2	1	.902	-6	3-38,2-14,S-12,/O-1R	-1.2
1947	Was-A	95	266	25	62	9	3	1	23	32	52	.233	.318	.301	618	74	-9	4	5	-1	.949	0	O-55(55-0-0),3-10/2-4	-1.4
1948	Was-A	71	187	19	46	11	3	2	22	24	26	.246	.335	.369	704	90	-3	8	0	2	.939	-1	O-51(1-1-49)	-0.4
1949	Was-A	110	374	59	94	17	3	11	42	42	35	.251	.329	.401	730	95	-5	10	3	1	.947	-8	2-71,3-19,O-13R	-0.8
1950	Was-A	71	123	19	32	3	3	2	16	22	18	.260	.372	.382	755	98	0	1	1	-0	.952	-9	O-14(0-0-14),2-12/3-1	-0.8
1951	Was-A	62	111	14	21	2	1	1	10	9	22	.189	.256	.252	508	38	-10	2	1	0	.949	3	O-22(1-0-21)	-0.7
1952	Was-A	1	0	0	0	0	0	0	0	0	0	—	—	—	—	—	0	0	0	0	.000	0	R	0.0
	Phi-A	43	60	8	12	3	0	0	5	21	15	.200	.407	.250	657	81	-0	1	2	-0	.958	-3	/2-8,O-7(0-0-7),3-2	-0.4
	Yr	44	60	8	12	3	0	0	5	21	15	.200	.407	.250	657	81	-0	1	2	-0	.958	-3	/2-8,O-7(0-0-7),3-2	-0.4
Total	10	597	1507	200	346	55	18	26	151	202	238	.230	.323	.342	664	83	-37	32	16	1	.946	-27	O-163R,2-109/3-98,S	-6.3

■ BILLY JO ROBIDOUX Robidoux, William Joseph b: 1/13/64, Ware, Mass. BL/TR, 6'1", 200 lbs. Deb: 9/11/85 Career OF: (12-LF 0-CF 0-RF)

YEAR	TM/L	G	AB	R	H	2B	3B	HR	RBI	BB	SO	AVG	OBP	SLG	OPS	OPS+	BR+	SB	CS	SBR	FA	FR	G/POS	TPR
1985	Mil-A	18	51	5	9	2	0	3	8	12	16	.176	.333	.392	725	98	0	0	0	0	1.000	-1	O-11(11-0-0)/1-6,D-1	-0.1
1986	Mil-A	56	181	15	41	8	0	1	21	33	36	.227	.346	.287	633	72	-6	0	0	0	.986	-2	1-43,D-10	-1.0
1987	Mil-A	23	62	9	12	0	0	0	4	8	17	.194	.286	.194	479	30	-6	0	1	-0	.983	-0	1-10,D-10	-0.7
1988	Mil-A	33	91	9	23	5	0	0	5	8	14	.253	.313	.308	621	74	-3	1	1	-0	.983	2	1-30/D-1	-0.3
1989	Chi-A	16	39	2	5	2	0	0	1	4	9	.128	.209	.179	389	11	-5	0	0	0	.990	-1	1-15/O-1(1-0-0)	-0.6
1990	Bos-A	27	44	3	8	4	0	1	4	6	14	.182	.294	.341	635	74	-2	0	0	0	.981	-0	1-11/D-4	-0.2
Total	6	173	468	43	98	21	0	5	43	71	106	.209	.315	.286	601	65	-21	1	2	-0	.986	-1	1-115/D-26,O-12L	-2.9

■ AARON ROBINSON Robinson, Aaron Andrew b: 6/23/15, Lancaster, S.C. d: 3/9/66, Lancaster, S.C. BL/TR, 6'2", 205 lbs. Deb: 5/6/43

YEAR	TM/L	G	AB	R	H	2B	3B	HR	RBI	BB	SO	AVG	OBP	SLG	OPS	OPS+	BR+	SB	CS	SBR	FA	FR	G/POS	TPR
1943	NY-A	1	1	0	0	0	0	0	0	0	1	.000	.000	.000	0	-99	-0	0	0	0	.000	0	H	0.0
1945	NY-A	50	160	19	45	6	1	8	24	21	23	.281	.368	.481	849	139	8	0	0	0	1.000	-3	C-45	0.8
1946	NY-A	100	330	32	98	17	2	16	64	48	39	.297	.388	.506	894	146	21	0	1	-0	.983	-11	C-95	1.5
1947	*NY-A☆	82	252	23	68	11	5	5	36	40	26	.270	.370	.413	783	119	7	0	1	-0	.997	-0	C-74	1.0
1948	Chi-A	98	326	47	82	14	2	8	39	46	30	.252	.344	.380	724	96	-2	0	1	-0	.989	-5	C-92	-0.2
1949	Det-A	110	331	38	89	12	0	13	56	73	21	.269	.402	.423	825	118	11	0	2	-1	.986	-1	*C-108	1.4
1950	Det-A	107	283	37	64	7	0	9	37	75	35	.226	.388	.346	735	86	-3	0	1	-0	.993	-3	*C-103	-0.1
1951	Det-A	36	82	3	17	6	0	0	9	17	9	.207	.343	.280	624	70	-3	0	0	0	1.000	-2	C-35	-0.4
	Bos-A	26	74	9	15	1	1	2	7	17	10	.203	.352	.324	676	76	-2	0	0	0	.983	-1	C-25	-0.1
	Yr	62	156	12	32	7	1	2	16	34	19	.205	.347	.301	649	73	-5	0	0	0	.991	-3	C-60	-0.5
Total	8	610	1839	208	478	74	11	61	272	337	194	.260	.375	.412	787	112	35	0	6	-2	.990	-26	C-577	3.9

■ VAL ROBINSON Robinson, Alfred Valentine Deb: 5/1/1872

YEAR	TM/L	G	AB	R	H	2B	3B	HR	RBI	BB	SO	AVG	OBP	SLG	OPS	OPS+	BR+	SB	CS	SBR	FA	FR	G/POS	TPR
1872	Oly-n	7	30	6	6	0	0	0	4	1	1	.200	.226	.200	426	34	-2	0	0	0	.750	-0	/O-7(0-0-7)	-0.1

■ BROOKS ROBINSON Robinson, Brooks Calbert b: 5/18/37, Little Rock, Ark. BR/TR, 6'1", 190 lbs. Deb: 9/17/55 CH

YEAR	TM/L	G	AB	R	H	2B	3B	HR	RBI	BB	SO	AVG	OBP	SLG	OPS	OPS+	BR+	SB	CS	SBR	FA	FR	G/POS	TPR
1955	Bal-A	6	22	0	2	0	0	0	1	0	10	.091	.091	.091	182	-55	-5	0	0	0	.833	-2	/3-6	-0.7
1956	Bal-A	15	44	5	10	4	0	1	1	1	5	.227	.244	.386	631	70	-2	0	0	0	.944	0	3-14/2-1	-0.2
1957	Bal-A	50	117	13	28	6	1	2	14	7	10	.239	.288	.359	647	81	-4	1	0	0	.971	4	3-47	0.0
1958	Bal-A	145	463	31	110	16	3	3	32	31	51	.238	.293	.305	597	68	-20	1	2	-0	.953	10	*3-140,2-16	-1.2

YEAR	TM/L	G	AB	R	H	2B	3B	HR	RBI	BB	SO	AVG	OBP	SLG	OPS	OPS+	BR+	SB	CS	SBR	FA	FR	G/POS	TPR
1959	Bal-A	88	313	29	89	15	2	4	24	17	37	.284	.325	.383	709	96	-2	2	2	-0	.955	7	3-87/2-1	0.4
1960	Bal-A★	152	595	74	175	27	9	14	88	35	49	.294	.333	.440	774	109	5	2	2	-0	**.977**	12	*3-152/2-3	1.7
1961	Bal-A★	163	668	89	192	38	7	7	61	47	57	.287	.338	.397	735	99	-2	1	3	-1	**.972**	-6	*3-163/2-2,S-1	-0.9
1962	Bal-A★	162	634	77	192	29	9	23	86	42	70	.303	.347	.486	833	129	24	3	1	0	**.979**	7	*3-162/S-3,2-2	3.0
1963	Bal-A★	161	589	67	148	26	4	11	67	46	84	.251	.307	.365	672	91	-8	2	3	-1	**.976**	9	*3-160/S-1	0.0
1964	Bal-A★	163	612	82	194	35	3	28	**118**	51	64	.317	.373	.521	895	146	37	1	0	0	**.972**	-2	*3-163	3.6
1965	Bal-A★	144	559	81	166	25	2	18	80	47	47	.297	.354	.445	799	123	17	3	0	1	.967	-6	*3-143	1.1
1966	*Bal-A★	157	620	91	167	35	2	23	100	56	36	.269	.335	.444	778	123	18	2	3	-1	**.976**	4	*3-157	2.2
1967	Bal-A★	158	610	88	164	25	5	22	77	54	54	.269	.332	.434	767	126	19	1	3	-1	**.980**	**31**	*3-158	5.2
1968	Bal-A★	162	608	65	154	36	6	17	75	44	55	.253	.308	.416	724	118	11	1	1	-0	**.970**	17	*3-162	3.1
1969	*Bal-A★	156	598	73	140	21	3	23	84	56	55	.234	.303	.395	698	93	-7	2	1	0	**.976**	19	*3-156	1.2
1970	*Bal-A★	158	608	84	168	31	4	18	94	53	53	.276	.338	.429	768	109	7	1	1	-0	.966	-1	*3-156	0.5
1971	*Bal-A★	156	589	67	160	21	1	20	92	63	50	.272	.345	.413	758	115	11	0	0	0	.968	7	*3-156	1.9
1972	Bal-A★	153	556	48	139	23	2	8	64	43	45	.250	.306	.342	648	90	-7	1	0	0	**.977**	6	*3-152	-0.2
1973	*Bal-A★	155	549	53	141	17	2	9	72	55	50	.257	.328	.344	672	90	-7	2	0	0	.970	9	*3-154	0.2
1974	*Bal-A★	153	553	46	159	27	0	7	59	56	47	.288	.356	.374	731	114	11	2	0	0	.967	21	*3-153	3.2
1975	Bal-A	144	482	50	97	15	1	6	53	44	33	.201	.269	.274	543	57	-27	0	0	0	**.979**	4	*3-143	-2.5
1976	Bal-A	71	218	16	46	8	2	3	11	8	24	.211	.242	.307	550	64	-11	0	0	0	.969	0	3-71	-1.2
1977	Bal-A	24	47	3	7	2	0	1	4	4	4	.149	.216	.255	471	30	-5	0	0	0	1.000	2	3-15	-0.3
Total	23	2896	10654	1232	2848	482	68	268	1357	860	990	.267	.325	.401	726	105	53	28	22	-2	.971	151	*3-2870/2-25,S-5	20.1
■ BRUCE ROBINSON Robinson, Bruce Philip b: 4/16/54, LaJolla, Cal. BL/TR, 6'1", 185 lbs. Deb: 8/19/78 F																								
1978	Oak-A	28	84	5	21	3	1	0	8	3	8	.250	.276	.310	585	68	-4	0	0	0	.965	7	C-28	0.5
1979	NY-A	6	12	0	2	0	0	0	2	1	0	.167	.231	.167	397	9	-2	0	0	0	.943	2	/C-6	0.1
1980	NY-A	4	5	0	0	0	0	0	0	0	4	.000	.000	.000	0	-99	-1	0	0	0	1.000	-0	/C-3	-0.2
Total	3	38	101	5	23	3	1	0	10	4	12	.228	.257	.277	534	52	-7	0	0	0	.962	9	/C-37	0.4
■ CHARLIE ROBINSON Robinson, Charles Henry b: 7/27/1856, Westerly, R.I. d: 5/18/13, BL/TR, Deb: 8/2/1884																								
1884	Ind-a	20	80	11	23	2	0	0		3		.287	.313	.313	626	108	1				.967	-1	C-17/S-3,O-1(0-0-1)	0.1
1885	Bro-a	11	40	5	6	2	1	0	4	3		.150	.209	.250	459	44	-3				.840	-4	C-11	-0.5
Total	2	31	120	16	29	4	1	0	4	6		.242	.278	.292	569	85	-2				.919	-5	/C-28,S-3,O-1(0-0-1)	-0.4
■ RABBIT ROBINSON Robinson, Clyde b: 3/5/1882, Wellsburg, W.Va. d: 4/9/15, Waterbury, Conn. BR/TR, 5'6", 148 lbs. Deb: 4/22/03 Career OF: (7-LF 14-CF 29-RF)																								
1903	Was-A	103	373	41	79	10	8	1	20	33		.212	.279	.290	569	69	-13	16			.917	2	2-45,O-30R,S-24,/3	-1.2
1904	Det-A	101	320	30	77	13	6	0	37	29		.241	.314	.319	632	103	2	14			.925	1	S-30,3-26,O-20R,2	0.5
1910	Cin-N	2	7	0	0	0	0	0	1	1	0	.000	.125	.000	125	-66	-1	0			1.000	-1	/3-2	-0.3
Total	3	206	700	71	156	23	14	1	58	63	0	.223	.294	.300	594	83	-13	30			.940	2	/2-64,S-54,O-50R,3	-1.0
■ CRAIG ROBINSON Robinson, Craig George b: 8/21/48, Abington, Pa. BR/TR, 5'10", 165 lbs. Deb: 9/9/72																								
1972	Phi-N	5	15	0	3	1	0	0	0	1	2	.200	.250	.267	517	46	-1	0	0	0	1.000	2	/S-4	0.2
1973	Phi-N	46	146	11	33	7	0	0	7	0	25	.226	.226	.274	500	37	-12	1	1	-0	.945	1	S-42/2-4	-0.8
1974	Atl-N	145	452	52	104	4	6	0	29	30	57	.230	.282	.265	548	52	-29	11	2	2	.956	-17	*S-142	-3.0
1975	Atl-N	10	17	1	1	0	0	0	0	0	5	.059	.059	.059	118	-65	-4	0	0	0	1.000	1	/S-7	-0.2
	SF-N	29	29	4	2	1	0	0	0	2	6	.069	.129	.103	232	-34	-5	0	0	0	.941	5	S-12/2-9	0.0
	Yr	39	46	5	3	1	0	0	0	2	11	.065	.104	.087	191	-45	-9	0	0	0	.967	6	S-19/2-9	-0.2
1976	SF-N	15	13	4	4	1	0	0	2	3	4	.308	.438	.385	822	131	1	0	1	-0	.952	4	/2-7,3-2,S-1	0.5
	Atl-N	15	17	4	4	0	0	0	3	5	2	.235	.409	.235	644	81	-0	0	0	0	.952	2	/2-5,S-2,3-1	0.2
	Yr	30	30	8	8	1	0	0	5	8	6	.267	.421	.300	721	102	1	0	1	-0	.952	6	2-12/3-3,S-3	0.7
1977	Atl-N	27	29	4	6	1	0	0	1	1	6	.207	.233	.241	475	25	-3	0	0	0	1.000	6	S-23	0.3
Total	6	292	718	80	157	15	6	0	42	42	107	.219	.265	.256	521	44	-54	12	4	1	.956	3	S-233/2-25,3-3	-2.8
■ DAVE ROBINSON Robinson, David Tanner b: 5/22/46, Minneapolis, Minn. BB/TL, 6'1", 186 lbs. Deb: 9/10/70 F																								
1970	SD-N	15	38	5	12	2	0	2	6	5	4	.316	.395	.526	922	151	3	2	0	0	1.000	1	O-13(12-1-0)	0.3
1971	SD-N	7	6	0	0	0	0	0	0	1	3	.000	.143	.000	143	-61	-1	0	0	0	.000	0	H	-0.1
Total	2	22	44	5	12	2	0	2	6	6	7	.273	.360	.455	815	124	1	2	0	0	1.000	1	/O-13(12-1-0)	0.2
■ EARL ROBINSON Robinson, Earl John b: 11/3/36, New Orleans, La. BR/TR, 6'1", 190 lbs. Deb: 9/10/58																								
1958	LA-N	8	15	3	3	0	0	0	0	1	4	.200	.250	.200	450	20	-2	0	0	0	1.000	1	/3-6	0.0
1961	Bal-A	96	222	37	59	12	3	8	30	31	54	.266	.356	.455	811	119	6	4	3	-0	.973	-3	O-82(6-1-78)	-0.2
1962	Bal-A	29	63	12	18	3	1	1	4	8	10	.286	.366	.413	779	116	2	2	0	0	1.000	0	O-17(1-0-16)	0.1
1964	Bal-A	37	121	11	33	5	1	3	10	7	24	.273	.313	.405	717	98	-1	1	2	-0	.986	1	O-34(16-20-0)	-0.1
Total	4	170	421	63	113	20	5	12	44	47	92	.268	.342	.425	767	109	5	7	5	-0	.980	-1	O-133(23-21-94)/3-6	-0.2
■ FLOYD ROBINSON Robinson, Floyd Andrew b: 5/9/36, Prescott, Ark. BL/TR, 5'9", 175 lbs. Deb: 8/10/60																								
1960	Chi-A	22	46	7	13	0	0	0	1	11	8	.283	.431	.283	714	98	1	2	3	-1	.960	-2	O-17(1-4-12)	-0.3
1961	Chi-A	132	432	69	134	20	7	11	59	52	32	.310	.389	.465	855	129	19	7	4	0	.991	4	*O-106(0-0-106)	1.5
1962	Chi-A	156	600	89	187	**45**	10	11	109	72	47	.312	.387	.475	862	131	27	4	2	0	.973	-10	*O-155(114-0-75)	0.8
1963	Chi-A	146	527	71	149	21	6	13	71	62	43	.283	.363	.419	782	120	16	4	3	-0	.984	-7	*O-137(36-0-119)	-0.1
1964	Chi-A	141	525	83	158	17	3	11	59	70	41	.301	.388	.408	796	125	20	9	5	0	.987	-12	*O-138(54-0-112)	-0.1
1965	Chi-A	156	577	70	153	15	6	14	66	76	51	.265	.356	.385	740	117	15	4	1	1	.985	-4	*O-153(6-1-148)	0.1
1966	Chi-A	127	342	44	81	11	2	5	35	44	32	.237	.332	.325	657	96	-1	8	2	1	.962	-14	*O-113(4-0-111)	-2.2
1967	Cin-N	55	130	19	31	6	2	1	10	14	14	.238	.313	.338	651	77	-3	3	1	0	.981	-4	O-39(4-0-35)	-1.0
1968	Oak-A	53	81	5	20	5	0	1	14	4	10	.247	.282	.346	628	94	-1	0	0	0	1.000	-1	O-18(18-0-0)	-0.3
	Bos-A	23	24	1	3	0	0	0	2	3	4	.125	.250	.125	375	15	-2	1	0	0	.833	-3	O-10(5-0-5)	-0.6
	Yr	76	105	6	23	5	0	1	16	7	14	.219	.274	.295	570	74	-3	1	0	0	.963	-4	O-28(23-0-5)	-0.9
Total	9	1011	3284	458	929	140	36	67	426	408	282	.283	.367	.409	775	118	91	42	21	2	.981	-53	O-886(242-5-723)	-2.2
■ FRANK ROBINSON Robinson, Frank b: 8/31/35, Beaumont, Tex. BR/TR, 6'1", 195 lbs. Deb: 4/17/56 MCH Career OF: (820-LF 99-CF 1281-RF)																								
1956	Cin-N★	152	572	**122**	166	27	6	38	83	64	95	.290	.381	.558	939	139	32	8	4	0	.976	6	*O-152(143-10-0)	2.9
1957	Cin-N★	150	611	97	197	29	5	29	75	44	92	.322	.379	.529	908	131	27	10	2	2	.989	19	*O-136(106-32-1),1-24	3.8
1958	Cin-N	148	554	90	149	25	6	31	83	62	80	.269	.350	.504	854	116	13	10	1	2	.991	9	*O-138(83-53-0),3-11	1.6
1959	Cin-N★	146	540	106	168	31	4	36	125	69	93	.311	.397	.583	980	152	41	18	8	1	.984	-9	*1-125,O-40(40-0-0)	2.4
1960	Cin-N	139	464	86	138	33	6	31	83	82	67	.297	.413	**.595**	**1007**	169	46	13	6	1	.993	7	1-78,O-51(51-0-0)/3-1	4.6
1961	*Cin-N★	153	545	117	176	32	7	37	124	71	64	.323	.411	**.611**	**1022**	164	51	22	3	**4**	.990	10	*O-150(52-3-99)/3-1	5.3
1962	Cin-N★	162	609	**134**	208	**51**	2	39	136	76	62	.342	**.424**	**.624**	**1048**	**172**	**62**	18	9	1	.994	9	*O-161(9-0-155)	5.9
1963	Cin-N	140	482	79	125	19	3	21	91	81	69	.259	.381	.442	823	132	23	26	10	2	.984	9	*O-139(116-1-31)/1-1	2.8
1964	Cin-N	156	568	103	174	38	6	29	96	79	67	.306	.399	.548	947	158	45	23	5	3	.986	2	*O-156(77-0-102)	4.3
1965	Cin-N★	156	582	109	172	33	5	33	113	70	100	.296	.388	.540	928	148	38	13	9	-0	.990	2	*O-155(7-0-152)	3.1
1966	*Bal-A★	155	576	**122**	182	34	2	**49**	**122**	87	90	**.316**	**.415**	**.637**	**1052**	**200**	**76**	8	5	0	.985	-4	*O-151(20-0-135)/1-3	**6.5**
1967	Bal-A†	129	479	83	149	23	7	30	94	71	84	.311	.408	.576	984	189	54	2	3	-1	.990	-2	*O-126(31-0-95)/1-2	4.7
1968	Bal-A	130	421	69	113	27	1	15	52	73	84	.268	.391	.444	835	153	30	11	2	2	.962	-8	*O-117(55-0-78)/1-3	1.8
1969	*Bal-A★	148	539	111	166	19	5	32	100	88	62	.308	.417	.540	957	164	49	9	3	1	.987	-1	*O-134(1-0-134),1-19	4.2
1970	*Bal-A★	132	471	88	144	24	1	25	78	69	70	.306	.402	.520	922	151	34	2	1	0	.987	6	*O-120(0-0-120)/1-7	3.4
1971	*Bal-A★	133	455	82	128	16	2	28	99	72	62	.281	.390	.510	900	154	34	3	0	1	.973	-4	O-92(1-0-91),1-37	2.4
1972	LA-N	103	342	41	86	6	1	19	59	55	76	.251	.358	.442	800	129	14	2	3	-1	.967	-1	O-95(9-0-88)	0.8
1973	Cal-A	147	534	85	142	29	0	30	97	82	93	.266	.374	.489	863	153	39	1	1	-0	.976	4	*D-127,O-17(17-0-0)	3.8
1974	Cal-A★	129	427	75	107	26	2	20	63	75	85	.251	.375	.461	836	148	29	5	1	1	.000	-0	*D-123/O-1(1-0-0)	2.7
	Cle-A	15	50	6	10	1	1	2	5	10	10	.200	.333	.380	713	106	1	0	1	-0	.958	-1	D-11/1-4	-0.1
	Yr	144	477	81	117	27	3	22	68	85	95	.245	.371	.453	823	143	29	5	2	0	.891	-1	*D-134/1-4,O-1(1-0-0)	2.6
1975	Cle-A	49	118	19	28	5	0	9	24	29	15	.237	.388	.508	896	152	9	0	0	0	.000	0	D-42,M	0.8

YEAR	TM/L	G	AB	R	H	2B	3B	HR	RBI	BB	SO	AVG	OBP	SLG	OPS	OPS+	BR+	SB	CS	SBR	FA	FR	G/POS	TPR
1976	Cle-A	36	67	5	15	0	0	3	10	11	12	.224	.333	.358	692	104	1	0	0	0	1.000	-1	D-18/1-2,O-1(1-0-0),M	-0.1
Total	21	2808	10006	1829	2943	528	72	586	1812	1420	1532	.294	.392	.537	929	154	746	204	77	18	.984	52	*O-2132R,D-321,1/3	67.6

■ FRED ROBINSON

Robinson, Frederic Henry b: 7/6/1856, South Acton, Mass. d: 12/18/33, Hudson, Mass. BR/TR, Deb: 4/17/1884 F

YEAR	TM/L	G	AB	R	H	2B	3B	HR	RBI	BB	SO	AVG	OBP	SLG	OPS	OPS+	BR+	SB	CS	SBR	FA	FR	G/POS	TPR
1884	Cin-U	3	13	1	3	0	0	0		0		.231	.231	.231	462	37	-1				.727	-3	/2-3	-0.4

■ JACKIE ROBINSON

Robinson, Jack Roosevelt b: 1/31/19, Cairo, Ga. d: 10/24/72, Stamford, Conn. BR/TR, 5'11", 204 lbs. Deb: 4/15/47 H Career OF: (161-LF 0-CF 1-RF)

YEAR	TM/L	G	AB	R	H	2B	3B	HR	RBI	BB	SO	AVG	OBP	SLG	OPS	OPS+	BR+	SB	CS	SBR	FA	FR	G/POS	TPR
1947	*Bro-N	151	590	125	175	31	5	12	48	74	36	.297	.383	.427	810	111	11	**29**			.989	-3	*1-151	0.3
1948	Bro-N	147	574	108	170	38	8	12	85	57	37	.296	.367	.453	820	117	13	22			**.980**	1	*2-116,1-30/3-6	2.0
1949	*Bro-N★	156	593	122	203	38	12	16	124	86	27	**.342**	.432	.528	960	150	45	**37**			.981	-1	*2-156	5.1
1950	Bro-N★	144	518	99	170	39	4	14	81	80	24	.328	.423	.500	923	139	32	12			**.986**	11	*2-144	**4.8**
1951	Bro-N★	153	548	106	185	33	7	19	88	79	27	.338	.429	.527	957	153	43	25	8	3	**.992**	17	*2-150	**6.9**
1952	*Bro-N★	149	510	104	157	17	3	19	75	106	40	.308	**.440**	.465	904	149	41	24	7	3	.974	4	*2-146	**5.6**
1953	*Bro-N★	136	484	109	159	34	7	12	95	74	30	.329	.425	.502	927	137	30	17	4	2	.981	8	O-76L,3-44/2-9,1S	3.4
1954	Bro-N★	124	386	62	120	22	4	15	59	63	20	.311	.417	.505	922	135	22	7	3	0	1.000	-9	O-74(73-0-1),3-50/2-4	1.0
1955	*Bro-N	105	317	51	81	6	2	8	36	61	18	.256	.381	.363	743	96	1	12	3	2	.966	7	3-84,O-10L/1-1,2-1	0.8
1956	*Bro-N	117	357	61	98	15	2	10	43	60	32	.275	.383	.412	795	106	5	12	5	1	.967	15	3-72,2-22/1-9,O-2L	2.1
Total	10	1382	4877	947	1518	273	54	137	734	740	291	.311	.410	.474	883	131	242	197	30		.983	49	2-748,3-256,1O/S	32.0

■ JACK ROBINSON

Robinson, John W. "Bridgeport" b: 7/15/1880, Portland, Maine d: 7/22/21, Macon, Ga. TR, Deb: 9/6/02

YEAR	TM/L	G	AB	R	H	2B	3B	HR	RBI	BB	SO	AVG	OBP	SLG	OPS	OPS+	BR+	SB	CS	SBR	FA	FR	G/POS	TPR
1902	NY-N	4	9	0	0	0	0	0	0	0		.000	.000	.000	0	-99	-2	0			1.000	1	/C-3	-0.1

■ KERRY ROBINSON

Robinson, Kerry Keith b: 10/3/73, St.Louis, Mo. BL/TL, 6', 175 lbs. Deb: 9/22/98

YEAR	TM/L	G	AB	R	H	2B	3B	HR	RBI	BB	SO	AVG	OBP	SLG	OPS	OPS+	BR+	SB	CS	SBR	FA	FR	G/POS	TPR
1998	TB-A	2	3	0	0	0	0	0	0	0	1	.000	.000	.000	0	-98	-1	0	0	0	1.000	0	/O-2(2-0-0)	-0.1
1999	Cin-N	9	1	4	0	0	0	0	0	0	1	.000	.000	.000	0	-97	-0	0	1	-0	.000	-1	/O-2(2-0-0)	-0.1
Total	2	11	4	4	0	0	0	0	0	0	2	.000	.000	.000	0	-98	-1	0	1	-0	1.000	-1	/O-4(4-0-0)	-0.2

■ WILBERT ROBINSON

Robinson, Wilbert "Uncle Robby" b: 6/29/1863, Bolton, Mass.
d: 8/8/34, Atlanta, Ga. BR/TR, 5'8.5", 215 lbs. Deb: 4/19/1886 FMCH Career OF: (0-LF 5-CF 3-RF)

YEAR	TM/L	G	AB	R	H	2B	3B	HR	RBI	BB	SO	AVG	OBP	SLG	OPS	OPS+	BR+	SB	CS	SBR	FA	FR	G/POS	TPR
1886	Phi-a	87	342	57	69	11	3	1	30	21		.202	.254	.260	514	61	-16	33			.893	-10	C-61,1-22/O-5(0-4-1)	-2.0
1887	Phi-a	68	278	28	74	6	2	1	24	14		.266	.269	.277	545	52	-17	15			.901	1	C-67/1-3,O-1(0-1-0)	-0.9
1888	Phi-a	66	254	32	62	7	2	1	31	9		.244	.270	.299	569	83	-5	11			.938	25	C-65/1-1	2.3
1889	Phi-a	69	264	31	61	13	2	0	28	6	34	.231	.251	.295	546	56	-16	9			.943	4	C-69	-0.5
1890	Phi-a	82	329	32	78	13	4	4	42	16		.237	.279	.337	616	82	-9	20			.930	-9	C-82	-1.0
	Bal-a	14	48	7	13	1	0	0	4	3		.271	.314	.292	605	75	-2	1			.989	6	C-11/1-3	0.5
	Yr	96	377	39	91	14	4	4	46	19		.241	.283	.332	615	81	-11	21			.938	-3	C-93/1-3	-0.5
1891	Bal-a	93	334	25	72	8	5	2	46	16	37	.216	.251	.287	539	54	-22	18			.954	3	C-92/O-1(0-0-1)	-1.0
1892	Bal-N	90	330	36	88	14	4	2	57	15	35	.267	.303	.352	654	95	-3	5			.921	-18	C-87/1-2,O-1(0-0-1)	-1.3
1893	Bal-N	95	359	49	120	21	3	3	57	26	22	.334	.382	.435	817	115	7	17			.942	-8	*C-93/1-1	0.6
1894	*Bal-N	109	414	69	146	21	4	1	98	46	18	.353	.421	.430	851	101	2	12			.944	-5	*C-109	0.5
1895	*Bal-N	77	282	38	74	19	1	0	48	12	19	.262	.295	.337	632	61	-17	11			**.979**	14	C-75	0.3
1896	*Bal-N	67	245	43	85	9	6	2	38	14	13	.347	.385	.457	842	120	6	9			.948	3	C-67	1.2
1897	Bal-N	48	181	25	57	9	0	0	23	8		.315	.347	.365	712	88	-3	0			.965	-2	C-48	-0.1
1898	Bal-N	79	289	29	80	12	2	0	38	16		.277	.317	.332	649	84	-6	3			.965	-5	C-77	-0.4
1899	Bal-N	108	356	40	101	15	2	0	47	31		.284	.344	.337	682	83	-8	5			.949	-18	*C-105	-1.5
1900	StL-N	60	210	26	52	5	1	0	28	11		.248	.291	.281	572	59	-12	7			.974	-1	C-54	-0.7
1901	Bal-A	68	239	32	72	12	3	0	26	10		.301	.335	.377	711	93	-3	9			.949	-2	C-67	0.2
1902	Bal-A	91	335	38	98	16	7	1	57	12		.293	.321	.391	712	93	-4	11			.949	-15	C-87,M	-1.0
Total	17	1371	5089	637	1402	212	51	18	722	286	178	.275	.316	.346	662	83	-129	196			.941	-36	*C-1316/1-32,O-8C	-4.8

■ EDDIE ROBINSON

Robinson, William Edward b: 12/15/20, Paris, Tex. BL/TR, 6'2.5", 210 lbs. Deb: 9/9/42 C

YEAR	TM/L	G	AB	R	H	2B	3B	HR	RBI	BB	SO	AVG	OBP	SLG	OPS	OPS+	BR+	SB	CS	SBR	FA	FR	G/POS	TPR
1942	Cle-A	8	8	1	1	0	0	0	2	1	0	.125	.222	.125	347	-1	-1	0	0	0	1.000	-0	/1-1	-0.1
1946	Cle-A	8	30	6	12	1	0	3	4	2	4	.400	.438	.733	1171	238	5	0	0	0	.988	-2	/1-8	0.3
1947	Cle-A	95	318	52	78	10	1	14	52	30	18	.245	.314	.415	729	105	0	1	0	0	.994	-3	1-87	-0.4
1948	*Cle-A	134	493	53	125	18	5	16	83	36	42	.254	.307	.408	715	91	-9	1	0	0	**.995**	-1	*1-131	-1.3
1949	Was-A★	143	527	66	155	27	3	18	78	67	30	.294	.381	.459	840	125	18	3	4	-1	.987	-2	*1-143	1.0
1950	Was-A	36	129	21	30	4	2	1	13	25	4	.233	.365	.318	683	80	-3	0	0	0	1.000	0	1-36	-0.4
	Chi-A	119	424	62	133	11	2	20	73	60	28	.314	.405	.491	895	132	21	0	0	0	.987	-7	*1-119	1.0
	Yr	155	553	83	163	15	4	21	86	85	32	.295	.395	.450	846	120	18	0	0	0	.990	-7	*1-155	0.6
1951	Chi-A★	151	564	85	159	23	5	29	117	77	54	.282	.371	.495	866	135	27	2	5	-1	.988	-6	*1-147	1.4
1952	Chi-A★	155	594	79	176	33	1	22	104	70	49	.296	.382	.466	848	134	27	2	0	0	.990	-8	*1-155	1.5
1953	Phi-A★	156	615	64	152	28	4	22	102	63	56	.247	.322	.413	735	94	-7	1	2	-0	.988	-14	*1-155	-3.1
1954	NY-A	85	142	11	37	9	0	3	27	19	21	.261	.348	.387	735	105	1	0	0	0	.980	1	1-29	0.0
1955	*NY-A	88	173	25	36	1	0	16	42	36	26	.208	.360	.491	851	129	7	0	0	0	.995	-2	1-46	0.3
1956	NY-A	26	54	7	12	1	0	5	11	5	3	.222	.323	.519	841	123	1	0	1	-0	1.000	-0	1-14	0.0
	KC-A	75	172	13	34	5	1	2	12	26	20	.198	.310	.273	583	55	-[illegible]1	0	0	0	.977	-4	1-47	-1.7
	Yr	101	226	20	46	6	1	7	23	31	23	.204	.313	.332	645	71	-10	0	1	-0	.983	-4	1-61	-1.7
1957	Det-A	13	9	0	0	0	0	0	0	3	0	.000	.308	.000	308	-9	-1	0	0	0	1.000	0	/1-1	-0.1
	Cle-A	19	27	1	6	1	0	1	3	0	3	.222	.250	.370	620	68	-1	0	0	0	1.000	0	/1-7	-0.1
	Bal-A	4	3	0	0	0	0	0	0	1	1	.000	.250	.000	250	-28	-1	0	0	0	.000	0	H	-0.1
	Yr	36	39	1	6	1	0	1	3	4	4	.154	.267	.256	523	44	-3	0	0	0	1.000	1	/1-8	-0.3
Total	13	1315	4282	546	1146	172	24	172	723	521	359	.268	.354	.440	793	113	74	10	12	-2	.990	-45	*1-1126	-1.8

■ YANK ROBINSON

Robinson, William H. b: 9/19/1859, Philadelphia, Pa. d: 8/25/1894, St.Louis, Mo. BR/TR, 5'6.5", 170 lbs. Deb: 8/24/1882 Career OF: (52-LF 2-CF 2-RF)

YEAR	TM/L	G	AB	R	H	2B	3B	HR	RBI	BB	SO	AVG	OBP	SLG	OPS	OPS+	BR+	SB	CS	SBR	FA	FR	G/POS	TPR
1882	Det-N	11	39	1	7	1	0	0	2	1	13	.179	.200	.205	405	30	-3				.800	-4	S-10/O-1(0-1-0),P-1	-0.6
1884	Bal-U	102	415	101	111	24	4	3		**37**		.267	.327	.366	694	100	-12				.831	16	3-71,S-14,C-11,P/2	0.9
1885	*StL-a	78	287	63	75	8	8	0	35	29		.261	.344	.345	689	113	5				.862	-6	O-52L,2-19/C-5,31	-0.1
1886	*StL-a	133	481	89	132	26	9	3	71	64		.274	.377	.385	761	132	20	51			.888	-4	*2-125/3-6,O-1C,SP	1.8
1887	*StL-a	125	522	102	223	32	4	1	74	92		.427	.445	.405	850	125	18	75			.899	-13	*2-117/3-6,O-2R,SCP	0.8
1888	*StL-a	134	455	111	105	17	6	3	53	**116**		.231	**.400**	.314	714	117	14	56			.895	-44	*2-102,S-34	-2.3
1889	StL-a	132	452	97	94	17	3	5	70	**118**	55	.208	.378	.292	671	81	-9	39			.887	-35	*2-132	-3.3
1890	Pit-P	98	306	59	70	10	3	0	38	101	33	.229	.434	.281	715	101	12	17			.887	-19	*2-98	-0.3
1891	Cin-a	97	342	48	61	9	4	1	37	68	51	.178	.328	.237	565	57	-18	23			.867	-11	*2-97	-2.3
	StL-a	1	3	0	0	0	0	0	0	0	0	.000	.000	.000	0	-87	-1	0			.750	-1	/2-1	-0.1
	Yr	98	345	48	61	9	4	1	37	68	51	.177	.325	.235	560	56	-19	23			.866	-12	2-98	-2.4
1892	Was-N	67	218	26	39	4	3	0	19	38	29	.179	.301	.225	526	61	-9	4			.852	-4	3-58/S-5,2-4	-1.1
Total	10	978	3520	697	917	148	44	16	399	664	181	.261	.375	.324	699	101	17	272			.887	-124	2-698,3-143/SOCP1	-6.6

■ BILL ROBINSON

Robinson, William Henry b: 6/26/43, McKeesport, Pa. BR/TR, 6'3", 205 lbs. Deb: 9/20/66 C Career OF: (479-LF 280-CF 364-RF)

YEAR	TM/L	G	AB	R	H	2B	3B	HR	RBI	BB	SO	AVG	OBP	SLG	OPS	OPS+	BR+	SB	CS	SBR	FA	FR	G/POS	TPR
1966	Atl-N	6	11	1	3	0	1	0	3	0	1	.273	.273	.455	727	96	-0	0	0	0	.800	-1	/O-5(2-0-3)	-0.2
1967	NY-A	116	342	31	67	6	1	7	29	28	56	.196	.261	.281	541	62	-16	2	2	-0	.968	-2	*O-102(20-33-53)	-2.6
1968	NY-A	107	342	34	82	16	7	6	40	26	54	.240	.297	.380	677	107	2	7	6	-1	.985	-3	O-98(6-51-44)	-0.6
1969	NY-A	87	222	23	38	11	2	3	21	16	39	.171	.227	.279	506	42	-18	3	1	0	.963	-3	O-62(17-19-29)/1-1	-2.5
1972	Phi-N	82	188	19	45	9	1	8	21	5	30	.239	.259	.426	685	89	-4	2	3	-1	.982	-8	O-72(13-30-32)	-1.6
1973	Phi-N	124	452	62	130	32	1	25	65	27	91	.288	.329	.529	858	131	16	5	4	-0	.979	-7	*O-113(13-44-75),3-14	0.5
1974	Phi-N	100	280	32	66	14	1	5	29	17	61	.236	.282	.346	628	72	-11	5	3	0	.971	-3	O-87(40-40-19)	-1.8
1975	*Pit-N	92	200	26	56	12	2	6	33	11	36	.280	.318	.450	768	112	2	3	1	0	.991	-2	O-57(31-15-13)	-0.1
1976	Pit-N	122	393	55	119	22	3	21	64	16	73	.303	.332	.534	866	142	18	2	6	-1	.993	-12	O-78R,3-37/1-3	0.2
1977	Pit-N	137	507	74	154	32	1	26	104	25	92	.304	.340	.525	865	125	16	12	6	1	.992	-14	1-86,O-43L,3-17	-0.5
1978	Pit-N	136	499	70	123	36	2	14	80	35	105	.246	.302	.411	713	93	-6	14	11	-1	.988	-4	*O-127L,3-29/1-3	-1.6
1979	*Pit-N	148	421	59	111	17	6	24	75	24	81	.264	.305	.504	808	111	4	13	2	2	.982	-13	*O-125L,1-28/3-3	-1.2

YEAR	TM/L	G	AB	R	H	2B	3B	HR	RBI	BB	SO	AVG	OBP	SLG	OPS	OPS+	BR+	SB	CS	SBR	FA	FR	G/POS	TPR
1980	Pit-N	100	272	28	78	10	1	12	36	15	45	.287	.324	.463	787	116	5	1	4	-1	.985	-10	1-49,O-41(28-0-14)	-1.2
1981	Pit-N	39	88	8	19	3	0	2	8	5	18	.216	.258	.318	576	61	-5	1	0	0	1.000	-0	1-23/O-7(1-0-6),3-1	-0.6
1982	Pit-N	31	71	8	17	3	0	4	12	5	19	.239	.289	.451	740	101	-0	0	1	-0	1.000	-1	O-22(12-0-11)	-0.2
	Phi-N	35	69	6	18	6	0	3	19	7	15	.261	.329	.478	807	121	2	1	1	-0	.960	-1	O-19(0-0-19)/1-5	0.0
	Yr	66	140	14	35	9	0	7	31	12	34	.250	.309	.464	773	111	1	1	2	-0	.984	-1	O-41(12-0-30)/1-5	-0.2
1983	Phi-N	10	7	0	1	0	0	0	2	1	4	.143	.250	.143	393	12	-1	0	0	0	1.000	-1	/1-3,3-2,O-1(1-0-0)	-0.2
Total	16	1472	4364	536	1127	229	29	166	641	263	820	.258	.303	.438	741	104	5	71	49	-2	.979	-84	*O-1059L,1-201,3-103	-14.2
■ **RAFAEL ROBLES**	Robles, Rafael Orlando (Natera) b: 10/20/47, San Pedro De Macoris, D.R. d: 8/13/98, New York, N.Y. BR/TR, 6', 170 lbs. Deb: 4/8/69																							
1969	SD-N	6	20	1	2	0	0	0	0	1	3	.100	.143	.100	243	-32	-4	1	1	-0	.895	-4	/S-6	-0.8
1970	SD-N	23	89	5	19	1	0	0	3	5	11	.213	.263	.225	488	33	-8	3	0	1	.968	2	S-23	-0.3
1972	SD-N	18	24	1	4	0	0	0	0	0	3	.167	.167	.167	333	-5	-3	0	0	0	.952	-2	S-15/3-1	-0.5
Total	3	47	133	7	25	1	0	0	3	6	17	.188	.229	.195	424	17	-15	4	1	1	.958	-4	/S-44,3-1	-1.6
■ **SERGIO ROBLES**	Robles, Sergio (Valenzuela) b: 4/16/46, Magdalena, Mexico BR/TR, 6'2", 190 lbs. Deb: 8/27/72																							
1972	Bal-A	2	5	0	1	0	0	0	0	0	0	.200	.200	.200	400	19	-0	0	0	0	1.000	-1	/C-1	-0.2
1973	Bal-A	8	13	0	1	0	0	0	0	3	1	.077	.250	.077	327	-4	-2	0	0	0	1.000	3	/C-8	0.1
1976	LA-N	6	3	0	0	0	0	0	0	0	2	.000	.000	.000	0	-99	-1	0	0	0	1.000	1	/C-6	0.0
Total	3	16	21	0	2	0	0	0	0	3	3	.095	.208	.095	304	-11	-3	0	0	0	1.000	2	/C-15	-0.1
■ **TOM ROBSON**	Robson, Thomas James b: 1/15/46, Rochester, N.Y. BR/TR, 6'3", 215 lbs. Deb: 9/14/74 C																							
1974	Tex-A	6	13	2	3	1	0	0	2	4	3	.231	.412	.308	719	112	0	0	0	0	1.000	-0	/1-1,D-5	0.0
1975	Tex-A	17	35	3	7	0	0	0	2	1	3	.200	.222	.200	422	20	-4	0	0	0	1.000	-0	/1-5,D-4	-0.4
Total	2	23	48	5	10	1	0	0	4	5	6	.208	.283	.229	512	48	-3	0	0	0	1.000	-0	/D-9,1-6	-0.4
■ **ADAM ROCAP**	Rocap, Adam b: 1854, Philadelphia, Pa. d: 3/29/1892, Philadelphia, Pa. 5'9", 170 lbs. Deb: 5/5/1875																							
1875	Ath-n	16	69	13	12	1	0	0	4	1	7	.174	.186	.188	374	27	-5	3	2	-0	.839	-1	O-12(0-5-7)/2-4	-0.6
■ **MICKEY ROCCO**	Rocco, Michael Dominick b: 3/2/16, St.Paul, Minn. d: 6/1/97, St.Paul, Minn. BL/TL, 5'11", 188 lbs. Deb: 6/5/43																							
1943	Cle-A	108	405	43	97	14	4	5	46	51	40	.240	.328	.331	658	99	-0	1	2	-0	**.995**	-5	*1-108	-1.3
1944	Cle-A	155	653	87	174	29	7	13	70	56	51	.266	.325	.392	717	108	5	4	8	-2	.993	17	*1-155	1.3
1945	Cle-A	143	565	81	149	28	6	10	56	52	40	.264	.326	.388	713	111	6	0	4	-1	**.992**	4	*1-141	0.2
1946	Cle-A	34	98	8	24	2	0	2	14	15	15	.245	.345	.327	672	94	-0	1	1	-0	.996	5	1-27	0.3
Total	4	440	1721	219	444	73	17	30	186	174	146	.258	.327	.372	700	106	11	6	15	-4	.994	21	1-431	0.5
■ **JACK ROCHE**	Roche, John Joseph "Red" b: 11/22/1890, Los Angeles, Cal. d: 3/30/83, Peoria, Ariz. BR/TR, 6'1", 178 lbs. Deb: 5/24/14																							
1914	StL-N	12	9	1	6	2	1	0	3	0	1	.667	.700	1.111	1811	441	4	1			.667	-2	/C-9	0.2
1915	StL-N	46	39	2	8	0	1	0	6	4	8	.205	.295	.256	552	68	-1	1			1.000	0	/C-4	-0.1
1917	StL-N	1	1	0	0	0	0	0	0	0	0	.000	.000	.000	0	-99	-0	0			.000	-1	/C-1	-0.1
Total	3	59	49	3	14	2	2	0	9	4	9	.286	.364	.408	772	133	2	2			.750	-2	/C-14	0.0
■ **BEN ROCHEFORT**	Rochefort, Bennett Harold (b: Bennett Harold Rochefort Gilbert) b: 8/15/1896, Camden, N.J. d: 4/2/81, Red Bank, N.J. BL/TR, 6'2", 185 lbs. Deb: 10/3/14																							
1914	Phi-A	1	2	0	1	0	0	0	0	0	1	.500	.500	.500	1000	209	0	0			1.000	0	/1-1	0.1
■ **LOU ROCHELLI**	Rochelli, Louis Joseph b: 1/11/19, Staunton, Ill. d: 10/23/92, Victoria, Tex. BR/TR, 6'1", 175 lbs. Deb: 8/25/44																							
1944	Bro-N	5	17	0	3	0	1	0	2	2	6	.176	.263	.294	557	58	-1	0			.964	-0	/2-5	-0.1
■ **LES ROCK**	Rock, Lester Henry (b: Lester Henry Schwarzrock) b: 8/19/12, Springfield, Minn. d: 9/9/91, Davis, Cal. BL/TR, 6'2", 184 lbs. Deb: 9/11/36																							
1936	Chi-A	2	1	0	0	0	0	0	1	0	0	.000	.000	.000	0	-97	-0	0	0	0	.000	0	/1-2	0.0
■ **IKE ROCKENFIELD**	Rockenfield, Isaac Broc b: 11/3/1876, Omaha, Neb. d: 2/21/27, San Diego, Cal. BR/TR, 5'7", 150 lbs. Deb: 5/5/05																							
1905	StL-A	95	322	40	70	12	0	0	16	46		.217	.340	.255	595	95	2	11			.926	-8	2-95	-0.6
1906	StL-A	27	89	3	21	4	0	0	8	1		.236	.277	.281	557	78	-2	0			.956	-5	2-26	-0.8
Total	2	122	411	43	91	16	0	0	24	47		.221	.328	.260	588	91	-1	11			.933	-14	2-121	-1.4
■ **PAT ROCKETT**	Rockett, Patrick Edward b: 1/9/55, San Antonio, Tex. BR/TR, 5'11", 170 lbs. Deb: 9/17/76																							
1976	Atl-N	4	5	0	1	0	0	0	0	0	1	.200	.200	.200	400	13	-1	0	0	0	1.000	-1	/S-2	-0.2
1977	Atl-N	93	264	27	67	10	0	1	24	27	32	.254	.330	.303	633	64	-12	1	2	-0	.940	-11	S-84	-1.6
1978	Atl-N	55	142	6	20	2	0	0	4	13	12	.141	.213	.155	368	4	-18	1	2	-0	.970	-10	S-51	-2.6
Total	3	152	411	33	88	12	0	1	28	40	45	.214	.289	.251	539	43	-31	2	4	-1	.949	-21	S-137	-4.4
■ **ANDRE RODGERS**	Rodgers, Kenneth Andre Ian "Andy" b: 12/2/34, Nassau, Bahamas BR/TR, 6'3", 200 lbs. Deb: 4/16/57																							
1957	NY-N	32	86	8	21	2	1	3	9	9	21	.244	.323	.395	718	92	-1	0	0	0	.950	5	S-20/3-8	0.6
1958	SF-N	22	63	7	13	3	1	2	11	4	14	.206	.254	.381	635	67	-3	0	0	0	.972	-3	S-18	-0.5
1959	SF-N	71	228	32	57	12	1	6	24	32	50	.250	.345	.390	735	98	-0	2	1	0	.933	-9	S-66	-0.4
1960	SF-N	81	217	22	53	8	5	2	22	24	44	.244	.328	.355	683	92	-2	1	1	-0	.953	-4	S-41,3-21/1-6,O-2L	-0.3
1961	Chi-N	73	214	27	57	17	0	6	23	25	54	.266	.346	.430	776	103	1	1	1	-0	.983	1	1-42,S-24/O-2R,2-1	0.1
1962	Chi-N	138	461	40	128	20	8	5	44	44	93	.278	.344	.388	733	93	-4	5	6	-1	.960	7	*S-133/1-1	1.3
1963	Chi-N	150	516	51	118	17	4	5	33	65	90	.229	.325	.306	632	79	-12	5	7	-1	.954	-3	*S-150	-0.3
1964	Chi-N	129	448	50	107	17	3	12	46	53	88	.239	.319	.371	690	90	-5	5	1	1	.965	19	*S-126	2.6
1965	Pit-N	75	178	17	51	12	0	2	25	18	28	.287	.352	.388	740	108	2	2	1	0	.950	-6	S-33,3-15/1-6,2-1	-0.2
1966	Pit-N	36	49	6	9	1	0	0	4	8	7	.184	.298	.204	502	43	-4	0	1	-0	.913	-1	/S-5,3-3,O-3L,1-2	-0.5
1967	Pit-N	47	61	8	14	3	0	2	4	8	18	.230	.319	.377	696	98	-0	1	1	-0	1.000	2	/1-9,3-5,S-3,2-2	0.2
Total	11	854	2521	268	628	112	23	45	245	290	507	.249	.331	.365	696	90	-28	22	20	-2	.956	9	S-619/1-66,3-52,O2	2.6
■ **BUCK RODGERS**	Rodgers, Robert Leroy b: 8/16/38, Delaware, Ohio BB/TR, 6'2", 195 lbs. Deb: 9/8/61 MC																							
1961	LA-A	16	56	8	18	2	0	2	13	1	6	.321	.333	.464	798	99	-0	0	0	0	.965	-1	C-14	0.0
1962	LA-A	155	565	65	146	34	6	6	61	45	68	.258	.313	.372	685	86	-12	1	8	-3	.989	1	*C-150	-0.6
1963	LA-A	100	300	24	70	6	0	4	23	29	35	.233	.305	.293	598	73	-10	2	2	-0	.979	-14	C-85	-2.2
1964	LA-A	148	514	38	125	18	3	4	54	40	71	.243	.303	.313	616	80	-14	4	3	-0	.987	14	*C-146	0.7
1965	Cal-A	132	411	33	86	14	3	1	32	35	61	.209	.276	.265	541	56	-23	4	5	-1	.991	6	*C-128	-1.4
1966	Cal-A	133	454	45	107	20	3	7	48	29	57	.236	.285	.339	624	81	-12	3	4	-1	.992	-4	*C-133	-1.2
1967	Cal-A	139	429	29	94	13	3	6	41	34	55	.219	.280	.305	585	76	-13	1	4	-1	.991	2	*C-134/O-1(1-0-0)	-0.7
1968	Cal-A	91	258	13	49	6	0	1	14	16	48	.190	.245	.225	470	45	-17	2	1	0	.985	0	C-87	-1.6
1969	Cal-A	18	46	4	9	1	0	0	2	5	8	.196	.288	.217	506	46	-3	0	0	0	1.000	-0	C-18	-0.3
Total	9	932	3033	259	704	114	18	31	288	234	409	.232	.291	.312	603	74	-106	17	27	-6	.988	3	C-895/O-1(1-0-0)	-7.3
■ **BILL RODGERS**	Rodgers, Wilbur Kincaid "Rawmeat Bill" b: 4/18/1887, Pleasant Ridge, O. d: 12/24/78, Goliad, Tex. BL/TR, 5'9.5", 170 lbs. Deb: 4/15/15 Career OF: (0-LF 0-CF 1-RF)																							
1915	Cle-A	16	45	8	14	2	0	0	7	8	7	.311	.415	.356	771	128	2	3	3	-0	.945	-4	2-13	-0.2
	Bos-A	11	6	2	0	0	0	0	0	3	2	.000	.333	.000	333	-0	-1	0			.900	1	/2-6	0.1
	Yr	27	51	10	14	2	0	0	7	11	9	.275	.403	.314	717	115	2	3	3	-0	.938	-3	2-19	-0.1
	Cin-N	72	213	20	51	13	4	0	12	11	29	.239	.299	.338	637	91	-3	8	5	0	.947	5	2-56/S-6,3-1,O-1R	0.4
1916	Cin-N	3	4	0	0	0	0	0	0	0	2	.000	.000	.000	0	-99	-1	0			1.000	-0	/S-1	-0.2
Total	2	102	268	30	65	15	4	0	19	22	40	.243	.316	.328	645	93	-2	11	8		.945	2	/2-75,S-7,O-1R,3-1	0.1
■ **BILL RODGERS**	Rodgers, William Sherman b: 12/5/22, Harrisburg, Pa. BL/TL, 6', 162 lbs. Deb: 9/27/44																							
1944	Pit-N	2	4	1	1	0	0	0	0	0	1	.250	.250	.250	500	39	-0	0			.000	-1	/O-1(0-0-1)	-0.1
1945	Pit-N	1	1	0	1	0	0	0	0	0	0	1.000	1.000	1.000	2000	440	0	0			.000	0	H	0.0
Total	2	3	5	1	2	0	0	0	0	0	1	.400	.400	.400	800	120	0	0			—	-1	/O-1(0-0-1)	-0.1

YEAR	TM/L	G	AB	R	H	2B	3B	HR	RBI	BB	SO	AVG	OBP	SLG	OPS	OPS+	BR+	SB	CS	SBR	FA	FR	G/POS	TPR
■ **ERIC RODIN**	Rodin, Eric Chapman b: 2/5/30, Orange, N.J. d: 1/4/91, Somerville, N.J. BR/TR, 6'2", 215 lbs. Deb: 9/7/54																							
1954	NY-N	5	6	0	0	0	0	0	0	0	2	.000	.000	.000	0	-99	-2	0	0	0	1.000	-1	/O-3(0-2-1)	-0.3
■ **ALEX RODRIGUEZ**	Rodriguez, Alexander Emmanuel b: 7/27/75, New York, N.Y. BR/TR, 6'3", 190 lbs. Deb: 7/8/94																							
1994	Sea-A	17	54	4	11	0	0	0	2	3	20	.204	.246	.204	449	17	-7	3	0	1	.915	1	S-17	-0.3
1995	*Sea-A	48	142	15	33	6	2	5	19	6	42	.232	.264	.408	672	71	-7	4	2	0	.953	-2	S-46/D-1	-0.5
1996	Sea-A★	146	601	**141**	215	**54**	1	36	123	59	104	**.358**	.419	.631	1049	160	55	15	4	2	.977	-10	*S-146	5.3
1997	*Sea-A★	141	587	100	176	40	3	23	84	41	99	.300	.351	.496	846	119	15	29	6	4	.962	-1	*S-140/D-1	2.9
1998	Sea-A★	161	686	123	**213**	35	5	42	124	45	121	.310	.362	.560	921	135	33	46	13	6	.975	-1	*S-160/D-1	4.8
1999	Sea-A	129	502	110	143	25	0	42	111	56	109	.285	.362	.586	948	140	28	21	7	2	.977	19	*S-129	5.4
2000	*Sea-A†	148	554	134	175	34	2	41	132	100	121	.316	.427	.606	1033	162	55	15	4	2	.986	18	*S-148	**7.7**
Total	7	790	3126	627	966	194	13	189	595	310	616	.309	.377	.561	938	138	172	133	36	17	.973	25	S-786/D-3	25.3
■ **AURELIO RODRIGUEZ**	Rodriguez, Aurelio (Ituarte) b: 12/28/47, Cananea, Mexico d: 9/23/2000, Detroit, Mich. BR/TR, 5'10", 180 lbs. Deb: 9/1/67																							
1967	Cal-A	29	130	14	31	3	1	1	8	2	21	.238	.250	.300	550	64	-6	1	0	0	.989	5	3-29	-0.2
1968	Cal-A	76	223	14	54	10	1	1	16	17	36	.242	.299	.309	608	88	-3	0	2	-1	.921	-7	3-70/2-2	-1.2
1969	Cal-A	159	561	47	130	17	2	7	49	32	88	.232	.276	.307	582	66	-27	5	3	0	.954	8	*3-159	-2.1
1970	Cal-A	17	63	6	17	2	2	0	7	3	6	.270	.313	.365	679	90	-1	0	1	-0	1.000	4	3-17	0.2
	Was-A	142	547	64	135	31	5	19	76	37	81	.247	.303	.426	729	104	0	15	5	2	.961	13	*3-136/S-7	1.5
	Yr	159	610	70	152	33	7	19	83	40	87	.249	.304	.420	724	102	-1	15	6	1	.965	17	*3-153/S-7	1.7
1971	Det-A	154	604	68	153	30	7	15	39	27	93	.253	.289	.401	689	90	-10	4	6	-1	.953	15	*3-153/S-1	0.3
1972	*Det-A	153	601	65	142	23	5	13	56	28	104	.236	.273	.356	629	83	-14	2	3	-1	.969	24	*3-153/S-2	1.0
1973	Det-A	160	555	46	123	27	3	9	58	31	85	.222	.267	.330	596	63	-28	3	1	0	.971	10	*3-160/S-1	-1.9
1974	Det-A	159	571	54	127	23	5	5	49	26	70	.222	.258	.306	564	60	-30	2	0	0	.961	22	*3-159	-1.0
1975	Det-A	151	507	47	124	20	6	13	60	30	63	.245	.287	.385	671	85	-12	1	1	-0	.953	21	*3-151	0.8
1976	Det-A	128	480	40	115	13	2	8	50	19	61	.240	.270	.325	595	71	-18	0	4	-1	**.978**	13	*3-128	-0.8
1977	Det-A	96	306	30	67	14	1	10	32	16	36	.219	.258	.369	627	65	-15	1	1	-0	.972	16	3-95/S-1	-0.1
1978	Det-A	134	385	40	102	25	2	7	43	19	37	.265	.305	.395	699	93	-5	0	1	-0	**.987**	2	*3-131	-0.5
1979	Det-A	106	343	27	87	18	0	5	36	11	40	.254	.279	.350	629	66	-17	0	2	-1	.956	5	*3-106/1-1	-1.4
1980	SD-N	89	175	7	35	7	2	2	13	6	26	.200	.227	.297	524	48	-13	1	1	-0	.965	10	3-88/S-2	-0.4
	*NY-A	52	164	14	36	6	1	3	14	7	35	.220	.251	.323	575	57	-10	0	0	0	.954	-5	3-49/2-6	-1.6
1981	*NY-A	27	52	4	18	2	0	2	8	2	10	.346	.370	.500	870	151	3	0	0	0	.951	4	3-20/2-3,1-1,D-2	0.7
1982	Chi-A	118	257	24	62	15	1	3	31	11	35	.241	.275	.342	618	68	-11	0	0	0	.969	19	*3-112/2-3,S-2	0.6
1983	Bal-A	45	67	0	8	0	0	0	2	0	13	.119	.132	.119	252	-31	-12	0	0	0	.969	2	3-45	-1.1
	*Chi-A	22	20	1	4	1	0	1	1	0	3	.200	.200	.400	600	58	-1	0	0	0	1.000	4	3-22	0.3
	Yr	67	87	1	12	1	0	1	3	0	16	.138	.148	.184	332	-9	-13	0	0	0	.978	6	3-67	-0.8
Total	17	2017	6611	612	1570	287	46	124	648	324	943	.237	.276	.351	627	75	-231	35	31	-3	.964	183	*3-1983/S-16,2-14,D1	-6.9
■ **CARLOS RODRIGUEZ**	Rodriguez, Carlos (Marquez) b: 11/1/67, Mexico City, Mexico BB/TR, 5'9", 160 lbs. Deb: 6/16/91																							
1991	NY-A	15	37	1	7	0	0	0	2	1	2	.189	.211	.189	400	11	-4	0	0	0	.957	1	S-11/2-3	-0.3
1994	Bos-A	57	174	15	50	14	1	1	13	11	13	.287	.330	.397	726	82	-5	1	0	0	.973	2	S-32,2-20/3-4	0.1
1995	Bos-A	13	30	5	10	2	0	0	5	2	2	.333	.394	.400	794	104	0	0	0	0	.960	3	/2-7,S-6,3-1	0.4
Total	3	85	241	21	67	16	1	1	20	14	17	.278	.320	.365	685	75	-9	1	0	0	.972	6	/S-49,2-30,3-5	0.2
■ **EDWIN RODRIGUEZ**	Rodriguez, Edwin (Morales) b: 8/14/60, Ponce, P.R. BR/TR, 5'11", 175 lbs. Deb: 9/28/82																							
1982	NY-A	3	9	2	3	0	0	0	1	1	1	.333	.400	.333	733	106	0	0	0	0	.875	1	/2-3	0.1
1983	SD-N	7	12	1	2	1	0	0	0	1	3	.167	.231	.250	481	34	-1	0	0	0	1.000	-1	/2-5,S-2,3-1	-0.2
1985	SD-N	1	1	0	0	0	0	0	0	0	0	.000	.000	.000	0	-99	-0	0	0	0	.000	0	/H	0.0
Total	3	11	22	3	5	1	0	0	1	2	4	.227	.292	.273	564	58	-1	0	0	0	.935	0	/2-8,S-2,3-1	-0.1
■ **ELLIE RODRIGUEZ**	Rodriguez, Eliseo (Delgado) b: 5/24/46, Fajardo, P.R. BR/TR, 5'11", 185 lbs. Deb: 5/26/68																							
1968	NY-A	9	24	1	5	0	0	0	1	3	3	.208	.296	.208	505	57	-1	0	0	0	1.000	0	/C-9	-0.1
1969	KC-A☆	95	267	27	63	10	0	2	20	31	26	.236	.333	.296	629	77	-7	3	2	-0	.990	-8	C-90	-1.2
1970	KC-A	80	231	25	52	8	2	1	15	27	35	.225	.317	.290	607	68	-9	2	1	0	.988	12	C-75	0.6
1971	Mil-A	115	319	28	67	10	1	1	30	41	51	.210	.315	.257	572	64	-13	1	1	-0	.992	6	*C-114	-0.3
1972	Mil-A☆	116	355	31	101	14	2	2	35	52	43	.285	.386	.352	739	123	13	1	4	-1	.983	-11	*C-114	0.7
1973	Mil-A	94	290	30	78	8	1	0	30	41	28	.269	.378	.303	682	96	1	4	3	-0	.986	4	C-75,D-14	0.8
1974	Cal-A	140	395	48	100	20	0	7	36	69	56	.253	.376	.357	733	119	13	4	5	-1	.992	-10	*C-137/D-1	0.9
1975	Cal-A	90	226	20	53	6	0	3	27	49	37	.235	.384	.301	685	103	4	2	2	-0	.991	-7	C-90	0.1
1976	LA-N	36	66	10	14	0	0	0	9	19	12	.212	.409	.212	621	82	0	0	0	0	.986	4	C-33	0.6
Total	9	775	2173	220	533	76	6	16	203	332	291	.245	.359	.308	667	94	1	17	18	-3	.989	-10	C-737/D-15	2.1
■ **HECTOR RODRIGUEZ**	Rodriguez, Hector Antonio (Ordenana) b: 6/13/20, Alquizar, Cuba BR/TR, 5'8", 165 lbs. Deb: 4/15/52																							
1952	Chi-A	124	407	55	108	14	0	1	40	47	22	.265	.346	.307	653	82	-8	7	6	-1	.959	2	*3-113	-0.8
■ **HENRY RODRIGUEZ**	Rodriguez, Henry Anderson (Lorenzo) b: 11/8/67, Santo Domingo, D.R. BL/TL, 6'1", 200 lbs. Deb: 7/5/92 Career OF: (676-LF 0-CF 94-RF)																							
1992	LA-N	53	146	11	32	7	0	3	14	8	30	.219	.260	.329	589	67	-7	0	0	0	.960	1	O-48(17-0-31)/1-1	-0.8
1993	LA-N	76	176	20	39	10	0	8	23	11	39	.222	.267	.415	682	84	-5	1	0	0	.984	-6	O-48(26-0-23),1-13	-1.3
1994	LA-N	104	306	33	82	14	2	8	49	17	58	.268	.311	.405	716	91	-5	0	1	-0	.986	0	O-86(85-0-6),1-17	-0.8
1995	LA-N	21	80	6	21	4	1	1	10	5	17	.262	.306	.375	681	86	-2	0	1	-0	1.000	-1	O-20(0-0-20)/1-1	-0.4
	Mon-N	24	58	7	12	0	0	1	5	6	11	.207	.281	.259	540	42	-5	0	0	0	1.000	-2	1-10/O-8(4-0-4)	-0.8
	Yr	45	138	13	33	4	1	2	15	11	28	.239	.295	.326	621	65	-7	0	1	-0	.977	-2	O-28(4-0-24),1-11	-1.2
1996	Mon-N★	145	532	81	147	42	1	36	103	37	160	.276	.327	.562	889	126	17	2	0	1	.947	-9	O-89(88-0-2),1-51	0.0
1997	Mon-N	132	476	55	116	28	3	26	83	42	149	.244	.308	.479	787	103	-1	3	3	-0	.985	-2	*O-126(126-0-1)/1-3	-0.7
1998	*Chi-N	128	415	56	104	21	1	31	85	54	113	.251	.337	.530	867	119	10	1	3	-1	.996	12	*O-114(114-0-0)/D-5	1.8
1999	Chi-N	130	447	72	136	29	0	26	87	56	113	.304	.382	.544	925	133	22	2	4	-1	.974	5	*O-122(122-0-0)/D-2	2.1
2000	Chi-N	76	259	37	65	15	1	18	51	22	76	.251	.317	.525	842	110	2	1	2	-0	.983	2	O-70(70-0-1)	0.2
	Fla-N	36	108	10	29	6	0	2	10	14	23	.269	.358	.380	737	91	-1	0	0	0	1.000	-2	O-29(24-0-6)	-0.4
	Yr	112	367	47	94	21	1	20	61	36	99	.256	.329	.482	812	105	1	1	2	-0	.987	1	O-99(94-0-7)	-0.2
Total	9	925	3003	388	783	176	9	160	520	272	789	.261	.324	.485	810	109	26	10	14	-3	.980	-1	O-760L/1-96,D-7	-1.1
■ **IVAN RODRIGUEZ**	Rodriguez, Ivan (Torres) "Pudge" b: 11/27/71, Manati, P.R. BR/TR, 5'9", 205 lbs. Deb: 6/20/91																							
1991	Tex-A	88	280	24	74	16	0	3	27	5	42	.264	.277	.354	631	75	-10	0	1	-0	.983	14	C-88	0.7
1992	Tex-A★	123	420	39	109	16	1	8	37	24	73	.260	.301	.360	661	87	-8	0	0	0	.983	8	*C-116/D-2	0.7
1993	Tex-A★	137	473	56	129	28	4	10	66	29	70	.273	.320	.412	732	99	-2	8	7	-1	.991	6	*C-134/D-1	1.1
1994	Tex-A★	99	363	56	108	19	1	16	57	31	42	.298	.364	.488	852	117	9	6	3	0	.992	-4	C-99	1.0
1995	Tex-A★	130	492	56	149	32	2	12	67	16	48	.303	.330	.449	779	98	-3	0	2	-1	.990	-1	*C-127/D-1	0.4
1996	*Tex-A★	153	639	116	192	47	3	19	86	38	55	.300	.344	.473	816	98	-3	5	0	1	.989	9	*C-146/D-6	1.5
1997	Tex-A★	150	597	98	187	34	4	20	77	38	89	.313	.362	.484	846	112	10	7	3	0	.992	5	*C-143/D-5	2.3
1998	*Tex-A★	145	579	88	186	40	4	21	91	32	88	.321	.360	.513	873	119	15	9	0	2	.994	-3	*C-139/D-6	2.1
1999	*Tex-A★	144	600	116	199	29	1	35	113	24	64	.332	.358	.558	917	124	19	25	12	1	.993	1	*C-141/D-1	2.8
2000	Tex-A★	91	363	66	126	27	4	27	83	19	48	.347	.381	.667	1048	153	27	5	5	-1	**.996**	-4	C-87/D-1	2.5
Total	10	1260	4806	715	1459	288	24	171	704	256	619	.304	.343	.480	823	110	55	65	33	3	.990	29	*C-1220/D-23	15.1
■ **JOSE RODRIGUEZ**	Rodriguez, Jose "El Hombre Goma" b: 2/23/1894, Havana, Cuba d: 1/21/53, Havana, Cuba BR/TR, 5'8", 150 lbs. Deb: 10/5/16																							
1916	NY-N	1	0	0	0	0	0	0	0	0	0	—	—	—	—	—	0	0			.000	0	R	0.0
1917	NY-N	7	20	2	4	0	1	0	2	2	1	.200	.273	.300	573	78	-1	2			1.000	-1	/1-7	-0.2
1918	NY-N	50	125	15	20	0	2	0	15	12	3	.160	.239	.192	431	33	-10	6			.978	4	2-40/1-8,3-2	-0.6
Total	3	58	145	17	24	0	3	0	17	14	4	.166	.244	.207	451	39	-10	8			.989	3	/2-40,1-15,3-2	-0.8

■ LIU RODRIGUEZ Rodriguez, Liubiemithz b: 11/5/76, Caracas, Venez. BB/TR, 5'9", 170 lbs. Deb: 6/9/99

YEAR	TM/L	G	AB	R	H	2B	3B	HR	RBI	BB	SO	AVG	OBP	SLG	OPS	OPS+	BR+	SB	CS	SBR	FA	FR	G/POS	TPR
1999	Chi-A	39	93	8	22	2	2	1	12	12	11	.237	.343	.333	676	73	-3	0	0	0	.985	-4	2-22,S-14/3-1	-0.5

■ TONY RODRIGUEZ Rodriguez, Luis Antonio b: 8/15/70, Rio Piedras, P.R. BR/TR, 5'11", 165 lbs. Deb: 7/6/96

YEAR	TM/L	G	AB	R	H	2B	3B	HR	RBI	BB	SO	AVG	OBP	SLG	OPS	OPS+	BR+	SB	CS	SBR	FA	FR	G/POS	TPR
1996	Bos-A	27	67	7	16	1	0	1	9	4	8	.239	.292	.299	590	49	-5	0	0	0	.979	5	S-21/3-5	0.2

■ RUBEN RODRIGUEZ Rodriguez, Ruben Dario (Martinez) b: 8/4/64, Cabrera, D.R. BR/TR, 6'3", 190 lbs. Deb: 9/17/86

YEAR	TM/L	G	AB	R	H	2B	3B	HR	RBI	BB	SO	AVG	OBP	SLG	OPS	OPS+	BR+	SB	CS	SBR	FA	FR	G/POS	TPR
1986	Pit-N	2	3	0	0	0	0	0	0	0	1	.000	.000	.000	0	-98	-1	0	0	0	1.000	1	/C-2	0.0
1988	Pit-N	2	5	1	1	0	1	0	1	0	2	.200	.200	.600	800	123	0	0	0	0	1.000	0	/C-2	0.0
Total	2	4	8	1	1	0	1	0	1	0	3	.125	.125	.375	500	36	-1	0	0	0	1.000	1	/C-4	0.0

■ STEVE RODRIGUEZ Rodriguez, Steven James b: 11/29/70, Las Vegas, Nev. BR/TR, 5'8", 170 lbs. Deb: 4/30/95

YEAR	TM/L	G	AB	R	H	2B	3B	HR	RBI	BB	SO	AVG	OBP	SLG	OPS	OPS+	BR+	SB	CS	SBR	FA	FR	G/POS	TPR
1995	Bos-A	6	8	1	1	0	0	0	0	1	1	.125	.222	.125	347	-6	-1	1	0	0	.667	-2	/S-4,2-1,D-1	-0.2
	Det-A	12	31	4	6	1	0	0	0	5	9	.194	.306	.226	531	41	-3	1	2	-0	.982	4	2-12/S-1	0.1
	Yr	18	39	5	7	1	0	0	0	6	10	.179	.289	.205	494	31	-4	2	2	-0	.983	2	2-13/S-5,D-1	-0.1

■ VIC RODRIGUEZ Rodriguez, Victor Manuel (Rivera) b: 7/14/61, New York, N.Y. BR/TR, 5'11", 173 lbs. Deb: 9/5/84

YEAR	TM/L	G	AB	R	H	2B	3B	HR	RBI	BB	SO	AVG	OBP	SLG	OPS	OPS+	BR+	SB	CS	SBR	FA	FR	G/POS	TPR
1984	Bal-A	11	17	4	7	3	0	0	2	0	2	.412	.412	.588	1000	177	2	0	0	0	.958	2	/2-7,D-1	0.4
1989	Min-A	6	11	2	5	2	0	0	0	0	1	.455	.455	.636	1091	191	1	0	0	0	.900	1	/3-5,D-1	0.2
Total	2	17	28	6	12	5	0	0	2	0	3	.429	.429	.607	1036	183	3	0	0	0	.958	3	/2-7,3-5,D-2	0.6

■ GARY ROENICKE Roenicke, Gary Steven b: 12/5/54, Covina, Cal. BR/TR, 6'3", 205 lbs. Deb: 6/8/76 F Career OF: (693-LF 113-CF 236-RF)

YEAR	TM/L	G	AB	R	H	2B	3B	HR	RBI	BB	SO	AVG	OBP	SLG	OPS	OPS+	BR+	SB	CS	SBR	FA	FR	G/POS	TPR
1976	Mon-N	29	90	9	20	3	1	2	5	4	18	.222	.263	.344	608	69	-4	0	0	0	.955	-1	O-25(3-0-22)	-0.6
1978	Bal-A	27	58	5	15	3	0	3	15	8	3	.259	.358	.466	824	138	3	0	1	-0	1.000	-3	O-20(20-0-0)	-0.1
1979	*Bal-A	133	376	60	98	16	1	25	64	61	74	.261	.381	.508	889	143	24	1	3	-1	.981	-8	*O-130(114-26-8)/D-2	1.0
1980	Bal-A	118	297	40	71	13	0	10	28	41	49	.239	.343	.384	727	100	1	2	0	0	**1.000**	-13	*O-113(86-13-38)	-1.6
1981	Bal-A	85	219	31	59	16	0	3	20	23	29	.269	.344	.384	728	110	3	1	2	-0	.983	-13	O-83(45-13-54)	-1.4
1982	Bal-A	137	393	58	106	25	1	21	74	70	73	.270	.392	.499	891	143	25	6	7	-1	.990	-9	*O-125(80-34-42),1-10	1.1
1983	*Bal-A	115	323	45	84	13	0	19	64	30	35	.260	.331	.477	807	121	9	2	2	-0	.982	-14	*O-100L/1-7,3-2,D-2	-0.9
1984	Bal-A	121	326	36	73	19	1	10	44	58	43	.224	.348	.380	728	104	3	1	2	-0	.995	-10	*O-117(85-6-32)	-1.2
1985	Bal-A	114	225	36	49	9	0	15	43	44	36	.218	.346	.458	804	121	7	2	2	-0	.993	-8	O-89(76-9-9),D-17	-0.4
1986	NY-A	69	136	11	36	5	0	3	18	27	30	.265	.390	.368	758	109	3	1	1	-0	1.000	-6	O-37L,D-15/3-3,1-2	-0.4
1987	Atl-N	67	151	25	33	8	0	9	28	32	23	.219	.359	.450	809	107	2	0	0	0	.968	-4	O-44(40-0-4)/1-9	-0.4
1988	Atl-N	49	114	11	26	5	0	1	7	8	15	.228	.279	.298	577	63	-5	0	0	0	1.000	-4	O-35(32-1-2)/1-1	-1.1
Total	12	1064	2708	367	670	135	4	121	410	406	428	.247	.354	.434	788	117	71	16	20	-3	.988	-92	O-918L/D-36,1-29,3	-6.0

■ RON ROENICKE Roenicke, Ronald Jon b: 8/19/56, Covina, Cal. BB/TL, 6', 180 lbs. Deb: 9/2/81 FC Career OF: (100-LF 169-CF 141-RF)

YEAR	TM/L	G	AB	R	H	2B	3B	HR	RBI	BB	SO	AVG	OBP	SLG	OPS	OPS+	BR+	SB	CS	SBR	FA	FR	G/POS	TPR
1981	LA-N	22	47	6	11	0	0	0	0	6	8	.234	.321	.234	555	62	-2	1	1	-0	1.000	-0	O-20(5-6-10)	-0.3
1982	LA-N	109	143	18	37	8	0	1	12	21	32	.259	.361	.336	697	99	1	5	0	1	.984	-19	O-72(21-18-39)	-2.0
1983	LA-N	81	145	12	32	4	0	2	12	14	26	.221	.289	.290	579	61	-8	3	2	-0	.987	-12	O-62(9-17-44)	-2.2
	Sea-A	59	198	23	50	12	0	4	23	33	22	.253	.365	.374	739	100	1	6	2	1	.993	7	O-54(16-38-4)/1-8,D-1	0.7
1984	*SD-N	12	20	4	6	1	0	1	2	2	5	.300	.364	.500	864	141	1	0	0	0	1.000	-2	O-10(7-2-2)	-0.2
1985	SF-N	65	133	23	34	9	1	3	13	35	27	.256	.411	.406	817	136	8	6	2	1	.984	-1	O-35(9-6-20)	0.7
1986	Phi-N	102	275	42	68	13	1	5	42	61	52	.247	.384	.356	740	102	3	2	2	-0	.989	-2	O-83(24-63-8)	0.0
1987	Phi-N	63	78	9	13	3	1	1	4	14	15	.167	.293	.269	563	49	-6	1	0	0	.964	-6	O-26(9-15-4)	-1.2
1988	Cin-N	14	37	4	5	1	0	0	5	4	8	.135	.238	.162	400	16	-4	0	0	0	1.000	-2	O-14(0-4-10)	-0.7
Total	8	527	1076	141	256	51	3	17	113	190	195	.238	.355	.338	693	92	-5	24	9	2	.989	-37	O-376C/1-8,D-1	-5.2

■ OSCAR ROETTGER Roettger, Oscar Frederick Louis "Okkie" b: 2/19/1900, St.Louis, Mo. d: 7/4/86, St.Louis, Mo. BR/TR, 6', 170 lbs. Deb: 7/7/23 F

YEAR	TM/L	G	AB	R	H	2B	3B	HR	RBI	BB	SO	AVG	OBP	SLG	OPS	OPS+	BR+	SB	CS	SBR	FA	FR	G/POS	TPR
1923	NY-A	5	2	0	0	0	0	0	0	0	0	.000	.000	.000	0	-98	-1	0	0	0	1.000	0	/P-5	0.0
1924	NY-A	1	0	0	0	0	0	0	0	0	0	—	—	—	—	—	0	0	0	0	.000	0	/P-1	0.0
1927	Bro-N	5	4	0	0	0	0	0	0	1	1	.000	.333	.000	333	-4	-0	0			.000	-1	/O-1(0-0-1)	-0.1
1932	Phi-A	26	60	7	14	1	0	0	6	5	4	.233	.292	.250	542	40	-5	0	0	0	.978	-2	1-15	-0.7
Total	4	37	66	7	14	1	0	0	6	6	5	.212	.288	.227	515	34	-6	0	0		1.000	-2	/1-15,P-6,O-1(0-0-1)	-0.8

■ WALLY ROETTGER Roettger, Walter Henry b: 8/28/02, St.Louis, Mo. d: 9/14/51, Champaign, Ill. BR/TR, 6'1.5", 190 lbs. Deb: 5/1/27 F

YEAR	TM/L	G	AB	R	H	2B	3B	HR	RBI	BB	SO	AVG	OBP	SLG	OPS	OPS+	BR+	SB	CS	SBR	FA	FR	G/POS	TPR
1927	StL-N	5	1	0	0	0	0	0	0	1	0	.000	.500	.000	500	42	0	0			.500	-1	/O-3(3-0-0)	-0.1
1928	StL-N	68	261	27	89	17	4	6	44	10	22	.341	.372	.506	878	125	9	2			.981	-1	O-66(33-0-34)	0.3
1929	StL-N	79	269	27	68	11	3	3	42	13	27	.253	.287	.349	637	56	-19	0			.993	-4	O-69(7-0-62)	-2.6
1930	NY-N	121	420	51	119	15	5	5	51	25	29	.283	.330	.379	708	72	-19	1			**.992**	-6	*O-114(28-85-4)	-2.7
1931	Cin-N	44	185	25	65	11	4	1	20	7	9	.351	.378	.470	849	135	8	1			.990	-1	O-44(18-2-24)	0.5
	*StL-N	45	151	16	43	12	2	0	17	9	14	.285	.337	.391	728	92	-2	0			.974	-6	O-42(8-7-27)	-1.0
	Yr	89	336	41	108	23	6	1	37	16	23	.321	.360	.435	794	114	6	1			.983	-7	O-86(26-9-51)	-0.5
1932	Cin-N	106	347	26	96	18	3	3	43	23	24	.277	.323	.372	695	89	-5	0			.991	0	O-94(89-5-0)	-1.1
1933	Cin-N	84	209	13	50	7	1	1	17	8	10	.239	.267	.297	564	62	-11	0			.977	0	O-55(26-1-28)	-1.4
1934	Pit-N	47	106	7	26	5	1	0	11	3	8	.245	.266	.311	577	53	-7	0			1.000	1	O-23(19-0-4)	-0.8
Total	8	599	1949	192	556	96	23	19	245	99	143	.285	.324	.387	711	85	-45	4			.986	-19	O-510(231-100-183)	-8.9

■ ED ROETZ Roetz, Edward Bernard b: 8/6/05, Philadelphia, Pa. d: 3/16/65, Philadelphia, Pa. BR/TR, 5'10", 160 lbs. Deb: 5/26/29

YEAR	TM/L	G	AB	R	H	2B	3B	HR	RBI	BB	SO	AVG	OBP	SLG	OPS	OPS+	BR+	SB	CS	SBR	FA	FR	G/POS	TPR
1929	StL-A	16	45	7	11	4	1	0	5	4	6	.244	.306	.378	684	72	-2	0	0	0	.909	-1	/S-8,1-5,2-2,3-1	-0.2

■ BILLY ROGELL Rogell, William George b: 11/24/04, Springfield, Ill. BB/TR, 5'10.5", 163 lbs. Deb: 4/14/25

YEAR	TM/L	G	AB	R	H	2B	3B	HR	RBI	BB	SO	AVG	OBP	SLG	OPS	OPS+	BR+	SB	CS	SBR	FA	FR	G/POS	TPR
1925	Bos-A	58	169	12	33	5	1	0	17	11	17	.195	.244	.237	481	22	-20	0	3	-1	.935	6	2-49/S-6	-1.3
1927	Bos-A	82	207	35	55	14	6	2	28	24	28	.266	.342	.420	762	99	-1	3	1	0	.966	6	3-53/2-2,O-2(1-0-1)	0.8
1928	Bos-A	102	296	33	69	10	4	0	29	22	47	.233	.295	.294	589	56	-19	2	6	-2	.935	-13	S-67,2-22/O-6R,3-3	-2.6
1930	Det-A	54	144	20	24	4	2	0	9	15	23	.167	.250	.222	472	20	-18	1	2	-0	.938	4	S-33,3-13/O-1(1-0-0)	-1.0
1931	Det-A	48	185	21	56	12	3	2	24	24	17	.303	.383	.432	815	110	3	8	8	-1	.958	11	S-48	1.5
1932	Det-A	144	554	88	150	29	6	9	61	50	38	.271	.332	.394	726	84	-14	14	6	1	.944	8	*S-139/3-4	0.5
1933	Det-A	155	587	67	173	42	11	0	57	79	33	.295	.381	.404	785	106	7	6	9	-2	.944	20	*S-155	3.4
1934	*Det-A	154	592	114	175	32	8	3	100	74	36	.296	.374	.392	766	97	-1	13	3	2	.962	9	*S-154	2.0
1935	*Det-A	150	560	88	154	23	11	6	71	80	29	.275	.367	.387	754	99	0	3	6	-1	**.971**	12	*S-150	2.1
1936	Det-A	146	585	85	160	27	5	6	68	73	41	.274	.357	.368	725	79	-19	14	10	-0	**.965**	-1	*S-146/3-1	-0.8
1937	Det-A	146	536	85	148	30	7	8	64	83	48	.276	.376	.403	779	94	-3	5	5	-1	**.967**	2	*S-146	0.8
1938	Det-A	136	501	76	130	22	8	3	55	86	37	.259	.373	.353	727	78	-14	9	2	1	.959	8	*S-134	0.4
1939	Det-A	74	174	24	40	6	3	2	23	26	14	.230	.330	.333	663	65	-9	3	1	0	.931	2	S-43,3-21/2-2	-0.3
1940	Chi-N	33	59	7	8	0	0	1	3	2	8	.136	.164	.186	350	-4	-8	1			.900	-5	S-14/3-9,2-3	-1.3
Total	14	1482	5149	755	1375	256	75	42	609	649	416	.267	.351	.370	722	84	-115	82	62		.956	68	*S-1235,3-104/2-78,O	4.2

■ EMMETT ROGERS Rogers, Emmett E. b: 11/8/1861, Ostelic, N.Y. BB, 5'10", 165 lbs. Deb: 4/19/1890

YEAR	TM/L	G	AB	R	H	2B	3B	HR	RBI	BB	SO	AVG	OBP	SLG	OPS	OPS+	BR+	SB	CS	SBR	FA	FR	G/POS	TPR
1890	Tol-a	35	110	18	19	3	3	0		7	14	.173	.266	.255	521	52	-7	2			.924	5	C-34/O-1(1-0-0)	0.1

■ FRALEY ROGERS Rogers, Fraley W. b: 1850, Brooklyn, N.Y. d: 5/10/1881, New York, N.Y. 5'8", 184 lbs. Deb: 4/30/1872

YEAR	TM/L	G	AB	R	H	2B	3B	HR	RBI	BB	SO	AVG	OBP	SLG	OPS	OPS+	BR+	SB	CS	SBR	FA	FR	G/POS	TPR
1872	Bos-n	45	204	39	56	7	1	1	28	1	4	.275	.278	.333	611	83	-5	2	0	0	.790	-2	*O-41(4-0-38)/1-6	-0.3
1873	Bos-n	1	6	1	2	1	0	0	2	0	1	.333	.333	.500	833	133	0	0	0	0	.813	-1	/1-1	0.0
Total	2 n	46	210	40	58	8	1	1	30	1	5	.276	.280	.338	618	84	-5	2	0	0	.893	-2	/O-41(4-0-38),1-7	-0.3

■ JIM ROGERS Rogers, James F. b: 4/9/1872, Hartford, Conn. 5'7.5", 180 lbs. Deb: 4/17/1896 M Career OF: (0-LF 1-CF 0-RF)

YEAR	TM/L	G	AB	R	H	2B	3B	HR	RBI	BB	SO	AVG	OBP	SLG	OPS	OPS+	BR+	SB	CS	SBR	FA	FR	G/POS	TPR
1896	Was-N	38	154	21	43	6	4	1	30	10	9	.279	.323	.390	713	87	-3	3			.882	-6	3-32/2-6,O-1(0-1-0)	-0.7
	Lou-N	72	290	39	75	8	6	0	38	15	14	.259	.297	.328	625	67	-14	13			.971	-2	1-60,S-12	-1.4
	Yr	110	444	60	118	14	10	1	68	25	23	.266	.306	.349	655	74	-17	16			.971	-8	1-60,3-32,S-12,/2O	-2.1
1897	Lou-N	42	153	22	22	3	2	2	22	23		.144	.260	.229	489	31	-15	4			.930	-3	2-40/1-3,M	-1.4
Total	2	152	597	82	140	17	12	3	90	48	23	.235	.294	.318	612	63	-33	20			.970	-11	/1-63,2-46,3-32,SO	-3.5

YEAR	TM/L	G	AB	R	H	2B	3B	HR	RBI	BB	SO	AVG	OBP	SLG	OPS	OPS+	BR+	SB	CS	SBR	FA	FR	G/POS	TPR
■ JAY ROGERS Rogers, Jay Lewis b: 8/3/1888, Sandusky, N.Y. d: 7/1/64, Carlisle, N.Y. BR/TR, 5'11.5", 178 lbs. Deb: 5/22/14																								
1914	NY-A	5	8	0	0	0	0	0	0	0	4	.000	.000	.000	0	-99	-2	0			.923	-0	/C-4	-0.2
■ PACKY ROGERS Rogers, Stanley Frank (b: Stanley Frank Hazinski) b: 4/26/13, Swoyersville, Pa. d: 5/15/98, Elmira, N.Y. BR/TR, 5'8", 175 lbs. Deb: 7/12/38																								
1938	Bro-N	23	37	3	7	1	1	0	5	6	6	.189	.302	.270	573	57	-2	0			1.000	-1	/S-9,3-8,2-3,O-1L	-0.2
■ MIKE ROGODZINSKI Rogodzinski, Michael George b: 2/22/48, Evanston, Ill. BL/TR, 6', 185 lbs. Deb: 5/4/73																								
1973	Phi-N	66	80	13	19	3	0	2	7	12	19	.237	.337	.350	687	88	-1	0	0	0	.947	-3	O-16(5-0-13)	-0.4
1974	Phi-N	17	15	1	1	0	0	0	1	2	3	.067	.176	.067	243	-29	-3	0	0	0	.000	-0	/O-1(0-0-1)	-0.3
1975	Phi-N	16	19	3	5	1	0	0	4	3	2	.263	.364	.316	679	86	-0	0	1	-0	.667	-1	/O-2(2-0-0)	-0.1
Total	3	99	114	17	25	4	0	2	12	17	24	.219	.321	.307	628	73	-4	0	1	-0	.909	-4	/O-19(7-0-14)	-0.8
■ DAVE ROHDE Rohde, David Grant b: 5/8/64, Los Altos, Cal. BB/TR, 6'2", 180 lbs. Deb: 4/9/90																								
1990	Hou-N	59	98	8	18	4	0	0	5	9	20	.184	.286	.224	510	44	-7	0	0	0	1.000	-0	2-32/3-4,S-2	-0.7
1991	Hou-N	29	41	3	5	0	0	0	0	5	8	.122	.217	.122	339	-2	-5	0	0	0	1.000	1	/2-4,3-3,S-3,1-1	-0.5
1992	Cle-A	5	7	0	0	0	0	0	0	2	3	.000	.222	.000	222	-34	-1	0	0	0	.900	1	/3-5	-0.1
Total	3	93	146	11	23	4	0	0	5	16	31	.158	.263	.185	448	27	-14	0	0	0	1.000	2	/2-36,3-12,S-5,1-1	-1.3
■ GEORGE ROHE Rohe, George Anthony "Whitey" b: 9/15/1875, Cincinnati, Ohio d: 6/10/57, Cincinnati, Ohio BR/TR, 5'9", 165 lbs. Deb: 5/7/01 Career OF: (1-LF 0-CF 0-RF)																								
1901	Bal-A	14	36	7	10	2	0	0	4	5		.278	.381	.333	714	95	0	1			.912	-3	/1-8,3-6	-0.2
1905	Chi-A	34	113	14	24	1	0	1	12	12		.212	.310	.248	558	81	-2	2			.934	-4	2-17,3-17	-0.6
1906	*Chi-A	77	225	14	58	5	1	0	25	16		.258	.316	.289	604	92	-2	8			.926	2	3-57/2-5,O-1(1-0-0)	0.2
1907	Chi-A	144	494	46	105	11	2	2	51	39		.213	.274	.255	529	71	-15	16			.898	-5	3-76,2-39,S-30	-1.9
Total	4	269	868	81	197	19	3	3	92	72		.227	.294	.266	561	79	-19	27			.917	-9	3-156/2-61,S-30,1O	-2.5
■ DAN ROHN Rohn, Daniel Jay b: 1/10/56, Alpena, Mich. BL/TR, 5'7", 165 lbs. Deb: 9/2/83																								
1983	Chi-N	23	31	3	12	3	2	0	6	2	2	.387	.424	.613	1037	176	3	1	0	0	.923	-0	/2-6,S-1	0.3
1984	Chi-N	25	31	1	4	0	0	1	3	1	6	.129	.156	.226	382	6	-4	0	0	0	1.000	0	/3-7,2-5,S-5	-0.4
1986	Cle-A	6	10	1	2	0	0	0	2	1	1	.200	.273	.200	473	32	-1	0	0	0	.900	1	/2-2,3-2,S-1	0.0
Total	3	54	72	5	18	3	2	1	11	4	9	.250	.289	.389	678	82	-2	1	0	0	.930	1	/2-13,3-9,S-7	-0.1
■ DAN ROHRMEIER Rohrmeier, Daniel b: 9/27/65, Cincinnati, O. BR/TR, 6', 185 lbs. Deb: 9/3/97																								
1997	Sea-A	7	9	4	3	0	0	0	2	2	4	.333	.455	.333	788	111	0	0	0	0	1.000	0	/1-3,D-4	0.1
■ RAY ROHWER Rohwer, Ray b: 6/5/1895, Dixon, Cal. d: 1/24/88, Davis, Cal. BL/TL, 5'10", 155 lbs. Deb: 4/13/21																								
1921	Pit-N	30	40	6	10	3	2	0	6	4	8	.250	.318	.425	743	93	-1	0	1	-0	.842	-1	O-10(0-3-7)	-0.2
1922	Pit-N	53	129	19	38	6	3	3	22	10	17	.295	.350	.457	807	105	1	1	0	0	.938	0	O-30(0-2-28)	-0.1
Total	2	83	169	25	48	9	5	3	28	14	25	.284	.342	.450	792	102	0	1	1	-0	.917	-1	/O-40(0-5-35)	-0.3
■ TONY ROIG Roig, Anton Ambrose b: 12/23/27, New Orleans, La. BR/TR, 6'1", 180 lbs. Deb: 9/13/53																								
1953	Was-A	3	8	0	1	1	0	0	0	0	1	.125	.125	.250	375	-1	-1	0	0	0	1.000	2	/2-2	0.0
1955	Was-A	29	57	3	13	1	1	0	4	2	15	.228	.254	.281	535	46	-4	0	0	0	.932	1	S-21/3-8,2-1	-0.3
1956	Was-A	44	119	11	25	5	2	0	7	20	29	.210	.324	.286	609	62	-6	2	0	0	.973	7	2-27,S-19	0.3
Total	3	76	184	14	39	7	3	0	11	22	45	.212	.296	.283	579	55	-12	2	0	0	.927	9	/S-40,2-30,3-8	0.0
■ COOKIE ROJAS Rojas, Octavio Victor (Rivas) b: 3/6/39, Havana, Cuba BR/TR, 5'10", 170 lbs. Deb: 4/10/62 MC Career OF: (79-LF 124-CF 10-RF)																								
1962	Cin-N	39	86	9	19	2	0	0	6	9	4	.221	.302	.244	546	47	-6	1	1	-0	.949	-2	2-30/3-1	-0.6
1963	Phi-N	64	77	18	17	0	1	1	2	3	8	.221	.259	.286	545	57	-4	4	1	1	.991	16	2-25/O-1(1-0-0)	1.5
1964	Phi-N	109	340	58	99	19	5	2	31	22	17	.291	.338	.394	732	107	3	1	3	-1	.967	-11	O-70C,2-20,S-18,/C3	-1.0
1965	Phi-N★	142	521	78	158	25	3	3	42	42	33	.303	.359	.380	739	110	8	5	5	-1	.986	-3	2-84,O-55C,S-11,/C1	1.0
1966	Phi-N	156	626	77	168	18	1	6	55	35	46	.268	.311	.329	640	78	-18	4	6	-1	.983	-9	*2-106,O-56L/S-2	-2.3
1967	Phi-N	147	528	60	137	21	2	4	45	30	58	.259	.299	.330	629	79	-14	8	4	0	.977	-4	*2-137/O-9L,C-3,SP3	-0.8
1968	Phi-N	152	621	53	144	19	0	9	48	16	55	.232	.251	.306	557	67	-26	4	8	-2	**.987**	11	*2-150/C-1	-0.5
1969	Phi-N	110	391	35	89	11	1	4	30	23	28	.228	.272	.292	564	60	-22	1	6	-2	.980	-3	2-95/O-2(2-0-0)	-2.2
1970	StL-N	23	47	2	5	0	0	0	2	3	4	.106	.176	.106	283	-22	-8	0	0	0	1.000	0	2-10/O-3(3-0-0),S-2	-0.7
	KC-A	98	384	36	100	13	3	2	28	20	29	.260	.297	.326	623	72	-15	3	7	-2	.982	-1	2-97	-1.1
1971	KC-A★	115	414	56	124	22	2	6	59	39	35	.300	.363	.406	768	118	10	8	3	1	**.991**	-12	*2-111/S-2,O-1(1-0-0)	0.7
1972	KC-A★	137	487	49	127	25	0	3	53	41	35	.261	.319	.331	650	94	-3	2	8	-2	.986	-2	*2-131/3-6,S-2	0.1
1973	KC-A★	139	551	78	152	29	3	6	69	37	38	.276	.323	.372	695	88	-9	18	4	3	.982	9	*2-137	1.2
1974	KC-A☆	144	542	52	147	17	1	6	60	30	43	.271	.313	.339	653	83	-12	8	4	0	**.987**	-24	*2-141	-2.8
1975	KC-A	120	406	34	103	18	2	2	37	30	24	.254	.305	.323	628	75	-13	4	5	-1	.980	-15	*2-117/D-1	-2.3
1976	*KC-A	63	132	11	32	6	0	0	16	8	15	.242	.286	.288	574	68	-5	2	0	0	1.000	-13	2-40/3-6,1-1,D-9	-1.7
1977	*KC-A	64	156	8	39	9	1	0	10	8	17	.250	.287	.321	607	65	-8	1	3	-1	.944	3	3-31,2-16/D-6	-0.5
Total	16	1822	6309	714	1660	254	25	54	593	396	489	.263	.309	.337	646	83	-143	74	68	-8	.984	-60	*2-1447,O-197C/3SDC1P	-12.0
■ STAN ROJEK Rojek, Stanley Andrew b: 4/21/19, N.Tonawanda, N.Y. d: 7/9/97, N.Tonawanda, N.Y. BR/TR, 5'10", 170 lbs. Deb: 9/22/42																								
1942	Bro-N	1	0	1	0	0	0	0	0	0	0	—	—	—	—	—	0	0			.000	0	R	0.0
1946	Bro-N	45	47	11	13	2	1	0	2	4	1	.277	.333	.362	695	96	-0	1			.974	5	S-15/2-6,3-4	0.6
1947	Bro-N	32	80	7	21	0	1	0	7	7	3	.262	.322	.287	609	61	-4	1			.971	8	S-17/3-9,2-7	0.4
1948	Pit-N	156	641	85	186	27	5	4	51	61	41	.290	.355	.367	721	94	-4	24			.962	-9	*S-156	-0.3
1949	Pit-N	144	557	72	136	19	2	0	31	50	31	.244	.309	.285	594	59	-31	4			.966	1	*S-144	-2.2
1950	Pit-N	76	230	28	59	12	1	0	17	18	13	.257	.313	.317	631	64	-12	2			.967	-15	S-68/2-3	-2.3
1951	Pit-N	8	16	0	3	0	0	0	0	0	1	.188	.188	.188	375	1	-2	0	0	0	.900	-1	/S-8	-0.3
	StL-N	51	186	21	51	7	3	0	14	10	10	.274	.318	.344	662	78	-6	0	3	-1	.974	1	S-51	-0.3
	Yr	59	202	21	54	7	3	0	14	10	11	.267	.308	.332	640	72	-8	0	3	-1	.968	-1	S-59	-0.6
1952	StL-A	9	7	0	1	0	0	0	0	2	0	.143	.333	.143	476	35	-1	0	0	0	1.000	2	/S-4,2-1	0.1
Total	8	522	1764	225	470	67	13	4	122	152	100	.266	.327	.326	653	74	-61	32	3		.965	-9	S-463/2-17,3-13	-4.3
■ SCOTT ROLEN Rolen, Scott Bruce b: 4/4/75, Evansville, Ind. BR/TR, 6'4", 210 lbs. Deb: 8/1/96																								
1996	Phi-N	37	130	10	33	7	0	4	18	13	27	.254	.326	.400	726	89	-2	0	2	-1	.954	-7	3-37	-1.0
1997	Phi-N	156	561	93	159	35	3	21	92	76	138	.283	.382	.469	850	121	19	16	6	1	.948	13	*3-155	3.4
1998	Phi-N	160	601	120	174	45	4	31	110	93	141	.290	.394	.532	927	139	36	14	7	1	.970	13	*3-159	4.9
1999	Phi-N	112	421	74	113	28	1	26	77	67	114	.268	.373	.525	898	120	13	12	2	2	.960	10	*3-112	2.4
2000	Phi-N	128	483	88	144	32	6	26	89	51	99	.298	.371	.551	922	127	19	8	1	1	.971	6	*3-128	2.5
Total	5	593	2196	385	623	147	14	108	386	300	519	.284	.378	.511	889	125	84	50	18	5	.961	36	3-591	12.2
■ RED ROLFE Rolfe, Robert Abial b: 10/17/08, Penacook, N.H. d: 7/8/69, Gilford, N.H. BL/TR, 5'11.5", 170 lbs. Deb: 6/29/31 MC																								
1931	NY-A	1	0	0	0	0	0	0	0	0	0	—	—	—	—	—	0	0	0	0	1.000	-0	/S-1	0.0
1934	NY-A	89	279	54	80	13	2	0	18	26	16	.287	.348	.348	695	86	-6	2	3	-1	.944	4	S-46,3-26	0.1
1935	NY-A	149	639	108	192	33	9	5	67	57	39	.300	.361	.404	764	103	3	7	3	0	**.964**	-7	*3-136,S-17	0.3
1936	*NY-A	135	568	116	181	39	**15**	10	70	68	38	.319	.392	.493	884	121	19	3	0	1	**.957**	3	*3-133	2.4
1937	*NY-A★	154	648	143	179	34	10	4	62	90	53	.276	.365	.378	743	87	-11	4	2	0	.962	5	*3-154	-0.1
1938	*NY-A☆	151	631	132	196	36	8	10	80	74	44	.311	.386	.441	826	107	8	13	1	3	.959	-7	*3-151	0.8
1939	*NY-A★	152	648	**139**	**213**	**46**	10	14	80	81	41	.329	.404	.495	899	131	31	7	6	-1	.958	-15	*3-152	1.9
1940	NY-A†	139	588	102	147	26	6	10	53	50	48	.250	.311	.366	677	78	-20	4	2	0	.949	-1	*3-138	-1.5
1941	*NY-A	136	561	106	148	22	5	8	42	57	38	.264	.332	.364	695	85	-12	3	2	-0	.946	-10	*3-134	-1.7
1942	*NY-A	69	265	42	58	8	2	8	25	23	18	.219	.281	.355	636	80	-8	1	1	-0	.959	5	3-60	-0.2
Total	10	1175	4827	942	1394	257	67	69	497	526	335	.289	.360	.413	773	100	3	44	20	3	.956	-22	*3-1084/S-64	2.0
■ NATE ROLISON Rolison, Natham Mardis b: 3/27/77, Hattiesburg, Miss. BL/TR, 6'6", 240 lbs. Deb: 9/5/2000																								
2000	Fla-N	8	13	0	1	0	0	0	2	1	4	.077	.143	.077	220	-45	-3	0	0	0	1.000	0	/1-4	-0.3

■ RAY ROLLING Rolling, Raymond Copeland b: 9/8/1886, Martinsburg, Mo. d: 8/25/66, St.Paul, Minn. BR/TR, 5'10.5", 160 lbs. Deb: 9/6/12

YEAR	TM/L	G	AB	R	H	2B	3B	HR	RBI	BB	SO	AVG	OBP	SLG	OPS	OPS+	BR+	SB	CS	SBR	FA	FR	G/POS	TPR
1912	StL-N	5	15	0	3	0	0	0	0	0	5	.200	.200	.200	400	10	-2	0			.947	-0	/2-4	-0.2

■ RED ROLLINGS Rollings, William Russell b: 3/21/04, Mobile, Ala. d: 12/31/64, Mobile, Ala. BL/TR, 5'11", 167 lbs. Deb: 4/17/27 Career OF: (2-LF 0-CF 2-RF)

YEAR	TM/L	G	AB	R	H	2B	3B	HR	RBI	BB	SO	AVG	OBP	SLG	OPS	OPS+	BR+	SB	CS	SBR	FA	FR	G/POS	TPR
1927	Bos-A	82	184	19	49	4	1	0	9	12	10	.266	.325	.299	624	64	-9	3	1	0	.938	-5	3-44,1-10/2-2	-1.2
1928	Bos-A	50	48	7	11	3	1	0	9	6	8	.229	.315	.333	648	72	-2	0	0	0	1.000	-2	/1-5,2-4,O-4L,3-1	-0.4
1930	Bos-N	52	123	10	29	6	0	0	10	9	5	.236	.288	.285	572	40	-12	2			.973	3	3-28,2-10	-0.7
Total	3	184	355	36	89	13	2	0	28	27	23	.251	.311	.299	609	57	-23	5	1		.947	-5	/3-73,2-16,1-15,O-4L	-2.3

■ JIMMY ROLLINS Rollins, James Calvin b: 11/27/78, Oakland, Cal. BB/TR, 5'8", 160 lbs. Deb: 9/17/2000

YEAR	TM/L	G	AB	R	H	2B	3B	HR	RBI	BB	SO	AVG	OBP	SLG	OPS	OPS+	BR+	SB	CS	SBR	FA	FR	G/POS	TPR
2000	Phi-N	14	53	5	17	1	1	0	5	2	7	.321	.345	.377	723	81	-1	3	0	1	.978	-5	S-13	-0.5

■ RICH ROLLINS Rollins, Richard John "Red" b: 4/16/38, Mount Pleasant, Pa. BR/TR, 5'10", 185 lbs. Deb: 6/16/61 Career OF: (1-LF 0-CF 0-RF)

YEAR	TM/L	G	AB	R	H	2B	3B	HR	RBI	BB	SO	AVG	OBP	SLG	OPS	OPS+	BR+	SB	CS	SBR	FA	FR	G/POS	TPR
1961	Min-A	13	17	3	5	1	0	0	3	2	2	.294	.400	.353	753	98	0	0	0	0	1.000	1	/2-5,3-4	0.1
1962	Min-A★	159	624	96	186	23	5	16	96	75	61	.298	.379	.428	807	112	13	3	1	0	.943	-5	*3-159/S-1	0.7
1963	Min-A	136	531	75	163	23	1	16	61	36	59	.307	.360	.444	804	122	15	2	0	0	.935	-7	*3-132/2-1	0.9
1964	Min-A	148	596	87	161	25	**10**	12	68	53	80	.270	.335	.406	741	104	3	2	5	-1	.947	-2	*3-146	0.0
1965	*Min-A	140	469	59	117	22	1	5	32	37	54	.249	.310	.333	642	79	-12	4	0	1	.958	-4	*3-112,2-16	-1.5
1966	Min-A	90	269	30	66	7	1	10	40	13	34	.245	.290	.390	681	88	-4	0	2	-1	.953	-4	3-65/2-2,O-1(1-0-0)	-1.0
1967	Min-A	109	339	31	83	11	2	6	39	27	58	.245	.306	.342	648	84	-6	1	1	-0	.963	-10	3-97	-1.8
1968	Min-A	93	203	14	49	5	0	6	30	10	34	.241	.287	.355	642	89	-3	3	1	0	.931	-2	3-56	-0.5
1969	Sea-A	58	187	15	42	7	0	4	21	7	19	.225	.271	.326	598	68	-9	2	0	0	.948	3	3-47/S-1	-0.6
1970	Mil-A	14	25	3	5	1	0	0	5	3	4	.200	.286	.240	526	46	-2	0	0	0	1.000	1	/3-7	-0.1
	Cle-A	42	43	6	10	0	0	2	4	3	5	.233	.283	.372	655	75	-2	0	0	0	.600	-1	/3-5	-0.3
	Yr	56	68	9	15	1	0	2	9	6	9	.221	.284	.324	607	65	-3	0	0	0	.900	-0	3-12	-0.4
Total	10	1002	3303	419	887	125	20	77	399	266	410	.269	.330	.388	719	98	-6	17	10	0	.947	-30	3-830/2-24,S-2,O-1L	-4.1

■ BILL ROLLINSON Rollinson, William (b: William Henry Winslow) b: 6/10/1856, Fairfield, Maine d: 9/28/38, Bristow, Va. Deb: 6/17/1884

YEAR	TM/L	G	AB	R	H	2B	3B	HR	RBI	BB	SO	AVG	OBP	SLG	OPS	OPS+	BR+	SB	CS	SBR	FA	FR	G/POS	TPR
1884	Was-U	1	3	0	0	0	0	0		0		.000	.000	.000	0	-99	-1				.714	0	/C-1	0.0

■ DAMIAN ROLLS Rolls, Damian Michael b: 9/15/77, Manhattan, Kan. BR/TR, 6'2", 205 lbs. Deb: 9/3/2000

YEAR	TM/L	G	AB	R	H	2B	3B	HR	RBI	BB	SO	AVG	OBP	SLG	OPS	OPS+	BR+	SB	CS	SBR	FA	FR	G/POS	TPR
2000	TB-A	4	3	0	1	0	0	0	0	0	1	.333	.333	.333	667	70	-0	0	0	0	.000	-0	/3-1,D-1	0.0

■ BILL ROMAN Roman, William Anthony b: 10/11/38, Detroit, Mich. BL/TL, 6'4", 190 lbs. Deb: 9/30/64

YEAR	TM/L	G	AB	R	H	2B	3B	HR	RBI	BB	SO	AVG	OBP	SLG	OPS	OPS+	BR+	SB	CS	SBR	FA	FR	G/POS	TPR
1964	Det-A	3	8	2	3	0	0	1	1	0	2	.375	.375	.750	1125	201	1	0	0	0	1.000	0	/1-2	0.1
1965	Det-A	21	27	0	2	0	0	0	0	2	7	.074	.138	.074	212	-38	-5	0	0	0	1.000	-0	/1-6	-0.6
Total	2	24	35	2	5	0	0	1	1	2	9	.143	.189	.229	418	17	-4	0	0	0	1.000	-0	/1-8	-0.5

■ JOHNNY ROMANO Romano, John Anthony "Honey" b: 8/23/34, Hoboken, N.J. BR/TR, 5'11", 205 lbs. Deb: 9/12/58

YEAR	TM/L	G	AB	R	H	2B	3B	HR	RBI	BB	SO	AVG	OBP	SLG	OPS	OPS+	BR+	SB	CS	SBR	FA	FR	G/POS	TPR
1958	Chi-A	4	7	1	2	0	0	0	1	1	0	.286	.375	.286	661	86	-0	0	0	0	1.000	1	/C-2	0.1
1959	*Chi-A	53	126	20	37	5	1	5	25	23	18	.294	.407	.468	875	141	8	0	1	-0	.979	1	C-38	1.0
1960	Cle-A	108	316	40	86	12	2	16	52	37	50	.272	.354	.475	829	126	11	0	0	0	.988	-11	C-99	0.5
1961	Cle-A★	142	509	76	152	29	1	21	80	61	60	.299	.379	.483	862	132	24	0	0	0	.989	-9	*C-141	2.2
1962	Cle-A★	135	459	71	120	19	3	25	81	73	64	.261	.369	.479	848	130	20	0	1	-0	.990	-9	*C-130	1.8
1963	Cle-A	89	255	28	55	5	2	10	34	38	49	.216	.322	.369	691	94	-2	4	3	-0	.993	-11	C-71/O-4(4-0-0)	-1.0
1964	Cle-A	106	352	46	85	18	1	19	47	51	83	.241	.349	.460	809	124	12	2	2	-0	.991	-5	C-96/1-1	1.2
1965	Chi-A	122	356	39	86	11	0	18	48	59	74	.242	.357	.424	781	129	15	0	2	-1	.992	4	*C-111/O-4(4-0-0),1-2	2.4
1966	Chi-A	122	329	33	76	12	0	15	47	58	72	.231	.348	.404	752	124	11	0	0	0	.993	3	*C-102	2.1
1967	StL-N	24	58	1	7	1	0	0	2	13	15	.121	.282	.138	420	24	-5	1	0	0	.983	-1	C-20	-0.5
Total	10	905	2767	355	706	112	10	129	417	414	485	.255	.358	.443	801	123	94	7	9	-2	.990	-36	C-810/O-8(8-0-0),1-3	9.8

■ TOM ROMANO Romano, Thomas Michael b: 10/25/58, Syracuse, N.Y. BR/TR, 5'10", 170 lbs. Deb: 9/1/87

YEAR	TM/L	G	AB	R	H	2B	3B	HR	RBI	BB	SO	AVG	OBP	SLG	OPS	OPS+	BR+	SB	CS	SBR	FA	FR	G/POS	TPR
1987	Mon-N	7	3	1	0	0	0	0	0	0	1	.000	.000	.000	0	-97	-1	0	0	0	.000	-1	/O-3(3-0-0)	-0.2

■ MANDY ROMERO Romero, Armando b: 10/29/67, Miami, Fla. BB/TR, 5'11", 200 lbs. Deb: 7/15/97

YEAR	TM/L	G	AB	R	H	2B	3B	HR	RBI	BB	SO	AVG	OBP	SLG	OPS	OPS+	BR+	SB	CS	SBR	FA	FR	G/POS	TPR
1997	SD-N	21	48	7	10	0	0	2	4	2	18	.208	.240	.333	573	52	-4	1	0	0	1.000	3	C-19	0.0
1998	SD-N	6	9	1	0	0	0	0	0	1	3	.000	.100	.000	100	-77	-2	0	0	0	.963	1	/C-6	-0.1
	Bos-A	12	13	2	3	1	0	0	1	3	3	.231	.375	.308	683	79	-0	0	0	0	1.000	0	/C-4,D-3	0.0
Total	2	39	70	10	13	1	0	2	5	6	24	.186	.250	.286	536	42	-6	1	0	0	.993	4	/C-29,D-3	-0.1

■ ED ROMERO Romero, Edgardo Ralph (Rivera) b: 12/9/57, Santurce, P.R. BR/TR, 5'11", 175 lbs. Deb: 7/16/77 Career OF: (17-LF 1-CF 14-RF)

YEAR	TM/L	G	AB	R	H	2B	3B	HR	RBI	BB	SO	AVG	OBP	SLG	OPS	OPS+	BR+	SB	CS	SBR	FA	FR	G/POS	TPR
1977	Mil-A	10	25	4	7	1	0	0	2	4	3	.280	.379	.320	699	93	-0	0	0	0	.971	0	S-10	0.1
1980	Mil-A	42	104	20	27	7	0	1	10	9	11	.260	.319	.356	674	87	-2	2	0	0	.894	4	S-22,2-15/3-3	0.5
1981	*Mil-A	44	91	6	18	3	0	1	10	4	9	.198	.232	.264	495	45	-7	0	2	-1	.949	10	S-22,2-18/3-3	0.5
1982	Mil-A	52	144	18	36	8	0	1	7	8	16	.250	.289	.326	616	73	-5	0	0	0	.975	-1	2-39,S-10/3-2,O-1L	-0.4
1983	Mil-A	59	145	17	46	7	0	1	18	8	8	.317	.353	.386	739	112	2	1	0	0	.962	-10	S-22,O-15L/3-5,2D	-0.6
1984	Mil-A	116	357	36	90	12	0	1	31	29	25	.252	.310	.294	604	71	-13	3	3	-0	.943	2	3-59,S-39,2-11,/1OD	-0.9
1985	Mil-A	88	251	24	63	11	1	0	21	26	20	.251	.321	.303	624	72	-9	1	1	-0	.977	8	S-43,2-31,O-14R,/3	0.5
1986	*Bos-A	100	233	41	49	11	0	2	23	18	16	.210	.273	.283	556	51	-16	2	0	0	.959	-8	S-75,3-18/2-4,O-1C	-1.7
1987	Bos-A	88	235	23	64	5	0	0	14	18	22	.272	.324	.294	618	64	-12	0	2	-1	.973	2	2-29,S-24,3-24,/1-8	-0.7
1988	*Bos-A	31	75	3	18	3	0	0	5	3	8	.240	.278	.280	558	55	-4	0	0	0	1.000	-1	3-15/S-8/2-5,1-1,D	-0.4
1989	Bos-A	46	113	14	24	4	0	0	6	7	7	.212	.264	.248	512	42	-8	0	2	-1	.983	13	2-22,3-14,S-10,/D-2	0.4
	Atl-N	7	19	1	5	1	0	1	1	0	0	.263	.263	.474	737	104	-0	0	0	0	.947	5	/2-4,S-2,3-1	0.5
	Mil-A	15	50	3	10	3	0	0	3	0	10	.200	.200	.260	460	29	-5	0	0	0	1.000	0	2-11/3-4,S-1	-0.4
1990	Det-A	32	70	8	16	3	0	0	4	6	4	.229	.289	.271	561	57	-4	0	0	0	.982	6	3-27/D-3	0.2
Total	12	730	1912	218	473	79	1	8	155	140	159	.247	.300	.302	603	67	-83	9	10	-2	.958	30	S-288,2-192,3/O1D	-2.4

■ KEVIN ROMINE Romine, Kevin Andrew b: 5/23/61, Exeter, N.H. BR/TR, 5'11", 185 lbs. Deb: 9/5/85 Career OF: (53-LF 112-CF 130-RF)

YEAR	TM/L	G	AB	R	H	2B	3B	HR	RBI	BB	SO	AVG	OBP	SLG	OPS	OPS+	BR+	SB	CS	SBR	FA	FR	G/POS	TPR
1985	Bos-A	24	28	3	6	2	0	0	1	1	4	.214	.241	.286	527	42	-2	1	0	0	1.000	-5	O-23(12-1-12)/D-1	-0.8
1986	Bos-A	35	35	6	9	2	0	0	2	3	9	.257	.316	.314	630	72	-1	2	0	0	1.000	-6	O-33(0-28-5)	-0.7
1987	Bos-A	9	24	5	7	2	0	0	2	2	6	.292	.346	.375	721	89	-0	0	0	0	1.000	-0	/O-7(1-4-3),D-2	-0.1
1988	*Bos-A	57	78	17	15	2	1	1	6	7	15	.192	.259	.282	541	49	-5	2	0	0	.957	-13	O-45(5-9-38)/D-5	-1.8
1989	Bos-A	92	274	30	75	13	0	1	23	21	53	.274	.330	.332	662	82	-6	1	1	-0	.982	-2	O-89(9-48-32)/D-2	-0.9
1990	Bos-A	70	136	21	37	7	0	2	14	12	27	.272	.336	.368	703	92	-1	4	0	1	.976	-11	O-64(16-18-30)/D-1	-1.3
1991	Bos-A	44	55	7	9	2	0	1	7	3	10	.164	.207	.255	461	26	-6	1	1	-0	.964	-4	O-23(10-4-10),D-14	-1.1
Total	7	331	630	89	158	30	1	5	55	49	124	.251	.308	.325	633	73	-22	11	2	2	.980	-41	O-284R/D-25	-6.7

■ MARC RONAN Ronan, Edward Marcus b: 9/19/69, Ozark, Ala. BL/TR, 6'2", 190 lbs. Deb: 9/21/93

YEAR	TM/L	G	AB	R	H	2B	3B	HR	RBI	BB	SO	AVG	OBP	SLG	OPS	OPS+	BR+	SB	CS	SBR	FA	FR	G/POS	TPR
1993	StL-N	6	12	0	1	0	0	0	0	0	5	.083	.083	.083	167	-56	-3	0	0	0	1.000	2	/C-6	-0.1

■ HENRI RONDEAU Rondeau, Henri Joseph b: 5/7/1887, Danielson, Conn. d: 5/28/43, Woonsocket, R.I. BR/TR, 5'11", 175 lbs. Deb: 4/11/13 Career OF: (42-LF 0-CF 17-RF)

YEAR	TM/L	G	AB	R	H	2B	3B	HR	RBI	BB	SO	AVG	OBP	SLG	OPS	OPS+	BR+	SB	CS	SBR	FA	FR	G/POS	TPR
1913	Det-A	36	70	5	13	2	0	0	5	14	16	.186	.321	.214	536	58	-3	1			1.000	-2	C-16/1-6	-0.4
1915	Was-A	14	40	3	7	0	0	0	4	4	3	.175	.250	.175	425	27	-4	1	2	-0	1.000	3	O-11(11-0-0)	-0.2
1916	Was-A	50	162	20	36	5	3	1	28	18	18	.222	.311	.309	620	87	-2	7			.958	3	O-48(31-0-17)	-0.1
Total	3	100	272	28	56	7	3	1	37	36	37	.206	.305	.265	570	71	-9	9	2		.967	4	/O-59L,C-16,1-6	-0.7

■ GENE ROOF Roof, Eugene Lawrence b: 1/13/58, Paducah, Ky. BB/TR, 6'2", 180 lbs. Deb: 9/3/81 F

YEAR	TM/L	G	AB	R	H	2B	3B	HR	RBI	BB	SO	AVG	OBP	SLG	OPS	OPS+	BR+	SB	CS	SBR	FA	FR	G/POS	TPR
1981	StL-N	23	60	11	18	6	0	0	3	12	16	.300	.417	.400	817	129	3	5	1	1	.950	-2	O-20(20-0-0)	0.1
1982	StL-N	11	15	3	4	0	0	0	2	1	4	.267	.313	.267	579	63	-1	2	0	0	1.000	-1	/O-5(4-0-2)	-0.2
1983	StL-N	6	3	1	0	0	0	0	0	0	0	.000	.000	.000	0	-99	-1	0	0	0	.000	-0	/O-1(1-0-0)	-0.1
	Mon-N	8	12	2	2	2	0	0	1	1	3	.167	.231	.333	564	55	-1	0	0	0	1.000	-1	/O-5(0-1-4)	-0.2

YEAR	TM/L	G	AB	R	H	2B	3B	HR	RBI	BB	SO	AVG	OBP	SLG	OPS	OPS+	BR+	SB	CS	SBR	FA	FR	G/POS	TPR
	Yr	14	15	3	2	2	0	0	1	1	3	.133	.188	.267	454	25	-2	0	0	0	1.000	-2	/O-6(1-1-4)	-0.3
Total	3	48	90	17	24	8	0	0	6	14	23	.267	.365	.356	721	102	1	7	1	1	.958	-5	/O-31(25-1-6)	-0.4
■ PHIL ROOF Roof, Phillip Anthony b: 3/5/41, Paducah, Ky. BR/TR, 6'3", 210 lbs. Deb: 4/29/61 FC																								
1961	Mil-N	1	0	0	0	0	0	0	0	0	0	—	—	—	—	—	0	0	0	0	1.000	0	/C-1	0.0
1964	Mil-N	1	2	0	0	0	0	0	0	0	1	.000	.000	.000	0	-99	-1	0	0	0	1.000	1	/C-1	0.1
1965	Cal-A	9	22	1	3	0	0	0	0	0	6	.136	.136	.136	273	-23	-3	0	0	0	.983	6	/C-9	0.2
	Cle-A	43	52	3	9	1	0	0	3	5	13	.173	.259	.192	451	30	-5	0	0	0	.994	13	C-41	1.0
	Yr	52	74	4	12	1	0	0	3	5	19	.162	.225	.176	401	15	-8	0	0	0	.992	19	C-50	1.2
1966	KC-A	127	369	33	77	14	3	7	44	37	95	.209	.286	.320	606	76	-11	2	5	-1	.985	-1	*C-123/1-2	-0.8
1967	KC-A	114	327	23	67	14	5	6	24	23	85	.205	.268	.333	601	79	-9	4	1	1	.991	-1	*C-113	-0.6
1968	Oak-A	34	64	5	12	0	0	1	2	2	15	.188	.212	.234	446	37	-5	1	0	0	.968	-1	C-32	-0.6
1969	Oak-A	106	247	19	58	6	1	2	19	33	55	.235	.337	.291	628	81	-5	1	0	0	.983	-1	*C-106	-0.2
1970	Mil-A	110	321	39	73	7	1	13	37	32	72	.227	.307	.377	684	87	-6	3	2	-0	.988	8	*C-107/1-1	0.6
1971	Mil-A	41	114	6	22	2	1	1	10	8	28	.193	.252	.254	506	44	-8	0	0	0	.975	3	C-39	-0.4
	Min-A	31	87	6	21	4	0	0	6	8	18	.241	.305	.287	593	67	-4	0	1	-0	.985	8	C-29	0.5
	Yr	72	201	12	43	6	1	1	16	16	46	.214	.275	.269	544	54	-12	0	1	-0	.980	11	C-68	0.1
1972	Min-A	61	146	16	30	11	1	3	12	6	27	.205	.237	.356	593	71	-6	0	1	-0	.978	-2	C-61	-0.7
1973	Min-A	47	117	10	23	4	1	1	15	13	27	.197	.277	.274	550	53	-7	0	0	0	.992	6	C-47	0.1
1974	Min-A	44	97	10	19	1	0	2	13	6	24	.196	.257	.268	525	50	-6	0	0	0	1.000	7	C-44	0.3
1975	Min-A	63	126	18	38	2	0	7	21	9	28	.302	.353	.484	837	133	5	0	0	0	.989	6	C-63	1.3
1976	Min-A	18	46	1	10	3	0	0	4	2	6	.217	.250	.283	533	55	-3	0	0	0	.962	5	C-12/D-1	0.3
	Chi-A	4	9	0	1	0	0	0	0	0	3	.111	.111	.111	222	-35	-2	0	0	0	1.000	-0	/C-4	-0.2
	Yr	22	55	1	11	3	0	0	4	2	9	.200	.228	.255	483	40	-4	0	0	0	.967	5	C-16/D-1	0.1
1977	Tor-A	3	5	0	0	0	0	0	0	0	1	.000	.000	.000	0	-99	-1	0	0	0	1.000	1	/C-3	0.0
Total	15	857	2151	190	463	69	13	43	210	184	504	.215	.284	.319	604	73	-77	11	10	-1	.986	58	C-835/1-3,D-1	0.9
■ GEORGE ROOKS Rooks, George Brinton McClellan (b: George Brinton Mc Clellan Ruckser) b: 10/21/1863, Chicago, Ill. d: 3/11/35, Chicago, Ill. BR/TR, 5'11", 170 lbs. Deb: 5/12/1891 F																								
1891	Bos-N	5	16	1	2	0	0	0	0	4	1	.125	.300	.125	425	23	-1	0			1.000	1	/O-5(5-0-0)	-0.1
■ ROLANDO ROOMES Roomes, Rolando Audley b: 2/15/62, Kingston, Jamaica BR/TR, 6'3", 180 lbs. Deb: 4/12/88																								
1988	Chi-N	17	16	3	3	0	0	0	0	0	4	.188	.188	.188	375	8	-2	0	1	-0	.833	-1	/O-5(4-0-1)	-0.4
1989	Cin-N	107	315	36	83	18	5	7	34	13	100	.263	.299	.419	718	100	-1	12	8	-0	.981	-3	*O-100(45-29-37)	-0.6
1990	Cin-N	30	61	5	13	0	0	2	7	0	20	.213	.213	.311	525	41	-5	0	0	0	1.000	-0	O-19(12-0-7)	-0.6
	Mon-N	16	14	1	4	0	1	0	1	1	6	.286	.333	.429	762	112	0	0	2	-1	1.000	-1	/O-6(3-2-1)	-0.2
	Yr	46	75	6	17	0	1	2	8	1	26	.227	.237	.333	570	54	-5	0	2	-1	1.000	-2	O-25(15-2-8)	-0.8
Total	3	170	406	45	103	18	6	9	42	14	130	.254	.284	.394	678	88	-8	12	11	-1	.980	-5	O-130(64-31-46)	-1.8
■ FRANK ROONEY Rooney, Frank (b: Frank Rovny) b: 10/12/1884, Podebrady, Bohemia (Austria-Hungary) d: 4/6/77, Bessemer, Mich. Deb: 4/18/14																								
1914	Ind-F	12	35	1	7	0	1	1	8	1	0	.200	.222	.343	565	47	-3	2			.980	-1	/1-9	-0.5
■ PAT ROONEY Rooney, Patrick Eugene b: 11/28/57, Chicago, Ill. BR/TR, 6'1", 190 lbs. Deb: 9/9/81																								
1981	Mon-N	4	5	0	0	0	0	0	0	0	3	.000	.000	.000	0	-99	-1	0	0	0	1.000	-1	/O-2(0-0-2)	-0.2
■ JORGE ROQUE Roque, Jorge (Vargas) b: 4/28/50, Ponce, P.R. BR/TR, 5'10", 158 lbs. Deb: 9/4/70																								
1970	StL-N	5	1	2	0	0	0	0	0	0	1	.000	.500	.000	500	45	0	0	0	0	.000	-0	/O-1(1-0-0)	0.0
1971	StL-N	3	10	2	3	0	0	0	1	0	3	.300	.300	.300	600	68	-0	1	0	0	1.000	-0	/O-3(0-3-0)	0.0
1972	StL-N	32	67	3	7	2	1	1	5	6	19	.104	.178	.209	387	10	-8	1	1	-0	.980	-1	O-24(0-21-3)	-1.1
1973	Mon-N	25	61	7	9	2	0	1	6	4	17	.148	.212	.230	442	22	-7	2	2	-0	.878	-3	O-24(1-23-0)	-1.0
Total	4	65	139	14	19	4	1	2	12	10	40	.137	.205	.223	428	20	-15	4	3	-0	.934	-4	/O-52(2-47-3)	-2.1
■ LUIS ROSADO Rosado, Luis (Robles) b: 12/6/55, Santurce, P.R. BR/TR, 6', 180 lbs. Deb: 9/8/77																								
1977	NY-N	9	24	1	5	1	0	0	3	1	3	.208	.269	.250	519	42	-2	0	0	0	.980	-0	/1-7,C-1	-0.3
1980	NY-N	2	4	0	0	0	0	0	0	0	1	.000	.000	.000	0	-99	-1	0	0	0	1.000	-0	/1-1	-0.1
Total	2	11	28	1	5	1	0	0	3	1	4	.179	.233	.214	448	23	-3	0	0	0	.983	-0	/1-8,C-1	-0.4
■ BUDDY ROSAR Rosar, Warren Vincent b: 7/3/14, Buffalo, N.Y. d: 3/13/94, Rochester, N.Y. BR/TR, 5'9", 190 lbs. Deb: 4/29/39																								
1939	NY-A	43	105	18	29	5	1	0	12	13	10	.276	.356	.343	699	81	-3	4	0	1	.980	4	C-35	0.4
1940	NY-A	73	228	34	68	11	3	4	37	19	11	.298	.357	.425	783	106	2	7	1	1	.983	1	C-63	0.7
1941	*NY-A	67	209	25	60	17	2	1	36	22	10	.287	.355	.402	757	101	0	0	0	0	.996	0	C-60	0.4
1942	*NY-A☆	69	209	18	48	10	0	2	34	17	20	.230	.288	.306	594	68	-9	1	2	-0	.996	4	C-58	-0.3
1943	Cle-A☆	115	382	53	108	17	1	1	41	33	12	.283	.340	.340	680	106	2	0	4	-1	.983	7	*C-114	1.5
1944	Cle-A	99	331	29	87	9	3	0	30	34	17	.263	.339	.308	647	89	-4	1	2	-0	**.989**	4	C-98	0.6
1945	Phi-A	92	300	23	63	12	1	1	25	20	16	.210	.262	.267	528	54	-18	2	1	0	.987	-0	C-85	-1.4
1946	Phi-A★	121	424	34	120	22	2	2	47	36	17	.283	.339	.358	698	96	-3	1	3	-1	**1.000**	7	*C-117	1.0
1947	Phi-A★	102	359	40	93	20	2	1	33	40	13	.259	.335	.334	669	85	-7	1	3	-1	**.996**	13	*C-102	1.1
1948	Phi-A★	90	302	30	77	13	0	4	41	39	12	.255	.344	.338	682	82	-7	0	2	-1	**.997**	-3	C-90	-0.6
1949	Phi-A	32	95	7	19	2	0	0	6	16	5	.200	.315	.221	536	45	-7	0	0	0	.992	-2	C-31	-0.8
1950	Bos-A	27	84	13	25	2	0	1	12	7	4	.298	.352	.357	709	75	-3	0	0	0	.991	-1	C-25	-0.2
1951	Bos-A	58	170	11	39	7	0	1	13	19	14	.229	.307	.288	595	56	-10	0	0	0	.996	0	C-56	-0.7
Total	13	988	3198	335	836	147	15	18	367	315	161	.261	.330	.334	663	84	-66	17	18	-3	.992	33	C-934	1.7
■ JIMMY ROSARIO Rosario, Angel Ramon (Ferrer) b: 5/5/45, Bayamon, P.R. BB/TR, 5'10", 155 lbs. Deb: 4/8/71																								
1971	*SF-N	92	192	26	43	6	1	0	13	33	35	.224	.341	.266	606	75	-5	7	4	0	1.000	-1	O-67(9-60-1)	-0.8
1972	SF-N	7	2	1	0	0	0	0	0	0	0	.000	.000	.000	0	-99	-1	0	1	-0	.000	-1	/O-1(0-1-0)	-0.1
1976	Mil-A	15	37	4	7	0	0	1	5	3	8	.189	.250	.270	520	53	-2	1	3	-1	1.000	-2	O-12(11-2-0)/D-2	-0.6
Total	3	114	231	31	50	6	1	1	18	36	43	.216	.325	.264	589	70	-8	8	8	-1	1.000	-4	/O-80(20-63-1),D-2	-1.5
■ MEL ROSARIO Rosario, Melvin Gregorio b: 5/25/73, Santo Domingo, D.R. BB/TR, 6', 191 lbs. Deb: 9/11/97																								
1997	Bal-A	4	3	0	0	0	0	0	0	0	1	.000	.000	.000	0	-99	-1	0	0	0	.875	0	/C-4	-0.1
■ SANTIAGO ROSARIO Rosario, Santiago b: 7/25/39, Guayanilla, P.R. BL/TL, 5'11", 165 lbs. Deb: 6/23/65																								
1965	KC-A	81	85	8	20	3	0	2	8	6	16	.235	.293	.341	635	81	-2	0	0	0	.991	-1	1-31/O-3(2-0-1)	-0.4
■ VICTOR ROSARIO Rosario, Victor Manuel (Rivera) b: 8/26/66, Hato Mayor Del Rey, D.R. BR/TR, 5'11", 155 lbs. Deb: 9/6/90																								
1990	Atl-N	9	7	3	1	0	0	0	0	1	1	.143	.250	.143	393	10	-1	0	0	0	1.000	1	/S-3,2-1	0.0
■ PETE ROSE Rose, Peter Edward Jr. b: 11/16/69, Cincinnati, O. BL/TR, 6'1", 180 lbs. Deb: 9/1/97 F																								
1997	Cin-N	11	14	2	2	0	0	0	0	2	9	.143	.250	.143	393	6	-2	0	0	0	.600	-1	/3-2,1-1	-0.2
■ PETE ROSE Rose, Peter Edward Sr. "Charlie Hustle" b: 4/14/41, Cincinnati, Ohio BB/TR, 5'11", 200 lbs. Deb: 4/8/63 FM Career OF: (671-LF 70-CF 594-RF)																								
1963	Cin-N	157	623	101	170	25	9	6	41	55	72	.273	.337	.371	708	101	1	13	15	-2	.971	-23	*2-157/O-1(1-0-0)	-1.1
1964	Cin-N	136	516	64	139	13	2	4	34	36	51	.269	.319	.326	645	79	-13	4	10	-3	.979	-14	*2-128	-2.0
1965	Cin-N★	162	670	117	**209**	35	11	11	81	69	76	.312	.383	.446	829	124	23	8	3	1	.975	-18	*2-162	2.1
1966	Cin-N	156	654	97	205	38	5	16	70	37	61	.313	.351	.460	811	113	12	4	9	-2	.981	-8	*2-140,3-16	1.5
1967	Cin-N★	148	585	86	176	32	8	12	76	56	66	.301	.365	.444	809	117	14	11	6	0	.982	-4	*O-123(123-1-0),2-35	0.8
1968	Cin-N†	149	626	94	**210**	42	6	10	49	56	76	**.335**	**.394**	.470	863	149	38	3	7	-2	.990	7	*O-148R/2-3,1-1	3.8
1969	Cin-N★	156	627	**120**	218	33	11	16	82	88	65	**.348**	.432	.512	944	155	49	7	10	-2	.988	5	*O-156(0-56-101)/2-2	4.7
1970	*Cin-N★	159	649	120	**205**	37	9	15	52	73	64	.316	.387	.470	857	128	26	12	7	0	**.997**	5	*O-159(1-5-155)	2.2
1971	Cin-N★	160	632	86	192	27	4	13	44	68	50	.304	.374	.421	795	127	24	13	9	-0	.994	4	*O-158(0-1-158)	2.0
1972	*Cin-N	154	645	107	**198**	31	11	6	57	73	46	.307	.383	.417	801	135	31	10	3	1	.994	16	*O-154(154-0-0)	4.1
1973	*Cin-N★	160	680	115	**230**	36	8	5	64	65	42	**.338**	.401	.437	838	139	37	10	7	-0	.992	17	*O-159(159-0-0)	4.5

YEAR	TM/L	G	AB	R	H	2B	3B	HR	RBI	BB	SO	AVG	OBP	SLG	OPS	OPS+	BR+	SB	CS	SBR	FA	FR	G/POS	TPR
1974	Cin-N★	163	652	**110**	185	**45**	7	3	51	106	54	.284	.388	.388	776	119	21	2	4	-1	**.997**	18	*O-163(163-0-0)	2.8
1975	*Cin-N★	162	662	**112**	210	**47**	4	7	74	89	50	.317	.407	.432	839	130	31	0	1	-0	.963	-36	*3-137,O-35(35-0-0)	-0.8
1976	*Cin-N★	162	665	**130**	**215**	**42**	6	10	63	86	54	.323	.406	.450	855	139	37	9	5	0	**.969**	-12	*3-159/O-1(0-0-1)	2.5
1977	Cin-N★	162	655	95	204	38	7	9	64	66	42	.311	.379	.432	811	115	15	16	4	2	.958	-24	*3-161	-0.9
1978	Cin-N★	159	655	103	198	**51**	3	7	52	62	30	.302	.365	.421	787	119	17	13	9	-0	.961	-26	*3-156/O-7(7-0-0),1-2	-1.2
1979	Phi-N★	163	628	90	208	40	5	4	59	95	32	.331	.421	.430	851	128	29	20	11	1	.995	-5	*1-159/3-5,2-1	1.5
1980	*Phi-N★	162	655	95	185	**42**	1	1	64	66	33	.282	.354	.354	708	93	-4	12	8	-0	**.997**	9	*1-162	-0.5
1981	*Phi-N★	107	431	73	**140**	18	5	0	33	46	26	.325	.394	.390	784	118	12	4	4	-1	.996	9	*1-107	1.4
1982	Phi-N★	162	634	80	172	25	4	3	54	66	32	.271	.347	.338	684	90	-6	8	8	-1	.995	6	*1-162	-1.3
1983	*Phi-N	151	493	52	121	14	3	0	45	52	28	.245	.320	.286	606	70	-19	7	7	-1	.990	-2	*1-112,O-35(0-0-35)	-3.0
1984	Mon-N	95	278	34	72	6	2	0	23	31	20	.259	.335	.295	630	82	-6	1	1	-0	.988	8	1-40,O-28(28-0-0)	-0.2
	Cin-N	26	96	9	35	9	0	0	11	9	7	.365	.430	.458	888	143	6	0	0	0	.990	-3	1-23/M	0.2
	Yr	121	374	43	107	15	2	0	34	40	27	.286	.360	.337	697	99	1	1	1	-0	.989	5	1-63,O-28(28-0-0)	0.0
1985	Cin-N★	119	405	60	107	12	2	2	46	86	35	.264	.398	.319	716	98	4	8	1	1	.995	0	*1-110/M	-0.1
1986	Cin-N	72	237	15	52	8	2	0	25	30	31	.219	.317	.270	587	61	-12	3	0	1	.990	-1	1-61/M	-1.6
Total	24	3562	14053	2165	4256	746	135	160	1314	1566	1143	.303	.377	.409	786	117	370	198	149	-9	.991	-71	*O-1327L,1-939,32	21.4

■ BOBBY ROSE

Rose, Robert Richard b: 3/15/67, Covina, Cal. BR/TR, 5′11″, 170 lbs. Deb: 8/12/89 Career OF: (6-LF 0-CF 1-RF)

YEAR	TM/L	G	AB	R	H	2B	3B	HR	RBI	BB	SO	AVG	OBP	SLG	OPS	OPS+	BR+	SB	CS	SBR	FA	FR	G/POS	TPR
1989	Cal-A	14	38	4	8	1	2	1	3	2	10	.211	.268	.421	689	93	-1	0	0	0	.920	-1	3-10/2-3	-0.2
1990	Cal-A	7	13	5	5	0	0	1	2	2	1	.385	.467	.615	1082	204	2	0	0	0	1.000	-1	/2-4,3-3	0.1
1991	Cal-A	22	65	5	18	5	1	1	8	3	13	.277	.309	.431	740	102	-0	0	0	0	1.000	-1	/2-8,O-7L,3-4,1-3	-0.1
1992	Cal-A	30	84	10	18	5	0	2	10	8	9	.214	.298	.345	643	79	-2	1	1	-0	.953	8	2-28/1-2	0.6
Total	4	73	200	24	49	11	3	5	23	15	33	.245	.307	.405	712	98	-1	1	1	-0	.965	6	/2-43,3-17,O-7L,1-5	0.4

■ JOHNNY ROSEBORO

Roseboro, John Junior b: 5/13/33, Ashland, Ohio BL/TR, 5′11.5″, 190 lbs. Deb: 6/14/57 C Career OF: (4-LF 1-CF 0-RF)

YEAR	TM/L	G	AB	R	H	2B	3B	HR	RBI	BB	SO	AVG	OBP	SLG	OPS	OPS+	BR+	SB	CS	SBR	FA	FR	G/POS	TPR
1957	Bro-N	35	69	6	10	2	0	2	6	10	20	.145	.253	.261	514	35	-6	0	0	0	.972	3	C-19/1-5	-0.3
1958	LA-N☆	114	384	52	104	11	9	14	43	36	56	.271	.336	.456	792	104	2	11	8	-0	.987	-16	*C-104/O-5(4-1-0)	-0.9
1959	*LA-N	118	397	39	92	14	7	10	38	52	69	.232	.325	.378	703	81	-10	7	5	-0	.991	6	*C-117	0.2
1960	LA-N	103	287	22	61	15	3	8	42	44	53	.213	.325	.369	695	84	-6	7	6	-1	.993	3	C-87/1-1,3-1	0.1
1961	LA-N★	128	394	59	99	16	6	18	59	56	62	.251	.350	.459	810	104	2	6	4	-0	.986	7	*C-125	1.5
1962	LA-N★	128	389	45	97	16	7	7	55	50	60	.249	.345	.380	726	101	1	12	3	2	.985	-2	*C-128	0.7
1963	*LA-N	135	470	50	111	13	7	9	49	36	50	.236	.295	.351	646	91	-6	7	6	-1	.992	-10	*C-134	-1.1
1964	LA-N	134	414	42	119	24	1	3	45	44	61	.287	.361	.372	733	115	10	3	3	-0	.993	1	*C-128	1.7
1965	*LA-N	136	437	42	102	10	0	8	57	34	51	.233	.292	.311	603	75	-15	1	6	-2	.994	-2	*C-131/3-1	-1.4
1966	*LA-N	142	445	47	123	23	2	9	53	44	51	.276	.346	.398	743	115	9	3	2	-0	.993	6	*C-138	2.3
1967	LA-N	116	334	37	91	18	2	4	24	38	33	.272	.350	.374	725	117	8	2	4	-1	.984	-11	*C-107	0.1
1968	Min-A	135	380	31	82	12	0	8	39	46	57	.216	.304	.311	614	82	-7	2	3	-1	.991	-5	*C-117	-0.8
1969	*Min-A★	115	361	33	95	12	0	3	32	39	44	.263	.335	.321	656	83	-8	5	5	-1	.980	0	*C-111	-0.4
1970	Was-A	46	86	7	20	4	0	1	6	18	10	.233	.365	.314	679	94	0	1	1	-0	1.000	-3	C-30	-0.2
Total	14	1585	4847	512	1206	190	44	104	548	547	677	.249	.329	.371	700	95	-26	67	56	-5	.989	-22	*C-1476/1-6,O-5L,3	1.5

■ BOB ROSELLI

Roselli, Robert Edward b: 12/10/31, San Francisco, Cal. BR/TR, 5′11″, 185 lbs. Deb: 8/16/55

YEAR	TM/L	G	AB	R	H	2B	3B	HR	RBI	BB	SO	AVG	OBP	SLG	OPS	OPS+	BR+	SB	CS	SBR	FA	FR	G/POS	TPR
1955	Mil-N	6	9	1	2	1	0	0	0	1	4	.222	.364	.333	697	91	-0	0	0	0	.917	0	/C-2	0.0
1956	Mil-N	4	2	1	1	0	0	1	1	0	1	.500	.500	2.000	2500	564	1	0	0	0	1.000	2	/C-3	0.3
1958	Mil-N	1	1	0	0	0	0	0	0	0	0	.000	.000	.000	0	-99	-0	0	0	0	.000	0	H	0.0
1961	Chi-A	22	38	2	10	3	0	0	4	0	11	.263	.263	.342	605	61	-2	0	0	0	1.000	-1	C-10	-0.3
1962	Chi-A	35	64	4	12	3	1	1	5	11	15	.188	.316	.313	628	70	-3	1	0	0	.988	-1	C-20	-0.3
Total	5	68	114	8	25	7	1	2	10	12	31	.219	.305	.351	656	76	-4	1	0	0	.986	-1	/C-35	-0.3

■ DAVE ROSELLO

Rosello, David (Rodriguez) b: 6/26/50, Mayaguez, P.R. BR/TR, 5′11″, 160 lbs. Deb: 9/10/72

YEAR	TM/L	G	AB	R	H	2B	3B	HR	RBI	BB	SO	AVG	OBP	SLG	OPS	OPS+	BR+	SB	CS	SBR	FA	FR	G/POS	TPR
1972	Chi-N	5	12	2	3	0	0	1	3	3	2	.250	.400	.500	900	139	1	0	0	0	.846	1	/S-5	0.2
1973	Chi-N	16	38	4	10	2	0	0	2	2	4	.263	.300	.316	616	66	-2	2	2	-0	.964	3	2-13/S-1	0.1
1974	Chi-N	62	148	9	30	7	0	0	10	10	28	.203	.253	.250	503	39	-12	1	1	-0	.972	3	2-49,S-12	-0.6
1975	Chi-N	19	58	7	15	2	0	1	8	9	8	.259	.358	.345	703	92	-0	0	1	-0	.952	1	S-19	0.2
1976	Chi-N	91	227	27	55	5	1	1	11	41	33	.242	.361	.286	647	78	-5	1	2	-0	.966	-7	S-86/2-1	-0.3
1977	Chi-N	56	82	18	18	2	1	1	9	12	12	.220	.319	.305	624	62	-4	0	0	0	.938	-3	3-21,S-10/2-3	-0.7
1979	Cle-A	59	107	20	26	6	1	3	14	15	27	.243	.336	.402	738	98	-0	1	0	0	.976	-5	2-33,3-14,S-11	-0.3
1980	Cle-A	71	117	16	29	3	0	2	12	9	19	.248	.302	.325	626	71	-5	0	0	0	.980	3	2-43,3-22/S-3,D-1	0.0
1981	Cle-A	43	84	11	20	4	0	1	7	7	12	.238	.297	.321	618	79	-2	0	1	-0	.979	3	2-26/3-8,S-4,D-4	0.1
Total	9	422	873	114	206	31	3	10	76	108	145	.236	.321	.313	633	73	-29	5	7	-1	.975	0	2-168,S-151/3-65,D	-1.3

■ CHIEF ROSEMAN

Roseman, James John b: 1856, New York, N.Y. d: 7/4/38, Brooklyn, N.Y. BR/TR, 5′7″, 167 lbs. Deb: 5/1/1882 M Career OF: (123-LF 351-CF 189-RF)

YEAR	TM/L	G	AB	R	H	2B	3B	HR	RBI	BB	SO	AVG	OBP	SLG	OPS	OPS+	BR+	SB	CS	SBR	FA	FR	G/POS	TPR
1882	Tro-N	82	331	41	78	21	6	1	29	3	41	.236	.243	.344	587	90	-3				.853	-3	*O-82(1-0-81)	-0.7
1883	NY-a	93	398	48	100	13	6	0		11		.251	.271	.314	585	84	-8				.855	-3	*O-91(3-8-80)/1-2	-1.1
1884	*NY-a	107	436	97	130	16	11	4		21		.298	.339	.413	752	148	23				.885	-2	*O-107(4-103-0)	1.6
1885	NY-a	101	410	72	114	13	14	4	46	25		.278	.335	.407	742	145	23				.865	-7	*O-101(1-99-1)/P-1	1.1
1886	NY-a	134	559	90	127	19	10	5	53	24		.227	.269	.324	593	89	-7	6			.891	-3	*O-134(88-44-3)/P-1	-1.2
1887	Phi-a	21	83	16	26	2	1	0	8	10		.313	.352	.274	626	76	-2	3			.821	-0	O-21(0-21-0)	-0.2
	NY-a	60	250	30	64	10	1	1	27	9		.256	.265	.290	555	57	-14	3			.868	-8	O-59(9-36-14)/1-3,P-2	-1.8
	Bro-a	1	3	2	1	0	0	0	1	0		.333	.500	.333	833	133	0	0			1.000	-3	/O-1(0-0-9)	-0.3
	Yr	82	336	48	91	12	2	1	36	19		.271	.290	.287	577	63	-15	6			.856	-11	O-81(9-57-23)/1-3,P-2	-2.3
1890	StL-a	80	302	47	103	26	0	2	58	30		.341	.449	.447	896	144	17	7			.819	-8	O-58(17-40-1),1-22,M	0.4
	Lou-a	2	8	0	2	0	0	0	0	0		.250	.250	.250	500	48	-1	0			.864	-1	/1-2	-0.1
	Yr	82	310	47	105	26	0	2	58	30		.339	.444	.442	886	142	17	7			.819	-9	O-58(17-40-1),1-24	0.3
Total	7	681	2780	443	745	120	49	17	222	133	41	.268	.312	.360	672	109	29	19			.866	-37	O-654C/1-29,P-4	-2.3

■ AL ROSEN

Rosen, Albert Leonard "Flip" b: 2/29/24, Spartanburg, S.C. BR/TR, 5′10.5″, 180 lbs. Deb: 9/10/47 Career OF: (1-LF 0-CF 0-RF)

YEAR	TM/L	G	AB	R	H	2B	3B	HR	RBI	BB	SO	AVG	OBP	SLG	OPS	OPS+	BR+	SB	CS	SBR	FA	FR	G/POS	TPR
1947	Cle-A	7	9	1	1	0	0	0	0	0	3	.111	.111	.111	222	-39	-2	0	0	0	.000	1	/3-2,O-1(1-0-0)	-0.1
1948	*Cle-A	5	5	0	1	0	0	0	0	0	2	.200	.200	.200	400	7	-1	0	0	0	1.000	0	/3-2	-0.1
1949	Cle-A	23	44	3	7	2	0	0	5	7	4	.159	.275	.205	479	28	-5	0	1	-0	1.000	-1	3-10	-0.6
1950	Cle-A	155	554	100	159	23	4	**37**	116	100	72	.287	.405	.543	948	146	38	5	7	-1	.969	1	*3-154	3.4
1951	Cle-A	154	573	82	152	30	1	24	102	85	71	.265	.362	.447	809	125	19	7	5	-0	.958	-15	*3-154	0.4
1952	Cle-A★	148	567	101	171	32	5	28	**105**	75	54	.302	.387	.524	911	162	46	8	6	-0	.958	-20	*3-147/1-4,S-3	2.6
1953	Cle-A★	155	599	**115**	201	27	5	**43**	**145**	85	48	.336	.422	**.613**	**1034**	**181**	**67**	8	7	-1	.964	1	*3-154/1-1,S-1	**6.5**
1954	*Cle-A★	137	466	76	140	20	2	24	102	85	43	.300	.412	.506	918	148	33	6	2	1	.959	-14	3-87,1-46/2-1,S-1	1.7
1955	Cle-A★	139	492	61	120	13	1	21	81	92	44	.244	.367	.402	770	103	4	4	2	0	.963	3	*3-106,1-41	0.4
1956	Cle-A	121	416	64	111	18	2	15	61	58	44	.267	.357	.428	784	104	2	1	3	-1	.945	-8	*3-116	-0.6
Total	10	1044	3725	603	1063	165	20	192	717	587	385	.285	.386	.495	882	138	203	39	33	-3	.961	-52	3-932/1-92,S-5,2O	13.6

■ GOODY ROSEN

Rosen, Goodwin George b: 8/28/12, Toronto, Ont., Can. d: 4/6/94, Toronto, Ont., Can. BL/TL, 5′10″, 155 lbs. Deb: 9/14/37

YEAR	TM/L	G	AB	R	H	2B	3B	HR	RBI	BB	SO	AVG	OBP	SLG	OPS	OPS+	BR+	SB	CS	SBR	FA	FR	G/POS	TPR
1937	Bro-N	22	77	10	24	5	1	0	6	6	6	.312	.361	.403	764	106	1	2			.981	1	O-21(8-13-0)	0.1
1938	Bro-N	138	473	75	133	17	11	4	51	65	43	.281	.368	.389	757	106	5	0			**.989**	13	*O-113(13-43-59)	1.3
1939	Bro-N	54	183	22	46	6	4	1	12	23	21	.251	.335	.344	679	80	-5	4			1.000	-3	O-47(1-40-7)	-0.9
1944	Bro-N	89	264	38	69	8	3	0	23	26	27	.261	.330	.314	644	83	-5	0			.991	12	O-65(1-62-3)	0.5
1945	Bro-N†	145	606	126	197	24	11	12	75	50	36	.325	.379	.460	840	134	26	4			.993	2	*O-141(0-141-0)	2.4
1946	Bro-N	3	3	0	1	0	0	0	0	0	1	.333	.333	.333	667	89	-0	0			.000	-1	/O-1(0-1-0)	-0.1
	NY-N	100	310	39	87	11	4	5	30	48	32	.281	.377	.390	767	117	8	2			.976	4	O-84(0-30-52)	1.0
	Yr	103	313	39	88	11	4	5	30	48	33	.281	.377	.390	767	117	8	2			.976	3	O-85(0-31-52)	0.9
Total	6	551	1916	310	557	71	34	22	197	218	166	.291	.364	.398	762	111	31	12			.989	28	O-472(23-330-121)	4.3

YEAR	TM/L	G	AB	R	H	2B	3B	HR	RBI	BB	SO	AVG	OBP	SLG	OPS	OPS+	BR+	SB	CS	SBR	FA	FR	G/POS	TPR
■ **HARRY ROSENBERG**	Rosenberg, Harry b: 6/22/09, San Francisco, Cal. d: 4/13/97, San Mateo, Cal. BR/TR, 5'9.5", 160 lbs. Deb: 7/15/30 F																							
1930	NY-N	9	5	1	0	0	0	0	0	1	4	.000	.167	.000	167	-56	-1	0			1.000	-1	/O-3(0-2-1)	-0.2
■ **LOU ROSENBERG**	Rosenberg, Louis b: 3/5/04, San Francisco, Cal. d: 9/8/91, Daly City, Cal. BR/TR, 5'7", 155 lbs. Deb: 5/22/23 F																							
1923	Chi-A	3	4	0	1	0	0	0	0	0	1	.250	.250	.250	500	32	-0	0	1	-0	1.000	-1	/2-2	-0.2
■ **MAX ROSENFELD**	Rosenfeld, Max b: 12/23/02, New York, N.Y. d: 3/10/69, Miami, Fla. BR/TR, 5'8", 175 lbs. Deb: 4/21/31																							
1931	Bro-N	3	9	0	2	1	0	0	0	1	1	.222	.300	.333	633	70	-0	0			1.000	-1	/O-3(0-3-0)	-0.1
1932	Bro-N	34	39	8	14	3	0	2	7	0	10	.359	.359	.590	949	153	3	2			.970	-9	O-30(1-10-19)	-0.7
1933	Bro-N	5	9	0	1	0	0	0	0	1	1	.111	.200	.111	311	-10	-1	0			1.000	0	/O-2(1-1-0)	-0.1
Total	3	42	57	8	17	4	0	2	7	2	12	.298	.322	.474	796	115	1	2			.978	-9	/O-35(2-14-19)	-0.9
■ **LARRY ROSENTHAL**	Rosenthal, Lawrence John b: 5/21/10, St.Paul, Minn. d: 3/4/92, Woodbury, Minn. BL/TL, 6'0.5", 190 lbs. Deb: 6/20/36 Career OF: (109-LF 177-CF 131-RF)																							
1936	Chi-A	85	317	71	89	15	8	3	46	59	37	.281	.394	.407	801	95	-1	2	0	0	.977	6	O-80(0-80-0)	0.3
1937	Chi-A	58	97	20	28	5	3	0	9	9	20	.289	.355	.402	757	90	-1	1	0	0	.980	-3	O-25(0-25-0)	-0.4
1938	Chi-A	61	105	14	30	5	1	1	12	12	13	.286	.359	.381	740	83	-3	0	1	-0	.959	-3	O-22(0-22-2)	-0.6
1939	Chi-A	107	324	50	86	21	5	10	51	53	46	.265	.369	.454	822	106	3	6	4	-0	.990	-3	O-93(0-20-75)	-0.4
1940	Chi-A	107	276	46	83	14	5	6	42	64	32	.301	.432	.453	885	128	15	2	3	-1	.977	-3	O-92(68-15-11)	0.7
1941	Chi-A	20	59	9	14	4	0	0	1	12	5	.237	.366	.305	671	80	-1	0	0	0	.938	-1	O-18(0-2-16)	-0.3
	Cle-A	45	75	10	14	3	1	1	8	9	10	.187	.274	.293	567	53	-5	1	0	0	1.000	0	O-14(5-8-1)/1-1	-0.5
	Yr	65	134	19	28	7	1	1	9	21	15	.209	.316	.299	615	66	-6	1	0	0	.971	-1	O-32(5-10-17)/1-1	-0.8
1944	NY-A	36	101	9	20	3	0	0	9	19	15	.198	.325	.228	553	57	-5	1	0	0	.986	3	O-26(10-5-11)	-0.4
	Phi-A	32	54	5	11	2	0	1	6	5	9	.204	.271	.296	567	63	-3	0	0	0	.960	-4	O-19(5-0-15)	-0.8
	Yr	68	155	14	31	5	0	1	15	24	24	.200	.307	.252	559	60	-7	1	0	0	.979	-2	O-45(15-5-26)	-1.2
1945	Phi-A	28	75	6	15	3	2	0	5	9	8	.200	.286	.293	579	68	-3	0	1	-0	1.000	-2	O-21(21-0-0)	-0.7
Total	8	579	1483	240	390	75	25	22	189	251	195	.263	.370	.392	762	96	-4	13	9	-0	.979	-11	O-410C/1-1	-3.1
■ **SI ROSENTHAL**	Rosenthal, Simon b: 11/13/03, Boston, Mass. d: 4/7/69, Boston, Mass. BL/TL, 5'9", 165 lbs. Deb: 9/8/25																							
1925	Bos-A	19	72	6	19	5	2	0	8	7	3	.264	.329	.389	718	82	-2	1	0	0	.919	0	O-17(7-0-10)	-0.3
1926	Bos-A	104	285	34	76	12	3	4	34	19	18	.267	.317	.372	689	82	-8	4	1	1	.962	-13	O-67(48-0-19)	-2.6
Total	2	123	357	40	95	17	5	4	42	26	21	.266	.319	.375	695	82	-11	5	1	1	.950	-13	/O-84(55-0-29)	-2.9
■ **BUNNY ROSER**	Roser, John William Joseph "Jack" b: 11/15/01, St.Louis, Mo. d: 5/6/79, Rocky Hill, Conn. BL/TL, 5'11", 175 lbs. Deb: 8/24/22																							
1922	Bos-N	32	113	13	27	3	4	0	16	10	19	.239	.306	.336	643	69	-5	2	1	0	.915	-2	O-32(32-0-0)	-1.0
■ **JOHN ROSKOS**	Roskos, John Edward b: 11/19/74, Victorville, Cal. BR/TR, 5'11", 198 lbs. Deb: 4/20/98																							
1998	Fla-N	10	10	1	1	0	0	0	0	0	5	.100	.100	.100	200	-50	-2	0	0	0	1.000	-0	/1-1	-0.2
1999	Fla-N	13	12	0	2	2	0	0	1	1	7	.167	.231	.333	564	43	-1	0	0	0	1.000	1	/C-1	0.0
2000	SD-N	14	27	0	1	1	0	0	1	3	7	.037	.133	.074	207	-49	-6	0	0	0	.875	-1	/O-6(4-0-2),1-2	-0.7
Total	3	37	49	1	4	3	0	0	2	4	19	.082	.151	.143	294	-26	-10	0	0	0	1.000	-0	/O-6(4-0-2),1-3,C-1	-0.9
■ **CHET ROSS**	Ross, Chester James b: 4/1/17, Buffalo, N.Y. d: 2/21/89, Buffalo, N.Y. BR/TR, 6'1", 195 lbs. Deb: 9/15/39																							
1939	Bos-N	11	31	4	10	1	1	0	0	2	10	.323	.364	.419	783	118	1	0			1.000	1	/O-8(1-1-7)	0.1
1940	Bos-N	149	569	84	160	23	14	17	89	59	127	.281	.352	.460	812	130	22	4			.962	7	*O-149(149-0-0)	2.0
1941	Bos-N	29	50	1	6	1	0	0	4	9	17	.120	.254	.140	394	14	-6	0			1.000	-1	O-12(12-0-0)	-0.7
1942	Bos-N	76	220	20	43	7	2	5	19	16	37	.195	.250	.314	564	66	-10	0			.992	-1	O-57(52-0-6)	-1.6
1943	Bos-N	94	285	27	62	12	2	7	32	26	67	.218	.285	.347	633	84	-7	1			.977	3	O-73(73-0-0)	-0.9
1944	Bos-N	54	154	20	35	9	2	5	26	12	23	.227	.287	.409	697	91	-3	1			1.000	3	O-38(25-0-15)	-0.2
Total	6	413	1309	156	316	53	21	34	170	124	281	.241	.309	.392	701	100	-3	6			.976	11	O-337(312-1-28)	-1.3
■ **DON ROSS**	Ross, Donald Raymond b: 7/16/14, Pasadena, Cal. d: 4/4/96, Arcadia, Cal. BR/TR, 6'2", 200 lbs. Deb: 4/19/38 Career OF: (11-LF 0-CF 104-RF)																							
1938	Det-A	77	265	22	69	7	1	1	30	29	11	.260	.333	.306	639	58	-17	1	0	0	.946	4	3-75	-0.9
1940	Bro-N	10	38	4	11	2	0	1	8	3	3	.289	.341	.421	763	103	0	1			.879	-0	3-10	0.0
1942	Det-A	87	226	29	62	10	2	3	30	36	16	.274	.379	.376	755	104	2	2	1	0	.964	-3	O-38(5-0-33),3-20	-0.3
1943	Det-A	89	247	19	66	13	0	0	18	20	3	.267	.325	.320	644	82	-5	2	0	0	.985	-8	O-38R,S-18/2-7,3-1	-1.4
1944	Det-A	66	167	14	35	5	0	2	15	14	9	.210	.275	.275	550	54	-10	2	1	0	.958	-1	O-37(0-0-37)/S-2,1-1	-1.4
1945	Det-A	8	29	3	11	4	0	0	4	5	1	.379	.471	.517	988	175	3	2	0	0	.960	-0	/3-8	0.3
	Cle-A	106	363	26	95	15	1	2	43	42	15	.262	.340	.325	665	97	-0	0	4	-1	.958	-13	*3-106	-1.5
	Yr	114	392	29	106	19	1	2	47	47	16	.270	.350	.339	689	104	3	2	4	-1	.958	-14	*3-114	-1.2
1946	Cle-A	55	153	12	41	7	0	3	14	17	12	.268	.341	.373	714	106	1	0	0	0	.944	-12	3-41/O-2(0-0-2)	-1.1
Total	7	498	1488	129	390	63	4	12	162	166	70	.262	.338	.334	672	86	-25	10	6		.946	-33	3-261,O-115R/S-20,21	-6.3
■ **JOE ROSSI**	Rossi, Joseph Anthony b: 3/13/21, Oakland, Cal. d: 2/20/99, Oakland, Cal. BR/TR, 6'1", 205 lbs. Deb: 4/20/52																							
1952	Cin-N	55	145	14	32	0	1	1	6	20	20	.221	.319	.255	574	61	-7	1	0	0	.982	2	C-46	-0.3
■ **CLAUDE ROSSMAN**	Rossman, Claude R. b: 6/17/1881, Philmont, N.Y. d: 1/16/28, Poughkeepsie, N.Y. BL/TL, 6', 188 lbs. Deb: 9/16/04																							
1904	Cle-A	18	62	5	13	5	0	0	6	0		.210	.210	.290	500	58	-3	0			.933	-4	O-17(0-1-16)	-0.9
1906	Cle-A	118	396	49	122	13	2	1	53	17		.308	.338	.359	697	120	8	11			.984	-8	*1-105/O-1(0-1-0)	-0.2
1907	*Det-A	153	571	60	158	21	8	0	69	33		.277	.318	.342	660	107	3	20			.981	-14	*1-153	-1.5
1908	*Det-A	138	524	45	154	33	13	2	71	27		.294	.330	.418	748	137	19	8			.981	6	*1-138	2.5
1909	Det-A	82	287	16	75	8	3	0	39	13		.261	.293	.310	603	87	-5	10			.981	-6	1-75	-1.4
	StL-A	2	8	0	1	0	0	0	0	0		.125	.125	.125	250	-23	-1	0			1.000	-0	/O-2(0-0-2)	-0.2
	Yr	84	295	16	76	8	3	0	39	13		.258	.289	.305	594	84	-6	10			.981	-6	1-75/O-2(0-0-2)	-1.6
Total	5	511	1848	175	523	80	26	3	238	90		.283	.318	.359	677	113	21	49			.982	-26	1-471/O-20(0-2-18)	-1.7
■ **RICO ROSSY**	Rossy, Elam Jose (Ramos) b: 2/16/64, San Juan, P.R. BR/TR, 5'10", 175 lbs. Deb: 9/11/91																							
1991	Atl-N	5	1	0	0	0	0	0	0	0	1	.000	.000	.000	0	-94	-0	0	0	0	.000	0	/S-1	0.0
1992	KC-A	59	149	21	32	8	1	1	12	20	20	.215	.312	.302	614	71	-5	0	3	-1	.961	5	S-51/3-9,2-3	0.2
1993	KC-A	46	86	10	19	4	0	2	12	9	11	.221	.302	.337	639	68	-4	0	0	0	.987	1	2-24,3-16,S-11	-0.1
1998	Sea-A	37	81	12	16	6	0	1	4	6	13	.198	.253	.309	562	45	-7	0	0	0	1.000	9	3-25/2-6,S-4,D-1	0.2
Total	4	147	317	43	67	18	1	4	28	35	45	.211	.294	.312	606	63	-16	0	3	-1	.967	15	/S-67,3-50,2-33,D-1	0.3
■ **FRANK ROTH**	Roth, Francis Charles b: 10/11/1878, Chicago, Ill. d: 3/27/55, Burlington, Wis. BR/TR, 5'10", 160 lbs. Deb: 4/18/03 FC Career OF: (1-LF 0-CF 0-RF)																							
1903	Phi-N	68	220	27	60	11	4	0	22	9		.273	.304	.359	663	92	-3	3			.935	-7	C-60/3-1	-0.4
1904	Phi-N	81	229	28	59	8	1	1	20	12		.258	.298	.314	612	92	-2	8			.958	-11	C-67/1-1,2-1	-0.8
1905	StL-A	35	107	9	25	3	0	0	7	6		.234	.274	.262	536	74	-3	1			.962	-6	C-29	-0.7
1906	Chi-A	16	51	4	10	1	1	0	7	3		.196	.241	.255	496	57	-3	1			.990	3	C-15	0.2
1909	Cin-N	56	147	12	35	7	2	0	16	6		.238	.287	.313	600	87	-3	5			.967	-3	C-54	-0.1
1910	Cin-N	26	29	3	7	2	0	0	3	0	2	.241	.267	.310	577	71	-1	1			.938	-0	/C-4,O-1(1-0-0)	-0.1
Total	6	282	783	83	196	32	8	1	75	36	2	.250	.289	.315	605	86	-15	19			.956	-24	C-229/O-1L,2-1,13	-1.9
■ **BRAGGO ROTH**	Roth, Robert Frank b: 8/28/1892, Burlington, Wis. d: 9/11/36, Chicago, Ill. BR/TR, 5'7.5", 170 lbs. Deb: 9/1/14 F Career OF: (42-LF 135-CF 550-RF)																							
1914	Chi-A	34	126	14	37	4	6	1	10	8	25	.294	.355	.444	800	142	6	3	3	-0	.924	2	O-34(0-12-22)	0.5
1915	Chi-A	70	240	44	60	6	10	3	35	29	50	.250	.338	.396	734	116	4	12	6	1	.837	-15	3-35,O-30(29-1-0)	-1.2
	Cle-A	39	144	23	43	4	7	4	20	22	22	.299	.399	.507	906	168	12	14	4	2	.878	-6	O-39(0-39-0)	0.5
	Yr	109	384	67	103	10	17	**7**	55	51	72	.268	.361	.438	799	135	16	26	10	2	.906	-21	O-69(29-40-0),3-35	-0.7
1916	Cle-A	125	409	50	117	19	7	4	72	38	48	.286	.350	.396	746	117	8	29	14	1	.954	3	*O-112(0-9-103)	0.7
1917	Cle-A	145	495	69	141	30	9	1	72	52	73	.285	.355	.388	743	118	10	51			.957	-0	*O-135(0-0-135)	0.4
1918	Cle-A	106	375	53	106	21	12	1	59	53	41	.283	.383	.411	794	127	14	35			.936	-3	*O-106(2-0-104)	0.5
1919	Phi-A	48	195	33	63	13	8	5	29	15	21	.323	.377	.549	926	156	13	11			.975	-5	O-48(0-0-48)	0.6
	Bos-A	63	227	32	58	9	4	0	23	24	32	.256	.337	.330	668	93	-2	9			.943	-4	O-58(1-57-0)	-1.0

YEAR	TM/L	G	AB	R	H	2B	3B	HR	RBI	BB	SO	AVG	OBP	SLG	OPS	OPS+	BR+	SB	CS	SBR	FA	FR	G/POS	TPR
	Yr	111	422	65	121	22	12	5	52	39	53	.287	.355	.431	787	124	12	20			.955	-9	*O-106(1-57-48)	-0.4
1920	Was-A	138	468	80	136	23	8	9	92	75	57	.291	.395	.432	827	122	17	24	12	1	.952	-10	*O-128(7-0-121)	0.2
1921	NY-A	43	152	29	43	9	2	2	10	19	20	.283	.370	.408	778	96	-1	1	2	-0	.923	-3	O-37(3-17-17)	-0.6
Total	8	811	2831	427	804	138	73	30	422	335	389	.284	.367	.416	783	122	82	189	41		.944	-42	O-727R/3-35	0.6
■ BOB ROTHEL	Rothel, Robert Burton b: 9/17/23, Columbia Station, Ohio d: 3/21/84, Huron, Ohio BR/TR, 5'10.5", 170 lbs. Deb: 4/22/45																							
1945	Cle-A	4	10	0	2	0	0	0	0	3	1	.200	.385	.200	585	75	-0	0	0	0	.875	-1	/3-4	-0.1
■ BOBBY ROTHERMEL	Rothermel, Edward Hill b: 12/18/1870, Fleetwood, Pa. d: 2/11/27, Detroit, Mich. Deb: 6/18/1899																							
1899	Bal-N	10	21	1	2	0	0	0	3	1		.095	.136	.095	232	-34	-4	0			.867	-2	/2-5,3-2,S-1	-0.6
■ JACK ROTHFUSS	Rothfuss, John Albert b: 4/18/1872, Newark, N.J. d: 4/20/47, Basking Ridge, N.J BR/TR, 5'11.5", 195 lbs. Deb: 8/2/1897																							
1897	Pit-N	35	115	20	36	3	1	2	18	5		.313	.352	.409	761	105	1	3			.984	-1	1-32	0.0
■ CLAUDE ROTHGEB	Rothgeb, Claude James b: 1/1/1880, Milford, Ill. d: 7/6/44, Manitowoc, Wis. BB, 6'0.5", 200 lbs. Deb: 6/17/05																							
1905	Was-A	7	16	2	2	0	0	0	0	0		.125	.125	.125	250	-22	-2	1			.833	-0	/O-4(0-0-4)	-0.3
■ JACK ROTHROCK	Rothrock, John Huston b: 3/14/05, Long Beach, Cal. d: 2/2/80, San Bernardino, Cal BB/TR, 5'11.5", 165 lbs. Deb: 7/28/25 Career OF: (138-LF 194-CF 311-RF)																							
1925	Bos-A	22	55	6	19	3	3	0	7	3	7	.345	.379	.509	888	124	2	0	0	0	.893	-4	S-22	0.0
1926	Bos-A	15	17	3	5	1	0	0	2	3	1	.294	.400	.353	753	101	0	0	0	0	.692	-2	/S-2	-0.1
1927	Bos-A	117	428	61	111	24	8	1	36	24	46	.259	.302	.360	662	73	-19	5	5	-1	.953	4	S-40,2-36,3-20,1-13	-0.9
1928	Bos-A	117	344	52	92	9	4	3	22	33	40	.267	.333	.343	676	79	-10	12	6	1	.979	-17	O-53L,3-17,1S/2PC	-2.9
1929	Bos-A	143	473	70	142	19	7	6	59	43	47	.300	.361	.408	769	100	0	23	13	1	.970	2	*O-128(0-126-2)	-0.2
1930	Bos-A	45	65	4	18	3	1	0	4	2	9	.277	.299	.354	652	67	-3	0	2	-1	.947	1	/O-9(1-0-8),3-1	-0.4
1931	Bos-A	133	475	81	132	32	3	4	42	47	48	.278	.343	.383	726	96	-3	13	7	0	.982	-1	O-79L,2-23/1-8,3S	-0.6
1932	Bos-A	12	48	3	10	1	0	0	0	5	5	.208	.283	.229	512	35	-5	3	0	1	.973	2	O-12(12-0-0)	-0.2
	Chi-A	39	64	8	12	2	1	0	6	5	9	.188	.246	.250	496	31	-7	1	0	0	.929	-9	O-19(12-1-6)/3-8,1-1	-1.4
	Yr	51	112	11	22	3	1	0	6	10	14	.196	.262	.241	503	33	-11	4	0	1	.961	-7	O-31(24-1-6)/3-8,1-1	-1.6
1934	*StL-N	154	647	106	184	35	3	11	72	49	56	.284	.336	.399	734	90	-9	10			.975	5	*O-154(5-0-149)/2-1	-1.3
1935	StL-N	129	502	76	137	18	5	3	56	57	29	.273	.347	.347	694	84	-10	7			.980	1	*O-127(1-1-125)	-1.7
1937	Phi-A	88	232	28	62	15	0	0	21	28	15	.267	.346	.332	678	73	-9	1	0	0	.992	-6	O-58(6-52-0)/2-1	-1.5
Total	11	1014	3350	498	924	162	35	28	327	299	312	.276	.336	.370	706	85	-72	75	33		.976	-24	O-639R/S-78,231CP	-11.2
■ EDD ROUSH	Roush, Edd J b: 5/8/1893, Oakland City, Ind. d: 3/21/88, Bradenton, Fla. BL/TL, 5'11", 170 lbs. Deb: 8/20/13 CH Career OF: (81-LF 1754-CF 13-RF)																							
1913	Chi-A	9	10	2	1	0	0	0	0	0	2	.100	.100	.100	200	-42	-2	0			1.000	-1	/O-2(0-2-0)	-0.3
1914	Ind-F	74	166	26	54	8	4	1	30	6	20	.325	.353	.440	792	104	-2	12			.989	2	O-43(38-4-1)/1-2	-0.2
1915	New-F	145	551	73	164	20	11	3	60	38	25	.298	.350	.390	740	115	1	28			.972	4	*O-144(0-143-1)	-0.5
1916	NY-N	39	69	4	13	0	1	0	5	1	4	.188	.200	.217	417	30	-6	4			.952	-1	O-15(0-5-10)	-0.9
	Cin-N	69	272	34	78	7	14	0	15	13	19	.287	.336	.415	751	133	10	15			.971	6	O-69(0-69-0)	1.3
	Yr	108	341	38	91	7	15	0	20	14	23	.267	.309	.375	685	114	4	19			.969	5	O-84(0-74-10)	0.4
1917	Cin-N	136	522	82	178	19	14	4	67	27	24	**.341**	.379	.454	833	162	36	21			.962	2	*O-134(0-134-0)	3.2
1918	Cin-N	113	435	61	145	18	10	5	62	22	10	.333	.368	**.455**	**823**	**153**	26	24			.960	8	*O-113(0-113-0)	2.9
1919	*Cin-N	133	504	73	162	19	12	4	71	42	19	**.321**	.380	.431	811	147	29	20			.989	10	*O-133(0-133-0)	3.3
1920	Cin-N	149	579	81	196	22	16	4	90	42	22	.339	.386	.453	839	142	31	36	24	-0	.975	16	*O-139C,1-11/2-1	3.8
1921	Cin-N	112	418	68	147	27	12	4	71	31	8	.352	.403	.502	905	145	27	19	17	-2	.980	2	*O-108(0-108-0)	2.2
1922	Cin-N	49	165	29	58	7	4	1	24	19	5	.352	.428	.461	888	132	9	5	3	0	.990	1	O-43(0-43-0)	0.7
1923	Cin-N	138	527	88	185	**41**	18	6	88	46	16	.351	.406	.531	938	149	36	10	15	-3	.970	-4	*O-137(0-137-0)	2.3
1924	Cin-N	121	483	67	168	23	**21**	3	72	22	11	.348	.376	.501	877	135	22	17	13	-1	.959	-5	*O-119(0-119-0)	1.2
1925	Cin-N	134	540	91	183	28	16	8	83	35	14	.339	.383	.494	878	125	20	22	20	-2	.978	1	*O-134(0-134-0)	1.2
1926	Cin-N	144	563	95	182	37	10	7	79	38	17	.323	.366	.462	828	125	18	8			.955	-12	*O-143(0-143-0)/1-1	0.0
1927	NY-N	140	570	83	173	27	4	7	58	26	15	.304	.335	.402	737	97	-4	18			.975	-4	*O-138(0-137-1)	-1.3
1928	NY-N	46	163	20	41	5	3	2	13	14	8	.252	.315	.356	670	75	-6	1			.955	2	O-39(0-39-0)	-0.6
1929	NY-N	115	450	76	146	19	7	8	52	45	16	.324	.390	.451	841	108	6	6			.982	-1	*O-107(0-107-0)	0.0
1931	Cin-N	101	376	46	102	12	5	1	41	17	5	.271	.308	.338	646	78	-12	2			.981	-4	O-88(43-45-0)	-2.0
Total	18	1967	7363	1099	2376	339	182	68	981	484	260	.323	.369	.446	815	126	241	268	92		.972	23	*O-1848C/1-14,2-1	16.3
■ PHIL ROUTCLIFFE	Routcliffe, Philip John "Chicken" b: 10/24/1870, Oswego, N.Y. d: 10/4/18, Oswego, N.Y. BR/TR, 6', 175 lbs. Deb: 4/21/1890																							
1890	Pit-N	1	4	1	1	0	0	0	1	0	0	.250	.400	.250	650	102	0	1			1.000	0	/O-1(1-0-0)	0.0
■ DAVE ROWAN	Rowan, David (b: David Drohan) b: 12/6/1882, Elora, Ont., Canada d: 7/30/55, Toronto, Ont., Can BL/TL, 5'11", 175 lbs. Deb: 5/27/11																							
1911	StL-A	18	65	7	25	1	1	0	11	4		.385	.420	.431	851	143	4	0			.945	-2	1-18	0.2
■ WADE ROWDON	Rowdon, Wade Lee b: 9/7/60, Riverhead, N.Y. BR/TR, 6'2", 180 lbs. Deb: 9/8/84 Career OF: (11-LF 0-CF 0-RF)																							
1984	Cin-N	4	7	0	2	0	0	0	0	0	1	.286	.286	.286	571	58	-0	0	0	0	1.000	1	/S-1,3-1	0.1
1985	Cin-N	5	9	2	2	0	0	0	2	2	1	.222	.364	.222	586	64	-0	0	0	0	.667	-1	/3-4	-0.2
1986	Cin-N	38	80	9	20	5	1	0	10	9	17	.250	.333	.338	671	82	-2	2	0	0	.889	-7	/3-7,S-6,O-5L,2-3	-0.8
1987	Chi-N	11	31	2	7	1	1	1	4	3	10	.226	.294	.419	713	83	-1	0	2	-1	.818	-1	/3-9	-0.3
1988	Bal-A	20	30	1	3	0	0	0	0	0	6	.100	.100	.100	200	-45	-6	1	1	-0	.947	1	/3-8,O-5(5-0-0),D-5	-0.5
Total	5	78	157	14	34	6	2	1	16	14	35	.217	.285	.299	584	59	-9	3	3	-0	.866	-7	/3-29,O-10L,S-7,D2	-1.7
■ DAVE ROWE	Rowe, David Elwood b: 10/9/1854, Harrisburg, Pa. d: 12/9/30, Glendale, Cal. BR/TR, 5'9", 180 lbs. Deb: 5/30/1877 FM Career OF: (9-LF 246-CF 51-RF)																							
1877	Chi-N	2	7	0	2	0	0	0	0	0	3	.286	.286	.286	571	72	-0				.667	-1	/O-2(0-0-2),P-1	-0.1
1882	Cle-N	24	97	13	25	4	3	1	17	4	9	.258	.287	.392	679	119	2				.837	-3	O-23(3-20-1)/P-1	-0.2
1883	Bal-a	59	256	40	80	11	6	0		2		.313	.318	.402	720	127	6				.798	-9	O-50R/S-7,1-3,P-1	-0.2
1884	StL-U	109	485	95	142	32	11	4		10		.293	.307	.429	736	117	-5				**.947**	-2	*O-92C,S-14/2-2,1P	-0.9
1885	StL-N	16	62	8	10	3	0	0	3	5	8	.161	.224	.210	434	44	-4				.906	-2	O-16(0-16-0)	-0.6
1886	KC-N	105	429	53	103	24	8	3	57	15	43	.240	.266	.354	620	82	-11	2			.851	-5	*O-90C,S-11/2-4,M	-1.7
1888	KC-a	32	122	14	21	3	4	0	13	6		.172	.217	.262	479	50	-7	2			.914	2	O-32(0-32-0),M	-0.6
Total	7	347	1458	223	383	77	32	8	90	42	63	.263	.284	.376	660	99	-18	4			.878	-19	O-305C/S-32,2-6,1P	-4.3
■ HARLAND ROWE	Rowe, Harland Stimson "Hypie" b: 4/20/1896, Springvale, Me. d: 5/26/69, Springvale, Maine BL/TR, 6'1", 170 lbs. Deb: 6/23/16																							
1916	Phi-A	17	36	2	5	1	0	0	3	2	8	.139	.184	.167	351	6	-4	0			.842	-3	/3-8,O-1(0-0-1)	-0.7
■ JACK ROWE	Rowe, John Charles b: 12/8/1856, Hamburg, Pa. d: 4/25/11, St.Louis, Mo. BL/TR, 5'8", 170 lbs. Deb: 9/6/1879 FM Career OF: (47-LF 32-CF 26-RF)																							
1879	Buf-N	8	34	8	12	1	0	0	8	0	1	.353	.353	.382	735	139	1				.905	2	/C-6,O-2(0-0-2)	0.3
1880	Buf-N	79	326	43	82	10	6	1	36	6	17	.252	.265	.328	593	98	-1				.897	-19	*C-60,O-25R/3-3	-1.9
1881	Buf-N	64	246	30	82	11	**11**	1	43	1	12	.333	.336	.480	816	156	15				.900	-7	C-46/S-7,3-7,O-5R	0.9
1882	Buf-N	75	308	43	82	14	5	1	42	12	0	.266	.294	.354	648	105	1				.950	-13	C-46,S-22/3-7,O-1C	-0.7
1883	Buf-N	87	374	65	104	18	7	1	38	15	14	.278	.306	.372	678	102	1				.899	-17	C-49,O-28L,S-18,/3	-1.1
1884	Buf-N	93	400	85	126	14	14	4	61	23	14	.315	.352	.450	802	146	20				**.943**	-10	C-65,O-30L/S-6	1.3
1885	Buf-N	98	421	62	122	28	8	2	51	13	19	.290	.311	.409	720	127	11				.834	-14	S-65,C-23,O-12C	0.0
1886	Det-N	111	468	97	142	21	9	6	87	26	27	.303	.340	.425	765	128	14	12			.880	-21	*S-110/C-3	-0.2
1887	*Det-N	124	576	135	210	30	10	6	96	39	11	.365	.368	.445	813	121	14	22			.907	-27	*S-124	-0.8
1888	Det-N	105	451	62	125	19	8	2	74	19	28	.277	.311	.368	679	116	7	10			.861	-9	*S-105	0.2
1889	Pit-N	75	317	57	82	14	3	2	32	22	16	.259	.313	.341	654	91	-3	5			.896	-10	S-75	-0.9
1890	Buf-P	125	504	77	126	22	7	2	76	48	18	.250	.324	.333	657	83	-11	10			**.901**	-2	*S-125,M	-0.7
Total	12	1044	4425	764	1295	202	88	28	644	224	177	.293	.323	.392	715	115	70	59			.882	-147	S-657,C-298,O-103L,/3	-3.6
■ SCHOOLBOY ROWE	Rowe, Lynwood Thomas b: 1/11/10, Waco, Tex. d: 1/8/61, ElDorado, Ark. BR/TR, 6'4.5", 210 lbs. Deb: 4/15/33 C																							
1933	Det-A	21	50	6	11	1	0	0	6	1	4	.220	.235	.240	475	26	-5	0	0	0	1.000	2	P-19	0.0
1934	*Det-A	51	109	15	33	8	1	2	22	6	20	.303	.339	.450	789	102	-0	0	0	0	**1.000**	-0	P-45	0.0

YEAR	TM/L	G	AB	R	H	2B	3B	HR	RBI	BB	SO	AVG	OBP	SLG	OPS	OPS+	BR+	SB	CS	SBR	FA	FR	G/POS	TPR
1935	*Det-A☆	45	109	19	34	3	2	3	28	12	12	.312	.380	.459	839	120	3	0	0	0	.981	-2	P-42	0.0
1936	Det-A★	45	90	16	23	2	1	1	12	13	15	.256	.356	.333	689	71	-4	0	0	0	.984	2	P-41	0.0
1937	Det-A	10	10	2	2	0	0	0	1	1	4	.200	.273	.200	473	21	-1	0	0	0	1.000	0	P-10	0.0
1938	Det-A	4	6	1	1	1	0	0	0	0	1	.167	.167	.333	500	21	-1	0	0	0	.889	1	/P-4	0.0
1939	Det-A	31	61	7	15	0	1	1	12	5	7	.246	.303	.328	631	57	-4	1	1	-0	.947	0	P-28	0.0
1940	*Det-A	27	67	7	18	6	1	1	18	5	13	.269	.319	.433	752	85	-2	1	1	-0	**1.000**	-0	P-27	0.0
1941	Det-A	32	55	10	15	0	3	1	12	5	8	.273	.333	.436	770	93	-1	0	0	0	.927	1	P-27	0.0
1942	Det-A	2	4	0	0	0	0	0	0	0	0	.000	.000	.000	0	-93	-1	0	0	0	1.000	0	/P-2	0.0
	Bro-N	14	19	2	4	0	0	0	2	1	4	.211	.250	.211	461	35	-2	0			1.000	0	/P-9	0.0
1943	Phi-N	82	120	14	36	7	0	4	18	15	21	.300	.382	.458	841	148	7	0			.981	0	P-27	0.0
1946	Phi-N	30	61	4	11	5	0	1	6	3	16	.180	.219	.311	530	51	-4	0			1.000	-2	P-17	0.0
1947	Phi-N★	43	79	9	22	2	0	2	11	13	18	.278	.380	.380	760	106	1	0			.974	-1	P-31	0.0
1948	Phi-N	31	52	3	10	0	0	1	4	4	10	.192	.250	.250	500	36	-5	1			.976	1	P-30	0.0
1949	Phi-N	23	17	1	4	1	0	1	1	2	4	.235	.316	.471	786	111	0	0			.870	1	P-23	0.0
Total	15	491	909	116	239	36	9	18	153	86	157	.263	.328	.382	710	87	-17	3	2		.974	2	P-382	0.0

■ BAMA ROWELL

Rowell, Carvel William b: 1/13/16, Citronelle, Ala. d: 8/16/93, Citronelle, Ala. BL/TR, 5′11″, 185 lbs. Deb: 9/4/39 Career OF: (191-LF 32-CF 18-RF)

YEAR	TM/L	G	AB	R	H	2B	3B	HR	RBI	BB	SO	AVG	OBP	SLG	OPS	OPS+	BR+	SB	CS	SBR	FA	FR	G/POS	TPR
1939	Bos-N	21	59	5	11	2	2	0	6	1	4	.186	.200	.288	488	32	-6	0			.853	-2	O-16(0-13-3)	-0.9
1940	Bos-N	130	486	46	148	19	8	3	58	18	22	.305	.331	.395	726	105	2	12			.953	-3	*2-115/O-7(0-1-6)	0.6
1941	Bos-N	138	483	49	129	23	6	7	60	39	36	.267	.322	.383	705	102	0	11			.935	-10	*2-112,O-14L/3-2	-0.4
1946	Bos-N	95	293	37	82	12	6	3	31	29	15	.280	.345	.392	737	108	3	5			.978	-0	O-85(71-14-0)	-0.3
1947	Bos-N	113	384	48	106	23	2	5	40	18	14	.276	.310	.385	696	86	-9	7			.945	-8	*O-100L/2-7,3-4	-2.3
1948	Phi-N	77	196	15	47	16	2	1	22	8	14	.240	.270	.357	627	70	-9	2			.821	-12	3-18,O-17L,2-12	-2.2
Total	6	574	1901	200	523	95	26	19	217	113	105	.275	.316	.382	699	95	-19	37			.945	-35	2-246,O-239L/3-24	-5.5

■ ED ROWEN

Rowen, W. Edward b: 10/22/1857, Bridgeport, Conn. d: 2/22/1892, Bridgeport, Conn. 5′6″, 155 lbs. Deb: 5/1/1882 Career OF: (0-LF 5-CF 51-RF)

YEAR	TM/L	G	AB	R	H	2B	3B	HR	RBI	BB	SO	AVG	OBP	SLG	OPS	OPS+	BR+	SB	CS	SBR	FA	FR	G/POS	TPR
1882	Bos-N	83	327	36	81	7	4	1	43	19	18	.248	.289	.303	592	90	-3				.885	-12	O-48R,C-34/S-6,3-1	-1.1
1883	Phi-a	49	196	28	43	10	1	0	21	11		.219	.261	.281	541	68	-7				.855	-2	C-44/O-8C,3-1,2-1	-0.5
1884	Phi-a	4	15	4	6	1	0	0	1	1		.400	.471	.467	937	194	2				.806	-3	/C-4	-0.1
Total	3	136	538	68	130	18	5	1	65	31	18	.242	.284	.299	583	85	-9				.866	-17	/C-82,O-56R,S-6,32	-1.7

■ CHUCK ROWLAND

Rowland, Charlie Leland b: 7/23/1899, Warrenton, N.C. d: 1/21/92, Raleigh, N.C. BR/TR, 6′1″, 185 lbs. Deb: 5/11/23

YEAR	TM/L	G	AB	R	H	2B	3B	HR	RBI	BB	SO	AVG	OBP	SLG	OPS	OPS+	BR+	SB	CS	SBR	FA	FR	G/POS	TPR
1923	Phi-A	5	6	0	0	0	0	0	0	0	2	.000	.000	.000	0	-99	-2	0	0	0	1.000	0	/C-4	-0.1

■ RICH ROWLAND

Rowland, Richard Garnet b: 2/25/64, Cloverdale, Cal. BR/TR, 6′1″, 215 lbs. Deb: 9/7/90

YEAR	TM/L	G	AB	R	H	2B	3B	HR	RBI	BB	SO	AVG	OBP	SLG	OPS	OPS+	BR+	SB	CS	SBR	FA	FR	G/POS	TPR
1990	Det-A	7	19	3	3	1	0	0	0	2	4	.158	.238	.211	449	26	-2	0	0	0	.967	-0	/C-5,D-2	-0.2
1991	Det-A	4	4	0	1	0	0	0	1	1	2	.250	.400	.250	650	83	-0	0	0	0	1.000	0	/C-2,D-1	0.0
1992	Det-A	6	14	2	3	0	0	0	0	3	3	.214	.353	.214	567	62	-1	0	0	0	1.000	0	/C-3,1-1,3-1,D-2	-0.1
1993	Det-A	21	46	2	10	3	0	0	4	5	16	.217	.294	.283	577	56	-3	0	0	0	.988	5	C-17/D-3	0.2
1994	Bos-A	46	118	14	27	3	0	9	20	11	35	.229	.295	.483	778	92	-2	0	0	0	.972	-1	C-39/1-1,D-4	-0.1
1995	Bos-A	14	29	1	5	1	0	0	1	0	11	.172	.172	.207	379	-2	-4	0	0	0	.977	2	C-11/D-3	-0.2
Total	6	98	230	22	49	8	0	9	26	22	71	.213	.282	.365	647	67	-12	0	0	0	.976	5	/C-77,D-15,1-2,3-1	-0.4

■ JIM ROXBURGH

Roxburgh, James A. b: 1/17/1858, San Francisco, Cal d: 2/21/34, San Francisco, Cal BR/TR, 5′10″, 170 lbs. Deb: 5/30/1884

YEAR	TM/L	G	AB	R	H	2B	3B	HR	RBI	BB	SO	AVG	OBP	SLG	OPS	OPS+	BR+	SB	CS	SBR	FA	FR	G/POS	TPR
1884	Bal-a	2	4	1	2	0	0	0		1		.500	.667	.500	1167	275	1				.824	-0	/C-2	0.1
1887	Phi-a	2	8	0	1	0	0	0	0	0		.125	.125	.125	250	-30	-1	0			.875	-2	/C-2,2-1	-0.2
Total	2	4	12	1	3	0	0	0	0	1		.250	.357	.250	607	81	-0	0			.840	-2	/C-4,2-1	-0.1

■ STAN ROYER

Royer, Stanley Dean b: 8/31/67, Olney, Ill. BR/TR, 6′3″, 195 lbs. Deb: 9/11/91

YEAR	TM/L	G	AB	R	H	2B	3B	HR	RBI	BB	SO	AVG	OBP	SLG	OPS	OPS+	BR+	SB	CS	SBR	FA	FR	G/POS	TPR
1991	StL-N	9	21	1	6	1	0	0	1	1	2	.286	.318	.333	652	83	-0	0	0	0	1.000	-2	/3-5	-0.2
1992	StL-N	13	31	6	10	2	0	2	9	1	4	.323	.344	.581	924	162	2	0	0	0	.900	-0	/3-5,1-4	0.2
1993	StL-N	24	46	4	14	2	0	1	8	2	14	.304	.333	.413	746	100	-0	0	1	-0	.857	-0	3-10/1-2	-0.1
1994	StL-N	39	57	3	10	5	0	1	2	0	18	.175	.175	.316	491	25	-6	0	0	0	.972	-1	1-11/3-5	-0.7
	Bos-A	4	9	0	1	0	0	0	1	0	3	.111	.111	.111	222	-41	-2	0	0	0	.833	-0	/3-3,1-1	-0.2
Total	4	89	164	14	41	10	0	4	21	4	41	.250	.268	.384	652	74	-7	0	1	-0	.895	-3	/3-28,1-18	-1.0

■ JERRY ROYSTER

Royster, Jeron Kennis b: 10/18/52, Sacramento, Cal. BR/TR, 6′, 165 lbs. Deb: 8/14/73 C Career OF: (123-LF 21-CF 9-RF)

YEAR	TM/L	G	AB	R	H	2B	3B	HR	RBI	BB	SO	AVG	OBP	SLG	OPS	OPS+	BR+	SB	CS	SBR	FA	FR	G/POS	TPR
1973	LA-N	10	19	1	4	0	0	0	2	0	5	.211	.211	.211	421	18	-2	1	0	0	.842	2	/3-6,2-1	0.0
1974	LA-N	6	0	2	0	0	0	0	0	0	0	—	—	—	—	—	0	0	0	0	1.000	1	/2-1,3-1,O-1(0-0-1)	0.1
1975	LA-N	13	36	2	9	2	1	0	1	1	3	.250	.270	.361	631	77	-1	1	0	0	1.000	-3	/O-7R,2-4,3-3,S-1	-0.4
1976	Atl-N	149	533	65	132	13	1	5	45	52	53	.248	.316	.304	620	72	-18	24	13	1	.962	17	*3-148/S-2	-0.2
1977	Atl-N	140	445	64	96	10	2	6	28	38	67	.216	.279	.288	567	47	-33	28	10	3	.953	-29	3-56,S-51,2-38,/O-1C	-5.5
1978	Atl-N	140	529	67	137	17	8	2	35	56	49	.259	.333	.333	666	78	-14	27	17	-0	.974	-13	2-75,S-60/3-1	-1.7
1979	Atl-N	154	601	103	164	25	6	3	51	62	59	.273	.341	.349	690	83	-13	35	8	5	.948	13	3-80,2-77	0.8
1980	Atl-N	123	392	42	95	17	5	1	20	37	48	.242	.309	.319	628	73	-13	22	13	0	.948	-11	2-49,3-48,O-41L	-2.5
1981	Atl-N	64	93	13	19	4	1	0	9	7	14	.204	.260	.269	529	49	-6	7	5	-0	.950	3	3-24,2-13	-0.3
1982	*Atl-N	108	261	43	77	13	2	2	25	22	36	.295	.354	.383	738	102	1	14	6	1	.943	-2	3-62,O-25L,2-16,S	0.0
1983	Atl-N	91	268	32	63	10	3	3	30	28	35	.235	.307	.328	636	71	-10	11	7	-0	.940	7	3-47,2-26,O-18L,S	-0.3
1984	Atl-N	81	227	22	47	13	2	1	21	15	41	.207	.259	.295	554	52	-15	6	4	-0	.973	5	2-29,3-17,S-16,O-11L	-0.8
1985	SD-N	90	249	31	70	13	2	5	31	32	31	.281	.365	.410	775	118	7	6	5	-0	.975	2	2-58,3-29/S-7,O-2C	1.1
1986	SD-N	118	257	31	66	12	0	5	26	32	45	.257	.339	.362	701	95	-1	3	5	-1	.931	-4	3-59,S-24,2-21,/O-7L	-0.5
1987	Chi-A	55	154	25	37	11	0	7	23	19	28	.240	.328	.448	776	101	-0	2	1	0	.969	-8	3-30,O-13L/2-5,D-4	-0.8
	NY-A	18	42	1	15	2	0	0	4	4	4	.357	.413	.405	818	120	1	2	1	0	.909	2	3-13/2-1,S-1,O-1L	0.4
	Yr	73	196	26	52	13	0	7	27	23	32	.265	.345	.439	784	104	1	4	2	0	.954	-5	3-43,O-14L/2-6,DS	-0.4
1988	Atl-N	68	102	8	18	3	0	0	1	6	16	.176	.222	.206	428	22	-10	0	0	0	1.000	-2	O-26C,3-10/2-2,S-2	-1.3
Total	16	1428	4208	552	1049	165	33	40	352	411	534	.249	.318	.333	650	76	-128	189	95	8	.951	-19	3-634,2-416,SO/D	-11.9

■ WILLIE ROYSTER

Royster, Willie Arthur b: 4/11/54, Clarksville, Va. BR/TR, 5′11″, 180 lbs. Deb: 9/3/81

YEAR	TM/L	G	AB	R	H	2B	3B	HR	RBI	BB	SO	AVG	OBP	SLG	OPS	OPS+	BR+	SB	CS	SBR	FA	FR	G/POS	TPR
1981	Bal-A	4	4	0	0	0	0	0	0	0	2	.000	.000	.000	0	-99	-1	0	0	0	1.000	-0	/C-4	-0.1

■ VIC ROZNOVSKY

Roznovsky, Victor Joseph b: 10/19/38, Shiner, Tex. BL/TR, 6′1″, 180 lbs. Deb: 6/28/64

YEAR	TM/L	G	AB	R	H	2B	3B	HR	RBI	BB	SO	AVG	OBP	SLG	OPS	OPS+	BR+	SB	CS	SBR	FA	FR	G/POS	TPR
1964	Chi-N	35	76	2	15	1	0	0	2	5	18	.197	.247	.211	457	29	-7	0	1	-0	.976	-6	C-26	-1.3
1965	Chi-N	71	172	9	38	4	1	3	15	16	30	.221	.298	.308	607	70	-7	1	0	0	.984	2	C-63	-0.3
1966	Bal-A	41	97	4	23	5	0	1	10	9	11	.237	.308	.320	628	82	-2	0	0	0	.995	-3	C-34	-0.4
1967	Bal-A	45	97	7	20	5	0	0	10	1	20	.206	.214	.258	472	39	-7	0	0	0	.993	-2	C-23	-0.9
1969	Phi-N	13	13	0	3	0	0	0	1	1	4	.231	.286	.231	516	47	-1	0	0	0	1.000	0	/C-2	-0.1
Total	5	205	455	22	99	15	1	4	38	32	83	.218	.275	.281	556	59	-24	1	1	-0	.988	-9	C-148	-3.0

■ AL RUBELING

Rubeling, Albert William b: 5/10/13, Baltimore, Md. d: 1/28/88, Baltimore, Md. BR/TR, 6′, 185 lbs. Deb: 4/16/40 Career OF: (9-LF 0-CF 9-RF)

YEAR	TM/L	G	AB	R	H	2B	3B	HR	RBI	BB	SO	AVG	OBP	SLG	OPS	OPS+	BR+	SB	CS	SBR	FA	FR	G/POS	TPR
1940	Phi-A	108	376	49	92	16	6	4	38	48	58	.245	.330	.351	681	78	-12	4	5	-1	.933	-7	3-98,2-10	-1.5
1941	Phi-A	6	19	0	5	0	0	0	2	2	1	.263	.333	.263	596	61	-1	0	0	0	.833	-2	/3-6	-0.2
1943	Pit-N	47	168	23	44	8	4	0	9	8	17	.262	.295	.357	653	85	-4	0			.974	-1	2-44/3-1	-0.2
1944	Pit-N	92	184	22	45	7	2	4	30	19	19	.245	.322	.370	692	90	-2	4			1.000	-1	O-18(9-0-9),2-17,3-16	-0.4
Total	4	253	747	94	186	31	12	8	79	77	95	.249	.321	.355	676	82	-19	8	5		.939	-10	3-121/2-71,O-18L	-2.3

■ SONNY RUBERTO

Ruberto, John Edward b: 1/2/46, Staten Island, N.Y. BR/TR, 5′11″, 175 lbs. Deb: 5/25/69 C

YEAR	TM/L	G	AB	R	H	2B	3B	HR	RBI	BB	SO	AVG	OBP	SLG	OPS	OPS+	BR+	SB	CS	SBR	FA	FR	G/POS	TPR
1969	SD-N	19	21	3	3	0	0	0	0	1	7	.143	.182	.143	325	-8	-3	0	0	0	1.000	4	C-15	0.1
1972	Cin-N	2	3	0	0	0	0	0	0	0	1	.000	.250	.000	250	-25	-0	0	0	0	1.000	-0	/C-2	-0.1
Total	2	21	24	3	3	0	0	0	0	1	8	.125	.192	.125	317	-10	-3	0	0	0	1.000	4	/C-17	0.0

■ ART RUBLE

Ruble, William Arthur "Speedy" b: 3/11/03, Knoxville, Tenn. d: 11/1/83, Maryville, Tenn. BL/TR, 5′10.5″, 168 lbs. Deb: 4/18/27

YEAR	TM/L	G	AB	R	H	2B	3B	HR	RBI	BB	SO	AVG	OBP	SLG	OPS	OPS+	BR+	SB	CS	SBR	FA	FR	G/POS	TPR
1927	Det-A	56	91	16	15	4	2	0	11	14	15	.165	.283	.253	536	39	-8	2	2	-0	.970	-7	O-43(24-13-7)	-1.7

YEAR	TM/L	G	AB	R	H	2B	3B	HR	RBI	BB	SO	AVG	OBP	SLG	OPS	OPS+	BR+	SB	CS	SBR	FA	FR	G/POS	TPR
1934	Phi-N	19	54	7	15	4	0	0	8	7	3	.278	.361	.352	713	81	-1	0			.839	-2	O-14(4-1-10)	-0.3
Total	2	75	145	23	30	8	2	0	19	21	18	.207	.311	.290	601	55	-9	2	2		.929	-9	/O-57(28-14-17)	-2.0
■ **JOHNNY RUCKER** Rucker, John Joel b: 1/15/17, Crabapple, Ga. d: 8/7/85, Moultrie, Ga. BL/TR, 6'2", 175 lbs. Deb: 4/16/40																								
1940	NY-N	86	277	38	82	7	5	4	23	7	32	.296	.313	.401	714	95	-3	4			.954	-3	O-57(0-57-0)	-0.8
1941	NY-N	143	622	95	179	38	9	1	42	29	61	.288	.320	.383	702	95	-6	8			.967	5	*O-142(0-142-0)	-0.4
1943	NY-N	132	505	56	138	19	4	2	46	22	44	.273	.304	.339	642	85	-11	4			.969	3	*O-117(0-117-0)	-1.3
1944	NY-N	144	587	79	143	14	8	6	39	24	48	.244	.275	.325	600	69	-26	8			.985	-6	*O-139(0-139-0)	-3.7
1945	NY-N	105	429	58	117	19	11	7	51	20	36	.273	.305	.417	722	98	-3	7			.978	-1	O-98(0-98-0)	-0.8
1946	NY-N	95	197	28	52	8	2	1	13	7	27	.264	.300	.340	640	81	-5	4			.948	-10	O-54(0-50-6)	-1.7
Total	6	705	2617	354	711	105	39	21	214	109	248	.272	.302	.366	668	87	-54	35			.971	-12	O-607(0-603-6)	-8.7
■ **JOHN RUDDERHAM** Rudderham, John Edmund b: 8/30/1863, Quincy, Mass. d: 4/3/42, Randolph, Mass. BR/TR, 5'8", 170 lbs. Deb: 9/18/1884																								
1884	Bos-U	1	4	0	1	0	0	0		0		.250	.250	.250	500	53	-0				.000	-1	/O-1(1-0-0)	-0.1
■ **JOE RUDI** Rudi, Joseph Oden b: 9/7/46, Modesto, Cal. BR/TR, 6'2", 200 lbs. Deb: 4/11/67 C Career OF: (1160-LF 2-CF 47-RF)																								
1967	KC-A	19	43	4	8	2	0	0	1	3	7	.186	.239	.233	472	41	-3	0	0	0	.984	-2	/1-9,O-6(6-0-0)	-0.6
1968	Oak-A	68	181	10	32	5	1	1	12	12	32	.177	.236	.232	468	44	-12	1	1	-0	.987	-3	O-56(55-1-1)	-2.1
1969	Oak-A	35	122	10	23	3	1	2	6	5	16	.189	.220	.279	499	41	-10	1	1	-0	1.000	2	O-18(18-0-0),1-11	-1.1
1970	Oak-A	106	350	40	108	23	2	11	42	16	61	.309	.342	.480	822	129	12	3	1	0	.982	-2	O-63(58-1-12),1-28	0.4
1971	*Oak-A	127	513	62	137	23	4	10	52	28	62	.267	.306	.386	692	97	-4	3	2	-0	.996	7	*O-121(115-0-9)/1-5	-0.5
1972	*Oak-A★	147	593	94	**181**	32	**9**	19	75	37	62	.305	.348	.486	834	154	36	3	4	-1	.992	-1	*O-147(147-0-0)/3-1	2.9
1973	*Oak-A	120	437	53	118	25	1	12	66	30	72	.270	.320	.414	734	111	5	0	0	0	.992	4	*O-117L/1-1,D-1	0.2
1974	*Oak-A★	158	593	73	174	**39**	4	22	99	34	92	.293	.337	.484	821	143	30	2	3	-1	.984	-7	*O-140L,1-27/D-2	1.3
1975	*Oak-A★	126	468	66	130	26	6	21	75	40	56	.278	.339	.494	832	136	20	2	1	0	.991	-12	1-91,O-44(44-0-0)/D-2	-0.1
1976	Oak-A	130	500	54	135	32	3	13	94	41	71	.270	.329	.424	753	124	14	6	1	1	.989	-1	*O-126L/1-2,D-2	0.6
1977	Cal-A	64	242	48	64	13	2	13	53	22	48	.264	.336	.496	832	128	9	1	0	0	1.000	5	O-61(61-0-0)/D-3	1.1
1978	Cal-A	133	497	58	127	27	1	17	79	28	82	.256	.298	.416	714	103	-0	2	1	0	.992	7	*O-111L,D-11,1-10	0.1
1979	Cal-A	90	330	35	80	11	3	11	61	24	61	.242	.296	.394	690	87	-7	0	0	0	.989	6	O-80(69-0-12)/1-5,D-3	-0.5
1980	Cal-A	104	372	42	88	17	1	16	53	17	84	.237	.279	.417	696	90	-7	1	0	0	.991	8	O-90(89-0-1)/1-6,D-3	-0.2
1981	Bos-A	49	122	14	22	3	0	6	24	8	29	.180	.242	.352	595	66	-6	0	0	0	1.000	-1	D-21/1-5,O-1(0-0-1)	-0.8
1982	Oak-A	71	193	21	41	6	1	5	18	24	35	.212	.303	.332	634	77	-6	0	0	0	.991	-7	1-49,O-14(4-0-10)/D-3	-1.6
Total	16	1547	5556	684	1468	287	39	179	810	369	870	.264	.314	.427	741	112	70	25	15	0	.991	3	*O-1195L,1-249/D-51,3	-0.9
■ **DUTCH RUDOLPH** Rudolph, John Herman b: 7/10/1882, Natrona, Pa. d: 4/17/67, Natrona, Pa. BL/TL, 5'10", 160 lbs. Deb: 7/3/03																								
1903	Phi-N	1	1	0	0	0	0	0	0	0		.000	.000	.000	0	-99	-0	0			.000	0	H	0.0
1904	Chi-N	2	3	0	1	0	0	0	0	0		.333	.333	.333	667	106	0	0			1.000	-1	/O-2(0-0-2)	-0.1
Total	2	3	4	0	1	0	0	0	0	0		.250	.250	.250	500	52	-0	0			1.000	-1	/O-2(0-0-2)	-0.1
■ **KEN RUDOLPH** Rudolph, Kenneth Victor b: 12/29/46, Rockford, Ill. BR/TR, 6'1", 185 lbs. Deb: 4/20/69																								
1969	Chi-N	27	34	7	7	1	0	1	6	6	11	.206	.325	.324	649	73	-1	0	0	0	.977	0	C-11/O-3(3-0-0)	-0.1
1970	Chi-N	20	40	1	4	1	0	0	2	1	12	.100	.122	.125	247	-30	-7	0	0	0	1.000	1	C-16	-0.5
1971	Chi-N	25	76	5	15	3	0	0	7	6	20	.197	.265	.237	502	38	-6	0	0	0	1.000	7	C-25	0.2
1972	Chi-N	42	106	10	25	1	1	2	9	6	14	.236	.283	.321	604	64	-5	1	2	-0	.966	5	C-41	0.2
1973	Chi-N	64	170	12	35	8	1	2	17	7	25	.206	.242	.300	542	46	-13	1	4	-1	.970	-3	C-64	-1.5
1974	SF-N	57	158	11	41	3	0	0	10	21	15	.259	.350	.278	628	74	-5	0	0	0	.996	3	C-56	0.1
1975	StL-N	44	80	5	16	2	0	1	6	3	10	.200	.229	.262	491	35	-7	0	0	0	.972	2	C-31	-0.5
1976	StL-N	27	50	1	8	3	0	0	5	1	7	.160	.176	.220	396	12	-6	0	0	0	.940	2	C-14	-0.4
1977	SF-N	11	15	1	3	0	0	0	0	1	3	.200	.250	.200	450	22	-2	0	0	0	.946	3	C-11	0.1
	Bal-A	11	14	2	4	1	0	0	2	0	4	.286	.286	.357	643	79	-0	0	0	0	1.000	5	C-11	0.4
Total	9	328	743	55	158	23	2	6	64	52	121	.213	.268	.273	541	48	-51	2	6	-2	.980	24	C-280/O-3(3-0-0)	-2.0
■ **MUDDY RUEL** Ruel, Herold Dominic b: 2/20/1896, St.Louis, Mo. d: 11/13/63, Palo Alto, Cal. BR/TR, 5'9", 150 lbs. Deb: 5/29/15 MC																								
1915	StL-A	10	14	0	0	0	0	0	1	5	5	.000	.263	.000	263	-22	-2	0			.958	-1	/C-6	-0.3
1917	NY-A	6	17	1	2	0	0	0	1	2	2	.118	.211	.118	328	0	-2	1			1.000	-1	/C-6	-0.2
1918	NY-A	3	6	0	2	0	0	0	0	2	1	.333	.500	.333	833	148	1	1			1.000	0	/C-2	0.1
1919	NY-A	79	233	18	56	6	0	0	31	34	26	.240	.340	.266	606	71	-8	4			.975	2	C-79	0.1
1920	NY-A	82	261	30	70	14	1	1	15	15	18	.268	.310	.341	651	70	-11	4	2	0	.984	0	C-80	-0.4
1921	Bos-A	113	358	41	99	21	1	1	45	41	15	.277	.352	.349	702	82	-9	2	7	-2	.977	-10	*C-109	-1.3
1922	Bos-A	116	361	34	92	15	1	0	28	41	26	.255	.333	.302	634	67	-17	4	2	0	.978	-2	*C-112	-1.0
1923	Was-A	136	449	63	142	24	3	0	54	55	21	.316	.394	.383	778	111	9	4	6	-1	.980	19	*C-133	3.4
1924	*Was-A	149	501	50	142	20	2	0	57	62	20	.283	.370	.331	702	84	-9	7	11	-2	.980	14	*C-147	1.2
1925	*Was-A	127	393	55	122	9	2	0	54	63	16	.310	.411	.344	754	95	1	4	5	-1	.982	12	*C-126/1-1	1.8
1926	Was-A	117	368	42	110	22	4	1	53	61	14	.299	.401	.389	790	109	8	7	6	-1	**.989**	2	*C-117	1.6
1927	Was-A	131	428	61	132	16	5	1	52	63	18	.308	.403	.376	779	104	6	9	6	-0	.988	-3	*C-128	1.1
1928	Was-A	108	350	31	90	18	2	0	55	44	14	.257	.342	.320	662	75	-11	12	10	-1	**.989**	7	*C-101/1-2	0.1
1929	Was-A	69	188	16	46	4	2	0	20	31	7	.245	.352	.287	639	66	-8	0	4	-1	.990	9	C-62	0.3
1930	Was-A	66	198	18	50	3	4	0	26	24	13	.253	.342	.308	650	66	-9	1	0	0	.986	4	C-60	-0.2
1931	Bos-A	33	83	6	25	5	0	0	6	9	6	.301	.370	.361	731	98	0	0	0	0	.945	1	C-30	0.2
	Det-A	14	50	1	6	1	0	0	3	5	1	.120	.200	.140	340	-9	-8	0	0	0	.975	3	C-14	-0.4
	Yr	47	133	7	31	6	0	0	9	14	7	.233	.306	.278	584	56	-8	0	0	0	.958	4	C-44	-0.2
1932	Det-A	51	136	10	32	4	2	0	18	17	6	.235	.320	.294	614	58	-8	1	0	0	.989	-2	C-49	-0.7
1933	StL-A	36	63	13	12	2	0	0	8	24	4	.190	.414	.222	636	68	-1	0	0	0	1.000	3	C-28	0.2
1934	Chi-A	22	57	4	12	3	0	0	7	8	5	.211	.308	.263	571	47	-4	0	0	0	.976	-2	C-21	-0.5
Total	19	1468	4514	494	1242	187	29	4	534	606	238	.275	.365	.332	697	84	-84	61	59		.982	53	*C-1410/1-3	5.0
■ **DUTCH RUETHER** Ruether, Walter Henry b: 9/13/1893, Alameda, Cal. d: 5/16/70, Phoenix, Ariz. BL/TL, 6'1.5", 180 lbs. Deb: 4/13/17																								
1917	Chi-N	31	44	3	12	1	3	0	11	8	11	.273	.385	.432	816	139	2	0			1.000	1	P-10/1-5	0.1
	Cin-N	19	24	1	5	2	0	0	1	3	6	.208	.296	.292	588	84	-0	1			.833	-0	/P-7	0.0
	Yr	50	68	4	17	3	3	0	12	11	17	.250	.354	.382	737	122	2	1			.920	0	P-17/1-5	0.1
1918	Cin-N	2	3	0	0	0	0	0	0	0	2	.000	.000	.000	0	-99	-1	0			1.000	-0	/P-2	0.0
1919	*Cin-N	42	92	8	24	2	3	0	6	4	18	.261	.292	.348	639	94	-1	1			.971	-3	P-33	0.0
1920	Cin-N	45	104	3	20	4	0	0	10	5	24	.192	.229	.231	460	33	-9	0	0	0	.952	0	P-37/1-1	0.0
1921	Bro-N	49	97	12	34	5	2	2	13	4	9	.351	.376	.505	881	127	3	1	0	0	.966	-1	P-36	0.0
1922	Bro-N	67	125	12	26	6	1	2	20	12	11	.208	.283	.320	603	56	-9	0	0	0	**1.000**	-0	P-35	0.0
1923	Bro-N	49	117	6	32	1	0	0	10	12	12	.274	.341	.282	623	68	-5	0	0	0	.968	-2	P-34/1-1	0.0
1924	Bro-N	34	62	5	15	1	1	0	4	5	2	.242	.299	.290	589	60	-3	0	0	0	.981	1	P-30	0.0
1925	*Was-A	55	108	18	36	3	2	1	15	10	8	.333	.390	.426	816	109	2	0	1	-0	.962	-3	P-30/1-1	0.0
1926	Was-A	47	92	6	23	2	0	1	11	6	10	.250	.296	.304	600	58	-6	0	0	0	.974	-2	P-23	0.0
	*NY-A	13	21	2	2	0	0	0	0	0	1	.095	.136	.095	232	-39	-4	0	0	0	.875	-1	/P-5	0.0
	Yr	60	113	8	25	2	0	1	11	6	11	.221	.267	.265	532	40	-10	0	0	0	.957	-3	P-28	0.0
1927	NY-A	35	80	7	21	3	0	1	10	8	15	.262	.330	.338	667	76	-3	0	0	0	**1.000**	0	P-27	0.0
Total	11	488	969	83	250	30	12	7	111	77	129	.258	.314	.335	649	76	-33	3	1		.970	-9	P-309/1-8	0.1
■ **RUDY RUFER** Rufer, Rudolph Joseph b: 10/28/26, Ridgewood, N.Y. BR/TR, 6'0.5", 165 lbs. Deb: 9/22/49																								
1949	NY-N	7	15	1	1	0	0	0	2	2	0	.067	.176	.067	243	-32	-3	0			.957	-1	/S-7	-0.3
1950	NY-N	15	11	1	1	0	0	0	0	0	1	.091	.091	.091	182	-52	-2	1			.889	1	/S-8	-0.1
Total	2	22	26	2	2	0	0	0	2	2	1	.077	.143	.077	220	-40	-5	1			.938	1	/S-15	-0.4
■ **RED RUFFING** Ruffing, Charles Herbert b: 5/3/04, Granville, Ill. d: 2/17/86, Mayfield Hts., O. BR/TR, 6'1.5", 205 lbs. Deb: 5/31/24 CH																								
1924	Bos-A	8	7	0	1	0	1	0	0	0	1	.143	.143	.429	571	44	-1	0	0	0	1.000	-1	/P-8	0.0

YEAR	TM/L	G	AB	R	H	2B	3B	HR	RBI	BB	SO	AVG	OBP	SLG	OPS	OPS+	BR+	SB	CS	SBR	FA	FR	G/POS	TPR
1925	Bos-A	37	79	6	17	4	2	0	11	1	22	.215	.235	.316	551	39	-8	0	0	0	.983	-1	P-37	0.0
1926	Bos-A	37	51	8	10	1	0	1	5	2	12	.196	.226	.275	501	31	-5	0	1	-0	.978	-1	P-37	0.0
1927	Bos-A	29	55	5	14	3	1	0	4	0	6	.255	.268	.345	613	59	-3	0	0	0	.978	0	P-26	0.0
1928	Bos-A	60	121	12	38	13	1	2	19	3	12	.314	.331	.488	818	115	2	0	0	0	.951	-3	P-42	0.0
1929	Bos-A	60	114	9	35	9	0	2	17	2	13	.307	.325	.439	763	97	-1	0	0	0	.946	-2	P-35/O-2(2-0-0)	-0.1
1930	Bos-A	6	11	2	3	2	0	0	1	0	1	.273	.273	.455	727	84	-0	0	0	0	.667	-1	/P-4	0.0
	NY-A	52	99	15	37	6	2	4	21	7	7	.374	.415	.596	1011	160	9	0	0	0	.938	-2	P-34	0.0
	Yr	58	110	17	40	8	2	4	22	7	8	.364	.402	.582	984	153	8	0	0	0	.914	-3	P-38	0.0
1931	NY-A	48	109	14	36	8	1	3	12	1	13	.330	.336	.505	841	125	3	0	0	0	**1.000**	-3	P-37/O-1(0-0-1)	0.0
1932	*NY-A	55	124	20	38	6	1	3	19	6	10	.306	.338	.444	782	106	1	0	0	0	.955	-2	P-35	0.0
1933	NY-A	55	115	10	29	3	1	2	13	7	15	.252	.295	.348	643	74	-5	0	0	0	.964	-0	P-35	0.0
1934	NY-A★	45	113	11	28	3	0	2	13	3	17	.248	.274	.327	601	58	-7	0	0	0	.933	-3	P-36	0.0
1935	NY-A	50	109	13	37	10	0	2	18	3	9	.339	.363	.486	849	125	3	0	0	0	**1.000**	-2	P-30	0.0
1936	*NY-A	53	127	14	37	5	0	5	22	11	12	.291	.348	.449	797	99	-1	0	0	0	.986	2	P-33	0.0
1937	*NY-A	54	129	11	26	3	0	1	10	13	24	.202	.275	.248	523	32	-13	0	0	0	.974	-4	P-31	0.0
1938	*NY-A☆	45	107	12	24	4	1	3	17	17	21	.224	.331	.364	695	74	-4	0	0	0	**1.000**	-2	P-31	0.0
1939	*NY-A★	44	114	12	35	1	0	1	20	7	18	.307	.347	.342	689	78	-4	1	0	0	.952	-2	P-28	0.0
1940	NY-A★	33	89	8	11	4	0	1	7	3	9	.124	.152	.202	354	-9	-15	0	0	0	.947	-3	P-30	0.0
1941	*NY-A☆	38	89	10	27	8	1	2	22	4	12	.303	.333	.483	816	115	1	0	0	0	**1.000**	-3	P-23	0.0
1942	*NY-A☆	30	80	8	20	4	0	1	13	5	13	.250	.302	.338	640	81	-2	0	0	0	.974	-2	P-24	0.0
1945	NY-A	21	46	4	10	0	1	1	5	0	8	.217	.217	.326	543	54	-3	0	0	0	.929	-2	P-11	0.0
1946	NY-A	8	25	1	3	1	0	0	1	1	8	.120	.154	.160	314	-12	-4	0	0	0	1.000	-1	/P-8	0.0
1947	Chi-A	14	24	2	5	0	0	0	3	1	3	.208	.240	.208	448	26	-2	0	0	0	1.000	-0	/P-9	0.0
Total	22	882	1937	207	521	98	13	36	273	97	266	.269	.306	.389	695	81	-59	1	1	-0	.968	-35	P-624/O-3(2-0-1)	-0.1
■ **CHICO RUIZ**	Ruiz, Hiraldo (Sablon) (b: (Hiraldo Sablon (Ruiz)) b: 12/5/38, Santo Domingo, Cuba d: 2/9/72, San Diego, Cal. BB/TR, 6′, 173 lbs. Deb: 4/13/64 Career OF: (11-LF 0-CF 3-RF)																							
1964	Cin-N	77	311	33	76	13	2	2	16	7	41	.244	.270	.318	589	63	-15	11	3	1	.942	-10	3-49,2-30	-2.3
1965	Cin-N	29	18	7	2	1	0	0	1	0	5	.111	.111	.167	278	-21	-3	1	2	-0	.875	2	/3-4,S-3	-0.1
1966	Cin-N	82	110	13	28	2	1	0	5	5	14	.255	.287	.291	578	56	-6	1	2	-0	.927	-1	3-27/O-8(7-0-1),S-6	-0.8
1967	Cin-N	105	250	32	55	12	4	0	13	11	35	.220	.259	.300	559	53	-15	9	4	1	.969	0	2-56,3-13,S-11,/O-5L	-1.0
1968	Cin-N	85	139	15	36	2	1	0	9	12	18	.259	.318	.288	606	78	-3	4	3	-0	.979	8	2-34,1-16/3-5,S-3	0.7
1969	Cin-N	88	196	19	48	4	1	0	13	14	28	.245	.295	.276	571	58	-11	4	2	0	.949	-7	2-39,S-29/3-7,1O	-1.3
1970	Cal-A	68	107	10	26	3	1	0	12	7	16	.243	.296	.290	585	64	-5	3	0	1	.985	0	3-27/2-3,S-3,1-2,C	-0.5
1971	Cal-A	31	19	4	5	0	0	0	0	2	7	.263	.333	.263	596	76	-1	1	0	0	1.000	2	/3-3,2-2	0.2
Total	8	565	1150	133	276	37	10	2	69	58	164	.240	.281	.295	575	60	-59	34	16	2	.966	-6	2-164,3-135/S-55,1OC	-5.1
■ **CHICO RUIZ**	Ruiz, Manuel (Cruz) b: 11/1/51, Santurce, P.R. BR/TR, 5′11.5″, 170 lbs. Deb: 7/29/78																							
1978	Atl-N	18	46	3	13	3	0	0	2	2	4	.283	.313	.348	660	76	-1	0	0	0	.984	1	2-14/3-1	0.1
1980	Atl-N	25	26	3	8	2	1	0	2	3	7	.308	.379	.462	841	129	1	0	1	-0	.875	2	3-16/S-4,2-2	0.3
Total	2	43	72	6	21	5	1	0	4	5	11	.292	.338	.389	727	95	-0	0	1	-0	.880	3	/3-17,2-16,S-4	0.4
■ **JOE RULLO**	Rullo, Joseph Vincent b: 6/16/16, New York, N.Y. d: 10/28/69, Philadelphia, Pa. BR/TR, 5′11″, 168 lbs. Deb: 9/22/43																							
1943	Phi-A	16	55	2	16	3	0	0	6	8	7	.291	.381	.345	726	114	1	0	0	0	.963	-1	2-16	0.1
1944	Phi-A	35	96	5	16	0	0	0	5	6	19	.167	.223	.167	390	12	-11	1	0	0	.954	3	2-33/1-1,O-1(0-1-0)	-0.6
Total	2	51	151	7	32	3	0	0	11	14	26	.212	.283	.232	515	50	-10	1	0	0	.957	2	/2-49,O-1(0-1-0),1-1	-0.5
■ **WILLIAM RUMLER**	Rumler, William George b: 3/27/1891, Milford, Neb. d: 5/26/66, Lincoln, Neb. BR/TR, 6′1″, 190 lbs. Deb: 5/4/14																							
1914	StL-A	34	46	2	8	1	0	0	6	3	12	.174	.240	.196	436	32	-4	2	2	-0	1.000	-3	C-10/O-6(0-0-6)	-0.8
1916	StL-A	27	37	6	12	3	0	0	10	3	7	.324	.375	.405	780	141	2	0			.971	0	/C-9	0.3
1917	StL-A	78	88	7	23	3	4	1	16	8	9	.261	.323	.420	743	132	3	2			.938	-0	/O-9(3-0-6)	0.3
Total	3	139	171	15	43	7	4	1	32	14	28	.251	.312	.357	669	107	1	4	2		.986	-3	/C-19,O-15(3-0-12)	-0.2
■ **PAUL RUNGE**	Runge, Paul William b: 5/21/58, Kingston, N.Y. BR/TR, 6′, 175 lbs. Deb: 9/25/81																							
1981	Atl-N	10	27	2	7	1	0	0	2	4	4	.259	.355	.296	651	84	-0	0	0	0	.911	-1	S-10	-0.1
1982	Atl-N	4	2	0	0	0	0	0	0	0	0	.000	.000	.000	0	-96	-1	0	0	0	.000	0	/H	-0.1
1983	Atl-N	5	8	0	2	0	0	0	1	1	4	.250	.333	.250	583	59	-0	0	0	0	1.000	-1	/2-2	-0.1
1984	Atl-N	28	90	5	24	3	1	0	3	10	14	.267	.340	.322	662	81	-2	5	3	0	.970	10	2-22/S-7,3-3	0.9
1985	Atl-N	50	87	15	19	3	0	1	5	18	18	.218	.352	.287	640	76	-2	0	1	-0	.929	4	3-28/S-5,2-2	0.1
1986	Atl-N	7	8	1	2	0	0	0	0	2	4	.250	.400	.250	650	79	-0	0	0	0	1.000	2	/2-5	0.2
1987	Atl-N	27	47	9	10	1	0	3	8	5	10	.213	.288	.426	714	82	-1	0	1	-0	.923	1	3-10/S-9,2-2	0.0
1988	Atl-N	52	76	11	16	5	0	0	7	14	21	.211	.333	.276	610	73	-2	0	0	0	1.000	-1	3-19/2-7,S-6	-0.4
Total	8	183	345	43	80	13	1	4	26	54	75	.232	.336	.310	646	77	-9	5	5	-1	.941	13	/3-60,2-40,S-37	0.5
■ **TOM RUNNELLS**	Runnells, Thomas William b: 4/17/55, Greeley, Colo. BB/TR, 6′, 175 lbs. Deb: 8/9/85 MC																							
1985	Cin-N	28	35	3	7	1	0	0	0	3	4	.200	.263	.229	492	37	-3	0	0	0	1.000	1	S-11/2-1	-0.2
1986	Cin-N	12	11	1	1	1	0	0	0	0	2	.091	.091	.182	273	-26	-2	0	0	0	1.000	1	/2-4,3-3	-0.1
Total	2	40	46	4	8	2	0	0	0	3	6	.174	.224	.217	442	23	-5	0	0	0	1.000	2	/S-11,2-5,3-3	-0.3
■ **PETE RUNNELS**	Runnels, James Edward (b: James Edward Runnells) b: 1/28/28, Lufkin, Tex. d: 5/20/91, Pasadena, Tex. BL/TR, 6′, 170 lbs. Deb: 7/1/51 MC Career OF: (1-LF 0-CF 0-RF)																							
1951	Was-A	78	273	31	76	12	2	0	25	31	24	.278	.354	.337	691	89	-3	0	3	-1	.949	-21	S-73	-2.1
1952	Was-A	152	555	70	158	18	3	1	64	72	55	.285	.368	.333	701	99	2	0	10	-4	.966	-15	*S-147/2-1	-0.7
1953	Was-A	137	486	64	125	15	5	2	50	64	36	.257	.347	.321	668	83	-9	3	4	-1	.958	-33	*S-121,2-11	-3.3
1954	Was-A	139	488	75	131	17	15	3	56	78	60	.268	.369	.383	752	112	10	2	3	-1	.953	-19	*S-107,2-27/O-1L	0.1
1955	Was-A	134	503	66	143	16	4	2	49	55	51	.284	.356	.344	700	94	-3	3	9	-2	.976	-3	*2-132/S-2	0.1
1956	Was-A	147	578	72	179	29	9	8	76	58	64	.310	.375	.433	807	113	11	5	5	-1	.995	0	1-81,2-69/S-3	1.0
1957	Was-A	134	473	53	109	18	4	2	35	55	51	.230	.313	.298	611	69	-20	2	3	-1	.995	2	1-72,3-32,2-23	-2.2
1958	Bos-A	147	568	103	183	32	5	8	59	87	49	.322	.418	.438	856	127	25	1	2	-0	.985	8	*2-106,1-42	3.9
1959	Bos-A★	147	560	95	176	33	6	6	57	95	48	.314	.415	.427	841	126	24	6	5	-0	.982	6	*2-101,1-44/S-9	3.5
1960	Bos-A★	143	528	80	169	29	2	2	35	71	51	**.320**	.403	.394	797	112	12	5	2	0	**.986**	9	*2-129,1-57/3-3	3.0
1961	Bos-A	143	360	49	114	20	3	3	38	46	32	.317	.399	.414	812	115	9	5	1	1	**.995**	1	*1-113,3-11/2-7,S-1	0.6
1962	Bos-A★	152	562	80	183	33	5	10	60	79	57	**.326**	.411	.456	867	129	26	3	4	-1	.993	-1	*1-151	1.4
1963	Hou-N	124	388	35	98	9	1	2	23	45	42	.253	.335	.296	631	89	-4	2	0	0	.993	-10	1-70,2-36/3-3	-1.7
1964	Hou-N	22	51	3	10	1	0	0	3	8	7	.196	.305	.216	521	53	-3	0	0	0	.986	-2	1-14	-0.6
Total	14	1799	6373	876	1854	282	64	49	630	844	627	.291	.376	.378	755	106	77	37	51	-10	.994	-78	1-644,2-642,S/3O	3.0
■ **JOHN RUSS**	Russ, John b: 4/1/1858, Cannelton, Ind. d: 1/18/12, Louisville, Ky. Deb: 7/4/1882																							
1882	Bal-a	1	3	0	1	0	0	0		0		.333	.333	.333	667	136	0				.000	-1	/O-1(0-1-0),P-1	0.0
■ **REB RUSSELL**	Russell, Ewell Albert b: 4/12/1889, Jackson, Miss. d: 9/30/73, Indianapolis, Ind BL/TL, 5′11″, 185 lbs. Deb: 4/18/13																							
1913	Chi-A	54	106	9	20	5	3	1	7	1	29	.189	.204	.321	524	54	-7	0			.953	-5	P-52	0.0
1914	Chi-A	46	64	6	17	1	1	0	7	1	14	.266	.277	.313	589	78	-2	0			.946	0	P-38	0.0
1915	Chi-A	45	86	11	21	2	3	0	7	4	14	.244	.293	.337	631	86	-2	1			.971	-2	P-41	0.0
1916	Chi-A	56	91	9	13	2	0	0	6	0	18	.143	.152	.165	317	-5	-12	1			.974	-2	P-56	0.0
1917	*Chi-A	39	68	4	19	3	3	0	9	2	10	.279	.300	.412	712	115	1	0			.984	-1	P-35/O-1(1-0-0)	0.0
1918	Chi-A	27	50	2	7	3	0	0	3	0	6	.140	.157	.200	357	8	-6	0			1.000	-2	P-19/O-1(0-0-1)	0.0
1919	Chi-A	1	0	0	0	0	0	0	0	0	0	—	—	—	—	—	0	0			.000	0	/P-1	0.0
1922	Pit-N	60	220	51	81	14	8	12	75	14	18	.368	.423	.668	1091	175	23	4	2	0	.968	-2	O-60(0-0-60)	1.6
1923	Pit-N	94	291	49	84	18	7	9	58	20	21	.289	.341	.491	832	115	5	3	1	0	.970	-2	O-76(4-0-72)	-0.3
Total	9	422	976	141	262	48	25	22	172	42	130	.268	.309	.436	745	104	0	9	3		.968	-15	P-242,O-138(5-0-133)	1.3

YEAR	TM/L	G	AB	R	H	2B	3B	HR	RBI	BB	SO	AVG	OBP	SLG	OPS	OPS+	BR+	SB	CS	SBR	FA	FR	G/POS	TPR
■ **RIP RUSSELL** Russell, Glen David b: 1/26/15, Los Angeles, Cal. d: 9/26/76, Los Alamitos, Cal BR/TR, 6′1″, 180 lbs. Deb: 5/5/39 Career OF: (3-LF 0-CF 0-RF)																								
1939	Chi-N	143	542	55	148	24	5	9	79	36	56	.273	.318	.386	704	87	-11	2			.988	-5	*1-143	-3.0
1940	Chi-N	68	215	15	53	7	2	5	33	8	23	.247	.277	.367	644	78	-7	1			.982	-6	1-51/3-3	-1.8
1941	Chi-N	6	17	1	5	1	0	0	1	1	5	.294	.333	.353	686	97	-0	0			.975	0	/1-5	-0.1
1942	Chi-N	102	302	32	73	9	0	8	41	17	21	.242	.282	.351	633	88	-6	0			.974	-12	1-35,2-24,3-10,/O-3L	-2.1
1946	*Bos-A	80	274	22	57	10	1	6	35	13	30	.208	.247	.318	564	54	-18	1	1	-0	.942	-1	3-70/2-3	-2.0
1947	Bos-A	26	52	8	8	1	0	1	3	8	7	.154	.267	.231	497	36	-4	0	0	0	.923	1	3-13	-0.3
Total	6	425	1402	133	344	52	8	29	192	83	142	.245	.289	.356	644	77	-46	4	1		.984	-22	1-234/3-96,2-27,O-3L	-9.3
■ **HARVEY RUSSELL** Russell, Harvey Holmes b: 1/10/1887, Marshall, Va. d: 1/8/80, Alexandria, Va. BL/TR, 5′9.5″, 163 lbs. Deb: 4/17/14																								
1914	Bal-F	81	168	18	39	3	2	0	13	18	17	.232	.310	.274	584	58	-12	2			.956	-17	C-47/S-1,O-1(1-1-0)	-2.7
1915	Bal-F	53	73	5	19	1	2	0	11	14	5	.260	.407	.329	735	105	1	1			.989	-4	C-21	-0.2
Total	2	134	241	23	58	4	4	0	24	32	22	.241	.342	.290	632	73	-11	3			.965	-22	/C-68,O-1(1-1-0),S-1	-2.9
■ **JIM RUSSELL** Russell, James William b: 10/1/18, Fayette City, Pa. d: 11/24/87, Pittsburgh, Pa. BB/TR, 6′1″, 181 lbs. Deb: 9/12/42 Career OF: (568-LF 360-CF 25-RF)																								
1942	Pit-N	5	14	2	1	0	0	0	0	1	4	.071	.133	.071	205	-38	-2	0			1.000	1	/O-3(0-3-0)	-0.2
1943	Pit-N	146	533	79	138	19	11	4	44	77	67	.259	.354	.358	712	102	4	12			.990	2	*O-134(133-2-2)/1-6	-0.3
1944	Pit-N	152	580	109	181	34	14	8	66	79	63	.312	.399	.460	859	136	29	6			.986	13	*O-149(139-6-4)	3.4
1945	Pit-N	146	510	88	145	24	8	12	77	71	40	.284	.377	.433	810	120	15	15			.973	3	*O-140(139-1-0)	1.0
1946	Pit-N	146	516	68	143	29	6	8	50	67	54	.277	.362	.403	765	114	10	11			.966	-2	*O-134(67-68-0)/1-5	0.1
1947	Pit-N	128	478	68	121	21	8	8	51	63	58	.253	.343	.381	723	89	-7	7			.980	11	*O-119(1-102-19)	0.1
1948	Bos-N	89	322	44	85	18	1	9	54	46	31	.264	.361	.410	771	110	5	4			.992	6	O-84(2-82-0)	0.9
1949	Bos-N	130	415	57	96	22	1	8	54	64	68	.231	.337	.347	684	88	-6	3			.975	-9	*O-120(30-93-0)	-1.9
1950	Bro-N	77	214	37	49	8	2	10	32	31	36	.229	.329	.425	755	95	-2	1			.993	4	O-55(53-3-0)	-0.2
1951	Bro-N	16	13	2	0	0	0	0	0	4	6	.000	.278	.000	278	-18	-2	0	0	0	1.000	-1	/O-4(4-0-0)	-0.3
Total	10	1035	3595	554	959	175	51	67	428	503	427	.267	.360	.400	760	108	44	59	0		.981	27	O-942L/1-11	2.6
■ **JOHN RUSSELL** Russell, John William b: 1/5/61, Oklahoma City, Okla. BR/TR, 6′, 200 lbs. Deb: 6/22/84 Career OF: (88-LF 0-CF 36-RF)																								
1984	Phi-N	39	99	11	28	8	1	2	11	12	33	.283	.360	.444	805	123	3	0	1	-0	1.000	-1	O-29(14-0-18)/C-2	0.0
1985	Phi-N	81	216	22	47	12	0	9	23	18	72	.218	.278	.398	676	85	-5	2	0	0	1.000	-6	O-49(49-0-0),1-18	-1.4
1986	Phi-N	93	315	35	76	21	2	13	60	25	103	.241	.303	.444	748	100	-1	0	1	-0	.976	-5	C-89	-0.3
1987	Phi-N	24	62	5	9	1	0	3	8	3	17	.145	.185	.306	491	26	-7	0	1	-0	.955	0	O-10(10-0-0)/C-7	-0.7
1988	Phi-N	22	49	5	12	1	0	2	4	3	15	.245	.302	.388	690	95	-0	0	0	0	.945	3	C-15	0.3
1989	Atl-N	74	159	14	29	2	0	2	9	8	53	.182	.226	.233	459	31	-14	0	0	0	.990	-7	C-45,O-14R/1-2,3P	-2.1
1990	Tex-A	68	128	16	35	4	0	2	8	11	41	.273	.331	.352	682	91	-1	1	0	0	.980	2	C-31,D-19/O-6L,13	0.1
1991	Tex-A	22	27	3	3	0	0	0	1	1	7	.111	.143	.111	254	-29	-5	0	0	0	1.000	-0	/O-8(6-0-2),C-5,D-5	-0.5
1992	Tex-A	7	10	1	1	0	0	0	2	1	4	.100	.250	.100	350	2	-1	0	0	0	1.000	1	/C-4,O-2(1-0-1),D-1	0.0
1993	Tex-A	18	22	1	5	1	0	1	3	2	10	.227	.292	.409	701	90	-0	0	0	0	1.000	-2	C-11/1-1,3-1,O-1L	-0.2
Total	10	448	1087	113	245	50	3	34	129	84	355	.225	.285	.371	655	79	-32	3	3	-0	.979	-16	C-209,O-119L/D13P	-4.8
■ **LLOYD RUSSELL** Russell, Lloyd Opal b: 4/10/13, Atoka, Okla. d: 5/24/68, Waco, Tex. BR/TR, 5′11″, 166 lbs. Deb: 4/26/38																								
1938	Cle-A	2	0	0	0	0	0	0	0	0	0	—	—	—	—	—	0	0	0	0	.000	0	R	0.0
■ **PAUL RUSSELL** Russell, Paul A. b: 1870, Reading, Pa. d: Pottstown, Pa. Deb: 7/29/1894																								
1894	StL-N	3	10	1	1	0	0	0	0	0	2	.100	.100	.100	200	-52	-2	0			1.000	0	/O-1(0-1-0),3-1,2-1	-0.2
■ **BILL RUSSELL** Russell, William Ellis b: 10/21/48, Pittsburg, Kan. BR/TR (BB 1971), 6′, 175 lbs. Deb: 4/7/69 MC Career OF: (62-LF 75-CF 179-RF)																								
1969	LA-N	98	212	35	48	6	2	5	15	22	45	.226	.302	.344	646	87	-4	4	1	1	.978	-7	O-86(7-24-62)	-1.4
1970	LA-N	81	278	30	72	11	9	0	28	16	28	.259	.306	.363	670	82	-8	9	1	2	.983	6	O-79(2-23-57)/S-1	-0.3
1971	LA-N	91	211	29	48	7	4	2	15	11	39	.227	.266	.327	593	71	-9	6	3	0	.964	-6	2-41,O-40(3-8-35)/S-6	-1.4
1972	LA-N	129	434	47	118	19	5	4	34	34	64	.272	.328	.366	694	99	-1	14	7	1	.949	15	*S-121/O-6(1-1-4)	3.1
1973	LA-N★	162	615	55	163	26	3	4	56	34	63	.265	.305	.337	641	81	-17	15	7	1	.963	9	*S-162	1.3
1974	*LA-N	160	553	61	149	18	6	5	65	53	53	.269	.338	.351	689	97	-2	14	5	1	.946	-19	*S-160/O-1(0-0-1)	-0.1
1975	LA-N	84	252	24	52	9	2	0	14	23	28	.206	.278	.258	536	52	-16	5	0	1	.967	-21	S-83	-2.9
1976	LA-N★	149	554	53	152	17	3	5	65	21	46	.274	.304	.343	647	85	-12	15	5	2	.963	-14	*S-149	-0.7
1977	*LA-N	153	634	84	176	28	6	4	51	24	43	.278	.306	.360	666	78	-20	16	7	1	.963	10	*S-153	0.7
1978	*LA-N	155	625	72	179	32	4	3	46	30	34	.286	.321	.365	686	92	-8	10	6	0	.962	12	*S-155	2.2
1979	LA-N	153	627	72	170	26	4	7	56	24	43	.271	.299	.359	658	80	-19	6	9	-2	.957	-26	*S-150	-3.2
1980	LA-N★	130	466	38	123	23	2	3	34	18	44	.264	.296	.341	637	79	-14	13	2	2	.968	-22	*S-129	-2.1
1981	*LA-N	82	262	20	61	9	2	0	22	19	20	.233	.287	.282	570	64	-12	2	1	0	.965	10	S-80	0.6
1982	LA-N	153	497	64	136	20	2	3	46	63	30	.274	.360	.340	700	99	2	10	2	2	.961	-4	*S-150	1.6
1983	*LA-N	131	451	47	111	13	1	1	30	33	31	.246	.303	.286	589	64	-21	13	9	-0	.964	1	*S-127	-0.8
1984	LA-N	89	262	25	70	12	1	0	19	25	24	.267	.331	.321	652	85	-5	4	4	-1	.965	-4	S-65,O-18(0-18-0)/2-5	-0.4
1985	LA-N	76	169	19	44	6	1	0	13	18	9	.260	.335	.308	643	83	-3	4	0	1	.919	-7	S-23,O-21L/2-8,3-5	-0.7
1986	LA-N	105	216	21	54	11	0	0	18	15	23	.250	.305	.301	606	73	-8	7	0	2	1.000	-7	O-48L,S-32/2-8,3-1	-1.2
Total	18	2181	7318	796	1926	293	57	46	627	483	667	.263	.312	.338	650	83	-176	167	69	13	.960	-74	*S-1746,O-299R/2-62,3	-5.7
■ **HANK RUSZKOWSKI** Ruszkowski, Henry Alexander b: 11/10/25, Cleveland, Ohio d: 5/31/2000, Cleveland, Ohio BR/TR, 6′, 190 lbs. Deb: 9/26/44																								
1944	Cle-A	3	8	1	3	0	0	0	1	0	1	.375	.375	.375	750	119	0	0	0	0	1.000	-0	/C-2	0.0
1945	Cle-A	14	49	2	10	0	0	0	5	4	9	.204	.264	.204	468	38	-4	0	0	0	.975	3	C-14	0.0
1947	Cle-A	23	27	5	7	2	0	3	4	2	6	.259	.310	.667	977	172	2	0	0	0	1.000	-2	C-16	0.1
Total	3	40	84	8	20	2	0	3	10	6	16	.238	.289	.369	658	91	-1	0	0	0	.981	1	/C-32	0.1
■ **BABE RUTH** Ruth, George Herman "The Bambino" or "The Sultan Of Swat" b: 2/6/1895, Baltimore, Md. d: 8/16/48, New York, N.Y. BL/TL (BB 1923 (part)), 6′2″, 215 lbs. Deb: 7/11/14 CH Career OF: (1057-LF 64-CF 1131-RF)																								
1914	Bos-A	5	10	1	2	1	0	0	2	0	4	.200	.200	.300	500	50	-1	0			1.000	-0	/P-4	0.0
1915	*Bos-A	42	92	16	29	10	1	4	21	9	23	.315	.376	.576	952	191	9	0			.976	1	P-32	0.0
1916	*Bos-A	67	136	18	37	5	3	3	15	10	23	.272	.322	.419	741	122	3	0			.973	0	P-44	0.0
1917	Bos-A	52	123	14	40	6	3	2	12	12	18	.325	.385	.472	857	163	9	0			.984	2	P-41	0.0
1918	*Bos-A	95	317	50	95	26	11	**11**	66	58	58	.300	.411	**.555**	966	195	36	6			.949	3	O-59L,P-20,1-13	2.7
1919	Bos-A	130	432	**103**	139	34	12	**29**	**114**	101	58	.322	**.456**	**.657**	**1114**	**224**	**74**	7			**.996**	5	*O-111L,P-17/1-5	**6.6**
1920	NY-A	142	458	**158**	172	36	9	**54**	**137**	**150**	80	.376	**.532**	**.847**	**1379**	**252**	**107**	14	14	-2	.936	-0	*O-141R/1-2,P-1	**9.1**
1921	*NY-A	152	540	**177**	204	44	16	**59**	**171**	**145**	81	.378	**.512**	**.846**	**1359**	**236**	**115**	17	13	-1	.966	4	*O-152L/P-2,1-2	**9.6**
1922	*NY-A	110	406	94	128	24	8	35	99	84	80	.315	.434	**.672**	**1106**	**181**	48	2	5	-1	.964	1	*O-110(71-0-40)/1-1	3.7
1923	*NY-A	152	522	**151**	205	45	13	**41**	**131**	**170**	93	.393	**.545**	**.764**	**1309**	**238**	**116**	17	21	-4	.973	16	*O-148(68-7-73)/1-4	**10.8**
1924	NY-A	153	529	**143**	200	39	7	**46**	121	**142**	81	**.378**	**.513**	**.739**	**1252**	**221**	**101**	9	13	-3	.962	7	*O-152(50-7-99)	**8.6**
1925	NY-A	98	359	61	104	12	2	25	66	59	68	.290	.393	.543	936	138	20	2	4	-1	.974	9	O-98(33-0-66)	1.8
1926	*NY-A	152	495	**139**	184	30	5	**47**	**146**	**144**	76	.372	**.516**	**.737**	**1253**	**228**	**100**	11	9	-1	.979	1	*O-149(82-0-68)/1-2	**8.4**
1927	*NY-A	151	540	**158**	192	29	8	**60**	164	**137**	89	.356	**.486**	**.772**	**1258**	**229**	106	7	6	-1	.963	5	*O-151(56-0-95)	**9.0**
1928	*NY-A	154	536	**163**	173	29	8	**54**	**142**	**137**	87	.323	.463	**.709**	**1172**	**211**	**90**	4	5	-1	.975	-3	*O-154(55-0-99)	**7.0**
1929	NY-A	135	499	121	172	26	6	**46**	154	72	60	.345	.430	**.697**	**1128**	**199**	**72**	5	3	0	.984	-9	*O-133(55-0-78)	**4.9**
1930	NY-A	145	518	150	186	28	9	**49**	153	**136**	61	.359	**.493**	**.732**	**1225**	**216**	**98**	10	10	-1	.965	-0	*O-144(53-0-91)/P-1	7.4
1931	NY-A	145	534	149	199	31	3	**46**	163	**128**	51	.373	**.495**	**.700**	**1195**	**223**	**102**	5	4	-0	.972	-12	*O-142(51-0-91)/1-1	**7.4**
1932	*NY-A	133	457	120	156	13	5	41	137	**130**	62	.341	**.489**	.661	1150	**206**	79	2	2	-0	.961	-7	*O-128(44-0-87)/1-1	5.8
1933	NY-A★	137	459	97	138	21	3	34	103	**114**	90	.301	.442	.582	1023	180	57	4	5	-1	.970	-7	*O-132R/P-1,1-1	3.9
1934	NY-A★	125	365	78	105	17	4	22	84	104	63	.288	.448	.537	985	164	40	1	3	-1	.962	-6	*O-111(34-0-77)	2.5
1935	Bos-N	28	72	13	13	0	0	6	12	20	24	.181	.359	.431	789	121	3	0			.952	-4	O-26(22-0-4)	-0.3
Total	22	2503	8399	2174	2873	506	136	714	2213	2062	1330	.342	.474	.690	1164	209	1386	123	117		.968	5	*O-2241R,P-163/1-32	108.9
■ **JIM RUTHERFORD** Rutherford, James Hollis b: 9/26/1886, Stillwater, Minn. d: 9/18/56, Cleveland, Ohio BL/TR, 6′1″, 180 lbs. Deb: 7/12/10																								
1910	Cle-A	1	2	0	1	0	0	0	0	0		.500	.500	.500	1000	210	0	0			1.000	-0	/O-1(0-1-0)	0.0

YEAR	TM/L	G	AB	R	H	2B	3B	HR	RBI	BB	SO	AVG	OBP	SLG	OPS	OPS+	BR+	SB	CS	SBR	FA	FR	G/POS	TPR
■ MICKEY RUTNER Rutner, Milton b: 3/18/20, Hempstead, N.Y. BR/TR, 5'11", 190 lbs. Deb: 9/11/47																								
1947	Phi-A	12	48	4	12	1	0	1	4	3	2	.250	.294	.333	627	73	-2	0	0	0	.885	-3	3-11	-0.5
■ MARK RYAL Ryal, Mark Dwayne b: 4/28/60, Henryetta, Okla. BL/TL, 6'1", 185 lbs. Deb: 9/7/82 Career OF: (27-LF 2-CF 25-RF)																								
1982	KC-A	6	13	0	1	0	0	0	0	1	3	.077	.143	.077	220	-38	-2	0	0	0	.900	-1	/O-5(4-1-0)	-0.3
1985	Chi-A	12	33	4	5	3	0	0	3	3	3	.152	.222	.242	465	26	-3	0	0	0	1.000	-1	O-12(12-1-0)	-0.5
1986	Cal-A	13	32	6	12	0	0	2	5	2	4	.375	.412	.563	974	164	3	1	0	0	.900	-1	/O-6(0-0-6),1-4,D-2	0.2
1987	Cal-A	58	100	7	20	6	0	5	18	3	15	.200	.223	.410	633	65	-5	0	0	0	.955	-6	O-21(6-0-15)/1-4,D-5	-1.1
1989	Phi-N	29	33	2	8	2	0	0	5	1	6	.242	.265	.303	568	62	-2	0	0	0	1.000	-1	/1-4,O-4(2-0-2)	-0.3
1990	Pit-N	9	12	0	1	0	0	0	0	0	3	.083	.083	.083	167	-56	-3	0	0	0	1.000	-1	/O-4(3-0-2)	-0.4
Total	6	127	223	19	47	11	0	7	31	10	34	.211	.245	.354	599	61	-13	1	0	0	.957	-11	/O-52L,1-12,D-7	-2.4
■ CONNIE RYAN Ryan, Cornelius Joseph b: 2/27/20, New Orleans, La. d: 1/3/96, Metairie, La. BR/TR, 5'11", 175 lbs. Deb: 4/14/42 MC Career OF: (0-LF 0-CF 1-RF)																								
1942	NY-N	11	27	4	5	0	0	0	2	4	3	.185	.290	.185	476	40	-2	1			.944	7	2-11	0.5
1943	Bos-N	132	457	52	97	10	2	1	24	58	56	.212	.301	.249	550	61	-22	7			.962	-20	*2-100,3-30	-3.8
1944	Bos-N★	88	332	56	98	18	5	4	25	36	40	.295	.364	.416	780	114	7	13			.974	13	2-80,3-14	2.4
1946	Bos-N	143	502	55	121	28	8	1	48	55	63	.241	.317	.335	652	84	-11	7			.968	-2	*2-120,3-24	-0.7
1947	Bos-N	150	544	60	144	33	5	5	69	71	60	.265	.351	.371	722	94	-4	5			.973	-7	*2-150/S-1	-0.2
1948	*Bos-N	51	122	14	26	3	0	0	10	21	16	.213	.333	.238	571	58	-6	0			.966	4	2-40/3-4	0.0
1949	Bos-N	85	208	28	52	13	1	6	20	21	30	.250	.319	.409	727	99	-1	1			.973	6	3-25,S-18,2-16,/1-3	0.7
1950	Bos-N	20	72	12	14	2	0	3	6	12	9	.194	.326	.347	673	82	-2	0			1.000	1	2-20	0.0
	Cin-N	106	367	45	95	18	5	3	43	52	46	.259	.352	.360	712	87	-5	4			.973	11	*2-103	1.0
	Yr	126	439	57	109	20	5	6	49	64	55	.248	.348	.358	705	87	-7	4			.978	12	*2-123	1.0
1951	Cin-N	136	473	75	112	17	4	16	53	79	72	.237	.350	.391	741	97	-0	11	6	0	.970	-3	*2-121/3-3,1-2,O-1R	0.4
1952	Phi-N	154	577	81	139	24	6	12	49	69	72	.241	.327	.366	693	93	-5	13	5	1	.972	-5	*2-154	-0.1
1953	Phi-N	90	247	47	73	14	6	5	26	30	35	.296	.372	.462	833	116	6	5	1	1	.958	-5	2-65/1-2	0.6
	Chi-A	17	54	6	12	1	0	0	6	9	12	.222	.333	.241	574	55	-3	2	0	0	.927	-1	3-16	-0.4
1954	Cin-N	1	0	0	0	0	0	0	0	1	0	—	1.000	—	1000	182	0	0	0	0	.000	0	H	0.0
Total	12	1184	3982	535	988	181	42	56	381	518	514	.248	.337	.357	694	90	-47	69	12		.970	-1	2-980,3-116/S-19,1O	0.4
■ CYCLONE RYAN Ryan, Daniel R. b: 1866, Cappagh White, Ireland d: 1/30/17, Medfield, Mass. TR, 6', 200 lbs. Deb: 8/8/1887																								
1887	NY-a	8	35	4	10	1	0	0	3	3		.286	.286	.250	536	52	-2	1			.938	-0	/1-8,P-2	-0.2
1891	Bos-N	1	1	0	0	0	0	0	0	0	0	.000	.000	.000	0	-89	-0	0			1.000	0	/P-1	0.0
Total	2	9	36	4	10	1	0	0	3	3	0	.278	.278	.242	520	48	-2	1			1.000	0	/1-8,P-3	-0.2
■ MIKE RYAN Ryan, J. b: St.Louis, Mo. Deb: 7/25/1895																								
1895	StL-N	2	2	0	0	0	0	0	0	0	0	.000	.000	.000	0	-99	-1	0			.000	-1	/3-2	-0.1
■ JIMMY RYAN Ryan, James Edward "Pony" b: 2/11/1863, Clinton, Mass. d: 10/26/23, Chicago, Ill. BR/TL, 5'9", 162 lbs. Deb: 10/8/1885 Career OF: (393-LF 956-CF 609-RF)																								
1885	Chi-N	3	13	2	6	1	0	0	2	1	1	.462	.500	.538	1038	207	1				.737	1	/S-2,O-1(0-1-0)	0.2
1886	*Chi-N	84	327	58	100	17	6	4	53	12	28	.306	.330	.431	762	114	3	10			.828	1	O-70L/S-6,3-6,2P	0.2
1887	Chi-N	126	561	117	198	23	10	11	74	53	19	.353	.360	.435	795	106	2	50			.857	-2	*O-122C/P-8,2-3	-0.5
1888	Chi-N	129	549	115	**182**	**33**	10	**16**	64	35	50	.332	.377	**.515**	892	170	41	60			.878	4	*O-128(0-127-1)/P-8	3.8
1889	Chi-N	135	576	140	177	31	14	17	72	70	62	.307	.388	.498	886	140	29	45			.926	6	*O-106(0-105-1),S-29	2.8
1890	Chi-P	118	486	99	165	32	5	6	89	60	36	.340	.416	.463	879	129	20	30			.919	2	*O-118(0-118-0)	1.5
1891	Chi-N	118	505	110	140	22	15	9	66	53	38	.277	.355	.434	789	129	18	27			.905	5	*O-117C/S-2,P-2	1.7
1892	Chi-N	128	505	105	148	21	11	10	65	61	41	.293	.375	.438	812	144	27	27			.921	5	*O-120(0-120-0)/S-9	2.2
1893	Chi-N	83	341	82	102	21	7	3	30	59	25	.299	.407	.428	835	124	14	8			.908	-1	O-73(1-73-1),S-10/P-1	0.7
1894	Chi-N	110	482	133	172	37	7	3	62	51	24	.357	.422	.481	903	111	9	11			.908	8	*O-110(0-5-106)	0.9
1895	Chi-N	108	438	83	139	22	8	6	49	48	22	.317	.392	.445	837	109	5	18			.937	2	*O-108(0-0-108)	0.1
1896	Chi-N	128	489	83	149	24	10	3	86	46	16	.305	.369	.413	782	102	1	29			.912	-0	*O-128(0-0-128)	-0.5
1897	Chi-N	136	520	103	156	33	17	5	85	50		.300	.369	.458	827	113	8	27			.945	7	*O-136(0-0-136)	0.7
1898	Chi-N	144	572	122	185	32	13	4	79	73		.323	.405	.446	850	144	34	29			.914	-7	*O-144(134-0-10)	1.4
1899	Chi-N	125	525	91	158	20	10	3	68	43		.301	.357	.394	752	109	6	9			.956	-1	*O-125(125-0-0)	-0.5
1900	Chi-N	105	415	66	115	25	4	5	59	29		.277	.329	.393	722	102	0	19			.913	-11	*O-105(49-9-57)	-1.7
1902	Was-A	120	484	92	155	32	6	6	44	43		.320	.384	.448	832	129	19	10			.949	3	*O-120(2-105-13)	1.5
1903	Was-A	114	437	42	109	25	4	7	46	17		.249	.290	.373	663	96	-3	9			.970	3	*O-114(0-114-0)	-0.6
Total	18	2014	8225	1643	2556	451	157	118	1093	804	362	.311	.374	.443	817	122	235	418			.918	25	*O-1945C/S-58,P23	13.9
■ JACK RYAN Ryan, John Bernard b: 11/12/1868, Haverhill, Mass. d: 8/21/52, Boston, Mass. BR/TR, 5'10.5", 165 lbs. Deb: 9/2/1889 C Career OF: (4-LF 4-CF 7-RF)																								
1889	Lou-a	21	79	8	14	1	0	0	2	3	17	.177	.207	.190	397	14	-9	2			.864	-6	C-15/O-4(0-3-1),3-2	-1.2
1890	*Lou-a	93	337	43	73	16	4	0	35	12		.217	.244	.288	531	58	-19	6			.932	5	C-89/O-3R,S-1,1-1	-0.6
1891	Lou-a	75	253	24	57	5	4	2	25	15	40	.225	.271	.300	572	64	-13	3			.930	-1	C-56,1-11/3-6,O2	-0.9
1894	Bos-N	53	201	39	54	12	7	1	29	13	16	.269	.316	.413	729	69	-12	3			.911	0	C-51/1-2	-0.5
1895	Bos-N	49	189	22	55	7	0	0	18	6	6	.291	.313	.328	641	61	-12	3			.951	1	C-43/2-5,O-1(0-0-1)	-0.5
1896	Bos-N	8	32	2	3	1	0	0	0	0	1	.094	.094	.125	219	-40	-7	0			.911	2	/C-8	-0.3
1898	Bro-N	87	301	39	57	11	4	0	24	15		.189	.233	.252	485	39	-24	5			.960	3	C-84/3-4,1-1	-1.3
1899	Bal-N	2	4	0	2	1	0	0	1	0		.500	.500	.750	1250	229	1	1			1.000	1	/C-2	0.2
1901	StL-N	83	300	27	59	6	5	0	31	7		.197	.218	.250	468	37	-24	5			.982	5	C-65/2-9,1-5,O-3R	-1.3
1902	StL-N	76	267	23	48	4	4	0	14	4		.180	.195	.225	420	31	-22	2			.966	-7	C-66/1-4,3-4,2-2,S	-2.4
1903	StL-N	67	227	18	54	5	1	1	10	10		.238	.273	.282	555	60	-12	2			.971	-9	C-47,1-18/S-2	-1.6
1912	Was-A	1	1	0	0	0	0	0	0	0		.000	.000	.000	0	-99	-0	0			1.000	0	/3-1	0.0
1913	Was-A	1	1	0	0	0	0	0	0	0	0	.000	.000	.000	0	-98	-0	0			1.000	0	/C-1	0.0
Total	13	616	2192	245	476	69	29	4	189	85	80	.217	.249	.281	529	50	-154	32			.947	-6	C-527/1-42,2-19,3OS	-10.4
■ BUDDY RYAN Ryan, John Budd b: 10/6/1885, Denver, Colo. d: 7/9/56, Sacramento, Cal. BL/TR, 5'9.5", 172 lbs. Deb: 4/11/12																								
1912	Cle-A	93	328	53	89	12	9	1	31	30		.271	.343	.372	715	101	0	12			.963	5	O-90(56-0-34)	0.1
1913	Cle-A	73	243	26	72	6	1	0	32	11	13	.296	.332	.329	661	91	-3	9			.986	-2	O-68(3-65-0)/1-1	-1.0
Total	2	166	571	79	161	18	10	1	63	41	13	.282	.339	.354	692	97	-3	21			.973	3	O-158(59-65-34)/1-1	-0.9
■ BLONDY RYAN Ryan, John Collins b: 1/4/06, Lynn, Mass d: 11/28/59, Swampscott, Mass. BR/TR, 6'1", 178 lbs. Deb: 7/13/30																								
1930	Chi-A	28	87	9	18	0	4	1	10	6	13	.207	.258	.333	591	50	-7	2	0	0	.875	-1	3-23/S-2,2-1	-0.6
1933	*NY-N	146	525	47	125	10	5	3	48	15	62	.238	.259	.293	553	58	-29	0			.950	17	*S-146	-0.1
1934	NY-N	110	385	35	93	19	0	2	41	19	68	.242	.277	.306	584	57	-23	3			.953	12	3-65,S-30,2-25	-0.6
1935	Phi-N	39	129	13	34	3	0	1	10	7	20	.264	.312	.310	622	61	-7	1			.912	2	S-35/2-1,3-1	-0.2
	NY-A	30	105	12	25	1	3	0	11	3	10	.238	.259	.305	564	48	-8	0	0	0	.908	-4	S-30	-1.0
1937	*NY-N	21	75	10	18	3	1	1	13	6	8	.240	.296	.347	643	73	-3	0			.941	1	S-19/2-1,3-1	-0.1
1938	NY-N	12	24	1	5	0	0	0	0	1	3	.208	.240	.208	448	24	-2	0			1.000	-1	/2-5,3-3,S-2	-0.3
Total	6	386	1330	127	318	36	13	8	133	57	184	.239	.271	.304	575	57	-79	6	0		.936	26	S-264/3-93,2-33	-2.9
■ JACK RYAN Ryan, John Francis b: 5/5/05, West Mineral, Kan. d: 9/2/67, Rochester, Minn. BR/TR, 6', 185 lbs. Deb: 6/18/29																								
1929	Bos-A	2	3	0	0	0	0	0	0	0	0	.000	.000	.000	0	-99	-1	0	0	0	1.000	-1	/O-2(1-0-1)	-0.2
■ JOHNNY RYAN Ryan, John Joseph b: 10/1853, Philadelphia, Pa. d: 3/22/02, Philadelphia, Pa. 5'7.5", 150 lbs. Deb: 8/19/1873 NA OF: (77-LF 1-CF 0-RF)																								
1873	Phi-n	2	8	1	2	0	0	0	1	0	0	.250	.250	.250	500	47	-1	0	0	0	.800	0	/1-1,O-1(0-1-0)	0.0
1874	Bal-n	47	181	29	35	8	1	0	19	5	13	.193	.215	.249	464	49	-10	3	0	1	.862	13	*O-47(47-0-0)/P-1	0.4
1875	NH-n	37	146	17	23	2	2	0	8	3	12	.158	.174	.199	373	34	-8	10	4	1	.796	-8	O-30L,P-10/C-4,S-1	-1.1
1876	Lou-N	64	247	32	61	5	1	1	18	6	23	.247	.271	.295	566	75	-8				.886	-7	*O-64(63-1-0)/P-1	-1.7
1877	Cin-N	6	26	2	4	0	1	0	2	1	5	.154	.185	.231	416	34	-2				.769	-1	/O-6(1-5-0)	-0.3
Total	3 n	86	335	47	60	10	3	0	28	8	25	.179	.198	.227	425	43	-18	13	4	1	.850	5	/O-78L,P-11,C-4,S1	-0.7
Total	2	70	273	34	65	5	2	1	20	7	28	.238	.263	.288	551	72	-10				.877	-9	/O-70(64-6-0),P-1	-2.0

YEAR	TM/L	G	AB	R	H	2B	3B	HR	RBI	BB	SO	AVG	OBP	SLG	OPS	OPS+	BR+	SB	CS	SBR	FA	FR	G/POS	TPR
■ JOHN RYAN	Ryan, John M. (Played 1 Game Under Real Name Of Daniel Sheehan) b: Washington, D.C. Deb: 6/11/1884																							
1884	Was-U	7	28	2	4	0	1	0		1		.143	.172	.214	387	17	-4				.667	-1	/O-7(2-3-2),3-1	-0.5
	Wil-U	2	6	0	1	0	0	0		1		.167	.286	.167	452	39	-1				.800	-0	/O-2(1-1-0)	-0.1
	Yr	9	34	2	5	0	1	0		2		.147	.194	.206	400	22	-4				.706	-1	/O-9(3-4-2),3-1	-0.6
■ MIKE RYAN	Ryan, Michael James b: 11/25/41, Haverhill, Mass. BR/TR, 6'2", 205 lbs. Deb: 10/3/64 C																							
1964	Bos-A	1	3	0	1	0	0	0	2	1	0	.333	.500	.333	833	131	0	0	0	0	1.000	-1	/C-1	0.0
1965	Bos-A	33	107	7	17	0	1	3	9	5	19	.159	.196	.262	458	27	-10	0	0	0	.981	0	C-33	-0.9
1966	Bos-A	116	369	27	79	15	3	2	32	29	68	.214	.271	.287	559	55	-21	1	0	0	.992	1	*C-114	-1.5
1967	*Bos-A	79	226	21	45	4	2	2	27	26	42	.199	.285	.261	546	58	-11	2	0	0	.988	1	C-79	-0.7
1968	Phi-N	96	296	12	53	6	1	1	15	15	59	.179	.219	.216	435	31	-25	0	3	-1	.991	-4	C-96	-2.9
1969	Phi-N	133	446	41	91	17	2	12	44	30	66	.204	.257	.332	589	66	-22	1	1	-0	.991	2	*C-132	-1.5
1970	Phi-N	46	134	14	24	8	0	2	11	16	24	.179	.267	.284	550	49	-10	0	0	0	.992	-12	C-46	-2.1
1971	Phi-N	43	134	9	22	5	1	3	6	10	32	.164	.222	.284	506	42	-10	0	0	0	1.000	12	C-43	0.3
1972	Phi-N	46	106	6	19	4	0	2	10	10	25	.179	.256	.274	530	49	-7	0	0	0	.992	6	C-46	0.0
1973	Phi-N	28	69	7	16	1	2	1	5	6	19	.232	.293	.348	641	75	-2	0	0	0	.992	1	C-27	-0.1
1974	Pit-N	15	30	2	3	0	0	0	0	4	16	.100	.206	.100	306	-13	-4	0	0	0	1.000	3	C-15	-0.1
Total	11	636	1920	146	370	60	12	28	161	152	370	.193	.253	.280	534	51	-123	4	4	-1	.991	10	C-632	-9.5
■ ROB RYAN	Ryan, Robert James b: 6/24/73, Havre, Mont. BL/TL, 5'11", 190 lbs. Deb: 8/20/99																							
1999	Ari-N	20	29	4	7	1	0	2	5	1	8	.241	.267	.483	749	84	-1	0	0	0	1.000	-1	/O-5(1-0-4)	-0.1
2000	Ari-N	27	27	4	8	1	1	0	2	4	7	.296	.406	.407	814	106	0	0	0	0	1.000	-1	/O-2(0-0-2),D-1	0.0
Total	2	47	56	8	15	2	1	2	7	5	15	.268	.339	.446	785	96	-0	0	0	0	1.000	-1	/O-7(1-0-6),D-1	-0.1
■ TOM RYDER	Ryder, Thomas BL, Deb: 7/22/1884																							
1884	StL-U	8	28	4	7	1	0	0		2		.250	.300	.286	586	76	-2				.650	-0	/O-8(5-3-0)	-0.2
■ GENE RYE	Rye, Eugene Rudolph "Half-Pint" (b: Eugene Rudolph Mercantelli) b: 11/15/06, Chicago, Ill. d: 1/21/80, Park Ridge, Ill. BL/TR, 5'6", 165 lbs. Deb: 4/22/31																							
1931	Bos-A	17	39	3	7	0	0	0	1	2	5	.179	.220	.179	399	6	-5	0	0	0	.944	-1	O-10(10-0-0)	-0.7
■ ALEX SABO	Sabo, Alexander "Giz" (b: Alexsander Szabo) b: 2/14/10, New Brunswick, N.J BR/TR, 6', 192 lbs. Deb: 8/1/36																							
1936	Was-A	4	8	1	3	0	0	0	1	0	2	.375	.375	.375	750	91	-0	0	0	0	.923	1	/C-4	0.1
1937	Was-A	1	0	0	0	0	0	0	0	0	0	—	—	—	—	—	0	0	0	0	1.000	-0	/C-1	0.0
Total	2	5	8	1	3	0	0	0	1	0	2	.375	.375	.375	750	91	-0	0	0	0	.929	1	/C-5	0.1
■ CHRIS SABO	Sabo, Christopher Andrew b: 1/19/62, Detroit, Mich. BR/TR, 6', 185 lbs. Deb: 4/4/88 Career OF: (9-LF 0-CF 13-RF)																							
1988	Cin-N★	137	538	74	146	40	2	11	44	29	52	.271	.316	.414	730	104	2	46	14	5	**.966**	19	*3-135/S-2	2.8
1989	Cin-N	82	304	40	79	21	1	6	29	25	33	.260	.318	.395	713	99	-1	14	9	-0	.943	-3	3-76	-0.4
1990	*Cin-N★	148	567	95	153	38	2	25	71	61	58	.270	.345	.476	821	118	14	25	10	2	**.966**	-6	*3-146	1.1
1991	Cin-N★	153	582	91	175	35	3	26	88	44	79	.301	.356	.505	861	134	25	19	6	2	.966	-15	*3-151	1.3
1992	Cin-N	96	344	42	84	19	3	12	43	30	54	.244	.307	.422	728	102	-0	4	5	-1	.961	-1	3-93	-0.2
1993	Cin-N	148	552	86	143	33	2	21	82	43	105	.259	.319	.440	760	101	-1	6	4	-0	.967	-15	*3-148	-1.5
1994	Bal-A	68	258	41	66	15	3	11	42	20	38	.256	.322	.465	787	95	-3	1	1	-0	.958	-11	3-37,O-22R,D-10	-1.4
1995	Chi-A	20	71	10	18	5	0	1	8	3	12	.254	.303	.366	669	76	-3	2	0	0	.909	-1	D-15/1-1,3-1	-0.3
	StL-N	5	13	0	2	1	0	0	3	1	2	.154	.214	.231	445	17	-2	1	0	0	.929	-1	/1-2,3-1	-0.3
1996	Cin-N	54	125	15	32	7	1	3	16	18	27	.256	.354	.400	754	98	-0	2	0	0	.961	6	3-43	0.6
Total	9	911	3354	494	898	214	17	116	426	274	460	.268	.329	.445	774	109	32	120	49	9	.963	-28	3-831/D-25,O-22R,1S	1.7
■ FRANK SACKA	Sacka, Frank b: 8/30/24, Romulus, Mich. d: 12/7/94, Dearborn, Mich. BR/TR, 6', 195 lbs. Deb: 4/29/51																							
1951	Was-A	7	16	1	4	0	0	0	3	0	5	.250	.250	.250	500	36	-1	0	0	0	.962	2	/C-6	0.0
1953	Was-A	7	18	2	5	0	0	0	3	3	1	.278	.381	.278	659	82	-0	0	0	0	1.000	2	/C-6	0.2
Total	2	14	34	3	9	0	0	0	6	3	6	.265	.324	.265	589	62	-2	0	0	0	.982	3	/C-12	0.2
■ MIKE SADEK	Sadek, Michael George b: 5/30/46, Minneapolis, Minn. BR/TR (BB 1979 (part)), 5'9", 165 lbs. Deb: 4/13/73																							
1973	SF-N	39	66	6	11	1	1	0	4	11	8	.167	.286	.212	498	38	-5	1	0	0	.981	7	C-35	0.3
1975	SF-N	42	106	14	25	5	2	0	9	14	14	.236	.325	.321	646	76	-3	1	0	0	.995	7	C-38	0.5
1976	SF-N	55	93	8	19	2	0	0	7	11	10	.204	.295	.226	521	48	-6	0	0	0	.985	8	C-51	0.3
1977	SF-N	61	126	12	29	7	0	1	15	12	5	.230	.297	.310	607	63	-6	2	1	0	.992	10	C-57	0.5
1978	SF-N	40	109	15	26	3	0	2	9	10	11	.239	.303	.321	624	77	-3	1	0	0	.975	2	C-37	0.0
1979	SF-N	63	126	14	30	5	0	1	11	15	24	.238	.324	.302	626	77	-4	1	0	0	.993	1	C-60/O-1(0-0-1)	-0.1
1980	SF-N	64	151	14	38	4	1	1	16	27	18	.252	.365	.311	676	93	-0	0	0	0	.974	4	C-59	0.6
1981	SF-N	19	36	5	6	3	0	0	3	8	7	.167	.318	.250	568	64	-1	0	0	0	.979	7	C-19	0.6
Total	8	383	813	88	184	30	4	5	74	108	97	.226	.319	.292	610	70	-30	6	1	1	.985	45	C-356/O-1(0-0-1)	2.7
■ DONNIE SADLER	Sadler, Donnie Lamont b: 6/17/75, Clifton, Tex. BR/TR, 5'6", 165 lbs. Deb: 4/1/98 Career OF: (4-LF 19-CF 2-RF)																							
1998	*Bos-A	58	124	21	28	4	4	3	15	6	28	.226	.278	.395	673	71	-6	4	0	1	.972	1	2-50/S-4,D-4	-0.2
1999	*Bos-A	49	107	18	30	5	1	0	4	5	20	.280	.313	.346	658	66	-5	2	1	0	.930	-1	S-14,2-10/3-9,OD	-0.5
2000	Bos-A	49	99	14	22	5	0	1	10	5	18	.222	.267	.303	570	42	-9	3	1	0	.958	4	S-19,O-17C,2-12,/3D	-0.3
Total	3	156	330	53	80	14	5	4	29	16	66	.242	.286	.352	637	60	-20	9	2	1	.970	3	/2-72,S-37,O-25C,3D	-1.0
■ ED SADOWSKI	Sadowski, Edward Roman b: 1/19/31, Pittsburgh, Pa. d: 11/6/93, Garden Grove, Cal. BR/TR, 5'11", 175 lbs. Deb: 4/20/60 F																							
1960	Bos-A	38	93	10	20	2	0	3	8	8	13	.215	.284	.333	618	64	-5	0	0	0	.995	6	C-36	0.2
1961	LA-A	69	164	16	38	13	0	4	12	11	33	.232	.280	.384	664	68	-8	2	3	-1	.987	8	C-56	0.2
1962	LA-A	27	55	4	11	4	0	1	3	2	14	.200	.228	.327	555	49	-4	1	0	0	.968	3	C-18	0.0
1963	LA-A	80	174	24	30	1	1	4	15	17	33	.172	.246	.259	505	44	-13	2	1	0	.997	20	C-68	1.0
1966	Atl-N	3	9	1	1	0	0	0	1	1	1	.111	.200	.111	311	-10	-1	0	0	0	1.000	1	/C-3	-0.1
Total	5	217	495	55	100	20	1	12	39	39	94	.202	.262	.319	581	56	-31	5	4	-0	.991	37	C-181	1.3
■ BOB SADOWSKI	Sadowski, Robert Frank "Sid" b: 1/15/37, St.Louis, Mo. BL/TR, 6', 175 lbs. Deb: 9/16/60 Career OF: (1-LF 0-CF 24-RF)																							
1960	StL-N	1	1	0	0	0	0	0	0	1	0	.000	.500	.000	500	47	0	0	0	0	.000	-1	/2-1	-0.1
1961	Phi-N	16	54	4	7	0	0	0	0	4	7	.130	.203	.130	333	-9	-8	1	0	0	.971	-1	3-14	-1.0
1962	Chi-A	79	130	22	30	3	3	6	24	13	22	.231	.301	.438	739	97	-1	0	0	0	.955	5	3-16,2-12	0.5
1963	LA-A	88	144	12	36	6	0	1	22	15	34	.250	.321	.313	633	83	-3	2	1	0	1.000	-3	O-25(1-0-24)/3-6,2-4	-0.8
Total	4	184	329	38	73	9	3	7	46	33	63	.222	.295	.331	626	73	-13	3	1	0	.953	-0	/3-36,O-25R,2-17	-1.4
■ OLMEDO SAENZ	Saenz, Olmedo (Sanchez) b: 10/8/70, Chitre Herrera, Pan. BR/TR, 6'2", 185 lbs. Deb: 5/28/94																							
1994	Chi-A	5	14	2	2	0	1	0	0	0	5	.143	.143	.286	429	7	-2	0	0	0	1.000	-0	/3-5	-0.2
1999	Oak-A	97	255	41	70	18	0	11	41	22	47	.275	.366	.475	841	117	7	1	1	-0	.938	0	3-56,1-28/D-8	0.5
2000	*Oak-A	76	214	40	67	12	2	9	33	25	40	.313	.402	.514	916	133	11	1	0	0	.923	-3	D-27,3-18,1-17	0.5
Total	3	178	483	83	139	30	3	20	74	47	92	.288	.377	.487	863	121	16	2	1	0	.938	-4	/3-79,1-45,D-35	0.8
■ TOM SAFFELL	Saffell, Thomas Judson b: 7/26/21, Etowah, Tenn. BL/TR, 5'11", 170 lbs. Deb: 7/2/49																							
1949	Pit-N	73	205	36	66	7	1	2	25	21	27	.322	.385	.395	780	107	3	5			.992	-3	O-53(0-52-2)	-0.2
1950	Pit-N	67	182	18	37	7	0	2	6	14	34	.203	.264	.275	539	41	-16	1			.993	6	O-43(0-42-2)	-1.1
1951	Pit-N	49	65	11	13	0	0	1	5	5	18	.200	.257	.246	503	35	-6	1	1	-0	.929	-4	O-17(1-13-3)	-1.0
1955	Pit-N	73	113	21	19	1	0	1	3	15	22	.168	.266	.204	469	27	-12	1	0	0	.964	-7	O-47(6-37-4)	-2.0
	KC-A	9	37	5	8	0	0	0	1	4	7	.216	.293	.216	509	38	-3	1	0	0	.962	-0	/O-9(0-9-0)	-0.3
Total	4	271	602	91	143	15	1	6	40	59	108	.238	.307	.296	602	60	-34	9	1		.980	-8	O-169(7-153-11)	-4.6
■ HARRY SAGE	Sage, Harry "Doc" b: 3/16/1864, Rock Island, Ill. d: 5/27/47, Rock Island, Ill. BR/TR, 5'10", 185 lbs. Deb: 4/17/1890																							
1890	Tol-a	81	275	40	41	8	4	2	25	29		.149	.235	.229	464	36	-23	10			.948	8	C-80/O-1(0-1-0)	-0.7

YEAR	TM/L	G	AB	R	H	2B	3B	HR	RBI	BB	SO	AVG	OBP	SLG	OPS	OPS+	BR+	SB	CS	SBR	FA	FR	G/POS	TPR
■ PONY SAGER	Sager, Samuel B. b: 1847, Marshalltown, Iowa 140 lbs. Deb: 5/6/1871																							
1871	Rok-n	8	39	9	11	0	0	0	5	2	2	.282	.317	.282	599	78	-1	5	1	1	.643	-4	/S-4,O-4(4-0-0)	-0.2
■ MARC SAGMOEN	Sagmoen, Marc Richard b: 4/16/71, Seattle, Wash. BL/TL, 5'11", 185 lbs. Deb: 4/15/97																							
1997	Tex-A	21	43	2	6	2	0	1	4	2	13	.140	.178	.256	434	11	-6	0	0	0	1.000	-3	O-17(2-0-16)/1-1,D-1	-0.9
■ VIC SAIER	Saier, Victor Sylvester b: 5/4/1891, Lansing, Mich. d: 5/14/67, E.Lansing, Mich. BL/TR, 5'11", 185 lbs. Deb: 5/3/11																							
1911	Chi-N	86	259	42	67	15	1	1	37	25	37	.259	.340	.336	676	89	-3	11			.980	-4	1-73	-0.9
1912	Chi-N	122	451	74	130	25	14	2	61	34	65	.288	.340	.419	759	107	3	11			.992	-5	*1-120	-0.5
1913	Chi-N	149	519	94	150	15	**21**	14	92	62	62	.289	.370	.480	850	141	27	26			.983	-5	*1-149	1.9
1914	Chi-N	153	537	87	129	24	8	18	72	94	61	.240	.357	.415	773	130	21	19			.986	-11	*1-153	0.7
1915	Chi-N	144	497	74	131	35	11	11	64	64	62	.264	.350	.445	795	140	23	29	9	**3**	.985	-5	*1-139	2.0
1916	Chi-N	147	498	60	126	25	3	7	50	79	68	.253	.356	.357	714	108	8	20	17	-2	.984	-0	*1-147	0.2
1917	Chi-N	6	21	5	5	1	0	0	2	2	1	.238	.304	.286	590	75	-1	0			1.000	2	/1-6	0.1
1919	Pit-N	58	166	19	37	3	3	2	17	18	13	.223	.306	.313	620	83	-3	5			.985	-5	1-51	-1.0
Total	8	865	2948	455	775	143	61	55	395	378	369	.263	.351	.409	760	119	76	121	26		.986	-33	1-838	2.5
■ EBBA ST.CLAIRE	St.Claire, Edward Joseph b: 8/5/21, Whitehall, N.Y. d: 8/22/82, Whitehall, N.Y. BB/TR, 6'1", 219 lbs. Deb: 4/17/51 F																							
1951	Bos-N	72	220	22	62	17	2	1	25	12	24	.282	.322	.391	713	98	-1	2	0	0	.977	3	C-62	0.5
1952	Bos-N	39	108	5	23	2	0	2	4	8	12	.213	.267	.287	554	56	-7	0	1	-0	.972	4	C-34	-0.1
1953	Mil-N	33	80	7	16	3	0	2	5	3	9	.200	.229	.313	541	42	-7	0	0	0	.992	3	C-27	-0.3
1954	NY-N	20	42	5	11	1	0	2	6	12	7	.262	.436	.429	865	126	2	0	0	0	.975	2	C-16	0.5
Total	4	164	450	39	112	23	2	7	40	35	52	.249	.306	.356	662	81	-13	2	1	0	.978	12	C-139	0.6
■ LENN SAKATA	Sakata, Lenn Haruki b: 6/8/54, Honolulu, Hawaii BR/TR, 5'9", 160 lbs. Deb: 7/21/77 Career OF: (1-LF 0-CF 0-RF)																							
1977	Mil-A	53	154	13	25	2	0	2	12	9	22	.162	.209	.214	423	16	-18	1	3	-1	.985	17	2-53	0.1
1978	Mil-A	30	78	8	15	4	0	0	3	8	11	.192	.267	.244	511	44	-6	1	0	0	.975	0	2-29	-0.4
1979	Mil-A	4	14	1	7	2	0	0	1	0	1	.500	.500	.643	1143	206	2	0	0	0	1.000	2	/2-4	0.4
1980	Bal-A	43	83	12	16	3	2	1	9	6	10	.193	.247	.313	560	53	-6	2	1	0	.984	6	2-34/S-4,D-1	0.2
1981	Bal-A	61	150	19	34	4	0	5	15	11	18	.227	.284	.353	637	83	-4	4	0	1	.963	2	S-42,2-20	0.3
1982	Bal-A	136	343	40	89	18	1	6	31	30	39	.259	.326	.370	697	91	-4	7	4	0	.977	-6	2-83,S-56	-0.1
1983	*Bal-A	66	134	23	34	7	0	3	12	16	17	.254	.338	.373	711	97	-0	8	4	0	.990	4	2-60/C-1,D-1	0.6
1984	Bal-A	81	157	23	30	1	0	3	11	6	15	.191	.221	.255	476	32	-15	4	1	1	.988	5	2-76/O-1(1-0-0)	-0.6
1985	Bal-A	55	97	15	22	3	0	3	6	6	15	.227	.279	.351	629	73	-4	3	2	-0	.960	-1	2-50/D-1	-0.3
1986	Oak-A	17	34	4	12	2	0	0	5	3	6	.353	.405	.412	817	133	2	0	1	-0	.984	5	2-16/D-1	0.6
1987	NY-A	19	45	5	12	0	1	2	4	2	4	.267	.313	.444	757	99	-0	0	1	-0	.929	1	3-12/2-6	0.0
Total	11	565	1289	163	296	46	4	25	109	97	158	.230	.288	.330	617	71	-52	30	17	1	.982	36	2-431,S-102/3-12,DOC	0.8
■ MARK SALAS	Salas, Mark Bruce b: 3/8/61, Montebello, Cal. BL/TR, 6', 205 lbs. Deb: 6/19/84																							
1984	StL-N	14	20	1	2	1	0	0	1	0	3	.100	.100	.150	250	-31	-3	0	0	0	1.000	-1	/C-4,O-3(2-0-1)	-0.5
1985	Min-A	120	360	51	108	20	5	9	41	18	37	.300	.335	.458	793	108	4	0	1	-0	.991	2	*C-115/D-3	1.0
1986	Min-A	91	258	28	60	7	4	8	33	18	32	.233	.285	.384	669	78	-8	3	1	0	.980	-6	C-69/D-8	-1.1
1987	Min-A	22	45	8	17	2	0	3	9	5	6	.378	.440	.622	1062	171	5	0	1	-0	.989	1	C-14	0.5
	NY-A	50	115	13	23	4	0	3	12	10	17	.200	.281	.313	594	58	-7	0	0	0	1.000	-3	C-41/O-1(1-0-0),D-4	-0.8
	Yr	72	160	21	40	6	0	6	21	15	23	.250	.326	.400	726	91	-2	0	1	-0	.996	-2	C-55/D-4,O-1(1-0-0)	-0.3
1988	Chi-A	75	196	17	49	7	0	3	9	12	17	.250	.303	.332	635	78	-6	0	0	0	.979	0	C-69/D-1	-0.2
1989	Cle-A	30	77	4	17	4	1	2	7	5	13	.221	.277	.377	654	81	-2	0	0	0	1.000	-0	D-20/C-5	-0.3
1990	Det-A	74	164	18	38	3	0	9	24	21	28	.232	.323	.415	737	104	1	0	0	0	.988	-4	C-57/3-1,D-3	-0.1
1991	Det-A	33	57	2	5	1	0	1	7	0	10	.088	.119	.158	277	-24	-10	0	0	0	1.000	0	C-11/1-5,D-8	-1.0
Total	8	509	1292	142	319	49	10	38	143	89	163	.247	.302	.389	690	86	-27	3	3	-0	.987	-11	C-385/D-47,1-5,O3	-2.5
■ ANGEL SALAZAR	Salazar, Argenis Antonio (Yepez) b: 11/4/61, Anaco, Venez. BR/TR, 6', 173 lbs. Deb: 8/10/83																							
1983	Mon-N	36	37	5	8	1	1	0	1	1	8	.216	.237	.297	534	47	-3	0	0	0	.966	2	S-34	0.1
1984	Mon-N	80	174	12	27	4	2	0	12	4	38	.155	.179	.201	380	7	-22	1	1	-0	.960	-3	S-80	-2.0
1986	KC-A	117	298	24	73	20	2	0	24	7	47	.245	.267	.326	593	59	-17	1	1	-0	.978	-5	*S-115/2-1	-1.2
1987	KC-A	116	317	24	65	7	0	2	21	6	46	.205	.220	.246	466	23	-35	4	4	-1	.981	22	*S-116	-0.3
1988	Chi-N	34	60	4	15	1	1	0	1	1	11	.250	.262	.300	562	58	-3	0	0	0	.966	7	S-29/2-2,3-1	0.5
Total	5	383	886	69	188	33	6	2	59	19	150	.212	.231	.270	501	36	-80	6	6	-1	.974	23	S-374/2-3,3-1	-2.9
■ LUIS SALAZAR	Salazar, Luis Ernesto (Garcia) b: 5/19/56, Barcelona, Venez. BR/TR, 5'9", 180 lbs. Deb: 8/15/80 Career OF: (161-LF 114-CF 36-RF)																							
1980	SD-N	44	169	28	57	4	7	1	25	9	25	.337	.374	.462	836	140	9	11	2	2	.944	-2	3-42/O-4(0-3-1)	0.8
1981	SD-N	109	400	37	121	19	6	3	38	16	72	.303	.331	.403	733	116	6	11	8	-0	.955	-1	3-94,O-23(1-10-14)	0.3
1982	SD-N	145	524	55	127	15	5	8	62	23	80	.242	.277	.336	613	75	-19	32	9	4	.938	16	*3-129,S-18/O-1C	0.0
1983	SD-N	134	481	52	124	16	2	14	45	17	80	.258	.286	.387	673	88	-10	24	9	2	.949	10	*3-118,S-19	0.2
1984	*SD-N	93	228	20	55	7	2	3	17	6	38	.241	.261	.329	590	65	-11	11	7	-0	.970	5	3-58,O-24(4-19-2)/S-4	-0.8
1985	Chi-A	122	327	39	80	18	2	10	45	12	60	.245	.271	.404	675	79	-10	14	4	2	.968	-19	O-84C,3-39/1-6,D-8	-3.0
1986	Chi-A	4	7	1	1	0	0	0	0	1	3	.143	.250	.143	393	10	-1	0	0	0	.000	0	/D-2	-0.1
1987	SD-N	84	189	13	48	5	0	3	17	14	30	.254	.305	.328	633	70	-8	3	3	-0	.957	-9	3-38,S-22,O-10C,/P1	-1.6
1988	Det-A	130	452	61	122	14	1	12	62	21	70	.270	.307	.385	692	96	-3	6	0	1	.992	-10	O-68L,S-37,3-31,/21	-1.1
1989	SD-N	95	246	27	66	7	2	8	22	11	44	.268	.302	.411	713	102	-0	1	3	-1	.968	7	3-72,O-14R/S-9,1-2	0.6
	*Chi-N	26	80	7	26	5	0	1	12	4	13	.325	.357	.425	782	114	1	0	1	-0	.921	-6	3-25/O-2(2-0-0)	-0.5
	Yr	121	326	34	92	12	2	9	34	15	57	.282	.316	.414	730	105	1	1	4	-1	.959	1	3-97,O-16R/S-9,1-2	0.1
1990	Chi-N	115	410	44	104	13	3	12	47	19	59	.254	.293	.388	681	80	-12	3	1	0	.950	-20	3-91,O-28(28-0-0)	-3.3
1991	Chi-N	103	333	34	86	14	1	14	38	15	45	.258	.292	.432	725	97	-3	0	3	-1	.956	-7	3-86/1-7,O-1(1-0-0)	-1.1
1992	Chi-N	98	255	20	53	7	2	5	25	11	34	.208	.241	.310	550	53	-16	1	1	-0	.935	3	3-40,O-34L,S-12,/1	-1.5
Total	13	1302	4101	438	1070	144	33	94	455	179	653	.261	.294	.381	675	88	-78	117	51	8	.950	-33	3-863,O-293L,S/1D2P	-11.1
■ ED SALES	Sales, Edward A. b: 1861, Harrisburg, Pa. d: 8/10/12, New Haven, Conn. BL/TR, Deb: 7/15/1890																							
1890	Pit-N	51	189	19	43	7	3	1	23	16	15	.228	.298	.312	610	88	-2	3			.871	-14	S-51	-1.3
■ BILL SALKELD	Salkeld, William Franklin b: 3/8/17, Pocatello, Idaho d: 4/22/67, Los Angeles, Cal. BL/TR, 5'10", 190 lbs. Deb: 4/18/45 F																							
1945	Pit-N	95	267	45	83	16	1	15	52	50	16	.311	.420	.547	966	161	23	2			.973	-9	C-86	1.9
1946	Pit-N	69	160	18	47	8	0	3	19	39	16	.294	.432	.400	832	133	9	2			.972	-1	C-51	1.2
1947	Pit-N	47	61	5	13	2	0	0	8	6	8	.213	.284	.246	529	41	-5	0			.971	-3	C-15	-0.7
1948	*Bos-N	78	198	26	48	8	1	8	28	42	37	.242	.378	.414	792	116	6	1			.990	5	C-59	1.4
1949	Bos-N	66	161	17	41	5	0	5	25	44	24	.255	.417	.379	796	121	8	1			.980	-4	C-63	0.7
1950	Chi-A	1	3	0	0	0	0	0	0	1	0	.000	.250	.000	250	-33	-1	0	0	0	1.000	-0	/C-1	-0.1
Total	6	356	850	111	232	39	2	31	132	182	101	.273	.402	.433	835	129	40	6	0		.979	-11	C-275	4.4
■ CHICO SALMON	Salmon, Ruthford Eduardo b: 12/3/40, Colon, Panama d: 9/17/2000, Docas Del Toro, Panama BR/TR, 5'10", 170 lbs. Deb: 6/28/64 Career OF: (56-LF 5-CF 64-RF)																							
1964	Cle-A	86	283	43	87	17	2	4	25	13	37	.307	.342	.424	766	113	4	10	6	0	1.000	-8	O-53R,2-32,1-13	-0.5
1965	Cle-A	79	120	20	29	8	0	3	12	5	19	.242	.283	.383	667	87	-2	7	4	0	.985	-6	1-28,O-17L/2-5,3-5	-1.0
1966	Cle-A	126	422	46	108	13	2	7	40	21	41	.256	.291	.346	637	82	-10	10	1	2	.958	-18	S-61,2-28,1-24,O/3	-2.2
1967	Cle-A	90	203	19	46	13	1	2	19	17	29	.227	.290	.330	620	82	-5	10	4	1	1.000	1	O-28L,1-24,2-24,S/3	-0.2
1968	Cle-A	103	276	24	59	8	1	3	12	12	30	.214	.254	.283	537	63	-13	7	7	-1	.971	-15	2-45,3-18,S-15,O1	-2.9
1969	*Bal-A	52	91	18	27	5	0	3	12	10	22	.297	.379	.451	829	130	4	0	0	0	1.000	-5	1-17/2-9,S-9,3-3,O	-0.1
1970	*Bal-A	63	172	19	43	4	0	7	22	8	30	.250	.287	.395	683	85	-4	2	2	-0	.946	-20	S-33,2-12,3-11,/1-2	-2.2
1971	Bal-A	42	84	11	15	1	0	2	7	3	21	.179	.207	.262	469	32	-8	0	0	0	1.000	-3	/1-9,2-9,3-6,S-5	-1.1
1972	Bal-A	17	16	2	1	1	0	0	0	0	4	.063	.063	.125	188	-44	-3	0	0	0	1.000	0	/1-2,3-1	-0.3
Total	9	658	1667	202	415	70	6	31	149	89	233	.249	.291	.354	645	84	-36	46	24	2	.959	-75	2-164,S-137,1O/3	-10.5

■ TIM SALMON
Salmon, Timothy James b: 8/24/68, Long Beach, Cal. BR/TR, 6'3", 220 lbs. Deb: 8/21/92

YEAR	TM/L	G	AB	R	H	2B	3B	HR	RBI	BB	SO	AVG	OBP	SLG	OPS	OPS+	BR+	SB	CS	SBR	FA	FR	G/POS	TPR
1992	Cal-A	23	79	8	14	1	0	2	6	11	23	.177	.286	.266	552	55	-5	1	1	-0	.953	-0	O-21(0-0-21)	-0.6
1993	Cal-A	142	515	93	146	35	1	31	95	82	135	.283	.387	.536	923	141	30	5	6	-1	.980	15	*O-140(0-1-140)/D-1	3.5
1994	Cal-A	100	373	67	107	18	2	23	70	54	102	.287	.384	.531	915	131	18	1	3	-1	.966	8	O-99(0-0-99)	1.8
1995	Cal-A	143	537	111	177	34	3	34	105	91	111	.330	.432	.594	1026	165	54	5	5	-1	.988	16	*O-142(0-0-142)/D-1	5.6
1996	Cal-A	156	581	90	166	27	4	30	98	93	125	.286	.388	.501	889	122	21	4	2	0	.975	8	*O-153(0-0-153)/D-3	1.9
1997	Ana-A	157	582	95	172	28	1	33	129	95	142	.296	.401	.517	918	138	34	9	12	-2	.971	19	*O-153(0-0-153)/D-4	4.0
1998	Ana-A	136	463	84	139	28	1	26	88	90	100	.300	.417	.533	951	144	33	0	1	-0	.959	2	*D-111,O-19(0-0-19)	2.5
1999	Ana-A	98	353	60	94	24	2	17	69	63	82	.266	.377	.490	867	120	11	4	1	1	.981	8	O-89(0-0-89)/D-9	1.4
2000	Ana-A	158	568	108	165	36	2	34	97	104	139	.290	.406	.540	946	136	33	0	2	-1	.979	12	*O-124(0-0-124),D-33	3.3
Total	9	1113	4051	716	1180	231	16	230	757	683	959	.291	.398	.527	925	136	230	29	33	-5	.977	86	O-940(0-1-940),D-162	23.4

■ JACK SALTZGAVER
Saltzgaver, Otto Hamlin b: 1/23/03, Croton, Iowa d: 2/1/78, Keokuk, Iowa BL/TR, 5'11", 165 lbs. Deb: 4/12/32

YEAR	TM/L	G	AB	R	H	2B	3B	HR	RBI	BB	SO	AVG	OBP	SLG	OPS	OPS+	BR+	SB	CS	SBR	FA	FR	G/POS	TPR
1932	NY-A	20	47	10	6	2	1	0	5	10	10	.128	.281	.213	493	31	-5	1	1	-0	.958	-3	2-16	-0.7
1934	NY-A	94	350	64	95	8	1	6	36	48	28	.271	.359	.351	711	90	-4	8	1	1	.953	-16	3-84/1-4	-1.5
1935	NY-A	61	149	17	39	6	0	3	18	23	12	.262	.368	.362	730	95	-0	0	2	-1	.937	-13	2-25,3-18/1-6	-1.2
1936	NY-A	34	90	14	19	5	0	1	13	13	18	.211	.311	.300	611	53	-7	0	0	0	.972	-5	3-16/2-6,1-4	-0.9
1937	NY-A	17	11	6	2	0	0	0	0	3	4	.182	.357	.182	539	40	-1	0	0	0	1.000	0	/1-4	-0.1
1945	Pit-N	52	117	20	38	5	3	0	10	8	8	.325	.368	.419	787	114	2	0			.963	-4	2-31/3-1	0.0
Total	6	278	764	131	199	26	5	10	82	105	80	.260	.351	.347	698	85	-15	9	4		.957	-40	3-119/2-78,1-18	-4.4

■ ED SAMCOFF
Samcoff, Edward William b: 9/1/24, Sacramento, Cal. BR/TR, 5'10", 165 lbs. Deb: 4/21/51

YEAR	TM/L	G	AB	R	H	2B	3B	HR	RBI	BB	SO	AVG	OBP	SLG	OPS	OPS+	BR+	SB	CS	SBR	FA	FR	G/POS	TPR
1951	Phi-A	4	11	0	0	0	0	0	0	1	2	.000	.083	.000	83	-75	-3	0	0	0	1.000	-2	/2-3	-0.4

■ RON SAMFORD
Samford, Ronald Edward b: 2/28/30, Dallas, Tex. BR/TR, 5'11", 156 lbs. Deb: 4/15/54

YEAR	TM/L	G	AB	R	H	2B	3B	HR	RBI	BB	SO	AVG	OBP	SLG	OPS	OPS+	BR+	SB	CS	SBR	FA	FR	G/POS	TPR
1954	NY-N	12	5	2	0	0	0	0	0	0	1	.000	.000	.000	0	-99	-1	0	1	-0	1.000	1	/2-3	0.0
1955	Det-A	1	1	0	0	0	0	0	0	0	1	.000	.000	.000	0	-99	-0	0	0	0	1.000	0	/S-1	0.0
1957	Det-A	54	91	6	20	1	2	0	5	6	15	.220	.276	.275	550	49	-6	1	0	0	.964	13	S-35,2-11/3-4	0.9
1959	Was-A	91	237	23	53	13	0	5	22	11	29	.224	.264	.342	606	65	-12	1	0	0	.947	0	S-64,2-23	-0.6
Total	4	158	334	31	73	14	2	5	27	17	46	.219	.263	.317	580	58	-20	2	1	0	.952	15	S-100/2-37,3-4	0.3

■ BILL SAMPLE
Sample, William Amos b: 4/2/55, Roanoke, Va. BR/TR, 5'9", 175 lbs. Deb: 9/2/78 Career OF: (532-LF 99-CF 97-RF)

YEAR	TM/L	G	AB	R	H	2B	3B	HR	RBI	BB	SO	AVG	OBP	SLG	OPS	OPS+	BR+	SB	CS	SBR	FA	FR	G/POS	TPR
1978	Tex-A	8	15	2	7	2	0	0	3	0	3	.467	.467	.600	1067	197	2	0	0	0	.000	-1	/O-2(2-0-0),D-3	0.1
1979	Tex-A	128	325	60	95	21	2	5	35	37	28	.292	.368	.415	784	112	6	8	6	-0	1.000	-4	*O-103(91-10-5)/D-9	-0.1
1980	Tex-A	99	204	29	53	10	0	4	19	18	15	.260	.338	.368	705	96	-1	8	5	0	.973	-9	O-72(15-18-40)/D-4	-1.2
1981	Tex-A	66	230	36	65	16	0	3	25	17	21	.283	.350	.391	742	120	6	4	1	1	.993	-1	O-64(62-5-0)	0.3
1982	Tex-A	97	360	56	94	14	2	10	29	27	35	.261	.318	.394	712	99	-1	10	2	2	.981	2	O-91(85-9-0)/D-1	-0.2
1983	Tex-A	147	554	80	152	28	3	12	57	44	46	.274	.333	.401	734	103	2	44	8	7	.988	6	*O-146(144-2-1)	0.9
1984	Tex-A	130	489	67	121	20	2	5	33	29	46	.247	.290	.327	617	68	-21	18	6	2	.986	0	*O-122(72-51-3)/D-2	-2.3
1985	NY-A	59	139	18	40	5	0	1	15	9	10	.288	.340	.345	685	90	-2	2	1	0	.989	-4	O-55(51-4-0)	-0.7
1986	Atl-N	92	200	23	57	11	0	6	14	14	26	.285	.341	.430	771	105	1	4	2	0	.986	-8	O-56(10-0-48)/2-1	-0.9
Total	9	826	2516	371	684	127	9	46	230	195	230	.272	.331	.384	715	98	-7	98	31	11	.987	-19	O-711L/D-19,2-1	-4.1

■ AMADO SAMUEL
Samuel, Amado Ruperto b: 12/6/38, San Pedro De Macoris, D.R. BR/TR, 6'1", 170 lbs. Deb: 4/10/62

YEAR	TM/L	G	AB	R	H	2B	3B	HR	RBI	BB	SO	AVG	OBP	SLG	OPS	OPS+	BR+	SB	CS	SBR	FA	FR	G/POS	TPR
1962	Mil-N	76	209	16	43	10	0	3	20	12	54	.206	.249	.297	546	47	-16	0	2	-1	.958	-4	S-36,2-28/3-3	-1.7
1963	Mil-N	15	17	0	3	1	0	0	0	0	4	.176	.176	.235	412	18	-2	0	1	-0	.786	2	/S-7,2-4	0.0
1964	NY-N	53	142	7	33	7	0	0	5	4	24	.232	.264	.282	545	55	-8	0	1	-0	.945	6	S-34,3-17/2-3	-0.1
Total	3	144	368	23	79	18	0	3	25	16	82	.215	.251	.288	539	49	-26	0	4	-1	.942	4	/S-77,2-35,3-20	-1.8

■ JUAN SAMUEL
Samuel, Juan Milton b: 12/9/60, San Pedro De Macoris, D.R. BR/TR, 5'11", 170 lbs. Deb: 8/24/83 C Career OF: (34-LF 197-CF 40-RF)

YEAR	TM/L	G	AB	R	H	2B	3B	HR	RBI	BB	SO	AVG	OBP	SLG	OPS	OPS+	BR+	SB	CS	SBR	FA	FR	G/POS	TPR
1983	*Phi-N	18	65	14	18	1	2	2	5	4	16	.277	.329	.446	775	114	1	3	2	-0	.916	3	2-18	0.5
1984	Phi-N☆	160	701	105	191	36	**19**	15	69	28	168	.272	.307	.442	749	107	3	72	15	11	.962	-22	*2-160	0.1
1985	Phi-N	161	663	101	175	31	13	19	74	33	141	.264	.305	.436	741	102	-0	53	19	5	.983	-2	*2-159	1.2
1986	Phi-N	145	591	90	157	36	12	16	78	26	142	.266	.306	.448	754	102	-1	42	14	4	.967	-9	*2-143	0.2
1987	Phi-N★	160	655	113	178	37	**15**	28	100	60	162	.272	.338	.502	840	115	13	35	15	2	.978	-19	*2-160	0.5
1988	Phi-N	157	629	68	153	32	9	12	67	39	151	.243	.300	.380	680	92	-7	33	10	4	.978	-26	*2-152/O-3(0-2-1),3-1	-2.7
1989	Phi-N	51	199	32	49	3	1	8	20	18	45	.246	.312	.392	704	100	-0	11	3	1	.993	5	O-50(0-50-0)	0.6
	NY-N	86	333	37	76	13	1	3	28	24	75	.228	.300	.300	600	76	-10	31	9	4	.986	7	O-84(0-84-0)	-0.1
	Yr	137	532	69	125	16	2	11	48	42	120	.235	.304	.335	639	85	-10	42	12	5	.989	11	*O-134(0-134-0)	0.5
1990	LA-N	143	492	62	119	24	3	13	52	51	126	.242	.319	.382	701	95	-4	38	20	1	.972	-5	*2-108,O-31(0-31-0)	-0.5
1991	LA-N★	153	594	74	161	22	6	12	58	49	133	.271	.330	.389	719	104	2	23	8	2	.978	4	*2-152	1.3
1992	LA-N	47	122	7	32	3	1	0	15	7	22	.262	.308	.303	611	75	-4	2	2	-0	.974	-2	2-38/O-1(0-0-1)	-0.5
	KC-A	29	102	15	29	5	3	0	8	7	27	.284	.336	.392	729	101	0	6	1	1	.903	-3	O-18(0-0-18),2-10	-0.3
1993	Cin-N	103	261	31	60	10	4	4	26	23	53	.230	.300	.345	644	72	-11	9	7	-0	.971	3	2-70/1-6,3-4,O-3L	-0.5
1994	Det-A	59	136	32	42	9	5	5	21	10	26	.309	.369	.559	928	134	7	5	2	0	1.000	3	O-27C,D-10/2-8,1-2	0.9
1995	Det-A	76	171	28	48	10	1	10	34	24	38	.281	.376	.526	902	132	8	5	4	-0	.983	-1	1-37,D-16/O-9L,2-6	0.3
	KC-A	15	34	3	6	0	0	2	5	5	11	.176	.282	.353	635	63	-2	1	0	0	1.000	-2	/O-5(5-0-0),1-1,D-7	-0.3
	Yr	91	205	31	54	10	1	12	39	29	49	.263	.360	.498	858	121	6	6	4	-0	.984	-3	1-38,D-23,O-14L,/2	0.0
1996	Tor-A	69	188	34	48	8	3	8	26	15	65	.255	.320	.457	778	94	-2	9	1	2	1.000	-8	O-24R,D-24,1-17	-1.1
1997	Tor-A	45	95	13	27	5	4	3	15	10	28	.284	.364	.516	880	126	3	5	3	0	1.000	-1	D-15/3-9,1-7,2-4,O	0.1
1998	Tor-A	43	50	14	9	2	0	1	2	7	13	.180	.293	.280	573	50	-4	13	8	0	.882	-0	D-11,O-10L/1-3,2-2	-0.5
Total	16	1720	6081	873	1578	287	102	161	703	440	1442	.259	.317	.420	737	101	-8	396	143	37	.973	-76	*2-1190,O-267C/D13	-0.8

■ IKE SAMULS
Samuls, Samuel Earl b: 2/20/1876, Chicago, Ill. d: 1/1/42, Los Angeles, Cal. BR/TR, Deb: 8/3/1895

YEAR	TM/L	G	AB	R	H	2B	3B	HR	RBI	BB	SO	AVG	OBP	SLG	OPS	OPS+	BR+	SB	CS	SBR	FA	FR	G/POS	TPR
1895	StL-N	24	74	5	17	2	0	0	5	5	7	.230	.278	.257	535	39	-7	5			.750	-3	3-21/S-3	-0.8

■ ALEJANDRO SANCHEZ
Sanchez, Alejandro (Pimentel) b: 2/14/59, San Pedro De Macoris, D.R. BR/TR, 6', 185 lbs. Deb: 9/6/82

YEAR	TM/L	G	AB	R	H	2B	3B	HR	RBI	BB	SO	AVG	OBP	SLG	OPS	OPS+	BR+	SB	CS	SBR	FA	FR	G/POS	TPR
1982	Phi-N	7	14	3	4	1	0	2	4	0	4	.286	.286	.786	1071	186	1	0	0	0	1.000	-0	/O-4(0-0-4)	0.1
1983	Phi-N	8	7	2	2	0	0	0	2	0	2	.286	.286	.286	571	59	-0	0	0	0	.500	-1	/O-2(0-0-2)	-0.1
1984	SF-N	13	41	3	8	0	1	0	2	0	12	.195	.195	.244	439	23	-4	2	3	-1	.952	0	O-11(3-0-9)	-0.5
1985	Det-A	71	133	19	33	6	2	6	12	0	39	.248	.248	.459	707	89	-3	2	2	-0	.923	-6	O-31(5-2-24),D-28	-1.0
1986	Min-A	8	16	1	2	0	0	0	1	1	8	.125	.176	.125	301	-16	-3	0	0	0	.000	-0	/O-1(1-0-0),D-3	-0.3
1987	Oak-A	2	3	0	0	0	0	0	0	0	1	.000	.000	.000	0	-99	-1	0	0	0	1.000	-0	/O-1(0-0-1),D-1	-0.1
Total	6	109	214	28	49	7	3	8	21	1	66	.229	.233	.402	634	71	-9	4	5	-1	.929	-7	/O-50(9-2-40),D-32	-1.9

■ CELERINO SANCHEZ
Sanchez, Celerino (Perez) b: 2/3/44, Veracruz, Mexico d: 5/1/92, Leon, Mexico BR/TR, 5'11", 160 lbs. Deb: 6/13/72 Career OF: (0-LF 0-CF 2-RF)

YEAR	TM/L	G	AB	R	H	2B	3B	HR	RBI	BB	SO	AVG	OBP	SLG	OPS	OPS+	BR+	SB	CS	SBR	FA	FR	G/POS	TPR
1972	NY-A	71	250	18	62	8	3	0	22	12	30	.248	.293	.304	597	81	-6	0	0	0	.939	4	3-68	-0.3
1973	NY-A	34	64	12	14	3	0	1	9	2	12	.219	.242	.313	555	57	-4	1	1	-0	1.000	1	3-11,D-11/S-2,O-2R	-0.3
Total	2	105	314	30	76	11	3	1	31	14	42	.242	.283	.306	589	76	-10	1	1	-0	.943	5	/3-79,D-11,O-2R,S-2	-0.6

■ ORLANDO SANCHEZ
Sanchez, Orlando (Marquez) b: 9/7/56, Canovanas, P.R. BL/TR, 6'1", 195 lbs. Deb: 5/6/81

YEAR	TM/L	G	AB	R	H	2B	3B	HR	RBI	BB	SO	AVG	OBP	SLG	OPS	OPS+	BR+	SB	CS	SBR	FA	FR	G/POS	TPR
1981	StL-N	27	49	5	14	2	1	0	6	2	6	.286	.314	.367	681	90	-1	1	0	0	.926	-2	C-18	-0.2
1982	StL-N	26	37	6	7	0	1	0	3	5	5	.189	.286	.243	529	49	-2	0	0	0	1.000	-1	C-15	-0.3
1983	StL-N	6	6	0	0	0	0	0	0	0	4	.000	.000	.000	0	-99	-2	0	0	0	1.000	-0	/C-1	-0.2
1984	KC-A	10	10	0	1	1	0	0	2	0	2	.100	.100	.200	300	-19	-2	0	0	0	1.000	-0	/C-1	-0.2
	Bal-A	4	8	0	2	0	0	0	1	0	2	.250	.250	.250	500	40	-1	0	0	0	1.000	-0	/C-4	-0.1
	Yr	14	18	0	3	1	0	0	3	0	4	.167	.167	.222	389	7	-2	0	0	0	1.000	-0	/C-5	-0.3
Total	4	73	110	11	24	3	2	0	12	7	19	.218	.265	.282	547	53	-7	1	0	0	.962	-3	/C-39	-1.0

■ REY SANCHEZ
Sanchez, Rey Francisco (Guadalupe) b: 10/5/67, Rio Piedras, P.R. BR/TR, 5'9", 170 lbs. Deb: 9/8/91

YEAR	TM/L	G	AB	R	H	2B	3B	HR	RBI	BB	SO	AVG	OBP	SLG	OPS	OPS+	BR+	SB	CS	SBR	FA	FR	G/POS	TPR
1991	Chi-N	13	23	1	6	0	0	0	2	4	3	.261	.370	.261	631	77	-0	0	0	0	1.000	2	S-10/2-2	0.2

YEAR	TM/L	G	AB	R	H	2B	3B	HR	RBI	BB	SO	AVG	OBP	SLG	OPS	OPS+	BR+	SB	CS	SBR	FA	FR	G/POS	TPR
1992	Chi-N	74	255	24	64	14	3	1	19	10	17	.251	.287	.341	628	75	-8	2	1	0	.974	14	S-68/2-4	1.1
1993	Chi-N	105	344	35	97	11	2	0	28	15	22	.282	.318	.326	643	74	-13	1	1	-0	.969	27	S-98	2.2
1994	Chi-N	96	291	26	83	13	1	0	24	20	29	.285	.346	.337	683	80	-8	2	5	-1	.993	**29**	2-50,S-30,3-17	2.3
1995	Chi-N	114	428	57	119	22	2	3	27	14	48	.278	.302	.360	662	75	-16	6	4	-0	.987	4	*2-111/S-4	-0.7
1996	Chi-N	95	289	28	61	9	0	1	12	22	42	.211	.274	.253	526	39	-25	7	1	1	.977	22	S-92	0.5
1997	Chi-N	97	205	14	51	9	0	1	12	11	26	.249	.287	.307	594	54	-14	4	2	0	.964	-0	S-63,2-32/3-1	-1.0
	*NY-A	38	138	21	43	12	0	1	15	5	21	.312	.340	.420	761	98	-1	0	4	-1	.976	-1	2-37/S-6	-0.1
1998	SF-N	109	316	44	90	14	2	2	30	16	47	.285	.327	.361	688	86	-7	0	0	0	.977	15	S-76,2-36	1.4
1999	KC-A	134	479	66	141	18	6	2	56	22	48	.294	.331	.370	700	77	-17	11	5	1	.982	**30**	*S-134	2.3
2000	KC-A	143	509	68	139	18	2	1	38	28	55	.273	.316	.322	638	62	-29	7	3	0	.994	**20**	*S-143	0.2
Total	10	1018	3277	384	894	140	18	12	263	167	358	.273	.314	.338	652	71	-137	40	26	-0	.979	161	S-724,2-272/3-18	8.4
■ **HEINIE SAND**	Sand, John Henry b: 7/3/1897, San Francisco, Cal d: 11/3/58, San Francisco, Cal. BR/TR, 5'8", 160 lbs. Deb: 4/17/23																							
1923	Phi-N	132	470	85	107	16	5	4	32	82	56	.228	.347	.309	656	67	-21	7	3	0	.934	-3	*S-120,3-11	-0.8
1924	Phi-N	137	539	79	132	21	6	6	40	52	57	.245	.316	.340	655	67	-24	5	4	-0	**.959**	2	*S-137	-0.8
1925	Phi-N	148	496	69	138	30	7	3	55	64	65	.278	.364	.385	749	84	-10	1	1	-0	.928	-6	*S-143	-0.1
1926	Phi-N	149	567	99	154	30	5	4	37	66	56	.272	.350	.363	713	88	-9	2			.939	-3	*S-149	0.4
1927	Phi-N	141	535	87	160	22	8	1	49	58	59	.299	.369	.376	744	98	0	5			.949	-15	S-86,3-58	-0.2
1928	Phi-N	141	426	38	90	26	1	0	38	60	47	.211	.310	.277	587	53	-28	1			.951	-1	*S-137	-1.5
Total	6	848	3033	457	781	145	32	18	251	382	340	.258	.343	.344	688	77	-91	21	8		.943	-26	S-772/3-69	-3.0
■ **GUS SANDBERG**	Sandberg, Gustave E. b: 2/23/1896, Long Island City, N.Y. d: 2/3/30, Los Angeles, Cal. BR/TR, 6'1", 189 lbs. Deb: 5/11/23																							
1923	Cin-N	7	17	1	3	1	0	0	1	1	1	.176	.222	.235	458	21	-2	0	0	0	1.000	-1	/C-5	-0.2
1924	Cin-N	24	52	1	9	0	0	0	3	2	7	.173	.204	.173	377	2	-7	0	0	0	1.000	0	C-24	-0.6
Total	2	31	69	2	12	1	0	0	4	3	8	.174	.208	.188	397	7	-9	0	0	0	1.000	-1	/C-29	-0.8
■ **RYNE SANDBERG**	Sandberg, Ryne Dee b: 9/18/59, Spokane, Wash. BR/TR, 6'2", 180 lbs. Deb: 9/2/81																							
1981	Phi-N	13	6	2	1	0	0	0	0	0	1	.167	.167	.167	333	-5	-1	0	0	0	1.000	4	/S-5,2-1	0.3
1982	Chi-N	156	635	103	172	33	5	7	54	36	90	.271	.314	.372	686	89	-10	32	12	3	.970	5	*3-133,2-24	-0.4
1983	Chi-N	158	633	94	165	25	4	8	48	51	79	.261	.319	.351	669	81	-15	37	11	4	**.986**	**41**	*2-157/S-1	4.0
1984	*Chi-N★	156	636	**114**	200	36	**19**	19	84	52	101	.314	.369	.520	889	135	29	32	7	5	**.993**	23	*2-156	**6.7**
1985	Chi-N★	153	609	113	186	31	6	26	83	57	97	.305	.366	.504	870	127	22	54	11	8	.986	8	*2-153/S-1	4.8
1986	Chi-N★	154	627	68	178	28	5	14	76	46	79	.284	.333	.411	744	97	-3	34	11	4	**.994**	5	*2-153	1.5
1987	Chi-N★	132	523	81	154	25	2	16	59	59	79	.294	.368	.442	810	109	8	21	2	4	.985	1	*2-131	2.0
1988	Chi-N★	155	618	77	163	23	8	19	69	54	91	.264	.324	.419	743	107	5	25	10	2	.987	11	*2-153	2.4
1989	*Chi-N★	157	606	**104**	176	25	5	30	76	59	85	.290	.357	.497	854	132	25	15	5	2	.992	1	*2-155	3.3
1990	Chi-N★	155	615	**116**	188	30	3	**40**	100	50	84	.306	.359	.559	918	138	30	25	7	3	.989	7	*2-154	4.5
1991	Chi-N★	158	585	104	170	32	2	26	100	87	89	.291	.384	.485	870	137	30	22	8	2	**.995**	11	*2-157	4.8
1992	Chi-N★	158	612	100	186	32	8	26	87	68	73	.304	.374	.510	884	145	35	17	6	2	.990	14	*2-157	5.8
1993	Chi-N★	117	456	67	141	20	0	9	45	37	62	.309	.364	.412	776	109	6	9	2	1	.988	-4	*2-115	0.9
1994	Chi-N	57	223	36	53	9	5	5	24	23	40	.238	.312	.390	702	83	-6	2	3	-1	.987	3	2-57	0.0
1996	Chi-N	150	554	85	135	28	4	25	92	54	116	.244	.319	.444	763	96	-4	12	8	-0	.991	-12	*2-146	-0.9
1997	Chi-N	135	447	54	118	26	0	12	64	28	94	.264	.310	.403	713	83	-12	7	4	0	.984	-25	*2-126/D-1	-3.1
Total	16	2164	8385	1318	2386	403	76	282	1061	761	1260	.285	.347	.452	798	113	138	344	107	38	.989	93	*2-1995,3-133/S-7,D	36.6
■ **BEN SANDERS**	Sanders, Alexander Bennett b: 2/16/1865, Catharpin, Va. d: 8/29/30, Memphis, Tenn. BR/TR, 6', 210 lbs. Deb: 6/6/1888 Career OF: (24-LF 11-CF 36-RF)																							
1888	Phi-N	57	236	26	58	11	2	1	25	8	12	.246	.276	.322	598	86	-4	13			.929	3	P-31,O-25(13-6-7)/3-1	-0.3
1889	Phi-N	44	169	21	47	8	2	0	21	6	11	.278	.307	.349	656	76	-6	4			.879	-3	P-44/O-3(1-2-0)	-0.1
1890	Phi-P	52	189	31	59	6	6	0	30	10	10	.312	.347	.407	754	99	-1	2			.924	1	P-43,O-10(0-3-7)	-0.1
1891	Phi-a	40	156	24	39	6	4	1	19	7	12	.250	.291	.359	650	86	-4	2			.839	-6	O-22(10-0-13),P-19	-0.6
1892	Lou-N	54	198	30	54	12	2	3	18	16	17	.273	.330	.399	729	131	7	6			.930	-3	P-31,1-15/O-9(0-0-9)	0.1
Total	5	247	948	132	257	43	16	5	113	47	62	.271	.310	.366	676	95	-8	27			.916	-8	P-168/O-69R,1-15,3	-1.0
■ **ANTHONY SANDERS**	Sanders, Anthony Marcus b: 3/2/74, Tucson, Ariz. BR/TR, 6'2", 200 lbs. Deb: 4/26/99																							
1999	Tor-A	3	7	1	2	1	0	0	2	0	2	.286	.286	.429	714	78	-0	0	0	0	1.000	-0	/O-1(1-0-0),D-2	0.0
2000	Sea-A	1	1	1	1	0	0	0	0	0	0	1.000	1.000	1.000	2000	419	0	0	0	0	1.000	-0	/O-1(0-0-1)	0.0
Total	2	4	8	2	3	1	0	0	2	0	2	.375	.375	.500	875	119	0	0	0	0	1.000	-0	/D-2,O-2(1-0-1)	0.0
■ **DEION SANDERS**	Sanders, Deion Luwynn b: 8/9/67, Ft.Myers, Fla. BL/TL, 6'1", 195 lbs. Deb: 5/31/89																							
1989	NY-A	14	47	7	11	2	0	2	7	3	8	.234	.280	.404	684	92	-1	1	0	0	.969	-0	O-14(3-11-0)	-0.1
1990	NY-A	57	133	24	21	2	2	3	9	13	27	.158	.238	.271	509	42	-11	8	2	1	.973	-4	O-42(29-15-0)/D-4	-1.5
1991	Atl-N	54	110	16	21	1	2	4	13	12	23	.191	.270	.345	616	68	-5	11	3	1	.952	-5	O-44(41-5-1)	-1.0
1992	*Atl-N	97	303	54	92	6	**14**	8	28	18	52	.304	.347	.495	842	128	10	26	9	3	.983	-1	O-75(12-60-9)	1.2
1993	*Atl-N	95	272	42	75	18	6	6	28	16	42	.276	.323	.452	775	104	1	19	7	2	.986	-0	O-60(5-55-0)	0.3
1994	Atl-N	46	191	32	55	10	0	4	21	16	28	.288	.346	.403	749	93	-2	19	7	2	.980	-2	O-46(0-46-0)	-0.1
	Cin-N	46	184	26	51	7	4	0	7	16	35	.277	.342	.359	700	84	-4	19	9	1	1.000	2	O-45(0-45-0)	0.0
	Yr	92	375	58	106	17	4	4	28	32	63	.283	.344	.381	725	88	-6	38	16	3	.991	0	O-91(0-91-0)	-0.1
1995	Cin-N	33	129	19	31	2	3	1	10	9	18	.240	.300	.326	626	65	-6	16	3	2	.968	4	O-33(0-33-0)	0.0
	SF-N	52	214	29	61	9	5	5	18	18	42	.285	.346	.444	790	110	3	8	6	-0	.984	1	O-52(0-52-0)	0.4
	Yr	85	343	48	92	11	8	6	28	27	60	.268	.329	.399	728	93	-4	24	9	2	.977	5	O-85(0-85-0)	0.4
1997	Cin-N	115	465	53	127	13	7	5	23	34	67	.273	.331	.363	694	81	-13	56	13	8	.984	6	*O-113(33-77-0)	0.1
Total	8	609	2048	302	545	70	43	38	164	155	342	.266	.324	.398	722	91	-27	183	59	20	.981	0	O-524(123-399-10)/D-4	-0.7
■ **JOHN SANDERS**	Sanders, John Frank b: 11/20/45, Grand Island, Neb. BR/TR, 6'2", 200 lbs. Deb: 4/13/65																							
1965	KC-A	1	0	0	0	0	0	0	0	0	0	—	—	—	—	—	0	0	0	0	.000	0	R	0.0
■ **RAY SANDERS**	Sanders, Raymond Floyd b: 12/4/16, Bonne Terre, Mo. d: 10/28/83, Washington, Mo. BL/TR, 6'2", 185 lbs. Deb: 4/14/42																							
1942	*StL-N	95	282	37	71	17	2	5	39	42	31	.252	.351	.379	730	106	3	2			.991	-4	1-77	-0.8
1943	*StL-N	144	478	69	134	21	5	11	73	77	33	.280	.381	.414	796	124	17	1			.995	-7	*1-141	0.3
1944	*StL-N	154	601	87	177	34	9	12	102	71	50	.295	.371	.441	812	126	21	2			**.994**	-13	*1-152	0.0
1945	StL-N	143	537	85	148	29	3	8	78	83	55	.276	.375	.385	760	109	9	3			.986	-5	*1-142	-0.3
1946	Bos-N	80	259	43	63	12	0	6	35	50	38	.243	.368	.359	727	105	3	0			.988	4	1-77	0.5
1948	*Bos-N	5	4	0	1	0	0	0	2	1	0	.250	.400	.250	650	81	-0	0			.000	0	H	0.0
1949	Bos-N	9	21	0	3	1	0	0	0	4	9	.143	.280	.190	470	30	-2	0			.984	2	/1-7	0.0
Total	7	630	2182	321	597	114	19	42	329	328	216	.274	.370	.401	771	115	51	8			.991	-22	1-596	-0.3
■ **REGGIE SANDERS**	Sanders, Reginald Jerome b: 9/9/49, Birmingham, Ala. BR/TR, 6'2", 205 lbs. Deb: 9/1/74																							
1974	Det-A	26	99	12	27	7	0	3	10	5	20	.273	.308	.434	742	108	1	1	0	0	.987	1	1-25/D-1	-0.1
■ **REGGIE SANDERS**	Sanders, Reginald Laverne b: 12/1/67, Florence, S.C. BR/TR, 6'1", 186 lbs. Deb: 8/22/91 Career OF: (219-LF 210-CF 654-RF)																							
1991	Cin-N	9	40	6	8	0	0	1	3	0	9	.200	.200	.275	475	31	-4	1	1	-0	1.000	1	/O-9(0-9-0)	-0.4
1992	Cin-N	116	385	62	104	26	6	12	36	48	98	.270	.357	.462	819	127	14	16	7	1	.978	5	*O-110(53-77-0)	1.9
1993	Cin-N	138	496	90	136	16	4	20	83	51	118	.274	.348	.444	791	110	7	27	10	2	.975	8	*O-137(0-4-135)	1.0
1994	Cin-N	107	400	66	105	20	8	17	62	41	114	.262	.334	.480	814	110	5	21	9	1	.975	12	*O-104(0-0-104)	1.2
1995	*Cin-N★	133	484	91	148	36	6	28	99	69	122	.306	.401	.579	980	155	39	36	12	4	.983	5	*O-130(0-16-125)	4.1
1996	Cin-N	81	287	49	72	17	1	14	33	44	86	.251	.354	.463	818	113	6	24	8	2	.988	7	O-80(0-0-80)	1.1
1997	Cin-N	86	312	52	79	19	2	19	56	42	93	.253	.347	.510	857	119	8	13	7	0	.974	8	O-85(0-0-85)	1.2
1998	Cin-N	135	481	83	129	18	6	14	59	51	137	.268	.347	.418	765	99	-0	20	9	1	.978	-6	*O-131(0-88-57)	-0.6
1999	SD-N	133	478	92	136	24	7	26	72	65	108	.285	.377	.527	904	136	26	36	13	3	.975	-7	*O-129(97-15-41)/D-1	1.7
2000	*Atl-N	103	340	43	79	23	1	11	37	32	78	.232	.302	.403	705	77	-13	21	4	3	.964	1	O-96(69-1-27)	-1.1
Total	10	1041	3703	634	996	199	41	162	540	443	963	.269	.353	.476	829	117	88	215	80	19	.977	33	*O-1011R/D-1	10.1

■ MIKE SANDLOCK
Sandlock, Michael Joseph b: 10/17/15, Old Greenwich, Conn. BB/TR (BL 1944), 6'1", 185 lbs. Deb: 9/19/42

YEAR	TM/L	G	AB	R	H	2B	3B	HR	RBI	BB	SO	AVG	OBP	SLG	OPS	OPS+	BR+	SB	CS	SBR	FA	FR	G/POS	TPR
1942	Bos-N	2	1	1	1	0	0	0	0	0	0	1.000	1.000	1.000	2000	496	0	0			.000	0	/S-2	0.1
1944	Bos-N	30	30	1	3	0	0	0	2	5	3	.100	.250	.100	350	1	-4	0			.956	7	3-22/S-7	0.3
1945	Bro-N	80	195	21	55	14	2	2	17	18	19	.282	.346	.405	751	109	2	2			.991	1	C-47,S-22/2-4,3-2	0.7
1946	Bro-N	19	34	1	5	0	0	0	0	3	4	.147	.216	.147	363	4	-4	0			.973	6	C-17/3-1	0.2
1953	Pit-N	64	186	10	43	5	0	0	12	12	19	.231	.281	.258	539	42	-16	0	0	0	.991	16	C-64	0.3
Total	5	195	446	34	107	19	2	2	31	38	45	.240	.304	.305	609	66	-21	2	0		.989	30	C-128/S-31,3-25,2-4	1.6

■ CHARLIE SANDS
Sands, Charles Duane b: 12/17/47, Newport News, Va. BL/TR, 6'2", 215 lbs. Deb: 6/21/67

YEAR	TM/L	G	AB	R	H	2B	3B	HR	RBI	BB	SO	AVG	OBP	SLG	OPS	OPS+	BR+	SB	CS	SBR	FA	FR	G/POS	TPR
1967	NY-A	1	1	0	0	0	0	0	0	0	1	.000	.000	.000	0	-99	-0	0	0	0	.000	0	H	0.0
1971	*Pit-N	28	25	4	5	2	0	1	5	7	6	.200	.375	.400	775	120	1	0	0	0	1.000	0	/C-3	0.1
1972	Pit-N	1	1	0	0	0	0	0	0	0	0	.000	.000	.000	0	-99	-0	0	0	0	.000	0	H	0.0
1973	Cal-A	17	33	5	9	2	1	1	5	5	10	.273	.368	.485	853	150	2	0	0	0	.917	-8	C-10	-0.5
1974	Cal-A	43	83	6	16	2	0	4	13	23	17	.193	.374	.361	735	119	3	0	0	0	1.000	-1	D-21/C-5	0.2
1975	Oak-A	3	2	0	1	0	0	0	0	1	1	.500	.667	.500	1167	239	1	0	0	0	.000	0	/D-1	0.1
Total	6	93	145	15	31	6	1	6	23	36	35	.214	.374	.393	767	125	6	0	0	0	.955	-8	/D-22,C-18	-0.1

■ TOMMY SANDT
Sandt, Thomas James b: 12/22/50, Brooklyn, N.Y. BR/TR, 5'11", 175 lbs. Deb: 6/29/75 C

YEAR	TM/L	G	AB	R	H	2B	3B	HR	RBI	BB	SO	AVG	OBP	SLG	OPS	OPS+	BR+	SB	CS	SBR	FA	FR	G/POS	TPR
1975	Oak-A	1	0	0	0	0	0	0	0	0	0	—	—	—	—	—	0	0	0	0	.000	0	/2-1	0.0
1976	Oak-A	41	67	6	14	1	0	0	3	7	9	.209	.284	.224	508	52	-4	0	0	0	.966	3	S-29/2-9,3-2	0.1
Total	2	42	67	6	14	1	0	0	3	7	9	.209	.284	.224	508	52	-4	0	0	0	1.000	3	/S-29,2-10,3-2	0.1

■ CHANCE SANFORD
Sanford, Chance Steven b: 6/2/72, Houston, Tex. BL/TR, 5'10", 165 lbs. Deb: 4/30/98

YEAR	TM/L	G	AB	R	H	2B	3B	HR	RBI	BB	SO	AVG	OBP	SLG	OPS	OPS+	BR+	SB	CS	SBR	FA	FR	G/POS	TPR
1998	Pit-N	14	28	3	4	1	1	0	3	1	6	.143	.172	.250	422	9	-4	0	0	0	.900	-3	/3-5,2-1,S-1	-0.7
1999	LA-N	5	8	1	2	0	0	0	2	0	1	.250	.250	.250	500	29	-1	0	0	0	1.000	-1	/2-2	-0.2
Total	2	19	36	4	6	1	1	0	5	1	7	.167	.189	.250	439	13	-5	0	0	0	.750	-4	/3-5,2-3,S-1	-0.9

■ JACK SANFORD
Sanford, John Doward b: 6/23/17, Chatham, Va. BR/TR, 6'3", 195 lbs. Deb: 8/24/40

YEAR	TM/L	G	AB	R	H	2B	3B	HR	RBI	BB	SO	AVG	OBP	SLG	OPS	OPS+	BR+	SB	CS	SBR	FA	FR	G/POS	TPR
1940	Was-A	34	122	5	24	4	2	0	10	6	17	.197	.234	.262	497	30	-13	0	0	0	.993	-2	1-34	-1.7
1941	Was-A	3	5	1	2	0	1	0	0	1	1	.400	.500	.800	1300	251	1	0	0	0	1.000	-0	/1-1	0.1
1946	Was-A	10	26	7	6	0	1	0	1	2	6	.231	.286	.308	593	70	-1	0	0	0	.971	-2	/1-6	-0.3
Total	3	47	153	13	32	4	4	0	11	9	24	.209	.253	.288	541	44	-13	0	0	0	.989	-4	/1-41	-1.9

■ MANNY SANGUILLEN
Sanguillen, Manuel De Jesus (Magan) b: 3/21/44, Colon, Panama BR/TR, 6', 193 lbs. Deb: 7/23/67 Career OF: (2-LF 0-CF 68-RF)

YEAR	TM/L	G	AB	R	H	2B	3B	HR	RBI	BB	SO	AVG	OBP	SLG	OPS	OPS+	BR+	SB	CS	SBR	FA	FR	G/POS	TPR
1967	Pit-N	30	96	6	26	4	0	0	8	4	12	.271	.300	.313	613	75	-3	0	1	-0	.986	-5	C-28	-0.8
1969	Pit-N	129	459	62	139	21	6	5	57	12	48	.303	.325	.407	732	106	2	8	4	0	.981	4	*C-113	1.2
1970	*Pit-N	128	486	63	158	19	9	7	61	17	45	.325	.348	.444	792	113	7	2	3	-1	.988	1	*C-125	1.3
1971	*Pit-N☆	138	533	60	170	26	5	7	81	19	32	.319	.346	.426	772	118	11	6	4	-0	.994	5	*C-135	2.4
1972	*Pit-N★	136	520	55	155	18	8	7	71	21	38	.298	.325	.404	729	108	4	1	2	-0	.988	-3	*C-127/O-2(2-0-0)	0.7
1973	Pit-N	149	589	64	166	26	7	12	65	17	29	.282	.305	.411	716	99	-3	2	5	-1	.983	4	C-89,O-59(0-0-59)	0.1
1974	*Pit-N	151	596	77	171	21	4	7	68	21	27	.287	.317	.371	688	95	-6	2	2	-0	.985	-6	*C-151	-0.6
1975	*Pit-N☆	133	481	60	158	24	4	9	58	48	31	.328	.393	.451	844	135	23	5	4	-0	.987	-5	*C-132	2.5
1976	Pit-N	114	389	52	113	16	6	2	36	28	18	.290	.341	.378	719	103	1	2	4	-1	.978	-7	*C-111	-0.1
1977	Oak-A	152	571	42	157	17	5	6	58	22	35	.275	.304	.354	658	80	-16	2	5	-1	.985	-8	C-77,D-58/O-9R,1-7	-2.5
1978	Pit-N	85	220	15	58	5	1	3	16	9	10	.264	.299	.336	635	74	-8	2	2	-0	1.000	-2	1-40,C-18	-1.3
1979	*Pit-N	56	74	8	17	5	2	0	4	2	5	.230	.250	.351	601	59	-4	0	0	0	.947	0	/C-8,1-5	-0.4
1980	Pit-N	47	48	2	12	3	0	0	2	3	1	.250	.294	.313	607	68	-2	3	2	-0	.956	0	/1-5	-0.2
Total	13	1448	5062	566	1500	205	57	65	585	223	331	.296	.329	.398	727	103	6	35	38	-6	.986	-23	*C-1114/O-70R,D-58,1	2.3

■ ED SANICKI
Sanicki, Edward Robert "Butch" b: 7/7/23, Wallington, N.J. d: 7/6/98, Old Bridge, N.J. BR/TR, 5'9", 175 lbs. Deb: 9/14/49

YEAR	TM/L	G	AB	R	H	2B	3B	HR	RBI	BB	SO	AVG	OBP	SLG	OPS	OPS+	BR+	SB	CS	SBR	FA	FR	G/POS	TPR
1949	Phi-N	7	13	4	3	0	0	3	7	1	4	.231	.286	.923	1209	217	2	0			1.000	-1	/O-6(0-1-5)	0.1
1951	Phi-N	13	4	1	2	1	0	0	1	1	1	.500	.600	.750	1350	265	1	1	0	0	1.000	-4	O-10(10-0-0)	-0.3
Total	2	20	17	5	5	1	0	3	8	2	5	.294	.368	.882	1251	231	3	1	0		1.000	-5	/O-16(10-1-5)	-0.2

■ BEN SANKEY
Sankey, Benjamin Turner b: 9/2/07, Nauvoo, Ala. BR/TR, 5'10", 155 lbs. Deb: 10/5/29

YEAR	TM/L	G	AB	R	H	2B	3B	HR	RBI	BB	SO	AVG	OBP	SLG	OPS	OPS+	BR+	SB	CS	SBR	FA	FR	G/POS	TPR
1929	Pit-N	2	7	1	1	0	0	0	0	0	1	.143	.143	.143	286	-28	-1	0			.909	-0	/S-2	-0.1
1930	Pit-N	13	30	6	5	0	0	0	0	2	3	.167	.219	.167	385	-5	-5	0			.871	-0	/S-6,2-4	-0.4
1931	Pit-N	57	132	14	30	2	5	0	14	14	10	.227	.301	.318	620	67	-6	0			.920	-9	S-49/2-2,3-2	-1.2
Total	3	72	169	21	36	2	5	0	14	16	14	.213	.281	.284	565	49	-13	0			.914	-10	/S-57,2-6,3-2	-1.7

■ ANDRES SANTANA
Santana, Andres Confesor (Belonis) b: 2/5/68, San Pedro De Macoris, D.R. BB/TR, 5'11", 160 lbs. Deb: 9/16/90

YEAR	TM/L	G	AB	R	H	2B	3B	HR	RBI	BB	SO	AVG	OBP	SLG	OPS	OPS+	BR+	SB	CS	SBR	FA	FR	G/POS	TPR
1990	SF-N	6	2	0	0	0	0	0	1	0	0	.000	.000	.000	0	-99	-1	0	0	0	1.000	1	/S-3	0.0

■ RAFAEL SANTANA
Santana, Rafael Francisco (De La Cruz) b: 1/31/58, LaRomana, D.R. BR/TR, 6'1", 165 lbs. Deb: 4/5/83

YEAR	TM/L	G	AB	R	H	2B	3B	HR	RBI	BB	SO	AVG	OBP	SLG	OPS	OPS+	BR+	SB	CS	SBR	FA	FR	G/POS	TPR
1983	StL-N	30	14	1	3	0	0	0	2	2	2	.214	.353	.214	567	61	-1	0	1	-0	.857	2	/2-9,S-6,3-4	0.1
1984	NY-N	51	152	14	42	11	1	1	12	9	17	.276	.317	.382	698	97	-1	0	3	-1	.970	-3	S-50	0.0
1985	NY-N	154	529	41	136	19	1	1	29	29	54	.257	.296	.302	598	69	-22	1	0	0	.965	-11	*S-153	-1.8
1986	*NY-N	139	394	38	86	11	0	1	28	36	43	.218	.287	.254	541	52	-25	0	0	0	.973	17	*S-137/2-1	0.4
1987	NY-N	139	439	41	112	21	2	5	44	29	57	.255	.303	.346	649	75	-16	1	1	-0	.973	15	*S-138	1.2
1988	NY-A	148	480	50	115	12	1	4	38	33	61	.240	.290	.294	584	64	-23	1	2	-0	.966	-9	*S-148	-2.2
1990	Cle-A	7	13	3	3	0	0	1	3	0	0	.231	.231	.462	692	89	-0	0	0	0	1.000	-2	/S-7	-0.2
Total	7	668	2021	188	497	74	5	13	156	138	234	.246	.296	.307	603	68	-88	3	7	-2	.969	9	S-639/2-10,3-4	-2.5

■ F. P. SANTANGELO
Santangelo, Frank-Paul b: 10/24/67, Livonia, Mich. BB/TR, 5'10", 165 lbs. Deb: 8/2/95 Career OF: (217-LF 190-CF 87-RF)

YEAR	TM/L	G	AB	R	H	2B	3B	HR	RBI	BB	SO	AVG	OBP	SLG	OPS	OPS+	BR+	SB	CS	SBR	FA	FR	G/POS	TPR
1995	Mon-N	35	98	11	29	5	1	1	9	12	9	.296	.384	.398	782	103	1	1	1	-0	.979	-1	O-25(20-2-7)/2-5	-0.1
1996	Mon-N	152	393	54	109	20	5	7	56	49	61	.277	.373	.407	780	103	3	5	2	0	.983	5	*O-124C,3-23/2-5,S	0.8
1997	Mon-N	130	350	56	87	19	5	5	31	50	73	.249	.381	.374	755	99	2	8	5	0	1.000	-7	O-99R,3-32/2-7,S-1	-0.7
1998	Mon-N	122	383	53	82	18	0	4	23	44	72	.214	.331	.292	624	67	-17	7	3	0	.983	-11	O-92L,2-35/3-1	-2.8
1999	SF-N	113	254	49	66	17	3	3	26	53	54	.260	.409	.386	795	111	7	12	4	1	.993	-11	O-81C,2-11/3-3,S-1	-0.2
2000	LA-N	81	142	19	28	4	0	1	9	21	33	.197	.325	.246	572	50	-10	3	2	-0	.983	-7	O-50(26-27-1)/2-7	-1.6
Total	6	633	1620	242	401	83	14	21	154	229	302	.248	.367	.355	722	90	-13	36	17	2	.988	-32	O-471L/2-70,3-59,S	-4.6

■ BENITO SANTIAGO
Santiago, Benito (Rivera) b: 3/9/65, Ponce, P.R. BR/TR, 6'1", 182 lbs. Deb: 9/14/86 Career OF: (2-LF 0-CF 0-RF)

YEAR	TM/L	G	AB	R	H	2B	3B	HR	RBI	BB	SO	AVG	OBP	SLG	OPS	OPS+	BR+	SB	CS	SBR	FA	FR	G/POS	TPR
1986	SD-N	17	62	10	18	2	0	3	6	2	12	.290	.313	.468	780	115	1	0	1	-0	.946	-6	C-17	-0.5
1987	SD-N	146	546	64	164	33	2	18	79	16	112	.300	.326	.467	793	111	6	21	12	0	.976	-7	*C-146	0.6
1988	SD-N	139	492	49	122	22	2	10	46	24	82	.248	.284	.362	646	86	-10	15	7	1	.985	-5	*C-136	-0.7
1989	SD-N★	129	462	50	109	16	3	16	62	26	89	.236	.278	.387	666	88	-9	11	6	0	.975	-6	*C-127	-0.7
1990	SD-N†	100	344	42	93	8	5	11	53	27	55	.270	.329	.419	747	103	1	5	5	-1	.980	-5	C-98	0.2
1991	SD-N★	152	580	60	155	22	3	17	87	23	114	.267	.300	.403	703	93	-7	8	10	-2	.985	-1	*C-151/O-1(1-0-0)	0.0
1992	SD-N★	106	386	37	97	21	0	10	42	21	52	.251	.290	.383	673	88	-7	2	5	-1	.982	-11	*C-103	-1.4
1993	Fla-N	139	469	49	108	19	6	13	50	37	88	.230	.294	.380	673	74	-18	10	7	-0	.987	-6	*C-136/O-1(1-0-0)	-1.6
1994	Fla-N	101	337	35	92	14	2	11	41	25	57	.273	.325	.424	749	91	-5	1	2	-0	.991	3	C-97	0.4
1995	*Cin-N	81	266	40	76	20	0	11	44	24	48	.286	.354	.485	839	119	7	2	2	-0	**.996**	3	C-75/1-8	1.3
1996	Phi-N	136	481	71	127	21	2	30	85	49	104	.264	.333	.503	836	116	9	2	0	0	.987	-8	*C-114,1-14	0.7
1997	Tor-A	97	341	31	83	10	0	13	42	17	80	.243	.283	.387	670	72	-15	1	0	0	.997	-3	C-95/D-1	-1.1
1998	Tor-A	15	29	3	9	5	0	0	4	1	6	.310	.333	.483	816	108	0	0	0	0	1.000	-2	C-15	-0.1
1999	Chi-N	109	350	28	87	18	3	7	36	32	71	.249	.315	.377	692	75	-14	1	1	-0	.990	-14	*C-107/1-1	-2.1
2000	Cin-N	89	252	22	66	11	1	8	45	19	45	.262	.316	.409	725	78	-9	2	2	-0	.994	4	C-84	-0.1
Total	15	1556	5397	591	1406	242	29	178	722	343	1015	.261	.308	.415	723	93	-67	81	60	-3	.985	-63	*C-1501/1-23,O-2L,D	-5.1

■ RON SANTO
Santo, Ronald Edward b: 2/25/40, Seattle, Wash. BR/TR, 6', 190 lbs. Deb: 6/26/60 Career OF: (7-LF 0-CF 1-RF)

YEAR	TM/L	G	AB	R	H	2B	3B	HR	RBI	BB	SO	AVG	OBP	SLG	OPS	OPS+	BR+	SB	CS	SBR	FA	FR	G/POS	TPR
1960	Chi-N	95	347	44	87	24	2	9	44	31	44	.251	.312	.409	721	97	-2	0	3	-1	.945	-19	3-94	-2.4

YEAR	TM/L	G	AB	R	H	2B	3B	HR	RBI	BB	SO	AVG	OBP	SLG	OPS	OPS+	BR+	SB	CS	SBR	FA	FR	G/POS	TPR
1961	Chi-N	154	578	84	164	32	6	23	83	73	77	.284	.364	.479	843	120	17	2	3	-1	.937	5	*3-153	2.1
1962	Chi-N	162	604	44	137	20	4	17	83	65	94	.227	.304	.358	662	74	-22	4	1	1	.955	11	*3-157/S-8	-1.1
1963	Chi-N★	162	630	79	187	29	6	25	99	42	92	.297	.345	.481	826	128	22	6	4	-0	.951	13	*3-162	3.6
1964	Chi-N☆	161	592	94	185	33	**13**	30	114	**86**	96	.313	**.401**	.564	966	162	50	3	4	-1	.963	17	*3-161	6.7
1965	Chi-N★	164	608	88	173	30	4	33	101	88	109	.285	.379	.510	889	144	37	3	1	0	.957	19	*3-164	5.7
1966	Chi-N★	155	561	93	175	21	8	30	94	**95**	78	.312	**.417**	.538	955	161	50	4	5	-1	.956	29	*3-152/S-8	**7.9**
1967	Chi-N	161	586	107	176	23	4	31	98	**96**	103	.300	.401	.512	913	153	43	1	5	-2	.957	**31**	*3-161	**7.5**
1968	Chi-N★	162	577	86	142	17	3	26	98	**96**	106	.246	.357	.421	778	124	20	3	4	-1	**.971**	17	*3-162	4.0
1969	Chi-N★	160	575	97	166	18	4	29	123	96	97	.289	.392	.485	877	128	24	1	3	-1	.947	6	*3-160	2.9
1970	Chi-N	154	555	83	148	30	4	26	114	92	108	.267	.372	.476	848	112	10	2	0	0	.945	13	*3-152/O-1(0-0-1)	2.3
1971	Chi-N★	154	555	77	148	22	1	21	88	79	95	.267	.358	.423	781	105	6	4	0	1	.958	-3	*3-149/O-6(6-0-0)	0.3
1972	Chi-N★	133	464	68	140	25	5	17	74	69	75	.302	.397	.487	884	135	23	1	4	-1	.948	6	*3-129/2-3,S-1,O-1L	3.0
1973	Chi-N★	149	536	65	143	29	2	20	77	63	97	.267	.348	.440	789	109	7	1	2	-0	.950	-12	*3-146	-0.7
1974	Chi-A	117	375	29	83	12	1	5	41	37	72	.221	.295	.299	593	69	-14	0	2	-1	.970	6	D-47,2-39,3-28,/1S	-0.9
Total	15	2243	8143	1138	2254	365	67	342	1331	1108	1343	.277	.366	.464	830	123	269	35	41	-7	.954	138	*3-2130/D-47,2SO1	40.9

■ RAFAEL SANTO DOMINGO

Santo Domingo, Rafael (Molina) b: 11/24/55, Orocovis, P.R. BB/TR, 6′, 160 lbs. Deb: 9/7/79

YEAR	TM/L	G	AB	R	H	2B	3B	HR	RBI	BB	SO	AVG	OBP	SLG	OPS	OPS+	BR+	SB	CS	SBR	FA	FR	G/POS	TPR
1979	Cin-N	7	6	0	1	0	0	0	0	1	3	.167	.286	.167	452	26	-1	0	0	0	.000	0	/H	-0.1

■ NELSON SANTOVENIA

Santovenia, Nelson Gil (Mayol) b: 7/27/61, Pinar Del Rio, Cuba BR/TR, 6′3″, 215 lbs. Deb: 9/16/87

YEAR	TM/L	G	AB	R	H	2B	3B	HR	RBI	BB	SO	AVG	OBP	SLG	OPS	OPS+	BR+	SB	CS	SBR	FA	FR	G/POS	TPR
1987	Mon-N	2	1	0	0	0	0	0	0	0	0	.000	.000	.000	0	-97	-0	0	0	0	1.000	-0	/C-1	0.0
1988	Mon-N	92	309	26	73	20	2	8	41	24	77	.236	.298	.392	689	92	-4	2	3	-1	.983	2	C-86/1-1	0.3
1989	Mon-N	97	304	30	76	14	1	5	31	24	37	.250	.311	.352	663	88	-5	2	1	0	.981	12	C-89/1-1	1.3
1990	Mon-N	59	163	13	31	3	1	6	28	8	31	.190	.228	.331	559	54	-11	0	3	-1	.980	2	C-51	-0.8
1991	Mon-N	41	96	7	24	5	0	2	14	2	18	.250	.265	.365	630	76	-3	0	0	0	.976	-4	C-30/1-7	-0.6
1992	Chi-A	2	3	1	1	0	0	1	2	0	0	.333	.333	1.333	1667	352	1	0	0	0	1.000	-0	/C-2	0.1
1993	KC-A	4	8	0	1	0	0	0	0	1	2	.125	.222	.125	347	-4	-1	0	0	0	1.000	0	/C-4	-0.1
Total	7	297	884	77	206	42	4	22	116	59	165	.233	.286	.364	650	82	-23	4	7	-2	.981	12	C-263/1-9	0.2

■ EDWARD SANTRY

Santry, Edward b: Chicago, Ill. d: 3/6/1899, Chicago, Ill. Deb: 8/7/1884

YEAR	TM/L	G	AB	R	H	2B	3B	HR	RBI	BB	SO	AVG	OBP	SLG	OPS	OPS+	BR+	SB	CS	SBR	FA	FR	G/POS	TPR
1884	Det-N	6	22	1	4	0	0	0	0	1	2	.182	.217	.182	399	29	-2				.821	-0	/S-5,2-1	-0.2

■ JOE SARGENT

Sargent, Joseph Alexander "Horse Belly" b: 9/24/1893, Rochester, N.Y. d: 7/5/50, Rochester, N.Y. BR/TR, 5′10″, 165 lbs. Deb: 4/27/21

YEAR	TM/L	G	AB	R	H	2B	3B	HR	RBI	BB	SO	AVG	OBP	SLG	OPS	OPS+	BR+	SB	CS	SBR	FA	FR	G/POS	TPR
1921	Det-A	66	178	21	45	8	5	2	22	24	26	.253	.342	.388	729	87	-4	2	3	-1	.927	3	2-24,3-23,S-19	0.2

■ BILL SARNI

Sarni, William Florine b: 9/19/27, Los Angeles, Cal. d: 4/15/83, Creve Coeur, Mo. BR/TR, 5′11″, 187 lbs. Deb: 5/9/51 C

YEAR	TM/L	G	AB	R	H	2B	3B	HR	RBI	BB	SO	AVG	OBP	SLG	OPS	OPS+	BR+	SB	CS	SBR	FA	FR	G/POS	TPR
1951	StL-N	36	86	7	15	1	0	0	2	9	13	.174	.253	.186	439	20	-10	1	0	0	.984	0	C-35	-0.8
1952	StL-N	3	5	0	1	0	0	0	0	0	1	.200	.200	.200	400	11	-1	0	0	0	1.000	2	/C-3	0.2
1954	StL-N	123	380	40	114	18	4	9	70	25	42	.300	.343	.439	783	101	0	3	3	-0	**.996**	-13	*C-118	-0.7
1955	StL-N	107	325	32	83	15	2	3	34	27	33	.255	.314	.342	656	74	-12	1	1	-0	.987	-6	C-99	-1.3
1956	StL-N	43	148	12	43	7	2	5	22	8	15	.291	.331	.466	797	111	2	1	0	-0	.992	3	C-41	0.7
	NY-N	78	238	16	55	9	3	5	23	20	31	.231	.293	.357	651	74	-9	0	1	-0	.993	-6	C-78	-1.2
	Yr	121	386	28	98	16	5	10	45	28	46	.254	.308	.399	707	88	-7	1	1	-0	.992	-3	*C-119	-0.5
Total	5	390	1182	107	311	50	11	22	151	89	135	.263	.316	.380	696	84	-29	6	5	-0	.991	-19	C-374	-3.1

■ MACKEY SASSER

Sasser, Mack Daniel b: 8/3/62, Fort Gaines, Ga. BL/TR, 6′1″, 210 lbs. Deb: 7/17/87 Career OF: (41-LF 0-CF 28-RF)

YEAR	TM/L	G	AB	R	H	2B	3B	HR	RBI	BB	SO	AVG	OBP	SLG	OPS	OPS+	BR+	SB	CS	SBR	FA	FR	G/POS	TPR
1987	SF-N	2	4	0	0	0	0	0	0	0	0	.000	.000	.000	0	-99	-1	0	0	0	1.000	0	/C-1	-0.1
	Pit-N	12	23	2	5	0	0	0	2	0	2	.217	.217	.217	435	16	-3	0	0	0	1.000	-1	/C-5	-0.4
	Yr	14	27	2	5	0	0	0	2	0	2	.185	.185	.185	370	-2	-4	0	0	0	1.000	-1	/C-6	-0.5
1988	*NY-N	60	123	9	35	10	1	1	17	6	9	.285	.318	.407	724	112	1	0	0	0	.977	9	C-42/3-1,O-1(0-0-1)	1.2
1989	NY-N	72	182	17	53	14	2	1	22	7	15	.291	.317	.407	724	111	2	0	1	-0	.992	0	C-62/3-1	0.5
1990	NY-N	100	270	31	83	14	0	6	41	15	19	.307	.346	.426	772	111	4	0	0	0	.975	-9	C-87/1-1	-0.1
1991	NY-N	96	228	18	62	14	2	5	35	9	19	.272	.303	.417	719	101	-1	0	2	-1	.994	-9	C-43,O-21R,1-10	-1.0
1992	NY-N	92	141	7	34	6	0	2	18	3	10	.241	.257	.326	583	65	-7	0	0	0	.989	-11	C-27,1-12/O-9(7-0-2)	-1.9
1993	Sea-A	83	188	18	41	10	2	1	21	15	30	.218	.279	.309	588	57	-12	1	0	0	.946	-3	O-37L,D-19/C-4,1-1	-1.6
1994	Sea-A	3	4	0	0	0	0	0	0	0	0	.000	.000	.000	0	-98	-1	0	0	0	.000	-0	/C-1,O-1(1-0-0)	-0.1
1995	Pit-N	14	26	1	4	1	0	0	0	0	0	.154	.154	.192	346	-9	-4	0	0	0	1.000	-1	C-11	-0.4
Total	9	534	1189	103	317	69	7	16	156	55	104	.267	.301	.377	678	89	-21	1	3	-1	.983	-24	C-283/O-69L,1-24,D3	-3.9

■ ROB SASSER

Sasser, Robert Doffell b: 3/9/75, Philadelphia, Pa. BR/TR, 6′3″, 205 lbs. Deb: 7/31/98

YEAR	TM/L	G	AB	R	H	2B	3B	HR	RBI	BB	SO	AVG	OBP	SLG	OPS	OPS+	BR+	SB	CS	SBR	FA	FR	G/POS	TPR
1998	Tex-A	1	1	0	0	0	0	0	0	0	0	.000	.000	.000	0	-96	-0	0	0	0	.000	0	/H	0.0

■ TOM SATRIANO

Satriano, Thomas Victor Nicholas b: 8/28/40, Pittsburgh, Pa. BL/TR, 6′1″, 190 lbs. Deb: 7/23/61

YEAR	TM/L	G	AB	R	H	2B	3B	HR	RBI	BB	SO	AVG	OBP	SLG	OPS	OPS+	BR+	SB	CS	SBR	FA	FR	G/POS	TPR
1961	LA-A	35	96	15	19	5	1	1	8	12	16	.198	.294	.302	596	53	-6	2	0	0	.915	0	3-23,2-10/S-1	-0.5
1962	LA-A	10	19	4	8	2	0	2	6	0	1	.421	.421	.842	1263	238	3	0	0	0	.833	-0	/3-5	0.3
1963	LA-A	23	50	1	9	1	0	0	2	9	10	.180	.305	.200	505	48	-3	0	0	0	.952	3	3-13/C-2,1-1	0.0
1964	LA-A	108	255	18	51	9	0	1	17	30	37	.200	.284	.247	531	55	-15	0	2	-1	.917	-2	3-38,1-32,C-25,/S2	-1.9
1965	Cal-A	47	79	8	13	2	0	1	4	10	10	.165	.258	.228	486	40	-6	1	1	-0	1.000	0	3-15,C-12,2-12,/1-3	-0.5
1966	Cal-A	103	226	16	54	5	3	0	24	27	32	.239	.320	.288	608	78	-6	3	3	-0	.991	-9	C-43,1-36,3-25,/2-4	-1.5
1967	Cal-A	90	201	13	45	7	0	4	21	28	25	.224	.319	.318	637	92	-1	1	0	0	.962	-7	3-38,C-23,2-15,/1-5	-0.8
1968	Cal-A	111	297	20	75	9	0	8	35	37	44	.253	.337	.364	701	117	6	0	0	0	.989	-9	C-85,2-14,3-11,/1-1	0.2
1969	Cal-A	41	108	5	28	2	0	1	16	18	15	.259	.370	.306	676	95	0	0	2	-1	1.000	-1	C-36/1-5,2-2	0.0
	Bos-A	47	127	9	24	2	0	0	11	22	12	.189	.318	.205	523	46	-8	0	0	0	.978	-2	C-44	-0.9
	Yr	88	235	14	52	4	0	1	27	40	27	.221	.342	.251	593	68	-8	0	2	-1	.987	-2	C-80/1-5,2-2	-0.9
1970	Bos-A	59	165	21	39	9	1	3	13	21	23	.236	.326	.358	684	83	-4	0	0	0	.985	0	C-51	-0.1
Total	10	674	1623	130	365	53	5	21	157	214	225	.225	.317	.303	620	79	-40	7	8	-1	.987	-26	C-321,3-168/1-83,2S	-5.7

■ LUIS SATURRIA

Saturria, Luis Arturo b: 7/21/76, San Pedro De Macoris, D.R. BR/TR, 6′2″, 165 lbs. Deb: 9/11/2000

YEAR	TM/L	G	AB	R	H	2B	3B	HR	RBI	BB	SO	AVG	OBP	SLG	OPS	OPS+	BR+	SB	CS	SBR	FA	FR	G/POS	TPR
2000	StL-N	12	5	1	0	0	0	0	0	1	3	.000	.167	.000	167	-53	-1	0	0	0	1.000	-3	/O-9(0-5-4)	-0.4

■ FRANK SAUCIER

Saucier, Francis Field b: 5/28/26, Leslie, Mo. BL/TR, 6′1″, 180 lbs. Deb: 7/21/51

YEAR	TM/L	G	AB	R	H	2B	3B	HR	RBI	BB	SO	AVG	OBP	SLG	OPS	OPS+	BR+	SB	CS	SBR	FA	FR	G/POS	TPR
1951	StL-A	18	14	4	1	1	0	0	1	3	4	.071	.278	.143	421	16	-2	0	0	0	.714	-1	/O-3(1-0-2)	-0.2

■ ED SAUER

Sauer, Edward "Horn" b: 1/3/19, Pittsburgh, Pa. d: 7/1/88, Thousand Oaks, Cal BR/TR, 6′1″, 188 lbs. Deb: 9/17/43 F

YEAR	TM/L	G	AB	R	H	2B	3B	HR	RBI	BB	SO	AVG	OBP	SLG	OPS	OPS+	BR+	SB	CS	SBR	FA	FR	G/POS	TPR
1943	Chi-N	14	55	3	15	3	0	0	9	3	6	.273	.322	.327	649	89	-1	1			1.000	2	O-13(13-0-0)	0.0
1944	Chi-N	23	50	3	11	4	0	0	5	2	6	.220	.250	.300	550	55	-3	0			.960	-0	O-12(12-0-0)	-0.4
1945	*Chi-N	49	93	8	24	4	1	2	11	8	23	.258	.317	.387	704	97	-1	2			1.000	-2	O-26(21-2-3)	-0.4
1949	StL-N	24	45	5	10	2	1	0	1	3	8	.222	.271	.311	582	53	-3	0			1.000	-2	O-10(4-0-7)	-0.5
	Bos-N	79	214	26	57	12	0	3	31	17	34	.266	.323	.364	688	89	-4	0			.972	-7	O-71(29-20-25)	-1.3
	Yr	103	259	31	67	14	1	3	32	20	42	.259	.314	.355	669	82	-7	0			.974	-9	O-81(33-20-32)	-1.8
Total	4	189	457	45	117	25	2	5	57	33	77	.256	.309	.352	661	83	-11	3			.981	-9	O-132(79-22-35)	-2.6

■ HANK SAUER

Sauer, Henry John b: 3/17/17, Pittsburgh, Pa. BR/TR, 6′4″, 199 lbs. Deb: 9/9/41 FC Career OF: (1029-LF 0-CF 208-RF)

YEAR	TM/L	G	AB	R	H	2B	3B	HR	RBI	BB	SO	AVG	OBP	SLG	OPS	OPS+	BR+	SB	CS	SBR	FA	FR	G/POS	TPR
1941	Cin-N	9	33	4	10	4	0	0	5	1	4	.303	.324	.424	748	109	0	0			.957	1	/O-8(8-0-0)	0.1
1942	Cin-N	7	20	4	5	0	0	2	4	2	2	.250	.318	.550	868	152	1	0			.976	0	/1-4	0.1
1945	Cin-N	31	116	18	34	1	0	5	20	6	16	.293	.328	.431	759	112	1	2			.972	1	O-28(28-0-0)/1-3	0.1
1948	Cin-N	145	530	78	138	22	1	35	97	60	85	.260	.340	.504	844	130	20	2			.973	4	*O-132(132-0-0),1-12	1.4
1949	Cin-N	42	152	22	36	6	0	4	16	18	19	.237	.318	.355	673	79	-4	0			.956	5	O-39(39-0-0)/1-1	-0.2
	Chi-N	96	357	59	104	17	1	27	83	37	47	.291	.363	.571	934	151	24	0			.981	2	O-96(96-0-0)	1.8
	Yr	138	509	81	140	23	1	31	99	55	66	.275	.349	.507	856	129	19	0			.972	7	*O-135(135-0-0)/1-1	1.6
1950	Chi-N★	145	540	85	148	32	2	32	103	60	67	.274	.350	.519	868	127	19	1			.965	-1	*O-125(125-0-0),1-18	0.7
1951	Chi-N	141	525	77	138	19	4	30	89	45	77	.263	.325	.486	810	113	7	2	1	0	.981	10	*O-132(131-0-1)	0.7

YEAR	TM/L	G	AB	R	H	2B	3B	HR	RBI	BB	SO	AVG	OBP	SLG	OPS	OPS+	BR+	SB	CS	SBR	FA	FR	G/POS	TPR
1952	Chi-N★	151	567	89	153	31	3	**37**	**121**	77	92	.270	.361	.531	892	143	32	1	2	-0	.983	17	*O-151(151-0-0)	3.7
1953	Chi-N	108	395	61	104	16	5	19	60	50	56	.263	.349	.473	822	109	5	0	0	0	.970	3	*O-105(42-0-64)	0.3
1954	Chi-N	142	520	98	150	18	1	41	103	70	68	.288	.379	.563	943	140	30	2	1	0	.963	-2	*O-141(9-0-140)	2.2
1955	Chi-N	79	261	29	55	8	1	12	28	26	47	.211	.287	.387	674	77	-9	0	0	0	.984	-1	O-68(67-0-1)	-1.5
1956	StL-N	75	151	11	45	4	0	5	24	25	31	.298	.408	.424	832	124	6	0	0	0	1.000	-1	O-37(35-0-2)	0.3
1957	NY-N	127	378	46	98	14	1	26	76	49	59	.259	.344	.508	852	126	13	1	0	0	.992	-12	O-98(98-0-0)	-0.4
1958	SF-N	88	236	27	59	8	0	12	46	35	37	.250	.356	.436	793	111	4	0	0	0	.950	-4	O-67(67-0-0)	-0.4
1959	SF-N	13	15	1	1	0	0	1	1	0	7	.067	.067	.267	333	-17	-3	0	0	0	.000	-0	/O-1(1-0-0)	-0.3
Total	15	1399	4796	709	1278	200	19	288	876	561	714	.266	.347	.496	844	123	146	11	4		.974	22	*O-1228L/1-38	8.6
■ **DOUG SAUNDERS**	Saunders, Douglas Long b: 12/13/69, Yorba Linda, Cal. BR/TR, 6', 172 lbs. Deb: 6/13/93																							
1993	NY-N	28	67	8	14	2	0	0	0	3	4	.209	.243	.239	482	30	-7	0	0	0	.956	1	2-22/3-4,S-1	-0.4
■ **RUSTY SAUNDERS**	Saunders, Russell Collier b: 3/12/06, Trenton, N.J. d: 11/24/67, Trenton, N.J. BR/TR, 6'2", 205 lbs. Deb: 9/24/27																							
1927	Phi-A	5	15	2	2	1	0	0	2	3	2	.133	.278	.200	478	24	-2	0	0	0	.818	0	/O-4(4-0-0)	-0.2
■ **AL SAUTERS**	Sauters, Al b: Philadelphia, Pa. Deb: 9/8/1890																							
1890	Phi-a	14	41	1	4	0	0	0	0	11		.098	.288	.098	386	14	-4	0			.850	-4	3-11/O-2(0-2-0),2-2	-0.7
■ **DON SAVAGE**	Savage, Donald Anthony b: 3/5/19, Bloomfield, N.J. d: 12/25/61, Montclair, N.J. BR/TR, 6', 180 lbs. Deb: 4/18/44																							
1944	NY-A	71	239	31	63	7	5	4	24	20	41	.264	.323	.385	708	98	-1	1	1	-0	.946	-10	3-60	-1.1
1945	NY-A	34	58	5	13	1	0	0	3	3	14	.224	.262	.241	504	44	-4	1	0	0	.891	1	3-14/O-2(2-0-0)	-0.3
Total	2	105	297	36	76	8	5	4	27	23	55	.256	.312	.357	668	88	-5	2	1	0	.935	-10	/3-74,O-2(2-0-0)	-1.4
■ **JIMMIE SAVAGE**	Savage, James Harold b: 8/29/1883, Southington, Conn. d: 6/26/40, New Castle, Pa. BB/TR, 5'5", 150 lbs. Deb: 9/3/12 Career OF: (22-LF 5-CF 69-RF)																							
1912	Phi-N	2	3	1	0	0	0	0	0	1	0	.000	.250	.000	250	-27	-1	0			.750	-0	/2-1	-0.1
1914	Pit-F	132	479	81	136	9	9	1	26	67	32	.284	.372	.347	718	97	-7	17			.963	-9	O-93R,3-29,S-11,/2	-1.9
1915	Pit-F	14	21	0	3	0	0	0	0	1	0	.143	.182	.143	325	-8	-3	0			1.000	-1	/O-3(0-0-3),3-1	-0.5
Total	3	148	503	82	139	9	9	1	26	69	32	.276	.364	.336	700	92	-10	17			.964	-10	/O-96R,3-30,S-11,2	-2.5
■ **TED SAVAGE**	Savage, Theodore Edmund (b: Ephesian Savage) b: 2/21/36, Venice, Ill. BR/TR, 6'1", 185 lbs. Deb: 4/9/62 Career OF: (219-LF 81-CF 172-RF)																							
1962	Phi-N	127	335	54	89	11	2	7	39	40	66	.266	.347	.373	721	96	-1	16	5	2	.974	1	*O-109(92-12-10)	-0.4
1963	Pit-N	85	149	22	29	2	1	5	14	14	31	.195	.268	.322	590	69	-6	4	3	-0	.943	-5	O-47(36-9-2)	-1.4
1965	StL-N	30	63	7	10	3	0	1	4	6	9	.159	.232	.254	486	34	-5	1	1	-0	.938	-2	O-20(0-0-20)	-0.9
1966	StL-N	16	29	4	5	2	1	0	3	4	7	.172	.273	.310	583	61	-2	4	0	1	1.000	-1	/O-7(0-2-5)	-0.2
1967	StL-N	9	8	1	1	0	0	0	0	1	3	.125	.222	.125	347	2	-1	0	0	0	.000	0	H	-0.1
	Chi-N	96	225	40	49	10	1	5	33	40	54	.218	.348	.338	686	93	-1	7	6	-1	.979	-5	O-86(0-23-66)/3-1	-1.2
	Yr	105	233	41	50	10	1	5	33	41	57	.215	.344	.330	675	90	-1	7	6	-1	.979	-5	O-86(0-23-66)/3-1	-1.3
1968	Chi-N	3	8	0	2	0	0	0	0	0	1	.250	.250	.250	500	47	-1	0	1	-0	1.000	-1	/O-2(0-1-2)	-0.2
	LA-N	61	126	7	26	6	1	2	7	10	20	.206	.270	.317	588	82	-3	1	2	-0	.985	0	O-39(18-0-24)	-0.6
	Yr	64	134	7	28	6	1	2	7	10	21	.209	.269	.313	582	80	-4	1	3	-1	.986	-1	O-41(18-1-26)	-0.8
1969	Cin-N	68	110	20	25	7	0	2	11	20	27	.227	.346	.345	692	90	-1	3	0	1	.983	-6	O-42(28-12-4)/2-1	-0.8
1970	Mil-A	114	276	43	77	10	5	12	50	57	44	.279	.406	.482	888	143	18	10	6	0	.953	-10	O-82(34-22-33)/1-1	0.5
1971	Mil-A	14	17	2	3	0	0	0	1	5	4	.176	.364	.176	540	58	-1	1	0	0	1.000	-2	/O-6(6-0-1)	-0.3
	KC-A	19	29	2	5	0	0	0	1	3	6	.172	.250	.172	422	22	-3	2	0	0	1.000	-2	/O-9(5-0-5)	-0.5
	Yr	33	46	4	8	0	0	0	2	8	10	.174	.296	.174	470	36	-4	3	0	1	1.000	-3	O-15(11-0-6)	-0.8
Total	9	642	1375	202	321	51	11	34	163	200	272	.233	.335	.361	696	94	-6	49	24	2	.970	-32	O-449L/1-1,2-1,3-1	-6.1
■ **BOB SAVERINE**	Saverine, Robert Paul "Rabbit" b: 6/2/41, Norwalk, Conn. BB/TR, 5'9", 165 lbs. Deb: 9/12/59 Career OF: (8-LF 60-CF 4-RF)																							
1959	Bal-A	1	0	1	0	0	0	0	0	0	0	—	—	—	—	—	0	0	0	0	.000	0	R	0.0
1962	Bal-A	8	21	2	5	2	0	0	3	1	3	.238	.273	.333	606	66	-1	0	2	-1	1.000	2	/2-7	0.0
1963	Bal-A	115	167	21	39	1	2	1	12	25	44	.234	.333	.281	615	77	-4	8	3	1	.976	-9	O-59C,2-19,S-13	-1.1
1964	Bal-A	46	34	14	5	1	0	0	0	3	6	.147	.216	.176	393	11	-4	3	1	0	1.000	5	S-15/O-2(0-2-0)	0.1
1966	Was-A	120	406	54	102	10	4	5	24	27	62	.251	.301	.333	634	83	-9	4	3	-0	.972	-19	2-70,3-26,S-11,/O-9L	-2.3
1967	Was-A	89	233	22	55	13	0	0	8	17	34	.236	.288	.292	580	75	-7	8	0	2	.957	-20	2-48,S-10/3-8,O-2L	-2.4
Total	6	379	861	114	206	27	6	6	47	73	149	.239	.300	.305	606	76	-26	23	9	2	.971	-40	2-144/O-72C,S-49,3	-5.7
■ **CARL SAWATSKI**	Sawatski, Carl Ernest "Swats" b: 11/4/27, Shickshinny, Pa. d: 11/24/91, Little Rock, Ark. BL/TR, 5'10", 210 lbs. Deb: 9/29/48																							
1948	Chi-N	2	2	0	0	0	0	0	0	0	0	.000	.000	.000	0	-99	-1	0			.000	0	H	-0.1
1950	Chi-N	38	103	4	18	1	0	1	7	11	19	.175	.254	.214	468	25	-11	0			.983	-1	C-32	-1.1
1953	Chi-N	43	59	5	13	3	0	1	5	7	7	.220	.303	.322	625	62	-3	0	0	0	.943	-1	C-15	-0.3
1954	Chi-A	43	109	6	20	3	3	1	12	15	20	.183	.282	.294	576	56	-7	0	0	0	.987	0	C-33	-0.5
1957	*Mil-N	58	105	13	25	4	0	6	17	10	15	.238	.316	.448	764	110	1	0	0	0	.986	6	C-28	0.9
1958	Mil-N	10	10	1	1	0	0	0	1	2	5	.100	.250	.100	350	-3	-1	0	0	0	1.000	1	/C-3	-0.1
	Phi-N	60	183	12	42	4	1	5	12	16	42	.230	.302	.344	646	72	-8	0	0	0	.986	-3	C-53	-0.9
	Yr	70	193	13	43	4	1	5	13	18	47	.223	.299	.332	631	68	-9	0	0	0	.987	-3	C-56	-1.0
1959	Phi-N	74	198	15	58	10	0	9	43	32	36	.293	.394	.480	874	129	9	0	0	0	.979	-14	C-69	-0.2
1960	StL-N	78	179	16	41	4	0	6	27	22	24	.229	.313	.352	665	75	-6	0	0	0	.993	-7	C-67	-1.1
1961	StL-N	86	174	23	52	8	0	10	33	25	17	.299	.387	.517	904	125	7	0	0	0	.996	-7	C-60/O-1(0-1-0)	0.2
1962	StL-N	85	222	26	56	9	1	13	42	36	38	.252	.357	.477	834	111	4	0	0	0	.997	-1	C-70	0.6
1963	StL-N	56	105	12	25	0	0	6	14	15	28	.238	.333	.410	743	103	1	2	0	0	.986	-5	C-27	-0.3
Total	11	633	1449	133	351	46	5	58	213	191	251	.242	.333	.401	734	92	-15	2	0		.988	-32	C-457/O-1(0-1-0)	-2.9
■ **CARL SAWYER**	Sawyer, Carl Everett "Huck" b: 10/19/1890, Seattle, Wash. d: 1/17/57, Los Angeles, Cal. BR/TR, 5'11", 160 lbs. Deb: 9/11/15																							
1915	Was-A	10	32	8	8	1	0	0	3	4	5	.250	.351	.281	633	88	-0	2			.964	-2	/2-6,S-4	-0.2
1916	Was-A	16	31	3	6	1	0	0	2	4	4	.194	.306	.226	531	60	-1	3			.963	2	/2-6,S-5,3-1	0.1
Total	2	26	63	11	14	2	0	0	5	8	9	.222	.329	.254	583	74	-2	5			.964	-1	/2-12,S-9,3-1	-0.1
■ **DAVE SAX**	Sax, David John b: 9/22/58, Sacramento, Cal. BR/TR, 6', 185 lbs. Deb: 9/1/82 F																							
1982	LA-N	2	2	0	0	0	0	0	0	0	0	.000	.000	.000	0	-99	-1	0	0	0	1.000	-0	/O-1(1-0-0)	-0.1
1983	LA-N	7	8	0	0	0	0	0	1	0	0	.000	.000	.000	0	-99	-2	0	0	0	.917	-0	/C-4	-0.2
1985	Bos-A	22	36	2	11	3	0	0	6	3	3	.306	.359	.389	748	101	0	0	1	-0	.985	-2	C-16/O-4(2-0-2)	-0.2
1986	Bos-A	4	11	1	5	1	0	1	1	0	1	.455	.455	.818	1273	237	2	0	0	0	1.000	-1	/C-2,1-1	0.1
1987	Bos-A	2	3	0	0	0	0	0	0	0	1	.000	.000	.000	0	-97	-1	0	0	0	1.000	1	/C-2	0.0
Total	5	37	60	3	16	4	0	1	8	3	5	.267	.302	.383	685	84	-1	0	1	-0	.980	-2	/C-24,O-5(3-0-2),1-1	-0.4
■ **OLLIE SAX**	Sax, Erik Oliver b: 11/5/04, Branford, Conn. d: 3/21/82, Newark, N.J. BR/TR, 5'8", 164 lbs. Deb: 4/13/28																							
1928	StL-A	16	17	4	3	0	0	0	0	5	3	.176	.364	.176	540	45	-1	0	0	0	.955	3	/3-9	0.2
■ **STEVE SAX**	Sax, Stephen Louis b: 1/29/60, Sacramento, Cal. BR/TR, 5'11", 185 lbs. Deb: 8/18/81 F Career OF: (27-LF 0-CF 6-RF)																							
1981	*LA-N	31	119	15	33	2	0	2	9	7	14	.277	.317	.345	662	91	-2	5	7	-1	.975	2	2-29	0.1
1982	LA-N★	150	638	88	180	23	7	4	47	49	53	.282	.335	.359	694	97	-3	49	19	4	.977	-9	*2-149	0.1
1983	*LA-N★	155	623	94	175	18	5	5	41	58	73	.281	.343	.350	693	93	-5	56	30	2	.961	-30	*2-152	-2.5
1984	LA-N	145	569	70	138	24	4	1	35	47	53	.243	.301	.304	606	71	-21	34	19	1	.973	12	*2-141	-0.1
1985	*LA-N	136	488	62	136	8	4	1	42	54	43	.279	.354	.318	672	92	-3	27	11	2	.969	-9	*2-135/3-1	-0.3
1986	LA-N★	157	633	91	210	43	4	6	56	59	58	.332	.391	.441	832	139	34	40	17	3	.980	-5	*2-154	4.1
1987	LA-N	157	610	84	171	22	7	6	46	44	61	.280	.332	.369	701	88	-11	37	11	4	.982	1	*2-152/3-1,O-1(1-0-0)	0.3
1988	*LA-N	160	632	70	175	19	4	5	57	45	51	.277	.326	.343	669	95	-4	42	12	5	.981	-19	*2-158	-1.5
1989	NY-A★	158	651	88	205	26	3	5	63	52	44	.315	.366	.387	754	114	13	43	17	4	**.987**	-10	*2-158	1.1
1990	NY-A★	155	615	70	160	24	2	4	42	49	46	.260	.319	.325	644	80	-16	43	9	6	.987	-13	*2-154	-1.9
1991	NY-A	158	652	85	198	38	2	10	56	41	38	.304	.348	.414	762	110	8	31	11	3	.990	-7	*2-149/3-5,D-4	0.8
1992	Chi-A	143	567	74	134	26	4	4	47	43	42	.236	.292	.317	610	72	-22	30	12	2	.972	-28	*2-141/D-1	-4.5

YEAR	TM/L	G	AB	R	H	2B	3B	HR	RBI	BB	SO	AVG	OBP	SLG	OPS	OPS+	BR+	SB	CS	SBR	FA	FR	G/POS	TPR
1993	Chi-A	57	119	20	28	5	0	1	8	8	6	.235	.283	.303	586	59	-7	7	3	0	1.000	-5	O-32(26-0-6),D-21/2-1	-1.3
1994	Oak-A	7	24	2	6	0	1	0	1	0	2	.250	.250	.333	583	53	-2	0	0	0	1.000	2	/2-6	0.1
Total	14	1769	6940	913	1949	278	47	54	550	556	584	.281	.336	.358	694	95	-40	444	178	35	.978	-117	*2-1679/O-33L,D-26,3	-5.5
■ **JIMMY SAY**	Say, James I. b: 1862, Baltimore, Md. d: 6/23/1894, Baltimore, Md. Deb: 7/22/1882 F																							
1882	Lou-a	1	4	1	1	0	0	0		0		.250	.250	.250	500	73	-0				.333	-1	/3-1	-0.1
	Phi-a	22	82	12	17	2	0	1		1		.207	.217	.268	485	56	-4				.884	1	S-22	-0.2
	Yr	23	86	13	18	2	0	1		1		.209	.218	.267	486	57	-4				.884	0	S-22/3-1	-0.3
1884	Wil-U	16	59	3	13	1	2	0		1		.220	.233	.305	538	60	-5				.733	-3	3-16	-0.7
	KC-U	2	8	0	2	0	0	0		0		.250	.250	.250	500	60	-1				.200	-2	/3-2	-0.3
	Yr	18	67	3	15	1	2	0		1		.224	.235	.299	534	60	-5				.680	-5	3-18	-1.0
1887	Cle-a	16	65	9	25	5	3	0	12	1		.385	.385	.547	931	163	5	0			.714	-4	3-16	0.1
Total	3	57	218	25	58	8	5	1	12	3		.266	.273	.359	632	90	-5	0			.690	-9	/3-35,S-22	-1.2
■ **LOU SAY**	Say, Louis I. b: 2/4/1854, Baltimore, Md. d: 6/5/30, Fallston, Md. BR/TR, 5'7", 145 lbs. Deb: 4/14/1873 F																							
1873	Mar-n	3	12	1	2	0	0	0	2	0	0	.167	.167	.167	333	-1	-1	0	0	0	.667	1	/S-2,O-1(0-0-1)	0.0
1874	Bal-n	18	66	4	14	3	0	0	5	0	1	.212	.212	.258	470	50	-3	0	0	0	.786	12	S-18	0.6
1875	Was-n	11	38	4	10	0	0	0	2	0	7	.263	.263	.263	526	87	-0	0	0	0	.698	-1	/S-8,2-2,O-1(0-1-0)	-0.1
1880	Cin-N	48	191	14	38	8	1	0	15	4	31	.199	.215	.251	467	58	-8				.832	1	S-48	-0.5
1882	Phi-a	49	199	35	45	4	3	1	28	8		.226	.256	.291	547	75	-6				.867	6	S-49	0.2
1883	Bal-a	74	324	52	83	13	2	1		10		.256	.278	.318	596	89	-4				.794	7	*S-74	0.4
1884	Bal-U	78	339	65	81	14	2	2		11		.239	.263	.310	573	66	-24				.795	2	*S-78	-1.8
	KC-U	17	70	6	14	2	0	1		2		.200	.222	.271	494	56	-6				.860	9	S-16/2-1	0.3
	Yr	95	409	71	95	16	2	3		13		.232	.256	.303	559	65	-30				.808	10	S-94/2-1	-1.5
Total	3 n	32	116	9	26	3	0	0	9	0	8	.224	.224	.250	474	57	-5	0	0	0	.750	12	/S-28,2-2,O-2(0-1-1)	0.5
Total	4	266	1123	172	261	41	8	5	43	35	31	.232	.256	.297	552	72	-48				.820	24	S-265/2-1	-1.4
■ **JERRY SCALA**	Scala, Gerard Michael b: 9/27/24, Bayonne, N.J. d: 12/14/93, Fallston, Md. BL/TR, 5'11", 178 lbs. Deb: 4/22/48																							
1948	Chi-A	3	6	1	0	0	0	0	0	0	3	.000	.000	.000	0	-99	-2	0	0	0	1.000	-0	/O-2(0-2-0)	-0.2
1949	Chi-A	37	120	17	30	7	1	1	13	17	19	.250	.348	.350	698	88	-2	3	3	-0	.988	-3	O-37(2-35-0)	-0.6
1950	Chi-A	40	67	8	13	2	1	0	6	10	10	.194	.299	.254	552	44	-6	0	0	0	1.000	-4	O-23(1-22-0)	-0.9
Total	3	80	193	26	43	9	2	1	19	27	32	.223	.321	.306	627	67	-9	3	3	-0	.993	-7	/O-62(3-59-0)	-1.7
■ **SKEETER SCALZI**	Scalzi, Frank John b: 6/16/13, Lafferty, Ohio d: 8/25/84, Pittsburgh, Pa. BR/TR, 5'6", 160 lbs. Deb: 7/21/39																							
1939	NY-N	11	18	3	6	0	0	0	0	3	2	.333	.429	.333	762	106	0	1			.875	2	/S-5,3-1	0.3
■ **JOHNNY SCALZI**	Scalzi, John Anthony b: 3/22/07, Stamford, Conn. d: 9/27/62, Port Chester, N.Y BR/TR, 5'7", 170 lbs. Deb: 6/19/31																							
1931	Bos-N	2	1	0	0	0	0	0	0	0	1	.000	.000	.000	0	-99	-0	0			.000	0	H	0.0
■ **MORT SCANLAN**	Scanlan, Mortimer J. b: 3/18/1861, Chicago, Ill. d: 12/29/28, Chicago, Ill. 6'1", 186 lbs. Deb: 4/21/1890																							
1890	NY-N	3	10	0	0	0	0	0	0	2	5	.000	.167	.000	167	-50	-2	1			1.000	-0	/1-3	-0.2
■ **PATRICK SCANLAN**	Scanlan, Patrick J. b: 3/25/1861, Nova Scotia, Can. d: 7/17/13, Springfield, Mass. Deb: 7/4/1884																							
1884	Bos-U	6	24	2	7	1	0	0		0		.292	.292	.333	625	90	-1				.800	0	/O-6(6-0-0)	-0.1
■ **PAT SCANLON**	Scanlon, James Patrick b: 9/23/52, Minneapolis, Minn. BL/TR, 6', 180 lbs. Deb: 9/27/74 Career OF: (1-LF 0-CF 0-RF)																							
1974	Mon-N	2	4	1	1	0	0	0	0	0	1	.250	.250	.250	500	38	-0	0	0	0	1.000	1	/3-1	0.0
1975	Mon-N	60	109	5	20	3	1	2	15	17	25	.183	.294	.284	578	58	-6	0	1	-0	.957	2	3-28/1-1	-0.5
1976	Mon-N	11	27	2	5	1	0	1	2	2	5	.185	.241	.333	575	59	-2	0	0	0	.842	-1	/3-7,1-1	-0.3
1977	SD-N	47	79	9	15	3	0	1	11	12	20	.190	.297	.266	563	58	-5	0	0	0	.957	-5	2-15,3-11/O-1(1-0-0)	-0.9
Total	4	120	219	17	41	7	1	4	28	31	51	.187	.288	.283	571	58	-12	0	1	-0	.938	-3	/3-47,2-15,1-2,O-1L	-1.7
■ **RUSS SCARRITT**	Scarritt, Stephen Russell Mallory b: 1/14/03, Pensacola, Fla. d: 12/4/94, Pensacola, Fla. BL/TR, 5'10.5", 165 lbs. Deb: 4/18/29																							
1929	Bos-A	151	540	69	159	26	17	1	71	34	38	.294	.337	.411	749	94	-6	13	11	-1	.944	1	*O-145(134-1-10)	-1.6
1930	Bos-A	113	447	48	129	17	8	2	48	12	49	.289	.312	.376	688	76	-17	4	7	-2	.967	4	*O-110(110-0-0)	-2.1
1931	Bos-A	10	39	2	6	1	0	0	1	2	2	.154	.195	.179	375	-1	-6	0	0	0	1.000	1	/O-9(9-0-0)	-0.5
1932	Phi-N	11	11	0	2	0	0	0	0	1	2	.182	.250	.182	432	16	-1	0			1.000	-0	/O-1(1-0-0)	-0.1
Total	4	285	1037	119	296	44	25	3	120	49	91	.285	.320	.385	705	82	-30	17	18		.956	6	O-265(254-1-10)	-4.3
■ **LES SCARSELLA**	Scarsella, Leslie George b: 11/23/13, Santa Cruz, Cal. d: 12/17/58, San Francisco, Cal BL/TL, 5'11", 185 lbs. Deb: 9/15/35																							
1935	Cin-N	6	10	4	2	1	0	0	0	3	1	.200	.385	.300	685	89	0	0			1.000	1	/1-2	0.0
1936	Cin-N	115	485	63	152	21	9	3	65	14	36	.313	.335	.412	748	107	3	6			.989	2	*1-115	-0.6
1937	Cin-N	110	329	35	81	11	4	3	34	17	26	.246	.285	.331	617	70	-14	5			.984	-5	1-65,O-14(12-0-2)	-2.6
1939	Cin-N	16	14	0	2	0	0	0	2	0	2	.143	.143	.143	286	-23	-2	0			.000	0	H	-0.2
1940	Bos-N	18	60	7	18	1	3	0	8	3	5	.300	.344	.417	760	115	1	2			.986	-1	1-15	-0.1
Total	5	265	898	109	255	34	16	6	109	37	70	.284	.315	.378	693	92	-12	13			.988	-4	1-197/O-14(12-0-2)	-3.5
■ **STEVE SCARSONE**	Scarsone, Steven Wayne b: 4/11/66, Anaheim, Cal. BR/TR, 6'2", 195 lbs. Deb: 5/15/92 Career OF: (1-LF 1-CF 0-RF)																							
1992	Phi-N	7	13	1	2	0	0	0	0	1	6	.154	.214	.154	368	6	-2	0	0	0	1.000	-2	/2-3	-0.4
	Bal-A	11	17	2	3	0	0	0	0	1	6	.176	.222	.176	399	13	-2	0	0	0	.889	-1	/2-5,3-2,S-1	-0.3
1993	SF-N	44	103	16	26	9	0	2	15	4	32	.252	.280	.398	678	82	-3	0	1	-0	1.000	-5	2-20/3-8,1-6	-0.8
1994	SF-N	52	103	21	28	8	0	2	13	10	20	.272	.336	.408	744	97	-0	0	2	-1	.990	9	2-22/3-8,1-6,S-1	0.9
1995	SF-N	80	233	33	62	10	3	11	29	18	82	.266	.335	.476	811	114	4	3	2	-0	.927	-5	3-50,2-13,1-11	-0.1
1996	SF-N	105	283	28	62	12	1	5	23	25	91	.219	.287	.322	609	63	-16	2	3	-1	.973	-4	2-74,3-14/1-1,S-1	-1.7
1997	StL-N	5	10	0	1	0	0	0	0	2	5	.100	.250	.100	350	-4	-2	1	0	0	1.000	-3	/2-2,O-2(1-1-0),3-1	-0.4
1999	KC-A	46	68	2	14	5	0	0	6	9	24	.206	.299	.279	578	48	-5	1	0	0	.977	3	S-16,1-12/2-9,3D	-0.1
Total	7	350	830	103	198	44	4	20	86	70	266	.239	.304	.373	677	80	-25	7	8	-1	.975	-8	2-148/3-86,1-36,SDO	-2.9
■ **PAUL SCHAAL**	Schaal, Paul b: 3/3/43, Pittsburgh, Pa. BR/TR, 5'11", 180 lbs. Deb: 9/3/64																							
1964	LA-A	17	32	3	4	0	0	0	0	2	5	.125	.176	.125	301	-16	-5	0	1	-0	1.000	-1	/2-9,3-9	-0.6
1965	Cal-A	155	483	48	108	12	2	9	45	61	88	.224	.312	.313	625	80	-12	6	3	0	.970	-10	*3-153/2-1	-2.4
1966	Cal-A	138	386	59	94	15	7	6	24	68	56	.244	.364	.365	729	113	9	6	4	-0	.948	-2	*3-131	0.7
1967	Cal-A	99	272	31	51	9	1	6	20	38	39	.188	.289	.294	584	76	-8	2	2	-0	.970	-2	3-88/S-2,2-1	-1.2
1968	Cal-A	60	219	22	46	7	1	2	16	29	25	.210	.308	.279	587	82	-4	5	7	-1	.958	9	3-58	0.4
1969	KC-A	61	205	22	54	6	0	1	13	25	27	.263	.349	.307	656	84	-3	2	1	0	.897	-19	3-49/2-6,S-6	-2.3
1970	KC-A	124	380	50	102	12	3	5	35	43	39	.268	.344	.355	700	93	-3	7	4	0	.938	-16	3-97,S-10/2-6	-1.9
1971	KC-A	161	548	80	150	31	6	11	63	103	51	.274	.391	.412	803	129	25	7	5	-0	.940	-12	*3-161	1.2
1972	KC-A	127	435	47	99	19	3	6	41	61	59	.228	.325	.326	652	95	-1	1	3	-1	.947	-16	*3-123/S-1	-2.2
1973	KC-A	121	396	61	114	14	3	8	42	63	45	.288	.392	.399	791	114	10	5	6	-1	.913	-12	*3-121	-0.4
1974	KC-A	12	34	3	6	2	0	1	4	5	5	.176	.300	.324	624	75	-1	0	0	0	.949	1	3-12	0.0
	Cal-A	53	165	10	41	5	0	2	20	18	27	.248	.322	.315	638	89	-2	2	2	-0	.903	-10	3-51	-1.3
	Yr	65	199	13	47	7	0	3	24	23	32	.236	.318	.317	635	86	-3	2	2	-0	.914	-9	3-63	-1.3
Total	11	1128	3555	436	869	132	26	57	323	516	466	.244	.344	.344	688	98	5	43	38	-4	.943	-91	*3-1053/2-23,S-19	-10.0
■ **GERMANY SCHAEFER**	Schaefer, Herman A. b: 2/4/1877, Chicago, Ill. d: 5/16/19, Saranac Lake, N.Y. BR/TR, 5'9", 175 lbs. Deb: 10/5/01 Career OF: (18-LF 13-CF 46-RF)																							
1901	Chi-N	2	5	0	3	1	0	0	0	2		.600	.714	.800	1514	352	2	0			1.000	1	/2-1,3-1	0.3
1902	Chi-N	81	291	32	57	2	3	0	14	19		.196	.250	.223	473	48	-18	12			.864	-8	3-75/1-3,O-2R,S-1	-2.6
1905	Det-A	153	554	64	135	17	9	2	47	45		.244	.302	.318	619	96	-3	19			.955	8	*2-151/S-3	0.7
1906	Det-A	124	446	48	106	14	3	2	42	32		.238	.290	.296	586	81	-10	31			.948	9	*2-114/S-7	0.0
1907	*Det-A	109	372	44	96	12	3	1	32	30		.258	.313	.315	628	97	-1	21			.961	-5	2-74,S-18,3-14,/O-1R	-0.5
1908	*Det-A	153	584	96	151	20	10	3	52	37		.259	.304	.342	646	106	2	40			.918	4	S-68,2-58,3-29	1.1
1909	Det-A	87	280	26	70	12	0	0	22	14		.250	.286	.293	579	79	-7	12			.966	14	2-86/O-1(0-0-1)	0.8

YEAR	TM/L	G	AB	R	H	2B	3B	HR	RBI	BB	SO	AVG	OBP	SLG	OPS	OPS+	BR+	SB	CS	SBR	FA	FR	G/POS	TPR
	Was-A	37	128	13	31	5	1	1	4	6		.242	.281	.320	602	94	-1	2			.941	0	2-32/3-1	-0.1
	Yr	124	408	39	101	17	1	1	26	20		.248	.284	.301	586	84	-8	14			.960	14	*2-118/O-1(0-0-1),3-1	0.7
1910	Was-A	74	229	27	63	6	5	0	14	25		.275	.352	.345	697	124	7	17			.953	-1	2-35,O-26(8-13-5)/3-2	0.6
1911	Was-A	125	440	73	147	14	7	0	45	57		.334	.412	.398	809	129	19	22			.980	0	*1-108/O-7(7-0-0)	1.6
1912	Was-A	60	166	21	41	7	3	0	19	23		.247	.342	.325	667	90	-2	11			.900	-11	O-19R,1-15,2-15,/P	-1.4
1913	Was-A	54	100	17	32	1	1	0	7	15	12	.320	.419	.350	769	123	4	6			.926	-2	2-16/1-6,3-2,P-1,O	0.2
1914	Was-A	30	29	6	7	1	0	0	2	3	5	.241	.313	.276	588	74	-1	4	1	1	1.000	0	/2-3,O-3(0-0-3)	0.0
1915	New-F	59	154	26	33	5	3	0	8	25	11	.214	.328	.286	613	78	-6	3			.952	-1	O-17R,1-13/3-9,2-2	-0.9
1916	NY-A	1	1	0	0	0	0	0	0	0	0	.000	.000	.000	0	-98	-0	0			.000	0	/O-1	0.0
1918	Cle-A	1	5	2	0	0	0	0	0	0	0	.000	.000	.000	0	-91	-1	1			1.000	-0	/2-1	-0.2
Total	15	1150	3784	495	972	117	48	9	308	333	28	.257	.319	.320	639	96	-15	201	1		.954	6	2-588,1-145,3/SOP	-0.4

■ **JEFF SCHAEFER** Schaefer, Jeffrey Scott b: 5/31/60, Patchogue, N.Y. BR/TR, 5'10", 170 lbs. Deb: 4/7/89

YEAR	TM/L	G	AB	R	H	2B	3B	HR	RBI	BB	SO	AVG	OBP	SLG	OPS	OPS+	BR+	SB	CS	SBR	FA	FR	G/POS	TPR
1989	Chi-A	15	10	2	1	0	0	0	0	0	2	.100	.100	.100	200	-45	-2	1	1	-0	.900	1	/S-5,2-4,3-4,D-1	-0.1
1990	Sea-A	55	107	11	22	3	0	0	6	3	11	.206	.241	.234	475	33	-10	4	1	1	.933	11	3-26,S-24/2-3	0.4
1991	Sea-A	84	164	19	41	7	1	1	11	5	25	.250	.272	.323	595	64	-8	3	1	0	.968	2	S-46,3-30,2-11,/D-1	-0.3
1992	Sea-A	65	70	5	8	2	0	1	3	2	10	.114	.139	.186	325	-10	-10	0	1	-0	.922	14	S-33,3-21/2-7,D-2	0.5
1994	Oak-A	6	8	0	1	0	0	0	0	0	1	.125	.125	.125	250	-39	-2	0	0	0	.800	-1	/3-3,S-2,1-1	-0.2
Total	5	225	359	37	73	12	1	2	20	10	49	.203	.229	.259	488	35	-32	8	4	0	.957	28	S-110/3-84,2-25,D1	0.3

■ **HARRY SCHAFER** Schafer, Harry C. "Silk Stocking" b: 8/14/1846, Philadelphia, Pa. d: 2/28/35, Philadelphia, Pa. BR/TR, 5'9.5", 143 lbs. Deb: 5/5/1871 NA OF: (18-LF 1-CF 0-RF) Career OF: (1-LF 0-CF 24-RF)

YEAR	TM/L	G	AB	R	H	2B	3B	HR	RBI	BB	SO	AVG	OBP	SLG	OPS	OPS+	BR+	SB	CS	SBR	FA	FR	G/POS	TPR
1871	Bos-n	31	149	38	42	7	5	0	28	3	1	.282	.296	.396	692	94	-2	13	4	1	.684	3	*3-31	0.1
1872	Bos-n	48	225	51	65	10	4	1	37	0	8	.289	.289	.382	671	99	-2	2	0	0	.795	4	*3-43/O-5(5-0-0),C-2	0.1
1873	Bos-n	60	295	65	79	12	3	2	46	3	1	.268	.275	.349	624	78	-10	3	4	-1	.732	-15	*3-47,O-13(13-0-0)	-1.9
1874	Bos-n	71	327	69	87	10	2	1	45	1	5	.266	.268	.318	586	83	-7	2	4	-1	.785	6	*3-71/S-1	-0.4
1875	Bos-n	52	222	49	64	9	0	0	17	1	8	.288	.291	.329	620	111	2	3	2	-0	.795	3	*3-51/O-1(0-1-0)	0.3
1876	Bos-N	70	290	47	72	11	0	0	35	4	11	.248	.262	.290	552	82	-5				.810	3	*3-70	0.0
1877	Bos-N	33	141	20	39	5	2	0	13	0	7	.277	.277	.340	617	90	-2				.621	-12	O-23(1-0-22)/3-9,S-1	-1.2
1878	Bos-N	2	8	0	1	0	0	0	0	0	1	.125	.125	.125	250	-16	-1				1.000	-1	/O-2(0-0-2)	-0.1
Total	5 n	262	1218	272	337	48	14	4	173	8	23	.277	.281	.349	630	91	-19	23	14	0	.764	0	3-243/O-19L,C-2,S-1	-1.8
Total	3	105	439	67	112	16	2	0	48	4	19	.255	.264	.303	568	83	-8				.810	-9	/3-79,O-25R,S-1	-1.3

■ **JIMMIE SCHAFFER** Schaffer, Jimmie Ronald b: 4/5/36, Limeport, Pa. BR/TR, 5'9", 185 lbs. Deb: 5/20/61 C

YEAR	TM/L	G	AB	R	H	2B	3B	HR	RBI	BB	SO	AVG	OBP	SLG	OPS	OPS+	BR+	SB	CS	SBR	FA	FR	G/POS	TPR
1961	StL-N	68	153	15	39	7	0	1	16	9	29	.255	.301	.320	621	59	-9	0	0	0	.996	4	C-68	-0.3
1962	StL-N	70	66	7	16	2	1	0	6	6	16	.242	.306	.303	609	58	-4	1	0	0	.993	7	C-69	0.4
1963	Chi-N	57	142	17	34	7	0	7	19	11	35	.239	.294	.437	731	102	0	0	0	0	.996	1	C-54	0.3
1964	Chi-N	54	122	9	25	6	1	2	9	17	17	.205	.307	.320	627	74	-4	2	4	-1	.970	-8	C-43	-1.1
1965	Chi-A	17	31	2	6	3	1	0	1	3	4	.194	.265	.355	620	79	-1	0	0	0	1.000	3	C-14	0.2
	NY-N	24	37	0	5	2	0	0	0	1	15	.135	.158	.189	347	-3	-5	0	0	0	.968	-1	C-21	-0.5
1966	Phi-N	8	15	2	2	1	0	1	4	1	7	.133	.188	.400	588	58	-1	0	0	0	.952	-1	/C-6	-0.1
1967	Phi-N	2	2	1	0	0	0	0	0	1	1	.000	.333	.000	333	3	-0	0	0	0	1.000	0	/C-1	0.0
1968	Cin-N	4	6	0	1	0	0	0	1	0	3	.167	.167	.167	333	0	-1	0	0	0	1.000	-1	/C-2	-0.2
Total	8	304	574	53	128	28	3	11	56	49	127	.223	.286	.340	626	69	-24	3	4	-1	.989	5	C-278	-1.3

■ **JOHNNY SCHAIVE** Schaive, John Edward b: 2/25/34, Springfield, Ill. BR/TR, 5'8", 175 lbs. Deb: 9/19/58

YEAR	TM/L	G	AB	R	H	2B	3B	HR	RBI	BB	SO	AVG	OBP	SLG	OPS	OPS+	BR+	SB	CS	SBR	FA	FR	G/POS	TPR
1958	Was-A	7	24	1	6	0	0	0	1	1	4	.250	.280	.250	530	48	-2	0	0	0	1.000	-1	/2-6	-0.2
1959	Was-A	16	59	3	9	2	0	0	2	0	7	.153	.167	.186	353	-3	-8	0	0	0	.977	4	2-16	-0.3
1960	Was-A	6	12	1	3	1	0	0	0	0	3	.250	.250	.333	583	57	-1	0	0	0	.917	-0	/2-4	-0.1
1962	Was-A	82	225	20	57	15	1	6	29	6	25	.253	.273	.409	682	81	-7	0	1	-0	.967	4	3-49/2-6	-0.3
1963	Was-A	3	3	0	0	0	0	0	0	0	1	.000	.000	.000	0	-99	-1	0	0	0	.000	0	H	-0.1
Total	5	114	323	25	75	18	1	6	32	7	40	.232	.251	.350	601	61	-18	0	1	-0	.980	7	/3-49,2-32	-1.0

■ **ROY SCHALK** Schalk, Le Roy John b: 11/9/08, Chicago, Ill. d: 3/11/90, Gainesville, Tex. BR/TR, 5'10", 168 lbs. Deb: 9/17/32

YEAR	TM/L	G	AB	R	H	2B	3B	HR	RBI	BB	SO	AVG	OBP	SLG	OPS	OPS+	BR+	SB	CS	SBR	FA	FR	G/POS	TPR
1932	NY-A	3	12	3	3	1	0	0	0	2	2	.250	.357	.333	690	84	-0	0	0	0	.867	-2	/2-3	-0.1
1944	Chi-A	146	587	47	129	14	4	1	44	45	52	.220	.276	.262	539	55	-34	5	4	-0	.964	-14	*2-142/S-5	-4.3
1945	Chi-A	133	513	50	127	23	1	1	65	32	41	.248	.293	.302	595	75	-17	3	6	-1	.977	6	*2-133	-0.6
Total	3	282	1112	100	259	38	5	2	109	79	95	.233	.285	.281	566	64	-52	8	10	-2	.970	-9	2-278/S-5	-5.0

■ **RAY SCHALK** Schalk, Raymond William "Cracker" b: 8/12/1892, Harvey, Ill. d: 5/19/70, Chicago, Ill. BR/TR, 5'9", 165 lbs. Deb: 8/11/12 MCH

YEAR	TM/L	G	AB	R	H	2B	3B	HR	RBI	BB	SO	AVG	OBP	SLG	OPS	OPS+	BR+	SB	CS	SBR	FA	FR	G/POS	TPR
1912	Chi-A	23	63	7	18	2	0	0	8	3		.286	.357	.317	675	96	-0	2			.917	4	C-23	0.5
1913	Chi-A	129	401	38	98	15	5	1	38	27	36	.244	.297	.314	611	80	-11	14			.980	-1	*C-125	-0.1
1914	Chi-A	136	392	30	106	13	2	0	36	38	24	.270	.347	.314	661	100	1	24	11	1	.974	6	*C-125	2.1
1915	Chi-A	135	413	46	110	14	4	1	54	62	21	.266	.366	.327	693	104	4	15	18	-3	**.984**	-3	*C-134	1.0
1916	Chi-A	129	410	36	95	12	9	0	41	41	31	.232	.311	.305	616	84	-8	30	13	2	**.988**	9	*C-124	1.5
1917	*Chi-A	140	424	48	96	12	5	2	51	59	27	.226	.331	.292	623	88	-4	19			.981	5	*C-139	1.5
1918	Chi-A	108	333	35	73	6	3	0	22	36	22	.219	.301	.255	556	67	-12	12			.978	-4	*C-106	-0.8
1919	*Chi-A	131	394	57	111	9	3	0	34	51	25	.282	.367	.320	687	93	-1	11			.981	1	*C-129	1.1
1920	Chi-A	151	485	64	131	25	5	1	61	68	19	.270	.362	.348	711	89	-6	10	4	1	**.986**	-1	*C-151	0.7
1921	Chi-A	128	416	32	105	24	4	0	47	40	36	.252	.328	.329	658	69	-19	3	4	-1	**.985**	8	*C-126	-0.4
1922	Chi-A	142	442	57	124	22	3	4	60	67	36	.281	.379	.371	750	97	0	12	4	1	**.989**	20	*C-142	3.0
1923	Chi-A	123	382	42	87	12	2	1	44	39	28	.228	.306	.277	583	55	-24	7	4	0	.983	5	*C-121	-1.1
1924	Chi-A	57	153	15	30	4	2	1	11	21	10	.196	.301	.268	569	49	-12	1	5	-2	.959	6	C-56	-0.3
1925	Chi-A	125	343	44	94	18	1	0	52	57	27	.274	.382	.332	714	87	-4	11	5	1	.983	3	*C-125	0.7
1926	Chi-A	82	226	26	60	9	1	0	32	27	11	.265	.349	.314	663	77	-7	5	1	1	.977	-6	C-80	-0.8
1927	Chi-A	16	26	2	6	2	0	0	2	2	1	.231	.286	.308	593	55	-2	0	0	0	1.000	1	C-15,M	0.0
1928	Chi-A	2	1	0	1	0	0	0	1	0	0	1.000	1.000	1.000	2000	433	0	1	0	0	1.000	1	/C-1,M	0.1
1929	NY-N	5	2	0	0	0	0	0	0	0	1	.000	.000	.000	0	-99	-1	0			1.000	1	/C-5	0.0
Total	18	1762	5306	579	1345	199	49	11	594	638	355	.253	.340	.316	656	83	-105	177	69		.981	54	*C-1727	8.7

■ **GENE SCHALL** Schall, Eugene David b: 6/5/70, Abington, Pa. BR/TR, 6'3", 190 lbs. Deb: 6/16/95

YEAR	TM/L	G	AB	R	H	2B	3B	HR	RBI	BB	SO	AVG	OBP	SLG	OPS	OPS+	BR+	SB	CS	SBR	FA	FR	G/POS	TPR
1995	Phi-N	24	65	2	15	2	0	0	5	6	16	.231	.306	.262	567	51	-4	0	0	0	.984	-1	1-14/O-4(4-0-0)	-0.7
1996	Phi-N	28	66	7	18	5	1	2	10	12	15	.273	.392	.470	862	125	3	0	0	0	.986	-2	1-19	0.0
Total	2	52	131	9	33	7	1	2	15	18	31	.252	.351	.366	717	89	-2	0	0	0	.985	-2	/1-33,O-4(4-0-0)	-0.7

■ **BIFF SCHALLER** Schaller, Walter b: 9/23/1889, Chicago, Ill. d: 10/9/39, Emeryville, Cal. BL/TR, 5'11", 168 lbs. Deb: 4/30/11

YEAR	TM/L	G	AB	R	H	2B	3B	HR	RBI	BB	SO	AVG	OBP	SLG	OPS	OPS+	BR+	SB	CS	SBR	FA	FR	G/POS	TPR
1911	Det-A	40	60	8	8	0	1	1	7	4		.133	.200	.217	417	15	-7	1			1.000	-1	O-16(7-9-0)/1-1	-0.8
1913	Chi-A	36	96	12	21	3	0	0	4	20	16	.219	.353	.250	603	78	-2	5			.918	-6	O-32(32-0-0)	-1.0
Total	2	76	156	20	29	3	1	1	11	24	16	.186	.298	.237	536	54	-9	6			.949	-7	/O-48(39-9-0),1-1	-1.8

■ **BOBBY SCHANG** Schang, Robert Martin b: 12/7/1886, Wales Center, N.Y. d: 8/29/66, Sacramento, Cal. BR/TR, 5'7", 165 lbs. Deb: 9/23/14 F

YEAR	TM/L	G	AB	R	H	2B	3B	HR	RBI	BB	SO	AVG	OBP	SLG	OPS	OPS+	BR+	SB	CS	SBR	FA	FR	G/POS	TPR
1914	Pit-N	11	35	0	8	1	1	0	1	0	10	.229	.229	.314	543	64	-2	0			.964	-2	C-10	-0.3
1915	Pit-N	56	125	13	23	6	3	0	4	14	32	.184	.271	.280	551	68	-5	2	2	-0	.974	-7	C-45	-1.0
	NY-N	12	21	1	3	0	0	0	1	4	5	.143	.280	.143	423	31	-2	1			.875	-3	/C-6	-0.4
	Yr	68	146	14	26	6	3	0	5	18	37	.178	.273	.260	533	63	-6	3	2	-0	.960	-10	C-51	-1.4
1927	StL-N	3	5	0	1	0	0	0	0	0	0	.200	.200	.200	400	7	-1	0			1.000	-0	/C-3	-0.1
Total	3	82	186	14	35	7	4	0	6	18	47	.188	.263	.269	532	62	-9	3	2		.962	-12	/C-64	-1.8

■ **WALLY SCHANG** Schang, Walter Henry b: 8/22/1889, S.Wales, N.Y. d: 3/6/65, St.Louis, Mo. BB/TR, 5'10", 180 lbs. Deb: 5/9/13 FC Career OF: (97-LF 65-CF 5-RF)

YEAR	TM/L	G	AB	R	H	2B	3B	HR	RBI	BB	SO	AVG	OBP	SLG	OPS	OPS+	BR+	SB	CS	SBR	FA	FR	G/POS	TPR
1913	*Phi-A	79	207	32	55	16	3	3	30	34	44	.266	.392	.415	807	139	12	4			.967	-5	C-72	1.3
1914	*Phi-A	107	307	44	88	11	8	3	45	32	33	.287	.371	.404	775	138	15	7	7	-1	.956	1	*C-100	2.5
1915	Phi-A	116	359	64	89	9	11	1	44	66	47	.248	.385	.343	728	122	14	18	3	3	.890	-1	3-43,O-41C,C-26	1.8

YEAR	TM/L	G	AB	R	H	2B	3B	HR	RBI	BB	SO	AVG	OBP	SLG	OPS	OPS+	BR+	SB	CS	SBR	FA	FR	G/POS	TPR
1916	Phi-A	110	338	41	90	15	8	7	38	38	44	.266	.358	.420	778	140	16	14			.966	5	O-61(58-3-0),C-36	2.3
1917	Phi-A	118	316	41	90	14	9	3	36	29	24	.285	.362	.415	776	139	14	6			.956	-10	C-80,3-12/O-6(2-0-4)	1.2
1918	*Bos-A	88	225	36	55	7	1	0	20	46	35	.244	.377	.284	662	101	3	4			.962	-13	C-57,O-16L/3-5,S-1	-0.6
1919	Bos-A	113	330	43	101	16	3	0	55	71	42	.306	.436	.373	809	136	22	15			.972	-4	*C-103	2.7
1920	Bos-A	122	387	58	118	30	7	4	51	64	37	.305	.413	.450	862	134	22	7	7	-1	.958	-3	C-73,O-40(0-39-1)	2.0
1921	*NY-A	134	424	77	134	30	5	6	55	78	35	.316	.428	.453	881	122	18	7	4	0	.969	-6	*C-132	1.9
1922	*NY-A	124	408	46	130	21	7	1	53	53	36	.319	.405	.412	816	111	9	12	6	1	.976	0	*C-119	1.7
1923	*NY-A	84	272	39	75	8	2	2	29	27	17	.276	.360	.342	702	84	-5	5	2	0	.970	-8	C-81	-0.8
1924	NY-A	114	356	46	104	19	7	5	52	48	43	.292	.382	.427	809	109	5	2	6	-2	.972	-2	*C-108	0.8
1925	NY-A	73	167	17	40	8	1	2	24	17	9	.240	.310	.335	645	65	-9	2	1	0	.974	2	C-58	-0.3
1926	StL-A	103	285	36	94	19	5	8	50	32	20	.330	.405	.516	921	133	14	5	5	-1	.968	-1	C-82/O-3(3-0-0)	1.6
1927	StL-A	97	264	40	84	15	2	5	42	41	33	.318	.414	.447	861	119	9	3	2	-0	.976	-9	C-75	0.5
1928	StL-A	91	245	41	70	10	5	3	39	68	26	.286	.448	.404	852	121	12	8	2	1	.984	-12	C-82	0.6
1929	StL-A	94	249	43	59	10	5	5	36	74	22	.237	.424	.378	802	104	6	1	4	-1	**.988**	-6	C-85	0.4
1930	Phi-A	45	92	16	16	4	1	1	9	17	15	.174	.309	.272	581	47	-7	0	0	0	.973	2	C-36	-0.3
1931	Det-A	30	76	9	14	2	0	0	2	14	11	.184	.311	.211	522	38	-6	1	0	0	.965	-0	C-30	-0.5
Total	19	1842	5307	769	1506	264	90	59	710	849	573	.284	.393	.401	794	117	161	121	49		.967	-69	*C-1435,O-167L/3-60,S	18.8
■ ART SCHAREIN Scharein, Arthur Otto "Scoop" b: 6/30/05, Decatur, Ill. d: 7/2/69, San Antonio, Tex. BR/TR, 5′11″, 155 lbs. Deb: 7/6/32 F																								
1932	StL-A	81	303	43	92	19	2	0	42	25	10	.304	.363	.380	742	87	-5	4	8	-2	.965	18	3-77/S-3,2-2	1.3
1933	StL-A	123	471	49	96	13	3	0	26	41	21	.204	.269	.244	513	35	-44	7	9	-2	.949	14	3-95,S-24/2-7	-2.5
1934	StL-A	1	2	0	1	0	0	0	2	0	0	.500	.500	.500	1000	146	0	0	0	0	.000	0	H	0.0
Total	3	205	776	92	189	32	5	0	70	66	31	.244	.306	.298	604	56	-49	11	17	-4	.956	32	3-172/S-27,2-9	-1.2
■ GEORGE SCHAREIN Scharein, George Albert "Tom" b: 11/21/14, Decatur, Ill. d: 12/23/81, Decatur, Ill. BR/TR, 6′1″, 174 lbs. Deb: 4/19/37 F																								
1937	Phi-N	146	511	44	123	20	1	0	57	36	47	.241	.293	.284	577	53	-32	13			.947	9	*S-146	-1.3
1938	Phi-N	117	390	47	93	16	4	1	29	16	33	.238	.268	.308	576	60	-22	11			.921	-2	S-77,2-39/3-1	-1.7
1939	Phi-N	118	399	35	95	17	1	1	33	13	40	.238	.262	.293	555	50	-28	4			.958	-9	*S-117	-3.0
1940	Phi-N	7	17	0	5	0	0	0	0	0	3	.294	.294	.294	588	65	-1	0			.839	-1	/S-7	-0.1
Total	4	388	1317	126	316	53	6	2	119	65	123	.240	.277	.294	571	54	-84	28			.943	-3	S-347/2-39,3-1	-6.1
■ NICK SCHARF Scharf, Edward T. b: 7/1858, Baltimore, Md. d: 5/12/37, Baltimore, Md. TR, Deb: 5/18/1882																								
1882	Bal-a	10	39	4	8	1	1	1		0		.205	.205	.359	564	94	-0				.727	-2	/O-9(1-7-1),3-1	-0.2
1883	Bal-a	3	13	1	2	1	0	0		1		.154	.214	.231	445	42	-1				.643	-3	/S-3	-0.3
Total	2	13	52	5	10	2	1	1		1		.192	.208	.327	534	79	-1				.727	-4	/O-9(1-7-1),S-3,3-1	-0.5
■ AL SCHEER Scheer, Allan G. b: 10/21/1888, Dayton, Ohio d: 5/6/59, Logansport, Ind. BL/TR, 5′9″, 165 lbs. Deb: 8/2/13 Career OF: (201-LF 2-CF 60-RF)																								
1913	Bro-N	6	22	3	5	0	0	0	0	2	4	.227	.292	.227	519	48	-1	1			.800	-1	/O-6(0-0-6)	-0.3
1914	Ind-F	120	363	63	111	23	6	3	45	49	39	.306	.396	.427	823	112	3	9			.926	-5	*O-102R/2-4,S-1	-0.7
1915	New-F	155	546	75	146	25	14	2	60	65	38	.267	.353	.375	728	111	1	31			.971	-2	*O-155(155-0-0)	-0.9
Total	3	281	931	141	262	48	20	5	105	116	81	.281	.368	.392	760	110	2	41			.953	-9	O-263L/2-4,S-1	-1.9
■ HEINIE SCHEER Scheer, Henry b: 7/31/1900, New York, N.Y. d: 3/21/76, New Haven, Conn. BR/TR, 5′8″, 146 lbs. Deb: 4/20/22																								
1922	Phi-A	51	135	10	23	3	0	4	12	3	25	.170	.188	.281	470	21	-16	1	0	0	.976	9	2-30,3-10	-0.6
1923	Phi-A	69	210	26	50	8	1	2	21	17	41	.238	.301	.314	616	61	-12	3	4	-1	.971	-9	2-61	-1.9
Total	2	120	345	36	73	11	1	6	33	20	66	.212	.259	.301	560	46	-28	4	4	-1	.973	0	/2-91,3-10	-2.5
■ FRITZ SCHEEREN Scheeren, Frederick "Dutch" b: 9/8/1891, Kokomo, Ind. d: 6/17/73, Oil City, Pa. BR/TR, 6′, 180 lbs. Deb: 9/14/14																								
1914	Pit-N	11	31	4	9	0	1	1	2	1	6	.290	.313	.452	764	132	1	1			.824	-3	O-10(0-4-7)	-0.3
1915	Pit-N	4	3	0	0	0	0	0	0	0	0	.000	.000	.000	0	-99	-1	0			.000	-1	/O-1(0-1-0)	-0.1
Total	2	15	34	4	9	0	1	1	2	1	6	.265	.286	.412	697	111	0	1			.824	-4	/O-11(0-5-7)	-0.4
■ BOB SCHEFFING Scheffing, Robert Boden b: 8/11/13, Overland, Mo. d: 10/26/85, Phoenix, Ariz. BR/TR, 6′2″, 189 lbs. Deb: 4/27/41 MC																								
1941	Chi-N	51	132	9	32	8	0	1	20	5	19	.242	.270	.326	596	70	-6	2			.966	-3	C-34	-0.7
1942	Chi-N	44	102	7	20	3	0	2	12	7	11	.196	.248	.284	532	58	-6	2			.986	4	C-32	-0.1
1946	Chi-N	63	115	8	32	4	1	0	18	12	18	.278	.346	.330	677	94	-1	0			1.000	-7	C-40	-0.6
1947	Chi-N	110	363	33	96	11	5	5	50	25	25	.264	.312	.364	675	82	-10	2			.984	-6	C-97	-1.1
1948	Chi-N	102	293	23	88	18	2	5	45	22	27	.300	.351	.427	778	114	5	0			.989	-5	C-78	0.5
1949	Chi-N	55	149	12	40	6	1	3	19	9	9	.268	.314	.383	697	88	-3	0			.977	-3	C-40	-0.4
1950	Chi-N	12	16	0	3	1	0	0	1	0	2	.188	.188	.250	438	14	-2	0			.917	0	/C-3	-0.2
	Cin-N	21	47	4	13	0	0	2	6	4	2	.277	.333	.404	738	93	-1	0			1.000	-4	C-11	-0.3
	Yr	33	63	4	16	1	0	2	7	4	4	.254	.299	.365	664	74	-3	0			.982	-3	C-14	-0.5
1951	Cin-N	47	122	9	31	2	0	2	14	16	9	.254	.345	.320	665	79	-3	0	0	0	.976	-4	C-41	-0.5
	StL-N	12	18	0	2	0	0	0	2	3	5	.111	.238	.111	349	-3	-3	0	0	0	1.000	1	C-11	-0.1
	Yr	59	140	9	33	2	0	2	16	19	14	.236	.331	.293	624	68	-6	0	0	0	.980	-2	C-52	-0.6
Total	8	517	1357	105	357	53	9	20	187	103	127	.263	.316	.360	676	86	-28	6	0		.984	-25	C-387	-3.5
■ TED SCHEFFLER Scheffler, Theodore J. b: 4/5/1864, New York, N.Y. d: 2/24/49, Jamaica, N.Y. BR/TR, 5′10″, 160 lbs. Deb: 8/7/1888																								
1888	Det-N	27	94	17	19	3	1	0	4	9	9	.202	.286	.255	541	74	-2	4			.847	-4	O-27(4-23-0)	-0.7
1890	Roc-a	119	445	111	109	12	6	3	34	78		.245	.374	.319	693	113	13	77			.911	9	*O-119(2-0-117)/C-1	1.9
Total	2	146	539	128	128	15	7	3	38	87	9	.237	.360	.308	668	106	11	81			.899	5	O-146(6-23-117)/C-1	1.2
■ FRANK SCHEIBECK Scheibeck, Frank S. b: 6/28/1865, Detroit, Mich. d: 10/22/56, Detroit, Mich. BR/TR, 5′7″, 145 lbs. Deb: 5/9/1887 Career OF: (8-LF 1-CF 0-RF)																								
1887	Cle-a	3	11	2	4	0	0	0	0	2		.364	.364	.222	586	67	-0	0			.500	-2	/S-1,3-1,P-1	-0.1
1888	Det-N	1	4	0	0	0	0	0	0	0	0	.000	.000	.000	0	-99	-1	0			.500	-1	/S-1	-0.3
1890	Tol-a	134	485	72	117	13	5	1	49	76		.241	.350	.295	645	88	-5	57			.883	1	*S-134	0.0
1894	Pit-N	28	102	20	36	2	3	1	10	11	9	.353	.416	.461	877	112	2	7			.891	-8	S-11/O-9L,3-3,2-2	-0.4
	Was-N	52	196	49	45	2	4	0	17	45	24	.230	.384	.281	664	64	-9	11			.876	5	S-52	-0.1
	Yr	80	298	69	81	4	7	1	27	56	33	.272	.394	.342	736	81	-7	18			.878	-3	S-63/O-9L,3-3,2-2	-0.5
1895	Was-N	49	172	18	31	5	2	0	25	17	23	.180	.258	.233	490	27	-19	5			.889	-1	S-45/3-2,2-2	-1.4
1899	Was-N	27	94	19	27	4	1	0	9	11		.287	.368	.351	719	99	0	5			.877	-11	S-27	-0.8
1901	Cle-A	93	329	33	70	11	3	0	38	18		.213	.258	.264	522	47	-23	3			.897	-14	S-92	-3.1
1906	Det-A	3	10	1	1	0	0	0	0	2		.100	.250	.100	350	11	-1	0			.889	-1	/2-3	-0.2
Total	8	390	1403	214	331	37	18	2	148	182	56	.236	.328	.291	620	69	-56	88			.884	-32	S-363/O-9L,2-7,3P	-6.4
■ RICHIE SCHEINBLUM Scheinblum, Richard Alan b: 11/5/42, New York, N.Y. BB/TR, 6′1″, 180 lbs. Deb: 9/1/65																								
1965	Cle-A	4	1	1	0	0	0	0	0	0	0	.000	.000	.000	0	-99	-0	0	0	0	.000	0	H	0.0
1967	Cle-A	18	66	8	21	4	2	0	6	5	10	.318	.366	.439	806	136	3	0	2	-1	.943	-0	O-18(0-0-18)	0.1
1968	Cle-A	19	55	3	12	5	0	0	5	5	8	.218	.295	.309	604	84	-1	0	0	0	1.000	1	O-16(6-0-11)	-0.1
1969	Cle-A	102	199	13	37	5	1	1	13	19	30	.186	.257	.236	493	37	-17	0	2	-1	.974	-1	O-50(32-3-15)	-2.2
1971	Was-A	27	49	5	7	3	0	0	4	8	5	.143	.263	.204	467	36	-4	0	0	0	.933	3	O-13(7-0-6)	-0.2
1972	KC-A★	134	450	60	135	21	4	8	66	58	40	.300	.385	.418	803	139	23	0	1	-0	.965	-3	*O-119(2-0-119)	1.6
1973	Cin-N	29	54	5	12	2	0	1	8	10	4	.222	.344	.315	659	88	-1	0	0	0	.960	-2	O-19(1-0-18)	-0.4
	Cal-A	77	229	28	75	10	2	3	21	35	27	.328	.419	.428	847	150	17	0	0	0	.969	-0	O-54(6-0-49)/D-7	1.4
1974	Cal-A	10	26	1	4	0	0	0	2	1	2	.154	.185	.154	339	-2	-3	0	0	0	.929	-1	/O-8(4-0-5),D-1	-0.5
	KC-A	36	83	7	15	2	0	0	2	8	8	.181	.253	.205	458	31	-7	0	1	-0	.000	-1	D-17/O-2(2-0-0)	-0.9
	Yr	46	109	8	19	2	0	0	4	9	10	.174	.237	.193	430	24	-10	0	1	-0	.929	-2	D-18,O-10(6-0-5)	-1.4
	StL-N	6	6	0	2	0	0	0	0	0	1	.333	.333	.333	667	88	-0	0	0	0	.000	0	H	0.0
Total	8	462	1218	131	320	52	9	13	127	149	135	.263	.346	.352	698	104	10	0	6	-2	.965	-4	O-299(60-3-241)/D-25	-1.2
■ DANNY SCHELL Schell, Clyde Daniel b: 12/26/27, Fostoria, Mich. d: 5/11/72, Mayville, Mich. BR/TR, 6′1″, 195 lbs. Deb: 4/13/54																								
1954	Phi-N	92	272	25	77	14	3	7	33	17	31	.283	.330	.434	764	97	-2	0	3	-1	.974	1	O-69(60-3-6)	-0.6

YEAR	TM/L	G	AB	R	H	2B	3B	HR	RBI	BB	SO	AVG	OBP	SLG	OPS	OPS+	BR+	SB	CS	SBR	FA	FR	G/POS	TPR
1955	Phi-N	2	2	0	0	0	0	0	0	0	1	.000	.000	.000	0	-99	-1	0	0	0	.000	0	H	-0.1
Total	2	94	274	25	77	14	3	7	33	17	32	.281	.328	.431	758	96	-2	0	3	-1	.974	1	/O-69(60-3-6)	-0.7
■ AL SCHELLHASE Schellhase, Albert Herman "Schelley" b: 9/13/1864, Evansville, Ind. d: 1/3/19, Evansville, Ind. BR/TR, 5'8", 148 lbs. Deb: 5/7/1890 Career OF: (0-LF 0-CF 5-RF)																								
1890	Bos-N	9	29	1	4	0	0	0	1	1	10	.138	.167	.138	305	-10	-4	0			.778	-1	/O-5R,C-2,S-1,3-1	-0.4
1891	Lou-a	6	16	3	2	0	0	0	0	1	1	.125	.176	.125	301	-14	-2	2			.929	-1	/C-6	-0.3
Total	2	15	45	4	6	0	0	0	1	2	11	.133	.170	.133	304	-11	-6	2			.909	-2	/C-8,O-5R,3-1,S-1	-0.7
■ FRED SCHEMANSKE Schemanske, Frederick George "Buck" b: 4/28/03, Detroit, Mich. d: 2/18/60, Detroit, Mich. BR/TR, 6'2", 190 lbs. Deb: 9/15/23																								
1923	Was-A	2	2	0	2	0	0	0	2	1	0	1.000	1.000	1.000	2000	450	1	0	0	0	.000	-0	/P-1	0.0
■ MIKE SCHEMER Schemer, Michael "Lefty" b: 11/20/17, Baltimore, Md. d: 4/22/83, Miami, Fla. BL/TL, 6', 180 lbs. Deb: 8/8/45																								
1945	NY-N	31	108	10	36	3	1	1	10	6	1	.333	.368	.407	776	114	2	2			.993	4	1-27	0.5
1946	NY-N	1	1	0	0	0	0	0	0	0	0	.000	.000	.000	0	-99	-0	0			.000	0	H	0.0
Total	2	32	109	10	36	3	1	1	10	6	1	.330	.365	.404	769	112	2	2			.993	4	/1-27	0.5
■ BILL SCHENCK Schenck, William G. b: 7/1854, Brooklyn, N.Y. d: 1/29/34, Brooklyn, N.Y. 5'7", 171 lbs. Deb: 5/29/1882																								
1882	Lou-a	60	231	37	60	11	3	0		8		.260	.285	.333	618	114	4				.814	-7	*3-58/S-2,P-2	-0.1
1884	Ric-a	42	151	14	31	4	0	3		1		.205	.216	.291	507	65	-6				.836	-5	S-40/2-2	-0.9
1885	Bro-a	1	4	0	0	0	0	0	0	0		.000	.000	.000	0	-99	-1				1.000	0	/3-1	-0.1
Total	3	103	386	51	91	15	3	3	0	9		.236	.255	.313	569	92	-3				.817	-12	/3-59,S-42,2-2,P-2	-1.1
■ HANK SCHENZ Schenz, Henry Leonard b: 4/11/19, New Richmond, Ohio d: 5/12/88, Cincinnati, Ohio BR/TR, 5'9.5", 175 lbs. Deb: 9/18/46																								
1946	Chi-N	6	11	0	2	0	0	0	1	0	0	.182	.182	.182	364	3	-1	1			1.000	0	/3-5	-0.2
1947	Chi-N	7	14	2	1	0	0	0	0	2	1	.071	.235	.071	307	-16	-2	0			.917	0	/3-5	-0.2
1948	Chi-N	96	337	43	88	17	1	1	14	18	15	.261	.306	.326	633	74	-12	3			.974	-5	2-78/3-5	-1.4
1949	Chi-N	7	14	2	6	0	0	0	1	1	0	.429	.467	.429	895	146	1	2			1.000	1	/3-5	0.2
1950	Pit-N	58	101	17	23	4	2	1	5	6	7	.228	.271	.337	608	57	-6	0			.987	3	2-21,3-12/S-4	-0.3
1951	Pit-N	25	61	5	13	1	0	0	3	0	2	.213	.226	.230	455	22	-7	0	2	-1	.961	-3	2-19/3-2	-0.9
	*NY-N	8	0	1	0	0	0	0	0	0	0	—	—	—	—	—	0	0	0	0	.000	0	R	0.0
	Yr	33	61	6	13	1	0	0	3	0	2	.213	.226	.230	455	22	-7	0	2	-1	.961	-3	2-19/3-2	-0.9
Total	6	207	538	70	133	22	3	2	24	27	25	.247	.291	.310	601	63	-28	6	2		.974	-5	2-118/3-34,S-4	-2.8
■ JOE SCHEPNER Schepner, Joseph Maurice "Gentleman Joe" b: 8/10/1895, Aliquippa, Pa. d: 7/25/59, Mobile, Ala. BR/TR, 5'10", 160 lbs. Deb: 9/11/19																								
1919	StL-A	14	48	2	10	4	0	0	6	1	5	.208	.224	.292	516	43	-4	0			.947	-1	3-13	-0.5
■ BOB SCHERBARTH Scherbarth, Robert Elmer b: 1/18/26, Milwaukee, Wis. BR/TR, 6', 180 lbs. Deb: 4/23/50																								
1950	Bos-A	1	0	0	0	0	0	0	0	0	0	—	—	—	—	—	0	0	0	0	.000	0	/C-1	0.0
■ HARRY SCHERER Scherer, Harry Deb: 7/24/1889																								
1889	Lou-a	1	3	0	1	0	0	0	0	0	0	.333	.333	.333	667	92	-0	0			.500	-1	/O-1(0-1-0)	-0.1
■ LOU SCHIAPPACASSE Schiappacasse, Louis Joseph b: 3/29/1881, Ann Arbor, Mich. d: 9/20/10, Ann Arbor, Mich. BR/TR, Deb: 9/7/02																								
1902	Det-A	2	5	0	0	0	0	0	1	1		.000	.167	.000	167	-50	-1	0			.000	-1	/O-2(0-0-2)	-0.2
■ MORRIE SCHICK Schick, Maurice Francis b: 4/17/1892, Chicago, Ill. d: 10/25/79, Hazel Crest, Ill. BR/TR, 5'11", 170 lbs. Deb: 4/15/17																								
1917	Chi-N	14	34	3	5	0	0	0	3	3	10	.147	.216	.147	363	11	-3	0			.960	0	O-12(2-10-0)	-0.4
■ CHUCK SCHILLING Schilling, Charles Thomas b: 10/25/37, Brooklyn, N.Y. BR/TR, 5'11", 170 lbs. Deb: 4/11/61																								
1961	Bos-A	158	646	87	167	25	2	5	62	78	77	.259	.340	.327	667	77	-19	7	6	-1	**.991**	15	*2-158	1.0
1962	Bos-A	119	413	48	95	17	1	7	35	29	48	.230	.287	.327	614	63	-22	1	0	0	.985	13	*2-118	0.2
1963	Bos-A	146	576	63	135	25	0	8	33	41	72	.234	.291	.319	610	69	-24	3	2	-0	.985	-14	*2-143	-2.7
1964	Bos-A	47	163	18	32	6	0	0	7	15	22	.196	.264	.233	497	38	-13	0	1	-0	.974	-0	2-42	-1.1
1965	Bos-A	71	171	14	41	3	2	3	9	13	17	.240	.293	.333	627	73	-6	0	1	-0	.976	10	2-41	0.7
Total	5	541	1969	230	470	76	5	23	146	176	236	.239	.305	.317	622	68	-83	11	10	-1	.985	24	2-502	-1.9
■ BILL SCHINDLER Schindler, William Gibbons b: 7/10/1896, Perryville, Mo. d: 2/6/79, Perryville, Mo. BR/TR, 5'11", 160 lbs. Deb: 9/3/20																								
1920	StL-N	1	2	0	0	0	0	0	0	0	1	.000	.000	.000	0	-99	-1	0	0	0	1.000	-0	/C-1	-0.1
■ DUTCH SCHIRICK Schirick, Harry Ernest b: 6/15/1890, Ruby, N.Y. d: 11/12/68, Kingston, N.Y. BR/TR, 5'8", 160 lbs. Deb: 9/17/14																								
1914	StL-A	1	0	0	0	0	0	0	0	1	0	—	1.000	—	1000	212	0	2			.000	0	H	0.1
■ LARRY SCHLAFLY Schlafly, Harry Linton b: 9/20/1878, Port Washington, Ohio d: 6/27/19, Canton, Ohio BR/TR, 5'11", 182 lbs. Deb: 9/18/02 M Career OF: (1-LF 0-CF 5-RF)																								
1902	Chi-N	10	31	5	10	0	3	0	5	6		.323	.432	.516	949	198	4	2			1.000	-4	/O-5(0-0-5),2-4,3-2	0.0
1906	Was-A	123	426	60	105	13	8	2	30	50		.246	.345	.329	674	117	11	29			.961	15	*2-123	2.9
1907	Was-A	24	74	10	10	0	0	1	4	22		.135	.354	.176	529	75	0	7			.928	-9	2-24	-1.0
1914	Buf-F	51	127	16	33	7	1	2	19	12	22	.260	.338	.378	716	93	-3	3			.951	2	2-23/1-7,C-1,3OM	-0.1
Total	4	208	658	91	158	20	12	5	58	90	22	.240	.349	.330	679	111	12	41			.954	4	2-174/1-7,O-6R,3C	1.8
■ ADMIRAL SCHLEI Schlei, George Henry b: 1/12/1878, Cincinnati, Ohio d: 1/24/58, Huntington, W.Va. BR/TR, 5'8.5", 179 lbs. Deb: 4/24/04																								
1904	Cin-N	97	291	25	69	8	3	0	32	17		.237	.297	.285	583	74	-9	7			.977	10	C-88	1.0
1905	Cin-N	99	314	32	71	8	3	1	36	22		.226	.285	.280	566	62	-15	9			.962	16	C-89/1-6	1.0
1906	Cin-N	116	388	44	95	13	8	4	54	29		.245	.304	.351	655	100	-1	7			.961	9	C-91,1-21	1.8
1907	Cin-N	84	246	28	67	3	2	0	27	28		.272	.347	.301	648	99	1	5			.980	7	C-67/1-3,O-2(1-0-1)	1.6
1908	Cin-N	92	300	31	66	6	4	1	22	22		.220	.278	.277	554	79	-7	2			.962	-8	C-88	-0.7
1909	NY-N	92	279	25	68	12	0	0	30	40		.244	.343	.287	629	94	-0	4			.963	3	C-89	1.3
1910	NY-N	55	99	10	19	2	1	0	8	14	10	.192	.304	.232	537	57	-5	4			.986	0	C-49	-0.2
1911	NY-N	1	1	0	0	0	0	0	0	0	1	.000	.000	.000	0	-97	-0	0			.000	0	H	0.0
Total	8	636	1918	195	455	52	21	6	209	172	11	.237	.307	.296	603	83	-37	38			.968	36	C-561/1-30,O-2(1-0-1)	5.8
■ RUDY SCHLESINGER Schlesinger, William Cordes b: 11/5/41, Cincinnati, Ohio BR/TR, 6'2", 175 lbs. Deb: 5/4/65																								
1965	Bos-A	1	1	0	0	0	0	0	0	0	0	.000	.000	.000	0	-94	-0	0	0	0	.000	0	H	0.0
■ DUTCH SCHLIEBNER Schliebner, Frederick Paul b: 5/19/1891, Charlottenburg, Germany d: 4/15/75, Toledo, Ohio BR/TR, 5'10", 180 lbs. Deb: 4/17/23																								
1923	Bro-N	19	76	11	19	4	0	0	4	5	7	.250	.296	.303	599	60	-4	1	0	0	.981	3	1-19	-0.3
	StL-A	127	444	50	122	19	6	4	52	39	60	.275	.339	.372	710	82	-12	3	2	-0	.989	-0	*1-127	-2.0
Total	1	146	520	61	141	23	6	4	56	44	67	.271	.333	.362	694	79	-16	4	2	0	.988	2	1-146	-2.3
■ JAY SCHLUETER Schlueter, Jay D b: 7/31/49, Phoenix, Ariz. BR/TR, 6', 182 lbs. Deb: 6/18/71																								
1971	Hou-N	7	3	1	1	0	0	0	0	0	1	.333	.333	.333	667	92	-0	0	0	0	1.000	-0	/O-2(2-0-0)	0.0
■ NORM SCHLUETER Schlueter, Norman John "Duke" b: 9/25/16, Belleville, Ill. BR/TR, 5'10", 175 lbs. Deb: 5/28/38																								
1938	Chi-A	35	118	11	27	5	1	0	7	4	15	.229	.254	.288	542	35	-12	1	0	0	.952	-3	C-34	-1.2
1939	Chi-A	34	56	5	13	2	1	0	8	1	11	.232	.246	.304	549	39	-5	2	0	0	.988	1	C-32	-0.3
1944	Cle-A	49	122	2	15	4	0	0	11	12	22	.123	.201	.156	357	3	-15	0	2	-1	.985	-8	C-43	-2.3
Total	3	118	296	18	55	11	2	0	26	17	48	.186	.230	.236	467	24	-33	3	2	-0	.974	-10	C-109	-3.8
■ RAY SCHMANDT Schmandt, Raymond Henry b: 1/25/1896, St.Louis, Mo. d: 2/2/69, St.Louis, Mo. BR/TR, 6'1", 175 lbs. Deb: 6/24/15																								
1915	StL-A	3	4	0	0	0	0	0	0	0	1	.000	.000	.000	0	-99	-1	0			1.000	-0	/1-1	-0.1
1918	Bro-N	34	114	11	35	5	4	0	18	7	7	.307	.347	.421	768	134	4	1			.934	-4	2-34	0.1
1919	Bro-N	47	127	8	21	4	0	0	10	4	13	.165	.191	.197	388	16	-13	0			.911	0	2-18,1-12/3-6	-1.4
1920	*Bro-N	28	63	7	15	2	1	0	7	3	4	.238	.273	.302	574	63	-3	1	1	-0	.995	3	1-20	0.0
1921	Bro-N	95	350	42	107	8	5	1	43	11	22	.306	.329	.366	694	81	-10	3	4	-1	.989	0	1-92	-1.6

YEAR	TM/L	G	AB	R	H	2B	3B	HR	RBI	BB	SO	AVG	OBP	SLG	OPS	OPS+	BR+	SB	CS	SBR	FA	FR	G/POS	TPR
1922	Bro-N	110	396	54	106	17	3	2	44	21	28	.268	.306	.341	647	67	-20	6	6	-1	.989	5	*1-110	-2.2
Total	6	317	1054	122	284	36	13	3	122	46	75	.269	.301	.337	638	72	-42	11	11		.990	5	1-235/2-52,3-6	-5.2

■ GEORGE SCHMEES

Schmees, George Edward "Rocky" b: 9/6/24, Cincinnati, Ohio d: 10/30/98, San Jose, Cal. BL/TL, 6', 190 lbs. Deb: 4/15/52

YEAR	TM/L	G	AB	R	H	2B	3B	HR	RBI	BB	SO	AVG	OBP	SLG	OPS	OPS+	BR+	SB	CS	SBR	FA	FR	G/POS	TPR
1952	StL-A	34	61	9	8	1	1	0	3	2	18	.131	.159	.180	339	-6	-9	0	0	0	.932	-1	O-19(9-2-8)/1-2	-1.0
	Bos-A	42	64	8	13	3	0	0	3	10	11	.203	.311	.250	561	53	-4	0	1	-0	1.000	-7	O-29(0-18-11)/P-2,1-2	-1.3
	Yr	76	125	17	21	4	1	0	6	12	29	.168	.241	.216	457	26	-12	0	1	-0	.960	-8	O-48(9-20-19)/1-4,P-2	-2.3

■ BOSS SCHMIDT

Schmidt, Charles b: 9/12/1880, Coal Hill, Ark. d: 11/14/32, Clarksville, Ark. BB/TR, 5'11", 200 lbs. Deb: 4/30/06 F

YEAR	TM/L	G	AB	R	H	2B	3B	HR	RBI	BB	SO	AVG	OBP	SLG	OPS	OPS+	BR+	SB	CS	SBR	FA	FR	G/POS	TPR
1906	Det-A	68	216	13	47	4	3	0	10	6		.218	.242	.264	506	57	-11	1			.958	7	C-67	0.3
1907	*Det-A	104	349	32	85	6	6	0	23	5		.244	.269	.295	564	77	-10	8			.944	3	*C-103	0.3
1908	*Det-A	122	419	45	111	14	3	1	38	16		.265	.297	.320	617	96	-3	5			.951	8	*C-121	2.0
1909	*Det-A	84	253	21	53	8	2	1	28	7		.209	.240	.269	508	58	-13	7			.955	-6	C-81/O-1(0-0-1)	-1.3
1910	Det-A	71	197	22	51	7	7	1	23	2		.259	.277	.381	658	99	-1	2			.973	-8	C-66	-0.4
1911	Det-A	28	46	4	13	2	1	0	2	0		.283	.298	.370	667	82	-1	0			1.000	-2	/C-9,O-1(0-0-1)	-0.3
Total	6	477	1480	137	360	41	22	3	124	36		.243	.270	.307	577	79	-39	23			.955	3	C-447/O-2(0-0-2)	0.6

■ BUTCH SCHMIDT

Schmidt, Charles John "Butcher Boy" b: 7/19/1886, Baltimore, Md. d: 9/4/52, Baltimore, Md. BL/TL, 6'1.5", 200 lbs. Deb: 5/11/09

YEAR	TM/L	G	AB	R	H	2B	3B	HR	RBI	BB	SO	AVG	OBP	SLG	OPS	OPS+	BR+	SB	CS	SBR	FA	FR	G/POS	TPR
1909	NY-A	1	2	0	0	0	0	0	0	0		.000	.000	.000	0	-99	-0	0			.500	-0	/P-1	0.0
1913	Bos-N	22	78	6	24	2	2	1	14	2	5	.308	.333	.423	756	113	1	1			.983	1	1-22	0.1
1914	*Bos-N	147	537	67	153	17	9	1	71	43	55	.285	.350	.356	706	111	8	14			.990	3	*1-147	0.7
1915	Bos-N	127	458	46	115	26	7	2	60	36	59	.251	.318	.352	670	107	4	3	10	-3	.987	-4	*1-127	-0.8
Total	4	297	1075	119	292	45	18	4	145	81	119	.272	.335	.358	693	109	12	18	10		.988	-1	1-296/P-1	0.0

■ DAVE SCHMIDT

Schmidt, David Frederick b: 12/22/56, Mesa, Ariz. BR/TR, 6'1", 190 lbs. Deb: 4/28/81

YEAR	TM/L	G	AB	R	H	2B	3B	HR	RBI	BB	SO	AVG	OBP	SLG	OPS	OPS+	BR+	SB	CS	SBR	FA	FR	G/POS	TPR
1981	Bos-A	15	42	6	10	1	0	2	3	7	17	.238	.347	.405	752	109	1	0	0	0	1.000	-4	C-15	-0.2

■ MIKE SCHMIDT

Schmidt, Michael Jack b: 9/27/49, Dayton, Ohio BR/TR, 6'2", 203 lbs. Deb: 9/12/72 H

YEAR	TM/L	G	AB	R	H	2B	3B	HR	RBI	BB	SO	AVG	OBP	SLG	OPS	OPS+	BR+	SB	CS	SBR	FA	FR	G/POS	TPR
1972	Phi-N	13	34	2	7	0	0	1	3	5	15	.206	.325	.294	619	75	-1	0	0	0	.964	2	3-11/2-1	0.1
1973	Phi-N	132	367	43	72	11	0	18	52	62	136	.196	.326	.373	700	91	-4	8	2	1	.954	**21**	*3-125/2-4,1-2,S-2	1.9
1974	Phi-N★	162	568	108	160	28	7	**36**	116	106	138	.282	.398	**.546**	944	156	43	23	12	1	.954	26	*3-162	**7.1**
1975	Phi-N	158	562	93	140	34	3	**38**	95	101	180	.249	.367	.523	890	139	30	29	12	2	.954	**24**	*3-151,S-10	5.7
1976	*Phi-N★	160	584	112	153	31	4	**38**	107	100	149	.262	.380	.524	904	150	39	14	9	-0	.961	**25**	*3-160	**6.5**
1977	*Phi-N★	154	544	114	149	27	11	38	101	104	122	.274	.399	.574	972	151	41	15	8	1	.964	29	*3-149/S-2,2-1	**6.7**
1978	*Phi-N	145	513	93	129	27	2	21	78	91	103	.251	.368	.435	803	122	17	19	6	2	.963	10	*3-139/S-1	2.9
1979	Phi-N★	160	541	109	137	25	4	45	114	**120**	115	.253	.392	.564	955	153	41	9	5	0	.954	18	*3-157/S-2	5.8
1980	*Phi-N†	150	548	104	157	25	8	**48**	**121**	89	119	.286	.388	**.624**	**1012**	**169**	**50**	12	5	1	.946	23	*3-149	**7.3**
1981	*Phi-N★	102	354	**78**	112	19	2	**31**	**91**	**73**	71	.316	**.439**	**.644**	**1083**	**195**	**46**	12	4	1	.956	23	*3-101	**7.0**
1982	Phi-N★	148	514	108	144	26	3	35	87	**107**	131	.280	**.407**	**.547**	**954**	**161**	**45**	14	7	1	.950	19	*3-148	**6.3**
1983	*Phi-N★	154	534	104	136	16	4	**40**	109	**128**	148	.255	**.402**	.524	926	**156**	**45**	7	8	-1	.959	23	*3-153/S-2	**6.6**
1984	Phi-N★	151	528	93	146	23	3	**36**	**106**	92	116	.277	.388	.536	**924**	**155**	**40**	5	7	-1	.941	12	*3-145/1-2,S-1	4.9
1985	Phi-N	158	549	89	152	31	5	33	93	87	117	.277	.379	.532	911	148	36	1	3	-1	.993	5	*1-106,3-54/S-1	3.4
1986	Phi-N★	160	552	97	160	29	1	**37**	**119**	89	84	.290	.395	**.547**	**942**	**152**	**40**	1	2	-0	**.980**	-7	*3-124,1-35	3.0
1987	Phi-N★	147	522	88	153	28	0	35	113	83	80	.293	.392	.548	940	141	32	2	1	0	.971	13	*3-138/1-9,S-3	4.1
1988	Phi-N	108	390	52	97	21	2	12	62	49	42	.249	.342	.405	747	111	6	3	0	1	.939	3	*3-104/1-3	1.1
1989	Phi-N†	42	148	19	30	7	0	6	28	21	17	.203	.302	.372	673	91	-2	0	1	-0	.918	-5	3-42	-0.8
Total	18	2404	8352	1506	2234	408	59	548	1595	1507	1883	.267	.384	.527	912	147	544	174	92	6	.955	265	*3-2212,1-157/S-24,2	79.6

■ BOB SCHMIDT

Schmidt, Robert Benjamin b: 4/22/33, St.Louis, Mo. BR/TR, 6'2", 205 lbs. Deb: 4/16/58

YEAR	TM/L	G	AB	R	H	2B	3B	HR	RBI	BB	SO	AVG	OBP	SLG	OPS	OPS+	BR+	SB	CS	SBR	FA	FR	G/POS	TPR
1958	SF-N☆	127	393	46	96	20	2	14	54	33	59	.244	.308	.412	720	90	-6	0	1	-0	.982	-3	*C-123	-0.4
1959	SF-N	71	181	17	44	7	1	5	20	13	24	.243	.297	.376	673	80	-6	0	2	-1	1.000	-0	C-70	-0.4
1960	SF-N	110	344	31	92	12	1	8	37	26	51	.267	.319	.378	697	96	-3	0	3	-1	.981	-3	*C-108	-0.2
1961	SF-N	2	6	0	1	0	0	0	1	0	1	.167	.167	.167	333	-12	-1	0	0	0	1.000	1	/C-2	0.0
	Cin-N	27	70	4	9	0	0	1	4	8	14	.129	.218	.171	389	5	-10	0	0	0	.993	1	C-27	-0.7
	Yr	29	76	4	10	0	0	1	5	8	15	.132	.214	.171	385	4	-10	0	0	0	.994	3	C-29	-0.7
1962	Was-A	88	256	28	62	14	0	10	31	14	37	.242	.284	.414	698	86	-6	0	0	0	**.997**	-2	C-88	-0.5
1963	Was-A	9	15	3	3	1	0	0	0	3	5	.200	.333	.267	600	71	-0	0	0	0	1.000	-1	/C-6	-0.1
1965	NY-A	20	40	4	10	1	0	1	3	3	8	.250	.302	.350	652	85	-1	0	0	0	.990	2	C-20	0.2
Total	7	454	1305	133	317	55	4	39	150	100	199	.243	.299	.381	680	84	-32	0	6	-2	.988	-5	C-444	-2.1

■ WALTER SCHMIDT

Schmidt, Walter Joseph b: 3/20/1887, Coal Hill, Ark. d: 7/4/73, Modesto, Cal. BR/TR, 5'9", 159 lbs. Deb: 4/13/16 F

YEAR	TM/L	G	AB	R	H	2B	3B	HR	RBI	BB	SO	AVG	OBP	SLG	OPS	OPS+	BR+	SB	CS	SBR	FA	FR	G/POS	TPR
1916	Pit-N	64	184	16	35	1	2	2	15	10	13	.190	.236	.250	486	49	-11	3			.976	0	C-57	-0.7
1917	Pit-N	72	183	9	45	7	0	0	17	11	11	.246	.296	.284	580	76	-5	4			.978	8	C-61	0.9
1918	Pit-N	105	323	31	77	6	3	0	27	17	19	.238	.281	.276	556	68	-12	7			.981	16	*C-104	1.3
1919	Pit-N	85	267	23	67	9	2	0	29	23	9	.251	.310	.300	610	81	-6	5			.982	1	C-85	0.3
1920	Pit-N	94	310	22	86	8	4	0	20	24	15	.277	.337	.329	666	89	-4	9	3	1	.971	-5	C-92	0.1
1921	Pit-N	114	393	30	111	9	3	0	38	12	13	.282	.307	.321	628	65	-19	10	6	0	**.986**	7	*C-111	-0.5
1922	Pit-N	40	152	21	50	11	1	0	22	1	5	.329	.333	.414	748	91	-2	2	1	0	.995	-6	C-40	-0.5
1923	Pit-N	97	335	39	83	7	2	0	37	22	12	.248	.300	.281	581	53	-22	10	5	0	.981	-9	C-96	-2.3
1924	Pit-N	58	177	16	43	3	2	1	20	13	5	.243	.295	.299	594	59	-10	6	1	1	.986	2	C-57	-0.4
1925	StL-N	37	87	9	22	2	1	0	9	4	3	.253	.293	.299	592	51	-6	1	0	0	.967	6	C-31	0.1
Total	10	766	2411	216	619	63	20	3	234	137	105	.257	.301	.303	604	68	-99	57	16		.980	20	C-734	-1.7

■ HANK SCHMULBACH

Schmulbach, Henry Alrives b: 1/17/25, E.St.Louis, Ill. BL/TR, 5'11", 165 lbs. Deb: 9/27/43

YEAR	TM/L	G	AB	R	H	2B	3B	HR	RBI	BB	SO	AVG	OBP	SLG	OPS	OPS+	BR+	SB	CS	SBR	FA	FR	G/POS	TPR
1943	StL-A	1	0	1	0	0	0	0	0	0	0	—	—	—	—	—	0	0	0	0	.000	0	R	0.0

■ DAVE SCHNECK

Schneck, David Lee b: 6/18/49, Allentown, Pa. BL/TL, 5'10", 200 lbs. Deb: 7/14/72

YEAR	TM/L	G	AB	R	H	2B	3B	HR	RBI	BB	SO	AVG	OBP	SLG	OPS	OPS+	BR+	SB	CS	SBR	FA	FR	G/POS	TPR
1972	NY-N	37	123	7	23	3	2	3	10	10	26	.187	.254	.317	571	63	-6	0	1	-0	.985	-1	O-33(1-17-16)	-1.0
1973	NY-N	13	36	2	7	0	1	0	0	1	4	.194	.216	.250	466	29	-3	0	0	0	1.000	0	O-12(0-12-0)	-0.4
1974	NY-N	93	254	23	52	11	1	5	25	16	43	.205	.255	.315	570	60	-15	4	1	1	.974	0	O-84(23-59-9)	-1.7
Total	3	143	413	32	82	14	4	8	35	27	73	.199	.251	.310	561	58	-24	4	2	0	.979	-0	O-129(24-88-25)	-3.1

■ BRIAN SCHNEIDER

Schneider, Brian Duncan b: 11/26/76, Jacksonville, Fla. BL/TR, 6'1", 200 lbs. Deb: 5/26/2000

YEAR	TM/L	G	AB	R	H	2B	3B	HR	RBI	BB	SO	AVG	OBP	SLG	OPS	OPS+	BR+	SB	CS	SBR	FA	FR	G/POS	TPR
2000	Mon-N	45	115	6	27	6	0	0	11	7	24	.235	.279	.287	566	43	-10	0	1	-0	.974	1	C-43	-0.7

■ RED SCHOENDIENST

Schoendienst, Albert Fred b: 2/2/23, Germantown, Ill. BB/TR, 6', 170 lbs. Deb: 4/17/45 MCH Career OF: (119-LF 4-CF 0-RF)

YEAR	TM/L	G	AB	R	H	2B	3B	HR	RBI	BB	SO	AVG	OBP	SLG	OPS	OPS+	BR+	SB	CS	SBR	FA	FR	G/POS	TPR
1945	StL-N	137	565	89	157	22	6	1	47	21	17	.278	.305	.343	648	78	-18	**26**			.983	3	*O-118L,S-10/2-1	-2.1
1946	*StL-N★	142	606	94	170	28	5	0	34	37	27	.281	.322	.343	665	85	-12	12			**.984**	-1	*2-128,3-12/S-4	-0.6
1947	StL-N	151	659	91	167	25	9	3	48	48	27	.253	.304	.332	636	66	-32	6			.976	-2	*2-142/3-5,O-1(1-0-0)	-2.6
1948	StL-N★	119	408	64	111	21	4	4	36	28	16	.272	.319	.373	691	82	-11	1			.980	1	2-96	-0.5
1949	StL-N★	151	640	102	190	25	2	3	54	51	18	.297	.351	.356	707	86	-11	8			**.987**	24	*2-138,S-14/3-6,O-2C	2.1
1950	StL-N★	153	642	81	177	**43**	9	7	63	33	32	.276	.313	.403	717	83	-17	3			.985	8	*2-143,S-10/3-1	0.0
1951	StL-N★	135	553	88	160	32	7	6	54	35	23	.289	.335	.405	740	98	-3	0	1	-0	.990	16	*2-124/S-8	2.0
1952	StL-N☆	152	620	91	188	40	7	7	67	42	30	.303	.347	.424	772	113	10	9	6	-0	.977	**33**	*2-142,3-11/S-3	5.1
1953	StL-N★	146	564	107	193	35	5	15	79	60	23	.342	.405	.502	907	135	30	3	3	-0	**.983**	25	*2-140	6.1
1954	StL-N★	148	610	98	192	38	8	5	79	54	22	.315	.371	.428	799	107	7	4	2	0	.980	**33**	*2-144	4.9
1955	StL-N★	145	553	68	148	21	3	11	51	54	28	.268	.337	.376	713	89	-8	7	7	-1	**.985**	-15	*2-142	-1.4
1956	StL-N	40	153	22	48	9	0	0	15	13	5	.314	.367	.373	740	100	0	0	1	-0	.995	-2	2-36	0.1
	NY-N	92	334	39	99	12	3	2	14	28	10	.296	.354	.368	723	95	-1	1	2	-0	.993	-11	2-85	-0.6
	Yr	132	487	61	147	21	3	2	29	41	15	.302	.358	.370	728	97	-1	1	3	-1	**.993**	-12	*2-121	-0.5
1957	NY-N	57	254	35	78	8	4	9	33	10	8	.307	.338	.476	815	116	5	2	1	0	.984	-2	2-57	0.8
	*Mil-N★	93	394	56	122	23	4	6	32	23	7	.310	.349	.434	783	117	9	2	3	-1	.987	4	2-92/O-2(0-2-0)	2.0

YEAR	TM/L	G	AB	R	H	2B	3B	HR	RBI	BB	SO	AVG	OBP	SLG	OPS	OPS+	BR+	SB	CS	SBR	FA	FR	G/POS	TPR
	Yr	150	648	91	**200**	31	8	15	65	33	15	.309	.345	.451	796	117	14	4	4	-1	.986	3	*2-149/O-2(0-2-0)	2.8
1958	*Mil-N	106	427	47	112	23	1	1	24	31	21	.262	.314	.328	642	77	-15	3	1	0	**.987**	1	*2-105	-0.6
1959	Mil-N	5	3	0	0	0	0	0	0	0	0	.000	.000	.000	0	-99	-1	0	0	0	.667	-0	/2-4	-0.1
1960	Mil-N	68	226	21	58	9	1	1	19	17	13	.257	.311	.319	630	79	-7	1	0	0	.964	-17	2-62	-2.0
1961	StL-N	72	120	9	36	9	0	1	12	12	6	.300	.364	.400	764	93	-1	1	0	0	.955	-11	2-32	-0.9
1962	StL-N	98	143	21	43	4	0	2	12	9	12	.301	.346	.371	717	84	-3	0	0	0	.986	-0	2-21/3-4	-0.2
1963	StL-N	6	5	0	0	0	0	0	0	0	1	.000	.000	.000	0	-91	-1	0	0	0	.000	0	H	-0.1
Total	19	2216	8479	1223	2449	427	78	84	773	606	346	.289	.338	.387	725	93	-80	89	27		.983	88	*2-1834,O-123L/S-49,3	11.4

■ **JUMBO SCHOENECK** Schoeneck, Louis N. b: 3/3/1862, Chicago, Ill. d: 1/20/30, Chicago, Ill. BR/TR, 6'3", 223 lbs. Deb: 4/20/1884

YEAR	TM/L	G	AB	R	H	2B	3B	HR	RBI	BB	SO	AVG	OBP	SLG	OPS	OPS+	BR+	SB	CS	SBR	FA	FR	G/POS	TPR
1884	CP-U	90	366	56	116	22	2	2		8		.317	.332	.404	736	123	-1				.956	0	*1-90	-0.8
	Bal-U	16	60	5	15	2	0	0		0		.250	.250	.283	533	56	-5				.962	2	1-16	-0.4
	Yr	106	426	61	131	24	2	2		8		.308	.320	.387	708	112	-6				**.957**	2	*1-106	-1.2
1888	Ind-N	48	169	15	40	4	0	0	20	9	24	.237	.283	.260	544	73	-5	11			.974	-1	1-48/P-2	-1.0
1889	Ind-N	16	62	3	15	2	2	0	8	3	3	.242	.299	.339	637	76	-2	1			.978	2	1-16	-0.1
Total	3	170	657	79	186	30	4	2	28	20	27	.283	.308	.350	658	99	-13	12			.964	3	1-170/P-2	-2.3

■ **DICK SCHOFIELD** Schofield, John Richard "Ducky" b: 1/7/35, Springfield, Ill. BB/TR, 5'9", 165 lbs. Deb: 7/3/53 F

YEAR	TM/L	G	AB	R	H	2B	3B	HR	RBI	BB	SO	AVG	OBP	SLG	OPS	OPS+	BR+	SB	CS	SBR	FA	FR	G/POS	TPR
1953	StL-N	33	39	9	7	0	0	2	4	2	11	.179	.220	.333	553	42	-3	0	0	0	.917	10	S-15	0.6
1954	StL-N	43	7	17	1	0	1	0	1	0	3	.143	.143	.429	571	42	-1	1	1	-0	1.000	2	S-11	0.1
1955	StL-N	12	4	3	0	0	0	0	0	0	1	.000	.000	.000	0	-99	-1	0	0	0	1.000	1	/S-3	-0.1
1956	StL-N	16	30	3	3	2	0	0	1	0	6	.100	.100	.167	267	-30	-5	0	0	0	.923	-1	/S-9	-0.6
1957	StL-N	65	56	10	9	0	0	0	1	7	13	.161	.254	.161	415	14	-7	1	3	-1	.948	10	S-23	0.3
1958	StL-N	39	108	16	23	4	0	1	8	23	15	.213	.351	.278	629	67	-4	0	2	-1	.932	-5	S-27	-0.8
	Pit-N	26	27	4	4	0	1	0	2	3	6	.148	.233	.222	456	22	-3	0	1	-0	1.000	0	/S-5,3-2	-0.3
	Yr	65	135	20	27	4	1	1	10	26	21	.200	.329	.267	596	59	-7	0	3	-1	.943	-5	S-32/3-2	-1.1
1959	Pit-N	81	145	21	34	10	1	1	9	16	22	.234	.311	.338	648	73	-5	1	1	-0	.980	10	2-28/S-8,O-3(0-0-3)	0.7
1960	*Pit-N	65	102	9	34	4	1	0	10	16	20	.333	.429	.392	821	126	5	0	1	-0	.947	8	S-23,2-10/3-1	1.5
1961	Pit-N	60	78	16	15	2	1	0	2	10	19	.192	.284	.244	528	42	-6	0	1	-0	.923	9	3-11/S-9,2-5,O-3L	0.3
1962	Pit-N	54	104	19	30	3	0	2	10	17	22	.288	.388	.375	763	106	2	0	1	-0	.933	-6	3-20/2-2,S-1	-0.5
1963	Pit-N	138	541	54	133	18	2	3	32	69	83	.246	.334	.303	638	84	-8	2	4	-1	.966	10	*S-117,2-20/3-1	1.4
1964	Pit-N	121	398	50	98	22	5	3	36	54	60	.246	.346	.349	696	97	0	1	2	-0	.950	2	*S-111	1.2
1965	Pit-N	31	109	13	25	5	0	0	6	15	19	.229	.323	.275	598	70	-4	1	0	0	.974	4	S-28	0.3
	SF-N	101	379	39	77	10	1	2	19	33	50	.203	.272	.251	523	47	-26	2	4	-1	.984	-6	S-93	-2.7
	Yr	132	488	52	102	15	1	2	25	48	69	.209	.284	.256	540	52	-30	3	4	-1	**.981**	-2	*S-121	-2.4
1966	SF-N	11	16	4	1	0	0	0	0	2	2	.063	.167	.063	229	-32	-3	0	0	0	1.000	2	/S-8	-0.1
	NY-A	25	58	5	9	2	0	0	2	9	8	.155	.269	.190	458	36	-5	0	0	0	.909	5	S-19	0.2
	LA-N	20	70	10	18	0	0	0	4	8	8	.257	.350	.257	607	78	-2	1	1	-0	.923	-3	3-19/S-3	-0.4
1967	LA-N	84	232	23	50	10	1	2	15	31	40	.216	.308	.293	601	79	-6	1	2	-0	.976	-0	S-69/2-4,3-2	-0.1
1968	*StL-N	69	127	14	28	7	1	1	8	13	31	.220	.303	.315	618	87	-2	1	2	-0	.973	9	S-43,2-23	1.1
1969	Bos-A	94	226	30	58	9	3	2	20	29	44	.257	.351	.350	701	92	-2	0	2	-1	.981	2	2-37,S-11/3-9,O-5L	0.3
1970	Bos-A	76	139	16	26	1	2	1	14	21	26	.187	.298	.245	543	48	-9	0	1	-0	.969	-4	2-15,3-15/S-3	-1.4
1971	Mil-A	23	28	2	3	2	0	0	1	2	8	.107	.194	.179	372	6	-4	0	0	0	1.000	-2	3-12/S-4,2-2	-0.5
	StL-N	34	60	7	13	2	0	1	6	10	9	.217	.347	.300	647	82	-1	0	0	0	.935	2	S-17,2-13/3-3	0.2
Total	19	1321	3083	394	699	113	20	21	211	390	526	.227	.319	.297	615	73	-100	12	29	-8	.961	58	S-660,2-159/3-95,O	0.7

■ **DICK SCHOFIELD** Schofield, Richard Craig b: 11/21/62, Springfield, Ill. BR/TR, 5'10", 178 lbs. Deb: 9/8/83 F

YEAR	TM/L	G	AB	R	H	2B	3B	HR	RBI	BB	SO	AVG	OBP	SLG	OPS	OPS+	BR+	SB	CS	SBR	FA	FR	G/POS	TPR
1983	Cal-A	21	54	4	11	2	0	3	4	6	8	.204	.295	.407	702	92	-1	0	0	0	.929	5	S-21	0.5
1984	Cal-A	140	400	39	77	10	3	4	21	33	79	.192	.264	.262	527	47	-29	5	2	0	**.982**	3	*S-140	-1.1
1985	Cal-A	147	438	50	96	19	3	8	41	35	70	.219	.289	.331	620	70	-18	11	4	1	.963	1	*S-147	-0.2
1986	*Cal-A	139	458	67	114	17	6	13	57	48	55	.249	.327	.397	724	97	-2	23	5	3	.972	15	*S-137	3.0
1987	Cal-A	134	479	52	120	17	3	9	46	37	63	.251	.307	.355	662	78	-16	19	3	3	**.984**	-18	*S-131/2-2,D-1	-1.6
1988	Cal-A	155	527	61	126	11	6	6	34	40	57	.239	.304	.317	621	76	-16	20	5	3	**.983**	23	*S-155	2.1
1989	Cal-A	91	302	42	69	11	2	4	26	28	47	.228	.300	.318	618	76	-10	9	3	1	.983	-8	S-90	-0.9
1990	Cal-A	99	310	41	79	8	1	1	18	52	61	.255	.365	.297	662	89	-2	3	4	-1	.966	12	S-99	1.7
1991	Cal-A	134	427	44	96	9	3	0	31	50	69	.225	.310	.260	570	60	-22	8	4	0	.975	12	*S-133	0.0
1992	Cal-A	1	3	0	1	0	0	0	0	1	0	.333	.500	.333	833	137	0	0	0	0	1.000	-1	/S-1	-0.1
	NY-N	142	420	52	86	18	2	4	36	60	82	.205	.311	.286	597	71	-14	11	4	1	**.988**	13	*S-141	1.1
1993	Tor-A	36	110	11	21	1	2	0	5	16	25	.191	.294	.236	530	44	-8	3	0	1	.977	3	S-36	-0.2
1994	Tor-A	95	325	38	83	14	1	4	32	34	62	.255	.333	.342	675	74	-12	7	7	-1	.972	-9	S-95	-1.3
1995	LA-N	9	10	0	1	0	0	0	0	1	3	.100	.182	.100	282	-25	-2	0	0	0	1.000	3	/S-3,3-1	0.1
	Cal-A	12	20	1	5	0	0	0	2	4	2	.250	.375	.250	625	67	-1	0	0	0	1.000	1	S-12	0.1
1996	Cal-A	13	16	3	4	0	0	0	0	1	1	.250	.294	.250	544	39	-1	1	0	0	.889	1	/S-7,2-2,3-1,D-1	0.0
Total	14	1368	4299	505	989	137	32	56	353	446	684	.230	.309	.316	625	73	-153	120	41	12	.976	56	*S-1348/2-4,3-2,D-2	3.2

■ **OTTO SCHOMBERG** Schomberg, Otto H. (b: Otto H. Shambrick) b: 11/14/1864, Milwaukee, Wis. d: 5/3/27, Ottawa, Kan. BL/TL, Deb: 7/7/1886

YEAR	TM/L	G	AB	R	H	2B	3B	HR	RBI	BB	SO	AVG	OBP	SLG	OPS	OPS+	BR+	SB	CS	SBR	FA	FR	G/POS	TPR
1886	Pit-a	72	246	53	67	6	6	1	29	57		.272	.417	.358	775	144	17	7			.966	-7	1-72	0.3
1887	Ind-N	112	475	91	185	18	16	5	83	56	32	.389	.397	.463	860	143	27	21			.958	-10	*1-112/O-1(0-0-1)	0.5
1888	Ind-N	30	112	11	24	5	1	1	10	10	12	.214	.290	.304	594	88	-1	6			.857	-5	O-15(0-0-15),1-15	-0.7
Total	3	214	833	155	276	29	23	7	122	123	44	.331	.389	.407	796	136	43	34			.961	-22	1-199/O-16(0-0-16)	0.1

■ **JERRY SCHOONMAKER** Schoonmaker, Jerald Lee b: 12/14/33, Seymour, Mo. BR/TR, 5'11", 190 lbs. Deb: 6/11/55

YEAR	TM/L	G	AB	R	H	2B	3B	HR	RBI	BB	SO	AVG	OBP	SLG	OPS	OPS+	BR+	SB	CS	SBR	FA	FR	G/POS	TPR
1955	Was-A	20	46	5	7	0	1	1	4	5	11	.152	.235	.261	496	35	-4	1	0	0	.960	-1	O-15(5-3-7)	-0.6
1957	Was-A	30	23	5	2	1	0	0	0	2	11	.087	.160	.130	290	-20	-4	0	0	0	1.000	-3	O-13(5-8-0)	-0.7
Total	2	50	69	10	9	1	1	1	4	7	22	.130	.211	.217	428	16	-8	1	0	0	.975	-4	/O-28(10-11-7)	-1.3

■ **GENE SCHOTT** Schott, Arthur Eugene b: 7/14/13, Batavia, Ohio d: 11/16/92, Sun City Center, Fla. BR/TR, 6'2", 185 lbs. Deb: 4/16/35

YEAR	TM/L	G	AB	R	H	2B	3B	HR	RBI	BB	SO	AVG	OBP	SLG	OPS	OPS+	BR+	SB	CS	SBR	FA	FR	G/POS	TPR
1935	Cin-N	36	60	6	12	2	0	0	2	3	13	.200	.238	.233	471	28	-6	0			.965	3	P-33	0.0
1936	Cin-N	39	60	10	18	3	1	1	8	5	18	.300	.354	.433	787	118	1	0			.947	1	P-31	0.0
1937	Cin-N	50	49	5	7	2	0	0	4	1	14	.143	.160	.184	344	-7	-7	0			.961	1	P-37	0.0
1938	Cin-N	31	24	3	3	0	0	0	0	1	4	.125	.160	.125	285	-21	-4	0			1.000	1	P-31	0.0
1939	Phi-N	8	6	3	2	0	1	0	0	0	0	.333	.333	.667	1000	168	0	0			.500	-1	/P-4	0.0
	Bro-N	1	0	0	0	0	0	0	0	0	0	—	—	—	—	—	0	0			.000	0	R	0.0
	Yr	9	6	3	2	0	1	0	0	0	0	.333	.333	.667	1000	166	0	0			.500	-1	/P-4	0.0
Total	5	165	199	27	42	7	2	1	14	10	49	.211	.249	.281	530	45	-15	0			.959	6	P-136	0.0

■ **PAUL SCHRAMKA** Schramka, Paul Edward b: 3/22/28, Milwaukee, Wis. BL/TL, 6', 185 lbs. Deb: 4/14/53

YEAR	TM/L	G	AB	R	H	2B	3B	HR	RBI	BB	SO	AVG	OBP	SLG	OPS	OPS+	BR+	SB	CS	SBR	FA	FR	G/POS	TPR
1953	Chi-N	2	0	0	0	0	0	0	0	0	0	—	—	—	—	—	0	0	0	0	.000	-0	/O-1(1-0-0)	0.0

■ **OSSEE SCHRECKENGOST** Schreckengost, Ossee Freeman (a.k.a. Ossee Schreck) b: 4/11/1875, New Bethlehem, Pa. d: 7/9/14, Philadelphia, Pa. BR/TR, 5'10", 180 lbs. Deb: 9/8/1897 Career OF: (0-LF 1-CF 2-RF)

YEAR	TM/L	G	AB	R	H	2B	3B	HR	RBI	BB	SO	AVG	OBP	SLG	OPS	OPS+	BR+	SB	CS	SBR	FA	FR	G/POS	TPR
1897	Lou-N	1	3	0	0	0	0	0	0	0		.000	.000	.000	0	-99	-1	0			1.000	-0	/C-1	-0.1
1898	Cle-N	10	35	5	11	2	3	0	10	0		.314	.314	.543	857	146	2	1			.860	0	/C-9	0.2
1899	StL-N	6	8	0	0	0	0	0	0	1		.000	.111	.000	111	-67	-2	0			1.000	-1	/1-1,O-1(0-0-1)	-0.2
	Cle-N	43	150	15	47	8	3	0	10	6		.313	.348	.407	755	115	3	4			.911	-5	C-39/1-1,S-1,O-1R	0.1
	StL-N	66	269	42	77	12	2	2	37	14		.286	.324	.368	692	88	-5	14			.963	-3	1-41,C-25/2-1	-0.6
	Yr	115	427	57	124	20	5	2	47	21		.290	.328	.375	703	94	-5	18			.927	-9	C-64,1-43/O-2R,S2	-0.7
1901	Bos-A	86	280	37	85	13	5	0	38	19		.304	.356	.386	742	108	3	6			.926	2	C-72/1-4	1.1
1902	Cle-A	18	74	5	25	0	0	0	9	0		.338	.338	.338	676	91	-1	2			.975	-1	1-17	-0.2
	Phi-A	79	284	45	92	17	2	2	43	9		.324	.347	.419	766	107	2	3			.960	22	C-71/1-7,O-1(0-1-0)	2.8
	Yr	97	358	50	117	17	2	2	52	9		.327	.345	.402	747	104	1	5			.960	21	C-71,1-24/O-1(0-1-0)	2.6

YEAR	TM/L	G	AB	R	H	2B	3B	HR	RBI	BB	SO	AVG	OBP	SLG	OPS	OPS+	BR+	SB	CS	SBR	FA	FR	G/POS	TPR
1903	Phi-A	92	306	26	78	13	4	3	30	11		.255	.285	.353	638	87	-5	0			.975	18	C-77,1-10	2.1
1904	Phi-A	95	311	23	58	9	1	1	21	5		.186	.199	.232	431	34	-23	3			.979	5	C-84/1-9	-1.1
1905	*Phi-A	123	420	30	114	19	6	0	45	3		.271	.278	.345	624	96	-4	9			**.984**	12	*C-114/1-2	2.1
1906	Phi-A	98	338	29	96	20	1	1	41	10		.284	.305	.358	663	104	0	5			.971	8	C-89/1-4	1.9
1907	Phi-A	101	356	30	97	16	3	0	38	17		.272	.306	.334	640	102	-0	4			**.985**	16	C-99/1-2	2.8
1908	Phi-A	71	207	16	46	7	1	0	16	6		.222	.248	.266	513	63	-9	1			.978	9	C-65/1-1	0.7
	Chi-A	6	16	1	3	0	0	0	0	1		.188	.235	.188	423	38	-1	0			.982	4	/C-6	0.4
	Yr	77	223	17	49	7	1	0	16	7		.220	.247	.260	507	61	-10	1			.978	13	C-71/1-1	1.1
Total	11	895	3057	304	829	136	31	9	338	102		.271	.297	.345	642	90	-42	52			.970	86	C-751/1-99,O-3R,2S	12.0

■ HANK SCHREIBER

Schreiber, Henry Walter b: 7/12/1891, Cleveland, Ohio d: 2/23/68, Indianapolis, Ind. BR/TR, 5'11", 165 lbs. Deb: 4/14/14 Career OF: (1-LF 0-CF 0-RF)

YEAR	TM/L	G	AB	R	H	2B	3B	HR	RBI	BB	SO	AVG	OBP	SLG	OPS	OPS+	BR+	SB	CS	SBR	FA	FR	G/POS	TPR
1914	Chi-A	1	2	0	0	0	0	0	0	0	1	.000	.000	.000	0	-99	-0	0			.000	-1	/O-1(1-0-0)	-0.1
1917	Bos-N	2	7	1	2	0	0	0	0	0	1	.286	.286	.286	571	80	-0	0			1.000	-1	/S-1,3-1	-0.1
1919	Cin-N	19	58	5	13	4	0	0	4	0	12	.224	.224	.293	517	56	-3	0			.984	7	3-17/S-2	0.4
1921	NY-N	4	6	2	2	0	0	0	2	1	1	.333	.429	.333	762	104	0	0			.500	-0	/2-2,S-2,3-1	0.0
1926	Chi-N	10	18	2	1	1	0	0	0	0	1	.056	.056	.111	167	-55	-4	0	0	0	1.000	1	/S-3,3-3,2-1	-0.3
Total	5	36	91	10	18	5	0	0	6	1	16	.198	.207	.253	459	34	-8	0	0		.986	6	/3-22,S-8,2-3,O-1L	-0.1

■ TED SCHREIBER

Schreiber, Theodore Henry b: 7/11/38, Brooklyn, N.Y. BR/TR, 5'11", 175 lbs. Deb: 4/14/63

YEAR	TM/L	G	AB	R	H	2B	3B	HR	RBI	BB	SO	AVG	OBP	SLG	OPS	OPS+	BR+	SB	CS	SBR	FA	FR	G/POS	TPR
1963	NY-N	39	50	1	8	0	0	0	2	4	14	.160	.236	.160	396	16	-5	0	1	-0	.977	8	3-17/S-9,2-3	0.3

■ POP SCHRIVER

Schriver, William Frederick b: 7/11/1865, Brooklyn, N.Y. d: 12/27/32, Brooklyn, N.Y. BR/TR, 5'9.5", 172 lbs. Deb: 4/29/1886 Career OF: (8-LF 10-CF 5-RF)

YEAR	TM/L	G	AB	R	H	2B	3B	HR	RBI	BB	SO	AVG	OBP	SLG	OPS	OPS+	BR+	SB	CS	SBR	FA	FR	G/POS	TPR
1886	Bro-a	8	21	2	1	0	0	0	0	2		.048	.130	.048	178	-43	-3	0			.667	0	/O-5(2-0-3),C-3	-0.3
1888	Phi-N	40	134	15	26	5	2	1	23	7	21	.194	.250	.284	534	66	-5	2			.870	-3	C-27/S-6,3-6,O-1R	-0.6
1889	Phi-N	55	211	24	56	10	0	1	19	16	8	.265	.323	.327	650	75	-7	5			.920	3	C-48/2-6,3-1	0.0
1890	Phi-N	57	223	37	61	9	6	0	35	22	15	.274	.339	.368	706	103	0	9			.916	-3	C-34,1-10/3-8,2O	0.0
1891	Chi-N	27	90	15	30	1	4	1	21	10	9	.333	.412	.467	878	156	7	1			.964	2	C-27/1-2	0.9
1892	Chi-N	92	326	40	73	10	6	1	34	27	25	.224	.297	.301	598	80	-8	4			.929	-9	C-82,O-10(0-10-0)	-0.9
1893	Chi-N	64	229	49	65	8	3	4	34	14	9	.284	.336	.397	733	96	-2	4			.926	2	C-56/O-5(4-0-1)	0.4
1894	Chi-N	98	354	56	97	12	3	3	49	32	21	.274	.344	.350	695	64	-21	9			.920	2	*C-90/S-3,3-3,1-2	-0.9
1895	NY-N	24	92	16	29	2	1	1	16	9	10	.315	.382	.391	774	102	1	3			.898	-3	C-18/1-6	-0.1
1897	Cin-N	61	178	29	54	12	4	1	30	19		.303	.374	.433	806	106	1	3			.959	-4	C-53	0.2
1898	Pit-N	95	315	25	72	15	3	0	32	23		.229	.287	.295	583	68	-13	0			.957	-5	C-92/1-1	-0.9
1899	Pit-N	92	302	31	85	19	5	1	49	24		.281	.344	.387	732	101	0	4			.958	5	C-78/1-9	1.1
1900	*Pit-N	37	92	12	27	7	0	1	12	10		.293	.381	.402	783	115	2	0			.959	-4	C-24/1-1	0.0
1901	StL-N	53	166	17	45	7	3	1	23	12		.271	.335	.367	703	109	2	2			.971	4	C-24,1-19	0.7
Total	14	803	2733	368	721	117	40	16	377	227	118	.264	.330	.353	683	88	-48	46			.934	-13	C-656/1-50,O-23C,32S	-0.4

■ BOB SCHRODER

Schroder, Robert James b: 12/30/44, Ridgefield, N.J. BL/TR, 6', 175 lbs. Deb: 4/20/65

YEAR	TM/L	G	AB	R	H	2B	3B	HR	RBI	BB	SO	AVG	OBP	SLG	OPS	OPS+	BR+	SB	CS	SBR	FA	FR	G/POS	TPR
1965	SF-N	31	9	4	2	0	0	0	1	1	1	.222	.300	.222	522	48	-1	0	0	0	1.000	3	/2-4,3-1	0.3
1966	SF-N	10	33	0	8	0	0	0	2	0	2	.242	.242	.242	485	34	-3	0	0	0	.963	-5	/S-9	-0.8
1967	SF-N	62	135	20	31	4	0	0	7	15	15	.230	.307	.259	566	64	-6	1	0	0	.993	-10	2-45/3-4	-1.4
1968	SF-N	35	44	5	7	1	1	0	2	7	3	.159	.288	.227	516	56	-2	0	0	0	.960	-3	2-12/S-4,3-2	-0.6
Total	4	138	221	29	48	5	1	0	12	23	21	.217	.294	.249	543	58	-11	1	0	0	.989	-15	/2-61,S-13,3-7	-2.5

■ BILL SCHROEDER

Schroeder, Alfred William b: 9/7/58, Baltimore, Md. BR/TR, 6'2", 200 lbs. Deb: 7/13/83

YEAR	TM/L	G	AB	R	H	2B	3B	HR	RBI	BB	SO	AVG	OBP	SLG	OPS	OPS+	BR+	SB	CS	SBR	FA	FR	G/POS	TPR
1983	Mil-A	23	73	7	13	2	1	3	7	3	23	.178	.221	.356	577	60	-4	0	1	-0	.980	-3	C-23	-0.7
1984	Mil-A	61	210	29	54	6	0	14	25	8	54	.257	.291	.486	777	115	3	0	1	-0	.987	-5	C-58/1-1,D-3	0.0
1985	Mil-A	53	194	18	47	8	0	8	25	12	61	.242	.293	.407	700	90	-3	0	1	-0	.987	-7	C-48/1-1,D-4	-0.9
1986	Mil-A	64	217	32	46	14	0	7	19	9	59	.212	.263	.373	636	69	-10	1	0	0	.995	-4	C-35,1-19,D-10	-1.3
1987	Mil-A	75	250	35	83	12	0	14	42	16	56	.332	.379	.548	927	138	13	5	2	0	.995	-6	C-67/1-4,D-2	0.9
1988	Mil-A	41	122	9	19	2	0	5	10	6	36	.156	.208	.295	503	39	-10	0	0	0	1.000	5	C-30,1-10/D-1	-0.4
1989	Cal-A	41	138	16	28	2	0	6	15	3	44	.203	.220	.348	568	59	-8	0	0	0	.991	10	C-33/1-8	0.3
1990	Cal-A	18	58	7	13	3	0	4	9	1	10	.224	.237	.483	720	98	-1	0	0	0	1.000	2	C-15/1-3	0.2
Total	8	376	1262	153	303	49	1	61	152	58	343	.240	.282	.426	708	91	-20	6	5	-0	.992	-8	C-309/1-46,D-20	-1.9

■ RICK SCHU

Schu, Richard Spencer b: 1/26/62, Philadelphia, Pa. BR/TR, 6', 170 lbs. Deb: 9/1/84 Career OF: (4-LF 0-CF 0-RF)

YEAR	TM/L	G	AB	R	H	2B	3B	HR	RBI	BB	SO	AVG	OBP	SLG	OPS	OPS+	BR+	SB	CS	SBR	FA	FR	G/POS	TPR
1984	Phi-N	17	29	12	8	2	1	2	5	6	6	.276	.400	.621	1021	180	3	0	0	0	.952	-0	3-15	0.3
1985	Phi-N	112	416	54	105	21	4	7	24	38	78	.252	.318	.373	691	90	-6	8	6	-0	.933	-10	*3-111	-1.9
1986	Phi-N	92	208	32	57	10	1	8	25	18	44	.274	.338	.447	785	111	3	2	2	-0	.913	1	3-58	0.3
1987	Phi-N	92	196	24	46	6	3	7	23	20	36	.235	.312	.403	715	85	-4	0	2	-1	.905	-1	3-45,1-28	-0.8
1988	Bal-A	89	270	22	69	9	4	4	20	21	49	.256	.316	.363	679	92	-3	6	4	-0	.937	-12	3-72/1-4,D-9	-1.5
1989	Bal-A	1	0	0	0	0	0	0	0	0	0	—	—	—	—	—	0	0	0	0	1.000	-0	/2-1	0.0
	Det-A	98	266	25	57	11	0	7	21	24	37	.214	.279	.335	614	74	-10	1	2	-0	.934	-2	3-83/2-5,1-3,S-3,D	-1.2
	Yr	99	266	25	57	11	0	7	21	24	37	.214	.279	.335	614	74	-10	1	2	-0	.934	-2	3-83/D-9,2-6,1-3,S	-1.2
1990	Cal-A	61	157	19	42	8	0	6	14	11	25	.268	.315	.433	749	110	1	0	0	0	.918	0	3-38,1-15/O-4L,2-1	0.1
1991	Phi-N	17	22	1	2	0	0	0	2	1	7	.091	.130	.091	221	-37	-4	0	0	0	.667	-1	/3-3,1-1	-0.5
1996	Mon-N	1	4	0	0	0	0	0	0	0	0	.000	.000	.000	0	-98	-1	0	0	0	.667	-0	/3-1	-0.2
Total	9	580	1568	189	386	67	13	41	134	139	282	.246	.311	.384	695	91	-20	17	16	-2	.926	-25	3-426/1-51,D-18,2OS	-5.4

■ HEINIE SCHUBLE

Schuble, Henry George b: 11/1/06, Houston, Tex. d: 10/2/90, Baytown, Tex. BR/TR, 5'9", 152 lbs. Deb: 7/8/27

YEAR	TM/L	G	AB	R	H	2B	3B	HR	RBI	BB	SO	AVG	OBP	SLG	OPS	OPS+	BR+	SB	CS	SBR	FA	FR	G/POS	TPR
1927	StL-N	65	218	29	56	6	2	4	28	7	27	.257	.283	.358	641	69	-10	0			.915	-7	S-65	-1.0
1929	Det-A	92	258	35	60	11	7	2	28	19	23	.233	.288	.353	640	64	-15	3	2	-0	.886	-10	S-86/3-2	-1.6
1932	Det-A	102	340	58	92	20	6	5	52	24	37	.271	.319	.409	728	84	-9	14	5	1	.941	8	3-76,S-16	0.4
1933	Det-A	49	96	12	21	4	1	0	6	5	17	.219	.257	.281	539	42	-8	2	0	0	.951	1	3-23/S-2,2-1	-0.5
1934	Det-A	11	15	2	4	2	0	0	2	1	4	.267	.313	.400	713	83	-0	0	0	0	1.000	0	/S-3,3-2,2-1	0.0
1935	Det-A	11	8	3	2	0	0	0	0	1	0	.250	.333	.250	583	55	-0	0	0	0	.714	1	/3-2,2-1	0.1
1936	StL-N	2	0	0	0	0	0	0	0	0	0	—	—	—	—	—	0	0			.000	0	/3-1	0.0
Total	7	332	935	139	235	43	16	11	116	57	108	.251	.296	.367	663	70	-43	19	7		.906	-6	S-172,3-106/2-3	-2.6

■ WES SCHULMERICH

Schulmerich, Edward Wesley b: 8/21/01, Hillsboro, Ore. d: 6/26/85, Corvallis, Ore. BR/TR, 5'11", 210 lbs. Deb: 5/1/31

YEAR	TM/L	G	AB	R	H	2B	3B	HR	RBI	BB	SO	AVG	OBP	SLG	OPS	OPS+	BR+	SB	CS	SBR	FA	FR	G/POS	TPR
1931	Bos-N	95	327	36	101	17	7	2	43	28	30	.309	.363	.422	785	115	7	0			.966	-4	O-87(0-0-87)	-0.3
1932	Bos-N	119	404	47	105	22	5	11	57	27	61	.260	.314	.421	735	99	-1	5			.968	3	*O-101(0-0-101)	-0.5
1933	Bos-N	29	85	10	21	6	1	1	13	5	10	.247	.289	.376	665	97	-1	0			.980	1	O-21(0-0-21)	-0.1
	Phi-N	97	365	53	122	19	4	8	59	32	45	.334	.394	.474	868	130	15	1			.977	-2	O-97(97-0-0)	0.8
	Yr	126	450	63	143	25	5	9	72	37	55	.318	.375	.456	830	126	16	1			.978	-1	*O-118(97-0-21)	0.7
1934	Phi-N	15	52	2	13	1	0	0	1	4	8	.250	.316	.269	585	51	-3	0			.963	-1	O-13(3-0-10)	-0.5
	Cin-N	74	209	21	55	8	3	5	19	22	43	.263	.333	.402	735	98	-1	1			.976	-2	O-56(13-0-43)	-0.6
	Yr	89	261	23	68	9	3	5	20	26	51	.261	.330	.375	705	88	-4	1			.974	-3	O-69(16-0-53)	-1.1
Total	4	429	1442	169	417	73	20	27	192	118	197	.289	.347	.424	771	109	16	7			.971	-6	O-375(113-0-262)	-1.2

■ ART SCHULT

Schult, Arthur William "Dutch" b: 6/20/28, Brooklyn, N.Y. BR/TR, 6'4", 220 lbs. Deb: 5/17/53

YEAR	TM/L	G	AB	R	H	2B	3B	HR	RBI	BB	SO	AVG	OBP	SLG	OPS	OPS+	BR+	SB	CS	SBR	FA	FR	G/POS	TPR
1953	NY-A	7	0	3	0	0	0	0	0	0	0	—	—	—	—	—	0	0	0	0	.000	0	R	0.0
1956	Cin-N	5	7	3	3	0	0	0	2	1	1	.429	.500	.429	929	144	1	0	0	0	.000	-0	/O-1(1-0-0)	0.0
1957	Cin-N	21	34	4	9	2	0	0	4	0	2	.265	.286	.324	609	59	-2	0	0	0	1.000	1	/O-5(5-0-0)	-0.2
	Was-A	77	247	30	65	14	0	4	35	14	30	.263	.305	.368	674	84	-6	0	1	-0	.987	-1	1-35,O-31(14-1-17)	-1.0
1959	Chi-N	42	118	17	32	7	0	2	14	7	14	.271	.323	.381	704	88	-2	0	0	0	.985	-4	1-23,O-15(12-0-6)	-0.8
1960	Chi-N	12	15	1	2	1	0	0	1	1	3	.133	.188	.200	388	6	-2	0	0	0	1.000	-1	/O-4(4-0-0),1-1	-0.3
Total	5	164	421	58	111	24	0	6	56	23	50	.264	.308	.363	671	81	-11	0	1	-0	.987	-5	/1-59,O-56(36-1-23)	-2.3

■ FRANK SCHULTE

Schulte, Frank M. "Wildfire" b: 9/17/1882, Cohocton, N.Y. d: 10/2/49, Oakland, Cal. BL/TR, 5'11", 170 lbs. Deb: 9/21/04

YEAR	TM/L	G	AB	R	H	2B	3B	HR	RBI	BB	SO	AVG	OBP	SLG	OPS	OPS+	BR+	SB	CS	SBR	FA	FR	G/POS	TPR
1904	Chi-N	20	84	16	24	4	3	2	13	2		.286	.310	.476	787	141	3	1			.949	0	O-20(20-0-0)	0.3

YEAR	TM/L	G	AB	R	H	2B	3B	HR	RBI	BB	SO	AVG	OBP	SLG	OPS	OPS+	BR+	SB	CS	SBR	FA	FR	G/POS	TPR
1905	Chi-N	123	493	67	135	15	14	1	47	32		.274	.326	.367	693	102	1	16			.981	-7	*O-123(107-0-16)	-1.4
1906	*Chi-N	146	563	77	158	18	**13**	7	60	31		.281	.324	.396	720	118	9	25			.975	0	*O-146(0-0-146)	0.3
1907	*Chi-N	97	342	44	98	14	7	2	32	22		.287	.339	.386	725	120	7	7			.973	-3	O-92(1-0-91)	0.0
1908	*Chi-N	102	386	42	91	20	2	1	43	29		.236	.294	.306	600	88	-5	15			.994	-6	*O-102(12-1-89)	-1.9
1909	Chi-N	140	538	57	142	16	11	4	60	24		.264	.298	.357	655	101	-2	23			.968	-13	*O-140(0-0-140)	-2.4
1910	*Chi-N	151	559	93	168	29	15	**10**	68	39	57	.301	.349	.460	809	137	22	22			.968	-6	*O-150(0-0-150)	1.0
1911	Chi-N	154	577	105	173	30	21	**21**	**107**	76	71	.300	.384	**.534**	918	**156**	**40**	23			.971	-5	*O-154(0-0-154)	2.7
1912	Chi-N	139	553	90	146	27	11	12	64	53	70	.264	.336	.418	754	106	3	17			.952	-4	*O-139(0-0-139)	-0.9
1913	Chi-N	132	497	85	138	28	6	9	68	39	68	.278	.336	.412	749	113	7	21			.956	-8	*O-130(1-0-129)	-0.8
1914	Chi-N	137	465	54	112	22	7	5	61	39	55	.241	.306	.351	657	95	-3	16			.954	-10	*O-134(134-0-2)	-2.0
1915	Chi-N	151	550	66	137	20	6	12	62	49	68	.249	.313	.373	686	107	4	19	17	-2	.962	5	*O-147(146-0-4)	0.0
1916	Chi-N	72	230	31	68	11	1	5	27	20	35	.296	.352	.417	769	123	6	9			.951	-3	O-67(66-0-1)	0.1
	Pit-N	55	177	12	45	5	3	0	14	17	19	.254	.323	.316	639	96	-0	5			.968	-2	O-48(20-0-28)	-0.5
	Yr	127	407	43	113	16	4	5	41	37	54	.278	.339	.373	713	111	6	14			.958	-5	*O-115(86-0-29)	-0.4
1917	Pit-N	30	103	11	22	5	1	0	7	10	14	.214	.283	.282	565	71	-3	5			.963	-0	O-28(3-0-25)	-0.6
	Phi-N	64	149	21	32	10	0	1	15	16	22	.215	.299	.302	601	81	-3	4			.923	-10	O-42(20-7-15)	-1.7
	Yr	94	252	32	54	15	1	1	22	26	36	.214	.293	.294	587	77	-6	9			.943	-10	O-70(23-7-40)	-2.3
1918	Was-A	93	267	35	77	14	3	0	44	47	36	.288	.406	.363	770	135	14	5			.969	1	O-75(14-1-60)	1.3
Total	15	1806	6533	906	1766	288	124	92	792	545	515	.270	.332	.395	726	114	99	233	17		.966	-70	*O-1737(544-9-1189)	-6.5

■ FRED SCHULTE

Schulte, Fred William "Fritz" (b: Fred William Schult) b: 1/13/01, Belvidere, Ill. d: 5/20/83, Belvidere, Ill. BR/TR, 6'1", 183 lbs. Deb: 4/15/27 Career OF: (17-LF 1016-CF 28-RF)

YEAR	TM/L	G	AB	R	H	2B	3B	HR	RBI	BB	SO	AVG	OBP	SLG	OPS	OPS+	BR+	SB	CS	SBR	FA	FR	G/POS	TPR
1927	StL-A	60	189	32	60	16	5	3	34	20	14	.317	.383	.503	885	124	6	5	3	0	.916	-3	O-49(0-49-0)	0.2
1928	StL-A	146	556	90	159	44	6	7	85	51	60	.286	.347	.424	771	99	-2	6	5	-0	.973	17	*O-143(0-143-0)	0.9
1929	StL-A	121	446	63	137	24	5	3	71	59	44	.307	.389	.404	793	101	2	8	3	1	**.989**	13	*O-116(0-116-0)	1.0
1930	StL-A	113	392	59	109	23	5	5	62	41	44	.278	.348	.401	748	86	-8	12	8	-0	.966	-2	O-98(0-98-0)/1-5	-1.3
1931	StL-A	134	553	100	168	32	7	9	65	56	49	.304	.369	.436	805	107	6	6	8	-1	.971	6	*O-134(0-134-0)	0.6
1932	StL-A	146	565	106	166	35	6	9	73	71	44	.294	.373	.425	797	100	1	5	9	-2	.986	0	*O-129(3-126-0)/1-5	-0.4
1933	*Was-A	144	550	98	162	30	7	5	87	61	27	.295	.366	.402	768	104	4	10	12	-2	.980	16	*O-142(0-142-0)	1.4
1934	Was-A	136	524	72	156	32	6	3	73	53	34	.298	.363	.399	762	100	1	3	7	-2	.986	-1	*O-134(0-134-0)	-0.5
1935	Was-A	76	226	33	60	6	4	2	23	26	22	.265	.344	.354	698	83	-5	0	3	-1	.980	-8	O-56(12-19-26)	-1.5
1936	Pit-N	74	238	28	62	7	3	1	17	20	20	.261	.320	.328	648	73	-9	1			.977	-3	O-55(1-54-0)	-1.3
1937	Pit-N	29	20	5	2	0	0	0	3	4	3	.100	.280	.100	380	7	-2	0			.800	-1	/O-4(1-1-2)	-0.4
Total	11	1179	4259	686	1241	249	54	47	593	462	361	.291	.362	.408	770	98	-6	56	58		.976	35	*O-1060C/1-10	-1.3

■ HAM SCHULTE

Schulte, Herman Joseph (b: Herman Joseph Schultehenrich) b: 9/1/12, St.Louis, Mo. d: 12/21/93, St.Charles, Mo. BR/TR, 5'8.5", 158 lbs. Deb: 4/16/40 F

YEAR	TM/L	G	AB	R	H	2B	3B	HR	RBI	BB	SO	AVG	OBP	SLG	OPS	OPS+	BR+	SB	CS	SBR	FA	FR	G/POS	TPR
1940	Phi-N	120	436	44	103	18	2	1	21	32	30	.236	.288	.294	582	63	-22	3			**.980**	-10	*2-119/S-1	-2.5

■ JOHNNY SCHULTE

Schulte, John Clement b: 9/8/1896, Fredericktown, Mo. d: 6/28/78, St.Louis, Mo. BL/TR, 5'11", 190 lbs. Deb: 4/18/23 C

YEAR	TM/L	G	AB	R	H	2B	3B	HR	RBI	BB	SO	AVG	OBP	SLG	OPS	OPS+	BR+	SB	CS	SBR	FA	FR	G/POS	TPR
1923	StL-A	7	3	1	0	0	0	0	1	4	0	.000	.571	.000	571	56	0	0	0	0	1.000	1	/C-1,1-1	0.1
1927	StL-N	64	156	35	45	8	2	9	32	47	19	.288	.456	.538	994	160	16	1			.956	3	C-59	2.1
1928	Phi-N	65	113	14	28	2	2	4	17	15	12	.248	.336	.407	743	90	-2	0			.949	-5	C-34	-0.5
1929	Chi-N	31	69	6	18	3	0	0	9	7	11	.261	.329	.304	633	58	-4	0			.978	-0	C-30	-0.3
1932	StL-A	15	24	2	5	2	0	0	3	1	6	.208	.240	.292	532	35	-2	0	0	0	.864	-1	/C-6	-0.2
	Bos-N	10	9	1	2	0	0	1	2	2	1	.222	.364	.556	919	149	1	0			1.000	1	C-10	0.2
Total	5	192	374	59	98	15	4	14	64	76	49	.262	.388	.436	824	112	8	1	0		.957	-2	C-140/1-1	1.4

■ JACK SCHULTE

Schulte, John Herman Frank b: 11/15/1881, Cincinnati, Ohio d: 8/17/75, Roseville, Mich. BR/TR, 5'9", 180 lbs. Deb: 8/19/06

YEAR	TM/L	G	AB	R	H	2B	3B	HR	RBI	BB	SO	AVG	OBP	SLG	OPS	OPS+	BR+	SB	CS	SBR	FA	FR	G/POS	TPR
1906	Bos-N	2	7	0	0	0	0	0	0	0		.000	.000	.000	0	-99	-2	0			1.000	-1	/S-2	-0.3

■ LEN SCHULTE

Schulte, Leonard Bernard (b: Leonard Bernard Schultehenrich) b: 12/5/16, St.Charles, Mo. d: 5/6/86, Orlando, Fla. BR/TR, 5'10", 160 lbs. Deb: 9/27/44 F

YEAR	TM/L	G	AB	R	H	2B	3B	HR	RBI	BB	SO	AVG	OBP	SLG	OPS	OPS+	BR+	SB	CS	SBR	FA	FR	G/POS	TPR
1944	StL-A	1	0	0	0	0	0	0	0	1	0	—	1.000	—	1000	188	0	0	0	0	.000	0	H	0.0
1945	StL-A	119	430	37	106	16	1	0	36	24	35	.247	.286	.288	575	64	-20	0	3	-1	.961	-8	3-71,2-37,S-14	-2.8
1946	StL-A	4	5	1	2	0	0	0	2	0	0	.400	.400	.400	800	118	0	0	0	0	1.000	1	/2-1,3-1	0.1
Total	3	124	435	38	108	16	1	0	38	25	35	.248	.289	.290	579	65	-20	0	3	-1	.962	-7	/3-72,2-38,S-14	-2.7

■ HOWIE SCHULTZ

Schultz, Howard Henry "Stretch" or "Steeple" b: 7/3/22, St.Paul, Minn. BR/TR, 6'6", 200 lbs. Deb: 8/16/43

YEAR	TM/L	G	AB	R	H	2B	3B	HR	RBI	BB	SO	AVG	OBP	SLG	OPS	OPS+	BR+	SB	CS	SBR	FA	FR	G/POS	TPR
1943	Bro-N	45	182	20	49	12	0	1	34	6	24	.269	.300	.352	652	88	-3	3			.986	2	1-45	-0.4
1944	Bro-N	138	526	59	134	32	3	11	83	24	67	.255	.290	.390	680	92	-8	6			.988	-0	*1-136	-1.6
1945	Bro-N	39	142	18	34	8	2	1	19	10	14	.239	.294	.345	639	78	-5	2			.984	3	1-38	-0.4
1946	Bro-N	90	249	27	63	14	1	3	27	16	34	.253	.298	.353	652	84	-6	2			.989	5	1-87	-0.4
1947	Bro-N	2	1	0	0	0	0	0	0	0	0	.000	.000	.000	0	-96	-0	0			1.000	-0	/1-1	0.0
	Phi-N	114	403	30	90	19	1	6	35	21	70	.223	.264	.320	584	56	-27	0			.993	-1	*1-114	-3.1
	Yr	116	404	30	90	19	1	6	35	21	70	.223	.263	.319	582	56	-27	0			.993	-1	*1-115	-3.1
1948	Phi-N	6	13	0	1	0	0	0	1	1	2	.077	.143	.077	220	-40	-3	0			1.000	0	/1-3	-0.3
	Cin-N	36	72	9	12	0	0	2	9	4	7	.167	.211	.250	461	25	-8	2			.982	-3	1-26	-1.1
	Yr	42	85	9	13	0	0	2	10	5	9	.153	.200	.224	424	15	-10	2			.984	-3	1-29	-1.4
Total	6	470	1588	163	383	85	7	24	208	82	218	.241	.281	.349	630	75	-59	15			.989	6	1-450	-7.3

■ JOHN SCHULTZ

Schultz, John b: St.Louis, Mo. Deb: 8/7/1891

YEAR	TM/L	G	AB	R	H	2B	3B	HR	RBI	BB	SO	AVG	OBP	SLG	OPS	OPS+	BR+	SB	CS	SBR	FA	FR	G/POS	TPR
1891	StL-a	1	2	0	0	0	0	0	0	0	0	.000	.000	.000	0	-87	-0	0			1.000	0	/C-1	0.0

■ JOE SCHULTZ

Schultz, Joseph Charles Jr. "Dode" b: 8/29/18, Chicago, Ill. d: 1/10/96, St.Louis, Mo. BL/TR, 5'11", 184 lbs. Deb: 9/27/39 FMC

YEAR	TM/L	G	AB	R	H	2B	3B	HR	RBI	BB	SO	AVG	OBP	SLG	OPS	OPS+	BR+	SB	CS	SBR	FA	FR	G/POS	TPR
1939	Pit-N	4	14	3	4	2	0	0	2	2	0	.286	.375	.429	804	117	0	0			1.000	1	/C-4	0.1
1940	Pit-N	16	36	2	7	0	1	0	4	2	1	.194	.237	.250	487	35	-3	0			.917	-3	C-13	-0.6
1941	Pit-N	2	2	1	1	0	0	0	0	0	0	.500	.500	.500	1000	183	0	0			.000	0	/C-2	0.0
1943	StL-A	46	92	6	22	5	0	0	8	9	8	.239	.307	.293	600	74	-3	0	1	-0	.979	-5	C-26	-0.8
1944	StL-A	3	8	1	2	0	0	0	0	0	1	.250	.250	.250	500	41	-1	0	0	0	.818	-1	/C-3	-0.1
1945	StL-A	41	44	1	13	2	0	0	8	3	1	.295	.340	.341	681	93	-0	0	0	0	.941	0	/C-4	0.0
1946	StL-A	42	57	1	22	4	0	0	14	11	2	.386	.485	.456	941	156	5	0	0	0	1.000	-5	C-17	0.1
1947	StL-A	43	38	3	7	0	0	1	1	4	5	.184	.262	.263	525	45	-3	0	0	0	.000	0	H	-0.3
1948	StL-A	43	37	0	7	0	0	0	9	6	3	.189	.302	.189	492	32	-3	0	0	0	.000	0	H	-0.3
Total	9	240	328	18	85	13	1	1	46	37	21	.259	.334	.314	648	81	-8	0	1		.964	-12	/C-69	-1.9

■ JOE SCHULTZ

Schultz, Joseph Charles Sr. "Germany" b: 7/24/1893, Pittsburgh, Pa. d: 4/13/41, Columbia, S.C. BR/TR, 5'11.5", 172 lbs. Deb: 9/28/12 F Career OF: (104-LF 9-CF 307-RF)

YEAR	TM/L	G	AB	R	H	2B	3B	HR	RBI	BB	SO	AVG	OBP	SLG	OPS	OPS+	BR+	SB	CS	SBR	FA	FR	G/POS	TPR
1912	Bos-N	4	12	1	3	1	0	0	4	0	2	.250	.250	.333	583	58	-1	0			.824	-0	/2-4	-0.1
1913	Bos-N	9	18	2	4	0	0	0	1	2	7	.222	.333	.222	556	59	-1	0			1.000	0	/O-5(0-2-3),2-1	-0.1
1915	Bro-N	56	120	13	35	3	2	0	4	10	18	.292	.346	.350	696	109	1	3	4	-1	.894	-4	3-27/S-1	-0.3
	Chi-N	7	8	1	2	0	0	0	3	0	2	.250	.250	.250	500	51	-0	0			.857	0	/2-2	0.0
	Yr	63	128	14	37	3	2	0	7	10	20	.289	.341	.344	684	106	1	3	4	-1	.894	-3	3-27/2-2,S-1	-0.3
1916	Pit-N	77	204	18	53	8	2	0	22	7	14	.260	.298	.319	616	88	-3	6			.840	-15	2-24,3-24/O-6L,S-1	-2.0
1919	StL-N	88	229	24	58	9	1	2	21	11	7	.253	.287	.328	615	90	-3	4			1.000	-7	O-49(2-2-46)/2-6,3-1	-1.4
1920	StL-N	99	320	38	84	5	5	0	32	21	11	.262	.308	.309	617	81	-8	5	4	-0	.945	-4	O-80(2-0-79)	-1.7
1921	StL-N	92	275	37	85	20	3	6	45	15	11	.309	.347	.469	816	116	6	4	3	-0	.977	-2	O-67(0-0-67)/3-3,1-2	-0.1
1922	StL-N	112	344	50	108	13	4	2	64	19	10	.314	.350	.392	742	96	-2	3	1	0	.976	2	O-89(33-3-53)	-0.7
1923	StL-N	2	7	0	2	0	0	0	1	1	0	.286	.375	.286	661	78	-0	0	0	0	1.000	0	/O-2(0-0-2)	0.0
1924	StL-N	12	12	0	2	0	0	0	2	3	0	.167	.333	.167	500	39	-1	0	0	0	1.000	-1	/O-2(1-1-0)	-0.2
	Phi-N	88	284	35	80	15	1	5	29	20	18	.282	.329	.394	723	83	-7	6	2	1	.960	-6	O-76(54-1-25)	-1.8
	Yr	100	296	35	82	15	1	5	31	23	18	.277	.329	.385	714	82	-7	6	2	1	.960	-7	O-78(55-2-25)	-2.0

YEAR	TM/L	G	AB	R	H	2B	3B	HR	RBI	BB	SO	AVG	OBP	SLG	OPS	OPS+	BR+	SB	CS	SBR	FA	FR	G/POS	TPR
1925	Phi-N	24	64	10	22	6	0	0	8	4	1	.344	.382	.438	820	100	0	1	1	-0	.923	-2	O-20(3-0-17)	-0.3
	Cin-N	33	62	6	20	3	1	0	13	3	1	.323	.354	.403	757	95	-0	3	1	0	.950	-4	O-15(5-0-12)/2-1	-0.5
	Yr	57	126	16	42	9	1	0	21	7	2	.333	.368	.421	789	99	-0	4	2	0	.932	-6	O-35(8-0-29)/2-1	-0.8
Total	11	703	1959	235	558	83	19	15	249	116	102	.285	.327	.370	696	93	-20	35	16		.966	-42	O-411R/3-55,2-38,1S	-9.2
■ **JEFF SCHULZ**	Schulz, Jeffrey Alan b: 6/2/61, Evansville, Ind. BL/TR, 6'1", 190 lbs. Deb: 9/2/89																							
1989	KC-A	7	9	0	2	0	0	0	1	0	2	.222	.222	.222	444	26	-1	0	0	0	1.000	-0	/O-5(4-0-0)	-0.1
1990	KC-A	30	66	5	17	5	1	0	6	6	13	.258	.319	.364	683	92	-1	0	0	0	.943	-3	O-22(8-0-16)/D-1	-0.4
1991	Pit-N	3	3	0	0	0	0	0	0	0	2	.000	.000	.000	0	-99	-1	0	0	0	.000	0	/H	-0.1
Total	3	40	78	5	19	5	1	0	7	6	17	.244	.298	.333	631	77	-2	0	0	0	.951	-4	/O-27(12-0-16),D-1	-0.6
■ **BILL SCHUSTER**	Schuster, William Charles "Broadway Bill" b: 8/4/12, Buffalo, N.Y. d: 6/28/87, ElMonte, Cal. BR/TR, 5'9", 164 lbs. Deb: 9/29/37																							
1937	Pit-N	3	6	2	3	0	0	0	1	1	0	.500	.571	.500	1071	193	1	0			1.000	1	/S-2	0.2
1939	Bos-N	2	3	0	0	0	0	0	0	0	1	.000	.000	.000	0	-99	-1	0			.833	-0	/S-1,3-1	-0.1
1943	Chi-N	13	51	3	15	2	1	0	0	3	2	.294	.333	.373	706	105	0	0			.977	7	S-13	0.8
1944	Chi-N	60	154	14	34	7	1	1	14	12	16	.221	.277	.299	576	62	-8	4			.946	-4	S-38/2-6	-1.0
1945	*Chi-N	45	47	8	9	2	1	0	2	7	4	.191	.296	.277	573	61	-2	2			.949	8	S-22/2-3,3-1	0.7
Total	5	123	261	27	61	11	3	1	17	23	23	.234	.296	.310	606	72	-10	6			.954	11	/S-76,2-9,3-2	0.6
■ **RANDY SCHWARTZ**	Schwartz, Douglas Randall b: 2/9/44, Los Angeles, Cal. BL/TL, 6'3", 230 lbs. Deb: 9/8/65																							
1965	KC-A	6	7	0	2	0	0	0	1	0	4	.286	.286	.286	571	64	-0	0	0	0	1.000	1	/1-2	0.0
1966	KC-A	10	11	0	1	0	0	0	1	1	3	.091	.167	.091	258	-24	-2	0	0	0	1.000	-0	/1-2	-0.2
Total	2	16	18	0	3	0	0	0	2	1	7	.167	.211	.167	377	10	-2	0	0	0	1.000	0	/1-4	-0.2
■ **BILL SCHWARTZ**	Schwartz, William August "Pop" or "Scooper Bill" b: 4/3/1864, Jamestown, Ky. d: 12/22/40, Newport, Ky. BR/TR, 6'1", 195 lbs. Deb: 5/3/1883 Career OF: (2-LF 1-CF 1-RF)																							
1883	Col-a	2	4	0	1	0	0	0		0		.250	.250	.250	500	67	-0				.600	-1	/1-1,C-1	-0.1
1884	Cin-U	29	106	14	25	4	0	1		3		.236	.257	.302	559	64	-8				.837	-4	C-25/O-3(2-1-1),3-1	-0.9
Total	2	31	110	14	26	4	0	1		3		.236	.257	.300	557	64	-8				.828	-6	/C-26,O-3L,3-1,1-1	-1.0
■ **BILL SCHWARTZ**	Schwartz, William Charles "Blab" b: 4/22/1884, Cleveland, Ohio d: 8/29/61, Nashville, Tenn. BR/TR, 6'2", 185 lbs. Deb: 5/2/04																							
1904	Cle-A	24	86	5	13	2	0	0	0	0		.151	.151	.174	326	3	-9	4			.980	-4	1-22/3-1	-1.6
■ **AL SCHWEITZER**	Schweitzer, Albert Caspar "Cheese" b: 12/23/1882, Cleveland, Ohio d: 1/27/69, Newark, Ohio BR/TR, 5'6", 170 lbs. Deb: 4/30/08																							
1908	StL-A	64	182	22	53	4	2	1	14	20		.291	.374	.352	725	135	8	6			.952	5	O-55(0-28-27)	1.2
1909	StL-A	27	76	7	17	2	0	0	2	5		.224	.298	.250	548	79	-2	3			.933	-3	O-22(6-7-9)	-0.6
1910	StL-A	113	379	37	87	11	2	2	37	36		.230	.303	.285	588	90	-4	26			.937	-4	*O-109(1-32-76)	-1.5
1911	StL-A	76	237	31	51	11	4	0	34	43		.215	.338	.295	633	80	-5	12			.934	-1	O-68(9-8-51)	-0.9
Total	4	280	874	97	208	28	8	3	87	104		.238	.327	.299	626	95	-2	47			.940	-3	O-254(16-75-163)	-1.8
■ **PI SCHWERT**	Schwert, Pius Louis b: 11/22/1892, Angola, N.Y. d: 3/11/41, Washington, D.C. BR/TR, 5'10.5", 160 lbs. Deb: 8/20/14																							
1914	NY-A	3	6	0	0	0	0	0	0	2	3	.000	.250	.000	250	-24	-1	0			.923	1	/C-3	0.0
1915	NY-A	9	18	6	5	3	0	0	6	1	6	.278	.316	.444	760	128	0	0			.972	0	/C-9	0.1
Total	2	12	24	6	5	3	0	0	6	3	9	.208	.296	.333	630	89	-0	0			.959	1	/C-12	0.1
■ **ART SCHWIND**	Schwind, Arthur Edwin b: 11/4/1889, Ft.Wayne, Ind. d: 1/13/68, Sullivan, Ill. BB/TR, 5'8", 150 lbs. Deb: 10/3/12																							
1912	Bos-N	1	2	0	1	0	0	0	0	0	0	.500	.500	.500	1000	171	0	0			.000	0	/3-1	0.0
■ **JERRY SCHYPINSKI**	Schypinski, Gerald Albert b: 9/16/31, Detroit, Mich. BL/TR, 5'10", 170 lbs. Deb: 8/31/55																							
1955	KC-A	22	69	7	15	2	0	0	5	1	6	.217	.229	.246	475	27	-7	0	0	0	.932	-2	S-21/2-2	-0.8
■ **MIKE SCIOSCIA**	Scioscia, Michael Lorri b: 11/27/58, Upper Darby, Pa. BL/TR, 6'2", 220 lbs. Deb: 4/20/80 MC																							
1980	LA-N	54	134	8	34	5	1	1	8	12	9	.254	.315	.328	643	81	-3	1	0	0	.992	3	C-54	0.2
1981	*LA-N	93	290	27	80	10	0	2	29	36	18	.276	.358	.331	689	100	1	0	2	-1	.987	-3	C-91	0.2
1982	LA-N	129	365	31	80	11	1	5	38	44	31	.219	.305	.296	601	70	-14	2	0	0	.986	-7	*C-123	-1.6
1983	LA-N	12	35	3	11	3	0	1	7	5	2	.314	.400	.486	886	145	2	0	0	0	1.000	-3	C-11	0.0
1984	LA-N	114	341	29	93	18	0	5	38	52	26	.273	.371	.370	740	110	6	2	1	0	.985	14	*C-112	2.5
1985	*LA-N	141	429	47	127	26	3	7	53	77	21	.296	.409	.420	829	136	25	3	3	-0	.986	2	*C-139	3.4
1986	LA-N	122	374	36	94	18	1	5	26	62	23	.251	.362	.345	707	103	4	3	3	-0	.982	-1	*C-119	0.8
1987	LA-N	142	461	44	122	26	1	6	38	55	23	.265	.344	.364	709	90	-5	7	4	0	.989	11	*C-138	1.1
1988	*LA-N	130	408	29	105	18	0	3	35	38	31	.257	.321	.324	644	88	-6	0	3	-1	.991	8	*C-123	0.9
1989	LA-N★	133	408	40	102	16	0	10	44	52	29	.250	.339	.363	702	102	2	0	2	-1	.988	18	*C-130	2.8
1990	LA-N★	135	435	46	115	25	0	12	66	55	31	.264	.351	.405	756	110	7	4	1	1	.989	5	*C-132	2.1
1991	LA-N	119	345	39	91	16	2	8	40	47	32	.264	.357	.391	748	113	7	4	3	-0	.990	9	*C-115	2.2
1992	LA-N	117	348	19	77	6	3	3	24	32	31	.221	.289	.282	570	63	-17	3	2	-0	.988	11	*C-108	0.1
Total	13	1441	4373	398	1131	198	12	68	446	567	307	.259	.347	.356	703	99	9	29	24	-2	.988	67	*C-1395	14.7
■ **LOU SCOFFIC**	Scoffic, Louis "Weaser" b: 5/20/13, Herrin, Ill. d: 8/28/97, Herrin, Ill. BR/TR, 5'10", 182 lbs. Deb: 4/16/36																							
1936	StL-N	4	7	2	3	0	0	0	2	1	2	.429	.500	.429	929	153	1	0			.875	-0	/O-3(0-0-3)	0.0
■ **DARYL SCONIERS**	Sconiers, Daryl Anthony b: 10/3/58, San Bernardino, Cal. BL/TL, 6'2", 195 lbs. Deb: 9/13/81																							
1981	Cal-A	15	52	6	14	1	1	1	7	1	10	.269	.283	.385	668	91	-1	0	0	0	1.000	1	1-12/D-3	-0.1
1982	Cal-A	12	13	0	2	0	0	0	2	2	1	.154	.267	.154	421	19	-1	0	0	0	1.000	0	/1-3,D-1	-0.1
1983	Cal-A	106	314	49	86	19	3	8	46	17	41	.274	.311	.430	741	102	0	4	2	0	.986	-5	1-57,D-27/O-1(1-0-0)	-0.8
1984	Cal-A	57	160	14	39	4	0	4	17	13	17	.244	.301	.344	644	78	-5	1	2	-0	.990	-1	1-41/D-1	-0.8
1985	Cal-A	44	98	14	28	6	1	2	12	15	18	.286	.381	.429	809	122	3	2	1	0	.973	-1	D-20/1-6	0.2
Total	5	234	637	83	169	30	5	15	84	48	87	.265	.317	.399	716	97	-3	7	5	-0	.989	-6	1-119/D-52,O-1(1-0-0)	-1.6
■ **SCOTT**	Scott Deb: 7/16/1884																							
1884	Bal-U	13	53	10	12	1	1	1		2		.226	.255	.340	594	71	-4				.909	-2	O-13(0-0-13)/3-1	-0.5
■ **TONY SCOTT**	Scott, Anthony b: 9/18/51, Cincinnati, Ohio BB/TR, 6', 175 lbs. Deb: 9/1/73																							
1973	Mon-N	11	1	2	0	0	0	0	0	0	1	.000	.000	.000	0	-97	-0	0	0	0	.000	-2	/O-3(1-1-1)	-0.2
1974	Mon-N	19	7	2	2	0	0	0	1	1	3	.286	.375	.286	661	82	-0	1	1	-0	1.000	-5	O-16(2-1-14)	-0.6
1975	Mon-N	92	143	19	26	4	2	0	11	12	38	.182	.259	.238	497	37	-12	5	6	-1	.962	-9	O-71(45-4-28)	-2.5
1977	StL-N	95	292	38	85	16	3	3	41	33	48	.291	.369	.397	766	107	4	13	10	-1	.996	5	O-89(3-82-6)	0.7
1978	StL-N	96	219	28	50	5	2	1	14	14	41	.228	.281	.283	564	59	-12	5	6	-1	.946	-9	O-77(38-31-10)	-2.6
1979	StL-N	153	587	69	152	22	10	6	68	34	92	.259	.305	.361	666	80	-16	37	17	2	.984	17	*O-151(0-140-14)	0.1
1980	StL-N	143	415	51	104	19	3	0	28	35	68	.251	.310	.311	621	72	-15	22	10	1	**.997**	1	*O-134(0-134-0)	-1.5
1981	StL-N	45	176	21	40	5	2	2	17	5	22	.227	.253	.313	565	58	-10	10	7	-0	1.000	1	O-44(0-44-0)	-1.1
	*Hou-N	55	225	28	66	13	2	2	22	15	32	.293	.338	.396	733	113	3	8	3	1	.985	1	O-55(0-55-0)	0.5
	Yr	100	401	49	106	18	4	4	39	20	54	.264	.301	.359	660	88	-7	18	10	0	.992	2	O-99(0-99-0)	-0.6
1982	Hou-N	132	460	43	110	16	3	1	29	15	56	.239	.265	.293	558	61	-25	18	4	3	.982	-3	*O-129(2-125-3)	-2.9
1983	Hou-N	80	186	20	42	6	1	2	17	11	39	.226	.269	.301	570	62	-10	5	4	-0	1.000	-12	O-61(17-30-28)	-2.5
1984	Hou-N	25	21	2	4	1	0	0	0	4	3	.190	.320	.238	558	63	-1	0	0	0	1.000	-1	/O-6(1-5-0)	-0.2
	Mon-N	45	71	8	18	4	0	0	5	7	21	.254	.321	.310	630	81	-2	1	1	-0	1.000	-2	O-17(16-1-2)	-0.4
	Yr	70	92	10	22	5	0	0	5	11	24	.239	.320	.293	614	78	-2	1	1	-0	1.000	-3	O-23(17-6-2)	-0.6
Total	11	991	2803	331	699	111	28	17	253	186	464	.249	.300	.327	627	75	-97	125	69	3	.986	-18	O-853(125-653-106)	-13.2
■ **DONNIE SCOTT**	Scott, Donald Malcolm b: 8/16/61, Dunedin, Fla. BB/TR, 5'11", 185 lbs. Deb: 9/30/83																							
1983	Tex-A	2	4	0	0	0	0	0	0	0	0	.000	.000	.000	0	-99	-1	0	0	0	1.000	1	/C-2	0.0
1984	Tex-A	81	235	16	52	9	0	3	20	20	44	.221	.282	.298	580	59	-13	0	1	-0	.974	4	C-80	-0.6
1985	Sea-A	80	185	18	41	13	0	4	23	15	41	.222	.280	.357	637	72	-7	1	1	-0	.981	-7	C-74	-1.2

YEAR	TM/L	G	AB	R	H	2B	3B	HR	RBI	BB	SO	AVG	OBP	SLG	OPS	OPS+	BR+	SB	CS	SBR	FA	FR	G/POS	TPR
1991	Cin-N	10	19	0	3	0	0	0	0	0	2	.158	.158	.158	316	-11	-3	0	0	0	1.000	-3	/C-8	-0.6
Total	4	173	443	34	96	22	0	7	43	35	87	.217	.274	.314	588	60	-24	1	2	-0	.977	-5	C-164	-2.4
■ PETE SCOTT	Scott, Floyd John b: 12/21/1898, Woodland, Cal. d: 5/3/53, Daly City, Cal. BR/TR, 5′11.5″, 175 lbs. Deb: 4/13/26 Career OF: (64-LF 1-CF 77-RF)																							
1926	Chi-N	77	189	34	54	13	1	3	34	22	31	.286	.363	.413	776	107	2	3			.968	-1	O-59(34-0-29)/3-1	-0.2
1927	Chi-N	71	156	28	49	18	1	0	21	19	18	.314	.392	.442	834	123	5	1			.986	-2	O-36(1-1-35)	0.0
1928	Pit-N	60	177	33	55	10	4	5	33	18	14	.311	.378	.497	875	122	5	1			.979	2	O-42(29-0-13)/1-8	0.4
Total	3	208	522	95	158	41	6	8	88	59	63	.303	.377	.450	827	117	13	5			.976	-1	O-137R/1-8,3-1	0.2
■ GARY SCOTT	Scott, Gary Thomas b: 8/22/68, New Rochelle, N.Y. BR/TR, 6′, 175 lbs. Deb: 4/9/91																							
1991	Chi-N	31	79	8	13	3	0	1	5	13	14	.165	.305	.241	546	53	-5	0	1	-0	.969	2	3-31	-0.3
1992	Chi-N	36	96	8	15	2	0	2	11	5	14	.156	.198	.240	438	23	-10	0	1	-0	.922	-2	3-29/S-2	-1.3
Total	2	67	175	16	28	5	0	3	16	18	28	.160	.250	.240	490	38	-14	0	2	-1	.946	-0	/3-60,S-2	-1.6
■ GEORGE SCOTT	Scott, George Charles "Boomer" b: 3/23/44, Greenville, Miss. BR/TR, 6′2″, 215 lbs. Deb: 4/12/66																							
1966	Bos-A★	162	601	73	147	18	7	27	90	65	152	.245	.326	.433	759	105	4	4	0	1	.991	3	*1-158/3-5	-0.2
1967	*Bos-A	159	565	74	171	21	7	19	82	63	119	.303	.377	.465	842	136	27	10	8	-1	.987	-5	*1-152/3-2	1.3
1968	Bos-A	124	350	23	60	14	0	3	25	26	88	.171	.239	.237	476	42	-24	3	5	-1	.987	1	*1-112/3-6	-3.4
1969	Bos-A	152	549	63	139	14	5	16	52	61	74	.253	.332	.384	717	95	-3	4	3	-0	.954	-6	*3-109,1-53	-1.4
1970	Bos-A	127	480	50	142	24	5	16	63	44	95	.296	.357	.467	824	117	11	4	11	-3	.934	-8	3-68,1-59	-0.5
1971	Bos-A	146	537	72	141	16	4	24	78	41	102	.263	.321	.441	762	106	3	0	3	-1	.992	-7	*1-143	-1.8
1972	Mil-A	152	578	71	154	24	4	20	88	43	130	.266	.322	.426	747	123	15	16	4	2	.992	-5	*1-139,3-23	0.1
1973	Mil-A	158	604	98	185	30	4	24	107	61	94	.306	.372	.488	860	144	34	9	5	0	.994	7	*1-157/D-1	2.8
1974	Mil-A	158	604	74	170	36	2	17	82	59	90	.281	.348	.432	780	124	18	9	9	-1	**.992**	8	*1-148/D-9	1.3
1975	Mil-A★	158	617	86	176	26	4	**36**	**109**	51	97	.285	.343	.515	858	139	29	6	5	-0	.989	3	*1-144,D-12/3-5	1.9
1976	Mil-A	156	606	73	166	21	5	18	77	53	118	.274	.337	.414	752	122	15	0	1	-0	.991	-2	*1-155	0.1
1977	Bos-A★	157	584	103	157	26	5	33	95	57	112	.269	.340	.500	840	112	9	1	1	-0	.985	0	*1-157	-0.1
1978	Bos-A	120	412	51	96	16	4	12	54	44	86	.233	.307	.379	686	83	-9	1	1	-0	.991	-8	*1-113/D-7	-2.6
1979	Bos-A	45	156	18	35	9	1	4	23	17	22	.224	.301	.372	672	76	-5	0	0	0	.986	-2	1-41	-1.0
	KC-A	44	146	19	39	8	2	1	20	12	32	.267	.331	.370	701	87	-3	1	1	-0	.989	-3	1-41/3-1,D-2	-0.8
	NY-A	16	44	9	14	3	1	1	6	2	7	.318	.348	.500	848	128	2	1	0	0	1.000	-0	D-15/1-1	0.1
	Yr	105	346	46	88	20	4	6	49	31	61	.254	.319	.387	707	87	-6	2	1	0	.987	-5	1-83,D-17/3-1	-1.7
Total	14	2034	7433	957	1992	306	60	271	1051	699	1418	.268	.335	.435	770	113	122	69	57	-5	.990	-25	*1-1773,3-219/D-46	-4.2
■ JIM SCOTT	Scott, James Walter b: 9/22/1888, Shenandoah, Pa. d: 5/12/72, S.Pasadena, Fla. BR/TR, 5′9.5″, 165 lbs. Deb: 4/22/14																							
1914	Pit-F	8	24	2	6	1	0	0	1	5	0	.250	.379	.292	671	85	-1	1			.800	-3	/S-8	-0.3
■ JOHN SCOTT	Scott, John Henry b: 1/24/52, Jackson, Miss. BR/TR, 6′2″, 165 lbs. Deb: 9/7/74																							
1974	SD-N	14	15	3	1	0	0	0	0	0	4	.067	.067	.067	133	-65	-3	1	0	0	1.000	-1	/O-8(5-2-1)	-0.4
1975	SD-N	25	9	6	0	0	0	0	0	0	2	.000	.000	.000	0	-99	-2	2	0	0	.000	-1	/O-1(0-1-0)	-0.3
1977	Tor-A	79	233	26	56	9	0	2	15	8	39	.240	.266	.305	570	54	-15	10	8	-1	.963	-5	O-67(27-41-0)/D-2	-2.2
Total	3	118	257	35	57	9	0	2	15	8	45	.222	.245	.280	525	43	-21	13	8	0	.965	-6	/O-76(32-44-1),D-2	-2.9
■ LE GRANT SCOTT	Scott, Le Grant Edward b: 7/25/10, Cleveland, Ohio d: 11/12/93, Birmingham, Ala. BL/TL, 5′8.5″, 170 lbs. Deb: 4/19/39																							
1939	Phi-N	76	232	31	65	15	1	1	26	22	14	.280	.343	.366	709	93	-2	5			.959	1	O-55(1-1-54)	-0.4
■ EVERETT SCOTT	Scott, Lewis Everett "Deacon" b: 11/19/1892, Bluffton, Ind. d: 11/2/60, Fort Wayne, Ind. BR/TR, 5′8″, 148 lbs. Deb: 4/14/14																							
1914	Bos-A	144	539	66	129	15	6	2	37	32	43	.239	.286	.301	586	76	-17	9	14	-3	.949	-11	*S-143	-2.3
1915	*Bos-A	100	359	25	72	11	0	0	28	17	21	.201	.237	.231	468	41	-27	4	7	-2	.961	4	*S-100	-1.9
1916	*Bos-A	123	366	37	85	19	2	0	27	23	24	.232	.283	.295	578	73	-13	8			**.967**	7	*S-121/2-1,3-1	0.1
1917	Bos-A	157	528	40	127	24	7	0	50	20	46	.241	.268	.313	581	78	-16	12			**.953**	8	*S-157	0.3
1918	*Bos-A	126	443	40	98	11	5	0	43	12	16	.221	.242	.269	510	55	-26	11			**.976**	18	*S-126	0.0
1919	Bos-A	138	507	41	141	19	0	0	38	19	26	.278	.306	.316	621	79	-15	8			**.976**	7	*S-138	0.1
1920	Bos-A	154	569	41	153	21	12	4	61	21	15	.269	.300	.369	669	80	-19	4	11	-3	**.973**	17	*S-154	0.6
1921	Bos-A	154	576	65	151	21	9	1	62	27	21	.262	.295	.335	630	62	-34	5	9	-2	**.972**	**38**	*S-154	1.8
1922	*NY-A	154	557	64	150	23	5	3	45	23	22	.269	.304	.345	649	67	-27	2	3	-1	**.966**	17	*S-154	0.6
1923	*NY-A	152	533	48	131	16	4	6	60	13	19	.246	.266	.325	591	54	-37	1	3	-1	**.961**	-11	*S-152	-3.2
1924	NY-A	153	548	56	137	12	6	4	64	21	15	.250	.278	.316	593	53	-40	3	7	-2	.966	10	*S-153	-1.5
1925	NY-A	22	60	3	13	0	0	0	4	2	2	.217	.242	.217	459	17	-8	0	1	-0	.988	3	S-18	-0.3
	Was-A	33	103	10	28	6	1	0	18	4	4	.272	.299	.350	649	65	-6	1	2	-0	.932	3	S-30/3-2	-0.1
	Yr	55	163	13	41	6	1	0	22	6	6	.252	.278	.301	579	48	-13	1	3	-1	.952	6	S-48/3-2	-0.4
1926	Chi-A	40	143	15	36	10	1	0	13	9	8	.252	.296	.336	632	67	-7	1	3	-1	.955	5	S-39	0.1
	Cin-N	4	6	1	4	0	0	0	1	0	0	.667	.667	.667	1333	267	1	0			.875	0	/S-4	0.2
Total	13	1654	5837	552	1455	208	58	20	551	243	282	.249	.281	.315	596	65	-290	69	60		.965	115	*S-1643/3-3,2-1	-5.5
■ MILT SCOTT	Scott, Milton Parker "Mikado Milt" b: 1/17/1866, Chicago, Ill. d: 11/3/38, Baltimore, Md. BR, 5′9″, 160 lbs. Deb: 9/30/1882																							
1882	Chi-N	1	5	1	2	0	0	0	0	0	0	.400	.400	.400	800	151	0				1.000	0	/1-1	0.0
1884	Det-N	110	438	29	108	17	5	3	50	9	62	.247	.262	.329	591	90	-5				.968	-1	*1-110	-1.4
1885	Det-N	38	148	14	39	7	0	0	12	4	16	.264	.283	.311	594	92	-2				.967	3	1-38	-0.2
	Pit-a	55	210	15	52	7	1	0	18	5		.248	.272	.290	562	79	-5				.986	3	1-55	-0.7
1886	Bal-a	137	484	48	92	11	4	2	52	22		.190	.239	.242	481	52	-26	11			.974	8	*1-137/P-1	-2.7
Total	4	341	1285	107	293	42	10	5	132	40	78	.228	.257	.288	545	74	-37	11			.973	13	1-341/P-1	-5.0
■ DICK SCOTT	Scott, Richard Edward b: 7/19/62, Ellsworth, Maine BR/TR, 6′1″, 170 lbs. Deb: 5/19/89																							
1989	Oak-A	3	2	0	0	0	0	0	1	0	0	.000	.000	.000	0	-99	-1	0	0	0	.000	0	/S-3	-0.1
■ RODNEY SCOTT	Scott, Rodney Darrell b: 10/16/53, Indianapolis, Ind. BB/TR (BR 1975), 6′, 160 lbs. Deb: 4/11/75 Career OF: (0-LF 10-CF 1-RF)																							
1975	KC-A	48	15	13	1	0	0	0	0	1	3	.067	.125	.067	192	-43	-3	4	2	0	1.000	6	D-22/2-9,S-8,R-0	0.3
1976	Mon-N	7	10	3	4	0	0	0	0	1	1	.400	.455	.400	855	138	1	2	0	0	1.000	-0	/2-6,S-3	0.1
1977	Oak-A	133	364	56	95	4	4	0	20	43	50	.261	.344	.294	638	77	-10	33	18	1	.963	-30	2-71,S-70/3-5,OD	-3.2
1978	Chi-N	78	227	41	64	5	1	0	15	43	41	.282	.403	.313	716	91	0	27	10	2	.929	-9	3-59,O-10C/2-6,S-6	-0.7
1979	Mon-N	151	562	69	134	12	5	3	42	66	82	.238	.321	.294	614	69	-22	39	12	4	.980	-15	*2-113,S-39	-2.3
1980	Mon-N	154	567	84	127	13	**13**	0	46	70	75	.224	.310	.293	603	69	-22	63	13	9	.982	-16	*2-129,S-21	-2.1
1981	*Mon-N	95	336	43	69	9	3	0	26	50	35	.205	.310	.250	560	60	-16	30	7	4	.983	-15	2-93	-2.4
1982	Mon-N	14	25	2	5	0	0	0	1	3	2	.200	.286	.200	486	37	-2	5	0	1	.971	-1	2-12	-0.2
	NY-A	10	26	5	5	0	0	0	0	4	2	.192	.300	.192	492	39	-2	2	0	0	.963	1	/S-6,2-4	0.0
Total	8	690	2132	316	504	43	26	3	150	281	291	.236	.328	.285	613	71	-76	205	62	23	.979	-81	2-443,S-153/3-64,DO	-10.5
■ JIM SCRANTON	Scranton, James Dean b: 4/5/60, Torrance, Cal. BR/TR, 6′, 175 lbs. Deb: 9/5/84																							
1984	KC-A	2	2	0	0	0	0	0	0	0	0	.000	.000	.000	0	-99	-1	0	0	0	1.000	-1	/S-1,3-1	-0.1
1985	KC-A	6	4	1	0	0	0	0	0	0	0	.000	.000	.000	0	-99	-1	0	0	0	1.000	2	/S-5	0.1
Total	2	8	6	1	0	0	0	0	0	0	0	.000	.000	.000	0	-99	-2	0	0	0	1.000	2	/S-6,3-1	0.0
■ CHUCK SCRIVENER	Scrivener, Wayne Allison b: 10/3/47, Alexandria, Va. BR/TR, 5′9″, 170 lbs. Deb: 9/18/75																							
1975	Det-A	4	16	0	4	1	0	0	0	0	1	.250	.250	.313	563	56	-1	1	0	0	1.000	-2	/3-3,S-2	-0.3
1976	Det-A	80	222	28	49	7	1	2	16	19	34	.221	.282	.288	570	65	-10	1	0	0	.976	7	2-43,S-37/3-5	0.4
1977	Det-A	61	72	10	6	0	0	0	2	5	9	.083	.143	.083	226	-35	-13	0	0	0	.981	10	S-50/2-8,3-3	-0.1
Total	3	145	310	38	59	8	1	2	18	24	44	.190	.249	.242	490	40	-24	2	0	0	.970	15	/S-89,2-51,3-11	-0.0
■ TONY SCRUGGS	Scruggs, Anthony Raymond b: 3/19/66, Riverside, Cal. BR/TR, 6′1″, 210 lbs. Deb: 4/8/91																							
1991	Tex-A	5	6	1	0	0	0	0	0	0	1	.000	.000	.000	0	-99	-2	0	0	0	1.000	-1	/O-5(5-1-0)	-0.3

■ KEN SEARS

Sears, Kenneth Eugene "Ziggy" b: 7/6/17, Streator, Ill. d: 7/17/68, Bridgeport, Tex. BL/TR, 6'1", 200 lbs. Deb: 5/2/43

YEAR	TM/L	G	AB	R	H	2B	3B	HR	RBI	BB	SO	AVG	OBP	SLG	OPS	OPS+	BR+	SB	CS	SBR	FA	FR	G/POS	TPR
1943	NY-A	60	187	22	52	7	0	2	22	11	18	.278	.328	.348	676	97	-1	1	3	-1	.974	1	C-50	0.2
1946	StL-A	7	15	1	5	0	0	0	1	3	0	.333	.444	.333	778	114	1	0	0	0	1.000	-3	/C-4	-0.2
Total	2	67	202	23	57	7	0	2	23	14	18	.282	.338	.347	684	99	-0	1	3	-1	.975	-2	/C-54	0.0

■ JIMMY SEBRING

Sebring, James Dennison b: 3/22/1882, Liberty, Pa. d: 12/22/09, Williamsport, Pa. BL/TR, 6', 180 lbs. Deb: 9/8/02

YEAR	TM/L	G	AB	R	H	2B	3B	HR	RBI	BB	SO	AVG	OBP	SLG	OPS	OPS+	BR+	SB	CS	SBR	FA	FR	G/POS	TPR
1902	Pit-N	19	80	15	26	4	4	0	15	5		.325	.365	.475	840	154	5	2			.974	4	O-19(0-0-19)	0.8
1903	*Pit-N	124	506	71	140	16	13	4	64	32		.277	.325	.383	708	98	-3	20			.927	7	*O-124(0-0-124)	-0.1
1904	Pit-N	80	305	28	82	11	7	0	32	17		.269	.307	.351	658	100	-1	8			.959	9	O-80(0-0-80)	0.5
	Cin-N	56	222	22	50	9	2	0	24	14		.225	.271	.284	555	65	-9	8			1.000	4	O-56(0-0-56)	-0.9
	Yr	136	527	50	132	20	9	0	56	31		.250	.292	.323	615	85	-10	16			.974	12	*O-136(0-0-136)	-0.4
1905	Cin-N	58	217	31	62	10	5	2	28	14		.286	.329	.406	735	107	1	11			.885	-6	O-56(0-0-56)	-0.8
1909	Bro-N	25	81	11	8	1	1	0	5	11		.099	.207	.136	342	7	-9	3			.951	-2	O-25(0-21-4)	-1.4
	Was-A	1	0	0	0	0	0	0	0	0		—	—	—	—		0	0			.000	-1	/O-1(0-1-0)	-0.1
Total	5	363	1411	178	368	51	32	6	168	93		.261	.308	.355	663	93	-15	52			.945	14	O-361(0-22-339)	-2.0

■ FRANK SECORY

Secory, Frank Edward b: 8/24/12, Mason City, Iowa d: 4/7/95, Port Huron, Mich. BR/TR, 6'1", 200 lbs. Deb: 4/28/40 U

YEAR	TM/L	G	AB	R	H	2B	3B	HR	RBI	BB	SO	AVG	OBP	SLG	OPS	OPS+	BR+	SB	CS	SBR	FA	FR	G/POS	TPR
1940	Det-A	1	1	0	0	0	0	0	0	0	1	.000	.000	.000	0	-91	-0	0	0	0	.000	0	H	0.0
1942	Cin-N	2	5	1	0	0	0	0	1	3	2	.000	.375	.000	375	14	-0	0			.857	0	/O-2(2-0-0)	0.0
1944	Chi-N	22	56	10	18	1	0	4	17	6	8	.321	.387	.554	941	163	5	1			1.000	0	O-17(17-1-0)	0.4
1945	*Chi-N	35	57	4	9	1	0	0	6	2	7	.158	.186	.175	362	1	-8	0			1.000	-1	O-12(10-0-2)	-1.0
1946	Chi-N	33	43	6	10	3	0	3	12	6	6	.233	.327	.512	838	139	2	0			.833	-3	/O-9(9-0-0)	-0.1
Total	5	93	162	21	37	5	0	7	36	17	24	.228	.302	.389	691	95	-2	1	0		.964	-4	/O-40(38-1-2)	-0.7

■ CHARLIE SEE

See, Charles Henry "Chad" b: 10/13/1896, Pleasantville, N.Y d: 7/19/48, Bridgeport, Conn. BL/TR, 5'10.5", 175 lbs. Deb: 8/6/19

YEAR	TM/L	G	AB	R	H	2B	3B	HR	RBI	BB	SO	AVG	OBP	SLG	OPS	OPS+	BR+	SB	CS	SBR	FA	FR	G/POS	TPR
1919	Cin-N	8	14	1	4	0	0	0	1	1	0	.286	.333	.286	619	89	-0	0			.833	-1	/O-4(2-2-0)	-0.2
1920	Cin-N	47	82	9	25	4	0	0	15	1	7	.305	.329	.354	683	97	-0	2	4	-1	1.000	3	O-17(0-14-4)/P-1	0.0
1921	Cin-N	37	106	11	26	5	1	1	7	7	5	.245	.298	.340	638	72	-4	3	2	-0	.954	-0	O-30(0-11-18)	-0.6
Total	3	92	202	21	55	9	1	1	23	9	12	.272	.313	.342	655	83	-5	5	6		.967	1	/O-51(2-27-22),P-1	-0.8

■ LARRY SEE

See, Ralph Laurence b: 6/20/60, Norwalk, Cal. BR/TR, 6'1", 195 lbs. Deb: 9/3/86

YEAR	TM/L	G	AB	R	H	2B	3B	HR	RBI	BB	SO	AVG	OBP	SLG	OPS	OPS+	BR+	SB	CS	SBR	FA	FR	G/POS	TPR
1986	LA-N	13	20	1	5	2	0	0	2	2	7	.250	.318	.350	668	90	-0	0	0	0	.979	1	/1-9	0.1
1988	Tex-A	13	23	0	3	0	0	0	0	1	8	.130	.167	.130	297	-15	-3	0	0	0	1.000	-0	/C-2,1-2/3-1,D-7	-0.4
Total	2	26	43	1	8	2	0	0	2	3	15	.186	.239	.233	472	32	-4	0	0	0	.967	1	/1-11,D-7,C-2,3-1	-0.3

■ BOB SEEDS

Seeds, Ira Robert "Suitcase Bob" b: 2/24/07, Ringgold, Tex. d: 10/28/93, Erick, Okla. BR/TR, 6', 180 lbs. Deb: 4/19/30 Career OF: (194-LF 160-CF 131-RF)

YEAR	TM/L	G	AB	R	H	2B	3B	HR	RBI	BB	SO	AVG	OBP	SLG	OPS	OPS+	BR+	SB	CS	SBR	FA	FR	G/POS	TPR
1930	Cle-A	85	277	37	79	11	3	3	32	12	22	.285	.315	.379	694	72	-12	1	3	-1	.953	2	O-70(48-21-1)	-1.4
1931	Cle-A	48	134	26	41	4	1	1	10	11	11	.306	.359	.373	732	88	-2	1	0	0	.966	-2	O-33(3-1-29)/1-2	-0.6
1932	Cle-A	2	4	0	0	0	0	0	0	0	0	.000	.000	.000	0	-94	-1	0	0	0	.000	-0	/O-1(0-0-1)	-0.2
	Chi-A	116	434	53	126	18	6	2	45	31	37	.290	.342	.373	715	91	-6	5	7	-1	.964	-9	*O-112(34-34-53)	-2.0
	Yr	118	438	53	126	18	6	2	45	31	37	.288	.339	.370	709	89	-7	5	7	-1	.964	-9	*O-113(34-34-54)	-2.2
1933	Bos-A	82	230	26	56	13	4	0	23	21	20	.243	.310	.335	644	71	-10	1	3	-1	.985	-5	1-41,O-32(17-0-16)	-1.9
1934	Bos-A	8	6	0	1	0	0	0	1	0	1	.167	.167	.167	333	-13	-1	0	0	0	.000	-0	/O-1(0-0-1)	-0.1
	Cle-A	61	186	28	46	8	1	0	18	21	13	.247	.327	.301	628	62	-10	2	1	0	.977	-4	O-48(26-2-21)	-1.5
	Yr	69	192	28	47	8	1	0	19	21	14	.245	.322	.297	619	59	-11	2	1	0	.977	-4	O-49(26-2-22)	-1.6
1936	*NY-A	13	42	12	11	1	0	4	10	5	3	.262	.340	.571	912	126	1	3	1	0	1.000	1	/O-9(1-0-8),3-3	0.2
1938	NY-N	81	296	35	86	12	3	9	52	20	33	.291	.338	.443	780	112	4	0			.987	-5	O-76(37-40-1)	-0.4
1939	NY-N	63	173	33	46	5	1	5	26	22	31	.266	.352	.393	745	99	0	1			.975	-8	O-50(12-38-0)	-0.9
1940	NY-N	56	155	18	45	5	2	4	16	17	19	.290	.371	.426	797	118	4	0			.985	-4	O-40(16-24-0)	-0.1
Total	9	615	1937	268	537	77	21	28	233	160	190	.277	.336	.382	718	89	-32	14	15		.970	-35	O-472L/1-43,3-3	-8.9

■ PAT SEEREY

Seerey, James Patrick b: 3/17/23, Wilburton, Okla. d: 4/28/86, Jennings, Mo. BR/TR, 5'10", 200 lbs. Deb: 6/9/43

YEAR	TM/L	G	AB	R	H	2B	3B	HR	RBI	BB	SO	AVG	OBP	SLG	OPS	OPS+	BR+	SB	CS	SBR	FA	FR	G/POS	TPR
1943	Cle-A	26	72	8	16	3	0	1	5	4	19	.222	.263	.306	569	70	-3	0	0	0	.974	1	O-16(16-0-0)	-0.3
1944	Cle-A	101	342	39	80	16	0	15	39	19	99	.234	.276	.412	689	99	-3	0	2	-1	.986	1	O-86(63-19-4)	-0.8
1945	Cle-A	126	414	56	98	22	2	14	56	66	97	.237	.342	.401	743	120	11	1	2	-0	.975	-15	*O-117(38-28-68)	-1.2
1946	Cle-A	117	404	57	91	17	2	26	62	65	101	.225	.334	.470	804	131	16	2	3	-1	.981	-5	*O-115(39-40-43)	0.6
1947	Cle-A	82	216	24	37	4	1	11	29	34	66	.171	.284	.352	636	78	-7	0	1	-0	.957	-8	O-68(53-1-16)	-2.0
1948	Cle-A	10	23	7	6	0	0	1	6	7	8	.261	.433	.391	825	123	1	0	0	0	1.000	-2	/O-7(0-0-7)	-0.1
	Chi-A	95	340	44	78	11	0	18	64	61	94	.229	.347	.421	767	107	3	0	0	0	.981	-0	O-93(82-12-0)	-0.4
	Yr	105	363	51	84	11	0	19	70	68	102	.231	.353	.419	771	108	4	0	0	0	.982	-2	*O-100(82-12-7)	-0.5
1949	Chi-A	4	4	1	0	0	0	0	0	3	1	.000	.429	.000	429	19	-0	0	0	0	1.000	-1	/O-2(0-0-2)	-0.1
Total	7	561	1815	236	406	73	5	86	261	259	485	.224	.321	.412	733	109	17	3	8	-2	.978	-27	O-504(291-100-140)	-4.3

■ EMMETT SEERY

Seery, John Emmett b: 2/13/1861, Princeville, Ill. d: 8/7/30, Saranac Lake, N.Y. BL/TR, Deb: 4/17/1884 Career OF: (778-LF 2-CF 138-RF)

YEAR	TM/L	G	AB	R	H	2B	3B	HR	RBI	BB	SO	AVG	OBP	SLG	OPS	OPS+	BR+	SB	CS	SBR	FA	FR	G/POS	TPR
1884	Bal-U	105	463	113	144	25	7	2		20		.311	.340	.408	748	114	-6				.828	7	*O-103L/C-3,3-2	-0.1
	KC-U	1	4	2	2	1	0	0		1		.500	.600	.750	1350	353	1				.000	-0	/O-1(1-0-0)	0.1
	Yr	106	467	115	146	26	7	2		21		.313	.342	.411	753	116	-5				.828	6	*O-104L/C-3,3-2	0.0
1885	StL-N	59	216	20	35	7	0	1	14	16	37	.162	.220	.208	428	42	-13				.874	5	O-59(49-0-10)/3-1	-0.9
1886	StL-N	126	453	73	108	22	6	2	48	57	82	.238	.324	.327	650	105	6	24			.883	-5	*O-126(126-0-0)/P-2	-0.2
1887	Ind-N	122	536	104	175	18	15	4	28	71	68	.326	.331	.353	684	93	-2	48			.891	7	*O-122(122-1-1)/S-1	0.2
1888	Ind-N	133	500	87	110	20	10	5	50	64	73	.220	.316	.330	646	104	4	80			.939	8	*O-133(133-0-0)/S-1	0.9
1889	Ind-N	127	526	123	165	26	12	8	59	67	59	.314	.401	.454	856	136	27	19			.909	1	*O-127(127-0-0)	2.1
1890	Bro-P	104	394	78	88	12	7	1	50	70	36	.223	.348	.297	645	69	-17	44			.894	7	*O-104(104-0-0)	-1.0
1891	Cin-a	97	372	77	106	15	10	4	36	81	52	.285	.423	.411	834	128	16	19			.898	3	*O-97(17-1-80)	1.5
1892	Lou-N	42	154	18	31	6	1	0	15	24	19	.201	.309	.253	562	76	-3	6			.961	3	O-42(0-0-42)	-0.2
Total	9	916	3618	695	964	152	68	27	300	471	426	.266	.345	.356	701	103	13	240			.896	36	O-914L/3-3,C-3,SP	2.4

■ KEVIN SEFCIK

Sefcik, Kevin John b: 2/10/71, Tinley Park, Ill. BR/TR, 5'11", 175 lbs. Deb: 9/8/95 Career OF: (91-LF 47-CF 46-RF)

YEAR	TM/L	G	AB	R	H	2B	3B	HR	RBI	BB	SO	AVG	OBP	SLG	OPS	OPS+	BR+	SB	CS	SBR	FA	FR	G/POS	TPR
1995	Phi-N	5	4	1	0	0	0	0	0	0	2	.000	.000	.000	0	-99	-1	0	0	0	1.000	0	/3-2	-0.1
1996	Phi-N	44	116	10	33	5	3	0	9	9	16	.284	.346	.379	726	90	-1	3	0	1	.986	1	S-21,3-20/2-1	0.1
1997	Phi-N	61	119	11	32	3	0	2	6	4	9	.269	.298	.345	643	68	-6	1	2	-0	.961	-3	2-22,S-10/3-4	-0.8
1998	Phi-N	104	169	27	53	7	2	3	20	25	32	.314	.423	.432	855	124	7	4	2	0	.989	-6	O-60(35-8-20)/3-2,2-1	0.0
1999	Phi-N	111	209	28	58	15	3	1	11	29	24	.278	.368	.392	761	90	-2	9	4	1	.986	-15	O-64(31-19-17),2-15	-1.6
2000	Phi-N	99	153	15	36	6	2	0	10	13	19	.235	.304	.301	604	52	-11	4	2	0	1.000	-6	O-50(25-20-9)/D-1	-1.7
Total	6	424	770	92	212	36	10	6	56	80	102	.275	.353	.371	725	86	-14	21	10	1	.991	-30	O-174L/2-39,S-31,3D	-4.1

■ KAL SEGRIST

Segrist, Kal Hill b: 4/14/31, Greenville, Tex. BR/TR, 6', 180 lbs. Deb: 7/16/52

YEAR	TM/L	G	AB	R	H	2B	3B	HR	RBI	BB	SO	AVG	OBP	SLG	OPS	OPS+	BR+	SB	CS	SBR	FA	FR	G/POS	TPR
1952	NY-A	13	23	3	1	0	0	0	1	3	1	.043	.154	.043	197	-46	-5	0	0	0	.971	0	2-11/3-1	-0.4
1955	Bal-A	7	9	1	3	0	0	0	0	2	0	.333	.455	.333	788	123	0	0	0	0	1.000	0	/3-3,1-1,2-1	0.1
Total	2	20	32	4	4	0	0	0	1	5	1	.125	.243	.125	368	4	-4	0	0	0	.971	1	/2-12,3-4,1-1	-0.3

■ DAVID SEGUI

Segui, David Vincent b: 7/19/66, Kansas City, Kan. BB/TL, 6'1", 202 lbs. Deb: 5/8/90 F Career OF: (71-LF 0-CF 29-RF)

YEAR	TM/L	G	AB	R	H	2B	3B	HR	RBI	BB	SO	AVG	OBP	SLG	OPS	OPS+	BR+	SB	CS	SBR	FA	FR	G/POS	TPR
1990	Bal-A	40	123	14	30	7	0	2	15	11	15	.244	.311	.350	661	87	-2	0	0	0	.990	1	1-36/D-4	-0.3
1991	Bal-A	86	212	15	59	7	0	2	22	12	19	.278	.317	.340	657	85	-4	1	1	-0	.996	1	1-42,O-33(28-0-5)/D-4	-0.6
1992	Bal-A	115	189	21	44	9	0	1	17	20	23	.233	.306	.296	603	68	-8	1	0	0	.998	2	1-95,O-18(3-0-15)	-0.8
1993	Bal-A	146	450	54	123	27	0	10	60	58	53	.273	.356	.400	756	99	0	2	1	0	.996	4	*1-144/D-1	-0.9
1994	NY-N	92	336	46	81	17	1	10	43	33	43	.241	.311	.387	698	81	-10	0	0	0	**.996**	-3	1-78,O-21(19-0-2)	-2.0
1995	NY-N	33	73	9	24	3	1	2	11	12	9	.329	.430	.479	910	144	5	1	3	-1	1.000	-2	O-18(18-0-0)/1-7	0.1
	Mon-N	97	383	59	117	22	3	10	57	28	38	.305	.356	.457	813	109	5	1	4	-1	.997	0	1-97/O-2(2-0-0)	-0.6
	Yr	130	456	68	141	25	4	12	68	40	47	.309	.369	.461	829	115	10	2	7	-2	.997	-2	*1-104,O-20(20-0-0)	-0.5
1996	Mon-N	115	416	69	119	30	1	11	58	60	54	.286	.376	.442	818	112	9	4	4	-1	.993	6	*1-113	0.3

YEAR	TM/L	G	AB	R	H	2B	3B	HR	RBI	BB	SO	AVG	OBP	SLG	OPS	OPS+	BR+	SB	CS	SBR	FA	FR	G/POS	TPR
1997	Mon-N	125	459	75	141	22	3	21	68	57	66	.307	.385	.505	890	131	21	1	0	0	.995	-1	*1-125	0.9
1998	Sea-A	143	522	79	159	36	1	19	84	49	80	.305	.364	.487	851	119	14	3	1	0	**.999**	14	*1-134/O-1(1-0-0)	1.4
1999	Sea-A	90	345	43	101	22	3	9	39	32	43	.293	.354	.452	807	106	3	1	2	-0	.996	4	1-90	-0.2
	Tor-A	31	95	14	30	5	0	5	13	8	17	.316	.369	.526	895	123	3	0	0	0	.955	-0	D-25/1-4	0.1
	Yr	121	440	57	131	27	3	14	52	40	60	.298	.358	.468	826	110	6	1	2	-0	.995	4	1-94,D-25	-0.1
2000	Tex-A	93	351	52	118	29	1	11	57	34	51	.336	.395	.519	913	125	13	0	1	-0	1.000	2	D-52,1-38	0.8
	Cle-A	57	223	41	74	13	0	8	46	19	33	.332	.387	.498	885	119	6	0	0	0	1.000	4	1-35,D-16/O-7(0-0-7)	0.5
	Yr	150	574	93	192	42	1	19	103	53	84	.334	.392	.510	902	122	20	0	1	-0	1.000	6	1-73,D-68/O-7(0-0-7)	1.3
Total	11	1263	4177	591	1220	249	14	121	590	433	544	.292	.360	.445	805	109	56	15	17	-3	.996	32	*1-1038,D-102,O-100L	-1.3

■ **FERNANDO SEGUIGNOL** Seguignol, Fernando Alfredo b: 1/19/75, Bocas Del Toro, Panama BB/TR, 6'5", 190 lbs. Deb: 9/5/98 Career OF: (31-LF 0-CF 18-RF)

YEAR	TM/L	G	AB	R	H	2B	3B	HR	RBI	BB	SO	AVG	OBP	SLG	OPS	OPS+	BR+	SB	CS	SBR	FA	FR	G/POS	TPR
1998	Mon-N	16	42	6	11	4	0	2	3	3	15	.262	.311	.500	811	111	0	0	0	0	1.000	2	/O-9(8-0-1),1-7	0.2
1999	Mon-N	35	105	14	27	9	0	5	10	5	33	.257	.333	.486	819	107	1	0	0	0	.989	-2	1-23/O-8(6-0-3)	-0.3
2000	Mon-N	76	162	22	45	8	0	10	22	9	46	.278	.328	.512	840	107	1	0	1	-0	.987	-8	1-30,O-30L/D-1	-1.0
Total	3	127	309	42	83	21	0	17	35	17	94	.269	.327	.502	829	107	2	0	1	-0	.990	-9	/1-60,O-47L,D-1	-1.1

■ **KURT SEIBERT** Seibert, Kurt Elliott b: 10/16/55, Cheverly, Md. BB/TR, 6', 165 lbs. Deb: 9/3/79

YEAR	TM/L	G	AB	R	H	2B	3B	HR	RBI	BB	SO	AVG	OBP	SLG	OPS	OPS+	BR+	SB	CS	SBR	FA	FR	G/POS	TPR
1979	Chi-N	7	2	2	0	0	0	0	0	0	1	.000	.000	.000	0	-91	-1	0	0	0	1.000	0	/2-1	0.0

■ **SOCKS SEIBOLD** Seibold, Harry b: 4/3/1896, Philadelphia, Pa. d: 9/21/65, Philadelphia, Pa. BR/TR, 5'8.5", 162 lbs. Deb: 9/18/15

YEAR	TM/L	G	AB	R	H	2B	3B	HR	RBI	BB	SO	AVG	OBP	SLG	OPS	OPS+	BR+	SB	CS	SBR	FA	FR	G/POS	TPR
1915	Phi-A	10	26	3	3	1	0	0	2	4	4	.115	.233	.154	387	16	-3	0			.714	-4	/S-7	-0.7
1916	Phi-A	5	12	0	2	1	0	0	1	0	4	.167	.167	.250	417	26	-1	0			1.000	2	/P-3,O-1(0-1-0)	0.0
1917	Phi-A	36	59	6	13	1	1	0	5	4	8	.220	.281	.271	552	70	-2	1			.978	-2	P-33/O-2(2-0-0)	-0.1
1919	Phi-A	15	13	1	2	0	0	0	1	0	4	.154	.154	.154	308	-13	-2	0			.941	0	P-14	0.0
1929	Bos-N	33	70	6	20	2	0	0	9	6	6	.286	.342	.314	656	67	-3	0			**1.000**	-1	P-33	0.0
1930	Bos-N	36	90	6	19	2	0	1	5	6	6	.211	.260	.267	527	29	-10	0			.941	-3	P-36	0.0
1931	Bos-N	33	70	3	9	0	0	0	2	1	9	.129	.141	.129	269	-28	-13	0			**1.000**	0	P-33	0.0
1932	Bos-N	28	46	2	7	0	0	0	2	2	0	.152	.188	.152	340	-8	-7	0			1.000	2	P-28	0.0
1933	Bos-N	11	9	0	1	0	0	0	0	2	2	.111	.273	.111	384	14	-1	0			1.000	0	P-11	0.0
Total	9	207	395	27	76	7	1	1	27	25	43	.192	.242	.223	465	25	-42	1			.982	-5	P-191/S-7,O-3(2-1-0)	-0.8

■ **RICKY SEILHEIMER** Seilheimer, Ricky Allen b: 8/30/60, Brenham, Tex. BL/TR, 5'11", 185 lbs. Deb: 7/5/80

YEAR	TM/L	G	AB	R	H	2B	3B	HR	RBI	BB	SO	AVG	OBP	SLG	OPS	OPS+	BR+	SB	CS	SBR	FA	FR	G/POS	TPR
1980	Chi-A	21	52	4	11	3	1	1	3	4	15	.212	.268	.365	633	72	-2	1	0	0	.946	-3	C-21	-0.4

■ **KEVIN SEITZER** Seitzer, Kevin Lee b: 3/26/62, Springfield, Ill. BR/TR, 5'11", 190 lbs. Deb: 9/3/86 Career OF: (14-LF 1-CF 1-RF)

YEAR	TM/L	G	AB	R	H	2B	3B	HR	RBI	BB	SO	AVG	OBP	SLG	OPS	OPS+	BR+	SB	CS	SBR	FA	FR	G/POS	TPR
1986	KC-A	28	96	16	31	4	1	2	11	19	14	.323	.440	.448	888	140	6	0	0	0	.987	1	1-22/O-5(5-0-0),3-3	0.6
1987	KC-A★	161	641	105	**207**	33	8	15	83	80	85	.323	.400	.470	869	126	27	12	7	0	.947	8	*3-141,1-25/O-3L,D	2.9
1988	KC-A	149	559	90	170	32	5	5	60	72	64	.304	.389	.406	795	122	19	10	8	-1	.938	3	*3-147/O-1(1-0-0),D-1	2.2
1989	KC-A	160	597	78	168	17	2	4	48	102	76	.281	.391	.337	727	107	11	17	8	1	.950	-11	*3-159/S-6,O-3L,1-2	0.2
1990	KC-A	158	622	91	171	31	5	6	38	67	66	.275	.347	.370	717	102	3	7	5	-0	.953	-9	*3-152,2-10	-0.6
1991	KC-A	85	234	28	62	11	3	1	25	29	21	.265	.351	.350	701	94	-1	4	1	1	.940	0	3-68/D-3	0.0
1992	Mil-A	148	540	74	146	35	1	5	71	57	44	.270	.342	.367	709	101	1	13	11	-1	**.969**	-13	*3-146/2-2,1-1	-1.3
1993	Oak-A	73	255	24	65	10	2	4	27	27	33	.255	.329	.357	685	90	-4	4	7	-2	.933	-9	3-46,1-24/O-3L,2PDS	-1.6
	Mil-A	47	162	21	47	6	0	7	30	17	15	.290	.361	.457	818	120	5	3	0	1	.942	-2	3-33/1-7,2-1,O-1R,D	0.3
	Yr	120	417	45	112	16	2	11	57	44	48	.269	.341	.396	737	102	1	7	7	-1	.937	-11	3-79,1-31/D-6,O2PS	-1.3
1994	Mil-A	80	309	44	97	24	2	5	49	30	38	.314	.378	.453	831	108	4	2	1	0	.924	-4	3-43,1-35/D-4	-0.3
1995	Mil-A★	132	492	56	153	33	3	5	69	64	57	.311	.397	.421	818	107	7	2	0	0	.968	-1	3-88,1-36,D-14	0.3
1996	Mil-A	132	490	74	155	25	3	12	62	73	68	.316	.409	.453	862	113	13	6	1	1	.996	0	1-65,D-56,3-12	0.4
	*Cle-A	22	83	11	32	10	0	1	16	14	11	.386	.480	.542	1022	159	8	0	0	0	1.000	2	D-17/1-5	0.8
	Yr	154	573	85	187	35	3	13	78	87	79	.326	.420	.466	886	120	21	6	1	1	.997	3	D-73,1-70,3-12	1.2
1997	*Cle-A	64	198	27	53	14	0	2	24	18	25	.268	.329	.369	697	79	-6	0	0	0	1.000	1	D-24,1-19,3-13	-0.8
Total	12	1439	5278	739	1557	285	35	74	613	669	617	.295	.378	.404	782	110	94	80	49	0	.949	-33	*3-1051,1-241,D/O2SP	3.1

■ **KIP SELBACH** Selbach, Albert Karl b: 3/24/1872, Columbus, Ohio d: 2/17/56, Columbus, Ohio BR/TR, 5'7", 190 lbs. Deb: 4/24/1894 Career OF: (1356-LF 66-CF 148-RF)

YEAR	TM/L	G	AB	R	H	2B	3B	HR	RBI	BB	SO	AVG	OBP	SLG	OPS	OPS+	BR+	SB	CS	SBR	FA	FR	G/POS	TPR
1894	Was-N	97	372	69	114	21	17	7	71	51	20	.306	.390	.511	901	119	11	21			.915	-9	O-80(45-2-33),S-19	-0.2
1895	Was-N	130	519	116	168	22	**22**	6	55	71	28	.324	.406	.486	892	131	25	31			.913	16	*O-119L/S-6,2-5	2.5
1896	Was-N	127	487	100	148	17	13	5	100	76	28	.304	.405	.423	828	118	16	49			.946	7	*O-126(124-0-2)	1.0
1897	Was-N	124	486	113	152	25	16	5	59	80		.313	.414	.461	875	131	24	46			.955	13	*O-124(124-0-0)	2.2
1898	Was-N	132	515	88	156	28	11	3	60	64		.303	.383	.417	801	130	21	25			.948	20	*O-131(127-4-0)/S-1	2.7
1899	Cin-N	141	525	105	156	28	11	3	87	70		.297	.386	.410	796	116	13	38			.953	17	*O-141(101-40-0)	1.6
1900	NY-N	141	523	98	176	29	12	4	68	72		.337	.425	.461	885	151	40	36			.951	10	*O-141(141-0-0)	3.3
1901	NY-N	125	502	89	145	29	6	1	56	45		.289	.350	.376	726	115	10	8			.942	-10	*O-125(125-0-0)	-0.7
1902	Bal-A	128	503	86	161	27	9	3	60	58		.320	.393	.427	820	122	16	22			.941	9	*O-127(127-0-0)	1.7
1903	Was-A	140	533	68	134	23	12	3	49	41		.251	.305	.356	661	96	-3	20			.956	-3	*O-140(120-0-20)/3-1	-1.4
1904	Was-A	48	178	15	49	8	4	0	14	24		.275	.361	.365	727	132	7	9			.931	3	O-48(48-0-0)	0.8
	Bos-A	98	376	50	97	19	8	0	30	48		.258	.347	.351	698	114	8	10			.961	1	O-98(98-0-0)	0.3
	Yr	146	554	65	146	27	12	0	44	72		.264	.351	.356	707	120	15	19			.950	4	*O-146(146-0-0)	1.1
1905	Bos-A	121	418	54	103	16	6	4	47	67		.246	.355	.342	697	120	12	12			.928	-1	*O-112(0-20-92)	0.6
1906	Bos-A	60	228	15	48	9	2	0	23	18		.211	.277	.268	545	71	-7	7			.966	1	O-58(58-0-0)	-1.1
Total	13	1612	6165	1066	1807	301	149	44	779	785	76	.293	.377	.412	788	121	193	334			.944	75	*O-1570L/S-26,2-5,3	13.3

■ **BILL SELBY** Selby, William Frank b: 6/11/70, Monroeville, Ala. BL/TR, 5'9", 190 lbs. Deb: 4/19/96 Career OF: (10-LF 0-CF 6-RF)

YEAR	TM/L	G	AB	R	H	2B	3B	HR	RBI	BB	SO	AVG	OBP	SLG	OPS	OPS+	BR+	SB	CS	SBR	FA	FR	G/POS	TPR
1996	Bos-A	40	95	12	26	4	0	3	6	9	11	.274	.337	.411	747	86	-2	1	1	-0	.980	-6	2-14,3-14/O-6(6-0-0)	-0.7
2000	Cle-A	30	46	8	11	1	0	0	4	1	9	.239	.271	.261	532	35	-5	0	0	0	1.000	-3	O-10R/2-6,3-4,D-6	-0.7
Total	2	70	141	20	37	5	0	3	10	10	20	.262	.316	.362	677	69	-7	1	1	-0	.982	-10	/2-20,3-18,O-16L,D	-1.4

■ **GEORGE SELKIRK** Selkirk, George Alexander "Twinkletoes"
b: 1/4/08, Huntsville, Ont., Canada d: 1/19/87, Ft.Lauderdale, Fla BL/TR, 6'1", 182 lbs. Deb: 8/12/34

YEAR	TM/L	G	AB	R	H	2B	3B	HR	RBI	BB	SO	AVG	OBP	SLG	OPS	OPS+	BR+	SB	CS	SBR	FA	FR	G/POS	TPR
1934	NY-A	46	176	23	55	7	1	5	38	15	17	.313	.370	.449	819	118	4	1	1	-0	.989	-2	O-46(43-0-7)	0.0
1935	NY-A	128	491	64	153	29	12	11	94	44	36	.312	.372	.487	859	128	18	2	7	-2	.975	6	*O-127(0-0-127)	1.4
1936	*NY-A★	137	493	93	152	28	9	18	107	94	60	.308	.420	.511	931	133	28	13	7	0	.974	3	*O-135(18-0-118)	2.1
1937	*NY-A	78	256	49	84	13	5	18	68	34	24	.328	.411	.629	1040	157	22	8	2	1	.987	5	O-69(0-0-69)	2.1
1938	*NY-A	99	335	58	85	12	5	10	62	68	52	.254	.384	.409	793	99	1	9	4	1	.973	-3	O-95(95-0-0)	-0.6
1939	*NY-A★	128	418	103	128	17	4	21	101	103	49	.306	.452	.517	969	149	37	12	5	1	**.989**	-4	*O-124(86-0-38)	2.4
1940	NY-A	118	379	68	102	17	5	19	71	84	43	.269	.406	.491	896	137	23	3	6	-1	.962	-3	*O-111(79-2-31)	1.2
1941	*NY-A	70	164	30	36	5	0	6	25	28	30	.220	.340	.360	700	86	-3	1	0	0	.967	-2	O-47(19-0-28)	-0.7
1942	*NY-A	42	78	15	15	3	0	0	10	16	8	.192	.330	.231	561	60	-3	0	0	0	1.000	-1	O-19(0-0-19)	-0.6
Total	9	846	2790	503	810	131	41	108	576	486	319	.290	.400	.483	883	128	128	49	32	-0	.977	-1	O-773(340-2-437)	7.3

■ **RUBE SELLERS** Sellers, Oliver b: 3/7/1881, Duquesne, Pa. d: 1/14/52, Pittsburgh, Pa. BR/TR, 5'10", 180 lbs. Deb: 8/12/10

YEAR	TM/L	G	AB	R	H	2B	3B	HR	RBI	BB	SO	AVG	OBP	SLG	OPS	OPS+	BR+	SB	CS	SBR	FA	FR	G/POS	TPR
1910	Bos-N	12	32	3	5	0	0	0	2	6	5	.156	.289	.156	446	29	-3	1			1.000	-2	/O-9(8-0-1)	-0.6

■ **FRANK SELMAN** Selman, Frank C. (a.k.a. Frank C. Williams 1871-75) b: Baltimore, Md. Deb: 5/4/1871

YEAR	TM/L	G	AB	R	H	2B	3B	HR	RBI	BB	SO	AVG	OBP	SLG	OPS	OPS+	BR+	SB	CS	SBR	FA	FR	G/POS	TPR
1871	Kek-n	14	65	14	15	3	0	1	10	4	0	.231	.275	.323	598	70	-3	1	0	0	.711	-3	3-14/C-5,S-2	-0.3
1872	Oly-n	9	42	3	10	2	0	0	1	0	1	.238	.238	.286	524	64	-2	0	2	-1	.788	-3	/C-7,3-2	-0.3
1873	Mar-n	1	3	1	1	0	0	0	0	0	0	.333	.333	.333	667	129	0	0	0	0	.000	-0	/P-1	0.0
1874	Bal-n	12	54	9	16	3	2	0	7	0	2	.296	.296	.426	722	130	2	2	0	0	.304	-18	/C-6,S-6,2-2,3-2,O	-1.3
1875	Was-n	1	3	0	1	0	0	0	0	0	0	.333	.333	.333	667	137	0	0	0	0	1.000	0	/1-1	0.0
Total	5 n	37	167	27	43	8	2	1	18	4	3	.257	.275	.347	622	88	-2	3	2	-0	.657	-23	/C-18,3-18,S-8,O21P	-1.9

■ **CAREY SELPH** Selph, Carey Isom b: 12/5/01, Donaldson, Ark. d: 2/24/76, Houston, Tex. BR/TR, 5'9.5", 175 lbs. Deb: 5/25/29

YEAR	TM/L	G	AB	R	H	2B	3B	HR	RBI	BB	SO	AVG	OBP	SLG	OPS	OPS+	BR+	SB	CS	SBR	FA	FR	G/POS	TPR
1929	StL-N	25	51	8	12	1	1	0	7	6	4	.235	.316	.294	610	52	-4	1			.981	-5	2-16	-0.8

YEAR	TM/L	G	AB	R	H	2B	3B	HR	RBI	BB	SO	AVG	OBP	SLG	OPS	OPS+	BR+	SB	CS	SBR	FA	FR	G/POS	TPR
1932	Chi-A	116	396	50	112	19	8	0	51	31	9	.283	.341	.371	712	90	-6	7	6	-1	.910	-6	3-71,2-26	-0.7
Total	2	141	447	58	124	20	9	0	58	37	13	.277	.338	.362	701	85	-9	8	6		.955	-11	/3-71,2-42	-1.5
■ **MIKE SEMBER** Sember, Michael David b: 2/24/53, Hammond, Ind. BR/TR, 6', 185 lbs. Deb: 8/18/77																								
1977	Chi-N	3	4	0	1	0	0	0	0	0	2	.250	.250	.250	500	31	-0	0	0	0	1.000	1	/2-1	0.0
1978	Chi-N	9	3	2	1	0	0	0	0	1	1	.333	.500	.333	833	122	0	0	0	0	.667	1	/3-7,S-1	0.1
Total	2	12	7	2	2	0	0	0	0	1	3	.286	.375	.286	661	74	-0	0	0	0	.667	1	/3-7,S-1,2-1	0.1
■ **ANDY SEMINICK** Seminick, Andrew Wasil b: 9/12/20, Pierce, W.Va. BR/TR, 5'11", 187 lbs. Deb: 9/14/43 C Career OF: (9-LF 0-CF 0-RF)																								
1943	Phi-N	22	72	9	13	2	0	2	5	7	22	.181	.253	.292	545	60	-4	0			.930	1	C-22/O-1(1-0-0)	-0.2
1944	Phi-N	22	63	9	14	2	1	0	4	6	17	.222	.300	.286	586	68	-3	2			.963	1	C-11/O-7(7-0-0)	-0.2
1945	Phi-N	80	188	18	45	7	2	6	26	18	38	.239	.313	.394	706	98	-1	3			.979	-0	C-70/3-4,O-1(1-0-0)	0.2
1946	Phi-N	124	406	55	107	15	5	12	52	39	86	.264	.334	.414	748	115	7	2			.974	-6	*C-118	0.7
1947	Phi-N	111	337	48	85	16	2	13	50	58	69	.252	.370	.427	797	115	9	4			.978	7	*C-107	2.0
1948	Phi-N	125	391	49	88	11	3	13	44	58	68	.225	.328	.368	696	90	-5	4			.965	6	*C-124	0.7
1949	Phi-N★	109	334	52	81	11	2	24	68	69	74	.243	.380	.503	883	138	19	0			.975	7	C-98	3.0
1950	*Phi-N	130	393	55	113	15	3	24	68	68	50	.288	.400	.524	925	143	26	0			.976	4	*C-124	3.6
1951	Phi-N	101	291	42	66	8	1	11	37	63	67	.227	.370	.375	744	102	3	1	0	0	.979	-3	C-91	0.5
1952	Cin-N	108	336	38	86	16	1	14	50	35	65	.256	.330	.435	764	111	4	1	3	-1	.973	-4	C-99	0.5
1953	Cin-N	119	387	46	91	12	0	19	64	49	82	.235	.323	.413	736	90	-6	2	2	-0	.982	-5	*C-112	-0.6
1954	Cin-N	86	247	25	58	9	4	7	30	48	39	.235	.364	.389	752	93	-1	0	0	0	.989	3	C-82	0.6
1955	Cin-N	6	15	1	2	0	0	1	1	0	3	.133	.133	.333	467	18	-2	0	0	0	1.000	2	/C-5	0.0
	Phi-N	93	289	32	71	12	1	11	34	32	59	.246	.333	.408	742	97	-1	1	2	-0	.994	10	C-88	1.3
	Yr	99	304	33	73	12	1	12	35	32	62	.240	.325	.405	729	93	-3	1	2	-0	**.994**	12	C-93	1.3
1956	Phi-N	60	161	16	32	3	1	7	23	31	38	.199	.332	.360	692	88	-2	3	0	1	.976	-8	C-54	-0.7
1957	Phi-N	8	11	0	1	0	0	0	0	1	3	.091	.167	.091	258	-29	-2	0	0	0	1.000	1	/C-8	-0.1
Total	15	1304	3921	495	953	139	26	164	556	582	780	.243	.347	.417	764	107	40	23	7		.977	15	*C-1213/O-9L,3-4	11.3
■ **SONNY SENERCHIA** Senerchia, Emanuel Robert b: 4/6/31, Newark, N.J. BR/TR, 6'1", 195 lbs. Deb: 8/22/52																								
1952	Pit-N	29	100	5	22	5	0	3	11	4	21	.220	.250	.360	610	66	-5	0	3	-1	.953	-8	3-28	-1.5
■ **COUNT SENSENDERFER** Sensenderfer, John Phillips Jenkins b: 12/28/1847, Philadelphia, Pa. d: 5/3/03, Philadelphia, Pa. 5'9", 170 lbs. Deb: 5/20/1871																								
1871	Ath-n	25	127	38	41	5	2	0	23	0	1	.323	.323	.394	717	106	1	5	3	0	.814	-1	*O-25(0-25-0)	0.0
1872	Ath-n	1	5	2	2	0	0	0	1	0	0	.400	.400	.400	800	146	0	0	1	-0	.000	-0	/O-1(0-0-1)	0.0
1873	Ath-n	20	86	12	24	1	0	0	8	0	2	.279	.279	.291	570	65	-4	0	2	-1	.827	0	O-19(0-19-0)/1-1	-0.3
1874	Ath-n	5	16	3	3	0	0	0	2	0	0	.188	.188	.188	375	19	-1	0	0	0	.625	-1	/O-5(0-1-4)	-0.2
Total	4 n	51	234	55	70	6	2	0	34	0	3	.299	.299	.342	641	85	-4	5	6	-1	.807	-2	/O-50(0-45-5),1-1	-0.5
■ **PAUL SENTELL** Sentell, Leopold Theodore b: 8/27/1879, New Orleans, La. d: 4/27/23, Cincinnati, Ohio BR/TR, 5'9", 176 lbs. Deb: 4/12/06 U Career OF: (0-LF 0-CF 3-RF)																								
1906	Phi-N	63	192	19	44	5	1	1	14	14		.229	.292	.281	573	79	-5	15			.887	-9	3-33,2-19/O-2R,S-1	-1.4
1907	Phi-N	3	3	0	0	0	0	0	0	1		.000	.250	.000	250	-22	-0	0			1.000	-2	/S-2,O-1(0-0-1)	-0.3
Total	2	66	195	19	44	5	1	1	14	15		.226	.291	.277	568	77	-5	15			1.000	-11	/3-33,2-19,S-3,O-3R	-1.7
■ **TED SEPKOWSKI** Sepkowski, Theodore Walter (b: Theodore Walter Sczepkowski) b: 11/9/23, Baltimore, Md. BL/TR, 5'11", 190 lbs. Deb: 9/9/42																								
1942	Cle-A	5	10	0	1	0	0	0	0	0	3	.100	.100	.100	200	-46	-2	0	0	0	.824	0	/2-2	-0.1
1946	Cle-A	2	8	2	4	1	0	0	1	0	0	.500	.500	.625	1125	228	1	0	0	0	.833	-1	/3-2	0.1
1947	Cle-A	10	8	0	1	1	0	0	0	1	1	.125	.222	.250	472	32	-1	0	0	0	.000	-0	/O-1(0-0-1)	-0.1
	NY-A	2	0	1	0	0	0	0	0	0	0	—	—	—	—	—	0	0	1	-0	.000	0	R	0.0
	Yr	12	8	1	1	1	0	0	0	1	1	.125	.222	.250	472	32	-1	0	1	-0	.000	-0	/O-1(0-0-1)	-0.1
Total	3	19	26	3	6	2	0	0	1	1	4	.231	.259	.308	567	61	-1	0	1	-0	.833	-1	/3-2,2-2,O-1(0-0-1)	-0.1
■ **BILL SERENA** Serena, William Robert b: 10/2/24, Alameda, Cal. d: 4/17/96, Hayward, Cal. BR/TR, 5'9.5", 175 lbs. Deb: 9/16/49																								
1949	Chi-N	12	37	3	8	3	0	1	7	7	9	.216	.341	.378	719	95	-0	0			.923	-4	3-11	-0.4
1950	Chi-N	127	435	56	104	20	4	17	61	65	75	.239	.339	.421	760	100	-0	1			.945	-2	*3-125	-0.2
1951	Chi-N	13	39	8	13	3	1	1	4	11	4	.333	.490	.538	1029	173	5	0	2	-1	.941	-4	3-12	0.0
1952	Chi-N	122	390	49	107	21	5	15	61	39	83	.274	.345	.469	814	122	11	1	0	0	.971	-1	3-58,2-49	1.3
1953	Chi-N	93	275	30	69	10	5	10	52	41	46	.251	.350	.433	783	100	0	0	0	0	.983	-15	2-49,3-28	-1.1
1954	Chi-N	41	63	8	10	0	1	4	13	14	18	.159	.321	.381	701	81	-2	0	0	0	.933	-3	3-12/2-2	-0.5
Total	6	408	1239	154	311	57	16	48	198	177	235	.251	.348	.439	787	108	14	2	2		.951	-30	3-246,2-100	-0.9
■ **PAUL SERNA** Serna, Paul David b: 11/16/58, ElCentro, Cal. BR/TR, 5'8", 170 lbs. Deb: 9/1/81																								
1981	Sea-A	30	94	11	24	2	0	4	9	3	11	.255	.293	.404	697	95	-1	2	3	-1	.954	-3	S-23/2-7	-0.2
1982	Sea-A	65	169	15	38	3	0	3	8	4	13	.225	.247	.296	543	47	-12	0	5	-2	.936	3	S-31,2-18,3-15,/D-2	-0.8
Total	2	95	263	26	62	5	0	7	17	7	24	.236	.264	.335	598	64	-13	2	8	-2	.945	1	/S-54,2-25,3-15,D-2	-1.0
■ **SCOTT SERVAIS** Servais, Scott Daniel b: 6/4/67, LaCrosse, Wis. BR/TR, 6'2", 195 lbs. Deb: 7/12/91																								
1991	Hou-N	16	37	0	6	3	0	0	6	4	8	.162	.244	.243	487	40	-3	0	0	0	.988	2	C-14	0.0
1992	Hou-N	77	205	12	49	9	0	0	15	11	25	.239	.294	.283	577	67	-9	0	0	0	.995	-2	C-73	-0.8
1993	Hou-N	85	258	24	63	11	0	11	32	22	45	.244	.316	.415	731	97	-2	0	0	0	.996	2	C-82	0.5
1994	Hou-N	78	251	27	49	15	1	9	41	10	44	.195	.238	.371	608	58	-17	0	0	0	.996	1	C-78	-1.2
1995	Hou-N	28	89	7	20	10	0	1	12	9	15	.225	.303	.371	674	82	-2	0	1	-0	.977	5	C-28	0.4
	Chi-N	52	175	31	50	12	0	12	35	23	37	.286	.375	.560	935	145	11	2	1	0	.981	-2	C-52	1.3
	Yr	80	264	38	70	22	0	13	47	32	52	.265	.351	.496	847	125	9	2	2	-0	.980	4	C-80	1.7
1996	Chi-N	129	445	42	118	20	0	11	63	30	75	.265	.331	.384	716	86	-9	0	2	-1	.988	1	*C-128/1-1	-0.1
1997	Chi-N	122	385	36	100	21	0	6	45	24	56	.260	.313	.361	674	74	-15	0	1	-0	.990	2	*C-118/1-1,D-2	-0.6
1998	*Chi-N	113	325	35	72	15	1	7	36	26	51	.222	.289	.338	628	62	-18	1	0	0	.994	-5	*C-110/1-1	-1.7
1999	SF-N	69	198	21	54	10	0	5	21	13	31	.273	.327	.399	726	89	-4	0	0	0	.992	-1	C-62/1-1	-0.1
2000	Col-N	33	101	6	22	4	0	1	13	7	16	.218	.275	.287	562	33	-10	0	1	-0	.987	10	C-32	0.1
	SF-N	7	8	1	2	0	0	0	0	2	1	.250	.400	.250	650	74	-0	0	0	0	1.000	0	/C-6	0.0
	Yr	40	109	7	24	4	0	1	13	9	17	.220	.286	.284	570	37	-10	0	1	-0	.988	10	C-38	0.1
Total	10	809	2477	242	605	130	2	63	319	181	404	.244	.308	.375	682	79	-77	3	6	-1	.991	12	C-783/1-4,D-2	-2.2
■ **WALTER SESSI** Sessi, Walter Anthony "Watsie" b: 7/23/18, Finleyville, Pa. d: 4/18/98, Mobile, Ala. BL/TL, 6'3", 225 lbs. Deb: 9/18/41																								
1941	StL-N	5	13	2	0	0	0	0	0	1	2	.000	.071	.000	71	-74	-3	0			.750	-1	/O-3(0-0-3)	-0.4
1946	StL-N	15	14	2	2	0	0	1	2	1	4	.143	.200	.357	557	54	-1	0			.000	0	H	-0.1
Total	2	20	27	4	2	0	0	1	2	2	6	.074	.138	.185	323	-9	-4	0			.750	-1	/O-3(0-0-3)	-0.5
■ **JOHN SEVCIK** Sevcik, John Joseph b: 7/11/42, Oak Park, Ill. BR/TR, 6'2", 205 lbs. Deb: 4/24/65																								
1965	Min-A	12	16	1	1	1	0	0	0	1	5	.063	.118	.125	243	-30	-3	0	0	0	1.000	3	C-11	0.0
■ **HANK SEVEREID** Severeid, Henry Levai b: 6/1/1891, Story City, Iowa d: 12/17/68, San Antonio, Tex. BR/TR, 6', 175 lbs. Deb: 5/15/11 Career OF: (6-LF 1-CF 0-RF)																								
1911	Cin-N	37	56	5	17	6	1	0	10	3	6	.304	.350	.446	796	127	2	0			.913	-3	C-22	0.0
1912	Cin-N	50	114	10	27	0	3	0	13	8	11	.237	.287	.289	576	60	-6	0			.943	-9	C-20/1-7,O-6(5-1-0)	-1.4
1913	Cin-N	8	6	0	0	0	0	0	0	1	1	.000	.143	.000	143	-58	-1	0			1.000	-1	/C-2,O-1(1-0-0)	-0.2
1915	StL-A	80	203	12	45	6	1	1	22	16	25	.222	.279	.276	554	69	-8	2	1	0	.966	-10	C-64	-1.4
1916	StL-A	100	293	23	80	8	2	0	34	26	17	.273	.341	.314	655	102	1	3			.976	-16	C-89/1-1,3-1	-0.9
1917	StL-A	143	501	45	133	23	4	1	57	28	20	.265	.306	.333	639	99	-3	6			.966	-19	*C-139/1-1	-1.0
1918	StL-A	51	133	8	34	4	0	0	11	18	4	.256	.357	.286	643	97	0	4			.946	-5	C-42	-0.2
1919	StL-A	112	351	16	87	12	2	0	36	21	13	.248	.298	.293	591	65	-16	2			.983	-5	*C-103	-1.3
1920	StL-A	123	422	46	117	14	5	2	49	33	11	.277	.336	.348	684	79	-12	5	3	0	.983	3	*C-117	0.0
1921	StL-A	143	472	66	153	23	7	2	78	42	9	.324	.379	.415	795	97	-2	7	2	1	.972	-3	*C-126	0.5
1922	StL-A	137	517	49	166	32	7	3	78	28	12	.321	.356	.427	783	100	-1	1	4	-1	.984	7	*C-133	1.4

YEAR	TM/L	G	AB	R	H	2B	3B	HR	RBI	BB	SO	AVG	OBP	SLG	OPS	OPS+	BR+	SB	CS	SBR	FA	FR	G/POS	TPR
1923	StL-A	122	432	50	133	27	6	3	51	31	11	.308	.356	.419	775	98	-2	3	0	1	**.993**	10	*C-116	1.5
1924	StL-A	137	432	37	133	23	2	4	48	36	15	.308	.362	.398	761	90	-6	1	6	-2	**.989**	-2	*C-130	-0.1
1925	StL-A	34	109	15	40	9	0	1	21	11	2	.367	.425	.477	902	122	4	0	2	-1	.993	-0	C-31	0.5
	*Was-A	50	110	11	39	8	1	0	14	13	6	.355	.423	.445	868	123	4	0	0	0	.986	2	C-35	0.7
	Yr	84	219	26	79	17	1	1	35	24	8	.361	.424	.461	885	123	9	0	2	-1	.990	2	C-66	1.2
1926	Was-A	22	34	2	7	1	0	0	4	3	2	.206	.270	.235	506	34	-3	0	0	0	.977	0	C-16	-0.2
	*NY-A	41	127	13	34	8	1	0	13	13	4	.268	.336	.346	682	79	-4	1	1	-0	.988	-3	C-40	-0.4
	Yr	63	161	15	41	9	1	0	17	16	6	.255	.322	.323	645	70	-7	1	1	-0	.985	-3	C-56	-0.6
Total	15	1390	4312	408	1245	204	42	17	539	331	169	.289	.342	.367	709	91	-54	35	19		.978	-56	*C-1225/1-9,O-7L,3	-2.5
■ RICH SEVERSON	Severson, Richard Allen b: 1/18/45, Artesia, Cal. BR/TR, 6', 174 lbs. Deb: 4/10/70																							
1970	KC-A	77	240	22	60	11	1	1	22	16	33	.250	.300	.317	616	70	-10	0	0	0	.962	1	S-50,2-25	-0.2
1971	KC-A	16	30	4	9	0	2	0	1	3	5	.300	.364	.433	797	126	1	0	0	0	1.000	6	/2-6,S-6,3-1	0.8
Total	2	93	270	26	69	11	3	1	23	19	38	.256	.307	.330	637	76	-9	0	0	0	.958	7	/S-56,2-31,3-1	0.6
■ ED SEWARD	Seward, Edward William (b: Edward William Sourhardt) b: 6/29/1867, Cleveland, Ohio d: 7/30/47, Cleveland, Ohio TR, 5'7", 175 lbs. Deb: 9/30/1885 U Career OF: (5-LF 33-CF 7-RF)																							
1885	Pro-N	1	3	0	0	0	0	0	0	0	2	.000	.000	.000	0	-99	-1				1.000	1	/P-1	0.0
1887	Phi-a	74	282	31	66	10	0	5	28	16		.234	.239	.282	521	45	-20	14			.901	-3	P-55,O-21(2-19-0)	-0.5
1888	Phi-a	64	225	27	32	3	3	2	14	18		.142	.215	.209	424	36	-16	12			.887	4	P-57/O-7(2-1-4)	-0.1
1889	Phi-a	46	143	22	31	5	3	2	17	22	19	.217	.333	.336	669	92	-1	6			.885	-4	P-39/O-8(0-6-2),2-1	-0.2
1890	Phi-a	26	72	7	10	4	0	0	2	8		.139	.244	.194	438	29	-6	3			.811	-2	P-21/O-6(0-6-0)	-0.2
1891	Cle-N	7	19	2	4	2	0	0	1	3	4	.211	.318	.316	634	81	-0	0			1.000	-2	/O-3(1-1-1),P-3,1-1	-0.2
Total	6	218	744	89	143	24	6	9	62	67	25	.192	.253	.261	514	51	-44	35			.882	-7	P-176/O-45C,1-1,2-1	-1.2
■ GEORGE SEWARD	Seward, George T. b: St.Louis, Mo. d: 3/28/04, St.Louis, Mo. 5'7.5", 145 lbs. Deb: 5/19/1875																							
1875	StL-n	25	96	12	24	2	0	0	8	1	1	.250	.258	.271	529	92	-0	1	0	0	.817	-2	C-18/O-7(3-1-3),2-2	-0.1
1876	NY-N	1	3	0	0	0	0	0	0	0	0	.000	.000	.000	0	-99	-1				1.000	1	/2-1	0.0
1882	StL-a	38	144	23	31	1	1	0		12		.215	.276	.236	512	71	-4				.776	-0	O-35(6-2-27)/C-5	-0.4
Total	2	39	147	23	31	1	1	0	0	12	0	.211	.270	.231	502	68	-5				.776	0	/O-35(6-2-27),C-5,2-1	-0.4
■ LUKE SEWELL	Sewell, James Luther b: 1/5/01, Titus, Ala. d: 5/14/87, Akron, Ohio BR/TR, 5'9", 160 lbs. Deb: 6/30/21 FMC Career OF: (4-LF 0-CF 5-RF)																							
1921	Cle-A	3	6	0	0	0	0	0	1	0	3	.000	.000	.000	0	-99	-2	0	0	0	1.000	1	/C-3	-0.1
1922	Cle-A	41	87	14	23	5	0	0	10	5	8	.264	.312	.322	634	65	-4	1	1	-0	.963	0	C-39	-0.3
1923	Cle-A	10	10	2	2	0	1	0	1	1	0	.200	.273	.400	673	76	-0	0	0	0	.833	0	/C-7	0.0
1924	Cle-A	63	165	27	48	9	1	0	17	22	13	.291	.387	.358	745	92	-1	1	0	0	.959	5	C-57	0.7
1925	Cle-A	74	220	30	51	10	2	0	18	33	18	.232	.337	.295	633	61	-12	6	2	1	.971	7	C-66/O-2(2-0-0)	-0.1
1926	Cle-A	126	433	41	103	16	4	0	46	36	27	.238	.302	.293	596	55	-28	9	3	1	.983	2	*C-125	-1.6
1927	Cle-A	128	470	52	138	27	6	0	53	20	23	.294	.328	.377	705	82	-13	4	8	-2	.963	-2	*C-126	-0.8
1928	Cle-A	122	411	52	111	16	9	3	52	26	27	.270	.318	.375	693	81	-12	3	4	-1	.972	13	*C-118	0.7
1929	Cle-A	124	406	41	96	16	3	1	39	29	26	.236	.287	.298	585	49	-31	6	6	-1	.966	4	*C-124	-1.8
1930	Cle-A	76	292	40	75	21	2	1	43	14	9	.257	.293	.353	646	61	-18	5	2	0	.974	-2	C-76	-1.3
1931	Cle-A	108	375	45	103	30	4	1	53	36	17	.275	.341	.384	725	86	-8	1	1	-0	.980	-8	*C-104	-0.9
1932	Cle-A	87	300	36	76	20	2	2	52	38	24	.253	.337	.353	691	74	-11	4	5	-1	.978	4	C-84	-0.3
1933	*Was-A	141	474	65	125	30	4	2	61	48	24	.264	.335	.357	692	84	-10	7	2	1	.990	-6	*C-141	-0.7
1934	Was-A	72	207	21	49	7	3	2	21	22	10	.237	.313	.329	642	68	-10	0	1	-0	.994	-1	C-50/O-7R,1-6,23	-0.9
1935	Chi-A	118	421	52	120	19	3	2	67	32	18	.285	.336	.359	694	78	-14	3	2	-0	.988	6	*C-112	-0.1
1936	Chi-A	128	451	59	113	20	5	5	73	54	16	.251	.332	.350	682	66	-24	11	2	2	.984	12	*C-126	-0.2
1937	Chi-A☆	122	412	51	111	21	6	1	61	46	18	.269	.343	.357	700	77	-14	4	5	-1	.985	6	*C-118	-0.1
1938	Chi-A	65	211	23	45	4	1	0	27	20	20	.213	.284	.242	526	32	-22	0	0	0	.985	7	C-65	-1.0
1939	Cle-A	16	20	1	3	1	0	0	1	3	1	.150	.261	.200	461	20	-2	0	0	0	.966	-1	C-15/1-1	-0.2
1942	StL-A	6	12	1	1	0	0	0	0	1	5	.083	.154	.083	237	-32	-2	0	0	0	.944	1	/C-6,M	-0.1
Total	20	1630	5383	653	1393	272	56	20	696	486	307	.259	.323	.341	665	70	-241	65	44	-1	.978	48	*C-1562/O-9R,1-7,32	-9.1
■ JOE SEWELL	Sewell, Joseph Wheeler b: 10/9/1898, Titus, Ala. d: 3/6/90, Mobile, Ala. BL/TR, 5'6.5", 155 lbs. Deb: 9/10/20 FCH																							
1920	*Cle-A	22	70	14	23	4	1	0	12	9	4	.329	.412	.414	827	116	2	1	0	0	.884	3	S-22	0.6
1921	Cle-A	154	572	101	182	36	12	4	93	80	17	.318	.412	.444	856	117	17	7	6	-1	.944	-3	*S-154	2.8
1922	Cle-A	153	558	80	167	28	7	2	83	73	20	.299	.386	.385	771	101	3	10	12	-2	.939	12	*S-139,2-12	2.8
1923	Cle-A	153	553	98	195	41	10	3	109	98	12	.353	.456	.479	935	147	43	9	6	-0	.930	6	*S-151	6.2
1924	Cle-A	153	594	99	188	**45**	5	4	106	67	13	.316	.388	.429	817	109	9	3	3	-0	.960	**21**	*S-153	4.3
1925	Cle-A	155	608	78	204	37	7	1	98	64	4	.336	.402	.424	827	109	10	7	6	-1	**.967**	16	*S-153/2-3	3.9
1926	Cle-A	154	578	91	187	41	5	4	85	65	6	.324	.399	.433	832	116	15	17	7	1	.955	3	*S-154	3.4
1927	Cle-A	153	569	83	180	48	5	1	92	51	7	.316	.382	.424	805	108	7	3	16	-5	**.962**	6	*S-153	2.4
1928	Cle-A	155	588	79	190	40	2	4	70	58	9	.323	.391	.418	809	111	11	7	1	1	**.963**	27	*S-137,3-19	5.3
1929	Cle-A	152	578	90	182	38	3	7	73	48	4	.315	.372	.427	800	102	2	6	6	-1	.975	15	*3-152	2.4
1930	Cle-A	109	353	44	102	17	6	0	48	41	3	.289	.374	.371	745	86	-6	1	4	-1	.950	0	3-97	-0.1
1931	NY-A	130	484	102	146	22	1	6	64	61	8	.302	.390	.388	778	111	11	1	1	-0	.952	-2	*3-121/2-1	1.2
1932	*NY-A	125	503	95	137	21	3	11	68	56	3	.272	.349	.392	740	96	-2	0	2	-1	.974	2	*3-123	0.3
1933	NY-A	135	524	87	143	18	1	2	54	71	4	.273	.361	.323	683	87	-7	2	2	-0	.964	3	*3-131	0.0
Total	14	1903	7132	1141	2226	436	68	49	1055	842	114	.312	.391	.413	804	109	117	74	72	-9	.951	107	*S-1216,3-643/2-16	35.5
■ TOMMY SEWELL	Sewell, Thomas Wesley b: 4/16/06, Titus, Ala. d: 7/30/56, Montgomery, Ala. BL/TR, 5'7.5", 155 lbs. Deb: 6/21/27 F																							
1927	Chi-N	1	1	0	0	0	0	0	0	0	0	.000	.000	.000	0	-99	-0	0			.000	0	H	0.0
■ RICHIE SEXSON	Sexson, Richmond Lockwood b: 12/29/74, Portland, Ore. BR/TR, 6'6", 205 lbs. Deb: 9/14/97 Career OF: (109-LF 0-CF 3-RF)																							
1997	Cle-A	5	11	1	3	0	0	0	0	0	2	.273	.273	.273	545	41	-1	0	0	0	1.000	0	/1-2,D-1	-0.1
1998	*Cle-A	49	174	28	54	14	1	11	35	6	42	.310	.344	.592	936	133	8	1	1	-0	.984	4	1-45/O-3(3-0-0),D-2	0.7
1999	*Cle-A	134	479	72	122	17	7	31	116	34	117	.255	.309	.514	823	100	-2	3	3	-0	.988	2	1-61,O-49L,D-25	-0.8
2000	Cle-A	91	324	45	83	16	1	16	44	25	96	.256	.317	.460	777	91	-5	1	0	0	1.000	1	O-58L,1-27,D-10	-0.8
	Mil-N	57	213	44	63	14	0	14	47	34	63	.296	.400	.559	959	142	14	1	1	-0	.991	10	1-57	1.7
Total	4	336	1201	190	325	61	9	72	242	99	320	.271	.333	.516	850	109	13	6	4	-0	.989	17	1-192,O-110L/D-38	0.7
■ CHRIS SEXTON	Sexton, Christopher Philip b: 8/3/71, Cincinnati, Ohio BR/TR, 5'11", 180 lbs. Deb: 5/3/99 Career OF: (3-LF 9-CF 1-RF)																							
1999	Col-N	35	59	9	14	0	1	1	7	11	10	.237	.357	.322	679	58	-4	4	2	0	1.000	-1	O-13(3-9-1),2-10/S-6	-0.3
2000	Cin-N	35	100	9	21	4	0	0	10	13	12	.210	.313	.250	563	43	-8	4	2	0	.954	-2	S-14,2-12/3-3	-0.9
Total	2	70	159	18	35	4	1	1	17	24	22	.220	.330	.277	606	49	-12	8	4	0	.976	-3	/2-22,S-20,O-13C,3	-1.2
■ JIMMY SEXTON	Sexton, Jimmy Dale b: 12/15/51, Mobile, Ala. BR/TR, 5'10", 175 lbs. Deb: 9/2/77																							
1977	Sea-A	14	37	5	8	1	1	1	3	2	6	.216	.256	.378	635	71	-2	1	1	-0	.929	3	S-12	0.2
1978	Hou-N	88	141	17	29	3	2	2	6	13	28	.206	.273	.298	571	64	-7	16	2	3	.981	-3	S-58/3-8,2-3	-0.3
1979	Hou-N	52	43	8	9	0	0	0	1	7	7	.209	.320	.209	529	50	-3	1	3	-1	.943	7	S-11/3-4,2-2	0.3
1981	Oak-A	7	3	3	0	0	0	0	0	0	2	.000	.000	.000	0	-99	-1	2	0	0	1.000	1	/3-1,D-1	0.1
1982	Oak-A	69	139	19	34	4	0	2	14	9	24	.245	.295	.317	612	71	-5	16	0	4	.957	-3	S-47/3-8,D-5	-0.2
1983	StL-N	6	9	1	1	1	0	0	0	1	4	.111	.200	.222	422	17	-1	0	0	0	1.000	1	/S-4,3-2	0.0
Total	6	236	372	53	81	9	3	5	24	32	71	.218	.281	.298	580	64	-19	36	6	6	.962	5	S-132/3-23,D-6,2-5	0.1
■ TOM SEXTON	Sexton, Thomas William b: 3/14/1865, Rock Island, Ill. d: 2/8/34, Rock Island, Ill. Deb: 9/27/1884																							
1884	Mil-U	12	47	9	11	2	0	0		4		.234	.294	.277	571	136	2				.853	-1	S-12	0.1
■ SOCKS SEYBOLD	Seybold, Ralph Orlando b: 11/23/1870, Washingtonville, O d: 12/22/21, Greensburg, Pa. BR/TR, 5'11", 175 lbs. Deb: 8/20/1899																							
1899	Cin-N	22	85	13	19	5	1	0	8	6		.224	.283	.306	588	60	-5	2			.917	1	O-22(3-0-19)	-0.5
1901	Phi-A	114	449	74	150	24	14	8	90	40		.334	.397	.503	901	142	25	15			.954	-5	*O-100(2-25-74),1-14	1.3

YEAR	TM/L	G	AB	R	H	2B	3B	HR	RBI	BB	SO	AVG	OBP	SLG	OPS	OPS+	BR+	SB	CS	SBR	FA	FR	G/POS	TPR
1902	Phi-A	137	522	91	165	27	12	**16**	97	43		.316	.375	.506	881	137	24	6			.963	2	*O-136(0-16-120)	1.9
1903	Phi-A	137	522	76	156	**45**	8	8	84	38		.299	.353	.462	815	137	23	5			.964	-2	*O-120(0-1-119),1-18	1.6
1904	Phi-A	143	510	56	149	26	9	3	64	42		.292	.351	.396	747	129	17	12			.975	1	*O-129(0-0-129),1-13	1.4
1905	*Phi-A	133	492	64	135	37	4	6	59	42		.274	.341	.402	744	133	18	5			.983	9	*O-133(0-0-133)	2.3
1906	Phi-A	116	411	41	130	23	2	5	59	30		.316	.367	.418	786	141	19	9			.925	-5	*O-114(0-0-114)	1.0
1907	Phi-A	147	564	58	153	29	4	5	92	40		.271	.324	.363	687	116	10	10			.973	1	*O-147(0-0-147)	0.4
1908	Phi-A	48	130	5	28	2	0	0	3	12		.215	.287	.231	517	64	-5	2			.921	-4	O-34(0-0-34)	-1.1
Total	9	997	3685	478	1085	218	54	51	556	293		.294	.353	.424	777	129	126	66			.961	-3	O-935(5-42-889)/1-45	8.3

■ CY SEYMOUR Seymour, James Bentley b: 12/9/1872, Albany, N.Y. d: 9/20/19, New York, N.Y. BL/TL, 6′, 200 lbs. Deb: 4/22/1896 Career OF: (20-LF 1094-CF 224-RF)

YEAR	TM/L	G	AB	R	H	2B	3B	HR	RBI	BB	SO	AVG	OBP	SLG	OPS	OPS+	BR+	SB	CS	SBR	FA	FR	G/POS	TPR
1896	NY-N	12	32	2	7	0	0	0	0	0	7	.219	.219	.219	438	16	-4	0			.857	0	P-11/O-1(0-1-0)	-0.1
1897	NY-N	45	141	13	34	5	1	2	14	4		.241	.262	.333	595	58	-9	3			.853	7	P-39/O-6(2-4-0)	-0.2
1898	NY-N	80	297	41	82	5	2	4	23	9		.276	.300	.347	646	88	-6	8			.887	7	P-45,O-35R/2-1	-0.6
1899	NY-N	50	159	25	52	3	2	2	27	4		.327	.344	.409	752	110	1	2			.839	3	P-32/O-8R,1-3,3-1	-0.2
1900	NY-N	23	40	9	12	0	0	0	2	3		.300	.349	.300	649	84	-1	0			.828	-0	P-13/O-3(1-1-2),1-1	-0.2
1901	Bal-A	134	547	84	166	19	8	1	77	28		.303	.337	.373	710	93	-6	38			.945	14	*O-133(4-0-131)/1-1	0.1
1902	Bal-A	72	280	38	75	8	8	3	41	18		.268	.317	.386	702	90	-4	12			.956	1	O-72(0-3-70)	-0.6
	Cin-N	62	244	27	83	8	2	2	37	12		.340	.378	.414	792	132	9	8			.920	4	O-61(0-61-0)/P-1,3-1	1.0
1903	Cin-N	135	558	85	191	25	15	7	72	33		.342	.382	.478	861	130	19	25			.902	5	*O-135(0-135-0)	1.7
1904	Cin-N	131	531	71	166	26	13	5	58	29		.313	.352	.439	790	132	18	11			.951	13	*O-130(0-130-0)	2.6
1905	Cin-N	149	581	95	**219**	**40**	**21**	8	**121**	51		**.377**	.429	**.559**	**988**	**175**	**51**	21			.947	12	*O-149(0-149-0)	5.7
1906	Cin-N	79	307	35	79	7	2	4	38	24		.257	.317	.332	650	98	-1	9			.968	10	O-79(0-79-0)	0.6
	NY-N	72	269	35	86	12	3	4	42	18		.320	.365	.431	796	145	13	20			.978	-2	O-72(0-72-0)	0.8
	Yr	151	576	70	165	19	5	8	80	42		.286	.339	.378	718	120	12	29			.972	8	*O-151(0-151-0)	1.4
1907	NY-N	131	473	46	139	25	8	3	75	36		.294	.350	.400	750	131	16	21			.975	3	*O-126(0-126-0)	1.5
1908	NY-N	156	587	60	157	23	2	5	92	30		.267	.306	.339	645	101	-0	18			.949	11	*O-155(0-155-0)	0.4
1909	NY-N	80	280	37	87	12	5	1	30	25		.311	.369	.400	769	137	12	14			.968	0	O-74(1-71-1)	0.9
1910	NY-N	79	287	32	76	9	4	1	40	23	18	.265	.324	.334	658	92	-3	10			.936	-6	O-76(0-76-0)	-1.4
1913	Bos-N	39	73	2	13	2	0	0	10	7	7	.178	.259	.205	465	33	-6	2			.950	0	O-18(0-18-0)	-0.7
Total	16	1529	5686	737	1724	229	96	52	799	354	32	.303	.347	.405	752	117	98	222			.945	82	*O-1333C,P-141/132	11.3

■ TILLIE SHAFER Shafer, Arthur Joseph b: 3/22/1889, Los Angeles, Cal. d: 1/10/62, Los Angeles, Cal. BB/TR, 5′10″, 165 lbs. Deb: 4/24/09

YEAR	TM/L	G	AB	R	H	2B	3B	HR	RBI	BB	SO	AVG	OBP	SLG	OPS	OPS+	BR+	SB	CS	SBR	FA	FR	G/POS	TPR
1909	NY-N	38	84	11	15	2	1	0	7	14		.179	.296	.226	522	61	-3	6			.750	-0	3-16,2-13/O-2(0-1-1)	-0.4
1910	NY-N	29	21	5	4	1	0	0	1	0	6	.190	.190	.238	429	25	-2	0			.889	5	/3-8,2-2,S-2	0.3
1912	*NY-N	78	163	48	47	4	1	0	23	30	19	.288	.408	.325	733	99	2	22			.879	-7	S-31,3-16,2-15	-0.3
1913	*NY-N	138	508	74	146	17	12	5	52	61	55	.287	.369	.398	767	118	13	32			.923	-9	3-79,2-25,S-16,O-15C	0.7
Total	4	283	776	138	212	24	14	5	83	105	80	.273	.366	.360	725	106	10	60			.903	-12	3-119/2-55,S-49,O	0.3

■ RALPH SHAFER Shafer, Ralph Newton b: 3/17/1894, Cincinnati, Ohio d: 2/5/50, Akron, Ohio 5′11″, Deb: 7/25/14

YEAR	TM/L	G	AB	R	H	2B	3B	HR	RBI	BB	SO	AVG	OBP	SLG	OPS	OPS+	BR+	SB	CS	SBR	FA	FR	G/POS	TPR
1914	Pit-N	1	0	0	0	0	0	0	0	0	0	—	—	—	—	—	0	0			.000	0	H	0.0

■ SHAFFER Shaffer Deb: 9/15/1875

YEAR	TM/L	G	AB	R	H	2B	3B	HR	RBI	BB	SO	AVG	OBP	SLG	OPS	OPS+	BR+	SB	CS	SBR	FA	FR	G/POS	TPR
1875	Atl-n	1	4	0	0	0	0	0	0	0	0	.000	.000	.000	0	-99	-1	0	0	0	.500	-0	/O-1(0-0-1)	-0.1

■ FRANK SHAFFER Shaffer, Frank Deb: 4/24/1884

YEAR	TM/L	G	AB	R	H	2B	3B	HR	RBI	BB	SO	AVG	OBP	SLG	OPS	OPS+	BR+	SB	CS	SBR	FA	FR	G/POS	TPR
1884	Alt-U	19	74	11	21	2	0	0		3		.284	.312	.311	622	88	-3				.889	-3	O-17(9-7-1)/C-2,3-1	-0.6
	KC-U	44	164	18	28	3	2	0		15		.171	.240	.213	454	44	-15				.768	-3	O-41R/C-2,2-1,S3	-1.6
	Bal-U	3	13	1	1	0	0	0		0		.077	.077	.077	154	-48	-3				.750	-1	/O-3(1-0-3)	-0.3
	Yr	66	251	30	50	5	2	0		18		.199	.253	.235	488	53	-21				.796	-6	O-61R/C-4,3-2,2S	-2.5

■ ORATOR SHAFFER Shaffer, George b: 1852, Philadelphia, Pa. BL/TR, 5′9″, 165 lbs. Deb: 5/23/1874 F Career OF: (9-LF 23-CF 807-RF)

YEAR	TM/L	G	AB	R	H	2B	3B	HR	RBI	BB	SO	AVG	OBP	SLG	OPS	OPS+	BR+	SB	CS	SBR	FA	FR	G/POS	TPR
1874	Har-n	9	35	6	8	0	0	1	3	0	4	.229	.229	.314	543	69	-1	0	0	0	.710	-1	/O-9(8-0-1)	-0.2
	Mut-n	1	5	1	1	0	0	0	0	0	0	.200	.200	.200	400	28	-0	0	0	0	.000	-0	/O-1(0-0-1)	-0.1
	Yr	10	40	7	9	0	0	1	3	0	4	.225	.225	.300	525	64	-2	0	0	0	.710	-2	O-10(8-0-2)	-0.3
1875	Phi-n	19	70	10	17	2	1	0	6	0	4	.243	.243	.300	543	84	-1	2	0	0	.769	-2	O-12(3-8-1)/3-5,1-2	-0.2
1877	Lou-N	61	260	38	74	9	5	3	34	9	17	.285	.309	.392	701	101	-1				.835	14	*O-60(0-1-60)/1-1	1.1
1878	Ind-N	63	266	48	90	19	6	0	30	13	20	.338	.369	.455	824	**196**	**29**				.842	8	*O-63(1-0-63)	**3.3**
1879	Chi-N	73	316	53	96	13	0	0	35	6	28	.304	.317	.345	662	111	3				.801	20	*O-72(0-0-72)/3-1	2.1
1880	Cle-N	83	338	62	90	14	9	0	21	17	36	.266	.301	.361	662	126	9				.901	17	*O-83(0-0-83)	2.6
1881	Cle-N	85	343	48	88	13	6	1	34	23	20	.257	.303	.338	641	107	4				.880	2	*O-85(0-0-85)	0.6
1882	Cle-N	84	313	37	67	14	2	3	28	27	27	.214	.276	.300	577	88	-3				.805	-9	*O-84(2-1-83)	-1.2
1883	Buf-N	95	401	67	117	11	3	0	41	27	39	.292	.336	.334	671	103	2				.861	20	*O-95(0-0-95)	1.8
1884	StL-U	106	467	130	168	**40**	10	2		30		.360	.398	.501	899	165	24				.870	-3	*O-100R/2-7,1-1	1.8
1885	StL-N	69	257	30	50	11	2	0	18	19	31	.195	.250	.253	503	67	-8				.918	11	O-69(0-1-68)	0.2
	Phi-a	2	9	1	2	0	1	0	1	1		.222	.300	.444	744	125	0				1.000	-1	/O-2(0-2-0)	0.0
1886	Phi-a	21	82	15	22	3	3	0	8	8		.268	.333	.378	711	121	2	3			.815	0	O-21(0-18-4)	0.2
1890	Phi-a	100	390	55	110	15	5	1	58	47		.282	.367	.354	720	113	7	29			**.958**	2	*O-98(0-0-98)/1-3	0.7
Total	2 n	29	110	17	26	2	1	1	9	0	8	.236	.236	.300	536	76	-3	2	0	0	.737	-4	/O-22(11-8-3),3-5,1-2	-0.5
Total	11	842	3442	584	974	162	52	10	308	227	218	.283	.328	.369	697	119	68	32			.865	81	O-832R/2-7,1-5,3-1	13.2

■ TAYLOR SHAFFER Shaffer, Taylor b: 7/1870, Philadelphia, Pa. Deb: 4/17/1890 F

YEAR	TM/L	G	AB	R	H	2B	3B	HR	RBI	BB	SO	AVG	OBP	SLG	OPS	OPS+	BR+	SB	CS	SBR	FA	FR	G/POS	TPR
1890	Phi-a	69	261	28	45	3	4	0	21	28		.172	.258	.215	472	40	-20	19			.921	4	2-69	-1.2

■ ART SHAMSKY Shamsky, Arthur Louis b: 10/14/41, St.Louis, Mo. BL/TL, 6′1″, 175 lbs. Deb: 4/17/65

YEAR	TM/L	G	AB	R	H	2B	3B	HR	RBI	BB	SO	AVG	OBP	SLG	OPS	OPS+	BR+	SB	CS	SBR	FA	FR	G/POS	TPR
1965	Cin-N	64	96	13	25	4	3	2	10	10	29	.260	.330	.427	757	104	1	1	0	0	.966	0	O-18(3-0-15)/1-1	0.0
1966	Cin-N	96	234	41	54	5	0	21	47	32	45	.231	.323	.521	845	120	6	0	2	-1	.973	-3	O-74(42-0-33)	-0.1
1967	Cin-N	76	147	6	29	3	1	3	13	15	34	.197	.276	.293	569	56	-8	0	1	-0	.984	-2	O-40(18-0-25)	-1.4
1968	NY-N	116	345	30	82	14	4	12	48	21	58	.238	.295	.406	701	108	3	1	0	0	.993	1	O-82(71-0-12),1-17	-0.2
1969	*NY-N	100	303	42	91	9	3	14	47	36	32	.300	.380	.488	869	139	16	1	2	-0	.992	-6	O-78(16-0-63)/1-9	0.5
1970	NY-N	122	403	48	118	19	2	11	49	49	33	.293	.374	.432	805	115	9	1	1	-0	1.000	1	O-58(4-0-54),1-56	0.3
1971	NY-N	68	135	13	25	6	2	5	18	21	18	.185	.299	.370	670	90	-2	1	1	-0	.984	2	O-38(12-0-27)/1-1	-0.2
1972	Chi-N	15	16	1	2	0	0	0	1	3	3	.125	.263	.125	388	12	-2	0	0	0	1.000	0	/1-4	-0.2
	Oak-A	8	7	0	0	0	0	0	0	1	2	.000	.125	.000	125	-64	-1	0	0	0	.000	0	H	-0.2
Total	8	665	1686	194	426	60	15	68	233	188	254	.253	.333	.427	760	109	21	5	7	-1	.987	-8	O-388(166-0-229)/1-88	-1.5

■ JIM SHANDLEY Shandley, James H. b: New York d: 11/4/04, Brooklyn, N.Y. Deb: 5/3/1876

YEAR	TM/L	G	AB	R	H	2B	3B	HR	RBI	BB	SO	AVG	OBP	SLG	OPS	OPS+	BR+	SB	CS	SBR	FA	FR	G/POS	TPR
1876	NY-N	2	8	0	1	0	0	0	0	0	0	.125	.125	.125	250	-19	-1				.600	-1	/O-2(0-1-1)	-0.1

■ WALLY SHANER Shaner, Walter Dedaker "Skinny" b: 5/24/1900, Lynchburg, Va. d: 11/13/92, Las Vegas, Nev. BR/TR, 6′2″, 195 lbs. Deb: 5/4/23 Career OF: (137-LF 25-CF 10-RF)

YEAR	TM/L	G	AB	R	H	2B	3B	HR	RBI	BB	SO	AVG	OBP	SLG	OPS	OPS+	BR+	SB	CS	SBR	FA	FR	G/POS	TPR
1923	Cle-A	3	4	1	1	0	0	0	0	1	1	.250	.400	.250	650	74	-0	0	0	0	1.000	-1	/O-2(2-0-0),3-1	-0.1
1926	Bos-A	69	191	20	54	12	2	0	21	17	13	.283	.348	.366	714	89	-3	1	0	0	.965	0	O-48(48-0-0)	-0.6
1927	Bos-A	122	406	54	111	33	6	3	49	21	35	.273	.311	.406	717	87	-10	11	4	1	.955	-8	*O-108(85-25-10)/1-1	-2.3
1929	Cin-N	13	28	5	9	0	0	1	4	4	5	.321	.406	.429	835	112	1	1			1.000	-1	/1-8,O-2(2-0-0)	0.0
Total	4	207	629	80	175	45	8	4	74	43	54	.278	.327	.394	722	89	-12	13	4		.959	-9	O-160L/1-9,3-1	-3.0

■ HOWIE SHANKS Shanks, Howard Samuel "Hank" b: 7/21/1890, Chicago, Ill. d: 7/30/41, Monaca, Pa. BR/TR, 5′11″, 170 lbs. Deb: 5/9/12 C Career OF: (602-LF 55-CF 44-RF)

YEAR	TM/L	G	AB	R	H	2B	3B	HR	RBI	BB	SO	AVG	OBP	SLG	OPS	OPS+	BR+	SB	CS	SBR	FA	FR	G/POS	TPR
1912	Was-A	116	399	52	92	14	7	1	48	40		.231	.305	.308	614	75	-13	21			.962	-2	*O-114(111-0-2)	-2.0
1913	Was-A	109	390	38	99	11	5	1	37	15	40	.254	.287	.315	602	75	-14	24			.978	3	*O-109(109-0-0)	-1.6
1914	Was-A	143	500	44	112	22	10	4	64	29	51	.224	.269	.332	601	78	-16	18	16	-2	.954	-0	*O-139(94-43-2)	-2.8
1915	Was-A	141	492	52	123	19	8	0	47	30	42	.250	.297	.321	618	83	-12	12	14	-2	.982	7	O-80L,3-49,2-10	-1.0
1916	Was-A	140	471	51	119	15	7	1	48	41	34	.253	.317	.321	637	92	-5	23	12	1	.987	10	O-88L,3-31/S-8,1-7	0.4

YEAR	TM/L	G	AB	R	H	2B	3B	HR	RBI	BB	SO	AVG	OBP	SLG	OPS	OPS+	BR+	SB	CS	SBR	FA	FR	G/POS	TPR
1917	Was-A	126	430	45	87	15	5	0	28	33	37	.202	.269	.260	529	62	-20	15			.929	13	S-90,O-26(21-5-0)/1-2	-0.2
1918	Was-A	120	436	42	112	19	4	1	56	31	21	.257	.312	.326	638	94	-4	23			.957	1	O-64(54-2-8),2-48/3-3	-0.6
1919	Was-A	135	491	33	122	8	7	1	54	25	48	.248	.289	.299	588	66	-23	13			.922	-11	S-94,2-34/O-6(6-0-0)	-2.9
1920	Was-A	128	444	56	119	16	7	4	37	29	43	.268	.316	.363	678	82	-13	11	6	0	.951	-6	3-63,O-35L,1-14,/2S	-1.8
1921	Was-A	154	562	81	170	24	**18**	7	69	57	38	.302	.370	.447	816	113	10	11	10	-1	**.960**	5	*3-154/2-1	2.2
1922	Was-A	84	272	35	77	10	9	1	32	25	25	.283	.352	.397	749	100	-0	6	0	1	.920	7	3-54,O-27(21-0-6)	0.9
1923	Bos-A	131	464	38	118	19	5	3	57	19	37	.254	.285	.336	621	63	-26	6	6	-1	.939	-19	3-83,2-38/O-6L,S-1	-3.9
1924	Bos-A	72	193	22	50	16	3	0	25	21	12	.259	.332	.373	705	81	-6	1	0	0	.972	7	S-41,3-22/O-4R,12	0.6
1925	NY-A	66	155	15	40	3	1	1	18	20	15	.258	.343	.310	653	68	-7	1	0	0	.938	-6	3-26,2-21/O-4(3-0-1)	-1.0
Total	14	1665	5699	604	1440	211	96	25	620	415	443	.253	.308	.337	644	82	-147	185	64		.971	10	O-702L,3-485,S2/1	-13.7

■ DOC SHANLEY Shanley, Harry Root b: 1890, Granbury, Tex. d: 12/13/34, St.Petersburg, Fla BR/TR, 6', 174 lbs. Deb: 9/15/12

YEAR	TM/L	G	AB	R	H	2B	3B	HR	RBI	BB	SO	AVG	OBP	SLG	OPS	OPS+	BR+	SB	CS	SBR	FA	FR	G/POS	TPR
1912	StL-A	5	8	1	0	0	0	0	1	2		.000	.200	.000	200	-43	-1	0			.833	-2	/S-4	-0.3

■ WARREN SHANNABROOK Shannabrook, Warren H. b: 11/30/1880, Massillon, Ohio d: 3/10/64, N.Canton, Ohio BR/TR, 6', 170 lbs. Deb: 8/13/06

YEAR	TM/L	G	AB	R	H	2B	3B	HR	RBI	BB	SO	AVG	OBP	SLG	OPS	OPS+	BR+	SB	CS	SBR	FA	FR	G/POS	TPR
1906	Was-A	1	2	0	0	0	0	0	0	0		.000	.000	.000	0	-99	-0	0			1.000	-1	/3-1	-0.1

■ DAN SHANNON Shannon, Daniel Webster b: 3/23/1865, Bridgeport, Conn. d: 10/24/13, Bridgeport, Conn. 5'9", 175 lbs. Deb: 4/17/1889 M

YEAR	TM/L	G	AB	R	H	2B	3B	HR	RBI	BB	SO	AVG	OBP	SLG	OPS	OPS+	BR+	SB	CS	SBR	FA	FR	G/POS	TPR
1889	Lou-a	121	498	90	128	22	12	4	48	42	52	.257	.315	.373	688	97	-3	26			.910	7	*2-121,M	0.7
1890	Phi-P	19	75	15	18	5	1	1	16	4	12	.240	.278	.373	652	72	-4	4			.926	-4	2-19	-0.6
	NY-P	83	324	59	70	7	8	3	44	25	34	.216	.274	.315	589	53	-24	21			.908	1	2-77/S-6	-1.6
	Yr	102	399	74	88	12	9	4	60	29	46	.221	.275	.326	601	56	-28	25			.911	-3	2-96/S-6	-2.2
1891	Was-a	19	67	7	9	2	0	0	3	6	9	.134	.205	.164	370	6	-8	3			.878	1	S-14/2-5,M	-0.6
Total	3	242	964	171	225	36	21	8	111	77	107	.233	.291	.339	630	73	-39	54			.911	5	2-222/S-20	-2.1

■ FRANK SHANNON Shannon, John Francis b: 12/3/1873, San Francisco, Cal. d: 2/27/34, Boston, Mass. 5'3", 155 lbs. Deb: 10/1/1892

YEAR	TM/L	G	AB	R	H	2B	3B	HR	RBI	BB	SO	AVG	OBP	SLG	OPS	OPS+	BR+	SB	CS	SBR	FA	FR	G/POS	TPR
1892	Was-N	1	4	0	1	0	0	0	2	0	2	.250	.250	.250	500	53	-0	0			.625	-1	/S-1	-0.1
1896	Lou-N	31	115	14	18	1	1	1	15	13	15	.157	.248	.209	457	22	-13	3			.830	-13	S-28/3-3	-2.2
Total	2	32	119	14	19	1	1	1	17	13	17	.160	.248	.210	458	23	-13	3			.820	-14	/S-29,3-3	-2.3

■ JOE SHANNON Shannon, Joseph Aloysius b: 2/11/1897, Jersey City, N.J. d: 7/28/55, Jersey City, N.J. BR/TR, 5'11", 170 lbs. Deb: 7/7/15 F

YEAR	TM/L	G	AB	R	H	2B	3B	HR	RBI	BB	SO	AVG	OBP	SLG	OPS	OPS+	BR+	SB	CS	SBR	FA	FR	G/POS	TPR
1915	Bos-N	5	10	3	2	0	0	0	1	0	3	.200	.200	.200	400	22	-1	0			.750	-0	/O-4(1-1-0),2-1	-0.1

■ RED SHANNON Shannon, Maurice Joseph b: 2/11/1897, Jersey City, N.J. d: 4/12/70, Jersey City, N.J. BB/TR, 5'11", 170 lbs. Deb: 10/7/15 F

YEAR	TM/L	G	AB	R	H	2B	3B	HR	RBI	BB	SO	AVG	OBP	SLG	OPS	OPS+	BR+	SB	CS	SBR	FA	FR	G/POS	TPR
1915	Bos-N	1	3	0	0	0	0	0	0	0	0	.000	.000	.000	0	-99	-1	0			.857	1	/2-1	0.0
1917	Phi-A	11	35	8	10	0	0	0	7	6	9	.286	.390	.286	676	108	1	2			.875	-0	S-10	0.1
1918	Phi-A	72	225	23	54	6	5	0	16	42	52	.240	.367	.311	678	103	3	5			.898	-4	S-45,2-26	0.3
1919	Phi-A	39	155	14	42	7	2	0	14	12	28	.271	.331	.342	673	88	-2	4			.948	-5	2-37	-0.7
	Bos-A	80	290	36	75	11	7	0	17	17	42	.259	.313	.345	658	90	-5	7			.973	-4	2-79	-0.8
	Yr	119	445	50	117	18	9	0	31	29	70	.263	.320	.344	663	89	-7	11			.965	-9	*2-116	-1.5
1920	Was-A	62	222	30	64	8	7	0	30	22	32	.288	.352	.387	740	99	-0	2	5	-1	.919	-19	S-31,2-16,3-15	-1.8
	Phi-A	25	88	4	15	1	1	0	3	4	12	.170	.207	.205	411	9	-12	1	1	-0	.945	-1	S-24	-1.1
	Yr	87	310	34	79	9	8	0	33	26	44	.255	.313	.335	648	73	-12	3	6	-1	.931	-21	S-55,2-16,3-15	-2.9
1921	Phi-A	1	1	0	0	0	0	0	0	0	0	.000	.000	.000	0	-99	-0	0	0	0	.000	0	H	0.0
1926	Chi-N	19	51	9	17	5	0	0	4	6	3	.333	.414	.431	845	126	2	0			.957	-2	S-13	0.2
Total	7	310	1070	124	277	38	22	0	91	109	178	.259	.334	.336	670	89	-14	21	6		.957	-35	2-159,S-123/3-15	-3.8

■ OWEN SHANNON Shannon, Owen Dennis Ignatius b: 12/22/1879, Omaha, Neb. d: 4/10/18, Omaha, Neb. BR/TR, Deb: 9/6/03

YEAR	TM/L	G	AB	R	H	2B	3B	HR	RBI	BB	SO	AVG	OBP	SLG	OPS	OPS+	BR+	SB	CS	SBR	FA	FR	G/POS	TPR
1903	StL-A	9	28	1	6	2	0	0	3	1		.214	.241	.286	527	59	-1	0			.957	-0	/C-8,1-1	-0.1
1907	Was-A	4	7	0	1	0	0	0	0	0		.143	.143	.143	286	-10	-1	0			1.000	3	/C-4	0.2
Total	2	13	35	1	7	2	0	0	3	1		.200	.222	.257	479	47	-2	0			.970	2	/C-12,1-1	0.1

■ MIKE SHANNON Shannon, Thomas Michael "Moonman" b: 7/5/39, St.Louis, Mo. BR/TR, 6'3", 195 lbs. Deb: 9/11/62 Career OF: (44-LF 30-CF 294-RF)

YEAR	TM/L	G	AB	R	H	2B	3B	HR	RBI	BB	SO	AVG	OBP	SLG	OPS	OPS+	BR+	SB	CS	SBR	FA	FR	G/POS	TPR
1962	StL-N	10	15	3	2	0	0	0	0	1	3	.133	.188	.133	321	-11	-2	0	0	0	1.000	-0	/O-7(5-0-2)	-0.3
1963	StL-N	32	26	3	8	0	0	1	2	0	6	.308	.333	.423	756	106	0	0	1	-0	.944	-5	O-26(13-1-12)	-0.6
1964	*StL-N	88	253	30	66	8	2	9	43	19	54	.261	.313	.415	728	95	-2	4	0	1	.983	-6	O-88(9-6-76)	-1.2
1965	StL-N	124	244	32	54	17	3	3	25	28	46	.221	.307	.352	659	78	-7	2	1	0	.994	-1	*O-101(1-14-87)/C-4	-1.2
1966	StL-N	137	459	61	132	20	6	16	64	37	106	.288	.341	.462	803	120	12	8	4	0	.985	6	*O-129(14-7-112)/C-1	1.1
1967	*StL-N	130	482	53	118	18	3	12	77	37	89	.245	.304	.369	673	93	-5	2	4	-1	.919	-11	*3-122/O-6(2-2-5)	-2.0
1968	*StL-N	156	576	62	153	29	2	15	79	37	114	.266	.312	.401	713	114	9	1	2	-0	.952	-7	*3-156	0.1
1969	StL-N	150	551	51	140	15	5	12	55	49	87	.254	.316	.365	681	90	-8	1	4	-1	.945	-19	*3-149	-3.0
1970	StL-N	55	174	18	37	9	2	0	22	16	20	.213	.279	.287	566	51	-12	1	1	-0	.919	-13	3-51	-2.6
Total	9	882	2780	313	710	116	23	68	367	224	525	.255	.313	.387	700	96	-15	19	17	-2	.938	-57	3-478,O-357R/C-5	-9.7

■ WALLY SHANNON Shannon, Walter Charles b: 1/23/33, Cleveland, Ohio d: 2/8/92, Creve Coeur, Mo. BL/TR, 6', 178 lbs. Deb: 7/9/59

YEAR	TM/L	G	AB	R	H	2B	3B	HR	RBI	BB	SO	AVG	OBP	SLG	OPS	OPS+	BR+	SB	CS	SBR	FA	FR	G/POS	TPR
1959	StL-N	47	95	5	27	5	0	0	5	0	12	.284	.292	.337	629	63	-5	0	0	0	1.000	-11	S-21,2-10	-1.4
1960	StL-N	18	23	2	4	0	0	0	1	3	6	.174	.296	.174	470	30	-2	0	0	0	1.000	2	2-15/S-1	0.0
Total	2	65	118	7	31	5	0	0	6	3	18	.263	.293	.305	598	56	-7	0	0	0	.955	-9	/2-25,S-22	-1.4

■ SPIKE SHANNON Shannon, William Porter b: 2/7/1878, Pittsburgh, Pa. d: 5/16/40, Minneapolis, Minn. BB/TR, 5'11", 180 lbs. Deb: 4/15/04 U

YEAR	TM/L	G	AB	R	H	2B	3B	HR	RBI	BB	SO	AVG	OBP	SLG	OPS	OPS+	BR+	SB	CS	SBR	FA	FR	G/POS	TPR
1904	StL-N	134	500	84	140	10	3	1	26	50		.280	.349	.318	667	111	9	34			**.978**	9	*O-133(13-3-117)	1.2
1905	StL-N	140	544	73	146	16	3	0	41	47		.268	.327	.309	635	92	-4	27			**.984**	0	*O-140(140-0-0)	-1.3
1906	StL-N	80	302	36	78	4	0	0	25	36		.258	.337	.272	609	94	-1	15			.972	6	O-80(80-0-0)	0.0
	NY-N	76	287	42	73	5	1	0	25	34		.254	.342	.279	620	91	-1	18			.958	-7	O-76(76-0-0)	-1.4
	Yr	156	589	78	151	9	1	0	50	70		.256	.339	.275	614	93	-2	33			.966	-1	*O-156(156-0-0)	-1.4
1907	NY-N	155	585	**104**	155	12	5	1	33	82		.265	.363	.308	671	107	9	33			.977	2	*O-155(155-0-0)	0.2
1908	NY-N	77	268	34	60	2	1	1	21	28		.224	.314	.250	564	77	-6	13			.976	-3	O-74(60-0-15)	-1.5
	Pit-N	32	127	10	25	0	2	0	12	9		.197	.250	.228	478	53	-7	5			.947	1	O-32(8-20-7)	-0.9
	Yr	109	395	44	85	2	3	1	33	37		.215	.294	.243	537	69	-12	18			.964	-2	*O-106(68-20-22)	-2.4
Total	5	694	2613	383	677	49	15	3	183	286		.259	.337	.293	630	96	-1	145			.974	8	O-690(532-23-139)	-3.7

■ BILLY SHANTZ Shantz, Wilmer Ebert b: 7/31/27, Pottstown, Pa. d: 12/13/93, Lauderhill, Fla. BR/TR, 6'1", 160 lbs. Deb: 4/13/54 F

YEAR	TM/L	G	AB	R	H	2B	3B	HR	RBI	BB	SO	AVG	OBP	SLG	OPS	OPS+	BR+	SB	CS	SBR	FA	FR	G/POS	TPR
1954	Phi-A	51	164	13	42	9	3	1	17	17	23	.256	.326	.366	692	89	-3	0	0	0	.975	-13	C-51	-1.4
1955	KC-A	79	217	18	56	4	1	1	12	11	14	.258	.294	.300	593	59	-13	0	0	0	.990	-10	C-78	-2.0
1960	NY-A	1	0	0	0	0	0	0	0	0	0	—	—	—	—	—	0	0	0	0	1.000	-0	/C-1	0.0
Total	3	131	381	31	98	13	4	2	29	28	37	.257	.308	.328	636	72	-15	0	0	0	.984	-23	C-130	-3.4

■ RALPH SHARMAN Sharman, Ralph Edward "Bally" b: 4/11/1895, Cleveland, Ohio d: 5/24/18, Camp Sheridan, Ala BR/TR, 5'11", 176 lbs. Deb: 9/10/17

YEAR	TM/L	G	AB	R	H	2B	3B	HR	RBI	BB	SO	AVG	OBP	SLG	OPS	OPS+	BR+	SB	CS	SBR	FA	FR	G/POS	TPR
1917	Phi-A	13	37	2	11	2	1	0	2	3	2	.297	.366	.405	771	137	2	1			.941	-1	O-10(2-3-5)	0.0

■ DICK SHARON Sharon, Richard Louis b: 4/15/50, San Mateo, Cal. BR/TR, 6'2", 195 lbs. Deb: 5/13/73

YEAR	TM/L	G	AB	R	H	2B	3B	HR	RBI	BB	SO	AVG	OBP	SLG	OPS	OPS+	BR+	SB	CS	SBR	FA	FR	G/POS	TPR
1973	Det-A	91	178	20	43	9	0	7	16	10	31	.242	.282	.410	692	87	-4	2	0	0	.970	-10	O-91(19-7-71)	-1.6
1974	Det-A	60	129	12	28	4	0	2	10	14	29	.217	.294	.295	588	67	-5	4	4	-1	.989	-5	O-56(23-14-19)	-1.4
1975	SD-N	91	160	14	31	7	0	4	20	26	35	.194	.306	.313	619	77	-5	0	2	-1	.948	-7	O-57(39-12-7)	-1.6
Total	3	242	467	46	102	20	0	13	46	50	95	.218	.294	.345	639	79	-14	6	6	-1	.969	-22	O-204(81-33-97)	-4.6

■ BILL SHARP Sharp, William Howard b: 1/18/50, Lima, Ohio BL/TL, 5'10", 178 lbs. Deb: 5/26/73

YEAR	TM/L	G	AB	R	H	2B	3B	HR	RBI	BB	SO	AVG	OBP	SLG	OPS	OPS+	BR+	SB	CS	SBR	FA	FR	G/POS	TPR
1973	Chi-A	77	196	23	54	8	3	4	22	19	28	.276	.349	.408	757	109	2	2	3	-1	.981	2	O-70(11-59-0)/D-1	0.2
1974	Chi-A	100	320	45	81	13	2	4	24	25	37	.253	.311	.344	655	86	-6	0	3	-1	.986	-1	O-99(13-7-85)	-1.3
1975	Chi-A	18	35	1	7	0	0	0	4	2	3	.200	.243	.200	443	26	-3	0	0	0	.941	-3	O-14(2-1-11)	-0.7
	Mil-A	125	373	37	95	27	3	1	34	19	26	.255	.293	.351	644	81	-10	0	3	-1	.994	-3	*O-124(43-82-23)	-1.9
	Yr	143	408	38	102	27	3	1	38	21	29	.250	.288	.338	627	76	-14	0	3	-1	.991	-6	*O-138(45-83-34)	-2.6

YEAR	TM/L	G	AB	R	H	2B	3B	HR	RBI	BB	SO	AVG	OBP	SLG	OPS	OPS+	BR+	SB	CS	SBR	FA	FR	G/POS	TPR
1976	Mil-A	78	180	16	44	4	0	0	11	10	15	.244	.288	.267	555	64	-8	1	3	-1	.975	0	O-56(11-10-37)/D-7	-1.1
Total	4	398	1104	122	281	52	8	9	95	75	109	.255	.306	.341	647	83	-25	3	12	-4	.985	-5	O-363(80-159-156)/D-8	-4.8
■ BUD SHARPE	Sharpe, Bayard Heston b: 8/6/1881, West Chester, Pa. d: 5/31/16, Haddock, Ga. BL/TR, Deb: 4/14/05 Career OF: (0-LF 0-CF 42-RF)																							
1905	Bos-N	46	170	8	31	3	2	0	11	7		.182	.215	.224	438	31	-15	0			.904	2	O-42(0-0-42)/C-3,1-1	-1.5
1910	Bos-N	115	439	30	105	14	3	0	29	14	31	.239	.264	.285	549	58	-25	4			.987	7	*1-113	-2.1
	Pit-N	4	16	2	3	0	1	0	1	0	2	.188	.188	.313	500	43	-1	0			1.000	0	/1-4	-0.1
	Yr	119	455	32	108	14	4	0	30	14	33	.237	.262	.286	547	57	-26	4			.987	8	*1-117	-2.2
Total	2	165	625	40	139	17	6	0	41	21	33	.222	.249	.269	518	50	-41	4			.987	9	1-118/O-42R,C-3	-3.7
■ MIKE SHARPERSON	Sharperson, Michael Tyrone b: 10/4/61, Orangeburg, S.C. d: 5/26/96, Las Vegas, Nev. BR/TR, 6'3", 191 lbs. Deb: 4/6/87 Career OF: (0-LF 0-CF 1-RF)																							
1987	Tor-A	32	96	4	20	4	1	0	9	7	15	.208	.269	.271	540	43	-8	2	1	0	.971	-5	2-32	-1.1
	LA-N	10	33	7	9	2	0	0	1	4	5	.273	.351	.333	685	85	-1	0	0	0	1.000	2	/3-7,2-6	0.1
1988	*LA-N	46	59	8	16	1	0	0	4	1	12	.271	.295	.288	583	70	-2	0	1	-0	.949	-0	2-20/3-6,S-4	-0.3
1989	LA-N	27	28	2	7	3	0	0	5	4	7	.250	.344	.357	701	102	0	0	1	-0	1.000	-0	/2-4,1-2,3-2,S-1	0.0
1990	LA-N	129	357	42	106	14	2	3	36	46	39	.297	.379	.373	751	111	7	15	6	1	.949	6	*3-106,S-15/2-9,1-6	1.4
1991	LA-N	105	216	24	60	11	2	2	20	25	24	.278	.355	.375	730	108	3	1	3	-1	.981	-5	3-68,S-16,1-10,/2-5	-0.3
1992	LA-N★	128	317	48	95	21	0	3	36	47	33	.300	.390	.394	784	125	12	2	2	-0	.979	1	2-63,3-60/S-2	1.5
1993	LA-N	73	90	13	23	4	0	2	10	5	17	.256	.302	.367	669	83	-2	2	0	0	.945	1	2-17/3-6,S-3,1-1,O	0.0
1995	Atl-N	7	7	1	1	1	0	0	2	0	2	.143	.143	.286	429	9	-1	0	0	0	.000	0	/3-1	-0.1
Total	8	557	1203	149	337	61	5	10	123	139	154	.280	.357	.364	721	103	8	22	14	-0	.952	-0	3-256,2-156/S-41,1O	1.2
■ JACK SHARROTT	Sharrott, John Henry b: 8/13/1869, Bangor, Me. d: 12/31/27, Los Angeles, Cal. BR/TR, 5'9", 165 lbs. Deb: 4/22/1890																							
1890	NY-N	32	109	16	22	3	2	0	14	0	14	.202	.202	.266	468	36	-9	6			.932	-2	P-25/O-9(5-0-4)	-0.5
1891	NY-N	10	30	5	10	2	0	1	7	1	2	.333	.355	.500	855	154	2	3			.950	1	P-10	0.0
1892	NY-N	4	8	1	1	0	0	0	0	0	1	.125	.125	.125	250	-25	-1	0			.333	-1	/O-3(0-0-3),P-1	-0.2
1893	Phi-N	50	152	25	38	4	3	1	22	8	14	.250	.287	.336	623	66	-8	6			.824	-8	O-33(24-9-5),P-12	-1.3
Total	4	96	299	47	71	9	5	2	43	9	31	.237	.260	.321	581	61	-17	15			.927	-10	/P-48,O-45(29-9-12)	-2.0
■ SHAG SHAUGHNESSY	Shaughnessy, Francis Joseph b: 4/8/1883, Amboy, Ill. d: 5/15/69, Montreal, Que., Can BR/TR, 6'1.5", 185 lbs. Deb: 4/17/05 C																							
1905	Was-A	1	3	0	0	0	0	0	0	0		.000	.250	.000	250	-19	-0	0			.667	-0	/O-1(0-0-1)	-0.1
1908	Phi-A	8	29	2	9	0	0	0	1	2		.310	.355	.310	665	109	0	3			1.000	-1	/O-8(0-8-0)	-0.1
Total	2	9	32	2	9	0	0	0	1	2		.281	.343	.281	624	97	-0	3			.938	-1	/O-9(0-8-1)	-0.2
■ JON SHAVE	Shave, Jonathan Taylor b: 11/4/67, Waycross, Ga. BR/TR, 6', 185 lbs. Deb: 5/15/93																							
1993	Tex-A	17	47	3	15	2	0	0	7	0	8	.319	.319	.362	681	86	-1	1	3	-1	.917	-2	/S-9,2-8	-0.3
1998	Min-A	19	40	7	10	3	0	1	5	3	10	.250	.302	.400	702	79	-1	1	2	-0	1.000	1	3-15/1-1,S-1,D-1	0.0
1999	Tex-A	43	73	10	21	4	0	0	9	5	17	.288	.350	.342	692	74	-3	1	0	0	.953	8	S-24/1-9,3-6,2-1,D	0.5
Total	3	79	160	20	46	9	0	1	21	8	35	.287	.329	.363	692	79	-5	3	5	-1	.942	7	/S-34,3-21,1-10,2D	0.2
■ AL SHAW	Shaw, Albert Simpson b: 3/1/1881, Toledo, Ill. d: 12/30/74, Danville, Ill. BL/TR, 5'8.5", 165 lbs. Deb: 9/28/07 Career OF: (122-LF 272-CF 24-RF)																							
1907	StL-N	9	25	2	7	0	0	0	1	3		.280	.379	.280	659	110	1	1			.947	-1	/O-9(0-9-0)	0.0
1908	StL-N	107	367	40	97	13	4	1	19	25		.264	.311	.330	641	110	3	9			.931	7	O-91(2-67-22)/S-4,3-1	0.7
1909	StL-N	114	331	45	82	12	7	2	34	55		.248	.355	.344	699	125	11	15			.940	-1	O-92(0-90-2)	0.7
1914	Bro-F	112	376	81	122	27	7	5	49	44	59	.324	.395	.473	869	137	14	24			.955	1	*O-102(0-102-0)	0.8
1915	KC-F	132	448	67	126	22	10	6	67	46	45	.281	.348	.415	763	119	4	15			.942	-14	*O-124(120-4-0)	-1.7
Total	5	474	1547	235	434	74	28	14	170	173	104	.281	.353	.392	745	123	33	64			.942	-8	O-418C/S-4,3-1	0.5
■ AL SHAW	Shaw, Alfred "Shoddy" b: 10/3/1874, Burslem, England d: 3/25/58, Uhrichsville, Ohio BR/TR, 5'8", 170 lbs. Deb: 6/8/01																							
1901	Det-A	55	171	20	46	7	0	1	23	10		.269	.321	.327	648	76	-5	2			.938	-0	C-42/1-9,3-2,S-1	-0.2
1907	Bos-A	76	198	10	38	1	3	0	7	18		.192	.269	.227	497	59	-9	4			.971	15	C-73/1-1	1.3
1908	Chi-A	32	49	0	4	1	0	0	2	2		.082	.118	.102	220	-29	-7	0			.953	2	C-29	-0.4
1909	Bos-N	18	41	1	4	0	0	0	0	5		.098	.213	.098	310	-3	-5	0			.975	4	C-14	0.0
Total	4	181	459	31	92	9	3	1	32	35		.200	.267	.240	507	53	-26	6			.961	20	C-158/1-10,3-2,S-1	0.7
■ BEN SHAW	Shaw, Benjamin Nathaniel b: 6/18/1893, LaCenter, Ky. d: 3/16/59, Cleveland, Ohio BR/TR, 5'11.5", 190 lbs. Deb: 4/11/17																							
1917	Pit-N	2	2	0	0	0	0	0	0	0	0	.000	.000	.000	0	-97	-0	0			.000	0	H	-0.1
1918	Pit-N	21	36	5	7	1	0	0	2	2	2	.194	.275	.222	497	51	-2	0			.981	-2	/1-9,C-5	-0.4
Total	2	23	38	5	7	1	0	0	2	2	2	.184	.262	.211	472	43	-2	0			.981	-2	/1-9,C-5	-0.5
■ HUNKY SHAW	Shaw, Royal N b: 9/29/1884, Yakima, Wash. d: 7/3/69, Yakima, Wash. BB/TR, 5'8", 165 lbs. Deb: 5/16/08																							
1908	Pit-N	1	1	0	0	0	0	0	0	0		.000	.000	.000	0	-99	-0	0			.000	0	H	0.0
■ MARTY SHAY	Shay, Arthur Joseph b: 4/25/1896, Boston, Mass. d: 2/20/51, Worcester, Mass. BR/TR, 5'7.5", 148 lbs. Deb: 9/16/16																							
1916	Chi-N	2	7	0	2	0	0	0	0	0	1	.286	.286	.286	571	68	-0	0			.917	0	/S-2	0.0
1924	Bos-N	19	68	4	16	3	1	0	2	5	5	.235	.297	.309	606	65	-3	2	1	0	.950	-12	2-19/S-1	-1.5
Total	2	21	75	4	18	3	1	0	2	5	6	.240	.296	.307	603	66	-4	2	1		.929	-12	/2-19,S-3	-1.5
■ DANNY SHAY	Shay, Daniel C. b: 11/8/1876, Springfield, Ohio d: 12/1/27, Kansas City, Mo. TR, 5'10", Deb: 4/30/01																							
1901	Cle-A	19	75	4	17	2	2	0	10	2		.227	.266	.307	572	61	-4	0			.901	-4	S-19	-0.7
1904	StL-N	99	340	45	87	11	1	1	18	39		.256	.338	.303	641	103	3	36			.911	-7	S-97/2-2	-0.1
1905	StL-N	78	281	30	67	12	1	0	28	35		.238	.331	.288	620	88	-3	11			.953	-13	2-39,S-39	-1.5
1907	NY-N	35	79	10	15	1	1	1	6	12		.190	.304	.266	570	76	-2	5			.931	-7	2-13/S-9,O-2(0-2-0)	-1.0
Total	4	231	775	89	186	26	5	2	62	88		.240	.325	.294	620	90	-6	52			.902	-31	S-164/2-54,O-2(0-2-0)	-3.3
■ GERRY SHEA	Shea, Gerald J. b: 7/26/1881, St.Louis, Mo. d: 5/3/64, Berkeley, Mo. TR, 5'7", 160 lbs. Deb: 10/1/05																							
1905	StL-N	2	6	0	2	0	0	0	0	0		.333	.333	.333	667	102	-0	0			.917	1	/C-2	0.1
■ NAP SHEA	Shea, John Edward "Napoleon" b: 5/23/1874, Ware, Mass. d: 7/8/68, Bloomfield Hills, Mich. BR/TR, 5'5", 155 lbs. Deb: 9/11/02																							
1902	Phi-N	3	8	1	1	0	0	0	0	1		.125	.300	.125	425	32	-1	0			1.000	-0	/C-3	-0.1
■ MERV SHEA	Shea, Mervyn David John b: 9/5/1900, San Francisco, Cal d: 1/27/53, Sacramento, Cal. BR/TR, 5'11", 175 lbs. Deb: 4/23/27 C																							
1927	Det-A	34	85	5	15	6	3	0	9	7	15	.176	.239	.318	557	43	-8	0	0	0	.949	-1	C-31	-0.6
1928	Det-A	39	85	8	20	2	3	0	9	9	11	.235	.316	.329	645	69	-4	2	2	-0	.951	4	C-30	0.1
1929	Det-A	50	162	23	47	6	0	3	24	19	18	.290	.365	.383	747	92	-1	2	1	0	.964	-6	C-46	-0.4
1933	Bos-A	16	56	1	8	3	0	0	8	4	7	.143	.200	.196	396	5	-8	0	0	0	1.000	-2	C-16	-0.8
	StL-A	94	279	26	73	11	1	1	27	43	26	.262	.360	.319	679	76	-8	2	0	0	.995	9	C-85	0.6
	Yr	110	335	27	81	14	1	1	35	47	33	.242	.335	.299	634	65	-15	2	0	0	**.996**	7	*C-101	-0.2
1934	Chi-A	62	176	8	28	3	0	0	5	24	19	.159	.260	.176	436	14	-22	0	1	-0	.972	1	C-60	-1.7
1935	Chi-A	46	122	8	28	2	0	0	13	30	9	.230	.382	.246	627	64	-5	0	0	0	.990	8	C-43	0.5
1936	Chi-A	14	24	3	3	0	0	0	2	6	5	.125	.300	.125	425	8	-3	0	0	0	1.000	1	C-14	-0.2
1937	Chi-A	25	71	7	15	1	0	0	5	15	10	.211	.349	.225	574	48	-5	1	0	0	.966	3	C-25	-0.1
1938	Bro-N	48	120	14	22	5	0	0	12	28	20	.183	.338	.225	563	56	-6	1			.977	-1	C-47	-0.5
1939	Det-A	4	2	0	0	0	0	0	0	0	1	.000	.000	.000	0	-93	-1	0	0	0	.500	-1	/C-4	-0.1
1944	Phi-N	7	15	2	4	0	0	1	1	4	4	.267	.421	.467	888	155	1	0			.952	-0	/C-6	0.1
Total	11	439	1197	105	263	39	7	5	115	189	145	.220	.327	.277	603	58	-70	8	4		.976	16	C-407	-3.1
■ DANNY SHEAFFER	Sheaffer, Danny Todd b: 8/2/61, Jacksonville, Fla. BR/TR, 6', 202 lbs. Deb: 4/9/87 Career OF: (20-LF 2-CF 9-RF)																							
1987	Bos-A	25	66	5	8	1	0	1	5	0	14	.121	.121	.182	303	-21	-11	0	0	0	.977	-3	C-25	-1.3
1989	Cle-A	7	16	1	1	0	0	0	0	2	2	.063	.167	.063	229	-32	-3	0	0	0	.000	0	/3-2,O-1(1-0-0),D-3	-0.3
1993	Col-N	82	216	26	60	9	1	4	32	8	15	.278	.307	.384	691	72	-8	2	3	-1	.994	-2	C-65/1-7,O-2L,3-1	-0.7
1994	Col-N	44	110	11	24	4	0	1	12	10	11	.218	.283	.282	565	41	-9	0	2	-1	.995	4	C-30/1-2,O-1(1-0-0)	-0.5
1995	StL-N	76	208	24	48	10	1	5	30	23	38	.231	.307	.361	668	76	-7	0	0	0	.993	10	C-67/1-3,3-1	0.6

YEAR	TM/L	G	AB	R	H	2B	3B	HR	RBI	BB	SO	AVG	OBP	SLG	OPS	OPS+	BR+	SB	CS	SBR	FA	FR	G/POS	TPR
1996	*StL-N	79	198	10	45	9	3	2	20	9	25	.227	.271	.333	605	59	-12	3	3	-0	.983	1	C-47,3-17/1-6,O-3L	-0.9
1997	StL-N	76	132	10	33	5	0	0	11	8	17	.250	.298	.288	586	55	-9	1	0	0	.957	-10	3-30,O-22L/C-9,2-3	-1.8
Total	7	389	946	87	219	38	5	13	110	60	122	.232	.281	.323	604	56	-60	6	8	-1	.990	1	C-243/3-51,O-29L,12D	-4.9

■ DAVE SHEAN Shean, David William b: 7/9/1883, Arlington, Mass. d: 5/22/63, Boston, Mass. BR/TR, 5'11", 175 lbs. Deb: 9/10/06

YEAR	TM/L	G	AB	R	H	2B	3B	HR	RBI	BB	SO	AVG	OBP	SLG	OPS	OPS+	BR+	SB	CS	SBR	FA	FR	G/POS	TPR
1906	Phi-A	22	75	7	16	3	2	0	3	5		.213	.280	.307	587	81	-2	6			.980	-2	2-22	-0.4
1908	Phi-N	14	48	4	7	2	0	0	2	1		.146	.180	.188	368	17	-5	1			.871	-6	S-14	-1.2
1909	Phi-N	36	112	14	26	2	2	0	4	14		.232	.323	.286	609	88	-1	3			.982	-2	2-14,1-11/O-3C,S-1	-0.4
	Bos-N	75	267	32	66	11	4	1	29	17		.247	.297	.330	627	90	-4	14			.956	8	2-72	0.5
	Yr	111	379	46	92	13	6	1	33	31		.243	.305	.317	622	90	-5	17			.960	6	2-86,1-11/O-3C,S-1	0.1
1910	Bos-N	150	543	52	130	12	7	3	36	42	45	.239	.294	.304	598	71	-21	16			.953	**43**	*2-148	2.4
1911	Chi-N	54	145	17	28	4	0	0	15	8	15	.193	.240	.221	461	29	-14	4			.947	1	2-23,S-19/3-1	-1.1
1912	Bos-N	4	10	1	3	0	0	0	0	1	2	.300	.417	.300	717	96	0	0			.917	-1	/S-4	-0.1
1917	Cin-N	131	442	36	93	9	5	2	35	22	39	.210	.249	.267	516	61	-21	10			.961	19	*2-131	0.0
1918	*Bos-A	115	425	58	112	16	3	0	34	40	25	.264	.331	.315	646	97	-1	11			.967	-9	*2-115	-0.9
1919	Bos-A	29	100	4	14	0	0	0	8	5	7	.140	.189	.140	329	-7	-14	1			.981	4	2-29	-1.0
Total	9	630	2167	225	495	59	23	6	166	155	133	.228	.284	.285	569	70	-82	66			.961	55	2-554/S-38,1-11,O3	-2.2

■ RAY SHEARER Shearer, Ray Solomon b: 9/19/29, Jacobus, Pa. d: 2/21/82, York, Pa. BR/TR, 6', 200 lbs. Deb: 9/18/57

YEAR	TM/L	G	AB	R	H	2B	3B	HR	RBI	BB	SO	AVG	OBP	SLG	OPS	OPS+	BR+	SB	CS	SBR	FA	FR	G/POS	TPR
1957	Mil-N	2	2	1	1	0	0	0	0	1	1	.500	.667	.500	1167	237	1	0	0	0	.000	-0	/O-1(1-0-0)	0.0

■ JOHN SHEARON Shearon, John M. b: 1870, Pittsburgh, Pa. d: 2/1/23, Bradford, Pa. Deb: 7/28/1891

YEAR	TM/L	G	AB	R	H	2B	3B	HR	RBI	BB	SO	AVG	OBP	SLG	OPS	OPS+	BR+	SB	CS	SBR	FA	FR	G/POS	TPR
1891	Cle-N	30	124	10	30	1	1	0	13	1	15	.242	.248	.266	514	48	-9	6			.814	-4	O-25(4-14-10)/P-6	-1.1
1896	Cle-N	16	64	6	11	0	1	0	3	4	6	.172	.221	.203	424	11	-8	3			.818	-4	O-16(0-0-16)	-1.2
Total	2	46	188	16	41	1	2	0	16	5	21	.218	.238	.245	483	34	-17	9			.815	-9	/O-41(4-14-26),P-6	-2.3

■ JIMMY SHECKARD Sheckard, Samuel James Tilden b: 11/23/1878, Upper Chanceford, Pa.
d: 1/15/47, Lancaster, Pa. BL/TR, 5'9", 175 lbs. Deb: 9/14/1897 Career OF: (1843-LF 22-CF 214-RF)

YEAR	TM/L	G	AB	R	H	2B	3B	HR	RBI	BB	SO	AVG	OBP	SLG	OPS	OPS+	BR+	SB	CS	SBR	FA	FR	G/POS	TPR
1897	Bro-N	13	49	12	14	3	2	3	14	6		.286	.364	.612	976	164	4	5			.753	-5	S-11/O-2(0-0-2)	0.0
1898	Bro-N	105	408	51	113	17	9	4	64	37		.277	.349	.392	741	113	6	8			.926	-4	*O-105(101-4-0)/3-1	-0.6
1899	Bal-N	147	536	104	158	18	10	3	75	56		.295	.380	.382	763	104	4	**77**			.943	21	*O-146(0-1-146)/1-1	1.6
1900	Bro-N	85	273	74	82	19	10	1	39	42		.300	.416	.454	870	132	13	30			.925	2	O-78(67-6-5)	0.8
1901	Bro-N	133	554	116	196	29	**19**	11	104	47		.354	.409	**.534**	944	168	47	35			.944	7	*O-121(120-1-0),3-12	4.5
1902	Bal-A	4	15	3	4	1	0	0	0	1		.267	.313	.333	646	76	-0	2			1.000	-1	/O-4(0-4-0)	-0.2
	Bro-N	123	486	86	129	20	10	4	37	57		.265	.349	.372	721	122	13	23			.964	8	*O-123(122-1-0)	1.5
1903	Bro-N	139	515	99	171	29	9	**9**	75	75		.332	.423	.476	899	161	**43**	**67**			.951	23	*O-139(139-0-0)	5.5
1904	Bro-N	143	507	70	121	23	6	1	46	56		.239	.317	.314	630	97	-0	21			.956	7	*O-141(141-0-0)/2-2	-0.1
1905	Bro-N	130	480	58	140	20	11	3	41	61		.292	.380	.398	777	142	27	23			.967	15	*O-129(129-0-0)	3.5
1906	*Chi-N	149	549	90	144	27	10	1	45	67		.262	.349	.353	702	112	9	30			.986	0	*O-149(149-0-0)	0.0
1907	*Chi-N	143	484	76	129	23	1	1	36	76		.267	.373	.324	697	112	10	31			.975	-10	*O-142(142-0-0)	-1.0
1908	*Chi-N	115	403	54	93	18	3	2	22	62		.231	.336	.305	641	101	3	18			.955	-2	*O-115(115-0-0)	-0.7
1909	Chi-N	148	525	81	134	29	5	1	43	72		.255	.346	.335	681	109	7	15			.967	-3	*O-148(148-0-0)	-0.6
1910	*Chi-N	144	507	82	130	27	6	5	51	83	53	.256	.366	.363	729	114	11	22			.976	7	*O-143(143-0-0)	1.0
1911	Chi-N	156	539	**121**	149	26	11	4	50	**147**	58	.276	**.434**	.388	822	130	32	32			.963	15	*O-156(156-0-0)	3.9
1912	Chi-N	146	523	85	128	22	10	3	47	**122**	81	.245	.392	.342	735	102	8	15			.962	7	*O-146(146-0-0)	0.9
1913	StL-N	52	136	18	27	2	1	0	17	41	25	.199	.388	.228	616	79	-1	5			.953	-3	O-46(16-0-36)	-0.7
	Cin-N	47	116	16	22	1	3	0	7	27	16	.190	.343	.250	593	71	-3	6			.969	-3	O-38(9-5-25)	-0.8
	Yr	99	252	34	49	3	4	0	24	68	41	.194	.368	.238	606	76	-4	11			.960	-6	O-84(25-5-61)	-1.5
Total	17	2122	7605	1296	2084	354	136	56	813	1135	233	.274	.375	.378	753	120	233	465			.958	82	*O-2071L/3-13,S21	18.5

■ JIM SHEEHAN Sheehan, James Thomas "Big Jim" b: 6/3/13, New Haven, Conn. BR/TR, 6'2", 196 lbs. Deb: 9/26/36

YEAR	TM/L	G	AB	R	H	2B	3B	HR	RBI	BB	SO	AVG	OBP	SLG	OPS	OPS+	BR+	SB	CS	SBR	FA	FR	G/POS	TPR
1936	NY-N	1	4	0	0	0	0	0	0	0	2	.000	.000	.000	0	-99	-1	0			.833	-0	/C-1	-0.1

■ JACK SHEEHAN Sheehan, John Thomas b: 4/15/1893, Chicago, Ill. d: 5/29/87, W.Palm Beach, Fla. BB/TR, 5'8.5", 165 lbs. Deb: 9/11/20

YEAR	TM/L	G	AB	R	H	2B	3B	HR	RBI	BB	SO	AVG	OBP	SLG	OPS	OPS+	BR+	SB	CS	SBR	FA	FR	G/POS	TPR
1920	*Bro-N	3	5	0	2	1	0	0	0	1	0	.400	.500	.600	1100	208	1	0	0	0	.875	0	/S-2,3-1	0.1
1921	Bro-N	5	12	2	0	0	0	0	0	0	1	.000	.000	.000	0	-97	-3	0	0	0	.900	-0	/2-2,S-1,3-1	-0.3
Total	2	8	17	2	2	1	0	0	0	1	1	.118	.167	.176	343	-7	-3	0	0	0	.909	0	/S-3,2-2,3-2	-0.2

■ TOMMY SHEEHAN Sheehan, Thomas H. b: 11/6/1877, Sacramento, Cal. d: 5/22/59, Panama City, Pan. BR/TR, 5'8", 160 lbs. Deb: 8/2/00

YEAR	TM/L	G	AB	R	H	2B	3B	HR	RBI	BB	SO	AVG	OBP	SLG	OPS	OPS+	BR+	SB	CS	SBR	FA	FR	G/POS	TPR
1900	NY-N	1	2	0	0	0	0	0	0	0		.000	.000	.000	0	-99	-1	0			.000	0	/S-1	-0.1
1906	Pit-N	95	315	28	76	6	3	1	34	18		.241	.284	.289	573	75	-9	13			.947	-5	3-90	-1.4
1907	Pit-N	75	226	23	62	2	3	0	25	23		.274	.341	.310	651	103	1	10			.941	-1	3-57,S-10	0.3
1908	Bro-N	146	468	45	100	18	2	0	29	53		.214	.302	.261	562	83	-7	9			.930	-6	*3-145	-1.1
Total	4	317	1011	96	238	26	8	1	88	94		.235	.305	.280	585	85	-16	32			.938	-12	3-292/S-11	-2.3

■ BIFF SHEEHAN Sheehan, Timothy James b: 2/13/1868, Hartford, Conn. d: 10/21/23, Hartford, Conn. TR, 5'9", 165 lbs. Deb: 7/22/1895

YEAR	TM/L	G	AB	R	H	2B	3B	HR	RBI	BB	SO	AVG	OBP	SLG	OPS	OPS+	BR+	SB	CS	SBR	FA	FR	G/POS	TPR
1895	StL-N	52	180	24	57	3	6	1	18	20	6	.317	.394	.417	811	111	3	7			.940	-2	O-41(0-2-39),1-11	0.0
1896	StL-N	6	19	0	3	0	0	0	1	4	0	.158	.304	.158	462	25	-2	0			1.000	-1	/O-6(1-0-5)	-0.2
Total	2	58	199	24	60	3	6	1	19	24	6	.302	.385	.392	777	103	2	7			.948	-3	/O-47(1-2-44),1-11	-0.2

■ EARL SHEELY Sheely, Earl Homer "Whitey" b: 2/12/1893, Bushnell, Ill. d: 9/16/52, Seattle, Wash. BR/TR, 6'3.5", 195 lbs. Deb: 4/14/21 F

YEAR	TM/L	G	AB	R	H	2B	3B	HR	RBI	BB	SO	AVG	OBP	SLG	OPS	OPS+	BR+	SB	CS	SBR	FA	FR	G/POS	TPR
1921	Chi-A	154	563	68	171	25	6	11	95	57	34	.304	.375	.428	803	106	5	4	9	-2	.988	5	*1-154	-0.2
1922	Chi-A	149	526	72	167	37	4	6	80	60	27	.317	.393	.437	830	117	14	4	6	-1	.993	2	*1-149	0.5
1923	Chi-A	156	570	74	169	25	3	4	88	79	30	.296	.387	.372	759	102	4	5	5	-1	.992	-1	*1-156	-0.7
1924	Chi-A	146	535	84	171	34	3	3	103	95	28	.320	.426	.411	837	120	21	7	4	0	.991	-10	*1-146	0.2
1925	Chi-A	153	600	93	189	43	3	9	111	68	23	.315	.389	.442	831	117	16	3	3	-0	.988	-5	*1-153	0.1
1926	Chi-A	145	525	77	157	40	2	6	89	75	13	.299	.394	.417	811	116	14	3	1	0	**.995**	0	*1-144	0.5
1927	Chi-A	45	129	11	27	3	0	2	16	20	5	.209	.320	.279	599	58	-8	1	3	-1	.982	-4	1-36	-1.4
1929	Pit-N	139	485	63	142	22	4	6	88	75	24	.293	.392	.392	784	93	-3	6			**.996**	-0	*1-139	-1.1
1931	Bos-N	147	538	30	147	15	2	1	77	34	21	.273	.319	.314	633	73	-20	0			.992	-3	*1-143	-3.6
Total	9	1234	4471	572	1340	244	27	48	747	563	205	.300	.383	.399	782	104	45	33	31		.991	-14	*1-1220	-5.7

■ BUD SHEELY Sheely, Hollis Kimball b: 11/26/20, Spokane, Wash. d: 10/17/85, Sacramento, Cal. BL/TR, 6'1", 200 lbs. Deb: 7/26/51 F

YEAR	TM/L	G	AB	R	H	2B	3B	HR	RBI	BB	SO	AVG	OBP	SLG	OPS	OPS+	BR+	SB	CS	SBR	FA	FR	G/POS	TPR
1951	Chi-A	34	89	2	16	2	0	0	7	6	7	.180	.240	.202	442	21	-10	0	0	0	.986	3	C-33	-0.5
1952	Chi-A	36	75	1	18	2	0	0	3	12	7	.240	.352	.267	619	73	-2	0	1	-0	.992	-2	C-31	-0.3
1953	Chi-A	31	46	4	10	1	0	0	2	9	8	.217	.345	.239	585	58	-2	0	0	0	1.000	0	C-17	-0.1
Total	3	101	210	7	44	5	0	0	12	27	22	.210	.305	.233	539	49	-14	0	1	-0	.991	2	/C-81	-0.9

■ CHUCK SHEERIN Sheerin, Charles Joseph b: 4/17/09, Brooklyn, N.Y. d: 9/27/86, Valley Stream, N.Y. BR/TR, 5'11.5", 198 lbs. Deb: 4/21/36

YEAR	TM/L	G	AB	R	H	2B	3B	HR	RBI	BB	SO	AVG	OBP	SLG	OPS	OPS+	BR+	SB	CS	SBR	FA	FR	G/POS	TPR
1936	Phi-N	39	72	4	19	4	0	0	4	7	18	.264	.329	.319	649	68	-3	0			.942	-3	2-17,3-13/S-5	-0.5

■ ANDY SHEETS Sheets, Andrew Mark b: 11/19/71, Baton Rouge, La. BR/TR, 6'2", 180 lbs. Deb: 4/22/96

YEAR	TM/L	G	AB	R	H	2B	3B	HR	RBI	BB	SO	AVG	OBP	SLG	OPS	OPS+	BR+	SB	CS	SBR	FA	FR	G/POS	TPR
1996	Sea-A	47	110	18	21	8	0	0	9	10	41	.191	.264	.264	528	34	-11	2	0	0	.947	8	3-25,2-18/S-7	-0.2
1997	*Sea-A	32	89	18	22	3	0	4	9	7	34	.247	.302	.416	718	86	-2	2	0	0	.872	-1	3-21/S-9,2-2	-0.1
1998	*SD-N	88	194	31	47	5	3	7	29	21	62	.242	.319	.407	727	97	-1	7	2	1	.964	6	S-39,3-23,2-22,/1-2	0.8
1999	Ana-A	87	244	22	48	10	0	3	29	14	59	.197	.240	.275	515	31	-26	1	2	-0	.966	-20	S-76/2-7,3-1	-3.8
2000	Bos-A	12	21	1	2	0	0	0	1	0	3	.095	.095	.095	190	-49	-5	0	0	0	1.000	3	S-10/1-1,D-2	-0.2
Total	5	266	658	90	140	26	3	14	77	52	199	.213	.272	.325	598	55	-45	12	4	1	.966	-5	S-141/3-70,2-49,1D	-3.5

■ LARRY SHEETS Sheets, Larry Kent b: 12/6/59, Staunton, Va. BL/TR, 6'3", 225 lbs. Deb: 9/18/84 Career OF: (192-LF 0-CF 144-RF)

YEAR	TM/L	G	AB	R	H	2B	3B	HR	RBI	BB	SO	AVG	OBP	SLG	OPS	OPS+	BR+	SB	CS	SBR	FA	FR	G/POS	TPR
1984	Bal-A	8	16	3	7	1	0	1	2	1	3	.438	.471	.688	1158	221	3	0	0	0	1.000	0	/O-7(0-0-7)	0.2
1985	Bal-A	113	328	43	86	8	0	17	50	28	52	.262	.324	.442	766	110	4	0	1	-0	.875	-2	D-93/O-9(1-0-8),1-1	-0.2

YEAR	TM/L	G	AB	R	H	2B	3B	HR	RBI	BB	SO	AVG	OBP	SLG	OPS	OPS+	BR+	SB	CS	SBR	FA	FR	G/POS	TPR
1986	Bal-A	112	338	42	92	17	1	18	60	21	56	.272	.319	.488	807	117	7	2	0	0	.984	-0	D-58,O-32L/C-6,13	0.4
1987	Bal-A	135	469	74	148	23	0	31	94	31	67	.316	.362	.563	925	144	28	1	1	-0	.975	-4	*O-124L/1-3,D-7	1.7
1988	Bal-A	136	452	38	104	19	1	10	47	42	72	.230	.304	.343	647	83	-10	1	6	-2	.974	1	O-76L,D-50/1-3	-1.5
1989	Bal-A	102	304	33	74	12	1	7	33	26	58	.243	.309	.359	668	90	-4	1	1	-0	.000	0	D-88	-0.7
1990	Det-A	131	360	40	94	17	2	10	52	24	42	.261	.311	.403	714	97	-2	1	3	-1	.981	-7	O-79(56-0-23),D-44	-1.4
1993	Sea-A	11	17	0	2	1	0	0	1	2	1	.118	.250	.176	426	17	-2	0	0	0	1.000	-0	/O-1(0-0-1),D-5	-0.2
Total	8	748	2284	273	607	98	5	94	339	175	351	.266	.323	.437	760	109	23	6	12	-3	.976	-12	D-345,O-328L/1-11,C3	-1.7

■ GARY SHEFFIELD

Sheffield, Gary Antonian b: 11/18/68, Tampa, Fla. BR/TR, 5'11", 190 lbs. Deb: 9/3/88 Career OF: (287-LF 0-CF 565-RF)

YEAR	TM/L	G	AB	R	H	2B	3B	HR	RBI	BB	SO	AVG	OBP	SLG	OPS	OPS+	BR+	SB	CS	SBR	FA	FR	G/POS	TPR
1988	Mil-A	24	80	12	19	1	0	4	12	7	7	.237	.299	.400	699	93	-1	3	1	0	.967	-10	S-24	-0.9
1989	Mil-A	95	368	34	91	18	0	5	32	27	33	.247	.306	.337	643	82	-9	10	6	0	.959	-17	S-70,3-21/D-4	-2.1
1990	Mil-A	125	487	67	143	30	1	10	67	44	41	.294	.356	.421	777	117	11	25	10	2	.934	-4	*3-125	0.9
1991	Mil-A	50	175	25	34	12	2	2	22	19	15	.194	.284	.320	604	69	-8	5	5	-1	.922	-12	3-43/D-5	-2.0
1992	SD-N★	146	557	87	184	34	3	33	100	48	40	**.330**	.390	.580	969	168	48	5	6	-1	.961	10	*3-144	6.0
1993	SD-N	68	258	34	76	12	2	10	36	18	30	.295	.348	.473	821	115	5	5	1	1	.905	-11	3-67	-0.5
	Fla-N★	72	236	33	69	8	3	10	37	29	34	.292	.384	.479	863	122	8	12	4	1	.894	-4	3-66	0.6
	Yr	140	494	67	145	20	5	20	73	47	64	.294	.365	.476	841	119	13	17	5	2	.899	-16	*3-133	0.1
1994	Fla-N	87	322	61	89	16	1	27	78	51	50	.276	.385	.584	969	144	21	12	6	1	.970	0	O-87(0-0-87)	1.7
1995	Fla-N	63	213	46	69	8	0	16	46	55	45	.324	.471	.587	1057	176	27	19	4	3	.942	0	O-61(3-0-59)	2.6
1996	Fla-N★	161	519	118	163	33	1	42	120	142	66	.314	**.469**	.624	**1094**	**192**	**78**	16	9	0	.976	-9	*O-161(0-0-161)	5.8
1997	*Fla-N	135	444	86	111	22	1	21	71	121	79	.250	.426	.446	872	135	30	11	7	-0	.980	8	*O-132(0-0-132)/D-1	3.0
1998	Fla-N	40	136	21	37	11	1	6	28	26	16	.272	.396	.500	896	141	9	4	2	0	.986	2	O-37(0-0-37)	0.9
	LA-N★	90	301	52	95	16	1	16	57	69	30	.316	.452	.535	987	168	34	18	5	2	.994	2	O-89(0-0-89)	3.3
	Yr	130	437	73	132	27	2	22	85	95	46	.302	.435	.524	959	160	43	22	7	2	.991	4	*O-126(0-0-126)	4.2
1999	LA-N★	152	549	103	165	20	0	34	101	101	64	.301	.413	.523	936	143	39	11	5	1	.972	-0	*O-145(145-0-0)/D-3	3.2
2000	LA-N★	141	501	105	163	24	3	43	109	101	71	.325	.442	.643	1085	178	63	4	6	-1	.954	-3	*O-139(139-0-0)/D-2	5.0
Total	13	1449	5146	884	1508	265	19	279	916	858	621	.293	.402	.515	916	145	356	160	77	8	.972	-50	O-851R,3-466/S-94,D	27.5

■ JOHN SHELBY

Shelby, John T. b: 2/23/58, Lexington, Ky. BB/TR, 6'1", 175 lbs. Deb: 9/15/81 C Career OF: (114-LF 781-CF 85-RF)

YEAR	TM/L	G	AB	R	H	2B	3B	HR	RBI	BB	SO	AVG	OBP	SLG	OPS	OPS+	BR+	SB	CS	SBR	FA	FR	G/POS	TPR
1981	Bal-A	7	2	2	0	0	0	0	0	0	1	.000	.000	.000	0	-99	-1	2	0	0	1.000	-2	/O-4(0-4-0)	-0.2
1982	Bal-A	26	35	8	11	3	0	1	2	0	5	.314	.314	.486	800	116	1	0	1	-0	1.000	-8	O-24(0-24-0)	-0.8
1983	*Bal-A	126	325	52	84	15	2	5	27	18	64	.258	.297	.363	660	82	-8	15	2	3	.981	-14	*O-115(0-115-0)/D-1	-2.1
1984	Bal-A	128	383	44	80	12	5	6	30	20	71	.209	.248	.313	561	55	-24	12	4	1	.993	-10	*O-124(0-118-9)	-3.4
1985	Bal-A	69	205	28	58	6	2	7	27	7	44	.283	.307	.434	741	103	0	5	1	1	.981	0	O-59(9-43-10)/2-1,D-3	0.0
1986	Bal-A	135	404	54	92	14	4	11	49	18	75	.228	.264	.364	628	70	-18	18	6	2	.978	-12	*O-121(49-56-31)/D-2	-3.1
1987	Bal-A	21	32	4	6	0	0	1	3	1	13	.188	.212	.281	493	30	-3	0	1	-0	1.000	-3	O-19(0-4-15)/D-1	-0.7
	LA-N	120	476	61	132	26	0	21	69	31	97	.277	.323	.464	787	108	4	16	6	1	.972	11	*O-117(0-117-0)	1.5
1988	*LA-N	140	494	65	130	23	6	10	64	44	128	.263	.323	.395	718	109	5	16	5	2	.982	7	*O-140(0-140-0)	1.3
1989	LA-N	108	345	28	63	11	1	1	12	25	92	.183	.238	.229	467	35	-29	10	7	-0	.991	0	O-98(0-98-0)	-3.3
1990	LA-N	25	24	2	6	1	0	0	2	0	7	.250	.250	.292	542	50	-2	1	0	0	1.000	-3	O-12(7-1-4)	-0.5
	Det-A	78	222	22	55	9	3	4	20	10	51	.248	.280	.369	650	80	-7	3	5	-1	.973	-1	O-68(24-35-13)/D-5	-1.0
1991	Det-A	53	143	19	22	8	1	3	8	8	23	.154	.204	.287	491	34	-13	0	2	-1	.982	-1	O-47(25-26-3)/D-4	-1.6
Total	11	1036	3090	389	739	128	24	70	313	182	671	.239	.282	.364	646	79	-95	98	40	8	.982	-36	O-948C/D-16,2-1	-13.9

■ BOB SHELDON

Sheldon, Bob Mitchell b: 11/27/50, Montebello, Cal. BL/TR, 6', 170 lbs. Deb: 4/10/74

YEAR	TM/L	G	AB	R	H	2B	3B	HR	RBI	BB	SO	AVG	OBP	SLG	OPS	OPS+	BR+	SB	CS	SBR	FA	FR	G/POS	TPR
1974	Mil-A	10	17	4	2	1	1	0	0	4	2	.118	.286	.294	580	67	-1	0	1	-0	1.000	-1	/2-3,D-4	-0.2
1975	Mil-A	53	181	17	52	3	3	0	14	13	14	.287	.342	.337	679	92	-2	0	3	-1	.977	-8	2-44/D-6	-0.8
1977	Mil-A	31	64	9	13	4	1	0	3	6	9	.203	.271	.297	568	55	-4	0	0	0	1.000	1	D-17/2-5	-0.4
Total	3	94	262	30	67	8	5	0	17	23	25	.256	.321	.324	645	81	-6	0	4	-1	.979	-9	/2-52,D-27	-1.4

■ SCOTT SHELDON

Sheldon, Scott Patrick b: 11/28/68, Hammond, Ind. BR/TR, 6'3", 185 lbs. Deb: 5/18/97 Career OF: (2-LF 1-CF 1-RF)

YEAR	TM/L	G	AB	R	H	2B	3B	HR	RBI	BB	SO	AVG	OBP	SLG	OPS	OPS+	BR+	SB	CS	SBR	FA	FR	G/POS	TPR
1997	Oak-A	13	24	2	6	0	0	1	2	1	6	.250	.308	.375	683	78	-1	0	0	0	.939	-1	S-12/2-1,3-1	-0.1
1998	Tex-A	7	16	0	2	0	0	0	1	1	6	.125	.176	.125	301	-19	-3	0	0	0	1.000	2	/3-3,S-2,1-1,D-1	0.0
1999	Tex-A	2	1	0	0	0	0	0	0	0	0	.000	.000	.000	0	-96	-0	0	0	0	1.000	1	/3-2	0.1
2000	Tex-A	58	124	21	35	11	0	4	19	10	37	.282	.341	.468	808	99	-0	0	0	0	.970	5	S-22,3-15,2-12,1/COP	0.5
Total	4	80	165	23	43	11	0	5	22	12	49	.261	.318	.418	737	84	-4	0	0	0	.957	8	/S-36,3-21,21COPD	0.5

■ HUGH SHELLEY

Shelley, Hubert Leneirre b: 10/26/10, Rogers, Tex. d: 6/16/78, Beaumont, Tex. BR/TR, 6', 170 lbs. Deb: 6/25/35

YEAR	TM/L	G	AB	R	H	2B	3B	HR	RBI	BB	SO	AVG	OBP	SLG	OPS	OPS+	BR+	SB	CS	SBR	FA	FR	G/POS	TPR
1935	Det-A	7	8	1	2	0	0	0	1	2	1	.250	.400	.250	650	74	-0	0	0	0	1.000	-1	/O-5(3-1-1)	-0.2

■ SKEETER SHELTON

Shelton, Andrew Kemper b: 6/29/1888, Huntington, W.Va. d: 1/9/54, Huntington, W.Va. BR/TR, 5'11", 175 lbs. Deb: 8/25/15

YEAR	TM/L	G	AB	R	H	2B	3B	HR	RBI	BB	SO	AVG	OBP	SLG	OPS	OPS+	BR+	SB	CS	SBR	FA	FR	G/POS	TPR
1915	NY-A	10	40	1	1	0	0	0	0	2	10	.025	.071	.025	96	-71	-8	0			1.000	0	O-10(0-10-0)	-1.0

■ BEN SHELTON

Shelton, Benjamin Davis b: 9/21/69, Chicago, Ill. BR/TL, 6'3", 210 lbs. Deb: 6/16/93

YEAR	TM/L	G	AB	R	H	2B	3B	HR	RBI	BB	SO	AVG	OBP	SLG	OPS	OPS+	BR+	SB	CS	SBR	FA	FR	G/POS	TPR
1993	Pit-N	15	24	3	6	1	0	2	7	3	3	.250	.333	.542	875	130	1	0	0	0	.889	-0	/O-6(6-0-0),1-2	0.0

■ STEVE SHEMO

Shemo, Stephen Michael b: 4/9/15, Swoyersville, Pa. d: 4/13/92, Eden, N.C. BR/TR, 5'11", 175 lbs. Deb: 4/18/44

YEAR	TM/L	G	AB	R	H	2B	3B	HR	RBI	BB	SO	AVG	OBP	SLG	OPS	OPS+	BR+	SB	CS	SBR	FA	FR	G/POS	TPR
1944	Bos-N	18	31	3	9	2	0	0	1	1	3	.290	.313	.355	667	84	-1	0			.966	3	2-16/3-2	0.3
1945	Bos-N	17	46	4	11	1	0	0	7	1	3	.239	.255	.261	516	43	-4	0			.921	-6	2-12/3-3,S-1	-0.9
Total	2	35	77	7	20	3	0	0	8	2	6	.260	.278	.299	577	60	-4	0			.948	-3	/2-28,3-5,S-1	-0.6

■ JACK SHEPARD

Shepard, Jack Leroy b: 5/13/32, Clovis, Cal. d: 12/31/94, Atherton, Cal. BR/TR, 6'2", 195 lbs. Deb: 6/19/53

YEAR	TM/L	G	AB	R	H	2B	3B	HR	RBI	BB	SO	AVG	OBP	SLG	OPS	OPS+	BR+	SB	CS	SBR	FA	FR	G/POS	TPR
1953	Pit-N	2	4	0	1	0	0	0	0	0	2	.250	.250	.250	500	31	-0	0	0	0	.750	-0	/C-2	-0.1
1954	Pit-N	82	227	24	69	8	2	3	22	26	33	.304	.375	.396	772	103	2	0	0	0	.977	2	C-67	0.6
1955	Pit-N	94	264	24	63	10	2	2	23	33	25	.239	.323	.314	638	71	-10	1	0	0	.982	-10	C-77	-1.7
1956	Pit-N	100	256	24	62	11	2	7	30	25	37	.242	.310	.383	692	87	-5	1	1	-0	.990	1	C-86/1-2	0.0
Total	4	278	751	72	195	29	6	12	75	84	97	.260	.334	.362	696	86	-14	2	1	0	.982	-8	C-232/1-2	-1.2

■ RAY SHEPARDSON

Shepardson, Raymond Francis b: 5/3/1897, Little Falls, N.Y. d: 11/8/75, Little Falls, N.Y. BR/TR, 5'11.5", 170 lbs. Deb: 9/19/24

YEAR	TM/L	G	AB	R	H	2B	3B	HR	RBI	BB	SO	AVG	OBP	SLG	OPS	OPS+	BR+	SB	CS	SBR	FA	FR	G/POS	TPR
1924	StL-N	3	6	1	0	0	0	0	0	0	3	.000	.000	.000	0	-99	-2	0	0	0	1.000	0	/C-3	-0.2

■ RON SHEPHERD

Shepherd, Ronald Wayne b: 10/27/60, Longview, Tex. BR/TR, 6'4", 175 lbs. Deb: 9/5/84

YEAR	TM/L	G	AB	R	H	2B	3B	HR	RBI	BB	SO	AVG	OBP	SLG	OPS	OPS+	BR+	SB	CS	SBR	FA	FR	G/POS	TPR
1984	Tor-A	12	4	0	0	0	0	0	0	0	3	.000	.000	.000	0	-97	-1	0	1	-0	1.000	-1	/O-5(5-0-0),D-4	-0.2
1985	Tor-A	38	35	7	4	2	0	0	1	2	12	.114	.162	.171	334	-8	-5	3	0	1	1.000	-4	O-16(3-13-1),D-15	-0.9
1986	Tor-A	65	69	16	14	4	0	2	4	3	22	.203	.236	.348	584	55	-4	0	0	0	1.000	-8	O-32(12-10-11),D-16	-1.4
Total	3	115	108	23	18	6	0	2	5	5	37	.167	.204	.278	481	29	-11	3	1	0	1.000	-13	/O-53(20-23-12),D-35	-2.5

■ JOHN SHEPPARD

Sheppard, John b: Baltimore, Md. Deb: 6/27/1873

YEAR	TM/L	G	AB	R	H	2B	3B	HR	RBI	BB	SO	AVG	OBP	SLG	OPS	OPS+	BR+	SB	CS	SBR	FA	FR	G/POS	TPR
1873	Mar-n	3	11	1	0	0	0	0	0	0	1	.000	.000	.000	0	-99	-3	0	0	0	.500	-1	/O-2(1-0-1),C-1	-0.3

■ SHERIDAN

Sheridan Deb: 10/9/1875

YEAR	TM/L	G	AB	R	H	2B	3B	HR	RBI	BB	SO	AVG	OBP	SLG	OPS	OPS+	BR+	SB	CS	SBR	FA	FR	G/POS	TPR
1875	Atl-n	1	4	0	0	0	0	0	0	0	1	.000	.000	.000	0	-99	-1	0	0	0	.000	-0	/O-1(1-0-0)	-0.1

■ RED SHERIDAN

Sheridan, Eugene Anthony b: 11/14/1896, Brooklyn, N.Y. d: 11/25/75, Queens Village, N.Y. BR/TR, 5'10.5", 160 lbs. Deb: 7/3/18

YEAR	TM/L	G	AB	R	H	2B	3B	HR	RBI	BB	SO	AVG	OBP	SLG	OPS	OPS+	BR+	SB	CS	SBR	FA	FR	G/POS	TPR
1918	Bro-N	2	4	0	1	0	0	0	0	1	0	.250	.400	.250	650	100	0	1			1.000	-1	/2-2	-0.1
1920	Bro-N	3	2	0	0	0	0	0	0	0	1	.000	.000	.000	0	-97	-0	0	0	0	1.000	1	/S-3	0.1
Total	2	5	6	0	1	0	0	0	0	1	1	.167	.286	.167	452	37	-0	1	0		1.000	1	/S-3,2-2	0.0

■ NEILL SHERIDAN

Sheridan, Neill Rawlins "Wild Horse" b: 11/20/21, Sacramento, Cal. BR/TR, 6'1.5", 195 lbs. Deb: 9/19/48

YEAR	TM/L	G	AB	R	H	2B	3B	HR	RBI	BB	SO	AVG	OBP	SLG	OPS	OPS+	BR+	SB	CS	SBR	FA	FR	G/POS	TPR
1948	Bos-A	2	1	0	0	0	0	0	0	0	1	.000	.000	.000	0	-95	-0	0	0	0	.000	0	H	0.0

■ PAT SHERIDAN

Sheridan, Patrick Arthur b: 12/4/57, Ann Arbor, Mich. BL/TR, 6'3", 175 lbs. Deb: 9/16/81 Career OF: (162-LF 173-CF 481-RF)

YEAR	TM/L	G	AB	R	H	2B	3B	HR	RBI	BB	SO	AVG	OBP	SLG	OPS	OPS+	BR+	SB	CS	SBR	FA	FR	G/POS	TPR
1981	KC-A	3	1	0	0	0	0	0	0	0	1	.000	.000	.000	0	-99	-0	0	0	0	1.000	-1	/O-3(1-0-2)	-0.1

YEAR	TM/L	G	AB	R	H	2B	3B	HR	RBI	BB	SO	AVG	OBP	SLG	OPS	OPS+	BR+	SB	CS	SBR	FA	FR	G/POS	TPR
1983	KC-A	109	333	43	90	12	2	7	36	20	64	.270	.312	.381	693	89	-5	12	3	2	.988	-2	*O-100(28-36-48)	-0.9
1984	*KC-A	138	481	64	136	24	4	8	53	41	91	.283	.340	.399	740	103	2	19	6	2	.986	-3	*O-134(0-35-101)	-0.4
1985	*KC-A	78	206	18	47	9	2	3	17	23	38	.228	.309	.335	644	76	-7	11	3	1	.983	-4	O-69(0-0-69)/D-1	-1.2
1986	Det-A	98	236	41	56	9	1	6	19	21	57	.237	.302	.360	662	80	-7	9	2	1	.977	-10	O-90(11-51-32)/D-5	-1.7
1987	*Det-A	141	421	57	109	19	3	6	49	44	90	.259	.330	.361	692	87	-7	18	13	-1	.976	-12	*O-137(0-26-124)	-2.4
1988	Det-A	127	347	47	88	9	5	11	47	44	64	.254	.341	.403	744	112	6	8	6	-0	.981	-6	*O-111(92-9-12)/D-3	-0.3
1989	Det-A	50	120	16	29	3	0	3	15	17	21	.242	.336	.342	677	93	-1	4	0	1	.982	-3	O-35(19-7-9)/D-8	-0.4
	*SF-N	70	161	20	33	3	4	3	14	13	45	.205	.264	.329	594	71	-7	4	1	1	.983	-4	O-66(8-3-58)	-1.2
1991	NY-A	62	113	13	23	3	0	4	7	13	30	.204	.286	.336	622	71	-5	1	1	-0	1.000	-3	O-34(3-6-26)/D-2	-0.8
Total	9	876	2419	319	611	91	21	51	257	236	501	.253	.321	.371	691	91	-30	86	35	7	.983	-48	O-779R/D-19	-9.4

■ ED SHERLING

Sherling, Edward Creech "Shine" b: 7/17/1897, Coalburg, Ala. d: 11/16/65, Enterprise, Cal. BR/TR, 6′1″, 185 lbs. Deb: 8/13/24

YEAR	TM/L	G	AB	R	H	2B	3B	HR	RBI	BB	SO	AVG	OBP	SLG	OPS	OPS+	BR+	SB	CS	SBR	FA	FR	G/POS	TPR
1924	Phi-A	4	2	2	1	1	0	0	0	0	0	.500	.500	1.000	1500	278	0	0	0	0	.000	0	H	0.0

■ MONK SHERLOCK

Sherlock, John Clinton b: 10/26/04, Buffalo, N.Y. d: 11/26/85, Buffalo, N.Y. BR/TR, 5′10″, 175 lbs. Deb: 4/20/30 F

YEAR	TM/L	G	AB	R	H	2B	3B	HR	RBI	BB	SO	AVG	OBP	SLG	OPS	OPS+	BR+	SB	CS	SBR	FA	FR	G/POS	TPR
1930	Phi-N	92	299	51	97	18	2	0	38	27	28	.324	.380	.398	778	83	-7	0			.990	4	1-70/2-5,O-1(0-1-0)	-0.7

■ VINCE SHERLOCK

Sherlock, Vincent Thomas "Baldy" b: 3/27/10, Buffalo, N.Y. d: 5/11/97, Cheektowaga, N.Y. BR/TR, 6′, 180 lbs. Deb: 9/18/35 F

YEAR	TM/L	G	AB	R	H	2B	3B	HR	RBI	BB	SO	AVG	OBP	SLG	OPS	OPS+	BR+	SB	CS	SBR	FA	FR	G/POS	TPR
1935	Bro-N	9	26	4	12	1	0	0	6	1	2	.462	.481	.500	981	168	3	1			.907	-1	/2-8	0.2

■ DARRELL SHERMAN

Sherman, Darrell Edward b: 12/4/67, Los Angeles, Cal. BL/TL, 5′9″, 160 lbs. Deb: 4/8/93

YEAR	TM/L	G	AB	R	H	2B	3B	HR	RBI	BB	SO	AVG	OBP	SLG	OPS	OPS+	BR+	SB	CS	SBR	FA	FR	G/POS	TPR
1993	SD-N	37	63	8	14	1	0	0	2	6	8	.222	.319	.238	558	51	-4	2	1	0	1.000	-3	O-26(24-6-1)	-0.8

■ DENNIS SHERRILL

Sherrill, Dennis Lee b: 3/3/56, Miami, Fla. BR/TR, 6′, 165 lbs. Deb: 9/4/78

YEAR	TM/L	G	AB	R	H	2B	3B	HR	RBI	BB	SO	AVG	OBP	SLG	OPS	OPS+	BR+	SB	CS	SBR	FA	FR	G/POS	TPR
1978	NY-A	2	1	1	0	0	0	0	0	0	1	.000	.000	.000	0	-99	-0	0	0	0	.000	-0	/3-1,D-1	-0.1
1980	NY-A	3	4	0	1	0	0	0	0	0	1	.250	.250	.250	500	38	-0	0	0	0	1.000	-0	/S-2,2-1	-0.1
Total	2	5	5	1	1	0	0	0	0	0	2	.200	.200	.200	400	11	-1	0	0	0	1.000	-1	/S-2,2-1,D-1,3-1	-0.2

■ NORM SHERRY

Sherry, Norman Burt b: 7/16/31, New York, N.Y. BR/TR, 5′11″, 181 lbs. Deb: 4/12/59 FMC

YEAR	TM/L	G	AB	R	H	2B	3B	HR	RBI	BB	SO	AVG	OBP	SLG	OPS	OPS+	BR+	SB	CS	SBR	FA	FR	G/POS	TPR
1959	LA-N	2	3	0	1	0	0	0	2	0	0	.333	.500	.333	833	119	0	0	0	0	1.000	-1	/C-2	-0.1
1960	LA-N	47	138	22	39	4	1	8	19	12	29	.283	.353	.500	853	122	4	0	0	0	.993	-4	C-44	0.2
1961	LA-N	47	121	10	31	2	0	5	21	9	30	.256	.308	.397	704	78	-4	0	0	0	.993	4	C-45	0.2
1962	LA-N	35	88	7	16	2	0	3	16	6	17	.182	.242	.307	549	49	-7	0	0	0	.992	9	C-34	0.3
1963	NY-N	63	147	6	20	1	0	2	11	10	26	.136	.206	.184	390	13	-16	1	0	0	.980	3	C-61	-1.2
Total	5	194	497	45	107	9	1	18	69	37	102	.215	.280	.346	627	69	-22	1	0	0	.989	11	C-186	-0.6

■ BARRY SHETRONE

Shetrone, Barry Stevan b: 7/6/38, Baltimore, Md. BL/TR, 6′2″, 190 lbs. Deb: 7/27/59

YEAR	TM/L	G	AB	R	H	2B	3B	HR	RBI	BB	SO	AVG	OBP	SLG	OPS	OPS+	BR+	SB	CS	SBR	FA	FR	G/POS	TPR
1959	Bal-A	33	79	8	16	1	1	0	5	5	9	.203	.250	.241	491	36	-7	3	0	1	.947	-4	O-23(5-17-1)	-1.2
1960	Bal-A	1	0	1	0	0	0	0	0	0	0	—	—	—	—	—	0	0	0	0	.000	0	R	0.0
1961	Bal-A	3	7	0	1	0	0	0	1	0	2	.143	.143	.143	286	-24	-1	0	0	0	1.000	-0	/O-2(0-2-0)	-0.2
1962	Bal-A	21	24	3	6	1	0	1	1	0	5	.250	.250	.417	667	81	-1	0	0	0	1.000	-0	/O-6(3-2-1)	-0.1
1963	Was-A	2	2	0	0	0	0	0	0	0	0	.000	.000	.000	0	-99	-1	0	0	0	.000	0	H	-0.1
Total	5	60	112	12	23	2	1	1	7	5	16	.205	.239	.268	507	39	-9	3	0	1	.962	-5	/O-31(8-21-2)	-1.6

■ JOHN SHETZLINE

Shetzline, John Henry b: 1850, Philadelphia, Pa. d: 12/15/1892, Philadelphia, Pa. 5′11.5″, 190 lbs. Deb: 5/2/1882

YEAR	TM/L	G	AB	R	H	2B	3B	HR	RBI	BB	SO	AVG	OBP	SLG	OPS	OPS+	BR+	SB	CS	SBR	FA	FR	G/POS	TPR
1882	Bal-a	73	282	23	62	8	3	0		5		.220	.233	.270	503	75	-6				.800	3	3-52,2-20/O-1C,S-1	-0.2

■ JIMMY SHEVLIN

Shevlin, James Cornelius b: 7/9/09, Cincinnati, Ohio d: 10/30/74, Ft.Lauderdale, Fla BL/TL, 5′10.5″, 155 lbs. Deb: 6/29/30

YEAR	TM/L	G	AB	R	H	2B	3B	HR	RBI	BB	SO	AVG	OBP	SLG	OPS	OPS+	BR+	SB	CS	SBR	FA	FR	G/POS	TPR
1930	Det-A	28	14	4	2	0	0	0	2	2	3	.143	.250	.143	393	2	-2	0	0	0	1.000	1	1-25	-0.2
1932	Cin-N	7	24	3	5	2	0	0	4	4	0	.208	.345	.292	636	76	-1	4			.985	-0	/1-7	-0.2
1934	Cin-N	18	39	6	12	2	0	0	6	6	5	.308	.400	.359	759	107	1	0			1.000	0	1-10	0.0
Total	3	53	77	13	19	4	0	0	12	12	8	.247	.356	.299	654	77	-2	4	0		.995	1	/1-42	-0.4

■ PETE SHIELDS

Shields, Francis Leroy b: 9/21/1891, Swiftwater, Miss. d: 2/11/61, Jackson, Miss. BR/TR, 6′, 175 lbs. Deb: 4/14/15

YEAR	TM/L	G	AB	R	H	2B	3B	HR	RBI	BB	SO	AVG	OBP	SLG	OPS	OPS+	BR+	SB	CS	SBR	FA	FR	G/POS	TPR
1915	Cle-A	23	72	4	15	6	0	0	6	4	14	.208	.250	.292	542	61	-4	3	3	-0	.974	0	1-23	-0.5

■ TOMMY SHIELDS

Shields, Thomas Charles b: 8/14/64, Fairfax, Va. BL/TR, 6′, 180 lbs. Deb: 7/25/92 Career OF: (1-LF 0-CF 0-RF)

YEAR	TM/L	G	AB	R	H	2B	3B	HR	RBI	BB	SO	AVG	OBP	SLG	OPS	OPS+	BR+	SB	CS	SBR	FA	FR	G/POS	TPR
1992	Bal-A	2	0	0	0	0	0	0	0	0	0	—	—	—	—	—	0	0	0	0	.000	0	/R	0.0
1993	Chi-N	20	34	4	6	1	0	0	1	2	10	.176	.222	.206	428	16	-4	0	0	0	1.000	2	/2-7,3-7,1-1,O-1L	-0.2
Total	2	22	34	4	6	1	0	0	1	2	10	.176	.222	.206	428	16	-4	0	0	0	1.000	2	/3-7,2-7,O-1L,1-1	-0.2

■ JIM SHILLING

Shilling, James Robert b: 5/14/14, Tulsa, Okla. d: 9/12/86, Tulsa, Okla. BR/TR, 5′11″, 175 lbs. Deb: 4/21/39 Career OF: (1-LF 0-CF 0-RF)

YEAR	TM/L	G	AB	R	H	2B	3B	HR	RBI	BB	SO	AVG	OBP	SLG	OPS	OPS+	BR+	SB	CS	SBR	FA	FR	G/POS	TPR
1939	Cle-A	31	98	8	27	7	2	0	12	7	9	.276	.324	.388	712	84	-3	1	0	0	.935	4	2-27/S-3	0.3
	Phi-N	11	33	3	10	1	3	0	4	1	4	.303	.324	.515	839	126	1	0			.944	-2	/2-5,S-3,3-3,O-1L	0.0
Total	1	42	131	11	37	8	5	0	16	8	13	.282	.324	.420	744	94	-2	1	0		.936	2	/2-32,S-6,3-3,O-1L	0.3

■ GINGER SHINAULT

Shinault, Enoch Erskine b: 9/7/1892, Benton, Ark. d: 12/29/30, Denver, Colo. BR/TR, 5′11″, 170 lbs. Deb: 7/4/21

YEAR	TM/L	G	AB	R	H	2B	3B	HR	RBI	BB	SO	AVG	OBP	SLG	OPS	OPS+	BR+	SB	CS	SBR	FA	FR	G/POS	TPR
1921	Cle-A	22	29	5	11	1	0	0	4	6	5	.379	.486	.414	900	129	2	1	0	0	.917	2	C-20	0.4
1922	Cle-A	13	15	1	2	1	0	0	0	0	2	.133	.133	.200	333	-14	-3	0	0	0	.400	-4	C-11	-0.6
Total	2	35	44	6	13	2	0	0	4	6	7	.295	.380	.341	721	85	-1	1	0	0	.868	-2	/C-31	-0.2

■ BILLY SHINDLE

Shindle, William b: 12/5/1860, Gloucester, N.J. d: 6/3/36, Lakeland, N.J. BR/TR, 5′8.5″, 155 lbs. Deb: 10/5/1886 Career OF: (1-LF 0-CF 0-RF)

YEAR	TM/L	G	AB	R	H	2B	3B	HR	RBI	BB	SO	AVG	OBP	SLG	OPS	OPS+	BR+	SB	CS	SBR	FA	FR	G/POS	TPR
1886	Det-N	7	26	4	7	0	0	0	4	0	5	.269	.269	.269	538	62	-1	2			.900	1	/S-7	0.0
1887	Det-N	22	91	17	31	3	2	0	12	7	10	.341	.341	.369	710	94	-1	13			.818	-5	3-21/O-1(1-0-0)	-0.4
1888	Bal-a	135	514	61	107	14	8	1	53	20		.208	.249	.272	521	69	-18	52			**.922**	**37**	*3-135	1.9
1889	Bal-a	138	567	122	178	24	7	3	64	42	37	.314	.369	.397	765	116	11	56			.862	20	*3-138	2.8
1890	Phi-P	132	584	127	189	21	21	10	90	40	30	.324	.371	.483	854	124	17	51			.856	8	*S-130/3-2	2.3
1891	Phi-N	103	415	68	87	13	1	0	38	33	39	.210	.278	.246	523	51	-26	17			.874	6	*3-100/S-3	-1.6
1892	Bal-N	143	619	100	156	20	18	3	50	35	34	.252	.301	.357	658	96	-6	24			.882	35	*3-134/S-9	3.0
1893	Bal-N	125	521	100	136	22	11	1	75	66	17	.261	.353	.351	704	86	-10	17			.885	8	*3-125	0.0
1894	Bro-N	117	480	94	142	22	9	4	96	29	21	.296	.344	.404	748	86	-11	19			.896	3	*3-117	-0.5
1895	Bro-N	117	481	92	135	21	2	3	69	47	28	.281	.358	.351	709	91	-4	17			.895	1	*3-117	-0.1
1896	Bro-N	131	516	75	144	24	9	1	61	24	20	.279	.316	.366	682	84	-13	24			.912	-12	*3-131	-1.9
1897	Bro-N	134	542	83	154	32	6	4	105	35		.284	.336	.387	723	96	-4	23			.904	-12	*3-134	-1.2
1898	Bro-N	120	466	50	105	10	3	1	41	10		.225	.249	.266	516	48	-32	3			.911	7	*3-120	-2.2
Total	13	1424	5822	993	1571	226	97	31	758	388	241	.270	.323	.357	680	88	-97	318			.892	97	*3-1274,S-149/O-1L	2.1

■ RAZOR SHINES

Shines, Anthony Raymond "Ray" b: 7/18/56, Durham, N.C. BB/TR, 6′1″, 210 lbs. Deb: 9/9/83 Career OF: (1-LF 0-CF 0-RF)

YEAR	TM/L	G	AB	R	H	2B	3B	HR	RBI	BB	SO	AVG	OBP	SLG	OPS	OPS+	BR+	SB	CS	SBR	FA	FR	G/POS	TPR
1983	Mon-N	3	2	0	1	0	0	0	0	0	0	.500	.500	.500	1000	179	0	0	0	0	.000	-0	/O-1(1-0-0)	0.0
1984	Mon-N	12	20	0	6	1	0	0	2	0	3	.300	.300	.350	650	86	-0	0	0	0	1.000	-1	/1-3,3-1	-0.2
1985	Mon-N	47	50	0	6	0	0	0	3	4	9	.120	.185	.120	305	-14	-8	0	1	-0	.950	0	/1-5,P-1	-0.8
1987	Mon-N	6	9	0	2	0	0	0	0	1	0	.222	.364	.222	586	58	-0	1	0	0	1.000	-0	/1-2	0.0
Total	4	68	81	0	15	1	0	0	5	5	12	.185	.241	.198	439	24	-8	1	1	-0	.975	-1	/1-10,P-1,3-1,O-1L	-1.0

■ RALPH SHINNERS

Shinners, Ralph Peter b: 10/4/1895, Monches, Wis. d: 7/23/62, Milwaukee, Wis. BR/TR, 6′, 180 lbs. Deb: 4/12/22

YEAR	TM/L	G	AB	R	H	2B	3B	HR	RBI	BB	SO	AVG	OBP	SLG	OPS	OPS+	BR+	SB	CS	SBR	FA	FR	G/POS	TPR
1922	NY-N	56	135	16	34	4	2	0	15	5	22	.252	.308	.311	619	60	-8	3	5	-1	.915	-4	O-37(1-30-6)	-1.4
1923	NY-N	33	13	5	2	1	0	0	0	2	1	.154	.267	.231	497	33	-1	0	0	0	1.000	-1	/O-6(2-1-3)	-0.2
1925	StL-N	74	251	39	74	9	2	7	36	12	19	.295	.330	.430	760	90	-4	8	5	0	.982	-3	O-66(3-56-7)	-1.0
Total	3	163	399	60	110	14	4	7	51	19	42	.276	.320	.383	703	78	-13	11	10	-1	.959	-8	O-109(6-87-16)	-2.6

■ TIM SHINNICK

Shinnick, Timothy James "Dandy" or "Good Eye" b: 11/6/1867, Exeter, N.H. d: 5/18/44, Exeter, N.H. BB/TR, 5′9″, 150 lbs. Deb: 4/19/1890

YEAR	TM/L	G	AB	R	H	2B	3B	HR	RBI	BB	SO	AVG	OBP	SLG	OPS	OPS+	BR+	SB	CS	SBR	FA	FR	G/POS	TPR
1890	*Lou-a	133	493	87	126	16	11	1	82	62		.256	.348	.339	687	105	5	62			.925	-25	*2-130/3-3	-1.3

YEAR	TM/L	G	AB	R	H	2B	3B	HR	RBI	BB	SO	AVG	OBP	SLG	OPS	OPS+	BR+	SB	CS	SBR	FA	FR	G/POS	TPR
1891	Lou-a	126	436	77	96	9	11	1	52	54	46	.220	.313	.298	611	76	-13	36			.913	-24	*2-118/3-7,S-1	-2.9
Total	2	259	929	164	222	25	22	2	134	116	46	.239	.332	.320	651	91	-9	98			.919	-49	2-248/3-10,S-1	-4.2
■ BILL SHIPKE	Shipke, William Martin "Skipper Bill" or "Muskrat Bill" (b: William Martin Shipkrethaver) b: 11/18/1882, St.Louis, Mo. d: 9/10/40, Omaha, Neb. BR/TR, 5'7", 145 lbs. Deb: 4/23/06																							
1906	Cle-A	2	6	0	0	0	0	0	0	0		.000	.000	.000	0	-99	-1	0			.933	2	/2-2	0.0
1907	Was-A	64	189	17	37	3	2	1	9	15		.196	.262	.249	511	68	-7	6			.944	7	3-63	0.3
1908	Was-A	111	341	40	71	7	8	0	20	38		.208	.297	.276	573	94	-1	15			.932	-7	*3-110/2-1	-0.6
1909	Was-A	9	16	2	2	1	0	0	0	2		.125	.222	.188	410	31	-1	0			.905	2	/3-6,S-2	0.1
Total	4	186	552	59	110	11	10	1	29	55		.199	.280	.261	541	81	-10	21			.935	4	3-179/2-3,S-2	-0.2
■ CRAIG SHIPLEY	Shipley, Craig Barry b: 1/7/63, Parramatta, Australia BR/TR, 6'1", 185 lbs. Deb: 6/22/86 Career OF: (4-LF 4-CF 4-RF)																							
1986	LA-N	12	27	3	3	1	0	0	4	2	5	.111	.200	.148	348	-3	-4	0	0	0	.914	-1	S-10/2-1,3-1	-0.4
1987	LA-N	26	35	3	9	1	0	0	2	0	6	.257	.257	.286	543	45	-3	0	0	0	.949	3	S-18/3-6	0.0
1989	NY-N	4	7	3	1	0	0	0	0	0	1	.143	.143	.143	286	-19	-1	0	0	0	1.000	-0	/S-3,3-2	-0.1
1991	SD-N	37	91	6	25	3	0	1	6	2	14	.275	.298	.341	639	77	-3	0	1	-0	.902	-1	S-19,2-14	-0.3
1992	SD-N	52	105	7	26	6	0	0	7	2	21	.248	.262	.305	566	59	-6	1	1	-1	.986	10	S-23,2-11/3-8	0.5
1993	SD-N	105	230	25	54	9	0	4	22	10	31	.235	.276	.326	602	59	-13	12	3	2	.964	-8	S-38,3-37,2-12,/O-5C	-1.7
1994	SD-N	81	240	32	80	14	4	4	30	9	28	.333	.365	.475	840	120	7	6	6	-1	.936	-8	3-53,S-14,2-13,/O1	0.0
1995	Hou-N	92	232	23	61	8	1	3	24	8	28	.263	.293	.345	638	73	-10	6	1	1	.982	-2	3-65,S-11/2-4,1-1	-1.0
1996	SD-N	33	92	13	29	5	0	1	7	2	15	.315	.344	.402	746	102	0	7	0	2	.985	0	2-17/S-7,3-4,O-3R	0.3
1997	SD-N	63	139	22	38	9	0	5	19	7	20	.273	.308	.446	754	102	-0	1	1	-0	.947	-6	S-21,2-16/1-4,3-2	-0.5
1998	Ana-A	77	147	18	38	7	1	2	17	5	22	.259	.306	.361	666	72	-6	0	4	-1	.963	1	3-48,2-11/1-8,SO	-0.5
Total	11	582	1345	155	364	63	6	20	138	47	191	.271	.304	.371	675	80	-39	33	17	1	.963	-13	3-226,S-169/2-99,10	-3.7
■ ART SHIRES	Shires, Charles Arthur "Art The Great" b: 8/13/07, Italy, Tex. d: 7/13/67, Italy, Tex. BL/TR, 6'1", 195 lbs. Deb: 8/20/28																							
1928	Chi-A	33	123	20	42	6	1	1	11	13	10	.341	.409	.431	840	122	5	0	3	-1	.990	3	1-32	0.5
1929	Chi-A	100	353	41	110	20	7	3	41	32	20	.312	.370	.433	804	108	4	4	5	-1	.991	0	1-90/2-3	-0.2
1930	Chi-A	37	128	14	33	5	1	1	18	6	6	.258	.291	.336	627	61	-8	2	0	0	.979	-2	1-33	-1.1
	Was-A	38	84	11	31	5	0	1	19	5	5	.369	.404	.464	869	119	3	1	3	-1	.982	0	1-21	0.1
	Yr	75	212	25	64	10	1	2	37	11	11	.302	.336	.387	723	84	-5	3	3	-0	.980	-2	1-54	-1.0
1932	Bos-N	82	298	32	71	9	3	5	30	25	21	.238	.299	.339	638	74	-11	1			.988	-2	1-80	-2.1
Total	4	290	986	118	287	45	12	11	119	81	62	.291	.347	.395	741	95	-8	8	11		.988	-1	1-256/2-3	-2.8
■ BART SHIRLEY	Shirley, Barton Arvin b: 1/4/40, Corpus Christi, Tex. BR/TR, 5'10", 183 lbs. Deb: 9/14/64																							
1964	LA-N	18	62	6	17	1	1	0	7	4	8	.274	.318	.323	641	87	-1	0	0	0	.900	1	3-10/S-8	0.0
1966	LA-N	12	5	2	1	0	0	0	0	0	2	.200	.200	.200	400	13	-1	0	0	0	1.000	1	/S-5	0.1
1967	NY-N	6	12	1	0	0	0	0	0	0	5	.000	.000	.000	0	-99	-3	0	0	0	.917	0	/2-3	-0.3
1968	LA-N	39	83	6	15	3	0	0	4	10	13	.181	.269	.217	486	51	-5	0	1	-0	.903	3	S-21,2-18	0.0
Total	4	75	162	15	33	4	1	0	11	14	28	.204	.267	.241	508	53	-9	0	1	-0	.936	5	/S-34,2-21,3-10	-0.2
■ MULE SHIRLEY	Shirley, Ernest Raeford b: 5/24/01, Snow Hill, N.C. d: 8/4/55, Goldsboro, N.C. BL/TL, 5'11", 180 lbs. Deb: 5/6/24																							
1924	*Was-A	30	77	12	18	2	2	0	16	3	7	.234	.262	.312	574	49	-6	0	0	0	.984	0	1-25	-0.7
1925	Was-A	14	23	2	3	1	0	0	2	1	7	.130	.167	.174	341	-14	-4	0	0	0	1.000	0	/1-9	-0.4
Total	2	44	100	14	21	3	2	0	18	4	14	.210	.240	.280	520	34	-10	0	0	0	.988	0	/1-34	-1.1
■ IVEY SHIVER	Shiver, Ivey Merwin "Chick" b: 1/22/06, Sylvester, Ga. d: 8/31/72, Savannah, Ga. BR/TR, 6'1.5", 190 lbs. Deb: 4/14/31																							
1931	Det-A	2	9	2	1	0	0	0	0	0	3	.111	.111	.111	222	-40	-2	0	0	0	1.000	-1	/O-2(0-2-0)	-0.2
1934	Cin-N	19	59	6	12	1	0	2	6	3	15	.203	.242	.322	564	51	-4	1			1.000	-2	O-15(0-0-15)	-0.7
Total	2	21	68	8	13	1	0	2	6	3	18	.191	.225	.294	519	38	-6	1	0		1.000	-3	/O-17(0-2-15)	-0.9
■ GEORGE SHOCH	Shoch, George Quintus b: 1/6/1859, Philadelphia, Pa. d: 9/30/37, Philadelphia, Pa. BR/TR, 5'6", 158 lbs. Deb: 9/10/1886 Career OF: (99-LF 41-CF 159-RF)																							
1886	Was-N	26	95	11	28	2	1	1	18	2	13	.295	.309	.368	678	112	1	2			.882	-5	O-25(1-0-24)/S-1	-0.3
1887	Was-N	70	285	47	84	9	1	1	18	21	16	.295	.304	.292	596	70	-10	29			.897	7	O-63(11-3-49)/S-6,2-1	-0.3
1888	Was-N	90	317	46	58	6	3	2	24	25	22	.183	.262	.240	502	64	-11	23			.900	4	S-52,O-35R/2-1,P-1	-0.6
1889	Was-N	30	109	12	26	2	0	0	11	20	5	.239	.385	.257	642	86	0	9			.905	3	O-29(16-0-13)/S-1	0.2
1891	Mil-a	34	127	29	40	7	1	1	16	18	5	.315	.435	.409	845	118	3	12			.932	3	S-25/3-9	0.6
1892	Bal-N	76	308	42	85	15	3	1	50	24	19	.276	.340	.354	694	107	2	14			.872	0	S-57,O-12(8-4-0)/3-7	0.4
1893	Bro-N	94	327	53	86	17	1	2	54	48	13	.263	.366	.339	705	92	-2	9			.892	-3	O-46L,3-37,S-11,/2	-0.6
1894	Bro-N	65	243	47	77	6	5	1	37	26	6	.317	.394	.395	789	98	1	16			.926	1	O-35C,3-14/2-9,S-7	0.1
1895	Bro-N	61	216	49	56	9	7	0	29	32	6	.259	.368	.366	733	97	1	7			.952	-6	O-39R,2-13/S-6,3-3	-0.6
1896	Bro-N	76	250	36	73	7	4	1	28	33	10	.292	.381	.364	745	103	3	11			.941	-13	2-62,O-10R/3-3,S-1	-0.7
1897	Bro-N	85	284	42	79	9	2	0	38	49		.278	.393	.324	717	96	2	6			.941	5	2-68,S-13/O-4(3-1-0)	0.9
Total	11	707	2561	414	692	89	28	10	323	298	115	.270	.354	.333	687	93	-9	138			.912	-4	O-298R,S-180,2/3P	-0.9
■ COSTEN SHOCKLEY	Shockley, John Costen b: 2/8/42, Georgetown, Del. BL/TL, 6'2", 200 lbs. Deb: 7/17/64																							
1964	Phi-N	11	35	4	8	0	0	1	2	2	8	.229	.270	.314	585	65	-2	0	0	0	.968	-1	/1-9	-0.3
1965	Cal-A	40	107	5	20	2	0	2	17	9	16	.187	.256	.262	518	49	-7	0	0	0	.996	0	1-31/O-1(0-0-1)	-0.9
Total	2	51	142	9	28	2	0	3	19	11	24	.197	.260	.275	534	53	-9	0	0	0	.991	-1	/1-40,O-1(0-0-1)	-1.2
■ CHARLIE SHOEMAKER	Shoemaker, Charles Landis b: 8/10/39, Los Angeles, Cal. d: 5/31/90, Mount Penn, Pa. BL/TR, 5'10", 155 lbs. Deb: 9/9/61																							
1961	KC-A	7	26	5	10	2	0	0	1	2	2	.385	.429	.462	890	135	1	0	0	0	1.000	0	/2-6	0.2
1962	KC-A	5	11	1	2	0	0	0	0	0	2	.182	.182	.182	364	-2	-2	0	0	0	1.000	1	/2-4	0.0
1964	KC-A	16	52	6	11	2	2	0	3	0	9	.212	.212	.327	538	46	-4	0	0	0	.964	-5	2-14	-0.8
Total	3	28	89	12	23	4	2	0	4	2	13	.258	.275	.348	623	67	-4	0	0	0	.981	-3	/2-24	-0.6
■ STRICK SHOFNER	Shofner, Frank Strickland b: 7/23/19, Crawford, Tex. d: 10/10/98, Crawford, Tex. BL/TR, 5'10.5", 187 lbs. Deb: 4/19/47																							
1947	Bos-A	5	13	1	2	0	1	0	0	0	3	.154	.154	.308	462	25	-1	0	0	0	1.000	1	/3-4	-0.1
■ EDDIE SHOKES	Shokes, Edward Christopher b: 1/27/20, Charleston, S.C. BL/TL, 6', 170 lbs. Deb: 6/9/41																							
1941	Cin-N	1	1	0	0	0	0	0	0	0	1	.000	.000	.000	0	-99	-0	0			.000	0	H	0.0
1946	Cin-N	31	83	3	10	1	0	0	5	18	21	.120	.277	.133	410	19	-8	1			.996	-1	1-29	-1.1
Total	2	32	84	3	10	1	0	0	5	18	22	.119	.275	.131	405	18	-8	1			.996	-1	/1-29	-1.1
■ RAY SHOOK	Shook, Raymond Curtis b: 11/18/1889, Perry, Ohio d: 9/16/70, South Bend, Ind. BR/TR, 5'7.5", 155 lbs. Deb: 4/16/16																							
1916	Chi-A	1	0	0	0	0	0	0	0	0	0	—	—	—	—	—	0	0			.000	0	R	0.0
■ RON SHOOP	Shoop, Ronald Lee b: 9/19/31, Rural Valley, Pa. BR/TR, 5'11", 180 lbs. Deb: 8/22/59																							
1959	Det-A	3	7	1	1	0	0	0	1	0	1	.143	.143	.143	286	-20	-1	0	0	0	1.000	-1	/C-3	-0.2
■ TOM SHOPAY	Shopay, Thomas Michael b: 2/21/45, Bristol, Conn. BL/TR, 5'9.5", 160 lbs. Deb: 9/17/67 Career OF: (53-LF 36-CF 37-RF)																							
1967	NY-A	8	27	2	8	1	0	2	6	1	5	.296	.321	.556	877	161	2	2	0	0	.917	1	/O-7(7-0-0)	0.3
1969	NY-A	28	48	2	4	0	1	0	0	2	10	.083	.120	.125	245	-33	-9	0	1	-0	1.000	1	O-11(7-0-5)	-0.9
1971	*Bal-A	47	74	10	19	2	0	0	5	3	7	.257	.286	.284	569	62	-4	2	1	0	1.000	-1	O-13(4-0-9)	-0.5
1972	Bal-A	49	40	3	9	0	0	0	2	5	12	.225	.311	.225	536	60	-2	0	0	0	1.000	-0	/O-3(3-0-0)	-0.2
1975	Bal-A	40	31	4	5	1	0	0	2	4	7	.161	.257	.194	451	31	-3	3	0	1	1.000	-3	O-13(1-6-6)/C-1,D-3	-0.5
1976	Bal-A	14	20	4	4	0	0	0	1	3	3	.200	.304	.200	504	53	-1	1	0	0	1.000	-4	O-11(6-2-3)/C-1	-0.5
1977	Bal-A	67	69	15	13	3	0	1	4	8	7	.188	.273	.275	548	53	-4	3	3	-0	1.000	-18	O-52(25-28-14)/D-2	-2.4
Total	7	253	309	40	62	7	1	3	20	26	51	.201	.263	.259	522	50	-21	11	5	1	.993	-24	O-110L/D-5,C-2	-4.7
■ DAVE SHORT	Short, David Orvis b: 5/11/17, Magnolia, Ark. d: 11/22/83, Shreveport, La. BL/TR, 5'11.5", 162 lbs. Deb: 9/16/40																							
1940	Chi-A	4	3	1	1	0	0	0	0	1	2	.333	.500	.333	833	119	0	0	0	0	.000	0	H	0.0

YEAR	TM/L	G	AB	R	H	2B	3B	HR	RBI	BB	SO	AVG	OBP	SLG	OPS	OPS+	BR+	SB	CS	SBR	FA	FR	G/POS	TPR
1941	Chi-A	3	8	0	0	0	0	0	0	2	1	.000	.200	.000	200	-44	-2	0	0	0	.800	-0	/O-2(2-0-0)	-0.2
Total	2	7	11	1	1	0	0	0	0	3	3	.091	.286	.091	377	3	-1	0	0	0	.800	-0	/O-2(2-0-0)	-0.2

■ CHICK SHORTEN

Shorten, Charles Henry b: 4/19/1892, Scranton, Pa. d: 10/23/65, Scranton, Pa. BL/TL, 6', 175 lbs. Deb: 9/22/15

YEAR	TM/L	G	AB	R	H	2B	3B	HR	RBI	BB	SO	AVG	OBP	SLG	OPS	OPS+	BR+	SB	CS	SBR	FA	FR	G/POS	TPR
1915	Bos-A	6	14	1	3	1	0	0	0	0	2	.214	.214	.286	500	51	-1	0			1.000	-1	/O-5(0-4-1)	-0.2
1916	*Bos-A	53	112	14	33	2	1	0	11	10	8	.295	.352	.330	683	105	1	1			1.000	-8	O-33(13-19-1)	-1.0
1917	Bos-A	69	168	12	30	4	2	0	16	10	10	.179	.229	.226	455	39	-12	2			.977	-5	O-43(16-20-7)	-2.2
1919	Det-A	95	270	37	85	9	3	0	22	22	13	.315	.366	.370	737	110	4	5			.973	-6	O-75(0-18-57)	-0.7
1920	Det-A	116	364	35	105	9	6	1	40	28	14	.288	.339	.354	694	86	-7	2	4	-1	.989	-1	O-99(0-31-68)	-1.5
1921	Det-A	92	217	33	59	11	3	0	23	20	11	.272	.333	.350	684	75	-8	2	3	-1	.981	-4	O-51(3-36-12)	-1.4
1922	StL-A	55	131	22	36	12	5	2	16	16	8	.275	.354	.489	842	114	2	0	1	-0	1.000	-2	O-31(4-16-12)	-0.2
1924	Cin-N	41	69	7	19	3	0	0	6	4	2	.275	.315	.319	634	71	-3	0	0	0	1.000	-4	O-15(11-0-4)	-0.7
Total	8	527	1345	161	370	51	20	3	134	110	68	.275	.330	.349	680	87	-25	12	8		.985	-31	O-352(47-144-162)	-7.9

■ BURT SHOTTON

Shotton, Burton Edwin "Barney" b: 10/18/1884, Brownhelm, Ohio d: 7/29/62, Lake Wales, Fla. BL/TR, 5'11", 175 lbs. Deb: 9/13/09 MC

YEAR	TM/L	G	AB	R	H	2B	3B	HR	RBI	BB	SO	AVG	OBP	SLG	OPS	OPS+	BR+	SB	CS	SBR	FA	FR	G/POS	TPR
1909	StL-A	17	61	5	16	0	1	0	0	5		.262	.328	.295	623	104	0	3			.915	1	O-17(2-15-0)	0.1
1911	StL-A	139	572	84	146	11	8	0	36	51		.255	.317	.302	620	76	-18	26			.950	7	*O-139(18-121-0)	-2.0
1912	StL-A	154	580	87	168	15	8	2	40	86		.290	.390	.353	743	117	18	35			.941	7	*O-154(0-154-0)	1.3
1913	StL-A	147	549	105	163	23	8	1	28	**99**	63	.297	.405	.373	779	132	27	43			.951	13	*O-146(0-146-0)	3.1
1914	StL-A	154	579	82	156	19	9	0	38	64	66	.269	.344	.333	678	108	6	40	29	-1	.940	2	*O-152(0-152-0)	-0.5
1915	StL-A	156	559	93	158	18	11	1	30	118	62	.283	.409	.360	769	135	32	43	32	-2	.931	-3	*O-154(138-5-11)	2.1
1916	StL-A	156	614	97	174	23	6	1	36	**110**	65	.283	.392	.345	738	128	26	41	28	-1	.950	10	*O-156(156-0-0)	3.1
1917	StL-A	118	398	48	89	9	1	1	20	62	47	.224	.330	.259	589	83	-6	16			.923	-12	*O-107(107-0-0)	-2.5
1918	Was-A	126	505	68	132	16	7	0	21	67	28	.261	.349	.321	670	104	4	25			.942	6	*O-122(67-1-54)	0.4
1919	StL-N	85	270	35	77	13	5	1	20	22	25	.285	.341	.381	723	125	8	16			.927	-5	O-67(67-0-0)	0.0
1920	StL-N	62	180	28	41	5	0	1	12	18	14	.228	.305	.272	577	69	-7	5	1	1	.959	1	O-51(41-2-6)	-0.8
1921	StL-N	38	48	9	12	1	1	1	7	7	4	.250	.357	.375	732	96	-0	0	2	-1	.958	-0	O-11(1-10-0)	-0.1
1922	StL-N	34	30	5	6	1	0	0	2	4	6	.200	.294	.233	527	39	-3	0	1	-0	1.000	-1	/O-3(1-1-1)	-0.4
1923	StL-N	1	0	1	0	0	0	0	0	0	0	—	—	—	—	—	0	0	0	0	.000	0	R	0.0
Total	14	1387	4945	747	1338	154	65	9	290	713	380	.271	.365	.333	698	110	89	293	93		.942	26	*O-1279(598-607-72)	3.8

■ JOHN SHOUPE

Shoupe, John F. b: 9/30/1851, Cincinnati, Ohio d: 2/13/20, Cincinnati, Ohio BL/TL, 5'7", 140 lbs. Deb: 5/3/1879

YEAR	TM/L	G	AB	R	H	2B	3B	HR	RBI	BB	SO	AVG	OBP	SLG	OPS	OPS+	BR+	SB	CS	SBR	FA	FR	G/POS	TPR
1879	Tro-N	11	44	5	4	0	0	0	1	0	3	.091	.091	.091	182	-43	-6				.820	-3	S-10/2-1	-0.9
1882	StL-a	2	7	1	0	0	0	0		0		.000	.000	.000	0	-96	-1				1.000	1	/2-2	0.0
1884	Was-U	1	4	1	3	0	0	0		0		.750	.750	.750	1500	368	1				.857	2	/O-1(0-1-0)	0.2
Total	3	14	55	7	7	0	0	0	1	0	3	.127	.127	.127	255	-17	-7				.857	-0	/S-10,2-3,O-1(0-1-0)	-0.7

■ JOHN SHOVLIN

Shovlin, John Joseph "Brode" b: 1/14/1891, Drifton, Pa. d: 2/16/76, Bethesda, Md. BR/TR, 5'7", 163 lbs. Deb: 6/21/11

YEAR	TM/L	G	AB	R	H	2B	3B	HR	RBI	BB	SO	AVG	OBP	SLG	OPS	OPS+	BR+	SB	CS	SBR	FA	FR	G/POS	TPR
1911	Pit-N	2	1	1	0	0	0	0	0	0	1	.000	.000	.000	0	-96	-0	0			.000	0	H	0.0
1919	StL-A	9	35	4	7	0	0	0	1	5	2	.200	.300	.200	500	41	-3	0			.936	-2	/2-9	-0.5
1920	StL-A	7	7	2	2	0	0	0	2	0	0	.286	.286	.286	571	50	-0	0	0	0	1.000	1	/S-5	0.0
Total	3	18	43	7	9	0	0	0	3	5	3	.209	.292	.209	501	39	-3	0	0		.936	-1	/2-9,S-5	-0.5

■ GEORGE SHUBA

Shuba, George Thomas "Shotgun" b: 12/13/24, Youngstown, Ohio BL/TR, 5'11", 180 lbs. Deb: 7/2/48

YEAR	TM/L	G	AB	R	H	2B	3B	HR	RBI	BB	SO	AVG	OBP	SLG	OPS	OPS+	BR+	SB	CS	SBR	FA	FR	G/POS	TPR
1948	Bro-N	63	161	21	43	6	0	4	32	34	31	.267	.395	.379	774	107	3	1			.936	-10	O-56(55-2-1)	-1.0
1949	Bro-N	1	1	0	0	0	0	0	0	0	0	.000	.000	.000	0	-96	-0	0			.000	0	H	0.0
1950	Bro-N	34	111	15	23	8	2	3	12	13	22	.207	.302	.396	698	80	-3	2			.984	3	O-27(27-0-0)	-0.3
1952	*Bro-N	94	256	40	78	12	1	9	40	38	29	.305	.395	.465	859	136	13	1	3	-1	.992	-2	O-67(66-0-1)	0.6
1953	*Bro-N	74	169	19	43	12	1	5	23	17	20	.254	.326	.426	752	92	-2	1	2	-0	.984	-5	O-44(43-0-1)	-1.0
1954	Bro-N	45	65	3	10	5	0	2	10	7	10	.154	.247	.323	570	46	-5	0	0	0	.913	-1	O-13(7-0-5)	-0.7
1955	*Bro-N	44	51	8	14	2	0	1	8	11	10	.275	.422	.373	794	110	1	0	0	0	.909	-2	/O-9(7-1-2)	-0.1
Total	7	355	814	106	211	45	4	24	125	120	122	.259	.359	.413	771	104	6	5	5		.967	-18	O-216(205-3-10)	-2.5

■ FRANK SHUGART

Shugart, Frank Harry (b: Frank Harry Shugarts)
b: 12/10/1866, Luthersburg, Pa. d: 9/9/44, Clearfield, Pa. BL/TR (BB 1897), 5'8", 170 lbs. Deb: 8/23/1890 Career OF: (0-LF 164-CF 19-RF)

YEAR	TM/L	G	AB	R	H	2B	3B	HR	RBI	BB	SO	AVG	OBP	SLG	OPS	OPS+	BR+	SB	CS	SBR	FA	FR	G/POS	TPR
1890	Chi-P	29	106	8	20	5	5	0	15	5	13	.189	.232	.330	562	47	-9	5			.881	-5	S-25/O-5(0-1-4)	-1.0
1891	Pit-N	75	320	57	88	19	8	3	33	20	26	.275	.324	.412	736	117	5	21			.902	4	S-75	1.0
1892	Pit-N	137	554	94	148	19	14	0	62	47	48	.267	.329	.352	681	105	3	28			.886	8	*S-134/C-2,O-1(0-0-1)	1.7
1893	Pit-N	52	210	37	55	7	3	1	32	19	15	.262	.332	.338	670	80	-6	12			.882	-3	S-51	-0.5
	StL-N	59	246	41	69	10	4	0	28	22	10	.280	.354	.354	708	88	-4	13			.907	-3	O-28(0-19-9),S-23/3-9	-0.6
	Yr	111	456	78	124	17	7	1	60	41	25	.272	.344	.346	690	84	-10	25			.868	-6	S-74,O-28(0-19-9)/3-9	-1.1
1894	StL-N	133	527	103	154	19	18	7	72	38	37	.292	.350	.436	787	89	-12	21			.912	-3	*O-122C/S-7,3-7	-1.8
1895	Lou-N	113	473	61	125	14	13	4	70	31	25	.264	.315	.374	689	82	-13	14			.874	-16	*S-88,O-27(0-22-5)	-2.2
1897	Phi-N	40	163	20	41	8	2	5	25	8		.252	.287	.417	704	87	-4	5			.872	-4	S-40	-0.5
1901	Chi-A	107	415	62	104	9	12	2	47	28		.251	.301	.345	646	81	-11	12			.885	-8	*S-107	-1.4
Total	8	745	3014	483	804	110	79	22	384	218	174	.267	.323	.378	700	90	-51	131			.883	-30	S-550,O-183C/3-16,C	-5.3

■ TERRY SHUMPERT

Shumpert, Terrance Darnell b: 8/16/66, Paducah, Ky. BR/TR, 5'11", 185 lbs. Deb: 5/1/90 Career OF: (48-LF 9-CF 5-RF)

YEAR	TM/L	G	AB	R	H	2B	3B	HR	RBI	BB	SO	AVG	OBP	SLG	OPS	OPS+	BR+	SB	CS	SBR	FA	FR	G/POS	TPR
1990	KC-A	32	91	7	25	6	1	0	8	2	17	.275	.298	.363	661	85	-2	3	3	-0	.977	2	2-27/D-3	0.1
1991	KC-A	144	369	45	80	16	4	5	34	30	75	.217	.285	.322	607	67	-17	17	11	-0	.975	3	*2-144	-1.1
1992	KC-A	36	94	6	14	5	1	1	11	3	17	.149	.175	.255	431	19	-10	2	2	-0	.969	1	2-33/S-1,D-1	-0.9
1993	KC-A	8	10	0	1	0	0	0	0	2	2	.100	.250	.100	350	-2	-1	1	0	0	1.000	2	/2-8	0.0
1994	KC-A	64	183	28	44	6	2	8	24	13	39	.240	.291	.426	717	79	-6	18	3	3	.964	-8	2-38,3-24/S-1,D-2	-0.9
1995	Bos-A	21	47	6	11	3	0	0	3	4	13	.234	.294	.298	592	53	-3	3	1	0	1.000	3	/2-8,3-5,S-3,D-1	0.1
1996	Chi-N	27	31	5	7	1	0	2	6	2	11	.226	.294	.452	746	91	-1	0	1	-0	.923	-0	3-10/2-4,S-1	-0.1
1997	SD-N	13	33	4	9	3	0	1	6	3	4	.273	.333	.455	788	112	0	0	0	0	.973	-1	/2-7,O-3(2-0-1),3-2	0.0
1998	Col-N	23	26	3	6	1	0	1	2	2	8	.231	.286	.385	670	61	-1	0	0	0	1.000	2	/2-6	0.1
1999	Col-N	92	262	58	91	26	3	10	37	31	41	.347	.420	.584	1004	119	8	14	0	3	.988	4	2-54,O-19C,3-14,/S	1.6
2000	Col-N	115	263	52	68	11	7	9	40	28	40	.259	.343	.456	800	78	-9	8	4	0	.967	-10	O-40L,2-23,3-15,/S1D	-1.8
Total	11	575	1409	214	356	78	18	37	171	120	267	.253	.318	.412	730	81	-43	66	25	6	.978	-3	2-352/3-70,O-62L,SD1	-2.9

■ VINCE SHUPE

Shupe, Vincent William b: 9/5/21, E.Canton, Ohio d: 4/5/62, Canton, Ohio BL/TL, 5'11", 180 lbs. Deb: 7/7/45

YEAR	TM/L	G	AB	R	H	2B	3B	HR	RBI	BB	SO	AVG	OBP	SLG	OPS	OPS+	BR+	SB	CS	SBR	FA	FR	G/POS	TPR
1945	Bos-N	78	283	22	76	8	0	0	15	17	16	.269	.312	.297	609	69	-11	3			.989	1	1-77	-1.4

■ ED SICKING

Sicking, Edward Joseph b: 3/30/1897, St.Bernard, Ohio d: 8/30/78, Madeira, Ohio BR/TR, 5'9.5", 165 lbs. Deb: 8/26/16

YEAR	TM/L	G	AB	R	H	2B	3B	HR	RBI	BB	SO	AVG	OBP	SLG	OPS	OPS+	BR+	SB	CS	SBR	FA	FR	G/POS	TPR
1916	Chi-N	1	1	0	0	0	0	0	0	0	0	.000	.000	.000	0	-90	-0	0			.000	0	H	0.0
1918	NY-N	46	132	9	33	4	0	0	12	6	11	.250	.283	.280	563	73	-4	2			.917	-8	3-24,2-18/S-3	-1.3
1919	NY-N	6	15	2	5	0	0	0	3	1	0	.333	.412	.333	745	127	1	0			.971	3	/S-6	0.4
	Phi-N	61	185	16	40	2	1	0	15	8	17	.216	.253	.238	490	45	-12	4			.925	5	S-35,2-22	-0.6
	Yr	67	200	18	45	2	1	0	18	9	17	.225	.265	.245	510	51	-12	4			.933	8	S-41,2-22	-0.2
1920	NY-N	46	134	11	23	3	1	0	9	10	10	.172	.234	.209	443	28	-12	6	2	1	.915	4	3-28,2-15/S-3	-0.8
	Cin-N	37	123	12	33	3	0	0	17	13	5	.268	.338	.293	631	83	-2	2	3	-1	.955	1	2-25/S-9,3-2	-0.1
	Yr	83	257	23	56	6	1	0	26	23	15	.218	.285	.249	534	55	-14	8	5	0	.952	4	2-40,3-30,S-12	-0.9
1927	Pit-N	6	7	1	1	1	0	0	3	1	0	.143	.250	.286	536	40	-1	0			1.000	2	/2-5	0.1
Total	5	203	597	51	135	13	2	0	59	39	43	.226	.277	.255	532	57	-31	14	5		.965	5	/2-85,S-56,3-54	-2.3

■ JOE SIDDALL

Siddall, Joseph Todd b: 10/25/67, Windsor, Ont., Can. BL/TR, 6'1", 197 lbs. Deb: 7/28/93

YEAR	TM/L	G	AB	R	H	2B	3B	HR	RBI	BB	SO	AVG	OBP	SLG	OPS	OPS+	BR+	SB	CS	SBR	FA	FR	G/POS	TPR
1993	Mon-N	19	20	0	2	1	0	0	1	1	5	.100	.143	.150	293	-21	-3	0	0	0	1.000	2	C-15/1-1,O-1(1-0-0)	-0.1
1995	Mon-N	7	10	4	3	0	0	0	1	3	3	.300	.500	.300	800	113	1	0	0	0	.882	-3	/C-7	-0.2
1996	Fla-N	18	47	0	7	1	0	0	3	2	8	.149	.184	.170	354	-6	-7	0	0	0	.977	-1	C-18	-0.7
1998	Det-A	29	65	3	12	3	0	1	6	7	25	.185	.264	.277	541	41	-6	0	0	0	.994	8	C-27/O-1(0-0-1)	0.3
Total	4	73	142	7	24	5	0	1	11	13	41	.169	.244	.225	469	24	-16	0	0	0	.983	6	/C-67,O-2(1-0-1),1-1	-0.7

■ NORM SIEBERN
Siebern, Norman Leroy b: 7/26/33, St.Louis, Mo. BL/TR, 6'3", 205 lbs. Deb: 6/15/56 Career OF: (402-LF 16-CF 11-RF)

YEAR	TM/L	G	AB	R	H	2B	3B	HR	RBI	BB	SO	AVG	OBP	SLG	OPS	OPS+	BR+	SB	CS	SBR	FA	FR	G/POS	TPR
1956	*NY-A	54	162	27	33	1	4	4	21	19	38	.204	.287	.333	621	66	-9	1	1	-0	.971	0	O-51(51-0-0)	-1.1
1958	*NY-A	134	460	79	138	19	5	14	55	66	87	.300	.389	.454	843	136	24	5	8	-2	.982	5	*O-133(127-11-0)	2.1
1959	NY-A	120	380	52	103	17	0	11	53	41	71	.271	.345	.403	748	108	4	3	1	0	.989	-2	O-93(82-5-9)/1-2	-0.3
1960	KC-A	144	520	69	145	31	6	19	69	72	68	.279	.369	.471	840	125	18	0	0	0	.987	-1	O-75(75-0-0),1-69	0.9
1961	KC-A	153	560	68	166	36	5	18	98	82	91	.296	.387	.475	862	127	23	2	4	-1	.989	-1	*1-109,O-47(47-0-0)	1.2
1962	KC-A★	162	600	114	185	25	6	25	117	110	88	.308	.416	.495	911	138	36	3	1	0	.994	5	*1-162	3.0
1963	KC-A☆	152	556	80	151	25	2	16	83	79	82	.272	.362	.410	772	110	9	1	4	-1	.991	4	*1-131,O-16(16-0-1)	0.3
1964	Bal-A★	150	478	92	117	24	2	12	56	**106**	87	.245	.384	.379	763	114	13	2	3	-1	.995	4	*1-149	0.8
1965	Bal-A	106	297	44	76	13	4	8	32	50	49	.256	.365	.407	772	117	8	1	2	-0	.991	1	1-76	0.4
1966	Cal-A	125	336	29	83	14	1	5	41	63	61	.247	.366	.339	705	107	6	0	1	-0	.992	1	1-99	0.1
1967	SF-N	46	58	6	9	1	1	0	4	14	13	.155	.319	.207	526	54	-3	0	0	0	1.000	-0	1-15/O-2(2-0-0)	-0.4
	*Bos-A	33	44	2	9	0	2	0	7	6	8	.205	.300	.295	595	71	-1	0	0	0	.981	1	1-13/O-1(1-0-0)	-0.2
1968	Bos-A	27	30	0	2	0	0	0	0	0	5	.067	.067	.067	133	-56	-5	0	0	0	1.000	-1	/1-2,O-2(1-0-1)	-0.7
Total	12	1406	4481	662	1217	206	38	132	636	708	748	.272	.372	.423	795	117	123	18	25	-5	.992	17	1-827,O-420L	6.1

■ DICK SIEBERT
Siebert, Richard Walther b: 2/19/12, Fall River, Mass. d: 12/9/78, Minneapolis, Minn. BL/TL, 6', 170 lbs. Deb: 9/7/32 F

YEAR	TM/L	G	AB	R	H	2B	3B	HR	RBI	BB	SO	AVG	OBP	SLG	OPS	OPS+	BR+	SB	CS	SBR	FA	FR	G/POS	TPR
1932	Bro-N	6	7	1	2	0	0	0	0	2	2	.286	.444	.286	730	104	0	0			1.000	-0	/1-2	0.0
1936	Bro-N	2	2	0	0	0	0	0	0	0	0	.000	.000	.000	0	-99	-1	0			1.000	0	/O-1(0-0-1)	0.0
1937	StL-N	22	38	3	7	2	0	0	2	4	8	.184	.279	.237	516	41	-3	1			.979	-1	/1-7	-0.4
1938	StL-N	1	1	0	1	0	0	0	0	0	0	1.000	1.000	1.000	2000	427	0	0			.000	0	H	0.0
	Phi-A	48	194	24	55	8	3	0	28	10	9	.284	.329	.356	684	73	-8	2	3	-1	1.000	5	1-46	-0.7
1939	Phi-A	101	402	58	118	28	3	6	47	21	22	.294	.329	.423	751	93	-6	4	1	1	.991	5	1-99	-0.9
1940	Phi-A	154	595	69	170	31	6	5	77	33	34	.286	.325	.383	709	85	-14	8	6	-0	.985	8	*1-154	-2.0
1941	Phi-A	123	467	63	156	28	8	5	79	37	22	.334	.385	.460	846	126	17	1	3	-1	.990	6	*1-123	1.1
1942	Phi-A	153	612	57	159	25	7	2	74	24	17	.260	.291	.333	624	76	-21	4	5	-1	.989	-2	*1-152	-4.0
1943	Phi-A★	146	558	50	140	26	7	1	72	33	21	.251	.295	.328	623	83	-14	6	7	-1	.990	4	*1-145	-2.1
1944	Phi-A	132	468	52	143	27	5	6	52	62	17	.306	.387	.423	810	133	21	2	0	0	.993	-4	1-74,O-58(42-0-17)	1.2
1945	Phi-A	147	573	62	153	29	1	7	51	50	33	.267	.328	.358	686	99	-1	2	7	-2	.991	10	*1-147	-0.1
Total	11	1035	3917	439	1104	204	40	32	482	276	185	.282	.332	.379	710	96	-29	30	32		.990	31	1-949/O-59(42-0-18)	-7.9

■ FRED SIEFKE
Siefke, Frederick Edwin b: 3/27/1870, New York, N.Y. d: 4/18/1893, New York, N.Y. 5'11", 168 lbs. Deb: 5/2/1890

YEAR	TM/L	G	AB	R	H	2B	3B	HR	RBI	BB	SO	AVG	OBP	SLG	OPS	OPS+	BR+	SB	CS	SBR	FA	FR	G/POS	TPR
1890	Bro-a	16	58	1	8	2	0	0	3	5		.138	.206	.172	379	12	-6	2			.811	0	3-16	-0.5

■ JOHN SIEGEL
Siegel, John b: York, Pa. Deb: 6/9/1884

YEAR	TM/L	G	AB	R	H	2B	3B	HR	RBI	BB	SO	AVG	OBP	SLG	OPS	OPS+	BR+	SB	CS	SBR	FA	FR	G/POS	TPR
1884	Phi-U	8	31	4	7	2	0	0		1		.226	.250	.290	540	68	-2				.533	-5	/3-8	-0.6

■ JOHNNY SIEGLE
Siegle, John Herbert b: 7/8/1874, Urbana, Ohio d: 2/12/68, Urbana, Ohio BR/TR, 5'10", 165 lbs. Deb: 9/15/05

YEAR	TM/L	G	AB	R	H	2B	3B	HR	RBI	BB	SO	AVG	OBP	SLG	OPS	OPS+	BR+	SB	CS	SBR	FA	FR	G/POS	TPR
1905	Cin-N	17	56	9	17	1	2	1	8	7		.304	.391	.446	837	135	2	0			.960	-1	O-16(0-0-16)	0.1
1906	Cin-N	22	68	4	8	2	2	0	7	3		.118	.178	.206	384	19	-7	0			.959	0	O-21(7-14-0)	-0.8
Total	2	39	124	13	25	3	4	1	15	10		.202	.277	.315	592	75	-4	0			.959	-1	/O-37(7-14-16)	-0.7

■ OSCAR SIEMER
Siemer, Oscar Sylvester "Cotton" b: 8/14/01, St.Louis, Mo. d: 12/5/59, St.Louis, Mo. BR/TR, 5'9", 162 lbs. Deb: 5/20/25

YEAR	TM/L	G	AB	R	H	2B	3B	HR	RBI	BB	SO	AVG	OBP	SLG	OPS	OPS+	BR+	SB	CS	SBR	FA	FR	G/POS	TPR
1925	Bos-N	16	46	5	14	0	1	1	6	1	0	.304	.319	.413	732	94	-1	0	0	0	.900	-2	C-16	-0.1
1926	Bos-N	31	73	3	15	1	0	0	5	2	7	.205	.227	.219	446	22	-8	0			.920	-2	C-30	-0.8
Total	2	47	119	8	29	1	1	1	11	3	7	.244	.262	.294	556	51	-9	0	0		.913	-4	/C-46	-0.9

■ RUBEN SIERRA
Sierra, Ruben Angel (Garcia) b: 10/6/65, Rio Piedras, P.R. BB/TR, 6'1", 200 lbs. Deb: 6/1/86 Career OF: (100-LF 31-CF 1342-RF)

YEAR	TM/L	G	AB	R	H	2B	3B	HR	RBI	BB	SO	AVG	OBP	SLG	OPS	OPS+	BR+	SB	CS	SBR	FA	FR	G/POS	TPR
1986	Tex-A	113	382	50	101	13	10	16	55	22	65	.264	.306	.476	783	106	2	7	8	-1	.972	-10	*O-107(44-21-68)/D-3	-1.3
1987	Tex-A	158	643	97	169	35	4	30	109	39	114	.263	.307	.470	777	102	-0	16	11	-0	.963	5	*O-157(0-4-156)	-0.4
1988	Tex-A	156	615	77	156	32	2	23	91	44	91	.254	.305	.424	729	99	-2	18	4	3	.979	6	*O-153(0-0-153)/D-1	0.2
1989	Tex-A★	162	634	101	194	35	**14**	29	**119**	43	82	.306	.352	**.543**	895	146	36	8	2	1	.973	6	*O-162(0-2-161)	3.8
1990	Tex-A	159	608	70	170	37	2	16	96	49	86	.280	.334	.426	760	111	8	9	0	2	.967	0	*O-151(0-0-151)/D-7	0.5
1991	Tex-A★	161	661	110	203	44	5	25	116	56	91	.307	.361	.502	863	139	33	16	4	2	.979	5	*O-161(0-3-161)	3.5
1992	Tex-A★	124	500	66	139	30	6	14	70	31	59	.278	.320	.446	766	117	9	12	4	1	.970	0	*O-119(0-0-119)/D-4	0.6
	*Oak-A	27	101	17	28	4	1	3	17	14	9	.277	.365	.426	791	128	4	2	0	0	1.000	1	O-25(0-0-25)/D-2	0.5
	Yr	151	601	83	167	34	7	17	87	45	68	.278	.328	.443	771	119	13	14	4	2	.976	1	*O-144(0-0-144)/D-6	1.1
1993	Oak-A	158	630	77	147	23	5	22	101	52	97	.233	.292	.390	682	87	-14	25	5	4	.977	7	*O-133(0-0-133),D-25	-1.2
1994	Oak-A★	110	426	71	114	21	1	23	92	23	64	.268	.305	.484	789	108	3	8	5	0	.948	-4	O-98(0-1-97),D-10	-0.6
1995	Oak-A	70	264	40	70	17	0	12	42	24	42	.265	.326	.466	792	109	3	4	4	-1	.957	-5	O-62(0-0-62)/D-7	-0.6
	*NY-A	56	215	33	56	15	0	7	44	22	34	.260	.329	.428	757	96	-2	1	0	0	.950	1	D-46,O-10(0-0-10)	-0.4
	Yr	126	479	73	126	32	0	19	86	46	76	.263	.328	.449	776	103	1	5	4	-0	.956	-5	O-72(0-0-72),D-53	-1.0
1996	NY-A	96	360	39	93	17	1	11	52	40	58	.258	.333	.403	735	85	-9	1	3	-1	.984	2	D-61,O-33(32-0-1)	-1.1
	Det-A	46	158	22	35	9	1	1	20	20	25	.222	.309	.310	619	57	-10	3	1	0	.914	1	O-23(4-0-19),D-20	-1.0
	Yr	142	518	61	128	26	2	12	72	60	83	.247	.325	.375	700	76	-19	4	4	-1	.950	4	D-81,O-56(36-0-20)	-2.1
1997	Cin-N	25	90	6	22	5	1	2	7	6	21	.244	.292	.389	681	75	-3	0	0	0	1.000	1	O-24(12-0-12)	-0.4
	Tor-A	14	48	4	10	0	2	1	5	3	13	.208	.255	.354	609	56	-3	0	0	0	.929	-1	/O-7(6-0-2),D-6	-0.4
1998	Chi-A	27	74	7	16	4	1	4	11	3	11	.216	.247	.459	706	80	-3	2	0	0	1.000	-1	O-14(2-0-12)/D-5	-0.4
2000	Tex-A	20	60	5	14	0	0	1	7	4	9	.233	.281	.283	565	42	-5	1	0	0	.000	0	D-14	-0.5
Total	14	1682	6469	892	1737	341	56	240	1054	495	971	.269	.321	.450	771	107	45	133	51	11	.971	14	*O-1439R,D-211	0.8

■ ROY SIEVERS
Sievers, Roy Edward "Squirrel" b: 11/18/26, St.Louis, Mo. BR/TR, 6'1", 195 lbs. Deb: 4/21/49 C Career OF: (676-LF 163-CF 4-RF)

YEAR	TM/L	G	AB	R	H	2B	3B	HR	RBI	BB	SO	AVG	OBP	SLG	OPS	OPS+	BR+	SB	CS	SBR	FA	FR	G/POS	TPR
1949	StL-A	140	471	84	144	28	1	16	91	70	75	.306	.398	.471	869	124	17	1	5	-2	.973	6	*O-125(51-76-0)/3-7	1.5
1950	StL-A	113	370	46	88	20	4	10	57	34	42	.238	.305	.395	700	75	-16	1	3	-1	.983	6	O-78(10-68-0),3-21	-1.2
1951	StL-A	31	89	10	20	2	1	1	11	9	21	.225	.303	.303	606	62	-5	0	0	0	.985	-2	O-25(9-19-0)	-0.7
1952	StL-A	11	30	3	6	3	0	0	5	1	4	.200	.226	.300	526	44	-2	0	0	0	.968	-1	/1-7	-0.4
1953	StL-A	92	285	37	77	15	0	8	35	32	47	.270	.344	.407	751	100	-0	0	1	-0	.992	-6	1-76	-1.1
1954	Was-A	145	514	75	119	26	6	24	102	80	77	.232	.337	.446	783	120	12	2	1	0	.971	9	*O-133(133-0-0)/1-8	1.3
1955	Was-A	144	509	74	138	20	8	25	106	73	66	.271	.367	.489	856	136	25	1	2	-0	.988	-1	*O-129L,1-17/3-2	1.4
1956	Was-A★	152	550	92	139	27	2	29	95	100	88	.253	.373	.467	840	121	17	0	0	0	.987	2	O-78(78-0-0),1-76	0.9
1957	Was-A☆	152	572	99	172	23	5	**42**	**114**	76	55	.301	.389	.579	968	163	49	1	1	-0	.985	4	*O-130(130-0-0),1-21	4.4
1958	Was-A	148	550	85	162	18	1	39	108	53	63	.295	.361	.544	904	148	34	3	1	0	.991	5	*O-114(114-0-0),1-33	3.0
1959	Was-A★	115	385	55	93	19	0	21	49	53	62	.242	.336	.455	791	116	8	1	1	-0	.989	5	1-93,O-13(13-0-0)	0.6
1960	Chi-A	127	444	87	131	22	0	28	93	74	69	.295	.399	.534	933	152	33	1	1	-0	.993	-7	*1-114/O-6(6-0-0)	1.9
1961	Chi-A★	141	492	76	145	26	6	27	92	61	62	.295	.379	.537	916	144	30	1	0	0	.993	0	*1-132	2.2
1962	Phi-N	144	477	61	125	19	5	21	80	56	80	.262	.348	.455	803	117	11	2	1	0	.991	1	*1-130/O-7(3-0-4)	0.5
1963	Phi-N	138	450	46	108	19	2	19	82	43	72	.240	.313	.418	731	110	5	0	2	-1	.989	-1	*1-126	-0.4
1964	Phi-N	49	120	7	22	3	1	4	16	13	20	.183	.269	.325	594	67	-5	0	0	0	.992	-1	1-33	-0.9
	Was-A	33	58	5	10	1	0	4	11	9	14	.172	.284	.397	680	87	-1	0	0	0	1.000	1	1-15	-0.1
1965	Was-A	12	21	3	4	1	0	0	0	4	3	.190	.320	.238	558	62	-1	0	0	0	1.000	-1	/1-7	-0.2
Total	17	1887	6387	945	1703	292	42	318	1147	841	920	.267	.357	.475	831	124	211	14	19	-4	.991	19	1-888,O-838L/3-30	12.7

■ FRANK SIFFELL
Siffell, Frank b: 1860, Germany d: 10/26/09, Philadelphia, Pa. Deb: 6/14/1884

YEAR	TM/L	G	AB	R	H	2B	3B	HR	RBI	BB	SO	AVG	OBP	SLG	OPS	OPS+	BR+	SB	CS	SBR	FA	FR	G/POS	TPR
1884	Phi-a	7	17	3	3	1	0	0	3	0		.176	.222	.235	458	46	-1				.875	-3	/C-7	-0.3
1885	Phi-a	3	10	0	1	0	0	0	0	0		.100	.100	.100	200	-35	-2				.750	-3	/C-2,O-1(0-0-1)	-0.4
Total	2	10	27	3	4	1	0	0	3	0		.148	.179	.185	364	16	-3				.841	-6	/C-9,O-1(0-0-1)	-0.7

■ FRANK SIGAFOOS
Sigafoos, Francis Leonard b: 3/21/04, Easton, Pa. d: 4/12/68, Indianapolis, Ind. BR/TR, 5'9", 170 lbs. Deb: 9/3/26

YEAR	TM/L	G	AB	R	H	2B	3B	HR	RBI	BB	SO	AVG	OBP	SLG	OPS	OPS+	BR+	SB	CS	SBR	FA	FR	G/POS	TPR
1926	Phi-A	13	43	4	11	0	0	0	2	0	3	.256	.256	.256	512	32	-4	0	0	0	.915	-3	S-12	-0.6
1929	Det-A	14	23	3	4	1	0	0	2	5	4	.174	.321	.217	539	41	-2	0	2	-1	.909	-2	/3-6,S-5	-0.4
	Chi-A	7	3	1	1	0	0	0	1	2	1	.333	.600	.333	933	148	1	0	0	0	1.000	1	/2-6	0.2

YEAR	TM/L	G	AB	R	H	2B	3B	HR	RBI	BB	SO	AVG	OBP	SLG	OPS	OPS+	BR+	SB	CS	SBR	FA	FR	G/POS	TPR
	Yr	21	26	4	5	1	0	0	3	7	5	.192	.364	.231	594	56	-1	0	2	-1	.909	-1	/3-6,2-6,S-5	-0.2
1931	Cin-N	21	65	6	11	2	0	0	8	0	6	.169	.182	.200	382	3	-9	0			.881	-3	3-15/S-2	-1.2
Total	3	55	134	14	27	3	0	0	13	7	14	.201	.246	.224	470	25	-15	0	2		.887	-7	/3-21,S-19,2-6	-2.0

■ PADDY SIGLIN Siglin, Wesley Peter b: 9/24/1891, Aurelia, Iowa d: 8/5/56, Oakland, Cal. BR/TR, 5'10", 160 lbs. Deb: 9/12/14

YEAR	TM/L	G	AB	R	H	2B	3B	HR	RBI	BB	SO	AVG	OBP	SLG	OPS	OPS+	BR+	SB	CS	SBR	FA	FR	G/POS	TPR
1914	Pit-N	14	39	4	6	0	0	0	2	4	6	.154	.233	.154	386	16	-4	1			.911	-6	2-11	-1.1
1915	Pit-N	6	7	1	2	0	0	0	0	1	2	.286	.375	.286	661	103	0	1			.800	-0	/2-1	0.0
1916	Pit-N	3	4	0	1	0	0	0	0	0	2	.250	.250	.250	500	53	-0	0			.857	0	/2-3	0.0
Total	3	23	50	5	9	0	0	0	2	5	10	.180	.255	.180	435	32	-4	2			.895	-5	/2-15	-1.1

■ TRIPP SIGMAN Sigman, Wesley Triplett b: 1/17/1899, Mooresville, N.C. d: 3/8/71, Augusta, Ga. BL/TR, 6', 180 lbs. Deb: 9/18/29

YEAR	TM/L	G	AB	R	H	2B	3B	HR	RBI	BB	SO	AVG	OBP	SLG	OPS	OPS+	BR+	SB	CS	SBR	FA	FR	G/POS	TPR
1929	Phi-N	10	29	8	15	1	0	2	9	3	1	.517	.563	.759	1321	210	5	0			.944	-2	O-10(5-5-0)	0.2
1930	Phi-N	52	100	15	27	4	1	4	6	6	9	.270	.324	.450	774	79	-4	1			.932	-1	O-19(3-16-0)	-0.5
Total	2	62	129	23	42	5	1	6	15	9	10	.326	.379	.519	898	108	1	1			.935	-3	/O-29(8-21-0)	-0.3

■ EDDIE SILBER Silber, Edward James b: 6/6/14, Philadelphia, Pa. d: 10/26/76, Dunedin, Fla. BR/TR, 5'11", 170 lbs. Deb: 9/3/37

YEAR	TM/L	G	AB	R	H	2B	3B	HR	RBI	BB	SO	AVG	OBP	SLG	OPS	OPS+	BR+	SB	CS	SBR	FA	FR	G/POS	TPR
1937	StL-A	22	83	10	26	2	0	0	4	5	13	.313	.352	.337	690	74	-3	0	2	-1	.871	-7	O-21(2-6-15)	-1.1
1939	StL-A	1	1	0	0	0	0	0	0	0	1	.000	.000	.000	0	-98	-0	0	0	0	.000	0	H	0.0
Total	2	23	84	10	26	2	0	0	4	5	14	.310	.348	.333	682	72	-3	0	2	-1	.871	-7	/O-21(2-6-15)	-1.1

■ ED SILCH Silch, Edward "Baldy" b: 2/22/1865, St.Louis, Mo. d: 1/15/1895, St.Louis, Mo. TR, 6'2", 180 lbs. Deb: 4/29/1888

YEAR	TM/L	G	AB	R	H	2B	3B	HR	RBI	BB	SO	AVG	OBP	SLG	OPS	OPS+	BR+	SB	CS	SBR	FA	FR	G/POS	TPR
1888	Bro-a	14	48	5	13	4	0	0	3	4		.271	.327	.354	681	118	1	4			.870	-2	O-14(0-6-8)	-0.1

■ DANNY SILVA Silva, Daniel James b: 10/5/1896, Everett, Mass. d: 4/4/74, Hyannis, Mass. BR/TR, 6', 170 lbs. Deb: 8/11/19

YEAR	TM/L	G	AB	R	H	2B	3B	HR	RBI	BB	SO	AVG	OBP	SLG	OPS	OPS+	BR+	SB	CS	SBR	FA	FR	G/POS	TPR
1919	Was-A	1	4	0	1	0	0	0	0	0	0	.250	.250	.250	500	41	-0	0			1.000	1	/3-1	0.0

■ AL SILVERA Silvera, Aaron Albert b: 8/26/35, San Diego, Cal. BR/TR, 6', 180 lbs. Deb: 6/12/55

YEAR	TM/L	G	AB	R	H	2B	3B	HR	RBI	BB	SO	AVG	OBP	SLG	OPS	OPS+	BR+	SB	CS	SBR	FA	FR	G/POS	TPR
1955	Cin-N	13	7	3	1	0	0	0	2	0	1	.143	.143	.143	286	-23	-1	0	0	0	.000	-0	/O-1(1-0-0)	-0.2
1956	Cin-N	1	0	0	0	0	0	0	0	0	0	—	—	—	—	—	0	0	0	0	.000	0	R	0.0
Total	2	14	7	3	1	0	0	0	2	0	1	.143	.143	.143	286	-23	-1	0	0	0	—	-0	/O-1(1-0-0)	-0.2

■ CHARLIE SILVERA Silvera, Charles Anthony Ryan "Swede" b: 10/13/24, San Francisco, Cal BR/TR, 5'10", 175 lbs. Deb: 9/29/48 C

YEAR	TM/L	G	AB	R	H	2B	3B	HR	RBI	BB	SO	AVG	OBP	SLG	OPS	OPS+	BR+	SB	CS	SBR	FA	FR	G/POS	TPR
1948	NY-A	4	14	1	8	0	1	0	1	0	1	.571	.571	.714	1286	243	3	0	0	0	1.000	0	/C-4	0.3
1949	*NY-A	58	130	8	41	2	0	0	13	18	5	.315	.403	.331	733	95	0	2	1	0	.985	4	C-51	0.6
1950	NY-A	18	25	2	4	0	0	0	1	1	2	.160	.192	.160	352	-9	-4	0	0	0	.959	3	C-15	-0.1
1951	NY-A	18	51	5	14	3	0	1	7	5	3	.275	.339	.392	731	101	-0	0	0	0	1.000	0	C-18	0.1
1952	NY-A	20	55	4	18	3	0	0	11	5	2	.327	.383	.382	765	121	2	0	3	-1	1.000	-3	C-20	-0.1
1953	NY-A	42	82	11	23	3	1	0	12	9	5	.280	.352	.341	693	91	-1	0	1	-0	.992	6	C-39/3-1	0.6
1954	NY-A	20	37	1	10	1	0	0	4	3	2	.270	.341	.297	639	79	-1	0	1	-0	.962	5	C-18	0.5
1955	NY-A	14	26	1	5	0	0	0	1	6	4	.192	.344	.192	536	48	-2	0	0	0	1.000	3	C-11	0.2
1956	NY-A	7	9	0	2	0	0	0	0	2	3	.222	.364	.222	586	60	-0	0	0	0	.909	-1	/C-7	-0.1
1957	Chi-N	26	53	1	11	3	0	0	2	4	5	.208	.263	.264	527	43	-4	0	0	0	.982	3	C-26	-0.1
Total	10	227	482	34	136	15	2	1	52	53	32	.282	.356	.328	683	86	-8	2	6	-2	.985	21	C-209/3-1	1.9

■ LUIS SILVERIO Silverio, Luis Pascual (Delmonte) b: 10/23/56, Villa Gonzalez, D.R. BR/TR, 5'11", 165 lbs. Deb: 9/9/78

YEAR	TM/L	G	AB	R	H	2B	3B	HR	RBI	BB	SO	AVG	OBP	SLG	OPS	OPS+	BR+	SB	CS	SBR	FA	FR	G/POS	TPR
1978	KC-A	8	11	7	6	2	1	0	3	2	3	.545	.615	.909	1524	315	3	1	1	-0	.833	-2	/O-6(4-0-2),D-2	0.1

■ TOM SILVERIO Silverio, Tomas Roberto (Veloz) b: 10/14/45, Santiago, D.R. BL/TL, 5'10", 170 lbs. Deb: 4/30/70

YEAR	TM/L	G	AB	R	H	2B	3B	HR	RBI	BB	SO	AVG	OBP	SLG	OPS	OPS+	BR+	SB	CS	SBR	FA	FR	G/POS	TPR
1970	Cal-A	15	15	1	0	0	0	0	0	2	4	.000	.118	.000	118	-67	-3	0	1	-0	1.000	-2	/O-5(1-4-0),1-1	-0.7
1971	Cal-A	3	3	0	1	0	0	0	0	0	0	.333	.333	.333	667	96	-0	0	0	0	.000	-1	/O-1(0-1-0)	-0.1
1972	Cal-A	13	12	1	2	0	0	0	0	0	5	.167	.167	.167	333	-1	-1	0	0	0	1.000	-1	/O-4(2-1-1)	-0.3
Total	3	31	30	2	3	0	0	0	0	2	9	.100	.156	.100	256	-27	-5	0	1	-0	1.000	-4	/O-10(3-6-1),1-1	-1.1

■ DAVE SILVESTRI Silvestri, David Joseph b: 9/29/67, St.Louis, Mo. BR/TR, 6', 196 lbs. Deb: 4/27/92 Career OF: (5-LF 1-CF 0-RF)

YEAR	TM/L	G	AB	R	H	2B	3B	HR	RBI	BB	SO	AVG	OBP	SLG	OPS	OPS+	BR+	SB	CS	SBR	FA	FR	G/POS	TPR
1992	NY-A	7	13	3	4	0	2	0	1	0	3	.308	.308	.615	923	154	1	0	0	0	.889	1	/S-6	0.2
1993	NY-A	7	21	4	6	1	0	1	4	5	3	.286	.423	.476	899	146	2	0	0	0	.955	2	/S-4,3-3	0.3
1994	NY-A	12	18	3	2	0	1	1	2	4	9	.111	.273	.389	662	71	-1	0	1	-0	1.000	1	/2-9,3-2,S-1	0.0
1995	NY-A	17	21	4	2	0	0	1	4	4	9	.095	.269	.238	507	34	-2	0	0	0	1.000	2	/2-7,1-4,S-1,D-4	-0.1
	Mon-N	39	72	12	19	6	0	2	7	9	27	.264	.346	.431	776	100	-0	2	0	0	1.000	-3	/S-9,3-8,1-4,2-3,O	-0.2
1996	Mon-N	86	162	16	33	4	0	1	17	34	41	.204	.342	.247	589	57	-9	2	1	0	.913	-2	3-47,S-10/O-2L,12	-1.0
1997	Tex-A	2	4	0	0	0	0	0	0	0	1	.000	.000	.000	0	-95	-1	0	0	0	.000	-1	/3-1,S-1	-0.2
1998	TB-A	8	14	0	1	0	0	0	0	0	2	.071	.071	.071	143	-61	-3	0	0	0	1.000	1	/3-3,2-2,S-1,D-2	-0.2
1999	Ana-A	3	11	0	1	1	0	0	1	0	1	.091	.091	.182	273	-33	-2	0	0	0	1.000	-1	/2-1,S-1,O-1(1-0-0)	-0.3
Total	8	181	336	42	68	12	3	6	36	56	96	.202	.318	.310	628	65	-16	4	2	0	.912	-1	/3-64,S-34,2-23,1OD	-1.5

■ KEN SILVESTRI Silvestri, Kenneth Joseph "Hawk" b: 5/3/16, Chicago, Ill. d: 3/31/92, Tallahassee, Fla. BB/TR, 6'1", 200 lbs. Deb: 4/18/39 MC

YEAR	TM/L	G	AB	R	H	2B	3B	HR	RBI	BB	SO	AVG	OBP	SLG	OPS	OPS+	BR+	SB	CS	SBR	FA	FR	G/POS	TPR
1939	Chi-A	22	75	6	13	3	0	2	5	6	13	.173	.244	.293	537	36	-8	0	1	-0	.947	-0	C-20	-0.6
1940	Chi-A	28	24	5	6	2	0	2	10	4	7	.250	.357	.583	940	138	1	0	0	0	1.000	-0	/C-1	0.1
1941	NY-A	17	40	6	10	5	0	1	4	7	6	.250	.362	.450	812	115	1	0	0	0	1.000	0	C-13	0.1
1946	NY-A	13	21	4	6	1	0	0	1	3	7	.286	.375	.333	708	98	0	0	0	0	.977	2	C-12	0.3
1947	NY-A	3	10	0	2	0	0	0	0	2	2	.200	.333	.200	533	51	-1	0	0	0	1.000	-2	/C-3	-0.2
1949	Phi-N	4	4	1	0	0	0	0	0	2	1	.000	.333	.000	333	-3	-0	0			1.000	0	/C-1,2-1,S-1	0.0
1950	*Phi-N	11	20	2	5	0	1	0	4	4	3	.250	.400	.350	750	101	0	0			1.000	-1	/C-9	-0.1
1951	Phi-N	4	9	2	2	0	0	0	1	3	2	.222	.417	.222	639	78	-0	0	0	0	1.000	-3	/C-3,2-1	-0.3
Total	8	102	203	26	44	11	1	5	25	31	41	.217	.326	.355	681	78	-6	0	1		.974	-3	/C-62,2-2,S-1	-0.7

■ AL SIMMONS Simmons, Aloysius Harry "Bucketfoot Al" (b: Aloys Szymanski)
b: 5/22/02, Milwaukee, Wis. d: 5/26/56, Milwaukee, Wis. BR/TR, 5'11", 190 lbs. Deb: 4/15/24 CH Career OF: (1377-LF 771-CF 1-RF)

YEAR	TM/L	G	AB	R	H	2B	3B	HR	RBI	BB	SO	AVG	OBP	SLG	OPS	OPS+	BR+	SB	CS	SBR	FA	FR	G/POS	TPR
1924	Phi-A	152	594	69	183	31	9	8	102	30	60	.308	.343	.431	774	98	-4	16	15	-2	.976	7	*O-152(51-101-0)	-0.7
1925	Phi-A	153	654	122	**253**	43	12	24	129	35	41	.387	.419	.599	1018	146	43	7	14	-3	.966	5	*O-153(0-153-0)	3.4
1926	Phi-A	147	583	90	199	53	10	19	109	48	49	.341	.392	.564	957	139	31	11	3	1	.975	-4	*O-147(0-147-0)	2.1
1927	Phi-A	106	406	86	159	36	11	15	108	31	30	.392	.436	.645	1081	168	39	10	2	2	.985	3	*O-105(10-94-1)	3.5
1928	Phi-A	119	464	78	163	33	9	15	107	31	30	.351	.396	.558	954	144	28	1	4	-1	.988	2	*O-114(114-0-0)	1.9
1929	*Phi-A	143	581	114	212	41	9	34	**157**	31	38	.365	.398	.642	1040	158	46	4	2	0	.989	17	*O-142(142-0-0)	4.8
1930	*Phi-A	138	554	**152**	211	41	16	36	165	39	34	**.381**	.423	.708	1130	173	58	9	2	1	**.990**	6	*O-136(129-7-0)	4.8
1931	*Phi-A	128	513	105	200	37	13	22	128	47	45	**.390**	.444	.641	1085	172	52	3	3	-0	.987	8	*O-128(125-3-0)	4.8
1932	Phi-A	154	670	144	**216**	28	9	35	151	47	76	.322	.368	.548	915	129	26	4	2	0	.980	-5	*O-154(154-1-0)	1.1
1933	Chi-A★	146	605	85	200	29	10	14	119	39	49	.331	.373	.481	854	130	24	5	1	1	.990	14	*O-145(144-1-0)	2.9
1934	Chi-A★	138	558	102	192	36	7	18	104	53	58	.344	.403	.530	933	135	28	3	2	-0	.987	5	*O-138(136-2-0)	2.3
1935	Chi-A★	128	525	68	140	22	7	16	79	33	43	.267	.313	.427	739	87	-12	4	6	-1	.981	1	*O-126(11-115-0)	-1.5
1936	Det-A	143	568	96	186	38	6	13	112	49	35	.327	.383	.484	867	112	10	6	4	-0	**.986**	-4	*O-138(7-134-0)/1-1	0.2
1937	Was-A	103	419	60	117	21	10	8	84	27	35	.279	.329	.434	763	95	-5	3	2	-0	.984	5	*O-102(98-4-0)	-0.5
1938	Was-A	125	470	79	142	23	6	21	95	38	40	.302	.357	.511	868	123	14	2	1	0	.983	-8	*O-117(112-8-0)	0.0
1939	Bos-N	93	330	39	93	17	5	7	43	22	40	.282	.331	.427	758	110	3	0			.982	-0	O-82(81-1-0)	-0.2
	*Cin-N	9	21	0	3	0	0	0	1	2	3	.143	.217	.143	360	-1	-3	0			.938	1	/O-5(5-0-0)	-0.2
	Yr	102	351	39	96	17	5	7	44	24	43	.274	.324	.410	734	103	0	0			.978	1	O-87(86-1-0)	-0.4
1940	Phi-A	37	81	7	25	4	0	1	19	4	8	.309	.341	.395	736	92	-1	0	0	0	.963	2	O-18(18-0-0)	0.0
1941	Phi-A	9	24	1	3	1	0	0	1	1	2	.125	.160	.167	327	-14	-4	0	0	0	1.000	1	/O-5(5-0-0)	-0.4
1943	Bos-A	40	133	9	27	5	0	1	12	8	21	.203	.248	.263	511	49	-9	0	1	-0	.986	-2	O-33(33-0-0)	-1.4
1944	Phi-A	4	6	1	3	0	0	0	2	0	0	.500	.500	.500	1000	189	1	0	0	0	1.000	-0	/O-2(2-0-0)	0.0
Total	20	2215	8759	1507	2927	539	149	307	1827	615	737	.334	.380	.535	915	132	363	88	64		.982	53	*O-2142L/1-1	26.9

YEAR	TM/L	G	AB	R	H	2B	3B	HR	RBI	BB	SO	AVG	OBP	SLG	OPS	OPS+	BR+	SB	CS	SBR	FA	FR	G/POS	TPR
■ **BRIAN SIMMONS**	Simmons, Brian Lee b: 9/4/73, Lebanon, Pa. BB/TR, 6'2", 185 lbs. Deb: 9/21/98																							
1998	Chi-A	5	19	4	7	0	0	2	6	0	2	.368	.368	.684	1053	170	2	0	1	-0	1.000	-0	/O-5(2-4-0)	0.1
1999	Chi-A	54	126	14	29	3	3	4	17	9	30	.230	.281	.397	678	70	-6	4	0	1	.976	-4	O-46(28-11-9)/D-3	-0.9
Total	2	59	145	18	36	3	3	6	23	9	32	.248	.292	.434	727	83	-4	4	1	1	.979	-4	/O-51(30-15-9),D-3	-0.8
■ **HACK SIMMONS**	Simmons, George Washington b: 1/29/1885, Brooklyn, N.Y. d: 4/26/42, Arverne, N.Y. BR/TR, 5'8", 179 lbs. Deb: 4/15/10 Career OF: (74-LF 1-CF 13-RF)																							
1910	Det-A	42	110	12	25	3	1	0	9	10		.227	.303	.273	576	75	-3	1			.984	-0	1-22/3-7,O-2(0-1-1)	-0.4
1912	NY-A	110	401	45	96	17	2	0	41	33		.239	.308	.292	600	68	-17	19			.946	-21	2-88,1-13/S-4	-3.6
1914	Bal-F	114	352	50	95	16	5	1	38	32	26	.270	.341	.352	693	86	-11	7			.894	-8	O-73L,2-26/1-4,S3	-2.3
1915	Bal-F	39	88	8	18	7	1	1	14	10	9	.205	.293	.341	634	76	-4	1			1.000	-3	2-13,O-13(13-0-0)	-0.9
Total	4	305	951	115	234	43	9	2	102	85	35	.246	.318	.317	635	76	-35	28			.953	-32	2-127/O-88L,1-39,3S	-7.2
■ **JOHN SIMMONS**	Simmons, John Earl b: 7/7/24, Birmingham, Ala. BR/TR, 6'1.5", 192 lbs. Deb: 4/22/49																							
1949	Was-A	62	93	12	20	0	0	0	5	11	6	.215	.298	.215	513	38	-8	0	0	0	1.000	-5	O-26(18-0-8)	-1.4
■ **JOE SIMMONS**	Simmons, Joseph S. b: 6/13/1845, New York, N.Y. 5'9", 166 lbs. Deb: 5/8/1871 M																							
1871	Chi-n	27	129	29	28	6	1	0	17	1	0	.217	.223	.279	502	39	-11	4	1	1	.894	-1	*O-25(0-9-17)/1-2	-0.7
1872	Cle-n	18	90	11	23	5	1	0	9	1	2	.256	.264	.333	597	87	-1	1	0	0	.938	0	1-15/O-3(1-0-2)	0.0
1875	Wes-n	13	53	5	9	1	0	0	4	0	2	.170	.170	.189	358	23	-4	1	2	-0	.733	-1	O-10(0-9-1)/1-3,M	-0.4
Total	3 n	58	272	45	60	12	2	0	30	2	4	.221	.226	.279	506	51	-16	6	3	0	.855	-1	/O-38(1-18-20),1-20	-1.1
■ **NELSON SIMMONS**	Simmons, Nelson Bernard b: 6/27/63, Washington, D.C. BB/TR, 6'1", 185 lbs. Deb: 9/4/84																							
1984	Det-A	9	30	4	13	2	0	0	3	2	5	.433	.469	.500	969	169	3	1	0	0	1.000	-1	/O-5(2-0-4),D-4	0.2
1985	Det-A	75	251	31	60	11	0	10	33	26	41	.239	.310	.402	713	94	-2	1	0	0	.945	-1	O-38(25-0-13),D-31	-0.6
1987	Bal-A	16	49	3	13	1	1	1	4	3	8	.265	.308	.388	695	85	-1	0	1	-0	1.000	1	O-13(0-0-13)/D-1	-0.1
Total	3	100	330	38	86	14	1	11	40	31	54	.261	.324	.409	733	99	-1	2	1	0	.963	-1	/O-56(27-0-30),D-36	-0.5
■ **TED SIMMONS**	Simmons, Ted Lyle b: 8/9/49, Highland Park, Mich. BB/TR, 6', 200 lbs. Deb: 9/21/68 Career OF: (37-LF 0-CF 3-RF)																							
1968	StL-N	2	3	0	1	0	0	0	0	1	1	.333	.500	.333	833	156	0	0	0	0	1.000	-0	/C-2	0.0
1969	StL-N	5	14	0	3	0	1	0	3	1	1	.214	.267	.357	624	73	-1	0	0	0	.957	-1	/C-4	-0.2
1970	StL-N	82	284	29	69	8	2	3	24	37	37	.243	.334	.317	651	74	-10	2	2	-0	.990	-3	C-79	-0.9
1971	StL-N	133	510	64	155	32	4	7	77	36	50	.304	.353	.424	777	115	10	1	3	-1	.989	-13	*C-130	0.2
1972	StL-N☆	152	594	70	180	36	6	16	96	29	57	.303	.338	.465	802	127	19	1	3	-1	.991	6	*C-135,1-15	3.1
1973	StL-N★	161	619	62	192	36	2	13	91	61	47	.310	.374	.438	812	124	21	2	2	-0	.987	10	*C-153/1-6,O-2(0-0-2)	3.8
1974	StL-N☆	152	599	66	163	33	6	20	103	47	35	.272	.331	.447	779	117	11	0	0	0	.986	-4	*C-141,1-12	1.3
1975	StL-N	157	581	80	193	32	3	18	100	63	35	.332	.398	.491	889	141	32	1	3	-1	.983	-6	*C-154/1-2,O-2(2-0-0)	3.3
1976	StL-N	150	546	60	159	35	3	5	75	73	35	.291	.375	.394	769	117	14	0	7	-2	.993	-9	*C-113,1-30/O-7L,3	0.5
1977	StL-N★	150	516	82	164	25	3	21	95	79	37	.318	.410	.500	910	145	35	2	6	-2	.987	-14	*C-143/O-1(0-0-1)	2.6
1978	StL-N★	152	516	71	148	40	5	22	80	77	39	.287	.383	.512	894	150	35	1	1	-0	.988	-6	*C-134,O-23(23-0-0)	3.6
1979	StL-N†	123	448	68	127	22	0	26	87	61	34	.283	.374	.507	881	137	23	0	1	-0	.985	-5	*C-122	2.3
1980	StL-N	145	495	84	150	33	2	21	98	59	45	.303	.379	.505	885	140	27	1	0	0	.985	-9	*C-129/O-5(5-0-0)	2.4
1981	*Mil-A★	100	380	45	82	13	3	14	61	23	32	.216	.266	.376	642	88	-8	0	1	-0	.980	-9	*C-75,D-22/1-4	-1.5
1982	*Mil-A	137	539	73	145	29	0	23	97	32	40	.269	.312	.451	763	114	8	0	0	0	**.995**	-1	*C-121,D-15	1.2
1983	Mil-A★	153	600	76	185	39	3	13	108	41	51	.308	.355	.448	803	129	23	4	2	0	.975	-4	C-86,D-66	2.1
1984	Mil-A	132	497	44	110	23	2	4	52	30	40	.221	.270	.300	570	60	-27	3	0	1	.995	-1	D-77,1-37,3-14	-3.4
1985	Mil-A	143	528	60	144	28	2	12	76	57	32	.273	.345	.402	746	104	4	1	1	-0	.992	-3	D-99,1-28,C-15,/3-2	-0.4
1986	Atl-N	76	127	14	32	5	0	4	25	12	14	.252	.321	.386	707	89	-2	1	0	0	.964	-3	1-14,C-10/3-9	-0.6
1987	Atl-N	73	177	20	49	8	0	4	30	21	23	.277	.354	.390	743	92	-2	1	1	-0	.984	-1	1-28,C-15/3-2	-0.4
1988	Atl-N	78	107	6	21	6	0	2	11	15	9	.196	.295	.308	603	70	-4	0	0	0	.993	-1	1-19,C-10	-0.6
Total	21	2456	8680	1074	2472	483	47	248	1389	855	694	.285	.352	.437	789	118	209	21	33	-7	.987	-79	*C-1771,D-279,1/O3	18.4
■ **MIKE SIMMS**	Simms, Michael Howard b: 1/12/67, Orange, Cal. BR/TR, 6'4", 185 lbs. Deb: 9/5/90 Career OF: (15-LF 0-CF 126-RF)																							
1990	Hou-N	12	13	3	4	1	0	1	2	0	4	.308	.308	.615	923	152	1	0	0	0	1.000	-0	/1-6	0.0
1991	Hou-N	49	123	18	25	5	0	3	16	18	38	.203	.305	.317	622	80	-3	1	0	0	.889	-5	O-41(1-0-41)	-1.0
1992	Hou-N	15	24	1	6	1	0	1	3	2	9	.250	.333	.417	750	116	0	0	0	0	1.000	-1	/O-9(0-0-9),1-1	-0.1
1994	Hou-N	6	12	1	1	1	0	0	0	0	5	.083	.083	.167	250	-39	-2	1	0	0	.857	-0	/O-3(0-0-3)	-0.3
1995	Hou-N	50	121	14	31	4	0	9	24	13	28	.256	.343	.512	855	131	5	1	2	-0	.995	-1	1-25,O-12(0-0-12)	0.1
1996	Hou-N	49	68	6	12	2	1	1	8	4	16	.176	.233	.279	512	37	-6	1	0	0	1.000	-1	O-12(9-0-3)/1-5	-0.7
1997	Tex-A	59	111	13	28	8	0	5	22	8	27	.252	.303	.459	762	90	-2	0	1	-0	.958	-4	D-28,O-19(2-0-17)/1-2	-0.8
1998	*Tex-A	86	186	36	55	11	0	16	46	24	47	.296	.385	.613	998	148	13	0	1	-0	1.000	-8	O-43R,D-26,1-16	0.1
1999	Tex-A	4	2	0	1	0	0	0	0	0	1	.500	.500	.500	1000	150	0	0	0	0	1.000	-0	/1-1,O-1(0-0-1),D-2	0.0
Total	9	330	660	92	163	33	1	36	121	69	175	.247	.326	.464	789	109	5	4	4	-1	.954	-20	O-140R/D-56,1-56	-2.6
■ **HANK SIMON**	Simon, Henry Joseph b: 8/25/1862, Hawkinsville, N.Y. d: 1/1/25, Albany, N.Y. BR/TR, Deb: 10/7/1887																							
1887	Cle-a	3	10	1	1	0	0	0	0	0		.100	.100	.100	200	-45	-2	0			1.000	-1	/O-3(3-0-0)	-0.2
1890	Bro-a	89	373	66	96	17	11	0	38	34		.257	.323	.362	685	105	2	23			.951	6	O-89(89-0-0)	0.5
	Syr-a	38	156	33	47	5	3	2	23	17		.301	.370	.410	780	145	9	12			.941	-3	O-38(36-2-0)	0.5
	Yr	127	529	99	143	22	14	2	61	51		.270	.337	.376	713	116	10	35			.948	3	*O-127(125-2-0)	1.0
Total	2	130	539	100	144	22	14	2	61	51		.267	.333	.371	704	113	9	35			.949	3	O-130(128-2-0)	0.8
■ **MIKE SIMON**	Simon, Michael Edward b: 4/13/1883, Hayden, Ind. d: 6/10/63, Los Angeles, Cal. BR/TR, 5'11", 188 lbs. Deb: 6/27/09																							
1909	Pit-N	12	18	2	3	0	0	0	2	1		.167	.211	.167	377	16	-2	0			.917	0	/C-9	-0.1
1910	Pit-N	22	50	3	10	0	1	0	5	1	2	.200	.216	.240	456	31	-4	1			1.000	-4	C-14	-0.8
1911	Pit-N	71	215	19	49	4	3	0	22	10	14	.228	.275	.274	550	52	-14	1			.968	0	C-68	-0.9
1912	Pit-N	42	113	10	34	2	1	0	11	5	9	.301	.331	.336	667	84	-3	1			.991	3	C-40	0.3
1913	Pit-N	92	255	23	63	6	2	1	17	10	15	.247	.281	.298	579	68	-11	3			.975	19	C-92	1.5
1914	StL-F	93	276	21	57	11	2	0	21	18	21	.207	.263	.261	523	41	-27	2			.984	12	C-78	-0.9
1915	Bro-F	47	142	7	25	5	1	0	12	9	12	.176	.225	.225	451	27	-16	1			.992	-0	C-45	-1.4
Total	7	379	1069	85	241	28	10	1	90	54	73	.225	.269	.273	542	51	-77	9			.979	30	C-346	-2.3
■ **RANDALL SIMON**	Simon, Randall Carlito b: 5/26/75, Willemstad, Curacao BL/TL, 6', 180 lbs. Deb: 9/1/97																							
1997	Atl-N	13	14	2	6	1	0	0	1	1	2	.429	.467	.500	967	150	1	0	0	0	1.000	0	/1-6	0.1
1998	Atl-N	7	16	2	3	0	0	0	4	0	1	.188	.188	.188	375	-1	-2	0	0	0	1.000	-0	/1-4	-0.3
1999	Atl-N	90	218	26	69	16	0	5	25	17	25	.317	.369	.459	827	108	3	2	2	-0	.994	-2	1-70	-0.5
Total	3	110	248	30	78	17	0	5	30	18	28	.315	.363	.444	807	103	1	2	2	-0	.995	-2	/1-80	-0.7
■ **SYL SIMON**	Simon, Sylvester Adam "Sammy" b: 12/14/1897, Evansville, Ind. d: 2/28/73, Chandler, Ind. BR/TR, 5'10.5", 170 lbs. Deb: 10/1/23																							
1923	StL-A	1	1	0	0	0	0	0	0	0	0	.000	.000	.000	0	-95	-0	0	0	0	.000	0	H	0.0
1924	StL-A	23	32	5	8	1	1	0	6	3	5	.250	.314	.344	658	66	-2	0	0	0	.889	-0	/3-6,S-5	-0.1
Total	2	24	33	5	8	1	1	0	6	3	5	.242	.306	.333	639	61	-2	0	0	0	.889	-0	/3-6,S-5	-0.1
■ **MEL SIMONS**	Simons, Melbern Ellis "Butch" b: 7/1/1900, Carlyle, Ill. d: 11/10/74, Paducah, Ky. BL/TR, 5'10", 175 lbs. Deb: 4/14/31																							
1931	Chi-A	68	189	24	52	9	0	0	12	12	17	.275	.318	.323	641	73	-7	1	1	-0	.950	-9	O-59(15-45-0)	-1.7
1932	Chi-A	7	5	0	0	0	0	0	0	0	1	.000	.000	.000	0	-99	-2	0	0	0	1.000	-3	/O-6(4-2-0)	-0.4
Total	2	75	194	24	52	9	0	0	12	12	18	.268	.311	.314	625	69	-9	1	1	-0	.951	-12	/O-65(19-47-0)	-2.1
■ **HARRY SIMPSON**	Simpson, Harry Leon "Suitcase" or "Goody" b: 12/3/25, Atlanta, Ga. d: 4/3/79, Akron, Ohio BL/TR, 6'1", 180 lbs. Deb: 4/21/51 Career OF: (44-LF 136-CF 415-RF)																							
1951	Cle-A	122	332	51	76	7	0	7	24	45	48	.229	.325	.313	638	77	-10	6	4	-0	.971	-4	O-68(5-8-58),1-50	-1.7
1952	Cle-A	146	545	66	145	21	10	10	65	56	82	.266	.337	.396	733	111	6	5	3	0	.988	-4	*O-127(0-11-117),1-28	-0.2
1953	Cle-A	82	242	25	55	3	1	7	22	18	27	.227	.284	.335	618	68	-11	0	0	0	.968	-6	O-69(1-7-62)/1-2	-2.0
1955	Cle-A	3	1	1	0	0	0	0	0	2	0	.000	.667	.000	667	88	0	0	0	0	.000	0	H	0.0

YEAR	TM/L	G	AB	R	H	2B	3B	HR	RBI	BB	SO	AVG	OBP	SLG	OPS	OPS+	BR+	SB	CS	SBR	FA	FR	G/POS	TPR
	KC-A	112	396	42	119	16	7	5	52	34	61	.301	.359	.414	773	106	3	3	5	-1	.978	1	*O-100(4-91-10)/1-3	-0.1
	Yr	115	397	43	119	16	7	5	52	36	61	.300	.361	.413	774	106	3	3	5	-1	.978	1	*O-100(4-91-10)/1-3	-0.1
1956	KC-A★	141	543	76	159	22	**11**	21	105	47	82	.293	.350	.490	840	119	13	2	3	-1	.965	-15	*O-111(0-19-96),1-32	-0.9
1957	KC-A	50	179	24	53	9	6	6	24	12	28	.296	.340	.514	854	128	6	0	1	-0	.996	1	1-27,O-21(0-0-21)	0.4
	*NY-A	75	224	27	56	7	3	7	39	19	36	.250	.309	.402	710	94	-2	1	0	0	.952	-2	O-42(16-0-26),1-21	-0.8
	Yr	125	403	51	109	16	**9**	13	63	31	64	.270	.323	.452	774	110	4	1	1	-0	.957	-2	O-63(16-0-47),1-48	-0.4
1958	NY-A	24	51	1	11	2	1	0	6	6	12	.216	.310	.294	604	70	-2	0	0	0	1.000	-3	O-15(8-0-9)	-0.5
	KC-A	78	212	21	56	7	1	7	27	26	33	.264	.345	.406	750	104	1	0	2	-1	.990	-3	1-43,O-11(9-0-2)	-0.5
	Yr	102	263	22	67	9	2	7	33	32	45	.255	.338	.384	722	98	-0	0	2	-1	.990	-5	1-43,O-26(17-0-11)	-1.0
1959	KC-A	8	14	1	4	0	0	1	2	2	4	.286	.412	.500	912	146	1	0	0	0	1.000	0	/1-4	0.1
	Chi-A	38	75	5	14	5	1	2	13	4	14	.187	.228	.360	588	59	-5	0	0	0	.947	-2	O-12(0-0-12)/1-1	-0.7
	Yr	46	89	6	18	5	1	3	15	6	18	.202	.260	.382	642	75	-3	0	0	0	.947	-2	O-12(0-0-12)/1-5	-0.6
	Pit-N	9	15	3	4	2	0	0	2	0	2	.267	.267	.400	667	75	-1	0	0	0	1.000	-0	/O-3(1-0-2)	-0.1
Total	8	888	2829	343	752	101	41	73	381	271	429	.266	.332	.408	740	102	-0	17	18	-3	.974	-37	O-579R,1-211	-7.0
■ **JOE SIMPSON** Simpson, Joe Allen b: 12/31/51, Purcell, Okla. BL/TL, 6'3", 175 lbs. Deb: 9/2/75 Career OF: (100-LF 226-CF 198-RF)																								
1975	LA-N	9	6	3	2	0	0	0	0	0	2	.333	.333	.333	667	89	-0	0	0	0	1.000	-2	/O-6(0-6-0)	-0.2
1976	LA-N	23	30	2	4	1	0	0	0	1	6	.133	.161	.167	328	-7	-4	0	1	-0	1.000	-4	O-20(5-6-9)	-1.0
1977	LA-N	29	23	2	4	0	0	0	1	2	6	.174	.240	.174	414	13	-3	1	1	-0	.957	-6	O-28(5-7-16)/1-1	-1.0
1978	LA-N	10	5	1	2	0	0	0	1	0	2	.400	.400	.400	800	125	0	0	0	0	1.000	-3	O-10(3-2-6)	-0.3
1979	Sea-A	120	265	29	75	11	0	2	27	11	21	.283	.314	.347	661	77	-9	6	3	0	.966	-5	*O-105(27-5-73)/D-3	-1.6
1980	Sea-A	129	365	42	91	15	3	3	34	28	43	.249	.305	.332	636	74	-13	17	4	2	.977	-8	*O-119(24-36-63)/1-3	-2.3
1981	Sea-A	91	288	32	64	11	3	2	30	15	41	.222	.263	.302	565	60	-15	12	3	2	.978	-0	O-88(0-86-2)	-1.5
1982	Sea-A	105	296	39	76	14	4	2	23	22	48	.257	.313	.351	664	80	-8	8	14	-3	.984	-7	O-97(32-59-10)	-2.0
1983	KC-A	91	119	16	20	2	2	0	8	11	21	.168	.250	.218	468	30	-11	1	1	-0	.995	-0	1-54,O-38C/P-2,D-1	-1.3
Total	9	607	1397	166	338	54	12	9	124	90	190	.242	.291	.317	608	67	-63	45	27	0	.978	-35	O-511C/1-58,D-4,P-2	-11.2
■ **MARTY SIMPSON** Simpson, Martin b: Baltimore, Md. Deb: 5/14/1873																								
1873	Mar-n	4	15	4	2	0	0	0	2	0	0	.133	.133	.133	267	-27	-2	0	0	0	.792	0	/2-3,C-1	-0.1
■ **DICK SIMPSON** Simpson, Richard Charles b: 7/28/43, Washington, D.C. BR/TR, 6'4", 176 lbs. Deb: 9/21/62																								
1962	LA-A	6	8	1	2	1	0	0	1	2	3	.250	.400	.375	775	114	0	0	0	0	1.000	-1	/O-4(4-0-1)	0.0
1964	LA-A	21	50	11	7	1	0	2	4	8	15	.140	.259	.280	539	55	-3	2	2	-0	1.000	-2	O-16(0-16-0)	-0.6
1965	Cal-A	8	27	2	6	1	0	0	3	2	8	.222	.276	.259	535	54	-2	1	0	0	.875	-1	/O-8(0-8-0)	-0.3
1966	Cin-N	92	84	26	20	2	0	4	14	10	32	.238	.333	.405	738	96	-0	0	1	-0	.921	-18	O-64(9-10-46)	-2.1
1967	Cin-N	44	54	8	14	3	0	1	6	7	11	.259	.344	.370	715	94	-0	0	1	-0	.973	-2	O-26(1-4-21)	-0.3
1968	StL-N	26	56	11	13	0	0	3	8	8	21	.232	.328	.393	721	117	1	0	1	-0	1.000	-3	O-22(0-0-22)	-0.4
	Hou-N	59	177	25	33	7	2	3	11	20	61	.186	.284	.299	583	77	-5	4	4	-1	.970	-6	O-49(13-16-23)	-1.6
	Yr	85	233	36	46	7	2	6	19	28	82	.197	.294	.322	616	86	-4	4	5	-1	.979	-9	O-71(13-16-45)	-2.0
1969	NY-A	6	11	2	3	2	0	0	4	3	6	.273	.429	.455	883	153	1	0	0	0	1.000	-1	/O-5(3-2-0)	0.0
	Sea-A	26	51	8	9	2	0	2	5	4	17	.176	.236	.333	570	59	-3	3	1	0	1.000	-3	O-17(1-16-0)	-0.6
	Yr	32	62	10	12	4	0	2	9	7	23	.194	.275	.355	630	77	-2	3	1	0	1.000	-4	O-22(4-18-0)	-0.6
Total	7	288	518	94	107	19	2	15	56	64	174	.207	.301	.338	639	84	-11	10	10	-1	.967	-35	O-211(31-72-113)	-5.9
■ **DUKE SIMS** Sims, Duane B b: 6/5/41, Salt Lake City, Ut. BL/TR, 6'2", 205 lbs. Deb: 9/22/64 Career OF: (35-LF 0-CF 19-RF)																								
1964	Cle-A	2	6	0	0	0	0	0	0	0	2	.000	.000	.000	0	-99	-2	0	0	0	1.000	1	/C-1	-0.1
1965	Cle-A	48	118	9	21	0	0	6	15	15	33	.178	.271	.331	601	69	-5	0	0	0	.980	-2	C-40	-0.5
1966	Cle-A	52	133	12	35	2	2	6	19	11	31	.263	.338	.444	781	122	4	0	1	-0	.975	-5	C-48	0.1
1967	Cle-A	88	272	25	55	8	2	12	37	30	64	.202	.295	.379	674	97	-1	3	3	-0	.989	-3	C-85	-0.1
1968	Cle-A	122	361	48	90	21	0	11	44	62	68	.249	.367	.399	766	134	17	1	3	-1	.983	-1	C-84,1-31/O-4(2-0-2)	2.0
1969	Cle-A	114	326	40	77	8	0	18	45	66	80	.236	.374	.426	801	120	10	1	2	-0	.991	-4	*C-102/O-3(2-0-1),1-1	1.1
1970	Cle-A	110	345	46	91	12	0	23	56	46	59	.264	.360	.499	859	128	13	0	4	-1	.993	-2	C-39,O-36L,1-29	0.9
1971	LA-N	90	230	23	63	7	2	6	25	30	39	.274	.360	.400	760	122	7	0	1	-0	.992	0	C-74	1.1
1972	LA-N	51	151	7	29	7	0	2	11	17	23	.192	.278	.278	556	60	-8	0	0	0	.989	-1	C-48	-0.8
	*Det-A	38	98	11	31	4	0	4	19	19	18	.316	.432	.480	912	166	9	0	0	0	.994	-3	C-25/O-4(0-0-4)	0.8
1973	Det-A	80	252	31	61	10	0	8	30	30	36	.242	.327	.377	704	92	-3	1	2	-0	.979	2	C-68/O-6(5-0-1)	0.1
	NY-A	4	9	3	3	0	0	1	1	3	1	.333	.500	.667	1167	234	2	0	0	0	1.000	1	/C-1,D-2	0.2
	Yr	84	261	34	64	10	0	9	31	33	37	.245	.334	.387	721	97	-1	1	2	-0	.979	2	C-69/O-6(5-0-1),D-2	0.3
1974	NY-A	5	15	1	2	1	0	0	2	1	5	.133	.188	.200	388	12	-2	0	0	0	1.000	-0	/C-1,D-3	-0.2
	Tex-A	39	106	7	22	0	0	3	6	8	24	.208	.282	.292	575	67	-4	0	0	0	.970	-3	C-30/O-1(0-0-1),D-2	-0.6
	Yr	44	121	8	24	1	0	3	8	9	29	.198	.271	.281	552	60	-6	0	0	0	.971	-3	C-31/D-5,O-1(0-0-1)	-0.8
Total	11	843	2422	263	580	80	6	100	310	338	483	.239	.341	.401	742	111	38	6	16	-4	.986	-20	C-646/1-61,O-54L,D	4.0
■ **GREG SIMS** Sims, Gregory Emmett b: 6/28/46, San Francisco, Cal BB/TR, 6', 190 lbs. Deb: 4/15/66																								
1966	Hou-N	7	6	1	1	0	0	0	0	1	3	.167	.286	.167	452	32	-1	0	0	0	.500	-0	/O-1(1-0-0)	-0.1
■ **MATT SINATRO** Sinatro, Matthew Stephen b: 3/22/60, Hartford, Conn. BR/TR, 5'9", 175 lbs. Deb: 9/22/81																								
1981	Atl-N	12	32	4	9	1	1	0	4	5	4	.281	.378	.375	753	111	1	1	0	0	1.000	4	C-12	0.6
1982	Atl-N	37	81	10	11	2	0	1	4	4	9	.136	.176	.198	374	4	-10	0	1	-0	1.000	4	C-35	-0.6
1983	Atl-N	7	12	0	2	0	0	0	2	2	1	.167	.286	.167	452	26	-1	0	0	0	.967	2	/C-7	0.1
1984	Atl-N	2	4	0	0	0	0	0	0	0	0	.000	.000	.000	0	-93	-1	0	0	0	1.000	-0	/C-2	-0.2
1987	Oak-A	6	3	0	0	0	0	0	0	0	1	.000	.000	.000	0	-99	-1	0	0	0	1.000	-0	/C-6	-0.1
1988	Oak-A	10	9	1	3	2	0	0	5	0	1	.333	.333	.556	889	149	1	0	0	0	1.000	2	/C-9	0.3
1989	Det-A	13	25	2	3	0	0	0	1	1	3	.120	.185	.120	305	-13	-4	0	0	0	1.000	0	C-13	-0.3
1990	Sea-A	30	50	2	15	1	0	0	4	4	10	.300	.352	.320	672	88	-1	1	0	0	.992	7	C-28	0.7
1991	Sea-A	5	8	1	2	0	0	0	1	1	1	.250	.333	.250	583	64	-0	0	0	0	1.000	1	/C-5	0.1
1992	Sea-A	18	28	0	3	0	0	0	0	0	5	.107	.107	.107	214	-40	-5	0	0	0	1.000	0	C-18	-0.5
Total	10	140	252	20	48	6	1	1	21	17	35	.190	.244	.234	479	34	-22	2	1	0	.996	19	C-135	0.1
■ **HOSEA SINER** Siner, Hosea John b: 3/20/1885, Shelburn, Ind. d: 6/10/48, Sullivan, Ind. BR/TR, 5'10.5", 185 lbs. Deb: 7/28/09																								
1909	Bos-N	10	23	1	3	0	0	0	1	2		.130	.200	.130	330	3	-3	0			.909	-1	/3-5,2-1,S-1	-0.4
■ **CHRIS SINGLETON** Singleton, Christopher Verdell b: 8/15/72, Martinez, Cal. BL/TL, 6'2", 195 lbs. Deb: 4/10/99																								
1999	Chi-A	133	496	72	149	31	6	17	72	22	45	.300	.331	.490	821	106	3	20	5	3	.990	17	*O-127(11-121-1)/D-2	2.1
2000	*Chi-A	147	511	83	130	22	5	11	62	35	85	.254	.303	.382	685	71	-23	22	7	2	.992	3	*O-145(19-143-0)	-1.5
Total	2	280	1007	155	279	53	11	28	134	57	130	.277	.317	.435	752	88	-21	42	12	5	.991	20	O-272(30-264-1)/D-2	0.6
■ **DUANE SINGLETON** Singleton, Duane Earl b: 8/6/72, Staten Island, N.Y. BL/TR, 6'1", 170 lbs. Deb: 8/4/94																								
1994	Mil-A	2	0	0	0	0	0	0	0	0	0	—	—	—	—	—	0	0	0	0	1.000	-1	/O-2(0-2-0)	-0.1
1995	Mil-A	13	31	0	2	0	0	0	0	1	10	.065	.094	.065	158	-55	-7	1	0	0	1.000	-1	O-11(3-9-0)	-0.7
1996	Det-A	18	56	5	9	1	0	0	3	4	15	.161	.230	.179	408	5	-8	0	2	-1	1.000	0	O-15(3-15-0)	-0.8
Total	3	33	87	5	11	1	0	0	3	5	25	.126	.183	.138	321	-16	-15	1	2	-0	1.000	-2	/O-28(6-26-0)	-1.6
■ **KEN SINGLETON** Singleton, Kenneth Wayne b: 6/10/47, New York, N.Y. BB/TR, 6'4", 213 lbs. Deb: 6/24/70 Career OF: (242-LF 4-CF 1313-RF)																								
1970	NY-N	69	198	22	52	8	0	5	26	30	48	.263	.362	.379	741	99	0	1	1	-0	.968	-0	O-51(26-0-26)	-0.3
1971	NY-N	115	298	34	73	5	0	13	46	61	64	.245	.377	.393	769	120	10	0	1	-0	.974	-5	O-96(10-3-85)	0.0
1972	Mon-N	142	507	77	139	23	2	14	50	70	99	.274	.364	.410	775	118	13	5	10	-2	.972	-0	*O-137(111-0-29)	0.2
1973	Mon-N	162	560	100	169	26	2	23	103	123	91	.302	**.429**	.479	908	146	41	2	8	-2	.983	3	*O-161(2-0-161)	3.4
1974	Mon-N	148	511	68	141	20	2	9	74	93	84	.276	.387	.376	763	108	9	5	2	0	.955	-9	*O-143(0-0-143)	-0.7
1975	Bal-A	155	586	88	176	37	4	15	55	118	82	.300	.418	.454	872	156	50	3	5	-1	.990	-6	*O-155(0-0-155)	3.4
1976	Bal-A	154	544	62	151	25	2	13	70	79	76	.278	.369	.403	772	134	25	2	2	-0	.983	-3	*O-134(80-0-63),D-19	1.5
1977	Bal-A★	152	536	90	176	24	0	24	99	107	101	.328	.442	.507	949	168	57	0	1	-0	.986	1	*O-150(0-0-150)/D-1	4.8

YEAR	TM/L	G	AB	R	H	2B	3B	HR	RBI	BB	SO	AVG	OBP	SLG	OPS	OPS+	BR+	SB	CS	SBR	FA	FR	G/POS	TPR
1978	Bal-A	149	502	67	147	21	2	20	81	98	94	.293	.410	.462	872	**154**	41	0	0	0	.976	-13	*O-140(4-0-139)/D-5	2.1
1979	*Bal-A★	159	570	93	168	29	1	35	111	109	118	.295	.409	.533	942	158	49	3	1	0	.981	-6	*O-143(7-0-136),D-16	3.5
1980	Bal-A	156	583	85	177	28	3	24	104	92	94	.304	.399	.485	885	143	37	0	2	-1	.984	-10	*O-151(0-0-151)/D-5	1.7
1981	Bal-A★	103	363	48	101	16	1	13	49	61	59	.278	.382	.435	817	135	18	0	0	0	**1.000**	-3	O-72(0-1-72),D-30	1.1
1982	Bal-A	156	561	71	141	27	2	14	77	86	93	.251	.353	.381	734	102	4	0	1	-0	1.000	-0	*D-148/O-5(2-0-3)	-0.1
1983	*Bal-A	151	507	52	140	21	3	18	84	99	83	.276	.395	.436	831	131	26	0	2	-1	.000	0	*D-150	2.0
1984	Bal-A	111	363	28	78	7	1	6	36	37	60	.215	.287	.289	577	61	-19	0	0	0	.000	0	*D-103	-2.2
Total	15	2082	7189	985	2029	317	25	246	1065	1263	1246	.282	.391	.436	827	132	361	21	36	-8	.980	-52	*O-1538R,D-477	20.4

■ **FRED SINGTON** Sington, Frederic William b: 2/24/10, Birmingham, Ala. d: 8/20/98, Birmingham, Ala. BR/TR, 6'2", 215 lbs. Deb: 9/23/34

YEAR	TM/L	G	AB	R	H	2B	3B	HR	RBI	BB	SO	AVG	OBP	SLG	OPS	OPS+	BR+	SB	CS	SBR	FA	FR	G/POS	TPR
1934	Was-A	9	35	2	10	2	0	0	6	4	3	.286	.359	.343	702	85	-1	0	1	-0	.933	-1	/O-9(3-0-6)	-0.2
1935	Was-A	20	22	1	4	0	0	0	3	5	1	.182	.333	.182	515	38	-2	0	0	0	.889	0	/O-4(2-0-2)	-0.2
1936	Was-A	25	94	13	30	8	0	1	28	15	9	.319	.413	.436	849	116	3	0	0	0	.946	-1	O-25(0-0-25)	0.0
1937	Was-A	78	228	27	54	15	4	3	36	37	33	.237	.348	.377	726	87	-4	1	1	-0	.961	-3	O-64(14-0-50)	-1.0
1938	Bro-N	17	53	10	19	6	1	2	5	13	5	.358	.493	.623	1115	200	8	1			1.000	-2	O-17(0-0-17)	0.5
1939	Bro-N	32	84	13	23	5	0	1	7	15	15	.274	.384	.369	753	100	1	0			.978	-1	O-22(7-0-15)	-0.1
Total	6	181	516	66	140	36	5	7	85	89	66	.271	.382	.401	783	104	5	2	2		.961	-7	O-141(26-0-115)	-1.0

■ **DICK SIPEK** Sipek, Richard Francis b: 1/16/23, Chicago, Ill. BL/TR, 5'9", 170 lbs. Deb: 4/28/45

YEAR	TM/L	G	AB	R	H	2B	3B	HR	RBI	BB	SO	AVG	OBP	SLG	OPS	OPS+	BR+	SB	CS	SBR	FA	FR	G/POS	TPR
1945	Cin-N	82	156	14	38	6	2	0	13	9	15	.244	.302	.308	609	71	-6	0			.972	-0	O-31(14-0-17)	-0.8

■ **JOHN SIPIN** Sipin, John White b: 8/29/46, Watsonville, Cal. BR/TR, 6'1.5", 175 lbs. Deb: 5/24/69

YEAR	TM/L	G	AB	R	H	2B	3B	HR	RBI	BB	SO	AVG	OBP	SLG	OPS	OPS+	BR+	SB	CS	SBR	FA	FR	G/POS	TPR
1969	SD-N	68	229	22	51	12	2	2	9	8	44	.223	.252	.319	571	61	-13	2	0	0	.976	-2	2-60	-1.1

■ **STEVE SISCO** Sisco, Steven Michael b: 12/2/69, Thousand Oaks, Cal. BR/TR, 5'10", 190 lbs. Deb: 5/6/2000

YEAR	TM/L	G	AB	R	H	2B	3B	HR	RBI	BB	SO	AVG	OBP	SLG	OPS	OPS+	BR+	SB	CS	SBR	FA	FR	G/POS	TPR
2000	Atl-N	25	27	4	5	0	0	1	2	3	4	.185	.267	.296	563	42	-2	0	0	0	1.000	-1	/O-6L,2-5,3-2,D-1	-0.3

■ **GEORGE SISLER** Sisler, George Harold "Georgeous George"
b: 3/24/1893, Manchester, Ohio d: 3/26/73, Richmond Heights, Mo. BL/TL, 5'11", 170 lbs. Deb: 6/28/15 FMCH Career OF: (12-LF 10-CF 15-RF)

YEAR	TM/L	G	AB	R	H	2B	3B	HR	RBI	BB	SO	AVG	OBP	SLG	OPS	OPS+	BR+	SB	CS	SBR	FA	FR	G/POS	TPR
1915	StL-A	81	274	28	78	10	2	3	29	7	27	.285	.307	.369	676	106	0	10	9	-1	.989	-3	1-36,O-29R,P-15	-0.6
1916	StL-A	151	580	83	177	21	11	4	76	40	37	.305	.355	.400	755	133	21	34	26	-2	.985	-2	*1-141/P-3,O-3C,3-2	1.4
1917	StL-A	135	539	60	190	30	9	2	52	30	19	.353	.390	.453	843	163	38	37			.985	4	*1-133/2-2	4.1
1918	StL-A	114	452	69	154	21	9	2	41	40	17	.341	.400	.440	841	159	31	**45**			.990	9	*1-114/P-2	4.0
1919	StL-A	132	511	96	180	31	15	10	83	27	20	.352	.390	.530	921	153	33	28			.991	13	*1-131	4.4
1920	StL-A	154	631	137	**257**	49	18	19	122	46	19	**.407**	.449	.632	1082	179	69	42	17	3	.990	15	*1-154/P-1	7.8
1921	StL-A	138	582	125	216	38	**18**	12	104	34	27	.371	.411	.560	971	137	31	**35**	11	**4**	.993	8	*1-138	3.1
1922	StL-A	142	586	**134**	**246**	42	**18**	8	105	49	14	**.420**	.467	.594	1061	169	**60**	**51**	19	**5**	.988	12	*1-141	**6.3**
1924	StL-A	151	636	94	194	27	10	9	74	31	29	.305	.340	.421	762	90	-11	19	17	-2	.984	1	*1-151,M	-2.1
1925	StL-A	150	649	100	224	21	15	12	105	27	24	.345	.371	.479	851	109	7	11	12	-2	.983	11	*1-150/P-1,M	0.5
1926	StL-A	150	613	78	178	21	12	7	71	30	30	.290	.327	.398	725	84	-16	12	8	-0	.987	-4	*1-149/P-1,M	-2.9
1927	StL-A	149	614	87	201	32	8	5	97	24	15	.327	.357	.430	787	100	-1	**27**	7	**3**	.984	11	*1-149	0.3
1928	Was-A	20	49	1	12	1	0	0	2	1	2	.245	.260	.265	525	39	-4	0	1	-0	1.000	-2	/1-5,O-5(5-0-0)	-0.7
	Bos-N	118	491	71	167	26	4	4	68	30	15	.340	.380	.434	814	119	13	11			.988	7	*1-118/P-1	1.2
1929	Bos-N	154	629	67	205	40	8	2	79	33	17	.326	.363	.424	788	98	-2	6			.982	3	*1-154	-0.8
1930	Bos-N	116	431	54	133	15	7	3	67	23	15	.309	.346	.397	743	82	-12	7			.987	5	*1-107	-1.3
Total	15	2055	8267	1284	2812	425	164	102	1175	472	327	.340	.379	.468	847	124	256	375	127		.987	88	*1-1971/O-37R,P23	24.7

■ **DICK SISLER** Sisler, Richard Allan b: 11/2/20, St.Louis, Mo. d: 11/20/98, Nashville, Tenn. BL/TR, 6'2", 205 lbs. Deb: 4/16/46 FMC

YEAR	TM/L	G	AB	R	H	2B	3B	HR	RBI	BB	SO	AVG	OBP	SLG	OPS	OPS+	BR+	SB	CS	SBR	FA	FR	G/POS	TPR
1946	*StL-N	83	235	17	61	11	2	3	42	14	28	.260	.307	.362	668	86	-5	0			.988	-2	1-37,O-29(29-0-0)	-1.1
1947	StL-N	46	74	4	15	2	1	0	9	3	8	.203	.234	.257	491	29	-8	0			.976	-0	1-10/O-5(5-0-0)	-0.8
1948	Phi-N	121	446	60	122	21	3	11	56	47	46	.274	.344	.408	752	105	3	1			.983	-4	*1-120	-0.5
1949	Phi-N	121	412	42	119	19	6	7	50	25	38	.289	.333	.415	748	102	0	0			.987	-9	1-96	-1.2
1950	*Phi-N★	141	523	79	155	29	4	13	83	64	50	.296	.373	.442	815	115	12	1			.987	2	*O-137(137-0-0)	0.4
1951	Phi-N	125	428	46	123	20	5	8	52	40	39	.287	.351	.414	765	107	4	1	0	0	.968	0	*O-111(111-0-0)	-0.4
1952	Cin-N	11	27	3	5	1	1	0	4	3	5	.185	.267	.296	563	56	-2	0	0	0	1.000	-1	/O-7(3-0-4)	-0.3
	StL-N	119	418	48	109	14	5	13	60	29	35	.261	.312	.411	723	99	-2	3	3	-0	.985	2	*1-114	-0.4
	Yr	130	445	51	114	15	6	13	64	32	40	.256	.309	.404	713	96	-3	3	3	-0	.985	1	*1-114/O-7(3-0-4)	-0.7
1953	StL-N	32	43	3	11	1	1	0	4	1	4	.256	.273	.326	598	55	-3	0	0	0	1.000	1	1-10	-0.2
Total	8	799	2606	302	720	118	28	55	360	226	253	.276	.336	.406	743	101	0	6	3		.985	-10	1-387,O-289(285-0-4)	-4.5

■ **SIBBY SISTI** Sisti, Sebastian Daniel b: 7/26/20, Buffalo, N.Y. BR/TR, 5'11", 175 lbs. Deb: 7/21/39 C Career OF: (29-LF 14-CF 35-RF)

YEAR	TM/L	G	AB	R	H	2B	3B	HR	RBI	BB	SO	AVG	OBP	SLG	OPS	OPS+	BR+	SB	CS	SBR	FA	FR	G/POS	TPR
1939	Bos-N	63	215	19	49	7	1	1	11	12	38	.228	.269	.284	552	52	-15	4			.994	0	2-34,3-17,S-10	-1.1
1940	Bos-N	123	459	73	115	19	5	6	34	36	64	.251	.311	.353	664	87	-8	4			.936	-2	*3-102,2-16	-0.6
1941	Bos-N	140	541	72	140	24	3	1	45	38	76	.259	.309	.320	628	81	-14	7			.916	-8	*3-137/2-2,S-2	-1.8
1942	Bos-N	129	407	50	86	11	4	4	35	45	55	.211	.296	.287	584	73	-14	5			.970	-4	*2-124/O-1(0-1-0)	-1.1
1946	Bos-N	1	0	0	0	0	0	0	0	0	0	—	—	—	—	—	0	0			.000	0	/3-1	0.0
1947	Bos-N	56	153	22	43	8	0	2	15	20	17	.281	.371	.373	744	100	1	2			.947	-9	S-51/2-1	-0.5
1948	*Bos-N	83	221	30	54	6	2	0	21	31	34	.244	.340	.290	630	73	-7	0			.972	-5	2-44,S-26	-0.9
1949	Bos-N	101	268	39	69	12	0	5	22	34	42	.257	.343	.358	701	93	-2	1			.989	-13	O-48L,2-21,S-18,/3	-1.5
1950	Bos-N	69	105	21	18	3	1	2	11	16	19	.171	.287	.276	563	52	-7	1			.931	0	S-23,2-19,3-13,/1O	-0.6
1951	Bos-N	114	362	46	101	20	2	2	38	32	50	.279	.341	.362	703	96	-2	4	5	-1	.944	-23	S-55,2-52/3-6,1O	-2.1
1952	Bos-N	90	245	19	52	10	1	4	24	14	43	.212	.255	.310	565	58	-15	2	0	0	.966	-12	2-33,O-23R,S-18,/3	-2.6
1953	Mil-N	38	23	8	5	1	0	0	4	5	2	.217	.357	.261	618	69	-1	0	0	0	1.000	4	2-13/S-6,3-4	0.4
1954	Mil-N	9	0	2	0	0	0	0	0	0	0	—	—	—	—	—	0	0	0	0	.000	0	R	0.0
Total	13	1016	2999	401	732	121	19	27	260	283	440	.244	.313	.324	637	79	-84	30	5		.973	-72	2-359,3-290,S/O1	-12.4

■ **ED SIXSMITH** Sixsmith, Edward b: 2/26/1863, Philadelphia, Pa. d: 12/12/26, Philadelphia, Pa. BR/TR, Deb: 9/11/1884

YEAR	TM/L	G	AB	R	H	2B	3B	HR	RBI	BB	SO	AVG	OBP	SLG	OPS	OPS+	BR+	SB	CS	SBR	FA	FR	G/POS	TPR
1884	Phi-N	1	2	0	0	0	0	0	0	0	0	.000	.000	.000	0	-99	-0				1.000	-1	/C-1	-0.1

■ **TED SIZEMORE** Sizemore, Theodore Crawford b: 4/15/45, Gadsden, Ala. BR/TR, 5'10", 165 lbs. Deb: 4/7/69 Career OF: (16-LF 0-CF 10-RF)

YEAR	TM/L	G	AB	R	H	2B	3B	HR	RBI	BB	SO	AVG	OBP	SLG	OPS	OPS+	BR+	SB	CS	SBR	FA	FR	G/POS	TPR
1969	LA-N	159	590	69	160	20	5	4	46	45	40	.271	.328	.342	670	95	-4	5	5	-1	.979	-6	*2-118,S-46/O-1L	0.2
1970	LA-N	96	340	40	104	10	1	1	34	34	19	.306	.369	.350	719	98	0	5	1	1	.984	-7	2-86/O-9(8-0-1),S-2	-0.1
1971	StL-N	135	478	53	126	14	5	3	42	42	26	.264	.324	.333	657	83	-10	4	6	-1	.976	-3	2-93,S-39,O-15R,/3	-0.4
1972	StL-N	120	439	53	116	17	4	2	38	37	36	.264	.327	.335	662	90	-6	8	3	1	.976	0	*2-111	0.3
1973	StL-N	142	521	69	147	22	1	1	54	68	34	.282	.367	.334	701	96	-0	6	4	-0	.981	9	*2-139/3-3	1.9
1974	StL-N	129	504	68	126	17	0	2	47	70	37	.250	.341	.296	637	80	-11	8	4	0	.980	13	*2-128/S-1,O-1(0-0-1)	1.1
1975	StL-N	153	562	56	135	23	1	3	49	45	37	.240	.299	.301	600	64	-27	1	5	-2	.972	-25	*2-153	-4.6
1976	LA-N	84	266	18	64	8	1	0	18	15	22	.241	.281	.278	559	60	-14	2	3	-1	.986	2	2-71/3-3,C-2	-0.9
1977	*Phi-N	152	519	64	146	20	3	4	47	52	40	.281	.348	.355	702	85	-9	8	11	-2	.986	9	*2-152	0.6
1978	*Phi-N	108	351	38	77	12	0	0	25	25	29	.219	.273	.254	527	48	-24	8	1	1	.978	4	*2-107	-1.4
1979	Chi-N	98	330	36	82	17	0	2	24	32	25	.248	.321	.318	639	68	-13	3	3	-0	.973	15	2-96	0.7
	Bos-A	26	88	12	23	7	0	1	6	4	5	.261	.301	.375	676	77	-3	1	0	0	.993	9	2-26/C-2	0.7
1980	Bos-A	9	23	1	5	1	0	0	0	0	0	.217	.217	.261	478	29	-2	0	0	0	.927	3	/2-8	0.1
Total	12	1411	5011	577	1311	188	21	23	430	469	350	.262	.327	.321	649	80	-124	59	46	-3	.979	25	*2-1288/S-88,O3C	-1.8

■ **FRANK SKAFF** Skaff, Francis Michael b: 9/30/13, LaCrosse, Wis. d: 4/12/88, Towson, Md. BR/TR, 5'10", 185 lbs. Deb: 9/11/35 MC

YEAR	TM/L	G	AB	R	H	2B	3B	HR	RBI	BB	SO	AVG	OBP	SLG	OPS	OPS+	BR+	SB	CS	SBR	FA	FR	G/POS	TPR
1935	Bro-N	6	11	4	6	1	1	0	3	0	2	.545	.545	.818	1364	267	2	0			.857	-0	/3-3	0.2
1943	Phi-A	32	64	8	18	2	1	1	8	6	11	.281	.343	.391	733	115	1	0	0	0	.976	1	1-18/3-3,S-1	0.2
Total	2	38	75	12	24	3	2	1	11	6	13	.320	.370	.453	824	138	4	0	0		.900	1	/1-18,3-6,S-1	0.4

■ **DAVE SKAGGS** Skaggs, David Lindsey b: 6/12/51, Santa Monica, Cal. BR/TR, 6'2", 200 lbs. Deb: 4/17/77

YEAR	TM/L	G	AB	R	H	2B	3B	HR	RBI	BB	SO	AVG	OBP	SLG	OPS	OPS+	BR+	SB	CS	SBR	FA	FR	G/POS	TPR
1977	Bal-A	80	216	22	62	9	1	1	24	20	34	.287	.347	.352	699	97	-0	0	0	0	.995	-1	C-80	0.2

YEAR	TM/L	G	AB	R	H	2B	3B	HR	RBI	BB	SO	AVG	OBP	SLG	OPS	OPS+	BR+	SB	CS	SBR	FA	FR	G/POS	TPR
1978	Bal-A	36	86	6	13	1	1	0	2	9	14	.151	.232	.186	418	20	-9	0	1	-0	.988	5	C-35	-0.4
1979	*Bal-A	63	137	9	34	8	0	1	14	13	14	.248	.313	.328	642	76	-4	0	0	0	.984	2	C-63	0.0
1980	Bal-A	2	5	0	1	0	0	0	0	0	1	.200	.200	.200	400	10	-1	0	0	0	1.000	1	/C-2	0.0
	Cal-A	24	66	7	13	0	0	1	9	9	13	.197	.293	.242	536	50	-4	0	0	0	.968	-10	C-24	-1.4
	Yr	26	71	7	14	0	0	1	9	9	14	.197	.287	.239	527	47	-5	0	0	0	.971	-9	C-26	-1.4
Total	4	205	510	44	123	18	2	3	49	51	76	.241	.310	.302	612	72	-19	0	1	-0	.988	-3	C-204	-1.6

■ BUD SKETCHLEY Sketchley, Harry Clement b: 3/30/19, Virden, Man., Can. d: 12/19/79, Los Angeles, Cal. BL/TL, 5′10″, 180 lbs. Deb: 4/14/42

YEAR	TM/L	G	AB	R	H	2B	3B	HR	RBI	BB	SO	AVG	OBP	SLG	OPS	OPS+	BR+	SB	CS	SBR	FA	FR	G/POS	TPR
1942	Chi-A	13	36	1	7	1	0	0	3	7	4	.194	.326	.222	548	57	-2	0	1	-0	.952	-1	O-12(0-0-12)	-0.4

■ ROE SKIDMORE Skidmore, Robert Roe b: 10/30/45, Decatur, Ill. BR/TR, 6′3″, 188 lbs. Deb: 9/17/70

YEAR	TM/L	G	AB	R	H	2B	3B	HR	RBI	BB	SO	AVG	OBP	SLG	OPS	OPS+	BR+	SB	CS	SBR	FA	FR	G/POS	TPR
1970	Chi-N	1	1	0	1	0	0	0	0	0	0	1.000	1.000	1.000	2000	390	0	0	0	0	.000	0	H	0.0

■ BILL SKIFF Skiff, William Franklin b: 10/16/1895, New Rochelle, N.Y. d: 12/25/76, Bronxville, N.Y. BR/TR, 5′10″, 170 lbs. Deb: 5/17/21

YEAR	TM/L	G	AB	R	H	2B	3B	HR	RBI	BB	SO	AVG	OBP	SLG	OPS	OPS+	BR+	SB	CS	SBR	FA	FR	G/POS	TPR
1921	Pit-N	16	45	7	13	2	0	0	11	0	4	.289	.289	.333	622	63	-2	1	1	-0	.982	-2	C-13	-0.3
1926	NY-A	6	11	0	1	0	0	0	0	0	1	.091	.091	.091	182	-53	-2	0	0	0	1.000	-1	/C-6	-0.3
Total	2	22	56	7	14	2	0	0	11	0	5	.250	.250	.286	536	40	-5	1	1	-0	.984	-3	/C-19	-0.6

■ ALEXANDER SKINNER Skinner, Alexander b: 8/14/1856, Chicago, Ill. d: 3/5/01, Washington, Mass. Deb: 7/12/1884

YEAR	TM/L	G	AB	R	H	2B	3B	HR	RBI	BB	SO	AVG	OBP	SLG	OPS	OPS+	BR+	SB	CS	SBR	FA	FR	G/POS	TPR
1884	Bal-U	1	3	0	1	0	0	0		0		.333	.333	.333	667	93	-0				1.000	0	/O-1(0-0-1)	0.0
	CP-U	1	3	1	1	0	0	0		0		.333	.333	.333	667	103	-0				.000	-0	/O-1(0-1-0)	0.0
	Yr	2	6	1	2	0	0	0		0		.333	.333	.333	667	98	-0				1.000	-0	/O-2(0-1-1)	0.0

■ CAMP SKINNER Skinner, Elisha Harrison b: 6/25/1897, Douglasville, Ga. d: 8/4/44, Douglasville, Ga. BL/TR, 5′11″, 165 lbs. Deb: 5/2/22

YEAR	TM/L	G	AB	R	H	2B	3B	HR	RBI	BB	SO	AVG	OBP	SLG	OPS	OPS+	BR+	SB	CS	SBR	FA	FR	G/POS	TPR
1922	NY-A	27	33	1	6	0	0	0	2	0	4	.182	.206	.182	388	2	-5	1	0	0	1.000	-0	/O-4(1-3-0)	-0.5
1923	Bos-A	7	13	1	3	2	0	0	1	0	0	.231	.231	.385	615	60	-1	0	0	0	.000	-1	/O-2(0-2-0)	-0.2
Total	2	34	46	2	9	2	0	0	3	0	4	.196	.213	.239	452	18	-6	1	0	0	1.000	-2	/O-6(1-5-0)	-0.7

■ JOEL SKINNER Skinner, Joel Patrick b: 2/21/61, LaJolla, Cal. BR/TR, 6′4″, 204 lbs. Deb: 6/12/83 F

YEAR	TM/L	G	AB	R	H	2B	3B	HR	RBI	BB	SO	AVG	OBP	SLG	OPS	OPS+	BR+	SB	CS	SBR	FA	FR	G/POS	TPR
1983	Chi-A	6	11	2	3	0	0	0	1	0	1	.273	.273	.273	545	49	-1	0	0	0	.960	2	/C-6	0.2
1984	Chi-A	43	80	4	17	2	0	0	3	7	19	.213	.276	.237	513	42	-6	1	0	0	.989	10	C-43	0.5
1985	Chi-A	22	44	9	15	4	1	1	5	5	13	.341	.408	.545	954	153	3	0	0	0	.971	4	C-21	0.7
1986	Chi-A	60	149	17	30	5	1	4	20	9	43	.201	.252	.329	580	55	-10	1	0	0	.988	-7	C-60	-1.4
	NY-A	54	166	6	43	4	0	1	17	7	40	.259	.289	.301	590	62	-9	0	4	-1	.981	6	C-54	-0.3
	Yr	114	315	23	73	9	1	5	37	16	83	.232	.271	.314	585	58	-18	1	4	-1	.984	-1	*C-114	-1.7
1987	NY-A	64	139	9	19	4	0	3	14	8	46	.137	.189	.230	419	11	-18	0	0	0	.984	-3	C-64	-1.8
1988	NY-A	88	251	23	57	15	0	4	23	14	72	.227	.268	.335	603	68	-11	0	0	0	.990	-7	C-85/O-2(1-0-1),1-1	-1.4
1989	Cle-A	79	178	10	41	10	0	1	13	9	42	.230	.271	.303	575	61	-9	1	1	-0	.990	-4	C-79	-1.1
1990	Cle-A	49	139	16	35	4	1	2	16	7	44	.252	.288	.338	626	75	-5	0	0	0	.996	0	C-49	-0.2
1991	Cle-A	99	284	23	69	14	0	1	24	14	67	.243	.281	.303	584	61	-15	0	2	-1	.991	1	C-99	-0.9
Total	9	564	1441	119	329	62	3	17	136	80	387	.228	.271	.311	582	60	-81	3	7	-2	.988	3	C-560/O-2(1-0-1),1-1	-5.7

■ BOB SKINNER Skinner, Robert Ralph b: 10/3/31, LaJolla, Cal. BL/TR, 6′4″, 190 lbs. Deb: 4/13/54 FMC Career OF: (893-LF 0-CF 58-RF)

YEAR	TM/L	G	AB	R	H	2B	3B	HR	RBI	BB	SO	AVG	OBP	SLG	OPS	OPS+	BR+	SB	CS	SBR	FA	FR	G/POS	TPR
1954	Pit-N	132	470	67	117	15	9	8	46	47	59	.249	.317	.370	687	80	-14	4	0	1	.986	-3	*1-118/O-2(0-0-2)	-2.3
1956	Pit-N	113	233	29	47	8	3	5	29	26	50	.202	.285	.326	611	65	-12	1	1	-0	.977	-9	O-36L,1-23/3-1	-2.5
1957	Pit-N	126	387	58	118	12	6	13	45	38	50	.305	.370	.468	838	127	15	10	4	1	.963	3	O-93(93-0-0)/1-9,3-1	1.3
1958	Pit-N★	144	529	93	170	33	9	13	70	58	55	.321	.390	.491	882	135	27	12	4	1	.977	9	*O-141(141-0-0)	2.9
1959	Pit-N	143	547	78	153	18	4	13	61	67	65	.280	.358	.399	757	102	3	10	7	-0	.964	6	*O-142(142-0-0)/1-1	0.0
1960	*Pit-N★	145	571	83	156	33	6	15	86	59	86	.273	.342	.431	773	109	7	11	8	-0	.981	7	*O-141(141-0-0)	0.5
1961	Pit-N	119	381	61	102	20	3	3	42	51	49	.268	.360	.360	720	91	-3	3	5	-1	.973	3	O-97(97-0-0)	-0.7
1962	Pit-N	144	510	87	154	29	7	20	75	76	89	.302	.397	.504	901	140	30	10	4	1	.960	1	*O-139(139-0-0)	2.3
1963	Pit-N	34	122	18	33	5	5	0	8	13	22	.270	.341	.393	734	110	2	4	1	1	.983	2	O-32(32-0-0)	0.2
	Cin-N	72	194	25	49	10	2	3	17	21	42	.253	.332	.371	703	99	0	1	2	-0	1.000	2	O-51(51-0-0)	-0.2
	Yr	106	316	43	82	15	7	3	25	34	64	.259	.335	.380	715	103	2	5	3	0	.993	3	O-83(83-0-0)	0.0
1964	Cin-N	25	59	6	13	3	0	3	5	4	12	.220	.270	.424	694	89	-1	0	0	0	.913	1	O-12(12-0-0)	-0.1
	*StL-N	55	118	10	32	5	0	1	16	11	20	.271	.333	.339	672	83	-2	0	0	0	.938	-1	O-31(4-0-27)	-0.5
	Yr	80	177	16	45	8	0	4	21	15	32	.254	.313	.367	680	85	-3	0	0	0	.930	-0	O-43(16-0-27)	-0.6
1965	StL-N	80	152	25	47	5	4	5	26	12	30	.309	.360	.493	853	126	5	1	0	0	.935	-4	O-33(15-0-19)	-0.1
1966	StL-N	49	45	2	7	1	0	1	5	2	17	.156	.208	.244	453	25	-5	0	0	0	.000	0	H	-0.5
Total	12	1381	4318	642	1198	197	58	103	531	485	646	.277	.353	.421	774	108	53	67	36	2	.969	14	O-950L,1-151/3-2	0.3

■ LOU SKIZAS Skizas, Louis Peter "The Nervous Greek" b: 6/2/32, Chicago, Ill. BR/TR, 5′11″, 175 lbs. Deb: 4/19/56

YEAR	TM/L	G	AB	R	H	2B	3B	HR	RBI	BB	SO	AVG	OBP	SLG	OPS	OPS+	BR+	SB	CS	SBR	FA	FR	G/POS	TPR
1956	NY-A	6	6	0	1	0	0	0	1	0	2	.167	.167	.167	333	-12	-1	0	0	0	.000	0	H	-0.1
	KC-A	83	297	39	94	11	3	11	39	15	17	.316	.349	.485	834	118	6	3	1	0	.975	5	O-74(57-0-18)	0.8
	Yr	89	303	39	95	11	3	11	40	15	19	.314	.346	.479	824	116	5	3	1	0	.975	5	O-74(57-0-18)	0.7
1957	KC-A	119	376	34	92	14	1	18	44	27	15	.245	.299	.431	730	95	-4	5	2	0	.976	-9	O-76(14-0-69),3-32	-1.6
1958	Det-A	23	33	4	8	2	0	1	2	5	1	.242	.342	.394	736	95	-0	0	0	0	.750	-3	/O-5(4-0-1),3-4	-0.3
1959	Chi-A	8	13	3	1	0	0	0	0	3	2	.077	.250	.077	327	-6	-2	0	0	0	1.000	-0	/O-6(5-0-1)	-0.2
Total	4	239	725	80	196	27	4	30	86	50	37	.270	.319	.443	762	102	-1	8	3	1	.973	-7	O-161(80-0-89)/3-36	-1.4

■ BILL SKOWRON Skowron, William Joseph "Moose" b: 12/18/30, Chicago, Ill. BR/TR, 5′11″, 195 lbs. Deb: 4/13/54

YEAR	TM/L	G	AB	R	H	2B	3B	HR	RBI	BB	SO	AVG	OBP	SLG	OPS	OPS+	BR+	SB	CS	SBR	FA	FR	G/POS	TPR
1954	NY-A	87	215	37	73	12	9	7	41	19	18	.340	.396	.577	972	170	19	2	1	0	.986	-1	1-61/3-5,2-2	1.7
1955	*NY-A	108	288	46	92	17	3	12	61	21	32	.319	.372	.524	896	141	15	1	1	-0	.989	-3	1-74/3-3	0.9
1956	*NY-A	134	464	78	143	21	6	23	90	50	60	.308	.383	.528	911	143	27	4	4	-1	.993	3	*1-120/3-2	2.3
1957	*NY-A★	122	457	54	139	15	5	17	88	31	60	.304	.352	.470	823	125	14	3	2	-0	.992	6	*1-115	1.4
1958	*NY-A★	126	465	61	127	22	3	14	73	28	69	.273	.320	.424	744	107	3	1	1	-0	**.993**	-2	*1-118/3-2	-0.7
1959	NY-A★	74	282	39	84	13	5	15	59	20	47	.298	.351	.539	890	145	16	1	0	0	.991	0	1-72	1.2
1960	*NY-A★	146	538	63	166	34	3	26	91	38	95	.309	.356	.528	884	144	30	2	3	-1	.991	9	*1-142	3.0
1961	*NY-A☆	150	561	76	150	23	4	28	89	35	108	.267	.320	.472	792	115	9	0	0	0	.993	-1	*1-149	-0.2
1962	*NY-A	140	478	63	129	16	6	23	80	36	99	.270	.328	.473	800	116	9	0	1	-0	.991	-5	*1-135	-0.4
1963	*LA-N	89	237	19	48	8	0	4	19	13	49	.203	.253	.287	540	59	-13	0	1	-0	.991	-1	1-66/3-1	-2.0
1964	Was-A	73	262	28	71	10	0	13	41	11	56	.271	.308	.458	766	110	3	0	0	0	.994	-2	1-66	-0.3
	Chi-A	73	273	19	80	11	3	4	38	19	36	.293	.341	.399	741	108	3	0	0	0	.998	-1	1-70	-0.2
	Yr	146	535	47	151	21	3	17	79	30	92	.282	.325	.428	753	109	5	0	0	0	.996	-3	*1-136	-0.5
1965	Chi-A†	146	559	63	153	24	3	18	78	32	77	.274	.319	.424	743	116	10	1	3	-1	.994	-6	*1-145	-0.6
1966	Chi-A	120	337	27	84	15	2	6	29	26	45	.249	.309	.359	668	98	-1	1	1	-0	.991	1	1-98	-0.6
1967	Chi-A	8	8	0	0	0	0	0	1	0	1	.000	.000	.000	0	-99	-2	0	0	0	.000	0	H	-0.2
	Cal-A	62	123	8	27	2	1	1	10	4	18	.220	.267	.276	544	63	-6	0	0	0	.988	-1	1-32	-0.9
	Yr	70	131	8	27	2	1	1	11	4	19	.206	.252	.260	511	53	-8	0	0	0	.988	-1	1-32	-1.1
Total	14	1658	5547	681	1566	243	53	211	888	383	870	.282	.335	.459	794	121	135	16	18	-3	.992	-3	*1-1463/3-13,2-2	4.4

■ BOB SKUBE Skube, Robert Jacob b: 10/8/57, Northridge, Cal. BL/TL, 6′, 180 lbs. Deb: 9/17/82

YEAR	TM/L	G	AB	R	H	2B	3B	HR	RBI	BB	SO	AVG	OBP	SLG	OPS	OPS+	BR+	SB	CS	SBR	FA	FR	G/POS	TPR
1982	Mil-A	4	3	0	2	0	0	0	0	0	0	.667	.667	.667	1333	285	1	0	0	0	.000	-1	/O-1(0-1-0),D-1	0.0
1983	Mil-A	12	25	2	5	1	1	0	9	4	7	.200	.310	.320	630	80	-1	0	0	0	1.000	-1	/O-8(0-4-4),1-1,D-2	-0.1
Total	2	16	28	2	7	1	1	0	9	4	7	.250	.344	.357	701	101	0	0	0	0	1.000	-1	/O-9(0-5-4),D-3,1-1	-0.1

■ GORDON SLADE Slade, Gordon Leigh "Oskie" b: 10/9/04, Salt Lake City, Utah d: 1/2/74, Long Beach, Cal. BR/TR, 5′10.5″, 160 lbs. Deb: 4/21/30 Career OF: (8-LF 0-CF 0-RF)

YEAR	TM/L	G	AB	R	H	2B	3B	HR	RBI	BB	SO	AVG	OBP	SLG	OPS	OPS+	BR+	SB	CS	SBR	FA	FR	G/POS	TPR
1930	Bro-N	25	37	8	8	2	0	1	2	3	5	.216	.275	.351	626	51	-3	0			.938	10	S-21	0.7
1931	Bro-N	85	272	27	65	13	2	1	29	23	28	.239	.310	.313	623	68	-12	2			.947	11	S-82/3-2	0.5
1932	Bro-N	79	250	23	60	15	1	1	23	11	26	.240	.280	.320	600	62	-13	3			.943	11	S-55,3-23	0.1
1933	StL-N	39	62	6	7	1	0	0	3	6	7	.113	.191	.129	320	-7	-8	1			.941	3	S-31/2-1	-0.5

YEAR	TM/L	G	AB	R	H	2B	3B	HR	RBI	BB	SO	AVG	OBP	SLG	OPS	OPS+	BR+	SB	CS	SBR	FA	FR	G/POS	TPR
1934	Cin-N	138	555	61	158	19	8	4	52	25	34	.285	.320	.369	690	86	-11	6			.952	2	S-97,2-39	0.0
1935	Cin-N	71	196	22	55	10	0	1	14	16	16	.281	.341	.347	688	88	-3	0			.927	-12	S-30,2-19/O-8L,3-7	-1.2
Total	6	437	1372	147	353	60	11	8	123	84	116	.257	.307	.335	641	73	-51	12			.945	25	S-316/2-59,3-32,O-8L	-0.4
■ ART SLADEN Sladen, Arthur b: 10/28/1860, Dracut, Mass. d: 2/28/14, Dracut, Mass. Deb: 4/22/1884																								
1884	Bos-U	2	7	0	0	0	0	0		0		.000	.000	.000	0	-99	-2				1.000	-1	/O-2(0-0-2)	-0.2
■ JIMMY SLAGLE Slagle, James Franklin "Rabbit" or "Shorty" b: 7/11/1873, Worthville, Pa. d: 5/10/56, Chicago, Ill. BL/TR, 5'7", 144 lbs. Deb: 4/17/1899																								
1899	Was-N	147	599	92	163	15	8	0	41	55		.272	.338	.324	662	83	-13	22			.953	20	*O-146(0-146-0)	-0.2
1900	Phi-N	141	574	115	165	16	9	0	45	60		.287	.358	.347	705	96	-2	34			.922	1	*O-141(141-0-0)	-1.3
1901	Phi-N	48	183	20	37	6	2	1	20	16		.202	.277	.273	550	59	-9	5			.930	6	O-48(48-0-0)	-0.6
	Bos-N	66	255	35	69	7	0	0	7	34		.271	.359	.298	657	84	-4	14			.935	-2	O-66(0-5-61)	-0.9
	Yr	114	438	55	106	13	2	1	27	50		.242	.325	.288	613	74	-13	19			.932	4	*O-114(48-5-61)	-1.5
1902	Chi-N	117	463	66	146	11	4	0	28	53		.315	.386	.356	742	133	20	41			.965	7	*O-115(94-22-0)	2.2
1903	Chi-N	139	543	104	162	20	6	0	44	81		.298	.393	.357	751	118	17	33			.936	2	*O-139(115-24-0)	1.0
1904	Chi-N	120	481	73	125	12	10	1	31	41		.260	.322	.333	655	102	1	28			.921	-3	*O-120(102-18-0)	-0.8
1905	Chi-N	155	568	96	153	19	4	0	37	97		.269	.379	.317	696	104	8	27			.962	3	*O-155(33-123-0)	0.3
1906	Chi-N	127	498	71	119	8	6	0	33	63		.239	.324	.279	604	83	-8	25			.976	2	*O-127(4-123-0)	-1.3
1907	*Chi-N	136	489	71	126	6	6	0	32	76		.258	.359	.294	653	99	3	28			.962	-10	*O-136(4-132-0)	-1.6
1908	Chi-N	104	352	38	78	4	1	0	26	43		.222	.306	.239	545	71	-10	17			.976	-6	*O-101(26-75-0)	-2.4
Total	10	1300	5005	781	1343	124	56	2	344	619		.268	.352	.317	668	97	4	274			.950	22	*O-1294(567-668-61)	-5.6
■ JACK SLATTERY Slattery, John Terrence b: 1/6/1878, S.Boston, Mass. d: 7/17/49, Boston, Mass. BR/TR, 6'2", 191 lbs. Deb: 9/28/01 MC																								
1901	Bos-A	1	3	1	1	0	0	0	1	1		.333	.500	.333	833	137	0	0			1.000	0	/C-1	0.0
1903	Cle-A	4	11	1	0	0	0	0	0	0		.000	.000	.000	0	-99	-3	0			.885	-1	/1-2	-0.4
	Chi-A	63	211	8	46	3	2	0	20	2		.218	.233	.251	484	47	-14	2			.974	-8	C-56/1-5	-1.7
	Yr	67	222	9	46	3	2	0	20	2		.207	.221	.239	460	40	-16	2			.974	-9	C-56/1-7	-2.1
1906	StL-N	3	7	0	2	0	0	0	0	1		.286	.375	.286	661	111	0	0			1.000	-1	/C-2	0.0
1909	Was-A	32	56	4	12	2	0	0	6	2		.214	.254	.250	504	62	-2	1			.953	-1	1-11/C-6	-0.4
Total	4	103	288	14	61	5	2	0	27	6		.212	.236	.243	479	47	-18	3			.974	-10	/C-65,1-18	-2.5
■ MIKE SLATTERY Slattery, Michael J. b: 11/26/1866, Boston, Mass. d: 10/16/04, Boston, Mass. BL/TL, 6'2", 210 lbs. Deb: 4/17/1884																								
1884	Bos-U	106	413	60	86	6	2	0		4		.208	.216	.232	448	36	-44				.802	6	*O-96(1-96-0),1-11	-3.7
1888	*NY-N	103	391	50	96	12	6	1	35	13	28	.246	.272	.315	586	87	-6	26			.919	1	*O-103(4-90-9)	-0.8
1889	*NY-N	12	48	7	14	2	0	1	12	4	3	.292	.346	.396	742	107	0	2			.852	-1	O-12(4-7-1)	-0.1
1890	NY-P	97	411	80	126	20	11	5	67	27	25	.307	.352	.445	798	103	-1	18			.905	-14	*O-97(53-39-9)	-1.4
1891	Cin-N	41	158	24	33	3	2	1	16	10	10	.209	.256	.272	528	53	-10	1			.941	-0	O-41(4-37-0)	-1.0
	Was-a	15	60	8	17	1	0	0	5	4	5	.283	.358	.300	658	93	-0	6			.862	-2	O-15(3-12-0)	-0.2
Total	5	374	1481	229	372	44	21	8	135	62	71	.251	.284	.325	610	77	-60	53			.883	-11	O-364(69-281-19)/1-11	-7.2
■ DON SLAUGHT Slaught, Donald Martin b: 9/11/58, Long Beach, Cal. BR/TR, 6'1", 190 lbs. Deb: 7/6/82																								
1982	KC-A	43	115	14	32	6	0	3	8	9	12	.278	.331	.409	739	102	0	0	0	0	.994	2	C-43	0.4
1983	KC-A	83	276	21	86	13	4	0	28	11	27	.312	.338	.388	726	99	-1	3	1	0	.964	-7	C-79/D-1	-0.4
1984	*KC-A	124	409	48	108	27	4	4	42	20	55	.264	.302	.379	681	86	-8	0	0	0	.982	-10	*C-123/D-1	-1.3
1985	Tex-A	102	343	34	96	17	4	8	35	20	41	.280	.331	.423	753	103	1	5	4	-0	.990	-11	*C-102	-0.6
1986	Tex-A	95	314	39	83	17	1	13	46	16	59	.264	.310	.449	759	101	-0	3	2	-0	.993	-6	C-91/D-2	-0.3
1987	Tex-A	95	237	25	53	15	2	8	16	24	51	.224	.298	.405	703	84	-6	0	3	-1	.985	-0	C-85/D-5	-0.4
1988	NY-A	97	322	33	91	25	1	9	43	24	54	.283	.338	.450	788	120	8	1	0	0	.979	-12	C-94/D-1	0.2
1989	NY-A	117	350	34	88	21	3	5	38	30	57	.251	.319	.371	691	95	-2	1	1	-0	.991	-5	*C-105/D-3	-0.2
1990	*Pit-N	84	230	27	69	18	3	4	29	27	27	.300	.381	.457	837	134	11	0	1	-0	.979	-3	C-78	1.2
1991	*Pit-N	77	220	19	65	17	1	1	29	21	32	.295	.365	.395	760	116	5	1	0	0	.987	-5	C-69/3-1	0.4
1992	*Pit-N	87	255	26	88	17	3	4	37	17	23	.345	.391	.482	873	147	16	2	2	-0	.988	-4	C-79	1.7
1993	Pit-N	116	377	34	113	19	2	10	55	29	56	.300	.359	.440	800	113	7	2	1	0	.993	-10	*C-105	0.3
1994	Pit-N	76	240	21	69	7	0	2	21	34	31	.287	.383	.342	724	90	-2	0	0	0	.994	-1	C-74	0.2
1995	Pit-N	35	112	13	34	6	0	0	13	9	8	.304	.361	.357	718	88	-2	0	0	0	.996	2	C-33	0.2
1996	Cal-A	62	207	23	67	9	0	6	32	13	20	.324	.369	.454	823	106	2	0	0	0	.992	-8	C-59/D-1	-0.2
	Chi-A	14	36	2	9	1	0	0	4	2	2	.250	.289	.278	567	47	-3	0	0	0	.986	1	C-12/D-1	-0.1
	Yr	76	243	25	76	10	0	6	36	15	22	.313	.358	.428	786	98	-1	0	0	0	.991	-7	C-71/D-2	-0.3
1997	SD-N	20	20	2	0	0	0	0	0	5	4	.000	.200	.000	200	-45	-4	0	0	0	1.000	-1	/C-6	-0.5
Total	16	1327	4063	415	1151	235	28	77	476	311	559	.283	.341	.412	752	104	22	18	15	-1	.987	-78	*C-1237/D-15,3-1	0.6
■ ENOS SLAUGHTER Slaughter, Enos Bradsher "Country" b: 4/27/16, Roxboro, N.C. BL/TR, 5'9", 192 lbs. Deb: 4/19/38 H																								
1938	StL-N	112	395	59	109	20	10	8	58	32	38	.276	.330	.438	768	104	1	1			.970	-2	O-92(1-20-75)	-0.6
1939	StL-N	149	604	95	193	**52**	5	12	86	44	53	.320	.371	.482	852	120	16	2			.968	**16**	*O-149(0-0-149)	2.3
1940	StL-N	140	516	96	158	25	13	17	73	50	35	.306	.370	.504	874	131	21	8			.989	3	*O-132(0-0-132)	1.7
1941	StL-N★	113	425	71	132	22	9	13	76	53	28	.311	.390	.496	886	139	22	4			.947	-8	*O-108(0-0-108)	0.7
1942	*StL-N★	152	591	100	**188**	31	**17**	13	98	88	30	.318	.412	.494	906	153	41	9			.987	4	*O-151(0-0-151)	3.8
1946	*StL-N★	156	609	100	183	30	8	18	**130**	69	41	.300	.374	.465	838	131	24	9			.981	6	*O-156(0-0-156)	2.6
1947	StL-N★	147	551	100	162	31	13	10	86	59	27	.294	.366	.452	818	111	9	4			.982	9	*O-142(110-0-32)	0.8
1948	StL-N★	146	549	91	176	27	11	11	90	81	29	.321	.409	.470	879	130	25	4			.971	6	*O-146(107-0-39)	2.1
1949	StL-N★	151	568	92	191	34	**13**	13	96	79	37	.336	.418	.511	929	141	35	3			.983	5	*O-150(150-0-0)	2.5
1950	StL-N★	148	556	82	161	26	7	10	101	66	33	.290	.367	.415	782	100	2	3			.978	-1	*O-145(20-0-125)	-0.5
1951	StL-N★	123	409	48	115	17	8	4	64	67	25	.281	.386	.391	777	109	8	7	2	1	.995	-0	*O-106(0-0-106)	0.5
1952	StL-N★	140	510	73	153	17	12	11	101	70	25	.300	.386	.445	831	130	22	6	1	1	.989	2	*O-137(0-0-137)	2.0
1953	StL-N★	143	492	64	143	34	9	6	89	80	28	.291	.395	.433	828	116	14	4	4	-1	**.996**	-6	*O-137(0-0-137)	0.3
1954	NY-A	69	125	19	31	4	2	1	19	28	8	.248	.386	.336	722	102	2	0	2	-1	.974	-6	O-30(3-0-29)	-0.6
1955	NY-A	10	9	1	1	0	0	0	1	1	1	.111	.200	.111	311	-15	-1	0	0	0	.000	0	H	-0.1
	KC-A	108	267	49	86	12	4	5	34	40	17	.322	.414	.453	867	132	13	2	3	-1	.985	-4	O-77(0-0-77)	0.6
	Yr	118	276	50	87	12	4	5	35	41	18	.315	.408	.442	850	127	12	2	3	-1	.985	-4	O-77(0-0-77)	0.5
1956	KC-A	91	223	37	62	14	3	2	23	29	20	.278	.364	.395	758	100	0	1	0	0	.981	-3	O-56(19-1-37)	-0.4
	*NY-A	24	83	15	24	4	2	0	4	5	6	.289	.330	.386	715	91	-1	1	1	-0	1.000	-2	O-20(17-0-4)	-0.4
	Yr	115	306	52	86	18	5	2	27	34	26	.281	.355	.392	747	97	-1	2	1	0	.985	-5	O-76(36-1-41)	-0.8
1957	*NY-A	96	209	24	53	7	1	5	34	40	19	.254	.373	.368	742	105	3	0	2	-1	1.000	-3	O-64(56-0-9)	-0.4
1958	*NY-A	77	138	21	42	4	1	4	19	21	16	.304	.396	.435	831	133	7	2	0	0	.957	-5	O-35(16-0-20)	0.1
1959	NY-A	74	99	10	17	2	0	6	21	13	19	.172	.268	.374	642	77	-4	1	0	0	.964	-5	O-26(9-0-18)	-0.9
	Mil-N	11	18	0	3	0	0	0	1	3	3	.167	.286	.167	452	27	-2	0	0	0	1.000	-1	/O-5(5-0-0)	-0.3
Total	19	2380	7946	1247	2383	413	148	169	1304	1018	538	.300	.382	.453	835	122	259	71	15		.980	-0	*O-2064(513-21-1541)	15.8
■ SCOTTIE SLAYBACK Slayback, Elbert b: 10/5/01, Paducah, Ky. d: 11/30/79, Cincinnati, Ohio BR/TR, 5'8", 165 lbs. Deb: 9/26/26																								
1926	NY-N	2	8	0	0	0	0	0	0	0	0	.000	.000	.000	0	-99	-2	0			.889	-1	/2-2	-0.4
■ BRUCE SLOAN Sloan, Bruce Adams "Fatso" b: 10/4/14, McAlester, Okla. d: 9/24/73, Oklahoma City, Okla. BL/TL, 5'9", 195 lbs. Deb: 4/29/44																								
1944	NY-N	59	104	7	28	4	1	1	9	13	8	.269	.350	.356	706	99	0	0			.935	-4	O-21(3-0-18)	-0.6
■ TOD SLOAN Sloan, Yale Yeastman b: 12/24/1890, Madisonville, Tenn d: 9/12/56, Akron, Ohio BL/TR, 6', 175 lbs. Deb: 9/22/13																								
1913	StL-A	7	26	2	7	1	0	0	2	1	9	.269	.321	.308	629	87	-0	1			.950	2	/O-7(0-0-7)	0.1
1917	StL-A	109	313	32	72	6	2	2	25	28	34	.230	.307	.281	589	83	-6	8			.963	-3	O-77(16-1-60)	-1.4
1919	StL-A	27	63	9	15	1	3	0	6	12	3	.238	.368	.349	718	99	0	0			.933	-1	O-20(0-0-20)	-0.1
Total	3	143	402	43	94	8	5	2	33	41	46	.234	.319	.294	612	86	-6	9			.957	-1	O-104(16-1-87)	-1.4
■ RON SLOCUM Slocum, Ronald Reece b: 7/2/45, Modesto, Cal. BR/TR, 6'2", 185 lbs. Deb: 9/8/69																								
1969	SD-N	13	24	6	7	1	0	1	5	0	5	.292	.292	.458	750	112	0	0	0	0	.938	-1	/2-4,3-4,S-1	-0.1

YEAR	TM/L	G	AB	R	H	2B	3B	HR	RBI	BB	SO	AVG	OBP	SLG	OPS	OPS+	BR+	SB	CS	SBR	FA	FR	G/POS	TPR
1970	SD-N	60	71	8	10	2	2	1	11	8	24	.141	.237	.268	505	37	-7	0	1	-0	.978	13	C-19,S-17,3-11,/2-9	0.6
1971	SD-N	7	18	1	0	0	0	0	0	0	8	.000	.053	.000	53	-90	-4	0	0	0	.905	1	/3-6	-0.3
Total	3	80	113	15	17	3	2	2	16	8	37	.150	.220	.265	485	33	-11	0	1	-0	.887	13	/3-21,C-19,S-18,2	0.2
■ CRAIG SMAJSTRLA Smajstrla, Craig Lee b: 6/19/62, Houston, Tex. BB/TR, 5'9", 165 lbs. Deb: 9/6/88																								
1988	Hou-N	8	3	2	0	0	0	0	0	0	1	.000	.000	.000	0	-99	-1	0	0	0	1.000	0	/2-2	-0.1
■ CHARLIE SMALL Small, Charles Albert b: 10/24/05, Auburn, Me. d: 1/14/53, Auburn, Me. BL/TR, 5'11", 180 lbs. Deb: 7/7/30																								
1930	Bos-A	25	18	1	3	1	0	0	0	2	5	.167	.250	.222	472	22	-2	1	0	0	1.000	-0	/O-1(0-1-0)	-0.2
■ HANK SMALL Small, George Henry b: 7/31/53, Atlanta, Ga. BR/TR, 6'3", 205 lbs. Deb: 9/27/78																								
1978	Atl-N	1	4	0	0	0	0	0	0	0	0	.000	.000	.000	0	-90	-1	0	0	0	1.000	0	/1-1	-0.1
■ JIM SMALL Small, James Arthur Patrick b: 3/8/37, Portland, Ore. BL/TL, 6'1.5", 180 lbs. Deb: 6/22/55																								
1955	Det-A	12	4	2	0	0	0	0	0	1	1	.000	.200	.000	200	-44	-1	0	0	0	1.000	-1	/O-4(3-0-1)	-0.1
1956	Det-A	58	91	13	29	4	2	0	10	6	10	.319	.361	.407	767	102	0	0	0	0	.940	-3	O-26(4-12-10)	-0.3
1957	Det-A	36	42	7	9	2	0	0	0	2	11	.214	.250	.262	512	39	-4	0	2	-1	1.000	-3	O-14(8-1-5)	-0.7
1958	KC-A	2	4	0	0	0	0	0	0	1	0	.000	.200	.000	200	-39	-1	0	0	0	1.000	0	/O-1(0-0-1)	-0.1
Total	4	108	141	22	38	6	2	0	10	10	22	.270	.318	.340	658	75	-5	0	2	-1	.957	-6	/O-45(15-13-17)	-1.2
■ ROY SMALLEY Smalley, Roy Frederick Iii b: 10/25/52, Los Angeles, Cal. BB/TR, 6'1", 185 lbs. Deb: 4/30/75 F																								
1975	Tex-A	78	250	22	57	8	0	3	33	30	42	.228	.311	.296	607	73	-8	4	0	1	.941	4	S-59,2-19/C-1	0.4
1976	Tex-A	41	129	15	29	2	0	1	8	29	27	.225	.367	.264	631	85	-1	2	0	0	.963	-6	2-38/S-5	-0.3
	Min-A	103	384	46	104	16	3	2	36	47	79	.271	.353	.344	697	103	3	0	4	-1	.967	5	*S-103	1.9
	Yr	144	513	61	133	18	3	3	44	76	106	.259	.357	.324	681	98	2	2	4	-1	.966	-1	*S-108,2-38	1.6
1977	Min-A	150	584	93	135	21	5	6	56	74	89	.231	.319	.315	634	75	-19	5	5	-1	.958	19	*S-150	1.5
1978	Min-A	158	586	80	160	31	3	19	77	85	70	.273	.366	.433	800	122	18	2	8	-2	.970	18	*S-157	**5.2**
1979	Min-A★	162	621	94	168	28	3	24	95	80	80	.271	.357	.441	799	110	9	2	3	-1	.968	**33**	*S-161/1-1	5.6
1980	Min-A	133	486	64	135	24	1	12	63	65	63	.278	.365	.405	771	103	4	3	3	-0	.975	21	*S-125/1-3,D-3	3.7
1981	Min-A	56	167	24	44	7	1	7	22	31	24	.263	.379	.443	822	128	7	0	0	0	.946	-17	S-37,D-15/1-1	-0.8
1982	Min-A	4	13	2	2	1	0	0	0	3	4	.154	.313	.231	543	51	-1	0	0	0	1.000	1	/S-4	0.0
	NY-A	142	486	55	125	14	2	20	67	68	100	.257	.348	.418	766	111	8	0	1	-0	.977	-19	S-89,3-53/2-1,D-4	-0.2
	Yr	146	499	57	127	15	2	20	67	71	104	.255	.347	.413	760	109	7	0	1	-0	.979	-18	S-93,3-53/D-4,2-1	-0.2
1983	NY-A	130	451	70	124	24	1	18	62	58	68	.275	.360	.452	812	127	17	3	3	-0	.959	-16	S-91,3-26,1-22	0.8
1984	NY-A	67	209	17	50	8	1	7	26	15	35	.239	.290	.388	678	89	-4	2	1	0	.905	0	3-35,S-13/1-5,D-5	-0.4
	Chi-A	47	135	15	23	4	0	4	13	22	30	.170	.287	.289	576	57	-8	1	1	-0	.947	-8	3-38/S-3,1-1,D-2	-1.6
	Yr	114	344	32	73	12	1	11	39	37	65	.212	.289	.349	638	76	-12	3	2	-0	.923	-7	3-73,S-16/D-7,1-6	-2.0
1985	Min-A	129	388	57	100	20	0	12	45	60	65	.258	.359	.402	761	102	2	0	2	-1	.987	-15	D-56,S-49,3-14,/1-1	-1.0
1986	Min-A	143	459	59	113	20	4	20	57	68	80	.246	.343	.438	781	108	6	1	3	-1	.963	-4	*D-114,S-19/3-8	-0.1
1987	*Min-A	110	309	32	85	16	1	8	34	36	52	.275	.353	.411	764	98	-0	2	0	0	.850	-3	D-73,3-14/S-4	-0.5
Total	13	1653	5657	745	1454	244	25	163	694	771	908	.257	.348	.395	743	103	33	27	34	-6	.966	14	*S-1069,D-272,3/21C	14.2
■ ROY SMALLEY Smalley, Roy Frederick Jr. b: 6/9/26, Springfield, Mo. BR/TR, 6'3", 190 lbs. Deb: 4/20/48 F																								
1948	Chi-N	124	361	25	78	11	4	4	36	23	76	.216	.265	.302	567	55	-23	0			.941	9	*S-124	-0.8
1949	Chi-N	135	477	57	117	21	10	8	35	36	77	.245	.304	.382	685	85	-12	2			.947	14	*S-132	1.1
1950	Chi-N	154	557	58	128	21	9	21	85	49	114	.230	.297	.413	710	85	-14	2			.945	**21**	*S-154	1.7
1951	Chi-N	79	238	24	55	7	4	8	31	25	53	.231	.304	.395	699	85	-6	0	0	0	.953	-13	S-74	-1.4
1952	Chi-N	87	261	36	58	14	1	5	30	29	58	.222	.305	.341	646	78	-8	0	0	0	.952	-11	S-82	-1.5
1953	Chi-N	82	253	20	63	9	0	6	25	28	57	.249	.329	.356	684	77	-8	0	0	0	.932	-6	S-77	-0.8
1954	Mil-N	25	36	5	8	0	0	1	7	4	9	.222	.317	.306	623	67	-2	0	0	0	.950	4	/S-9,2-7,1-2	0.3
1955	Phi-N	92	260	33	51	11	1	7	39	39	58	.196	.306	.327	633	69	-11	0	0	0	.974	-16	S-87/2-1,3-1	-2.1
1956	Phi-N	65	168	14	38	9	3	0	16	23	29	.226	.323	.315	638	74	-6	0	0	0	.949	-1	S-60	-0.3
1957	Phi-N	28	31	5	5	0	1	1	1	1	9	.161	.212	.323	535	42	-3	0	0	0	.941	1	S-20	-0.2
1958	Phi-N	1	2	0	0	0	0	0	0	0	1	.000	.000	.000	0	-99	-1	0	0	0	.714	0	/S-1	0.0
Total	11	872	2644	277	601	103	33	61	305	257	541	.227	.300	.360	661	77	-92	4	0		.947	3	S-820/2-8,1-2,3-1	-4.0
■ WILL SMALLEY Smalley, William Darwin "Deacon" b: 6/27/1871, Oakland, Cal. d: 10/11/1891, Bay City, Mich. BR/TR, Deb: 4/19/1890																								
1890	Cle-N	136	502	62	107	11	1	0	42	60	44	.213	.303	.239	542	60	-23	10			.895	17	*3-136	-0.4
1891	Was-a	11	38	5	6	0	1	0	3	5	2	.158	.256	.211	466	35	-3	0			.762	-2	/3-9,2-2	-0.4
Total	2	147	540	67	113	11	2	0	45	65	46	.209	.300	.237	537	58	-27	10			.887	15	3-145/2-2	-0.8
■ JOE SMAZA Smaza, Joseph Paul b: 7/7/23, Detroit, Mich. d: 5/30/79, Royal Oak, Mich. BL/TL, 5'11", 175 lbs. Deb: 9/18/46																								
1946	Chi-A	2	5	2	1	0	0	0	0	0	0	.200	.200	.200	400	12	-1	0	0	0	.000	-1	/O-1(0-0-1)	-0.1
■ BILL SMILEY Smiley, William B. b: 1856, Baltimore, Md. d: 7/11/1884, Baltimore, Md. Deb: 10/13/1874																								
1874	Bal-n	2	7	0	0	0	0	0	0	0	0	.000	.000	.000	0	-99	-1	0	0	0	.786	1	/3-2	-0.1
1882	StL-a	59	240	30	51	4	2	0		6		.213	.232	.246	478	59	-10				.885	-7	*2-57/O-2(1-0-1)	-1.4
	Bal-a	16	61	3	9	0	0	0		0		.148	.148	.148	295	-0	-6				.843	2	2-16/S-2	-0.4
	Yr	75	301	33	60	4	2	0		6		.199	.215	.226	441	48	-16				.874	-5	2-73/O-2(1-0-1),S-2	-1.8
■ EDGAR SMITH Smith, Albert Edgar b: 10/15/1860, North Haven, Conn. TR, 6', 200 lbs. Deb: 6/20/1883																								
1883	Bos-N	30	115	10	25	5	3	0	16	5	11	.217	.250	.313	563	68	-4				.905	-0	O-30(0-30-0)/C-1	-0.5
■ ALECK SMITH Smith, Alexander Benjamin "Broadway Aleck" b: 1871, New York, N.Y. d: 7/9/19, New York, N.Y. TR, Deb: 4/23/1897 Career OF: (35-LF 13-CF 10-RF)																								
1897	Bro-N	66	237	36	71	13	1	1	39	4		.300	.317	.376	692	87	-5	12			.903	-6	C-43,O-18(14-2-2)/1-6	-0.7
1898	Bro-N	52	199	25	52	6	5	0	23	3		.261	.276	.342	618	77	-7	7			.909	-10	O-26L,C-20/3-2,21	-1.6
1899	Bro-N	17	61	6	11	0	1	0	6	2		.180	.206	.213	419	15	-7	0			.917	-3	C-17	-0.8
	Bal-N	41	120	17	46	6	4	0	25	4		.383	.417	.500	917	144	7	7			.951	-4	C-36/O-2(0-0-2),1-1	0.5
	Yr	58	181	23	57	6	5	0	31	6		.315	.347	.403	751	101	-0	7			.939	-7	C-53/O-2(0-0-2),1-1	-0.3
1900	Bro-N	7	25	2	6	0	0	0	3	1		.240	.269	.240	509	39	-2	2			.875	-2	/3-6,C-1	-0.4
1901	NY-N	26	78	5	11	0	0	0	6	0		.141	.141	.141	282	-19	-12	2			.962	-2	C-24	-1.1
1902	Bal-A	41	145	10	34	3	0	0	21	8		.234	.275	.255	530	45	-11	5			.947	-6	C-27/1-7,O-4L,23	-1.4
1903	Bos-A	11	33	4	10	1	0	0	4	0		.303	.303	.333	636	86	-1	0			.932	0	C-10	0.0
1904	Chi-N	10	29	2	6	1	0	0	1	3		.207	.281	.241	523	62	-1	1			.778	-2	/O-6(0-6-0),C-1,3-1	-0.3
1906	NY-N	16	28	0	5	0	0	0	2	1		.179	.207	.179	385	20	-3	1			1.000	-1	/C-8,1-3,O-1(0-0-1)	-0.3
Total	9	287	955	107	252	30	11	1	130	26		.264	.288	.321	609	69	-41	37			.933	-35	C-187/O-57L,1-18,32	-6.1
■ AL SMITH Smith, Alphonse Eugene "Fuzzy" b: 2/7/28, Kirkwood, Mo. BR/TR, 6', 191 lbs. Deb: 7/10/53 Career OF: (399-LF 87-CF 679-RF)																								
1953	Cle-A	47	150	28	36	9	0	3	14	20	25	.240	.341	.360	701	92	-1	2	0	0	.920	-3	O-39(4-0-35)/3-2	-0.6
1954	*Cle-A	131	481	101	135	29	6	11	50	88	65	.281	.399	.435	834	126	20	2	9	-3	.984	-3	*O-109L,3-21/S-4	0.9
1955	Cle-A★	154	607	**123**	186	27	4	22	77	93	77	.306	.411	.473	884	132	31	11	6	0	.977	-17	*O-120R,3-45/S-5,2	0.9
1956	Cle-A	141	526	87	144	26	5	16	71	84	72	.274	.382	.433	815	112	11	6	3	0	.981	-7	*O-122R,3-28/2-1	-0.1
1957	Cle-A	135	507	78	125	23	5	11	49	79	70	.247	.353	.377	729	100	2	12	6	1	.913	-16	3-84,O-58(18-41-6)	-1.7
1958	Chi-A	139	480	61	121	23	5	12	58	48	77	.252	.326	.396	722	100	-0	3	3	-0	.970	-1	*O-138(77-2-63)/3-1	-0.9
1959	*Chi-A	129	472	65	112	16	4	17	55	46	74	.237	.312	.396	708	94	-5	7	5	-0	.980	10	*O-128(84-3-45)/3-1	-0.2
1960	Chi-A★	142	536	80	169	31	3	12	72	50	65	.315	.377	.451	828	124	18	8	3	1	.966	-5	*O-141(3-5-139)	0.8
1961	Chi-A	147	532	88	148	29	4	28	93	56	67	.278	.352	.506	858	128	20	4	4	-1	.948	-11	3-80,O-71(10-3-59)	0.4
1962	Chi-A	142	511	62	149	23	8	16	82	57	60	.292	.366	.462	828	122	16	3	3	-0	.935	-23	*3-105,O-39(38-0-2)	-1.0
1963	Bal-A	120	368	45	100	17	1	10	39	32	74	.272	.335	.405	740	110	5	9	0	2	.971	-4	O-97(7-0-92)	-0.4
1964	Cle-A	61	136	15	22	1	1	4	9	8	32	.162	.214	.272	486	34	-12	0	1	-0	1.000	-3	O-48(1-1-46)/3-1	-1.9
	Bos-A	29	51	10	11	4	0	2	7	13	10	.216	.385	.412	796	116	2	0	0	0	.917	-2	3-10/O-8(2-0-6)	0.0

YEAR	TM/L	G	AB	R	H	2B	3B	HR	RBI	BB	SO	AVG	OBP	SLG	OPS	OPS+	BR+	SB	CS	SBR	FA	FR	G/POS	TPR
	Yr	90	187	25	33	5	1	6	16	21	42	.176	.267	.310	577	59	-10	0	1	-0	.987	-4	O-56(3-1-52),3-11	-1.9
Total	12	1517	5357	843	1458	258	46	164	676	674	768	.272	.360	.429	790	113	106	67	43	-0	.974	-84	*O-1118R,3-378/S-9,2	-3.8
■ TONY SMITH Smith, Anthony b: 5/14/1884, Chicago, Ill. d: 2/27/64, Galveston, Tex. BR/TR, 5'9", 150 lbs. Deb: 8/12/07																								
1907	Was-A	51	139	12	26	1	1	0	8	18		.187	.285	.209	493	63	-5	3			.920	-9	S-51	-1.4
1910	Bro-N	106	321	31	58	10	1	1	16	69	53	.181	.329	.227	556	65	-11	9			.941	12	*S-101/3-6	0.5
1911	Bro-N	13	40	3	6	1	0	0	2	8	7	.150	.292	.175	467	33	-3	1			.870	0	S-10/2-3	-0.2
Total	3	170	500	46	90	12	2	1	26	95	60	.180	.314	.218	532	62	-19	13			.931	3	S-162/3-6,2-3	-1.1
■ KLONDIKE SMITH Smith, Armstrong Frederick b: 1/4/1887, London, England d: 11/15/59, Springfield, Mass. BL/TL, 5'9", 160 lbs. Deb: 9/28/12																								
1912	NY-A	7	27	0	5	1	0	0	0	0		.185	.185	.222	407	15	-3	1			1.000	-1	/O-7(0-5-2)	-0.5
■ BILLY SMITH Smith, Billy Edward b: 7/14/53, Jonesboro, La. BB/TR, 6'2.5", 185 lbs. Deb: 4/13/75																								
1975	Cal-A	59	143	10	29	5	1	0	14	12	27	.203	.265	.252	516	50	-9	1	3	-1	.932	-9	S-50/1-6,3-2,D-4	-1.5
1976	Cal-A	13	8	0	3	0	0	0	0	0	2	.375	.375	.375	750	128	0	0	0	0	.625	-1	S-10/D-1	0.0
1977	Bal-A	109	367	44	79	12	2	5	29	33	71	.215	.282	.300	582	62	-19	3	2	-0	.991	4	*2-104/S-5,1-2,3-1	-0.9
1978	Bal-A	85	250	29	65	12	2	5	30	27	40	.260	.335	.384	719	108	3	3	0	1	.986	-1	2-83/S-2	0.6
1979	*Bal-A	68	189	18	47	9	4	6	33	15	33	.249	.311	.434	745	102	0	1	0	0	.980	-8	2-63/S-5	-0.4
1981	SF-N	36	61	6	11	0	0	1	5	9	16	.180	.286	.230	515	48	-4	0	0	0	.971	-0	S-21/2-5,3-3	-0.3
Total	6	370	1018	107	234	38	9	17	111	96	189	.230	.299	.335	634	79	-29	8	5	0	.987	-15	2-255/S-93,1-8,3D	-2.5
■ BOBBY GENE SMITH Smith, Bobby Gene b: 5/28/34, Hood River, Ore. BR/TR, 5'11", 185 lbs. Deb: 4/16/57																								
1957	StL-N	93	185	24	39	7	1	3	18	13	35	.211	.263	.308	571	52	-13	1	1	-0	.973	-8	O-79(0-61-18)	-2.4
1958	StL-N	28	88	8	25	3	0	2	5	2	18	.284	.308	.386	694	79	-3	1	0	0	1.000	-1	O-27(0-25-2)	-0.4
1959	StL-N	43	60	11	13	1	1	1	7	1	9	.217	.230	.317	546	41	-5	0	0	0	.971	-4	O-32(11-6-15)	-1.0
1960	Phi-N	98	217	24	62	5	2	4	27	10	28	.286	.317	.382	700	90	-3	2	3	-1	1.000	1	O-70(65-6-0)/3-1	-0.6
1961	Phi-N	79	174	16	44	7	0	2	18	15	32	.253	.316	.328	643	72	-7	0	1	-0	.971	6	O-47(33-3-12)	-0.3
1962	NY-N	8	22	1	3	0	1	0	2	3	2	.136	.240	.227	467	26	-2	0	1	-0	1.000	-1	/O-6(0-3-4)	-0.4
	Chi-N	13	29	3	5	0	0	1	2	2	6	.172	.226	.276	502	33	-3	0	1	-0	1.000	-1	/O-7(0-6-1)	-0.4
	StL-N	91	130	13	30	9	0	0	12	7	14	.231	.270	.300	570	48	-9	1	1	-0	1.000	-14	O-80(66-13-7)	-2.5
	Yr	112	181	17	38	9	1	1	16	12	22	.210	.259	.287	546	43	-15	1	3	-1	1.000	-15	O-93(66-22-12)	-3.3
1965	Cal-A	23	57	1	13	3	0	0	5	2	10	.228	.267	.281	547	57	-3	0	1	-0	1.000	-0	O-15(14-0-1)	-0.5
Total	7	476	962	101	234	35	5	13	96	55	154	.243	.286	.331	617	64	-48	5	9	-2	.986	-22	O-363(189-123-60)/3-1	-8.5
■ BRICK SMITH Smith, Brick Dudley b: 5/2/59, Charlotte, N.C. BR/TR, 6'4", 225 lbs. Deb: 9/13/87																								
1987	Sea-A	5	8	1	1	0	0	0	0	2	4	.125	.300	.125	425	18	-1	0	0	0	.963	0	/1-3,D-1	-0.1
1988	Sea-A	4	10	1	1	0	0	0	1	0	1	.100	.100	.100	200	-42	-2	0	0	0	1.000	1	/1-4	-0.1
Total	2	9	18	2	2	0	0	0	1	2	5	.111	.200	.111	311	-12	-3	0	0	0	.983	1	/1-7,D-1	-0.2
■ BERNIE SMITH Smith, Calvin Bernard b: 9/4/41, Ponchatoula, La. BR/TR, 5'9", 164 lbs. Deb: 7/31/70																								
1970	Mil-A	44	76	8	21	3	1	1	6	11	12	.276	.382	.382	764	110	2	1	3	-1	.979	-7	O-39(2-11-27)	-0.7
1971	Mil-A	15	36	1	5	1	0	1	3	0	5	.139	.162	.250	412	15	-4	0	0	0	.923	-3	O-12(3-1-9)	-0.8
Total	2	59	112	9	26	4	1	2	9	11	17	.232	.317	.339	657	83	-3	1	3	-1	.967	-9	/O-51(5-12-36)	-1.5
■ REGGIE SMITH Smith, Carl Reginald b: 4/2/45, Shreveport, La. BB/TR, 6', 195 lbs. Deb: 9/18/66 C Career OF: (3-LF 808-CF 874-RF)																								
1966	Bos-A	6	26	1	4	1	0	0	0	0	5	.154	.154	.192	346	-1	-3	0	0	0	.944	1	/O-6(0-6-0)	-0.3
1967	*Bos-A	158	565	78	139	24	6	15	61	57	95	.246	.316	.389	706	99	-0	16	6	1	.983	17	*O-144(0-144-0)/2-6	1.5
1968	Bos-A	155	558	78	148	**37**	5	15	69	64	77	.265	.345	.430	775	125	18	22	18	-1	.985	10	*O-155(0-155-0)	2.4
1969	Bos-A★	143	543	87	168	29	7	25	93	54	67	.309	.373	.527	900	142	29	7	13	-3	.959	6	*O-139(3-136-0)	3.0
1970	Bos-A	147	580	109	176	32	7	22	74	51	60	.303	.364	.497	860	126	20	10	7	-0	.977	16	*O-145(0-145-0)	3.3
1971	Bos-A	159	618	85	175	**33**	2	30	96	63	82	.283	.354	.489	843	128	22	11	3	1	.966	16	*O-159(0-87-74)	3.5
1972	Bos-A★	131	467	75	126	25	4	21	74	68	63	.270	.367	.475	843	142	25	15	4	2	.981	5	*O-129(0-4-125)	2.8
1973	Bos-A	115	423	79	128	23	2	21	69	68	49	.303	.400	.515	916	148	28	3	2	-0	.983	7	*O-104C/1-1,D-8	3.2
1974	StL-N★	143	517	79	160	26	9	23	100	71	70	.309	.394	.528	922	158	39	4	3	-0	.976	6	*O-132(0-0-132)/1-1	3.9
1975	StL-N★	135	477	67	144	26	3	19	76	63	59	.302	.387	.488	875	137	24	9	7	-0	.963	-5	O-69(0-1-68),1-66/3-1	1.1
1976	StL-N	47	170	20	37	7	1	8	23	14	28	.218	.281	.412	693	94	-2	1	2	-0	.986	7	1-17,O-16R,3-13	0.3
	LA-N	65	225	35	63	8	4	10	26	18	42	.280	.336	.484	821	133	9	2	0	0	.985	3	O-58(0-1-57)/3-1	1.0
	Yr	112	395	55	100	15	5	18	49	32	70	.253	.312	.453	766	116	6	3	2	-0	.989	10	O-74R,1-17,3-14	1.3
1977	*LA-N★	148	488	104	150	27	4	32	87	104	76	.307	**.432**	.576	1008	**168**	51	7	5	-0	.980	-7	*O-140(0-9-138)	3.6
1978	*LA-N★	128	447	82	132	27	2	29	93	70	90	.295	.392	.559	951	**164**	38	12	5	1	.950	-4	*O-126(0-1-126)	3.0
1979	LA-N	68	234	41	64	13	1	10	32	31	50	.274	.363	.466	829	126	9	6	5	-0	.988	8	O-62(0-5-59)	1.3
1980	LA-N★	92	311	47	100	13	0	15	55	41	63	.322	.402	.508	910	155	24	5	6	-1	.994	6	O-84(0-7-82)	2.6
1981	*LA-N	41	35	5	7	1	0	1	8	7	8	.200	.333	.314	648	88	-0	0	0	0	1.000	0	/1-2	0.0
1982	SF-N	106	349	51	99	11	0	18	56	46	46	.284	.367	.470	837	133	15	7	0	2	.982	2	1-99	1.3
Total	17	1987	7033	1123	2020	363	57	314	1092	890	1030	.287	.370	.489	859	136	344	137	86	0	.976	93	*O-1668R,1-186/3D2	37.5
■ CHARLIE SMITH Smith, Charles J. b: 12/11/1840, Brooklyn, N.Y. d: 11/15/1897, Great Neck, N.Y. 5'10.5", 150 lbs. Deb: 5/18/1871																								
1871	Mut-n	14	72	15	19	2	1	0	5	1	1	.264	.274	.319	593	77	-1	6	0	1	.688	-1	3-12/2-3	-0.1
■ POP SMITH Smith, Charles Marvin b: 10/12/1856, Digby, N.S., Canada d: 4/18/27, Boston, Mass. BR/TR, 5'11", 170 lbs. Deb: 5/1/1880 U																								
1880	Cin-N	83	334	35	69	10	9	0	27	6	36	.207	.221	.290	511	72	-9				.855	-11	*2-83	-1.6
1881	Cle-N	10	34	1	4	0	0	0	3	0	8	.118	.118	.118	235	-27	-5				.838	-2	3-10	-0.6
	Buf-N	3	11	3	0	0	0	0	1	3	5	.000	.214	.000	214	-27	-1				.840	-1	/2-3	-0.2
	Wor-N	11	41	1	3	0	0	0	2	3	5	.073	.136	.073	210	-31	-6				.955	2	/O-8(1-4-3),2-3	-0.4
	Yr	24	86	5	7	0	0	0	6	6	18	.081	.141	.081	223	-28	-12				.838	-1	3-10/O-8(1-4-3),2-6	-1.2
1882	Phi-a	20	65	10	6	0	0	0	2	12		.092	.234	.092	326	12	-6				.732	2	3-11/S-4,O-3C,2-2	-0.3
	Lou-a	3	11	1	2	0	0	0		0		.182	.182	.182	364	24	-1				.778	-0	/S-3	-0.1
	Yr	23	76	11	8	0	0	0	2	12		.105	.227	.105	333	14	-7				.732	2	3-11/S-7,O-3C,2-2	-0.4
1883	Col-a	97	405	82	106	14	**17**	4		22		.262	.300	.410	710	137	18				.889	18	*2-73,3-24/P-3	3.4
1884	Col-a	108	445	78	106	18	10	6		20		.238	.289	.364	653	122	12				.905	29	*2-108	4.1
1885	Pit-a	106	453	85	113	11	13	0	35	25		.249	.293	.331	624	98	-1				.922	33	*2-106	3.2
1886	Pit-a	126	483	75	105	20	9	2	57	42		.217	.288	.308	597	87	-7	38			**.895**	21	*S-98,2-28/C-1	1.6
1887	Pit-N	122	486	69	128	12	7	2	54	30	48	.263	.283	.285	568	62	-22	30			.914	-6	*2-89,S-33	-2.0
1888	Pit-N	131	481	61	99	15	2	4	52	22	78	.206	.248	.270	518	71	-15	37			.901	-2	S-75,2-56	-1.2
1889	Pit-N	72	258	26	54	10	2	5	27	24	38	.209	.292	.322	613	79	-7	12			.897	-0	S-58/2-9,3-3,O-3R	-0.4
	Bos-N	59	208	21	54	13	4	0	32	23	30	.260	.345	.361	705	92	-2	11			.890	-0	S-59	-0.1
	Yr	131	466	47	108	23	6	5	59	47	68	.232	.315	.339	655	85	-9	23			.894	-0	*S-117/2-9,3-3,O-3R	-0.5
1890	Bos-N	134	463	82	106	16	12	1	53	80	81	.229	.353	.322	675	90	-5	39			.918	-20	*2-134/S-1	-1.7
1891	Was-a	27	90	13	16	2	2	0	13	13	16	.178	.295	.244	540	57	-5	2			.919	7	2-19/S-5,3-4	0.3
Total	12	1112	4268	643	971	141	87	24	358	325	345	.228	.287	.313	600	86	-61	169			.903	70	2-713,S-336/3-52,OPC	4.0
■ CHARLEY SMITH Smith, Charles William b: 9/15/37, Charleston, S.C. d: 11/29/94, Reno, Nev. BR/TR, 6', 177 lbs. Deb: 9/8/60 Career OF: (13-LF 0-CF 0-RF)																								
1960	LA-N	18	60	2	10	1	1	0	5	1	15	.167	.180	.217	397	8	-8	0	0	0	.953	0	3-18	-0.8
1961	LA-N	9	24	4	6	1	0	2	3	1	6	.250	.280	.542	822	103	-0	0	0	0	1.000	-0	/3-4,S-3	0.0
	Phi-N	112	411	43	102	13	4	9	47	23	76	.248	.296	.365	661	75	-15	3	4	-1	.924	-2	3-94,S-14	-1.7
	Yr	121	435	47	108	14	4	11	50	24	82	.248	.295	.375	670	77	-15	3	4	-1	.926	-3	3-98,S-17	-1.7
1962	Chi-A	65	145	11	30	4	0	2	17	9	32	.207	.258	.276	534	44	-12	0	1	-0	.944	2	3-54	-1.0
1963	Chi-A	4	7	0	2	0	1	0	1	0	2	.286	.286	.571	857	136	0	0	0	0	1.000	2	/S-1	0.2
1964	Chi-A	2	7	1	1	0	1	0	0	1	1	.143	.250	.429	679	87	-0	0	0	0	1.000	3	/3-2	0.3
	NY-N	127	443	44	106	12	0	20	58	19	101	.239	.275	.402	677	90	-7	2	2	-0	.917	-12	3-85,S-36,O-13L	-1.9
1965	NY-N	135	499	49	122	20	3	16	62	17	123	.244	.275	.393	668	89	-9	2	1	0	.957	10	*3-131/S-6,2-1	0.1
1966	StL-N	116	391	34	104	13	4	10	43	22	81	.266	.305	.396	702	93	-4	0	2	-1	.964	-1	*3-107/S-1	-0.6

YEAR	TM/L	G	AB	R	H	2B	3B	HR	RBI	BB	SO	AVG	OBP	SLG	OPS	OPS+	BR+	SB	CS	SBR	FA	FR	G/POS	TPR
1967	NY-A	135	425	38	95	15	3	9	38	32	110	.224	.279	.336	616	84	-9	0	2	-1	.947	11	*3-115	0.0
1968	NY-A	46	70	2	16	4	1	1	7	5	18	.229	.280	.357	637	95	-1	0	0	0	.961	4	3-13	0.3
1969	Chi-N	2	2	0	0	0	0	0	0	0	0	.000	.000	.000	0	-89	-0	0	0	0	.000	0	H	-0.1
Total	10	771	2484	228	594	83	18	69	281	130	565	.239	.281	.370	651	82	-65	7	12	-3	.945	16	3-623/S-61,O-13L,2	-5.2
■ CHRIS SMITH	Smith, Christopher William b: 7/18/57, Torrance, Cal. BB/TR, 6', 185 lbs. Deb: 5/14/81 Career OF: (4-LF 0-CF 0-RF)																							
1981	Mon-N	7	7	0	0	0	0	0	0	0	2	.000	.000	.000	0	-99	-2	0	0	0	1.000	0	/2-1	-0.2
1982	Mon-N	2	2	0	0	0	0	0	0	0	1	.000	.000	.000	0	-98	-1	0	0	0	.000	0	/H	-0.1
1983	SF-N	22	67	13	22	6	1	1	11	7	12	.328	.408	.493	900	153	5	0	0	0	.976	-2	1-15/O-4(4-0-0),3-1	0.2
Total	3	31	76	13	22	6	1	1	11	7	15	.289	.365	.434	799	124	3	0	0	0	.976	-2	/1-15,O-4L,3-1,2-1	-0.1
■ EARL SMITH	Smith, Earl Calvin b: 3/14/28, Sunnyside, Wash. BR/TR, 6', 185 lbs. Deb: 4/14/55																							
1955	Pit-N	5	16	1	1	0	0	0	0	4	2	.063	.286	.063	348	-1	-2	0	0	0	1.000	-0	/O-5(0-5-0)	-0.3
■ EARL SMITH	Smith, Earl Leonard "Sheriff" b: 1/20/1891, Oak Hill, Ohio d: 3/14/43, Portsmouth, Ohio BB/TR, 5'11", 170 lbs. Deb: 9/12/16 Career OF: (136-LF 68-CF 114-RF)																							
1916	Chi-N	14	27	2	7	1	1	0	4	2	5	.259	.310	.370	681	98	-0	1			.800	-3	/O-7(6-0-1)	-0.3
1917	StL-A	52	199	31	56	7	7	0	10	15	21	.281	.332	.387	719	124	5	5			.977	5	O-51(22-29-0)	0.7
1918	StL-A	89	286	28	77	10	5	0	32	13	16	.269	.303	.339	642	97	-3	13			.952	1	O-81(54-25-2)	-0.6
1919	StL-A	88	252	21	63	12	5	1	36	18	27	.250	.300	.349	649	80	-7	1			.971	10	O-68(0-4-64)	-0.1
1920	StL-A	103	353	45	108	21	8	3	55	13	18	.306	.336	.436	772	100	-1	11	4	1	.916	-5	3-70,O-15(4-2-9)	-0.4
1921	StL-A	25	78	7	26	4	2	2	14	3	4	.333	.366	.513	879	115	1	0	0	0	.878	-3	3-13/O-4(0-4-0)	-0.1
	Was-A	59	180	20	39	5	2	2	12	10	19	.217	.266	.300	566	46	-15	1	0	0	.949	4	O-43(3-4-36)/3-1	-1.4
	Yr	84	258	27	65	9	4	4	26	13	23	.252	.296	.364	660	69	-13	1	0	0	.944	0	O-47(3-8-36),3-14	-1.5
1922	Was-A	65	205	22	53	12	2	1	23	8	17	.259	.293	.351	644	71	-9	4	4	-1	.917	1	O-49(47-0-2)/3-2	-1.2
Total	7	495	1580	176	429	72	32	9	186	82	127	.272	.311	.375	686	90	-29	36	8		.952	10	O-318L/3-86	-3.4
■ EARL SMITH	Smith, Earl Sutton "Oil" b: 2/14/1897, Hot Springs, Ark. d: 6/8/63, Little Rock, Ark. BL/TR, 5'10.5", 180 lbs. Deb: 4/24/19																							
1919	NY-N	21	36	5	9	2	1	0	8	3	3	.250	.308	.361	669	102	0	1			.973	-3	C-14/2-1	-0.2
1920	NY-N	91	262	20	77	7	1	1	30	18	16	.294	.344	.340	684	98	-0	5	2	0	.976	-5	C-82	0.1
1921	*NY-N	89	229	35	77	8	4	10	51	27	8	.336	.409	.537	946	148	16	4	3	-0	.965	-10	C-78	1.0
1922	*NY-N	90	234	29	65	11	4	9	39	37	12	.278	.383	.474	858	119	7	1	1	-0	.978	-2	C-75	0.9
1923	NY-N	24	34	2	7	1	1	1	4	4	1	.206	.289	.382	672	77	-1	0	0	0	.975	2	C-12	0.1
	Bos-N	72	191	22	55	15	1	3	19	22	10	.288	.364	.424	789	112	3	0	1	-0	.975	-4	C-54	0.3
	Yr	96	225	24	62	16	2	4	23	26	11	.276	.353	.418	771	106	2	0	1	-0	.975	-2	C-66	0.4
1924	Bos-N	33	59	1	16	3	0	0	8	6	3	.271	.338	.322	660	81	-1	0	1	-0	.946	-1	C-13	-0.2
	Pit-N	39	111	12	41	10	1	4	21	13	4	.369	.435	.586	1021	168	11	2	0	0	.974	0	C-35	1.3
	Yr	72	170	13	57	13	1	4	29	19	7	.335	.402	.494	896	140	10	2	1	0	.967	-1	C-48	1.1
1925	*Pit-N	109	329	34	103	22	3	8	64	31	13	.313	.374	.471	845	107	4	4	1	1	.968	11	C-96	2.0
1926	Pit-N	105	292	29	101	17	2	2	46	28	7	.346	.407	.438	845	121	10	1			.964	4	C-98	1.9
1927	*Pit-N	66	189	16	51	3	1	5	25	21	11	.270	.346	.376	722	87	-3	0			.986	-4	C-61	-0.4
1928	Pit-N	32	85	8	21	6	0	2	11	11	7	.247	.333	.388	722	85	-2	0			.967	-4	C-28	-0.4
	*StL-N	24	58	3	13	2	0	0	7	5	4	.224	.286	.259	544	42	-5	0			1.000	-1	C-18	-0.5
	Yr	56	143	11	34	8	0	2	18	16	11	.238	.314	.336	650	68	-7	0			.980	-5	C-46	-0.9
1929	StL-N	57	145	9	50	8	0	1	22	18	6	.345	.417	.421	838	107	3	0			.962	-5	C-50	0.0
1930	StL-N	8	10	0	0	0	0	0	0	3	1	.000	.231	.000	231	-36	-2	0			.913	1	/C-6	-0.1
Total	12	860	2264	225	686	115	19	46	355	247	106	.303	.374	.432	806	111	38	18	9		.971	-20	C-720/2-1	5.8
■ EDGAR SMITH	Smith, Edgar Eugene b: 6/12/1862, Providence, R.I. d: 11/3/1892, Providence, R.I. BR/TR, 5'10", 160 lbs. Deb: 5/25/1883 Career OF: (3-LF 0-CF 14-RF)																							
1883	Pro-N	2	9	2	2	1	0	0	1	0	2	.222	.222	.333	556	64	-0				1.000	-0	/1-2,O-2(2-0-0)	-0.1
	Phi-N	1	4	1	3	0	0	0	1	0	0	.750	.750	.750	1500	393	1				.000	-1	/P-1,O-1(1-0-0)	0.0
	Yr	3	13	3	5	1	0	0	2	0	2	.385	.385	.462	846	158	1				1.000	-1	/O-3(3-0-0),1-2,P-1	-0.1
1884	Was-a	14	57	5	5	0	1	0		1		.088	.103	.123	226	-30	-8				.794	5	O-12(0-0-12)/P-3	-0.2
1885	Pro-N	1	4	0	1	0	0	0	0	0	0	.250	.250	.250	500	64	-0				.750	0	/P-1	0.0
1890	Cle-N	8	24	2	7	0	1	0	4	4	1	.292	.393	.375	768	126	1	0			.900	1	/P-6,O-2(0-0-2)	0.0
Total	4	26	98	10	18	1	2	0	6	5	3	.184	.223	.235	458	47	-6	0			.821	5	/O-17R,P-11,1-2	-0.3
■ MAYO SMITH	Smith, Edward Mayo b: 1/17/15, New London, Mo. d: 11/24/77, Boynton Beach, Fla BL/TR, 6', 183 lbs. Deb: 6/24/45 M																							
1945	Phi-A	73	203	18	43	5	0	0	11	36	13	.212	.333	.236	570	67	-7	0	1	-0	.976	-8	O-65(33-27-7)	-1.9
■ ELMER SMITH	Smith, Elmer Ellsworth b: 3/23/1868, Pittsburgh, Pa. d: 11/3/45, Pittsburgh, Pa. BL/TL, 5'11", 178 lbs. Deb: 9/10/1886 Career OF: (927-LF 39-CF 123-RF)																							
1886	Cin-a	9	28	6	8	1	1	0	2	9		.286	.459	.393	852	163	3	0			.600	-2	P-9/O-1(1-0-0)	0.0
1887	Cin-a	52	197	26	58	10	6	0	23	11		.294	.298	.371	669	84	-5	5			.851	-6	P-52/O-2(0-2-0)	-0.1
1888	Cin-a	40	129	15	29	4	1	0	9	20		.225	.329	.271	600	88	-1	2			.838	-6	P-40/O-2(0-2-0)	-0.1
1889	Cin-a	29	83	12	23	3	1	2	17	7	18	.277	.348	.410	757	112	1	1			.821	-4	P-29	0.0
1892	Pit-N	138	511	86	140	16	14	4	63	82	43	.274	.375	.384	759	129	20	22			.885	-5	*O-124(115-2-7),P-17	0.3
1893	Pit-N	128	518	121	179	26	23	7	103	77	23	.346	.435	.525	960	158	44	26			.921	3	*O-128(128-0-0)	2.9
1894	Pit-N	126	490	128	175	33	19	6	74	68	12	.357	.440	.539	979	136	30	34			.933	4	*O-126(121-5-0)/P-1	1.8
1895	Pit-N	125	484	89	146	15	12	1	81	55	25	.302	.380	.388	768	104	5	34			.897	-3	*O-124(124-0-0)	-0.7
1896	Pit-N	122	484	121	175	21	14	6	94	74	18	.362	.454	.500	954	158	45	33			.946	9	*O-122(122-0-0)	3.6
1897	Pit-N	123	467	99	145	19	17	6	54	70		.310	.408	.463	871	135	26	25			.904	3	*O-123(123-0-0)	1.5
1898	Cin-N	123	486	79	166	21	10	1	66	69		.342	.425	.432	858	136	25	20			.949	4	*O-123(123-0-0)/P-1	1.6
1899	Cin-N	88	343	65	101	13	6	1	24	47		.294	.381	.376	757	106	4	10			.923	-1	O-88(38-28-22)	-0.3
1900	Cin-N	29	111	14	31	4	4	1	18	18		.279	.389	.414	804	125	4	5			.930	0	O-27(27-0-0)	0.2
	NY-N	85	312	47	81	9	7	2	34	24		.260	.317	.353	669	89	-5	14			.953	-8	O-83(0-0-83)	-1.6
	Yr	114	423	61	112	13	11	3	52	42		.265	.337	.369	706	99	-1	19			.944	-8	*O-110(27-0-83)	-1.4
1901	Pit-N	4	4	0	0	0	0	0	0	2		.000	.333	.000	333	1	-0	0			1.000	-0	/O-1(1-0-0)	-0.1
	Bos-N	16	57	5	10	2	1	0	3	6		.175	.254	.246	500	41	-4	2			.833	-3	O-15(4-0-11)	-0.8
	Yr	20	61	5	10	2	1	0	3	8		.164	.261	.230	490	40	-5	2			.846	-3	O-16(5-0-11)	-0.9
Total	14	1237	4704	913	1467	197	136	37	665	639	139	.312	.398	.434	831	126	192	233			.922	-17	*O-1089L,P-149	8.2
■ ELMER SMITH	Smith, Elmer John b: 9/21/1892, Sandusky, Ohio d: 8/3/84, Columbia, Ky. BL/TR, 5'10", 165 lbs. Deb: 9/20/14																							
1914	Cle-A	13	53	5	17	3	0	0	8	2	11	.321	.345	.377	723	113	1	1	1	-0	1.000	1	O-13(0-13-0)	0.1
1915	Cle-A	144	476	37	118	23	12	3	67	36	75	.248	.301	.366	666	97	-4	10	11	-2	.923	0	*O-123(21-0-102)	-1.2
1916	Cle-A	79	213	25	59	15	3	3	40	18	35	.277	.336	.418	754	119	4	3			.966	-2	O-57(1-0-56)	0.0
	Was-A	45	168	12	36	10	3	2	27	18	28	.214	.298	.345	643	94	-2	4			.988	1	O-45(10-0-35)	-0.3
	Yr	124	381	37	95	25	6	5	67	36	63	.249	.319	.386	705	108	2	7			.976	-1	*O-102(11-0-91)	-0.3
1917	Was-A	35	117	8	26	4	3	0	17	5	14	.222	.260	.308	568	74	-4	1			.901	-0	O-29(27-0-2)	-0.6
	Cle-A	64	161	21	42	5	1	3	22	13	18	.261	.316	.360	676	99	-1	6			.986	-1	O-40(8-0-32)	-0.4
	Yr	99	278	29	68	9	4	3	39	18	32	.245	.293	.338	631	89	-5	7			.943	-1	O-69(35-0-34)	-1.0
1919	Cle-A	114	395	60	110	24	6	9	54	41	30	.278	.354	.438	792	115	7	15			.957	-6	*O-111(0-0-111)	-0.5
1920	*Cle-A	129	456	82	144	37	10	12	103	53	35	.316	.391	.520	910	135	22	5	4	-0	.970	-8	*O-129(0-0-129)	0.8
1921	Cle-A	129	431	98	125	28	9	16	85	56	46	.290	.374	.508	882	121	13	0	2	-1	.971	-8	*O-127(1-0-126)	-0.4
1922	Bos-A	73	231	43	66	13	6	6	32	25	21	.286	.358	.472	830	116	5	0	3	-1	.947	2	O-58(0-1-57)	0.1
	*NY-A	21	27	1	5	0	0	1	5	3	5	.185	.267	.296	563	46	-2	0	0	0	.933	-2	O-11(2-0-9)	-0.4
	Yr	94	258	44	71	13	6	7	37	28	26	.275	.348	.453	802	108	2	0	3	-1	.945	1	O-69(2-1-66)	-0.3
1923	NY-A	70	183	30	56	6	2	7	35	21	21	.306	.377	.475	853	121	5	3	1	0	.948	-2	O-47(0-0-47)	0.0
1925	Cin-N	96	284	47	77	13	7	8	46	28	20	.271	.339	.451	789	102	0	6	5	-0	.967	-5	O-80(53-2-26)	-1.0
Total	10	1012	3195	469	881	181	62	70	541	319	359	.276	.344	.437	781	112	44	54	27		.957	-29	O-870(123-16-732)	-3.8
■ MIKE SMITH	Smith, Elwood Hope b: 11/16/04, Norfolk, Va. d: 5/31/81, Chesapeake, Va. BL/TR, 5'11.5", 170 lbs. Deb: 9/4/26																							
1926	NY-N	4	7	0	1	0	0	0	0	0	2	.143	.143	.143	286	-23	-1	0			1.000	0	/O-1(1-0-0)	-0.1

YEAR	TM/L	G	AB	R	H	2B	3B	HR	RBI	BB	SO	AVG	OBP	SLG	OPS	OPS+	BR+	SB	CS	SBR	FA	FR	G/POS	TPR
■ CARR SMITH	Smith, Emanuel Carr b: 4/8/01, Kernersville, N.C. d: 4/14/89, Miami, Fla. BR/TR, 6'1", 175 lbs. Deb: 9/23/23																							
1923	Was-A	5	9	0	1	1	0	0	1	0	0	.111	.111	.222	333	-14	-2	0	0	0	1.000	-1	/O-4(0-4-0)	-0.3
1924	Was-A	5	10	1	2	0	0	0	0	0	3	.200	.200	.200	400	3	-1	0	0	0	1.000	-1	/O-4(0-0-4)	-0.3
Total	2	10	19	1	3	1	0	0	1	0	3	.158	.158	.211	368	-5	-3	0	0	0	1.000	-3	/O-8(0-4-4)	-0.6
■ ERNIE SMITH	Smith, Ernest Henry "Kansas City Kid" b: 10/11/1899, Totowa, N.J. d: 4/6/73, Brooklyn, N.Y. BR/TR, 5'8", 155 lbs. Deb: 4/17/30																							
1930	Chi-A	24	79	5	19	3	0	0	3	5	6	.241	.286	.278	564	45	-7	2	0	0	.920	0	S-21	-0.4
■ FRANK SMITH	Smith, Frank L. b: 11/24/1857, Canada d: 10/11/28, Canandaigua, N.Y. Deb: 8/6/1884																							
1884	Pit-a	10	36	3	9	0	1	0		0		.250	.250	.306	556	81	-1				.930	-3	/C-7,O-3(0-3-0)	-0.3
■ FRED SMITH	Smith, Fred Vincent b: 7/29/1886, Cleveland, Ohio d: 5/28/61, Cleveland, Ohio BR/TR, 5'11.5", 185 lbs. Deb: 4/17/13 F																							
1913	Bos-N	92	285	35	65	9	3	0	27	29	55	.228	.302	.281	582	65	-12	7			.920	-14	3-59,2-14,S-11,/O-4L	-2.6
1914	Buf-F	145	473	48	104	12	10	2	45	49	78	.220	.297	.300	597	62	-33	24			.930	-0	*3-127,S-19/1-1	-2.9
1915	Buf-F	35	114	8	27	2	4	0	11	13	15	.237	.320	.325	645	80	-5	2			.920	3	S-32/3-1	0.1
	Bro-F	110	385	41	95	16	6	5	58	25	49	.247	.298	.358	656	85	-15	21			.920	1	S-94,3-15	-0.7
	Yr	145	499	49	122	18	10	5	69	38	64	.244	.303	.351	654	84	-19	23			.920	5	*S-126,3-16	-0.6
1917	StL-N	56	165	11	30	0	2	1	17	17	22	.182	.262	.224	487	51	-9	4			.950	7	3-51/2-2,S-1	-0.1
Total	4	438	1422	143	321	39	25	8	158	133	219	.226	.296	.305	601	69	-73	58			.932	-3	3-253,S-157/2-16,O1	-6.2
■ GEORGE SMITH	Smith, George Cornelius b: 7/7/37, St.Petersburg, Fla. d: 6/15/87, St.Petersburg, Fla. BR/TR, 5'10", 170 lbs. Deb: 8/4/63																							
1963	Det-A	52	171	16	37	8	2	0	17	18	34	.216	.298	.287	585	63	-8	4	0	1	.982	11	2-52	0.8
1964	Det-A	5	7	1	2	0	0	0	2	1	4	.286	.375	.286	661	86	-0	1	0	0	1.000	1	/2-3	0.1
1965	Det-A	32	53	6	5	0	0	1	1	3	18	.094	.143	.151	294	-16	-8	0	0	0	.984	3	2-22/S-3,3-3	-0.5
1966	Bos-A	128	403	41	86	19	4	8	37	37	86	.213	.284	.340	624	71	-15	4	0	1	.969	16	*2-109,S-19	1.3
Total	4	217	634	64	130	27	6	9	57	59	142	.205	.278	.309	587	62	-31	9	0	2	.974	30	2-186/S-22,3-3	1.7
■ HEINIE SMITH	Smith, George Henry b: 10/24/1871, Pittsburgh, Pa. d: 6/25/39, Buffalo, N.Y. BR/TR, 5'9.5", 160 lbs. Deb: 9/8/1897 M																							
1897	Lou-N	21	76	7	20	3	0	1	7	3		.263	.300	.342	642	72	-3	1			.928	-3	2-21	-0.4
1898	Lou-N	35	121	14	23	4	0	0	13	6		.190	.246	.223	469	35	-10	6			.910	-6	2-33	-1.4
1899	Pit-N	15	53	9	15	3	1	0	12	5		.283	.345	.377	722	98	-0	2			.851	-3	2-15/S-1	-0.3
1901	NY-N	9	29	5	6	2	1	1	4	1		.207	.233	.448	682	99	-0	1			.969	-1	/2-7,P-2	-0.1
1902	NY-N	140	517	48	129	19	2	0	34	17		.250	.277	.294	571	77	-15	32			.954	7	*2-140,M	-0.7
1903	Det-A	93	336	36	75	11	3	1	22	19		.223	.271	.283	554	68	-13	12			.928	-2	2-93	-1.4
Total	6	313	1132	119	268	42	7	3	92	51		.237	.276	.294	570	71	-42	54			.935	-8	2-309/P-2,S-1	-4.3
■ GERMANY SMITH	Smith, George J. b: 4/21/1863, Pittsburgh, Pa. d: 12/1/27, Altoona, Pa. BR/TR, 6', 175 lbs. Deb: 4/17/1884																							
1884	Alt-U	25	108	9	34	8	1	0		1		.315	.321	.407	729	118	-1				.871	6	S-25/P-1	0.5
	Cle-N	72	291	31	74	14	4	4	26	2	45	.254	.259	.371	631	93	-3				.879	9	2-42,S-30	0.8
1885	Bro-a	108	419	63	108	17	11	4	62	10		.258	.275	.379	655	105	1				.884	**40**	*S-108	3.9
1886	Bro-a	105	426	66	105	17	6	2	45	19		.246	.279	.329	607	89	-7	22			.860	13	*S-105/O-1(1-0-0),C-1	0.8
1887	Bro-a	103	448	79	141	19	16	4	72	13		.315	.316	.439	755	108	2	26			**.886**	**32**	*S-101/3-2	3.0
1888	Bro-a	103	402	47	86	10	7	3	61	22		.214	.255	.296	551	76	-11	27			.844	6	*S-103/2-1	-0.2
1889	*Bro-a	121	446	89	103	22	3	3	53	40	42	.231	.296	.314	610	73	-16	35			.899	-4	*S-120/O-1(0-0-1)	-1.4
1890	*Bro-N	129	481	76	92	6	5	1	47	42	23	.191	.260	.231	491	43	-35	24			.904	4	*S-129	-2.4
1891	Cin-N	138	512	50	103	11	5	3	53	38	32	.201	.258	.260	517	50	-33	16			.909	11	*S-138	-1.6
1892	Cin-N	139	506	58	123	13	6	8	63	42	52	.243	.301	.340	641	95	-4	19			.920	25	*S-139	2.5
1893	Cin-N	130	500	63	118	18	6	4	56	38	20	.236	.293	.320	613	61	-30	14			**.934**	20	*S-130	-0.3
1894	Cin-N	129	492	73	130	34	6	3	79	41	28	.264	.323	.376	699	66	-30	15			.910	25	*S-129	0.1
1895	Cin-N	127	503	75	151	23	6	4	74	34	24	.300	.345	.394	738	86	-12	13			.923	3	*S-127	-0.2
1896	Cin-N	120	456	65	131	21	9	3	71	28	22	.287	.330	.393	722	84	-12	22			.926	-10	*S-120	-1.4
1897	Bro-N	112	428	47	86	17	3	0	29	14		.201	.233	.255	488	30	-44	1			.908	-11	*S-112	-4.3
1898	StL-N	51	157	16	25	2	1	1	9	24		.159	.275	.204	479	37	-12	1			.904	-5	S-51	-1.4
Total	15	1712	6575	907	1610	252	95	47	800	408	288	.245	.289	.332	622	74	-247	235			.902	162	*S-1667/2-43,3-2,OCP	-1.6
■ JUD SMITH	Smith, Grant Judson b: 1/13/1869, Green Oak, Mich. d: 12/7/47, Los Angeles, Cal. BR/TR, Deb: 5/21/1893 Career OF: (1-LF 0-CF 8-RF)																							
1893	Cin-N	17	43	7	10	1	0	1	5	9	5	.233	.365	.326	691	82	-1	1			.750	-2	/O-9(1-0-8),3-6,S-1	-0.3
	StL-N	4	13	1	1	0	0	0	0	1	2	.077	.200	.077	277	-25	-2	0			.889	1	/3-4	-0.1
	Yr	21	56	8	11	1	0	1	5	10	7	.196	.328	.268	596	58	-3	1			.844	-1	3-10/O-9(1-0-8),S-1	-0.4
1896	Pit-N	10	35	6	12	2	1	0	4	2	2	.343	.395	.457	852	129	1	3			.909	2	3-10	0.3
1898	Was-N	66	234	33	71	7	5	3	28	22		.303	.378	.415	792	127	8	11			.903	-10	3-47,S-10/1-7,2-1	0.0
1901	Pit-N	6	21	1	3	1	0	0	0	3		.143	.250	.190	440	28	-2	0			.947	0	/3-6	-0.2
Total	4	103	346	48	97	11	6	4	37	37	9	.280	.363	.382	745	109	5	15			.900	-9	/3-73,S-11,O-9R,12	-0.3
■ GREG SMITH	Smith, Gregory Alan b: 4/5/67, Baltimore, Md. BB/TR, 5'11", 170 lbs. Deb: 9/2/89																							
1989	Chi-N	4	5	1	2	0	0	0	2	0	0	.400	.500	.400	900	149	0	0	0	0	.778	0	/2-2	0.1
1990	Chi-N	18	44	4	9	2	1	0	5	2	5	.205	.239	.295	535	43	-3	1	0	0	1.000	4	/2-7,S-7	0.1
1991	LA-N	5	3	1	0	0	0	0	0	0	2	.000	.000	.000	0	-99	-1	0	0	0	.000	0	/2-1	-0.1
Total	3	27	52	6	11	2	1	0	7	2	7	.212	.255	.288	543	47	-4	1	0	0	.944	4	/2-10,S-7	0.1
■ HAL SMITH	Smith, Harold Raymond "Cura" b: 6/1/31, Barling, Ark. BR/TR, 5'11", 189 lbs. Deb: 5/2/56 C																							
1956	StL-N	75	227	27	64	12	0	5	23	15	22	.282	.326	.401	727	94	-2	1	0	0	.982	-2	C-66	-0.1
1957	StL-N☆	100	333	25	93	12	3	2	37	18	18	.279	.316	.351	668	78	-10	2	2	-0	.990	-1	C-97	-0.7
1958	StL-N	77	220	13	50	4	1	1	24	14	14	.227	.274	.268	542	42	-18	0	0	0	.989	-1	C-71	-1.6
1959	StL-N★	142	452	35	122	15	3	13	50	15	28	.270	.295	.403	698	78	-14	2	6	-2	.989	5	*C-141	-0.5
1960	StL-N	127	337	20	77	16	0	2	28	29	33	.228	.292	.294	585	56	-20	1	0	0	.990	18	*C-124	0.4
1961	StL-N	45	125	6	31	4	1	0	10	11	12	.248	.314	.296	610	57	-7	0	0	0	.993	17	C-45	1.2
1965	Pit-N	4	3	0	0	0	0	0	0	0	1	.000	.000	.000	0	-99	-1	0	0	0	1.000	2	/C-4	0.1
Total	7	570	1697	126	437	63	8	23	172	102	128	.258	.301	.345	646	69	-72	6	8	-1	.989	38	C-548	-1.2
■ HAL SMITH	Smith, Harold Wayne b: 12/7/30, W.Frankfort, Ill. BR/TR, 6', 195 lbs. Deb: 4/11/55																							
1955	Bal-A	135	424	41	115	23	4	4	52	30	21	.271	.322	.373	695	93	-6	1	3	-1	.986	-3	*C-125	-0.3
1956	Bal-A	77	229	16	60	14	0	3	18	17	22	.262	.316	.362	678	85	-6	1	0	0	.994	3	C-71	0.1
	KC-A	37	142	15	39	9	2	2	24	3	12	.275	.290	.408	698	82	-4	1	1	-0	.986	1	C-37	-0.1
	Yr	114	371	31	99	23	2	5	42	20	34	.267	.306	.380	686	85	-10	2	1	0	.991	5	*C-108	0.0
1957	KC-A	107	360	41	109	26	0	13	41	14	44	.303	.331	.483	814	118	7	2	2	-0	.983	-1	*C-103	1.1
1958	KC-A	99	315	32	86	19	2	5	46	25	47	.273	.330	.394	724	97	-2	0	0	0	.949	-1	3-43,C-31,1-14	-0.2
1959	KC-A	108	292	36	84	12	0	5	31	34	39	.288	.368	.380	748	104	3	0	3	-1	.953	7	3-77,C-22	0.9
1960	*Pit-N	77	258	37	76	18	2	11	45	22	48	.295	.355	.508	862	132	11	1	1	-0	.985	-6	C-71	0.8
1961	Pit-N	67	193	12	43	10	0	3	26	11	38	.223	.268	.321	590	55	-13	0	0	0	.990	-1	C-65	-1.0
1962	Hou-N	109	345	32	81	14	0	12	35	24	55	.235	.288	.380	668	84	-9	0	0	0	.986	2	C-92/3-6,1-2	-0.3
1963	Hou-N	31	58	1	14	2	0	0	2	4	15	.241	.290	.276	566	68	-2	0	0	0	.985	-3	C-11	-0.5
1964	Cin-N	32	66	6	8	1	0	0	3	12	20	.121	.256	.136	393	14	-7	1	0	0	.983	-3	C-20	-1.0
Total	10	879	2682	269	715	148	10	58	323	196	361	.267	.320	.394	714	94	-28	7	10	-2	.986	-3	C-648,3-126/1-16	-0.5
■ HARRY SMITH	Smith, Harry Thomas b: 10/31/1874, Yorkshire, England d: 2/17/33, Salem, N.J. BR/TR, 5'8.5", 165 lbs. Deb: 7/11/01 M																							
1901	Phi-A	11	34	3	11	1	0	0	3	2		.324	.378	.353	731	99	0	1			.969	-3	/C-9,O-1(0-0-1)	-0.2
1902	Pit-N	50	185	14	35	4	1	0	12	4		.189	.211	.222	432	32	-15	4			.972	-2	C-50	-1.3
1903	*Pit-N	61	212	15	37	3	2	0	19	12		.175	.222	.208	430	22	-22	2			.974	-4	C-60/O-1(0-0-1)	-1.9
1904	Pit-N	47	141	17	35	3	1	0	18	16		.248	.346	.284	629	92	-0	5			.964	-4	C-44/O-3(2-0-1)	0.0
1905	Pit-N	1	3	0	0	0	0	0	1	0		.000	.000	.000	0	-98	-1	1			1.000	0	/C-1	-0.1

YEAR	TM/L	G	AB	R	H	2B	3B	HR	RBI	BB	SO	AVG	OBP	SLG	OPS	OPS+	BR+	SB	CS	SBR	FA	FR	G/POS	TPR
1906	Pit-N	1	1	0	0	0	0	0	0	0		.000	.000	.000	0	-96	-0	0			.800	0	/C-1	0.0
1907	Pit-N	18	38	4	10	1	0	0	1	4		.263	.364	.289	653	103	0	0			.939	-3	C-18	-0.1
1908	Bos-N	41	130	13	32	2	2	1	16	7		.246	.295	.315	610	96	-1	2			.975	0	C-38	0.4
1909	Bos-N	43	113	9	19	4	1	0	4	5		.168	.203	.221	425	30	-9	3			.972	2	C-31,M	-0.5
1910	Bos-N	70	147	8	35	4	0	1	15	5	14	.238	.263	.286	549	57	-8	5			.949	3	C-38	-0.2
Total	10	343	1004	83	214	22	7	2	89	55	14	.213	.262	.255	517	54	-56	23			.967	-9	C-290/O-5(2-0-3)	-3.9

■ HARRY SMITH

Smith, Harry W. b: 2/5/1856, N.Vernon, Ind. d: 6/4/1898, Queensville, Ind. BR/TR, 6', 175 lbs. Deb: 5/8/1877 Career OF: (0-LF 11-CF 3-RF)

YEAR	TM/L	G	AB	R	H	2B	3B	HR	RBI	BB	SO	AVG	OBP	SLG	OPS	OPS+	BR+	SB	CS	SBR	FA	FR	G/POS	TPR
1877	Chi-N	24	94	7	19	1	0	0	3	4	6	.202	.235	.213	447	37	-7				.853	-7	2-14,O-10(0-7-3)	-1.3
	Cin-N	10	36	4	9	2	1	0	3	1	5	.250	.270	.361	631	109	1				.879	1	/C-8,2-3,O-3(0-3-0)	0.1
	Yr	34	130	11	28	3	1	0	6	5	11	.215	.244	.254	498	54	-7				.837	-7	2-17,O-13(0-10-3)/C-8	-1.2
1889	Lou-a	1	2	0	1	0	0	0	1	0	1	.500	.500	.500	1000	189	0	0			.000	-2	/O-1(0-1-0),C-1	-0.1
Total	2	35	132	11	29	3	1	0	7	5	12	.220	.248	.258	506	56	-6	0			.720	-8	/2-17,O-14C,C-9	-1.3

■ HARVEY SMITH

Smith, Harvey Fetterhoff b: 7/24/1871, Union Deposit, Pa d: 11/12/62, Harrisburg, Pa. BL/TR, 5'8", 160 lbs. Deb: 8/19/1896

YEAR	TM/L	G	AB	R	H	2B	3B	HR	RBI	BB	SO	AVG	OBP	SLG	OPS	OPS+	BR+	SB	CS	SBR	FA	FR	G/POS	TPR
1896	Was-N	36	131	21	36	7	2	0	17	12	7	.275	.345	.359	704	86	-3	9			.861	3	3-36	0.1

■ HAPPY SMITH

Smith, Henry Joseph b: 7/14/1883, Coquille, Ore. d: 2/26/61, San Jose, Cal. BL/TR, 6', 185 lbs. Deb: 4/15/10

YEAR	TM/L	G	AB	R	H	2B	3B	HR	RBI	BB	SO	AVG	OBP	SLG	OPS	OPS+	BR+	SB	CS	SBR	FA	FR	G/POS	TPR
1910	Bro-N	35	76	6	18	2	0	0	5	4	14	.237	.275	.263	538	59	-4	4			.974	2	O-16(0-5-11)	-0.2

■ JACK SMITH

Smith, Jack b: 6/23/1895, Chicago, Ill. d: 5/2/72, Westchester, Ill. BL/TL, 5'8", 165 lbs. Deb: 9/30/15

YEAR	TM/L	G	AB	R	H	2B	3B	HR	RBI	BB	SO	AVG	OBP	SLG	OPS	OPS+	BR+	SB	CS	SBR	FA	FR	G/POS	TPR
1915	StL-N	4	16	2	3	0	1	0	0	1	5	.188	.235	.313	548	65	-1	0			1.000	-1	/O-4(3-1-0)	-0.2
1916	StL-N	130	357	43	87	6	5	6	34	20	50	.244	.291	.339	630	94	-3	24	16	-0	.949	-11	*O-120(1-109-11)	-2.5
1917	StL-N	137	462	64	137	16	11	3	34	38	65	.297	.351	.398	750	133	18	25			.961	-10	*O-128(27-65-37)	0.1
1918	StL-N	42	166	24	35	2	1	0	4	7	21	.211	.260	.235	495	53	-9	5			.941	1	O-42(0-42-0)	-1.3
1919	StL-N	119	408	47	91	16	3	0	15	26	29	.223	.271	.277	548	69	-15	30			.960	-0	*O-111(1-36-76)	-2.5
1920	StL-N	91	313	53	104	22	5	1	28	25	23	.332	.385	.444	829	143	17	14	9	-0	.963	-10	O-83(18-57-14)	0.3
1921	StL-N	116	411	86	135	22	9	7	33	21	24	.328	.361	.477	838	122	12	11	6	0	.955	-6	*O-103(0-19-84)	-0.1
1922	StL-N	143	510	117	158	23	12	8	46	50	30	.310	.375	.449	824	117	13	18	7	2	.951	-8	*O-136(17-79-40)	-0.1
1923	StL-N	124	407	98	126	16	6	5	41	27	20	.310	.356	.415	771	105	3	32	11	3	.974	4	*O-109(77-10-23)	0.2
1924	StL-N	124	459	91	130	18	6	2	33	33	27	.283	.333	.362	694	88	-8	24	16	-0	.968	10	*O-114(25-14-77)	-0.7
1925	StL-N	80	243	53	61	11	4	4	31	19	13	.251	.308	.379	687	73	-10	20	2	4	.958	-3	O-64(5-38-28)	-1.2
1926	StL-N	1	1	0	0	0	0	0	0	0	1	.000	.000	.000	0	-96	-0	0			.000	0	H	0.0
	Bos-N	96	322	46	100	15	2	2	25	28	12	.311	.369	.388	758	114	7	11			.973	2	O-83(10-59-15)	0.4
	Yr	97	323	46	100	15	2	2	25	28	13	.310	.368	.387	755	113	7	11			.973	2	O-83(10-59-15)	0.4
1927	Bos-N	84	183	27	58	6	4	1	24	16	12	.317	.375	.410	785	119	5	8			.950	-1	O-48(3-14-32)	0.2
1928	Bos-N	96	254	30	71	9	2	1	32	21	14	.280	.335	.343	677	82	-7	6			.988	1	O-65(18-40-7)	-0.9
1929	Bos-N	19	20	2	5	0	0	0	2	2	2	.250	.318	.250	568	45	-2	0			.833	-3	/O-9(2-4-3)	-0.5
Total	15	1406	4532	783	1301	182	71	40	382	334	348	.287	.339	.385	724	103	19	228	67		.961	-36	*O-1219(207-587-447)	-8.8

■ STUB SMITH

Smith, James A. b: 11/26/1876, Elmwood, Ill. BL/TR, 5'6", 145 lbs. Deb: 9/10/1898

YEAR	TM/L	G	AB	R	H	2B	3B	HR	RBI	BB	SO	AVG	OBP	SLG	OPS	OPS+	BR+	SB	CS	SBR	FA	FR	G/POS	TPR
1898	Bos-N	3	10	1	1	0	0	0	0	0		.100	.100	.100	200	-41	-2	0			.933	1	/S-3	-0.1

■ RED SMITH

Smith, James Carlisle b: 4/6/1890, Greenville, S.C. d: 10/11/66, Atlanta, Ga. BR/TR, 5'11", 165 lbs. Deb: 9/5/11

YEAR	TM/L	G	AB	R	H	2B	3B	HR	RBI	BB	SO	AVG	OBP	SLG	OPS	OPS+	BR+	SB	CS	SBR	FA	FR	G/POS	TPR
1911	Bro-N	28	111	10	29	6	1	0	19	5	13	.261	.299	.333	632	80	-3	5			.900	-2	3-28	-0.5
1912	Bro-N	128	486	75	139	28	6	4	57	54	51	.286	.362	.393	755	111	8	22			.938	5	*3-125	1.6
1913	Bro-N	151	540	70	160	**40**	10	6	76	45	67	.296	.358	.441	799	124	16	22			.933	-1	*3-151	2.0
1914	Bro-N	90	330	39	81	10	8	4	48	30	26	.245	.310	.361	671	97	-2	11			.937	12	3-90	1.4
	Bos-N	60	207	30	65	17	1	3	37	28	24	.314	.401	.449	850	153	14	4			.937	10	3-60	2.8
	Yr	150	537	69	146	27	9	7	85	58	50	.272	.346	.395	741	119	12	15			.937	23	*3-150	4.2
1915	Bos-N	157	549	66	145	34	4	2	65	67	49	.264	.345	.352	697	116	12	10	5	0	.947	-7	*3-157	1.1
1916	Bos-N	150	509	48	132	16	10	3	60	53	55	.259	.333	.348	680	114	9	13			.928	-4	*3-150	1.0
1917	Bos-N	147	505	60	149	31	6	2	62	53	61	.295	.369	.392	761	142	26	16			.925	-21	*3-147	1.0
1918	Bos-N	119	429	55	128	20	3	2	65	45	47	.298	.373	.373	746	133	18	8			.922	4	*3-119	2.8
1919	Bos-N	87	241	24	59	6	0	1	25	40	22	.245	.359	.282	641	98	2	6			.981	-0	O-48(17-30-3),3-23	0.0
Total	9	1117	3907	477	1087	208	49	27	514	420	415	.278	.353	.377	731	120	100	117	5		.932	-3	*3-1050/O-48(17-30-3)	13.2

■ HARRY SMITH

Smith, James Harry b: 5/15/1890, Baltimore, Md. d: 4/1/22, Charlotte, N.C. BR/TR, 5'10", 180 lbs. Deb: 9/21/14

YEAR	TM/L	G	AB	R	H	2B	3B	HR	RBI	BB	SO	AVG	OBP	SLG	OPS	OPS+	BR+	SB	CS	SBR	FA	FR	G/POS	TPR
1914	NY-N	5	7	0	3	0	0	0	2	3	1	.429	.600	.429	1029	215	1	1			1.000	2	/C-4	0.3
1915	NY-N	21	32	1	4	0	1	0	3	6	12	.125	.263	.188	451	40	-2	0	1	-0	.967	-3	C-18	-0.5
	Bro-F	28	65	5	13	0	0	1	4	7	16	.200	.278	.246	524	48	-5	2			.967	-5	C-19/O-1(0-0-1)	-1.0
1917	Cin-N	8	17	0	2	0	0	0	1	2	7	.118	.211	.118	328	2	-2	0			.978	4	/C-7	0.3
1918	Cin-N	13	27	4	5	1	2	0	4	3	6	.185	.267	.370	637	95	-0	1			1.000	-2	/C-6,O-1(0-1-0)	-0.2
Total	4	75	148	10	27	1	3	1	14	21	42	.182	.284	.250	534	59	-8	4	1		.975	-4	/C-54,O-2(0-1-1)	-1.1

■ JIMMY SMITH

Smith, James Lawrence "Greenfield Jimmy" b: 5/15/1895, Pittsburgh, Pa. d: 1/1/74, Pittsburgh, Pa. BB/TR (BR 1914), 5'9", 152 lbs. Deb: 9/26/14

YEAR	TM/L	G	AB	R	H	2B	3B	HR	RBI	BB	SO	AVG	OBP	SLG	OPS	OPS+	BR+	SB	CS	SBR	FA	FR	G/POS	TPR
1914	Chi-F	3	6	1	3	1	0	0	1	0	0	.500	.500	.667	1167	229	1	0			1.000	1	/S-3	0.2
1915	Chi-F	95	318	32	69	11	4	4	30	14	65	.217	.250	.314	564	62	-23	4			.904	-14	S-92/2-1	-3.4
	Bal-F	33	108	9	19	1	1	1	11	11	23	.176	.258	.231	490	37	-11	3			.883	-4	S-33	-1.3
	Yr	128	426	41	88	12	5	5	41	25	88	.207	.252	.293	546	55	-34	7			.898	-18	*S-125/2-1	-4.7
1916	Pit-N	36	96	4	18	1	1	0	5	6	22	.188	.257	.219	476	46	-6	0			.929	1	S-27/3-6	-0.4
1917	NY-N	36	96	12	22	5	1	0	9	9	18	.229	.295	.302	597	86	-2	6			.971	-2	2-29/S-7	-0.4
1918	Bos-N	34	102	8	23	3	4	1	14	3	13	.225	.255	.363	617	91	-2	1			1.000	-1	2-10/S-9,O-6C,3-5	-0.2
1919	*Cin-N	28	40	9	11	1	3	1	10	4	8	.275	.341	.525	866	163	3	1			1.000	-2	/3-6,S-5,2-4,O-4R	0.2
1921	Phi-N	67	247	31	57	8	1	4	22	11	28	.231	.266	.320	586	50	-18	2	8	-2	.971	8	2-66	-1.0
1922	Phi-N	38	114	13	25	1	0	1	6	5	9	.219	.258	.254	513	30	-12	1	3	-1	.952	-3	S-23,2-13/3-1	-1.3
Total	8	370	1127	119	247	32	15	12	108	63	186	.219	.265	.306	571	60	-68	18	11		.910	-16	S-199,2-123/3-18,O	-7.6

■ JIM SMITH

Smith, James Lorne b: 9/8/54, Santa Monica, Cal. BR/TR, 6'3", 185 lbs. Deb: 4/12/82

YEAR	TM/L	G	AB	R	H	2B	3B	HR	RBI	BB	SO	AVG	OBP	SLG	OPS	OPS+	BR+	SB	CS	SBR	FA	FR	G/POS	TPR
1982	Pit-N	42	42	5	10	2	1	0	4	5	7	.238	.319	.333	652	80	-1	0	1	-0	.929	8	S-29/2-3,3-1	0.8

■ JOHN SMITH

Smith, John b: Baltimore, Md. Deb: 4/14/1873

YEAR	TM/L	G	AB	R	H	2B	3B	HR	RBI	BB	SO	AVG	OBP	SLG	OPS	OPS+	BR+	SB	CS	SBR	FA	FR	G/POS	TPR
1873	Mar-n	5	19	2	2	0	0	0	1	0	1	.105	.105	.105	211	-49	-3	0	0	0	.773	-2	/S-3,O-2(2-0-0)	-0.3
1874	Bal-n	6	21	2	4	1	0	0	1	0	1	.190	.190	.238	429	37	-1	0	0	0	.731	-10	/S-6	-0.9
1875	NH-n	1	3	0	0	0	0	0	0	1	0	.000	.250	.000	250	-6	-0	0	0	0	.500	-1	/S-1	-0.1
Total	3 n	12	43	4	6	1	0	0	2	1	2	.140	.159	.163	322	1	-4	0	0	0	.722	-12	/S-10,O-2(2-0-0)	-1.3

■ DWIGHT SMITH

Smith, John Dwight b: 11/8/63, Tallahassee, Fla. BL/TR, 5'11", 175 lbs. Deb: 5/1/89

YEAR	TM/L	G	AB	R	H	2B	3B	HR	RBI	BB	SO	AVG	OBP	SLG	OPS	OPS+	BR+	SB	CS	SBR	FA	FR	G/POS	TPR
1989	*Chi-N	109	343	52	111	19	6	9	52	31	51	.324	.383	.493	876	138	17	9	4	1	.975	1	*O-102(75-0-32)	1.7
1990	Chi-N	117	290	34	76	15	0	6	27	28	46	.262	.331	.376	707	88	-4	11	6	0	.986	-4	O-81(59-3-22)	-1.0
1991	Chi-N	90	167	16	38	7	2	3	21	11	32	.228	.279	.347	627	72	-6	2	3	-1	.962	-3	O-42(5-13-28)	-1.1
1992	Chi-N	109	217	28	60	10	3	3	24	13	40	.276	.320	.392	712	98	-1	9	8	-1	.979	-10	O-63(20-27-22)	-1.4
1993	Chi-N	111	310	51	93	17	5	11	35	25	51	.300	.358	.494	852	127	11	8	6	-0	.955	-8	O-89(14-53-28)	0.2
1994	Cal-A	45	122	19	32	5	1	5	18	7	20	.262	.302	.443	745	88	-3	2	3	-1	.912	-2	O-31(31-0-0)/D-2	-0.6
	Bal-A	28	74	12	23	2	1	3	12	5	17	.311	.363	.486	849	111	1	0	1	-0	.939	-4	O-22(20-2-1)/D-3	-0.4
	Yr	73	196	31	55	7	2	8	30	12	37	.281	.325	.459	785	97	-1	2	4	-1	.922	-6	O-53(51-2-1)/D-5	-1.0
1995	*Atl-N	103	131	16	33	8	2	3	21	13	35	.252	.329	.412	741	91	-2	0	3	-1	.923	-4	O-25(11-0-14)	-0.8
1996	Atl-N	101	153	16	31	5	0	3	16	17	42	.203	.287	.294	581	51	-11	1	3	-1	.962	-0	O-29(3-0-26)	-1.3
Total	8	813	1807	244	497	88	20	46	226	150	334	.275	.335	.422	757	101	3	42	37	-4	.964	-34	O-484(238-98-173)/D-5	-4.7

■ JOHN SMITH

Smith, John J. b: 1858, New York, N.Y. 5'11", 210 lbs. Deb: 5/1/1882

YEAR	TM/L	G	AB	R	H	2B	3B	HR	RBI	BB	SO	AVG	OBP	SLG	OPS	OPS+	BR+	SB	CS	SBR	FA	FR	G/POS	TPR
1882	Tro-N	35	149	27	36	4	3	0	14	3	24	.242	.257	.309	565	84	-2				.960	-0	1-35	-0.5

YEAR	TM/L	G	AB	R	H	2B	3B	HR	RBI	BB	SO	AVG	OBP	SLG	OPS	OPS+	BR+	SB	CS	SBR	FA	FR	G/POS	TPR
	Wor-N	19	70	10	17	3	2	0	5	5	10	.243	.293	.343	636	101	0				.939	1	1-19	-0.1
	Yr	54	219	37	53	7	5	0	19	8	34	.242	.269	.320	588	90	-2				.952	1	1-54	-0.6
■ JACK SMITH	Smith, John Joseph (b: John Joseph Coffey) b: 8/8/1893, Oswayo, Pa. d: 12/4/62, New York, N.Y. BR/TR, 5'9", Deb: 5/18/12																							
1912	Det-A	1	0	0	0	0	0	0	0	0		—	—	—	—	—	0	0			1.000	1	/3-1	0.1
■ JOHN SMITH	Smith, John Marshall b: 9/27/06, Washington, D.C. d: 5/9/82, Silver Spring, Md. BB/TR, 6'1", 180 lbs. Deb: 9/17/31																							
1931	Bos-A	4	15	2	2	0	0	0	1	2	1	.133	.235	.133	369	-1	-2	1	0	0	1.000	-1	/1-4	-0.3
■ KEITH SMITH	Smith, Keith Lavarne b: 5/3/53, Palmetto, Fla. BR/TR, 5'9", 178 lbs. Deb: 8/2/77																							
1977	Tex-A	23	67	13	16	4	0	2	6	4	7	.239	.301	.388	689	85	-1	2	0	0	.975	-1	O-22(22-0-0)	-0.3
1979	StL-N	6	13	1	3	0	0	0	0	0	1	.231	.231	.231	462	26	-1	0	1	-0	1.000	2	/O-5(5-0-0)	0.0
1980	StL-N	24	31	3	4	1	0	0	2	2	2	.129	.182	.161	343	-3	-4	0	0	0	1.000	-1	/O-7(4-1-2)	-0.6
Total	3	53	111	17	23	5	0	2	8	6	10	.207	.261	.306	567	54	-7	2	1	0	.985	0	/O-34(31-1-2)	-0.9
■ KEN SMITH	Smith, Kenneth Earl b: 2/12/58, Youngstown, Ohio BL/TR, 6'1", 195 lbs. Deb: 9/22/81																							
1981	Atl-N	5	3	0	1	1	0	0	0	0	1	.333	.333	.667	1000	174	0	0	0	0	1.000	0	/1-4	0.1
1982	Atl-N	48	41	6	12	1	0	0	3	6	13	.293	.383	.317	700	94	-0	0	0	0	1.000	-1	/1-6,O-3(3-0-0)	-0.2
1983	Atl-N	30	12	2	2	0	0	1	2	1	5	.167	.231	.417	647	71	-1	1	0	0	1.000	2	1-13	0.2
Total	3	83	56	8	15	2	0	1	5	7	19	.268	.349	.357	706	93	-0	1	0	0	1.000	1	/1-23,O-3(3-0-0)	0.1
■ L. SMITH	Smith, L. Deb: 9/7/1882																							
1882	Bal-a	1	3	0	0	0	0	0		0		.000	.000	.000	0	-99	-1				1.000	-0	/O-1(0-0-1)	-0.1
■ PADDY SMITH	Smith, Lawrence Patrick b: 5/16/1894, Pelham, N.Y. d: 12/2/90, New Rochelle, N.Y. BL/TR, 6', 195 lbs. Deb: 7/6/20																							
1920	Bos-A	2	2	0	0	0	0	0	0	0	1	.000	.000	.000	0	-99	-1	0	0	0	.000	0	/C-1	-0.1
■ BULL SMITH	Smith, Lewis Oscar b: 8/20/1880, Plum, W.Va. d: 5/1/28, Charleston, W.Va. BR/TR, 6', 180 lbs. Deb: 8/30/04																							
1904	Pit-N	13	42	2	6	0	1	0	0	1		.143	.163	.190	353	9	-5	0			.857	-0	O-13(11-0-2)	-0.6
1906	Chi-N	1	1	0	0	0	0	0	0	0		.000	.000	.000	0	-95	-0	0			.000	0	H	0.0
1911	Was-A	1	0	0	0	0	0	0	0	0		—	—	—	—	—	0	0			.000	0	R	0.0
Total	3	15	43	2	6	0	1	0	0	1		.140	.159	.186	345	6	-5	0			.857	-0	/O-13(11-0-2)	-0.6
■ LEO SMITH	Smith, Lionel H. b: 5/13/1859, Brooklyn, N.Y. d: 8/30/35, Brooklyn, N.Y. 5'6", 142 lbs. Deb: 8/28/1890																							
1890	Roc-a	35	112	11	21	1	3	0	11	14		.188	.283	.250	533	62	-5	1			.948	8	S-35	0.4
■ LONNIE SMITH	Smith, Lonnie b: 12/22/55, Chicago, Ill. BR/TR, 5'9", 170 lbs. Deb: 9/2/78 Career OF: (1257-LF 77-CF 54-RF)																							
1978	Phi-N	17	4	6	0	0	0	0	0	4	3	.000	.500	.000	500	50	0	4	0	1	1.000	-3	O-11(10-1-1)	-0.2
1979	Phi-N	17	30	4	5	2	0	0	3	1	7	.167	.194	.233	427	15	-4	2	1	0	1.000	-1	O-11(3-5-4)	-0.5
1980	*Phi-N	100	298	69	101	14	4	3	20	26	48	.339	.399	.443	842	128	12	33	13	3	.969	-9	O-82(52-9-23)	0.3
1981	*Phi-N	62	176	40	57	14	3	2	11	18	14	.324	.402	.472	874	141	10	21	10	1	.971	2	O-51(8-23-24)	1.2
1982	*StL-N★	156	592	**120**	182	35	8	8	69	64	74	.307	.383	.434	818	127	23	68	26	6	.970	-1	*O-149(135-36-0)	2.3
1983	StL-N	130	492	83	158	31	5	8	45	41	55	.321	.384	.453	837	131	21	43	18	3	.941	3	*O-126(126-0-0)	2.2
1984	StL-N	145	504	77	126	20	4	6	49	70	90	.250	.352	.341	693	98	1	50	13	6	.948	-3	*O-140(140-0-0)	-0.1
1985	StL-N	28	96	15	25	2	2	0	7	15	20	.260	.377	.323	700	98	1	12	6	1	1.000	-1	O-28(29-0-0)	-0.1
	*KC-A	120	448	77	115	23	4	6	41	41	69	.257	.325	.366	691	88	-7	40	7	6	.958	-3	*O-119(119-0-0)	-0.9
1986	KC-A	134	508	80	146	25	7	8	44	46	78	.287	.358	.411	770	107	6	26	9	3	.965	4	*O-118(118-0-0),D-10	0.6
1987	KC-A	48	167	26	42	7	1	3	8	24	31	.251	.359	.359	718	89	-2	9	4	1	.915	-2	O-32(32-0-0),D-15	-0.5
1988	Atl-N	43	114	14	27	3	0	3	9	10	25	.237	.298	.342	640	79	-3	4	2	0	.968	-1	O-35(35-0-0)	-0.5
1989	Atl-N	134	482	89	152	34	4	21	79	76	95	.315	**.420**	.533	953	166	44	25	12	1	.993	9	*O-132(132-0-0)	5.2
1990	Atl-N	135	466	72	142	27	9	9	42	58	69	.305	.389	.459	848	125	17	10	10	-1	.956	5	*O-122(122-0-0)	1.8
1991	*Atl-N	122	353	58	97	19	1	7	44	50	64	.275	.379	.394	772	111	7	9	5	0	.965	-8	O-99(99-0-0)	-0.3
1992	*Atl-N	84	158	23	39	8	2	6	33	17	37	.247	.331	.437	768	109	2	4	0	1	.954	0	O-35(35-0-0)	0.2
1993	Pit-N	94	199	35	57	5	4	6	24	43	42	.286	.425	.442	867	133	12	9	4	1	.981	-4	O-60(58-3-0)	0.7
	Bal-A	9	24	8	5	1	0	2	3	8	10	.208	.406	.500	906	136	2	0	0	0	1.000	0	/O-4(4-0-0),D-5	0.2
1994	Bal-A	35	59	13	12	3	0	0	2	11	18	.203	.338	.254	592	53	-4	1	0	0	1.000	0	D-30/O-2(0-0-2)	-0.5
Total	17	1613	5170	909	1488	273	58	98	533	623	849	.288	.374	.420	794	117	139	370	140	32	.964	-12	*O-1356L/D-60	11.1
■ MARK SMITH	Smith, Mark Edward b: 5/7/70, Pasadena, Cal. BR/TR, 6'3", 205 lbs. Deb: 5/14/94 Career OF: (93-LF 0-CF 84-RF)																							
1994	Bal-A	3	7	0	1	0	0	0	2	0	2	.143	.143	.143	286	-25	-1	0	0	0	1.000	0	/O-3(0-0-3)	-0.1
1995	Bal-A	37	104	11	24	5	0	3	15	12	22	.231	.316	.365	682	76	-4	3	0	1	1.000	2	O-32(15-0-17)/D-3	-0.3
1996	Bal-A	27	78	9	19	2	0	4	10	3	20	.244	.298	.423	721	80	-3	0	2	-1	.980	2	O-20(12-0-8)/D-6	-0.2
1997	Pit-N	71	193	29	55	13	1	9	35	28	36	.285	.376	.503	878	125	7	3	1	0	1.000	-2	O-42(21-0-22)/1-9,D-5	0.4
1998	Pit-N	59	128	18	25	6	0	2	13	10	26	.195	.270	.289	559	46	-10	7	0	2	.977	-0	O-24(16-0-9)/1-6,D-3	-1.0
2000	Fla-N	104	192	22	47	8	1	5	27	17	54	.245	.313	.375	688	77	-7	2	0	0	1.000	-3	O-49(29-0-25)/D-1	-1.1
Total	6	301	702	89	171	34	2	23	102	70	160	.244	.320	.396	716	84	-18	15	3	2	.993	-2	O-170L/D-18,1-15	-2.3
■ RED SMITH	Smith, Marvin Harold b: 7/17/1900, Ashley, Ill. d: 2/19/61, Los Angeles, Cal. BL/TR, 5'7", 165 lbs. Deb: 4/14/25																							
1925	Phi-A	20	14	1	4	0	0	0	1	2	5	.286	.375	.286	661	65	-1	0	0	0	.864	1	S-16/3-2	0.1
■ MILT SMITH	Smith, Milton b: 3/27/29, Columbus, Ga. d: 4/11/97, San Diego, Cal. BR/TR, 5'10", 165 lbs. Deb: 7/21/55																							
1955	Cin-N	36	102	15	20	3	1	3	8	13	24	.196	.293	.333	626	62	-6	2	2	-0	.915	-2	3-28/2-5	-0.8
■ NATE SMITH	Smith, Nathaniel Beverly b: 4/26/35, Chicago, Ill. BR/TR, 5'11", 170 lbs. Deb: 9/19/62																							
1962	Bal-A	5	9	3	2	1	0	0	0	1	4	.222	.364	.333	697	95	0	0	0	0	1.000	1	/C-3	0.1
■ OLLIE SMITH	Smith, Oliver H. b: 1868, Mt.Vernon, Ohio BL/TL, Deb: 7/11/1894																							
1894	Lou-N	39	137	27	41	6	1	3	20	29	15	.299	.432	.423	855	115	5	13			.883	-2	O-39(0-0-39)	0.1
■ OZZIE SMITH	Smith, Osborne Earl b: 12/26/54, Mobile, Ala. BB/TR, 5'11", 150 lbs. Deb: 4/7/78																							
1978	SD-N	159	590	69	152	17	6	1	46	47	43	.258	.312	.312	624	81	-15	40	12	5	.970	26	*S-159	3.3
1979	SD-N	156	587	77	124	18	6	0	27	37	37	.211	.260	.262	523	46	-44	28	7	4	.976	21	*S-155	-0.4
1980	SD-N	158	609	67	140	18	5	0	35	71	49	.230	.315	.276	591	70	-22	57	15	7	.974	**41**	*S-158	4.4
1981	SD-N★	110	450	53	100	11	2	0	21	41	37	.222	.294	.256	550	62	-22	22	12	1	**.976**	**26**	*S-110	1.7
1982	*StL-N★	140	488	58	121	24	1	2	43	68	32	.248	.342	.314	656	84	-8	25	5	4	**.984**	**33**	*S-139	4.5
1983	StL-N★	159	552	69	134	30	6	3	50	64	36	.243	.323	.335	658	82	-12	34	7	5	.975	18	*S-158	2.7
1984	StL-N★	124	412	53	106	20	5	1	44	56	17	.257	.349	.337	686	96	-0	35	7	5	**.982**	**26**	*S-124	4.5
1985	*StL-N★	158	537	70	148	22	3	6	54	65	27	.276	.356	.361	717	102	3	31	8	4	**.983**	16	*S-158	4.1
1986	StL-N★	153	514	67	144	19	4	0	54	79	27	.280	.378	.333	711	99	3	31	7	4	**.978**	-9	*S-144	1.4
1987	*StL-N★	158	600	104	182	40	4	0	75	89	36	.303	.394	.383	778	105	8	43	9	6	**.987**	19	*S-158	4.9
1988	StL-N★	153	575	80	155	27	1	3	51	74	43	.270	.354	.336	689	98	1	57	9	**9**	.972	**23**	*S-150	4.7
1989	StL-N★	155	593	82	162	30	8	2	50	55	37	.273	.337	.361	698	96	-2	29	7	4	.976	6	*S-153	2.1
1990	StL-N★	143	512	61	130	21	1	1	50	61	33	.254	.336	.305	640	77	-14	32	6	5	.980	-13	*S-140	-1.2
1991	StL-N★	150	550	96	157	30	3	3	50	83	36	.285	.380	.367	747	110	11	35	9	5	**.987**	-21	*S-150	0.6
1992	StL-N★	132	518	73	153	20	2	0	31	59	34	.295	.367	.342	709	105	6	43	9	6	.985	8	*S-132	3.2
1993	StL-N	141	545	75	157	22	6	1	53	43	18	.288	.341	.356	697	89	-8	21	8	2	.974	18	*S-134	2.3
1994	StL-N★	98	381	51	100	18	3	3	30	38	26	.262	.329	.349	678	79	-12	6	3	0	**.982**	-2	S-96	-0.5
1995	StL-N†	44	156	16	31	5	1	0	11	17	12	.199	.286	.244	529	41	-13	4	3	-0	.964	1	S-41	-0.8
1996	*StL-N★	82	227	36	64	10	2	2	18	25	9	.282	.358	.370	728	93	-1	7	5	-0	.969	6	S-52	0.9
Total	19	2573	9396	1257	2460	402	69	28	793	1072	589	.262	.339	.328	668	87	-143	580	148	76	.978	243	*S-2511	42.4
■ KEITH SMITH	Smith, Patrick Keith b: 10/20/61, Los Angeles, Cal. BB/TR, 6'1", 175 lbs. Deb: 4/12/84																							
1984	NY-A	2	4	0	0	0	0	0	0	0	2	.000	.200	.000	200	-41	-1	0	0	0	.923	2	/S-2	0.2

YEAR	TM/L	G	AB	R	H	2B	3B	HR	RBI	BB	SO	AVG	OBP	SLG	OPS	OPS+	BR+	SB	CS	SBR	FA	FR	G/POS	TPR
1985	NY-A	4	0	1	0	0	0	0	0	0	0	—	—	—	—	—	0	0	0	0	1.000	0	/S-3	0.0
Total	2	6	4	1	0	0	0	0	0	0	2	.000	.200	.000	200	-41	-1	0	0	0	.929	3	/S-5	0.2
■ PAUL SMITH	Smith, Paul Leslie b: 3/19/31, New Castle, Pa. BL/TL, 5′8″, 165 lbs. Deb: 4/14/53																							
1953	Pit-N	118	389	41	110	12	7	4	44	24	23	.283	.329	.380	710	85	-9	3	0	1	.985	-2	1-74,O-19(19-0-0)	-1.4
1957	Pit-N	81	150	12	38	4	0	3	11	12	17	.253	.313	.340	653	78	-5	0	2	-1	1.000	-3	O-33(16-1-20)/1-1	-1.0
1958	Pit-N	6	3	0	1	0	0	0	0	3	0	.333	.667	.333	1000	180	1	0	0	0	.000	0	H	0.1
	Chi-N	18	20	1	3	0	0	0	1	3	4	.150	.261	.150	411	13	-2	0	0	0	.941	0	/1-4	-0.3
	Yr	24	23	1	4	0	0	0	1	6	4	.174	.345	.174	519	44	-2	0	0	0	.941	0	/1-4	-0.2
Total	3	223	562	54	152	16	7	7	56	42	44	.270	.326	.361	687	81	-15	3	2	-0	.984	-5	/1-79,O-52(35-1-20)	-2.6
■ PAUL SMITH	Smith, Paul Stoner b: 5/7/1888, Mt.Zion, Ill. d: 7/3/58, Decatur, Ill. BL/TR, 6′1″, 190 lbs. Deb: 9/19/16																							
1916	Cin-N	10	44	5	10	0	1	0	1	1	8	.227	.244	.273	517	60	-2	3			1.000	-1	O-10(10-0-0)	-0.4
■ RAY SMITH	Smith, Raymond Edward b: 9/18/55, Glendale, Cal. BR/TR, 6′1″, 185 lbs. Deb: 4/9/81																							
1981	Min-A	15	40	4	8	1	0	1	1	0	3	.200	.200	.300	500	40	-3	0	0	0	1.000	1	C-15	-0.1
1982	Min-A	9	23	1	5	0	1	0	1	1	3	.217	.250	.304	554	50	-2	0	0	0	1.000	1	/C-9	0.0
1983	Min-A	59	152	11	34	5	0	0	8	10	12	.224	.276	.257	533	46	-11	1	0	0	.984	11	C-59	0.2
Total	3	83	215	16	47	6	1	1	10	11	18	.219	.260	.270	530	45	-16	1	0	0	.988	14	/C-83	0.1
■ DICK SMITH	Smith, Richard Arthur b: 5/17/39, Lebanon, Ore. BR/TR, 6′2″, 205 lbs. Deb: 7/20/63																							
1963	NY-N	20	42	4	10	0	1	0	3	5	10	.238	.319	.286	605	74	-1	3	2	-0	1.000	-2	O-10(3-7-0)/1-2	-0.3
1964	NY-N	46	94	14	21	6	1	0	3	1	29	.223	.247	.309	556	57	-6	6	2	1	.987	-3	1-18,O-13(12-1-1)	-1.1
1965	LA-N	10	6	0	0	0	0	0	1	0	3	.000	.000	.000	0	-99	-2	0	0	0	1.000	-3	/O-9(5-4-1)	-0.6
Total	3	76	142	18	31	6	2	0	7	6	42	.218	.260	.289	549	56	-8	9	4	1	1.000	-8	/O-32(20-12-2),1-20	-2.0
■ DICK SMITH	Smith, Richard Harrison b: 7/21/27, Blandburg, Pa. BR/TR, 5′8″, 160 lbs. Deb: 9/14/51																							
1951	Pit-N	12	46	2	8	0	0	0	4	8	8	.174	.296	.174	470	29	-4	0	2	-1	.936	2	3-12	-0.3
1952	Pit-N	29	66	8	7	1	0	0	5	9	3	.106	.213	.121	335	-5	-9	0	0	0	.958	5	3-16/2-4,S-4	-0.5
1953	Pit-N	13	43	4	7	0	1	0	2	6	6	.163	.265	.209	475	26	-5	0	1	-0	.961	5	S-13	0.1
1954	Pit-N	12	31	2	3	1	1	0	0	6	5	.097	.243	.194	437	16	-4	0	0	0	.933	2	/3-9	-0.2
1955	Pit-N	4	0	1	0	0	0	0	0	1	0	—	1.000	—	1000	198	0	0	0	0	.000	0	/S-1	0.0
Total	5	70	186	17	25	2	2	0	11	30	22	.134	.255	.167	421	15	-22	0	3	-1	.944	14	/3-37,S-18,2-4	-0.9
■ DICK SMITH	Smith, Richard Kelly b: 8/25/44, Lincolnton, N.C. BR/TR, 6′5″, 200 lbs. Deb: 8/20/69																							
1969	Was-A	21	28	2	3	0	0	0	0	4	7	.107	.242	.107	350	1	-4	0	0	0	.909	-2	/O-9(9-0-0)	-0.6
■ RED SMITH	Smith, Richard Paul b: 5/18/04, Brokaw, Wis. d: 3/8/78, Sylvania, Ohio BR/TR, 5′10″, 185 lbs. Deb: 5/31/27 C																							
1927	NY-N	1	0	0	0	0	0	0	0	0	0	—	—	—	—	—	0	0			1.000	-0	/C-1	0.0
■ BOB SMITH	Smith, Robert Eldridge b: 4/22/1895, Rogersville, Tenn. d: 7/19/87, Waycross, Ga. BR/TR, 5′10″, 175 lbs. Deb: 4/19/23 Career OF: (0-LF 1-CF 0-RF)																							
1923	Bos-N	115	375	30	94	16	3	0	40	17	35	.251	.285	.309	594	59	-22	4	9	-2	.944	14	*S-101/2-8	0.0
1924	Bos-N	106	347	32	79	12	3	2	38	15	26	.228	.260	.297	556	51	-25	5	2	0	.958	8	S-80,3-23	-0.7
1925	Bos-N	58	174	17	49	9	4	0	23	5	6	.282	.302	.379	681	80	-6	2	2	-0	.906	3	S-21,2-15,P-13,/O-1C	0.0
1926	Bos-N	40	84	10	25	6	2	0	13	2	4	.298	.314	.417	731	105	0	0			.972	2	P-33	0.0
1927	Bos-N	54	109	10	27	3	1	1	10	2	4	.248	.261	.321	582	60	-7	0			.966	2	P-41	0.0
1928	Bos-N	39	92	11	23	2	0	1	8	1	6	.250	.258	.304	562	49	-7	2			.965	3	P-38	0.0
1929	Bos-N	39	99	12	17	4	2	1	8	2	8	.172	.188	.283	471	16	-14	1			.986	4	P-34/S-5	0.2
1930	Bos-N	39	81	7	19	2	0	0	4	0	5	.235	.235	.259	494	20	-10	0			.984	2	P-38	0.0
1931	Chi-N	36	87	7	19	2	0	0	4	5	2	.218	.261	.241	502	35	-8	0			**1.000**	1	P-36	0.0
1932	*Chi-N	36	42	5	10	4	1	0	4	0	2	.238	.238	.381	619	64	-2	1			1.000	3	P-34/2-2	0.2
1933	Cin-N	23	25	2	5	1	0	0	1	1	0	.200	.231	.240	471	35	-2	1			.882	-1	P-16/S-1	0.0
	Bos-N	14	20	1	4	0	1	0	2	0	1	.200	.200	.300	500	45	-2	0			1.000	1	P-14	0.0
	Yr	37	45	3	9	1	1	0	3	1	1	.200	.217	.267	484	39	-4	1			.946	0	P-30/S-1	0.0
1934	Bos-N	42	36	5	9	1	0	0	3	0	1	.250	.250	.278	528	44	-3	0			1.000	1	P-39	0.0
1935	Bos-N	47	63	3	17	0	0	0	4	1	5	.270	.281	.270	551	53	-4	0			.980	-1	P-46	0.0
1936	Bos-N	35	45	1	10	2	0	0	4	0	4	.222	.222	.267	489	33	-4	0			1.000	1	P-35	0.0
1937	Bos-N	19	10	1	2	0	0	0	0	1	1	.200	.273	.200	473	33	-1	0			1.000	-1	P-18	0.0
Total	15	742	1689	154	409	64	17	5	166	52	110	.242	.265	.309	574	53	-116	16	13		.981	42	P-435,S-208/2-25,3O	-0.3
■ BOBBY SMITH	Smith, Robert Eugene b: 4/10/74, Oakland, Cal. BR/TR, 6′3″, 190 lbs. Deb: 4/3/98																							
1998	TB-A	117	370	44	102	15	3	11	55	34	110	.276	.346	.422	768	97	-2	5	3	0	.963	11	3-97/S-7,2-6,D-7	1.0
1999	TB-A	68	199	18	36	4	1	3	19	16	64	.181	.245	.256	502	28	-22	4	4	-1	.933	12	3-59,2-13	-0.9
2000	TB-A	49	175	21	41	8	0	6	26	14	59	.234	.295	.383	678	70	-8	2	2	-0	.970	1	2-45/3-5	-0.5
Total	3	234	744	83	179	27	4	20	100	64	233	.241	.308	.368	676	72	-32	11	9	-1	.951	24	3-161/2-64,D-7,S-7	-0.4
■ JOE SMITH	Smith, Salvatore (b: Salvatore Persico) b: 12/29/1893, New York, N.Y. d: 1/12/74, Yonkers, N.Y. BR/TR, 5′7″, 170 lbs. Deb: 7/7/13																							
1913	NY-A	14	32	1	5	0	0	0	2	1	14	.156	.182	.156	338	-1	-4	1			.952	0	C-14	-0.3
■ SKYROCKET SMITH	Smith, Samuel J. b: 3/19/1868, St.Louis, Mo. d: 4/26/16, St.Louis, Mo. BR, 6′2″, 170 lbs. Deb: 4/18/1888																							
1888	Lou-a	58	206	27	49	9	4	1	31	24		.238	.349	.335	683	122	7	5			.970	-0	1-58	0.1
■ SYD SMITH	Smith, Sydney E. b: 8/31/1883, Smithville, S.C. d: 6/5/61, Orangeburg, S.C. BR/TR, 5′10″, 190 lbs. Deb: 4/14/08 Career OF: (0-LF 1-CF 0-RF)																							
1908	Phi-A	46	128	8	26	8	0	1	10	4		.203	.233	.289	522	65	-5	0			.975	-0	C-31/1-6,O-1(0-1-0)	-0.3
	StL-A	27	76	6	14	4	0	0	5	4		.184	.225	.237	462	50	-4	2			.977	8	C-24	0.7
	Yr	73	204	14	40	12	0	1	15	8		.196	.230	.270	500	60	-9	2			.976	8	C-55/1-6,O-1(0-1-0)	0.4
1910	Cle-A	9	27	1	9	1	0	0	3	3		.333	.400	.370	770	140	1	0			.958	0	/C-9	0.2
1911	Cle-A	58	154	8	46	8	1	1	21	11		.299	.353	.383	736	104	1	0			.979	9	C-48/1-1,3-1	1.3
1914	Pit-N	5	11	1	3	0	0	0	1	0	1	.273	.273	.273	545	65	-1	0			1.000	-0	/C-3	0.0
1915	Pit-N	1	1	0	0	0	0	0	0	0	0	.000	.000	.000	0	-99	-0	0			.000	0	H	0.0
Total	5	146	397	24	98	21	1	2	40	22	1	.247	.291	.320	611	83	-8	2			.977	16	C-115/1-7,3-1,O-1C	1.9
■ TOM SMITH	Smith, Thomas N. b: 1851, Guelph, Ontario, Canada d: 3/28/1889, Detroit, Mich. 5′8″, 141 lbs. Deb: 9/15/1875																							
1875	Atl-n	3	13	0	1	0	0	0	1	0	0	.077	.077	.077	154	-53	-2	0	0	0	.783	0	/2-3	-0.2
■ TOMMY SMITH	Smith, Tommy Alexander b: 8/1/48, Albemarle, N.C. BL/TR, 6′3″, 215 lbs. Deb: 9/6/73																							
1973	Cle-A	14	41	6	10	2	0	2	3	1	2	.244	.262	.439	701	93	-1	1	0	0	1.000	-1	O-13(1-11-1)	-0.2
1974	Cle-A	23	31	4	3	1	0	0	0	2	7	.097	.176	.129	306	-11	-4	0	0	0	.938	-2	O-17(9-4-4)/D-1	-0.7
1975	Cle-A	8	8	0	1	0	0	0	2	0	1	.125	.125	.125	250	-29	-1	0	0	0	1.000	-1	/O-3(1-0-2),D-3	-0.2
1976	Cle-A	55	164	17	42	3	1	2	12	8	8	.256	.291	.323	614	80	-4	8	0	2	.979	-0	O-50(12-0-38)/D-2	-0.5
1977	Sea-A	21	27	1	7	1	1	0	4	0	6	.259	.259	.370	630	70	-1	0	1	-0	1.000	-2	O-14(1-0-14)	-0.3
Total	5	121	271	28	63	7	2	4	21	11	24	.232	.265	.317	582	68	-12	9	1	2	.977	-5	/O-97(24-15-59),D-6	-1.9
■ VINNIE SMITH	Smith, Vincent Ambrose b: 12/7/15, Richmond, Va. d: 12/14/79, Virginia Beach, Va BR/TR, 6′1″, 176 lbs. Deb: 9/10/41 U																							
1941	Pit-N	9	33	3	10	1	0	0	5	1	5	.303	.324	.333	657	86	-1	0			.941	-2	/C-9	-0.2
1946	Pit-N	7	21	2	4	0	0	0	0	1	5	.190	.227	.190	418	19	-2	0			.967	1	/C-7	-0.1
Total	2	16	54	5	14	1	0	0	5	2	10	.259	.286	.278	563	59	-3	0			.953	-1	/C-16	-0.3
■ WALLY SMITH	Smith, Wallace H. b: 3/13/1889, Philadelphia, Pa. d: 6/10/30, Florence, Ariz. BR/TR, 5′11.5″, 180 lbs. Deb: 4/17/11 Career OF: (0-LF 1-CF 1-RF)																							
1911	StL-N	81	194	23	42	6	5	2	19	21	33	.216	.303	.330	633	79	-6	5			.936	2	3-26,S-25/2-8,O-1C	-0.2
1912	StL-N	75	219	22	56	5	5	0	26	29	27	.256	.351	.324	675	87	-3	4			.949	-1	3-32,S-22/1-6	-0.2
1914	Was-A	45	97	11	19	4	1	0	8	3	12	.196	.235	.258	493	46	-7	3	4	-1	.955	-4	2-12/1-7,S-7,3-5,O	-1.2
Total	3	201	510	56	117	15	11	2	53	53	72	.229	.312	.314	625	77	-15	12	4		.947	-3	/3-63,S-54,2-20,1O	-1.6

YEAR	TM/L	G	AB	R	H	2B	3B	HR	RBI	BB	SO	AVG	OBP	SLG	OPS	OPS+	BR+	SB	CS	SBR	FA	FR	G/POS	TPR
■ **WIB SMITH** Smith, Wilbur Floyd b: 8/30/1886, Evart, Mich. d: 11/18/59, Fargo, N.D. BL/TR, 5'10.5", 165 lbs. Deb: 5/31/09																								
1909	StL-A	17	42	3	8	0	0	0	2	0		.190	.190	.190	381	22	-4	0			.836	-9	C-13/1-1	-1.4
■ **RED SMITH** Smith, Willard Jehu b: 4/11/1892, Logansport, Ind. d: 7/17/72, Noblesville, Ind. BR/TR, 5'8", 165 lbs. Deb: 9/17/17																								
1917	Pit-N	11	21	1	3	1	0	0	2	3	4	.143	.250	.190	440	35	-2	1			1.000	2	/C-6	0.1
1918	Pit-N	15	24	1	4	1	0	0	3	3	0	.167	.259	.208	468	42	-2	0			.939	-1	C-10	-0.2
Total	2	26	45	2	7	2	0	0	5	6	4	.156	.255	.200	455	39	-3	1			.969	1	/C-16	-0.1
■ **BILL SMITH** Smith, William E. b: Cleveland, Ohio d: 8/9/1886, Toronto, Ont., Can. 5'11", 178 lbs. Deb: 9/17/1884																								
1884	Cle-N	1	3	0	0	0	0	0	0	0	2	.000	.000	.000	0	-97	-1				.000	-0	/O-1(1-0-0)	-0.1
■ **BILL SMITH** Smith, William J. b: Baltimore, Md. d: 8/9/1886, Deb: 4/14/1873 M																								
1873	Mar-n	6	22	2	4	0	0	0	1	0	0	.174	.174	.174	348	5	-2	0	0	0	.500	-3	/O-3(0-3-0),C-2,2-1,M	-0.3
■ **WILLIE SMITH** Smith, Willie b: 2/11/39, Anniston, Ala. BL/TL, 6', 190 lbs. Deb: 6/18/63 Career OF: (288-LF 3-CF 56-RF)																								
1963	Det-A	17	8	2	1	0	0	0	0	0	1	.125	.125	.125	250	-29	-1	0	0	0	1.000	0	P-11	0.0
1964	LA-A	118	359	46	108	14	6	11	51	8	39	.301	.320	.465	785	128	11	7	5	-0	.977	-6	O-87(58-3-31),P-15	-0.1
1965	Cal-A	136	459	52	120	14	9	14	57	32	60	.261	.311	.423	734	109	4	9	8	-1	.980	-0	*O-123(123-0-1)/1-2	-0.4
1966	Cal-A	90	195	18	36	3	2	1	20	12	37	.185	.243	.236	479	39	-15	1	0	0	.974	-3	O-52(32-0-22)	-2.3
1967	Cle-A	21	32	0	7	2	0	0	2	1	10	.219	.242	.281	524	54	-2	0	2	-1	.800	-1	/O-4(4-0-0),1-3	-0.4
1968	Cle-A	33	42	1	6	2	0	0	3	3	14	.143	.217	.190	408	25	-4	0	0	0	1.000	-0	/1-7,P-2,O-1(1-0-0)	-0.5
	Chi-N	55	142	13	39	8	2	5	25	12	33	.275	.335	.465	800	129	5	0	0	0	1.000	-3	O-38(38-0-0)/1-4,P-1	-0.1
1969	Chi-N	103	195	21	48	9	1	9	25	25	49	.246	.332	.441	773	102	0	1	0	0	.929	-7	O-33(32-0-1),1-24	-1.0
1970	Chi-N	87	167	15	36	9	1	5	24	11	32	.216	.268	.371	639	62	-9	2	1	0	.994	-5	1-43/O-1(0-0-1)	-1.7
1971	Cin-N	31	55	3	9	2	0	1	4	3	9	.164	.207	.255	461	31	-5	0	0	0	1.000	1	1-10	-0.5
Total	9	691	1654	171	410	63	21	46	211	107	284	.248	.297	.395	692	94	-16	20	16	-1	.975	-24	O-339L/1-93,P-29	-7.0
■ **HOMER SMOOT** Smoot, Homer Vernon "Doc" b: 3/23/1878, Galestown, Md. d: 3/25/28, Salisbury, Md. BL/TR, 5'10", 180 lbs. Deb: 4/17/02																								
1902	StL-N	129	518	58	161	19	4	3	48	23		.311	.350	.380	730	131	17	20			.931	-0	*O-129(0-129-0)	1.1
1903	StL-N	129	500	67	148	22	8	4	49	32		.296	.342	.396	738	114	8	17			.942	-7	*O-129(0-129-0)	-0.5
1904	StL-N	137	520	58	146	23	6	3	66	37		.281	.331	.365	696	120	12	23			.966	2	*O-137(0-137-0)	0.8
1905	StL-N	139	534	73	166	21	16	4	58	33		.311	.359	.433	791	140	24	21			.975	1	*O-138(0-138-0)	1.9
1906	StL-N	86	343	41	85	9	10	0	31	11		.248	.289	.332	622	98	-2	3			.953	2	O-86(0-55-31)	-0.6
	Cin-N	60	220	11	57	8	1	1	17	13		.259	.315	.318	633	93	-2	0			.944	1	O-59(4-55-0)	-0.5
	Yr	146	563	52	142	17	11	1	48	24		.252	.300	.327	626	96	-4	3			.950	2	*O-145(4-110-31)	-1.1
Total	5	680	2635	308	763	102	45	15	269	149		.290	.336	.380	715	120	57	84			.953	-2	O-678(4-643-31)	2.2
■ **HENRY SMOYER** Smoyer, Henry Neitz "Hennie" (b: Henry Neitz Smowery) b: 4/24/1890, Fredericksburg, Pa. d: 2/28/58, DuBois, Pa. BR/TR, 5'6", Deb: 8/14/12																								
1912	StL-A	6	14	1	3	0	0	0	0	2		.214	.313	.214	527	53	-1	0			1.000	-0	/S-4,3-2	-0.1
■ **FRANK SMYKAL** Smykal, Frank John (b: Frank John Smejkal) b: 10/13/1889, Chicago, Ill. d: 8/11/50, Chicago, Ill. BR/TR, 5'7", 150 lbs. Deb: 8/30/16																								
1916	Pit-N	6	10	1	3	0	0	0	2	3	1	.300	.500	.300	800	147	1	1			.842	-1	/S-5,3-1	0.1
■ **CLANCY SMYRES** Smyres, Clarence Melvin b: 5/24/22, Culver City, Cal. BB/TR, 5'11.5", 175 lbs. Deb: 4/18/44																								
1944	Bro-N	5	2	1	0	0	0	0	0	0	0	.000	.000	.000	0	-99	-1	0			.000	0	H	-0.1
■ **RED SMYTH** Smyth, James Daniel b: 1/30/1893, Holly Springs, Miss. d: 4/14/58, Inglewood, Cal. BL/TR, 5'9", 152 lbs. Deb: 8/11/15 Career OF: (20-LF 8-CF 28-RF)																								
1915	Bro-N	19	22	3	3	1	0	0	3	4	2	.136	.269	.182	451	37	-2	1	2	-0	1.000	-1	/O-9(6-2-1)	-0.3
1916	Bro-N	2	5	0	0	0	0	0	0	0	3	.000	.000	.000	0	-97	-1	0			1.000	-0	/2-2	-0.2
1917	Bro-N	29	24	5	3	0	0	0	1	4	6	.125	.250	.125	375	16	-2	0			.667	-1	/3-4,O-2(0-2-0)	-0.3
	StL-N	38	72	5	15	0	2	0	4	4	9	.208	.269	.264	533	66	-3	3			.889	-5	O-23(12-4-5)	-1.0
	Yr	67	96	10	18	0	2	0	5	8	15	.188	.264	.229	493	52	-5	3			.871	-6	O-25(12-6-5)/3-4	-1.3
1918	StL-N	40	113	19	24	1	2	0	4	16	11	.212	.315	.257	572	78	-2	3			.956	-0	O-25(2-0-22),2-11	-0.4
Total	4	128	236	32	45	2	4	0	12	28	31	.191	.285	.233	518	60	-10	7	<u>2</u>		.934	-7	/O-59R,2-13,3-4	-2.2
■ **JOHN SNEED** Sneed, Jonathon L. b: Columbus, Ohio d: 1/4/1899, Memphis, Tenn. 5'8", 160 lbs. Deb: 5/1/1884																								
1884	Ind-a	27	102	14	22	4	0	1		6		.216	.259	.284	544	79	-2				.817	-0	O-27(0-21-6)	-0.3
1890	Tol-a	9	30	3	6	0	0	0	4	8		.200	.368	.200	568	66	-1	5			.889	2	/O-9(0-0-9)	0.1
	Col-a	128	484	114	141	13	15	2	65	63		.291	.383	.393	776	138	26	39			.883	-8	*O-126(26-3-97)/S-2	1.5
	Yr	137	514	117	147	13	15	2	69	71		.286	.382	.381	763	133	25	44			.883	-5	*O-135(26-3-106)/S-2	1.6
1891	Col-a	99	366	66	94	9	6	1	61	55	29	.257	.366	.322	688	103	5	24			.894	-4	*O-99(0-0-99)	0.0
Total	3	263	982	197	263	26	21	4	<u>130</u>	132	<u>29</u>	.268	.364	.349	714	117	28	68			.879	-10	O-261(26-24-211)/S-2	1.3
■ **CHARLIE SNELL** Snell, Charles Anthony (b: Charles Anthony Schnell) b: 11/29/1893, Hampstead, Md. d: 4/4/88, Reading, Pa. BR/TR, 5'11", 160 lbs. Deb: 7/19/12																								
1912	StL-A	8	19	0	4	1	0	0	0	3		.211	.348	.263	611	78	-0	0			.941	2	/C-8	0.2
■ **WALLY SNELL** Snell, Walter Henry "Doc" b: 5/19/1889, W.Bridgewater, Mass. d: 7/23/80, Providence, R.I. BR/TR, 5'10", 170 lbs. Deb: 8/1/13																								
1913	Bos-A	6	12	1	3	0	0	0	0	0	1	.250	.250	.250	500	45	-1	1			.923	1	/C-2	0.0
■ **DUKE SNIDER** Snider, Edwin Donald "The Silver Fox" b: 9/19/26, Los Angeles, Cal. BL/TR, 6', 190 lbs. Deb: 4/17/47 CH																								
1947	Bro-N	40	83	6	20	3	1	0	5	3	24	.241	.276	.301	577	51	-6	2			.980	-2	O-25(4-13-7)	-0.9
1948	Bro-N	53	160	22	39	6	6	5	21	12	27	.244	.297	.450	747	96	-2	4			.989	-3	O-47(0-41-7)	-0.6
1949	*Bro-N	146	552	100	161	28	7	23	92	56	92	.292	.361	.493	854	122	16	12			.984	4	*O-145(0-145-0)	1.5
1950	Bro-N★	152	620	109	**199**	31	10	31	107	58	79	.321	.379	.553	932	139	33	16			.983	9	*O-151(0-151-0)	3.7
1951	Bro-N★	150	606	96	168	26	6	29	101	62	97	.277	.344	.483	828	118	14	14	10	-0	.987	3	*O-150(0-150-0)	1.2
1952	*Bro-N☆	144	534	80	162	25	7	21	92	55	77	.303	.368	.494	863	136	25	7	4	0	.992	1	*O-141(0-141-0)	2.3
1953	*Bro-N★	153	590	**132**	198	38	4	42	126	82	90	.336	.419	**.627**	**1046**	165	56	16	7	1	.987	-3	*O-151(0-151-0)	4.5
1954	Bro-N★	149	584	**120**	199	39	10	40	130	84	96	.341	.427	.647	1074	170	60	6	6	-1	.981	-5	*O-148(0-148-0)	4.6
1955	*Bro-N★	148	538	**126**	166	34	6	42	**136**	104	87	.309	.421	.628	1050	169	55	9	7	-0	.989	1	*O-146(0-146-0)	4.7
1956	*Bro-N★	151	542	112	158	33	2	**43**	101	**99**	101	.292	**.402**	**.598**	**1000**	152	42	3	3	-0	.984	-0	*O-150(0-150-0)	3.4
1957	Bro-N	139	508	91	139	25	7	40	92	77	104	.274	.370	.587	957	139	28	3	4	-1	.990	-6	*O-136(0-136-0)	1.4
1958	LA-N	106	327	45	102	12	3	15	58	32	49	.312	.375	.505	880	126	12	2	2	-0	.987	-13	O-92(6-78-11)	-0.5
1959	*LA-N	126	370	59	114	11	2	23	88	58	71	.308	.402	.535	937	137	21	1	5	-2	.975	-17	*O-107(0-53-71)	-0.2
1960	LA-N	101	235	38	57	13	5	14	36	46	54	.243	.369	.519	888	131	11	1	0	0	.965	-12	O-75(0-48-35)	-0.4
1961	LA-N	85	233	35	69	8	3	16	56	29	43	.296	.376	.562	939	133	11	1	1	-0	.975	-2	O-66(0-24-51)	0.6
1962	LA-N	80	158	28	44	11	3	5	30	36	32	.278	.418	.481	899	150	13	2	0	0	.967	-1	O-39(15-2-24)	1.0
1963	NY-N★	129	354	44	86	8	3	14	45	56	74	.243	.348	.401	749	113	7	0	1	-0	.986	-10	*O-106(34-13-62)	-0.9
1964	SF-N	91	167	16	35	7	0	4	17	22	40	.210	.302	.323	625	74	-5	0	0	0	.979	-5	O-43(19-0-25)	-1.3
Total	18	2143	7161	1259	2116	358	85	407	1333	971	1237	.295	.381	.540	921	138	390	99	<u>50</u>		.985	-62	*O-1918(78-1590-293)	24.1
■ **VAN SNIDER** Snider, Van Voorhees b: 8/11/63, Birmingham, Ala. BL/TR, 6'3", 185 lbs. Deb: 9/2/88																								
1988	Cin-N	11	28	4	6	1	0	1	6	0	13	.214	.214	.357	571	59	-2	0	1	-0	1.000	-1	/O-8(6-0-3)	-0.3
1989	Cin-N	8	7	1	1	0	0	0	0	0	5	.143	.143	.143	286	-17	-1	0	0	0	1.000	-2	/O-6(5-0-2)	-0.3
Total	2	19	35	5	7	1	0	1	6	0	18	.200	.200	.314	514	44	-3	0	1	-0	1.000	-2	/O-14(11-0-5)	-0.6
■ **ROXY SNIPES** Snipes, Wyatt Eure "Rock" b: 10/28/1896, Marion, S.C. d: 5/1/41, Fayetteville, N.C. BL/TR, 6', 185 lbs. Deb: 7/15/23																								
1923	Chi-A	1	1	0	0	0	0	0	0	0	0	.000	.000	.000	0	-99	-0	0	0	0	.000	0	H	0.0
■ **CHAPPIE SNODGRASS** Snodgrass, Amzie Beal b: 3/18/1870, Springfield, Ohio d: 9/9/51, New York, N.Y. BR/TR, 5'10", 165 lbs. Deb: 5/15/01																								
1901	Bal-A	3	10	0	1	0	0	0	1	0		.100	.100	.100	200	-43	-2	0			.500	-1	/O-2(2-0-0)	-0.3

■ FRED SNODGRASS

Snodgrass, Frederick Carlisle "Snow" b: 10/19/1887, Ventura, Cal. d: 4/5/74, Ventura, Cal. BR/TR, 5'11.5", 175 lbs. Deb: 6/4/08 Career OF: (108-LF 666-CF 73-RF)

YEAR	TM/L	G	AB	R	H	2B	3B	HR	RBI	BB	SO	AVG	OBP	SLG	OPS	OPS+	BR+	SB	CS	SBR	FA	FR	G/POS	TPR
1908	NY-N	6	4	2	1	0	0	0	1	0		.250	.250	.250	500	57	-0	1			1.000	1	/C-3	0.1
1909	NY-N	28	70	10	21	5	0	1	6	7		.300	.387	.414	802	146	4	10			.921	-1	O-20(15-3-1)/C-2,1-1	0.3
1910	NY-N	123	396	69	127	22	8	2	44	71	52	.321	.440	.432	871	154	32	33			.970	-8	*O-101C/1-9,C-1,3-1	2.0
1911	*NY-N	151	534	83	157	27	10	1	77	72	59	.294	.393	.388	781	115	13	51			.973	9	*O-149C/1-1,3-1	1.2
1912	*NY-N	146	535	91	144	24	9	3	69	70	65	.269	.362	.364	727	96	-1	43			.948	-3	*O-116C,1-27/2-1	-1.2
1913	*NY-N	141	457	65	133	21	6	3	49	53	44	.291	.373	.383	756	115	11	27			.968	6	*O-133C/1-3,2-1	0.7
1914	NY-N	113	392	54	103	20	4	0	44	37	43	.263	.336	.334	670	103	2	25			.977	5	O-96C,1-14/2-1,3-1	0.0
1915	NY-N	80	252	36	49	9	0	0	20	35	33	.194	.307	.230	537	68	-8	11	12	-2	.935	4	O-75(0-68-5)	-1.2
	Bos-N	23	79	10	22	2	0	0	9	7	9	.278	.352	.304	656	104	1	0	4	-1	.938	-2	O-18(0-20-0)/1-5	-0.4
	Yr	103	331	46	71	11	0	0	29	42	42	.215	.318	.248	565	76	-7	11	16	-3	.935	2	O-93(0-88-5)/1-5	-1.6
1916	Bos-N	112	382	33	95	13	5	1	32	34	54	.249	.318	.317	635	100	0	14			.983	13	*O-110(0-110-0)	0.7
Total	9	923	3101	453	852	143	42	11	351	386	359	.275	.367	.359	725	110	53	215	16		.965	24	O-818C/1-60,C-6,23	2.2

■ CHRIS SNOPEK

Snopek, Christopher Charles b: 9/20/70, Cynthiana, Ky. BR/TR, 6'1", 185 lbs. Deb: 7/31/95 Career OF: (0-LF 0-CF 1-RF)

YEAR	TM/L	G	AB	R	H	2B	3B	HR	RBI	BB	SO	AVG	OBP	SLG	OPS	OPS+	BR+	SB	CS	SBR	FA	FR	G/POS	TPR
1995	Chi-A	22	68	12	22	4	0	1	7	9	12	.324	.403	.426	829	121	3	1	0	0	1.000	-0	3-17/S-6	0.3
1996	Chi-A	46	104	18	27	6	1	6	18	6	16	.260	.306	.510	816	106	0	0	1	-0	.939	4	3-27,S-12/D-3	0.4
1997	Chi-A	86	298	27	65	15	0	5	35	18	51	.218	.265	.319	584	54	-21	3	2	-0	.915	-15	3-82/S-4	-3.4
1998	Chi-A	53	125	17	26	2	0	1	4	14	24	.208	.293	.248	541	44	-10	3	0	1	.972	6	S-33,2-12/3-3,1OD	-0.1
	Bos-A	8	12	2	2	0	0	0	2	2	5	.167	.286	.167	452	21	-1	0	0	0	.750	-2	/2-3,3-3,D-2	-0.3
	Yr	61	137	19	28	2	0	1	6	16	29	.204	.292	.241	533	42	-11	3	0	1	.972	5	S-33,2-15/3-6,D1O	-0.4
Total	4	215	607	76	142	27	1	13	66	49	108	.234	.294	.346	640	68	-29	7	3	0	.928	-7	3-132/S-55,2-15,DO1	-3.1

■ CHARLIE SNOW

Snow, Charles M. b: 8/3/1849, Lowell, Mass. Deb: 10/1/1874

YEAR	TM/L	G	AB	R	H	2B	3B	HR	RBI	BB	SO	AVG	OBP	SLG	OPS	OPS+	BR+	SB	CS	SBR	FA	FR	G/POS	TPR
1874	Atl-n	1	1	0	1	0	0	0	0	0	0	1.000	1.000	1.000	2000	615	1	0	0	0	.000	-1	/C-1	0.0

■ J. T. SNOW

Snow, Jack Thomas b: 2/26/68, Long Beach, Cal. BB/TL (BL 1999), 6'2", 202 lbs. Deb: 9/20/92

YEAR	TM/L	G	AB	R	H	2B	3B	HR	RBI	BB	SO	AVG	OBP	SLG	OPS	OPS+	BR+	SB	CS	SBR	FA	FR	G/POS	TPR
1992	NY-A	7	14	1	2	1	0	0	2	5	5	.143	.368	.214	583	67	-0	0	0	0	1.000	-0	/1-6,D-1	-0.1
1993	Cal-A	129	419	60	101	18	2	16	57	55	88	.241	.332	.408	740	95	-3	3	0	1	.995	-2	*1-129	-1.6
1994	Cal-A	61	223	22	49	4	0	8	30	19	48	.220	.290	.345	635	62	-13	0	1	-0	.996	-1	1-61	-1.9
1995	Cal-A	143	544	80	157	22	1	24	102	52	91	.289	.354	.465	819	112	9	2	1	0	.997	-17	*1-143	-2.0
1996	Cal-A	155	575	69	148	20	1	17	67	56	96	.257	.329	.384	713	79	-18	1	6	-2	.993	1	*1-154	-3.1
1997	*SF-N	157	531	81	149	36	1	28	104	96	124	.281	.392	.510	902	138	31	6	4	-0	.995	-2	*1-156	1.4
1998	SF-N	138	435	65	108	29	1	15	79	58	84	.248	.337	.423	760	104	3	1	2	-0	**.999**	5	*1-136	-0.4
1999	SF-N	161	570	93	156	25	2	24	98	86	121	.274	.374	.451	825	116	15	0	4	-1	.996	11	*1-160	1.0
2000	*SF-N	155	536	82	152	33	2	19	96	66	129	.284	.374	.459	833	117	15	1	3	-1	.995	0	*1-153	0.1
Total	9	1106	3847	553	1022	188	10	151	635	493	786	.266	.354	.437	791	106	37	14	21	-4	.996	-5	*1-1098/D-1	-6.6

■ BERNIE SNYDER

Snyder, Bernard Austin b: 8/25/13, Philadelphia, Pa. d: 4/15/99, Havertown, Pa. BR/TR, 6', 165 lbs. Deb: 9/15/35

YEAR	TM/L	G	AB	R	H	2B	3B	HR	RBI	BB	SO	AVG	OBP	SLG	OPS	OPS+	BR+	SB	CS	SBR	FA	FR	G/POS	TPR
1935	Phi-A	10	32	5	11	1	0	0	3	1	2	.344	.364	.375	739	92	-0	0	0	0	.880	-3	/2-5,S-4	-0.2

■ CHARLES SNYDER

Snyder, Charles b: Camden, N.J. d: 3/3/01, Philadelphia, Pa. BR/TR, Deb: 9/19/1890

YEAR	TM/L	G	AB	R	H	2B	3B	HR	RBI	BB	SO	AVG	OBP	SLG	OPS	OPS+	BR+	SB	CS	SBR	FA	FR	G/POS	TPR
1890	Phi-a	9	33	5	9	1	0	0	4	2		.273	.314	.303	617	82	-1	0			.583	-3	/O-5(1-0-4),C-5	-0.4

■ POP SNYDER

Snyder, Charles N. b: 10/6/1854, Washington, D.C. d: 10/29/24, Washington, D.C. BR/TR, 5'11.5", 184 lbs. Deb: 6/16/1873 MU Career OF: (0-LF 4-CF 13-RF)

YEAR	TM/L	G	AB	R	H	2B	3B	HR	RBI	BB	SO	AVG	OBP	SLG	OPS	OPS+	BR+	SB	CS	SBR	FA	FR	G/POS	TPR
1873	Was-n	28	108	16	21	2	0	0	4	3	3	.194	.216	.213	429	29	-9	0	1	-0	.848	-1	C-28/O-3(0-3-0)	-0.7
1874	Bal-n	39	151	24	33	4	0	1	17	1	2	.219	.224	.265	489	56	-7	0	0	0	.789	-0	C-39	-0.6
1875	Phi-n	66	263	38	64	8	2	1	25	4	4	.243	.255	.300	555	89	-3	3	8	-2	.825	4	*C-66/1-1	-0.1
1876	Lou-N	56	226	21	44	4	1	1	9	2	7	.195	.204	.237	440	39	-16				.833	11	*C-55/O-4(0-3-1)	-0.3
1877	Lou-N	61	248	23	64	7	2	2	28	3	14	.258	.267	.327	594	73	-9				**.910**	15	*C-61/O-1(0-0-1),S-1	0.7
1878	Bos-N	60	226	21	48	5	0	0	14	1	19	.212	.216	.235	450	44	-14				**.912**	5	*C-58/O-2(0-0-2)	-0.6
1879	Bos-N	81	329	42	78	16	3	2	35	5	31	.237	.249	.322	571	85	-6				**.925**	**24**	*C-80/O-2(0-0-2)	1.9
1881	Bos-N	62	219	14	50	8	0	0	16	3	23	.228	.239	.265	504	61	-9				.897	3	*C-60/O-1R,S-1,2-1	-0.4
1882	Cin-a	72	309	49	90	12	2	1	50	9		.291	.311	.353	664	117	5				.916	19	*C-70/1-2,O-1R,M	2.7
1883	Cin-a	58	250	38	64	14	6	0	34	8		.256	.279	.360	639	99	-1				.919	14	C-57/S-2,M	1.5
1884	Cin-a	67	268	32	69	9	9	0	39	7		.257	.276	.358	635	101	-1				.922	28	C-65/1-2,O-1(0-0-1),M	2.9
1885	Cin-a	39	152	13	36	4	3	1	19	6		.237	.270	.322	593	85	-3				.880	3	C-38/1-1	0.3
1886	Cin-a	60	220	33	41	8	3	0	28	13		.186	.242	.250	492	52	-12	11			.874	-5	C-41,1-19/O-1(0-1-0)	-1.4
1887	Cle-a	74	291	33	81	12	6	0	27	9		.278	.281	.340	621	75	-10	5			.905	19	C-63,1-13	1.1
1888	Cle-a	64	237	22	51	7	3	0	14	6		.215	.238	.270	508	64	-10	9			.901	8	C-58/1-4,O-3(0-0-3)	0.3
1889	Cle-N	22	83	5	16	3	0	0	12	2	12	.193	.221	.229	450	26	-8	4			.907	2	C-22	-0.4
1890	Cle-P	13	48	5	9	1	0	0	12	1	9	.188	.220	.208	428	16	-6	1			.958	3	C-13	-0.1
1891	Was-a	8	27	4	5	0	1	0	2	0	3	.185	.241	.259	501	45	-2	0			1.000	0	/1-4,C-3,O-1(0-0-1),M	-0.2
Total	3 n	133	522	78	118	14	2	2	46	8	9	.226	.238	.272	510	66	-19	3	9	-2	.819	3	C-133/O-3(0-3-0),1-1	-1.4
Total	15	797	3133	355	746	110	39	7	339	75	118	.238	.256	.303	559	73	-101	30			.904	148	C-744/1-45,O-17R,S2	8.0

■ REDLEG SNYDER

Snyder, Emanuel Sebastian (b: Emanuel Sebastian Schneider) b: 12/12/1854, Camden, N.J. d: 11/24/32, Camden, N.J. BR/TR, 5'10", 175 lbs. Deb: 4/25/1876

YEAR	TM/L	G	AB	R	H	2B	3B	HR	RBI	BB	SO	AVG	OBP	SLG	OPS	OPS+	BR+	SB	CS	SBR	FA	FR	G/POS	TPR
1876	Cin-N	55	206	10	31	3	1	0	12	1	19	.150	.155	.176	331	12	-17				.825	5	*O-55(54-0-1)	-1.4
1884	Wil-U	17	52	4	10	0	0	0		1		.192	.208	.192	400	21	-6				.976	1	1-16/O-1(1-0-0)	-0.6
Total	2	72	258	14	41	3	1	0	12	2	19	.159	.166	.179	345	14	-23				.825	6	/O-56(55-0-1),1-16	-2.0

■ COONEY SNYDER

Snyder, Frank C. b: Toronto, Ontario, Canada d: 3/9/17, Toronto, Ont., Can. 6'3", 180 lbs. Deb: 5/19/1898

YEAR	TM/L	G	AB	R	H	2B	3B	HR	RBI	BB	SO	AVG	OBP	SLG	OPS	OPS+	BR+	SB	CS	SBR	FA	FR	G/POS	TPR
1898	Lou-N	17	61	4	10	0	0	0	6	3		.164	.215	.164	379	9	-7	0			.935	-6	C-17	-1.1

■ FRANK SNYDER

Snyder, Frank Elton "Pancho" b: 5/27/1893, San Antonio, Tex. d: 1/5/62, San Antonio, Tex. BR/TR, 6'2", 185 lbs. Deb: 8/25/12 C

YEAR	TM/L	G	AB	R	H	2B	3B	HR	RBI	BB	SO	AVG	OBP	SLG	OPS	OPS+	BR+	SB	CS	SBR	FA	FR	G/POS	TPR
1912	StL-N	11	18	2	2	0	0	0	0	2	7	.111	.200	.111	311	-14	-3	1			.919	0	C-11	-0.2
1913	StL-N	7	21	1	4	0	1	0	2	0	4	.190	.190	.286	476	35	-2	0			.956	2	/C-7	0.0
1914	StL-N	100	326	19	75	15	4	1	25	13	28	.230	.262	.310	572	71	-13	1			**.979**	5	C-98	0.0
1915	StL-N	144	473	41	141	22	7	2	55	39	49	.298	.353	.387	740	124	13	3	6	-1	.983	6	*C-142	3.2
1916	StL-N	132	406	23	105	12	4	0	39	18	31	.259	.290	.308	598	84	-8	7			.973	9	C-72,1-46/S-1	1.7
1917	StL-N	115	313	18	74	9	2	1	33	27	43	.236	.301	.288	589	83	-6	4			.975	0	C-94/2-1	0.2
1918	StL-N	39	112	5	28	7	1	0	10	6	13	.250	.288	.330	618	92	-1	4			.959	2	C-27/1-3	0.3
1919	StL-N	50	154	7	28	4	2	0	14	5	13	.182	.213	.234	446	36	-12	2			.983	5	C-48/1-1	-0.4
	NY-N	32	92	7	21	6	0	0	11	8	9	.228	.297	.293	591	79	-2	1			.983	-4	C-31	-0.5
	Yr	82	246	14	49	10	2	0	25	13	22	.199	.245	.256	501	53	-14	3			.983	1	C-79/1-1	-0.9
1920	NY-N	87	264	26	66	13	4	3	27	17	18	.250	.295	.364	659	89	-4	2	2	-0	.978	1	C-84	0.4
1921	*NY-N	108	309	36	99	13	2	8	45	27	24	.320	.382	.453	835	120	9	3	4	-1	.985	5	*C-101	1.9
1922	*NY-N	104	318	34	109	21	5	5	51	23	25	.343	.387	.487	875	123	11	1	5	-2	.980	-3	C-97	1.1
1923	*NY-N	120	402	37	103	13	6	5	63	24	29	.256	.298	.356	654	73	-17	5	3	0	**.990**	3	*C-112	-0.6
1924	*NY-N	118	354	37	107	18	3	5	53	30	43	.302	.357	.412	769	109	4	3	0	1	.987	-16	*C-110	-0.4
1925	NY-N	107	325	21	78	9	1	11	51	20	49	.240	.286	.375	662	70	-16	0	0	0	**.985**	2	C-96	-0.7
1926	NY-N	55	148	10	32	3	2	5	16	13	13	.216	.280	.365	644	73	-6	0			.981	-0	C-55	-0.3
1927	StL-N	63	194	7	50	5	0	1	30	9	18	.258	.293	.299	590	56	-12	0			.981	0	C-62	-0.8
Total	16	1392	4229	331	1122	170	44	47	525	281	416	.265	.313	.360	672	90	-64	37	20		.981	15	*C-1247/1-50,2-1,S	3.9

■ JERRY SNYDER

Snyder, Gerald George b: 7/21/29, Jenks, Okla. BR/TR, 6', 170 lbs. Deb: 5/8/52

YEAR	TM/L	G	AB	R	H	2B	3B	HR	RBI	BB	SO	AVG	OBP	SLG	OPS	OPS+	BR+	SB	CS	SBR	FA	FR	G/POS	TPR
1952	Was-A	36	57	5	9	2	0	0	2	5	8	.158	.226	.193	419	18	-6	1	0	0	.965	7	2-19/S-4	0.2
1953	Was-A	29	62	10	21	4	0	0	4	5	8	.339	.388	.403	791	117	2	0	1	-0	.988	7	S-17/2-4	0.9
1954	Was-A	64	154	17	36	3	1	0	17	15	18	.234	.302	.266	568	60	-8	3	0	1	.978	9	S-48/2-3	0.5
1955	Was-A	46	107	7	24	5	0	0	5	6	6	.224	.265	.271	537	47	-8	1	1	-0	.977	1	2-22,S-20	-0.5

YEAR	TM/L	G	AB	R	H	2B	3B	HR	RBI	BB	SO	AVG	OBP	SLG	OPS	OPS+	BR+	SB	CS	SBR	FA	FR	G/POS	TPR
1956	Was-A	43	148	14	40	3	1	2	14	10	9	.270	.321	.345	665	76	-5	1	0	0	.968	-5	S-35/2-7	-0.6
1957	Was-A	42	93	6	14	1	0	1	4	4	9	.151	.186	.194	379	4	-12	0	1	-0	.966	1	S-15,2-13/3-1	-1.1
1958	Was-A	6	9	1	1	0	0	0	1	1	1	.111	.200	.111	311	-12	-1	0	0	0	1.000	-1	/2-2,S-1	-0.2
Total	7	266	630	60	145	18	2	3	47	46	59	.230	.284	.279	563	54	-40	7	3	0	.971	20	S-140/2-70,3-1	-0.8

■ JIM SNYDER Snyder, James C. A. b: 9/15/1847, Brooklyn, N.Y. d: 12/1/22, Rockaway Beach, N.Y 5'7", 130 lbs. Deb: 5/7/1872

YEAR	TM/L	G	AB	R	H	2B	3B	HR	RBI	BB	SO	AVG	OBP	SLG	OPS	OPS+	BR+	SB	CS	SBR	FA	FR	G/POS	TPR
1872	Eck-n	26	107	16	28	2	2	0	11	0	1	.262	.262	.318	579	91	1	0	0	0	.763	4	S-25/C-1,O-1(0-0-1)	0.3

■ CORY SNYDER Snyder, James Cory b: 11/11/62, Inglewood, Cal. BR/TR, 6'3", 185 lbs. Deb: 6/13/86 Career OF: (99-LF 17-CF 793-RF)

YEAR	TM/L	G	AB	R	H	2B	3B	HR	RBI	BB	SO	AVG	OBP	SLG	OPS	OPS+	BR+	SB	CS	SBR	FA	FR	G/POS	TPR
1986	Cle-A	103	416	58	113	21	1	24	69	16	123	.272	.299	.500	799	115	6	2	3	-1	.987	-7	O-74R,S-34,3-11,/D	-0.2
1987	Cle-A	157	577	74	136	24	2	33	82	31	166	.236	.276	.456	732	89	-12	5	1	1	.971	2	*O-139(15-0-134),S-18	-1.4
1988	Cle-A	142	511	71	139	24	3	26	75	42	101	.272	.329	.483	812	121	13	5	1	1	.985	14	*O-141(1-3-139)/D-1	2.3
1989	Cle-A	132	489	49	105	17	0	18	59	23	134	.215	.253	.360	613	70	-21	6	5	-0	**.997**	19	*O-125R/S-7,D-2	-0.7
1990	Cle-A	123	438	46	102	27	3	14	55	21	118	.233	.271	.404	675	87	-10	1	4	-1	.975	2	*O-120(0-0-120)/S-5	-1.3
1991	Chi-A	50	117	10	22	4	0	3	11	6	41	.188	.228	.299	527	46	-9	0	0	0	.981	-2	O-29(13-0-17),1-18	-1.3
	Tor-A	21	49	4	7	0	1	0	6	3	19	.143	.192	.184	376	4	-6	0	0	0	1.000	-3	O-14R/1-4,3-3,D-3	-0.9
	Yr	71	166	14	29	4	1	3	17	9	60	.175	.217	.265	482	33	-15	0	0	0	.985	-5	O-43R,1-22/3-3,D-3	-2.2
1992	SF-N	124	390	48	105	22	2	14	57	23	96	.269	.313	.444	757	119	8	4	4	-1	.992	-5	O-70R,1-27,3-14,/2S	-0.1
1993	LA-N	143	516	61	137	33	1	11	56	47	147	.266	.332	.397	729	100	-0	4	1	1	.979	-8	*O-115R,3-23,1-12,/S	-1.3
1994	LA-N	73	153	18	36	6	0	6	18	14	47	.235	.304	.392	696	85	-4	1	0	0	.967	-8	O-50L/1-9,3-6,S2	-1.3
Total	9	1068	3656	439	902	178	13	149	488	226	992	.247	.293	.425	718	95	-36	28	19	-0	.983	3	O-877R/S-73,1-70,32D	-6.2

■ JIM SNYDER Snyder, James Robert b: 8/15/32, Dearborn, Mich. BR/TR, 6'1", 185 lbs. Deb: 9/15/61 MC

YEAR	TM/L	G	AB	R	H	2B	3B	HR	RBI	BB	SO	AVG	OBP	SLG	OPS	OPS+	BR+	SB	CS	SBR	FA	FR	G/POS	TPR
1961	Min-A	3	5	0	0	0	0	0	0	0	1	.000	.000	.000	0	-95	-1	0	0	0	1.000	0	/2-3	-0.1
1962	Min-A	12	10	1	1	0	0	0	1	0	0	.100	.100	.100	200	-44	-2	0	1	-0	.941	-6	/2-5,1-1	-0.8
1964	Min-A	26	71	3	11	2	0	1	9	4	11	.155	.211	.225	436	21	-8	0	0	0	.990	-4	2-25	-1.0
Total	3	41	86	4	12	2	0	1	10	4	12	.140	.187	.198	384	6	-11	0	1	-0	.984	-10	/2-33,1-1	-1.9

■ JACK SNYDER Snyder, John William b: 10/6/1886, Lincoln, Pa. d: 12/13/81, Brownsville, Pa. BR/TR, 5'9", 168 lbs. Deb: 6/13/14

YEAR	TM/L	G	AB	R	H	2B	3B	HR	RBI	BB	SO	AVG	OBP	SLG	OPS	OPS+	BR+	SB	CS	SBR	FA	FR	G/POS	TPR
1914	Buf-F	1	0	0	0	0	0	0	0	1	0	—	1.000	—	1000	183	0	0			.000	0	/C-1	0.0
1917	Bro-N	7	11	1	3	0	0	0	1	0	2	.273	.273	.273	545	66	-0	0			1.000	0	/C-5	0.0
Total	2	8	11	1	3	0	0	0	1	1	2	.273	.333	.273	606	84	-0	0			1.000	0	/C-6	0.0

■ JOSH SNYDER Snyder, Joshua M. b: 3/1844, Brooklyn, N.Y. d: 4/21/1881, Brooklyn, N.Y. Deb: 5/18/1872

YEAR	TM/L	G	AB	R	H	2B	3B	HR	RBI	BB	SO	AVG	OBP	SLG	OPS	OPS+	BR+	SB	CS	SBR	FA	FR	G/POS	TPR
1872	Eck-n	9	37	2	6	2	0	0	1	1	1	.162	.184	.216	400	27	-2	0	0	0	.778	2	/O-9(9-0-0)	0.0

■ RUSS SNYDER Snyder, Russell Henry b: 6/22/34, Oak, Neb. BL/TR, 6'1", 190 lbs. Deb: 4/18/59 Career OF: (442-LF 424-CF 390-RF)

YEAR	TM/L	G	AB	R	H	2B	3B	HR	RBI	BB	SO	AVG	OBP	SLG	OPS	OPS+	BR+	SB	CS	SBR	FA	FR	G/POS	TPR
1959	KC-A	73	243	41	76	13	2	3	21	19	29	.313	.367	.420	787	113	5	6	2	1	.986	3	O-64(27-30-12)	0.5
1960	KC-A	125	304	45	79	10	5	4	26	20	28	.260	.308	.365	673	81	-9	7	3	0	.986	-10	O-91(21-16-62)	-2.2
1961	Bal-A	115	312	46	91	13	5	1	13	20	32	.292	.334	.375	709	92	-4	5	3	0	.966	-16	*O-108(75-28-22)	-2.4
1962	Bal-A	139	416	47	127	19	4	9	40	17	46	.305	.336	.435	771	113	6	7	4	0	.974	-3	*O-121(43-41-45)	-0.2
1963	Bal-A	148	429	51	110	21	2	7	36	40	48	.256	.323	.364	686	95	-2	18	5	2	.988	-18	*O-130(32-74-57)	-2.5
1964	Bal-A	56	93	11	27	3	0	1	7	11	22	.290	.365	.355	720	102	1	0	2	-1	.971	-9	O-40(31-8-3)	-1.1
1965	Bal-A	132	345	49	93	11	2	1	29	27	38	.270	.324	.322	646	83	-7	3	4	-1	1.000	-7	*O-106(36-36-52)	-2.2
1966	*Bal-A	117	373	66	114	21	5	3	41	38	37	.306	.370	.413	783	127	13	2	1	0	.986	-13	*O-104(59-86-4)	-0.4
1967	Bal-A	108	275	40	65	8	2	4	23	32	48	.236	.318	.324	642	91	-3	5	2	0	.985	-1	O-69(24-25-27)	-0.8
1968	Chi-A	38	82	2	11	2	0	1	5	4	16	.134	.174	.195	370	12	-9	0	0	0	1.000	-5	O-22(9-1-16)	-1.8
	Cle-A	68	217	30	61	8	2	2	23	25	21	.281	.355	.364	719	120	6	1	1	-0	.991	4	O-54(5-11-43)/1-1	0.7
	Yr	106	299	32	72	10	2	3	28	29	37	.241	.308	.318	626	90	-3	1	1	-0	.992	-1	O-76(14-12-59)/1-1	-1.1
1969	Cle-A	122	266	26	66	10	0	2	24	25	33	.248	.313	.308	621	72	-10	3	2	-0	.961	-4	O-84(37-28-21)	-1.7
1970	Mil-A	124	276	34	64	11	0	4	31	16	40	.232	.274	.315	589	62	-15	1	3	-1	.966	-16	*O-106(43-40-26)	-3.6
Total	12	1365	3631	488	984	150	29	42	319	294	438	.271	.327	.363	690	94	-27	58	32	2	.981	-96	*O-1099L/1-1	-17.7

■ CHIEF SOCKALEXIS Sockalexis, Louis Francis b: 10/24/1871, Old Town, Maine d: 12/24/13, Burlington, Maine BL/TR, 5'11", 185 lbs. Deb: 4/22/1897

YEAR	TM/L	G	AB	R	H	2B	3B	HR	RBI	BB	SO	AVG	OBP	SLG	OPS	OPS+	BR+	SB	CS	SBR	FA	FR	G/POS	TPR
1897	Cle-N	66	278	43	94	9	8	3	42	18		.338	.385	.460	845	116	6	16			.888	1	O-66(0-1-66)	0.3
1898	Cle-N	21	67	11	15	2	0	0	10	1		.224	.246	.254	500	44	-5	0			.964	2	O-16(4-4-8)	-0.4
1899	Cle-N	7	22	0	6	1	0	0	3	1		.273	.304	.318	623	76	-1	0			.818	1	/O-5(0-0-5)	0.0
Total	3	94	367	54	115	12	8	3	55	20		.313	.355	.414	770	103	-0	16			.896	4	/O-87(4-5-79)	-0.1

■ BILL SODD Sodd, William b: 9/18/14, Ft.Worth, Tex. d: 5/14/98, Fort Worth, Tex. BR/TR, 6'2", 210 lbs. Deb: 9/27/37

YEAR	TM/L	G	AB	R	H	2B	3B	HR	RBI	BB	SO	AVG	OBP	SLG	OPS	OPS+	BR+	SB	CS	SBR	FA	FR	G/POS	TPR
1937	Cle-A	1	1	0	0	0	0	0	0	0	1	.000	.000	.000	0	-99	-0	0	0	0	.000	0	H	0.0

■ ERIC SODERHOLM Soderholm, Eric Thane b: 9/24/48, Cortland, N.Y. BR/TR, 5'11", 187 lbs. Deb: 9/3/71

YEAR	TM/L	G	AB	R	H	2B	3B	HR	RBI	BB	SO	AVG	OBP	SLG	OPS	OPS+	BR+	SB	CS	SBR	FA	FR	G/POS	TPR
1971	Min-A	21	64	9	10	4	0	1	4	10	17	.156	.299	.266	564	59	-3	0	1	-0	.942	3	3-20	0.0
1972	Min-A	93	287	28	54	10	0	13	39	19	48	.188	.246	.359	605	75	-10	3	3	-0	.942	2	3-79	-1.0
1973	Min-A	35	111	22	33	7	2	1	9	21	16	.297	.414	.423	837	131	6	1	2	-0	.921	0	3-33/S-1	0.5
1974	Min-A	141	464	63	128	18	3	10	51	48	68	.276	.350	.392	742	110	6	7	3	0	.956	-4	*3-130/S-1	0.3
1975	Min-A	117	419	62	120	17	2	11	58	53	66	.286	.367	.415	782	119	11	3	5	-1	.969	12	*3-113/D-3	2.1
1977	Chi-A	130	460	77	129	20	3	25	67	47	47	.280	.352	.500	852	129	18	2	4	-1	**.978**	0	*3-126/D-3	1.5
1978	Chi-A	143	457	57	118	17	1	20	67	39	44	.258	.322	.431	753	109	4	2	2	-0	.964	0	*3-128,D-11/2-1	0.2
1979	Chi-A	56	210	31	53	8	2	6	34	19	19	.252	.314	.395	710	90	-3	0	1	-0	.986	15	3-56	1.0
	Tex-A	63	147	15	40	6	0	4	19	12	9	.272	.331	.395	726	96	-1	0	0	0	.944	0	3-37,D-14/1-2	-0.1
	Yr	119	357	46	93	14	2	10	53	31	28	.261	.321	.395	716	93	-4	0	1	-0	.975	15	3-93,D-14/1-2	0.9
1980	*NY-A	95	275	38	79	13	1	11	35	27	25	.287	.353	.462	815	123	9	0	0	0	.952	-1	D-51,3-37	0.5
Total	9	894	2894	402	764	120	14	102	383	295	359	.264	.337	.421	758	110	37	18	21	-3	.962	27	3-759/D-82,1-2,S2	5.0

■ RICK SOFIELD Sofield, Richard Michael b: 12/16/56, Cheyenne, Wyo. BL/TR, 6'1", 195 lbs. Deb: 4/6/79

YEAR	TM/L	G	AB	R	H	2B	3B	HR	RBI	BB	SO	AVG	OBP	SLG	OPS	OPS+	BR+	SB	CS	SBR	FA	FR	G/POS	TPR
1979	Min-A	35	93	8	28	5	0	0	12	12	27	.301	.381	.355	736	96	0	2	3	-1	.954	-3	O-35(7-6-22)	-0.5
1980	Min-A	131	417	52	103	18	4	9	49	24	92	.247	.291	.374	665	75	-15	4	5	-1	.979	-5	*O-126(74-49-9)/D-2	-2.4
1981	Min-A	41	102	9	18	2	0	0	5	8	22	.176	.236	.196	432	24	-10	3	2	-0	.983	-1	O-34(33-0-1)	-1.2
Total	3	207	612	69	149	25	4	9	66	44	141	.243	.296	.342	638	71	-24	9	10	-2	.975	-8	O-195(114-55-32)/D-2	-4.1

■ LUIS SOJO Sojo, Luis Beltran (Sojo) b: 1/3/66, Caracas, Venez. BR/TR, 5'11", 174 lbs. Deb: 7/14/90 Career OF: (12-LF 0-CF 0-RF)

YEAR	TM/L	G	AB	R	H	2B	3B	HR	RBI	BB	SO	AVG	OBP	SLG	OPS	OPS+	BR+	SB	CS	SBR	FA	FR	G/POS	TPR
1990	Tor-A	33	80	14	18	3	0	1	9	5	5	.225	.271	.300	571	58	-4	1	1	-0	.969	-3	2-15/S-5,O-5L,3D	-0.7
1991	Cal-A	113	364	38	94	14	1	3	20	14	26	.258	.295	.327	622	72	-14	4	2	0	.981	20	*2-107/S-2,3-1,OD	0.8
1992	Cal-A	106	368	37	100	12	3	7	43	14	24	.272	.300	.378	678	88	-7	7	11	-2	.985	2	2-96/3-9,S-5	-0.4
1993	Tor-A	19	47	5	8	2	0	0	6	4	2	.170	.235	.213	448	21	-5	0	0	0	1.000	-1	/2-8,S-8,3-3	-0.5
1994	Sea-A	63	213	32	59	9	2	6	22	8	25	.277	.309	.423	732	85	-5	2	1	0	.973	18	2-40,S-24/3-1,D-2	1.4
1995	*Sea-A	102	339	50	98	18	2	7	39	23	19	.289	.336	.416	752	93	-4	4	2	0	.983	-14	S-80,2-19/O-6(6-0-0)	-1.0
1996	Sea-A	77	247	20	52	8	1	1	16	10	13	.211	.244	.263	507	28	-27	2	2	-0	.940	10	3-33,2-27,S-19	-1.4
	*NY-A	18	40	3	11	2	0	0	5	1	4	.275	.293	.325	618	56	-3	0	0	0	1.000	3	2-14/S-4,3-1	0.1
	Yr	95	287	23	63	10	1	1	21	11	17	.220	.251	.272	523	32	-30	2	2	-0	.986	13	2-41,3-34,S-23	-1.3
1997	NY-A	77	215	27	66	6	1	2	25	16	14	.307	.358	.372	730	92	-2	3	1	0	.982	-5	2-72/S-4,3-3,1-2	-0.3
1998	*NY-A	54	147	16	34	3	1	0	14	4	15	.231	.252	.265	517	36	-14	1	0	0	.973	5	S-20,1-19/2-8,3D	-0.8
1999	*NY-A	49	127	20	32	6	0	2	16	4	17	.252	.275	.346	621	58	-8	1	0	0	.974	5	3-20,2-16/S-6,1D	-0.3
2000	Pit-N	61	176	14	50	11	0	5	20	11	16	.284	.330	.432	762	91	-3	1	0	0	.960	4	3-50/2-1	0.2
	*NY-A	34	125	19	36	7	1	2	17	6	6	.288	.321	.408	729	84	-3	1	0	0	.989	-4	2-25,3-10/1-7,S-2	-0.6
Total	11	806	2488	295	658	101	12	36	252	120	186	.264	.302	.358	660	73	-99	27	20	-1	.981	39	2-448,S-179,3/1OD	-3.5

■ TONY SOLAITA Solaita, Tolia b: 1/15/47, Nuuuli, Amer.Samoa d: 2/10/90, Tafuna, Amer.Samoa BL/TL, 6', 215 lbs. Deb: 9/16/68 Career OF: (0-LF 0-CF 1-RF)

YEAR	TM/L	G	AB	R	H	2B	3B	HR	RBI	BB	SO	AVG	OBP	SLG	OPS	OPS+	BR+	SB	CS	SBR	FA	FR	G/POS	TPR
1968	NY-A	1	1	0	0	0	0	0	0	0	1	.000	.000	.000	0	-99	-0	0	0	0	1.000	-0	/1-1	0.0
1974	KC-A	96	239	31	64	12	0	7	30	35	70	.268	.364	.406	769	115	5	0	3	-1	.991	3	1-65,D-14/O-1(0-0-1)	0.3

YEAR	TM/L	G	AB	R	H	2B	3B	HR	RBI	BB	SO	AVG	OBP	SLG	OPS	OPS+	BR+	SB	CS	SBR	FA	FR	G/POS	TPR
1975	KC-A	93	231	35	60	11	0	16	44	39	79	.260	.371	.515	886	145	14	0	1	-0	.994	3	D-37,1-35	1.4
1976	KC-A	31	68	4	16	4	0	0	9	6	17	.235	.297	.294	591	73	-2	0	0	0	.974	0	D-14/1-5	-0.3
	Cal-A	63	215	25	58	9	0	9	33	34	44	.270	.369	.437	807	145	13	1	1	-0	.998	8	1-54/D-7	1.7
	Yr	94	283	29	74	13	0	9	42	40	61	.261	.353	.403	756	126	10	1	1	-0	.996	8	1-59,D-21	1.4
1977	Cal-A	116	324	40	78	15	0	14	53	56	77	.241	.353	.417	769	113	7	1	3	-1	.990	1	1-91/D-6	0.2
1978	Cal-A	60	94	10	21	3	0	1	14	16	25	.223	.336	.287	624	80	-2	0	0	0	1.000	1	D-18,1-11	-0.2
1979	Mon-N	29	42	5	12	4	0	1	7	11	16	.286	.434	.452	886	143	3	0	0	0	.989	0	1-13	0.3
	Tor-A	36	102	14	27	8	1	2	13	17	16	.265	.370	.422	791	112	2	0	0	0	1.000	0	D-26/1-6	0.1
Total	7	525	1316	164	336	66	1	50	203	214	345	.255	.361	.421	782	120	40	2	8	-2	.993	17	1-281,D-122/O-1R	3.5
■ MOSE SOLOMON Solomon, Mose Hirsch "The Rabbi Of Swat" b: 12/8/1900, New York, N.Y. d: 6/25/66, Miami, Fla. BL/TL, 5'9.5", 180 lbs. Deb: 9/30/23																								
1923	NY-N	2	8	0	3	1	0	0	1	0	1	.375	.375	.500	875	131	0	0	0	0	.833	-0	/O-2(0-0-2)	0.0
■ MOOSE SOLTERS Solters, Julius Joseph (b: Julius Joseph Soltesz) b: 3/22/06, Pittsburgh, Pa. d: 9/28/75, Pittsburgh, Pa. BR/TR, 6', 190 lbs. Deb: 4/17/34																								
1934	Bos-A	101	365	61	109	25	4	7	58	18	50	.299	.333	.447	780	93	-5	9	4	1	.933	2	O-89(6-57-26)	-0.6
1935	Bos-A	24	79	15	19	6	1	0	8	2	7	.241	.268	.342	610	53	-6	1	1	-0	.966	3	O-21(10-0-11)	-0.4
	StL-A	127	552	79	182	39	6	18	104	34	35	.330	.369	.520	889	122	15	10	1	2	.989	16	*O-127(116-12-0)	2.5
	Yr	151	631	94	201	45	7	18	112	36	42	.319	.356	.498	854	113	10	11	2	2	.985	19	*O-148(126-12-11)	2.1
1936	StL-A	152	628	100	183	45	7	17	134	41	76	.291	.336	.467	802	93	-10	3	0	1	.956	12	*O-147(145-6-0)	-0.5
1937	Cle-A	152	589	90	190	42	11	20	109	42	56	.323	.372	.533	905	125	19	6	9	-2	.953	2	*O-149(149-0-0)	1.0
1938	Cle-A	67	199	30	40	6	3	2	22	13	28	.201	.250	.291	541	36	-21	4	1	1	.969	1	O-46(40-0-6)	-1.9
1939	Cle-A	41	102	19	28	7	2	2	19	9	15	.275	.333	.441	775	100	-0	2	1	0	.915	-3	O-25(17-0-8)	-0.4
	StL-A	40	131	14	27	6	1	0	14	10	20	.206	.262	.267	530	35	-13	1	0	0	.935	0	O-30(22-1-7)	-1.3
	Yr	81	233	33	55	13	3	2	33	19	35	.236	.294	.343	637	63	-14	3	1	0	.927	-3	O-55(39-1-15)	-1.7
1940	Chi-A	116	428	65	132	28	3	12	80	27	54	.308	.351	.472	823	110	5	3	3	-0	.971	5	*O-107(107-0-0)	0.4
1941	Chi-A	76	251	24	65	9	4	4	43	18	31	.259	.311	.375	686	82	-7	3	2	-0	.966	1	O-63(62-0-1)	-1.0
1943	Chi-A	42	97	6	15	0	0	1	8	7	5	.155	.212	.186	397	17	-10	0	1	-0	.941	-3	O-21(13-0-8)	-1.7
Total	9	938	3421	503	990	213	42	83	599	221	377	.289	.334	.449	783	96	-32	42	23	1	.960	36	O-825(687-76-67)	-3.9
■ JOCK SOMERLOTT Somerlott, John Wesley b: 10/26/1882, Flint, Ind. d: 4/21/65, Butler, Ind. BR/TR, 6', 160 lbs. Deb: 9/19/10																								
1910	Was-A	16	63	6	14	0	0	0	2	3		.222	.258	.222	480	53	-3	2			.994	0	1-16	-0.4
1911	Was-A	13	40	2	7	0	0	0	2	0		.175	.195	.175	370	4	-5	2			.992	2	1-12	-0.4
Total	2	29	103	8	21	0	0	0	4	3		.204	.234	.204	438	32	-9	4			.993	2	/1-28	-0.8
■ ED SOMERVILLE Somerville, Edward G. b: 3/1/1853, Philadelphia, Pa. d: 10/1/1877, London, Ont., Canada BR/TR, 5'7", 158 lbs. Deb: 4/30/1875																								
1875	Cen-n	14	57	6	13	3	0	0	6	1	3	.228	.241	.281	522	88	-0	1	0	0	.771	-6	2-14/S-1	-0.6
	NH-n	33	136	14	29	5	0	0	7	1	3	.213	.219	.250	469	72	-2	1	2	-0	.802	13	2-29/3-2,1-1,S-1	0.7
	Yr	47	193	20	42	8	0	0	13	2	6	.218	.226	.259	485	77	-3	2	2	-0	.794	7	2-43/S-2,3-2,1-1	0.1
1876	Lou-N	64	257	29	48	5	1	0	14	1	6	.187	.191	.215	406	30	-20				.870	**30**	*2-64	1.1
■ JOE SOMMER Sommer, Joseph John b: 11/20/1858, Covington, Ky. d: 1/16/38, Cincinnati, Ohio BR/TR, Deb: 7/8/1880 Career OF: (567-LF 15-CF 132-RF)																								
1880	Cin-N	24	88	10	16	1	0	0	6	0	2	.182	.182	.193	375	28	-6				.913	-1	O-22L/S-1,3-1,C-1	-0.8
1882	Cin-a	80	354	82	102	12	6	1	29	24		.288	.333	.364	698	128	10				**.925**	4	*O-80(80-0-0)	1.1
1883	Cin-a	97	413	79	115	5	7	3	52	20		.278	.312	.346	658	106	2				.854	-1	*O-94L/3-3,P-1	-0.1
1884	Bal-a	107	479	96	129	11	10	4		8		.269	.293	.359	652	107	3				.841	6	*3-97/O-9(0-2-7),2-1	0.9
1885	Bal-a	110	471	84	118	23	6	1	44	24		.251	.291	.331	622	98	-1				.921	12	*O-107L/S-2,3-2,P1	0.8
1886	Bal-a	139	560	79	117	18	4	1	52	24		.209	.245	.261	506	60	-26	31			.900	13	*O-95L,2-32,3-11,/SP	-1.2
1887	Bal-a	131	526	88	186	11	5	0	65	63		.354	.358	.311	670	93	0	29			.902	0	*O-110L,2-13,3/SP	-0.1
1888	Bal-a	79	297	31	65	10	0	0	35	18		.219	.266	.253	518	68	-10	13			.871	-4	O-44L,S-34/2-2,1-1	-1.3
1889	Bal-a	106	386	51	85	13	2	1	36	42	49	.220	.298	.272	570	62	-19	18			.929	9	*O-105(4-3-99)/S-1	-0.9
1890	Cle-N	9	35	4	8	1	0	0	0	2	2	.229	.270	.257	527	55	-2	0			.789	-2	/O-9(9-0-0),P-1	-0.4
	Bal-a	38	129	13	33	4	2	0	23	13		.256	.324	.318	642	85	-3	10			.892	1	O-38(38-0-0)	-0.2
Total	10	920	3738	617	974	109	42	11	342	238	53	.261	.297	.309	607	88	-53	101			.901	38	O-713L,3-124/2SP1C	-2.2
■ PETE SOMMERS Sommers, Joseph Andrews b: 10/26/1866, Cleveland, Ohio d: 7/22/08, Cleveland, Ohio BR/TR, 5'11.5", 181 lbs. Deb: 4/27/1887																								
1887	NY-a	33	123	9	28	3	0	1	12	7		.228	.234	.233	467	32	-10	6			.830	-8	C-31/O-1(0-0-1),1-1	-1.4
1888	Bos-N	4	13	1	3	1	0	0	0	0	3	.231	.231	.308	538	69	-0	0			.880	-0	/C-4	-0.1
1889	Chi-N	12	45	5	10	5	0	0	8	2	8	.222	.271	.333	604	65	-2	0			.836	-5	C-11/O-1(0-0-1)	-0.6
	Ind-N	23	84	12	21	2	2	2	14	1	16	.250	.267	.393	660	82	-3	2			.905	-2	C-21/O-2(0-2-0)	-0.3
	Yr	35	129	17	31	7	2	2	22	3	24	.240	.269	.372	641	76	-5	2			.882	-7	C-32/O-3(0-2-1)	-0.9
1890	NY-N	17	47	4	5	1	1	0	1	4	13	.106	.192	.170	363	6	-6	0			.837	1	C-11/1-5,O-2(0-0-2)	-0.4
	Cle-N	9	34	4	7	1	1	0	1	2	3	.206	.250	.294	544	60	-2	0			.906	1	/C-8,O-1(0-1-0)	-0.1
	Yr	26	81	8	12	2	2	0	2	6	16	.148	.216	.222	438	28	-8	0			.865	1	C-19/1-5,O-3(0-1-2)	-0.5
Total	4	98	346	35	74	13	4	3	36	16	43	.214	.242	.286	528	50	-23	8			.860	-15	/C-86,O-7(0-3-4),1-6	-2.9
■ BILL SOMMERS Sommers, William Dunn b: 2/17/23, Brooklyn, N.Y. BR/TR, 6', 180 lbs. Deb: 4/25/50																								
1950	StL-A	65	137	24	35	5	1	0	14	25	14	.255	.370	.307	677	72	-5	0	1	-0	.917	-9	3-37,2-21	-1.3
■ ALFONSO SORIANO Soriano, Alfonso Guilleard b: 1/7/78, San Pedro De Macoris, D.R. BR/TR, 6'1", 160 lbs. Deb: 9/14/99																								
1999	NY-A	9	8	2	1	0	0	1	1	0	3	.125	.125	.500	625	50	-1	0	1	-0	.500	0	/S-1,D-6	-0.1
2000	NY-A	22	50	5	9	3	0	2	3	1	15	.180	.196	.360	556	37	-5	2	0	0	.846	-5	3-10/S-9,2-1,D-1	-0.8
Total	2	31	58	7	10	3	0	3	4	1	18	.172	.186	.379	566	39	-6	2	1	0	.833	-5	/3-10,S-10,D-7,2-1	-0.9
■ BILL SORRELL Sorrell, William b: 10/14/40, Morehead, Ky. BL/TR, 6', 190 lbs. Deb: 9/2/65																								
1965	Phi-N	10	13	2	5	0	0	1	2	2	1	.385	.467	.615	1082	206	2	0	0	0	.000	0	/3-1	0.2
1967	SF-N	18	17	1	3	1	0	0	1	3	2	.176	.300	.235	535	56	-1	0	0	0	1.000	-2	/O-5(5-0-0)	-0.3
1970	KC-A	57	135	12	36	2	0	4	14	10	13	.267	.317	.370	688	89	-2	1	0	0	.873	-6	3-29/O-4(2-0-2),1-3	-0.9
Total	3	85	165	15	44	3	0	5	17	15	16	.267	.328	.376	704	95	-1	1	0	0	.873	-8	/3-30,O-9(7-0-2),1-3	-1.0
■ CHICK SORRELLS Sorrells, Raymond Edwin b: 7/31/1896, Stringtown, Okla. d: 7/20/83, Terrell, Tex. BR/TR, 5'9", 155 lbs. Deb: 9/18/22																								
1922	Cle-A	2	1	0	0	0	0	0	0	0	0	.000	.000	.000	0	-99	-0	0	0	0	1.000	1	/S-1	0.1
■ PAUL SORRENTO Sorrento, Paul Anthony b: 11/17/65, Somerville, Mass. BL/TR, 6'2", 200 lbs. Deb: 9/8/89 Career OF: (61-LF 0-CF 17-RF)																								
1989	Min-A	14	21	2	5	0	0	0	1	5	4	.238	.385	.238	623	74	-0	0	0	0	1.000	-0	/1-5,D-5	-0.1
1990	Min-A	41	121	11	25	4	1	5	13	12	31	.207	.284	.380	664	79	-4	1	1	-0	.992	-1	D-23,1-15	-0.6
1991	*Min-A	26	47	6	12	2	0	4	13	4	11	.255	.314	.553	867	129	2	0	0	0	1.000	1	1-13/D-2	0.2
1992	Cle-A	140	458	52	123	24	1	18	60	51	89	.269	.343	.443	786	121	12	0	3	-1	.993	-1	*1-121,D-11	0.1
1993	Cle-A	148	463	75	119	26	1	18	65	58	121	.257	.342	.434	776	108	5	3	1	0	.995	-0	*1-144/O-3(0-0-3),D-1	-0.6
1994	Cle-A	95	322	43	90	14	0	14	62	34	68	.280	.348	.453	802	104	2	0	1	-0	.995	1	1-86/D-8	-0.5
1995	*Cle-A	104	323	50	76	14	0	25	79	51	71	.235	.340	.511	850	116	7	1	1	-0	.992	-2	1-91,D-11	-0.4
1996	Sea-A	143	471	67	136	32	1	23	93	57	103	.289	.374	.507	881	120	14	0	2	-1	.990	-2	*1-138	0.0
1997	*Sea-A	146	457	68	123	19	0	31	80	51	112	.269	.346	.514	861	122	14	0	2	-1	.996	5	*1-139/D-1	0.6
1998	TB-A	137	435	40	98	27	0	17	57	54	133	.225	.315	.405	720	84	-11	2	3	-1	1.000	1	D-86,1-27,O-18R	-1.7
1999	TB-A	99	294	40	69	14	1	11	42	49	101	.235	.352	.401	753	91	-4	1	1	-0	.957	-6	O-57(57-0-0),1-27/D-9	-1.2
Total	11	1093	3412	454	876	176	5	166	565	426	844	.257	.343	.457	800	108	36	8	15	-3	.994	-3	1-806,D-157/O-78L	-4.2
■ JUAN SOSA Sosa, Juan Luis (Encarnacion) b: 8/19/75, San Francisco De Macoris, D.R. BR/TR, 6'1", 175 lbs. Deb: 9/10/99																								
1999	Col-N	11	9	3	2	0	0	0	0	2	2	.222	.364	.222	586	42	-1	0	0	0	1.000	-1	/O-6(1-5-0),S-2	-0.1
■ SAMMY SOSA Sosa, Samuel Peralta b: 11/12/68, San Pedro De Macoris, D.R. BR/TR, 6', 185 lbs. Deb: 6/16/89 Career OF: (13-LF 233-CF 1362-RF)																								
1989	Tex-A	25	84	8	20	3	0	1	3	0	20	.238	.238	.310	548	52	-5	0	2	-1	.944	-2	O-19(12-8-1)/D-6	-0.9
	Chi-A	33	99	19	27	5	0	3	10	11	27	.273	.357	.414	771	120	3	7	3	0	.969	-5	O-33(1-25-9)	-0.2

YEAR	TM/L	G	AB	R	H	2B	3B	HR	RBI	BB	SO	AVG	OBP	SLG	OPS	OPS+	BR+	SB	CS	SBR	FA	FR	G/POS	TPR
	Yr	58	183	27	47	8	0	4	13	11	47	.257	.306	.366	672	89	-3	7	5	-0	.960	-7	O-52(13-33-10)/D-6	-1.1
1990	Chi-A	153	532	72	124	26	10	15	70	33	150	.233	.285	.404	690	93	-7	32	16	1	.962	9	*O-152(0-1-152)	-0.1
1991	Chi-A	116	316	39	64	10	1	10	33	14	98	.203	.241	.335	576	59	-19	13	6	1	.973	-3	*O-111(0-13-102)/D-2	-2.3
1992	Chi-N	67	262	41	68	7	2	8	25	19	63	.260	.319	.393	712	98	-1	15	7	1	.961	-3	O-67(0-67-0)	-0.4
1993	Chi-N	159	598	92	156	25	5	33	93	38	135	.261	.309	.485	794	111	6	36	11	4	.976	0	*O-158(0-70-114)	0.6
1994	Chi-N	105	426	59	128	17	6	25	70	25	92	.300	.342	.545	887	128	16	22	13	0	.973	5	*O-105(0-15-98)	1.6
1995	Chi-N★	144	564	89	151	17	3	36	119	58	134	.268	.341	.500	841	121	15	34	7	5	.962	14	*O-143(0-0-143)	2.6
1996	Chi-N	124	498	84	136	21	2	40	100	34	134	.273	.326	.564	890	126	16	18	5	2	.964	12	*O-124(0-0-124)	2.3
1997	Chi-N	162	642	90	161	31	4	36	119	45	174	.251	.302	.480	782	98	-5	22	12	1	.977	17	*O-161(0-0-161)	0.4
1998	*Chi-N†	159	643	**134**	198	20	0	66	**158**	73	171	.308	.379	.647	1026	158	52	18	9	1	.975	16	*O-159(0-7-156)	5.8
1999	Chi-N★	162	625	114	180	24	2	63	141	78	171	.288	.370	.635	1005	150	45	7	8	-1	.978	16	*O-162(0-25-146)	4.8
2000	Chi-N★	156	604	106	193	38	1	**50**	138	91	168	.320	.410	.634	1044	162	58	7	4	0	.970	2	*O-156(0-2-156)	4.8
Total	12	1565	5893	947	1606	244	36	386	1079	519	1537	.273	.335	.523	858	123	173	231	103	15	.971	78	*O-1550R/D-8	19.0

■ DENNY SOTHERN

Sothern, Dennis Elwood b: 1/20/04, Washington, D.C. d: 12/7/77, Durham, N.C. BR/TR, 5′11″, 175 lbs. Deb: 9/10/26

YEAR	TM/L	G	AB	R	H	2B	3B	HR	RBI	BB	SO	AVG	OBP	SLG	OPS	OPS+	BR+	SB	CS	SBR	FA	FR	G/POS	TPR
1926	Phi-N	14	53	5	13	1	0	3	10	4	10	.245	.310	.434	744	94	-1	0			.975	2	O-13(11-3-0)	0.0
1928	Phi-N	141	579	82	165	27	5	5	38	34	53	.285	.327	.375	702	80	-17	17			.964	8	*O-136(8-127-1)	-1.5
1929	Phi-N	76	294	52	90	21	3	5	27	16	24	.306	.346	.449	795	90	-5	13			.967	3	O-71(2-63-6)	-0.5
1930	Phi-N	90	347	66	97	26	1	5	36	22	37	.280	.326	.403	730	70	-17	6			.967	8	O-84(3-81-0)	-1.1
	Pit-N	17	51	4	9	4	0	1	4	3	4	.176	.222	.314	536	28	-6	2			.971	-1	O-13(0-12-1)	-0.7
	Yr	107	398	70	106	30	1	6	40	25	41	.266	.313	.392	705	65	-23	8			.967	8	O-97(3-93-1)	-1.8
1931	Bro-N	19	31	10	5	1	0	0	0	4	8	.161	.257	.194	451	23	-3	0			.958	-1	O-10(3-7-0)	-0.4
Total	5	357	1355	219	379	80	9	19	115	83	136	.280	.325	.394	719	77	-50	38			.966	20	O-327(27-293-8)	-4.2

■ STEVE SOUCHOCK

Souchock, Stephen "Bud" b: 3/3/19, Yatesboro, Pa. BR/TR, 6′2.5″, 203 lbs. Deb: 5/25/46 Career OF: (133-LF 1-CF 114-RF)

YEAR	TM/L	G	AB	R	H	2B	3B	HR	RBI	BB	SO	AVG	OBP	SLG	OPS	OPS+	BR+	SB	CS	SBR	FA	FR	G/POS	TPR
1946	NY-A	47	86	15	26	3	3	2	10	7	13	.302	.362	.477	838	131	3	0	3	-1	.964	-2	1-20	0.0
1948	NY-A	44	118	11	24	3	1	3	11	7	13	.203	.248	.322	570	51	-9	3	0	1	.988	-2	1-32	-1.1
1949	Chi-A	84	252	29	59	13	5	7	37	25	38	.234	.303	.409	712	90	-6	5	2	0	.951	2	O-39(39-0-0),1-30	-0.7
1951	Det-A	91	188	33	46	10	3	11	28	18	27	.245	.314	.505	819	118	3	0	2	-1	.941	-6	O-59L/3-3,1-1,2-1	-0.6
1952	Det-A	92	265	40	66	16	4	13	45	21	28	.249	.304	.487	791	117	4	1	0	0	.964	1	O-56R,3-13/1-9	0.2
1953	Det-A	89	278	29	84	13	3	11	46	8	35	.302	.326	.489	816	119	5	5	1	1	.962	-1	O-80(39-0-44)/1-1	0.2
1954	Det-A	25	39	6	7	0	1	3	8	2	10	.179	.220	.462	681	84	-1	1	1	-0	1.000	-1	/O-9(9-0-0),3-2	-0.3
1955	Det-A	1	1	0	1	0	0	0	1	0	0	1.000	1.000	1.000	2000	449	0	0	0	0	.000	0	H	0.0
Total	8	473	1227	163	313	58	20	50	186	88	164	.255	.307	.457	764	106	1	15	9	0	.957	-10	O-243L/1-93,3-18,2	-2.3

■ CLYDE SOUTHWICK

Southwick, Clyde Aubra b: 11/3/1886, Maxwell, Iowa d: 10/14/61, Freeport, Ill. BL/TR, 6′, 180 lbs. Deb: 8/22/11

YEAR	TM/L	G	AB	R	H	2B	3B	HR	RBI	BB	SO	AVG	OBP	SLG	OPS	OPS+	BR+	SB	CS	SBR	FA	FR	G/POS	TPR
1911	StL-A	4	12	3	3	0	0	0	0	1		.250	.308	.250	558	58	-1	0			.938	-1	/C-4	-0.1

■ BILL SOUTHWORTH

Southworth, William Frederick b: 11/10/45, Madison, Wis. BR/TR, 6′2″, 205 lbs. Deb: 10/2/64

YEAR	TM/L	G	AB	R	H	2B	3B	HR	RBI	BB	SO	AVG	OBP	SLG	OPS	OPS+	BR+	SB	CS	SBR	FA	FR	G/POS	TPR
1964	Mil-N	3	7	2	2	0	0	1	2	0	3	.286	.444	.714	1159	219	1	0	0	0	1.000	-1	/3-2	0.0

■ BILLY SOUTHWORTH

Southworth, William Harrison b: 3/9/1893, Harvard, Neb.
d: 11/15/69, Columbus, Ohio BL/TR, 5′9″, 170 lbs. Deb: 8/4/13 MC Career OF: (93-LF 214-CF 805-RF)

YEAR	TM/L	G	AB	R	H	2B	3B	HR	RBI	BB	SO	AVG	OBP	SLG	OPS	OPS+	BR+	SB	CS	SBR	FA	FR	G/POS	TPR
1913	Cle-A	1	0	0	0	0	0	0	0	0	0	—	—	—	—	—	0	0			.000	0	/O-1	0.0
1915	Cle-A	60	177	25	39	2	5	0	8	36	12	.220	.352	.288	640	90	-1	2	4	-1	.942	1	O-44(10-30-4)	-0.3
1918	Pit-N	64	246	37	84	5	7	2	43	26	9	.341	.409	.443	852	154	17	19			.980	9	O-64(0-0-64)	2.4
1919	Pit-N	121	453	56	127	14	**14**	4	61	32	22	.280	.329	.400	729	114	7	23			.968	5	*O-121(75-0-46)	0.7
1920	Pit-N	146	546	64	155	17	13	2	53	52	20	.284	.348	.374	722	104	4	23	25	-4	**.991**	10	*O-142(0-0-142)	0.3
1921	Bos-N	141	569	86	175	25	15	7	79	36	13	.308	.351	.441	792	115	11	22	20	-2	.975	9	*O-141(0-0-141)	0.6
1922	Bos-N	43	158	27	51	4	4	4	18	18	1	.323	.392	.475	867	128	7	4	1	1	.955	5	O-41(0-0-41)	0.8
1923	Bos-N	153	611	95	195	29	16	6	78	61	23	.319	.383	.448	831	124	21	14	16	-3	.943	6	*O-151(0-0-151)/2-2	1.2
1924	*NY-N	94	281	40	72	13	0	3	36	32	16	.256	.332	.335	667	81	-7	1	6	-2	.935	-3	O-75(1-51-19)	-1.5
1925	NY-N	123	473	79	138	19	5	6	44	51	11	.292	.363	.391	754	97	-1	6	13	-3	.964	-8	*O-119(0-117-2)	-1.7
1926	NY-N	36	116	23	38	6	1	5	30	7	1	.328	.366	.526	892	139	6	1			.970	-2	O-29(7-16-8)	0.2
	*StL-N	99	391	76	124	22	6	11	69	26	9	.317	.364	.488	853	123	12	13			.971	-3	O-99(0-0-99)	0.1
	Yr	135	507	99	162	28	7	16	99	33	10	.320	.365	.497	862	127	17	14			.971	-5	*O-128(7-16-107)	0.3
1927	StL-N	92	306	52	92	15	5	2	39	23	7	.301	.350	.402	752	98	-1	10			.970	-7	O-83(0-0-83)	-1.5
1929	StL-N	19	32	1	6	2	0	0	3	2	4	.188	.235	.250	485	20	-4	0			1.000	-0	/O-5(0-0-5),M	-0.4
Total	13	1192	4359	661	1296	173	91	52	561	402	148	.297	.359	.415	773	111	70	138	85		.965	23	*O-1115R/2-2	0.9

■ JOHN SOWDERS

Sowders, John b: 12/10/1866, Louisville, Ky. d: 7/29/39, Indianapolis, Ind BR/TL, 6′, Deb: 6/28/1887 F

YEAR	TM/L	G	AB	R	H	2B	3B	HR	RBI	BB	SO	AVG	OBP	SLG	OPS	OPS+	BR+	SB	CS	SBR	FA	FR	G/POS	TPR
1887	Ind-N	1	2	0	0	0	0	0	0	0	1	.000	.000	.000	0	-99	-1	0			1.000	-1	/O-1(0-0-1),P-1	0.0
1889	KC-a	28	87	11	19	3	0	0	6	4	20	.218	.269	.253	522	46	-6	1			.842	-3	P-25/O-3(3-0-0)	-0.1
1890	Bro-P	40	132	14	25	3	0	1	20	10	12	.189	.246	.235	481	27	-14	0			.921	-2	P-39/O-3(0-0-3)	-0.1
Total	3	69	221	25	44	6	0	1	26	14	33	.199	.253	.240	493	33	-21	1			.884	-6	/P-65,O-7(3-0-4)	-0.2

■ LEN SOWDERS

Sowders, Leonard b: 6/29/1861, Louisville, Ky. d: 11/19/1888, Indianapolis, Ind. 5′11.5″, 172 lbs. Deb: 9/10/1886 F

YEAR	TM/L	G	AB	R	H	2B	3B	HR	RBI	BB	SO	AVG	OBP	SLG	OPS	OPS+	BR+	SB	CS	SBR	FA	FR	G/POS	TPR
1886	Bal-a	23	76	10	20	3	1	0	14	12		.263	.364	.329	693	121	2	6			.889	-1	O-23(0-23-0)/1-1	0.1

■ AL SPALDING

Spalding, Albert Goodwill b: 9/2/1850, Byron, Ill. d: 9/9/15, San Diego, Cal. BR/TR, 6′1″, 170 lbs. Deb: 5/5/1871 MH NA OF: (1-LF 44-CF 9-RF)

YEAR	TM/L	G	AB	R	H	2B	3B	HR	RBI	BB	SO	AVG	OBP	SLG	OPS	OPS+	BR+	SB	CS	SBR	FA	FR	G/POS	TPR
1871	Bos-n	31	144	43	39	10	1	1	31	8	1	.271	.309	.375	684	93	-2	2	0	0	.776	-3	*P-31/O-9(0-9-0)	-0.2
1872	Bos-n	48	237	60	84	11	5	0	47	3	1	.354	.363	.443	806	139	9	3	0	1	.902	-3	*P-48/O-7(0-7-0)	-0.2
1873	Bos-n	60	322	83	106	18	2	1	60	3	1	.329	.335	.407	742	110	2	1	0	0	.855	6	*P-60,O-13(0-13-0)	-0.4
1874	Bos-n	71	362	80	119	13	1	0	54	3	0	.329	.334	.370	704	119	6	2	1	0	**.854**	5	*P-71/O-6(0-6-0)	-0.1
1875	Bos-n	74	343	68	107	15	3	0	56	3	3	.312	.318	.373	691	134	10	2	2	-0	.906	-1	*P-72,O-18(1-9-9)/1-4	-0.3
1876	Chi-N	66	298	54	91	14	2	0	44	6	3	.305	.326	.373	699	118	4				.951	1	*P-61,O-10L/1-3,SM	-0.2
1877	Chi-N	60	254	29	65	7	6	0	35	3	16	.256	.265	.331	595	77	-8				.959	6	*1-45,2-13/P-4,3M	-0.3
1878	Chi-N	1	4	0	2	0	0	0	0	0	0	.500	.500	.500	1000	215	0				.429	-2	/2-1	-0.1
Total	5 n	284	1408	334	455	67	12	2	248	20	6	.323	.333	.392	725	121	25	10	3	1	.868	5	P-282/O-53C,1-4	-1.2
Total	3	127	556	83	158	21	8	0	79	9	19	.284	.299	.355	653	100	-3				.948	5	/P-65,1-48,2-14,O3S	-0.6

■ DICK SPALDING

Spalding, Charles Harry b: 10/13/1893, Philadelphia, Pa. d: 2/3/50, Philadelphia, Pa. BL/TL, 5′11″, 185 lbs. Deb: 4/18/27 C

YEAR	TM/L	G	AB	R	H	2B	3B	HR	RBI	BB	SO	AVG	OBP	SLG	OPS	OPS+	BR+	SB	CS	SBR	FA	FR	G/POS	TPR
1927	Phi-N	115	442	68	131	16	3	0	25	38	40	.296	.352	.346	698	86	-7	5			**.992**	3	*O-113(113-0-0)	-1.3
1928	Was-A	16	23	1	8	0	0	0	0	0	4	.348	.348	.348	696	84	-1	0	2	-1	1.000	-3	O-11(8-0-3)	-0.5
Total	2	131	465	69	139	16	3	0	25	38	44	.299	.352	.346	698	86	-8	5	2		.993	-0	O-124(121-0-3)	-1.8

■ AL SPANGLER

Spangler, Albert Donald b: 7/8/33, Philadelphia, Pa. BL/TL, 6′, 175 lbs. Deb: 9/16/59 C

YEAR	TM/L	G	AB	R	H	2B	3B	HR	RBI	BB	SO	AVG	OBP	SLG	OPS	OPS+	BR+	SB	CS	SBR	FA	FR	G/POS	TPR
1959	Mil-N	6	12	3	5	0	1	0	0	1	1	.417	.462	.583	1045	192	2	1	0	0	1.000	-1	/O-4(1-3-0)	0.1
1960	Mil-N	101	105	26	28	5	2	0	6	14	17	.267	.358	.352	711	103	1	6	2	1	.989	-14	O-92(90-1-1)	-1.4
1961	Mil-N	68	97	23	26	2	0	0	6	28	9	.268	.432	.289	721	102	3	4	2	0	1.000	-7	O-44(23-21-1)	-0.5
1962	Hou-N	129	418	51	119	10	9	5	35	70	46	.285	.391	.388	779	119	14	7	6	-1	.960	-0	*O-121(93-28-0)	0.8
1963	Hou-N	120	430	52	121	25	4	4	27	50	38	.281	.358	.386	744	122	13	5	8	-2	.987	3	*O-113(87-33-3)	0.9
1964	Hou-N	135	449	51	110	18	5	4	38	41	43	.245	.314	.334	648	88	-7	7	8	-1	.964	-5	*O-127(113-18-0)	-2.2
1965	Hou-N	38	112	18	24	1	1	1	7	14	8	.214	.302	.268	569	66	-5	1	1	-0	.956	-1	O-33(31-1-1)	-0.8
	Cal-A	51	96	17	25	1	0	0	1	8	9	.260	.317	.271	588	70	-4	4	0	1	.973	-4	O-24(4-17-6)	-0.8
1966	Cal-A	6	9	2	6	0	0	0	0	2	2	.667	.727	.667	1394	312	3	0	0	0	1.000	-1	/O-3(0-0-3)	0.2
1967	Chi-N	62	130	18	33	7	0	0	13	23	17	.254	.366	.308	674	91	-0	2	2	-0	.986	-3	O-41(0-7-34)	-0.6
1968	Chi-N	88	177	21	48	9	3	2	18	20	24	.271	.348	.390	738	114	3	0	1	-0	.973	-5	O-48(1-7-42)	-0.5
1969	Chi-N	82	213	23	45	8	1	4	23	21	16	.211	.285	.315	600	60	-11	0	2	-1	.950	-7	O-58(0-1-57)	-2.3
1970	Chi-N	21	14	2	2	1	0	1	1	3	3	.143	.294	.429	723	81	-0	0	0	0	1.000	-1	/O-6(3-0-3)	-0.2
1971	Chi-N	5	5	0	2	0	0	0	0	0	1	.400	.400	.400	800	111	0	0	0	0	.000	0	H	0.0
Total	13	912	2267	307	594	87	26	21	175	295	234	.262	.350	.351	701	100	11	37	32	-3	.973	-45	O-714(446-137-151)	-7.3

YEAR	TM/L	G	AB	R	H	2B	3B	HR	RBI	BB	SO	AVG	OBP	SLG	OPS	OPS+	BR+	SB	CS	SBR	FA	FR	G/POS	TPR
■ **BOB SPEAKE**	Speake, Robert Charles "Spook" b: 8/22/30, Springfield, Mo. BL/TL, 6'1", 178 lbs. Deb: 4/16/55																							
1955	Chi-N	95	261	36	57	9	5	12	43	28	71	.218	.301	.429	730	91	-4	3	4	-1	.959	-3	O-55(49-0-8)/1-8	-1.2
1957	Chi-N	129	418	65	97	14	5	16	50	38	68	.232	.301	.404	705	89	-8	5	6	-1	.974	6	O-60(20-40-0),1-39	-0.8
1958	SF-N	66	71	9	15	3	0	3	10	13	15	.211	.333	.380	714	90	-1	0	1	-0	.938	0	O-10(10-0-0)	-0.1
1959	SF-N	15	11	0	1	0	0	0	1	1	4	.091	.167	.091	258	-30	-2	0	0	0	.000	0	H	-0.2
Total	4	305	761	110	170	26	10	31	104	80	158	.223	.302	.406	708	88	-14	8	11	-2	.966	3	O-125(79-40-8)/1-47	-2.3
■ **TRIS SPEAKER**	Speaker, Tristram E "The Grey Eagle" b: 4/4/1888, Hubbard, Tex. d: 12/8/58, Lake Whitney, Tex. BL/TL, 5'11.5", 193 lbs. Deb: 9/14/07 MH Career OF: (2-LF 2690-CF 6-RF)																							
1907	Bos-A	7	19	0	3	0	0	0	1	1		.158	.200	.158	358	14	-2	0			1.000	1	/O-4(0-0-4)	-0.1
1908	Bos-A	31	116	12	26	2	2	0	9	4		.224	.262	.276	538	73	-4	3			1.000	5	O-31(1-30-0)	0.0
1909	Bos-A	143	544	73	168	26	13	7	77	38		.309	.362	.443	805	151	30	35			.973	**23**	*O-142(0-142-0)	5.1
1910	Bos-A	141	538	92	183	20	14	7	65	52		.340	.404	.468	873	169	42	35			.957	15	*O-140(0-140-0)	5.5
1911	Bos-A	141	500	88	167	34	13	8	70	59		.334	.418	.502	920	158	39	25			.956	6	*O-138(0-138-0)	3.5
1912	*Bos-A	153	580	136	222	**53**	12	**10**	90	82		.383	**.464**	.567	1031	185	65	52			.958	22	*O-153(0-153-0)	**7.4**
1913	Bos-A	141	520	94	189	35	22	3	71	65	22	.363	.441	.533	974	180	53	46			.942	24	*O-139(0-139-0)	**6.9**
1914	Bos-A	158	571	101	**193**	**46**	18	4	90	77	25	.338	.423	.503	**926**	178	55	42	29	-1	.968	28	*O-156C/P-1,1-1	**7.6**
1915	*Bos-A	150	547	108	176	25	12	0	69	81	14	.322	.416	.411	827	152	38	29	25	-2	.976	13	*O-150(0-150-0)	4.1
1916	Cle-A	151	546	102	**211**	**41**	8	2	79	82	20	**.386**	**.470**	**.502**	**972**	**181**	**57**	35	27	-2	.975	9	*O-151(0-151-0)	**5.8**
1917	Cle-A	142	523	90	184	42	11	2	60	67	14	.352	.432	.486	918	168	43	30			.980	8	*O-142(0-142-0)	4.5
1918	Cle-A	127	471	73	150	**33**	11	0	61	64	9	.318	.403	.435	839	140	24	27			.973	11	*O-127(0-127-0)	2.9
1919	Cle-A	134	494	83	146	38	12	2	63	73	12	.296	.395	.433	828	125	18	15			.983	19	*O-134(0-134-0),M	2.9
1920	*Cle-A	150	552	137	214	**50**	11	8	107	97	13	.388	.483	.562	1045	171	61	10	13	-2	.977	10	*O-148(0-148-0),M	5.5
1921	Cle-A	132	506	107	183	**52**	14	3	75	68	12	.362	.439	.538	977	146	37	2	4	-1	**.984**	10	*O-128(0-128-0),M	3.7
1922	Cle-A	131	426	85	161	**48**	8	11	71	77	11	.378	**.474**	.606	1080	178	52	8	3	1	**.983**	8	*O-109(0-109-0),M	5.3
1923	Cle-A	150	574	133	218	**59**	11	17	130	93	15	.380	.469	.610	1079	183	71	8	9	-1	.968	10	*O-150(0-150-0),M	6.9
1924	Cle-A	135	486	94	167	36	9	9	65	72	13	.344	.432	.510	943	141	31	5	7	-1	.963	5	*O-128(0-127-1),M	2.7
1925	Cle-A	117	429	79	167	35	5	12	87	70	12	.389	**.479**	.578	1057	166	46	5	2	0	.967	10	*O-109(0-109-0),M	**4.7**
1926	Cle-A	150	539	96	164	52	8	7	86	94	15	.304	.408	.469	877	127	23	6	1	1	.981	10	*O-149(0-149-0),M	2.7
1927	Was-A	141	523	71	171	43	6	2	73	55	8	.327	.395	.444	839	119	15	9	8	-1	.967	1	*O-120(0-119-1),1-17	0.9
1928	Phi-A	64	191	28	51	22	2	3	30	10	5	.267	.310	.450	761	95	-2	5	1	1	.975	1	O-50(1-49-0)	-0.3
Total	22	2789	10195	1882	3514	792	222	117	1529	1381	220	.345	.428	.500	928	156	795	432	129		.970	248	*O-2698C/1-18,P-1	88.2
■ **HORACE SPEED**	Speed, Horace Arthur b: 10/4/51, Los Angeles, Cal. BR/TR, 6'1", 180 lbs. Deb: 4/10/75																							
1975	SF-N	17	15	2	2	1	0	0	1	1	8	.133	.235	.200	435	21	-2	0	0	0	.900	-2	/O-9(5-0-5)	-0.4
1978	Cle-A	70	106	13	24	4	1	0	4	14	31	.226	.322	.283	605	72	-3	2	4	-1	.977	-12	O-61(12-23-30)/D-3	-1.8
1979	Cle-A	26	14	6	2	0	0	0	1	5	7	.143	.368	.143	511	44	-1	2	1	0	.875	-5	O-16(10-3-3)/D-4	-0.5
Total	3	113	135	21	28	5	1	0	6	20	46	.207	.318	.259	578	63	-6	4	5	-1	.956	-19	/O-86(27-26-38),D-7	-2.7
■ **TIM SPEHR**	Spehr, Timothy Joseph b: 7/2/66, Excelsior Springs, Mo. BR/TR, 6'2", 200 lbs. Deb: 7/18/91																							
1991	KC-A	37	74	7	14	5	0	3	14	9	18	.189	.286	.378	664	82	-2	1	0	0	.986	12	C-37	1.1
1993	Mon-N	53	87	14	20	6	0	2	10	6	20	.230	.287	.368	655	71	-4	2	0	0	.954	9	C-49	0.7
1994	Mon-N	52	36	8	9	3	1	0	5	4	11	.250	.325	.389	714	84	-1	2	0	0	1.000	10	C-46/O-2(2-0-0)	1.0
1995	Mon-N	41	35	4	9	5	0	1	3	6	7	.257	.366	.486	852	118	1	0	0	0	.990	8	C-38	0.9
1996	Mon-N	63	44	4	4	1	0	1	3	3	15	.091	.167	.182	348	-8	-7	1	0	0	.985	8	C-58/O-1(0-0-1)	0.1
1997	KC-A	17	35	3	6	0	0	1	2	2	12	.171	.237	.257	494	28	-4	0	0	0	1.000	5	C-17	0.1
	Atl-N	8	14	2	3	1	0	1	4	0	4	.214	.214	.500	714	78	-1	1	0	0	.947	3	/C-7	0.2
1998	NY-N	21	51	3	7	1	0	0	3	7	16	.137	.267	.157	424	15	-6	1	0	0	1.000	5	C-21/1-1	-0.1
	KC-A	11	25	5	6	2	0	1	2	8	3	.240	.457	.440	897	131	2	0	0	0	1.000	-1	C-11	0.1
1999	KC-A	60	155	26	32	7	0	9	26	22	47	.206	.328	.426	754	88	-3	1	0	0	.990	-3	C-59	-0.2
Total	8	363	556	76	110	31	1	19	72	67	153	.198	.300	.360	660	71	-24	9	0	2	.985	53	C-343/O-3(2-0-1),1-1	3.9
■ **CHRIS SPEIER**	Speier, Chris Edward b: 6/28/50, Alameda, Cal. BR/TR (BB 1972 (part)), 6'1", 182 lbs. Deb: 4/7/71 FC																							
1971	*SF-N	157	601	74	141	17	6	8	46	56	90	.235	.307	.323	630	80	-16	4	7	-2	.958	-12	*S-156	-1.1
1972	SF-N★	150	562	74	151	25	2	15	71	82	92	.269	.365	.400	765	116	14	9	4	1	.974	-5	*S-150	3.0
1973	SF-N★	153	542	58	135	17	4	11	71	66	69	.249	.333	.356	689	87	-8	4	5	-1	.956	-10	*S-150/2-1	-0.1
1974	SF-N☆	141	501	55	125	19	5	9	53	62	64	.250	.337	.361	698	91	-5	3	2	-0	.969	3	*S-135/2-4	1.5
1975	SF-N	141	487	60	132	30	5	10	69	70	50	.271	.364	.415	779	111	8	4	5	-1	**.982**	1	*S-136/3-1	2.6
1976	SF-N	145	495	51	112	18	4	3	40	60	52	.226	.315	.297	612	72	-17	2	2	-0	.974	-1	*S-135/2-7,3-5,1-1	-0.1
1977	SF-N	6	17	1	3	1	0	0	0	0	3	.176	.176	.235	412	9	-2	0	0	0	.920	2	/S-5	0.0
	Mon-N	139	531	58	125	30	6	5	38	67	78	.235	.322	.343	665	81	-14	1	2	-0	.970	-12	*S-138	-1.1
	Yr	145	548	59	128	31	6	5	38	67	81	.234	.318	.339	658	79	-16	1	2	-0	.968	-10	*S-143	-1.1
1978	Mon-N	150	501	47	126	18	3	5	51	60	75	.251	.333	.329	662	87	-8	1	0	0	.975	1	*S-148	0.9
1979	Mon-N	113	344	31	78	13	1	7	26	43	45	.227	.318	.331	649	78	-10	0	0	0	.970	4	*S-112	0.6
1980	Mon-N	128	388	35	103	14	4	1	32	52	38	.265	.352	.330	682	91	-3	0	3	-1	.965	-0	*S-127/3-1	0.9
1981	*Mon-N	96	307	33	69	10	2	2	25	38	29	.225	.310	.290	600	70	-11	1	2	-0	.964	-11	S-96	-1.3
1982	Mon-N	156	530	41	136	26	4	7	60	47	67	.257	.318	.360	679	88	-9	1	6	-2	.982	-21	*S-155	-1.6
1983	Mon-N	88	261	31	67	12	2	2	22	29	37	.257	.336	.341	677	88	-4	2	1	0	.962	-11	S-74,3-12/2-2	-0.8
1984	Mon-N	25	40	1	6	0	0	0	1	1	8	.150	.171	.150	321	-10	-6	0	0	0	.960	-2	S-13/3-4	-0.7
	StL-N	38	118	9	21	7	1	3	8	9	19	.178	.242	.331	573	61	-7	0	0	0	.983	10	S-34/3-2	0.7
	Yr	63	158	10	27	7	1	3	9	10	27	.171	.225	.285	510	44	-12	0	0	0	.980	8	S-47/3-6	0.0
	Min-A	12	33	2	7	0	0	0	1	3	7	.212	.278	.212	490	36	-3	0	0	0	.977	-3	S-12	-0.5
1985	Chi-N	106	218	16	53	11	0	4	24	17	34	.243	.298	.349	646	72	-8	1	3	-1	.964	2	S-58,3-31,2-13	-0.3
1986	Chi-N	95	155	21	44	8	0	6	23	15	32	.284	.351	.452	802	111	2	2	2	-0	.984	9	3-53,S-23/2-7	1.2
1987	*SF-N	111	317	39	79	13	0	11	39	42	51	.249	.343	.394	737	99	0	4	7	-2	.989	2	2-55,3-44,S-22	0.3
1988	SF-N	82	171	26	37	9	1	3	18	23	39	.216	.313	.333	646	89	-2	3	3	-0	.985	3	2-45,3-22,S-12	0.2
1989	SF-N	28	37	7	9	4	0	0	2	5	9	.243	.333	.351	685	99	0	0	0	0	1.000	-2	/3-9,S-9,2-4,1-1	-0.2
Total	19	2260	7156	770	1759	302	50	112	720	847	988	.246	.329	.349	678	88	-106	42	54	-10	.970	-52	*S-1900,3-184,2/1	4.1
■ **BOB SPENCE**	Spence, John Robert b: 2/10/46, San Diego, Cal. BL/TR, 6'4", 215 lbs. Deb: 9/5/69																							
1969	Chi-A	12	26	0	4	1	0	0	3	0	9	.154	.154	.192	346	-4	-4	0	0	0	1.000	-0	/1-6	-0.5
1970	Chi-A	46	130	11	29	4	1	4	15	11	32	.223	.289	.362	650	75	-5	0	0	0	.994	3	1-37	-0.4
1971	Chi-A	14	27	2	4	0	0	0	1	5	6	.148	.281	.148	429	24	-3	0	0	0	.986	-1	/1-7	-0.4
Total	3	72	183	13	37	5	1	4	19	16	47	.202	.270	.306	576	57	-11	0	0	0	.993	2	/1-50	-1.3
■ **STAN SPENCE**	Spence, Stanley Orville b: 3/20/15, S.Portsmouth, Ky. d: 1/9/83, Kinston, N.C. BL/TL, 5'10.5", 180 lbs. Deb: 6/8/40 Career OF: (90-LF 801-CF 104-RF)																							
1940	Bos-A	51	68	5	19	2	1	2	13	4	9	.279	.319	.426	746	88	-1	0	1	-0	1.000	-4	O-15(6-0-9)	-0.6
1941	Bos-A	86	203	22	47	10	3	2	28	18	14	.232	.304	.340	643	68	-10	1	0	0	1.000	-1	O-52(27-10-16)/1-1	-1.3
1942	Was-A☆	149	629	94	203	27	**15**	4	79	62	16	.323	.384	.432	817	131	26	5	2	0	.973	-3	*O-149(0-149-0)	2.0
1943	Was-A	149	570	72	152	23	10	12	88	84	39	.267	.366	.405	771	130	23	8	1	1	.983	3	*O-148(0-148-0)	2.5
1944	Was-A★	153	592	83	187	31	8	18	100	69	28	.316	.391	.486	877	157	43	3	7	-2	.989	19	*O-150(0-150-0)/1-3	5.7
1946	Was-A★	152	578	83	169	50	10	16	87	62	31	.292	.365	.497	861	148	35	1	7	-2	.982	8	*O-150(0-150-0)	3.8
1947	Was-A★	147	506	62	141	22	6	16	73	81	41	.279	.378	.441	819	131	22	2	2	-0	.984	8	*O-142(0-142-0)	2.6
1948	Bos-A	114	391	71	92	17	4	12	61	82	33	.235	.368	.391	759	97	-0	0	2	-1	.977	-1	O-92(24-0-70),1-14	-0.6
1949	Bos-A	7	20	3	3	1	0	0	1	6	1	.150	.346	.200	546	43	-1	0	0	0	1.000	1	/O-5(0-2-3)	0.0
	StL-A	104	314	46	77	13	3	13	45	52	36	.245	.356	.430	786	103	1	1	1	-0	.995	3	O-87(33-50-6)/1-1	-0.1
	Yr	111	334	49	80	14	3	13	46	58	37	.240	.355	.416	771	99	-1	1	1	-0	.996	4	O-92(33-52-9)/1-1	-0.1
Total	9	1112	3871	541	1090	196	60	95	575	520	248	.282	.369	.437	806	126	136	21	23	-3	.984	34	O-990C/1-19	14.0
■ **SPENCER**	Spencer Deb: 6/3/1872																							
1872	Nat-n	1	4	1	0	0	0	0	0	0	0	.000	.000	.000	0	-86	-1	0	0	0	.429	-1	/S-1	-0.1

YEAR	TM/L	G	AB	R	H	2B	3B	HR	RBI	BB	SO	AVG	OBP	SLG	OPS	OPS+	BR+	SB	CS	SBR	FA	FR	G/POS	TPR
■ CHET SPENCER Spencer, Chester Arthur b: 3/4/1883, S.Webster, Ohio d: 11/10/38, Portsmouth, Ohio BL/TR, 6', 180 lbs. Deb: 8/22/06																								
1906	Bos-N	8	27	1	4	1	0	0	0	0		.148	.148	.185	333	4	-3	0			.875	-1	/O-8(1-3-3)	-0.5
■ DARYL SPENCER Spencer, Daryl Dean "Big Dee" b: 7/13/29, Wichita, Kan. BR/TR, 6'2", 190 lbs. Deb: 9/17/52																								
1952	NY-N	7	17	0	5	0	1	0	3	1	4	.294	.333	.412	745	105	0	0	0	0	1.000	1	/S-3,3-3	0.2
1953	NY-N	118	408	55	85	18	5	20	56	42	74	.208	.287	.424	711	81	-13	0	1	-0	.927	-10	S-53,3-36,2-32	-1.6
1956	NY-N	146	489	46	108	13	2	14	42	35	65	.221	.277	.342	619	66	-24	1	3	-1	.974	-2	2-70,S-66,3-12	-1.8
1957	NY-N	148	534	65	133	31	2	11	50	50	50	.249	.315	.376	691	85	-11	3	1	0	.950	14	*S-110,2-36/3-6	1.4
1958	SF-N	148	539	71	138	20	5	17	74	73	60	.256	.348	.406	754	101	2	1	0	0	.955	-1	*S-134,2-17	1.3
1959	SF-N	152	555	59	147	20	1	12	62	58	67	.265	.334	.369	704	89	-8	5	0	1	.970	-4	*2-151/S-4	0.0
1960	StL-N	148	507	70	131	20	3	16	58	81	74	.258	.366	.404	770	102	4	1	1	-0	.946	-24	*S-138,2-16	-0.9
1961	StL-N	37	130	19	33	4	0	4	21	23	17	.254	.366	.377	743	89	-1	1	0	0	.956	-1	S-37	0.1
	LA-N	60	189	27	46	7	0	8	27	20	35	.243	.329	.407	736	86	-4	0	1	-0	.964	5	3-57/S-3	0.1
	Yr	97	319	46	79	11	0	12	48	43	52	.248	.344	.395	739	88	-5	1	1	-0	.964	4	3-57,S-40	0.2
1962	LA-N	77	157	24	37	5	1	2	12	32	31	.236	.365	.318	684	91	-1	0	0	0	.925	7	3-57,S-10	0.6
1963	LA-N	7	9	0	1	0	0	0	0	3	2	.111	.333	.111	444	37	-1	0	0	0	1.000	-0	/3-3	-0.1
	Cin-N	50	155	21	37	7	0	1	23	31	37	.239	.369	.303	672	93	0	1	0	0	.979	3	3-48	0.3
	Yr	57	164	21	38	7	0	1	23	34	39	.232	.367	.293	660	91	-0	1	0	0	.979	2	3-51	0.2
Total	10	1098	3689	457	901	145	20	105	428	449	516	.244	.329	.380	709	88	-58	13	7	0	.953	-13	S-558,2-322,3-222	-0.4
■ TUBBY SPENCER Spencer, Edward Russell b: 1/26/1884, Oil City, Pa. d: 2/1/45, San Francisco, Cal. BR/TR, 5'10", 215 lbs. Deb: 7/23/05																								
1905	StL-A	35	115	6	27	1	2	0	11	7		.235	.285	.278	563	83	-2	2			.962	-6	C-34	-0.6
1906	StL-A	58	188	15	33	6	1	0	17	7		.176	.205	.218	423	34	-14	4			.935	-5	C-54	-1.6
1907	StL-A	71	230	27	61	11	1	1	25	7		.265	.299	.335	634	102	-0	1			.957	-2	C-63	0.5
1908	StL-A	91	286	19	60	6	1	0	28	17		.210	.254	.238	492	60	-13	1			.983	-1	C-88	-0.6
1909	Bos-A	28	74	6	12	1	0	0	9	6		.162	.225	.176	401	26	-6	2			.992	-4	C-26	-0.9
1911	Phi-N	11	32	2	5	1	0	1	3	3	7	.156	.229	.281	510	42	-3	0			.925	-1	C-11	-0.3
1916	Det-A	19	54	7	20	1	1	1	10	6	6	.370	.443	.481	924	172	5	2			.988	-7	C-19	0.0
1917	Det-A	70	192	13	46	8	3	0	22	15	15	.240	.324	.313	637	95	-1	0			.978	-2	C-62	0.2
1918	Det-A	66	155	11	34	8	1	0	8	19	18	.219	.313	.284	596	83	-3	1			.966	-12	C-48/1-1	-1.3
Total	9	449	1326	106	298	43	10	3	133	87	46	.225	.281	.279	560	76	-37	13			.966	-40	C-405/1-1	-4.6
■ TOM SPENCER Spencer, Hubert Thomas b: 2/28/51, Gallipolis, Ohio BR/TR, 6', 170 lbs. Deb: 7/17/78 C																								
1978	Chi-A	29	65	3	12	1	0	0	4	2	9	.185	.209	.200	409	15	-7	0	1	-0	1.000	-1	O-27(6-19-2)/D-2	-1.0
■ JIM SPENCER Spencer, James Lloyd b: 7/30/47, Hanover, Pa. BL/TL, 6'2", 195 lbs. Deb: 9/7/68 F Career OF: (24-LF 0-CF 0-RF)																								
1968	Cal-A	19	68	2	13	1	0	0	5	3	10	.191	.236	.206	442	36	-5	0	0	0	.994	3	1-19	-0.4
1969	Cal-A	113	386	39	98	14	3	10	31	26	53	.254	.304	.383	688	96	-4	1	0	0	.991	-1	*1-107	-1.4
1970	Cal-A	146	511	61	140	20	4	12	68	28	61	.274	.312	.399	711	98	-3	0	2	-1	**.995**	-1	*1-142	-1.6
1971	Cal-A	148	510	50	121	21	2	18	59	48	63	.237	.307	.392	699	104	1	0	1	-0	**.996**	2	*1-145	-0.9
1972	Cal-A	82	212	13	47	5	0	1	14	12	25	.222	.263	.259	523	59	-11	0	1	-0	.990	-2	1-35,O-24(24-0-0)	-2.0
1973	Cal-A	29	87	10	21	4	2	2	11	9	9	.241	.320	.402	722	111	1	0	0	0	1.000	-2	1-26/D-2	-0.3
	Tex-A★	102	352	35	94	12	3	4	43	34	41	.267	.333	.352	686	97	-1	0	3	-1	.999	5	1-99/D-1	-0.4
	Yr	131	439	45	115	16	5	6	54	43	50	.262	.331	.362	693	100	0	0	3	-1	**.999**	3	*1-125/D-3	-0.7
1974	Tex-A	118	352	36	98	11	4	7	44	22	27	.278	.326	.392	718	109	3	1	2	-0	.998	1	1-60,D-54	-0.1
1975	Tex-A	132	403	50	107	18	1	11	47	35	43	.266	.327	.397	724	105	2	0	1	-0	.995	5	1-99,D-25	0.0
1976	Chi-A	150	518	53	131	13	2	14	70	49	52	.253	.319	.367	685	100	-0	6	4	-0	**.998**	8	*1-143/D-2	-0.4
1977	Chi-A	128	470	56	116	16	1	18	69	36	50	.247	.303	.400	703	90	-7	1	2	-0	.991	2	*1-125	-1.3
1978	*NY-A	71	150	12	34	9	1	7	24	15	32	.227	.297	.440	737	107	1	0	1	-0	1.000	1	D-35,1-15	0.0
1979	NY-A	106	295	60	85	15	3	23	53	38	25	.288	.369	.593	963	158	23	0	2	-1	.992	-0	D-71,1-26	1.8
1980	*NY-A	97	259	38	61	9	0	13	43	30	44	.236	.317	.421	738	102	0	1	0	0	.990	2	1-75,D-15	-0.2
1981	NY-A	25	63	6	9	2	0	2	4	9	7	.143	.250	.270	520	50	-4	0	0	0	1.000	2	1-25	-0.3
	*Oak-A	54	171	14	35	6	0	2	9	10	20	.205	.249	.275	523	53	-11	1	0	0	.997	2	1-48	-1.1
	Yr	79	234	20	44	8	0	4	13	19	27	.188	.249	.274	523	52	-15	1	0	0	.998	5	1-73	-1.4
1982	Oak-A	33	101	6	17	3	1	2	5	3	20	.168	.192	.277	470	28	-10	0	0	0	.992	2	1-32	-1.0
Total	15	1553	4908	541	1227	179	27	146	599	407	582	.250	.310	.387	696	98	-25	11	19	-4	.995	30	*1-1221,D-205/O-24L	-9.6
■ BEN SPENCER Spencer, Lloyd Benjamin b: 5/15/1890, Patapsco, Md. d: 9/1/70, Finksburg, Md. BL/TL, 5'8", 160 lbs. Deb: 9/8/13 F																								
1913	Was-A	8	21	2	6	1	1	0	2	2	4	.286	.348	.429	776	124	1	0			.917	-1	/O-8(7-1-0)	-0.1
■ SHANE SPENCER Spencer, Michael Shane b: 2/20/72, Key West, Fla. BR/TR, 5'11", 210 lbs. Deb: 4/10/98 Career OF: (88-LF 0-CF 44-RF)																								
1998	*NY-A	27	67	18	25	6	0	10	27	5	12	.373	.417	.910	1327	241	13	0	1	-0	1.000	-4	O-22(9-0-15)/1-1,D-4	0.8
1999	*NY-A	71	205	25	48	8	0	8	20	18	51	.234	.302	.390	692	76	-8	0	4	-1	1.000	-1	O-64(46-0-22)/D-3	-1.1
2000	NY-A	73	248	33	70	11	3	9	40	19	45	.282	.338	.460	798	101	-0	1	2	-0	.989	3	O-40(33-0-7),D-33	0.0
Total	3	171	520	76	143	25	3	27	87	42	108	.275	.334	.490	824	108	5	1	7	-2	.996	-1	O-126L/D-40,1-1	-0.3
■ ROY SPENCER Spencer, Roy Hampton b: 2/22/1900, Scranton, N.C. d: 2/8/73, Port Charlotte, Fla BR/TR, 5'10", 168 lbs. Deb: 4/19/25																								
1925	Pit-N	14	28	1	6	1	0	0	2	1	3	.214	.241	.250	491	24	-3	1	0	0	.905	-2	C-11	-0.4
1926	Pit-N	28	43	5	17	3	0	0	4	1	0	.395	.409	.465	874	128	2	0			.970	-1	C-12	0.2
1927	*Pit-N	38	92	9	26	3	1	0	13	3	3	.283	.305	.337	642	67	-4	0			.974	2	C-34	-0.1
1929	Was-A	50	116	18	18	4	0	1	9	8	15	.155	.222	.216	438	13	-15	0	0	0	.967	-2	C-41	-1.4
1930	Was-A	93	321	32	82	11	4	0	36	18	27	.255	.303	.315	618	57	-21	3	0	1	.989	5	C-93	-0.9
1931	Was-A	145	483	48	133	16	3	1	60	35	21	.275	.327	.327	654	72	-19	0	0	0	.985	7	*C-145	-0.3
1932	Was-A	102	317	28	78	9	0	1	41	24	17	.246	.301	.284	585	53	-22	0	1	-0	.978	-10	C-98	-2.4
1933	Cle-A	75	227	26	46	5	2	0	23	23	17	.203	.282	.242	524	38	-20	0	0	0	.990	5	C-72	-1.0
1934	Cle-A	5	7	0	1	1	0	0	2	0	1	.143	.143	.286	429	8	-1	0	0	0	1.000	1	/C-4	0.0
1936	NY-N	19	18	3	5	1	0	0	3	2	3	.278	.350	.333	683	86	-0	0			1.000	1	C-14	0.1
1937	Bro-N	51	117	5	24	2	2	0	4	8	17	.205	.256	.256	512	39	-10	0			1.000	9	C-45	0.1
1938	Bro-N	16	45	2	12	1	1	0	6	5	6	.267	.340	.333	673	84	-1	0			.968	-0	C-16	0.0
Total	12	636	1814	177	448	57	13	3	203	128	130	.247	.301	.298	598	56	-115	4	1		.984	16	C-585	-6.1
■ VERN SPENCER Spencer, Vernon Murray b: 2/4/1894, Wixom, Mich. d: 6/3/71, Wixom, Mich. BL/TR, 5'7", 165 lbs. Deb: 7/4/20																								
1920	NY-N	45	140	15	28	2	3	0	19	11	17	.200	.258	.257	515	49	-9	4	3	-0	.932	-1	O-40(38-1-2)	-1.3
■ PAUL SPERAW Speraw, Paul Bachman "Polly" or "Birdie" b: 10/5/1893, Annville, Pa. d: 2/22/62, Cedar Rapids, Iowa BR/TR, 5'8.5", 145 lbs. Deb: 9/15/20																								
1920	StL-A	1	2	0	0	0	0	0	0	0	0	.000	.000	.000	0	-97	-1	0	0	0	1.000	0	/3-1	0.0
■ ED SPERBER Sperber, Edwin George b: 1/21/1895, Cincinnati, Ohio d: 1/5/76, Cincinnati, Ohio BL/TL, 5'11", 175 lbs. Deb: 4/16/24																								
1924	Bos-N	24	59	8	17	2	0	1	12	10	9	.288	.400	.373	773	113	2	3	1	0	.897	-3	O-17(2-1-14)	-0.2
1925	Bos-N	2	2	0	0	0	0	0	0	0	0	.000	.000	.000	0	-99	-1	0	0	0	.000	0	H	-0.1
Total	2	26	61	8	17	2	0	1	12	10	9	.279	.389	.361	750	106	1	3	1	0	.897	-3	/O-17(2-1-14)	-0.3
■ ROB SPERRING Sperring, Robert Walter b: 10/10/49, San Francisco, Cal. BR/TR, 6'1", 185 lbs. Deb: 8/11/74																								
1974	Chi-N	42	107	9	22	3	0	1	5	9	28	.206	.267	.262	529	46	-8	1	2	-0	.952	5	2-35/S-8	-0.1
1975	Chi-N	65	144	25	30	4	1	1	9	16	31	.208	.292	.271	563	54	-9	0	2	-1	.946	12	3-22,2-17,S-16,/O-8R	0.4
1976	Chi-N	43	93	8	24	3	0	0	7	9	25	.258	.324	.290	614	69	-3	0	2	-1	.955	-9	3-20,S-15/2-4,O-3L	-1.3
1977	Hou-N	58	129	6	24	3	0	1	9	12	23	.186	.255	.233	488	35	-12	0	0	0	.940	-2	S-22,2-20,3-11	-1.2
Total	4	208	473	48	100	13	1	3	30	46	107	.211	.283	.262	545	51	-32	1	6	-2	.964	6	/2-76,S-61,3-53,O	-2.2
■ STAN SPERRY Sperry, Stanley Kenneth b: 2/19/14, Evansville, Wis. d: 9/27/62, Evansville, Wis. BL/TR, 5'10.5", 164 lbs. Deb: 7/28/36																								
1936	Phi-N	20	37	2	5	3	0	0	4	3	5	.135	.200	.216	416	11	-5	0			.900	-4	2-15	-0.8

YEAR	TM/L	G	AB	R	H	2B	3B	HR	RBI	BB	SO	AVG	OBP	SLG	OPS	OPS+	BR+	SB	CS	SBR	FA	FR	G/POS	TPR
1938	Phi-A	60	253	28	69	6	3	0	27	15	9	.273	.313	.320	634	61	-15	1	2	-0	.959	-8	2-60	-1.9
Total	2	80	290	30	74	9	3	0	31	18	14	.255	.299	.307	606	54	-20	1	2		.951	-12	/2-75	-2.7

■ BILL SPIERS Spiers, William James b: 6/5/66, Orangeburg, S.C. BL/TR, 6'2", 190 lbs. Deb: 4/7/89 Career OF: (33-LF 11-CF 20-RF)

YEAR	TM/L	G	AB	R	H	2B	3B	HR	RBI	BB	SO	AVG	OBP	SLG	OPS	OPS+	BR+	SB	CS	SBR	FA	FR	G/POS	TPR
1989	Mil-A	114	345	44	88	9	3	4	33	21	63	.255	.300	.333	633	79	-10	10	2	2	.962	14	S-89,3-12/2-4,1D	1.2
1990	Mil-A	112	363	44	88	15	3	2	36	16	45	.242	.276	.317	593	66	-17	11	6	0	.976	-7	*S-111	-1.5
1991	Mil-A	133	414	71	117	13	6	8	54	34	55	.283	.340	.401	741	107	4	14	8	0	.970	-11	*S-128/O-1(0-1-0),D-2	0.2
1992	Mil-A	12	16	2	5	2	0	0	2	1	4	.313	.353	.438	790	123	0	1	1	-0	1.000	-2	/S-5,2-4,3-1,D-1	-0.2
1993	Mil-A	113	340	43	81	8	4	2	36	29	51	.238	.306	.303	609	65	-16	9	8	-1	.971	-24	*2-104/O-7R,S-4,D-1	-3.6
1994	Mil-A	73	214	27	54	10	1	0	17	19	42	.252	.316	.308	625	59	-13	7	1	1	.947	-4	3-35,S-35/O-2R,1D	-1.2
1995	NY-N	63	72	5	15	2	1	0	11	12	15	.208	.321	.264	585	58	-4	0	1	-0	.794	3	3-11/2-6	-0.1
1996	Hou-N	122	218	27	55	10	1	6	26	20	34	.252	.321	.390	711	94	-2	7	0	2	.959	4	3-77/2-7,1-4,S-4,O	0.4
1997	*Hou-N	132	291	51	93	27	4	4	48	61	42	.320	.439	.481	920	146	23	10	5	0	.935	11	3-84,S-28/1-8,2-4	3.5
1998	*Hou-N	123	384	66	105	27	4	4	43	45	62	.273	.357	.396	753	101	1	11	2	2	.966	-6	3-99/2-9,1-7,S-2	-0.3
1999	*Hou-N	127	393	56	113	18	5	4	39	47	45	.288	.364	.389	753	92	-4	10	5	0	.958	5	3-71,O-31L,S-13,/21	0.2
2000	Hou-N	124	355	41	107	17	3	3	43	49	38	.301	.388	.392	779	92	-2	7	4	0	.959	2	3-51,S-27,2-26,O-10L	0.2
Total	12	1248	3405	477	921	158	35	37	388	354	496	.270	.342	.370	712	90	-40	97	43	6	.970	-16	S-446,3-441,2/O1D	-1.2

■ HARRY SPIES Spies, Henry b: 6/12/1866, New Orleans, La. d: 7/7/42, Los Angeles, Cal. BL/TR, 5'9", 170 lbs. Deb: 4/20/1895

YEAR	TM/L	G	AB	R	H	2B	3B	HR	RBI	BB	SO	AVG	OBP	SLG	OPS	OPS+	BR+	SB	CS	SBR	FA	FR	G/POS	TPR
1895	Cin-N	14	50	2	11	0	1	0	5	3	2	.220	.264	.260	524	34	-5	0			.867	2	C-12/1-2	-0.2
	Lou-N	72	276	42	74	14	7	2	35	11	19	.268	.313	.391	704	86	-6	4			.981	-3	1-47,C-26/S-1	-0.6
	Yr	86	326	44	85	14	8	2	40	14	21	.261	.305	.371	677	78	-12	4			.979	-2	1-49,C-38/S-1	-0.8

■ ED SPIEZIO Spiezio, Edward Wayne b: 10/31/41, Joliet, Ill. BR/TR, 5'11", 180 lbs. Deb: 7/23/64 F

YEAR	TM/L	G	AB	R	H	2B	3B	HR	RBI	BB	SO	AVG	OBP	SLG	OPS	OPS+	BR+	SB	CS	SBR	FA	FR	G/POS	TPR
1964	StL-N	12	12	0	4	0	0	0	0	0	1	.333	.333	.333	667	81	-0	0	0	0	.000	0	H	0.0
1965	StL-N	10	18	0	3	0	0	0	5	1	4	.167	.250	.167	417	18	-2	0	0	0	1.000	0	/3-3	-0.2
1966	StL-N	26	73	4	16	5	1	2	10	5	11	.219	.269	.397	666	82	-2	1	0	0	.885	-4	3-19	-0.6
1967	*StL-N	55	105	9	22	2	0	3	10	7	18	.210	.265	.314	580	66	-5	2	1	0	.962	-0	3-19/O-7(2-0-6)	-0.6
1968	*StL-N	29	51	1	8	0	0	0	2	5	6	.157	.232	.157	389	19	-5	1	1	-0	1.000	0	O-11(3-0-9)/3-2	-0.6
1969	SD-N	121	355	29	83	9	0	13	43	38	64	.234	.315	.369	684	95	-3	1	2	-0	.939	1	3-98/O-1(1-0-0)	-0.3
1970	SD-N	110	316	45	90	18	1	12	42	43	42	.285	.377	.462	839	129	13	4	0	1	.953	2	3-93	1.6
1971	SD-N	97	308	16	71	10	1	7	36	22	50	.231	.290	.338	628	83	-8	6	5	-0	.962	1	3-91/O-1(1-0-0)	-0.9
1972	SD-N	20	29	2	4	2	0	0	4	1	6	.138	.167	.207	374	6	-4	1	0	0	1.000	-2	/3-5	-0.6
	Chi-A	74	277	20	66	10	1	2	22	13	43	.238	.277	.303	581	71	-10	0	1	-0	.952	7	3-74	-0.5
Total	9	554	1544	126	367	56	4	39	174	135	245	.238	.306	.355	661	88	-24	16	10	0	.949	4	3-404/O-20(7-0-15)	-2.7

■ SCOTT SPIEZIO Spiezio, Scott Edward b: 9/21/72, Joliet, Ill. BB/TR, 6'2", 205 lbs. Deb: 9/14/96 F Career OF: (8-LF 0-CF 2-RF)

YEAR	TM/L	G	AB	R	H	2B	3B	HR	RBI	BB	SO	AVG	OBP	SLG	OPS	OPS+	BR+	SB	CS	SBR	FA	FR	G/POS	TPR
1996	Oak-A	9	29	6	9	2	0	2	8	4	4	.310	.394	.586	980	146	2	0	1	-0	.846	-1	/3-5,D-4	0.1
1997	Oak-A	147	538	58	131	28	4	14	65	44	75	.243	.302	.388	690	80	-17	9	3	1	**.990**	0	*2-146/3-1	-0.8
1998	Oak-A	114	406	54	105	19	1	9	50	44	56	.259	.334	.377	711	87	-8	1	3	-1	.975	-7	*2-112/D-1	-0.9
1999	Oak-A	89	247	31	60	24	0	8	33	29	36	.243	.327	.437	765	97	-2	0	0	0	.984	4	2-42,3-31,1-10,/D-6	0.4
2000	Ana-A	123	297	47	72	11	2	17	49	40	56	.242	.338	.465	803	100	-0	1	2	-0	.993	-9	D-50,1-29,3-15,O/2	-1.4
Total	5	482	1517	196	377	84	7	50	205	161	227	.249	.324	.412	736	90	-25	11	9	-1	.984	-13	2-302/D-61,3-52,1O	-2.6

■ CHARLIE SPIKES Spikes, Leslie Charles b: 1/23/51, Bogalusa, La. BR/TR, 6'3", 220 lbs. Deb: 9/1/72

YEAR	TM/L	G	AB	R	H	2B	3B	HR	RBI	BB	SO	AVG	OBP	SLG	OPS	OPS+	BR+	SB	CS	SBR	FA	FR	G/POS	TPR
1972	NY-A	14	34	2	5	1	0	0	3	1	13	.147	.171	.176	348	4	-4	0	1	-0	1.000	0	/O-9(0-0-9)	-0.6
1973	Cle-A	140	506	68	120	12	3	23	73	45	103	.237	.306	.409	715	98	-3	5	3	0	.964	5	*O-111(90-0-22),D-26	-0.5
1974	Cle-A	155	568	63	154	23	1	22	80	34	100	.271	.320	.431	752	116	9	10	7	-0	.968	0	*O-154(0-0-154)	0.1
1975	Cle-A	111	345	41	79	13	3	11	33	30	51	.229	.291	.380	670	88	-6	7	6	-1	.974	1	*O-103(31-0-72)/D-2	-1.1
1976	Cle-A	101	334	34	79	11	5	3	31	23	50	.237	.296	.326	622	83	-7	5	6	-1	.985	1	O-98(2-96)/D-2	-1.3
1977	Cle-A	32	95	13	22	2	0	3	11	11	17	.232	.324	.347	671	86	-2	0	2	-1	.972	-3	O-27(0-0-27)/D-2	-0.7
1978	Det-A	10	28	1	7	1	0	0	2	2	6	.250	.344	.286	629	77	-1	0	0	0	.909	-1	/O-9(0-0-9)	-0.3
1979	Atl-N	66	93	12	26	8	0	3	21	5	30	.280	.316	.462	779	102	0	0	0	0	.842	-3	O-15(12-0-3)	-0.4
1980	Atl-N	41	36	6	10	1	0	0	2	3	18	.278	.350	.306	656	82	-1	0	0	0	1.000	-2	/O-7(1-0-6)	-0.3
Total	9	670	2039	240	502	72	12	65	256	154	388	.246	.306	.389	695	96	-14	27	25	-3	.969	-2	O-533(136-0-398)/D-32	-5.1

■ HARRY SPILMAN Spilman, William Harry b: 7/18/54, Albany, Ga. BL/TR, 6'1", 190 lbs. Deb: 9/11/78 C Career OF: (4-LF 0-CF 0-RF)

YEAR	TM/L	G	AB	R	H	2B	3B	HR	RBI	BB	SO	AVG	OBP	SLG	OPS	OPS+	BR+	SB	CS	SBR	FA	FR	G/POS	TPR
1978	Cin-N	4	4	1	1	0	0	0	0	0	1	.250	.250	.250	500	40	-0	0	0	0	.000	0	H	0.0
1979	*Cin-N	43	56	7	12	3	0	0	5	7	5	.214	.323	.268	591	63	-3	0	0	0	1.000	-0	1-12/3-4	-0.3
1980	Cin-N	65	101	14	27	4	0	4	19	9	19	.267	.333	.426	759	110	1	0	0	0	.986	0	1-18/O-2L,C-1,3-1	0.0
1981	Cin-N	23	24	4	4	1	0	0	3	3	7	.167	.259	.208	468	33	-2	0	0	0	1.000	0	/3-3,1-2	-0.2
	*Hou-N	28	34	5	10	0	0	0	1	2	3	.294	.333	.294	627	83	-1	0	1	-0	1.000	-0	1-13	-0.2
	Yr	51	58	9	14	1	0	0	4	5	10	.241	.302	.259	560	61	-3	0	1	-0	.984	-0	1-15/3-3	-0.4
1982	Hou-N	38	61	7	17	2	0	3	11	5	10	.279	.333	.459	792	129	2	0	0	0	.989	-1	1-11	0.1
1983	Hou-N	42	78	7	13	3	0	1	9	5	12	.167	.217	.244	460	29	-8	0	0	0	1.000	-2	1-19/C-6	-1.1
1984	Hou-N	32	72	14	19	2	0	2	15	12	10	.264	.369	.375	744	118	2	0	0	0	.978	-3	1-18/C-8	-0.2
1985	Hou-N	44	66	3	9	1	0	1	4	3	7	.136	.174	.197	371	4	-9	0	0	0	1.000	-1	1-19/C-2	-1.1
1986	Det-A	24	49	6	12	2	0	3	8	3	8	.245	.288	.469	758	102	-0	0	0	0	1.000	0	D-11/3-2,C-1,1-1	0.0
	SF-N	58	94	12	27	7	0	2	22	12	13	.287	.368	.426	793	124	3	0	0	0	.994	0	1-19/3-5,C-1,2-1,O	0.2
1987	*SF-N	83	90	5	24	5	0	1	14	9	20	.267	.333	.356	689	87	-2	1	1	-0	.875	-2	3-10/1-9,C-1	-0.5
1988	SF-N	40	40	4	7	1	1	1	3	4	6	.175	.250	.325	575	67	-2	0	0	0	1.000	1	/1-6,C-2,O-1(1-0-0)	-0.2
	Hou-N	7	5	0	0	0	0	0	0	0	3	.000	.000	.000	0	-99	-1	0	0	0	1.000	0	/1-1	-0.1
	Yr	47	45	4	7	1	1	1	3	4	9	.156	.224	.289	513	48	-3	0	0	0	1.000	1	/1-7,C-2,O-1(1-0-0)	-0.3
1989	Hou-N	32	36	7	10	3	0	0	3	7	2	.278	.395	.361	756	122	1	0	0	0	1.000	0	/1-9,C-1	0.1
Total	12	563	810	96	192	34	1	18	117	81	126	.237	.309	.348	657	85	-17	1	2	-0	.991	-8	1-157/3-25,C-23,DO2	-3.5

■ HAL SPINDEL Spindel, Harold Stewart b: 5/27/13, Chandler, Okla. BR/TR, 6', 185 lbs. Deb: 4/23/39

YEAR	TM/L	G	AB	R	H	2B	3B	HR	RBI	BB	SO	AVG	OBP	SLG	OPS	OPS+	BR+	SB	CS	SBR	FA	FR	G/POS	TPR
1939	StL-A	48	119	13	32	3	1	0	11	8	7	.269	.315	.311	626	59	-7	0	2	-1	.993	-0	C-32	-0.6
1945	Phi-N	36	87	7	20	3	0	0	8	6	7	.230	.280	.264	544	53	-5	0			.964	0	C-31	-0.4
1946	Phi-N	1	3	0	1	0	0	0	1	0	0	.333	.333	.333	667	92	-0	0			1.000	-0	/C-1	0.0
Total	3	85	209	20	53	6	1	0	20	14	14	.254	.300	.292	592	57	-13	0	2		.980	0	/C-64	-1.0

■ ANDY SPOGNARDI Spognardi, Andrea Ettore b: 10/18/08, Boston, Mass. d: 1/1/2000, Dedham, Mass. BR/TR, 5'9.5", 160 lbs. Deb: 9/2/32

YEAR	TM/L	G	AB	R	H	2B	3B	HR	RBI	BB	SO	AVG	OBP	SLG	OPS	OPS+	BR+	SB	CS	SBR	FA	FR	G/POS	TPR
1932	Bos-A	17	34	9	10	1	0	0	1	6	6	.294	.400	.324	724	92	-0	0	0	0	.979	3	/2-9,S-3,3-2	0.3

■ AL SPOHRER Spohrer, Alfred Ray b: 12/3/02, Philadelphia, Pa. d: 7/17/72, Plymouth, N.H. BR/TR, 5'10.5", 175 lbs. Deb: 4/13/28

YEAR	TM/L	G	AB	R	H	2B	3B	HR	RBI	BB	SO	AVG	OBP	SLG	OPS	OPS+	BR+	SB	CS	SBR	FA	FR	G/POS	TPR
1928	NY-N	2	2	0	0	0	0	0	0	0	0	.000	.000	.000	0	-99	-1	0			1.000	0	/C-2	-0.1
	Bos-N	51	124	15	27	3	0	0	9	5	11	.218	.254	.242	496	32	-12	1			.976	-5	C-48	-1.5
	Yr	53	126	15	27	3	0	0	9	5	11	.214	.250	.238	488	30	-13	1			.977	-5	C-50	-1.6
1929	Bos-N	114	342	42	93	21	8	2	48	26	35	.272	.327	.398	725	82	-10	1			.954	-10	*C-109	-1.2
1930	Bos-N	112	356	44	113	22	8	2	37	22	24	.317	.361	.441	802	96	-3	3			.957	-18	*C-108	-1.2
1931	Bos-N	114	350	23	84	17	5	0	27	22	27	.240	.285	.317	602	64	-18	2			.982	-0	*C-111	-1.2
1932	Bos-N	104	335	31	90	12	2	0	33	15	26	.269	.300	.316	616	69	-15	2			.991	10	*C-100	0.1
1933	Bos-N	67	184	11	46	6	1	1	12	11	13	.250	.292	.310	602	78	-5	3			.972	-6	C-65	-0.9
1934	Bos-N	100	265	25	59	15	0	0	17	14	18	.223	.262	.279	541	49	-20	1			.977	0	C-98	-1.4
1935	Bos-N	92	260	22	63	7	1	1	16	9	12	.242	.273	.288	562	55	-16	0			.958	-10	C-90	-2.2
Total	8	756	2218	213	575	103	25	6	199	124	166	.259	.301	.336	637	70	-100	13			.972	-39	C-731	-9.6

■ JIM SPOTTS Spotts, James Russell b: 4/10/09, Honey Brook, Pa. d: 6/15/64, Medford, N.J. BR/TR, 5'10.5", 175 lbs. Deb: 4/23/30

YEAR	TM/L	G	AB	R	H	2B	3B	HR	RBI	BB	SO	AVG	OBP	SLG	OPS	OPS+	BR+	SB	CS	SBR	FA	FR	G/POS	TPR
1930	Phi-N	3	2	1	0	0	0	0	0	0	1	.000	.000	.000	0	-93	-1	0			1.000	0	/C-2	0.0

■ CHARLIE SPRAGUE Sprague, Charles Wellington b: 10/10/1864, Cleveland, Ohio d: 12/31/12, Des Moines, Iowa BL/TL, 5'11", 150 lbs. Deb: 9/17/1887

YEAR	TM/L	G	AB	R	H	2B	3B	HR	RBI	BB	SO	AVG	OBP	SLG	OPS	OPS+	BR+	SB	CS	SBR	FA	FR	G/POS	TPR
1887	Chi-N	3	13	0	2	0	0	0	0	0	2	.154	.154	.154	308	-13	-2	0			.667	-1	/P-3,O-1(0-1-0)	-0.1
1889	Cle-N	2	7	2	1	0	0	0	1	1	0	.143	.250	.143	393	11	-1	1			.857	1	/P-2	0.0
1890	Tol-a	55	199	25	47	5	6	1	19	16		.236	.303	.337	639	86	-4	10			.892	-6	O-40(24-10-6),P-19	-0.7
Total	3	60	219	27	50	5	6	1	20	17	2	.228	.293	.320	613	77	-7	11			.892	-6	/O-41(24-11-6),P-24	-0.8

■ ED SPRAGUE Sprague, Edward Nelson Jr. b: 7/25/67, Castro Valley, Cal. BR/TR, 6'2", 210 lbs. Deb: 5/8/91 F Career OF: (6-LF 0-CF 1-RF)

YEAR	TM/L	G	AB	R	H	2B	3B	HR	RBI	BB	SO	AVG	OBP	SLG	OPS	OPS+	BR+	SB	CS	SBR	FA	FR	G/POS	TPR
1991	Tor-A	61	160	17	44	7	0	4	20	19	43	.275	.363	.394	756	105	2	0	3	-1	.870	-1	3-35,1-22/C-2,D-2	-0.1
1992	*Tor-A	22	47	6	11	2	0	1	7	3	7	.234	.280	.340	620	70	-2	0	0	0	.985	1	C-15/1-4,3-1,D-2	-0.1
1993	*Tor-A	150	546	50	142	31	1	12	73	32	85	.260	.313	.386	699	86	-11	1	0	0	.955	-9	*3-150	-1.9
1994	Tor-A	109	405	38	97	19	1	11	44	23	95	.240	.298	.373	671	71	-18	1	0	0	.946	-12	*3-107/1-3	-2.8
1995	Tor-A	144	521	77	127	27	2	18	74	58	96	.244	.337	.407	744	93	-5	0	0	0	.958	-1	*3-139/1-7,D-2	-0.5
1996	Tor-A	159	591	88	146	35	2	36	101	60	146	.247	.329	.496	825	105	2	0	0	0	.956	-14	*3-148,D-10	-1.1
1997	Tor-A	138	504	63	115	29	4	14	48	51	102	.228	.307	.385	692	79	-16	0	1	-0	.945	-12	*3-129/D-8	-2.7
1998	Tor-A	105	382	49	91	20	0	17	51	24	73	.238	.302	.424	726	86	-9	0	2	-1	.924	-9	*3-105	-1.7
	Oak-A	27	87	8	13	5	0	3	7	2	17	.149	.187	.310	497	27	-10	1	0	0	.909	0	3-23/1-1	-0.9
	Yr	132	469	57	104	25	0	20	58	26	90	.222	.281	.403	684	75	-18	1	2	-0	.921	-9	*3-128/1-1	-2.6
1999	Pit-N★	137	490	71	131	27	2	22	81	50	93	.267	.355	.465	821	106	4	3	6	-1	.920	-1	*3-134	0.2
2000	SD-N	53	117	17	32	10	0	10	25	10	28	.274	.341	.615	956	143	7	0	0	0	.964	-8	1-24/3-5,O-5(4-0-1)	-0.2
	Bos-A	33	111	11	24	4	0	2	9	12	18	.216	.293	.306	599	50	-8	0	0	0	.972	-0	3-31/1-3,D-1	-0.8
	SD-N	20	40	2	9	2	0	0	2	3	12	.225	.295	.275	570	48	-3	0	0	0	1.000	-5	/3-5,O-2L,1-1,2-1	-0.7
Total	10	1158	4001	497	982	218	12	150	542	347	815	.245	.320	.418	738	89	-68	6	12	-3	.942	-72	*3-1012/1-65,DCO2	-13.3

■ HARRY SPRATT Spratt, Henry Lee b: 7/10/1887, Broadford, Va. d: 7/3/69, Washington, D.C. BL/TR, 5'8.5", 175 lbs. Deb: 4/13/11 Career OF: (0-LF 3-CF 1-RF)

YEAR	TM/L	G	AB	R	H	2B	3B	HR	RBI	BB	SO	AVG	OBP	SLG	OPS	OPS+	BR+	SB	CS	SBR	FA	FR	G/POS	TPR
1911	Bos-N	62	154	22	37	4	4	2	13	13	25	.240	.299	.357	657	77	-5	1			.892	-8	S-26/2-5,3-4,O-4C	-1.2
1912	Bos-N	27	89	6	23	3	2	3	15	7	11	.258	.313	.438	751	102	-0	2			.842	-13	S-23	-1.2
Total	2	89	243	28	60	7	6	5	28	20	36	.247	.304	.387	691	86	-6	3			.871	-21	/S-49,2-5,O-4C,3-4	-2.4

■ GEORGE SPRIGGS Spriggs, George Herman b: 5/22/41, Jewell, Md. BL/TR, 5'11", 175 lbs. Deb: 9/15/65

YEAR	TM/L	G	AB	R	H	2B	3B	HR	RBI	BB	SO	AVG	OBP	SLG	OPS	OPS+	BR+	SB	CS	SBR	FA	FR	G/POS	TPR
1965	Pit-N	9	2	5	1	0	0	0	0	0	0	.500	.500	.500	1000	182	0	2	0	0	.000	-0	/O-1(0-0-1)	0.0
1966	Pit-N	9	7	0	1	0	0	0	0	0	3	.143	.143	.143	286	-20	-1	0	0	0	.000	0	H	-0.1
1967	Pit-N	38	57	14	10	1	1	0	5	6	20	.175	.254	.228	482	39	-4	3	0	1	1.000	-2	O-13(10-0-3)	-0.7
1969	KC-A	23	29	4	4	2	1	0	0	3	8	.138	.242	.276	518	44	-2	0	0	0	1.000	-1	/O-6(4-1-1)	-0.4
1970	KC-A	51	130	12	27	2	3	1	7	14	32	.208	.285	.292	577	59	-7	4	3	-0	.953	1	O-36(0-0-36)	-0.9
Total	5	130	225	35	43	5	5	1	12	23	63	.191	.269	.271	540	51	-15	9	3	1	.965	-3	/O-56(14-1-41)	-2.1

■ STEVE SPRINGER Springer, Steven Michael b: 2/11/61, Long Beach, Cal. BR/TR, 6', 190 lbs. Deb: 5/22/90

YEAR	TM/L	G	AB	R	H	2B	3B	HR	RBI	BB	SO	AVG	OBP	SLG	OPS	OPS+	BR+	SB	CS	SBR	FA	FR	G/POS	TPR
1990	Cle-A	4	12	1	2	0	0	0	1	0	6	.167	.167	.167	333	-7	-2	0	0	0	1.000	-1	/3-3,D-1	-0.2
1992	NY-N	4	5	0	2	1	0	0	0	0	1	.400	.400	.600	1000	182	0	0	0	0	1.000	-0	/2-1,3-1	0.0
Total	2	8	17	1	4	1	0	0	1	0	7	.235	.235	.294	529	48	-1	0	0	0	1.000	-1	/3-4,2-1,D-1	-0.2

■ JOE SPRINZ Sprinz, Joseph Conrad "Mule" b: 8/3/02, St.Louis, Mo. d: 1/11/94, Fremont, Cal. BR/TR, 5'11", 185 lbs. Deb: 7/16/30

YEAR	TM/L	G	AB	R	H	2B	3B	HR	RBI	BB	SO	AVG	OBP	SLG	OPS	OPS+	BR+	SB	CS	SBR	FA	FR	G/POS	TPR
1930	Cle-A	17	45	5	8	1	0	0	2	4	4	.178	.245	.200	445	14	-6	0	0	0	1.000	6	C-17	0.1
1931	Cle-A	1	3	0	0	0	0	0	0	0	0	.000	.000	.000	0	-95	-1	0	0	0	1.000	0	/C-1	-0.1
1933	StL-N	3	5	1	1	0	0	0	0	1	1	.200	.333	.200	533	53	-0	0			1.000	2	/C-3	0.2
Total	3	21	53	6	9	1	0	0	2	5	5	.170	.241	.189	430	12	-7	0	0		1.000	8	/C-21	0.2

■ FREDDY SPURGEON Spurgeon, Fred b: 10/9/1900, Wabash, Ind. d: 11/5/70, Kalamazoo, Mich. BR/TR, 5'11.5", 160 lbs. Deb: 9/19/24

YEAR	TM/L	G	AB	R	H	2B	3B	HR	RBI	BB	SO	AVG	OBP	SLG	OPS	OPS+	BR+	SB	CS	SBR	FA	FR	G/POS	TPR
1924	Cle-A	3	7	0	1	1	0	0	0	0	0	.143	.250	.286	536	37	-1	0	0	0	.882	1	/2-3	0.0
1925	Cle-A	107	376	50	108	9	3	0	32	15	21	.287	.315	.327	642	62	-22	8	5	0	.927	-4	3-56,2-46/S-3	-2.0
1926	Cle-A	149	614	101	181	31	3	0	49	27	36	.295	.327	.355	682	77	-21	7	2	1	.962	-8	*2-149	-2.3
1927	Cle-A	57	179	30	45	6	1	1	19	18	14	.251	.323	.313	636	65	-9	8	1	1	.938	-8	2-52	-1.3
Total	4	316	1176	181	335	47	7	1	100	60	71	.285	.322	.339	661	70	-53	23	8	2	.958	-19	2-250/3-56,S-3	-5.6

■ ED SPURNEY Spurney, Edward Frederick b: 1/19/1872, Cleveland, Ohio d: 10/12/32, Cleveland, Ohio Deb: 6/26/1891

YEAR	TM/L	G	AB	R	H	2B	3B	HR	RBI	BB	SO	AVG	OBP	SLG	OPS	OPS+	BR+	SB	CS	SBR	FA	FR	G/POS	TPR
1891	Pit-N	3	7	2	2	1	0	0	0	2	1	.286	.444	.429	873	158	1	0			.889	-1	/S-3	0.0

■ MIKE SQUIRES Squires, Michael Lynn b: 3/5/52, Kalamazoo, Mich. BL/TL, 5'11", 185 lbs. Deb: 9/1/75 C

YEAR	TM/L	G	AB	R	H	2B	3B	HR	RBI	BB	SO	AVG	OBP	SLG	OPS	OPS+	BR+	SB	CS	SBR	FA	FR	G/POS	TPR
1975	Chi-A	20	65	5	15	0	0	0	4	8	5	.231	.315	.231	546	55	-3	3	0	1	.988	0	1-20	-0.4
1977	Chi-A	3	3	0	0	0	0	0	0	0	1	.000	.000	.000	0	-99	-1	0	0	0	1.000	0	/1-1	0.0
1978	Chi-A	46	150	25	42	9	2	0	19	16	21	.280	.349	.367	716	101	0	4	4	-1	.997	-2	1-45	-0.5
1979	Chi-A	122	295	44	78	10	1	2	22	22	9	.264	.320	.325	645	74	-10	15	5	2	.995	4	*1-110/O-1(1-0-0)	-0.9
1980	Chi-A	131	343	38	97	11	3	2	33	33	24	.283	.347	.350	697	92	-3	8	9	-1	.995	4	*1-114/C-2	-0.6
1981	Chi-A	92	294	35	78	9	0	0	25	22	17	.265	.316	.296	612	79	-8	7	2	1	.992	2	1-88/O-1(1-0-0)	-1.0
1982	Chi-A	116	195	33	52	9	3	1	21	14	13	.267	.316	.359	675	85	-4	3	3	-0	.995	7	*1-109	-0.1
1983	*Chi-A	143	153	21	34	4	1	1	11	22	11	.222	.328	.281	609	67	-6	3	3	-0	**.996**	6	*1-124/3-1,D-5	-0.3
1984	Chi-A	104	82	9	15	1	0	0	6	6	7	.183	.239	.195	434	21	-9	2	2	-0	1.000	4	1-77,3-13/O-3C,P-1	-0.6
1985	Chi-A	2	0	1	0	0	0	0	0	0	0	—	—	—	—	—	0	0	0	0	.000	0	/R	0.0
Total	10	779	1580	211	411	53	10	6	141	143	108	.260	.323	.318	641	78	-43	45	28	0	.995	25	1-688/3-14,D-5,OCP	-4.4

■ MARV STAEHLE Staehle, Marvin Gustave b: 3/13/42, Oak Park, Ill. BL/TR, 5'10", 172 lbs. Deb: 9/15/64

YEAR	TM/L	G	AB	R	H	2B	3B	HR	RBI	BB	SO	AVG	OBP	SLG	OPS	OPS+	BR+	SB	CS	SBR	FA	FR	G/POS	TPR
1964	Chi-A	6	5	0	2	0	0	0	2	0	0	.400	.400	.400	800	127	0	1	0	0	.000	0	H	0.0
1965	Chi-A	7	7	0	3	0	0	0	2	0	0	.429	.429	.429	857	154	0	0	0	0	.000	0	H	0.0
1966	Chi-A	8	15	2	2	0	0	0	0	4	2	.133	.316	.133	449	37	-1	1	0	0	1.000	1	/2-6	0.0
1967	Chi-A	32	54	1	6	1	0	0	1	4	8	.111	.172	.130	302	-10	-7	1	1	-0	1.000	1	2-17/S-5	-0.6
1969	Mon-N	6	17	4	7	2	0	1	1	2	0	.412	.474	.706	1180	226	3	0	0	0	.944	-1	/2-4	0.2
1970	Mon-N	104	321	41	70	9	1	0	26	39	21	.218	.309	.252	561	52	-21	1	3	-1	.963	-13	2-91/S-1	-2.9
1971	Atl-N	22	36	5	4	0	0	0	1	5	4	.111	.238	.111	349	2	-5	0	0	0	1.000	4	/2-7,3-1	0.0
Total	7	185	455	53	94	12	1	1	33	54	35	.207	.296	.244	540	50	-30	4	4	-1	.971	-8	2-125/S-6,3-1	-3.3

■ HEINIE STAFFORD Stafford, Henry Alexander b: 11/1/1891, Orleans, Vt. d: 1/29/72, Lake Worth, Fla. BR/TR, 5'7", 160 lbs. Deb: 10/5/16

YEAR	TM/L	G	AB	R	H	2B	3B	HR	RBI	BB	SO	AVG	OBP	SLG	OPS	OPS+	BR+	SB	CS	SBR	FA	FR	G/POS	TPR
1916	NY-N	1	1	0	0	0	0	0	0	0	0	.000	.000	.000	0	-99	-0	0			.000	0	H	0.0

■ GENERAL STAFFORD Stafford, James Joseph "Jamsey" b: 7/9/1868, Webster, Mass. d: 9/18/23, Worcester, Mass. BR/TR, 5'8", 165 lbs. Deb: 8/27/1890 F Career OF: (96-LF 111-CF 44-RF)

YEAR	TM/L	G	AB	R	H	2B	3B	HR	RBI	BB	SO	AVG	OBP	SLG	OPS	OPS+	BR+	SB	CS	SBR	FA	FR	G/POS	TPR
1890	Buf-P	15	49	11	7	1	0	0	3	7	8	.143	.250	.163	413	13	-6	2			.893	-2	P-12/O-4(1-1-2)	-0.2
1893	NY-N	67	281	58	79	7	4	5	27	25	31	.281	.344	.388	732	94	-3	19			.901	-7	O-67(0-67-0)	-1.2
1894	NY-N	14	46	10	10	1	1	0	4	10	7	.217	.368	.283	651	59	-3	2			.750	-3	/3-6,O-5R,2-1,1-1	-0.5
1895	NY-N	123	463	79	129	12	5	3	73	40	32	.279	.344	.346	689	80	-13	42			.911	-9	*2-109,O-12L/3-2	-1.4
1896	NY-N	59	230	28	66	9	1	0	40	13	18	.287	.333	.335	668	79	-7	15			.897	-5	O-53(53-0-0)/S-6	-1.3
1897	NY-N	7	23	0	2	0	0	0	3	3		.087	.192	.087	279	-26	-4	0			1.000	-3	/O-5(5-0-0),S-2	-0.7
	Lou-N	113	441	68	122	16	5	7	54	31		.277	.328	.383	712	91	-7	15			.886	-9	*S-105/O-7(4-2-1),3-1	-0.9
	Yr	120	464	68	124	16	5	7	57	34		.267	.321	.369	690	85	-11	15			.881	-12	*S-107,O-12L/3-1	-1.6
1898	Lou-N	49	181	26	54	3	0	1	25	19		.298	.368	.331	700	103	1	7			.901	-8	2-28,O-22(6-7-9)/3-1	-0.7
	Bos-N	37	123	21	32	2	0	1	8	4		.260	.289	.301	590	66	-6	3			.909	-3	O-35(9-1-25)/1-1	-1.0
	Yr	86	304	47	86	5	0	2	33	23		.283	.337	.319	656	87	-5	10			.924	-12	O-57R,2-28/3-1,1-1	-1.7
1899	Bos-N	55	182	29	55	4	2	3	40	7		.302	.328	.396	724	89	-4	9			.956	-9	O-41(6-33-2)/2-5,S-5	-1.3
	Was-N	31	118	11	29	5	1	1	14	5		.246	.276	.331	607	67	-6	4			.951	-5	2-17,S-13/3-2	-0.9
	Yr	86	300	40	84	9	3	4	54	12		.280	.308	.370	678	81	-9	13			.956	-14	O-41C,2-22,S-18,/3	-2.2
Total	8	570	2137	341	585	60	19	21	291	164	96	.274	.330	.349	680	82	-56	118			.911	-63	O-251C,2-160,S/3P1	-10.1

BOB STAFFORD Stafford, Robert M. b: 6/26/1872, Oak Ridge, N.C. d: 8/20/16, Moores Springs, N.C. Deb: 10/12/1890

YEAR	TM/L	G	AB	R	H	2B	3B	HR	RBI	BB	SO	AVG	OBP	SLG	OPS	OPS+	BR+	SB	CS	SBR	FA	FR	G/POS	TPR
1890	Phi-a	1	2	0	0	0	0	0	0	0		.000	.000	.000	0	-99	-0	0			1.000	1	/O-1(1-0-0)	0.0

STEVE STAGGS Staggs, Stephen Robert b: 5/6/51, Anchorage, Alaska BR/TR, 5'9", 150 lbs. Deb: 7/1/77

YEAR	TM/L	G	AB	R	H	2B	3B	HR	RBI	BB	SO	AVG	OBP	SLG	OPS	OPS+	BR+	SB	CS	SBR	FA	FR	G/POS	TPR
1977	Tor-A	72	290	37	75	11	6	2	28	36	38	.259	.340	.359	699	90	-3	5	9	-2	.965	-14	2-72	-1.6
1978	Oak-A	47	78	10	19	2	2	0	0	19	17	.244	.392	.321	712	108	2	2	3	-1	.976	-3	2-40/S-2,3-2,D-2	0.0
Total	2	119	368	47	94	13	8	2	28	55	55	.255	.352	.351	703	94	-1	7	12	-3	.968	-17	2-112/D-2,3-2,S-2	-1.6

CHICK STAHL Stahl, Charles Sylvester b: 1/10/1873, Avilla, Ind. d: 3/28/07, W.Baden, Ind. BL/TL, 5'10", 160 lbs. Deb: 4/19/1897 M Career OF: (74-LF 777-CF 446-RF)

YEAR	TM/L	G	AB	R	H	2B	3B	HR	RBI	BB	SO	AVG	OBP	SLG	OPS	OPS+	BR+	SB	CS	SBR	FA	FR	G/POS	TPR
1897	*Bos-N	114	469	112	166	30	13	4	97	38		.354	.406	.499	905	130	19	18			.928	-3	*O-111(1-0-110)	0.9
1898	Bos-N	125	467	72	144	21	8	3	52	46		.308	.375	.407	782	118	10	6			.968	-2	*O-125(8-0-118)	0.2
1899	Bos-N	148	576	122	202	23	19	7	52	72		.351	.426	.493	919	138	31	33			.969	6	*O-148(1-1-146)/P-1	2.6
1900	Bos-N	136	553	88	163	23	16	5	82	34		.295	.336	.421	757	96	-5	27			**.968**	9	*O-135(64-1-71)	-0.6
1901	Bos-A	131	515	105	156	20	16	6	72	54		.303	.377	.439	816	128	20	29			.957	-1	*O-131(0-130-1)	1.2
1902	Bos-A	127	508	92	164	22	11	2	58	37		.323	.375	.421	796	117	12	24			.953	-5	*O-125(0-125-0)	0.1
1903	*Bos-A	77	299	60	82	12	6	2	44	28		.274	.338	.375	713	108	3	10			.961	-2	O-74(0-74-0)	-0.3
1904	Bos-A	157	587	83	170	27	**19**	3	67	64		.290	.366	.416	782	139	27	11			.961	-14	*O-157(0-157-0)	0.6
1905	Bos-A	134	500	61	129	17	4	0	47	50		.258	.332	.308	640	102	3	18			.977	-6	*O-134(0-134-0)	-1.1
1906	Bos-A	155	595	63	170	24	6	4	51	47		.286	.346	.366	713	123	16	13			.961	10	*O-155(0-155-0),M	2.0
Total	10	1304	5069	858	1546	219	118	36	622	470		.305	.369	.416	785	121	136	189			.961	-8	*O-1295C/P-1	5.6

JAKE STAHL Stahl, Garland b: 4/13/1879, Elkhart, Ill. d: 9/18/22, Monrovia, Cal. BR/TR, 6'2", 195 lbs. Deb: 4/20/03 M Career OF: (65-LF 27-CF 0-RF)

YEAR	TM/L	G	AB	R	H	2B	3B	HR	RBI	BB	SO	AVG	OBP	SLG	OPS	OPS+	BR+	SB	CS	SBR	FA	FR	G/POS	TPR
1903	Bos-A	40	92	14	22	3	5	2	8	4		.239	.286	.446	731	111	1	1			.956	-2	C-28/O-1(1-0-0)	0.1
1904	Was-A	142	520	54	136	29	12	3	50	21		.262	.309	.381	690	119	10	25			.978	6	*1-119,O-23(0-23-0)	1.4
1905	Was-A	141	501	66	125	22	12	5	66	28		.250	.311	.371	683	121	11	41			.986	2	*1-140,M	1.1
1906	Was-A	137	482	38	107	9	8	0	51	21		.222	.266	.274	540	73	-16	30			.983	-2	*1-136,M	-2.2
1908	NY-A	75	274	34	70	18	5	2	42	11		.255	.304	.380	683	120	5	17			.933	4	O-68(64-4-0)/1-6	0.6
	Bos-A	78	262	29	64	9	11	0	23	20		.244	.333	.363	696	123	7	13			.984	-2	1-78	0.4
	Yr	153	536	63	134	27	16	2	65	31		.250	.319	.371	690	122	12	30			.984	2	1-84,O-68(64-4-0)	1.0
1909	Bos-A	127	435	62	128	19	12	6	60	43		.294	.377	.434	812	153	27	16			.986	-11	*1-126	1.5
1910	Bos-A	144	531	68	144	19	16	**10**	77	42		.271	.334	.424	758	134	19	22			.985	-7	*1-142	1.0
1912	*Bos-A	95	326	40	98	21	6	3	60	31		.301	.372	.429	801	123	9	13			.980	-2	1-92,M	0.5
1913	Bos-A	2	2	0	0	0	0	0	0	0	1	.000	.000	.000	0	-98	-0	0			.000	0	HM	-0.1
Total	9	981	3425	405	894	149	87	31	437	221	1	.261	.323	.382	706	120	73	178			.983	-14	1-839/O-92L,C-28	4.3

LARRY STAHL Stahl, Larry Floyd b: 6/29/41, Belleville, Ill. BL/TL, 6'1", 185 lbs. Deb: 9/11/64 Career OF: (217-LF 106-CF 160-RF)

YEAR	TM/L	G	AB	R	H	2B	3B	HR	RBI	BB	SO	AVG	OBP	SLG	OPS	OPS+	BR+	SB	CS	SBR	FA	FR	G/POS	TPR
1964	KC-A	15	46	7	12	1	0	3	6	1	10	.261	.277	.478	755	102	-0	0	0	0	.955	1	O-10(5-4-1)	0.0
1965	KC-A	28	81	9	16	2	1	4	14	5	16	.198	.253	.395	648	82	-2	1	0	0	1.000	1	O-21(8-12-4)	-0.2
1966	KC-A	119	312	37	78	11	5	5	34	17	63	.250	.291	.365	656	90	-5	5	3	0	.980	-4	O-94(69-2-27)	-1.4
1967	NY-N	71	155	9	37	5	0	1	18	8	25	.239	.285	.290	575	66	-7	2	2	-0	.969	3	O-43(3-32-8)	-0.6
1968	NY-N	53	183	15	43	7	2	3	10	21	38	.235	.314	.344	658	97	-0	3	0	1	.983	1	O-47(13-30-19)/1-9	-0.2
1969	SD-N	95	162	10	32	6	2	3	10	17	31	.198	.278	.315	593	68	-7	3	3	-0	.981	2	O-37(27-4-5),1-13	-0.8
1970	SD-N	52	66	5	12	2	0	0	3	2	14	.182	.206	.212	418	13	-8	2	2	-0	1.000	-3	O-20(17-0-4)	-1.2
1971	SD-N	114	308	27	78	13	4	8	36	26	59	.253	.311	.399	711	107	2	4	3	-0	.987	6	O-75(46-8-26)/1-7	0.3
1972	SD-N	107	297	31	67	9	3	7	20	31	67	.226	.299	.347	646	89	-5	1	3	-1	.986	-1	O-76(26-10-42)/1-1	-1.1
1973	*Cin-N	76	111	17	25	2	2	2	12	14	34	.225	.317	.333	651	85	-2	1	0	0	1.000	-6	O-29(3-4-24)/1-2	-0.9
Total	10	730	1721	167	400	58	19	36	163	142	357	.232	.293	.351	644	86	-35	22	16	-1	.983	-1	O-452L/1-32	-6.1

SCOTT STAHOVIAK Stahoviak, Scott Edmund b: 3/6/70, Waukegan, Ill. BL/TR, 6'5", 210 lbs. Deb: 9/10/93 Career OF: (0-LF 0-CF 1-RF)

YEAR	TM/L	G	AB	R	H	2B	3B	HR	RBI	BB	SO	AVG	OBP	SLG	OPS	OPS+	BR+	SB	CS	SBR	FA	FR	G/POS	TPR
1993	Min-A	20	57	1	11	4	0	0	1	3	22	.193	.233	.263	496	33	-5	0	2	-1	.922	3	3-19	-0.3
1995	Min-A	94	263	28	70	19	0	3	23	30	61	.266	.344	.373	716	86	-5	5	1	1	.998	7	1-69,3-22/D-1	-0.2
1996	Min-A	130	405	72	115	30	3	13	61	59	114	.284	.378	.469	847	111	7	3	3	-0	.994	10	*1-114/D-9	0.7
1997	Min-A	91	275	33	63	17	0	10	33	24	73	.229	.305	.400	705	81	-8	5	2	0	.990	4	1-81/D-5	-1.0
1998	Min-A	9	19	1	2	0	0	1	1	0	7	.105	.105	.263	368	-8	-3	0	0	0	.975	0	/1-4,O-1(0-0-1)	-0.3
Total	5	344	1019	135	261	70	3	27	119	116	277	.256	.337	.410	748	91	-14	13	8	0	.994	24	1-268/3-41,D-15,O-1R	-1.1

ROY STAIGER Staiger, Roy Joseph b: 1/6/50, Tulsa, Okla. BR/TR, 6', 195 lbs. Deb: 9/12/75

YEAR	TM/L	G	AB	R	H	2B	3B	HR	RBI	BB	SO	AVG	OBP	SLG	OPS	OPS+	BR+	SB	CS	SBR	FA	FR	G/POS	TPR
1975	NY-N	13	19	2	3	1	0	0	0	0	4	.158	.158	.211	368	2	-3	0	0	0	1.000	1	3-13	-0.1
1976	NY-N	95	304	23	67	8	1	2	26	25	35	.220	.282	.273	555	62	-15	3	3	-0	.967	19	3-93/S-1	0.3
1977	NY-N	40	123	16	31	9	0	2	11	4	20	.252	.276	.374	650	76	-5	1	0	0	.934	6	3-36/S-1	0.1
1979	NY-A	4	11	1	3	1	0	0	1	1	0	.273	.333	.364	697	90	-0	0	0	0	1.000	0	/3-4	0.0
Total	4	152	457	42	104	19	1	4	38	30	59	.228	.277	.300	576	64	-23	4	3	-0	.960	26	3-146/S-2	0.3

TUCK STAINBACK Stainback, George Tucker b: 8/4/11, Los Angeles, Cal. d: 11/29/92, Camarillo, Cal. BR/TR, 5'11.5", 175 lbs. Deb: 4/17/34 Career OF: (182-LF 284-CF 168-RF)

YEAR	TM/L	G	AB	R	H	2B	3B	HR	RBI	BB	SO	AVG	OBP	SLG	OPS	OPS+	BR+	SB	CS	SBR	FA	FR	G/POS	TPR
1934	Chi-N	104	359	47	110	14	3	2	46	8	42	.306	.327	.379	706	90	-5	7			.955	-6	O-96(60-22-15)/3-1	-1.6
1935	Chi-N	47	94	16	24	4	0	3	11	0	13	.255	.271	.394	664	76	-4	1			.932	-5	O-28(1-1-26)	-0.9
1936	Chi-N	44	75	13	13	3	0	1	5	6	14	.173	.235	.253	488	31	-7	1			1.000	-4	O-26(15-6-5)	-1.2
1937	Chi-N	72	160	18	37	7	1	0	14	7	16	.231	.268	.287	555	49	-11	3			.981	-2	O-49(9-39-1)	-1.4
1938	StL-N	6	10	2	0	0	0	0	0	0	3	.000	.000	.000	0	-95	-3	0			1.000	1	/O-2(1-1-0)	-0.2
	Phi-N	30	81	9	21	3	0	1	11	3	3	.259	.294	.333	627	74	-3	1			.980	-2	O-25(13-4-9)	-0.6
	Bro-N	35	104	15	34	6	3	0	20	2	4	.327	.346	.442	788	113	1	1			.981	-1	O-23(2-21-0)	0.0
	Yr	71	195	26	55	9	3	1	31	5	10	.282	.307	.374	681	86	-4	2			.982	-3	O-50(16-26-9)	-0.8
1939	Bro-N	68	201	22	54	7	0	3	19	4	23	.269	.290	.348	638	68	-9	0			.938	-5	O-55(10-39-7)	-1.6
1940	Det-A	15	40	4	9	2	0	0	0	1	9	.225	.262	.275	537	36	-4	0	0	0	.968	4	/O-9(1-8-0)	-0.1
1941	Det-A	94	200	19	49	8	1	2	10	3	21	.245	.260	.325	585	49	-15	6	3	0	.948	-15	O-80(39-6-36)	-3.2
1942	*NY-A	15	10	0	2	0	0	0	0	0	2	.200	.200	.200	400	13	-1	0	0	0	1.000	-0	/O-3(2-0-1)	-0.1
1943	*NY-A	71	231	31	60	11	2	0	10	7	16	.260	.285	.325	609	77	-7	3	3	-0	.993	-1	O-60(12-43-5)	-1.2
1944	NY-A	30	78	13	17	3	0	0	5	3	7	.218	.247	.256	503	42	-6	1	0	0	.957	-3	O-24(4-4-17)	-1.0
1945	NY-A	95	327	40	84	12	2	5	32	13	20	.257	.289	.352	641	82	-9	0	4	-1	.968	9	O-83(2-72-9)	-0.4
1946	Phi-A	91	291	35	71	10	2	0	20	7	20	.244	.264	.292	556	56	-18	3	2	-0	.963	3	O-66(11-18-37)	-1.9
Total	13	817	2261	284	585	90	14	17	204	64	213	.259	.284	.333	618	68	-100	27	12		.965	-29	O-629C/3-1	-15.4

MATT STAIRS Stairs, Matthew Wade b: 2/27/68, St.John, N.B., Canada BL/TR, 5'9", 175 lbs. Deb: 5/29/92 Career OF: (83-LF 2-CF 341-RF)

YEAR	TM/L	G	AB	R	H	2B	3B	HR	RBI	BB	SO	AVG	OBP	SLG	OPS	OPS+	BR+	SB	CS	SBR	FA	FR	G/POS	TPR
1992	Mon-N	13	30	2	5	2	0	0	5	7	7	.167	.324	.233	558	61	-1	0	0	0	.933	-1	O-10(10-0-0)	-0.3
1993	Mon-N	6	8	1	3	1	0	0	2	0	1	.375	.375	.500	875	126	0	0	0	0	1.000	-0	/O-1(1-0-0)	0.0
1995	*Bos-A	39	88	8	23	7	1	1	17	4	14	.261	.301	.398	699	77	-3	0	1	-0	.913	-4	O-23(17-0-6)/D-2	-0.8
1996	Oak-A	61	137	21	38	5	1	10	23	19	23	.277	.369	.547	917	130	6	1	1	-0	.985	1	O-44(16-0-29)/1-1,D-5	0.5
1997	Oak-A	133	352	62	105	19	0	27	73	50	60	.298	.390	.582	973	152	27	3	2	-0	.977	-9	O-89R,D-16/1-7	1.2
1998	Oak-A	149	523	88	154	33	1	26	106	59	93	.294	.372	.511	883	130	23	8	3	1	1.000	3	*D-120,O-12L/1-6	1.8
1999	Oak-A	146	531	94	137	26	3	38	102	89	124	.258	.367	.533	900	131	25	2	7	-2	.981	-0	*O-139R/1-1,D-5	1.4
2000	*Oak-A	143	476	74	108	26	0	21	81	78	122	.227	.337	.414	751	91	-6	5	2	0	.979	-1	*O-103R,D-37/1-1	-1.3
Total	8	690	2145	350	573	119	6	123	409	306	444	.267	.362	.500	863	122	70	19	16	-1	.978	-12	O-421R,D-185/1-16	2.5

GALE STALEY Staley, George Gaylord b: 5/2/1899, DePere, Wis. d: 4/19/89, Walnut Creek, Cal. BL/TR, 5'8.5", 167 lbs. Deb: 9/16/25

YEAR	TM/L	G	AB	R	H	2B	3B	HR	RBI	BB	SO	AVG	OBP	SLG	OPS	OPS+	BR+	SB	CS	SBR	FA	FR	G/POS	TPR
1925	Chi-N	7	26	2	11	2	0	0	3	2	1	.423	.464	.500	964	144	2	0	1	-0	.979	4	/2-7	0.5

VIRGIL STALLCUP Stallcup, Thomas Virgil "Red" b: 1/3/22, Ravensford, N.C. d: 5/2/89, Greenville, S.C. BR/TR, 6'3", 185 lbs. Deb: 4/18/47

YEAR	TM/L	G	AB	R	H	2B	3B	HR	RBI	BB	SO	AVG	OBP	SLG	OPS	OPS+	BR+	SB	CS	SBR	FA	FR	G/POS	TPR
1947	Cin-N	8	1	1	0	0	0	0	0	0	1	.000	.000	.000	0	-99	-0	0			.000	0	/S-1	0.0
1948	Cin-N	149	539	40	123	30	4	3	65	18	52	.228	.253	.315	569	55	-36	2			.956	-0	*S-148	-2.7
1949	Cin-N	141	575	49	146	28	5	3	45	9	44	.254	.268	.336	604	60	-33	1			.962	-10	*S-141	-3.4

YEAR	TM/L	G	AB	R	H	2B	3B	HR	RBI	BB	SO	AVG	OBP	SLG	OPS	OPS+	BR+	SB	CS	SBR	FA	FR	G/POS	TPR
1950	Cin-N	136	483	44	121	23	2	8	54	17	39	.251	.276	.356	632	65	-26	4			**.973**	-5	*S-136	-2.3
1951	Cin-N	121	428	33	103	17	2	8	49	6	40	.241	.251	.346	597	58	-26	2	4	-1	**.969**	-8	*S-117	-2.9
1952	Cin-N	2	1	0	0	0	0	0	0	0	0	.000	.000	.000	0	-99	-0	0	0	0	.000	0	/S-1	0.0
	StL-N	29	31	4	4	1	0	0	1	1	5	.129	.156	.161	318	-12	-5	0	0	0	1.000	2	S-12	-0.3
	Yr	31	32	4	4	1	0	0	1	1	5	.125	.152	.156	308	-15	-5	0	0	0	1.000	2	S-13	-0.3
1953	StL-N	1	1	0	0	0	0	0	0	0	0	.000	.000	.000	0	-99	-0	0	0	0	.000	0	H	0.0
Total	7	587	2059	171	497	99	13	22	214	51	181	.241	.260	.334	595	58	-127	9	4		.965	-21	S-556	-11.6

■ GEORGE STALLER

Staller, George Walborn "Stopper" b: 4/1/16, Rutherford Heights, Pa. d: 7/3/92, Harrisburg, Pa. BL/TL, 5'11", 190 lbs. Deb: 9/14/43 C

YEAR	TM/L	G	AB	R	H	2B	3B	HR	RBI	BB	SO	AVG	OBP	SLG	OPS	OPS+	BR+	SB	CS	SBR	FA	FR	G/POS	TPR
1943	Phi-A	21	85	14	23	1	3	3	12	5	6	.271	.326	.459	785	129	3	1	0	0	.977	-1	O-20(0-0-20)	0.1

■ GEORGE STALLINGS

Stallings, George Tweedy "Gentleman George"
b: 11/17/1867, Augusta, Ga. d: 5/13/29, Haddock, Ga. BR/TR, 6'1", 187 lbs. Deb: 5/22/1890 M

YEAR	TM/L	G	AB	R	H	2B	3B	HR	RBI	BB	SO	AVG	OBP	SLG	OPS	OPS+	BR+	SB	CS	SBR	FA	FR	G/POS	TPR
1890	Bro-N	4	11	1	0	0	0	0	0	1	3	.000	.154	.000	154	-54	-2	0			.933	-1	/C-4	-0.3
1897	Phi-N	2	9	1	2	1	0	0	0	0		.222	.222	.333	556	47	-1	0			1.000	1	/O-1(0-0-1),1-1,M	0.0
1898	Phi-N	1	0	1	0	0	0	0	0	0		—	—	—	—	—	0	0			.000	0	/HM	0.0
Total	3	7	20	3	2	1	0	0	0	1	3	.100	.182	.150	332	-7	-3	0			.933	-1	/C-4,1-1,O-1(0-0-1)	-0.3

■ OSCAR STANAGE

Stanage, Oscar Harland b: 3/17/1883, Tulare, Cal. d: 11/11/64, Detroit, Mich. BR/TR, 5'9.5", 185 lbs. Deb: 5/19/06 C

YEAR	TM/L	G	AB	R	H	2B	3B	HR	RBI	BB	SO	AVG	OBP	SLG	OPS	OPS+	BR+	SB	CS	SBR	FA	FR	G/POS	TPR
1906	Cin-N	1	1	0	0	0	0	0	0	0		.000	.000	.000	0	-96	-0	0			1.000	-0	/C-1	0.0
1909	*Det-A	77	252	17	66	8	6	0	21	11		.262	.298	.341	639	98	-1	2			.964	-8	C-77	-0.2
1910	Det-A	88	275	24	57	7	4	2	25	20		.207	.266	.284	550	68	-11	1			.952	-4	C-84	-0.6
1911	Det-A	141	503	45	133	13	7	3	51	20		.264	.297	.336	633	73	-20	3			.952	-13	*C-141	-2.0
1912	Det-A	121	394	35	103	9	4	0	41	34		.261	.326	.305	631	83	-8	3			.950	-28	*C-120	-2.6
1913	Det-A	80	241	19	54	13	2	0	21	21	35	.224	.292	.295	586	73	-9	5			.960	-8	C-77	-1.1
1914	Det-A	122	400	16	77	8	4	0	25	24	58	.192	.242	.233	474	41	-29	2	1	0	.960	-6	*C-122	-2.7
1915	Det-A	100	300	27	67	9	2	1	31	20	41	.223	.274	.277	551	62	-15	5	1	1	.964	-9	*C-100	-1.6
1916	Det-A	94	291	16	69	17	3	0	30	17	48	.237	.286	.316	602	78	-9	3			.969	-9	C-94	-1.1
1917	Det-A	99	297	19	61	14	1	0	30	20	35	.205	.262	.259	522	59	-15	3			.977	-4	C-95	-1.3
1918	Det-A	54	186	9	47	4	0	1	14	11	18	.253	.294	.290	585	80	-5	2			.980	-8	C-47/1-5,S-1	-1.1
1919	Det-A	38	120	9	29	4	1	1	15	7	12	.242	.295	.317	611	73	-4	1			.974	1	C-36/1-1	-0.1
1920	Det-A	78	238	12	55	17	0	0	17	14	21	.231	.277	.303	579	55	-16	0	0	0	.958	-10	C-77	-1.9
1925	Det-A	3	5	0	1	0	0	0	0	0	0	.200	.200	.200	400	2	-1	0	0	0	1.000	-1	/C-3	-0.1
Total	14	1096	3503	248	819	123	34	8	321	219	268	.234	.284	.295	579	69	-142	30	2		.961	-107	*C-1074/1-6,S-1	-16.4

■ JERRY STANDAERT

Standaert, Jerome John b: 11/2/01, Chicago, Ill. d: 8/4/64, Chicago, Ill. BR/TR, 5'10", 168 lbs. Deb: 4/16/25

YEAR	TM/L	G	AB	R	H	2B	3B	HR	RBI	BB	SO	AVG	OBP	SLG	OPS	OPS+	BR+	SB	CS	SBR	FA	FR	G/POS	TPR
1925	Bro-N	1	1	0	0	0	0	0	0	0	1	.000	.000	.000	0	-99	-0	0	0	0	.000	0	H	0.0
1926	Bro-N	66	113	13	39	8	2	0	14	5	7	.345	.378	.451	829	124	4	0			.918	-11	2-21,3-14/S-6	-0.6
1929	Bos-A	19	18	1	3	2	0	0	4	3	2	.167	.286	.278	563	47	-1	0	0	0	.958	-0	1-10	-0.2
Total	3	86	132	14	42	10	2	0	18	8	10	.318	.362	.424	786	111	2	0	0		.918	-11	/2-21,3-14,1-10,S-6	-0.8

■ PETE STANICEK

Stanicek, Peter Louis b: 4/18/63, Harvey, Ill. BB/TR, 5'11", 175 lbs. Deb: 9/1/87 F Career OF: (65-LF 0-CF 0-RF)

YEAR	TM/L	G	AB	R	H	2B	3B	HR	RBI	BB	SO	AVG	OBP	SLG	OPS	OPS+	BR+	SB	CS	SBR	FA	FR	G/POS	TPR
1987	Bal-A	30	113	9	31	3	0	0	9	8	19	.274	.333	.301	634	72	-4	8	1	1	.975	-6	2-19,D-10/3-2	-0.8
1988	Bal-A	83	261	29	60	7	1	4	17	28	45	.230	.314	.310	624	78	-7	12	6	1	.985	-5	O-65(65-0-0),2-16/D-1	-1.3
Total	2	113	374	38	91	10	1	4	26	36	64	.243	.320	.307	627	76	-11	20	7	2	.967	-10	/O-65L,2-35,D-11,3	-2.1

■ STEVE STANICEK

Stanicek, Stephen Blair b: 6/19/61, Lake Forest, Ill. BR/TR, 6' ", 190 lbs. Deb: 9/16/87 F

YEAR	TM/L	G	AB	R	H	2B	3B	HR	RBI	BB	SO	AVG	OBP	SLG	OPS	OPS+	BR+	SB	CS	SBR	FA	FR	G/POS	TPR
1987	Mil-A	4	7	2	2	0	0	0	0	0	2	.286	.286	.286	571	51	-0	0	0	0	.000	0	/D-1	0.0
1989	Phi-N	9	9	0	1	0	0	0	1	0	3	.111	.111	.111	222	-36	-2	0	0	0	.000	0	H	-0.2
Total	2	13	16	2	3	0	0	0	1	0	5	.188	.188	.188	375	4	-2	0	0	0		0	/D-1	-0.2

■ TOM STANKARD

Stankard, Thomas Francis b: 3/20/1882, Waltham, Mass. d: 6/13/58, Waltham, Mass. BR/TR, 6', 190 lbs. Deb: 7/2/04

YEAR	TM/L	G	AB	R	H	2B	3B	HR	RBI	BB	SO	AVG	OBP	SLG	OPS	OPS+	BR+	SB	CS	SBR	FA	FR	G/POS	TPR
1904	Pit-N	2	2	0	0	0	0	0	0	0		.000	.000	.000	0	-97	-0	0			1.000	-1	/S-1,3-1	-0.1

■ ANDY STANKIEWICZ

Stankiewicz, Andrew Neal b: 8/10/64, Inglewood, Cal. BR/TR, 5'9", 165 lbs. Deb: 4/11/92

YEAR	TM/L	G	AB	R	H	2B	3B	HR	RBI	BB	SO	AVG	OBP	SLG	OPS	OPS+	BR+	SB	CS	SBR	FA	FR	G/POS	TPR
1992	NY-A	116	400	52	107	22	2	2	25	38	42	.268	.339	.348	686	93	-3	9	5	0	.973	6	S-81,2-34/D-1	1.1
1993	NY-A	16	9	5	0	0	0	0	0	1	1	.000	.100	.000	100	-73	-2	0	0	0	1.000	6	/2-6,3-4,S-1,D-1	0.4
1994	Hou-N	37	54	10	14	3	0	1	5	12	12	.259	.403	.370	773	109	1	1	1	-0	1.000	-0	S-17/2-6,3-1	0.2
1995	Hou-N	43	52	6	6	1	0	0	7	12	19	.115	.281	.135	416	15	-6	4	2	0	.985	12	S-14/2-6,3-3	0.6
1996	Mon-N	64	77	12	22	5	1	0	9	6	12	.286	.360	.377	737	92	-1	1	0	0	.969	1	2-19,S-13/3-1	0.2
1997	Mon-N	76	107	11	24	9	0	1	5	4	22	.224	.252	.336	589	53	-8	1	1	-0	.957	6	2-25,S-14/3-3,D-2	-0.1
1998	Ari-N	77	145	9	30	5	0	0	8	7	33	.207	.253	.241	495	31	-14	1	0	0	.994	-4	2-61	-1.6
Total	7	429	844	105	203	45	3	4	59	80	141	.241	.314	.315	630	72	-32	17	9	1	.986	27	2-157,S-140/3-12,D	0.8

■ EDDIE STANKY

Stanky, Edward Raymond "The Brat" or "Muggsy" b: 9/3/16, Philadelphia, Pa. d: 6/6/99, Fairhope, Ala. BR/TR, 5'8", 170 lbs. Deb: 4/21/43 MC

YEAR	TM/L	G	AB	R	H	2B	3B	HR	RBI	BB	SO	AVG	OBP	SLG	OPS	OPS+	BR+	SB	CS	SBR	FA	FR	G/POS	TPR
1943	Chi-N	142	510	92	125	15	1	0	47	92	42	.245	.363	.278	641	88	-3	4			.966	12	*2-131,S-12/3-2	1.8
1944	Chi-N	13	25	4	6	0	1	0	0	2	2	.240	.296	.320	616	74	-1	1			.875	2	/2-3,S-3,3-3	0.1
	Bro-N	89	261	32	72	9	2	0	16	44	13	.276	.382	.326	708	102	3	3			.961	-18	2-58,S-35/3-1	-1.0
	Yr	102	286	36	78	9	3	0	16	46	15	.273	.375	.325	701	100	2	4			.958	-16	2-61,S-38/3-4	-0.9
1945	Bro-N	153	555	**128**	143	29	5	1	39	**148**	42	.258	.417	.333	751	111	18	6			.962	9	*2-153/S-1	3.5
1946	Bro-N	144	483	98	132	24	7	0	36	**137**	56	.273	**.436**	.352	788	124	25	8			.977	-5	*2-141	2.9
1947	*Bro-N★	146	559	97	141	24	5	3	53	103	39	.252	.373	.329	702	85	-8	3			**.985**	7	*2-146	0.6
1948	*Bos-N†	67	247	49	79	14	2	2	29	61	13	.320	.455	.417	872	140	18	3			.981	5	2-66	2.6
1949	Bos-N	138	506	90	144	24	5	1	42	113	41	.285	.417	.358	775	116	19	3			.979	-9	*2-135	1.7
1950	NY-N☆	152	527	115	158	25	5	8	51	**144**	50	.300	**.460**	.412	872	131	35	9			.976	2	*2-151	4.3
1951	*NY-N	145	515	88	127	17	2	14	43	127	63	.247	.401	.369	770	108	12	8	5	0	.977	-1	*2-140	1.9
1952	StL-N	53	83	13	19	4	0	0	7	19	9	.229	.373	.277	650	83	-1	0	0	0	1.000	-1	2-20,M	-0.1
1953	StL-N	17	30	5	8	0	0	0	1	6	4	.267	.405	.267	672	80	-0	0	0	0	1.000	1	/2-8,M	0.1
Total	11	1259	4301	811	1154	185	35	29	364	996	374	.268	.410	.348	758	109	117	48	5		.975	4	*2-1152/S-51,3-6	18.4

■ FRED STANLEY

Stanley, Frederick Blair "Chicken" b: 8/13/47, Farnhamville, Iowa BR/TR (BB 1969-71), 5'10", 167 lbs. Deb: 9/11/69 C

YEAR	TM/L	G	AB	R	H	2B	3B	HR	RBI	BB	SO	AVG	OBP	SLG	OPS	OPS+	BR+	SB	CS	SBR	FA	FR	G/POS	TPR
1969	Sea-A	17	43	2	12	2	1	0	4	3	8	.279	.326	.372	698	96	-0	1	0	0	.962	-4	S-15/2-1	-0.3
1970	Mil-A	6	0	1	0	0	0	0	0	0	0	—	—	—	—	—	0	0	0	0	1.000	1	/2-2	0.1
1971	Cle-A	60	129	14	29	4	0	2	12	27	25	.225	.363	.302	665	83	-2	1	0	0	.971	7	S-55/2-3	1.1
1972	Cle-A	6	12	1	2	1	0	0	0	2	3	.167	.286	.250	536	58	-1	0	0	0	.917	-3	/S-5,2-1	-0.4
	SD-N	39	85	15	17	2	0	0	2	12	19	.200	.306	.224	530	57	-4	1	0	0	.989	3	2-21,S-17/3-4	0.1
1973	NY-A	26	66	6	14	0	1	1	5	7	16	.212	.288	.288	576	65	-3	0	0	0	.981	3	S-21/2-3	0.2
1974	NY-A	33	38	2	7	0	0	0	3	3	2	.184	.244	.184	428	25	-4	1	2	-0	.973	12	S-19,2-15	0.9
1975	NY-A	117	252	34	56	5	1	0	15	21	27	.222	.285	.250	535	53	-15	3	1	0	.977	4	S-83,2-33/3-1	-0.2
1976	*NY-A	110	260	32	62	2	2	1	20	34	29	.238	.329	.273	602	78	-6	1	0	0	.983	-24	*S-110/2-3	-2.0
1977	*NY-A	48	46	6	12	0	0	1	7	8	6	.261	.370	.326	696	93	-0	1	1	-0	.958	3	S-42/3-3,2-2	0.4
1978	*NY-A	81	160	14	35	7	0	1	9	25	31	.219	.324	.281	606	73	-5	0	0	0	.959	-5	S-71,2-11/3-4	-0.4
1979	NY-A	57	100	9	20	1	0	2	14	5	17	.200	.238	.270	508	38	-9	0	1	-0	.978	13	S-31,3-16/2-8,1O	0.5
1980	NY-A	49	86	13	18	3	0	0	5	5	5	.209	.269	.244	513	42	-7	0	0	0	.923	7	S-19,2-17,3-12	0.2
1981	*Oak-A	66	145	15	28	4	0	0	7	15	23	.193	.269	.221	489	44	-10	2	0	0	.986	-17	S-62/2-6	-2.2
1982	Oak-A	101	228	33	44	7	0	2	17	29	32	.193	.287	.250	537	51	-15	0	1	-0	.963	-20	S-98/2-2	-2.7
Total	14	816	1650	197	356	38	5	10	120	196	243	.216	.302	.263	565	62	-80	11	6	0	.971	-19	S-648,2-128/3-40,O1	-4.7

■ JIM STANLEY

Stanley, James F. b: 1889, BB/TR, 5'6", 148 lbs. Deb: 4/19/14

YEAR	TM/L	G	AB	R	H	2B	3B	HR	RBI	BB	SO	AVG	OBP	SLG	OPS	OPS+	BR+	SB	CS	SBR	FA	FR	G/POS	TPR
1914	Chi-F	54	98	13	19	3	0	0	4	19	14	.194	.347	.224	572	61	-6	2			.878	-10	S-40/3-3,2-1,O-1L	-1.5

YEAR	TM/L	G	AB	R	H	2B	3B	HR	RBI	BB	SO	AVG	OBP	SLG	OPS	OPS+	BR+	SB	CS	SBR	FA	FR	G/POS	TPR
■ **JOE STANLEY**	Stanley, Joseph b: New Jersey Deb: 4/24/1884																							
1884	Bal-U	6	21	3	5	1	0	0		0		.238	.238	.286	524	53	-2				.444	-2	/O-6(0-4-2)	-0.4
■ **JOE STANLEY**	Stanley, Joseph Bernard b: 4/2/1881, Washington, D.C. d: 9/13/67, Detroit, Mich. BB/TR, 5′9.5″, 150 lbs. Deb: 9/11/1897 F Career OF: (33-LF 52-CF 106-RF)																							
1897	Was-N	1	1	0	0	0	0	0	0	0		.000	.000	.000	0	-99	-0	0			.000	-0	/P-1	0.0
1902	Was-A	3	12	2	4	0	0	0	1	0		.333	.333	.333	667	85	-0	0			.833	-1	/O-3(3-0-0)	-0.1
1903	Bos-N	86	308	40	77	12	5	1	47	18		.250	.306	.331	637	85	-6	10			.902	3	O-77R/P-1,S-1	-0.6
1904	Bos-N	3	8	0	0	0	0	0	0	0		.000	.000	.000	0	-99	-2	0			.800	1	/O-3(1-0-2)	-0.2
1905	Was-A	28	92	13	24	2	1	1	17	7		.261	.313	.337	650	111	1	4			.944	0	O-27(13-9-5)	0.0
1906	Was-A	73	221	18	36	0	4	0	9	20		.163	.236	.199	435	38	-15	6			.934	-5	O-63(0-7-56)/P-1	-2.6
1909	Chi-N	22	52	4	7	1	0	0	2	6		.135	.224	.154	378	17	-5	0			.947	-4	O-16(5-4-9)	-1.1
Total	7	216	694	77	148	15	10	2	76	51		.213	.275	.272	547	66	-28	20			.918	-6	O-189R/P-3,S-1	-4.6
■ **MICKEY STANLEY**	Stanley, Mitchell Jack b: 7/20/42, Grand Rapids, Mich BR/TR, 6′1″, 195 lbs. Deb: 9/13/64 Career OF: (44-LF 1171-CF 82-RF)																							
1964	Det-A	4	11	3	3	0	0	0	1	0	1	.273	.273	.273	545	52	-1	0	0	0	1.000	-1	/O-4(3-1-1)	-0.2
1965	Det-A	30	117	14	28	6	0	3	13	3	12	.239	.258	.368	626	75	-4	1	0	0	.986	3	O-29(0-29-0)	-0.2
1966	Det-A	92	235	28	68	15	4	3	19	17	20	.289	.337	.426	763	115	4	2	1	0	1.000	2	O-82(0-82-0)	0.5
1967	Det-A	145	333	38	70	7	3	7	24	29	46	.210	.273	.312	586	71	-12	9	2	1	.982	-8	*O-129(2-126-2)/1-8	-2.5
1968	*Det-A	153	583	88	151	16	6	11	60	42	57	.259	.313	.364	677	102	1	4	3	-0	**1.000**	3	*O-130C,1-15/S-9,2	0.0
1969	Det-A	149	592	73	139	28	1	16	70	52	56	.235	.299	.367	665	82	-15	8	4	0	.985	-19	*O-101C,S-59/1-4	-3.1
1970	Det-A	142	568	83	143	21	11	13	47	45	56	.252	.307	.396	703	92	-8	10	1	2	**1.000**	6	*O-132(0-132-0)/1-9	-0.4
1971	Det-A	139	401	43	117	14	5	7	41	24	44	.292	.332	.404	736	103	1	1	3	-1	.988	6	*O-139(0-139-0)	0.4
1972	*Det-A	142	435	45	102	16	6	14	55	29	49	.234	.282	.395	678	97	-3	1	0	0	.994	6	*O-139(0-139-0)	0.0
1973	Det-A	157	602	81	147	23	5	17	57	48	65	.244	.300	.384	684	86	-12	0	4	-1	.993	13	*O-157(0-157-0)	-0.6
1974	Det-A	99	394	40	87	13	2	8	34	26	63	.221	.271	.325	596	68	-17	5	3	0	.992	6	O-91(1-90-0),1-12/2-1	-1.5
1975	Det-A	52	164	26	42	7	3	3	19	15	27	.256	.322	.390	712	96	-1	1	1	-0	.983	-1	O-28C,1-14/3-7,D-1	-0.5
1976	Det-A	84	214	34	55	17	1	4	29	14	19	.257	.303	.402	705	101	-0	2	0	0	.969	-2	O-38C,1-17,3-11,/S2D	-0.4
1977	Det-A	75	222	30	51	9	1	8	23	18	30	.230	.287	.387	675	78	-7	0	0	0	.972	-6	O-57R/1-3,S-3,D-2	-1.6
1978	Det-A	53	151	15	40	9	0	3	8	9	19	.265	.306	.384	690	90	-2	0	1	-0	.960	-6	O-34(2-4-28),1-12	-1.0
Total	15	1516	5022	641	1243	201	48	117	500	371	564	.248	.300	.377	677	89	-77	44	23	2	.991	2	*O-1290C/1-94,S3D2	-11.1
■ **MIKE STANLEY**	Stanley, Robert Michael b: 6/25/63, Ft.Lauderdale, Fla BR/TR, 6′1″, 185 lbs. Deb: 6/24/86 Career OF: (4-LF 0-CF 0-RF)																							
1986	Tex-A	15	30	4	10	3	0	1	1	3	7	.333	.394	.533	927	146	2	1	0	0	.857	-1	/3-7,C-4,O-1L,D-3	0.1
1987	Tex-A	78	216	34	59	8	1	6	37	31	48	.273	.367	.403	770	104	2	3	0	1	.980	-11	C-61,1-12/O-1L,D-5	-0.6
1988	Tex-A	94	249	21	57	8	0	3	27	37	62	.229	.329	.297	626	75	-7	0	0	0	.991	-3	C-64,D-18/1-6,3-2	-0.8
1989	Tex-A	67	122	9	30	3	1	1	11	12	29	.246	.324	.311	635	78	-3	1	0	0	.978	-4	C-25,D-21/1-7,3-3	-0.7
1990	Tex-A	103	189	21	47	8	1	2	19	30	25	.249	.352	.333	685	92	-1	1	0	0	.985	-3	C-63,D-14/3-8,1-6	-0.2
1991	Tex-A	95	181	25	45	13	1	3	25	34	44	.249	.373	.381	754	111	4	0	0	0	.980	-10	C-58,1-12/3-6,OD	-0.4
1992	NY-A	68	173	24	43	7	0	8	27	33	45	.249	.372	.428	800	124	7	0	0	0	.980	5	C-55/1-4,D-6	1.4
1993	NY-A	130	423	70	129	17	1	26	84	57	85	.305	.394	.534	928	152	31	1	1	-0	**.996**	-9	*C-122/D-2	2.9
1994	NY-A	82	290	54	87	20	0	17	57	39	56	.300	.387	.545	932	142	18	0	0	0	.993	-0	C-72/1-7,D-4	2.0
1995	*NY-A★	118	399	63	107	29	1	18	83	57	106	.268	.367	.481	848	120	12	1	1	-0	.993	-3	*C-107,D-10	1.4
1996	Bos-A	121	397	73	107	20	1	24	69	69	62	.270	.384	.506	891	120	13	2	0	0	.985	-28	*C-105,D-10	-0.8
1997	Bos-A	97	260	45	78	17	0	13	53	39	50	.300	.403	.515	919	135	14	0	1	-0	.996	-1	D-53,1-31,C-15	0.8
	*NY-A	28	87	16	25	8	0	3	12	15	22	.287	.392	.483	875	128	4	0	0	0	1.000	-1	D-16,1-12	0.1
	Yr	125	347	61	103	25	0	16	65	54	72	.297	.400	.507	908	133	18	0	1	-0	.997	-2	D-69,1-43,C-15	0.9
1998	Tor-A	98	341	49	82	13	0	22	47	56	86	.240	.356	.472	828	112	7	2	1	0	.995	-1	D-73,1-22/O-1(1-0-0)	-0.1
	*Bos-A	47	156	25	45	12	0	7	32	26	43	.288	.397	.500	897	129	7	1	0	0	1.000	-1	D-34,1-13	0.3
	Yr	145	497	74	127	25	0	29	79	82	129	.256	.369	.481	849	118	14	3	1	0	.981	-2	*D-107,1-35/O-1L	0.2
1999	*Bos-A	136	427	59	120	22	0	19	72	70	94	.281	.396	.466	862	115	12	0	0	0	.988	0	*1-111,D-22	0.1
2000	Bos-A	58	185	22	41	5	0	10	28	30	44	.222	.330	.411	741	83	-5	0	0	0	.997	4	1-39,D-18	-0.4
	Oak-A	32	97	11	26	7	0	4	18	14	21	.268	.366	.464	830	111	2	0	0	0	.988	1	1-19/D-8	0.1
	Yr	90	282	33	67	12	0	14	46	44	65	.238	.343	.429	772	92	-3	0	0	0	.993	5	1-58,D-26	-0.3
Total	15	1467	4222	625	1138	220	7	187	702	652	929	.270	.373	.458	831	117	118	13	4	1	.988	-65	C-751,D-323,1/3O	5.2
■ **JACK STANSBURY**	Stansbury, John James b: 12/6/1885, Phillipsburg, N.J. d: 12/26/70, Easton, Pa. BR/TR, 5′9″, 165 lbs. Deb: 6/30/18																							
1918	Bos-A	20	47	3	6	1	0	0	2	6	3	.128	.241	.149	390	18	-5	0			.980	2	3-18/O-2(0-2-0)	-0.2
■ **BUCK STANTON**	Stanton, George Washington b: 6/19/06, Stantonsburg, N.C d: 1/1/92, San Antonio, Tex. BL/TL, 5′10″, 150 lbs. Deb: 9/5/31																							
1931	StL-A	13	15	3	3	2	0	0	0	0	6	.200	.200	.333	533	37	-1	0	0	0	.750	-0	/O-1(0-0-1)	-0.1
■ **HARRY STANTON**	Stanton, Harry Andrew b: St.Louis, Mo. TR, Deb: 10/14/00																							
1900	StL-N	1	0	0	0	0	0	0	0	0		—	—	—	—	—	0	0			.000	0	/C-1	0.0
■ **LEROY STANTON**	Stanton, Leroy Bobby b: 4/10/46, Latta, S.C. BR/TR, 6′1″, 195 lbs. Deb: 9/10/70 Career OF: (107-LF 49-CF 553-RF)																							
1970	NY-N	4	4	0	1	0	1	0	0	0	0	.250	.250	.750	1000	157	0	0	0	0	1.000	-0	/O-1(0-1-0)	0.0
1971	NY-N	5	21	2	4	1	0	0	2	2	4	.190	.261	.238	499	43	-2	0	0	0	1.000	-0	/O-5(0-0-5)	-0.2
1972	Cal-A	127	402	44	101	15	3	12	39	22	100	.251	.297	.393	690	110	3	2	3	-1	.983	2	*O-124(0-2-123)	-0.2
1973	Cal-A	119	306	41	72	9	2	8	34	27	88	.235	.301	.356	658	92	-4	3	3	-0	.965	-7	*O-107(36-0-76)	-1.6
1974	Cal-A	118	415	48	111	21	2	11	62	33	107	.267	.329	.407	736	117	9	10	8	-1	.975	4	*O-114(0-10-110)	0.6
1975	Cal-A	137	440	67	115	20	3	14	82	52	85	.261	.347	.416	763	124	14	18	6	2	.961	2	*O-131(0-5-127)/D-1	1.2
1976	Cal-A	93	231	12	44	13	1	2	25	24	57	.190	.270	.281	551	66	-10	2	6	-2	.985	-15	O-79(33-31-27)/D-4	-3.2
1977	Sea-A	133	454	56	125	24	1	27	90	42	115	.275	.343	.511	854	131	18	0	1	-0	.953	5	O-91(8-0-84),D-33	1.6
1978	Sea-A	93	302	24	55	11	0	3	24	34	80	.182	.267	.248	515	46	-21	1	0	0	1.000	-0	D-59,O-30(30-0-1)	-2.5
Total	9	829	2575	294	628	114	13	77	358	236	636	.244	.313	.388	701	103	7	36	27	-2	.972	-9	O-682R/D-97	-4.3
■ **TOM STANTON**	Stanton, Thomas Patrick b: 10/25/1874, St.Louis, Mo. d: 1/17/57, St.Louis, Mo. BB/TR, 5′10″, 175 lbs. Deb: 4/19/04																							
1904	Chi-N	1	3	0	0	0	0	0	0	0		.000	.000	.000	0	-99	-1	0			1.000	-0	/C-1	-0.1
■ **JOE STAPLES**	Staples, Joseph F. b: Buffalo, N.Y. Deb: 9/19/1885																							
1885	Buf-N	7	22	0	1	0	0	0	0	0	9	.045	.045	.045	91	-68	-4				.545	-3	/O-6(0-6-1),2-1	-0.7
■ **DAVE STAPLETON**	Stapleton, David Leslie b: 1/16/54, Fairhope, Ala. BR/TR, 6′1″, 178 lbs. Deb: 5/30/80 Career OF: (5-LF 0-CF 2-RF)																							
1980	Bos-A	106	449	61	144	33	5	7	45	13	32	.321	.341	.463	805	112	6	3	2	-0	.979	10	2-94/1-8,O-6L,3D	2.1
1981	Bos-A	93	355	45	101	17	1	10	42	21	22	.285	.326	.423	749	108	3	0	4	-1	.948	-7	S-33,3-25,2-23,1/D	-0.3
1982	Bos-A	150	538	66	142	28	1	14	65	31	40	.264	.308	.398	705	87	-10	2	4	-1	.991	2	*1-106,S-27/2-9,3OD	-1.3
1983	Bos-A	151	542	54	134	31	1	10	66	40	44	.247	.301	.363	665	76	-17	1	1	-0	.993	-2	*1-145/2-5	-2.9
1984	Bos-A	13	39	4	9	2	0	0	1	3	3	.231	.286	.282	568	55	-2	0	0	0	1.000	1	1-10/D-1	-0.2
1985	Bos-A	30	66	4	15	6	0	0	2	4	11	.227	.271	.318	590	58	-4	0	0	0	1.000	1	2-14/1-8,D-5	-0.2
1986	*Bos-A	39	39	4	5	1	0	0	3	2	10	.128	.171	.154	325	-11	-6	0	0	0	1.000	3	1-29/2-6,3-2	-0.4
Total	7	582	2028	238	550	118	8	41	224	114	162	.271	.312	.398	710	90	-30	6	11	-3	.993	7	1-318,2-151/S-60,3DO	-3.2
■ **WILLIE STARGELL**	Stargell, Wilver Dornel b: 3/6/40, Earlsboro, Okla. BL/TL, 6′2.5″, 225 lbs. Deb: 9/16/62 CH Career OF: (1225-LF 8-CF 72-RF)																							
1962	Pit-N	10	31	1	9	3	1	0	4	3	10	.290	.353	.452	805	114	1	0	1	-0	.929	-0	/O-9(2-1-6)	-0.1
1963	Pit-N	108	304	34	74	11	6	11	47	19	85	.243	.292	.428	720	104	1	0	2	-1	.953	-8	O-65(35-6-24),1-16	-1.3
1964	Pit-N★	117	421	53	115	19	7	21	78	17	92	.273	.305	.501	806	123	11	1	1	-0	.900	-7	O-59(57-1-2),1-50	-0.3
1965	Pit-N★	144	533	68	145	25	8	27	107	39	127	.272	.330	.501	831	130	19	1	1	-0	.965	0	*O-137(125-0-19)/1-7	1.2
1966	Pit-N★	140	485	84	153	30	0	33	102	48	109	.315	.384	.581	965	164	41	2	3	-1	.945	-4	*O-127(121-0-7),1-15	3.0
1967	Pit-N	134	462	54	125	18	6	20	73	67	103	.271	.367	.465	832	136	23	1	0	0	.938	-2	O-98(92-0-6),1-37	1.5
1968	Pit-N	128	435	57	103	15	1	24	67	47	105	.237	.320	.441	761	129	14	5	0	1	.945	-3	*O-113(108-0-5),1-13	0.6
1969	Pit-N	145	522	89	160	31	6	29	92	61	120	.307	.385	.556	941	164	44	1	0	0	.970	-2	*O-116(115-0-1),1-23	3.4

YEAR	TM/L	G	AB	R	H	2B	3B	HR	RBI	BB	SO	AVG	OBP	SLG	OPS	OPS+	BR+	SB	CS	SBR	FA	FR	G/POS	TPR
1970	*Pit-N	136	474	70	125	18	3	31	85	44	119	.264	.333	.511	843	125	14	0	1	-0	.976	7	*O-125(123-0-2)/1-1	1.4
1971	*Pit-N★	141	511	104	151	26	0	**48**	125	83	154	.295	.401	.628	1029	188	**59**	0	0	0	.984	3	*O-138(138-0-0)	**5.6**
1972	*Pit-N★	138	495	75	145	28	2	33	112	65	129	.293	.377	.558	935	166	42	1	1	-0	.984	-13	*1-101,O-32(32-0-0)	2.1
1973	Pit-N★	148	522	106	156	**43**	3	**44**	**119**	80	129	.299	.395	**.646**	**1041**	**189**	**61**	0	0	0	.975	7	*O-142(142-0-0)	6.1
1974	*Pit-N	140	508	90	153	37	4	25	96	87	106	.301	.409	.537	**947**	**169**	**49**	0	2	-1	.967	2	*O-135(135-0-0)/1-1	4.3
1975	*Pit-N	124	461	71	136	32	2	22	90	58	109	.295	.377	.516	894	147	29	0	0	0	.992	-10	*1-122	0.9
1976	Pit-N	117	428	54	110	20	3	20	65	50	101	.257	.342	.458	800	124	13	2	0	0	.988	-10	*1-111	-0.6
1977	Pit-N	63	186	29	51	12	0	13	35	31	55	.274	.386	.548	935	144	12	0	1	-0	.986	-1	1-55	0.7
1978	Pit-N★	122	390	60	115	18	2	28	97	50	93	.295	.385	.567	951	156	29	3	2	-0	.994	-2	*1-112	2.2
1979	*Pit-N	126	424	60	119	19	0	32	82	47	105	.281	.357	.552	908	138	21	0	1	-0	**.997**	-6	*1-113	0.8
1980	Pit-N	67	202	28	53	10	1	11	38	26	52	.262	.352	.485	837	129	8	0	0	0	.992	0	1-54	0.5
1981	Pit-N	38	60	2	17	4	0	0	9	5	9	.283	.338	.350	688	93	-0	0	0	0	1.000	-2	/1-9	-0.4
1982	Pit-N	74	73	6	17	4	0	3	17	10	24	.233	.325	.411	736	102	0	0	0	0	1.000	0	/1-8	0.0
Total	21	2360	7927	1195	2232	423	55	475	1540	937	1936	.282	.363	.529	892	147	488	17	16	-2	.961	-51	*O-1296L,1-848	31.6

■ MATT STARK

Stark, Matthew Scott b: 1/21/65, Whittier, Cal. BR/TR, 6'4", 225 lbs. Deb: 4/8/87

YEAR	TM/L	G	AB	R	H	2B	3B	HR	RBI	BB	SO	AVG	OBP	SLG	OPS	OPS+	BR+	SB	CS	SBR	FA	FR	G/POS	TPR
1987	Tor-A	5	12	0	1	0	0	0	0	0	0	.083	.083	.083	167	-55	-3	0	0	0	1.000	1	/C-5	-0.2
1990	Chi-A	8	16	0	4	1	0	0	3	1	6	.250	.294	.313	607	71	-1	0	0	0	.000	0	/D-6	-0.1
Total	2	13	28	0	5	1	0	0	3	1	6	.179	.207	.214	421	15	-3	0	0	0	1.000	1	/D-6,C-5	-0.3

■ DOLLY STARK

Stark, Monroe Randolph b: 1/19/1885, Ripley, Miss. d: 12/1/24, Memphis, Tenn. BR/TR, 5'9", 160 lbs. Deb: 9/12/09

YEAR	TM/L	G	AB	R	H	2B	3B	HR	RBI	BB	SO	AVG	OBP	SLG	OPS	OPS+	BR+	SB	CS	SBR	FA	FR	G/POS	TPR
1909	Cle-A	19	60	4	12	0	0	0	1	6		.200	.273	.200	473	48	-3	4			.875	-10	S-19	-1.5
1910	Bro-N	30	103	7	17	3	0	0	8	7	19	.165	.225	.194	419	23	-10	2			.893	-1	S-30	-1.1
1911	Bro-N	70	193	25	57	4	1	0	19	20	24	.295	.370	.326	697	100	1	6			.910	-3	S-34,2-18/3-3	0.0
1912	Bro-N	8	22	2	4	0	0	0	2	1	3	.182	.217	.182	399	10	-3	2			.892	0	/S-7	-0.2
Total	4	127	378	38	90	7	1	0	30	34	46	.238	.308	.262	570	66	-15	14			.896	-14	/S-90,2-18,3-3	-2.8

■ GEORGE STARNAGLE

Starnagle, George Henry (b: George Henry Steuernagel) b: 10/6/1873, Belleville, Ill. d: 2/15/46, Belleville, Ill. BR/TR, 5'11", 175 lbs. Deb: 9/14/02

YEAR	TM/L	G	AB	R	H	2B	3B	HR	RBI	BB	SO	AVG	OBP	SLG	OPS	OPS+	BR+	SB	CS	SBR	FA	FR	G/POS	TPR
1902	Cle-A	1	3	0	0	0	0	0	0	0		.000	.000	.000	0	-99	-1	0			.667	-1	/C-1	-0.1

■ CHARLIE STARR

Starr, Charles Watkin b: 8/30/1878, Pike Co., Ohio d: 10/18/37, Pasadena, Cal. TR, 5'10.5", 165 lbs. Deb: 4/29/05

YEAR	TM/L	G	AB	R	H	2B	3B	HR	RBI	BB	SO	AVG	OBP	SLG	OPS	OPS+	BR+	SB	CS	SBR	FA	FR	G/POS	TPR
1905	StL-A	26	97	9	20	0	0	0	6	7		.206	.260	.206	466	51	-5	0			.938	-4	2-18/3-6	-1.0
1908	Pit-N	20	59	8	11	2	0	0	8	13		.186	.342	.220	563	80	-0	6			.926	-5	2-12/S-5,3-2	-0.6
1909	Bos-N	61	216	16	48	2	3	0	6	31		.222	.333	.259	593	80	-3	7			.931	-9	2-54/S-6,3-3	-1.3
	Phi-N	3	3	0	0	0	0	0	0	0		.000	.000	.000	0	-99	-1	0			.000	0	H	-0.1
	Yr	64	219	16	48	2	3	0	6	31		.219	.329	.256	585	78	-4	7			.931	-9	2-54/S-6,3-3	-1.4
Total	3	110	375	33	79	4	3	0	20	51		.211	.315	.237	552	72	-10	13			.931	-18	/2-84,S-11,3-11	-3.0

■ BILL STARR

Starr, William b: 2/26/11, Brooklyn, N.Y. d: 8/12/91, LaJolla, Cal. BR/TR, 6'1", 175 lbs. Deb: 8/23/35

YEAR	TM/L	G	AB	R	H	2B	3B	HR	RBI	BB	SO	AVG	OBP	SLG	OPS	OPS+	BR+	SB	CS	SBR	FA	FR	G/POS	TPR
1935	Was-A	12	24	1	5	0	0	0	1	0	1	.208	.208	.208	417	8	-3	0	0	0	.971	2	C-12	-0.1
1936	Was-A	1	0	0	0	0	0	0	0	0	0	—	—	—	—	—	0	0	0	0	.000	0	/C-1	0.0
Total	2	13	24	1	5	0	0	0	1	0	1	.208	.208	.208	417	8	-3	0	0	0	.971	2	/C-13	-0.1

■ JOE START

Start, Joseph "Old Reliable" or "Rocks" b: 10/14/1842, New York, N.Y. d: 3/27/27, Providence, R.I. BL/TL, 5'9", 165 lbs. Deb: 5/18/1871 M

YEAR	TM/L	G	AB	R	H	2B	3B	HR	RBI	BB	SO	AVG	OBP	SLG	OPS	OPS+	BR+	SB	CS	SBR	FA	FR	G/POS	TPR
1871	Mut-n	33	161	35	58	5	1	1	34	3	0	.360	.372	.422	794	140	10	4	2	0	.921	-2	*1-33	0.6
1872	Mut-n	55	282	62	76	4	0	0	50	0	0	.270	.270	.284	553	75	-6	3	3	-0	**.955**	2	*1-55	-0.3
1873	Mut-n	53	251	42	67	8	3	1	28	4	0	.267	.278	.335	613	82	-5	1	0	0	.943	5	*1-53/O-2(0-0-2),M	0.1
1874	Mut-n	63	306	67	96	13	3	2	46	4	0	.314	.323	.395	718	125	8	5	0	1	**.961**	4	*1-63/O-2(1-1-0)	1.1
1875	Mut-n	69	314	58	90	10	5	4	30	3	0	.287	.293	.389	682	128	7	1	4	-1	.948	2	*1-69	0.8
1876	NY-N	56	265	40	73	6	0	0	21	1	2	.275	.279	.299	578	107	3				**.964**	3	*1-56	0.4
1877	Har-N	60	271	55	90	3	6	1	21	6	2	.332	.347	.399	745	150	16				**.964**	-2	*1-60	1.0
1878	Chi-N	61	285	58	**100**	12	5	1	27	2	3	.351	.355	.439	794	150	14				.957	-2	*1-61	0.9
1879	Pro-N	66	317	70	101	11	5	2	37	7	4	.319	.333	.404	737	144	15				**.973**	0	*1-65/O-1(0-0-1)	1.1
1880	Pro-N	82	345	53	96	14	6	0	27	13	20	.278	.304	.354	658	126	10				.971	-3	*1-82	0.3
1881	Pro-N	79	348	56	114	12	6	0	29	9	7	.328	.345	.397	741	135	13				.963	-4	*1-79	0.5
1882	Pro-N	82	356	58	117	8	10	0	48	11	7	.329	.349	.407	756	142	16				.974	2	*1-82	0.9
1883	Pro-N	87	370	63	105	16	7	1	57	22	16	.284	.324	.373	697	108	4				.957	-1	*1-87	-0.5
1884	*Pro-N	93	381	80	105	10	5	2	32	35	25	.276	.337	.344	680	117	9				**.980**	1	*1-93	0.1
1885	Pro-N	101	374	47	103	11	4	0	41	39	10	.275	.344	.326	670	121	11				.972	3	*1-101	0.4
1886	Was-N	31	122	10	27	4	1	0	17	5	13	.221	.252	.270	522	63	-5	4			.973	-2	1-31	-0.9
Total	5 n	273	1314	264	387	40	12	8	188	14	0	.295	.302	.361	663	108	14	14	9	-0	.948	11	1-273/O-4(1-1-2)	2.3
Total	11	798	3434	590	1031	107	55	7	357	150	109	.300	.330	.370	699	127	104	4			.968	-5	1-797/O-1(0-0-1)	4.2

■ DAVE STATON

Staton, David Alan b: 4/12/68, Seattle, Wash. BR/TR, 6'5", 215 lbs. Deb: 9/8/93

YEAR	TM/L	G	AB	R	H	2B	3B	HR	RBI	BB	SO	AVG	OBP	SLG	OPS	OPS+	BR+	SB	CS	SBR	FA	FR	G/POS	TPR
1993	SD-N	17	42	7	11	3	0	5	9	3	12	.262	.326	.690	1017	161	3	0	0	0	1.000	3	1-12	0.5
1994	SD-N	29	66	6	12	2	0	4	6	10	18	.182	.289	.394	683	78	-2	0	0	0	1.000	4	1-20	0.0
Total	2	46	108	13	23	5	0	9	15	13	30	.213	.303	.509	813	110	1	0	0	0	1.000	7	/1-32	0.5

■ JOE STATON

Staton, Joseph b: 3/8/48, Seattle, Wash. BL/TL, 6'3", 175 lbs. Deb: 9/5/72

YEAR	TM/L	G	AB	R	H	2B	3B	HR	RBI	BB	SO	AVG	OBP	SLG	OPS	OPS+	BR+	SB	CS	SBR	FA	FR	G/POS	TPR
1972	Det-A	6	2	1	0	0	0	0	0	0	1	.000	.000	.000	0	-97	-0	0	1	-0	1.000	0	/1-2	-0.1
1973	Det-A	9	17	2	4	0	0	0	3	0	3	.235	.235	.235	471	31	-2	1	0	0	.969	2	/1-5	0.0
Total	2	15	19	3	4	0	0	0	3	0	4	.211	.211	.211	421	18	-2	1	1	-0	.973	2	/1-7	-0.1

■ JIGGER STATZ

Statz, Arnold John b: 10/20/1897, Waukegan, Ill. d: 3/16/88, Corona Del Mar, Cal. BR/TR (BB 1922 (part)), 5'7.5", 150 lbs. Deb: 7/30/19

YEAR	TM/L	G	AB	R	H	2B	3B	HR	RBI	BB	SO	AVG	OBP	SLG	OPS	OPS+	BR+	SB	CS	SBR	FA	FR	G/POS	TPR
1919	NY-N	21	60	7	18	2	1	0	6	3	8	.300	.333	.367	700	112	1	2			.977	-1	O-18(3-7-8)/2-5	-0.1
1920	NY-N	16	30	0	4	0	1	0	5	2	9	.133	.188	.200	388	11	-3	0	1	-0	.944	-3	O-12(0-12-0)	-0.8
	Bos-A	2	3	0	0	0	0	0	0	0	0	.000	.000	.000	0	-99	-1	0	0	0	1.000	-1	/O-2(0-0-2)	-0.2
1922	Chi-N	110	462	77	137	19	5	1	34	41	31	.297	.355	.366	721	85	-10	16	13	-1	.959	9	*O-110(0-110-0)	-0.6
1923	Chi-N	154	655	110	209	33	8	10	70	56	42	.319	.375	.440	815	114	14	29	23	-2	.975	18	*O-154(0-154-0)	2.2
1924	Chi-N	135	549	69	152	22	5	3	49	37	50	.277	.325	.352	676	80	-15	13	9	-0	.961	15	*O-131(0-131-0)/2-1	-0.6
1925	Chi-N	38	148	21	38	6	3	2	14	11	16	.257	.317	.378	695	76	-6	4	0	1	.943	2	O-37(0-37-0)	-0.4
1927	Bro-N	130	507	64	139	24	7	1	21	26	43	.274	.310	.355	665	77	-17	10			.990	15	*O-122(3-118-1)/2-1	-0.7
1928	Bro-N	77	171	28	40	8	1	0	16	18	12	.234	.311	.292	603	59	-10	3			.965	-6	O-52(2-49-1)/2-1	-1.7
Total	8	683	2585	376	737	114	31	17	215	194	211	.285	.337	.373	710	87	-47	77	46		.969	49	O-638(8-618-12)/2-8	-2.9

■ RUSTY STAUB

Staub, Daniel Joseph b: 4/1/44, New Orleans, La. BL/TR, 6'2", 200 lbs. Deb: 4/9/63 C Career OF: (75-LF 11-CF 1604-RF)

YEAR	TM/L	G	AB	R	H	2B	3B	HR	RBI	BB	SO	AVG	OBP	SLG	OPS	OPS+	BR+	SB	CS	SBR	FA	FR	G/POS	TPR
1963	Hou-N	150	513	43	115	17	4	6	45	59	58	.224	.310	.308	618	84	-10	0	0	0	.989	-1	*1-109,O-49(0-1-48)	-2.1
1964	Hou-N	89	292	26	63	10	2	8	35	21	31	.216	.275	.346	621	78	-9	1	1	-0	.992	-1	1-49,O-38(0-7-31)	-1.6
1965	Hou-N	131	410	43	105	20	1	14	63	52	57	.256	.343	.412	755	120	11	3	0	1	.951	4	*O-112(1-2-110)/1-1	0.9
1966	Hou-N	153	554	60	155	28	3	13	81	58	61	.280	.349	.412	761	119	14	2	1	0	.962	9	*O-148(55-1-105)/1-1	1.4
1967	Hou-N★	149	546	71	182	**44**	1	10	74	60	47	.333	.402	.473	875	155	40	0	4	-1	.962	7	*O-144(0-0-144)	3.7
1968	Hou-N★	161	591	54	172	37	1	6	72	73	57	.291	.376	.387	763	132	26	2	0	0	.992	-1	*1-147,O-15(0-0-15)	1.7
1969	Mon-N☆	158	549	89	166	26	5	29	79	110	61	.302	.427	.526	953	165	52	3	4	-1	.966	7	*O-156(0-0-156)	5.1
1970	Mon-N★	160	569	98	156	23	7	30	94	112	93	.274	.396	.497	894	138	33	12	11	-1	.985	11	*O-160(0-0-160)	3.4
1971	Mon-N☆	162	599	94	186	34	6	19	97	74	42	.311	.394	.482	877	147	38	9	5	0	.945	5	*O-162(1-0-162)	3.6
1972	NY-N	66	239	32	70	11	0	9	38	31	13	.293	.379	.452	831	139	13	0	1	-0	.982	0	O-65(0-0-65)	1.0
1973	*NY-N	152	585	77	163	36	1	15	76	74	52	.279	.363	.421	783	118	15	1	1	-0	.978	11	*O-152(0-0-152)	1.8
1974	NY-N	151	561	65	145	22	2	19	78	77	39	.258	.351	.406	757	113	10	2	1	0	.983	9	*O-147(0-0-147)	1.2
1975	NY-N	155	574	93	162	30	4	19	105	77	55	.282	.376	.448	823	134	27	2	0	0	.986	8	*O-153(0-0-153)	2.8
1976	Det-A★	161	589	73	176	28	3	15	96	83	49	.299	.392	.433	825	136	29	3	1	0	.970	-6	*O-126(0-0-126),D-36	1.7
1977	Det-A	158	623	84	173	34	3	22	101	59	47	.278	.341	.448	789	107	6	1	1	-0	.000	0	*D-156	0.1

YEAR	TM/L	G	AB	R	H	2B	3B	HR	RBI	BB	SO	AVG	OBP	SLG	OPS	OPS+	BR+	SB	CS	SBR	FA	FR	G/POS	TPR
1978	Det-A	162	642	75	175	30	1	24	121	76	35	.273	.352	.435	787	117	15	3	1	0	.000	0	*D-162	1.0
1979	Det-A	68	246	32	58	12	1	9	40	32	18	.236	.336	.402	738	95	-1	1	0	0	.000	0	D-66	-0.3
	Mon-N	38	86	9	23	3	0	3	14	14	10	.267	.370	.407	777	113	2	0	0	0	.994	-2	1-22/O-1(0-0-1)	-0.2
1980	Tex-A	109	340	42	102	23	2	9	55	39	18	.300	.375	.459	834	131	15	1	1	-0	.977	-2	D-57,1-30,O-14R	0.9
1981	NY-N	70	161	9	51	9	0	5	21	22	12	.317	.402	.466	868	148	11	1	0	0	.989	-2	1-41	0.7
1982	NY-N	112	219	11	53	9	0	3	27	24	10	.242	.317	.324	641	80	-5	0	0	0	.959	2	O-27(12-0-15),1-18	-0.6
1983	NY-N	104	115	5	34	6	0	3	28	14	10	.296	.377	.426	803	123	4	0	0	0	.976	-1	/1-5,O-5(3-0-2)	0.2
1984	NY-N	78	72	2	19	4	0	1	18	4	9	.264	.303	.361	664	87	-1	0	0	0	1.000	-0	/1-3	-0.2
1985	NY-N	54	45	2	12	3	0	1	8	10	4	.267	.400	.400	800	128	2	0	0	0	1.000	-0	/O-1(0-0-1)	0.2
Total	23	2951	9720	1189	2716	499	47	292	1466	1255	888	.279	.366	.431	797	125	336	47	33	-1	.969	55	*O-1675R,D-477,1-426	26.4

■ **ECKY STEARNS** Stearns, Daniel Eckford b: 10/17/1861, Buffalo, N.Y. d: 6/28/44, Glendale, Cal. BL/TR, 6′1″, 185 lbs. Deb: 8/17/1880 Career OF: (7-LF 3-CF 28-RF)

YEAR	TM/L	G	AB	R	H	2B	3B	HR	RBI	BB	SO	AVG	OBP	SLG	OPS	OPS+	BR+	SB	CS	SBR	FA	FR	G/POS	TPR
1880	Buf-N	28	104	8	19	6	1	0	13	3	23	.183	.206	.260	465	55	-5				.774	-9	O-20R/C-8,3-5,S-1	-1.4
1881	Det-N	3	11	1	1	1	0	0	0	0	2	.091	.091	.182	273	-16	-1				.714	-1	/S-3	-0.2
1882	Cin-a	49	214	28	55	10	2	0	35	6		.257	.277	.322	600	96	-1				.931	-2	1-35,O-12R/2-2,S-1	-0.6
1883	Bal-a	93	382	54	94	10	9	1		**34**		.246	.308	.327	635	101	1				.947	3	*1-92/O-1(1-0-0)	-0.4
1884	Bal-a	100	396	61	94	12	3	3		28		.237	.298	.306	603	94	-3				.949	4	*1-100/2-1	-0.7
1885	Bal-a	67	253	40	47	3	8	1	29	38		.186	.306	.273	579	85	-2				.973	1	1-63/O-3(0-2-1),C-2	-0.6
	Buf-N	30	105	7	21	6	1	0	9	8	23	.200	.257	.276	533	70	-3				.821	-7	S-19,1-12/C-2	-1.0
1889	KC-a	139	560	96	160	24	12	3	87	56	69	.286	.351	.387	738	104	1	67			.967	0	*1-135/3-4	-0.9
Total	7	509	2025	295	491	72	36	8	173	173	117	.242	.306	.325	631	94	-14	67			.956	-10	1-437/O-36R,S-24,C32	-5.8

■ **JOHN STEARNS** Stearns, John Hardin b: 8/21/51, Denver, Col. BR/TR, 6′, 185 lbs. Deb: 9/22/74 C Career OF: (6-LF 0-CF 0-RF)

YEAR	TM/L	G	AB	R	H	2B	3B	HR	RBI	BB	SO	AVG	OBP	SLG	OPS	OPS+	BR+	SB	CS	SBR	FA	FR	G/POS	TPR
1974	Phi-N	1	2	0	1	0	0	0	0	0	0	.500	.500	.500	1000	173	0	0	0	0	1.000	-1	/C-1	0.0
1975	NY-N	59	169	25	32	5	1	3	10	17	15	.189	.271	.284	555	57	-10	4	1	1	.994	6	C-54	-0.1
1976	NY-N	32	103	13	27	6	0	2	10	16	11	.262	.367	.379	745	119	3	1	2	-0	.987	3	C-30	0.8
1977	NY-N★	139	431	52	108	25	1	12	55	77	76	.251	.373	.397	770	112	10	9	8	-1	.982	4	*C-127/1-6	1.8
1978	NY-N	143	477	65	126	24	1	15	73	70	57	.264	.368	.413	781	122	16	25	13	1	.985	-3	*C-141/3-1	2.1
1979	NY-N☆	155	538	58	131	29	2	9	66	52	57	.243	.315	.355	670	86	-11	15	15	-2	.983	5	*C-121,1-16,3-11,/O	-0.5
1980	NY-N★	91	319	42	91	25	1	0	45	33	24	.285	.354	.370	724	105	3	7	3	0	.985	5	C-74,1-16/3-1	1.1
1981	NY-N	80	273	25	74	12	1	1	24	24	17	.271	.330	.333	663	90	-3	12	2	2	.983	-2	C-66/1-9,3-4	-0.2
1982	NY-N★	98	352	46	103	25	3	4	28	30	35	.293	.352	.415	766	114	7	17	7	1	.987	-7	C-81,3-12	0.5
1983	NY-N	4	0	2	0	0	0	0	0	0	0	—	—	—	—	—	0	0	0	0	.000	0	/R	0.0
1984	NY-N	8	17	6	3	1	0	0	1	4	2	.176	.333	.235	569	63	-1	1	0	0	1.000	-1	/C-4,1-2	-0.1
Total	11	810	2681	334	696	152	10	46	312	323	294	.260	.345	.375	720	102	13	91	51	2	.985	10	C-699/1-49,3-29,O-6L	5.4

■ **JOHN STEDRONSKY** Stedronsky, John b: Troy, N.Y. Deb: 9/25/1879

YEAR	TM/L	G	AB	R	H	2B	3B	HR	RBI	BB	SO	AVG	OBP	SLG	OPS	OPS+	BR+	SB	CS	SBR	FA	FR	G/POS	TPR
1879	Chi-N	4	12	0	1	0	0	0	0	0	3	.083	.083	.083	167	-42	-2				.789	1	/3-4	0.0

■ **FARMER STEELMAN** Steelman, Morris James b: 6/29/1875, Millville, N.J. d: 9/16/44, Merchantville, N.J. TR, Deb: 9/15/1899

YEAR	TM/L	G	AB	R	H	2B	3B	HR	RBI	BB	SO	AVG	OBP	SLG	OPS	OPS+	BR+	SB	CS	SBR	FA	FR	G/POS	TPR
1899	Lou-N	4	15	2	1	0	1	0	2	2		.067	.176	.200	376	3	-2	0			.929	-2	/C-4	-0.3
1900	Bro-N	1	4	0	0	0	0	0	0	0		.000	.000	.000	0	-94	-1	0			1.000	0	/C-1	-0.1
1901	Bro-N	1	3	0	1	0	0	0	0	0		.333	.333	.333	667	91	-0	0			.875	1	/C-1	0.1
	Phi-A	27	88	5	23	2	0	0	7	10		.261	.350	.284	634	74	-3	4			1.000	2	C-14,O-12(0-0-12)	0.0
1902	Phi-A	10	32	1	6	1	0	0	6	2		.188	.235	.219	454	25	-3	2			1.000	1	/C-5,O-5(0-0-5)	-0.2
Total	4	43	142	8	31	3	1	0	15	14		.218	.297	.254	551	52	-9	6			.985	2	/C-25,O-17(0-0-17)	-0.5

■ **JIM STEELS** Steels, James Earl b: 5/30/61, Jackson, Miss. BL/TL, 5′10″, 185 lbs. Deb: 4/6/87 Career OF: (26-LF 7-CF 15-RF)

YEAR	TM/L	G	AB	R	H	2B	3B	HR	RBI	BB	SO	AVG	OBP	SLG	OPS	OPS+	BR+	SB	CS	SBR	FA	FR	G/POS	TPR
1987	SD-N	62	68	9	13	1	1	0	6	11	14	.191	.304	.235	539	47	-5	3	2	-0	.960	-6	O-28(17-6-7)	-1.2
1988	Tex-A	36	53	4	10	1	0	0	5	0	15	.189	.189	.208	396	11	-6	2	0	0	1.000	-5	O-17(9-1-7)/1-7,D-7	-1.1
1989	SF-N	13	12	0	1	0	0	0	0	2	4	.083	.214	.083	298	-12	-2	0	0	0	1.000	0	/1-3,O-1(0-0-1)	-0.2
Total	3	111	133	13	24	2	1	0	11	13	33	.180	.253	.211	464	28	-13	5	2	0	.973	-11	/O-46L,1-10,D-7	-2.5

■ **GENE STEERE** Steere, Frederick Eugene b: 8/16/1872, S.Scituate, R.I. d: 3/13/42, San Francisco, Cal Deb: 8/29/1894

YEAR	TM/L	G	AB	R	H	2B	3B	HR	RBI	BB	SO	AVG	OBP	SLG	OPS	OPS+	BR+	SB	CS	SBR	FA	FR	G/POS	TPR
1894	Pit-N	10	39	3	8	0	0	0	4	2	1	.205	.244	.205	449	9	-6	2			.896	-2	S-10	-0.6

■ **JOHN STEFERO** Stefero, John Robert b: 9/22/59, Sumter, S.C. BL/TR, 5′8″, 185 lbs. Deb: 6/24/83

YEAR	TM/L	G	AB	R	H	2B	3B	HR	RBI	BB	SO	AVG	OBP	SLG	OPS	OPS+	BR+	SB	CS	SBR	FA	FR	G/POS	TPR
1983	Bal-A	9	11	2	5	1	0	0	4	3	2	.455	.571	.545	1117	213	2	0	0	0	.920	0	/C-9	0.2
1986	Bal-A	52	120	14	28	2	0	2	13	16	25	.233	.324	.300	624	72	-4	0	1	-0	.984	-2	C-50/2-1	-0.5
1987	Mon-N	18	56	4	11	0	0	1	3	3	17	.196	.237	.250	487	28	-6	0	0	0	.981	-0	C-17	-0.5
Total	3	79	187	20	44	3	0	3	20	22	44	.235	.316	.299	615	67	-8	0	1	-0	.979	-2	/C-76,2-1	-0.8

■ **DAVE STEGMAN** Stegman, David William b: 1/30/54, Inglewood, Cal. BR/TR, 5′11″, 190 lbs. Deb: 9/4/78

YEAR	TM/L	G	AB	R	H	2B	3B	HR	RBI	BB	SO	AVG	OBP	SLG	OPS	OPS+	BR+	SB	CS	SBR	FA	FR	G/POS	TPR
1978	Det-A	8	14	3	4	2	0	1	3	1	2	.286	.333	.643	976	164	1	0	0	0	1.000	-2	/O-7(0-5-3)	-0.1
1979	Det-A	12	31	6	6	0	0	3	5	2	3	.194	.242	.484	726	88	-1	1	1	-0	1.000	1	O-12(0-11-1)	0.0
1980	Det-A	65	130	12	23	5	0	2	9	14	23	.177	.257	.262	518	41	-10	1	1	-0	.988	-13	O-57(14-27-23)/D-2	-2.6
1982	NY-A	2	0	0	0	0	0	0	0	0	0	—	—	—	—	—	0	0	0	0	.000	0	/D-1	0.0
1983	Chi-A	30	53	5	9	2	0	0	4	10	9	.170	.302	.208	509	42	-4	0	1	-0	1.000	-7	O-29(5-19-5)	-1.2
1984	Chi-A	55	92	13	24	1	2	2	11	4	18	.261	.306	.380	687	85	-2	3	0	1	.985	-9	O-46(11-27-8)/D-3	-1.1
Total	6	172	320	39	66	10	2	8	32	31	55	.206	.280	.325	605	64	-16	5	3	0	.991	-31	O-151(30-89-40)/D-6	-5.0

■ **JUSTIN STEIN** Stein, Justin Marion “Ott” b: 8/9/11, St.Louis, Mo. d: 5/1/92, Creve Coeur, Mo. BR/TR, 5′11″, 180 lbs. Deb: 5/28/38

YEAR	TM/L	G	AB	R	H	2B	3B	HR	RBI	BB	SO	AVG	OBP	SLG	OPS	OPS+	BR+	SB	CS	SBR	FA	FR	G/POS	TPR
1938	Phi-N	11	39	6	10	0	1	0	2	2	4	.256	.293	.308	600	67	-2	0			.880	0	/3-7,2-3	-0.1
	Cin-N	11	18	3	6	1	0	0	1	0	1	.333	.333	.389	722	101	-0	0			.857	1	/S-7,2-2	0.1
	Yr	22	57	9	16	1	1	0	3	2	5	.281	.305	.333	638	78	-2	0			.857	1	/3-7,S-7,2-5	0.0

■ **BILL STEIN** Stein, William Allen b: 1/21/47, Battle Creek, Mich. BR/TR, 5′10″, 170 lbs. Deb: 9/6/72 Career OF: (15-LF 0-CF 14-RF)

YEAR	TM/L	G	AB	R	H	2B	3B	HR	RBI	BB	SO	AVG	OBP	SLG	OPS	OPS+	BR+	SB	CS	SBR	FA	FR	G/POS	TPR
1972	StL-N	14	35	2	11	0	1	2	3	0	7	.314	.314	.543	857	141	2	1	0	0	1.000	-3	/3-4,O-4(4-0-1)	-0.2
1973	StL-N	32	55	4	12	2	0	0	2	7	18	.218	.306	.255	561	57	-3	0	0	0	1.000	-2	O-10(2-0-8)/1-2,3-1	-0.6
1974	Chi-A	13	43	5	12	1	0	0	5	7	8	.279	.380	.302	682	96	0	0	0	0	.871	-2	3-11/D-2	-0.2
1975	Chi-A	76	226	23	61	7	1	3	21	18	32	.270	.327	.350	676	90	-3	2	2	-0	.974	3	2-28,3-24,D-18,/O-1L	0.1
1976	Chi-A	117	392	32	105	15	2	4	36	22	67	.268	.310	.347	657	92	-5	4	2	0	.960	-11	2-58,3-58/1-1,SOD	-1.3
1977	Sea-A	151	556	53	144	26	5	13	67	29	79	.259	.302	.394	696	89	-10	3	4	-1	.964	-11	*3-147/S-2,D-3	-2.4
1978	Sea-A	114	403	41	105	24	4	4	37	37	56	.261	.323	.370	692	95	-3	1	0	0	.929	-6	*3-111/D-1	-1.1
1979	Sea-A	88	250	28	62	9	2	7	27	17	28	.248	.301	.384	685	82	-7	1	2	-0	.959	11	3-67,2-17/S-3	0.3
1980	Sea-A	67	198	16	53	5	1	5	27	16	25	.268	.326	.379	704	92	-2	1	1	-0	.972	5	3-34,2-14/1-8,D-5	0.3
1981	Tex-A	53	115	21	38	6	0	2	22	7	15	.330	.369	.435	804	138	5	1	2	-0	1.000	1	1-20/O-8L,3-7,2S	0.5
1982	Tex-A	85	184	14	44	8	0	1	16	12	23	.239	.293	.299	592	66	-8	0	0	0	.957	3	2-34,3-28/S-6,1OD	-0.4
1983	Tex-A	78	232	21	72	15	1	2	33	8	31	.310	.333	.409	743	105	1	2	3	-1	.975	0	2-32,1-23,3-10,/D-6	0.1
1984	Tex-A	27	43	3	12	1	0	0	3	5	9	.279	.354	.302	656	81	-1	0	0	0	.967	-3	2-11/1-3,3-3,D-4	-0.3
1985	Tex-A	44	79	5	20	3	1	1	12	1	15	.253	.272	.354	626	69	-3	0	0	0	.952	1	3-11/1-8,2-3,O-3R,D	-0.3
Total	14	959	2811	268	751	122	18	44	311	186	413	.267	.316	.370	686	91	-37	16	16	-2	.950	-13	3-516,2-200/1-67,DOS	-5.5

■ **TERRY STEINBACH** Steinbach, Terry Lee b: 3/2/62, New Ulm, Minn. BR/TR, 6′1″, 195 lbs. Deb: 9/12/86 Career OF: (7-LF 0-CF 8-RF)

YEAR	TM/L	G	AB	R	H	2B	3B	HR	RBI	BB	SO	AVG	OBP	SLG	OPS	OPS+	BR+	SB	CS	SBR	FA	FR	G/POS	TPR
1986	Oak-A	6	15	3	5	0	0	2	4	1	0	.333	.375	.733	1108	208	2	0	0	0	.962	-0	/C-5	0.2
1987	Oak-A	122	391	66	111	16	3	16	56	32	66	.284	.352	.463	815	122	12	1	2	-0	.986	-12	*C-107,3-10/1-1,D-8	0.4
1988	*Oak-A★	104	351	42	93	19	1	9	51	33	47	.265	.338	.402	740	110	5	3	0	1	.983	5	C-84/3-9,1-8,O-1L,D	1.5
1989	*Oak-A★	130	454	37	124	13	1	7	42	30	66	.273	.321	.352	673	93	-4	1	2	-0	.985	-7	*C-103,O-14R,1/3D	-0.7
1990	*Oak-A	114	379	32	95	15	2	9	57	19	66	.251	.294	.372	666	89	-7	0	1	-0	.988	-4	C-83,D-25/1-3	-0.7
1991	Oak-A	129	456	50	125	31	1	6	67	22	70	.274	.318	.386	703	99	-1	2	2	-0	.980	-24	*C-117/1-9,D-2	-1.9
1992	*Oak-A	128	438	48	122	20	1	12	53	45	58	.279	.347	.411	758	118	10	2	3	-1	.985	-4	*C-124/1-5,D-2	1.3
1993	Oak-A★	104	389	47	111	19	1	10	43	25	65	.285	.333	.416	750	107	3	3	3	-0	.989	-22	C-86,1-15/D-6	-1.5

YEAR	TM/L	G	AB	R	H	2B	3B	HR	RBI	BB	SO	AVG	OBP	SLG	OPS	OPS+	BR+	SB	CS	SBR	FA	FR	G/POS	TPR
1994	Oak-A	103	369	51	105	21	2	11	57	26	62	.285	.332	.442	773	106	3	2	1	0	**.998**	-2	C-93/1-6,D-6	0.5
1995	Oak-A	114	406	43	113	26	1	15	65	25	74	.278	.325	.458	783	107	3	1	3	-1	.993	-1	*C-111/1-2	0.7
1996	Oak-A	145	514	79	140	25	1	35	100	49	115	.272	.343	.529	872	118	12	0	1	-0	.991	-9	*C-137/1-1,D-4	1.0
1997	Min-A	122	447	60	111	27	1	12	54	35	106	.248	.304	.394	698	79	-14	6	1	1	.993	-10	*C-116/1-2,D-1	-1.5
1998	Min-A	124	422	45	102	25	2	14	54	38	89	.242	.310	.410	720	84	-11	0	1	-0	.990	-10	*C-119/D-3	-1.3
1999	Min-A	101	338	35	96	16	4	4	42	38	54	.284	.360	.391	750	88	-5	2	2	-0	.991	-11	C-96/D-1	-1.0
Total	14	1546	5369	638	1453	273	21	162	745	418	938	.271	.329	.420	749	102	7	23	22	-3	.989	-110	*C-1381/D-69,1-62,3O	-3.0
■ HANK STEINBACHER	Steinbacher, Henry John b: 3/22/13, Sacramento, Cal. d: 4/3/77, Sacramento, Cal. BL/TR, 5′11″, 180 lbs. Deb: 4/21/37																							
1937	Chi-A	26	73	13	19	4	1	1	9	4	7	.260	.299	.384	682	71	-4	2	0	0	.960	-2	O-15(15-0-0)	-0.6
1938	Chi-A	106	399	59	132	23	8	4	61	41	19	.331	.393	.459	852	110	7	1	3	-1	.963	-4	*O-101(0-8-93)	-0.4
1939	Chi-A	71	111	16	19	2	1	1	15	21	8	.171	.303	.234	537	38	-10	0	0	0	1.000	-2	O-22(1-0-21)	-1.2
Total	3	203	583	88	170	29	10	6	85	66	34	.292	.364	.407	770	92	-7	3	3	-0	.968	-8	O-138(16-8-114)	-2.2
■ GENE STEINBRENNER	Steinbrenner, Eugene Gass b: 11/17/1892, Pittsburgh, Pa. d: 4/25/70, Pittsburgh, Pa. BR/TR, 5′8.5″, 155 lbs. Deb: 4/25/12																							
1912	Phi-N	3	9	0	2	1	0	0	1	0	3	.222	.222	.333	556	48	-1	0			.900	-1	/2-3	-0.1
■ BILL STEINECKE	Steinecke, William Robert b: 2/7/07, Cincinnati, Ohio d: 7/20/86, St.Augustine, Fla BR/TR, 5′8.5″, 175 lbs. Deb: 9/16/31																							
1931	Pit-N	4	4	0	0	0	0	0	0	0	1	.000	.000	.000	0	-99	-1	0			.000	0	/C-1	-0.1
■ BEN STEINER	Steiner, Benjamin Saunders b: 7/28/21, Alexandria, Va. d: 10/27/88, Venice, Fla. BL/TR, 5′11″, 165 lbs. Deb: 4/17/45																							
1945	Bos-A	78	304	39	78	8	3	3	20	31	29	.257	.327	.332	660	89	-4	10	6	0	.967	-4	2-77	-0.4
1946	Bos-A	3	4	1	1	0	0	0	0	0	0	.250	.250	.250	500	38	-0	0	0	0	.750	0	/3-1	0.0
1947	Det-A	1	0	1	0	0	0	0	0	0	0	—	—	—	—		0	0	0	0	.000	0	R	0.0
Total	3	82	308	41	79	8	3	3	20	31	29	.256	.326	.331	658	89	-4	10	6	0	.967	-4	/2-77,3-1	-0.4
■ RED STEINER	Steiner, James Harry b: 1/7/15, Los Angeles, Cal. BL/TR, 6′, 185 lbs. Deb: 5/11/45																							
1945	Cle-A	12	20	0	3	0	0	0	2	1	4	.150	.190	.150	340	-1	-3	0	0	0	1.000	1	/C-4	-0.2
	Bos-A	26	59	6	12	1	0	0	4	14	2	.203	.356	.220	577	67	-2	0	0	0	.986	-5	C-24	-0.6
	Yr	38	79	6	15	1	0	0	6	15	6	.190	.319	.203	522	52	-4	0	0	0	.989	-4	C-28	-0.8
■ HARRY STEINFELDT	Steinfeldt, Harry M. b: 9/29/1877, St.Louis, Mo. d: 8/17/14, Bellevue, Ky. BR/TR, 5′9.5″, 180 lbs. Deb: 4/22/1898 Career OF: (15-LF 16-CF 4-RF)																							
1898	Cin-N	88	308	47	91	18	6	0	43	27		.295	.354	.393	747	107	2	9			.917	-1	2-31,O-29C,3-22,/S1	0.1
1899	Cin-N	108	390	63	96	16	8	0	43	40		.246	.326	.328	654	78	-12	19			.888	-3	3-60,2-40/S-8,O-2C	-1.1
1900	Cin-N	134	510	57	125	29	7	2	66	27		.245	.292	.341	633	76	-18	14			.922	**36**	3-67,2-64/O-2R,S-2	2.0
1901	Cin-N	105	382	40	95	18	7	6	47	28		.249	.303	.380	683	104	1	10			.886	10	3-55,2-50	1.3
1902	Cin-N	129	479	53	133	20	7	1	49	24		.278	.316	.355	671	98	-2	12			.912	22	*3-129/O-1(0-0-1)	2.4
1903	Cin-N	118	439	71	137	**32**	12	6	83	47		.312	.386	.481	867	132	17	6			.937	7	*3-104,S-14	2.6
1904	Cin-N	99	349	35	85	11	6	1	52	29		.244	.313	.318	631	87	-5	16			.887	-7	3-98	-1.0
1905	Cin-N	114	384	49	104	16	9	1	39	30		.271	.329	.367	696	97	-2	15			.919	14	*3-103/1-1,2-1,O-1L	1.5
1906	*Chi-N	151	539	81	**176**	27	10	3	**83**	47		.327	.395	.430	825	149	31	29			**.954**	-17	*3-150/2-1	1.9
1907	*Chi-N	152	542	52	144	25	5	1	70	37		.266	.323	.336	659	100	-0	19			**.967**	-5	*3-151	-0.1
1908	*Chi-N	150	539	63	130	20	6	1	62	36		.241	.294	.306	600	88	-8	12			.940	-12	*3-150	-1.8
1909	Chi-N	151	528	73	133	27	6	2	59	57		.252	.331	.337	668	105	3	22			.940	2	*3-151	1.0
1910	*Chi-N	129	448	70	113	21	1	2	58	36	29	.252	.323	.317	640	88	-7	10			**.946**	0	*3-128	-0.4
1911	Bos-N	19	63	5	16	4	0	1	8	6	3	.254	.338	.365	703	89	-1	1			.810	-5	3-19	-0.5
Total	14	1647	5900	759	1578	284	90	27	762	471	32	.267	.330	.360	690	101	-1	194			.926	42	*3-1387,2-187/OS1	7.9
■ BILL STELLBAUER	Stellbauer, William Jennings b: 3/20/1894, Bremond, Tex. d: 2/16/74, New Braunfels, Tex BR/TR, 5′10″, 175 lbs. Deb: 4/12/16																							
1916	Phi-A	25	48	2	13	2	1	0	5	6	7	.271	.352	.354	706	118	1	2			.857	-4	O-14(14-0-0)	-0.3
■ RICK STELMASZEK	Stelmaszek, Richard Francis b: 10/8/48, Chicago, Ill. BL/TR, 6′1″, 195 lbs. Deb: 6/25/71 C																							
1971	Was-A	6	9	0	0	0	0	0	0	0	3	.000	.000	.000	0	-99	-2	0	0	0	1.000	-1	/C-3	-0.3
1973	Tex-A	7	9	0	1	0	0	0	0	1	2	.111	.200	.111	311	-11	-1	0	0	0	1.000	-0	/C-7	-0.1
	Cal-A	22	26	2	4	1	0	0	3	6	7	.154	.313	.192	505	49	-2	0	0	0	1.000	-2	C-22	-0.3
	Yr	29	35	2	5	1	0	0	3	7	9	.143	.286	.171	457	34	-3	0	0	0	1.000	-2	C-29	-0.4
1974	Chi-N	25	44	2	10	2	0	1	7	10	6	.227	.370	.341	711	96	0	0	0	0	.983	-6	C-16	-0.5
Total	3	60	88	4	15	3	0	1	10	17	18	.170	.305	.239	543	55	-5	0	0	0	.993	-9	/C-48	-1.2
■ FRED STEM	Stem, Frederick Boothe b: 9/22/1885, Oxford, N.C. d: 9/5/64, Darlington, S.C. BL/TR, 6′2″, 160 lbs. Deb: 9/15/08																							
1908	Bos-N	20	72	9	20	0	1	0	3	2		.278	.297	.306	603	94	-1	1			.995	-1	1-19	-0.2
1909	Bos-N	73	245	13	51	2	3	0	11	12		.208	.254	.241	495	51	-14	5			.989	10	1-68	-0.6
Total	2	93	317	22	71	2	4	0	14	14		.224	.263	.256	519	60	-15	6			.990	10	/1-87	-0.8
■ CASEY STENGEL	Stengel, Charles Dillon "The Old Professor" b: 7/30/1890, Kansas City, Mo. d: 9/29/75, Glendale, Cal. BL/TL, 5′11″, 175 lbs. Deb: 9/17/12 MCH																							
1912	Bro-N	17	57	9	18	1	0	1	13	15	9	.316	.466	.386	852	140	5	5			.902	-2	O-17(0-17-0)	0.1
1913	Bro-N	124	438	60	119	16	8	7	43	56	58	.272	.356	.393	748	110	7	19			.960	2	*O-119(0-117-2)	0.0
1914	Bro-N	126	412	55	130	13	10	4	60	56	55	.316	**.404**	.425	829	143	24	19			.964	-8	*O-121(0-2-119)	1.0
1915	Bro-N	132	459	52	109	20	12	3	50	34	46	.237	.294	.353	647	94	-4	5	10	-2	.959	1	*O-129(1-0-128)	-1.4
1916	*Bro-N	127	462	66	129	27	8	8	53	33	51	.279	.329	.424	753	127	13	11			.965	3	*O-121(0-0-121)	1.1
1917	Bro-N	150	549	69	141	23	12	6	73	60	62	.257	.336	.375	711	115	10	18			.969	13	*O-150(0-1-149)	1.7
1918	Pit-N	39	122	18	30	4	1	1	12	16	14	.246	.343	.320	663	99	1	11			.973	2	O-37(0-0-37)	0.1
1919	Pit-N	89	321	38	94	10	10	4	43	35	35	.293	.364	.424	788	131	13	12			.957	3	O-87(0-0-87)	1.2
1920	Phi-N	129	445	53	130	25	6	9	50	38	35	.292	.356	.436	792	121	12	7	13	-3	.954	-3	*O-118(1-5-113)	0.0
1921	Phi-N	24	59	7	18	3	1	0	4	6	7	.305	.369	.390	759	94	-0	1	1	-0	.969	2	O-15(0-0-15)	0.1
	NY-N	18	22	4	5	1	0	0	2	1	5	.227	.261	.273	534	41	-2	0	1	-0	.875	-3	/O-8(0-2-6)	-0.5
	Yr	42	81	11	23	4	1	0	6	7	12	.284	.341	.358	699	81	-2	1	2	-0	.950	-0	O-23(0-2-21)	-0.4
1922	*NY-N	84	250	48	92	8	10	7	48	21	17	.368	.436	.564	1000	155	21	4	2	0	.969	-4	O-77(0-75-2)	1.3
1923	*NY-N	75	218	39	74	11	5	5	43	20	18	.339	.400	.505	905	139	12	6	2	1	.983	-7	O-57(6-51-0)	0.4
1924	Bos-N	131	461	57	129	20	6	5	39	45	39	.280	.348	.382	730	100	0	13	13	-2	.978	-7	*O-126(0-5-121)	-1.8
1925	Bos-N	12	13	0	1	0	0	0	2	1	2	.077	.143	.077	220	-46	-3	0	1	-0	1.000	-0	/O-1(0-0-1)	-0.3
Total	14	1277	4288	575	1219	182	89	60	535	437	453	.284	.356	.410	766	119	108	131	43		.964	-8	*O-1183(8-275-901)	3.0
■ MIKE STENHOUSE	Stenhouse, Michael Steven b: 5/29/58, Pueblo, Colo. BL/TR, 6′1″, 195 lbs. Deb: 10/3/82 F Career OF: (43-LF 0-CF 37-RF)																							
1982	Mon-N	1	1	0	0	0	0	0	0	0	1	.000	.000	.000	0	-98	-0	0	0	0	.000	0	/H	0.0
1983	Mon-N	24	40	2	5	1	0	0	2	4	10	.125	.205	.150	355	-0	-5	0	0	0	1.000	-3	/O-9(3-0-7),1-5	-0.9
1984	Mon-N	80	175	14	32	8	0	4	16	26	32	.183	.292	.297	589	69	-7	0	0	0	.986	-3	O-48(30-0-19),1-14	-1.3
1985	Min-A	81	179	23	40	5	0	5	21	29	18	.223	.332	.335	667	79	-5	1	0	0	.929	0	D-27,O-16(8-0-9)/1-8	-0.6
1986	Bos-A	21	21	1	2	1	0	0	1	12	5	.095	.424	.143	567	63	-0	0	0	0	1.000	-0	/O-4(2-0-2),1-3	-0.1
Total	5	207	416	40	79	15	0	9	40	71	66	.190	.309	.291	600	67	-18	1	0	0	.973	-5	/O-77L,1-30,D-27	-2.9
■ RENNIE STENNETT	Stennett, Renaldo Antonio (Porte) b: 4/5/51, Colon, Panama BR/TR, 5′11″, 175 lbs. Deb: 7/10/71 Career OF: (34-LF 5-CF 14-RF)																							
1971	Pit-N	50	153	24	54	5	4	1	15	7	9	.353	.381	.458	839	137	7	1	1	-0	.954	2	2-36	1.2
1972	*Pit-N	109	370	43	106	14	5	3	30	9	43	.286	.307	.376	683	95	-4	4	3	-0	.977	6	2-49,O-41L/S-6	0.4
1973	Pit-N	128	466	45	113	18	3	10	55	16	63	.242	.268	.358	626	74	-18	2	3	-1	.981	-0	2-84,S-43/O-5(3-0-2)	-0.9
1974	*Pit-N	157	673	84	196	29	3	7	56	32	51	.291	.325	.374	700	99	-3	8	9	-1	.980	13	*2-154/O-2(0-0-2)	1.9
1975	*Pit-N	148	616	89	176	25	7	7	62	33	42	.286	.326	.383	709	97	-4	5	4	-0	.979	13	*2-144	1.9
1976	Pit-N	157	654	59	168	31	9	2	60	19	32	.257	.279	.341	620	75	-23	18	6	2	.981	17	*2-157/S-4	0.7
1977	Pit-N	116	453	53	152	20	4	5	51	29	24	.336	.378	.430	809	113	9	28	18	-0	.982	-7	*2-113	0.8
1978	Pit-N	106	333	30	81	9	2	3	35	13	22	.243	.276	.309	585	60	-18	2	1	0	.971	-12	2-80/3-6	-2.7
1979	*Pit-N	108	319	31	76	13	2	0	24	24	25	.238	.292	.292	583	57	-19	1	4	-1	.974	6	*2-102	-0.9

YEAR	TM/L	G	AB	R	H	2B	3B	HR	RBI	BB	SO	AVG	OBP	SLG	OPS	OPS+	BR+	SB	CS	SBR	FA	FR	G/POS	TPR
1980	SF-N	120	397	34	97	13	2	2	37	22	31	.244	.287	.302	590	66	-18	4	4	-1	.973	-13	*2-111	-2.8
1981	SF-N	38	87	8	20	0	0	1	7	3	6	.230	.264	.264	528	51	-6	2	1	0	1.000	-2	2-19	-0.7
Total	11	1237	4521	500	1239	177	41	41	432	207	348	.274	.308	.359	667	85	-96	75	54	-2	.978	23	*2-1049/S-53,O-48L,3	-1.1

■ JAKE STENZEL

Stenzel, Jacob Charles (b: Jacob Charles Stelzle)
b: 6/24/1867, Cincinnati, Ohio d: 1/6/19, Cincinnati, Ohio BR/TR, 5'10", 168 lbs. Deb: 6/16/1890 Career OF: (18-LF 692-CF 33-RF)

YEAR	TM/L	G	AB	R	H	2B	3B	HR	RBI	BB	SO	AVG	OBP	SLG	OPS	OPS+	BR+	SB	CS	SBR	FA	FR	G/POS	TPR
1890	Chi-N	11	41	3	11	1	0	0	3	1	0	.268	.286	.293	578	66	-2	0			.857	-4	/O-6(0-0-6),C-6	-0.4
1892	Pit-N	3	9	0	0	0	0	0	0	1	3	.000	.100	.000	100	-69	-2	1			1.000	0	/O-2(1-1-0),C-1	-0.1
1893	Pit-N	60	224	57	81	13	4	4	37	24	17	.362	.423	.509	932	150	16	16			.905	-9	O-45R,C-12/S-1,2-1	0.4
1894	Pit-N	132	525	150	185	39	20	13	121	76	13	.352	.440	.577	1017	145	39	61			.926	-1	*O-132(5-127-0)	2.2
1895	Pit-N	130	518	114	192	38	13	7	97	57	25	.371	.444	.535	978	160	49	53			.909	-6	*O-130(0-130-0)	2.8
1896	Pit-N	114	479	104	173	26	14	2	82	32	13	.361	.410	.486	897	141	29	57			.922	-3	*O-114(0-114-0)/1-1	1.5
1897	*Bal-N	131	536	113	189	**43**	7	4	116	36		.353	.404	.481	885	133	25	69			.932	-11	*O-131(0-131-0)	0.5
1898	Bal-N	35	138	33	35	5	2	0	22	12		.254	.340	.319	659	87	-2	4			.926	-2	O-35(0-35-0)	-0.6
	StL-N	108	404	64	114	15	11	1	33	41		.282	.367	.381	748	112	7	21			.943	0	*O-108(0-108-0)	0.0
	Yr	143	542	97	149	20	13	1	55	53		.275	.360	.365	725	106	5	25			.940	-2	*O-143(0-143-0)	-0.6
1899	StL-N	35	128	21	35	9	0	1	19	16		.273	.367	.367	735	99	0	8			.949	-1	O-33(8-21-4)	-0.3
	Cin-N	9	29	5	9	1	0	0	3	4		.310	.412	.345	757	106	1	2			1.000	-1	/O-7(0-7-0)	-0.1
	Yr	44	157	26	44	10	0	1	22	20		.280	.376	.363	739	101	1	10			.957	-2	O-40(8-28-4)	-0.4
Total	9	768	3031	664	1024	190	71	32	533	300	71	.338	.408	.479	887	135	159	292			.927	-37	O-743C/C-19,1-1,2S	5.9

■ RAY STEPHENS

Stephens, Carl Ray b: 9/22/62, Houston, Tex. BR/TR, 6', 190 lbs. Deb: 9/20/90

YEAR	TM/L	G	AB	R	H	2B	3B	HR	RBI	BB	SO	AVG	OBP	SLG	OPS	OPS+	BR+	SB	CS	SBR	FA	FR	G/POS	TPR
1990	StL-N	5	15	2	2	1	0	1	1	0	3	.133	.133	.400	533	41	-1	0	0	0	1.000	2	/C-5	0.1
1991	StL-N	6	7	0	2	0	0	0	0	1	3	.286	.375	.286	661	88	-0	0	0	0	1.000	0	/C-6	0.1
1992	Tex-A	8	13	0	2	0	0	0	0	0	5	.154	.154	.154	308	-14	-2	0	0	0	1.000	-0	/C-6,D-1	-0.2
Total	3	19	35	2	6	1	0	1	1	1	11	.171	.194	.286	480	32	-3	0	0	0	1.000	3	/C-17,D-1	0.0

■ GENE STEPHENS

Stephens, Glen Eugene b: 1/20/33, Gravette, Ark. BL/TR, 6'3.5", 175 lbs. Deb: 4/16/52

YEAR	TM/L	G	AB	R	H	2B	3B	HR	RBI	BB	SO	AVG	OBP	SLG	OPS	OPS+	BR+	SB	CS	SBR	FA	FR	G/POS	TPR
1952	Bos-A	21	53	10	12	5	0	0	5	3	8	.226	.268	.321	589	59	-3	4	2	0	.962	0	O-13(2-0-11)	-0.3
1953	Bos-A	78	221	30	45	6	2	3	18	29	56	.204	.302	.290	591	57	-13	3	3	-0	.966	-7	O-72(71-0-3)	-2.4
1955	Bos-A	109	157	25	46	9	4	3	18	20	34	.293	.380	.459	838	114	3	0	0	0	.947	-11	O-75(71-4-0)	-1.0
1956	Bos-A	104	63	22	17	2	0	1	7	12	12	.270	.387	.349	736	85	-1	1	1	-0	.983	-17	O-71(69-2-2)	-1.8
1957	Bos-A	120	173	25	46	6	4	3	26	26	20	.266	.362	.399	761	102	1	0	2	-1	.987	-19	O-90(75-6-11)	-2.1
1958	Bos-A	134	270	38	59	10	1	9	25	22	46	.219	.280	.363	643	71	-11	1	2	-0	.975	-16	*O-110(92-26-3)	-3.2
1959	Bos-A	92	270	34	75	13	1	3	39	29	33	.278	.356	.367	723	95	-1	5	2	0	.981	1	O-85(62-17-7)	-0.4
1960	Bos-A	35	109	9	25	4	0	2	11	14	22	.229	.317	.321	638	71	-4	5	1	1	.951	-1	O-31(21-4-8)	-0.6
	Bal-A	84	193	38	46	11	0	5	11	25	25	.238	.329	.373	702	91	-2	4	2	0	.992	-10	O-77(36-19-42)	-1.5
	Yr	119	302	47	71	15	0	7	22	39	47	.235	.325	.354	679	83	-7	9	3	1	.979	-11	*O-108(57-23-50)	-2.1
1961	Bal-A	32	58	4	11	2	0	0	2	14	7	.190	.347	.224	571	58	-3	1	1	-0	1.000	-6	O-30(27-5-5)	-1.0
	KC-A	62	183	22	38	6	1	4	26	16	27	.208	.279	.317	596	58	-11	3	2	-0	.968	1	O-54(6-28-25)	-1.2
	Yr	94	241	26	49	8	1	4	28	30	34	.203	.297	.295	591	59	-14	4	3	-0	.975	-5	O-84(33-33-30)	-2.2
1962	KC-A	5	4	0	0	0	0	0	0	1	1	.000	.200	.000	200	-39	-1	0	0	0	.000	0	H	-0.1
1963	Chi-A	6	18	5	7	0	0	1	2	1	3	.389	.421	.556	977	174	2	0	0	0	.909	1	/O-5(2-0-3)	0.3
1964	Chi-A	82	141	21	33	4	2	3	17	21	28	.234	.341	.355	696	97	-0	1	2	-0	.969	-5	O-59(32-25-6)	-0.8
Total	12	964	1913	283	460	78	15	37	207	233	322	.240	.327	.355	682	82	-45	27	20	-1	.973	-87	O-772(566-136-126)	-16.1

■ JIM STEPHENS

Stephens, James Walter "Little Nemo" b: 12/10/1883, Salineville, Ohio d: 1/2/65, Oxford, Ala. BR/TR, 5'6.5", 157 lbs. Deb: 4/11/07

YEAR	TM/L	G	AB	R	H	2B	3B	HR	RBI	BB	SO	AVG	OBP	SLG	OPS	OPS+	BR+	SB	CS	SBR	FA	FR	G/POS	TPR
1907	StL-A	58	173	15	35	6	3	0	11	15		.202	.270	.272	542	73	-5	3			.967	-4	C-56	-0.4
1908	StL-A	47	150	14	30	4	1	0	6	9		.200	.255	.240	495	61	-6	0			.960	-0	C-45	-0.2
1909	StL-A	79	223	18	49	5	0	3	18	13		.220	.278	.283	561	83	-5	5			.980	3	C-72	0.6
1910	StL-A	99	289	24	62	3	7	0	23	16		.215	.261	.273	534	72	-10	2			.971	2	C-96	0.1
1911	StL-A	70	212	11	49	5	5	0	17	17		.231	.300	.302	602	71	-8	1			.949	-2	C-66	-0.5
1912	StL-A	75	205	13	51	7	5	0	22	7		.249	.274	.332	605	76	-7	3			.954	4	C-66	0.2
Total	6	428	1252	95	276	30	21	3	97	77		.220	.273	.285	558	73	-42	14			.965	3	C-401	-0.2

■ VERN STEPHENS

Stephens, Vernon Decatur "Junior" or "Buster"
b: 10/23/20, McAlister, N.Mex. d: 11/3/68, Long Beach, Cal. BR/TR, 5'10", 185 lbs. Deb: 9/13/41 Career OF: (9-LF 0-CF 3-RF)

YEAR	TM/L	G	AB	R	H	2B	3B	HR	RBI	BB	SO	AVG	OBP	SLG	OPS	OPS+	BR+	SB	CS	SBR	FA	FR	G/POS	TPR
1941	StL-A	3	2	0	1	0	0	0	0	0	0	.500	.500	.500	1000	160	0	0	0	0	.500	-0	/S-1	0.0
1942	StL-A	145	575	84	169	26	6	14	92	41	53	.294	.341	.433	774	115	9	1	3	-1	.944	-10	*S-144	1.0
1943	StL-A★	137	512	75	148	27	3	22	91	54	73	.289	.357	.482	839	142	25	3	2	-0	.943	-25	*S-123,O-11(9-0-3)	0.9
1944	*StL-A★	145	559	91	164	32	1	20	**109**	62	54	.293	.365	.462	826	128	20	2	2	-0	.954	-4	*S-143	2.8
1945	StL-A†	149	571	90	165	27	3	**24**	89	55	70	.289	.352	.473	825	132	21	2	1	0	**.961**	-17	*S-144/3-4	1.7
1946	StL-A★	115	450	67	138	19	4	14	64	35	49	.307	.357	.460	817	121	12	0	1	-0	.950	0	*S-112	1.9
1947	StL-A	150	562	74	157	18	4	15	83	70	61	.279	.359	.406	765	110	8	8	4	0	.970	12	*S-149	3.0
1948	Bos-A★	155	635	114	171	25	8	29	137	77	56	.269	.350	.471	821	112	8	1	0	0	.971	10	*S-155	2.7
1949	Bos-A★	155	610	113	177	31	2	39	**159**	101	73	.290	.391	.539	930	135	29	2	2	-0	.966	4	*S-155	4.0
1950	Bos-A☆	149	628	125	185	34	6	30	**144**	65	43	.295	.361	.511	872	110	7	1	0	0	.981	-0	*S-146	1.5
1951	Bos-A★	109	377	62	113	21	2	17	78	38	33	.300	.364	.501	865	120	10	1	2	-0	.978	14	3-89/S-2	2.2
1952	Bos-A	92	295	35	75	13	2	7	44	39	31	.254	.343	.383	726	95	-2	2	2	-0	.957	4	S-53,3-29	0.5
1953	Chi-A	44	129	14	24	6	0	1	14	13	18	.186	.261	.256	516	39	-11	2	0	0	.990	-3	3-38/S-3	-1.4
	StL-A	46	165	16	53	8	0	4	17	18	24	.321	.388	.442	830	121	5	0	0	0	.954	-2	3-46	0.3
	Yr	90	294	30	77	14	0	5	31	31	42	.262	.332	.361	693	85	-6	2	0	0	.968	-5	3-84/S-3	-1.1
1954	Bal-A	101	365	31	104	17	1	8	46	17	36	.285	.317	.403	719	104	-0	0	3	-1	.966	-6	3-96	-0.8
1955	Bal-A	3	6	0	1	0	0	0	0	0	0	.167	.286	.167	452	26	-1	0	0	0	1.000	-1	/3-2	-0.1
	Chi-A	22	56	10	14	3	0	3	7	7	11	.250	.333	.464	798	110	1	0	0	0	1.000	4	3-18	0.5
	Yr	25	62	10	15	3	0	3	7	7	11	.242	.329	.435	764	102	0	0	0	0	1.000	4	3-20	0.4
Total	15	1720	6497	1001	1859	307	42	247	1174	692	685	.286	.355	.460	816	118	139	25	22	-2	.960	-20	*S-1330,3-322/O-11L	20.7

■ RIGGS STEPHENSON

Stephenson, Jackson Riggs "Old Hoss" b: 1/5/1898, Akron, Ala.
d: 11/15/85, Tuscaloosa, Ala. BR/TR, 5'10", 185 lbs. Deb: 4/13/21 Career OF: (885-LF 0-CF 28-RF)

YEAR	TM/L	G	AB	R	H	2B	3B	HR	RBI	BB	SO	AVG	OBP	SLG	OPS	OPS+	BR+	SB	CS	SBR	FA	FR	G/POS	TPR
1921	Cle-A	65	206	45	68	17	2	2	34	23	15	.330	.408	.461	869	119	7	4	1	1	.942	-1	2-54/3-2	0.7
1922	Cle-A	86	233	47	79	24	5	2	32	27	18	.339	.421	.511	932	141	15	3	0	1	.952	-6	3-34,2-25/O-3(2-0-1)	1.1
1923	Cle-A	91	301	48	96	20	6	5	65	15	25	.319	.357	.475	832	118	6	5	5	-1	.970	11	2-66/O-3(0-0-3),3-2	1.8
1924	Cle-A	71	240	33	89	20	0	4	44	27	10	.371	.439	.504	943	141	15	1	2	-0	.961	-13	2-58/O-7(0-0-7)	0.3
1925	Cle-A	19	54	8	16	3	1	1	9	7	3	.296	.387	.444	832	110	1	1	1	-0	.946	1	O-16(0-0-16)	0.1
1926	Chi-N	82	281	40	95	18	3	3	44	31	16	.338	.404	.456	859	129	12	2			.950	-4	O-74(73-0-1)	0.3
1927	Chi-N	152	579	101	199	**46**	9	7	82	65	28	.344	.415	.491	906	142	36	8			.975	4	*O-146(146-0-0)/3-6	2.7
1928	Chi-N	137	512	75	166	36	9	8	90	68	29	.324	.407	.477	883	132	25	8			.982	0	*O-135(135-0-0)	1.5
1929	*Chi-N	136	495	91	179	36	6	17	110	67	21	.362	.445	.562	1006	147	39	10			.984	-0	*O-130(130-0-0)	2.5
1930	Chi-N	109	341	56	125	21	1	5	68	32	20	.367	.421	.478	899	116	10	2			.958	-5	O-80(80-0-0)	-0.1
1931	Chi-N	80	263	34	84	14	4	1	52	37	14	.319	.405	.414	820	119	9	1			.985	-2	O-66(66-0-0)	0.3
1932	*Chi-N	147	583	86	189	49	4	4	85	54	27	.324	.383	.443	826	123	20	3			.984	-5	*O-147(147-0-0)	0.6
1933	Chi-N	97	346	45	114	17	4	4	51	34	16	.329	.397	.436	834	138	18	5			.985	-2	O-91(91-0-0)	1.2
1934	Chi-N	38	74	5	16	0	0	0	7	7	5	.216	.293	.216	509	39	-6	0			1.000	1	O-15(15-0-0)	-0.6
Total	14	1310	4508	714	1515	321	54	63	773	494	247	.336	.407	.473	880	130	207	53	9		.978	-21	O-913L,2-203/3-44	12.4

■ JOHN STEPHENSON

Stephenson, John Herman b: 4/13/41, S.Portsmouth, Ky. BL/TR, 5'11", 180 lbs. Deb: 4/14/64 Career OF: (7-LF 3-CF 2-RF)

YEAR	TM/L	G	AB	R	H	2B	3B	HR	RBI	BB	SO	AVG	OBP	SLG	OPS	OPS+	BR+	SB	CS	SBR	FA	FR	G/POS	TPR
1964	NY-N	37	57	2	9	0	0	1	2	4	18	.158	.226	.211	436	24	-6	0	0	0	.800	-4	3-14/O-8(5-3-0)	-1.1
1965	NY-N	62	121	9	26	5	0	4	15	8	19	.215	.264	.355	619	75	-4	0	1	-0	.981	-9	C-47/O-2(0-0-2)	-1.3
1966	NY-N	63	143	17	28	1	1	1	11	8	28	.196	.248	.238	486	37	-12	0	0	0	.973	-1	C-52/O-1(1-0-0)	-1.2
1967	Chi-N	18	49	3	11	3	1	0	5	1	6	.224	.255	.327	581	62	-2	0	0	0	1.000	1	C-13	-0.1

YEAR	TM/L	G	AB	R	H	2B	3B	HR	RBI	BB	SO	AVG	OBP	SLG	OPS	OPS+	BR+	SB	CS	SBR	FA	FR	G/POS	TPR
1968	Chi-N	2	2	0	0	0	0	0	0	0	0	.000	.000	.000	0	-94	-0	0	0	0	.000	0	H	-0.1
1969	SF-N	22	27	2	6	2	0	0	3	0	4	.222	.222	.296	519	45	-2	0	0	0	.941	-3	/C-9,3-1	-0.5
1970	SF-N	23	43	3	3	1	0	0	6	2	7	.070	.111	.093	204	-45	-9	0	0	0	1.000	2	/C-9,O-1(1-0-0)	-0.6
1971	Cal-A	98	279	24	61	17	0	3	25	22	21	.219	.283	.312	595	74	-10	0	0	0	.992	-9	C-88	-1.6
1972	Cal-A	66	146	14	40	3	1	2	17	11	8	.274	.342	.349	691	112	2	0	0	0	.993	-7	C-56	-0.3
1973	Cal-A	60	122	9	30	5	0	1	9	7	7	.246	.292	.311	604	76	-4	0	0	0	.980	-8	C-56	-1.1
Total	10	451	989	83	214	37	3	12	93	63	118	.216	.272	.296	568	64	-48	0	1	-0	.986	-38	C-330/3-15,O-12L	-7.9
■ JOE STEPHENSON	Stephenson, Joseph Chester b: 6/30/21, Detroit, Mich. BR/TR, 6'2", 185 lbs. Deb: 9/19/43 F																							
1943	NY-N	9	24	4	6	1	0	0	1	0	5	.250	.250	.292	542	56	-1	0			.973	2	/C-6	0.1
1944	Chi-N	4	8	1	1	0	0	0	0	1	3	.125	.222	.125	347	-1	-1	1			1.000	1	/C-3	0.0
1947	Chi-A	16	35	3	5	0	0	0	3	1	7	.143	.211	.143	353	-1	-5	0	0	0	.959	0	C-13	-0.4
Total	3	29	67	8	12	1	0	0	4	2	15	.179	.225	.194	419	19	-7	1	0		.970	3	/C-22	-0.3
■ PHIL STEPHENSON	Stephenson, Phillip Raymond b: 9/19/60, Guthrie, Okla. BL/TL, 6'1", 195 lbs. Deb: 4/5/89																							
1989	Chi-N	17	21	0	3	0	0	0	0	2	3	.143	.217	.143	360	5	-3	1	0	0	1.000	-1	/O-3(3-0-0)	-0.3
	SD-N	10	17	4	6	0	0	2	2	3	2	.353	.450	.706	1156	225	3	0	0	0	.977	0	/1-8	0.3
	Yr	27	38	4	9	0	0	2	2	5	5	.237	.326	.395	720	100	0	1	0	0	.977	-0	/1-8,O-3(3-0-0)	0.0
1990	SD-N	103	182	26	38	9	1	4	19	30	43	.209	.321	.335	656	80	-5	2	1	0	.997	3	1-60	-0.5
1991	SD-N	11	7	0	2	0	0	0	0	2	3	.286	.444	.286	730	106	0	0	0	0	.000	0	/H	0.0
1992	SD-N	53	71	5	11	2	1	0	8	10	11	.155	.259	.211	471	34	-6	0	0	0	1.000	-3	O-15(10-0-6)/1-7	-1.0
Total	4	194	298	35	60	11	2	6	29	47	62	.201	.310	.312	622	73	-10	3	1	0	.993	-1	/1-75,O-18(13-0-6)	-1.5
■ DUMMY STEPHENSON	Stephenson, Reuben Crandol b: 9/22/1869, Petersburg, N.J. d: 12/1/24, Trenton, N.J. BR/TR, 5'11.5", 180 lbs. Deb: 9/9/1892																							
1892	Phi-N	8	37	4	10	3	0	0	5	0	2	.270	.289	.351	641	94	-0	0			.800	-2	/O-8(0-8-0)	-0.2
■ BOB STEPHENSON	Stephenson, Robert Lloyd b: 8/11/28, Blair, Okla. BR/TR, 6', 165 lbs. Deb: 4/14/55																							
1955	StL-N	67	111	19	27	3	0	0	6	5	18	.243	.276	.270	546	46	-9	2	1	0	.938	-1	S-48/2-7,3-1	-0.7
■ WALTER STEPHENSON	Stephenson, Walter McQueen "Tarzan" b: 3/27/11, Saluda, N.C. d: 7/4/93, Shreveport, La. BR/TR, 6', 180 lbs. Deb: 4/29/35																							
1935	*Chi-N	16	26	2	10	1	1	0	2	1	5	.385	.407	.500	907	142	1	0			1.000	2	/C-6	0.3
1936	Chi-N	6	12	0	1	0	0	0	1	0	5	.083	.083	.083	167	-54	-3	0			1.000	-0	/C-4	-0.3
1937	Phi-N	10	23	1	6	0	0	0	2	2	3	.261	.320	.261	581	55	-1	0			.967	0	/C-7	-0.1
Total	3	32	61	3	17	1	1	0	5	3	13	.279	.313	.328	640	70	-2	0			.984	2	/C-17	-0.1
■ DUTCH STERRETT	Sterrett, Charles Hurlbut b: 10/1/1889, Milroy, Pa. d: 12/9/65, Baltimore, Md. BR/TR, 5'11.5", 165 lbs. Deb: 6/20/12 Career OF: (0-LF 31-CF 6-RF)																							
1912	NY-A	66	230	30	61	4	7	1	32	11		.265	.310	.357	667	85	-5	8			.972	-7	O-37C,1-17,C-10,/2	-1.4
1913	NY-A	21	35	0	6	0	0	0	3	1	5	.171	.216	.171	388	14	-4	1			1.000	-1	/1-6,C-1	-0.5
Total	2	87	265	30	67	4	7	1	35	12	5	.253	.298	.332	630	77	-9	9			.986	-8	/O-37C,1-23,C-11,2	-1.9
■ CHUCK STEVENS	Stevens, Charles Augustus b: 7/10/18, Van Houten, N.Mex BB/TL, 6'1", 180 lbs. Deb: 9/16/41																							
1941	StL-A	4	13	2	2	0	0	0	2	0	1	.154	.154	.154	308	-18	-2	0	0	0	.966	-1	/1-4	-0.3
1946	StL-A	122	432	53	107	17	4	3	27	47	62	.248	.324	.326	651	78	-12	4	6	-1	**.995**	3	*1-120	-1.5
1948	StL-A	85	287	34	75	12	4	1	26	41	26	.261	.354	.341	695	83	-6	2	2	-0	.991	1	1-85	-0.8
Total	3	211	732	89	184	29	8	4	55	88	89	.251	.333	.329	663	79	-20	6	8	-1	.993	3	1-209	-2.6
■ LEE STEVENS	Stevens, De Wain Lee b: 7/10/67, Kansas City, Mo. BL/TL, 6'4", 219 lbs. Deb: 7/16/90 Career OF: (9-LF 0-CF 34-RF)																							
1990	Cal-A	67	248	28	53	10	0	7	32	22	75	.214	.278	.339	616	73	-9	1	1	-0	.994	-4	1-67	-1.8
1991	Cal-A	18	58	8	17	7	0	0	9	6	12	.293	.359	.414	773	113	1	1	2	-0	.989	-1	1-11/O-9(1-0-8)	-0.1
1992	Cal-A	106	312	25	69	19	0	7	37	29	64	.221	.289	.349	639	78	-10	1	4	-1	.995	-4	1-91/D-2	-2.2
1996	Tex-A	27	78	6	18	2	3	3	12	6	22	.231	.294	.449	743	80	-3	0	0	0	.994	0	1-18/O-5(5-0-0)	-0.4
1997	Tex-A	137	426	58	128	24	2	21	74	23	83	.300	.338	.514	852	112	6	1	3	-1	.994	-5	1-62,D-38,O-22R	-0.7
1998	*Tex-A	120	344	52	91	17	4	20	59	31	93	.265	.325	.512	837	109	3	0	2	-1	.996	-1	D-72,1-37/O-7(0-0-7)	-0.5
1999	*Tex-A	146	517	76	146	31	1	24	81	52	132	.282	.348	.485	833	105	3	2	3	-1	.994	-7	*1-133/D-8	-1.6
2000	Mon-N	123	449	60	119	27	2	22	75	48	105	.265	.339	.481	820	103	1	0	0	0	.991	2	*1-123	-0.8
Total	8	744	2432	313	641	137	12	104	379	217	586	.264	.325	.458	783	100	-7	6	15	-4	.993	-18	1-542,D-120/O-43R	-8.1
■ ED STEVENS	Stevens, Edward Lee "Big Ed" b: 1/12/25, Galveston, Tex. BL/TL, 6'1", 190 lbs. Deb: 8/9/45 C																							
1945	Bro-N	55	201	29	55	14	3	4	29	32	20	.274	.376	.433	809	125	7	0			.987	0	1-55	0.5
1946	Bro-N	103	310	34	75	13	7	10	60	27	44	.242	.303	.426	728	104	0	2			.986	-4	1-99	-0.7
1947	Bro-N	5	13	0	2	1	0	0	0	1	5	.154	.214	.231	445	18	-2	0			.971	1	/1-4	-0.1
1948	Pit-N	128	429	47	109	19	6	10	69	35	53	.254	.313	.396	710	89	-7	4			**.996**	5	*1-117	-0.6
1949	Pit-N	67	221	22	58	10	1	4	32	22	24	.262	.332	.371	703	86	-4	1			.995	10	1-58	0.4
1950	Pit-N	17	46	2	9	2	0	0	3	4	5	.196	.260	.239	499	31	-5	0			1.000	1	1-12	-0.4
Total	6	375	1220	134	308	59	17	28	193	121	151	.252	.322	.398	719	95	-10	7			.992	13	1-345	-0.9
■ R C STEVENS	Stevens, R C b: 7/22/34, Moultrie, Ga. BL/TR, 6'5", 219 lbs. Deb: 4/15/58																							
1958	Pit-N	59	90	16	24	3	1	7	18	5	25	.267	.320	.556	875	129	3	0	0	0	.991	3	1-52	0.5
1959	Pit-N	3	7	2	2	0	0	1	1	0	0	.286	.286	.714	1000	157	0	0	0	0	1.000	0	/1-1	0.1
1960	Pit-N	9	3	1	0	0	0	0	0	0	1	.000	.000	.000	0	-99	-1	0	0	0	1.000	1	/1-7	0.0
1961	Was-A	33	62	2	8	1	0	0	2	7	15	.129	.217	.145	363	-1	-9	1	0	0	1.000	4	1-25	-0.6
Total	4	104	162	21	34	4	1	8	21	12	41	.210	.273	.395	668	77	-6	1	0	0	.995	7	/1-85	0.0
■ ROBERT STEVENS	Stevens, Robert Deb: 5/4/1875																							
1875	Was-n	1	4	0	1	0	0	0	0	0	0	.250	.250	.250	500	77	-0	0	0	0	.000	-1	/O-1(0-0-1)	0.0
■ BOBBY STEVENS	Stevens, Robert Jordan b: 4/17/07, Chevy Chase, Md. BL/TR, 5'8", 149 lbs. Deb: 7/3/31																							
1931	Phi-N	12	35	3	12	0	0	0	4	2	2	.343	.410	.343	753	97	0	0			.870	-5	S-10	-0.5
■ TODD STEVERSON	Steverson, Todd Anthony b: 11/15/71, Los Angeles, Cal. BR/TR, 6'2", 195 lbs. Deb: 4/28/95																							
1995	Det-A	30	42	11	11	0	0	2	6	6	10	.262	.354	.405	759	97	-0	2	0	0	1.000	-6	O-27(17-1-10)/D-1	-0.6
1996	SD-N	1	1	0	0	0	0	0	0	0	1	.000	.000	.000	0	-99	-0	0	0	0	.000	0	/H	0.0
Total	2	31	43	11	11	0	0	2	6	6	11	.256	.347	.395	742	93	-0	2	0	0	1.000	-6	/O-27(17-1-10),D-1	-0.6
■ ANDY STEWART	Stewart, Andrew David b: 12/5/70, Oshawa, Ont., Canada BR/TR, 5'11", 205 lbs. Deb: 9/6/97																							
1997	KC-A	5	8	1	2	1	0	0	0	0	0	.250	.250	.375	625	59	-0	0	0	0	1.000	1	/C-4,D-1	0.0
■ ACE STEWART	Stewart, Asa b: 2/14/1869, Terre Haute, Ind. d: 4/17/12, Terre Haute, Ind. BR/TR, 5'10", 176 lbs. Deb: 4/18/1895																							
1895	Chi-N	97	365	52	88	8	10	8	76	39	40	.241	.314	.384	698	75	-16	14			.911	-8	*2-97	-1.6
■ TUFFY STEWART	Stewart, Charles Eugene b: 7/31/1883, Chicago, Ill. d: 11/18/34, Chicago, Ill. BL/TL, 5'10", 167 lbs. Deb: 8/8/13																							
1913	Chi-N	9	8	1	1	1	0	0	2	2	5	.125	.300	.250	550	58	-0	1			1.000	0	/O-1(0-0-1)	0.0
1914	Chi-N	2	1	0	0	0	0	0	0	0	0	.000	.000	.000	0	-99	-0	0			.000	0	H	0.0
Total	2	11	9	1	1	1	0	0	2	2	5	.111	.273	.222	495	43	-1	1			1.000	0	/O-1(0-0-1)	0.0
■ BUD STEWART	Stewart, Edward Perry b: 6/15/16, Sacramento, Cal. d: 6/21/2000, Palo Alto, Cal. BL/TR, 5'11", 170 lbs. Deb: 4/19/41 Career OF: (281-LF 58-CF 222-RF)																							
1941	Pit-N	73	172	27	46	7	0	0	10	12	17	.267	.315	.308	623	76	-5	3			.962	-2	O-41(15-4-24)	-0.9
1942	Pit-N	82	183	21	40	8	4	0	20	22	16	.219	.302	.306	608	76	-5	2			1.000	-4	O-34L,3-10/2-6	-1.1
1948	NY-A	6	5	1	1	1	0	0	0	0	0	.200	.200	.400	600	58	-0	0	0	0	.000	0	H	0.0
	Was-A	118	401	56	112	17	13	7	69	49	27	.279	.361	.439	800	115	8	8	9	-1	.975	-4	*O-114(10-37-72)	-0.1
	Yr	124	406	57	113	18	13	7	69	49	27	.278	.359	.438	797	115	7	8	9	-1	.975	-4	*O-114(10-37-72)	-0.1
1949	Was-A	118	388	58	110	23	4	8	43	49	33	.284	.368	.425	793	112	6	6	4	-0	.982	-7	*O-105(75-16-20)	-0.7
1950	Was-A	118	378	46	101	15	6	4	35	46	33	.267	.348	.370	719	88	-7	5	4	-0	.991	-3	*O-100(42-0-66)	-1.4

YEAR	TM/L	G	AB	R	H	2B	3B	HR	RBI	BB	SO	AVG	OBP	SLG	OPS	OPS+	BR+	SB	CS	SBR	FA	FR	G/POS	TPR
1951	Chi-A	95	217	40	60	13	5	6	40	29	9	.276	.367	.465	832	127	8	1	6	-2	.983	-7	O-63(52-1-14)	-0.4
1952	Chi-A	92	225	23	60	10	0	5	30	28	17	.267	.350	.378	728	102	1	3	0	1	.982	-4	O-60(57-0-3)	-0.7
1953	Chi-A	53	59	16	16	2	0	2	13	14	3	.271	.411	.407	818	118	2	1	0	0	1.000	-4	O-16(11-0-5)	-0.2
1954	Chi-A	18	13	0	1	0	0	0	0	3	2	.077	.250	.077	327	-7	-2	0	0	0	1.000	-0	/O-2(0-0-2)	-0.2
Total	9	773	2041	288	547	96	32	32	260	252	157	.268	.351	.393	744	102	5	29	23		.982	-35	O-535L/3-10,2-6	-5.7

■ GLEN STEWART

Stewart, Glen Weldon "Gabby" b: 9/29/12, Tullahoma, Tenn. d: 2/11/97, Memphis, Tenn. BR/TR, 6', 175 lbs. Deb: 6/26/40

YEAR	TM/L	G	AB	R	H	2B	3B	HR	RBI	BB	SO	AVG	OBP	SLG	OPS	OPS+	BR+	SB	CS	SBR	FA	FR	G/POS	TPR
1940	NY-N	15	29	1	4	1	0	0	0	1	2	.138	.167	.172	339	-6	-4	0			.875	1	/3-6,S-5	-0.3
1943	Phi-N	110	336	23	71	10	1	2	24	32	41	.211	.284	.265	549	61	-16	1			.947	-9	S-77,2-18/1-8,C-1	-2.1
1944	Phi-N	118	377	32	83	11	5	0	29	28	40	.220	.274	.276	550	57	-22	0			.963	5	3-83,S-32/2-1	-1.5
Total	3	243	742	56	158	22	6	2	53	61	83	.213	.275	.267	541	56	-42	1			.953	-4	S-114/3-89,2-19,1C	-3.9

■ JIMMY STEWART

Stewart, James Franklin b: 6/11/39, Opelika, Ala. BB/TR, 6', 165 lbs. Deb: 9/3/63 Career OF: (176-LF 43-CF 11-RF)

YEAR	TM/L	G	AB	R	H	2B	3B	HR	RBI	BB	SO	AVG	OBP	SLG	OPS	OPS+	BR+	SB	CS	SBR	FA	FR	G/POS	TPR
1963	Chi-N	13	37	1	11	2	0	0	1	1	7	.297	.316	.351	667	87	-1	1	1	-0	.973	1	/S-9,2-1	0.1
1964	Chi-N	132	415	59	105	17	0	3	33	49	61	.253	.335	.316	650	81	-9	10	8	-1	.981	-7	2-61,S-45/O-4C,3-1	-0.8
1965	Chi-N	116	282	26	63	9	4	0	19	30	53	.223	.303	.284	586	65	-12	13	3	2	.955	-11	O-55(47-8-0),S-48	-2.4
1966	Chi-N	57	90	4	16	4	1	0	4	7	12	.178	.253	.244	497	38	-7	1	1	-0	1.000	-1	O-15C/2-4,S-2,3-2	-1.0
1967	Chi-N	6	6	1	1	0	0	0	1	0	0	.167	.167	.167	333	-4	-1	0	0	0	.000	0	H	-0.1
	Chi-A	24	18	5	3	0	0	0	1	1	6	.167	.211	.167	377	13	-2	1	0	0	1.000	0	/O-6(6-0-0),2-5,S-2	-0.2
1969	Cin-N	119	221	26	56	3	4	4	24	19	33	.253	.313	.357	670	83	-5	4	2	0	.973	-9	O-66L,2-18/3-6,S-1	-1.6
1970	*Cin-N	101	105	15	28	3	1	1	8	8	13	.267	.325	.343	667	79	-3	5	3	0	1.000	-11	O-48L,2-18/3-9,C1	-1.4
1971	Cin-N	80	82	7	19	2	2	0	9	9	12	.232	.308	.305	613	76	-3	3	1	0	1.000	-10	O-19(11-6-3)/3-9,2-6	-1.3
1972	Hou-N	68	96	14	21	5	2	0	9	6	9	.219	.265	.313	577	65	-5	0	1	-0	1.000	-5	O-11L/1-9,2-8,3-2	-1.2
1973	Hou-N	61	68	6	13	0	0	0	3	9	12	.191	.295	.191	486	37	-5	0	0	0	1.000	0	/3-8,O-3(3-0-0),2-1	-0.6
Total	10	777	1420	164	336	45	14	8	112	139	218	.237	.308	.305	613	71	-53	38	20	1	.969	-53	O-227L,2-122,S/31C	-10.5

■ STUFFY STEWART

Stewart, John Franklin b: 1/31/1894, Jasper, Fla. d: 12/30/80, Lake City, Fla. BR/TR, 5'9.5", 160 lbs. Deb: 9/3/16

YEAR	TM/L	G	AB	R	H	2B	3B	HR	RBI	BB	SO	AVG	OBP	SLG	OPS	OPS+	BR+	SB	CS	SBR	FA	FR	G/POS	TPR
1916	StL-N	9	17	0	3	0	0	0	1	0	3	.176	.176	.176	353	9	-2	0			.833	-2	/2-8	-0.4
1917	StL-N	13	9	4	0	0	0	0	0	0	4	.000	.000	.000	0	-99	-2	0			1.000	-3	/O-7(2-3-2),2-2	-0.5
1922	Pit-N	3	13	3	2	0	0	0	0	0	1	.154	.154	.154	308	-20	-2	0	0	0	.875	-1	/2-3	-0.3
1923	Bro-N	4	11	3	4	1	0	1	1	1	1	.364	.417	.727	1144	202	2	0	0	0	.786	-1	/2-3	0.0
1925	Was-A	7	17	3	6	1	0	0	3	1	2	.353	.389	.412	801	105	0	1	0	0	.929	1	/3-5,2-1	0.1
1926	Was-A	62	63	27	17	6	1	0	9	6	6	.270	.333	.397	730	92	-1	8	4	0	.975	7	2-25/3-1	0.6
1927	Was-A	56	129	24	31	6	2	0	4	8	15	.240	.285	.318	603	57	-8	12	2	2	.939	1	2-37/3-2	-0.5
1929	Was-A	22	6	10	0	0	0	0	0	1	0	.000	.143	.000	143	-60	-1	0	1	-0	1.000	2	/2-3	0.0
Total	8	176	265	74	63	14	3	1	18	17	32	.238	.284	.325	608	61	-15	21	7		.932	4	/2-82,3-8,O-7(2-3-2)	-1.0

■ MARK STEWART

Stewart, Mark "Big Slick" b: 10/11/1889, Whitlock, Tenn. d: 1/17/32, Memphis, Tenn. BL/TR, 6'1", 180 lbs. Deb: 10/4/13

YEAR	TM/L	G	AB	R	H	2B	3B	HR	RBI	BB	SO	AVG	OBP	SLG	OPS	OPS+	BR+	SB	CS	SBR	FA	FR	G/POS	TPR
1913	Cin-N	1	1	0	0	0	0	0	0	0	0	.000	.000	.000	0	-99	-0	0			.000	0	/C-1	0.0

■ SHANNON STEWART

Stewart, Shannon Harold b: 2/25/74, Cincinnati, Ohio BR/TR, 6', 175 lbs. Deb: 9/2/95

YEAR	TM/L	G	AB	R	H	2B	3B	HR	RBI	BB	SO	AVG	OBP	SLG	OPS	OPS+	BR+	SB	CS	SBR	FA	FR	G/POS	TPR
1995	Tor-A	12	38	2	8	0	0	0	1	5	5	.211	.318	.211	529	41	-3	2	0	0	.955	-1	O-12(0-12-0)	-0.4
1996	Tor-A	7	17	2	3	1	0	0	2	1	4	.176	.222	.235	458	16	-2	1	0	0	.800	-2	/O-6(0-6-0)	-0.4
1997	Tor-A	44	168	25	48	13	7	0	22	19	24	.286	.372	.446	818	112	3	10	3	1	.980	1	O-41(2-39-0)/D-1	0.5
1998	Tor-A	144	516	90	144	29	3	12	55	67	77	.279	.378	.417	795	106	7	51	18	5	.980	-2	*O-144(110-44-0)	0.6
1999	Tor-A	145	608	102	185	28	2	11	67	59	83	.304	.373	.411	785	98	0	37	14	3	.981	-6	*O-142(140-7-0)/D-2	-0.7
2000	Tor-A	136	583	107	186	43	5	21	69	37	79	.319	.366	.518	884	119	16	20	5	3	.993	8	*O-136(136-1-0)	2.0
Total	6	488	1930	328	574	114	17	44	216	188	272	.297	.370	.442	812	106	21	121	40	13	.983	-4	O-481(388-109-0)/D-3	1.6

■ NEB STEWART

Stewart, Walter Nesbitt b: 5/21/18, S.Charleston, Ohio d: 6/8/90, London, Ohio BR/TR, 6'1", 195 lbs. Deb: 9/8/40

YEAR	TM/L	G	AB	R	H	2B	3B	HR	RBI	BB	SO	AVG	OBP	SLG	OPS	OPS+	BR+	SB	CS	SBR	FA	FR	G/POS	TPR
1940	Phi-N	10	31	3	4	0	0	0	0	1	5	.129	.156	.129	285	-21	-5	0			.944	0	/O-9(8-1-0)	-0.5

■ BILL STEWART

Stewart, William Wayne b: 4/15/28, Bay City, Mich. BR/TR, 5'11", 200 lbs. Deb: 4/17/55

YEAR	TM/L	G	AB	R	H	2B	3B	HR	RBI	BB	SO	AVG	OBP	SLG	OPS	OPS+	BR+	SB	CS	SBR	FA	FR	G/POS	TPR
1955	KC-A	11	18	2	2	1	0	0	0	1	6	.111	.158	.167	325	-13	-3	0	0	0	1.000	-0	/O-6(4-0-2)	-0.3

■ ROYLE STILLMAN

Stillman, Royle Eldon b: 1/2/51, Santa Monica, Cal. BL/TL, 5'11", 180 lbs. Deb: 6/22/75 Career OF: (19-LF 1-CF 9-RF)

YEAR	TM/L	G	AB	R	H	2B	3B	HR	RBI	BB	SO	AVG	OBP	SLG	OPS	OPS+	BR+	SB	CS	SBR	FA	FR	G/POS	TPR
1975	Bal-A	13	14	1	6	0	0	0	1	1	3	.429	.467	.429	895	165	1	0	0	0	1.000	-0	/O-2(0-1-1)	0.1
1976	Bal-A	20	22	0	2	0	0	0	1	3	4	.091	.200	.091	291	-14	-3	0	0	0	1.000	-0	/1-2,D-5	-0.3
1977	Chi-A	56	119	18	25	7	1	3	13	17	21	.210	.309	.361	670	82	-3	2	1	0	.977	-3	O-26(19-0-8),D-13/1-1	-0.7
Total	3	89	155	19	33	7	1	3	15	21	28	.213	.307	.329	636	77	-5	2	1	0	.978	-3	/O-28L,D-18,1-3	-0.9

■ KURT STILLWELL

Stillwell, Kurt Andrew b: 6/4/65, Glendale, Cal. BB/TR, 5'11", 175 lbs. Deb: 4/13/86 F

YEAR	TM/L	G	AB	R	H	2B	3B	HR	RBI	BB	SO	AVG	OBP	SLG	OPS	OPS+	BR+	SB	CS	SBR	FA	FR	G/POS	TPR
1986	Cin-N	104	279	31	64	6	1	0	26	30	47	.229	.309	.258	567	56	-16	6	2	1	.951	-2	S-80	-1.1
1987	Cin-N	131	395	54	102	20	7	4	33	32	50	.258	.317	.375	692	79	-12	4	6	-1	.914	-21	S-51,2-37,3-20	-2.8
1988	KC-A★	128	459	63	115	28	5	10	53	47	76	.251	.324	.399	723	100	0	6	5	-0	.976	-18	*S-124	-0.9
1989	KC-A	130	463	52	121	20	7	7	54	42	64	.261	.327	.380	707	99	-1	9	6	-0	.970	-32	*S-130	-2.4
1990	KC-A	144	506	60	126	35	4	3	51	39	60	.249	.308	.352	660	85	-10	0	2	-1	.957	-20	*S-141	-2.1
1991	KC-A	122	385	44	102	17	1	6	51	33	56	.265	.325	.361	686	89	-6	3	4	-1	.959	-25	*S-118	-2.4
1992	SD-N	114	379	35	86	15	3	2	24	26	58	.227	.278	.298	576	62	-19	4	1	1	.970	-14	*2-111	-3.3
1993	SD-N	57	121	9	26	4	0	1	11	11	22	.215	.286	.273	558	49	-9	4	3	-0	.921	-5	S-30/3-3	-1.2
	Cal-A	22	61	2	16	2	2	0	3	4	11	.262	.308	.361	668	76	-2	2	0	0	.952	-4	2-18/S-7	-0.4
1996	Tex-A	46	77	12	21	4	0	1	4	10	11	.273	.364	.364	727	81	-2	0	0	0	.964	-9	2-21/S-9,3-6,1-1,D	-0.9
Total	9	998	3125	362	779	151	30	34	310	274	455	.249	.313	.349	663	82	-76	38	29	-2	.958	-151	S-690,2-187/3-29,D1	-17.5

■ RON STILLWELL

Stillwell, Ronald Roy b: 12/3/39, Los Angeles, Cal. BR/TR, 5'11", 165 lbs. Deb: 7/3/61 F

YEAR	TM/L	G	AB	R	H	2B	3B	HR	RBI	BB	SO	AVG	OBP	SLG	OPS	OPS+	BR+	SB	CS	SBR	FA	FR	G/POS	TPR
1961	Was-A	8	16	3	2	1	0	0	1	1	4	.125	.176	.188	364	-3	-2	0	0	0	.929	-1	/S-5	-0.3
1962	Was-A	6	22	5	6	0	0	0	2	2	2	.273	.333	.273	606	66	-1	0	0	0	1.000	-2	/2-6,S-1	-0.3
Total	2	14	38	8	8	1	0	0	3	3	6	.211	.268	.237	505	37	-3	0	0	0	.929	-3	/2-6,S-6	-0.6

■ CRAIG STIMAC

Stimac, Craig Steven b: 11/18/54, Oak Park, Ill. BR/TR, 6'2", 185 lbs. Deb: 8/12/80

YEAR	TM/L	G	AB	R	H	2B	3B	HR	RBI	BB	SO	AVG	OBP	SLG	OPS	OPS+	BR+	SB	CS	SBR	FA	FR	G/POS	TPR
1980	SD-N	20	50	5	11	2	0	0	7	1	6	.220	.235	.260	495	40	-4	0	0	0	.982	4	C-11/3-2	0.0
1981	SD-N	9	9	0	1	0	0	0	0	0	3	.111	.111	.111	222	-40	-2	0	0	0	.000	0	/H	-0.2
Total	2	29	59	5	12	2	0	0	7	1	9	.203	.217	.237	454	29	-6	0	0	0	.982	4	/C-11,3-2	-0.2

■ KELLY STINNETT

Stinnett, Kelly Lee b: 2/14/70, Lawton, Okla. BR/TR, 5'11", 195 lbs. Deb: 4/5/94

YEAR	TM/L	G	AB	R	H	2B	3B	HR	RBI	BB	SO	AVG	OBP	SLG	OPS	OPS+	BR+	SB	CS	SBR	FA	FR	G/POS	TPR
1994	NY-N	47	150	20	38	6	2	2	14	11	28	.253	.325	.360	685	79	-4	2	0	0	.979	-5	C-44	-0.6
1995	NY-N	77	196	23	43	8	1	4	18	29	65	.219	.338	.332	669	80	-5	2	0	0	.983	1	C-67	0.0
1996	Mil-A	14	26	1	2	0	0	0	0	2	11	.077	.172	.077	249	-33	-5	0	0	0	.960	-1	C-14/D-1	-0.4
1997	Mil-A	30	36	2	9	4	0	0	3	3	9	.250	.308	.361	669	73	-1	0	0	0	.989	5	C-25/D-1	0.4
1998	Ari-N	92	274	35	71	14	1	11	34	35	74	.259	.356	.438	794	108	3	0	1	-0	.984	-7	C-86/D-1	0.1
1999	*Ari-N	88	284	36	66	13	0	14	38	24	83	.232	.304	.426	730	81	-9	2	1	0	.990	-5	C-86	-0.8
2000	Ari-N	76	240	22	52	7	0	8	33	19	56	.217	.291	.346	636	59	-15	0	1	-0	.990	8	C-74	-0.3
Total	7	424	1206	139	281	52	4	39	140	123	326	.233	.319	.380	699	80	-37	6	3	0	.986	-2	C-396/D-3	-1.6

■ BOB STINSON

Stinson, Gorrell Robert b: 10/11/45, Elkin, N.C. BB/TR (BR 1969 BL 1980 (part)), 5'11.5", 185 lbs. Deb: 9/23/69 Career OF: (3-LF 0-CF 4-RF)

YEAR	TM/L	G	AB	R	H	2B	3B	HR	RBI	BB	SO	AVG	OBP	SLG	OPS	OPS+	BR+	SB	CS	SBR	FA	FR	G/POS	TPR
1969	LA-N	4	8	1	3	0	0	0	2	0	2	.375	.375	.375	750	119	0	0	1	-0	.952	1	/C-4	0.1
1970	LA-N	4	3	1	0	0	0	0	0	0	1	.000	.000	.000	0	-99	-1	0	0	0	1.000	-0	/C-3	-0.1
1971	StL-N	17	19	3	4	1	0	0	1	1	7	.211	.250	.263	513	44	-1	0	0	0	.971	2	/C-6,O-3(1-0-2)	0.1
1972	Hou-N	27	35	3	6	1	0	0	2	1	6	.171	.216	.200	416	19	-4	0	0	0	.964	-4	C-12/O-3(2-0-1)	-0.9
1973	Mon-N	48	111	12	29	6	1	3	12	17	15	.261	.374	.414	788	114	3	0	1	-0	.979	-3	C-35/3-1	0.0
1974	Mon-N	38	87	4	15	2	0	1	6	15	16	.172	.294	.230	524	45	-6	1	1	-0	1.000	1	C-29	-0.5
1975	KC-A	63	147	18	39	9	1	1	9	18	29	.265	.349	.361	710	98	0	1	0	0	.993	7	C-59/1-1,2-1,O-1R,D	1.0

YEAR	TM/L	G	AB	R	H	2B	3B	HR	RBI	BB	SO	AVG	OBP	SLG	OPS	OPS+	BR+	SB	CS	SBR	FA	FR	G/POS	TPR
1976	*KC-A	79	209	26	55	7	1	2	25	25	29	.263	.345	.335	680	99	0	3	1	0	.979	-6	C-79	-0.2
1977	Sea-A	105	297	27	80	11	1	8	32	37	50	.269	.362	.394	756	107	4	0	3	-1	.984	-7	C-99/D-1	0.0
1978	Sea-A	124	364	46	94	14	3	11	55	45	42	.258	.349	.404	753	112	6	2	1	0	.987	-18	*C-123/D-1	-0.6
1979	Sea-A	95	247	19	60	8	0	6	28	33	38	.243	.342	.348	690	85	-4	1	2	-0	.978	-7	C-91	-0.8
1980	Sea-A	48	107	6	23	2	0	1	8	9	19	.215	.282	.262	544	50	-7	0	0	0	.979	-9	C-45	-1.5
Total	12	652	1634	166	408	61	7	33	180	201	254	.250	.340	.356	696	93	-10	8	10	-2	.984	-44	C-585/O-7R,D-3,213	-3.4

■ GAT STIRES

Stires, Garrett b: 10/13/1849, Hunterdon Co., N.J d: 6/13/33, Byron, Ill. BL/TR, 5'8", 180 lbs. Deb: 5/6/1871

YEAR	TM/L	G	AB	R	H	2B	3B	HR	RBI	BB	SO	AVG	OBP	SLG	OPS	OPS+	BR+	SB	CS	SBR	FA	FR	G/POS	TPR
1871	Rok-n	25	110	23	30	4	6	2	24	7	5	.273	.316	.473	789	129	5	3	0	1	.837	1	*O-25(0-0-25)	0.5

■ SNUFFY STIRNWEISS

Stirnweiss, George Henry b: 10/26/18, New York, N.Y. d: 9/15/58, Newark Bay, N.J. BR/TR, 5'8.5", 175 lbs. Deb: 4/22/43

YEAR	TM/L	G	AB	R	H	2B	3B	HR	RBI	BB	SO	AVG	OBP	SLG	OPS	OPS+	BR+	SB	CS	SBR	FA	FR	G/POS	TPR
1943	*NY-A	83	274	34	60	8	4	1	25	47	37	.219	.333	.288	622	82	-5	11	9	-1	.938	-6	S-68/2-4	-0.7
1944	NY-A	154	643	**125**	**205**	35	**16**	8	43	73	87	.319	.389	.460	849	137	32	**55**	11	**8**	**.982**	19	*2-154	6.9
1945	NY-A†	152	632	**107**	**195**	32	**22**	10	64	78	62	**.309**	.385	**.476**	**862**	**143**	**34**	**33**	17	1	.970	26	*2-152	**7.2**
1946	NY-A★	129	487	75	122	19	7	0	37	66	58	.251	.340	.318	658	83	-9	18	6	2	.991	-6	3-79,2-46/S-4	-1.1
1947	*NY-A	148	571	102	146	18	8	5	41	89	47	.256	.358	.342	700	96	-1	5	3	0	.983	-11	*2-148	-0.3
1948	NY-A	141	515	90	130	20	7	3	32	86	62	.252	.360	.336	696	87	-8	5	4	-0	**.993**	-11	*2-141	-1.1
1949	*NY-A	70	157	29	41	8	2	0	11	29	20	.261	.380	.338	717	90	-1	3	2	-0	.974	4	2-51/3-4	0.5
1950	NY-A	7	2	0	0	0	0	0	0	0	0	.000	.000	.000	0	-99	-1	0	0	0	1.000	1	/2-4	0.0
	StL-A	93	326	32	71	16	2	1	24	51	49	.218	.324	.288	612	56	-21	3	3	-0	.975	-24	2-62,3-31/S-5	-4.1
	Yr	100	328	32	71	16	2	1	24	51	49	.216	.322	.287	608	55	-22	3	3	-0	.975	-23	2-66,3-31/S-5	-4.1
1951	Cle-A	50	88	10	19	1	0	1	4	22	25	.216	.373	.261	634	78	-1	1	0	0	.992	7	2-25/3-2	0.7
1952	Cle-A	1	0	0	0	0	0	0	0	0	0	—	—	—	—		0	0	0	0	.000	0	/3-1	0.0
Total	10	1028	3695	604	989	157	68	29	281	541	447	.268	.362	.371	733	102	20	134	55	10	.980	-1	2-787,3-117/S-77	8.0

■ JACK STIVETTS

Stivetts, John Elmer "Happy Jack" b: 3/31/1868, Ashland, Pa. d: 4/18/30, Ashland, Pa. BR/TR, 6'2", 185 lbs. Deb: 6/26/1889 Career OF: (41-LF 34-CF 68-RF)

YEAR	TM/L	G	AB	R	H	2B	3B	HR	RBI	BB	SO	AVG	OBP	SLG	OPS	OPS+	BR+	SB	CS	SBR	FA	FR	G/POS	TPR
1889	StL-a	27	79	12	18	2	2	0	7	3	13	.228	.265	.304	569	55	-5	0			.896	-1	P-26/O-1(0-1-0)	-0.1
1890	StL-a	67	226	36	65	15	6	7	43	16		.288	.337	.500	837	128	5	2			.894	4	P-54,O-10(0-10-0)/1-3	0.1
1891	StL-a	85	302	45	92	10	2	7	54	10	32	.305	.331	.421	752	100	-3	4			.898	2	P-64,O-24(1-0-23)	-0.1
1892	*Bos-N	71	240	40	71	14	2	3	36	27	28	.296	.369	.408	778	124	6	8			.904	-0	P-54,O-18(16-2-0)/1-1	-0.1
1893	Bos-N	50	172	32	51	5	6	3	25	12	14	.297	.342	.448	790	101	-1	6			.955	-4	P-38/O-8(3-0-5),3-3	-0.2
1894	Bos-N	68	244	55	80	12	7	8	64	16	21	.328	.369	.533	902	107	0	3			.943	-4	P-45,O-16(8-2-6)/1-4	-0.1
1895	Bos-N	46	158	20	30	6	4	0	24	6	18	.190	.220	.278	498	26	-18	1			.961	-1	P-38/1-5,O-2(0-1-1)	-0.3
1896	Bos-N	67	222	43	77	9	6	3	49	12	10	.347	.383	.482	865	120	5	4			.946	-6	P-42,O-12R/1-5,3-1	-0.2
1897	*Bos-N	61	199	41	73	9	9	2	37	15		.367	.417	.533	949	141	11	2			.926	-3	O-29R,P-18/2-2,1-2	0.1
1898	Bos-N	41	111	16	28	1	1	2	16	10		.252	.314	.333	647	81	-3	1			.909	-5	O-14R,1-10/S-4,2P	-0.8
1899	Cle-N	18	39	8	8	1	1	0	2	6		.205	.326	.282	608	73	-1	0			1.000	1	/O-7R,P-7,S-1,3-1	-0.2
Total	11	601	1992	348	593	84	46	35	357	133	136	.298	.344	.439	783	104	-4	31			.924	-17	P-388,O-141R/1S32	-1.9

■ MILT STOCK

Stock, Milton Joseph b: 7/11/1893, Chicago, Ill. d: 7/16/77, Fairhope, Ala. BR/TR, 5'8", 154 lbs. Deb: 9/29/13 C

YEAR	TM/L	G	AB	R	H	2B	3B	HR	RBI	BB	SO	AVG	OBP	SLG	OPS	OPS+	BR+	SB	CS	SBR	FA	FR	G/POS	TPR
1913	NY-N	7	17	2	3	1	0	0	1	2	2	.176	.263	.235	498	43	-1	2			.838	2	/S-7	0.1
1914	NY-N	115	365	52	96	17	1	3	41	34	21	.263	.333	.340	672	103	2	11			.939	15	*3-113/S-1	2.1
1915	*Phi-N	69	227	37	59	7	3	1	15	22	26	.260	.325	.330	656	98	-0	6	2	1	.971	2	3-55/S-4	0.4
1916	Phi-N	132	509	61	143	25	6	1	43	27	33	.281	.320	.360	679	105	2	21	26	-4	.955	-6	*3-117,S-15	-0.5
1917	Phi-N	150	564	76	149	27	6	3	53	51	34	.264	.326	.349	676	103	2	25			.942	-9	*3-133,S-19	-0.2
1918	Phi-N	123	481	62	132	14	1	1	42	35	22	.274	.325	.314	639	89	-6	20			.946	-5	*3-123	-0.8
1919	StL-N	135	492	56	151	16	4	0	52	49	21	.307	.371	.356	727	127	17	17			.966	17	2-77,3-58	4.1
1920	StL-N	155	639	85	204	28	6	0	76	40	27	.319	.360	.382	742	117	14	15	17	-3	.939	-8	*3-155	0.9
1921	StL-N	149	587	96	180	27	6	3	84	48	26	.307	.360	.388	748	100	1	11	3	1	.940	-22	*3-149	-1.0
1922	StL-N	151	581	85	177	33	9	5	79	42	29	.305	.352	.418	770	103	2	7	12	-3	.950	-9	*3-149/S-1	0.0
1923	StL-N	151	603	63	174	33	3	2	96	40	21	.289	.334	.363	697	86	-12	9	6	-0	.955	-14	*3-150/2-1	-1.7
1924	Bro-N	142	561	66	136	14	4	2	52	26	32	.242	.277	.292	570	54	-36	3	8	-2	.931	-23	*3-142	-5.3
1925	Bro-N	146	615	98	202	28	9	1	62	38	28	.328	.368	.408	776	101	1	8	1	1	.978	1	*2-141/3-5	0.7
1926	Bro-N	3	8	0	0	0	0	0	0	1	0	.000	.111	.000	111	-69	-2	0			.923	-1	/2-3	-0.2
Total	14	1628	6249	839	1806	270	58	22	696	455	321	.289	.339	.361	700	98	-16	155	75		.945	-59	*3-1349,2-222/S-47	-1.4

■ KEVIN STOCKER

Stocker, Kevin Douglas b: 2/13/70, Spokane, Wash. BB/TR, 6'1", 175 lbs. Deb: 7/7/93

YEAR	TM/L	G	AB	R	H	2B	3B	HR	RBI	BB	SO	AVG	OBP	SLG	OPS	OPS+	BR+	SB	CS	SBR	FA	FR	G/POS	TPR
1993	*Phi-N	70	259	46	84	12	3	2	31	30	43	.324	.411	.417	828	124	11	5	0	1	.958	-1	S-70	1.7
1994	Phi-N	82	271	38	74	11	2	2	28	44	41	.273	.388	.351	739	92	-1	2	2	-0	.959	-2	S-82	0.4
1995	Phi-N	125	412	42	90	14	3	1	32	43	75	.218	.306	.274	580	54	-26	6	1	1	.969	8	*S-125	-0.7
1996	Phi-N	119	394	46	100	22	6	5	41	43	89	.254	.339	.378	717	88	-6	6	4	-0	.975	5	*S-119	0.8
1997	Phi-N	149	504	51	134	23	5	4	40	51	91	.266	.336	.355	691	81	-13	11	6	0	.981	-18	*S-147	-1.8
1998	TB-A	112	336	37	70	11	3	6	25	27	80	.208	.283	.313	596	54	-23	5	3	0	.979	20	*S-110	0.5
1999	TB-A	79	254	39	76	11	2	1	27	24	41	.299	.369	.370	739	88	-4	9	7	-0	.957	-1	S-76	0.2
2000	TB-A	40	114	20	30	7	1	2	8	19	27	.263	.378	.395	773	97	-0	1	2	-0	.933	-6	S-40	-0.3
	Ana-A	70	229	21	45	13	3	0	16	32	54	.197	.300	.279	580	48	-18	0	3	-1	.978	-6	S-69	-1.7
	Yr	110	343	41	75	20	4	2	24	51	81	.219	.327	.318	644	64	-18	1	5	-2	.962	-11	*S-109	-2.0
Total	8	846	2773	340	703	124	28	23	248	313	541	.254	.340	.343	683	78	-80	45	28	0	.969	0	S-838	-0.9

■ LEN STOCKWELL

Stockwell, Leonard Clark b: 8/25/1859, Cordova, Ill. d: 1/28/05, Niles, Cal. BR/TR, 5'11", 165 lbs. Deb: 5/17/1879

YEAR	TM/L	G	AB	R	H	2B	3B	HR	RBI	BB	SO	AVG	OBP	SLG	OPS	OPS+	BR+	SB	CS	SBR	FA	FR	G/POS	TPR
1879	Cle-N	2	6	0	0	0	0	0	0	0	2	.000	.000	.000	0	-99	-1				1.000	1	/O-2(0-1-1)	0.0
1884	Lou-a	2	9	0	1	0	0	0		0		.111	.111	.111	222	-29	-1				.667	-1	/O-2(1-1-0),C-1	-0.2
1890	Cle-N	2	7	2	2	1	0	0	0	0	3	.286	.286	.429	714	110	0	0			1.000	0	/O-1(1-0-0),1-1	0.0
Total	3	6	22	2	3	1	0	0	0	0	5	.136	.136	.182	318	-1	-2	0			.900	1	/O-5(2-2-1),1-1,C-1	-0.2

■ STODDARD

Stoddard Deb: 9/25/1875

YEAR	TM/L	G	AB	R	H	2B	3B	HR	RBI	BB	SO	AVG	OBP	SLG	OPS	OPS+	BR+	SB	CS	SBR	FA	FR	G/POS	TPR
1875	Atl-n	2	9	1	1	1	0	0	0	0	1	.111	.111	.222	333	15	-1	0	0	0	.800	-0	/O-2(1-1-0)	-0.1

■ AL STOKES

Stokes, Albert John (b: Albert John Stocek) b: 1/1/1900, Chicago, Ill. d: 12/19/86, Grantham, N.H. BR/TR, 5'9", 175 lbs. Deb: 5/10/25

YEAR	TM/L	G	AB	R	H	2B	3B	HR	RBI	BB	SO	AVG	OBP	SLG	OPS	OPS+	BR+	SB	CS	SBR	FA	FR	G/POS	TPR
1925	Bos-A	17	52	7	11	0	1	0	1	4	8	.212	.268	.250	518	32	-5	0	0	0	.969	3	C-17	-0.2
1926	Bos-A	30	86	7	14	3	3	0	6	8	28	.163	.234	.267	501	32	-9	0	0	0	.931	-4	C-29	-1.1
Total	2	47	138	14	25	3	4	0	7	12	36	.181	.247	.261	508	32	-14	0	0	0	.946	-1	/C-46	-1.3

■ GENE STONE

Stone, Eugene Daniel b: 1/16/44, Burbank, Cal. BL/TL, 5'11", 190 lbs. Deb: 5/13/69

YEAR	TM/L	G	AB	R	H	2B	3B	HR	RBI	BB	SO	AVG	OBP	SLG	OPS	OPS+	BR+	SB	CS	SBR	FA	FR	G/POS	TPR
1969	Phi-N	18	28	4	6	0	1	0	0	4	9	.214	.313	.286	598	70	-1	0	0	0	1.000	-1	/1-5	-0.2

■ GEORGE STONE

Stone, George Robert b: 9/3/1877, Lost Nation, Iowa d: 1/3/45, Clinton, Iowa BL/TL, 5'9", 175 lbs. Deb: 4/20/03

YEAR	TM/L	G	AB	R	H	2B	3B	HR	RBI	BB	SO	AVG	OBP	SLG	OPS	OPS+	BR+	SB	CS	SBR	FA	FR	G/POS	TPR
1903	Bos-A	2	2	0	0	0	0	0	0	0		.000	.000	.000	0	-95	-0	0			.000	0	H	0.0
1905	StL-A	154	632	76	**187**	25	13	7	52	44		.296	.347	.410	756	147	32	26			.954	2	*O-154(154-0-0)	2.7
1906	StL-A	154	581	91	208	25	20	6	71	52		**.358**	**.417**	**.501**	**918**	**195**	**63**	35			.968	-1	*O-154(154-0-0)	5.7
1907	StL-A	155	596	77	191	13	11	4	59	59		.320	.387	.399	787	151	36	23			.970	-3	*O-155(155-0-0)	2.6
1908	StL-A	148	588	89	165	21	8	5	31	55		.281	.345	.369	714	131	21	20			.947	-0	*O-148(148-0-0)	1.3
1909	StL-A	83	310	33	89	5	4	1	15	24		.287	.340	.339	679	123	8	8			.928	2	O-81(63-0-18)	0.6
1910	StL-A	152	562	60	144	17	12	0	40	48		.256	.315	.329	644	108	5	20			.972	-2	*O-145(139-1-5)	-0.6
Total	7	848	3271	426	984	106	68	23	268	282		.301	.360	.396	756	145	165	132			.958	-3	O-837(813-1-23)	12.3

■ RON STONE

Stone, Harry Ronald b: 9/9/42, Corning, Cal. BL/TL, 6'2", 195 lbs. Deb: 4/13/66

YEAR	TM/L	G	AB	R	H	2B	3B	HR	RBI	BB	SO	AVG	OBP	SLG	OPS	OPS+	BR+	SB	CS	SBR	FA	FR	G/POS	TPR
1966	KC-A	26	22	2	6	1	0	0	0	0	2	.273	.273	.318	591	71	-1	1	1	-0	1.000	-1	/O-4(2-2-1),1-3	-0.3
1969	Phi-N	103	222	22	53	7	1	1	24	29	28	.239	.335	.293	627	79	-5	3	1	0	.978	-3	O-69(37-2-32)	-1.2
1970	Phi-N	123	321	30	84	12	5	3	39	38	45	.262	.342	.358	700	90	-4	5	6	-1	.968	-3	O-99(51-0-48)/1-6	-1.3
1971	Phi-N	95	185	16	42	8	1	2	23	25	36	.227	.319	.314	633	80	-4	2	2	-0	.964	-4	O-51(22-1-33)/1-3	-1.2

YEAR	TM/L	G	AB	R	H	2B	3B	HR	RBI	BB	SO	AVG	OBP	SLG	OPS	OPS+	BR+	SB	CS	SBR	FA	FR	G/POS	TPR
1972	Phi-N	41	54	3	9	0	1	0	3	9	11	.167	.286	.204	489	40	-4	0	0	0	1.000	1	O-15(6-1-9)	-0.4
Total	5	388	804	73	194	28	8	6	89	101	122	.241	.329	.318	647	81	-18	11	10	-1	.973	-11	O-238(118-6-123)/1-12	-4.4

■ JEFF STONE Stone, Jeffrey Glen b: 12/26/60, Kennett, Mo. BL/TR, 6', 175 lbs. Deb: 9/9/83

YEAR	TM/L	G	AB	R	H	2B	3B	HR	RBI	BB	SO	AVG	OBP	SLG	OPS	OPS+	BR+	SB	CS	SBR	FA	FR	G/POS	TPR
1983	Phi-N	9	4	2	3	0	2	0	3	0	1	.750	.750	1.750	2500	580	2	4	0	1	.000	-0	/O-1(0-1-0)	0.3
1984	Phi-N	51	185	27	67	4	6	1	15	9	26	.362	.398	.465	863	139	10	27	5	4	.916	-2	O-46(46-0-0)	1.0
1985	Phi-N	88	264	36	70	4	3	3	11	15	50	.265	.307	.337	644	78	-8	15	5	2	.966	-6	O-69(69-0-0)	-1.6
1986	Phi-N	82	249	32	69	6	4	6	19	20	52	.277	.341	.406	746	101	1	19	6	2	.982	2	O-58(37-25-0)	0.3
1987	Phi-N	66	125	19	32	7	1	1	16	8	38	.256	.316	.352	668	74	-5	3	1	0	1.000	-1	O-25(20-5-1)	-0.6
1988	Bal-A	26	61	4	10	1	0	0	1	4	11	.164	.215	.180	396	12	-7	4	1	1	.963	-2	O-21(18-0-3)/D-1	-0.9
1989	Tex-A	22	36	5	6	1	2	0	5	3	5	.167	.250	.306	556	55	-2	2	1	0	.000	-1	D-15/O-3(1-1-1)	-0.4
	Bos-A	18	15	3	3	0	0	0	1	1	2	.200	.250	.200	450	27	-1	1	0	0	1.000	-3	O-11(0-4-7)/D-3	-0.5
	Yr	40	51	8	9	1	2	0	6	4	7	.176	.250	.275	525	46	-4	3	1	0	1.000	-5	D-18,O-14(1-5-8)	-0.9
1990	Bos-A	10	2	1	1	0	0	0	1	0	1	.500	.500	.500	1000	173	0	0	1	-0	.000	0	/D-2	0.0
Total	8	372	941	129	261	23	18	11	72	60	186	.277	.328	.375	703	92	-10	75	20	10	.963	-14	O-234(191-36-12)/D-21	-2.4

■ JOHN STONE Stone, John Thomas "Rocky" b: 10/10/05, Mulberry, Tenn. d: 11/30/55, Shelbyville, Tenn. BL/TR, 6'1", 178 lbs. Deb: 8/31/28

YEAR	TM/L	G	AB	R	H	2B	3B	HR	RBI	BB	SO	AVG	OBP	SLG	OPS	OPS+	BR+	SB	CS	SBR	FA	FR	G/POS	TPR
1928	Det-A	26	113	20	40	10	3	2	21	5	8	.354	.387	.549	935	141	6	1	0	0	.962	-1	O-26(26-0-0)	0.3
1929	Det-A	51	150	23	39	11	2	2	15	11	13	.260	.311	.400	711	81	-5	1	1	-0	.986	-1	O-36(35-0-2)	-0.8
1930	Det-A	127	425	60	132	29	11	3	56	32	49	.311	.360	.452	812	102	1	6	9	-2	.966	0	*O-109(93-11-6)	-0.7
1931	Det-A	147	584	86	191	28	11	10	76	56	48	.327	.388	.464	852	119	16	13	13	-2	.959	4	*O-147(143-5-0)	1.0
1932	Det-A	145	582	106	173	35	12	17	108	58	64	.297	.361	.486	847	113	10	2	1	0	.961	3	*O-142(90-53-0)	0.6
1933	Det-A	148	574	86	161	33	11	11	80	54	37	.280	.344	.434	778	103	1	1	4	-1	.970	1	*O-141(18-0-124)	-0.7
1934	Was-A	113	419	77	132	28	7	7	67	52	26	.315	.395	.465	860	126	17	1	2	-0	.966	7	*O-112(0-16-98)	1.6
1935	Was-A	125	455	78	143	27	18	1	78	39	29	.314	.372	.459	832	118	11	4	5	-1	.955	0	*O-114(19-7-90)	0.4
1936	Was-A	123	437	95	149	22	11	15	90	60	26	.341	.421	.545	965	145	31	8	0	2	.967	7	*O-114(109-0-6)	2.9
1937	Was-A	139	542	84	179	33	15	6	88	66	36	.330	.403	.480	883	127	23	6	4	-0	.984	7	*O-137(37-7-95)	2.0
1938	Was-A	56	213	24	52	12	4	3	28	30	16	.244	.337	.380	718	85	-5	2	1	0	.974	-2	O-53(29-1-26)	-0.9
Total	11	1200	4494	739	1391	268	105	77	707	463	352	.310	.376	.467	843	116	107	45	40	-4	.967	24	*O-1131(599-100-447)	5.7

■ TIGE STONE Stone, William Arthur b: 9/18/01, Macon, Ga. d: 1/1/60, Jacksonville, Fla. BR/TR, 5'8", 145 lbs. Deb: 8/23/23

YEAR	TM/L	G	AB	R	H	2B	3B	HR	RBI	BB	SO	AVG	OBP	SLG	OPS	OPS+	BR+	SB	CS	SBR	FA	FR	G/POS	TPR
1923	StL-N	5	1	0	1	0	0	0	0	2	0	1.000	1.000	1.000	2000	438	1	0	0	0	.000	-2	/O-4(2-2-0),P-1	-0.2

■ JOHN STONEHAM Stoneham, John Andrew b: 11/8/08, Wood River, Ill. BL/TR, 5'9.5", 168 lbs. Deb: 9/18/33

YEAR	TM/L	G	AB	R	H	2B	3B	HR	RBI	BB	SO	AVG	OBP	SLG	OPS	OPS+	BR+	SB	CS	SBR	FA	FR	G/POS	TPR
1933	Chi-A	10	25	4	3	0	0	1	3	2	2	.120	.185	.240	425	12	-3	0	0	0	1.000	-2	/O-9(1-1-7)	-0.5

■ HOWIE STORIE Storie, Howard Edward "Sponge" b: 5/15/11, Pittsfield, Mass. d: 7/27/68, Pittsfield, Mass. BR/TR, 5'10", 175 lbs. Deb: 9/7/31

YEAR	TM/L	G	AB	R	H	2B	3B	HR	RBI	BB	SO	AVG	OBP	SLG	OPS	OPS+	BR+	SB	CS	SBR	FA	FR	G/POS	TPR
1931	Bos-A	6	17	2	2	0	0	0	0	3	2	.118	.250	.118	368	-1	-2	0	0	0	1.000	0	/C-6	-0.2
1932	Bos-A	6	8	0	3	0	0	0	0	0	0	.375	.375	.375	750	98	-0	0	0	0	1.000	0	/C-5	0.0
Total	2	12	25	2	5	0	0	0	0	3	2	.200	.286	.200	486	31	-2	0	0	0	1.000	1	/C-11	-0.2

■ ALAN STORKE Storke, Alan Marshall b: 9/27/1884, Auburn, N.Y. d: 3/18/10, Newton, Mass. BR/TR, 6'1", Deb: 9/24/06

YEAR	TM/L	G	AB	R	H	2B	3B	HR	RBI	BB	SO	AVG	OBP	SLG	OPS	OPS+	BR+	SB	CS	SBR	FA	FR	G/POS	TPR
1906	Pit-N	5	12	1	3	1	0	0	1	1		.250	.308	.333	641	96	-0	1			1.000	0	/3-2,S-1	0.0
1907	Pit-N	112	357	24	92	6	6	1	39	16		.258	.295	.317	612	90	-5	6			.925	-13	3-67,1-23/2-7,S-5	-1.8
1908	Pit-N	64	202	20	51	5	3	1	12	9		.252	.284	.322	606	93	-2	4			.988	-6	1-49/3-6,2-1	-1.0
1909	Pit-N	37	118	12	30	5	2	0	12	7		.254	.302	.331	632	89	-2	1			.994	-0	1-18,3-14	-0.2
	StL-N	48	174	11	49	5	0	0	10	12		.282	.328	.310	638	105	1	5			.958	-1	S-44/2-4,1-1	0.1
	Yr	85	292	23	79	10	2	0	22	19		.271	.317	.318	636	97	-1	6			.958	-2	S-44,1-19,3-14,/2-4	-0.1
Total	4	266	863	68	225	22	11	2	74	45		.261	.300	.319	619	94	-8	17			.990	-20	/1-91,3-89,S-50,2	-2.9

■ LIN STORTI Storti, Lindo Ivan b: 12/5/06, Santa Monica, Cal. d: 7/24/82, Ontario, Cal. BB/TR, 5'11", 165 lbs. Deb: 9/18/30

YEAR	TM/L	G	AB	R	H	2B	3B	HR	RBI	BB	SO	AVG	OBP	SLG	OPS	OPS+	BR+	SB	CS	SBR	FA	FR	G/POS	TPR
1930	StL-A	7	28	6	9	1	1	0	2	2	6	.321	.367	.429	795	98	-0	0	0	0	.975	1	/2-6	0.1
1931	StL-A	86	273	32	60	15	4	3	26	15	50	.220	.263	.337	600	55	-19	0	2	-1	.926	9	3-67/2-7	-0.8
1932	StL-A	53	193	19	50	11	2	3	26	5	20	.259	.278	.383	661	66	-10	1	0	0	.956	-4	3-51	-1.2
1933	StL-A	70	210	26	41	7	4	3	21	25	31	.195	.281	.310	590	53	-15	2	2	-0	.934	-2	3-32,2-24	-1.4
Total	4	216	704	83	160	34	11	9	75	47	107	.227	.277	.345	622	59	-44	3	4	-1	.936	4	3-150/2-37	-3.3

■ TOM STOUCH Stouch, Thomas Carl b: 12/2/1869, Perrysville, Ohio d: 10/7/56, Lancaster, Pa. BR/TR, 6'2", 165 lbs. Deb: 7/7/1898

YEAR	TM/L	G	AB	R	H	2B	3B	HR	RBI	BB	SO	AVG	OBP	SLG	OPS	OPS+	BR+	SB	CS	SBR	FA	FR	G/POS	TPR
1898	Lou-N	4	16	4	5	1	0	0	6	1		.313	.353	.375	728	110	0	0			.850	-2	/2-4	-0.2

■ DA ROND STOVALL Stovall, Da Rond Tyrone b: 1/3/73, St.Louis, Mo. BB/TL, 6'1", 185 lbs. Deb: 4/1/98

YEAR	TM/L	G	AB	R	H	2B	3B	HR	RBI	BB	SO	AVG	OBP	SLG	OPS	OPS+	BR+	SB	CS	SBR	FA	FR	G/POS	TPR
1998	Mon-N	62	78	11	16	2	1	2	6	6	29	.205	.262	.333	595	56	-5	1	0	0	.925	-10	O-47(27-14-7)	-1.5

■ GEORGE STOVALL Stovall, George Thomas "Firebrand" b: 11/23/1878, Leeds, Mo. d: 11/5/51, Burlington, Iowa BR/TR, 6'2", 180 lbs. Deb: 7/4/04 FM

YEAR	TM/L	G	AB	R	H	2B	3B	HR	RBI	BB	SO	AVG	OBP	SLG	OPS	OPS+	BR+	SB	CS	SBR	FA	FR	G/POS	TPR
1904	Cle-A	52	181	18	54	10	1	1	31	2		.298	.317	.381	698	121	4	3			.978	-2	1-38/2-9,O-3L,3-1	0.1
1905	Cle-A	112	423	41	115	31	1	1	47	13		.272	.295	.357	652	105	1	13			.973	-5	1-60,2-46/O-4(0-3-0)	-0.6
1906	Cle-A	116	443	54	121	19	5	0	37	8		.273	.288	.339	626	97	-3	15			.985	-5	1-55,3-30,2-19	-0.9
1907	Cle-A	124	466	38	110	17	6	1	36	18		.236	.267	.305	572	82	-11	13			.983	-4	*1-122/3-2	-1.9
1908	Cle-A	138	534	71	156	29	6	2	45	17		.292	.316	.380	697	126	13	14			**.990**	3	*1-132/O-5(0-5-0),S-1	1.5
1909	Cle-A	145	565	60	139	17	10	2	49	6		.246	.259	.322	581	80	-15	25			**.988**	10	*1-145	-0.9
1910	Cle-A	142	521	49	136	19	4	0	52	14		.261	.284	.313	597	86	-10	16			**.988**	7	*1-132/2-2	-0.7
1911	Cle-A	126	458	48	124	17	7	0	79	21		.271	.306	.338	644	79	-14	11			**.986**	7	*1-118/2-2,M	-1.0
1912	StL-A	116	398	35	101	17	5	0	45	14		.254	.286	.322	608	76	-14	11			.983	5	1-94,M	-1.1
1913	StL-A	89	303	34	87	14	3	1	24	7	23	.287	.305	.363	669	98	-2	7			.988	8	1-76,M	0.3
1914	KC-F	124	450	51	128	20	5	7	75	23	35	.284	.325	.398	723	100	-9	6			.989	4	*1-116/3-1,M	-0.8
1915	KC-F	130	480	48	111	21	3	0	44	31	36	.231	.286	.287	574	64	-31	8			.987	5	*1-129,M	-3.2
Total	12	1414	5222	547	1382	231	56	15	564	174	94	.265	.293	.339	632	91	-92	142			.986	32	*1-1217/2-78,3-34,OS	-9.2

■ HARRY STOVEY Stovey, Harry Duffield (b: Harry Duffield Stowe)
b: 12/20/1856, Philadelphia, Pa. d: 9/20/37, New Bedford, Mass BR/TR, 5'11.5", 175 lbs. Deb: 5/1/1880 M Career OF: (519-LF 176-CF 251-RF)

YEAR	TM/L	G	AB	R	H	2B	3B	HR	RBI	BB	SO	AVG	OBP	SLG	OPS	OPS+	BR+	SB	CS	SBR	FA	FR	G/POS	TPR
1880	Wor-N	83	355	76	94	21	**14**	**6**	28	12	46	.265	.289	.454	742	136	12				.860	-5	O-46(5-42-0),1-37/P-2	0.3
1881	Wor-N	75	341	57	92	25	7	2	30	12	23	.270	.295	.402	696	111	3				.955	-5	*1-57,O-18(1-0-17),M	-0.4
1882	Wor-N	84	360	90	104	13	10	5	26	22	34	.289	.330	.422	752	136	14				.956	4	1-43,O-41(41-0-0)	1.2
1883	Phi-a	94	421	**110**	128	**31**	6	**14**	66	27		.304	.346	**.506**	852	156	24				**.965**	0	*1-93/O-3(0-3-0),P-1	1.4
1884	Phi-a	104	448	**124**	146	22	**23**	10	83	26		.326	.368	.545	913	182	38				.960	-1	*1-104	2.5
1885	Phi-a	112	486	**130**	153	27	9	**13**	75	39		.315	.371	.488	858	160	31				.967	4	*1-82,O-30(0-30-0),M	2.4
1886	Phi-a	123	489	115	144	28	11	7	59	64		.294	.377	.440	817	154	31	**68**			.870	3	O-63C,1-62/P-1	2.3
1887	Phi-a	124	553	125	198	31	12	4	77	56		.358	.366	.421	787	119	13	74			.902	12	O-80(49-29-2),1-46	1.5
1888	Phi-a	130	530	127	152	25	**20**	9	65	62		.287	.365	.460	825	165	**39**	87			.943	4	*O-118(118-0-0),1-13	3.5
1889	Phi-a	137	556	**152**	171	38	13	**19**	**119**	77	68	.308	.393	**.525**	918	162	45	63			.897	18	*O-137(137-0-0)/1-1	**4.9**
1890	Bos-P	118	481	142	144	25	11	12	84	81	38	.299	.406	.472	878	126	17	**97**			.921	2	*O-117(1-0-116)/1-1	1.4
1891	Bos-N	134	544	118	152	31	**20**	**16**	95	79	69	.279	.373	**.498**	871	137	22	57			.910	9	*O-134(39-0-96)/1-1	2.6
1892	Bos-N	38	146	21	24	8	1	0	12	14	19	.164	.252	.233	484	43	-10	20			.901	0	O-38(38-0-0)	-1.3
	Bal-N	74	283	58	77	14	11	4	55	40	32	.272	.364	.442	806	140	13	20			.913	-3	O-64(64-0-0),1-10	0.3
	Yr	112	429	79	101	22	12	4	67	54	51	.235	.326	.371	697	105	2	40			.908	-3	*O-102(102-0-0),1-10	-1.0
1893	Bal-N	8	26	4	4	2	0	0	5	8	3	.154	.353	.231	584	55	-1	1			.864	0	/O-7(7-0-0)	-0.1
	Bro-N	48	175	43	44	6	6	1	29	44	11	.251	.402	.371	773	111	5	22			.901	-3	O-48(19-26-3)	-0.1
	Yr	56	201	47	48	8	6	1	34	52	14	.239	.395	.353	748	103	4	23			.895	-2	O-55(26-26-3)	-0.2
Total	14	1486	6194	1492	1827	347	174	122	908	663	343	.295	.361	.461	822	141	296	509			.896	40	O-944L,1-550/P-4	22.4

■ RAY STOVIAK Stoviak, Raymond Thomas b: 6/6/15, Scottdale, Pa. d: 2/23/98, Nicoya, Costa Rica BL/TL, 6'1", 195 lbs. Deb: 6/5/38

YEAR	TM/L	G	AB	R	H	2B	3B	HR	RBI	BB	SO	AVG	OBP	SLG	OPS	OPS+	BR+	SB	CS	SBR	FA	FR	G/POS	TPR
1938	Phi-N	10	10	1	0	0	0	0	0	0	3	.000	.000	.000	0	-99	-3	0			1.000	-1	/O-4(0-0-4)	-0.4

YEAR	TM/L	G	AB	R	H	2B	3B	HR	RBI	BB	SO	AVG	OBP	SLG	OPS	OPS+	BR+	SB	CS	SBR	FA	FR	G/POS	TPR
■ CHRIS STOWERS	Stowers, Christopher James b: 8/18/74, St.Louis, Mo. BL/TL, 6'3", 195 lbs. Deb: 7/10/99																							
1999	Mon-N	4	2	0	0	0	0	0	0	0	0	.000	.000	.000	0	-99	-1	0	0	0	1.000	-1	/O-2(0-1-1)	-0.1
■ JOE STRAIN	Strain, Joseph Allan b: 4/30/54, Denver, Colo. BR/TR, 5'10", 169 lbs. Deb: 6/28/79																							
1979	SF-N	67	257	27	62	8	1	1	12	13	21	.241	.286	.292	578	62	-14	8	4	0	.982	-1	2-67/3-1	-1.1
1980	SF-N	77	189	26	54	6	0	0	16	10	10	.286	.322	.317	639	81	-5	1	2	-0	.989	-11	2-42/3-6,S-1	-1.5
1981	Chi-N	25	74	7	14	1	0	0	1	5	7	.189	.250	.203	453	28	-7	0	0	0	.975	7	2-20	0.2
Total	3	169	520	60	130	15	1	1	29	28	38	.250	.293	.288	582	64	-25	9	6	-0	.983	-5	2-129/3-7,S-1	-2.4
■ PAUL STRAND	Strand, Paul Edward b: 12/19/1893, Carbonado, Wash. d: 7/2/74, Salt Lake City, Utah BR/TL, 6'0.5", 190 lbs. Deb: 5/15/13																							
1913	Bos-N	7	6	0	1	0	0	0	0	0	0	.167	.167	.167	333	-5	-1	0			.875	0	/P-7	0.0
1914	Bos-N	18	24	2	8	2	0	0	3	0	2	.333	.333	.417	750	123	1	0			.813	-0	P-16	0.0
1915	Bos-N	24	22	3	2	0	0	0	2	0	4	.091	.091	.091	182	-47	-4	0			.750	-1	/P-6,O-5(2-1-0)	-0.2
1924	Phi-A	47	167	15	38	9	4	0	13	4	9	.228	.254	.329	584	49	-13	3	3	-0	.988	-6	O-44(0-39-5)	-2.1
Total	4	96	219	20	49	11	4	0	18	4	15	.224	.244	.311	555	47	-18	3	3		.989	-7	/O-49(2-40-5),P-29	-2.3
■ LARRY STRANDS	Strands, John Lawrence b: 12/5/1885, Chicago, Ill. d: 1/19/57, Forest Park, Ill. BR/TR, 5'10.5", 165 lbs. Deb: 4/25/15																							
1915	New-F	35	75	7	14	3	1	1	11	6	11	.187	.247	.293	540	55	-6	1			.852	-7	3-12/2-9,O-2(0-0-2)	-1.4
■ SAMMY STRANG	Strang, Samuel Nicklin "The Dixie Thrush" (b: Samuel Strang Nicklin) b: 12/16/1876, Chattanooga, Tenn. d: 3/13/32, Chattanooga, Tenn. BB/TR, 5'8", 160 lbs. Deb: 7/10/1896 Career OF: (11-LF 63-CF 92-RF)																							
1896	Lou-N	14	46	6	12	0	0	0	7	6	6	.261	.346	.261	607	64	-2	4			.803	-8	S-14	-0.8
1900	Chi-N	27	102	15	29	3	0	0	9	8		.284	.348	.314	662	86	-1	1			.887	-11	3-16/S-9,2-2	-1.1
1901	NY-N	135	493	55	139	14	6	1	34	59		.282	.364	.341	705	109	9	40			.877	2	3-91,2-37/O-5R,S-4	1.3
1902	Chi-A	137	536	108	158	18	5	3	46	76		.295	.387	.364	751	114	15	38			.890	5	*3-137	2.2
	Chi-N	3	11	1	4	0	0	0	0	0		.364	.364	.364	727	128	0	1			1.000	-1	/2-2,3-2	0.0
1903	Bro-N	135	508	101	138	21	5	0	38	75		.272	.376	.333	709	106	8	46			.914	-7	*3-124/O-8(0-8-0),2-3	0.3
1904	Bro-N	77	271	28	52	11	0	1	9	45		.192	.316	.244	559	75	-6	16			.910	-32	2-63,3-12/S-1	-4.0
1905	*NY-N	111	294	51	76	9	4	3	29	58		.259	.389	.347	736	117	10	23			.915	-17	2-47,O-38R/S-9,13	-0.8
1906	NY-N	113	313	50	100	16	4	4	49	54		.319	.423	.435	857	164	26	21			.944	3	2-57,O-39C/S-4,31	3.0
1907	NY-N	123	306	56	77	20	4	4	30	60		.252	.388	.382	770	137	16	21			.947	-1	O-70R,2-13/3-7,1S	1.4
1908	NY-N	28	53	8	5	0	0	0	2	23		.094	.385	.094	479	52	-1	5			.863	-3	2-14/O-5(1-3-2),S-3	-0.4
Total	10	903	2933	479	790	112	28	16	253	464	6	.269	.377	.343	720	113	73	216			.891	-70	3-393,2-238,O/S1	1.1
■ ALAN STRANGE	Strange, Alan Cochrane "Inky" b: 11/7/06, Philadelphia, Pa. d: 6/27/94, Seattle, Wash. BR/TR, 5'9", 162 lbs. Deb: 4/17/34																							
1934	StL-A	127	430	39	100	17	2	1	45	48	28	.233	.310	.288	598	51	-31	3	1	0	.955	4	*S-125	-1.7
1935	StL-A	49	147	8	34	6	1	0	17	17	7	.231	.311	.286	597	53	-10	0	0	0	.960	2	S-49	-0.5
	Was-A	20	54	3	10	2	1	0	5	4	1	.185	.241	.259	501	30	-6	0	0	0	.974	3	S-16	-0.2
	Yr	69	201	11	44	8	2	0	22	21	8	.219	.293	.279	571	47	-16	0	0	0	.963	5	S-65	-0.7
1940	StL-A	54	167	26	31	8	3	0	6	22	12	.186	.284	.269	554	43	-14	2	1	0	.962	3	S-35/2-4	-0.8
1941	StL-A	45	112	14	26	4	0	0	11	15	5	.232	.323	.268	591	56	-7	1	0	0	.973	2	S-32/1-2,3-1	-0.3
1942	StL-A	19	37	3	10	2	0	0	5	3	1	.270	.325	.324	649	82	-1	0	1	-0	.935	5	3-10/S-3,2-1	0.4
Total	5	314	947	93	211	39	7	1	89	109	54	.223	.304	.282	586	50	-68	6	3	0	.959	18	S-260/3-11,2-5,1-2	-3.1
■ DOUG STRANGE	Strange, Joseph Douglas b: 4/13/64, Greenville, S.C. BB/TR, 6'1", 185 lbs. Deb: 7/13/89 Career OF: (18-LF 0-CF 2-RF)																							
1989	Det-A	64	196	16	42	4	1	1	14	17	36	.214	.280	.260	541	54	-12	3	3	-0	.878	1	3-54/2-9,S-9,D-1	-1.1
1991	Chi-N	3	9	0	4	1	0	0	1	0	1	.444	.500	.556	1056	188	1	1	0	0	.800	-1	/3-3	0.0
1992	Chi-N	52	94	7	15	1	0	1	5	10	15	.160	.240	.202	443	26	-9	1	0	0	.900	-0	3-33,2-12	-1.0
1993	Tex-A	145	484	58	124	29	0	7	60	43	69	.256	.321	.360	680	86	-10	6	4	-0	.980	-9	*2-135/3-9,S-1	-1.2
1994	Tex-A	73	226	26	48	12	1	5	26	15	38	.212	.270	.341	611	56	-15	1	3	-1	.970	7	2-53,3-13/O-3(2-0-1)	-0.7
1995	*Sea-A	74	155	19	42	9	2	2	21	10	25	.271	.323	.394	717	85	-4	0	3	-1	.948	6	3-41/2-5,O-4L,D-1	0.1
1996	Sea-A	88	183	19	43	7	1	3	23	14	31	.235	.293	.333	626	58	-12	1	0	0	.961	-7	3-39,O-11L,D-10,/12	-1.8
1997	Mon-N	118	327	40	84	16	2	12	47	36	76	.257	.334	.428	762	98	-1	0	2	-1	.947	2	*3-105/2-3,O-2L,1-1	0.0
1998	Pit-N	90	185	9	32	8	0	0	14	10	39	.173	.219	.216	436	15	-23	1	0	0	.940	-3	3-42/2-9,1-3	-2.6
Total	9	707	1859	194	434	87	7	31	211	155	330	.233	.297	.338	635	69	-84	14	15	-2	.927	-6	3-339,2-229/ODS1	-8.3
■ ASA STRATTON	Stratton, Asa Evans b: 2/10/1853, Grafton, Mass. d: 8/14/25, Fitchburg, Mass. Deb: 6/17/1881																							
1881	Wor-N	1	4	0	1	0	0	0	0	0	2	.250	.250	.250	500	55	-0				.333	-1	/S-1	-0.2
■ SCOTT STRATTON	Stratton, C. Scott b: 10/2/1869, Campbellsburg, Ky. d: 3/8/39, Louisville, Ky. BL/TR, 6', 180 lbs. Deb: 4/21/1888 Career OF: (41-LF 23-CF 68-RF)																							
1888	Lou-a	67	249	35	64	8	1	1	29	12		.257	.310	.309	619	101	0	10			.821	-5	O-38(28-7-3),P-33	-0.5
1889	Lou-a	62	229	30	66	7	5	4	34	13	36	.288	.332	.415	747	114	3	10			.915	5	O-29R,P-19,1-17	0.3
1890	*Lou-a	55	189	29	61	3	5	0	24	16		.323	.385	.392	776	132	8	8			**.977**	5	P-50/O-5(0-5-0)	0.0
1891	Pit-N	2	8	1	1	0	0	0	0	0	3	.125	.125	.125	250	-28	-1	0			.900	1	/P-2	0.0
	Lou-a	34	115	9	27	2	0	0	8	11	13	.235	.307	.252	559	61	-6	8			.939	2	P-20/1-8,O-6(2-3-1)	-0.3
1892	Lou-N	63	219	22	56	2	9	0	23	17	21	.256	.318	.347	665	110	3	9			.915	1	P-42,O-17(1-0-16)/1-6	-0.1
1893	Lou-N	61	221	34	50	8	5	0	16	25	15	.226	.308	.308	615	69	-9	6			.975	6	P-37,O-24(0-0-23)/1-1	-0.4
1894	Lou-N	13	37	9	12	1	2	0	4	4	2	.324	.390	.459	850	112	1	1			.929	2	/P-7,O-5(0-0-5)	0.1
	Chi-N	24	99	30	37	5	4	3	23	7	1	.374	.421	.596	1017	135	5	3			.938	-1	P-16/O-5(0-0-5),1-2	0.0
	Yr	37	136	39	49	6	6	3	27	11	3	.360	.412	.559	971	131	6	4			.935	1	P-23,O-10(0-0-10)/1-2	0.1
1895	Chi-N	10	24	3	7	1	1	0	2	4	2	.292	.393	.417	810	102	0	1			.833	-1	/P-5,O-4(0-4-0)	-0.1
Total	8	391	1390	202	381	37	32	8	163	109	93	.274	.335	.364	699	103	4	56			.938	15	P-231,O-133R/1-34	-1.0
■ JOE STRAUB	Straub, Joseph b: 1/19/1858, Germany d: 2/13/29, Pueblo, Colo. BR/TR, 5'10", 160 lbs. Deb: 6/24/1880																							
1880	Tro-N	3	12	1	3	0	0	0	3	1	3	.250	.308	.250	558	87	-0				.815	0	/C-3	0.0
1882	Phi-a	8	32	2	6	2	0	0	1	1		.188	.212	.250	462	50	-2				.830	-1	/C-7,O-1(0-0-1)	-0.2
1883	Col-a	27	100	4	13	0	0	0		4		.130	.163	.130	293	-5	-11				.860	-3	C-14,1-12/O-1(0-1-0)	-1.3
Total	3	38	144	7	22	2	0	0	4	6	3	.153	.187	.167	353	17	-13				.843	-4	/C-24,1-12,O-2(0-1-1)	-1.5
■ JOE STRAUSS	Strauss, Joseph "Dutch" or "The Socker" (b: Joseph Strasser) b: 11/16/1858, Cincinnati, Ohio d: 6/24/06, Cincinnati, Ohio BR/TR, Deb: 7/27/1884 Career OF: (83-LF 8-CF 1-RF)																							
1884	KC-U	16	60	4	12	3	0	0		1		.200	.213	.250	463	46	-6				.833	-1	O-10L/C-3,2-2,3-1	-0.6
1885	Lou-a	2	6	0	1	0	0	0	0	0		.167	.167	.167	333	6	-1				.000	-2	/O-1(1-0-0),C-1	-0.2
1886	Lou-a	74	297	36	64	5	6	1	31	8		.215	.239	.283	521	60	-15	25			.857	4	O-73(67-6-1)/P-2,C-1	-1.1
	Bro-a	9	36	6	9	1	1	0	5	1		.250	.270	.333	604	88	-1	4			1.000	1	/O-7(7-0-0),C-2	0.0
	Yr	83	333	42	73	6	7	1	36	9		.219	.242	.288	530	63	-16	29			.866	5	O-80(74-6-1)/C-3,P-2	-1.1
Total	3	101	399	46	86	9	7	1	36	10		.216	.237	.281	517	59	-22	29			.861	2	/O-91L,C-7,P-2,23	-1.9
■ DARRYL STRAWBERRY	Strawberry, Darryl Eugene b: 3/12/62, Los Angeles, Cal. BL/TL, 6'6", 200 lbs. Deb: 5/6/83 Career OF: (54-LF 48-CF 1308-RF)																							
1983	NY-N	122	420	63	108	15	7	26	74	47	128	.257	.338	.512	849	134	17	19	6	2	.984	6	*O-117(0-0-117)	2.0
1984	NY-N★	147	522	75	131	27	4	26	97	75	131	.251	.345	.467	812	128	19	27	8	3	.980	4	*O-146(0-21-134)	2.1
1985	NY-N★	111	393	78	109	15	4	29	79	73	96	.277	.392	.557	949	167	36	26	11	2	.991	-4	*O-110(0-27-100)	3.0
1986	*NY-N★	136	475	76	123	27	5	27	93	72	141	.259	.363	.507	871	142	27	28	12	2	.975	2	*O-131(1-0-130)	2.5
1987	NY-N★	154	532	108	151	32	5	39	104	97	122	.284	.401	.583	984	165	51	36	12	4	.972	1	*O-151(0-0-151)	4.8
1988	*NY-N★	153	543	101	146	27	3	**39**	101	85	127	.269	.371	**.545**	**916**	**168**	48	29	14	1	.971	7	*O-150(0-0-150)	5.4
1989	NY-N†	134	476	69	107	26	1	29	77	61	105	.225	.314	.466	781	126	15	11	4	1	.972	9	*O-131(0-0-131)	2.2
1990	NY-N★	152	542	92	150	18	1	37	108	70	110	.277	.364	.518	882	140	29	15	8	1	.989	6	*O-149(0-0-149)	3.2
1991	LA-N†	139	505	86	134	22	4	28	99	75	125	.265	.364	.491	855	141	28	10	8	-1	.978	-2	*O-136(0-0-136)	2.1
1992	LA-N	43	156	20	37	8	0	5	25	19	34	.237	.324	.385	708	101	0	3	1	0	.986	-1	O-42(2-0-40)	-0.2
1993	LA-N	32	100	12	14	2	0	5	12	16	19	.140	.271	.310	581	59	-6	1	0	0	.905	-4	O-29(4-0-25)	-1.2
1994	SF-N	29	92	13	22	3	1	4	17	19	22	.239	.369	.424	793	111	2	0	3	-1	.969	2	O-27(0-0-27)	0.1
1995	*NY-A	32	87	15	24	4	1	3	13	10	22	.276	.364	.448	812	111	1	0	0	0	.909	1	D-15,O-11(1-0-10)	0.1

YEAR	TM/L	G	AB	R	H	2B	3B	HR	RBI	BB	SO	AVG	OBP	SLG	OPS	OPS+	BR+	SB	CS	SBR	FA	FR	G/POS	TPR
1996	*NY-A	63	202	35	53	13	0	11	36	31	55	.262	.363	.490	853	113	4	6	5	-0	1.000	-3	O-34(26-0-8),D-26	-0.2
1997	NY-A	11	29	1	3	1	0	0	2	3	9	.103	.188	.138	325	-13	-5	0	0	0	1.000	-1	/O-4(4-0-0),D-4	-0.5
1998	NY-A	101	295	44	73	11	2	24	57	46	90	.247	.355	.542	897	134	14	8	7	-1	.905	-3	D-81,O-16(16-0-0)	0.5
1999	*NY-A	24	49	10	16	5	0	3	6	17	16	.327	.500	.612	1112	184	7	2	0	0	.000	0	D-17	0.6
Total	17	1583	5418	898	1401	256	38	335	1000	816	1352	.259	.360	.505	865	139	289	221	99	14	.977	20	*O-1384R,D-143	26.5

■ GABBY STREET

Street, Charles Evard "Old Sarge" b: 9/30/1882, Huntsville, Ala. d: 2/6/51, Joplin, Mo. BR/TR, 5'11", 180 lbs. Deb: 9/13/04 MC

YEAR	TM/L	G	AB	R	H	2B	3B	HR	RBI	BB	SO	AVG	OBP	SLG	OPS	OPS+	BR+	SB	CS	SBR	FA	FR	G/POS	TPR
1904	Cin-N	11	33	1	4	1	0	0	0	1		.121	.147	.152	299	-7	-4	2			.973	4	C-11	0.1
1905	Cin-N	2	2	0	0	0	0	0	0	2		.000	.500	.000	500	48	0	0			1.000	1	/C-1	0.1
	Bos-N	3	12	0	2	0	0	0	0	0		.167	.167	.167	333	-1	-1	1			.778	-2	/C-3	-0.4
	Cin-N	29	91	8	23	5	1	0	8	6		.253	.306	.330	636	81	-2	1			.975	3	C-26	0.4
	Yr	34	105	8	25	5	1	0	8	8		.238	.298	.305	603	73	-4	2			.957	2	C-30	0.1
1908	Was-A	131	394	31	81	12	7	1	32	40		.206	.289	.279	568	92	-2	5			.973	-1	*C-128	1.0
1909	Was-A	137	407	25	86	12	1	0	29	26		.211	.262	.246	508	63	-17	2			.981	11	*C-137	0.8
1910	Was-A	89	257	13	52	6	0	1	16	23		.202	.273	.237	510	63	-11	1			**.978**	9	C-86	0.7
1911	Was-A	72	216	16	48	7	1	0	14	14		.222	.279	.264	543	53	-14	4			.973	7	C-71	-0.1
1912	NY-A	29	88	4	16	1	1	0	6	7		.182	.258	.216	474	34	-8	1			.958	0	C-29	-0.5
1931	StL-N	1	1	0	0	0	0	0	0	0	0	.000	.000	.000	0	-96	-0	0			1.000	0	/C-1,M	0.0
Total	8	504	1501	98	312	44	11	2	105	119	0	.208	.273	.256	529	66	-59	17			.974	32	C-493	2.1

■ WALT STREULI

Streuli, Walter Herbert b: 9/26/35, Memphis, Tenn. BR/TR, 6'2", 195 lbs. Deb: 9/25/54

YEAR	TM/L	G	AB	R	H	2B	3B	HR	RBI	BB	SO	AVG	OBP	SLG	OPS	OPS+	BR+	SB	CS	SBR	FA	FR	G/POS	TPR
1954	Det-A	1	0	0	0	0	0	0	0	1	0	—	1.000	—	1000	195	0	0	0	0	1.000	-0	/C-1	0.0
1955	Det-A	2	4	1	1	1	0	0	1	0	0	.250	.250	.500	750	100	-0	0	0	0	1.000	0	/C-2	0.0
1956	Det-A	3	8	0	2	1	0	0	1	1	2	.250	.333	.375	708	87	-0	0	0	0	.933	0	/C-3	0.0
Total	3	6	12	1	3	2	0	0	2	2	2	.250	.357	.417	774	106	0	0	0	0	.957	0	/C-6	0.0

■ JOHN STRICK

Strick, John Quincy Adams Deb: 5/18/1882

YEAR	TM/L	G	AB	R	H	2B	3B	HR	RBI	BB	SO	AVG	OBP	SLG	OPS	OPS+	BR+	SB	CS	SBR	FA	FR	G/POS	TPR
1882	Lou-a	32	110	17	18	6	1	0		9		.164	.227	.236	463	60	-4				.898	-0	C-21/O-6C,2-6,S1	-0.2

■ CUB STRICKER

Stricker, John A. (b: John A. Streaker) b: 2/15/1860, Philadelphia, Pa. d: 11/19/37, Philadelphia, Pa. BR/TR, 5'3", 138 lbs. Deb: 5/2/1882 M Career OF: (0-LF 1-CF 19-RF)

YEAR	TM/L	G	AB	R	H	2B	3B	HR	RBI	BB	SO	AVG	OBP	SLG	OPS	OPS+	BR+	SB	CS	SBR	FA	FR	G/POS	TPR
1882	Phi-a	72	272	34	59	6	1	0	18	15		.217	.258	.246	504	63	-11				.904	**23**	*2-72/P-2,O-1(0-0-1)	1.3
1883	Phi-a	89	330	67	90	8	0	1	40	19		.273	.312	.306	618	91	-4				.837	-20	*2-88/C-2	-1.8
1884	Phi-a	107	399	59	92	16	11	1		19		.231	.267	.333	601	89	-6				.870	-35	*2-107/O-1C,C-1,P-1	-3.4
1885	Phi-a	106	398	71	93	9	3	1	41	21		.234	.284	.279	563	74	-12				.879	-13	*2-106	-1.9
1887	Cle-a	131	587	122	194	19	4	2	53	53		.330	.334	.326	660	87	-7	86			.912	10	*2-126/S-6,P-3	0.6
1888	Cle-a	127	493	80	115	13	6	1	33	50		.233	.311	.290	602	96	-0	60			.929	23	*2-122/O-6(0-0-6),P-2	2.5
1889	Cle-N	136	566	83	142	10	4	1	47	58	18	.251	.323	.288	611	73	-19	32			.932	7	*2-135/S-1	-0.6
1890	Cle-P	127	544	93	133	19	8	2	65	54	16	.244	.318	.320	638	77	-16	24			.905	5	*2-109,S-20	-0.5
1891	Bos-a	139	514	96	111	15	4	0	46	63	34	.216	.309	.261	569	64	-23	54			.942	**24**	*2-139	0.6
1892	StL-N	28	98	12	20	1	0	0	11	10	7	.204	.297	.214	512	58	-4	5			.939	-4	2-27/S-1,M	-0.7
	Bal-N	75	269	45	71	5	5	3	37	32	18	.264	.344	.353	698	108	3	13			.918	2	2-75	0.8
	Yr	103	367	57	91	6	5	3	48	42	25	.248	.332	.316	648	95	-1	18			.923	-2	*2-102/S-1	0.1
1893	Was-N	59	218	28	39	7	1	0	20	20	12	.179	.248	.220	468	25	-23	4			.903	7	2-39,O-12R/S-4,3-4	-1.3
Total	11	1196	4688	790	1159	128	47	12	411	414	105	.247	.306	.294	600	78	-123	278			.907	30	*2-1145/S-32,OP3C	-4.4

■ GEORGE STRICKLAND

Strickland, George Bevan "Bo" b: 1/10/26, New Orleans, La. BR/TR, 6'1", 180 lbs. Deb: 5/7/50 MC

YEAR	TM/L	G	AB	R	H	2B	3B	HR	RBI	BB	SO	AVG	OBP	SLG	OPS	OPS+	BR+	SB	CS	SBR	FA	FR	G/POS	TPR
1950	Pit-N	23	27	0	3	0	0	0	2	3	8	.111	.226	.111	337	-8	-4	0			.978	3	S-19/3-1	-0.1
1951	Pit-N	138	454	59	98	12	7	9	47	65	83	.216	.318	.333	651	73	-16	4	2	0	.943	12	*S-125,2-13	0.4
1952	Pit-N	76	232	17	41	6	2	5	22	21	45	.177	.248	.284	533	46	-17	4	2	0	.953	15	2-45,S-28/1-1,3-1	0.2
	Cle-A	31	88	8	19	4	0	1	8	14	15	.216	.324	.295	619	78	-2	0	0	0	.964	10	S-30/2-1	0.9
1953	Cle-A	123	419	43	119	17	4	5	47	51	52	.284	.362	.379	741	103	3	0	0	0	.974	16	*S-122/1-1	2.8
1954	*Cle-A	112	361	42	77	12	3	6	37	55	62	.213	.319	.313	632	72	-13	2	1	0	.961	-12	*S-112	-1.6
1955	Cle-A	130	388	34	81	9	5	2	34	49	60	.209	.302	.273	575	54	-25	1	0	0	**.976**	8	*S-128	-0.6
1956	Cle-A	85	171	22	36	1	2	3	17	22	27	.211	.301	.292	593	56	-11	0	1	-0	.986	16	2-28,S-28,3-26	0.8
1957	Cle-A	89	201	21	47	8	2	1	19	26	29	.234	.325	.308	633	75	-7	0	3	-1	.980	15	2-48,S-23,3-19	1.1
1959	Cle-A	132	441	55	105	15	2	3	48	51	64	.238	.317	.302	619	74	-15	1	1	-0	.971	-9	3-80,S-50/2-4	-2.0
1960	Cle-A	32	42	4	7	0	0	1	3	4	8	.167	.255	.238	493	35	-4	0	0	0	.962	1	S-14,3-12/2-2	-0.3
Total	10	971	2824	305	633	84	27	36	284	361	453	.224	.314	.311	626	70	-112	12	10		.963	74	S-679,2-141,3-139,/1	1.6

■ GEORGE STRIEF

Strief, George Andrew b: 10/16/1856, Cincinnati, Ohio d: 4/1/46, Cleveland, Ohio BR/TR, 5'7", 172 lbs. Deb: 5/1/1879 U Career OF: (61-LF 60-CF 8-RF)

YEAR	TM/L	G	AB	R	H	2B	3B	HR	RBI	BB	SO	AVG	OBP	SLG	OPS	OPS+	BR+	SB	CS	SBR	FA	FR	G/POS	TPR
1879	Cle-N	71	264	24	46	7	1	0	15	10	23	.174	.204	.208	413	37	-17				.918	-9	O-55(1-54-1),2-16	-2.6
1882	Pit-a	79	297	45	58	9	6	2		13		.195	.229	.286	515	76	-6				.917	0	*2-78/S-1	-0.3
1883	StL-a	82	302	22	68	9	0	1	22	12		.225	.255	.265	520	64	-12				.899	6	*2-67,O-15(11-1-3)	-0.3
1884	StL-a	48	184	22	37	5	2	2		13		.201	.254	.283	536	72	-6				.848	-3	O-44(43-1-0)/2-3,1-1	-0.9
	KC-U	15	56	5	6	5	0	0		4		.107	.167	.196	363	11	-8				.900	8	2-15	0.1
	CP-U	15	53	6	11	5	0	0		3		.208	.250	.302	552	67	-4				.905	-2	2-15	-0.4
	Yr	30	109	11	17	10	0	0		7		.156	.207	.248	455	40	-11				.902	7	2-30	-0.3
	Cle-N	8	29	2	7	2	0	0	0	0	5	.241	.241	.310	552	70	-1				1.000	-0	/O-6(6-0-0),3-2	-0.1
1885	Phi-a	44	175	19	48	8	5	0	27	9		.274	.310	.377	687	110	1				.828	-2	3-19,S-10/O-8C,2-7	0.0
Total	5	362	1360	145	281	50	14	5	64	64	28	.207	.242	.275	517	67	-53				.899	-1	2-201,O-128L/3-21,S1	-4.5

■ LOU STRINGER

Stringer, Louis Bernard b: 5/13/17, Grand Rapids, Mich BR/TR, 5'11", 173 lbs. Deb: 4/15/41

YEAR	TM/L	G	AB	R	H	2B	3B	HR	RBI	BB	SO	AVG	OBP	SLG	OPS	OPS+	BR+	SB	CS	SBR	FA	FR	G/POS	TPR
1941	Chi-N	145	512	59	126	31	4	5	53	59	86	.246	.324	.352	676	94	-4	3			.960	20	*2-137/S-7	2.5
1942	Chi-N	121	406	45	96	10	5	9	41	31	55	.236	.292	.352	644	92	-6	3			.955	2	*2-113/3-1	0.3
1946	Chi-N	80	209	26	51	3	1	3	19	26	34	.244	.328	.311	639	83	-4	0			.956	-5	2-62/S-1,3-1	-0.6
1948	Bos-A	4	11	1	1	0	0	1	1	0	3	.091	.091	.364	455	17	-1	0	0	0	.947	2	/2-2	0.1
1949	Bos-A	35	41	10	11	4	0	1	6	5	10	.268	.348	.439	787	100	-0	0	0	0	.978	3	/2-9	0.3
1950	Bos-A	24	17	7	5	1	0	0	2	0	4	.294	.294	.353	647	59	-1	1	0	0	.778	3	/3-3,2-1,S-1	0.2
Total	6	409	1196	148	290	49	10	19	122	121	192	.242	.313	.348	660	90	-17	7	0		.958	25	2-324/S-9,3-5	2.8

■ JOE STRIPP

Stripp, Joseph Valentine "Jersey Joe" b: 2/3/03, Harrison, N.J. d: 6/10/89, Orlando, Fla. BR/TR, 5'11.5", 175 lbs. Deb: 7/2/28 Career OF: (10-LF 0-CF 12-RF)

YEAR	TM/L	G	AB	R	H	2B	3B	HR	RBI	BB	SO	AVG	OBP	SLG	OPS	OPS+	BR+	SB	CS	SBR	FA	FR	G/POS	TPR
1928	Cin-N	42	139	18	40	7	3	1	17	8	8	.288	.340	.403	743	95	-1	0			.931	-7	O-21R,3-17/S-1	-0.8
1929	Cin-N	64	187	24	40	3	2	3	20	24	15	.214	.313	.299	613	55	-13	2			.960	8	3-55/2-2	-0.1
1930	Cin-N	130	464	74	142	37	6	3	64	51	37	.306	.377	.431	808	100	1	15			.996	0	1-75,3-48	-0.1
1931	Cin-N	105	426	71	138	26	2	3	42	21	31	.324	.359	.415	774	114	8	5			.957	4	3-96/1-9	1.4
1932	Bro-N	138	534	94	162	36	9	6	64	36	30	.303	.350	.438	788	113	9	14			.954	16	3-93,1-43	2.4
1933	Bro-N	141	537	69	149	20	7	1	51	26	23	.277	.312	.346	658	92	-6	5			.967	5	*3-140	0.3
1934	Bro-N	104	384	50	121	19	6	1	40	22	20	.315	.354	.404	757	108	4	2			.941	-6	3-96/1-7,S-1	0.1
1935	Bro-N	109	373	44	114	13	5	3	43	22	15	.306	.344	.391	736	99	-0	2			.962	7	3-88,1-15/O-1(0-0-1)	0.8
1936	Bro-N	110	439	51	139	31	1	1	60	22	12	.317	.351	.399	749	100	0	2			**.968**	8	*3-106	1.1
1937	Bro-N	90	300	37	73	10	2	1	26	20	18	.243	.291	.300	591	60	-17	1			.971	-6	3-66,1-14/S-3	-2.2
1938	StL-N	54	199	24	57	7	0	0	18	18	10	.286	.349	.322	670	81	-5	0			.977	-8	3-51	-1.1
	Bos-N	59	229	19	63	10	0	1	19	10	7	.275	.305	.332	637	84	-6	2			.966	1	3-58	-0.3
	Yr	113	428	43	120	17	0	1	37	28	17	.280	.326	.327	653	82	-10	2			**.971**	-7	*3-109	-1.4
Total	11	1146	4211	575	1238	219	43	24	464	280	226	.294	.340	.384	724	96	-26	50			.961	21	3-914,1-163/O-22R,S2	1.5

■ MARK STRITTMATTER

Strittmatter, Mark Arthur b: 4/4/69, Huntington, N.Y. BR/TR, 6'1", 210 lbs. Deb: 9/3/98

YEAR	TM/L	G	AB	R	H	2B	3B	HR	RBI	BB	SO	AVG	OBP	SLG	OPS	OPS+	BR+	SB	CS	SBR	FA	FR	G/POS	TPR
1998	Col-N	4	4	0	0	0	0	0	0	0	3	.000	.000	.000	0	-82	-1	0	0	0	1.000	1	/C-3	0.0

■ ALLIE STROBEL

Strobel, Albert Irving b: 6/11/1884, Boston, Mass. d: 2/10/55, Hollywood, Fla. BR/TR, 6', 160 lbs. Deb: 8/29/05 Career OF: (1-LF 1-CF 0-RF)

YEAR	TM/L	G	AB	R	H	2B	3B	HR	RBI	BB	SO	AVG	OBP	SLG	OPS	OPS+	BR+	SB	CS	SBR	FA	FR	G/POS	TPR
1905	Bos-N	5	19	1	2	0	0	0	2	0		.105	.105	.105	211	-38	-3	0			1.000	-0	/3-4,O-1(1-0-0)	-0.4

YEAR	TM/L	G	AB	R	H	2B	3B	HR	RBI	BB	SO	AVG	OBP	SLG	OPS	OPS+	BR+	SB	CS	SBR	FA	FR	G/POS	TPR
1906	Bos-N	100	317	28	64	10	3	1	24	29		.202	.273	.262	535	69	-12	2			.946	-6	2-93/S-6,O-1(0-1-0)	-1.8
Total	2	105	336	29	66	10	3	1	26	29		.196	.264	.253	517	63	-15	2			1.000	-6	/2-93,S-6,3-4,O-2L	-2.2
■ **JIM STRONER** Stroner, James Melvin b: 5/29/01, Chicago, Ill. d: 12/6/75, Tarboro, N.C. BR/TR, 5′10″, 175 lbs. Deb: 5/1/29																								
1929	Pit-N	6	8	0	3	1	0	0	0	1	0	.375	.444	.500	944	130	0	0			.571	-0	/3-2	0.0
■ **ED STROUD** Stroud, Edwin Marvin b: 10/31/39, Lapine, Ala. BL/TR, 5′11″, 180 lbs. Deb: 9/11/66																								
1966	Chi-A	12	36	3	6	2	0	0	1	2	8	.167	.231	.222	453	33	-3	3	0	1	1.000	-0	O-11(4-0-7)	-0.4
1967	Chi-A	20	27	6	8	0	1	0	3	1	5	.296	.345	.370	715	116	1	7	2	1	1.000	-1	O-12(11-0-5)	0.0
	Was-A	87	204	36	41	5	3	1	10	25	29	.201	.291	.270	561	69	-7	8	6	-0	.983	-13	O-79(1-79-0)	-2.5
	Yr	107	231	42	49	5	4	1	13	26	34	.212	.297	.281	579	75	-7	15	8	1	.985	-14	O-91(12-79-5)	-2.5
1968	Was-A	105	306	41	73	10	10	4	23	20	50	.239	.285	.376	661	102	-0	9	3	1	.979	-4	O-84(25-7-58)	-1.0
1969	Was-A	123	206	35	52	5	6	4	29	30	33	.252	.353	.393	746	114	4	12	2	2	.982	-11	O-85(28-1-58)	-0.8
1970	Was-A	129	433	69	115	11	5	5	32	40	79	.266	.332	.349	681	92	-4	29	8	4	.993	2	*O-118(9-106-9)	-0.2
1971	Chi-A	53	141	19	25	4	3	0	2	11	20	.177	.237	.248	485	36	-12	4	5	-1	1.000	-11	O-44(8-22-20)	-2.8
Total	6	529	1353	209	320	37	28	14	100	129	224	.237	.307	.336	643	87	-22	72	26	7	.988	-38	O-433(86-215-157)	-7.7
■ **STEVE STROUGHTER** Stroughter, Stephen Lewis b: 3/15/52, Visalia, Cal. BL/TR, 6′2″, 190 lbs. Deb: 4/7/82																								
1982	Sea-A	26	47	4	8	1	0	1	3	3	9	.170	.235	.255	491	34	-4	0	0	0	1.000	1	/O-3(3-0-0),D-9	-0.3
■ **AMOS STRUNK** Strunk, Amos Aaron b: 1/22/1889, Philadelphia, Pa. d: 7/22/79, Llanerch, Pa. BL/TL, 5′11.5″, 175 lbs. Deb: 9/24/08 Career OF: (143-LF 954-CF 228-RF)																								
1908	Phi-A	12	34	4	8	1	0	0	0	4		.235	.316	.265	580	83	-0	0			.903	1	O-11(1-10-0)	0.0
1909	Phi-A	11	35	1	4	0	0	0	2	1		.114	.139	.114	253	-20	-5	2			1.000	-1	/O-9(1-8-0)	-0.7
1910	*Phi-A	16	48	9	16	0	1	0	2	3		.333	.373	.375	748	135	2	4			1.000	1	O-14(0-14-0)	0.2
1911	*Phi-A	74	215	42	55	7	2	1	21	35		.256	.363	.321	683	93	-1	13			.958	1	O-62(19-43-0)/1-2	-0.3
1912	Phi-A	122	412	58	119	13	12	3	63	47		.289	.366	.400	766	123	13	29			**.990**	11	*O-116(65-51-0)	1.8
1913	*Phi-A	94	292	30	89	11	12	0	46	29	23	.305	.368	.425	792	135	12	14			.962	-2	O-81(0-80-0)	0.6
1914	*Phi-A	122	404	58	111	15	3	2	45	57	38	.275	.364	.342	706	117	10	25	22	-2	**.987**	9	*O-120(12-108-0)	1.0
1915	Phi-A	132	485	76	144	28	16	1	45	56	45	.297	.371	.427	798	144	25	17	19	-3	.980	12	*O-111(0-59-52),1-19	2.8
1916	Phi-A	150	544	71	172	30	9	3	49	66	59	.316	.393	.421	814	152	35	21	23	-3	.978	2	*O-143(6-119-18)/1-7	2.6
1917	Phi-A	148	540	83	152	26	7	1	45	68	37	.281	.363	.361	724	123	16	16			**.986**	-2	*O-146(0-146-0)	0.3
1918	*Bos-A	114	413	50	106	18	9	0	35	36	13	.257	.316	.344	660	101	-1	20			**.988**	-5	*O-113(1-112-0)	-1.5
1919	Bos-A	48	184	27	50	11	3	0	17	13	13	.272	.323	.364	687	98	-1	3			.968	-1	O-48(0-48-0)	-0.6
	Phi-A	60	194	15	41	6	4	0	13	23	15	.211	.298	.284	582	63	-9	3			.981	1	O-52(0-10-42)	-1.2
	Yr	108	378	42	91	17	7	0	30	36	28	.241	.310	.323	633	79	-10	6			.974	-1	*O-100(0-58-42)	-1.8
1920	Phi-A	58	202	23	60	9	3	0	20	21	9	.297	.363	.371	735	94	-1	0	6	-2	.990	-4	O-54(6-10-38)	-1.1
	Chi-A	53	188	33	45	8	1	1	16	28	15	.239	.338	.309	646	72	-7	1	0	0	.981	-1	O-49(3-7-38)	-1.0
	Yr	111	390	56	105	17	4	1	36	49	24	.269	.351	.341	692	83	-8	1	6	-2	.985	-5	*O-103(9-17-76)	-2.1
1921	Chi-A	121	401	68	133	19	10	3	69	38	27	.332	.391	.451	842	116	10	7	10	-2	.970	-8	*O-111(9-69-33)	-0.5
1922	Chi-A	92	311	36	90	11	4	0	33	33	28	.289	.358	.350	708	85	-6	9	6	-0	.989	2	O-74(14-56-4)/1-7	-0.8
1923	Chi-A	54	54	7	17	0	0	0	8	8	5	.315	.403	.315	718	92	-0	1	0	0	1.000	-0	/O-5(2-3-0),1-2	0.0
1924	Chi-A	1	1	0	0	0	0	0	0	0	0	.000	.000	.000	0	-99	-0	0	0	0	.000	0	H	0.0
	Phi-A	30	42	5	6	0	0	0	1	7	4	.143	.265	.143	408	7	-6	0	0	0	1.000	-3	/O-8(4-1-3)	-0.8
	Yr	31	43	5	6	0	0	0	1	7	4	.140	.260	.140	400	5	-6	0	0	0	1.000	-3	/O-8(4-1-3)	-0.8
Total	17	1512	4999	696	1418	213	96	15	530	573	331	.284	.359	.374	732	112	86	185	86		.980	13	*O-1327C/1-37	0.8
■ **AL STRUEVE** Strueve, Albert Frederick b: 6/26/1860, Cincinnati, Ohio d: 1/28/29, Buckskin Township, O. Deb: 6/22/1884																								
1884	StL-a	2	7	2	2	0	0	0		0		.286	.286	.286	571	84	-0				.000	1	/O-1(0-1-0),C-1	0.1
■ **LUKE STUART** Stuart, Luther Lane b: 5/23/1892, Alamance Co., N.C. d: 6/15/47, Winston-Salem, N.C. BR/TR, 5′8″, 165 lbs. Deb: 7/28/21																								
1921	StL-A	3	3	2	1	0	0	1	2	0	1	.333	.333	1.333	1667	291	1	0	0	0	1.000	-1	/2-3	0.0
■ **DICK STUART** Stuart, Richard Lee "Dr. Strangeglove" b: 11/7/32, San Francisco, Cal. BR/TR, 6′4″, 212 lbs. Deb: 7/10/58 Career OF: (2-LF 0-CF 0-RF)																								
1958	Pit-N	67	254	38	68	12	5	16	48	11	75	.268	.311	.543	854	124	7	0	0	0	.973	0	1-64	0.3
1959	Pit-N	118	397	64	118	15	2	27	78	42	86	.297	.367	.549	916	141	22	1	1	-0	.976	1	*1-105/O-1(1-0-0)	1.7
1960	*Pit-N	122	438	48	114	17	5	23	83	39	107	.260	.321	.479	800	115	8	0	0	0	.986	-1	*1-108	0.0
1961	Pit-N★	138	532	83	160	28	8	35	117	34	121	.301	.347	.581	928	140	28	0	3	-1	.983	-2	*1-132/O-1(1-0-0)	1.7
1962	Pit-N	114	394	52	90	11	4	16	64	32	94	.228	.290	.398	688	83	-11	0	1	-0	.982	2	*1-101	-1.6
1963	Bos-A	157	612	81	160	25	4	42	**118**	44	144	.261	.312	.521	833	125	18	0	0	0	.979	8	*1-155	1.7
1964	Bos-A	156	603	73	168	27	1	33	114	37	130	.279	.323	.491	814	117	12	0	0	0	.981	1	*1-155	0.4
1965	Phi-N	149	538	53	126	19	1	28	95	39	136	.234	.290	.429	719	101	-1	1	0	0	.986	3	*1-143/3-1	-0.6
1966	NY-N	31	87	7	19	0	0	4	13	9	26	.218	.292	.356	648	81	-2	0	1	-0	.974	-1	1-23	-0.6
	*LA-N	38	91	4	24	1	0	3	9	11	17	.264	.356	.374	729	112	2	0	1	-0	.991	3	1-25	0.3
	Yr	69	178	11	43	1	0	7	22	20	43	.242	.325	.365	690	97	-1	0	2	-1	.982	2	1-48	-0.3
1969	Cal-A	22	51	3	8	2	0	1	4	3	21	.157	.204	.255	459	29	-5	0	0	0	.991	-1	1-13	-0.8
Total	10	1112	3997	506	1055	157	30	228	743	301	957	.264	.319	.489	808	117	78	2	7	-2	.982	13	*1-1024/O-2L,3-1	2.5
■ **BILL STUART** Stuart, William Alexander "Chauncey" b: 8/28/1873, Boalsburg, Pa. d: 10/14/28, Fort Worth, Tex. 5′11″, 170 lbs. Deb: 8/15/1895																								
1895	Pit-N	19	77	5	19	3	0	0	10	2	6	.247	.275	.286	561	47	-6	2			.913	-1	S-17/2-2	-0.5
1899	NY-N	1	3	0	0	0	0	0	0	0		.000	.000	.000	0	-99	-1	0			1.000	-0	/2-1	-0.1
Total	2	20	80	5	19	3	0	0	10	2	6	.237	.265	.275	540	42	-7	2			.909	-1	/S-17,2-3	-0.6
■ **FRANKLIN STUBBS** Stubbs, Franklin Lee b: 10/21/60, Richlands, N.C. BL/TL, 6′2″, 215 lbs. Deb: 4/28/84 Career OF: (247-LF 32-CF 49-RF)																								
1984	LA-N	87	217	22	42	2	3	8	17	24	63	.194	.274	.341	615	73	-8	2	2	-0	.993	-1	1-51,O-20(6-3-13)	-1.3
1985	LA-N	10	9	0	2	0	0	0	2	0	3	.222	.222	.222	444	25	-1	0	0	0	1.000	-0	/1-4	-0.1
1986	LA-N	132	420	55	95	11	1	23	58	37	107	.226	.292	.421	713	101	-1	7	1	1	.969	-4	*O-124L,1-13	-1.0
1987	LA-N	129	386	48	90	16	3	16	52	31	85	.233	.292	.415	706	87	-9	8	1	1	**.994**	7	*1-111,O-18(13-0-6)	-0.7
1988	*LA-N	115	242	30	54	13	0	8	34	23	61	.223	.293	.376	669	94	-2	11	3	1	.978	2	1-84,O-13(7-1-6)	-0.4
1989	LA-N	69	103	11	30	6	0	4	15	16	27	.291	.387	.466	853	145	6	3	2	-0	.948	1	O-28(22-5-3)/1-7	0.7
1990	Hou-N	146	448	59	117	23	2	23	71	48	114	.261	.335	.475	811	124	13	19	6	2	.991	-9	1-72,O-71(67-0-5)	0.0
1991	Mil-A	103	362	48	77	16	2	11	38	35	71	.213	.286	.359	645	79	-11	13	4	1	.991	5	1-92/O-4(4-0-0),D-4	-1.1
1992	Mil-A	92	288	37	66	11	1	9	42	27	68	.229	.297	.368	666	87	-5	11	8	-0	.987	6	1-68,D-16/O-1(0-0-1)	-0.5
1995	Det-A	62	116	13	29	11	0	2	19	19	27	.250	.360	.397	757	97	-0	0	1	-0	.972	-7	1-20,O-20(20-0-0)/D-3	-0.9
Total	10	945	2591	323	602	109	12	104	348	260	626	.232	.305	.404	709	97	-19	74	28	6	.989	-1	1-522,O-299L/D-23	-5.3
■ **MOOSE STUBING** Stubing, Lawrence George b: 3/31/38, Bronx, N.Y. BL/TL, 6′3″, 220 lbs. Deb: 4/14/67 MC																								
1967	Cal-A	5	5	0	0	0	0	0	0	0	4	.000	.000	.000	0	-99	-1	0	0	0	.000	0	H	-0.1
■ **SEEM STUDLEY** Studley, Seymour L. "Warhorse" b: Washington, D.C. d: 1874, Washington, D.C. Deb: 4/20/1872																								
1872	Nat-n	5	21	3	2	0	0	0	2	0	1	.095	.095	.095	190	-35	-4	0	0	0	.571	-1	/O-5(0-5-0)	-0.4
■ **GEORGE STUMPF** Stumpf, George Frederick b: 12/15/10, New Orleans, La. d: 3/6/93, Metairie, La. BL/TL, 5′8″, 155 lbs. Deb: 9/19/31																								
1931	Bos-A	7	28	2	7	1	1	0	4	1	2	.250	.276	.357	633	69	-1	0	0	0	1.000	-1	/O-7(6-2-0)	-0.3
1932	Bos-A	79	169	18	34	2	2	1	18	18	21	.201	.278	.254	533	40	-15	1	1	-0	.952	-7	O-51(17-2-32)	-2.3
1933	Bos-A	22	41	8	14	3	0	0	5	4	2	.341	.400	.415	815	117	1	4	0	1	1.000	-3	O-15(3-8-4)	-0.1
1936	Chi-A	10	22	3	6	1	0	0	5	2	1	.273	.333	.318	652	59	-1	0	0	0	1.000	1	/O-4(4-0-0)	-0.1
Total	4	118	260	31	61	7	3	1	32	25	26	.235	.302	.296	598	57	-17	5	1	1	.969	-11	/O-77(30-12-36)	-2.8
■ **BILL STUMPF** Stumpf, William Frederick b: 3/21/1892, Baltimore, Md. d: 2/14/66, Crownsville, Md. BR/TR, 6′0.5″, 175 lbs. Deb: 5/11/12																								
1912	NY-A	42	129	8	31	0	0	0	10	6		.240	.279	.240	520	46	-9	5			.892	-6	S-26/2-8,3-5,1-1,O	-1.3
1913	NY-A	12	29	5	6	1	0	0	1	3	3	.207	.281	.241	523	53	-2	0			.818	-3	/S-6,2-4,O-1(0-0-1)	-0.5
Total	2	54	158	13	37	1	0	0	11	9	3	.234	.280	.241	520	47	-11	5			.877	-9	/S-32,2-12,3-5,O1	-1.8

■ GUY STURDY
Sturdy, Guy R. b: 8/7/1899, Sherman, Tex. d: 5/4/65, Marshall, Tex. BL/TL, 6′0.5″, 180 lbs. Deb: 9/30/27

YEAR	TM/L	G	AB	R	H	2B	3B	HR	RBI	BB	SO	AVG	OBP	SLG	OPS	OPS+	BR+	SB	CS	SBR	FA	FR	G/POS	TPR
1927	StL-A	5	21	5	9	1	0	0	5	1	0	.429	.455	.476	931	137	1	2	0	0	.974	-1	/1-5	0.1
1928	StL-A	54	45	3	10	1	0	1	8	8	4	.222	.340	.311	651	70	-2	1	0	0	1.000	-0	/1-1	-0.2
Total	2	59	66	8	19	2	0	1	13	9	4	.288	.373	.364	737	91	-1	3	0	1	.975	-1	/1-6	-0.1

■ BOBBY STURGEON
Sturgeon, Robert Howard b: 8/6/19, Clinton, Ind. BR/TR, 6′, 175 lbs. Deb: 4/16/40

YEAR	TM/L	G	AB	R	H	2B	3B	HR	RBI	BB	SO	AVG	OBP	SLG	OPS	OPS+	BR+	SB	CS	SBR	FA	FR	G/POS	TPR
1940	Chi-N	7	21	1	4	1	0	0	2	0	1	.190	.190	.238	429	18	-2	0			.848	2	/S-7	0.0
1941	Chi-N	129	433	45	106	15	3	0	25	9	30	.245	.260	.293	553	58	-25	5			.956	-4	*S-126/2-1,3-1	-2.1
1942	Chi-N	63	162	8	40	7	1	0	7	4	13	.247	.269	.302	572	70	-7	2			.988	21	2-32,S-29/3-2	1.8
1946	Chi-N	100	294	26	87	12	2	1	21	10	18	.296	.319	.361	680	94	-3	0			.934	-13	S-72,2-21	-1.3
1947	Chi-N	87	232	16	59	10	5	0	21	7	12	.254	.276	.341	617	66	-12	0			.975	13	S-45,2-30/3-5	0.4
1948	Bos-N	34	78	10	17	3	1	0	4	4	5	.218	.256	.282	538	46	-6	0			.938	-3	2-18/S-4,3-4	-0.9
Total	6	420	1220	106	313	48	12	1	80	34	79	.257	.277	.318	595	68	-56	7			.951	14	S-283,2-102/3-12	-2.1

■ DEAN STURGIS
Sturgis, Dean Donnell b: 12/1/1892, Beloit, Kan. d: 6/4/50, Uniontown, Pa. BR/TR, 6′1″, 180 lbs. Deb: 5/1/14

YEAR	TM/L	G	AB	R	H	2B	3B	HR	RBI	BB	SO	AVG	OBP	SLG	OPS	OPS+	BR+	SB	CS	SBR	FA	FR	G/POS	TPR
1914	Phi-A	4	4	1	1	0	0	0	0	1	2	.250	.400	.250	650	100	0	0			1.000	0	/C-1	0.0

■ JOHNNY STURM
Sturm, John Peter Joseph b: 1/23/16, St.Louis, Mo. BL/TL, 6′1″, 185 lbs. Deb: 4/14/41

YEAR	TM/L	G	AB	R	H	2B	3B	HR	RBI	BB	SO	AVG	OBP	SLG	OPS	OPS+	BR+	SB	CS	SBR	FA	FR	G/POS	TPR
1941	*NY-A	124	524	58	125	17	3	3	36	37	50	.239	.293	.300	592	58	-32	3	5	-1	.990	-2	*1-124	-4.7

■ GEORGE STUTZ
Stutz, George "Kid" or "Satan" b: 2/12/1893, Philadelphia, Pa. d: 12/29/30, Philadelphia, Pa. BL/TR, 5′5″, 150 lbs. Deb: 8/17/26

YEAR	TM/L	G	AB	R	H	2B	3B	HR	RBI	BB	SO	AVG	OBP	SLG	OPS	OPS+	BR+	SB	CS	SBR	FA	FR	G/POS	TPR
1926	Phi-N	6	9	0	0	0	0	0	0	0	2	.000	.000	.000	0	-95	-2	0			.938	1	/S-5	-0.1

■ LENA STYLES
Styles, William Graves b: 11/27/1899, Gurley, Ala. d: 3/14/56, Hunstville, Ala. BR/TR, 6′1″, 185 lbs. Deb: 9/10/19

YEAR	TM/L	G	AB	R	H	2B	3B	HR	RBI	BB	SO	AVG	OBP	SLG	OPS	OPS+	BR+	SB	CS	SBR	FA	FR	G/POS	TPR
1919	Phi-A	8	22	0	6	1	0	0	5	1	6	.273	.304	.318	623	74	-1	0			.974	0	/C-8	0.0
1920	Phi-A	24	50	5	13	3	1	0	5	6	7	.260	.339	.360	699	84	-1	1	0	0	.966	2	/C-9,1-7	0.1
1921	Phi-A	4	5	0	1	0	0	0	0	0	2	.200	.200	.200	400	2	-1	0	0	0	.333	-1	/C-2	-0.2
1930	Cin-N	7	12	2	3	0	1	0	1	1	2	.250	.357	.417	774	91	-0	0			.875	0	/C-5,1-1	0.0
1931	Cin-N	34	87	7	21	3	0	0	5	8	7	.241	.313	.276	588	63	-4	0			.949	-7	C-31	-0.9
Total	5	77	176	14	44	7	2	0	16	16	24	.250	.320	.313	632	71	-7	1	0		.929	-6	/C-55,1-8	-1.0

■ CHRIS STYNES
Stynes, Christopher Desmond b: 1/19/73, Queens, N.Y. BR/TR, 5′9″, 170 lbs. Deb: 5/19/95 Career OF: (131-LF 2-CF 22-RF)

YEAR	TM/L	G	AB	R	H	2B	3B	HR	RBI	BB	SO	AVG	OBP	SLG	OPS	OPS+	BR+	SB	CS	SBR	FA	FR	G/POS	TPR
1995	KC-A	22	35	7	6	1	0	0	2	4	3	.171	.256	.200	456	20	-4	0	0	0	.982	6	2-17/D-2	0.2
1996	KC-A	36	92	8	27	6	0	0	6	2	5	.293	.309	.359	667	68	-4	5	2	0	.939	-2	O-19L/2-5,3-2,D-3	-0.6
1997	Cin-N	49	198	31	69	7	1	6	28	11	13	.348	.394	.485	879	127	8	11	2	2	.976	5	O-38(38-0-0)/2-8,3-3	1.4
1998	Cin-N	123	347	52	88	10	1	6	27	32	36	.254	.324	.340	664	74	-13	15	1	3	1.000	-8	O-80L,3-22,2-11,/S	-1.9
1999	Cin-N	73	113	18	27	1	0	2	14	12	13	.239	.312	.301	613	55	-8	5	2	0	.956	-2	2-43/3-8,O-4(4-0-0)	-0.8
2000	Cin-N	119	380	71	127	24	1	12	40	32	54	.334	.389	.497	886	117	10	5	2	0	.966	-14	3-77,2-15/O-8(6-0-2)	-0.3
Total	6	422	1165	187	344	49	3	26	117	93	124	.295	.353	.409	762	93	-11	41	9	6	.984	-15	O-149L,3-112/2-99,DS	-2.0

■ NEIL STYNES
Stynes, Cornelius William b: 12/10/1868, Arlington, Mass. d: 3/26/44, Somerville, Mass. BR/TR, 6′, 165 lbs. Deb: 9/8/1890

YEAR	TM/L	G	AB	R	H	2B	3B	HR	RBI	BB	SO	AVG	OBP	SLG	OPS	OPS+	BR+	SB	CS	SBR	FA	FR	G/POS	TPR
1890	Cle-P	2	8	0	0	0	0	0	0	0	0	.000	.000	.000	0	-99	-2	0			.846	-0	/C-2	-0.2

■ KEN SUAREZ
Suarez, Kenneth Raymond b: 4/12/43, Tampa, Fla. BR/TR, 5′9″, 175 lbs. Deb: 4/14/66 Career OF: (1-LF 0-CF 0-RF)

YEAR	TM/L	G	AB	R	H	2B	3B	HR	RBI	BB	SO	AVG	OBP	SLG	OPS	OPS+	BR+	SB	CS	SBR	FA	FR	G/POS	TPR
1966	KC-A	35	69	5	10	0	1	0	2	15	26	.145	.298	.174	472	41	-5	2	0	0	.954	5	C-34	0.2
1967	KC-A	39	63	7	15	5	0	2	9	16	21	.238	.392	.413	805	143	4	1	0	0	.979	7	C-36	1.3
1968	Cle-A	17	10	1	1	0	0	0	0	1	3	.100	.182	.100	282	-13	-1	0	0	0	1.000	1	C-12/2-1,3-1,O-1L	0.0
1969	Cle-A	36	85	7	25	5	0	1	9	15	12	.294	.400	.388	788	117	3	1	0	0	.991	6	C-36	1.0
1971	Cle-A	50	123	10	25	7	0	1	9	18	15	.203	.315	.285	599	65	-5	0	1	-0	.993	9	C-48	0.5
1972	Tex-A	25	33	2	5	1	0	0	4	1	4	.152	.176	.182	358	7	-4	0	0	0	.965	1	C-17	-0.3
1973	Tex-A	93	278	25	69	11	0	1	27	33	16	.248	.339	.299	637	84	-5	1	2	-0	.989	3	C-90	0.2
Total	7	295	661	57	150	29	1	5	60	99	97	.227	.334	.297	630	81	-13	5	3	0	.984	31	C-273/O-1L,3-1,2-1	2.9

■ LUIS SUAREZ
Suarez, Luis Abelardo b: 8/24/16, Alto Songo, Cuba d: 6/5/91, Havana, Cuba BR/TR, 5′11″, 170 lbs. Deb: 5/28/44

YEAR	TM/L	G	AB	R	H	2B	3B	HR	RBI	BB	SO	AVG	OBP	SLG	OPS	OPS+	BR+	SB	CS	SBR	FA	FR	G/POS	TPR
1944	Was-A	1	2	0	0	0	0	0	0	0	0	.000	.000	.000	0	-99	-1	0	0	0	1.000	0	/3-1	0.0

■ TONY SUCK
Suck, Anthony (b: Charles Anthony Zuck) b: 6/11/1858, Chicago, Ill. d: 1/29/1895, Chicago, Ill. 5′9″, 164 lbs. Deb: 8/9/1883 Career OF: (2-LF 10-CF 1-RF)

YEAR	TM/L	G	AB	R	H	2B	3B	HR	RBI	BB	SO	AVG	OBP	SLG	OPS	OPS+	BR+	SB	CS	SBR	FA	FR	G/POS	TPR
1883	Buf-N	2	7	1	0	0	0	0	0	1	4	.000	.125	.000	125	-56	-1				.000	-2	/O-1(1-0-0),C-1	-0.3
1884	CP-U	53	188	18	28	2	0	0		13		.149	.204	.160	364	12	-26				.904	-5	C-28,S-15,O-12C,/3	-2.5
	Bal-U	3	10	2	3	0	0	0		0		.300	.300	.300	600	75	-1				.882	2	/C-3	0.1
	Yr	56	198	20	31	2	0	0		13		.157	.209	.167	375	15	-26				.901	-3	C-31,S-15,O-12C,/3	-2.4
Total	2	58	205	21	31	2	0	0	0	14	4	.151	.205	.161	366	12	-27				.894	-5	/C-32,S-15,O-13C,3	-2.7

■ BILL SUDAKIS
Sudakis, William Paul "Suds" b: 3/27/46, Joliet, Ill. BB/TR, 6′1″, 190 lbs. Deb: 9/3/68 Career OF: (1-LF 0-CF 6-RF)

YEAR	TM/L	G	AB	R	H	2B	3B	HR	RBI	BB	SO	AVG	OBP	SLG	OPS	OPS+	BR+	SB	CS	SBR	FA	FR	G/POS	TPR
1968	LA-N	24	87	11	24	4	2	3	12	15	14	.276	.382	.471	854	168	8	1	0	0	.953	4	3-24	1.3
1969	LA-N	132	462	50	108	17	5	14	53	40	94	.234	.296	.383	679	96	-4	3	2	-0	.946	11	*3-121	0.6
1970	LA-N	94	269	37	71	11	0	14	44	35	46	.264	.355	.461	816	122	8	4	0	1	.983	-6	C-38,3-37/O-3R,1-1	0.5
1971	LA-N	41	83	10	16	3	0	3	7	12	22	.193	.302	.337	639	86	-2	0	1	-0	1.000	1	C-19/3-3,1-1,O-1L	-0.1
1972	NY-N	18	49	3	7	0	0	1	7	6	14	.143	.236	.204	440	27	-5	0	0	0	.967	1	/1-7,C-5	-0.5
1973	Tex-A	82	235	32	60	11	0	15	43	23	53	.255	.322	.494	815	132	9	0	1	-0	.962	-4	3-29,1-24/C-9,OD	0.3
1974	NY-A	89	259	26	60	8	0	7	39	25	48	.232	.302	.344	645	87	-5	0	0	0	.990	2	D-39,1-33/3-3,C-1	-0.7
1975	Cal-A	30	58	4	7	2	0	1	6	12	15	.121	.282	.207	489	43	-4	1	1	-0	.941	-1	D-13/C-5,1-2	-0.6
	Cle-A	20	46	4	9	0	0	1	3	4	7	.196	.260	.261	521	48	-3	0	1	-0	1.000	-1	1-12/C-6	-0.5
	Yr	50	104	8	16	2	0	2	9	16	22	.154	.273	.231	503	45	-7	1	2	-0	1.000	-2	1-14,D-13,C-11	-1.1
Total	8	530	1548	177	362	56	7	59	214	172	313	.234	.313	.393	707	102	2	9	6	-0	.942	6	3-217/C-83,1-80,DO	0.3

■ PETE SUDER
Suder, Peter "Pecky" b: 4/16/16, Aliquippa, Pa. BR/TR, 6′, 175 lbs. Deb: 4/15/41 Career OF: (0-LF 0-CF 2-RF)

YEAR	TM/L	G	AB	R	H	2B	3B	HR	RBI	BB	SO	AVG	OBP	SLG	OPS	OPS+	BR+	SB	CS	SBR	FA	FR	G/POS	TPR
1941	Phi-A	139	531	45	130	20	9	4	52	19	47	.245	.271	.339	610	62	-31	1	3	-1	.957	-7	*3-136/S-3	-3.3
1942	Phi-A	128	476	46	122	20	4	4	54	24	39	.256	.293	.340	634	78	-15	4	4	-1	.954	3	S-69,3-34,2-31	-0.5
1943	Phi-A	131	475	30	105	14	5	3	41	14	40	.221	.243	.291	534	56	-28	1	1	-0	.971	-8	2-95,3-32/S-5	-3.3
1946	Phi-A	128	455	38	128	20	3	2	50	18	37	.281	.309	.352	660	85	-10	1	1	-0	.959	1	S-67,3-33,2-12,/1O	-0.6
1947	Phi-A	145	528	45	127	28	4	5	60	35	44	.241	.290	.337	627	73	-21	0	3	-1	**.986**	-17	*2-140/S-3,3-2	-3.2
1948	Phi-A	148	519	64	125	23	5	7	60	60	60	.241	.321	.345	666	77	-18	1	3	-1	.988	-1	*2-148	-1.1
1949	Phi-A	118	445	44	119	24	6	10	75	23	35	.267	.306	.416	722	93	-8	0	1	-0	.975	7	2-89,3-36/S-2	0.3
1950	Phi-A	77	248	34	61	10	0	8	35	23	31	.246	.310	.383	693	78	-9	2	2	-0	.979	1	2-47,3-11,S-10,/1-4	-0.6
1951	Phi-A	123	440	46	108	18	1	1	42	30	42	.245	.295	.298	593	59	-25	5	5	-1	**.987**	10	*2-103,S-18/3-3	-1.0
1952	Phi-A	74	228	22	55	7	2	1	20	16	17	.241	.291	.303	594	61	-12	1	1	-0	.991	3	2-43,S-17,3-16	-0.6
1953	Phi-A	115	454	44	130	11	3	4	35	17	35	.286	.312	.350	662	76	-16	3	3	-0	.974	4	3-72,2-38/S-7	-0.9
1954	Phi-A	69	205	8	41	11	1	0	16	7	16	.200	.226	.263	490	34	-19	0	0	0	.961	9	2-35,3-20/S-2	-0.9
1955	KC-A	26	81	3	17	4	1	0	1	2	13	.210	.229	.284	513	37	-7	0	1	-0	.990	-3	2-24	-0.9
Total	13	1421	5085	469	1268	210	44	49	541	288	456	.249	.291	.337	627	71	-220	19	28	-6	.982	2	2-805,3-395,S/1O	-16.6

■ WILLIAM SUERO
Suero, Williams (Urban) b: 11/7/66, Santo Domingo, D.R. d: 11/30/95, Santo Domingo, D.R. BR/TR, 5′9″, 175 lbs. Deb: 4/9/92

YEAR	TM/L	G	AB	R	H	2B	3B	HR	RBI	BB	SO	AVG	OBP	SLG	OPS	OPS+	BR+	SB	CS	SBR	FA	FR	G/POS	TPR
1992	Mil-A	18	16	4	3	1	0	0	0	2	1	.188	.316	.250	566	62	-1	1	1	-0	.971	4	2-15/S-1,D-2	0.3
1993	Mil-A	15	14	0	4	0	0	0	0	1	3	.286	.333	.286	619	69	-1	0	1	-0	.944	3	/2-8,3-1	0.2
Total	2	33	30	4	7	1	0	0	0	3	4	.233	.324	.267	590	65	-1	1	2	-0	.962	7	/2-23,D-2,3-1,S-1	0.5

■ JOE SUGDEN
Sugden, Joseph b: 7/31/1870, Philadelphia, Pa. d: 6/28/59, Philadelphia, Pa. BB/TR, 5′10″, 180 lbs. Deb: 7/20/1893 C Career OF: (0-LF 6-CF 18-RF)

YEAR	TM/L	G	AB	R	H	2B	3B	HR	RBI	BB	SO	AVG	OBP	SLG	OPS	OPS+	BR+	SB	CS	SBR	FA	FR	G/POS	TPR
1893	Pit-N	27	92	20	24	4	3	0	12	10	11	.261	.340	.370	709	90	-1	1			.956	-0	C-27	0.1
1894	Pit-N	39	139	23	46	13	2	2	23	14	2	.331	.404	.496	900	117	4	3			.910	-5	C-31/3-4,S-3,O-1C	0.1
1895	Pit-N	50	158	28	48	4	1	1	17	16	12	.304	.379	.361	739	96	0	4			.901	4	C-50	0.7
1896	Pit-N	80	301	42	89	5	7	0	36	19	9	.296	.348	.359	706	90	-4	5			.952	1	C-70/1-7,O-4(0-4-0)	0.3

YEAR	TM/L	G	AB	R	H	2B	3B	HR	RBI	BB	SO	AVG	OBP	SLG	OPS	OPS+	BR+	SB	CS	SBR	FA	FR	G/POS	TPR
1897	Pit-N	84	288	31	64	6	4	0	38	18		.222	.275	.271	546	46	-22	9			.941	-4	C-81/1-3	-1.6
1898	StL-N	89	289	29	73	7	1	0	34	23		.253	.314	.284	598	70	-11	5			.937	0	C-60,O-15(0-1-14)/1-8	-0.5
1899	Cle-N	76	250	19	69	5	1	0	14	11		.276	.307	.304	611	73	-9	2			.935	-0	C-66/O-4R,1-3,3-1	-0.3
1901	Chi-A	48	153	21	42	7	1	0	19	13		.275	.339	.333	673	89	-2	4			.970	4	C-42/1-5	0.6
1902	StL-A	68	200	25	50	7	2	0	15	20		.250	.330	.305	635	78	-5	2			.956	-2	C-61/1-4,P-1	-0.1
1903	StL-A	79	241	18	51	4	0	0	22	25		.212	.288	.228	517	58	-11	4			.983	6	C-66/1-8	0.1
1904	StL-A	105	348	25	93	6	3	0	30	28		.267	.331	.302	632	107	4	6			**.989**	-1	C-79,1-28	1.2
1905	StL-A	90	266	21	46	4	0	0	23	23		.173	.247	.188	435	41	-17	3			.983	19	C-76/1-9	1.0
1912	Det-A	1	4	1	1	0	0	0	0	0		.250	.250	.250	500	44	-0	0			.941	1	/1-1	0.0
Total	13	836	2729	303	696	72	25	3	283	220	34	.255	.318	.303	621	78	-75	48			.957	23	C-709/1-76,O-24R,3SP	1.6

■ GUS SUHR

Suhr, August Richard b: 1/3/06, San Francisco, Cal. BL/TR, 6', 180 lbs. Deb: 4/15/30

YEAR	TM/L	G	AB	R	H	2B	3B	HR	RBI	BB	SO	AVG	OBP	SLG	OPS	OPS+	BR+	SB	CS	SBR	FA	FR	G/POS	TPR
1930	Pit-N	151	542	93	155	26	14	17	107	80	56	.286	.380	.480	860	106	5	11			.992	-7	*1-151	-1.0
1931	Pit-N	87	270	26	57	13	4	4	32	38	25	.211	.308	.333	642	73	-10	4			.993	0	1-76	-1.6
1932	Pit-N	154	581	78	153	31	16	5	81	63	39	.263	.337	.398	735	99	-1	7			.988	-10	*1-154	-2.5
1933	Pit-N	154	566	72	151	31	11	10	75	72	52	.267	.350	.413	763	117	14	2			.991	-4	*1-154	-0.5
1934	Pit-N	151	573	67	162	36	13	13	103	66	52	.283	.360	.459	819	115	12	4			.994	-5	*1-151	-0.7
1935	Pit-N	153	529	68	144	33	12	10	81	70	54	.272	.357	.437	794	109	7	6			.989	-7	*1-149/O-2(0-0-2)	-1.3
1936	Pit-N☆	156	583	111	182	33	12	11	118	95	34	.312	.410	.467	877	133	30	8			**.993**	-4	*1-156	1.1
1937	Pit-N	151	575	69	160	28	14	5	97	83	42	.278	.369	.402	771	109	9	2			.993	-4	*1-151	-0.9
1938	Pit-N	145	530	82	156	35	14	3	64	87	37	.294	.394	.430	824	126	21	4			.993	-8	*1-145	-0.1
1939	Pit-N	63	204	23	59	10	2	1	31	25	23	.289	.367	.373	739	101	1	4			.993	-4	1-52	-0.8
	Phi-N	60	198	21	63	12	2	3	24	34	14	.318	.421	.444	865	137	12	1			.995	1	1-60	0.7
	Yr	123	402	44	122	22	4	4	55	59	37	.303	.394	.408	802	118	13	5			.994	-4	*1-112	-0.1
1940	Phi-N	10	25	4	4	0	0	2	5	5	5	.160	.300	.400	700	95	-0	0			.967	-2	/1-7	-0.2
Total	11	1435	5176	714	1446	288	114	84	818	718	433	.279	.368	.428	796	112	101	53			.992	-53	*1-1406/O-2(0-0-2)	-7.8

■ CLYDE SUKEFORTH

Sukeforth, Clyde Leroy "Sukey" b: 11/30/01, Washington, Me. d: 9/3/2000, Waldoboro, Me. BL/TR, 5'10", 155 lbs. Deb: 5/23/26 MC

YEAR	TM/L	G	AB	R	H	2B	3B	HR	RBI	BB	SO	AVG	OBP	SLG	OPS	OPS+	BR+	SB	CS	SBR	FA	FR	G/POS	TPR
1926	Cin-N	1	1	0	0	0	0	0	0	0	1	.000	.000	.000	0	-99	-0	0			.000	0	H	0.0
1927	Cin-N	38	58	12	11	2	0	0	2	7	2	.190	.277	.224	501	37	-5	2			.970	1	C-24	-0.3
1928	Cin-N	33	53	5	7	2	1	0	3	3	5	.132	.179	.208	386	1	-8	0			.966	1	C-26	-0.6
1929	Cin-N	84	237	31	84	16	2	1	33	17	6	.354	.398	.451	849	115	6	8			.981	-8	C-76	0.2
1930	Cin-N	94	296	30	84	9	3	1	19	17	12	.284	.325	.345	669	65	-16	1			.976	-3	C-82	-1.2
1931	Cin-N	112	351	22	90	15	4	0	25	38	13	.256	.334	.322	656	82	-8	0			.965	-8	*C-106	-0.9
1932	Bro-N	59	111	14	26	4	4	0	12	6	10	.234	.280	.342	622	68	-5	1			.991	-3	C-36	-0.7
1933	Bro-N	20	36	1	2	0	0	0	0	2	1	.056	.105	.056	161	-55	-7	0			.983	3	C-18	-0.4
1934	Bro-N	27	43	5	7	1	0	0	1	1	6	.163	.182	.186	368	-1	-6	0			1.000	-1	C-18	-0.6
1945	Bro-N	18	51	2	15	1	0	0	1	4	1	.294	.345	.314	659	85	-1	0			.947	-3	C-13	-0.3
Total	10	486	1237	122	326	50	14	2	96	95	57	.264	.319	.331	650	71	-51	12			.974	-20	C-399	-4.8

■ GUY SULARZ

Sularz, Guy Patrick b: 11/7/55, Minneapolis, Minn. BR/TR, 5'11", 165 lbs. Deb: 9/2/80

YEAR	TM/L	G	AB	R	H	2B	3B	HR	RBI	BB	SO	AVG	OBP	SLG	OPS	OPS+	BR+	SB	CS	SBR	FA	FR	G/POS	TPR
1980	SF-N	25	65	3	16	1	1	0	3	9	6	.246	.338	.292	630	79	-1	1	0	0	.975	12	2-21/3-5	1.2
1981	SF-N	10	20	0	4	0	0	0	2	2	4	.200	.304	.200	504	46	-1	0	1	-0	1.000	4	/2-6,3-1	0.3
1982	SF-N	63	101	15	23	3	0	1	7	9	11	.228	.291	.287	578	62	-5	3	0	1	.961	10	S-37,3-14/2-9	0.9
1983	SF-N	10	20	3	2	0	0	0	0	3	2	.100	.217	.100	317	-10	-3	0	0	0	.917	3	/S-6,3-4	0.0
Total	4	108	206	21	45	4	1	1	12	23	23	.218	.300	.262	562	59	-11	4	1	1	.954	29	/S-43,2-36,3-24	2.4

■ ERNIE SULIK

Sulik, Ernest Richard "Dave" b: 7/7/10, San Francisco, Cal. d: 5/31/63, Oakland, Cal. BL/TL, 5'10", 178 lbs. Deb: 4/15/36

YEAR	TM/L	G	AB	R	H	2B	3B	HR	RBI	BB	SO	AVG	OBP	SLG	OPS	OPS+	BR+	SB	CS	SBR	FA	FR	G/POS	TPR
1936	Phi-N	122	404	69	116	14	4	6	36	40	22	.287	.353	.386	739	90	-5	4			.971	-6	*O-105(41-65-1)	-1.5

■ SULLIVAN

Sullivan b: Bristol, R.I. Deb: 5/14/1875

YEAR	TM/L	G	AB	R	H	2B	3B	HR	RBI	BB	SO	AVG	OBP	SLG	OPS	OPS+	BR+	SB	CS	SBR	FA	FR	G/POS	TPR
1875	NH-n	2	8	3	3	0	0	0	2	0	1	.375	.375	.375	750	185	1	1	0	0	1.000	-1	/O-2(0-0-2)	0.1

■ ANDY SULLIVAN

Sullivan, Andrew R. b: 8/30/1884, Southborough, Mass d: 2/14/20, Framingham, Mass. TR, Deb: 9/13/04

YEAR	TM/L	G	AB	R	H	2B	3B	HR	RBI	BB	SO	AVG	OBP	SLG	OPS	OPS+	BR+	SB	CS	SBR	FA	FR	G/POS	TPR
1904	Bos-N	1	1	0	0	0	0	0	0	1		.000	.500	.000	500	61	0	0			1.000	-0	/S-1	0.0

■ JACKIE SULLIVAN

Sullivan, Carl Mancel b: 2/22/18, Princeton, Tex. d: 10/15/92, Dallas, Tex. BR/TR, 5'11", 172 lbs. Deb: 7/6/44

YEAR	TM/L	G	AB	R	H	2B	3B	HR	RBI	BB	SO	AVG	OBP	SLG	OPS	OPS+	BR+	SB	CS	SBR	FA	FR	G/POS	TPR
1944	Det-A	1	1	0	0	0	0	0	0	0	0	.000	.000	.000	0	-95	-0	0	0	0	1.000	-0	/2-1	0.0

■ DAN SULLIVAN

Sullivan, Daniel C. "Link" b: 5/9/1857, Providence, R.I. d: 10/26/1893, Providence, R.I. TR, 5'11", 194 lbs. Deb: 5/2/1882 Career OF: (1-LF 5-CF 1-RF)

YEAR	TM/L	G	AB	R	H	2B	3B	HR	RBI	BB	SO	AVG	OBP	SLG	OPS	OPS+	BR+	SB	CS	SBR	FA	FR	G/POS	TPR
1882	Lou-a	67	286	44	78	8	2	0		9		.273	.295	.315	610	112	4				.878	7	*C-54,3-10/O-4C,S-1	1.5
1883	Lou-a	36	145	8	31	5	2	0		3		.214	.230	.276	506	67	-5				.900	-6	C-31/O-2C,3-2,S-1	-0.7
1884	Lou-a	63	247	27	59	8	6	0	26	9		.239	.268	.320	588	95	-1				.930	-14	C-63/O-1(1-0-0)	-0.9
1885	Lou-a	13	44	3	8	1	0	0	4	2		.182	.234	.205	439	40	-3				.948	-3	C-13	-0.5
	StL-a	17	60	4	7	2	0	0	3	6		.117	.197	.150	347	10	-6				.956	1	C-13/1-4	-0.4
	Yr	30	104	7	15	3	0	0	7	8		.144	.212	.173	385	22	-9				.952	-2	C-26/1-4	-0.9
1886	Pit-a	1	4	0	0	0	0	0	0	0		.000	.000	.000	0	-99	-1	0			.600	-1	/C-1	-0.2
Total	5	197	786	86	183	24	10	0	33	29		.233	.262	.289	551	84	-11	0			.909	-17	C-175/3-12,O-7C,1S	-1.2

■ DENNY SULLIVAN

Sullivan, Dennis J. b: 6/26/1858, Boston, Mass. d: 12/31/25, Boston, Mass. TR, 5'9", 170 lbs. Deb: 8/25/1879

YEAR	TM/L	G	AB	R	H	2B	3B	HR	RBI	BB	SO	AVG	OBP	SLG	OPS	OPS+	BR+	SB	CS	SBR	FA	FR	G/POS	TPR
1879	Pro-N	5	19	5	5	2	0	0	2	1	1	.263	.300	.368	668	121	0				.429	-4	/3-4,O-1(0-0-1)	-0.3
1880	Bos-N	1	4	1	1	0	0	0	1	0	1	.250	.250	.250	500	72	-0				.857	-1	/C-1	-0.1
Total	2	6	23	6	6	2	0	0	3	1	2	.261	.292	.348	639	113	0				.429	-4	/3-4,C-1,O-1(0-0-1)	-0.4

■ DENNY SULLIVAN

Sullivan, Dennis William b: 9/28/1882, Hillsboro, Wis. d: 6/2/56, W.Los Angeles, Cal BL/TR, 5'10", Deb: 4/22/05

YEAR	TM/L	G	AB	R	H	2B	3B	HR	RBI	BB	SO	AVG	OBP	SLG	OPS	OPS+	BR+	SB	CS	SBR	FA	FR	G/POS	TPR
1905	Was-A	3	11	0	0	0	0	0	0	1		.000	.083	.000	83	-76	-2	0			1.000	-1	/O-3(0-0-3)	-0.3
1907	Bos-A	144	551	73	135	18	0	1	26	44		.245	.315	.283	598	92	-4	16			.975	1	*O-143(0-143-0)	-1.1
1908	Bos-A	101	355	33	85	7	8	0	25	14		.239	.276	.304	580	86	-6	14			.981	7	O-97(0-92-5)	-0.4
	Cle-A	4	6	0	0	0	0	0	0	0		.000	.000	.000	0	-99	-1	0			1.000	-0	/O-2(1-0-1)	-0.2
	Yr	105	361	33	85	7	8	0	25	14		.235	.272	.299	571	83	-7	14			.982	7	O-99(1-92-6)	-0.6
1909	Cle-A	3	2	0	1	0	0	0	0	0		.500	.500	.500	1000	207	0	0			.000	-1	/O-2(0-0-2)	-0.1
Total	4	255	925	106	221	25	8	1	51	59		.239	.296	.286	582	87	-13	30			.978	7	O-247(1-235-11)	-2.1

■ HAYWOOD SULLIVAN

Sullivan, Haywood Cooper b: 12/15/30, Donalsonville, Ga. BR/TR, 6'4", 215 lbs. Deb: 9/20/55 FM

YEAR	TM/L	G	AB	R	H	2B	3B	HR	RBI	BB	SO	AVG	OBP	SLG	OPS	OPS+	BR+	SB	CS	SBR	FA	FR	G/POS	TPR
1955	Bos-A	2	6	1	0	0	0	0	0	0	1	.000	.000	.000	0	-92	-2	0	0	0	1.000	1	/C-2	-0.1
1957	Bos-A	2	1	0	0	0	0	0	0	0	0	.000	.000	.000	0	-95	-0	0	0	0	1.000	0	/C-1	0.0
1959	Bos-A	4	2	0	0	0	0	0	0	1	1	.000	.333	.000	333	-0	-0	0	0	0	1.000	1	/C-2	0.0
1960	Bos-A	52	124	9	20	1	0	3	10	16	24	.161	.257	.242	499	35	-11	0	0	0	.992	6	C-50	-0.4
1961	KC-A	117	331	42	80	16	2	6	40	46	45	.242	.334	.356	691	83	-7	1	0	0	.984	-6	C-88,1-16/O-5(2-0-3)	-0.9
1962	KC-A	95	274	33	68	7	2	4	29	31	54	.248	.327	.332	659	74	-9	1	0	0	.980	-9	C-94/1-1	-1.4
1963	KC-A	40	113	9	24	6	1	0	8	15	15	.212	.305	.283	588	62	-5	0	0	0	.992	8	C-37	0.4
Total	7	312	851	94	192	30	5	13	87	109	140	.226	.314	.318	633	69	-35	2	0	0	.985	1	C-274/1-17,O-5(2-0-3)	-2.4

■ JOHN SULLIVAN

Sullivan, John Eugene b: 2/16/1873, Illinois d: 6/5/24, St.Paul, Minn. BR/TR, 5'10", 170 lbs. Deb: 4/19/05

YEAR	TM/L	G	AB	R	H	2B	3B	HR	RBI	BB	SO	AVG	OBP	SLG	OPS	OPS+	BR+	SB	CS	SBR	FA	FR	G/POS	TPR
1905	Det-A	13	32	4	5	0	0	0	4	4		.156	.250	.156	406	29	-2	0			.964	4	C-12	0.2
1908	Pit-N	1	1	0	0	0	0	0	0	0		.000	.000	.000	0	-99	-0	0			1.000	0	/C-1	0.0
Total	2	14	33	4	5	0	0	0	4	4		.152	.243	.152	395	26	-3	0			.965	4	/C-13	0.2

■ CHUB SULLIVAN

Sullivan, John Frank b: 1/12/1856, Boston, Mass. d: 9/12/1881, Boston, Mass. BR/TR, 6', 164 lbs. Deb: 9/24/1877

YEAR	TM/L	G	AB	R	H	2B	3B	HR	RBI	BB	SO	AVG	OBP	SLG	OPS	OPS+	BR+	SB	CS	SBR	FA	FR	G/POS	TPR
1877	Cin-N	8	32	4	8	0	0	0	4	1	0	.250	.273	.250	523	74	-1				.944	-1	/1-8	-0.1
1878	Cin-N	61	244	29	63	4	2	0	20	2	9	.258	.264	.291	555	91	-2				**.975**	5	*1-61	0.1

YEAR	TM/L	G	AB	R	H	2B	3B	HR	RBI	BB	SO	AVG	OBP	SLG	OPS	OPS+	BR+	SB	CS	SBR	FA	FR	G/POS	TPR
1880	Wor-N	43	166	22	43	6	3	0	0	4	6	.259	.276	.331	608	97	-1				.983	3	1-43	0.0
Total	3	112	442	55	114	10	5	0	24	7	15	.258	.269	.303	573	92	-3				.976	7	1-112	0.0
■ JOHN SULLIVAN Sullivan, John Lawrence b: 3/21/1890, Williamsport, Pa. d: 4/1/66, Milton, Pa. BR/TR, 5'11", 180 lbs. Deb: 4/18/20																								
1920	Bos-N	81	250	36	74	14	4	1	28	29	29	.296	.374	.396	770	126	9	3	2	-0	.977	-2	O-66(16-5-45)/1-6	0.4
1921	Bos-N	5	5	0	0	0	0	0	0	0	0	.000	.000	.000	0	-99	-1	0	0	0	.000	0	H	-0.1
	Chi-N	76	240	28	79	14	4	4	41	19	26	.329	.381	.471	852	124	8	3	5	-1	.962	-7	O-66(63-1-1)	-0.4
	Yr	81	245	28	79	14	4	4	41	19	26	.322	.374	.461	835	120	7	3	5	-1	.962	-7	O-66(63-1-1)	-0.5
Total	2	162	495	64	153	28	8	5	69	48	55	.309	.374	.428	802	123	16	6	7	-1	.969	-9	O-132(79-6-46)/1-6	-0.1
■ JOHN SULLIVAN Sullivan, John Paul b: 11/2/20, Chicago, Ill. BR/TR, 5'10", 170 lbs. Deb: 6/7/42 C																								
1942	Was-A	94	357	38	84	16	1	0	42	25	30	.235	.285	.286	571	61	-19	2	0	0	.936	-11	S-92	-2.3
1943	Was-A	134	456	49	95	12	2	1	55	57	59	.208	.298	.250	548	63	-20	6	2	1	.946	11	*S-133	0.2
1944	Was-A	138	471	49	118	12	1	0	30	52	43	.251	.325	.280	605	77	-13	3	3	-0	.934	-14	*S-138	-1.7
1947	Was-A	49	133	13	34	0	1	0	5	22	14	.256	.361	.271	632	79	-3	0	2	-1	.963	8	S-40/2-1	0.7
1948	Was-A	85	173	25	36	4	1	0	12	22	25	.208	.297	.243	540	46	-13	2	2	-0	.951	2	S-57/2-4	-0.8
1949	StL-A	105	243	29	55	8	3	0	18	38	35	.226	.331	.284	615	61	-13	5	2	0	.942	-9	S-71,3-23/2-6	-1.8
Total	6	605	1833	203	422	52	9	1	162	216	206	.230	.312	.270	582	66	-80	18	11	0	.942	-13	S-531/3-23,2-11	-5.7
■ JOHN SULLIVAN Sullivan, John Peter b: 1/3/41, Somerville, N.J. BL/TR, 6', 195 lbs. Deb: 9/20/63																								
1963	Det-A	3	5	0	0	0	0	0	0	2	1	.000	.286	.000	286	-11	-1	0	0	0	1.000	0	/C-2	0.0
1964	Det-A	2	3	0	0	0	0	0	0	0	1	.000	.000	.000	0	-99	-1	0	0	0	1.000	0	/C-2	-0.1
1965	Det-A	34	86	5	23	0	0	2	11	9	13	.267	.344	.337	681	93	-0	0	0	0	.994	1	C-29	0.2
1967	NY-N	65	147	4	32	5	0	0	6	6	26	.218	.248	.252	500	44	-11	0	2	-1	.991	-11	C-57	-2.2
1968	Phi-N	12	18	0	4	0	0	0	1	2	4	.222	.300	.222	522	59	-1	0	0	0	.967	-0	/C-8	-0.1
Total	5	116	259	9	59	5	0	2	18	19	45	.228	.283	.270	553	59	-13	0	2	-1	.991	-10	/C-98	-2.2
■ JOE SULLIVAN Sullivan, Joseph Daniel b: 1/6/1870, Charlestown, Mass. d: 11/2/1897, Charlestown, Mass. 5'10", 178 lbs. Deb: 4/27/1893 Career OF: (56-LF 39-CF 2-RF)																								
1893	Was-N	128	508	72	134	16	13	2	64	36	24	.264	.322	.358	681	83	-13	7			.860	-29	*S-128	-2.9
1894	Was-N	17	60	7	15	3	0	0	5	6	2	.250	.357	.300	657	62	-3	3			.900	-3	/2-8,S-6,3-1,O-1R	-0.4
	Phi-N	77	312	65	110	10	8	3	63	24	10	.353	.408	.465	872	113	7	12			.886	-13	S-77	-0.1
	Yr	94	372	72	125	13	8	3	68	30	12	.336	.399	.438	837	104	4	15			.883	-16	S-83/2-8,3-1,O-1R	-0.5
1895	Phi-N	94	373	75	126	7	3	2	50	24	20	.338	.395	.389	783	102	2	15			.879	-16	*S-89/O-6(3-2-1)	-0.8
1896	Phi-N	48	191	45	48	5	3	2	24	18	12	.251	.347	.340	687	82	-4	9			.962	-4	O-45(8-37-0)/S-2,3-2	-0.9
	StL-N	51	212	25	62	4	2	2	21	9	12	.292	.351	.358	709	91	-2	5			.955	-6	O-45(45-0-0)/2-7	-1.0
	Yr	99	403	70	110	9	5	4	45	27	24	.273	.349	.350	699	87	-7	14			.959	-10	O-90L/2-7,S-2,3-2	-1.9
Total	4	415	1656	289	495	45	29	11	227	117	80	.299	.362	.381	743	93	-14	51			.871	-70	S-302/O-97L,2-15,3	-6.1
■ MARC SULLIVAN Sullivan, Marc Cooper b: 7/25/58, Quincy, Mass. BR/TR, 6'4", 205 lbs. Deb: 10/1/82 F																								
1982	Bos-A	2	6	0	2	0	0	0	0	0	2	.333	.333	.333	667	79	-0	0	0	0	1.000	1	/C-2	0.1
1984	Bos-A	2	6	1	3	0	0	0	1	1	0	.500	.571	.500	1071	191	1	0	0	0	.950	1	/C-2	0.2
1985	Bos-A	32	69	10	12	2	0	2	3	6	15	.174	.240	.290	530	43	-6	0	0	0	.993	4	C-32	-0.1
1986	Bos-A	41	119	15	23	4	0	1	14	7	32	.193	.262	.252	514	40	-10	0	0	0	.986	-5	C-41	-1.3
1987	Bos-A	60	160	11	27	5	0	2	10	4	43	.169	.199	.237	436	15	-20	0	0	0	.994	0	C-60	-1.7
Total	5	137	360	37	67	11	0	5	28	18	92	.186	.237	.258	495	33	-34	0	0	0	.990	1	C-137	-2.8
■ MARTY SULLIVAN Sullivan, Martin C. b: 10/20/1862, Lowell, Mass. d: 1/6/1894, Lowell, Mass. BR/TR, Deb: 4/30/1887 Career OF: (322-LF 67-CF 3-RF)																								
1887	Chi-N	115	508	98	170	13	16	7	77	36	53	.335	.340	.424	764	98	-4	35			.847	-7	*O-115(111-3-1)/P-1	-1.1
1888	Chi-N	75	314	40	74	12	6	7	39	15	32	.236	.273	.379	652	99	-1	9			.927	3	O-75(74-1-0)	0.0
1889	Ind-N	69	256	45	73	11	3	4	35	50	31	.285	.404	.398	802	122	10	15			.910	-5	O-64(0-63-1)/1-5	0.1
1890	Bos-N	121	505	82	144	19	7	6	61	56	48	.285	.357	.386	743	108	4	33			.951	4	*O-120(120-0-0)/3-1	0.4
1891	Bos-N	17	67	15	15	1	0	2	7	5	3	.224	.288	.328	616	71	-3	7			.926	-2	O-17(17-0-0)	-0.5
	Cle-N	1	4	0	1	0	0	0	1	0	1	.250	.250	.250	500	44	-0	0			.000	-0	/O-1(0-0-1)	-0.1
	Yr	18	71	15	16	1	0	2	8	5	4	.225	.286	.324	610	69	-3	7			.926	-3	O-18(17-0-1)	-0.6
Total	5	398	1654	280	477	56	32	26	220	162	168	.288	.341	.395	736	104	5	99			.909	-8	O-392L/1-5,3-1,P-1	-1.2
■ MIKE SULLIVAN Sullivan, Michael Joseph b: 6/10/1860, Webster, Mass. d: 6/16/29, Webster, Mass. BR/TR, 5'8.5", 165 lbs. Deb: 4/26/1888																								
1888	Phi-a	28	112	20	31	5	6	1	19	3		.277	.296	.455	751	140	4	10			.742	-6	O-18(16-0-2),3-10	-0.2
■ PAT SULLIVAN Sullivan, Patrick J. b: 12/22/1862, Milwaukee, Wis. TR, 5'11", 165 lbs. Deb: 8/30/1884																								
1884	KC-U	31	114	15	22	3	1	0		4		.193	.220	.237	457	44	-11				.767	1	3-21/O-9C,C-1,P-1	-0.8
■ RUSS SULLIVAN Sullivan, Russell Guy b: 2/19/23, Fredericksburg, Va BL/TR, 6', 196 lbs. Deb: 9/8/51																								
1951	Det-A	7	26	2	5	1	0	1	1	2	1	.192	.250	.346	596	60	-2	0	0	0	.938	0	/O-7(6-0-1)	-0.2
1952	Det-A	15	52	7	17	2	1	3	5	3	5	.327	.375	.577	952	161	4	1	0	0	.826	-2	O-14(6-0-9)	0.2
1953	Det-A	23	72	7	18	5	1	1	6	13	5	.250	.379	.389	768	109	1	0	0	0	.958	3	O-20(20-0-0)	0.3
Total	3	45	150	16	40	8	2	5	12	18	11	.267	.357	.447	803	118	4	1	0	0	.920	1	/O-41(32-0-10)	0.3
■ SUTER SULLIVAN Sullivan, Suter G. b: 10/14/1872, Baltimore, Md. d: 4/19/25, Baltimore, Md. 6', 170 lbs. Deb: 7/24/1898 Career OF: (1-LF 0-CF 30-RF)																								
1898	StL-N	42	144	10	32	3	0	0	12	13		.222	.300	.243	543	55	-8	1			.875	-13	S-23,O-10R/2-6,1P	-1.8
1899	Cle-N	127	473	37	116	16	3	0	55	25		.245	.297	.292	589	67	-21	16			.938	5	*3-101,O-20R/S-3,12	-1.4
Total	2	169	617	47	148	19	3	0	67	38		.240	.298	.280	578	64	-29	17			.889	-8	3-101/O-30R,S-26,21P	-3.2
■ TOM SULLIVAN Sullivan, Thomas Brandon b: 12/19/06, Nome, Alaska d: 8/16/44, Seattle, Wash. BR/TR, 6', 190 lbs. Deb: 6/14/25																								
1925	Cin-N	1	1	0	0	0	0	0	0	0	0	.000	.000	.000	0	-99	-0	0	0	0	1.000	-0	/C-1	0.0
■ SLEEPER SULLIVAN Sullivan, Thomas Jefferson "Old Iron Hands" b: 1859, Ireland. d: 10/13/09, St.Louis, Mo. BR/TR, 175 lbs. Deb: 5/3/1881																								
1881	Buf-N	35	121	13	23	4	0	0	15	1	21	.190	.197	.223	420	32	-9				.853	-12	C-31/O-5(0-2-4)	-2.0
1882	StL-a	51	188	24	34	3	3	0		3		.181	.194	.229	422	40	-12				.840	-18	C-51	-2.4
1883	StL-a	8	27	2	6	0	1	0		0		.222	.222	.296	519	62	-1				.939	5	/C-6,O-2(0-1-1)	0.4
	Lou-a	1	2	0	0	0	0	0		0		.000	.000	.000	0	-99	-0				.667	-1	/C-1	-0.1
	Yr	9	29	2	6	0	1	0		0		.207	.207	.276	483	52	-2				.923	5	/C-7,O-2(0-1-1)	0.3
1884	StL-U	2	9	0	1	0	0	0		0		.111	.111	.111	222	-31	-2				.000	-1	/O-1(0-0-1),C-1,P-1	-0.2
Total	4	97	347	39	64	7	4	0	15	4	21	.184	.194	.228	421	36	-24				.851	-27	/C-90,O-8(0-3-6),P-1	-4.3
■ TED SULLIVAN Sullivan, Timothy Paul b: 1851, County Clare, Ireland d: 7/5/29, Washington, D.C. Deb: 9/9/1884 MU																								
1884	KC-U	3	9	0	3	0	0	0		1		.333	.400	.333	733	143	0				1.000	-2	/O-2(0-0-2),S-1,M	-0.1
■ BILL SULLIVAN Sullivan, William b: 7/4/1853, Holyoke, Mass. d: 11/13/1884, Holyoke, Mass. Deb: 8/9/1878																								
1878	Chi-N	2	6	1	1	0	0	0	0	0	0	.167	.167	.167	333	9	-1				1.000	-1	/O-2(2-0-0)	-0.1
■ BILLY SULLIVAN Sullivan, William Joseph Jr. b: 10/23/10, Chicago, Ill. d: 1/4/94, Sarasota, Fla. BL/TR, 6', 170 lbs. Deb: 6/9/31 F Career OF: (33-LF 0-CF 33-RF)																								
1931	Chi-A	92	363	48	100	16	5	2	33	20	14	.275	.315	.364	679	83	-10	4	4	-1	.912	-9	3-83/O-2(0-0-2),1-1	-1.5
1932	Chi-A	93	307	31	97	16	1	1	45	20	9	.316	.358	.384	742	99	-0	1	3	-1	.990	-3	1-52,3-17/C-5,O-3R	-0.8
1933	Chi-A	54	125	9	24	0	1	0	13	10	5	.192	.252	.208	460	24	-14	0	0	0	.982	-3	1-22/C-8	-1.7
1935	Cin-N	85	241	29	64	9	4	2	36	19	16	.266	.324	.361	685	87	-4	4			.992	2	1-40,3-15/2-6	-0.4
1936	Cle-A	93	319	39	112	32	6	2	48	16	9	.351	.382	.508	890	117	7	5	2	0	.968	-2	C-72/3-5,1-3,O-1L	0.9
1937	Cle-A	72	168	26	48	12	3	3	22	17	7	.286	.355	.446	801	100	-0	1	4	-1	.949	-6	C-38/1-5,3-1	-0.5
1938	StL-A	111	375	35	104	16	1	7	49	20	10	.277	.316	.381	697	74	-16	8	5	0	**.990**	-1	C-99/1-6	-1.1
1939	StL-A	118	332	53	96	17	5	5	50	34	18	.289	.362	.416	778	96	-2	3	3	-0	.954	4	O-59L,C-19/1-4	-0.1
1940	*Det-A	78	220	36	68	14	4	3	41	31	11	.309	.399	.450	849	109	4	2	0	0	.976	1	C-57/3-6	0.9
1941	Det-A	85	234	29	66	15	1	3	29	35	11	.282	.375	.393	769	94	-1	0	3	-1	.976	5	C-63	0.6
1942	Bro-N	43	101	11	27	2	1	1	14	12	6	.267	.345	.337	682	98	0	1			.962	-0	C-41	0.2

YEAR	TM/L	G	AB	R	H	2B	3B	HR	RBI	BB	SO	AVG	OBP	SLG	OPS	OPS+	BR+	SB	CS	SBR	FA	FR	G/POS	TPR
1947	Pit-N	38	55	1	14	3	0	0	8	6	3	.255	.328	.309	637	68	-2	1			1.000	1	C-12	-0.1
Total	12	962	2840	347	820	152	32	29	388	240	119	.289	.346	.395	742	91	-38	30	24		.972	-11	C-414,1-133,3/O2	-3.6
■ **BILLY SULLIVAN** Sullivan, William Joseph Sr. b: 2/1/1875, Oakland, Wis. d: 1/28/65, Newberg, Ore. BR/TR, 5'9", 155 lbs. Deb: 9/13/1899 FM Career OF: (1-LF 0-CF 1-RF)																								
1899	Bos-N	22	74	10	20	2	0	2	12	1		.270	.308	.378	686	80	-2	2			.952	5	C-22	0.4
1900	Bos-N	72	238	36	65	6	0	8	41	9		.273	.302	.399	702	83	-7	4			.974	0	C-66/S-1,2-1	-0.1
1901	Chi-A	98	367	54	90	15	6	4	56	10		.245	.271	.351	623	74	-14	12			**.967**	-1	C-97/3-1	-0.5
1902	Chi-A	76	263	36	64	12	3	1	26	6		.243	.268	.323	592	66	-12	11			.967	-3	C-70/1-2,O-2(1-0-1)	-0.8
1903	Chi-A	32	111	10	21	4	0	1	7	5		.189	.224	.252	476	45	-7	3			.988	-2	C-31	-0.7
1904	Chi-A	108	371	29	85	18	4	1	44	12		.229	.255	.307	562	81	-9	11			.964	2	*C-107	0.4
1905	Chi-A	98	323	25	65	10	3	2	26	13		.201	.239	.269	508	64	-14	14			.974	-4	C-92/1-2,3-1	-1.0
1906	*Chi-A	118	387	37	83	18	4	2	33	22		.214	.262	.297	559	77	-11	10			**.974**	-4	*C-118	-0.4
1907	Chi-A	112	329	30	59	8	4	0	36	21		.179	.235	.228	463	49	-19	6			.983	-1	*C-108/2-1	-1.1
1908	Chi-A	137	430	40	82	8	4	0	29	22		.191	.235	.228	463	51	-23	15			**.985**	-20	*C-137	-3.4
1909	Chi-A	97	265	11	43	3	0	0	16	17		.162	.226	.174	400	28	-21	9			.983	5	C-97,M	-0.9
1910	Chi-A	45	142	10	26	4	1	0	6	7		.183	.227	.225	452	43	-9	0			.976	12	C-45	0.8
1911	Chi-A	89	256	26	55	9	3	0	31	16		.215	.266	.273	540	52	-17	1			**.986**	1	C-89	-0.8
1912	Chi-A	41	91	9	19	2	1	0	15	9		.209	.287	.253	540	57	-5	0			.975	1	C-41	-0.1
1914	Chi-A	1	0	0	0	0	0	0	0	0	0	—	—	—	—	—	0	0			1.000	-0	/C-1	0.0
1916	Det-A	1	0	0	0	0	0	0	0	0	0	—	—	—	—	—	0	0			.000	0	/C-1	0.0
Total	16	1147	3647	363	777	119	33	21	378	170	0	.213	.254	.281	535	63	-171	98			.976	-8	*C-1122/1-4,O-2L,32S	-8.2
■ **HOMER SUMMA** Summa, Homer Wayne b: 11/3/1898, Gentry, Mo. d: 1/29/66, Los Angeles, Cal. BL/TR, 5'10.5", 170 lbs. Deb: 9/13/20																								
1920	Pit-N	10	22	1	7	1	1	0	1	3	1	.318	.400	.455	855	141	1	1	0	0	.950	1	/O-6(1-5-0)	0.2
1922	Cle-A	12	46	9	16	3	3	1	6	1	1	.348	.400	.609	1009	159	4	1	2	-0	1.000	0	O-12(0-0-12)	0.2
1923	Cle-A	137	525	92	172	27	6	3	69	33	20	.328	.374	.419	793	109	6	9	13	-3	.951	-13	*O-136(0-3-133)	-1.9
1924	Cle-A	111	390	55	113	21	6	2	38	11	16	.290	.311	.390	701	79	-14	4	2	0	.941	-6	O-95(0-3-92)	-2.5
1925	Cle-A	75	224	28	74	10	1	0	25	13	6	.330	.375	.384	759	92	-2	3	2	-0	.966	-9	O-54(18-1-35)/3-2	-1.4
1926	Cle-A	154	581	74	179	31	6	4	76	47	9	.308	.368	.403	771	100	0	15	8	1	.975	7	*O-154(0-0-154)	-0.4
1927	Cle-A	145	574	72	164	41	7	4	74	32	18	.286	.331	.402	734	89	-11	6	5	-0	.955	-8	*O-145(0-1-144)	-3.0
1928	Cle-A	134	504	60	143	26	3	3	57	20	15	.284	.319	.365	684	78	-16	4	2	0	.971	-4	*O-132(0-0-132)	-3.0
1929	*Phi-A	37	81	12	22	4	0	0	10	2	1	.272	.298	.321	619	57	-5	1	1	-0	.980	-5	O-24(18-0-16)	-1.1
1930	Phi-A	25	54	10	15	2	1	1	5	4	1	.278	.339	.407	746	85	-1	0	0	0	.938	0	O-15(3-0-12)	-0.2
Total	10	840	3001	413	905	166	34	18	361	166	88	.302	.346	.398	743	92	-38	44	35	-3	.961	-36	O-773(40-13-730)/3-2	-13.1
■ **CHAMP SUMMERS** Summers, John Junior b: 6/15/46, Bremerton, Wash. BL/TR, 6'2", 205 lbs. Deb: 5/4/74 C Career OF: (103-LF 0-CF 160-RF)																								
1974	Oak-A	20	24	2	3	1	0	0	3	1	5	.125	.160	.167	327	-6	-3	0	0	0	1.000	-4	O-12(8-0-4)/D-2	-0.8
1975	Chi-N	76	91	14	21	5	1	1	16	10	13	.231	.314	.341	654	78	-3	0	0	0	.889	-4	O-18(15-0-3)	-0.8
1976	Chi-N	83	126	11	26	2	0	3	13	13	31	.206	.286	.294	579	59	-7	1	0	0	.964	-5	O-26(19-0-7),1-10/C-1	-1.4
1977	Cin-N	59	76	11	13	4	0	3	6	6	16	.171	.241	.342	583	53	-5	0	0	0	1.000	-1	O-16(3-0-13)/3-1	-0.7
1978	Cin-N	13	35	4	9	2	0	1	3	7	4	.257	.381	.400	781	118	1	2	1	0	.933	-2	O-12(0-0-12)	-0.2
1979	Cin-N	27	60	10	12	2	1	1	11	13	15	.200	.351	.317	668	83	-1	0	1	-0	.941	-2	O-13(4-0-9)/1-6	-0.4
	Det-A	90	246	47	77	12	1	20	51	40	33	.313	.415	.614	1029	168	24	7	6	-1	.989	-10	O-69(2-0-67),D-10/1-4	1.0
1980	Det-A	120	347	61	103	19	1	17	60	52	52	.297	.396	.504	900	142	21	4	3	-0	.953	-8	D-64,O-47R/1-1	0.9
1981	Det-A	64	165	16	42	8	0	3	21	19	35	.255	.342	.358	700	98	0	1	1	-0	.964	-2	D-37,O-18(0-0-18)	-0.4
1982	SF-N	70	125	15	31	5	0	4	19	16	17	.248	.347	.384	731	105	1	0	1	-0	.913	-3	O-31(30-0-1)/1-3	-0.4
1983	SF-N	29	22	3	3	0	0	0	3	7	8	.136	.345	.136	481	39	-1	0	0	0	1.000	0	/O-1(1-0-0)	-0.1
1984	*SD-N	47	54	5	10	3	0	1	12	4	15	.185	.254	.296	551	54	-3	0	0	0	1.000	-1	/1-8	-0.5
Total	11	698	1371	199	350	63	4	54	218	188	244	.255	.353	.425	778	111	24	15	13	-1	.959	-41	O-263R,D-113/1-32,3C	-3.8
■ **KID SUMMERS** Summers, William b: Toronto, Ont., Canada d: 10/16/1895, Toronto, Ont., Can. TR, 5'10", 169 lbs. Deb: 8/5/1893																								
1893	StL-N	2	1	1	0	0	0	0	0	0	0	.000	.500	.000	500	37	0	0			.500	-0	/O-1(1-0-0),C-1	0.0
■ **CARL SUMNER** Sumner, Carl Ringdahl "Lefty" b: 9/28/08, Cambridge, Mass. d: 2/8/99, Chatham, Mass. BL/TL, 5'8", 170 lbs. Deb: 7/28/28																								
1928	Bos-A	16	29	6	8	1	1	0	3	5	6	.276	.382	.379	762	103	0	0	0	0	.923	-3	O-10(5-4-1)	-0.3
■ **ART SUNDAY** Sunday, Arthur (b: August Wacher) b: 1/21/1862, Springfield, Ohio BL/TL, 5'9", 193 lbs. Deb: 5/5/1890																								
1890	Bro-P	24	83	26	22	5	1	0	13	15	9	.265	.419	.349	768	100	1	0			.909	-5	O-24(0-5-20)	-0.4
■ **BILLY SUNDAY** Sunday, William Ashley "Parson" or "The Evangelist" b: 11/19/1862, Ames, Iowa d: 11/6/35, Chicago, Ill. BL/TR, 5'10", 160 lbs. Deb: 5/22/1883																								
1883	Chi-N	14	54	6	13	4	0	0	5	1	18	.241	.255	.315	569	66	-2				.647	-5	O-14(1-0-13)	-0.6
1884	Chi-N	43	176	25	39	4	1	4	28	4	36	.222	.239	.324	563	70	-7				.663	-9	O-43(0-9-34)	-1.5
1885	*Chi-N	46	172	36	44	3	3	2	20	12	33	.256	.304	.343	647	96	-1				.825	-9	O-46(1-4-43)	-1.0
1886	Chi-N	28	103	16	25	2	2	0	6	7	26	.243	.291	.301	592	70	-4	10			.914	-0	O-28(1-0-27)	-0.4
1887	Chi-N	50	220	41	79	6	6	3	32	21	20	.359	.362	.427	789	105	1	34			.766	-8	O-50(2-23-25)	-0.7
1888	Pit-N	120	505	69	119	14	3	0	15	12	36	.236	.256	.275	532	75	-14	71			.939	17	*O-120(1-117-3)	-0.1
1889	Pit-N	81	321	62	77	10	6	2	25	27	33	.240	.307	.327	634	85	-6	47			.946	8	O-81(1-0-80)	0.2
1890	Pit-N	86	358	58	92	9	2	1	33	32	20	.257	.327	.302	628	94	-0	56			.883	11	O-86(0-51-35)/P-1	0.8
	Phi-N	31	119	26	31	3	1	0	6	18	7	.261	.367	.303	669	93	-0	28			.950	3	O-31(0-31-0)	0.2
	Yr	117	477	84	123	12	3	1	39	50	27	.258	.337	.302	639	94	-1	84			.900	15	*O-117(0-82-35)/P-1	1.0
Total	8	499	2028	339	519	55	24	12	170	134	229	.256	.300	.317	617	86	-34	246			.883	9	O-499(7-235-260)/P-1	-3.1
■ **JIM SUNDBERG** Sundberg, James Howard b: 5/18/51, Galesburg, Ill. BR/TR, 6', 195 lbs. Deb: 4/4/74 Career OF: (3-LF 0-CF 0-RF)																								
1974	Tex-A☆	132	368	45	91	13	3	3	36	62	61	.247	.356	.323	679	99	2	2	4	-1	.990	6	*C-132	1.3
1975	Tex-A	155	472	45	94	9	0	6	36	51	77	.199	.283	.256	539	54	-28	3	1	0	.981	5	*C-155	-1.6
1976	Tex-A	140	448	33	102	24	2	3	34	37	61	.228	.287	.310	597	73	-15	0	0	0	**.991**	17	*C-140	0.8
1977	Tex-A	149	453	61	132	20	3	6	65	53	77	.291	.368	.389	757	105	5	2	3	-1	**.994**	23	*C-149	3.3
1978	Tex-A★	149	518	54	144	23	6	6	58	64	70	.278	.361	.380	741	108	7	2	5	-1	**.997**	16	*C-148/D-1	2.9
1979	Tex-A	150	495	50	136	23	4	5	64	51	51	.275	.348	.368	716	94	-3	3	3	-0	**.995**	9	*C-150	1.2
1980	Tex-A	151	505	59	138	24	1	10	63	64	67	.273	.356	.384	740	106	6	2	2	-0	.993	6	*C-151	1.8
1981	Tex-A	102	339	42	94	17	2	3	28	50	48	.277	.372	.366	738	120	10	2	5	-1	.996	-3	C-98/O-2(2-0-0)	1.1
1982	Tex-A	139	470	37	118	22	5	10	47	49	57	.251	.323	.383	706	98	-1	2	6	-2	.991	-2	*C-132/O-1(1-0-0)	0.1
1983	Tex-A	131	378	30	76	14	0	2	28	35	64	.201	.272	.254	526	47	-27	0	4	-1	.993	5	*C-131	-1.8
1984	Mil-A★	110	348	43	91	19	4	7	43	38	63	.261	.334	.399	734	106	3	1	1	-0	**.995**	7	*C-109	1.4
1985	*KC-A	115	367	38	90	12	4	10	35	33	67	.245	.309	.381	691	88	-6	0	2	-1	.992	1	*C-112	-0.1
1986	KC-A	140	429	41	91	9	1	12	42	57	91	.212	.305	.322	626	69	-18	1	1	-0	**.995**	-1	*C-134	-1.4
1987	Chi-N	61	139	9	28	2	0	4	15	19	40	.201	.306	.302	608	60	-8	0	0	0	.994	9	C-57	0.2
1988	Chi-N	24	54	8	13	1	0	2	9	8	15	.241	.339	.370	709	99	0	0	0	0	1.000	-1	C-20	0.0
	Tex-A	38	91	13	26	4	0	4	13	5	17	.286	.323	.462	784	114	1	0	0	0	1.000	0	C-36	0.3
1989	Tex-A	76	147	13	29	7	1	2	8	23	37	.197	.306	.299	605	70	-5	0	0	0	.992	1	C-73/D-1	-0.1
Total	16	1962	6021	621	1493	243	36	95	624	699	963	.248	.328	.348	676	89	-77	20	37	-9	.993	96	*C-1927/O-3L,D-2	9.4
■ **B.J. SURHOFF** Surhoff, William James b: 8/4/64, Bronx, N.Y. BL/TR, 6'1", 200 lbs. Deb: 4/8/87 F Career OF: (671-LF 5-CF 28-RF)																								
1987	Mil-A	115	395	50	118	22	3	7	68	36	30	.299	.357	.423	780	103	2	11	10	-1	.984	6	C-98,3-10/1-1,D-7	1.1
1988	Mil-A	139	493	47	121	21	0	5	38	31	49	.245	.294	.318	613	71	-19	21	6	3	.990	-8	*C-106,3-31/1-2,SO	-1.8
1989	Mil-A	126	436	42	108	17	4	5	55	25	29	.248	.293	.339	633	79	-13	14	12	-1	.985	-5	*C-106,D-12/3-6	-1.4
1990	Mil-A	135	474	55	131	21	4	6	59	41	37	.276	.335	.376	711	99	-0	18	7	2	.985	-6	*C-125,3-11	0.3
1991	Mil-A	143	505	57	146	19	4	5	68	26	33	.289	.324	.372	696	94	-4	5	8	-2	.995	-4	*C-127/3-5,O-2C,2D	-0.2
1992	Mil-A	139	480	63	121	19	1	4	62	46	41	.252	.320	.321	641	82	-11	14	8	0	.990	6	*C-109,1-17/O-7L,3D	0.0
1993	Mil-A	148	552	66	151	38	3	7	79	36	47	.274	.320	.391	712	92	-7	12	9	-1	.949	-7	*3-121,O-24R/1-8,CD	-1.5
1994	Mil-A	40	134	20	35	11	2	5	22	16	14	.261	.340	.485	825	105	1	0	1	-0	.923	-4	3-18,C-12/1-8,OD	-0.3

YEAR	TM/L	G	AB	R	H	2B	3B	HR	RBI	BB	SO	AVG	OBP	SLG	OPS	OPS+	BR+	SB	CS	SBR	FA	FR	G/POS	TPR
1995	Mil-A	117	415	72	133	26	3	13	73	37	43	.320	.382	.492	873	118	11	7	3	0	.993	2	O-60L,1-55,C-18,/D	0.9
1996	*Bal-A	143	537	74	157	27	6	21	82	47	79	.292	.353	.482	835	109	6	0	1	-0	.948	-7	*3-106,O-27L,D-10,/1	-0.2
1997	*Bal-A	147	528	80	150	30	4	18	88	49	60	.284	.351	.458	809	112	9	1	1	-0	.992	7	*O-133L/1-3,3-3,D-9	1.1
1998	Bal-A	162	573	79	160	34	1	22	92	49	81	.279	.337	.457	794	106	4	9	7	-0	.989	-0	*O-157(157-0-0)/1-1	-0.2
1999	Bal-A★	162	673	104	207	38	1	28	107	43	78	.308	.351	.492	843	116	15	5	1	1	**1.000**	10	*O-148L,D-13/3-2	1.9
2000	Bal-A	103	411	56	120	27	0	13	57	29	46	.292	.342	.453	794	102	1	7	2	1	.987	8	*O-102(102-0-0)/D-1	0.5
	*Atl-N	44	128	13	37	9	2	1	11	12	12	.289	.355	.414	769	94	-1	3	0	1	1.000	0	O-32(32-0-0)	-0.1
Total	14	1863	6734	878	1895	359	38	160	961	523	679	.281	.336	.417	753	100	-8	127	76	1	.988	-1	C-704,O-696L,3/1D2S	0.1

■ GEORGE SUSCE Susce, George Cyril Methodius "Good Kid" b: 8/13/07, Pittsburgh, Pa. d: 2/25/86, Sarasota, Fla. BR/TR, 5'11.5", 200 lbs. Deb: 4/23/29 FC

YEAR	TM/L	G	AB	R	H	2B	3B	HR	RBI	BB	SO	AVG	OBP	SLG	OPS	OPS+	BR+	SB	CS	SBR	FA	FR	G/POS	TPR
1929	Phi-N	17	17	5	5	3	0	1	1	1	2	.294	.368	.647	1015	137		0			.900	-2	C-11	-0.1
1932	Det-A	2	0	0	0	0	0	0	0	0	0	—	—	—	—	—	0	0	0	0	1.000	-0	/C-2	0.0
1939	Pit-N	31	75	8	17	3	1	1	4	12	5	.227	.333	.333	667	81	-2	0			.984	2	C-31	0.2
1940	StL-A	61	113	6	24	4	0	0	13	9	9	.212	.282	.248	530	38	-10	1	0	0	.984	6	C-61	-0.1
1941	Cle-A	1	0	0	0	0	0	0	0	0	0	—	—	—	—	—	0	0	0	0	1.000	-0	/C-1	0.0
1942	Cle-A	2	1	1	1	0	0	0	0	1	0	1.000	1.000	1.000	2000	492	1	0	0	0	1.000	-0	/C-2	0.1
1943	Cle-A	3	1	0	0	0	0	0	0	0	0	.000	.000	.000	0	-99	-0	0	0	0	1.000	1	/C-3	0.0
1944	Cle-A	29	61	3	14	1	0	0	4	2	5	.230	.254	.246	500	45	-4	0	0	0	.948	1	C-29	-0.2
Total	8	146	268	23	61	11	1	2	22	25	21	.228	.301	.299	599	60	-15	1	0		.974	8	C-140	-0.1

■ PETE SUSKO Susko, Peter Jonathan b: 7/2/04, Laura, Ohio d: 5/22/78, Jacksonville, Fla. BL/TL, 5'11", 172 lbs. Deb: 8/1/34

YEAR	TM/L	G	AB	R	H	2B	3B	HR	RBI	BB	SO	AVG	OBP	SLG	OPS	OPS+	BR+	SB	CS	SBR	FA	FR	G/POS	TPR
1934	Was-A	58	224	25	64	5	3	2	25	18	10	.286	.342	.362	703	85	-5	3	4	-1	.988	3	1-58	-0.8

■ BUTCH SUTCLIFFE Sutcliffe, Charles Inigo b: 7/22/15, Fall River, Mass. d: 3/2/94, Fall River, Mass. BR/TR, 5'8.5", 165 lbs. Deb: 8/28/38

YEAR	TM/L	G	AB	R	H	2B	3B	HR	RBI	BB	SO	AVG	OBP	SLG	OPS	OPS+	BR+	SB	CS	SBR	FA	FR	G/POS	TPR
1938	Bos-N	4	4	1	1	0	0	0	2	2	1	.250	.500	.250	750	124	0	0			.800	0	/C-3	0.1

■ SY SUTCLIFFE Sutcliffe, Elmer Ellsworth b: 4/15/1862, Wheaton, Ill. d: 2/13/1893, Wheaton, Ill. BL/TR, 6'2", 170 lbs. Deb: 10/2/1884 Career OF: (10-LF 5-CF 43-RF)

YEAR	TM/L	G	AB	R	H	2B	3B	HR	RBI	BB	SO	AVG	OBP	SLG	OPS	OPS+	BR+	SB	CS	SBR	FA	FR	G/POS	TPR
1884	Chi-N	4	15	4	3	1	0	0	2	2	4	.200	.294	.267	561	72	-0				.976	2	/C-4	0.2
1885	Chi-N	11	43	5	8	1	1	0	4	2	5	.186	.222	.256	478	48	-3				.838	-5	C-11/O-1(0-0-1)	-0.6
	StL-N	16	49	2	6	1	0	0	4	5	10	.122	.204	.143	347	15	-4				.881	-2	C-14/O-2(0-0-2)	-0.5
	Yr	27	92	7	14	2	1	0	8	7	15	.152	.212	.196	408	32	-7				.862	-7	C-25/O-3(0-0-3)	-1.1
1888	Det-N	49	191	17	49	5	3	0	23	5	14	.257	.276	.314	590	88	-3	6			.901	7	S-24,C-14/1-5,O2	0.6
1889	Cle-N	46	161	17	40	3	2	1	21	14	6	.248	.309	.311	619	75	-5	5			.892	9	C-37/1-8,O-1(0-0-1)	0.6
1890	Cle-P	99	386	62	127	14	8	2	60	33	16	.329	.382	.422	804	125	15	10			.883	-5	C-84,O-15R/S-4,3-2	1.3
1891	Was-a	53	201	29	71	8	3	2	33	17	17	.353	.409	.453	862	154	14	8			.918	-4	O-35R,C-22/S-3,3-1	0.9
1892	Bal-N	66	276	41	77	10	7	1	27	14	15	.279	.316	.377	693	106	1	12			.958	-7	1-66	-0.6
Total	7	344	1322	177	381	43	24	6	174	92	87	.288	.336	.371	707	107	14	41			.887	-5	C-186/1-79,O-58R,S32	1.9

■ GARY SUTHERLAND Sutherland, Gary Lynn b: 9/27/44, Glendale, Cal. BR/TR, 6', 185 lbs. Deb: 9/17/66 F

YEAR	TM/L	G	AB	R	H	2B	3B	HR	RBI	BB	SO	AVG	OBP	SLG	OPS	OPS+	BR+	SB	CS	SBR	FA	FR	G/POS	TPR
1966	Phi-N	3	3	0	0	0	0	0	0	0	0	.000	.000	.000	0	-99	-1	0	0	0	1.000	1	/S-1	0.0
1967	Phi-N	103	231	23	57	12	1	1	19	17	22	.247	.298	.320	619	76	-7	0	3	-1	.928	-16	S-66,O-25(25-0-0)	-2.2
1968	Phi-N	67	138	16	38	7	0	0	15	8	15	.275	.315	.326	641	93	-1	0	0	0	.968	-3	2-17,S-10,3-10,/O-7R	-0.3
1969	Mon-N	141	544	63	130	26	1	3	35	37	31	.239	.290	.307	597	67	-24	5	7	-1	.971	10	*2-139,S-15/O-1R	-0.6
1970	Mon-N	116	359	37	74	10	0	3	26	31	22	.206	.273	.259	532	43	-29	2	2	-0	.975	3	2-97,S-15/3-1	-2.0
1971	Mon-N	111	304	25	78	7	2	4	26	18	12	.257	.302	.332	635	79	-8	3	4	-1	.963	-1	2-56,S-46/O-4L,3-2	-0.3
1972	Hou-N	5	8	0	1	0	0	0	1	0	0	.125	.125	.125	250	-29	-1	0	0	0	.000	-1	/2-1,3-1	-0.2
1973	Hou-N	16	54	8	14	5	0	0	3	3	5	.259	.298	.352	650	80	-2	0	0	0	.971	-4	2-14/S-1	-0.5
1974	Det-A	149	619	60	157	20	1	5	49	26	37	.254	.284	.313	597	69	-25	1	3	-1	.976	-23	*2-147,S-10/3-4	-4.1
1975	Det-A	129	503	51	130	12	3	6	39	45	41	.258	.323	.330	653	81	-12	0	2	-1	.968	-7	*2-128	-1.1
1976	Det-A	42	117	10	24	5	2	0	6	7	12	.205	.250	.282	532	53	-7	0	1	-0	.984	1	2-42	-0.4
	Mil-A	59	115	9	25	2	0	1	9	8	7	.217	.274	.261	535	58	-6	0	2	-1	.955	-0	2-45/1-2,D-8	-0.5
	Yr	101	232	19	49	7	2	1	15	15	19	.211	.262	.272	534	56	-13	0	3	-1	.970	1	2-87/D-8,1-2	-0.9
1977	SD-N	80	103	5	25	3	0	1	11	7	15	.243	.291	.301	592	66	-5	0	0	0	.943	-4	2-30,3-21/1-4	-0.9
1978	StL-N	10	6	1	1	0	0	0	0	0	0	.167	.167	.167	333	-7	-1	0	0	0	1.000	1	/2-1	0.0
Total	13	1031	3104	308	754	109	10	24	239	207	219	.243	.292	.308	600	69	-128	11	24	-6	.971	-42	2-717,S-164/3-39,OD1	-13.1

■ LEO SUTHERLAND Sutherland, Leonardo (Cantin) b: 4/6/58, Santiago De Cuba, Cuba BL/TL, 5'10", 165 lbs. Deb: 8/11/80

YEAR	TM/L	G	AB	R	H	2B	3B	HR	RBI	BB	SO	AVG	OBP	SLG	OPS	OPS+	BR+	SB	CS	SBR	FA	FR	G/POS	TPR
1980	Chi-A	34	89	9	23	3	0	0	5	1	11	.258	.267	.292	559	53	-6	4	1	1	.943	-1	O-23(16-7-0)	-0.7
1981	Chi-A	11	12	6	2	0	0	0	0	3	1	.167	.333	.167	500	49	-1	2	1	0	1.000	-3	/O-7(4-4-0)	-0.3
Total	2	45	101	15	25	3	0	0	5	4	12	.248	.276	.277	553	53	-6	6	2	1	.949	-4	/O-30(20-11-0)	-1.0

■ GLENN SUTKO Sutko, Glenn Edward b: 5/9/68, Atlanta, Ga. BR/TR, 6'3", 225 lbs. Deb: 10/3/90

YEAR	TM/L	G	AB	R	H	2B	3B	HR	RBI	BB	SO	AVG	OBP	SLG	OPS	OPS+	BR+	SB	CS	SBR	FA	FR	G/POS	TPR
1990	Cin-N	1	1	0	0	0	0	0	0	0	1	.000	.000	.000	0	-96	-0	0	0	0	1.000	0	/C-1	0.0
1991	Cin-N	10	10	0	1	0	0	0	1	2	6	.100	.250	.100	350	2	-1	0	0	0	.875	0	/C-9	-0.1
Total	2	11	11	0	1	0	0	0	1	2	7	.091	.231	.091	322	-6	-2	0	0	0	.889	0	/C-10	-0.1

■ EZRA SUTTON Sutton, Ezra Ballou b: 9/17/1850, Palmyra, N.Y. d: 6/20/07, Braintree, Mass. BR/TR, 5'8.5", 153 lbs. Deb: 5/4/1871 NA OF: (0-LF 1-CF 2-RF) Career OF: (29-LF 7-CF 30-RF)

YEAR	TM/L	G	AB	R	H	2B	3B	HR	RBI	BB	SO	AVG	OBP	SLG	OPS	OPS+	BR+	SB	CS	SBR	FA	FR	G/POS	TPR
1871	Cle-n	29	128	35	45	3	7	3	23	1	0	.352	.357	.555	911	166	11	3	1	0	**.795**	-1	*3-29/O-2(0-1-1),C-1	0.6
1872	Cle-n	22	107	30	30	6	1	0	10	1	0	.280	.287	.355	642	102	1	1	0	0	.718	-5	3-22	-0.3
1873	Ath-n	51	242	51	81	7	6	0	33	2	2	.335	.340	.413	753	114	2	1	3	-1	.806	1	*3-43/S-8,2-2	0.1
1874	Ath-n	55	243	54	71	10	3	0	28	0	2	.292	.292	.358	650	99	-2	6	4	-0	.827	-1	3-36,S-20	-0.4
1875	Ath-n	75	358	83	116	11	7	1	59	1	3	.324	.326	.402	728	136	10	13	10	-1	.803	14	*3-73/P-2,1-2,SO	1.8
1876	Phi-N	54	239	45	70	12	7	1	31	3	2	.293	.305	.419	725	141	10				.915	-4	1-29,2-15/3-8,O-4R	0.5
1877	Bos-N	58	253	43	74	10	6	0	39	4	10	.292	.304	.379	683	110	2				.882	-9	S-36,3-22	-0.4
1878	Bos-N	60	239	31	54	9	3	1	29	2	14	.226	.232	.301	534	69	-8				.888	-1	*3-59/S-1	-0.7
1879	Bos-N	84	339	54	84	13	4	0	34	2	18	.248	.252	.310	562	82	-7				.884	-12	S-51,3-33	-1.4
1880	Bos-N	76	288	41	72	9	2	0	25	7	7	.250	.268	.295	563	94	-2				.896	4	S-39,3-37	0.5
1881	Bos-N	83	333	43	97	12	4	0	31	13	9	.291	.318	.351	669	116	6				.877	-3	*3-81/S-2	0.5
1882	Bos-N	81	319	44	80	8	1	2	38	24	25	.251	.303	.301	604	94	-1				.856	-4	*3-77/S-4	-0.4
1883	Bos-N	94	414	101	134	28	15	3	73	17	12	.324	.350	.486	836	147	22				.866	-1	*3-93/O-1(0-0-1),S-1	2.0
1884	Bos-N	110	468	102	**162**	28	7	3	61	29	22	.346	.384	.455	839	164	34				**.908**	-4	*3-110	2.8
1885	Bos-N	110	457	78	143	23	8	4	47	17	25	.313	.338	.425	762	151	25				.875	-0	*3-91,S-16/2-2,1-1	2.4
1886	Bos-N	116	499	83	138	21	6	3	48	26	21	.277	.312	.361	673	108	5	18			.859	-5	O-43L,S-28,3-28,2	0.1
1887	Bos-N	77	339	58	112	14	9	3	46	13	6	.330	.342	.429	771	113	5	17			.875	15	S-37,O-18L,2-13,3	1.8
1888	Bos-N	28	110	16	24	3	1	1	16	7	3	.218	.277	.291	568	80	-2	10			.859	-5	3-27/S-1	-0.7
Total	5 n	232	1078	253	343	37	24	4	153	5	8	.318	.321	.408	729	122	23	24	18	-1	.796	7	3-203/S-29,O-3R,1P2C	1.8
Total	13	1031	4297	739	1244	190	73	21	518	164	174	.290	.315	.381	696	118	89	45			.871	-30	3-677,S-216/O-66R,21	7.0

■ LARRY SUTTON Sutton, Larry James b: 5/14/70, West Covina, Cal. BL/TL, 5'11", 175 lbs. Deb: 8/17/97 Career OF: (43-LF 0-CF 49-RF)

YEAR	TM/L	G	AB	R	H	2B	3B	HR	RBI	BB	SO	AVG	OBP	SLG	OPS	OPS+	BR+	SB	CS	SBR	FA	FR	G/POS	TPR
1997	KC-A	27	69	9	20	2	0	2	8	5	12	.290	.338	.406	744	91	-1	0	0	0	1.000	-0	1-12/O-1(1-0-0),D-3	-0.2
1998	KC-A	111	310	29	76	14	2	5	42	29	46	.245	.316	.352	667	71	-13	3	3	-0	.987	-2	O-79(39-0-47)/1-6,D-3	-1.8
1999	KC-A	43	102	14	23	6	0	2	15	13	17	.225	.313	.343	656	66	-5	1	0	0	.987	-1	1-30/O-1(0-0-1),D-5	-0.8
2000	StL-N	23	25	5	8	0	0	1	6	5	7	.320	.433	.440	873	121	1	0	0	0	1.000	-0	/1-6,O-4(3-0-1)	0.0
Total	4	204	506	57	127	22	2	10	71	52	82	.251	.324	.362	686	75	-18	4	3	-0	.987	-4	/O-85R,1-54,D-11	-2.8

■ DALE SVEUM Sveum, Dale Curtis b: 11/23/63, Richmond, Cal. BB/TR, 6'3", 185 lbs. Deb: 5/12/86 Career OF: (2-LF 0-CF 0-RF)

YEAR	TM/L	G	AB	R	H	2B	3B	HR	RBI	BB	SO	AVG	OBP	SLG	OPS	OPS+	BR+	SB	CS	SBR	FA	FR	G/POS	TPR
1986	Mil-A	91	317	35	78	13	2	7	35	32	63	.246	.317	.366	683	83	-7	4	3	-0	.865	-8	3-65,2-13,S-13	-1.5
1987	Mil-A	153	535	86	135	27	3	25	95	40	133	.252	.306	.454	760	95	-5	2	6	-2	.965	-13	*S-142,2-13	-0.4
1988	Mil-A	129	467	41	113	14	4	9	51	21	122	.242	.276	.347	623	73	-18	1	0	0	.955	-6	*S-127/2-1,D-1	-1.4
1990	Mil-A	48	117	15	23	7	0	1	12	12	30	.197	.282	.282	564	59	-6	0	1	-0	.918	-6	3-22,2-16/1-5,S-5	-1.2
1991	Mil-A	90	266	33	64	19	1	4	43	32	78	.241	.324	.365	689	93	-2	2	4	-1	.968	-7	S-51,3-38/2-2,D-3	-0.7

YEAR	TM/L	G	AB	R	H	2B	3B	HR	RBI	BB	SO	AVG	OBP	SLG	OPS	OPS+	BR+	SB	CS	SBR	FA	FR	G/POS	TPR
1992	Phi-N	54	135	13	24	4	0	2	16	16	39	.178	.265	.252	517	47	-9	0	0	0	.948	2	S-34/3-5,1-4	-0.6
	Chi-A	40	114	15	25	9	0	2	12	12	29	.219	.294	.351	645	81	-3	1	1	-0	.944	-10	S-37/1-2,3-2	-1.1
1993	Oak-A	30	79	12	14	2	1	2	6	16	21	.177	.316	.304	620	72	-3	0	0	0	.976	-4	1-14/3-7,2-4,SOD	-0.8
1994	Sea-A	10	27	3	5	0	0	1	2	2	10	.185	.241	.296	538	37	-3	0	0	0	.909	1	/3-3,D-4	-0.2
1996	Pit-N	12	34	9	12	5	0	1	5	6	6	.353	.450	.588	1038	167	3	0	0	0	.913	-1	3-10	0.3
1997	Pit-N	126	306	30	80	20	1	12	47	27	81	.261	.321	.451	772	98	-2	0	3	-1	.941	-7	3-47,S-28,1-21,/2-2	-0.8
1998	NY-A	30	58	6	9	0	0	0	3	4	16	.155	.210	.155	365	-3	-9	0	0	0	.975	1	1-21/3-6,D-3	-0.9
1999	Pit-N	49	71	7	15	5	1	3	13	7	28	.211	.282	.437	719	78	-3	0	0	0	.944	-1	3-12/1-4,S-4,2-2,O	-0.3
Total	12	862	2526	305	597	125	13	69	340	227	656	.236	.301	.378	679	82	-67	10	18	-4	.960	-59	S-442,3-217/1-71,2DO	-9.6
■ HARRY SWACINA	Swacina, Harry Joseph "Swats" b: 8/22/1881, St.Louis, Mo. d: 6/21/44, Birmingham, Ala. BR/TR, 6'2", 190 lbs. Deb: 9/13/07																							
1907	Pit-N	26	95	9	19	1	1	0	10	4		.200	.240	.232	472	47	-6	1			.996	-1	1-26	-0.8
1908	Pit-N	53	176	7	38	6	1	0	13	5		.216	.238	.261	499	59	-8	4			.983	-5	1-50	-1.7
1914	Bal-F	158	617	70	173	26	8	0	90	14	23	.280	.297	.348	646	73	-33	15			.985	10	*1-158	-2.9
1915	Bal-F	85	301	24	74	13	1	1	38	9	11	.246	.268	.306	573	59	-21	9			.986	6	1-75/2-1	-1.9
Total	4	322	1189	110	304	46	11	1	151	32	34	.256	.276	.315	592	66	-69	29			.986	10	1-309/2-1	-7.3
■ ANDY SWAN	Swan, Andrew J. Deb: 7/23/1884																							
1884	Was-a	5	21	3	3	1	0	0		0		.143	.143	.190	333	9	-2				.824	-3	/1-3,3-2	-0.5
	Ric-a	3	10	2	5	0	0	0		0		.500	.500	.500	1000	230	1				1.000	-0	/1-3	0.1
	Yr	8	31	5	8	1	0	0		0		.258	.258	.290	548	85	-0				.902	-3	/1-6,3-2	-0.4
■ MARTY SWANDELL	Swandell, John Martin (b: Martin Schwendel) b: 1841, Baden, Germany d: 10/25/06, Brooklyn, N.Y. TL, 5'10.5", 146 lbs. Deb: 5/7/1872 U Career OF: (0-LF 4-CF 0-RF)																							
1872	Eck-n	14	55	7	11	0	0	0	4	2	1	.200	.228	.200	428	38	-3	0	0	0	.625	-2	/3-8,O-4C,1-1,2-1	-0.4
1873	Res-n	2	9	1	1	0	0	0	1	0	0	.111	.111	.111	222	-37	-1	0	0	0	.909	-0	/1-2	-0.1
Total	2 n	16	64	8	12	0	0	0	5	2	1	.188	.212	.188	400	27	-4	0	0	0	.944	-3	/3-8,O-4C,1-3,2-1	-0.5
■ PINKY SWANDER	Swander, Edward O. b: 7/4/1880, Portsmouth, Ohio d: 10/24/44, Springfield, Mass. BL/TL, 5'9", 180 lbs. Deb: 9/18/03																							
1903	StL-A	14	51	9	14	2	2	0	6	10		.275	.413	.392	805	146	4	0			.833	-2	O-14(0-0-14)	0.1
1904	StL-A	1	1	0	0	0	0	0	0	0		.000	.000	.000	0	-99	-0	0			.000	0	H	0.0
Total	2	15	52	9	14	2	2	0	6	10		.269	.406	.385	791	142	3	0			.833	-2	/O-14(0-0-14)	0.1
■ PEDRO SWANN	Swann, Pedro Maurice b: 10/27/70, Wilmington, Del. BL/TR, 6', 195 lbs. Deb: 9/9/2000																							
2000	Atl-N	4	2	0	0	0	0	0	0	0	2	.000	.000	.000	0	-99	-1	0	0	0	.000	-2	/O-3(1-1-2)	-0.2
■ EVAR SWANSON	Swanson, Ernest Evar b: 10/15/02, DeKalb, Ill. d: 7/17/73, Galesburg, Ill. BR/TR, 5'9", 170 lbs. Deb: 4/18/29																							
1929	Cin-N	148	574	100	172	35	12	4	43	41	47	.300	.353	.423	776	96	-4	33			.970	-3	*O-142(91-51-0)	-1.6
1930	Cin-N	95	301	43	93	15	3	2	22	11	17	.309	.335	.399	734	81	-10	4			.963	0	O-71(3-68-0)	-1.1
1932	Chi-A	14	52	9	16	3	1	0	8	8	3	.308	.400	.404	804	116	2	3	1	0	.960	-2	O-14(14-0-0)	-0.1
1933	Chi-A	144	539	102	165	25	7	1	63	93	35	.306	.411	.384	795	117	18	19	11	0	.973	-5	*O-139(6-8-129)	0.5
1934	Chi-A	117	426	71	127	9	5	0	34	59	31	.298	.385	.343	727	86	-6	10	3	1	.980	-3	*O-105(4-1-100)	-1.4
Total	5	518	1892	325	573	87	28	7	170	212	133	.303	.376	.390	766	98	-0	69	15		.971	-14	O-471(118-128-229)	-3.7
■ KARL SWANSON	Swanson, Karl Edward b: 12/17/1900, N.Henderson, Ill. BL/TR, 5'10", 155 lbs. Deb: 8/12/28																							
1928	Chi-A	22	64	2	9	1	0	0	6	4	7	.141	.191	.156	347	-8	-10	3	0	1	.943	1	2-21	-0.7
1929	Chi-A	2	1	0	0	0	0	0	0	0	0	.000	.000	.000	0	-99	-0	0	0	0	.000	0	H	0.0
Total	2	24	65	2	9	1	0	0	6	4	7	.138	.188	.154	342	-9	-10	3	0	1	.943	1	/2-21	-0.7
■ STAN SWANSON	Swanson, Stanley Lawrence b: 5/19/44, Yuba City, Cal. BR/TR, 5'11", 168 lbs. Deb: 6/23/71																							
1971	Mon-N	49	106	14	26	3	0	2	11	10	13	.245	.310	.330	641	81	-3	1	3	-1	1.000	-6	O-38(24-16-2)	-1.2
■ BILL SWANSON	Swanson, William Andrew b: 10/12/1888, New York, N.Y. d: 10/14/54, New York, N.Y. BB/TR, 5'6", 156 lbs. Deb: 9/2/14																							
1914	Bos-A	11	20	0	4	2	0	0	0	3	4	.200	.304	.300	604	82	-0	0	1	-0	.875	-3	/2-6,3-3,S-1	-0.4
■ ED SWARTWOOD	Swartwood, Cyrus Edward b: 1/12/1859, Rockford, Ill. d: 5/15/24, Pittsburgh, Pa. BL/TR, 5'11", 198 lbs. Deb: 8/11/1881 U Career OF: (47-LF 89-CF 502-RF)																							
1881	Buf-N	1	3	0	1	0	0	0	0	1	0	.333	.500	.333	833	170	0				.500	-1	/O-1(0-0-1)	0.0
1882	Pit-a	76	325	**86**	107	**18**	11	4		21		.329	.370	.489	859	197	33				.788	-8	*O-73(0-29-44)/1-4	2.1
1883	Pit-a	94	412	86	**147**	24	8	3		25		**.357**	**.394**	.476	**869**	**186**	**40**				.936	2	1-60,O-37(0-31-6)/C-3	3.0
1884	Pit-a	102	399	74	115	19	6	0		33		.288	.365	.366	731	141	20				.804	-3	*O-79R,1-22/3-1,P-1	1.2
1885	Bro-a	99	399	80	106	8	9	0	49	36		.266	.334	.331	665	110	6				.851	-10	*O-95R/1-4,S-1,C-1	-0.6
1886	Bro-a	122	471	95	132	13	10	3	58	**70**		.280	.377	.369	746	133	20	37			.884	7	*O-122(0-20-103)/C-1	2.3
1887	Bro-a	91	409	72	138	14	8	1	54	46		.337	.342	.344	687	91	-4	29			.835	2	O-91(0-0-91)	-0.3
1890	Tol-a	126	462	106	151	23	11	3	64	80		.327	.444	.444	887	157	37	53			.925	8	*O-126(0-7-119)/P-1	3.8
1892	Pit-N	13	42	8	10	1	0	0	4	13	11	.238	.418	.262	680	106	1	1			.933	4	O-13(0-0-13)	0.4
Total	9	724	2922	607	907	120	63	14	229	325	11	.310	.379	.400	778	142	154	120			.856	0	O-637R/1-90,C-5,PS3	11.9
■ CHARLIE SWEASY	Sweasy, Charles James (b: Charles James Swasey) b: 11/2/1847, Newark, N.J. d: 3/30/08, Newark, N.J. BR/TR, 5'9", 172 lbs. Deb: 5/19/1871 M																							
1871	Oly-n	5	19	5	4	1	0	0	4	1	0	.211	.250	.263	513	50	-1	0	0	0	.788	-1	/2-5	-0.1
1872	Cle-n	12	57	8	16	0	0	0	6	2	1	.281	.305	.281	586	86	-0	1	0	0	.833	3	2-11/O-1(0-0-1)	0.2
1873	Bos-n	1	4	0	1	0	0	0	0	0	0	.250	.250	.250	500	45	-0	0	0	0	.714	-1	/2-1	-0.1
1874	Bal-n	8	33	2	8	0	0	0	4	2	0	.242	.286	.242	528	72	-1	0	0	0	.646	-6	/2-8,O-1(0-0-1)	-0.6
	Atl-n	10	44	4	5	1	0	0	3	0	0	.114	.114	.136	250	-23	-5	0	0	0	.879	5	2-10	-0.1
	Yr	18	77	6	13	1	0	0	7	2	0	.169	.190	.182	372	21	-6	0	0	0	.781	-1	2-18/O-1(0-0-1)	-0.7
1875	RS-n	19	76	7	13	1	0	0	4	3	1	.171	.203	.184	387	39	-4	2	4	-1	.828	-5	2-19,M	-0.9
1876	Cin-N	56	227	18	46	5	2	0	10	2	5	.203	.211	.244	456	60	-7				.864	2	*2-55/O-1(0-0-1)	-0.2
1878	Pro-N	55	212	23	37	3	0	0	8	7	23	.175	.201	.189	390	29	-16				.846	-9	*2-55	-2.0
Total	5 n	55	233	26	47	3	0	0	21	8	2	.202	.228	.215	443	47	-12	3	4	-1	.808	-4	/2-54,O-2(0-0-2)	-1.6
Total	2	111	439	41	83	8	2	0	18	9	28	.189	.206	.217	424	44	-23				.855	-6	2-110/O-1(0-0-1)	-2.2
■ BUCK SWEENEY	Sweeney, Charles Francis b: 4/15/1890, Pittsburgh, Pa. d: 3/13/55, Pittsburgh, Pa. Deb: 9/28/14																							
1914	Phi-A	1	1	0	0	0	0	0	0	0	1	.000	.000	.000	0	-99	-0	0			1.000	-0	/O-1(1-0-0)	-0.1
■ CHARLIE SWEENEY	Sweeney, Charles J. b: 4/13/1863, San Francisco, Cal d: 4/4/02, San Francisco, Cal. BR/TR, 5'10.5", 181 lbs. Deb: 5/11/1882 Career OF: (30-LF 31-CF 31-RF)																							
1882	Pro-N	1	4	0	0	0	0	0	0	0	1	.000	.000	.000	0	-99	-1				.500	0	/O-1(0-0-1)	-0.1
1883	Pro-N	22	87	9	19	3	0	0	15	2	10	.218	.236	.253	489	47	-5				.863	3	P-20/O-7(2-3-2)	0.0
1884	Pro-N	41	168	24	50	9	0	1	19	11	17	.298	.341	.369	710	126	5				.940	-2	P-27,O-17(0-5-13)/1-1	-0.2
	StL-U	45	171	31	54	14	2	1		10		.316	.354	.439	792	134	2				**.943**	4	P-33,O-13(13-0-0)/1-1	-0.1
1885	StL-N	71	267	27	55	7	1	0	24	12	33	.206	.240	.240	480	59	-11				.827	-3	O-39(14-19-6),P-35	-1.0
1886	StL-N	17	64	4	16	2	0	0	7	3	10	.250	.284	.281	565	77	-2	0			.929	-0	P-11/O-4(0-4-0),S-2	-0.1
1887	Cle-a	36	154	22	51	4	4	0	19	21		.331	.331	.316	647	83	-2	11			.936	-4	1-20,O-10R/P-3,S3	-0.7
Total	6	233	915	117	245	39	7	2	84	59	71	.268	.297	.317	614	90	-14	11			.909	-3	P-129/O-91C,1-22,S3	-2.2
■ DAN SWEENEY	Sweeney, Daniel J. b: 1/28/1868, Philadelphia, Pa. d: 7/13/13, Louisville, Ky. 5'5", 160 lbs. Deb: 4/18/1895																							
1895	Lou-N	22	90	18	24	5	0	1	16	17	2	.267	.389	.356	744	99	1	2			.794	-4	O-22(0-1-21)	-0.4
■ ED SWEENEY	Sweeney, Edward Francis "Jeff" b: 7/19/1888, Chicago, Ill. d: 7/4/47, Chicago, Ill. BR/TR, 6'1", 200 lbs. Deb: 5/16/08																							
1908	NY-A	32	82	4	12	2	0	0	2	5		.146	.195	.171	366	19	-7	0			.955	-0	C-25/1-1,O-1(0-0-1)	-0.6
1909	NY-A	67	176	18	47	3	0	0	21	16		.267	.328	.284	612	93	-1	3			.947	3	C-62/1-3	0.9
1910	NY-A	78	215	25	43	4	4	0	13	17		.200	.271	.256	527	62	-9	12			.974	5	C-77	0.3
1911	NY-A	83	229	17	53	6	5	0	18	14		.231	.299	.301	600	63	-11	8			.964	-3	C-83	-0.8

YEAR	TM/L	G	AB	R	H	2B	3B	HR	RBI	BB	SO	AVG	OBP	SLG	OPS	OPS+	BR+	SB	CS	SBR	FA	FR	G/POS	TPR
1912	NY-A	110	351	37	94	12	1	0	30	27		.268	.325	.308	633	77	-10	6			.955	-1	*C-108	-0.2
1913	NY-A	117	351	35	93	10	2	2	40	37	41	.265	.348	.322	670	96	-1	11			.964	9	*C-112/1-1,O-1(0-1-0)	1.8
1914	NY-A	87	258	25	55	8	1	1	22	35	30	.213	.316	.264	580	75	-7	19	6	2	.980	2	C-78	0.4
1915	NY-A	53	137	12	26	2	0	0	5	25	12	.190	.319	.204	523	57	-6	3	3	-0	.975	-6	C-53	-0.8
1919	Pit-N	17	42	0	4	1	0	0	0	5	6	.095	.191	.119	311	-5	-5	1			.944	-3	C-15	-0.8
Total	9	644	1841	173	427	48	13	3	151	181	89	.232	.310	.277	587	73	-58	63	9		.964	6	C-613/1-5,O-2(0-1-1)	0.2
■ HANK SWEENEY	Sweeney, Henry Leon b: 12/28/15, Franklin, Tenn. d: 5/6/80, Columbia, Tenn. BL/TL, 6', 185 lbs. Deb: 10/1/44																							
1944	Pit-N	1	2	0	0	0	0	0	0	0	1	.000	.000	.000	0	-96	-1	0			1.000	0	/1-1	0.0
■ JERRY SWEENEY	Sweeney, Jeremiah H. b: 1860, Boston, Mass. d: 8/25/1891, Boston, Mass. 5'9.5", 157 lbs. Deb: 8/22/1884																							
1884	KC-U	31	129	16	34	3	0	0		4		.264	.286	.287	573	85	-6				.958	3	1-31	-0.5
■ ROONEY SWEENEY	Sweeney, John J. b: 1860, New York, N.Y. 5'8", 155 lbs. Deb: 7/25/1883 Career OF: (1-LF 7-CF 13-RF)																							
1883	Bal-a	25	101	13	21	5	2	0		4		.208	.238	.297	535	69	-4				.878	-1	C-23/O-3(0-0-3)	-0.2
1884	Bal-U	48	186	37	42	7	1	0		15		.226	.284	.274	558	63	-14				.917	-8	C-33,O-16(0-6-10)/3-1	-1.7
1885	StL-N	3	11	1	1	0	0	0	0	0	4	.091	.091	.091	182	-44	-2				.750	-0	/O-2(1-1-0),C-1	-0.2
Total	3	76	298	51	64	12	3	0	0	19	4	.215	.262	.275	537	62	-19				.905	-9	/C-57,O-21R,3-1	-2.1
■ MARK SWEENEY	Sweeney, Mark Patrick b: 10/26/69, Framingham, Mass. BL/TL, 6'1", 195 lbs. Deb: 8/4/95 Career OF: (62-LF 1-CF 64-RF)																							
1995	StL-N	37	77	5	21	2	0	2	13	10	15	.273	.356	.377	733	94	-0	1	1	-0	.994	-1	1-19/O-1(1-0-0)	-0.3
1996	*StL-N	98	170	32	45	9	0	3	22	33	29	.265	.387	.371	758	102	2	3	0	1	.984	-5	O-43(36-0-7),1-15	-0.4
1997	StL-N	44	61	5	13	3	0	0	4	9	14	.213	.324	.262	586	56	-4	0	1	-0	1.000	-5	O-25(10-0-15)/1-4	-0.9
	SD-N	71	103	11	33	4	0	2	19	11	18	.320	.386	.417	803	119	3	2	2	-0	.944	-5	O-20(6-1-13)/1-7	-0.3
	Yr	115	164	16	46	7	0	2	23	20	32	.280	.362	.360	722	94	-1	2	3	-1	.976	-9	O-45(16-1-28),1-11	-1.2
1998	*SD-N	122	192	17	45	8	3	2	15	26	37	.234	.329	.339	667	82	-5	1	2	-0	1.000	-7	O-34(5-0-29),1-21/D-1	-1.4
1999	Cin-N	37	31	6	11	3	0	2	7	4	9	.355	.429	.645	1074	162	3	0	0	0	1.000	-0	/1-1,O-1(1-0-0)	0.3
2000	Mil-N	71	73	9	16	6	0	1	6	12	18	.219	.337	.342	680	74	-3	0	0	0	1.000	0	/O-3(3-0-0),1-2,D-4	-0.3
Total	6	480	707	85	184	35	3	12	86	105	140	.260	.359	.369	728	94	-3	7	6	-1	.980	-21	O-127R/1-69,D-5	-3.3
■ MIKE SWEENEY	Sweeney, Michael John b: 7/22/73, Orange, Cal. BR/TR, 6'1", 195 lbs. Deb: 9/14/95																							
1995	KC-A	4	4	1	1	0	0	0	0	0	0	.250	.250	.250	500	30	-0	0	0	0	.875	-0	/C-4	-0.1
1996	KC-A	50	165	23	46	10	0	4	24	18	21	.279	.364	.412	776	96	-1	1	2	-0	.994	0	C-26,D-22	-0.1
1997	KC-A	84	240	30	58	8	0	7	31	17	33	.242	.308	.363	670	72	-10	3	2	-0	.993	6	C-76/D-3	0.0
1998	KC-A	92	282	32	73	18	0	8	35	24	38	.259	.321	.408	729	86	-6	2	3	-1	.984	-8	C-91	-0.9
1999	KC-A	150	575	101	185	44	2	22	102	54	48	.322	.390	.520	910	127	23	6	1	1	.981	-8	D-75,1-74/C-4	0.5
2000	KC-A★	159	618	105	206	30	0	29	144	71	67	.333	.415	.523	937	134	34	8	3	1	.991	4	*1-114,D-45	2.3
Total	6	539	1884	292	569	110	2	70	336	184	207	.302	.375	.474	849	113	40	20	11	1	.988	-5	C-201,1-188,D-145	1.7
■ PETE SWEENEY	Sweeney, Peter Jay b: 12/31/1863, California d: 8/22/01, San Francisco, Cal BR/TR, Deb: 9/28/1888 Career OF: (3-LF 4-CF 4-RF)																							
1888	Was-N	11	44	3	8	0	1	0	5	0	4	.182	.182	.227	409	32	-3	0			.784	-0	/3-8,O-3(3-0-0)	-0.4
1889	Was-N	49	193	13	44	7	3	1	23	11	26	.228	.284	.311	595	70	-8	8			.802	-10	3-47/2-1,O-1(0-0-1)	-1.5
	StL-a	9	38	8	14	2	0	0	8	1	5	.368	.415	.421	836	122	1	2			.780	-1	/3-8,O-1(0-0-1)	0.0
1890	StL-a	49	190	23	34	3	2	0	10	17		.179	.271	.216	487	38	-15	8			.880	-5	2-23,3-21/1-3,O-2R	-1.8
	Lou-a	2	7	1	1	1	0	0	1	1		.143	.250	.286	536	59	-0	1			.889	-1	/S-2	-0.2
	Phi-a	14	49	5	8	1	1	0	0	7		.163	.281	.224	505	49	-3	0			.915	-6	/2-9,O-4(0-4-0),3-2	-0.7
	Yr	65	246	29	43	5	3	0	11	25		.175	.272	.220	492	41	-19	9			.889	-12	2-32,3-23/O-6C,1S	-2.7
Total	3	134	521	53	109	14	7	1	47	37	35	.209	.280	.269	548	57	-29	19			.799	-24	/3-86,2-33,O-11C,1S	-4.6
■ BILL SWEENEY	Sweeney, William John b: 3/6/1886, Covington, Ky. d: 5/26/48, Cambridge, Mass. BR/TR, 5'11", 175 lbs. Deb: 6/14/07 Career OF: (9-LF 1-CF 1-RF)																							
1907	Chi-N	3	10	1	1	0	0	0	1	1		.100	.182	.100	282	-11	-1	1			.571	-4	/S-3	-0.6
	Bos-N	58	191	24	50	2	0	0	18	15		.262	.316	.272	588	85	-3	8			.871	0	3-23,S-15,O-11L,/21	-0.3
	Yr	61	201	25	51	2	0	0	19	16		.254	.309	.264	572	79	-4	9			.871	-4	3-23,S-18,O-11L,/21	-0.9
1908	Bos-N	127	418	44	102	15	3	0	40	45		.244	.317	.294	612	97	-0	17			.930	12	*3-123/S-3,2-1	1.7
1909	Bos-N	138	493	44	120	19	3	1	36	37		.243	.296	.300	596	81	-11	25			.903	8	*3-112,S-26	0.1
1910	Bos-N	150	499	43	133	22	4	5	46	61	28	.267	.349	.357	705	101	1	25			.903	-1	*S-110,3-21,1-17	0.4
1911	Bos-N	137	523	92	164	33	6	3	63	77	26	.314	.404	.417	820	120	16	33			.944	11	*2-136	2.9
1912	Bos-N	153	593	84	204	31	13	1	100	68	34	.344	.416	.445	861	133	29	27			.959	**30**	*2-153	5.9
1913	Bos-N	139	502	65	129	17	6	0	47	66	50	.257	.347	.315	662	88	-6	18			.939	1	*2-137	-0.3
1914	Chi-N	134	463	45	101	14	5	1	38	53	15	.218	.298	.276	575	71	-15	18			.954	15	*2-134	0.2
Total	8	1039	3692	442	1004	153	40	11	389	423	153	.272	.349	.344	693	100	9	172			.949	72	2-566,3-279,S/1O	10.0
■ BILL SWEENEY	Sweeney, William Joseph b: 12/29/04, Cleveland, Ohio d: 4/18/57, San Diego, Cal. BR/TR, 5'11", 180 lbs. Deb: 4/13/28																							
1928	Det-A	89	309	47	78	15	5	0	19	15	28	.252	.287	.333	620	62	-18	12	9	-1	.993	4	1-75/O-3(3-0-0)	-1.9
1930	Bos-A	88	243	32	75	13	0	4	30	9	15	.309	.333	.412	745	91	-4	5	3	0	.997	-1	1-56/3-1	-0.7
1931	Bos-A	131	498	48	147	30	3	1	58	20	30	.295	.322	.373	696	87	-10	5	12	-3	**.993**	10	*1-124	-1.4
Total	3	308	1050	127	300	58	8	5	107	44	73	.286	.314	.370	685	80	-32	22	24	-4	.994	13	1-255/O-3(3-0-0),3-1	-4.0
■ RICK SWEET	Sweet, Ricky Joe b: 9/7/52, Longview, Wash. BB/TR (BL 1978 (part)), 6'1", 200 lbs. Deb: 4/8/78 C																							
1978	SD-N	88	226	15	50	8	0	1	11	27	22	.221	.307	.270	577	68	-9	1	4	-1	.984	3	C-76	-0.5
1982	NY-N	3	3	0	1	0	0	0	0	0	1	.333	.333	.333	667	88	-0	0	0	0	.000	0	/H	0.0
	Sea-A	88	258	29	66	6	1	4	24	20	24	.256	.314	.333	648	76	-8	3	0	1	.993	-6	C-83	-1.1
1983	Sea-A	93	249	18	55	9	0	1	22	13	26	.221	.260	.269	529	44	-19	2	2	-0	.987	-3	C-85	-1.8
Total	3	272	736	62	172	23	1	6	57	60	73	.234	.294	.292	586	63	-36	6	6	-1	.988	-7	C-244	-3.4
■ HAM SWEIGERT	Sweigert, Hampton Deb: 10/12/1890																							
1890	Phi-a	1	1	0	0	0	0	0	0	1		.000	.500	.000	500	48	0	1			.000	-0	/O-1(0-0-1)	0.0
■ AUGIE SWENTOR	Swentor, August William b: 11/21/1899, Seymour, Conn. d: 11/10/69, Waterbury, Conn. BR/TR, 6', 185 lbs. Deb: 9/12/22																							
1922	Chi-A	1	1	0	0	0	0	0	0	0	1	.000	.000	.000	0	-99	-0	0	0	0	.000	0	H	0.0
■ STEVE SWETONIC	Swetonic, Stephen Albert b: 8/13/03, Mt.Pleasant, Pa. d: 4/22/74, Canonsburg, Pa. BR/TR, 5'11", 185 lbs. Deb: 4/17/29																							
1929	Pit-N	42	48	11	13	3	1	0	2	2	6	.271	.314	.375	689	68	-2	0			.960	2	P-41	0.0
1930	Pit-N	23	36	2	4	2	0	0	2	1	5	.111	.135	.167	302	-27	-8	0			1.000	-1	P-23	0.0
1931	Pit-N	14	7	0	1	0	0	0	0	1	3	.143	.250	.143	393	8	-1	0			1.000	-0	P-14	0.0
1932	Pit-N	24	54	1	5	1	0	0	2	2	7	.093	.125	.111	236	-37	-10	0			**1.000**	-1	P-24	0.0
1933	Pit-N	31	55	3	11	0	2	0	4	1	7	.200	.214	.273	487	38	-4	0			.950	-1	P-31	0.0
1935	Pit-N	1	0	1	0	0	0	0	0	0	0	—	—	—	—	—	0	0			.000	0	R	0.0
Total	6	135	200	18	34	6	3	0	10	7	28	.170	.202	.230	432	13	-26	0			.973	-2	P-133	0.0
■ POP SWETT	Swett, William E. b: 4/16/1870, San Francisco, Cal d: 11/22/34, San Francisco, Cal 6', 175 lbs. Deb: 5/3/1890																							
1890	Bos-P	37	94	16	18	4	3	1	12	16	26	.191	.321	.330	651	69	-4	4			.820	-8	C-34/O-3(0-0-3)	-0.8
■ BOB SWIFT	Swift, Robert Virgil b: 3/6/15, Salina, Kan. d: 10/17/66, Detroit, Mich. BR/TR, 5'11.5", 180 lbs. Deb: 4/16/40 MC																							
1940	StL-A	130	398	37	97	20	1	0	39	28	39	.244	.295	.299	594	53	-27	1	0	0	.980	-20	*C-128	-3.8
1941	StL-A	63	170	13	44	7	0	0	21	22	11	.259	.344	.300	644	69	-7	2	0	0	.985	-4	C-58	-0.7
1942	StL-A	29	76	3	15	4	0	1	8	3	5	.197	.228	.289	517	44	-6	0	2	-1	1.000	-1	C-28	-0.7
	Phi-A	60	192	9	44	3	0	0	15	13	17	.229	.278	.245	523	48	-13	1	2	-0	.970	2	C-60	-0.8
	Yr	89	268	12	59	7	0	1	23	16	22	.220	.264	.257	522	47	-19	1	4	-1	.977	1	C-88	-1.5
1943	Phi-A	77	224	16	43	5	1	1	11	35	16	.192	.301	.237	538	58	-11	0	0	0	.976	-3	C-77	-1.0
1944	Det-A	80	247	15	63	11	1	1	19	27	27	.255	.331	.320	651	82	-5	2	0	0	.982	1	C-76	0.1
1945	*Det-A	95	279	19	65	5	0	0	24	26	22	.233	.298	.251	549	56	-15	1	0	0	.988	1	C-94	-0.8

YEAR	TM/L	G	AB	R	H	2B	3B	HR	RBI	BB	SO	AVG	OBP	SLG	OPS	OPS+	BR+	SB	CS	SBR	FA	FR	G/POS	TPR
1946	Det-A	42	107	13	25	2	0	2	10	14	7	.234	.322	.308	631	72	-4	0	0	0	.980	-4	C-42	-0.7
1947	Det-A	97	279	23	70	11	0	1	21	33	16	.251	.330	.301	631	74	-9	2	2	-0	.989	-0	C-97	-0.5
1948	Det-A	113	292	23	65	6	0	4	33	51	29	.223	.338	.284	622	65	-14	1	0	0	.991	6	*C-112	-0.2
1949	Det-A	74	189	16	45	6	0	2	18	26	20	.238	.330	.302	632	68	-9	0	0	0	.989	1	C-69	-0.5
1950	Det-A	67	132	14	30	4	0	2	9	25	6	.227	.350	.303	653	66	-6	0	0	0	.995	8	C-66	0.4
1951	Det-A	44	104	8	20	0	0	0	5	12	10	.192	.276	.192	468	28	-10	0	0	0	.982	2	C-43	-0.7
1952	Det-A	28	58	3	8	1	0	0	4	7	7	.138	.242	.155	398	12	-7	0	0	0	.977	6	C-28	0.0
1953	Det-A	2	3	0	1	1	0	0	1	2	1	.333	.600	.667	1267	245	1	0	0	0	1.000	1	/C-2	0.2
Total	14	1001	2750	212	635	86	3	14	238	324	233	.231	.313	.280	592	61	-141	10	6	0	.985	-5	C-980	-9.7

■ JOSH SWINDELL

Swindell, Joshua Ernest b: 7/5/1883, Rose Hill, Kan. d: 3/19/69, Fruita, Colo. BR/TR, 6′, 180 lbs. Deb: 9/16/11

YEAR	TM/L	G	AB	R	H	2B	3B	HR	RBI	BB	SO	AVG	OBP	SLG	OPS	OPS+	BR+	SB	CS	SBR	FA	FR	G/POS	TPR
1911	Cle-A	4	4	0	1	0	0	0	0	0		.250	.250	.250	500	39	-0	0			.800	-0	/P-4	0.0
1913	Cle-A	1	0	0	0	0	0	0	0	0	0	—	—	—	—	—	0	0			.000	0	R	0.0
Total	2	5	4	0	1	0	0	0	0	0	0	.250	.250	.250	500	39	-0	0			.800	-0	/P-4	0.0

■ CHARLIE SWINDELLS

Swindells, Charles Jay "Swin" b: 10/26/1878, Rockford, Ill. d: 7/22/40, Portland, Ore. BR/TR, 5′11.5″, 180 lbs. Deb: 9/7/04

YEAR	TM/L	G	AB	R	H	2B	3B	HR	RBI	BB	SO	AVG	OBP	SLG	OPS	OPS+	BR+	SB	CS	SBR	FA	FR	G/POS	TPR
1904	StL-N	3	8	0	1	0	0	0	0	0		.125	.125	.125	250	-24	-1	0			1.000	-0	/C-3	-0.1

■ STEVE SWISHER

Swisher, Steven Eugene b: 8/9/51, Parkersburg, W.Va. BR/TR, 6′2″, 205 lbs. Deb: 6/14/74

YEAR	TM/L	G	AB	R	H	2B	3B	HR	RBI	BB	SO	AVG	OBP	SLG	OPS	OPS+	BR+	SB	CS	SBR	FA	FR	G/POS	TPR
1974	Chi-N	90	280	21	60	5	0	5	27	37	63	.214	.310	.286	596	65	-12	0	3	-1	.987	-1	C-90	-1.1
1975	Chi-N	93	254	20	54	16	2	1	22	30	57	.213	.306	.303	609	66	-11	1	0	0	.979	-8	C-93	-1.6
1976	Chi-N☆	109	377	25	89	13	3	5	42	20	82	.236	.278	.326	604	65	-17	2	1	0	.983	-3	*C-107	-1.7
1977	Chi-N	74	205	21	39	7	0	5	15	9	47	.190	.231	.298	529	37	-18	0	0	0	.976	-3	C-72	-1.9
1978	StL-N	45	115	11	32	5	1	1	10	8	14	.278	.331	.365	696	96	-1	1	0	0	.991	6	C-42	0.7
1979	StL-N	38	73	4	11	1	1	1	3	6	17	.151	.215	.233	448	22	-8	0	0	0	.974	1	C-33	-0.6
1980	StL-N	18	24	2	6	1	0	0	2	1	7	.250	.280	.292	572	58	-1	0	0	0	.957	0	/C-8	-0.1
1981	SD-N	16	28	2	4	0	0	0	0	2	11	.143	.200	.143	343	-2	-4	0	0	0	.971	-0	C-10	-0.4
1982	SD-N	26	58	2	10	1	0	2	3	5	24	.172	.238	.293	531	50	-4	0	0	0	.981	1	C-26	-0.2
Total	9	509	1414	108	305	49	7	20	124	118	322	.216	.281	.303	584	59	-77	4	4	-1	.982	-5	C-481	-6.9

■ RON SWOBODA

Swoboda, Ronald Alan "Rocky" b: 6/30/44, Baltimore, Md. BR/TR, 6′2″, 205 lbs. Deb: 4/12/65 Career OF: (201-LF 57-CF 524-RF)

YEAR	TM/L	G	AB	R	H	2B	3B	HR	RBI	BB	SO	AVG	OBP	SLG	OPS	OPS+	BR+	SB	CS	SBR	FA	FR	G/POS	TPR
1965	NY-N	135	399	52	91	15	3	19	50	33	102	.228	.292	.424	716	102	-0	2	3	-1	.947	1	*O-112(73-26-15)	-0.5
1966	NY-N	112	342	34	76	9	4	8	50	31	76	.222	.296	.342	638	79	-10	4	2	0	.987	0	O-97(88-0-10)	-1.5
1967	NY-N	134	449	47	126	17	3	13	53	41	96	.281	.342	.419	761	119	11	3	1	0	.957	3	*O-108(0-0-108),1-20	0.6
1968	NY-N	132	450	46	109	14	6	11	59	52	113	.242	.326	.373	699	109	6	8	1	1	.975	4	*O-125(0-0-125)	0.3
1969	*NY-N	109	327	38	77	10	2	9	52	43	90	.235	.328	.361	689	91	-3	1	1	-0	.988	0	O-97(22-0-77)	-0.9
1970	NY-N	115	245	29	57	8	2	9	40	40	72	.233	.343	.392	734	96	-1	2	4	-1	.984	-12	*O-100(1-0-100)	-1.8
1971	Mon-N	39	75	7	19	4	3	0	6	11	16	.253	.364	.387	750	112	2	0	1	-0	.977	-3	O-26(10-17-3)	-0.2
	NY-A	54	138	17	36	2	1	2	20	27	35	.261	.393	.333	726	114	4	0	0	0	.965	-3	O-47(7-1-39)	-0.1
1972	NY-A	63	113	9	28	8	0	1	12	17	29	.248	.346	.345	691	110	2	0	1	-0	.983	-5	O-35(0-5-35)/1-2	-0.5
1973	NY-A	35	43	6	5	0	0	1	2	4	18	.116	.191	.186	378	7	-5	0	0	0	1.000	-4	O-20(0-8-12)/D-4	-1.0
Total	9	928	2581	285	624	87	24	73	344	299	647	.242	.325	.379	704	101	4	20	14	-1	.972	-18	O-767R/1-22,D-4	-5.6

■ LOU SYLVESTER

Sylvester, Louis J. b: 2/14/1855, Springfield, Ill. BR/TR, 5′3″, 165 lbs. Deb: 4/18/1884 Career OF: (73-LF 62-CF 38-RF)

YEAR	TM/L	G	AB	R	H	2B	3B	HR	RBI	BB	SO	AVG	OBP	SLG	OPS	OPS+	BR+	SB	CS	SBR	FA	FR	G/POS	TPR
1884	Cin-U	82	333	67	89	13	8	2		18		.267	.305	.372	677	97	-11				.792	0	*O-81L/P-6,S-2	-1.0
1886	Lou-a	45	154	41	35	5	3	0	17	29		.227	.350	.299	648	98	0	3			.913	-0	O-45(0-45-0)	-0.1
	Cin-a	17	55	10	10	0	0	3	8	7		.182	.286	.345	631	94	-0	2			.909	1	O-17(7-7-3)	0.0
	Yr	62	209	51	45	5	3	3	25	36		.215	.333	.311	644	97	0	5			.912	1	O-62(7-52-3)	-0.1
1887	StL-a	29	125	20	38	4	3	1	18	13		.304	.310	.339	649	73	-5	13			.923	2	O-29(12-4-13)/2-1	-0.2
Total	3	173	667	138	172	22	14	6	43	67		.258	.315	.347	662	92	-16	18			.854	3	O-172L/P-6,S-2,2-1	-1.3

■ JOE SZEKELY

Szekely, Joseph b: 2/2/25, Cleveland, Ohio BR/TR, 5′11″, 180 lbs. Deb: 9/13/53

YEAR	TM/L	G	AB	R	H	2B	3B	HR	RBI	BB	SO	AVG	OBP	SLG	OPS	OPS+	BR+	SB	CS	SBR	FA	FR	G/POS	TPR
1953	Cin-N	5	13	0	1	0	0	0	0	0	3	.077	.077	.077	154	-59	-3	0	0	0	1.000	1	/O-3(0-0-3)	-0.2

■ KEN SZOTKIEWICZ

Szotkiewicz, Kenneth John b: 2/25/47, Wilmington, Del. BL/TR, 6′, 165 lbs. Deb: 4/7/70

YEAR	TM/L	G	AB	R	H	2B	3B	HR	RBI	BB	SO	AVG	OBP	SLG	OPS	OPS+	BR+	SB	CS	SBR	FA	FR	G/POS	TPR
1970	Det-A	47	84	9	9	1	0	3	9	12	29	.107	.219	.226	445	23	-9	0	0	0	.971	9	S-44	0.4

■ JERRY TABB

Tabb, Jerry Lynn b: 3/17/52, Altus, Okla. BL/TR, 6′2″, 195 lbs. Deb: 9/8/76

YEAR	TM/L	G	AB	R	H	2B	3B	HR	RBI	BB	SO	AVG	OBP	SLG	OPS	OPS+	BR+	SB	CS	SBR	FA	FR	G/POS	TPR
1976	Chi-N	11	24	2	7	0	0	0	0	3	2	.292	.370	.292	662	82	-0	0	0	0	1.000	-1	/1-6	-0.1
1977	Oak-A	51	144	8	32	3	0	6	19	10	26	.222	.273	.368	641	74	-6	0	1	-0	.993	-2	1-36/D-5	-1.0
1978	Oak-A	12	9	0	1	0	0	0	1	2	5	.111	.273	.111	384	12	-1	0	0	0	1.000	-0	/1-2,D-2	-0.1
Total	3	74	177	10	40	3	0	6	20	15	33	.226	.286	.345	631	72	-7	0	1	-0	.994	-3	/1-44,D-7	-1.2

■ PAT TABLER

Tabler, Patrick Sean b: 2/2/58, Hamilton, Ohio BR/TR, 6′2″, 200 lbs. Deb: 8/21/81 Career OF: (204-LF 0-CF 80-RF)

YEAR	TM/L	G	AB	R	H	2B	3B	HR	RBI	BB	SO	AVG	OBP	SLG	OPS	OPS+	BR+	SB	CS	SBR	FA	FR	G/POS	TPR
1981	Chi-N	35	101	11	19	3	1	1	5	13	26	.188	.281	.267	548	54	-6	0	1	-0	.982	1	2-35	-0.4
1982	Chi-N	25	85	9	20	4	2	1	7	6	20	.235	.293	.365	658	81	-2	0	0	0	.949	-5	3-25	-0.8
1983	Cle-A	124	430	56	125	23	5	6	65	56	63	.291	.374	.409	783	111	8	2	4	-1	.948	-3	O-88L,3-25/2-2,D-6	-0.1
1984	Cle-A	144	473	66	137	21	3	10	68	47	62	.290	.358	.410	768	110	7	3	1	0	.998	-13	1-67,O-43L,3-36,/2D	-1.1
1985	Cle-A	117	404	47	111	18	3	5	59	27	55	.275	.323	.371	695	90	-5	0	6	-2	.983	1	1-92,D-18/3-4,2-1	-1.2
1986	Cle-A	130	473	61	154	29	2	6	48	29	75	.326	.368	.433	802	119	13	3	1	0	.990	1	*1-107,D-18	0.7
1987	Cle-A★	151	553	66	170	34	3	11	86	51	84	.307	.372	.439	812	113	12	5	2	0	.984	5	1-82,D-66	1.0
1988	Cle-A	41	143	16	32	5	1	1	17	23	27	.224	.335	.294	629	76	-4	1	0	0	1.000	-1	D-29,1-10	-0.6
	KC-A	89	301	37	93	17	2	1	49	23	41	.309	.362	.389	751	109	4	2	3	-1	.986	-2	D-40,O-37L/1-7,3-1	-0.1
	Yr	130	444	53	125	22	3	2	66	46	68	.282	.353	.358	711	98	0	3	3	-0	.986	-2	D-69,O-37L,1-17,/3	-0.7
1989	KC-A	123	390	36	101	11	1	2	42	37	42	.259	.326	.308	634	80	-9	0	0	0	.970	2	O-55R,D-39,1-20,/23	-1.2
1990	KC-A	75	195	12	53	14	0	1	19	20	21	.272	.343	.359	702	98	-0	0	2	-1	.986	-0	O-42R,D-15/3-6,1-5	-0.3
	NY-N	17	43	6	12	1	1	1	10	3	8	.279	.340	.419	759	108	0	0	0	0	1.000	1	O-10(3-0-8)	0.1
1991	*Tor-A	82	185	20	40	5	1	1	21	29	21	.216	.326	.270	596	64	-8	0	0	0	.985	0	D-57,1-20/O-1(1-0-0)	-1.1
1992	*Tor-A	49	135	11	34	5	0	0	16	11	14	.252	.308	.289	597	65	-6	0	0	0	1.000	-1	1-34/O-8L,3-1,D-2	-1.0
Total	12	1202	3911	454	1101	190	25	47	512	375	559	.282	.348	.379	727	99	3	16	20	-3	.988	-14	1-444,D-291,O/32	-6.1

■ GREG TABOR

Tabor, Gregory Steven b: 5/21/61, Castro Valley, Cal. BR/TR, 6′ ", 165 lbs. Deb: 9/10/87

YEAR	TM/L	G	AB	R	H	2B	3B	HR	RBI	BB	SO	AVG	OBP	SLG	OPS	OPS+	BR+	SB	CS	SBR	FA	FR	G/POS	TPR
1987	Tex-A	9	9	4	1	1	0	0	1	0	4	.111	.111	.222	333	-15	-1	0	0	0	.938	4	/2-4,D-1	0.2

■ JIM TABOR

Tabor, James Reubin "Rawhide" b: 11/5/16, New Hope, Ala. d: 8/22/53, Sacramento, Cal. BR/TR, 6′2″, 175 lbs. Deb: 8/2/38

YEAR	TM/L	G	AB	R	H	2B	3B	HR	RBI	BB	SO	AVG	OBP	SLG	OPS	OPS+	BR+	SB	CS	SBR	FA	FR	G/POS	TPR
1938	Bos-A	19	57	8	18	3	2	1	8	1	6	.316	.328	.491	819	98	-1	0	1	-0	.889	1	3-11/S-2	0.1
1939	Bos-A	149	577	76	167	33	8	14	95	40	54	.289	.337	.447	784	95	-6	16	10	0	.923	7	*3-148	0.5
1940	Bos-A	120	459	73	131	28	6	21	81	42	58	.285	.345	.510	855	114	8	14	10	-0	.926	5	*3-120	1.6
1941	Bos-A	126	498	65	139	29	3	16	101	36	48	.279	.328	.446	773	100	-2	17	9	1	.930	2	*3-125	0.5
1942	Bos-A	139	508	56	128	18	2	12	75	37	47	.252	.303	.366	669	85	-12	6	13	-3	.924	-9	*3-138	-1.9
1943	Bos-A	137	537	57	130	26	3	13	85	43	54	.242	.299	.374	674	95	-5	7	7	-1	.938	-8	*3-133/O-2(2-0-0)	-1.4
1944	Bos-A	116	438	58	125	25	3	13	72	31	38	.285	.334	.445	779	123	11	4	4	-1	.950	3	*3-114	1.6
1946	Phi-N	124	463	53	124	15	2	10	50	36	51	.268	.322	.374	696	100	-1	3			.954	-3	*3-124	-0.5
1947	Phi-N	75	251	27	59	14	0	4	31	20	21	.235	.297	.339	635	71	-11	2			.916	-17	3-67	-2.8
Total	9	1005	3788	473	1021	191	29	104	598	286	377	.270	.322	.418	739	99	-19	69	54		.933	-19	3-980/O-2(2-0-0),S-2	-2.3

■ JEFF TACKETT

Tackett, Jeffrey Wilson b: 12/1/65, Fresno, Cal. BR/TR, 6′2″, 200 lbs. Deb: 9/11/91

YEAR	TM/L	G	AB	R	H	2B	3B	HR	RBI	BB	SO	AVG	OBP	SLG	OPS	OPS+	BR+	SB	CS	SBR	FA	FR	G/POS	TPR
1991	Bal-A	6	8	1	1	0	0	0	0	2	2	.125	.300	.125	425	23	-1	0	0	0	1.000	0	/C-6	0.0
1992	Bal-A	65	179	21	43	8	1	5	24	17	28	.240	.313	.380	693	91	-2	0	0	0	.997	6	C-64/3-1	0.7
1993	Bal-A	39	87	8	15	3	0	0	9	13	28	.172	.280	.207	487	32	-8	0	0	0	.989	5	C-38/P-1	-0.2
1994	Bal-A	26	53	5	12	3	1	2	9	5	13	.226	.317	.434	751	87	-1	0	0	0	.980	2	C-26	0.1
Total	4	136	327	35	71	14	2	7	42	37	71	.217	.304	.336	641	72	-12	0	0	0	.992	13	C-134/P-1,3-1	0.6

YEAR	TM/L	G	AB	R	H	2B	3B	HR	RBI	BB	SO	AVG	OBP	SLG	OPS	OPS+	BR+	SB	CS	SBR	FA	FR	G/POS	TPR
■ **DOUG TAITT** Taitt, Douglas John "Poco" b: 8/3/02, Bay City, Mich. d: 12/12/70, Portland, Ore. BL/TR, 6', 176 lbs. Deb: 4/10/28																								
1928	Bos-A	143	482	51	144	28	14	3	61	36	32	.299	.350	.434	784	107	4	13	6	1	.975	5	*O-139(9-0-130)/P-1	-0.1
1929	Bos-A	26	65	6	18	4	0	0	6	8	5	.277	.365	.338	703	84	-1	0	1	-0	.955	-0	O-21(11-0-11)	-0.3
	Chi-A	47	124	11	21	7	0	0	12	8	13	.169	.220	.226	446	15	-16	0	0	0	.966	0	O-30(0-0-30)	-1.7
	Yr	73	189	17	39	11	0	0	18	16	18	.206	.272	.265	536	39	-17	0	1	-0	.961	0	O-51(11-0-41)	-2.0
1931	Phi-N	38	151	13	34	4	2	1	15	4	14	.225	.245	.298	543	42	-12	0			.990	5	O-38(38-0-0)	-0.9
1932	Phi-N	4	2	0	0	0	0	0	1	2	0	.000	.500	.000	500	43	0	0			.000	0	H	0.0
Total	4	258	824	81	217	43	16	4	95	58	64	.263	.314	.369	683	79	-26	13	7		.975	10	O-228(58-0-171)/P-1	-3.0
■ **BOB TALBOT** Talbot, Robert Dale b: 6/6/27, Visalia, Cal. BR/TR, 6', 170 lbs. Deb: 9/16/53																								
1953	Chi-N	8	30	5	10	0	1	0	0	0	4	.333	.333	.400	733	88	-1	1	0	0	1.000	3	/O-7(0-7-0)	0.2
1954	Chi-N	114	403	45	97	15	4	1	19	16	25	.241	.275	.305	580	50	-29	3	6	-1	.985	-6	*O-111(0-111-0)	-4.2
Total	2	122	433	50	107	15	5	1	19	16	29	.247	.279	.312	591	53	-30	4	6	-1	.986	-4	O-118(0-118-0)	-4.0
■ **TIM TALTON** Talton, Marion Lee b: 1/14/39, Pikeville, N.C. BL/TR, 6'3", 200 lbs. Deb: 7/8/66																								
1966	KC-A	37	53	8	18	3	1	2	6	1	5	.340	.364	.547	911	163	4	0	1	-0	1.000	-1	C-14/1-9	0.3
1967	KC-A	46	59	7	15	3	1	0	5	7	13	.254	.333	.339	672	102	0	0	0	0	.971	-5	C-22/1-1	-0.4
Total	2	83	112	15	33	6	2	2	11	8	18	.295	.347	.438	785	131	4	0	1	-0	.980	-6	/C-36,1-10	-0.1
■ **JOHN TAMARGO** Tamargo, John Felix b: 11/7/51, Tampa, Fla. BB/TR, 5'10", 180 lbs. Deb: 9/3/76 C																								
1976	StL-N	10	10	2	3	0	0	0	1	3	0	.300	.462	.300	762	118	1	0	0	0	1.000	-1	/C-1	0.0
1977	StL-N	4	4	0	0	0	0	0	0	0	2	.000	.000	.000	0	-99	-1	0	0	0	1.000	-0	/C-1	-0.1
1978	StL-N	6	6	0	0	0	0	0	0	0	2	.000	.000	.000	0	-99	-2	0	0	0	.000	0	/C-1	-0.2
	SF-N	36	92	6	22	4	1	1	8	18	7	.239	.364	.337	701	101	1	1	1	-0	.965	-2	C-31	0.0
	Yr	42	98	6	22	4	1	1	8	18	9	.224	.345	.316	661	89	-1	1	1	-0	.965	-2	C-32	-0.2
1979	SF-N	30	60	7	12	3	0	2	6	4	8	.200	.250	.350	600	66	-3	0	0	0	.985	-6	C-17	-0.9
	Mon-N	12	21	0	8	2	0	0	5	3	3	.381	.458	.476	935	157	2	0	0	0	1.000	-1	/C-4	0.1
	Yr	42	81	7	20	5	0	2	11	7	11	.247	.307	.383	690	92	-1	0	0	0	.989	-7	C-21	-0.8
1980	Mon-N	37	51	4	14	3	0	1	13	6	5	.275	.351	.392	743	107	1	0	0	0	.975	-2	C-12	-0.1
Total	5	135	244	19	59	12	1	4	33	34	27	.242	.335	.348	683	92	-2	1	1	-0	.974	-12	/C-67	-1.2
■ **LEO TANKERSLEY** Tankersley, Lawrence William b: 6/8/01, Terrell, Tex. d: 9/18/80, Dallas, Tex. BR/TR, 6', 176 lbs. Deb: 7/2/25																								
1925	Chi-A	1	3	0	0	0	0	0	0	0	0	.000	.000	.000	0	-99	-1	0	0	0	1.000	-1	/C-1	-0.2
■ **JESSE TANNEHILL** Tannehill, Jesse Niles "Powder" b: 7/14/1874, Dayton, Ky. d: 9/22/56, Dayton, Ky. BB/TL (BL 1903), 5'8", 150 lbs. Deb: 6/17/1894 FC																								
1894	Cin-N	5	11	0	0	0	0	0	1	1	2	.000	.083	.000	83	-76	-3	0			.600	-1	/P-5	0.0
1897	Pit-N	56	184	22	49	8	2	0	22	18		.266	.338	.332	670	80	-5	4			.900	7	O-33(4-27-2),P-21	-0.1
1898	Pit-N	60	152	25	44	9	3	1	17	7		.289	.321	.408	729	111	1	4			.956	4	P-43/O-7(3-4-0)	0.0
1899	Pit-N	48	136	18	34	5	3	0	11	8		.250	.301	.331	632	74	-5	2			.955	4	P-41/O-1(1-0-0)	-0.1
1900	Pit-N	34	110	19	37	7	0	0	17	5		.336	.365	.400	765	110	1	2			.924	1	P-29/O-4(0-0-4)	0.0
1901	Pit-N	42	135	19	33	3	3	1	12	6		.244	.277	.333	610	74	-5	0			.917	-2	P-32,O-10(9-0-1)	-0.1
1902	Pit-N	44	148	27	43	6	1	1	17	12		.291	.348	.365	713	116	3	3			.969	-3	P-26,O-16(5-0-11)	-0.2
1903	NY-A	40	111	18	26	6	2	1	13	8		.234	.292	.351	643	87	-2	1			.969	1	P-32/O-5(4-1-0)	-0.2
1904	Bos-A	45	122	14	24	2	6	0	6	9		.197	.252	.311	563	73	-4	1			.991	2	P-33/O-2(2-0-0)	-0.1
1905	Bos-A	37	93	11	21	2	0	1	12	16		.226	.339	.280	619	96	0	1			.946	2	P-37	0.0
1906	Bos-A	31	79	12	22	2	2	0	4	6		.278	.329	.354	684	114	1	1			.948	0	P-27	0.0
1907	Bos-A	21	51	2	10	3	1	0	6	2		.196	.241	.294	535	71	-2	0			.981	0	P-18	0.0
1908	Bos-A	1	2	0	1	0	0	0	0	0		.500	.500	.500	1000	219	0	0			1.000	0	/P-1	0.0
	Was-A	26	43	1	11	1	0	0	3	2		.256	.289	.279	568	92	-0	0			.897	1	P-10	0.0
	Yr	27	45	1	12	1	0	0	3	2		.267	.298	.289	587	99	-0	0			.907	2	P-11	0.0
1909	Was-A	16	36	2	6	1	0	0	1	5		.167	.286	.194	480	55	-2	0			1.000	-0	/O-9(0-0-9),P-3	-0.3
1911	Cin-N	1	1	0	0	0	0	0	0	0	1	.000	.000	.000	0	-99	-0	0			1.000	0	/P-1	0.0
Total	15	507	1414	190	361	55	23	5	142	105	3	.255	.310	.337	648	89	-21	19			.953	17	P-359/O-87(28-32-27)	-1.1
■ **LEE TANNEHILL** Tannehill, Lee Ford b: 10/26/1880, Dayton, Ky. d: 2/16/38, Live Oak, Fla. BR/TR, 5'11", 170 lbs. Deb: 4/22/03 F																								
1903	Chi-A	138	503	48	113	14	3	2	50	25		.225	.263	.276	539	65	-21	10			.908	-5	*S-138	-2.2
1904	Chi-A	153	547	50	125	31	5	0	61	20		.229	.260	.303	563	81	-13	14			.947	**28**	*3-153	2.1
1905	Chi-A	142	480	38	96	17	2	0	39	45		.200	.274	.244	518	67	-17	8			.931	28	*3-142	1.7
1906	*Chi-A	116	378	26	69	8	3	0	33	31		.183	.254	.220	473	50	-21	7			.951	**39**	3-99,S-17	2.3
1907	Chi-A	33	108	9	26	2	0	0	11	8		.241	.293	.259	552	79	-2	3			.912	5	3-31/S-2	0.4
1908	Chi-A	141	482	44	104	15	3	0	35	25		.216	.257	.259	517	69	-17	6			.935	18	*3-136/S-5	0.6
1909	Chi-A	155	531	39	118	21	5	0	47	31		.222	.269	.281	550	77	-15	12			.941	7	3-91,S-64	-0.4
1910	Chi-A	67	230	17	51	10	0	1	21	11		.222	.263	.278	542	73	-8	3			.947	3	S-38,1-23/3-6	-0.4
1911	Chi-A	141	516	60	131	17	6	0	49	32		.254	.300	.310	610	73	-20	0			.957	**43**	*S-102,2-27/3-7,1-5	3.0
1912	Chi-A	4	3	0	0	0	0	0	0	1		.000	.400	.000	400	18	-0	0			.667	-1	/3-3,S-1	-0.1
Total	10	1090	3778	331	833	135	27	3	346	229		.220	.269	.273	542	70	-133	63			.938	165	3-668,S-367/1-28,2	7.0
■ **CHUCK TANNER** Tanner, Charles William b: 7/4/29, New Castle, Pa. BL/TL, 6', 185 lbs. Deb: 4/12/55 FM																								
1955	Mil-N	97	243	27	60	9	3	6	27	27	32	.247	.322	.383	705	91	-3	0	0	0	.981	-4	O-62(52-0-11)	-1.1
1956	Mil-N	60	63	6	15	2	0	1	4	10	10	.238	.342	.317	660	84	-1	0	0	0	.800	-3	/O-8(7-0-1)	-0.4
1957	Mil-N	22	69	5	17	3	0	2	6	5	4	.246	.297	.377	674	86	-2	0	0	0	1.000	-0	O-18(18-0-0)	-0.3
	Chi-N	95	318	42	91	16	2	7	42	23	20	.286	.338	.415	753	103	1	0	2	-1	.988	-1	O-82(59-25-0)	-0.5
	Yr	117	387	47	108	19	2	9	48	28	24	.279	.331	.408	739	100	-0	0	2	-1	.990	-1	*O-100(77-25-0)	-0.8
1958	Chi-N	73	103	10	27	6	0	4	17	9	10	.262	.321	.437	758	100	-0	1	0	0	.955	-2	O-15(2-3-10)	-0.3
1959	Cle-A	14	48	6	12	2	0	1	5	2	9	.250	.280	.354	634	76	-2	0	0	0	1.000	-1	O-10(3-7-0)	-0.3
1960	Cle-A	21	25	2	7	1	0	0	4	4	6	.280	.379	.320	699	94	-0	1	0	0	1.000	-1	/O-4(4-0-0)	-0.1
1961	LA-A	7	8	0	1	0	0	0	0	2	2	.125	.300	.125	425	16	-1	0	0	0	.000	-0	/O-1(0-0-1)	-0.1
1962	LA-A	7	8	0	1	0	0	0	0	0	0	.125	.125	.125	250	-34	-1	0	0	0	.000	-1	/O-2(1-0-1)	-0.2
Total	8	396	885	98	231	39	5	21	105	82	93	.261	.325	.388	713	93	-9	2	2	-0	.983	-13	O-202(146-35-24)	-3.3
■ **WALTER TAPPAN** Tappan, Walter Van Dorn "Tap" b: 10/8/1890, Carlinville, Ill. d: 12/19/67, Lynwood, Cal. BR/TR, 5'8", 158 lbs. Deb: 4/16/14																								
1914	KC-F	18	39	1	8	1	0	1	3	1	0	.205	.225	.308	533	46	-4	1			.875	-3	/S-8,3-6,2-1	-0.7
■ **EL TAPPE** Tappe, Elvin Walter b: 5/21/27, Quincy, Ill. d: 10/10/98, Quincy, Ill. BR/TR, 5'11", 180 lbs. Deb: 4/24/54 MC																								
1954	Chi-N	46	119	5	22	3	0	0	4	10	9	.185	.248	.210	458	21	-14	0	0	0	.986	6	C-46	-0.6
1955	Chi-N	2	0	0	0	0	0	0	0	0	0	—	—	—	—	—	0	0	0	0	1.000	1	/C-2	0.1
1956	Chi-N	3	1	0	0	0	0	0	0	1	0	.000	.500	.000	500	51	0	0	0	0	1.000	0	/C-3	0.0
1958	Chi-N	17	28	2	6	0	0	0	4	3	1	.214	.290	.214	505	37	-2	0	0	0	.962	-1	C-16	-0.3
1960	Chi-N	51	103	11	24	7	0	0	3	11	12	.233	.313	.301	614	70	-4	0	1	-0	.992	9	C-49	0.6
1962	Chi-N	26	53	3	11	0	0	0	6	4	3	.208	.288	.208	496	34	-5	0	0	0	1.000	4	C-26,M	0.0
Total	6	145	304	21	63	10	0	0	17	29	25	.207	.283	.240	523	41	-25	0	1	-0	.989	19	C-142	-0.2
■ **TED TAPPE** Tappe, Theodore Nash b: 2/2/31, Seattle, Wash. BL/TR, 6'3", 185 lbs. Deb: 9/14/50																								
1950	Cin-N	7	5	1	1	0	0	1	1	1	1	.200	.333	.800	1133	187	1	0			.000	0	H	0.1
1951	Cin-N	4	3	0	1	0	0	0	0	0	0	.333	.333	.333	667	79	-0	0	0	0	.000	0	H	0.0
1955	Chi-N	23	50	12	13	2	0	4	10	11	11	.260	.413	.540	953	151	4	0	0	0	1.000	-2	O-15(0-0-15)	0.2
Total	3	34	58	13	15	2	0	5	11	12	12	.259	.403	.552	955	151	5	0	0		1.000	-2	/O-15(0-0-15)	0.3
■ **TONY TARASCO** Tarasco, Anthony Giacinto b: 12/9/70, New York, N.Y. BL/TR, 6'1", 205 lbs. Deb: 4/30/93																								
1993	*Atl-N	24	35	6	8	2	0	0	2	0	5	.229	.250	.286	536	43	-3	0	1	-0	1.000	-3	O-12(4-0-8)	-0.6
1994	Atl-N	87	132	16	36	6	0	5	19	9	17	.273	.319	.432	751	91	-2	5	0	1	1.000	-8	O-45(26-0-22)	-0.9

YEAR	TM/L	G	AB	R	H	2B	3B	HR	RBI	BB	SO	AVG	OBP	SLG	OPS	OPS+	BR+	SB	CS	SBR	FA	FR	G/POS	TPR
1995	Mon-N	126	438	64	109	18	4	14	40	51	78	.249	.330	.404	734	89	-7	24	3	4	.979	6	*O-116(11-0-105)	-0.2
1996	*Bal-A	31	84	14	20	3	0	1	9	7	15	.238	.297	.310	606	54	-6	5	3	0	1.000	1	O-23(0-1-22)/D-6	-0.5
1997	Bal-A	100	166	26	34	8	1	7	26	25	33	.205	.313	.392	704	85	-4	2	2	-0	.991	-10	O-81(7-8-68)/D-2	-1.5
1998	Cin-N	15	24	5	5	2	0	1	4	3	5	.208	.296	.417	713	84	-1	0	0	0	1.000	-1	/O-7(4-1-2)	-0.1
1999	NY-A	14	31	5	5	2	0	0	3	3	5	.161	.235	.226	461	19	-4	1	0	0	1.000	-3	O-12(9-0-5)	-0.7
Total	7	397	910	136	217	41	5	28	103	98	158	.238	.315	.387	702	81	-26	37	9	5	.987	-16	O-296(61-10-232)/D-8	-4.5
■ ARLIE TARBERT	Tarbert, Wilbur Arlington b: 9/10/04, Cleveland, Ohio d: 11/27/46, Cleveland, Ohio BR/TR, 6′, 160 lbs. Deb: 6/18/27																							
1927	Bos-A	33	69	5	13	1	0	0	5	3	12	.188	.253	.203	456	20	-8	0	0	0	.944	-4	O-27(10-3-14)	-1.3
1928	Bos-A	6	17	1	3	1	0	0	2	1	1	.176	.222	.235	458	21	-2	1	0	0	.900	-0	/O-6(0-0-6)	-0.3
Total	2	39	86	6	16	2	0	0	7	4	13	.186	.247	.209	457	20	-10	1	0	0	.935	-5	/O-33(10-3-20)	-1.6
■ DANNY TARTABULL	Tartabull, Danilo (Mora) b: 10/30/62, San Juan, P.R. BR/TR, 6′1″, 205 lbs. Deb: 9/7/84 F Career OF: (15-LF 0-CF 904-RF)																							
1984	Sea-A	10	20	3	6	1	0	2	7	2	3	.300	.391	.650	1041	185	2	0	0	0	.931	2	/S-8,2-1	0.4
1985	Sea-A	19	61	8	20	7	1	1	7	8	14	.328	.406	.525	930	152	4	1	0	0	.940	-3	S-16/3-4	0.4
1986	Sea-A	137	511	76	138	25	6	25	96	61	157	.270	.349	.489	838	124	17	4	8	-2	.953	1	*O-101R,2-31/3-1,D	1.2
1987	KC-A	158	582	95	180	27	3	34	101	79	136	.309	.393	.541	934	141	35	9	4	1	.976	-6	*O-149(0-0-150)/D-6	2.0
1988	KC-A	146	507	80	139	38	3	26	102	76	119	.274	.373	.515	888	145	31	8	5	0	.963	-4	*O-130(0-0-130),D-13	2.2
1989	KC-A	133	441	54	118	22	0	18	62	69	123	.268	.370	.440	810	128	18	4	2	0	.982	-7	O-71(0-0-73),D-55	0.7
1990	KC-A	88	313	41	84	19	0	15	60	36	93	.268	.344	.473	817	128	11	1	1	-0	.965	-4	O-52(0-0-52),D-32	0.5
1991	KC-A★	132	484	78	153	35	3	31	100	65	121	.316	.400	**.593**	993	170	46	6	3	0	.965	-10	*O-124(0-0-124)/D-6	3.2
1992	NY-A	123	421	72	112	19	0	25	85	103	115	.266	.410	.489	900	152	33	2	2	-0	.980	1	O-69(1-0-68),D-53	3.1
1993	NY-A	138	513	87	128	33	2	31	102	92	156	.250	.366	.503	869	135	26	0	0	0	.978	-1	D-88,O-50(0-0-50)	1.6
1994	NY-A	104	399	68	102	24	1	19	67	66	111	.256	.363	.464	826	115	10	1	1	-0	1.000	-2	D-78,O-26(0-0-26)	0.2
1995	NY-A	59	192	25	43	12	0	6	28	33	54	.224	.341	.380	721	88	-3	0	0	0	1.000	-0	D-39,O-18(0-0-18)	-0.6
	Oak-A	24	88	9	23	4	0	2	7	10	28	.261	.337	.375	712	90	-1	0	2	-1	1.000	-0	D-22/O-1(0-0-1)	-0.3
	Yr	83	280	34	66	16	0	8	35	43	82	.236	.340	.379	718	89	-4	0	2	-1	.938	-1	D-61,O-19(0-0-19)	-0.9
1996	Chi-A	132	472	58	120	23	3	27	101	64	128	.254	.343	.487	831	112	8	1	2	-0	.973	3	*O-122(0-0-122),D-10	0.3
1997	Phi-N	3	7	2	0	0	0	0	0	4	4	.000	.364	.000	364	5	-1	0	0	0	1.000	-1	/O-3(0-0-3)	-0.2
Total	14	1406	5011	756	1366	289	22	262	925	768	1362	.273	.371	.496	867	133	236	37	30	-2	.971	-32	O-916R,D-405/2-32,S3	14.7
■ JOSE TARTABULL	Tartabull, Jose Milages (Guzman) b: 11/27/38, Cienfuegos, Cuba BL/TL, 5′11″, 165 lbs. Deb: 4/10/62 F																							
1962	KC-A	107	310	49	86	6	5	0	22	20	19	.277	.323	.329	652	73	-11	19	5	2	.974	4	O-85(1-85-0)	-0.8
1963	KC-A	79	242	27	58	8	5	1	19	17	17	.240	.290	.326	616	68	-10	16	1	3	.986	-3	O-71(1-70-0)	-1.3
1964	KC-A	104	100	9	20	2	0	0	3	5	12	.200	.238	.220	458	28	-10	4	0	1	.978	-12	O-59(44-13-5)	-2.3
1965	KC-A	68	218	28	68	11	4	1	19	18	20	.312	.364	.413	777	122	6	11	5	1	.986	7	O-54(26-27-8)	1.2
1966	KC-A	37	127	13	30	2	3	0	4	11	13	.236	.297	.299	596	74	-4	8	1	1	1.000	0	O-32(1-32-0)	-0.4
	Bos-A	68	195	28	54	7	4	0	11	6	11	.277	.299	.354	652	79	-5	11	3	1	.989	-2	O-47(0-47-0)	-0.8
	Yr	105	322	41	84	9	7	0	15	17	24	.261	.298	.332	630	77	-10	19	4	3	.994	-2	O-79(1-79-0)	-1.2
1967	*Bos-A	115	247	36	55	1	2	0	10	23	26	.223	.289	.243	532	54	-13	6	6	-1	.989	-12	O-83(12-19-55)	-3.3
1968	Bos-A	72	139	24	39	6	0	0	6	6	5	.281	.310	.324	634	87	-2	2	3	-1	.984	-4	O-43(12-11-20)	-1.0
1969	Oak-A	75	266	28	71	11	1	0	11	9	11	.267	.291	.316	607	73	-10	3	4	-1	.993	1	O-63(28-36-0)	-1.4
1970	Oak-A	24	13	5	3	2	0	0	2	0	2	.231	.231	.385	615	69	-1	1	0	0	1.000	-2	/O-6(4-2-0)	-0.2
Total	9	749	1857	247	484	56	24	2	107	115	136	.261	.304	.320	624	74	-61	81	28	8	.986	-24	O-543(129-342-88)	-10.3
■ LA SCHELLE TARVER	Tarver, La Schelle b: 1/30/59, Modesto, Cal. BL/TL, 5′11″, 165 lbs. Deb: 7/12/86																							
1986	Bos-A	13	25	3	3	0	0	0	1	1	4	.120	.154	.120	274	-24	-4	0	1	-0	1.000	-1	/O-9(3-7-0)	-0.6
■ WILLIE TASBY	Tasby, Willie b: 1/8/33, Shreveport, La. BR/TR, 5′11″, 175 lbs. Deb: 9/9/58 Career OF: (65-LF 460-CF 48-RF)																							
1958	Bal-A	18	50	6	10	3	0	1	1	7	15	.200	.310	.320	630	78	-1	1	1	-0	1.000	-4	O-16(6-12-5)	-0.6
1959	Bal-A	142	505	69	126	16	5	13	48	34	80	.250	.305	.378	683	88	-9	3	5	-1	.968	3	*O-137(5-132-1)	-1.3
1960	Bal-A	39	85	9	18	2	1	0	3	9	12	.212	.295	.259	554	52	-6	1	0	0	.980	-8	O-36(17-9-18)	-1.5
	Bos-A	105	385	68	108	17	1	7	37	51	54	.281	.372	.384	756	101	2	3	1	0	.979	3	*O-102(0-102-0)	0.1
	Yr	144	470	77	126	19	2	7	40	60	66	.268	.358	.362	720	93	-3	4	1	1	.979	-5	*O-138(17-111-18)	-1.4
1961	Was-A	141	494	54	124	13	2	17	63	58	94	.251	.332	.389	721	93	-5	4	10	-3	.985	2	*O-139(0-138-1)	-0.9
1962	Was-A	11	34	4	7	0	0	0	0	2	6	.206	.250	.206	456	24	-4	0	0	0	.933	-2	O-10(7-3-0)	-0.6
	Cle-A	75	199	25	48	7	0	4	17	25	41	.241	.326	.337	663	81	-5	0	2	-1	1.000	-12	O-66(12-57-10)/3-1	-2.0
	Yr	86	233	29	55	7	0	4	17	27	47	.236	.315	.318	633	73	-9	0	2	-1	.992	-14	O-76(19-60-10)/3-1	-2.6
1963	Cle-A	52	116	11	26	3	1	4	5	15	25	.224	.318	.371	689	93	-1	0	1	-0	.981	-5	O-37(18-7-13)/2-1	-0.8
Total	6	583	1868	246	467	61	10	46	174	201	327	.250	.328	.367	695	89	-28	12	20	-4	.980	-22	O-543C/2-1,3-1	-7.6
■ POP TATE	Tate, Edward Christopher "Dimples" b: 12/22/1860, Richmond, Va. d: 6/25/32, Richmond, Va. BR/TL, 5′10″, 178 lbs. Deb: 9/26/1885																							
1885	Bos-N	4	13	1	2	0	0	0	2	1	3	.154	.214	.154	368	21	-1				.865	1	/C-4	0.0
1886	Bos-N	31	106	13	24	3	1	0	3	7	17	.226	.274	.274	548	70	-4	0			.885	-4	C-31	-0.4
1887	Bos-N	60	239	34	68	5	3	0	27	8	9	.285	.296	.307	604	68	-10	7			.924	13	C-53/O-8(0-0-8)	0.6
1888	Bos-N	41	148	18	34	7	1	1	6	8	7	.230	.278	.311	589	86	-2	3			.854	-3	C-41/O-1(0-0-1)	-0.2
1889	Bal-a	72	253	28	46	6	3	1	27	13	37	.182	.236	.241	477	35	-22	4			.938	-3	C-62,1-10	-1.7
1890	Bal-a	19	71	7	13	1	1	0	6	4		.183	.284	.225	509	48	-5	3			.923	-2	C-11/1-8	-0.6
Total	6	227	830	101	187	22	9	2	71	41	73	.225	.269	.274	543	58	-43	17			.905	3	C-202/1-18,O-9(0-0-9)	-2.3
■ BENNIE TATE	Tate, Henry Bennett b: 12/3/01, Whitwell, Tenn. d: 10/27/73, W.Frankfort, Ill. BL/TR, 5′8″, 165 lbs. Deb: 4/29/24																							
1924	*Was-A	21	43	2	13	2	0	0	7	1	2	.302	.318	.349	667	74	-2	0	0	0	.841	-3	C-14	-0.4
1925	Was-A	16	27	0	13	3	0	0	7	2	2	.481	.517	.593	1110	185	4	0	0	0	.955	2	C-14	0.5
1926	Was-A	59	142	17	38	5	2	1	13	15	1	.268	.338	.352	690	82	-4	0	0	0	.960	-5	C-45	-0.6
1927	Was-A	61	131	12	41	5	1	1	24	8	4	.313	.357	.389	746	95	-1	0	3	-1	.977	4	C-39	0.4
1928	Was-A	57	122	10	30	6	0	0	15	10	4	.246	.303	.295	598	58	-7	0	4	-1	.985	2	C-30	-0.4
1929	Was-A	81	265	26	78	12	3	0	30	16	8	.294	.335	.362	697	79	-8	2	5	-1	.971	-2	C-74	-0.6
1930	Was-A	14	20	1	5	0	0	0	2	0	1	.250	.250	.250	500	27	-2	0	0	0	.933	-1	/C-9	-0.2
	Chi-A	72	230	26	73	11	2	0	27	18	10	.317	.367	.383	750	94	-2	2	1	0	.981	-10	C-70	-0.6
	Yr	86	250	27	78	11	2	0	29	18	11	.312	.358	.372	730	88	-4	2	1	0	.978	-11	C-79	-0.8
1931	Chi-A	89	273	27	73	12	3	0	22	26	10	.267	.331	.333	664	80	-8	1	1	-0	.987	7	C-85	0.4
1932	Chi-A	4	10	1	1	0	0	0	0	1	0	.100	.182	.100	282	-27	-2	0	0	0	1.000	0	/C-4	-0.1
	Bos-A	81	273	21	67	12	5	2	26	20	6	.245	.297	.348	645	68	-13	0	1	-0	.974	-5	C-76	-1.3
	Yr	85	283	22	68	12	5	2	26	21	6	.240	.293	.339	632	65	-15	0	1	-0	.975	-5	C-80	-1.4
1934	Chi-N	11	24	1	3	0	0	0	0	1	3	.125	.160	.125	285	-23	-4	0			1.000	-3	/C-8	-0.7
Total	10	566	1560	144	435	68	16	4	173	118	51	.279	.330	.351	681	78	-49	5	15		.974	-14	C-468	-3.6
■ HUGHIE TATE	Tate, Hugh Henry b: 5/19/1880, Everett, Pa. d: 8/7/56, Greenville, Pa. BR/TR, 5′11″, 190 lbs. Deb: 9/21/05																							
1905	Was-A	4	13	1	4	0	1	0	2	0		.308	.308	.462	769	149	1	1			1.000	0	/O-3(3-0-0)	0.1
■ LEE TATE	Tate, Lee Willie "Skeeter" b: 3/18/32, Black Rock, Ark. BR/TR, 5′10″, 165 lbs. Deb: 9/12/58																							
1958	StL-N	10	35	4	7	2	0	0	1	4	3	.200	.282	.257	539	42	-3	0	0	0	.950	-4	/S-9	-0.7
1959	StL-N	41	50	5	7	1	1	1	4	5	7	.140	.232	.260	492	29	-5	0	0	0	.927	1	S-39/2-2,3-2	-0.3
Total	2	51	85	9	14	3	1	1	5	9	10	.165	.253	.259	511	34	-8	0	0	0	.934	-4	/S-48,3-2,2-2	-1.0
■ FERNANDO TATIS	Tatis, Fernando b: 1/1/75, San Pedro De Macoris, D.R. BR/TR, 6′1″, 175 lbs. Deb: 7/26/97																							
1997	Tex-A	60	223	29	57	9	0	8	29	14	42	.256	.300	.404	703	77	-8	3	0	1	.951	-11	3-60	-1.7
1998	Tex-A	95	330	41	89	17	2	3	32	12	66	.270	.303	.361	664	69	-15	6	2	1	.945	10	3-94	-0.3
	StL-N	55	202	28	58	16	2	8	26	24	57	.287	.368	.505	873	128	8	7	3	0	.928	-0	3-55/S-3	0.9
1999	StL-N	149	537	104	160	31	2	34	107	82	128	.298	.406	.553	959	139	34	21	9	1	.958	-2	*3-147	3.2
2000	*StL-N	96	324	59	82	21	1	18	64	57	94	.253	.381	.491	872	118	10	2	3	-1	.953	-16	3-91/1-1,D-2	-0.6
Total	4	455	1616	261	446	94	7	71	258	189	387	.276	.363	.475	838	111	28	39	17	3	.949	-18	3-447/S-3,D-2,1-1	1.5

YEAR	TM/L	G	AB	R	H	2B	3B	HR	RBI	BB	SO	AVG	OBP	SLG	OPS	OPS+	BR+	SB	CS	SBR	FA	FR	G/POS	TPR
■ JIM TATUM Tatum, James Ray b: 10/9/67, Grossmont, Cal. BR/TR, 6'2", 200 lbs. Deb: 9/18/92 Career OF: (8-LF 0-CF 1-RF)																								
1992	Mil-A	5	8	0	1	0	0	0	0	1	2	.125	.222	.125	347	-0	-1	0	0	0	1.000	-0	/3-5	-0.1
1993	Col-N	92	98	7	20	5	0	1	12	5	27	.204	.250	.286	536	37	-9	0	0	0	.978	-2	1-12/3-6,O-3(2-0-1)	-1.1
1995	Col-N	34	34	4	8	1	1	0	4	1	7	.235	.257	.324	581	40	-3	0	0	0	1.000	-1	/O-2(2-0-0),C-1	-0.3
1996	Bos-A	2	8	1	1	0	0	0	0	0	2	.125	.125	.125	250	-36	-2	0	0	0	1.000	-0	/3-2	-0.2
	SD-N	5	3	0	0	0	0	0	0	0	1	.000	.000	.000	0	-99	-1	0	0	0	.000	0	/3-1	-0.1
1998	NY-N	35	50	4	9	1	2	2	13	3	19	.180	.226	.400	626	61	-3	0	0	0	1.000	-1	/1-9,C-4,O-4L,3D	-0.4
Total	5	173	201	16	39	7	3	3	29	10	58	.194	.236	.303	539	37	-18	0	0	0	.987	-4	/1-21,3-17,O-9L,CD	-2.2
■ JARVIS TATUM Tatum, Jarvis b: 10/11/46, Fresno, Cal. BR/TR, 6', 185 lbs. Deb: 9/7/68																								
1968	Cal-A	17	51	7	9	1	0	0	2	0	9	.176	.176	.196	373	13	-5	0	0	0	1.000	-0	O-11(0-11-0)	-0.7
1969	Cal-A	10	22	2	7	0	0	0	0	0	6	.318	.318	.318	636	83	-1	0	1	-0	.857	-1	/O-5(0-0-5)	-0.2
1970	Cal-A	75	181	28	43	7	0	0	6	17	35	.238	.303	.276	579	63	-9	1	0	0	.982	-5	O-58(8-43-12)	-1.6
Total	3	102	254	37	59	8	0	0	8	17	50	.232	.280	.264	544	56	-15	1	1	-0	.979	-6	/O-74(8-54-17)	-2.5
■ TOMMY TATUM Tatum, V T b: 7/16/19, Decatur, Tex. d: 11/7/89, Oklahoma City, Okla BR/TR, 6', 185 lbs. Deb: 8/1/41																								
1941	Bro-N	8	12	1	2	1	0	0	1	1	3	.167	.231	.250	481	34	-1	0			1.000	-1	/O-4(1-3-0)	-0.2
1947	Bro-N	4	6	0	0	0	0	0	0	0	1	.000	.000	.000	0	-96	-2	0			1.000	-1	/O-3(2-0-1)	-0.3
	Cin-N	69	176	19	48	5	2	1	16	16	16	.273	.333	.341	674	80	-5	7			1.000	4	O-49(9-37-4)/2-1	-0.2
	Yr	73	182	19	48	5	2	1	16	16	17	.264	.323	.330	653	74	-7	7			1.000	3	O-52(11-37-5)/2-1	-0.5
Total	2	81	194	20	50	6	2	1	17	17	20	.258	.318	.325	642	72	-8	7			1.000	2	/O-56(12-40-5),2-1	-0.7
■ EDDIE TAUBENSEE Taubensee, Edward Kenneth b: 10/31/68, Beeville, Tex. BL/TR, 6'4", 205 lbs. Deb: 5/18/91 Career OF: (6-LF 0-CF 5-RF)																								
1991	Cle-A	26	66	5	16	2	1	0	8	5	16	.242	.296	.303	599	66	-3	0	0	0	.979	-7	C-25	-0.9
1992	Hou-N	104	297	23	66	15	0	5	28	31	78	.222	.300	.323	623	80	-8	2	1	0	.992	4	*C-103	0.1
1993	Hou-N	94	288	26	72	11	1	9	42	21	44	.250	.301	.389	690	86	-6	1	0	0	.992	4	C-90	0.3
1994	Hou-N	5	10	0	1	0	0	0	0	0	3	.100	.100	.100	200	-50	-2	0	0	0	1.000	1	/C-5	-0.1
	Cin-N	61	177	29	52	8	2	8	21	15	28	.294	.349	.497	846	118	4	2	0	0	.990	-1	C-61	0.7
	Yr	66	187	29	53	8	2	8	21	15	31	.283	.337	.476	813	110	2	2	0	0	.990	-0	C-66	0.6
1995	*Cin-N	80	218	32	62	14	2	9	44	22	52	.284	.355	.491	846	121	6	2	2	-0	.983	-9	C-65/1-3	0.0
1996	Cin-N	108	327	46	95	20	0	12	48	26	64	.291	.343	.462	805	109	4	3	4	-1	.981	-10	C-94	-0.2
1997	Cin-N	108	254	26	68	18	0	10	34	22	66	.268	.329	.457	785	102	0	0	1	-0	.987	-8	C-64,O-11L/1-7,D-3	-0.6
1998	Cin-N	130	431	61	120	27	0	11	72	52	93	.278	.356	.418	774	101	2	1	0	0	.988	-15	*C-126	-0.6
1999	Cin-N	126	424	58	132	22	2	21	87	30	67	.311	.358	.521	879	116	9	0	2	-1	.989	-1	*C-124	1.4
2000	Cin-N	81	266	29	71	12	0	6	24	21	44	.267	.325	.380	705	74	-10	0	0	0	.989	-7	C-76	-1.2
Total	10	923	2758	335	755	149	8	91	408	245	555	.274	.335	.433	767	100	-5	11	10	-1	.988	-50	C-833/O-11L,1-10,D	-1.1
■ FRED TAUBY Tauby, Frederick Joseph (b: Frederick Joseph Taubensee) b: 3/27/06, Canton, Ohio d: 11/23/55, Concord, Cal. BR/TR, 5'9.5", 168 lbs. Deb: 9/1/35																								
1935	Chi-A	13	32	5	4	1	0	0	2	2	3	.125	.176	.156	333	-13	-5	0	0	0	1.000	2	/O-7(1-1-5)	-0.4
1937	Phi-N	11	20	2	0	0	0	0	3	0	5	.000	.000	.000	0	-93	-5	1			1.000	-2	/O-7(3-3-1)	-0.7
Total	2	24	52	7	4	1	0	0	5	2	8	.077	.111	.096	207	-43	-11	1	0		1.000	-0	/O-14(4-4-6)	-1.1
■ DON TAUSSIG Taussig, Donald Franklin b: 2/19/32, New York, N.Y. BR/TR, 6', 180 lbs. Deb: 4/23/58																								
1958	SF-N	39	50	10	10	0	0	1	4	3	8	.200	.245	.260	505	35	-5	0	0	0	1.000	-9	O-36(27-0-11)	-1.4
1961	StL-N	98	188	27	54	14	5	2	25	16	34	.287	.343	.447	790	98	-1	2	2	-0	.992	-9	O-87(48-20-30)	-1.2
1962	Hou-N	16	25	1	5	0	0	1	1	2	11	.200	.259	.320	579	59	-2	0	0	0	1.000	1	/O-4(4-0-0)	-0.1
Total	3	153	263	38	69	14	5	4	30	21	53	.262	.317	.399	716	84	-7	2	2	-0	.994	-17	O-127(79-20-41)	-2.7
■ JESUS TAVAREZ Tavarez, Jesus Rafael (Alcantaras) b: 3/26/71, Santo Domingo, D.R. BB/TR, 6', 170 lbs. Deb: 5/23/94																								
1994	Fla-N	17	39	4	7	0	0	0	4	1	5	.179	.200	.179	379	-0	-6	1	1	-0	1.000	2	O-11(1-2-8)	-0.4
1995	Fla-N	63	190	31	55	6	2	2	13	16	27	.289	.348	.374	722	90	-2	7	5	-0	1.000	-10	O-61(4-47-32)	-1.3
1996	Fla-N	98	114	14	25	3	0	0	6	7	18	.219	.264	.246	510	37	-10	5	1	1	1.000	-15	O-65(25-30-12)	-2.4
1997	Bos-A	42	69	12	12	3	1	0	9	4	9	.174	.219	.246	466	21	-8	0	0	0	.980	-7	O-35(4-29-4)/D-2	-1.5
1998	Bal-A	8	11	2	2	0	0	1	1	2	3	.182	.308	.455	762	96	-0	0	1	-0	1.000	-3	/O-8(0-5-4)	-0.3
Total	5	228	423	63	101	12	3	3	33	30	62	.239	.291	.303	593	56	-27	13	8		.996	-32	O-180(34-113-60)/D-2	-5.9
■ JACKIE TAVENER Tavener, John Adam "Rabbit" b: 12/27/1897, Celina, Ohio d: 9/14/69, Fort Worth, Tex. BL/TR, 5'5", 138 lbs. Deb: 9/24/21																								
1921	Det-A	2	4	0	0	0	0	0	0	0	1	.000	.000	.000	0	-99	-1	0	0	0	1.000	1	/S-2	0.0
1925	Det-A	134	453	45	111	11	11	0	47	39	60	.245	.309	.318	627	60	-28	5	4	-0	.963	7	*S-134	-0.7
1926	Det-A	156	532	65	141	22	14	1	58	52	53	.265	.332	.365	696	80	-16	8	7	-1	.952	9	*S-156	0.9
1927	Det-A	116	419	60	115	22	9	5	59	36	38	.274	.333	.406	739	90	-7	19	8	1	.948	4	*S-114	1.0
1928	Det-A	132	473	59	123	24	15	5	52	33	51	.260	.314	.406	720	86	-11	13	8	0	.944	14	*S-131	1.7
1929	Cle-A	92	250	25	53	9	4	2	27	26	28	.212	.289	.304	593	51	-19	1	4	-1	.945	23	S-89	1.1
Total	6	632	2131	254	543	88	53	13	243	186	231	.255	.318	.364	682	75	-81	46	31	-1	.951	58	S-626	4.0
■ ALEX TAVERAS Taveras, Alejandro Antonio (Betances) b: 10/9/55, Santiago, D.R. BR/TR, 5'10", 155 lbs. Deb: 9/9/76																								
1976	Hou-N	14	46	3	10	0	0	0	2	2	1	.217	.250	.217	467	37	-4	1	2	-0	.923	1	/2-7,S-7	-0.2
1982	LA-N	11	3	1	1	1	0	0	2	0	1	.333	.333	.667	1000	178	0	0	0	0	1.000	4	/2-4,3-4,S-2	0.4
1983	LA-N	10	4	0	0	0	0	0	0	0	1	.000	.000	.000	0	-99	-1	0	0	0	.000	2	/S-3,2-2,3-1	0.1
Total	3	35	53	4	11	1	0	0	4	2	3	.208	.236	.226	463	34	-5	1	2	-0	.938	7	/2-13,S-12,3-5	0.3
■ FRANK TAVERAS Taveras, Franklin Crisostomo (Fabian) b: 12/24/49, Las Matas De Santa Cruz, D.R. BR/TR, 6', 168 lbs. Deb: 9/25/71																								
1971	Pit-N	1	0	0	0	0	0	0	0	0	0	—	—	—	—	—	0	0	0	0	.000	0	R	0.0
1972	Pit-N	4	3	0	0	0	0	0	0	1	1	.000	.250	.000	250	-24	-0	0	0	0	1.000	-1	/S-4	-0.1
1974	*Pit-N	126	333	33	82	4	2	0	26	25	41	.246	.303	.270	573	63	-16	13	4	1	.941	-17	*S-124	-2.0
1975	*Pit-N	134	378	44	80	9	4	0	23	37	42	.212	.285	.257	542	52	-24	17	6	2	.953	-15	*S-132	-2.4
1976	Pit-N	144	519	76	134	8	6	0	24	44	79	.258	.321	.297	618	75	-16	58	11	9	.952	-5	*S-141	0.6
1977	Pit-N	147	544	72	137	20	10	1	29	38	71	.252	.308	.331	639	69	-23	**70**	18	**9**	.962	-22	*S-146	-2.2
1978	Pit-N	157	654	81	182	31	9	0	38	29	60	.278	.314	.353	667	82	-16	46	25	1	.946	-29	*S-157	-2.8
1979	Pit-N	11	45	4	11	3	0	0	1	0	2	.244	.244	.311	556	48	-3	2	1	0	.935	-4	S-11	-0.7
	NY-N	153	635	89	167	26	9	1	33	33	72	.263	.301	.337	639	77	-21	42	19	3	.966	-21	*S-153	-2.5
	Yr	164	680	93	178	29	9	1	34	33	74	.262	.298	.335	633	75	-25	44	20	3	.964	-25	*S-164	-3.2
1980	NY-N	141	562	65	157	27	0	0	25	23	64	.279	.309	.327	636	80	-16	32	18	1	.959	-39	*S-140	-4.2
1981	NY-N	84	283	30	65	11	3	0	11	12	36	.230	.266	.290	556	58	-16	16	4	2	.931	-22	S-79	-3.0
1982	Mon-N	48	87	9	14	5	1	0	4	7	6	.161	.223	.241	465	29	-8	4	0	1	.947	-1	S-26,2-19	-0.7
Total	11	1150	4043	503	1029	144	44	2	214	249	474	.255	.302	.313	615	71	-159	300	106	29	.953	-175	*S-1113/2-19	-20.0
■ TONY TAYLOR Taylor, Antonio Nemesio (Sanchez) b: 12/19/35, Central Alara, Cuba BR/TR, 5'9", 179 lbs. Deb: 4/15/58 C Career OF: (19-LF 0-CF 0-RF)																								
1958	Chi-N	140	497	63	117	15	3	6	27	40	93	.235	.301	.314	615	64	-25	21	6	3	.968	9	*2-137/3-1	-0.4
1959	Chi-N	150	624	96	175	30	8	8	38	45	86	.280	.335	.393	727	94	-5	23	9	2	.970	10	*2-149/S-2	1.8
1960	Chi-N	19	76	14	20	3	3	1	9	8	12	.263	.341	.421	762	108	1	2	0	0	.977	-2	2-19	0.1
	Phi-N★	127	505	66	145	22	4	4	35	33	86	.287	.333	.370	704	92	-5	24	11	1	.968	-6	*2-123/3-4	-0.1
	Yr	146	581	80	165	25	7	5	44	41	98	.284	.334	.377	711	94	-4	26	11	2	.969	-8	*2-142/3-4	0.0
1961	Phi-N	106	400	47	100	17	3	2	26	29	59	.250	.304	.322	626	67	-19	11	5	1	.980	0	2-91/3-3	-1.0
1962	Phi-N	152	625	87	162	21	5	7	43	68	82	.259	.337	.342	679	85	-12	20	9	3	.972	-15	*2-150/S-2	-1.3
1963	Phi-N	157	640	102	180	20	10	5	49	42	99	.281	.332	.367	700	102	2	23	9	2	**.986**	-9	*2-149,3-13	0.9
1964	Phi-N	154	570	62	143	13	6	4	46	46	74	.251	.321	.316	637	81	-13	13	7	0	.977	-21	*2-150	-2.2
1965	Phi-N	106	323	41	74	14	3	3	27	22	58	.229	.303	.319	621	77	-10	5	4	-0	.958	-2	2-86/3-5	-0.6
1966	Phi-N	125	434	47	105	14	8	5	40	31	56	.242	.294	.346	640	77	-14	8	4	0	.988	4	2-68,3-52	-0.4
1967	Phi-N	132	462	55	110	16	6	2	34	42	74	.238	.308	.312	620	77	-13	10	9	-1	.991	-8	1-58,3-44,2-42,/S-3	-2.5
1968	Phi-N	145	547	59	137	20	2	3	38	39	60	.250	.304	.311	615	85	-10	22	5	3	.966	16	*3-138/2-5,1-1	1.0

YEAR	TM/L	G	AB	R	H	2B	3B	HR	RBI	BB	SO	AVG	OBP	SLG	OPS	OPS+	BR+	SB	CS	SBR	FA	FR	G/POS	TPR
1969	Phi-N	138	557	68	146	24	5	3	30	42	62	.262	.318	.339	658	87	-10	19	10	1	.967	-2	3-71,2-57,1-10	-0.9
1970	Phi-N	124	439	74	132	26	9	9	55	50	67	.301	.376	.462	838	127	17	9	11	-2	.996	0	2-59,3-38,O-18L,/S	1.8
1971	Phi-N	36	107	9	25	2	1	1	5	9	10	.234	.293	.299	592	68	-4	2	2	-0	1.000	5	2-14,3-11/1-2	0.0
	Det-A	55	181	27	52	10	2	3	19	12	11	.287	.335	.414	749	107	1	5	1	1	.995	1	2-51/3-3	0.6
1972	*Det-A	78	228	33	69	12	4	1	20	14	34	.303	.348	.404	752	119	5	5	1	1	.966	-8	2-67/3-8,1-1	0.2
1973	Det-A	84	275	35	63	9	3	5	24	17	29	.229	.276	.338	615	68	-12	9	5	0	.987	-14	2-72/1-6,3-4,O-1L,D	-2.2
1974	Phi-N	62	64	5	21	4	0	2	13	6	6	.328	.394	.484	879	139	3	0	0	0	1.000	-1	/1-7,3-5,2-4	0.2
1975	Phi-N	79	103	13	25	5	1	1	17	17	18	.243	.355	.340	695	90	-1	3	3	-0	.913	1	3-16/1-4,2-3	0.0
1976	Phi-N	26	23	2	6	1	0	0	3	1	7	.261	.320	.304	624	76	-1	0	0	0	.000	-0	/2-2,3-1	-0.1
Total	19	2195	7680	1005	2007	298	86	75	598	613	1083	.261	.322	.352	674	88	-123	234	111	13	.976	-41	*2-1498,3-417/1OSD	-5.1

■ BEN TAYLOR

Taylor, Benjamin Eugene b: 9/30/24, Metropolis, Ill. d: 5/11/99, Alma, Okla. BL/TL, 6', 185 lbs. Deb: 7/29/51

YEAR	TM/L	G	AB	R	H	2B	3B	HR	RBI	BB	SO	AVG	OBP	SLG	OPS	OPS+	BR+	SB	CS	SBR	FA	FR	G/POS	TPR
1951	StL-A	33	93	14	24	2	1	3	6	9	22	.258	.337	.398	734	95	-1	1	1	-0	.972	-2	1-25	-0.4
1952	Det-A	7	18	0	3	0	0	0	0	0	5	.167	.167	.167	333	-7	-3	0	0	0	1.000	-0	/1-4	-0.3
1955	Mil-N	12	10	2	1	0	0	0	0	2	4	.100	.250	.100	350	-3	-1	0	0	0	1.000	-0	/1-1	-0.2
Total	3	52	121	16	28	2	1	3	6	11	31	.231	.306	.339	645	73	-5	1	1	-0	.976	-2	/1-30	-0.9

■ CHINK TAYLOR

Taylor, C L b: 2/9/1898, Burnet, Tex. d: 7/7/80, Temple, Tex. BR/TR, 5'9", 160 lbs. Deb: 4/18/25

YEAR	TM/L	G	AB	R	H	2B	3B	HR	RBI	BB	SO	AVG	OBP	SLG	OPS	OPS+	BR+	SB	CS	SBR	FA	FR	G/POS	TPR
1925	Chi-N	8	6	2	0	0	0	0	0	0	0	.000	.000	.000	0	-99	-2	0	0	0	1.000	-1	/O-2(1-0-1)	-0.2

■ CARL TAYLOR

Taylor, Carl Means b: 1/20/44, Sarasota, Fla. BR/TR, 6'2", 207 lbs. Deb: 4/11/68 Career OF: (27-LF 0-CF 79-RF)

YEAR	TM/L	G	AB	R	H	2B	3B	HR	RBI	BB	SO	AVG	OBP	SLG	OPS	OPS+	BR+	SB	CS	SBR	FA	FR	G/POS	TPR
1968	Pit-N	44	71	5	15	1	0	0	7	10	10	.211	.309	.225	534	63	-3	1	0	0	.979	-6	C-29/O-2(1-0-1)	-0.9
1969	Pit-N	104	221	30	77	10	1	4	33	31	36	.348	.435	.457	892	153	17	0	1	-0	.914	-1	O-36(19-0-19),1-24	1.3
1970	StL-N	104	245	39	61	12	2	6	45	41	30	.249	.359	.388	747	98	0	5	2	0	.986	-4	O-46(0-0-46),1-15/3-1	-0.6
1971	Pit-N	7	12	1	2	0	1	0	0	0	5	.167	.167	.333	500	39	-1	0	0	0	1.000	0	/O-1(0-0-1)	-0.1
	KC-A	20	39	3	7	0	0	0	3	5	13	.179	.273	.179	452	30	-3	0	1	-0	.964	1	O-12(6-0-6)	-0.4
1972	KC-A	63	113	17	30	2	1	0	11	17	16	.265	.366	.301	667	101	1	4	1	1	.982	-5	C-21/O-7R,1-6,3-5	-0.4
1973	KC-A	69	145	18	33	6	1	0	16	32	20	.228	.367	.283	650	79	-3	2	2	-0	.980	2	C-63/1-2,D-1	0.1
Total	6	411	846	113	225	31	6	10	115	136	130	.266	.371	.352	723	103	9	12	7	0	.980	-14	C-113,O-104R/1-47,3D	-1.0

■ DANNY TAYLOR

Taylor, Daniel Turney b: 12/23/1900, Lash, Pa. d: 10/11/72, Latrobe, Pa. BR/TR, 5'10", 190 lbs. Deb: 6/30/26

YEAR	TM/L	G	AB	R	H	2B	3B	HR	RBI	BB	SO	AVG	OBP	SLG	OPS	OPS+	BR+	SB	CS	SBR	FA	FR	G/POS	TPR
1926	Was-A	21	50	10	15	0	1	1	5	5	7	.300	.364	.400	764	102	0	1	2	-0	1.000	-1	O-12(0-1-11)	-0.3
1929	Chi-N	2	3	0	0	0	0	0	0	1	1	.000	.250	.000	250	-32	-1	0			1.000	-0	/O-1(0-0-1)	-0.1
1930	Chi-N	74	219	43	62	14	3	2	37	27	34	.283	.364	.402	766	84	-5	6			.971	-1	O-52(52-0-0)	-0.9
1931	Chi-N	88	270	48	81	13	6	5	41	31	46	.300	.372	.448	820	117	7	4			.989	4	O-67(39-22-4)	0.8
1932	Chi-N	6	22	3	5	2	0	0	3	3	1	.227	.320	.318	638	73	-1	1			.900	-0	/O-6(0-4-2)	-0.1
	Bro-N	105	395	84	128	22	7	11	48	33	41	.324	.378	.499	876	136	20	13			.989	4	O-96(0-96-0)	2.1
	Yr	111	417	87	133	24	7	11	51	36	42	.319	.374	.489	864	133	19	14			.983	4	*O-102(0-100-2)	2.0
1933	Bro-N	103	358	75	102	21	9	9	40	47	45	.285	.368	.469	837	144	21	11			.977	2	O-91(0-91-0)	2.1
1934	Bro-N	120	405	62	121	24	6	7	57	63	47	.299	.396	.440	835	130	19	12			.975	-8	*O-108(89-21-0)	0.6
1935	Bro-N	112	352	51	102	19	5	7	59	46	32	.290	.372	.432	804	118	10	6			.970	-6	O-99(99-0-0)	-0.1
1936	Bro-N	43	116	12	34	6	0	2	15	11	14	.293	.359	.397	756	102	1	2			.981	-3	O-31(31-0-0)	-0.3
Total	9	674	2190	388	650	121	37	44	305	267	268	.297	.374	.446	821	121	71	56	2		.979	-10	O-563(310-235-18)	3.8

■ DWIGHT TAYLOR

Taylor, Dwight Bernard b: 3/24/60, Los Angeles, Cal. BL/TL, 5'9", 166 lbs. Deb: 4/14/86

YEAR	TM/L	G	AB	R	H	2B	3B	HR	RBI	BB	SO	AVG	OBP	SLG	OPS	OPS+	BR+	SB	CS	SBR	FA	FR	G/POS	TPR
1986	KC-A	4	2	1	0	0	0	0	0	0	0	.000	.000	.000	0	-98	-1	0	0	0	.000	-1	/O-1(0-1-0),D-2	-0.1

■ ED TAYLOR

Taylor, Edward James b: 11/17/01, Chicago, Ill. d: 1/30/92, Chula Vista, Cal. BR/TR, 5'6.5", 160 lbs. Deb: 4/14/26

YEAR	TM/L	G	AB	R	H	2B	3B	HR	RBI	BB	SO	AVG	OBP	SLG	OPS	OPS+	BR+	SB	CS	SBR	FA	FR	G/POS	TPR
1926	Bos-N	92	272	37	73	8	2	0	33	38	26	.268	.368	.313	681	93	-0	4			.945	-1	3-62,S-33	0.5

■ LIVE OAK TAYLOR

Taylor, Edward S. Deb: 8/21/1877

YEAR	TM/L	G	AB	R	H	2B	3B	HR	RBI	BB	SO	AVG	OBP	SLG	OPS	OPS+	BR+	SB	CS	SBR	FA	FR	G/POS	TPR
1877	Har-N	2	8	0	3	0	0	0	0	0	2	.375	.375	.375	750	153	0				1.000	-1	/O-2(2-0-0)	0.0
1884	Pit-a	41	152	22	32	4	1	0		6		.211	.255	.250	505	66	-5				.798	-1	O-41(0-41-0)	-0.7
Total	2	43	160	22	35	4	1	0	0	6	2	.219	.260	.256	517	70	-5				.802	-1	/O-43(2-41-0)	-0.7

■ FRED TAYLOR

Taylor, Frederick Rankin b: 12/3/24, Zanesville, Ohio BL/TR, 6'3", 201 lbs. Deb: 9/12/50

YEAR	TM/L	G	AB	R	H	2B	3B	HR	RBI	BB	SO	AVG	OBP	SLG	OPS	OPS+	BR+	SB	CS	SBR	FA	FR	G/POS	TPR
1950	Was-A	6	16	1	2	0	0	0	0	1	2	.125	.176	.125	301	-23	-3	0	0	0	.968	0	/1-3	-0.3
1951	Was-A	6	12	1	2	1	0	0	0	0	4	.167	.167	.250	417	12	-2	0	0	0	.962	-0	/1-2	-0.2
1952	Was-A	10	19	3	5	1	0	0	4	3	2	.263	.364	.316	679	93	-0	0	0	0	1.000	1	/1-5	0.1
Total	3	22	47	5	9	2	0	0	4	4	8	.191	.255	.234	489	33	-5	0	0	0	.979	1	/1-10	-0.4

■ HARRY TAYLOR

Taylor, Harry Leonard b: 4/4/1866, Halsey Valley, N.Y. d: 7/12/55, Buffalo, N.Y. BL, 6'2", 160 lbs. Deb: 4/18/1890 Career OF: (23-LF 0-CF 50-RF)

YEAR	TM/L	G	AB	R	H	2B	3B	HR	RBI	BB	SO	AVG	OBP	SLG	OPS	OPS+	BR+	SB	CS	SBR	FA	FR	G/POS	TPR
1890	*Lou-a	134	553	115	169	7	7	0	53	68		.306	.383	.344	726	117	14	45			.982	5	*1-118,S-12/2-4,C-1	0.8
1891	Lou-a	91	348	80	103	7	3	2	35	55	30	.296	.398	.351	749	116	10	15			.978	2	1-90/3-1,2-1,C-1	0.4
1892	Lou-N	125	493	66	128	7	1	0	34	58	23	.260	.342	.278	620	96	1	24			.923	-8	O-73R,1-34,2-14,/3S	-1.0
1893	Bal-N	88	360	50	102	9	1	1	54	32	11	.283	.347	.322	669	77	-12	24			.976	-3	*1-88	-1.2
Total	4	438	1754	311	502	30	12	3	176	213	64	.286	.367	.322	689	102	14	108			.979	-3	1-330/O-73R,2-19,S3C	-1.0

■ HARRY TAYLOR

Taylor, Harry Warren b: 12/26/07, McKeesport, Pa. d: 4/27/69, Toledo, Ohio BL/TL, 6'1.5", 185 lbs. Deb: 4/14/32

YEAR	TM/L	G	AB	R	H	2B	3B	HR	RBI	BB	SO	AVG	OBP	SLG	OPS	OPS+	BR+	SB	CS	SBR	FA	FR	G/POS	TPR
1932	Chi-N	10	8	1	1	0	0	0	0	1	1	.125	.222	.125	347	-4	-1	0			1.000	-0	/1-1	-0.1

■ SANDY TAYLOR

Taylor, James B. 5'10.5", 175 lbs. Deb: 8/11/1879

YEAR	TM/L	G	AB	R	H	2B	3B	HR	RBI	BB	SO	AVG	OBP	SLG	OPS	OPS+	BR+	SB	CS	SBR	FA	FR	G/POS	TPR
1879	Tro-N	24	97	10	21	4	0	0	8	1	8	.216	.224	.258	482	63	-4				.765	-3	O-24(24-0-0)	-0.8

■ ZACK TAYLOR

Taylor, James Wren b: 7/27/1898, Yulee, Fla. d: 9/19/74, Orlando, Fla. BR/TR, 5'11.5", 180 lbs. Deb: 6/15/20 MC

YEAR	TM/L	G	AB	R	H	2B	3B	HR	RBI	BB	SO	AVG	OBP	SLG	OPS	OPS+	BR+	SB	CS	SBR	FA	FR	G/POS	TPR
1920	Bro-N	9	13	3	5	2	0	0	5	0	2	.385	.385	.538	923	158	1	0	1	-0	.882	-1	/C-9	0.0
1921	Bro-N	30	102	6	20	0	2	0	8	1	8	.196	.212	.235	447	17	-12	2	0	0	.965	0	C-30	-0.9
1922	Bro-N	7	14	0	3	0	0	0	2	1	1	.214	.267	.214	481	26	-2	0	0	0	.950	-1	/C-6	-0.2
1923	Bro-N	96	337	29	97	11	6	0	46	9	13	.288	.312	.356	668	78	-11	2	5	-1	.967	14	C-84	0.7
1924	Bro-N	99	345	36	100	9	4	1	39	14	14	.290	.319	.348	667	81	-9	0	1	-0	**.988**	-8	C-93	-1.1
1925	Bro-N	109	352	33	109	16	4	3	44	17	19	.310	.343	.403	747	92	-4	0	0	0	.959	-9	C-96	-0.7
1926	Bos-N	125	432	36	110	22	3	0	42	28	27	.255	.303	.319	622	74	-16	1			.985	2	*C-123	-0.6
1927	Bos-N	30	96	8	23	2	1	1	14	8	5	.240	.298	.313	611	69	-4	0			.988	12	C-27	0.9
	NY-N	83	258	18	60	7	3	0	21	17	20	.233	.283	.283	566	52	-17	2			.972	-4	C-81	-1.6
	Yr	113	354	26	83	9	4	1	35	25	25	.234	.287	.291	578	56	-22	2			.978	8	*C-108	-0.7
1928	Bos-N	125	399	36	100	15	1	2	30	33	29	.251	.313	.308	621	66	-19	2			.985	-12	*C-124	-2.3
1929	Bos-N	34	101	8	25	7	0	0	10	7	9	.248	.303	.317	620	56	-7	0			.965	6	C-31	0.1
	*Chi-N	64	215	29	59	16	3	1	31	19	18	.274	.336	.391	727	79	-7	0			.979	-1	C-64	-0.4
	Yr	98	316	37	84	23	3	1	41	26	27	.266	.326	.367	693	72	-14	0			.974	5	C-95	-0.3
1930	Chi-N	32	95	12	22	2	1	1	11	2	12	.232	.255	.305	560	34	-10	0			1.000	-1	C-28	-0.8
1931	Chi-N	8	4	0	1	0	0	0	0	2	1	.250	.500	.250	750	106	0	0			1.000	1	/C-5	0.1
1932	Chi-N	21	30	2	6	1	0	0	3	1	4	.200	.226	.233	459	24	-3	0			1.000	3	C-14	0.0
1933	Chi-N	16	11	0	0	0	0	0	0	0	1	.000	.000	.000	0	-99	-3	0			1.000	-0	C-12	-0.3
1934	NY-A	4	7	0	1	0	0	0	0	0	1	.143	.143	.143	286	-28	-1	0	0	0	1.000	-0	/C-3	-0.1
1935	Bro-N	26	54	2	7	3	0	0	5	2	8	.130	.175	.185	361	-3	-8	0			.970	0	C-26	-0.7
Total	16	918	2865	258	748	113	28	9	311	161	192	.261	.304	.329	634	68	-134	9	7		.977	1	C-856	-7.9

■ JOE TAYLOR

Taylor, Joe Cephus b: 3/2/26, Chapman, Ala. d: 3/18/93, Pittsburgh, Pa. BR/TR, 6'1", 185 lbs. Deb: 8/26/54

YEAR	TM/L	G	AB	R	H	2B	3B	HR	RBI	BB	SO	AVG	OBP	SLG	OPS	OPS+	BR+	SB	CS	SBR	FA	FR	G/POS	TPR
1954	Phi-A	18	58	5	13	1	1	1	8	2	9	.224	.250	.328	578	57	-4	0	1	-0	.943	-0	O-16(9-0-8)	-0.5
1957	Cin-N	33	107	14	28	7	0	4	9	6	24	.262	.301	.439	740	89	-2	0	1	-0	.971	4	O-27(19-0-8)	0.0
1958	StL-N	18	23	2	7	3	0	1	3	2	4	.304	.360	.565	925	135	1	0	0	0	1.000	-0	/O-5(2-2-1)	0.1
	Bal-A	36	77	11	21	4	0	2	9	7	19	.273	.333	.403	736	107	1	0	0	0	.972	-2	O-21(3-4-15)	-0.2

YEAR	TM/L	G	AB	R	H	2B	3B	HR	RBI	BB	SO	AVG	OBP	SLG	OPS	OPS+	BR+	SB	CS	SBR	FA	FR	G/POS	TPR
1959	Bal-A	14	32	2	5	1	0	1	2	11	5	.156	.372	.281	653	84	-0	0	0	0	1.000	-3	O-12(2-0-10)	-0.3
Total	4	119	297	34	74	16	1	9	31	28	61	.249	.314	.401	715	92	-4	0	2	-1	.969	-1	/O-81(35-6-42)	-0.9
■ LEO TAYLOR	Taylor, Leo Thomas "Chink" b: 5/13/01, Walla Walla, Wash. d: 5/20/82, Seattle, Wash. BR/TR, 5'10.5", 150 lbs. Deb: 5/3/23																							
1923	Chi-A	1	0	0	0	0	0	0	0	0	0	—	—	—	—	—	0	0	0	0	.000	0	R	0.0
■ REGGIE TAYLOR	Taylor, Reginald Tremain b: 1/12/77, Newberry, S.C. BL/TR, 6'1", 175 lbs. Deb: 9/17/2000																							
2000	Phi-N	9	11	1	1	0	0	0	0	0	8	.091	.091	.091	182	-53	-3	1	0	0	.800	-1	/O-3(0-3-0)	-0.3
■ HAWK TAYLOR	Taylor, Robert Dale b: 4/3/39, Metropolis, Ill. BR/TR, 6'2", 190 lbs. Deb: 6/9/57 Career OF: (37-LF 3-CF 22-RF)																							
1957	Mil-N	7	1	2	0	0	0	0	0	0	0	.000	.000	.000	0	-99	-0	0	0	0	.000	0	/C-1	0.0
1958	Mil-N	4	8	1	1	1	0	0	0	0	3	.125	.125	.250	375	-4	-1	0	0	0	1.000	-0	/O-4(4-0-0)	-0.2
1961	Mil-N	20	26	1	5	0	0	1	1	3	11	.192	.276	.308	584	58	-2	0	1	-0	1.000	0	/O-5(4-0-1),C-1	-0.2
1962	Mil-N	20	47	3	12	0	0	0	2	2	10	.255	.286	.255	541	48	-3	0	1	-0	.960	1	O-11(7-0-4)	-0.3
1963	Mil-N	16	29	1	2	0	0	0	0	1	12	.069	.100	.069	169	-51	-6	0	0	0	1.000	-0	/O-8(4-3-1)	-0.7
1964	NY-N	92	225	20	54	8	0	4	23	8	33	.240	.272	.329	601	70	-9	0	0	0	.981	1	C-45,O-16(16-0-0)	-0.8
1965	NY-N	25	46	5	7	0	0	4	10	1	8	.152	.170	.413	583	61	-3	0	0	0	.962	-2	C-15/1-1	-0.5
1966	NY-N	53	109	5	19	2	0	3	12	3	19	.174	.204	.275	479	32	-10	0	1	-0	1.000	-4	C-29,1-13	-1.5
1967	NY-N	13	37	3	9	3	0	0	4	2	8	.243	.282	.324	606	74	-1	0	0	0	.955	5	C-12	0.4
	Cal-A	23	52	5	16	3	0	1	3	4	8	.308	.357	.423	780	135	2	0	0	0	1.000	2	C-19	0.5
1969	KC-A	64	89	7	24	5	0	3	21	6	18	.270	.316	.427	743	105	0	0	0	0	.909	-4	O-18(2-0-16)/C-6	-0.4
1970	KC-A	57	55	3	9	3	0	0	6	6	16	.164	.258	.218	476	33	-5	0	0	0	1.000	0	/C-3,1-1	-0.5
Total	11	394	724	56	158	25	0	16	82	36	146	.218	.259	.319	578	62	-38	0	3	-1	.984	-1	C-131/O-62L,1-15	-4.2
■ BOB TAYLOR	Taylor, Robert Lee b: 3/20/44, Leland, Miss. BL/TR, 5'9", 170 lbs. Deb: 4/9/70																							
1970	SF-N	63	84	12	16	0	0	2	10	12	13	.190	.320	.262	582	58	-5	0	0	0	1.000	-3	O-26(22-0-5)/C-1	-0.9
■ SAMMY TAYLOR	Taylor, Samuel Douglas b: 2/27/33, Woodruff, S.C. BL/TR, 6'2", 185 lbs. Deb: 4/27/58																							
1958	Chi-N	96	301	30	78	12	2	6	36	27	46	.259	.320	.372	692	84	-7	2	1	0	.988	-11	C-87	-1.4
1959	Chi-N	110	353	41	95	13	2	13	43	35	47	.269	.337	.428	765	103	1	1	0	0	.982	-15	*C-109	-0.8
1960	Chi-N	74	150	14	31	9	0	3	17	6	18	.207	.242	.327	569	55	-10	0	1	-0	.978	-9	C-43	-1.9
1961	Chi-N	89	235	26	56	8	2	8	23	23	39	.238	.317	.391	708	86	-5	0	0	0	.989	-8	C-75	-1.0
1962	Chi-N	7	15	0	2	1	0	0	1	3	3	.133	.278	.200	478	30	-1	0	0	0	1.000	-1	/C-6	-0.3
	NY-N	68	158	12	35	4	2	3	20	23	17	.222	.328	.329	657	76	-5	0	0	0	.991	-9	C-50	-1.2
	Yr	75	173	12	37	5	2	3	21	26	20	.214	.323	.318	641	72	-6	0	0	0	.992	-10	C-56	-1.5
1963	NY-N	22	35	3	9	0	1	0	6	5	7	.257	.350	.314	664	91	-0	0	0	0	1.000	0	C-13	0.1
	Cin-N	3	6	0	0	0	0	0	0	0	2	.000	.000	.000	0	-97	-1	0	0	0	.833	-1	/C-2	-0.3
	Yr	25	41	3	9	0	1	0	6	5	9	.220	.304	.268	573	65	-2	0	0	0	.984	-1	C-15	-0.2
	Cle-A	4	10	1	3	0	0	0	1	0	2	.300	.300	.300	600	69	-0	0	0	0	1.000	-1	/C-2	-0.1
Total	6	473	1263	127	309	47	9	33	147	122	181	.245	.315	.375	690	84	-29	3	2	-0	.986	-55	C-387	-6.9
■ TOMMY TAYLOR	Taylor, Thomas Livingstone Carlton b: 9/17/1892, Mexia, Tex. d: 4/5/56, Greenville, Miss. BR/TR, 5'8.5", 160 lbs. Deb: 7/9/24																							
1924	*Was-A	26	73	11	19	3	1	0	10	2	8	.260	.289	.329	618	61	-4	2	0	0	.923	-5	3-16/2-2,O-1(0-1-0)	-0.8
■ BILLY TAYLOR	Taylor, William H. b: 12/1870, Butler, Ky. d: 9/12/05, Cincinnati, Ohio 5'10", 160 lbs. Deb: 9/19/1898																							
1898	Lou-N	9	24	2	6	1	0	0	2	1		.250	.308	.292	599	73	-1	1			.909	-1	/3-7,2-1	-0.2
■ BILLY TAYLOR	Taylor, William Henry "Bollicky Bill" b: 1855, Washington, D.C. d: 5/14/1900, Jacksonville, Fla. BR/TR, 5'11.5", 204 lbs. Deb: 5/21/1881 Career OF: (24-LF 15-CF 38-RF)																							
1881	Wor-N	6	28	3	3	1	0	0	2	0	2	.107	.107	.143	250	-21	-4				.882	1	/O-5(0-0-5),P-1	-0.2
	Det-N	1	4	0	2	2	0	0	1	0	0	.500	.500	1.000	1500	346	1				.750	-0	/3-1	0.1
	Cle-N	24	103	6	25	1	0	0	12	0	8	.243	.243	.252	495	59	-5				.859	-1	O-23(23-0-0)/P-1,3-1	-0.7
	Yr	31	135	9	30	4	0	0	15	0	10	.222	.222	.252	474	50	-7				.864	-0	O-28(23-0-5)/P-2,3-2	-0.8
1882	Pit-a	70	299	40	84	16	13	3		7		.281	.297	.452	749	157	17				.862	-11	C-27,1-23,3-14,/OP	0.7
1883	Pit-a	83	369	43	96	13	7	2		9		.260	.278	.350	627	105	2				.747	-15	O-37R,C-33,P-19,/1	-0.9
1884	StL-U	43	186	44	68	23	1	3		7		.366	.389	.548	937	175	11				.872	1	P-33,1-10/O-4(1-1-2)	0.4
	Phi-a	30	111	8	28	6	2	0		2		.252	.272	.342	614	93	-1				.784	2	P-30	0.0
1885	Phi-a	6	21	0	4	0	0	0	2	0		.190	.190	.190	381	19	-2				.556	-1	/P-6	0.0
1886	Bal-a	10	39	4	12	0	1	0	8	1		.308	.325	.359	684	117	1	1			.800	-1	/P-8,1-1,C-1	0.0
1887	Phi-a	1	4	0	1	0	0	0	1	0		.250	.250	.250	500	40	-0	0			1.000	-0	/P-1	0.0
Total	7	274	1164	148	323	62	24	8	26	26	10	.277	.294	.393	686	121	21	1			.820	-26	P-100/O-77R,C-61,13	-0.6
■ BILL TAYLOR	Taylor, William Michael b: 12/30/29, Alhambra, Cal. BL/TR, 6'3", 212 lbs. Deb: 4/14/54																							
1954	NY-N	55	65	4	12	1	0	2	10	3	15	.185	.243	.292	535	38	-6	0	0	0	1.000	-3	/O-9(7-0-2)	-0.9
1955	NY-N	65	64	9	17	4	0	4	12	1	16	.266	.277	.516	793	104	-0	0	0	0	.000	-1	/O-2(0-0-2)	-0.1
1956	NY-N	1	4	0	1	1	0	0	0	0	1	.250	.250	.500	750	96	-0	0	0	0	1.000	-0	/O-1(0-0-1)	0.0
1957	NY-N	11	9	0	0	0	0	0	0	1	2	.000	.100	.000	100	-70	-2	0	0	0	.000	0	H	-0.2
	Det-A	9	23	4	8	2	0	1	3	0	3	.348	.348	.565	913	142	1	0	0	0	1.000	-1	/O-5(5-0-0)	0.0
1958	Det-A	8	8	0	3	0	0	0	1	0	2	.375	.375	.375	750	100	0	0	0	0	1.000	-0	/O-1(0-0-1)	0.0
Total	5	149	173	17	41	8	0	7	26	5	39	.237	.267	.405	671	74	-7	0	0	0	1.000	-5	/O-18(12-0-6)	-1.2
■ ZACHARY TAYLOR	Taylor, Zachary H. Deb: 9/10/1874																							
1874	Bal-n	13	48	3	12	0	0	0	3	0	1	.250	.250	.250	500	61	-2	0	0	0	.914	-1	1-13	-0.2
■ BIRDIE TEBBETTS	Tebbetts, George Robert b: 11/10/12, Burlington, Vt. d: 3/24/99, Manatee, Fla. BR/TR, 5'11.5", 170 lbs. Deb: 9/16/36 M																							
1936	Det-A	10	33	7	10	1	2	1	4	5	3	.303	.395	.545	940	129	1	0	0	0	.982	2	C-10	0.4
1937	Det-A	50	162	15	31	4	3	2	16	10	13	.191	.238	.290	528	32	-18	0	0	0	.963	-4	C-48	-1.7
1938	Det-A	53	143	16	42	6	2	1	25	12	13	.294	.348	.385	733	79	-5	1	2	-0	.985	-5	C-53	-0.7
1939	Det-A	106	341	37	89	22	2	4	53	25	20	.261	.315	.372	688	70	-16	2	1	0	.970	15	*C-100	0.4
1940	*Det-A	111	379	46	112	24	4	4	46	35	14	.296	.357	.412	768	90	-5	4	5	-1	.975	18	*C-107	1.8
1941	Det-A☆	110	359	28	102	19	4	2	47	38	29	.284	.354	.376	730	85	-7	1	2	-0	.977	7	C-98	0.5
1942	Det-A★	99	308	24	76	11	0	1	27	39	17	.247	.335	.292	627	71	-10	4	0	1	.977	7	C-97	0.3
1946	Det-A	87	280	20	68	11	2	1	34	28	23	.243	.312	.307	619	69	-11	1	3	-1	.982	-1	C-87	-0.9
1947	Det-A	20	53	1	5	1	0	0	2	3	3	.094	.143	.113	256	-27	-9	0	1	-0	1.000	8	C-20	-0.1
	Bos-A	90	291	22	87	10	0	1	28	21	30	.299	.346	.344	690	86	-5	2	4	-1	.974	-3	C-89	-0.4
	Yr	110	344	23	92	11	0	1	30	24	33	.267	.315	.308	623	69	-14	2	5	-1	.980	5	*C-109	-0.5
1948	Bos-A★	128	446	54	125	26	2	5	68	62	32	.280	.371	.381	752	95	-2	5	2	0	.981	-9	*C-126	-0.3
1949	Bos-A★	122	403	42	109	14	0	5	48	62	22	.270	.369	.342	712	83	-8	8	1	1	.980	-6	*C-118	-0.6
1950	Bos-A	79	268	33	83	10	1	8	45	29	26	.310	.377	.444	821	100	-0	1	1	-0	.988	-6	C-74	-0.2
1951	Cle-A	55	137	8	36	6	0	2	18	8	7	.263	.308	.350	659	82	-4	0	0	0	.977	-1	C-44	-0.3
1952	Cle-A	42	101	4	25	4	0	1	8	12	9	.248	.339	.317	656	89	-1	0	1	-0	.986	-4	C-37	-0.4
Total	14	1162	3704	357	1000	169	22	38	469	389	261	.270	.341	.358	700	81	-100	29	23	-2	.978	19	*C-1108	-2.2
■ PUSSY TEBEAU	Tebeau, Charles Alston b: 2/22/1870, Worcester, Mass. d: 3/25/50, Pittsfield, Mass. BR/TR, 5'10", 175 lbs. Deb: 7/22/1895																							
1895	Cle-N	2	6	3	3	0	0	0	1	2	1	.500	.625	.500	1125	182	1	1			1.000	1	/O-2(0-0-2)	0.1
■ GEORGE TEBEAU	Tebeau, George E. "White Wings" b: 12/26/1861, St.Louis, Mo. d: 2/4/23, Denver, Colo. BR/TR, 5'9", 175 lbs. Deb: 4/16/1887 F Career OF: (349-LF 170-CF 51-RF)																							
1887	Cin-a	85	349	57	125	12	5	4	33	31		.358	.364	.403	766	111	4	37			.887	4	O-84(80-1-3)/P-1	0.5
1888	Cin-a	121	411	72	94	12	12	3	51	61		.229	.338	.338	676	111	6	37			.911	4	*O-121(121-0-0)	0.6
1889	Cin-a	135	496	110	125	21	11	7	70	69	62	.252	.350	.381	731	105	3	61			.887	-5	*O-134(134-0-0)/1-1	-0.5
1890	Tol-a	94	381	71	102	16	10	1	36	51		.268	.359	.370	729	112	6	55			.951	3	*O-94(1-93-0)/P-1	0.4

YEAR	TM/L	G	AB	R	H	2B	3B	HR	RBI	BB	SO	AVG	OBP	SLG	OPS	OPS+	BR+	SB	CS	SBR	FA	FR	G/POS	TPR
1894	Was-N	61	222	41	50	10	6	0	28	37	20	.225	.341	.324	665	63	-13	17			.857	-9	O-61(8-53-0)	-2.0
	Cle-N	40	150	32	47	9	4	0	25	25	18	.313	.411	.427	838	98	0	9			.928	-6	O-27(4-23-0),1-12/3-1	-0.6
	Yr	101	372	73	97	19	10	0	53	62	38	.261	.369	.366	735	78	-12	26			.880	-15	O-88C,1-12/3-1	-2.6
1895	Cle-N	92	341	58	111	16	6	0	68	50	29	.326	.413	.408	821	106	4	12			.873	-9	O-49(1-0-48),1-43	-0.5
Total	6	628	2350	441	654	96	54	15	311	324	129	.278	.364	.376	740	103	11	228			.900	-19	O-570L/1-56,P-2,3-1	-2.1

■ PATSY TEBEAU

Tebeau, Oliver Wendell b: 12/5/1864, St.Louis, Mo. d: 5/15/18, St.Louis, Mo. BR/TR, 5′8″, 163 lbs. Deb: 9/20/1887 FM Career OF: (1-LF 0-CF 0-RF)

YEAR	TM/L	G	AB	R	H	2B	3B	HR	RBI	BB	SO	AVG	OBP	SLG	OPS	OPS+	BR+	SB	CS	SBR	FA	FR	G/POS	TPR
1887	Chi-N	20	72	8	15	3	0	0	10	4	4	.208	.208	.206	414	14	-8	8			.855	-3	3-20	-1.0
1889	Cle-N	136	521	72	147	20	6	8	76	37	41	.282	.332	.390	722	103	1	26			.897	0	*3-136	0.3
1890	Cle-P	110	450	86	134	26	6	5	74	34	20	.298	.351	.416	767	114	9	14			**.872**	13	*3-110,M	1.9
1891	Cle-N	61	249	38	65	8	3	1	41	16	13	.261	.313	.329	643	84	-6	12			.884	6	3-61/O-1(1-0-0),M	0.1
1892	*Cle-N	86	340	47	83	13	3	2	49	23	34	.244	.307	.318	625	86	-7	6			.911	-2	3-74/2-5,1-4,S-3,M	-0.6
1893	Cle-N	116	486	90	160	32	8	2	102	32	11	.329	.375	.440	816	110	4	19			.980	6	1-57,3-56/2-3,M	0.9
1894	Cle-N	125	523	82	158	23	7	3	89	35	35	.302	.347	.390	737	75	-23	30			.977	-5	*1-115,2-10/3-2,SM	-2.2
1895	*Cle-N	63	264	50	84	13	2	2	52	16	18	.318	.362	.405	767	92	-4	8			.992	6	1-49/2-9,3-6,M	0.2
1896	*Cle-N	132	543	56	146	22	6	2	94	21	22	.269	.300	.343	642	65	-29	20			.985	7	*1-122/3-7,2-5,SPM	-1.9
1897	Cle-N	109	412	62	110	15	9	0	59	30		.267	.323	.347	670	73	-17	11			**.994**	0	*1-92,2-18/3-2,SM	-1.4
1898	Cle-N	131	477	53	123	11	4	1	63	53		.258	.341	.304	645	86	-7	5			.984	3	1-91,2-34/S-7,3M	-0.2
1899	StL-N	77	281	27	69	10	3	1	26	18		.246	.303	.313	616	67	-13	5			.980	-3	1-65,S-11/3-1,2M	-1.4
1900	StL-N	1	4	0	0	0	0	0	0	0		.000	.000	.000	0	-99	-1	0			.700	-1	/S-1,M	-0.1
Total	13	1167	4622	671	1294	196	57	27	735	319	198	.280	.332	.364	696	86	-99	164			.984	28	1-595,3-478/2-85,SPO	-5.4

■ DICK TEED

Teed, Richard Leroy b: 3/8/26, Springfield, Mass. BB/TR, 5′11″, 180 lbs. Deb: 7/24/53

YEAR	TM/L	G	AB	R	H	2B	3B	HR	RBI	BB	SO	AVG	OBP	SLG	OPS	OPS+	BR+	SB	CS	SBR	FA	FR	G/POS	TPR
1953	Bro-N	1	1	0	0	0	0	0	0	0	1	.000	.000	.000	0	-98	-0	0	0	0	.000	0	H	0.0

■ MIGUEL TEJADA

Tejada, Miguel Odalis (Martinez) b: 5/25/76, Bani, D.R. BR/TR, 5′10″, 170 lbs. Deb: 8/27/97

YEAR	TM/L	G	AB	R	H	2B	3B	HR	RBI	BB	SO	AVG	OBP	SLG	OPS	OPS+	BR+	SB	CS	SBR	FA	FR	G/POS	TPR
1997	Oak-A	26	99	10	20	3	2	2	10	2	22	.202	.240	.333	574	48	-8	2	0	0	.968	-2	S-26	-0.7
1998	Oak-A	105	365	53	85	20	1	11	45	28	86	.233	.300	.384	684	78	-12	5	6	-1	.951	1	*S-104	-0.3
1999	Oak-A	159	593	93	149	33	4	21	84	57	94	.251	.327	.427	754	94	-6	8	7	-1	.973	4	*S-159/D-1	1.0
2000	*Oak-A	160	607	105	167	32	1	30	115	66	102	.275	.350	.479	829	110	8	6	0	1	.972	7	*S-160	2.7
Total	4	450	1664	261	421	88	8	64	254	153	304	.253	.325	.431	756	94	-18	21	13	0	.967	10	S-449/D-1	2.7

■ WILFREDO TEJADA

Tejada, Wilfredo Aristides (Andujar) b: 11/12/62, Santo Domingo, D.R. BR/TR, 6′, 175 lbs. Deb: 9/9/86

YEAR	TM/L	G	AB	R	H	2B	3B	HR	RBI	BB	SO	AVG	OBP	SLG	OPS	OPS+	BR+	SB	CS	SBR	FA	FR	G/POS	TPR
1986	Mon-N	10	25	1	6	1	0	0	2	2	8	.240	.296	.280	576	60	-1	0	0	0	1.000	-1	C-10	-0.2
1988	Mon-N	8	15	1	4	2	0	0	2	0	4	.267	.267	.400	667	85	-0	0	0	0	1.000	3	/C-7	0.3
Total	2	18	40	2	10	3	0	0	4	2	12	.250	.286	.325	611	70	-2	0	0	0	1.000	2	/C-17	0.1

■ JOHNNY TEMPLE

Temple, John Ellis b: 8/8/27, Lexington, N.C. d: 1/9/94, Anderson, S.C. BR/TR, 5′11″, 175 lbs. Deb: 4/15/52 C

YEAR	TM/L	G	AB	R	H	2B	3B	HR	RBI	BB	SO	AVG	OBP	SLG	OPS	OPS+	BR+	SB	CS	SBR	FA	FR	G/POS	TPR
1952	Cin-N	30	97	8	19	3	0	1	5	5	1	.196	.235	.258	493	37	-8	2	1	0	.984	-1	2-22	-0.8
1953	Cin-N	63	110	14	29	4	0	1	9	7	12	.264	.314	.327	641	67	-5	1	0	0	.964	10	2-44	0.6
1954	Cin-N	146	505	60	155	14	8	0	44	62	24	.307	.385	.366	751	94	-1	21	7	2	.973	-10	*2-144	0.2
1955	Cin-N	150	588	94	165	20	3	0	50	80	32	.281	.368	.325	693	81	-13	19	4	3	.971	-3	*2-149/S-1	-0.1
1956	Cin-N★	154	632	88	180	18	3	2	41	58	40	.285	.346	.332	678	78	-17	14	4	2	.981	-7	*2-154/O-1(0-0-1)	-1.1
1957	Cin-N★	145	557	85	158	24	4	0	37	**94**	34	.284	.391	.341	732	92	-1	19	5	**2**	.974	-21	*2-145	-0.9
1958	Cin-N	141	542	82	166	31	6	3	47	91	41	.306	.406	.402	808	109	11	15	8	1	.979	-19	*2-141/1-1	0.4
1959	Cin-N★	149	598	102	186	35	6	8	67	72	40	.311	.387	.430	817	114	14	14	3	2	.974	-26	*2-149	0.2
1960	Cle-A	98	381	50	102	13	1	2	19	32	20	.268	.326	.323	649	79	-11	11	5	1	.974	-30	2-77,3-17	-3.6
1961	Cle-A★	129	518	73	143	22	3	3	30	61	36	.276	.352	.347	700	90	-6	9	5	0	.969	-30	*2-129	-2.4
1962	Bal-A	78	270	28	71	8	1	1	17	36	22	.263	.352	.311	663	85	-4	7	4	0	.981	-19	2-71	-1.7
	Hou-N	31	95	14	25	4	0	0	12	7	11	.263	.314	.305	619	72	-4	1	0	0	.941	-8	2-26/3-1	-1.0
1963	Hou-N	100	322	22	85	12	1	1	17	41	24	.264	.347	.317	664	99	1	7	2	1	.970	-20	2-61,3-29	-1.5
1964	Cin-N	6	3	0	0	0	0	0	0	2	1	.000	.400	.000	400	23	-0	0	0	0	.000	0	H	0.0
Total	13	1420	5218	720	1484	208	36	22	395	648	338	.284	.365	.351	716	91	-44	140	48	14	.974	-183	*2-1312/3-47,1-1,OS	-11.7

■ GARRY TEMPLETON

Templeton, Garry Lewis b: 3/24/56, Lockney, Tex. BB/TR, 5′11″, 190 lbs. Deb: 8/9/76

YEAR	TM/L	G	AB	R	H	2B	3B	HR	RBI	BB	SO	AVG	OBP	SLG	OPS	OPS+	BR+	SB	CS	SBR	FA	FR	G/POS	TPR
1976	StL-N	53	213	32	62	8	2	1	17	7	33	.291	.317	.362	678	91	-3	11	7	-0	.922	1	S-53	0.5
1977	StL-N★	153	621	94	200	19	**18**	8	79	15	70	.322	.339	.449	788	111	8	28	24	-2	.958	-3	*S-151	1.9
1978	StL-N	155	647	82	181	31	**13**	2	47	22	87	.280	.304	.377	682	91	-10	34	11	4	.953	23	*S-155	3.5
1979	StL-N†	154	672	105	**211**	32	**19**	9	62	18	91	.314	.333	.458	791	113	9	26	10	2	.960	18	*S-150	4.6
1980	StL-N	118	504	83	161	19	9	4	43	18	43	.319	.343	.417	760	108	4	31	15	2	.959	28	*S-115	4.7
1981	StL-N	80	333	47	96	16	8	1	33	14	55	.288	.317	.393	710	98	-2	8	12	-2	.960	5	S-76	1.0
1982	SD-N	141	563	76	139	25	8	6	64	26	82	.247	.281	.352	633	80	-17	27	16	0	.961	-24	*S-136	-2.8
1983	SD-N	126	460	39	121	20	2	3	40	21	57	.263	.295	.335	630	77	-15	16	6	1	.960	-14	*S-123	-1.6
1984	*SD-N	148	493	40	127	19	3	2	35	39	81	.258	.313	.320	634	79	-14	8	3	1	.960	-23	*S-146	-2.2
1985	SD-N★	148	546	63	154	30	2	6	55	41	88	.282	.333	.377	711	100	-0	16	6	1	.968	-7	*S-148	1.0
1986	SD-N	147	510	42	126	21	2	2	44	35	86	.247	.297	.308	605	68	-22	10	5	0	.966	-28	*S-144	-3.7
1987	SD-N	148	510	42	113	13	5	5	48	42	92	.222	.282	.296	578	55	-33	14	3	2	.972	9	*S-146	-0.7
1988	SD-N	110	362	35	90	15	7	3	36	20	50	.249	.288	.354	642	85	-8	8	2	1	.968	15	*S-105/3-2	1.7
1989	SD-N	142	506	43	129	26	3	6	40	23	80	.255	.287	.354	641	82	-13	1	3	-1	.970	13	*S-140	1.0
1990	SD-N	144	505	45	125	25	3	9	59	24	59	.248	.282	.362	644	75	-18	1	4	-1	.957	-9	*S-135	-1.9
1991	SD-N	32	57	5	11	1	1	1	6	1	9	.193	.207	.298	505	39	-5	0	1	-0	.950	-3	3-15/S-1	-0.8
	NY-N	80	219	20	50	9	1	2	20	9	29	.228	.259	.306	565	59	-12	3	1	0	.963	5	S-40,1-25/3-2,O-2R	-0.6
	Yr	112	276	25	61	10	2	3	26	10	38	.221	.248	.304	553	54	-17	3	2	-0	.963	3	S-41,1-25,3-17,/O-2R	-1.4
Total	16	2079	7721	893	2096	329	106	70	728	375	1092	.271	.306	.369	675	87	-150	242	129	8	.961	7	*S-1964/1-25,3-19,O	5.6

■ GENE TENACE

Tenace, Fury Gene (b: Fiore Gino Tennaci) b: 10/10/46, Russellton, Pa. BR/TR, 6′, 190 lbs. Deb: 5/29/69 MC

YEAR	TM/L	G	AB	R	H	2B	3B	HR	RBI	BB	SO	AVG	OBP	SLG	OPS	OPS+	BR+	SB	CS	SBR	FA	FR	G/POS	TPR
1969	Oak-A	16	38	1	6	0	0	1	2	1	15	.158	.200	.237	437	23	-4	0	0	0	1.000	-0	C-13	-0.4
1970	Oak-A	38	105	19	32	6	0	7	20	23	30	.305	.430	.562	992	178	12	0	2	-1	.990	4	C-30	1.7
1971	*Oak-A	65	179	26	49	7	0	7	25	29	34	.274	.381	.430	811	132	8	2	1	0	.994	-6	C-52/O-1(1-0-0)	0.5
1972	*Oak-A	82	227	22	51	5	3	5	32	24	42	.225	.307	.339	646	97	-1	0	0	0	.979	-8	C-49/O-9R,1-7,23	-0.8
1973	*Oak-A	160	510	83	132	18	2	24	84	101	94	.259	.391	.443	834	142	33	2	2	-0	.989	-11	*1-134,C-33/2-1,D-3	1.2
1974	*Oak-A	158	484	71	102	17	1	26	73	**110**	105	.211	.370	.411	781	133	25	2	9	-3	.995	-9	*1-106,C-79/2-3	1.0
1975	*Oak-A★	158	498	83	127	17	0	29	87	106	127	.255	.398	.464	862	146	35	7	4	0	.984	-16	*C-125,1-68/D-1	2.2
1976	Oak-A	128	417	64	104	19	1	22	66	81	91	.249	.376	.458	835	150	28	5	4	-0	.995	-20	1-70,C-65/D-2	0.6
1977	SD-N	147	437	66	102	24	4	15	61	**125**	119	.233	.417	.410	827	137	32	5	3	0	.980	-7	C-99,1-36,3-14	2.7
1978	SD-N	142	401	60	90	18	4	16	61	101	98	.224	.394	.409	803	135	24	6	5	-0	.993	-3	1-80,C-71/3-1	2.0
1979	SD-N	151	463	61	122	16	4	20	67	105	106	.263	.407	.445	852	141	31	2	6	-2	**.998**	-3	C-94,1-72	2.7
1980	SD-N	133	316	46	70	11	1	17	50	92	63	.222	.403	.424	827	139	22	4	4	-1	.979	-7	*C-104,1-19	1.8
1981	StL-N	58	129	26	30	7	0	5	22	38	26	.233	.421	.403	824	131	8	0	0	0	.980	-6	C-38/1-7	0.3
1982	*StL-N	66	124	18	32	9	0	7	18	36	31	.258	.439	.500	939	160	12	1	1	-0	.994	1	C-37/1-7	1.5
1983	Pit-N	53	62	7	11	5	0	0	6	12	17	.177	.346	.258	604	68	-2	0	1	-0	.989	-2	1-19/C-3,O-1(0-0-1)	-0.5
Total	15	1555	4390	653	1060	179	20	201	674	984	998	.241	.391	.429	819	137	263	36	42	-7	.986	-92	C-892,1-625/3-17,OD2	16.5

■ JOHN TENER

Tener, John Kinley b: 7/25/1863, County Tyrone, Ireland d: 5/19/46, Pittsburgh, Pa. BR/TR, 6′4″, 180 lbs. Deb: 6/8/1885 Career OF: (4-LF 0-CF 6-RF)

YEAR	TM/L	G	AB	R	H	2B	3B	HR	RBI	BB	SO	AVG	OBP	SLG	OPS	OPS+	BR+	SB	CS	SBR	FA	FR	G/POS	TPR
1885	Bal-a	1	4	0	0	0	0	0	0	0		.000	.000	.000	0	-99	-1				.000	-1	/O-1(0-0-1)	-0.2
1888	Chi-N	12	46	4	9	1	0	0	1	1	15	.196	.229	.217	447	40	-3	1			.892	0	P-12/O-1(1-0-0)	0.0
1889	Chi-N	42	150	18	41	4	2	1	19	7	22	.273	.306	.347	652	78	-5	2			.929	3	P-35/O-6(1-0-5),1-2	-0.1
1890	Pit-P	18	63	7	12	0	0	2	5	7	10	.190	.301	.286	587	62	-3	1			.966	2	P-14/O-2(2-0-0),3-2	-0.2
Total	4	73	263	29	62	5	2	3	25	15	47	.236	.287	.304	591	66	-12	4			.933	4	/P-61,O-10R,3-2,1-2	-0.5

YEAR	TM/L	G	AB	R	H	2B	3B	HR	RBI	BB	SO	AVG	OBP	SLG	OPS	OPS+	BR+	SB	CS	SBR	FA	FR	G/POS	TPR
■ **TOM TENNANT** Tennant, Thomas Francis b: 7/3/1882, Monroe, Wis. d: 2/15/55, San Carlos, Cal. BL/TL, 5'11", 165 lbs. Deb: 4/18/12																								
1912	StL-A	2	2	1	0	0	0	0	0	0		.000	.000	.000	0	-99	-1	0			.000	0	H	-0.1
■ **FRED TENNEY** Tenney, Fred Clay b: 7/9/1859, Marlborough, N.H. d: 6/15/19, Fall River, Mass. Deb: 4/28/1884																								
1884	Was-U	32	119	17	28	3	1	0		6		.235	.272	.277	549	69	-8				.867	-1	O-27(0-1-26)/1-6	-0.8
	Bos-U	4	17	1	2	0	0	0		0		.118	.118	.118	235	-29	-3				.750	-1	/P-4	0.0
	Wil-U	1	3	0	0	0	0	0		0		.000	.000	.000	0	-97	-1				1.000	0	/P-1	0.0
	Yr	37	139	18	30	3	1	0		6		.216	.248	.252	500	53	-12				.867	-1	O-27(0-1-26)/1-6,P-5	-0.8
■ **FRED TENNEY** Tenney, Frederick b: 11/26/1871, Georgetown, Mass. d: 7/3/52, Boston, Mass. BL/TL, 5'9", 155 lbs. Deb: 6/16/1894 M Career OF: (35-LF 7-CF 62-RF)																								
1894	Bos-N	27	86	23	34	7	1	2	21	12	9	.395	.469	.570	1039	138	5	6			.893	-0	C-20/O-6(3-2-1),1-1	0.5
1895	Bos-N	49	173	35	47	9	1	1	21	24	5	.272	.360	.353	713	78	-6	6			.885	-3	O-28(25-3-0),C-21	-0.8
1896	Bos-N	88	348	64	117	14	3	2	49	36	12	.336	.400	.411	811	108	4	18			.957	0	O-60(7-0-53),C-27	0.3
1897	*Bos-N	132	566	125	180	24	3	1	85	49		.318	.376	.376	753	93	-5	34			.988	5	*1-128/O-4(0-0-4)	-0.1
1898	Bos-N	117	488	106	160	25	5	0	62	33		.328	.370	.400	770	114	8	23			.980	5	*1-117/C-1	1.2
1899	Bos-N	150	603	115	209	19	17	1	67	63		.347	.411	.439	851	122	18	28			.978	10	*1-150	2.5
1900	Bos-N	112	437	77	122	13	5	1	56	39		.279	.346	.339	685	80	-12	17			.981	9	*1-111	-0.4
1901	Bos-N	115	451	66	127	13	1	1	22	37		.282	.340	.322	662	85	-8	15			.976	7	*1-113/C-2	-0.3
1902	Bos-N	134	489	88	154	18	3	2	30	73		.315	.409	.376	785	141	28	21			**.985**	12	*1-134	3.9
1903	Bos-N	122	447	79	140	22	3	3	41	70		.313	.415	.396	811	137	26	21			.974	8	*1-122	3.1
1904	Bos-N	147	533	76	144	17	9	1	37	57		.270	.351	.341	692	118	14	17			.986	8	*1-144/O-4(0-1-3)	2.0
1905	Bos-N	149	549	84	158	18	3	0	28	67		.288	.368	.332	700	111	11	17			.982	22	*1-148/P-1,M	3.1
1906	Bos-N	143	544	61	154	12	8	1	28	58		.283	.357	.340	698	121	15	17			.983	10	*1-143,M	2.4
1907	Bos-N	150	554	83	151	18	8	0	26	82		.273	.371	.334	705	121	17	15			.989	9	*1-149,M	2.6
1908	NY-N	156	583	**101**	149	20	1	2	49	72		.256	.344	.304	648	102	4	17			.990	10	*1-156	1.4
1909	NY-N	101	375	43	88	8	2	3	30	52		.235	.333	.291	623	92	-2	8			.986	8	1-98	0.5
1911	Bos-N	102	369	52	97	13	4	1	36	50	17	.263	.352	.328	680	84	-7	5			.985	2	1-96/O-2(0-1-1),M	-0.7
Total	17	1994	7595	1278	2231	270	77	22	688	874	43	.294	.371	.358	730	109	111	285			.983	123	*1-1810,O-104R/C-71,P	21.2
■ **FRANK TEPEDINO** Tepedino, Frank Ronald b: 11/23/47, Brooklyn, N.Y. BL/TL, 5'11", 192 lbs. Deb: 5/12/67																								
1967	NY-A	9	5	0	2	0	0	0	0	1	1	.400	.500	.400	900	175	1	0	0	0	1.000	0	/1-1	0.1
1969	NY-A	13	39	6	9	0	0	0	4	4	4	.231	.302	.231	533	53	-2	1	0	0	.950	-1	O-13(0-0-13)	-0.4
1970	NY-A	16	19	2	6	2	0	0	2	1	2	.316	.350	.421	771	118	0	0	1	-0	1.000	-1	/1-1,O-1(1-0-0)	-0.1
1971	NY-A	6	6	0	0	0	0	0	0	0	0	.000	.000	.000	0	-99	-2	0	0	0	1.000	-0	/O-1(1-0-0)	-0.2
	Mil-A	53	106	11	21	1	0	2	7	4	17	.198	.234	.264	498	41	-8	2	2	-0	.986	3	1-28	-0.8
	Yr	59	112	11	21	1	0	2	7	4	17	.188	.222	.250	472	34	-10	2	2	-0	.986	3	1-28/O-1(1-0-0)	-1.0
1972	NY-A	8	8	0	0	0	0	0	0	0	1	.000	.000	.000	0	-99	-2	0	0	0	.000	0	H	-0.2
1973	Atl-N	74	148	20	45	5	0	4	29	13	21	.304	.360	.419	779	107	2	0	0	0	.992	2	1-58	0.1
1974	Atl-N	78	169	11	39	5	1	0	16	9	13	.231	.274	.272	546	51	-11	1	2	-0	.988	1	1-46	-1.4
1975	Atl-N	8	7	0	0	0	0	0	0	1	2	.000	.125	.000	125	-61	-2	0	0	0	.000	0	H	-0.2
Total	8	265	507	50	122	13	1	6	58	33	61	.241	.290	.306	595	65	-24	4	5	-1	.989	4	1-134/O-15(2-0-13)	-3.1
■ **JOE TEPSIC** Tepsic, Joseph John b: 9/18/23, Slovan, Pa. BR/TR, 5'9", 170 lbs. Deb: 7/12/46																								
1946	Bro-N	15	5	2	0	0	0	0	0	1	1	.000	.167	.000	167	-50	-1	0			1.000	-0	/O-1(1-0-0)	-0.1
■ **JERRY TERRELL** Terrell, Jerry Wayne b: 7/13/46, Waseca, Minn. BR/TR (BB 1974 (part)), 6', 170 lbs. Deb: 4/14/73 Career OF: (12-LF 1-CF 11-RF)																								
1973	Min-A	124	438	43	116	15	2	1	32	21	56	.265	.300	.315	615	71	-17	13	7	0	.962	-14	S-81,3-30,2-14,/OD	-2.2
1974	Min-A	116	229	43	56	4	6	0	19	11	27	.245	.279	.314	594	68	-10	3	2	-0	.960	**23**	S-34,2-26,3-21,D/O1	1.7
1975	Min-A	108	385	48	110	16	2	1	36	19	27	.286	.324	.345	670	88	-6	4	4	-1	.947	-3	S-41,2-39,1-15,3/OD	-0.4
1976	Min-A	89	171	29	42	3	1	0	8	9	15	.246	.287	.275	562	64	-8	11	2	2	.988	7	2-31,3-26,S-16,D/O	0.3
1977	Min-A	93	214	32	48	6	0	1	20	11	21	.224	.265	.266	532	46	-16	10	4	1	.953	5	3-59,2-14/S-7,1OD	-1.0
1978	KC-A	73	133	14	27	1	0	0	8	4	13	.203	.226	.211	437	23	-13	8	4	0	1.000	6	2-31,3-25,S-11,/1-5	-0.6
1979	KC-A	31	40	5	12	3	0	1	2	1	1	.300	.317	.450	767	102	-0	1	0	0	.963	3	3-19/2-7,P-1,S-1,D	0.3
1980	KC-A	23	16	4	1	0	0	0	0	0	0	.063	.063	.063	125	-65	-4	0	0	0	1.000	2	/O-7L,1-3,2-3,PD	-0.2
Total	8	657	1626	218	412	48	11	4	125	76	160	.253	.289	.304	593	66	-73	50	23	3	.961	28	3-192,S-191,2/D1OP	-2.1
■ **TOM TERRELL** Terrell, John Thomas b: 6/19/1867, Louisville, Ky. d: 7/9/1893, Louisville, Ky. Deb: 10/5/1886																								
1886	Lou-a	1	4	0	1	0	0	0	0	0		.250	.250	.250	500	54	-0	0			.000	-2	/O-1(1-0-0),C-1	-0.2
■ **TERRY** Terry b: Attleborough, Pa. Deb: 4/26/1875																								
1875	Was-n	6	22	0	4	0	1	0	2	0	1	.182	.182	.273	455	58	-1	0	0	0	.810	-3	/1-4,O-3(0-1-2)	-0.3
■ **ADONIS TERRY** Terry, William H b: 8/7/1864, Westfield, Mass. d: 2/24/15, Milwaukee, Wis. BR/TR, 5'11.5", 168 lbs. Deb: 5/1/1884 U Career OF: (94-LF 43-CF 79-RF)																								
1884	Bro-a	67	236	15	55	10	3	0		8		.233	.258	.301	559	81	-5				.764	-1	P-56,O-13(2-7-4)	0.1
1885	Bro-a	71	264	23	45	1	3	1	20	10		.170	.201	.208	409	29	-21				.883	2	O-47L,P-25/3-1	-1.3
1886	Bro-a	75	299	34	71	8	9	2	39	10		.237	.265	.344	609	89	-5	17			.934	4	P-34,O-32C,S-13	-0.3
1887	Bro-a	86	368	56	119	6	10	3	65	16		.323	.323	.392	715	98	-2	27			.895	3	O-49R,P-40/S-2	-0.4
1888	Bro-a	30	115	13	29	6	0	0	8	5		.252	.283	.304	588	89	-2	7			.909	1	P-23/O-7(2-4-1),1-2	0.0
1889	*Bro-a	49	160	29	48	6	6	2	26	14	14	.300	.356	.450	806	129	5	8			.963	5	P-41,1-10	-0.1
1890	*Bro-N	99	363	63	101	17	9	4	59	40	34	.278	.356	.408	764	122	10	32			.930	-1	O-54(42-5-7),P-46/1-1	0.2
1891	Bro-N	30	91	10	19	7	1	0	6	9	26	.209	.301	.308	609	78	-3	4			.957	-2	P-25/O-5(0-0-5)	-0.1
1892	Bal-N	1	4	0	0	0	0	0	0	0	1	.000	.000	.000	0	-97	-1	0			1.000	0	/P-1	0.0
	Pit-N	31	100	10	16	0	4	2	11	10	11	.160	.236	.300	536	62	-5	2			.938	-0	P-30/O-1(0-1-0)	-0.1
	Yr	32	104	10	16	0	4	2	11	10	12	.154	.228	.288	517	56	-6	2			.940	-0	P-31/O-1(0-1-0)	-0.1
1893	Pit-N	26	71	9	18	4	3	0	11	3	12	.254	.293	.394	688	84	-2	1			.920	0	P-26	0.0
1894	Pit-N	1	0	0	0	0	0	0	0	0	0	—	—	—	—	—	0	0			.000	0	/P-1	0.0
	Chi-N	30	95	19	33	4	2	0	17	11	12	.347	.415	.432	847	99	0	3			.875	-2	P-23/O-7(0-0-7),1-2	-0.1
	Yr	31	95	19	33	4	2	0	17	11	12	.347	.415	.432	847	99	0	3			.875	-2	P-24/O-7(0-0-7),1-2	-0.1
1895	Chi-N	40	137	18	30	3	2	1	10	2	17	.219	.236	.292	528	33	-14	1			.895	2	P-38/O-1(0-0-1),S-1	-0.1
1896	Chi-N	30	99	14	26	4	2	0	15	8	12	.263	.324	.343	668	73	-4	4			.968	-2	P-30	0.0
1897	Chi-N	1	3	1	0	0	0	0	0	0		.000	.000	.000	0	-96	-1	0			.750	0	/P-1	0.0
Total	14	667	2405	314	610	76	54	15	287	146	139	.254	.295	.344	639	85	-50	106			.903	10	P-440,O-216L/S-16,13	-2.2
■ **BILL TERRY** Terry, William Harold "Memphis Bill" b: 10/30/1898, Atlanta, Ga. d: 1/9/89, Jacksonville, Fla. BL/TL, 6'1", 200 lbs. Deb: 9/24/23 MH																								
1923	NY-N	3	7	1	1	0	0	0	0	2	2	.143	.333	.143	476	30	-1	0	0	0	1.000	0	/1-2	-0.1
1924	*NY-N	77	163	26	39	7	2	5	24	17	18	.239	.311	.399	710	91	-2	1	1	-0	.988	-2	1-35	-0.6
1925	NY-N	133	489	75	156	31	6	11	70	42	52	.319	.374	.474	848	120	14	4	5	-1	.990	4	*1-126	0.8
1926	NY-N	98	225	26	65	12	5	5	43	22	17	.289	.352	.453	806	117	5	3			.979	4	1-38,O-14(1-0-13)	0.5
1927	NY-N	150	580	101	189	32	13	20	121	46	53	.326	.377	.529	907	141	31	1			.993	5	*1-150	2.6
1928	NY-N	149	568	100	185	36	11	17	101	64	36	.326	.394	.518	912	136	29	7			.993	-2	*1-149	1.7
1929	NY-N	150	607	103	226	39	5	14	117	48	35	.372	.418	.522	941	132	31	10			.994	7	*1-149/O-1(1-0-0)	2.5
1930	NY-N	154	633	139	**254**	39	15	23	129	57	33	**.401**	.452	.619	1071	159	61	8			.990	13	*1-154	5.5
1931	NY-N	153	611	**121**	213	43	**20**	9	112	47	36	.349	.397	.529	926	150	**42**	8			.990	9	*1-153	3.6
1932	NY-N	154	643	124	225	42	11	28	117	32	23	.350	.382	.580	962	158	49	4			.991	14	*1-154,M	4.7
1933	*NY-N★	123	475	68	153	20	5	6	58	40	23	.322	.375	.423	798	129	19	3			.992	1	*1-117,M	0.9
1934	NY-N★	153	602	109	213	30	6	8	83	60	47	.354	.414	.463	878	138	34	0			**.994**	6	*1-153,M	2.5
1935	NY-N★	145	596	91	203	32	8	6	64	41	55	.341	.383	.451	834	126	22	7			**.996**	6	*1-143,M	1.4
1936	*NY-N	79	229	36	71	10	5	2	39	19	19	.310	.363	.424	786	112	4	0			.996	3	1-56,M	0.1
Total	14	1721	6428	1120	2193	373	112	154	1078	537	449	.341	.393	.506	899	137	338	56	6		.992	67	*1-1579/O-15(2-0-13)	26.1

■ ZEB TERRY
Terry, Zebulon Alexander b: 6/17/1891, Denison, Tex. d: 3/14/88, Los Angeles, Cal. BR/TR, 5'8", 129 lbs. Deb: 4/12/16

YEAR	TM/L	G	AB	R	H	2B	3B	HR	RBI	BB	SO	AVG	OBP	SLG	OPS	OPS+	BR+	SB	CS	SBR	FA	FR	G/POS	TPR
1916	Chi-A	94	269	20	51	8	4	0	17	33	36	.190	.292	.249	541	62	-12	4			.935	-10	S-93	-1.8
1917	Chi-A	2	1	0	0	0	0	0	0	2	0	.000	.667	.000	667	102	0	0			1.000	-1	/S-1	0.0
1918	Bos-N	28	105	17	32	2	2	0	8	8	14	.305	.360	.362	722	125	3	1			.977	8	S-27	1.4
1919	Pit-N	129	472	46	107	12	6	0	27	31	26	.227	.280	.278	558	65	-19	12			**.960**	-31	*S-127	-4.7
1920	Chi-N	133	496	56	139	26	9	0	52	44	22	.280	.341	.369	710	102	2	12	16	-3	.962	14	S-70,2-63	2.0
1921	Chi-N	123	488	59	134	18	1	2	45	27	19	.275	.318	.328	646	71	-20	1	13	-4	.972	6	*2-122	-1.5
1922	Chi-N	131	496	56	142	24	2	0	67	34	16	.286	.335	.343	677	74	-19	2	11	-3	.964	9	*2-125/S-4,3-3	-0.9
Total	7	640	2327	254	605	90	24	2	216	179	133	.260	.318	.322	640	78	-64	32	40		.956	-5	S-322,2-310/3-3	-5.5

■ WAYNE TERWILLIGER
Terwilliger, Willard Wayne "Twig" b: 6/27/25, Clare, Mich. BR/TR, 5'11", 170 lbs. Deb: 8/6/49 C

YEAR	TM/L	G	AB	R	H	2B	3B	HR	RBI	BB	SO	AVG	OBP	SLG	OPS	OPS+	BR+	SB	CS	SBR	FA	FR	G/POS	TPR
1949	Chi-N	36	112	11	25	2	1	2	10	16	22	.223	.326	.313	638	74	-4	0			.978	4	2-34	0.2
1950	Chi-N	133	480	63	116	22	3	10	32	43	63	.242	.311	.363	673	77	-16	13			.967	-9	*2-126/1-1,3-1,O-1C	-1.7
1951	Chi-N	50	192	26	41	6	0	0	10	29	21	.214	.317	.245	562	52	-12	3	1	0	.969	-4	2-49	-1.3
	Bro-N	37	50	11	14	1	0	0	4	8	7	.280	.390	.300	690	87	-0	1	0	0	.949	6	2-24/3-1	0.7
	Yr	87	242	37	55	7	0	0	14	37	28	.227	.332	.256	588	59	-12	4	1	1	.964	3	2-73/3-1	-0.6
1953	Was-A	134	464	62	117	24	4	4	46	64	65	.252	.343	.347	690	89	-6	7	4	0	.982	5	*2-133	0.8
1954	Was-A	106	337	42	70	10	1	3	24	32	40	.208	.282	.270	552	55	-21	3	3	-0	.972	13	2-90,3-10/S-3	-0.3
1955	NY-N	80	257	29	66	16	1	1	18	36	42	.257	.350	.339	689	84	-5	2	4	-1	.985	26	2-78/S-1,3-1	2.5
1956	NY-N	14	18	0	4	1	0	0	0	0	5	.222	.222	.278	500	34	-2	0	0	0	.958	2	/2-6	0.1
1959	KC-A	74	180	27	48	11	0	2	18	19	31	.267	.337	.361	698	90	-2	2	2	-0	.972	20	2-63/S-2,3-1	2.1
1960	KC-A	2	1	0	0	0	0	0	0	0	0	.000	.000	.000	0	-99	-0	0	0	0	1.000	0	/2-2	0.0
Total	9	666	2091	271	501	93	10	22	162	247	296	.240	.323	.325	648	76	-69	31	14		.974	64	2-605/3-14,S-6,O1	3.1

■ AL TESCH
Tesch, Albert John "Tiny" b: 1/27/1891, Jersey City, N.J. d: 8/3/47, Jersey City, N.J. BB/TR, 5'10", 155 lbs. Deb: 8/21/15

YEAR	TM/L	G	AB	R	H	2B	3B	HR	RBI	BB	SO	AVG	OBP	SLG	OPS	OPS+	BR+	SB	CS	SBR	FA	FR	G/POS	TPR
1915	Bro-F	8	7	2	2	1	0	0	2	0	0	.286	.286	.429	714	100	-0	0			.867	3	/2-3	0.3

■ NICK TESTA
Testa, Nicholas b: 6/29/28, New York, N.Y. BR/TR, 5'8", 180 lbs. Deb: 4/23/58 C

YEAR	TM/L	G	AB	R	H	2B	3B	HR	RBI	BB	SO	AVG	OBP	SLG	OPS	OPS+	BR+	SB	CS	SBR	FA	FR	G/POS	TPR
1958	SF-N	1	0	0	0	0	0	0	0	0	0	—	—	—	—	—	0	0	0	0	.000	-1	/C-1	0.0

■ DICK TETTELBACH
Tettelbach, Richard Morley "Tut" b: 6/26/29, New Haven, Conn. d: 1/26/95, E.Harwich, Mass. BR/TR, 6', 195 lbs. Deb: 9/25/55

YEAR	TM/L	G	AB	R	H	2B	3B	HR	RBI	BB	SO	AVG	OBP	SLG	OPS	OPS+	BR+	SB	CS	SBR	FA	FR	G/POS	TPR
1955	NY-A	2	5	0	0	0	0	0	0	0	0	.000	.000	.000	0	-99	-1	0	0	0	1.000	0	/O-2(2-0-0)	-0.2
1956	Was-A	18	64	10	10	1	2	1	9	14	15	.156	.308	.281	589	56	-4	0	1	-0	1.000	2	O-18(18-0-0)	-0.3
1957	Was-A	9	11	2	2	0	0	0	1	4	2	.182	.400	.182	582	65	-0	0	0	0	.900	-0	/O-3(2-2-0)	-0.1
Total	3	29	80	12	12	1	2	1	10	18	17	.150	.306	.250	556	49	-6	0	1	-0	.980	2	/O-23(22-2-0)	-0.6

■ MICKEY TETTLETON
Tettleton, Mickey Lee b: 9/16/60, Oklahoma City, Okla. BB/TR, 6'2", 212 lbs. Deb: 6/30/84 Career OF: (24-LF 0-CF 120-RF)

YEAR	TM/L	G	AB	R	H	2B	3B	HR	RBI	BB	SO	AVG	OBP	SLG	OPS	OPS+	BR+	SB	CS	SBR	FA	FR	G/POS	TPR
1984	Oak-A	33	76	10	20	2	1	1	5	11	21	.263	.356	.355	712	105	1	0	0	0	.992	0	C-32	0.2
1985	Oak-A	78	211	23	53	12	0	3	15	28	59	.251	.344	.351	695	98	0	2	2	-0	.989	-1	C-76/D-1	0.2
1986	Oak-A	90	211	26	43	9	0	10	35	39	51	.204	.331	.389	719	103	1	7	1	1	.984	-2	C-89	0.3
1987	Oak-A	82	211	19	41	3	0	8	26	30	65	.194	.295	.322	617	68	-10	1	1	-0	.987	4	C-80/1-1,D-1	-0.3
1988	Bal-A	86	283	31	74	11	1	11	37	28	70	.261	.332	.424	756	113	5	0	1	-0	.992	-10	C-80	0.0
1989	Bal-A★	117	411	72	106	21	2	26	65	73	117	.258	.371	.509	880	150	28	3	2	-0	.994	-7	C-75,D-43	2.4
1990	Bal-A	135	444	68	99	21	2	15	51	106	160	.223	.378	.381	759	117	15	2	4	-1	.991	-13	C-90,D-40/1-5,O-1R	0.4
1991	Det-A	154	501	85	132	17	2	31	89	101	131	.263	.389	.491	880	140	30	3	3	-0	.990	-15	*C-125,D-24/O-3L,1	2.1
1992	Det-A	157	525	82	125	25	0	32	83	**122**	137	.238	.383	.469	851	137	29	0	6	-2	**.996**	-18	*C-113,D-40/1-3,O-2L	1.4
1993	Det-A	152	522	79	128	25	4	32	110	109	139	.245	.376	.492	868	132	25	3	7	-2	.992	-17	1-59,C-56,O-55R,/D	0.3
1994	Det-A★	107	339	57	84	18	2	17	51	97	98	.248	.422	.463	885	127	18	0	1	-0	.992	-15	C-53,1-24,D-22,O-18R	0.3
1995	Tex-A	134	429	76	102	19	1	32	78	107	110	.238	.398	.510	908	131	22	0	0	0	.972	-3	O-63R,D-58/1-9,C-3	1.2
1996	*Tex-A	143	491	78	121	26	1	24	83	95	137	.246	.372	.450	822	101	2	2	1	0	.977	-2	*D-115,1-23	-0.8
1997	Tex-A	17	44	5	4	1	0	3	4	3	12	.091	.167	.318	485	22	-5	0	0	0	.000	0	D-13	-0.6
Total	14	1485	4698	711	1132	210	16	245	732	949	1307	.241	.372	.449	821	122	162	23	29	-5	.991	-100	C-872,D-361,O-1421R,1	7.1

■ TIM TEUFEL
Teufel, Timothy Shawn b: 7/7/58, Greenwich, Conn. BR/TR, 6', 175 lbs. Deb: 9/3/83

YEAR	TM/L	G	AB	R	H	2B	3B	HR	RBI	BB	SO	AVG	OBP	SLG	OPS	OPS+	BR+	SB	CS	SBR	FA	FR	G/POS	TPR
1983	Min-A	21	78	11	24	7	1	3	6	2	8	.308	.325	.538	863	128	3	0	0	0	.990	-1	2-18/S-1,D-1	0.2
1984	Min-A	157	568	76	149	30	3	14	61	76	73	.262	.351	.400	751	103	3	1	3	-1	.984	-12	*2-157	0.0
1985	Min-A	138	434	58	113	24	3	10	50	48	70	.260	.338	.399	737	95	-2	4	2	0	.980	-33	*2-137/D-1	-2.8
1986	*NY-N	93	279	35	69	20	1	4	31	32	42	.247	.327	.369	696	94	-2	1	2	-0	.971	-18	2-84/1-3,3-1	-1.8
1987	NY-N	97	299	55	92	29	0	14	61	44	53	.308	.400	.545	945	155	24	3	2	-0	.972	-11	2-92/1-1	1.7
1988	*NY-N	90	273	35	64	20	0	4	31	29	41	.234	.310	.352	662	94	-2	0	1	-0	.981	12	2-84/1-3	1.2
1989	NY-N	83	219	27	56	7	2	2	15	32	50	.256	.353	.333	687	102	2	1	3	-1	.960	-1	2-40,1-33	-0.1
1990	NY-N	80	175	28	43	11	0	10	24	15	33	.246	.305	.480	785	113	2	0	0	0	.991	-4	1-24,2-24,3-10	-0.3
1991	NY-N	20	34	2	4	0	0	1	2	2	8	.118	.167	.206	373	4	-4	1	1	-0	1.000	0	/1-6,3-5,2-1	-0.5
	SD-N	97	307	39	70	16	0	11	42	49	69	.228	.336	.388	724	100	1	8	2	1	.987	-14	2-65,3-48	-1.2
	Yr	117	341	41	74	16	0	12	44	51	77	.217	.321	.370	690	91	-3	9	3	1	.987	-14	2-66,3-53/1-6	-1.7
1992	SD-N	101	246	23	55	10	0	6	25	31	45	.224	.313	.337	650	83	-5	2	1	0	.987	-3	2-52,3-26/1-5	-0.8
1993	SD-N	96	200	26	50	11	2	7	31	27	39	.250	.339	.430	769	102	1	2	2	-0	.990	-3	2-52/3-9,1-8	0.0
Total	11	1073	3112	415	789	185	12	86	379	387	531	.254	.338	.404	742	104	20	23	19	-2	.980	-88	2-806/3-99,1-83,DS	-4.4

■ GEORGE TEXTOR
Textor, George Bernhardt b: 12/27/1888, Newport, Ky. d: 3/10/54, Massillon, Ohio BB/TR, 5'10.5", 174 lbs. Deb: 4/19/14

YEAR	TM/L	G	AB	R	H	2B	3B	HR	RBI	BB	SO	AVG	OBP	SLG	OPS	OPS+	BR+	SB	CS	SBR	FA	FR	G/POS	TPR
1914	Ind-F	22	57	2	10	0	0	0	4	2	9	.175	.230	.175	405	10	-8	0			.955	2	C-21	-0.5
1915	New-F	3	6	1	2	0	0	0	0	0	0	.333	.333	.333	667	93	-0	0			1.000	-1	/C-3	-0.1
Total	2	25	63	3	12	0	0	0	4	2	9	.190	.239	.190	429	17	-8	0			.957	1	/C-24	-0.6

■ MOE THACKER
Thacker, Morris Benton b: 5/21/34, Louisville, Ky. d: 11/13/97, Louisville, Ky. BR/TR, 6'3", 210 lbs. Deb: 4/20/58

YEAR	TM/L	G	AB	R	H	2B	3B	HR	RBI	BB	SO	AVG	OBP	SLG	OPS	OPS+	BR+	SB	CS	SBR	FA	FR	G/POS	TPR
1958	Chi-N	11	24	4	6	1	0	2	3	1	7	.250	.280	.542	822	113	0	0	0	0	.952	1	/C-9	0.1
1960	Chi-N	54	90	5	14	1	0	0	6	14	20	.156	.269	.167	436	23	-9	1	1	-0	.980	5	C-50	-0.4
1961	Chi-N	25	35	3	6	0	0	0	2	11	11	.171	.383	.171	554	53	-2	0	0	0	.973	-1	C-25	-0.2
1962	Chi-N	65	107	8	20	5	0	0	9	14	40	.187	.287	.234	521	40	-9	0	1	-0	.996	13	C-65	0.6
1963	StL-N	3	4	0	0	0	0	0	0	0	3	.000	.000	.000	0	-91	-1	0	0	0	1.000	1	/C-3	0.0
Total	5	158	260	20	46	7	0	2	20	40	81	.177	.291	.227	518	41	-20	1	2	-0	.984	18	C-152	0.1

■ AL THAKE
Thake, Albert b: 9/21/1849, Wymondham, England d: 9/1/1872, Brooklyn, N.Y. 6', Deb: 6/13/1872

YEAR	TM/L	G	AB	R	H	2B	3B	HR	RBI	BB	SO	AVG	OBP	SLG	OPS	OPS+	BR+	SB	CS	SBR	FA	FR	G/POS	TPR
1872	Atl-n	18	78	14	23	2	2	0	15	0	2	.295	.295	.372	667	88	-2	2	0	0	.808	-1	O-18(18-0-0)/2-1	-0.2

■ RON THEOBALD
Theobald, Ronald Merrill b: 7/28/43, Oakland, Cal. BR/TR, 5'8", 165 lbs. Deb: 4/12/71

YEAR	TM/L	G	AB	R	H	2B	3B	HR	RBI	BB	SO	AVG	OBP	SLG	OPS	OPS+	BR+	SB	CS	SBR	FA	FR	G/POS	TPR
1971	Mil-A	126	388	50	107	12	2	1	23	38	39	.276	.345	.325	670	92	-3	11	8	-0	.973	1	*2-111/S-1,3-1	0.5
1972	Mil-A	125	391	45	86	11	0	1	19	68	38	.220	.343	.256	598	81	-5	0	7	-2	.988	-13	*2-113	-1.6
Total	2	251	779	95	193	23	2	2	42	106	77	.248	.344	.290	634	87	-9	11	15	-3	.980	-12	2-224/3-1,S-1	-1.1

■ GEORGE THEODORE
Theodore, George Basil b: 11/13/47, Salt Lake City, Ut. BR/TR, 6'4", 190 lbs. Deb: 4/14/73

YEAR	TM/L	G	AB	R	H	2B	3B	HR	RBI	BB	SO	AVG	OBP	SLG	OPS	OPS+	BR+	SB	CS	SBR	FA	FR	G/POS	TPR
1973	*NY-N	45	116	14	30	4	0	1	15	10	13	.259	.323	.319	642	80	-3	1	0	0	.984	2	O-33(28-4-1)/1-4	-0.3
1974	NY-N	60	76	7	12	1	0	1	1	8	14	.158	.247	.211	458	29	-7	0	0	0	.990	-5	1-14,O-12(8-0-4)	-1.4
Total	2	105	192	21	42	5	0	2	16	18	27	.219	.292	.276	568	60	-10	1	0	0	.958	-3	/O-45(36-4-5),1-18	-1.7

■ TOMMY THEVENOW
Thevenow, Thomas Joseph b: 9/6/03, Madison, Ind. d: 7/29/57, Madison, Ind. BR/TR, 5'10", 155 lbs. Deb: 9/4/24

YEAR	TM/L	G	AB	R	H	2B	3B	HR	RBI	BB	SO	AVG	OBP	SLG	OPS	OPS+	BR+	SB	CS	SBR	FA	FR	G/POS	TPR
1924	StL-N	23	89	4	18	4	1	0	7	1	6	.202	.211	.270	481	28	-9	1	3	-1	.951	8	S-23	0.0
1925	StL-N	50	175	17	47	7	2	0	17	7	12	.269	.301	.331	632	60	-11	3	0	1	.950	3	S-50	-0.2
1926	*StL-N	156	563	64	144	15	5	2	63	27	26	.256	.291	.311	602	60	-32	8			.956	18	*S-156	0.4
1927	StL-N	59	191	23	37	6	1	0	4	14	8	.194	.249	.236	484	29	-19	2			.945	7	S-59	-0.6
1928	*StL-N	69	171	11	35	8	3	0	13	20	12	.205	.288	.287	575	50	-13	0			.931	-4	S-64/3-3,1-1	-1.1
1929	Phi-N	90	317	30	72	11	0	0	35	25	25	.227	.288	.262	550	35	-32	3			.953	3	S-90	-1.8

YEAR	TM/L	G	AB	R	H	2B	3B	HR	RBI	BB	SO	AVG	OBP	SLG	OPS	OPS+	BR+	SB	CS	SBR	FA	FR	G/POS	TPR
1930	Phi-N	156	573	57	164	21	1	0	78	23	26	.286	.316	.326	642	52	-44	1			.941	-2	*S-156	-2.6
1931	Pit-N	120	404	35	86	12	1	0	38	28	22	.213	.266	.248	513	39	-34	0			.964	9	*S-120	-1.7
1932	Pit-N	59	194	12	46	3	3	0	26	7	12	.237	.264	.284	547	48	-14	0			.918	-1	S-29,3-22	-1.2
1933	Pit-N	73	253	20	79	5	1	0	34	3	5	.312	.320	.340	660	89	-4	2			.975	-13	2-61/S-3,3-1	-1.3
1934	Pit-N	122	446	37	121	16	2	0	54	20	20	.271	.306	.316	622	65	-21	0			.969	-18	2-75,3-44/S-1	-3.3
1935	Pit-N	110	408	38	97	9	9	0	47	12	23	.238	.261	.304	565	50	-29	1			.951	4	3-82,S-13/2-8	-2.0
1936	Cin-N	106	321	25	75	7	2	0	36	15	23	.234	.268	.268	536	48	-24	2			.945	-9	S-68,2-33,3-12	-2.6
1937	Bos-N	21	34	5	4	0	1	0	2	4	2	.118	.211	.176	387	7	-4	0			.969	1	S-12/3-6,2-2	-0.3
1938	Pit-N	15	25	2	5	0	0	0	2	4	0	.200	.333	.200	533	49	-1	0			1.000	3	/2-9,S-4,3-1	0.2
Total	15	1229	4164	380	1030	124	32	2	456	210	222	.247	.285	.294	579	52	-291	23	3		.950	9	S-848,2-188,3-171,/1	-18.1

■ HENRY THIELMAN Thielman, Henry Joseph b: 10/3/1880, St.Cloud, Minn. d: 9/2/42, New York, N.Y. BR/TR, 5'11", 175 lbs. Deb: 4/17/02 F

YEAR	TM/L	G	AB	R	H	2B	3B	HR	RBI	BB	SO	AVG	OBP	SLG	OPS	OPS+	BR+	SB	CS	SBR	FA	FR	G/POS	TPR
1902	NY-N	6	9	0	1	0	0	0	0	2		.111	.273	.111	384	19	-1	1			.800	1	/P-2,O-3(0-2-1)	0.0
	Cin-N	28	91	6	12	0	2	0	4	5		.132	.177	.176	353	8	-10	0			.910	-2	P-25/O-3(3-0-0)	-0.2
	Yr	34	100	6	13	0	2	0	4	7		.130	.187	.170	357	10	-11	1			.903	-1	P-27/O-6(3-2-1)	-0.2
1903	Bro-N	9	23	3	5	1	0	1	2	5		.217	.357	.391	748	117	1	0			.750	-0	/O-5(0-4-0),P-4	-0.1
Total	2	43	123	9	18	1	2	1	6	12		.146	.222	.211	434	30	-10	1			.918	-1	/P-31,O-11(3-6-1)	-0.3

■ ANDRES THOMAS Thomas, Andres Perez (b: Andres Perez (Thomas)) b: 11/10/63, Boca Chica, D.R. BR/TR, 6'1", 185 lbs. Deb: 9/3/85

YEAR	TM/L	G	AB	R	H	2B	3B	HR	RBI	BB	SO	AVG	OBP	SLG	OPS	OPS+	BR+	SB	CS	SBR	FA	FR	G/POS	TPR
1985	Atl-N	15	18	6	5	0	0	0	2	0	2	.278	.278	.278	556	53	-1	0	0	0	.920	3	S-10	0.2
1986	Atl-N	102	323	26	81	17	2	6	32	8	49	.251	.269	.372	640	71	-13	4	6	-1	.958	26	S-97	2.0
1987	Atl-N	82	324	29	75	11	0	5	39	14	50	.231	.268	.312	579	50	-23	6	5	-0	.953	9	S-81	-0.5
1988	Atl-N	153	606	54	153	22	2	13	68	14	95	.252	.271	.360	630	76	-20	7	3	0	.959	-8	*S-150	-1.8
1989	Atl-N	141	554	41	118	18	0	13	57	12	62	.213	.230	.316	546	53	-35	3	3	-0	.956	6	*S-138	-2.0
1990	Atl-N	84	278	26	61	8	0	5	30	11	43	.219	.249	.302	551	48	-20	2	1	0	.967	3	S-72/3-5	-1.2
Total	6	577	2103	182	493	76	4	42	228	59	301	.234	.256	.334	591	61	-112	22	18	-1	.958	38	S-548/3-5	-3.3

■ PINCH THOMAS Thomas, Chester David b: 1/24/1888, Camp Point, Ill. d: 12/24/53, Modesto, Cal. BL/TR, 5'9.5", 173 lbs. Deb: 4/24/12

YEAR	TM/L	G	AB	R	H	2B	3B	HR	RBI	BB	SO	AVG	OBP	SLG	OPS	OPS+	BR+	SB	CS	SBR	FA	FR	G/POS	TPR
1912	Bos-A	13	30	0	6	0	0	0	5	2		.200	.250	.200	450	28	-3	1			.966	2	/C-8	0.0
1913	Bos-A	38	91	6	26	1	2	1	15	2	11	.286	.309	.374	682	97	-1	1			.983	1	C-31	0.3
1914	Bos-A	66	130	9	25	1	0	0	5	18	17	.192	.291	.200	491	48	-8	1			.966	-2	C-64/1-1	-0.7
1915	*Bos-A	86	203	21	48	4	4	0	21	13	20	.236	.286	.296	581	76	-6	3	2	-0	.969	4	C-82	0.3
1916	*Bos-A	99	216	21	57	10	1	1	21	33	13	.264	.364	.333	697	109	4	4			.981	-8	C-90	0.2
1917	Bos-A	83	202	24	48	7	0	0	24	27	9	.238	.333	.272	606	86	-2	2			**.986**	3	C-77	0.7
1918	Cle-A	32	73	2	18	0	1	0	5	6	6	.247	.304	.274	578	68	-3	0			.948	1	C-24	0.0
1919	Cle-A	34	46	2	5	0	0	0	2	4	3	.109	.180	.109	289	-17	-7	0			.980	-2	C-21	-0.8
1920	*Cle-A	9	9	2	3	1	0	0	0	3	1	.333	.500	.444	944	147	1	0	0	0	1.000	1	/C-7	0.2
1921	Cle-A	21	35	1	9	3	0	0	4	10	2	.257	.422	.343	765	96	0	0	0	0	.882	-6	C-19	-0.5
Total	10	481	1035	88	245	27	8	2	102	118	82	.237	.318	.284	602	78	-25	12	2		.973	-5	C-423/1-1	-0.3

■ DAN THOMAS Thomas, Danny Lee b: 5/9/51, Birmingham, Ala. d: 6/12/80, Mobile, Ala. BR/TR, 6'2", 190 lbs. Deb: 9/2/76

YEAR	TM/L	G	AB	R	H	2B	3B	HR	RBI	BB	SO	AVG	OBP	SLG	OPS	OPS+	BR+	SB	CS	SBR	FA	FR	G/POS	TPR
1976	Mil-A	32	105	13	29	5	1	4	15	14	28	.276	.372	.457	829	145	6	1	2	-0	.955	-0	O-32(32-0-0)	0.4
1977	Mil-A	22	70	11	19	3	2	2	11	8	11	.271	.354	.457	812	119	2	0	2	-1	1.000	1	/O-9(9-0-0),D-9	0.2
Total	2	54	175	24	48	8	3	6	26	22	39	.274	.365	.457	822	134	8	1	4	-1	.966	0	/O-41(41-0-0),D-9	0.6

■ DERREL THOMAS Thomas, Derrel Osbon b: 1/14/51, Los Angeles, Cal. BB/TR, 6', 160 lbs. Deb: 9/14/71 Career OF: (93-LF 394-CF 65-RF)

YEAR	TM/L	G	AB	R	H	2B	3B	HR	RBI	BB	SO	AVG	OBP	SLG	OPS	OPS+	BR+	SB	CS	SBR	FA	FR	G/POS	TPR
1971	Hou-N	5	5	0	0	0	0	0	0	0	2	.000	.000	.000	0	-99	-1	0	1	-0	1.000	1	/2-1	-0.1
1972	SD-N	130	500	48	115	15	5	5	36	41	73	.230	.291	.310	601	76	-16	9	9	-1	.967	-18	2-83,S-49/O-3(0-2-1)	-2.6
1973	SD-N	113	404	41	96	7	1	0	22	34	52	.238	.300	.260	560	61	-21	15	5	2	.914	-14	S-74,2-47	-2.3
1974	SD-N	141	523	48	129	24	6	3	41	51	58	.247	.315	.333	647	85	-11	7	8	-1	.976	6	*2-104,3-22,O-20C,/S	0.0
1975	SF-N	144	540	99	149	21	9	6	48	57	56	.276	.348	.381	730	98	-1	28	13	2	.974	-7	*2-141/O-1(0-0-1)	0.3
1976	SF-N	81	272	38	63	5	4	2	19	29	26	.232	.315	.301	616	73	-9	10	11	-2	.964	2	2-69/O-2C,S-1,3-1	-0.4
1977	SF-N	148	506	75	135	13	10	8	44	46	70	.267	.330	.379	710	90	-7	15	13	-1	.991	10	O-78C,2-27,S-26,/31	0.4
1978	SD-N	128	352	36	80	10	2	3	26	35	37	.227	.303	.293	595	73	-13	11	6	0	.991	3	O-77C,2-40,3-26,1	-1.0
1979	LA-N	141	406	47	104	15	4	5	44	41	49	.256	.332	.350	682	87	-6	18	5	2	.996	2	*O-119C,3-18/2-5,S1	-0.3
1980	LA-N	117	297	32	79	18	3	1	22	26	48	.266	.327	.357	684	93	-3	7	9	-2	.987	-1	O-52C,S-49,2-18,/C3	-0.2
1981	*LA-N	80	218	25	54	4	0	4	24	25	23	.248	.325	.321	646	87	-3	7	2	1	.986	-10	2-30,S-26,O-18C,3	-1.0
1982	LA-N	66	98	13	26	2	1	0	2	10	12	.265	.333	.306	639	82	-2	2	3	-1	1.000	-7	O-28C,2-18,3-14,/S	-1.0
1983	*LA-N	118	192	38	48	6	6	2	8	27	36	.250	.348	.375	723	101	1	9	3	1	.990	-12	O-82C,S-13/2-9,3-7	-1.1
1984	Mon-N	108	243	26	62	12	2	0	20	20	33	.255	.312	.321	633	82	-6	0	4	-1	.963	-38	S-62,O-48L,2-15,/31	-4.2
	Cal-A	14	29	3	4	0	1	0	2	3	4	.138	.219	.207	426	19	-3	0	0	0	.889	-5	/O-7(2-2-4),S-4,3-3	-0.8
1985	Phi-N	63	92	16	19	2	0	4	12	11	14	.207	.291	.359	650	79	-3	2	0	0	.906	-8	S-21/O-7L,C-1,23	-0.9
Total	15	1597	4677	585	1163	154	54	43	370	456	593	.249	.319	.332	651	83	-104	140	92	-1	.970	-94	2-608,O-542C,S3/1C	-15.2

■ FRANK THOMAS Thomas, Frank Edward "The Big Hurt" b: 5/27/68, Columbus, Ga. BR/TR, 6'5", 257 lbs. Deb: 8/2/90

YEAR	TM/L	G	AB	R	H	2B	3B	HR	RBI	BB	SO	AVG	OBP	SLG	OPS	OPS+	BR+	SB	CS	SBR	FA	FR	G/POS	TPR
1990	Chi-A	60	191	39	63	11	3	7	31	44	54	.330	.460	.529	989	180	23	0	1	-0	.989	-5	1-51/D-8	1.4
1991	Chi-A	158	559	104	178	31	2	32	109	**138**	112	.318	**.454**	.553	**1007**	**181**	**69**	1	2	-0	.996	-4	*D-101,1-56	5.6
1992	Chi-A	160	573	108	185	**46**	2	24	115	**122**	88	.323	**.446**	.536	**981**	176	**64**	6	3	0	.992	-10	*1-158/D-2	4.3
1993	*Chi-A★	153	549	106	174	36	0	41	128	112	54	.317	.434	.607	1041	180	66	4	2	0	.989	-9	*1-150/D-4	4.1
1994	Chi-A★	113	399	**106**	141	34	1	38	101	**109**	61	.353	**.494**	**.729**	**1223**	**214**	**74**	2	3	-1	.991	-8	1-99,D-13	**5.0**
1995	Chi-A★	145	493	102	152	27	0	40	111	**136**	74	.308	.463	.606	1069	184	69	3	2	-0	.991	-13	1-90,D-54	4.1
1996	Chi-A†	141	527	110	184	26	0	40	134	109	70	.349	.465	.626	1091	181	**71**	1	1	-0	.992	-4	*1-139	4.8
1997	Chi-A†	146	530	110	184	35	0	35	125	109	69	**.347**	**.461**	.611	**1072**	**184**	**71**	1	1	-0	.986	-7	1-97,D-49	4.8
1998	Chi-A	160	585	109	155	35	2	29	109	110	93	.265	.387	.480	867	127	26	7	0	2	.984	-2	*D-146,1-14	1.5
1999	Chi-A	135	486	74	148	36	0	15	77	87	66	.305	.419	.471	890	126	23	3	3	-0	.990	-5	D-83,1-49	0.8
2000	*Chi-A	159	582	115	191	44	0	43	143	112	94	.328	.441	.625	1066	164	60	1	3	-1	.996	-2	*D-127,1-30	4.3
Total	11	1530	5474	1083	1755	361	10	344	1183	1188	835	.321	.446	.579	1024	171	617	29	21	-1	.991	-67	1-933,D-587	40.7

■ FRANK THOMAS Thomas, Frank Joseph b: 6/11/29, Pittsburgh, Pa. BR/TR, 6'3", 205 lbs. Deb: 8/17/51 Career OF: (709-LF 308-CF 48-RF)

YEAR	TM/L	G	AB	R	H	2B	3B	HR	RBI	BB	SO	AVG	OBP	SLG	OPS	OPS+	BR+	SB	CS	SBR	FA	FR	G/POS	TPR
1951	Pit-N	39	148	21	39	9	2	2	16	9	15	.264	.306	.392	698	84	-4	0	2	-1	1.000	1	O-37(0-37-0)	-0.4
1952	Pit-N	6	21	1	2	0	0	0	0	1	1	.095	.136	.095	232	-34	-4	0	0	0	1.000	-0	/O-5(0-5-0)	-0.5
1953	Pit-N	128	455	68	116	22	1	30	102	50	93	.255	.331	.505	837	115	8	1	2	-0	.976	10	*O-118(6-96-16)	1.2
1954	Pit-N★	153	577	81	172	32	7	23	94	51	74	.298	.365	.497	863	124	19	3	2	-0	.989	12	*O-153(48-109-0)	2.2
1955	Pit-N★	142	510	72	125	16	2	25	72	60	76	.245	.327	.431	758	101	-0	2	0	0	.984	-0	*O-139(86-59-0)	-0.8
1956	Pit-N	157	588	69	166	24	3	25	80	36	61	.282	.329	.461	790	112	8	0	5	-2	.942	-8	*3-111,O-56L/2-4	-0.4
1957	Pit-N	151	594	72	172	30	1	23	89	44	66	.290	.342	.460	801	116	12	3	1	0	.977	-1	1-71,O-59L,3-31	0.4
1958	Pit-N★	149	562	89	158	26	4	35	109	42	79	.281	.339	.528	867	129	21	0	1	-0	.926	-32	*3-139/O-8(5-0-3),1-2	-1.2
1959	Cin-N	108	374	41	84	18	2	12	47	27	56	.225	.282	.380	662	72	-16	0	2	-1	.927	-13	3-64,O-33L,1-14	-3.3
1960	Chi-N	135	479	54	114	12	1	21	64	28	74	.238	.280	.399	679	84	-12	1	0	0	.983	-10	1-50,O-49L,3-33	-2.8
1961	Chi-N	15	50	7	13	2	0	2	6	2	8	.260	.288	.420	708	84	-1	0	0	0	1.000	-1	O-10(10-0-0)/1-6	-0.3
	Mil-N	124	423	58	120	13	3	25	67	29	70	.284	.338	.506	844	128	15	2	4	-1	.954	-0	*O-109(109-0-0),1-11	0.8
	Yr	139	473	65	133	15	3	27	73	31	78	.281	.333	.497	830	123	14	2	4	-1	.956	-1	*O-119(119-0-0),1-17	0.5
1962	NY-N	156	571	69	152	23	3	34	94	48	95	.266	.332	.496	827	117	12	2	1	0	.962	8	*O-126L,1-11,3-10	1.1
1963	NY-N	126	420	34	109	9	1	15	60	33	48	.260	.318	.393	711	102	1	0	0	0	.988	5	O-96(96-0-0),1-15/3-1	0.0
1964	NY-N	60	197	19	50	6	1	3	19	10	29	.254	.297	.340	637	81	-5	1	1	-0	1.000	4	O-31(31-0-0),1-19/3-2	-0.4
	Phi-N	39	143	20	42	11	0	7	26	5	12	.294	.318	.517	835	132	5	0	1	-0	.976	1	1-36	0.4
	Yr	99	340	39	92	17	1	10	45	15	41	.271	.305	.415	720	103	0	1	2	-0	.982	5	1-55,O-31(31-0-0)/3-2	0.0
1965	Phi-N	35	77	7	20	4	0	1	7	4	10	.260	.296	.351	647	83	-2	0	0	0	1.000	-3	O-12(9-0-4),1-11/3-1	-0.6
	Hou-N	23	58	7	10	2	0	3	9	3	15	.172	.213	.362	575	63	-3	0	0	0	.984	-2	1-16/3-2,O-1(1-0-0)	-0.6
	Mil-N	15	33	3	7	3	0	0	1	2	11	.212	.257	.303	560	57	-2	0	0	0	.979	-1	/1-6,O-3(3-0-0)	-0.4
	Yr	73	168	17	37	9	0	4	17	9	36	.220	.260	.345	605	71	-7	0	0	0	.985	-6	1-33,O-16(13-0-4)/3-3	-1.6

YEAR	TM/L	G	AB	R	H	2B	3B	HR	RBI	BB	SO	AVG	OBP	SLG	OPS	OPS+	BR+	SB	CS	SBR	FA	FR	G/POS	TPR
1966	Chi-N	5	5	0	0	0	0	0	0	0	1	.000	.000	.000	0	-99	-1	0	0	0	.000	0	H	-0.1
Total	16	1766	6285	792	1671	262	31	286	962	484	894	.266	.323	.454	777	108	52	15	22	-4	.978	-31	*O-1045L,3-394,1/2	-5.7

■ FRED THOMAS

Thomas, Frederick Harvey "Tommy" b: 12/19/1892, Milwaukee, Wis. d: 1/15/86, Rice Lake, Wis. BR/TR, 5'10", 160 lbs. Deb: 4/22/18

YEAR	TM/L	G	AB	R	H	2B	3B	HR	RBI	BB	SO	AVG	OBP	SLG	OPS	OPS+	BR+	SB	CS	SBR	FA	FR	G/POS	TPR
1918	*Bos-A	44	144	19	37	2	1	1	11	15	20	.257	.331	.306	637	94	-1	4			.968	5	3-41/S-1	0.6
1919	Phi-A	124	453	42	96	11	10	2	23	43	52	.212	.283	.294	577	61	-24	12			.945	-5	*3-124	-2.7
1920	Phi-A	76	255	27	59	6	3	1	11	26	17	.231	.307	.290	598	58	-15	8	4	0	.960	1	3-61,S-12	-1.1
	Was-A	3	7	0	1	0	0	0	0	0	1	.143	.143	.143	286	-25	-1	0	1	-0	1.000	2	/3-2	0.0
	Yr	79	262	27	60	6	3	1	11	26	18	.229	.303	.286	590	56	-16	8	5	0	.962	3	3-63,S-12	-1.1
Total	3	247	859	88	193	19	14	4	45	84	90	.225	.297	.293	591	65	-41	24	5		.954	3	3-228/S-13	-3.2

■ GEORGE THOMAS

Thomas, George Edward b: 11/29/37, Minneapolis, Minn. BR/TR, 6'3.5", 190 lbs. Deb: 9/11/57 C Career OF: (136-LF 170-CF 186-RF)

YEAR	TM/L	G	AB	R	H	2B	3B	HR	RBI	BB	SO	AVG	OBP	SLG	OPS	OPS+	BR+	SB	CS	SBR	FA	FR	G/POS	TPR
1957	Det-A	1	1	0	0	0	0	0	0	0	1	.000	.000	.000	0	-97	-0	0	0	0	.000	-0	/3-1	-0.1
1958	Det-A	1	0	0	0	0	0	0	0	0	0	—	—	—	—	—	0	0	0	0	.000	-0	/O-1(0-0-1)	0.0
1961	Det-A	17	6	2	0	0	0	0	0	0	4	.000	.000	.000	0	-97	-2	0	0	0	.000	0	/O-2(0-0-2),S-1	-0.1
	LA-A	79	282	39	79	12	1	13	59	21	66	.280	.337	.468	805	101	0	3	6	-1	.986	-11	O-45(24-17-4),3-38	-1.4
	Yr	96	288	41	79	12	1	13	59	21	70	.274	.330	.458	788	99	-1	3	6	-1	.986	-10	O-47L,3-38/S-1	-1.5
1962	LA-A	56	181	13	43	10	2	4	12	21	37	.238	.320	.381	701	91	-2	0	0	0	.957	1	O-51(3-8-45)	-0.4
1963	LA-A	53	167	14	35	7	1	4	15	9	32	.210	.254	.335	590	68	-8	0	0	0	.941	-2	O-39(3-1-35),3-10/1-4	-1.3
	Det-A	49	109	13	26	4	1	1	11	11	22	.239	.314	.321	635	76	-3	2	1	0	1.000	-2	O-40(2-30-9)/2-1	-0.6
	Yr	102	276	27	61	11	2	5	26	20	54	.221	.279	.330	608	71	-11	2	1	0	.974	-4	O-79R,3-10/1-4,2-1	-1.9
1964	Det-A	105	308	39	88	15	2	12	44	18	53	.286	.331	.464	796	117	6	4	1	1	.988	-2	O-90(17-57-19)/3-1	0.1
1965	Det-A	79	169	19	36	5	1	3	10	12	39	.213	.273	.308	581	64	-8	2	3	-1	.948	-3	O-59(5-26-28)/2-1	-1.4
1966	Bos-A	69	173	25	41	4	0	5	20	23	33	.237	.333	.347	680	87	-2	1	0	0	1.000	0	O-48C/3-6,C-2,1-2	-0.4
1967	*Bos-A	65	89	10	19	2	0	1	6	3	23	.213	.255	.270	525	51	-5	0	1	-0	.973	-8	O-43(20-3-20)/1-3,C-1	-1.6
1968	Bos-A	12	10	3	2	0	0	1	1	1	3	.200	.273	.500	773	122	0	1	0	0	1.000	-2	/O-9(5-2-2)	-0.1
1969	Bos-A	29	51	9	18	3	1	0	8	3	11	.353	.400	.451	851	131	2	0	0	0	1.000	-4	O-12L,1-10/C-1,3-1	-0.2
1970	Bos-A	38	99	13	34	8	0	2	13	11	12	.343	.420	.485	904	139	6	0	0	0	.972	-5	O-26(25-0-1)/3-6	0.0
1971	Bos-A	9	13	0	1	0	0	0	1	1	4	.077	.143	.077	220	-34	-2	0	0	0	1.000	-2	/O-5(3-0-2)	-0.4
	Min-A	23	30	4	8	1	0	0	2	4	3	.267	.353	.300	653	84	-0	0	0	0	1.000	-4	O-11(11-0-0)/1-1,3-1	-0.5
	Yr	32	43	4	9	1	0	0	3	5	7	.209	.292	.233	524	48	-3	0	0	0	1.000	-5	O-16(14-0-2)/1-1,3-1	-0.9
Total	13	685	1688	203	430	71	9	46	202	138	343	.255	.318	.389	707	92	-19	13	12	-1	.976	-42	O-481R/3-64,1-20,C2S	-8.4

■ HERB THOMAS

Thomas, Herbert Mark b: 5/26/02, Sampson City, Fla. d: 12/4/91, Starke, Fla. BR/TR, 5'4.5", 157 lbs. Deb: 8/28/24 Career OF: (1-LF 32-CF 2-RF)

YEAR	TM/L	G	AB	R	H	2B	3B	HR	RBI	BB	SO	AVG	OBP	SLG	OPS	OPS+	BR+	SB	CS	SBR	FA	FR	G/POS	TPR
1924	Bos-N	32	127	12	28	4	1	1	8	9	8	.220	.288	.291	579	58	-8	5	2	0	.983	8	O-32(0-32-0)	-0.1
1925	Bos-N	5	17	2	4	0	1	0	0	2	0	.235	.350	.353	703	88	-0	0	1	-0	.963	-1	/2-5	-0.1
1927	Bos-N	24	74	11	17	6	1	0	6	3	9	.230	.269	.338	607	67	-4	2			.972	-11	2-17/S-2	-1.4
	NY-N	13	17	2	3	1	1	0	1	1	1	.176	.263	.353	616	64	-1	0			.900	0	/O-3(1-0-2),S-1	-0.1
	Yr	37	91	13	20	7	2	0	7	4	10	.220	.268	.341	609	65	-5	2			.972	-11	2-17/S-3,O-3(1-0-2)	-1.5
Total	3	74	235	27	52	11	4	1	15	15	18	.221	.285	.315	600	63	-12	7	3		.976	-4	/O-35C,2-22,S-3	-1.7

■ IRA THOMAS

Thomas, Ira Felix b: 1/22/1881, Ballston Spa, N.Y. d: 10/11/58, Philadelphia, Pa. BR/TR, 6'2", 200 lbs. Deb: 5/18/06 C

YEAR	TM/L	G	AB	R	H	2B	3B	HR	RBI	BB	SO	AVG	OBP	SLG	OPS	OPS+	BR+	SB	CS	SBR	FA	FR	G/POS	TPR
1906	NY-A	44	115	12	23	1	2	0	15	8		.200	.258	.243	502	52	-6	2			.938	-5	C-42	-0.8
1907	NY-A	80	208	20	40	5	4	1	24	10		.192	.240	.269	509	58	-10	5			.953	8	C-61/1-2	0.3
1908	*Det-A	40	101	6	31	1	0	0	8	5		.307	.346	.317	663	111	1	0			.972	-5	C-29	-0.2
1909	Phi-A	84	256	22	57	9	3	0	31	18		.223	.292	.281	573	79	-6	4			**.985**	12	C-84	1.6
1910	*Phi-A	60	180	14	50	8	2	1	19	6		.278	.301	.361	662	108	1	2			.967	8	C-60	1.5
1911	*Phi-A	103	297	33	81	14	3	0	39	23		.273	.341	.340	682	92	-3	4			.974	6	*C-103	1.1
1912	Phi-A	48	139	14	30	4	2	1	13	8		.216	.268	.295	563	63	-7	3			.971	-1	C-48	-0.4
1913	Phi-A	22	53	3	15	4	1	0	6	4	8	.283	.333	.396	730	116	1	0			.983	3	C-21	0.5
1914	Phi-A	2	3	0	0	0	0	0	0	0	0	.000	.000	.000	0	-99	-1	0			1.000	0	/C-1	0.0
1915	Phi-A	1	0	0	0	0	0	0	0	0	0	—	—	—	—	—	0	0			1.000	0	/C-1	0.0
Total	10	484	1352	124	327	46	17	3	155	82	8	.242	.296	.308	604	82	-30	20			.970	26	C-450/1-2	3.6

■ GORMAN THOMAS

Thomas, James Gorman b: 12/12/50, Charleston, S.C. BR/TR, 6'2", 210 lbs. Deb: 4/6/73 Career OF: (66-LF 967-CF 133-RF)

YEAR	TM/L	G	AB	R	H	2B	3B	HR	RBI	BB	SO	AVG	OBP	SLG	OPS	OPS+	BR+	SB	CS	SBR	FA	FR	G/POS	TPR
1973	Mil-A	59	155	16	29	7	1	2	11	14	61	.187	.254	.284	538	53	-10	5	5	-1	.957	-4	O-50(4-1-46)/3-1,D-3	-1.7
1974	Mil-A	17	46	10	12	4	0	2	11	8	15	.261	.370	.478	849	143	3	4	0	1	1.000	-1	O-13(4-1-8)/D-2	0.2
1975	Mil-A	121	240	34	43	12	2	10	28	31	84	.179	.273	.371	644	80	-7	4	2	0	.961	-13	*O-113(23-92-1)/D-6	-2.3
1976	Mil-A	99	227	27	45	9	2	8	36	31	67	.198	.297	.361	659	94	-2	2	3	-1	.986	-5	O-94(1-66-29)/3-1,D-1	-1.0
1978	Mil-A	137	452	70	111	24	1	32	86	73	133	.246	.353	.515	868	141	24	3	4	-1	.983	-4	*O-137(0-137-0)	1.9
1979	Mil-A	156	557	97	136	29	0	**45**	123	98	175	.244	.359	.539	898	138	30	1	5	-2	.991	4	*O-152(0-152-0)/D-4	2.9
1980	Mil-A	162	628	78	150	26	3	38	105	58	170	.239	.305	.471	777	113	8	8	5	0	.985	3	*O-160(0-160-0)/D-2	1.0
1981	*Mil-A★	103	363	54	94	22	0	21	65	50	85	.259	.352	.493	845	149	22	4	5	-1	.979	3	O-97(0-49-49)/D-6	2.2
1982	*Mil-A	158	567	96	139	29	1	**39**	112	84	143	.245	.347	.506	853	139	30	3	7	-2	.991	10	*O-157(0-157-0)	3.7
1983	Mil-A	46	164	21	30	6	1	5	18	23	50	.183	.287	.323	610	73	-6	2	1	0	.992	-0	O-46(0-46-0)	-0.6
	Cle-A	106	371	51	82	17	0	17	51	57	98	.221	.326	.404	731	96	-2	8	3	1	.982	12	*O-106(0-106-0)	1.0
	Yr	152	535	72	112	23	1	22	69	80	148	.209	.314	.379	694	90	-7	10	4	1	.985	11	*O-152(0-152-0)	0.4
1984	Sea-A	35	108	6	17	3	0	1	13	28	27	.157	.336	.213	549	56	-5	0	3	-1	1.000	-3	O-34(34-0-0)/D-1	-1.1
1985	Sea-A	135	484	76	104	16	1	32	87	84	126	.215	.332	.450	783	111	8	3	2	-0	.000	0	*D-133	0.4
1986	Sea-A	57	170	24	33	4	0	10	26	27	55	.194	.308	.394	702	89	-3	1	2	-0	.000	0	D-52	-0.5
	Mil-A	44	145	21	26	4	1	6	10	31	50	.179	.324	.345	669	80	-4	2	2	-0	.980	-1	D-36/1-6	-0.6
	Yr	101	315	45	59	8	1	16	36	58	105	.187	.316	.371	687	85	-6	3	4	-1	.980	-1	D-88/1-6	-1.1
Total	13	1435	4677	681	1051	212	13	268	782	697	1339	.225	.328	.448	775	114	87	50	49	-6	.984	1	*O-1159C,D-246/1-6,3	5.5

■ LEE THOMAS

Thomas, James Leroy b: 2/5/36, Peoria, Ill. BL/TR, 6'2", 198 lbs. Deb: 4/22/61 C Career OF: (83-LF 20-CF 392-RF)

YEAR	TM/L	G	AB	R	H	2B	3B	HR	RBI	BB	SO	AVG	OBP	SLG	OPS	OPS+	BR+	SB	CS	SBR	FA	FR	G/POS	TPR
1961	NY-A	2	2	0	1	0	0	0	0	0	0	.500	.500	.500	1000	177	0	0	0	0	.000	0	H	0.0
	LA-A	130	450	77	128	11	5	24	70	47	74	.284	.355	.491	846	111	7	0	5	-2	.966	-3	O-86(26-0-65),1-34	-0.5
	Yr	132	452	77	129	11	5	24	70	47	74	.285	.355	.491	846	111	7	0	5	-2	.966	-3	O-86(26-0-65),1-34	-0.5
1962	LA-A★	160	583	88	169	21	2	26	104	55	74	.290	.357	.467	824	124	19	6	1	1	.982	-10	1-90,O-74(17-18-42)	0.0
1963	LA-A	149	528	52	116	12	6	9	55	53	82	.220	.302	.316	618	78	-15	6	0	1	.996	3	*1-104,O-43(2-0-41)	-2.1
1964	LA-A	47	172	14	47	8	1	2	24	18	22	.273	.342	.366	708	108	2	1	0	0	.949	-1	O-47(1-0-46)/1-1	-0.2
	Bos-A	107	401	44	103	19	2	13	42	34	29	.257	.321	.411	733	97	-1	2	1	0	.995	3	*O-107(0-0-107)/1-1	-0.6
	Yr	154	573	58	150	27	3	15	66	52	51	.262	.328	.398	725	100	0	3	1	0	.981	3	*O-154(1-0-153)/1-2	-0.8
1965	Bos-A	151	521	74	141	27	4	22	75	72	42	.271	.362	.464	827	126	18	6	2	1	.984	5	*1-127,O-20(14-0-6)	1.6
1966	Atl-N	39	126	11	25	1	1	6	15	10	15	.198	.263	.365	628	71	-5	1	1	-0	.987	2	1-36	-0.5
	Chi-N	75	149	15	36	4	0	1	9	14	15	.242	.319	.289	608	70	-6	0	0	0	.992	-1	1-20,O-17(16-1-0)	-0.9
	Yr	114	275	26	61	5	1	7	24	24	30	.222	.294	.324	617	71	-11	1	1	-0	.989	1	1-56,O-17(16-1-0)	-1.4
1967	Chi-N	77	191	16	42	4	1	2	23	15	22	.220	.287	.283	570	61	-9	1	0	0	.969	-4	O-43(0-1-43),1-10	-1.8
1968	Hou-N	90	201	14	39	4	0	1	11	14	22	.194	.250	.229	479	45	-13	2	1	0	.973	-1	O-48(7-0-42)/1-2	-2.0
Total	8	1027	3324	405	847	111	22	106	428	332	397	.255	.328	.397	725	99	-4	25	11	2	.975	-7	O-485R,1-425	-7.0

■ BUD THOMAS

Thomas, John Tillman b: 3/10/29, Sedalia, Mo. BR/TR, 6', 180 lbs. Deb: 9/2/51

YEAR	TM/L	G	AB	R	H	2B	3B	HR	RBI	BB	SO	AVG	OBP	SLG	OPS	OPS+	BR+	SB	CS	SBR	FA	FR	G/POS	TPR
1951	StL-A	14	20	3	7	0	0	1	1	0	3	.350	.350	.500	850	124	1	2	0	0	1.000	1	S-14	0.2

■ KITE THOMAS

Thomas, Keith Marshall b: 4/27/23, Kansas City, Kan. d: 1/7/95, Rocky Mount, N.C. BR/TR, 6'1.5", 195 lbs. Deb: 4/19/52

YEAR	TM/L	G	AB	R	H	2B	3B	HR	RBI	BB	SO	AVG	OBP	SLG	OPS	OPS+	BR+	SB	CS	SBR	FA	FR	G/POS	TPR
1952	Phi-A	75	116	24	29	6	1	6	18	20	27	.250	.365	.474	839	124	4	0	1	-0	.957	-3	O-29(12-0-17)	-0.1
1953	Phi-A	24	49	1	6	0	0	0	2	3	6	.122	.173	.122	296	-18	-8	0	0	0	1.000	-0	O-15(6-0-9)	-0.9
	Was-A	38	58	10	17	3	2	1	12	11	7	.293	.414	.466	880	141	4	0	0	0	1.000	-2	/O-8(3-0-5),C-1	0.2
	Yr	62	107	11	23	3	2	1	14	14	13	.215	.311	.308	620	68	-5	0	0	0	1.000	-2	O-23(9-0-14)/C-1	-0.7
Total	2	137	223	35	52	9	3	7	32	34	40	.233	.340	.395	734	98	-0	0	1	-0	.978	-5	/O-52(21-0-31),C-1	-0.8

YEAR	TM/L	G	AB	R	H	2B	3B	HR	RBI	BB	SO	AVG	OBP	SLG	OPS	OPS+	BR+	SB	CS	SBR	FA	FR	G/POS	TPR
■ LEO THOMAS Thomas, Leo Raymond "Tommy" b: 7/26/23, Turlock, Cal. BR/TR, 5'11.5", 178 lbs. Deb: 4/29/50																								
1950	StL-A	35	121	19	24	6	0	1	9	20	14	.198	.312	.273	585	49	-9	0	1	-0	.964	-4	3-35	-1.3
1952	StL-A	41	124	12	29	5	1	0	12	17	7	.234	.336	.290	626	73	-4	2	0	0	.934	4	3-37/S-3,2-1	0.0
	Chi-A	19	24	1	4	0	0	0	6	6	4	.167	.333	.167	500	42	-2	0	0	0	.952	1	/3-9	-0.1
	Yr	60	148	13	33	5	1	0	18	23	11	.223	.335	.270	606	68	-5	2	0	0	.936	4	3-46/S-3,2-1	-0.1
Total	2	95	269	32	57	11	1	1	27	43	25	.212	.325	.271	596	59	-15	2	1	0	.948	1	/3-81,S-3,2-1	-1.4
■ RAY THOMAS Thomas, Raymond Joseph b: 7/9/10, Dover, N.H. d: 12/6/93, Wilson, N.C. BR/TR, 5'10.5", 175 lbs. Deb: 7/21/38																								
1938	Bro-N	1	3	1	1	0	0	0	0	0	0	.333	.333	.333	667	82	-0	0			1.000	0	/C-1	0.0
■ RED THOMAS Thomas, Robert William b: 4/25/1898, Hargrove, Ala. d: 3/29/62, Fremont, Ohio BR/TR, 5'11", 165 lbs. Deb: 9/13/21																								
1921	Chi-N	8	30	5	8	3	0	1	5	4	5	.267	.371	.467	838	120	1	0	1	-0	.962	1	/O-8(0-8-0)	0.1
■ ROY THOMAS Thomas, Roy Allen b: 3/24/1874, Norristown, Pa. d: 11/20/59, Norristown, Pa. BL/TL, 5'11", 150 lbs. Deb: 4/14/1899 FC Career OF: (75-LF 1349-CF 11-RF)																								
1899	Phi-N	150	547	137	178	12	4	0	47	115		.325	.457	.362	819	130	35	42			.952	4	*O-135(0-135-0),1-14	2.7
1900	Phi-N	140	531	**132**	168	4	3	0	33	**115**		.316	.451	.335	786	119	26	37			.958	-2	*O-139(0-139-0)/P-1	1.3
1901	Phi-N	129	479	102	148	5	2	1	28	**100**		.309	.437	.334	771	123	22	27			.967	-2	*O-129(0-129-0)	1.4
1902	Phi-N	138	500	89	143	4	7	0	24	**107**		.286	**.414**	.322	736	127	24	17			.974	6	*O-138(0-138-0)	2.4
1903	Phi-N	130	477	88	156	11	2	1	27	**107**		.327	**.453**	.365	818	139	34	17			.963	14	*O-130(0-130-0)	4.0
1904	Phi-N	139	496	92	144	6	6	3	29	**102**		.290	.416	.345	761	141	32	28			.974	15	*O-139(0-139-0)	4.2
1905	Phi-N	147	562	118	178	11	6	0	31	93		.317	.417	.358	775	137	32	23			.983	19	*O-147(0-147-0)	4.5
1906	Phi-N	142	493	81	125	10	7	0	16	**107**		.254	.393	.302	695	117	17	22			**.986**	10	*O-142(0-142-0)	2.2
1907	Phi-N	121	419	70	102	15	3	1	23	**83**		.243	.374	.301	674	113	11	11			.980	5	*O-121(0-121-0)	1.2
1908	Phi-N	6	24	2	4	0	0	0	0	2		.167	.231	.167	397	26	-2	0			1.000	-1	/O-6(0-6-0)	-0.3
	Pit-N	102	386	52	99	11	10	1	24	49		.256	.348	.345	692	121	11	11			.975	5	*O-101(0-101-0)	1.2
	Yr	108	410	54	103	11	10	1	24	51		.251	.341	.334	675	116	9	11			.976	4	*O-107(0-107-0)	0.9
1909	Bos-N	82	281	36	74	9	1	0	11	47		.263	.369	.302	671	104	3	5			.976	-2	O-76(75-2-0)	-0.3
1910	Phi-N	23	71	7	13	0	2	0	4	7	5	.183	.266	.239	505	46	-5	4			.952	-2	O-20(0-20-0)	-0.8
1911	Phi-N	21	30	5	5	2	0	0	2	8	6	.167	.342	.233	575	61	-1	0			1.000	1	O-11(0-0-11)	-0.1
Total	13	1470	5296	1011	1537	100	53	7	299	1042	11	.290	.413	.333	747	124	240	244			.972	71	*O-1434C/1-14,P-1	23.6
■ VALMY THOMAS Thomas, Valmy b: 10/21/28, Santurce, P.R. BR/TR, 5'9", 165 lbs. Deb: 4/16/57																								
1957	NY-N	88	241	30	60	10	3	6	31	16	29	.249	.298	.390	688	83	-6	0	0	0	.991	2	C-88	0.0
1958	SF-N	63	143	14	37	5	0	3	16	13	24	.259	.325	.357	681	82	-4	1	0	0	.992	2	C-61	0.1
1959	Phi-N	66	140	5	28	2	0	1	7	9	19	.200	.253	.236	489	31	-14	1	0	0	.980	15	C-65/3-1	0.4
1960	Bal-A	8	16	0	1	0	0	0	0	1	0	.063	.118	.063	180	-51	-3	0	1	-0	1.000	1	/C-8	-0.3
1961	Cle-A	27	86	7	18	3	0	2	6	6	7	.209	.261	.314	575	54	-6	0	0	0	.988	9	C-27	0.4
Total	5	252	626	56	144	20	3	12	60	45	79	.230	.285	.329	614	64	-32	2	1	0	.988	29	C-249/3-1	0.6
■ BILL THOMAS Thomas, William Miskey b: 12/8/1877, Norristown, Pa. d: 1/14/50, Evansburg, Pa. BR/TR, 5'10", 190 lbs. Deb: 5/1/02 F																								
1902	Phi-N	6	17	1	2	0	0	0	0	1		.118	.167	.118	284	-12	-2	0			.500	-1	/O-3(2-0-1),1-1,2-1	-0.4
■ WALT THOMAS Thomas, William Walter "Tommy" b: 4/28/1884, Foot Of Ten, Pa. d: 6/6/50, Altoona, Pa. BR/TR, 5'8", Deb: 9/18/08																								
1908	Bos-N	5	13	2	2	0	0	0	1	3		.154	.313	.154	466	51	-1	2			.864	-1	/S-5	-0.2
■ ART THOMASON Thomason, Arthur Wilson b: 2/12/1889, Liberty, Mo. d: 5/2/44, Kansas City, Mo. BL/TL, 5'8", 150 lbs. Deb: 8/10/10																								
1910	Cle-A	20	70	4	12	0	1	0	2	5		.171	.227	.200	427	33	-5	3			.944	2	O-20(0-1-19)	-0.5
■ GARY THOMASSON Thomasson, Gary Leah b: 7/29/51, San Diego, Cal. BL/TL, 6'1", 180 lbs. Deb: 9/5/72 Career OF: (182-LF 247-CF 206-RF)																								
1972	SF-N	10	27	5	9	1	1	0	1	1	7	.333	.357	.444	802	125	1	0	0	0	1.000	-2	/1-7,O-2(2-0-0)	-0.1
1973	SF-N	112	235	35	67	10	4	4	30	22	43	.285	.346	.413	759	105	2	2	0	1	.992	-3	1-47,O-43(23-11-9)	-0.4
1974	SF-N	120	315	41	77	14	3	2	29	38	56	.244	.326	.327	653	79	-8	7	1	1	.981	1	O-76(20-32-26),1-15	-1.0
1975	SF-N	114	326	44	74	12	3	7	32	37	48	.227	.308	.347	654	78	-10	9	3	1	.978	7	O-74(27-34-18),1-17	-0.6
1976	SF-N	103	328	45	85	20	5	8	38	30	45	.259	.323	.424	747	107	2	8	3	1	.959	-7	O-54(5-35-19),1-39	-0.9
1977	SF-N	145	446	63	114	24	6	17	71	75	102	.256	.364	.451	815	118	12	16	4	2	.959	-5	*O-113(62-49-20),1-31	0.5
1978	Oak-A	47	154	17	31	4	1	5	16	15	44	.201	.272	.338	610	74	-6	4	1	1	.969	6	O-44(0-0-44)/1-5	-0.6
	*NY-A	55	116	20	32	4	1	3	20	13	22	.276	.349	.405	754	114	2	0	2	-1	.972	0	O-50(24-16-12)/D-1	0.1
	Yr	102	270	37	63	8	2	8	36	28	66	.233	.305	.367	672	92	-3	4	3	-0	.971	2	O-94R/1-5,D-1	-0.5
1979	LA-N	115	315	39	78	11	1	14	45	43	70	.248	.340	.422	762	108	4	4	2	0	.980	-12	*O-100(10-61-43)/1-1	-1.1
1980	LA-N	80	111	6	24	3	0	1	12	17	26	.216	.326	.270	596	69	-4	0	0	0	.974	-6	O-31(9-9-15)/1-1	-1.2
Total	9	901	2373	315	591	103	25	61	294	291	463	.249	.332	.391	723	98	-5	50	16	5	.970	-24	O-587C,1-163/D-1	-5.3
■ JIM THOME Thome, James Howard b: 8/27/70, Peoria, Ill. BL/TR, 6'4", 220 lbs. Deb: 9/4/91																								
1991	Cle-A	27	98	7	25	4	2	1	9	5	16	.255	.298	.367	665	82	-2	1	1	-0	.900	1	3-27	-0.1
1992	Cle-A	40	117	8	24	3	1	2	12	10	34	.205	.279	.299	578	63	-6	2	0	0	.882	-6	3-40	-1.2
1993	Cle-A	47	154	28	41	11	0	7	22	29	36	.266	.396	.474	870	133	8	2	1	0	.950	-2	3-47	0.6
1994	Cle-A	98	321	58	86	20	1	20	52	46	84	.268	.360	.523	883	124	11	3	3	-0	.940	-1	3-94	1.0
1995	*Cle-A	137	452	92	142	29	3	25	73	97	113	.314	.440	.558	998	155	41	4	3	-0	.948	-14	*3-134/D-1	2.6
1996	*Cle-A	151	505	122	157	28	5	38	116	123	141	.311	.451	.612	1063	166	56	2	2	-0	.953	-6	*3-150/D-1	4.6
1997	*Cle-A★	147	496	104	142	25	0	40	102	**120**	146	.286	.428	.579	1007	154	43	1	1	-0	.993	1	*1-145	2.9
1998	*Cle-A★	123	440	89	129	34	2	30	85	89	141	.293	.417	.584	1001	151	35	1	0	0	.991	1	*1-117/D-6	2.4
1999	*Cle-A★	146	494	101	137	27	2	33	108	**127**	171	.277	.429	.540	969	139	33	0	0	0	.994	8	*1-111,D-36	2.6
2000	Cle-A	158	557	106	150	33	1	37	106	118	171	.269	.401	.531	932	130	28	1	0	0	.995	11	*1-107,D-48	2.3
Total	10	1074	3634	715	1033	214	17	233	685	764	1053	.284	.413	.545	958	142	248	17	11	-0	.940	-6	3-492,1-480/D-92	17.7
■ ANDY THOMPSON Thompson, Andrew John b: 10/8/75, Oconomowoc, Wis. BR/TR, 6'3", 210 lbs. Deb: 5/2/2000																								
2000	Tor-A	2	6	2	1	0	0	0	1	3	2	.167	.444	.167	611	63	-0	0	0	0	1.000	-0	/O-2(2-0-0)	-0.1
■ ANDREW THOMPSON Thompson, Andrew M. b: 1845, Illinois Deb: 4/26/1875 M																								
1875	Was-n	11	41	3	4	0	1	0	3	0	1	.098	.098	.146	244	-17	-4	0	0	0	.624	-7	C-11/O-1(0-0-1)	-1.0
■ BOBBY THOMPSON Thompson, Bobby La Rue b: 11/3/53, Charlotte, N.C. BB/TR, 5'11", 175 lbs. Deb: 4/16/78																								
1978	Tex-A	64	120	23	27	3	3	2	12	9	26	.225	.290	.350	640	79	-3	7	2	1	.982	-5	O-52(8-37-10)/D-3	-0.9
■ TIM THOMPSON Thompson, Charles Lemoine b: 3/1/24, Coalport, Pa. BL/TR, 5'11", 190 lbs. Deb: 4/28/54 C																								
1954	Bro-N	10	13	2	2	1	0	0	1	1	1	.154	.214	.231	445	15	-2	0	0	0	.909	-1	/C-2,O-1(1-0-0)	-0.2
1956	KC-A	92	268	21	73	13	2	1	27	17	23	.272	.321	.347	668	76	-9	2	4	-1	.981	2	C-68	-0.5
1957	KC-A	81	230	25	47	10	0	7	19	18	26	.204	.262	.339	601	62	-13	0	0	0	.993	-3	C-62	-1.3
1958	Det-A	4	6	1	1	0	0	0	0	3	2	.167	.444	.167	611	70	-0	0	0	0	1.000	-1	/C-4	-0.1
Total	4	187	517	49	123	24	2	8	47	39	52	.238	.294	.338	632	68	-24	2	4	-1	.986	-3	C-136/O-1(1-0-0)	-2.1
■ DANNY THOMPSON Thompson, Danny Leon b: 2/1/47, Wichita, Kan. d: 12/10/76, Rochester, Minn. BR/TR, 6', 183 lbs. Deb: 6/25/70																								
1970	*Min-A	96	302	25	66	9	0	0	22	7	39	.219	.236	.248	485	33	-27	0	0	0	.986	-12	2-81,3-37/S-6	-3.6
1971	Min-A	48	57	10	15	2	0	0	7	7	12	.263	.344	.298	642	81	-1	0	0	0	.897	1	3-17/2-3,S-1	0.0
1972	Min-A	144	573	54	158	22	6	4	48	34	57	.276	.319	.356	675	96	-3	3	4	-1	.957	-9	*S-144	0.6
1973	Min-A	99	347	29	78	13	2	1	36	16	41	.225	.263	.282	545	52	-22	1	0	0	.950	7	S-95/3-1,D-1	-0.5
1974	Min-A	97	264	25	66	6	1	4	25	22	29	.250	.313	.326	638	81	-6	1	1	-0	.963	-21	S-88/3-5,D-1	-1.9
1975	Min-A	112	355	25	96	11	2	5	37	18	30	.270	.306	.355	661	85	-8	0	3	-1	.941	-17	*S-100/3-7,2-1,D-3	-1.5
1976	Min-A	34	124	9	29	4	0	0	6	3	8	.234	.258	.266	524	53	-7	1	1	-0	.988	-1	S-34	-0.5
	Tex-A	64	196	12	42	3	0	1	13	13	19	.214	.267	.245	512	49	-12	2	2	-0	.976	-7	3-39,2-14,S-10,/D-1	-2.0
	Yr	98	320	21	71	7	0	1	19	16	27	.222	.263	.253	516	51	-20	3	3	-0	.981	-9	S-44,3-39,2-14,/D-1	-2.5
Total	7	694	2218	189	550	70	11	15	194	120	235	.248	.289	.310	599	70	-88	8	11	-2	.956	-60	S-478,3-106/2-99,D	-9.4

■ DON THOMPSON

Thompson, Donald Newlin b: 12/28/23, Swepsonville, N.C. BL/TL, 6', 185 lbs. Deb: 4/24/49

YEAR	TM/L	G	AB	R	H	2B	3B	HR	RBI	BB	SO	AVG	OBP	SLG	OPS	OPS+	BR+	SB	CS	SBR	FA	FR	G/POS	TPR
1949	Bos-N	7	11	0	2	0	0	0	0	0	2	.182	.182	.182	364	-2	-2	0			.800	-0	/O-2(0-0-2)	-0.2
1951	Bro-N	80	118	25	27	3	0	0	6	12	12	.229	.305	.254	560	51	-8	2	8	-2	.987	-11	O-61(56-6-0)	-2.4
1953	*Bro-N	96	153	25	37	5	0	1	12	14	13	.242	.310	.294	604	57	-9	2	3	-1	.989	-14	O-81(51-8-25)	-2.5
1954	Bro-N	34	25	2	1	0	0	0	1	5	5	.040	.226	.040	266	-25	-5	0	0	0	1.000	-9	O-29(27-2-0)	-1.4
Total	4	217	307	52	67	8	0	1	19	31	32	.218	.296	.254	550	46	-23	4	11		.984	-35	O-173(134-16-27)	-6.5

■ FRANK THOMPSON

Thompson, Frank Deb: 9/11/1875

YEAR	TM/L	G	AB	R	H	2B	3B	HR	RBI	BB	SO	AVG	OBP	SLG	OPS	OPS+	BR+	SB	CS	SBR	FA	FR	G/POS	TPR
1875	Atl-n	1	5	1	2	0	0	0	1	0	0	.400	.400	.400	800	205	1	0	0	0	.000	-1	/O-1(0-0-1)	0.0

■ FRANK THOMPSON

Thompson, Frank E b: 7/2/1895, Springfield, Mo. d: 6/27/40, Jasper Co., Mo. BR/TR, 5'8", 155 lbs. Deb: 5/6/20

YEAR	TM/L	G	AB	R	H	2B	3B	HR	RBI	BB	SO	AVG	OBP	SLG	OPS	OPS+	BR+	SB	CS	SBR	FA	FR	G/POS	TPR
1920	StL-A	22	53	7	9	0	0	0	5	13	10	.170	.343	.170	513	38	-4	1	1	-0	.878	-4	3-14/2-2	-0.8

■ HANK THOMPSON

Thompson, Henry Curtis b: 12/8/25, Oklahoma City, Okla d: 9/30/69, Fresno, Cal. BL/TR, 5'9", 174 lbs. Deb: 7/17/47 Career OF: (30-LF 53-CF 21-RF)

YEAR	TM/L	G	AB	R	H	2B	3B	HR	RBI	BB	SO	AVG	OBP	SLG	OPS	OPS+	BR+	SB	CS	SBR	FA	FR	G/POS	TPR
1947	StL-A	27	78	10	20	1	1	0	5	10	7	.256	.341	.295	636	76	-2	2	1	0	.957	1	2-19	0.0
1949	NY-N	75	275	51	77	10	4	9	34	42	30	.280	.377	.444	821	120	8	5			.961	-8	2-69/3-1	0.5
1950	NY-N	148	512	82	148	17	6	20	91	83	60	.289	.391	.463	854	123	19	8			.944	5	*3-138,O-10(0-2-9)	2.3
1951	*NY-N	87	264	37	62	8	4	8	33	43	23	.235	.342	.386	728	95	-1	1	2	-0	.925	-14	3-71	-1.6
1952	NY-N	128	423	67	110	13	9	17	67	50	38	.260	.344	.454	798	119	10	4	4	-1	.979	9	O-72C,3-46/2-4	1.6
1953	NY-N	114	388	80	117	15	8	24	74	60	39	.302	.400	.567	967	146	27	6	5	-0	.956	-3	*3-101/O-9(1-0-8),2-1	2.2
1954	*NY-N	136	448	76	118	18	1	26	86	90	58	.263	.392	.482	874	126	19	3	0	1	.945	-4	*3-130/2-2,O-1(1-0-0)	1.5
1955	NY-N	135	432	65	106	13	1	17	63	84	56	.245	.373	.398	771	105	5	2	2	-0	.943	2	*3-124/2-7,S-1	0.7
1956	NY-N	83	183	24	43	9	0	8	29	31	26	.235	.349	.415	764	105	2	2	1	0	.908	0	3-44,O-10(8-0-3)/S-1	0.2
Total	9	933	3003	492	801	104	34	129	482	493	337	.267	.374	.453	827	118	87	33	15		.941	-13	3-655,O-102C,2-102,/S	7.4

■ HOMER THOMPSON

Thompson, Homer Thomas b: 6/1/1891, Spring City, Tenn. d: 9/12/57, Atlanta, Ga. BR/TR, 5'9", 160 lbs. Deb: 10/5/12 F

YEAR	TM/L	G	AB	R	H	2B	3B	HR	RBI	BB	SO	AVG	OBP	SLG	OPS	OPS+	BR+	SB	CS	SBR	FA	FR	G/POS	TPR
1912	NY-A	1	0	0	0	0	0	0	0	0		—	—	—	—	—	0	0			.500	-0	/C-1	0.0

■ SHAG THOMPSON

Thompson, James Alfred b: 4/29/1893, Haw River, N.C. d: 1/7/90, Black Mountain, N.C BL/TR, 5'8.5", 165 lbs. Deb: 6/8/14

YEAR	TM/L	G	AB	R	H	2B	3B	HR	RBI	BB	SO	AVG	OBP	SLG	OPS	OPS+	BR+	SB	CS	SBR	FA	FR	G/POS	TPR
1914	Phi-A	16	29	3	5	0	1	0	2	7	8	.172	.351	.241	593	82	-0	1			.941	1	/O-8(2-6-0)	0.1
1915	Phi-A	17	33	5	11	2	0	0	2	4	6	.333	.405	.394	799	144	2	0	1	-0	1.000	0	/O-7(0-7-0)	0.2
1916	Phi-A	15	17	4	0	0	0	0	0	7	6	.000	.292	.000	292	-12	-2	1			1.000	-1	/O-8(1-6-1)	-0.3
Total	3	48	79	12	16	2	1	0	4	18	20	.203	.357	.253	610	87	-0	2	1		.978	1	/O-23(3-19-1)	0.0

■ JASON THOMPSON

Thompson, Jason Dolph b: 7/6/54, Hollywood, Cal. BL/TL, 6'3", 210 lbs. Deb: 4/23/76

YEAR	TM/L	G	AB	R	H	2B	3B	HR	RBI	BB	SO	AVG	OBP	SLG	OPS	OPS+	BR+	SB	CS	SBR	FA	FR	G/POS	TPR
1976	Det-A	123	412	45	90	12	1	17	54	68	72	.218	.331	.376	707	103	2	2	4	-1	.994	2	*1-117	-0.7
1977	Det-A☆	158	585	87	158	24	5	31	105	73	91	.270	.352	.487	839	120	16	0	1	-0	.991	-7	*1-158	-0.2
1978	Det-A★	153	589	79	169	25	3	26	96	74	96	.287	.367	.472	839	130	24	0	0	0	.993	-5	*1-151	0.9
1979	Det-A	145	492	58	121	16	1	20	79	70	90	.246	.341	.404	746	97	-1	2	0	0	.994	0	*1-140/D-2	-0.9
1980	Det-A	36	126	10	27	5	0	4	20	13	26	.214	.293	.349	642	73	-5	0	1	-0	1.000	4	1-36	-0.3
	Cal-A	102	312	59	99	14	0	17	70	70	60	.317	.442	.526	968	168	33	2	0	0	1.000	-3	1-47,D-45	2.6
	Yr	138	438	69	126	19	0	21	90	83	86	.288	.402	.475	877	141	28	2	1	0	1.000	1	1-83,D-45	2.3
1981	Pit-N	86	223	36	54	13	0	15	42	59	49	.242	.401	.502	903	150	17	0	0	0	.989	-1	1-78	1.2
1982	Pit-N★	156	550	87	156	32	0	31	101	101	107	.284	.397	.511	908	148	37	1	0	0	.993	-1	*1-155	2.8
1983	Pit-N	152	517	70	134	20	1	18	76	99	128	.259	.379	.406	785	115	14	1	0	0	.993	-6	*1-151	-0.1
1984	Pit-N	154	543	61	138	22	0	17	74	87	73	.254	.359	.389	748	110	9	0	0	0	.990	-10	*1-152	-1.1
1985	Pit-N	123	402	42	97	17	1	12	61	84	58	.241	.372	.378	751	111	9	0	0	0	.992	2	*1-114	0.5
1986	Mon-N	30	51	6	10	4	0	0	4	18	12	.196	.406	.275	680	92	1	0	1	-0	.962	-3	1-15	-0.4
Total	11	1418	4802	640	1253	204	12	208	782	816	862	.261	.369	.438	808	121	156	8	7	-1	.992	-28	*1-1314/D-47	4.3

■ JASON THOMPSON

Thompson, Jason Michael b: 6/13/71, Orlando, Fla. BL/TL, 6'4", 200 lbs. Deb: 6/9/96

YEAR	TM/L	G	AB	R	H	2B	3B	HR	RBI	BB	SO	AVG	OBP	SLG	OPS	OPS+	BR+	SB	CS	SBR	FA	FR	G/POS	TPR
1996	SD-N	13	49	4	11	4	0	2	6	1	14	.224	.240	.429	669	76	-2	0	0	0	.964	1	1-13	-0.2

■ TUG THOMPSON

Thompson, John P. b: London, Ontario, Canada BL/TR, 5'8", 160 lbs. Deb: 8/31/1882

YEAR	TM/L	G	AB	R	H	2B	3B	HR	RBI	BB	SO	AVG	OBP	SLG	OPS	OPS+	BR+	SB	CS	SBR	FA	FR	G/POS	TPR
1882	Cin-a	1	5	0	1	0	0	0		0		.200	.200	.200	400	33	-0				.000	-1	/O-1(0-1-0)	-0.1
1884	Ind-a	24	97	10	20	3	0	0		2		.206	.222	.237	459	51	-5				.429	-11	O-12(0-7-5),C-12	-1.4
Total	2	25	102	10	21	3	0	0		2		.206	.221	.235	456	50	-5				.409	-11	/O-13(0-8-5),C-12	-1.5

■ FRESCO THOMPSON

Thompson, Lafayette Fresco "Tommy" b: 6/6/02, Centreville, Ala. d: 11/20/68, Fullerton, Cal. BR/TR, 5'8", 150 lbs. Deb: 9/5/25

YEAR	TM/L	G	AB	R	H	2B	3B	HR	RBI	BB	SO	AVG	OBP	SLG	OPS	OPS+	BR+	SB	CS	SBR	FA	FR	G/POS	TPR
1925	Pit-N	14	37	4	9	2	1	0	8	4	1	.243	.317	.351	668	66	-2	2	1	0	.977	-2	2-12	-0.3
1926	NY-N	2	8	1	5	0	0	0	1	2	0	.625	.700	.625	1325	262	2	1			1.000	-1	/2-2	0.1
1927	Phi-N	153	597	78	181	32	14	1	70	34	36	.303	.343	.409	752	99	-1	19			.963	-5	*2-153	-0.2
1928	Phi-N	152	634	99	182	34	11	3	50	42	27	.287	.332	.390	722	85	-14	19			.966	9	*2-152	-0.1
1929	Phi-N	148	623	115	202	41	3	4	53	75	34	.324	.398	.419	817	96	-1	16			.965	12	*2-148	1.4
1930	Phi-N	122	478	77	135	34	4	4	46	35	29	.282	.331	.395	727	70	-24	7			.955	1	*2-112	-1.8
1931	Bro-N	74	181	26	48	6	1	1	21	23	16	.265	.351	.326	677	84	-3	5			.946	-3	2-43,S-10/3-5	-0.4
1932	Bro-N	3	1	0	0	0	0	0	0	0	0	.000	.000	.000	0	-99	-0	0			.000	0	H	0.0
1934	NY-N	1	1	0	0	0	0	0	0	0	0	.000	.000	.000	0	-99	-0	0			.000	0	H	0.0
Total	9	669	2560	400	762	149	34	13	249	215	143	.298	.353	.398	751	88	-44	69	1		.962	10	2-622/S-10,3-5	-1.3

■ MILT THOMPSON

Thompson, Milton Bernard b: 1/5/59, Washington, D.C. BL/TR, 5'11", 170 lbs. Deb: 9/4/84

YEAR	TM/L	G	AB	R	H	2B	3B	HR	RBI	BB	SO	AVG	OBP	SLG	OPS	OPS+	BR+	SB	CS	SBR	FA	FR	G/POS	TPR
1984	Atl-N	25	99	16	30	1	0	2	4	11	11	.303	.373	.374	746	103	1	14	2	2	.956	3	O-25(25-0-0)	0.5
1985	Atl-N	73	182	17	55	7	2	0	6	7	36	.302	.339	.363	701	91	-2	9	4	1	.964	-5	O-49(23-5-27)	-0.9
1986	Phi-N	96	299	38	75	7	1	6	23	26	62	.251	.313	.341	654	78	-9	19	4	3	.991	4	O-89(0-89-0)	-0.3
1987	Phi-N	150	527	86	159	26	9	7	43	42	87	.302	.353	.425	778	102	2	46	10	7	.989	9	*O-146(1-145-1)	1.5
1988	Phi-N	122	378	53	109	16	2	2	33	39	59	.288	.356	.357	714	103	3	17	9	1	.983	5	*O-112(0-112-5)	0.8
1989	StL-N	155	545	60	158	28	8	4	68	39	91	.290	.342	.393	734	106	4	27	8	3	.978	2	*O-147(23-123-3)	0.9
1990	StL-N	135	418	42	91	14	7	6	30	39	60	.218	.292	.328	620	70	-17	25	5	4	.971	-4	*O-116(12-14-96)	-2.1
1991	StL-N	115	326	55	100	16	5	6	34	32	53	.307	.369	.442	810	126	11	16	9	0	.991	9	O-91(72-12-12)	1.9
1992	StL-N	109	208	31	61	9	1	4	17	16	39	.293	.350	.404	753	116	4	18	6	2	.974	-3	O-45(35-1-11)	0.2
1993	*Phi-N	129	340	42	89	14	2	4	44	40	57	.262	.343	.350	693	87	-5	9	4	1	.994	-3	*O-106(102-4-0)	-1.1
1994	Phi-N	87	220	29	60	7	0	3	30	23	28	.273	.350	.345	695	80	-6	7	2	1	1.000	-6	O-79(72-12-0)	-1.2
	Hou-N	9	21	5	6	0	0	1	3	1	2	.286	.318	.429	747	97	-0	2	0	0	1.000	-0	/O-6(0-0-6)	0.0
	Yr	96	241	34	66	7	0	4	33	24	30	.274	.347	.353	700	82	-6	9	2	1	1.000	-6	O-85(72-12-6)	-1.2
1995	Hou-N	92	132	14	29	9	0	2	19	14	37	.220	.299	.333	633	71	-6	4	2	0	.979	-3	O-34(15-1-21)	-0.9
1996	LA-N	48	51	2	6	1	0	0	1	6	10	.118	.211	.137	348	-6	-8	1	1	-0	1.000	-3	O-17(17-0-0)	-1.1
	Col-N	14	15	1	1	1	0	0	2	1	3	.067	.125	.133	258	-26	-3	0	0	0	1.000	0	/O-1(1-0-0)	-0.3
	Yr	62	66	3	7	2	0	0	3	7	13	.106	.192	.136	328	-12	-11	1	1	-0	1.000	-3	O-18(18-0-0)	-1.4
Total	13	1359	3761	491	1029	156	37	47	357	336	635	.274	.337	.372	709	94	-30	214	66	24	.984	4	*O-1063(398-518-182)	-2.1

■ ROBBY THOMPSON

Thompson, Robert Randall b: 5/10/62, W.Palm Beach, Fla. BR/TR, 5'11", 170 lbs. Deb: 4/8/86 C

YEAR	TM/L	G	AB	R	H	2B	3B	HR	RBI	BB	SO	AVG	OBP	SLG	OPS	OPS+	BR+	SB	CS	SBR	FA	FR	G/POS	TPR
1986	SF-N	149	549	73	149	27	3	7	47	42	112	.271	.329	.370	699	97	-3	12	15	-3	.976	1	*2-149/S-1	0.4
1987	*SF-N	132	420	62	110	26	5	10	44	40	91	.262	.338	.419	757	104	2	16	11	-0	.972	6	*2-126	1.4
1988	SF-N†	138	477	66	126	24	6	7	48	40	111	.264	.326	.384	710	108	4	14	5	1	.978	-9	*2-134	0.0
1989	*SF-N	148	547	91	132	26	**11**	13	50	51	133	.241	.321	.400	721	108	5	12	2	2	.989	5	*2-148	1.7
1990	SF-N	144	498	67	122	22	3	15	56	34	96	.245	.301	.392	693	92	-7	14	4	2	.989	**28**	*2-142	2.7
1991	SF-N	144	492	74	129	24	5	19	48	63	95	.262	.353	.447	800	128	18	14	7	1	.985	10	*2-144	3.4
1992	SF-N	128	443	54	115	25	1	14	49	43	75	.260	.336	.415	751	118	10	5	9	-2	.978	20	*2-120	3.4
1993	SF-N†	128	494	85	154	30	2	19	65	45	97	.312	.377	.496	873	136	25	10	4	1	.988	11	*2-128	4.2
1994	SF-N	35	129	13	27	8	2	2	7	15	32	.209	.292	.349	641	69	-6	3	1	0	.989	4	2-35	0.0
1995	SF-N	95	336	51	75	15	0	8	23	42	76	.223	.317	.339	656	75	-12	1	2	-0	.993	-16	2-91	-2.4

YEAR	TM/L	G	AB	R	H	2B	3B	HR	RBI	BB	SO	AVG	OBP	SLG	OPS	OPS+	BR+	SB	CS	SBR	FA	FR	G/POS	TPR
1996	SF-N	63	227	35	48	11	1	5	21	24	69	.211	.301	.335	636	70	-10	2	2	-0	.976	-10	2-62	-1.7
Total	11	1304	4612	671	1187	238	39	119	458	439	987	.257	.331	.403	734	105	28	103	62	1	.983	50	*2-1279/S-1	13.1
■ TOMMY THOMPSON	Thompson, Rupert Lockhart b: 5/19/10, Elkhart, Ill. d: 5/24/71, Auburn, Cal. BL/TR, 5'9.5", 155 lbs. Deb: 9/3/33																							
1933	Bos-N	24	97	6	18	1	0	0	6	4	6	.186	.218	.196	414	21	-10	0			1.000	2	O-24(1-13-10)	-0.9
1934	Bos-N	105	343	40	91	12	3	0	37	13	19	.265	.300	.318	618	71	-14	2			.964	10	O-82(6-1-75)	-0.9
1935	Bos-N	112	297	34	81	7	1	4	30	36	17	.273	.353	.343	697	96	-0	2			.965	1	O-85(12-12-62)	-0.4
1936	Bos-N	106	266	37	76	9	0	4	36	31	12	.286	.362	.365	727	103	2	3			1.000	0	O-39(10-22-7),1-25	-0.1
1938	Chi-A	19	18	2	2	0	0	0	2	1	2	.111	.158	.111	269	-31	-4	0	0	0	1.000	-0	/1-1	-0.3
1939	Chi-A	1	0	0	0	0	0	0	1	0	0	—	—	—	—	—	-0	0	0	0	.000	0	H	0.0
	StL-A	30	86	23	26	5	0	1	7	23	7	.302	.455	.395	850	117	4	0	0	0	.977	-0	O-23(0-0-23)	0.2
	Yr	31	86	23	26	5	0	1	8	23	7	.302	.455	.395	850	117	4	0	0	0	.977	-0	O-23(0-0-23)	0.2
Total	6	397	1107	142	294	34	4	9	119	108	63	.266	.335	.328	663	84	-23	7	0		.975	13	O-253(29-48-177)/1-26	-2.4
■ RYAN THOMPSON	Thompson, Ryan Orlando b: 11/4/67, Chestertown, Md. BR/TR, 6'3", 200 lbs. Deb: 9/1/92																							
1992	NY-N	30	108	15	24	7	1	3	10	8	24	.222	.276	.389	665	88	-2	2	2	-0	.988	0	O-29(0-26-10)	-0.3
1993	NY-N	80	288	34	72	19	2	11	26	19	81	.250	.303	.444	748	98	-2	2	7	-2	.987	10	O-76(0-76-0)	0.7
1994	NY-N	98	334	39	75	14	1	18	59	28	94	.225	.304	.434	738	90	-6	1	1	-0	.989	8	O-98(0-98-0)	0.4
1995	NY-N	75	267	39	67	13	0	7	31	19	77	.251	.310	.378	689	83	-7	3	1	0	.985	8	O-74(11-38-31)	0.0
1996	Cle-A	8	22	2	7	0	0	1	5	1	6	.318	.348	.455	802	101	0	0	0	0	1.000	-3	/O-8(0-8-0)	-0.3
1999	Hou-N	12	20	2	4	1	0	1	5	2	7	.200	.273	.400	673	68	-1	0	0	0	.800	-3	O-10(2-5-3)	-0.4
2000	NY-A	33	50	12	13	3	0	3	14	5	12	.260	.339	.500	839	111	1	0	1	-0	1.000	-8	O-31(20-9-6)	-0.7
Total	7	336	1089	143	262	57	4	44	150	82	301	.241	.304	.421	726	91	-17	8	12	-2	.987	14	O-326(33-260-50)	-0.6
■ SAM THOMPSON	Thompson, Samuel Luther "Big Sam" b: 3/5/1860, Danville, Ind. d: 11/7/22, Detroit, Mich. BL/TL, 6'2", 207 lbs. Deb: 7/2/1885 H																							
1885	Det-N	63	254	58	77	11	9	7	44	16	22	.303	.344	.500	844	170	19				.885	7	O-63(0-0-63)	2.3
1886	Det-N	122	503	101	156	18	13	8	89	35	31	.310	.355	.445	800	138	22	13			.945	10	*O-122(0-0-122)	2.8
1887	*Det-N	127	577	118	235	29	**23**	10	**166**	32	19	.407	.416	**.565**	982	165	46	22			.909	7	*O-127(0-0-127)	**4.3**
1888	Det-N	56	238	51	67	10	8	6	40	23	10	.282	.352	.466	819	159	16	5			.882	-7	O-56(0-0-56)	0.9
1889	Phi-N	128	533	103	158	36	4	**20**	111	36	22	.296	.348	.492	839	123	12	24			.901	-7	*O-128(0-0-128)	0.3
1890	Phi-N	132	549	116	**172**	**41**	9	4	102	42	29	.313	.371	.443	813	133	21	25			.939	2	*O-132(0-0-132)	2.0
1891	Phi-N	133	554	108	163	23	10	7	90	52	20	.294	.363	.410	773	122	15	29			.937	19	*O-133(0-2-131)	2.9
1892	Phi-N	153	609	109	186	28	11	9	104	59	19	.305	.377	.432	809	145	33	28			.937	5	*O-153(3-0-150)	2.7
1893	Phi-N	131	600	130	**222**	**37**	13	11	126	50	17	.370	.424	.530	954	153	44	18			.931	-11	*O-131(0-0-131)/1-1	2.1
1894	Phi-N	102	451	114	187	32	28	13	**147**	41	13	.415	.465	**.696**	1161	**181**	58	27			**.972**	-5	*O-102(0-0-102)	3.6
1895	Phi-N	119	538	131	211	45	21	**18**	**165**	31	11	.392	.430	**.654**	1085	177	56	27			.943	12	*O-118(0-0-118)	5.0
1896	Phi-N	119	517	103	154	28	7	12	100	28	13	.298	.341	.449	790	108	4	12			**.974**	18	*O-119(0-0-119)	1.3
1897	Phi-N	3	13	2	3	0	1	0	3	1		.231	.286	.385	670	78	-0	0			.833	0	/O-3(0-0-3)	0.0
1898	Phi-N	14	63	14	22	5	3	1	15	4		.349	.388	.571	959	182	6	2			1.000	2	O-14(0-0-14)	0.7
1906	Det-A	8	31	4	7	0	1	0	3	1		.226	.250	.290	540	67	-1	0			1.000	-0	/O-8(0-0-8)	-0.2
Total	15	1410	6030	1262	2020	343	161	126	1305	451	226	.335	.384	.505	890	146	348	232			.934	52	*O-1409(3-2-1404)/1-1	30.7
■ SCOT THOMPSON	Thompson, Vernon Scot b: 12/7/55, Grove City, Pa. BL/TL, 6'3", 195 lbs. Deb: 9/3/78 Career OF: (61-LF 66-CF 150-RF)																							
1978	Chi-N	19	36	7	15	3	0	0	2	2	4	.417	.447	.500	947	147	2	0	0	0	1.000	-2	/O-5(0-5-1),1-2	0.1
1979	Chi-N	128	346	36	100	13	5	2	29	17	37	.289	.324	.373	697	82	-8	4	3	-0	.971	-9	*O-100(12-26-72)	-2.2
1980	Chi-N	102	226	26	48	10	1	2	13	28	31	.212	.302	.292	594	62	-11	6	6	-1	.963	-6	O-66(1-14-52),1-12	-2.1
1981	Chi-N	57	115	8	19	5	0	0	8	7	8	.165	.213	.209	422	19	-12	2	0	0	.980	-5	O-30(3-20-8)/1-3	-1.9
1982	Chi-N	49	74	11	27	5	1	0	7	5	4	.365	.405	.459	865	138	4	0	1	-0	1.000	-1	O-23(20-1-4)/1-4	0.2
1983	Chi-N	53	88	4	17	3	1	0	10	3	14	.193	.220	.250	470	28	-8	0	0	0	1.000	-5	O-29(23-0-6)/1-1	-1.6
1984	SF-N	120	245	30	75	7	1	1	31	30	26	.306	.382	.355	737	112	5	5	3	0	.998	-1	1-87/O-6(2-0-4)	0.1
1985	SF-N	64	111	8	23	5	0	0	6	2	10	.207	.221	.252	473	34	-10	0	0	0	.995	2	1-24	-1.0
	Mon-N	34	32	2	9	1	0	0	4	3	7	.281	.343	.313	655	90	-0	0	0	0	1.000	-0	/1-3,O-3(0-0-3)	-0.1
	Yr	98	143	10	32	6	0	0	10	5	17	.224	.250	.266	516	47	-10	0	0	0	.995	2	1-27/O-3(0-0-3)	-1.1
Total	8	626	1273	132	333	52	9	5	110	97	141	.262	.315	.328	643	76	-39	17	13	-1	.973	-27	O-262R,1-136	-8.5
■ BOBBY THOMSON	Thomson, Robert Brown "The Staten Island Scot" b: 10/25/23, Glasgow, Scotland BR/TR, 6'2", 185 lbs. Deb: 9/9/46 Career OF: (511-LF 982-CF 59-RF)																							
1946	NY-N	18	54	8	17	4	1	2	9	4	5	.315	.362	.537	899	152	3	0			.935	0	3-16	0.3
1947	NY-N	138	545	105	154	26	5	29	85	40	78	.283	.336	.508	844	121	13	1			.980	9	*O-127(0-127-0)/2-9	1.8
1948	NY-N★	138	471	75	117	20	2	16	63	30	77	.248	.296	.401	697	87	-11	2			.970	6	*O-125(64-57-4)	-1.1
1949	NY-N★	156	641	99	198	35	9	27	109	44	45	.309	.355	.518	873	132	26	10			.982	20	*O-156(0-156-0)	4.0
1950	NY-N	149	563	79	142	22	7	25	85	55	45	.252	.324	.449	774	101	-1	3			.978	10	*O-149(0-149-0)	0.5
1951	*NY-N	148	518	89	152	27	8	32	101	73	57	.293	.385	.562	947	150	36	5	5	-1	.966	-11	O-77(33-43-3),3-69	2.1
1952	NY-N★	153	608	89	164	29	**14**	24	108	52	74	.270	.331	.482	813	122	16	5	2	0	.940	-7	3-91,O-63(0-63-0)	0.8
1953	NY-N	154	608	80	175	22	6	26	106	43	57	.288	.338	.472	810	106	4	4	2	0	.983	3	*O-154(0-153-1)	0.0
1954	Mil-N	43	99	7	23	3	0	2	15	12	29	.232	.315	.323	639	71	-4	0	0	0	.980	1	O-26(26-0-0)	-0.5
1955	Mil-N	101	343	40	88	12	3	12	56	34	52	.257	.324	.414	738	99	-1	2	1	0	.969	0	O-91(88-3-0)	-0.6
1956	Mil-N	142	451	59	106	10	4	20	74	43	75	.235	.304	.408	712	95	-4	2	4	-1	.974	-4	*O-136(128-18-0)/3-3	-1.7
1957	Mil-N	41	148	15	35	5	3	4	23	8	27	.236	.285	.392	677	86	-4	2	1	0	.988	-1	O-38(36-5-1)	-0.7
	NY-N	81	215	24	52	7	4	8	38	19	39	.242	.303	.423	727	93	-3	1	2	-0	.992	-4	O-71(54-3-17)/3-1	-1.0
	Yr	122	363	39	87	12	7	12	61	27	66	.240	.296	.410	706	90	-6	3	3	-0	.990	-5	*O-109(90-8-18)/3-1	-1.7
1958	Chi-N	152	547	67	155	27	5	21	82	56	76	.283	.354	.466	820	117	13	0	2	-1	.989	4	*O-148(7-143-1)/3-4	0.9
1959	Chi-N	122	374	55	97	15	2	11	52	35	50	.259	.326	.398	724	93	-4	1	0	0	.987	-7	*O-116(62-49-29)	-1.6
1960	Bos-A	40	114	12	30	3	1	5	20	11	15	.263	.328	.439	767	102	0	0	1	-0	.971	2	O-27(12-13-2)/1-1	0.0
	Bal-A	3	6	0	0	0	0	0	0	0	3	.000	.000	.000	0	-99	-2	0	0	0	.000	-1	/O-2(1-0-1)	-0.3
	Yr	43	120	12	30	3	1	5	20	11	18	.250	.313	.417	730	93	-2	0	1	-0	.971	1	O-29(13-13-3)/1-1	-0.3
Total	15	1779	6305	903	1705	267	74	264	1026	559	804	.270	.333	.462	795	111	77	38	20		.980	20	*O-1506C,3-184/2-9,1	2.9
■ DICKIE THON	Thon, Richard William b: 6/20/58, South Bend, Ind. BR/TR, 5'11", 175 lbs. Deb: 5/22/79																							
1979	*Cal-A	35	56	6	19	3	0	0	8	5	10	.339	.393	.393	786	117	2	0	0	0	.923	3	2-24/S-8,3-1,D-1	0.5
1980	Cal-A	80	267	32	68	12	2	0	15	10	28	.255	.284	.315	599	65	-13	7	5	-0	.928	-12	S-22,2-21,D-15,3/1	-2.3
1981	*Hou-N	49	95	13	26	6	0	0	3	9	13	.274	.337	.337	673	96	-0	6	1	1	.950	-5	2-28,S-13/3-5	-0.3
1982	Hou-N	136	496	73	137	31	**10**	3	36	37	48	.276	.328	.397	725	110	5	37	8	5	.975	5	*S-119/3-8,2-1	2.9
1983	Hou-N★	154	619	81	177	28	9	20	79	54	73	.286	.345	.457	802	128	22	34	16	2	.966	21	*S-154	6.2
1984	Hou-N	5	17	3	6	0	1	0	1	0	4	.353	.389	.471	859	151	1	0	1	-0	1.000	-0	/S-5	0.1
1985	Hou-N	84	251	26	63	6	1	6	29	18	50	.251	.301	.355	656	85	-5	8	3	1	.967	7	S-79	1.0
1986	*Hou-N	106	278	24	69	13	1	3	21	29	49	.248	.319	.335	654	83	-6	6	5	-0	.972	-2	*S-104	-0.1
1987	Hou-N	32	66	6	14	1	0	1	3	16	13	.212	.366	.273	639	75	-2	3	0	1	.925	-8	S-31	-0.6
1988	SD-N	95	258	36	68	12	2	1	18	33	49	.264	.349	.337	687	100	1	19	4	3	.954	-20	S-70/2-2,3-1	-1.2
1989	Phi-N	136	435	45	118	18	4	15	60	33	81	.271	.323	.434	757	115	7	6	3	0	.972	16	*S-129	3.4
1990	Phi-N	149	552	54	141	20	4	8	48	37	77	.255	.306	.350	655	80	-15	12	5	1	.964	3	*S-148	0.0
1991	Phi-N	146	539	44	136	18	4	9	44	25	84	.252	.285	.351	636	79	-16	11	5	1	.969	-8	*S-146	-1.4
1992	Tex-A	95	275	30	68	15	3	4	37	20	40	.247	.298	.367	666	89	-5	12	2	2	.958	0	S-87	0.3
1993	Mil-A	85	245	23	66	10	1	1	33	22	39	.269	.330	.331	660	79	-7	6	5	-0	.966	-11	S-28,3-25,2-22,D-14	-1.6
Total	15	1387	4449	496	1176	193	42	71	435	348	658	.264	.319	.374	693	95	-32	167	63	15	.965	-13	*S-1143/2-98,3-50,D1	6.9
■ JACK THONEY	Thoney, John "Bullet Jack" (b: John Thoeny) b: 12/8/1879, Ft.Thomas, Ky. d: 10/24/48, Covington, Ky. BR/TR, 5'10", 175 lbs. Deb: 4/26/02 Career OF: (97-LF 52-CF 15-RF)																							
1902	Cle-A	28	105	14	30	7	1	0	11	9		.286	.342	.371	714	102	0	4			.891	-15	2-14,S-11/O-2(0-0-2)	-1.4
	Bal-A	3	11	1	0	0	0	0	0	1		.000	.083	.000	83	-72	-3	1			.778	-2	/3-3	-0.4
	Yr	31	116	15	30	7	1	0	11	10		.259	.317	.336	654	84	-2	5			.891	-17	2-14,S-11/3-3,O-2R	-1.8
1903	Cle-A	32	122	10	25	3	0	1	9	2		.205	.218	.254	472	42	-9	7			.889	1	O-24(0-23-1)/2-5,3-2	-0.9

YEAR	TM/L	G	AB	R	H	2B	3B	HR	RBI	BB	SO	AVG	OBP	SLG	OPS	OPS+	BR+	SB	CS	SBR	FA	FR	G/POS	TPR
1904	Was-A	17	70	6	21	3	0	0	6	1		.300	.310	.343	653	108	0	2			.860	2	O-17(0-8-9)	0.2
	NY-A	36	128	17	24	4	2	0	12	8		.188	.241	.250	491	53	-7	9			.826	1	3-26,O-10(0-10-0)	-0.7
	Yr	53	198	23	45	7	2	0	18	9		.227	.264	.283	547	71	-7	11			.886	3	O-27(0-18-9),3-26	-0.5
1908	Bos-A	109	416	58	106	5	9	2	30	13		.255	.282	.325	607	94	-4	16			.948	8	*O-101(87-11-3)	-0.2
1909	Bos-A	13	40	1	5	1	0	0	3	2		.125	.167	.150	317	0	-5	2			.960	1	O-10(10-0-0)	-0.5
1911	Bos-A	26	20	5	5	0	0	0	2	0		.250	.250	.250	500	40	-2	1			.000	0	H	-0.2
Total	6	264	912	112	216	23	12	3	73	36		.237	.269	.298	567	75	-27	42			.929	-4	O-164L/3-31,2-19,S	-4.1

■ **ANDY THORNTON** Thornton, Andre b: 8/13/49, Tuskegee, Ala. BR/TR, 6′2″, 205 lbs. Deb: 7/28/73 Career OF: (0-LF 0-CF 11-RF)

YEAR	TM/L	G	AB	R	H	2B	3B	HR	RBI	BB	SO	AVG	OBP	SLG	OPS	OPS+	BR+	SB	CS	SBR	FA	FR	G/POS	TPR
1973	Chi-N	17	35	3	7	3	0	0	2	7	9	.200	.333	.286	619	68	-1	0	0	0	.989	2	/1-9	0.0
1974	Chi-N	107	303	41	79	16	4	10	46	48	50	.261	.369	.439	808	120	9	2	1	0	.992	8	1-90/3-1	1.1
1975	Chi-N	120	372	70	109	21	4	18	60	88	63	.293	.433	.516	949	156	32	3	2	-0	.988	3	*1-113/3-2	2.6
1976	Chi-N	27	85	8	17	6	0	2	14	20	14	.200	.364	.341	706	93	-0	2	0	0	.987	1	1-25	-0.1
	Mon-N	69	183	20	35	5	2	9	24	28	32	.191	.308	.388	696	93	-2	2	1	0	.994	-0	1-43,O-11(0-0-11)	-0.6
	Yr	96	268	28	52	11	2	11	38	48	46	.194	.327	.373	700	93	-2	4	1	1	.991	1	1-68,O-11(0-0-11)	-0.7
1977	Cle-A	131	433	77	114	20	5	28	70	70	82	.263	.379	.527	906	149	30	3	4	-1	.995	-3	*1-117/D-9	2.0
1978	Cle-A	145	508	97	133	22	4	33	105	93	72	.262	.382	.516	898	152	37	4	7	-2	.995	5	*1-145	3.1
1979	Cle-A	143	515	89	120	31	1	26	93	90	93	.233	.351	.449	800	114	11	5	4	-0	.994	-3	*1-130,D-13	-0.1
1981	Cle-A	69	226	22	54	12	0	6	30	23	37	.239	.309	.372	681	97	-1	3	1	0	.986	-1	D-53,1-11	-0.4
1982	Cle-A★	161	589	90	161	26	1	32	116	109	81	.273	.389	.484	872	139	34	6	7	-1	1.000	0	*D-152/1-8	2.8
1983	Cle-A	141	508	78	143	27	1	17	77	87	72	.281	.389	.439	828	123	18	4	2	0	.991	2	*D-114,1-27	1.5
1984	Cle-A★	155	587	91	159	26	0	33	99	91	79	.271	.371	.484	854	132	27	6	5	-0	.979	0	*D-144,1-11	2.1
1985	Cle-A	124	461	49	109	13	0	22	88	47	75	.236	.307	.408	715	94	-4	3	2	-0	.000	0	*D-122	-0.8
1986	Cle-A	120	401	49	92	14	0	17	66	65	67	.229	.338	.392	730	100	1	4	1	1	.000	0	*D-110	-0.2
1987	Cle-A	36	85	8	10	2	0	0	5	10	25	.118	.211	.141	352	-4	-13	1	0	0	.000	0	D-21	-1.3
Total	14	1565	5291	792	1342	244	22	253	895	876	851	.254	.364	.452	815	123	178	48	37	-2	.992	14	D-738,1-729/O-11R,3	11.7

■ **JOHN THORNTON** Thornton, John b: 1870, Washington, D.C. 5′10.5″, 175 lbs. Deb: 8/14/1889

YEAR	TM/L	G	AB	R	H	2B	3B	HR	RBI	BB	SO	AVG	OBP	SLG	OPS	OPS+	BR+	SB	CS	SBR	FA	FR	G/POS	TPR
1889	Was-N	1	4	0	0	0	0	0	1	0	1	.000	.000	.000	0	-99	-1	0			1.000	-0	/P-1	0.0
1891	Phi-N	39	123	7	17	3	0	0	6	2	10	.138	.152	.163	315	-8	-17	1			.881	-0	P-37/O-3(1-2-0)	-0.2
1892	Phi-N	5	13	1	5	0	0	0	2	0	0	.385	.385	.385	769	133	0	0			.857	-1	/P-3,O-2(0-2-0)	-0.1
	StL-N	1	3	0	0	0	0	0	0	0	2	.000	.000	.000	0	-99	-1	0			.000	-0	/O-1(0-0-1)	-0.1
	Yr	6	16	1	5	0	0	0	2	0	2	.313	.313	.313	625	90	-0	0			.500	-1	/P-3,O-3(0-2-1)	-0.2
Total	3	46	143	8	22	3	0	0	9	2	13	.154	.166	.175	340	-1	-18	1			.881	-1	/P-41,O-6(1-4-1)	-0.4

■ **LOU THORNTON** Thornton, Louis b: 4/26/63, Montgomery, Ala. BL/TR, 6′2″, 185 lbs. Deb: 4/8/85

YEAR	TM/L	G	AB	R	H	2B	3B	HR	RBI	BB	SO	AVG	OBP	SLG	OPS	OPS+	BR+	SB	CS	SBR	FA	FR	G/POS	TPR
1985	*Tor-A	56	72	18	17	1	1	1	8	2	24	.236	.267	.319	586	58	-4	1	0	0	.957	-7	O-35(16-0-20),D-16	-1.2
1987	Tor-A	12	2	5	1	0	0	0	0	1	0	.500	.667	.500	1167	212	0	0	1	-0	.000	-2	/O-4(4-0-0),D-6	-0.1
1988	Tor-A	11	2	1	0	0	0	0	0	0	0	.000	.000	.000	0	-99	-1	0	0	0	1.000	-4	O-10(9-0-1)/D-1	-0.5
1989	NY-N	13	13	5	4	1	0	0	1	0	1	.308	.308	.385	692	102	-0	2	0	0	1.000	-1	/O-6(3-1-2)	0.0
1990	NY-N	3	0	0	0	0	0	0	0	0	0	—	—	—	—		0	0	0	0	1.000	-1	/O-2(0-1-1)	-0.1
Total	5	95	89	29	22	2	1	1	9	3	25	.247	.280	.326	605	65	-4	3	1	0	.965	-13	/O-57(32-2-24),D-23	-1.9

■ **OTIS THORNTON** Thornton, Otis Benjamin b: 6/30/45, Docena, Ala. BR/TR, 6′1″, 186 lbs. Deb: 7/6/73

YEAR	TM/L	G	AB	R	H	2B	3B	HR	RBI	BB	SO	AVG	OBP	SLG	OPS	OPS+	BR+	SB	CS	SBR	FA	FR	G/POS	TPR
1973	Hou-N	2	3	0	0	0	0	0	1	0	2	.000	.000	.000	0	-99	-1	0	0	0	1.000	0	/C-2	-0.1

■ **WALTER THORNTON** Thornton, Walter Miller b: 2/18/1875, Lewiston, Maine d: 7/14/60, Los Angeles, Cal. BL/TL, 6′1″, 180 lbs. Deb: 7/1/1895 Career OF: (50-LF 36-CF 10-RF)

YEAR	TM/L	G	AB	R	H	2B	3B	HR	RBI	BB	SO	AVG	OBP	SLG	OPS	OPS+	BR+	SB	CS	SBR	FA	FR	G/POS	TPR
1895	Chi-N	8	22	4	7	1	0	1	7	3	1	.318	.400	.500	900	123	1	0			.900	-1	/P-7,1-1	0.0
1896	Chi-N	9	22	6	8	0	1	0	1	5	2	.364	.481	.455	936	142	2	2			.800	-1	/P-5,O-3(0-2-1)	0.0
1897	Chi-N	75	265	39	85	9	6	0	55	30		.321	.402	.400	802	108	4	13			.781	-11	O-59(48-8-3),P-16	-1.1
1898	Chi-N	62	210	34	62	5	2	0	14	22		.295	.362	.338	700	101	1	8			.877	-3	O-34(2-26-6),P-28	-0.3
Total	4	154	519	83	162	15	9	1	77	60	3	.312	.390	.382	771	108	7	23			.821	-15	/O-96L,P-56,1-1	-1.4

■ **BOB THORPE** Thorpe, Benjamin Robert b: 11/19/26, Caryville, Fla. d: 10/30/96, Waveland, Miss. BR/TR, 6′1.5″, 190 lbs. Deb: 4/19/51

YEAR	TM/L	G	AB	R	H	2B	3B	HR	RBI	BB	SO	AVG	OBP	SLG	OPS	OPS+	BR+	SB	CS	SBR	FA	FR	G/POS	TPR
1951	Bos-N	2	2	1	1	0	1	0	1	0	0	.500	.500	1.500	2000	448	1	0	0	0	.000	0	H	0.1
1952	Bos-N	81	292	20	76	8	2	3	26	5	42	.260	.275	.332	607	70	-13	3	1	0	.972	0	O-72(8-0-70)	-1.6
1953	Mil-N	27	37	1	6	1	0	0	5	1	6	.162	.184	.189	373	-3	-6	0	1	-0	1.000	-5	O-18(10-0-8)	-1.1
Total	3	110	331	22	83	9	3	3	32	6	48	.251	.266	.323	590	64	-17	3	2	-0	.975	-5	/O-90(18-0-78)	-2.6

■ **JIM THORPE** Thorpe, James Francis b: 5/28/1887, Prague, Okla. d: 3/28/53, Long Beach, Cal. BR/TR (BB 1915), 6′1″, 185 lbs. Deb: 4/14/13

YEAR	TM/L	G	AB	R	H	2B	3B	HR	RBI	BB	SO	AVG	OBP	SLG	OPS	OPS+	BR+	SB	CS	SBR	FA	FR	G/POS	TPR
1913	NY-N	19	35	6	5	0	0	1	2	1	9	.143	.167	.229	395	12	-4	2			.944	-1	/O-9(3-7-0)	-0.5
1914	NY-N	30	31	5	6	1	0	0	2	0	4	.194	.194	.226	419	25	-3	1			.750	-2	/O-4(0-2-2)	-0.5
1915	NY-N	17	52	8	12	3	1	0	1	2	16	.231	.259	.327	586	82	-1	4	2	0	.933	-2	O-15(0-13-2)	-0.5
1917	Cin-N	77	251	29	62	2	8	4	36	6	35	.247	.267	.367	634	98	-2	11			.962	2	O-69(38-0-33)	-0.4
	*NY-N	26	57	12	11	3	2	0	4	8	10	.193	.303	.316	619	93	-0	1			.939	-3	O-18(6-1-13)	-0.5
	Yr	103	308	41	73	5	10	4	40	14	45	.237	.275	.357	632	97	-2	12			.958	-1	O-87(44-1-46)	-0.9
1918	NY-N	58	113	15	28	4	4	1	11	4	18	.248	.286	.381	666	105	0	3			.983	-12	O-44(2-33-12)	-1.5
1919	NY-N	2	3	0	1	0	0	0	1	0	0	.333	.333	.333	667	102	-0	0			1.000	-1	/O-2(1-1-0)	-0.1
	Bos-N	60	156	16	51	7	3	1	25	6	30	.327	.360	.429	789	143	7	7			.926	-7	O-38(22-12-7)/1-2	-0.1
	Yr	62	159	16	52	7	3	1	26	6	30	.327	.359	.428	787	142	7	7			.928	-7	O-40(23-13-7)/1-2	-0.2
Total	6	289	698	91	176	20	18	7	82	27	122	.252	.286	.362	648	99	-3	29	2		.951	-25	O-199(72-69-69)/1-2	-4.1

■ **BUCK THRASHER** Thrasher, Frank Edward b: 8/6/1889, Watkinsville, Ga. d: 6/12/38, Cleveland, Ohio BL/TR, 5′11″, 182 lbs. Deb: 9/27/16

YEAR	TM/L	G	AB	R	H	2B	3B	HR	RBI	BB	SO	AVG	OBP	SLG	OPS	OPS+	BR+	SB	CS	SBR	FA	FR	G/POS	TPR
1916	Phi-A	7	29	4	9	2	1	0	4	2	1	.310	.355	.448	803	148	1	0			1.000	-1	/O-7(0-0-7)	0.0
1917	Phi-A	23	77	5	18	2	1	0	2	3	12	.234	.272	.286	557	71	-3	0			.938	-3	O-22(0-0-22)	-0.8
Total	2	30	106	9	27	4	2	0	6	5	13	.255	.295	.330	625	92	-1	0			.951	-4	/O-29(0-0-29)	-0.8

■ **MARV THRONEBERRY** Throneberry, Marvin Eugene "Marvelous Marv" b: 9/2/33, Collierville, Tenn. d: 6/23/94, Fisherville, Tenn. BL/TL, 6′, 197 lbs. Deb: 9/25/55 F

YEAR	TM/L	G	AB	R	H	2B	3B	HR	RBI	BB	SO	AVG	OBP	SLG	OPS	OPS+	BR+	SB	CS	SBR	FA	FR	G/POS	TPR
1955	NY-A	1	2	1	2	1	0	0	3	0	0	1.000	1.000	1.500	2500	574	1	1	0	0	1.000	0	/1-1	0.2
1958	*NY-A	60	150	30	34	5	2	7	19	19	40	.227	.318	.427	744	107	1	1	1	-0	.991	-1	1-40/O-5(0-0-5)	-0.2
1959	NY-A	80	192	27	46	5	0	8	22	18	51	.240	.305	.391	695	93	-2	0	0	0	.989	-1	1-54,O-13(1-0-12)	-0.6
1960	KC-A	104	236	29	59	9	2	11	41	23	60	.250	.317	.445	762	103	0	0	0	0	.991	1	1-71	-0.2
1961	KC-A	40	130	17	31	2	1	6	24	19	30	.238	.336	.408	743	96	-1	0	0	0	.996	1	1-30,O-10(0-0-10)	-0.2
	Bal-A	56	96	9	20	3	0	5	11	12	20	.208	.296	.396	692	86	-2	0	0	0	.923	-3	O-15(0-0-15),1-11	-0.6
	Yr	96	226	26	51	5	1	11	35	31	50	.226	.319	.403	722	93	-3	0	0	0	.991	-2	1-41,O-25(0-0-25)	-0.8
1962	Bal-A	9	9	1	0	0	0	0	0	4	6	.000	.308	.000	308	-9	-1	0	0	0	1.000	-0	/O-2(0-0-2)	-0.2
	NY-N	116	357	29	87	11	3	16	49	34	83	.244	.309	.426	735	94	-4	1	3	-1	.981	4	1-97	-0.7
1963	NY-N	14	14	0	2	1	0	0	1	1	5	.143	.200	.214	414	19	-1	0	0	0	1.000	-0	/1-3	-0.2
Total	7	480	1186	143	281	37	8	53	170	130	295	.237	.313	.416	729	96	-10	3	4	-1	.987	1	1-307/O-45(1-0-44)	-2.7

■ **FAYE THRONEBERRY** Throneberry, Maynard Faye b: 6/22/31, Fisherville, Tenn. d: 4/26/99, Memphis, Tenn. BL/TR, 6′, 190 lbs. Deb: 4/15/52 F

YEAR	TM/L	G	AB	R	H	2B	3B	HR	RBI	BB	SO	AVG	OBP	SLG	OPS	OPS+	BR+	SB	CS	SBR	FA	FR	G/POS	TPR
1952	Bos-A	98	310	38	80	11	3	5	23	33	67	.258	.331	.361	693	86	-6	16	7	1	.955	-0	O-86(11-4-71)	-0.8
1955	Bos-A	60	144	20	37	7	3	6	27	14	31	.257	.327	.472	799	104	0	0	0	0	.960	1	O-34(32-0-3)	-0.1
1956	Bos-A	24	50	6	11	2	0	1	3	3	16	.220	.264	.320	584	48	-4	0	0	0	.909	-2	O-13(8-2-3)	-0.6
1957	Bos-A	1	1	0	0	0	0	0	0	0	1	.000	.000	.000	0	-95	-0	0	0	0	.000	0	H	0.0
	Was-A	68	195	21	36	8	2	2	12	17	37	.185	.254	.277	530	45	-15	0	1	-0	.983	-6	O-58(14-48-2)	-2.5
	Yr	69	196	21	36	8	2	2	12	17	38	.184	.252	.276	528	45	-15	0	1	-0	.983	-6	O-58(14-48-2)	-2.5
1958	Was-A	44	87	12	16	1	1	4	7	4	28	.184	.245	.356	601	64	-5	0	1	-0	1.000	-3	O-26(5-13-8)	-1.0
1959	Was-A	117	327	36	82	11	2	10	42	33	61	.251	.325	.388	713	95	-2	6	4	-0	.953	-2	O-86(16-1-71)	-0.7
1960	Was-A	85	157	18	39	7	1	1	23	18	33	.248	.330	.325	654	78	-4	1	1	-0	.947	-3	O-34(12-7-17)	-0.9

YEAR	TM/L	G	AB	R	H	2B	3B	HR	RBI	BB	SO	AVG	OBP	SLG	OPS	OPS+	BR+	SB	CS	SBR	FA	FR	G/POS	TPR
1961	LA-A	24	31	1	6	1	0	0	0	5	10	.194	.306	.226	531	40	-3	0	0	0	1.000	1	/O-5(3-0-2)	-0.2
Total	8	521	1302	152	307	48	12	29	137	127	284	.236	.309	.358	666	79	-38	23	14	0	.962	-15	O-342(101-75-177)	-6.8
■ GARY THURMAN	Thurman, Gary Montez b: 11/12/64, Indianapolis, Ind. BR/TR, 5'10", 175 lbs. Deb: 8/30/87 Career OF: (132-LF 84-CF 147-RF)																							
1987	KC-A	27	81	12	24	2	0	0	5	8	20	.296	.360	.321	681	81	-2	7	2	1	.971	4	O-27(22-6-0)	0.2
1988	KC-A	35	66	6	11	1	0	0	2	4	20	.167	.214	.182	396	12	-8	5	1	1	.949	-7	O-32(22-11-0)/D-1	-1.5
1989	KC-A	72	87	24	17	2	1	0	5	15	26	.195	.314	.241	555	59	-4	16	0	4	.949	-17	O-60(12-28-24)/D-4	-1.9
1990	KC-A	23	60	5	14	3	0	0	3	2	12	.233	.258	.283	541	52	-4	1	1	-0	1.000	-2	O-21(5-2-15)	-0.7
1991	KC-A	80	184	24	51	9	0	2	13	11	42	.277	.321	.359	680	87	-3	15	5	2	.970	-5	O-72(39-9-29)	-0.8
1992	KC-A	88	200	25	49	6	3	0	20	9	34	.245	.281	.305	586	62	-10	9	6	-0	.986	2	O-67(7-2-59)/D-9	-1.0
1993	Det-A	75	89	22	19	2	2	0	13	11	30	.213	.300	.281	581	58	-5	7	0	2	.950	-12	O-53(17-21-15)/D-9	-1.5
1995	Sea-A	13	25	3	8	2	0	0	3	1	3	.320	.346	.400	746	93	-0	5	2	0	1.000	-1	/O-9(5-1-4)	-0.1
1997	NY-N	11	6	0	1	0	0	0	0	0	0	.167	.167	.167	333	-13	-1	0	1	-0	1.000	-3	/O-7(3-4-1)	-0.4
Total	9	424	798	121	194	27	6	2	64	61	187	.243	.298	.299	598	65	-37	65	18	8	.971	-40	O-348R/D-23	-7.7
■ BOB THURMAN	Thurman, Robert Burns b: 5/14/17, Wichita, Kan. d: 10/31/98, Wichita, Kan. BL/TL, 6'1", 205 lbs. Deb: 4/14/55																							
1955	Cin-N	82	152	19	33	2	3	7	22	17	26	.217	.296	.408	704	80	-5	0	2	-1	.949	-4	O-36(36-0-0)	-1.1
1956	Cin-N	80	139	25	41	5	2	8	22	10	14	.295	.342	.532	875	123	4	0	0	0	.953	-3	O-29(9-0-20)	0.0
1957	Cin-N	74	190	38	47	4	2	16	40	15	33	.247	.306	.542	848	114	3	0	0	0	.987	-0	O-44(29-0-15)	0.0
1958	Cin-N	94	178	23	41	7	4	4	20	20	38	.230	.322	.382	704	81	-5	1	2	-0	.976	2	O-41(33-0-8)	-0.5
1959	Cin-N	4	4	1	1	0	0	0	2	0	1	.250	.250	.250	500	33	-0	0	0	0	.000	0	H	0.0
Total	5	334	663	106	163	18	11	35	106	62	112	.246	.315	.465	780	99	-3	1	4	-1	.970	-5	O-150(107-0-43)	-1.6
■ EDDIE TIEMEYER	Tiemeyer, Edward Carl b: 5/9/1885, Cincinnati, Ohio d: 9/27/46, Cincinnati, Ohio BR/TR, 5'11.5", 185 lbs. Deb: 8/19/06																							
1906	Cin-N	5	11	3	2	0	0	0	0	1		.182	.250	.182	432	33	-1	0			1.000	0	/3-3,P-1	0.0
1907	Cin-N	1	0	1	0	0	0	0	0	1		—	1.000	—	1000	206	0	0			.000	0	H	0.0
1909	NY-A	3	8	1	3	1	0	0	0	1		.375	.444	.500	944	197	1	0			.962	-1	/1-3	0.0
Total	3	9	19	5	5	1	0	0	0	3		.263	.364	.316	679	110	0	0			.962	-0	/1-3,3-3,P-1	0.0
■ MIKE TIERNAN	Tiernan, Michael Joseph "Silent Mike" b: 1/21/1867, Trenton, N.J. d: 11/9/18, New York, N.Y. BL/TL, 5'11", 165 lbs. Deb: 4/30/1887 Career OF: (170-LF 148-CF 1160-RF)																							
1887	NY-N	103	439	82	149	13	12	10	62	32	31	.339	.344	.452	796	125	14	28			.865	-9	*O-103(34-11-58)/P-5	0.3
1888	*NY-N	113	443	75	130	16	8	9	52	42	42	.293	.364	.427	790	153	28	52			**.960**	-0	*O-113(0-1-112)	2.5
1889	*NY-N	122	499	**147**	167	23	14	10	73	**96**	32	.335	.447	.497	944	163	47	33			.896	-3	*O-122(0-1-122)	3.7
1890	NY-N	133	553	132	168	25	21	**13**	59	68	53	.304	.385	**.495**	**880**	**156**	**38**	56			.896	-15	*O-133(2-131-1)	1.6
1891	NY-N	134	542	111	166	30	12	**16**	73	69	32	.306	.388	.494	**882**	**163**	**43**	53			.901	-9	*O-134(0-4-130)	2.9
1892	NY-N	116	450	79	130	16	10	5	66	57	46	.289	.371	.402	774	136	20	20			.899	-3	*O-116(0-0-116)	1.0
1893	NY-N	125	511	114	158	19	12	14	102	72	24	.309	.399	.476	874	131	23	26			.927	-9	*O-125(0-0-125)	0.6
1894	*NY-N	113	429	87	120	20	13	5	78	55	21	.280	.363	.422	785	89	-8	28			.923	-11	*O-112(0-0-112)	-1.9
1895	NY-N	120	476	127	165	23	21	7	70	66	19	.347	.427	.527	955	149	36	36			.946	-5	*O-119(0-0-119)	2.0
1896	NY-N	133	521	132	192	24	16	7	89	77	18	.369	.452	.516	968	159	48	35			.970	-2	*O-133(0-0-133)	3.3
1897	NY-N	128	532	123	174	29	10	5	72	61		.327	.397	.447	845	126	21	40			.931	-11	*O-128(38-0-90)	0.2
1898	NY-N	103	415	90	116	15	11	5	49	43		.280	.357	.405	762	122	12	19			.973	-12	*O-103(96-0-7)	-0.9
1899	NY-N	35	137	17	35	4	2	0	7	10		.255	.306	.314	620	73	-5	2			.938	-4	O-35(0-0-35)	-1.0
Total	13	1478	5947	1316	1870	257	162	106	852	748	318	.314	.392	.463	855	138	316	428			.924	-91	*O-1476R/P-5	14.3
■ COTTON TIERNEY	Tierney, James Arthur b: 2/10/1894, Kansas City, Kan. d: 4/18/53, Kansas City, Mo. BR/TR, 5'8", 175 lbs. Deb: 9/23/20 Career OF: (3-LF 0-CF 10-RF)																							
1920	Pit-N	12	46	4	11	5	0	0	8	3	4	.239	.286	.348	634	79	-1	1	1	-0	.964	-2	2-10/S-2	-0.3
1921	Pit-N	117	442	49	132	22	8	3	52	24	31	.299	.338	.405	743	93	-5	4	6	-1	.965	-27	2-72,3-32/O-4R,S-3	-2.9
1922	Pit-N	122	441	58	152	26	14	7	86	22	40	.345	.378	.515	893	127	16	7	8	-1	.964	-37	*2-105/O-2R,S-1,3-1	-1.9
1923	Pit-N	29	120	22	35	5	2	2	23	2	10	.292	.309	.417	726	88	-3	2	1	0	.941	-3	2-29	-0.5
	Phi-N	121	480	68	152	31	1	11	65	24	42	.317	.352	.454	806	100	-1	3	4	-1	.975	17	*2-115/O-7(3-0-4),3-2	1.8
	Yr	150	600	90	187	36	3	13	88	26	52	.312	.343	.447	790	97	-3	5	5	-1	.968	14	*2-144/O-7(3-0-4),3-2	1.3
1924	Bos-N	136	505	38	131	16	1	6	58	22	37	.259	.296	.331	626	71	-22	11	8	-0	.964	-2	*2-115,3-22	-1.9
1925	Bro-N	93	265	27	68	14	4	2	39	12	23	.257	.294	.362	656	68	-13	0	3	-1	.963	-1	3-61/1-1,2-1	-1.1
Total	6	630	2299	266	681	119	30	31	331	109	187	.296	.332	.415	746	93	-28	28	31	-5	.966	-54	2-447,3-118/O-13R,S1	-6.8
■ BILL TIERNEY	Tierney, William J. b: 5/14/1858, Boston, Mass. d: 9/21/1898, Boston, Mass. Deb: 5/2/1882																							
1882	Cin-a	1	5	1	0	0	0	0		0		.000	.000	.000	0	-95	-1				.917	0	/1-1	-0.1
1884	Bal-U	1	3	0	1	0	0	0		1		.333	.500	.333	833	142	0				1.000	-0	/O-1(0-0-1)	0.0
Total	2	2	8	1	1	0	0	0		1		.125	.222	.125	347	13	-1				1.000	0	/O-1(0-0-1),1-1	-0.1
■ JOHN TILLEY	Tilley, John C. b: New York, N.Y. BR, 5'7", 154 lbs. Deb: 8/23/1882																							
1882	Cle-N	15	56	2	5	1	1	0	4	2	11	.089	.121	.143	264	-16	-7				.857	2	O-15(14-1-0)	-0.5
1884	Tol-a	17	56	5	10	2	0	0		4		.179	.246	.214	460	50	-3				.632	-4	O-17(17-0-0)	-0.7
	StP-U	9	26	2	4	1	0	0		3		.154	.241	.192	434	61	-2				.938	0	/O-9(9-0-0)	-0.1
Total	2	41	138	9	19	4	1	0	4	9	11	.138	.196	.181	377	23	-11				.818	-2	/O-41(40-1-0)	-1.3
■ BOB TILLMAN	Tillman, John Robert b: 3/24/37, Nashville, Tenn. d: 6/23/2000, Gallatin, Tenn. BR/TR, 6'4", 205 lbs. Deb: 4/15/62																							
1962	Bos-A	81	249	28	57	6	4	14	38	19	65	.229	.286	.454	740	93	-4	0	0	0	.983	-4	C-66	-0.4
1963	Bos-A	96	307	24	69	10	2	8	32	34	64	.225	.304	.349	653	80	-8	0	0	0	.992	1	C-95	-0.2
1964	Bos-A	131	425	43	118	18	1	17	61	49	74	.278	.352	.445	797	114	9	0	0	0	.989	-8	*C-131	0.7
1965	Bos-A	111	368	20	79	10	3	6	35	40	69	.215	.292	.307	599	66	-16	0	0	0	.988	-7	*C-106	-1.8
1966	Bos-A	78	204	12	47	8	0	3	24	22	35	.230	.305	.314	619	71	-7	0	0	0	.990	-3	C-72	-0.8
1967	Bos-A	30	64	4	12	1	0	1	4	3	18	.188	.224	.250	474	37	-5	0	0	0	.977	2	C-26	-0.3
	NY-A	22	63	5	16	1	0	2	9	7	17	.254	.329	.365	694	109	1	0	0	0	.970	0	C-15	0.2
	Yr	52	127	9	28	2	0	3	13	10	35	.220	.277	.307	584	70	-5	0	0	0	.974	2	C-41	-0.1
1968	Atl-N	86	236	16	52	4	0	5	20	16	55	.220	.278	.301	579	74	-8	1	0	0	.990	-1	C-75	-0.6
1969	*Atl-N	69	190	18	37	5	0	12	29	18	47	.195	.264	.411	675	86	-4	0	0	0	.988	-10	C-69	-1.2
1970	Atl-N	71	223	19	53	5	0	11	30	20	66	.238	.300	.408	708	83	-6	0	0	0	.988	-2	C-70	-0.5
Total	9	775	2329	189	540	68	10	79	282	228	510	.232	.302	.371	673	85	-48	1	0	0	.988	-31	C-725	-4.9
■ RUSTY TILLMAN	Tillman, Kerry Jerome b: 8/29/60, Jacksonville, Fla. BR/TR, 6', 185 lbs. Deb: 6/6/82																							
1982	NY-N	12	13	4	2	1	0	0	0	0	4	.154	.154	.231	385	6	-2	1	0	0	1.000	-1	/O-3(0-0-3)	-0.2
1986	Oak-A	22	39	6	10	1	0	1	6	3	11	.256	.310	.359	668	88	-1	2	0	0	.952	-3	O-17(8-0-10)	-0.4
1988	SF-N	4	4	1	1	0	0	1	3	2	1	.250	.500	1.000	1500	335	1	0	0	0	1.000	-0	/O-1(1-0-0)	0.1
Total	3	38	56	11	13	2	0	2	9	5	16	.232	.295	.375	670	88	-1	3	0	1	.958	-4	/O-21(9-0-13)	-0.5
■ OZZIE TIMMONS	Timmons, Osborne Llewellyn b: 9/18/70, Tampa, Fla. BR/TR, 6'2", 205 lbs. Deb: 4/26/95 Career OF: (89-LF 0-CF 40-RF)																							
1995	Chi-N	77	171	30	45	10	1	8	28	13	32	.263	.315	.474	789	107	1	3	0	1	.970	-6	O-55(49-0-6)	-0.5
1996	Chi-N	65	140	18	28	4	0	7	16	15	30	.200	.282	.379	661	70	-6	1	0	0	1.000	-3	O-47(25-0-22)	-1.1
1997	Cin-N	6	9	1	3	1	0	0	0	0	1	.333	.333	.444	778	100	-0	0	0	0	.000	-1	/O-1(1-0-0)	-0.1
1999	Sea-A	26	44	4	5	2	0	1	3	4	12	.114	.188	.227	415	5	-7	0	1	-0	1.000	-5	O-17(12-0-5)/1-1,D-5	-1.1
2000	TB-A	12	41	9	14	3	0	4	13	1	7	.341	.357	.707	1064	161	3	0	0	0	1.000	-2	/O-9(2-0-7),D-1	0.1
Total	5	186	405	62	95	20	1	20	60	33	82	.235	.294	.437	731	88	-9	4	1	1	.980	-16	O-129L/D-6,1-1	-2.7
■ BEN TINCUP	Tincup, Austin Ben b: 12/14/1890, Adair, Okla. d: 7/5/80, Claremore, Okla. BL/TR, 6'1", 180 lbs. Deb: 5/22/14 C																							
1914	Phi-N	31	53	3	9	1	1	0	1	0	18	.170	.170	.226	396	16	-6	0			.926	1	P-28	0.0
1915	Phi-N	11	9	1	0	0	0	0	0	0	3	.000	.000	.000	0	-99	-2	0			1.000	0	P-10	0.0
1916	Phi-N	1	1	0	0	0	0	0	0	0	0	.000	.000	.000	0	-97	-0	0			.000	0	H	0.0
1918	Phi-N	11	8	0	1	1	0	0	0	0	4	.125	.125	.250	375	13	-1	0			.800	1	/P-8,O-1(0-0-1)	0.0

YEAR	TM/L	G	AB	R	H	2B	3B	HR	RBI	BB	SO	AVG	OBP	SLG	OPS	OPS+	BR+	SB	CS	SBR	FA	FR	G/POS	TPR
1928	Chi-N	2	3	0	0	0	0	0	0	0	0	.000	.000	.000	0	-99	-1	0			1.000	0	/P-2	0.0
Total	5	56	74	4	10	2	1	0	1	0	25	.135	.135	.189	324	-4	-10	0			.917	2	/P-48,O-1(0-0-1)	0.0
■ **RON TINGLEY**	Tingley, Ronald Irvin b: 5/27/59, Presque Isle, Maine BR/TR, 6'2", 194 lbs. Deb: 9/25/82																							
1982	SD-N	8	20	0	2	0	0	0	0	0	7	.100	.100	.100	200	-46	-4	0	0	0	.957	3	/C-8	-0.1
1988	Cle-A	9	24	1	4	0	0	1	2	2	8	.167	.231	.292	522	44	-2	0	0	0	1.000	3	/C-9	0.2
1989	Cal-A	4	3	0	1	0	0	0	0	1	0	.333	.500	.333	833	142	0	0	0	0	.889	0	/C-4	0.1
1990	Cal-A	5	3	0	0	0	0	0	0	1	1	.000	.250	.000	250	-25	-0	0	0	0	1.000	1	/C-5	0.0
1991	Cal-A	45	115	11	23	7	0	1	13	8	34	.200	.258	.287	545	51	-8	1	1	-0	.988	10	C-45	0.4
1992	Cal-A	71	127	15	25	2	1	3	8	13	35	.197	.282	.299	581	62	-6	0	1	-0	.987	11	C-69	0.7
1993	Cal-A	58	90	7	18	7	0	0	12	9	22	.200	.280	.278	558	49	-6	1	2	-0	.995	9	C-58	0.4
1994	Fla-N	19	52	4	9	3	1	1	2	5	18	.173	.246	.327	573	46	-4	0	0	0	.990	2	C-18	-0.1
	Chi-A	5	5	0	0	0	0	0	0	0	2	.000	.000	.000	0	-99	-1	0	0	0	1.000	1	/C-5	0.0
1995	Det-A	54	124	14	28	8	1	4	18	15	38	.226	.309	.403	713	84	-3	0	1	-0	.991	-5	C-53/1-1	-0.6
Total	9	278	563	52	110	27	3	10	55	54	165	.195	.271	.307	578	56	-35	2	5	-1	.989	36	C-274/1-1	1.0
■ **JOE TINKER**	Tinker, Joseph Bert b: 7/27/1880, Muscotah, Kan. d: 7/27/48, Orlando, Fla. BR/TR, 5'9", 175 lbs. Deb: 4/17/02 MH																							
1902	Chi-N	133	501	55	132	19	5	2	55	26		.263	.300	.333	633	98	-2	27			.908	10	*S-126/3-8	1.2
1903	Chi-N	124	460	67	134	21	7	2	70	37		.291	.345	.380	726	110	6	27			.906	0	*S-107,3-19	0.9
1904	Chi-N	141	488	55	108	12	13	3	41	29		.221	.268	.318	585	80	-12	41			.925	19	*S-140/O-1(0-0-1)	1.2
1905	Chi-N	149	547	70	135	18	8	2	66	34		.247	.292	.320	612	79	-15	31			.940	17	*S-149	0.7
1906	*Chi-N	148	523	75	122	18	4	1	64	43		.233	.293	.289	581	77	-14	30			**.944**	4	*S-147/3-1	-0.6
1907	*Chi-N	117	402	36	89	11	3	1	36	25		.221	.269	.271	540	65	-17	20			.939	16	*S-113	0.3
1908	*Chi-N	157	548	67	146	22	14	6	68	32		.266	.307	.391	697	117	8	30			**.958**	30	*S-157	5.0
1909	Chi-N	143	516	56	132	26	11	4	57	17		.256	.280	.372	652	100	-4	23			**.940**	20	*S-143	2.3
1910	*Chi-N	134	473	48	136	25	9	3	69	24	35	.288	.322	.397	719	110	3	20			.942	16	*S-132	2.4
1911	Chi-N	144	536	61	149	24	12	4	69	39	31	.278	.327	.390	717	100	-2	30			**.937**	**23**	*S-143	3.1
1912	Chi-N	142	550	80	155	24	7	0	75	38	21	.282	.331	.351	681	87	-11	25			.943	25	*S-142	2.4
1913	Cin-N	110	382	47	121	20	13	1	57	20	26	.317	.352	.445	797	127	12	10			.968	17	*S-101/3-9,M	3.7
1914	Chi-F	126	438	50	112	21	7	2	46	38	30	.256	.317	.349	666	86	-16	19			.947	19	*S-125,M	1.1
1915	Chi-F	31	67	7	18	2	1	0	9	13	5	.269	.387	.328	716	109	0	3			.914	-2	S-16/2-5,3-4,M	-0.1
1916	Chi-N	7	10	0	1	0	0	0	1	1	1	.100	.182	.100	282	-11	-1	0			.909	-0	/S-4,3-2,M	-0.2
Total	15	1806	6441	774	1690	263	114	31	783	416	149	.262	.308	.353	661	95	-64	336			.938	214	*S-1745/3-43,2-5,O	23.4
■ **LEE TINSLEY**	Tinsley, Lee Owen b: 3/4/69, Shelbyville, Ky. BB/TR, 5'10", 185 lbs. Deb: 4/6/93																							
1993	Sea-A	11	19	2	3	1	0	1	2	2	9	.158	.238	.368	607	60	-1	0	0	0	.900	-1	/O-6(5-1-1),D-2	-0.2
1994	Bos-A	78	144	27	32	4	0	2	14	19	36	.222	.317	.292	609	56	-9	13	0	3	.991	-5	O-60(27-26-11),D-10	-1.2
1995	*Bos-A	100	341	61	97	17	1	7	41	39	74	.284	.360	.402	761	95	-2	18	8	1	.979	0	O-97(0-97-0)	0.0
1996	Phi-N	31	52	1	7	0	0	0	2	4	22	.135	.196	.135	331	-11	-8	2	4	-1	.960	-4	O-22(18-7-0)	-1.4
	Bos-A	92	192	28	47	6	1	3	14	13	56	.245	.300	.333	633	59	-12	6	8	-1	.993	-6	O-83(4-79-0)	-1.8
1997	Sea-A	49	122	12	24	6	2	0	6	11	34	.197	.263	.279	542	42	-10	2	0	0	1.000	-1	O-41(34-6-2)/D-5	-1.1
Total	5	361	870	131	210	34	4	13	79	88	231	.241	.314	.334	648	66	-43	41	20	2	.985	-18	O-309(88-216-14)/D-17	-5.7
■ **JIM TIPPER**	Tipper, James b: 6/18/1849, Middletown, Conn. d: 4/21/1895, New Haven, Conn. 5'5.5", 148 lbs. Deb: 4/26/1872																							
1872	Man-n	24	112	23	31	5	1	0	15	0	0	.277	.277	.339	616	94	-0	0	0	0	.778	-1	O-19(19-0-0)/3-5	0.0
1874	Har-n	45	197	36	60	8	0	0	19	1	7	.305	.308	.345	653	104	0	0	1	-0	.812	-1	*O-45(45-0-0)	0.0
1875	NH-n	41	159	10	25	1	0	0	4	1	6	.157	.162	.164	326	16	-11	1	0	0	.790	-3	O-41(8-32-3)	-1.2
Total	3 n	110	468	69	116	14	1	0	38	2	13	.248	.251	.282	533	76	-12	1	1	-0	.799	-5	O-105(72-32-3)/3-5	-1.2
■ **ERIC TIPTON**	Tipton, Eric Gordon "Dukie" or "Blue Devil" b: 4/20/15, Petersburg, Va. BR/TR, 5'11", 190 lbs. Deb: 6/9/39																							
1939	Phi-A	47	104	12	24	4	2	1	14	13	7	.231	.316	.337	653	68	-5	2	0	0	.942	-5	O-34(33-0-2)	-1.0
1940	Phi-A	2	8	2	1	0	1	0	0	1	1	.125	.222	.375	597	53	-1	0	0	0	1.000	-0	/O-2(2-0-0)	-0.1
1941	Phi-A	1	4	0	2	0	0	0	0	0	0	.500	.500	.500	1000	169	0	0	0	0	1.000	-0	/O-1(1-0-0)	0.0
1942	Cin-N	63	207	22	46	5	5	4	18	25	14	.222	.309	.353	662	94	-2	1			.977	-1	O-58(38-20-1)	-0.6
1943	Cin-N	140	493	82	142	26	7	9	49	85	36	.288	.395	.424	819	138	27	1			.984	-1	*O-139(139-0-0)	1.9
1944	Cin-N	140	479	62	144	28	3	3	36	59	32	.301	.380	.390	770	121	15	5			.983	3	*O-139(139-0-0)	1.0
1945	Cin-N	108	331	32	80	17	1	5	34	40	37	.242	.327	.344	671	89	-5	11			.970	-1	O-83(83-0-0)	-1.1
Total	7	501	1626	212	439	80	19	22	151	223	127	.270	.360	.383	744	112	31	20	0		.977	-6	O-456(435-20-3)	0.1
■ **JOE TIPTON**	Tipton, Joe Hicks b: 2/18/22, McCaysville, Ga. d: 3/1/94, Birmingham, Ala. BR/TR, 5'11", 185 lbs. Deb: 5/2/48																							
1948	*Cle-A	47	90	11	26	3	0	1	13	4	10	.289	.333	.356	689	85	-2	0	0	0	.971	0	C-40	0.0
1949	Chi-A	67	191	20	39	5	3	3	19	27	17	.204	.306	.309	615	65	-10	1	1	-0	.992	2	C-53	-0.5
1950	Phi-A	64	184	15	49	5	1	6	20	19	16	.266	.335	.402	737	90	-3	0	0	0	.987	-4	C-59	-0.4
1951	Phi-A	72	213	23	51	9	0	3	20	51	25	.239	.389	.324	713	92	0	1	1	-0	.969	2	C-72	0.6
1952	Phi-A	23	68	6	13	4	0	3	8	15	10	.191	.337	.382	720	94	-0	0	0	0	.990	-2	C-23	-0.1
	Cle-A	43	105	15	26	2	0	6	22	21	21	.248	.383	.438	821	137	6	1	0	0	.971	-8	C-35	-0.1
	Yr	66	173	21	39	6	0	9	30	36	31	.225	.365	.416	781	119	5	1	0	0	.979	-11	C-58	-0.2
1953	Cle-A	47	109	17	25	2	0	6	13	19	13	.229	.359	.413	772	111	2	0	0	0	1.000	-7	C-46	-0.3
1954	Was-A	54	157	9	35	6	1	1	10	30	30	.223	.354	.293	647	83	-2	0	1	-0	.992	3	C-52	0.3
Total	7	417	1117	116	264	36	5	29	125	186	142	.236	.351	.355	706	91	-10	3	3	-0	.984	-14	C-380	-0.5
■ **TOM TISCHINSKI**	Tischinski, Thomas Arthur b: 7/12/44, Kansas City, Mo. BR/TR, 5'10", 190 lbs. Deb: 4/11/69																							
1969	Min-A	37	47	2	9	0	0	0	2	8	8	.191	.309	.191	501	42	-3	0	0	0	1.000	0	C-32	-0.3
1970	Min-A	24	46	6	9	0	0	1	2	9	6	.196	.327	.261	588	63	-2	0	0	0	.990	1	C-22	0.0
1971	Min-A	21	23	0	3	2	0	0	2	1	4	.130	.200	.217	417	18	-3	0	0	0	.982	3	C-21	0.1
Total	3	82	116	8	21	2	0	1	6	18	18	.181	.296	.224	520	46	-8	0	0	0	.992	4	/C-75	-0.2
■ **JOHN TITUS**	Titus, John Franklin "Silent John" b: 2/21/1876, St.Clair, Pa. d: 1/8/43, St.Clair, Pa. BL/TL, 5'9", 156 lbs. Deb: 6/8/03																							
1903	Phi-N	72	280	38	80	15	6	2	34	19		.286	.340	.404	744	115	5	5			.952	3	O-72(34-2-36)	0.4
1904	Phi-N	146	504	60	148	25	5	4	55	46		.294	.362	.387	749	136	22	15			.952	8	*O-140(105-2-33)	2.4
1905	Phi-N	147	548	99	169	36	14	2	89	69		.308	.397	.436	834	154	39	11			.962	9	*O-147(0-0-147)	4.1
1906	Phi-N	145	484	67	129	22	5	1	57	78		.267	.378	.339	717	124	17	12			.974	7	*O-142(0-8-134)	2.0
1907	Phi-N	145	523	72	144	23	12	3	63	47		.275	.345	.382	728	130	18	9			.928	-5	*O-142(0-0-142)	0.8
1908	Phi-N	149	539	75	154	24	5	2	48	53		.286	.365	.360	725	127	18	27			.963	-3	*O-149(0-0-149)	1.0
1909	Phi-N	151	540	69	146	22	6	3	46	66		.270	.367	.350	717	121	16	23			.971	5	*O-149(0-0-149)	1.6
1910	Phi-N	143	535	91	129	26	5	3	35	93	44	.241	.358	.325	683	96	0	20			.976	1	*O-142(1-0-142)	-0.5
1911	Phi-N	76	236	35	67	14	1	8	26	32	16	.284	.372	.453	825	129	9	3			.979	-1	O-60(1-0-59)	0.5
1912	Phi-N	45	157	43	43	9	5	3	22	33	14	.274	.403	.452	855	125	6	6			.917	-7	O-42(0-0-42)	-0.3
	Bos-N	96	345	56	112	23	6	2	48	49	20	.325	.422	.443	865	134	19	5			.965	-5	O-96(1-0-96)	0.9
	Yr	141	502	99	155	32	11	5	70	82	34	.309	.416	.446	862	131	25	11			.952	-11	*O-138(1-0-138)	0.6
1913	Bos-N	87	269	33	80	14	2	5	38	35	22	.297	.392	.420	812	129	12	4			.919	-7	O-75(0-0-75)	0.1
Total	11	1402	4960	738	1401	253	72	38	561	620	116	.282	.373	.385	758	127	181	140			.959	7	*O-1356(142-12-1204)	13.0
■ **JIM TOBIN**	Tobin, James Anthony "Abba Dabba" b: 12/27/12, Oakland, Cal. d: 5/19/69, Oakland, Cal. BR/TR, 6', 185 lbs. Deb: 4/30/37 F																							
1937	Pit-N	21	34	7	15	4	0	0	6	4	3	.441	.500	.559	1059	187	4	0			.938	-2	P-20	0.0
1938	Pit-N	56	103	8	25	6	1	0	11	9	12	.243	.310	.320	630	73	-4	0			**1.000**	-2	P-40	0.0
1939	Pit-N	43	74	9	18	3	1	2	11	2	12	.243	.263	.392	655	75	-3	0			1.000	-1	P-25	0.0
1940	Bos-N	20	43	5	12	3	0	0	3	1	10	.279	.295	.349	644	82	-1	0			.957	-1	P-15	0.0
1941	Bos-N	43	103	6	19	5	0	0	9	10	31	.184	.257	.233	490	40	-8	1			.966	4	P-33	0.0
1942	Bos-N	47	114	14	28	2	0	6	15	16	23	.246	.344	.421	765	126	4	0			.947	6	P-37	0.0
1943	Bos-N	46	107	8	30	4	0	2	12	6	16	.280	.319	.374	692	101	-0	0			.927	2	P-33/1-1	0.0

YEAR	TM/L	G	AB	R	H	2B	3B	HR	RBI	BB	SO	AVG	OBP	SLG	OPS	OPS+	BR+	SB	CS	SBR	FA	FR	G/POS	TPR
1944	Bos-N★	62	116	13	22	5	1	2	18	16	28	.190	.288	.302	590	63	-6	0			.972	7	P-43	0.0
1945	Bos-N	41	77	9	11	3	0	3	12	15	22	.143	.290	.299	589	64	-4	0			**1.000**	4	P-27	0.0
	*Det-A	17	25	2	3	0	0	2	5	1	5	.120	.154	.360	514	44	-2	0	0	0	.950	1	P-14	0.0
Total	9	396	796	81	183	35	3	17	102	80	162	.230	.303	.345	648	82	-20	1	0		.965	17	P-287/1-1	0.0
■ JOHNNY TOBIN Tobin, John Martin "Tip" b: 9/15/06, Jamaica Plain, Mass. d: 8/6/83, Rhinebeck, N.Y. BR/TR, 6'3", 187 lbs. Deb: 9/22/32																								
1932	NY-N	1	1	0	0	0	0	0	0	0	0	.000	.000	.000	0	-99	-0	0			.000	0	H	0.0
■ JOHNNY TOBIN Tobin, John Patrick "Jackie" b: 1/8/21, Oakland, Cal. d: 1/18/82, Oakland, Cal. BL/TR, 6', 165 lbs. Deb: 4/20/45 F																								
1945	Bos-A	84	278	25	70	6	2	0	21	26	24	.252	.320	.288	608	75	-8	2	6	-2	.951	9	3-72/2-5,O-1(0-1-0)	0.0
■ JACK TOBIN Tobin, John Thomas b: 5/4/1892, St.Louis, Mo. d: 12/10/69, St.Louis, Mo. BL/TL, 5'8", 142 lbs. Deb: 4/16/14 C Career OF: (220-LF 137-CF 1139-RF)																								
1914	StL-F	139	529	81	143	24	10	7	35	51	53	.270	.340	.393	733	94	-12	20			.952	5	*O-132(12-7-113)	-1.4
1915	StL-F	158	625	92	**184**	26	13	6	51	68	42	.294	.366	.406	773	111	2	31			.965	3	*O-158(0-31-128)	-0.4
1916	StL-A	77	150	16	32	4	1	0	10	12	13	.213	.272	.253	525	61	-7	7			.842	-9	O-41(0-6-35)	-2.0
1918	StL-A	122	480	59	133	19	5	0	36	48	26	.277	.349	.338	686	111	7	13			.971	-1	*O-122(43-78-1)	-0.2
1919	StL-A	127	486	54	159	22	7	6	57	36	24	.327	.376	.438	814	125	15	8			.953	2	*O-123(123-0-0)	1.2
1920	StL-A	147	593	94	202	34	10	4	62	39	23	.341	.383	.452	835	117	14	21	13	0	.960	5	*O-147(34-0-113)	1.0
1921	StL-A	150	671	132	236	31	**18**	8	59	45	22	.352	.395	.487	882	117	17	7	12	-3	.956	8	*O-150(0-8-143)	1.0
1922	StL-A	146	625	122	207	34	8	13	66	56	22	.331	.388	.474	862	119	18	7	9	-2	.940	-8	*O-145(0-1-144)	-0.4
1923	StL-A	151	637	91	202	32	15	13	73	42	13	.317	.363	.476	839	113	10	8	7	-1	.969	-8	*O-151(0-0-151)	-1.1
1924	StL-A	136	569	87	170	30	8	2	48	50	12	.299	.357	.390	748	87	-11	6	10	-2	.957	2	*O-132(1-1-130)	-2.0
1925	StL-A	77	193	25	58	11	0	2	27	9	5	.301	.335	.389	724	79	-6	8	2	1	1.000	-5	O-39(1-1-38)/1-3	-1.3
1926	Was-A	27	33	5	7	0	1	0	3	0	0	.212	.212	.273	485	26	-4	0	0	0	1.000	-2	/O-7(0-4-3)	-0.5
	Bos-A	51	209	26	57	9	0	1	14	16	3	.273	.324	.330	655	73	-8	6	5	-0	.966	-3	O-51(1-0-51)	-1.6
	Yr	78	242	31	64	9	1	1	17	16	3	.264	.310	.322	632	67	-12	6	5	-0	.970	-5	O-58(1-4-54)	-2.1
1927	Bos-A	111	374	52	116	18	3	2	40	36	9	.310	.371	.390	761	100	0	5	4	-0	.947	-5	O-93(5-0-89)	-1.2
Total	13	1619	6174	936	1906	294	99	64	581	508	267	.309	.364	.420	784	106	34	147	62		.957	-14	*O-1491R/1-3	-8.9
■ BILL TOBIN Tobin, William F. b: 10/10/1854, Hartford, Conn. d: 10/10/12, Hartford, Conn. BL, Deb: 7/21/1880																								
1880	Wor-N	5	16	1	2	0	0	0	3	0	5	.125	.125	.125	250	-14	-2				1.000	-0	/1-5	-0.2
	Tro-N	33	136	14	22	1	1	0	8	4	20	.162	.186	.184	370	24	-10				.950	-1	1-33	-1.2
	Yr	38	152	15	24	1	1	0	11	4	25	.158	.179	.178	357	20	-12				.958	-1	1-38	-1.4
■ JORGE TOCA Toca, Jorge Luis b: 1/7/75, Remedios, Cuba BR/TR, 6'3", 220 lbs. Deb: 9/12/99																								
1999	NY-N	4	3	0	1	0	0	0	0	0	2	.333	.333	.333	667	72	-0	0	0	0	1.000	0	/1-1	0.0
2000	NY-N	8	7	1	3	1	0	0	4	0	1	.429	.429	.571	1000	155	1	0	0	0	1.000	-1	/1-5,O-1(1-0-0)	0.0
Total	2	12	10	1	4	1	0	0	4	0	3	.400	.400	.500	900	130	0	0	0	0	1.000	-1	/1-6,O-1(1-0-0)	0.0
■ AL TODD Todd, Alfred Chester b: 1/7/02, Troy, N.Y. d: 3/8/85, Elmira, N.Y. BR/TR, 6'1", 198 lbs. Deb: 4/25/32																								
1932	Phi-N	33	70	8	16	5	0	0	9	1	9	.229	.260	.300	560	45	-5	1			.899	-4	C-25	-0.9
1933	Phi-N	73	136	13	28	4	0	0	10	4	18	.206	.239	.235	475	32	-12	1			.983	5	C-34/O-2(2-0-0)	-0.6
1934	Phi-N	91	302	33	96	22	2	4	41	10	39	.318	.344	.444	788	96	-2	3			.976	-2	C-82	0.1
1935	Phi-N	107	328	40	95	18	3	3	42	19	35	.290	.334	.390	725	85	-7	3			.968	-12	C-87	-1.3
1936	Pit-N	76	267	28	73	10	5	2	28	11	24	.273	.307	.371	678	80	-8	4			.976	1	C-70	-0.2
1937	Pit-N	133	514	51	158	18	10	8	86	16	36	.307	.330	.428	758	104	1	2			.972	-2	*C-128	0.8
1938	Pit-N	133	491	52	130	19	7	7	75	18	31	.265	.296	.375	671	83	-13	2			.985	10	*C-132	0.6
1939	Bro-N	86	245	28	68	10	0	5	32	13	16	.278	.317	.380	696	83	-6	1			.985	8	C-73	0.6
1940	Chi-N	104	381	31	97	13	2	6	42	11	29	.255	.283	.346	629	74	-14	1			.984	-6	*C-104	-1.4
1941	Chi-N	6	6	1	1	0	0	0	0	0	1	.167	.167	.167	333	-6	-1	0			.000	0	H	-0.1
1943	Chi-N	21	45	1	6	0	0	0	1	1	5	.133	.152	.133	286	-17	-7	0			.986	4	C-17	-0.3
Total	11	863	2785	286	768	119	29	35	366	104	243	.276	.307	.377	684	82	-72	18			.977	1	C-752/O-2(2-0-0)	-2.7
■ PHIL TODT Todt, Philip Julius "Hook" b: 8/9/01, St.Louis, Mo. d: 11/15/73, St.Louis, Mo. BL/TL, 6', 175 lbs. Deb: 4/25/24																								
1924	Bos-A	52	103	17	27	8	2	1	14	6	9	.262	.309	.408	717	84	-3	0	1	-0	.983	-3	1-18/O-4(0-2-2)	-0.7
1925	Bos-A	141	544	62	151	29	13	11	75	44	29	.278	.333	.439	782	97	-4	3	2	-0	.991	3	*1-140	-1.0
1926	Bos-A	154	599	56	153	19	12	7	69	40	38	.255	.306	.362	669	76	-23	3	2	-0	.988	10	*1-154	-2.2
1927	Bos-A	140	516	55	122	22	6	6	52	28	23	.236	.280	.337	617	61	-32	6	2	1	.991	9	*1-139	-3.0
1928	Bos-A	144	539	61	136	31	8	12	73	26	47	.252	.290	.406	697	83	-16	6	5	-0	**.997**	3	*1-144	-2.2
1929	Bos-A	153	534	49	140	38	10	4	64	31	28	.262	.305	.393	698	80	-17	6	7	-1	.991	3	*1-153	-2.4
1930	Bos-A	111	383	49	103	22	5	11	62	24	33	.269	.312	.439	751	92	-7	4	1	1	.993	3	*1-104	-0.9
1931	*Phi-A	62	197	23	48	14	2	5	44	8	22	.244	.273	.411	684	73	-9	1	1	-0	.995	-4	1-52	-1.6
Total	8	957	3415	372	880	183	58	57	453	207	229	.258	.305	.395	700	81	-111	29	21	-1	.992	24	1-904/O-4(0-2-2)	-14.0
■ BOBBY TOLAN Tolan, Robert b: 11/19/45, Los Angeles, Cal. BL/TL, 5'11", 170 lbs. Deb: 9/3/65 C Career OF: (131-LF 561-CF 348-RF)																								
1965	StL-N	17	69	8	13	2	0	0	6	0	4	.188	.200	.217	417	16	-7	2	1	0	.970	-1	O-17(0-0-17)	-1.0
1966	StL-N	43	93	10	16	5	1	1	6	6	15	.172	.238	.280	517	43	-7	1	1	-0	.952	-1	O-26(10-0-16)/1-1	-1.1
1967	*StL-N	110	265	35	67	7	3	6	32	19	43	.253	.313	.370	682	96	-2	12	7	0	.992	-9	O-80(6-54-25),1-13	-1.5
1968	*StL-N	92	278	28	64	12	1	5	17	13	42	.230	.272	.335	607	82	-7	9	5	0	.967	-2	O-67(2-9-57)/1-9	-1.4
1969	Cin-N	152	637	104	194	25	10	21	93	27	92	.305	.348	.474	822	122	17	26	12	2	.974	11	*O-150(0-88-62)	2.4
1970	*Cin-N	152	589	112	186	34	6	16	80	62	94	.316	.388	.475	864	130	25	**57**	20	6	.978	8	*O-150(0-150-0)	3.4
1972	*Cin-N	149	604	88	171	28	5	8	82	44	88	.283	.338	.386	724	112	8	42	15	4	.990	13	*O-149(0-149-0)	2.2
1973	Cin-N	129	457	42	94	14	2	9	51	27	68	.206	.255	.304	559	57	-28	15	10	-0	.966	-4	*O-120(0-76-65)	-3.8
1974	SD-N	95	357	45	95	16	1	8	40	20	41	.266	.321	.384	705	101	-1	7	9	-2	.971	-2	O-88(1-9-81)	-0.9
1975	SD-N	147	506	58	129	19	4	5	43	28	45	.255	.307	.338	645	84	-12	11	13	-2	.971	-2	*O-120(90-16-19),1-27	-2.5
1976	*Phi-N	110	272	32	71	7	0	5	35	7	39	.261	.290	.342	632	76	-9	10	5	0	.992	-12	1-50,O-35(20-10-5)	-2.7
1977	Phi-N	15	16	1	2	0	0	0	1	1	4	.125	.176	.125	301	-17	-3	0	0	0	.944	-0	/1-5	-0.3
	Pit-N	49	74	7	15	4	0	2	9	4	10	.203	.244	.338	581	53	-5	1	1	-0	1.000	-0	1-20/O-2(2-0-0)	-0.6
	Yr	64	90	8	17	4	0	2	10	5	14	.189	.232	.300	532	40	-8	1	1	-0	.992	-0	1-25/O-2(2-0-0)	-0.9
1979	SD-N	22	21	2	4	0	1	0	2	0	2	.190	.190	.286	476	30	-2	0	0	0	1.000	-0	/1-5,O-1(0-0-1)	-0.2
Total	13	1282	4238	572	1121	173	34	86	497	258	587	.265	.317	.382	699	96	-31	193	100	7	.976	-1	*O-1005C,1-130	-8.0
■ JOSE TOLENTINO Tolentino, Jose (Franco) b: 6/3/61, Mexico City, Mexico BL/TL, 6'1", 195 lbs. Deb: 7/28/91																								
1991	Hou-N	44	54	6	14	4	0	1	6	4	9	.259	.310	.389	699	101	-0	0	0	0	.982	1	1-10/O-1(1-0-0)	0.1
■ WAYNE TOLLESON Tolleson, Jimmy Wayne b: 11/22/55, Spartanburg, S.C. BB/TR, 5'9", 160 lbs. Deb: 9/1/81 Career OF: (1-LF 2-CF 0-RF)																								
1981	Tex-A	14	24	6	4	0	0	0	1	1	5	.167	.200	.167	367	7	-3	2	0	0	1.000	-1	/3-6,S-2	-0.3
1982	Tex-A	38	70	6	8	1	0	0	2	5	14	.114	.173	.129	302	-16	-11	1	1	-0	.958	5	S-26/3-4,2-1	-0.4
1983	Tex-A	134	470	64	122	13	2	3	20	40	68	.260	.320	.315	635	77	-14	33	10	4	.972	-10	*2-112,S-26/D-1	-1.2
1984	Tex-A	118	338	35	72	9	2	0	9	27	47	.213	.277	.251	529	46	-24	22	4	3	.979	-7	*2-109/S-7,3-5,OD	-2.2
1985	Tex-A	123	323	45	101	9	5	1	18	21	46	.313	.355	.381	735	100	0	21	12	0	.972	-4	S-81,2-29,3-12,/D-6	0.5
1986	Chi-A	81	260	39	65	7	3	3	29	38	43	.250	.346	.335	680	84	-5	13	6	1	.955	-10	3-65,S-18/O-2L,D-2	-1.4
	NY-A	60	215	22	61	9	2	0	14	14	33	.284	.333	.344	678	86	-4	4	4	1	.981	6	S-56/3-7,2-3	0.7
	Yr	141	475	61	126	16	5	3	43	52	76	.265	.340	.339	679	85	-9	17	10	0	.981	-4	S-74,3-72/2-3,OD	-0.7
1987	NY-A	121	349	48	77	4	0	1	22	43	72	.221	.306	.241	547	48	-25	5	3	0	.970	-3	*S-119/3-3	-1.5
1988	NY-A	21	59	8	15	2	0	0	5	8	12	.254	.343	.288	631	79	-1	1	0	0	.981	6	2-12,3-10/S-1	0.5
1989	NY-A	80	140	16	23	5	2	1	9	16	23	.164	.255	.250	505	43	-10	5	1	1	.912	10	3-28,S-28,2-13,D-10	0.1
1990	NY-A	73	74	12	11	1	1	0	4	6	21	.149	.213	.189	402	13	-9	1	0	0	.983	15	S-45,2-13/3-3,D-5	0.8
Total	10	863	2322	301	559	60	17	9	133	219	384	.241	.308	.293	601	66	-106	108	41	9	.974	7	S-409,2-292,3/DO	-4.4
■ TIM TOLMAN Tolman, Timothy Lee b: 4/20/56, Santa Monica, Cal. BR/TR, 6', 195 lbs. Deb: 9/9/81 Career OF: (19-LF 0-CF 16-RF)																								
1981	Hou-N	4	8	0	1	0	0	0	0	0	0	.125	.125	.125	250	-30	-1	0	0	0	1.000	-1	/O-3(3-0-1)	-0.3

YEAR	TM/L	G	AB	R	H	2B	3B	HR	RBI	BB	SO	AVG	OBP	SLG	OPS	OPS+	BR+	SB	CS	SBR	FA	FR	G/POS	TPR
1982	Hou-N	15	26	4	5	2	0	1	3	4	3	.192	.300	.385	685	98	-0	0	0	0	1.000	-0	/O-5(4-0-1),1-1	-0.1
1983	Hou-N	43	56	4	11	4	0	2	10	6	9	.196	.274	.375	649	83	-2	0	1	-0	1.000	-2	/1-7,O-3(3-0-0)	-0.4
1984	Hou-N	14	17	2	3	1	0	0	0	0	3	.176	.176	.235	412	16	-2	0	0	0	1.000	-0	/O-3(1-0-2),1-1	-0.3
1985	Hou-N	31	43	4	6	1	0	2	8	1	10	.140	.178	.302	480	33	-4	0	1	-0	1.000	-1	/O-9(6-0-3),1-6	-0.6
1986	Det-A	16	34	4	6	1	0	0	2	6	4	.176	.300	.206	506	41	-3	1	1	-0	1.000	-1	/O-4(0-0-4),1-3,D-9	-0.4
1987	Det-A	9	12	3	1	1	0	0	1	7	2	.083	.450	.167	617	77	0	0	0	0	1.000	-1	/O-7(2-0-5),D-2	-0.1
Total	7	132	196	21	33	10	0	5	24	24	31	.168	.266	.296	562	58	-11	1	3	-1	1.000	-6	/O-34L,1-18,D-11	-2.2

■ CHICK TOLSON
Tolson, Charles Julius "Toby" b: 11/6/1898, Washington, D.C. d: 4/16/65, Washington, D.C. BR/TR, 6', 185 lbs. Deb: 7/3/25

YEAR	TM/L	G	AB	R	H	2B	3B	HR	RBI	BB	SO	AVG	OBP	SLG	OPS	OPS+	BR+	SB	CS	SBR	FA	FR	G/POS	TPR
1925	Cle-A	3	12	0	3	0	0	0	0	2	1	.250	.357	.250	607	56	-1	0	0	0	1.000	0	/1-3	-0.1
1926	Chi-N	57	80	4	25	6	1	1	8	5	8	.313	.353	.450	803	113	1	0			.991	0	1-13	0.1
1927	Chi-N	39	54	6	16	4	0	2	17	4	9	.296	.345	.481	826	119	1	0			1.000	0	/1-8	0.1
1929	*Chi-N	32	109	13	28	5	0	1	19	9	16	.257	.325	.330	655	63	-6	0			.978	-2	1-31	-0.9
1930	Chi-N	13	20	0	6	1	0	0	1	6	5	.300	.462	.350	812	99	0	1			.979	1	/1-5	0.1
Total	5	144	275	23	78	16	1	4	45	26	39	.284	.350	.393	743	90	-4	1	0		.985	-1	/1-60	-0.7

■ ANDY TOMBERLIN
Tomberlin, Andy Lee b: 11/7/66, Monroe, N.C. BL/TL, 5'11", 160 lbs. Deb: 8/12/93 Career OF: (30-LF 18-CF 37-RF)

YEAR	TM/L	G	AB	R	H	2B	3B	HR	RBI	BB	SO	AVG	OBP	SLG	OPS	OPS+	BR+	SB	CS	SBR	FA	FR	G/POS	TPR
1993	Pit-N	27	42	4	12	0	1	1	5	2	14	.286	.333	.405	738	97	-0	0	0	0	1.000	-0	/O-7(6-0-1)	-0.1
1994	Bos-A	18	36	1	7	0	1	1	1	6	12	.194	.310	.333	643	63	-2	1	0	0	1.000	-0	O-11(5-0-6)/P-1,D-5	-0.2
1995	Oak-A	46	85	15	18	0	0	4	10	5	22	.212	.256	.353	608	60	-5	4	1	1	.979	-9	O-42(5-18-20)/D-2	-1.3
1996	NY-N	63	66	12	17	4	0	3	10	9	27	.258	.355	.455	810	117	2	0	0	0	1.000	-4	O-17(9-0-8)/1-1	-0.2
1997	NY-N	6	7	0	2	0	0	0	0	1	3	.286	.375	.286	661	79	-0	0	0	0	1.000	-0	/O-2(1-0-1)	-0.1
1998	Det-A	32	69	8	15	2	0	2	12	3	25	.217	.280	.333	613	58	-4	1	0	0	1.000	-1	D-22/O-5(4-0-1)	-0.6
Total	6	192	305	40	71	6	2	11	38	26	103	.233	.304	.374	677	77	-10	6	1	1	.989	-15	/O-84R,D-29,1-1,P-1	-2.5

■ GEORGE TOMER
Tomer, George Clarence b: 11/26/1895, Perry, Iowa d: 12/15/84, Perry, Iowa BL/TR, 6', 180 lbs. Deb: 9/17/13

YEAR	TM/L	G	AB	R	H	2B	3B	HR	RBI	BB	SO	AVG	OBP	SLG	OPS	OPS+	BR+	SB	CS	SBR	FA	FR	G/POS	TPR
1913	StL-A	1	1	0	0	0	0	0	0	0	1	.000	.000	.000	0	-99	-0	0			.000	0	H	0.0

■ PHIL TOMNEY
Tomney, Philip Howard "Buster" b: 7/17/1863, Reading, Pa. d: 3/18/1892, Reading, Pa. BR/TR, 5'7", 155 lbs. Deb: 9/7/1888

YEAR	TM/L	G	AB	R	H	2B	3B	HR	RBI	BB	SO	AVG	OBP	SLG	OPS	OPS+	BR+	SB	CS	SBR	FA	FR	G/POS	TPR
1888	Lou-a	34	120	15	18	3	0	0	4	7		.150	.197	.175	372	20	-11	11			.882	6	S-34	-0.3
1889	Lou-a	112	376	61	80	8	5	4	38	46	47	.213	.304	.293	596	71	-13	26			.857	27	*S-112	1.4
1890	*Lou-a	108	386	72	107	21	7	1	58	43		.277	.357	.376	733	119	9	27			**.902**	18	*S-108	2.6
Total	3	254	882	148	205	32	12	5	100	96	47	.232	.313	.313	626	86	-14	64			.878	50	S-254	3.7

■ TONY TONNEMAN
Tonneman, Charles Richard b: 9/10/1881, Chicago, Ill. d: 8/7/51, Prescott, Ariz. BR/TR, 5'10.5", 175 lbs. Deb: 9/19/11

YEAR	TM/L	G	AB	R	H	2B	3B	HR	RBI	BB	SO	AVG	OBP	SLG	OPS	OPS+	BR+	SB	CS	SBR	FA	FR	G/POS	TPR
1911	Bos-A	2	5	0	1	1	0	0	3	1		.200	.333	.400	733	105	0	0			.900	1	/C-2	0.1

■ BERT TOOLEY
Tooley, Albert R. b: 8/30/1886, Howell, Mich. d: 8/17/76, Marshall, Mich. BR/TR, 5'10", 155 lbs. Deb: 4/12/11

YEAR	TM/L	G	AB	R	H	2B	3B	HR	RBI	BB	SO	AVG	OBP	SLG	OPS	OPS+	BR+	SB	CS	SBR	FA	FR	G/POS	TPR
1911	Bro-N	119	433	55	89	11	3	1	29	53	63	.206	.295	.252	547	56	-25	18			.925	-8	*S-114	-2.6
1912	Bro-N	77	265	34	62	6	5	2	37	19	21	.234	.285	.317	602	67	-13	12			.885	-15	S-76	-2.3
Total	2	196	698	89	151	17	8	3	66	72	84	.216	.291	.277	568	60	-37	30			.909	-24	S-190	-4.9

■ SPECS TOPORCER
Toporcer, George b: 2/9/1899, New York, N.Y. d: 5/17/89, Huntington Station, N.Y. BL/TR, 5'10.5", 165 lbs. Deb: 4/13/21 Career OF: (0-LF 0-CF 1-RF)

YEAR	TM/L	G	AB	R	H	2B	3B	HR	RBI	BB	SO	AVG	OBP	SLG	OPS	OPS+	BR+	SB	CS	SBR	FA	FR	G/POS	TPR
1921	StL-N	22	53	4	14	1	0	0	2	3	4	.264	.304	.283	587	57	-3	1	0	0	.938	0	2-12/S-2	-0.2
1922	StL-N	116	352	56	114	25	6	3	36	24	18	.324	.370	.455	825	117	8	2	1	0	.939	-23	S-91/3-6,2-1,O-1R	-0.5
1923	StL-N	97	303	45	77	11	3	3	35	41	14	.254	.349	.340	689	84	-6	4	3	-0	.945	-13	2-52,S-33/1-1,3-1	-1.4
1924	StL-N	70	198	30	62	10	3	1	24	11	14	.313	.362	.409	771	108	2	2	3	-1	.974	-16	3-33,S-25/2-3	-1.0
1925	StL-N	83	268	38	76	13	4	2	26	36	15	.284	.373	.384	757	92	-2	7	2	1	.960	-3	S-66/2-7	0.3
1926	*StL-N	64	88	13	22	3	2	0	9	8	9	.250	.327	.330	656	74	-3	1			.983	-9	2-27/S-5,3-1	-1.2
1927	StL-N	86	290	37	72	13	4	0	19	27	16	.248	.314	.321	635	68	-13	5			.980	-11	3-54,S-27/2-2,1-1	-1.8
1928	StL-N	8	14	0	0	0	0	0	0	0	3	.000	.000	.000	0	-98	-4	0			1.000	0	/1-1,2-1	-0.4
Total	8	546	1566	223	437	76	22	9	151	150	93	.279	.347	.373	720	90	-20	22	9		.946	-74	S-249,2-105/3-95,1O	-6.2

■ JEFF TORBORG
Torborg, Jeffrey Allen b: 11/26/41, Plainfield, N.J. BR/TR, 6'0.5", 195 lbs. Deb: 5/10/64 MC

YEAR	TM/L	G	AB	R	H	2B	3B	HR	RBI	BB	SO	AVG	OBP	SLG	OPS	OPS+	BR+	SB	CS	SBR	FA	FR	G/POS	TPR
1964	LA-N	28	43	4	10	1	1	0	4	3	8	.233	.298	.302	600	75	-1	0	0	0	.977	-2	C-27	-0.3
1965	LA-N	56	150	8	36	5	1	3	13	10	26	.240	.292	.347	639	85	-3	0	0	0	.991	4	C-53	0.3
1966	LA-N	46	120	4	27	3	0	1	13	10	23	.225	.285	.275	560	61	-6	0	0	0	.986	6	C-45	0.2
1967	LA-N	76	196	11	42	4	1	2	12	13	31	.214	.267	.276	542	60	-10	1	3	-1	.989	12	C-75	0.4
1968	LA-N	37	93	2	15	2	0	0	4	6	10	.161	.212	.183	395	21	-9	0	0	0	.991	10	C-37	0.3
1969	LA-N	51	124	7	23	4	0	0	7	9	17	.185	.241	.218	458	31	-11	1	0	0	.996	11	C-50	0.1
1970	LA-N	64	134	11	31	8	0	1	17	14	15	.231	.304	.313	617	69	-6	1	1	-0	.983	10	C-63	0.5
1971	Cal-A	55	123	6	25	5	0	0	5	3	6	.203	.222	.244	466	34	-11	0	0	0	.987	5	C-49	-0.5
1972	Cal-A	59	153	5	32	3	0	0	8	14	21	.209	.280	.229	509	56	-8	0	0	0	.998	16	C-58	1.1
1973	Cal-A	102	255	20	56	7	0	1	18	21	32	.220	.279	.259	538	57	-15	0	2	-1	.991	8	*C-102	-0.3
Total	10	574	1391	78	297	42	3	8	101	103	189	.214	.270	.265	535	56	-81	3	6	-1	.990	79	C-559	1.8

■ EARL TORGESON
Torgeson, Clifford Earl "The Earl Of Snohomish" b: 1/1/24, Snohomish, Wash. d: 11/8/90, Everett, Wash. BL/TL, 6'3", 180 lbs. Deb: 4/15/47 C

YEAR	TM/L	G	AB	R	H	2B	3B	HR	RBI	BB	SO	AVG	OBP	SLG	OPS	OPS+	BR+	SB	CS	SBR	FA	FR	G/POS	TPR
1947	Bos-N	128	399	73	112	20	6	16	78	82	59	.281	.403	.481	885	137	24	11			.984	-1	*1-117	1.9
1948	*Bos-N	134	438	70	111	23	5	10	67	81	54	.253	.372	.397	770	110	9	19			.993	1	*1-129	0.6
1949	Bos-N	25	100	17	26	5	1	4	19	13	4	.260	.345	.450	795	118	2	4			.988	-3	1-25	-0.2
1950	Bos-N	156	576	**120**	167	30	3	23	87	119	69	.290	.412	.472	885	141	39	15			.986	-0	*1-156	3.2
1951	Bos-N	155	581	99	153	21	4	24	92	102	70	.263	.375	.437	812	127	24	20	11	1	.988	-1	*1-155	1.8
1952	Bos-N	122	382	49	88	17	0	5	34	81	38	.230	.366	.314	681	94	0	11	7	-0	.989	-1	*1-105/O-5(2-0-3)	-0.5
1953	Phi-N	111	379	58	104	25	8	11	64	53	57	.274	.366	.470	836	117	10	7	1	1	.987	-3	*1-105	0.2
1954	Phi-N	135	490	63	133	22	6	5	54	75	52	.271	.368	.371	740	93	-3	7	1	1	.990	-10	*1-133	-1.9
1955	Phi-N	47	150	29	40	5	3	1	17	32	20	.267	.396	.360	756	104	2	2	3	-1	.995	-1	1-43	-0.2
	Det-A	89	300	58	85	10	1	9	50	61	29	.283	.404	.413	818	123	12	9	0	**2**	.992	-0	1-83	0.9
1956	Det-A	117	318	61	84	9	3	12	42	78	47	.264	.409	.425	834	120	12	6	4	-0	.992	-7	1-83	0.1
1957	Det-A	30	50	5	12	2	1	1	5	12	10	.240	.387	.380	767	108	1	0	0	0	1.000	0	1-17	0.1
	Chi-A	86	251	53	74	11	2	7	46	49	44	.295	.410	.438	848	131	13	7	3	0	.998	-5	1-70/O-1(0-0-1)	0.4
	Yr	116	301	58	86	13	3	8	51	61	54	.286	.406	.429	835	127	14	7	3	0	.999	-5	1-87/O-1(0-0-1)	0.5
1958	Chi-A	96	188	37	50	8	0	10	30	48	29	.266	.415	.468	883	146	14	7	2	1	.978	-2	1-73	1.0
1959	*Chi-A	127	277	40	61	5	3	9	45	62	55	.220	.363	.357	720	100	2	7	6	-1	.983	-6	*1-103	-0.9
1960	Chi-A	68	57	12	15	2	0	2	9	21	8	.263	.462	.404	865	137	5	1	0	0	.983	0	1-10	0.5
1961	Chi-A	20	15	1	1	0	0	0	1	3	5	.067	.222	.067	289	-19	-3	0	0	0	1.000	-0	/1-1	-0.3
	NY-A	22	18	3	2	0	0	0	0	8	3	.111	.385	.111	496	42	-1	0	1	-0	.969	-0	/1-8	-0.2
	Yr	42	33	4	3	0	0	0	1	11	8	.091	.318	.091	409	16	-4	0	1	-0	.970	-0	/1-9	-0.5
Total	15	1668	4969	848	1318	215	46	149	740	980	653	.265	.387	.417	804	118	163	133	39		.989	-39	*1-1416/O-6(2-0-4)	6.5

■ RED TORPHY
Torphy, Walter Anthony b: 11/6/1891, Fall River, Mass. d: 2/11/80, Fall River, Mass. BR/TR, 5'11", 169 lbs. Deb: 9/25/20

YEAR	TM/L	G	AB	R	H	2B	3B	HR	RBI	BB	SO	AVG	OBP	SLG	OPS	OPS+	BR+	SB	CS	SBR	FA	FR	G/POS	TPR
1920	Bos-N	3	15	1	3	2	0	0	2	0	1	.200	.200	.333	533	54	-1	0	0	0	.969	-1	/1-3	-0.2

■ FRANK TORRE
Torre, Frank Joseph b: 12/30/31, Brooklyn, N.Y. BL/TL, 6'3", 205 lbs. Deb: 4/20/56 F

YEAR	TM/L	G	AB	R	H	2B	3B	HR	RBI	BB	SO	AVG	OBP	SLG	OPS	OPS+	BR+	SB	CS	SBR	FA	FR	G/POS	TPR
1956	Mil-N	111	159	17	41	6	0	0	16	11	4	.258	.306	.296	601	67	-7	1	0	0	.993	6	1-89	-0.4
1957	*Mil-N	129	364	46	99	19	5	5	40	29	19	.272	.341	.393	734	104	2	0	0	0	**.996**	1	*1-117	-0.2
1958	*Mil-N	138	372	41	115	22	5	6	55	42	14	.309	.390	.444	833	131	18	2	0	0	**.994**	6	*1-122	1.8
1959	Mil-N	115	263	23	60	15	1	1	33	35	12	.228	.326	.304	630	75	-9	0	0	0	.994	-0	1-87	-1.3
1960	Mil-N	21	44	2	9	1	0	0	5	3	2	.205	.255	.227	483	36	-4	0	0	0	1.000	-1	1-17	-0.6
1962	Phi-N	108	168	13	52	8	2	0	20	24	6	.310	.408	.381	789	117	5	1	1	-0	.980	3	1-76	0.6
1963	Phi-N	92	112	8	28	7	2	1	10	11	7	.250	.333	.375	708	105	1	0	0	0	.989	5	1-56	0.5
Total	7	714	1482	150	404	78	15	13	179	155	64	.273	.352	.372	724	101	6	4	1	1	.993	19	1-564	0.4

YEAR	TM/L	G	AB	R	H	2B	3B	HR	RBI	BB	SO	AVG	OBP	SLG	OPS	OPS+	BR+	SB	CS	SBR	FA	FR	G/POS	TPR
■ JOE TORRE	Torre, Joseph Paul b: 7/18/40, Brooklyn, N.Y. BR/TR, 6'2", 212 lbs. Deb: 9/25/60 FM																							
1960	Mil-N	2	2	0	1	0	0	0	0	0	1	.500	.500	.500	1000	189	0	0	0	0	.000	0	H	0.0
1961	Mil-N	113	406	40	113	21	4	10	42	28	60	.278	.331	.424	755	105	2	3	5	-1	.982	-8	*C-112	-0.2
1962	Mil-N	80	220	23	62	8	1	5	26	24	24	.282	.358	.395	753	105	2	1	0	0	.986	6	C-63	1.1
1963	Mil-N☆	142	501	57	147	19	4	14	71	42	79	.293	.354	.431	785	126	17	1	5	-2	.994	-7	*C-105,1-37/O-2L	1.2
1964	Mil-N★	154	601	87	193	36	5	20	109	36	67	.321	.366	.498	864	140	31	2	4	-1	**.995**	-8	C-96,1-70	2.4
1965	Mil-N★	148	523	68	152	21	1	27	80	61	79	.291	.373	.489	863	140	28	0	1	-0	.991	-6	*C-100,1-49	2.6
1966	Atl-N★	148	546	83	172	20	3	36	101	60	61	.315	.385	.560	945	157	41	0	4	-1	.984	-3	*C-114,1-36	4.2
1967	Atl-N★	135	477	67	132	18	1	20	68	49	75	.277	.348	.444	792	127	16	2	2	-0	.991	-5	*C-114,1-23	1.6
1968	Atl-N	115	424	45	115	11	2	10	55	34	72	.271	.333	.377	710	112	7	1	0	0	**.996**	-11	C-92,1-29	-0.1
1969	StL-N	159	602	72	174	29	6	18	101	66	85	.289	.364	.447	811	126	21	0	0	0	.996	-3	*1-144,C-17	0.7
1970	StL-N★	161	624	89	203	27	9	21	100	70	91	.325	.399	.498	898	136	33	2	2	-0	.987	-8	C-90,3-73/1-1	2.8
1971	StL-N★	161	634	97	**230**	34	8	24	**137**	63	70	**.363**	.424	.555	979	169	57	4	1	1	.951	-17	*3-161	4.2
1972	StL-N★	149	544	71	157	26	6	11	81	54	64	.289	.361	.419	781	123	17	3	0	1	.963	-15	*3-117,1-27	0.0
1973	StL-N★	141	519	67	149	17	2	13	69	65	78	.287	.377	.403	780	116	14	2	0	0	.993	-12	*1-114,3-58	-0.6
1974	StL-N	147	529	59	149	28	1	11	70	69	88	.282	.373	.401	774	117	14	1	2	-0	.992	3	*1-139,3-18	0.6
1975	NY-N	114	361	33	89	16	3	6	35	35	55	.247	.317	.357	674	91	-5	0	0	0	.950	-1	3-83,1-24	-0.8
1976	NY-N	114	310	36	95	10	3	5	31	21	35	.306	.360	.406	767	124	10	1	3	-1	.989	3	1-78/3-4	0.6
1977	NY-N	26	51	2	9	3	0	1	9	2	10	.176	.208	.294	502	34	-5	0	0	0	.988	-1	1-16/3-1,M	-0.7
Total	18	2209	7874	996	2342	344	59	252	1185	779	1094	.297	.367	.452	819	129	299	23	29	-5	.990	-93	C-903,1-787,3-515,/O	19.6
■ GIL TORRES	Torres, Don Gilberto (Nunez) b: 8/23/15, Regla, Cuba d: 1/10/83, Regla, Cuba BR/TR, 6', 155 lbs. Deb: 4/25/40 F																							
1940	Was-A	2	0	0	0	0	0	0	0	0	0	—	—	—	—	—	0	0	0	0	1.000	0	/P-2	0.0
1944	Was-A	134	524	42	140	20	6	0	58	21	24	.267	.297	.328	625	82	-14	10	7	-0	.952	9	*3-123,2-10/1-4	-0.4
1945	Was-A	147	562	39	133	12	5	0	48	21	29	.237	.264	.276	540	62	-29	7	4	0	.953	-21	*S-145/3-2	-4.2
1946	Was-A	63	185	18	47	8	0	0	13	11	12	.254	.296	.297	593	70	-8	3	2	-0	.939	2	S-31,3-18/2-7,P-3	-0.4
Total	4	346	1271	99	320	40	11	0	119	53	65	.252	.282	.301	583	72	-51	20	13	-0	.951	-11	S-176,3-143/2-17,P1	-5.0
■ FELIX TORRES	Torres, Felix (Sanchez) b: 5/1/32, Ponce, P.R. BR/TR, 5'11", 165 lbs. Deb: 4/10/62																							
1962	LA-A	127	451	44	117	19	4	11	74	28	73	.259	.308	.392	701	90	-7	0	0	0	.938	-3	*3-123	-1.1
1963	LA-A	138	463	40	121	32	1	4	51	30	73	.261	.310	.361	671	93	-5	1	0	0	.939	-4	*3-122/1-2	-1.0
1964	LA-A	100	277	25	64	10	0	12	28	13	56	.231	.268	.397	665	91	-5	1	3	-1	.970	-0	3-72/1-3	-0.7
Total	3	365	1191	109	302	61	5	27	153	71	202	.254	.300	.381	681	91	-17	2	3	-1	.945	-8	3-317/1-5	-2.8
■ HECTOR TORRES	Torres, Hector Epitacio (Marroquin) b: 9/16/45, Monterrey, Mexico BR/TR, 6', 175 lbs. Deb: 4/10/68 C																							
1968	Hou-N	128	466	44	104	11	1	1	24	18	64	.223	.252	.258	510	54	-26	2	3	-1	.958	-4	*S-127/2-1	-2.4
1969	Hou-N	34	69	5	11	1	0	1	8	2	12	.159	.183	.217	400	12	-8	0	0	0	.944	0	S-22	-0.7
1970	Hou-N	31	65	6	16	1	2	0	5	6	8	.246	.310	.323	633	73	-3	0	0	0	.947	1	S-22/2-6	0.0
1971	Chi-N	31	58	4	13	3	0	0	2	4	10	.224	.274	.276	550	49	-4	0	0	0	.962	1	S-18/2-4	-0.2
1972	Mon-N	83	181	14	28	4	1	2	7	13	26	.155	.215	.221	436	24	-18	0	2	-1	.965	14	2-60,S-16/O-2L,P3	-0.1
1973	Hou-N	38	66	3	6	1	0	0	2	7	13	.091	.189	.106	295	-16	-10	0	1	-0	.952	7	S-22,2-13	-0.2
1975	SD-N	112	352	31	91	12	0	5	26	22	32	.259	.302	.335	637	82	-10	2	3	-1	.971	11	S-75,3-42,2-16	1.0
1976	SD-N	74	215	8	42	6	0	4	15	16	31	.195	.254	.279	533	56	-13	2	1	0	.949	-16	S-63/3-4,2-3	-2.4
1977	Tor-A	91	266	33	64	7	3	5	26	16	33	.241	.286	.346	632	70	-11	1	1	-0	.980	-2	S-68,2-23/3-2	-0.7
Total	9	622	1738	148	375	46	7	18	115	104	229	.216	.262	.281	543	55	-103	7	11	-2	.962	11	S-433,2-126/3-49,OP	-5.7
■ RICARDO TORRES	Torres, Ricardo J. (Martinez) b: 4/16/1891, Regla, Cuba d: 4/17/60, Regla, Cuba BR/TR, 5'11", 160 lbs. Deb: 5/18/20 F																							
1920	Was-A	16	30	8	10	1	0	0	3	1	4	.333	.355	.367	722	94	-0	0	0	0	1.000	-1	/1-7,C-5	-0.1
1921	Was-A	2	3	1	1	0	0	0	0	1	1	.333	.500	.333	833	122	0	0	0	0	.750	-1	/C-2	-0.1
1922	Was-A	4	4	0	0	0	0	0	0	0	1	.000	.000	.000	0	-99	-1	0	0	0	1.000	1	/C-3	0.0
Total	3	22	37	9	11	1	0	0	3	2	6	.297	.333	.324	658	76	-1	0	0	0	.955	-1	/C-10,1-7	-0.2
■ RUSTY TORRES	Torres, Rosendo (Hernandez) b: 9/30/48, Aguadilla, P.R. BB/TR, 5'10", 180 lbs. Deb: 9/20/71 Career OF: (96-LF 251-CF 240-RF)																							
1971	NY-A	9	26	5	10	3	0	2	3	0	8	.385	.385	.731	1115	223	4	0	1	-0	1.000	0	/O-5(0-1-4)	0.4
1972	NY-A	80	199	15	42	7	0	3	13	18	44	.211	.280	.291	571	73	-7	0	4	-1	.978	-6	O-62(1-1-60)	-2.0
1973	Cle-A	122	312	31	64	8	1	7	28	50	62	.205	.321	.304	625	76	-9	6	5	-0	.976	-5	*O-114(1-37-77)	-1.9
1974	Cle-A	108	150	19	28	2	0	3	12	13	24	.187	.252	.260	512	48	-10	2	1	0	.959	-19	O-94(35-38-24)/D-1	-3.3
1976	Cal-A	120	264	37	54	16	3	6	27	36	39	.205	.300	.356	656	98	-1	4	4	-1	.990	-11	*O-105C/3-1,D-6	-1.5
1977	Cal-A	58	77	9	12	1	1	3	10	10	18	.156	.253	.312	565	55	-5	0	1	-0	.984	-12	O-54(4-40-10)	-1.8
1978	Chi-A	16	44	7	14	3	0	3	6	6	7	.318	.400	.591	991	174	4	0	1	-0	.964	-2	O-14(4-5-8)	0.1
1979	Chi-A	90	170	26	43	5	0	8	24	23	37	.253	.349	.424	772	107	2	0	0	0	.976	-13	O-85(36-17-35)	-1.3
1980	KC-A	51	72	10	12	0	0	0	3	8	7	.167	.250	.167	417	16	-8	1	3	-1	.973	-4	O-40(15-8-21)/D-1	-1.4
Total	9	654	1314	159	279	45	5	35	126	164	246	.212	.303	.334	637	82	-30	13	20	-4	.977	-73	O-573C/D-8,3-1	-12.7
■ KELVIN TORVE	Torve, Kelvin Curtis b: 1/10/60, Rapid City, S.Dak. BL/TR, 6'3", 205 lbs. Deb: 6/25/88																							
1988	Min-A	12	16	1	3	0	0	1	2	1	2	.188	.235	.375	610	66	-1	0	1	-0	1.000	0	/1-4,D-1	-0.1
1990	NY-N	20	38	0	11	4	0	0	2	4	9	.289	.386	.395	781	116	1	0	0	0	1.000	-2	/1-9,O-1(1-0-0)	-0.2
1991	NY-N	10	8	0	0	0	0	0	0	0	1	.000	.000	.000	0	-99	-2	0	0	0	1.000	1	/1-1	-0.1
Total	3	42	62	1	14	4	0	1	4	5	12	.226	.304	.339	643	78	-2	0	1	-0	1.000	-2	/1-14,O-1(1-0-0),D-1	-0.4
■ CESAR TOVAR	Tovar, Cesar Leonardo "Pepito" (b: Cesar Leonard Perez (Tovar)) b: 7/3/40, Caracas, Venez. d: 7/14/94, Caracas, Venez. BR/TR, 5'9", 155 lbs. Deb: 4/12/65 Career OF: (378-LF 471-CF 205-RF)																							
1965	Min-A	18	25	3	5	1	0	0	2	2	3	.200	.259	.240	499	41	-2	2	0	0	.800	1	/2-4,3-2,O-2C,S-1	-0.1
1966	Min-A	134	465	57	121	19	5	2	41	44	50	.260	.329	.335	665	86	-7	16	6	1	.978	-8	2-76,S-31,O-24C	-0.6
1967	Min-A	164	649	98	173	32	7	6	47	46	51	.267	.328	.365	693	97	-2	19	11	0	.994	-4	O-74C,3-70,2-36,/S	-0.7
1968	Min-A	157	613	89	167	31	6	6	47	34	41	.272	.328	.372	700	106	5	35	13	3	.966	-2	O-78L,3-75,S2/PC1	0.6
1969	*Min-A	158	535	99	154	25	5	11	52	37	37	.288	.344	.415	759	109	6	45	12	6	.983	9	*O-113C,2-41,3-20	2.0
1970	*Min-A	161	650	120	195	**36**	**13**	10	54	52	47	.300	.359	.442	801	118	16	30	15	1	.977	0	*O-151C/2-8,3-4	1.2
1971	Min-A	157	657	94	**204**	29	3	1	45	45	39	.311	.357	.368	726	103	3	18	14	-1	.986	4	*O-154L/3-7,2-2	-0.2
1972	Min-A	141	548	86	145	20	6	2	31	39	39	.265	.329	.334	663	93	-3	21	10	1	.983	7	*O-139(38-5-101)	-0.4
1973	Phi-N	97	328	49	88	18	4	1	21	29	35	.268	.337	.357	694	90	-4	6	4	-0	.928	-15	3-46,O-24R,2-22	-2.0
1974	Tex-A	138	562	78	164	24	6	4	58	47	33	.292	.356	.377	733	114	11	13	9	-0	.980	-1	*O-135(66-87-11)/D-3	0.4
1975	Tex-A	102	427	53	110	16	0	3	28	27	25	.258	.306	.316	623	77	-13	16	11	-0	.919	-3	D-66,O-31(25-6-1)/2-1	-2.1
	*Oak-A	19	26	5	6	1	0	0	3	3	3	.231	.310	.269	580	66	-1	4	0	1	1.000	-0	/2-4,3-3,S-1,D-7	0.0
	Yr	121	453	58	116	17	0	3	31	30	28	.256	.307	.313	620	76	-14	20	11	1	.887	-3	D-73,O-31L/2-5,3S	-2.1
1976	Oak-A	29	45	1	8	0	0	0	4	4	4	.178	.275	.178	452	36	-3	1	2	-0	.958	-5	O-20(14-2-4)/D-4	-1.0
	NY-A	13	39	2	6	1	0	0	2	4	3	.154	.250	.179	429	27	-3	0	1	-0	1.000	1	D-10/2-3	-0.3
	Yr	42	84	3	14	1	0	0	6	8	7	.167	.263	.179	442	32	-7	1	3	-1	.958	-4	O-20(14-2-4),D-14/2-3	-1.3
Total	12	1488	5569	834	1546	253	55	46	435	413	410	.278	.337	.368	705	99	1	226	108	12	.980	-18	O-945C,3-227,2/DS1CP	-3.2
■ BABE TOWNE	Towne, Jay King b: 3/12/1880, Coon Rapids, Iowa d: 10/29/38, Des Moines, Iowa BR/TR, 5'10", 180 lbs. Deb: 8/1/06																							
1906	*Chi-A	14	36	3	10	0	0	0	6	7		.278	.395	.278	673	115	1	0			.923	-4	C-13	-0.2
■ GEORGE TOWNSEND	Townsend, George Hodgson "Sleepy" b: 6/4/1867, Hartsdale, N.Y. d: 3/15/30, New Haven, Conn. BR/TR, 5'7.5", 180 lbs. Deb: 6/25/1887																							
1887	Phi-a	31	112	12	24	3	0	0	14	3		.214	.214	.220	434	21	-12	8			.865	-7	C-28/O-3(1-0-2)	-1.4
1888	Phi-a	42	161	13	25	6	0	0	12	4		.155	.181	.193	373	20	-14	2			.912	-2	C-42	-1.2
1890	Bal-a	18	67	6	16	4	1	0	9	4		.239	.282	.328	610	76	-2	3			.930	2	C-18	0.1
1891	Bal-a	61	204	29	39	5	4	0	18	20	21	.191	.279	.255	534	53	-13	3			.909	-11	C-58/O-3(0-1-2)	-1.6
Total	4	152	544	60	104	18	5	0	53	31	21	.191	.239	.238	477	40	-41	16			.905	-17	C-146/O-6(1-1-4)	-4.1

YEAR	TM/L	G	AB	R	H	2B	3B	HR	RBI	BB	SO	AVG	OBP	SLG	OPS	OPS+	BR+	SB	CS	SBR	FA	FR	G/POS	TPR
■ **JIM TOY** Toy, James Madison b: 2/20/1858, Beaver Falls, Pa. d: 3/13/19, Cresson, Pa. 5′6″, 160 lbs. Deb: 4/20/1887 Career OF: (2-LF 2-CF 7-RF)																								
1887	Cle-a	109	440	56	111	20	5	1	56	17		.252	.256	.300	556	56	-25	8			.975	3	1-82,O-11R,C-10,/3S	-2.4
1890	Bro-a	44	160	11	29	3	0	0	7	11		.181	.238	.200	438	30	-14	2			.867	-1	C-44	-0.9
Total	2	153	600	67	140	23	5	1	63	28		.233	.251	.273	524	50	-39	10			.859	3	/1-82,C-54,O-11R,3S	-3.3
■ **JIM TRABER** Traber, James Joseph b: 12/26/61, Columbus, Ohio BL/TL, 6′, 194 lbs. Deb: 9/21/84 Career OF: (9-LF 0-CF 9-RF)																								
1984	Bal-A	10	21	3	5	0	0	0	2	2	4	.238	.304	.238	542	54	-1	0	0	0	.000	0	/D-9	-0.2
1986	Bal-A	65	212	28	54	7	0	13	44	18	31	.255	.328	.472	799	116	4	0	0	0	.988	1	1-29,D-21/O-8(7-0-1)	0.3
1988	Bal-A	103	352	25	78	6	0	10	45	19	42	.222	.263	.324	587	65	-17	1	2	-0	.990	8	1-57,D-30,O-11(2-0-8)	-1.5
1989	Bal-A	86	234	14	49	8	0	4	26	19	41	.209	.269	.295	564	61	-12	4	3	-0	.998	5	1-69/D-5	-1.2
Total	4	264	819	70	186	21	0	27	117	58	118	.227	.283	.352	635	77	-26	5	5	-1	.993	15	1-155/D-65,O-19L	-2.6
■ **DICK TRACEWSKI** Tracewski, Richard Joseph b: 2/3/35, Eynon, Pa. BR/TR, 5′11″, 167 lbs. Deb: 4/12/62 MC																								
1962	LA-N	15	2	3	0	0	0	0	0	2	0	.000	.500	.000	500	50	0	0	0	0	1.000	2	/S-4	0.2
1963	*LA-N	104	217	23	49	2	1	1	10	19	39	.226	.288	.258	546	63	-10	2	3	-1	.957	19	S-81,2-23	1.4
1964	LA-N	106	304	31	75	13	4	1	26	31	61	.247	.316	.326	642	88	-5	3	3	-0	.970	-0	2-56,3-30,S-19	0.0
1965	*LA-N	78	186	17	40	6	0	1	20	25	30	.215	.315	.263	578	69	-7	2	6	-2	.950	8	3-53,2-14/S-7	0.1
1966	Det-A	81	124	15	24	1	1	0	7	10	32	.194	.254	.218	471	36	-10	1	1	-0	.947	11	2-70/S-3	0.3
1967	Det-A	74	107	19	30	4	2	1	9	8	20	.280	.330	.383	714	107	1	1	1	-0	.965	9	S-44,2-12,3-10	1.3
1968	*Det-A	90	212	30	33	3	1	4	15	24	51	.156	.242	.236	477	44	-14	3	0	1	.982	-5	S-51,3-16,2-14	-1.7
1969	Det-A	66	79	10	11	2	0	0	4	15	20	.139	.277	.165	441	25	-8	3	0	1	.957	16	S-41,2-13/3-6	1.2
Total	8	614	1231	148	262	31	9	8	91	134	253	.213	.291	.272	563	65	-52	15	14	-2	.958	60	S-250,2-202,3-115	2.8
■ **ANDY TRACY** Tracy, Andrew Michael b: 12/11/73, Bowling Green, Ohio BL/TR, 6′3″, 220 lbs. Deb: 4/25/2000																								
2000	Mon-N	83	192	29	50	8	1	11	32	22	61	.260	.343	.484	827	105	1	1	0	0	.882	-11	3-34,1-27	-1.1
■ **JIM TRACY** Tracy, James Edwin b: 12/31/55, Hamilton, Ohio BL/TR, 6′, 185 lbs. Deb: 7/20/80																								
1980	Chi-N	42	122	12	31	3	3	3	9	13	37	.254	.326	.402	728	95	-1	2	2	-0	.950	-7	O-31(22-0-14)/1-1	-1.0
1981	Chi-N	45	63	6	15	2	1	0	5	12	14	.238	.360	.302	662	85	-1	1	0	0	1.000	-1	O-11(10-0-1)	-0.2
Total	2	87	185	18	46	5	4	3	14	25	51	.249	.338	.368	706	92	-1	3	2	-0	.964	-8	/O-42(32-0-15),1-1	-1.2
■ **JOHN TRAFFLEY** Traffley, John M. b: 1862, Chicago, Ill. d: 5/15/1900, Baltimore, Md. 5′9″, 180 lbs. Deb: 6/15/1889 F																								
1889	Lou-a	1	2	0	1	0	0	0	0	0	0	.500	.500	.500	1000	189	0	0			.000	-1	/O-1(0-0-1)	0.0
■ **BILL TRAFFLEY** Traffley, William Franklin b: 12/21/1859, Staten Island, N.Y d: 6/23/08, Des Moines, Iowa BR/TR, 5′11.5″, 185 lbs. Deb: 7/27/1878 F Career OF: (0-LF 5-CF 11-RF)																								
1878	Chi-N	2	9	1	1	0	0	0	1	0	1	.111	.111	.111	222	-25	-1				1.000	-1	/C-2	-0.2
1883	Cin-a	30	105	17	21	5	0	0	8	4		.200	.229	.248	477	51	-6				.851	2	C-29/S-2	-0.2
1884	Bal-a	53	210	25	37	4	6	0		3		.176	.192	.252	444	42	-13				.926	-8	C-47/O-6(0-0-6),1-1	-1.6
1885	Bal-a	69	254	27	39	4	5	1	20	17		.154	.215	.220	436	38	-17				**.943**	2	C-61,O-10(0-5-5)/2-3	-0.9
1886	Bal-a	25	85	15	18	0	1	0	7	10		.212	.295	.235	530	68	-3	8			.952	-3	C-25	-0.3
Total	5	179	663	85	116	13	12	1	36	34	1	.175	.220	.235	455	45	-40	8			.927	-8	C-164/O-16R,2-3,S1	-3.2
■ **WALT TRAGESSER** Tragesser, Walter Joseph b: 6/14/1887, Lafayette, Ind. d: 12/14/70, Lafayette, Ind. BR/TR, 6′, 175 lbs. Deb: 7/30/13																								
1913	Bos-N	2	0	0	0	0	0	0	0	0	0	—	—	—	—	—	0	0			1.000	-0	/C-2	0.0
1915	Bos-N	7	7	1	0	0	0	0	0	0	2	.000	.000	.000	0	-99	-2	0			.944	1	/C-7	-0.1
1916	Bos-N	41	54	3	11	1	0	0	4	5	10	.204	.283	.222	506	59	-2	0			.971	4	C-29	0.3
1917	Bos-N	98	297	23	66	10	2	0	25	15	36	.222	.264	.269	534	68	-12	5			.971	-2	C-94	-0.6
1918	Bos-N	7	1	0	0	0	0	0	0	0	0	.000	.000	.000	0	-99	-0	0			.833	1	/C-7	0.0
1919	Bos-N	20	40	3	7	2	0	0	3	2	10	.175	.233	.225	458	39	-3	1			.959	-0	C-14	-0.3
	Phi-N	35	114	7	27	7	0	0	8	9	31	.237	.298	.298	597	74	-3	4			.953	4	C-34	0.4
	Yr	55	154	10	34	9	0	0	11	11	41	.221	.281	.279	561	67	-6	5			.954	4	C-48	0.1
1920	Phi-N	62	176	17	37	11	1	6	26	4	36	.210	.236	.386	623	73	-7	4	0	1	.944	-13	C-52	-1.6
Total	7	272	689	54	148	31	3	6	66	35	125	.215	.260	.295	555	67	-29	14	0		.961	-6	C-239	-1.9
■ **RED TRAMBACK** Tramback, Stephen Joseph b: 11/1/15, Iselin, Pa. d: 12/28/79, Buffalo, N.Y. BL/TL, 6′, 175 lbs. Deb: 9/15/40																								
1940	NY-N	2	4	0	1	0	0	0	0	1	1	.250	.400	.250	650	82	-0	1			.667	-0	/O-1(0-0-1)	0.0
■ **ALAN TRAMMELL** Trammell, Alan Stuart b: 2/21/58, Garden Grove, Cal. BR/TR, 6′, 175 lbs. Deb: 9/9/77 C Career OF: (5-LF 4-CF 0-RF)																								
1977	Det-A	19	43	6	8	0	0	0	0	4	12	.186	.255	.186	441	21	-5	0	0	0	.961	-7	S-19	-1.0
1978	Det-A	139	448	49	120	14	6	2	34	45	56	.268	.337	.339	677	88	-6	3	1	0	.979	6	*S-139	1.5
1979	Det-A	142	460	68	127	11	4	6	50	43	55	.276	.338	.357	694	85	-9	17	14	-1	.961	-14	*S-142	-0.9
1980	Det-A★	146	560	107	168	21	5	9	65	69	63	.300	.380	.404	783	112	12	12	12	-2	.980	-27	*S-144	-0.2
1981	Det-A	105	392	52	101	15	3	2	31	49	31	.258	.345	.327	671	91	-3	10	3	1	.983	6	*S-105	1.6
1982	Det-A	157	489	66	126	34	3	9	57	52	47	.258	.329	.395	724	97	-2	19	8	1	.978	-8	*S-157	0.8
1983	Det-A	142	505	83	161	31	2	14	66	57	64	.319	.388	.471	859	139	28	30	10	3	.979	-18	*S-140	2.8
1984	*Det-A†	139	555	85	174	34	5	14	69	60	63	.314	.383	.468	852	135	27	19	13	-0	.980	-12	*S-114,D-22	2.7
1985	Det-A★	149	605	79	156	21	7	13	57	50	71	.258	.317	.380	697	90	-8	14	5	1	.977	-16	*S-149	-0.6
1986	Det-A	151	574	107	159	33	7	21	75	59	57	.277	.350	.469	818	121	16	25	12	1	.969	6	*S-149/D-2	3.8
1987	*Det-A★	151	597	109	205	34	3	28	105	60	47	.343	.406	.551	957	157	50	21	2	4	.971	-10	*S-149	5.5
1988	Det-A†	128	466	73	145	24	1	15	69	46	46	.311	.378	.464	841	140	25	7	4	0	.980	-7	*S-125	2.8
1989	Det-A	121	449	54	109	20	3	5	43	45	45	.243	.317	.334	651	86	-8	10	2	2	.985	12	*S-117/D-2	1.5
1990	Det-A★	146	559	71	170	37	1	14	89	68	55	.304	.381	.449	830	130	24	12	10	-1	.979	1	*S-142/D-3	3.4
1991	Det-A	101	375	57	93	20	0	9	55	37	39	.248	.320	.373	694	90	-5	11	2	2	.979	4	S-92/D-6	0.7
1992	Det-A	29	102	11	28	7	1	1	11	15	4	.275	.373	.392	765	114	2	2	2	-0	.977	-1	S-27/D-1	0.4
1993	Det-A	112	401	72	132	25	3	12	60	38	38	.329	.390	.496	886	137	21	12	8	-0	.989	-13	S-63,3-35/O-8L,D-6	1.3
1994	Det-A	76	292	38	78	17	1	8	28	16	35	.267	.307	.414	722	84	-8	3	0	1	.968	-4	S-63,D-11	-0.6
1995	Det-A	74	223	28	60	12	0	2	23	27	19	.269	.348	.350	698	83	-5	3	1	0	.980	-6	S-60/D-6	-0.6
1996	Det-A	66	193	16	45	2	0	1	16	10	27	.233	.271	.259	530	35	-19	6	0	1	.976	-4	S-43,2-11/3-8,O-1L	-1.6
Total	20	2293	8288	1231	2365	412	55	185	1003	850	874	.285	.354	.415	770	110	127	236	109	14	.977	-111	*S-2139/D-59,3-43,2O	23.3
■ **BUBBA TRAMMELL** Trammell, Thomas Bubba b: 11/6/71, Knoxville, Tenn. BR/TR, 6′3″, 205 lbs. Deb: 4/1/97																								
1997	Det-A	44	123	14	28	5	0	4	13	15	35	.228	.312	.366	677	77	-4	3	1	0	1.000	-1	O-28(13-0-16),D-15	-0.6
1998	TB-A	59	199	28	57	18	1	12	35	16	45	.286	.340	.568	907	128	7	0	2	-1	1.000	-3	O-37(23-0-16),D-19	0.1
1999	TB-A	82	283	49	82	19	0	14	39	43	37	.290	.385	.505	891	123	10	0	2	-1	.993	-2	O-74(61-0-20)/D-7	0.5
2000	TB-A	66	189	19	52	11	2	7	33	21	30	.275	.354	.466	819	106	2	3	0	1	1.000	-5	O-48(26-0-24)/D-9	-0.4
	*NY-N	36	56	9	13	2	0	3	12	8	19	.232	.328	.429	757	93	-1	1	0	0	.963	-4	O-25(11-0-16)	-0.5
Total	4	287	850	119	232	55	3	40	132	103	166	.273	.354	.486	839	112	14	7	5	-0	.994	-16	O-212(134-0-92)/D-50	-0.9
■ **CECIL TRAVIS** Travis, Cecil Howell b: 8/8/13, Riverdale, Ga. BL/TR, 6′1.5″, 185 lbs. Deb: 5/16/33 Career OF: (17-LF 0-CF 52-RF)																								
1933	Was-A	18	43	7	13	1	0	0	2	2	5	.302	.348	.326	673	80	-1	0	0	0	.974	4	3-15	0.3
1934	Was-A	109	392	48	125	22	4	1	53	24	37	.319	.361	.403	764	101	0	1	5	-2	.937	3	3-99	0.5
1935	Was-A	138	534	85	170	27	8	0	61	41	28	.318	.377	.399	776	104	4	4	2	0	.963	21	*3-114,O-16(16-0-0)	2.7
1936	Was-A	138	517	77	164	34	10	2	92	39	21	.317	.366	.433	800	102	1	4	4	-1	.938	-13	S-71,O-53R/2-4,3-2	-0.8
1937	Was-A	135	526	72	181	27	7	3	66	39	34	.344	.395	.439	834	115	13	3	2	-0	.965	-11	*S-129	1.0
1938	Was-A☆	146	567	96	190	30	5	5	67	58	22	.335	.401	.432	833	117	16	6	5	-0	.950	3	*S-143	2.6
1939	Was-A	130	476	55	139	20	9	5	63	34	25	.292	.342	.403	745	97	-3	0	3	-1	.958	-4	*S-118	0.1
1940	Was-A★	136	528	60	170	37	11	2	76	48	23	.322	.381	.445	826	121	17	0	1	-0	.934	16	*3-113,S-23	3.5
1941	Was-A★	152	608	106	**218**	39	19	7	101	52	25	.359	.410	.520	930	152	44	2	2	-0	.964	2	*S-136,3-16	5.3
1945	Was-A	15	54	4	13	2	1	0	10	4	5	.241	.293	.315	608	83	-1	0	1	-0	.920	0	3-14	-0.1
1946	Was-A	137	465	45	117	22	3	1	56	45	47	.252	.323	.318	641	85	-9	2	4	-1	.959	-19	S-75,3-56	-2.6

YEAR	TM/L	G	AB	R	H	2B	3B	HR	RBI	BB	SO	AVG	OBP	SLG	OPS	OPS+	BR+	SB	CS	SBR	FA	FR	G/POS	TPR
1947	Was-A	74	204	10	44	4	1	1	10	16	19	.216	.273	.260	533	50	-14	1	3	-1	.932	-2	3-39,S-15	-1.7
Total	12	1328	4914	665	1544	265	78	27	657	402	291	.314	.370	.416	786	109	66	23	32	-6	.955	0	S-710,3-468/O-69R,2	10.8
■ BRIAN TRAXLER	Traxler, Brian Lee b: 9/26/67, Waukegan, Ill. BL/TL, 5'10", 200 lbs. Deb: 4/24/90																							
1990	LA-N	9	11	0	1	1	0	0	0	0	4	.091	.091	.182	273	-28	-2	0	0	0	1.000	1	/1-3	-0.2
■ JIM TRAY	Tray, James (b: James Trahey) b: 2/14/1860, Jackson, Mich. d: 7/28/05, Jackson, Mich. 5'11", 180 lbs. Deb: 9/6/1884																							
1884	Ind-a	6	21	2	6	0	0	0		2		.286	.348	.286	634	112	0				.857	-2	/C-4,1-2	-0.1
■ PIE TRAYNOR	Traynor, Harold Joseph b: 11/11/1899, Framingham, Mass. d: 3/16/72, Pittsburgh, Pa. BR/TR, 6', 170 lbs. Deb: 9/15/20 MH																							
1920	Pit-N	17	52	6	11	3	1	0	2	3	6	.212	.268	.308	576	63	-3	1	3	-1	.860	-6	S-17	-0.9
1921	Pit-N	7	19	0	5	0	0	0	2	1	2	.263	.300	.263	563	49	-1	0	0	0	.917	1	/3-3,S-1	-0.1
1922	Pit-N	142	571	89	161	17	12	4	81	27	28	.282	.319	.375	694	77	-20	17	3	3	.945	-6	*3-124,S-18	-1.2
1923	Pit-N	153	616	108	208	19	**19**	12	101	34	19	.338	.377	.489	866	124	20	28	13	2	.950	8	*3-152/S-1	3.8
1924	Pit-N	142	545	86	160	26	13	5	82	37	26	.294	.340	.417	756	100	-1	24	18	-1	.968	9	*3-141	1.6
1925	*Pit-N	150	591	114	189	39	14	6	106	52	19	.320	.377	.464	840	106	6	15	9	0	**.957**	23	*3-150/S-1	3.6
1926	Pit-N	152	574	83	182	25	17	3	92	38	14	.317	.361	.436	796	108	6	8			.952	7	*3-148/S-3	2.1
1927	*Pit-N	149	573	93	196	32	9	5	106	22	11	.342	.370	.455	825	112	9	11			.962	13	*3-143/S-9	3.1
1928	Pit-N	144	569	91	192	38	12	3	124	28	10	.337	.370	.462	832	112	9	12			.946	4	*3-144	2.1
1929	Pit-N	130	540	94	192	27	12	4	108	30	7	.356	.393	.472	865	111	9	13			.951	-1	*3-130	1.4
1930	Pit-N	130	497	90	182	22	11	9	119	48	19	.366	.423	.509	932	124	21	7			.941	5	*3-130	3.0
1931	Pit-N	155	615	81	183	37	15	2	103	54	28	.298	.354	.416	771	107	6	6			.925	-9	*3-155	0.3
1932	Pit-N	135	513	74	169	27	10	2	68	32	20	.329	.373	.433	806	118	13	6			.936	-3	*3-127	1.5
1933	Pit-N★	154	624	85	190	27	6	1	82	35	24	.304	.342	.372	714	104	3	5			.946	-1	*3-154	0.8
1934	Pit-N★	119	444	62	137	22	10	1	61	21	27	.309	.341	.410	751	98	-2	3			.954	-10	*3-110,M	-0.8
1935	Pit-N	57	204	24	57	10	3	1	36	10	17	.279	.323	.373	695	84	-5	2			.888	-3	3-49/1-1,M	-0.6
1937	Pit-N	5	12	3	2	0	0	0	0	0	1	.167	.167	.167	333	-9	-2	0			1.000	1	/3-3,M	0.0
Total	17	1941	7559	1183	2416	371	164	58	1273	472	278	.320	.362	.435	797	107	69	158	46		.947	31	*3-1863/S-50,1-1	19.7
■ FRED TREACEY	Treacey, Frederick S. b: 1847, Brooklyn, N.Y. 5'9.5", 145 lbs. Deb: 5/16/1871 F																							
1871	Chi-n	25	124	39	42	7	5	**4**	33	2	5	.339	.349	.573	922	144	5	13	5	1	**.918**	7	*O-25(25-0-0)	0.9
1872	Ath-n	47	236	53	65	7	3	2	29	5	10	.275	.290	.356	646	97	-1	7	5	-0	.814	-2	*O-47(0-47-0)	-0.2
1873	Phi-n	51	243	49	62	7	2	1	32	5	6	.255	.270	.313	583	70	-9	2	3	-1	.771	3	*O-51(1-51-0)	-0.5
1874	Chi-n	35	148	18	28	5	0	0	12	2	6	.189	.200	.223	423	35	-10	4	4	-1	.790	7	O-35(2-11-24)	-0.2
1875	Cen-n	11	46	9	12	3	0	0	2	2	0	.261	.292	.326	618	124	1	1	0	0	.848	1	O-11(11-0-0)	0.3
	Phi-n	43	179	23	38	3	3	0	15	1	3	.212	.217	.263	479	63	-7	6	3	0	.858	2	O-43(42-1-0)	-0.2
	Yr	54	225	32	50	6	3	0	17	3	3	.222	.232	.276	508	75	-6	7	3	0	.856	4	O-54(53-1-0)	0.1
1876	NY-N	57	257	47	54	5	1	0	18	1	5	.210	.214	.238	452	58	-9				.844	12	*O-57(52-0-5)	0.0
Total	5 n	212	976	191	247	32	13	7	123	17	30	.253	.266	.334	600	84	-21	33	20	0	.826	19	O-212(81-110-24)	0.1
■ PETE TREACEY	Treacey, Peter b: 1852, Brooklyn, N.Y. Deb: 8/5/1876 F																							
1876	NY-N	2	6	1	0	0	0	0	0	1	0	.000	.167	.000	167	-46	-1				.750	-1	/S-2	-0.1
■ RAY TREADAWAY	Treadaway, Edgar Raymond b: 10/31/07, Ragland, Ala. d: 10/12/35, Chattanooga, Tenn. BL/TR, 5'7", 150 lbs. Deb: 9/17/30																							
1930	Was-A	6	19	1	4	2	0	0	1	0	3	.211	.211	.316	526	31	-2	0	0	0	.833	-1	/3-4	-0.3
■ GEORGE TREADWAY	Treadway, George B. BL/TL, 6', 185 lbs. Deb: 4/27/1893																							
1893	Bal-N	115	458	78	119	16	17	1	67	58	50	.260	.348	.376	724	91	-7	24			.901	9	*O-115(1-0-114)	-0.3
1894	Bro-N	124	482	125	159	28	26	4	102	73	43	.330	.420	.521	941	135	30	27			.893	1	*O-123(121-0-2)/1-1	1.5
1895	Bro-N	87	343	56	89	14	3	8	54	33	22	.259	.328	.388	716	92	-4	9			.886	-10	O-87(0-0-87)	-1.5
1896	Lou-N	2	7	0	1	0	0	0	1	1	0	.143	.250	.143	393	5	-1	0			.500	-1	/O-1(0-0-1),1-1	-0.2
Total	4	328	1290	259	368	58	46	13	224	165	115	.285	.370	.432	802	108	18	60			.891	-1	O-326(122-0-204)/1-2	-0.5
■ JEFF TREADWAY	Treadway, Hugh Jeffery b: 1/22/63, Columbus, Ga. BL/TR, 5'11", 170 lbs. Deb: 9/4/87																							
1987	Cin-N	23	84	9	28	4	0	2	4	2	6	.333	.356	.452	809	108	1	1	0	0	.958	-7	2-21	-0.5
1988	Cin-N	103	301	30	76	19	4	2	23	27	30	.252	.320	.362	682	92	-3	2	0	0	.984	3	2-97/3-2	0.2
1989	Atl-N	134	473	58	131	18	3	8	40	30	38	.277	.320	.378	699	96	-3	3	2	-0	.981	3	*2-123/3-6	0.4
1990	Atl-N	128	474	56	134	20	2	11	59	25	42	.283	.323	.403	726	93	-5	3	4	-1	.976	10	*2-122	0.8
1991	*Atl-N	106	306	41	98	17	2	3	32	23	19	.320	.372	.418	790	115	6	2	2	-0	.960	-8	2-93	0.0
1992	*Atl-N	61	126	5	28	6	1	0	5	9	16	.222	.274	.286	560	55	-7	1	2	-0	.993	0	2-45/3-1	-0.8
1993	Cle-A	97	221	25	67	14	1	2	27	14	21	.303	.350	.403	753	102	1	1	1	-0	.933	1	3-42,2-19/D-4	0.2
1994	LA-N	52	67	14	20	3	0	0	5	5	8	.299	.356	.343	699	89	-1	1	1	-0	.950	-1	2-24/3-3	-0.1
1995	LA-N	17	17	2	2	0	1	0	3	0	2	.118	.118	.235	353	-11	-3	0	0	0	.000	-1	/3-2,2-1	-0.3
	Mon-N	41	50	4	12	2	0	0	10	5	2	.240	.309	.280	589	55	-3	0	1	-0	1.000	-2	2-11/3-1	-0.5
	Yr	58	67	6	14	2	1	0	13	5	4	.209	.264	.269	533	41	-6	0	1	-0	1.000	-2	2-12/3-3	-0.8
Total	9	762	2119	244	596	103	14	28	208	140	184	.281	.329	.383	712	94	-17	14	13	-1	.975	-1	2-556/3-57,D-4	-0.6
■ RED TREADWAY	Treadway, Thadford Leon b: 4/28/20, Athlone, N.C. d: 5/26/94, Atlanta, Ga. BL/TR, 5'10", 175 lbs. Deb: 7/25/44																							
1944	NY-N	50	170	23	51	5	2	0	5	13	11	.300	.350	.353	703	98	-0	2			.957	1	O-38(10-2-27)	-0.2
1945	NY-N	88	224	31	54	4	2	4	23	20	13	.241	.303	.330	634	75	-8	3			.940	-9	O-60(27-18-18)	-2.0
Total	2	138	394	54	105	9	4	4	28	33	24	.266	.323	.340	663	85	-8	5			.948	-8	/O-98(37-20-45)	-2.2
■ FRANK TRECHOCK	Trechock, Frank Adam b: 12/24/15, Windber, Pa. d: 1/16/89, Minneapolis, Minn. BR/TR, 5'10", 175 lbs. Deb: 9/19/37																							
1937	Was-A	1	4	0	2	0	0	0	0	0	1	.500	.500	.500	1000	160	0	0	0	0	.750	0	/S-1	0.1
■ NICK TREMARK	Tremark, Nicholas Joseph b: 10/15/12, Yonkers, N.Y. BL/TL, 5'5", 150 lbs. Deb: 8/9/34																							
1934	Bro-N	17	28	3	7	1	0	0	6	2	2	.250	.300	.286	586	61	-2	0			1.000	-1	/O-9(8-1-0)	-0.3
1935	Bro-N	10	13	1	3	1	0	0	3	1	1	.231	.286	.308	593	61	-1	0			1.000	-1	/O-4(0-0-4)	-0.1
1936	Bro-N	8	32	6	8	2	0	0	1	3	2	.250	.333	.313	646	74	-1	0			1.000	1	/O-8(0-2-6)	0.0
Total	3	35	73	10	18	4	0	0	10	6	5	.247	.313	.301	614	67	-3	0			1.000	-0	/O-21(8-3-10)	-0.4
■ CHRIS TREMIE	Tremie, Christopher James b: 10/17/69, Houston, Tex. BR/TR, 6', 200 lbs. Deb: 7/1/95																							
1995	Chi-A	10	24	0	4	0	0	0	0	1	2	.167	.200	.167	367	-3	-4	0	0	0	.976	-1	/C-9,D-1	-0.4
1998	Tex-A	2	3	2	1	1	0	0	0	1	1	.333	.500	.667	1167	192	0	0	0	0	.000	0	/D-2	0.0
1999	Pit-N	9	14	1	1	0	0	0	1	2	4	.071	.188	.071	259	-31	-3	0	0	0	1.000	1	/C-8	-0.2
Total	3	21	41	3	6	1	0	0	1	4	7	.146	.222	.171	393	3	-6	0	0	0	.986	-0	/C-17,D-3	-0.6
■ OVERTON TREMPER	Tremper, Carlton Overton b: 3/22/06, Brooklyn, N.Y. d: 1/9/96, Clearwater, Fla. BR/TR, 5'10", 163 lbs. Deb: 6/16/27																							
1927	Bro-N	26	60	4	14	0	0	0	4	0	2	.233	.246	.233	479	29	-6	0			1.000	-4	O-18(18-0-0)	-1.1
1928	Bro-N	10	31	1	6	2	1	0	1	0	1	.194	.194	.323	516	33	-3	0			1.000	-0	/O-9(7-1-1)	-0.4
Total	2	36	91	5	20	2	1	0	5	0	3	.220	.228	.264	492	30	-9	0			1.000	-4	/O-27(25-1-1)	-1.5
■ GEORGE TRENWITH	Trenwith, George W. b: 1851, Philadelphia, Pa. d: 2/1/1890, Philadelphia, Pa. Deb: 4/30/1875																							
1875	Cen-n	10	45	5	8	2	0	0	4	1	2	.178	.196	.222	418	49	-2	0	0	0	.583	-6	3-10	-0.8
	NH-n	6	25	1	6	2	0	0	3	0	1	.240	.240	.320	560	106	0	0	0	0	.692	-2	/3-6	-0.1
	Yr	16	70	6	14	4	0	0	7	1	3	.200	.211	.257	468	69	-2	0	0	0	.629	-8	3-16	-0.9
■ MIKE TRESH	Tresh, Michael b: 2/23/14, Hazleton, Pa. d: 10/4/66, Detroit, Mich. BR/TR, 5'11", 170 lbs. Deb: 9/4/38 F																							
1938	Chi-A	10	29	3	7	2	0	0	2	8	4	.241	.405	.310	716	80	-1	0	0	0	.978	2	C-10	0.1
1939	Chi-A	119	352	49	91	5	2	0	38	64	30	.259	.377	.284	661	70	-13	3	2	-0	.985	2	*C-119	-0.4
1940	Chi-A	135	480	62	135	15	5	1	64	49	40	.281	.349	.340	689	78	-14	3	10	-3	.983	7	*C-135	-0.1
1941	Chi-A	115	390	38	98	10	1	0	33	38	27	.251	.319	.282	601	61	-21	1	0	0	.981	10	*C-115	-0.3
1942	Chi-A	72	233	21	54	8	1	0	15	28	24	.232	.314	.275	589	68	-9	2	0	0	.977	-6	C-72	-1.0

YEAR	TM/L	G	AB	R	H	2B	3B	HR	RBI	BB	SO	AVG	OBP	SLG	OPS	OPS+	BR+	SB	CS	SBR	FA	FR	G/POS	TPR
1943	Chi-A	86	279	20	60	3	0	0	20	37	20	.215	.307	.226	533	57	-14	2	1	0	.982	-1	C-85	-1.0
1944	Chi-A	93	312	22	81	8	1	0	25	37	15	.260	.342	.292	634	83	-5	0	3	-1	.981	-3	C-93	-0.4
1945	Chi-A†	150	458	50	114	12	0	0	47	65	37	.249	.342	.275	617	82	-8	6	3	0	.984	-2	*C-150	0.0
1946	Chi-A	80	217	28	47	5	2	0	21	36	24	.217	.336	.258	594	70	-7	0	2	-1	.995	14	C-79	1.0
1947	Chi-A	90	274	19	66	6	2	0	20	26	26	.241	.311	.277	589	67	-12	2	0	0	.975	-7	C-89	-1.4
1948	Chi-A	39	108	10	27	1	0	1	11	9	9	.250	.308	.287	595	61	-6	0	0	0	.983	-1	C-34	-0.5
1949	Cle-A	38	37	4	8	0	0	0	1	5	7	.216	.310	.216	526	41	-3	0	0	0	1.000	6	C-38	0.3
Total	12	1027	3169	326	788	75	14	2	297	402	263	.249	.335	.283	619	71	-113	19	21	-3	.983	22	*C-1019	-3.7

■ **TOM TRESH** Tresh, Thomas Michael b: 9/20/37, Detroit, Mich. BB/TR, 6', 191 lbs. Deb: 9/3/61 F Career OF: (516-LF 293-CF 28-RF)

YEAR	TM/L	G	AB	R	H	2B	3B	HR	RBI	BB	SO	AVG	OBP	SLG	OPS	OPS+	BR+	SB	CS	SBR	FA	FR	G/POS	TPR
1961	NY-A	9	8	1	2	0	0	0	0	0	1	.250	.250	.250	500	36	-1	0	0	0	1.000	3	/S-3	0.2
1962	*NY-A★	157	622	94	178	26	5	20	93	67	74	.286	.363	.441	803	119	17	4	8	-2	.970	-11	*S-111,O-43(43-0-0)	1.1
1963	*NY-A★	145	520	91	140	28	5	25	71	83	79	.269	.374	.487	861	140	29	3	3	-0	.981	2	*O-144(46-101-0)	2.7
1964	*NY-A	153	533	75	131	25	5	16	73	73	110	.246	.344	.402	746	105	5	13	0	3	**.996**	-14	*O-146(106-69-6)	-1.4
1965	NY-A	156	602	94	168	29	6	26	74	59	92	.279	.348	.477	825	133	25	5	2	0	.970	-21	*O-154(100-105-18)	-0.3
1966	NY-A	151	537	76	125	12	4	27	68	86	89	.233	.345	.421	766	123	18	5	4	-0	.985	28	O-84(69-18-0),3-64	4.3
1967	NY-A	130	448	45	98	23	3	14	53	50	86	.219	.303	.377	680	104	2	1	0	0	.972	4	*O-118(118-0-0)	-0.2
1968	NY-A	152	507	60	99	18	3	11	52	76	97	.195	.305	.308	613	89	-5	10	5	0	.951	9	*S-119,O-27(27-0-0)	1.5
1969	NY-A	45	143	13	26	5	2	1	9	17	23	.182	.269	.266	534	52	-9	2	1	0	.980	0	S-41	-0.4
	Det-A	94	331	46	74	13	1	13	37	39	47	.224	.309	.387	696	90	-5	2	2	-0	.965	-18	S-77,O-11(7-0-4)/3-1	-1.6
	Yr	139	474	59	100	18	3	14	46	56	70	.211	.297	.350	647	79	-14	4	3	-0	.971	-18	*S-118,O-11L/3-1	-2.0
Total	9	1192	4251	595	1041	179	34	153	530	550	698	.245	.337	.411	748	113	75	45	25	1	.979	-19	O-727L,S-351/3-65	5.9

■ **ALEX TREVINO** Trevino, Alejandro (Castro) b: 8/26/57, Monterrey, Mex. BR/TR, 5'11", 170 lbs. Deb: 9/11/78 F

YEAR	TM/L	G	AB	R	H	2B	3B	HR	RBI	BB	SO	AVG	OBP	SLG	OPS	OPS+	BR+	SB	CS	SBR	FA	FR	G/POS	TPR
1978	NY-N	6	12	3	3	0	0	0	0	1	2	.250	.308	.250	558	60	-1	0	0	0	1.000	0	/C-5,3-1	-0.1
1979	NY-N	79	207	24	56	11	1	0	20	20	27	.271	.338	.333	671	87	-3	2	2	-0	.976	10	C-36,3-27/2-8	0.8
1980	NY-N	106	355	26	91	11	2	0	37	13	41	.256	.285	.299	583	65	-17	0	3	-1	.977	-5	C-86,3-14/2-1	-2.1
1981	NY-N	56	149	17	39	2	0	0	10	13	19	.262	.325	.275	600	73	-5	3	0	1	.963	2	C-45/2-4,O-2L,3-1	0.0
1982	Cin-N	120	355	24	89	10	3	1	33	34	34	.251	.321	.304	626	74	-11	3	1	0	.979	4	*C-116/3-2	-0.2
1983	Cin-N	74	167	14	36	8	1	1	13	17	20	.216	.288	.293	581	59	-9	0	0	0	.987	11	C-63/3-4,2-1	0.4
1984	Cin-N	6	6	0	1	0	0	0	0	0	2	.167	.167	.167	333	-6	-1	0	0	0	1.000	-0	/C-4	-0.1
	Atl-N	79	266	36	65	16	0	3	28	16	27	.244	.290	.338	628	71	-10	5	2	0	.989	7	C-79	0.0
	Yr	85	272	36	66	16	0	3	28	16	29	.243	.287	.335	622	69	-11	5	2	0	.989	6	C-83	-0.1
1985	SF-N	57	157	17	34	10	1	6	19	20	24	.217	.305	.408	713	103	0	0	0	0	.978	-0	C-55/3-1	0.2
1986	LA-N	89	202	31	53	13	0	4	26	27	35	.262	.352	.386	738	111	3	0	0	0	.969	-4	C-63/1-1	0.2
1987	LA-N	72	144	16	32	7	1	3	16	6	28	.222	.273	.347	620	65	-8	1	0	0	.987	-3	C-45/O-2(1-0-1),3-1	-0.9
1988	Hou-N	78	193	19	48	17	0	2	13	24	29	.249	.341	.368	709	108	2	5	2	0	.977	-9	C-74/O-1(1-0-0)	-0.2
1989	Hou-N	59	131	15	38	7	1	2	16	7	18	.290	.331	.405	736	113	2	0	0	0	.989	-3	C-32/1-2,3-2	0.0
1990	Hou-N	42	69	3	13	3	0	1	10	6	11	.188	.273	.275	548	53	-4	0	1	-0	.992	6	C-30/1-1	0.2
	NY-N	9	10	0	3	1	0	0	2	1	0	.300	.364	.400	764	110	0	0	0	0	.929	0	/C-7	0.1
	Cin-N	7	7	0	3	1	0	0	1	0	0	.429	.500	.571	1071	186	1	0	0	0	1.000	1	/C-2	0.2
	Yr	58	86	3	19	5	0	1	13	7	11	.221	.302	.314	616	71	-3	0	1	-0	.982	7	C-39/1-1	0.5
Total	13	939	2430	245	604	117	10	23	244	205	317	.249	.312	.333	645	81	-60	19	11	0	.979	16	C-742/3-53,2-14,O1	-1.5

■ **BOBBY TREVINO** Trevino, Carlos (Castro) b: 8/15/43, Monterrey, Mexico BR/TR, 6'2", 185 lbs. Deb: 5/22/68 F

YEAR	TM/L	G	AB	R	H	2B	3B	HR	RBI	BB	SO	AVG	OBP	SLG	OPS	OPS+	BR+	SB	CS	SBR	FA	FR	G/POS	TPR
1968	Cal-A	17	40	1	9	1	0	0	1	2	9	.225	.262	.250	512	58	-2	0	1	-0	.962	-0	O-11(1-7-5)	-0.3

■ **GUS TRIANDOS** Triandos, Gus b: 7/30/30, San Francisco, Cal BR/TR, 6'3", 215 lbs. Deb: 8/13/53

YEAR	TM/L	G	AB	R	H	2B	3B	HR	RBI	BB	SO	AVG	OBP	SLG	OPS	OPS+	BR+	SB	CS	SBR	FA	FR	G/POS	TPR
1953	NY-A	18	51	5	8	2	0	1	6	3	9	.157	.204	.255	459	24	-6	0	0	0	.991	0	1-12/C-5	-0.6
1954	NY-A	2	1	0	0	0	0	0	0	0	1	.000	.000	.000	0	-99	-0	0	0	0	.000	0	/C-1	0.0
1955	Bal-A	140	481	47	133	17	3	12	65	40	55	.277	.335	.399	734	104	1	0	0	0	.989	0	*1-103,C-36/3-1	-0.3
1956	Bal-A	131	452	47	126	18	1	21	88	48	73	.279	.351	.462	813	122	13	0	0	0	.989	10	C-89,1-52	2.3
1957	Bal-A☆	129	418	44	106	21	1	19	72	38	73	.254	.320	.445	765	114	6	0	0	0	.992	-2	*C-120	1.1
1958	Bal-A★	137	474	59	116	10	0	30	79	60	65	.245	.331	.456	787	120	12	1	0	0	.987	1	*C-132	2.1
1959	Bal-A★	126	393	43	85	7	1	25	73	65	56	.216	.332	.430	762	110	5	0	0	0	.981	2	*C-125	1.3
1960	Bal-A	109	364	36	98	18	0	12	54	41	62	.269	.345	.418	762	107	3	0	0	0	.989	-7	*C-105	0.1
1961	Bal-A	115	397	35	97	21	0	17	63	44	60	.244	.321	.426	747	101	-0	0	0	0	.989	4	*C-114	0.9
1962	Bal-A	66	207	20	33	7	0	6	23	29	43	.159	.263	.280	543	49	-15	0	0	0	.985	-2	C-63	-1.4
1963	Det-A	106	327	28	78	13	0	14	41	32	67	.239	.318	.407	725	98	-1	0	0	0	**.998**	-6	C-90	-0.2
1964	Phi-N	73	188	17	47	9	0	8	33	26	41	.250	.344	.426	770	117	5	0	0	0	.985	2	C-64/1-1	1.0
1965	Phi-N	30	82	3	14	2	0	0	4	9	17	.171	.253	.195	448	29	-8	0	0	0	.975	-5	C-28	-1.3
	Hou-N	24	72	5	13	2	0	2	7	5	14	.181	.244	.292	535	54	-5	0	0	0	.970	-2	C-20	-0.6
	Yr	54	154	8	27	4	0	2	11	14	31	.175	.249	.240	489	40	-12	0	0	0	.973	-7	C-48	-1.9
Total	13	1206	3907	389	954	147	6	167	608	440	636	.244	.324	.413	737	103	11	1	0	0	.987	-4	C-992,1-168/3-1	4.4

■ **MANNY TRILLO** Trillo, Jesus Manuel Marcano (b: Jesus Manuel Marcano (Trillo)) b: 12/25/50, Caripito, Ven. BR/TR, 6'1", 164 lbs. Deb: 6/28/73

YEAR	TM/L	G	AB	R	H	2B	3B	HR	RBI	BB	SO	AVG	OBP	SLG	OPS	OPS+	BR+	SB	CS	SBR	FA	FR	G/POS	TPR
1973	Oak-A	17	12	0	3	2	0	0	3	0	4	.250	.250	.417	667	90	-0	0	0	0	.941	5	2-16	0.5
1974	*Oak-A	21	33	3	5	0	0	0	2	2	8	.152	.222	.152	374	10	-4	0	0	0	.949	6	2-21	0.3
1975	Chi-N	154	545	55	135	12	2	7	70	45	78	.248	.309	.316	624	70	-21	1	7	-2	.967	16	*2-153/S-1	0.3
1976	Chi-N	158	582	42	139	24	3	4	59	53	70	.239	.306	.311	617	69	-23	17	6	2	.981	18	*2-156/S-1	0.8
1977	Chi-N★	152	504	51	141	18	5	7	57	44	58	.280	.344	.377	721	84	-10	3	5	-1	.970	30	*2-149	2.7
1978	Chi-N	152	552	53	144	17	5	4	55	50	67	.261	.325	.332	656	75	-17	0	7	-2	.978	**29**	*2-149	1.8
1979	Phi-N	118	431	40	112	22	1	6	42	20	59	.260	.299	.357	656	76	-15	4	7	-2	.985	6	*2-118	-0.4
1980	*Phi-N	141	531	68	155	25	9	7	43	32	46	.292	.336	.412	748	102	1	8	3	1	.987	19	*2-140	3.0
1981	*Phi-N★	94	349	37	100	14	3	6	36	26	37	.287	.341	.395	737	104	2	10	4	1	.987	11	2-94	2.0
1982	Phi-N★	149	549	52	149	24	1	0	39	33	53	.271	.316	.319	635	76	-17	8	10	-2	**.994**	5	*2-149	-0.5
1983	Cle-A★	88	320	33	87	13	1	1	29	21	46	.272	.317	.328	645	75	-11	1	3	-1	.989	3	2-87	-0.3
	Mon-N	31	121	16	32	8	0	2	16	10	18	.264	.331	.380	711	97	-0	0	0	0	.979	-6	2-31	-0.5
1984	SF-N	98	401	45	102	21	1	4	36	25	55	.254	.303	.342	645	84	-9	0	0	0	.988	-8	2-96/3-4	-1.2
1985	SF-N	125	451	36	101	16	2	3	25	40	44	.224	.289	.288	577	65	-21	2	0	0	.981	4	*2-120/3-1	-1.1
1986	Chi-N	81	152	22	45	10	0	1	19	16	21	.296	.363	.382	745	98	0	0	2	-1	.949	-0	3-53,1-11/2-6	-0.2
1987	Chi-N	108	214	27	63	8	0	8	26	25	37	.294	.368	.444	812	110	3	0	3	-1	.994	-4	1-47,3-35,2-10,/S-6	-0.4
1988	Chi-N	76	164	15	41	5	0	1	14	8	32	.250	.285	.299	584	65	-7	2	0	0	.994	1	1-24,3-17,2-13,/S-7	-0.7
1989	Cin-N	17	39	3	8	0	0	0	0	2	9	.205	.262	.205	467	34	-3	0	0	0	1.000	-4	2-10/1-3,S-1	-0.8
Total	17	1780	5950	598	1562	239	33	61	571	452	742	.263	.318	.345	663	80	-153	56	57	-8	.981	129	*2-1518,3-110/1-85,S	5.3

■ **COAKER TRIPLETT** Triplett, Herman Coaker b: 12/18/11, Boone, N.C. d: 1/30/92, Boone, N.C. BR/TR, 5'11", 185 lbs. Deb: 4/19/38

YEAR	TM/L	G	AB	R	H	2B	3B	HR	RBI	BB	SO	AVG	OBP	SLG	OPS	OPS+	BR+	SB	CS	SBR	FA	FR	G/POS	TPR
1938	Chi-N	12	36	4	9	2	1	0	2	0	1	.250	.250	.361	611	65	-2	0			1.000	-1	/O-9(6-2-1)	-0.3
1941	StL-N	76	185	29	53	6	3	3	21	18	27	.286	.350	.400	750	104	1	0			.965	-3	O-46(38-0-8)	-0.4
1942	StL-N	64	154	18	42	7	4	1	23	17	15	.273	.345	.390	735	107	1	1			.966	-3	O-46(45-0-1)	-0.4
1943	StL-N	9	25	1	2	0	0	1	4	1	6	.080	.115	.200	315	-9	-4	0			1.000	-0	/O-6(2-0-4)	-0.5
	Phi-N	105	360	45	98	16	4	14	52	28	28	.272	.325	.456	780	129	11	2			.970	2	O-90(90-0-0)	0.8
	Yr	114	385	46	100	16	4	15	56	29	34	.260	.312	.439	751	120	7	2			.972	1	O-96(92-0-4)	0.3
1944	Phi-N	84	184	15	43	5	1	1	25	19	10	.234	.305	.288	593	70	-7	1			.989	-1	O-44(41-1-2)	-1.0
1945	Phi-N	120	363	36	87	11	1	7	46	40	27	.240	.315	.333	648	83	-9	6			.945	-3	O-92(92-0-2)	-1.7
Total	6	470	1307	148	334	47	14	27	173	123	114	.256	.320	.375	694	97	-8	10			.965	-9	O-333(314-3-18)	-3.5

■ **HAL TROSKY** Trosky, Harold Arthur Sr. (b: Harold Arthur Troyavesky Sr.)
b: 11/11/12, Norway, Iowa d: 6/18/79, Cedar Rapids, Iowa BL/TR (BB 1935 (part)), 6'2", 207 lbs. Deb: 9/11/33 F

YEAR	TM/L	G	AB	R	H	2B	3B	HR	RBI	BB	SO	AVG	OBP	SLG	OPS	OPS+	BR+	SB	CS	SBR	FA	FR	G/POS	TPR
1933	Cle-A	11	44	6	13	1	2	1	8	2	12	.295	.340	.477	818	110	0	0	0	0	.990	-1	1-11	-0.1
1934	Cle-A	154	625	117	206	45	9	35	142	58	49	.330	.388	.598	987	149	42	2	2	-0	.986	0	*1-154	2.4

YEAR	TM/L	G	AB	R	H	2B	3B	HR	RBI	BB	SO	AVG	OBP	SLG	OPS	OPS+	BR+	SB	CS	SBR	FA	FR	G/POS	TPR
1935	Cle-A	154	632	84	171	33	7	26	113	46	60	.271	.321	.468	789	100	-4	1	2	-0	.993	1	*1-153	-1.7
1936	Cle-A	151	629	124	216	45	9	42	**162**	36	58	.343	.382	.644	1026	148	41	6	5	-0	.985	1	*1-151/2-1	2.4
1937	Cle-A	153	601	104	179	36	9	32	128	65	60	.298	.367	.547	915	127	21	3	1	0	.993	-2	*1-152	0.5
1938	Cle-A	150	554	106	185	40	9	19	110	67	40	.334	.407	.542	948	138	32	5	1	1	.993	4	*1-148	2.1
1939	Cle-A	122	448	89	150	31	4	25	104	52	28	.335	.405	.589	994	157	37	2	3	-1	.992	11	*1-118	3.3
1940	Cle-A	140	522	85	154	39	4	25	93	79	45	.295	.392	.529	920	140	31	1	2	-0	.991	-7	*1-139	1.0
1941	Cle-A	89	310	43	91	17	0	11	51	44	21	.294	.383	.455	838	127	12	1	2	-0	.989	-3	1-85	0.1
1944	Chi-A	135	497	55	120	32	2	10	70	62	30	.241	.327	.374	701	101	1	3	2	-0	.993	-9	*1-130	-1.6
1946	Chi-A	88	299	22	76	12	3	2	31	34	37	.254	.330	.334	665	89	-4	4	3	-0	.991	-8	1-80	-1.6
Total	11	1347	5161	835	1561	331	58	228	1012	545	440	.302	.371	.522	892	130	210	28	23	-2	.991	-12	*1-1321/2-1	6.8
■ MIKE TROST Trost, Michael J. b: 1866, Philadelphia, Pa. d: 3/24/01, Philadelphia, Pa. TR, 6'0.5", 180 lbs. Deb: 8/21/1890																								
1890	StL-a	17	51	10	13	2	0	1	7	6		.255	.345	.353	698	93	-1	4			.890	1	C-13/O-4(0-3-1)	0.0
1895	Lou-N	3	12	1	1	0	0	0	1	0	1	.083	.083	.083	167	-61	-3	1			1.000	-1	/1-3	-0.3
Total	2	20	63	11	14	2	0	1	8	6	1	.222	.300	.302	602	66	-4	5			.890	0	/C-13,O-4(0-3-1),1-3	-0.3
■ SAM TROTT Trott, Samuel W. b: 3/1859, Maryland d: 6/5/25, Catonsville, Md. BL/TL, 5'9", 190 lbs. Deb: 5/29/1880 M Career OF: (8-LF 5-CF 14-RF)																								
1880	Bos-N	39	125	14	26	4	1	0	9	3	5	.208	.227	.256	483	65	-4				.893	6	C-36/O-4(1-3-0)	0.3
1881	Det-N	6	25	3	5	2	1	0	2	1	3	.200	.231	.360	591	80	-1				.868	-2	/C-6	-0.3
1882	Det-N	32	129	11	31	7	1	0	12	0	13	.240	.240	.310	550	75	-4				.890	7	C-23/S-3,2-3,1O3	0.4
1883	Det-N	75	295	27	72	14	1	0	29	10	23	.244	.269	.298	567	76	-8				.882	-17	2-42,C-34/O-6R,1-1	-1.8
1884	Bal-a	71	284	36	73	17	9	3		4		.257	.272	.412	684	116	4				.931	16	C-60/2-6,O-5(1-1-3)	2.3
1885	Bal-a	21	88	12	24	2	2	0	12	5		.273	.312	.341	653	108	1				.882	-5	C-17/O-4R,2-2,S-1	-0.2
1887	Bal-a	85	327	44	104	16	3	0	37	27		.318	.322	.330	652	87	-4	8			.915	5	C-69,2-11/O-3L,1S	0.6
1888	Bal-a	31	108	19	30	11	4	0	22	4		.278	.304	.454	757	145	5	1			.908	-4	C-27/O-3R,2-1,1-1	0.3
Total	8	360	1381	166	365	73	22	3	123	54	44	.264	.280	.343	623	93	-11	9			.906	6	C-272/2-65,O-27R,1S3	1.6
■ QUINCY TROUPPE Trouppe, Quincy Thomas b: 12/25/12, Dublin, Ga. d: 8/12/93, Creve Coeur, Mo. BB/TR, 6'2.5", 225 lbs. Deb: 4/30/52																								
1952	Cle-A	6	10	1	1	0	0	0	0	1	3	.100	.182	.100	282	-22	-2	0	0	0	1.000	2	/C-6	0.1
■ DASHER TROY Troy, John Joseph b: 5/8/1856, New York, N.Y. d: 3/30/38, Ozone Park, N.Y. BR/TR, 5'5", 154 lbs. Deb: 8/23/1881 Career OF: (0-LF 0-CF 2-RF)																								
1881	Det-N	11	44	2	15	3	0	0	4	3	8	.341	.383	.409	792	143	2				.792	-4	/3-7,2-4	-0.1
1882	Det-N	40	152	22	37	7	2	0	14	5	10	.243	.268	.316	583	86	-2				.847	-19	2-31,S-11	-1.9
	Pro-N	4	17	1	4	0	0	0	1	0	1	.235	.235	.235	471	52	-1				.750	-1	/S-4	-0.2
	Yr	44	169	23	41	7	2	0	15	5	11	.243	.264	.308	572	83	-3				.847	-21	2-31,S-15	-2.1
1883	NY-N	85	316	37	68	7	5	0	20	9	33	.215	.237	.269	506	54	-17				.879	-14	*2-73,S-12	-2.5
1884	*NY-a	107	421	80	111	22	10	2		19		.264	.300	.378	678	123	11				.879	-20	*2-107	-0.5
1885	NY-a	45	177	24	39	3	3	2	12	5		.220	.258	.305	563	84	-3				.866	-13	2-42/O-2(0-0-2),S-1	-1.2
Total	5	292	1127	166	274	42	20	4	51	41	52	.243	.274	.327	601	92	-10				.873	-71	2-257/S-28,3-7,O-2R	-6.4
■ FRED TRUAX Truax, Frederick W. b: 1868, d: 12/18/1899, Omaha, Neb. Deb: 8/18/1890																								
1890	Pit-N	1	3	0	1	0	0	0	1	1	1	.333	.500	.333	833	163	0	0			1.000	0	/O-1(1-0-0)	0.0
■ CHRIS TRUBY Truby, Christopher John b: 12/9/73, Palm Springs, Cal. BR/TR, 6'2", 190 lbs. Deb: 6/16/2000																								
2000	Hou-N	78	258	28	67	15	4	11	59	10	56	.260	.300	.477	777	87	-6	2	1	0	.926	5	3-74	-0.1
■ HARRY TRUBY Truby, Harry Garvin "Bird Eye" b: 5/12/1870, Ironton, Ohio d: 3/21/53, Ironton, Ohio TR, 5'11", 185 lbs. Deb: 8/21/1895 U																								
1895	Chi-N	33	119	17	40	3	0	0	16	10	7	.336	.402	.361	763	92	-1	7			.950	0	2-33	0.0
1896	Chi-N	29	109	13	28	2	2	2	31	6	5	.257	.314	.367	681	76	-4	4			.935	1	2-28	-0.2
	Pit-N	8	32	1	5	0	0	0	3	2	4	.156	.206	.156	362	-4	-5	1			.949	-4	/2-8	-0.7
	Yr	37	141	14	33	2	2	2	34	8	9	.234	.289	.319	609	59	-9	5			.938	-3	2-36	-0.9
Total	2	70	260	31	73	5	2	2	50	18	16	.281	.342	.338	680	75	-10	12			.944	-3	/2-69	-0.9
■ FRANK TRUESDALE Truesdale, Frank Day b: 3/31/1884, St.Louis, Mo. d: 8/27/43, Albuquerque, N.Mex. BB/TR, 5'8", 145 lbs. Deb: 4/27/10																								
1910	StL-A	123	415	39	91	7	2	1	25	48		.219	.303	.253	556	79	-8	29			.914	-5	*2-122	-1.3
1911	StL-A	1	0	1	0	0	0	0	0	0		—	—	—	—	—	0	0			.000	0	R	0.0
1914	NY-A	77	217	22	46	4	0	0	13	39	35	.212	.340	.230	570	72	-5	11	11	-1	.947	-2	2-67/3-4	-0.8
1918	Bos-A	15	36	6	10	1	0	0	2	4	5	.278	.350	.306	656	100	0	1			.913	-1	2-10	-0.1
Total	4	216	668	68	147	12	2	1	40	91	40	.220	.318	.249	567	78	-13	41	11		.924	-7	2-199/3-4	-2.2
■ ED TRUMBULL Trumbull, Edward J. (b: Edward J. Trembly) b: 11/3/1860, Chicopee, Mass. d: 1/14/37, Kingston, Pa. Deb: 5/10/1884																								
1884	Was-a	25	86	5	10	2	0	0		2		.116	.136	.140	276	-11	-10				.828	-0	O-15(2-8-5),P-10	-0.5
■ GREG TUBBS Tubbs, Gregory Alan b: 8/31/62, Smithville, Tenn. BR/TR, 5'9", 185 lbs. Deb: 8/1/93																								
1993	Cin-N	35	59	10	11	0	0	1	2	14	10	.186	.351	.237	589	61	-3	3	1	0	.975	-4	O-21(11-14-2)	-0.6
■ EDDIE TUCKER Tucker, Eddie Jack "Scooter" b: 11/18/66, Greenville, Miss. BR/TR, 6'2", 205 lbs. Deb: 6/14/92																								
1992	Hou-N	20	50	5	6	1	0	0	3	3	13	.120	.200	.140	340	-2	-7	1	1	-0	.976	-6	C-19	-1.3
1993	Hou-N	9	26	1	5	1	0	0	3	2	3	.192	.250	.231	481	31	-3	0	0	0	1.000	2	/C-8	0.0
1995	Hou-N	5	7	1	2	0	0	1	1	0	0	.286	.286	.714	1000	164	1	0	0	0	1.000	-0	/C-3	0.0
	Cle-A	17	20	2	0	0	0	0	0	5	4	.000	.231	.000	231	-33	-4	0	0	0	.982	1	C-17	-0.2
Total	3	51	103	9	13	2	0	1	7	10	20	.126	.224	.175	399	11	-13	1	1	-0	.986	-3	/C-47	-1.5
■ MICHAEL TUCKER Tucker, Michael Anthony b: 6/25/71, S.Boston, Va. BL/TR, 6'2", 185 lbs. Deb: 4/26/95 Career OF: (152-LF 42-CF 472-RF)																								
1995	KC-A	62	177	23	46	10	0	4	17	18	51	.260	.332	.384	716	84	-4	2	3	-1	.986	1	O-36(30-1-5),D-22	-0.6
1996	KC-A	108	339	55	88	18	4	12	53	40	69	.260	.350	.442	792	99	-1	10	4	1	.989	-2	O-98(28-0-73)/1-9,D-5	-0.6
1997	*Atl-N	138	499	80	141	25	7	14	56	44	116	.283	.348	.445	793	104	2	12	7	0	.980	-5	*O-129(53-0-102)	-0.8
1998	*Atl-N	130	414	54	101	27	3	13	46	49	112	.244	.328	.418	746	94	-4	8	3	1	.995	1	*O-118(0-0-118)	-0.8
1999	Cin-N	133	296	55	75	8	5	11	44	37	81	.253	.342	.426	768	90	-4	11	4	1	.990	-6	*O-114(0-13-107)	-1.2
2000	Cin-N	148	270	55	72	13	4	15	36	44	64	.267	.383	.511	894	118	8	13	6	1	.969	-22	*O-120(41-28-67)/2-1	-1.4
Total	6	719	1995	322	523	101	23	69	252	232	493	.262	.347	.440	787	99	-2	56	27	3	.985	-33	O-615R/D-27,1-9,2-1	-5.4
■ OLLIE TUCKER Tucker, Oliver Dinwiddie b: 1/27/02, Radiant, Va. d: 7/13/40, Radiant, Va. BL/TR, 5'11", 180 lbs. Deb: 4/17/27																								
1927	Was-A	20	24	1	5	2	0	0	8	4	2	.208	.321	.292	613	61	-1	0	0	0	1.000	-0	/O-5(0-0-5)	-0.2
1928	Cle-A	14	47	5	6	0	0	1	2	7	3	.128	.255	.191	446	19	-6	0	2	-1	1.000	-0	O-14(0-0-14)	-0.7
Total	2	34	71	6	11	2	0	1	10	11	5	.155	.277	.225	502	33	-7	0	2	-1	1.000	-1	/O-19(0-0-19)	-0.9
■ TOMMY TUCKER Tucker, Thomas Joseph "Foghorn" b: 10/28/1863, Holyoke, Mass. d: 10/22/35, Montague, Mass. BB/TR, 5'11", 165 lbs. Deb: 4/16/1887 Career OF: (2-LF 12-CF 6-RF)																								
1887	Bal-a	136	553	114	173	15	9	6	84	29		.313	.347	.372	719	107	7	85			.976	4	*1-136	-0.1
1888	Bal-a	136	520	74	149	17	12	6	61	16		.287	.330	.400	730	137	21	43			.975	4	*1-129/O-7(2-0-5),P-1	1.1
1889	Bal-a	134	527	103	**196**	22	11	5	99	42	26	**.372**	**.450**	.484	**934**	**163**	**46**	63			.964	-1	*1-123,O-12(0-11-1)	2.8
1890	Bos-N	132	539	104	159	17	8	1	62	56	22	.295	.387	.362	749	110	8	43			**.979**	-2	*1-132	-0.5
1891	Bos-N	140	548	103	148	16	5	2	69	37	30	.270	.349	.328	677	87	-9	26			.976	-3	*1-140/P-1	-2.3
1892	*Bos-N	149	542	85	153	15	7	1	62	45	35	.282	.365	.341	707	104	3	22			.972	-12	*1-149	-0.9
1893	Bos-N	121	486	83	138	13	2	7	91	27	31	.284	.347	.362	709	82	-14	8			.980	-11	*1-121	-2.1
1894	Bos-N	123	500	112	165	24	6	3	100	53	21	.330	.412	.420	832	94	-5	18			**.985**	2	*1-123/O-1(0-1-0)	-0.3
1895	Bos-N	126	465	87	115	19	6	3	73	63	29	.247	.360	.333	693	74	-18	15			.978	6	*1-126	-1.0
1896	Bos-N	122	474	74	144	27	5	2	72	30	29	.304	.363	.395	757	94	-5	6			.985	3	*1-122	-0.2
1897	Bos-N	4	14	0	3	2	0	0	4	2		.214	.313	.357	670	72	-1	0			.957	1	/1-4	0.0
	Was-N	93	352	52	119	18	5	5	61	27		.338	.403	.460	863	128	15	18			.984	-3	*1-93	1.0
	Yr	97	366	52	122	20	5	5	65	29		.333	.399	.456	855	126	14	18			.982	-3	1-97	1.0
1898	Bro-N	73	283	35	79	9	4	1	34	12		.279	.325	.350	674	94	-3	1			.991	7	1-73	0.4

YEAR	TM/L	G	AB	R	H	2B	3B	HR	RBI	BB	SO	AVG	OBP	SLG	OPS	OPS+	BR+	SB	CS	SBR	FA	FR	G/POS	TPR
	StL-N	72	252	18	60	7	2	0	20	18		.238	.319	.282	601	71	-9	1			.973	-0	1-72	-0.9
	Yr	145	535	53	139	16	6	1	54	30		.260	.322	.318	640	83	-12	2			.982	7	*1-145	-0.5
1899	Cle-N	127	456	40	110	19	3	0	40	24		.241	.297	.296	593	68	-20	3			.977	-1	*1-127	-1.9
Total	13	1688	6511	1084	1911	240	85	42	932	481	223	.294	.364	.373	737	101	16	352			.978	-8	*1-1670/O-20C,P-2	-4.9

■ THURMAN TUCKER Tucker, Thurman Lowell "Joe E." b: 9/26/17, Gordon, Tex. d: 5/7/93, Oklahoma City, Okla. BL/TR, 5'11", 170 lbs. Deb: 4/14/42

YEAR	TM/L	G	AB	R	H	2B	3B	HR	RBI	BB	SO	AVG	OBP	SLG	OPS	OPS+	BR+	SB	CS	SBR	FA	FR	G/POS	TPR
1942	Chi-A	7	24	2	3	0	1	0	1	0	4	.125	.125	.208	333	-7	-3	0	0	0	.900	-1	/O-5(0-5-0)	-0.5
1943	Chi-A	139	528	81	124	15	6	3	39	79	72	.235	.336	.303	639	87	-6	29	17	0	.988	15	*O-132(0-132-0)	0.6
1944	Chi-A★	124	446	59	128	15	6	2	46	57	40	.287	.368	.361	729	110	7	13	12	-1	**.991**	18	*O-120(0-120-0)	2.1
1946	Chi-A	121	438	62	126	20	3	1	36	54	45	.288	.367	.354	721	106	5	9	10	-2	.990	2	*O-110(0-110-0)	0.2
1947	Chi-A	89	254	28	60	9	4	1	17	38	25	.236	.336	.315	651	85	-5	10	4	1	.978	-1	O-65(0-65-0)	-0.7
1948	*Cle-A	83	242	52	63	13	2	1	19	31	17	.260	.347	.343	690	86	-5	11	2	2	1.000	-1	O-66(0-66-0)	-0.5
1949	Cle-A	80	197	28	48	5	2	0	14	18	19	.244	.307	.289	596	59	-12	4	2	0	.984	2	O-42(4-38-0)	-1.0
1950	Cle-A	57	101	13	18	2	0	1	7	14	14	.178	.284	.228	512	34	-10	1	0	0	.968	-5	O-34(15-16-4)	-1.5
1951	Cle-A	1	1	0	0	0	0	0	0	0	1	.000	.000	.000	0	-99	-0	0	0	0	.000	0	H	0.0
Total	9	701	2231	325	570	79	24	9	179	291	237	.255	.342	.325	667	89	-28	77	47	0	.988	29	O-574(19-552-4)	-1.3

■ BRIAN TURANG Turang, Brian Craig b: 6/14/67, Long Beach, Cal. BR/TR, 5'10", 170 lbs. Deb: 8/13/93 Career OF: (46-LF 26-CF 1-RF)

YEAR	TM/L	G	AB	R	H	2B	3B	HR	RBI	BB	SO	AVG	OBP	SLG	OPS	OPS+	BR+	SB	CS	SBR	FA	FR	G/POS	TPR
1993	Sea-A	40	140	22	35	11	1	0	7	17	20	.250	.340	.343	682	83	-3	6	2	1	.986	-2	O-38L/3-2,2-1,D-1	-0.5
1994	Sea-A	38	112	9	21	5	1	1	8	7	25	.188	.242	.277	518	33	-11	3	1	0	.978	-4	O-30(20-12-0)/2-5,D-4	-1.5
Total	2	78	252	31	56	16	2	1	15	24	45	.222	.297	.313	611	60	-14	9	3	1	.983	-6	/O-68L,2-6,D-5,3-2	-2.0

■ JERRY TURBIDY Turbidy, Jeremiah b: 7/4/1852, Dudley, Mass. d: 9/5/20, Webster, Mass. 5'8", 165 lbs. Deb: 7/27/1884

YEAR	TM/L	G	AB	R	H	2B	3B	HR	RBI	BB	SO	AVG	OBP	SLG	OPS	OPS+	BR+	SB	CS	SBR	FA	FR	G/POS	TPR
1884	KC-U	13	49	5	11	4	0	0		3		.224	.269	.306	575	85	-2				.830	6	S-13	0.4

■ EDDIE TURCHIN Turchin, Edward Lawrence "Smiley" b: 2/10/17, New York, N.Y. d: 2/8/82, Brookhaven, N.Y. BR/TR, 5'10", 165 lbs. Deb: 5/9/43

YEAR	TM/L	G	AB	R	H	2B	3B	HR	RBI	BB	SO	AVG	OBP	SLG	OPS	OPS+	BR+	SB	CS	SBR	FA	FR	G/POS	TPR
1943	Cle-A	11	13	4	3	0	0	0	1	3	1	.231	.375	.231	606	84	-0	0	0	0	1.000	1	/3-4,S-2	0.2

■ PETE TURGEON Turgeon, Eugene Joseph b: 1/3/1897, Minneapolis, Minn. d: 1/24/77, Wichita Falls, Tex BR/TR, 5'6", 145 lbs. Deb: 9/20/23

YEAR	TM/L	G	AB	R	H	2B	3B	HR	RBI	BB	SO	AVG	OBP	SLG	OPS	OPS+	BR+	SB	CS	SBR	FA	FR	G/POS	TPR
1923	Chi-N	3	6	1	1	0	0	0	0	0	0	.167	.167	.167	333	-12	-1	0	0	0	.875	0	/S-2	-0.1

■ CHRIS TURNER Turner, Christopher Wan b: 3/23/69, Bowling Green, Ky. BR/TR, 6'1", 190 lbs. Deb: 8/27/93 Career OF: (1-LF 0-CF 1-RF)

YEAR	TM/L	G	AB	R	H	2B	3B	HR	RBI	BB	SO	AVG	OBP	SLG	OPS	OPS+	BR+	SB	CS	SBR	FA	FR	G/POS	TPR
1993	Cal-A	25	75	9	21	5	0	1	13	9	16	.280	.365	.387	751	99	0	1	1	-0	.992	-4	C-25	-0.2
1994	Cal-A	58	149	23	36	7	1	1	12	10	29	.242	.294	.322	616	58	-9	3	0	1	.997	4	C-57	-0.2
1995	Cal-A	5	10	0	1	0	0	0	1	0	3	.100	.100	.100	200	-48	-2	0	0	0	1.000	1	/C-4,D-1	-0.1
1996	Cal-A	4	3	1	1	0	0	0	1	1	0	.333	.500	.333	833	116	0	0	0	0	1.000	-0	/C-3,O-1(1-0-0)	0.0
1997	Ana-A	13	23	4	6	1	1	1	2	5	8	.261	.393	.522	915	136	1	0	0	0	1.000	-2	/C-8,1-2,O-1R,D-1	0.0
1998	KC-A	4	9	0	0	0	0	0	0	0	4	.000	.100	.000	100	-69	-2	0	0	0	1.000	-1	/C-4	-0.3
1999	Cle-A	12	21	3	4	0	0	0	0	1	8	.190	.227	.190	418	8	-3	1	0	0	.964	2	C-12	0.0
2000	NY-A	37	89	9	21	3	0	1	7	10	21	.236	.320	.303	623	60	-5	0	1	-0	1.000	0	C-36/1-1	-0.4
Total	8	158	379	49	90	16	2	4	36	36	89	.237	.310	.322	632	63	-20	5	2	0	.994	1	C-149/1-3,O-2L,D-2	-1.2

■ EARL TURNER Turner, Earl Edwin b: 5/6/23, Pittsfield, Mass. d: 10/20/99, Lee, Mass. BR/TR, 5'9", 170 lbs. Deb: 9/25/48

YEAR	TM/L	G	AB	R	H	2B	3B	HR	RBI	BB	SO	AVG	OBP	SLG	OPS	OPS+	BR+	SB	CS	SBR	FA	FR	G/POS	TPR
1948	Pit-N	2	1	0	0	0	0	0	0	0	0	.000	.000	.000	0	-98	-0	0			.000	0	/C-1	0.0
1950	Pit-N	40	74	10	18	0	0	3	5	4	13	.243	.282	.365	647	66	-4	1			.974	2	C-34	-0.1
Total	2	42	75	10	18	0	0	3	5	4	13	.240	.278	.360	638	64	-4	1			.974	2	/C-35	-0.1

■ TUCK TURNER Turner, George A. b: 2/13/1873, W.New Brighton, N.Y. d: 7/16/45, Staten Island, N.Y. BB/TL, 5'6.5", 155 lbs. Deb: 8/18/1893

YEAR	TM/L	G	AB	R	H	2B	3B	HR	RBI	BB	SO	AVG	OBP	SLG	OPS	OPS+	BR+	SB	CS	SBR	FA	FR	G/POS	TPR
1893	Phi-N	36	155	32	50	4	3	1	13	9	19	.323	.364	.406	770	105	1	7			.933	-2	O-36(1-35-0)	-0.3
1894	Phi-N	82	347	95	145	21	9	1	84	24	13	.418	.458	.539	997	143	25	11			.902	-9	O-80(56-3-22)/P-1	0.8
1895	Phi-N	59	210	51	81	8	6	2	43	25	11	.386	.453	.510	963	147	16	14			.847	-8	O-55(31-9-15)	0.3
1896	Phi-N	13	32	12	7	2	0	0	0	8	5	.219	.375	.281	656	75	-1	6			.905	2	/O-8(1-7-0)	0.0
	StL-N	51	203	30	50	7	8	1	27	14	21	.246	.298	.374	673	80	-7	6			.961	-5	O-51(0-0-51)	-1.3
	Yr	64	235	42	57	9	8	1	27	22	26	.243	.310	.362	672	79	-8	12			.948	-4	O-59(1-7-51)	-1.3
1897	StL-N	103	416	58	121	17	12	2	41	35		.291	.350	.404	754	101	-0	8			.945	-7	*O-102(0-0-102)	-1.1
1898	StL-N	35	141	20	28	8	0	0	7	14	—	.199	.280	.255	536	52	-9	1			.929	-3	O-34(0-0-34)	-1.3
Total	6	379	1504	298	482	67	38	7	215	129	69	.320	.378	.430	807	111	26	53			.916	-33	O-366(89-54-224)/P-1	-2.9

■ JERRY TURNER Turner, John Webber b: 1/17/54, Texarkana, Ark. BL/TL, 5'9", 180 lbs. Deb: 9/2/74

YEAR	TM/L	G	AB	R	H	2B	3B	HR	RBI	BB	SO	AVG	OBP	SLG	OPS	OPS+	BR+	SB	CS	SBR	FA	FR	G/POS	TPR
1974	SD-N	17	48	4	14	1	0	0	2	3	5	.292	.333	.313	646	85	-1	2	1	0	1.000	-1	O-13(13-0-0)	-0.3
1975	SD-N	11	22	1	6	0	0	0	0	2	1	.273	.333	.273	606	74	-1	0	0	0	.909	0	/O-4(4-0-0)	-0.1
1976	SD-N	105	281	41	75	16	5	5	37	32	38	.267	.342	.413	755	123	8	12	6	1	.960	-2	O-74(74-0-0)	0.3
1977	SD-N	118	289	43	71	16	1	10	48	31	43	.246	.319	.412	731	105	1	12	4	1	.947	3	O-69(65-4-2)	0.3
1978	SD-N	106	225	28	63	9	1	8	37	21	32	.280	.349	.436	785	128	8	6	4	-0	.970	-7	O-58(28-17-24)	-0.1
1979	SD-N	138	448	55	111	23	2	9	61	34	58	.248	.304	.368	672	88	-9	4	2	0	.958	-1	*O-115(114-0-2)	-1.5
1980	SD-N	85	153	22	44	5	0	3	18	10	18	.288	.339	.379	718	106	1	8	3	1	1.000	-4	O-34(5-0-30)	-0.4
1981	SD-N	33	31	5	7	0	0	2	6	4	3	.226	.314	.419	734	115	1	0	1	-0	.833	-1	/O-4(0-0-4)	-0.1
	Chi-A	10	12	1	2	0	0	0	2	1	2	.167	.231	.167	397	16	-1	0	0	0	1.000	0	/O-1(0-0-1)	-0.1
1982	Det-A	85	210	21	52	3	0	8	27	20	37	.248	.313	.376	689	88	-4	1	3	-1	.909	-4	D-50,O-13(2-0-12)	-1.0
1983	SD-N	25	23	1	3	0	0	0	0	1	8	.130	.167	.130	297	-17	-4	0	0	0	.000	-0	/O-1(0-0-1)	-0.4
Total	10	733	1742	222	448	73	9	45	238	159	245	.257	.322	.387	709	101	0	45	24	2	.959	-18	O-386(305-21-76)/D-50	-3.4

■ SHANE TURNER Turner, Shane Lee b: 1/8/63, Los Angeles, Cal. BL/TR, 5'10", 180 lbs. Deb: 8/19/88 Career OF: (15-LF 0-CF 1-RF)

YEAR	TM/L	G	AB	R	H	2B	3B	HR	RBI	BB	SO	AVG	OBP	SLG	OPS	OPS+	BR+	SB	CS	SBR	FA	FR	G/POS	TPR
1988	Phi-N	18	35	1	6	0	0	0	1	5	9	.171	.275	.171	446	30	-3	0	0	0	.941	-2	/3-8,S-5	-0.6
1991	Bal-A	4	1	0	0	0	0	0	0	0	0	.000	.000	.000	0	-99	-0	0	0	0	1.000	-0	/2-1,D-1	0.0
1992	Sea-A	34	74	8	20	5	0	0	5	9	15	.270	.349	.338	687	93	-0	2	1	0	.881	-5	3-18,O-15(15-0-1)	-0.5
Total	3	56	110	9	26	5	0	0	6	14	24	.236	.323	.282	604	71	-4	2	1	0	.898	-7	/3-26,O-15L,S-5,D2	-1.1

■ TERRY TURNER Turner, Terrence Lamont "Cotton Top" b: 2/28/1881, Sandy Lake, Pa. d: 7/18/60, Cleveland, Ohio BR/TR, 5'8", 149 lbs. Deb: 8/25/01 C

YEAR	TM/L	G	AB	R	H	2B	3B	HR	RBI	BB	SO	AVG	OBP	SLG	OPS	OPS+	BR+	SB	CS	SBR	FA	FR	G/POS	TPR
1901	Pit-N	2	7	0	3	0	0	0	1	0		.429	.429	.429	857	145	0	0			.833	1	/3-2	0.2
1904	Cle-A	111	404	41	95	9	6	1	45	11		.235	.255	.295	550	74	-13	5			.940	3	*S-111	-0.7
1905	Cle-A	155	586	49	155	16	14	4	72	14		.265	.289	.360	649	104	0	17			.946	-26	*S-155	-2.2
1906	Cle-A	147	584	85	170	27	7	2	62	35		.291	.338	.372	709	124	15	27			**.960**	23	*S-147	4.6
1907	Cle-A	140	524	57	127	20	7	0	46	19		.242	.272	.307	579	84	-11	27			**.950**	-4	*S-139	-1.1
1908	Cle-A	60	201	21	48	11	1	0	19	15		.239	.298	.303	602	95	-1	18			.952	-4	O-36(0-2-34),S-17	-0.7
1909	Cle-A	53	208	25	52	7	4	0	16	14		.250	.304	.322	626	94	-2	14			.969	10	2-26,S-26	1.1
1910	Cle-A	150	574	71	132	14	6	0	33	53		.230	.301	.275	576	79	-13	31			.973	2	S-94,3-46/2-9	-0.7
1911	Cle-A	117	417	59	105	16	9	0	28	34		.252	.310	.333	643	78	-13	29			.970	1	3-94,2-14,S-10	-0.8
1912	Cle-A	103	370	54	114	14	4	0	33	31		.308	.363	.368	731	106	3	19			**.951**	-2	*3-103	0.3
1913	Cle-A	120	388	60	96	13	4	0	44	55	35	.247	.348	.302	650	88	-4	13			.954	16	3-71,2-25,S-21	1.7
1914	Cle-A	121	428	43	105	14	9	1	33	44	36	.245	.319	.327	646	91	-5	17	13	-1	**.963**	21	*3-104,2-17	2.0
1915	Cle-A	75	262	35	66	14	1	0	14	29	13	.252	.329	.313	642	90	-3	12	11	-1	.965	-9	2-51,3-20	-1.2
1916	Cle-A	124	428	52	112	15	3	0	38	40	29	.262	.325	.311	636	86	-7	15			.963	5	3-77,2-42	0.1
1917	Cle-A	69	180	16	37	7	0	0	15	14	19	.206	.263	.244	507	51	-11	4			.980	-2	3-40,2-23/S-1	-1.3
1918	Cle-A	74	233	24	58	7	2	0	23	22	15	.249	.316	.296	613	77	-6	6			.969	-4	3-46,2-26/S-1	-0.9
1919	Phi-A	38	127	7	24	3	0	0	6	5	9	.189	.220	.213	432	21	-13	2			.946	1	S-19,2-17/3-1	-1.1
Total	17	1659	5921	699	1499	207	77	8	528	435	156	.253	.308	.318	626	89	-82	256	24		.952	33	S-741,3-604,2-250,/O	-0.7

■ TOM TURNER Turner, Thomas Richard b: 9/8/16, Custer Co., Okla. d: 5/14/86, Kennewick, Wash. BR/TR, 6'2", 195 lbs. Deb: 4/25/40

YEAR	TM/L	G	AB	R	H	2B	3B	HR	RBI	BB	SO	AVG	OBP	SLG	OPS	OPS+	BR+	SB	CS	SBR	FA	FR	G/POS	TPR
1940	Chi-A	37	96	11	20	1	2	0	6	3	12	.208	.240	.260	500	29	-10	1	0	0	.969	2	C-29	-0.6
1941	Chi-A	38	126	7	30	5	0	0	8	9	15	.238	.289	.278	567	51	-9	2	0	0	.979	5	C-35	-0.1
1942	Chi-A	56	182	18	44	9	1	3	21	19	15	.242	.313	.352	665	89	-3	0	1	-0	.971	-1	C-54	-0.1

YEAR	TM/L	G	AB	R	H	2B	3B	HR	RBI	BB	SO	AVG	OBP	SLG	OPS	OPS+	BR+	SB	CS	SBR	FA	FR	G/POS	TPR
1943	Chi-A	51	154	16	37	7	1	2	11	13	21	.240	.299	.338	637	86	-3	1	0	0	.978	4	C-49	0.5
1944	Chi-A	36	113	9	26	6	0	2	13	5	16	.230	.263	.336	599	71	-5	0	1	-0	.958	-2	C-36	-0.6
	*StL-A	15	25	2	8	1	0	0	4	2	5	.320	.370	.360	730	103	0	0	0	0	.969	-1	C-11	0.0
	Yr	51	138	11	34	7	0	2	17	7	21	.246	.283	.341	623	77	-5	0	1	-0	.960	-3	C-47	-0.6
Total	5	233	696	63	165	29	4	7	63	51	84	.237	.290	.320	611	70	-29	4	2	0	.972	7	C-214	-0.9

■ BILL TUTTLE Tuttle, William Robert b: 7/4/29, Elwood, Ill. d: 7/27/98, Anoka, Minn. BR/TR, 6', 190 lbs. Deb: 9/10/52 Career OF: (4-LF 1139-CF 67-RF)

YEAR	TM/L	G	AB	R	H	2B	3B	HR	RBI	BB	SO	AVG	OBP	SLG	OPS	OPS+	BR+	SB	CS	SBR	FA	FR	G/POS	TPR
1952	Det-A	7	25	2	6	0	0	0	2	0	1	.240	.240	.240	480	34	-2	0	0	0	1.000	1	/O-6(3-3-0)	-0.2
1954	Det-A	147	530	64	141	20	11	7	58	62	60	.266	.345	.385	730	102	1	5	8	-2	.985	4	*O-145(1-144-0)	-0.4
1955	Det-A	154	603	102	168	23	4	14	78	76	54	.279	.360	.400	760	107	6	6	3	0	.985	15	*O-154(0-154-0)	1.4
1956	Det-A	140	546	61	138	22	4	9	65	38	48	.253	.303	.357	660	73	-22	5	4	-0	.976	10	*O-137(0-137-0)	-1.9
1957	Det-A	133	451	49	113	12	4	5	47	44	41	.251	.319	.328	647	75	-15	2	6	-2	.982	4	*O-128(0-128-0)	-1.9
1958	KC-A	148	511	77	118	14	9	11	51	74	58	.231	.329	.358	687	88	-8	7	9	-2	.988	1	*O-145(0-107-46)	-1.5
1959	KC-A	126	463	74	139	19	6	7	43	48	38	.300	.371	.413	783	113	9	10	6	0	.984	12	*O-121(0-121-0)	1.5
1960	KC-A	151	559	75	143	21	3	8	40	66	52	.256	.337	.347	684	85	-11	1	5	-2	.988	17	*O-148(0-148-0)	-0.2
1961	KC-A	25	84	15	22	2	2	0	8	9	9	.262	.333	.333	667	77	-3	0	0	0	.951	-1	O-25(0-25-0)	-0.4
	Min-A	113	370	38	91	12	3	5	38	43	41	.246	.324	.335	660	73	-14	1	3	-1	.943	-13	3-85,O-64(0-63-6)/2-2	-2.9
	Yr	138	454	53	113	14	5	5	46	52	50	.249	.326	.335	661	73	-16	1	3	-1	.970	-14	O-89(0-88-6),3-85/2-2	-3.3
1962	Min-A	110	123	21	26	4	1	1	13	19	14	.211	.322	.285	606	62	-6	1	0	0	.973	-31	*O-104(0-95-15)	-3.9
1963	Min-A	16	3	0	0	0	0	0	0	1	0	.000	.250	.000	250	-22	-0	0	0	0	1.000	-4	O-14(0-14-0)	-0.5
Total	11	1270	4268	578	1105	149	47	67	443	480	416	.259	.336	.363	699	88	-64	38	44	-7	.983	14	*O-1191C/3-85,2-2	-10.9

■ GUY TUTWILER Tutwiler, Guy Isbel "King Tut" b: 7/17/1888, Coalburg, Ala. d: 8/15/30, Birmingham, Ala. BL/TR, 6', 175 lbs. Deb: 8/29/11

YEAR	TM/L	G	AB	R	H	2B	3B	HR	RBI	BB	SO	AVG	OBP	SLG	OPS	OPS+	BR+	SB	CS	SBR	FA	FR	G/POS	TPR
1911	Det-A	13	32	3	6	2	0	0	3	2		.188	.235	.250	485	34	-3	0			.778	-4	/2-6,O-3(3-0-0)	-0.7
1913	Det-A	14	47	4	10	0	1	0	7	4	12	.213	.275	.255	530	56	-3	2			.987	1	1-14	-0.2
Total	2	27	79	7	16	2	1	0	10	6	12	.203	.259	.253	512	47	-6	2			.987	-3	/1-14,2-6,O-3(3-0-0)	-0.9

■ ART TWINEHAM Twineham, Arthur W. "Old Hoss" b: 11/26/1866, Galesburg, Ill. BL/TL, 6'1.5", 190 lbs. Deb: 9/11/1893

YEAR	TM/L	G	AB	R	H	2B	3B	HR	RBI	BB	SO	AVG	OBP	SLG	OPS	OPS+	BR+	SB	CS	SBR	FA	FR	G/POS	TPR
1893	StL-N	14	48	8	15	2	0	0	11	1	2	.313	.340	.354	694	84	-1	0			.928	2	C-14	0.2
1894	StL-N	38	127	22	40	4	1	1	16	9	11	.315	.387	.386	773	87	-2	2			.939	4	C-38	0.4
Total	2	52	175	30	55	6	1	1	27	10	13	.314	.375	.377	752	86	-3	2			.936	7	/C-52	0.6

■ LARRY TWITCHELL Twitchell, Lawrence Grant b: 2/18/1864, Cleveland, Ohio d: 8/23/30, Cleveland, Ohio BR/TR, 6', 185 lbs. Deb: 4/30/1886 Career OF: (511-LF 10-CF 88-RF)

YEAR	TM/L	G	AB	R	H	2B	3B	HR	RBI	BB	SO	AVG	OBP	SLG	OPS	OPS+	BR+	SB	CS	SBR	FA	FR	G/POS	TPR
1886	Det-N	4	16	0	1	0	0	0	0	0	2	.063	.063	.063	125	-60	-3	0			1.000	0	/P-4,O-2(1-1-0)	-0.1
1887	*Det-N	65	272	44	96	14	6	0	51	8	19	.353	.358	.432	789	115	4	12			.871	-6	O-53(44-9-0),P-15	-0.2
1888	Det-N	131	524	71	128	19	4	5	67	28	45	.244	.286	.324	611	95	-3	14			.885	-9	*O-131(131-0-0)/P-2	-1.5
1889	Cle-N	134	549	73	151	16	11	4	95	29	37	.275	.315	.366	681	92	-7	17			.916	-10	*O-134(134-0-0)/P-1	-1.8
1890	Cle-P	56	233	33	52	6	3	2	36	17	17	.223	.279	.300	579	60	-13	4			.821	-9	O-56(1-0-56)	-1.9
	Buf-P	44	172	24	38	3	1	2	17	23	12	.221	.316	.285	601	67	-7	4			.918	-1	O-32(4-0-28),P-13/1-3	-0.7
	Yr	100	405	57	90	9	4	4	53	40	29	.222	.295	.294	589	63	-20	8			.857	-10	O-88(5-0-84),P-13/1-3	-2.6
1891	Col-a	57	224	32	62	9	4	2	35	20	28	.277	.341	.379	721	113	3	10			.887	-10	O-56(56-0-0)/P-6	-0.7
1892	Was-N	51	192	20	42	9	5	0	20	11	31	.219	.275	.318	593	82	-5	8			.897	-5	O-48(46-0-2)/S-3,3-1	-1.3
1893	Lou-N	45	187	37	58	11	3	2	31	17	20	.310	.377	.433	810	125	7	7			.874	-2	O-45(43-0-2)	0.1
1894	Lou-N	52	210	28	56	16	3	2	32	15	20	.267	.316	.400	716	77	-9	8			.908	7	O-51(51-0-0)/P-1	-0.5
Total	9	639	2579	362	684	103	40	19	384	168	231	.265	.313	.356	669	91	-33	84			.890	-45	O-608L/P-42,S-3,13	-8.6

■ BABE TWOMBLY Twombly, Clarence Edward b: 1/18/1896, Jamaica Plain, Mass. d: 11/23/74, San Clemente, Cal. BL/TR, 5'10", 165 lbs. Deb: 4/14/20 F

YEAR	TM/L	G	AB	R	H	2B	3B	HR	RBI	BB	SO	AVG	OBP	SLG	OPS	OPS+	BR+	SB	CS	SBR	FA	FR	G/POS	TPR
1920	Chi-N	78	183	25	43	1	1	2	14	17	20	.235	.303	.284	588	68	-7	5	9	-2	.970	0	O-45(5-15-25)/2-2	-1.2
1921	Chi-N	87	175	22	66	8	1	1	18	11	10	.377	.414	.451	865	129	8	4	6	-1	.968	0	O-45(10-29-6)	0.5
Total	2	165	358	47	109	9	2	3	32	28	30	.304	.357	.366	723	98	0	9	15	-3	.969	1	/O-90(15-44-31),2-2	-0.7

■ GEORGE TWOMBLY Twombly, George Frederick "Silent George" b: 6/4/1892, Boston, Mass. d: 2/17/75, Lexington, Mass. BR/TR, 5'9", 165 lbs. Deb: 7/9/14 F

YEAR	TM/L	G	AB	R	H	2B	3B	HR	RBI	BB	SO	AVG	OBP	SLG	OPS	OPS+	BR+	SB	CS	SBR	FA	FR	G/POS	TPR
1914	Cin-N	68	240	22	56	0	5	0	19	14	27	.233	.284	.275	559	64	-10	12			.968	1	O-68(68-0-1)	-1.4
1915	Cin-N	46	66	5	13	0	1	0	5	8	8	.197	.293	.227	521	57	-3	5	3	0	1.000	-4	O-24(10-13-1)	-0.9
1916	Cin-N	3	5	0	0	0	0	0	0	1	1	.000	.167	.000	167	-48	-1	0			1.000	-0	/O-1(1-0-0)	-0.1
1917	Bos-N	32	102	8	19	1	1	0	9	18	5	.186	.314	.216	530	68	-3	4			.943	-5	O-29(1-21-7)/1-1	-1.1
1919	Was-A	1	4	0	0	0	0	0	0	0	0	.000	.000	.000	0	-99	-1	0			.000	-1	/O-1(1-0-0)	-0.2
Total	5	150	417	35	88	1	7	0	33	41	41	.211	.289	.247	536	62	-18	21	3		.967	-9	O-123(81-34-9)/1-1	-3.7

■ JIM TYACK Tyack, James Frederick b: 1/9/11, Florence, Mont. d: 1/3/95, Bakersfield, Cal. BL/TR, 6'2", 195 lbs. Deb: 4/20/43

YEAR	TM/L	G	AB	R	H	2B	3B	HR	RBI	BB	SO	AVG	OBP	SLG	OPS	OPS+	BR+	SB	CS	SBR	FA	FR	G/POS	TPR
1943	Phi-A	54	155	11	40	8	1	0	23	14	9	.258	.320	.323	642	88	-2	1	1	-0	.977	1	O-38(9-2-27)	-0.4

■ FRED TYLER Tyler, Frederick Franklin "Clancy" b: 12/16/1891, Derry, N.H. d: 10/14/45, E.Derry, N.H. BR/TR, 5'10.5", 180 lbs. Deb: 4/14/14 F

YEAR	TM/L	G	AB	R	H	2B	3B	HR	RBI	BB	SO	AVG	OBP	SLG	OPS	OPS+	BR+	SB	CS	SBR	FA	FR	G/POS	TPR
1914	Bos-N	6	19	2	2	0	0	0	2	1	5	.105	.150	.105	255	-24	-3	0			1.000	-1	/C-6	-0.3

■ JOHNNIE TYLER Tyler, John Anthony "Ty Ty" or "Katz" (b: John Tylka) b: 7/30/06, Mt.Pleasant, Pa. d: 7/11/72, Mt.Pleasant, Pa. BB/TR, 6', 175 lbs. Deb: 9/16/34

YEAR	TM/L	G	AB	R	H	2B	3B	HR	RBI	BB	SO	AVG	OBP	SLG	OPS	OPS+	BR+	SB	CS	SBR	FA	FR	G/POS	TPR
1934	Bos-N	3	6	0	1	0	0	0	1	0	3	.167	.167	.167	333	-11	-1	0			1.000	1	/O-1(0-1-0)	0.0
1935	Bos-N	13	47	7	16	2	1	2	11	4	3	.340	.404	.553	957	168	4	0			.893	-0	O-11(11-0-0)	0.3
Total	2	16	53	7	17	2	1	2	12	4	6	.321	.379	.509	889	148	4	0			.906	1	/O-12(11-1-0)	0.3

■ JASON TYNER Tyner, Jason Renyt b: 4/23/77, Bedford, Tex. BL/TL, 6'1", 170 lbs. Deb: 6/5/2000

YEAR	TM/L	G	AB	R	H	2B	3B	HR	RBI	BB	SO	AVG	OBP	SLG	OPS	OPS+	BR+	SB	CS	SBR	FA	FR	G/POS	TPR
2000	NY-N	13	41	3	8	2	0	0	5	1	4	.195	.233	.244	476	21	-5	1	1	-0	.920	0	O-12(12-2-0)	-0.5
	TB-A	37	83	6	20	2	0	0	8	4	12	.241	.284	.265	549	40	-7	6	1	1	1.000	0	O-31(27-4-0)/D-1	-0.6
Total	1	50	124	9	28	4	0	0	13	5	16	.226	.267	.258	525	34	-12	7	2	1	.975	0	/O-43(39-6-0),D-1	-1.1

■ EARL TYREE Tyree, Earl Carlton "Ty" b: 3/4/1890, Huntsville, Ill. d: 5/17/54, Rushville, Ill. BR/TR, 5'8", 160 lbs. Deb: 10/5/14

YEAR	TM/L	G	AB	R	H	2B	3B	HR	RBI	BB	SO	AVG	OBP	SLG	OPS	OPS+	BR+	SB	CS	SBR	FA	FR	G/POS	TPR
1914	Chi-N	1	4	1	0	0	0	0	0	0	0	.000	.000	.000	0	-99	-1	0			1.000	-1	/C-1	-0.2

■ JIM TYRONE Tyrone, James Vernon b: 1/29/49, Alice, Tex. BR/TR, 6'1", 185 lbs. Deb: 8/27/72 F Career OF: (42-LF 5-CF 83-RF)

YEAR	TM/L	G	AB	R	H	2B	3B	HR	RBI	BB	SO	AVG	OBP	SLG	OPS	OPS+	BR+	SB	CS	SBR	FA	FR	G/POS	TPR
1972	Chi-N	13	8	1	0	0	0	0	0	0	3	.000	.000	.000	0	-90	-2	1	0	0	1.000	0	/O-4(3-0-1)	-0.1
1974	Chi-N	57	81	19	15	0	1	3	3	6	8	.185	.241	.321	562	54	-5	1	1	-0	.962	-8	O-32(21-1-12)/3-1	-1.5
1975	Chi-N	11	22	0	5	0	1	0	3	1	4	.227	.261	.318	579	58	-1	1	1	-0	1.000	-1	/O-8(8-0-0)	-0.3
1977	Oak-A	96	294	32	72	11	1	5	26	25	62	.245	.304	.340	644	76	-10	3	1	0	.950	1	O-81R/1-1,S-1,D-4	-1.2
Total	4	177	405	52	92	11	3	8	32	32	77	.227	.284	.328	612	67	-18	6	3	0	.955	-7	O-125R/D-4,S-1,13	-3.1

■ WAYNE TYRONE Tyrone, Oscar Wayne b: 8/1/50, Alice, Tex. BR/TR, 6'1", 185 lbs. Deb: 7/15/76 F

YEAR	TM/L	G	AB	R	H	2B	3B	HR	RBI	BB	SO	AVG	OBP	SLG	OPS	OPS+	BR+	SB	CS	SBR	FA	FR	G/POS	TPR
1976	Chi-N	30	57	3	13	1	0	1	8	3	21	.228	.267	.298	565	55	-3	0	0	0	1.000	-3	/O-7(6-0-1),1-5,3-5	-0.7

■ TY TYSON Tyson, Albert Thomas b: 6/1/1892, Wilkes-Barre, Pa. d: 8/16/53, Buffalo, N.Y. BR/TR, 5'11", 169 lbs. Deb: 4/13/26

YEAR	TM/L	G	AB	R	H	2B	3B	HR	RBI	BB	SO	AVG	OBP	SLG	OPS	OPS+	BR+	SB	CS	SBR	FA	FR	G/POS	TPR
1926	NY-N	97	335	40	98	16	1	3	35	15	28	.293	.329	.373	702	90	-5	6			.980	3	O-92(12-83-0)	-0.7
1927	NY-N	43	159	24	42	7	2	1	17	10	19	.264	.308	.352	660	76	-5	5			.929	-3	O-41(40-1-2)	-1.1
1928	Bro-N	59	210	25	57	11	1	1	21	10	14	.271	.317	.348	665	75	-8	3			.965	0	O-55(1-41-14)	-1.0
Total	3	199	704	89	197	34	4	5	73	35	61	.280	.320	.361	681	82	-19	14			.966	0	O-188(53-125-16)	-2.8

■ TURKEY TYSON Tyson, Cecil Washington "Slim" b: 12/6/14, Elm City, N.C. d: 2/17/2000, Elm City, N.C. BL/TR, 6'5.5", 225 lbs. Deb: 4/23/44

YEAR	TM/L	G	AB	R	H	2B	3B	HR	RBI	BB	SO	AVG	OBP	SLG	OPS	OPS+	BR+	SB	CS	SBR	FA	FR	G/POS	TPR
1944	Phi-N	1	1	0	0	0	0	0	0	0	0	.000	.000	.000	0	-99	-0	0			.000	0	H	0.0

■ MIKE TYSON Tyson, Michael Ray b: 1/13/50, Rocky Mount, N.C. BR/TR (BB 1972, 76, 79, 80 (partS)), 5'9", 170 lbs. Deb: 9/5/72

YEAR	TM/L	G	AB	R	H	2B	3B	HR	RBI	BB	SO	AVG	OBP	SLG	OPS	OPS+	BR+	SB	CS	SBR	FA	FR	G/POS	TPR
1972	StL-N	13	37	1	7	1	0	0	0	1	9	.189	.211	.216	427	22	-4	0	1	-0	.981	4	2-11/S-2	0.1
1973	StL-N	144	469	48	114	15	4	1	33	23	66	.243	.281	.299	580	61	-25	2	5	-1	.944	-19	*S-128,2-16	-3.0
1974	StL-N	151	422	35	94	14	5	1	37	22	70	.223	.266	.287	553	55	-26	4	2	0	.955	15	*S-143,2-12	0.5

YEAR	TM/L	G	AB	R	H	2B	3B	HR	RBI	BB	SO	AVG	OBP	SLG	OPS	OPS+	BR+	SB	CS	SBR	FA	FR	G/POS	TPR
1975	StL-N	122	368	45	98	16	3	2	37	24	39	.266	.316	.342	659	80	-10	5	2	0	.971	-12	S-95,2-24/3-5	-1.1
1976	StL-N	76	245	26	70	12	9	3	28	16	34	.286	.330	.445	774	117	5	3	1	0	.971	8	2-74	1.8
1977	StL-N	138	418	42	103	15	2	7	57	30	48	.246	.300	.342	642	73	-16	3	4	-1	.979	22	*2-135	1.2
1978	StL-N	125	377	26	88	16	0	3	26	24	41	.233	.279	.300	579	63	-19	2	0	0	.977	0	*2-124	-1.3
1979	StL-N	75	190	18	42	8	2	5	20	13	28	.221	.275	.363	638	72	-8	2	1	0	.975	8	2-71	0.4
1980	Chi-N	123	341	34	81	19	3	3	23	15	61	.238	.274	.337	611	65	-16	1	2	-0	.968	9	*2-117	-0.2
1981	Chi-N	50	92	6	17	2	0	2	8	7	15	.185	.250	.272	522	46	-7	1	0	0	.940	0	2-36/S-1	-0.5
Total	10	1017	2959	281	714	118	28	27	269	175	411	.241	.287	.327	614	69	-126	23	18	-1	.973	36	2-620,S-369/3-5	-2.1
■ BOB UECKER Uecker, Robert George b: 1/26/35, Milwaukee, Wis. BR/TR, 6'1", 190 lbs. Deb: 4/13/62																								
1962	Mil-N	33	64	5	16	2	0	1	8	7	15	.250	.324	.328	652	78	-2	0	0	0	.982	4	C-24	0.3
1963	Mil-N	13	16	3	4	2	0	0	0	2	5	.250	.333	.375	708	105	0	0	0	0	.958	1	/C-6	0.1
1964	StL-N	40	106	8	21	1	0	1	6	17	24	.198	.315	.236	550	53	-6	0	1	-0	.987	5	C-40	0.0
1965	StL-N	53	145	17	33	7	0	2	10	24	27	.228	.345	.317	662	80	-3	0	1	-0	.985	-1	C-49	-0.2
1966	Phi-N	78	207	15	43	6	0	7	30	22	36	.208	.284	.338	622	72	-8	0	0	0	.985	1	C-76	-0.4
1967	Phi-N	18	35	3	6	2	0	0	7	5	9	.171	.275	.229	504	45	-2	0	0	0	.973	0	C-17	-0.2
	Atl-N	62	158	14	23	2	0	3	13	19	51	.146	.237	.215	452	31	-14	0	1	-0	.972	5	C-59	-0.8
	Yr	80	193	17	29	4	0	3	20	24	60	.150	.244	.218	462	33	-16	0	1	-0	.972	5	C-76	-1.0
Total	6	297	731	65	146	22	0	14	74	96	167	.200	.295	.287	582	63	-35	0	3	-1	.981	14	C-271	-1.2
■ FRENCHY UHALT Uhalt, Bernard Bartholomew b: 4/27/10, Bakersfield, Cal. BL/TR, 5'10", 180 lbs. Deb: 4/17/34																								
1934	Chi-A	57	165	28	40	5	1	0	16	29	12	.242	.359	.285	644	66	-7	6	5	-0	.935	-1	O-40(4-14-22)	-1.0
■ TED UHLAENDER Uhlaender, Theodore Otto b: 10/21/40, Chicago Heights, Ill. BL/TR, 6'2", 190 lbs. Deb: 9/4/65 C																								
1965	Min-A	13	22	1	4	0	0	0	1	0	2	.182	.182	.182	364	3	-3	1	0	0	1.000	1	/O-4(4-0-0)	-0.2
1966	Min-A	105	367	39	83	12	2	2	22	27	33	.226	.281	.286	567	60	-19	10	2	2	.985	12	*O-100(4-96-0)	-0.9
1967	Min-A	133	415	41	107	19	7	6	49	13	45	.258	.285	.381	666	88	-7	4	4	-1	**.996**	7	*O-118(0-118-0)	-0.4
1968	Min-A	140	488	52	138	21	5	7	52	28	46	.283	.326	.389	715	110	6	16	7	1	.986	-2	*O-129(0-129-0)	0.1
1969	*Min-A	152	554	93	151	18	2	8	62	44	52	.273	.331	.356	686	90	-7	15	9	0	.997	-6	*O-150(44-108-1)	-1.8
1970	Cle-A	141	473	56	127	21	2	11	46	39	44	.268	.326	.391	717	92	-5	3	6	-1	.991	-14	*O-134(24-116-8)	-2.6
1971	Cle-A	141	500	52	144	20	3	2	47	38	44	.288	.338	.352	690	88	-7	3	6	-1	.992	1	*O-131(87-33-13)	-1.5
1972	*Cin-N	73	113	9	18	3	0	0	6	13	11	.159	.246	.186	432	26	-11	0	1	-0	.976	-2	O-27(3-2-23)	-1.6
Total	8	898	2932	343	772	114	21	36	285	202	277	.263	.313	.353	667	86	-53	52	35	-1	.991	-3	O-793(166-602-45)	-8.9
■ GEORGE UHLE Uhle, George Ernest "The Bull" b: 9/18/1898, Cleveland, Ohio d: 2/26/85, Lakewood, Ohio BR/TR, 6', 190 lbs. Deb: 4/30/19 C																								
1919	Cle-A	26	43	7	13	2	1	0	6	1	5	.302	.318	.395	714	94	-0	0			.915	0	P-26	0.0
1920	*Cle-A	27	32	4	11	0	0	0	2	2	2	.344	.382	.344	726	91	-0	1	0	0	1.000	0	P-27	0.0
1921	Cle-A	48	94	21	23	2	3	1	18	6	9	.245	.290	.362	652	64	-5	0	0	0	.938	-3	P-41	0.0
1922	Cle-A	56	109	21	29	8	2	0	14	13	6	.266	.350	.376	726	88	-2	1	2	-0	.932	-3	P-50	0.0
1923	Cle-A	58	144	23	52	10	3	0	22	7	10	.361	.391	.472	863	127	5	2	1	0	.982	0	P-54	0.0
1924	Cle-A	59	107	10	33	6	1	1	19	4	8	.308	.339	.411	751	92	-2	0	1	-0	**1.000**	1	P-28	0.0
1925	Cle-A	55	101	10	29	3	3	0	13	7	7	.287	.339	.376	716	81	-3	0	0	0	.943	-3	P-29	0.0
1926	Cle-A	50	132	16	30	3	0	1	11	10	12	.227	.287	.273	559	46	-10	2	2	-0	.933	-0	P-39	0.0
1927	Cle-A	43	79	4	21	7	1	0	14	5	12	.266	.310	.380	689	78	-3	0	1	-0	.974	-1	P-25	0.0
1928	Cle-A	55	98	9	28	3	2	1	17	8	4	.286	.340	.388	727	90	-2	0	0	0	.972	3	P-31	0.0
1929	Det-A	40	108	18	37	1	1	0	13	6	6	.343	.377	.370	748	93	-1	0	0	0	.929	-3	P-32	0.0
1930	Det-A	59	117	15	36	4	2	2	21	8	13	.308	.352	.427	779	95	-1	0	0	0	.975	-3	P-33	0.0
1931	Det-A	53	90	8	22	6	0	2	7	8	8	.244	.306	.378	684	76	-3	0	1	-0	**1.000**	-1	P-29	0.0
1932	Det-A	38	55	2	10	3	1	0	4	6	5	.182	.262	.273	535	37	-5	0	0	0	1.000	-1	P-33	0.0
1933	Det-A	1	0	0	0	0	0	0	0	0	0	—	—	—		—	0	0	0	0	.000	0	/P-1	0.0
	NY-N	8	5	1	0	0	0	0	0	1	3	.000	.167	.000	167	-50	-1	0			1.000	0	/P-6	0.0
	NY-A	12	20	1	8	1	0	0	1	4	2	.400	.500	.450	950	163	2	0	0	0	1.000	-1	P-12	0.0
1934	NY-A	10	5	1	3	0	1	0	1	0	0	.600	.600	1.000	1600	329	2	0	0	0	1.000	-0	P-10	0.0
1936	Cle-A	24	21	1	8	1	0	1	4	2	0	.381	.435	.571	1006	145	1	0	0	0	.000	-1	/P-7	0.0
Total	17	722	1360	172	393	60	21	9	187	98	112	.289	.339	.384	722	86	-28	6	8		.960	-15	P-513	0.0
■ MAURY UHLER Uhler, Maurice William b: 12/14/1886, Pikesville, Md. d: 5/4/18, Baltimore, Md. BR/TR, 5'11", 165 lbs. Deb: 4/14/14																								
1914	Cin-N	46	56	12	12	2	0	0	3	5	11	.214	.279	.250	529	56	-3	4			.932	-8	O-36(22-11-3)	-1.3
■ CHARLIE UHLIR Uhlir, Charles Karel b: 7/30/12, Chicago, Ill. d: 7/9/84, Spirit Lake, Iowa BL/TL, 5'7.5", 150 lbs. Deb: 8/3/34																								
1934	Chi-A	14	27	3	4	0	0	0	3	2	6	.148	.207	.148	355	-7	-4	0	0	0	1.000	-1	/O-6(6-0-0)	-0.5
■ MIKE ULISNEY Ulisney, Michael Edward "Slugs" b: 9/28/17, Greenwald, Pa. BR/TR, 5'9", 165 lbs. Deb: 5/5/45																								
1945	Bos-N	11	18	4	7	1	0	1	4	1	0	.389	.421	.611	1032	184	2	0			.714	-2	/C-4	0.0
■ SCOTT ULLGER Ullger, Scott Matthew b: 6/10/56, New York, N.Y. BR/TR, 6'2", 186 lbs. Deb: 4/17/83																								
1983	Min-A	35	79	8	15	4	0	0	5	5	21	.190	.247	.241	488	34	-7	0	2	-1	.990	-2	1-30/3-3,D-1	-1.1
■ GEORGE ULRICH Ulrich, George T. b: 6/5/1869, Philadelphia, Pa. Deb: 5/1/1892 Career OF: (11-LF 1-CF 0-RF)																								
1892	Was-N	6	24	1	7	1	0	0	0	0	4	.292	.292	.333	625	91	-0	2			.889	-1	/3-3,S-2,C-2	-0.1
1893	Cin-N	1	3	0	0	0	0	0	0	0	0	.000	.250	.000	250	-31	-1	1			1.000	-0	/O-1(0-1-0)	-0.1
1896	NY-N	14	45	4	8	1	0	0	1	1	1	.178	.229	.200	429	14	-6	0			.920	0	O-11(11-0-0)/3-3	-0.5
Total	3	21	72	5	15	2	0	0	1	1	5	.208	.250	.236	486	35	-7	3			.923	-1	/O-12L,3-6,C-2,S-2	-0.7
■ TOM UMPHLETT Umphlett, Thomas Mullen b: 5/12/30, Scotland Neck, N.C BR/TR, 6'2", 180 lbs. Deb: 4/16/53																								
1953	Bos-A	137	495	53	140	27	5	3	59	34	30	.283	.331	.376	707	86	-10	4	2	0	.983	6	*O-136(0-136-0)	-1.0
1954	Was-A	114	342	21	75	8	3	1	33	17	42	.219	.256	.269	525	46	-26	1	2	-0	.989	0	*O-101(12-4-86)	-3.1
1955	Was-A	110	323	34	70	10	0	2	19	24	35	.217	.271	.266	537	47	-24	2	1	0	.988	4	*O-103(18-62-23)	-2.5
Total	3	361	1160	108	285	45	8	6	111	75	107	.246	.293	.314	606	65	-60	7	5	-0	.986	10	O-340(30-202-109)	-6.6
■ BOB UNGLAUB Unglaub, Robert Alexander b: 7/31/1881, Baltimore, Md. d: 11/29/16, Baltimore, Md. BR/TR, 5'11", 178 lbs. Deb: 4/15/04 M																								
1904	NY-A	6	19	2	4	0	0	0	2	0		.211	.211	.211	421	32	-1	0			.786	-1	/3-4,S-1	-0.3
	Bos-A	9	13	1	2	1	0	0	2	1		.154	.214	.231	445	39	-1	0			.625	-2	/2-3,3-2,S-1	-0.3
	Yr	15	32	3	6	1	0	0	4	1		.188	.212	.219	431	35	-2	0			.842	-3	/3-6,2-3,S-2	-0.6
1905	Bos-A	43	121	18	27	5	1	0	11	6		.223	.260	.281	541	71	-4	2			.928	1	3-21/2-7,1-2	-0.3
1907	Bos-A	139	544	49	138	17	13	1	62	23		.254	.284	.338	622	99	-3	14			.986	-1	*1-139,M	-0.7
1908	Bos-A	72	266	23	70	11	3	1	25	7		.263	.287	.338	626	100	-1	6			.980	2	1-72	-0.1
	Was-A	72	276	23	85	10	5	0	29	8		.308	.327	.380	708	142	11	8			.928	11	3-39,2-27/1-4	2.5
	Yr	144	542	46	155	21	8	1	54	15		.286	.308	.360	667	120	9	14			.981	12	1-76,3-39,2-27	2.4
1909	Was-A	130	480	43	127	14	9	3	41	22		.265	.301	.350	651	111	4	15			.992	1	1-57,O-42R,2-25,/3	0.2
1910	Was-A	124	431	29	101	9	4	0	44	21		.234	.270	.274	544	74	-14	21			.985	6	*1-124	-1.2
Total	6	595	2150	188	554	67	35	5	216	88		.258	.288	.328	617	99	-9	66			.986	15	1-398/3-70,2-62,OS	-0.2
■ TIM UNROE Unroe, Timothy Brian b: 10/7/70, Round Lake Beach, Ill. BR/TR, 6'3", 200 lbs. Deb: 5/30/95 Career OF: (7-LF 0-CF 9-RF)																								
1995	Mil-A	2	4	0	1	0	0	0	0	0	0	.250	.250	.250	500	29	-0	0	0	0	1.000	-0	/1-2	-0.1
1996	Mil-A	14	16	5	3	0	0	0	0	4	5	.188	.350	.188	538	40	-1	0	1	-0	.976	1	1-11/3-3,O-1L,D-1	-0.1
1997	Mil-A	32	16	3	4	1	0	2	5	2	9	.250	.333	.688	1021	156	1	2	0	0	.969	2	1-23/3-2,O-2L,2-1	0.3
1999	Ana-A	27	54	5	13	2	0	1	6	4	16	.241	.305	.333	638	63	-3	0	0	0	1.000	-3	O-12R/3-3,2-1,D-9	-0.6
2000	Atl-N	4	5	0	0	0	0	0	0	1	2	.000	.167	.000	167	-54	-1	0	0	0	1.000	0	/1-2,O-1(1-0-0)	-0.1
Total	5	79	95	13	21	3	0	3	11	11	32	.221	.308	.347	656	67	-5	2	1	0	.977	-1	/1-38,O-16R,D-10,32	-0.6

■ AL UNSER

Unser, Albert Bernard b: 10/12/12, Morrisonville, Ill. d: 7/7/95, Decatur, Ill. BR/TR, 6'1", 175 lbs. Deb: 9/14/42 F

YEAR	TM/L	G	AB	R	H	2B	3B	HR	RBI	BB	SO	AVG	OBP	SLG	OPS	OPS+	BR+	SB	CS	SBR	FA	FR	G/POS	TPR
1942	Det-A	4	8	2	3	0	0	0	0	0	2	.375	.375	.375	750	103	0	0	0	0	1.000	1	/C-4	0.1
1943	Det-A	38	101	14	25	5	0	0	4	15	15	.248	.350	.297	647	84	-1	0	1	-0	.982	-3	C-37	-0.3
1944	Det-A	11	25	2	3	0	1	1	5	3	2	.120	.214	.320	534	49	-2	0	0	0	.864	-4	/2-5,C-1	-0.6
1945	Cin-N	67	204	23	54	10	3	3	21	14	24	.265	.318	.387	705	98	-1	0			.956	0	C-61	0.3
Total	4	120	338	41	85	15	4	4	30	32	43	.251	.322	.355	677	90	-5	0	1		.967	-7	C-103/2-5	-0.5

■ DEL UNSER

Unser, Delbert Bernard b: 12/9/44, Decatur, Ill. BL/TL, 6'1", 180 lbs. Deb: 4/10/68 FC Career OF: (118-LF 1112-CF 226-RF)

YEAR	TM/L	G	AB	R	H	2B	3B	HR	RBI	BB	SO	AVG	OBP	SLG	OPS	OPS+	BR+	SB	CS	SBR	FA	FR	G/POS	TPR
1968	Was-A	156	635	66	146	13	7	1	30	46	66	.230	.284	.277	561	73	-21	11	6	0	.988	19	*O-156(0-156-0)/1-1	-0.7
1969	Was-A	153	581	69	166	19	**8**	7	57	58	54	.286	.351	.382	733	111	8	8	10	-2	.972	6	*O-149(0-149-0)	0.9
1970	Was-A	119	322	37	83	5	1	5	30	30	29	.258	.321	.326	647	83	-7	1	1	-0	.984	-3	*O-103(11-43-50)	-1.5
1971	Was-A	153	581	63	148	19	6	9	41	59	68	.255	.326	.355	680	98	-2	11	6	0	.981	3	*O-151(8-105-68)	-0.4
1972	Cle-A	132	383	29	91	12	0	1	17	28	46	.238	.291	.277	568	67	-15	5	9	-2	.989	2	*O-119(14-85-23)	-2.1
1973	Phi-N	136	440	64	127	20	4	11	52	47	55	.289	.359	.427	786	114	9	5	8	-2	.988	17	*O-132(0-132-0)	2.1
1974	Phi-N	142	454	72	120	18	5	11	61	50	62	.264	.339	.399	737	101	1	6	4	-0	.981	6	*O-135(0-135-0)	0.3
1975	NY-N	147	531	65	156	18	2	10	53	37	76	.294	.340	.392	732	107	4	4	3	-0	.987	12	*O-144(0-144-0)	1.3
1976	NY-N	77	276	28	63	13	2	5	25	18	40	.228	.278	.344	622	80	-8	4	4	-1	.995	4	O-77(2-75-0)	-0.7
	Mon-N	69	220	29	50	6	2	7	15	11	44	.227	.264	.368	632	75	-8	3	3	-0	.983	-6	O-65(29-13-34)	-1.9
	Yr	146	496	57	113	19	4	12	40	29	84	.228	.272	.355	627	78	-16	7	7	-1	.990	-3	*O-142(31-88-34)	-2.6
1977	Mon-N	113	289	33	79	14	1	12	40	33	41	.273	.348	.453	801	116	6	2	5	-1	.976	-7	O-72(11-34-27),1-27	-0.4
1978	Mon-N	130	179	16	35	5	0	2	15	24	29	.196	.294	.257	551	56	-10	2	0	0	.994	1	1-64,O-33(7-12-14)	-1.1
1979	Phi-N	95	141	26	42	8	0	6	29	14	33	.298	.361	.482	844	124	5	2	0	0	.978	-4	O-30(16-11-3),1-22	-0.1
1980	*Phi-N	96	110	15	29	6	4	0	10	10	21	.264	.325	.391	716	94	-1	0	1	-0	1.000	3	1-31,O-23(13-12-1)	0.1
1981	Phi-N	62	59	5	9	3	0	0	6	13	9	.153	.306	.203	509	45	-4	0	0	0	1.000	-3	1-18,O-16(7-6-4)	-0.7
1982	Phi-N	19	14	0	0	0	0	0	0	3	2	.000	.176	.000	176	-46	-3	0	0	0	1.000	-1	/1-5,O-2(0-0-2)	-0.4
Total	15	1799	5215	617	1344	179	42	87	481	481	675	.258	.321	.358	680	93	-46	64	60	-7	.984	48	*O-1407C,1-168	-5.3

■ JOHN UPHAM

Upham, John Leslie b: 12/29/41, Windsor, Ont., Can. BL/TL, 6', 180 lbs. Deb: 4/16/67

YEAR	TM/L	G	AB	R	H	2B	3B	HR	RBI	BB	SO	AVG	OBP	SLG	OPS	OPS+	BR+	SB	CS	SBR	FA	FR	G/POS	TPR
1967	Chi-N	8	3	1	2	0	0	0	0	0	0	.667	.667	.667	1333	270	1	0	0	0	.000	0	/P-5	0.0
1968	Chi-N	13	10	0	2	0	0	0	0	0	3	.200	.200	.200	400	19	-1	0	0	0	1.000	-1	/P-2,O-2(1-1-0)	-0.1
Total	2	21	13	1	4	0	0	0	0	0	3	.308	.308	.308	615	78	-0	0	0	0	1.000	-1	/P-7,O-2(1-1-0)	-0.1

■ DIXIE UPRIGHT

Upright, Roy T. b: 5/30/26, Kannapolis, N.C. d: 11/13/86, Concord, N.C. BL/TL, 6', 175 lbs. Deb: 4/18/53

YEAR	TM/L	G	AB	R	H	2B	3B	HR	RBI	BB	SO	AVG	OBP	SLG	OPS	OPS+	BR+	SB	CS	SBR	FA	FR	G/POS	TPR
1953	StL-A	9	8	3	2	0	0	1	1	1	3	.250	.333	.625	958	151	0	0	0	0	.000	0	H	0.0

■ WILLIE UPSHAW

Upshaw, Willie Clay b: 4/27/57, Blanco, Tex. BL/TL, 6', 185 lbs. Deb: 4/9/78 C Career OF: (52-LF 6-CF 9-RF)

YEAR	TM/L	G	AB	R	H	2B	3B	HR	RBI	BB	SO	AVG	OBP	SLG	OPS	OPS+	BR+	SB	CS	SBR	FA	FR	G/POS	TPR
1978	Tor-A	95	224	26	53	8	2	1	17	21	35	.237	.302	.304	606	69	-9	4	6	-1	.943	-6	O-52L,D-18,1-10	-1.9
1980	Tor-A	34	61	10	13	3	1	1	5	6	14	.213	.284	.344	628	68	-3	1	0	0	.983	1	1-14,D-12/O-1(1-0-0)	-0.2
1981	Tor-A	61	111	15	19	3	1	4	10	11	16	.171	.252	.324	576	61	-6	2	1	0	1.000	-2	D-15,1-14,O-14(6-0-8)	-0.9
1982	Tor-A	160	580	77	155	25	7	21	75	52	91	.267	.329	.443	772	100	-0	8	8	-1	.989	-1	*1-155/D-5	-1.3
1983	Tor-A	160	579	99	177	26	7	27	104	61	98	.306	.377	.515	891	134	27	10	7	-0	.985	3	*1-159/D-1	2.0
1984	Tor-A	152	569	79	158	31	9	19	84	55	86	.278	.347	.464	811	118	13	10	4	1	.990	-3	*1-151/D-1	0.2
1985	*Tor-A	148	501	79	138	31	5	15	65	48	71	.275	.344	.447	791	112	8	8	8	-1	.992	1	*1-147/D-1	0.0
1986	Tor-A	155	573	85	144	28	6	9	60	78	87	.251	.343	.368	711	91	-5	23	5	3	.992	5	*1-154/D-1	-0.7
1987	Tor-A	150	512	68	125	22	4	15	58	58	78	.244	.325	.391	715	87	-10	10	11	-2	.993	12	*1-146	-0.8
1988	Cle-A	149	493	58	121	22	3	11	50	62	66	.245	.332	.369	701	94	-3	12	9	-1	.991	1	*1-144	-1.3
Total	10	1264	4203	596	1103	199	45	123	528	452	642	.262	.337	.419	756	102	13	88	59	-1	.990	11	*1-1094/O-67L,D-54	-4.9

■ TOM UPTON

Upton, Thomas Herbert "Muscles" b: 12/29/26, Esther, Mo. BR/TR, 6', 160 lbs. Deb: 4/19/50 F

YEAR	TM/L	G	AB	R	H	2B	3B	HR	RBI	BB	SO	AVG	OBP	SLG	OPS	OPS+	BR+	SB	CS	SBR	FA	FR	G/POS	TPR
1950	StL-A	124	389	50	92	5	6	2	30	52	45	.237	.328	.296	624	58	-24	7	2	1	.946	-10	*S-115/2-2,3-1	-2.5
1951	StL-A	52	131	9	26	4	3	0	12	12	22	.198	.271	.275	546	46	-10	1	1	-0	.949	-4	S-47	-1.2
1952	Was-A	5	5	1	0	0	0	0	0	1	0	.000	.167	.000	167	-53	-1	0	0	0	1.000	2	/S-3	0.1
Total	3	181	525	60	118	9	9	2	42	65	67	.225	.313	.288	600	55	-35	8	3	1	.948	-13	S-165/2-2,3-1	-3.6

■ LUKE URBAN

Urban, Louis John b: 3/22/1898, Fall River, Mass. d: 12/7/80, Somerset, Mass. BR/TR, 5'8", 168 lbs. Deb: 7/19/27

YEAR	TM/L	G	AB	R	H	2B	3B	HR	RBI	BB	SO	AVG	OBP	SLG	OPS	OPS+	BR+	SB	CS	SBR	FA	FR	G/POS	TPR
1927	Bos-N	35	111	11	32	5	0	0	10	3	6	.288	.313	.333	646	79	-3	1			.947	-8	C-34	-0.9
1928	Bos-N	15	17	0	3	0	0	0	2	0	1	.176	.222	.176	399	6	-2	0			1.000	1	C-10	-0.1
Total	2	50	128	11	35	5	0	0	12	3	7	.273	.301	.313	613	69	-6	1			.955	-7	/C-44	-1.0

■ BILLY URBANSKI

Urbanski, William Michael b: 6/5/03, Linoleumville, N.Y d: 7/12/73, Perth Amboy, N.J. BR/TR, 5'8", 165 lbs. Deb: 7/4/31

YEAR	TM/L	G	AB	R	H	2B	3B	HR	RBI	BB	SO	AVG	OBP	SLG	OPS	OPS+	BR+	SB	CS	SBR	FA	FR	G/POS	TPR
1931	Bos-N	82	303	22	72	13	4	0	17	10	32	.238	.274	.307	581	58	-18	3			.961	11	3-68,S-19	-0.4
1932	Bos-N	136	563	80	153	25	8	8	46	28	60	.272	.307	.387	695	89	-10	8			.946	1	*S-136	0.2
1933	Bos-N	144	566	65	142	21	4	0	35	33	48	.251	.298	.302	600	78	-16	4			.953	-4	*S-143	-1.0
1934	Bos-N	146	605	104	177	30	6	7	53	56	37	.293	.357	.397	754	110	9	4			**.961**	-10	*S-146	1.0
1935	Bos-N	132	514	53	118	17	0	4	30	40	32	.230	.286	.286	572	59	-29	3			.939	-27	*S-129	-4.6
1936	Bos-N	122	494	55	129	17	5	0	26	31	42	.261	.310	.316	626	74	-18	2			.937	-18	S-80,3-38	-2.8
1937	Bos-N	1	1	0	0	0	0	0	0	0	1	.000	.000	.000	0	-99	-0	0			.000	0	H	0.0
Total	7	763	3046	379	791	123	27	19	207	198	252	.260	.309	.337	646	81	-83	24			.949	-47	S-653,3-106	-7.6

■ JOSE URIBE

Uribe, Jose Altagracia (Played Under Real Name Of Jose Altagracia Gonzalez (Uribe) In 1984)
b: 1/21/59, San Cristobal, D.R. BB/TR (BR 1984, 89 (part)), 5'10", 165 lbs. Deb: 9/13/84

YEAR	TM/L	G	AB	R	H	2B	3B	HR	RBI	BB	SO	AVG	OBP	SLG	OPS	OPS+	BR+	SB	CS	SBR	FA	FR	G/POS	TPR
1984	StL-N	8	19	4	4	0	0	0	3	0	2	.211	.211	.211	421	19	-2	1	0	0	.955	0	/S-5,2-1	-0.1
1985	SF-N	147	476	46	113	20	4	3	26	30	57	.237	.285	.315	601	71	-19	8	2	1	.961	-2	*S-145/2-1	-0.6
1986	SF-N	157	453	46	101	15	1	3	43	61	76	.223	.315	.280	596	69	-18	22	11	1	.977	12	*S-156	1.1
1987	*SF-N	95	309	44	90	16	5	5	30	24	35	.291	.344	.424	768	107	3	12	2	2	.971	11	S-95	2.4
1988	SF-N	141	493	47	124	10	7	3	35	36	69	.252	.302	.318	621	82	-12	14	10	-0	.970	-3	*S-140	-0.5
1989	*SF-N	151	453	34	100	12	6	1	30	34	74	.221	.275	.280	556	61	-23	6	6	-1	.973	8	*S-150	-0.5
1990	SF-N	138	415	35	103	8	6	1	24	29	49	.248	.297	.304	601	68	-18	5	9	-2	.965	16	*S-134	0.4
1991	SF-N	90	231	23	51	8	4	1	12	20	33	.221	.283	.303	586	67	-10	3	4	-1	.966	6	S-87	0.0
1992	SF-N	66	162	24	39	9	1	2	13	14	25	.241	.301	.346	647	88	-3	2	2	-0	.971	9	S-62	1.0
1993	Hou-N	45	53	4	13	1	0	0	3	8	5	.245	.355	.264	619	71	-2	1	0	0	.944	6	S-41	0.6
Total	10	1038	3064	307	738	99	34	19	219	256	425	.241	.300	.314	614	75	-104	74	46	0	.969	62	*S-1015/2-2	3.8

■ LON URY

Ury, Louis Newton "Old Sleep" b: 1877, Ft.Scott, Kan. d: 3/4/18, Kansas City, Mo. TR, 6', Deb: 9/9/03

YEAR	TM/L	G	AB	R	H	2B	3B	HR	RBI	BB	SO	AVG	OBP	SLG	OPS	OPS+	BR+	SB	CS	SBR	FA	FR	G/POS	TPR
1903	StL-N	2	7	0	1	0	0	0	0	0		.143	.143	.143	286	-19	-1	0			1.000	0	/1-2	-0.1

■ BOB USHER

Usher, Robert Royce b: 3/1/25, San Diego, Cal. BR/TR, 6'1.5", 180 lbs. Deb: 4/16/46

YEAR	TM/L	G	AB	R	H	2B	3B	HR	RBI	BB	SO	AVG	OBP	SLG	OPS	OPS+	BR+	SB	CS	SBR	FA	FR	G/POS	TPR
1946	Cin-N	92	152	16	31	5	1	1	14	13	27	.204	.271	.270	541	56	-9	2			.982	-12	O-80(23-32-25)/3-1	-2.5
1947	Cin-N	9	22	2	4	0	0	1	1	2	2	.182	.250	.318	568	50	-2	0			1.000	0	/O-8(3-5-0)	-0.2
1950	Cin-N	106	321	51	83	17	0	6	35	27	38	.259	.316	.368	684	79	-10	3			.985	-5	O-93(4-80-12)	-1.7
1951	Cin-N	114	303	27	63	12	2	5	25	19	36	.208	.257	.310	567	51	-21	4	5	-1	.974	-3	O-98(14-82-2)	-2.9
1952	Chi-N	1	0	0	0	0	0	0	0	1	0	—	1.000	—	1000	197	0	0	0	0	.000	0	H	0.0
1957	Cle-A	10	8	1	1	0	0	0	0	1	3	.125	.222	.125	347	-3	-1	0	0	0	1.000	-2	/O-4(1-3-0),3-1	-0.3
	Was-A	96	295	36	77	7	1	5	27	27	30	.261	.327	.342	670	84	-6	0	0	0	.979	3	O-95(1-93-2)	-0.7
	Yr	106	303	37	78	7	1	5	27	28	33	.257	.324	.337	661	82	-7	0	0	0	.979	2	O-99(2-96-2)/3-1	-1.0
Total	6	428	1101	133	259	41	4	18	102	90	136	.235	.295	.329	624	69	-49	9	5		.980	-19	O-378(46-295-41)/3-2	-8.3

■ DUTCH USSAT

Ussat, William August b: 4/11/04, Dayton, Ohio d: 5/29/59, Dayton, Ohio BR/TR, 6'1", 170 lbs. Deb: 9/13/25

YEAR	TM/L	G	AB	R	H	2B	3B	HR	RBI	BB	SO	AVG	OBP	SLG	OPS	OPS+	BR+	SB	CS	SBR	FA	FR	G/POS	TPR
1925	Cle-A	1	1	0	0	0	0	0	0	0	0	.000	.000	.000	0	-99	-0	0	0	0	1.000	0	/2-1	0.0
1927	Cle-A	4	16	4	3	0	1	0	2	2	1	.188	.278	.313	590	53	-1	0	0	0	1.000	-1	/3-4	-0.2
Total	2	5	17	4	3	0	1	0	2	2	1	.176	.263	.294	557	44	-1	0	0	0	1.000	-1	/3-4,2-1	-0.2

YEAR	TM/L	G	AB	R	H	2B	3B	HR	RBI	BB	SO	AVG	OBP	SLG	OPS	OPS+	BR+	SB	CS	SBR	FA	FR	G/POS	TPR
■ TEX VACHE Vache, Ernest Lewis b: 11/17/1894, Santa Monica, Cal. d: 6/11/53, Los Angeles, Cal. BR/TR, 6'1", 200 lbs. Deb: 4/16/25																								
1925	Bos-A	110	252	41	79	15	7	3	48	21	33	.313	.382	.464	846	114	5	2	2	-0	.908	-12	O-53(57-0-1)	-1.0
■ GENE VADEBONCOEUR Vadeboncoeur, Onesime Eugene b: 7/15/1858, Louiseville, Que., Can. d: 10/16/35, Haverhill, Mass. BR/TR, 5'6", 150 lbs. Deb: 7/11/1884																								
1884	Phi-N	4	14	1	3	0	0	0	3	1	2	.214	.267	.214	481	56	-1				.846	-1	/C-4	-0.1
■ HARRY VAHRENHORST Vahrenhorst, Harry Henry "Van" b: 2/13/1885, St.Louis, Mo. d: 10/10/43, St.Louis, Mo. BR/TR, 6'1", 175 lbs. Deb: 9/21/04																								
1904	StL-A	1	1	0	0	0	0	0	0	0		.000	.000	.000	0	-99	-0	0			.000	0	H	0.0
■ MIKE VAIL Vail, Michael Lewis b: 11/10/51, San Francisco, Cal. BR/TR, 6', 185 lbs. Deb: 8/18/75 Career OF: (124-LF 1-CF 278-RF)																								
1975	NY-N	38	162	17	49	8	1	3	17	9	37	.302	.339	.420	759	115	3	0	0	0	.971	11	O-36(35-1-0)	1.2
1976	NY-N	53	143	8	31	5	1	0	9	6	19	.217	.248	.266	514	49	-10	0	1	-0	.941	-1	O-35(2-0-33)	-1.4
1977	NY-N	108	279	29	73	12	1	8	35	19	58	.262	.313	.398	711	94	-3	0	7	-2	.965	2	O-85(2-0-83)	-0.7
1978	Cle-A	14	34	2	8	2	1	0	2	1	9	.235	.257	.353	610	71	-1	1	1	-0	1.000	-0	/O-9(2-0-7),D-1	-0.2
	Chi-N	74	180	15	60	6	2	4	33	3	24	.333	.344	.456	800	109	2	0	1	-0	.981	-9	O-45(7-0-39)/3-1	-1.0
1979	Chi-N	87	179	28	60	8	2	7	35	14	27	.335	.383	.520	903	131	8	0	2	-1	.964	-4	O-39(1-0-38)/3-2	0.1
1980	Chi-N	114	312	30	93	17	2	6	47	14	77	.298	.330	.423	753	101	0	2	5	-1	.963	-4	O-77(19-0-61)	-0.9
1981	Cin-N	31	31	1	5	0	0	0	3	0	9	.161	.161	.161	323	-8	-4	0	0	0	1.000	-1	/O-3(0-0-3)	-0.5
1982	Cin-N	78	189	9	48	10	1	4	29	6	33	.254	.277	.381	658	81	-5	0	0	0	.988	0	O-52(50-0-2)	-0.7
1983	SF-N	18	26	1	4	1	0	0	3	0	7	.154	.185	.192	377	5	-3	0	0	0	1.000	-1	/1-4,O-2(2-0-0)	-0.5
	Mon-N	34	53	5	15	2	0	2	4	8	10	.283	.387	.434	821	128	2	0	0	0	.958	1	O-15(3-0-12)/1-1,3-1	0.3
	Yr	52	79	6	19	3	0	2	7	8	17	.241	.326	.354	680	90	-1	0	0	0	.960	-0	O-17(5-0-12)/1-5,3-1	-0.2
1984	LA-N	16	16	1	1	0	0	0	2	1	7	.063	.118	.063	180	-49	-3	0	0	0	.000	-0	/O-1(1-0-0)	-0.4
Total	10	665	1604	146	447	71	11	34	219	81	317	.279	.315	.400	716	95	-16	3	17	-5	.968	-5	O-399R/1-5,3-4,D-1	-4.7
■ PEDRO VALDES Valdes, Pedro Jose (Manzo) b: 6/29/73, Fajardo, P.R. BL/TL, 6'1", 180 lbs. Deb: 5/15/96																								
1996	Chi-N	9	8	2	1	1	0	0	1	1	5	.125	.222	.250	472	24	-1	0	0	0	1.000	-1	/O-2(0-0-2)	-0.2
1998	Chi-N	14	23	1	5	1	1	0	2	1	3	.217	.250	.348	598	53	-2	0	1	-0	1.000	-0	/O-7(6-0-1)	-0.2
2000	Tex-A	30	54	4	15	5	0	1	5	6	7	.278	.350	.426	776	92	-1	0	0	0	1.000	-2	O-14(1-0-13)/D-5	-0.3
Total	3	53	85	7	21	7	1	1	8	8	15	.247	.312	.388	700	76	-3	0	1	-0	1.000	-3	/O-23(7-0-16),D-5	-0.7
■ ROY VALDES Valdes, Rogelio Lazaro (Rojas) b: 2/20/20, Havana, Cuba BR/TR, 5'11", 185 lbs. Deb: 5/3/44																								
1944	Was-A	1	1	0	0	0	0	0	0	0	0	.000	.000	.000	0	-99	-0	0	0	0	.000	0	H	0.0
■ SANDY VALDESPINO Valdespino, Hilario (Borroto) b: 1/14/39, San Jose De Las Lajas, Cuba BL/TL, 5'8", 170 lbs. Deb: 4/12/65																								
1965	*Min-A	108	245	38	64	8	2	1	22	20	28	.261	.322	.322	645	80	-6	7	4	0	.990	0	O-57(43-0-17)	-0.9
1966	Min-A	52	108	11	19	1	1	2	9	4	24	.176	.212	.259	472	33	-9	2	2	-0	1.000	-1	O-23(22-1-0)	-1.3
1967	Min-A	99	97	9	16	2	0	1	3	5	22	.165	.206	.216	422	23	-9	3	1	0	.977	-11	O-65(64-0-1)	-2.4
1968	Atl-N	36	86	8	20	1	0	1	4	10	20	.233	.320	.279	599	81	-2	0	0	0	.976	1	O-20(20-0-0)	-0.2
1969	Hou-N	41	119	17	29	4	0	0	12	15	19	.244	.328	.277	606	73	-4	2	2	-0	.976	1	O-29(29-0-0)	-0.5
	Sea-A	20	38	3	8	1	0	0	2	1	7	.211	.250	.237	487	37	-3	0	1	-0	.889	2	/O-7(7-0-0)	-0.2
1970	Mil-A	8	9	0	0	0	0	0	0	0	4	.000	.000	.000	0	-99	-2	0	0	0	.000	-0	/O-1(1-0-0)	-0.3
1971	KC-A	18	63	10	20	6	0	2	15	2	5	.317	.338	.508	846	138	3	0	0	0	.950	-2	O-15(13-0-2)	0.0
Total	7	382	765	96	176	23	3	7	67	57	129	.230	.288	.295	583	66	-33	14	10	-0	.974	-10	O-217(199-1-20)	-5.8
■ JULIO VALDEZ Valdez, Julio Julian (b: Julio Julian Castillo (Valdez) b: 6/3/56, San Cristobal, D.R. BB/TR (BR 1980), 6'2", 160 lbs. Deb: 9/2/80																								
1980	Bos-A	8	19	4	5	1	0	1	4	0	5	.263	.300	.474	774	103	-0	2	0	0	.935	7	/S-8	0.8
1981	Bos-A	17	23	1	5	0	0	0	3	0	2	.217	.217	.217	435	24	-2	0	1	-0	.955	3	S-17	0.1
1982	Bos-A	28	20	3	5	1	0	0	1	0	7	.250	.250	.300	550	48	-1	1	0	0	.976	7	S-22/D-3	0.6
1983	Bos-A	12	25	3	3	0	0	0	0	1	4	.120	.185	.120	305	-13	-4	0	0	0	.939	-1	/2-9,S-2,D-1	-0.5
Total	4	65	87	11	18	2	0	1	8	1	18	.207	.233	.264	498	36	-7	3	1	0	.955	16	/S-49,2-9,D-4	1.0
■ MARIO VALDEZ Valdez, Mario A. b: 11/19/74, Obregon, Mex. BL/TL, 6'2", 190 lbs. Deb: 6/15/97																								
1997	Chi-A	54	115	11	28	7	0	1	13	17	39	.243	.356	.330	686	84	-2	1	0	0	1.000	-3	1-47/3-1,D-2	-0.7
2000	Oak-A	5	12	0	0	0	0	0	0	0	3	.000	.000	.000	0	-99	-4	0	0	0	1.000	0	/1-4	-0.4
Total	2	59	127	11	28	7	0	1	13	17	42	.220	.327	.299	626	67	-6	1	0	0	1.000	-2	/1-51,D-2,3-1	-1.1
■ JOSE VALDIVIELSO Valdivielso, Jose (Lopez) (b: Jose Martinez De Valdivielso (Lopez)) b: 5/22/34, Matanzas, Cuba BR/TR, 6'1", 175 lbs. Deb: 6/21/55																								
1955	Was-A	94	294	32	65	12	5	2	28	21	38	.221	.280	.316	596	63	-16	1	2	-0	.956	9	S-94	0.1
1956	Was-A	90	246	18	58	8	2	4	29	29	36	.236	.319	.333	652	72	-10	3	1	0	.947	16	S-90	1.3
1959	Was-A	24	14	1	4	0	0	0	0	1	3	.286	.333	.286	619	72	-0	0	0	0	1.000	5	S-21	0.5
1960	Was-A	117	268	23	57	1	1	2	19	20	36	.213	.277	.246	524	43	-21	1	2	-0	.954	9	*S-115/3-1	-0.5
1961	Min-A	76	149	15	29	5	0	1	9	8	19	.195	.236	.248	484	28	-15	1	1	-0	.971	-2	S-43,2-15,3-14	-1.4
Total	5	401	971	89	213	26	8	9	85	79	132	.219	.284	.290	574	55	-62	6	6	-1	.955	37	S-363/2-15,3-15	0.0
■ JOHN VALENTIN Valentin, John William b: 2/18/67, Mineola, N.Y. BR/TR, 6', 185 lbs. Deb: 7/27/92																								
1992	Bos-A	58	185	21	51	13	0	5	25	20	17	.276	.353	.427	780	110	3	1	0	0	.963	5	S-58	1.2
1993	Bos-A	144	468	50	130	40	3	11	66	49	77	.278	.349	.447	795	106	3	3	4	-1	.971	5	*S-144	1.9
1994	Bos-A	84	301	53	95	26	2	9	49	42	38	.316	.405	.505	910	127	13	3	1	0	.979	1	S-83/D-1	2.0
1995	*Bos-A	135	520	108	155	37	2	27	102	81	67	.298	.403	.533	935	136	29	20	5	3	.973	6	*S-135	4.5
1996	Bos-A	131	527	84	156	29	3	13	59	63	59	.296	.379	.436	815	103	4	9	10	-2	.971	6	*S-118,3-12/D-1	1.7
1997	Bos-A	143	575	95	176	**47**	5	18	77	58	66	.306	.375	.499	874	123	19	7	4	0	.976	18	2-79,3-64	3.9
1998	*Bos-A	153	588	113	145	44	1	23	73	77	82	.247	.343	.442	785	100	0	4	5	-1	.965	13	*3-153/2-1	1.3
1999	*Bos-A	113	450	58	114	27	1	12	70	40	68	.253	.320	.398	718	79	-15	0	1	-0	.954	6	*3-111/D-2	-0.7
2000	Bos-A	10	35	6	9	1	0	2	2	2	5	.257	.297	.457	754	84	-1	0	1	-0	1.000	-4	3-10	-0.5
Total	9	971	3649	588	1031	264	17	120	523	432	479	.283	.365	.463	828	110	56	47	31	-1	.972	54	S-538,3-350/2-80,D	15.3
■ JOSE VALENTIN Valentin, Jose Antonio b: 10/12/69, Manati, P.R. BB/TR, 5'10", 175 lbs. Deb: 9/17/92 F Career OF: (0-LF 0-CF 1-RF)																								
1992	Mil-A	4	3	1	0	0	0	0	1	0	0	.000	.000	.000	0	-99	-1	0	0	0	.667	-1	/2-1,S-1	-0.2
1993	Mil-A	19	53	10	13	1	2	1	7	7	16	.245	.344	.396	740	100	0	1	0	0	.922	-0	S-19	0.1
1994	Mil-A	97	285	47	68	19	0	11	46	38	75	.239	.332	.421	753	89	-5	12	3	2	.954	**28**	S-83,2-18/3-1	2.9
1995	Mil-A	112	338	62	74	23	3	11	49	37	83	.219	.296	.402	698	75	-13	16	8	1	.971	20	*S-104/3-1,D-4	1.4
1996	Mil-A	154	552	90	143	33	7	24	95	66	145	.259	.338	.475	813	99	-2	17	4	2	.950	-3	*S-151	0.9
1997	Mil-A	136	494	58	125	23	1	17	58	39	109	.253	.313	.407	720	85	-11	19	8	1	.967	1	*S-134/D-1	0.2
1998	Mil-N	151	428	65	96	24	0	16	49	63	105	.224	.325	.393	718	88	-8	10	7	-0	.963	0	*S-139/D-1	0.3
1999	Mil-N	89	256	45	58	9	5	10	38	48	52	.227	.353	.418	771	95	-1	3	2	-0	.937	-5	S-85	0.0
2000	*Chi-A	144	568	107	155	37	6	25	92	59	106	.273	.345	.491	837	107	5	19	2	3	.950	12	*S-141/O-1(0-0-1)	2.9
Total	9	906	2977	485	732	169	24	115	435	357	691	.246	.329	.435	764	93	-37	97	34	9	.956	51	S-857/2-19,D-6,3O	8.5
■ JAVIER VALENTIN Valentin, Jose Javier (Rosario) b: 9/19/75, Manati, P.R. BB/TR, 5'10", 198 lbs. Deb: 9/13/97 F																								
1997	Min-A	4	7	1	2	0	0	0	0	0	3	.286	.286	.286	571	49	-1	0	0	0	1.000	1	/C-4	0.0
1998	Min-A	55	162	11	32	7	1	3	18	11	30	.198	.249	.309	557	43	-14	0	0	0	.983	-1	C-53/D-1	-1.1
1999	Min-A	78	218	22	54	12	1	5	28	22	39	.248	.320	.381	700	75	-8	0	0	0	.998	2	C-76	-0.2
Total	3	137	387	34	88	19	2	8	46	33	72	.227	.290	.349	639	62	-23	0	0	0	.992	2	C-133/D-1	-1.3
■ ELLIS VALENTINE Valentine, Ellis Clarence b: 7/30/54, Helena, Ark. BR/TR, 6'4", 207 lbs. Deb: 9/3/75																								
1975	Mon-N	12	33	2	12	4	0	1	3	2	4	.364	.400	.576	976	161	3	0	0	0	.867	-1	O-11(0-0-11)	0.1
1976	Mon-N	94	305	36	85	15	2	7	39	30	51	.279	.343	.410	753	108	3	14	1	3	.972	0	O-88(2-55-31)	0.3
1977	Mon-N★	127	508	63	149	28	2	25	76	30	58	.293	.333	.504	837	124	15	13	5	1	.972	1	*O-126(0-0-126)	1.0
1978	Mon-N	151	570	75	165	35	2	25	76	35	88	.289	.333	.489	822	129	19	13	8	0	.970	14	*O-146(0-3-145)	2.7
1979	Mon-N	146	548	73	151	29	3	21	82	22	74	.276	.305	.454	759	105	1	11	9	-1	.983	1	*O-144(0-0-144)	-0.6

YEAR	TM/L	G	AB	R	H	2B	3B	HR	RBI	BB	SO	AVG	OBP	SLG	OPS	OPS+	BR+	SB	CS	SBR	FA	FR	G/POS	TPR
1980	Mon-N	86	311	40	98	22	2	13	67	25	44	.315	.372	.524	896	147	19	5	5	-1	.970	1	O-83(0-0-83)	1.6
1981	Mon-N	22	76	8	16	3	0	3	15	6	11	.211	.268	.368	637	78	-2	0	1	-0	1.000	-0	O-21(0-0-21)	-0.4
	NY-N	48	169	15	35	8	1	5	21	5	38	.207	.230	.355	585	65	-9	0	3	-1	.957	3	O-47(0-0-47)	-1.0
	Yr	70	245	23	51	11	1	8	36	11	49	.208	.242	.359	601	69	-11	0	4	-1	.969	3	O-68(0-0-68)	-1.4
1982	NY-N	111	337	33	97	14	1	8	48	5	38	.288	.300	.407	707	97	-3	1	3	-1	.983	1	O-98(14-4-82)	-0.7
1983	Cal-A	86	271	30	65	10	2	13	43	18	48	.240	.287	.435	723	97	-2	2	1	0	.963	-7	O-85(11-0-80)	-1.3
1985	Tex-A	11	38	5	8	1	0	2	4	2	8	.211	.250	.395	645	72	-2	0	1	-0	1.000	-1	/O-7(0-0-7),D-4	-0.4
Total	10	894	3166	380	881	169	15	123	474	180	462	.278	.319	.458	776	113	42	59	37	0	.972	10	O-856(27-62-777)/D-4	1.3

■ FRED VALENTINE
Valentine, Fred Lee "Squeaky" b: 1/19/35, Clarksdale, Miss. BB/TR, 6'1", 190 lbs. Deb: 9/7/59

YEAR	TM/L	G	AB	R	H	2B	3B	HR	RBI	BB	SO	AVG	OBP	SLG	OPS	OPS+	BR+	SB	CS	SBR	FA	FR	G/POS	TPR
1959	Bal-A	12	19	0	6	0	0	0	1	3	4	.316	.409	.316	725	104	0	0	1	-0	.889	-2	/O-8(3-0-6)	-0.2
1963	Bal-A	26	41	5	11	1	0	0	1	8	5	.268	.388	.293	680	98	0	0	0	0	1.000	-1	O-10(1-0-10)	-0.2
1964	Was-A	102	212	20	48	5	0	4	20	21	44	.226	.305	.307	612	71	-8	4	2	0	.978	-4	O-57(22-14-22)	-1.5
1965	Was-A	12	29	6	7	0	0	0	1	4	5	.241	.353	.241	594	73	-1	3	0	1	1.000	-0	O-11(5-6-1)	-0.1
1966	Was-A	146	508	77	140	29	7	16	59	51	63	.276	.353	.455	808	132	21	22	10	1	.980	-4	*O-138(32-63-70)/1-2	1.2
1967	Was-A	151	457	52	107	16	1	11	44	56	76	.234	.331	.346	677	104	4	17	3	3	.989	-6	*O-136(26-70-55)	-0.6
1968	Was-A	37	101	11	24	2	0	3	7	6	11	.238	.294	.347	640	96	-1	1	0	0	1.000	-1	O-27(0-1-26)	-0.4
	Bal-A	47	91	9	17	3	2	2	5	7	20	.187	.253	.330	582	75	-3	0	0	0	.972	-1	O-26(6-6-14)	-0.6
	Yr	84	192	20	41	5	2	5	12	13	31	.214	.274	.339	613	86	-4	1	0	0	.986	-3	O-53(6-7-40)	-1.0
Total	7	533	1458	180	360	56	10	36	138	156	228	.247	.331	.373	704	106	13	47	16	5	.983	-20	O-413(95-160-204)/1-2	-2.4

■ BOB VALENTINE
Valentine, Robert Deb: 5/20/1876

YEAR	TM/L	G	AB	R	H	2B	3B	HR	RBI	BB	SO	AVG	OBP	SLG	OPS	OPS+	BR+	SB	CS	SBR	FA	FR	G/POS	TPR
1876	NY-N	1	3	0	0	0	0	0	0	0	0	.000	.000	.000	0	-99	-1				.400	-0	/C-1	-0.1

■ BOBBY VALENTINE
Valentine, Robert John b: 5/13/50, Stamford, Conn. BR/TR, 5'10", 189 lbs. Deb: 9/2/69 MC Career OF: (87-LF 18-CF 26-RF)

YEAR	TM/L	G	AB	R	H	2B	3B	HR	RBI	BB	SO	AVG	OBP	SLG	OPS	OPS+	BR+	SB	CS	SBR	FA	FR	G/POS	TPR
1969	LA-N	5	0	3	0	0	0	0	0	0	0	—	—	—	—		0	0	0	0	.000	0	R	0.0
1971	LA-N	101	281	32	70	10	2	1	25	15	20	.249	.292	.310	602	75	-10	5	3	0	.961	-1	S-37,3-23,2-21,O-11R	-0.8
1972	LA-N	119	391	42	107	11	2	3	32	27	33	.274	.324	.335	659	90	-5	5	5	-1	.976	0	2-49,3-39,O-16C,S	-0.2
1973	Cal-A	32	126	12	38	5	2	1	13	5	9	.302	.328	.397	725	112	2	6	1	1	.948	0	S-25/O-8(1-7-0)	0.5
1974	Cal-A	117	371	39	97	10	3	3	39	25	25	.261	.313	.329	642	90	-5	8	5	0	.950	-8	O-62L,S-36,3-15,/2D	-1.3
1975	Cal-A	26	57	5	16	2	0	0	5	4	3	.281	.339	.316	654	92	-0	0	2	-1	.958	-2	D-13/1-3,3-2,O-2L	-0.4
	SD-N	7	15	1	2	0	0	1	1	4	0	.133	.316	.333	649	86	-0	1	0	0	1.000	-1	/O-4(4-0-0)	-0.1
1976	SD-N	15	49	3	18	4	0	0	4	6	2	.367	.436	.449	885	165	4	0	1	-0	1.000	-1	O-10(7-0-5)/1-4	0.4
1977	SD-N	44	67	5	12	3	0	1	10	7	10	.179	.257	.269	525	46	-5	0	0	0	.962	-1	S-10,3-10/1-1	-0.6
	NY-N	42	83	8	11	1	0	1	3	6	9	.133	.191	.181	372	0	-12	0	0	0	1.000	-1	1-15,S-14/3-4	-1.3
	Yr	86	150	13	23	4	0	2	13	13	19	.153	.221	.220	441	20	-17	0	0	0	.969	-2	S-24,1-16,3-14	-1.9
1978	NY-N	69	160	17	43	7	0	1	18	19	18	.269	.350	.331	681	95	-1	1	1	-0	.977	-9	2-45/3-9	-0.8
1979	Sea-A	62	98	9	27	6	0	0	7	22	5	.276	.408	.337	745	102	2	1	2	-0	.971	-6	S-29,O-15R/2-4,3CD	-0.4
Total	10	639	1698	176	441	59	9	12	157	140	134	.260	.319	.326	646	86	-31	27	20	-1	.957	-27	S-161,O-128L,23/1DC	-5.0

■ BENNY VALENZUELA
Valenzuela, Benjamin Beltran "Papelero" b: 6/2/33, Los Mochis, Mexico BR/TR, 5'10", 175 lbs. Deb: 4/27/58

YEAR	TM/L	G	AB	R	H	2B	3B	HR	RBI	BB	SO	AVG	OBP	SLG	OPS	OPS+	BR+	SB	CS	SBR	FA	FR	G/POS	TPR
1958	StL-N	10	14	0	3	1	0	0	0	1	0	.214	.267	.286	552	45	-1	0	0	0	.875	0	/3-3	-0.1

■ YOHANNY VALERA
Valera, Yohanny b: 8/17/76, Santo Domingo, D.R. BR/TR, 6'1", 205 lbs. Deb: 9/13/2000

YEAR	TM/L	G	AB	R	H	2B	3B	HR	RBI	BB	SO	AVG	OBP	SLG	OPS	OPS+	BR+	SB	CS	SBR	FA	FR	G/POS	TPR
2000	Mon-N	7	10	1	0	0	0	0	1	1	5	.000	.167	.000	167	-52	-2	0	0	0	1.000	1	/C-7	-0.2

■ DAVE VALLE
Valle, David b: 10/30/60, Bayside, N.Y. BR/TR, 6'2", 200 lbs. Deb: 9/7/84 Career OF: (0-LF 0-CF 1-RF)

YEAR	TM/L	G	AB	R	H	2B	3B	HR	RBI	BB	SO	AVG	OBP	SLG	OPS	OPS+	BR+	SB	CS	SBR	FA	FR	G/POS	TPR
1984	Sea-A	13	27	4	8	1	0	1	4	1	5	.296	.321	.444	766	111	0	0	0	0	1.000	2	C-13	0.3
1985	Sea-A	31	70	2	11	1	0	0	4	1	17	.157	.181	.171	352	-3	-10	0	0	0	.976	-1	C-31	-1.0
1986	Sea-A	22	53	10	18	3	0	5	15	7	7	.340	.417	.679	1096	191	7	0	0	0	.982	-4	C-12/1-4	0.3
1987	Sea-A	95	324	40	83	16	3	12	53	15	46	.256	.295	.435	731	86	-7	2	0	1	.989	1	C-75,D-14/1-2,O-1R	-0.3
1988	Sea-A	93	290	29	67	15	2	10	50	18	38	.231	.297	.400	697	89	-5	0	1	-0	.989	6	C-84/1-1,D-3	0.6
1989	Sea-A	94	316	32	75	10	3	7	34	29	32	.237	.313	.354	668	85	-6	0	0	0	.993	-3	C-93	-0.3
1990	Sea-A	107	308	37	66	15	0	7	33	45	48	.214	.328	.331	659	84	-6	1	2	-0	**.997**	-0	*C-104/1-1	0.0
1991	Sea-A	132	324	38	63	8	1	8	32	34	49	.194	.289	.299	588	63	-16	0	2	-1	.992	9	*C-129/1-2	-0.2
1992	Sea-A	124	367	39	88	16	1	9	30	27	58	.240	.306	.362	668	86	-7	0	0	0	.990	-3	*C-122	-0.4
1993	Sea-A	135	423	48	109	19	0	13	63	48	56	.258	.357	.395	751	100	1	1	0	0	.995	9	*C-135	1.8
1994	Bos-A	30	76	6	12	2	1	1	5	9	18	.158	.256	.250	506	30	-8	0	1	-0	.982	-1	C-28/1-2	-0.7
	Mil-A	16	36	8	14	6	0	1	5	9	4	.389	.522	.639	1161	189	5	0	1	-0	1.000	0	C-12/D-2	0.5
	Yr	46	112	14	26	8	1	2	10	18	22	.232	.348	.375	723	83	-3	0	2	-1	.986	-1	C-40/1-2,D-2	-0.2
1995	Tex-A	36	75	7	18	3	0	0	5	6	18	.240	.305	.280	585	52	-5	1	0	0	.993	7	C-29/1-7	0.3
1996	Tex-A	42	86	14	26	6	1	3	17	9	17	.302	.368	.500	868	111	1	0	0	0	.994	8	C-35/1-5,D-1	1.0
Total	13	970	2775	314	658	121	12	77	350	258	413	.237	.316	.373	689	86	-55	5	7	-1	.992	29	C-902/1-24,D-20,O-1R	1.9

■ HECTOR VALLE
Valle, Hector Jose b: 10/27/40, Vega Baja, P.R. BR/TR, 5'9", 180 lbs. Deb: 6/6/65

YEAR	TM/L	G	AB	R	H	2B	3B	HR	RBI	BB	SO	AVG	OBP	SLG	OPS	OPS+	BR+	SB	CS	SBR	FA	FR	G/POS	TPR
1965	LA-N	9	13	1	4	0	0	0	2	2	3	.308	.400	.308	708	110	0	0	0	0	1.000	-0	/C-6	0.0

■ ELMER VALO
Valo, Elmer William b: 3/5/21, Ribnik, Czech. d: 7/19/98, Palmerton, Pa. BL/TR, 5'11", 190 lbs. Deb: 9/22/40 C

YEAR	TM/L	G	AB	R	H	2B	3B	HR	RBI	BB	SO	AVG	OBP	SLG	OPS	OPS+	BR+	SB	CS	SBR	FA	FR	G/POS	TPR
1940	Phi-A	6	23	6	8	0	0	0	0	3	0	.348	.423	.348	771	104	0	2	0	0	1.000	1	/O-6(6-0-0)	0.1
1941	Phi-A	15	50	13	21	0	1	2	6	4	2	.420	.463	.580	1043	179	6	0	0	0	1.000	-1	O-10(10-0-0)	0.4
1942	Phi-A	133	459	64	115	13	10	2	40	70	21	.251	.355	.336	690	95	-1	13	8	0	.964	1	*O-122(1-1-120)	-0.8
1943	Phi-A	77	249	31	55	6	2	3	18	35	13	.221	.319	.297	616	81	-5	2	6	-2	.986	-1	O-63(9-0-54)	-1.3
1946	Phi-A	108	348	59	107	21	6	1	31	60	18	.307	.411	.411	822	131	17	9	8	-1	.974	1	O-90(5-0-85)	1.5
1947	Phi-A	112	370	60	111	12	6	5	36	64	21	.300	.406	.405	811	123	14	11	3	1	.973	-1	*O-104(0-0-104)	1.2
1948	Phi-A	113	383	72	117	17	4	3	46	81	13	.305	.432	.394	826	120	16	10	6	0	.983	-1	*O-109(0-0-109)	1.2
1949	Phi-A	150	547	86	155	27	12	5	85	119	32	.283	.413	.404	817	121	21	14	11	-1	.981	10	*O-150(150-0-0)	1.9
1950	Phi-A	129	446	62	125	16	5	10	46	82	22	.280	.400	.406	806	109	9	12	7	0	.982	4	*O-117(33-0-85)	0.7
1951	Phi-A	123	444	75	134	27	8	7	55	75	20	.302	.412	.446	858	129	21	11	6	0	.981	-0	*O-116(1-22-95)	1.7
1952	Phi-A	129	388	69	109	26	4	5	47	101	16	.281	.432	.407	839	126	20	12	11	-1	.962	-3	*O-121(2-11-108)	1.3
1953	Phi-A	50	85	15	19	3	0	0	9	22	7	.224	.383	.259	642	73	-2	0	1	-0	1.000	-1	O-25(10-0-15)	-0.4
1954	Phi-A	95	224	28	48	11	6	1	33	51	18	.214	.360	.330	690	90	-1	2	1	0	.965	2	O-62(34-0-30)	-0.3
1955	KC-A	112	283	50	103	17	4	3	37	52	18	.364	.463	.484	947	153	24	5	3	0	.987	2	O-72(46-4-23)	2.2
1956	KC-A	9	9	1	2	0	0	0	2	1	1	.222	.300	.222	522	40	-1	0	0	0	.000	-0	/O-1(1-0-0)	-0.1
	Phi-N	98	291	40	84	13	3	5	37	48	21	.289	.395	.405	800	118	9	7	6	-1	.966	-0	O-87(0-0-87)	0.6
1957	Bro-N	81	161	14	44	10	1	4	26	25	16	.273	.374	.422	797	104	2	0	1	-0	1.000	-4	O-36(26-0-14)	-0.5
1958	LA-N	65	101	9	25	2	1	1	14	12	11	.248	.327	.317	644	69	-4	0	1	-0	1.000	-6	O-26(16-0-13)	-1.1
1959	Cle-A	34	24	3	7	0	0	0	5	7	0	.292	.452	.292	743	113	1	0	0	0	1.000	-1	/O-2(0-0-2)	0.1
1960	NY-A	8	5	1	0	0	0	0	0	2	1	.000	.286	.000	286	-17	-1	0	0	0	.000	-1	/O-2(0-0-2)	-0.2
	Was-A	76	64	6	18	3	0	0	16	17	4	.281	.439	.328	767	112	2	0	0	0	1.000	-1	/O-6(1-0-5)	0.2
	Yr	84	69	7	18	3	0	0	16	19	5	.261	.427	.304	731	103	2	0	0	0	1.000	-1	/O-8(1-0-7)	0.0
1961	Min-A	33	32	0	5	2	0	0	4	3	3	.156	.250	.219	469	25	-3	0	0	0	1.000	0	/O-1(1-0-0)	-0.3
	Phi-N	50	43	4	8	2	0	1	8	8	6	.186	.327	.302	629	69	-2	0	0	0	.000	-0	/O-1(0-0-1)	-0.2
Total	20	1806	5029	768	1420	228	73	58	601	942	284	.282	.399	.391	791	114	143	110	79	-3	.977	1	*O-1329(352-38-952)	7.9

■ DEACON Van BUREN
Van Buren, Edward Eugene b: 12/14/1870, LaSalle Co., Ill. d: 6/29/57, Portland, Ore. BL/TR, 5'10", 175 lbs. Deb: 4/21/04

YEAR	TM/L	G	AB	R	H	2B	3B	HR	RBI	BB	SO	AVG	OBP	SLG	OPS	OPS+	BR+	SB	CS	SBR	FA	FR	G/POS	TPR
1904	Bro-N	1	1	0	1	0	0	0	0	0		1.000	1.000	1.000	2000	531	0	0			.000	0	H	0.0
	Phi-N	12	43	2	10	2	0	0	3	3		.233	.283	.279	562	76	-1	2			.962	1	O-12(12-0-0)	-0.1
	Yr	13	44	2	11	2	0	0	3	3		.250	.298	.295	593	86	-1	2			.962	1	O-12(12-0-0)	-0.1

■ TY Van BURKLEO
Van Burkleo, Tyler Lee b: 10/7/63, Oakland, Cal. BL/TL, 6'5", 225 lbs. Deb: 7/28/93

YEAR	TM/L	G	AB	R	H	2B	3B	HR	RBI	BB	SO	AVG	OBP	SLG	OPS	OPS+	BR+	SB	CS	SBR	FA	FR	G/POS	TPR
1993	Cal-A	12	33	2	5	3	0	1	1	6	9	.152	.282	.333	615	63	-2	1	0	0	1.000	-2	1-12	-0.4

YEAR	TM/L	G	AB	R	H	2B	3B	HR	RBI	BB	SO	AVG	OBP	SLG	OPS	OPS+	BR+	SB	CS	SBR	FA	FR	G/POS	TPR
1994	Col-N	2	5	0	0	0	0	0	0	0	1	.000	.000	.000	0	-86	-1	0	0	0	1.000	0	/1-2	-0.1
Total	2	14	38	2	5	3	0	1	1	6	10	.132	.250	.289	539	42	-3	1	0	0	1.000	-1	/1-14	-0.5

■ AL Van CAMP Van Camp, Albert Joseph b: 9/7/03, Moline, Ill. d: 2/2/81, Davenport, Iowa BR/TR, 5'11.5", 175 lbs. Deb: 9/11/28

YEAR	TM/L	G	AB	R	H	2B	3B	HR	RBI	BB	SO	AVG	OBP	SLG	OPS	OPS+	BR+	SB	CS	SBR	FA	FR	G/POS	TPR
1928	Cle-A	5	17	0	4	1	0	0	2	0	1	.235	.235	.294	529	38	-2	1	0	0	.980	-1	/1-5	-0.2
1931	Bos-A	101	324	34	89	15	4	0	33	20	24	.275	.319	.346	665	79	-10	3	2	-0	.973	-5	O-59(58-3-2),1-25	-1.9
1932	Bos-A	34	103	10	23	4	2	0	6	4	17	.223	.252	.301	553	44	-9	0	0	0	.985	1	1-25	-1.0
Total	3	140	444	44	116	20	6	0	41	24	42	.261	.301	.333	634	69	-20	4	2	0	.991	-5	/O-59(58-3-2),1-55	-3.1

■ CARL VANDAGRIFT Vandagrift, Carl William b: 4/22/1883, Cantrall, Ill. d: 10/9/20, Fort Wayne, Ind. BR/TR, 5'8", 155 lbs. Deb: 5/19/14

YEAR	TM/L	G	AB	R	H	2B	3B	HR	RBI	BB	SO	AVG	OBP	SLG	OPS	OPS+	BR+	SB	CS	SBR	FA	FR	G/POS	TPR
1914	Ind-F	43	136	25	34	4	0	0	9	9	15	.250	.301	.279	581	53	-11	7			.925	-6	2-28,3-12/S-5	-1.7

■ JOHN VANDER WAL Vander Wal, John Henry b: 4/29/66, Grand Rapids, Mich. BL/TL, 6'2", 190 lbs. Deb: 9/6/91 Career OF: (201-LF 2-CF 120-RF)

YEAR	TM/L	G	AB	R	H	2B	3B	HR	RBI	BB	SO	AVG	OBP	SLG	OPS	OPS+	BR+	SB	CS	SBR	FA	FR	G/POS	TPR
1991	Mon-N	21	61	4	13	4	1	1	8	1	18	.213	.226	.361	586	63	-3	0	0	0	1.000	-1	O-17(17-0-0)	-0.5
1992	Mon-N	105	213	21	51	8	2	4	20	24	36	.239	.316	.352	669	90	-3	3	0	1	.981	0	O-57(55-0-4)/1-7	-0.4
1993	Mon-N	106	215	34	50	7	4	5	30	27	30	.233	.321	.372	693	81	-6	6	3	0	.988	-12	1-42,O-38(27-2-10)	-2.1
1994	Col-N	91	110	12	27	3	1	5	15	16	31	.245	.341	.427	769	85	-2	2	1	0	1.000	-2	1-14/O-7(5-0-2)	-0.5
1995	*Col-N	105	101	15	35	8	1	5	21	16	23	.347	.436	.594	1030	131	5	1	1	-0	.957	-1	1-10,O-10(7-0-3)	0.3
1996	Col-N	104	151	20	38	6	2	5	31	19	38	.252	.339	.417	756	79	-4	2	2	-0	1.000	-3	O-26(25-0-1),1-10	-0.8
1997	Col-N	76	92	7	16	2	0	1	11	10	33	.174	.255	.228	483	23	-10	1	1	-0	.923	-2	/O-9(2-0-7),1-5,D-2	-1.3
1998	Col-N	89	104	18	30	10	1	5	20	16	29	.288	.383	.548	931	116	3	0	0	0	1.000	-4	O-25(3-0-22)/1-2	-0.2
	*SD-N	20	25	3	6	3	0	0	0	6	5	.240	.387	.360	747	106	1	0	0	0	1.000	0	/O-5(2-0-3),1-3,D-3	0.0
	Yr	109	129	21	36	13	1	5	20	22	34	.279	.384	.512	896	114	3	0	0	0	1.000	-4	O-30(5-0-25)/1-5,D-3	-0.2
1999	SD-N	132	246	26	67	18	0	6	41	37	59	.272	.372	.419	791	108	4	2	1	0	1.000	-2	O-48(45-0-3),1-28/D-1	-0.1
2000	Pit-N	134	384	74	115	29	0	24	94	72	92	.299	.413	.563	975	144	28	11	2	2	.965	-7	O-78R,1-33/D-3	1.6
Total	10	983	1702	234	448	98	12	61	291	244	394	.263	.358	.442	800	102	11	28	11	2	.981	-33	O-320L,1-154/D-9	-4.0

■ FRED Van DUSEN Van Dusen, Frederick William b: 7/31/37, Jackson Heights, N.Y. BL/TL, 6'3", 180 lbs. Deb: 9/11/55

YEAR	TM/L	G	AB	R	H	2B	3B	HR	RBI	BB	SO	AVG	OBP	SLG	OPS	OPS+	BR+	SB	CS	SBR	FA	FR	G/POS	TPR
1955	Phi-N	1	0	0	0	0	0	0	0	0	0	—	1.000	—	1000	199	0	0	0	0	.000	0	H	0.0

■ BILL Van DYKE Van Dyke, William Jennings b: 12/15/1863, Paris, Ill. d: 5/5/33, ElPaso, Tex. BR/TR, 5'8", 170 lbs. Deb: 4/17/1890 Career OF: (112-LF 5-CF 0-RF)

YEAR	TM/L	G	AB	R	H	2B	3B	HR	RBI	BB	SO	AVG	OBP	SLG	OPS	OPS+	BR+	SB	CS	SBR	FA	FR	G/POS	TPR
1890	Tol-a	129	502	74	129	14	11	2	54	25		.257	.296	.341	637	85	-12	73			.924	-7	*O-110L,3-18/2-2,C	-1.9
1892	StL-N	4	16	2	2	0	0	0	1	0	1	.125	.125	.125	250	-26	-2	0			.875	-1	/O-4(0-4-0)	-0.3
1893	Bos-N	3	12	2	3	1	0	0	1	0	1	.250	.250	.333	583	50	-1	1			1.000	-1	/O-3(3-0-0)	-0.2
Total	3	136	530	78	134	15	11	2	56	25	2	.253	.290	.334	624	81	-15	74			.924	-8	O-117L/3-18,2-2,C-1	-2.4

■ DAVE Van GORDER Van Gorder, David Thomas b: 3/27/57, Los Angeles, Cal. BR/TR, 6'2", 205 lbs. Deb: 6/15/82

YEAR	TM/L	G	AB	R	H	2B	3B	HR	RBI	BB	SO	AVG	OBP	SLG	OPS	OPS+	BR+	SB	CS	SBR	FA	FR	G/POS	TPR
1982	Cin-N	51	137	4	25	3	1	0	7	14	19	.182	.263	.219	482	35	-12	1	0	0	.986	-2	C-51	-1.2
1984	Cin-N	38	101	10	23	2	0	0	6	12	17	.228	.310	.248	557	56	-5	0	0	0	1.000	2	C-36/1-1	-0.3
1985	Cin-N	73	151	12	36	7	0	2	24	9	19	.238	.286	.325	610	67	-7	0	0	0	.989	-3	C-70	-0.9
1986	Cin-N	9	10	0	0	0	0	0	0	1	2	.000	.091	.000	91	-70	-2	0	0	0	1.000	1	/C-7	-0.2
1987	Bal-A	12	21	4	5	0	0	1	1	3	6	.238	.333	.381	714	91	-0	0	0	0	.978	1	C-12	0.1
Total	5	183	420	30	89	12	1	3	38	39	63	.212	.282	.267	549	52	-26	1	0	0	.990	-2	C-176/1-1	-2.5

■ GEORGE Van HALTREN Van Haltren, George Edward Martin "Rip" b: 3/30/1866, St.Louis, Mo. d: 9/29/45, Oakland, Cal. BL/TL, 5'11", 170 lbs. Deb: 6/27/1887 M Career OF: (313-LF 1376-CF 149-RF)

YEAR	TM/L	G	AB	R	H	2B	3B	HR	RBI	BB	SO	AVG	OBP	SLG	OPS	OPS+	BR+	SB	CS	SBR	FA	FR	G/POS	TPR
1887	Chi-N	45	187	30	50	4	0	3	17	15	15	.267	.271	.279	550	47	-13	12			.927	-3	O-27(4-0-23),P-20	-0.9
1888	Chi-N	81	318	46	90	9	14	4	34	22	34	.283	.329	.437	767	133	11	21			.872	-2	O-57(47-4-7),P-30	0.2
1889	Chi-N	134	543	126	168	20	10	9	81	82	41	.309	.405	.433	838	128	22	28			.898	-3	*O-130L/S-3,2-1	1.3
1890	Bro-P	92	376	84	126	8	9	5	54	41	23	.335	.405	.444	849	119	10	35			.896	5	O-67R,P-28/S-3	0.6
1891	Bal-a	139	566	136	180	14	15	9	83	71	46	.318	.398	.443	841	139	29	75			.882	-12	O-81L,S-59/P-6,2-2	1.4
1892	Bal-N	135	556	105	168	20	12	7	57	70	34	.302	.382	.419	801	138	26	49			.850	0	*O-129C/P-4,3-3,1SM	1.6
	Pit-N	13	55	10	11	2	2	0	5	6	0	.200	.279	.309	588	77	-2	6			.905	-2	O-13(0-13-0)	-0.4
	Yr	148	611	115	179	22	14	7	62	76	34	.293	.373	.409	782	133	25	55			.854	-2	*O-142C/P-4,3-3,1S	1.2
1893	Pit-N	124	529	129	179	14	11	3	79	75	25	.338	.422	.423	846	127	24	37			.869	-6	*O-111C,S-12/2-2	0.9
1894	*NY-N	139	528	109	175	22	4	7	104	55	23	.331	.399	.428	827	100	1	43			.915	-2	*O-139(0-139-0)	-0.7
1895	NY-N	131	521	113	177	23	19	8	103	57	29	.340	.408	.503	911	137	29	32			.914	-4	*O-131(0-131-0)/P-1	1.4
1896	NY-N	133	562	136	197	18	**21**	5	74	55	36	.351	.410	.484	894	139	32	39			.952	4	*O-133(0-133-0)/P-2	2.3
1897	NY-N	130	566	119	186	22	9	3	64	42		.329	.376	.415	791	112	10	50			.938	9	*O-130(0-130-0)	0.9
1898	NY-N	156	654	129	204	28	16	2	68	59		.312	.372	.413	785	129	24	36			.917	-2	*O-156(17-138-3)	1.1
1899	NY-N	152	607	118	183	22	3	2	58	75		.301	.379	.357	737	106	8	31			.932	2	*O-152(23-129-0)	0.0
1900	NY-N	141	571	114	180	30	7	1	51	50		.315	.371	.398	769	118	14	**45**			.939	10	*O-141(0-141-0)/P-1	1.3
1901	NY-N	135	543	82	182	23	6	1	47	51		.335	.396	.405	801	138	28	24			.941	4	*O-135(0-135-0)/P-1	2.4
1902	NY-N	26	96	14	24	1	2	0	7	17		.250	.363	.302	665	106	2	6			.929	2	O-26(3-13-10)	0.2
1903	NY-N	84	280	42	72	6	1	0	28	28		.257	.327	.286	613	72	-9	14			.959	-6	O-75(3-70-2)	-1.8
Total	17	1990	8058	1642	2552	286	161	69	1014	871	306	.317	.385	.417	802	121	246	583			.915	-5	*O-1833C/P-93,S231	11.8

■ JOHN VANN Vann, John Silas b: 6/7/1893, Fairland, Okla. d: 6/10/58, Shreveport, La. BR/TR, Deb: 6/11/13

YEAR	TM/L	G	AB	R	H	2B	3B	HR	RBI	BB	SO	AVG	OBP	SLG	OPS	OPS+	BR+	SB	CS	SBR	FA	FR	G/POS	TPR
1913	StL-N	1	1	0	0	0	0	0	0	0	1	.000	.000	.000	0	-99	-0	0			.000	0	H	0.0

■ JAY Van NOY Van Noy, Jay Lowell b: 11/4/28, Garland, Utah BL/TR, 6'1", 200 lbs. Deb: 6/18/51

YEAR	TM/L	G	AB	R	H	2B	3B	HR	RBI	BB	SO	AVG	OBP	SLG	OPS	OPS+	BR+	SB	CS	SBR	FA	FR	G/POS	TPR
1951	StL-N	6	7	1	0	0	0	0	0	1	6	.000	.125	.000	125	-63	-2	0	0	0	1.000	-0	/O-1(0-0-1)	-0.2

■ MAURICE Van ROBAYS Van Robays, Maurice Rene "Bomber" b: 11/15/14, Detroit, Mich. d: 3/1/65, Detroit, Mich. BR/TR, 6'0.5", 190 lbs. Deb: 9/7/39 Career OF: (403-LF 3-CF 64-RF)

YEAR	TM/L	G	AB	R	H	2B	3B	HR	RBI	BB	SO	AVG	OBP	SLG	OPS	OPS+	BR+	SB	CS	SBR	FA	FR	G/POS	TPR
1939	Pit-N	27	105	13	33	9	0	2	16	6	10	.314	.351	.457	808	118	2	0			.919	-4	O-25(25-0-0)/3-1	-0.3
1940	Pit-N	145	572	82	156	27	7	11	116	33	58	.273	.316	.402	718	98	-3	2			.963	-4	*O-143(137-0-6)/1-1	-1.6
1941	Pit-N	129	457	62	129	23	5	4	78	41	29	.282	.343	.381	723	104	2	0			.974	7	*O-121(121-0-0)	0.3
1942	Pit-N	100	328	29	76	13	5	1	46	30	24	.232	.298	.311	609	76	-10	0			.986	5	O-84(84-0-0)	-1.0
1943	Pit-N	69	236	32	68	17	7	1	35	18	19	.288	.344	.432	776	119	5	0			.940	-3	O-60(15-0-45)	-0.1
1946	Pit-N	59	146	14	31	5	3	1	12	11	15	.212	.272	.308	580	63	-7	0			.955	-5	O-37(21-3-13)/1-2	-1.5
Total	6	529	1844	232	493	94	27	20	303	139	155	.267	.321	.380	702	97	-11	2			.966	-3	O-470L/1-3,3-1	-4.2

■ ANDY Van SLYKE Van Slyke, Andrew James b: 12/21/60, Utica, N.Y. BL/TR, 6'2", 192 lbs. Deb: 6/17/83 Career OF: (89-LF 1119-CF 316-RF)

YEAR	TM/L	G	AB	R	H	2B	3B	HR	RBI	BB	SO	AVG	OBP	SLG	OPS	OPS+	BR+	SB	CS	SBR	FA	FR	G/POS	TPR
1983	StL-N	101	309	51	81	15	5	8	38	46	64	.262	.360	.421	780	115	7	21	7	2	.974	-10	O-69L,3-30/1-9	-0.4
1984	StL-N	137	361	45	88	16	4	7	50	63	71	.244	.356	.368	725	107	5	28	5	4	1.000	-12	O-81R,3-32,1-30	-0.7
1985	*StL-N	146	424	61	110	25	6	13	55	47	54	.259	.336	.439	775	116	9	34	6	5	.996	-2	*O-142(4-10-133)/1-2	0.7
1986	StL-N	137	418	48	113	23	7	13	61	47	85	.270	.345	.452	798	119	10	21	8	2	.969	3	*O-110(1-27-87),1-38	1.0
1987	Pit-N	157	564	93	165	36	11	21	82	56	122	.293	.361	.507	868	126	20	34	8	5	.988	10	*O-150(0-114-37)/1-1	3.1
1988	Pit-N★	154	587	101	169	23	**15**	25	100	57	126	.288	.352	.506	858	146	33	30	9	3	.991	17	*O-152(0-152-0)	**5.5**
1989	Pit-N	130	476	64	113	18	9	9	53	47	100	.237	.310	.370	680	97	-2	16	4	2	.989	14	*O-123(0-123-0)/1-2	1.3
1990	*Pit-N	136	493	67	140	26	6	17	77	66	89	.284	.370	.465	834	133	23	14	4	2	.976	3	*O-133(0-133-0)	2.7
1991	*Pit-N	138	491	87	130	24	7	17	83	71	85	.265	.362	.446	808	128	19	10	3	1	.996	1	*O-135(0-135-0)	2.1
1992	*Pit-N★	154	614	103	**199**	**45**	12	14	89	58	99	.324	.386	.505	891	152	41	12	3	2	.989	11	*O-154(0-154-0)	5.6
1993	Pit-N†	83	323	42	100	13	4	8	50	24	40	.310	.361	.449	810	116	7	11	2	2	.995	3	O-78(0-78-0)	1.3
1994	Pit-N	105	374	41	92	18	3	6	30	52	72	.246	.341	.358	699	82	-9	7	0	2	.992	6	O-99(0-99-0)	-0.1
1995	Bal-A	17	63	6	10	1	0	3	8	5	15	.159	.221	.317	538	37	-6	0	0	0	.978	2	O-17(0-16-1)	-0.4
	Phi-N	63	214	26	52	10	2	3	16	28	41	.243	.336	.350	687	81	-5	7	0	2	.984	3	O-56(0-56-0)	-0.1
Total	13	1658	5711	835	1562	293	91	164	792	667	1063	.274	.352	.443	795	120	151	245	59	33	.988	48	*O-1499C/1-82,3-62	21.6

■ IKE Van ZANDT Van Zandt, Charles Isaac b: 2/1876, Brooklyn, N.Y. d: 9/14/08, Nashua, N.H. BL, Deb: 8/5/01 Career OF: (1-LF 29-CF 46-RF)

YEAR	TM/L	G	AB	R	H	2B	3B	HR	RBI	BB	SO	AVG	OBP	SLG	OPS	OPS+	BR+	SB	CS	SBR	FA	FR	G/POS	TPR
1901	NY-N	3	6	1	1	0	0	0	0	0		.167	.167	.167	333	-3	-1	0			.333	-2	/P-2,O-1(1-0-0)	-0.1

YEAR	TM/L	G	AB	R	H	2B	3B	HR	RBI	BB	SO	AVG	OBP	SLG	OPS	OPS+	BR+	SB	CS	SBR	FA	FR	G/POS	TPR
1904	Chi-N	3	11	0	0	0	0	0	0	0		.000	.000	.000	0	-99	-3	0			1.000	0	/O-3(0-0-1)	-0.3
1905	StL-A	94	322	31	75	15	1	1	20	7		.233	.252	.295	547	77	-9	7			.874	-13	O-75(0-29-45)/P-1,1-1	-2.9
Total	3	100	339	32	76	15	1	1	20	7		.224	.242	.283	525	69	-13	7			.868	-14	/O-79R,P-3,1-1	-3.3
■ DICK Van ZANT	Van Zant, Richard "Foghorn Dick" b: 11/1864, Indiana d: 8/6/12, Wayne Co., Ind. Deb: 10/4/1888																							
1888	Cle-a	10	31	1	8	1	0	0	1	1		.258	.303	.290	593	93	-0	1			.784	0	3-10	0.0
■ EDDIE VARGAS	Vargas, Hediberto (Rodriguez) b: 2/23/59, Guanica, P.R. BR/TR, 6'4", 205 lbs. Deb: 9/8/82																							
1982	Pit-N	8	8	1	3	1	0	0	3	0	2	.375	.375	.500	875	139	0	0	0	0	1.000	0	/1-5	0.0
1984	Pit-N	18	31	3	7	2	0	0	2	3	5	.226	.294	.290	584	65	-1	0	0	0	.982	-0	1-13	-0.2
Total	2	26	39	4	10	3	0	0	5	3	7	.256	.310	.333	643	80	-1	0	0	0	.986	-0	/1-18	-0.2
■ JASON VARITEK	Varitek, Jason A. b: 4/11/72, Rochester, Minn. BB/TR, 6'2", 210 lbs. Deb: 9/24/97																							
1997	Bos-A	1	1	0	1	0	0	0	0	0	0	1.000	1.000	1.000	2000	416	0	0	0	0	1.000	-0	/C-1	0.0
1998	*Bos-A	86	221	31	56	13	0	7	33	17	45	.253	.313	.407	720	84	-6	2	2	-0	.988	1	C-75/D-3	-0.2
1999	*Bos-A	144	483	70	130	39	2	20	76	46	85	.269	.335	.482	818	102	0	1	2	-0	.990	21	*C-140/D-2	2.7
2000	Bos-A	139	448	55	111	31	1	10	65	60	84	.248	.344	.388	733	82	-12	1	1	-0	.992	8	*C-128/D-1	0.3
Total	4	370	1153	156	298	83	3	37	174	123	214	.258	.335	.432	767	91	-17	4	5	-1	.990	30	C-344/D-6	2.8
■ BUCK VARNER	Varner, Glen Gann b: 8/17/30, Hixson, Tenn. BL/TR, 5'10", 170 lbs. Deb: 9/19/52																							
1952	Was-A	2	4	0	0	0	0	0	0	1	1	.000	.200	.000	200	-43	-1	0	0	0	1.000	-0	/O-1(0-0-1)	-0.1
■ PETE VARNEY	Varney, Richard Fred b: 4/10/49, Roxbury, Mass. BR/TR, 6'3", 235 lbs. Deb: 8/26/73																							
1973	Chi-A	5	4	0	0	0	0	0	0	1	0	.000	.200	.000	200	-38	-1	0	0	0	1.000	0	/C-5	0.0
1974	Chi-A	9	28	1	7	0	0	0	2	1	8	.250	.276	.250	526	51	-2	0	0	0	.981	1	/C-9	0.0
1975	Chi-A	36	107	12	29	5	1	2	8	6	28	.271	.316	.393	708	98	-1	2	0	0	.988	-1	C-34/D-2	0.0
1976	Chi-A	14	41	5	10	2	0	3	5	2	9	.244	.279	.512	791	128	1	0	0	0	.988	1	C-14	0.3
	Atl-N	5	10	0	1	0	0	0	0	0	2	.100	.100	.100	200	-41	-2	0	0	0	1.000	-1	/C-5	-0.2
Total	4	69	190	18	47	7	1	5	15	10	47	.247	.289	.374	662	86	-4	2	0	0	.988	1	/C-67,D-2	0.1
■ GARY VARSHO	Varsho, Gary Andrew b: 6/20/61, Marshfield, Wis. BL/TR, 5'11", 190 lbs. Deb: 7/6/88																							
1988	Chi-N	46	73	6	20	3	0	0	5	1	6	.274	.284	.315	599	69	-3	5	0	1	.906	-2	O-18(10-0-8)	-0.4
1989	Chi-N	61	87	10	16	4	2	0	6	4	13	.184	.220	.276	496	38	-7	3	0	1	.929	-3	O-21(17-0-4)	-1.0
1990	Chi-N	46	48	10	12	4	0	0	1	1	6	.250	.265	.333	599	59	-3	2	0	0	1.000	-1	/O-3(2-0-1)	-0.3
1991	*Pit-N	99	187	23	51	11	2	4	23	19	34	.273	.346	.417	763	115	4	9	2	1	.989	-4	O-54(5-5-45)/1-3	0.0
1992	*Pit-N	103	162	22	36	6	3	4	22	10	32	.222	.267	.370	638	80	-5	5	2	0	.984	-5	O-44(14-2-28)	-1.1
1993	Cin-N	77	95	8	22	6	0	2	11	9	19	.232	.305	.358	663	77	-3	1	0	0	1.000	-2	O-22(13-0-9)	-0.6
1994	Pit-N	67	82	15	21	6	3	0	5	4	19	.256	.307	.402	709	82	-2	0	1	-0	.926	-10	O-36(18-2-18)/1-1	-1.3
1995	Phi-N	72	103	7	26	1	1	0	11	7	17	.252	.313	.282	594	58	-6	2	0	0	.939	-4	O-25(9-0-16)	-1.0
Total	8	571	837	101	204	41	11	10	84	55	146	.244	.296	.355	651	78	-25	27	5	4	.963	-30	O-223(88-9-129)/1-4	-5.7
■ JIM VATCHER	Vatcher, James Ernest b: 5/27/65, Santa Monica, Cal. BR/TR, 5'9", 165 lbs. Deb: 5/30/90																							
1990	Phi-N	36	46	5	12	1	0	1	4	4	6	.261	.320	.348	668	84	-1	0	0	0	1.000	-6	O-24(12-0-12)	-0.8
	Atl-N	21	27	2	7	1	1	0	3	1	9	.259	.286	.370	656	75	-1	0	0	0	1.000	-1	/O-6(2-0-4)	-0.2
	Yr	57	73	7	19	2	1	1	7	5	15	.260	.308	.356	664	80	-2	0	0	0	1.000	-7	O-30(14-0-16)	-1.0
1991	SD-N	17	20	3	4	0	0	0	2	4	6	.200	.333	.200	533	52	-1	1	0	0	.900	-2	O-11(2-0-9)	-0.3
1992	SD-N	13	16	1	4	1	0	0	2	3	6	.250	.368	.313	681	93	-0	0	0	0	1.000	-2	O-13(0-1-12)	-0.2
Total	3	87	109	11	27	3	1	1	11	12	27	.248	.322	.321	643	77	-3	1	0	0	.980	-11	/O-54(16-1-37)	-1.5
■ GLENN VAUGHAN	Vaughan, Glenn Edward "Sparky" b: 2/15/44, Compton, Cal. BB/TR, 5'11", 170 lbs. Deb: 9/20/63																							
1963	Hou-N	9	30	1	5	0	0	0	0	2	5	.167	.219	.167	385	14	-3	1	0	0	.914	-3	/S-9,3-1	-0.7
■ ARKY VAUGHAN	Vaughan, Joseph Floyd b: 3/9/12, Clifty, Ark. d: 8/30/52, Eagleville, Cal. BL/TR, 5'10.5", 175 lbs. Deb: 4/17/32 H Career OF: (60-LF 0-CF 0-RF)																							
1932	Pit-N	129	497	71	158	15	10	4	61	39	26	.318	.375	.412	787	113	11	10			.934	-20	*S-128	0.0
1933	Pit-N	152	573	85	180	29	**19**	9	97	64	23	.314	.388	.478	866	146	35	3			.945	-9	*S-152	3.9
1934	Pit-N★	149	558	115	186	41	11	12	94	**94**	38	.333	**.431**	.511	942	148	42	10			.952	3	*S-149	**5.3**
1935	Pit-N★	137	499	108	192	34	10	19	99	**97**	18	**.385**	**.491**	**.607**	**1098**	**187**	**67**	4			.950	-11	*S-137	**6.3**
1936	Pit-N☆	156	568	**122**	190	30	11	9	78	**118**	21	.335	**.453**	.474	927	146	44	6			.945	-11	*S-156	4.3
1937	Pit-N★	126	469	71	151	17	**17**	5	72	54	22	.322	.394	.463	857	132	22	7			.956	0	*S-108,O-12(12-0-0)	2.9
1938	Pit-N☆	148	541	88	174	35	5	7	68	104	21	.322	.433	.444	876	140	36	14			.961	18	*S-147	**6.4**
1939	Pit-N★	152	595	94	182	30	11	6	62	70	20	.306	.385	.424	808	119	18	12			.962	9	*S-152	3.7
1940	Pit-N★	156	594	**113**	178	40	**15**	7	95	88	25	.300	.393	.453	846	134	30	12			.942	8	*S-155/3-2	**4.9**
1941	Pit-N★	106	374	69	118	20	7	6	38	50	13	.316	.399	.455	854	141	21	8			.958	-12	S-97/3-3	1.6
1942	Bro-N★	128	495	82	137	18	4	2	49	51	17	.277	.348	.341	689	100	1	8			.959	-10	*3-119/S-5,2-1	-0.5
1943	Bro-N	149	610	**112**	186	39	6	5	66	60	13	.305	.370	.413	783	126	20	**20**			.965	-24	S-99,3-55	0.5
1947	*Bro-N	64	126	24	41	5	2	2	25	27	11	.325	.444	.444	889	132	7	4			1.000	1	O-22(22-0-0),3-10	0.7
1948	Bro-N	65	123	19	30	3	0	3	22	21	8	.244	.354	.341	696	86	-2	0			1.000	1	O-26(26-0-0)/3-8	-0.3
Total	14	1817	6622	1173	2103	356	128	96	926	937	276	.318	.406	.453	859	136	352	118			.951	-59	*S-1485,3-197/O-60L,2	39.7
■ FRED VAUGHN	Vaughn, Frederick Thomas "Muscles" b: 10/18/18, Coalinga, Cal. d: 3/2/64, Near Lake Wales, Fla. BR/TR, 5'10", 185 lbs. Deb: 8/20/44																							
1944	Was-A	30	109	10	28	2	1	1	21	9	24	.257	.319	.321	640	87	-2	2	2	-0	.942	-2	2-26/3-3	-0.2
1945	Was-A	80	268	28	63	7	4	1	25	23	48	.235	.298	.302	600	81	-7	0	3	-1	.946	-5	2-76/S-1	-1.0
Total	2	110	377	38	91	9	5	2	46	32	72	.241	.304	.308	612	83	-9	2	5	-1	.945	-6	2-102/3-3,S-1	-1.2
■ GREG VAUGHN	Vaughn, Gregory Lamont b: 7/3/65, Sacramento, Cal. BR/TR, 6', 193 lbs. Deb: 8/10/89 Career OF: (1167-LF 4-CF 2-RF)																							
1989	Mil-A	38	113	18	30	3	0	5	23	13	23	.265	.341	.425	766	116	2	4	1	1	.943	-3	O-24(23-0-0),D-13	-0.1
1990	Mil-A	120	382	51	84	26	2	17	61	33	91	.220	.284	.432	716	98	-3	7	4	0	.967	-1	*O-106(106-0-0)/D-8	-0.6
1991	Mil-A	145	542	81	132	24	5	27	98	62	125	.244	.322	.456	778	116	10	2	2	-0	.994	13	*O-135(134-0-1),D-10	1.8
1992	Mil-A	141	501	77	114	18	2	23	78	60	123	.228	.316	.409	725	104	2	15	15	-2	.990	3	*O-131(131-0-1)/D-7	-0.1
1993	Mil-A★	154	569	97	152	28	2	30	97	89	118	.267	.371	.482	853	129	24	10	7	-0	.986	4	O-94(94-0-0),D-58	2.1
1994	Mil-A	95	370	59	94	24	1	19	55	51	93	.254	.346	.478	824	105	2	9	5	0	.982	-0	O-81(81-1-0),D-14	-0.1
1995	Mil-A	108	392	67	88	19	1	17	59	55	89	.224	.320	.408	728	83	-10	10	4	1	.000	0	*D-104	-1.5
1996	Mil-A☆	102	375	78	105	16	0	31	95	58	99	.280	.382	.571	953	132	18	5	2	0	.980	-2	*O-100(98-3-0)/D-1	1.2
	*SD-N	43	141	20	29	3	1	10	22	24	31	.206	.329	.454	783	110	2	4	1	1	.974	3	O-39(39-0-0)	0.4
1997	SD-N	120	361	60	78	10	0	18	57	56	110	.216	.325	.393	718	94	-4	7	4	0	.994	2	O-94(94-0-0)/D-3	-0.4
1998	*SD-N★	158	573	112	156	28	4	50	119	79	121	.272	.365	.597	962	160	48	11	4	1	.993	10	*O-151(151-0-0)/D-4	5.2
1999	Cin-N	153	550	104	135	20	2	45	118	85	137	.245	.350	.535	884	116	12	15	2	3	.986	7	*O-144(144-0-0)/D-6	1.6
2000	TB-A	127	461	83	117	27	1	28	74	80	128	.254	.366	.499	865	117	12	8	1	1	.993	4	O-72(72-0-0),D-52	1.1
Total	12	1504	5330	907	1314	246	21	320	956	745	1288	.247	.342	.481	823	116	115	107	52	5	.986	41	*O-1171L,D-280	10.6
■ FARMER VAUGHN	Vaughn, Harry Francis b: 3/1/1864, Ruraldale, Ohio d: 2/21/14, Cincinnati, Ohio BR/TR, 6'3", 177 lbs. Deb: 10/7/1886 Career OF: (59-LF 14-CF 35-RF)																							
1886	Cin-a	1	3	0	0	0	0	0	0	0		.000	.250	.000	250	-19	-0	0			.917	1	/C-1	0.0
1888	Lou-a	51	189	15	37	4	2	1	21	4		.196	.216	.254	470	52	-10	4			.863	-2	O-28(22-1-5),C-25	-1.0
1889	Lou-a	90	360	39	86	11	5	3	45	7	41	.239	.253	.322	576	65	-18	13			.900	3	C-54,O-20C,1-18,/3	-1.1
1890	NY-P	44	166	27	44	7	0	1	22	10	9	.265	.307	.325	632	63	-9	6			.877	-12	C-30,O-12L/3-1,2-1	-1.6
1891	Cin-a	51	175	21	45	7	1	1	14	14	15	.257	.316	.326	642	77	-6	7			.923	7	C-44/O-6L,1-2,3P	0.3
	Mil-a	25	99	13	33	7	0	0	9	4	5	.333	.359	.404	763	98	-1	1			.924	2	C-20/1-4,O-1(1-0-0)	0.2
	Yr	76	274	34	78	14	1	1	23	18	20	.285	.331	.354	685	85	-7	8			.923	9	C-64/O-7L,1-6,3P	0.5
1892	Cin-N	91	346	45	88	10	5	2	50	16	13	.254	.295	.329	625	90	-5	10			.929	-13	C-67,1-14,O-11R,/3	-1.2
1893	Cin-N	121	483	68	135	17	12	1	108	35	17	.280	.332	.371	703	85	-12	16			**.969**	1	C-80,O-23L,1-21	-0.5
1894	Cin-N	72	284	50	88	15	5	8	64	12	11	.310	.338	.482	820	92	-6	5			.918	-1	C-43,1-27/O-8L,S-3	-0.2
1895	Cin-N	92	334	60	102	23	5	1	48	17	10	.305	.339	.413	752	90	-7	15			.934	11	C-77,1-15/3-1,2-1	0.9

YEAR	TM/L	G	AB	R	H	2B	3B	HR	RBI	BB	SO	AVG	OBP	SLG	OPS	OPS+	BR+	SB	CS	SBR	FA	FR	G/POS	TPR
1896	Cin-N	114	433	71	127	20	9	2	66	16	7	.293	.320	.395	715	82	-13	7			.984	3	1-57,C-57	-0.4
1897	Cin-N	54	199	21	58	13	5	0	30	2		.291	.299	.407	706	80	-7	2			.986	-0	1-35,C-15	-0.5
1898	Cin-N	78	275	35	84	12	4	1	46	11		.305	.339	.389	728	101	-1	4			.979	-3	1-39,C-33	0.0
1899	Cin-N	31	108	9	19	1	0	0	2	3		.176	.198	.185	383	5	-14	2			.982	3	1-21/C-7,O-1(0-0-1)	-0.9
Total	13	915	3454	474	946	147	53	21	525	151	128	.274	.307	.365	672	80	-111	92			.926	-0	C-553,1-253,O/3S2P	-6.0

■ **MO VAUGHN** Vaughn, Maurice Samuel b: 12/15/67, Norwalk, Conn. BL/TR, 6'1", 230 lbs. Deb: 6/27/91

YEAR	TM/L	G	AB	R	H	2B	3B	HR	RBI	BB	SO	AVG	OBP	SLG	OPS	OPS+	BR+	SB	CS	SBR	FA	FR	G/POS	TPR
1991	Bos-A	74	219	21	57	12	0	4	32	26	43	.260	.344	.370	714	93	-2	2	1	0	.985	-2	1-49,D-16	-0.7
1992	Bos-A	113	355	42	83	16	2	13	57	47	67	.234	.328	.400	728	97	-1	3	3	-0	.982	-2	1-85,D-20	-1.1
1993	Bos-A	152	539	86	160	34	1	29	101	79	130	.297	.395	.525	920	136	29	4	3	-0	.987	-9	*1-131,D-19	0.6
1994	Bos-A	111	394	65	122	25	1	26	82	57	112	.310	.410	.576	986	144	27	4	4	-1	.989	-5	*1-106/D-1	1.0
1995	*Bos-A★	140	550	98	165	28	3	39	**126**	68	150	.300	.391	.575	965	142	34	11	4	1	.992	-3	*1-138/D-2	1.8
1996	Bos-A★	161	635	118	207	29	1	44	143	95	154	.326	.425	.583	1007	148	49	2	0	0	.988	-10	*1-146,D-15	2.3
1997	Bos-A	141	527	91	166	24	0	35	96	86	154	.315	.422	.560	982	151	42	2	2	-0	.988	-6	*1-131/D-9	2.2
1998	*Bos-A†	154	609	107	205	31	2	40	115	61	144	.337	.404	.591	995	151	46	0	0	0	.991	-3	*1-142,D-12	2.7
1999	Ana-A	139	524	63	147	20	0	33	108	54	127	.281	.360	.508	868	119	14	0	0	0	.995	-2	1-72,D-70	0.1
2000	Ana-A	161	614	93	167	31	0	36	117	79	181	.272	.368	.498	866	116	15	2	0	0	.990	-11	*1-147,D-14	-0.9
Total	10	1346	4966	784	1479	250	10	299	977	652	1262	.298	.390	.533	923	134	252	30	17	1	.989	-51	*1-1147,D-178	8.0

■ **BOBBY VAUGHN** Vaughn, Robert b: 6/4/1885, Stamford, N.Y. d: 4/11/65, Seattle, Wash. BR/TR, 5'9", 150 lbs. Deb: 6/12/09

YEAR	TM/L	G	AB	R	H	2B	3B	HR	RBI	BB	SO	AVG	OBP	SLG	OPS	OPS+	BR+	SB	CS	SBR	FA	FR	G/POS	TPR
1909	NY-A	5	14	1	2	0	0	0	0	1		.143	.200	.143	343	8	-1	1			.882	-3	/2-4,S-1	-0.5
1915	StL-F	144	521	69	146	19	9	0	32	58	38	.280	.356	.351	707	94	-10	24			.953	-8	*2-127,S-12/3-8	-1.6
Total	2	149	535	70	148	19	9	0	32	59	38	.277	.352	.346	698	92	-11	25			.951	-11	2-131/S-13,3-8	-2.1

■ **BOBBY VEACH** Veach, Robert Hayes b: 6/29/1888, Island, Ky. d: 8/7/45, Detroit, Mich. BL/TR, 5'11", 160 lbs. Deb: 8/6/12 Career OF: (1671-LF 14-CF 65-RF)

YEAR	TM/L	G	AB	R	H	2B	3B	HR	RBI	BB	SO	AVG	OBP	SLG	OPS	OPS+	BR+	SB	CS	SBR	FA	FR	G/POS	TPR
1912	Det-A	23	79	8	27	5	1	0	15	5		.342	.388	.430	819	138	4	2			.927	2	O-22(22-0-0)	0.5
1913	Det-A	137	491	54	132	22	10	0	64	53	31	.269	.346	.354	700	107	5	22			.917	-5	*O-135(135-0-0)	-0.7
1914	Det-A	149	531	56	146	19	14	1	72	50	29	.275	.341	.369	710	110	6	20	20	-3	.965	3	*O-145(145-0-0)	0.0
1915	Det-A	152	569	81	178	**40**	10	3	**112**	68	43	.313	.390	.434	824	140	27	16	19	-3	.975	2	*O-152(152-0-0)	2.1
1916	Det-A	150	566	92	173	33	15	3	91	52	41	.306	.367	.433	800	135	23	24	15	0	.967	4	*O-150(150-0-0)	2.2
1917	Det-A	154	571	79	182	31	12	8	**103**	61	44	.319	.393	.457	850	160	40	21			.956	5	*O-154(154-0-0)	4.2
1918	Det-A	127	499	59	139	21	13	3	**78**	35	23	.279	.331	.391	722	123	11	21			.977	3	*O-127(124-1-2)/P-1	1.0
1919	Det-A	139	538	87	**191**	**45**	**17**	3	101	33	33	.355	.398	.519	916	160	40	19			.967	11	*O-138(138-0-0)	4.6
1920	Det-A	154	612	92	188	39	15	11	113	36	22	.307	.353	.474	827	121	15	11	7	-0	.967	15	*O-154(154-0-0)	2.2
1921	Det-A	150	612	110	207	43	13	16	128	48	31	.338	.387	.529	917	133	28	14	10	-0	.974	15	*O-149(149-0-0)	2.9
1922	Det-A	155	618	96	202	34	13	9	126	42	27	.327	.377	.468	845	123	20	9	1	2	.982	8	*O-154(154-0-0)	1.6
1923	Det-A	114	293	45	94	13	3	2	39	29	21	.321	.388	.406	794	111	5	10	3	1	.943	-14	O-85(46-13-26)	-1.2
1924	Bos-A	142	519	77	153	35	9	5	99	47	18	.295	.359	.426	785	102	0	5	5	-1	.956	-4	*O-130(130-0-0)	-1.4
1925	Bos-A	1	5	0	1	0	0	0	2	1	1	.200	.333	.200	533	38	-0	0	0	0	1.000	0	/O-1(1-0-0)	0.0
	NY-A	56	116	13	41	10	2	0	15	8	0	.353	.400	.474	874	123	4	1	4	-1	.957	-7	O-33(13-0-30)	-0.6
	*Was-A	18	37	4	9	3	0	0	8	3	3	.243	.300	.324	624	60	-2	0	0	0	.923	-3	O-11(4-0-7)	-0.5
	Yr	75	158	17	51	13	2	0	25	12	4	.323	.374	.430	805	106	1	1	4	-1	.952	-10	O-45(18-0-37)	-1.1
Total	14	1821	6656	953	2063	393	147	64	1166	571	367	.310	.370	.442	812	127	226	195	84		.964	36	*O-1740L/P-1	16.9

■ **PEEK-A-BOO VEACH** Veach, William Walter b: 6/15/1862, Indianapolis, Ind d: 11/12/37, Indianapolis, Ind. Deb: 8/24/1884 Career OF: (11-LF 2-CF 1-RF)

YEAR	TM/L	G	AB	R	H	2B	3B	HR	RBI	BB	SO	AVG	OBP	SLG	OPS	OPS+	BR+	SB	CS	SBR	FA	FR	G/POS	TPR
1884	KC-U	27	82	9	11	1	0	1		9		.134	.220	.183	403	27	-9				.833	-1	O-14L,P-12/2-1,1-1	-0.6
1887	Lou-a	1	4	0	1	0	0	0	0	1		.250	.250	.000	250	-26	-0	0			.750	-0	/P-1	0.0
1890	Cle-N	64	238	24	56	10	5	0	32	33	28	.235	.336	.319	655	93	-1	9			.971	6	1-64	-0.1
	Pit-N	8	30	6	9	1	1	2	5	8	3	.300	.447	.600	1047	231	6	0			.968	0	/1-8	0.4
	Yr	72	268	30	65	11	6	2	37	41	31	.243	.349	.351	700	107	4	9			.971	7	1-72	0.3
Total	3	100	354	39	77	12	6	3	37	51	31	.218	.319	.309	628	89	-6	9			.971	6	/1-73,O-14L,P-13,2	-0.3

■ **COOT VEAL** Veal, Orville Inman b: 7/9/32, Sandersville, Ga. BR/TR, 6'1", 165 lbs. Deb: 7/30/58

YEAR	TM/L	G	AB	R	H	2B	3B	HR	RBI	BB	SO	AVG	OBP	SLG	OPS	OPS+	BR+	SB	CS	SBR	FA	FR	G/POS	TPR
1958	Det-A	58	207	29	53	10	2	0	16	14	21	.256	.306	.324	630	69	-9	1	1	-0	.981	-8	S-58	-1.3
1959	Det-A	77	89	12	18	1	0	1	15	8	7	.202	.276	.247	523	42	-7	0	0	0	.962	10	S-72	0.5
1960	Det-A	27	64	8	19	5	1	0	8	11	7	.297	.400	.406	806	115	2	0	0	0	.988	-2	S-22/3-3,2-1	0.1
1961	Was-A	69	218	21	44	10	0	0	8	19	29	.202	.275	.248	523	41	-18	1	8	-3	.974	0	S-63	-1.5
1962	Pit-N	1	1	0	0	0	0	0	0	0	1	.000	.000	.000	0	-99	-0	0	0	0	.000	0	H	0.0
1963	Det-A	15	32	5	7	0	0	0	4	4	4	.219	.306	.219	524	48	-2	0	0	0	.980	4	S-12	0.2
Total	6	247	611	75	141	26	3	1	51	56	69	.231	.301	.288	589	59	-34	2	9	-3	.976	4	S-227/3-3,2-1	-2.0

■ **JESUS VEGA** Vega, Jesus Anthony (Morales) b: 10/14/55, Bayamon, P.R. BR/TR, 6'1", 176 lbs. Deb: 9/5/79

YEAR	TM/L	G	AB	R	H	2B	3B	HR	RBI	BB	SO	AVG	OBP	SLG	OPS	OPS+	BR+	SB	CS	SBR	FA	FR	G/POS	TPR
1979	Min-A	4	7	0	0	0	0	0	0	0	2	.000	.000	.000	0	-96	-2	0	0	0	.000	0	/D-3	-0.2
1980	Min-A	12	30	3	5	0	0	0	4	3	7	.167	.242	.167	409	13	-3	1	0	0	1.000	0	/1-2,D-9	-0.3
1982	Min-A	71	199	23	53	6	0	5	29	8	19	.266	.295	.372	667	80	-6	6	1	1	.974	-1	D-39,1-18/O-1(1-0-0)	-0.8
Total	3	87	236	26	58	6	0	5	33	11	28	.246	.279	.335	614	65	-11	7	1	1	.975	-1	/D-51,1-20,O-1(1-0-0)	-1.3

■ **JORGE VELANDIA** Velandia, Jorge Luis (Macias) b: 1/12/75, Caracas, Venez. BR/TR, 5'9", 160 lbs. Deb: 6/20/97

YEAR	TM/L	G	AB	R	H	2B	3B	HR	RBI	BB	SO	AVG	OBP	SLG	OPS	OPS+	BR+	SB	CS	SBR	FA	FR	G/POS	TPR
1997	SD-N	14	29	0	3	2	0	0	0	1	7	.103	.133	.172	306	-22	-5	0	0	0	.941	2	/S-6,2-5,3-3	-0.3
1998	Oak-A	8	4	0	1	0	0	0	0	0	1	.250	.250	.250	500	31	-0	0	0	0	.909	3	/S-7,2-1	0.3
1999	Oak-A	63	48	4	9	1	0	0	2	2	13	.188	.235	.208	444	15	-6	2	0	0	.989	23	2-52/S-8,3-2,D-1	1.6
2000	Oak-A	18	24	1	3	1	0	0	2	0	6	.125	.160	.167	327	-17	-4	0	0	0	1.000	4	2-14/S-4	0.0
	NY-N	15	7	1	0	0	0	0	0	2	2	.000	.222	.000	222	-39	-2	0	0	0	1.000	-0	/2-7,S-7,3-3	-0.1
Total	4	118	112	6	16	4	0	0	4	5	29	.143	.193	.179	372	-4	-18	2	0	0	.987	32	/2-79,S-32,3-8,D-1	1.5

■ **RANDY VELARDE** Velarde, Randy Lee b: 11/24/62, Midland, Tex. BR/TR, 6', 190 lbs. Deb: 8/20/87 Career OF: (95-LF 4-CF 9-RF)

YEAR	TM/L	G	AB	R	H	2B	3B	HR	RBI	BB	SO	AVG	OBP	SLG	OPS	OPS+	BR+	SB	CS	SBR	FA	FR	G/POS	TPR
1987	NY-A	8	22	1	4	0	0	0	1	0	6	.182	.182	.182	364	-3	-3	0	0	0	.933	0	/S-8	-0.2
1988	NY-A	48	115	18	20	6	0	5	12	8	24	.174	.240	.357	597	65	-6	1	1	-0	.967	8	2-24,S-14,3-11	0.4
1989	NY-A	33	100	12	34	4	2	2	11	7	14	.340	.389	.480	869	145	6	0	3	-1	.954	2	3-27/S-9	0.7
1990	NY-A	95	229	21	48	6	2	5	19	20	53	.210	.276	.319	595	66	-11	0	3	-1	.945	9	3-74,S-15/O-5L,2D	-0.2
1991	NY-A	80	184	19	45	11	1	1	15	18	43	.245	.322	.332	653	81	-4	3	1	0	.935	7	3-50,S-31/O-2(2-0-0)	0.4
1992	NY-A	121	412	57	112	24	1	7	46	38	78	.272	.336	.386	722	103	1	7	2	1	.974	-8	S-75,3-26,O-23L,/2	0.0
1993	NY-A	85	226	28	68	13	2	7	24	18	39	.301	.363	.469	832	126	8	2	2	-0	.932	-1	O-50L,S-26,3-16,/D	0.7
1994	NY-A	77	280	47	78	16	1	9	34	22	61	.279	.340	.439	779	103	1	4	2	0	.944	1	S-49,3-27/O-7L,2-5	0.6
1995	*NY-A	111	367	60	102	19	1	7	46	55	64	.278	.378	.392	770	102	3	5	1	1	.976	-15	2-62,S-28,O-20L,3	-0.6
1996	Cal-A	136	530	82	151	27	3	14	54	70	118	.285	.374	.426	800	101	3	7	7	-1	.982	-26	*2-114,3-28/S-7	-1.7
1997	Ana-A	1	0	0	0	0	0	0	0	0	0	—	—	—	—	—	0	0	0	0	.000	0	/R	0.0
1998	Ana-A	51	188	29	49	13	1	4	26	34	42	.261	.377	.404	781	103	2	7	2	1	.982	-8	2-51	-0.2
1999	Ana-A	95	376	57	115	15	4	9	48	43	56	.306	.383	.439	822	110	7	13	4	1	.986	1	2-95	1.3
	Oak-A	61	255	48	85	10	3	7	28	27	42	.333	.401	.478	880	129	12	11	4	1	.977	-4	2-61	1.1
	Yr	156	631	105	200	25	7	16	76	70	98	.317	.390	.455	845	117	18	24	8	2	.983	-3	*2-156	2.4
2000	*Oak-A	122	485	82	135	23	0	12	41	54	95	.278	.354	.400	754	93	-4	9	3	1	.982	13	*2-122	1.4
Total	14	1124	3769	561	1046	187	21	89	405	414	735	.278	.355	.409	764	101	13	69	35	3	.980	-20	2-540,3-278,SO/D	3.7

■ **GUILLERMO VELASQUEZ** Velasquez, Guillermo (Burgara) b: 4/23/68, Mexicali, Mexico BL/TR, 6'3", 220 lbs. Deb: 9/14/92

YEAR	TM/L	G	AB	R	H	2B	3B	HR	RBI	BB	SO	AVG	OBP	SLG	OPS	OPS+	BR+	SB	CS	SBR	FA	FR	G/POS	TPR
1992	SD-N	15	23	1	7	0	0	1	5	1	7	.304	.333	.435	768	114	0	0	0	0	.933	-1	/1-3,O-2(2-0-0)	-0.1
1993	SD-N	79	143	7	30	2	0	3	20	13	35	.210	.276	.287	562	50	-10	0	0	0	.984	-1	1-38/O-6(4-0-2)	-1.4
Total	2	94	166	8	37	2	0	4	25	14	42	.223	.283	.307	591	58	-10	0	0	0	.981	-2	/1-41,O-8(6-0-2)	-1.5

■ **FREDDIE VELAZQUEZ** Velazquez, Federico Antonio (Velasquez) b: 12/6/37, Santo Domingo, D.R. BR/TR, 6'1", 185 lbs. Deb: 4/20/69

YEAR	TM/L	G	AB	R	H	2B	3B	HR	RBI	BB	SO	AVG	OBP	SLG	OPS	OPS+	BR+	SB	CS	SBR	FA	FR	G/POS	TPR
1969	Sea-A	6	16	1	2	2	0	0	2	1	3	.125	.176	.250	426	18	-2	0	0	0	1.000	-1	/C-5	-0.2

YEAR	TM/L	G	AB	R	H	2B	3B	HR	RBI	BB	SO	AVG	OBP	SLG	OPS	OPS+	BR+	SB	CS	SBR	FA	FR	G/POS	TPR
1973	Atl-N	15	23	2	8	1	0	0	3	1	3	.348	.375	.391	766	105	0	0	0	0	.975	2	C-11	0.2
Total	2	21	39	3	10	3	0	0	5	2	6	.256	.293	.333	626	71	-2	0	0	0	.985	1	/C-16	0.0
■ OTTO VELEZ	Velez, Otoniel (Franceschi) b: 11/29/50, Ponce, P.R. BR/TR, 6', 195 lbs. Deb: 9/4/73 Career OF: (88-LF 0-CF 197-RF)																							
1973	NY-A	23	77	9	15	4	0	2	7	15	24	.195	.326	.325	651	87	-1	0	1	-0	.959	1	O-23(0-0-23)	-0.2
1974	NY-A	27	67	9	14	1	1	2	10	15	24	.209	.354	.343	697	103	1	0	0	0	.986	-4	1-21/O-3(0-0-3),3-2	-0.5
1975	NY-A	6	8	0	2	0	0	0	1	2	0	.250	.400	.250	650	89	0	0	0	0	1.000	-0	/1-1,D-1	0.0
1976	*NY-A	49	94	11	25	6	0	2	10	23	26	.266	.410	.394	804	137	6	0	0	0	.979	-3	O-24R/1-8,3-1,D-5	0.2
1977	Tor-A	120	360	50	92	19	3	16	62	65	87	.256	.371	.458	829	123	13	4	2	0	.973	0	O-79(0-0-79),D-28	0.8
1978	Tor-A	91	248	29	66	14	2	9	38	45	41	.266	.383	.448	831	130	11	1	3	-1	.982	7	O-74(39-0-39)/1-1,D-9	1.4
1979	Tor-A	99	274	45	79	21	0	15	48	46	45	.288	.396	.529	925	145	18	0	1	-0	.971	-5	O-73(43-0-34)/1-6,D-9	0.9
1980	Tor-A	104	357	54	96	12	3	20	62	54	86	.269	.368	.487	855	126	13	0	0	0	.975	0	D-97/1-3	1.0
1981	Tor-A	80	240	32	51	9	2	11	28	55	60	.213	.366	.404	770	114	6	0	3	-1	1.000	-0	D-74/1-1	0.3
1982	Tor-A	28	52	4	10	1	0	1	5	13	15	.192	.354	.269	623	68	-2	1	0	0	.000	0	D-24	-0.2
1983	Cle-A	10	25	1	2	0	0	0	1	3	6	.080	.179	.080	259	-25	-4	0	0	0	.000	0	/D-8	-0.5
Total	11	637	1802	244	452	87	11	78	272	336	414	.251	.372	.441	813	122	61	6	10	-2	.973	-4	O-276R,D-255/1-41,3	3.2
■ PAT VELTMAN	Veltman, Arthur Patrick b: 3/24/06, Mobile, Ala. d: 10/1/80, San Antonio, Tex. BR/TR, 6', 175 lbs. Deb: 4/17/26																							
1926	Chi-A	5	4	1	1	0	0	0	0	1	1	.250	.400	.250	650	75	-0	0	0	0	1.000	0	/S-1	0.0
1928	NY-N	1	3	1	1	0	1	0	0	1	0	.333	.500	1.000	1500	282	1	0			1.000	-0	/O-1(0-1-0)	0.1
1929	NY-N	2	1	1	0	0	0	0	0	2	0	.000	.667	.000	667	81	0	0			1.000	-0	/C-1	0.0
1931	Bos-N	1	1	0	0	0	0	0	0	0	0	.000	.000	.000	0	-99	-0	0			.000	0	H	0.0
1932	NY-N	2	1	0	0	0	0	0	0	0	1	.000	.000	.000	0	-99	-0	0			.000	0	H	0.0
1934	Pit-N	12	28	1	3	0	0	0	2	0	1	.107	.107	.107	214	-41	-6	0			1.000	-2	C-11	-0.7
Total	6	23	38	4	5	0	1	0	2	4	3	.132	.214	.184	398	7	-5	0	0		1.000	-2	/C-12,O-1(0-1-0),S-1	-0.6
■ MAX VENABLE	Venable, William McKinley b: 6/6/57, Phoenix, Ariz. BL/TR, 5'10", 185 lbs. Deb: 4/8/79 Career OF: (247-LF 141-CF 113-RF)																							
1979	SF-N	55	85	12	14	1	1	0	3	10	18	.165	.260	.200	460	29	-8	3	3	-0	.914	-5	O-25(6-2-21)	-1.5
1980	SF-N	64	138	13	37	5	0	0	10	15	22	.268	.340	.304	644	83	-3	8	2	1	1.000	-5	O-40(16-14-11)	-0.9
1981	SF-N	18	32	2	6	0	2	0	1	4	3	.188	.278	.313	590	68	-1	3	1	0	1.000	0	/O-5(0-2-3)	-0.1
1982	SF-N	71	125	17	28	2	1	1	7	7	16	.224	.265	.280	545	53	-8	9	3	1	.986	-4	O-53(33-12-8)	-1.3
1983	SF-N	94	228	28	50	7	4	6	27	22	34	.219	.296	.364	660	85	-5	15	2	3	.993	3	O-66(32-25-14)	-0.2
1984	Mon-N	38	71	7	17	2	0	2	7	3	7	.239	.280	.352	632	80	-2	1	0	0	1.000	-4	O-27(23-3-3)	-0.7
1985	Cin-N	77	135	21	39	12	3	0	10	6	17	.289	.319	.422	741	101	-0	11	3	1	1.000	-1	O-39(31-7-3)	-0.1
1986	Cin-N	108	147	17	31	7	1	2	15	17	24	.211	.293	.313	606	64	-7	7	2	1	.969	-10	O-57(49-8-3)	-1.9
1987	Cin-N	7	7	2	1	0	0	0	2	0	0	.143	.143	.143	286	-23	-1	0	0	0	1.000	-1	/O-4(0-4-0)	-0.2
1989	Cal-A	20	53	7	19	4	0	0	4	1	16	.358	.370	.434	804	128	2	0	0	0	1.000	-3	O-13(4-4-7)	-0.1
1990	Cal-A	93	189	26	49	9	3	4	21	24	31	.259	.343	.402	745	110	3	5	1	1	.975	-12	O-77(40-33-10)/D-1	-1.0
1991	Cal-A	82	187	24	46	8	2	3	21	11	30	.246	.295	.358	653	80	-5	2	1	0	.967	-11	O-65(13-27-30)/D-3	-1.7
Total	12	727	1397	176	337	57	17	18	128	120	218	.241	.304	.345	649	81	-37	64	18	8	.982	-54	O-471L/D-4	-9.7
■ ROBIN VENTURA	Ventura, Robin Mark b: 7/14/67, Santa Maria, Cal. BL/TR, 6'1", 198 lbs. Deb: 9/12/89																							
1989	Chi-A	16	45	5	8	3	0	0	7	8	6	.178	.315	.244	559	61	-2	0	0	0	.962	2	3-16	0.0
1990	Chi-A	150	493	48	123	17	1	5	54	55	53	.249	.326	.318	645	83	-10	1	4	-1	.939	-0	*3-147/1-1	-1.2
1991	Chi-A	157	606	92	172	25	1	23	100	80	67	.284	.371	.442	813	127	24	2	4	-1	.959	1	*3-151,1-31	2.3
1992	Chi-A★	157	592	85	167	38	1	16	93	93	71	.282	.380	.431	810	128	25	2	4	-1	.957	24	*3-157/1-2	**4.8**
1993	*Chi-A	157	554	85	145	27	1	22	94	105	82	.262	.382	.433	815	121	20	1	6	-2	.965	-5	*3-155/1-4	1.4
1994	Chi-A	109	401	57	113	15	1	18	78	61	69	.282	.379	.459	838	117	11	3	1	0	.935	-4	*3-108/1-3,S-1	0.8
1995	Chi-A	135	492	79	145	22	0	26	93	75	98	.295	.389	.498	887	135	27	4	3	-0	.948	-3	*3-121,1-18/D-1	2.1
1996	Chi-A	158	586	96	168	31	2	34	105	78	81	.287	.372	.520	893	129	25	1	3	-1	.974	-0	*3-150,1-14	2.2
1997	Chi-A	54	183	27	48	10	1	6	26	34	21	.262	.378	.426	804	114	5	0	0	0	.956	1	3-54	0.6
1998	Chi-A	161	590	84	155	31	4	21	91	79	111	.263	.351	.436	786	106	6	1	1	-0	.966	19	*3-161	2.4
1999	*NY-N	161	588	88	177	38	0	32	120	74	109	.301	.382	.529	911	131	28	1	1	-0	**.980**	20	*3-160/1-1	4.5
2000	*NY-N	141	469	61	109	23	1	24	84	75	91	.232	.341	.439	780	99	-1	3	5	-1	.954	11	*3-137/1-1	0.9
Total	12	1556	5599	807	1530	280	13	227	945	817	859	.273	.368	.450	817	118	156	19	32	-7	.959	64	*3-1517/1-75,D-1,S	20.8
■ VINCE VENTURA	Ventura, Vincent b: 4/18/17, New York, N.Y. BR/TR, 6'1.5", 190 lbs. Deb: 5/8/45																							
1945	Was-A	18	58	4	12	0	0	0	2	4	4	.207	.258	.207	465	39	-5	0	0	0	.886	-1	O-15(15-0-0)	-0.7
■ QUILVIO VERAS	Veras, Quilvio Alberto (Perez) b: 4/3/71, Santo Domingo, D.R. BB/TR, 5'9", 170 lbs. Deb: 4/25/95																							
1995	Fla-N	124	440	86	115	20	7	5	32	80	68	.261	.386	.373	758	101	4	**56**	21	5	.986	7	*2-122/O-2(0-1-1)	2.1
1996	Fla-N	73	253	40	64	8	1	4	14	51	42	.253	.382	.340	722	96	1	8	8	-1	.986	6	2-67	0.9
1997	SD-N	145	539	74	143	23	1	3	45	72	84	.265	.359	.328	688	88	-7	33	12	3	.984	-6	*2-142	-0.2
1998	*SD-N	138	517	79	138	24	2	6	45	84	78	.267	.376	.356	732	102	5	24	9	2	.987	13	*2-131	2.6
1999	SD-N	132	475	95	133	25	2	6	41	65	88	.280	.369	.379	748	97	-0	30	17	1	.981	8	*2-118	1.3
2000	Atl-N	84	298	56	92	15	0	5	37	51	50	.309	.418	.409	827	112	8	25	12	1	.984	-8	2-82	0.5
Total	6	696	2522	430	685	115	13	29	214	403	410	.272	.379	.362	741	99	11	176	79	11	.984	21	2-662/O-2(0-1-1)	7.2
■ WILTON VERAS	Veras, Wilton Andres b: 1/19/78, Monte Cristi, D.R. BR/TR, 6'2", 186 lbs. Deb: 7/1/99																							
1999	Bos-A	36	118	14	34	5	1	2	13	5	14	.288	.328	.398	726	82	-3	0	2	-1	.929	1	3-35	-0.2
2000	Bos-A	49	164	21	40	7	1	0	14	7	20	.244	.283	.299	582	46	-13	0	0	0	.907	3	3-49	-0.9
Total	2	85	282	35	74	12	2	2	27	12	34	.262	.302	.340	642	61	-17	0	2	-1	.916	4	/3-84	-1.1
■ EMIL VERBAN	Verban, Emil Matthew "Dutch" or "Antelope" b: 8/27/15, Lincoln, Ill. d: 6/8/89, Quincy, Ill. BR/TR, 5'11", 165 lbs. Deb: 4/18/44 Career OF: (0-LF 1-CF 0-RF)																							
1944	*StL-N	146	498	51	128	14	2	0	43	19	14	.257	.287	.293	580	62	-25	0			.968	-6	*2-146	-2.4
1945	StL-N†	155	597	59	166	22	8	0	72	19	15	.278	.304	.342	645	77	-19	4			**.978**	-19	*2-155	-3.0
1946	StL-N	1	1	0	0	0	0	0	0	0	0	.000	.000	.000	0	-96	-0	0			.000	0	H	0.0
	Phi-N★	138	473	44	130	17	5	0	34	21	18	.275	.306	.332	638	83	-12	5			.963	-3	*2-138	-0.8
	Yr	139	474	44	130	17	5	0	34	21	18	.274	.305	.331	636	83	-12	5			.963	-3	*2-138	-0.8
1947	Phi-N★	155	540	50	154	14	8	0	42	23	8	.285	.316	.341	656	77	-18	5			.982	17	*2-155	0.7
1948	Phi-N	55	169	14	39	5	1	0	11	11	5	.231	.282	.272	554	51	-11	0			.975	-4	2-54	-1.3
	Chi-N	56	248	37	73	15	1	1	16	4	7	.294	.308	.375	683	88	-5	4			.964	6	2-56	0.4
	Yr	111	417	51	112	20	2	1	27	15	12	.269	.297	.333	631	72	-17	4			.969	2	*2-110	-0.9
1949	Chi-N	98	343	38	99	11	1	0	22	8	2	.289	.309	.327	635	72	-14	3			.965	3	2-88	-0.6
1950	Chi-N	45	37	7	4	1	0	0	1	3	5	.108	.175	.135	310	-17	-6	0			.966	6	/2-8,S-3,3-1,O-1C	-0.1
	Bos-N	4	5	1	0	0	0	0	0	0	0	.000	.000	.000	0	-99	-1	0			.833	1	/2-2	0.0
	Yr	49	42	8	4	1	0	0	1	3	5	.095	.156	.119	275	-27	-8	0			.927	7	2-10/S-3,3-1,O-1C	-0.1
Total	7	853	2911	301	793	99	26	1	241	108	74	.272	.301	.325	626	73	-113	21			.971	1	2-802/S-3,O-1C,3-1	-7.1
■ GENE VERBLE	Verble, Gene Kermit "Satchel" b: 6/29/28, Concord, N.C. BR/TR, 5'10", 163 lbs. Deb: 4/17/51																							
1951	Was-A	68	177	16	36	3	2	0	15	18	10	.203	.277	.243	520	42	-14	1	1	-0	.978	-2	S-28,2-19/3-1	-1.3
1953	Was-A	13	21	4	4	0	0	0	2	2	1	.190	.261	.190	451	24	-2	0	0	0	1.000	2	/S-8	0.0
Total	2	81	198	20	40	3	2	0	17	20	11	.202	.275	.237	513	40	-16	1	1	-0	.981	1	/S-36,2-19,3-1	-1.3
■ FRANK VERDI	Verdi, Frank Michael b: 6/2/26, Brooklyn, N.Y. BR/TR, 5'10.5", 170 lbs. Deb: 5/10/53																							
1953	NY-A	1	0	0	0	0	0	0	0	0	0	—	—	—	—	—	0	0	0	0	.000	0	/S-1	0.0
■ JOHNNY VERGEZ	Vergez, John Louis b: 7/9/06, Oakland, Cal. d: 7/15/91, Davis, Cal. BR/TR, 5'8", 165 lbs. Deb: 4/14/31																							
1931	NY-N	152	565	67	157	24	2	13	81	29	65	.278	.320	.396	716	94	-6	11			.932	-3	*3-152	-0.4
1932	NY-N	118	376	42	98	21	3	6	43	25	36	.261	.310	.380	690	86	-8	1			.935	5	*3-111/S-1	0.1
1933	NY-N	123	458	57	124	21	6	16	72	39	66	.271	.332	.448	780	123	13	1			.928	-14	*3-123	0.4
1934	NY-N	108	320	31	64	18	1	7	27	28	55	.200	.269	.328	597	60	-19	1			.943	10	*3-104	-0.5

YEAR	TM/L	G	AB	R	H	2B	3B	HR	RBI	BB	SO	AVG	OBP	SLG	OPS	OPS+	BR+	SB	CS	SBR	FA	FR	G/POS	TPR
1935	Phi-N	148	546	56	136	27	4	9	63	46	67	.249	.312	.363	675	73	-20	8			**.953**	-7	*3-148/S-2	-2.1
1936	Phi-N	15	40	4	11	2	0	1	5	3	11	.275	.326	.400	726	86	-1	0			.964	0	3-12	0.0
	StL-N	8	18	1	3	1	0	0	1	1	3	.167	.211	.222	433	17	-2	0			.929	0	/3-8	-0.2
	Yr	23	58	5	14	3	0	1	6	4	14	.241	.290	.345	635	66	-3	0			.952	0	3-20	-0.2
Total	6	672	2323	258	593	114	16	52	292	171	303	.255	.311	.385	696	87	-43	22			.939	-8	3-658/S-3	-2.7

■ MICKEY VERNON Vernon, James Barton b: 4/22/18, Marcus Hook, Pa. BL/TL, 6'2", 180 lbs. Deb: 7/8/39 MC

YEAR	TM/L	G	AB	R	H	2B	3B	HR	RBI	BB	SO	AVG	OBP	SLG	OPS	OPS+	BR+	SB	CS	SBR	FA	FR	G/POS	TPR
1939	Was-A	76	276	23	71	15	4	1	30	24	28	.257	.317	.351	668	76	-10	1	1	-0	.985	-3	1-75	-1.9
1940	Was-A	5	19	0	3	0	0	0	0	0	3	.158	.158	.158	316	-19	-3	0	0	0	1.000	-0	/1-4	-0.4
1941	Was-A	138	531	73	159	27	11	9	93	43	51	.299	.352	.443	794	114	9	9	3	1	.992	-6	*1-132	-0.9
1942	Was-A	151	621	76	168	34	6	9	86	59	63	.271	.337	.388	725	104	3	25	6	3	.982	-8	*1-151	-1.6
1943	Was-A	145	553	89	148	29	8	7	70	67	55	.268	.357	.387	744	122	16	24	8	2	.990	-11	*1-143	0.0
1946	Was-A★	148	587	88	207	**51**	8	8	85	49	64	**.353**	.403	.508	910	163	47	14	10	-0	.990	-1	*1-147	4.2
1947	Was-A	154	600	77	159	29	12	7	85	49	42	.265	.320	.388	709	99	-3	12	12	-2	.987	-4	*1-154	-1.4
1948	Was-A★	150	558	78	135	27	7	3	48	54	43	.242	.310	.332	641	73	-23	15	11	-1	.989	5	*1-150	-2.3
1949	Cle-A	153	584	72	170	27	4	18	83	58	51	.291	.357	.443	801	113	9	9	7	-0	.991	19	*1-153	2.1
1950	Cle-A	28	90	8	17	0	0	0	10	12	10	.189	.284	.189	473	24	-10	2	0	0	.996	1	1-25	-0.9
	Was-A	90	327	47	100	17	3	9	65	50	29	.306	.404	.459	863	127	14	6	1	1	.990	1	1-85	1.3
	Yr	118	417	55	117	17	3	9	75	62	39	.281	.379	.400	779	104	4	8	1	1	**.991**	3	*1-110	0.4
1951	Was-A	141	546	69	160	30	7	9	87	53	45	.293	.358	.423	781	112	9	7	6	-1	**.994**	-4	*1-137	0.0
1952	Was-A	154	569	71	143	33	9	10	80	89	66	.251	.353	.394	746	111	9	7	7	-1	**.993**	1	*1-153	0.4
1953	Was-A★	152	608	101	205	**43**	11	15	115	63	57	**.337**	.403	.518	921	151	43	4	6	-1	.992	-3	*1-152	2.9
1954	Was-A★	151	597	90	173	**33**	14	20	97	61	61	.290	.360	.492	853	140	30	1	4	-1	**.992**	-9	*1-148	1.1
1955	Was-A★	150	538	74	162	23	8	14	85	74	50	.301	.389	.452	840	133	25	0	4	-1	.994	-8	*1-144	0.7
1956	Bos-A★	119	403	67	125	28	4	15	84	57	40	.310	.405	.511	916	125	15	1	0	0	.989	-3	*1-108	0.6
1957	Bos-A	102	270	36	65	18	1	7	38	41	35	.241	.351	.393	744	97	-0	0	0	0	.992	4	1-70	0.0
1958	Cle-A★	119	355	49	104	22	3	8	55	44	56	.293	.374	.439	814	126	13	0	4	-1	.987	-2	1-96	0.5
1959	Mil-N	74	91	8	20	4	0	3	14	7	20	.220	.283	.363	645	77	-3	0	0	0	.983	1	1-10/O-4(2-0-2)	-0.3
1960	Pit-N	9	8	0	1	0	0	0	1	1	0	.125	.222	.125	347	-2	-1	0	0	0	.000	0	H	-0.1
Total	20	2409	8731	1196	2495	490	120	172	1311	955	869	.286	.359	.428	788	116	189	137	90	-1	.990	-32	*1-2237/O-4(2-0-2)	4.0

■ ZOILO VERSALLES Versalles, Zoilo Casanova (Rodriguez) "Zorro"
b: 12/18/39, Veldado, Cuba d: 6/9/95, Bloomington, Minn. BR/TR, 5'10", 150 lbs. Deb: 8/1/59

YEAR	TM/L	G	AB	R	H	2B	3B	HR	RBI	BB	SO	AVG	OBP	SLG	OPS	OPS+	BR+	SB	CS	SBR	FA	FR	G/POS	TPR
1959	Was-A	29	59	4	9	0	0	1	1	4	15	.153	.219	.203	422	17	-7	1	0	0	.943	3	S-29	-0.2
1960	Was-A	15	45	2	6	2	2	0	4	2	5	.133	.170	.267	437	16	-5	0	0	0	.935	-1	S-15	-0.5
1961	Min-A	129	510	65	143	25	5	7	53	25	61	.280	.315	.390	705	83	-13	16	9	0	.952	-2	*S-129	-0.3
1962	Min-A	160	568	69	137	18	3	17	67	37	71	.241	.290	.373	663	74	-21	5	5	-1	.970	32	*S-160	2.3
1963	Min-A★	159	621	74	162	31	**13**	10	54	33	66	.261	.303	.401	704	94	-6	7	4	0	.961	-2	*S-159	0.6
1964	Min-A	160	659	94	171	33	**10**	20	64	42	88	.259	.312	.431	743	103	2	14	4	2	.957	-17	*S-160	0.0
1965	*Min-A★	160	666	**126**	182	**45**	**12**	19	77	41	122	.273	.322	.462	785	115	11	27	5	4	.950	2	*S-160	3.3
1966	Min-A	137	543	73	135	20	6	7	36	40	85	.249	.308	.346	655	82	-12	10	12	-2	.942	-17	*S-135	-2.0
1967	Min-A	160	581	63	116	16	7	6	50	33	113	.200	.250	.282	532	53	-34	5	3	0	.958	2	*S-159	-2.0
1968	LA-N	122	403	29	79	16	3	2	24	26	84	.196	.245	.266	510	57	-22	6	4	-0	.954	8	*S-119	-0.4
1969	Cle-A	72	217	21	49	11	1	1	13	21	47	.226	.300	.300	600	66	-10	3	1	0	.975	-11	2-46,3-30/S-3	-1.9
	Was-A	31	75	9	20	2	1	0	6	3	13	.267	.304	.320	624	79	-2	1	0	0	.935	-1	S-13/2-6,3-5	-0.2
	Yr	103	292	30	69	13	2	1	19	24	60	.236	.301	.305	606	69	-12	4	1	1	.978	-12	2-52,3-35,S-16	-2.1
1971	Atl-N	66	194	21	37	11	0	5	22	11	40	.191	.234	.325	559	53	-12	2	1	0	.902	-14	3-30,S-24/2-1	-2.6
Total	12	1400	5141	650	1246	230	63	95	471	318	810	.242	.292	.367	659	82	-131	97	48	5	.956	-20	*S-1265/3-65,2-53	-3.9

■ TOM VERYZER Veryzer, Thomas Martin b: 2/11/53, Port Jefferson, N.Y BR/TR, 6'1", 185 lbs. Deb: 8/14/73

YEAR	TM/L	G	AB	R	H	2B	3B	HR	RBI	BB	SO	AVG	OBP	SLG	OPS	OPS+	BR+	SB	CS	SBR	FA	FR	G/POS	TPR
1973	Det-A	18	20	1	6	0	1	0	2	2	4	.300	.364	.400	764	108	0	0	0	0	.857	-5	S-18	-0.4
1974	Det-A	22	55	4	13	2	0	2	9	5	8	.236	.300	.382	682	92	-1	1	0	0	.927	-10	S-20	-0.9
1975	Det-A	128	404	37	102	13	1	5	48	23	76	.252	.301	.327	628	74	-14	2	6	-2	.960	-4	*S-128	-0.4
1976	Det-A	97	354	31	83	8	2	1	25	21	44	.234	.289	.277	566	64	-16	1	4	-1	.966	-1	S-97	-0.7
1977	Det-A	125	350	31	69	12	1	2	28	16	44	.197	.232	.254	487	31	-33	0	1	-0	.969	10	*S-124	-1.1
1978	Cle-A	130	421	48	114	18	4	1	32	13	36	.271	.301	.340	640	81	-11	1	2	-0	.963	-4	*S-129	-0.3
1979	Cle-A	149	449	41	99	9	3	0	34	34	54	.220	.281	.254	535	45	-34	2	5	-1	.974	4	*S-148	-1.6
1980	Cle-A	109	358	28	97	12	0	2	28	10	25	.271	.306	.321	627	72	-14	0	5	-2	.971	-1	*S-108	-0.5
1981	Cle-A	75	221	13	54	4	0	0	14	10	10	.244	.280	.262	543	58	-12	1	0	0	.970	-7	S-75	-1.1
1982	NY-N	40	54	6	18	2	0	0	4	3	4	.333	.368	.370	739	108	1	1	0	0	.962	-1	2-26,S-16	0.1
1983	Chi-N	59	88	5	18	3	0	1	3	3	13	.205	.231	.273	503	37	-7	0	0	0	.978	7	S-28,3-17	0.1
1984	*Chi-N	44	74	5	14	1	0	0	4	3	11	.189	.259	.203	462	29	-7	0	0	0	.966	-2	S-36/3-5,2-4	-0.7
Total	12	996	2848	250	687	84	12	14	231	143	329	.241	.285	.294	579	61	-148	9	23	-6	.966	-14	S-927/2-30,3-22	-7.5

■ ERNIE VICK Vick, Henry Arthur b: 7/2/1900, Toledo, Ohio d: 7/16/80, Ann Arbor, Mich. BR/TR, 5'9.5", 185 lbs. Deb: 6/29/22

YEAR	TM/L	G	AB	R	H	2B	3B	HR	RBI	BB	SO	AVG	OBP	SLG	OPS	OPS+	BR+	SB	CS	SBR	FA	FR	G/POS	TPR
1922	StL-N	3	6	1	2	2	0	0	0	0	0	.333	.333	.667	1000	159	0	0	0	0	.875	-0	/C-3	0.0
1924	StL-N	16	23	2	8	1	0	0	0	3	3	.348	.423	.391	814	122	1	0	0	0	.974	3	C-16	0.4
1925	StL-N	14	32	3	6	2	1	0	3	3	1	.188	.257	.313	570	44	-3	0	0	0	.929	0	/C-9	-0.2
1926	StL-N	24	51	6	10	2	0	0	4	3	4	.196	.241	.235	476	27	-5	0			.944	-1	C-23	-0.5
Total	4	57	112	12	26	7	1	0	7	9	8	.232	.289	.313	602	58	-7	0	0		.944	2	/C-51	-0.3

■ SAMMY VICK Vick, Samuel Bruce b: 4/12/1895, Batesville, Miss. d: 8/17/86, Memphis, Tenn. BR/TR, 5'10.5", 163 lbs. Deb: 9/20/17

YEAR	TM/L	G	AB	R	H	2B	3B	HR	RBI	BB	SO	AVG	OBP	SLG	OPS	OPS+	BR+	SB	CS	SBR	FA	FR	G/POS	TPR
1917	NY-A	10	36	4	10	3	0	0	2	1	6	.278	.297	.361	658	100	-0	2			.882	-1	O-10(0-0-10)	-0.2
1918	NY-A	2	3	1	2	0	0	0	1	0	0	.667	.667	.667	1333	296	1	0			.000	-1	/O-1(0-0-1)	0.0
1919	NY-A	106	407	59	101	15	9	2	27	35	55	.248	.308	.344	652	82	-10	9			.952	-4	*O-100(0-0-100)	-2.1
1920	NY-A	51	118	21	26	7	1	0	11	14	20	.220	.313	.297	610	60	-7	1	1	-0	.949	-4	O-33(4-1-28)	-1.2
1921	Bos-A	44	77	5	20	3	1	0	9	1	10	.260	.269	.325	594	52	-6	0	1	-0	1.000	-1	O-14(0-0-14)	-0.8
Total	5	213	641	90	159	28	11	2	50	51	91	.248	.305	.335	641	76	-22	12	2		.951	-11	O-158(4-1-153)	-4.3

■ GEORGE VICO Vico, George Steve "Sam" b: 8/9/23, San Fernando, Cal. d: 1/13/94, Redondo Beach, Cal. BL/TR, 6'4", 200 lbs. Deb: 4/20/48

YEAR	TM/L	G	AB	R	H	2B	3B	HR	RBI	BB	SO	AVG	OBP	SLG	OPS	OPS+	BR+	SB	CS	SBR	FA	FR	G/POS	TPR
1948	Det-A	144	521	50	139	23	9	8	58	39	39	.267	.326	.392	718	88	-11	2	2	-0	.988	-3	*1-142	-1.8
1949	Det-A	67	142	15	27	5	2	4	18	21	17	.190	.311	.338	649	72	-6	0	0	0	.985	2	1-53	-0.5
Total	2	211	663	65	166	28	11	12	76	60	56	.250	.323	.380	703	85	-17	2	2	-0	.987	-1	1-195	-2.3

■ JOSE VIDAL Vidal, Jose (Nicolas) "Papito" b: 4/3/40, Batey Lechuga, D.R. BR/TR, 6', 190 lbs. Deb: 9/5/66

YEAR	TM/L	G	AB	R	H	2B	3B	HR	RBI	BB	SO	AVG	OBP	SLG	OPS	OPS+	BR+	SB	CS	SBR	FA	FR	G/POS	TPR
1966	Cle-A	17	32	4	6	1	1	0	3	5	11	.188	.297	.281	579	67	-1	0	1	-0	1.000	-1	O-11(0-3-8)	-0.3
1967	Cle-A	16	34	4	4	0	0	0	0	7	12	.118	.268	.118	386	17	-3	0	1	-0	1.000	-1	O-10(8-6-1)	-0.5
1968	Cle-A	37	54	5	9	0	0	2	5	2	15	.167	.196	.278	474	43	-4	3	0	1	1.000	-5	O-26(11-0-15)/1-1	-1.0
1969	Sea-A	18	26	7	5	0	1	1	2	4	8	.192	.323	.385	707	99	-0	1	1	-0	.917	-0	/O-6(1-0-5)	-0.1
Total	4	88	146	20	24	1	2	3	10	18	46	.164	.261	.260	521	53	-8	4	3	-0	.985	-7	/O-53(20-9-29),1-1	-1.9

■ JOSE VIDRO Vidro, Jose Angel (Cetty) b: 8/27/74, Mayaguez, P.R. BB/TR, 5'11", 175 lbs. Deb: 6/8/97 Career OF: (3-LF 0-CF 0-RF)

YEAR	TM/L	G	AB	R	H	2B	3B	HR	RBI	BB	SO	AVG	OBP	SLG	OPS	OPS+	BR+	SB	CS	SBR	FA	FR	G/POS	TPR
1997	Mon-N	67	169	19	42	12	1	2	17	11	20	.249	.302	.367	669	74	-7	1	0	0	.958	-6	3-36/2-5,D-5	-1.2
1998	Mon-N	83	205	24	45	12	0	0	18	27	33	.220	.322	.278	600	61	-11	2	2	-0	.975	-17	2-56/3-7	-2.5
1999	Mon-N	140	494	67	150	45	2	12	59	29	51	.304	.347	.476	823	108	5	0	4	-1	.982	2	*2-121,1-14/O-3L,3	0.9
2000	Mon-N★	153	605	101	200	51	2	24	97	49	68	.331	.383	.540	923	128	25	5	4	-0	.986	8	*2-153	3.8
Total	4	443	1473	211	437	120	5	38	191	116	172	.297	.353	.462	815	107	13	8	10	-2	.983	-13	2-335/3-45,1-14,DO	1.0

■ HECTOR VILLANUEVA Villanueva, Hector (Balasquide) b: 10/2/64, Rio Piedras, P.R. BR/TR, 6'1", 220 lbs. Deb: 6/1/90

YEAR	TM/L	G	AB	R	H	2B	3B	HR	RBI	BB	SO	AVG	OBP	SLG	OPS	OPS+	BR+	SB	CS	SBR	FA	FR	G/POS	TPR
1990	Chi-N	52	114	14	31	4	1	7	18	4	27	.272	.308	.509	817	112	1	1	0	0	.991	-4	C-23,1-14	-0.2
1991	Chi-N	71	192	23	53	10	1	13	32	21	30	.276	.347	.542	889	140	9	0	0	0	.979	-9	C-55/1-6	0.4

YEAR	TM/L	G	AB	R	H	2B	3B	HR	RBI	BB	SO	AVG	OBP	SLG	OPS	OPS+	BR+	SB	CS	SBR	FA	FR	G/POS	TPR
1992	Chi-N	51	112	9	17	6	0	2	13	11	24	.152	.228	.259	487	37	-9	0	0	0	.978	6	C-28/1-6	-0.2
1993	StL-N	17	55	7	8	1	0	3	9	4	17	.145	.203	.327	531	40	-5	0	0	0	1.000	-1	C-17	-0.5
Total	4	191	473	53	109	21	2	25	72	40	98	.230	.293	.442	735	98	-3	1	0	0	.984	-7	C-123/1-26	-0.5

■ **FERNANDO VINA** Vina, Fernando b: 4/16/69, Sacramento, Cal. BL/TR, 5'9", 170 lbs. Deb: 4/10/93

YEAR	TM/L	G	AB	R	H	2B	3B	HR	RBI	BB	SO	AVG	OBP	SLG	OPS	OPS+	BR+	SB	CS	SBR	FA	FR	G/POS	TPR
1993	Sea-A	24	45	5	10	2	0	0	2	4	3	.222	.327	.267	594	61	-2	6	0	1	1.000	6	2-16/S-4,D-2	0.5
1994	NY-N	79	124	20	31	6	0	0	6	12	11	.250	.372	.298	670	78	-3	3	1	0	.979	2	2-13,3-12/S-9,O-6L	0.0
1995	Mil-A	113	288	46	74	7	7	3	29	22	28	.257	.329	.361	690	75	-10	6	3	0	.983	10	2-99/S-6,3-2	0.4
1996	Mil-A	140	554	94	157	19	10	7	46	38	35	.283	.344	.392	735	82	-15	16	7	1	.979	8	*2-137	0.2
1997	Mil-A	79	324	37	89	12	2	4	28	12	23	.275	.315	.361	676	75	-12	8	7	-1	.982	2	2-77/D-1	-0.6
1998	Mil-N★	159	637	101	198	39	7	7	45	54	46	.311	.387	.427	814	114	15	22	16	-1	.986	29	*2-158	4.9
1999	Mil-N	37	154	17	41	7	0	1	16	14	6	.266	.343	.331	674	73	-6	5	2	0	.995	1	2-37	-0.3
2000	*StL-N	123	487	81	146	24	6	4	31	36	36	.300	.381	.398	779	97	-0	10	8	-1	**.988**	5	*2-122	0.9
Total	8	754	2613	401	746	116	32	26	203	192	188	.285	.358	.384	742	90	-33	76	44	1	.985	62	2-659/S-19,3-14,OD	6.0

■ **CHARLIE VINSON** Vinson, Charles Anthony "Chuck" b: 1/5/44, Washington, D.C. BL/TL, 6'3", 207 lbs. Deb: 9/19/66

YEAR	TM/L	G	AB	R	H	2B	3B	HR	RBI	BB	SO	AVG	OBP	SLG	OPS	OPS+	BR+	SB	CS	SBR	FA	FR	G/POS	TPR
1966	Cal-A	13	22	3	4	2	0	1	6	5	9	.182	.357	.409	766	123	1	0	0	0	1.000	-1	1-11	0.0

■ **RUBE VINSON** Vinson, Ernest Augustus b: 3/20/1879, Dover, Del. d: 10/12/51, Chester, Pa. 5'9", 168 lbs. Deb: 9/27/04

YEAR	TM/L	G	AB	R	H	2B	3B	HR	RBI	BB	SO	AVG	OBP	SLG	OPS	OPS+	BR+	SB	CS	SBR	FA	FR	G/POS	TPR
1904	Cle-A	15	49	12	15	1	0	0	2	10		.306	.433	.327	760	143	3	2			1.000	3	O-15(15-0-0)	0.6
1905	Cle-A	39	134	12	26	3	1	0	9	7		.194	.245	.231	476	51	-7	4			.930	-3	O-36(27-9-0)	-1.4
1906	Chi-A	10	24	2	6	0	0	0	3	2		.250	.308	.250	558	77	-1	1			.600	-3	/O-7(7-0-0)	-0.4
Total	3	64	207	26	47	4	1	0	14	19		.227	.301	.256	557	77	-5	7			.919	-3	/O-58(49-9-0)	-1.2

■ **JIM VIOX** Viox, James Harry b: 12/30/1890, Lockland, Ohio d: 1/6/69, Erlanger, Ky. BR/TR, 5'7", 150 lbs. Deb: 5/9/12 Career OF: (0-LF 2-CF 5-RF)

YEAR	TM/L	G	AB	R	H	2B	3B	HR	RBI	BB	SO	AVG	OBP	SLG	OPS	OPS+	BR+	SB	CS	SBR	FA	FR	G/POS	TPR
1912	Pit-N	33	70	8	13	2	3	1	7	3	9	.186	.219	.343	562	53	-5	2			.957	-4	3-10/S-8,O-3R,2-1	-0.9
1913	Pit-N	137	492	86	156	32	8	2	65	64	28	.317	.399	.427	826	142	29	14			.959	-43	*2-124,S-10	-1.2
1914	Pit-N	143	506	52	134	18	5	1	57	63	33	.265	.351	.326	677	106	6	9			.939	-25	*2-138/S-2,O-2(0-0-2)	-1.8
1915	Pit-N	150	503	56	129	17	8	2	45	75	31	.256	.357	.334	691	111	10	12	8	-0	.954	-26	*2-134,3-13/O-2C	-1.5
1916	Pit-N	43	132	12	33	7	0	1	17	17	11	.250	.340	.326	666	104	1	2			.937	-16	2-25,3-11	-1.6
Total	5	506	1703	214	465	76	24	7	191	222	112	.273	.361	.358	719	116	41	39	8		.949	-114	2-422/3-34,S-20,O-7R	-7.0

■ **BILL VIRDON** Virdon, William Charles b: 6/9/31, Hazel Park, Mich. BL/TR, 6', 175 lbs. Deb: 4/12/55 MC

YEAR	TM/L	G	AB	R	H	2B	3B	HR	RBI	BB	SO	AVG	OBP	SLG	OPS	OPS+	BR+	SB	CS	SBR	FA	FR	G/POS	TPR
1955	StL-N	144	534	58	150	18	6	17	68	36	64	.281	.327	.433	760	100	-1	2	4	-1	.966	-0	*O-142(1-109-34)	-0.9
1956	StL-N	24	71	10	15	2	0	2	9	5	8	.211	.273	.324	597	60	-4	0	1	-0	.982	-1	O-24(0-24-0)	-0.7
	Pit-N	133	509	67	170	21	10	8	37	33	63	.334	.376	.462	837	126	19	6	6	-1	.989	4	*O-130(0-130-0)	1.6
	Yr	157	580	77	185	23	10	10	46	38	71	.319	.363	.445	808	118	14	6	7	-1	.988	3	*O-154(0-154-0)	0.9
1957	Pit-N	144	561	59	141	28	11	8	50	33	69	.251	.293	.383	676	82	-15	3	3	-0	.986	12	*O-141(0-141-0)	-1.1
1958	Pit-N	144	604	75	161	24	11	9	46	52	70	.267	.326	.387	713	90	-9	5	3	0	.993	11	*O-143(0-143-0)	-0.5
1959	Pit-N	144	519	67	132	24	2	8	41	55	65	.254	.328	.355	683	83	-12	7	4	0	.979	**24**	*O-144(0-144-0)	0.5
1960	*Pit-N	120	409	60	108	16	9	8	40	40	44	.264	.330	.406	735	99	-0	8	2	1	.983	7	*O-109(0-109-0)	0.3
1961	Pit-N	146	599	81	156	22	8	9	58	49	45	.260	.316	.369	685	81	-16	5	8	-2	.985	11	*O-145(0-145-0)	-1.2
1962	Pit-N	156	663	82	164	27	**10**	6	47	36	65	.247	.287	.345	633	69	-30	5	13	-3	.976	6	*O-156(0-156-0)	-3.3
1963	Pit-N	142	554	58	149	22	6	8	53	43	55	.269	.322	.374	695	99	-1	1	2	-0	.988	6	*O-142(0-142-0)	0.0
1964	Pit-N	145	473	59	115	11	3	3	27	30	48	.243	.288	.298	586	66	-21	1	5	-2	.976	-7	*O-134(0-134-0)	-3.5
1965	Pit-N	135	481	58	134	22	5	4	24	30	49	.279	.322	.370	692	94	-4	4	3	-0	.970	-2	*O-128(1-127-0)	-1.0
1968	Pit-N	6	3	1	1	0	0	1	2	0	2	.333	.333	1.333	1667	388	1	0	0	0	1.000	-1	/O-4(1-0-3)	-0.1
Total	12	1583	5980	735	1596	237	81	91	502	442	647	.267	.318	.379	697	89	-95	47	54	-9	.982	69	*O-1542(3-1504-37)	-9.9

■ **OZZIE VIRGIL** Virgil, Osvaldo Jose Jr. b: 12/7/56, Mayaguez, P.R. BR/TR, 6'1", 205 lbs. Deb: 10/5/80 F

YEAR	TM/L	G	AB	R	H	2B	3B	HR	RBI	BB	SO	AVG	OBP	SLG	OPS	OPS+	BR+	SB	CS	SBR	FA	FR	G/POS	TPR
1980	Phi-N	1	5	1	1	1	0	0	0	0	1	.200	.200	.400	600	60	-0	0	0	0	1.000	-1	/C-1	-0.1
1981	Phi-N	6	6	0	0	0	0	0	0	0	2	.000	.000	.000	0	-96	-2	0	0	0	1.000	0	/C-1	-0.2
1982	Phi-N	49	101	11	24	6	0	3	8	10	26	.238	.306	.386	692	91	-1	0	1	-0	.964	4	C-35	0.3
1983	*Phi-N	55	140	11	30	7	0	6	23	8	34	.214	.272	.393	664	83	-4	0	2	-1	.966	-5	C-51	-0.8
1984	Phi-N	141	456	61	119	21	2	18	68	45	91	.261	.334	.434	768	113	7	1	1	-0	.992	-3	*C-137	1.0
1985	Phi-N★	131	426	47	105	16	3	19	55	49	85	.246	.331	.432	763	109	5	0	0	0	**.994**	-4	*C-120	0.6
1986	Atl-N	114	359	45	80	9	0	15	48	63	73	.223	.345	.373	718	93	-2	1	0	0	.984	14	*C-111	1.8
1987	Atl-N★	123	429	57	106	13	1	27	72	47	81	.247	.331	.471	802	104	2	0	1	-0	.989	-2	*C-122	0.5
1988	Atl-N	107	320	23	82	10	0	9	31	22	54	.256	.314	.372	686	92	-3	2	0	0	.990	-11	C-96	-0.9
1989	Tor-A	9	11	2	2	1	0	1	2	4	3	.182	.400	.545	945	167	1	0	0	0	1.000	-0	/C-1,D-6	0.1
1990	Tor-A	3	5	0	0	0	0	0	0	0	3	.000	.000	.000	0	-98	-1	0	0	0	1.000	-0	/C-2,D-1	-0.1
Total	11	739	2258	258	549	84	6	98	307	248	453	.243	.326	.416	742	101	1	4	5	-1	.987	-8	C-677/D-7	2.2

■ **OZZIE VIRGIL** Virgil, Osvaldo Jose Sr. (Pichardo) b: 5/17/33, Monte Cristi, D.R. BR/TR, 6', 175 lbs. Deb: 9/23/56 FC Career OF: (8-LF 0-CF 18-RF)

YEAR	TM/L	G	AB	R	H	2B	3B	HR	RBI	BB	SO	AVG	OBP	SLG	OPS	OPS+	BR+	SB	CS	SBR	FA	FR	G/POS	TPR
1956	NY-N	3	12	2	5	1	1	0	2	0	0	.417	.417	.667	1083	186	1	1	0	0	.800	-2	/3-3	0.0
1957	NY-N	96	226	26	53	0	2	4	24	14	27	.235	.279	.305	584	57	-14	2	3	-1	.926	9	3-62,O-24(8-0-16)/S-1	-0.6
1958	Det-A	49	193	19	47	10	2	3	19	8	20	.244	.274	.363	636	69	-8	1	0	0	.981	3	3-49	-0.6
1960	Det-A	62	132	16	30	4	2	3	13	4	14	.227	.250	.356	606	60	-8	1	1	-0	.974	8	3-42/2-8,S-5,C-1	0.1
1961	Det-A	20	30	1	4	0	0	1	1	1	5	.133	.161	.233	395	4	-4	0	0	0	.938	-1	/3-9,C-3,2-1,S-1	-0.5
	KC-A	11	21	1	3	0	0	0	0	0	3	.143	.143	.143	286	-23	-4	0	0	0	.818	0	/3-4,C-3	-0.3
	Yr	31	51	2	7	0	0	1	1	1	8	.137	.154	.196	350	-7	-8	0	0	0	.889	-1	3-13/C-6,2-1,S-1	-0.8
1962	Bal-A	1	0	0	0	0	0	0	0	1	0	—	1.000	—	1000	209	0	0	0	0	.000	0	H	0.0
1965	Pit-N	39	49	3	13	2	0	1	5	2	10	.265	.294	.367	661	85	-1	0	0	0	1.000	2	C-15/3-7,2-5	0.1
1966	SF-N	42	89	7	19	2	0	2	9	4	12	.213	.247	.303	551	51	-6	1	1	-0	.984	0	C-13,3-13/1-5,2O	-0.6
1969	SF-N	1	1	0	0	0	0	0	0	0	0	.000	.000	.000	0	-99	-0	0	0	0	.000	0	H	0.0
Total	9	324	753	75	174	19	7	14	73	34	91	.231	.264	.331	595	59	-43	6	5	-0	.951	19	3-189/C-35,O-26R,2S1	-2.4

■ **JAKE VIRTUE** Virtue, Jacob Kitchline "Guesses" b: 3/2/1865, Philadelphia, Pa. d: 2/3/43, Camden, N.J. BB/TL, 5'9.5", 165 lbs. Deb: 7/21/1890 Career OF: (0-LF 25-CF 9-RF)

YEAR	TM/L	G	AB	R	H	2B	3B	HR	RBI	BB	SO	AVG	OBP	SLG	OPS	OPS+	BR+	SB	CS	SBR	FA	FR	G/POS	TPR
1890	Cle-N	62	223	39	68	6	5	2	25	49	15	.305	.432	.404	836	147	16	9			.982	0	1-62	1.0
1891	Cle-N	139	517	82	135	19	14	2	72	75	40	.261	.363	.364	727	107	6	15			.972	-10	*1-139	-1.5
1892	*Cle-N	147	557	98	157	15	20	2	89	84	68	.282	.380	.391	771	128	20	14			.984	-4	*1-147	1.4
1893	Cle-N	97	378	87	100	16	10	1	60	54	14	.265	.358	.368	726	88	-7	11			.975	1	1-73,O-13C/S-5,3P	-0.5
1894	Cle-N	29	89	15	23	4	1	0	10	13	3	.258	.359	.326	685	64	-5	1			.885	-2	O-21C/2-3,1-2,P-1	-0.6
Total	5	474	1764	321	483	60	50	7	256	275	140	.274	.376	.376	753	111	31	50			.978	-15	1-423/O-34C,3-5,S2P	-0.2

■ **JOE VISNER** Visner, Joseph Paul (b: Joseph Paul Vezina) b: 9/27/1859, Minneapolis, Minn.
d: 6/17/45, Fosston, Minn. BL/TR, 5'11", 180 lbs. Deb: 7/4/1885 Career OF: (2-LF 2-CF 179-RF)

YEAR	TM/L	G	AB	R	H	2B	3B	HR	RBI	BB	SO	AVG	OBP	SLG	OPS	OPS+	BR+	SB	CS	SBR	FA	FR	G/POS	TPR
1885	Bal-a	4	13	2	3	0	0	0	2	2		.231	.333	.231	564	82	-0				.750	-1	/O-4(0-2-2)	-0.1
1889	*Bro-a	80	295	56	76	12	10	8	68	36	36	.258	.346	.447	794	125	9	13			.871	-16	C-53,O-29(2-0-27)	-0.2
1890	Pit-P	127	521	110	139	15	**22**	3	71	76	44	.267	.369	.397	766	114	14	18			.893	-6	*O-127(0-0-127)	0.5
1891	Was-a	18	68	13	19	2	3	1	7	8	7	.279	.355	.441	796	134	3	2			.806	-2	O-17(0-0-17)/C-1,3-1	0.0
	StL-a	6	27	2	4	0	1	0	1	0	3	.148	.148	.222	370	5	-4	0			1.000	0	/O-6(0-0-6)	-0.3
	Yr	24	95	15	23	2	4	1	8	8	10	.242	.301	.379	680	94	-1	2			.846	-2	O-23(0-0-23)/C-1,3-1	-0.3
Total	4	235	924	183	241	29	36	12	149	122	90	.261	.354	.409	764	115	22	33			.892	-25	O-183R/C-54,3-1	-0.1

■ **JOE VITELLI** Vitelli, Antonio Joseph b: 4/12/08, McKees Rocks, Pa. d: 2/7/67, Pittsburgh, Pa. BR/TR, 6'1", 195 lbs. Deb: 5/30/44

YEAR	TM/L	G	AB	R	H	2B	3B	HR	RBI	BB	SO	AVG	OBP	SLG	OPS	OPS+	BR+	SB	CS	SBR	FA	FR	G/POS	TPR
1944	Pit-N	4	3	0	0	0	0	0	0	0	0	.000	.000	.000	0	-96	-1	0			.750	0	/P-4	0.0
1945	Pit-N	1	0	1	0	0	0	0	0	0	0	—	—	—	—	—	0	0			.000	0	R	0.0
Total	2	5	3	1	0	0	0	0	0	0	0	.000	.000	.000	0	-96	-1	0			.750	0	/P-4	0.0

■ **JOE VITIELLO** Vitiello, Joseph David b: 4/11/70, Cambridge, Mass. BR/TR, 6'2", 215 lbs. Deb: 4/29/95 Career OF: (12-LF 0-CF 18-RF)

YEAR	TM/L	G	AB	R	H	2B	3B	HR	RBI	BB	SO	AVG	OBP	SLG	OPS	OPS+	BR+	SB	CS	SBR	FA	FR	G/POS	TPR
1995	KC-A	53	130	13	33	4	0	7	21	8	25	.254	.317	.446	763	95	-1	0	0	0	.982	-0	D-38/1-8	-0.4

YEAR	TM/L	G	AB	R	H	2B	3B	HR	RBI	BB	SO	AVG	OBP	SLG	OPS	OPS+	BR+	SB	CS	SBR	FA	FR	G/POS	TPR
1996	KC-A	85	257	29	62	15	1	8	40	38	69	.241	.346	.401	746	88	-4	2	0	0	1.000	0	D-70/1-9,O-1(0-0-1)	-0.7
1997	KC-A	51	130	11	31	6	0	5	18	14	37	.238	.322	.400	722	85	-3	0	0	0	.980	-3	O-28R,D-12/1-1	-0.7
1998	KC-A	3	7	0	1	0	0	0	0	1	2	.143	.250	.143	393	6	-1	0	0	0	.000	0	/D-2	-0.1
1999	KC-A	13	41	4	6	1	0	1	4	2	9	.146	.222	.244	466	18	-5	0	0	0	1.000	1	1-10/D-2	-0.5
2000	SD-N	39	52	7	13	3	0	2	8	10	9	.250	.371	.423	794	106	1	0	0	0	.966	-0	1-17/O-1(0-0-1)	-0.1
Total	6	244	617	64	146	29	1	23	91	73	151	.237	.328	.399	727	85	-14	2	0	0	.985	-2	D-124/1-45,O-30R	-2.5

■ OSSIE VITT Vitt, Oscar Joseph b: 1/4/1890, San Francisco, Cal. d: 1/31/63, Oakland, Cal. BR/TR, 5′10″, 150 lbs. Deb: 4/11/12 M Career OF: (30-LF 6-CF 1-RF)

YEAR	TM/L	G	AB	R	H	2B	3B	HR	RBI	BB	SO	AVG	OBP	SLG	OPS	OPS+	BR+	SB	CS	SBR	FA	FR	G/POS	TPR
1912	Det-A	76	273	39	67	4	4	0	19	18		.245	.297	.289	586	70	-11	17			.929	0	O-28L,3-24,2-15	-1.1
1913	Det-A	99	359	45	86	11	3	2	33	31	18	.240	.304	.304	607	79	-10	5			.960	5	2-78,3-17/O-2(0-2-0)	-0.4
1914	Det-A	66	195	35	49	7	0	0	8	31	8	.251	.354	.287	641	90	-1	10	8	-1	.964	2	2-36,3-16/O-2L,S-1	0.2
1915	Det-A	152	560	116	140	18	13	1	48	80	22	.250	.348	.334	682	99	1	26	18	-1	**.964**	14	*3-151/2-2	2.0
1916	Det-A	153	597	88	135	17	12	0	42	75	28	.226	.314	.295	608	80	-14	18			**.964**	28	*3-151/S-2	2.0
1917	Det-A	140	512	65	130	13	6	0	47	56	15	.254	.329	.303	631	93	-3	18			.940	-17	*3-140	-1.9
1918	Det-A	81	267	29	64	5	2	0	17	32	6	.240	.321	.273	594	83	-5	5			.953	4	3-66/2-9,O-3(0-3-0)	0.1
1919	Bos-A	133	469	64	114	10	3	0	40	44	11	.243	.309	.277	587	69	-18	9			**.970**	14	*3-133	0.0
1920	Bos-A	87	296	50	65	10	4	1	28	43	10	.220	.321	.291	611	66	-14	5	4	-0	.986	-6	3-64,2-21	-1.8
1921	Bos-A	78	232	29	44	11	1	0	13	45	13	.190	.321	.246	567	48	-17	1	2	-0	.962	-4	3-71/O-3(3-0-0),1-2	-1.7
Total	10	1065	3760	560	894	106	48	4	295	455	131	.238	.322	.295	617	80	-92	114	32		.960	40	3-833,2-161/O-38L,S1	-2.6

■ JOSE VIZCAINO Vizcaino, Jose Luis (Pimental) b: 3/26/68, San Cristobal, D.R. BB/TR, 6′1″, 180 lbs. Deb: 9/10/89 Career OF: (1-LF 0-CF 0-RF)

YEAR	TM/L	G	AB	R	H	2B	3B	HR	RBI	BB	SO	AVG	OBP	SLG	OPS	OPS+	BR+	SB	CS	SBR	FA	FR	G/POS	TPR
1989	LA-N	7	10	2	2	0	0	0	0	0	1	.200	.200	.200	400	15	-1	0	0	0	.882	2	/S-5	0.1
1990	LA-N	37	51	3	14	1	1	0	2	4	8	.275	.327	.333	661	85	-1	1	1	-0	.956	3	S-11/2-6	0.2
1991	Chi-N	93	145	7	38	5	0	0	10	5	18	.262	.287	.297	583	61	-7	2	1	0	.947	7	3-57,S-33/2-9	0.1
1992	Chi-N	86	285	25	64	10	4	1	17	14	35	.225	.261	.298	559	57	-16	3	0	1	.969	2	S-50,3-29/2-5	-1.1
1993	Chi-N	151	551	74	158	19	4	4	54	46	71	.287	.345	.358	703	90	-7	12	9	-1	.968	8	S-81,3-44,2-34	0.8
1994	NY-N	103	410	47	105	13	3	3	33	33	62	.256	.315	.324	639	68	-19	1	11	-4	.970	-12	*S-102	-2.6
1995	NY-N	135	509	66	146	21	5	3	56	35	76	.287	.334	.365	699	87	-9	8	3	1	**.984**	10	*S-134/2-1	1.2
1996	NY-N	96	363	47	110	12	6	1	32	28	58	.303	.358	.377	735	99	-0	9	5	0	.986	2	2-93	0.6
	*Cle-A	48	179	23	51	5	2	0	13	7	24	.285	.312	.335	647	64	-10	6	2	1	.981	2	2-45/S-4,D-1	-0.4
1997	*SF-N	151	568	77	151	19	7	5	50	48	87	.266	.323	.350	673	78	-18	8	8	-1	.976	7	*S-147/2-5	0.1
1998	LA-N	67	237	30	62	9	0	3	29	17	35	.262	.314	.338	651	76	-8	7	3	0	.985	-6	S-66	-0.8
1999	LA-N	94	266	27	67	9	0	1	29	20	23	.252	.307	.297	604	57	-17	2	1	0	.966	5	S-44,2-30/3-9,O-1L	-0.7
2000	LA-N	40	93	9	19	2	1	0	4	10	15	.204	.288	.247	536	39	-9	1	0	0	1.000	-1	S-19,3-12/2-3,1D	-0.7
	*NY-A	73	174	23	48	8	1	0	10	12	28	.276	.323	.333	656	68	-8	5	7	-1	.990	-1	2-62/3-6,S-2,D-4	-0.8
Total	12	1181	3841	460	1035	133	34	21	339	279	541	.269	.321	.338	659	76	-131	65	51	-4	.975	28	S-698,2-293,3/D1O	-4.0

■ OMAR VIZQUEL Vizquel, Omar Enrique (Gonzalez) b: 4/24/67, Caracas, Venez. BB/TR, 5′9″, 165 lbs. Deb: 4/3/89 Career OF: (0-LF 0-CF 1-RF)

YEAR	TM/L	G	AB	R	H	2B	3B	HR	RBI	BB	SO	AVG	OBP	SLG	OPS	OPS+	BR+	SB	CS	SBR	FA	FR	G/POS	TPR
1989	Sea-A	143	387	45	85	7	3	1	20	28	40	.220	.274	.261	535	50	-25	1	4	-1	.971	11	*S-143	-0.7
1990	Sea-A	81	255	19	63	3	2	2	18	18	22	.247	.297	.298	595	66	-11	4	1	1	.980	-3	S-81	-0.8
1991	Sea-A	142	426	42	98	16	4	1	41	45	37	.230	.304	.293	597	66	-19	7	2	1	.980	24	*S-138/2-1	1.5
1992	Sea-A	136	483	49	142	20	4	0	21	32	38	.294	.340	.352	692	94	-4	15	13	-1	**.989**	0	*S-136	0.6
1993	Sea-A	158	560	68	143	14	2	2	31	50	71	.255	.321	.298	619	67	-25	12	14	-2	.980	**23**	*S-155/D-2	0.8
1994	Cle-A	69	286	39	78	10	1	1	33	23	23	.273	.327	.325	652	69	-13	13	4	1	.981	-1	S-69	-0.5
1995	*Cle-A	136	542	87	144	28	0	6	56	59	59	.266	.339	.351	689	79	-16	29	11	3	.986	-3	*S-136	-0.4
1996	*Cle-A	151	542	98	161	36	1	9	64	56	42	.297	.367	.417	784	98	-0	35	9	5	.971	-1	*S-150	1.5
1997	*Cle-A	153	565	89	158	23	6	5	49	57	58	.280	.348	.368	716	84	-12	43	12	5	.985	5	*S-152	1.1
1998	*Cle-A★	151	576	86	166	30	6	2	50	62	64	.288	.361	.372	733	88	-8	37	12	4	**.993**	5	*S-151	1.3
1999	*Cle-A★	144	574	112	191	36	4	5	66	65	50	.333	.402	.436	837	109	10	42	9	6	.976	-4	*S-143/O-1(0-0-1)	2.2
2000	Cle-A	156	613	101	176	27	3	7	66	87	72	.287	.380	.375	755	90	-6	22	10	1	**.995**	-5	*S-156	0.3
Total	12	1620	5809	835	1605	250	36	41	515	582	576	.276	.345	.353	698	83	-130	260	101	22	.982	52	*S-1610/D-2,O-1R,2	6.9

■ OTTO VOGEL Vogel, Otto Henry b: 10/26/1899, Mendota, Ill. d: 7/19/69, Iowa City, Iowa BR/TR, 6′, 195 lbs. Deb: 6/5/23

YEAR	TM/L	G	AB	R	H	2B	3B	HR	RBI	BB	SO	AVG	OBP	SLG	OPS	OPS+	BR+	SB	CS	SBR	FA	FR	G/POS	TPR
1923	Chi-N	41	81	10	17	0	1	1	6	7	11	.210	.297	.272	568	51	-6	2	3	-1	.929	-2	O-24(3-0-21)/3-1	-1.0
1924	Chi-N	70	172	28	46	11	2	1	24	10	26	.267	.319	.372	691	84	-4	4	4	-1	.956	1	O-53(12-1-40)/3-2	-0.7
Total	2	111	253	38	63	11	3	2	30	17	37	.249	.312	.340	652	73	-10	6	7	-1	.948	-1	/O-77(15-1-61),3-3	-1.7

■ JACK VOIGT Voigt, John David b: 5/17/66, Sarasota, Fla. BR/TR, 6′1″, 175 lbs. Deb: 8/3/92 Career OF: (93-LF 13-CF 85-RF)

YEAR	TM/L	G	AB	R	H	2B	3B	HR	RBI	BB	SO	AVG	OBP	SLG	OPS	OPS+	BR+	SB	CS	SBR	FA	FR	G/POS	TPR
1992	Bal-A	1	0	0	0	0	0	0	0	0	0	—	—	—	—	—	0	0	0	0	.000	0	/R	0.0
1993	Bal-A	64	152	32	45	11	1	6	23	25	33	.296	.395	.500	895	133	8	1	0	0	.987	-1	O-43R/1-5,3-3,D-9	0.5
1994	Bal-A	59	141	15	34	5	0	3	20	18	25	.241	.331	.340	672	70	-6	0	0	0	.989	-4	O-54(17-1-37)/1-6,D-2	-1.1
1995	Bal-A	3	1	1	1	0	0	0	0	0	0	1.000	1.000	1.000	2000	416	0	0	0	0	1.000	0	/1-1,D-1	0.1
	Tex-A	33	62	8	10	3	0	2	8	10	14	.161	.278	.306	584	51	-5	0	0	0	1.000	-2	O-25(8-0-17)/1-5,D-2	-0.7
	Yr	36	63	9	11	3	0	2	8	10	14	.175	.288	.317	605	56	-4	0	0	0	1.000	-2	O-25(8-0-17)/1-6,D-3	-0.6
1996	Tex-A	5	9	1	1	0	0	0	0	0	2	.111	.111	.111	222	-41	-2	0	0	0	1.000	0	/O-3(2-0-1),3-1	-0.2
1997	Mil-A	72	151	20	37	9	2	8	22	19	36	.245	.333	.490	823	110	2	1	2	-0	.985	-2	O-40L,1-19/3-6,D-1	-0.2
1998	Oak-A	57	72	7	10	4	0	1	10	6	19	.139	.205	.236	441	15	-9	5	1	1	.987	-3	1-27,O-20C/3-2,D-3	-1.1
Total	7	294	588	84	138	32	3	20	83	78	129	.235	.326	.401	728	87	-12	7	3	0	.990	-12	O-185L/1-63,D-18,3	-2.7

■ CLYDE VOLLMER Vollmer, Clyde Frederick b: 9/24/21, Cincinnati, Ohio BR/TR, 6′1″, 190 lbs. Deb: 5/31/42

YEAR	TM/L	G	AB	R	H	2B	3B	HR	RBI	BB	SO	AVG	OBP	SLG	OPS	OPS+	BR+	SB	CS	SBR	FA	FR	G/POS	TPR
1942	Cin-N	12	43	2	4	0	0	1	4	1	5	.093	.114	.163	276	-20	-7	0			1.000	1	O-11(10-1-0)	-0.6
1946	Cin-N	9	22	1	4	0	0	0	1	1	3	.182	.217	.182	399	14	-2	2			1.000	-3	/O-7(5-3-1)	-0.6
1947	Cin-N	78	155	19	34	10	0	1	13	9	18	.219	.267	.303	570	51	-11	0			.984	-7	O-66(8-58-0)	-1.9
1948	Cin-N	7	9	0	1	0	0	0	0	1	1	.111	.200	.111	311	-14	-1	0			.000	-1	/O-2(0-1-1)	-0.2
	Was-A	1	5	1	2	0	0	0	0	0	1	.400	.400	.400	800	116	0	0	0	0	1.000	0	/O-1(0-1-0)	0.0
1949	Was-A	129	443	58	112	17	1	14	59	53	62	.253	.335	.391	726	94	-6	1	2	-0	.982	4	*O-114(0-99-15)	-0.5
1950	Was-A	6	14	4	4	0	0	0	1	2	3	.286	.375	.286	661	75	-0	1	0	0	1.000	0	/O-3(3-0-0)	0.0
	Bos-A	57	169	35	48	10	0	7	37	21	35	.284	.363	.467	831	102	0	1	0	0	.954	-2	O-39(17-11-11)	-0.3
	Yr	63	183	39	52	10	0	7	38	23	38	.284	.364	.454	818	100	-0	2	0	0	.957	-1	O-42(20-11-11)	-0.3
1951	Bos-A	115	386	66	97	9	2	22	85	55	66	.251	.346	.456	802	105	2	0	0	0	.986	0	*O-106(2-8-97)	-0.1
1952	Bos-A	90	250	35	66	12	4	11	50	39	47	.264	.370	.476	846	124	8	2	2	-0	1.000	-1	O-70(43-9-21)	0.3
1953	Bos-A	1	0	0	0	0	0	0	0	1	0	—	1.000	—	1000	180	0	0	0	0	.000	0	H	0.0
	Was-A	118	408	54	106	15	3	11	74	48	59	.260	.342	.392	734	100	0	0	2	-1	.979	7	*O-106(104-0-2)	0.0
	Yr	119	408	54	106	15	3	11	74	49	59	.260	.343	.392	736	101	0	0	2	-1	.979	7	*O-106(104-0-2)	0.0
1954	Was-A	62	117	8	30	4	0	2	15	12	28	.256	.331	.342	673	89	-2	0	0	0	1.000	-3	O-26(5-0-21)	-0.6
Total	10	685	2021	283	508	77	10	69	339	243	328	.251	.335	.402	737	95	-18	7	6		.984	-3	O-551(197-191-169)	-4.5

■ FRITZ Von KOLNITZ Von Kolnitz, Alfred Holmes b: 5/20/1893, Charleston, S.C. d: 3/18/48, Mount Pleasant, S.C. BR/TR, 5′10.5″, 175 lbs. Deb: 4/18/14 Career OF: (2-LF 7-CF 3-RF)

YEAR	TM/L	G	AB	R	H	2B	3B	HR	RBI	BB	SO	AVG	OBP	SLG	OPS	OPS+	BR+	SB	CS	SBR	FA	FR	G/POS	TPR
1914	Cin-N	41	104	8	23	2	0	0	6	6	16	.221	.270	.240	511	51	-6	4			.914	-4	3-20,O-11C/C-2,1-1	-1.1
1915	Cin-N	50	78	6	15	4	1	0	6	7	11	.192	.259	.269	528	59	-4	1	3	-1	.933	-6	3-18/S-6,1-3,C-2,O	-1.1
1916	Chi-A	24	44	1	10	3	0	0	7	2	6	.227	.261	.295	556	66	-2	0			.909	-5	3-13	-0.7
Total	3	115	226	15	48	9	1	0	19	15	33	.212	.264	.261	526	56	-12	5	3		.918	-15	/3-51,O-12C,S-6,1C	-2.9

■ JOE VOSMIK Vosmik, Joseph Franklin b: 4/4/10, Cleveland, Ohio d: 1/27/62, Cleveland, Ohio BR/TR, 6′, 185 lbs. Deb: 9/13/30

YEAR	TM/L	G	AB	R	H	2B	3B	HR	RBI	BB	SO	AVG	OBP	SLG	OPS	OPS+	BR+	SB	CS	SBR	FA	FR	G/POS	TPR
1930	Cle-A	9	26	1	6	2	0	0	4	1	1	.231	.259	.308	567	42	-2	0	0	0	.933	1	/O-5(1-4-0)	-0.2
1931	Cle-A	149	591	80	189	36	14	7	117	38	30	.320	.363	.464	827	110	7	7	7	-1	.970	6	*O-147(147-1-0)	0.4
1932	Cle-A	153	621	106	194	39	12	10	97	58	42	.312	.376	.462	838	109	8	2	3	-1	**.989**	24	*O-153(153-0-0)	2.1
1933	Cle-A	119	438	53	115	20	10	4	56	42	13	.263	.331	.381	713	84	-10	0	2	-1	.985	6	*O-113(113-0-0)	-1.1
1934	Cle-A	104	405	71	138	33	2	6	78	35	10	.341	.393	.477	870	122	13	1	1	-0	.976	-2	*O-104(104-0-0)	0.4
1935	Cle-A★	152	620	93	**216**	**47**	**20**	10	110	59	30	.348	.408	.537	946	140	36	2	1	0	.986	1	*O-150(150-0-0)	2.6

YEAR	TM/L	G	AB	R	H	2B	3B	HR	RBI	BB	SO	AVG	OBP	SLG	OPS	OPS+	BR+	SB	CS	SBR	FA	FR	G/POS	TPR
1936	Cle-A	138	506	76	145	29	7	7	94	79	21	.287	.383	.413	796	96	-2	5	1	1	.978	-1	*O-136(136-0-1)	-0.8
1937	StL-A	144	594	81	193	47	9	4	93	49	38	.325	.377	.455	832	108	7	2	3	-1	.972	8	*O-143(143-0-0)	0.5
1938	Bos-A	146	621	121	**201**	37	6	9	86	59	26	.324	.384	.446	830	103	3	0	3	-1	.978	3	*O-146(146-1-0)	-0.3
1939	Bos-A	145	554	89	153	29	6	7	84	66	33	.276	.356	.388	744	87	-10	4	3	-0	.974	-4	*O-144(144-0-0)	-2.1
1940	Bro-N	116	404	45	114	14	6	1	42	22	21	.282	.321	.354	675	81	-10	0			.976	0	O-99(39-9-51)	-1.6
1941	Bro-N	25	56	0	11	0	0	0	4	4	4	.196	.250	.196	446	26	-5	0			1.000	-5	O-18(2-0-16)	-1.2
1944	Was-A	14	36	2	7	2	0	0	9	2	3	.194	.237	.250	487	41	-3	0	0	0	1.000	-2	O-12(5-0-7)	-0.6
Total	13	1414	5472	818	1682	335	92	65	874	514	272	.307	.369	.438	807	104	30	23	24		.979	34	*O-1370(1283-15-75)	-1.9
■ ALEX VOSS	Voss, Alexander b: 5/16/1858, Roswell, Ga. d: 8/31/06, Cincinnati, Ohio BR/TR, 6'1", 180 lbs. Deb: 4/17/1884																							
1884	Was-U	63	245	33	47	9	0	0		5		.192	.208	.229	437	33	-27				.848	4	P-27,3-16,1-15,O/S	-1.6
	KC-U	14	45	1	4	0	0	0		0		.089	.089	.089	178	-53	-10				.867	1	/O-8(5-3-0),P-7	-0.4
	Yr	77	290	34	51	9	0	0		5		.176	.190	.207	397	21	-36				.859	5	P-34,O-21C,3-16,1/S	-2.0
■ BILL VOSS	Voss, William Edward b: 10/31/43, Glendale, Cal. BL/TL, 6'2", 160 lbs. Deb: 9/14/65																							
1965	Chi-A	11	33	4	6	0	1	1	3	3	5	.182	.250	.333	583	68	-1	0	0	0	1.000	-1	O-10(0-0-10)	-0.4
1966	Chi-A	2	2	0	0	0	0	0	0	0	2	.000	.000	.000	0	-99	-1	0	0	0	1.000	-0	/O-1(1-0-0)	-0.1
1967	Chi-A	13	22	4	2	0	0	0	0	0	1	.091	.091	.091	182	-48	-4	1	1	-0	1.000	-2	O-11(1-2-9)	-0.7
1968	Chi-A	61	167	14	26	2	1	2	15	16	34	.156	.238	.216	453	38	-12	5	3	0	.963	-4	O-55(5-2-53)	-2.2
1969	Cal-A	133	349	33	91	11	4	2	40	35	40	.261	.328	.332	661	90	-5	5	3	0	.995	1	*O-111(6-4-104)/1-2	-0.9
1970	Cal-A	80	181	21	44	4	3	3	30	23	18	.243	.335	.348	683	92	-2	2	1	0	.979	2	O-55(0-0-55)	-0.2
1971	Mil-A	97	275	31	69	4	0	10	30	24	45	.251	.313	.375	688	95	-2	2	2	-0	.987	-4	O-79(4-13-67)	-1.1
1972	Mil-A	27	36	1	3	1	0	0	1	5	4	.083	.195	.111	306	-7	-5	0	1	-0	.929	-3	O-11(3-0-9)	-0.9
	Oak-A	40	97	10	22	5	1	1	5	9	16	.227	.299	.330	629	92	-1	0	0	0	1.000	-1	O-34(1-13-21)	-0.4
	Yr	67	133	11	25	6	1	1	6	14	20	.188	.270	.271	541	64	-6	0	1	-0	.987	-4	O-45(4-13-30)	-1.3
	StL-N	11	15	1	4	2	0	0	3	2	2	.267	.353	.400	753	115	0	0	0	0	1.000	-0	/O-2(0-2-0)	0.0
Total	8	475	1177	119	267	29	10	19	127	117	167	.227	.300	.317	617	78	-32	15	11	-1	.986	-11	O-369(21-36-328)/1-2	-6.9
■ PHIL VOYLES	Voyles, Philip Vance b: 5/12/1900, Murphy, N.C. d: 11/3/72, Marlborough, Mass. BL/TR, 5'11.5", 175 lbs. Deb: 9/4/29																							
1929	Bos-N	20	68	9	16	0	2	0	14	6	8	.235	.297	.294	591	49	-5	0			.922	-2	O-20(1-19-0)	-0.8
■ GEORGE VUKOVICH	Vukovich, George Stephen b: 6/24/56, Chicago, Ill. BL/TR, 6', 198 lbs. Deb: 4/13/80																							
1980	*Phi-N	78	58	6	13	1	1	0	8	6	9	.224	.297	.276	573	58	-3	0	0	0	.933	-9	O-28(13-0-15)	-1.3
1981	*Phi-N	20	26	5	10	0	0	1	4	1	0	.385	.407	.500	907	150	2	1	0	0	1.000	-2	/O-9(3-1-5)	0.0
1982	Phi-N	123	335	41	91	18	2	6	42	32	47	.272	.335	.391	726	100	0	2	9	-3	.977	-6	*O-102(15-0-100)	-1.3
1983	Cle-A	124	312	31	77	13	2	3	44	24	37	.247	.305	.330	635	72	-12	3	4	-1	.986	-13	*O-122(20-3-107)	-3.0
1984	Cle-A	134	437	38	133	22	5	9	60	34	61	.304	.356	.439	795	117	10	1	4	-1	.994	14	*O-130(16-0-124)	1.6
1985	Cle-A	149	434	43	106	22	0	8	45	30	75	.244	.295	.350	645	76	-14	2	2	-0	.988	-7	*O-137(10-0-131)	-2.8
Total	6	628	1602	164	430	76	10	27	203	127	229	.268	.324	.379	703	92	-18	9	19	-5	.987	-22	O-528(77-4-482)	-6.8
■ JOHN VUKOVICH	Vukovich, John Christopher b: 7/31/47, Sacramento, Cal. BR/TR, 6'1", 190 lbs. Deb: 9/11/70 MC																							
1970	Phi-N	3	8	1	1	0	0	0	0	1	0	.125	.222	.125	347	-5	-1	0	0	0	.778	1	/S-2,3-1	0.0
1971	Phi-N	74	217	11	36	5	0	0	14	12	34	.166	.213	.189	402	15	-24	2	1	0	.956	10	3-74	-1.6
1973	Mil-A	55	128	10	16	3	0	2	9	9	40	.125	.182	.195	378	7	-16	0	2	-1	.948	-4	3-40,1-13/S-1	-2.2
1974	Mil-A	38	80	5	15	1	0	3	11	1	16	.188	.198	.313	510	45	-6	2	1	0	.945	2	S-12,3-12,2-11,/1-4	-0.2
1975	Cin-N	31	38	4	8	3	0	0	2	4	5	.211	.286	.289	575	59	-2	0	0	0	.925	7	3-31	0.5
1976	Phi-N	4	8	2	1	0	0	1	2	0	2	.125	.125	.500	625	69	-0	0	0	0	1.000	-0	/3-4,1-1	-0.1
1977	Phi-N	2	2	0	0	0	0	0	0	0	1	.000	.000	.000	0	-96	-1	0	0	0	.000	0	H	-0.1
1979	Phi-N	10	15	0	3	1	0	0	1	0	3	.200	.200	.267	467	25	-2	0	0	0	1.000	2	/3-7,2-3	0.0
1980	Phi-N	49	62	4	10	1	1	0	5	2	7	.161	.200	.210	410	14	-7	0	1	-0	.958	0	3-34/2-9,S-5,1-1	-0.8
1981	Phi-N	11	1	0	0	0	0	0	0	0	1	.000	.000	.000	0	-96	-0	0	0	0	.800	1	/3-9,1-1,2-1	0.0
Total	10	277	559	37	90	14	1	6	44	29	109	.161	.205	.222	427	20	-59	4	5	-1	.951	18	3-212/2-24,1-20,S	-4.5
■ FRANK WADDEY	Waddey, Frank Orum b: 8/21/05, Memphis, Tenn. d: 10/21/90, Knoxville, Tenn. BL/TL, 5'10.5", 185 lbs. Deb: 4/16/31																							
1931	StL-A	14	22	3	6	1	0	0	2	2	3	.273	.333	.318	652	70	-1	0	0	0	1.000	-3	/O-7(1-5-1)	-0.3
■ HAM WADE	Wade, Abraham Lincoln b: 12/20/1880, Spring City, Pa. d: 7/21/68, Riverside, N.J. BR/TR, 5'8", 155 lbs. Deb: 9/9/07																							
1907	NY-N	1	0	0	0	0	0	0	0	0		—	1.000	—	1000	208	0	0			1.000	0	/O-1(1-0-0)	0.0
■ GALE WADE	Wade, Galeard Lee b: 1/20/29, Hollister, Mo. BL/TR, 6'1.5", 185 lbs. Deb: 4/11/55																							
1955	Chi-N	9	33	5	6	1	0	1	1	4	3	.182	.270	.303	573	52	-2	0	0	0	.867	-2	/O-9(0-9-0)	-0.5
1956	Chi-N	10	12	0	0	0	0	0	0	1	0	.000	.077	.000	77	-78	-3	0	0	0	.875	-0	/O-3(0-3-0)	-0.4
Total	2	19	45	5	6	1	0	1	1	5	3	.133	.220	.222	442	18	-5	0	0	0	.870	-2	/O-12(0-12-0)	-0.9
■ RIP WADE	Wade, Richard Frank b: 1/12/1898, Duluth, Minn. d: 7/15/57, Duluth, Minn. BL/TR, 5'11", 174 lbs. Deb: 4/19/23																							
1923	Was-A	33	69	8	16	2	2	2	14	5	10	.232	.284	.406	690	84	-2	0	0	0	.967	-2	O-19(5-12-2)	-0.5
■ WOODY WAGENHORST	Wagenhorst, Ellwood Otto b: 6/3/1863, Kutztown, Pa. d: 2/12/46, Washington, D.C. 5'11", 165 lbs. Deb: 6/25/1888																							
1888	Phi-N	2	8	2	1	0	0	0	0	0	1	.125	.125	.125	250	-19	-1	0			.800	-1	/3-2	-0.2
■ BUTTS WAGNER	Wagner, Albert b: 9/17/1871, Chartiers, Pa. d: 11/26/28, Pittsburgh, Pa. BR/TR, 5'10", 170 lbs. Deb: 4/27/1898 F																							
1898	Was-N	63	223	20	50	11	2	1	31	14		.224	.279	.305	584	67	-10	4			.833	-11	3-39,O-10C/S-8,2-5	-1.9
	Bro-N	11	38	2	9	1	1	0	3	2		.237	.275	.316	591	69	-2	0			.813	-3	3-11	-0.4
	Yr	74	261	22	59	12	3	1	34	16		.226	.279	.307	585	68	-12	4			.828	-14	3-50,O-10C/S-8,2-5	-2.3
■ HEINIE WAGNER	Wagner, Charles F. b: 9/23/1880, New York, N.Y. d: 3/20/43, New Rochelle, N.Y. BR/TR, 5'9", 183 lbs. Deb: 7/1/02 MC Career OF: (1-LF 0-CF 0-RF)																							
1902	NY-N	17	56	4	12	1	0	0	2	0		.214	.214	.232	446	38	-4	3			.862	-3	S-17	-0.7
1906	Bos-A	9	32	1	9	0	0	0	4	1		.281	.303	.281	584	83	-1	2			.943	1	/2-9	0.1
1907	Bos-A	111	385	29	82	10	4	2	21	31		.213	.275	.275	550	76	-10	20			.931	2	*S-109/2-1,3-1	-0.4
1908	Bos-A	153	526	62	130	11	5	1	46	27		.247	.288	.293	581	86	-8	20			.939	32	*S-153	3.2
1909	Bos-A	124	430	53	110	16	7	1	49	35		.256	.316	.333	649	103	1	18			.933	14	*S-123/2-1	2.2
1910	Bos-A	142	491	61	134	26	7	1	52	44		.273	.335	.360	696	115	8	26			.927	-12	*S-140	0.1
1911	Bos-A	80	261	34	67	13	8	1	38	29		.257	.340	.379	719	101	0	15			.946	-4	2-40,S-32	0.0
1912	*Bos-A	144	504	75	138	25	6	2	68	62		.274	.358	.359	717	100	1	21			.922	-13	*S-144	-0.2
1913	Bos-A	110	365	43	83	14	8	2	34	40	29	.227	.316	.326	642	86	-7	9			.937	3	*S-103/2-5,3-1	0.4
1915	Bos-A	84	267	38	64	11	2	0	29	37	34	.240	.339	.296	635	93	-1	8	4	0	.927	-16	2-79/3-1,O-1(1-0-0)	-1.6
1916	Bos-A	6	8	2	4	1	0	0	0	3	0	.500	.636	.625	1261	278	2	2			1.000	2	/3-4,2-1,S-1	0.5
1918	Bos-A	3	8	0	1	0	0	0	0	1	0	.125	.222	.125	347	5	-1	0			.900	-0	/2-2,3-1	-0.1
Total	12	983	3333	402	834	128	47	10	343	310	63	.250	.319	.326	645	95	-19	144	4		.928	7	S-822,2-138/3-8,O-1L	3.5
■ HAL WAGNER	Wagner, Harold Edward b: 7/2/15, E.Riverton, N.J. d: 8/7/79, Riverside, N.J. BL/TR, 6', 165 lbs. Deb: 10/3/37																							
1937	Phi-A	1	0	0	0	0	0	0	0	0	0	—	—	—	—	—	0	0	0	0	1.000	0	/C-1	0.0
1938	Phi-A	33	88	10	20	2	1	0	8	8	9	.227	.299	.273	572	45	-7	0	0	0	.972	-1	C-30	-0.7
1939	Phi-A	5	8	0	1	0	0	0	0	0	3	.125	.125	.125	250	-37	-2	0	0	0	1.000	2	/C-5	0.0
1940	Phi-A	34	75	9	19	5	1	0	10	11	6	.253	.356	.347	703	85	-1	0	0	0	.964	3	C-28	0.2
1941	Phi-A	46	131	18	29	8	2	1	15	19	9	.221	.320	.336	656	75	-5	1	0	0	.976	2	C-42	0.0
1942	Phi-A☆	104	288	26	68	17	1	1	30	24	29	.236	.304	.313	616	74	-10	1	0	0	.986	-2	C-94	-0.7
1943	Phi-A	111	289	22	69	17	1	1	26	36	17	.239	.327	.315	642	89	-4	3	3	-0	.980	-8	C-99	-0.7
1944	Phi-A	5	4	0	1	0	0	0	0	0	0	.250	.250	.250	500	44	-0	0	0	0	1.000	0	/C-1	0.0
	Bos-A	66	223	21	74	13	4	1	38	29	14	.332	.418	.439	857	147	15	1	1	-0	.970	0	C-64	1.9
	Yr	71	227	21	75	13	4	1	38	29	14	.330	.415	.436	852	145	15	1	1	-0	.971	0	C-65	1.9
1946	*Bos-A★	117	370	39	85	12	2	6	52	69	32	.230	.354	.322	675	85	-5	3	1	0	.983	-7	*C-116	-0.6

YEAR	TM/L	G	AB	R	H	2B	3B	HR	RBI	BB	SO	AVG	OBP	SLG	OPS	OPS+	BR+	SB	CS	SBR	FA	FR	G/POS	TPR
1947	Bos-A	21	65	5	15	3	0	0	6	9	5	.231	.324	.277	601	63	-3	0	0	0	.978	-1	C-21	-0.3
	Det-A	71	191	19	55	10	0	5	33	28	16	.288	.382	.419	801	119	5	0	1	-0	.990	-4	C-71	0.5
	Yr	92	256	24	70	13	0	5	39	37	21	.273	.367	.383	750	105	2	0	1	-0	.987	-5	C-92	0.2
1948	Det-A	54	109	10	22	3	0	0	10	20	11	.202	.326	.229	555	48	-8	1	0	0	.989	-4	C-52	-0.9
	Phi-N	3	4	0	0	0	0	0	0	0	0	.000	.000	.000	0	-99	-1	0			1.000	1	/C-1	0.0
1949	Phi-N	1	4	0	0	0	0	0	0	0	1	.000	.000	.000	0	-99	-1	0			.750	-1	/C-1	-0.2
Total	12	672	1849	179	458	90	12	15	228	253	152	.248	.343	.334	677	87	-26	10	6		.981	-21	C-626	-1.5

■ HONUS WAGNER

Wagner, John Peter "The Flying Dutchman"
b: 2/24/1874, Chartiers, Pa. d: 12/6/55, Carnegie, Pa. BR/TR (BB 1909 (part)), 5'11", 200 lbs. Deb: 7/19/1897 FMCH Career OF: (35-LF 67-CF 272-RF)

YEAR	TM/L	G	AB	R	H	2B	3B	HR	RBI	BB	SO	AVG	OBP	SLG	OPS	OPS+	BR+	SB	CS	SBR	FA	FR	G/POS	TPR
1897	Lou-N	62	242	38	81	18	4	2	39	15		.335	.376	.467	843	126	8	20			.912	4	O-53(1-53-0)/2-9	0.8
1898	Lou-N	151	588	80	176	29	3	10	105	31		.299	.341	.410	751	117	10	27			.972	-4	1-75,3-65,2-10	0.7
1899	Lou-N	148	575	100	196	45	13	7	114	40		.341	.395	.501	895	145	33	37			.920	2	3-76,O-61R/2-7,1-4	3.0
1900	*Pit-N	135	527	107	201	**45**	**22**	4	100	41		**.381**	.434	**.573**	**1007**	**175**	52	38			.965	-8	*O-118R/3-9,2-7,1P	3.5
1901	Pit-N	140	549	101	194	37	11	6	**126**	53		.353	.417	.494	911	159	41	**49**			.918	10	S-61,O-54R,3-24,/2	5.0
1902	Pit-N	136	534	**105**	176	**30**	16	3	**91**	43		.330	.394	**.463**	**857**	**159**	**36**	**42**			1.000	8	O-61R,S-44,1-32,/P2	4.4
1903	*Pit-N	129	512	97	182	30	**19**	5	101	44		**.355**	.414	.518	931	160	39	46			.933	25	*S-111,O-12R/1-6	**6.2**
1904	Pit-N	132	490	97	171	**44**	14	4	75	59		**.349**	**.423**	**.520**	**944**	**186**	**50**	**53**			.929	-6	*S-121/O-8L,1-3,2-2	**4.9**
1905	Pit-N	147	548	114	199	32	14	6	101	54		.363	.427	.505	932	173	49	57			.935	20	*S-145/O-2(2-0-0)	**7.5**
1906	Pit-N	142	516	**103**	175	**38**	9	2	71	58		**.339**	.416	.459	**875**	166	40	53			.941	24	*S-137/O-2(0-0-2),3-1	**7.4**
1907	Pit-N	142	515	98	180	**38**	14	6	82	46		**.350**	**.408**	**.513**	**921**	**186**	**49**	**61**			.938	4	*S-138/1-4	**6.4**
1908	Pit-N	151	568	100	**201**	**39**	**19**	10	**109**	54		**.354**	**.415**	**.542**	**957**	**205**	**65**	**53**			.943	-7	*S-151	**7.2**
1909	*Pit-N	137	495	92	168	**39**	10	5	**100**	66		**.339**	**.420**	**.489**	**909**	**168**	**40**	35			.940	6	*S-136/O-1(1-0-0)	**5.4**
1910	Pit-N	150	556	90	**178**	34	8	4	81	59	47	.320	.390	.432	822	132	23	24			.935	3	*S-138,1-11/2-2	3.2
1911	Pit-N	130	473	87	158	23	16	9	89	67	34	**.334**	.423	.507	**930**	154	35	20			.932	4	*S-101,1-28/O-1C	**4.4**
1912	Pit-N	145	558	91	181	35	20	7	**102**	59	38	.324	.395	.496	891	145	34	26			**.962**	23	*S-143	**6.4**
1913	Pit-N	114	413	51	124	18	4	3	56	26	40	.300	.349	.385	734	114	7	21			**.962**	13	*S-105	2.8
1914	Pit-N	150	552	60	139	15	9	1	50	51	51	.252	.317	.317	634	93	-5	23			**.950**	7	*S-132,3-17/1-1	1.2
1915	Pit-N	156	566	68	155	32	17	6	78	39	64	.274	.325	.422	747	127	16	22	15	-0	**.948**	-9	*S-131,2-12,1-10	1.8
1916	Pit-N	123	432	45	124	15	9	1	39	34	36	.287	.350	.370	721	120	11	11			.942	-15	S-92,1-24/2-4	0.2
1917	Pit-N	74	230	15	61	7	1	0	24	24	17	.265	.337	.304	642	94	-1	5			.985	-4	1-47,3-18/2-2,SM	-0.6
Total	21	2794	10439	1739	3420	643	252	101	1733	963	327	.328	.391	.467	858	150	635	723	15		.940	99	*S-1887,O-373R,13/2P	81.8

■ JOE WAGNER

Wagner, Joseph Bernard b: 4/24/1889, New York, N.Y. d: 11/15/48, Bronx, N.Y. BR/TR, 5'11", 165 lbs. Deb: 4/25/15

YEAR	TM/L	G	AB	R	H	2B	3B	HR	RBI	BB	SO	AVG	OBP	SLG	OPS	OPS+	BR+	SB	CS	SBR	FA	FR	G/POS	TPR
1915	Cin-N	75	197	17	35	5	2	0	13	8	35	.178	.210	.223	433	31	-17	4	6	-1	.961	6	2-46,S-12/3-2	-1.2

■ LEON WAGNER

Wagner, Leon Lamar "Daddy Wags" b: 5/13/34, Chattanooga, Tenn. BL/TR, 6'1", 195 lbs. Deb: 6/22/58

YEAR	TM/L	G	AB	R	H	2B	3B	HR	RBI	BB	SO	AVG	OBP	SLG	OPS	OPS+	BR+	SB	CS	SBR	FA	FR	G/POS	TPR
1958	SF-N	74	221	31	70	9	0	13	35	18	34	.317	.371	.534	905	139	12	1	0	0	.949	-0	O-57(57-0-0)	0.9
1959	SF-N	87	129	20	29	4	3	5	22	25	24	.225	.363	.419	782	110	2	0	0	0	.941	-2	O-28(28-0-0)	0.0
1960	StL-N	39	98	12	21	2	0	4	11	17	17	.214	.336	.357	693	83	-2	0	1	-0	.963	1	O-32(29-0-4)	-0.4
1961	LA-A	133	453	74	127	19	2	28	79	48	65	.280	.353	.517	870	116	10	5	1	1	.971	2	*O-116(104-0-14)	0.5
1962	LA-A★	160	612	96	164	21	5	37	107	50	87	.268	.328	.500	828	123	17	7	5	-0	.972	-7	*O-156(102-0-62)	0.1
1963	LA-A★	149	550	73	160	11	1	26	90	49	73	.291	.356	.456	813	134	24	5	7	-1	.960	-2	*O-141(136-0-7)	1.4
1964	Cle-A	163	641	94	162	19	2	31	100	56	121	.253	.319	.434	752	108	6	14	2	2	.959	-1	*O-163(163-0-0)	-0.2
1965	Cle-A	144	517	91	152	18	1	28	79	60	52	.294	.371	.495	866	143	29	12	2	2	.957	-9	*O-134(134-0-0)	1.5
1966	Cle-A	150	549	70	153	20	0	23	66	46	69	.279	.336	.441	776	121	14	5	2	0	.990	-8	*O-139(139-0-0)	-0.2
1967	Cle-A	135	433	56	105	15	1	15	54	37	76	.242	.320	.386	705	107	4	3	3	-0	.980	-7	*O-117(117-0-0)	-1.2
1968	Cle-A	38	49	5	9	4	0	0	6	6	6	.184	.273	.265	538	65	-2	0	0	0	.500	-3	O-10(7-0-3)	-0.7
	Chi-A	69	162	14	46	8	0	1	18	21	31	.284	.366	.352	718	117	4	2	1	0	.941	-8	O-46(9-1-36)	-0.7
	Yr	107	211	19	55	12	0	1	24	27	37	.261	.345	.332	676	106	2	2	1	0	.895	-11	O-56(16-1-39)	-1.4
1969	SF-N	11	12	0	4	0	0	0	2	2	1	.333	.467	.333	800	130	1	0	0	0	1.000	0	/O-1(1-0-0)	0.1
Total	12	1352	4426	636	1202	150	15	211	669	435	656	.272	.343	.455	798	121	118	54	24	3	.964	-44	*O-1140(1026-1-126)	1.1

■ MARK WAGNER

Wagner, Mark Duane b: 3/4/54, Conneaut, Ohio BR/TR, 6'1", 175 lbs. Deb: 8/20/76

YEAR	TM/L	G	AB	R	H	2B	3B	HR	RBI	BB	SO	AVG	OBP	SLG	OPS	OPS+	BR+	SB	CS	SBR	FA	FR	G/POS	TPR
1976	Det-A	39	115	9	30	2	3	0	12	6	18	.261	.298	.330	628	81	-3	0	2	-1	.947	10	S-39	1.1
1977	Det-A	22	48	4	7	0	1	1	3	4	12	.146	.226	.250	476	28	-5	0	1	-0	.923	-1	S-21/2-1	-0.4
1978	Det-A	39	109	10	26	1	2	0	6	3	11	.239	.272	.284	556	55	-6	1	0	0	.964	-6	S-35/2-4	-1.0
1979	Det-A	75	146	16	40	3	0	1	13	16	25	.274	.346	.315	661	77	-4	3	2	-0	.974	8	S-41,2-29/3-2,D-1	0.7
1980	Det-A	45	72	5	17	1	0	0	3	7	11	.236	.304	.250	554	52	-4	0	1	-0	.935	2	S-28/3-9,2-6	-0.1
1981	Tex-A	50	85	15	22	4	1	1	14	8	13	.259	.323	.365	687	103	0	1	1	-0	.964	2	S-43/2-4,3-2	0.5
1982	Tex-A	60	179	14	43	4	1	0	8	10	28	.240	.280	.274	554	56	-11	1	0	0	.955	-0	S-60	-0.5
1983	Tex-A	2	2	0	0	0	0	0	0	0	1	.000	.000	.000	0	-99	-1	0	0	0	1.000	1	/S-2	0.1
1984	Oak-A	82	87	8	20	5	1	0	12	7	11	.230	.287	.310	598	70	-4	2	0	0	.951	12	S-57,3-15/2-8,PD	1.0
Total	9	414	843	81	205	20	9	3	71	61	130	.243	.297	.299	596	66	-37	8	7	-1	.953	26	S-326/2-52,3-28,DP	1.4

■ BILL WAGNER

Wagner, William Joseph b: 1/2/1894, Jesup, Iowa d: 1/11/51, Waterloo, Iowa BR/TR, 6', 187 lbs. Deb: 7/16/14

YEAR	TM/L	G	AB	R	H	2B	3B	HR	RBI	BB	SO	AVG	OBP	SLG	OPS	OPS+	BR+	SB	CS	SBR	FA	FR	G/POS	TPR
1914	Pit-N	3	1	0	0	0	0	0	0	0	0	.000	.000	.000	0	-99	-0	0			1.000	0	/C-3	0.0
1915	Pit-N	5	5	0	0	0	0	0	0	1	2	.000	.167	.000	167	-48	-1	0			1.000	2	/C-3	0.1
1916	Pit-N	19	38	2	9	0	2	0	2	5	8	.237	.326	.342	668	104	0	0			.936	2	C-15	0.3
1917	Pit-N	53	151	15	31	7	2	0	9	11	22	.205	.264	.278	542	64	-6	1			.958	-4	C-37,1-12	-0.8
1918	Bos-N	13	47	2	10	0	0	1	7	4	5	.213	.275	.277	551	71	-2	0			.917	-5	C-13	-0.6
Total	5	93	242	19	50	7	4	1	18	21	37	.207	.273	.281	554	69	-9	1			.947	-5	/C-71,1-12	-1.0

■ KERMIT WAHL

Wahl, Kermit Emerson b: 11/18/22, Columbia, S.Dak. d: 9/16/87, Tucson, Ariz. BR/TR, 5'11", 170 lbs. Deb: 6/23/44

YEAR	TM/L	G	AB	R	H	2B	3B	HR	RBI	BB	SO	AVG	OBP	SLG	OPS	OPS+	BR+	SB	CS	SBR	FA	FR	G/POS	TPR
1944	Cin-N	4	1	0	0	0	0	0	0	0	0	.000	.000	.000	0	-99	-0	0			.000	0	/3-1	0.0
1945	Cin-N	71	194	18	39	8	2	0	10	23	22	.201	.286	.263	549	54	-12	2			.948	5	2-32,S-31/3-7	-0.4
1947	Cin-N	39	81	8	14	0	0	1	4	6	12	.173	.239	.210	449	20	-9	0			.964	6	3-20/S-9,2-2	-0.3
1950	Phi-A	89	280	26	72	12	3	2	27	30	30	.257	.331	.343	674	74	-11	1	1	-0	.946	11	3-61,S-18/2-2	0.1
1951	Phi-A	20	59	4	11	2	0	0	6	9	5	.186	.294	.220	514	40	-5	0	0	0	.967	2	3-18	-0.3
	StL-A	8	27	2	9	1	1	0	3	0	3	.333	.333	.444	778	106	0	0	0	0	.950	1	/3-6	0.1
	Yr	28	86	6	20	3	1	0	9	9	8	.233	.305	.291	596	60	-5	0	0	0	.962	3	3-24	-0.2
Total	5	231	642	58	145	23	6	3	50	68	72	.226	.302	.294	596	60	-37	3	1		.949	25	3-113/S-58,2-36	-0.8

■ EDDIE WAITKUS

Waitkus, Edward Stephen b: 9/4/19, Cambridge, Mass. d: 9/15/72, Jamaica Plain, Mass. BL/TL, 6'1", 175 lbs. Deb: 4/15/41

YEAR	TM/L	G	AB	R	H	2B	3B	HR	RBI	BB	SO	AVG	OBP	SLG	OPS	OPS+	BR+	SB	CS	SBR	FA	FR	G/POS	TPR
1941	Chi-N	12	28	1	5	0	0	0	0	0	3	.179	.207	.179	385	10	-3	0			.949	-1	/1-9	-0.5
1946	Chi-N	113	441	50	134	24	5	4	55	23	14	.304	.340	.408	748	114	6	3			.996	4	*1-106	0.7
1947	Chi-N	130	514	60	150	28	6	2	35	32	17	.292	.336	.381	717	94	-5	3			.994	8	*1-126	-0.1
1948	Chi-N★	139	562	87	166	27	10	7	44	43	19	.295	.348	.416	764	110	7	11			.992	7	*1-116,O-20(20-0-0)	0.8
1949	Phi-N†	54	209	41	64	16	3	1	28	33	12	.306	.403	.426	829	126	9	3			.994	1	1-54	0.8
1950	*Phi-N	154	641	102	182	32	5	2	44	55	29	.284	.341	.359	700	86	-12	3			.993	-2	*1-154	-2.0
1951	Phi-N	145	610	65	157	27	4	1	46	53	22	.257	.317	.320	636	73	-23	0	3	-1	.992	-2	*1-144	-3.1
1952	Phi-N	146	499	51	144	29	4	2	49	64	23	.289	.371	.375	745	108	7	2	2	-0	.991	-2	*1-146	0.1
1953	Phi-N	81	247	24	72	9	2	1	16	13	23	.291	.330	.356	686	79	-7	1	1	-0	.989	-1	1-59	-1.2
1954	Bal-A	95	311	35	88	17	4	2	33	28	25	.283	.344	.383	727	107	2	0	1	-0	1.000	1	1-78	-0.2
1955	Bal-A	38	85	2	22	1	1	0	9	11	10	.259	.344	.294	638	78	-2	2	0	0	.974	-2	1-26	-0.5
	Phi-N	33	107	10	30	5	0	2	14	17	7	.280	.379	.383	762	105	1	0	1	-0	.996	0	1-31	-0.1
Total	11	1140	4254	528	1214	215	44	24	373	372	204	.285	.344	.374	718	96	-20	28	8		.993	10	*1-1049/O-20(20-0-0)	-5.3

■ CHARLIE WAITT

Waitt, Charles C. b: 10/14/1853, Hallowell, Me. d: 10/21/12, San Francisco, Cal. TR, 5'11", 165 lbs. Deb: 5/25/1875

YEAR	TM/L	G	AB	R	H	2B	3B	HR	RBI	BB	SO	AVG	OBP	SLG	OPS	OPS+	BR+	SB	CS	SBR	FA	FR	G/POS	TPR
1875	StL-n	30	113	14	23	10	0	0	12	2	7	.204	.217	.292	509	83	-1	3	2	-0	.787	-3	O-28(2-7-23)/1-4	-0.3
1877	Chi-N	10	41	2	4	0	0	0	2	0	3	.098	.098	.098	195	-34	-6				.793	2	O-10(0-0-10)	-0.4

YEAR	TM/L	G	AB	R	H	2B	3B	HR	RBI	BB	SO	AVG	OBP	SLG	OPS	OPS+	BR+	SB	CS	SBR	FA	FR	G/POS	TPR
1882	Bal-a	72	250	19	39	4	0	0		13		.156	.198	.172	370	28	-17				.874	0	*O-72(60-0-12)	-1.7
1883	Phi-N	1	3	0	1	0	0	0	0	0	1	.333	.333	.333	667	114	0				.333	-1	/O-1(0-1-0)	-0.1
Total	3	83	294	21	44	4	0	0	2	13	4	.150	.186	.163	349	18	-23				.855	1	/O-83(60-1-22)	-2.2
■ **DON WAKAMATSU** Wakamatsu, Wilbur Donald b: 2/22/63, Hood River, Ore. BR/TR, 6'2", 200 lbs. Deb: 5/22/91																								
1991	Chi-A	18	31	2	7	0	0	0	0	1	6	.226	.250	.226	476	33	-3	0	0	0	1.000	-0	C-18	-0.3
■ **HOWARD WAKEFIELD** Wakefield, Howard John b: 4/2/1884, Bucyrus, Ohio d: 4/16/41, Chicago, Ill. BR/TR, 6'1", 185 lbs. Deb: 9/18/05 F																								
1905	Cle-A	10	26	3	4	0	0	0	1	0		.154	.185	.154	339	8	-3	0			.926	-3	/C-8	-0.6
1906	Was-A	77	211	17	59	9	2	1	21	7		.280	.303	.355	658	111	2	6			.946	-15	C-60	-0.8
1907	Cle-A	26	37	4	5	2	0	0	3	3		.135	.200	.189	389	24	-3	0			.930	-0	C-11	-0.3
Total	3	113	274	24	68	11	2	1	25	10		.248	.277	.314	591	89	-4	6			.943	-18	/C-79	-1.7
■ **DICK WAKEFIELD** Wakefield, Richard Cummings b: 5/6/21, Chicago, Ill. d: 8/26/85, Redford, Mich. BL/TR, 6'4", 210 lbs. Deb: 6/26/41 F																								
1941	Det-A	7	7	0	1	0	0	0	0	0	1	.143	.143	.143	286	-22	-1	0	0	0	1.000	-0	/O-1(0-0-1)	-0.1
1943	Det-A★	155	633	91	**200**	**38**	8	7	79	62	60	.316	.377	.434	811	127	22	4	5	-1	.959	-6	*O-155(140-0-15)	0.6
1944	Det-A	78	276	53	98	15	5	12	53	55	29	.355	.464	.576	1040	186	33	2	2	-0	.963	-4	O-78(78-0-0)	2.4
1946	Det-A	111	396	64	106	11	5	12	59	59	55	.268	.364	.412	776	110	6	3	5	-1	.964	0	*O-104(104-0-0)	-0.3
1947	Det-A	112	368	59	104	15	5	8	51	80	44	.283	.412	.416	828	127	17	1	4	-1	.950	-2	*O-101(101-0-0)	0.6
1948	Det-A	110	322	50	89	20	5	11	53	70	55	.276	.406	.472	878	129	15	0	1	-0	.948	0	O-86(86-0-0)	0.8
1949	Det-A	59	126	17	26	3	1	6	19	32	24	.206	.367	.389	756	100	2	0	0	0	1.000	2	O-32(32-0-0)	0.0
1950	NY-A	3	2	0	1	0	0	0	1	1	1	.500	.667	.500	1167	208	1	0	0	0	.000	0	H	0.0
1952	NY-N	3	2	0	0	0	0	0	0	1	1	.000	.333	.000	333	-0	-0	0	0	0	.000	0	H	0.0
Total	9	638	2132	334	625	102	29	56	315	360	270	.293	.396	.447	843	130	92	10	17	-4	.959	-11	O-557(541-0-16)	4.0
■ **MATT WALBECK** Walbeck, Matthew Lovick b: 10/2/69, Sacramento, Cal. BB/TR, 5'11", 190 lbs. Deb: 4/7/93																								
1993	Chi-N	11	30	2	6	2	0	1	6	1	6	.200	.226	.367	592	56	-2	0	0	0	1.000	-0	C-11	-0.2
1994	Min-A	97	338	31	69	12	0	5	35	17	37	.204	.246	.284	531	36	-32	1	1	-0	.993	-7	C-95/D-1	-3.1
1995	Min-A	115	393	40	101	18	1	1	44	25	71	.257	.303	.316	619	61	-22	3	1	0	.991	-15	*C-113	-2.8
1996	Min-A	63	215	25	48	10	0	2	24	9	34	.223	.254	.298	552	38	-20	3	1	0	.994	-5	C-61	-2.0
1997	Det-A	47	137	18	38	3	0	3	10	12	19	.277	.336	.365	701	83	-3	3	3	-0	.988	-2	C-44	-0.3
1998	Ana-A	108	338	41	87	15	2	6	46	30	68	.257	.322	.367	688	78	-11	1	1	-0	.990	7	*C-104/D-2	0.2
1999	Ana-A	107	288	26	69	8	1	3	22	26	46	.240	.309	.306	615	58	-18	2	3	-1	.989	-10	C-97/D-1	-2.2
2000	Ana-A	47	146	17	29	5	0	6	12	7	22	.199	.240	.356	596	48	-12	0	1	-0	.991	0	C-44/1-2,D-1	-0.9
Total	8	595	1885	200	447	73	4	27	199	127	303	.237	.288	.323	612	57	-121	13	11	-1	.991	-31	C-569/D-5,1-2	-11.3
■ **ED WALCZAK** Walczak, Edwin Joseph "Husky" b: 9/21/18, Arctic, R.I. d: 3/10/98, Norwich, Conn. BR/TR, 5'11", 180 lbs. Deb: 9/3/45																								
1945	Phi-N	20	57	6	12	3	0	0	2	6	9	.211	.286	.263	549	55	-3	0			.966	1	2-17/S-2	-0.2
■ **FRED WALDEN** Walden, Thomas Fred b: 6/25/1890, Fayette, Mo. d: 9/27/55, Jefferson Barracks, Mo. BR/TR, Deb: 6/3/12																								
1912	StL-A	1	0	0	0	0	0	0	0	0		—	—	—	—	—	0	0			.000	-1	/C-1	-0.1
■ **IRV WALDRON** Waldron, Irving J. b: 1/21/1876, Hillside, N.Y. d: 7/22/44, Worcester, Mass. BL/TR, 5'5.5", 155 lbs. Deb: 4/25/01																								
1901	Mil-A	62	266	48	79	8	6	0	29	16		.297	.342	.372	714	103	1	12			.883	-2	O-62(0-0-62)	-0.3
	Was-A	79	332	54	107	14	3	0	23	22		.322	.368	.383	751	110	5	8			.955	-5	O-78(0-69-9)	-0.4
	Yr	141	598	102	186	22	9	0	52	38		.311	.356	.378	734	107	6	20			.923	-7	*O-140(0-69-71)	-0.7
■ **JIM WALEWANDER** Walewander, James b: 5/2/62, Chicago, Ill. BB/TR, 5'10", 160 lbs. Deb: 5/31/87																								
1987	Det-A	53	54	24	13	3	1	1	4	7	6	.241	.328	.389	717	93	-0	2	1	0	1.000	15	2-24,3-17/S-3,D-8	1.4
1988	Det-A	88	175	23	37	5	0	0	6	12	26	.211	.262	.240	502	43	-13	11	4	1	.977	14	2-61/S-8,3-3,D-9	0.4
1990	NY-A	9	5	1	1	1	0	0	1	0	0	.200	.200	.400	600	64	-0	1	1	-0	1.000	1	/2-2,3-2,S-1,D-2	0.1
1993	Cal-A	12	8	2	1	0	0	0	3	5	1	.125	.462	.125	587	64	0	1	1	-0	1.000	6	/S-6,2-2,D-3	0.6
Total	4	162	242	50	52	9	1	1	14	24	33	.215	.286	.273	558	57	-14	15	7	1	.982	37	/2-89,D-22,3-22,S	2.5
■ **RUBE WALKER** Walker, Albert Bluford b: 5/16/26, Lenoir, N.C. d: 12/12/92, Morganton, N.C. BL/TR, 6'1", 185 lbs. Deb: 4/20/48 C																								
1948	Chi-N	79	171	17	47	8	0	5	26	24	17	.275	.371	.409	780	115	4	0			.980	-3	C-44	0.3
1949	Chi-N	56	172	11	42	4	1	3	22	9	18	.244	.282	.331	613	66	-9	0			.964	-5	C-43	-1.1
1950	Chi-N	74	213	19	49	7	1	6	16	18	34	.230	.290	.357	647	70	-10	0			.975	1	C-62	-0.5
1951	Chi-N	37	107	9	25	4	0	2	5	12	13	.234	.311	.327	638	71	-4	0	0	0	.969	-4	C-31	-0.7
	Bro-N	36	74	6	18	4	0	2	9	6	14	.243	.300	.378	678	80	-2	0	0	0	.972	-5	C-23	-0.6
	Yr	73	181	15	43	8	0	4	14	18	27	.238	.307	.348	655	74	-7	0	0	0	.970	-9	C-54	-1.3
1952	Bro-N	46	139	9	36	8	0	1	19	8	17	.259	.304	.338	642	77	-4	0	0	0	.987	5	C-40	0.3
1953	Bro-N	43	95	5	23	6	0	3	9	7	11	.242	.301	.400	701	79	-3	0	0	0	.978	1	C-28	-0.1
1954	Bro-N	50	155	12	28	7	0	5	23	24	17	.181	.294	.323	617	59	-9	0	0	0	.996	-2	C-47	-0.6
1955	Bro-N	48	103	6	26	5	0	2	13	15	11	.252	.347	.359	707	86	-2	1	0	0	.987	2	C-35	0.1
1956	*Bro-N	54	146	5	31	6	1	3	20	7	18	.212	.248	.329	577	50	-10	0	1	-0	.986	-1	C-43	-1.1
1957	Bro-N	60	166	12	30	8	0	2	23	15	33	.181	.249	.265	514	35	-15	2	0	0	.992	-6	C-50	-1.9
1958	LA-N	25	44	3	5	2	0	1	7	5	10	.114	.204	.227	431	14	-6	0	0	0	.985	-2	C-20	-0.7
Total	11	608	1585	114	360	69	3	35	192	150	213	.227	.296	.341	637	68	-71	3	1		.982	-15	C-466	-6.6
■ **TONY WALKER** Walker, Anthony Bruce b: 7/1/59, San Diego, Cal. BR/TR, 6'2", 205 lbs. Deb: 4/8/86																								
1986	Hou-N	84	90	19	20	7	0	2	10	11	15	.222	.307	.367	674	87	-2	11	3	1	.986	-14	O-68(0-69-0)	-1.5
■ **FRANK WALKER** Walker, Charles Franklin b: 9/22/1894, Enoree, S.C. d: 9/16/74, Bristol, Tenn. BR/TR, 5'11", 165 lbs. Deb: 9/6/17																								
1917	Det-A	2	2	0	0	0	0	0	0	0	1	.000	.000	.000	0	-99	-0	0			.000	0	H	-0.1
1918	Det-A	55	167	10	33	10	3	1	20	7	29	.198	.234	.311	546	67	-8	3			.922	-2	O-45(3-34-9)	-1.4
1920	Phi-A	24	91	10	21	2	2	0	10	5	14	.231	.286	.297	582	54	-6	0	2	-1	.983	-1	O-24(0-24-0)	-1.0
1921	Phi-A	19	66	6	15	3	0	1	6	8	11	.227	.311	.318	629	60	-4	1	0	0	.961	1	O-19(3-16-0)	-0.4
1925	NY-N	39	81	12	18	1	0	1	5	9	11	.222	.308	.272	579	51	-6	1	1	-0	.960	-2	O-21(0-21-0)	-0.8
Total	5	139	407	38	87	16	5	3	41	29	66	.214	.273	.300	572	58	-24	5	3		.949	-4	O-109(6-95-10)	-3.7
■ **TILLY WALKER** Walker, Clarence William b: 9/4/1887, Telford, Tenn. d: 9/20/59, Unicoi, Tenn BR/TR, 5'11", 165 lbs. Deb: 6/10/11 Career OF: (725-LF 577-CF 43-RF)																								
1911	Was-A	95	356	44	99	6	4	2	39	15		.278	.311	.334	645	82	-10	12			.917	-1	O-94(94-0-0)	-1.5
1912	Was-A	39	110	22	30	2	1	0	9	8		.273	.333	.309	642	83	-2	11			.837	-3	O-34(3-6-22)/2-1	-0.6
1913	StL-A	23	85	7	25	4	1	0	11	2	9	.294	.310	.365	675	100	-0	5			.911	-0	O-23(23-0-0)	-0.2
1914	StL-A	151	517	67	154	24	16	6	78	51	72	.298	.365	.441	806	148	28	29	17	0	.972	16	*O-145(145-0-0)	4.1
1915	StL-A	144	510	53	137	20	7	5	49	36	77	.269	.323	.365	688	110	4	20	17	-2	.940	15	*O-139(1-119-19)	0.8
1916	*Bos-A	128	467	68	124	29	11	3	46	23	45	.266	.303	.394	697	109	2	14			.959	-4	*O-128(3-125-0)	-1.1
1917	Bos-A	106	337	41	83	18	7	2	37	25	38	.246	.300	.359	659	102	-1	6			.972	6	O-96(0-96-0)	-0.2
1918	Phi-A	114	414	56	122	20	0	**11**	48	41	44	.295	.360	.423	782	135	16	8			.953	5	*O-109(0-109-0)	1.4
1919	Phi-A	125	456	47	133	30	6	10	64	26	41	.292	.330	.450	779	116	7	8			.933	-4	*O-115(28-85-2)	-0.4
1920	Phi-A	149	585	79	157	23	7	17	82	41	59	.268	.321	.419	739	94	-8	8	3	1	.940	6	*O-149(123-26-0)	-0.8
1921	Phi-A	142	556	89	169	32	5	23	101	73	41	.304	.389	.504	892	125	21	3	5	-1	.955	9	*O-142(142-0-0)	1.6
1922	Phi-A	153	565	111	160	31	4	37	99	61	67	.283	.357	.549	906	130	21	4	3	-0	.956	-2	*O-148(137-11-0)	0.8
1923	Phi-A	52	109	12	30	5	2	2	16	14	11	.275	.368	.413	781	104	1	1	2	-0	1.000	-2	O-26(26-0-0)	-0.3
Total	13	1421	5067	696	1423	244	71	118	679	416	504	.281	.339	.427	766	115	80	129	47		.949	41	*O-1348L/2-1	3.6
■ **CHICO WALKER** Walker, Cleotha b: 11/25/58, Jackson, Miss. BB/TR, 5'9", 179 lbs. Deb: 9/2/80 Career OF: (87-LF 66-CF 42-RF)																								
1980	Bos-A	19	57	3	12	0	0	1	5	6	10	.211	.297	.263	560	52	-4	3	2	-0	.958	1	2-11/D-7	-0.3
1981	Bos-A	6	17	3	6	0	0	0	2	1	2	.353	.389	.353	742	108	0	0	2	-1	1.000	-2	/2-5	-0.2
1983	Bos-A	4	5	2	2	0	2	0	1	0	0	.400	.400	1.200	1600	299	1	0	0	0	1.000	0	/O-3(3-0-0)	0.1
1984	Bos-A	3	2	0	0	0	0	0	1	0	1	.000	.000	.000	0	-96	-1	0	0	0	1.000	0	/2-1	0.0

YEAR	TM/L	G	AB	R	H	2B	3B	HR	RBI	BB	SO	AVG	OBP	SLG	OPS	OPS+	BR+	SB	CS	SBR	FA	FR	G/POS	TPR
1985	Chi-N	21	12	3	1	0	0	0	0	0	5	.083	.083	.083	167	-48	-2	1	0	0	1.000	-2	/O-6(3-0-3),2-2	-0.4
1986	Chi-N	28	101	21	28	3	2	1	7	10	20	.277	.342	.376	719	91	-1	15	4	2	.956	-5	O-26(1-11-22)	-0.5
1987	Chi-N	47	105	15	21	4	0	0	7	12	23	.200	.282	.238	520	38	-9	11	4	1	.974	-5	O-33(25-3-5)/3-2	-1.4
1988	Cal-A	33	78	8	12	1	0	0	2	6	15	.154	.214	.167	381	8	-9	2	1	0	.933	-2	O-17(5-12-0)/2-7,3-2	-1.2
1991	Chi-N	124	374	51	96	10	1	6	34	33	57	.257	.317	.337	654	80	-9	13	5	1	.929	-23	3-57,O-53C/2-6	-3.4
1992	Chi-N	19	26	2	3	0	0	0	2	3	4	.115	.207	.115	322	-6	-4	1	0	0	1.000	0	/O-6(6-0-1),2-2,3-2	-0.4
	NY-N	107	227	24	70	12	1	4	36	24	46	.308	.375	.423	797	127	8	14	1	3	.971	-7	3-36,2-16,O-15(9-4-2)	0.4
	Yr	126	253	26	73	12	1	4	38	27	50	.289	.357	.391	748	113	5	15	1	3	.960	-7	3-38,O-21L,2-18	0.0
1993	NY-N	115	213	18	48	7	1	5	19	14	29	.225	.273	.338	611	63	-11	7	0	2	.976	-4	2-24,3-23,O-15L	-1.3
Total	11	526	1217	150	299	37	7	17	116	109	212	.246	.308	.329	638	75	-41	67	19	8	.968	-49	O-174L,3-122/2-74,D	-8.6

■ **DUANE WALKER** Walker, Duane Allen b: 3/13/57, Pasadena, Tex. BL/TL, 6', 185 lbs. Deb: 5/25/82 Career OF: (148-LF 15-CF 93-RF)

YEAR	TM/L	G	AB	R	H	2B	3B	HR	RBI	BB	SO	AVG	OBP	SLG	OPS	OPS+	BR+	SB	CS	SBR	FA	FR	G/POS	TPR
1982	Cin-N	86	239	26	52	10	0	5	22	27	58	.218	.302	.322	624	73	-8	9	3	1	.992	0	O-69(40-2-31)	-1.1
1983	Cin-N	109	225	14	53	12	1	2	29	20	43	.236	.298	.324	622	70	-9	6	3	0	.956	0	O-60(35-0-26)	-1.1
1984	Cin-N	83	195	35	57	10	3	10	28	33	35	.292	.395	.528	923	150	14	7	3	0	.950	-5	O-68(51-13-9)	0.8
1985	Cin-N	37	48	5	8	2	1	2	6	6	18	.167	.259	.375	634	72	-2	1	0	0	.882	-1	O-10(8-0-2)	-0.3
	Tex-A	53	132	14	23	2	0	5	11	15	29	.174	.264	.303	567	54	-8	2	1	0	1.000	1	O-32(12-0-23),D-10	-0.9
1988	StL-N	24	22	1	4	1	0	0	3	2	7	.182	.250	.227	477	38	-2	0	0	0	.000	-2	/O-4(2-0-2),1-1	-0.4
Total	5	392	861	95	197	37	5	24	99	103	190	.229	.313	.367	680	86	-16	25	10	2	.967	-6	O-243L/D-10,1-1	-3.0

■ **ERNIE WALKER** Walker, Ernest Robert b: 9/17/1890, Blossburg, Ala. d: 4/1/65, Pell City, Ala. BL/TR, 6', 165 lbs. Deb: 4/13/13 F

YEAR	TM/L	G	AB	R	H	2B	3B	HR	RBI	BB	SO	AVG	OBP	SLG	OPS	OPS+	BR+	SB	CS	SBR	FA	FR	G/POS	TPR
1913	StL-A	7	14	0	3	0	0	0	2	0	5	.214	.214	.214	429	26	-1	0			1.000	-0	/O-2(0-2-0)	-0.2
1914	StL-A	74	131	19	39	5	3	1	14	13	26	.298	.366	.405	770	137	6	6	4	-0	.960	-6	O-38(19-9-9)	-0.2
1915	StL-A	50	109	15	23	4	2	0	9	23	32	.211	.348	.284	633	93	0	5	8	-2	.881	-6	O-33(3-3-27)	-1.0
Total	3	131	254	34	65	9	5	1	25	36	63	.256	.351	.343	693	112	4	11	12		.928	-12	/O-73(22-14-36)	-1.4

■ **DIXIE WALKER** Walker, Fred "The People's Cherce" b: 9/24/10, Villa Rica, Ga.
d: 5/17/82, Birmingham, Ala. BL/TR, 6'1", 175 lbs. Deb: 4/28/31 FC Career OF: (249-LF 312-CF 1204-RF)

YEAR	TM/L	G	AB	R	H	2B	3B	HR	RBI	BB	SO	AVG	OBP	SLG	OPS	OPS+	BR+	SB	CS	SBR	FA	FR	G/POS	TPR
1931	NY-A	2	10	1	3	2	0	0	1	0	4	.300	.300	.500	800	113	0	0	0	0	1.000	-0	/O-2(1-0-1)	0.0
1933	NY-A	98	328	68	90	15	7	15	51	26	28	.274	.330	.500	830	125	9	2	2	-0	.962	5	O-77(15-60-3)	1.1
1934	NY-A	17	17	2	2	0	0	0	0	1	3	.118	.167	.118	284	-27	-3	0	0	0	1.000	-0	/O-1(1-0-0)	-0.3
1935	NY-A	8	13	1	2	1	0	0	1	0	1	.154	.154	.231	385	-2	-2	0	0	0	.750	-1	/O-2(2-0-0)	-0.3
1936	NY-A	6	20	3	7	0	2	1	5	1	3	.350	.381	.700	1081	167	2	1	1	-0	1.000	-1	/O-5(0-5-0)	0.0
	Chi-A	26	70	12	19	2	0	0	11	14	6	.271	.400	.300	700	73	-2	1	0	0	1.000	1	O-17(0-16-1)	-0.1
	Yr	32	90	15	26	2	2	1	16	15	9	.289	.396	.389	785	92	-1	2	1	0	1.000	-0	O-22(0-21-1)	-0.1
1937	Chi-A	154	593	105	179	28	**16**	9	95	78	26	.302	.383	.449	832	109	9	1	2	-0	.952	-10	*O-154(0-0-154)	-1.0
1938	Det-A	127	454	84	140	27	6	6	43	65	32	.308	.396	.434	830	102	3	5	4	-0	.979	-9	*O-114(94-26-0)	-1.1
1939	Det-A	43	154	30	47	4	5	4	19	15	8	.305	.367	.474	841	106	1	4	1	1	.970	4	O-37(23-4-11)	0.3
	Bro-N	61	225	27	63	6	4	2	38	20	10	.280	.339	.369	708	87	-4	1			.968	2	O-59(0-59-0)	-0.3
1940	Bro-N	143	556	75	171	37	8	6	66	42	21	.308	.357	.435	793	111	8	3			.973	2	*O-136(14-112-20)	0.6
1941	*Bro-N	148	531	88	165	32	8	9	71	70	18	.311	.391	.452	843	131	23	4			.976	11	*O-146(22-22-105)	2.7
1942	Bro-N	118	393	57	114	28	1	6	54	47	15	.290	.367	.412	780	126	13	1			.986	-1	*O-110(0-7-104)	0.6
1943	Bro-N★	138	540	83	163	32	6	5	71	49	24	.302	.363	.411	774	123	16	3			.969	3	*O-136(57-0-82)	1.0
1944	Bro-N★	147	535	77	191	37	8	13	91	72	27	**.357**	.434	.529	963	173	53	6			.962	-3	*O-140(19-0-125)	4.2
1945	Bro-N†	154	607	102	182	42	9	8	**124**	75	16	.300	.381	.438	820	128	24	6			.992	12	*O-153(0-0-153)	2.6
1946	Bro-N★	150	576	80	184	29	9	9	116	67	28	.319	.391	.448	839	136	28	14			.969	-8	*O-149(0-0-149)	1.6
1947	*Bro-N★	148	529	77	162	31	3	9	94	97	26	.306	.415	.427	842	119	19	6			.964	-8	*O-147(0-0-147)	0.6
1948	Pit-N	129	408	39	129	19	3	2	54	52	18	.316	.393	.392	786	111	8	1			.977	-12	*O-112(1-1-110)	-0.7
1949	Pit-N	88	181	26	51	4	1	1	18	26	11	.282	.372	.331	703	88	-2	0			.984	-4	O-39(0-0-39)/1-3	-0.7
Total	18	1905	6740	1037	2064	376	96	105	1023	817	325	.306	.383	.437	820	121	203	59	10		.972	-16	*O-1736R/1-3	10.8

■ **GEE WALKER** Walker, Gerald Holmes b: 3/19/08, Gulfport, Miss. d: 3/20/81, Whitfield, Miss. BR/TR, 5'11", 188 lbs. Deb: 4/14/31 FC Career OF: (742-LF 463-CF 420-RF)

YEAR	TM/L	G	AB	R	H	2B	3B	HR	RBI	BB	SO	AVG	OBP	SLG	OPS	OPS+	BR+	SB	CS	SBR	FA	FR	G/POS	TPR
1931	Det-A	59	189	20	56	17	2	1	28	14	21	.296	.345	.423	768	98	-1	10	7	-0	.953	-3	O-44(1-41-1)	-0.5
1932	Det-A	127	480	71	155	32	6	8	78	13	38	.323	.345	.465	809	104	1	30	6	**5**	.949	4	*O-116(39-79-0)	0.5
1933	Det-A	127	483	68	135	29	7	9	64	15	49	.280	.304	.424	728	89	-10	26	9	**3**	.942	-1	*O-113(92-8-13)	-1.3
1934	*Det-A	98	347	54	104	19	2	6	39	19	20	.300	.340	.418	758	94	-4	20	9	1	.947	2	O-80(9-48-23)	-0.3
1935	*Det-A	98	362	52	109	22	6	7	53	15	21	.301	.329	.453	782	104	0	6	4	-0	.954	-3	O-85(29-45-11)	-0.6
1936	Det-A	134	550	105	194	55	5	12	93	23	30	.353	.387	.536	924	125	19	17	8	1	.948	5	*O-125(2-21-103)	1.6
1937	Det-A†	151	635	105	213	42	4	18	113	41	74	.335	.380	.499	880	117	15	23	7	3	.956	-6	*O-151(88-11-54)	0.3
1938	Chi-A	120	442	69	135	23	6	16	87	38	32	.305	.360	.493	854	109	5	9	4	1	.958	-5	*O-107(50-0-57)	-0.6
1939	Chi-A	149	598	95	174	30	11	13	111	28	43	.291	.330	.443	773	94	-8	17	6	2	.967	9	*O-147(147-0-0)	-0.5
1940	Was-A	140	595	87	175	29	7	13	96	24	58	.294	.325	.432	757	101	-2	21	4	3	.967	-2	*O-140(140-0-0)	-0.8
1941	Cle-A	121	445	56	126	26	11	6	48	18	46	.283	.313	.431	744	100	-3	12	6	1	.982	8	*O-105(103-2-0)	-0.1
1942	Cin-N	119	422	40	97	20	2	5	50	31	44	.230	.290	.322	613	79	-12	11			.973	4	*O-110(20-74-19)	-1.2
1943	Cin-N	114	429	48	105	23	2	3	54	12	38	.245	.270	.329	599	74	-16	6			.980	-5	*O-106(15-75-17)	-2.8
1944	Cin-N	121	478	56	133	21	3	5	62	23	48	.278	.318	.366	684	96	-4	7			.967	-7	*O-117(1-59-61)	-1.7
1945	Cin-N	106	316	28	80	11	2	2	21	16	38	.253	.289	.320	609	71	-13	8			.962	-7	O-67(6-0-61)/3-3	-2.5
Total	15	1784	6771	954	1991	399	76	124	997	330	600	.294	.331	.430	761	99	-32	223	70		.961	-7	*O-1613L/3-3	-10.5

■ **GREG WALKER** Walker, Gregory Lee b: 10/6/59, Douglas, Ga. BL/TR, 6'3", 210 lbs. Deb: 9/18/82

YEAR	TM/L	G	AB	R	H	2B	3B	HR	RBI	BB	SO	AVG	OBP	SLG	OPS	OPS+	BR+	SB	CS	SBR	FA	FR	G/POS	TPR
1982	Chi-A	11	17	3	7	2	1	2	7	2	3	.412	.474	1.000	1474	292	4	0	0	0	.000	0	/D-4	0.4
1983	*Chi-A	118	307	32	83	16	3	10	55	28	57	.270	.335	.440	775	107	3	2	1	0	.985	-7	1-59,D-21	-0.8
1984	Chi-A	136	442	62	130	29	2	24	75	35	66	.294	.349	.532	880	134	19	8	5	0	.995	-5	*1-101,D-21	0.8
1985	Chi-A	163	601	77	155	38	4	24	92	44	100	.258	.311	.454	765	102	0	5	2	0	.994	-3	*1-151/D-7	-1.1
1986	Chi-A	78	282	37	78	10	6	13	51	29	44	.277	.348	.493	841	122	8	1	2	-0	.993	-1	1-77/D-1	0.2
1987	Chi-A	157	566	85	145	33	2	27	94	75	112	.256	.348	.465	813	110	9	2	1	0	.994	-14	*1-154/D-3	-1.4
1988	Chi-A	99	377	45	93	22	1	8	42	29	77	.247	.306	.374	680	90	-6	0	1	-0	.993	-14	1-98	-2.8
1989	Chi-A	77	233	25	49	14	0	5	26	23	50	.210	.290	.335	624	77	-7	0	0	0	.987	-6	1-48,D-23	-1.7
1990	Chi-A	2	5	0	1	0	0	0	0	0	2	.200	.200	.200	400	12	-1	0	0	0	1.000	0	/1-1,D-1	0.0
	Bal-A	14	34	2	5	0	0	0	2	3	9	.147	.237	.147	384	10	-4	1	0	0	.000	0	D-11	-0.4
	Yr	16	39	2	6	0	0	0	2	3	11	.154	.233	.154	386	10	-5	1	0	0	1.000	0	D-12/1-1	-0.4
Total	9	855	2864	368	746	164	19	113	444	268	520	.260	.328	.449	777	108	26	19	12	-0	.993	-49	1-689/D-92	-6.8

■ **HARRY WALKER** Walker, Harry William "Harry The Hat" b: 10/22/16, Pascagoula, Miss.
d: 8/8/99, Birmingham, Ala. BL/TR, 6'2", 190 lbs. Deb: 9/25/40 FMC Career OF: (116-LF 522-CF 53-RF)

YEAR	TM/L	G	AB	R	H	2B	3B	HR	RBI	BB	SO	AVG	OBP	SLG	OPS	OPS+	BR+	SB	CS	SBR	FA	FR	G/POS	TPR
1940	StL-N	7	27	2	5	2	0	0	6	0	2	.185	.185	.259	444	20	-3	0			1.000	2	/O-7(2-5-1)	-0.1
1941	StL-N	7	15	3	4	1	0	0	1	2	1	.267	.353	.333	686	88	-0	0			.875	-1	/O-5(5-0-0)	-0.2
1942	*StL-N	74	191	38	60	12	2	0	16	11	14	.314	.355	.398	753	112	3	2			.968	-1	O-56(12-43-3)/2-2	0.0
1943	*StL-N★	148	564	76	166	28	6	2	53	40	24	.294	.341	.376	717	102	1	5			.965	-5	*O-144(0-143-1)/2-1	-0.9
1946	*StL-N	112	346	53	82	14	6	3	27	30	29	.237	.300	.338	638	77	-11	12			.974	5	O-92(13-79-0)/1-8	-0.9
1947	StL-N	10	25	2	5	1	0	0	0	4	2	.200	.310	.240	550	46	-2	0			.938	-2	O-10(2-7-0)	-0.4
	Phi-N★	130	488	79	181	28	16	1	41	59	37	.371	.443	.500	943	156	41	13			.966	14	*O-127(0-127-0)/1-4	4.9
	Yr	140	513	81	186	29	**16**	1	41	63	39	**.363**	.436	.487	924	150	39	13			.964	12	*O-137(2-134-0)/1-4	4.5
1948	Phi-N	112	332	34	97	11	2	2	23	33	30	.292	.358	.355	713	95	-1	4			.981	2	O-81(21-58-3)/1-4,3-1	-0.3
1949	Chi-N	42	159	20	42	6	3	1	14	11	6	.264	.312	.358	670	81	-4	2			.947	-3	O-39(27-0-13)	-1.0
	Cin-N	86	314	53	100	15	2	1	23	34	17	.318	.385	.389	774	107	4	4			.963	2	O-77(22-26-29)/1-1	0.2
	Yr	128	473	73	142	21	5	2	37	45	23	.300	.361	.378	739	99	-0	6			.959	-2	*O-116(49-26-42)/1-1	-0.8
1950	StL-N	60	150	17	31	5	0	0	7	18	12	.207	.292	.240	532	40	-13	0			.969	-1	O-46(9-30-3)/1-2	-1.5
1951	StL-N	8	26	6	8	1	0	0	2	2	1	.308	.357	.346	703	90	-0	0	0	0	1.000	-1	/O-6(2-4-0),1-1	-0.2
1955	StL-N	11	14	2	5	2	0	0	1	1	0	.357	.400	.500	900	137	1	0	0	0	1.000	1	/O-1(1-0-0),M	0.2
Total	11	807	2651	385	786	126	37	10	214	245	175	.296	.358	.383	741	103	16	42	0		.968	10	O-691C/1-20,2-3,3-1	-0.2

YEAR	TM/L	G	AB	R	H	2B	3B	HR	RBI	BB	SO	AVG	OBP	SLG	OPS	OPS+	BR+	SB	CS	SBR	FA	FR	G/POS	TPR
■ HUB WALKER	Walker, Harvey Willos b: 8/17/06, Gulfport, Miss. d: 11/26/82, San Jose, Cal. BL/TR, 5'10.5", 175 lbs. Deb: 4/15/31 F Career OF: (51-LF 154-CF 7-RF)																							
1931	Det-A	90	252	27	72	13	1	0	16	23	25	.286	.355	.345	700	82	-6	10	1	2	.961	-0	O-66(4-60-2)	-0.6
1935	Det-A	9	25	4	4	3	0	0	1	3	4	.160	.250	.280	530	38	-2	0	0	0	1.000	-0	/O-7(0-7-0)	-0.3
1936	Cin-N	92	258	49	71	18	1	4	23	35	32	.275	.366	.399	765	113	6	8			.970	-4	O-73(25-47-2)/C-1,1-1	-0.1
1937	Cin-N	78	221	33	55	9	4	1	19	34	24	.249	.349	.339	688	92	-1	7			.993	4	O-58(17-40-1)/2-3	0.0
1945	*Det-A	28	23	4	3	0	0	0	1	9	4	.130	.375	.130	505	46	-1	1	0	0	1.000	-2	/O-7(5-0-2)	-0.3
Total	5	297	779	117	205	43	6	5	60	104	89	.263	.354	.353	707	92	-5	26	1		.975	-4	O-211C/2-3,1-1,C-1	-1.3
■ JOHNNY WALKER	Walker, John Miles b: 12/11/1896, Toulon, Ill. d: 8/19/76, Hollywood, Fla. BR/TR, 6', 175 lbs. Deb: 9/19/19																							
1919	Phi-A	3	9	0	0	0	0	0	0	0	2	.000	.000	.000	0	-99	-2	0			.941	-0	/C-3	-0.2
1920	Phi-A	9	22	0	5	1	0	0	5	0	1	.227	.227	.273	500	32	-2	0	0	0	.960	-1	/C-6	-0.2
1921	Phi-A	113	423	41	109	14	5	2	46	9	29	.258	.278	.329	607	54	-30	5	0	1	.989	-6	1-99/C-7	-4.0
Total	3	125	454	41	114	15	5	2	51	9	32	.251	.270	.319	590	50	-35	5	0		.968	-7	/1-99,C-16	-4.4
■ SPEED WALKER	Walker, Joseph Richard b: 1/23/1898, Munhall, Pa. d: 6/20/59, W.Mifflin, Pa. BR/TR, 6', 170 lbs. Deb: 9/15/23																							
1923	StL-N	2	7	1	2	0	0	0	0	0	1	.286	.286	.286	571	52	-0	0	0	0	1.000	-0	/1-2	-0.1
■ LARRY WALKER	Walker, Larry Kenneth Robert b: 12/1/66, Maple Ridge, B.C., Canada BL/TR, 6'3", 215 lbs. Deb: 8/16/89 Career OF: (33-LF 68-CF 1175-RF)																							
1989	Mon-N	20	47	4	8	0	0	0	4	5	13	.170	.264	.170	434	26	-4	1	1	-0	1.000	0	O-15(2-0-13)	-0.5
1990	Mon-N	133	419	59	101	18	3	19	51	49	112	.241	.328	.434	762	112	6	21	7	2	.985	9	*O-124(0-0-123)	1.4
1991	Mon-N	137	487	59	141	30	2	16	64	42	102	.290	.352	.458	810	128	17	14	9	-0	.991	9	*O-102(0-5-99),1-39	2.1
1992	Mon-N★	143	528	85	159	31	4	23	93	41	97	.301	.358	.506	864	143	28	18	6	2	.993	14	*O-139(0-0-139)	4.2
1993	Mon-N	138	490	85	130	24	5	22	86	80	76	.265	.375	.469	844	119	15	29	7	4	.979	10	*O-132(0-0-132)/1-4	2.1
1994	Mon-N	103	395	76	127	**44**	2	19	86	47	74	.322	.399	.587	986	151	30	15	5	2	.973	4	O-68(0-0-68),1-35	2.7
1995	*Col-N	131	494	96	151	31	5	36	101	49	72	.306	.384	.607	991	121	15	16	3	2	.988	1	*O-129(0-4-129)	1.2
1996	Col-N	83	272	58	75	18	4	18	58	20	58	.276	.346	.570	915	110	3	18	2	3	.994	-3	O-83(0-54-33)	0.2
1997	Col-N★	153	568	143	208	46	4	**49**	130	78	90	.366	**.455**	**.720**	**1175**	164	54	33	8	4	.992	-4	*O-151R/1-3,D-1	4.5
1998	Col-N★	130	454	113	165	46	3	23	67	64	61	**.363**	.446	.630	1076	147	33	14	4	2	.984	2	*O-123R/2-1,3-1,D-1	3.0
1999	Col-N★	127	438	108	166	26	4	37	115	57	52	**.379**	**.464**	**.710**	**1174**	151	35	11	4	1	.982	7	*O-114(0-0-114)/D-1	3.4
2000	Col-N	87	314	64	97	21	7	9	51	46	40	.309	.412	.506	918	102	2	5	5	-1	.994	10	O-83(31-0-52)/D-3	0.8
Total	12	1385	4906	950	1528	335	43	271	906	578	847	.311	.394	.563	957	134	235	195	61	22	.987	57	*O-1263R/1-81,D-6,32	25.1
■ FLEET WALKER	Walker, Moses Fleetwood b: 10/7/1856, Mt.Pleasant, Ohio d: 5/11/24, Cleveland, Ohio BR/TR, 159 lbs. Deb: 5/1/1884 F																							
1884	Tol-a	42	152	23	40	2	3	0		8		.263	.325	.316	641	106	1				.887	-6	C-41/O-1(1-0-0)	-0.1
■ OSCAR WALKER	Walker, Oscar b: 3/18/1854, Brooklyn, N.Y. d: 5/20/1889, Brooklyn, N.Y. BL/TL, 5'10", 166 lbs. Deb: 9/17/1875 Career OF: (20-LF 124-CF 5-RF)																							
1875	Atl-n	1	2	0	0	0	0	0	0	1	0	.000	.333	.000	333	30	-0	0	0	0	.400	-0	/1-1,O-1(0-0-1)	0.0
1879	Buf-N	72	287	35	79	15	6	1	35	8	38	.275	.295	.380	675	118	5				.946	3	*1-72	0.4
1880	Buf-N	34	126	12	29	4	2	1	15	6	18	.230	.265	.317	583	95	-1				.917	-2	1-24,O-11(3-7-1)	-0.3
1882	StL-a	76	318	48	76	15	7	**7**		10		.239	.262	.396	658	115	4				.846	8	*O-75(1-74-0)/2-1,1-1	0.8
1884	Bro-a	95	382	59	103	12	8	2		9		.270	.292	.359	651	110	4				.868	0	O-59(16-43-0),1-36	-0.1
1885	Bal-a	4	13	1	0	0	0	0	1	0		.000	.000	.000	0	-99	-3				.667	-1	/O-4(0-0-4)	-0.4
Total	5	281	1126	155	287	46	23	11	51	33	56	.255	.278	.366	644	109	9				.850	8	O-149C,1-133/2-1	0.4
■ TODD WALKER	Walker, Todd Arthur b: 5/25/73, Bakersfield, Cal. BL/TR, 6', 180 lbs. Deb: 8/30/96																							
1996	Min-A	25	82	8	21	6	0	0	6	4	13	.256	.291	.329	620	55	-6	2	0	0	.956	-0	3-20/2-4,D-1	-0.5
1997	Min-A	52	156	15	37	7	1	3	16	11	30	.237	.292	.353	644	66	-8	7	0	2	.969	2	3-40/2-8,D-2	-0.4
1998	Min-A	143	528	85	167	41	3	12	62	47	65	.316	.374	.473	848	117	13	19	7	2	.978	-23	*2-140/D-1	-0.1
1999	Min-A	143	531	62	148	37	4	6	46	52	83	.279	.344	.397	742	85	-11	18	10	0	.984	-15	*2-103,D-40	-2.2
2000	Min-A	23	77	14	18	1	0	2	8	7	10	.234	.298	.325	622	55	-5	3	0	1	.946	-8	2-19/D-2	-1.1
	Col-N	57	171	28	54	10	4	7	36	20	19	.316	.391	.544	934	104	1	4	1	1	.975	-3	2-52	0.1
Total	5	443	1545	212	445	102	12	30	174	141	220	.288	.349	.428	777	93	-15	53	18	5	.978	-47	2-326/3-60,D-46	-4.2
■ WALT WALKER	Walker, Walter S. b: 3/12/1860, Berlin, Mich. d: 2/28/22, Pontiac, Mich. TR, 5'10.5", 162 lbs. Deb: 5/8/1884																							
1884	Det-N	1	4	1	1	0	0	0	0	0	0	.250	.250	.250	500	61	-0				.750	-1	C-1	-0.1
■ WELDAY WALKER	Walker, Welday Wilberforce b: 6/1859, Steubenville, Ohio d: 11/23/37, Steubenville, Ohio Deb: 7/15/1884 F																							
1884	Tol-a	5	18	1	4	1	0	0	2	0		.222	.222	.278	500	60	-1				.667	-1	/O-5(4-1-0)	-0.2
■ CURT WALKER	Walker, William Curtis b: 7/3/1896, Beeville, Tex. d: 12/9/55, Beeville, Tex. BL/TR, 5'9.5", 170 lbs. Deb: 9/17/19 Career OF: (105-LF 95-CF 1120-RF)																							
1919	NY-A	1	1	0	0	0	0	0	0	0	0	.000	.000	.000	0	-99	-0	0			.000	0	H	0.0
1920	NY-N	8	14	0	1	0	0	0	0	1	3	.071	.133	.071	205	-41	-3	0	0	0	1.000	-1	/O-4(1-2-1)	-0.4
1921	NY-N	64	192	30	55	13	5	3	35	15	8	.286	.338	.453	791	107	2	4	3	-0	.978	1	O-58(0-46-13)	-0.1
	Phi-N	21	77	11	26	2	1	0	8	5	5	.338	.378	.390	768	96	-0	0	2	-1	.970	-5	O-21(7-7-10)	-0.7
	Yr	85	269	41	81	15	6	3	43	20	13	.301	.349	.435	784	104	1	4	5	-1	.976	-4	O-79(7-53-23)	-0.8
1922	Phi-N	148	581	102	196	36	11	12	89	56	46	.337	.399	.499	899	119	17	11	4	1	.955	6	*O-147(0-0-147)	1.1
1923	Phi-N	140	527	66	148	26	5	5	66	45	31	.281	.337	.378	715	79	-15	12	12	-2	.947	5	*O-137(12-0-125)/1-1	-2.2
1924	Phi-N	24	71	11	21	6	1	1	8	7	4	.296	.359	.451	810	103	0	0	1	-0	.900	-4	O-20(0-0-20)	-0.5
	Cin-N	109	397	55	119	21	10	4	46	44	15	.300	.371	.433	804	117	10	7	5	-0	.978	0	*O-109(3-23-86)	0.2
	Yr	133	468	66	140	27	11	5	54	51	19	.299	.369	.436	805	114	10	7	6	-1	.969	-4	*O-129(3-23-106)	-0.3
1925	Cin-N	145	509	86	162	22	16	6	71	57	31	.318	.387	.460	847	118	15	14	11	-1	**.983**	2	*O-141(4-15-124)	0.5
1926	Cin-N	155	571	83	175	24	20	6	78	60	31	.306	.372	.450	823	124	19	3			.961	4	*O-152(1-0-151)	1.0
1927	Cin-N	146	527	60	154	16	10	6	80	47	19	.292	.350	.395	745	102	2	5			.957	3	*O-141(0-0-141)	-0.7
1928	Cin-N	123	427	64	119	15	12	6	73	49	14	.279	.354	.412	766	101	1	19			.955	4	*O-122(0-0-122)	-0.5
1929	Cin-N	141	492	76	154	28	15	7	83	85	17	.313	.416	.474	890	126	23	17			.969	-6	*O-138(0-0-138)	0.6
1930	Cin-N	134	472	74	145	26	11	8	51	64	30	.307	.391	.460	851	110	9	4			.965	-6	*O-120(77-2-42)	-0.5
Total	12	1359	4858	718	1475	235	117	64	688	535	254	.304	.374	.440	813	110	79	96	38		.963	2	*O-1310R/1-1	-2.2
■ HOWARD WALL	Wall, Howard C. b: 1855, Washington, D.C. d: 3/15/09, Washington, D.C. Deb: 9/13/1873																							
1873	Was-n	1	4	1	1	0	0	0	0	0	0	.250	.250	.250	500	51	-0	0	0	0	.000	0	/S-1	0.0
■ JOE WALL	Wall, Joseph Francis "Gummy" b: 7/24/1873, Brooklyn, N.Y. d: 7/17/36, Brooklyn, N.Y. BL/TL, Deb: 9/22/01																							
1901	NY-N	4	8	0	4	0	0	0	1	0		.500	.500	.500	1000	198	1	0			1.000	-3	/C-2,O-1(0-0-1)	-0.1
1902	NY-N	6	14	2	5	2	0	0	0	2		.357	.438	.500	938	191	2	0			1.000	-0	/O-3(0-0-3)	0.1
	Bro-N	5	18	0	3	0	0	0	0	3		.167	.318	.167	485	50	-1	0			.893	-3	/C-5	-0.4
	Yr	11	32	2	8	2	0	0	0	5		.250	.368	.313	681	111	1	0			.893	-3	/C-5,O-3(0-0-3)	-0.3
Total	2	15	40	2	12	2	0	0	1	5		.300	.391	.350	741	127	2	0			.903	-6	/C-7,O-4(0-0-4)	-0.4
■ JACK WALLACE	Wallace, Clarence Eugene b: 8/6/1890, Winnfield, La. d: 10/15/60, Winnfield, La. BR/TR, 5'10.5", 175 lbs. Deb: 9/27/15																							
1915	Chi-N	2	7	1	2	0	0	0	1	0	2	.286	.375	.286	661	101	0	0			1.000	2	/C-2	0.2
■ DON WALLACE	Wallace, Donald Allen b: 8/25/40, Sapulpa, Okla. BL/TR, 5'8", 165 lbs. Deb: 4/12/67																							
1967	Cal-A	23	6	2	0	0	0	0	0	3	2	.000	.333	.000	333	6	-1	0	1	-0	1.000	2	/2-4,1-1,3-1	0.1
■ DOC WALLACE	Wallace, Frederick Renshaw "Jesse" b: 9/30/1893, Church Hill, Md. d: 12/31/64, Haverford, Pa. BR/TR, 5'6.5", 135 lbs. Deb: 5/2/19																							
1919	Phi-N	2	4	0	1	0	0	0	0	0	1	.250	.250	.250	500	47	-0	0			.875	0	/S-2	0.0
■ JIM WALLACE	Wallace, James L. b: 11/14/1881, Boston, Mass. d: 5/16/53, Revere, Mass. BL/TL, 5'9", 150 lbs. Deb: 8/24/05																							
1905	Pit-N	7	29	3	6	1	0	0	3	3		.207	.281	.241	523	55	-2	2			.929	1	/O-7(0-0-7)	-0.1
■ BOBBY WALLACE	Wallace, Rhoderick John b: 11/4/1873, Pittsburgh, Pa. d: 11/3/60, Torrance, Cal. BR/TR, 5'8", 170 lbs. Deb: 9/15/1894 MUCH Career OF: (4-LF 6-CF 16-RF)																							
1894	Cle-N	4	13	0	2	1	0	0	1	0	1	.154	.154	.231	385	-8	-2	0			1.000	1	/P-4	0.0

YEAR	TM/L	G	AB	R	H	2B	3B	HR	RBI	BB	SO	AVG	OBP	SLG	OPS	OPS+	BR+	SB	CS	SBR	FA	FR	G/POS	TPR
1895	Cle-N	30	98	16	21	2	3	0	10	6	17	.214	.274	.296	570	44	-9	0			.910	3	P-30	0.0
1896	*Cle-N	45	149	19	35	6	3	1	17	11	21	.235	.287	.336	623	60	-9	2			.950	-2	O-23(3-6-15),P-22/1-1	-0.7
1897	Cle-N	130	516	99	173	33	21	4	112	48		.335	.394	.504	898	129	20	14			.928	3	*3-130/O-1(1-0-0)	2.1
1898	Cle-N	154	593	81	160	25	13	3	99	63		.270	.344	.371	715	106	5	7			.936	17	*3-141,2-13	2.3
1899	StL-N	151	577	91	170	28	14	12	108	54		.295	.357	.454	811	119	13	17			.919	39	*S-100,3-52	5.1
1900	StL-N	126	485	70	130	25	9	4	70	40		.268	.328	.381	709	96	-3	7			.934	3	*S-126/3-1	0.5
1901	StL-N	134	550	69	178	34	15	2	91	20		.324	.351	.451	802	138	24	15			.929	**30**	*S-134	**5.6**
1902	StL-A	133	494	71	141	32	9	1	63	45		.285	.350	.393	743	107	5	18			.948	11	*S-131/P-1,O-1(0-0-1)	1.9
1903	StL-A	135	511	63	136	21	7	1	54	28		.266	.309	.341	650	97	-2	10			.924	18	*S-135	2.1
1904	StL-A	139	541	57	149	29	4	2	69	42		.275	.330	.355	685	124	15	20			**.947**	8	*S-139	3.1
1905	StL-A	156	587	67	159	25	9	1	59	45		.271	.324	.349	673	120	13	13			.935	20	*S-156	4.1
1906	StL-A	139	476	64	123	21	7	2	67	58		.258	.344	.345	688	121	13	24			.949	3	*S-138	2.2
1907	StL-A	147	538	56	138	20	7	0	70	54		.257	.328	.320	647	107	5	16			.941	7	*S-147	1.9
1908	StL-A	137	487	59	123	24	4	1	60	52		.253	.327	.324	652	111	7	5			**.951**	18	*S-137	3.3
1909	StL-A	116	403	36	96	12	2	0	35	38		.238	.310	.278	588	92	-3	7			.946	11	S-87,3-29	1.3
1910	StL-A	138	508	47	131	19	7	0	37	49		.258	.324	.323	647	110	6	12			.948	22	S-99,3-39	3.5
1911	StL-A	125	410	35	95	12	2	0	31	46		.232	.312	.271	583	66	-18	8			.943	2	*S-124/2-1,M	-0.8
1912	StL-A	100	323	39	78	14	5	0	31	43		.241	.332	.316	648	89	-4	3			.942	8	S-87,3-10/2-2,M	1.1
1913	StL-A	55	147	11	31	5	0	0	21	14	16	.211	.293	.245	538	59	-7	1			.931	-5	S-39/3-7	-1.0
1914	StL-A	26	73	3	16	2	1	0	5	5	13	.219	.269	.274	543	66	-3	1	1	-0	.889	-11	S-19/3-2	-1.5
1915	StL-A	9	13	1	3	0	1	0	4	5	0	.231	.444	.385	829	154	1	0	1	-0	.848	1	/S-9	0.2
1916	StL-A	14	18	0	5	0	0	0	1	2	1	.278	.350	.278	628	93	-0	0			.958	5	/3-9,S-5	0.6
1917	StL-N	8	10	0	1	0	0	0	2	0	1	.100	.100	.100	200	-40	-2	0			1.000	-1	/3-5,S-2	-0.3
1918	StL-N	32	98	3	15	1	0	0	4	6	9	.153	.202	.163	365	12	-10	1			.959	2	2-17,S-12/3-1	-0.9
Total	25	2383	8618	1057	2309	391	143	34	1121	774	79	.268	.332	.358	690	106	55	201	2		.938	212	*S-1826,3-426/P2O1	35.7

■ **TIM WALLACH** Wallach, Timothy Charles b: 9/14/57, Huntington Park, Cal. BR/TR, 6'3", 200 lbs. Deb: 9/6/80 Career OF: (4-LF 0-CF 36-RF)

YEAR	TM/L	G	AB	R	H	2B	3B	HR	RBI	BB	SO	AVG	OBP	SLG	OPS	OPS+	BR+	SB	CS	SBR	FA	FR	G/POS	TPR
1980	Mon-N	5	11	1	2	0	0	1	2	1	5	.182	.250	.455	705	93	-0	0	0	0	1.000	-1	/O-3(2-0-1),1-1	-0.2
1981	*Mon-N	71	212	19	50	9	1	4	13	15	37	.236	.299	.344	643	81	-5	0	1	-0	1.000	-4	O-35R,1-16,3-15	-1.4
1982	Mon-N	158	596	89	160	31	3	28	97	36	81	.268	.314	.471	786	115	9	6	4	-0	.948	-6	*3-156/O-2(1-0-1),1-1	0.1
1983	Mon-N	156	581	54	156	33	3	19	70	55	97	.269	.338	.434	772	113	9	0	3	-1	.956	-7	*3-156	-0.1
1984	Mon-N★	160	582	55	143	25	4	18	72	50	101	.246	.313	.395	708	102	0	3	7	-2	.959	16	*3-160/S-1	1.3
1985	Mon-N★	155	569	70	148	36	3	22	81	38	79	.260	.312	.450	762	117	10	9	9	-1	.967	37	*3-154	4.5
1986	Mon-N	134	480	50	112	22	1	18	71	44	72	.233	.311	.396	707	94	-5	8	4	0	.958	15	*3-132	0.9
1987	Mon-N★	153	593	89	177	**42**	4	26	123	37	98	.298	.347	.514	861	121	16	9	5	0	.952	-0	*3-150/P-1	1.4
1988	Mon-N	159	592	52	152	32	5	12	69	38	88	.257	.305	.389	693	93	-6	2	6	-2	.962	12	*3-153/2-1	0.5
1989	Mon-N★	154	573	76	159	**42**	0	13	77	58	81	.277	.345	.419	764	116	12	3	7	-2	.958	6	*3-153/P-1	1.7
1990	Mon-N★	161	626	69	185	37	5	21	98	42	80	.296	.343	.471	814	126	20	6	9	-2	.954	4	*3-161	2.3
1991	Mon-N	151	577	60	130	22	1	13	73	50	100	.225	.294	.334	628	77	-18	2	4	-1	**.968**	6	*3-149	-1.3
1992	Mon-N	150	537	53	120	29	1	9	59	50	90	.223	.299	.331	631	79	-15	2	2	-0	.964	18	3-85,1-71	-0.2
1993	LA-N	133	477	42	106	19	1	12	62	32	70	.222	.275	.342	617	68	-23	0	2	-1	.958	0	*3-130/1-1	-2.3
1994	LA-N	113	414	68	116	21	1	23	78	46	80	.280	.358	.502	860	130	17	0	2	-1	.959	-10	*3-113	0.7
1995	*LA-N	97	327	24	87	22	2	9	38	27	69	.266	.330	.428	758	107	3	0	0	0	**.976**	-11	3-96/1-1	-0.7
1996	Cal-A	57	190	23	45	7	0	8	20	18	47	.237	.306	.400	706	76	-7	1	0	0	.941	2	3-46/1-3,D-8	-0.4
	*LA-N	45	162	14	37	3	1	4	22	12	32	.228	.286	.333	619	68	-8	0	1	-0	.971	-7	3-45	-1.5
Total	17	2212	8099	908	2085	432	36	260	1125	649	1307	.257	.319	.416	735	103	11	51	66	-12	.959	71	*3-2054/1-94,ODP2S	5.3

■ **JACK WALLAESA** Wallaesa, John b: 8/31/19, Easton, Pa. d: 12/27/86, Easton, Pa. BB/TR (BR 1940), 6'3", 191 lbs. Deb: 9/22/40 Career OF: (23-LF 0-CF 0-RF)

YEAR	TM/L	G	AB	R	H	2B	3B	HR	RBI	BB	SO	AVG	OBP	SLG	OPS	OPS+	BR+	SB	CS	SBR	FA	FR	G/POS	TPR
1940	Phi-A	6	20	0	3	0	0	0	2	0	2	.150	.150	.150	300	-22	-4	0	0	0	.903	1	/S-6	-0.2
1942	Phi-A	36	117	13	30	4	1	2	13	8	26	.256	.315	.359	674	90	-2	0	1	-0	.920	-7	S-36	-0.7
1946	Phi-A	63	194	16	38	4	2	5	11	14	47	.196	.250	.314	564	57	-12	1	0	0	.916	-16	S-59	-2.6
1947	Chi-A	81	205	25	40	9	1	7	32	23	51	.195	.279	.351	631	78	-7	2	2	-0	.968	13	S-27,O-22(22-0-0)/3-1	0.6
1948	Chi-A	33	48	2	9	0	0	1	3	1	12	.188	.204	.250	454	21	-6	0	0	0	1.000	-0	/S-5,O-1(1-0-0)	-0.5
Total	5	219	584	56	120	17	4	15	61	46	138	.205	.267	.325	592	65	-30	3	3	-0	.933	-10	S-133/O-23L,3-1	-3.4

■ **NORM WALLEN** Wallen, Norman Edward (b: Norman Edward Walentoski) b: 2/13/17, Milwaukee, Wis. BR/TR, 5'11.5", 175 lbs. Deb: 4/20/45

YEAR	TM/L	G	AB	R	H	2B	3B	HR	RBI	BB	SO	AVG	OBP	SLG	OPS	OPS+	BR+	SB	CS	SBR	FA	FR	G/POS	TPR
1945	Bos-N	4	15	1	2	0	1	0	1	1	1	.133	.188	.267	454	25	-2	0			.800	-2	/3-4	-0.3

■ **TY WALLER** Waller, Elliott Tyrone b: 3/14/57, Fresno, Cal. BR/TR, 6', 180 lbs. Deb: 9/6/80 C Career OF: (2-LF 10-CF 1-RF)

YEAR	TM/L	G	AB	R	H	2B	3B	HR	RBI	BB	SO	AVG	OBP	SLG	OPS	OPS+	BR+	SB	CS	SBR	FA	FR	G/POS	TPR
1980	StL-N	5	12	3	1	0	0	0	0	1	5	.083	.154	.083	237	-31	-2	0	0	0	1.000	-2	/3-5	-0.5
1981	Chi-N	30	71	10	19	2	1	3	13	4	18	.268	.307	.451	757	108	0	2	0	0	.978	-2	3-22/2-3,O-3(0-3-0)	-0.2
1982	Chi-N	17	21	4	5	0	0	0	1	2	5	.238	.304	.238	542	52	-1	0	0	0	1.000	-2	/O-7(1-5-1),3-1	-0.3
1987	Hou-N	11	6	1	1	1	0	0	0	0	3	.167	.167	.333	500	30	-1	0	0	0	1.000	-1	/O-3(1-2-0)	-0.1
Total	4	63	110	18	26	3	1	3	14	7	31	.236	.282	.364	646	78	-4	2	0	0	.961	-7	/3-28,O-13C,2-3	-1.1

■ **DENNY WALLING** Walling, Dennis Martin b: 4/17/54, Neptune, N.J. BL/TR, 6'1", 185 lbs. Deb: 9/7/75 C Career OF: (131-LF 27-CF 135-RF)

YEAR	TM/L	G	AB	R	H	2B	3B	HR	RBI	BB	SO	AVG	OBP	SLG	OPS	OPS+	BR+	SB	CS	SBR	FA	FR	G/POS	TPR
1975	Oak-A	6	8	0	1	1	0	0	2	0	4	.125	.125	.250	375	4	-1	0	0	0	1.000	-1	/O-3(1-2-0)	-0.2
1976	Oak-A	3	11	1	3	0	0	0	0	0	3	.273	.273	.273	545	63	-1	0	0	0	.889	-1	/O-3(2-2-0)	-0.1
1977	Hou-N	6	21	1	6	0	1	0	6	2	4	.286	.348	.381	729	105	0	0	1	-0	1.000	1	/O-5(2-1-2)	0.0
1978	Hou-N	120	247	30	62	11	3	3	36	30	24	.251	.335	.356	691	101	0	9	2	1	.980	2	O-78(66-7-4)	0.1
1979	Hou-N	82	147	21	48	8	4	3	31	17	21	.327	.396	.497	893	151	10	3	2	-0	.985	-3	O-42(7-0-35)	0.6
1980	*Hou-N	100	284	30	85	6	5	3	29	35	26	.299	.376	.387	763	123	10	4	3	-0	.989	-7	1-63,O-19(1-0-18)	-0.2
1981	*Hou-N	65	158	23	37	6	0	5	23	28	17	.234	.349	.367	717	109	2	2	1	0	.990	-5	1-27,O-27(5-1-21)	-0.5
1982	Hou-N	85	146	22	30	4	1	1	14	23	19	.205	.314	.267	581	69	-5	4	2	0	1.000	-4	O-32(4-11-18),1-20	-1.2
1983	Hou-N	100	135	24	40	5	3	3	19	15	16	.296	.367	.444	811	132	6	2	2	-0	.992	-4	1-42,3-13,O-13R	0.0
1984	Hou-N	87	249	37	70	11	5	3	31	16	28	.281	.327	.402	729	112	3	7	1	1	.956	-1	3-52,1-16/O-6(3-3-0)	0.2
1985	Hou-N	119	345	44	93	20	1	7	45	25	26	.270	.319	.394	713	101	-0	5	2	0	.938	-2	3-51,1-46,O-13(6-0-7)	-0.6
1986	*Hou-N	130	382	54	119	23	1	13	58	36	31	.312	.371	.479	850	136	18	1	1	-0	.960	2	*3-102,O-11L/1-4	1.9
1987	Hou-N	110	325	45	92	21	4	5	33	39	37	.283	.360	.418	778	110	5	5	1	1	.948	-4	3-79,1-16/O-7(6-0-2)	-0.1
1988	Hou-N	65	176	19	43	10	2	1	20	15	18	.244	.304	.341	645	88	-3	1	0	0	.950	9	3-51/1-3,O-1(1-0-0)	0.6
	StL-N	19	58	3	13	3	0	0	1	2	7	.224	.250	.276	526	50	-4	1	0	0	1.000	-2	O-11(10-0-1)/3-5,1-1	-0.7
	Yr	84	234	22	56	13	2	1	21	17	25	.239	.291	.325	616	79	-7	2	0	0	.941	6	3-56,O-12(11-0-1)/1-4	-0.1
1989	StL-N	69	79	9	24	7	0	1	11	14	12	.304	.409	.430	839	136	4	0	0	0	.969	-2	1-20/3-9,O-6(3-0-3)	0.2
1990	StL-N	78	127	7	28	5	0	1	19	8	15	.220	.267	.283	550	51	-8	0	0	0	1.000	1	1-15,3-11/O-8(3-0-5)	-0.9
1991	Tex-A	24	44	1	4	1	0	0	2	3	8	.091	.184	.114	297	-16	-7	0	0	0	.950	-3	3-14/O-5(3-0-2)	-1.0
1992	Hou-N	3	3	1	1	0	0	0	0	0	0	.333	.333	.333	667	94	-0	0	0	0	.000	0	/H	0.0
Total	18	1271	2945	372	799	142	30	49	380	308	316	.271	.341	.390	731	107	30	44	18	3	.947	-25	3-387,O-290R,1-273	-1.9

■ **JOE WALLIS** Wallis, Harold Joseph b: 1/9/52, E.St.Louis, Ill. BB/TR, 5'10", 195 lbs. Deb: 9/2/75

YEAR	TM/L	G	AB	R	H	2B	3B	HR	RBI	BB	SO	AVG	OBP	SLG	OPS	OPS+	BR+	SB	CS	SBR	FA	FR	G/POS	TPR
1975	Chi-N	16	56	9	16	2	2	1	4	5	14	.286	.344	.446	791	113	1	2	0	0	1.000	-0	O-15(0-14-1)	0.1
1976	Chi-N	121	338	51	86	11	5	5	21	33	62	.254	.323	.361	684	86	-6	3	9	-2	.976	2	O-90(10-68-16)	-1.0
1977	Chi-N	56	80	14	20	3	0	2	8	16	25	.250	.375	.363	738	89	-1	0	1	-0	.974	-8	O-35(0-35-0)	-0.9
1978	Chi-N	28	55	7	17	2	1	1	6	5	13	.309	.367	.436	803	110	1	0	2	-1	1.000	-4	O-25(0-25-0)	-0.4
	Oak-A	85	279	28	66	16	1	6	26	26	42	.237	.302	.366	667	91	-4	1	4	-1	.980	3	O-80(5-55-23)/D-1	-0.4
1979	Oak-A	23	78	6	11	2	0	1	3	10	18	.141	.247	.205	452	25	-8	1	0	0	1.000	-1	O-23(0-1-23)	-1.0
Total	5	329	886	115	216	36	9	16	68	95	174	.244	.318	.359	677	86	-17	7	16	-4	.982	-9	O-268(15-198-63)/D-1	-3.6

■ **LEE WALLS** Walls, Ray Lee b: 1/6/33, San Diego, Cal. d: 10/11/93, Los Angeles, Cal. BR/TR, 6'3", 205 lbs. Deb: 4/21/52 C Career OF: (208-LF 58-CF 352-RF)

YEAR	TM/L	G	AB	R	H	2B	3B	HR	RBI	BB	SO	AVG	OBP	SLG	OPS	OPS+	BR+	SB	CS	SBR	FA	FR	G/POS	TPR
1952	Pit-N	32	80	6	15	0	1	2	5	8	22	.188	.261	.287	549	51	-5	0	0	0	1.000	0	O-19(1-18-0)	-0.6
1956	Pit-N	143	474	72	130	20	11	11	54	50	83	.274	.346	.432	778	110	7	3	5	-1	.967	6	*O-133(74-10-56)/3-1	0.5
1957	Pit-N	8	22	3	4	1	0	0	0	2	5	.182	.250	.227	477	30	-2	1	0	0	1.000	1	/O-7(7-0-0)	-0.2

YEAR	TM/L	G	AB	R	H	2B	3B	HR	RBI	BB	SO	AVG	OBP	SLG	OPS	OPS+	BR+	SB	CS	SBR	FA	FR	G/POS	TPR
	Chi-N	117	366	42	88	10	5	6	33	27	67	.240	.294	.344	639	72	-15	5	3	0	.984	-5	O-94(67-29-6)/3-1	-2.5
	Yr	125	388	45	92	11	5	6	33	29	72	.237	.292	.338	629	70	-17	6	3	0	.985	-4	*O-101(74-29-6)/3-1	-2.7
1958	Chi-N★	136	513	80	156	19	3	24	72	47	62	.304	.371	.493	865	128	21	4	4	-1	.992	5	*O-132(0-0-132)	2.1
1959	Chi-N	120	354	43	91	18	3	8	33	42	73	.257	.344	.393	737	97	-1	0	2	-1	.967	-8	*O-119(0-0-119)	-1.3
1960	Cin-N	29	84	12	23	3	2	1	7	17	20	.274	.396	.393	789	115	2	2	0	0	.960	1	O-24(12-0-12)/1-2	0.2
	Phi-N	65	181	19	36	6	1	3	19	14	32	.199	.256	.293	549	50	-13	3	2	-0	.947	-9	3-34,O-13(8-0-5)/1-7	-2.3
	Yr	94	265	31	59	9	3	4	26	31	52	.223	.304	.325	629	72	-10	5	2	0	.958	-8	O-37L,3-34/1-9	-2.1
1961	Phi-N	91	261	32	73	6	4	8	30	19	48	.280	.329	.425	754	99	-1	2	2	-0	.987	-6	1-28,3-26,O-17L	-0.9
1962	LA-N	60	109	9	29	3	1	0	17	10	21	.266	.328	.312	640	77	-3	1	0	0	.929	-4	O-17(15-0-3),1-11/3-4	-0.8
1963	LA-N	64	86	12	20	1	0	3	11	7	25	.233	.290	.349	639	89	-1	0	0	0	1.000	-2	O-18(10-0-8)/1-5,3-2	-0.4
1964	LA-N	37	28	1	5	1	0	0	3	2	12	.179	.233	.214	448	29	-3	0	0	0	1.000	-2	/O-6(3-0-3),C-1	-0.5
Total	10	902	2558	331	670	88	31	66	284	245	470	.262	.330	.398	728	96	-14	21	18	-2	.977	-23	O-599R/3-68,1-53,C	-6.7

■ **AUSTIN WALSH** Walsh, Austin Edward b: 9/1/1891, Cambridge, Mass. d: 1/26/55, Glendale, Cal. BL/TL, 5'11", 175 lbs. Deb: 4/19/14

YEAR	TM/L	G	AB	R	H	2B	3B	HR	RBI	BB	SO	AVG	OBP	SLG	OPS	OPS+	BR+	SB	CS	SBR	FA	FR	G/POS	TPR
1914	Chi-F	57	121	14	29	6	1	1	10	4	25	.240	.264	.331	595	65	-8	0			1.000	-3	O-30(21-1-8)	-1.3

■ **JIMMY WALSH** Walsh, James Charles b: 9/22/1885, Kallila, Ireland d: 7/3/62, Syracuse, N.Y. BL/TR, 5'10.5", 170 lbs. Deb: 8/26/12 Career OF: (162-LF 169-CF 165-RF)

YEAR	TM/L	G	AB	R	H	2B	3B	HR	RBI	BB	SO	AVG	OBP	SLG	OPS	OPS+	BR+	SB	CS	SBR	FA	FR	G/POS	TPR
1912	Phi-A	31	107	11	27	8	2	0	15	12		.252	.328	.364	692	101	0	7			.947	0	O-30(30-0-0)	-0.1
1913	Phi-A	97	303	56	77	16	5	0	27	38	40	.254	.341	.340	681	102	1	15			.961	1	O-90(38-43-12)	-0.3
1914	NY-A	43	136	13	26	1	3	1	11	29	21	.191	.333	.265	598	80	-2	6	9	-2	.977	-1	O-41(37-4-0)	-0.7
	*Phi-A	68	216	35	51	11	6	3	36	30	27	.236	.340	.384	724	123	6	6	12	-3	.966	-0	O-56C/1-3,3-3,S-1	0.0
	Yr	111	352	48	77	12	9	4	47	59	48	.219	.337	.338	675	106	4	12	21	-5	.971	-1	O-97L/1-3,3-3,S-1	-0.7
1915	Phi-A	117	417	48	86	15	6	1	20	57	64	.206	.306	.278	584	78	-11	22	12	1	.976	7	*O-109C/3-2,1-1	-1.0
1916	Phi-A	114	390	42	91	13	6	1	27	54	36	.233	.330	.305	635	95	-1	27	14	1	.939	-0	*O-113(0-6-107)/1-1	-0.8
	*Bos-A	14	17	5	3	1	0	0	2	4	2	.176	.333	.235	569	71	-0	3	2	-0	1.000	-3	/O-6(1-3-2),3-2	-0.4
	Yr	128	407	47	94	14	6	1	29	58	38	.231	.330	.302	632	94	-2	30	16	1	.940	-3	*O-119R/3-2,1-1	-1.2
1917	Bos-A	57	185	25	49	6	3	0	12	25	14	.265	.352	.330	682	109	3	6			.982	-0	O-47(2-43-2)	-0.1
Total	6	541	1771	235	410	71	31	6	150	249	204	.232	.330	.317	647	96	-4	92	49		.964	4	O-492C/3-7,1-5,S-1	-3.4

■ **JOHN WALSH** Walsh, John Gabriel b: 3/25/1879, Wilkes-Barre, Pa. d: 4/25/47, Jamaica, N.Y. BR/TR, 5'8.5", 162 lbs. Deb: 6/22/03

YEAR	TM/L	G	AB	R	H	2B	3B	HR	RBI	BB	SO	AVG	OBP	SLG	OPS	OPS+	BR+	SB	CS	SBR	FA	FR	G/POS	TPR
1903	Phi-N	1	3	0	0	0	0	0	0	0		.000	.000	.000	0	-99	-1	0			1.000	-0	/3-1	-0.1

■ **JOE WALSH** Walsh, Joseph Francis b: 10/14/1886, Minersville, Pa. d: 1/6/67, Buffalo, N.Y. BR/TR, 6'2", 170 lbs. Deb: 10/8/10

YEAR	TM/L	G	AB	R	H	2B	3B	HR	RBI	BB	SO	AVG	OBP	SLG	OPS	OPS+	BR+	SB	CS	SBR	FA	FR	G/POS	TPR
1910	NY-A	1	4	0	2	1	0	0	2	0		.500	.500	.750	1250	275	1	0			.900	-0	/C-1	0.1
1911	NY-A	4	9	2	2	1	0	0	0	0		.222	.222	.333	556	51	-1	0			1.000	-3	/C-4	-0.3
Total	2	5	13	2	4	2	0	0	2	0		.308	.308	.462	769	114	0	0			.933	-3	/C-5	-0.2

■ **JOE WALSH** Walsh, Joseph Patrick "Tweet" b: 3/13/17, Boston, Mass. d: 10/5/96, Boston, Mass. BR/TR, 5'10", 155 lbs. Deb: 7/1/38

YEAR	TM/L	G	AB	R	H	2B	3B	HR	RBI	BB	SO	AVG	OBP	SLG	OPS	OPS+	BR+	SB	CS	SBR	FA	FR	G/POS	TPR
1938	Bos-N	4	8	0	0	0	0	0	0	0	2	.000	.000	.000	0	-99	-2	0			.900	-2	/S-4	-0.4

■ **JOE WALSH** Walsh, Joseph R. "Reddy" b: 11/5/1864, Chicago, Ill. d: 8/8/11, Omaha, Neb. BL/TR, Deb: 9/3/1891

YEAR	TM/L	G	AB	R	H	2B	3B	HR	RBI	BB	SO	AVG	OBP	SLG	OPS	OPS+	BR+	SB	CS	SBR	FA	FR	G/POS	TPR
1891	Bal-a	26	100	14	21	0	1	1	10	6	18	.210	.255	.260	515	47	-7	4			.865	6	S-13,2-13	0.0

■ **DEE WALSH** Walsh, Leo Thomas b: 3/28/1890, St.Louis, Mo. d: 7/14/71, St.Louis, Mo. BB/TR, 5'9.5", 165 lbs. Deb: 4/10/13 Career OF: (0-LF 21-CF 24-RF)

YEAR	TM/L	G	AB	R	H	2B	3B	HR	RBI	BB	SO	AVG	OBP	SLG	OPS	OPS+	BR+	SB	CS	SBR	FA	FR	G/POS	TPR
1913	StL-A	23	53	8	9	0	1	0	5	6	11	.170	.302	.208	509	51	-3	3			.933	2	S-22/3-1	0.0
1914	StL-A	7	23	1	2	0	0	0	1	2	4	.087	.160	.087	247	-27	-4	1	1	-0	.919	-0	/S-7	-0.4
1915	StL-A	59	150	13	33	5	0	0	6	14	25	.220	.308	.253	561	71	-5	6	6	-1	.951	1	O-45R/3-2,P-1,2S	-0.7
Total	3	89	226	22	44	5	1	0	12	22	40	.195	.292	.226	517	56	-11	10	7		.924	3	/O-45R,S-30,3-3,2P	-1.1

■ **JIMMY WALSH** Walsh, Michael Timothy "Runt" b: 3/25/1886, Lima, Ohio d: 1/21/47, Baltimore, Md. BR/TR, 5'9", 174 lbs. Deb: 4/25/10 Career OF: (29-LF 16-CF 33-RF)

YEAR	TM/L	G	AB	R	H	2B	3B	HR	RBI	BB	SO	AVG	OBP	SLG	OPS	OPS+	BR+	SB	CS	SBR	FA	FR	G/POS	TPR
1910	Phi-N	88	242	28	60	8	3	3	31	25	38	.248	.323	.343	666	91	-3	5			.947	-2	2-26,O-26C/S-9,3-5	-0.5
1911	Phi-N	94	289	29	78	20	3	1	31	21	30	.270	.324	.370	694	93	-4	5			.962	-6	O-48R,2-14/S-9,3CP1	-1.0
1912	Phi-N	51	150	16	40	6	3	2	19	8	20	.267	.304	.387	690	83	-4	3			.944	0	2-31,3-12/C-5	-0.3
1913	Phi-N	26	30	3	10	4	0	0	5	1	5	.333	.355	.467	822	128	1	1			1.000	-1	/2-6,S-3,3-1,O-1R	0.1
1914	Bal-F	120	428	54	132	25	4	10	65	22	56	.308	.345	.456	801	113	0	18			.932	3	*3-113/2-1,S-1,O-1R	0.6
1915	Bal-F	106	401	43	121	20	1	9	60	21	44	.302	.340	.424	764	111	-1	12			.936	-9	*3-106	-0.8
	StL-F	17	31	5	6	1	0	0	1	3	4	.194	.306	.226	531	48	-2	1			.913	-1	/3-9	-0.3
	Yr	123	432	48	127	21	1	9	61	24	48	.294	.337	.410	747	106	-4	13			.934	-10	*3-115	-1.1
Total	6	502	1571	178	447	84	14	25	212	101	197	.285	.332	.404	735	102	-13	45			.925	-14	3-253/2-78,OSC1P	-2.2

■ **TOM WALSH** Walsh, Thomas Joseph b: 2/28/1886, Davenport, Iowa d: 3/16/63, Naples, Fla. BR/TR, 5'11", 170 lbs. Deb: 8/15/06

YEAR	TM/L	G	AB	R	H	2B	3B	HR	RBI	BB	SO	AVG	OBP	SLG	OPS	OPS+	BR+	SB	CS	SBR	FA	FR	G/POS	TPR
1906	Chi-N	2	1	0	0	0	0	0	0	0		.000	.000	.000	0	-95	-0	0			1.000	0	/C-2	0.0

■ **WALT WALSH** Walsh, Walter William b: 4/30/1897, Newark, N.J. d: 1/15/66, Avon By The Sea, N.J. BR/TR, 5'11", 170 lbs. Deb: 5/4/20

YEAR	TM/L	G	AB	R	H	2B	3B	HR	RBI	BB	SO	AVG	OBP	SLG	OPS	OPS+	BR+	SB	CS	SBR	FA	FR	G/POS	TPR
1920	Phi-N	2	0	0	0	0	0	0	0	0	0	—	—	—	—	—	0	0	0	0	.000	0	R	0.0

■ **ROXY WALTERS** Walters, Alfred John b: 11/5/1892, San Francisco, Cal. d: 6/3/56, Alameda, Cal. BR/TR, 5'8.5", 160 lbs. Deb: 9/16/15 Career OF: (0-LF 0-CF 9-RF)

YEAR	TM/L	G	AB	R	H	2B	3B	HR	RBI	BB	SO	AVG	OBP	SLG	OPS	OPS+	BR+	SB	CS	SBR	FA	FR	G/POS	TPR
1915	NY-A	2	3	0	1	0	0	0	0	0	0	.333	.333	.333	667	100	-0	0			1.000	2	/C-2	0.2
1916	NY-A	66	203	13	54	9	3	0	23	14	42	.266	.320	.340	660	96	-1	2			.974	17	C-65	2.2
1917	NY-A	61	171	16	45	2	0	0	14	9	22	.263	.304	.275	579	76	-5	2			.968	11	C-57	1.2
1918	NY-A	64	191	18	38	5	1	0	12	9	18	.199	.239	.236	474	42	-14	3			.953	-5	C-50/O-9(0-0-9)	-1.7
1919	Bos-A	48	135	7	26	2	0	0	9	7	15	.193	.259	.207	466	33	-12	1			.982	5	C-47	-0.4
1920	Bos-A	88	258	25	51	11	1	0	28	30	21	.198	.303	.248	551	49	-18	2	2	-0	.980	8	C-85/1-2	-0.3
1921	Bos-A	54	169	17	34	4	1	0	14	10	11	.201	.254	.237	491	27	-19	3	0	1	.990	15	C-54	0.1
1922	Bos-A	38	98	4	19	2	0	0	6	6	8	.194	.240	.214	455	19	-12	0	0	0	.967	6	C-36	-0.4
1923	Bos-A	40	104	9	26	4	0	0	5	2	6	.250	.264	.288	553	45	-8	0	2	-1	.974	7	C-36/2-1	-0.1
1924	Cle-A	32	74	10	19	2	0	0	5	10	6	.257	.345	.284	629	63	-4	0	1	-0	.979	6	C-25/2-7	0.3
1925	Cle-A	5	20	0	4	0	0	0	0	0	2	.200	.200	.200	400	2	-3	0	0	0	1.000	-0	/C-5	-0.3
Total	11	498	1426	119	317	41	6	0	116	97	151	.222	.281	.259	541	51	-95	13	5		.975	70	C-462/O-9R,2-8,1-2	0.8

■ **DAN WALTERS** Walters, Daniel Gene b: 8/15/66, Brunswick, Maine BR/TR, 6'4", 225 lbs. Deb: 6/1/92

YEAR	TM/L	G	AB	R	H	2B	3B	HR	RBI	BB	SO	AVG	OBP	SLG	OPS	OPS+	BR+	SB	CS	SBR	FA	FR	G/POS	TPR
1992	SD-N	57	179	14	45	11	1	4	22	10	28	.251	.298	.391	689	92	-2	1	0	0	.992	7	C-55	0.8
1993	SD-N	27	94	6	19	3	0	1	10	7	13	.202	.257	.266	523	40	-8	0	0	0	.970	-3	C-26	-0.9
Total	2	84	273	20	64	14	1	5	32	17	41	.234	.284	.348	632	73	-10	1	0	0	.985	4	/C-81	-0.1

■ **FRED WALTERS** Walters, Fred James "Whale" b: 9/4/12, Laurel, Miss. d: 2/1/80, Laurel, Miss. BR/TR, 6'1", 210 lbs. Deb: 4/17/45

YEAR	TM/L	G	AB	R	H	2B	3B	HR	RBI	BB	SO	AVG	OBP	SLG	OPS	OPS+	BR+	SB	CS	SBR	FA	FR	G/POS	TPR
1945	Bos-A	40	93	2	16	2	0	0	5	10	9	.172	.252	.194	446	29	-8	1	1	-0	.993	6	C-38	-0.1

■ **KEN WALTERS** Walters, Kenneth Rogers b: 11/11/33, Fresno, Cal. BR/TR, 6'1", 180 lbs. Deb: 4/12/60 Career OF: (16-LF 6-CF 179-RF)

YEAR	TM/L	G	AB	R	H	2B	3B	HR	RBI	BB	SO	AVG	OBP	SLG	OPS	OPS+	BR+	SB	CS	SBR	FA	FR	G/POS	TPR
1960	Phi-N	124	426	42	102	10	0	8	37	16	50	.239	.269	.319	588	60	-24	4	3	-0	.988	6	*O-119(5-2-116)	-2.3
1961	Phi-N	86	180	23	41	8	2	2	14	5	25	.228	.253	.328	580	53	-12	2	2	-0	.975	-6	O-56(0-4-53)/1-5,3-1	-2.1
1963	Cin-N	49	75	6	14	2	0	1	7	4	14	.187	.237	.253	491	40	-6	0	2	-1	.889	-5	O-21(11-0-10)/1-1	-1.3
Total	3	259	681	71	157	20	2	11	58	25	89	.231	.261	.314	575	56	-42	6	7	-1	.979	-5	O-196R/1-6,3-1	-5.7

■ **BUCKY WALTERS** Walters, William Henry b: 4/19/09, Philadelphia, Pa. d: 4/20/91, Abington, Pa. BR/TR, 6'1", 180 lbs. Deb: 9/18/31 MC

YEAR	TM/L	G	AB	R	H	2B	3B	HR	RBI	BB	SO	AVG	OBP	SLG	OPS	OPS+	BR+	SB	CS	SBR	FA	FR	G/POS	TPR
1931	Bos-N	9	38	2	8	2	0	0	0	0	3	.211	.211	.263	474	28	-4	0			.947	0	/3-6,2-3	-0.3
1932	Bos-N	22	75	8	14	3	0	0	4	2	18	.187	.208	.253	461	24	-8	0			.910	2	3-22	-0.5
1933	Bos-A	52	195	27	50	8	3	4	28	19	24	.256	.326	.390	715	90	-3	1	1	-0	.940	1	3-43/2-7	0.0
1934	Bos-A	23	88	10	19	4	4	4	18	3	12	.216	.242	.489	730	79	-4	0	0	0	.906	6	3-23	0.2
	Phi-N	83	300	36	78	20	3	4	38	19	54	.260	.308	.387	695	75	-11	1			.950	-7	3-80/2-3,P-2	-1.4
1935	Phi-N	49	96	14	24	2	1	0	6	9	12	.250	.314	.292	606	58	-5	0			1.000	1	P-24/O-5L,2-2,3-1	-0.2
1936	Phi-N	64	121	12	29	10	1	1	16	7	15	.240	.281	.364	645	66	-6	0			.974	9	P-40/2-1,3-1	0.0
1937	Phi-N★	56	137	15	38	6	0	1	16	5	16	.277	.303	.343	646	69	-6	1			.988	5	P-37/3-8	-0.1

YEAR	TM/L	G	AB	R	H	2B	3B	HR	RBI	BB	SO	AVG	OBP	SLG	OPS	OPS+	BR+	SB	CS	SBR	FA	FR	G/POS	TPR
1938	Phi-N	15	35	6	10	2	0	1	3	1	5	.286	.306	.429	734	103	-0	1			.955	0	P-12	0.0
	Cin-N	36	64	10	9	1	0	0	5	7	18	.141	.236	.156	392	10	-8	0			.981	2	P-27	0.0
	Yr	51	99	16	19	3	0	1	8	8	23	.192	.259	.253	512	42	-8	1			.973	3	P-39	0.0
1939	*Cin-N☆	40	120	16	39	8	1	1	16	5	12	.325	.357	.433	790	111	2	1			.979	4	P-39	0.0
1940	*Cin-N★	37	117	11	24	3	0	1	18	4	14	.205	.231	.256	488	34	-11	2			.945	-1	P-36	0.0
1941	Cin-N★	39	106	6	20	6	0	0	9	7	13	.189	.239	.245	484	36	-9	0			.977	2	P-37	0.0
1942	Cin-N★	40	99	13	24	6	1	2	13	3	13	.242	.265	.384	649	89	-2	0			.961	1	P-34/O-1(1-0-0)	-0.1
1943	Cin-N	37	90	11	24	7	1	1	12	6	15	.267	.313	.400	713	107	0	1			.971	1	P-34	0.0
1944	Cin-N★	37	107	9	30	4	0	0	13	8	18	.280	.330	.318	648	86	-2	0			**1.000**	1	P-34	0.0
1945	Cin-N	24	61	11	14	3	0	3	8	3	14	.230	.266	.426	692	93	-1	2			.975	-0	P-22	0.0
1946	Cin-N	24	55	6	7	2	0	0	5	4	12	.127	.186	.164	350	-0	-7	2			.940	2	P-22	0.0
1947	Cin-N	20	45	3	12	2	0	0	4	2	13	.267	.298	.311	609	62	-2	0			.962	-1	P-20	0.0
1948	Cin-N	7	15	1	4	0	0	0	2	0	2	.267	.267	.267	533	46	-1	0			1.000	1	/P-7,M	0.0
1950	Bos-N	1	2	0	0	0	0	0	0	0	0	.000	.000	.000	0	-99	-1	0			1.000	-0	/P-1	0.0
Total	19	715	1966	227	477	99	16	23	234	114	303	.243	.286	.344	630	69	-89	12	1		.974	28	P-428,3-184/2-16,O	-2.4

■ DANNY WALTON

Walton, Daniel James "Mickey" b: 7/14/47, Los Angeles, Cal. BR/TR (BB 1975-80), 6', 200 lbs. Deb: 4/20/68 Career OF: (172-LF 1-CF 6-RF)

YEAR	TM/L	G	AB	R	H	2B	3B	HR	RBI	BB	SO	AVG	OBP	SLG	OPS	OPS+	BR+	SB	CS	SBR	FA	FR	G/POS	TPR
1968	Hou-N	2	2	0	0	0	0	0	0	0	1	.000	.000	.000	0	-99	-0	0	0	0	.000	0	H	-0.1
1969	Sea-A	23	92	12	20	1	2	3	10	5	26	.217	.280	.370	650	82	-3	2	0	0	.976	-1	O-23(23-0-0)	-0.5
1970	Mil-A	117	397	32	102	20	1	17	66	51	126	.257	.350	.441	791	116	9	2	3	-1	.965	-6	*O-114(114-0-0)	-0.4
1971	Mil-A	30	69	5	14	3	0	2	9	7	22	.203	.286	.333	619	76	-2	0	0	0	.923	-4	O-19(19-1-0)/3-1	-0.7
	NY-A	5	14	1	2	0	0	1	2	0	7	.143	.143	.357	500	40	-1	0	0	0	1.000	-1	/O-4(1-0-3)	-0.3
	Yr	35	83	6	16	3	0	3	11	7	29	.193	.264	.337	601	71	-3	0	0	0	.933	-4	O-23(20-1-3)/3-1	-1.0
1973	Min-A	37	96	13	17	1	1	4	8	17	28	.177	.301	.333	634	75	-3	0	0	0	1.000	-3	O-18(15-0-3),D-11/3-1	-0.8
1975	Min-A	42	63	4	11	2	0	1	8	4	18	.175	.224	.254	478	34	-6	0	0	0	.962	-1	/1-7,C-2,D-6	-0.7
1976	LA-N	18	15	0	2	0	0	0	2	1	2	.133	.188	.133	321	-8	-2	0	0	0	.000	0	H	-0.3
1977	Hou-N	13	21	0	4	0	0	0	1	0	5	.190	.190	.190	381	3	-3	0	0	0	.956	-0	/1-5	-0.3
1980	Tex-A	10	10	2	2	0	0	0	1	3	5	.200	.385	.200	585	67	-0	0	0	0	.000	0	/D-1	0.0
Total	9	297	779	69	174	27	4	28	107	88	240	.223	.310	.376	686	90	-12	4	3	-0	.966	-15	O-178L/D-18,1-12,C3	-4.1

■ JEROME WALTON

Walton, Jerome O'Terrell b: 7/8/65, Newnan, Ga. BR/TR, 6'1", 175 lbs. Deb: 4/4/89 Career OF: (111-LF 373-CF 36-RF)

YEAR	TM/L	G	AB	R	H	2B	3B	HR	RBI	BB	SO	AVG	OBP	SLG	OPS	OPS+	BR+	SB	CS	SBR	FA	FR	G/POS	TPR
1989	*Chi-N	116	475	64	139	23	3	5	46	27	77	.293	.339	.385	724	99	-0	24	7	3	.990	4	*O-115(0-115-0)	0.6
1990	Chi-N	101	392	63	103	16	2	2	21	50	70	.263	.352	.329	681	82	-7	14	7	1	.977	3	O-98(0-99-0)	-0.5
1991	Chi-N	123	270	42	59	13	1	5	17	19	55	.219	.277	.330	607	67	-12	7	3	0	.983	-10	*O-101(0-100-1)	-2.4
1992	Chi-N	30	55	7	7	0	1	0	1	9	13	.127	.273	.164	436	26	-5	1	2	-0	.944	-3	O-24(22-1-1)	-1.0
1993	Cal-A	5	2	2	0	0	0	0	0	1	2	.000	.333	.000	333	-2	-0	1	0	0	1.000	0	/O-1(1-0-0),D-4	0.0
1994	Cin-N	46	68	10	21	4	0	1	9	4	12	.309	.347	.412	759	98	-0	1	3	-1	1.000	-6	O-26(16-5-6)/1-7	-0.8
1995	*Cin-N	102	162	32	47	12	1	8	22	17	25	.290	.372	.525	896	134	8	10	7	-0	.982	-15	O-89(36-50-8)/1-3	-0.8
1996	Atl-N	37	47	9	16	5	0	1	4	5	10	.340	.404	.511	914	132	2	0	0	0	1.000	-3	O-28(23-1-5)	-0.1
1997	*Bal-A	26	68	8	20	1	0	3	9	4	10	.294	.333	.441	775	103	0	0	0	0	1.000	-3	O-19(9-2-11)/1-5,D-2	-0.4
1998	TB-A	12	34	4	11	3	0	0	3	2	6	.324	.361	.412	773	99	-0	0	0	0	1.000	1	/O-8(4-0-4),D-3	0.1
Total	10	598	1573	241	423	77	8	25	132	138	280	.269	.335	.376	711	92	-15	58	29	3	.984	-33	O-509C/1-15,D-9	-5.3

■ REGGIE WALTON

Walton, Reginald Sherard b: 10/24/52, Kansas City, Mo. BR/TR, 6'3", 205 lbs. Deb: 6/13/80

YEAR	TM/L	G	AB	R	H	2B	3B	HR	RBI	BB	SO	AVG	OBP	SLG	OPS	OPS+	BR+	SB	CS	SBR	FA	FR	G/POS	TPR
1980	Sea-A	31	83	8	23	6	0	2	9	3	10	.277	.310	.422	732	98	-1	2	2	-0	.929	-2	O-17(6-0-11),D-11	-0.4
1981	Sea-A	12	6	1	0	0	0	0	0	1	2	.000	.143	.000	143	-54	-1	0	0	0	.000	-2	/O-4(3-0-1),D-1	-0.3
1982	Pit-N	13	15	1	3	1	0	0	0	1	1	.200	.294	.267	561	56	-1	0	0	0	.000	-1	/O-2(2-0-0)	-0.2
Total	3	56	104	10	26	7	0	2	9	5	13	.250	.297	.375	672	83	-3	2	2	-0	.929	-5	/O-23(11-0-12),D-12	-0.9

■ BILL WAMBSGANSS

Wambsganss, William Adolph b: 3/19/1894, Cleveland, Ohio d: 12/8/85, Lakewood, Ohio BR/TR, 5'11", 175 lbs. Deb: 8/4/14

YEAR	TM/L	G	AB	R	H	2B	3B	HR	RBI	BB	SO	AVG	OBP	SLG	OPS	OPS+	BR+	SB	CS	SBR	FA	FR	G/POS	TPR
1914	Cle-A	43	143	12	31	6	2	0	12	8	24	.217	.277	.287	564	67	-6	2	7	-2	.921	-1	S-36/2-4	-0.7
1915	Cle-A	121	375	30	73	4	4	0	21	36	50	.195	.272	.227	499	48	-23	8	9	-1	.938	7	2-78,3-35	-1.7
1916	Cle-A	136	475	57	117	14	4	0	45	41	40	.246	.313	.293	605	77	-13	13			.925	-8	*S-106,2-24/3-5	-1.5
1917	Cle-A	141	499	52	127	17	6	0	43	37	42	.255	.315	.313	628	85	-9	16			.951	15	*2-137/1-3	1.0
1918	Cle-A	87	315	34	93	15	2	0	40	21	21	.295	.345	.356	701	102	0	16			.952	-2	2-87	0.0
1919	Cle-A	139	526	60	146	17	6	2	60	32	24	.278	.323	.344	667	82	-13	18			.963	11	*2-139	0.1
1920	*Cle-A	153	565	83	138	16	11	1	55	54	26	.244	.316	.317	633	66	-27	9	18	-4	.960	8	*2-153	-2.0
1921	Cle-A	107	410	80	117	28	5	2	47	44	27	.285	.359	.393	752	90	-6	13	7	0	.963	-18	*2-103/3-2	-1.9
1922	Cle-A	142	538	89	141	22	6	0	47	60	26	.262	.341	.325	666	74	-19	17	10	0	.961	-9	*2-125,S-16	-2.3
1923	Cle-A	101	345	59	100	20	4	1	59	43	15	.290	.373	.380	753	99	0	10	9	-1	.963	5	2-88/3-4	0.7
1924	Bos-A	156	636	93	174	41	5	0	49	54	33	.274	.334	.354	688	77	-22	14	8	0	.963	14	*2-156	-0.2
1925	Bos-A	111	360	50	83	12	4	1	41	52	21	.231	.329	.294	624	59	-22	3	5	-1	.957	4	*2-103/1-6	-1.5
1926	Phi-A	54	54	11	19	3	0	0	1	8	8	.352	.444	.407	852	117	2	1	1	-0	.923	0	S-17/2-8	0.3
Total	13	1491	5241	710	1359	215	59	7	520	490	357	.259	.328	.327	655	78	-157	140	74		.958	26	*2-1205,S-175/3-46,1	-9.7

■ LLOYD WANER

Waner, Lloyd James "Little Poison" b: 3/16/06, Harrah, Okla. d: 7/22/82, Oklahoma City, Okla. BL/TR, 5'9", 150 lbs. Deb: 4/12/27 FH Career OF: (124-LF 1663-CF 33-RF)

YEAR	TM/L	G	AB	R	H	2B	3B	HR	RBI	BB	SO	AVG	OBP	SLG	OPS	OPS+	BR+	SB	CS	SBR	FA	FR	G/POS	TPR
1927	*Pit-N	150	629	**133**	223	17	6	2	27	37	23	.355	.396	.410	806	108	9	14			.976	-1	*O-150(42-109-0)/2-1	0.0
1928	Pit-N	152	659	121	221	22	14	5	61	40	13	.335	.377	.434	811	107	7	8			.980	7	*O-152(10-143-0)	0.7
1929	Pit-N	151	662	134	234	28	**20**	5	74	37	20	.353	.395	.479	874	113	14	6			.987	16	*O-151(0-151-0)	2.0
1930	Pit-N	68	260	32	94	8	3	1	36	5	5	.362	.376	.427	803	93	-2	3			.983	2	O-65(0-65-0)	-0.3
1931	Pit-N	154	681	90	**214**	25	13	4	57	39	16	.314	.352	.407	759	104	4	7			.979	**18**	*O-153(0-153-0)/2-1	1.8
1932	Pit-N	134	565	90	188	27	11	2	38	31	11	.333	.367	.430	798	116	12	6			.986	12	*O-131(0-131-0)	2.1
1933	Pit-N	121	500	59	138	14	5	0	26	22	8	.276	.307	.324	631	80	-13	3			.982	1	*O-114(65-49-0)	-1.8
1934	Pit-N	140	611	95	173	27	6	1	48	38	12	.283	.326	.352	678	80	-17	6			.979	12	*O-139(0-139-0)	-0.9
1935	Pit-N	122	537	83	166	22	14	0	46	22	10	.309	.336	.402	739	95	-4	1			.989	6	*O-121(0-121-0)	-0.2
1936	Pit-N	106	414	67	133	13	8	1	31	31	5	.321	.369	.399	767	104	3	1			.984	1	O-92(0-92-0)	0.1
1937	Pit-N	129	537	80	177	23	4	1	45	34	12	.330	.370	.393	762	107	6	3			.988	6	*O-123(0-123-0)	0.9
1938	Pit-N☆	147	619	79	194	25	7	5	57	28	11	.313	.343	.401	744	103	2	5			.986	2	*O-144(0-144-0)	0.0
1939	Pit-N	112	379	49	108	15	3	0	24	17	13	.285	.321	.340	661	79	-11	0			.992	6	O-92(0-92-0)/3-1	-0.7
1940	Pit-N	72	166	30	43	3	0	0	3	5	5	.259	.285	.277	562	56	-10	2			.989	-1	O-42(1-41-0)	-1.2
1941	Pit-N	3	4	2	1	0	0	0	1	2	0	.250	.500	.250	750	116	0	0			1.000	0	/O-1(0-1-0)	0.1
	Bos-N	19	51	7	21	1	0	0	4	2	0	.412	.434	.431	865	151	3	1			.969	-1	O-15(3-11-1)	0.2
	Cin-N	55	164	17	42	4	1	0	6	8	0	.256	.291	.293	583	64	-8	0			.986	-3	O-44(0-13-31)	-1.4
	Yr	77	219	26	64	5	1	0	11	12	0	.292	.329	.324	653	85	-4	1			.981	-4	O-60(3-25-32)	-1.1
1942	Phi-N	101	287	23	75	7	3	0	10	16	6	.261	.300	.307	607	82	-7	1			.967	-1	O-75(0-75-0)	-1.0
1944	Bro-N	15	14	3	4	0	0	0	1	3	0	.286	.412	.286	697	101	0	0			1.000	-2	/O-4(0-4-0)	-0.2
	Pit-N	19	14	2	5	0	0	0	2	2	0	.357	.438	.357	795	120	1	0			1.000	-2	/O-7(1-6-0)	-0.2
	Yr	34	28	5	9	0	0	0	3	5	0	.321	.424	.321	746	110	1	0			1.000	-4	O-11(1-10-0)	-0.4
1945	Pit-N	23	19	5	5	0	0	0	1	1	3	.263	.300	.263	563	55	-1	0			1.000	-0	/O-3(2-0-1)	-0.1
Total	18	1993	7772	1201	2459	281	118	27	598	420	173	.316	.353	.393	747	99	-13	67			.983	76	*O-1818C/2-2,3-1	-0.1

■ PAUL WANER

Waner, Paul Glee "Big Poison" b: 4/16/03, Harrah, Okla. d: 8/29/65, Sarasota, Fla. BL/TL, 5'8.5", 153 lbs. Deb: 4/13/26 FCH Career OF: (18-LF 18-CF 2256-RF)

YEAR	TM/L	G	AB	R	H	2B	3B	HR	RBI	BB	SO	AVG	OBP	SLG	OPS	OPS+	BR+	SB	CS	SBR	FA	FR	G/POS	TPR
1926	Pit-N	144	536	101	180	35	**22**	8	79	66	19	.336	**.413**	.528	941	144	34	11			.976	8	*O-139(6-0-133)	3.0
1927	*Pit-N	155	623	114	**237**	42	**18**	9	**131**	60	14	**.380**	.437	.549	986	152	47	5			.980	8	*O-143(0-0-143),1-14	4.0
1928	Pit-N	152	602	**142**	223	**50**	19	6	86	77	16	.370	.446	.547	992	152	48	6			.975	5	*O-131(0-0-131),1-24	3.9
1929	Pit-N	151	596	131	200	43	15	15	100	89	24	.336	.424	.534	958	133	32	15			.986	2	*O-143(0-0-143)/1-7	2.0
1930	Pit-N	145	589	117	217	32	18	8	77	57	18	.368	.428	.525	952	128	29	18			.959	-3	*O-143(0-5-138)	1.3
1931	Pit-N	150	559	88	180	35	10	6	70	73	21	.322	.404	.453	857	131	27	6			.976	15	*O-138(0-0-138),1-10	3.2
1932	Pit-N	154	630	107	215	**62**	10	8	82	56	24	.341	.397	.510	906	144	39	13			.974	3	*O-154(0-9-145)	3.2
1933	Pit-N★	154	618	101	191	38	16	7	70	60	20	.309	.372	.456	828	136	29	3			.981	5	*O-154(0-0-154)	2.5

YEAR	TM/L	G	AB	R	H	2B	3B	HR	RBI	BB	SO	AVG	OBP	SLG	OPS	OPS+	BR+	SB	CS	SBR	FA	FR	G/POS	TPR
1934	Pit-N★	146	599	**122**	**217**	32	16	14	90	68	24	**.362**	.429	.539	968	154	47	8			.985	7	*O-145(0-0-145)	4.4
1935	Pit-N★	139	549	98	176	29	12	11	78	61	22	.321	.392	.477	869	128	23	2			.983	3	*O-136(0-0-136)	1.7
1936	Pit-N	148	585	107	218	53	9	5	94	74	29	**.373**	.446	.520	965	156	48	7			.960	9	*O-145(0-0-145)	4.7
1937	Pit-N★	154	619	94	219	30	9	2	74	63	34	.354	.413	.441	855	132	30	4			.970	1	*O-150(0-0-150)/1-3	2.1
1938	Pit-N	148	625	77	175	31	6	6	69	47	28	.280	.331	.378	709	94	-5	2			.977	-3	*O-147(0-1-148)	-1.7
1939	Pit-N	125	461	62	151	30	6	3	45	35	18	.328	.375	.438	813	120	13	0			.978	2	*O-106(0-0-106)	0.8
1940	Pit-N	89	238	32	69	16	1	1	32	23	14	.290	.352	.378	731	102	1	0			.985	-5	O-45(0-0-45)/1-8	-0.7
1941	Bro-N	11	35	5	6	0	0	0	4	8	0	.171	.326	.171	497	41	-2	0			.923	-2	/O-9(0-0-9)	-0.5
	Bos-N	95	294	40	82	10	2	2	46	47	14	.279	.378	.347	725	110	6	1			.965	-4	O-77(10-3-66)/1-7	-0.3
	Yr	106	329	45	88	10	2	2	50	55	14	.267	.372	.328	701	102	3	1			.961	-6	O-86(10-3-75)/1-7	-0.8
1942	Bos-N	114	333	43	86	17	1	1	39	62	20	.258	.376	.324	701	108	6	2			.969	-8	O-94(0-0-94)	-0.8
1943	Bro-N	82	225	29	70	16	0	1	26	35	9	.311	.406	.396	802	132	11	0			.960	-1	O-57(1-0-56)	0.7
1944	Bro-N	83	136	16	39	4	1	0	16	27	7	.287	.405	.331	736	111	4	0			.983	-2	O-32(1-0-31)	0.0
	NY-A	9	7	1	1	0	0	0	1	2	1	.143	.333	.143	476	37	-0	1	0	0	.000	0	H	0.0
1945	NY-A	1	0	0	0	0	0	0	0	1	0	—	1.000	—	1000	191	0	0	0	0	.000	0	H	0.0
Total	20	2549	9459	1627	3152	605	191	113	1309	1091	376	.333	.404	.473	878	133	466	104	0		.975	40	*O-2288R/1-73	33.5
■ **JACK WANNER** Wanner, Clarence Curtis "Johnny" b: 11/29/1885, Geneseo, Ill. d: 5/28/19, Geneseo, Ill. BR/TR, 5′11.5″, 190 lbs. Deb: 9/28/09																								
1909	NY-A	3	8	0	1	0	0	0	0	2		.125	.300	.125	425	35	-0	1			.600	-2	/S-2	-0.3
■ **PEE-WEE WANNINGER** Wanninger, Paul Louis b: 12/12/02, Birmingham, Ala. d: 3/7/81, N.Augusta, S.C. BL/TR, 5′7″, 150 lbs. Deb: 4/22/25																								
1925	NY-A	117	403	35	95	13	6	1	22	11	34	.236	.256	.305	561	43	-36	3	5	-1	.944	-6	*S-111/3-3,2-1	-3.0
1927	Bos-A	18	60	4	12	0	0	0	1	6	2	.200	.284	.200	484	28	-6	2	4	-1	.890	-1	S-15	-0.7
	Cin-N	28	93	14	23	2	2	0	8	6	7	.247	.293	.312	605	64	-5	0			.953	6	S-28	0.4
Total	2	163	556	53	130	15	8	1	31	23	43	.234	.266	.295	560	45	-47	5	9		.941	-1	S-154/3-3,2-1	-3.3
■ **AARON WARD** Ward, Aaron Lee b: 8/28/1896, Booneville, Ark. d: 1/30/61, New Orleans, La. BR/TR, 5′10.5″, 160 lbs. Deb: 8/14/17 Career OF: (0-LF 4-CF 0-RF)																								
1917	NY-A	8	26	0	3	0	0	0	1	1	5	.115	.148	.115	264	-19	-4	0			.926	-2	/S-7	-0.6
1918	NY-A	20	32	2	4	1	0	0	1	2	7	.125	.176	.156	333	0	-4	1			.941	4	S-12/O-4(0-4-0),2-3	0.0
1919	NY-A	27	34	5	7	2	0	0	2	5	6	.206	.308	.265	572	61	-2	0			1.000	2	/1-5,3-3,S-2,2-1	0.0
1920	NY-A	127	496	62	127	18	7	11	54	33	84	.256	.304	.387	691	79	-17	7	5	-0	.965	22	*3-114,S-12	0.9
1921	*NY-A	153	556	77	170	30	10	5	75	42	68	.306	.363	.423	786	98	-2	6	8	-1	.961	19	*2-124,3-33	1.9
1922	*NY-A	154	558	69	149	19	5	7	68	45	64	.267	.328	.357	685	77	-19	6	4	-0	.974	3	*2-152/3-2	-1.2
1923	*NY-A	152	567	79	161	26	11	10	82	56	65	.284	.351	.422	773	101	-0	8	8	-1	**.980**	13	*2-152	1.6
1924	NY-A	120	400	42	101	13	10	8	66	40	45	.253	.324	.395	719	85	-11	1	4	-1	.973	8	*2-120/S-1	-0.1
1925	NY-A	125	439	41	108	22	3	4	38	49	49	.246	.326	.337	663	70	-20	1	4	-1	.966	-11	*2-113,3-10	-2.7
1926	NY-A	22	31	5	10	2	0	0	3	2	6	.323	.364	.387	751	97	-0	0	0	0	1.000	-4	/2-4,3-1	-0.4
1927	Chi-A	145	463	75	125	25	8	5	56	63	56	.270	.360	.391	751	97	-1	6	5	-0	.963	-19	*2-139/3-6	-1.6
1928	Cle-A	6	9	0	1	0	0	0	0	1	2	.111	.200	.111	311	-16	-2	0	0	0	.818	2	/3-3,S-2,2-1	0.1
Total	12	1059	3611	457	966	158	54	50	446	339	457	.268	.335	.383	717	85	-81	36	38		.970	35	2-809,3-172/S-36,1O	-2.1
■ **CHUCK WARD** Ward, Charles William b: 7/30/1894, St.Louis, Mo. d: 4/4/69, Indian Rocks, Fla. BR/TR, 5′11.5″, 170 lbs. Deb: 4/11/17																								
1917	Pit-N	125	423	25	100	12	3	0	43	32	43	.236	.302	.279	581	76	-11	5			.912	-27	*S-112/2-8,3-5	-3.4
1918	Bro-N	2	6	0	2	0	0	0	3	0	0	.333	.333	.333	667	104	0	0			1.000	-1	/3-2	-0.1
1919	Bro-N	45	150	7	35	1	2	0	8	7	11	.233	.277	.267	543	62	-7	0			.920	-6	3-45	-1.3
1920	Bro-N	19	71	7	11	1	0	0	4	3	3	.155	.200	.169	369	6	-8	1	0	0	.928	-9	S-19	-1.8
1921	Bro-N	12	28	1	2	1	0	0	0	4	2	.071	.188	.107	295	-19	-5	0	0	0	.937	4	S-12	0.0
1922	Bro-N	33	91	12	25	5	1	0	14	5	8	.275	.320	.352	671	74	-4	1	1	-0	.934	-3	S-31/3-2	-0.4
Total	6	236	769	52	175	20	6	0	72	51	67	.228	.286	.269	555	63	-34	7	1		.919	-41	S-174/3-54,2-8	-7.0
■ **CHRIS WARD** Ward, Chris Gilbert b: 5/18/49, Oakland, Cal. BL/TL, 6′, 180 lbs. Deb: 9/10/72																								
1972	Chi-N	1	1	0	0	0	0	0	0	0	0	.000	.000	.000	0	-90	-0	0	0	0	.000	0	H	0.0
1974	Chi-N	92	137	8	28	4	0	1	15	18	13	.204	.297	.255	552	53	-8	0	2	-1	.977	1	O-22(21-0-1)/1-6	-0.9
Total	2	93	138	8	28	4	0	1	15	18	13	.203	.295	.254	548	52	-8	0	2	-1	.977	1	/O-22(21-0-1),1-6	-0.9
■ **DARYLE WARD** Ward, Daryle Lamar b: 6/27/75, Lynwood, Cal. BL/TL, 6′2″, 240 lbs. Deb: 5/14/98 F Career OF: (74-LF 0-CF 4-RF)																								
1998	Hou-N	4	3	1	1	0	0	0	0	1	2	.333	.500	.333	833	128	0	0	0	0	.000	0	/H	0.0
1999	*Hou-N	64	150	11	41	6	0	8	30	9	31	.273	.314	.473	788	97	-1	0	0	0	.944	-5	O-31(31-0-0),1-10/D-3	-0.7
2000	Hou-N	119	264	36	68	10	2	20	47	15	61	.258	.297	.538	835	99	-2	0	0	0	.986	-4	O-47(43-0-4),1-19/D-4	-0.7
Total	3	187	417	48	110	16	2	28	77	25	94	.264	.305	.513	819	99	-3	0	0	0	.972	-8	/O-78L,1-29,D-7	-1.4
■ **PIGGY WARD** Ward, Frank Gray b: 4/16/1867, Chambersburg, Pa. d: 10/24/12, Altoona, Pa. BB/TR, 5′9.5″, 196 lbs. Deb: 6/12/1883 F Career OF: (21-LF 4-CF 85-RF)																								
1883	Phi-N	1	5	0	0	0	0	0	0	0	2	.000	.000	.000	0	-99	-1				1.000	-1	/3-1	-0.2
1889	Phi-N	7	25	0	4	1	0	0	4	0	7	.160	.160	.200	360	0	-3	1			.848	-2	/2-6,O-1(0-1-0)	-0.5
1891	Pit-N	6	18	3	6	0	0	0	2	3	3	.333	.455	.333	788	134	1	3			.833	-1	/O-5(5-0-0)	0.0
1892	Bal-N	56	186	28	54	6	5	1	33	31	18	.290	.403	.392	795	137	10	10			.892	1	O-43R/2-7,S-5,C-1	0.9
1893	Bal-N	11	49	11	12	1	3	0	5	5	2	.245	.327	.388	715	88	-1	4			.846	-1	/O-9(9-0-0),1-2	-0.2
	Cin-N	42	150	44	42	4	1	0	10	37	10	.280	.440	.320	760	101	3	27			.827	-2	O-40(1-0-39)/1-1	-0.1
	Yr	53	199	55	54	5	4	0	15	42	12	.271	.415	.337	752	99	2	31			.832	-3	O-49(10-0-39)/1-3	-0.3
1894	Was-N	98	347	86	105	11	7	0	36	80	31	.303	.447	.375	822	103	9	41			.900	-23	2-79,O-12L/S-3,3-1	-0.9
Total	6	221	780	172	223	23	16	1	90	156	73	.286	.419	.360	779	105	17	86			.852	-29	O-110R/2-92,S-8,13C	-1.0
■ **GARY WARD** Ward, Gary Lamell b: 12/6/53, Los Angeles, Cal. BR/TR, 6′2″, 202 lbs. Deb: 9/3/79 Career OF: (848-LF 181-CF 111-RF)																								
1979	Min-A	10	14	2	4	0	0	0	1	3	3	.286	.412	.286	697	89	-0	0	1	-0	1.000	-1	/O-5(1-0-4),D-3	-0.1
1980	Min-A	13	41	11	19	6	2	1	10	3	6	.463	.500	.780	1280	228	7	0	0	0	1.000	-2	O-12(12-0-0)	0.4
1981	Min-A	85	295	42	78	7	6	3	29	28	48	.264	.328	.359	687	92	-3	5	2	0	.975	6	O-80(61-19-1)/D-2	0.0
1982	Min-A	152	570	85	165	33	7	28	91	37	105	.289	.334	.519	853	127	19	13	1	3	.989	13	*O-150(127-4-25)/D-2	2.7
1983	Min-A★	157	623	76	173	34	5	19	88	44	98	.278	.328	.440	768	105	4	8	1	1	.978	**26**	*O-152(152-0-0)/D-2	2.4
1984	Tex-A	155	602	97	171	21	7	21	79	55	95	.284	.344	.447	791	113	10	7	5	-0	.987	12	*O-148(58-59-36)/D-5	1.8
1985	Tex-A★	154	593	77	170	28	7	15	70	39	97	.287	.332	.433	765	106	4	26	7	3	.969	2	*O-153(139-21-1)/D-1	0.3
1986	Tex-A	105	380	54	120	15	2	5	51	31	72	.316	.373	.405	779	109	6	12	8	-0	.996	13	*O-104(102-4-0)/D-1	1.4
1987	NY-A	146	529	65	131	22	1	16	78	33	101	.248	.293	.384	677	78	-17	9	1	2	.985	-4	O-94L,D-36,1-15	-2.4
1988	NY-A	91	231	26	52	8	0	4	24	24	41	.225	.304	.312	615	73	-8	0	1	-0	.992	-4	O-54C,1-11/3-2,D-9	-1.4
1989	NY-A	8	17	3	5	1	0	0	1	3	5	.294	.400	.353	753	115	1	0	0	0	1.000	-1	/O-6(0-0-6),D-1	-0.1
	Det-A	105	275	24	69	10	2	9	29	21	54	.251	.304	.400	704	99	-1	1	3	-1	.990	0	O-51L,1-26,D-26	-0.5
	Yr	113	292	27	74	11	2	9	30	24	59	.253	.310	.397	707	100	-1	1	3	-1	.991	-1	O-57L,D-27,1-26	-0.6
1990	Det-A	106	309	32	79	11	2	9	46	30	50	.256	.324	.392	715	98	-1	2	0	0	.988	-4	O-85L,D-13/1-2	-0.8
Total	12	1287	4479	594	1236	196	41	130	597	351	775	.276	.330	.425	755	104	20	83	30	8	.984	55	*O-1094L,D-101/1-54,3	3.7
■ **JIM WARD** Ward, James H. H. b: 3/2/1855, Boston, Mass. d: 6/4/1886, Boston, Mass. Deb: 8/3/1876																								
1876	Phi-N	1	4	1	2	0	0	0	1	0	1	.500	.500	.500	1000	236	1				.750	-0	/C-1	0.0
■ **RUBE WARD** Ward, John Andrew b: 2/6/1879, New Lexington, Ohio d: 1/17/45, Akron, Ohio Deb: 4/28/02																								
1902	Bro-N	13	31	4	9	1	0	0	2	2		.290	.333	.323	656	102	0	0			.850	-1	O-11(6-1-4)	-0.2
■ **JOHN WARD** Ward, John E. b: Washington, D.C. Deb: 5/23/1884																								
1884	Was-U	1	4	0	1	0	0	0		0		.250	.250	.250	500	54	-0				.000	-1	/O-1(0-1-0)	-0.1
■ **JAY WARD** Ward, John Francis b: 9/9/38, Brookfield, Mo. BR/TR, 6′1″, 185 lbs. Deb: 5/6/63 C Career OF: (4-LF 0-CF 0-RF)																								
1963	Min-A	9	15	0	1	1	0	0	2	1	5	.067	.125	.133	258	-27	-3	0	0	0	1.000	-1	/3-4,O-1(1-0-0)	-0.3
1964	Min-A	12	31	4	7	2	0	0	2	6	13	.226	.351	.290	642	80	-1	0	0	0	.977	0	/2-9,O-3(3-0-0)	0.0

YEAR	TM/L	G	AB	R	H	2B	3B	HR	RBI	BB	SO	AVG	OBP	SLG	OPS	OPS+	BR+	SB	CS	SBR	FA	FR	G/POS	TPR
1970	Cin-N	6	3	0	0	0	0	0	0	2	1	.000	.400	.000	400	17	-0	0	0	0	1.000	-0	/3-2,1-1,2-1	0.0
Total	3	27	49	4	8	3	0	0	4	9	19	.163	.293	.224	518	46	-3	0	0	0	.977	-1	/2-10,3-6,O-4L,1-1	-0.3

■ JOHN WARD

Ward, John Montgomery b: 3/3/1860, Bellefonte, Pa. d: 3/4/25, Augusta, Ga. BL/TR (BB 1888), 5'9", 165 lbs. Deb: 7/15/1878 MH Career OF: (4-LF 110-CF 100-RF)

YEAR	TM/L	G	AB	R	H	2B	3B	HR	RBI	BB	SO	AVG	OBP	SLG	OPS	OPS+	BR+	SB	CS	SBR	FA	FR	G/POS	TPR
1878	Pro-N	37	138	14	27	5	4	1	15	2	13	.196	.207	.312	519	69	-5				.866	2	P-37	0.0
1879	Pro-N	83	364	71	104	9	4	2	41	7	14	.286	.299	.349	648	115	6				.938	3	*P-70,3-16/O-8(4-0-4)	0.1
1880	Pro-N	86	356	53	81	12	2	0	27	6	16	.228	.240	.272	513	76	-8				.983	14	*P-70,3-25/O-2R,M	0.7
1881	Pro-N	85	357	56	87	18	6	0	53	5	10	.244	.254	.328	582	83	-7				.887	6	O-40R,P-39,S-13	-0.2
1882	Pro-N	83	355	58	87	10	3	1	39	13	22	.245	.272	.299	570	83	-7				.824	10	O-49(0-2-47),P-34/S-4	0.1
1883	NY-N	88	380	76	97	18	7	7	54	8	25	.255	.271	.395	665	100	-0				.859	19	O-56C,P-34/3-5,S2	1.2
1884	NY-N	113	482	98	122	11	8	2	51	28	47	.253	.294	.322	616	91	-5				.847	8	O-59C,2-47/P-9,M	0.2
1885	NY-N	111	446	72	101	8	9	0	37	17	39	.226	.255	.285	540	75	-12				.904	6	*S-111	-0.2
1886	NY-N	122	491	82	134	17	5	2	81	19	46	.273	.300	.340	640	93	-5	36			.870	-3	*S-122	-0.3
1887	NY-N	129	574	114	213	16	5	1	53	29	12	.371	.375	.391	766	119	15	**111**			**.919**	30	*S-129	4.1
1888	*NY-N	122	510	70	128	14	5	2	49	9	13	.251	.265	.310	575	84	-10	38			.857	-3	*S-122	-0.9
1889	*NY-N	114	479	87	143	13	4	1	67	27	7	.299	.339	.349	687	92	-5	62			.890	6	*S-108/2-7	0.3
1890	Bro-P	128	561	134	188	15	12	4	60	51	22	.335	.393	.426	819	112	8	63			.878	21	*S-128,M	2.6
1891	Bro-N	105	441	85	122	13	5	0	39	36	10	.277	.335	.329	664	94	-3	57			.878	-0	S-87,2-18,M	0.0
1892	Bro-N	148	614	109	163	13	3	1	47	82	19	.265	.355	.301	656	103	6	**88**			.920	3	*2-148,M	1.4
1893	NY-N	135	588	129	193	27	9	2	77	47	5	.328	.379	.415	794	111	8	46			.918	7	*2-134,M	1.7
1894	*NY-N	138	549	102	146	12	5	0	79	35	6	.266	.311	.306	617	50	-45	39			.923	8	*2-138,M	-2.4
Total	17	1827	7685	1410	2136	231	96	26	869	421	326	.278	.314	.341	655	93	-68	540			.885	136	S-826,2-493,PO/3	8.4

■ JOE WARD

Ward, Joseph A. b: 9/2/1884, Philadelphia, Pa. d: 8/11/34, Philadelphia, Pa. TR, Deb: 4/24/06 Career OF: (1-LF 1-CF 0-RF)

YEAR	TM/L	G	AB	R	H	2B	3B	HR	RBI	BB	SO	AVG	OBP	SLG	OPS	OPS+	BR+	SB	CS	SBR	FA	FR	G/POS	TPR
1906	Phi-N	35	129	12	38	8	6	0	11	5		.295	.321	.450	771	140	5	2			.929	-6	3-27/2-3,S-1	0.0
1909	NY-A	9	28	3	5	0	0	0	0	1		.179	.233	.179	412	30	-2	2			.846	-5	/2-7,1-1	-0.9
	Phi-N	74	184	21	49	8	2	0	23	9		.266	.304	.332	636	96	-1	7			.944	-10	2-48/S-8,1-5,O-2L	-1.2
1910	Phi-N	48	124	11	18	2	1	0	13	3	11	.145	.178	.177	356	4	-15	1			.975	2	1-32/S-1,3-1	-1.5
Total	3	166	465	47	110	18	9	0	47	18	11	.237	.271	.314	585	78	-14	12			.929	-20	/2-58,1-38,3-28,SO	-3.6

■ HAP WARD

Ward, Joseph Nichols b: 11/15/1885, Leesburg, N.J. d: 9/13/79, Elmer, N.J. Deb: 5/18/12

YEAR	TM/L	G	AB	R	H	2B	3B	HR	RBI	BB	SO	AVG	OBP	SLG	OPS	OPS+	BR+	SB	CS	SBR	FA	FR	G/POS	TPR
1912	Det-A	1	2	0	0	0	0	0	0	0		.000	.000	.000	0	-99	-1	0			1.000	0	/O-1	0.0

■ KEVIN WARD

Ward, Kevin Michael b: 9/28/61, Lansdale, Pa. BR/TR, 6'1", 195 lbs. Deb: 5/10/91

YEAR	TM/L	G	AB	R	H	2B	3B	HR	RBI	BB	SO	AVG	OBP	SLG	OPS	OPS+	BR+	SB	CS	SBR	FA	FR	G/POS	TPR
1991	SD-N	44	107	13	26	7	2	2	8	9	27	.243	.308	.402	710	95	-1	1	4	-1	.982	-2	O-33(31-0-2)	-0.5
1992	SD-N	81	147	12	29	5	0	3	12	14	38	.197	.276	.293	569	60	-8	2	3	-1	.946	-6	O-51(36-9-8)	-1.7
Total	2	125	254	25	55	12	2	5	20	23	65	.217	.289	.339	628	75	-9	3	7	-2	.961	-9	/O-84(67-9-10)	-2.2

■ PETE WARD

Ward, Peter Thomas b: 7/26/39, Montreal, Que., Can BL/TR, 6'1", 200 lbs. Deb: 9/21/62 C Career OF: (139-LF 0-CF 54-RF)

YEAR	TM/L	G	AB	R	H	2B	3B	HR	RBI	BB	SO	AVG	OBP	SLG	OPS	OPS+	BR+	SB	CS	SBR	FA	FR	G/POS	TPR
1962	Bal-A	8	21	1	3	2	0	0	2	4	5	.143	.280	.238	518	44	-2	0	0	0	1.000	-0	/O-6(2-0-4)	-0.2
1963	Chi-A	157	600	80	177	34	6	22	84	52	77	.295	.356	.482	838	135	27	7	6	-1	.923	-5	*3-154/2-1,S-1	2.1
1964	Chi-A	144	539	61	152	28	3	23	94	56	76	.282	.352	.473	825	131	22	1	1	-0	.958	13	*3-138	3.5
1965	Chi-A	138	507	62	125	25	3	10	57	56	83	.247	.329	.367	696	104	3	2	4	-1	.952	9	*3-134/2-1	1.1
1966	Chi-A	84	251	22	55	7	1	3	28	24	49	.219	.295	.291	586	74	-8	3	1	0	.989	-2	O-59L,3-16/1-5	-1.4
1967	Chi-A	146	467	49	109	16	2	18	62	61	109	.233	.336	.392	728	119	12	3	2	-0	.991	-17	O-89L,1-39,3-22	-1.3
1968	Chi-A	125	399	43	86	15	0	15	50	76	85	.216	.355	.366	721	117	11	4	3	-0	.946	-9	3-77,1-31,O-22L	-0.1
1969	Chi-A	105	199	22	49	7	0	6	32	33	38	.246	.362	.372	734	101	1	0	0	0	.994	-2	1-25,3-21/O-9(3-0-6)	-0.3
1970	NY-A	66	77	5	20	2	2	1	18	9	17	.260	.337	.377	714	102	0	0	0	0	1.000	-1	1-13	-0.1
Total	9	973	3060	345	776	136	17	98	427	371	539	.254	.342	.405	747	116	66	20	17	-2	.945	-14	3-562,O-185L,1/2S	3.3

■ PRESTON WARD

Ward, Preston Meyer b: 7/24/27, Columbia, Mo. BL/TR, 6'3", 198 lbs. Deb: 4/20/48 Career OF: (17-LF 27-CF 51-RF)

YEAR	TM/L	G	AB	R	H	2B	3B	HR	RBI	BB	SO	AVG	OBP	SLG	OPS	OPS+	BR+	SB	CS	SBR	FA	FR	G/POS	TPR
1948	Bro-N	42	146	9	38	9	2	1	21	15	23	.260	.329	.370	699	86	-3	0			.990	-2	1-38	-0.6
1950	Chi-N	80	285	31	72	11	2	6	33	27	42	.253	.317	.368	686	81	-8	3			.995	10	1-76	-0.1
1953	Chi-N	33	100	10	23	5	0	4	12	18	21	.230	.347	.400	747	92	-1	3	1	0	.961	-7	O-27(0-27-0)/1-7	-0.9
	Pit-N	88	281	35	59	7	1	8	27	44	39	.210	.319	.327	646	69	-12	1	3	-1	.991	4	1-78	-1.3
	Yr	121	381	45	82	12	1	12	39	62	60	.215	.327	.346	673	76	-13	4	4	-1	.991	-2	1-85,O-27(0-27-0)	-2.2
1954	Pit-N	117	360	37	97	16	2	7	48	39	61	.269	.341	.383	724	90	-5	0	0	0	.984	5	1-48,O-42R,3-11	-0.4
1955	Pit-N	84	179	16	38	7	4	5	25	22	28	.212	.299	.380	678	80	-6	0	0	0	.998	2	1-48/O-1(0-0-1)	-0.6
1956	Pit-N	16	30	3	10	0	1	1	11	6	4	.333	.444	.500	944	157	3	0	0	0	1.000	-5	/3-5,O-5(0-0-5)	-0.2
	Cle-A	87	150	18	38	10	0	6	21	16	20	.253	.325	.440	765	98	-1	0	0	0	.988	2	1-60,O-17(14-0-3)	-0.1
1957	Cle-A	10	11	2	2	1	0	0	0	0	2	.182	.182	.273	455	23	-1	0	0	0	1.000	-0	/1-1	-0.1
1958	Cle-A	48	148	22	50	3	1	4	21	10	27	.338	.384	.453	836	133	6	0	1	-0	.957	-3	3-24,1-21	0.2
	KC-A	81	268	28	68	10	1	6	24	27	36	.254	.322	.366	688	87	-5	0	1	-0	.989	-7	1-39,3-34/O-2(2-0-0)	-1.5
	Yr	129	416	50	118	13	2	10	45	37	63	.284	.344	.397	740	103	2	0	2	-1	.992	-10	1-60,3-58/O-2(2-0-0)	-1.3
1959	KC-A	58	109	8	27	4	1	2	19	7	12	.248	.293	.358	651	76	-4	0	0	0	.982	-3	1-22/O-1(1-0-0)	-0.8
Total	9	744	2067	219	522	83	15	50	262	231	315	.253	.328	.380	708	88	-36	7	6		.992	-3	1-438/O-95R,3-74	-6.4

■ TURNER WARD

Ward, Turner Max b: 4/11/65, Orlando, Fla. BB/TR, 6'2", 200 lbs. Deb: 9/10/90 Career OF: (169-LF 182-CF 220-RF)

YEAR	TM/L	G	AB	R	H	2B	3B	HR	RBI	BB	SO	AVG	OBP	SLG	OPS	OPS+	BR+	SB	CS	SBR	FA	FR	G/POS	TPR
1990	Cle-A	14	46	10	16	2	1	1	10	3	8	.348	.388	.500	888	147	3	3	0	1	.957	0	O-13(0-0-13)/D-1	0.3
1991	Cle-A	40	100	11	23	7	0	0	5	10	16	.230	.300	.300	600	66	-4	0	0	0	1.000	-2	O-38(0-2-36)	-0.7
	Tor-A	8	13	1	4	0	0	0	2	1	2	.308	.357	.308	665	83	-0	0	0	0	1.000	-1	/O-6(1-0-5)	-0.2
	Yr	48	113	12	27	7	0	0	7	11	18	.239	.306	.301	607	68	-5	0	0	0	1.000	-3	O-44(1-2-41)	-0.9
1992	Tor-A	18	29	7	10	3	0	1	3	4	4	.345	.424	.552	976	164	3	0	1	-0	1.000	-1	O-12(2-4-6)	0.1
1993	Tor-A	72	167	20	32	4	2	4	28	23	26	.192	.293	.311	605	62	-9	3	3	-0	.990	-7	O-65(33-10-22)/1-1	-1.7
1994	Mil-A	102	367	55	85	15	2	9	45	52	68	.232	.332	.357	689	74	-14	6	2	1	.985	3	O-99(35-52-25)/3-1	-1.1
1995	Mil-A	44	129	19	34	3	1	4	16	14	21	.264	.340	.395	736	86	-3	6	1	1	.989	-2	O-40(26-7-19)/D-1	-0.5
1996	Mil-A	43	67	7	12	2	1	2	10	13	17	.179	.313	.328	641	60	-4	3	0	1	1.000	-4	O-32(15-3-18)/D-1	-0.7
1997	Pit-N	71	167	33	59	16	1	7	33	18	17	.353	.422	.587	1009	158	14	4	1	1	1.000	-10	O-54(11-31-23)	0.4
1998	Pit-N	123	282	33	74	13	3	9	46	27	40	.262	.335	.426	761	97	-1	5	4	-0	.983	-5	O-97(41-48-22)/D-1	-0.7
1999	Pit-N	49	91	2	19	2	0	0	8	13	9	.209	.314	.231	545	41	-8	2	2	-0	.955	-8	O-34(5-22-13)	-1.6
	*Ari-N	10	23	6	8	1	0	2	7	2	6	.348	.400	.652	1052	159	2	0	0	0	1.000	-0	/O-5(0-2-4)	0.2
	Yr	59	114	8	27	3	0	2	15	15	15	.237	.331	.316	647	65	-6	2	2	-0	.964	-8	O-39(5-24-17)	-1.4
2000	Ari-N	15	52	5	9	4	0	0	4	5	7	.173	.246	.250	496	25	-6	1	1	-0	1.000	1	O-15(0-1-14)	-0.5
Total	11	609	1533	209	385	72	11	39	217	185	241	.251	.336	.389	725	87	-27	33	15	2	.988	-36	O-510R/D-4,3-1,1-1	-6.7

■ BUZZY WARES

Wares, Clyde Ellsworth b: 3/23/1886, Vandalia, Mich. d: 5/26/64, South Bend, Ind. BR/TR, 5'10", 150 lbs. Deb: 9/15/13 C

YEAR	TM/L	G	AB	R	H	2B	3B	HR	RBI	BB	SO	AVG	OBP	SLG	OPS	OPS+	BR+	SB	CS	SBR	FA	FR	G/POS	TPR
1913	StL-A	11	35	5	10	2	0	0	1	1	3	.286	.306	.343	648	92	-1	2			.973	-4	/2-9	-0.5
1914	StL-A	81	215	20	45	10	1	0	23	28	35	.209	.300	.265	566	73	-7	10	10	-1	.903	-2	S-68/2-8	-0.6
Total	2	92	250	25	55	12	1	0	24	29	38	.220	.301	.276	577	76	-7	12	10		.973	-6	/S-68,2-17	-1.1

■ FRED WARNER

Warner, Frederick John Rodney b: 1855, Philadelphia, Pa. d: 2/13/1886, Philadelphia, Pa. 5'7", 155 lbs. Deb: 4/30/1875 Career OF: (15-LF 8-CF 2-RF)

YEAR	TM/L	G	AB	R	H	2B	3B	HR	RBI	BB	SO	AVG	OBP	SLG	OPS	OPS+	BR+	SB	CS	SBR	FA	FR	G/POS	TPR
1875	Cen-n	14	57	11	14	4	0	0	2	1	2	.246	.259	.316	574	107	-1	0	0	0	.784	-0	O-14(0-14-0)	0.1
1876	Phi-N	1	3	0	0	0	0	0	0	0	0	.000	.000	.000	0	-99	-1				.600	-0	/O-1(0-1-0)	-0.1
1878	Ind-N	43	165	19	41	4	0	0	10	2	15	.248	.257	.273	530	86	-2				.907	-3	*S-41/O-2(2-0-0)	-0.3
1879	Cle-N	76	316	32	77	11	4	0	22	2	20	.244	.248	.304	552	82	-6				.827	0	3-54,O-21(13-7-1)/1-1	-0.5
1883	Phi-N	39	141	13	32	6	1	0	13	5	21	.227	.253	.284	537	69	-5				.775	-9	3-38/O-1(0-0-1)	-1.1
1884	Bro-a	84	352	40	78	4	0	1		17		.222	.259	.241	501	64	-13				.824	-6	*3-84	-1.7
Total	5	243	977	104	228	25	5	1	45	26	56	.233	.254	.272	526	73	-26				.815	-18	3-176/S-41,O-25L,1	-3.7

■ HOOKS WARNER

Warner, Hoke Hayden b: 5/22/1894, Del Rio, Tex. d: 2/19/47, San Francisco, Cal BL/TR, 5'10.5", 170 lbs. Deb: 8/21/16

YEAR	TM/L	G	AB	R	H	2B	3B	HR	RBI	BB	SO	AVG	OBP	SLG	OPS	OPS+	BR+	SB	CS	SBR	FA	FR	G/POS	TPR
1916	Pit-N	44	168	12	40	1	1	2	14	6	19	.238	.264	.292	556	70	-6	6			.899	-11	3-42/2-1	-1.9

YEAR	TM/L	G	AB	R	H	2B	3B	HR	RBI	BB	SO	AVG	OBP	SLG	OPS	OPS+	BR+	SB	CS	SBR	FA	FR	G/POS	TPR
1917	Pit-N	3	5	0	1	0	0	0	0	0	1	.200	.200	.200	400	22	-0	0			1.000	1	/3-1	0.1
1919	Pit-N	6	8	0	1	0	0	0	2	3	1	.125	.364	.125	489	48	-0	0			.818	1	/3-3	0.0
1921	Chi-N	14	38	4	8	1	0	0	3	2	1	.211	.268	.237	505	35	-3	1	1	-0	.957	-1	3-10	-0.4
Total	4	67	219	16	50	2	1	2	19	11	22	.228	.268	.274	542	61	-10	7	1		.906	-10	/3-56,2-1	-2.2
■ **JOHN WARNER** Warner, John Joseph b: 8/15/1872, New York, N.Y. d: 12/21/43, Far Rockaway, N.Y. BL/TR, 5'11", 165 lbs. Deb: 4/23/1895 Career OF: (1-LF 0-CF 0-RF)																								
1895	Bos-N	3	7	2	1	0	0	0	1	1	0	.143	.333	.143	476	24	-1	0			.917	1	/C-3	0.0
	Lou-N	67	232	20	62	4	2	1	20	11	16	.267	.320	.315	635	68	-10	10			.931	-10	C-64/1-3,2-1	-1.2
	Yr	70	239	22	63	4	2	1	21	12	16	.264	.320	.310	630	67	-11	10			.930	-10	C-67/1-3,2-1	-1.2
1896	Lou-N	33	110	9	25	1	1	0	10	10	10	.227	.303	.255	558	50	-8	3			.939	9	C-32/1-1	0.3
	NY-N	19	54	9	14	1	0	0	3	3	7	.259	.310	.278	588	57	-3	1			.922	-1	C-19	-0.2
	Yr	52	164	18	39	2	1	0	13	13	17	.238	.306	.262	568	52	-11	4			.934	9	C-51/1-1	0.1
1897	NY-N	111	400	50	109	6	3	2	51	26		.273	.342	.318	659	77	-12	8			.953	18	*C-111	1.4
1898	NY-N	110	373	40	96	14	5	0	42	22		.257	.316	.322	638	86	-7	9			.968	15	*C-109/O-1(1-0-0)	1.7
1899	NY-N	88	293	38	78	8	1	0	19	15		.266	.315	.300	616	72	-11	15			.952	12	C-82/1-3	0.7
1900	NY-N	34	108	15	27	4	0	0	13	8		.250	.319	.287	606	71	-4	1			.948	3	C-31	0.1
1901	NY-N	87	291	19	70	6	1	0	20	3		.241	.268	.268	536	58	-16	3			.967	-3	C-84	-1.1
1902	Bos-A	65	222	19	52	5	7	0	12	13		.234	.286	.320	606	66	-10	0			.979	4	C-64	0.0
1903	NY-N	89	285	38	81	8	5	0	34	7		.284	.322	.347	670	87	-5	5			**.986**	12	C-85	1.4
1904	NY-N	86	287	29	57	5	1	1	15	14		.199	.253	.233	487	48	-17	7			**.982**	2	C-86	-0.8
1905	StL-N	41	137	9	35	2	2	1	12	6		.255	.301	.321	623	88	-2	2			.958	3	C-41	0.5
	Det-A	36	119	12	24	2	3	0	7	8		.202	.252	.269	521	65	-5	2			.974	1	C-36	0.0
1906	Det-A	50	153	15	37	4	2	0	10	12		.242	.326	.294	620	92	-1	4			.978	9	C-49	1.3
	Was-A	32	103	5	21	4	1	1	9	2		.204	.226	.291	518	65	-5	3			.968	9	C-32	0.8
	Yr	82	256	20	58	8	3	1	19	14		.227	.288	.293	581	82	-5	7			.974	18	C-81	2.1
1907	Was-A	72	207	11	53	5	0	0	17	12		.256	.306	.280	586	95	-1	3			.971	-8	C-64	-0.4
1908	Was-A	51	116	8	28	2	1	0	8	8		.241	.313	.276	588	100	0	7			.982	1	C-41/1-1	0.6
Total	14	1074	3497	348	870	81	35	6	303	181	33	.249	.303	.297	600	73	-118	83			.966	75	*C-1033/1-8,O-1L,2	5.1
■ **JACKIE WARNER** Warner, John Joseph b: 8/1/43, Monrovia, Cal. BR/TR, 6', 180 lbs. Deb: 4/12/66																								
1966	Cal-A	45	123	22	26	4	1	7	16	9	55	.211	.265	.431	696	99	-1	0	0	0	.984	-2	O-37(0-0-37)	-0.5
■ **JACK WARNER** Warner, John Ralph b: 8/29/03, Evansville, Ind. d: 3/13/86, Mt.Vernon, Ill. BR/TR, 5'9.5", 165 lbs. Deb: 9/24/25																								
1925	Det-A	10	39	7	13	0	0	0	2	3	6	.333	.381	.333	714	84	-1	0	0	0	1.000	-2	3-10	-0.2
1926	Det-A	100	311	41	78	8	6	0	34	38	24	.251	.342	.315	657	71	-12	8	4	0	.956	-4	3-95/S-3	-1.0
1927	Det-A	139	559	78	149	22	9	1	45	47	45	.267	.330	.343	674	74	-21	14	4	2	.947	-5	*3-138	-1.5
1928	Det-A	75	206	33	44	4	4	0	13	16	15	.214	.274	.272	545	43	-17	4	4	-1	.944	6	3-52/S-7	-0.8
1929	Bro-N	17	62	3	17	2	0	0	4	7	6	.274	.348	.306	654	65	-3	3			.945	-2	S-17	-0.3
1930	Bro-N	21	25	4	8	1	0	0	0	2	7	.320	.370	.360	730	79	-1	1			1.000	2	/3-8	0.1
1931	Bro-N	9	4	2	2	0	0	0	0	1	1	.500	.600	.500	1100	200	1	0			1.000	2	/S-2,3-1	0.3
1933	Phi-N	107	340	31	76	15	1	0	22	28	33	.224	.285	.274	558	53	-20	1			.973	3	2-71,3-30/S-1	-1.2
Total	8	478	1546	199	387	52	20	1	120	142	137	.250	.319	.312	630	65	-74	31	12		.950	0	3-334/2-71,S-30	-4.6
■ **HAL WARNOCK** Warnock, Harold Charles b: 1/6/12, New York, N.Y. d: 2/8/97, Tucson, Ariz. BL/TR, 6'2", 180 lbs. Deb: 9/2/35																								
1935	StL-A	6	7	1	2	2	0	0	0	0	3	.286	.286	.571	857	112	0	0	0	0	1.000	-1	/O-2(1-1-0)	-0.1
■ **BENNIE WARREN** Warren, Bennie Louis b: 3/2/12, Elk City, Okla. d: 5/11/94, Oklahoma City, Okla. BR/TR, 6'1", 184 lbs. Deb: 9/13/39																								
1939	Phi-N	18	56	4	13	0	0	1	7	7	7	.232	.317	.286	603	65	-3	0			.958	-4	C-17	-0.5
1940	Phi-N	106	289	33	71	6	1	12	34	40	46	.246	.339	.398	737	107	3	1			.975	-4	C-97/1-1	0.5
1941	Phi-N	121	345	34	74	13	2	9	35	44	66	.214	.309	.342	651	86	-6	0			.973	-4	*C-110	-0.4
1942	Phi-N	90	225	19	47	6	3	7	20	24	36	.209	.288	.356	644	92	-3	0			.972	-2	C-78/1-1	-0.1
1946	NY-N	39	69	7	11	1	1	4	8	14	21	.159	.301	.377	678	91	-1	0			.965	1	C-30	0.2
1947	NY-N	3	5	0	1	0	0	0	0	0	1	.200	.200	.200	400	6	-1	0			1.000	-1	/C-3	-0.1
Total	6	377	989	97	217	26	7	33	104	129	177	.219	.313	.360	673	92	-10	1			.972	-13	C-335/1-2	-0.4
■ **BILL WARREN** Warren, William Hackney "Hack" b: 2/11/1883, Missouri d: 1/28/60, Whiteville, Tenn. BR/TR, 5'8", 165 lbs. Deb: 4/30/14																								
1914	Ind-F	26	50	5	12	2	0	0	5	5	7	.240	.309	.280	589	55	-4	2			.931	-5	C-23	-0.8
1915	New-F	5	3	0	1	0	0	0	1	0	0	.333	.333	.333	667	93	-0	0			1.000	-0	/C-1,1-1	0.0
Total	2	31	53	5	13	2	0	0	6	5	7	.245	.310	.283	593	57	-4	2			.932	-5	/C-24,1-1	-0.8
■ **RABBIT WARSTLER** Warstler, Harold Burton b: 9/13/03, N.Canton, Ohio d: 5/31/64, N.Canton, Ohio BR/TR, 5'7.5", 150 lbs. Deb: 7/24/30																								
1930	Bos-A	54	162	16	30	2	3	1	13	20	21	.185	.275	.253	528	36	-16	0	2	-1	.947	-3	S-54	-1.3
1931	Bos-A	66	181	20	44	5	3	0	10	15	27	.243	.308	.304	612	65	-9	2	3	-1	.933	1	2-42,S-19/3-1	-0.5
1932	Bos-A	115	388	26	82	15	5	0	34	22	43	.211	.259	.276	535	40	-35	9	6	-0	.939	**28**	*S-107	0.0
1933	Bos-A	92	322	44	70	13	1	1	17	42	36	.217	.308	.273	581	55	-20	2	4	-1	.951	1	S-87	-1.3
1934	Phi-A	117	419	56	99	19	3	1	36	51	30	.236	.321	.303	624	64	-22	9	3	1	.969	16	*2-107/S-2	0.2
1935	Phi-A	138	496	62	124	20	7	3	59	56	53	.250	.326	.337	663	72	-20	8	4	0	.959	2	*2-136/3-2	-0.8
1936	Phi-A	66	236	27	59	8	6	1	24	36	16	.250	.354	.347	701	75	-9	0	0	0	.973	11	2-66	0.6
	Bos-N	74	304	27	64	6	0	0	17	22	33	.211	.266	.230	496	37	-27	2			.948	13	S-74	-0.8
1937	Bos-N	149	555	57	124	20	0	3	36	51	62	.223	.291	.276	567	60	-30	4			.942	-11	*S-149	-3.0
1938	Bos-N	142	467	37	108	10	4	0	40	48	38	.231	.303	.270	573	65	-22	3			.937	-7	*S-135/2-7	-1.9
1939	Bos-N	114	342	34	83	11	3	0	24	24	31	.243	.292	.292	585	62	-19	2			.953	1	S-49,2-43,3-21	-1.1
1940	Bos-N	33	57	6	12	0	0	0	4	10	5	.211	.328	.211	539	54	-3	0			.974	-1	2-24/3-2,S-1	-0.3
	Chi-N	45	159	19	36	4	1	1	18	8	19	.226	.263	.283	546	52	-11	1			.939	-1	S-28,2-17	-0.9
	Yr	78	216	25	48	4	1	1	22	18	24	.222	.282	.264	546	53	-14	1			.960	-2	2-41,S-29/3-2	-1.2
Total	11	1205	4088	431	935	133	36	11	332	405	414	.229	.300	.287	587	59	-241	42	22		.942	49	S-705,2-442/3-26	-11.1
■ **CARL WARWICK** Warwick, Carl Wayne b: 2/27/37, Dallas, Tex. BR/TL, 5'10", 170 lbs. Deb: 4/11/61																								
1961	LA-N	19	11	2	1	0	0	0	1	2	3	.091	.231	.091	322	-9	-2	0	0	0	1.000	-4	O-12(6-5-1)	-0.6
	StL-N	55	152	27	38	6	2	4	16	18	33	.250	.329	.395	724	83	-4	3	0	1	.970	-5	O-48(15-34-10)	-1.0
	Yr	74	163	29	39	6	2	4	17	20	36	.239	.322	.374	697	77	-5	3	0	1	.970	-10	O-60(21-39-11)	-1.6
1962	StL-N	13	23	4	8	0	0	1	4	2	2	.348	.400	.478	878	123	1	2	0	0	1.000	-1	O-10(1-0-9)	0.0
	Hou-N	130	477	63	124	17	1	16	60	38	77	.260	.315	.400	715	98	-3	2	3	-1	.986	1	*O-128(15-116-9)	-0.7
	Yr	143	500	67	132	17	1	17	64	40	79	.264	.319	.404	723	98	-2	4	3	-0	.986	-0	*O-138(16-116-18)	-0.7
1963	Hou-N	150	528	49	134	19	5	7	47	49	70	.254	.320	.348	668	98	-1	3	3	-0	.988	-2	*O-141(23-11-114)/1-2	-1.4
1964	*StL-N	88	158	14	41	7	1	3	15	11	30	.259	.308	.373	681	83	-3	2	0	0	.933	-6	O-49(11-0-41)	-1.2
1965	StL-N	50	77	3	12	2	1	0	6	4	18	.156	.198	.208	405	13	-9	1	0	0	.960	-3	O-21(4-2-15)/1-4	-1.4
	Bal-A	9	14	3	0	0	0	0	0	3	2	.000	.176	.000	176	-44	-3	0	0	0	1.000	-1	/O-3(1-0-2)	-0.4
1966	Chi-N	16	22	3	5	0	0	0	0	0	6	.227	.227	.227	455	27	-2	0	0	0	1.000	-2	O-10(3-7-0)	-0.4
Total	6	530	1462	168	363	51	10	31	149	127	241	.248	.309	.360	670	87	-25	13	6	1	.980	-24	O-422(79-175-201)/1-6	-7.1
■ **BILL WARWICK** Warwick, Firmin Newton b: 11/26/1897, Philadelphia, Pa. d: 12/19/84, San Antonio, Tex. BR/TR, 6'0.5", 180 lbs. Deb: 7/18/21																								
1921	Pit-N	1	1	0	0	0	0	0	0	0	0	.000	.000	.000	0	-97	-0	0	0	0	.500	-0	/C-1	0.0
1925	StL-N	13	41	8	12	1	2	1	6	5	5	.293	.370	.488	857	114	1	0	1	-0	1.000	-4	C-13	-0.3
1926	StL-N	9	14	0	5	0	0	0	2	0	2	.357	.357	.357	714	89	-0	0			.923	2	/C-9	0.2
Total	3	23	56	8	17	1	2	1	8	5	7	.304	.361	.446	807	105	0	0	1		.954	-2	/C-23	-0.1
■ **JIMMY WASDELL** Wasdell, James Charles b: 5/15/14, Cleveland, Ohio d: 8/6/83, New Port Richey, Fla. BL/TL, 5'11", 185 lbs. Deb: 9/3/37 Career OF: (227-LF 43-CF 210-RF)																								
1937	Was-A	32	110	13	28	4	4	2	12	7	13	.255	.299	.418	717	82	-4	0	1	-0	.995	-0	1-21/O-7(3-0-4)	-0.6
1938	Was-A	53	140	19	33	2	1	2	16	12	12	.236	.296	.307	603	55	-10	5	2	0	.996	-1	1-26/O-6(0-0-6)	-1.2
1939	Was-A	29	109	12	33	5	1	0	13	9	16	.303	.361	.367	728	94	-1	3	1	0	.964	-2	1-28	-0.5
1940	Was-A	10	35	3	3	1	0	0	0	2	7	.086	.135	.114	249	-37	-7	0	0	0	1.000	-1	/1-8	-0.9

YEAR	TM/L	G	AB	R	H	2B	3B	HR	RBI	BB	SO	AVG	OBP	SLG	OPS	OPS+	BR+	SB	CS	SBR	FA	FR	G/POS	TPR
	Bro-N	77	230	35	64	14	4	3	37	18	24	.278	.333	.413	746	99	-1	4			.947	-7	O-42(1-1-40),1-17	-1.1
1941	*Bro-N	94	265	39	79	14	3	4	48	16	15	.298	.345	.419	764	110	3	2			.956	-6	O-54(8-0-46),1-15	-0.8
1942	Pit-N	122	409	44	106	11	2	3	38	47	22	.259	.337	.318	655	90	-4	1			.957	-3	O-97(36-2-61)/1-7	-1.5
1943	Pit-N	4	2	0	1	0	0	0	1	2	0	.500	.750	.500	1250	256	1	0			.000	0	H	0.1
	Phi-N	141	522	54	136	19	6	4	67	46	22	.261	.323	.343	666	96	-3	6			.988	-8	1-82,O-56(39-22-5)	-1.9
	Yr	145	524	54	137	19	6	4	68	48	22	.261	.326	.344	669	97	-2	6			.988	-8	1-82,O-56(39-22-5)	-1.8
1944	Phi-N	133	451	47	125	20	3	3	40	45	17	.277	.344	.355	699	100	1	0			.980	-9	*O-121(118-5-3)/1-4	-1.6
1945	Phi-N	134	500	65	150	19	8	7	60	32	11	.300	.346	.412	758	113	7	7			.967	-2	O-65(17-13-37),1-63	-0.2
1946	Phi-N	26	51	7	13	0	2	1	5	3	2	.255	.309	.392	701	101	-0	0			.923	-2	O-11(4-0-6)/1-2	-0.3
	Cle-A	32	41	1	11	0	0	0	4	4	4	.268	.333	.268	602	74	-1	1	0	0	.939	-2	/1-4,O-3(1-0-2)	-0.3
1947	Cle-A	1	1	0	0	0	0	0	0	0	0	.000	.000	.000	0	-99	-0	0	0	0	.000	0	H	0.0
Total	11	888	2866	339	782	109	34	29	341	243	165	.273	.332	.365	697	96	-19	29	4		.966	-45	O-462L,1-277	-10.8

■ **LINK WASEM** Wasem, Lincoln William b: 1/30/11, Birmingham, Ohio d: 3/6/79, S.Laguna, Cal. BR/TR, 5′9.5″, 180 lbs. Deb: 5/5/37

YEAR	TM/L	G	AB	R	H	2B	3B	HR	RBI	BB	SO	AVG	OBP	SLG	OPS	OPS+	BR+	SB	CS	SBR	FA	FR	G/POS	TPR
1937	Bos-N	2	1	0	0	0	0	0	0	0	0	.000	.000	.000	0	-99	-0	0			1.000	0	/C-2	0.0

■ **LIBE WASHBURN** Washburn, Libeus b: 6/16/1874, Lyme, N.H. d: 3/22/40, Malone, N.Y. BB/TL, 5′10″, 180 lbs. Deb: 5/30/02

YEAR	TM/L	G	AB	R	H	2B	3B	HR	RBI	BB	SO	AVG	OBP	SLG	OPS	OPS+	BR+	SB	CS	SBR	FA	FR	G/POS	TPR
1902	NY-N	6	9	1	4	0	0	0	0	2		.444	.615	.444	1060	230	2	1			1.000	-1	/O-3(0-2-1)	0.1
1903	Phi-N	8	18	1	3	0	0	0	1	1		.167	.211	.167	377	8	-2	0			1.000	-1	/P-4,O-2(1-0-0)	-0.1
Total	2	14	27	2	7	0	0	0	1	3		.259	.375	.259	634	89	-0	1			1.000	-1	/O-5(1-2-1),P-4	0.0

■ **CLAUDELL WASHINGTON** Washington, Claudell b: 8/31/54, Los Angeles, Cal. BL/TL, 6′, 190 lbs. Deb: 7/5/74 Career OF: (324-LF 320-CF 1101-RF)

YEAR	TM/L	G	AB	R	H	2B	3B	HR	RBI	BB	SO	AVG	OBP	SLG	OPS	OPS+	BR+	SB	CS	SBR	FA	FR	G/POS	TPR
1974	*Oak-A	73	221	16	63	10	5	0	19	13	44	.285	.328	.376	703	109	2	6	8	-1	.985	-1	D-38,O-32(14-10-10)	-0.3
1975	*Oak-A★	148	590	86	182	24	7	10	77	32	80	.308	.349	.424	773	120	14	40	15	4	.978	-3	*O-148(112-35-11)	0.7
1976	Oak-A	134	490	65	126	20	6	5	53	30	90	.257	.304	.353	657	96	-4	37	20	1	.963	-2	*O-126(0-30-105)/D-4	-1.1
1977	Tex-A	129	521	63	148	31	2	12	68	25	112	.284	.321	.420	741	99	-2	21	8	2	.978	-1	*O-127(93-41-4)/D-1	-0.5
1978	Tex-A	12	42	1	7	0	0	0	2	1	12	.167	.186	.167	353	-0	-6	0	1	-0	.917	-1	/O-7(1-0-6),D-4	-0.8
	Chi-A	86	314	33	83	16	5	6	31	12	57	.264	.294	.404	698	94	-4	5	5	-1	.959	-2	O-82(15-8-63)/D-1	-1.0
	Yr	98	356	34	90	16	5	6	33	13	69	.253	.281	.376	657	83	-9	5	6	-1	.957	-3	O-89(16-8-69)/D-5	-1.8
1979	Chi-A	131	471	79	132	33	5	13	66	28	93	.280	.325	.454	779	108	4	19	11	0	.974	4	*O-122(0-1-121)/D-3	0.1
1980	Chi-A	32	90	15	26	4	2	1	12	5	19	.289	.333	.411	744	103	0	4	2	0	.933	-2	O-23(21-0-3)/D-2	-0.2
	NY-N	79	284	38	78	16	4	10	42	20	63	.275	.325	.465	789	121	7	17	5	2	.978	2	O-70(23-1-58)	0.7
1981	Atl-N	85	320	37	93	22	3	5	37	15	47	.291	.330	.425	755	110	3	12	6	1	.993	2	O-79(0-0-79)	0.1
1982	*Atl-N	150	563	94	150	24	6	16	80	50	107	.266	.333	.416	748	104	3	33	10	4	.950	-4	*O-139(0-0-139)	-0.6
1983	Atl-N	134	496	75	138	24	8	9	44	35	103	.278	.326	.413	739	96	-3	31	9	4	.974	2	*O-128(0-0-128)	-0.4
1984	Atl-N★	120	416	62	119	21	2	17	61	59	77	.286	.376	.469	845	127	16	21	9	1	.967	-5	*O-107(0-0-107)	0.6
1985	Atl-N	122	398	62	110	14	6	15	43	40	66	.276	.344	.455	799	115	8	14	4	2	.962	-14	O-99(0-0-99)	-1.0
1986	Atl-N	40	137	17	37	11	0	5	14	14	26	.270	.338	.460	798	112	2	4	7	-2	.957	-5	O-38(0-0-38)	-0.7
	NY-A	54	135	19	32	5	0	6	16	7	33	.237	.285	.407	692	87	-3	6	1	1	.985	-6	O-39(11-20-9)	-0.8
1987	NY-A	102	312	42	87	17	0	9	44	27	54	.279	.336	.420	756	100	-0	10	1	2	.988	0	O-72(2-69-1),D-13	0.1
1988	NY-A	126	455	62	140	22	3	11	64	24	74	.308	.345	.442	787	120	11	15	6	1	.984	2	*O-117(13-103-8)	1.3
1989	Cal-A	110	418	53	114	18	4	13	42	27	84	.273	.320	.428	748	111	5	13	5	1	.975	-3	*O-100(0-2-99)/D-7	0.0
1990	Cal-A	12	34	3	6	1	0	1	3	2	8	.176	.222	.294	516	44	-3	1	0	0	1.000	1	/O-9(0-0-9)	-0.2
	NY-A	33	80	4	13	1	1	0	6	2	17	.162	.183	.200	383	7	-10	3	1	0	1.000	1	O-21(19-0-4)/D-2	-1.0
	Yr	45	114	7	19	2	1	1	9	4	25	.167	.195	.228	423	18	-13	4	1	1	1.000	2	O-30(19-0-13)/D-2	-1.2
Total	17	1912	6787	926	1884	334	69	164	824	468	1266	.278	.328	.420	747	106	41	312	134	22	.973	-37	*O-1685R/D-75	-5.0

■ **HERB WASHINGTON** Washington, Herbert Lee b: 11/16/51, Belzoni, Miss. BR/TR, 6′, 170 lbs. Deb: 4/4/74

YEAR	TM/L	G	AB	R	H	2B	3B	HR	RBI	BB	SO	AVG	OBP	SLG	OPS	OPS+	BR+	SB	CS	SBR	FA	FR	G/POS	TPR
1974	*Oak-A	92	0	29	0	0	0	0	0	0	0	—	—	—	—	—	0	29	16	1	.000	0	R	-0.2
1975	Oak-A	13	0	4	0	0	0	0	0	0	0	—	—	—	—	—	0	2	1	0	.000	0	R	0.0
Total	2	105	0	33	0	0	0	0	0	0	0	—	—	—	—	—	0	31	17	1		0	-0,-0	-0.2

■ **LA RUE WASHINGTON** Washington, La Rue b: 9/7/53, Long Beach, Cal. BR/TR, 6′, 170 lbs. Deb: 9/7/78 Career OF: (0-LF 12-CF 1-RF)

YEAR	TM/L	G	AB	R	H	2B	3B	HR	RBI	BB	SO	AVG	OBP	SLG	OPS	OPS+	BR+	SB	CS	SBR	FA	FR	G/POS	TPR
1978	Tex-A	3	3	0	0	0	0	0	0	0	1	.000	.000	.000	0	-99	-1	0	0	0	1.000	2	/2-2,D-1	0.1
1979	Tex-A	25	18	5	5	0	0	0	2	4	0	.278	.409	.278	687	90	0	2	1	0	1.000	-3	O-13(0-12-1)/3-1,D-1	-0.3
Total	2	28	21	5	5	0	0	0	2	4	1	.238	.360	.238	598	67	-1	2	1	0	1.000	-1	/O-13C,D-2,2-2,3-1	-0.2

■ **RON WASHINGTON** Washington, Ronald b: 4/29/52, New Orleans, La. BR/TR, 5′11″, 163 lbs. Deb: 9/10/77 C Career OF: (2-LF 2-CF 0-RF)

YEAR	TM/L	G	AB	R	H	2B	3B	HR	RBI	BB	SO	AVG	OBP	SLG	OPS	OPS+	BR+	SB	CS	SBR	FA	FR	G/POS	TPR
1977	LA-N	10	19	4	7	0	0	0	1	0	2	.368	.400	.368	768	108	0	1	1	-0	.857	-2	S-10	-0.1
1981	Min-A	28	84	8	19	3	1	0	5	4	14	.226	.270	.286	555	56	-5	4	1	1	.951	6	S-26/O-2(0-2-0)	0.5
1982	Min-A	119	451	48	122	17	6	5	39	14	79	.271	.292	.368	661	78	-14	3	3	-0	.972	-44	S-91,2-37/3-1	-4.9
1983	Min-A	99	317	28	78	7	3	4	26	22	50	.246	.297	.325	622	69	-13	10	5	0	.962	-17	S-81,2-14/3-1,D-1	-2.1
1984	Min-A	88	197	25	58	11	5	3	23	4	31	.294	.312	.447	759	102	0	1	1	-0	.978	-16	S-71/2-9,3-2,D-4	-1.1
1985	Min-A	70	135	24	37	6	4	1	14	8	15	.274	.315	.400	715	89	-2	5	1	1	.951	-4	S-31,2-24/3-7,1D	-0.3
1986	Min-A	48	74	15	19	3	0	4	11	3	21	.257	.286	.459	745	96	-1	1	2	-0	.917	0	2-16,D-15/S-7,3-3	-0.1
1987	Bal-A	26	79	7	16	3	1	1	6	1	15	.203	.213	.304	516	36	-7	0	1	-0	1.000	2	3-20/2-3,O-2L,SD	-0.6
1988	Cle-A	69	223	30	57	14	2	2	21	9	35	.256	.300	.363	663	82	-5	3	3	-0	.933	-14	S-54/3-8,2-7,D-1	-1.6
1989	Hou-N	7	7	1	1	1	0	0	0	0	4	.143	.143	.286	429	20	-1	0	0	0	.000	-0	/2-1,3-1	-0.1
Total	10	564	1586	190	414	65	22	20	146	65	266	.261	.294	.368	662	79	-48	28	18	-0	.958	-88	S-372,2-111/3-43,DO1	-10.4

■ **GEORGE WASHINGTON** Washington, Sloan Vernon "Vern" b: 6/4/07, Linden, Tex. d: 2/17/85, Linden, Tex. BL/TR, 5′11.5″, 190 lbs. Deb: 4/17/35

YEAR	TM/L	G	AB	R	H	2B	3B	HR	RBI	BB	SO	AVG	OBP	SLG	OPS	OPS+	BR+	SB	CS	SBR	FA	FR	G/POS	TPR
1935	Chi-A	108	339	40	96	22	3	8	47	10	18	.283	.310	.437	746	89	-7	1	0	0	.974	0	O-79(0-0-79)	-1.1
1936	Chi-A	20	49	6	8	2	0	1	5	1	4	.163	.180	.265	445	8	-7	0	0	0	.938	-2	O-12(0-0-12)	-0.9
Total	2	128	388	46	104	24	3	9	52	11	22	.268	.294	.415	708	78	-15	1	0	0	.970	-2	/O-91(0-0-91)	-2.0

■ **U L WASHINGTON** Washington, U L b: 10/27/53, Stringtown, Okla. BB/TR, 5′11″, 175 lbs. Deb: 9/6/77

YEAR	TM/L	G	AB	R	H	2B	3B	HR	RBI	BB	SO	AVG	OBP	SLG	OPS	OPS+	BR+	SB	CS	SBR	FA	FR	G/POS	TPR
1977	KC-A	10	20	0	4	1	1	0	1	5	4	.200	.360	.350	710	94	-0	1	0	0	.872	0	/S-9	0.1
1978	KC-A	69	129	10	34	2	1	0	9	10	20	.264	.317	.295	611	71	-5	12	6	1	.927	-11	S-49,2-19/D-1	-1.2
1979	KC-A	101	268	32	68	12	5	2	25	20	44	.254	.306	.358	664	77	-9	10	7	-0	.970	3	S-50,2-46/3-1,D-3	0.0
1980	*KC-A	153	549	79	150	16	11	6	53	53	78	.273	.337	.375	712	94	-4	20	7	2	.957	-26	*S-152	-1.2
1981	*KC-A	98	339	40	77	19	1	2	29	41	43	.227	.311	.307	617	79	-8	10	10	-1	.973	-21	S-98	-2.2
1982	KC-A	119	437	64	125	19	3	10	60	38	48	.286	.343	.412	755	106	4	23	7	3	.961	-11	*S-117/D-1	0.8
1983	KC-A	144	547	76	129	19	6	5	41	48	78	.236	.299	.320	619	70	-22	40	7	6	.947	-10	*S-140/D-1	-1.1
1984	*KC-A	63	170	18	38	6	0	1	10	14	31	.224	.283	.276	559	55	-10	4	6	-1	.961	0	S-61	-0.6
1985	Mon-N	68	193	24	48	9	4	1	17	15	33	.249	.303	.352	655	88	-4	6	3	0	.978	-10	2-43/S-9,3-3	-1.1
1986	Pit-N	72	135	14	27	0	4	0	10	15	27	.200	.280	.259	539	49	-9	6	0	1	.947	-8	S-51/2-3	-1.2
1987	Pit-N	10	10	1	3	0	0	0	0	2	3	.300	.417	.300	717	93	0	0	0	0	.833	-0	/S-1,3-1	0.0
Total	11	907	2797	358	703	103	36	27	255	261	409	.251	.315	.343	658	82	-67	132	53	10	.956	-93	S-737,2-111/D-6,3-5	-7.7

■ **MARK WASINGER** Wasinger, Mark Thomas b: 8/4/61, Monterey, Cal. BR/TR, 6′, 165 lbs. Deb: 5/27/86

YEAR	TM/L	G	AB	R	H	2B	3B	HR	RBI	BB	SO	AVG	OBP	SLG	OPS	OPS+	BR+	SB	CS	SBR	FA	FR	G/POS	TPR
1986	SD-N	3	8	0	0	0	0	0	1	0	2	.000	.000	.000	0	-99	-2	0	0	0	.500	-1	/3-3,2-1	-0.4
1987	SF-N	44	80	16	22	3	0	1	3	8	14	.275	.341	.350	691	88	-1	2	0	0	.973	3	3-21,2-10/S-2	0.2
1988	SF-N	3	2	1	0	0	0	0	0	0	0	.000	.000	.000	0	-99	-1	0	0	0	.000	0	/3-1	-0.1
Total	3	50	90	17	22	3	0	1	4	8	16	.244	.306	.311	617	68	-4	2	0	0	.907	2	/3-25,2-11,S-2	-0.3

■ **B.J. WASZGIS** Waszgis, Robert Michael b: 8/24/70, Omaha, Neb. BR/TR, 6′2″, 215 lbs. Deb: 7/29/2000

YEAR	TM/L	G	AB	R	H	2B	3B	HR	RBI	BB	SO	AVG	OBP	SLG	OPS	OPS+	BR+	SB	CS	SBR	FA	FR	G/POS	TPR
2000	Tex-A	24	45	6	10	1	0	0	4	4	10	.222	.300	.244	544	39	-4	0	0	0	1.000	-2	C-23/1-3	-0.5

■ **FRED WATERMAN** Waterman, Frederick A. b: 12/1845, New York, N.Y. d: 12/16/1899, Cincinnati, Ohio 5′7.5″, 148 lbs. Deb: 5/5/1871 M Career OF: (0-LF 3-CF 1-RF)

YEAR	TM/L	G	AB	R	H	2B	3B	HR	RBI	BB	SO	AVG	OBP	SLG	OPS	OPS+	BR+	SB	CS	SBR	FA	FR	G/POS	TPR
1871	Oly-n	32	158	46	50	7	4	0	17	10	0	.316	.357	.411	769	127	7	11	3	1	.695	2	*3-28/C-6	0.6
1872	Oly-n	9	45	13	17	1	2	0	6	0	0	.378	.378	.489	867	173	4	0	0	0	.843	3	/3-7,C-2,M	0.5
1873	Was-n	15	80	20	28	1	1	0	12	1	1	.350	.358	.387	746	125	3	0	0	0	.617	-6	/S-9,O-4(0-3-1),3-2	-0.3

YEAR	TM/L	G	AB	R	H	2B	3B	HR	RBI	BB	SO	AVG	OBP	SLG	OPS	OPS+	BR+	SB	CS	SBR	FA	FR	G/POS	TPR
1875	Chi-n	5	20	2	6	0	0	0	3	0	2	.300	.300	.300	600	108	0	0	1	-0	.545	-3	/3-5	-0.3
Total	4 n	61	303	81	101	9	7	0	38	11	3	.333	.357	.409	766	132	13	11	4	1	.713	-4	/3-42,S-9,C-8,O-4C	0.5

■ JOHN WATHAN
Wathan, John David b: 10/4/49, Cedar Rapids, Iowa BR/TR, 6'2", 205 lbs. Deb: 5/26/76 MC Career OF: (28-LF 0-CF 37-RF)

YEAR	TM/L	G	AB	R	H	2B	3B	HR	RBI	BB	SO	AVG	OBP	SLG	OPS	OPS+	BR+	SB	CS	SBR	FA	FR	G/POS	TPR
1976	*KC-A	27	42	5	12	1	0	0	5	2	5	.286	.333	.310	643	88	-1	0	2	-1	.984	-1	C-23/1-3	-0.2
1977	*KC-A	55	119	18	39	5	3	2	21	5	8	.328	.355	.471	825	122	3	2	0	0	.993	-2	C-35/1-5,D-2	0.2
1978	*KC-A	67	190	19	57	10	1	2	28	3	12	.300	.325	.395	720	99	-1	2	1	0	1.000	1	1-47,C-21	-0.1
1979	KC-A	90	199	26	41	7	3	2	28	7	24	.206	.233	.302	535	42	-16	2	1	0	.993	-2	1-49,C-23,D-11,/O-3L	-2.0
1980	*KC-A	126	453	57	138	14	7	6	58	50	42	.305	.377	.406	784	114	10	17	3	3	.982	-11	C-77,O-35L,1-12	0.3
1981	*KC-A	89	301	24	76	9	3	1	19	19	23	.252	.301	.312	614	78	-9	11	6	0	.979	-11	C-73,O-16(3-0-13)/1-1	-1.7
1982	KC-A	121	448	79	121	11	3	3	51	48	46	.270	.343	.328	671	85	-7	36	9	5	.980	-17	*C-120/1-3	-1.5
1983	KC-A	128	437	49	107	18	3	2	32	27	56	.245	.290	.314	604	66	-20	28	7	4	.985	-4	C-92,1-37/O-9(3-0-6)	-1.8
1984	*KC-A	97	171	17	31	7	1	2	10	21	34	.181	.271	.269	540	50	-12	6	6	-1	.975	5	C-59,1-33/O-1L,D-4	-0.6
1985	*KC-A	60	145	11	34	8	1	1	9	17	15	.234	.319	.324	643	76	-4	1	1	-0	.986	12	C-49/1-6,D-2	0.9
Total	10	860	2505	305	656	90	25	21	261	199	265	.262	.320	.343	663	83	-56	105	36	11	.982	-31	C-572,1-196/O-64R,D	-6.5

■ DAVE WATKINS
Watkins, David Roger b: 3/15/44, Owensboro, Ky. BR/TR, 5'10", 185 lbs. Deb: 4/9/69

YEAR	TM/L	G	AB	R	H	2B	3B	HR	RBI	BB	SO	AVG	OBP	SLG	OPS	OPS+	BR+	SB	CS	SBR	FA	FR	G/POS	TPR
1969	Phi-N	69	148	17	26	2	1	4	12	22	53	.176	.291	.284	574	63	-7	2	3	-1	.981	-5	C-54/O-5(5-0-1),3-1	-1.1

■ GEORGE WATKINS
Watkins, George Archibald b: 6/4/1900, Freestone Co., Tex d: 6/1/70, Houston, Tex. BL/TR, 6', 175 lbs. Deb: 4/15/30 Career OF: (266-LF 118-CF 434-RF)

YEAR	TM/L	G	AB	R	H	2B	3B	HR	RBI	BB	SO	AVG	OBP	SLG	OPS	OPS+	BR+	SB	CS	SBR	FA	FR	G/POS	TPR
1930	*StL-N	119	391	85	146	32	7	17	87	24	49	.373	.415	.621	1037	141	25	5			.956	-6	O-89(3-1-85),1-13/2-1	1.1
1931	*StL-N	131	503	93	145	30	13	13	51	31	66	.288	.336	.477	813	112	7	15			.958	-6	*O-129(0-9-121)	-0.6
1932	StL-N	127	458	67	143	35	3	9	63	45	46	.312	.384	.461	844	122	16	18			.949	3	*O-120(38-19-62)	1.1
1933	StL-N	138	525	66	146	24	5	5	62	39	62	.278	.342	.371	713	98	0	11			.953	1	*O-135(0-0-135)	-0.8
1934	NY-N	105	296	38	73	18	3	6	33	24	34	.247	.316	.389	704	90	-5	2			.944	-10	O-81(8-68-5)	-1.6
1935	Phi-N	150	600	80	162	25	5	17	76	40	78	.270	.320	.413	733	87	-12	3			.958	5	*O-148(128-20-1)	-1.4
1936	Phi-N	19	70	7	17	4	0	2	5	5	13	.243	.293	.386	679	74	-3	2			.889	-3	O-17(17-0-0)	-0.6
	Bro-N	105	364	54	93	24	6	4	43	38	34	.255	.334	.387	722	93	-4	5			.969	-4	O-98(72-1-25)	-1.3
	Yr	124	434	61	110	28	6	6	48	43	47	.253	.328	.387	715	90	-6	7			.959	-7	*O-115(89-1-25)	-1.9
Total	7	894	3207	490	925	192	42	73	420	246	382	.288	.347	.443	790	105	25	61			.954	-20	O-817R/1-13,2-1	-4.1

■ ED WATKINS
Watkins, James Edward b: 6/21/1877, Philadelphia, Pa. d: 3/29/33, Kelvin, Ariz. Deb: 9/6/02

YEAR	TM/L	G	AB	R	H	2B	3B	HR	RBI	BB	SO	AVG	OBP	SLG	OPS	OPS+	BR+	SB	CS	SBR	FA	FR	G/POS	TPR
1902	Phi-N	1	3	0	0	0	0	0	0	1		.000	.250	.000	250	-22	-0	0			1.000	-0	/O-1(1-0-0)	-0.1

■ BILL WATKINS
Watkins, William Henry b: 5/5/1858, Brantford, Ont., Can d: 6/9/37, Port Huron, Mich. 5'10", 156 lbs. Deb: 8/1/1884 M

YEAR	TM/L	G	AB	R	H	2B	3B	HR	RBI	BB	SO	AVG	OBP	SLG	OPS	OPS+	BR+	SB	CS	SBR	FA	FR	G/POS	TPR
1884	Ind-a	34	127	16	26	4	0	0		5		.205	.241	.236	477	58	-6				.845	-6	3-23/2-9,S-2,M	-1.0

■ PAT WATKINS
Watkins, William Patrick b: 9/2/72, Raleigh, N.C. BR/TR, 6'2", 185 lbs. Deb: 9/9/97

YEAR	TM/L	G	AB	R	H	2B	3B	HR	RBI	BB	SO	AVG	OBP	SLG	OPS	OPS+	BR+	SB	CS	SBR	FA	FR	G/POS	TPR
1997	Cin-N	17	29	2	6	2	0	0	0	0	5	.207	.207	.276	483	25	-3	1	0	0	1.000	-3	O-15(0-15-0)	-0.6
1998	Cin-N	83	147	11	39	8	1	2	15	8	26	.265	.308	.374	682	77	-5	1	3	-1	.971	-12	O-77(13-39-28)	-1.9
1999	Col-N	16	19	2	1	0	0	0	0	2	5	.053	.143	.053	195	-38	-4	0	0	0	1.000	-2	O-10(4-1-5)	-0.6
Total	3	116	195	15	46	10	1	2	15	10	36	.236	.277	.328	605	55	-12	2	3	-1	.976	-17	O-102(17-55-33)	-3.1

■ NEAL WATLINGTON
Watlington, Julius Neal b: 12/25/22, Yanceyville, N.C. BL/TR, 6', 195 lbs. Deb: 7/10/53

YEAR	TM/L	G	AB	R	H	2B	3B	HR	RBI	BB	SO	AVG	OBP	SLG	OPS	OPS+	BR+	SB	CS	SBR	FA	FR	G/POS	TPR
1953	Phi-A	21	44	4	7	1	0	0	3	3	8	.159	.213	.182	395	7	-6	0	1	-0	.978	0	/C-9	-0.5

■ ART WATSON
Watson, Arthur Stanhope "Watty" b: 1/11/1884, Jeffersonville, Ind. d: 5/9/50, Buffalo, N.Y. BL/TR, 5'10", 175 lbs. Deb: 5/19/14

YEAR	TM/L	G	AB	R	H	2B	3B	HR	RBI	BB	SO	AVG	OBP	SLG	OPS	OPS+	BR+	SB	CS	SBR	FA	FR	G/POS	TPR
1914	Bro-F	22	46	7	13	4	1	1	3	1	6	.283	.298	.478	776	110	-0	0			.977	2	C-18	0.3
1915	Bro-F	9	19	4	5	0	3	0	1	3	4	.263	.364	.579	943	164	1	0			.957	-3	/C-7	-0.1
	Buf-F	22	30	6	14	1	0	1	13	0	4	.467	.467	.600	1067	195	3	0			.778	-4	/C-6,O-1(1-0-0)	-0.1
	Yr	31	49	10	19	1	3	1	14	3	8	.388	.423	.592	1015	182	4	0			.878	-7	C-13/O-1(1-0-0)	-0.2
Total	2	53	95	17	32	5	4	2	17	4	14	.337	.364	.537	900	147	4	0			.946	-5	/C-31,O-1(1-0-0)	0.1

■ JOHNNY WATSON
Watson, John Thomas b: 1/16/08, Tazewell, Va. d: 4/29/65, Huntington, W.Va. BL/TR, 6', 175 lbs. Deb: 9/26/30

YEAR	TM/L	G	AB	R	H	2B	3B	HR	RBI	BB	SO	AVG	OBP	SLG	OPS	OPS+	BR+	SB	CS	SBR	FA	FR	G/POS	TPR
1930	Det-A	4	12	1	3	2	0	0	3	1	2	.250	.308	.417	724	80	-0	0	0	0	.933	-1	/S-4	-0.1

■ BOB WATSON
Watson, Robert Jose "Bull" b: 4/10/46, Los Angeles, Cal. BR/TR, 6'2", 205 lbs. Deb: 9/9/66 C Career OF: (570-LF 0-CF 1-RF)

YEAR	TM/L	G	AB	R	H	2B	3B	HR	RBI	BB	SO	AVG	OBP	SLG	OPS	OPS+	BR+	SB	CS	SBR	FA	FR	G/POS	TPR
1966	Hou-N	1	1	0	0	0	0	0	0	0	0	.000	.000	.000	0	-99	-0	0	0	0	.000	0	H	0.0
1967	Hou-N	6	14	1	3	0	0	1	2	0	3	.214	.214	.429	643	82	-0	0	0	0	.958	0	/1-3	-0.1
1968	Hou-N	45	140	13	32	7	0	2	8	13	32	.229	.299	.321	620	88	-2	1	0	0	.885	-5	O-40(40-0-1)	-1.1
1969	Hou-N	20	40	3	11	3	0	0	3	6	5	.275	.396	.350	746	113	1	0	0	0	1.000	-1	/O-6(6-0-0),1-5,C-1	0.0
1970	Hou-N	97	327	48	89	19	2	11	61	24	59	.272	.330	.443	773	110	3	1	1	-0	.992	-8	1-83/C-6,O-1(1-0-0)	-1.1
1971	Hou-N	129	468	49	135	17	3	9	67	41	56	.288	.348	.395	744	113	8	0	3	-1	.985	-10	O-87(87-0-0),1-45	-1.2
1972	Hou-N	147	548	74	171	27	4	16	86	53	83	.312	.381	.464	844	142	30	1	1	-0	.978	-6	*O-143(143-0-0)/1-2	1.6
1973	Hou-N★	158	573	97	179	24	3	16	94	85	73	.312	.405	.449	853	137	31	1	4	-1	.969	-1	*O-142L,1-26/C-3	2.1
1974	Hou-N	150	524	69	156	19	4	11	67	60	61	.298	.373	.412	785	125	18	3	4	-1	.981	-10	*O-140(140-0-0),1-35	-0.1
1975	Hou-N★	132	485	67	157	27	1	18	85	40	50	.324	.379	.495	874	152	32	3	5	-1	.993	-2	*1-118/O-9(9-0-0)	2.0
1976	Hou-N	157	585	76	183	31	3	16	102	62	64	.313	.382	.458	841	151	39	3	3	-0	.990	-2	*1-155	2.5
1977	Hou-N	151	554	77	160	38	6	22	110	57	69	.289	.362	.498	861	141	31	5	0	1	.994	12	*1-146	3.5
1978	Hou-N	139	461	51	133	25	4	14	79	51	57	.289	.364	.451	816	137	22	3	1	0	.992	10	*1-128	2.6
1979	Hou-N	49	163	15	39	4	0	3	18	16	23	.239	.307	.319	626	75	-6	0	0	0	.993	3	1-44	-0.6
	Bos-A	84	312	48	105	19	4	13	53	29	33	.337	.402	.548	950	145	20	3	2	-0	.988	2	1-58,D-26	1.7
1980	*NY-A	130	469	62	144	25	3	13	68	48	56	.307	.373	.456	829	128	18	2	1	0	.990	-2	*1-104,D-21	1.0
1981	*NY-A	59	156	15	33	3	3	6	12	24	17	.212	.317	.385	701	103	1	0	0	0	.997	-1	1-50/D-6	-0.3
1982	NY-A	7	17	3	4	3	0	0	3	3	0	.235	.350	.412	762	110	0	0	0	0	1.000	-1	/1-6,D-1	-0.1
	Atl-N	57	114	16	28	3	1	5	22	14	20	.246	.328	.421	749	104	1	1	1	-0	1.000	-4	1-27/O-2(2-0-0)	-0.5
1983	Atl-N	65	149	14	46	9	0	6	37	18	23	.309	.383	.490	873	131	6	0	2	-1	.984	-3	1-34	0.1
1984	Atl-N	49	85	4	18	4	0	2	12	9	12	.212	.287	.329	617	68	-4	0	0	0	.983	1	1-19	-0.4
Total	19	1832	6185	802	1826	307	41	184	989	653	796	.295	.367	.447	814	130	250	27	28	-4	.991	-27	*1-1088,O-570L/D-54,C	11.6

■ ALLIE WATT
Watt, Albert Bailey b: 12/12/1899, Philadelphia, Pa. d: 3/15/68, Norfolk, Va. BR/TR, 5'8", 154 lbs. Deb: 10/3/20 F

YEAR	TM/L	G	AB	R	H	2B	3B	HR	RBI	BB	SO	AVG	OBP	SLG	OPS	OPS+	BR+	SB	CS	SBR	FA	FR	G/POS	TPR
1920	Was-A	1	1	0	1	1	0	0	1	0	0	1.000	1.000	2.000	3000	700	1	0	0	0	1.000	0	/2-1	0.1

■ JOHNNY WATWOOD
Watwood, John Clifford "Lefty" b: 8/17/05, Alexander City, Ala. d: 3/1/80, Goodwater, Ala. BL/TL, 6'1", 186 lbs. Deb: 4/16/29

YEAR	TM/L	G	AB	R	H	2B	3B	HR	RBI	BB	SO	AVG	OBP	SLG	OPS	OPS+	BR+	SB	CS	SBR	FA	FR	G/POS	TPR
1929	Chi-A	85	278	33	84	12	6	2	28	22	21	.302	.355	.410	766	98	-1	6	3	0	.942	-2	O-77(1-53-23)	-0.6
1930	Chi-A	133	427	75	129	25	4	2	51	52	35	.302	.382	.393	775	100	2	5	7	-1	.989	3	1-62,O-52(1-36-14)	-0.3
1931	Chi-A	128	367	51	104	16	6	1	47	56	30	.283	.380	.368	748	103	4	9	3	1	.944	3	*O-102(4-76-24)/1-4	0.5
1932	Chi-A	13	49	5	15	2	0	0	0	1	3	.306	.333	.347	680	82	-1	0	0	0	.960	-2	O-13(4-1-11)	-0.4
	Bos-A	95	266	26	66	11	0	0	30	20	11	.248	.301	.289	590	55	-17	7	4	0	.945	-1	O-46(7-25-14),1-18	-2.1
	Yr	108	315	31	81	13	0	0	30	21	14	.257	.306	.298	604	59	-19	7	4	0	.948	-4	O-59(11-26-25),1-18	-2.5
1933	Bos-A	13	30	2	4	0	0	0	2	3	3	.133	.212	.133	345	-7	-5	0	0	0	.950	-1	/O-9(5-0-4)	-0.5
1939	Phi-N	2	6	0	1	0	0	0	0	0	0	.167	.167	.167	333	-11	-1	0			.933	-1	/1-2	-0.2
Total	6	469	1423	192	403	66	16	5	158	154	103	.283	.356	.363	718	89	-19	27	17		.948	-0	O-299(22-191-90)/1-86	-3.6

■ BOB WAY
Way, Robert Clinton b: 4/2/06, Emlenton, Pa. d: 6/20/74, Pittsburgh, Pa. BR/TR, 5'10.5", 168 lbs. Deb: 4/12/27

YEAR	TM/L	G	AB	R	H	2B	3B	HR	RBI	BB	SO	AVG	OBP	SLG	OPS	OPS+	BR+	SB	CS	SBR	FA	FR	G/POS	TPR
1927	Chi-A	5	3	3	1	0	0	0	1	0	0	.333	.333	.333	667	75	-0	0	0	0	1.000	0	/2-1	0.0

■ ROY WEATHERLY
Weatherly, Cyril Roy "Stormy" b: 2/25/15, Warren, Tex. d: 1/19/91, Woodville, Tex. BL/TR, 5'6.5", 170 lbs. Deb: 6/27/36

YEAR	TM/L	G	AB	R	H	2B	3B	HR	RBI	BB	SO	AVG	OBP	SLG	OPS	OPS+	BR+	SB	CS	SBR	FA	FR	G/POS	TPR
1936	Cle-A	84	349	64	117	28	6	8	53	16	29	.335	.364	.519	883	115	6	3	8	-2	.973	4	O-84(3-5-80)	0.3
1937	Cle-A	53	134	19	27	4	0	5	13	6	14	.201	.246	.343	590	47	-12	1	1	-0	.964	-3	O-38(7-0-32)/3-1	-1.6
1938	Cle-A	83	210	32	55	14	3	2	18	14	14	.262	.308	.386	694	74	-9	8	5	0	.975	-1	O-55(6-41-8)	-1.1
1939	Cle-A	95	323	43	100	16	6	1	32	19	23	.310	.348	.406	754	95	-3	7	2	1	.961	-8	O-76(36-27-14)	-1.2

YEAR	TM/L	G	AB	R	H	2B	3B	HR	RBI	BB	SO	AVG	OBP	SLG	OPS	OPS+	BR+	SB	CS	SBR	FA	FR	G/POS	TPR
1940	Cle-A	135	578	90	175	35	11	12	59	27	26	.303	.335	.464	799	108	4	9	8	-1	.969	6	*O-135(1-134-0)	0.6
1941	Cle-A	102	363	59	105	21	5	3	37	32	20	.289	.350	.399	750	103	1	2	5	-1	.968	-8	O-88(0-87-1)	-1.0
1942	Cle-A	128	473	61	122	23	7	5	39	35	25	.258	.310	.368	678	96	-4	8	13	-3	.991	2	*O-117(0-117-0)	-0.8
1943	*NY-A	77	280	37	74	8	3	7	28	18	9	.264	.311	.389	700	104	0	4	7	-2	.983	-2	O-68(0-68-0)	-0.6
1946	NY-A	2	2	0	1	0	0	0	0	0	0	.500	.500	.500	1000	178	0	0	0	0	.000	0	H	0.0
1950	NY-N	52	69	10	18	3	3	0	11	13	10	.261	.378	.391	769	102	1	0			1.000	-1	O-15(12-1-2)	-0.1
Total	10	811	2781	415	794	152	44	43	290	180	170	.286	.331	.418	749	99	-15	42	49		.975	-10	O-676(65-480-137)/3-1	-5.5

■ ART WEAVER

Weaver, Arthur Coggshall "Six O'Clock" b: 4/7/1879, Wichita, Kan. d: 3/23/17, Denver, Colo. TR, 6'1", 160 lbs. Deb: 9/14/02

YEAR	TM/L	G	AB	R	H	2B	3B	HR	RBI	BB	SO	AVG	OBP	SLG	OPS	OPS+	BR+	SB	CS	SBR	FA	FR	G/POS	TPR
1902	StL-N	11	33	2	6	2	0	0	3	1		.182	.206	.242	448	40	-2	0			.983	2	C-11	0.0
1903	StL-N	16	49	4	12	0	0	0	5	4		.245	.302	.245	547	58	-3	1			.969	3	C-16	0.2
	Pit-N	16	48	8	11	0	1	0	3	2		.229	.260	.271	531	50	-3	0			.978	-1	C-11/1-5	-0.3
	Yr	32	97	12	23	0	1	0	8	6		.237	.282	.258	539	54	-6	1			.972	2	C-27/1-5	-0.1
1905	StL-A	28	92	5	11	2	1	0	3	1		.120	.129	.163	292	-8	-11	0			.962	5	C-28	-0.4
1908	Chi-A	15	35	1	7	1	0	0	1	1		.200	.222	.229	451	47	-2	0			.953	-5	C-15	-0.7
Total	4	86	257	20	47	5	2	0	15	9		.183	.211	.218	428	31	-22	1			.967	4	/C-81,1-5	-1.2

■ BUCK WEAVER

Weaver, George Daniel b: 8/18/1890, Pottstown, Pa. d: 1/31/56, Chicago, Ill. BB/TR (BR 1912), 5'11", 170 lbs. Deb: 4/11/12

YEAR	TM/L	G	AB	R	H	2B	3B	HR	RBI	BB	SO	AVG	OBP	SLG	OPS	OPS+	BR+	SB	CS	SBR	FA	FR	G/POS	TPR
1912	Chi-A	147	523	55	117	21	8	1	43	9		.224	.245	.300	546	58	-31	12			.915	-6	*S-147	-2.7
1913	Chi-A	151	533	51	145	17	8	4	52	15	60	.272	.302	.356	659	94	-7	20			.929	**34**	*S-151	3.9
1914	Chi-A	136	541	64	133	20	9	2	28	20	40	.246	.279	.327	606	83	-14	14	20	-4	.928	5	*S-134	-0.4
1915	Chi-A	148	563	83	151	18	11	3	49	32	58	.268	.316	.355	671	98	-4	24	20	-2	.939	1	*S-148	0.6
1916	Chi-A	151	582	78	132	27	6	3	38	30	48	.227	.280	.309	589	76	-19	22	13	0	.941	7	3-85,S-66	-0.5
1917	*Chi-A	118	447	64	127	16	5	3	32	27	29	.284	.332	.362	694	110	4	19			**.949**	9	*3-107,S-10	1.8
1918	Chi-A	112	420	37	126	12	5	0	29	11	24	.300	.323	.352	675	103	-1	20			.941	-0	S-98,3-11/2-1	0.7
1919	*Chi-A	140	571	89	169	33	9	3	75	11	21	.296	.315	.401	716	100	-3	22			.963	0	3-97,S-43	0.3
1920	Chi-A	151	629	102	208	34	8	2	74	28	23	.331	.365	.420	785	107	6	19	17	-2	.933	-10	*3-127,S-25	-0.1
Total	9	1254	4809	623	1308	198	69	21	420	183	303	.272	.307	.355	662	92	-68	172	70		.935	39	S-822,3-427/2-1	3.6

■ JIM WEAVER

Weaver, James Francis b: 10/10/59, Kingston, N.Y. BL/TL, 6'3", 190 lbs. Deb: 4/10/85

YEAR	TM/L	G	AB	R	H	2B	3B	HR	RBI	BB	SO	AVG	OBP	SLG	OPS	OPS+	BR+	SB	CS	SBR	FA	FR	G/POS	TPR
1985	Det-A	12	7	2	1	1	0	0	0	1	4	.143	.250	.286	536	47	-1	0	1	-0	1.000	-2	/O-4(0-3-1),D-4	-0.3
1987	Sea-A	7	4	2	0	0	0	0	0	2	3	.000	.333	.000	333	-1	-1	1	1	-0	1.000	-1	/O-4(1-2-2)	-0.1
1989	SF-N	12	20	2	4	3	0	0	2	0	7	.200	.200	.350	550	56	-1	1	0	0	1.000	-2	/O-8(1-0-7)	-0.3
Total	3	31	31	6	5	4	0	0	2	3	14	.161	.235	.290	526	47	-2	2	2	-0	1.000	-4	/O-16(2-5-10),D-4	-0.7

■ FARMER WEAVER

Weaver, William B. b: 3/23/1865, Parkersburg, W.Va. d: 1/23/43, Akron, Ohio BL, 5'10", 170 lbs. Deb: 9/16/1888 Career OF: (132-LF 406-CF 111-RF)

YEAR	TM/L	G	AB	R	H	2B	3B	HR	RBI	BB	SO	AVG	OBP	SLG	OPS	OPS+	BR+	SB	CS	SBR	FA	FR	G/POS	TPR
1888	Lou-a	26	112	12	28	1	1	0	8	3		.250	.276	.277	553	79	-3	12			.878	-2	O-26(0-26-0)	-0.5
1889	Lou-a	124	499	62	145	17	6	0	60	40	22	.291	.352	.349	700	102	2	21			.918	-1	*O-123C/C-2,3-1,2-1	-0.2
1890	*Lou-a	130	557	101	161	27	9	3	67	29		.289	.333	.386	719	115	8	45			.933	-1	*O-127C/S-2,3-1	0.2
1891	Lou-a	133	556	74	157	25	7	1	53	33	23	.282	.335	.358	693	100	-2	30			**.958**	16	*O-130(0-130-0)/C-4	0.9
1892	Lou-N	138	551	58	140	15	4	0	57	40	17	.254	.315	.296	611	92	-4	30			.902	-11	*O-122L,C-15/1-1	-2.3
1893	Lou-N	106	439	79	128	17	7	2	49	27	12	.292	.348	.376	724	100	0	17			.913	-1	O-85(20-0-65),C-21	-0.3
1894	Lou-N	64	244	19	54	5	2	3	24	7	11	.221	.249	.295	544	33	-27	3			.958	-0	O-35R,C-17,1-10,/2	-2.2
	Pit-N	30	115	16	40	7	2	0	24	6	1	.348	.405	.443	848	105	1	4			.943	-10	C-14,S-12/3-5,O-1L	-0.5
	Yr	94	359	35	94	12	4	3	48	13	12	.262	.301	.343	643	58	-25	7			.947	-10	O-36R,C-31,S-12,1/32	-2.7
Total	7	751	3073	421	853	114	38	9	342	185	86	.278	.330	.348	678	95	-24	162			.927	-9	O-649C/C-73,S-14,132	-4.9

■ SKEETER WEBB

Webb, James Laverne b: 11/4/09, Meridian, Miss. d: 7/8/86, Meridian, Miss. BR/TR, 5'9.5", 150 lbs. Deb: 7/20/32

YEAR	TM/L	G	AB	R	H	2B	3B	HR	RBI	BB	SO	AVG	OBP	SLG	OPS	OPS+	BR+	SB	CS	SBR	FA	FR	G/POS	TPR
1932	StL-N	1	0	0	0	0	0	0	0	0	0	—	—	—	—	—	0	0			.000	0	/S-1	0.0
1938	Cle-A	20	58	11	16	2	0	0	2	8	7	.276	.364	.310	674	72	-2	1	0	0	.964	-2	S-13/3-3,2-2	-0.3
1939	Cle-A	81	269	28	71	14	1	2	26	15	24	.264	.305	.346	651	68	-13	1	1	-0	.932	-9	S-81	-1.5
1940	Chi-A	84	334	33	79	11	2	1	29	30	33	.237	.299	.290	590	53	-23	3	6	-1	.969	-10	2-74/S-7,3-1	-2.7
1941	Chi-A	29	84	7	16	2	0	0	6	3	9	.190	.227	.214	442	18	-10	1	0	0	.940	6	2-18/S-5,3-3	-0.3
1942	Chi-A	32	94	5	16	2	1	0	4	4	13	.170	.204	.213	417	18	-10	1	2	-0	.961	2	2-29	-0.8
1943	Chi-A	58	213	15	50	5	2	0	22	6	19	.235	.256	.277	533	56	-12	5	4	-0	.953	-3	2-54	-1.4
1944	Chi-A	139	513	44	108	19	6	0	30	20	39	.211	.242	.271	513	47	-37	7	3	0	.944	-5	*S-135/2-5	-3.2
1945	*Det-A	118	407	43	81	12	2	0	21	30	35	.199	.254	.238	492	41	-31	8	7	-1	.957	23	*S-104,2-11	0.0
1946	Det-A	64	169	12	37	1	1	0	17	9	18	.219	.258	.237	495	37	-14	3	3	-0	.972	15	2-50/S-8	0.3
1947	Det-A	50	79	13	16	3	0	0	6	7	9	.203	.267	.241	508	41	-6	3	0	1	.992	12	2-30/S-6	0.8
1948	Phi-A	23	54	5	8	2	0	0	3	0	9	.148	.148	.185	333	-12	-9	0	0	0	1.000	3	/2-9,S-8	-0.5
Total	12	699	2274	216	498	73	15	3	166	132	215	.219	.263	.268	531	46	-167	33	26		.946	32	S-368,2-282/3-7	-9.6

■ EARL WEBB

Webb, William Earl b: 9/17/1897, Bon Air, Tenn. d: 5/23/65, Jamestown, Tenn. BL/TR, 6'1", 185 lbs. Deb: 8/13/25

YEAR	TM/L	G	AB	R	H	2B	3B	HR	RBI	BB	SO	AVG	OBP	SLG	OPS	OPS+	BR+	SB	CS	SBR	FA	FR	G/POS	TPR
1925	NY-N	4	3	0	0	0	0	0	0	1	1	.000	.250	.000	250	-31	-1	0	0	0	.000	0	H	-0.1
1927	Chi-N	102	332	58	100	18	4	14	52	48	31	.301	.391	.506	897	138	18	3			.959	2	O-86(8-0-78)	1.3
1928	Chi-N	62	140	22	35	7	3	3	23	14	17	.250	.318	.407	725	90	-3	0			.986	2	O-31(0-0-31)	-0.3
1930	Bos-A	127	449	61	145	30	6	16	66	44	56	.323	.385	.523	908	133	22	2	1	0	.959	-5	*O-116(0-0-116)	0.6
1931	Bos-A	151	589	96	196	**67**	3	14	103	70	51	.333	.404	.528	932	151	44	2	2	-0	.948	-2	*O-151(0-0-151)	3.0
1932	Bos-A	52	192	23	54	9	1	5	27	25	15	.281	.364	.417	781	105	2	0	0	0	.964	-3	O-50(0-0-50)/1-2	-0.4
	Det-A	88	338	49	97	19	8	3	51	39	18	.287	.361	.417	778	97	-1	1	1	-0	.955	0	O-85(0-0-85)	-0.6
	Yr	140	530	72	151	28	9	8	78	64	33	.285	.362	.417	779	100	0	1	1	-0	.958	-2	*O-135(0-0-135)/1-2	-1.0
1933	Det-A	6	11	1	3	0	0	0	3	3	0	.273	.429	.273	701	87	0	0	0	0	1.000	-1	/O-2(0-0-2)	-0.1
	Chi-A	58	107	16	31	5	0	1	8	16	13	.290	.382	.364	747	103	1	0	0	0	1.000	-4	O-16(5-0-11),1-10	-0.4
	Yr	64	118	17	34	5	0	1	11	19	13	.288	.387	.356	743	101	1	0	0	0	1.000	-5	O-18(5-0-13),1-10	-0.5
Total	7	650	2161	326	661	155	25	56	333	260	202	.306	.381	.478	859	125	82	8	4		.958	-11	O-537(13-0-524)/1-12	3.0

■ BILL WEBB

Webb, William Joseph b: 6/25/1895, Chicago, Ill. d: 1/12/43, Chicago, Ill. BR/TR, 5'10", 161 lbs. Deb: 9/17/17 C

YEAR	TM/L	G	AB	R	H	2B	3B	HR	RBI	BB	SO	AVG	OBP	SLG	OPS	OPS+	BR+	SB	CS	SBR	FA	FR	G/POS	TPR
1917	Pit-N	5	15	1	3	0	0	0	0	2	3	.200	.294	.200	494	51	-1	0			1.000	1	/2-4,S-1	0.0

■ HARRY WEBER

Weber, Henry J. b: 3/1862, New York d: 12/22/26, Indianapolis, Ind. Deb: 7/22/1884

YEAR	TM/L	G	AB	R	H	2B	3B	HR	RBI	BB	SO	AVG	OBP	SLG	OPS	OPS+	BR+	SB	CS	SBR	FA	FR	G/POS	TPR
1884	Ind-a	3	8	0	0	0	0	0		0		.000	.111	.000	111	-62	-1				.794	1	/C-3	0.0

■ JOE WEBER

Weber, Joseph Edward b: 2/15/1862, Hamilton, Ont., Canada d: 12/15/21, Hamilton, Ont., Canada Deb: 5/30/1884

YEAR	TM/L	G	AB	R	H	2B	3B	HR	RBI	BB	SO	AVG	OBP	SLG	OPS	OPS+	BR+	SB	CS	SBR	FA	FR	G/POS	TPR
1884	Det-N	2	8	0	0	0	0	0	0	0	2	.000	.000	.000	0	-99	-2				.750	0	/O-2(1-0-1)	-0.2

■ LENNY WEBSTER

Webster, Leonard Irell b: 2/10/65, New Orleans, La. BR/TR, 5'9", 191 lbs. Deb: 9/1/89

YEAR	TM/L	G	AB	R	H	2B	3B	HR	RBI	BB	SO	AVG	OBP	SLG	OPS	OPS+	BR+	SB	CS	SBR	FA	FR	G/POS	TPR
1989	Min-A	14	20	3	6	2	0	0	1	3	2	.300	.391	.400	791	116	1	0	0	0	1.000	-2	C-14	-0.1
1990	Min-A	2	6	1	2	1	0	0	0	1	1	.333	.429	.500	929	149	0	0	0	0	1.000	-1	/C-2	0.0
1991	Min-A	18	34	7	10	1	0	3	8	6	10	.294	.400	.588	988	162	3	0	0	0	.986	4	C-17	0.7
1992	Min-A	53	118	10	33	10	1	1	13	9	11	.280	.331	.407	737	102	0	0	2	-1	.995	1	C-49/D-1	0.3
1993	Min-A	49	106	14	21	2	0	1	8	11	8	.198	.274	.245	519	40	-9	1	0	0	1.000	3	C-45/D-1	-0.4
1994	Mon-N	57	143	13	39	10	0	5	23	16	24	.273	.370	.448	817	111	3	0	0	0	.996	-1	C-46	0.4
1995	Phi-N	49	150	18	40	9	0	4	14	16	27	.267	.337	.407	744	94	-1	0	0	0	.990	0	C-43	0.2
1996	Mon-N	78	174	18	40	10	0	2	17	25	21	.230	.333	.322	655	72	-6	0	0	0	.998	10	C-63	0.7
1997	*Bal-A	98	259	29	66	8	1	7	37	22	46	.255	.318	.375	693	82	-7	0	1	-0	.995	9	C-97/D-1	0.6
1998	Bal-A	108	309	37	88	16	0	10	46	15	38	.285	.318	.434	752	94	-3	0	0	0	.993	-5	*C-102/D-4	-0.3
1999	Bal-A	16	36	1	6	1	0	0	3	8	5	.167	.333	.194	528	41	-3	0	0	0	.986	2	C-12/D-2	0.0
	Bos-A	6	14	0	0	0	0	0	1	2	2	.000	.176	.000	176	-48	-3	0	0	0	1.000	-0	/C-6	-0.3
	Yr	22	50	1	6	1	0	0	4	10	7	.120	.290	.140	430	15	-6	0	0	0	.990	2	C-18/D-2	-0.3
2000	Mon-N	39	81	6	17	3	0	0	5	6	14	.210	.264	.247	511	30	-9	0	0	0	1.000	-2	C-32	-0.9
Total	12	587	1450	157	368	73	2	33	176	140	209	.254	.325	.375	700	84	-35	1	3	-1	.995	19	C-528/D-9	0.9

YEAR	TM/L	G	AB	R	H	2B	3B	HR	RBI	BB	SO	AVG	OBP	SLG	OPS	OPS+	BR+	SB	CS	SBR	FA	FR	G/POS	TPR
■ MITCH WEBSTER Webster, Mitchell Dean b: 5/16/59, Larned, Kan. BB/TL, 6'1", 185 lbs. Deb: 9/2/83 Career OF: (275-LF 425-CF 393-RF)																								
1983	Tor-A	11	11	2	2	0	0	0	0	1	1	.182	.250	.182	432	20	-1	0	0	0	1.000	-3	/O-7(0-7-0),D-2	-0.4
1984	Tor-A	26	22	9	5	2	1	0	4	1	7	.227	.261	.409	670	79	-1	0	0	0	.875	-3	O-10(3-7-0)/1-1,D-9	-0.3
1985	Tor-A	4	1	0	0	0	0	0	0	0	0	.000	.000	.000	0	-98	-0	0	1	-0	.000	-1	/O-2(2-0-0),D-2	-0.1
	Mon-N	74	212	32	58	8	2	11	30	20	33	.274	.336	.486	822	135	9	15	9	0	.993	-5	O-64(4-52-20)	0.3
1986	Mon-N	151	576	89	167	31	**13**	8	49	57	78	.290	.358	.431	788	117	14	36	15	3	.977	4	*O-146(8-118-44)	1.7
1987	Mon-N	156	588	101	165	30	8	15	63	70	95	.281	.363	.435	798	107	7	33	10	4	.982	1	*O-153(0-0-153)	0.3
1988	Mon-N	81	259	33	66	5	2	2	13	36	37	.255	.357	.313	669	90	-2	12	10	-1	.994	-3	O-71(12-53-12)	-0.7
	Chi-N	70	264	36	70	11	6	4	26	19	50	.265	.322	.398	719	101	0	10	4	1	.971	2	O-65(8-52-10)	0.2
	Yr	151	523	69	136	16	8	6	39	55	87	.260	.340	.356	695	95	-2	22	14	-0	.982	-1	*O-136(20-105-22)	-0.5
1989	*Chi-N	98	272	40	70	12	4	3	19	30	55	.257	.333	.364	697	92	-2	14	2	2	.965	-1	O-74(52-13-21)	-0.3
1990	Cle-A	128	437	58	110	20	6	12	55	20	61	.252	.289	.407	696	93	-6	22	6	3	.991	9	*O-118C/1-3,D-3	0.5
1991	Cle-A	13	32	2	4	0	0	0	0	3	9	.125	.200	.125	325	-8	-5	2	2	-0	1.000	-1	O-10(6-1-6)	-0.6
	Pit-N	36	97	9	17	3	4	1	9	9	31	.175	.245	.320	565	59	-6	0	0	0	.963	-2	O-29(2-9-20)	-0.8
	LA-N	58	74	12	21	5	1	1	10	9	21	.284	.361	.419	780	122	2	0	1	-0	1.000	-8	O-36(29-4-7)/1-1	-0.7
	Yr	94	171	21	38	8	5	2	19	18	52	.222	.296	.363	659	86	-3	0	1	-0	.978	-10	O-65(31-13-27)/1-1	-1.5
1992	LA-N	135	262	33	70	12	5	6	35	27	49	.267	.340	.420	760	116	5	11	5	1	.977	-12	O-90(36-8-56)	-0.9
1993	LA-N	88	172	26	42	6	2	2	14	11	24	.244	.297	.337	635	74	-7	4	6	-1	.950	-9	O-56(32-2-27)	-1.9
1994	LA-N	82	84	16	23	4	0	4	12	8	13	.274	.344	.464	808	116	2	1	2	-0	1.000	-12	O-48(45-0-6)	-1.1
1995	*LA-N	54	56	6	10	1	1	1	3	4	14	.179	.246	.286	532	44	-5	0	0	0	1.000	-7	O-25(11-4-11)	-1.2
Total	13	1265	3419	504	900	150	55	70	342	325	578	.263	.332	.401	733	101	6	160	73	10	.980	-50	*O-1004C/D-16,1-5	-6.0
■ RAY WEBSTER Webster, Ramon Alberto b: 8/31/42, Colon, Panama BL/TL, 6', 185 lbs. Deb: 4/11/67																								
1967	KC-A	122	360	41	92	15	4	11	51	32	44	.256	.320	.411	731	118	7	5	3	0	.989	-3	1-83,O-15(14-0-2)	0.0
1968	Oak-A	66	196	17	42	11	1	3	23	12	24	.214	.260	.327	586	81	-5	3	0	1	.988	-1	1-55	-1.0
1969	Oak-A	64	77	5	20	0	1	1	13	12	8	.260	.367	.325	691	99	0	0	0	0	1.000	1	1-13	0.1
1970	SD-N	95	116	12	30	3	0	2	11	11	12	.259	.323	.336	659	80	-3	1	1	-0	.981	-1	1-15/O-1(1-0-0)	-0.5
1971	SD-N	10	8	0	1	0	0	0	0	2	1	.125	.300	.125	425	26	-1	0	0	0	.000	0	H	-0.1
	Oak-A	7	5	0	0	0	0	0	0	0	2	.000	.000	.000	0	-99	-1	0	0	0	1.000	0	/1-1	-0.1
	Chi-N	16	16	1	5	2	0	0	0	1	3	.313	.353	.438	790	107	0	0	0	0	1.000	0	/1-1	0.0
Total	5	380	778	76	190	31	6	17	98	70	94	.244	.309	.365	674	99	-2	9	4	1	.989	-4	1-168/O-16(15-0-2)	-1.6
■ RAY WEBSTER Webster, Raymond George b: 11/15/37, Grass Valley, Cal. BR/TR, 6', 175 lbs. Deb: 4/17/59																								
1959	Cle-A	40	74	10	15	2	1	2	10	5	7	.203	.253	.338	591	63	-4	1	0	0	.929	0	2-24/3-4	-0.3
1960	Bos-A	7	3	1	0	0	0	0	0	1	1	.000	.250	.000	250	-25	-1	0	0	0	1.000	1	/2-1	0.0
Total	2	47	77	11	15	2	1	2	11	6	7	.195	.253	.325	578	59	-5	1	0	0	.931	1	/2-25,3-4	-0.3
■ PETE WECKBECKER Weckbecker, Peter b: 8/30/1864, Butler, Pa. d: 5/16/35, Hampton, Va. 5'7", 150 lbs. Deb: 10/5/1889																								
1889	Ind-N	1	1	0	0	0	0	0	2	0	0	.000	.000	.000	0	-98	-0	0			1.000	0	/C-1	0.0
1890	*Lou-a	32	101	17	24	1	0	0	11	8		.238	.300	.248	548	63	-4	7			.941	1	C-32	-0.1
Total	2	33	102	17	24	1	0	0	13	8	0	.235	.297	.245	542	61	-5	7			.941	1	/C-33	-0.1
■ ERIC WEDGE Wedge, Eric Michael b: 1/27/68, Fort Wayne, Ind. BR/TR, 6'3", 215 lbs. Deb: 10/5/91																								
1991	Bos-A	1	1	0	1	0	0	0	0	0	0	1.000	1.000	1.000	2000	434	0	0	0	0	.000	0	/D-1	0.0
1992	Bos-A	27	68	11	17	2	0	5	11	13	18	.250	.370	.500	870	133	3	0	0	0	1.000	-0	D-20/C-5	0.3
1993	Col-N	9	11	2	2	0	0	0	1	0	4	.182	.182	.182	364	-2	-2	0	0	0	1.000	1	/C-1	-0.1
1994	Bos-A	2	6	0	0	0	0	0	0	1	3	.000	.143	.000	143	-56	-1	0	0	0	.000	0	/D-2	-0.1
Total	4	39	86	13	20	2	0	5	12	14	25	.233	.340	.430	770	104	1	0	0	0	1.000	0	/D-23,C-6	0.1
■ BERT WEEDEN Weeden, Charles Albert b: 12/21/1882, Northwood, N.H. d: 1/7/39, Northwood, N.H. BL/TL, 6', 200 lbs. Deb: 6/4/11																								
1911	Bos-N	1	1	0	0	0	0	0	0	0	0	.000	.000	.000	0	-93	-0	0			.000	0	H	0.0
■ JOHNNY WEEKLY Weekly, Johnny b: 6/14/37, Waterproof, La. d: 11/24/74, Walnut Creek, Cal. BR/TR, 6' ", 200 lbs. Deb: 4/13/62																								
1962	Hou-N	13	26	3	5	1	0	2	2	7	4	.192	.364	.462	825	129	1	0	0	0	1.000	-1	/O-7(4-0-4)	0.0
1963	Hou-N	34	80	4	18	3	0	3	14	7	14	.225	.295	.375	670	98	-0	0	0	0	1.000	1	O-23(15-0-8)	-0.1
1964	Hou-N	6	15	0	2	0	0	0	3	1	3	.133	.188	.133	321	-8	-2	0	0	0	1.000	1	/O-5(0-0-5)	-0.2
Total	3	53	121	7	25	4	0	5	19	15	21	.207	.299	.364	663	92	-1	0	0	0	1.000	1	/O-35(19-0-17)	-0.3
■ JOHN WEHNER Wehner, John Paul b: 6/29/67, Pittsburgh, Pa. BR/TR, 6'3", 205 lbs. Deb: 7/17/91 Career OF: (66-LF 28-CF 49-RF)																								
1991	Pit-N	37	106	15	36	7	0	0	7	7	17	.340	.381	.406	786	123	3	3	0	1	.936	7	3-36	1.2
1992	*Pit-N	55	123	11	22	6	0	0	4	12	22	.179	.252	.228	479	37	-10	3	0	1	.961	5	3-34,1-13/2-5	-0.6
1993	Pit-N	29	35	3	5	0	0	0	0	6	10	.143	.268	.143	411	14	-4	0	0	0	1.000	-1	O-13(4-8-2)/2-3,3-3	-0.5
1994	Pit-N	2	4	1	1	1	0	0	3	0	1	.250	.250	.500	750	88	-0	0	0	0	1.000	0	/3-1	0.0
1995	Pit-N	52	107	13	33	0	3	0	5	10	17	.308	.368	.364	732	92	-1	3	1	0	1.000	-4	O-23L,3-19/C-1,S-1	-0.4
1996	Pit-N	86	139	19	36	9	1	2	13	8	22	.259	.299	.381	681	76	-5	1	5	-2	.971	-1	O-29C,3-24,2-12,/C	-0.7
1997	*Fla-N	44	36	8	10	2	0	0	2	2	5	.278	.333	.333	667	79	-1	1	0	0	1.000	-8	O-27(10-1-19)/3-6	-0.9
1998	Fla-N	53	88	10	20	2	0	0	5	7	12	.227	.284	.250	534	44	-7	1	0	0	1.000	-3	O-23(12-2-11)/3-8	-1.0
1999	Pit-N	39	65	6	12	2	0	1	4	7	12	.185	.264	.262	525	34	-7	1	0	0	.958	-4	O-17L/3-2,S-2,2-1	-1.0
2000	Pit-N	21	50	10	15	3	0	1	9	4	6	.300	.352	.420	772	95	-0	0	0	0	.973	1	3-16/O-1(1-0-0)	0.0
Total	10	418	753	96	190	32	4	4	52	63	124	.252	.311	.321	632	70	-32	13	6	1	.967	-7	3-149,O-133L/21SC	-3.9
■ RALPH WEIGEL Weigel, Ralph Richard "Wig" b: 10/2/21, Coldwater, Ohio d: 4/15/92, Memphis, Tenn. BR/TR, 6'1", 180 lbs. Deb: 9/18/46																								
1946	Cle-A	6	12	0	2	0	0	0	0	0	2	.167	.167	.167	333	-7	-2	1	0	0	1.000	-1	/C-6	-0.3
1948	Chi-A	66	163	8	38	7	3	0	26	13	18	.233	.294	.313	607	64	-9	1	2	-0	.969	-7	C-39/O-2(2-0-0)	-1.4
1949	Was-A	34	60	4	14	2	0	0	4	8	6	.233	.324	.267	590	58	-3	0	1	-0	.985	1	C-21	-0.2
Total	3	106	235	12	54	9	3	0	30	21	26	.230	.296	.294	589	59	-14	2	3	-1	.976	-8	/C-66,O-2(2-0-0)	-1.9
■ PODGE WEIHE Weihe, John Garibaldi b: 11/13/1862, Cincinnati, Ohio d: 4/15/14, Cincinnati, Ohio BR/TR, 5'11", 175 lbs. Deb: 8/6/1883 Career OF: (1-LF 24-CF 35-RF)																								
1883	Cin-a	1	4	1	1	0	0	0		0		.250	.250	.250	500	58	-0				1.000	0	/O-1(0-1-0)	0.0
1884	Ind-a	63	256	29	65	13	2	4		9		.254	.279	.367	646	112	3				.860	-0	O-58(1-23-35)/2-4,1-3	0.2
Total	2	64	260	30	66	13	2	4		9		.254	.279	.365	644	111	3				.864	0	/O-59R,2-4,1-3	0.2
■ DICK WEIK Weik, Richard Henry "Legs" b: 11/17/27, Waterloo, Iowa d: 4/21/91, Harvey, Ill. BR/TR, 6'3.5", 184 lbs. Deb: 9/8/48																								
1948	Was-A	3	4	1	3	0	1	0	0	0	0	.750	.750	1.250	2000	439	2	0	0	0	1.000	-0	/P-3	0.0
1949	Was-A	28	28	3	5	0	0	0	2	1	8	.179	.207	.179	385	2	-4	0	0	0	.964	1	P-27	0.0
1950	Was-A	14	13	0	2	0	0	0	0	0	3	.154	.154	.154	308	-22	-2	0	0	0	1.000	-1	P-14	0.0
	Cle-A	11	5	0	1	1	0	0	0	0	4	.200	.200	.400	600	52	-0	0	0	0	1.000	0	P-11	0.0
	Yr	25	18	0	3	1	0	0	0	0	7	.167	.167	.222	389	-1	-3	0	0	0	1.000	-1	P-25	0.0
1953	Cle-A	1	0	1	0	0	0	0	0	0	0	—	—	—	—	—	0	0	0	0	.000	0	R	0.0
	Det-A	12	2	1	1	1	0	0	0	0	1	.500	.500	1.000	1500	300	1	0	0	0	1.000	0	P-12	0.0
	Yr	13	2	2	1	1	0	0	0	0	1	.500	.500	1.000	1500	301	1	0	0	0	1.000	0	P-12	0.0
1954	Det-A	9	1	0	0	0	0	0	0	0	0	.000	.000	.000	0	-99	-0	0	0	0	.500	-1	/P-9	0.0
Total	5	78	53	6	12	2	1	0	3	1	16	.226	.241	.302	543	43	-5	0	0	0	.958	0	/P-76	0.0
■ ELMER WEINGARTNER Weingartner, Elmer William "Dutch" b: 8/13/18, Cleveland, Ohio BR/TR, 5'11", 178 lbs. Deb: 4/19/45																								
1945	Cle-A	20	39	5	9	1	0	0	1	4	11	.231	.302	.256	559	66	-2	0	0	0	.871	-3	S-20	-0.3
■ PHIL WEINTRAUB Weintraub, Philip "Mickey" b: 10/12/07, Chicago, Ill. d: 6/21/87, Palm Springs, Cal BL/TL, 6'1", 195 lbs. Deb: 9/5/33																								
1933	NY-N	8	15	3	3	0	0	1	1	3	2	.200	.333	.400	733	110	0	0			.667	-3	/O-6(0-0-6)	-0.3
1934	NY-N	31	74	13	26	2	0	0	15	15	10	.351	.461	.378	839	130	4	0			.944	-4	O-20(12-9-0)	0.0
1935	NY-N	64	112	18	27	3	3	1	6	17	13	.241	.341	.348	689	87	-2	0			.975	-3	1-19/O-7(1-0-6)	-0.6
1937	Cin-N	49	177	27	48	10	4	3	20	19	25	.271	.345	.424	769	113	3	1			.976	-2	O-47(41-0-6)	-0.2

YEAR	TM/L	G	AB	R	H	2B	3B	HR	RBI	BB	SO	AVG	OBP	SLG	OPS	OPS+	BR+	SB	CS	SBR	FA	FR	G/POS	TPR
	NY-N	6	9	3	3	2	0	0	1	1	1	.333	.400	.556	956	155	1	0			1.000	-0	/O-1(1-0-0)	0.0
	Yr	55	186	30	51	12	4	3	21	20	26	.274	.348	.430	778	115	4	1			.976	-3	O-48(42-0-6)	-0.2
1938	Phi-N	100	351	51	109	23	2	4	45	64	43	.311	.422	.422	844	137	21	1			.988	2	1-98	1.4
1944	NY-N	104	361	55	114	18	9	13	77	59	59	.316	.412	.524	935	162	31	0			.992	3	1-99	2.9
1945	NY-N	82	283	45	77	9	1	10	42	54	29	.272	.389	.417	806	122	10	2			.993	3	1-77	0.9
Total	7	444	1382	215	407	67	19	32	207	232	182	.295	.398	.440	838	133	69	4			.990	-4	1-293/O-81(55-9-18)	4.1

■ AL WEIS
Weis, Albert John b: 4/2/38, Franklin Square, N.Y BB/TR (BR 1969-71), 6', 170 lbs. Deb: 9/15/62 Career OF: (0-LF 4-CF 0-RF)

YEAR	TM/L	G	AB	R	H	2B	3B	HR	RBI	BB	SO	AVG	OBP	SLG	OPS	OPS+	BR+	SB	CS	SBR	FA	FR	G/POS	TPR
1962	Chi-A	7	12	2	1	0	0	0	0	2	3	.083	.267	.083	350	-1	-2	1	0	0	.882	-1	/S-4,2-1,3-1	-0.2
1963	Chi-A	99	210	41	57	9	0	0	18	18	37	.271	.335	.314	649	85	-4	15	1	3	.990	14	2-48,S-27/3-1	1.8
1964	Chi-A	133	328	36	81	4	4	2	23	22	41	.247	.300	.302	602	70	-13	22	7	2	.966	12	*2-116/S-9,O-2(0-2-0)	0.9
1965	Chi-A	103	135	29	40	4	3	1	12	12	22	.296	.362	.393	755	122	4	4	1	1	.975	25	2-74/S-7,3-2,O-2C	3.4
1966	Chi-A	129	187	20	29	4	1	0	9	17	50	.155	.233	.187	420	24	-18	3	5	-1	.987	**37**	2-96,S-18	2.4
1967	Chi-A	50	53	9	13	2	0	0	4	1	7	.245	.273	.283	556	67	-2	3	3	-0	.986	11	2-32,S-13	1.0
1968	NY-N	90	274	15	47	6	0	1	14	21	63	.172	.236	.204	440	33	-22	3	1	0	.958	7	S-59,2-29/3-2	-1.0
1969	*NY-N	103	247	20	53	9	2	2	23	15	51	.215	.260	.291	551	53	-16	3	3	-0	.960	13	S-52,2-43/3-1	0.3
1970	NY-N	75	121	20	25	7	1	1	11	7	21	.207	.256	.306	562	50	-9	1	1	-0	.952	2	2-44,S-15	-0.4
1971	NY-N	11	11	3	0	0	0	0	1	2	4	.000	.154	.000	154	-54	-2	0	0	0	1.000	1	/2-5,3-2	-0.2
Total	10	800	1578	195	346	45	11	7	115	117	299	.219	.279	.275	554	59	-84	55	22	4	.975	121	2-488,S-204/3-9,O-4C	8.0

■ BUTCH WEIS
Weis, Arthur John b: 3/2/01, St.Louis, Mo. d: 5/4/97, St.Louis, Mo. BL/TL, 5'11", 180 lbs. Deb: 4/15/22

YEAR	TM/L	G	AB	R	H	2B	3B	HR	RBI	BB	SO	AVG	OBP	SLG	OPS	OPS+	BR+	SB	CS	SBR	FA	FR	G/POS	TPR
1922	Chi-N	2	2	2	1	0	0	0	0	0	0	.500	.500	.500	1000	156	0	0	0	0	.000	0	H	0.0
1923	Chi-N	22	26	2	6	1	0	0	2	5	8	.231	.355	.269	624	67	-1	0	1	-0	1.000	-1	/O-6(4-0-2)	-0.3
1924	Chi-N	37	133	19	37	8	1	0	23	15	14	.278	.356	.353	709	90	-1	4	5	-1	.978	6	O-36(14-0-22)	0.1
1925	Chi-N	67	180	16	48	5	3	2	25	23	22	.267	.350	.361	711	81	-5	2	4	-1	.964	-5	O-47(45-0-2)	-1.3
Total	4	128	341	39	92	14	4	2	50	43	44	.270	.353	.352	705	84	-7	6	10	-2	.973	0	/O-89(63-0-26)	-1.5

■ BUD WEISER
Weiser, Harry Budson b: 1/8/1891, Shamokin, Pa. d: 7/31/61, Shamokin, Pa. BR/TR, 5'11", 165 lbs. Deb: 4/29/15

YEAR	TM/L	G	AB	R	H	2B	3B	HR	RBI	BB	SO	AVG	OBP	SLG	OPS	OPS+	BR+	SB	CS	SBR	FA	FR	G/POS	TPR
1915	Phi-N	37	64	6	9	2	0	0	8	7	12	.141	.236	.172	408	24	-6	2	2	-0	.897	-5	O-20(4-16-0)	-1.4
1916	Phi-N	4	10	1	3	1	0	0	1	0	3	.300	.300	.400	700	110	0	0			1.000	-1	/O-4(4-0-0)	-0.1
Total	2	41	74	7	12	3	0	0	9	7	15	.162	.244	.203	447	36	-6	2	2		.912	-6	/O-24(8-16-0)	-1.5

■ GARY WEISS
Weiss, Gary Lee b: 12/27/55, Brenham, Tex. BB/TR (BR 1980), 5'10", 170 lbs. Deb: 9/13/80

YEAR	TM/L	G	AB	R	H	2B	3B	HR	RBI	BB	SO	AVG	OBP	SLG	OPS	OPS+	BR+	SB	CS	SBR	FA	FR	G/POS	TPR
1980	LA-N	8	0	2	0	0	0	0	0	0	0	—	—	—	—	—	0	0	0	0	.000	0	/R	0.0
1981	LA-N	14	19	2	2	0	0	0	1	1	4	.105	.150	.105	255	-28	-3	0	0	0	.920	-1	S-13	-0.4
Total	2	22	19	4	2	0	0	0	1	1	4	.105	.150	.105	255	-28	-3	0	0	0	.920	-1	/S-13	-0.4

■ JOE WEISS
Weiss, Joseph Harold b: 1/27/1894, Chicago, Ill. d: 7/7/67, Cedar Rapids, Iowa BR/TR, 6', 165 lbs. Deb: 8/29/15

YEAR	TM/L	G	AB	R	H	2B	3B	HR	RBI	BB	SO	AVG	OBP	SLG	OPS	OPS+	BR+	SB	CS	SBR	FA	FR	G/POS	TPR
1915	Chi-F	29	85	6	19	1	2	0	11	3	24	.224	.250	.282	532	53	-7	0			.992	-1	1-29	-1.0

■ WALT WEISS
Weiss, Walter William b: 11/28/63, Tuxedo, N.Y. BB/TR, 6', 175 lbs. Deb: 7/12/87

YEAR	TM/L	G	AB	R	H	2B	3B	HR	RBI	BB	SO	AVG	OBP	SLG	OPS	OPS+	BR+	SB	CS	SBR	FA	FR	G/POS	TPR
1987	Oak-A	16	26	3	12	4	0	0	1	2	2	.462	.500	.615	1115	208	4	1	2	-0	.974	5	S-11/D-2	0.8
1988	*Oak-A	147	452	44	113	17	3	3	39	35	56	.250	.317	.321	637	82	-10	4	4	-1	.979	10	*S-147	1.0
1989	*Oak-A	84	236	30	55	11	0	3	21	21	39	.233	.298	.318	616	76	-7	6	1	1	.953	-14	S-84	-1.5
1990	*Oak-A	138	445	50	118	17	1	2	35	46	53	.265	.339	.321	661	89	-5	9	3	1	.979	-26	*S-137	-2.0
1991	Oak-A	40	133	15	30	6	1	0	13	12	14	.226	.290	.286	575	63	-7	6	0	1	.970	-10	S-40	-1.3
1992	*Oak-A	103	316	36	67	5	2	0	21	43	39	.212	.308	.241	549	59	-16	6	3	0	.956	-14	*S-103	-2.3
1993	Fla-N	158	500	50	133	14	2	1	39	79	73	.266	.369	.308	677	79	-11	7	3	0	.977	-18	*S-153	-1.6
1994	Col-N	110	423	58	106	11	4	1	32	56	58	.251	.338	.303	641	59	-23	12	7	0	.973	3	*S-110	-1.1
1995	*Col-N	137	427	65	111	17	3	1	25	98	57	.260	.404	.321	725	73	-13	15	3	2	.974	12	*S-136	1.2
1996	Col-N	155	517	89	146	20	2	8	48	80	78	.282	.385	.375	760	82	-11	10	2	2	.957	-7	*S-155	-0.4
1997	Col-N	121	393	52	106	23	5	4	38	66	56	.270	.377	.384	762	81	-9	5	2	0	.983	20	*S-119	2.0
1998	*Atl-N★	96	347	64	97	18	2	0	27	59	53	.280	.389	.343	732	94	0	7	1	1	.967	-7	S-96	0.2
1999	*Atl-N	110	279	38	63	13	4	2	29	35	48	.226	.319	.323	641	63	-16	7	3	0	.963	-5	*S-102	-1.3
2000	*Atl-N	80	192	29	50	6	2	0	18	26	32	.260	.357	.313	670	72	-7	1	1	-0	.949	19	S-69	1.5
Total	14	1495	4686	623	1207	182	31	25	386	658	658	.258	.354	.326	679	77	-130	96	35	9	.970	-33	*S-1462/D-2	-4.8

■ JOHNNY WELAJ
Welaj, John Ludwig b: 5/27/14, Moss Creek, Pa. BR/TR, 6', 164 lbs. Deb: 5/2/39

YEAR	TM/L	G	AB	R	H	2B	3B	HR	RBI	BB	SO	AVG	OBP	SLG	OPS	OPS+	BR+	SB	CS	SBR	FA	FR	G/POS	TPR
1939	Was-A	63	201	23	55	11	2	1	33	13	20	.274	.318	.363	681	80	-7	13	2	2	.975	-4	O-55(13-17-26)	-1.0
1940	Was-A	88	215	31	55	9	0	3	21	19	20	.256	.322	.340	662	77	-7	8	7	-1	.978	-1	O-53(15-35-3)	-1.0
1941	Was-A	49	96	16	20	4	0	0	5	6	16	.208	.255	.250	505	36	-9	3	1	0	.979	-0	O-19(13-3-3)	-1.0
1943	Phi-A	93	281	45	68	16	1	0	15	15	17	.242	.280	.306	586	72	-11	12	5	1	.960	0	O-72(15-27-32)	-1.4
Total	4	293	793	115	198	40	3	4	74	53	73	.250	.298	.323	621	71	-34	36	15	3	.970	-5	O-199(56-82-64)	-4.4

■ CURT WELCH
Welch, Curtis Benton b: 2/10/1862, Williamsport, O. d: 8/29/1896, E.Liverpool, Ohio BR/TR, 5'10", 175 lbs. Deb: 5/1/1884 Career OF: (17-LF 1059-CF 0-RF)

YEAR	TM/L	G	AB	R	H	2B	3B	HR	RBI	BB	SO	AVG	OBP	SLG	OPS	OPS+	BR+	SB	CS	SBR	FA	FR	G/POS	TPR
1884	Tol-a	109	425	61	95	24	5	0		10		.224	.248	.304	552	76	-12				.888	16	*O-107C/2-2,C-2,1-1	0.1
1885	*StL-a	112	432	84	117	18	8	3	69	23		.271	.318	.370	689	112	5				**.946**	14	*O-112(0-112-0)	1.3
1886	*StL-a	138	563	114	158	31	13	2	95	29		.281	.332	.393	724	121	11	59			**.952**	14	*O-138(0-138-0)/2-2	1.8
1887	*StL-a	131	569	98	176	32	7	3	108	25		.309	.322	.379	701	86	-14	89			.941	19	*O-123C/2-8,1-1	0.1
1888	Phi-a	136	549	125	155	22	8	1	61	33		.282	.355	.357	712	129	20	95			.952	4	*O-135(0-135-0)/2-3	1.8
1889	Phi-a	125	516	134	140	**39**	6	0	39	67	30	.271	.375	.370	746	114	13	66			.923	8	*O-125(0-125-0)	1.4
1890	Phi-a	103	396	100	106	21	4	2	40	49		.268	.392	.356	748	121	14	64			.919	14	*O-103(0-103-0)/P-1	2.1
	Bal-a	19	68	16	9	4	0	0	5	9		.132	.253	.191	444	30	-6	8			.974	2	O-17(0-17-0)/1-2	-0.4
	Yr	122	464	116	115	25	4	2	45	58		.248	.372	.332	704	107	8	72			.926	16	*O-120C/1-2,P-1	1.7
1891	Bal-a	132	514	122	138	22	10	3	55	77	42	.268	.400	.368	768	119	17	50			.946	19	*O-113C,2-21/S-2	2.8
1892	Bal-N	63	237	42	56	1	3	1	22	36	9	.236	.363	.278	641	92	-0	14			.905	-4	O-63(0-63-0)	-0.8
	Cin-N	25	94	14	19	0	2	1	7	7	8	.202	.299	.277	576	75	-3	7			.925	-0	O-25(1-25-0)	-0.4
	Yr	88	331	56	75	1	5	2	29	43	17	.227	.345	.278	623	88	-3	21			.911	-4	O-88(1-88-0)	-1.2
1893	Lou-N	14	47	5	8	1	0	0	2	16	4	.170	.400	.191	591	64	-1	1			.912	-0	O-14(14-0-0)	-0.2
Total	10	1107	4410	915	1177	215	66	16	503	381	93	.267	.345	.353	698	107	45	453			.933	107	*O-1075C/2-36,1SCP	9.6

■ FRANK WELCH
Welch, Frank Tiguer "Bugger" b: 8/10/1897, Birmingham, Ala. d: 7/25/57, Birmingham, Ala. BR/TR, 5'9", 175 lbs. Deb: 9/9/19

YEAR	TM/L	G	AB	R	H	2B	3B	HR	RBI	BB	SO	AVG	OBP	SLG	OPS	OPS+	BR+	SB	CS	SBR	FA	FR	G/POS	TPR
1919	Phi-A	15	54	5	9	1	1	2	7	7	10	.167	.262	.333	596	66	-3	0			.909	0	O-15(0-15-0)	-0.4
1920	Phi-A	100	360	43	93	17	5	4	40	26	41	.258	.312	.367	679	78	-12	2	9	-3	.937	-6	O-97(0-84-16)	-2.6
1921	Phi-A	115	403	48	115	18	6	7	45	34	43	.285	.347	.412	759	92	-5	6	0	1	.943	3	*O-104(3-93-8)	-0.5
1922	Phi-A	114	375	43	97	17	3	11	49	40	40	.259	.335	.408	743	90	-6	3	4	-1	.949	-0	*O-104(4-6-94)	-1.4
1923	Phi-A	125	421	56	125	19	9	4	55	48	40	.297	.374	.413	788	106	4	1	4	-1	.967	3	*O-117(0-0-117)	-0.3
1924	Phi-A	94	293	47	85	13	2	5	31	35	27	.290	.372	.399	771	98	-0	2	3	-1	.985	1	O-74(0-2-72)	-0.6
1925	Phi-A	85	202	40	56	5	4	4	41	29	14	.277	.373	.401	774	90	-3	2	1	0	.968	-3	O-57(0-0-57)	-0.9
1926	Phi-A	75	174	26	49	8	1	4	23	26	9	.282	.381	.408	789	100	1	2	5	-1	.975	-5	O-49(28-3-20)	-0.9
1927	Bos-A	15	28	2	5	2	0	0	4	5	1	.179	.303	.250	553	46	-2	0	2	-1	1.000	2	/O-6(0-0-6)	-0.2
Total	9	738	2310	310	634	100	31	41	295	250	225	.274	.350	.398	748	92	-26	18	28		.955	-5	O-623(35-203-390)	-7.8

■ HERB WELCH
Welch, Herbert M. "Dutch" b: 10/19/1898, RoEllen, Tenn. d: 4/13/67, Memphis, Tenn. BL/TR, 5'6", 154 lbs. Deb: 9/15/25

YEAR	TM/L	G	AB	R	H	2B	3B	HR	RBI	BB	SO	AVG	OBP	SLG	OPS	OPS+	BR+	SB	CS	SBR	FA	FR	G/POS	TPR
1925	Bos-A	13	38	2	11	0	1	0	2	0	6	.289	.289	.342	632	60	-2	0	0	0	.893	5	S-13	0.4

■ TUB WELCH
Welch, James T. b: 7/3/1866, St.Louis, Mo. TR, 5'11", 230 lbs. Deb: 6/12/1890

YEAR	TM/L	G	AB	R	H	2B	3B	HR	RBI	BB	SO	AVG	OBP	SLG	OPS	OPS+	BR+	SB	CS	SBR	FA	FR	G/POS	TPR
1890	Tol-a	35	108	15	31	3	1	1	14	8		.287	.358	.361	719	109	1	7			.930	0	C-25,1-10	0.2
1895	Lou-N	47	153	18	37	4	1	1	8	13	7	.242	.310	.301	610	62	-8	2			.888	-1	C-28,1-20	-0.6
Total	2	82	261	33	68	7	2	2	22	21	7	.261	.330	.326	656	80	-7	9			.911	-1	/C-53,1-30	-0.4

YEAR	TM/L	G	AB	R	H	2B	3B	HR	RBI	BB	SO	AVG	OBP	SLG	OPS	OPS+	BR+	SB	CS	SBR	FA	FR	G/POS	TPR
■ **MILT WELCH**	Welch, Milton Edward b: 7/26/24, Farmersville, Ill BR/TR, 5'10", 175 lbs. Deb: 6/5/45																							
1945	Det-A	1	2	0	0	0	0	0	0	0	1	.000	.000	.000	0	-94	-0	0	0	0	1.000	1	/C-1	0.0
■ **HARRY WELCHONCE**	Welchonce, Harry Monroe "Welch" b: 11/20/1883, North Point, Pa. d: 2/26/77, Arcadia, Cal. BL/TR, 6', 170 lbs. Deb: 4/17/11																							
1911	Phi-N	26	66	9	14	4	0	0	6	7	8	.212	.288	.273	560	56	-4	0			.929	-3	O-17(1-6-11)	-0.8
■ **MIKE WELDAY**	Welday, Lyndon Earl b: 12/19/1879, Conway, Iowa d: 5/28/42, Leavenworth, Kan. BL/TL, Deb: 4/21/07																							
1907	Chi-A	24	35	2	8	1	1	0	0	6		.229	.341	.314	656	113	1	0			.938	-3	O-15(4-8-3)	-0.3
1909	Chi-A	29	74	3	14	0	0	0	5	4		.189	.231	.189	420	34	-5	2			.886	1	O-20(7-10-3)	-0.7
Total	2	53	109	5	22	1	1	0	5	10		.202	.269	.229	498	60	-5	2			.900	-2	/O-35(11-18-6)	-1.0
■ **OLLIE WELF**	Welf, Oliver Henry b: 1/17/1889, Cleveland, Ohio d: 6/15/67, Cleveland, Ohio BR/TL, 5'9", 160 lbs. Deb: 8/30/16																							
1916	Cle-A	1	0	0	0	0	0	0	0	0	0	—	—	—	—	—	0	0			.000	0	R	0.0
■ **BRAD WELLMAN**	Wellman, Brad Eugene b: 8/17/59, Lodi, Cal. BR/TR, 6', 170 lbs. Deb: 9/4/82																							
1982	SF-N	6	4	1	1	0	0	0	0	0	1	.250	.250	.250	500	40	-0	0	0	0	1.000	0	/2-2	0.0
1983	SF-N	82	182	15	39	3	0	1	16	22	39	.214	.299	.247	546	55	-11	5	3	0	.965	2	2-74/S-2	-0.6
1984	SF-N	93	265	23	60	9	1	2	25	19	41	.226	.278	.291	569	62	-14	10	5	0	.977	16	2-54,S-34/3-9	0.8
1985	SF-N	71	174	16	41	11	1	0	16	4	33	.236	.269	.310	580	65	-9	5	2	0	.983	-2	2-36,3-25/S-3	-1.0
1986	SF-N	12	13	0	2	0	0	0	1	1	2	.154	.214	.154	368	3	-2	0	0	0	1.000	-0	/S-8,2-1,3-1	-0.2
1987	LA-N	3	4	1	1	0	0	0	1	0	1	.250	.250	.250	500	34	-0	0	0	0	1.000	1	/2-1,S-1,3-1	0.0
1988	KC-A	71	107	11	29	3	0	1	6	6	23	.271	.322	.327	649	81	-3	1	2	-0	.972	15	2-46,S-15/3-4,D-3	1.3
1989	KC-A	103	178	30	41	4	0	2	12	7	36	.230	.263	.287	550	55	-11	5	3	0	.995	19	2-64,S-34/3-3,D-1	1.1
Total	8	441	927	97	214	30	2	6	77	59	176	.231	.282	.287	569	61	-48	26	15	0	.978	50	2-278/S-97,3-43,D-4	1.4
■ **BOB WELLMAN**	Wellman, Robert Joseph b: 7/15/25, Norwood, Ohio d: 12/20/94, Villa Hills, Ky. BR/TR, 6'4", 210 lbs. Deb: 9/23/48																							
1948	Phi-A	4	10	1	2	0	1	0	0	3	2	.200	.385	.400	785	109	0	0	0	0	1.000	0	/1-2,O-1(0-0-1)	0.0
1950	Phi-A	11	15	1	5	0	0	1	1	0	3	.333	.333	.533	867	121	0	0	0	0	1.000	-0	/O-2(0-0-2)	0.0
Total	2	15	25	2	7	0	1	1	1	3	5	.280	.357	.480	837	117	1	0	0	0	.889	0	/O-3(0-0-3),1-2	0.0
■ **GREG WELLS**	Wells, Gregory De Wayne b: 4/25/54, McIntosh, Ala. BR/TR, 6'5", 218 lbs. Deb: 8/10/81																							
1981	Tor-A	32	73	7	18	5	0	0	5	5	12	.247	.295	.315	610	71	-3	0	2	-1	.994	-0	1-22/D-3	-0.5
1982	Min-A	15	54	5	11	1	2	0	3	1	8	.204	.218	.296	514	39	-5	0	0	0	.962	-2	1-10/D-5	-0.8
Total	2	47	127	12	29	6	2	0	8	6	20	.228	.263	.307	570	58	-7	0	2	-1	.983	-2	/1-32,D-8	-1.3
■ **JAKE WELLS**	Wells, Jacob b: 8/9/1863, Memphis, Tenn. d: 3/16/27, Hendersonville, N.C. BR/TR, 5'11", 167 lbs. Deb: 8/10/1888																							
1888	Det-N	16	57	5	9	1	0	0	2	0	5	.158	.158	.175	333	6	-6	0			.917	5	•C-16	0.0
1890	StL-a	30	105	17	25	3	0	0	12	10		.238	.333	.267	600	67	-4	1			.941	2	C-28/O-3(3-0-0)	0.0
Total	2	46	162	22	34	4	0	0	14	10	5	.210	.277	.235	511	50	-10	1			.932	6	/C-44,O-3(3-0-0)	0.0
■ **LEO WELLS**	Wells, Leo Donald b: 7/18/17, Kansas City, Kan. BR/TR, 5'9", 170 lbs. Deb: 4/16/42																							
1942	Chi-A	35	62	8	12	2	0	1	4	4	5	.194	.242	.274	517	46	-5	1	0	0	1.000	11	S-12/3-6	0.7
1946	Chi-A	45	127	11	24	4	1	1	11	12	34	.189	.259	.260	519	47	-9	3	4	-1	.942	8	3-38/S-2	-0.2
Total	2	80	189	19	36	6	1	2	15	16	39	.190	.254	.265	518	47	-14	4	4	-1	.938	19	/3-44,S-14	0.5
■ **VERNON WELLS**	Wells, Vernon M. b: 12/8/78, Shreveport, La. BR/TR, 6'1", 195 lbs. Deb: 8/30/99																							
1999	Tor-A	24	88	8	23	5	0	1	8	4	18	.261	.293	.352	646	63	-5	1	1	-0	1.000	2	O-24(0-24-0)	-0.3
2000	Tor-A	3	2	0	0	0	0	0	0	0	0	.000	.000	.000	0	-99	-1	0	0	0	1.000	-1	/O-3(0-3-0)	-0.2
Total	2	27	90	8	23	5	0	1	8	4	18	.256	.287	.344	632	59	-6	1	1	-0	1.000	1	/O-27(0-27-0)	-0.5
■ **JIMMY WELSH**	Welsh, James Daniel b: 10/9/02, Denver, Colo. d: 10/30/70, Oakland, Cal. BL/TR, 6'1", 174 lbs. Deb: 4/14/25 Career OF: (45-LF 398-CF 252-RF)																							
1925	Bos-N	122	484	69	151	25	8	7	63	20	24	.312	.350	.440	790	110	6	7	4	0	.960	6	*O-116(7-1-109)/2-3	0.3
1926	Bos-N	134	490	69	136	18	11	3	57	33	28	.278	.333	.378	711	100	-0	6			.965	10	*O-129(0-0-129)	-0.1
1927	Bos-N	131	497	72	143	26	7	9	54	23	27	.288	.330	.423	752	109	4	11			.969	13	*O-129(1-121-11)/1-1	1.1
1928	NY-N	124	476	77	146	22	5	9	54	29	30	.307	.357	.431	787	104	3	4			.981	-0	*O-117(6-110-1)	-0.3
1929	NY-N	38	129	25	32	7	0	2	8	9	3	.248	.331	.349	680	69	-6	3			.940	-6	O-35(30-7-0)	-1.4
	Bos-N	53	186	24	54	8	7	2	16	13	9	.290	.350	.441	791	98	-1	1			.979	9	O-51(1-49-2)	0.5
	Yr	91	315	49	86	15	7	4	24	22	12	.273	.342	.403	745	86	-7	4			.970	2	O-86(31-56-2)	-0.9
1930	Bos-N	113	422	51	116	21	9	3	36	29	23	.275	.327	.389	716	75	-18	5			.980	11	*O-110(0-110-0)	-1.0
Total	6	715	2684	387	778	127	47	35	288	156	144	.290	.340	.411	751	98	-12	37	4		.971	42	O-687C/2-3,1-1	-0.9
■ **LEW WENDELL**	Wendell, Lewis Charles b: 3/22/1892, New York, N.Y. d: 7/11/53, Brooklyn, N.Y. BR/TR, 5'11", 178 lbs. Deb: 6/10/15																							
1915	NY-N	20	36	0	8	1	1	0	5	2	7	.222	.263	.306	569	76	-1	0			.920	-5	C-18	-0.6
1916	NY-N	2	2	0	0	0	0	0	0	0	2	.000	.000	.000	0	-99	-0	0			.000	0	H	-0.1
1924	Phi-N	21	32	3	8	1	0	0	2	3	5	.250	.314	.281	596	54	-2	0	0	0	1.000	-1	C-17	-0.3
1925	Phi-N	18	26	0	2	0	0	0	3	1	3	.077	.111	.077	188	-47	-6	0	0	0	.909	-1	/C-9	-0.6
1926	Phi-N	1	4	0	0	0	0	0	0	0	0	.000	.000	.000	0	-95	-1	0			.333	-1	/C-1	-0.2
Total	5	62	100	3	18	2	1	0	10	6	17	.180	.226	.220	446	23	-10	0	0		.925	-8	/C-45	-1.8
■ **JACK WENTZ**	Wentz, John George (b: John George Wernz) b: 3/4/1863, Louisville, Ky. d: 9/14/07, Louisville, Ky. BR/TR, 5'10.5", 175 lbs. Deb: 4/15/1891																							
1891	Lou-a	1	4	0	1	0	0	0	0	0	0	.250	.250	.250	500	44	-0	0			.667	-1	/2-1	-0.1
■ **STAN WENTZEL**	Wentzel, Stanley Aaron b: 1/13/17, Lorane, Pa. d: 11/28/91, St.Lawrence, Pa. BR/TR, 6'1", 200 lbs. Deb: 9/23/45																							
1945	Bos-N	4	19	3	4	0	1	0	6	0	3	.211	.211	.316	526	45	-1	1			1.000	-1	/O-4(0-4-0)	-0.3
■ **JULIE WERA**	Wera, Julian Valentine b: 2/9/02, Winona, Minn. d: 12/12/75, Rochester, Minn. BR/TR, 5'8", 164 lbs. Deb: 4/14/27																							
1927	NY-A	38	42	7	10	3	0	1	8	1	5	.238	.273	.381	654	70	-2	0	0	0	1.000	3	3-19	0.1
1929	NY-A	5	12	1	5	0	0	0	2	1	1	.417	.462	.417	878	137	1	0	0	0	1.000	-1	/3-4	0.0
Total	2	43	54	8	15	3	0	1	10	2	6	.278	.316	.389	705	85	-1	0	0	0	1.000	2	/3-23	0.1
■ **BILLY WERBER**	Werber, William Murray b: 6/20/08, Berwyn, Md. BR/TR, 5'10", 170 lbs. Deb: 6/25/30 Career OF: (39-LF 2-CF 7-RF)																							
1930	NY-A	4	14	5	4	0	0	0	2	3	1	.286	.412	.286	697	84	-0	0	0	0	.955	1	/S-3,3-1	0.1
1933	NY-A	3	2	0	0	0	0	0	0	0	0	.000	.000	.000	0	-99	-1	0	0	0	.000	0	/3-1	-0.1
	Bos-A	108	425	64	110	30	6	3	39	33	39	.259	.312	.379	691	83	-11	15	5	2	.910	-17	S-71,3-38/2-2	-1.9
	Yr	111	427	64	110	30	6	3	39	33	39	.258	.311	.377	688	82	-12	15	5	2	.910	-17	S-71,3-39/2-2	-2.0
1934	Bos-A	152	623	129	200	41	10	11	67	77	37	.321	.397	.472	868	115	15	**40**	15	4	.941	20	*3-130,S-22	4.1
1935	Bos-A	124	462	84	118	30	3	14	61	69	41	.255	.357	.424	781	95	-4	**29**	7	4	.942	17	*3-123	2.0
1936	Bos-A	145	535	89	147	29	6	10	67	89	37	.275	.382	.407	790	90	-7	23	13	1	.935	-12	*3-101,O-45L/2-1	-1.6
1937	Phi-A	128	493	85	144	31	4	7	70	74	39	.292	.386	.414	799	103	4	**35**	13	3	.958	0	*3-125/O-3(1-2-0)	1.1
1938	Phi-A	134	499	92	129	22	7	11	69	93	37	.259	.377	.397	774	96	-1	19	15	-1	.935	0	*3-134	0.3
1939	*Cin-N	147	599	**115**	173	35	5	5	57	91	46	.289	.388	.389	777	109	11	15			.933	13	*3-147	2.9
1940	*Cin-N	143	584	105	162	35	5	12	48	68	40	.277	.361	.416	777	113	11	16			**.962**	3	*3-143	1.9
1941	Cin-N	109	418	56	100	9	2	4	46	53	24	.239	.328	.299	627	77	-11	14			.959	13	*3-107	0.5
1942	NY-N	98	370	51	76	9	2	1	13	51	22	.205	.308	.249	557	64	-15	9			.927	10	3-93	-0.2
Total	11	1295	5024	875	1363	271	50	78	539	701	363	.271	.364	.392	756	97	-9	215	68		.944	49	*3-1143/S-96,O-48L,2	9.1
■ **PERRY WERDEN**	Werden, Percival Wheritt b: 7/21/1865, St.Louis, Mo. d: 1/9/34, Minneapolis, Minn. BR/TR, 6'2", 220 lbs. Deb: 4/24/1884 Career OF: (7-LF 5-CF 3-RF)																							
1884	StL-U	18	76	7	18	2	0	0		2		.237	.256	.263	520	56	-6				.893	-1	P-16/O-6(4-1-1)	-0.2
1888	Was-N	3	10	0	3	0	0	0	2	1	4	.300	.364	.300	664	120	0	0			.857	-0	/O-3(3-0-0)	0.0
1890	Tol-a	128	498	113	147	22	**20**	6	72	78		.295	.404	.456	860	149	32	59			.972	6	*1-124/O-5(0-4-1)	2.3
1891	Bal-a	139	552	102	160	20	18	6	104	52	59	.290	.363	.424	787	124	15	46			.980	1	*1-139	0.3
1892	StL-N	149	598	73	154	22	6	8	84	59	52	.258	.328	.355	683	112	9	20			.982	12	*1-149	1.8
1893	StL-N	125	500	73	138	22	**29**	1	94	49	25	.276	.349	.442	791	109	4	11			.968	3	*1-124/O-1(0-0-1)	0.5

YEAR	TM/L	G	AB	R	H	2B	3B	HR	RBI	BB	SO	AVG	OBP	SLG	OPS	OPS+	BR+	SB	CS	SBR	FA	FR	G/POS	TPR
1897	Lou-N	133	512	76	154	21	14	5	83	41		.301	.366	.426	792	113	9	15			.984	19	*1-133	2.4
Total	7	695	2746	444	774	109	87	26	439	282	140	.282	.359	.413	772	119	63	151			.978	39	1-669/P-16,O-15L	7.1
■ **JOHNNY WERHAS** Werhas, John Charles "Peaches" b: 2/7/38, Highland Park, Mich. BR/TR, 6'2", 200 lbs. Deb: 4/14/64																								
1964	LA-N	29	83	6	16	2	1	0	8	13	12	.193	.302	.241	543	59	-4	0	0	0	.952	4	3-28	-0.1
1965	LA-N	4	3	1	0	0	0	0	0	1	2	.000	.250	.000	250	-24	-0	0	0	0	1.000	-0	/1-1	-0.1
1967	LA-N	7	7	0	1	0	0	0	0	0	3	.143	.143	.143	286	-20	-1	0	0	0	.000	0	H	-0.1
	Cal-A	49	75	8	12	1	1	2	6	10	22	.160	.267	.280	547	64	-3	0	0	0	.963	1	3-30/1-4,O-1(1-0-0)	-0.3
Total	3	89	168	15	29	3	2	2	14	24	39	.173	.280	.250	530	57	-9	0	0	0	.956	4	/3-58,1-5,O-1(1-0-0)	-0.6
■ **DON WERNER** Werner, Donald Paul b: 3/8/53, Appleton, Wis. BR/TR, 6'1", 185 lbs. Deb: 9/2/75																								
1975	Cin-N	7	8	0	1	0	0	0	0	0	0	.125	.222	.125	347	-2	-1	0	0	0	.923	0	/C-7	-0.1
1976	Cin-N	3	4	0	2	1	0	0	1	1	1	.500	.600	.750	1350	275	1	0	0	0	1.000	1	/C-3	0.2
1977	Cin-N	10	23	3	4	0	0	2	4	2	3	.174	.240	.435	675	75	-1	0	1	-0	1.000	1	C-10	0.0
1978	Cin-N	50	113	7	17	2	1	0	11	14	30	.150	.250	.186	436	23	-11	1	0	0	.987	5	C-49	-0.5
1980	Cin-N	24	64	2	11	2	0	0	5	7	10	.172	.264	.203	467	32	-6	1	0	0	.962	1	C-24	-0.4
1981	Tex-A	2	8	1	2	0	0	0	0	0	2	.250	.250	.250	500	47	-1	0	1	-0	.000	0	/D-2	-0.1
1982	Tex-A	22	59	4	12	2	0	0	3	3	7	.203	.242	.237	479	34	-5	0	0	0	.980	1	C-22	-0.4
Total	7	118	279	17	49	7	1	2	24	27	53	.176	.256	.229	485	36	-24	2	2	-0	.979	9	C-115/D-2	-1.3
■ **JOE WERRICK** Werrick, Joseph Abraham b: 10/25/1861, St.Paul, Minn. d: 5/10/43, St.Peter, Minn. BR/TR, 5'9", 151 lbs. Deb: 9/27/1884 Career OF: (3-LF 0-CF 0-RF)																								
1884	StP-U	9	27	3	2	0	0	0		1		.074	.107	.074	181	-81	-7				.756	-0	/S-9	-0.6
1886	Lou-a	136	561	75	140	20	14	3	62	33		.250	.294	.351	645	96	-5	19			.853	-1	*3-136	-0.3
1887	Lou-a	136	571	90	190	21	13	7	99	38		.333	.336	.413	749	106	2	49			.831	-0	*3-136	0.4
1888	Lou-a	111	413	49	89	12	7	0	51	30		.215	.274	.278	552	79	-9	15			.811	-13	3-89,S-11/2-8,O-3L	-1.8
Total	4	392	1572	217	421	53	34	10	212	102		.268	.300	.348	648	94	-19	83			.834	-14	3-361/S-20,2-8,O-3L	-2.3
■ **DON WERT** Wert, Donald Ralph b: 7/29/38, Strasburg, Pa. BR/TR, 5'9", 165 lbs. Deb: 5/11/63																								
1963	Det-A	78	251	31	65	6	2	7	25	24	51	.259	.329	.382	711	95	-1	3	3	-0	.957	3	3-47,2-21/S-8	0.4
1964	Det-A	148	525	63	135	18	5	9	55	50	74	.257	.329	.362	691	91	-6	3	4	-1	.965	0	*3-142/S-4	-0.7
1965	Det-A	162	609	81	159	22	2	12	54	73	71	.261	.343	.363	706	100	1	5	6	-1	**.976**	5	*3-161/S-3,2-1	0.5
1966	Det-A	150	559	56	150	20	2	11	70	64	69	.268	.346	.370	716	103	4	6	3	0	.972	-18	*3-150	-1.6
1967	Det-A	142	534	60	137	23	2	6	40	44	59	.257	.321	.341	662	93	-4	1	1	-0	.978	-5	*3-140/S-1	-1.0
1968	*Det-A★	150	536	44	107	15	1	12	37	37	79	.200	.258	.299	556	66	-22	0	3	-1	.966	-6	*3-150/S-2	-3.5
1969	Det-A	132	423	46	95	11	1	14	50	49	60	.225	.307	.355	661	81	-11	3	1	0	.966	-0	*3-129	-1.2
1970	Det-A	128	363	34	79	13	0	6	33	44	56	.218	.309	.303	612	69	-15	1	3	-1	.953	-2	*3-117/2-2	-1.9
1971	Was-A	20	40	2	2	1	0	0	2	4	10	.050	.156	.075	231	-35	-7	0	0	0	1.000	-4	/S-7,3-7,2-1	-1.1
Total	9	1110	3840	417	929	129	15	77	366	389	529	.242	.317	.343	660	87	-61	22	24	-4	.968	-27	*3-1043/S-25,2-25	-10.1
■ **DENNIS WERTH** Werth, Dennis Dean b: 12/29/52, Lincoln, Ill. BR/TR, 6'1", 200 lbs. Deb: 9/17/79 Career OF: (7-LF 0-CF 9-RF)																								
1979	NY-A	3	4	1	1	0	0	0	0	0	0	.250	.250	.250	500	36	-0	0	0	0	1.000	0	/1-1	0.0
1980	NY-A	39	65	15	20	3	0	3	12	12	19	.308	.416	.492	908	150	5	0	1	-0	1.000	-2	1-12/O-8R,C-1,3D	0.2
1981	NY-A	34	55	7	6	1	0	0	1	12	12	.109	.269	.127	396	18	-5	1	0	0	1.000	0	1-19/O-8L,C-3,D-4	-0.6
1982	KC-A	41	15	5	2	0	0	0	2	4	2	.133	.316	.133	449	29	-1	0	0	0	.990	2	1-35/C-2	0.1
Total	4	117	139	28	29	4	0	3	15	28	33	.209	.341	.302	643	82	-2	1	1	-0	.996	1	/1-67,O-16R,D-12,C3	-0.3
■ **DEL WERTZ** Wertz, Dwight Lyman Moody b: 10/11/1888, Canton, Ohio d: 5/26/58, Sarasota, Fla. BR/TR, 5'10", 160 lbs. Deb: 5/23/14																								
1914	Buf-F	3	0	1	0	0	0	0	0	0	0	—	—	—	—	—	0	0			1.000	0	/S-1	0.0
■ **VIC WERTZ** Wertz, Victor Woodrow b: 2/9/25, York, Pa. d: 7/7/83, Detroit, Mich. BL/TR, 6', 186 lbs. Deb: 4/15/47 Career OF: (105-LF 4-CF 783-RF)																								
1947	Det-A	102	333	60	96	22	4	6	44	47	66	.288	.376	.432	809	121	10	2	0	0	.965	-2	O-83(38-2-43)	0.4
1948	Det-A	119	391	49	97	19	9	7	67	48	70	.248	.335	.396	731	92	-6	0	0	0	.954	1	O-98(64-1-36)	-1.0
1949	Det-A★	155	608	96	185	26	6	20	133	80	61	.304	.385	.465	851	124	20	2	3	-1	.981	2	*O-155(0-0-155)	1.6
1950	Det-A	149	559	99	172	37	4	27	123	91	55	.308	.408	.533	941	135	30	0	1	-0	.967	-8	*O-145(0-0-145)	1.5
1951	Det-A★	138	501	86	143	24	4	27	94	78	61	.285	.383	.511	894	139	27	0	3	-1	.989	3	*O-131(0-0-131)	2.4
1952	Det-A☆	85	285	46	70	15	3	17	51	46	44	.246	.352	.498	851	134	12	1	0	0	.986	3	O-79(0-0-79)	1.3
	StL-A	37	130	22	45	5	0	6	19	23	20	.346	.444	.523	968	164	12	0	0	0	.955	-3	O-36(0-0-36)	0.9
	Yr	122	415	68	115	20	3	23	70	69	64	.277	.381	.506	887	143	24	1	0	0	.976	0	*O-115(0-0-115)	2.2
1953	StL-A	128	440	61	118	18	6	19	70	72	44	.268	.376	.466	842	124	15	1	4	-1	.974	7	*O-121(0-1-120)	1.7
1954	Bal-A	29	94	5	19	1	0	1	13	11	17	.202	.286	.245	530	50	-6	0	0	0	.963	2	O-27(0-0-27)	-0.6
	*Cle-A	94	295	33	81	14	2	14	48	34	40	.275	.350	.478	828	123	8	0	2	-1	.989	2	1-83/O-5(2-0-3)	0.5
	Yr	123	389	38	100	15	2	15	61	45	57	.257	.334	.422	756	106	2	0	2	-1	.989	4	1-83,O-32(2-0-30)	-0.1
1955	Cle-A	74	257	30	65	11	2	14	55	32	33	.253	.338	.475	813	112	4	1	1	-0	.984	-3	1-63/O-9(1-0-8)	-0.3
1956	Cle-A	136	481	65	127	22	0	32	106	75	87	.264	.369	.509	878	127	18	0	0	0	.991	1	*1-133	1.1
1957	Cle-A★	144	515	84	145	21	0	28	105	78	88	.282	.378	.485	864	136	26	2	3	-1	.988	-2	*1-139	1.6
1958	Cle-A	25	43	5	12	1	0	3	12	5	7	.279	.354	.512	866	139	2	0	0	0	.980	0	/1-8	0.2
1959	Bos-A	94	247	38	68	13	0	7	49	22	32	.275	.339	.413	752	101	0	0	0	0	.992	2	1-64	-0.1
1960	Bos-A	131	443	45	125	22	0	19	103	37	54	.282	.339	.460	799	110	5	0	2	-1	.987	3	*1-117	0.1
1961	Bos-A	99	317	33	83	16	2	11	60	38	43	.262	.345	.429	774	103	1	0	0	0	.991	3	1-86	0.0
	Det-A	8	6	0	1	0	0	0	1	0	1	.167	.167	.167	333	-10	-1	0	0	0	.000	0	H	-0.1
	Yr	107	323	33	84	16	2	11	61	38	44	.260	.342	.424	766	101	0	0	0	0	.991	3	1-86	-0.1
1962	Det-A	74	105	7	34	2	0	5	18	5	13	.324	.360	.486	846	121	3	0	0	0	.988	0	1-16	0.2
1963	Det-A	6	5	0	0	0	0	0	0	0	1	.000	.000	.000	0	-97	-1	0	0	0	.000	0	H	-0.1
	Min-A	35	44	3	6	0	0	3	7	6	5	.136	.240	.341	581	59	-3	0	0	0	1.000	1	/1-6	-0.2
	Yr	41	49	3	6	0	0	3	7	6	6	.122	.218	.306	524	44	-4	0	0	0	1.000	1	/1-6	-0.3
Total	17	1862	6099	867	1692	289	42	266	1178	828	842	.277	.366	.469	836	121	177	9	19	-5	.973	12	O-889R,1-715	11.1
■ **JIM WESSINGER** Wessinger, James Michael b: 9/25/55, Utica, N.Y. BR/TR, 5'10", 165 lbs. Deb: 8/4/79																								
1979	Atl-N	10	7	2	0	0	0	0	0	1	4	.000	.125	.000	125	-59	-2	0	0	0	.833	1	/2-2	-0.1
■ **MAX WEST** West, Max Edward b: 11/28/16, Dexter, Mo. BL/TR, 6'1.5", 182 lbs. Deb: 4/19/38 Career OF: (342-LF 115-CF 171-RF)																								
1938	Bos-N	123	418	47	98	16	5	10	63	38	38	.234	.300	.368	668	92	-6	5			.986	-9	*O-109(75-0-36)/1-7	-2.1
1939	Bos-N	130	449	67	128	26	6	19	82	51	55	.285	.364	.497	861	139	24	1			.974	-7	*O-124(44-46-54)	1.1
1940	Bos-N★	139	524	72	137	27	5	7	72	65	54	.261	.344	.372	716	103	3	2			.975	1	*O-102(4-59-49),1-36	-0.4
1941	Bos-N	138	484	63	134	28	4	12	68	72	68	.277	.373	.426	798	130	20	5			.981	6	*O-132(126-5-5)	2.0
1942	Bos-N	134	452	54	115	22	0	16	56	68	59	.254	.354	.409	764	126	15	4			.991	-1	1-85,O-50(36-2-13)	0.4
1946	Bos-N	1	1	0	0	0	0	0	0	0	1	.000	.000	.000	0	-99	-0	0			1.000	-0	/1-1	0.0
	Cin-N	72	202	16	43	13	0	5	18	32	36	.213	.323	.351	675	95	-1	1			.952	-1	O-58(54-3-1)	-0.7
	Yr	73	203	16	43	13	0	5	18	32	37	.212	.322	.350	672	94	-2	1			.952	-1	O-58(54-3-1)/1-1	-0.7
1948	Pit-N	87	146	19	26	4	0	8	21	27	29	.178	.310	.370	680	82	-4	1			.991	-4	1-32,O-16(3-0-13)	-0.9
Total	7	824	2676	338	681	136	20	77	380	353	340	.254	.344	.407	751	114	51	19			.975	-15	O-591L,1-161	-0.6
■ **BUCK WEST** West, Milton Douglas b: 8/29/1860, Spring Mill, Ohio d: 1/13/29, Mansfield, Ohio BL/TR, 5'10", 200 lbs. Deb: 8/24/1884																								
1884	Cin-a	33	131	20	32	2	8	1	15	2		.244	.256	.405	660	107	0				.825	-6	O-33(0-33-0)	-0.6
1890	Cle-N	37	151	20	37	6	1	2	29	7	11	.245	.283	.338	621	82	-4	4			.831	-1	O-37(0-4-33)	-0.5
Total	2	70	282	40	69	8	9	3	44	9	11	.245	.271	.369	639	94	-4	4			.828	-7	/O-70(0-37-33)	-1.1
■ **DICK WEST** West, Richard Thomas b: 11/24/15, Louisville, Ky. d: 3/13/96, Fort Wayne, Ind. BR/TR, 6'2", 180 lbs. Deb: 9/28/38																								
1938	Cin-N	1	1	0	0	0	0	0	0	0	0	.000	.000	.000	0	-99	-0	0			.000	0	H	0.0
1939	Cin-N	8	19	1	4	0	0	0	4	1	4	.211	.250	.211	461	25	-2	0			1.000	-1	/O-5(5-0-0),C-1	-0.3
1940	Cin-N	7	28	4	11	2	0	1	6	0	2	.393	.393	.571	964	161	2	1			1.000	-3	/C-7	0.0
1941	Cin-N	67	172	15	37	5	2	1	17	6	23	.215	.246	.285	531	49	-12	4			.970	-3	C-64	-1.3

YEAR	TM/L	G	AB	R	H	2B	3B	HR	RBI	BB	SO	AVG	OBP	SLG	OPS	OPS+	BR+	SB	CS	SBR	FA	FR	G/POS	TPR
1942	Cin-N	33	79	9	14	3	0	1	8	5	13	.177	.226	.253	479	40	-6	1			.989	-3	C-17/O-6(6-0-0)	-0.3
1943	Cin-N	3	0	1	0	0	0	0	0	0	0	—	—	—	—	—	0	0			.000	0	R	0.0
Total	6	119	299	30	66	10	2	3	35	12	42	.221	.253	.298	551	55	-18	6			.977	-4	/C-89,O-11(11-0-0)	-1.9
■ **SAM WEST**	West, Samuel Filmore b: 10/5/04, Longview, Tex. d: 11/23/85, Lubbock, Tex. BL/TL, 5′11″, 165 lbs. Deb: 4/17/27 C Career OF: (92-LF 1454-CF 31-RF)																							
1927	Was-A	38	67	9	16	4	1	0	6	8	8	.239	.320	.328	648	69	-3	1	0	0	.939	-1	O-18(5-8-5)	-0.5
1928	Was-A	125	378	59	114	30	7	3	40	20	23	.302	.338	.442	780	104	1	5	6	-1	**.996**	-10	*O-116(53-60-6)	-1.5
1929	Was-A	142	510	60	136	16	8	3	75	45	41	.267	.326	.347	673	73	-20	9	8	-1	.978	15	*O-139(4-136-0)	-1.1
1930	Was-A	120	411	75	135	22	10	6	67	37	34	.328	.385	.474	860	116	10	5	5	-1	.972	3	*O-118(1-117-0)	0.8
1931	Was-A	132	526	77	175	43	13	3	91	30	37	.333	.369	.481	850	121	14	6	8	-1	.990	21	*O-127(0-127-0)	2.8
1932	Was-A	146	554	88	159	27	12	6	83	48	57	.287	.345	.412	756	96	-3	4	5	-1	.979	19	*O-143(0-143-0)	1.1
1933	StL-A★	133	517	93	155	25	12	11	48	59	49	.300	.373	.458	831	112	9	10	8	-1	.988	8	*O-127(0-127-0)	1.3
1934	StL-A★	122	482	90	157	22	10	9	55	62	55	.326	.403	.469	871	115	11	3	5	-1	.972	7	*O-120(0-120-0)	1.3
1935	StL-A☆	138	527	93	158	37	4	10	70	75	46	.300	.388	.442	830	109	8	1	6	-2	**.989**	17	*O-135(0-135-0)	1.8
1936	StL-A	152	533	78	148	26	4	7	70	94	70	.278	.386	.381	767	87	-8	2	0	0	.983	9	*O-148(0-148-0)	-0.2
1937	StL-A★	122	457	68	150	37	4	7	58	46	28	.328	.390	.473	862	115	11	1	1	-0	.987	12	*O-105(0-105-0)	1.8
1938	StL-A	44	165	17	51	8	2	1	27	14	9	.309	.363	.400	763	91	-2	1	0	0	.971	-3	O-41(0-41-0)	-0.5
	Was-A	92	344	51	104	19	5	5	47	33	21	.302	.363	.430	794	105	2	1	1	-0	.983	-3	O-85(1-84-0)	-0.2
	Yr	136	509	68	155	27	7	6	74	47	30	.305	.363	.420	784	100	0	2	1	0	.979	-6	*O-126(1-125-0)	-0.7
1939	Was-A	115	390	52	110	20	8	3	52	67	29	.282	.387	.397	785	109	8	1	1	-0	.992	3	O-89(23-55-11),1-17	0.5
1940	Was-A	57	99	7	25	6	1	1	18	16	13	.253	.357	.364	720	93	-1	0	2	-1	.990	-1	1-12/O-9(0-3-6)	-0.3
1941	Was-A	26	37	3	10	0	0	0	6	11	2	.270	.438	.270	708	95	1	1	0	0	1.000	-0	/O-8(4-1-3)	0.0
1942	Chi-A	49	151	14	35	5	0	0	25	31	18	.232	.363	.265	628	80	-2	2	0	0	.983	-3	O-45(1-44-0)	-0.6
Total	16	1753	6148	934	1838	347	101	75	838	696	540	.299	.371	.425	796	103	36	53	56	-8	.983	93	*O-1573C/1-29	6.5
■ **MAX WEST**	West, Walter Maxwell b: 7/14/04, Sunset, Tex. d: 4/25/71, Houston, Tex. BR/TR, 5′11″, 165 lbs. Deb: 9/18/28																							
1928	Bro-N	7	21	4	6	1	1	0	1	4	1	.286	.400	.429	829	118	1	0			.882	1	/O-6(1-4-1)	0.2
1929	Bro-N	5	8	1	2	1	0	0	1	1	0	.250	.333	.375	708	77	-0	0			1.000	-1	/O-2(1-1-0)	-0.1
Total	2	12	29	5	8	2	1	0	2	5	1	.276	.382	.414	796	107	0	0			.895	1	/O-8(2-5-1)	0.1
■ **BILLY WEST**	West, William Nelson b: 8/21/1840, Philadelphia, Pa. Deb: 5/22/1874																							
1874	Atl-n	9	35	4	8	1	0	0	2	1	2	.229	.250	.257	507	71	-1	0	0	0	.707	-1	/2-9,C-1,S-1	-0.2
1876	NY-N	1	4	0	0	0	0	0	0	0	0	.000	.000	.000	0	-99	-1				1.000	-0	/2-1	-0.1
■ **OSCAR WESTERBERG**	Westerberg, Oscar William b: 7/8/1882, Alameda, Cal. d: 4/17/09, Alameda, Cal. BB/TR, Deb: 9/5/07																							
1907	Bos-N	2	6	0	2	0	0	0	1	1		.333	.429	.333	762	139	0	0			1.000	-1	/S-2	0.0
■ **JIM WESTLAKE**	Westlake, James Patrick b: 7/3/30, Sacramento, Cal. BL/TL, 6′1″, 190 lbs. Deb: 4/16/55 F																							
1955	Phi-N	1	1	0	0	0	0	0	0	0	1	.000	.000	.000	0	-99	-0	0	0	0	.000	0	H	0.0
■ **WALLY WESTLAKE**	Westlake, Waldon Thomas b: 11/8/20, Gridley, Cal. BR/TR, 6′, 186 lbs. Deb: 4/15/47 F Career OF: (137-LF 344-CF 385-RF)																							
1947	Pit-N	112	407	59	111	17	4	17	69	27	63	.273	.324	.459	784	103	0	5			.988	4	*O-109(0-12-97)	0.1
1948	Pit-N	132	428	78	122	10	6	17	65	46	40	.285	.360	.456	815	117	10	2			.976	-0	*O-125(1-67-57)	0.6
1949	Pit-N	147	525	77	148	24	8	23	104	45	69	.282	.345	.490	835	118	12	6			.982	5	*O-143(0-51-92)	1.3
1950	Pit-N	139	477	69	136	15	6	24	95	48	78	.285	.359	.493	852	118	11	1			**.991**	4	*O-123(5-97-26)	1.1
1951	Pit-N	50	181	28	51	4	0	16	45	9	26	.282	.323	.569	892	131	7	0	1	-0	.908	5	3-34,O-11(10-1-0)	1.0
	StL-N★	73	267	36	68	8	5	6	39	24	42	.255	.325	.390	715	91	-4	1	2	-0	.982	2	O-68(11-29-28)	-0.5
	Yr	123	448	64	119	12	5	22	84	33	68	.266	.324	.462	786	107	3	1	3	-1	.984	7	O-79(21-30-28),3-34	0.5
1952	StL-N	21	74	7	16	3	0	0	10	8	11	.216	.293	.257	549	53	-5	1	1	-0	1.000	6	O-15(0-15-0)	0.1
	Cin-N	59	183	29	37	4	0	3	14	31	29	.202	.324	.273	597	67	-7	0	2	-1	.992	-2	O-56(5-43-10)	-1.2
	Yr	80	257	36	53	7	0	3	24	39	40	.206	.315	.268	584	63	-12	1	3	-1	.995	5	O-71(5-58-10)	-1.1
	Cle-A	29	69	11	16	4	1	1	9	8	16	.232	.312	.362	674	93	-1	1	0	0	1.000	-3	O-28(12-4-20)	-0.5
1953	Cle-A	82	218	42	72	7	1	9	46	35	29	.330	.427	.495	923	153	17	2	0	0	.963	-11	O-72(38-12-36)	0.4
1954	*Cle-A	85	240	36	63	9	2	11	42	26	37	.262	.340	.454	794	114	4	0	1	-0	.964	-7	O-70(49-10-14)	-0.7
1955	Cle-A	16	20	2	5	1	0	0	1	3	5	.250	.348	.300	648	73	-1	0	0	0	1.000	-0	/O-7(4-3-0)	-0.1
	Bal-A	8	24	0	3	1	0	0	0	6	5	.125	.300	.167	467	30	-2	0	0	0	1.000	-1	/O-7(2-0-5)	-0.4
	Yr	24	44	2	8	2	0	0	1	9	10	.182	.321	.227	548	49	-3	0	0	0	1.000	-2	O-14(6-3-5)	-0.5
1956	Phi-N	5	4	0	0	0	0	0	0	1	3	.000	.200	.000	200	-41	-1	0	0	0	.000	0	H	-0.1
Total	10	958	3117	474	848	107	33	127	539	317	453	.272	.346	.450	795	111	41	19	7		.983	1	O-834R/3-34	1.1
■ **AL WESTON**	Weston, Alfred John b: 12/11/05, Lynn, Mass. d: 11/13/97, San Diego, Cal. BR/TR, 6′, 195 lbs. Deb: 7/7/29																							
1929	Bos-N	3	3	0	0	0	0	0	0	0	2	.000	.000	.000	0	-99	-1	0			.000	0	H	-0.1
■ **WES WESTRUM**	Westrum, Wesley Noreen b: 11/28/22, Clearbrook, Minn. BR/TR, 5′11″, 185 lbs. Deb: 9/17/47 MC																							
1947	NY-N	6	12	1	5	1	0	0	2	0	2	.417	.417	.500	917	142	1	0			1.000	0	/C-2	0.1
1948	NY-N	66	125	14	20	3	1	4	16	20	36	.160	.276	.296	572	54	-8	3			.981	8	C-63	0.2
1949	NY-N	64	169	23	41	4	1	7	28	37	39	.243	.385	.402	787	111	4	1			.980	-0	C-62	0.7
1950	NY-N	140	437	68	103	13	3	23	71	92	73	.236	.371	.437	808	111	9	2			**.999**	10	*C-139	2.6
1951	*NY-N	124	361	59	79	12	0	20	70	104	93	.219	.400	.418	818	119	14	1	0	0	.987	8	*C-122	2.9
1952	NY-N☆	114	322	47	71	11	0	14	43	76	68	.220	.374	.385	759	110	7	1	2	-0	.978	-4	*C-112	0.9
1953	NY-N☆	107	290	40	65	5	0	12	30	56	73	.224	.352	.366	717	86	-5	2	0	0	.982	4	*C-106/3-1	0.4
1954	*NY-N	98	246	25	46	3	1	8	27	45	60	.187	.320	.305	625	63	-13	0	1	-0	.985	12	C-98	0.3
1955	NY-N	69	137	11	29	1	0	4	18	24	18	.212	.333	.307	640	71	-5	0	1	-0	.987	10	C-68	0.7
1956	NY-N	68	132	10	29	5	2	3	8	25	28	.220	.348	.356	704	91	-1	0	0	0	.982	13	C-67	1.4
1957	NY-N	63	91	4	15	1	0	1	2	10	24	.165	.255	.209	464	27	-9	0	1	-0	.966	2	C-63	-0.6
Total	11	919	2322	302	503	59	8	96	315	489	514	.217	.357	.373	730	95	-6	10	5		.985	64	C-902/3-1	9.6
■ **JEFF WETHERBY**	Wetherby, Jeffrey Barrett b: 10/18/63, Granada Hills, Cal. BL/TL, 6′2″, 195 lbs. Deb: 6/7/89																							
1989	Atl-N	52	48	5	10	2	1	1	7	4	6	.208	.269	.354	623	75	-2	1	0	0	1.000	-2	/O-9(7-0-2)	-0.4
■ **DUTCH WETZEL**	Wetzel, Franklin Burton b: 7/7/1893, Columbus, Ind. d: 3/5/42, Hollywood, Cal. BR/TR, 5′9.5″, 177 lbs. Deb: 9/15/20																							
1920	StL-A	7	21	5	9	1	1	0	5	4	1	.429	.520	.571	1091	183	3	0	1	-0	.875	0	/O-6(5-1-0)	0.2
1921	StL-A	61	119	16	25	2	0	2	10	9	20	.210	.271	.277	549	38	-11	0	0	0	.981	-2	O-27(12-4-11)	-1.4
Total	2	68	140	21	34	3	1	2	15	13	21	.243	.312	.321	633	59	-8	0	1	-0	.957	-2	/O-33(17-5-11)	-1.2
■ **BILL WHALEY**	Whaley, William Carl b: 2/10/1899, Indianapolis, Ind. d: 3/3/43, Indianapolis, Ind. BR/TR, 5′11″, 178 lbs. Deb: 4/18/23																							
1923	StL-A	23	50	5	12	2	1	0	1	4	2	.240	.309	.320	629	62	-3	0	0	0	1.000	-0	O-13(4-9-0)	-0.4
■ **BERT WHALING**	Whaling, Albert James b: 6/22/1888, Los Angeles, Cal. d: 1/21/65, Sawtelle, Cal. BR/TR, 6′, 185 lbs. Deb: 4/22/13																							
1913	Bos-N	79	211	22	51	8	2	0	25	10	32	.242	.283	.299	581	65	-10	3			**.990**	1	C-77	-0.4
1914	Bos-N	60	172	18	36	7	0	0	12	21	28	.209	.303	.250	553	65	-7	2			.981	12	C-59	1.0
1915	Bos-N	72	190	10	42	6	2	0	13	8	38	.221	.264	.274	537	66	-8	0	1	-0	.986	1	C-69	-0.3
Total	3	211	573	50	129	21	4	0	50	39	98	.225	.283	.276	558	65	-25	5	1		.986	13	C-205	0.3
■ **MACK WHEAT**	Wheat, McKinley Davis b: 6/9/1893, Polo, Mo. d: 8/14/79, Los Banos, Cal. BR/TR, 5′11.5″, 167 lbs. Deb: 4/14/15 F																							
1915	Bro-N	8	14	0	1	0	0	0	0	0	5	.071	.071	.071	143	-56	-3	0			.957	-0	/C-8	-0.3
1916	Bro-N	2	2	0	0	0	0	0	0	0	1	.000	.000	.000	0	-97	-0	0			1.000	0	/C-2	0.0
1917	Bro-N	29	60	2	8	1	0	0	0	1	12	.133	.161	.150	311	-4	-7	1			.968	1	C-18/O-9(9-1-0)	-0.6
1918	Bro-N	57	157	11	34	7	1	1	3	8	24	.217	.255	.293	548	67	-6	2			.966	-1	C-38/O-7(1-1-4)	-0.5
1919	Bro-N	41	112	5	23	3	0	0	8	2	22	.205	.246	.232	478	43	-8	1			.944	-4	C-38	-0.9
1920	Phi-N	78	230	15	52	10	3	3	20	8	35	.226	.261	.335	596	67	-10	3	1	0	.961	9	C-74	0.5

YEAR	TM/L	G	AB	R	H	2B	3B	HR	RBI	BB	SO	AVG	OBP	SLG	OPS	OPS+	BR+	SB	CS	SBR	FA	FR	G/POS	TPR
1921	Phi-N	10	27	1	5	2	1	0	4	0	3	.185	.241	.333	575	47	-2	0	0	0	.980	5	/C-9	0.3
Total	7	225	602	34	123	23	5	4	35	19	102	.204	.241	.279	520	52	-37	7	1		.961	9	C-187/O-16(10-2-4)	-1.5

■ ZACK WHEAT
Wheat, Zachary Davis "Buck" b: 5/23/1888, Hamilton, Mo. d: 3/11/72, Sedalia, Mo. BL/TR, 5'10", 170 lbs. Deb: 9/11/09 FH

YEAR	TM/L	G	AB	R	H	2B	3B	HR	RBI	BB	SO	AVG	OBP	SLG	OPS	OPS+	BR+	SB	CS	SBR	FA	FR	G/POS	TPR
1909	Bro-N	26	102	15	31	7	3	0	4	6		.304	.343	.431	774	145	5	1			.952	2	O-26(25-1-0)	0.5
1910	Bro-N	156	606	78	172	36	15	2	55	47	80	.284	.341	.403	744	120	13	16			.962	6	*O-156(156-0-0)	1.1
1911	Bro-N	140	534	55	153	26	13	5	76	29	58	.287	.332	.412	744	112	6	21			.955	-3	*O-136(135-1-0)	-0.3
1912	Bro-N	123	453	70	138	28	7	8	65	39	40	.305	.367	.450	818	128	16	16			.968	2	*O-120(120-0-0)	1.3
1913	Bro-N	138	535	64	161	28	10	7	58	25	45	.301	.335	.430	764	114	8	19			.978	9	*O-135(135-0-0)	1.1
1914	Bro-N	145	533	66	170	26	9	9	89	47	50	.319	.377	.452	830	143	27	20			.962	18	*O-144(144-0-0)	4.2
1915	Bro-N	146	528	64	136	15	12	5	66	52	42	.258	.330	.360	690	107	5	21	14	-0	.953	11	*O-144(144-0-0)	1.0
1916	*Bro-N	149	568	76	177	32	13	9	73	43	49	.312	.366	**.461**	828	149	32	19			.975	9	*O-149(149-1-0)	3.9
1917	Bro-N	109	362	38	113	15	11	1	41	20	18	.312	.352	.423	774	133	13	5			.979	6	O-98(98-0-0)	1.8
1918	Bro-N	105	409	39	137	15	3	0	51	16	17	**.335**	.369	.386	755	131	14	9			.979	4	*O-105(105-0-0)	1.5
1919	Bro-N	137	536	70	159	23	11	5	62	33	27	.297	.344	.409	753	123	14	15			.971	-1	*O-137(137-0-0)	0.8
1920	*Bro-N	148	583	89	191	26	13	9	73	48	21	.328	.385	.463	848	138	29	8	10	-2	.971	-4	*O-148(148-0-0)	1.8
1921	Bro-N	148	568	91	182	31	10	14	85	44	19	.320	.372	.484	857	121	16	11	8	-0	.965	-4	*O-148(148-0-0)	0.0
1922	Bro-N	152	600	92	201	29	12	16	112	45	22	.335	.388	.503	891	129	25	9	6	-0	**.991**	2	*O-152(152-0-0)	1.4
1923	Bro-N	98	349	63	131	13	5	8	65	23	12	.375	.417	.510	927	148	24	3	3	-0	.908	-11	O-87(85-0-2)	0.5
1924	Bro-N	141	566	92	212	41	8	14	97	49	18	.375	.428	.549	978	165	52	3	4	-1	.965	5	*O-139(139-0-0)	4.4
1925	Bro-N	150	616	125	221	42	14	14	103	45	22	.359	.403	.541	944	143	38	3	1	0	.962	0	*O-149(149-0-0)	2.5
1926	Bro-N	111	411	68	119	31	2	5	35	21	14	.290	.326	.411	737	99	-2	4			.955	2	*O-102(102-0-0)	-0.9
1927	Phi-A	88	247	34	80	12	1	1	38	18	5	.324	.379	.393	772	95	-1	2	3	-1	.983	-3	O-62(57-2-3)	-0.9
Total	19	2410	9106	1289	2884	476	172	132	1248	650	559	.317	.367	.450	817	129	336	205	49		.966	50	*O-2337(2328-5-5)	25.7

■ WOODY WHEATON
Wheaton, Elwood Pierce b: 10/3/14, Philadelphia, Pa. d: 12/11/95, Lancaster, Pa. BL/TL, 5'8.5", 160 lbs. Deb: 9/28/43

YEAR	TM/L	G	AB	R	H	2B	3B	HR	RBI	BB	SO	AVG	OBP	SLG	OPS	OPS+	BR+	SB	CS	SBR	FA	FR	G/POS	TPR
1943	Phi-A	7	30	2	6	2	0	0	2	3	2	.200	.294	.267	561	65	-1	0	0	0	1.000	1	/O-7(0-7-0)	-0.1
1944	Phi-A	30	59	1	11	2	0	0	5	5	3	.186	.250	.220	470	35	-5	1	2	-0	1.000	2	P-11/O-8(0-8-0)	-0.1
Total	2	37	89	3	17	4	0	0	7	8	5	.191	.265	.236	501	45	-6	1	2	-0	.981	3	/O-15(0-15-0),P-11	-0.2

■ DON WHEELER
Wheeler, Donald Wesley "Scott" b: 9/29/22, Minneapolis, Minn BR/TR, 5'10", 175 lbs. Deb: 4/23/49

YEAR	TM/L	G	AB	R	H	2B	3B	HR	RBI	BB	SO	AVG	OBP	SLG	OPS	OPS+	BR+	SB	CS	SBR	FA	FR	G/POS	TPR
1949	Chi-A	67	192	17	46	9	2	1	22	27	19	.240	.333	.323	656	76	-6	2	0	0	.976	3	C-58	0.0

■ ED WHEELER
Wheeler, Edward b: 6/15/1878, Sherman, Mich. d: 8/15/60, Ft.Worth, Tex. BB/TR, 5'10", 160 lbs. Deb: 5/10/02

YEAR	TM/L	G	AB	R	H	2B	3B	HR	RBI	BB	SO	AVG	OBP	SLG	OPS	OPS+	BR+	SB	CS	SBR	FA	FR	G/POS	TPR
1902	Bro-N	30	96	4	12	0	0	0	5	3		.125	.152	.125	277	-14	-13	1			.863	-3	3-11,2-10/S-5	-1.6

■ ED WHEELER
Wheeler, Edward Raymond b: 5/24/15, Los Angeles, Cal. d: 8/4/83, Centralia, Wash. BR/TR, 5'9", 160 lbs. Deb: 4/19/45

YEAR	TM/L	G	AB	R	H	2B	3B	HR	RBI	BB	SO	AVG	OBP	SLG	OPS	OPS+	BR+	SB	CS	SBR	FA	FR	G/POS	TPR
1945	Cle-A	46	72	12	14	2	0	0	2	8	13	.194	.275	.222	497	47	-5	1	1	-0	.912	-6	3-14,S-11/2-3	-1.1

■ GEORGE WHEELER
Wheeler, George Harrison "Heavy" b: 11/10/1881, Shelburn, Ind. d: 6/14/18, Clinton, Ind. BL/TR, 5'9.5", 180 lbs. Deb: 7/27/10

YEAR	TM/L	G	AB	R	H	2B	3B	HR	RBI	BB	SO	AVG	OBP	SLG	OPS	OPS+	BR+	SB	CS	SBR	FA	FR	G/POS	TPR
1910	Cin-N	3	3	0	0	0	0	0	0	0	2	.000	.000	.000	0	-99	-1	0			.000	0	H	-0.1

■ HARRY WHEELER
Wheeler, Harry Eugene b: 3/3/1858, Versailles, Ind.
d: 10/9/1900, Cincinnati, Ohio BR/TR, 5'11", 165 lbs. Deb: 6/19/1878 M Career OF: (115-LF 40-CF 82-RF)

YEAR	TM/L	G	AB	R	H	2B	3B	HR	RBI	BB	SO	AVG	OBP	SLG	OPS	OPS+	BR+	SB	CS	SBR	FA	FR	G/POS	TPR
1878	Pro-N	7	27	7	4	0	0	0	1	2	15	.148	.207	.148	355	18	-2				.875	-2	/P-7	0.0
1879	Cin-N	1	3	0	0	0	0	0	0	0	2	.000	.000	.000	0	-99	-1				1.000	-0	/O-1(0-0-1),P-1	-0.1
1880	Cle-N	1	4	0	1	0	0	0	0	0	0	.250	.250	.250	500	72	-0				1.000	-0	/O-1(1-0-0)	0.0
	Cin-N	17	65	1	6	2	0	0	2	0	15	.092	.092	.123	215	-28	-8				.750	1	O-17(16-1-0)	-0.8
	Yr	18	69	1	7	2	0	0	2	0	15	.101	.101	.130	232	-22	-8				.759	1	O-18(17-1-0)	-0.8
1882	Cin-a	76	344	59	86	11	11	1	29	7		.250	.265	.355	620	102	-0				.808	-5	*O-64R,1-12/P-4	-0.7
1883	Col-a	82	371	42	84	6	7	0		6		.226	.239	.280	519	72	-10				.803	-2	*O-82(82-0-0)/2-1,P-1	-1.2
1884	StL-a	5	19	0	5	2	0	0		1		.263	.300	.368	668	113	0				.600	-1	/O-5(4-1-0)	-0.1
	KC-U	14	62	11	16	1	0	0		3		.258	.292	.274	567	83	-3				.769	0	O-13(12-0-1)/P-1,M	-0.3
	CP-U	37	158	29	36	5	3	1		4		.228	.247	.316	563	70	-11				.774	-5	O-37(0-37-0)	-1.5
	Bal-U	17	69	3	18	2	0	0		0		.261	.261	.290	551	60	-5				.815	-1	O-17(0-1-16)	-0.5
	Yr	68	289	43	70	8	3	1		7		.242	.260	.301	561	70	-19				.781	-5	O-67(12-38-17)/P-1	-2.3
Total	6	257	1122	152	256	29	21	2	32	23	32	.228	.244	.297	540	74	-40				.791	-14	O-237L/P-14,1-12,2	-5.2

■ DICK WHEELER
Wheeler, Richard (b: Richard Wheeler Maynard) b: 1/14/1898, Keene, N.H. d: 2/12/62, Lexington, Mass. BR/TR, 5'11", 185 lbs. Deb: 6/17/18

YEAR	TM/L	G	AB	R	H	2B	3B	HR	RBI	BB	SO	AVG	OBP	SLG	OPS	OPS+	BR+	SB	CS	SBR	FA	FR	G/POS	TPR
1918	StL-N	3	6	0	0	0	0	0	0	0	3	.000	.000	.000	0	-99	-1	0			.000	-1	/O-2(0-0-2)	-0.3

■ BOBBY WHEELOCK
Wheelock, Warren H. b: 8/6/1864, Charlestown, Mass. d: 3/13/28, Boston, Mass. BR/TR, 5'8", 160 lbs. Deb: 5/19/1887 Career OF: (9-LF 1-CF 18-RF)

YEAR	TM/L	G	AB	R	H	2B	3B	HR	RBI	BB	SO	AVG	OBP	SLG	OPS	OPS+	BR+	SB	CS	SBR	FA	FR	G/POS	TPR
1887	Bos-N	48	181	32	57	4	2	2	15	15	15	.315	.315	.337	652	81	-4	20			.878	-7	O-28(9-1-18),S-20/2-4	-0.9
1890	Col-a	52	190	24	45	6	1	1	16	25		.237	.326	.295	620	89	-2	34			.885	-1	S-52	-0.1
1891	Col-a	136	498	82	114	15	1	0	39	78	55	.229	.336	.263	599	76	-11	52			.899	19	*S-136	1.0
Total	3	236	869	138	216	25	4	3	70	118	70	.249	.330	.285	614	80	-17	106			.894	11	S-208/O-28R,2-4	0.0

■ JIMMY WHELAN
Whelan, James Francis b: 5/11/1890, Kansas City, Mo. d: 11/29/29, Dayton, Ohio BR/TR, 5'8.5", 165 lbs. Deb: 4/24/13

YEAR	TM/L	G	AB	R	H	2B	3B	HR	RBI	BB	SO	AVG	OBP	SLG	OPS	OPS+	BR+	SB	CS	SBR	FA	FR	G/POS	TPR
1913	StL-N	1	1	0	0	0	0	0	0	0	0	.000	.000	.000	0	-99	-0	0			.000	0	H	0.0

■ TOM WHELAN
Whelan, Thomas Joseph b: 1/3/1894, Lynn, Mass. d: 6/26/57, Boston, Mass. BR/TR, 5'11", 175 lbs. Deb: 8/13/20

YEAR	TM/L	G	AB	R	H	2B	3B	HR	RBI	BB	SO	AVG	OBP	SLG	OPS	OPS+	BR+	SB	CS	SBR	FA	FR	G/POS	TPR
1920	Bos-N	1	1	0	0	0	0	0	0	1	1	.000	.500	.000	500	54	0	0	0	0	1.000	0	/1-1	0.0

■ PETE WHISENANT
Whisenant, Thomas Peter b: 12/14/29, Asheville, N.C.
d: 3/22/96, Port Charlotte, Fla. BR/TR, 6'2", 200 lbs. Deb: 4/16/52 C Career OF: (122-LF 142-CF 92-RF)

YEAR	TM/L	G	AB	R	H	2B	3B	HR	RBI	BB	SO	AVG	OBP	SLG	OPS	OPS+	BR+	SB	CS	SBR	FA	FR	G/POS	TPR
1952	Bos-N	24	52	3	10	2	0	0	7	4	13	.192	.250	.231	481	35	-5	1	1	-0	.973	2	O-14(9-5-0)	-0.3
1955	StL-N	58	115	10	22	5	1	2	9	5	29	.191	.225	.304	529	39	-10	2	0	0	.964	-1	O-40(12-11-19)	-1.2
1956	Chi-N	103	314	37	75	16	3	11	46	24	53	.239	.295	.414	709	89	-5	8	2	1	.992	6	O-93(6-84-0)	-0.3
1957	Cin-N	67	90	18	19	3	2	5	11	5	24	.211	.253	.456	708	80	-3	0	1	-0	.982	-9	O-43(24-9-12)	-1.3
1958	Cin-N	85	203	33	48	9	2	11	40	18	37	.236	.299	.463	762	93	-3	3	0	1	1.000	-1	O-66(26-2-42)/2-1	-0.6
1959	Cin-N	36	71	13	17	2	0	5	11	8	18	.239	.316	.479	795	105	0	0	0	0	.966	-2	O-21(5-0-16)	-0.2
1960	Cin-N	1	1	0	0	0	0	0	0	0	0	.000	.000	.000	0	-98	-0	0	0	0	.000	0	H	0.0
	Cle-A	7	6	0	1	0	0	0	0	0	2	.167	.167	.167	333	-10	-1	0	0	0	1.000	-1	/O-2(2-0-0)	-0.2
	Was-A	58	115	19	26	9	0	3	9	19	14	.226	.336	.383	718	95	-1	2	1	0	1.000	-9	O-47(23-31-1)	-1.2
	Yr	65	121	19	27	9	0	3	9	19	16	.223	.329	.372	700	90	-2	2	1	0	1.000	-10	O-49(25-31-1)	-1.4
1961	Min-A	10	6	1	0	0	0	0	0	1	2	.000	.143	.000	143	-55	-1	0	0	0	1.000	-2	/O-5(5-0-0)	-0.3
	Cin-N	26	15	6	3	0	0	0	1	2	4	.200	.294	.200	494	34	-1	1	0	0	1.000	-4	O-12(10-0-2)/C-1,3-1	-0.5
Total	8	475	988	140	221	46	8	37	134	86	196	.224	.287	.399	685	80	-30	17	5	2	.988	-20	O-343C/3-1,C-1,2-1	-6.1

■ LARRY WHISENTON
Whisenton, Larry b: 7/3/56, St.Louis, Mo. BL/TL, 6'1", 190 lbs. Deb: 9/17/77

YEAR	TM/L	G	AB	R	H	2B	3B	HR	RBI	BB	SO	AVG	OBP	SLG	OPS	OPS+	BR+	SB	CS	SBR	FA	FR	G/POS	TPR
1977	Atl-N	4	4	1	1	0	0	0	1	0	3	.250	.250	.250	500	31	-0	0	0	0	.000	0	H	-0.1
1978	Atl-N	6	16	1	3	1	0	0	2	1	2	.188	.235	.250	485	32	-1	0	0	0	1.000	-1	/O-4(0-0-4)	-0.2
1979	Atl-N	13	37	3	9	2	1	0	1	3	3	.243	.300	.351	651	72	-1	1	0	0	1.000	3	O-13(9-0-4)	0.1
1981	Atl-N	9	5	1	1	0	0	0	0	2	1	.200	.429	.200	629	81	0	0	0	0	.000	-1	/O-2(1-0-1)	-0.1
1982	*Atl-N	84	143	21	34	7	2	4	17	23	33	.238	.343	.399	742	103	1	2	2	-0	.964	-2	O-34(29-0-5)	-0.3
Total	5	116	205	27	48	10	3	4	21	29	42	.234	.329	.371	700	90	-2	3	2	-0	.968	-1	/O-53(39-0-14)	-0.6

■ LEW WHISTLER
Whistler, Lewis W. (b: Lewis Wissler) b: 3/10/1868, St.Louis, Mo.
d: 12/30/59, St.Louis, Mo. TR, 5'10.5", 178 lbs. Deb: 8/7/1890 Career OF: (15-LF 5-CF 12-RF)

YEAR	TM/L	G	AB	R	H	2B	3B	HR	RBI	BB	SO	AVG	OBP	SLG	OPS	OPS+	BR+	SB	CS	SBR	FA	FR	G/POS	TPR
1890	NY-N	45	170	27	49	9	7	2	29	20	37	.288	.366	.459	825	140	8	8			.982	-2	1-45	0.2
1891	NY-N	72	265	39	65	8	7	3	38	24	45	.245	.315	.362	677	101	0	4			.852	-16	S-33,O-22L/1-7,23	-1.4
1892	Bal-N	52	209	32	47	6	6	2	21	18	22	.225	.296	.340	635	90	-3	12			.973	-1	1-51/O-1(1-0-0)	-0.4
	Lou-N	80	285	42	67	4	7	5	34	30	45	.235	.312	.351	663	109	3	14			.978	-2	1-72,2-10	0.2

YEAR	TM/L	G	AB	R	H	2B	3B	HR	RBI	BB	SO	AVG	OBP	SLG	OPS	OPS+	BR+	SB	CS	SBR	FA	FR	G/POS	TPR
	Yr	132	494	74	114	10	13	7	55	48	67	.231	.305	.346	651	101	-0	26			.976	-3	*1-123,2-10/O-1L	-0.2
1893	Lou-N	13	47	5	10	1	1	0	9	5	5	.213	.302	.277	578	59	-3	1			.946	-0	1-13	-0.3
	StL-N	10	38	5	9	1	0	0	2	3	2	.237	.293	.263	556	48	-3	0			.923	-1	/O-9(0-0-9),1-1	-0.4
	Yr	23	85	10	19	2	1	0	11	8	7	.224	.298	.271	568	54	-6	1			.949	-2	1-14/O-9(0-0-9)	-0.7
Total	4	272	1014	150	247	29	28	12	133	100	156	.244	.318	.363	681	103	3	39			.976	-22	1-189/S-33,O-32L,23	-2.1
■ LOU WHITAKER Whitaker, Louis Rodman b: 5/12/57, Brooklyn, N.Y. BL/TR, 5'11", 160 lbs. Deb: 9/9/77																								
1977	Det-A	11	32	5	8	1	0	0	2	4	6	.250	.333	.281	615	66	-1	2	2	-0	1.000	-3	/2-9	-0.5
1978	Det-A	139	484	71	138	12	7	3	58	61	65	.285	.366	.357	724	101	3	7	7	-1	.978	12	*2-136/D-2	2.2
1979	Det-A	127	423	75	121	14	8	3	42	78	66	.286	.398	.378	777	107	8	20	10	1	.986	1	*2-126	1.6
1980	Det-A	145	477	68	111	19	1	1	45	73	79	.233	.335	.283	618	69	-18	8	4	0	.985	-3	*2-143	-1.3
1981	Det-A	109	335	48	88	14	4	5	36	40	42	.263	.343	.373	716	103	2	5	3	0	.985	6	*2-108	1.4
1982	Det-A	152	560	76	160	22	8	15	65	48	58	.286	.343	.434	777	111	8	11	3	1	**.988**	12	*2-149/D-1	3.0
1983	Det-A★	161	643	94	206	40	6	12	72	67	70	.320	.385	.457	842	134	31	17	10	0	.983	-13	*2-160	2.6
1984	*Det-A★	143	558	90	161	25	1	13	56	62	63	.289	.360	.407	766	112	10	6	5	-0	.979	-11	*2-142	0.7
1985	Det-A★	152	609	102	170	29	8	21	73	80	56	.279	.365	.456	821	124	21	6	4	-0	.985	-16	*2-150	1.3
1986	Det-A★	144	584	95	157	26	6	20	73	63	70	.269	.340	.437	777	110	8	13	8	0	.984	-1	*2-141	1.5
1987	*Det-A†	149	604	110	160	38	6	16	59	71	108	.265	.343	.427	770	107	7	13	5	1	.976	-14	*2-148	0.2
1988	Det-A	115	403	54	111	18	2	12	55	66	61	.275	.377	.419	797	128	17	2	0	0	.984	-23	*2-110	-0.3
1989	Det-A	148	509	77	128	21	1	28	85	89	59	.251	.366	.462	828	135	25	6	3	0	.985	-1	*2-146/D-2	2.8
1990	Det-A	132	472	75	112	22	2	18	60	74	71	.237	.341	.407	747	107	5	8	2	1	.991	12	*2-130/D-1	2.2
1991	Det-A	138	470	94	131	26	2	23	78	90	45	.279	.397	.489	886	142	29	4	2	0	**.994**	-11	*2-135/D-3	2.1
1992	Det-A	130	453	77	126	26	0	19	71	81	46	.278	.389	.461	850	137	24	6	4	-0	.984	-15	*2-119,D-10	1.3
1993	Det-A	119	383	72	111	32	1	9	67	78	46	.290	.415	.449	864	133	22	3	3	-0	.981	14	*2-110	3.9
1994	Det-A	92	322	67	97	21	2	12	43	41	47	.301	.382	.491	873	122	11	2	0	0	.970	-3	2-83/D-5	1.2
1995	Det-A	84	249	36	73	14	0	14	44	31	41	.293	.376	.518	894	130	11	4	0	1	.985	-11	2-63/D-8	0.4
Total	19	2390	8570	1386	2369	420	65	244	1084	1197	1099	.276	.366	.426	792	117	224	143	75	5	.984	-69	*2-2308/D-32	26.3
■ STEVE WHITAKER Whitaker, Stephen Edward b: 5/7/43, Tacoma, Wash. BL/TR, 6'1", 187 lbs. Deb: 8/23/66																								
1966	NY-A	31	114	15	28	3	2	7	15	9	24	.246	.306	.491	798	130	4	0	0	0	.955	-0	O-31(4-20-10)	0.3
1967	NY-A	122	441	37	107	12	3	11	50	23	89	.243	.285	.358	643	92	-6	2	5	-1	.982	6	*O-114(26-12-78)	-0.9
1968	NY-A	28	60	3	7	2	0	0	3	8	18	.117	.221	.150	371	14	-6	0	1	-0	.917	-1	O-14(6-7-2)	-1.0
1969	Sea-A	69	116	15	29	2	1	6	13	12	29	.250	.326	.440	765	114	2	2	0	0	.962	-2	O-39(22-0-18)	-0.1
1970	SF-N	16	27	3	3	1	0	0	4	2	14	.111	.172	.148	321	-13	-4	0	0	0	.857	-2	/O-9(9-0-0)	-0.7
Total	5	266	758	73	174	20	6	24	85	54	174	.230	.285	.367	652	92	-10	4	6	-1	.967	0	O-207(67-39-108)	-2.4
■ FUZZ WHITE White, Albert Eugene b: 6/27/18, Springfield, Mo. BL/TR, 6', 175 lbs. Deb: 9/17/40																								
1940	StL-A	2	2	0	0	0	0	0	0	0	0	.000	.000	.000	0	-98	-1	0	0	0	.000	0	H	-0.1
1947	NY-N	7	13	3	3	0	0	0	0	0	0	.231	.231	.231	462	23	-1	0			1.000	0	/O-5(0-0-5)	-0.2
Total	2	9	15	3	3	0	0	0	0	0	0	.200	.200	.200	400	6	-2	0	0		1.000	0	/O-5(0-0-5)	-0.3
■ C. B. WHITE White, C. B. b: Wakeman, Ohio Deb: 6/1/1883																								
1883	Phi-N	1	1	0	0	0	0	0	0	0	0	.000	.000	.000	0	-99	-0				.667	0	/S-1,3-1	0.0
■ CHARLIE WHITE White, Charles b: 8/12/28, Kinston, N.C. d: 5/26/98, Seattle, Wash. BL/TR, 5'11", 192 lbs. Deb: 4/18/54																								
1954	Mil-N	50	93	14	22	4	0	1	8	9	8	.237	.304	.312	616	65	-5	0	0	0	.981	-2	C-28	-0.6
1955	Mil-N	12	30	3	7	1	0	0	4	5	7	.233	.361	.267	628	74	-1	0	0	0	1.000	-2	C-10	-0.2
Total	2	62	123	17	29	5	0	1	12	14	15	.236	.319	.301	620	67	-6	0	0	0	.986	-4	/C-38	-0.8
■ DERRICK WHITE White, Derrick Ramon b: 10/12/69, San Rafael, Cal. BR/TR, 6'1", 220 lbs. Deb: 7/22/93 Career OF: (8-LF 0-CF 5-RF)																								
1993	Mon-N	17	49	6	11	3	0	2	4	2	12	.224	.269	.408	677	75	-2	2	0	0	.993	-0	1-17	-0.3
1995	Det-A	39	48	3	9	2	0	0	2	0	7	.188	.188	.229	417	8	-6	1	0	0	.981	-1	1-16,D-11/O-9(4-0-5)	-0.8
1998	Chi-N	11	10	1	1	0	0	1	2	0	5	.100	.100	.400	500	23	-1	0	0	0	.000	-1	/O-1(2-0-0)	-0.2
	Col-N	9	9	0	0	0	0	0	0	0	4	.000	.000	.000	0	-82	-2	0	0	0	1.000	-1	/O-2(2-0-0),D-1	-0.3
	Yr	20	19	1	1	0	0	1	2	0	9	.053	.053	.211	263	-31	-4	0	0	0	1.000	-1	/O-3(4-0-0),D-1	-0.5
Total	3	76	116	10	21	5	0	3	8	2	28	.181	.202	.302	503	30	-12	3	0	1	.990	-3	/1-33,O-12L,D-12	-1.6
■ DEVON WHITE White, Devon Markes b: 12/29/62, Kingston, Jamaica BB/TR, 6'2", 182 lbs. Deb: 9/2/85 Career OF: (37-LF 1636-CF 128-RF)																								
1985	Cal-A	21	7	7	1	0	0	0	0	1	3	.143	.333	.143	476	37	-1	3	1	0	1.000	-5	O-16(14-1-3)	-0.5
1986	*Cal-A	29	51	8	12	1	1	1	3	6	8	.235	.316	.353	669	83	-1	6	0	1	.961	-3	O-28(17-7-5)	-0.3
1987	Cal-A	159	639	103	168	33	5	24	87	39	135	.263	.307	.443	750	99	-3	32	11	3	.980	14	*O-159(6-64-120)	0.8
1988	Cal-A	122	455	76	118	22	2	11	51	23	84	.259	.298	.389	687	93	-5	17	8	1	.976	15	*O-116(0-116-0)	1.0
1989	Cal-A★	156	636	86	156	18	13	12	56	31	129	.245	.283	.371	654	84	-15	44	16	4	.989	15	*O-154(0-154-0)/D-1	0.3
1990	Cal-A	125	443	57	96	17	3	11	44	44	116	.217	.292	.343	635	79	-13	21	6	3	.972	8	*O-122(0-122-0)	-0.3
1991	*Tor-A	156	642	110	181	40	10	17	60	55	135	.282	.345	.455	800	115	12	33	10	4	**.998**	17	*O-156(0-156-0)	3.1
1992	*Tor-A	153	641	98	159	26	7	17	60	47	133	.248	.304	.390	694	89	-10	37	4	7	.985	15	*O-152(0-152-0)/D-1	1.0
1993	*Tor-A★	146	598	116	163	42	6	15	52	57	127	.273	.343	.438	781	108	6	34	4	6	.993	13	*O-145(0-145-0)	2.6
1994	Tor-A	100	403	67	109	24	6	13	49	21	80	.270	.315	.457	771	95	-4	11	3	1	.978	8	O-98(0-98-0)	0.6
1995	Tor-A	101	427	61	121	23	5	10	53	29	97	.283	.336	.431	767	99	-2	11	2	2	.989	8	O-99(0-99-0)	0.9
1996	Fla-N	146	552	77	151	37	6	17	84	38	99	.274	.329	.455	784	108	5	22	6	3	.987	2	*O-139(0-139-0)	1.1
1997	*Fla-N	74	265	37	65	13	1	6	34	32	65	.245	.342	.370	712	90	-3	13	5	1	.987	8	O-71(0-71-0)	0.3
1998	Ari-N★	146	563	84	157	32	1	22	85	42	102	.279	.339	.456	795	107	5	22	8	2	.987	8	*O-144(0-144-0)	1.7
1999	LA-N	134	474	60	127	20	2	14	68	39	88	.268	.338	.407	745	93	-6	19	5	2	.986	-2	*O-128(0-128-0)/D-1	-0.3
2000	LA-N	47	158	26	42	5	1	4	13	9	30	.266	.310	.386	696	78	-6	3	6	-1	.972	-4	O-40(0-40-0)	-1.0
Total	16	1815	6954	1073	1826	353	69	194	799	513	1431	.263	.320	.417	737	97	-41	328	95	39	.985	116	*O-1767C/D-3	11.0
■ DON WHITE White, Donald William b: 1/8/19, Everett, Wash. d: 6/15/87, Carlsbad, Cal. BR/TR, 6'1", 195 lbs. Deb: 4/19/48																								
1948	Phi-A	86	253	29	62	14	2	1	28	19	16	.245	.303	.328	631	68	-12	0	1	-0	.957	-4	O-54(33-7-17),3-17	-1.9
1949	Phi-A	57	169	12	36	6	0	0	10	14	12	.213	.273	.249	522	40	-15	2	0	0	.989	-2	O-48(6-0-43)/3-4	-1.8
Total	2	143	422	41	98	20	2	1	38	33	28	.232	.291	.296	587	57	-27	2	1	0	.971	-6	O-102(39-7-60)/3-21	-3.7
■ ED WHITE White, Edward Perry b: 4/6/26, Anniston, Ala. d: 9/28/82, Lakeland, Fla. BR/TR, 6'2", 200 lbs. Deb: 9/16/55																								
1955	Chi-A	3	4	0	2	0	0	0	0	1	1	.500	.600	.500	1100	193	1	0	0	0	1.000	-0	/O-2(0-0-2)	0.0
■ ELDER WHITE White, Elder Lafayette b: 12/23/34, Colerain, N.C. BR/TR, 5'11", 165 lbs. Deb: 4/10/62																								
1962	Chi-N	23	53	4	8	2	0	0	1	8	11	.151	.274	.189	463	26	-5	3	0	1	.986	0	S-15/3-1	-0.3
■ ELMER WHITE White, Elmer b: 5/23/1850, Caton, N.Y. d: 3/17/1872, Caton, N.Y. Deb: 5/4/1871																								
1871	Cle-n	15	70	13	18	2	0	0	9	1	6	.257	.268	.286	553	63	-3	0	1	-0	.783	-1	O-15(0-0-15)/C-3	-0.2
■ FRANK WHITE White, Frank b: 9/4/50, Greenville, Miss. BR/TR, 5'11", 170 lbs. Deb: 6/12/73 C Career OF: (0-LF 1-CF 1-RF)																								
1973	KC-A	51	139	20	31	6	1	0	5	8	23	.223	.265	.281	546	50	-9	3	1	0	.937	7	S-37,2-11	0.2
1974	KC-A	99	204	19	45	6	3	1	18	5	33	.221	.239	.294	533	50	-13	3	4	-1	.962	25	2-50,S-29,3-16,/D-3	1.5
1975	KC-A	111	304	43	76	10	2	7	36	20	39	.250	.298	.365	664	84	-7	11	3	1	.987	15	2-67,S-42/3-4,CD	1.7
1976	*KC-A	152	446	39	102	17	6	2	46	19	42	.229	.265	.307	572	67	-19	20	11	-1	.973	**21**	*2-130,S-37	1.3
1977	*KC-A	152	474	59	116	21	5	5	50	25	67	.245	.285	.342	627	70	-20	23	5	3	**.989**	-3	*2-152/S-4	-1.2
1978	*KC-A★	143	461	66	127	24	6	7	50	26	59	.275	.318	.399	717	98	-2	13	10	-1	.978	-17	*2-140	-1.2
1979	KC-A★	127	467	73	124	26	4	10	48	25	54	.266	.304	.403	707	87	-9	28	8	3	.982	-23	*2-125	-2.2
1980	*KC-A	154	560	70	148	23	4	7	60	19	69	.264	.291	.357	648	76	-19	19	6	2	.988	-7	*2-153	-1.7
1981	*KC-A★	94	364	35	91	17	1	9	38	19	50	.250	.287	.376	664	91	-5	4	2	0	.988	-16	2-93	-1.7
1982	KC-A★	145	524	71	156	45	6	11	56	16	65	.298	.321	.469	790	114	8	10	7	-0	.978	-15	*2-144	0.1
1983	KC-A	146	549	52	143	35	6	11	77	20	51	.260	.286	.406	693	88	-11	13	5	1	**.990**	9	*2-145	0.7

YEAR	TM/L	G	AB	R	H	2B	3B	HR	RBI	BB	SO	AVG	OBP	SLG	OPS	OPS+	BR+	SB	CS	SBR	FA	FR	G/POS	TPR
1984	*KC-A	129	479	58	130	22	5	17	56	27	72	.271	.313	.445	758	106	3	5	5	-1	.985	13	*2-129	2.2
1985	*KC-A	149	563	62	140	25	1	22	69	28	86	.249	.285	.414	699	88	-11	10	4	1	.980	14	*2-149	1.2
1986	KC-A★	151	566	76	154	37	3	22	84	43	88	.272	.326	.465	790	110	6	4	4	-1	.987	-0	*2-151/S-1,3-1	1.4
1987	KC-A	154	563	67	138	32	2	17	78	51	86	.245	.310	.400	710	84	-13	1	3	-1	.987	8	*2-152/D-1	0.2
1988	KC-A	150	537	48	126	25	1	8	58	21	67	.235	.269	.330	598	66	-25	7	3	0	**.994**	7	*2-148/D-3	-1.4
1989	KC-A	135	418	34	107	22	1	2	36	30	52	.256	.309	.328	637	80	-11	3	2	-0	.985	7	*2-132/O-1(0-1-0)	-0.1
1990	KC-A	82	241	20	52	14	1	2	21	10	32	.216	.256	.307	563	58	-14	1	0	0	.978	1	2-79/O-1(0-0-1)	-1.1
Total	18	2324	7859	912	2006	407	58	160	886	412	1035	.255	.295	.383	678	85	-173	178	83	10	.984	45	*2-2150,S-150/3DOC	-0.1
■ **DOC WHITE**	White, Guy Harris b: 4/9/1879, Washington, D.C. d: 2/19/69, Silver Spring, Md. BL/TL, 6'1", 150 lbs. Deb: 4/22/01 Career OF: (20-LF 51-CF 14-RF)																							
1901	Phi-N	31	98	15	27	3	1	1	10	2		.276	.297	.357	654	87	-2	1			.951	2	P-31/O-1(1-0-0)	0.0
1902	Phi-N	61	179	17	47	3	1	1	15	11		.263	.305	.307	613	89	-2	5			.931	-2	P-36,O-19(17-0-2)	-0.6
1903	Chi-A	38	99	10	20	3	0	0	5	19		.202	.331	.232	563	74	-2	1			.969	3	P-37/O-1(0-1-0)	0.0
1904	Chi-A	33	76	7	12	2	0	0	2	10		.158	.256	.184	440	42	-5	3			.951	1	P-30/O-2(0-2-0)	-0.1
1905	Chi-A	37	90	7	15	4	1	0	7	4		.167	.202	.233	435	40	-6	3			.953	2	P-36/O-1(1-0-0)	0.1
1906	*Chi-A	29	65	11	12	1	1	0	3	13		.185	.321	.231	551	75	-1	3			.922	2	P-28/O-1(0-1-0)	0.0
1907	Chi-A	48	90	12	20	1	0	0	2	12		.222	.314	.233	547	77	-2	2			**.986**	4	P-46/O-2(0-0-2),2-1	-0.1
1908	Chi-A	51	109	12	25	1	0	0	10	12		.229	.306	.239	544	79	-2	4			**.986**	6	P-41/O-3(0-2-1)	-0.1
1909	Chi-A	72	192	24	45	1	5	0	7	33		.234	.347	.292	638	106	3	7			.926	-4	O-40(1-35-4),P-24	-0.3
1910	Chi-A	56	126	14	25	1	2	0	8	14		.198	.279	.238	517	65	-5	2			.972	1	P-33,O-14(0-10-4)	-0.3
1911	Chi-A	39	78	12	20	1	1	0	6	7		.256	.318	.295	613	74	-3	1			.919	-1	P-34/1-2,O-1(0-0-1)	0.0
1912	Chi-A	32	56	5	7	1	1	0	0	7		.125	.222	.179	401	15	-6	0			**1.000**	-1	P-32	0.0
1913	Chi-A	21	25	1	3	0	0	0	0	3	1	.120	.214	.120	334	-2	-3	0			.959	2	P-19/1-1	0.0
Total	13	548	1283	147	278	22	13	2	75	147	1	.217	.298	.259	556	74	-36	32			.959	15	P-427/O-85C,1-3,2-1	-1.4
■ **DEACON WHITE**	White, James Laurie b: 12/7/1847, Caton, N.Y. d: 7/7/39, Aurora, Ill. BL/TR, 5'11", 175 lbs. Deb: 5/4/1871 FM NA OF: (2-LF 1-CF 48-RF) Career OF: (8-LF 5-CF 101-RF)																							
1871	Cle-n	29	146	40	47	6	5	1	21	4	1	.322	.340	.452	792	132	7	2	2	-0	.821	-5	*C-29/S-2,2-1,3O	0.1
1872	Cle-n	22	109	21	37	2	2	0	22	4	1	.339	.363	.394	757	140	6	0	0	0	.882	1	C-14/2-7,O-5(2-1-3),M	0.5
1873	Bos-n	60	310	79	121	15	6	0	**66**	0	2	.390	.390	.477	868	144	14	6	2	1	.845	2	*C-56/O-9(0-0-9)	1.2
1874	Bos-n	70	352	75	106	5	7	3	52	5	0	.301	.311	.381	692	114	4	1	1	-0	.839	-0	*C-58,O-21R/1-1	0.4
1875	Bos-n	80	371	76	136	23	3	1	60	3	2	**.367**	.372	.453	824	178	27	2	3	-1	.880	15	*C-75,O-14R/1-1	3.5
1876	Chi-N	66	310	66	104	18	1	1	**60**	7	3	.335	.358	.419	777	141	11				.844	7	*C-63/O-3L,1-3,3P	1.7
1877	Bos-N	59	266	51	**103**	14	**11**	2	**49**	8	3	**.387**	.405	**.545**	**950**	**190**	**26**				.963	1	1-35,O-19(0-0-19)/C-7	2.2
1878	Cin-N	61	258	41	81	4	1	0	29	10	5	.314	.340	.337	677	136	11				.909	-4	*C-48,O-16R/3-1	0.8
1879	Cin-N	78	333	55	110	16	6	1	52	6	9	.330	.342	.423	766	159	21				.901	2	*C-59,O-21R/1-2,M	2.2
1880	Cin-N	35	141	21	42	4	2	0	7	9	7	.298	.340	.355	695	137	6				.738	-3	O-33(0-1-33)/1-3,2-1	0.2
1881	Buf-N	78	319	58	99	24	4	0	53	9	8	.310	.329	.411	740	133	12				.943	-9	1-26,2-25,O-17R,/3C	0.3
1882	Buf-N	83	337	51	95	17	0	1	33	15	16	.282	.313	.341	654	108	3				.837	-10	*3-63,C-20	-0.4
1883	Buf-N	94	391	62	114	14	5	0	47	23	18	.292	.331	.353	684	106	3				.797	-10	*3-77,C-22	-0.3
1884	Buf-N	110	452	82	147	16	11	5	74	32	13	.325	.370	.442	812	149	25				.825	-7	*3-108/C-3	1.8
1885	Buf-N	98	404	54	118	6	6	0	57	12	11	.292	.313	.337	649	106	2				.888	1	*3-98	0.4
1886	Det-N	124	491	65	142	19	5	1	76	31	35	.289	.331	.354	686	106	3	9			.847	-9	*3-124	-0.3
1887	*Det-N	111	475	71	162	20	11	3	75	26	15	.341	.353	.416	770	109	5	20			.848	-0	*3-106/O-3(3-0-0),1-2	0.6
1888	Det-N	125	527	75	157	22	5	4	71	21	24	.298	.336	.381	717	128	16	12			.857	-3	*3-125	1.6
1889	Pit-N	55	225	35	57	10	1	0	26	16	18	.253	.314	.307	621	82	-5	2			.872	-10	3-52/1-3	-1.2
1890	Buf-P	122	439	62	114	13	4	0	47	67	30	.260	.381	.308	688	93	2	3			.905	19	3-64,1-57/S-1,P-1	1.4
Total	5 n	261	1288	291	447	51	23	5	221	16	6	.347	.355	.434	789	143	58	11	8	-0	.855	12	C-232/O-50R,2-8,1S3	5.7
Total	15	1299	5368	849	1645	217	73	18	756	292	215	.306	.344	.382	726	123	140	46			.853	-33	3-826,C-226,1O/2PS	11.0
■ **JERRY WHITE**	White, Jerome Cardell b: 8/23/52, Shirley, Mass. BB/TR, 5'11", 165 lbs. Deb: 9/16/74 C																							
1974	Mon-N	9	10	0	4	1	1	0	2	0	0	.400	.400	.700	1100	193	1	3	0	1	1.000	-2	/O-7(5-2-0)	0.0
1975	Mon-N	39	97	14	29	4	1	2	7	10	7	.299	.364	.423	787	113	2	5	2	0	.976	2	O-30(7-24-0)	0.3
1976	Mon-N	114	278	32	68	11	1	2	21	27	31	.245	.316	.313	629	76	-8	15	7	1	.982	-10	O-92(27-67-0)	-2.1
1977	Mon-N	16	21	4	4	0	0	0	1	1	3	.190	.227	.190	418	14	-3	1	0	0	1.000	-2	/O-8(7-0-1)	-0.5
1978	Mon-N	18	10	2	2	0	0	0	0	1	3	.200	.273	.200	473	34	-1	1	0	0	.000	-1	/O-3(1-0-2)	-0.2
	Chi-N	59	136	22	37	6	0	1	10	23	16	.272	.377	.338	716	90	-1	4	3	-0	.981	-3	O-54(0-54-0)	-0.4
	Yr	77	146	24	39	6	0	1	10	24	19	.267	.371	.329	699	89	-1	5	3	0	.981	-4	O-57(1-54-2)	-0.6
1979	Mon-N	88	138	30	41	7	1	3	18	21	23	.297	.394	.428	821	125	6	8	4	0	.983	-8	O-43(6-13-26)	-0.3
1980	Mon-N	110	214	22	56	9	3	7	23	30	37	.262	.355	.430	785	118	5	8	7	-1	.946	-12	O-84(62-7-18)	-1.0
1981	*Mon-N	59	119	11	26	5	1	3	11	13	17	.218	.295	.353	648	82	-3	5	2	0	.952	-5	O-39(7-13-20)	-0.9
1982	Mon-N	69	115	13	28	6	1	2	13	8	26	.243	.304	.365	669	85	-2	3	3	-0	1.000	-4	O-30(21-9-2)	-0.8
1983	Mon-N	40	34	4	5	1	0	0	0	12	8	.147	.383	.176	559	60	-1	4	0	1	1.000	-3	O-13(2-5-6)	-0.3
1986	StL-N	25	24	1	3	0	0	1	3	2	3	.125	.192	.250	442	21	-3	0	0	0	1.000	-1	/O-6(3-0-3)	-0.4
Total	11	646	1196	155	303	50	9	21	109	148	174	.253	.339	.363	702	94	-7	57	28	3	.974	-48	O-409(148-194-78)	-6.6
■ **JACK WHITE**	White, John Peter b: 8/31/05, New York, N.Y. d: 6/19/71, Flushing, N.Y. BB/TR, 5'7.5", 150 lbs. Deb: 6/22/27																							
1927	Cin-N	5	4	1	0	0	0	0	0	0	0	.000	.000	.000	0	-99	-1	0			1.000	0	/2-3,S-2	-0.1
1928	Cin-N	1	3	0	0	0	0	0	0	0	1	.000	.000	.000	0	-99	-1	0			.833	-1	/2-1	-0.1
Total	2	6	7	1	0	0	0	0	0	0	1	.000	.000	.000	0	-99	-2	0			.929	-0	/2-4,S-2	-0.2
■ **JACK WHITE**	White, John Wallace b: 1/19/1878, Traders Point, Ind. d: 9/30/63, Indianapolis, Ind BR/TR, 5'6", Deb: 6/26/04																							
1904	Bos-N	1	5	1	0	0	0	0	0	0		.000	.000	.000	0	-99	-1	0			1.000	1	/O-1(1-0-0)	-0.1
■ **JO-JO WHITE**	White, Joyner Clifford b: 6/1/09, Red Oak, Ga. d: 10/9/86, Tacoma, Wash. BL/TR, 5'11", 165 lbs. Deb: 4/15/32 FMC																							
1932	Det-A	80	208	25	54	6	3	2	21	22	19	.260	.330	.346	677	73	-8	6	8	-1	.962	-0	O-48(16-17-16)	-1.1
1933	Det-A	91	234	43	59	9	5	2	34	27	26	.252	.337	.359	696	83	-6	5	5	-1	.977	0	O-54(16-32-6)	-0.8
1934	*Det-A	115	384	97	120	18	5	0	44	69	39	.313	.419	.385	804	108	9	28	6	**4**	.959	-0	*O-100(1-93-6)	0.9
1935	*Det-A	114	412	82	99	13	12	2	32	68	42	.240	.348	.345	693	83	-9	19	10	1	.962	-2	O-98(0-98-0)	-1.2
1936	Det-A	58	51	11	14	3	0	0	6	9	10	.275	.383	.333	717	78	-1	2	0	0	.938	-7	O-18(0-18-1)	-0.7
1937	Det-A	94	305	50	75	5	7	0	21	50	40	.246	.354	.308	662	67	-14	12	7	0	.973	-3	O-82(3-79-0)	-1.8
1938	Det-A	78	206	40	54	6	1	0	15	30	15	.262	.359	.301	660	63	-11	3	4	-1	.967	0	O-55(21-34-1)	-1.2
1943	Phi-A	139	500	69	124	17	7	1	30	61	51	.248	.335	.316	651	91	-4	12	4	1	.966	-4	*O-133(2-131-0)	-1.1
1944	Phi-A	85	267	30	59	4	2	1	21	40	27	.221	.329	.262	591	71	-8	5	4	-0	.949	-1	O-74(10-9-57)/S-1	-1.5
	Cin-N	24	85	9	20	2	0	0	5	10	7	.235	.316	.259	575	65	-4	0			1.000	1	O-23(4-11-10)	-0.4
Total	9	878	2652	456	678	83	42	8	229	386	276	.256	.353	.328	681	82	-57	92	48		.965	-16	O-685(73-522-97)/S-1	-8.9
■ **MIKE WHITE**	White, Joyner Michael b: 12/18/38, Detroit, Mich. BR/TR, 5'8", 160 lbs. Deb: 9/21/63 F Career OF: (9-LF 55-CF 8-RF)																							
1963	Hou-N	3	7	0	2	0	0	0	0	0	0	.286	.286	.286	571	69	-0	0	0	0	1.000	1	/2-2	0.1
1964	Hou-N	89	280	30	76	11	3	0	27	20	47	.271	.320	.332	652	89	-4	1	1	-0	.978	2	O-72(9-55-8),2-10/3-3	-0.4
1965	Hou-N	8	9	0	0	0	0	0	0	1	2	.000	.100	.000	100	-74	-2	0	0	0	1.000	-0	/3-1	-0.3
Total	3	100	296	30	78	11	3	0	27	21	49	.264	.312	.321	633	84	-6	1	1	-0	.985	3	/O-72C,2-12,3-4	-0.6
■ **MYRON WHITE**	White, Myron Alan b: 8/1/57, Long Beach, Cal. BL/TL, 5'11", 180 lbs. Deb: 9/4/78																							
1978	LA-N	7	4	1	2	0	0	0	1	0	1	.500	.500	.500	1000	181	0	0	1	-0	1.000	-1	/O-4(1-0-3)	-0.1
■ **RONDELL WHITE**	White, Rondell Bernard b: 2/23/72, Milledgeville, Ga. BR/TR, 6'1", 205 lbs. Deb: 9/1/93																							
1993	Mon-N	23	73	9	19	3	1	2	15	7	16	.260	.325	.411	736	91	-1	1	2	-0	1.000	-3	O-21(19-5-0)	-0.5
1994	Mon-N	40	97	16	27	10	1	2	13	9	18	.278	.358	.464	822	111	2	1	1	-0	.946	-3	O-29(25-4-0)	-0.2
1995	Mon-N	130	474	87	140	33	4	13	57	41	87	.295	.359	.464	823	111	8	25	5	4	.986	6	*O-119(8-111-0)	1.8
1996	Mon-N	88	334	35	98	19	4	6	41	22	53	.293	.341	.428	769	99	-1	14	6	1	.990	5	O-86(0-86-0)	0.5

YEAR	TM/L	G	AB	R	H	2B	3B	HR	RBI	BB	SO	AVG	OBP	SLG	OPS	OPS+	BR+	SB	CS	SBR	FA	FR	G/POS	TPR
1997	Mon-N	151	592	84	160	29	5	28	82	31	111	.270	.318	.478	796	105	2	16	8	1	**.992**	17	*O-151(0-151-0)	2.1
1998	Mon-N	97	357	54	107	21	2	17	58	30	57	.300	.365	.513	878	130	15	16	7	1	.996	16	O-96(15-83-0)/D-1	3.1
1999	Mon-N	138	539	83	168	26	6	22	64	32	85	.312	.363	.505	867	120	15	10	6	0	.964	-8	*O-135(102-73-0)	0.5
2000	Mon-N	75	290	52	89	24	0	11	54	28	67	.307	.372	.503	875	117	7	5	1	1	.994	10	O-74(74-0-0)	1.5
	Chi-N	19	67	7	22	2	0	2	7	5	12	.328	.392	.448	840	114	2	0	2	-1	1.000	2	O-18(18-0-0)	0.2
	Yr	94	357	59	111	26	0	13	61	33	79	.311	.376	.493	869	117	9	5	3	0	.995	12	O-92(92-0-0)	1.7
Total	8	761	2823	427	830	167	23	103	391	205	506	.294	.351	.479	830	113	48	88	38	6	.986	42	O-729(261-513-0)/D-1	9.0
■ ROY WHITE	White, Roy Hilton b: 12/27/43, Los Angeles, Cal. BB/TR, 5'10", 172 lbs. Deb: 9/7/65 C Career OF: (1520-LF 63-CF 56-RF)																							
1965	NY-A	14	42	7	14	2	0	0	3	4	7	.333	.404	.381	785	125	2	2	1	0	1.000	-1	O-10(0-1-9)/2-1	0.0
1966	NY-A	115	316	39	71	13	2	7	20	37	43	.225	.308	.345	653	91	-4	14	7	1	.957	0	O-82(72-12-0)/2-2	-0.7
1967	NY-A	70	214	22	48	8	0	2	18	19	25	.224	.291	.290	580	75	-7	10	4	1	.968	-6	O-36(5-0-31),3-17	-1.7
1968	NY-A	159	577	89	154	20	7	17	62	73	50	.267	.352	.414	766	136	25	20	11	1	.997	10	*O-154(119-25-12)	3.1
1969	NY-A★	130	448	55	130	30	5	7	74	81	51	.290	.400	.426	826	136	25	18	10	0	.989	11	*O-126(126-0-0)	3.0
1970	NY-A☆	162	609	109	180	30	6	22	94	95	66	.296	.391	.473	864	144	38	24	10	2	.994	7	*O-161(161-0-1)	3.8
1971	NY-A	147	524	86	153	22	7	19	84	86	66	.292	.399	.469	868	154	40	14	7	1	**1.000**	10	*O-145(145-0-0)	4.4
1972	NY-A	155	556	76	150	29	0	10	54	**99**	59	.270	.385	.376	761	131	26	23	7	3	.994	9	*O-155(155-0-0)	3.2
1973	NY-A	162	639	88	157	22	3	18	60	78	81	.246	.330	.374	704	101	1	16	9	0	.977	4	*O-162(162-0-0)	-0.4
1974	NY-A	136	473	68	130	19	8	7	43	67	44	.275	.369	.393	763	121	15	15	6	1	.993	3	O-67(67-0-0),D-53	1.5
1975	NY-A	148	556	81	161	32	5	12	59	72	50	.290	.373	.430	803	129	22	16	15	-2	.984	11	*O-135L/1-7,D-2	2.3
1976	*NY-A	156	626	**104**	179	29	3	14	65	83	52	.286	.370	.409	778	129	24	31	13	2	.987	6	*O-156(140-21-1)	2.5
1977	*NY-A	143	519	72	139	25	2	14	52	75	58	.268	.360	.405	765	109	8	18	11	0	.981	10	*O-135(133-1-2)/D-4	1.2
1978	*NY-A	103	346	44	93	13	3	8	43	42	35	.269	.351	.393	744	112	6	10	4	1	.992	-4	O-74(73-3-0),D-23	-0.1
1979	NY-A	81	205	24	44	6	0	3	27	23	21	.215	.294	.288	582	59	-12	2	2	-0	1.000	0	D-29,O-27(27-0-0)	-1.3
Total	15	1881	6650	964	1803	300	51	160	758	934	708	.271	.363	.404	767	122	212	233	117	10	.988	71	*O-1625L,D-111/312	20.8
■ SAMMY WHITE	White, Samuel Charles b: 7/7/27, Wenatchee, Wash. d: 8/5/91, Princeville, Hawaii BR/TR, 6'3", 195 lbs. Deb: 9/26/51																							
1951	Bos-A	4	11	0	2	0	0	0	0	0	3	.182	.182	.182	364	-1	-2	0	0	0	1.000	1	/C-4	-0.1
1952	Bos-A	115	381	35	107	20	2	10	49	16	43	.281	.310	.423	732	95	-4	2	3	-1	.983	-2	*C-110	-0.1
1953	Bos-A☆	136	476	59	130	34	2	13	64	29	48	.273	.318	.435	752	96	-4	3	2	-0	.986	9	*C-131	1.1
1954	Bos-A	137	493	46	139	25	2	14	75	21	50	.282	.311	.426	737	90	-8	1	3	-1	.979	13	*C-133	1.1
1955	Bos-A	143	544	65	142	30	4	11	64	44	58	.261	.324	.392	716	84	-13	1	2	-0	.984	-0	*C-143	-0.6
1956	Bos-A	114	392	28	96	15	2	5	44	35	40	.245	.307	.332	638	61	-22	2	1	0	.984	7	*C-114	-0.9
1957	Bos-A	111	340	24	73	10	1	3	31	25	38	.215	.268	.276	545	46	-25	0	1	-0	.985	-4	*C-111	-2.5
1958	Bos-A	102	328	25	85	15	3	6	35	21	37	.259	.306	.378	684	81	-8	1	1	-0	.988	-2	*C-102	-0.6
1959	Bos-A	119	377	34	107	13	4	1	42	23	39	.284	.327	.347	674	81	-9	4	2	0	.990	0	*C-119	-0.3
1961	Mil-N	21	63	1	14	1	0	1	5	2	9	.222	.246	.286	532	43	-5	0	0	0	.974	4	C-20	0.0
1962	Phi-N	41	97	7	21	4	0	2	12	2	16	.216	.240	.320	560	50	-7	0	0	0	.975	5	C-40	-0.1
Total	11	1043	3502	324	916	167	20	66	421	218	381	.262	.307	.377	684	79	-107	14	15	-2	.984	30	*C-1027	-3.0
■ SAM WHITE	White, Samuel Lambeth b: 8/23/1892, Greater Preston, Yorkshire, England d: 11/11/29, Philadelphia, Pa. BL/TR, 6', 185 lbs. Deb: 9/8/19																							
1919	Bos-N	1	1	0	0	0	0	0	0	0	0	.000	.000	.000	0	-99	-0	0			1.000	2	/C-1	0.1
■ BARNEY WHITE	White, William Barney "Bear" b: 6/25/23, Paris, Tex. BR/TR, 5'11", 186 lbs. Deb: 6/5/45																							
1945	Bro-N	4	1	2	0	0	0	0	0	1	1	.000	.500	.000	500	46	0	0			1.000	0	/S-1,3-1	0.0
■ BILL WHITE	White, William De Kova b: 1/28/34, Lakewood, Fla. BL/TL, 6', 195 lbs. Deb: 5/7/56 Career OF: (99-LF 37-CF 21-RF)																							
1956	NY-N	138	508	63	130	23	7	22	59	47	72	.256	.324	.459	782	108	5	15	8	1	.989	2	*1-138/O-2(1-0-1)	-0.1
1958	SF-N	26	29	5	7	1	0	1	4	7	5	.241	.389	.379	768	107	1	1	0	0	1.000	-1	/1-3,O-2(1-0-1)	0.0
1959	StL-N☆	138	517	77	156	33	9	12	72	34	61	.302	.347	.470	817	108	6	15	10	-0	.962	-2	O-92(86-9-0),1-71	-0.4
1960	StL-N★	144	554	81	157	27	10	16	79	42	83	.283	.336	.455	791	105	4	12	6	1	.990	-6	*1-123,O-29(3-28-0)	-1.0
1961	StL-N★	153	591	89	169	28	11	20	90	64	84	.286	.357	.472	829	107	6	8	11	-2	.989	-2	*1-151	-0.7
1962	StL-N	159	614	93	199	31	3	20	102	58	69	.324	.388	.482	870	120	19	9	7	-0	.993	1	*1-146,O-27(8-0-19)	1.0
1963	StL-N★	162	658	106	200	26	8	27	109	59	100	.304	.361	.491	852	131	26	10	9	-1	.991	-2	*1-162	1.4
1964	*StL-N★	160	631	92	191	37	4	21	102	52	103	.303	.357	.474	831	121	18	7	6	-1	**.996**	-1	*1-160	0.7
1965	StL-N	148	543	82	157	26	3	24	73	63	86	.289	.367	.481	848	125	19	3	3	-0	.992	6	*1-144	1.6
1966	Phi-N	159	577	85	159	23	6	22	103	68	109	.276	.355	.451	806	122	18	16	6	1	**.994**	7	*1-158	1.7
1967	Phi-N	110	308	29	77	6	2	8	33	52	61	.250	.364	.360	724	107	5	6	1	1	.993	0	1-95	0.1
1968	Phi-N	127	385	34	92	16	2	9	40	39	79	.239	.312	.361	673	102	1	0	1	-0	.994	4	*1-111	-0.2
1969	StL-N	49	57	7	12	1	0	0	4	11	15	.211	.338	.228	566	61	-2	1	0	0	1.000	1	1-15	-0.2
Total	13	1673	5972	843	1706	278	65	202	870	596	927	.286	.353	.455	809	115	123	103	68	-1	.992	8	*1-1477,O-152L	3.9
■ BILL WHITE	White, William Dighton b: 5/1/1860, Bridgeport, Ohio d: 12/29/24, Bellaire, Ohio TR, Deb: 5/3/1884 Career OF: (0-LF 0-CF 4-RF)																							
1884	Pit-a	74	291	25	66	7	10	0		13		.227	.262	.320	582	90	-3				.807	-11	S-60,3-10/O-4(0-0-4)	-1.1
1886	Lou-a	135	557	96	143	17	10	1	66	37		.257	.304	.329	633	93	-7	14			.871	17	*S-135/P-1	1.3
1887	Lou-a	132	559	85	176	7	9	2	79	47		.315	.315	.313	627	74	-18	41			.869	22	*S-132	0.6
1888	Lou-a	49	198	35	55	6	5	1	30	7		.278	.313	.374	686	122	4	15			.816	-3	S-38,3-11	0.3
	*StL-a	76	275	31	48	2	3	2	30	21		.175	.238	.225	464	44	-18	6			.892	-3	S-74/2-2	-1.7
	Yr	125	473	66	103	8	8	3	60	28		.218	.269	.288	556	74	-15	21			.864	-6	*S-112,3-11/2-2	-1.4
Total	4	466	1880	272	488	39	37	6	205	125		.260	.292	.312	604	82	-41	76			.860	22	S-439/3-21,O-4R,2P	-0.6
■ BILL WHITE	White, William Edward b: Milner, Ga. Deb: 6/21/1879																							
1879	Pro-N	1	4	1	1	0	0	0	0	0	1	.250	.250	.250	500	67	-0				1.000	0	/1-1	0.0
■ WARREN WHITE	White, William Warren (a.k.a. William Warren) b: 1837, Washington, D.C. 5'10.5", 170 lbs. Deb: 6/17/1871 M Career OF: (0-LF 5-CF 0-RF)																							
1871	Oly-n	1	4	0	0	0	0	0	0	0	0	.000	.000	.000	0	-99	-1	0	0	0	1.000	-1	/2-1	-0.1
1872	Nat-n	10	45	7	13	0	0	0	4	0	0	.289	.289	.289	578	67	-2	0	0	0	.861	8	/3-9,S-1,M	0.4
1873	Was-n	39	160	29	43	3	4	0	21	0	1	.269	.269	.338	606	82	-3	1	1	-0	.717	5	*3-37/S-3	0.0
1874	Bal-n	45	211	21	57	1	0	0	17	2	2	.270	.277	.275	552	78	-5	1	0	0	.782	**25**	*3-45/C-3,M	1.5
1875	Chi-n	69	287	37	71	9	0	0	23	0	3	.247	.247	.279	526	82	-5	5	10	-2	.813	7	*3-59/S-5,O-5C,2-2	-0.2
1884	Was-U	4	18	2	1	0	0	0		0		.056	.056	.056	111	-68	-4				.692	-1	/3-2,S-1,2-1	-0.5
Total	5 n	164	707	94	184	13	4	0	65	2	6	.260	.262	.290	552	78	-17	7	11	-2	.779	44	3-150/S-9,O-5C,C2	1.6
■ ED WHITED	Whited, Edward Morris b: 2/9/64, Bristol, Pa. BR/TR, 6'3", 195 lbs. Deb: 7/5/89																							
1989	Atl-N	36	74	5	12	3	0	1	4	6	15	.162	.225	.243	468	33	-6	1	0	0	.914	-0	3-29/1-3	-0.7
■ BURGESS WHITEHEAD	Whitehead, Burgess Urquhart "Whitey" b: 6/29/10, Tarboro, N.C. d: 11/25/93, Windsor, N.C. BR/TR, 5'10.5", 160 lbs. Deb: 4/30/33																							
1933	StL-N	12	7	2	2	0	0	0	1	0	1	.286	.286	.286	571	60	-0	0			1.000	0	/S-9,2-3	0.0
1934	*StL-N	100	332	55	92	13	5	1	24	12	19	.277	.310	.355	666	73	-13	5			.962	-1	2-48,S-29,3-28	-0.8
1935	StL-N★	107	338	45	89	10	2	0	33	11	14	.263	.289	.305	593	57	-20	5			.980	5	2-80/3-8,S-6	-1.0
1936	*NY-N	154	632	99	176	31	3	4	47	29	32	.278	.317	.356	673	82	-16	14			.969	29	*2-153	2.2
1937	*NY-N★	152	574	64	164	15	6	5	52	28	20	.286	.323	.359	682	84	-13	7			**.974**	26	*2-152	2.3
1939	NY-N	95	335	31	80	6	3	2	24	24	19	.239	.299	.293	592	59	-19	1			.970	21	2-91/S-4,3-1	0.8
1940	NY-N	133	568	68	160	9	6	4	36	26	17	.282	.319	.340	659	81	-15	9			.947	13	3-74,2-57/S-4	0.4
1941	NY-N	116	403	41	92	15	4	1	23	14	10	.228	.258	.293	551	54	-25	7			.970	-0	*2-104/3-1	-2.0
1946	Pit-N	55	127	10	28	1	2	0	5	6	6	.220	.261	.260	521	47	-9	3			.963	-6	2-30/3-4,S-1	-1.5
Total	9	924	3316	415	883	100	31	17	245	150	138	.266	.304	.331	634	72	-130	51			.972	86	2-718,3-116/S-53	0.4
■ MILT WHITEHEAD	Whitehead, Milton P. b: 1862, Canada d: 8/15/01, Highland, Cal. BB, Deb: 4/20/1884																							
1884	StL-U	99	393	61	83	15	1	1		8		.211	.227	.262	489	46	-37				.803	-11	*S-94/O-2C,P-1,23	-4.0
	KC-U	5	22	2	3	0	0	0		0		.136	.136	.136	273	-20	-4				.857	-1	/2-3,C-1,S-1,3-1	-0.4
	Yr	104	415	63	86	15	1	1		8		.207	.222	.255	478	43	-41				.804	-12	S-95/2-4,O-2C,3PC	-4.4

YEAR	TM/L	G	AB	R	H	2B	3B	HR	RBI	BB	SO	AVG	OBP	SLG	OPS	OPS+	BR+	SB	CS	SBR	FA	FR	G/POS	TPR
■ GIL WHITEHOUSE Whitehouse, Gilbert Arthur b: 10/15/1893, Somerville, Mass. d: 2/14/26, Brewer, Me. BB/TR, 5'10", 170 lbs. Deb: 6/20/12																								
1912	Bos-N	2	3	0	0	0	0	0	0	0	3	.000	.000	.000	0	-98	-1	0			.667	-1	/C-2	-0.2
1915	New-F	35	120	16	27	6	2	0	9	6	16	.225	.268	.308	576	66	-8	3			.949	-1	O-28(0-2-26)/P-1,C-1	-1.1
Total	2	37	123	16	27	6	2	0	9	6	19	.220	.262	.301	562	61	-9	3			.846	-2	/O-28(0-2-26),C-3,P-1	-1.3
■ GURDON WHITELEY Whiteley, Gurdon W. b: 10/5/1859, Ashaway, R.I. d: 11/24/24, Cranston, R.I. 5'11", 190 lbs. Deb: 8/7/1884																								
1884	Cle-N	8	34	4	5	0	0	0	0	1	8	.147	.171	.147	318	1	-4				.800	1	/O-8(4-3-1)	-0.3
1885	Bos-N	33	135	14	25	2	2	1	7	1	25	.185	.191	.252	443	44	-8				.781	-2	O-32(8-0-24)/C-1	-1.0
Total	2	41	169	18	30	2	2	1	7	2	33	.178	.187	.231	418	34	-12				.785	-1	/O-40(12-3-25),C-1	-1.3
■ GEORGE WHITEMAN Whiteman, George "Lucky" b: 12/23/1882, Peoria, Ill. d: 2/10/47, Houston, Tex. BR/TR, 5'7", 160 lbs. Deb: 9/13/07																								
1907	Bos-A	4	12	0	2	0	0	0	1	0		.167	.167	.167	333	6	-1	0			1.000	-1	/O-2(2-0-0)	-0.2
1913	NY-A	11	32	8	11	3	1	0	2	7	2	.344	.462	.500	962	181	4	2			.938	1	O-11(4-4-3)	0.4
1918	*Bos-A	71	214	24	57	14	0	1	28	20	9	.266	.335	.346	681	107	2	9			.935	-11	O-69(65-0-4)	-1.4
Total	3	86	258	32	70	17	1	1	31	27	11	.271	.345	.357	702	113	4	11			.936	-11	/O-82(71-4-7)	-1.2
■ MARK WHITEN Whiten, Mark Anthony b: 11/25/66, Pensacola, Fla. BB/TR, 6'3", 215 lbs. Deb: 7/12/90 Career OF: (131-LF 67-CF 696-RF)																								
1990	Tor-A	33	88	12	24	1	1	2	7	7	14	.273	.326	.375	701	94	-1	2	0	0	1.000	2	O-30(3-0-27)/D-2	0.1
1991	Tor-A	46	149	12	33	4	3	2	19	11	35	.221	.280	.329	608	65	-7	0	1	-0	1.000	3	O-42(0-0-42)	-0.6
	Cle-A	70	258	34	66	14	4	7	26	19	50	.256	.312	.422	734	100	-0	4	2	0	.962	11	O-67(0-8-63)/D-3	0.9
	Yr	116	407	46	99	18	7	9	45	30	85	.243	.300	.388	688	87	-8	4	3	-0	.975	14	*O-109(0-8-105)/D-3	0.3
1992	Cle-A	148	508	73	129	19	4	9	43	72	102	.254	.349	.360	709	101	2	16	12	-1	.980	13	*O-144(0-0-144)/D-2	1.0
1993	StL-N	152	562	81	142	13	4	25	99	58	110	.253	.325	.423	748	100	-0	15	8	1	.971	1	*O-148(0-22-138)	-0.6
1994	StL-N	92	334	57	98	18	2	14	53	37	75	.293	.366	.485	851	122	10	10	5	0	.964	15	O-90(0-0-90)	2.1
1995	Bos-A	32	108	13	20	3	0	1	10	8	23	.185	.241	.241	482	25	-12	1	0	0	1.000	2	O-31(0-0-31)/D-1	-1.1
	Phi-N	60	212	38	57	10	1	11	37	31	63	.269	.365	.481	846	120	6	7	0	2	.965	2	O-55(0-0-55)	0.6
1996	Phi-N	60	182	33	43	8	0	7	21	33	62	.236	.356	.396	752	97	-0	13	3	2	.945	3	O-51(0-8-44)	0.3
	Atl-N	36	90	12	23	5	1	3	17	16	25	.256	.368	.433	801	105	1	2	5	-1	.933	-2	O-29(0-0-29)	-0.4
	Yr	96	272	45	66	13	1	10	38	49	87	.243	.360	.408	768	99	1	15	8	1	.942	1	O-80(0-8-73)	-0.1
	Sea-A	40	140	31	42	7	0	12	33	21	40	.300	.399	.607	1006	149	11	2	1	0	.969	4	O-39(36-0-4)	1.2
1997	NY-A	69	215	34	57	11	0	5	24	30	47	.265	.360	.386	746	96	-1	4	2	0	.954	-3	O-57(44-0-16)/D-6	-0.5
1998	*Cle-A	88	226	31	64	14	0	6	29	29	60	.283	.372	.425	797	103	2	2	1	0	.970	-4	O-72L/P-1,D-5	-0.3
1999	Cle-A	8	25	2	4	1	0	1	4	3	4	.160	.250	.320	570	42	-2	0	0	0	1.000	0	/O-7(5-2-0)	-0.2
2000	Cle-A	6	7	2	2	1	0	0	1	3	2	.286	.500	.429	929	135	1	0	0	0	1.000	-2	/O-5(0-5-0)	-0.1
Total	11	940	3104	465	804	129	20	105	423	378	712	.259	.343	.415	758	101	9	78	40	3	.970	45	O-867R/D-19,P-1	2.4
■ FRED WHITFIELD Whitfield, Fred Dwight b: 1/7/38, Vandiver, Ala. BL/TL, 6'1", 190 lbs. Deb: 5/27/62																								
1962	StL-N	73	158	20	42	7	1	8	34	7	30	.266	.301	.475	776	95	-2	1	0	0	.987	1	1-38	-0.2
1963	Cle-A	109	346	44	87	17	3	21	54	24	61	.251	.307	.500	807	123	9	0	1	-0	.987	-3	1-92	0.0
1964	Cle-A	101	293	29	79	13	1	10	29	12	58	.270	.303	.423	726	100	-1	0	5	-2	.992	-2	1-79	-0.9
1965	Cle-A	132	468	49	137	23	1	26	90	16	42	.293	.319	.513	832	131	16	2	2	-0	.993	4	*1-122	1.4
1966	Cle-A	137	502	59	121	15	2	27	78	27	76	.241	.285	.440	725	105	1	1	2	-0	.991	-4	*1-132	-1.2
1967	Cle-A	100	257	24	56	10	0	9	31	25	45	.218	.290	.362	652	91	-3	3	3	-0	.993	4	1-66	-0.4
1968	Cin-N	87	171	15	44	8	0	6	32	9	29	.257	.302	.409	712	105	-0	0	3	-1	.981	-1	1-41	-0.3
1969	Cin-N	74	74	2	11	0	0	1	8	18	27	.149	.315	.189	504	42	-5	0	0	0	.985	1	1-14	-0.5
1970	Mon-N	4	15	0	1	0	0	0	0	1	3	.067	.125	.067	192	-47	-3	0	0	0	.976	2	/1-4	-0.2
Total	9	817	2284	242	578	93	8	108	356	139	371	.253	.301	.443	743	107	14	7	16	-4	.990	3	1-588	-2.3
■ TERRY WHITFIELD Whitfield, Terry Bertland b: 1/12/53, Blythe, Cal. BL/TR, 6'1", 197 lbs. Deb: 9/29/74																								
1974	NY-A	2	5	0	1	0	0	0	0	0	1	.200	.200	.200	400	16	-1	0	0	0	.000	-1	/O-1(0-1-0)	-0.1
1975	NY-A	28	81	9	22	1	1	0	7	1	17	.272	.280	.309	589	67	-4	1	0	0	.978	0	O-25(2-0-23)/D-1	-0.5
1976	NY-A	1	0	0	0	0	0	0	0	0	0	—	—	—	—	—	0	0	0	0	.000	-1	/O-1(1-0-0)	-0.1
1977	SF-N	114	326	41	93	21	3	7	36	20	46	.285	.330	.433	763	103	1	2	3	-1	.972	-3	O-84(22-22-49)	-0.6
1978	SF-N	149	488	70	141	20	2	10	32	33	69	.289	.337	.400	736	109	5	5	11	-3	.988	0	*O-140(138-5-0)	-0.3
1979	SF-N	133	394	52	113	20	4	5	44	36	47	.287	.353	.396	748	111	6	5	4	-0	.957	2	*O-106(105-1-0)	0.3
1980	SF-N	118	321	38	95	16	2	4	26	20	44	.296	.339	.396	735	107	3	4	2	0	.987	-0	O-95(95-0-0)	-0.1
1984	LA-N	87	180	15	44	8	0	4	18	17	35	.244	.313	.356	669	88	-3	1	4	-1	.988	-5	O-58(23-2-37)	-1.1
1985	*LA-N	79	104	8	27	7	0	3	16	6	27	.260	.300	.413	713	101	-0	0	0	0	.926	-5	O-28(21-1-7)	-0.6
1986	LA-N	19	14	0	1	0	0	0	0	5	2	.071	.316	.071	387	14	-1	0	0	0	1.000	-0	/O-1(1-0-0)	-0.2
Total	10	730	1913	233	537	93	12	33	179	138	288	.281	.332	.394	726	103	6	18	24	-4	.976	-12	O-539(408-32-116)/D-1	-3.3
■ ED WHITING Whiting, Edward C. (a.k.a. Harry Zieber) b: 1860, Philadelphia, Pa. BL/TR, 188 lbs. Deb: 5/2/1882 Career OF: (2-LF 6-CF 2-RF)																								
1882	Bal-a	74	308	43	80	14	5	0		7		.260	.276	.338	614	115	5				.834	-7	*C-72/1-3,O-2(1-0-1)	0.4
1883	Lou-a	58	240	35	70	16	4	2		9		.292	.317	.417	734	145	12				.884	-8	C-50/O-6C,2-2,31	0.7
1884	Lou-a	42	157	16	35	7	3	0	18	9		.223	.274	.306	580	93	-1				.891	-1	C-40/O-2(1-0-1),1-2	0.1
1886	Was-N	6	21	0	0	0	0	0	0	1	12	.000	.045	.000	45	-90	-5	0			.919	-3	/C-6	-0.7
Total	4	180	726	94	185	37	12	2	18	26	12	.255	.282	.347	630	114	12	0			.866	-20	C-168/O-10C,1-6,23	0.5
■ DICK WHITMAN Whitman, Dick Corwin b: 11/9/20, Woodburn, Ore. BL/TR, 5'11", 170 lbs. Deb: 4/16/46																								
1946	Bro-N	104	265	39	69	15	3	2	31	22	19	.260	.317	.362	679	92	-3	5			1.000	-2	O-85(30-54-1)	-0.9
1947	Bro-N	4	10	1	4	0	0	0	2	1	0	.400	.455	.400	855	124	0	0			1.000	0	/O-3(2-0-1)	0.0
1948	Bro-N	60	165	24	48	13	0	0	20	14	12	.291	.346	.370	716	91	-2	4			.990	-1	O-48(12-4-34)	-0.5
1949	*Bro-N	23	49	8	9	2	0	0	2	4	4	.184	.245	.224	470	26	-5	0			.952	-1	O-11(10-0-1)	-0.7
1950	*Phi-N	75	132	21	33	7	0	0	12	10	10	.250	.317	.303	620	65	-6	1			.983	-4	O-32(7-13-15)	-1.1
1951	Phi-N	19	17	0	2	0	0	0	0	0	1	.118	.118	.118	235	-37	-3	0	0	0	.000	-3	/O-6(5-1-0)	-0.6
Total	6	285	638	93	165	37	3	2	67	51	46	.259	.316	.335	652	78	-20	10	0		.992	-11	O-185(66-72-52)	-3.8
■ FRANK WHITMAN Whitman, Walter Franklin "Hooker" b: 8/15/24, Marengo, Ind. d: 2/6/94, Maryville, Ill. BR/TR, 6'2", 175 lbs. Deb: 6/30/46																								
1946	Chi-A	17	16	7	1	0	0	0	1	2	6	.063	.211	.063	273	-22	-3	0	1	-0	1.000	4	/S-6,1-1,2-1	0.1
1948	Chi-A	3	6	0	0	0	0	0	0	0	3	.000	.000	.000	0	-99	-2	0	0	0	.500	-1	/S-1	-0.3
Total	2	20	22	7	1	0	0	0	1	2	9	.045	.160	.045	205	-43	-4	0	1	-0	.885	3	/S-7,2-1,1-1	-0.2
■ DAN WHITMER Whitmer, Daniel Charles b: 11/23/55, Redlands, Cal. BR/TR, 6'3", 195 lbs. Deb: 7/20/80 C																								
1980	Cal-A	48	87	8	21	3	0	0	7	4	21	.241	.275	.276	551	53	-6	1	0	0	1.000	4	C-48	0.0
1981	Tor-A	7	9	0	1	1	0	0	0	1	2	.111	.200	.222	422	20	-1	0	0	0	1.000	1	/C-7	0.0
Total	2	55	96	8	22	4	0	0	7	5	23	.229	.267	.271	538	49	-7	1	0	0	1.000	5	/C-55	0.0
■ DARRELL WHITMORE Whitmore, Darrell Lamont b: 11/18/68, Front Royal, Va. BL/TR, 6'1", 210 lbs. Deb: 6/25/93																								
1993	Fla-N	76	250	24	51	8	2	4	19	10	72	.204	.249	.300	549	44	-20	4	2	0	.979	2	O-69(1-0-69)	-2.2
1994	Fla-N	9	22	1	5	1	0	0	0	3	5	.227	.320	.273	593	55	-1	0	1	-0	1.000	1	/O-6(5-0-1)	-0.1
1995	Fla-N	27	58	6	11	2	0	1	2	5	15	.190	.254	.276	530	40	-5	0	0	0	.960	-3	O-16(0-14-3)	-0.8
Total	3	112	330	31	67	11	2	5	21	18	92	.203	.255	.294	549	44	-27	4	3	-0	.978	-0	/O-91(6-14-73)	-3.1
■ PINKY WHITNEY Whitney, Arthur Carter b: 1/2/05, San Antonio, Tex. d: 9/1/87, Center, Tex. BR/TR, 5'10", 165 lbs. Deb: 4/11/28																								
1928	Phi-N	151	585	73	176	35	4	10	103	36	30	.301	.342	.426	768	96	-4	3			.955	3	*3-149	0.8
1929	Phi-N	154	612	89	200	43	14	8	115	61	35	.327	.390	.482	872	108	8	7			.967	**21**	*3-154	3.5
1930	Phi-N	149	606	87	207	41	5	8	117	40	41	.342	.383	.465	849	97	-2	3			.965	20	*3-148	2.4
1931	Phi-N	130	501	64	144	36	5	9	74	30	38	.287	.331	.433	765	96	-3	6			.948	-6	*3-128	-0.5
1932	Phi-N	154	624	93	186	33	11	13	124	35	66	.298	.335	.449	784	97	-3	6			**.960**	5	*3-151/2-5	0.8
1933	Phi-N	31	121	12	32	4	0	3	19	8	8	.264	.310	.372	682	83	-3	1			.963	-4	3-30	-0.6
	Bos-N	100	382	42	94	17	2	8	49	25	23	.246	.296	.364	660	95	-3	2			.971	1	3-85,2-18	0.2

YEAR	TM/L	G	AB	R	H	2B	3B	HR	RBI	BB	SO	AVG	OBP	SLG	OPS	OPS+	BR+	SB	CS	SBR	FA	FR	G/POS	TPR
	Yr	131	503	54	126	21	2	11	68	33	31	.250	.299	.366	665	92	-6	3			.969	-4	*3-115,2-18	-0.4
1934	Bos-N	146	563	58	146	26	2	12	79	25	54	.259	.294	.377	671	85	-14	7			**.968**	3	*3-111,2-36/S-2	-0.5
1935	Bos-N	126	458	41	125	23	4	4	60	24	36	.273	.312	.367	679	89	-8	2			.958	6	3-74,2-49	0.3
1936	Bos-N	10	40	1	7	0	0	0	5	2	4	.175	.233	.175	408	12	-5	0			.971	1	3-10	-0.3
	Phi-N★	114	411	44	121	17	3	6	59	37	33	.294	.354	.394	748	92	-4	2			.955	10	*3-111/2-1	1.0
	Yr	124	451	45	128	17	3	6	64	39	37	.284	.343	.375	718	86	-8	2			.956	11	*3-121/2-1	0.7
1937	Phi-N	138	487	56	166	19	4	8	79	43	44	.341	.395	.446	841	118	13	6			**.982**	3	*3-130	2.1
1938	Phi-N	102	300	27	83	9	1	3	38	27	22	.277	.336	.343	680	90	-4	0			.934	-2	3-75/1-4,2-2	-0.3
1939	Phi-N	34	75	9	14	0	1	1	6	7	4	.187	.256	.253	509	38	-7	0			.991	1	1-12/2-8,3-2	-0.7
Total	12	1539	5765	696	1701	303	56	93	927	400	438	.295	.343	.415	758	96	-39	45			.961	62	*3-1358,2-119/1-16,S	8.2

■ **ART WHITNEY** Whitney, Arthur Wilson b: 1/16/1858, Brockton, Mass. d: 8/15/43, Lowell, Mass. BR/TR, 5'8", 155 lbs. Deb: 5/1/1880 F Career OF: (3-LF 1-CF 0-RF)

YEAR	TM/L	G	AB	R	H	2B	3B	HR	RBI	BB	SO	AVG	OBP	SLG	OPS	OPS+	BR+	SB	CS	SBR	FA	FR	G/POS	TPR
1880	Wor-N	76	302	38	67	13	5	1	36	9	15	.222	.244	.308	552	79	-7				.860	-1	*3-76	-0.5
1881	Det-N	58	214	23	39	7	5	0	9	7	15	.182	.208	.262	470	45	-13				.849	7	*3-58	-0.4
1882	Pro-N	11	40	2	3	0	0	0	1	2	11	.075	.119	.075	194	-36	-6				.784	-2	S-11	-0.7
	Det-N	31	115	10	21	0	0	0	4	1	12	.183	.190	.183	372	20	-10				.854	1	3-22/S-8,P-3	-0.6
	Yr	42	155	12	24	0	0	0	5	3	23	.155	.171	.155	326	5	-16				.854	-1	3-22,S-19/P-3	-1.3
1884	Pit-a	23	94	10	28	4	0	0		1		.298	.305	.340	646	112	1				.916	4	3-21/O-1(0-1-0),S-1	0.4
1885	Pit-a	90	373	53	87	10	4	0	28	16		.233	.267	.282	548	74	-11				**.918**	-14	*S-75/3-8,2-4,O-3L	-2.0
1886	Pit-a	136	511	70	122	13	4	0	55	51		.239	.315	.280	595	87	-6	15			**.906**	11	*3-95,S-42/P-1	0.8
1887	Pit-N	119	486	57	167	11	4	0	51	55	18	.344	.346	.304	650	87	-4	10			**.924**	-4	*3-119	-0.5
1888	*NY-N	90	328	28	72	1	4	1	28	8	22	.220	.240	.256	496	59	-15	7			.887	7	3-90	-0.7
1889	*NY-N	129	473	71	103	12	2	1	59	56	39	.218	.303	.258	561	57	-26	19			.882	0	*3-129/P-1	-2.0
1890	NY-P	119	442	71	97	12	3	0	45	64	19	.219	.322	.260	582	52	-31	8			.865	-12	3-88,S-31	-3.2
1891	Cin-a	93	347	42	69	6	1	3	33	31	20	.199	.270	.248	518	45	-26	8			.903	-5	3-93	-2.6
	StL-a	3	11	0	0	0	0	0	0	1	2	.000	.083	.000	83	-66	-2	0			.867	2	/3-3	-0.1
	Yr	96	358	42	69	6	1	3	33	32	22	.193	.265	.240	505	41	-29	8			**.902**	-3	3-96	-2.7
Total	11	978	3736	475	875	89	32	6	349	302	173	.234	.285	.269	554	64	-156	67			.888	-6	3-802,S-168/P-5,2O	-12.1

■ **FRANK WHITNEY** Whitney, Frank Thomas "Jumbo" b: 2/18/1856, Brockton, Mass. d: 10/30/43, Baltimore, Md. BR/TR, 5'7.5", 152 lbs. Deb: 5/17/1876 F

YEAR	TM/L	G	AB	R	H	2B	3B	HR	RBI	BB	SO	AVG	OBP	SLG	OPS	OPS+	BR+	SB	CS	SBR	FA	FR	G/POS	TPR
1876	Bos-N	34	140	27	33	7	1	0	15	1	3	.236	.243	.302	545	79	-3				.818	3	O-34(24-0-10)/2-1	-0.2

■ **JIM WHITNEY** Whitney, James Evans "Grasshopper Jim" b: 11/10/1857, Conklin, N.Y. d: 5/21/1891, Binghamton, N.Y. BL/TR, 6'2", 172 lbs. Deb: 5/2/1881 Career OF: (5-LF 74-CF 52-RF)

YEAR	TM/L	G	AB	R	H	2B	3B	HR	RBI	BB	SO	AVG	OBP	SLG	OPS	OPS+	BR+	SB	CS	SBR	FA	FR	G/POS	TPR
1881	Bos-N	75	282	37	72	17	3	0	32	19	18	.255	.302	.337	639	106	3				.808	-9	*P-66,O-15R/1-2	-0.5
1882	Bos-N	61	251	49	81	18	7	5	48	24	13	.323	.382	.510	892	183	24				.886	-3	P-49/O-9(0-1-9),1-6	-0.1
1883	Bos-N	96	409	78	115	27	10	5	57	25	29	.281	.323	.433	755	124	11				.921	-4	P-62,O-40C/1-2	0.0
1884	Bos-N	66	270	41	70	17	5	3	40	16	38	.259	.301	.393	693	117	5				**1.000**	-1	P-38,O-15C,1-15,/3	-0.4
1885	Bos-N	72	290	35	68	8	4	0	36	17	24	.234	.277	.290	567	86	-4				.901	5	P-51,O-17(2-13-2)/1-5	-0.3
1886	KC-N	67	247	25	59	13	3	2	23	29	39	.239	.319	.340	659	94	-2	5			.927	6	P-46,O-22(2-9-11)/3-1	-0.1
1887	Was-N	54	219	29	71	9	6	2	22	18	24	.324	.324	.398	722	105	2	10			.905	2	P-47/O-7(1-6-0)	-0.2
1888	Was-N	42	141	13	24	0	0	1	17	7	20	.170	.209	.191	401	30	-11	3			.882	-2	P-39/O-3(0-0-3),1-1	-0.2
1889	Ind-N	10	32	6	12	4	1	0	4	5	6	.375	.474	.563	1036	185	4	2			1.000	-1	/P-9,O-1(0-0-1)	0.0
1890	Phi-a	7	21	3	5	0	0	0	1	1		.238	.273	.238	511	51	-1	0			.900	-1	/P-6,O-1(0-1-0)	0.0
Total	10	550	2162	316	577	113	39	18	280	161	211	.267	.313	.375	688	112	31	20			.900	-9	P-413,O-130C/1-31,3	-1.8

■ **ERNIE WHITT** Whitt, Leo Ernest b: 6/13/52, Detroit, Mich. BL/TR, 6'2", 200 lbs. Deb: 9/12/76

YEAR	TM/L	G	AB	R	H	2B	3B	HR	RBI	BB	SO	AVG	OBP	SLG	OPS	OPS+	BR+	SB	CS	SBR	FA	FR	G/POS	TPR
1976	Bos-A	8	18	4	4	2	0	1	3	2	2	.222	.300	.500	800	117	0	0	0	0	1.000	-1	/C-8	0.0
1977	Tor-A	23	41	4	7	3	0	0	6	2	12	.171	.209	.244	453	23	-4	0	0	0	1.000	1	C-14	-0.3
1978	Tor-A	2	4	0	0	0	0	0	0	1	1	.000	.200	.000	200	-38	-1	0	0	0	1.000	0	/C-1	0.0
1980	Tor-A	106	295	23	70	12	2	6	34	22	30	.237	.290	.353	643	72	-12	1	3	-1	.986	6	*C-105	-0.2
1981	Tor-A	74	195	16	46	9	0	1	16	20	30	.236	.307	.297	604	70	-7	5	2	0	.991	9	C-72	0.5
1982	Tor-A	105	284	28	74	14	2	11	42	26	34	.261	.323	.440	763	98	-1	3	1	0	.982	1	C-98/D-1	0.3
1983	Tor-A	123	344	53	88	15	2	17	56	50	55	.256	.350	.459	810	114	7	1	1	-0	.992	6	*C-119	1.7
1984	Tor-A	124	315	35	75	12	1	15	46	43	49	.238	.331	.425	757	104	2	0	3	-1	.994	12	*C-118	1.7
1985	*Tor-A★	139	412	55	101	21	2	19	64	47	59	.245	.324	.444	768	105	2	3	6	-1	.988	6	*C-134	1.2
1986	Tor-A	131	395	48	106	19	2	16	56	35	39	.268	.328	.448	776	106	3	0	1	-0	.991	-4	*C-129	0.4
1987	Tor-A	135	446	57	120	24	1	19	75	44	50	.269	.336	.455	791	105	3	0	1	-0	.994	6	*C-131	1.3
1988	Tor-A	127	398	63	100	11	2	16	70	61	38	.251	.352	.410	762	112	8	4	2	0	.994	-6	*C-123	0.9
1989	*Tor-A	129	385	42	101	24	1	11	53	52	53	.262	.350	.416	766	117	9	5	4	-0	.992	-2	*C-115/D-8	1.4
1990	Atl-N	67	180	14	31	8	0	2	10	23	27	.172	.266	.250	516	40	-14	0	2	-1	.991	2	C-59	-1.1
1991	Bal-A	35	62	5	15	2	0	0	3	8	12	.242	.329	.274	603	71	-2	0	0	0	1.000	-1	C-20/D-2	-0.2
Total	15	1328	3774	447	938	176	15	134	534	436	491	.249	.327	.410	737	98	-8	22	26	-4	.991	36	*C-1246/D-11	7.6

■ **POSSUM WHITTED** Whitted, George Bostic b: 2/4/1890, Durham, N.C. d: 10/16/62, Wilmington, N.C. BR/TR, 5'8.5", 168 lbs. Deb: 9/16/12 Career OF: (442-LF 94-CF 117-RF)

YEAR	TM/L	G	AB	R	H	2B	3B	HR	RBI	BB	SO	AVG	OBP	SLG	OPS	OPS+	BR+	SB	CS	SBR	FA	FR	G/POS	TPR
1912	StL-N	12	46	7	12	3	0	0	7	3	5	.261	.306	.326	632	75	-2	1			.857	-3	3-12	-0.4
1913	StL-N	123	404	44	89	10	5	0	38	31	44	.220	.282	.270	552	59	-21	9			.989	5	O-41L,S-38,3-22,/21	-1.5
1914	StL-N	20	31	3	4	1	0	0	1	0	3	.129	.129	.161	290	-14	-4	1			.889	-3	/3-5,O-3(2-0-2),2-1	-0.8
	*Bos-N	66	218	36	57	11	4	2	31	18	18	.261	.326	.376	703	109	2	10			.967	4	O-38C,2-15/1-4,3S	0.5
	Yr	86	249	39	61	12	4	2	32	18	21	.245	.304	.349	653	95	-2	11			.957	1	O-41C,2-16/3-9,1S	-0.3
1915	*Phi-N	128	448	46	126	17	3	1	43	29	47	.281	.328	.339	667	101	0	24	15	0	.978	4	*O-119(53-66-0)/1-7	-0.3
1916	Phi-N	147	526	68	148	20	12	6	68	19	46	.281	.309	.399	708	113	6	29	17	0	.964	5	*O-136(136-0-0),1-16	0.6
1917	Phi-N	149	553	69	155	24	9	3	70	30	56	.280	.317	.373	690	107	3	10			.977	4	*O-141L,1-10/3-7,2	0.1
1918	Phi-N	24	86	7	21	4	0	0	3	4	10	.244	.278	.291	568	69	-3	4			.982	2	O-22(22-0-0)/1-1	-0.2
1919	Phi-N	78	289	32	72	14	1	3	32	14	20	.249	.284	.336	619	80	-7	5			.955	0	O-47(47-0-0),2-26/1-2	-1.0
	Pit-N	35	131	15	51	7	7	0	21	6	4	.389	.420	.550	970	183	13	7			.988	3	1-33/3-2,O-1(1-0-0)	1.5
	Yr	113	420	47	123	21	8	3	53	20	24	.293	.327	.402	729	112	5	12			.955	3	O-48L,1-35,2-26,/3	0.5
1920	Pit-N	134	494	53	129	11	12	1	74	35	36	.261	.314	.338	652	85	-10	11	11	-1	.961	-3	*3-125,1-10/O-1L	-1.2
1921	Pit-N	108	403	60	114	23	7	7	63	26	21	.283	.328	.427	755	96	-3	5	10	-2	.988	9	*O-102(15-0-87)/1-7	-0.5
1922	Bro-N	1	1	0	0	0	0	0	0	0	0	.000	.000	.000	0	-99	-0	0	0	0	.000	0	H	0.0
Total	11	1025	3630	440	978	145	60	23	451	215	310	.269	.313	.361	675	95	-26	116	53		.975	27	O-651L,3-177/1-92,2S	-3.2

■ **FLOYD WICKER** Wicker, Floyd Euliss b: 9/12/43, Burlington, N.C. BL/TR, 6'2", 175 lbs. Deb: 6/23/68

YEAR	TM/L	G	AB	R	H	2B	3B	HR	RBI	BB	SO	AVG	OBP	SLG	OPS	OPS+	BR+	SB	CS	SBR	FA	FR	G/POS	TPR
1968	StL-N	5	4	2	2	0	0	0	0	0	0	.500	.500	.500	1000	204	0	0	0	0	.000	0	H	0.1
1969	Mon-N	41	39	2	4	0	0	0	2	2	20	.103	.146	.103	249	-29	-7	0	0	0	1.000	-2	O-11(2-7-2)	-0.9
1970	Mil-A	15	41	3	8	1	0	1	3	1	8	.195	.214	.293	507	38	-4	0	0	0	1.000	-1	O-12(8-0-4)	-0.5
1971	Mil-A	11	8	0	1	0	0	0	0	2	0	.125	.300	.125	425	24	-1	0	0	0	.000	0	H	-0.1
	SF-N	9	21	3	3	0	0	0	1	2	5	.143	.250	.143	393	14	-2	0	0	0	1.000	1	/O-7(7-0-0)	-0.2
Total	4	81	113	10	18	1	0	1	6	7	33	.159	.215	.195	410	15	-13	0	0	0	1.000	-3	/O-30(17-7-6)	-1.6

■ **AL WICKLAND** Wickland, Albert b: 1/27/1888, Chicago, Ill. d: 3/14/80, Port Washington, Wis. BL/TL, 5'7", 155 lbs. Deb: 8/21/13

YEAR	TM/L	G	AB	R	H	2B	3B	HR	RBI	BB	SO	AVG	OBP	SLG	OPS	OPS+	BR+	SB	CS	SBR	FA	FR	G/POS	TPR
1913	Cin-N	26	79	7	17	5	5	0	8	6	19	.215	.279	.405	684	94	-1	3			.983	1	O-24(0-24-0)	-0.2
1914	Chi-F	157	536	74	148	31	10	6	68	**81**	58	.276	.375	.405	780	119	8	17			.962	-1	*O-157(30-1-129)	-0.2
1915	Chi-F	30	86	11	21	2	2	1	5	13	11	.244	.343	.349	692	101	-1	3			.946	-2	O-24(5-0-20)	-0.4
	Pit-F	110	389	63	117	12	8	1	30	52	47	.301	.386	.380	766	117	5	23			.968	4	*O-109(109-0-1)	0.4
	Yr	140	475	74	138	14	10	2	35	65	58	.291	.378	.375	753	114	4	26			.966	2	*O-133(114-0-21)	0.0
1918	Bos-N	95	332	55	87	7	13	4	32	53	39	.262	.367	.398	765	139	17	12			.975	3	O-95(1-0-94)	1.6
1919	NY-A	26	46	2	7	1	0	0	1	2	10	.152	.188	.174	361	2	-6	0			1.000	-4	O-15(0-0-15)	-1.1
Total	5	444	1468	212	397	58	38	12	144	207	184	.270	.364	.386	750	117	22	58			.968	-1	O-424(145-25-259)	0.1

YEAR	TM/L	G	AB	R	H	2B	3B	HR	RBI	BB	SO	AVG	OBP	SLG	OPS	OPS+	BR+	SB	CS	SBR	FA	FR	G/POS	TPR
■ CHRIS WIDGER Widger, Christopher Jon b: 5/21/71, Wilmington, Del. BR/TR, 6'3", 195 lbs. Deb: 6/23/95 Career OF: (2-LF 0-CF 2-RF)																								
1995	*Sea-A	23	45	2	9	0	0	1	2	3	11	.200	.250	.267	517	34	-4	0	0	0	1.000	-5	C-19/O-3(2-0-1),D-1	-0.8
1996	Sea-A	8	11	1	2	0	0	0	0	0	5	.182	.250	.182	432	12	-1	0	0	0	.905	-0	/C-7	-0.2
1997	Mon-N	91	278	30	65	20	3	7	37	22	59	.234	.292	.403	695	80	-9	2	0	0	.981	-8	C-85	-1.2
1998	Mon-N	125	417	36	97	18	1	15	53	29	85	.233	.283	.388	671	75	-16	6	1	1	.983	2	*C-123	-0.6
1999	Mon-N	124	383	42	101	24	1	14	56	28	86	.264	.325	.441	767	94	-5	1	4	-1	.992	1	*C-118	0.1
2000	Mon-N	86	281	31	67	17	2	12	34	29	61	.238	.312	.441	753	86	-7	1	2	-0	.985	-5	C-85	-0.6
	Sea-A	10	11	1	1	0	0	1	1	1	2	.091	.167	.364	530	30	-1	0	0	0	1.000	-1	/C-6,1-2,O-1(0-0-1)	-0.2
Total	6	467	1426	143	342	79	7	50	183	112	309	.240	.300	.410	710	81	-44	10	7	-0	.985	-16	C-443/O-4L,1-2,D-1	-3.5
■ TOM WIEDENBAUER Wiedenbauer, Thomas John b: 11/5/58, Menomonie, Wis. BR/TR, 6'1", 180 lbs. Deb: 9/14/79																								
1979	Hou-N	4	6	0	4	1	0	0	2	0	2	.667	.667	.833	1500	326	2	0	0	0	1.000	-1	/O-3(1-1-1)	0.1
■ STUMP WIEDMAN Wiedman, George Edward b: 2/17/1861, Rochester, N.Y. d: 3/2/05, New York, N.Y. BR/TR, 5'7.5", 165 lbs. Deb: 8/26/1880 U Career OF: (13-LF 21-CF 87-RF)																								
1880	Buf-N	23	78	8	8	1	0	0	3	2	11	.103	.125	.115	240	-18	-9				.893	-3	P-17,O-13(1-11-1)	-0.5
1881	Det-N	13	47	8	12	1	0	0	5	2	2	.255	.286	.277	562	75	-1				**1.000**	-2	P-13	0.0
1882	Det-N	50	193	20	42	7	1	0	20	2	19	.218	.226	.264	490	57	-9				.906	0	P-46/O-6(1-2-2),S-1	0.0
1883	Det-N	79	313	34	58	6	1	1	24	4	38	.185	.196	.220	416	27	-26				.909	-2	P-52,O-35(1-5-29)/2-4	-1.2
1884	Det-N	81	300	24	49	6	0	0	26	13	41	.163	.198	.183	381	22	-25				.846	-3	O-53R,P-26/S-1,2-1	-1.9
1885	Det-N	44	153	7	24	2	1	1	14	8	32	.157	.199	.203	401	30	-12				.869	-5	P-38/O-7(6-1-0),2-1	-0.3
1886	KC-N	51	179	13	30	2	0	0	7	5	46	.168	.190	.179	369	12	-19	3			.936	3	P-51/O-3(1-2-0)	-0.1
1887	Det-N	21	85	12	20	2	0	1	11	3	3	.235	.235	.268	504	38	-7	6			.837	-1	P-21/O-2(2-0-0)	-0.1
	NY-a	14	50	5	11	1	1	0	1	4		.220	.220	.217	437	23	-5	2			.882	2	P-12/O-3(1-0-2)	0.0
	NY-N	1	3	0	1	0	0	0	0	0	0	.333	.333	.333	667	90	-0	0			.500	-0	/P-1	0.0
1888	NY-N	2	7	1	0	0	0	0	1	2	1	.000	.222	.000	222	-24	-1	0			.714	-0	/P-2	0.0
Total	9	379	1408	132	255	28	4	3	112	45	193	.181	.203	.209	412	28	-114	11			.885	-10	P-279,O-122R/2-6,S	-4.1
■ TOM WIEGHAUS Wieghaus, Thomas Robert b: 2/1/57, Chicago Heights, Ill BR/TR, 6', 195 lbs. Deb: 10/4/81																								
1981	Mon-N	1	1	0	0	0	0	0	0	0	0	.000	.000	.000	0	-99	-0	0	0	0	1.000	1	/C-1	0.1
1983	Mon-N	1	0	0	0	0	0	0	0	0	0	—	—	—	—	—	0	0	0	0	1.000	-0	/C-1	0.0
1984	Hou-N	6	10	0	0	0	0	0	1	1	3	.000	.091	.000	91	-78	-2	0	0	0	1.000	2	/C-6	0.0
Total	3	8	11	0	0	0	0	0	1	1	3	.000	.083	.000	83	-80	-3	0	0	0	1.000	3	/C-8	0.1
■ WHITEY WIETELMANN Wietelmann, William Frederick b: 3/15/19, Zanesville, Ohio BB/TR (BR 1939-41), 6', 170 lbs. Deb: 9/6/39 C																								
1939	Bos-N	23	69	2	14	1	0	0	5	2	9	.203	.225	.217	443	21	-8	1			.953	2	S-22/2-1	-0.5
1940	Bos-N	35	41	3	8	1	0	0	1	5	5	.195	.283	.220	502	43	-3	0			.962	3	2-15/3-9,S-3	0.0
1941	Bos-N	16	33	1	3	0	0	0	0	1	2	.091	.118	.091	209	-43	-6	0			1.000	3	2-10/S-5,3-2	-0.3
1942	Bos-N	13	34	4	7	2	0	0	0	4	5	.206	.289	.265	554	64	-1	0			.941	-1	S-11/2-1	-0.1
1943	Bos-N	153	534	33	115	14	1	0	39	46	40	.215	.281	.245	527	53	-31	9			.957	20	*S-153	0.1
1944	Bos-N	125	417	46	100	18	1	2	32	33	25	.240	.300	.302	602	67	-18	0			.954	-6	*S-103,2-23/3-1	-1.5
1945	Bos-N	123	428	53	116	15	3	4	33	39	27	.271	.335	.348	683	89	-6	4			.972	3	2-87,S-39/3-2,P-1	0.4
1946	Bos-N	44	78	7	16	0	0	0	5	14	8	.205	.326	.205	531	52	-4	0			.915	-6	S-16/3-8,2-4,P-3	-0.9
1947	Pit-N	48	128	21	30	4	1	1	7	12	10	.234	.300	.305	605	59	-7	0			.885	-13	S-22,2-14/3-6,1-1	-1.9
Total	9	580	1762	170	409	55	6	7	122	156	131	.232	.298	.282	580	63	-85	14			.952	4	S-374,2-155/3-28,P1	-4.7
■ ALAN WIGGINS Wiggins, Alan Anthony b: 2/17/58, Los Angeles, Cal. d: 1/6/91, Los Angeles, Cal. BB/TR, 6'2", 160 lbs. Deb: 9/4/81 Career OF: (123-LF 67-CF 20-RF)																								
1981	SD-N	15	14	4	5	0	0	0	0	1	0	.357	.400	.357	757	125	0	2	0	0	.750	-1	/O-4(4-0-0)	0.0
1982	SD-N	72	254	40	65	3	3	1	15	13	19	.256	.295	.303	598	71	-10	33	6	5	.967	1	O-68(51-19-6)/2-1	-0.6
1983	SD-N	144	503	83	139	20	2	0	22	65	43	.276	.360	.324	684	94	-1	66	13	10	.992	-1	*O-105(63-48-14),1-45	0.2
1984	*SD-N	158	596	106	154	19	7	3	34	75	57	.258	.344	.329	673	90	-6	70	21	8	.962	-29	*2-157	-1.9
1985	SD-N	10	37	3	2	1	0	0	0	2	4	.054	.103	.081	184	-49	-7	0	1	-0	1.000	-3	/2-9	-1.2
	Bal-A	76	298	43	85	11	4	0	21	29	16	.285	.353	.349	702	96	-1	30	13	2	.960	-24	2-76	-1.9
1986	Bal-A	71	239	30	60	3	1	0	11	22	20	.251	.314	.272	586	62	-12	21	7	2	.978	-19	2-66/D-1	-2.5
1987	Bal-A	85	306	37	71	4	2	1	15	28	34	.232	.299	.268	566	53	-20	20	7	2	.983	-0	D-44,2-33/O-5(5-0-0)	-1.7
Total	7	631	2247	346	581	61	19	5	118	235	193	.259	.331	.309	640	80	-57	242	68	29	.967	-76	2-342,O-182L/D-45,1	-9.6
■ DEL WILBER Wilber, Delbert Quentin "Babe" b: 2/24/19, Lincoln Park, Mich BR/TR, 6'3", 200 lbs. Deb: 4/21/46 MC																								
1946	StL-N	4	4	0	0	0	0	0	0	1	1	.000	.200	.000	200	-39	-1	0			1.000	1	/C-4	0.0
1947	StL-N	51	99	7	23	8	1	0	12	5	13	.232	.269	.333	603	57	-6	0			.983	1	C-34	-0.4
1948	StL-N	27	58	5	11	2	0	0	10	4	9	.190	.242	.224	466	25	-6	0			.949	-3	C-26	-0.8
1949	StL-N	2	4	0	1	0	0	0	0	0	0	.250	.250	.250	500	33	-0	0			1.000	0	/C-2	0.0
1951	Phi-N	84	245	30	68	7	3	8	34	17	26	.278	.324	.429	753	102	0	0	1	-0	.978	4	C-73	0.7
1952	Phi-N	2	2	0	0	0	0	0	0	0	1	.000	.000	.000	0	-99	-1	0	0	0	.000	0	H	-0.1
	Bos-A	47	135	7	36	10	1	3	23	7	20	.267	.308	.422	730	94	-2	1	0	0	.995	1	C-39	0.1
1953	Bos-A	58	112	16	27	6	1	7	29	6	21	.241	.286	.500	786	103	-0	0	0	0	.980	-3	C-28/1-2	-0.2
1954	Bos-A	24	61	2	8	2	1	1	7	4	6	.131	.185	.246	431	15	-7	0	0	0	.950	-5	C-18	-1.3
Total	8	299	720	67	174	35	7	19	115	44	96	.242	.287	.389	676	79	-23	1	1		.978	-4	C-224/1-2	-2.0
■ CLAUDE WILBORN Wilborn, Claude Edward b: 9/1/12, Woodsdale, N.C. d: 11/13/92, Roxboro, N.C. BL/TR, 6'1", 180 lbs. Deb: 9/8/40																								
1940	Bos-N	5	7	0	0	0	0	0	0	0	1	.000	.000	.000	0	-99	-2	0			.500	-1	/O-3(0-0-3)	-0.4
■ TED WILBORN Wilborn, Thaddeaus Iglehart b: 12/16/58, Waco, Tex. BB/TR, 6', 165 lbs. Deb: 4/5/79																								
1979	Tor-A	22	12	3	0	0	0	0	0	1	7	.000	.077	.000	77	-76	-3	0	1	-0	.875	-2	/O-7(4-1-2),D-4	-0.5
1980	NY-A	8	8	2	2	0	0	0	1	0	1	.250	.250	.250	500	38	-1	0	0	0	1.000	1	/O-3(1-1-1)	0.0
Total	2	30	20	5	2	0	0	0	1	1	8	.100	.143	.100	243	-33	-4	0	1	-0	.933	-1	/O-10(5-2-3),D-4	-0.5
■ JOHN WILEY Wiley, John Deb: 6/23/1884																								
1884	Was-U	1	4	0	0	0	0	0		0		.000	.000	.000	0	-99	-1				.333	-1	/3-1	-0.2
■ ROB WILFONG Wilfong, Robert Donald b: 9/1/53, Pasadena, Cal. BL/TR, 6'1", 185 lbs. Deb: 4/10/77																								
1977	Min-A	73	171	22	42	1	1	1	13	17	26	.246	.321	.281	602	67	-7	10	4	1	.959	4	2-66/D-1	0.0
1978	Min-A	92	199	23	53	8	0	1	11	19	27	.266	.336	.322	658	84	-4	8	4	0	.986	6	2-80/D-5	0.6
1979	Min-A	140	419	71	131	22	6	9	59	29	54	.313	.360	.458	818	115	8	11	4	1	.979	21	*2-133/O-3(1-1-1)	3.5
1980	Min-A	131	416	55	103	16	5	8	45	34	61	.248	.309	.368	677	79	-12	10	6	0	**.995**	-4	*2-120/O-6(0-6-0)	-1.0
1981	Min-A	93	305	32	75	11	3	3	19	29	43	.246	.311	.331	643	80	-8	2	4	-1	.980	4	2-93	-0.1
1982	Min-A	25	81	7	13	1	0	0	5	7	13	.160	.236	.173	409	14	-9	0	2	-1	.980	-0	2-22	-0.9
	*Cal-A	55	102	17	25	4	2	1	11	7	17	.245	.294	.353	647	77	-3	4	0	1	.982	9	2-28/3-5,O-3C,SD	0.7
	Yr	80	183	24	38	5	2	1	16	14	30	.208	.268	.273	541	49	-13	4	2	0	.981	9	2-50/3-5,O-3C,SD	-0.2
1983	Cal-A	65	177	17	45	7	1	2	17	10	25	.254	.294	.339	633	74	-6	0	2	-1	.995	12	2-39,3-13/S-6,D-1	0.6
1984	Cal-A	108	307	31	76	13	2	6	33	20	53	.248	.298	.362	659	82	-8	3	2	-0	.975	3	2-97/S-4,D-1	0.0
1985	Cal-A	83	217	16	41	3	0	4	13	16	32	.189	.245	.258	503	38	-19	4	1	1	.986	21	2-69/D-2	0.6
1986	*Cal-A	92	288	25	63	11	3	3	33	16	34	.219	.265	.309	574	56	-18	1	4	-1	.982	9	2-90	-0.6
1987	SF-N	2	8	2	1	0	0	1	2	1	2	.125	.222	.500	722	89	-0	1	0	0	.833	-2	/2-2	-0.2
Total	11	959	2690	318	668	97	23	39	261	205	387	.248	.305	.345	650	77	-86	54	33	0	.982	80	2-839/3-18,S-12,OD	3.2
■ SPIDER WILHELM Wilhelm, Charles Ernest b: 5/23/29, Baltimore, Md. d: 10/20/92, Venice, Fla. BR/TR, 5'9", 170 lbs. Deb: 9/6/53																								
1953	Phi-A	7	7	1	2	1	0	0	0	0	3	.286	.286	.429	714	87	-0	0	0	0	.875	-0	/S-6	0.0
■ JIM WILHELM Wilhelm, James Webster b: 9/20/52, San Rafael, Cal. BR/TR, 6'3", 190 lbs. Deb: 9/4/78																								
1978	SD-N	10	19	2	7	2	0	0	4	0	2	.368	.400	.474	874	155	1	1	0	0	1.000	-3	O-10(3-7-0)	-0.1

YEAR	TM/L	G	AB	R	H	2B	3B	HR	RBI	BB	SO	AVG	OBP	SLG	OPS	OPS+	BR+	SB	CS	SBR	FA	FR	G/POS	TPR
1979	SD-N	39	103	8	25	4	3	0	8	2	12	.243	.257	.340	597	65	-5	1	1	-0	.985	0	O-30(4-25-1)	-0.6
Total	2	49	122	10	32	6	3	0	12	2	14	.262	.280	.361	641	79	-4	2	1	0	.987	-2	/O-40(7-32-1)	-0.7

■ JOE WILHOIT

Wilhoit, Joseph William b: 12/20/1885, Hiawatha, Kan. d: 9/25/30, Santa Barbara, Cal. BL/TR, 6'2", 175 lbs. Deb: 4/12/16

YEAR	TM/L	G	AB	R	H	2B	3B	HR	RBI	BB	SO	AVG	OBP	SLG	OPS	OPS+	BR+	SB	CS	SBR	FA	FR	G/POS	TPR
1916	Bos-N	116	383	44	88	13	4	2	38	27	45	.230	.282	.300	582	82	-8	18			.979	2	*O-108(1-1-106)	-1.4
1917	Bos-N	54	186	20	51	5	0	1	10	17	15	.274	.335	.317	652	107	2	5			.928	-3	O-52(0-0-52)	-0.4
	Pit-N	9	10	0	2	0	0	0	0	1	1	.200	.273	.200	473	45	-1	0			1.000	-0	/O-3(1-0-2),1-1	-0.1
	*NY-N	34	50	9	17	2	2	0	8	8	5	.340	.431	.460	891	179	5	0			1.000	-2	O-11(0-2-10)	0.3
	Yr	97	246	29	70	7	2	1	18	26	21	.285	.353	.341	694	118	6	5			.941	-5	O-66(1-2-64)/1-1	-0.2
1918	NY-N	64	135	13	37	3	3	0	15	17	14	.274	.355	.341	696	115	3	4			.975	-8	O-55(3-34-15)	-0.8
1919	Bos-A	6	18	7	6	0	0	0	2	5	2	.333	.478	.333	812	138	1	1			1.000	-1	/O-5(0-0-5)	0.1
Total	4	283	782	93	201	23	9	3	73	75	82	.257	.323	.321	644	101	2	28			.969	-11	O-234(5-37-190)/1-1	-2.3

■ DENNEY WILIE

Wilie, Dennis Ernest b: 9/22/1890, Mt.Calm, Tex. d: 6/20/66, Hayward, Cal. BL/TL, 5'8", 155 lbs. Deb: 7/27/11

YEAR	TM/L	G	AB	R	H	2B	3B	HR	RBI	BB	SO	AVG	OBP	SLG	OPS	OPS+	BR+	SB	CS	SBR	FA	FR	G/POS	TPR
1911	StL-N	28	51	10	12	3	1	0	3	8	11	.235	.361	.333	694	97	0	3			1.000	-3	O-15(11-3-2)	-0.3
1912	StL-N	30	48	2	11	0	1	0	6	7	9	.229	.351	.271	622	73	-1	0			.917	-3	O-16(3-1-12)	-0.5
1915	Cle-A	45	131	14	33	4	1	2	10	26	18	.252	.384	.344	727	115	4	2	6	-2	.910	-2	O-35(11-24-0)	-0.3
Total	3	103	230	26	56	7	3	2	19	41	38	.243	.372	.326	698	102	2	5	6		.925	-8	/O-66(25-28-14)	-1.1

■ HARRY WILKE

Wilke, Henry Joseph b: 12/14/1900, Cincinnati, Ohio d: 6/21/91, Hamilton, Ohio BR/TR, 5'10.5", 171 lbs. Deb: 5/12/27

YEAR	TM/L	G	AB	R	H	2B	3B	HR	RBI	BB	SO	AVG	OBP	SLG	OPS	OPS+	BR+	SB	CS	SBR	FA	FR	G/POS	TPR
1927	Chi-N	3	9	0	0	0	0	0	0	0	1	.000	.000	.000	0	-99	-3	0			1.000	0	/3-3	-0.2

■ CURTIS WILKERSON

Wilkerson, Curtis Vernon b: 4/26/61, Petersburg, Va. BB/TR, 5'9", 158 lbs. Deb: 9/10/83 Career OF: (2-LF 0-CF 0-RF)

YEAR	TM/L	G	AB	R	H	2B	3B	HR	RBI	BB	SO	AVG	OBP	SLG	OPS	OPS+	BR+	SB	CS	SBR	FA	FR	G/POS	TPR
1983	Tex-A	16	35	7	6	0	1	0	1	2	5	.171	.216	.229	445	23	-4	3	0	1	1.000	2	/S-9,2-2,3-2	-0.1
1984	Tex-A	153	484	47	120	12	0	1	26	22	72	.248	.283	.279	562	55	-29	12	10	-1	.944	-28	*S-116,2-47	-4.6
1985	Tex-A	129	360	35	88	11	6	0	22	22	63	.244	.295	.308	604	65	-17	14	7	1	.957	3	*S-110,2-19/D-2	-0.3
1986	Tex-A	110	236	27	56	10	3	0	15	11	42	.237	.274	.305	579	56	-14	9	7	-0	.968	15	2-60,S-56/D-2	0.5
1987	Tex-A	85	138	28	37	5	3	2	14	6	16	.268	.308	.391	700	84	-3	6	3	0	.946	11	S-33,2-28,3-18,/D-4	0.9
1988	Tex-A	117	338	41	99	12	5	0	28	26	43	.293	.347	.358	705	95	-1	9	4	1	.970	10	2-87,S-24,3-11,/D-1	1.3
1989	*Chi-N	77	160	18	39	4	2	1	10	8	33	.244	.280	.313	592	64	-7	4	2	0	.881	4	3-26,2-15/S-7,O-1L	-0.3
1990	Chi-N	77	186	21	41	5	1	0	16	7	36	.220	.249	.258	507	37	-16	2	2	-0	.888	-4	3-52,2-14/S-1,O-1L	-2.0
1991	*Pit-N	85	191	20	36	9	1	2	18	15	40	.188	.248	.277	525	48	-13	2	1	0	.992	3	2-30,S-15,3-14	-0.9
1992	KC-A	111	296	27	74	10	1	2	29	18	47	.250	.295	.311	606	68	-13	18	7	2	.968	-4	S-69,2-39/3-5,D-1	-1.0
1993	KC-A	12	28	1	4	0	0	0	0	1	6	.143	.172	.143	315	-13	-4	2	0	0	1.000	-1	2-10/S-4	-0.4
Total	11	972	2452	272	600	78	23	8	179	138	403	.245	.288	.305	593	63	-123	81	43	3	.957	11	S-444,2-351,3/DO	-6.9

■ RICK WILKINS

Wilkins, Richard David b: 6/4/67, Jacksonville, Fla. BL/TR, 6'2", 210 lbs. Deb: 6/6/91

YEAR	TM/L	G	AB	R	H	2B	3B	HR	RBI	BB	SO	AVG	OBP	SLG	OPS	OPS+	BR+	SB	CS	SBR	FA	FR	G/POS	TPR
1991	Chi-N	86	203	21	45	9	0	6	22	19	56	.222	.307	.355	662	82	-5	3	3	-0	.993	9	C-82	0.8
1992	Chi-N	83	244	20	66	9	1	8	22	28	53	.270	.346	.414	760	111	4	0	2	-1	.993	10	C-73	1.8
1993	Chi-N	136	446	78	135	23	1	30	73	50	99	.303	.377	.561	937	149	30	2	1	0	.996	5	*C-133	4.2
1994	Chi-N	100	313	44	71	25	2	7	39	40	86	.227	.318	.387	705	84	-8	4	3	-0	.993	-5	C-95/1-2	-0.7
1995	Chi-N	50	162	24	31	2	0	6	14	36	51	.191	.342	.315	657	76	-5	0	0	0	.988	-6	C-49/1-2	-0.8
	Hou-N	15	40	6	10	1	0	1	5	10	10	.250	.400	.350	750	107	1	0	0	0	1.000	-1	C-13	0.1
	Yr	65	202	30	41	3	0	7	19	46	61	.203	.353	.322	675	82	-4	0	0	0	.990	-7	C-62/1-2	-0.7
1996	Hou-N	84	254	34	54	8	2	6	23	46	81	.213	.336	.331	666	83	-5	0	1	-0	.990	-7	C-82	-0.7
	SF-N	52	157	19	46	10	0	8	36	21	40	.293	.376	.510	886	136	8	0	2	-1	.991	-7	C-42/1-7	0.2
	Yr	136	411	53	100	18	2	14	59	67	121	.243	.351	.399	750	104	3	0	3	-1	.990	-14	*C-124/1-7	-0.5
1997	SF-N	66	190	18	37	5	0	6	23	17	65	.195	.261	.316	577	51	-14	0	0	0	.986	0	C-57	-1.0
	*Sea-A	5	12	2	3	1	0	1	4	1	2	.250	.308	.583	891	127	0	0	0	0	1.000	-0	/C-3,D-2	0.0
1998	Sea-A	19	41	5	8	1	1	1	4	4	14	.195	.267	.341	608	57	-3	0	0	0	1.000	-1	/C-6,1-6,D-2	-0.3
	NY-N	5	15	3	2	0	0	0	1	2	2	.133	.235	.133	369	0	-2	0	0	0	.957	-2	/C-4	-0.4
1999	LA-N	3	4	0	0	0	0	0	0	0	2	.000	.000	.000	0	-99	-1	0	0	0	1.000	-1	/C-1	-0.2
2000	*StL-N	4	11	3	3	0	0	0	1	2	2	.273	.385	.273	657	70	-0	0	0	0	1.000	2	/C-3	0.1
Total	10	708	2092	277	511	94	7	80	267	276	563	.244	.336	.411	747	100	1	9	12	-2	.992	-2	C-643/1-17,D-4	3.1

■ BOBBY WILKINS

Wilkins, Robert Linwood b: 8/11/22, Denton, N.C. BR/TR, 5'9", 165 lbs. Deb: 4/18/44

YEAR	TM/L	G	AB	R	H	2B	3B	HR	RBI	BB	SO	AVG	OBP	SLG	OPS	OPS+	BR+	SB	CS	SBR	FA	FR	G/POS	TPR
1944	Phi-A	24	25	7	6	0	0	0	3	1	4	.240	.296	.240	536	55	-1	0	0	0	.943	5	/S-9	0.4
1945	Phi-A	62	154	22	40	6	0	0	4	10	17	.260	.305	.299	604	76	-5	2	4	-1	.923	0	S-40/O-4(4-0-0)	-0.3
Total	2	86	179	29	46	6	0	0	7	11	21	.257	.304	.291	594	73	-6	2	4	-1	.926	5	/S-49,O-4(4-0-0)	0.1

■ ED WILKINSON

Wilkinson, Edward Henry b: 6/20/1890, Jacksonville, Ore d: 4/9/18, Tucson, Ariz. BR/TR, 6', 170 lbs. Deb: 7/4/11

YEAR	TM/L	G	AB	R	H	2B	3B	HR	RBI	BB	SO	AVG	OBP	SLG	OPS	OPS+	BR+	SB	CS	SBR	FA	FR	G/POS	TPR
1911	NY-A	10	13	2	3	0	0	0	1	0		.231	.231	.231	462	27	-1	0			.800	-1	/O-3(3-0-0),2-1	-0.2

■ BOB WILL

Will, Robert Lee "Butch" b: 7/15/31, Berwyn, Ill. BL/TL, 5'10.5", 175 lbs. Deb: 4/16/57

YEAR	TM/L	G	AB	R	H	2B	3B	HR	RBI	BB	SO	AVG	OBP	SLG	OPS	OPS+	BR+	SB	CS	SBR	FA	FR	G/POS	TPR
1957	Chi-N	70	112	13	25	3	0	1	10	5	21	.223	.256	.277	533	44	-9	1	0	0	.963	-5	O-30(0-30-0)	-1.5
1958	Chi-N	6	4	1	1	0	0	0	0	2	0	.250	.500	.250	750	108	0	0	0	0	.000	0	/O-1(0-0-1)	0.0
1960	Chi-N	138	475	58	121	20	9	6	53	47	54	.255	.323	.373	696	91	-6	1	5	-2	.992	2	*O-121(4-0-117)	-1.0
1961	Chi-N	86	113	9	29	9	0	0	8	15	19	.257	.344	.336	680	80	-3	0	1	-0	1.000	-6	O-30(9-0-22)/1-1	-1.0
1962	Chi-N	87	92	6	22	3	0	2	15	13	22	.239	.333	.337	670	78	-3	0	0	0	1.000	-1	/O-9(0-0-9)	-0.4
1963	Chi-N	23	23	0	4	0	0	0	1	1	3	.174	.208	.174	382	11	-3	0	0	0	1.000	-0	/1-1	-0.3
Total	6	410	819	87	202	35	9	9	87	83	119	.247	.317	.344	661	80	-22	2	6	-2	.988	-10	O-191(13-30-148)/1-2	-4.2

■ JERRY WILLARD

Willard, Gerald Duane b: 3/14/60, Oxnard, Cal. BL/TR, 6'2", 195 lbs. Deb: 4/11/84

YEAR	TM/L	G	AB	R	H	2B	3B	HR	RBI	BB	SO	AVG	OBP	SLG	OPS	OPS+	BR+	SB	CS	SBR	FA	FR	G/POS	TPR
1984	Cle-A	87	246	21	55	8	1	10	37	26	55	.224	.298	.386	684	86	-5	1	0	0	.981	-1	C-76/D-1	-0.2
1985	Cle-A	104	300	39	81	13	0	7	36	28	59	.270	.334	.383	718	97	-1	0	0	0	.990	0	C-96/D-1	0.3
1986	Oak-A	75	161	17	43	7	0	4	26	22	28	.267	.362	.385	747	112	3	0	1	-0	.994	-11	C-71/D-1	-0.6
1987	Oak-A	7	6	1	1	0	0	0	0	2	1	.167	.375	.167	542	55	-0	0	0	0	1.000	-0	/1-1,3-1,D-3	-0.1
1990	Chi-A	3	3	0	0	0	0	0	0	0	2	.000	.000	.000	0	-99	-1	0	0	0	.000	0	/C-1	-0.1
1991	*Atl-N	17	14	1	3	0	0	1	4	2	5	.214	.313	.429	741	100	-0	0	0	0	1.000	0	/C-1	0.0
1992	Atl-N	26	23	2	8	1	0	2	7	1	3	.348	.375	.652	1027	175	2	0	0	0	1.000	0	/C-1	0.3
	Mon-N	21	25	0	3	0	0	0	1	1	7	.120	.154	.120	274	-22	-4	0	0	0	.952	0	/1-5	-0.4
	Yr	47	48	2	11	1	0	2	8	2	10	.229	.260	.375	635	76	-2	0	0	0	.952	1	/1-5,C-1	-0.1
1994	Sea-A	6	5	1	1	0	0	1	3	1	1	.200	.333	.800	1133	177	1	0	0	0	.000	-0	/C-1,D-1	0.0
Total	8	346	783	82	195	29	1	25	114	83	161	.249	.323	.384	708	95	-5	1	1	-0	.988	-11	C-247/D-7,1-6,3-1	-0.8

■ RIP WILLIAMS

Williams, Alva Mitchel "Buff" b: 1/31/1882, Carthage, Ill. d: 7/23/33, Keokuk, Iowa BR/TR, 6'0.5", 187 lbs. Deb: 4/12/11 Career OF: (0-LF 1-CF 5-RF)

YEAR	TM/L	G	AB	R	H	2B	3B	HR	RBI	BB	SO	AVG	OBP	SLG	OPS	OPS+	BR+	SB	CS	SBR	FA	FR	G/POS	TPR
1911	Bos-A	95	284	36	68	8	5	0	31	24		.239	.314	.303	617	73	-10	9			.975	1	1-57,C-38	-0.7
1912	Was-A	60	157	14	50	11	4	0	22	7		.318	.352	.439	791	125	4	2			.978	4	C-48	1.1
1913	Was-A	66	106	9	30	6	2	1	12	9	16	.283	.339	.406	745	115	2	3			.985	-4	C-18/1-9,O-5(0-1-4)	-0.2
1914	Was-A	81	169	17	47	6	4	1	22	13	19	.278	.341	.379	719	112	2	2	2	-0	.975	-5	C-44/1-8,O-1(0-0-1)	0.0
1915	Was-A	91	197	14	48	8	4	0	31	18	20	.244	.320	.325	645	91	-2	4	3	-0	.967	8	C-40,1-15/3-1	0.9
1916	Was-A	76	202	16	54	10	2	0	20	15	19	.267	.324	.337	661	100	-0	5			.982	-9	1-34,C-23/3-1	-0.9
1918	Cle-A	28	71	5	17	2	2	0	7	9	6	.239	.325	.324	649	87	-1	2			.980	-2	1-21/C-1	-0.3
Total	7	497	1186	111	314	51	23	2	145	95	80	.265	.328	.352	680	97	-6	27	5		.977	-6	C-212,1-144/O-6R,3	-0.1

■ ART WILLIAMS

Williams, Arthur Franklin b: 8/26/1877, Somerville, Mass. d: 5/16/41, Arlington, Va. TR, Deb: 5/7/02

YEAR	TM/L	G	AB	R	H	2B	3B	HR	RBI	BB	SO	AVG	OBP	SLG	OPS	OPS+	BR+	SB	CS	SBR	FA	FR	G/POS	TPR
1902	Chi-N	49	167	20	38	3	0	0	14	17		.228	.310	.246	556	74	-4	9			.921	-3	O-26(4-0-22),1-19	-1.0

■ GUS WILLIAMS

Williams, August Joseph "Gloomy Gus" b: 5/7/1888, Omaha, Neb. d: 4/16/64, Sterling, Ill. BL/TL, 6', 185 lbs. Deb: 4/12/11 F

YEAR	TM/L	G	AB	R	H	2B	3B	HR	RBI	BB	SO	AVG	OBP	SLG	OPS	OPS+	BR+	SB	CS	SBR	FA	FR	G/POS	TPR
1911	StL-A	9	26	1	7	3	0	0	4	0		.269	.296	.385	681	93	-0	0			.867	-1	/O-7(7-0-0)	-0.2
1912	StL-A	64	216	32	63	13	7	2	32	27		.292	.370	.444	815	138	10	18			.930	2	O-62(0-0-62)	0.9
1913	StL-A	148	538	72	147	21	16	5	53	57	87	.273	.346	.400	746	121	13	31			.951	4	*O-143(0-0-143)	1.0

YEAR	TM/L	G	AB	R	H	2B	3B	HR	RBI	BB	SO	AVG	OBP	SLG	OPS	OPS+	BR+	SB	CS	SBR	FA	FR	G/POS	TPR
1914	StL-A	144	499	51	126	19	6	4	47	36	120	.253	.308	.339	647	98	-3	35	20	1	.933	2	*O-142(0-0-141)	-0.8
1915	StL-A	45	119	15	24	2	2	1	11	6	16	.202	.246	.277	523	59	-7	11	1	2	.949	-5	O-35(0-0-35)	-1.2
Total	5	410	1398	171	367	58	31	12	147	126	223	.263	.327	.374	702	110	14	95	21		.939	2	O-389(7-0-381)	-0.3

■ BERNIE WILLIAMS

Williams, Bernabe (Figueroa) b: 9/13/68, San Juan, P.R. BB/TR, 6'2", 205 lbs. Deb: 7/7/91 Career OF: (4-LF 1213-CF 4-RF)

YEAR	TM/L	G	AB	R	H	2B	3B	HR	RBI	BB	SO	AVG	OBP	SLG	OPS	OPS+	BR+	SB	CS	SBR	FA	FR	G/POS	TPR
1991	NY-A	85	320	43	76	19	4	3	34	48	57	.237	.339	.350	689	91	-3	10	5	0	.979	6	O-85(0-85-0)	0.2
1992	NY-A	62	261	39	73	14	2	5	26	29	36	.280	.354	.406	760	113	5	7	6	-1	.995	8	O-62(4-55-4)	1.2
1993	NY-A	139	567	67	152	31	4	12	68	53	106	.268	.335	.400	735	100	-0	9	9	-1	.989	6	*O-139(0-139-0)	0.6
1994	NY-A	108	408	80	118	29	1	12	57	61	54	.289	.386	.453	839	120	14	16	9	0	.990	5	*O-107(0-107-0)	1.9
1995	*NY-A	144	563	93	173	29	9	18	82	75	98	.307	.393	.487	880	129	25	8	6	-0	.982	16	*O-144(0-144-0)	3.9
1996	*NY-A	143	551	108	168	26	7	29	102	82	72	.305	.395	.535	930	132	28	17	4	2	.986	9	*O-140(0-140-0)/D-2	3.7
1997	*NY-A★	129	509	107	167	35	6	21	100	73	80	.328	.413	.544	958	148	38	15	8	1	.993	-5	*O-128(0-128-0)	3.2
1998	*NY-A†	128	499	101	169	30	5	26	97	74	81	**.339**	.425	.575	1000	163	48	15	9	0	.990	2	*O-123(0-123-0)/D-5	4.8
1999	*NY-A★	158	591	116	202	28	6	25	115	100	95	.342	.438	.536	974	149	47	9	10	-2	.987	9	*O-155(0-155-0)/D-2	5.2
2000	*NY-A★	141	537	108	165	37	6	30	121	71	84	.307	.393	.566	959	141	34	13	5	1	**1.000**	6	*O-137(0-137-0)/D-4	3.9
Total	10	1237	4806	862	1463	278	50	181	802	666	763	.304	.392	.496	888	132	236	119	71	1	.989	61	*O-1220C/D-13	28.6

■ BERNIE WILLIAMS

Williams, Bernard b: 10/8/48, Alameda, Cal. BR/TR, 6'1", 175 lbs. Deb: 9/7/70

YEAR	TM/L	G	AB	R	H	2B	3B	HR	RBI	BB	SO	AVG	OBP	SLG	OPS	OPS+	BR+	SB	CS	SBR	FA	FR	G/POS	TPR
1970	SF-N	7	16	2	5	2	0	0	1	2	1	.313	.389	.438	826	122	1	1	1	-0	1.000	1	/O-6(6-0-0)	0.1
1971	SF-N	35	73	8	13	1	0	1	5	12	24	.178	.294	.233	527	52	-4	1	1	-0	.933	-5	O-27(22-0-5)	-1.1
1972	SF-N	46	68	12	13	3	1	3	9	7	22	.191	.267	.397	664	85	-2	0	0	0	1.000	2	O-15(14-1-0)	-0.1
1974	SD-N	14	15	1	2	0	0	0	0	0	6	.133	.133	.133	267	-26	-3	0	0	0	1.000	-1	/O-3(1-2-0)	-0.4
Total	4	102	172	23	33	6	1	4	15	21	53	.192	.280	.308	588	66	-8	2	2	-0	.974	-3	/O-51(43-3-5)	-1.5

■ BILLY WILLIAMS

Williams, Billy Leo b: 6/15/38, Whistler, Ala. BL/TR, 6'1", 175 lbs. Deb: 8/6/59 CH Career OF: (1738-LF 30-CF 384-RF)

YEAR	TM/L	G	AB	R	H	2B	3B	HR	RBI	BB	SO	AVG	OBP	SLG	OPS	OPS+	BR+	SB	CS	SBR	FA	FR	G/POS	TPR
1959	Chi-N	18	33	0	5	0	1	0	2	1	7	.152	.176	.212	389	3	-5	0	0	0	1.000	-0	O-10(10-0-0)	-0.5
1960	Chi-N	12	47	4	13	0	2	2	7	5	12	.277	.346	.489	836	127	2	0	0	0	.962	0	O-12(12-0-0)	0.1
1961	Chi-N	146	529	75	147	20	7	25	86	45	70	.278	.340	.484	824	114	10	6	0	1	.954	-2	*O-135(110-0-27)	0.1
1962	Chi-N★	159	618	94	184	22	8	22	91	70	72	.298	.373	.466	839	119	18	9	9	-1	.967	16	*O-159(158-0-1)	2.2
1963	Chi-N	161	612	87	175	36	9	25	95	68	78	.286	.359	.497	856	136	29	7	6	-1	.987	16	*O-160(160-0-0)	3.7
1964	Chi-N★	162	645	100	201	39	2	33	98	59	84	.312	.371	.532	903	145	38	10	7	-0	.950	1	*O-162(162-2-0)	3.0
1965	Chi-N★	164	645	115	203	39	6	34	108	65	76	.315	.380	.552	932	155	46	10	1	2	.968	0	*O-164(34-28-106)	4.0
1966	Chi-N	162	648	100	179	23	5	29	91	69	61	.276	.350	.461	811	122	19	6	3	0	.976	8	*O-162(11-0-152)	1.7
1967	Chi-N	162	634	92	176	21	12	28	84	68	67	.278	.349	.481	831	129	24	6	3	0	.989	-3	*O-162(161-0-6)	1.2
1968	Chi-N★	163	642	91	185	30	8	30	98	48	53	.288	.340	.500	840	140	30	4	1	1	.967	-11	*O-163(137-0-47)	1.0
1969	Chi-N	163	642	103	188	33	10	21	95	59	70	.293	.356	.474	830	116	13	3	2	-0	.957	2	*O-159(153-0-28)	0.6
1970	Chi-N	161	636	**137**	**205**	34	4	42	129	72	65	.322	.393	.586	979	142	37	7	1	1	.989	8	*O-160(155-0-9)	3.5
1971	Chi-N	157	594	86	179	27	5	28	93	77	44	.301	.384	.505	889	131	26	7	5	-0	.977	7	*O-154(151-0-4)	2.4
1972	Chi-N★	150	574	95	191	34	6	37	122	62	59	**.333**	.403	**.606**	**1010**	166	49	3	1	0	.984	-3	*O-144(144-0-0)/1-5	3.9
1973	Chi-N★	156	576	72	166	22	2	20	86	76	72	.288	.372	.438	810	115	13	4	3	-0	.985	12	*O-138(138-0-0),1-19	1.6
1974	Chi-N	117	404	55	113	22	0	16	68	67	44	.280	.383	.453	836	128	16	4	5	-1	.986	2	1-65,O-43(41-0-4)	1.1
1975	*Oak-A	155	520	68	127	20	1	23	81	76	68	.244	.343	.419	762	117	12	0	0	0	.971	-0	*D-145/1-7	0.8
1976	Oak-A	120	351	36	74	12	0	11	41	58	44	.211	.323	.339	662	98	0	4	2	0	.000	-0	*D-106/O-1(1-0-0)	-0.3
Total	18	2488	9350	1410	2711	434	88	426	1475	1045	1046	.290	.364	.492	856	131	376	90	49	3	.973	52	*O-2088L,D-251/1-96	30.1

■ DALLAS WILLIAMS

Williams, Dallas McKinley b: 2/28/58, Brooklyn, N.Y. BL/TL, 5'11", 165 lbs. Deb: 9/19/81 C

YEAR	TM/L	G	AB	R	H	2B	3B	HR	RBI	BB	SO	AVG	OBP	SLG	OPS	OPS+	BR+	SB	CS	SBR	FA	FR	G/POS	TPR
1981	Bal-A	2	2	0	1	0	0	0	0	0	0	.500	.500	.500	1000	189	0	0	0	0	1.000	-0	/O-1(1-0-0)	0.0
1983	Cin-N	18	36	2	2	0	0	0	1	3	6	.056	.128	.056	184	-46	-7	0	0	0	1.000	-1	O-12(6-3-3)	-0.9
Total	2	20	38	2	3	0	0	0	1	3	6	.079	.146	.079	225	-35	-7	0	0	0	1.000	-2	/O-13(7-3-3)	-0.9

■ DANA WILLIAMS

Williams, Dana Lamont b: 3/20/63, Weirton, W.Va. BR/TR, 5'10", 170 lbs. Deb: 6/21/89 C

YEAR	TM/L	G	AB	R	H	2B	3B	HR	RBI	BB	SO	AVG	OBP	SLG	OPS	OPS+	BR+	SB	CS	SBR	FA	FR	G/POS	TPR
1989	Bos-A	8	5	1	1	1	0	0	0	0	1	.200	.333	.400	733	100	0	0	0	0	1.000	0	/O-1(1-0-0),D-2	0.0

■ DAVEY WILLIAMS

Williams, David Carlous b: 11/2/27, Dallas, Tex. BR/TR, 5'10", 160 lbs. Deb: 9/16/49 C

YEAR	TM/L	G	AB	R	H	2B	3B	HR	RBI	BB	SO	AVG	OBP	SLG	OPS	OPS+	BR+	SB	CS	SBR	FA	FR	G/POS	TPR
1949	NY-N	13	50	7	12	1	1	1	5	7	4	.240	.333	.360	693	86	-1	0			.953	-10	2-13	-0.1
1951	*NY-N	30	64	17	17	1	0	2	8	5	8	.266	.319	.375	694	85	-1	1	1	-0	1.000	2	2-22	0.1
1952	NY-N	138	540	70	137	26	3	13	55	48	63	.254	.324	.385	709	95	-4	2	3	-1	.973	-15	*2-138	-1.2
1953	NY-N★	112	340	51	101	11	2	3	34	44	19	.297	.382	.368	750	95	-1	2	5	-1	.982	0	2-95	0.4
1954	*NY-N	142	544	65	121	18	3	9	46	43	33	.222	.285	.316	602	56	-35	1	1	-0	**.982**	-7	*2-142	-3.2
1955	NY-N	82	247	25	62	4	1	4	15	17	17	.251	.305	.324	628	67	-12	0	2	-1	.968	-8	2-71	-1.6
Total	6	517	1785	235	450	61	10	32	163	164	144	.252	.321	.351	673	79	-54	6	12		.978	-38	2-481	-6.6

■ KEITH WILLIAMS

Williams, David Keith b: 4/21/72, Bedford, Pa. BR/TR, 6', 190 lbs. Deb: 6/7/96

YEAR	TM/L	G	AB	R	H	2B	3B	HR	RBI	BB	SO	AVG	OBP	SLG	OPS	OPS+	BR+	SB	CS	SBR	FA	FR	G/POS	TPR
1996	SF-N	9	20	0	5	0	0	0	0	0	6	.250	.250	.250	500	34	-2	0	0	0	1.000	0	/O-4(1-0-3)	-0.2

■ DEWEY WILLIAMS

Williams, Dewey Edgar "Dee" b: 2/5/16, Durham, N.C. d: 3/19/2000, Williston, N.Dak. BR/TR, 6', 160 lbs. Deb: 6/28/44

YEAR	TM/L	G	AB	R	H	2B	3B	HR	RBI	BB	SO	AVG	OBP	SLG	OPS	OPS+	BR+	SB	CS	SBR	FA	FR	G/POS	TPR
1944	Chi-N	79	262	23	63	7	2	0	27	23	18	.240	.302	.282	584	65	-12	2			.981	4	C-77	-0.3
1945	*Chi-N	59	100	16	28	2	2	2	5	13	13	.280	.363	.400	763	114	2	0			.978	2	C-54	0.6
1946	Chi-N	4	5	0	1	0	0	0	0	0	2	.200	.200	.200	400	14	-1	0			1.000	0	/C-2	0.0
1947	Chi-N	3	2	0	0	0	0	0	0	0	1	.000	.000	.000	0	-99	-1	0			.000	0	/C-1	-0.1
1948	Cin-N	48	95	9	16	2	0	1	5	10	18	.168	.248	.221	469	29	-9	0			.961	-3	C-47	-1.1
Total	5	193	464	48	108	11	4	3	37	46	52	.233	.302	.293	595	67	-20	2			.976	3	C-181	-0.9

■ EARL WILLIAMS

Williams, Earl Baxter b: 1/27/03, Cumberland Gap, Tenn. d: 3/10/58, Knoxville, Tenn. BR/TR, 6'0.5", 185 lbs. Deb: 5/27/28

YEAR	TM/L	G	AB	R	H	2B	3B	HR	RBI	BB	SO	AVG	OBP	SLG	OPS	OPS+	BR+	SB	CS	SBR	FA	FR	G/POS	TPR
1928	Bos-N	3	2	0	0	0	0	0	0	0	1	.000	.000	.000	0	-99	-1	0			1.000	0	/C-1	-0.1

■ EARL WILLIAMS

Williams, Earl Craig b: 7/14/48, Newark, N.J. BR/TR, 6'3", 220 lbs. Deb: 9/13/70

YEAR	TM/L	G	AB	R	H	2B	3B	HR	RBI	BB	SO	AVG	OBP	SLG	OPS	OPS+	BR+	SB	CS	SBR	FA	FR	G/POS	TPR
1970	Atl-N	10	19	4	7	4	0	0	5	3	4	.368	.455	.579	1033	165	2	0	0	0	1.000	1	/1-4,3-3	0.3
1971	Atl-N	145	497	64	129	14	1	33	87	42	80	.260	.326	.491	817	121	12	0	1	-0	.981	-8	C-72,3-42,1-31	0.5
1972	Atl-N	151	565	72	146	24	2	28	87	62	118	.258	.338	.457	795	113	10	0	0	0	.980	-19	*C-116,3-21,1-20	-0.6
1973	*Bal-A	132	459	58	109	18	1	22	83	66	107	.237	.337	.425	762	114	9	0	2	-1	.987	-9	C-95,1-42/D-2	0.1
1974	*Bal-A	118	413	47	105	16	0	14	52	40	79	.254	.330	.395	725	111	6	0	2	-1	.983	-14	C-75,1-47/D-1	-0.9
1975	Atl-N	111	383	42	92	13	0	11	50	34	63	.240	.307	.360	667	82	-10	0	0	0	.989	-5	1-90,C-11	-2.2
1976	Atl-N	61	184	18	39	3	0	9	26	19	33	.212	.289	.375	664	82	-5	0	0	0	.995	-9	C-38,1-17	-1.3
	Mon-N	61	190	17	45	10	2	8	29	14	32	.237	.289	.437	726	100	-1	0	0	0	.981	6	1-47,C-13	0.3
	Yr	122	374	35	84	13	2	17	55	33	65	.225	.289	.406	696	91	-6	0	0	0	.986	-2	1-64,C-51	-1.0
1977	Oak-A	100	348	39	84	13	0	13	38	18	58	.241	.288	.391	679	84	-8	2	0	1	.989	-4	D-45,C-36,1-29	-1.3
Total	8	889	3058	361	756	115	6	138	457	298	574	.247	.321	.424	745	105	15	2	5	-1	.984	-60	C-456,1-327/3-66,D	-5.1

■ EDDIE WILLIAMS

Williams, Edward Laquan b: 11/1/64, Shreveport, La. BR/TR, 6', 185 lbs. Deb: 4/18/86

YEAR	TM/L	G	AB	R	H	2B	3B	HR	RBI	BB	SO	AVG	OBP	SLG	OPS	OPS+	BR+	SB	CS	SBR	FA	FR	G/POS	TPR
1986	Cle-A	5	7	2	1	0	0	0	1	0	3	.143	.143	.143	286	-22	-1	0	0	0	.000	-2	/O-4(4-0-0)	-0.3
1987	Cle-A	22	64	9	11	4	0	1	4	9	19	.172	.284	.281	565	50	-5	0	0	0	.982	2	3-22	-0.3
1988	Cle-A	10	21	3	4	0	0	0	1	0	3	.190	.227	.190	418	18	-2	0	0	0	1.000	3	3-10	0.0
1989	Chi-A	66	201	25	55	8	0	3	10	18	31	.274	.345	.358	704	101	1	1	2	-0	.909	1	3-65	0.1
1990	SD-N	14	42	5	12	3	0	3	4	5	6	.286	.362	.571	933	151	3	0	1	-0	.897	-1	3-13	0.2
1994	SD-N	49	175	32	58	11	1	11	42	15	26	.331	.394	.594	988	158	14	0	1	-0	.988	-2	1-46/3-1	0.8
1995	SD-N	97	296	35	77	11	1	12	47	23	47	.260	.322	.426	748	99	-1	0	0	0	.989	-1	1-81	-0.9
1996	Det-A	77	215	22	43	5	0	6	26	18	50	.200	.268	.307	575	45	-18	0	2	-1	1.000	-0	D-52/1-7,3-3,O-2R	-2.1
1997	LA-N	8	7	0	1	0	0	0	1	1	1	.143	.250	.143	393	7	-1	0	0	0	.000	0	/H	-0.1
	Pit-N	30	89	12	22	5	0	3	11	10	24	.247	.337	.404	741	91	-1	1	0	0	.991	-3	1-26	-0.6
	Yr	38	96	12	23	5	0	3	12	11	25	.240	.330	.385	716	87	-2	1	0	0	.991	-3	1-26	-0.7

YEAR	TM/L	G	AB	R	H	2B	3B	HR	RBI	BB	SO	AVG	OBP	SLG	OPS	OPS+	BR+	SB	CS	SBR	FA	FR	G/POS	TPR
1998	SD-N	17	28	1	4	0	0	0	3	2	6	.143	.200	.143	343	-9	-4	0	0	0	1.000	-0	/1-7	-0.5
Total	10	395	1145	146	288	47	2	39	150	101	216	.252	.321	.398	720	91	-16	2	6	-2	.989	-4	1-167,3-114/D-52,O	-3.7

■ DIB WILLIAMS Williams, Edwin Dibrell b: 1/19/10, Greenbrier, Ark. d: 4/2/92, Searcy, Ark. BR/TR, 5′11.5″, 175 lbs. Deb: 4/27/30 Career OF: (1-LF 0-CF 0-RF)

YEAR	TM/L	G	AB	R	H	2B	3B	HR	RBI	BB	SO	AVG	OBP	SLG	OPS	OPS+	BR+	SB	CS	SBR	FA	FR	G/POS	TPR
1930	Phi-A	67	191	24	50	10	3	3	22	15	19	.262	.322	.393	715	77	-7	2	1	0	.951	4	2-39,S-19/3-1	0.0
1931	*Phi-A	86	294	41	79	12	2	6	40	19	21	.269	.313	.384	697	78	-10	2	0	0	.931	7	S-72,2-10/O-1(1-0-0)	0.3
1932	Phi-A	62	215	30	54	10	1	4	24	22	23	.251	.329	.363	692	76	-8	0	1	-0	.952	7	2-53/S-3	0.2
1933	Phi-A	115	408	52	118	20	5	11	73	32	35	.289	.342	.444	786	106	2	1	0	0	.921	-9	S-84,2-29/1-2	0.0
1934	Phi-A	66	205	25	56	10	1	2	17	21	18	.273	.341	.361	702	84	-5	0	1	-0	.956	-0	2-53/S-2	-0.2
1935	Phi-A	4	10	0	1	0	0	0	0	0	1	.100	.100	.100	200	-49	-2	0	0	0	1.000	-2	/2-2	-0.4
	Bos-A	75	251	26	63	12	0	3	25	24	23	.251	.319	.335	654	65	-13	2	0	0	.952	-5	3-30,2-29,S-15,/1-1	-1.4
	Yr	79	261	26	64	12	0	3	25	24	24	.245	.311	.326	637	61	-15	2	0	0	.973	-7	2-31,3-30,S-15,/1-1	-1.8
Total	6	475	1574	198	421	74	12	29	201	133	140	.267	.327	.385	712	82	-42	7	3	0	.955	1	2-215,S-195/3-31,1O	-1.5

■ DENNY WILLIAMS Williams, Evon Daniel b: 12/13/1899, Portland, Ore. d: 3/23/29, San Clemente, Cal. BL/TR, 5′8.5″, 150 lbs. Deb: 4/15/21

YEAR	TM/L	G	AB	R	H	2B	3B	HR	RBI	BB	SO	AVG	OBP	SLG	OPS	OPS+	BR+	SB	CS	SBR	FA	FR	G/POS	TPR
1921	Cin-N	10	7	0	0	0	0	0	0	0	2	.000	.000	.000	0	-99	-2	0	1	-0	1.000	-0	/O-1(1-0-0)	-0.3
1924	Bos-A	25	85	17	31	3	0	0	4	10	5	.365	.438	.400	838	117	3	3	3	-0	.972	-2	O-19(19-0-0)	-0.1
1925	Bos-A	69	218	28	50	1	3	0	13	17	11	.229	.285	.261	547	39	-20	2	6	-2	.953	-2	O-52(42-11-0)	-2.6
1928	Bos-A	16	18	1	4	0	0	0	1	1	1	.222	.263	.222	485	29	-2	0	0	0	1.000	-2	/O-6(0-5-1)	-0.4
Total	4	120	328	46	85	4	3	0	18	28	19	.259	.319	.290	609	56	-21	5	10	-2	.959	-7	/O-78(62-16-1)	-3.4

■ CY WILLIAMS Williams, Fred b: 12/21/1887, Wadena, Ind. d: 4/23/74, Eagle River, Wis. BL/TL, 6′2″, 180 lbs. Deb: 7/18/12

YEAR	TM/L	G	AB	R	H	2B	3B	HR	RBI	BB	SO	AVG	OBP	SLG	OPS	OPS+	BR+	SB	CS	SBR	FA	FR	G/POS	TPR
1912	Chi-N	28	62	3	15	1	1	0	1	6	14	.242	.309	.290	599	65	-3	2			1.000	-2	O-22(5-17-0)	-0.6
1913	Chi-N	49	156	17	35	3	3	4	32	5	26	.224	.262	.359	621	76	-6	5			.976	-5	O-44(36-9-0)	-1.3
1914	Chi-N	55	94	12	19	2	2	0	5	13	13	.202	.312	.266	578	73	-3	2			.941	-3	O-27(22-7-0)	-0.7
1915	Chi-N	151	518	59	133	22	6	13	64	26	49	.257	.305	.398	703	112	5	15	10	-0	.968	5	*O-149(0-149-0)	0.0
1916	Chi-N	118	405	55	113	19	9	**12**	66	51	64	.279	.372	.459	**831**	140	20	6			.989	-4	*O-116(0-115-1)	0.9
1917	Chi-N	138	468	53	113	22	4	5	42	38	78	.241	.308	.338	646	91	-5	8			.960	12	*O-136(0-136-0)	-0.2
1918	Phi-N	94	351	49	97	14	1	6	39	27	30	.276	.337	.373	710	109	4	10			.968	0	O-91(0-91-0)	-0.3
1919	Phi-N	109	435	54	121	21	1	9	39	30	43	.278	.335	.393	728	111	6	9			.970	4	*O-108(0-108-0)	0.2
1920	Phi-N	148	590	88	192	36	10	**15**	72	32	45	.325	.364	.497	861	139	28	18	12	-0	.972	10	*O-147(0-147-0)	2.9
1921	Phi-N	146	562	67	180	28	6	18	75	30	32	.320	.357	.488	844	112	9	5	15	-4	.979	16	*O-146(0-146-0)	1.5
1922	Phi-N	151	584	98	180	30	6	26	92	74	49	.308	.392	.514	905	120	18	11	14	-2	.973	2	*O-150(0-150-0)	1.0
1923	Phi-N	136	535	98	157	22	3	**41**	114	59	57	.293	.371	.576	947	131	22	11	10	-1	.981	-3	*O-135(0-135-0)	1.2
1924	Phi-N	148	558	101	183	31	11	24	93	67	49	.328	.403	.552	955	137	29	7	12	-3	.962	-3	*O-145(0-145-0)	1.7
1925	Phi-N	107	314	78	104	11	5	13	60	53	34	.331	.435	.522	958	132	17	4	9	-2	.989	-5	O-96(0-0-96)	0.3
1926	Phi-N	107	336	63	116	13	4	18	53	38	35	.345	.418	**.568**	986	155	26	2			.963	-8	O-93(0-0-93)	1.1
1927	Phi-N	131	492	86	135	18	2	**30**	98	61	57	.274	.365	.502	867	128	19	0			.970	1	*O-130(0-0-130)	0.9
1928	Phi-N	99	238	31	61	9	0	12	37	54	34	.256	.400	.445	845	117	8	0			1.000	-2	O-69(20-9-40)	0.1
1929	Phi-N	66	65	11	19	2	0	5	21	22	9	.292	.471	.554	1025	144	5	0			.966	-0	O-11(1-9-1)	0.4
1930	Phi-N	21	17	1	8	2	0	0	2	4	3	.471	.571	.588	1160	169	2	0			1.000	-1	/O-3(1-1-1)	0.1
Total	19	2002	6780	1024	1981	306	74	251	1005	690	721	.292	.365	.470	835	123	202	115	82		.973	16	*O-1818(85-1374-362)	9.2

■ PAPA WILLIAMS Williams, Fred b: 7/17/13, Meridian, Miss. d: 11/2/93, Meridian, Miss. BR/TR, 6′1″, 200 lbs. Deb: 4/19/45

YEAR	TM/L	G	AB	R	H	2B	3B	HR	RBI	BB	SO	AVG	OBP	SLG	OPS	OPS+	BR+	SB	CS	SBR	FA	FR	G/POS	TPR
1945	Cle-A	16	19	0	4	0	0	0	0	1	2	.211	.250	.211	461	36	-2	0	0	0	1.000	0	/1-3	-0.1

■ GEORGE WILLIAMS Williams, George b: 10/23/39, Detroit, Mich. BR/TR, 5′11″, 165 lbs. Deb: 7/16/61 Career OF: (2-LF 0-CF 0-RF)

YEAR	TM/L	G	AB	R	H	2B	3B	HR	RBI	BB	SO	AVG	OBP	SLG	OPS	OPS+	BR+	SB	CS	SBR	FA	FR	G/POS	TPR
1961	Phi-N	17	36	4	9	0	0	0	1	4	4	.250	.325	.250	575	56	-2	0	0	0	.967	2	2-15	0.1
1962	Hou-N	5	8	1	3	1	0	0	2	0	1	.375	.375	.500	875	143	0	0	0	0	1.000	0	/2-3	0.1
1964	KC-A	37	91	10	19	6	0	0	2	6	12	.209	.265	.275	540	49	-6	0	0	0	.970	-3	2-20/S-2,3-2,O-2L	-0.8
Total	3	59	135	15	31	7	0	0	5	10	17	.230	.288	.281	569	56	-8	0	0	0	.970	-1	/2-38,O-2L,3-2,S-2	-0.6

■ GEORGE WILLIAMS Williams, George Erik b: 4/22/69, LaCrosse, Wis. BB/TR, 5′10″, 190 lbs. Deb: 7/14/95

YEAR	TM/L	G	AB	R	H	2B	3B	HR	RBI	BB	SO	AVG	OBP	SLG	OPS	OPS+	BR+	SB	CS	SBR	FA	FR	G/POS	TPR
1995	Oak-A	29	79	13	23	5	1	3	14	11	21	.291	.391	.494	885	136	4	0	0	0	.956	-3	C-13,D-10	0.2
1996	Oak-A	56	132	17	20	5	0	3	10	28	32	.152	.313	.258	570	47	-10	0	0	0	.982	-3	C-43,D-11	-1.1
1997	Oak-A	76	201	30	58	9	1	3	22	35	46	.289	.399	.388	787	108	4	0	1	-0	.984	-12	C-67/D-1	-0.4
2000	SD-N	11	16	2	3	0	0	1	2	0	4	.188	.235	.375	610	54	-1	0	0	0	1.000	-1	/C-6	-0.2
Total	4	172	428	62	104	19	2	10	48	74	103	.243	.365	.367	732	92	-3	0	1	-0	.981	-19	C-129/D-22	-1.5

■ GERALD WILLIAMS Williams, Gerald Floyd b: 8/10/66, New Orleans, La. BR/TR, 6′2″, 190 lbs. Deb: 9/15/92 Career OF: (391-LF 345-CF 166-RF)

YEAR	TM/L	G	AB	R	H	2B	3B	HR	RBI	BB	SO	AVG	OBP	SLG	OPS	OPS+	BR+	SB	CS	SBR	FA	FR	G/POS	TPR
1992	NY-A	15	27	7	8	2	0	3	6	0	3	.296	.296	.704	1000	174	2	2	0	0	.913	-1	O-12(0-0-12)	0.2
1993	NY-A	42	67	11	10	2	3	0	6	1	14	.149	.186	.269	454	21	-8	2	0	0	.956	-8	O-37(10-17-12)/D-1	-1.6
1994	NY-A	57	86	19	25	8	0	4	13	4	17	.291	.322	.523	845	118	2	1	3	-1	.957	-11	O-43(26-8-12)/D-2	-0.9
1995	*NY-A	100	182	33	45	18	2	6	28	22	34	.247	.332	.467	799	106	1	4	2	0	.993	-6	O-92(70-2-26)/D-2	-0.6
1996	NY-A	99	233	37	63	15	4	5	30	15	39	.270	.325	.433	759	90	-4	7	8	-1	.978	-11	O-92(70-14-10)/D-2	-1.6
	Mil-A	26	92	6	19	4	0	0	4	4	18	.207	.247	.250	497	25	-10	3	1	0	.987	4	O-26(0-25-1)	-0.5
	Yr	125	325	43	82	19	4	5	34	19	57	.252	.304	.382	685	71	-15	10	9	-1	.981	-7	*O-118(70-39-11)/D-2	-2.1
1997	Mil-A	155	566	73	143	32	2	10	41	19	90	.253	.284	.369	654	68	-27	23	9	2	.992	3	*O-154(39-129-0)/D-1	-2.1
1998	*Atl-N	129	266	46	81	19	2	10	44	17	48	.305	.353	.504	857	122	8	11	5	1	.970	-12	*O-120(56-11-61)	-0.6
1999	*Atl-N	143	422	76	116	24	1	17	68	33	67	.275	.336	.457	794	98	-2	19	11	0	.985	-10	*O-139(120-1-32)	-1.5
2000	TB-A	146	632	87	173	30	2	21	89	34	103	.274	.314	.427	741	86	-15	12	12	-2	.983	5	*O-138(0-138-0)/D-7	-1.0
Total	9	912	2573	395	683	154	16	76	329	149	433	.265	.312	.426	739	88	-54	84	51	1	.982	-47	O-853L/D-15	-10.2

■ HARRY WILLIAMS Williams, Harry Peter b: 6/23/1890, Omaha, Neb. d: 12/21/63, Huntington Park, Cal. BR/TR, 6′1.5″, 200 lbs. Deb: 8/7/13 F

YEAR	TM/L	G	AB	R	H	2B	3B	HR	RBI	BB	SO	AVG	OBP	SLG	OPS	OPS+	BR+	SB	CS	SBR	FA	FR	G/POS	TPR
1913	NY-A	27	82	18	21	3	1	1	12	15	10	.256	.378	.354	731	114	2	6			.981	-2	1-27	-0.1
1914	NY-A	59	178	9	29	5	2	1	17	26	26	.163	.287	.230	517	56	-9	3	6	-1	.976	-5	1-58	-1.9
Total	2	86	260	27	50	8	3	2	29	41	36	.192	.316	.269	585	75	-7	9	6		.977	-7	/1-85	-2.0

■ JIM WILLIAMS Williams, James Alfred b: 4/29/47, Zachary, La. BR/TR, 6′2″, 190 lbs. Deb: 9/8/69

YEAR	TM/L	G	AB	R	H	2B	3B	HR	RBI	BB	SO	AVG	OBP	SLG	OPS	OPS+	BR+	SB	CS	SBR	FA	FR	G/POS	TPR
1969	SD-N	13	25	4	7	1	0	0	2	3	11	.280	.357	.320	677	95	-0	0	0	0	.900	-0	/O-6(6-0-0)	-0.1
1970	SD-N	11	14	4	4	0	0	0	0	1	3	.286	.333	.286	619	70	-1	1	0	0	1.000	-1	/O-6(1-0-5)	-0.2
Total	2	24	39	8	11	1	0	0	2	4	14	.282	.349	.308	657	86	-1	1	0	0	.938	-2	/O-12(7-0-5)	-0.3

■ JIMY WILLIAMS Williams, James Francis b: 10/4/43, Santa Maria, Cal. BR/TR, 5′10″, 170 lbs. Deb: 4/26/66 MC

YEAR	TM/L	G	AB	R	H	2B	3B	HR	RBI	BB	SO	AVG	OBP	SLG	OPS	OPS+	BR+	SB	CS	SBR	FA	FR	G/POS	TPR
1966	StL-N	13	11	1	3	0	0	0	1	1	5	.273	.333	.273	606	71	-0	0	0	0	1.000	-2	/S-7,2-3	-0.2
1967	StL-N	1	2	0	0	0	0	0	0	0	1	.000	.000	.000	0	-99	-1	0	0	0	1.000	1	/S-1	0.0
Total	2	14	13	1	3	0	0	0	1	1	6	.231	.286	.231	516	46	-1	0	0	0	1.000	-1	/S-8,2-3	-0.2

■ JIMMY WILLIAMS Williams, James Thomas b: 12/20/1876, St.Louis, Mo. d: 1/16/65, St.Petersburg, Fla BR/TR, 5′9″, 175 lbs. Deb: 4/15/1899

YEAR	TM/L	G	AB	R	H	2B	3B	HR	RBI	BB	SO	AVG	OBP	SLG	OPS	OPS+	BR+	SB	CS	SBR	FA	FR	G/POS	TPR
1899	Pit-N	153	621	126	220	28	**27**	9	116	60		.354	.416	.530	946	159	49	26			.900	7	*3-153	5.2
1900	*Pit-N	106	416	73	110	15	11	5	68	32		.264	.323	.389	712	95	-4	18			.889	6	*3-103/S-4	0.4
1901	Bal-A	130	501	113	159	26	**21**	7	96	56		.317	.388	.495	883	138	25	21			.935	-2	*2-130	2.1
1902	Bal-A	125	498	83	156	27	**21**	8	83	36		.313	.361	.500	861	131	19	14			.945	4	*2-104,3-19/1-1	2.3
1903	NY-A	132	502	60	134	30	12	3	82	39		.267	.326	.392	718	108	5	9			**.957**	16	*2-132	2.2
1904	NY-A	146	559	62	147	31	7	2	74	38		.263	.314	.354	669	106	4	14			.951	17	*2-146	2.4
1905	NY-A	129	470	54	107	20	8	6	62	50		.228	.306	.343	648	95	-3	14			**.964**	6	*2-129	0.4
1906	NY-A	139	501	61	139	25	7	3	77	44		.277	.342	.373	715	112	7	8			.958	11	*2-139	2.1
1907	NY-A	139	504	53	136	17	11	2	63	35		.270	.319	.359	678	107	3	14			.966	-3	*2-139	0.2
1908	StL-A	148	539	63	127	20	7	4	53	55		.236	.310	.321	631	104	3	7			.963	5	*2-148	1.1
1909	StL-A	110	374	32	73	3	6	0	22	29		.195	.257	.235	492	60	-17	6			.962	-6	*2-109	-2.5
Total	11	1457	5485	780	1508	242	138	49	796	474		.275	.337	.396	733	114	92	151			.955	61	*2-1176,3-275/S-4,1	15.9

YEAR	TM/L	G	AB	R	H	2B	3B	HR	RBI	BB	SO	AVG	OBP	SLG	OPS	OPS+	BR+	SB	CS	SBR	FA	FR	G/POS	TPR
■ **KEN WILLIAMS**	Williams, Kenneth Roy b: 6/28/1890, Grants Pass, Ore. d: 1/22/59, Grants Pass, Ore. BL/TR, 6', 170 lbs. Deb: 7/14/15 Career OF: (1132-LF 158-CF 10-RF)																							
1915	Cin-N	71	219	22	53	10	4	0	16	15	20	.242	.297	.324	621	86	-4	4	3	-0	.948	2	O-62(54-8-0)	-0.5
1916	Cin-N	10	27	1	3	0	0	0	1	2	5	.111	.172	.111	284	-12	-4	1			.955	1	O-10(8-1-0)	-0.3
1918	StL-A	2	1	0	0	0	0	0	1	1	0	.000	.500	.000	500	53	0	0			.000	0	H	0.0
1919	StL-A	65	227	32	68	10	5	6	35	26	25	.300	.376	.467	843	133	10	7			.937	4	O-63(0-63-0)	0.9
1920	StL-A	141	521	90	160	34	13	10	72	41	26	.307	.362	.480	842	118	12	18	8	1	.961	8	*O-138(104-34-0)	1.3
1921	StL-A	146	547	115	190	31	7	24	117	74	42	.347	.429	.561	990	142	35	20	17	-2	.932	7	*O-145(145-0-0)	2.7
1922	StL-A	153	585	128	194	34	11	**39**	**155**	74	31	.332	.413	.627	1040	162	51	37	20	1	.970	7	*O-153(137-17-0)	4.6
1923	StL-A	147	555	106	198	37	12	29	91	79	32	.357	.439	.623	1062	168	54	18	17	-2	.967	12	*O-145(145-0-0)	4.9
1924	StL-A	114	398	78	129	21	4	18	84	69	17	.324	.425	.533	958	138	23	20	11	1	.968	6	*O-109(109-0-0)	2.0
1925	StL-A	102	411	83	136	31	5	25	105	37	14	.331	.390	**.613**	1003	144	24	10	5	0	.955	5	*O-102(102-0-0)	1.9
1926	StL-A	108	347	55	97	15	7	17	74	39	23	.280	.354	.510	864	118	7	5	4	-0	.948	1	O-92(91-1-0)/2-1	0.1
1927	StL-A	131	423	70	136	23	6	17	74	57	30	.322	.403	.525	928	135	22	9	7	-0	.965	6	*O-113(110-4-0)	1.8
1928	Bos-A	133	462	59	140	25	1	8	67	37	15	.303	.356	.413	769	104	2	4	9	-2	.971	-3	*O-127(127-0-0)	-1.3
1929	Bos-A	74	139	21	48	14	2	3	21	15	7	.345	.409	.540	949	146	9	1	5	-2	.963	-5	O-39(0-30-10)/1-2	0.1
Total	14	1397	4862	860	1552	285	77	196	913	566	287	.319	.393	.530	924	136	242	154	106		.958	50	*O-1298L/1-2,2-1	18.2
■ **KENNY WILLIAMS**	Williams, Kenneth Royal b: 4/6/64, Berkeley, Cal. BR/TR, 6'2", 187 lbs. Deb: 9/2/86 Career OF: (71-LF 189-CF 111-RF)																							
1986	Chi-A	15	31	2	4	0	0	1	1	1	11	.129	.182	.226	408	10	-4	1	1	-0	1.000	0	O-10(1-4-5)/D-1	-0.4
1987	Chi-A	116	391	48	110	18	2	11	50	10	83	.281	.315	.422	737	91	-6	21	10	1	.981	6	*O-115(0-111-4)	0.0
1988	Chi-A	73	220	18	35	4	2	8	28	10	64	.159	.223	.305	527	46	-16	6	5	-0	.959	-4	O-38R,3-32/D-3	-2.2
1989	Det-A	94	258	29	53	5	1	6	23	18	63	.205	.270	.302	573	63	-13	9	4	1	.979	4	O-87C/1-1,D-1	-1.1
1990	Det-A	57	83	10	11	2	0	0	5	3	24	.133	.172	.157	329	-7	-12	2	2	-0	1.000	-3	O-47(17-13-19)/D-6	-1.6
	Tor-A	49	72	13	14	6	1	0	8	7	18	.194	.275	.306	581	61	-4	7	2	1	1.000	-7	O-30(15-9-8)/D-9	-1.0
	Yr	106	155	23	25	8	1	0	13	10	42	.161	.222	.226	447	25	-16	9	4	1	1.000	-10	O-77(32-22-27),D-15	-2.6
1991	Tor-A	13	29	5	6	2	0	1	3	4	5	.207	.324	.379	703	90	-0	1	0	0	1.000	-0	/O-9(1-1-8),D-2	0.0
	Mon-N	34	70	11	19	5	2	0	1	3	22	.271	.311	.400	711	100	-0	2	1	0	.957	1	O-24(9-4-11)	0.0
Total	6	451	1154	136	252	42	8	27	119	56	290	.218	.271	.339	610	66	-55	49	25	2	.981	-3	O-360C/3-32,D-22,1	-6.3
■ **MARK WILLIAMS**	Williams, Mark Westley b: 7/28/53, Elmira, N.Y. BL/TL, 6', 180 lbs. Deb: 5/20/77																							
1977	Oak-A	3	2	0	0	0	0	0	1	1	1	.000	.333	.000	333	0	-0	0	0	0	1.000	-0	/O-1(0-0-1)	0.0
■ **MATT WILLIAMS**	Williams, Matthew Derrick b: 11/28/65, Bishop, Cal. BR/TR, 6'2", 210 lbs. Deb: 4/11/87																							
1987	SF-N	84	245	28	46	9	2	8	21	16	68	.188	.240	.339	579	54	-17	4	3	-0	.975	20	S-70,3-17	0.9
1988	SF-N	52	156	17	32	6	1	8	19	8	41	.205	.253	.410	663	91	-3	0	1	-0	.967	10	3-43,S-14	0.8
1989	*SF-N	84	292	31	59	18	1	18	50	14	72	.202	.244	.455	699	98	-3	1	2	-0	.961	6	3-73,S-30	0.4
1990	SF-N★	159	617	87	171	27	2	33	**122**	33	138	.277	.321	.488	809	124	17	7	4	0	.959	4	*3-159	2.1
1991	SF-N	157	589	72	158	24	5	34	98	33	128	.268	.314	.499	813	129	19	5	5	-1	.964	9	*3-155/S-4	2.9
1992	SF-N	146	529	58	120	13	5	20	66	39	109	.227	.287	.384	671	94	-6	7	7	-1	.945	7	*3-144	0.0
1993	SF-N	145	579	105	170	33	4	38	110	27	80	.294	.330	.561	891	137	27	1	3	-1	.970	3	*3-144	3.0
1994	SF-N★	112	445	74	119	16	3	**43**	96	33	87	.267	.321	.607	928	141	23	1	0	0	.963	9	*3-110	3.2
1995	SF-N†	76	283	53	95	17	1	23	65	30	58	.336	.403	.647	1050	177	30	2	0	0	.958	6	3-74	3.6
1996	SF-N†	105	404	69	122	16	1	22	85	39	91	.302	.372	.510	882	135	20	1	2	-0	.951	2	3-92,1-13/S-1	2.0
1997	*Cle-A	151	596	86	157	32	3	32	105	34	108	.263	.308	.488	796	100	-2	12	4	1	.970	7	*3-151	0.7
1998	Ari-N	135	510	72	136	26	1	20	71	43	102	.267	.327	.439	767	100	-1	5	1	1	.972	8	*3-134	0.8
1999	*Ari-N★	154	627	98	190	37	2	35	142	41	93	.303	.348	.536	884	118	15	2	0	1	.977	12	*3-153	2.7
2000	Ari-N	96	371	43	102	18	2	12	47	20	51	.275	.317	.431	749	86	-9	1	2	-0	.964	4	3-94/D-1	-0.5
Total	14	1656	6243	893	1677	292	33	346	1097	410	1226	.269	.319	.492	811	116	109	49	34	-1	.963	108	*3-1543,S-119/1-13,D	22.6
■ **OTTO WILLIAMS**	Williams, Otto George b: 11/2/1877, Newark, N.J. d: 3/19/37, Omaha, Neb. BR/TR, 5'8", 165 lbs. Deb: 10/5/02 C Career OF: (0-LF 8-CF 13-RF)																							
1902	StL-N	2	5	0	2	0	0	0	2	1		.400	.500	.400	900	186	1	1			.813	1	/S-2	0.2
1903	StL-N	53	187	10	38	4	2	0	9	9		.203	.240	.246	486	40	-15	6			.885	-5	S-52/2-1	-1.8
	Chi-N	38	130	14	29	5	0	0	13	4		.223	.246	.262	508	46	-9	8			.937	5	S-26/2-7,1-3,3-1	-0.4
	Yr	91	317	24	67	9	2	0	22	13		.211	.242	.252	495	42	-24	14			.904	0	S-78/2-8,1-3,3-1	-2.2
1904	Chi-N	57	185	21	37	4	1	0	8	13		.200	.256	.232	489	51	-10	9			.973	-0	O-21R,1-11,S-10,/23	-1.2
1906	Was-A	20	51	3	7	0	0	0	2	2		.137	.185	.137	322	1	-6	0			.897	1	/S-8,2-6,1-2,3-1	-0.6
Total	4	170	558	48	113	13	3	0	34	29		.203	.244	.237	481	43	-40	24			.905	1	/S-98,O-21R,2-20,13	-3.8
■ **REGGIE WILLIAMS**	Williams, Reginald Bernard b: 5/5/66, Laurens, S.C. BB/TR, 6'1", 180 lbs. Deb: 9/8/92																							
1992	Cal-A	14	26	5	6	1	1	0	2	1	10	.231	.259	.346	605	68	-1	0	2	-1	1.000	-1	O-12(0-12-0)/D-2	-0.3
1995	LA-N	15	11	2	1	0	0	0	1	2	3	.091	.231	.091	322	-12	-2	0	0	0	1.000	-4	O-14(10-1-4)	-0.6
1998	Ana-A	29	36	7	13	1	0	1	5	7	11	.361	.477	.472	949	147	3	3	3	-0	1.000	-6	O-24(19-5-2)/D-2	-0.3
1999	Ana-A	30	63	8	14	1	2	1	6	5	21	.222	.290	.349	639	62	-4	2	1	0	.974	-1	O-24(4-3-18)/D-4	-0.5
Total	4	88	136	22	34	3	3	2	14	15	45	.250	.333	.360	694	82	-4	5	6	-1	.989	-12	/O-74(33-21-24),D-8	-1.7
■ **REGGIE WILLIAMS**	Williams, Reginald Dewayne b: 8/29/60, Memphis, Tenn. BR/TR, 5'11", 185 lbs. Deb: 9/2/85																							
1985	LA-N	22	9	4	3	0	0	0	0	0	4	.333	.333	.333	667	90	-0	1	0	0	.900	-3	O-15(12-2-1)	-0.4
1986	LA-N	128	303	35	84	14	2	4	32	23	57	.277	.332	.376	709	102	1	9	3	1	.984	-16	*O-124(26-79-35)	-1.7
1987	LA-N	39	36	6	4	0	0	0	4	5	9	.111	.220	.111	331	-9	-6	1	1	-0	.913	-8	O-30(16-6-9)	-1.4
1988	Cle-A	11	31	7	7	2	0	1	3	0	6	.226	.226	.387	613	66	-1	0	0	0	1.000	-2	O-11(10-0-3)	-0.4
Total	4	200	379	52	98	16	2	5	39	28	76	.259	.313	.351	664	87	-7	11	4	1	.974	-29	O-180(64-87-48)	-3.9
■ **DICK WILLIAMS**	Williams, Richard Hirschfeld b: 5/7/29, St.Louis, Mo. BR/TR, 6', 190 lbs. Deb: 6/10/51 MC Career OF: (283-LF 156-CF 64-RF)																							
1951	Bro-N	23	60	5	12	3	1	1	5	4	10	.200	.250	.333	583	54	-4	0	0	0	1.000	-2	O-15(15-0-0)	-0.7
1952	Bro-N	36	68	13	21	4	1	0	11	2	10	.309	.329	.397	726	99	-0	0	0	0	1.000	-2	O-25(19-6-0)/1-1,3-1	-0.3
1953	*Bro-N	30	55	4	12	2	0	2	5	3	10	.218	.271	.364	635	62	-3	0	0	0	.923	-7	O-24(17-2-9)	-1.1
1954	Bro-N	16	34	5	5	0	0	1	2	2	7	.147	.194	.235	430	11	-5	0	0	0	1.000	-4	O-14(13-2-0)	-0.9
1956	Bro-N	7	7	0	2	0	0	0	0	0	1	.286	.286	.286	571	50	-0	0	0	0	.000	0	H	0.0
	Bal-A	87	353	45	101	18	4	11	37	30	40	.286	.342	.453	795	117	7	5	5	-1	.990	-3	O-81C,1-10,2-10,/3	0.0
1957	Bal-A	47	167	16	39	10	2	1	17	14	21	.234	.293	.335	628	76	-6	0	1	-0	1.000	0	O-26L,3-15,1-12	-0.8
	Cle-A	67	205	33	58	7	0	6	17	12	19	.283	.326	.405	731	99	-1	3	4	-1	.973	-3	O-37(18-20-0),3-19	-0.6
	Yr	114	372	49	97	17	2	7	34	26	40	.261	.311	.374	684	89	-6	3	5	-1	.984	-2	O-63C,3-34,1-12	-1.4
1958	Bal-A	128	409	36	113	17	0	4	32	37	47	.276	.339	.347	686	94	-3	0	6	-2	1.000	-9	O-70C,3-45,1-26,/2	-1.9
1959	KC-A	130	488	72	130	33	1	16	75	28	60	.266	.313	.436	749	102	-0	4	1	1	.957	-8	3-80,1-32,O-23L,/2	-1.1
1960	KC-A	127	420	47	121	31	0	12	65	39	68	.288	.350	.448	798	113	7	0	0	0	.951	5	3-57,1-34,O-25L	0.9
1961	Bal-A	103	310	37	64	15	2	8	24	20	38	.206	.255	.345	600	61	-19	0	4	-1	.968	-10	O-75(73-2-2),1-20/3-2	-3.5
1962	Bal-A	82	178	20	44	7	1	1	18	14	26	.247	.306	.315	620	72	-7	0	0	0	1.000	-2	O-29(21-0-9),1-21/3-4	-1.2
1963	Bos-A	79	136	15	35	8	0	2	12	15	25	.257	.331	.360	691	91	-1	0	0	0	.976	-6	3-17,1-11/O-7(7-0-0)	-0.9
1964	Bos-A	61	69	10	11	2	0	5	11	7	10	.159	.247	.406	653	74	-3	0	0	0	1.000	5	1-21,3-13/O-5(4-1-0)	0.2
Total	13	1023	2959	358	768	157	12	70	331	227	392	.260	.315	.392	707	92	-37	12	21	-5	.989	-46	O-456L,3-257,1-188,/2	-11.9
■ **RINALDO WILLIAMS**	Williams, Rinaldo Lewis b: 12/18/1893, Santa Cruz, Cal. d: 4/24/66, Cottonwood, Ariz. BL/TR, Deb: 10/8/14																							
1914	Bro-F	4	15	1	4	2	0	0	0	0	0	.267	.267	.400	667	81	-1	0			.923	-0	/3-4	-0.1
■ **BOB WILLIAMS**	Williams, Robert Elias b: 4/27/1884, Monday, Ohio d: 8/6/62, Nelsonville, Ohio BR/TR, 6', 190 lbs. Deb: 7/3/11																							
1911	NY-A	20	47	3	9	2	0	0	8	5		.191	.269	.234	503	38	-4	1			.942	-1	C-20	-0.3
1912	NY-A	20	44	7	6	1	0	0	3	9		.136	.283	.159	442	26	-4	0			.930	-2	C-20	-0.5
1913	NY-A	6	19	0	3	0	0	0	0	1	3	.158	.200	.158	358	5	-2	0			.971	0	/C-6	-0.2
Total	3	46	110	10	18	3	0	0	11	15	3	.164	.264	.191	455	28	-10	1			.941	-2	/C-46	-1.0

YEAR	TM/L	G	AB	R	H	2B	3B	HR	RBI	BB	SO	AVG	OBP	SLG	OPS	OPS+	BR+	SB	CS	SBR	FA	FR	G/POS	TPR
■ TED WILLIAMS	Williams, Theodore Samuel "The Kid," "The Thumper" or "The Splendid Splinter" b: 8/30/18, San Diego, Cal. BL/TR, 6'3", 205 lbs. Deb: 4/20/39 MH Career OF: (1984-LF 0-CF 169-RF)																							
1939	Bos-A	149	565	131	185	44	11	31	**145**	107	64	.327	.436	.609	1045	158	51	2	1	0	.945	2	*O-149(0-0-149)	4.0
1940	Bos-A★	144	561	**134**	193	43	14	23	113	96	54	.344	**.442**	.594	1036	159	52	4	4	-1	.960	1	*O-143(128-0-16)/P-1	4.0
1941	Bos-A★	143	456	**135**	185	33	3	**37**	120	**145**	27	**.406**	**.551**	**.735**	**1286**	**232**	**98**	2	4	-1	.961	-5	*O-133(130-0-4)	**8.0**
1942	Bos-A★	150	522	**141**	186	34	5	**36**	**137**	**145**	51	**.356**	**.499**	**.648**	**1147**	**214**	**87**	3	2	-0	.988	3	*O-150(150-0-0)	**8.0**
1946	*Bos-A★	150	514	**142**	176	37	8	38	123	**156**	44	.342	**.497**	**.667**	**1164**	**211**	**85**	0	0	0	.971	-0	*O-150(150-0-0)	**7.5**
1947	Bos-A★	156	528	**125**	181	40	9	**32**	**114**	**162**	47	**.343**	**.499**	**.634**	**1133**	**199**	**80**	0	1	-0	.975	1	*O-156(156-0-0)	**6.9**
1948	Bos-A★	137	509	124	188	**44**	3	25	127	**126**	41	**.369**	**.497**	**.615**	**1112**	**185**	**68**	4	0	1	.983	0	*O-134(134-0-0)	5.6
1949	Bos-A★	155	566	**150**	194	**39**	3	**43**	**159**	**162**	48	.343	**.490**	**.650**	**1141**	**187**	**77**	1	1	-0	.983	3	*O-155(155-0-0)	**6.4**
1950	Bos-A★	89	334	82	106	24	1	28	97	82	21	.317	.452	.647	1099	163	33	3	0	1	.956	-4	O-86(86-0-0)	2.1
1951	Bos-A★	148	531	109	169	28	4	30	126	**144**	45	.318	**.464**	**.556**	**1019**	159	**50**	1	1	-0	.988	3	*O-147(147-0-0)	**4.0**
1952	Bos-A	6	10	2	4	0	1	1	3	2	2	.400	.500	.900	1400	264	2	0	0	0	1.000	-0	/O-2(2-0-0)	0.2
1953	Bos-A†	37	91	17	37	6	0	13	34	19	10	.407	.509	.901	1410	261	21	0	1	-0	.970	-4	O-26(26-0-0)	1.5
1954	Bos-A★	117	386	93	133	23	1	29	89	**136**	32	.345	**.516**	.635	**1151**	**193**	**58**	0	0	0	.982	-3	*O-115(115-0-0)	4.9
1955	Bos-A★	98	320	77	114	21	3	28	83	91	24	.356	.501	.703	1204	203	50	2	0	1	.989	-1	O-93(93-0-0)	4.3
1956	Bos-A★	136	400	71	138	28	2	24	82	102	39	.345	**.479**	.605	1084	164	42	0	0	0	.973	-4	*O-110(110-0-0)	3.0
1957	Bos-A★	132	420	96	163	28	1	38	87	119	43	**.388**	**.528**	**.731**	**1259**	**227**	82	0	1	-0	.995	-3	*O-125(125-0-0)	7.1
1958	Bos-A★	129	411	81	135	23	2	26	85	98	49	**.328**	**.462**	.584	**1046**	174	47	1	0	0	.957	-12	*O-114(114-0-0)	2.8
1959	Bos-A★	103	272	32	69	15	0	10	43	52	27	.254	.377	.419	796	113	6	0	0	0	.970	-8	O-76(76-0-0)	-0.6
1960	Bos-A★	113	310	56	98	15	0	29	72	75	41	.316	.454	.645	1099	187	41	1	1	-0	.993	-2	O-87(87-0-0)	3.3
Total	19	2292	7706	1798	2654	525	71	521	1839	2019	709	.344	.483	.634	1116	186	1029	24	17	-1	.974	-34	*O-2151L/P-1	83.0
■ WALT WILLIAMS	Williams, Walter Allen "No-Neck" b: 12/19/43, Brownwood, Tex. BR/TR, 5'6", 185 lbs. Deb: 4/21/64 C Career OF: (242-LF 13-CF 338-RF)																							
1964	Hou-N	10	9	1	0	0	0	0	0	0	2	.000	.000	.000	0	-99	-2	1	0	0	1.000	-1	/O-5(5-0-0)	-0.3
1967	Chi-A	104	275	35	66	16	3	3	15	17	20	.240	.289	.353	642	92	-3	3	2	-0	.983	-2	O-73(59-0-21)	-1.1
1968	Chi-A	63	133	6	32	6	0	1	8	4	17	.241	.273	.308	582	75	-4	0	1	-0	1.000	-2	O-34(9-0-28)	-1.0
1969	Chi-A	135	471	59	143	22	1	3	32	26	33	.304	.344	.374	718	96	-2	6	2	1	.985	2	*O-111(34-0-83)	-0.6
1970	Chi-A	110	315	43	79	18	1	3	15	19	30	.251	.298	.343	640	73	-12	3	3	-0	.949	2	O-79(13-3-64)	-1.5
1971	Chi-A	114	361	43	106	17	3	8	35	24	27	.294	.346	.424	770	114	6	5	5	-1	1.000	-2	O-90(35-0-62)/3-1	-0.2
1972	Chi-A	77	221	22	55	7	1	2	11	13	20	.249	.291	.317	607	79	-6	6	1	1	.990	1	O-57(5-0-53)/3-1	-0.8
1973	Cle-A	104	350	43	101	15	1	8	38	14	29	.289	.318	.406	724	101	-1	9	4	1	.970	5	O-61(61-0-0),D-26	0.1
1974	NY-A	43	53	5	6	0	0	0	3	1	10	.113	.130	.113	243	-30	-9	1	0	0	.955	-6	O-24(13-0-13)/D-3	-1.6
1975	NY-A	82	185	27	52	5	1	5	16	8	23	.281	.321	.400	721	105	1	0	1	-0	.982	-3	O-31R,D-17/2-6	-0.4
Total	10	842	2373	284	640	106	11	33	173	126	211	.270	.311	.365	677	91	-33	34	19	1	.981	-6	O-565R/D-46,2-6,3-2	-7.4
■ WASH WILLIAMS	Williams, Washington J. b: Philadelphia, Pa. d: 1/1890, Philadelphia, Pa. 5'11", 180 lbs. Deb: 8/5/1884																							
1884	Ric-a	2	8	0	2	0	0	0		0		.250	.250	.250	500	64	-0				.500	-1	/O-2(0-0-2)	-0.1
1885	Chi-N	1	4	0	1	0	0	0	0	0	0	.250	.250	.250	500	54	-0				.500	-0	/O-1(0-0-1),P-1	-0.1
Total	2	3	12	0	3	0	0	0	0	0	0	.250	.250	.250	500	61	-1				.500	-1	/O-3(0-0-3),P-1	-0.2
■ BILLY WILLIAMS	Williams, William b: 6/13/33, Newberry, S.C. BL/TR, 6'3", 195 lbs. Deb: 8/15/69																							
1969	Sea-A	4	10	1	0	0	0	0	0	1	3	.000	.167	.000	167	-51	-2	0	0	0	1.000	1	/O-3(0-0-3)	-0.2
■ WOODY WILLIAMS	Williams, Woodrow Wilson b: 8/21/12, Pamplin, Va. d: 2/24/95, Appomattox, Va. BR/TR, 5'11", 175 lbs. Deb: 9/5/38																							
1938	Bro-N	20	51	6	17	1	1	0	6	4	1	.333	.382	.392	774	111	1	1			.931	-7	S-18/3-1	-0.5
1943	Cin-N	30	69	8	26	2	1	0	11	1	3	.377	.386	.435	820	139	3	0			.986	1	2-12/3-7,S-5	0.5
1944	Cin-N	155	653	73	157	23	3	1	35	44	24	.240	.290	.289	580	66	-30	7			**.971**	15	*2-155	-0.6
1945	Cin-N	133	482	46	114	14	0	0	27	39	24	.237	.296	.266	562	58	-27	6			.969	-10	*2-133	-3.0
Total	4	338	1255	133	314	40	5	1	79	88	52	.250	.301	.292	594	69	-52	14			.971	-1	2-300/S-23,3-8	-3.6
■ ANTONE WILLIAMSON	Williamson, Anthony Joseph b: 7/18/73, Harbor City, Cal. BL/TR, 6'1", 195 lbs. Deb: 5/31/97																							
1997	Mil-A	24	54	2	11	3	0	0	6	4	8	.204	.259	.259	518	35	-5	0	1	-0	.977	-1	1-14/D-4	-0.7
■ NED WILLIAMSON	Williamson, Edward Nagle b: 10/24/1857, Philadelphia, Pa. d: 3/3/1894, Mountain Valley Springs, Ark BR/TR, 5'11", 210 lbs. Deb: 5/1/1878																							
1878	Ind-N	63	250	31	58	10	2	1	19	5	15	.232	.247	.300	547	91	-1				.867	-4	*3-63	-0.3
1879	Chi-N	80	320	66	94	20	13	1	36	24	31	.294	.343	.447	790	149	17				**.871**	17	*3-70/1-6,C-4	3.2
1880	Chi-N	75	311	65	78	20	2	0	31	15	26	.251	.285	.328	613	101	0				**.893**	12	*3-63,C-11/2-3	1.4
1881	Chi-N	82	343	56	92	12	6	1	48	19	19	.268	.307	.347	654	100	-0				**.909**	22	*3-76/2-4,P-3,SC	2.3
1882	Chi-N	83	348	66	98	27	4	3	60	27	21	.282	.333	.408	741	130	12				**.881**	16	*3-83/P-1	2.6
1883	Chi-N	98	402	83	111	**49**	5	2	59	22	48	.276	.314	.438	751	116	6				.807	18	*3-97/C-3,P-1	2.2
1884	Chi-N	107	417	84	116	18	8	**27**	84	42	56	.278	.344	.554	898	164	29				.861	24	*3-99,C-10/P-2	4.8
1885	*Chi-N	113	407	87	97	16	5	3	65	**75**	60	.238	.357	.324	681	107	4				**.892**	12	*3-113/P-2,C-1	1.6
1886	*Chi-N	121	430	69	93	17	8	6	58	80	71	.216	.339	.335	674	92	-4	13			.869	-2	*S-121/C-4,P-2	-0.2
1887	Chi-N	127	512	77	190	20	14	9	78	73	57	.371	.377	.437	815	111	6	45			.890	-31	*S-127/P-1	-1.8
1888	Chi-N	132	452	75	113	9	14	8	73	65	71	.250	.352	.385	737	126	15	25			.884	-12	*S-132	0.7
1889	Chi-N	47	173	16	41	3	1	1	30	23	22	.237	.340	.283	623	71	-6	2			.844	-24	S-47	-2.5
1890	Chi-P	73	261	34	51	7	3	2	26	36	35	.195	.311	.268	580	53	-17	3			.809	-20	3-52,S-21	-2.9
Total	13	1201	4626	809	1232	228	85	64	667	506	532	.266	.332	.384	716	111	59	88			.866	28	3-716,S-450/C-34,P21	11.1
■ HOWIE WILLIAMSON	Williamson, Nathaniel Howard b: 12/23/04, Little Rock, Ark. d: 8/15/69, Texarkana, Ark. BL/TL, 6', 170 lbs. Deb: 7/7/28																							
1928	StL-N	10	9	0	2	0	0	0	0	1	4	.222	.300	.222	522	38	-1	0			.000	0	H	-0.1
■ JULIUS WILLIGROD	Willigrod, Julius b: Iowa d: 11/27/06, San Francisco, Cal BL, Deb: 7/15/1882																							
1882	Det-N	1	3	0	1	0	0	0	1	0	1	.333	.333	.333	667	115	0				1.000	-1	/S-1	-0.1
	Cle-N	9	36	5	5	1	1	0	2	3	7	.139	.205	.222	427	38	-2				.813	-3	/O-9(0-9-1)	-0.5
	Yr	10	39	5	6	1	1	0	3	3	8	.154	.214	.231	445	44	-2				.813	-3	/O-9(0-9-1),S-1	-0.6
■ HUGH WILLINGHAM	Willingham, Thomas Hugh b: 5/30/06, Dalhart, Tex. d: 6/15/88, ElReno, Okla. BR/TR, 6', 180 lbs. Deb: 9/13/30 Career OF: (1-LF 0-CF 0-RF)																							
1930	Chi-A	3	4	2	1	0	0	0	0	2	1	.250	.500	.250	750	100	0	0	0	0	1.000	-0	/2-1	0.0
1931	Phi-N	23	35	5	9	2	1	1	3	2	9	.257	.297	.457	754	93	-0	0			.875	0	/S-8,3-2,O-1(1-0-0)	0.0
1932	Phi-N	4	2	0	0	0	0	0	0	0	0	.000	.000	.000	0	-89	-1	0			.000	0	H	-0.1
1933	Phi-N	1	1	0	0	0	0	0	0	0	0	.000	.000	.000	0	-89	-0	0			.000	0	H	0.0
Total	4	31	42	7	10	2	1	1	3	4	10	.238	.304	.405	709	82	-1	0	0		.875	-0	/S-8,3-2,O-1L,2-1	-0.1
■ WILLS	Wills Deb: 5/14/1884																							
1884	Was-a	4	15	1	2	2	0	0		0		.133	.133	.267	400	31	-1				.889	2	/O-4(1-3-0)	0.0
	KC-U	5	21	2	3	1	0	0		0		.143	.143	.190	333	0	-3				1.000	1	/O-5(0-5-0)	-0.3
Total	1	9	36	3	5	3	0	0		0		.139	.139	.222	361	13	-4				.938	2	/O-9(1-8-0)	-0.3
■ DAVE WILLS	Wills, Davis Bowles b: 1/26/1877, Charlottesville, Va. d: 10/12/59, Washington, D.C. BL/TL, Deb: 6/8/1899																							
1899	Lou-N	24	94	15	21	3	1	0	12	2		.223	.240	.277	516	41	-8	1			.957	-3	1-24	-1.0
■ BUMP WILLS	Wills, Elliott Taylor b: 7/27/52, Washington, D.C. BB/TR, 5'9", 177 lbs. Deb: 4/7/77 F																							
1977	Tex-A	152	541	87	155	28	6	9	62	65	96	.287	.363	.410	773	109	8	28	12	2	.982	3	*2-150/S-2,1-1,D-1	2.1
1978	Tex-A	157	539	78	135	17	4	9	57	63	91	.250	.333	.347	680	91	-5	52	14	7	.981	21	*2-156	3.2
1979	Tex-A	146	543	90	148	21	3	5	46	53	58	.273	.342	.350	692	88	-8	35	11	4	.976	8	*2-146	1.2
1980	Tex-A	146	578	102	152	31	5	5	58	51	71	.263	.326	.360	686	90	-7	34	9	4	.984	19	*2-144	2.3
1981	Tex-A	102	410	51	103	13	2	2	41	32	49	.251	.307	.307	614	82	-9	12	9	-1	.983	9	*2-101/D-1	0.4
1982	Chi-N	128	419	64	114	18	4	6	38	46	76	.272	.351	.377	728	101	2	35	10	4	.963	-18	*2-103	-0.7
Total	6	831	3030	472	807	128	24	36	302	310	441	.266	.338	.360	698	94	-20	196	65	20	.979	41	2-800/D-2,S-2,1-1	8.5

YEAR	TM/L	G	AB	R	H	2B	3B	HR	RBI	BB	SO	AVG	OBP	SLG	OPS	OPS+	BR+	SB	CS	SBR	FA	FR	G/POS	TPR
■ **MAURY WILLS** Wills, Maurice Morning b: 10/2/32, Washington, D.C. BB/TR, 5′11″, 170 lbs. Deb: 6/6/59 FM																								
1959	*LA-N	83	242	27	63	5	2	0	7	13	27	.260	.298	.298	596	55	-15	7	3	0	.966	2	S-82	-0.6
1960	LA-N	148	516	75	152	15	2	0	27	35	47	.295	.343	.331	674	80	-12	**50**	12	**7**	.945	21	*S-145	2.7
1961	LA-N★	148	613	105	173	12	10	1	31	59	50	.282	.346	.339	686	76	-19	**35**	15	2	.959	12	*S-148	0.8
1962	LA-N★	165	695	130	208	13	**10**	6	48	51	57	.299	.349	.373	722	100	0	**104**	13	**18**	.956	-5	*S-165	2.8
1963	*LA-N☆	134	527	83	159	19	3	0	34	44	48	.302	.357	.349	706	112	9	**40**	19	2	.959	-5	*S-109,3-33	1.6
1964	LA-N	158	630	81	173	15	5	2	34	41	73	.275	.319	.324	643	88	-10	**53**	17	**6**	.963	-8	*S-149/3-6	0.1
1965	*LA-N★	158	650	92	186	14	7	0	33	40	64	.286	.331	.329	661	93	-6	**94**	31	**10**	.970	21	*S-155	4.0
1966	*LA-N★	143	594	60	162	14	2	1	39	34	60	.273	.314	.308	622	80	-16	38	24	-0	.967	9	*S-139/3-4	0.6
1967	Pit-N	149	616	92	186	12	9	3	45	31	44	.302	.336	.365	702	100	0	29	10	3	.948	9	*3-144/S-2	1.3
1968	Pit-N	153	627	76	174	12	6	0	31	45	57	.278	.327	.316	643	95	-3	52	21	4	.957	-9	*3-141,S-10	-0.9
1969	Mon-N	47	189	23	42	3	0	0	8	20	21	.222	.297	.238	535	51	-12	15	6	1	.950	-3	S-46/2-1	-0.8
	LA-N	104	434	57	129	7	8	4	39	39	40	.297	.357	.378	734	114	8	25	15	0	.969	7	*S-104	2.9
	Yr	151	623	80	171	10	8	4	47	59	61	.274	.338	.335	674	94	-4	40	21	1	.963	4	*S-150/2-1	2.1
1970	LA-N	132	522	77	141	19	3	0	34	50	34	.270	.334	.318	652	79	-14	28	13	2	.959	-19	*S-126/3-4	-1.7
1971	LA-N	149	601	73	169	14	3	3	44	40	44	.281	.326	.329	656	92	-7	15	8	1	.978	1	*S-144/3-4	1.3
1972	LA-N	71	132	16	17	3	1	0	4	10	18	.129	.190	.167	357	2	-17	1	1	-0	.984	-4	S-31,3-26	-1.9
Total	14	1942	7588	1067	2134	177	71	20	458	552	684	.281	.331	.331	662	88	-114	586	208	56	.963	30	*S-1555,3-362/2-1	12.2
■ **KID WILLSON** Willson, Frank Hoxie b: 11/3/1895, Bloomington, Neb. d: 4/17/64, Union Gap, Wash. BL/TL, 6′1″, 190 lbs. Deb: 7/2/18																								
1918	Chi-A	4	1	2	0	0	0	0	0	1	1	.000	.500	.000	500	50	0	0			.000	0	H	0.0
1927	Chi-A	7	10	1	1	0	0	0	1	0	2	.100	.100	.100	200	-49	-2	0	0	0	1.000	0	/O-2(1-1-0)	-0.2
Total	2	11	11	3	1	0	0	0	1	1	3	.091	.167	.091	258	-31	-2	0	0		1.000	0	/O-2(1-1-0)	-0.2
■ **WALT WILMOT** Wilmot, Walter Robert b: 10/18/1863, Plover, Wis. d: 2/1/29, Chicago, Ill. BB/TR, 5′9″, 165 lbs. Deb: 4/20/1888																								
1888	Was-N	119	473	61	106	16	9	4	43	23	55	.224	.263	.321	584	91	-5	46			.872	11	*O-119(119-0-0)	0.3
1889	Was-N	108	432	88	125	19	**19**	9	57	51	32	.289	.367	.484	851	146	26	40			.927	15	*O-108(107-1-0)	3.2
1890	Chi-N	139	571	114	159	15	13	**13**	99	64	44	.278	.353	.419	772	120	13	76			.938	13	*O-139(27-112-0)	1.8
1891	Chi-N	121	498	102	137	14	10	11	71	55	21	.275	.353	.410	763	122	13	42			.922	-5	*O-121(62-60-0)	0.4
1892	Chi-N	92	380	47	82	7	7	2	35	40	20	.216	.297	.287	584	76	-11	31			.903	2	O-92(92-0-0)	-1.6
1893	Chi-N	94	392	69	118	14	14	3	61	40	8	.301	.367	.431	798	114	7	39			.873	-0	*O-93(84-10-0)	-0.2
1894	Chi-N	135	604	136	199	45	12	5	130	36	27	.329	.368	.469	837	95	-8	76			.870	-7	*O-135(135-0-0)	-2.1
1895	Chi-N	108	466	86	132	16	6	8	72	30	19	.283	.327	.395	721	80	-16	28			.914	4	*O-108(108-0-0)	-1.8
1897	NY-N	11	34	8	9	2	0	1	4	2		.265	.306	.412	717	91	-1	1			.938	0	/O-9(5-1-3)	-0.1
1898	NY-N	35	138	16	33	4	2	2	22	9		.239	.286	.341	626	82	-4	4			.886	-5	O-34(6-0-29)	-1.0
Total	10	962	3988	727	1100	152	92	58	594	350	226	.276	.337	.404	741	105	15	383			.903	27	O-958(745-184-32)	-1.1
■ **ARCHIE WILSON** Wilson, Archie Clifton b: 11/25/23, Los Angeles, Cal. BR/TR, 6′, 175 lbs. Deb: 9/18/51																								
1951	NY-A	4	4	0	0	0	0	0	0	0	0	.000	.200	.000	200	-44	-1	0	0	0	1.000	-0	/O-2(0-0-2)	-0.1
1952	NY-A	3	2	0	1	0	0	0	1	0	0	.500	.500	.500	1000	190	0	0	0	0	.000	0	H	0.0
	Was-A	26	96	8	20	2	3	0	14	5	11	.208	.255	.292	547	54	-6	0	0	0	.971	1	O-24(14-10-0)	-0.7
	Bos-A	18	38	1	10	3	0	0	2	2	3	.263	.300	.342	642	73	-1	0	0	0	.944	-2	O-13(2-2-9)	-0.4
	Yr	47	136	9	31	5	3	0	17	7	14	.228	.271	.309	580	61	-8	0	0	0	.966	-1	O-37(16-12-9)	-1.1
Total	2	51	140	9	31	5	3	0	17	7	14	.221	.268	.300	568	58	-8	0	0	0	.967	-1	/O-39(16-12-11)	-1.2
■ **ART WILSON** Wilson, Arthur Earl "Dutch" b: 12/11/1885, Macon, Ill. d: 6/12/60, Chicago, Ill. BR/TR, 5′8″, 170 lbs. Deb: 9/29/08																								
1908	NY-N	1	0	0	0	0	0	0	0	0		—	—	—	—	—	0	0			.000	0	R	0.0
1909	NY-N	19	42	4	10	2	1	0	5	4		.238	.304	.333	638	96	-0	0			.985	-4	C-19	-0.4
1910	NY-N	26	52	10	14	4	1	0	5	9	6	.269	.387	.385	772	125	2	2			.975	-1	C-25/1-1	0.3
1911	*NY-N	66	109	17	33	9	1	1	17	19	12	.303	.411	.431	842	132	5	6			.963	-6	C-64	0.2
1912	*NY-N	65	121	17	35	6	0	3	19	13	14	.289	.358	.413	771	107	1	2			.960	1	C-61	0.5
1913	*NY-N	54	79	5	15	0	1	0	8	11	11	.190	.289	.215	504	45	-5	1			.965	6	C-49	0.3
1914	Chi-F	137	440	78	128	31	8	10	64	70	80	.291	.394	.466	860	142	20	13			.974	14	*C-132	4.6
1915	Chi-F	96	269	44	82	11	2	7	31	65	38	.305	.442	.439	880	157	21	8			.980	-8	C-87	2.1
1916	Pit-N	53	128	11	33	5	2	1	12	13	27	.258	.331	.352	683	109	2	4			.981	-9	C-39	-0.5
	Chi-N	36	114	5	22	3	1	0	5	6	14	.193	.233	.237	470	40	-8	1			.953	-4	C-34	-1.0
	Yr	89	242	16	55	8	3	1	17	19	41	.227	.286	.298	584	76	-7	5			.967	-13	C-73	-1.5
1917	Chi-N	81	211	17	45	9	2	2	25	32	36	.213	.322	.303	626	85	-3	6			.968	7	C-75	1.2
1918	Bos-N	89	280	15	69	8	2	0	19	24	31	.246	.310	.289	600	87	-4	5			.977	-10	C-85	-0.8
1919	Bos-N	71	191	14	49	8	1	0	16	25	19	.257	.346	.309	655	102	1	2			.977	-2	C-64/1-1	0.5
1920	Bos-N	16	19	0	1	0	0	0	0	1	1	.053	.143	.053	195	-44	-4	0	0	0	1.000	-2	/3-6,C-2	-0.5
1921	Cle-A	2	1	0	0	0	0	0	0	0	0	.000	.000	.000	0	-99	-0	0	0	0	1.000	0	/C-2	0.0
Total	14	812	2056	237	536	96	22	24	226	292	289	.261	.357	.364	721	110	29	50	0		.972	-18	C-738/3-6,1-2	6.5
■ **ARTIE WILSON** Wilson, Arthur Lee b: 10/28/20, Springfield, Ala. BL/TR, 5′10″, 162 lbs. Deb: 4/18/51																								
1951	NY-N	19	22	2	4	0	0	0	1	2	1	.182	.250	.182	432	18	-2	2	0	0	1.000	3	/2-3,S-3,1-2	0.1
■ **CHARLIE WILSON** Wilson, Charles Woodrow "Swamp Baby" b: 1/13/05, Clinton, S.C. d: 12/19/70, Rochester, N.Y. BB/TR, 5′10.5″, 178 lbs. Deb: 4/14/31																								
1931	Bos-N	16	58	7	11	4	0	1	11	3	5	.190	.230	.310	540	45	-5	0			.917	-2	3-14	-0.7
1932	StL-N	24	96	7	19	3	3	1	2	3	8	.198	.222	.323	545	43	-8	0			.935	-7	S-24	-1.3
1933	StL-N	1	1	0	0	0	0	0	0	0	1	.000	.000	.000	0	-95	-0	0			.000	0	/S-1	0.0
1935	StL-N	16	31	1	10	0	0	0	1	2	2	.323	.364	.323	686	83	-1	0			.933	-1	/3-8	-0.1
Total	4	57	186	15	40	7	3	2	14	8	16	.215	.247	.317	565	50	-13	0			.935	-10	/S-25,3-22	-2.1
■ **CRAIG WILSON** Wilson, Craig b: 11/28/64, Annapolis, Md. BR/TR, 5′11″, 175 lbs. Deb: 9/6/89 Career OF: (13-LF 0-CF 10-RF)																								
1989	StL-N	6	4	1	1	0	0	0	1	1	2	.250	.400	.250	650	87	-0	0	0	0	.500	-0	/3-2	0.0
1990	StL-N	55	121	13	30	2	0	0	7	8	14	.248	.295	.264	559	55	-7	0	2	-1	.971	-0	3-13,O-13L/2-9,1-1	-0.9
1991	StL-N	60	82	5	14	2	0	0	13	6	10	.171	.227	.195	422	20	-9	0	0	0	.905	-1	3-12/O-5L,1-4,2-3	-1.1
1992	StL-N	61	106	6	33	6	0	0	13	10	18	.311	.371	.368	739	113	2	1	2	-0	.970	-3	3-18,2-11/O-3(0-0-3)	-0.1
1993	KC-A	21	49	6	13	1	0	1	3	7	6	.265	.357	.347	704	85	-1	1	1	-0	1.000	-3	3-15/2-1,O-1(1-0-0)	-0.4
Total	5	203	362	31	91	11	0	1	37	32	50	.251	.312	.290	602	68	-15	2	5	-1	.957	-8	/3-60,2-24,O-22L,1	-2.5
■ **CRAIG WILSON** Wilson, Craig Franklin b: 9/3/70, Chicago, Ill. BR/TR, 6′, 185 lbs. Deb: 9/5/98																								
1998	Chi-A	13	47	14	22	5	0	3	10	3	6	.468	.500	.766	1266	229	9	1	0	0	1.000	-3	/S-8,2-4,3-2	0.6
1999	Chi-A	98	252	28	60	8	1	4	26	23	22	.238	.302	.325	627	60	-15	1	1	-0	.969	4	3-72,S-22/2-7,1D	-0.9
2000	Chi-A	28	73	12	19	3	0	0	4	5	11	.260	.316	.301	618	57	-5	1	0	0	.938	8	3-15,S-10/2-4	0.4
Total	3	139	372	54	101	16	1	7	40	31	39	.272	.329	.376	706	80	-11	3	1	0	.964	9	/3-89,S-40,2-15,D1	0.1
■ **DAN WILSON** Wilson, Daniel Allen b: 3/25/69, Arlington Heights, Ill. BR/TR, 6′3″, 190 lbs. Deb: 9/7/92																								
1992	Cin-N	12	25	2	9	1	0	0	3	3	8	.360	.429	.400	829	132	1	0	0	0	1.000	0	/C-9	0.2
1993	Cin-N	36	76	6	17	3	0	0	8	9	16	.224	.306	.263	569	54	-5	0	0	0	.994	-0	C-35	-0.4
1994	Sea-A	91	282	24	61	14	2	3	27	10	57	.216	.246	.312	558	42	-25	1	2	-0	.986	6	C-91	-1.4
1995	*Sea-A	119	399	40	111	22	3	9	51	33	63	.278	.336	.416	752	94	-4	2	1	0	.995	10	*C-119	1.3
1996	Sea-A★	138	491	51	140	24	0	18	83	32	88	.285	.333	.444	777	94	-5	1	2	-0	.996	-2	*C-135	0.0
1997	*Sea-A	146	508	66	137	31	1	15	74	39	72	.270	.328	.423	751	95	-4	7	2	1	.995	1	*C-144	0.6
1998	Sea-A	96	325	39	82	17	1	9	44	24	56	.252	.314	.394	707	82	-9	2	1	0	.994	-9	C-94	-1.1
1999	Sea-A	123	414	46	110	23	2	7	38	29	83	.266	.317	.382	698	79	-13	5	0	1	.995	3	*C-121/1-5	-0.3
2000	*Sea-A	90	268	31	63	12	0	5	27	22	51	.235	.293	.336	629	60	-16	1	2	-0	.990	-1	C-88/1-1,3-1	-1.2
Total	9	851	2788	305	730	147	9	66	355	201	494	.262	.316	.392	708	81	-81	19	10	1	.994	8	C-836/1-6,3-1	-2.3

YEAR	TM/L	G	AB	R	H	2B	3B	HR	RBI	BB	SO	AVG	OBP	SLG	OPS	OPS+	BR+	SB	CS	SBR	FA	FR	G/POS	TPR
■ DESI WILSON	Wilson, Desi Bernard b: 5/9/69, Glen Cove, N.Y. BL/TL, 6'7", 230 lbs. Deb: 8/7/96																							
1996	SF-N	41	118	10	32	2	0	2	12	12	27	.271	.338	.339	677	83	-3	0	2	-1	.984	-1	1-33	-0.7
■ EDDIE WILSON	Wilson, Edward Francis b: 9/7/09, Hamden, Conn. d: 4/11/79, Hamden, Conn. BL/TL, 5'11", 165 lbs. Deb: 6/21/36																							
1936	Bro-N	52	173	28	60	8	1	3	25	14	25	.347	.402	.457	859	129	7	3			.926	-5	O-47(0-0-47)	-0.1
1937	Bro-N	36	54	11	12	4	1	1	8	17	14	.222	.408	.389	797	116	2	1			.966	-3	O-21(0-1-20)	-0.2
Total	2	88	227	39	72	12	2	4	33	31	39	.317	.404	.441	844	126	10	4			.936	-9	/O-68(0-1-67)	-0.3
■ ENRIQUE WILSON	Wilson, Enrique (Martes) b: 7/27/75, Santo Domingo, D.R. BB/TR, 5'11", 160 lbs. Deb: 9/24/97																							
1997	Cle-A	5	15	2	5	0	0	0	1	0	2	.333	.333	.333	667	72	-1	0	0	0	.941	2	/S-4,2-1	0.1
1998	*Cle-A	32	90	13	29	6	0	2	12	4	8	.322	.358	.456	813	106	1	2	4	-1	.989	2	2-22,S-10/3-2	0.3
1999	*Cle-A	113	332	41	87	22	1	2	24	25	41	.262	.316	.352	668	67	-16	5	4	-0	.965	-15	3-61,S-35,2-21,/D-1	-2.7
2000	Cle-A	40	117	16	38	9	0	2	12	7	11	.325	.363	.453	816	102	0	2	1	0	.950	-2	3-12/2-7,S-7,D-8	-0.1
	Pit-N	40	122	11	32	6	1	3	15	11	13	.262	.323	.402	725	82	-3	0	1	-0	.925	-4	3-16,2-11/S-8	-0.6
Total	4	230	676	83	191	43	2	9	64	47	75	.283	.331	.392	723	81	-19	9	10	-2	.954	-18	/3-91,S-64,2-62,D-9	-3.0
■ FRANK WILSON	Wilson, Francis Edward "Squash" b: 4/20/01, Malden, Mass. d: 11/25/74, Leicester, Mass. BL/TR, 6', 185 lbs. Deb: 6/20/24																							
1924	Bos-N	61	215	20	51	7	0	1	15	23	22	.237	.311	.284	595	63	-11	3	4	-1	.973	3	O-55(35-20-0)	-1.2
1925	Bos-N	12	31	3	13	1	1	0	0	4	1	.419	.486	.516	1002	171	4	2	1	0	1.000	1	O-10(9-0-1)	0.3
1926	Bos-N	87	236	22	56	11	3	0	23	20	21	.237	.300	.309	609	70	-10	3			.934	1	O-56(50-1-6)	-1.3
1928	Cle-A	2	1	0	0	0	0	0	0	1	0	.000	.500	.000	500	41	0	0	0	0	.000	0	H	0.0
	StL-A	6	5	1	0	0	0	0	0	0	0	.000	.000	.000	0	-97	-1	0	0	0	.000	-0	/O-1(0-0-1)	-0.2
	Yr	8	6	1	0	0	0	0	0	1	0	.000	.143	.000	143	-58	-1	0	0	0	.000	-0	/O-1(0-0-1)	-0.2
Total	4	168	488	46	120	19	4	1	38	48	44	.246	.315	.307	622	72	-18	8	5		.958	4	O-122(94-21-8)	-2.4
■ TUG WILSON	Wilson, George Archer b: 1860, Brooklyn, N.Y. d: 11/28/14, New York, N.Y. 5'8", 175 lbs. Deb: 5/9/1884																							
1884	Bro-a	24	82	13	19	4	0	0	5			.232	.276	.280	556	81	-2				.826	-3	O-12C,C-10/1-3,2-1	-0.4
■ SQUANTO WILSON	Wilson, George Francis b: 3/29/1889, Old Town, Me. d: 3/26/67, Winthrop, Maine BB/TR, 5'9.5", 170 lbs. Deb: 10/2/11																							
1911	Det-A	5	16	2	3	0	0	0	0	2		.188	.278	.188	465	29	-1	0			.900	-1	/C-5	-0.2
1914	Bos-A	1	0	0	0	0	0	0	0	0	0	—	—	—	—	—	0	0			.000	0	/1-1	0.0
Total	2	6	16	2	3	0	0	0	0	2	0	.188	.278	.188	465	29	-1	0			.900	-1	/C-5,1-1	-0.2
■ ICEHOUSE WILSON	Wilson, George Peacock b: 9/14/12, Maricopa, Cal. d: 10/13/73, Moraga, Cal. BR/TR, 6', 186 lbs. Deb: 5/31/34																							
1934	Det-A	1	1	0	0	0	0	0	0	0	0	.000	.000	.000	0	-99	-0	0	0	0	.000	0	H	0.0
■ GEORGE WILSON	Wilson, George Washington "Teddy" b: 8/30/25, Cherryville, N.C. d: 10/29/74, Gastonia, N.C. BL/TR, 6'1.5", 185 lbs. Deb: 4/15/52																							
1952	Chi-A	8	9	0	1	0	0	0	1	1	2	.111	.200	.111	311	-12	-1	0	0	0	1.000	0	/O-1(0-0-1)	-0.1
	NY-N	62	112	9	27	7	0	2	16	3	14	.241	.261	.357	618	69	-5	0	0	0	.923	-3	O-21(16-1-4)/1-2	-0.9
1953	NY-N	11	8	0	1	0	0	0	0	2	2	.125	.364	.125	489	34	-1	0	0	0	.000	0	H	-0.1
1956	NY-N	53	68	5	9	1	0	1	2	5	14	.132	.192	.191	383	3	-9	0	0	0	1.000	0	/O-8(2-0-6)	-1.0
	*NY-A	11	12	1	2	0	0	0	0	3	0	.167	.333	.167	500	37	-1	0	0	0	.750	-2	/O-6(1-0-5)	-0.3
Total	3	145	209	15	40	8	0	3	19	14	32	.191	.246	.273	518	41	-17	0	0	0	.932	-5	/O-36(19-1-16),1-2	-2.4
■ GLENN WILSON	Wilson, Glenn Dwight b: 12/22/58, Baytown, Tex. BR/TR, 6'1", 190 lbs. Deb: 4/15/82 Career OF: (118-LF 90-CF 941-RF)																							
1982	Det-A	84	322	39	94	15	1	12	34	15	51	.292	.323	.457	780	111	4	2	3	-1	.987	7	O-80(2-71-8)/D-4	0.9
1983	Det-A	144	503	55	135	25	6	11	65	25	79	.268	.307	.408	715	97	-3	1	1	-0	.988	-7	*O-143(0-8-140)	-1.7
1984	Phi-N	132	341	28	82	21	3	6	31	17	56	.240	.279	.372	651	80	-10	7	1	1	.968	-12	*O-109(92-3-18)/3-4	-2.6
1985	Phi-N★	161	608	73	167	39	5	14	102	35	117	.275	.314	.424	738	102	-0	7	4	0	.968	20	*O-158(2-0-157)	1.3
1986	Phi-N	155	584	70	158	30	4	15	84	42	91	.271	.324	.413	736	98	-2	5	1	1	.989	21	*O-154(1-0-153)	1.2
1987	Phi-N	154	569	55	150	21	2	14	54	38	82	.264	.311	.381	692	80	-17	3	6	-1	.968	15	*O-154(0-0-154)/P-1	-1.1
1988	Sea-A	78	284	28	71	10	1	3	17	15	52	.250	.288	.324	612	68	-12	1	1	-0	.980	1	O-75(0-0-75)/D-2	-1.5
	Pit-N	37	126	11	34	8	0	2	15	3	18	.270	.292	.381	673	93	-2	0	0	0	.985	-1	O-35(0-4-32)	-0.4
1989	Pit-N	100	330	42	93	20	4	9	49	32	39	.282	.347	.448	796	130	12	1	4	-1	.977	1	O-85(0-1-85),1-10	1.0
	Hou-N	28	102	8	22	6	0	2	15	5	14	.216	.252	.333	586	68	-5	0	1	-0	.966	5	O-25(0-0-25)	-0.1
	Yr	128	432	50	115	26	4	11	64	37	53	.266	.326	.421	747	116	8	1	5	-2	.974	6	*O-110(0-1-110),1-10	0.9
1990	Hou-N	118	368	42	90	14	0	10	55	26	64	.245	.296	.364	660	83	-9	0	3	-1	.975	7	*O-108(21-0-92)/1-1	-0.6
1993	Pit-N	10	14	0	2	0	0	0	0	0	9	.143	.143	.143	286	-23	-2	0	0	0	.875	0	/O-5(0-3-2)	-0.2
Total	10	1201	4151	451	1098	209	26	98	521	253	672	.265	.309	.398	707	93	-46	27	25	-3	.977	57	*O-1131R/1-11,D-6,3P	-3.8
■ GRADY WILSON	Wilson, Grady Herbert b: 11/23/22, Columbus, Ga. BR/TR, 6'0.5", 170 lbs. Deb: 5/15/48																							
1948	Pit-N	12	10	1	1	1	0	0	1	0	3	.100	.100	.200	300	-20	-2	0			.846	1	/S-7	-0.1
■ HENRY WILSON	Wilson, Henry C. b: 4/8/1877, Baltimore, Md. Deb: 10/12/1898																							
1898	Bal-N	1	2	0	0	0	0	0	0	1		.000	.333	.000	333	-2	-0	0			1.000	0	/C-1	0.0
■ JIMMIE WILSON	Wilson, James "Ace" b: 7/23/1900, Philadelphia, Pa. d: 5/31/47, Bradenton, Fla. BR/TR, 6'1.5", 200 lbs. Deb: 4/17/23 MC Career OF: (1-LF 1-CF 1-RF)																							
1923	Phi-N	85	252	27	66	9	0	1	25	4	17	.262	.276	.310	586	49	-18	4	2	0	.960	-3	C-69/O-2(1-1-0)	-1.7
1924	Phi-N	95	280	32	78	16	3	6	39	17	12	.279	.322	.421	744	87	-5	5	4	-0	.968	5	C-82/1-2,O-1(0-0-1)	0.5
1925	Phi-N	108	335	42	110	19	3	3	54	32	25	.328	.390	.430	820	100	1	5	3	0	.982	-9	C-89/O-1(1-0-0)	-0.2
1926	Phi-N	90	279	40	85	10	2	4	32	25	20	.305	.362	.398	760	99	0	3			.950	0	C-79	0.5
1927	Phi-N	128	443	50	122	15	2	2	45	34	15	.275	.330	.332	662	77	-14	13			.975	-19	*C-124	-2.4
1928	Phi-N	21	70	11	21	4	1	0	13	9	8	.300	.380	.386	765	97	0	3			.990	1	C-20	0.3
	*StL-N	120	411	45	106	26	2	2	50	45	24	.258	.333	.345	678	76	-14	9			.983	1	*C-120	-0.5
	Yr	141	481	56	127	30	3	2	63	54	32	.264	.340	.351	691	79	-14	12			.985	2	*C-140	-0.2
1929	StL-N	120	394	59	128	27	8	4	71	43	19	.325	.394	.464	859	111	7	4			.972	5	*C-119	1.8
1930	*StL-N	107	362	54	115	25	7	1	58	28	17	.318	.368	.434	802	90	-5	8			.987	10	C-99	1.0
1931	*StL-N	115	383	45	105	20	2	0	51	28	15	.274	.332	.337	669	77	-12	5			.985	11	*C-110	0.6
1932	StL-N	92	274	36	68	16	2	2	28	15	18	.248	.290	.343	633	67	-13	9			.982	2	C-75/1-3,2-1	-0.6
1933	StL-N★	113	369	34	94	17	0	1	45	23	33	.255	.300	.309	609	71	-14	6			.982	2	*C-107	-0.5
1934	Phi-N	91	277	25	81	11	0	3	35	14	10	.292	.326	.365	691	75	-9	1			.987	2	C-77/1-1,2-1,M	-0.3
1935	Phi-N★	93	290	38	81	20	0	1	37	19	19	.279	.326	.359	684	76	-9	4			.982	8	C-78/2-1,M	0.3
1936	Phi-N	85	230	25	64	12	0	1	27	12	21	.278	.314	.343	658	70	-10	5			.960	-6	C-63/1-1,M	-1.2
1937	Phi-N	39	87	15	24	3	0	1	8	6	4	.276	.323	.345	667	75	-3	1			.978	-1	C-22/1-2,M	-0.3
1938	Phi-N	3	2	0	0	0	0	0	0	0	1	.000	.000	.000	0	-99	-1	0			1.000	0	/C-1,M	0.0
1939	Cin-N	4	3	0	1	0	0	0	0	0	1	.333	.333	.333	667	79	-0	0			.000	-0	/C-1	0.0
1940	*Cin-N	16	37	2	9	2	0	0	3	2	1	.243	.282	.297	579	59	-2	1			.982	3	C-16	0.1
Total	18	1525	4778	580	1358	252	32	32	621	356	280	.284	.336	.370	707	82	-120	86	9		.977	11	*C-1351/1-9,O-4L,2	-2.6
■ GARY WILSON	Wilson, James Garrett b: 1/12/1877, Baltimore, Md. d: 5/1/69, Randallstown, Md. BR/TR, 5'7", 168 lbs. Deb: 9/27/02																							
1902	Bos-A	2	8	0	1	0	0	0	1	0		.125	.125	.125	250	-30	-1	0			.800	0	/2-2	-0.1
■ JIM WILSON	Wilson, James George b: 12/29/60, Corvallis, Ore. BR/TR, 6'3", 230 lbs. Deb: 9/13/85																							
1985	Cle-A	4	14	2	5	0	0	0	4	1	3	.357	.400	.357	757	110	0	0	0	0	1.000	-1	/1-2,D-2	-0.1
1989	Sea-A	5	8	0	0	0	0	0	0	0	3	.000	.000	.000	0	-97	-2	0	0	0	.000	0	/D-5	-0.2
Total	2	9	22	2	5	0	0	0	4	1	6	.227	.261	.227	488	36	-2	0	0	0	1.000	-1	/D-7,1-2	-0.3
■ CHIEF WILSON	Wilson, John Owen b: 8/21/1883, Austin, Tex. d: 2/22/54, Bertram, Tex. BL/TR, 6'2", 185 lbs. Deb: 4/15/08																							
1908	Pit-N	144	529	47	120	8	7	3	43	22		.227	.260	.285	546	74	-16	12			.955	1	*O-144(1-34-109)	-2.6
1909	*Pit-N	154	569	64	155	22	12	4	59	19		.272	.303	.374	677	102	-2	17			.957	6	*O-154(0-0-154)	-0.3
1910	Pit-N	146	536	59	148	14	13	4	50	21	68	.276	.312	.373	685	94	-6	8			.972	3	*O-146(1-7-138)	-1.0
1911	Pit-N	148	544	72	163	34	12	12	**107**	41	55	.300	.353	.472	826	125	15	10			.977	7	*O-146(0-2-145)	1.4

YEAR	TM/L	G	AB	R	H	2B	3B	HR	RBI	BB	SO	AVG	OBP	SLG	OPS	OPS+	BR+	SB	CS	SBR	FA	FR	G/POS	TPR
1912	Pit-N	152	583	80	175	19	**36**	11	95	35	67	.300	.342	.513	855	134	22	16			.961	1	*O-152(0-87-69)	1.4
1913	Pit-N	155	580	71	154	12	14	10	73	32	62	.266	.307	.386	694	102	-1	9			.969	6	*O-155(0-3-153)	-0.4
1914	StL-N	154	580	64	150	27	12	9	73	32	66	.259	.302	.393	695	107	2	14			**.983**	17	*O-154(0-9-148)	1.2
1915	StL-N	107	348	33	96	13	6	3	39	19	43	.276	.321	.374	694	110	3	8	15	-3	**.984**	12	*O-105(3-70-33)	0.7
1916	StL-N	120	355	30	85	8	2	3	32	20	46	.239	.289	.299	588	81	-8	4			.955	-11	*O-113(0-58-61)	-2.9
Total	9	1280	4624	520	1246	157	114	59	571	241	407	.269	.311	.391	702	105	10	98	15		.968	42	*O-1269(5-270-1010)	-2.5

■ LES WILSON

Wilson, Lester Wilbur "Tug" b: 7/17/1885, St.Louis, Mich. d: 4/4/69, Edmonds, Wash. BL/TR, 5'11", 170 lbs. Deb: 7/15/11

YEAR	TM/L	G	AB	R	H	2B	3B	HR	RBI	BB	SO	AVG	OBP	SLG	OPS	OPS+	BR+	SB	CS	SBR	FA	FR	G/POS	TPR
1911	Bos-A	5	7	0	0	0	0	0	0	2		.000	.222	.000	222	-36	-1	0			1.000	-1	/O-3(2-0-1)	-0.2

■ HACK WILSON

Wilson, Lewis Robert b: 4/26/1900, Ellwood City, Pa. d: 11/23/48, Baltimore, Md. BR/TR, 5'6", 190 lbs. Deb: 9/29/23 H Career OF: (190-LF 925-CF 148-RF)

YEAR	TM/L	G	AB	R	H	2B	3B	HR	RBI	BB	SO	AVG	OBP	SLG	OPS	OPS+	BR+	SB	CS	SBR	FA	FR	G/POS	TPR
1923	NY-N	3	10	0	2	0	0	0	0	0	1	.200	.200	.200	400	6	-1	0	0	0	.857	-1	/O-3(1-2-0)	-0.2
1924	*NY-N	107	383	62	113	19	12	10	57	44	46	.295	.369	.486	855	131	16	4	3	-0	.967	-7	*O-103(14-90-1)	0.4
1925	NY-N	62	180	28	43	7	4	6	30	21	33	.239	.322	.422	744	92	-3	5	2	0	.975	-11	O-50(27-23-4)	-1.5
1926	Chi-N	142	529	97	170	36	8	**21**	109	**69**	61	.321	.406	.539	**944**	**150**	**38**	10			.973	2	*O-140(0-140-0)	**3.3**
1927	Chi-N	146	551	119	175	30	12	**30**	129	71	70	.318	.401	.579	980	160	45	13			.967	-1	*O-146(0-146-0)	3.8
1928	Chi-N	145	520	89	163	32	9	**31**	120	77	94	.313	.404	.588	992	159	44	4			.960	-10	*O-143(0-143-0)	2.7
1929	*Chi-N	150	574	135	198	30	5	39	**159**	78	83	.345	.425	.618	1044	155	49	3			.970	-3	*O-150(0-150-0)	3.6
1930	Chi-N	155	585	146	208	35	6	**56**	**191**	**105**	84	.356	.454	**.723**	**1177**	**177**	**74**	3			.951	-7	*O-155(0-155-0)	5.2
1931	Chi-N	112	395	66	103	22	4	13	61	63	69	.261	.362	.435	798	112	7	1			.978	-5	*O-103(40-60-3)	-0.2
1932	Bro-N	135	481	77	143	37	5	23	123	51	85	.297	.366	.538	904	142	28	2			.955	-9	*O-125(1-8-116)	1.1
1933	Bro-N	117	360	41	96	13	2	9	54	52	50	.267	.359	.389	748	119	10	7			.963	-7	O-90(75-8-7)/2-5	-0.1
1934	Bro-N	67	172	24	45	5	0	6	27	40	33	.262	.401	.395	796	120	7	0			.974	-3	O-43(27-0-16)	0.2
	Phi-N	7	20	0	2	0	0	0	3	3	4	.100	.217	.100	317	-11	-3	0			1.000	-1	/O-6(5-0-1)	-0.4
	Yr	74	192	24	47	5	0	6	30	43	37	.245	.383	.365	748	105	3	0			.977	-4	O-49(32-0-17)	-0.2
Total	12	1348	4760	884	1461	266	67	244	1063	674	713	.307	.395	.545	940	145	312	52	5		.965	-62	*O-1257C/2-5	17.9

■ TACK WILSON

Wilson, Michael b: 5/16/55, Shreveport, La. BR/TR, 5'10", 185 lbs. Deb: 4/9/83

YEAR	TM/L	G	AB	R	H	2B	3B	HR	RBI	BB	SO	AVG	OBP	SLG	OPS	OPS+	BR+	SB	CS	SBR	FA	FR	G/POS	TPR
1983	Min-A	5	4	4	1	1	0	0	1	0	0	.250	.250	.500	750	97	-0	0	0	0	1.000	-0	/O-1(0-1-0),D-2	0.0
1987	Cal-A	7	2	5	1	0	0	0	0	1	0	.500	.667	.500	1167	224	1	0	0	0	1.000	-1	/O-4(4-0-0),D-2	-0.1
Total	2	12	6	9	2	1	0	0	1	1	0	.333	.429	.500	929	150	0	0	0	0	1.000	-2	/O-5(4-1-0),D-4	-0.1

■ NIGEL WILSON

Wilson, Nigel Edward b: 1/12/70, Oshawa, Ont., Can. BL/TL, 6'1", 185 lbs. Deb: 9/8/93

YEAR	TM/L	G	AB	R	H	2B	3B	HR	RBI	BB	SO	AVG	OBP	SLG	OPS	OPS+	BR+	SB	CS	SBR	FA	FR	G/POS	TPR
1993	Fla-N	7	16	0	0	0	0	0	0	0	11	.000	.000	.000	0	-95	-4	0	0	0	1.000	-0	/O-3(3-0-0)	-0.5
1995	Cin-N	5	7	0	0	0	0	0	0	0	4	.000	.000	.000	0	-99	-2	0	0	0	1.000	-0	/O-2(2-0-0)	-0.2
1996	*Cle-A	10	12	2	3	0	0	2	5	1	6	.250	.308	.750	1058	157	1	0	0	0	.000	-0	/O-1(1-0-0),D-3	0.0
Total	3	22	35	2	3	0	0	2	5	1	21	.086	.111	.257	368	-7	-5	0	0	0	1.000	-1	/O-6(6-0-0),D-3	-0.7

■ PARKE WILSON

Wilson, Parke Asel b: 10/26/1867, Keithsburg, Ill. d: 12/20/34, Hermosa Beach, Cal BR/TR, 5'11", 166 lbs. Deb: 7/19/1893 Career OF: (3-LF 4-CF 5-RF)

YEAR	TM/L	G	AB	R	H	2B	3B	HR	RBI	BB	SO	AVG	OBP	SLG	OPS	OPS+	BR+	SB	CS	SBR	FA	FR	G/POS	TPR
1893	NY-N	31	114	16	28	4	1	2	21	7	9	.246	.289	.351	640	70	-6	5			.969	-7	C-31	-0.8
1894	NY-N	51	181	35	59	5	5	1	32	15	6	.326	.384	.425	809	96	-1	9			.841	-8	C-35,1-16	-0.5
1895	NY-N	67	238	32	56	9	0	0	30	14	16	.235	.281	.273	554	44	-20	11			.938	3	C-53,1-11/3-3	-1.0
1896	NY-N	75	253	33	60	2	0	0	23	13	14	.237	.277	.245	522	39	-22	9			.936	-4	C-71/1-2	-1.6
1897	NY-N	47	158	29	47	9	3	0	23	15		.297	.362	.392	754	102	1	6			.929	-1	C-30,1-11/O-4C,2-1	0.1
1898	NY-N	1	4	0	0	0	0	0	0	0		.000	.000	.000	0	-99	-1	0			1.000	0	/O-1(0-0-1)	-0.1
1899	NY-N	98	332	49	89	8	6	0	42	43		.268	.359	.328	687	92	-2	16			.925	-9	C-31,1-29,S-19,3/O	-0.6
Total	7	370	1280	194	339	37	15	3	171	107	45	.265	.326	.324	650	72	-50	56			.925	-26	C-251/1-69,S-19,3O2	-4.5

■ PRESTON WILSON

Wilson, Preston James Richard b: 7/19/74, Bamberg, S.C. BR/TR, 6'2", 193 lbs. Deb: 5/7/98 F

YEAR	TM/L	G	AB	R	H	2B	3B	HR	RBI	BB	SO	AVG	OBP	SLG	OPS	OPS+	BR+	SB	CS	SBR	FA	FR	G/POS	TPR
1998	NY-N	8	20	3	6	2	0	0	2	2	8	.300	.364	.400	764	102	0	1	1	-0	.909	-1	/O-7(4-2-1)	-0.1
	Fla-N	14	31	4	2	0	0	1	1	4	13	.065	.194	.161	356	-5	-5	0	0	0	1.000	-2	O-11(3-7-1)	-0.7
	Yr	22	51	7	8	2	0	1	3	6	21	.157	.259	.255	514	37	-5	1	1	-0	.958	-3	O-18(7-9-2)	-0.8
1999	Fla-N	149	482	67	135	21	4	26	71	46	156	.280	.354	.502	856	120	13	11	4	1	.973	4	*O-136(23-111-15)	1.8
2000	Fla-N	161	605	94	160	35	3	31	121	55	187	.264	.334	.486	820	109	6	36	14	3	.988	10	*O-158(0-158-0)	2.0
Total	3	332	1138	168	303	58	7	58	195	107	364	.266	.339	.482	821	111	15	48	19	4	.980	12	O-312(30-278-17)	3.0

■ BOB WILSON

Wilson, Robert b: 2/22/25, Dallas, Tex. d: 4/23/85, Dallas, Tex. BR/TR, 5'11", 197 lbs. Deb: 5/17/58

YEAR	TM/L	G	AB	R	H	2B	3B	HR	RBI	BB	SO	AVG	OBP	SLG	OPS	OPS+	BR+	SB	CS	SBR	FA	FR	G/POS	TPR
1958	LA-N	3	5	0	1	0	0	0	0	0	1	.200	.200	.200	400	6	-1	0	0	0	1.000	-0	/O-1(0-0-1)	-0.1

■ RED WILSON

Wilson, Robert James b: 3/7/29, Milwaukee, Wis. BR/TR, 6', 200 lbs. Deb: 9/22/51

YEAR	TM/L	G	AB	R	H	2B	3B	HR	RBI	BB	SO	AVG	OBP	SLG	OPS	OPS+	BR+	SB	CS	SBR	FA	FR	G/POS	TPR
1951	Chi-A	4	11	1	3	1	0	0	0	1	2	.273	.333	.364	697	90	-0	0	0	0	1.000	-1	/C-4	-0.1
1952	Chi-A	2	3	0	0	0	0	0	0	0	1	.000	.000	.000	0	-99	-1	0	0	0	1.000	1	/C-2	0.0
1953	Chi-A	71	164	21	41	6	1	0	10	26	12	.250	.353	.299	651	75	-5	2	3	-1	.981	10	C-63	0.7
1954	Chi-A	8	20	2	4	0	0	1	1	1	2	.200	.238	.350	588	58	-1	0	0	0	1.000	4	/C-8	0.3
	Det-A	54	170	22	48	11	1	2	22	27	12	.282	.381	.394	775	115	4	3	1	0	.996	2	C-53	0.9
	Yr	62	190	24	52	11	1	3	23	28	14	.274	.367	.389	756	108	3	3	1	0	.997	6	C-61	1.2
1955	Det-A	78	241	26	53	9	0	2	17	26	23	.220	.296	.282	578	57	-14	1	2	-0	.984	-6	C-72	-1.8
1956	Det-A	78	228	32	66	12	2	7	38	42	18	.289	.400	.452	852	124	9	2	1	0	.991	3	C-78	1.5
1957	Det-A	60	180	21	43	8	1	3	13	25	19	.239	.341	.344	686	86	-3	2	3	-1	1.000	1	C-60	0.0
1958	Det-A	103	298	31	89	13	1	3	29	35	30	.299	.376	.379	755	101	2	10	0	2	.992	7	*C-101	1.6
1959	Det-A	67	228	28	60	17	2	4	35	10	23	.263	.300	.408	708	88	-4	2	2	-0	.988	2	C-64	0.0
1960	Det-A	45	134	17	29	4	0	1	14	16	14	.216	.300	.269	569	54	-8	3	0	1	.980	-0	C-45	-0.6
	Cle-A	32	88	5	19	3	0	1	10	6	7	.216	.274	.284	558	53	-6	0	0	0	.989	7	C-30	0.3
	Yr	77	222	22	48	7	0	2	24	22	21	.216	.290	.275	565	53	-14	3	0	1	.984	7	C-75	-0.3
Total	10	602	1765	206	455	84	8	24	189	215	163	.258	.341	.355	696	87	-28	25	12	1	.990	31	C-580	2.8

■ MIKE WILSON

Wilson, Samuel Marshall b: 12/2/1896, Edge Hill, Pa. d: 5/16/78, Boynton Beach, Fla BR/TR, 5'10.5", 160 lbs. Deb: 6/4/21

YEAR	TM/L	G	AB	R	H	2B	3B	HR	RBI	BB	SO	AVG	OBP	SLG	OPS	OPS+	BR+	SB	CS	SBR	FA	FR	G/POS	TPR
1921	Pit-N	5	4	0	0	0	0	0	0	0	0	.000	.000	.000	0	-97	-1	0	0	0	.833	0	/C-5	-0.1

■ NEIL WILSON

Wilson, Samuel O'Neil b: 6/14/35, Lexington, Tenn. BL/TR, 6'1", 175 lbs. Deb: 4/17/60

YEAR	TM/L	G	AB	R	H	2B	3B	HR	RBI	BB	SO	AVG	OBP	SLG	OPS	OPS+	BR+	SB	CS	SBR	FA	FR	G/POS	TPR
1960	SF-N	6	10	0	0	0	0	0	0	1	2	.000	.091	.000	91	-77	-2	0	0	0	.958	0	/C-6	-0.2

■ TOM WILSON

Wilson, Thomas G. "Slats" b: 6/3/1890, Fleming, Kan. d: 3/7/53, San Pedro, Cal. BB/TR, 6'1.5", 160 lbs. Deb: 9/8/14

YEAR	TM/L	G	AB	R	H	2B	3B	HR	RBI	BB	SO	AVG	OBP	SLG	OPS	OPS+	BR+	SB	CS	SBR	FA	FR	G/POS	TPR
1914	Was-A	1	1	0	0	0	0	0	0	0	0	.000	.000	.000	0	-96	-0	0			.000	0	/C-1	0.0

■ VANCE WILSON

Wilson, Vance Allen b: 3/17/73, Mesa, Ariz. BR/TR, 5'11", 190 lbs. Deb: 4/24/99

YEAR	TM/L	G	AB	R	H	2B	3B	HR	RBI	BB	SO	AVG	OBP	SLG	OPS	OPS+	BR+	SB	CS	SBR	FA	FR	G/POS	TPR
1999	NY-N	1	0	0	0	0	0	0	0	0	0	—	—	—	—	—	0	0	0	0	.000	0	/C-1	0.0
2000	NY-N	4	4	0	0	0	0	0	0	0	2	.000	.000	.000	0	-99	-1	0	0	0	1.000	2	/C-3	0.0
Total	2	5	4	0	0	0	0	0	0	0	2	.000	.000	.000	0	-99	-1	0	0	0	1.000	2	/C-4	0.0

■ BILL WILSON

Wilson, William Donald b: 11/6/28, Central City, Neb. BR/TR, 6'2", 200 lbs. Deb: 9/24/50

YEAR	TM/L	G	AB	R	H	2B	3B	HR	RBI	BB	SO	AVG	OBP	SLG	OPS	OPS+	BR+	SB	CS	SBR	FA	FR	G/POS	TPR
1950	Chi-A	3	6	0	0	0	0	0	0	2	2	.000	.250	.000	250	-33	-1	0	0	0	1.000	-1	/O-2(0-2-0)	-0.2
1953	Chi-A	9	17	1	1	0	0	0	1	0	7	.059	.111	.059	170	-51	-4	0	0	0	1.000	0	/O-3(0-3-0)	-0.4
1954	Chi-A	20	35	4	6	1	0	2	5	7	5	.171	.310	.371	681	83	-1	0	1	-0	.943	-2	O-19(15-0-4)	-0.4
	Phi-A	94	323	43	77	10	1	15	33	39	59	.238	.335	.415	750	104	1	1	2	-0	.989	8	O-91(0-91-0)	0.5
	Yr	114	358	47	83	11	1	17	38	46	64	.232	.333	.411	743	102	0	1	3	-1	.984	6	*O-110(15-91-4)	0.1
1955	KC-A	98	273	39	61	12	0	15	38	24	63	.223	.289	.432	721	91	-5	1	1	-0	.969	-3	O-82(23-57-4)/P-1	-1.2
Total	4	224	654	87	145	23	1	32	77	72	136	.222	.308	.407	715	92	-10	2	4	-1	.979	3	O-197(38-153-8)/P-1	-1.7

■ BILL WILSON

Wilson, William G. b: 10/28/1867, Hannibal, Mo. d: 5/9/24, St.Paul, Minn. TR, Deb: 4/30/1890 Career OF: (4-LF 8-CF 13-RF)

YEAR	TM/L	G	AB	R	H	2B	3B	HR	RBI	BB	SO	AVG	OBP	SLG	OPS	OPS+	BR+	SB	CS	SBR	FA	FR	G/POS	TPR
1890	Pit-N	83	304	30	65	11	3	0	21	22	50	.214	.271	.270	541	65	-13	5			.874	2	C-38,O-25R,1-18,/S	-0.8
1897	Lou-N	107	389	44	83	12	4	1	41	18		.213	.257	.272	530	41	-34	9			.940	2	*C-105/3-1	-1.9

YEAR	TM/L	G	AB	R	H	2B	3B	HR	RBI	BB	SO	AVG	OBP	SLG	OPS	OPS+	BR+	SB	CS	SBR	FA	FR	G/POS	TPR
1898	Lou-N	29	102	5	17	1	2	1	13	5		.167	.213	.245	458	32	-9	3			.895	-4	C-28/1-1	-1.0
Total	3	219	795	79	165	24	9	2	75	45	50	.208	.257	.268	525	48	-56	17			.913	-0	C-171/O-25R,1-19,3S	-3.7

■ **MOOKIE WILSON** Wilson, William Hayward b: 2/9/56, Bamberg, S.C. BB/TR, 5'10", 170 lbs. Deb: 9/2/80 FC Career OF: (198-LF 1067-CF 90-RF)

YEAR	TM/L	G	AB	R	H	2B	3B	HR	RBI	BB	SO	AVG	OBP	SLG	OPS	OPS+	BR+	SB	CS	SBR	FA	FR	G/POS	TPR
1980	NY-N	27	105	16	26	5	3	0	4	12	19	.248	.325	.352	677	91	-1	7	7	-1	.973	2	O-26(1-26-0)	0.0
1981	NY-N	92	328	49	89	8	8	3	14	20	59	.271	.317	.372	689	96	-2	24	12	1	.983	6	O-80(6-68-10)	0.4
1982	NY-N	159	639	90	178	25	9	5	55	32	102	.279	.315	.369	684	91	-8	58	16	7	.988	17	*O-156(0-156-0)	1.5
1983	NY-N	152	638	91	176	25	6	7	51	18	103	.276	.300	.367	667	85	-15	54	16	6	.984	13	*O-148(0-148-0)	0.3
1984	NY-N	154	587	88	162	28	10	10	54	26	90	.276	.309	.409	718	102	-1	46	9	7	.990	17	*O-146(0-146-0)	2.2
1985	NY-N	93	337	56	93	16	8	6	26	28	52	.276	.332	.424	756	113	5	24	9	2	.964	2	O-83(4-83-0)	0.9
1986	*NY-N	123	381	61	110	17	5	9	45	32	72	.289	.345	.430	776	116	8	25	7	3	.979	-6	*O-114(78-65-3)	0.2
1987	NY-N	124	385	58	115	19	7	9	34	35	85	.299	.360	.455	815	120	11	21	6	3	.963	-8	*O-109(20-88-14)	0.4
1988	*NY-N	112	378	61	112	17	5	8	41	27	63	.296	.346	.431	778	128	13	15	4	2	.976	-7	*O-104(16-83-18)	0.7
1989	NY-N	80	249	22	51	10	1	3	18	10	47	.205	.238	.289	528	53	-16	7	4	0	.975	-3	O-71(13-44-25)	-2.1
	*Tor-A	54	238	32	71	9	1	2	17	3	37	.298	.313	.370	683	93	-3	12	1	2	.991	-3	O-54(16-22-20)	-0.5
1990	Tor-A	147	588	81	156	36	4	3	51	31	102	.265	.302	.355	658	82	-15	23	4	4	.992	8	*O-141(8-133-0)/D-6	-0.5
1991	*Tor-A	86	241	26	58	12	4	2	28	8	35	.241	.280	.349	628	70	-10	11	3	1	.973	-1	O-41(36-5-0),D-34	-1.2
Total	12	1403	5094	731	1397	227	71	67	438	282	866	.274	.315	.386	701	96	-35	327	98	38	.982	38	*O-1273C/D-40	2.3

■ **WILLIE WILSON** Wilson, Willie James b: 7/9/55, Montgomery, Ala. BB/TR (BR 1976), 6'3", 195 lbs. Deb: 9/4/76 Career OF: (673-LF 1356-CF 31-RF)

YEAR	TM/L	G	AB	R	H	2B	3B	HR	RBI	BB	SO	AVG	OBP	SLG	OPS	OPS+	BR+	SB	CS	SBR	FA	FR	G/POS	TPR
1976	KC-A	12	6	0	1	0	0	0	0	0	2	.167	.167	.167	333	-2	-1	2	1	0	.875	-2	/O-6(0-6-0)	-0.2
1977	KC-A	13	34	10	11	2	0	0	1	1	8	.324	.343	.382	725	97	-0	6	3	0	.960	0	/O-9(0-9-0),D-2	0.0
1978	*KC-A	127	198	43	43	8	2	0	16	16	33	.217	.282	.278	560	57	-11	46	12	6	.978	-14	*O-112(82-35-0)/D-6	-2.2
1979	KC-A	154	588	113	185	18	13	6	49	28	92	.315	.353	.420	773	106	4	**83**	12	**14**	.985	15	*O-152(130-23-5)/D-2	2.6
1980	*KC-A	161	705	**133**	**230**	28	**15**	3	49	28	81	.326	.357	.421	779	112	11	79	10	**14**	.988	22	*O-159(102-62-0)	4.0
1981	*KC-A	102	439	54	133	10	7	1	32	18	42	.303	.336	.364	701	103	1	34	8	5	.987	22	*O-101(83-19-0)	2.5
1982	KC-A★	136	585	87	194	19	**15**	3	46	26	81	**.332**	.366	.431	797	118	14	37	11	4	.987	15	*O-135(119-19-0)	2.7
1983	KC-A★	137	576	90	159	22	8	2	33	33	75	.276	.316	.352	669	84	-13	59	8	10	.975	1	*O-136(63-75-0)	-0.5
1984	*KC-A	128	541	81	163	24	9	2	44	39	56	.301	.352	.390	742	104	3	47	5	**9**	.990	10	*O-128(0-128-0)	2.1
1985	*KC-A	141	605	87	168	25	**21**	4	43	29	94	.278	.316	.408	724	96	-4	43	11	6	.995	3	*O-140(0-140-0)	0.3
1986	KC-A	156	631	77	170	20	7	9	44	31	97	.269	.313	.366	679	82	-16	34	8	5	.993	5	*O-155(0-155-0)	-0.7
1987	KC-A	146	610	97	170	18	**15**	4	30	32	88	.279	.321	.377	698	82	-16	59	11	**9**	**.997**	3	*O-143(0-143-0)/D-2	-0.5
1988	KC-A	147	591	81	155	17	**11**	1	37	22	106	.262	.291	.333	624	74	-21	35	7	5	.989	-0	*O-142(0-143-0)	-1.8
1989	KC-A	112	383	58	97	17	7	3	43	27	78	.253	.304	.358	662	86	-7	24	6	3	.977	-3	*O-108(0-108-0)/D-1	-0.8
1990	KC-A	115	307	49	89	13	3	2	42	30	57	.290	.357	.371	728	106	3	24	6	3	1.000	-6	*O-106(54-48-4)/D-1	-0.2
1991	Oak-A	113	294	38	70	14	4	0	28	18	43	.238	.291	.313	604	71	-12	20	5	3	.983	-4	O-87(40-33-19)/D-9	-1.4
1992	*Oak-A	132	396	38	107	15	5	0	37	35	65	.270	.331	.333	664	91	-4	28	8	3	.981	7	*O-120(0-118-3)/D-5	0.5
1993	Chi-N	105	221	29	57	11	3	1	11	11	40	.258	.302	.348	651	75	-8	7	2	1	.991	-18	O-82(0-82-0)	-2.5
1994	Chi-N	17	21	4	5	0	2	0	0	1	6	.238	.273	.429	701	80	-1	1	0	0	1.000	-3	O-10(0-10-0)	-0.4
Total	19	2154	7731	1169	2207	281	147	41	585	425	1144	.285	.328	.376	704	93	-77	668	134	100	.987	53	*O-2031C/D-28	3.5

■ **ED WINCENIAK** Winceniak, Edward Joseph b: 4/16/29, Chicago, Ill. BR/TR, 5'9", 165 lbs. Deb: 4/25/56

YEAR	TM/L	G	AB	R	H	2B	3B	HR	RBI	BB	SO	AVG	OBP	SLG	OPS	OPS+	BR+	SB	CS	SBR	FA	FR	G/POS	TPR
1956	Chi-N	15	17	1	2	0	0	0	0	1	3	.118	.167	.118	284	-22	-3	0	0	0	.889	-0	/3-4,2-1	-0.3
1957	Chi-N	17	50	5	12	3	0	1	8	2	9	.240	.269	.360	629	68	-2	0	0	0	1.000	-3	/S-5,3-4,2-3	-0.5
Total	2	32	67	6	14	3	0	1	8	3	12	.209	.243	.299	541	45	-5	0	0	0	.955	-3	/3-8,S-5,2-4	-0.8

■ **GORDIE WINDHORN** Windhorn, Gordon Ray b: 12/19/33, Watseka, Ill. BR/TR, 6'1", 185 lbs. Deb: 9/10/59

YEAR	TM/L	G	AB	R	H	2B	3B	HR	RBI	BB	SO	AVG	OBP	SLG	OPS	OPS+	BR+	SB	CS	SBR	FA	FR	G/POS	TPR
1959	NY-A	7	11	0	0	0	0	0	0	0	3	.000	.000	.000	0	-99	-3	0	0	0	1.000	-1	/O-4(4-0-0)	-0.4
1961	LA-N	34	33	10	8	2	1	2	6	4	3	.242	.324	.545	870	115	1	0	1	-0	.944	-2	O-17(5-3-9)	-0.2
1962	KC-A	14	19	1	3	1	0	0	1	0	3	.158	.158	.211	368	-2	-3	0	0	0	1.000	-2	/O-7(7-0-0)	-0.4
	LA-A	40	45	9	8	6	0	0	1	7	10	.178	.288	.311	600	63	-2	1	1	-0	1.000	-7	O-27(22-3-5)	-1.0
	Yr	54	64	10	11	7	0	0	2	7	13	.172	.254	.281	535	44	-5	1	1	-0	1.000	-9	O-34(29-3-5)	-1.4
Total	3	95	108	20	19	9	1	2	8	11	19	.176	.252	.333	585	55	-7	1	2	-0	.981	-12	/O-55(38-6-14)	-2.0

■ **BILL WINDLE** Windle, Willis Brewer b: 12/13/04, Galena, Kan. d: 12/8/81, Corpus Christi, Tex BL/TL, 5'11.5", 170 lbs. Deb: 9/27/28

YEAR	TM/L	G	AB	R	H	2B	3B	HR	RBI	BB	SO	AVG	OBP	SLG	OPS	OPS+	BR+	SB	CS	SBR	FA	FR	G/POS	TPR
1928	Pit-N	1	1	1	1	1	0	0	0	0	0	1.000	1.000	2.000	3000	641	1	0			1.000	0	/1-1	0.1
1929	Pit-N	2	1	0	0	0	0	0	0	0	1	.000	.000	.000	0	-98	-0	0			1.000	-0	/1-2	0.0
Total	2	3	2	1	1	1	0	0	0	0	1	.500	.500	1.000	1500	264	0	0			1.000	-0	/1-3	0.1

■ **ROBBIE WINE** Wine, Robert Paul Jr. b: 7/13/62, Norristown, Pa. BR/TR, 6'2", 190 lbs. Deb: 9/2/86 F

YEAR	TM/L	G	AB	R	H	2B	3B	HR	RBI	BB	SO	AVG	OBP	SLG	OPS	OPS+	BR+	SB	CS	SBR	FA	FR	G/POS	TPR
1986	Hou-N	9	12	2	3	1	0	0	0	1	4	.250	.308	.333	641	79	-0	0	0	0	1.000	3	/C-8	0.3
1987	Hou-N	14	29	1	3	1	0	0	0	1	10	.103	.133	.138	271	-29	-5	0	0	0	.979	-1	C-12	-0.6
Total	2	23	41	3	6	2	0	0	0	2	14	.146	.186	.195	381	2	-6	0	0	0	.988	2	/C-20	-0.3

■ **BOBBY WINE** Wine, Robert Paul Sr. b: 9/17/38, New York, N.Y. BR/TR, 6'1", 187 lbs. Deb: 9/20/60 FMC

YEAR	TM/L	G	AB	R	H	2B	3B	HR	RBI	BB	SO	AVG	OBP	SLG	OPS	OPS+	BR+	SB	CS	SBR	FA	FR	G/POS	TPR
1960	Phi-N	4	14	1	2	0	0	0	0	0	2	.143	.143	.143	286	-22	-2	0	0	0	1.000	0	/S-4	-0.2
1962	Phi-N	112	311	30	76	15	0	4	25	11	49	.244	.270	.331	601	62	-17	2	0	0	.979	7	S-89,3-20	-0.4
1963	Phi-N	142	418	29	90	14	3	6	44	14	83	.215	.242	.306	549	58	-23	1	3	-1	.971	15	*S-132/3-8	0.1
1964	Phi-N	126	283	28	60	8	3	4	34	25	37	.212	.276	.304	580	64	-13	1	0	0	.965	7	*S-108,3-16	0.1
1965	Phi-N	139	394	31	90	8	1	5	33	31	69	.228	.285	.292	577	64	-19	0	0	0	.967	22	*S-135/1-4	1.4
1966	Phi-N	46	89	8	21	5	0	0	5	6	13	.236	.292	.292	584	63	-4	0	1	-0	.974	12	S-40/O-2(2-0-0)	1.0
1967	Phi-N	135	363	27	69	12	5	2	28	29	77	.190	.250	.267	517	48	-25	3	2	-0	**.980**	29	*S-134/1-2	1.5
1968	Phi-N	27	71	5	12	3	0	2	7	6	17	.169	.234	.296	530	58	-4	0	0	0	.972	3	S-25/3-1	0.1
1969	Mon-N	121	370	23	74	8	1	3	25	28	49	.200	.256	.251	508	43	-28	0	0	0	.949	17	*S-118/1-1,3-1	0.2
1970	Mon-N	159	501	40	116	21	3	3	51	39	94	.232	.288	.303	592	59	-29	0	1	-0	.976	20	*S-159	0.8
1971	Mon-N	119	340	25	68	9	0	1	16	25	46	.200	.255	.235	490	39	-27	0	0	0	.982	2	*S-119	-1.3
1972	Mon-N	34	18	2	4	1	0	0	0	0	2	.222	.222	.278	500	41	-1	0	0	0	1.000	5	3-21/S-4,2-1	0.4
Total	12	1164	3172	249	682	104	16	30	268	214	538	.215	.265	.286	552	54	-193	7	7	-1	.971	137	*S-1067/3-67,1-7,O2	3.7

■ **RALPH WINEGARNER** Winegarner, Ralph Lee b: 10/29/09, Benton, Kan. d: 4/14/88, Wichita, Kan. BR/TR, 6', 182 lbs. Deb: 9/20/30 C Career OF: (4-LF 0-CF 1-RF)

YEAR	TM/L	G	AB	R	H	2B	3B	HR	RBI	BB	SO	AVG	OBP	SLG	OPS	OPS+	BR+	SB	CS	SBR	FA	FR	G/POS	TPR
1930	Cle-A	5	22	5	10	1	0	0	2	1	7	.455	.478	.500	978	143	2	0	0	0	.857	1	/3-5	0.2
1932	Cle-A	7	7	1	1	0	0	0	0	0	5	.143	.143	.143	286	-24	-1	0	0	0	.750	-0	/P-5	0.0
1934	Cle-A	32	51	9	10	2	0	1	5	3	11	.196	.241	.294	535	37	-5	0	0	0	1.000	1	P-22/O-1(0-0-1)	0.0
1935	Cle-A	65	84	11	26	4	1	3	17	9	12	.310	.376	.488	864	120	2	1	1	-0	.944	2	P-25/O-4L,3-3,1-1	0.2
1936	Cle-A	18	16	0	2	0	0	0	2	1	6	.125	.176	.125	301	-24	-3	0	0	0	1.000	-0	/P-9	0.0
1949	StL-A	9	5	2	2	0	0	1	2	1	2	.400	.500	1.000	1500	280	1	0	0	0	1.000	-0	/P-9	0.0
Total	6	136	185	28	51	7	1	5	28	15	43	.276	.330	.405	735	86	-4	1	1	-0	.952	2	/P-70,3-8,O-5L,1-1	0.4

■ **DAVE WINFIELD** Winfield, David Mark b: 10/3/51, St.Paul, Minn. BR/TR, 6'6", 220 lbs. Deb: 6/19/73 Career OF: (466-LF 219-CF 1879-RF)

YEAR	TM/L	G	AB	R	H	2B	3B	HR	RBI	BB	SO	AVG	OBP	SLG	OPS	OPS+	BR+	SB	CS	SBR	FA	FR	G/POS	TPR
1973	SD-N	56	141	9	39	4	1	3	12	12	19	.277	.333	.383	716	107	1	0	0	0	.956	-1	O-36(34-2-1)/1-1	-0.2
1974	SD-N	145	498	57	132	18	4	20	75	40	96	.265	.321	.438	759	116	8	9	7	-0	.960	7	*O-131(81-25-34)	0.8
1975	SD-N	143	509	74	136	20	2	15	76	69	82	.267	.358	.403	761	118	13	23	4	4	.972	10	*O-138(0-0-138)	2.0
1976	SD-N	137	492	81	139	26	4	13	69	65	78	.283	.370	.431	801	138	25	26	7	3	.982	12	*O-134(0-10-127)	3.5
1977	SD-N★	157	615	104	169	29	7	25	92	58	75	.275	.337	.467	804	126	20	16	7	1	.972	20	*O-156(0-0-156)	3.3
1978	SD-N★	158	587	88	181	30	5	24	97	55	81	.308	.370	.499	869	153	39	21	9	1	.979	-19	*O-154(1-84-112)/1-2	1.8
1979	SD-N★	159	597	97	184	27	10	34	**118**	85	71	.308	.396	.558	954	**167**	**55**	15	9	0	.986	11	*O-157(0-0-157)	**5.8**
1980	SD-N★	162	558	89	154	25	6	20	87	79	83	.276	.368	.450	818	135	27	23	7	3	.987	-4	*O-159(0-20-154)	1.9
1981	*NY-A★	105	388	52	114	25	1	13	68	43	41	.294	.366	.464	830	140	20	11	1	2	.985	-6	*O-102(80-23-0)/D-1	1.3
1982	NY-A★	140	539	84	151	24	8	37	106	45	64	.280	.336	.560	896	143	29	5	3	0	.974	12	*O-135(135-0-0)/D-4	3.5
1983	NY-A★	152	598	99	169	26	8	32	116	58	77	.283	.348	.513	861	139	30	15	6	1	.978	-11	*O-151(122-39-9)	1.4
1984	NY-A★	141	567	106	193	34	4	19	100	53	71	.340	.397	.515	912	156	43	6	4	-0	.994	2	*O-140(1-16-127)	3.8

YEAR	TM/L	G	AB	R	H	2B	3B	HR	RBI	BB	SO	AVG	OBP	SLG	OPS	OPS+	BR+	SB	CS	SBR	FA	FR	G/POS	TPR
1985	NY-A★	155	633	105	174	34	6	26	114	52	96	.275	.330	.471	801	119	15	19	7	2	.991	12	*O-152(0-0-152)/D-2	1.9
1986	NY-A★	154	565	90	148	31	5	24	104	77	106	.262	.352	.462	814	121	17	6	5	-0	.984	5	*O-145R/3-2,D-6	1.3
1987	NY-A★	156	575	83	158	22	1	27	97	76	96	.275	.359	.457	817	116	14	5	6	-1	.989	-4	*O-145(0-0-145)/D-8	0.1
1988	NY-A★	149	559	96	180	37	2	25	107	69	88	.322	.398	.530	928	159	44	9	4	1	.989	-3	*O-141(0-0-141)/D-4	3.7
1990	NY-A	20	61	7	13	3	0	2	6	4	13	.213	.273	.361	633	75	-2	0	0	0	1.000	-3	O-12(12-0-0)/D-7	-0.5
	Cal-A	112	414	63	114	18	2	19	72	48	68	.275	.352	.466	818	130	16	0	1	-0	.989	-6	*O-108(0-0-108)/D-3	0.7
	Yr	132	475	70	127	21	2	21	78	52	81	.267	.342	.453	795	122	14	0	1	-0	.989	-8	*O-120(12-0-108),D-10	0.2
1991	Cal-A	150	568	75	149	27	4	28	86	56	109	.262	.330	.472	801	119	13	7	2	1	.990	-1	*O-115(0-0-115),D-34	0.8
1992	*Tor-A	156	583	92	169	33	3	26	108	82	89	.290	.378	.491	869	136	28	2	3	-1	1.000	1	*D-130,O-26(0-0-26)	2.4
1993	Min-A	143	547	72	148	27	2	21	76	45	106	.271	.326	.442	768	104	2	2	3	-1	1.000	0	*D-105,O-31R/1-5	-0.6
1994	Min-A	77	294	35	74	15	3	10	43	31	51	.252	.323	.425	748	91	-5	2	1	0	1.000	0	D-76/O-1(0-0-1)	-0.8
1995	Cle-A	46	115	11	22	5	0	2	4	14	26	.191	.285	.287	572	49	-9	1	0	0	.000	0	D-39	-1.0
Total	22	2973	11003	1669	3110	540	88	465	1833	1216	1686	.283	.355	.475	830	130	443	223	96	15	.982	34	*O-2469R,D-419/1-8,3	36.9

■ AL WINGO Wingo, Absalom Holbrook "Red" b: 5/6/1898, Norcross, Ga. d: 10/9/64, Detroit, Mich. BL/TR, 5'11", 180 lbs. Deb: 9/9/19 F

YEAR	TM/L	G	AB	R	H	2B	3B	HR	RBI	BB	SO	AVG	OBP	SLG	OPS	OPS+	BR+	SB	CS	SBR	FA	FR	G/POS	TPR
1919	Phi-A	15	59	9	18	1	3	0	2	4	12	.305	.349	.424	773	115	1	0			.815	-3	O-15(15-0-0)	-0.3
1924	Det-A	78	150	21	43	12	2	1	26	21	13	.287	.374	.413	788	105	1	2	5	-1	.925	-8	O-43(30-7-6)	-1.0
1925	Det-A	130	440	104	163	34	10	5	68	69	31	.370	.456	.527	983	151	37	14	13	-1	.971	8	*O-122(120-2-0)	3.1
1926	Det-A	108	298	45	84	19	0	1	45	52	32	.282	.389	.356	744	94	-1	4	2	0	.923	4	O-74(61-0-14)/3-2	-0.2
1927	Det-A	75	137	15	32	8	2	0	20	25	14	.234	.352	.321	673	74	-5	1	0	0	.891	-3	O-34(9-4-21)	-0.9
1928	Det-A	87	242	30	69	13	2	2	30	40	17	.285	.389	.380	769	101	2	2	2	-0	.968	-3	O-71(35-28-6)	-0.6
Total	6	493	1326	224	409	87	19	9	191	211	119	.308	.404	.423	827	114	36	23	22		.944	-6	O-359(270-41-47)/3-2	0.1

■ ED WINGO Wingo, Edmond Armand (b: Edmond Armand La Riviere)
b: 10/8/1895, St.Anne De Bellevue, Que., Canada d: 12/5/64, Lachine, Que., Can. BR/TR, 5'6", 145 lbs. Deb: 10/2/20

YEAR	TM/L	G	AB	R	H	2B	3B	HR	RBI	BB	SO	AVG	OBP	SLG	OPS	OPS+	BR+	SB	CS	SBR	FA	FR	G/POS	TPR
1920	Phi-A	1	4	0	1	0	0	0	1	0	0	.250	.250	.250	500	32	-0	0	0	0	1.000	1	/C-1	0.0

■ IVEY WINGO Wingo, Ivey Brown b: 7/8/1890, Gainesville, Ga. d: 3/1/41, Waycross, Ga. BL/TR, 5'10", 160 lbs. Deb: 4/20/11 FMC Career OF: (7-LF 1-CF 5-RF)

YEAR	TM/L	G	AB	R	H	2B	3B	HR	RBI	BB	SO	AVG	OBP	SLG	OPS	OPS+	BR+	SB	CS	SBR	FA	FR	G/POS	TPR
1911	StL-N	25	57	4	12	2	0	0	3	3	7	.211	.250	.246	496	40	-5	0			.916	0	C-18	-0.3
1912	StL-N	100	310	38	82	18	8	2	44	23	45	.265	.317	.394	711	96	-3	8			.957	4	C-92	0.8
1913	StL-N	112	307	25	78	5	8	2	35	17	41	.254	.295	.342	637	83	-8	18			.945	-4	C-98/1-5,O-1(1-1-0)	-0.4
1914	StL-N	80	237	24	71	8	5	4	26	18	17	.300	.352	.426	778	132	9	15			.958	-3	C-70/O-4(0-0-4)	1.2
1915	Cin-N	119	339	26	75	11	6	3	29	13	33	.221	.250	.316	566	69	-14	10	11	-2	.966	3	C-98/O-1(2-0-0)	-0.5
1916	Cin-N	119	347	30	85	8	11	2	40	25	27	.245	.298	.349	646	100	-0	4			.958	7	*C-107,M	1.7
1917	Cin-N	121	399	37	106	16	11	2	39	25	13	.266	.311	.376	687	115	6	9			.967	-5	*C-120	1.3
1918	Cin-N	100	323	35	82	15	6	0	31	19	18	.254	.297	.337	635	95	-3	6			.973	-6	C-93/O-5(3-0-1)	0.0
1919	*Cin-N	76	245	30	67	12	6	0	27	23	19	.273	.336	.371	707	115	5	4			.969	3	C-75	1.6
1920	Cin-N	108	364	32	96	11	5	2	38	19	13	.264	.300	.338	638	84	-8	6	4	-0	.958	-10	*C-107/2-2	-1.0
1921	Cin-N	97	295	20	79	7	6	3	38	21	14	.268	.319	.363	681	84	-7	3	2	-0	.959	5	C-92/O-1(1-0-0)	0.4
1922	Cin-N	80	260	24	74	13	3	3	45	23	11	.285	.343	.392	735	91	-4	1	4	-1	.964	4	C-78	0.4
1923	Cin-N	61	171	10	45	9	2	1	24	9	11	.263	.304	.357	661	75	-6	1	1	-0	.969	3	C-57	0.0
1924	Cin-N	66	192	21	55	5	4	1	23	14	8	.286	.338	.370	708	91	-2	1	1	-0	.989	5	C-65/1-1	0.6
1925	Cin-N	55	146	6	30	7	0	0	12	11	8	.205	.261	.253	515	33	-15	1	2	-0	.965	3	C-55	-0.8
1926	Cin-N	7	10	0	2	0	0	0	1	1	0	.200	.333	.200	533	48	-1	0			1.000	-0	/C-7	-0.1
1929	Cin-N	1	1	0	0	0	0	0	0	0	0	.000	.000	.000	0	-99	-0	0			.000	0	/C-1	0.0
Total	17	1327	4003	362	1039	147	81	25	455	264	285	.260	.307	.355	662	91	-56	87	25		.962	11	*C-1233/O-12L,1-6,2	4.9

■ GEORGE WINKELMAN Winkelman, George Edward b: 2/18/1865, Washington, D.C. d: 5/19/60, Washington, D.C. BL/TL, Deb: 8/4/1883

YEAR	TM/L	G	AB	R	H	2B	3B	HR	RBI	BB	SO	AVG	OBP	SLG	OPS	OPS+	BR+	SB	CS	SBR	FA	FR	G/POS	TPR
1883	Lou-a	4	13	2	0	0	0	0		1		.000	.071	.000	71	-81	-2				.625	0	/O-4(3-1-0)	-0.2
1886	Was-N	1	5	0	1	0	0	0	0	0	1	.200	.200	.200	400	23	-0	0			.000	-1	/O-1(0-0-1),P-1	0.0
Total	2	5	18	2	1	0	0	0	0	1	1	.056	.105	.056	161	-51	-3	0			.625	-0	/O-5(3-1-1),P-1	-0.2

■ RANDY WINN Winn, Dwight Randolph b: 6/9/74, Los Angeles, Cal. BB/TR (BR 2000 (part)), 6'2", 175 lbs. Deb: 5/11/98

YEAR	TM/L	G	AB	R	H	2B	3B	HR	RBI	BB	SO	AVG	OBP	SLG	OPS	OPS+	BR+	SB	CS	SBR	FA	FR	G/POS	TPR
1998	TB-A	109	338	51	94	9	9	1	17	29	69	.278	.337	.367	704	82	-9	26	12	2	.980	-3	O-96(16-70-12)/D-4	-1.0
1999	TB-A	79	303	44	81	16	4	2	24	17	63	.267	.308	.366	675	70	-14	9	9	-1	.995	2	O-77(0-77-0)	-1.1
2000	TB-A	51	159	28	40	5	0	1	16	26	25	.252	.364	.302	666	71	-6	6	7	-1	.990	1	O-47(29-18-0)/D-1	-0.6
Total	3	239	800	123	215	30	13	4	57	72	157	.269	.332	.354	686	76	-28	41	28	-1	.988	-0	O-220(45-165-12)/D-5	-2.7

■ HERM WINNINGHAM Winningham, Herman Son b: 12/1/61, Orangeburg, S.C. BL/TR, 5'11", 185 lbs. Deb: 9/1/84 Career OF: (106-LF 547-CF 32-RF)

YEAR	TM/L	G	AB	R	H	2B	3B	HR	RBI	BB	SO	AVG	OBP	SLG	OPS	OPS+	BR+	SB	CS	SBR	FA	FR	G/POS	TPR
1984	NY-N	14	27	5	11	1	1	0	5	1	7	.407	.429	.519	947	167	2	2	1	0	1.000	-4	O-10(1-9-1)	-0.1
1985	Mon-N	125	312	30	74	6	5	3	21	28	72	.237	.300	.317	617	77	-10	20	9	1	.983	-4	*O-116(1-115-0)	-1.4
1986	Mon-N	90	185	23	40	6	3	4	11	18	51	.216	.286	.346	632	74	-7	12	7	0	.980	-7	O-66(3-56-7)/S-1	-1.5
1987	Mon-N	137	347	34	83	20	3	4	41	34	68	.239	.307	.349	656	71	-14	29	10	3	.975	-8	*O-131(0-131-0)	-2.0
1988	Mon-N	47	90	10	21	2	1	0	6	12	18	.233	.324	.278	601	71	-3	4	5	-1	.982	-3	O-30(0-29-1)	-0.8
	Cin-N	53	113	6	26	1	3	0	15	5	27	.230	.263	.292	555	57	-6	8	3	1	1.000	-3	O-42(14-21-8)	-1.0
	Yr	100	203	16	47	3	4	0	21	17	45	.232	.291	.286	577	63	-9	12	8	-0	.992	-7	O-72(14-50-9)	-1.8
1989	Cin-N	115	251	40	63	11	3	3	13	24	50	.251	.316	.355	671	88	-4	14	5	1	.980	-7	O-85(34-41-13)	-1.1
1990	*Cin-N	84	160	20	41	8	5	3	17	14	31	.256	.316	.425	741	98	-1	6	4	-0	1.000	-9	O-64(5-58-1)	-1.1
1991	Cin-N	98	169	17	38	6	1	1	4	11	40	.225	.272	.290	562	56	-10	4	4	-1	.953	-8	O-66(12-55-1)	-2.0
1992	Bos-A	105	234	27	55	8	1	1	14	10	53	.235	.266	.291	557	52	-15	6	5	-0	.975	-4	O-67(36-32-0)/D-6	-2.1
Total	9	868	1888	212	452	69	26	19	147	157	417	.239	.298	.334	631	74	-67	105	53	5	.980	-58	O-677C/D-6,S-1	-13.1

■ TOM WINSETT Winsett, John Thomas "Long Tom" b: 11/24/09, McKenzie, Tenn. d: 7/20/87, Memphis, Tenn. BL/TR, 6'2", 190 lbs. Deb: 4/20/30

YEAR	TM/L	G	AB	R	H	2B	3B	HR	RBI	BB	SO	AVG	OBP	SLG	OPS	OPS+	BR+	SB	CS	SBR	FA	FR	G/POS	TPR
1930	Bos-A	1	1	0	0	0	0	0	0	0	1	.000	.000	.000	0	-99	-0	0	0	0	.000	0	H	0.0
1931	Bos-A	64	76	6	15	1	0	1	7	4	21	.197	.247	.250	497	33	-8	0	0	0	1.000	-2	/O-8(8-0-0)	-0.8
1933	Bos-A	6	12	1	1	0	0	0	0	1	6	.083	.154	.083	237	-36	-2	0	0	0	1.000	-2	/O-4(2-0-2)	-0.4
1935	StL-N	7	12	2	6	1	0	0	2	2	3	.500	.571	.583	1155	203	2	0	0	0	.000	-1	/O-2(0-0-2)	0.1
1936	Bro-N	22	85	13	20	7	0	1	18	11	14	.235	.330	.353	683	83	-2	0			1.000	-1	O-21(21-0-0)	-0.2
1937	Bro-N	118	350	32	83	15	5	5	42	45	64	.237	.329	.351	681	84	-7	3			.960	1	*O-101(100-1-0)/P-1	-1.1
1938	Bro-N	12	30	6	9	1	0	1	7	6	4	.300	.417	.433	850	131	2	0			.882	-2	/O-9(5-0-4)	0.0
Total	7	230	566	60	134	25	5	8	76	69	113	.237	.325	.341	666	79	-16	3	0		.963	-2	O-145(136-1-8)/P-1	-2.4

■ MATT WINTERS Winters, Matthew Littleton b: 3/18/60, Buffalo, N.Y. BL/TR, 6'3", 215 lbs. Deb: 5/30/89

YEAR	TM/L	G	AB	R	H	2B	3B	HR	RBI	BB	SO	AVG	OBP	SLG	OPS	OPS+	BR+	SB	CS	SBR	FA	FR	G/POS	TPR
1989	KC-A	42	107	14	25	6	0	2	9	14	23	.234	.322	.346	668	89	-1	0	0	0	.939	-4	O-31(0-0-31)/D-3	-0.6

■ KETTLE WIRTS Wirts, Elwood Vernon b: 10/31/1897, Consumne, Cal. d: 7/12/68, Sacramento, Cal. BR/TR, 5'11", 170 lbs. Deb: 7/20/21

YEAR	TM/L	G	AB	R	H	2B	3B	HR	RBI	BB	SO	AVG	OBP	SLG	OPS	OPS+	BR+	SB	CS	SBR	FA	FR	G/POS	TPR
1921	Chi-N	7	11	0	2	0	0	0	1	0	3	.182	.182	.182	364	-3	-2	0	0	0	1.000	1	/C-5	-0.1
1922	Chi-N	31	58	7	10	2	0	1	6	12	15	.172	.314	.259	573	48	-4	0	0	0	.968	-5	C-27	-0.8
1923	Chi-N	5	5	2	1	0	0	0	1	2	0	.200	.429	.200	629	71	-0	0	0	0	1.000	1	/C-3	0.1
1924	Chi-A	6	12	0	1	0	0	0	0	2	2	.083	.214	.083	298	-22	-2	1	0	0	1.000	1	/C-5	-0.1
Total	4	49	86	9	14	2	0	1	8	16	20	.163	.294	.221	515	35	-8	1	0	0	.981	-3	/C-40	-0.9

■ HUGHIE WISE Wise, Hugh Edward b: 3/9/06, Campbellsville, Ky. d: 7/21/87, Plantation, Fla. BB/TR, 6', 178 lbs. Deb: 9/26/30

YEAR	TM/L	G	AB	R	H	2B	3B	HR	RBI	BB	SO	AVG	OBP	SLG	OPS	OPS+	BR+	SB	CS	SBR	FA	FR	G/POS	TPR
1930	Det-A	2	6	0	2	0	0	0	0	0	0	.333	.333	.333	667	68	-0	0	0	0	1.000	1	/C-2	0.1

■ CASEY WISE Wise, Kendall Cole b: 9/8/32, Lafayette, Ind. BB/TR, 6', 170 lbs. Deb: 4/16/57

YEAR	TM/L	G	AB	R	H	2B	3B	HR	RBI	BB	SO	AVG	OBP	SLG	OPS	OPS+	BR+	SB	CS	SBR	FA	FR	G/POS	TPR
1957	Chi-N	43	106	12	19	3	1	0	7	11	14	.179	.256	.226	483	32	-10	0	0	0	.940	3	2-31/S-5	-0.5
1958	*Mil-N	31	71	8	14	1	0	0	0	4	8	.197	.240	.211	451	23	-8	1	1	-0	1.000	-0	2-10/S-7,3-1	-0.7
1959	Mil-N	22	76	11	13	2	0	1	5	10	5	.171	.267	.237	504	39	-7	0	0	0	.989	-7	2-20/S-5	-1.3
1960	Det-A	30	68	6	10	0	2	2	5	4	9	.147	.194	.294	489	29	-7	1	0	0	.983	3	2-17,S-10/3-1	-0.3
Total	4	126	321	37	56	6	3	3	17	29	36	.174	.243	.240	483	31	-32	2	1	0	.968	-2	/2-78,S-27,3-2	-2.8

YEAR	TM/L	G	AB	R	H	2B	3B	HR	RBI	BB	SO	AVG	OBP	SLG	OPS	OPS+	BR+	SB	CS	SBR	FA	FR	G/POS	TPR
DEWAYNE WISE	Wise, Larry Dewayne b: 2/24/78, Columbia, S.C. BL/TL, 6'1", 180 lbs. Deb: 4/6/2000																							
2000	Tor-A	28	22	3	3	0	0	0	0	1	5	.136	.208	.136	345	-10	-4	1	0	0	1.000	-3	O-18(14-1-3)	-0.6
NICK WISE	Wise, Nicholas Joseph b: 6/15/1866, Boston, Mass. d: 1/15/23, Boston, Mass. BR/TR, 5'11", 194 lbs. Deb: 6/20/1888																							
1888	Bos-N	1	3	0	0	0	0	0	0	0	0	.000	.000	.000	0	-98	-1	0			.000	-0	/O-1(0-0-1),C-1	-0.1
SAM WISE	Wise, Samuel Washington "Modoc" b: 8/18/1857, Akron, Ohio d: 1/22/10, Akron, Ohio BL/TR, 5'10.5", 170 lbs. Deb: 7/30/1881 Career OF: (12-LF 0-CF 36-RF)																							
1881	Det-N	1	4	0	2	0	0	0	0	0	2	.500	.500	.500	1000	207	0				.571	-0	/3-1	0.0
1882	Bos-N	78	298	44	66	11	4	4	34	5	45	.221	.234	.326	560	77	-8				.852	-13	*S-72/3-6	-1.7
1883	Bos-N	96	406	73	110	25	7	4	58	13	74	.271	.294	.397	690	105	2				.823	-2	*S-96	0.2
1884	Bos-N	114	426	60	91	15	9	4	41	25	104	.214	.257	.319	576	81	-9				.884	6	*S-107/2-7	0.0
1885	Bos-N	107	424	71	120	20	10	4	46	25	61	.283	.323	.406	729	139	18				.858	13	*S-79,2-22/O-6(4-0-2)	3.2
1886	Bos-N	96	387	71	112	19	12	4	72	33	61	.289	.345	.432	777	140	19	31			.956	-24	1-57,2-20,S-18,/O-1R	-0.8
1887	Bos-N	113	503	103	192	27	17	9	92	36	44	.382	.390	.522	913	151	32	43			.869	-6	S-72,O-27R,2-16	2.4
1888	Bos-N	105	417	66	100	19	12	4	40	34	66	.240	.306	.372	678	113	6	33			.888	10	S-89/3-6,1-5,O-4L,2	1.8
1889	Was-N	121	472	79	118	15	8	4	62	61	62	.250	.341	.341	682	97	0	24			.916	-23	2-72,S-26,3-13,O-10R	-1.7
1890	Buf-P	119	505	95	148	29	11	5	102	46	45	.293	.359	.424	783	119	14	19			.906	5	*2-119	1.9
1891	Bal-a	103	388	70	96	14	5	1	48	62	52	.247	.364	.317	681	94	-1	33			.888	-13	*2-99/S-4	-0.9
1893	Was-N	122	521	102	162	27	17	5	77	49	27	.311	.375	.457	831	124	16	20			.924	14	*2-91,3-31	2.9
Total	12	1175	4751	834	1317	221	112	48	672	389	643	.277	.332	.397	729	114	90	203			.859	-33	S-563,2-448/1-62,3O	7.3
PHIL WISNER	Wisner, Philip N. b: 7/1869, Washington, D.C. d: 7/5/36, Washington, D.C. TR, Deb: 8/30/1895																							
1895	Was-N	1	0	0	0	0	0	0	0	0	0	—	—	—	—	—	0	0			.250	-1	/S-1	0.0
DAVE WISSMAN	Wissman, David Alvin b: 2/17/41, Greenfield, Mass. BL/TR, 6'2", 178 lbs. Deb: 9/15/64																							
1964	Pit-N	16	27	2	4	0	0	0	0	1	9	.148	.179	.148	327	-7	-4	0	0	0	1.000	-1	O-10(7-3-0)	-0.6
TEX WISTERZIL	Wisterzil, George John b: 3/7/1891, Detroit, Mich. d: 6/27/64, San Antonio, Tex. BR/TR, 5'9.5", 150 lbs. Deb: 4/14/14																							
1914	Bro-F	149	534	54	137	18	10	0	66	34	47	.257	.314	.328	642	76	-27	17			**.956**	16	*3-149	-0.7
1915	Bro-F	36	106	13	33	3	3	0	21	21	7	.311	.438	.396	835	137	5	8			.949	3	3-31	0.9
	Chi-F	7	20	3	4	1	0	0	0	3	2	.200	.304	.250	554	60	-1	0			.955	0	/3-6	-0.1
	StL-F	8	24	1	5	1	0	0	4	2	2	.208	.296	.250	546	52	-2	2			.939	2	/3-8	0.1
	Chi-F	42	144	12	36	3	1	0	14	5	10	.250	.280	.285	565	63	-10	2			.968	8	3-42	0.0
	Yr	93	294	29	78	8	4	0	39	31	21	.265	.345	.320	665	90	-7	12			.958	14	3-87	0.9
Total	2	242	828	83	215	26	14	0	105	65	68	.260	.326	.325	651	81	-34	29			.957	29	3-236	0.2
MICKEY WITEK	Witek, Nicholas Joseph b: 12/19/15, Luzerne, Pa. d: 8/24/90, Kingston, Pa. BR/TR, 5'10", 170 lbs. Deb: 4/16/40																							
1940	NY-N	119	433	34	111	7	0	3	31	24	17	.256	.295	.293	589	62	-22	2			.958	**19**	S-89,2-32	0.5
1941	NY-N	26	94	11	34	5	0	1	16	4	2	.362	.388	.447	835	132	4	0			.933	2	2-23	0.7
1942	NY-N	148	553	72	144	19	6	5	48	36	20	.260	.306	.344	649	89	-9	2			**.978**	-1	*2-147	0.0
1943	NY-N	153	622	68	195	17	0	6	55	41	23	.314	.356	.370	726	109	7	1			.967	16	*2-153	3.3
1946	NY-N	82	284	32	75	13	2	4	29	28	10	.264	.330	.366	696	97	-1	1			.962	-12	2-42,3-35	-1.3
1947	NY-N	51	160	22	35	4	1	3	17	15	12	.219	.286	.313	598	58	-10	1			.983	11	2-40/3-3	0.3
1949	NY-A	2	1	0	1	0	0	0	0	0	0	1.000	1.000	1.000	2000	430	0	0	0	0	.000	0	H	0.0
Total	7	581	2147	239	595	65	9	22	196	148	84	.277	.324	.347	670	90	-30	7	0		.969	34	2-437/S-89,3-38	3.5
FRANK WITHROW	Withrow, Frank Blaine "Kid" b: 6/14/1891, Greenwood, Mo. d: 9/5/66, Omaha, Neb. BR/TR, 5'11.5", 187 lbs. Deb: 4/15/20																							
1920	Phi-N	48	132	8	24	4	1	0	12	8	26	.182	.239	.227	467	33	-11	0	0	0	.973	3	C-48	-0.5
1922	Phi-N	10	21	3	7	2	0	0	3	3	5	.333	.417	.429	845	108	0	0	0	0	.909	1	/C-8	0.2
Total	2	58	153	11	31	6	1	0	15	11	31	.203	.265	.255	520	45	-11	0	0	0	.965	4	/C-56	-0.3
CORKY WITHROW	Withrow, Raymond Wallace b: 11/28/37, High Coal, W.Va. BR/TR, 6'3.5", 197 lbs. Deb: 9/6/63																							
1963	StL-N	6	9	0	0	0	0	0	1	0	2	.000	.000	.000	0	-91	-2	0	0	0	1.000	-0	/O-2(1-0-1)	-0.3
RON WITMEYER	Witmeyer, Ronald Herman b: 6/28/67, West Islip, N.Y. BL/TL, 6'3", 215 lbs. Deb: 8/25/91																							
1991	Oak-A	11	19	0	1	0	0	0	0	0	5	.053	.053	.053	105	-75	-4	0	0	0	1.000	0	/1-8	-0.5
KEVIN WITT	Witt, Kevin Joseph b: 1/5/76, High Point, N.C. BL/TR, 6'4", 195 lbs. Deb: 9/15/98																							
1998	Tor-A	5	7	0	1	0	0	0	0	0	3	.143	.143	.143	286	-25	-1	0	0	0	1.000	0	/1-1	-0.1
1999	Tor-A	15	34	3	7	1	0	1	5	2	9	.206	.250	.324	574	44	-3	0	0	0	.000	0	D-10	-0.3
Total	2	20	41	3	8	1	0	1	5	2	12	.195	.233	.293	525	33	-4	0	0	0	1.000	0	/D-10,1-1	-0.4
WHITEY WITT	Witt, Lawton Walter (b: Ladislaw Waldemar Wittkowski) b: 9/28/1895, Orange, Mass. d: 7/14/88, Salem Co., N.J. BL/TR, 5'7", 150 lbs. Deb: 4/12/16 Career OF: (50-LF 447-CF 232-RF)																							
1916	Phi-A	143	563	64	138	16	15	2	36	55	71	.245	.315	.337	652	101	-1	19			.902	-1	*S-142	0.9
1917	Phi-A	128	452	62	114	13	4	0	28	65	45	.252	.346	.299	645	98	1	12			.935	5	*S-111/O-7(7-0-0),3-6	1.5
1919	Phi-A	122	460	56	123	15	6	0	33	46	26	.267	.334	.326	660	85	-9	11			.972	-3	O-59L,2-56/3-2	-1.4
1920	Phi-A	65	218	29	70	11	3	1	25	27	16	.321	.396	.413	809	113	5	2	3	-1	.960	-8	O-50(0-5-45),2-10/S-2	-0.6
1921	Phi-A	154	629	100	198	31	11	4	45	77	52	.315	.390	.418	809	106	7	16	15	-2	.959	-2	*O-154(0-0-154)	-0.9
1922	*NY-A	140	528	98	157	11	6	4	40	**89**	29	.297	.400	.364	763	98	3	5	8	-2	.976	-5	*O-139(0-109-30)	-1.1
1923	*NY-A	146	596	113	187	18	10	6	56	67	42	.314	.386	.408	794	107	8	2	7	-2	**.979**	2	*O-144(0-144-0)	0.1
1924	NY-A	147	600	88	178	26	5	1	36	45	20	.297	.346	.362	707	83	-15	9	7	-0	.976	-1	*O-144(0-144-0)	-2.2
1925	NY-A	31	40	9	8	2	1	0	0	6	2	.200	.304	.300	604	55	-3	1	1	-0	1.000	-1	O-10(0-9-1)	-0.4
1926	Bro-N	63	85	13	22	1	1	0	3	12	6	.259	.351	.294	645	76	-2	1			.920	-2	O-22(3-17-2)	-0.4
Total	10	1139	4171	632	1195	144	62	18	302	489	309	.287	.362	.364	726	97	-6	78	41		.971	-16	O-729C,S-255/2-66,3	-4.5
JERRY WITTE	Witte, Jerome Charles b: 7/30/15, St.Louis, Mo. BR/TR, 6'1", 190 lbs. Deb: 9/10/46																							
1946	StL-A	18	73	7	14	2	0	2	4	0	18	.192	.192	.301	493	35	-7	0	0	0	.967	-2	1-18	-1.0
1947	StL-A	34	99	4	14	2	1	2	12	11	22	.141	.227	.242	470	30	-10	0	0	0	.983	-1	1-27	-1.3
Total	2	52	172	11	28	4	1	4	16	11	40	.163	.213	.267	481	32	-16	0	0	0	.977	-4	/1-45	-2.3
JOHN WOCKENFUSS	Wockenfuss, Johnny Bilton b: 2/27/49, Welch, W.Va. BR/TR, 6', 190 lbs. Deb: 8/11/74 Career OF: (42-LF 0-CF 69-RF)																							
1974	Det-A	13	29	1	4	1	0	0	2	3	2	.138	.219	.172	391	13	-3	0	0	0	.932	-1	C-13	-0.4
1975	Det-A	35	118	15	27	6	3	4	13	10	15	.229	.289	.432	721	97	-1	0	0	0	.982	4	C-34	0.5
1976	Det-A	60	144	18	32	7	2	3	10	17	14	.222	.309	.361	670	92	-1	0	3	-1	.941	-7	C-59	-0.8
1977	Det-A	53	164	26	45	8	1	9	25	14	18	.274	.331	.500	831	117	3	0	0	0	.985	-7	C-37/O-9(6-0-3),D-3	-0.2
1978	Det-A	71	187	23	53	5	0	7	22	21	14	.283	.359	.422	781	116	4	0	1	-0	.978	-8	O-60(6-0-55)/D-2	-0.7
1979	Det-A	87	231	27	61	9	1	15	46	18	40	.264	.323	.506	829	116	4	2	2	-0	.996	0	1-31,C-20,D-18,/O-6L	0.3
1980	Det-A	126	372	56	102	13	2	16	65	68	64	.274	.391	.449	839	126	16	1	4	-1	.983	0	1-52,D-28,C-25,O-23L	1.2
1981	Det-A	70	172	20	37	4	0	9	25	28	22	.215	.325	.395	720	103	1	0	0	0	.984	-3	D-39,1-25/C-5,O-1L	-0.4
1982	Det-A	70	193	28	58	9	0	8	32	29	21	.301	.392	.472	863	135	10	0	0	0	.981	-3	C-24,1-17,D-17,O/3	0.6
1983	Det-A	92	245	32	66	8	1	9	44	31	37	.269	.351	.420	772	114	5	1	1	-0	1.000	4	D-39,C-29,1-13,/3O	0.8
1984	Phi-N	86	180	20	52	3	1	6	24	30	24	.289	.390	.417	807	125	7	1	0	0	.996	-7	1-39,C-21/3-2	0.0
1985	Phi-N	32	37	1	6	0	0	0	2	8	7	.162	.311	.162	473	35	-3	0	0	0	1.000	-1	/1-7,C-2	-0.4
Total	12	795	2072	267	543	73	11	86	310	277	278	.262	.351	.432	783	114	42	5	11	-3	.972	-27	C-269,1-184,DO/3	0.5
ANDY WOEHR	Woehr, Andrew Emil b: 2/4/1896, Fort Wayne, Ind. d: 7/24/90, Fort Wayne, Ind. BR/TR, 5'11", 165 lbs. Deb: 9/15/23																							
1923	Phi-N	13	41	3	14	2	0	0	3	1	1	.341	.357	.390	747	87	-1	0	0	0	.975	3	3-13	0.3
1924	Phi-N	50	152	11	33	4	5	0	17	5	8	.217	.252	.309	561	44	-12	2	2	-0	.920	-5	3-44/2-1	-1.5
Total	2	63	193	14	47	6	5	0	20	6	9	.244	.274	.326	600	53	-13	2	2	-0	.935	-2	/3-57,2-1	-1.2

■ **JOE WOERLIN** Woerlin, Joseph b: 10/9/1864, France d: 6/22/19, St.Louis, Mo. Deb: 7/21/1895

YEAR	TM/L	G	AB	R	H	2B	3B	HR	RBI	BB	SO	AVG	OBP	SLG	OPS	OPS+	BR+	SB	CS	SBR	FA	FR	G/POS	TPR
1895	Was-N	1	3	1	1	0	0	0	0	0	0	.333	.333	.333	667	73	-0	0			1.000	-1	/S-1	0.0

■ **JIM WOHLFORD** Wohlford, James Eugene b: 2/28/51, Visalia, Cal. BR/TR, 5'11", 175 lbs. Deb: 9/1/72 Career OF: (616-LF 35-CF 268-RF)

YEAR	TM/L	G	AB	R	H	2B	3B	HR	RBI	BB	SO	AVG	OBP	SLG	OPS	OPS+	BR+	SB	CS	SBR	FA	FR	G/POS	TPR
1972	KC-A	15	25	3	6	1	0	0	0	2	6	.240	.321	.280	601	80	-1	0	0	0	.950	-2	/2-8	-0.3
1973	KC-A	45	109	21	29	1	3	2	10	11	12	.266	.333	.385	719	95	-1	1	1	-0	1.000	3	D-19,O-13(12-0-1)	0.1
1974	KC-A	143	501	55	136	16	7	2	44	39	74	.271	.328	.343	671	88	-7	16	13	-1	.982	1	*O-138(126-0-16)/D-1	-1.6
1975	KC-A	116	353	45	90	10	5	0	30	34	37	.255	.322	.312	634	78	-10	12	7	0	.953	-6	*O-102(43-0-66)/D-4	-2.1
1976	*KC-A	107	293	47	73	10	2	1	24	29	24	.249	.319	.307	626	83	-6	22	16	-1	.975	-1	O-93(84-2-8)/2-1,D-3	-1.2
1977	Mil-A	129	391	41	97	16	3	2	36	21	49	.248	.288	.320	608	65	-19	17	16	-2	.981	-2	*O-125L/2-1,D-1	-2.7
1978	Mil-A	46	118	16	35	7	2	1	19	6	10	.297	.331	.415	746	108	1	3	2	-0	.982	-5	O-35(21-4-12)/D-4	-0.5
1979	Mil-A	63	175	19	46	13	1	1	17	8	28	.263	.295	.366	661	77	-6	6	2	1	.969	-2	O-55(35-14-8)/D-5	-0.9
1980	SF-N	91	193	17	54	6	4	1	24	13	23	.280	.329	.368	696	96	-1	1	4	-1	.989	-2	O-49(40-4-8)/3-1	-0.6
1981	SF-N	50	68	4	11	3	0	1	7	4	9	.162	.208	.250	458	30	-6	0	0	0	1.000	-3	O-10(10-0-0)	-1.0
1982	SF-N	97	250	37	64	12	1	2	25	30	36	.256	.336	.336	672	89	-3	8	3	1	.992	-2	O-72(68-0-6)	-0.7
1983	Mon-N	83	141	7	39	8	0	1	14	5	14	.277	.301	.355	656	82	-4	0	0	0	.988	-11	O-61(18-6-48)	-1.7
1984	Mon-N	95	213	20	64	13	2	5	29	14	19	.300	.344	.451	794	127	7	3	0	1	.989	-2	O-59(44-1-14)/3-2	0.3
1985	Mon-N	70	125	7	24	5	1	1	15	16	18	.192	.284	.272	556	60	-7	0	2	-1	1.000	-5	O-43(8-0-36)	-1.4
1986	Mon-N	70	94	10	25	4	2	1	11	9	17	.266	.330	.383	713	97	-0	0	2	-1	1.000	-3	O-22(10-0-12)/3-6	-0.5
Total	15	1220	3049	349	793	125	33	21	305	241	376	.260	.316	.343	659	85	-62	89	68	-4	.980	-41	O-877L/D-37,2-10,3	-14.8

■ **JOHN WOJCIK** Wojcik, John Joseph b: 4/6/42, Olean, N.Y. BL/TR, 6' ", 175 lbs. Deb: 9/9/62

YEAR	TM/L	G	AB	R	H	2B	3B	HR	RBI	BB	SO	AVG	OBP	SLG	OPS	OPS+	BR+	SB	CS	SBR	FA	FR	G/POS	TPR
1962	KC-A	16	43	8	13	4	0	0	9	13	4	.302	.474	.395	869	131	3	3	0	1	1.000	-1	O-12(10-0-5)	0.2
1963	KC-A	19	59	7	11	0	0	0	2	8	8	.186	.284	.186	470	33	-5	2	0	0	1.000	0	O-17(10-2-6)	-0.5
1964	KC-A	6	22	1	3	0	0	0	0	2	8	.136	.208	.136	345	-2	-3	0	0	0	1.000	0	/O-6(6-0-0)	-0.4
Total	3	41	124	16	27	4	0	0	11	23	20	.218	.345	.250	595	64	-5	5	0	1	1.000	-1	/O-35(26-2-11)	-0.7

■ **RAY WOLF** Wolf, Raymond Bernard "Grandpa" b: 7/15/04, Chicago, Ill. d: 10/6/79, Fort Worth, Tex. BR/TR, 5'11", 175 lbs. Deb: 7/27/27

YEAR	TM/L	G	AB	R	H	2B	3B	HR	RBI	BB	SO	AVG	OBP	SLG	OPS	OPS+	BR+	SB	CS	SBR	FA	FR	G/POS	TPR
1927	Cin-N	1	1	0	0	0	0	0	0	0	0	.000	.000	.000	0	-99	-0	0			1.000	-0	/1-1	0.0

■ **JIMMY WOLF** Wolf, William Van Winkle "Chicken" b: 5/12/1862, Louisville, Ky. d: 5/16/03, Louisville, Ky. BR/TR, 5'9", 190 lbs. Deb: 5/2/1882 M Career OF: (17-LF 3-CF 1024-RF)

YEAR	TM/L	G	AB	R	H	2B	3B	HR	RBI	BB	SO	AVG	OBP	SLG	OPS	OPS+	BR+	SB	CS	SBR	FA	FR	G/POS	TPR
1882	Lou-a	78	318	46	95	11	8	0		9		.299	.318	.384	702	144	15				.902	-2	*O-70R/S-9,1-1,P-1	1.1
1883	Lou-a	98	389	59	102	17	9	1		5		.262	.272	.360	631	110	5				.890	17	*O-78R,C-20/S-5,2-1	2.0
1884	Lou-a	110	486	79	146	24	11	3	73	4		.300	.310	.414	724	140	20				.884	0	*O-101R,C-11/S-1,31	1.9
1885	Lou-a	112	483	79	141	23	17	1	52	11		.292	.309	.416	725	128	13				.917	-0	*O-111R/C-2,3-1,P-1	1.1
1886	Lou-a	130	545	93	148	17	12	3	61	27		.272	.310	.363	673	105	0	23			.934	9	*O-122R/1-8,C-3,2P	0.7
1887	Lou-a	137	603	103	194	27	13	2	102	34		.322	.331	.385	715	97	-4	45			.940	8	*O-128(8-1-120),1-11	0.2
1888	Lou-a	128	538	80	154	28	11	0	67	25		.286	.320	.379	700	126	15	41			.886	7	O-85R,S-39/3-4,C1	2.0
1889	Lou-a	130	546	72	159	20	9	3	57	29	34	.291	.333	.377	710	104	2	18			.946	-1	O-88R,1-16,2-13,S/3M	-0.1
1890	*Lou-a	134	543	100	**197**	29	11	4	98	43		**.363**	.421	.479	900	169	46	46			.939	-2	*O-123(0-0-123),3-12	3.8
1891	Lou-a	136	528	67	135	16	8	1	81	42	36	.256	.320	.322	642	85	-11	13			.922	5	*O-131R/1-5,3-1	-0.6
1892	StL-N	3	14	1	2	0	0	0	1	0	1	.143	.143	.143	286	-14	-2	0			1.000	-1	/O-3(0-0-3)	-0.3
Total	11	1196	4993	779	1473	212	109	18	592	229	71	.295	.327	.388	715	118	99	186			.918	41	*O-1040R/S-64,1C32P	11.8

■ **HARRY WOLFE** Wolfe, Harold "Whitey" b: 11/24/1890, Massachusetts d: 7/28/71, Fort Wayne, Ind. BR/TR, 5'8", 160 lbs. Deb: 4/15/17

YEAR	TM/L	G	AB	R	H	2B	3B	HR	RBI	BB	SO	AVG	OBP	SLG	OPS	OPS+	BR+	SB	CS	SBR	FA	FR	G/POS	TPR
1917	Chi-N	9	5	1	2	0	0	0	1	1	1	.400	.500	.400	900	164	0	0			1.000	0	/O-2(1-0-0),S-1	0.1
	Pit-N	3	5	0	0	0	0	0	0	1	4	.000	.167	.000	167	-45	-1	0			.875	1	/2-1,S-1	0.0
	Yr	12	10	1	2	0	0	0	1	2	5	.200	.333	.200	533	61	-0	0			1.000	1	/O-2(1-0-0),S-2,2-1	0.1

■ **LARRY WOLFE** Wolfe, Laurence Marcy b: 3/2/53, Melbourne, Fla. BR/TR, 5'11", 170 lbs. Deb: 9/16/77

YEAR	TM/L	G	AB	R	H	2B	3B	HR	RBI	BB	SO	AVG	OBP	SLG	OPS	OPS+	BR+	SB	CS	SBR	FA	FR	G/POS	TPR
1977	Min-A	8	25	3	6	1	0	0	6	1	0	.240	.269	.280	549	51	-2	0	0	0	1.000	0	/3-8	-0.2
1978	Min-A	88	235	25	55	10	1	3	25	36	27	.234	.336	.323	659	85	-4	0	1	-0	.953	6	3-81/S-7	0.1
1979	Bos-A	47	78	12	19	4	0	3	15	17	21	.244	.385	.410	796	109	2	0	0	0	.963	6	2-27/3-9,S-2,C1D	0.8
1980	Bos-A	18	23	3	3	1	0	1	4	0	5	.130	.130	.304	435	15	-3	0	0	0	1.000	1	3-14/D-4	-0.2
Total	4	161	361	43	83	16	1	7	50	54	53	.230	.332	.338	670	84	-7	0	1	-0	.957	13	3-112/2-27,S-9,D1C	0.5

■ **POLLY WOLFE** Wolfe, Roy Chamberlain b: 9/1/1888, Knoxville, Ill. d: 11/21/38, Morris, Ill. BL/TR, 5'10", 170 lbs. Deb: 9/22/12

YEAR	TM/L	G	AB	R	H	2B	3B	HR	RBI	BB	SO	AVG	OBP	SLG	OPS	OPS+	BR+	SB	CS	SBR	FA	FR	G/POS	TPR
1912	Chi-A	1	1	0	0	0	0	0	0	0		.000	.000	.000	0	-99	-0	0			.000	0	H	0.0
1914	Chi-A	8	28	0	6	0	0	0	0	3	6	.214	.290	.214	505	53	-2	1	1	-0	.875	-1	/O-7(0-0-7)	-0.4
Total	2	9	29	0	6	0	0	0	0	3	6	.207	.281	.207	488	47	-2	1	1		.875	-1	/O-7(0-0-7)	-0.4

■ **ABE WOLSTENHOLME** Wolstenholme, Abraham Lincoln b: 3/4/1861, Philadelphia, Pa. d: 3/4/16, Philadelphia, Pa. Deb: 6/4/1883

YEAR	TM/L	G	AB	R	H	2B	3B	HR	RBI	BB	SO	AVG	OBP	SLG	OPS	OPS+	BR+	SB	CS	SBR	FA	FR	G/POS	TPR
1883	Phi-N	3	11	0	1	1	0	0	0	0	0	.091	.091	.182	273	-22	-2				.727	-3	/C-2,O-1(1-0-0)	-0.4

■ **HARRY WOLTER** Wolter, Harry Meigs b: 7/11/1884, Monterey, Cal. d: 7/7/70, Palo Alto, Cal. BL/TL, 5'10", 175 lbs. Deb: 5/14/07 Career OF: (5-LF 126-CF 361-RF)

YEAR	TM/L	G	AB	R	H	2B	3B	HR	RBI	BB	SO	AVG	OBP	SLG	OPS	OPS+	BR+	SB	CS	SBR	FA	FR	G/POS	TPR
1907	Cin-N	4	15	1	2	0	0	0	1	0		.133	.133	.133	267	-16	-2	0			1.000	-0	/O-4(0-0-4)	-0.3
	Pit-N	1	1	0	0	0	0	0	0	0		.000	.000	.000	0	-99	-0	0			.000	-0	/P-1	0.0
	StL-N	16	47	4	16	0	0	0	6	3		.340	.380	.340	720	130	2	1			.962	3	O-12(1-6-2)/P-3	0.5
	Yr	21	63	5	18	0	0	0	7	3		.286	.318	.286	604	91	-1	1			.969	3	O-16(1-6-6)/P-4	0.2
1909	Bos-A	54	121	14	29	2	4	2	10	9		.240	.292	.372	664	107	1	2			.978	-1	1-17,P-11/O-9(0-0-9)	0.0
1910	NY-A	135	479	84	128	15	9	4	42	66		.267	.364	.361	725	120	13	39			.940	-3	*O-129(1-0-128)/1-2	0.5
1911	NY-A	122	434	78	132	17	15	4	36	62		.304	.396	.440	836	125	15	28			.951	4	*O-113(0-7-106)/1-2	1.3
1912	NY-A	12	32	8	11	2	1	0	1	10		.344	.512	.469	980	171	4	5			.923	-1	/O-9(0-5-4)	0.2
1913	NY-A	127	425	53	108	18	6	2	43	80	50	.254	.377	.339	716	109	9	13			.946	-7	*O-121(0-106-14)	-0.8
1917	Chi-N	117	353	44	88	15	7	0	28	38	40	.249	.324	.331	655	94	-2	7			.942	-4	O-97(3-2-94)/1-1	-1.2
Total	7	588	1907	286	514	69	42	12	167	268	90	.270	.365	.369	733	114	39	95			.941	-10	O-494R/1-22,P-15	0.2

■ **HARRY WOLVERTON** Wolverton, Harry Sterling "Fighting Harry" b: 12/6/1873, Mt.Vernon, Ohio d: 2/4/37, Oakland, Cal. BL/TR, 5'11", 205 lbs. Deb: 9/25/1898 M

YEAR	TM/L	G	AB	R	H	2B	3B	HR	RBI	BB	SO	AVG	OBP	SLG	OPS	OPS+	BR+	SB	CS	SBR	FA	FR	G/POS	TPR
1898	Chi-N	13	49	4	16	1	0	0	2	1		.327	.353	.347	700	101	0	1			.848	3	3-13	0.3
1899	Chi-N	99	389	50	111	14	11	1	49	30		.285	.350	.386	736	105	2	14			.860	-6	3-98/S-1	-0.2
1900	Chi-N	3	11	2	2	0	0	0	0	2		.182	.308	.182	490	38	-1	1			.875	-2	/3-3	-0.2
	Phi-N	101	383	42	108	10	8	3	58	20		.282	.323	.373	696	92	-5	4			.881	-9	*3-101	-1.2
	Yr	104	394	44	110	10	8	3	58	22		.279	.322	.368	690	91	-6	5			.881	-11	*3-104	-1.4
1901	Phi-N	93	379	42	117	15	4	0	43	22		.309	.356	.369	726	108	4	13			**.921**	3	3-93	1.0
1902	Was-A	59	249	35	62	8	3	1	23	13		.249	.292	.317	609	68	-11	8			.904	3	3-59	-0.6
	Phi-N	34	136	12	40	3	2	0	16	9		.294	.347	.346	693	114	2	3			.931	9	3-34	1.3
1903	Phi-N	123	494	72	152	13	12	0	53	18		.308	.342	.383	725	110	5	10			**.941**	1	*3-123	0.9
1904	Phi-N	102	398	43	106	15	5	0	49	26		.266	.321	.329	650	105	2	18			.925	1	*3-102	0.6
1905	Bos-N	122	463	38	104	15	7	2	55	23		.225	.276	.300	576	73	-16	10			.934	4	*3-122	-0.9
1912	NY-A	34	50	6	15	1	1	0	4	2		.300	.340	.360	700	94	-0	1			.821	-1	/3-8,M	-0.1
Total	9	783	3001	346	833	95	53	7	352	166		.278	.326	.352	677	96	-16	83			.909	6	3-756/S-1	0.9

■ **TONY WOMACK** Womack, Anthony Darrell b: 9/25/69, Chatham, Va. BL/TR, 5'9", 160 lbs. Deb: 9/10/93 Career OF: (0-LF 16-CF 125-RF)

YEAR	TM/L	G	AB	R	H	2B	3B	HR	RBI	BB	SO	AVG	OBP	SLG	OPS	OPS+	BR+	SB	CS	SBR	FA	FR	G/POS	TPR
1993	Pit-N	15	24	5	2	0	0	0	0	3	3	.083	.185	.083	269	-25	-4	2	0	0	.971	5	/S-6	0.2
1994	Pit-N	5	12	4	4	0	0	0	1	2	3	.333	.429	.333	762	101	0	0	0	0	.750	-3	/2-3,S-2	-0.3
1996	Pit-N	17	30	11	10	3	1	0	7	6	1	.333	.459	.500	959	149	3	2	0	0	1.000	-4	/O-6(0-5-1),2-4	-0.1
1997	Pit-N★	155	641	85	178	26	9	6	50	43	109	.278	.326	.374	700	81	-17	**60**	7	**11**	.974	3	*2-152/S-4	0.4
1998	Pit-N	159	655	85	185	26	7	3	45	38	94	.282	.322	.357	679	77	-21	**58**	8	**10**	.978	7	*2-152/O-5(0-5-0),S-2	0.4
1999	*Ari-N	144	614	111	170	25	10	4	41	52	68	.277	.335	.370	705	78	-20	**72**	13	**11**	.992	-9	*O-123R,2-19,S-19	-2.0

YEAR	TM/L	G	AB	R	H	2B	3B	HR	RBI	BB	SO	AVG	OBP	SLG	OPS	OPS+	BR+	SB	CS	SBR	FA	FR	G/POS	TPR
2000	Ari-N	146	617	95	167	21	**14**	7	57	30	74	.271	.310	.384	694	73	-26	45	11	6	.970	-15	*S-143/O-2(0-0-2)	-2.1
Total	7	641	2593	396	716	101	41	20	201	174	352	.276	.324	.370	694	78	-86	239	39	39	.974	-16	2-330,S-176,O-136R	-3.5
■ **SID WOMACK**	Womack, Sidney Kirk "Tex" b: 10/2/1896, Greensburg, La. d: 8/28/58, Jackson, Miss. BR/TR, 5'10.5", 185 lbs. Deb: 8/15/26																							
1926	Bos-N	1	3	0	0	0	0	0	1	0	0	.000	.000	.000	0	-99	-1	0			1.000	0	/C-1	-0.1
■ **WOOD**	Wood Deb: 9/30/1874																							
1874	Bal-n	1	5	0	0	0	0	0	0	0	1	.000	.000	.000	0	-99	-1	0	0	0	.000	-2	/2-1	-0.3
■ **DOC WOOD**	Wood, Charles Spencer b: 2/28/1900, Batesville, Miss. d: 11/3/74, New Orleans, La. BR/TR, 5'10", 150 lbs. Deb: 7/21/23																							
1923	Phi-A	3	3	0	1	0	0	0	0	0	0	.333	.333	.333	667	75	-0	0	0	0	.833	1	/S-3	0.1
■ **TED WOOD**	Wood, Edward Robert b: 1/4/67, Mansfield, Ohio BL/TL, 6'2", 178 lbs. Deb: 9/4/91																							
1991	SF-N	10	25	0	3	0	0	0	1	2	11	.120	.185	.120	305	-13	-4	0	0	0	.909	-1	/O-8(0-0-8)	-0.6
1992	SF-N	24	58	5	12	2	0	1	3	6	15	.207	.292	.293	585	70	-2	0	0	0	.972	1	O-16(6-0-10)	-0.2
1993	Mon-N	13	26	4	5	1	0	0	3	3	3	.192	.276	.231	507	36	-2	0	0	0	1.000	-0	/O-8(8-0-1)	-0.3
Total	3	47	109	9	20	3	0	1	7	11	29	.183	.264	.239	503	42	-8	0	0	0	.968	-1	/O-32(14-0-19)	-1.1
■ **FRED WOOD**	Wood, Fred S. b: 1863, Hamilton, Ont., Canada d: 8/23/33, New York, N.Y. 5'5", 150 lbs. Deb: 5/14/1884 F																							
1884	Det-N	12	42	4	2	0	0	0	1	3	18	.048	.111	.048	159	-51	-7				.889	-1	/C-7,O-6(0-0-6),S-1	-0.7
1885	Buf-N	1	4	0	1	0	0	0	0	0	0	.250	.250	.250	500	60	-0				.833	-0	/C-1	0.0
Total	2	13	46	4	3	0	0	0	1	3	18	.065	.122	.065	188	-41	-7				.883	-1	/C-8,O-6(0-0-6),S-1	-0.7
■ **GEORGE WOOD**	Wood, George A. "Dandy" b: 11/9/1858, Boston, Mass. d: 4/4/24, Harrisburg, Pa. BL/TR, 5'10.5", 175 lbs. Deb: 5/1/1880 MU Career OF: (1192-LF 5-CF 36-RF)																							
1880	Wor-N	81	327	37	80	16	5	0	28	10	37	.245	.267	.324	591	91	-4				.887	-7	*O-80(80-0-0)/3-2,1-1	-1.5
1881	Det-N	80	337	54	100	18	9	2	32	19	32	.297	.334	.421	756	131	11				.862	-2	*O-80(80-0-0)	0.4
1882	Det-N	84	375	69	101	12	12	**7**	29	14	30	.269	.296	.421	717	127	11				.884	2	*O-84(84-0-0)	1.0
1883	Det-N	99	441	81	133	26	11	5	47	25	37	.302	.339	.444	784	142	23				.876	9	*O-99(96-3-0)/P-1	2.5
1884	Det-N	114	473	79	119	16	10	8	29	39	75	.252	.309	.378	687	122	14				.896	3	*O-114(114-0-1)/3-1	1.2
1885	Det-N	82	362	62	105	19	8	5	28	13	19	.290	.315	.428	743	138	14				.885	1	O-70L,3-12/S-1,P-1	1.2
1886	Phi-N	106	450	81	123	18	15	4	50	23	75	.273	.309	.407	715	115	7	9			.904	-5	*O-97(96-1-0)/S-6,3-3	0.0
1887	Phi-N	113	531	118	182	22	19	14	66	40	51	.343	.350	.497	847	125	15	19			.873	-10	*O-104L/S-3,3-3,2-3	0.2
1888	Phi-N	106	433	67	99	19	6	6	51	39	44	.229	.303	.342	645	100	0	20			.905	0	*O-104L/3-2,P-2	-0.2
1889	Phi-N	97	422	77	106	21	4	5	53	53	33	.251	.336	.355	692	86	-9	17			.915	-4	O-92(92-0-0)/S-6,P-1	-1.3
	Bal-a	3	10	1	2	0	0	0	1	0	2	.200	.200	.200	400	14	-1	1			1.000	-0	/O-3(0-0-3)	-0.1
1890	Phi-P	132	539	115	156	20	14	9	102	51	35	.289	.360	.429	788	108	4	20			.895	14	*O-132(128-0-4)/3-1	1.2
1891	Phi-a	132	528	105	163	18	14	3	61	72	52	.309	.399	.413	812	132	23	22			.939	7	*O-122L/3-6,S-5,M	2.4
1892	Bal-N	21	76	9	17	1	1	0	10	10	8	.224	.330	.263	593	78	-2	1			.911	2	O-21(21-0-0)	-0.1
	Cin-N	30	107	10	21	2	4	0	14	10	17	.196	.271	.290	561	71	-4	4			.863	-2	O-30(1-1-28)	-0.7
	Yr	51	183	19	38	3	5	0	24	20	25	.208	.296	.279	575	74	-6	5			.885	1	O-51(22-1-28)	-0.8
Total	13	1280	5411	965	1507	228	132	68	601	418	547	.279	.329	.403	732	116	103	113			.895	11	*O-1232L/3-30,SP21	6.2
■ **HARRY WOOD**	Wood, Harold Austin b: 2/10/1881, Waterville, Maine d: 5/18/55, Bethesda, Md. BL/TR, 5'10", 155 lbs. Deb: 4/19/03																							
1903	Cin-N	2	3	0	0	0	0	0	0	1		.000	.250	.000	250	-24	-0	0			.000	-1	/O-2(1-0-1)	-0.1
■ **JAKE WOOD**	Wood, Jacob b: 6/22/37, Elizabeth, N.J. BR/TR, 6'1", 170 lbs. Deb: 4/11/61																							
1961	Det-A	162	663	96	171	17	**14**	11	69	58	141	.258	.321	.376	697	83	-16	30	9	3	.969	-27	*2-162	-2.5
1962	Det-A	111	367	68	83	10	5	8	30	33	59	.226	.292	.346	638	68	-16	24	3	**4**	.950	-31	2-90	-3.6
1963	Det-A	85	351	50	95	11	2	11	27	24	61	.271	.330	.407	737	102	1	18	5	2	.958	-11	2-81/3-1	-0.1
1964	Det-A	64	125	11	29	2	2	1	7	4	24	.232	.256	.304	560	54	-8	0	0	0	.989	-1	1-11,2-10/3-6,O-1L	-1.0
1965	Det-A	58	104	12	30	3	0	2	7	10	19	.288	.357	.375	732	107	1	3	3	-0	.977	-2	2-20/1-1,S-1,3-1	0.0
1966	Det-A	98	230	39	58	9	3	2	27	28	48	.252	.336	.343	679	94	-1	4	3	-0	.968	-13	2-52/3-4,1-2	-1.1
1967	Det-A	14	20	2	1	1	0	0	0	1	7	.050	.095	.100	195	-41	-3	0	0	0	1.000	-0	/1-2,2-2	-0.4
	Cin-N	16	17	1	2	0	0	0	1	1	3	.118	.167	.118	284	-15	-2	0	0	0	1.000	-0	/O-2(0-0-2)	-0.3
Total	7	608	1877	279	469	53	26	35	168	159	362	.250	.313	.362	675	82	-45	79	23	9	.963	-85	2-417/1-16,3-12,OS	-9.0
■ **JIMMY WOOD**	Wood, James Leon b: 12/1/1844, Brooklyn, N.Y. d: 11/30/1886, TR, 5'8.5", 150 lbs. Deb: 5/8/1871 M																							
1871	Chi-n	28	135	45	51	10	6	1	29	11	3	.378	.425	.563	988	163	9	18	2	**3**	**.887**	9	*2-28,M	1.3
1872	Tro-n	25	113	40	38	11	4	2	27	2	1	.336	.348	.558	905	172	9	3	0	1	.886	-0	2-25,M	0.5
	Eck-n	7	30	10	6	1	1	0	0	4	1	.200	.294	.300	594	98	1	1	0	0	.840	-1	/2-7,M	0.0
	Yr	32	143	50	44	12	5	2	27	6	2	.308	.336	.503	839	158	10	4	0	1	.875	-1	2-32	0.5
1873	Phi-n	42	209	67	67	11	1	0	27	8	1	.321	.346	.383	728	112	3	8	3	1	.850	4	*2-42	0.3
Total	3 n	102	487	162	162	33	12	3	83	25	6	.333	.365	.468	833	140	22	30	5	5	.868	12	2-102	2.1
■ **JASON WOOD**	Wood, Jason William b: 12/16/69, San Bernardino, Cal. BR/TR, 6'1", 170 lbs. Deb: 4/1/98																							
1998	Oak-A	3	1	1	0	0	0	0	0	0	1	.000	.000	.000	0	-99	-0	0	0	0	1.000	1	/S-2,3-1	0.1
	Det-A	10	23	5	8	2	0	1	1	3	4	.348	.423	.565	988	153	2	0	1	-0	1.000	-1	/1-6,S-1,D-3	0.1
	Yr	13	24	6	8	2	0	1	1	3	5	.333	.407	.542	949	144	2	0	1	-0	1.000	0	/1-6,S-3,D-3,3-1	0.2
1999	Det-A	27	44	5	7	1	0	1	8	2	13	.159	.196	.250	446	13	-6	0	0	0	.909	-5	/3-9,S-9,1-5,2-1,D	-1.0
Total	2	40	68	11	15	3	0	2	9	5	18	.221	.274	.353	627	60	-4	0	1	-0	.875	-5	/S-12,1-11,3-10,D2	-0.8
■ **JOE WOOD**	Wood, Joe "Smokey Joe" (b: Howard Ellsworth Wood) b: 10/25/1889, Kansas City, Mo. d: 7/27/85, West Haven, Conn BR/TR, 5'11", 180 lbs. Deb: 8/24/08 F Career OF: (106-LF 31-CF 295-RF)																							
1908	Bos-A	6	7	1	0	0	0	0	0	0		.000	.000	.000	0	-97	-1	0			.889	-0	/P-6	0.0
1909	Bos-A	24	55	4	9	0	1	0	3	2		.164	.207	.200	407	28	-5	0			.971	-4	P-24	0.0
1910	Bos-A	35	69	9	18	2	1	1	5	5		.261	.311	.362	673	108	0	0			.975	2	P-35	0.0
1911	Bos-A	44	88	15	23	4	2	2	11	10		.261	.343	.420	764	114	1	1			.947	2	P-44	0.0
1912	*Bos-A	43	124	16	36	13	1	1	13	11		.290	.348	.435	784	118	2	0			.974	8	P-43	0.0
1913	Bos-A	25	56	10	15	5	0	0	10	4	7	.268	.317	.357	674	95	-1	1			.955	4	P-23	0.0
1914	Bos-A	21	43	2	6	1	0	0	1	3	14	.140	.213	.163	376	13	-5	1			1.000	1	P-18	0.0
1915	Bos-A	29	54	6	14	1	1	1	7	5	10	.259	.322	.370	692	111	1	1	1	-0	.982	1	P-25	0.0
1917	Cle-A	10	6	1	0	0	0	0	0	0	3	.000	.000	.000	0	-93	-1	0			1.000	0	/P-5	0.0
1918	Cle-A	119	422	41	125	22	4	5	66	36	38	.296	.356	.403	759	118	8	8			.962	0	O-95L,2-19/1-4	0.5
1919	Cle-A	72	192	30	49	10	6	0	27	32	21	.255	.367	.370	737	101	1	3			.932	-8	O-64(15-6-43)/P-1	-1.0
1920	*Cle-A	61	137	25	37	11	2	1	30	25	16	.270	.390	.401	792	107	2	1	1	-0	.987	-6	O-55(5-2-48)/P-1	-0.6
1921	Cle-A	66	194	32	71	16	5	4	60	25	17	.366	.438	.562	1000	151	15	2	0	0	.973	-13	O-64(0-21-56)	-0.1
1922	Cle-A	142	505	74	150	33	8	8	92	50	63	.297	.367	.442	809	109	7	5	1	1	.960	2	*O-141(2-1-138)	-0.1
Total	14	697	1952	266	553	118	31	23	325	208	189	.283	.357	.411	768	110	26	23	3		.962	-11	O-419R,P-225/2-19,1	-1.3
■ **JOE WOOD**	Wood, Joseph Perry "J.P." or "Little Joe" b: 10/3/19, Houston, Tex. d: 3/25/85, Houston, Tex. BR/TR, 5'9.5", 160 lbs. Deb: 5/2/43																							
1943	Det-A	60	164	22	53	4	4	1	17	6	13	.323	.347	.415	762	114	2	2	2	-0	.896	-16	2-22,3-18	-1.3
■ **KEN WOOD**	Wood, Kenneth Lanier b: 7/1/24, Lincolnton, N.C. BR/TR, 6', 200 lbs. Deb: 4/28/48																							
1948	StL-A	10	24	2	2	0	1	0	2	1	4	.083	.120	.167	287	-24	-4	0	0	0	1.000	1	/O-5(0-0-5)	-0.4
1949	StL-A	7	6	0	0	0	0	0	0	1	2	.000	.143	.000	143	-58	-1	0	0	0	.000	-1	/O-3(2-0-1)	-0.3
1950	StL-A	128	369	42	83	24	0	13	62	38	58	.225	.299	.396	695	74	-17	0	4	-1	.952	-2	O-94(7-0-88)	-2.2
1951	StL-A	109	333	40	79	19	0	15	44	27	49	.237	.296	.429	726	92	-6	1	2	-0	.959	-4	*O-100(29-4-69)	-1.4
1952	Bos-A	15	20	0	2	0	0	0	0	3	4	.100	.217	.100	317	-9	-3	0	0	0	.889	-4	O-13(1-0-12)	-0.7
	Was-A	61	210	26	50	8	6	6	32	30	21	.238	.333	.419	752	112	3	0	1	-0	.954	8	O-56(54-3-1)	0.7
	Yr	76	230	26	52	8	6	6	32	33	25	.226	.323	.391	714	99	-1	0	1	-0	.951	5	O-69(55-3-13)	0.0

YEAR	TM/L	G	AB	R	H	2B	3B	HR	RBI	BB	SO	AVG	OBP	SLG	OPS	OPS+	BR+	SB	CS	SBR	FA	FR	G/POS	TPR
1953	Was-A	12	33	0	7	1	0	0	3	2	3	.212	.257	.242	500	36	-3	0	0	0	1.000	1	/O-7(7-0-0)	-0.3
Total	6	342	995	110	223	52	7	34	143	102	141	.224	.298	.393	691	81	-31	1	7	-2	.956	-1	O-278(100-7-176)	-4.6

■ BOB WOOD Wood, Robert Lynn b: 7/28/1865, Thorn Hill, Ohio d: 5/22/43, Churchill, Ohio BR/TR, 5'8.5", 153 lbs. Deb: 5/2/1898

YEAR	TM/L	G	AB	R	H	2B	3B	HR	RBI	BB	SO	AVG	OBP	SLG	OPS	OPS+	BR+	SB	CS	SBR	FA	FR	G/POS	TPR
1898	Cin-N	39	109	14	30	6	0	0	16	9		.275	.331	.330	661	84	-2	1			.943	1	C-29/O-1(1-0-0),1-1	0.1
1899	Cin-N	63	195	34	61	11	7	0	24	25		.313	.404	.441	845	129	9	3			.937	-10	C-53/O-2L,3-2,1-1	0.3
1900	Cin-N	45	139	17	37	8	1	0	22	10		.266	.320	.338	658	84	-3	3			.967	-6	C-18,3-15/O-1(0-1-0)	-0.7
1901	Cle-A	98	346	45	101	23	3	1	49	12		.292	.327	.384	711	101	-0	6			.952	-1	C-84/3-4,O-3R,12S	0.7
1902	Cle-A	81	258	23	76	18	2	0	40	27		.295	.375	.380	754	114	6	1			.941	-7	C-52,1-16/O-2R,23	0.4
1904	Det-A	49	175	15	43	6	2	1	17	5		.246	.271	.320	591	89	-3	1			.974	10	C-47	1.3
1905	Det-A	8	24	1	2	1	0	0	0	1		.083	.120	.125	245	-22	-3	0			.886	-0	/C-7	-0.3
Total	7	383	1246	149	350	73	15	2	168	89		.281	.338	.368	707	101	3	15			.951	-14	C-290/3-22,1-19,O2S	1.8

■ ROY WOOD Wood, Roy Winton "Woody" b: 8/29/1892, Monticello, Ark. d: 4/6/74, Fayetteville, Ark. BR/TR, 6', 175 lbs. Deb: 6/16/13

YEAR	TM/L	G	AB	R	H	2B	3B	HR	RBI	BB	SO	AVG	OBP	SLG	OPS	OPS+	BR+	SB	CS	SBR	FA	FR	G/POS	TPR
1913	Pit-N	14	35	4	10	4	0	0	2	1	8	.286	.306	.400	706	105	0	0			.895	1	/O-8(8-0-0),1-1	0.1
1914	Cle-A	72	220	24	52	6	3	1	15	13	26	.236	.300	.305	605	79	-6	6	9	-2	.946	-1	O-40(5-13-23),1-20	-1.2
1915	Cle-A	33	78	5	15	2	1	0	3	2	13	.192	.232	.244	475	41	-6	1	2	-0	.990	-2	1-21/O-2(1-0-1)	-0.9
Total	3	119	333	33	77	12	4	1	20	16	47	.231	.285	.300	585	73	-12	7	11		.936	-1	/O-50(14-13-24),1-42	-2.0

■ LARRY WOODALL Woodall, Charles Lawrence b: 7/26/1894, Staunton, Va. d: 5/16/63, Cambridge, Mass. BR/TR, 5'9", 165 lbs. Deb: 5/20/20 C

YEAR	TM/L	G	AB	R	H	2B	3B	HR	RBI	BB	SO	AVG	OBP	SLG	OPS	OPS+	BR+	SB	CS	SBR	FA	FR	G/POS	TPR
1920	Det-A	18	49	4	12	1	0	0	5	2	6	.245	.275	.265	540	45	-4	0	0	0	.988	2	C-15	0.0
1921	Det-A	46	80	10	29	4	1	0	14	6	7	.363	.407	.438	844	117	2	1	0	0	.966	-7	C-25	-0.4
1922	Det-A	50	125	19	43	2	2	0	18	8	11	.344	.388	.392	780	107	2	0	1	-0	.977	-10	C-40	-0.6
1923	Det-A	71	148	20	41	12	2	1	19	22	9	.277	.371	.405	776	106	2	2	1	0	.983	-5	C-60	0.0
1924	Det-A	67	165	23	51	9	2	0	25	21	5	.309	.387	.388	775	102	1	0	0	0	.986	0	C-62	0.4
1925	Det-A	75	171	20	35	4	1	0	13	24	8	.205	.303	.240	542	39	-15	1	0	0	.967	-7	C-75	-1.8
1926	Det-A	67	146	18	34	5	0	0	15	15	2	.233	.304	.267	571	49	-11	0	0	0	.979	-4	C-59	-1.1
1927	Det-A	88	246	28	69	8	6	0	39	37	9	.280	.375	.362	736	90	-2	9	1	2	**.997**	4	C-86	0.8
1928	Det-A	65	186	19	39	7	1	0	13	24	10	.210	.300	.258	558	47	-14	3	1	0	.992	4	C-62	-0.5
1929	Det-A	1	1	0	0	0	0	0	0	0	0	.000	.000	.000	0	-99	-0	0	0	0	.000	0	H	0.0
Total	10	548	1317	161	353	52	15	1	161	159	67	.268	.347	.333	680	77	-40	16	4	2	.984	-22	C-484	-3.2

■ DARRELL WOODARD Woodard, Darrell Lee b: 12/10/56, Wilmar, Ark. BR/TR, 5'11", 160 lbs. Deb: 8/6/78

YEAR	TM/L	G	AB	R	H	2B	3B	HR	RBI	BB	SO	AVG	OBP	SLG	OPS	OPS+	BR+	SB	CS	SBR	FA	FR	G/POS	TPR
1978	Oak-A	33	9	10	0	0	0	0	0	1	1	.000	.100	.000	100	-73	-2	3	4	-1	.964	9	2-14/3-1,D-1	0.6

■ MIKE WOODARD Woodard, Michael Cary b: 3/2/60, Melrose Park, Ill. BL/TR, 5'9", 155 lbs. Deb: 9/11/85

YEAR	TM/L	G	AB	R	H	2B	3B	HR	RBI	BB	SO	AVG	OBP	SLG	OPS	OPS+	BR+	SB	CS	SBR	FA	FR	G/POS	TPR
1985	SF-N	24	82	12	20	1	0	0	9	5	3	.244	.287	.256	543	56	-5	6	1	1	.990	-5	2-23	-0.9
1986	SF-N	48	79	14	20	2	1	1	5	10	9	.253	.337	.342	679	92	-1	7	2	1	.986	-2	2-23/S-2,3-2	-0.1
1987	SF-N	10	19	0	4	1	0	0	1	0	1	.211	.211	.263	474	26	-2	0	0	0	1.000	2	/2-8	0.0
1988	Chi-A	18	45	3	6	0	1	0	4	1	5	.133	.170	.178	348	-2	-6	1	1	-0	.975	4	2-14/D-2	-0.2
Total	4	100	225	29	50	4	2	1	19	16	18	.222	.277	.271	548	55	-14	14	4	2	.985	-1	/2-68,D-2,3-2,S-2	-1.2

■ RED WOODHEAD Woodhead, James b: 7/9/1851, Chelsea, Mass. d: 9/7/1881, Boston, Mass. 5'6", 160 lbs. Deb: 4/15/1873

YEAR	TM/L	G	AB	R	H	2B	3B	HR	RBI	BB	SO	AVG	OBP	SLG	OPS	OPS+	BR+	SB	CS	SBR	FA	FR	G/POS	TPR
1873	Mar-n	1	5	1	0	0	0	0	0	0	0	.000	.000	.000	0	-99	-1	0	0	0	.900	2	/S-1	0.0
1879	Syr-N	34	131	4	21	1	0	0	2	0	23	.160	.160	.168	328	9	-12				.792	-7	3-34	-1.7

■ GENE WOODLING Woodling, Eugene Richard b: 8/16/22, Akron, Ohio BL/TR, 5'9.5", 195 lbs. Deb: 9/23/43 C

YEAR	TM/L	G	AB	R	H	2B	3B	HR	RBI	BB	SO	AVG	OBP	SLG	OPS	OPS+	BR+	SB	CS	SBR	FA	FR	G/POS	TPR
1943	Cle-A	8	25	5	8	2	1	1	5	1	3	.320	.346	.600	946	186	2	0	0	0	1.000	-1	/O-6(0-1-5)	0.2
1946	Cle-A	61	133	8	25	1	4	0	9	16	13	.188	.280	.256	536	54	-8	1	2	-0	1.000	-3	O-37(6-31-0)	-1.3
1947	Pit-N	22	79	7	21	2	2	0	10	7	5	.266	.326	.342	667	75	-3	0			.968	1	O-21(1-20-0)	-0.2
1949	*NY-A	112	296	60	80	13	7	5	44	52	21	.270	.381	.412	793	110	5	2	2	-0	.982	-10	O-98(82-12-5)	-1.1
1950	*NY-A	122	449	81	127	20	10	6	60	70	31	.283	.381	.412	793	106	5	5	3	0	.993	10	*O-118(117-2-0)	0.6
1951	*NY-A	120	420	65	118	15	8	15	71	62	37	.281	.373	.462	835	130	17	0	4	-1	.993	1	*O-116(101-17-0)	0.9
1952	*NY-A	122	408	58	126	19	6	12	63	59	31	.309	.397	.473	870	151	28	1	4	-1	**.996**	6	*O-118(112-6-0)	2.5
1953	*NY-A	125	395	64	121	26	4	10	58	82	29	.306	**.429**	.468	898	147	30	2	7	-2	**.996**	4	*O-119(119-0-0)	2.5
1954	NY-A	97	304	33	76	12	5	3	40	53	35	.250	.361	.352	713	99	1	3	4	-1	.983	-1	O-89(89-0-0)	-0.6
1955	Bal-A	47	145	22	32	6	2	3	18	24	18	.221	.335	.352	687	91	-2	1	1	-0	1.000	-8	O-44(26-4-25)	-1.1
	Cle-A	79	259	33	72	15	1	5	35	36	15	.278	.372	.402	774	104	2	2	4	-1	.993	-3	O-70(64-0-16)	-0.5
	Yr	126	404	55	104	21	3	8	53	60	33	.257	.359	.384	743	100	1	3	5	-1	.995	-11	*O-114(90-4-41)	-1.6
1956	Cle-A	100	317	56	83	17	0	8	38	69	29	.262	.398	.391	790	107	6	2	6	-2	.981	-0	O-85(85-0-2)	-0.1
1957	Cle-A	133	430	74	138	25	2	19	78	64	35	.321	.412	.521	933	155	34	0	5	-2	.992	11	*O-113(113-0-0)	3.6
1958	Bal-A	133	413	57	114	16	1	15	65	66	49	.276	.378	.429	807	128	18	4	2	0	.974	-10	*O-116(61-0-68)	0.2
1959	Bal-A★	140	440	63	132	22	2	14	77	78	35	.300	.405	.455	860	139	26	1	1	-0	.981	-13	*O-124(85-0-57)	0.8
1960	Bal-A	140	435	68	123	18	3	11	62	84	40	.283	.403	.414	817	123	18	3	0	1	.995	-3	*O-124(124-0-1)	0.9
1961	Was-A	110	342	39	107	16	4	10	57	50	24	.313	.404	.471	874	135	18	1	0	0	.988	-3	O-90(15-0-77)	1.0
1962	Was-A	44	107	19	30	4	0	5	16	24	5	.280	.421	.458	879	138	7	1	0	0	.953	-4	O-30(3-0-27)	0.1
	NY-N	81	190	18	52	8	1	5	24	24	22	.274	.358	.405	763	103	1	0	0	0	.986	-4	O-48(27-0-21)	-0.5
Total	17	1796	5587	830	1585	257	63	147	830	921	477	.284	.388	.431	819	123	207	29	45		.989	-29	*O-1566(1230-93-304)	7.9

■ SAM WOODRUFF Woodruff, Orville Francis b: 12/27/1876, Chilo, Ohio d: 7/22/37, Cincinnati, Ohio BR/TR, 5'9", 160 lbs. Deb: 4/14/04 Career OF: (0-LF 0-CF 1-RF)

YEAR	TM/L	G	AB	R	H	2B	3B	HR	RBI	BB	SO	AVG	OBP	SLG	OPS	OPS+	BR+	SB	CS	SBR	FA	FR	G/POS	TPR
1904	Cin-N	87	306	20	58	14	3	0	20	19		.190	.244	.255	499	50	-18	9			.932	-4	3-61,2-17/S-8,O-1R	-2.2
1910	Cin-N	21	61	6	9	1	0	0	2	7	8	.148	.235	.164	399	18	-6	2			.933	-1	3-17/2-4	-0.7
Total	2	108	367	26	67	15	3	0	22	26	8	.183	.242	.240	482	45	-25	11			.932	-5	/3-78,2-21,S-8,O-1R	-2.9

■ PETE WOODRUFF Woodruff, Peter Frank b: 6/1873, New York BR/TR, Deb: 9/19/1899

YEAR	TM/L	G	AB	R	H	2B	3B	HR	RBI	BB	SO	AVG	OBP	SLG	OPS	OPS+	BR+	SB	CS	SBR	FA	FR	G/POS	TPR
1899	NY-N	20	61	11	15	1	1	2	7	9		.246	.343	.393	736	105	0	3			1.000	-1	O-19(0-0-19)/1-1	-0.1

■ AL WOODS Woods, Alvis b: 8/8/53, Oakland, Cal. BL/TL, 6'3", 195 lbs. Deb: 4/7/77

YEAR	TM/L	G	AB	R	H	2B	3B	HR	RBI	BB	SO	AVG	OBP	SLG	OPS	OPS+	BR+	SB	CS	SBR	FA	FR	G/POS	TPR
1977	Tor-A	122	440	58	125	17	4	6	35	36	38	.284	.338	.382	720	94	-3	8	7	-1	.969	-2	*O-115(106-0-15)/D-4	-1.1
1978	Tor-A	62	220	19	53	12	3	3	25	11	23	.241	.280	.364	644	78	-7	1	2	-0	.978	3	O-60(60-0-0)	-0.7
1979	Tor-A	132	436	57	121	24	4	5	36	40	28	.278	.340	.385	725	94	-3	6	4	-0	.967	3	*O-127(127-0-0)/D-2	-0.5
1980	Tor-A	109	373	54	112	18	2	15	47	37	35	.300	.365	.480	845	124	12	4	4	-1	.991	6	O-88(88-0-0),D-13	1.3
1981	Tor-A	85	288	20	71	15	0	1	21	19	31	.247	.293	.309	602	69	-11	3	4	-1	.973	3	O-77(77-0-0)/D-2	-1.4
1982	Tor-A	85	201	20	47	11	1	3	24	21	20	.234	.306	.343	650	71	-8	1	3	-1	.970	-7	O-64(64-0-0),D-10	-1.8
1986	Min-A	23	28	5	9	1	0	2	8	3	5	.321	.387	.571	959	153	2	0	0	0	.000	0	/D-7	0.2
Total	7	618	1986	233	538	98	14	35	196	167	180	.271	.328	.387	716	93	-18	23	24	-3	.974	6	O-531(522-0-15)/D-38	-4.0

■ GARY WOODS Woods, Gary Lee b: 7/20/54, Santa Barbara, Cal BR/TR, 6'2", 190 lbs. Deb: 9/14/76 Career OF: (164-LF 175-CF 107-RF)

YEAR	TM/L	G	AB	R	H	2B	3B	HR	RBI	BB	SO	AVG	OBP	SLG	OPS	OPS+	BR+	SB	CS	SBR	FA	FR	G/POS	TPR
1976	Oak-A	6	8	0	1	0	0	0	0	0	3	.125	.125	.125	250	-28	-1	0	0	0	1.000	-1	/O-4(1-2-1),D-1	-0.2
1977	Tor-A	60	227	21	49	9	1	0	17	7	38	.216	.246	.264	510	38	-19	5	4	-0	.994	3	O-60(0-60-0)	-1.7
1978	Tor-A	8	19	1	3	1	0	0	0	1	1	.158	.200	.211	411	15	-2	1	0	0	1.000	-0	/O-6(0-1-5)	-0.3
1980	*Hou-N	19	53	8	20	5	0	2	15	2	9	.377	.400	.585	985	186	6	1	0	0	1.000	-2	O-14(4-0-12)	0.4
1981	*Hou-N	54	110	10	23	4	1	0	12	11	22	.209	.281	.264	545	58	-6	2	1	0	.984	-3	O-40(2-3-35)	-1.1
1982	Chi-N	117	245	28	66	15	1	4	30	21	48	.269	.327	.388	715	97	-1	3	3	-0	1.000	-14	*O-103(37-67-12)	-1.9
1983	Chi-N	93	190	25	46	9	0	4	22	15	27	.242	.298	.353	650	76	-6	5	3	0	.971	-11	O-73(40-27-13)/2-1	-2.0
1984	*Chi-N	87	98	13	23	4	1	3	10	15	21	.235	.336	.388	724	94	-1	2	1	0	1.000	-13	O-62(36-11-18)/2-3	-1.5
1985	Chi-N	81	82	11	20	3	0	0	4	14	18	.244	.354	.280	635	72	-2	0	1	-0	1.000	-13	O-56(44-4-11)	-1.8
Total	9	525	1032	117	251	50	4	13	110	86	187	.243	.303	.337	640	76	-33	19	13	-0	.992	-54	O-418C/2-4,D-1	-10.1

■ JIM WOODS Woods, James Jerome "Woody" b: 9/17/39, Chicago, Ill. BR/TR, 6', 175 lbs. Deb: 9/27/57

YEAR	TM/L	G	AB	R	H	2B	3B	HR	RBI	BB	SO	AVG	OBP	SLG	OPS	OPS+	BR+	SB	CS	SBR	FA	FR	G/POS	TPR
1957	Chi-N	2	0	1	0	0	0	0	0	0	0	—	—	—	—	—	0	0	0	0	.000	0	R	0.0
1960	Phi-N	11	34	4	6	0	0	1	3	3	13	.176	.243	.265	508	39	-3	0	0	0	.939	2	3-11	-0.1

YEAR	TM/L	G	AB	R	H	2B	3B	HR	RBI	BB	SO	AVG	OBP	SLG	OPS	OPS+	BR+	SB	CS	SBR	FA	FR	G/POS	TPR
1961	Phi-N	23	48	6	11	3	0	2	9	4	15	.229	.302	.417	719	89	-1	0	0	0	.968	-1	3-15	-0.1
Total	3	36	82	11	17	3	0	3	12	7	28	.207	.278	.354	631	69	-4	0	0	0	.953	1	/3-26	-0.2
■ RON WOODS Woods, Ronald Lawrence b: 2/1/43, Hamilton, Ohio BR/TR, 5'10", 173 lbs. Deb: 4/22/69																								
1969	Det-A	17	15	3	4	0	0	1	3	2	3	.267	.353	.467	820	122	0	0	0	0	1.000	-2	/O-7(7-1-0)	-0.2
	NY-A	72	171	18	30	5	2	1	7	22	29	.175	.273	.246	519	48	-12	2	0	0	1.000	-3	O-67(1-66-0)	-1.6
	Yr	89	186	21	34	5	2	2	10	24	32	.183	.280	.263	543	54	-11	2	0	0	1.000	-5	O-74(8-67-0)	-1.8
1970	NY-A	95	225	30	51	5	3	8	27	33	35	.227	.326	.382	708	100	-0	4	2	0	.974	-6	O-78(2-9-70)	-1.0
1971	NY-A	25	32	4	8	1	0	1	2	4	2	.250	.333	.375	708	107	0	0	0	0	.929	-1	/O-9(3-0-6)	-0.1
	Mon-N	51	138	26	41	7	3	1	17	19	18	.297	.382	.413	795	125	5	0	2	-1	.989	-1	O-45(32-23-0)	0.2
1972	Mon-N	97	221	21	57	5	1	10	31	22	33	.258	.325	.425	750	110	2	3	3	-0	.991	-11	O-73(8-58-10)	-1.2
1973	Mon-N	135	318	45	73	11	3	3	31	56	34	.230	.345	.311	656	80	-7	12	6	1	.977	-9	*O-114(29-91-4)	-1.9
1974	Mon-N	90	127	15	26	0	0	1	12	17	17	.205	.303	.228	532	48	-8	6	5	-0	.987	-12	O-61(40-20-5)	-2.3
Total	6	582	1247	162	290	34	12	26	130	175	171	.233	.328	.342	670	87	-19	27	18	-0	.984	-45	O-454(122-268-95)	-8.1
■ TRACY WOODSON Woodson, Tracy Michael b: 10/5/62, Richmond, Va. BR/TR, 6'3", 215 lbs. Deb: 4/7/87																								
1987	LA-N	53	136	14	31	8	1	1	11	9	21	.228	.286	.324	609	63	-7	1	1	-0	.958	-1	3-45/1-7	-0.9
1988	*LA-N	65	173	15	43	4	1	3	15	7	32	.249	.282	.335	617	79	-5	1	2	-0	.938	-5	3-41,1-25	-1.2
1989	LA-N	4	6	0	0	0	0	0	0	0	1	.000	.000	.000	0	-99	-2	0	0	0	1.000	0	/3-1	-0.2
1992	StL-N	31	114	9	35	8	0	1	22	3	10	.307	.331	.404	734	110	1	0	0	0	.945	-6	3-26/1-3	-0.5
1993	StL-N	62	77	4	16	2	0	0	2	1	14	.208	.218	.234	452	21	-9	0	0	0	.909	2	3-28,1-11	-0.7
Total	5	215	506	42	125	22	2	5	50	20	78	.247	.281	.328	609	70	-21	2	3	-1	.943	-10	3-141/1-46	-3.5
■ CHRIS WOODWARD Woodward, Christopher Michael b: 6/27/76, Covina, Cal. BR/TR, 6', 160 lbs. Deb: 6/7/99																								
1999	Tor-A	14	26	1	6	1	0	0	2	2	6	.231	.286	.269	555	42	-2	0	0	0	.939	2	S-10/3-2	0.0
2000	Tor-A	37	104	16	19	7	0	3	14	10	28	.183	.254	.337	591	47	-9	1	0	0	.955	6	S-22/3-9,1-3,2-3	-0.1
Total	2	51	130	17	25	8	0	3	16	12	34	.192	.261	.323	584	46	-11	1	0	0	.950	8	/S-32,3-11,2-3,1-3	-0.1
■ WOODY WOODWARD Woodward, William Frederick b: 9/23/42, Miami, Fla. BR/TR, 6'2", 185 lbs. Deb: 9/9/63																								
1963	Mil-N	10	2	1	0	0	0	0	0	0	0	.000	.000	.000	0	-99	-1	0	0	0	1.000	3	/S-5	0.2
1964	Mil-N	77	115	18	24	2	1	0	11	6	28	.209	.260	.243	504	43	-9	0	1	-0	.958	13	2-40,S-18/3-7,1-1	0.7
1965	Mil-N	112	265	17	55	7	4	0	11	10	50	.208	.236	.264	501	41	-21	2	2	-0	.977	11	*S-107/2-8	-0.4
1966	Atl-N	144	455	46	120	23	3	0	43	37	54	.264	.325	.327	652	81	-11	2	2	-0	.973	-6	2-79,S-73	-0.6
1967	Atl-N	136	429	30	97	15	2	0	25	37	51	.226	.289	.270	559	62	-21	0	6	-2	**.982**	9	*2-120,S-16	-0.3
1968	Atl-N	12	24	2	4	1	0	0	1	1	6	.167	.200	.208	408	23	-2	1	0	0	.973	3	/S-6,3-2,2-1	0.1
	Cin-N	56	119	13	29	2	0	0	10	7	23	.244	.297	.261	557	64	-5	1	0	0	.968	-3	S-41/2-9,1-1	-0.6
	Yr	68	143	15	33	3	0	0	11	8	29	.231	.281	.252	533	58	-7	2	0	0	.969	-1	S-47,2-10/3-2,1-1	-0.5
1969	Cin-N	97	241	36	63	12	0	0	15	24	40	.261	.333	.311	645	77	-6	3	2	-0	.966	-2	S-93/2-2	0.1
1970	*Cin-N	100	264	23	59	8	3	1	14	20	21	.223	.283	.288	571	53	-17	1	2	-0	.973	2	S-77,3-20,2-10,/1-2	-0.8
1971	Cin-N	136	273	22	66	9	1	0	18	27	28	.242	.310	.282	592	70	-10	4	0	1	.987	-5	S-85,3-63/2-9	-0.7
Total	9	880	2187	208	517	79	14	1	148	169	301	.236	.295	.287	582	64	-102	14	15	-2	.974	23	S-521,2-278/3-92,1	-2.3
■ JUNIOR WOOTEN Wooten, Earl Hazwell b: 1/16/24, Pelzer, S.C. BR/TL, 5'11", 160 lbs. Deb: 9/16/47 Career OF: (1-LF 61-CF 22-RF)																								
1947	Was-A	6	24	0	2	0	0	0	1	0	4	.083	.083	.083	167	-55	-5	1	0	0	.905	-1	/O-6(1-6-0)	-0.6
1948	Was-A	88	258	34	66	8	3	1	23	24	21	.256	.324	.322	646	74	-10	2	1	0	.979	1	O-73(0-55-22)/1-6,P-1	-1.0
Total	2	94	282	34	68	8	3	1	24	24	25	.241	.305	.301	607	64	-15	3	1	0	.972	1	/O-79C,1-6,P-1	-1.6
■ SHAWN WOOTEN Wooten, William Shawn b: 7/24/72, Glendora, Cal. BR/TR, 5'10", 205 lbs. Deb: 8/18/2000																								
2000	Ana-A	7	9	2	5	1	0	0	1	0	0	.556	.556	.667	1222	207	1	0	0	0	1.000	-0	/C-4,1-3	0.1
■ FAVEL WORDSWORTH Wordsworth, Favel Perry b: 12/22/1850, New York, N.Y. d: 8/12/1888, New York, N.Y. Deb: 4/28/1873																								
1873	Res-n	12	42	5	10	0	0	0	3	2	1	.238	.273	.238	511	58	-2	0	0	0	.643	-3	S-11/O-1(0-0-1)	-0.4
■ CHUCK WORKMAN Workman, Charles Thomas b: 1/6/15, Leeton, Mo. d: 1/3/53, Kansas City, Mo. BL/TR, 6', 175 lbs. Deb: 9/18/38 Career OF: (22-LF 8-CF 300-RF)																								
1938	Cle-A	2	5	1	2	0	0	0	0	0	0	.400	.400	.400	800	103	0	0	0	0	.500	-0	/O-1(0-0-1)	0.0
1941	Cle-A	9	4	2	0	0	0	0	0	1	1	.000	.200	.000	200	-45	-1	0	0	0	.000	0	H	-0.1
1943	Bos-N	153	615	71	153	17	1	10	67	53	72	.249	.311	.328	640	86	-11	12			.988	6	*O-149R/1-3,3-1	-1.7
1944	Bos-N	140	418	46	87	18	3	11	53	42	41	.208	.287	.344	631	74	-15	1			.983	-3	*O-103(0-0-103),3-19	-2.4
1945	Bos-N	139	514	77	141	16	2	25	87	51	58	.274	.347	.459	806	122	14	9			.910	-17	*3-107,O-24(0-0-24)	-0.3
1946	Bos-N	25	48	5	8	2	0	2	7	3	11	.167	.231	.333	564	58	-3	0			.920	-1	O-12(3-8-1)	-0.5
	Pit-N	58	145	11	32	4	1	2	16	11	19	.221	.280	.303	584	64	-7	2			1.000	6	O-40(3-0-38)/3-1	-0.2
	Yr	83	193	16	40	6	1	4	23	14	30	.207	.268	.311	579	63	-10	2			.986	5	O-52(6-8-39)/3-1	-0.7
Total	6	526	1749	213	423	57	7	50	230	161	202	.242	.311	.368	679	91	-23	24	0		.985	-8	O-329R,3-128/1-3	-5.2
■ HANK WORKMAN Workman, Henry Kilgariff b: 2/5/26, Los Angeles, Cal. BL/TR, 6'1", 185 lbs. Deb: 9/4/50																								
1950	NY-A	2	5	1	1	0	0	0	0	0	1	.200	.200	.200	400	3	-1	0	0	0	1.000	-0	/1-1	-0.1
■ HERB WORTH Worth, Herbert b: 5/2/1847, Brooklyn, N.Y. d: 4/27/14, Brooklyn, N.Y. Deb: 7/29/1872																								
1872	Atl-n	1	5	1	1	1	0	0	1	0	0	.200	.200	.400	600	68	-0	0	0	0	1.000	0	/O-1(0-0-1)	0.0
■ CRAIG WORTHINGTON Worthington, Craig Richard b: 4/17/65, Los Angeles, Cal. BR/TR, 6', 200 lbs. Deb: 4/26/88																								
1988	Bal-A	26	81	5	15	2	0	2	4	9	24	.185	.267	.284	551	56	-5	1	0	0	.961	1	3-26	-0.4
1989	Bal-A	145	497	57	123	23	0	15	70	61	114	.247	.335	.384	719	105	4	1	2	-0	.951	-10	*3-145	-0.6
1990	Bal-A	133	425	46	96	17	0	8	44	63	96	.226	.330	.322	652	86	-6	1	2	-0	.945	-12	*3-131/D-2	-1.9
1991	Bal-A	31	102	11	23	3	0	4	12	12	14	.225	.313	.373	686	93	-1	0	1	-0	.975	-3	3-30	-0.4
1992	Cle-A	9	24	0	4	0	0	0	2	2	4	.167	.231	.167	397	13	-3	0	1	-0	.857	2	/3-9	-0.2
1995	Cin-N	10	18	1	5	1	0	1	2	2	1	.278	.350	.500	850	122	1	0	0	0	1.000	0	/1-4,3-2	0.0
	Tex-A	26	68	4	15	4	0	2	6	7	8	.221	.293	.368	661	69	-3	0	0	0	.980	-0	3-26	-0.3
1996	Tex-A	13	19	2	3	0	0	1	4	6	3	.158	.360	.316	676	69	-1	0	0	0	.917	1	/3-7,1-6	0.0
Total	7	393	1234	126	284	50	0	33	144	162	264	.230	.323	.351	674	90	-14	3	6	-1	.950	-21	3-376/1-10,D-2	-3.8
■ RED WORTHINGTON Worthington, Robert Lee b: 4/24/06, Alhambra, Cal. d: 12/8/63, Sepulveda, Cal. BR/TR, 5'11", 170 lbs. Deb: 4/14/31																								
1931	Bos-N	128	491	47	143	25	10	4	44	26	38	.291	.328	.407	736	100	-1	1			**.988**	-3	*O-124(114-0-10)	-1.1
1932	Bos-N	105	435	62	132	35	8	8	61	15	24	.303	.330	.476	806	118	9	1			.987	-1	*O-104(104-0-0)	0.2
1933	Bos-N	17	45	3	7	4	0	0	0	1	3	.156	.174	.244	418	20	-5	0			.900	-1	O-10(3-0-7)	-0.7
1934	Bos-N	41	65	6	16	5	0	0	6	6	5	.246	.319	.323	643	78	-2	0			.920	-1	O-11(0-0-11)	-0.4
	StL-N	1	1	0	0	0	0	0	0	0	1	.000	.000	.000	0	-94	-0	0			.000	0	H	0.0
	Yr	42	66	6	16	5	0	0	6	6	6	.242	.315	.318	633	75	-2	0			.920	-1	O-11(0-0-11)	-0.4
Total	4	292	1037	118	298	69	18	12	111	48	71	.287	.321	.423	745	103	1	2			.981	-7	O-249(221-0-28)	-2.0
■ CHUCK WORTMAN Wortman, William Lewis b: 1/5/1892, Baltimore, Md. d: 8/19/77, Las Vegas, Nev. BR/TR, 5'7", 150 lbs. Deb: 7/20/16																								
1916	Chi-N	69	234	17	47	4	2	2	16	18	22	.201	.258	.261	519	54	-12	4			.908	-21	S-69	-3.3
1917	Chi-N	75	190	24	33	4	1	0	9	18	23	.174	.245	.205	450	36	-14	6			.918	-8	S-65/2-1,3-1	-2.1
1918	*Chi-N	17	17	4	2	0	0	1	3	1	2	.118	.167	.294	461	39	-1	3			.864	2	/2-8,S-4	0.1
Total	3	161	441	45	82	8	3	3	28	37	47	.186	.249	.238	487	46	-28	13			.913	-27	S-138/2-9,3-1	-5.3
■ RON WOTUS Wotus, Ronald Allan b: 3/3/61, Colchester, Conn. BR/TR, 6'1", 164 lbs. Deb: 9/3/83 C																								
1983	Pit-N	5	3	0	0	0	0	0	0	0	1	.000	.000	.000	0	-98	-1	0	0	0	1.000	1	/S-2,2-1	0.0
1984	Pit-N	27	55	4	12	6	0	0	2	6	8	.218	.295	.327	622	75	-2	0	0	0	.976	9	S-17/2-7	0.9
Total	2	32	58	4	12	6	0	0	2	6	9	.207	.281	.310	592	66	-3	0	0	0	.976	10	/S-19,2-8	0.9
■ JIMMY WOULFE Woulfe, James Joseph b: 11/25/1859, New Orleans, La. d: 12/20/24, New Orleans, La. TR, 5'11", Deb: 5/16/1884																								
1884	Cin-a	8	34	3	5	0	1	0	2	1		.147	.171	.206	377	22	-3				.625	-3	/O-7(1-0-6),3-1	-0.6

YEAR	TM/L	G	AB	R	H	2B	3B	HR	RBI	BB	SO	AVG	OBP	SLG	OPS	OPS+	BR+	SB	CS	SBR	FA	FR	G/POS	TPR
	Pit-a	15	53	7	6	1	0	0	1	0		.113	.113	.132	245	-20	-7				.893	1	O-15(0-14-1)	-0.6
	Yr	23	87	10	11	1	1	0	3	1		.126	.136	.161	297	-3	-10				.795	-2	O-22(1-14-7)/3-1	-1.2

■ AL WRIGHT Wright, Albert Edgar "A-1" b: 11/11/12, San Francisco, Cal d: 11/13/98, Oakland, Cal. BR/TR, 6'1.5", 170 lbs. Deb: 4/25/33

YEAR	TM/L	G	AB	R	H	2B	3B	HR	RBI	BB	SO	AVG	OBP	SLG	OPS	OPS+	BR+	SB	CS	SBR	FA	FR	G/POS	TPR
1933	Bos-N	4	1	0	1	0	0	0	0	0	0	1.000	1.000	1.000	2000	515	1	0			.500	-0	/2-3	0.0

■ AB WRIGHT Wright, Albert Owen b: 11/16/06, Terlton, Okla. d: 5/23/95, Muskogee, Okla. BR/TR, 6'3", 200 lbs. Deb: 4/20/35

YEAR	TM/L	G	AB	R	H	2B	3B	HR	RBI	BB	SO	AVG	OBP	SLG	OPS	OPS+	BR+	SB	CS	SBR	FA	FR	G/POS	TPR
1935	Cle-A	67	160	17	38	11	1	2	18	10	17	.237	.291	.356	647	65	-9	2	1	0	.984	-8	O-47(5-5-38)	-1.7
1944	Bos-N	71	195	20	50	9	0	7	35	18	31	.256	.326	.410	736	102	0	0			.968	-4	O-47(35-0-12)	-0.7
Total	2	138	355	37	88	20	1	9	53	28	48	.248	.310	.386	696	85	-9	2	1		.974	-11	/O-94(40-5-50)	-2.4

■ CY WRIGHT Wright, Ceylon b: 8/16/1893, Minneapolis, Minn. d: 11/7/47, Hines, Ill. BL/TR, 5'9", 150 lbs. Deb: 6/30/16

YEAR	TM/L	G	AB	R	H	2B	3B	HR	RBI	BB	SO	AVG	OBP	SLG	OPS	OPS+	BR+	SB	CS	SBR	FA	FR	G/POS	TPR
1916	Chi-A	8	18	0	0	0	0	0	0	1	7	.000	.053	.000	53	-83	-4	0			.844	-1	/S-8	-0.5

■ GLENN WRIGHT Wright, Forest Glenn "Buckshot" b: 2/6/01, Archie, Mo. d: 4/6/84, Olathe, Kan. BR/TR, 5'11", 170 lbs. Deb: 4/15/24 Career OF: (0-LF 0-CF 1-RF)

YEAR	TM/L	G	AB	R	H	2B	3B	HR	RBI	BB	SO	AVG	OBP	SLG	OPS	OPS+	BR+	SB	CS	SBR	FA	FR	G/POS	TPR
1924	Pit-N	153	616	80	177	28	18	7	111	27	52	.287	.318	.425	744	96	-5	14	6	1	.946	11	*S-153	2.3
1925	*Pit-N	153	614	97	189	32	10	18	121	31	32	.308	.341	.480	822	100	-1	3	7	-2	.939	0	*S-153/3-1	1.3
1926	Pit-N	119	458	73	141	15	15	8	77	19	26	.308	.335	.459	794	106	2	6			.927	-13	*S-116	0.2
1927	*Pit-N	143	570	78	160	26	4	9	105	39	46	.281	.328	.388	716	85	-12	4			.942	-17	*S-143	-1.3
1928	Pit-N	108	407	63	126	20	8	8	66	21	53	.310	.343	.457	800	103	1	3			.927	-24	*S-101/1-1,O-1(0-0-1)	-1.2
1929	Bro-N	24	25	4	5	0	0	1	6	3	6	.200	.286	.320	606	51	-2	0			.667	-3	/S-3	-0.4
1930	Bro-N	135	532	83	171	28	12	22	126	32	70	.321	.360	.543	903	116	11	2			.964	-2	*S-134	2.2
1931	Bro-N	77	268	36	76	9	4	9	32	14	35	.284	.324	.448	772	106	1	1			.942	6	S-75	1.3
1932	Bro-N	127	446	50	122	31	5	11	60	12	57	.274	.293	.439	732	96	-4	4			.939	8	*S-122/1-2	1.2
1933	Bro-N	71	192	19	49	13	0	1	18	11	24	.255	.299	.339	638	85	-4	1			.936	-4	S-51/1-9,3-2	-0.6
1935	Chi-A	9	25	1	3	1	0	0	1	0	6	.120	.120	.160	280	-27	-5	0	0	0	.943	0	/2-7	-0.4
Total	11	1119	4153	584	1219	203	76	94	723	209	407	.294	.328	.447	775	99	-18	38	13		.941	-37	*S-1051/1-12,2-7,3O	4.6

■ GEORGE WRIGHT Wright, George b: 1/28/1847, Yonkers, N.Y. d: 8/21/37, Boston, Mass. BR/TR, 5'9.5", 150 lbs. Deb: 5/5/1871 FMH

YEAR	TM/L	G	AB	R	H	2B	3B	HR	RBI	BB	SO	AVG	OBP	SLG	OPS	OPS+	BR+	SB	CS	SBR	FA	FR	G/POS	TPR
1871	Bos-n	16	80	33	33	7	5	0	11	6	1	.412	.453	.625	1078	200	10	9	1	2	.816	5	S-15/1-1	1.0
1872	Bos-n	48	255	87	86	16	6	2	32	3	1	.337	.345	.471	816	141	10	14	4	2	.838	22	*S-48	2.2
1873	Bos-n	59	325	99	126	19	8	3	50	8	2	.388	.402	.523	925	160	21	3	5	-1	**.808**	15	*S-59	2.3
1874	Bos-n	60	313	76	103	10	**15**	2	44	5	6	.329	.340	.476	816	150	15	2	0	0	.821	4	*S-60/3-1	1.4
1875	Bos-n	79	408	106	136	20	7	2	61	2	6	.333	.337	.431	768	159	22	13	6	1	.861	4	*S-79/P-2	2.1
1876	Bos-N	70	343	72	100	18	6	1	34	8	9	.292	.315	.397	712	134	11				.888	13	*S-68/2-2,P-1	2.4
1877	Bos-N	61	290	58	80	15	1	0	35	9	15	.276	.298	.334	632	95	-2				.878	9	*2-58/S-3	0.9
1878	Bos-N	59	267	35	60	5	1	0	12	6	22	.225	.242	.251	493	58	-12				**.947**	11	*S-59	0.1
1879	Pro-N	85	388	79	107	15	10	1	42	13	20	.276	.299	.374	673	122	9				.924	21	*S-85,M	3.0
1880	Bos-N	1	4	2	1	0	0	0	0	0	0	.250	.250	.250	500	72	-0				1.000	-0	/S-1	0.0
1881	Bos-N	7	25	4	5	0	0	0	0	3	1	.200	.286	.200	486	58	-1				.963	-3	/S-7	-0.3
1882	Pro-N	46	185	14	30	1	2	0	9	4	36	.162	.180	.189	369	19	-16				.873	-7	S-46	-2.1
Total	5 n	262	1381	401	484	72	41	9	198	24	16	.350	.362	.482	843	156	78	41	16	3	.831	50	S-261/P-2,3-1,1-1	9.0
Total	7	329	1502	264	383	54	20	2	132	43	103	.255	.277	.323	600	93	-11				.911	42	S-269/2-60,P-1	4.0

■ GEORGE WRIGHT Wright, George De Witt b: 12/22/58, Oklahoma City, Okla BB/TR, 5'11", 180 lbs. Deb: 4/10/82 Career OF: (20-LF 444-CF 114-RF)

YEAR	TM/L	G	AB	R	H	2B	3B	HR	RBI	BB	SO	AVG	OBP	SLG	OPS	OPS+	BR+	SB	CS	SBR	FA	FR	G/POS	TPR
1982	Tex-A	150	557	69	147	20	5	11	50	30	78	.264	.305	.377	682	91	-8	3	7	-2	.981	11	*O-149(0-147-3)	0.0
1983	Tex-A	162	634	79	175	28	6	18	80	41	82	.276	.322	.424	746	106	4	8	7	-1	.985	10	*O-161(0-161-0)	1.2
1984	Tex-A	101	383	40	93	19	4	9	48	15	54	.243	.275	.384	659	78	-12	0	2	-1	.983	-3	O-80(0-54-26),D-18	-1.9
1985	Tex-A	109	363	21	69	13	0	2	18	25	49	.190	.242	.242	485	33	-33	4	7	-2	.991	-1	*O-102(0-53-55)/D-4	-3.9
1986	Tex-A	49	106	10	23	3	1	2	7	4	23	.217	.252	.321	573	53	-7	3	5	-1	.969	-5	O-42(10-8-27)	-1.4
	Mon-N	56	117	12	22	5	2	0	5	11	28	.188	.264	.265	529	47	-9	1	1	-0	1.000	-2	O-32(10-21-3)	-1.2
Total	5	627	2160	231	529	88	18	42	208	126	314	.245	.289	.361	650	78	-66	19	29	-6	.984	10	O-566C/D-22	-7.2

■ JOE WRIGHT Wright, Joseph S. b: 1873, Pittsburgh, Pa. BL/TL, 5'8", 175 lbs. Deb: 7/14/1895

YEAR	TM/L	G	AB	R	H	2B	3B	HR	RBI	BB	SO	AVG	OBP	SLG	OPS	OPS+	BR+	SB	CS	SBR	FA	FR	G/POS	TPR
1895	Lou-N	60	228	30	63	10	4	1	30	12	28	.276	.315	.368	684	81	-7	7			.963	-3	O-60(0-43-17)	-1.0
1896	Lou-N	2	7	0	2	0	0	0	0	0	1	.286	.286	.286	571	53	-0	0			1.000	-0	/O-2(0-0-2)	-0.1
	Pit-N	15	52	5	16	2	1	0	6	1	2	.308	.321	.385	705	89	-1	1			.958	-2	O-12(0-12-0)/3-1	-0.3
	Yr	17	59	5	18	2	1	0	6	1	3	.305	.317	.373	690	85	-1	1			.962	-2	O-14(0-12-2)/3-1	-0.4
Total	2	77	287	35	81	12	5	1	36	13	31	.282	.316	.369	685	82	-8	8			.963	-5	/O-74(0-55-19),3-1	-1.4

■ PAT WRIGHT Wright, Patrick Francis b: 7/5/1865, Pottsville, Pa. d: 5/29/43, Springfield, Ill. BB/TR, 6'2", 190 lbs. Deb: 7/11/1890

YEAR	TM/L	G	AB	R	H	2B	3B	HR	RBI	BB	SO	AVG	OBP	SLG	OPS	OPS+	BR+	SB	CS	SBR	FA	FR	G/POS	TPR
1890	Chi-N	1	2	0	0	0	0	0	0	1	0	.000	.333	.000	333	-1	-0	0			1.000	0	/2-1	0.0

■ SAM WRIGHT Wright, Samuel b: 11/25/1848, New York, N.Y. d: 5/6/28, Boston, Mass. BR/TR, 5'7.5", 146 lbs. Deb: 4/21/1875 F

YEAR	TM/L	G	AB	R	H	2B	3B	HR	RBI	BB	SO	AVG	OBP	SLG	OPS	OPS+	BR+	SB	CS	SBR	FA	FR	G/POS	TPR
1875	NH-n	33	127	10	24	4	0	0	5	1	1	.189	.195	.220	416	51	-5	1	0	0	.807	12	S-33	0.6
1876	Bos-N	2	8	0	1	0	0	0	0	0	0	.125	.125	.125	250	-16	-1				.778	-0	/S-2	-0.1
1880	Cin-N	9	34	0	3	0	0	0	0	0	5	.088	.088	.088	176	-40	-5				.889	-2	/S-9	-0.6
1881	Bos-N	1	4	0	1	0	0	0	0	0	0	.250	.250	.250	500	60	-0				.667	-1	/S-1	-0.1
Total	3	12	46	0	5	0	0	0	0	0	5	.109	.109	.109	217	-27	-6				.843	-3	/S-12	-0.8

■ TAFFY WRIGHT Wright, Taft Shedron b: 8/10/11, Tabor City, N.C. d: 10/22/81, Orlando, Fla. BL/TR, 5'10", 180 lbs. Deb: 4/18/38

YEAR	TM/L	G	AB	R	H	2B	3B	HR	RBI	BB	SO	AVG	OBP	SLG	OPS	OPS+	BR+	SB	CS	SBR	FA	FR	G/POS	TPR
1938	Was-A	100	263	37	92	18	10	2	36	13	17	.350	.389	.517	906	134	13	1	2	-0	.982	-4	O-60(14-1-45)	0.4
1939	Was-A	129	499	77	154	29	11	4	93	38	19	.309	.359	.435	794	110	7	1	2	-0	.950	-3	*O-123(39-0-84)	-0.4
1940	Chi-A	147	581	79	196	31	9	5	88	43	25	.337	.385	.448	832	114	12	4	7	-2	.963	-4	*O-144(0-0-144)	-0.2
1941	Chi-A	136	513	71	165	35	5	10	97	60	27	.322	.399	.468	867	130	23	5	4	-0	.973	-2	*O-134(0-0-134)	1.2
1942	Chi-A	85	300	43	100	13	5	0	47	48	9	.333	.432	.410	842	141	19	1	8	-3	.968	-1	O-81(81-0-1)	1.1
1946	Chi-A	115	422	46	116	19	4	7	52	42	17	.275	.342	.389	731	108	4	10	3	1	.991	-3	*O-107(8-0-99)	-0.2
1947	Chi-A	124	401	48	130	13	0	4	54	48	17	.324	.398	.387	784	123	14	8	6	-0	.971	-4	*O-100(35-0-66)	0.5
1948	Chi-A	134	455	50	127	15	6	4	61	38	18	.279	.341	.365	706	91	-6	2	1	0	.987	1	*O-114(6-0-108)	-1.0
1949	Phi-A	59	149	14	35	2	5	2	25	16	6	.235	.321	.356	677	82	-4	0	0	0	.970	-0	O-35(0-0-35)	-0.6
Total	9	1029	3583	465	1115	175	55	38	553	346	155	.311	.376	.423	799	116	81	32	33	-5	.972	-21	O-898(183-1-716)	0.8

■ TOM WRIGHT Wright, Thomas Everette b: 9/22/23, Shelby, N.C. BL/TR, 5'11.5", 180 lbs. Deb: 9/15/48

YEAR	TM/L	G	AB	R	H	2B	3B	HR	RBI	BB	SO	AVG	OBP	SLG	OPS	OPS+	BR+	SB	CS	SBR	FA	FR	G/POS	TPR
1948	Bos-A	3	2	1	1	0	1	0	0	0	0	.500	.500	1.500	2000	400	1	0	0	0	.000	0	H	0.1
1949	Bos-A	5	4	1	1	1	0	0	1	1	1	.250	.400	.500	900	128	0	0	0	0	.000	0	H	0.0
1950	Bos-A	54	107	17	34	7	0	0	20	6	18	.318	.360	.383	743	82	-3	0	0	0	.953	-2	O-24(5-0-19)	-0.6
1951	Bos-A	28	63	8	14	1	1	1	9	11	8	.222	.347	.317	664	73	-2	0	0	0	.950	-4	O-18(1-0-17)	-0.6
1952	StL-A	29	66	6	16	0	0	1	6	12	20	.242	.359	.288	647	79	-1	1	1	-0	.976	1	O-18(18-0-0)	-0.2
	Chi-A	60	132	15	34	10	2	1	21	16	16	.258	.342	.386	729	102	0	1	0	0	.969	-2	O-34(22-0-13)	-0.3
	Yr	89	198	21	50	10	2	2	27	28	36	.253	.348	.354	702	94	-1	2	1	0	.971	-1	O-52(40-0-13)	-0.5
1953	Chi-A	77	132	14	33	5	3	2	25	12	21	.250	.322	.379	701	86	-3	0	0	0	.978	-5	O-33(10-0-24)	-0.9
1954	Was-A	76	171	13	42	4	4	1	17	18	38	.246	.325	.333	658	85	-4	0	0	0	1.000	-2	O-43(15-0-28)	-0.7
1955	Was-A	7	7	0	0	0	0	0	0	0	1	.000	.000	.000	0	-99	-2	0	0	0	.000	0	H	-0.2
1956	Was-A	2	1	0	0	0	0	0	0	0	0	.000	.000	.000	0	-99	-0	0	0	0	.000	0	H	0.0
Total	9	341	685	75	175	28	11	6	99	76	123	.255	.336	.355	691	85	-13	2	1	0	.977	-13	O-170(71-0-101)	-3.4

■ DICK WRIGHT Wright, Willard James b: 5/5/1890, Worcester, N.Y. d: 1/24/52, Bethlehem, Pa. BR/TR, 5'10", 170 lbs. Deb: 6/30/15

YEAR	TM/L	G	AB	R	H	2B	3B	HR	RBI	BB	SO	AVG	OBP	SLG	OPS	OPS+	BR+	SB	CS	SBR	FA	FR	G/POS	TPR
1915	Bro-F	4	5	0	0	0	0	0	0	0	0	.000	.000	.000	0	-99	-1	0			.833	-1	/C-3	-0.2

■ HARRY WRIGHT Wright, William Henry b: 1/10/1835, Sheffield, England
d: 10/3/1895, Atlantic City, N.J. BR/TR, 5'9.5", 157 lbs. Deb: 5/5/1871 FMH NA OF: (0-LF 176-CF 1-RF)

YEAR	TM/L	G	AB	R	H	2B	3B	HR	RBI	BB	SO	AVG	OBP	SLG	OPS	OPS+	BR+	SB	CS	SBR	FA	FR	G/POS	TPR
1871	Bos-n	31	147	42	44	5	2	0	26	13	2	.299	.356	.361	717	103	1	7	1	1	.855	-0	*O-30C/P-9,S-1,M	0.1

YEAR	TM/L	G	AB	R	H	2B	3B	HR	RBI	BB	SO	AVG	OBP	SLG	OPS	OPS+	BR+	SB	CS	SBR	FA	FR	G/POS	TPR
1872	Bos-n	48	208	39	52	5	1	0	23	9	2	.250	.281	.284	565	70	-8	0	0	0	.866	-5	*O-48(0-48-0)/P-7,M	-0.8
1873	Bos-n	58	266	57	67	10	4	2	35	10	3	.252	.279	.342	621	77	-9	1	1	-0	.837	-4	*O-58(0-58-0),P-13,M	-0.9
1874	Bos-n	40	184	44	58	4	2	2	27	4	3	.315	.330	.391	721	123	4	1	0	0	.827	-2	*O-40(0-40-0)/P-6,M	0.1
1875	Bos-n	1	4	1	1	0	0	0	0	0	1	.250	.250	.250	500	72	-0	0	0	0	1.000	-0	/O-1(0-0-1),M	0.0
1876	Bos-N	1	3	0	0	0	0	0	0	0	1	.000	.000	.000	0	-98	-1				.000	-0	/O-1(0-0-1),M	-0.1
1877	Bos-N	1	4	0	0	0	0	0	0	0	1	.000	.000	.000	0	-97	-1				.667	1	/O-1(0-1-0),M	0.0
Total	5 n	178	809	183	222	24	9	4	111	36	11	.274	.305	.341	646	90	-13	9	2	1	.846	-11	O-177C/P-35,S-1	-1.5
Total	2	2	7	0	0	0	0	0	0	0	2	.000	.000	.000	0	-97	-1				.667	0	/O-2(0-1-1)	-0.1

■ BILL WRIGHT

Wright, William Hiram Deb: 9/16/1887

YEAR	TM/L	G	AB	R	H	2B	3B	HR	RBI	BB	SO	AVG	OBP	SLG	OPS	OPS+	BR+	SB	CS	SBR	FA	FR	G/POS	TPR
1887	Was-N	1	3	0	2	0	0	0	0	0	0	.667	.667	.667	1333	286	1	0			.778	-0	/C-1	0.0

■ RASTY WRIGHT

Wright, William Smith b: 1/31/1863, Birmingham, Mich. d: 10/14/22, Duluth, Minn. BL, 6'1", 185 lbs. Deb: 4/17/1890

YEAR	TM/L	G	AB	R	H	2B	3B	HR	RBI	BB	SO	AVG	OBP	SLG	OPS	OPS+	BR+	SB	CS	SBR	FA	FR	G/POS	TPR
1890	Syr-a	88	348	82	106	10	6	0	27	69		.305	.428	.368	796	150	29	30			.907	4	O-88(0-70-18)	2.6
	Cle-N	13	45	7	5	1	0	0	2	12	4	.111	.298	.133	432	27	-4	3			.917	-1	O-13(0-0-13)	-0.4
Total	1	101	393	89	111	11	6	0	29	81	4	.282	.412	.341	753	135	26	33			.908	3	O-101(0-70-31)	2.2

■ RUSS WRIGHTSTONE

Wrightstone, Russell Guy b: 3/18/1893, Bowmansdale, Pa.
d: 2/25/69, Harrisburg, Pa. BL/TR, 5'10.5", 176 lbs. Deb: 4/19/20 Career OF: (85-LF 0-CF 33-RF)

YEAR	TM/L	G	AB	R	H	2B	3B	HR	RBI	BB	SO	AVG	OBP	SLG	OPS	OPS+	BR+	SB	CS	SBR	FA	FR	G/POS	TPR
1920	Phi-N	76	206	23	54	6	1	3	17	10	25	.262	.303	.345	647	82	-5	3	2	-0	.934	6	3-56/S-2,2-1	0.2
1921	Phi-N	109	372	59	110	13	4	9	51	18	20	.296	.332	.425	756	92	-5	4	4	-1	.922	4	3-54,O-37(34-0-3)/2-4	-0.1
1922	Phi-N	99	331	56	101	18	6	5	33	28	17	.305	.365	.441	806	98	-1	4	5	-1	.973	13	3-40,S-35/1-2	1.5
1923	Phi-N	119	392	59	107	21	7	7	57	21	19	.273	.315	.416	731	82	-11	5	2	0	.942	-4	3-72,S-21/2-9	-0.8
1924	Phi-N	118	388	55	119	24	4	7	58	27	15	.307	.363	.443	806	102	2	5	4	-0	.944	-8	3-97/2-9,S-5,O-1R	-0.1
1925	Phi-N	92	286	48	99	18	5	14	61	19	18	.346	.389	.591	980	135	14	0	3	-1	.937	-19	O-45L,S-12,3-11,2/1	-0.7
1926	Phi-N	112	368	55	113	23	1	7	57	27	11	.307	.356	.432	788	106	3	5			.977	-0	1-53,3-37,2-13,/O-5L	0.1
1927	Phi-N	141	533	62	163	24	5	6	75	48	20	.306	.365	.403	769	104	4	9			.989	1	*1-136/2-1,3-1	-0.4
1928	Phi-N	33	91	7	19	5	1	1	11	14	5	.209	.321	.319	639	65	-4	0			.936	-4	O-26(9-0-19)/1-4	-1.0
	NY-N	30	25	3	4	0	0	1	5	3	2	.160	.250	.280	530	38	-2	0			1.000	-0	/1-2	-0.2
	Yr	63	116	10	23	5	1	2	16	17	7	.198	.306	.310	616	60	-7	0			.936	-4	O-26(9-0-19)/1-6	-1.2
Total	9	929	2992	427	889	152	34	60	425	215	152	.297	.349	.431	780	99	-7	35	20		.942	-12	3-368,1-203,O/S2	-1.5

■ ZEKE WRIGLEY

Wrigley, George Watson b: 1/18/1874, Philadelphia, Pa. d: 9/28/52, Philadelphia, Pa. 5'8.5", 150 lbs. Deb: 8/31/1896 Career OF: (4-LF 15-CF 20-RF)

YEAR	TM/L	G	AB	R	H	2B	3B	HR	RBI	BB	SO	AVG	OBP	SLG	OPS	OPS+	BR+	SB	CS	SBR	FA	FR	G/POS	TPR
1896	Was-N	5	9	1	1	0	0	0	2	1	1	.111	.200	.111	311	-17	-2	0			.909	3	/2-3,S-1	0.1
1897	Was-N	104	388	65	110	14	8	3	64	21		.284	.320	.384	704	86	-9	5			.885	-2	O-36R,S-33,3-30,/2	-0.9
1898	Was-N	111	400	50	98	9	10	2	39	20		.245	.283	.333	615	76	-14	10			.895	11	S-97,2-11/O-3C,3-1	0.2
1899	NY-N	4	15	1	3	0	0	0	1	1		.200	.250	.200	450	25	-2	1			.818	-1	/3-5	-0.3
	Bro-N	15	49	4	10	2	2	0	11	3		.204	.250	.327	577	56	-3	2			.870	-4	S-14/3-1	-0.6
	Yr	19	64	5	13	2	2	0	12	4		.203	.250	.297	547	49	-5	3			.870	-5	S-14/3-6	-0.9
Total	4	239	861	121	222	25	20	5	117	46	1	.258	.296	.351	647	78	-29	18			.892	7	S-145/O-39R,3-37,2	-1.5

■ RICK WRONA

Wrona, Richard James b: 12/10/63, Tulsa, Okla. BR/TR, 6'1", 185 lbs. Deb: 9/3/88

YEAR	TM/L	G	AB	R	H	2B	3B	HR	RBI	BB	SO	AVG	OBP	SLG	OPS	OPS+	BR+	SB	CS	SBR	FA	FR	G/POS	TPR
1988	Chi-N	4	6	0	0	0	0	0	0	0	1	.000	.000	.000	0	-96	-1	0	0	0	1.000	1	/C-2	0.0
1989	*Chi-N	38	92	11	26	2	1	2	14	2	21	.283	.305	.391	697	91	-1	0	0	0	.983	2	C-37	0.3
1990	Chi-N	16	29	3	5	0	0	0	0	2	11	.172	.226	.172	398	10	-3	1	0	0	.970	3	C-16	0.0
1992	Cin-N	11	23	0	4	0	0	0	0	0	3	.174	.174	.174	348	-1	-3	0	0	0	.965	3	C-10/1-1	0.0
1993	Chi-A	4	8	0	1	0	0	0	1	0	4	.125	.125	.125	250	-33	-1	0	0	0	1.000	-1	/C-4	-0.2
1994	Mil-A	6	10	2	5	4	0	1	3	1	1	.500	.545	1.200	1745	319	3	0	0	0	.923	-1	/C-5,1-1	0.2
Total	6	79	168	16	41	6	1	3	18	5	41	.244	.270	.345	615	68	-7	1	0	0	.976	8	/C-74,1-2	0.3

■ YATS WUESTLING

Wuestling, George b: 10/18/03, St.Louis, Mo. d: 4/26/70, St.Louis, Mo. BR/TR, 5'11", 167 lbs. Deb: 6/15/29

YEAR	TM/L	G	AB	R	H	2B	3B	HR	RBI	BB	SO	AVG	OBP	SLG	OPS	OPS+	BR+	SB	CS	SBR	FA	FR	G/POS	TPR
1929	Det-A	54	150	13	30	4	1	0	16	9	24	.200	.250	.240	490	27	-16	1	3	-1	.943	-2	S-52/2-1,3-1	-1.4
1930	Det-A	4	9	0	0	0	0	0	0	2	3	.000	.182	.000	182	-48	-2	0	0	0	.842	1	/S-4	-0.1
	NY-A	25	58	5	11	0	1	0	3	4	14	.190	.242	.224	466	20	-7	0	1	-0	.918	4	S-21/3-3	-0.2
	Yr	29	67	5	11	0	1	0	3	6	17	.164	.233	.194	427	10	-9	0	1	-0	.904	5	S-25/3-3	-0.3
Total	2	83	217	18	41	4	2	0	19	15	41	.189	.245	.226	470	21	-26	1	4	-1	.931	2	/S-77,3-4,2-1	-1.7

■ JOE WYATT

Wyatt, Loral John b: 4/6/1900, Petersburg, Ind. d: 12/5/70, Oblong, Ill. BR/TR, 6'1", 175 lbs. Deb: 9/11/24

YEAR	TM/L	G	AB	R	H	2B	3B	HR	RBI	BB	SO	AVG	OBP	SLG	OPS	OPS+	BR+	SB	CS	SBR	FA	FR	G/POS	TPR
1924	Cle-A	4	12	1	2	0	0	0	1	2	1	.167	.286	.167	452	18	-1	0	0	0	.833	-1	/O-4(0-0-4)	-0.3

■ REN WYLIE

Wylie, James Renwick b: 12/14/1861, Elizabeth, Pa. d: 8/17/51, Wilkinsburg, Pa. BR/TR, 5'11", 155 lbs. Deb: 8/11/1882

YEAR	TM/L	G	AB	R	H	2B	3B	HR	RBI	BB	SO	AVG	OBP	SLG	OPS	OPS+	BR+	SB	CS	SBR	FA	FR	G/POS	TPR
1882	Pit-a	1	3	0	0	0	0	0		0		.000	.000	.000	0	-99	-1				1.000	0	/O-1(0-1-0)	0.0

■ FRANK WYMAN

Wyman, Frank H. b: 5/10/1862, Haverhill, Mass. d: 2/4/16, Everett, Mass. Deb: 6/10/1884

YEAR	TM/L	G	AB	R	H	2B	3B	HR	RBI	BB	SO	AVG	OBP	SLG	OPS	OPS+	BR+	SB	CS	SBR	FA	FR	G/POS	TPR
1884	KC-U	30	124	16	27	4	0	0		3		.218	.236	.250	486	55	-10				.743	5	O-25L/P-3,1-3,3-3	-0.5
	CP-U	2	8	1	3	0	0	0		0		.375	.375	.375	750	129	0				.846	-0	/1-2	0.0
	Yr	32	132	17	30	4	0	0		3		.227	.244	.258	502	60	-10				.743	4	O-25L/1-5,P-3,3-3	-0.5

■ BUTCH WYNEGAR

Wynegar, Harold Delano b: 3/14/56, York, Pa. BB/TR, 6', 194 lbs. Deb: 4/9/76

YEAR	TM/L	G	AB	R	H	2B	3B	HR	RBI	BB	SO	AVG	OBP	SLG	OPS	OPS+	BR+	SB	CS	SBR	FA	FR	G/POS	TPR
1976	Min-A★	149	534	58	139	21	2	10	69	79	63	.260	.358	.363	721	109	9	0	0	0	.978	-10	*C-137,D-15	0.5
1977	Min-A★	144	532	76	139	22	3	10	79	68	61	.261	.347	.370	717	97	-1	2	3	-1	.993	-11	*C-142/3-1	-0.6
1978	Min-A	135	454	36	104	22	1	4	45	47	42	.229	.310	.308	618	73	-15	1	0	0	.988	-3	*C-131/3-1	-1.3
1979	Min-A	149	504	74	136	20	0	7	57	74	36	.270	.366	.351	717	91	-4	2	2	-0	.992	-4	*C-146/D-2	-0.2
1980	Min-A	146	486	61	124	18	3	5	57	63	36	.255	.343	.335	678	81	-11	3	1	0	.988	4	*C-142/D-1	-0.1
1981	Min-A	47	150	11	37	5	0	0	10	17	9	.247	.327	.280	607	72	-5	0	1	-0	.995	-1	C-37/D-9	-0.5
1982	Min-A	24	86	9	18	4	0	1	8	10	12	.209	.292	.291	582	59	-5	0	0	0	.986	-2	C-24	-0.5
	NY-A	63	191	27	56	8	1	3	20	40	21	.293	.418	.393	811	126	9	0	1	-0	.993	-1	C-62	1.1
	Yr	87	277	36	74	12	1	4	28	50	33	.267	.381	.361	742	106	4	0	1	-0	.991	-2	C-86	0.6
1983	NY-A	94	301	40	89	18	2	6	42	52	29	.296	.401	.429	830	133	16	1	1	-0	.985	-13	C-93	0.7
1984	NY-A	129	442	48	118	13	1	6	45	65	35	.267	.361	.342	703	99	2	1	4	-1	.993	-4	*C-126	0.3
1985	NY-A	102	309	27	69	15	0	5	32	64	43	.223	.357	.320	677	89	-2	0	0	0	.990	2	C-96	0.3
1986	NY-A	61	194	19	40	4	1	7	29	30	21	.206	.313	.345	658	80	-5	0	0	0	.994	-2	C-57	-0.5
1987	Cal-A	31	92	4	19	2	0	0	5	9	13	.207	.277	.228	505	37	-8	0	0	0	.994	3	C-28/D-1	-0.4
1988	Cal-A	27	55	8	14	4	1	1	8	8	7	.255	.349	.418	767	117	1	0	0	0	.981	-0	C-26	0.2
Total	13	1301	4330	498	1102	176	15	65	506	626	428	.255	.351	.347	698	93	-19	10	13	-2	.989	-43	*C-1247/D-28,3-2	-1.0

■ EARLY WYNN

Wynn, Early "Gus" b: 1/6/20, Hartford, Ala. d: 4/4/99, Venice, Fla. BB/TR (BR 1941-44), 6', 200 lbs. Deb: 9/13/39 CH

YEAR	TM/L	G	AB	R	H	2B	3B	HR	RBI	BB	SO	AVG	OBP	SLG	OPS	OPS+	BR+	SB	CS	SBR	FA	FR	G/POS	TPR
1939	Was-A	3	6	0	1	0	0	0	1	1	1	.167	.286	.167	452	20	-1	0	0	0	1.000	-1	/P-3	0.0
1941	Was-A	5	15	1	2	1	0	0	0	0	5	.133	.133	.200	333	-14	-2	0	0	0	.917	0	/P-5	0.0
1942	Was-A	30	69	4	15	2	0	0	7	3	13	.217	.250	.246	496	40	-6	0	0	0	.953	-1	P-30	0.0
1943	Was-A	38	98	6	29	3	1	1	11	1	11	.296	.303	.378	681	102	-0	0	0	0	.947	-2	P-37	0.0
1944	Was-A	43	92	4	19	2	0	1	6	3	21	.207	.232	.261	492	42	-7	0	0	0	.972	-2	P-33	0.0
1946	Was-A	25	47	4	15	2	0	1	9	5	7	.319	.385	.426	810	134	2	0	0	0	.962	-0	P-17	0.0
1947	Was-A☆	54	120	6	33	6	0	2	13	1	19	.275	.281	.375	656	84	-3	0	0	0	.980	-1	P-33	0.0
1948	Was-A	73	106	9	23	3	1	0	16	14	22	.217	.308	.264	572	55	-7	0	0	0	.950	-1	P-33	0.0
1949	Cle-A	35	70	3	10	1	0	1	7	4	10	.143	.189	.200	389	3	-10	0	0	0	**1.000**	1	P-26	0.0
1950	Cle-A	39	77	12	18	5	1	2	10	10	12	.234	.322	.403	724	87	-2	0	0	0	.932	0	P-32	0.0
1951	Cle-A	41	108	8	20	8	1	1	13	7	9	.185	.235	.306	540	48	-8	0	0	0	.982	-1	P-37	0.0
1952	Cle-A	44	99	5	22	2	0	0	10	9	15	.222	.287	.242	529	52	-6	0	0	0	.943	-1	P-42	0.0
1953	Cle-A	37	91	11	25	2	0	3	10	7	17	.275	.327	.396	722	97	-1	0	0	0	**1.000**	-1	P-36	0.0
1954	*Cle-A	40	93	10	17	3	0	0	4	7	13	.183	.240	.215	455	25	-10	0	0	0	.957	-3	P-40	0.0
1955	Cle-A★	34	84	8	15	3	0	1	7	6	17	.179	.233	.250	483	29	-9	0	0	0	.944	-3	P-32	0.0

YEAR	TM/L	G	AB	R	H	2B	3B	HR	RBI	BB	SO	AVG	OBP	SLG	OPS	OPS+	BR+	SB	CS	SBR	FA	FR	G/POS	TPR
1956	Cle-A★	38	101	5	23	5	0	1	15	7	22	.228	.278	.307	585	53	-7	1	0	0	.955	1	P-38	0.0
1957	Cle-A★	40	86	4	10	0	0	0	4	11	23	.116	.216	.116	333	-7	-13	0	0	0	**1.000**	-1	P-40	0.0
1958	Chi-A★	40	75	7	15	1	0	0	11	10	25	.200	.294	.213	507	43	-6	0	0	0	**1.000**	-2	P-40	0.0
1959	*Chi-A★	37	90	11	22	7	0	2	8	9	18	.244	.320	.389	709	95	-1	0	0	0	.957	-1	P-37	0.0
1960	Chi-A★	36	75	8	15	2	1	1	7	14	17	.200	.333	.293	627	72	-3	0	0	0	.972	-2	P-36	0.0
1961	Chi-A	17	37	4	6	0	0	0	2	3	11	.162	.225	.162	387	5	-5	0	0	0	1.000	-2	P-17	0.0
1962	Chi-A	27	54	5	7	1	0	0	2	7	17	.130	.230	.148	378	4	-7	0	0	0	**1.000**	-2	P-27	0.0
1963	Cle-A	20	11	1	3	0	0	0	0	2	5	.273	.385	.273	657	89	-0	0	0	0	1.000	-0	P-20	0.0
Total	23	796	1704	136	365	59	5	17	173	141	330	.214	.275	.285	560	54	-110	1	0	0	.967	-25	P-691	0.0

■ JIMMY WYNN

Wynn, James Sherman "The Toy Cannon" b: 3/12/42, Hamilton, Ohio BR/TR, 5'9", 170 lbs. Deb: 7/10/63 Career OF: (298-LF 1181-CF 355-RF)

YEAR	TM/L	G	AB	R	H	2B	3B	HR	RBI	BB	SO	AVG	OBP	SLG	OPS	OPS+	BR+	SB	CS	SBR	FA	FR	G/POS	TPR
1963	Hou-N	70	250	31	61	10	5	4	27	30	53	.244	.325	.372	697	107	2	4	2	0	.963	-2	O-53L,S-21/3-2	-0.2
1964	Hou-N	67	219	19	49	7	0	5	18	24	58	.224	.303	.324	627	81	-5	5	5	-1	.958	5	O-64(13-51-0)	-0.3
1965	Hou-N	157	564	90	155	30	7	22	73	84	126	.275	.374	.470	844	146	36	43	4	8	.978	20	*O-155(0-155-0)	6.1
1966	Hou-N	105	418	62	107	21	1	18	62	41	81	.256	.324	.440	764	118	9	13	10	-1	.978	11	*O-104(0-104-0)	1.7
1967	Hou-N★	158	594	102	148	29	3	37	107	74	137	.249	.334	.495	829	139	29	16	4	2	.968	9	*O-157(0-157-0)	3.7
1968	Hou-N	156	542	85	146	23	5	26	67	90	131	.269	.378	.474	853	158	40	11	17	-4	.988	15	*O-153(56-93-7)	5.1
1969	Hou-N	149	495	113	133	17	1	33	87	**148**	142	.269	.440	.507	947	168	53	23	7	3	.985	11	*O-149(0-149-0)	**6.4**
1970	Hou-N	157	554	82	156	32	2	27	88	106	96	.282	.398	.493	891	143	36	24	5	4	.987	10	*O-151(66-87-0)	4.3
1971	Hou-N	123	404	38	82	16	0	7	45	56	63	.203	.303	.295	598	72	-14	10	5	0	.988	2	*O-116(1-48-72)	-1.8
1972	Hou-N	145	542	117	148	29	3	24	90	103	99	.273	.391	.470	862	147	36	17	7	1	.983	6	*O-144(0-12-132)	3.8
1973	Hou-N	139	481	90	106	14	5	20	55	91	102	.220	.349	.395	744	106	6	14	11	-1	.986	3	*O-133(2-10-125)	0.1
1974	*LA-N★	150	535	104	145	17	4	32	108	108	104	.271	.393	.497	891	154	41	18	15	-1	.992	11	*O-148(0-148-0)	4.8
1975	LA-N★	130	412	80	102	16	0	18	58	110	77	.248	.407	.417	825	135	25	7	3	0	.983	-1	*O-120(21-107-0)	2.1
1976	Atl-N	148	449	75	93	19	1	17	66	**127**	111	.207	.382	.367	749	107	9	16	6	1	.971	11	*O-138(90-50-0)	1.6
1977	NY-A	30	77	7	11	2	1	1	3	15	16	.143	.283	.234	516	43	-6	1	0	0	1.000	2	D-15/O-8(5-0-3)	-0.5
	Mil-A	36	117	10	23	3	1	0	10	17	31	.197	.299	.239	538	49	-8	3	0	1	.967	-1	O-17(1-0-16),D-15	-1.0
	Yr	66	194	17	34	5	2	1	13	32	47	.175	.292	.237	529	46	-14	4	0	1	.981	1	D-30,O-25(6-0-19)	-1.5
Total	15	1920	6653	1105	1665	285	39	291	964	1224	1427	.250	.369	.436	805	129	290	225	101	14	.981	110	*O-1810C/D-30,S-21,3	35.9

■ MARVELL WYNNE

Wynne, Marvell b: 12/17/59, Chicago, Ill. BL/TL, 5'11", 185 lbs. Deb: 6/15/83

YEAR	TM/L	G	AB	R	H	2B	3B	HR	RBI	BB	SO	AVG	OBP	SLG	OPS	OPS+	BR+	SB	CS	SBR	FA	FR	G/POS	TPR
1983	Pit-N	103	366	66	89	16	2	7	26	38	52	.243	.319	.355	675	85	-7	12	10	-1	.983	-0	*O-102(0-102-0)	-1.0
1984	Pit-N	154	653	77	174	24	11	0	39	42	81	.266	.311	.337	648	82	-16	24	19	-1	.990	5	*O-154(0-154-0)	-1.5
1985	Pit-N	103	337	21	69	6	3	2	18	18	48	.205	.247	.258	505	42	-26	10	5	0	.987	6	O-99(0-100-0)	-2.2
1986	SD-N	137	288	34	76	19	2	7	37	15	45	.264	.303	.417	719	98	-2	11	11	-1	.986	-11	*O-125(0-125-0)	-1.5
1987	SD-N	98	188	17	47	8	2	2	24	20	37	.250	.322	.346	668	80	-5	11	6	0	.981	-10	O-71(33-40-5)	-1.6
1988	SD-N	128	333	37	88	13	4	11	42	31	62	.264	.327	.426	753	117	7	3	4	-1	.987	-11	*O-113(37-84-10)	-0.8
1989	SD-N	105	294	19	74	11	1	6	35	12	41	.252	.283	.357	641	82	-8	4	1	1	.971	-7	O-96(39-41-25)	-1.7
	*Chi-N	20	48	8	9	2	1	1	4	1	7	.188	.220	.333	553	52	-3	2	0	0	.944	-2	O-13(4-6-3)	-0.6
	Yr	125	342	27	83	13	2	7	39	13	48	.243	.275	.354	628	77	-11	6	1	1	.968	-10	*O-109(43-47-28)	-2.3
1990	Chi-N	92	186	21	38	8	2	4	19	14	25	.204	.264	.333	597	59	-11	3	2	-0	.991	-9	O-66(13-54-4)	-2.1
Total	8	940	2693	300	664	107	28	40	244	191	398	.247	.298	.352	650	81	-71	80	58	-3	.985	-41	O-839(126-706-47)	-13.0

■ JOHNNY WYROSTEK

Wyrostek, John Barney b: 7/12/19, Fairmont City, Ill. d: 12/12/86, St.Louis, Mo. BL/TR, 6'2", 180 lbs. Deb: 9/10/42 Career OF: (49-LF 396-CF 674-RF)

YEAR	TM/L	G	AB	R	H	2B	3B	HR	RBI	BB	SO	AVG	OBP	SLG	OPS	OPS+	BR+	SB	CS	SBR	FA	FR	G/POS	TPR
1942	Pit-N	9	35	0	4	0	1	0	3	3	2	.114	.184	.171	356	4	-4	0			1.000	1	/O-8(8-0-0)	-0.4
1943	Pit-N	51	79	7	12	3	0	0	1	3	15	.152	.183	.190	373	7	-9	0			.919	-5	O-20R/3-2,1-1,2-1	-1.6
1946	Phi-N	145	545	73	153	30	4	6	45	70	42	.281	.366	.383	749	116	13	7			.981	17	*O-142(6-138-0)	2.7
1947	Phi-N	128	454	68	124	24	7	5	51	61	45	.273	.364	.390	754	104	4	7			.971	1	*O-126(0-27-100)	0.1
1948	Cin-N	136	512	74	140	24	9	17	76	52	63	.273	.344	.455	799	119	12	7			.977	4	*O-130(0-130-0)	1.2
1949	Cin-N	134	474	54	118	20	4	9	46	58	63	.249	.333	.365	698	86	-9	7			.971	1	*O-129(2-60-67)	-1.2
1950	Cin-N★	131	509	70	145	34	5	8	76	52	38	.285	.357	.418	775	103	2	1			.980	-2	*O-129(11-9-115)/1-4	-0.4
1951	Cin-N★	142	537	52	167	31	3	2	61	54	54	.311	.376	.391	767	105	5	2	1	0	.970	-7	*O-139(1-0-139)	-0.6
1952	Cin-N	30	106	12	25	1	3	1	10	18	7	.236	.347	.330	677	89	-1	1	2	-0	1.000	2	O-29(0-25-6)/1-1	-0.1
	Phi-N	98	321	45	88	16	3	1	37	44	26	.274	.363	.352	715	100	2	1	7	-2	.972	8	O-88(2-1-87)	0.4
	Yr	128	427	57	113	17	6	2	47	62	33	.265	.359	.347	706	97	0	2	9	-3	.980	10	*O-117(2-26-93)/1-1	0.3
1953	Phi-N	125	409	42	111	14	2	6	47	38	43	.271	.339	.359	699	83	-10	0	3	-1	.962	2	*O-110(8-0-102)	-1.3
1954	Phi-N	92	259	28	62	12	4	3	28	29	39	.239	.318	.351	670	74	-10	0	0	0	.990	-5	O-55(0-6-49),1-22	-1.8
Total	11	1221	4240	525	1149	209	45	58	481	482	437	.271	.349	.383	731	98	-5	33	13		.975	16	*O-1105R/1-28,3-2,2	-3.0

■ HENRY YAIK

Yaik, Henry b: 3/1/1864, Detroit, Mich. d: 9/21/35, Detroit, Mich. BL, 5'11", 185 lbs. Deb: 10/3/1888

YEAR	TM/L	G	AB	R	H	2B	3B	HR	RBI	BB	SO	AVG	OBP	SLG	OPS	OPS+	BR+	SB	CS	SBR	FA	FR	G/POS	TPR
1888	Pit-N	2	6	0	2	0	0	0	1	1	0	.333	.429	.333	762	158	0	0			.625	2	/O-1(1-0-0),C-1	0.2

■ AD YALE

Yale, William M. b: 4/17/1870, Bristol, Conn. d: 4/27/48, Bridgeport, Conn. Deb: 9/18/05

YEAR	TM/L	G	AB	R	H	2B	3B	HR	RBI	BB	SO	AVG	OBP	SLG	OPS	OPS+	BR+	SB	CS	SBR	FA	FR	G/POS	TPR
1905	Bro-N	4	13	1	1	0	0	0	1	1		.077	.143	.077	220	-37	-2	0			1.000	-0	/1-4	-0.3

■ HUGH YANCY

Yancy, Hugh b: 10/16/49, Sarasota, Fla. BR/TR, 5'11", 170 lbs. Deb: 7/5/72

YEAR	TM/L	G	AB	R	H	2B	3B	HR	RBI	BB	SO	AVG	OBP	SLG	OPS	OPS+	BR+	SB	CS	SBR	FA	FR	G/POS	TPR
1972	Chi-A	3	9	0	1	0	0	0	0	0	0	.111	.111	.111	222	-33	-1	0	1	-0	1.000	0	/3-3	-0.2
1974	Chi-A	1	0	0	0	0	0	0	0	0	0	—	—	—	—		-0	0	0	0	.000	0	/D-1	0.0
1976	Chi-A	3	10	0	1	1	0	0	0	0	3	.100	.100	.200	300	-14	-1	0	0	0	1.000	-1	/2-3	-0.2
Total	3	7	19	0	2	1	0	0	0	0	3	.105	.105	.158	263	-23	-3	0	1	-0	1.000	-0	/2-3,3-3,D-1	-0.4

■ GEORGE YANKOWSKI

Yankowski, George Edward b: 11/19/22, Cambridge, Mass. BR/TR, 6', 180 lbs. Deb: 8/17/42

YEAR	TM/L	G	AB	R	H	2B	3B	HR	RBI	BB	SO	AVG	OBP	SLG	OPS	OPS+	BR+	SB	CS	SBR	FA	FR	G/POS	TPR
1942	Phi-A	6	13	0	2	1	0	0	2	0	2	.154	.154	.231	385	7	-2	0	0	0	1.000	0	/C-6	-0.1
1949	Chi-A	12	18	0	3	1	0	0	2	0	2	.167	.167	.222	389	3	-3	0	0	0	1.000	1	/C-6	-0.1
Total	2	18	31	0	5	2	0	0	4	0	4	.161	.161	.226	387	5	-4	0	0	0	1.000	1	/C-12	-0.2

■ GEORGE YANTZ

Yantz, George Webb b: 7/27/1886, Louisville, Ky. d: 2/26/67, Louisville, Ky. BR/TR, 5'6.5", 168 lbs. Deb: 9/30/12

YEAR	TM/L	G	AB	R	H	2B	3B	HR	RBI	BB	SO	AVG	OBP	SLG	OPS	OPS+	BR+	SB	CS	SBR	FA	FR	G/POS	TPR
1912	Chi-N	1	1	0	1	0	0	0	0	0	0	1.000	1.000	1.000	2000	450	0	0			.000	0	/C-1	0.0

■ YAM YARYAN

Yaryan, Clarence Everett b: 11/5/1892, Knowlton, Iowa d: 11/16/64, Birmingham, Ala. BR/TR, 5'10.5", 180 lbs. Deb: 4/23/21

YEAR	TM/L	G	AB	R	H	2B	3B	HR	RBI	BB	SO	AVG	OBP	SLG	OPS	OPS+	BR+	SB	CS	SBR	FA	FR	G/POS	TPR
1921	Chi-A	45	102	11	31	8	2	0	15	9	16	.304	.366	.422	788	102	0	0	0	0	.933	-6	C-34	-0.4
1922	Chi-A	36	71	9	14	2	0	2	9	6	10	.197	.269	.310	579	51	-5	1	0	0	.966	-1	C-26	-0.5
Total	2	81	173	20	45	10	2	2	24	15	26	.260	.326	.376	702	81	-5	1	0	0	.948	-8	/C-60	-0.9

■ CARL YASTRZEMSKI

Yastrzemski, Carl Michael "Yaz" b: 8/22/39, Southampton, N.Y. BL/TR, 5'11", 182 lbs. Deb: 4/11/61 H Career OF: (1917-LF 159-CF 7-RF)

YEAR	TM/L	G	AB	R	H	2B	3B	HR	RBI	BB	SO	AVG	OBP	SLG	OPS	OPS+	BR+	SB	CS	SBR	FA	FR	G/POS	TPR
1961	Bos-A	148	583	71	155	31	6	11	80	50	96	.266	.327	.396	723	90	-9	6	5	-0	.963	1	*O-147(147-0-0)	-1.7
1962	Bos-A	160	646	99	191	43	6	19	94	66	82	.296	.364	.469	833	118	17	7	4	0	.969	16	*O-160(160-0-0)	2.3
1963	Bos-A★	151	570	91	**183**	**40**	3	14	68	**95**	72	**.321**	**.419**	.475	894	145	**39**	8	5	0	.980	13	*O-151(151-1-0)	**4.5**
1964	Bos-A	151	567	77	164	29	9	15	67	75	90	.289	.374	.451	826	122	19	6	5	-0	.973	28	*O-148(18-131-0)/3-2	4.2
1965	Bos-A†	133	494	78	154	**45**	3	20	72	70	58	.312	**.398**	**.536**	**935**	**154**	**36**	7	6	-1	.987	6	*O-130(125-7-1)	**3.6**
1966	Bos-A☆	160	594	81	165	**39**	2	16	80	84	60	.278	.368	.431	799	117	15	8	9	-1	.985	17	*O-158(157-1-0)	2.3
1967	*Bos-A★	161	579	**112**	**189**	31	4	**44**	**121**	91	69	**.326**	**.421**	**.622**	**1043**	**189**	**66**	10	8	-1	.978	13	*O-161(161-1-0)	**7.4**
1968	Bos-A★	157	539	90	162	32	2	23	74	**119**	90	**.301**	**.429**	.495	**924**	168	**50**	13	6	1	.991	17	*O-155(154-1-0)/1-3	**6.6**
1969	Bos-A★	162	603	96	154	28	2	40	111	101	91	.255	.363	.507	871	134	27	15	7	1	.985	10	*O-143(140-3-0),1-22	2.9
1970	Bos-A★	161	566	**125**	186	29	0	40	102	128	66	.329	**.453**	**.592**	**1045**	**174**	**62**	23	13	1	.990	2	1-94,O-69(67-3-0)	**5.4**
1971	Bos-A★	148	508	75	129	21	2	15	70	106	60	.254	.384	.392	775	112	12	8	7	-1	.993	14	*O-146(146-0-0)	1.8
1972	Bos-A★	125	455	70	120	18	2	12	68	67	44	.264	.363	.391	754	118	12	5	4	-0	.974	8	O-83(83-0-0),1-42	1.3
1973	Bos-A†	152	540	82	160	25	4	19	95	105	58	.296	.411	.463	874	138	31	9	7	-0	.994	-5	*1-107,3-31,O-14L	1.6
1974	Bos-A★	148	515	**93**	155	25	2	15	79	104	48	.301	.421	.445	866	139	31	12	7	0	.997	-7	1-84,O-63(63-0-0)/D-4	1.5
1975	*Bos-A★	149	543	91	146	30	1	14	60	87	67	.269	.372	.405	777	110	9	8	4	0	.996	-1	*1-140/O-8(8-0-0),D-2	-0.3
1976	Bos-A★	155	546	71	146	23	2	21	102	80	67	.267	.362	.432	794	118	13	5	6	-1	.998	-8	1-94,O-51L,D-10	-0.7
1977	Bos-A★	150	558	99	165	27	3	28	102	73	40	.296	.378	.505	884	124	19	11	1	2	**1.000**	14	*O-140L/1-7,D-6	2.8

YEAR	TM/L	G	AB	R	H	2B	3B	HR	RBI	BB	SO	AVG	OBP	SLG	OPS	OPS+	BR+	SB	CS	SBR	FA	FR	G/POS	TPR
1978	Bos-A†	144	523	70	145	21	2	17	81	76	44	.277	.372	.423	795	111	10	4	5	-1	.986	6	O-71L,1-50,D-27	0.8
1979	Bos-A★	147	518	69	140	28	1	21	87	62	46	.270	.351	.450	800	108	6	3	3	-0	.996	6	D-56,1-51,O-36L	0.5
1980	Bos-A	105	364	49	100	21	1	15	50	44	38	.275	.353	.462	814	115	8	0	2	-1	1.000	-3	D-49,O-39L,1-16	0.0
1981	Bos-A	91	338	36	83	14	1	7	53	49	28	.246	.341	.355	696	95	-1	0	1	-0	.992	3	D-48,1-39	-0.3
1982	Bos-A★	131	459	53	126	22	1	16	72	59	50	.275	.360	.431	791	110	7	0	1	-0	1.000	0	*D-102,1-14/O-2C	0.3
1983	Bos-A★	119	380	38	101	24	0	10	56	54	29	.266	.360	.408	768	103	3	0	0	0	1.000	-1	*D-107/1-2,O-1(1-0-0)	-0.1
Total	23	3308	11988	1816	3419	646	59	452	1844	1845	1393	.285	.382	.462	844	128	482	168	116	-4	.981	149	*O-2076L,1-765,D/3	46.7

■ AL YATES
Yates, Albert Arthur b: 5/26/45, Jersey City, N.J. BR/TR, 6'2", 210 lbs. Deb: 5/13/71

YEAR	TM/L	G	AB	R	H	2B	3B	HR	RBI	BB	SO	AVG	OBP	SLG	OPS	OPS+	BR+	SB	CS	SBR	FA	FR	G/POS	TPR
1971	Mil-A	24	47	5	13	2	0	1	4	3	7	.277	.320	.383	703	100	-0	1	0	0	1.000	1	O-12(3-0-9)	0.0

■ BERT YEABSLEY
Yeabsley, Robert Watkins b: 12/17/1893, Philadelphia, Pa. d: 2/8/61, Philadelphia, Pa. BR/TR, 5'9.5", 175 lbs. Deb: 5/28/19

YEAR	TM/L	G	AB	R	H	2B	3B	HR	RBI	BB	SO	AVG	OBP	SLG	OPS	OPS+	BR+	SB	CS	SBR	FA	FR	G/POS	TPR
1919	Phi-N	3	0	0	0	0	0	0	0	1	0	—	1.000	—	1000	200	0	0			.000	0	H	0.0

■ GEORGE YEAGER
Yeager, George J. "Doc" b: 6/5/1874, Cincinnati, Ohio d: 7/5/40, Cincinnati, Ohio BR/TR, 5'10", 190 lbs. Deb: 9/25/1896 Career OF: (8-LF 5-CF 13-RF)

YEAR	TM/L	G	AB	R	H	2B	3B	HR	RBI	BB	SO	AVG	OBP	SLG	OPS	OPS+	BR+	SB	CS	SBR	FA	FR	G/POS	TPR
1896	Bos-N	2	5	1	1	0	0	0	0	0	1	.200	.200	.200	400	5	-1	0			1.000	-0	/1-2	-0.1
1897	*Bos-N	30	95	20	23	2	3	2	15	7		.242	.294	.389	684	75	-4	2			.970	1	C-13,O-10R/2-4,3-1	-0.2
1898	Bos-N	68	221	37	59	13	1	3	24	16		.267	.328	.376	703	96	-2	1			.951	-3	C-37,1-17/O-9L,S-2	-0.2
1899	Bos-N	3	8	1	1	0	0	0	0	1		.125	.222	.125	347	-3	-1	0			1.000	0	/O-2(0-1-1),C-1	-0.1
1901	Cle-A	39	139	13	31	5	0	0	14	4		.223	.250	.259	509	43	-11	2			.964	3	C-25/1-5,O-3R,2-2	-0.5
	Pit-N	26	91	9	24	2	1	0	10	4		.264	.302	.308	610	75	-3	1			.971	-2	C-20/3-4,1-1	-0.2
1902	NY-N	39	108	6	22	2	1	0	9	11		.204	.277	.241	518	61	-5	1			.946	-1	C-27/1-3,O-1(0-0-1)	-0.4
	Bal-A	11	38	3	7	1	0	0	1	2		.184	.225	.211	436	20	-4	0			.930	1	C-11	-0.2
Total	6	218	705	90	168	25	6	5	73	45	1	.238	.290	.312	602	69	-30	7			.953	-2	C-134/1-28,O-25R,23S	-1.9

■ JOE YEAGER
Yeager, Joseph F. "Little Joe" b: 8/28/1875, Philadelphia, Pa. d: 7/2/37, Detroit, Mich. BR/TR, 5'10", 160 lbs. Deb: 4/22/1898 Career OF: (10-LF 1-CF 7-RF)

YEAR	TM/L	G	AB	R	H	2B	3B	HR	RBI	BB	SO	AVG	OBP	SLG	OPS	OPS+	BR+	SB	CS	SBR	FA	FR	G/POS	TPR
1898	Bro-N	43	134	12	23	5	1	0	15	7		.172	.218	.224	442	27	-13	1			.908	6	P-36/O-4L,S-2,2-1	-0.1
1899	Bro-N	23	47	12	9	0	1	0	4	6		.191	.333	.234	567	55	-3	0			.914	3	S-11,P-10/O-1L,3-1	0.1
1900	Bro-N	3	9	0	3	0	0	0	0	0		.333	.333	.333	667	79	-0	0			1.000	-1	/P-2,3-1	0.0
1901	Det-A	41	125	18	37	7	1	2	17	4		.296	.343	.416	759	105	1	3			.919	5	P-26,S-12/2-1	0.3
1902	Det-A	50	161	17	39	6	5	1	23	5		.242	.282	.360	643	76	-6	0			.957	-1	P-19,O-13L,2-12,/S3	-0.8
1903	Det-A	109	402	36	103	15	6	0	43	18		.256	.303	.323	626	91	-4	9			.921	-9	*3-107/P-1,S-1	-1.1
1905	NY-A	115	401	54	107	16	7	0	42	25		.267	.330	.342	672	102	1	8			.923	0	3-91,S-21	0.5
1906	NY-A	57	123	20	37	6	1	0	12	13		.301	.407	.366	773	129	5	3			.905	-1	S-22,2-13/3-3	0.5
1907	StL-A	123	436	32	104	21	7	1	44	31		.239	.294	.326	619	98	-2	11			.938	7	3-91,2-17,S-10	1.0
1908	StL-A	10	15	3	5	1	0	0	1	1		.333	.474	.400	874	183	2	2			1.000	0	/2-4,S-1	0.2
Total	10	574	1853	204	467	77	29	4	201	110		.252	.312	.331	643	92	-19	37			.927	10	3-295/P-94,S-83,2O	0.6

■ STEVE YEAGER
Yeager, Stephen Wayne b: 11/24/48, Huntington, W.Va. BR/TR, 6', 190 lbs. Deb: 8/2/72

YEAR	TM/L	G	AB	R	H	2B	3B	HR	RBI	BB	SO	AVG	OBP	SLG	OPS	OPS+	BR+	SB	CS	SBR	FA	FR	G/POS	TPR
1972	LA-N	35	106	18	29	0	1	4	15	16	26	.274	.374	.406	780	124	4	0	0	0	.984	9	C-35	1.5
1973	LA-N	54	134	18	34	5	0	2	10	15	33	.254	.342	.336	678	93	-1	1	0	0	.981	5	C-50	0.6
1974	*LA-N	94	316	41	84	16	1	12	41	32	77	.266	.337	.437	774	120	7	2	2	-0	.992	13	C-93	2.5
1975	LA-N	135	452	34	103	16	1	12	54	40	75	.228	.302	.347	649	83	-11	2	5	-1	.992	12	*C-135	0.6
1976	LA-N	117	359	42	77	11	3	11	35	30	84	.214	.288	.354	642	83	-9	3	1	0	.985	9	*C-115	0.6
1977	*LA-N	125	387	53	99	21	2	16	55	43	84	.256	.336	.444	781	108	4	1	3	-1	.977	12	*C-123	2.0
1978	*LA-N	94	228	19	44	7	0	4	23	36	41	.193	.303	.276	579	63	-11	0	0	0	.988	11	C-91	0.4
1979	LA-N	105	310	33	67	9	2	13	41	29	68	.216	.283	.384	667	81	-9	1	0	0	.984	11	*C-103	0.6
1980	LA-N	96	227	20	48	8	0	2	20	20	54	.211	.275	.273	548	55	-14	2	3	-1	.984	4	C-95	-0.8
1981	*LA-N	42	86	5	18	2	0	3	7	6	14	.209	.261	.337	598	71	-4	0	0	0	.994	1	C-40	-0.1
1982	LA-N	82	196	13	48	5	2	2	18	13	28	.245	.295	.321	617	74	-7	0	0	0	.990	7	C-76	0.3
1983	*LA-N	113	335	31	68	8	3	15	41	23	57	.203	.256	.379	635	74	-13	1	1	-0	.985	-6	*C-112	-1.5
1984	LA-N	74	197	16	45	4	0	4	29	20	38	.228	.300	.310	609	72	-7	1	2	-0	.994	-6	C-65	-1.2
1985	*LA-N	53	121	4	25	4	1	0	9	7	24	.207	.250	.256	506	43	-9	0	1	-0	.992	9	C-48	0.0
1986	Sea-A	50	130	10	27	2	0	2	12	12	23	.208	.275	.269	544	48	-9	0	0	0	1.000	-0	C-49	-0.7
Total	15	1269	3584	357	816	118	16	102	410	342	726	.228	.300	.355	655	83	-88	14	18	-3	.987	90	*C-1230	4.8

■ BILL YEATMAN
Yeatman, William Suter b: 3/1839, Alexandria, Va. d: 4/20/01, York, Pa. Deb: 4/20/1872

YEAR	TM/L	G	AB	R	H	2B	3B	HR	RBI	BB	SO	AVG	OBP	SLG	OPS	OPS+	BR+	SB	CS	SBR	FA	FR	G/POS	TPR
1872	Nat-n	1	4	0	0	0	0	0	0	0	1	.000	.000	.000	0	-86	-1	0	0	0	.000	-0	/O-1(0-0-1)	-0.1

■ ERIC YELDING
Yelding, Eric Girard b: 2/22/65, Montrose, Ala. BR/TR, 5'11", 165 lbs. Deb: 4/9/89 Career OF: (14-LF 92-CF 10-RF)

YEAR	TM/L	G	AB	R	H	2B	3B	HR	RBI	BB	SO	AVG	OBP	SLG	OPS	OPS+	BR+	SB	CS	SBR	FA	FR	G/POS	TPR
1989	Hou-N	70	90	19	21	2	0	0	9	7	19	.233	.296	.256	551	61	-4	11	5	1	1.000	6	S-15,2-13/O-8(1-4-3)	0.3
1990	Hou-N	142	511	69	130	9	5	1	28	39	87	.254	.307	.297	605	69	-21	64	25	5	.971	-6	O-94C,S-40,2-10,/3	-2.0
1991	Hou-N	78	276	19	67	11	1	1	20	13	46	.243	.277	.301	578	66	-13	11	9	-1	.939	-14	S-72/O-4(0-3-1)	-2.4
1992	Hou-N	9	8	1	2	0	0	0	0	0	3	.250	.250	.250	500	44	-1	0	0	0	.000	-1	/S-2,O-2(2-1-0)	-0.2
1993	Chi-N	69	108	14	22	5	1	1	10	11	22	.204	.277	.296	574	54	-7	3	2	-0	.984	12	2-32/3-7,S-1,O-1C	0.6
Total	5	368	993	122	242	27	7	3	67	70	177	.244	.294	.294	588	66	-46	89	41	5	.948	-3	S-130,O-109C/2-55,3	-3.7

■ ARCHIE YELLE
Yelle, Archie Joseph b: 6/11/1892, Saginaw, Mich. d: 5/2/83, Woodland, Cal. BR/TR, 5'10.5", 170 lbs. Deb: 5/12/17

YEAR	TM/L	G	AB	R	H	2B	3B	HR	RBI	BB	SO	AVG	OBP	SLG	OPS	OPS+	BR+	SB	CS	SBR	FA	FR	G/POS	TPR
1917	Det-A	25	51	4	7	1	0	0	0	5	4	.137	.214	.157	371	13	-5	2			.975	-1	C-24	-0.6
1918	Det-A	56	144	7	25	3	0	0	7	9	15	.174	.227	.194	422	28	-13	0			.948	7	C-52	-0.2
1919	Det-A	6	4	1	0	0	0	0	0	1	0	.000	.200	.000	200	-42	-1	0			.833	-1	/C-6	-0.1
Total	3	87	199	12	32	4	0	0	7	15	19	.161	.223	.181	404	23	-19	2			.952	5	/C-82	-0.9

■ STEVE YERKES
Yerkes, Stephen Douglas b: 5/15/1888, Hatboro, Pa. d: 1/31/71, Lansdale, Pa. BR/TR, 5'9", 165 lbs. Deb: 9/29/09

YEAR	TM/L	G	AB	R	H	2B	3B	HR	RBI	BB	SO	AVG	OBP	SLG	OPS	OPS+	BR+	SB	CS	SBR	FA	FR	G/POS	TPR
1909	Bos-A	5	7	0	2	0	0	0	0	0		.286	.286	.286	571	79	-0	0			1.000	-1	/S-2	-0.1
1911	Bos-A	142	502	70	140	24	3	1	57	52		.279	.354	.345	698	96	-2	14			.927	-20	*S-116,2-14,3-11	-1.3
1912	*Bos-A	131	523	73	132	22	6	0	42	41		.252	.312	.317	629	76	-17	4			.943	-15	*2-131	-3.0
1913	Bos-A	137	483	67	129	29	6	1	48	50	32	.267	.338	.358	696	101	1	11			.957	-19	*2-129	-1.7
1914	Bos-A	92	293	23	64	17	2	1	23	14	23	.218	.259	.300	559	68	-13	5	6	-1	.972	4	2-91	-1.0
	Pit-F	39	142	18	48	9	5	1	25	11	13	.338	.386	.493	879	139	5	2			.974	8	S-39	1.6
1915	Pit-F	121	434	44	125	17	8	1	49	30	27	.288	.337	.371	708	100	-7	17			**.967**	-3	*2-114/S-8	-0.8
1916	Chi-N	44	137	12	36	6	2	1	10	9	7	.263	.308	.358	666	94	-1	1			.919	1	2-41	0.1
Total	7	711	2521	307	676	124	32	6	254	207	102	.268	.328	.350	677	93	-33	54	6		.956	-45	2-520,S-165/3-11	-6.2

■ TOM YEWCIC
Yewcic, Thomas "Kibby" b: 5/9/32, Conemaugh, Pa. BR/TR, 5'11", 180 lbs. Deb: 6/27/57

YEAR	TM/L	G	AB	R	H	2B	3B	HR	RBI	BB	SO	AVG	OBP	SLG	OPS	OPS+	BR+	SB	CS	SBR	FA	FR	G/POS	TPR
1957	Det-A	1	1	0	0	0	0	0	0	0	0	.000	.000	.000	0	-97	-0	0	0	0	.833	1	/C-1	0.0

■ ED YEWELL
Yewell, Edwin Leonard b: 8/22/1862, Washington, D.C. d: 9/15/40, Washington, D.C. Deb: 5/12/1884 Career OF: (1-LF 2-CF 5-RF)

YEAR	TM/L	G	AB	R	H	2B	3B	HR	RBI	BB	SO	AVG	OBP	SLG	OPS	OPS+	BR+	SB	CS	SBR	FA	FR	G/POS	TPR
1884	Was-a	27	93	14	23	3	1	0		1		.247	.263	.301	564	95	-0				.885	-3	2-11/O-8R,3-7,S-2	-0.2
	Was-U	1	4	0	0	0	0	0		0		.000	.000	.000	0	-99	-1				.571	-0	/3-1	-0.1
Total	1	28	97	14	23	3	1	0		1		.237	.253	.289	541	85	-1				.773	-3	/2-11,3-8,O-8R,S-2	-0.3

■ JOE YINGLING
Yingling, Joseph Granville b: 7/23/1866, Westminster, Md. d: 10/24/46, Manchester, Md. BR/TL, 5'7.5", 145 lbs. Deb: 5/28/1886

YEAR	TM/L	G	AB	R	H	2B	3B	HR	RBI	BB	SO	AVG	OBP	SLG	OPS	OPS+	BR+	SB	CS	SBR	FA	FR	G/POS	TPR
1886	Was-N	1	2	0	0	0	0	0	0	0	1	.000	.000	.000	0	-99	-0	0			.500	0	/P-1	0.0
1894	Phi-N	1	4	0	1	0	0	0	0	0	1	.250	.250	.250	500	21	-0	0			1.000	-1	/S-1	-0.1
Total	2	2	6	0	1	0	0	0	0	0	2	.167	.167	.167	333	-14	-1	0			1.000	-1	/S-1,P-1	-0.1

■ BILL YOHE
Yohe, William Clyde b: 9/2/1878, Mt.Erie, Ill. d: 12/24/38, Bremerton, Wash. TR, 5'8", 180 lbs. Deb: 8/30/09

YEAR	TM/L	G	AB	R	H	2B	3B	HR	RBI	BB	SO	AVG	OBP	SLG	OPS	OPS+	BR+	SB	CS	SBR	FA	FR	G/POS	TPR
1909	Was-A	21	72	6	15	2	0	0	4	3		.208	.240	.236	476	53	-4	2			.921	3	3-19	-0.1

■ RUDY YORK
York, Preston Rudolph b: 8/17/13, Ragland, Ala. d: 2/5/70, Rome, Ga. BR/TR, 6'1", 209 lbs. Deb: 8/22/34 MC

YEAR	TM/L	G	AB	R	H	2B	3B	HR	RBI	BB	SO	AVG	OBP	SLG	OPS	OPS+	BR+	SB	CS	SBR	FA	FR	G/POS	TPR
1934	Det-A	3	6	0	1	0	0	0	0	1	3	.167	.286	.167	452	19	-1	0	0	0	1.000	-0	/C-2	-0.1

YEAR	TM/L	G	AB	R	H	2B	3B	HR	RBI	BB	SO	AVG	OBP	SLG	OPS	OPS+	BR+	SB	CS	SBR	FA	FR	G/POS	TPR
1937	Det-A	104	375	72	115	18	3	35	103	41	52	.307	.375	.651	1026	150	26	3	2	-0	.960	-19	C-54,3-41/1-2	1.0
1938	Det-A★	135	463	85	138	27	2	33	127	92	74	.298	.417	.579	995	139	28	1	2	-0	.990	-1	*C-116,O-14L/1-1	3.0
1939	Det-A	102	329	66	101	16	1	20	68	41	50	.307	.387	.544	931	126	12	5	0	1	.985	-8	C-67,1-19	0.7
1940	*Det-A	155	588	105	186	46	6	33	134	89	88	.316	.410	.583	993	141	36	3	2	-0	.990	5	*1-155	2.4
1941	Det-A★	155	590	91	153	29	3	27	111	92	88	.259	.360	.456	816	104	3	3	1	0	.986	-1	*1-155	-1.2
1942	Det-A★	153	577	81	150	26	4	21	90	73	71	.260	.343	.428	771	107	5	3	3	-0	.988	15	*1-152	0.5
1943	Det-A★	155	571	90	155	22	11	**34**	**118**	84	88	.271	.366	**.527**	893	148	33	5	5	-1	.990	18	*1-155	4.5
1944	Det-A☆	151	583	77	161	27	7	18	98	68	73	.276	.353	.439	792	119	14	5	3	0	.989	5	*1-151	1.2
1945	*Det-A	155	595	71	157	25	5	18	87	60	85	.264	.331	.413	745	109	5	6	6	-1	.988	-2	*1-155	-0.6
1946	*Bos-A★	154	579	78	160	30	6	17	119	86	93	.276	.371	.437	808	118	16	3	2	-0	.994	6	*1-154	1.6
1947	Bos-A	48	184	16	39	7	0	6	27	22	32	.212	.296	.348	644	73	-7	0	0	0	.995	1	1-48	-0.8
	Chi-A☆	102	400	40	97	18	4	15	64	36	55	.243	.305	.420	725	104	-0	1	0	0	.995	-1	*1-102	-0.5
	Yr	150	584	56	136	25	4	21	91	58	87	.233	.302	.397	699	94	-8	1	0	0	**.995**	0	*1-150	-1.3
1948	Phi-A	31	51	4	8	0	0	0	6	7	15	.157	.259	.157	415	12	-6	0	0	0	.988	-1	1-14	-0.7
Total	13	1603	5891	876	1621	291	52	277	1152	792	867	.275	.362	.483	845	121	163	38	26	-1	.990	16	*1-1263,C-239/3-41,O	11.0

■ TOM YORK York, Thomas Jefferson b: 7/13/1851, Brooklyn, N.Y. d: 2/17/36, New York, N.Y. BL, 5'9", 165 lbs. Deb: 5/9/1871 MU

YEAR	TM/L	G	AB	R	H	2B	3B	HR	RBI	BB	SO	AVG	OBP	SLG	OPS	OPS+	BR+	SB	CS	SBR	FA	FR	G/POS	TPR
1871	Tro-n	29	145	36	37	5	7	2	23	9	1	.255	.299	.428	726	104	0	2	2	-0	.855	3	*O-29(0-29-0)	0.2
1872	Bal-n	51	248	66	66	10	4	1	41	4	1	.266	.278	.351	629	88	-5	2	1	0	.916	11	*O-51(51-0-1)	0.5
1873	Bal-n	57	277	70	84	10	7	2	49	3	3	.303	.311	.412	722	113	4	3	1	0	**.872**	11	*O-57(56-1-0)	1.2
1874	Phi-n	50	224	36	56	4	7	0	37	5	4	.250	.266	.330	597	87	-4	1	0	0	.861	8	*O-50(49-1-0)	0.5
1875	Har-n	86	375	68	111	14	7	0	37	3	6	.296	.302	.371	672	126	8	7	3	0	.868	4	*O-86(86-0-0)	1.3
1876	Har-N	67	273	47	68	12	7	1	39	10	4	.249	.286	.369	655	108	1				.899	2	*O-67(66-1-0)	-0.1
1877	Har-N	56	237	43	67	16	7	1	37	3	11	.283	.292	.422	714	137	10				.865	0	*O-56(56-0-0)	0.6
1878	Pro-N	62	269	56	83	19	**10**	1	26	8	19	.309	.329	.465	793	159	16				.873	4	*O-62(62-0-0),M	1.5
1879	Pro-N	81	342	69	106	25	5	1	50	19	28	.310	.346	.421	767	154	20				.898	-4	*O-81(81-0-0)	0.9
1880	Pro-N	53	203	21	43	9	2	0	18	8	29	.212	.242	.276	518	77	-4				.934	-3	O-53(50-1-2)	-1.0
1881	Pro-N	85	316	57	96	23	5	2	47	29	26	.304	.362	.427	790	150	19				.859	-2	*O-85(85-0-0),M	1.1
1882	Pro-N	81	321	48	86	23	7	1	40	19	14	.268	.309	.393	701	123	8				.873	-3	*O-81(81-0-0)	0.4
1883	Cle-N	100	381	56	99	29	5	2	46	**37**	55	.260	.325	.378	703	114	8				.864	0	*O-100(100-0-0)	0.5
1884	Bal-a	83	314	64	70	14	7	1		34		.223	.318	.322	640	105	3				.843	-5	*O-83(68-0-15)	-0.4
1885	Bal-a	22	87	6	23	4	2	0	12	8		.264	.326	.356	683	117	2				.938	1	O-22(2-1-19)	0.3
Total	5 n	273	1269	276	354	43	32	5	187	24	15	.279	.292	.375	667	106	5	15	7	1	.875	37	O-273(242-31-1)	3.7
Total	10	690	2743	467	741	174	57	10	315	175	186	.270	.317	.387	705	126	83				.878	-8	O-690(651-3-36)	3.8

■ TONY YORK York, Tony Batton b: 11/27/12, Irene, Tex. d: 4/18/70, Hillsboro, Tex. BR/TR, 5'10", 165 lbs. Deb: 4/18/44

YEAR	TM/L	G	AB	R	H	2B	3B	HR	RBI	BB	SO	AVG	OBP	SLG	OPS	OPS+	BR+	SB	CS	SBR	FA	FR	G/POS	TPR
1944	Chi-N	28	85	4	20	1	0	0	7	4	11	.235	.270	.247	517	46	-6	0			.940	10	S-15,3-12	0.5

■ NED YOST Yost, Edgar Frederick b: 8/19/54, Eureka, Cal. BR/TR, 6'1", 190 lbs. Deb: 4/12/80 C

YEAR	TM/L	G	AB	R	H	2B	3B	HR	RBI	BB	SO	AVG	OBP	SLG	OPS	OPS+	BR+	SB	CS	SBR	FA	FR	G/POS	TPR
1980	Mil-A	15	31	0	5	0	0	0	0	0	6	.161	.161	.161	323	-12	-5	0	0	0	1.000	2	C-15	-0.2
1981	Mil-A	18	27	4	6	0	0	3	3	3	6	.222	.300	.556	856	150	1	0	0	0	.956	2	C-16	0.4
1982	*Mil-A	40	98	13	27	6	3	1	8	7	20	.276	.324	.429	752	111	1	3	1	0	.977	-2	C-39/D-1	0.1
1983	Mil-A	61	196	21	44	5	1	6	28	5	36	.224	.244	.352	596	67	-10	1	0	0	.971	-6	C-61	-1.3
1984	Tex-A	80	242	15	44	4	0	6	25	6	47	.182	.202	.273	474	29	-23	1	2	-0	.995	-5	C-78	-2.7
1985	Mon-N	5	11	1	2	0	0	0	0	0	2	.182	.182	.182	364	2	-1	0	0	0	.962	1	/C-5	-0.1
Total	6	219	605	54	128	15	4	16	64	21	117	.212	.238	.329	567	56	-36	5	3	0	.982	-8	C-214/D-1	-3.8

■ EDDIE YOST Yost, Edward Frederick Joseph "The Walking Man" b: 10/13/26, Brooklyn, N.Y. BR/TR, 5'10", 170 lbs. Deb: 8/16/44 MC Career OF: (3-LF 0-CF 8-RF)

YEAR	TM/L	G	AB	R	H	2B	3B	HR	RBI	BB	SO	AVG	OBP	SLG	OPS	OPS+	BR+	SB	CS	SBR	FA	FR	G/POS	TPR
1944	Was-A	7	14	3	2	0	0	0	0	1	2	.143	.200	.143	343	-1	-2	0	0	0	.917	-1	/3-3,S-2	-0.2
1946	Was-A	8	25	2	2	1	0	0	1	5	5	.080	.233	.120	353	1	-3	2	1	0	1.000	1	/3-7	-0.3
1947	Was-A	115	428	52	102	17	3	0	14	45	57	.238	.314	.292	606	71	-16	3	5	-1	.958	-9	*3-114	-2.8
1948	Was-A	145	555	74	138	32	11	2	50	82	51	.249	.349	.357	706	91	-7	4	3	-0	.966	-13	*3-145	-2.0
1949	Was-A	124	435	57	110	19	7	9	45	91	41	.253	.383	.391	774	107	7	3	3	-0	.954	-2	*3-122	0.4
1950	Was-A	155	573	114	169	26	2	11	58	**141**	63	.295	.440	.405	845	123	30	6	6	-1	.945	-2	*3-155	2.5
1951	Was-A	154	568	109	161	**36**	4	12	65	126	55	.283	.423	.424	847	132	32	6	4	-0	.954	-27	*3-152/O-3(3-0-0)	0.5
1952	Was-A☆	157	587	92	137	32	3	12	49	**129**	73	.233	.378	.359	738	110	13	4	3	-0	.962	-35	*3-157	-2.4
1953	Was-A	152	577	107	157	30	7	9	45	**123**	59	.272	.403	.395	799	119	21	7	4	0	.965	-13	*3-152	0.8
1954	Was-A	155	539	101	138	26	4	11	47	131	71	.256	.406	.380	786	123	24	7	3	0	.968	3	*3-155	2.8
1955	Was-A	122	375	64	91	17	5	7	48	95	54	.243	.410	.371	780	117	15	4	3	-0	.943	-6	*3-107	0.9
1956	Was-A	152	515	94	119	17	2	11	53	**151**	82	.231	.412	.336	748	100	9	8	5	0	.963	11	*3-135/O-8(0-0-8)	1.9
1957	Was-A	110	414	47	104	13	5	9	38	73	49	.251	.370	.372	742	104	5	1	11	-4	.952	-11	*3-107	-1.0
1958	Was-A	134	406	55	91	16	0	8	37	81	43	.224	.365	.323	688	93	-0	3	6	-1	**.964**	-15	*3-114/O-4(4-0-0),1-2	-1.8
1959	Det-A	148	521	**115**	145	19	0	21	61	**135**	77	.278	**.437**	.436	873	133	32	9	2	1	**.962**	-11	*3-146/2-1	2.2
1960	Det-A	143	497	78	129	23	2	14	47	**125**	69	.260	**.416**	.398	814	118	19	5	4	-0	.933	-27	*3-142	-0.9
1961	LA-A	76	213	29	43	4	0	3	15	50	48	.202	.358	.263	621	62	-10	0	1	-0	.964	-10	3-67	-2.1
1962	LA-A	52	104	22	25	9	1	0	10	30	21	.240	.415	.346	761	111	4	0	2	-1	.950	-3	3-28/1-7	0.0
Total	18	2109	7346	1215	1863	337	56	139	683	1614	920	.254	.395	.371	766	109	174	72	66	-7	.957	-169	*3-2008/O-15R,1-9,S2	-1.5

■ ELMER YOTER Yoter, Elmer Elsworth b: 6/26/1900, Plainfield, Pa. d: 7/26/66, Camp Hill, Pa. BR/TR, 5'7", 155 lbs. Deb: 9/9/21

YEAR	TM/L	G	AB	R	H	2B	3B	HR	RBI	BB	SO	AVG	OBP	SLG	OPS	OPS+	BR+	SB	CS	SBR	FA	FR	G/POS	TPR
1921	Phi-A	3	3	0	0	0	0	0	0	0	0	.000	.000	.000	0	-99	-1	0	0	0	.000	0	H	-0.1
1924	Cle-A	19	66	3	18	1	1	0	7	5	8	.273	.324	.318	642	65	-3	0	0	0	.905	-2	3-19	-0.4
1927	Chi-N	13	27	2	6	1	1	0	5	4	4	.222	.323	.333	656	76	-1	0			.947	-0	3-11	-0.1
1928	Chi-N	1	0	0	0	0	0	0	0	0	0	—	—	—	—	0	0	0			.000	0	/3-1	0.0
Total	4	36	96	5	24	2	2	0	12	9	12	.250	.314	.313	627	63	-5	0	0		.915	-2	/3-31	-0.6

■ DEL YOUNG Young, Delmer Edward b: 5/11/12, Cleveland, Ohio d: 12/8/79, San Francisco, Cal. BB/TR, 5'11", 168 lbs. Deb: 4/19/37 F

YEAR	TM/L	G	AB	R	H	2B	3B	HR	RBI	BB	SO	AVG	OBP	SLG	OPS	OPS+	BR+	SB	CS	SBR	FA	FR	G/POS	TPR
1937	Phi-N	109	360	36	70	9	2	0	24	18	55	.194	.235	.231	465	25	-37	6			.950	10	*2-108	-2.1
1938	Phi-N	108	340	27	78	13	2	0	31	20	35	.229	.276	.279	556	55	-21	0			.933	-2	S-87,2-17	-1.7
1939	Phi-N	77	217	22	57	9	2	3	20	8	24	.263	.289	.364	653	77	-8	1			.946	-18	S-55,2-17	-2.2
1940	Phi-N	15	33	2	8	0	1	0	1	2	1	.242	.286	.303	589	65	-2	0			.962	-0	/S-6,2-5	-0.1
Total	4	309	950	87	213	31	7	3	76	48	115	.224	.264	.281	545	48	-68	7			.938	-10	S-148,2-147	-6.1

■ DEL YOUNG Young, Delmer John b: 10/24/1885, Macon, Mo. d: 12/17/59, Cleveland, Ohio BL/TR, 5'11", 195 lbs. Deb: 9/24/09 F

YEAR	TM/L	G	AB	R	H	2B	3B	HR	RBI	BB	SO	AVG	OBP	SLG	OPS	OPS+	BR+	SB	CS	SBR	FA	FR	G/POS	TPR
1909	Cin-N	2	7	0	2	0	0	0	0	1	1	.286	.375	.286	661	106	0	0			1.000	0	/O-2(1-0-1)	0.0
1914	Buf-F	80	174	17	48	5	5	4	22	3	13	.276	.288	.431	719	92	-6	0			.944	-6	O-41(7-2-32)	-1.4
1915	Buf-F	12	15	0	2	0	0	0	1	0	1	.133	.188	.133	321	-9	-2	1			.667	-1	/O-3(0-1-2)	-0.4
Total	3	94	196	17	52	5	5	4	23	5	13	.265	.284	.403	687	85	-8	1			.933	-7	/O-46(8-3-35)	-1.8

■ DMITRI YOUNG Young, Dmitri Dell b: 10/11/73, Vicksburg, Miss. BB/TR, 6'2", 215 lbs. Deb: 8/29/96 Career OF: (234-LF 0-CF 100-RF)

YEAR	TM/L	G	AB	R	H	2B	3B	HR	RBI	BB	SO	AVG	OBP	SLG	OPS	OPS+	BR+	SB	CS	SBR	FA	FR	G/POS	TPR
1996	*StL-N	16	29	3	7	0	0	0	2	4	5	.241	.353	.241	594	61	-1	0	1	-0	.976	-2	1-10	-0.4
1997	StL-N	110	333	38	86	14	3	5	34	38	63	.258	.338	.363	701	85	-7	6	5	-0	.985	-0	1-74,O-17(9-0-10)/D-1	-1.4
1998	Cin-N	144	536	81	166	48	1	14	83	47	94	.310	.368	.481	849	120	15	2	4	-1	.940	-6	*O-105(91-0-14),1-44	0.1
1999	Cin-N	127	373	63	112	30	2	14	56	30	71	.300	.356	.504	860	111	6	3	1	0	.976	-5	O-91(23-0-75)/1-9,D-1	-0.3
2000	Cin-N	152	548	68	166	37	6	18	88	36	80	.303	.349	.491	840	105	3	0	3	-1	.978	-4	*O-111L,1-36/D-4	-0.8
Total	5	549	1819	253	537	129	12	51	263	155	313	.295	.354	.463	817	106	15	11	14	-2	.962	-17	O-324L,1-173/D-6	-2.8

■ DON YOUNG Young, Donald Wayne b: 10/18/45, Houston, Tex. BR/TR, 6'2", 185 lbs. Deb: 9/9/65

YEAR	TM/L	G	AB	R	H	2B	3B	HR	RBI	BB	SO	AVG	OBP	SLG	OPS	OPS+	BR+	SB	CS	SBR	FA	FR	G/POS	TPR
1965	Chi-N	11	35	1	2	0	0	1	2	0	11	.057	.057	.143	200	-45	-7	0	0	0	.933	-2	O-11(0-11-0)	-1.0
1969	Chi-N	101	272	36	65	12	3	6	27	38	74	.239	.343	.371	714	89	-3	1	5	-2	.975	-4	*O-100(3-94-8)	-1.2
Total	2	112	307	37	67	12	3	7	29	38	85	.218	.314	.345	660	76	-10	1	5	-2	.972	-6	O-111(3-105-8)	-2.2

YEAR	TM/L	G	AB	R	H	2B	3B	HR	RBI	BB	SO	AVG	OBP	SLG	OPS	OPS+	BR+	SB	CS	SBR	FA	FR	G/POS	TPR
■ ERIC YOUNG	Young, Eric Orlando b: 5/18/67, New Brunswick, N.J. BR/TR, 5'9", 180 lbs. Deb: 7/30/92 Career OF: (125-LF 10-CF 0-RF)																							
1992	LA-N	49	132	9	34	1	0	1	11	8	9	.258	.300	.288	588	68	-5	6	1	1	.957	10	2-43	0.7
1993	Col-N	144	490	82	132	16	8	3	42	63	41	.269	.357	.353	710	78	-13	42	19	3	.962	-10	2-79,O-52(46-10-0)	-1.8
1994	Col-N	90	228	37	62	13	1	7	30	38	17	.272	.381	.430	810	95	-1	18	7	2	.981	1	O-60(60-0-0)/2-1	0.1
1995	*Col-N	120	366	68	116	21	**9**	6	36	49	29	.317	.405	.473	877	101	2	35	12	4	.973	-6	2-77,O-19(19-0-0)	0.4
1996	Col-N★	141	568	113	184	23	4	8	74	47	31	.324	.396	.421	817	94	-3	**53**	19	5	.985	**28**	*2-139	3.6
1997	Col-N	118	468	78	132	29	6	6	45	57	37	.282	.366	.408	774	83	-10	32	12	3	.978	21	*2-117	2.0
	LA-N	37	154	28	42	4	2	2	16	14	17	.273	.349	.364	712	94	-1	13	2	2	.979	-14	2-37	-1.1
	Yr	155	622	106	174	33	8	8	61	71	54	.280	.362	.397	759	85	-11	45	14	5	.978	7	*2-154	0.9
1998	LA-N	117	452	78	129	24	1	8	43	45	32	.285	.357	.396	753	104	3	42	13	5	.976	-10	*2-113/D-1	0.3
1999	LA-N	119	456	73	128	24	2	2	41	63	26	.281	.374	.355	729	91	-4	51	22	4	.984	-6	*2-116	0.0
2000	Chi-N	153	607	98	180	40	2	6	47	63	39	.297	.370	.399	769	97	-2	54	7	**9**	.979	3	*2-150	1.7
Total	9	1088	3921	664	1139	195	35	49	385	447	278	.290	.372	.396	767	91	-32	346	114	36	.977	17	2-872,O-131L/D-1	5.9
■ ERNIE YOUNG	Young, Ernest Wesley b: 7/8/69, Chicago, Ill. BR/TR, 6'1", 190 lbs. Deb: 5/17/94																							
1994	Oak-A	11	30	2	2	1	0	0	3	1	8	.067	.097	.100	197	-54	-7	0	0	0	.958	0	O-10(7-3-1)/D-1	-0.6
1995	Oak-A	26	50	9	10	3	0	2	5	8	12	.200	.310	.380	690	83	-1	0	0	0	.946	-3	O-24(7-7-10)	-0.5
1996	Oak-A	141	462	72	112	19	4	19	64	52	118	.242	.328	.424	752	90	-8	7	5	-0	.997	-1	*O-140(8-133-17)	-0.8
1997	Oak-A	71	175	22	39	7	0	5	15	19	57	.223	.306	.349	655	72	-7	1	3	-1	.980	-4	O-66(2-59-12)/D-1	-1.1
1998	KC-A	25	53	2	10	3	0	1	3	2	9	.189	.232	.302	534	36	-5	2	1	0	1.000	-1	O-24(1-5-19)	-0.6
1999	Ari-N	6	11	1	2	0	0	0	0	3	2	.182	.400	.182	582	54	-1	0	0	0	1.000	2	/O-4(1-0-3)	0.1
Total	6	280	781	108	175	33	4	27	90	85	206	.224	.309	.380	689	77	-29	10	9	-1	.989	-7	O-268(26-207-62)/D-2	-3.5
■ GEORGE YOUNG	Young, George Joseph b: 4/1/1890, Brooklyn, N.Y. d: 3/13/50, Brightwaters, N.Y. BL/TR, 6', 185 lbs. Deb: 8/10/13																							
1913	Cle-A	2	2	0	0	0	0	0	0	0	0	.000	.000	.000	0	-97	-0	0			.000	0	H	-0.1
■ GERALD YOUNG	Young, Gerald Anthony b: 10/22/64, Tela, Honduras BB/TR, 6'2", 185 lbs. Deb: 7/8/87																							
1987	Hou-N	71	274	44	88	9	2	1	15	26	27	.321	.382	.380	762	107	4	26	9	3	.980	5	O-67(0-67-0)	1.0
1988	Hou-N	149	576	79	148	21	9	0	37	66	66	.257	.336	.325	661	94	-3	65	27	5	.992	13	*O-145(0-145-0)	1.5
1989	Hou-N	146	533	71	124	17	3	0	38	74	60	.233	.328	.276	604	77	-13	34	25	-1	**.998**	26	*O-143(0-143-0)	1.1
1990	Hou-N	57	154	15	27	4	1	1	4	20	23	.175	.270	.234	504	41	-12	6	3	0	.990	-2	O-50(0-50-0)	-1.4
1991	Hou-N	108	142	26	31	3	1	1	11	24	17	.218	.331	.275	606	77	-4	16	5	2	1.000	-14	O-84(6-76-5)	-1.7
1992	Hou-N	74	76	14	14	1	1	0	4	10	11	.184	.279	.224	503	46	-5	6	2	1	.964	-15	O-57(6-14-43)	-2.2
1993	Col-N	19	19	5	1	0	0	0	1	4	1	.053	.217	.053	270	-20	-3	0	1	-0	.882	-3	O-11(4-3-5)	-0.6
1994	StL-N	16	41	5	13	3	2	0	3	3	8	.317	.364	.488	851	122	1	2	1	0	1.000	-1	O-11(3-6-2)	0.0
Total	8	640	1815	259	446	58	19	3	113	227	213	.246	.332	.304	635	82	-35	155	73	9	.990	9	O-568(19-504-55)	-2.3
■ HERMAN YOUNG	Young, Herman John b: 4/14/1886, Boston, Mass. d: 12/13/66, Ipswich, Mass. BR/TR, 5'8", 155 lbs. Deb: 6/11/11																							
1911	Bos-N	9	25	2	6	0	0	0	0	0	3	.240	.269	.240	509	40	-2	0			.905	4	/3-5,S-3	0.2
■ JOHN YOUNG	Young, John Thomas b: 2/9/49, Los Angeles, Cal. BL/TL, 6'3", 210 lbs. Deb: 9/9/71																							
1971	Det-A	2	4	1	2	1	0	0	1	0	0	.500	.500	.750	1250	241	1	0	0	0	1.000	-0	/1-1	0.1
■ KEVIN YOUNG	Young, Kevin Stacey b: 6/16/69, Alpena, Mich. BR/TR, 6'2", 219 lbs. Deb: 7/12/92 Career OF: (13-LF 0-CF 17-RF)																							
1992	Pit-N	10	7	2	4	0	0	0	4	2	0	.571	.667	.571	1238	256	2	1	0	0	.750	-1	/3-7,1-1	0.1
1993	Pit-N	141	449	38	106	24	3	6	47	36	82	.236	.306	.343	649	73	-17	2	2	-0	**.998**	7	*1-135/3-6	-2.2
1994	Pit-N	59	122	15	25	7	2	1	11	8	34	.205	.260	.320	579	49	-9	0	2	-1	1.000	1	1-37,3-17/O-1(1-0-1)	-1.0
1995	Pit-N	56	181	13	42	9	0	6	22	8	53	.232	.272	.381	653	69	-9	1	3	-1	.919	6	3-48/1-6	-0.3
1996	KC-A	55	132	20	32	6	0	8	23	11	32	.242	.301	.470	770	91	-2	3	3	-0	1.000	-3	1-27,O-17R/3-7,D-3	-0.8
1997	Pit-N	97	333	59	100	18	3	18	74	16	89	.300	.340	.535	874	123	9	11	2	2	.997	1	1-77,3-12,O-11L	0.5
1998	Pit-N	159	592	88	160	40	2	27	108	44	127	.270	.332	.481	814	109	7	15	7	1	.994	-12	*1-157	-1.9
1999	Pit-N	156	584	103	174	41	6	26	106	75	124	.298	.389	.522	911	128	26	22	10	1	.985	-4	*1-155	0.8
2000	Pit-N	132	496	77	128	27	0	20	88	32	96	.258	.313	.433	747	87	-12	8	3	1	.986	-11	*1-129/D-1	-3.2
Total	9	865	2896	415	771	172	16	112	483	232	637	.266	.331	.453	783	100	-5	63	32	3	.992	-17	1-724/3-97,O-29R,D	-8.0
■ PEP YOUNG	Young, Lemuel Floyd b: 8/29/07, Jamestown, N.C. d: 1/14/62, Jamestown, N.C. BR/TR, 5'9", 162 lbs. Deb: 4/25/33 Career OF: (1-LF 0-CF 5-RF)																							
1933	Pit-N	25	20	3	6	1	1	0	0	0	5	.300	.300	.450	750	112	0	0			1.000	0	/2-1,S-1	0.1
1934	Pit-N	19	17	3	4	0	0	0	2	0	6	.235	.235	.235	471	26	-2	0			1.000	2	/2-2,S-2	0.1
1935	Pit-N	128	494	60	131	25	10	7	82	21	59	.265	.298	.399	697	83	-13	2			.952	-12	*2-107/3-6,O-6R,S-4	-1.7
1936	Pit-N	125	475	47	118	23	10	6	77	29	52	.248	.293	.377	670	77	-16	3			.966	-24	*2-123	-3.2
1937	Pit-N	113	408	43	106	20	3	9	54	26	63	.260	.306	.390	695	88	-8	4			.942	18	S-45,3-39,2-30	1.6
1938	Pit-N	149	562	58	156	36	5	4	79	40	64	.278	.329	.381	710	94	-5	7			.973	**32**	*2-149	3.6
1939	Pit-N	84	293	34	81	14	3	3	29	23	29	.276	.333	.375	709	92	-4	1			.967	3	2-84	0.5
1940	Pit-N	54	136	19	34	8	2	2	20	12	23	.250	.320	.382	702	94	-1	1			.909	-5	2-33/S-7,3-5	-0.4
1941	Cin-N	4	12	2	2	0	0	0	0	0	1	.167	.231	.167	397	13	-1	0			.923	1	/3-3	-0.1
	StL-N	2	2	0	0	0	0	0	0	0	2	.000	.000	.000	0	-94	-1	0			.000	0	H	-0.1
	Yr	6	14	2	2	0	0	0	0	0	3	.143	.200	.143	343	-2	-2	0			.923	1	/3-3	-0.2
1945	StL-N	27	47	5	7	1	0	1	4	1	8	.149	.167	.234	401	10	-6	0			.978	1	S-11/3-9,2-3	-0.5
Total	10	730	2466	274	645	128	34	32	347	152	312	.262	.308	.380	688	85	-56	18			.964	17	2-532/S-70,3-62,O-6R	-0.1
■ MIKE YOUNG	Young, Michael B. b: 10/19/76, Covina, Cal. BR/TR, 6', 175 lbs. Deb: 9/30/2000																							
2000	Tex-A	2	2	0	0	0	0	0	0	0	1	.000	.000	.000	0	-97	-1	0	0	0	.000	-0	/2-1	-0.1
■ MIKE YOUNG	Young, Michael Darren b: 3/20/60, Oakland, Cal. BB/TR, 6'2", 195 lbs. Deb: 9/14/82 Career OF: (266-LF 8-CF 153-RF)																							
1982	Bal-A	6	2	2	0	0	0	0	0	0	1	.000	.000	.000	0	-99	-1	0	0	0	1.000	-0	/O-1(1-0-0),D-2	-0.1
1983	Bal-A	25	36	5	6	2	1	0	2	2	8	.167	.231	.278	509	40	-3	1	0	0	.929	-4	O-22(14-0-8)/D-3	-0.8
1984	Bal-A	123	401	59	101	17	2	17	52	58	110	.252	.356	.431	788	119	12	6	2	1	.982	-9	*O-115(40-1-85)/D-1	-0.3
1985	Bal-A	139	450	72	123	22	1	28	81	48	104	.273	.349	.513	862	136	21	1	5	-2	.975	-0	O-90(83-0-20),D-37	1.4
1986	Bal-A	117	369	43	93	15	1	9	42	49	90	.252	.344	.371	716	96	-1	3	1	0	.962	2	O-69(69-0-0),D-38	-0.2
1987	Bal-A	110	363	46	87	10	1	16	39	46	91	.240	.328	.405	733	96	-2	10	7	-0	.975	-3	O-60(54-7-0),D-47	-0.8
1988	Phi-N	75	146	13	33	14	0	1	14	26	43	.226	.347	.342	689	96	0	0	0	0	.938	-2	O-42(3-0-39)	-0.3
	Mil-A	8	14	2	0	0	0	0	0	2	5	.000	.176	.000	176	-46	-3	0	0	0	.000	-1	/O-2(1-0-1),D-5	-0.4
1989	Cle-A	32	59	2	11	0	0	1	5	6	13	.186	.273	.237	510	44	-4	1	2	-0	1.000	-0	D-15/O-1(1-0-0)	-0.6
Total	8	635	1840	244	454	80	6	72	235	237	465	.247	.339	.414	753	107	20	22	17	-1	.969	-18	O-402L,D-148	-2.1
■ BABE YOUNG	Young, Norman Robert b: 7/1/15, Astoria, N.Y. d: 12/25/83, Everett, Mass. BL/TL, 6'2.5", 185 lbs. Deb: 9/26/36																							
1936	NY-N	1	1	0	0	0	0	0	0	0	0	.000	.000	.000	0	-99	-0	0			.000	0	H	0.0
1939	NY-N	22	75	8	23	4	0	3	14	5	6	.307	.373	.480	853	127	3	0			.982	-2	1-22	-0.1
1940	NY-N	149	556	75	159	27	4	17	101	69	28	.286	.367	.441	807	121	16	4			.992	-2	*1-147	0.0
1941	NY-N	152	574	90	152	28	5	25	104	66	39	.265	.346	.462	807	124	17	1			.986	-4	*1-150	-0.1
1942	NY-N	101	287	37	80	17	1	11	59	34	22	.279	.365	.460	825	140	14	1			.972	-4	O-54(0-54-0),1-18	0.8
1946	NY-N	104	291	30	81	11	0	7	33	30	21	.278	.346	.388	734	107	3	3			.988	-8	1-49,O-24(0-17-7)	-0.8
1947	NY-N	14	14	0	1	1	0	0	0	0	1	.071	.071	.143	214	-44	-3	0			.000	0	H	-0.3
	Cin-N	95	364	55	103	21	3	14	79	35	26	.283	.349	.473	822	117	8	0			.990	-2	1-93	0.3
	Yr	109	378	55	104	22	3	14	79	35	27	.275	.340	.460	800	111	5	0			.990	-2	1-93	0.0
1948	Cin-N	49	130	11	30	7	2	1	12	19	12	.231	.329	.338	667	84	-3	0			.993	0	1-31/O-1(0-0-1)	-0.3
	StL-N	41	111	14	27	5	2	1	13	16	6	.243	.339	.351	690	82	-2	0			.996	-4	1-35	-0.8
	Yr	90	241	25	57	12	4	2	25	35	18	.237	.333	.344	678	83	-5	0			.995	-4	1-66/O-1(0-0-1)	-1.1
Total	8	728	2403	320	656	121	17	79	415	274	161	.273	.352	.436	788	117	52	9			.989	-25	1-545/O-79(0-71-8)	-1.3

YEAR	TM/L	G	AB	R	H	2B	3B	HR	RBI	BB	SO	AVG	OBP	SLG	OPS	OPS+	BR+	SB	CS	SBR	FA	FR	G/POS	TPR
■ RALPH YOUNG Young, Ralph Stuart b: 9/19/1889, Philadelphia, Pa. d: 1/24/65, Philadelphia, Pa. BB/TR, 5'5", 165 lbs. Deb: 4/10/13																								
1913	NY-A	7	15	2	1	0	0	0	0	3	3	.067	.222	.067	289	-15	-2	2			.857	1	/S-7	-0.1
1915	Det-A	123	378	44	92	6	5	0	31	53	31	.243	.339	.286	625	83	-6	12	11	-1	.950	8	*2-119	0.2
1916	Det-A	153	528	60	139	16	6	1	45	62	43	.263	.342	.322	664	96	-1	20	20	-3	.966	-1	*2-146/S-6,3-1	-0.3
1917	Det-A	141	503	64	116	18	2	1	35	61	35	.231	.317	.280	598	83	-9	8			.958	8	*2-141	0.1
1918	Det-A	91	298	31	56	7	1	0	21	54	17	.188	.313	.218	531	63	-11	15			.939	-12	2-91	-2.4
1919	Det-A	125	456	63	96	13	5	1	25	53	32	.211	.294	.268	562	60	-24	8			.970	17	*2-120/S-5	-0.4
1920	Det-A	150	594	84	173	21	6	0	33	85	30	.291	.382	.347	729	96	1	8	13	-3	.969	-11	*2-150	-1.0
1921	Det-A	107	401	70	120	8	3	0	29	69	23	.299	.406	.334	740	91	-1	11	9	-1	.947	-23	*2-106	-2.0
1922	Phi-A	125	470	62	105	19	2	1	35	55	21	.223	.309	.279	587	53	-32	8	6	-0	.960	-15	*2-120	-4.3
Total	9	1022	3643	480	898	108	30	4	254	495	235	.247	.339	.296	635	79	-85	92	59		.959	-28	2-993/S-18,3-1	-10.2
■ DICK YOUNG Young, Richard Ennis b: 6/3/28, Seattle, Wash. BL/TR (BB 1952), 5'11", 175 lbs. Deb: 9/11/51																								
1951	Phi-N	15	68	7	16	5	0	0	2	3	6	.235	.268	.309	576	55	-4	0	1	-0	.922	-9	2-15	-1.3
1952	Phi-N	5	9	3	2	1	0	0	0	1	3	.222	.300	.333	633	76	-0	1	0	0	.900	-0	/2-2	0.0
Total	2	20	77	10	18	6	0	0	2	4	9	.234	.272	.312	583	58	-5	1	1	-0	.919	-9	/2-17	-1.3
■ BOBBY YOUNG Young, Robert George b: 1/22/25, Granite, Md. d: 1/28/85, Baltimore, Md. BL/TR, 6'1", 175 lbs. Deb: 7/28/48																								
1948	StL-N	3	1	0	0	0	0	0	0	0	1	.000	.000	.000	0	-95	-0	0			1.000	0	/3-1	0.0
1951	StL-A	147	611	75	159	13	9	1	31	44	51	.260	.310	.316	626	67	-28	8	7	-1	.980	1	*2-147	-1.9
1952	StL-A	149	575	59	142	15	9	4	39	56	48	.247	.314	.325	639	76	-19	3	3	-0	.984	-9	*2-149	-2.1
1953	StL-A	148	537	48	137	22	2	4	25	41	40	.255	.309	.326	635	70	-22	2	1	0	.977	-17	*2-148	-2.8
1954	Bal-A	130	432	43	106	13	6	4	24	54	42	.245	.331	.331	662	88	-7	4	4	-1	.976	-14	*2-127	-1.3
1955	Bal-A	59	186	5	37	3	0	1	8	11	23	.199	.244	.231	475	30	-19	1	4	-1	.985	3	2-58	-1.4
	Cle-A	18	45	7	14	1	1	0	6	1	2	.311	.326	.378	704	86	-1	0	0	0	.983	7	2-11/3-1	0.6
	Yr	77	231	12	51	4	1	1	14	12	25	.221	.259	.260	519	42	-19	1	4	-1	.985	9	2-69/3-1	-0.8
1956	Cle-A	1	0	0	0	0	0	0	0	0	0	—	—	—	—		0	0	0	0	.000	0	R	0.0
1958	Phi-N	32	60	7	14	1	1	1	4	1	5	.233	.246	.333	579	52	-4	0	0	0	.968	-2	2-21	-0.6
Total	8	687	2447	244	609	68	28	15	137	208	212	.249	.308	.318	626	71	-100	18	19		.980	-32	2-661/3-2	-9.5
■ RUSS YOUNG Young, Russell Charles b: 9/15/02, Bryan, Ohio d: 5/13/84, Roseville, Cal. BB/TR, 6', 175 lbs. Deb: 4/16/31																								
1931	StL-A	16	34	2	4	0	0	1	2	2	4	.118	.167	.206	373	-3	-5	0	0	0	1.000	2	C-16	-0.2
■ JOEL YOUNGBLOOD Youngblood, Joel Randolph b: 8/28/51, Houston, Tex. BR/TR, 6', 180 lbs. Deb: 4/13/76 C Career OF: (233-LF 107-CF 454-RF)																								
1976	Cin-N	55	57	8	11	1	1	0	1	2	8	.193	.233	.246	479	35	-5	1	0	0	.938	-1	/O-9L,3-6,C-1,2-1	-0.6
1977	StL-N	25	27	1	5	2	0	0	1	3	5	.185	.267	.259	526	43	-2	0	2	-1	1.000	-3	O-11(10-0-1)/3-6	-0.6
	NY-N	70	182	16	46	11	1	0	11	13	40	.253	.303	.324	627	72	-7	1	3	-1	.954	2	2-33,O-22R,3-10	-0.6
	Yr	95	209	17	51	13	1	0	12	16	45	.244	.298	.316	614	67	-10	1	5	-2	1.000	-1	O-33L,2-33,3-16	-1.2
1978	NY-N	113	266	40	67	12	8	7	30	16	39	.252	.297	.436	733	106	1	4	0	1	.989	2	O-50R,2-39/3-9,S-1	0.3
1979	NY-N	158	590	90	162	37	5	16	60	60	84	.275	.349	.436	784	117	13	18	13	-1	.985	4	*O-147R,2-13,3-12	1.0
1980	NY-N	146	514	58	142	26	2	8	69	52	69	.276	.345	.381	726	105	4	14	11	-1	.984	15	*O-121R,3-21/2-6	1.4
1981	NY-N★	43	143	16	50	10	2	4	25	12	19	.350	.408	.531	939	167	12	2	5	-1	.962	2	O-41(4-2-36)	1.2
1982	NY-N	80	202	21	52	12	0	3	21	8	37	.257	.302	.361	664	85	-4	0	4	-1	.969	-9	O-63R/2-8,S-1,3-1	-1.7
	Mon-N	40	90	16	18	2	0	0	8	9	21	.200	.294	.222	516	45	-6	2	1	0	1.000	-3	O-35(0-2-33)	-1.1
	Yr	120	292	37	70	14	0	3	29	17	58	.240	.300	.318	618	73	-10	2	5	-1	.979	-12	O-98R/2-8,S-1,3-1	-2.8
1983	SF-N	124	373	59	109	20	3	17	53	33	59	.292	.358	.499	856	139	19	7	4	0	.948	-30	2-64,3-28,O-22L	-1.0
1984	SF-N	134	469	50	119	17	1	10	51	48	86	.254	.328	.358	686	96	-2	5	6	-1	.887	-26	*3-117,O-11R/2-5	-3.3
1985	SF-N	95	230	24	62	6	0	4	24	30	37	.270	.356	.348	704	103	2	3	2	-0	.955	-0	O-56(7-17-34)/3-1	-0.1
1986	SF-N	97	184	20	47	12	0	5	28	18	34	.255	.325	.402	727	105	1	1	1	-0	1.000	-6	O-45L/1-7,3-5,2S	-0.7
1987	SF-N	69	91	9	23	3	0	3	11	5	13	.253	.299	.385	684	83	-2	1	1	-0	1.000	-3	O-22(9-1-14)/3-2	-0.6
1988	SF-N	83	123	12	31	4	0	0	16	10	17	.252	.313	.285	598	76	-4	1	1	-0	.980	-11	O-45(22-9-18)	-1.7
1989	Cin-N	76	118	13	25	5	0	3	13	13	21	.212	.301	.331	631	78	-3	0	1	-0	.970	-10	O-45(35-0-10)	-1.6
Total	14	1408	3659	453	969	180	23	80	422	332	589	.265	.332	.392	724	103	15	60	55	-6	.981	-78	O-745R,3-218,2/1SC	-9.7
■ HENRY YOUNGMAN Youngman, Henry b: 1865, Indiana, Pa. d: 1/24/36, Pittsburgh, Pa. TR, Deb: 4/19/1890																								
1890	Pit-N	13	47	6	6	1	1	0	4	6	9	.128	.226	.191	418	25	-4	1			.750	-2	/3-7,2-6	-0.5
■ ROSS YOUNGS Youngs, Ross Middlebrook "Pep" (b: Royce Middlebrook Youngs) b: 4/10/1897, Shiner, Tex. d: 10/22/27, San Antonio, Tex. BL/TR, 5'8", 162 lbs. Deb: 9/25/17 H Career OF: (1-LF 6-CF 1192-RF)																								
1917	NY-N	7	26	5	9	2	3	0	1	1	5	.346	.370	.654	1024	218	3	1			1.000	1	/O-7(1-6-0)	0.4
1918	NY-N	121	474	70	143	16	8	1	25	44	49	.302	.368	.376	744	129	18	10			.950	-6	*O-120(0-0-120)/2-7	0.6
1919	NY-N	130	489	73	152	**31**	7	2	43	51	47	.311	.384	.415	799	142	26	24			.942	2	*O-130(0-0-130)	2.3
1920	NY-N	153	581	92	204	27	14	6	78	75	55	.351	.427	.477	904	161	48	18	18	-2	.935	3	*O-153(0-0-153)	4.2
1921	*NY-N	141	504	90	165	24	16	3	102	71	47	.327	.411	.456	868	129	24	21	17	-1	.978	-4	*O-137(0-0-137)	0.8
1922	*NY-N	149	559	105	185	34	10	7	86	55	50	.331	.398	.465	863	121	18	17	9	1	.942	4	*O-147(0-0-147)	1.0
1923	*NY-N	152	596	**121**	200	33	12	3	87	73	36	.336	.412	.446	859	128	27	13	19	-4	.959	1	*O-152(0-0-152)	1.1
1924	*NY-N	133	526	112	187	33	12	10	74	77	31	.356	.441	.521	962	161	49	11	9	-1	.955	-1	*O-132(0-0-132)/2-2	3.5
1925	NY-N	130	500	82	132	24	6	6	53	66	51	.264	.354	.372	726	89	-7	17	11	-0	.952	-7	*O-127(0-0-127)/2-3	-2.3
1926	NY-N	95	372	62	114	12	5	4	43	37	19	.306	.372	.398	770	109	5	21			.974	2	O-94(0-0-94)	-0.1
Total	10	1211	4627	812	1491	236	93	42	592	550	390	.322	.399	.441	839	131	212	153	83		.953	-5	*O-1199R/2-12	11.5
■ EDDIE YOUNT Yount, Floyd Edwin b: 12/19/16, Newton, N.C. d: 10/26/73, Newton, N.C. BR/TR, 6'1", 185 lbs. Deb: 9/9/37																								
1937	Phi-A	4	7	1	2	0	0	0	1	0	1	.286	.286	.286	571	45	-1	0	0	0	1.000	-0	/O-2(1-1-0)	-0.1
1939	Pit-N	2	2	0	0	0	0	0	0	0	2	.000	.000	.000	0	-99	-1	0			.000	0	H	-0.1
Total	2	6	9	1	2	0	0	0	1	0	3	.222	.222	.222	444	14	-1	0	0		1.000	-0	/O-2(1-1-0)	-0.2
■ ROBIN YOUNT Yount, Robin R b: 9/16/55, Danville, Ill. BR/TR, 6', 170 lbs. Deb: 4/5/74 FH Career OF: (69-LF 1150-CF 0-RF)																								
1974	Mil-A	107	344	48	86	14	5	3	26	12	46	.250	.277	.346	623	79	-10	7	7	-1	.962	-11	*S-107	-1.1
1975	Mil-A	147	558	67	149	28	2	8	52	33	69	.267	.309	.367	677	90	-8	12	4	1	.939	-23	*S-145	-1.3
1976	Mil-A	161	638	59	161	19	3	2	54	38	69	.252	.294	.301	595	76	-20	16	11	-0	.963	-5	*S-161/O-1(0-1-0)	-0.6
1977	Mil-A	154	605	66	174	34	4	4	49	41	80	.288	.335	.377	712	94	-5	16	7	1	.964	-9	*S-153	0.4
1978	Mil-A	127	502	66	147	23	9	9	71	24	43	.293	.326	.428	755	110	5	16	5	2	.959	22	*S-125	4.3
1979	Mil-A	149	577	72	154	26	5	8	51	35	52	.267	.310	.371	681	83	-15	11	8	-0	.969	5	*S-149	0.6
1980	Mil-A★	143	611	121	179	**49**	10	23	87	26	67	.293	.323	.519	842	131	22	20	5	3	.961	0	*S-133/D-9	3.9
1981	*Mil-A	96	377	50	103	15	5	10	49	22	37	.273	.317	.419	736	116	7	4	1	1	**.985**	28	S-93/D-3	4.6
1982	*Mil-A★	156	635	129	**210**	**46**	12	29	114	54	63	.331	.384	**.578**	**962**	**171**	**59**	14	3	2	.969	-4	*S-154/D-1	**7.2**
1983	Mil-A★	149	578	102	178	42	**10**	17	80	72	58	.308	.387	.503	891	155	44	12	5	1	.973	-5	*S-139/D-8	5.4
1984	Mil-A	160	624	105	186	27	7	16	80	67	67	.298	.367	.441	808	127	24	14	4	2	.971	15	*S-120,D-39	5.1
1985	Mil-A	122	466	76	129	26	3	15	68	49	56	.277	.348	.442	790	115	10	10	4	1	.970	4	*O-108L,D-12/1-2	1.0
1986	Mil-A	140	522	82	163	31	7	9	46	62	73	.312	.389	.450	840	124	19	14	5	1	**.997**	12	*O-131C/1-3,D-6	3.0
1987	Mil-A	158	635	99	198	25	9	21	103	76	94	.312	.386	.479	865	124	23	19	9	1	.987	8	*O-150(0-150-0)/D-8	2.9
1988	Mil-A	162	621	92	190	38	**11**	13	91	63	63	.306	.373	.465	838	132	27	22	4	3	.996	15	*O-158(0-158-0)/D-4	4.4
1989	Mil-A	160	614	101	195	38	9	21	103	63	71	.318	.387	.511	898	153	42	19	3	3	.981	4	*O-143(0-143-0),D-17	4.8
1990	Mil-A	158	587	98	145	17	5	17	77	78	89	.247	.341	.380	721	102	3	15	8	1	.991	6	*O-157(0-157-0)/D-1	0.8
1991	Mil-A	130	503	66	131	20	4	10	77	54	79	.260	.337	.376	713	99	0	6	4	-0	.994	4	*O-117(0-117-0),D-13	0.2
1992	Mil-A	150	557	71	147	40	3	8	77	53	81	.264	.331	.390	721	103	2	15	6	1	.995	2	*O-139(0-139-0),D-11	0.4
1993	Mil-A	127	454	62	117	25	3	8	51	44	93	.258	.330	.379	709	91	-5	9	2	1	.997	4	*O-114C/1-7,D-6	0.0
Total	20	2856	11008	1632	3142	583	126	251	1406	966	1350	.285	.346	.430	775	115	224	271	105	23	.964	71	*S-1479,*O-1218C,D/1	46.0
■ JEFF YURAK Yurak, Jeffrey Lynn b: 2/26/54, Pasadena, Cal. BB/TR, 6'3", 195 lbs. Deb: 9/15/78																								
1978	Mil-A	5	5	0	0	0	0	0	0	1	0	.000	.167	.000	167	-49	-1	0	0	0	1.000	0	/O-1(1-0-0)	-0.1

YEAR	TM/L	G	AB	R	H	2B	3B	HR	RBI	BB	SO	AVG	OBP	SLG	OPS	OPS+	BR+	SB	CS	SBR	FA	FR	G/POS	TPR
■ SAL YVARS Yvars, Salvador Anthony b: 2/20/24, New York, N.Y. BR/TR, 5'10", 187 lbs. Deb: 9/27/47																								
1947	NY-N	1	5	0	1	0	0	0	0	0	2	.200	.200	.200	400	6	-1	0			1.000	-0	/C-1	-0.1
1948	NY-N	15	38	4	8	1	0	1	6	3	1	.211	.286	.316	602	62	-2	0			1.000	3	C-15	0.1
1949	NY-N	3	8	0	0	0	0	0	0	1	1	.000	.111	.000	111	-68	-2	0			1.000	1	/C-2	-0.1
1950	NY-N	9	14	0	2	0	0	0	0	1	2	.143	.200	.143	343	-8	-2	0			.963	2	/C-9	0.0
1951	*NY-N	25	41	9	13	2	0	2	3	5	7	.317	.417	.512	929	147	3	0	0	0	.942	-3	C-23	0.0
1952	NY-N	66	151	15	37	3	0	4	18	10	16	.245	.296	.344	641	77	-5	0	0	0	.988	7	C-59	0.4
1953	NY-N	23	47	1	13	0	0	0	1	7	1	.277	.370	.277	647	71	-2	0	0	0	1.000	1	C-20	0.0
	StL-N	30	57	4	14	2	0	1	6	4	6	.246	.306	.333	640	67	-3	0	1	-0	.989	2	C-26	0.0
	Yr	53	104	5	27	2	0	1	7	11	7	.260	.336	.308	644	69	-4	0	1	-0	.994	3	C-46	0.0
1954	StL-N	38	57	8	14	4	0	2	8	6	5	.246	.328	.421	749	93	-1	1	0	0	1.000	-2	C-21	-0.2
Total	8	210	418	41	102	12	0	10	42	37	41	.244	.315	.344	659	76	-14	1	1		.987	10	C-176	0.1
■ ELMER ZACHER Zacher, Elmer Henry "Silver" b: 9/17/1883, Buffalo, N.Y. d: 12/20/44, Buffalo, N.Y. BR/TR, 5'9", 190 lbs. Deb: 4/30/10																								
1910	NY-N	1	0	0	0	0	0	0	0	0	0	—	—	—	—	—	0	0			1.000	-0	/O-1(0-1-0)	0.0
	StL-N	47	132	7	28	5	1	0	10	10	19	.212	.278	.265	543	61	-7	3			.966	3	O-36(11-12-13)/2-1	-0.6
	Yr	48	132	7	28	5	1	0	10	10	19	.212	.278	.265	543	61	-7	3			.966	2	O-37(11-13-13)/2-1	-0.6
■ FRED ZAHNER Zahner, Frederick Joseph b: 6/5/1870, Louisville, Ky. d: 7/24/1900, Louisville, Ky. Deb: 7/23/1894 Career OF: (0-LF 0-CF 2-RF)																								
1894	Lou-N	14	49	7	10	0	1	0	4	3	6	.204	.250	.245	495	21	-6	2			.778	-5	C-10/O-2R,1-1,S-1	-0.8
1895	Lou-N	21	49	7	11	1	1	0	6	6	4	.224	.321	.286	607	61	-3	0			.824	-6	C-21	-0.6
Total	2	35	98	14	21	1	2	0	10	9	10	.214	.287	.265	552	41	-9	2			.805	-11	/C-31,O-2R,S-1,1-1	-1.4
■ FRANKIE ZAK Zak, Frank Thomas b: 2/22/22, Passaic, N.J. d: 2/6/72, Passaic, N.J. BR/TR, 5'10", 150 lbs. Deb: 4/21/44																								
1944	Pit-N☆	87	160	33	48	3	1	0	11	22	18	.300	.385	.331	716	99	1	6			.948	6	S-67	1.0
1945	Pit-N	15	28	2	4	2	0	0	3	3	5	.143	.226	.214	440	22	-3	0			.971	1	S-10/2-1	-0.2
1946	Pit-N	21	20	8	4	0	0	0	0	1	0	.200	.238	.200	438	24	-2	0			.929	9	S-10	0.7
Total	3	123	208	43	56	5	1	0	14	26	23	.269	.350	.303	653	82	-4	6			.948	15	/S-87,2-1	1.5
■ JACK ZALUSKY Zalusky, John Francis b: 6/22/1879, Minneapolis, Minn d: 8/11/35, Minneapolis, Minn. BR/TR, 5'11.5", 172 lbs. Deb: 9/4/03																								
1903	NY-A	7	16	2	5	0	0	0	1	1		.313	.353	.313	665	95	-0	0			1.000	-1	/C-6,1-1	-0.1
■ EDUARDO ZAMBRANO Zambrano, Eduardo Jose (Guerra) b: 2/1/66, Maracaibo, Venez. BR/TR, 6'2", 175 lbs. Deb: 9/19/93 Career OF: (10-LF 0-CF 21-RF)																								
1993	Chi-N	8	17	1	5	0	0	0	2	1	3	.294	.333	.294	627	71	-1	0	0	0	1.000	-2	/O-4(1-0-3),1-2	-0.3
1994	Chi-N	67	116	17	30	7	0	6	18	16	29	.259	.353	.474	828	115	3	2	1	0	.944	-4	O-27(9-0-18)/1-9,3-4	-0.3
Total	2	75	133	18	35	7	0	6	20	17	32	.263	.351	.451	802	109	2	2	1	0	.946	-6	/O-31R,1-11,3-4	-0.6
■ JOE ZAPUSTAS Zapustas, Joseph John b: 7/25/07, Boston, Mass. BR/TR, 6'1", 185 lbs. Deb: 9/28/33																								
1933	Phi-A	2	5	0	1	0	0	0	0	0	0	.200	.200	.200	400	6	-1	0	0	0	1.000	-1	/O-2(1-1-0)	-0.1
■ JOSE ZARDON Zardon, Jose Antonio (Sanchez) "Guineo" b: 5/20/23, Havana, Cuba BR/TR, 6', 150 lbs. Deb: 4/18/45																								
1945	Was-A	54	131	13	38	5	3	0	13	7	11	.290	.326	.374	700	112	1	3	1	0	.972	-1	O-43(16-25-3)	-0.1
■ AL ZARILLA Zarilla, Allen Lee "Zeke" b: 5/1/19, Los Angeles, Cal. d: 9/4/96, Honolulu, Hawaii BL/TR, 5'11", 180 lbs. Deb: 6/30/43 C																								
1943	StL-A	70	228	27	58	7	1	2	17	17	20	.254	.309	.320	629	82	-5	1	1	-0	.962	-2	O-60(0-6-56)	-1.2
1944	*StL-A	100	288	43	86	13	6	6	45	29	33	.299	.375	.448	823	127	10	1	1	-0	.977	-2	O-79(74-2-4)	0.4
1946	StL-A	125	371	46	96	14	9	4	43	27	37	.259	.311	.377	688	87	-7	3	5	-1	.973	3	*O-107(46-17-51)	-1.0
1947	StL-A	127	380	34	85	15	6	3	38	40	45	.224	.303	.318	621	71	-15	3	6	-1	.986	-10	*O-110(23-22-72)	-3.2
1948	StL-A★	144	529	77	174	39	3	12	74	48	48	.329	.389	.482	871	128	20	11	6	0	.962	-9	*O-136(26-58-61)	0.6
1949	StL-A	15	56	10	14	1	0	1	6	8	2	.250	.354	.321	675	76	-2	1	1	-0	1.000	-5	O-15(10-1-8)	-0.8
	Bos-A	124	474	68	133	32	4	9	71	48	51	.281	.352	.422	774	97	-3	4	4	-1	.984	-2	*O-122(2-2-119)	-0.9
	Yr	139	530	78	147	33	4	10	77	56	53	.277	.352	.411	763	95	-5	5	5	-1	.985	-7	*O-137(12-3-127)	-1.7
1950	Bos-A	130	471	92	153	32	10	9	74	76	47	.325	.423	.493	915	122	17	2	3	-1	.976	-4	*O-128(0-0-128)	0.8
1951	Chi-A	120	382	56	98	21	2	10	60	60	57	.257	.363	.401	764	109	5	2	4	-1	.983	-12	*O-117(7-0-112)	-1.1
1952	Chi-A	39	99	14	23	4	1	2	7	14	6	.232	.333	.354	687	90	-1	1	0	0	.974	-6	O-32(17-0-18)	-0.9
	StL-A	48	130	20	31	6	0	1	9	27	15	.238	.373	.308	681	88	-1	2	1	0	.976	0	O-35(21-10-8)	-0.2
	Bos-A	21	60	9	11	0	1	2	8	7	8	.183	.269	.317	585	58	-4	2	0	0	.941	-1	O-19(0-6-14)	-0.5
	Yr	108	289	43	65	10	2	5	24	48	29	.225	.339	.325	664	83	-6	5	1	1	.968	-7	O-86(38-16-40)	-1.6
1953	Bos-A	57	67	11	13	2	0	0	4	14	13	.194	.333	.224	557	50	-4	0	1	-0	.947	-5	O-18(3-7-9)	-1.0
Total	10	1120	3535	507	975	186	43	61	456	415	382	.276	.357	.405	761	102	11	33	33	-4	.974	-53	O-978(229-131-660)	-9.0
■ NORM ZAUCHIN Zauchin, Norbert Henry b: 11/17/29, Royal Oak, Mich. d: 1/31/99, Birmingham, Ala. BR/TR, 6'4.5", 220 lbs. Deb: 9/23/51																								
1951	Bos-A	5	12	0	2	1	0	0	0	0	4	.167	.167	.250	417	11	-2	0	1	-0	.957	-0	/1-4	-0.2
1955	Bos-A	130	477	65	114	10	0	27	93	69	105	.239	.339	.430	769	97	-3	3	0	1	**.995**	1	*1-126	-0.8
1956	Bos-A	44	84	12	18	2	0	2	11	14	22	.214	.333	.310	643	63	-4	0	0	0	.990	-1	1-31	-0.6
1957	Bos-A	52	91	11	24	3	0	3	14	9	13	.264	.343	.396	739	96	-0	0	0	0	.972	0	1-36	-0.2
1958	Was-A	96	303	35	69	8	2	15	37	38	68	.228	.316	.416	732	101	0	0	0	0	.995	2	1-91	-0.3
1959	Was-A	19	71	11	15	4	0	3	4	7	14	.211	.291	.394	686	87	-1	2	0	0	.995	-2	1-19	-0.5
Total	6	346	1038	134	242	28	2	50	159	137	226	.233	.327	.408	736	93	-10	5	1	1	.993	0	1-307	-2.6
■ GREGG ZAUN Zaun, Gregory Owen b: 4/14/71, Glendale, Cal. BB/TR, 5'10", 170 lbs. Deb: 6/24/95																								
1995	Bal-A	40	104	18	27	5	0	3	14	16	14	.260	.358	.394	753	94	-1	1	1	-0	.987	4	C-39/D-1	0.5
1996	Bal-A	50	108	16	25	8	1	1	13	11	15	.231	.314	.352	666	68	-5	0	0	0	.987	1	C-49	-0.2
	Fla-N	10	31	4	9	1	0	1	2	3	5	.290	.353	.419	772	106	0	1	0	0	1.000	1	C-10	0.2
1997	*Fla-N	58	143	21	43	10	2	2	20	26	18	.301	.415	.441	856	130	8	1	0	0	.978	4	C-50/1-1	1.4
1998	Fla-N	106	298	19	56	12	2	5	29	35	52	.188	.275	.292	567	52	-21	5	2	0	.986	-6	C-88/2-1	-2.1
1999	Tex-A	43	93	12	23	2	1	1	12	10	7	.247	.320	.323	643	62	-5	1	0	0	.984	7	C-37/D-2	0.3
2000	KC-A	83	234	36	64	11	0	7	33	43	34	.274	.393	.410	803	103	3	7	3	0	.988	-10	C-76/1-1,2-1	-0.2
Total	6	390	1011	126	247	49	6	20	123	144	145	.244	.343	.364	707	84	-22	16	6	1	.985	-0	C-349/D-3,2-2,1-2	-0.1
■ ZAY Zay Deb: 10/7/1886																								
1886	Bal-a	1	1	0	0	0	0	0	0	0		.000	.000	.000	0	-99	-0	0			.000	-0	/O-1(0-1-0),P-1	0.0
■ JOE ZDEB Zdeb, Joseph Edmund b: 6/27/53, Compton, Ill. BR/TR, 5'11", 185 lbs. Deb: 4/7/77 Career OF: (137-LF 1-CF 23-RF)																								
1977	*KC-A	105	195	26	58	5	2	2	23	16	23	.297	.351	.374	725	97	-1	6	5	-0	.970	-18	O-93(88-1-8)/3-1,D-4	-2.1
1978	KC-A	60	127	18	32	2	3	0	11	7	18	.252	.291	.315	606	69	-5	3	0	1	.957	-9	O-52L/2-1,3-1,D-1	-1.6
1979	KC-A	15	23	3	4	1	1	0	0	2	4	.174	.240	.304	544	45	-2	1	0	0	1.000	-1	/O-9(6-0-3)	-0.3
Total	3	180	345	47	94	8	6	2	34	25	45	.272	.322	.348	669	83	-8	10	5	0	.967	-29	O-154L/D-5,3-2,2-1	-4.0
■ DAVE ZEARFOSS Zearfoss, David William Tilden b: 1/1/1868, Schenectady, N.Y. d: 9/12/45, Wilmington, Del. TR, 5'9", Deb: 4/17/1896																								
1896	NY-N	19	60	5	13	1	1	0	6	5	5	.217	.288	.267	555	48	-4	2			.893	-4	C-19	-0.6
1897	NY-N	5	10	1	3	0	1	0	0	0		.300	.300	.500	800	112	0	0			.880	2	/C-5	0.2
1898	NY-N	1	1	0	1	0	0	0	0	0		1.000	1.000	1.000	2000	489	0	0			1.000	1	/C-1	0.1
1904	StL-N	27	80	7	17	2	0	0	9	10		.213	.300	.237	538	70	-2	0			.966	-2	C-25	-0.2
1905	StL-N	20	51	2	8	0	1	0	2	4		.157	.218	.196	414	24	-5	0			.966	-0	C-19	-0.4
Total	5	72	202	15	42	3	3	0	17	19	5	.208	.279	.252	532	56	-11	2			.943	-3	/C-69	-0.9
■ GEORGE ZEBER Zeber, George William b: 8/29/50, Ellwood City, Pa. BB/TR, 5'11", 170 lbs. Deb: 5/7/77																								
1977	*NY-A	25	65	8	21	3	0	3	10	9	11	.323	.405	.508	913	149	5	0	0	0	.961	1	2-21/S-2,3-2,D-1	0.6
1978	NY-A	3	6	0	0	0	0	0	0	0	0	.000	.000	.000	0	-99	-2	0	0	0	.750	-1	/2-1	-0.3
Total	2	28	71	8	21	3	0	3	10	9	11	.296	.375	.465	840	129	3	0	0	0	.953	-0	/2-22,3-2,S-2,D-1	0.3

YEAR	TM/L	G	AB	R	H	2B	3B	HR	RBI	BB	SO	AVG	OBP	SLG	OPS	OPS+	BR+	SB	CS	SBR	FA	FR	G/POS	TPR
■ **ROLLIE ZEIDER** Zeider, Rollie Hubert "Bunions" b: 11/16/1883, Auburn, Ind. d: 9/12/67, Garrett, Ind. BR/TR, 5'10", 162 lbs. Deb: 4/14/10 Career OF: (6-LF 1-CF 1-RF)																								
1910	Chi-A	136	498	57	108	9	2	0	31	62		.217	.305	.243	548	75	-12	49			.931	-2	2-87,S-45/3-4	-1.3
1911	Chi-A	73	217	39	55	3	0	2	21	29		.253	.347	.295	642	82	-4	28			.997	-5	1-29,S-17,3-10,/2-9	-0.8
1912	Chi-A	130	420	57	103	12	10	1	42	50		.245	.330	.329	658	91	-4	47			.979	6	1-66,3-56/S-1	0.2
1913	Chi-A	16	20	4	7	0	0	0	2	4	1	.350	.458	.350	808	139	1	3			1.000	2	/3-6,1-3,2-1	0.4
	NY-A	50	159	15	37	2	0	0	12	25	9	.233	.341	.245	586	72	-4	3			.901	-14	S-24,2-19/1-4,3-2	-1.7
	Yr	66	179	19	44	2	0	0	14	29	10	.246	.354	.257	611	79	-3	6			.901	-11	S-24,2-20/3-8,1-7	-1.3
1914	Chi-F	119	452	60	124	13	2	1	36	44	28	.274	.344	.319	663	86	-15	35			.936	-0	*3-117/S-1	-1.2
1915	Chi-F	129	494	65	112	22	2	0	34	43	24	.227	.297	.279	576	66	-30	16			.941	1	2-83,3-30,S-21	-2.8
1916	Chi-N	98	345	29	81	11	2	1	22	26	26	.235	.294	.287	581	71	-11	9			.928	-8	3-55,2-33/O-7L,S1	-2.0
1917	Chi-N	108	354	36	86	14	2	0	27	28	30	.243	.302	.294	596	77	-9	17			.901	-21	S-48,3-26,2-24,/1O	-2.9
1918	*Chi-N	82	251	31	56	3	2	0	26	23	20	.223	.288	.251	539	63	-10	16			.956	-11	2-79/1-1,3-1	-2.3
Total	9	941	3210	393	769	89	22	5	253	334	138	.240	.315	.286	601	77	-98	223			.945	-52	2-335,3-307,S1/O	-14.4
■ **TODD ZEILE** Zeile, Todd Edward b: 9/9/65, Van Nuys, Cal. BR/TR, 6'1", 190 lbs. Deb: 8/18/89 Career OF: (3-LF 0-CF 0-RF)																								
1989	StL-N	28	82	7	21	3	1	1	8	9	14	.256	.330	.354	683	92	-1	0	0	0	.971	-2	C-23	-0.1
1990	StL-N	144	495	62	121	25	3	15	57	67	77	.244	.337	.398	735	101	1	2	4	-1	.988	-11	*C-105,3-24,1-11,/O	-0.5
1991	StL-N	155	565	76	158	36	3	11	81	62	94	.280	.356	.412	768	115	12	17	11	-0	.943	-7	*3-154	0.5
1992	StL-N	126	439	51	113	18	4	7	48	68	70	.257	.357	.364	721	108	7	7	10	-2	.960	-7	*3-124	-0.2
1993	StL-N	157	571	82	158	36	1	17	103	70	76	.277	.356	.433	788	112	10	5	4	-0	.923	-5	*3-153	0.6
1994	StL-N	113	415	62	111	25	1	19	75	52	56	.267	.353	.470	823	114	9	1	3	-1	.960	3	*3-112	1.1
1995	StL-N	34	127	16	37	6	0	5	22	18	23	.291	.384	.457	840	121	4	1	0	0	.980	1	1-34	0.2
	Chi-N	79	299	34	68	16	0	9	30	16	53	.227	.274	.371	645	69	-14	0	0	0	.939	-10	3-75/O-2(2-0-0),1-1	-2.4
	Yr	113	426	50	105	22	0	14	52	34	76	.246	.308	.397	705	85	-10	1	0	0	.939	-9	3-75,1-35/O-2(2-0-0)	-2.2
1996	Phi-N	134	500	61	134	24	0	20	80	67	88	.268	.356	.436	792	106	5	1	1	-0	.962	-14	*3-106,1-28	-1.1
	*Bal-A	29	117	17	28	8	0	5	19	15	16	.239	.326	.436	762	91	-2	0	0	0	.964	3	3-29	0.1
1997	LA-N	160	575	89	154	17	0	31	90	85	112	.268	.368	.459	827	124	21	8	7	-1	.931	-22	*3-160	0.0
1998	LA-N	40	158	22	40	6	1	7	27	10	24	.253	.302	.437	738	97	-1	1	1	-0	.929	-12	3-40/1-1	-1.4
	Fla-N	66	234	37	68	12	1	6	39	31	34	.291	.378	.427	806	117	7	2	3	-1	.971	-3	3-65	0.3
	Yr	106	392	59	108	18	2	13	66	41	58	.276	.349	.431	780	110	5	3	4	-1	.957	-15	*3-105/1-1	-1.1
	*Tex-A	52	180	26	47	14	1	6	28	28	32	.261	.364	.450	814	106	2	1	0	0	.915	-2	3-52	0.0
1999	*Tex-A	156	588	80	172	41	1	24	98	56	94	.293	.358	.488	846	108	7	1	2	-0	.941	3	*3-155/1-1,D-1	1.0
2000	*NY-N	153	544	67	146	36	3	22	79	74	85	.268	.358	.467	825	110	8	3	4	-1	.992	1	*1-151	-0.5
Total	12	1626	5889	789	1576	323	20	205	884	728	948	.268	.351	.434	785	108	74	50	50	-7	.943	-84	*3-1249,1-227,C/OD	-2.4
■ **BART ZELLER** Zeller, Barton Wallace b: 7/22/41, Chicago Heights, Ill. BR/TR, 6'1", 185 lbs. Deb: 5/21/70 C																								
1970	StL-N	1	0	0	0	0	0	0	0	0	0	—	—	—	—		0	0	0	0	1.000	-0	/C-1	0.0
■ **GUS ZERNIAL** Zernial, Gus Edward "Ozark Ike" b: 6/27/23, Beaumont, Tex. BR/TR, 6'2.5", 210 lbs. Deb: 4/19/49 Career OF: (1006-LF 0-CF 1-RF)																								
1949	Chi-A	73	198	29	63	17	2	5	38	15	26	.318	.366	.500	866	132	8	0	1	-0	1.000	-5	O-46(46-0-0)	-0.1
1950	Chi-A	143	543	75	152	16	4	29	93	38	110	.280	.330	.484	815	110	3	0	2	-1	.969	2	*O-137(137-0-0)	-0.6
1951	Chi-A	4	19	2	2	0	0	0	4	2	2	.105	.190	.105	296	-19	-3	0	0	0	.933	1	/O-4(4-0-0)	-0.2
	Phi-A	139	552	90	151	30	5	33	125	61	99	.274	.350	.525	875	132	21	2	2	-0	.974	10	*O-138(138-0-0)	1.9
	Yr	143	571	92	153	30	5	**33**	**129**	63	101	.268	.345	.511	856	127	18	2	2	-0	.972	11	*O-142(142-0-0)	1.7
1952	Phi-A	145	549	76	144	15	1	29	100	70	87	.262	.347	.452	799	114	9	5	1	1	.972	-1	*O-141(141-0-0)	-0.1
1953	Phi-A★	147	556	85	158	21	3	42	108	57	79	.284	.355	.559	914	138	27	4	0	1	.972	13	*O-141(141-0-0)	3.2
1954	Phi-A	97	336	42	84	8	2	14	62	30	60	.250	.319	.411	730	98	-2	0	0	0	.953	-1	O-90(90-0-0)/1-2	-0.9
1955	KC-A	120	413	62	105	9	3	30	84	30	90	.254	.309	.508	818	116	6	1	0	0	.964	8	*O-103(103-0-0)	0.8
1956	KC-A	109	272	36	61	12	0	16	44	33	66	.224	.317	.445	762	99	-2	2	0	0	.984	2	O-69(69-0-0)	-0.4
1957	KC-A	131	437	56	103	20	1	27	69	34	84	.236	.292	.471	764	104	-0	1	1	-0	.952	0	*O-113(113-0-0)/1-1	-0.8
1958	Det-A	66	124	8	40	7	1	5	23	6	25	.323	.354	.516	870	127	4	0	0	0	.939	-2	O-24(24-0-0)	0.0
1959	Det-A	60	132	11	30	4	0	7	26	7	27	.227	.266	.417	683	80	-4	0	0	0	.972	-3	1-32/O-1(0-0-1)	-0.9
Total	11	1234	4131	572	1093	159	22	237	776	383	755	.265	.331	.486	816	115	67	15	7	1	.968	24	*O-1007L/1-35	1.9
■ **CHARLIE ZIEGLER** Ziegler, Charles Wallace b: 1/13/1875, Canton, Ohio d: 4/18/04, Canton, Ohio Deb: 9/23/1899																								
1899	Cle-N	2	8	2	2	0	0	0	0	0		.250	.250	.250	500	40	-1	0			.750	-1	/S-1,2-1	-0.2
1900	Phi-N	3	11	0	3	0	0	0	1	0		.273	.273	.273	545	51	-1	0			.889	-1	/3-3	-0.2
Total	2	5	19	2	5	0	0	0	1	0		.263	.263	.263	526	47	-1	0			.889	-2	/3-3,2-1,S-1	-0.4
■ **BENNY ZIENTARA** Zientara, Benedict Joseph b: 2/14/20, Chicago, Ill. d: 4/16/85, Lake Elsinore, Cal. BR/TR, 5'9", 165 lbs. Deb: 9/11/41																								
1941	Cin-N	9	21	3	6	0	0	0	2	1	3	.286	.318	.286	604	71	-1	0			.914	1	/2-6	0.1
1946	Cin-N	78	280	26	81	10	2	0	16	14	11	.289	.323	.339	662	91	-4	3			.970	24	2-39,3-36	2.3
1947	Cin-N	117	418	60	108	18	1	2	24	23	23	.258	.297	.321	618	64	-22	2			.976	-17	*2-100,3-13	-3.3
1948	Cin-N	74	187	17	35	1	2	0	7	12	11	.187	.236	.214	450	23	-20	0			.990	12	2-60/3-3,S-2	-0.5
Total	4	278	906	106	230	29	5	2	49	50	48	.254	.293	.304	596	64	-46	5			.976	20	2-205/3-52,S-2	-1.4
■ **BILL ZIES** Zies, William BL, Deb: 8/9/1891																								
1891	StL-a	2	3	0	1	0	0	0	0	0	0	.333	.333	.333	667	79	-0	0			1.000	0	/C-2	0.0
■ **CHIEF ZIMMER** Zimmer, Charles Louis b: 11/23/1860, Marietta, Ohio d: 8/22/49, Cleveland, Ohio BR/TR, 6', 190 lbs. Deb: 7/18/1884 MU Career OF: (0-LF 1-CF 4-RF)																								
1884	Det-N	8	29	0	2	1	0	0	0	1	14	.069	.100	.103	203	-38	-4				.830	-1	/C-6,O-2(0-0-2)	-0.5
1886	NY-a	6	19	1	3	0	0	0	1	1		.158	.238	.158	396	26	-2	0			.893	3	/C-6	0.2
1887	Cle-a	14	56	9	16	5	0	0	4	4		.286	.298	.327	625	76	-2	1			.923	-4	C-12/1-2	-0.4
1888	Cle-a	65	212	27	51	11	4	0	22	18		.241	.312	.330	642	109	3	15			.917	7	C-59/O-3R,1-3,S-1	1.3
1889	Cle-N	84	259	47	67	9	9	1	21	44	35	.259	.368	.375	743	110	5	14			.931	7	C-81/1-3	1.6
1890	Cle-N	125	444	54	95	16	6	2	57	46	54	.214	.303	.291	594	75	-14	15			.937	12	*C-125	0.8
1891	Cle-N	116	440	55	112	21	4	3	69	33	49	.255	.312	.341	653	87	-9	15			.936	18	*C-116/3-1	1.7
1892	*Cle-N	111	413	63	109	29	13	1	64	32	47	.264	.327	.404	732	116	6	18			.938	12	*C-111	2.6
1893	Cle-N	57	227	27	70	13	7	2	41	16	15	.308	.357	.454	810	108	1	4			.968	8	C-56/3-1	1.2
1894	Cle-N	90	341	55	97	20	5	4	65	17	31	.284	.328	.408	735	74	-17	14			**.963**	10	*C-89	0.1
1895	*Cle-N	88	315	60	107	21	2	5	56	33	30	.340	.417	.467	884	121	10	14			.975	8	C-84/1-3	2.1
1896	*Cle-N	91	336	46	93	18	3	3	46	31	48	.277	.354	.375	729	87	-7	4			**.972**	9	*C-91/3-1	0.9
1897	Cle-N	80	294	50	93	22	3	0	40	25		.316	.378	.412	789	103	1	8			.976	7	C-80	1.3
1898	Cle-N	20	63	5	15	2	0	0	4	5		.238	.304	.270	574	66	-3	2			.970	4	C-19	0.3
1899	Cle-N	20	73	9	25	2	1	2	14	5		.342	.407	.479	887	154	5	1			.957	-1	C-20	0.6
	Lou-N	75	262	43	78	11	3	2	29	22		.298	.370	.385	755	107	3	9			.985	2	C-62,1-11	0.9
	Yr	95	335	52	103	13	4	4	43	27		.307	.378	.406	784	117	8	10			**.978**	1	C-82,1-11	1.5
1900	*Pit-N	82	271	27	80	7	10	0	35	17		.295	.361	.395	756	108	3	4			.961	5	C-78/1-2	1.4
1901	Pit-N	69	236	17	52	7	3	0	21	20		.220	.292	.275	568	63	-11	6			.975	-7	C-68	-1.1
1902	Pit-N	42	142	13	38	4	2	0	17	11		.268	.338	.324	662	101	0	4			.969	-1	C-41/1-1	0.3
1903	Phi-N	37	118	9	26	3	1	1	19	9		.220	.292	.288	580	68	-5	3			.968	4	C-35,M	0.3
Total	19	1280	4550	617	1229	222	76	26	625	390	323	.270	.339	.369	708	95	-33	151			.952	102	*C-1239/1-25,O-5R,3S	15.6
■ **DON ZIMMER** Zimmer, Donald William b: 1/17/31, Cincinnati, Ohio BR/TR, 5'9", 177 lbs. Deb: 7/2/54 MC Career OF: (4-LF 0-CF 4-RF)																								
1954	Bro-N	24	33	3	6	0	1	0	0	3	8	.182	.270	.242	513	34	-3	2	0	0	.939	3	S-13	0.1
1955	*Bro-N	88	280	38	67	10	1	15	50	19	66	.239	.292	.443	735	89	-5	5	3	0	.976	9	2-62,S-21/3-8	0.9
1956	Bro-N	17	20	4	6	1	0	0	2	0	7	.300	.333	.350	683	78	-1	0	1	-0	.944	2	/S-8,3-3,2-1	0.1
1957	Bro-N	84	269	23	59	9	1	6	19	16	63	.219	.263	.327	590	52	-18	1	3	-1	.957	9	3-39,S-37/2-5	-0.7
1958	LA-N	127	455	52	119	15	2	17	60	28	92	.262	.306	.415	721	86	-10	14	2	2	.965	**33**	*S-114,3-12/2-1,O-1L	3.4
1959	*LA-N	97	249	21	41	7	1	4	28	37	56	.165	.275	.249	524	38	-22	3	1	0	.972	2	S-88/3-5,2-1	-1.3
1960	Chi-N	132	368	37	95	16	7	6	35	27	56	.258	.309	.389	697	90	-5	8	6	-0	.980	6	2-75,3-45/S-5,O-2L	0.6

YEAR	TM/L	G	AB	R	H	2B	3B	HR	RBI	BB	SO	AVG	OBP	SLG	OPS	OPS+	BR+	SB	CS	SBR	FA	FR	G/POS	TPR
1961	Chi-N★	128	477	57	120	25	4	13	40	25	70	.252	.292	.403	694	81	-14	5	1	1	.973	0	*2-116/3-5,O-1(0-0-1)	-0.4
1962	NY-N	14	52	3	4	1	0	0	1	3	10	.077	.127	.096	223	-38	-10	0	1	-0	.961	5	3-14	-0.6
	Cin-N	63	192	16	48	11	2	2	16	14	30	.250	.304	.359	664	75	-7	1	2	-0	.949	-1	3-43,2-17/S-1	-0.8
	Yr	77	244	19	52	12	2	2	17	17	40	.213	.267	.303	570	51	-17	1	3	-1	.952	4	3-57,2-17/S-1	-1.4
1963	LA-N	22	23	4	5	1	0	1	2	3	10	.217	.308	.391	699	107	0	0	0	0	.933	2	3-10/2-1,S-1	0.2
	Was-A	83	298	37	74	12	1	13	44	18	57	.248	.296	.426	722	100	-1	3	2	-0	.935	3	3-78/2-2	0.1
1964	Was-A	121	341	38	84	16	2	12	38	27	94	.246	.302	.411	712	96	-2	1	3	-1	.955	-13	3-87/O-4R,C-2,2-1	-1.8
1965	Was-A	95	226	20	45	6	0	2	17	26	59	.199	.287	.252	540	56	-13	2	0	0	.966	-7	C-33,3-26,2-12	-1.9
Total	12	1095	3283	353	773	130	22	91	352	246	678	.235	.291	.372	663	76	-111	45	25	1	.941	53	3-375,2-294,S/CO	-2.1

■ EDDIE ZIMMERMAN

Zimmerman, Edward Desmond b: 1/4/1883, Oceanic, N.J. d: 5/6/45, Emmaus, Pa. BR/TR, 5'9", 160 lbs. Deb: 9/29/06

YEAR	TM/L	G	AB	R	H	2B	3B	HR	RBI	BB	SO	AVG	OBP	SLG	OPS	OPS+	BR+	SB	CS	SBR	FA	FR	G/POS	TPR
1906	StL-N	5	14	0	3	0	0	0	1	0		.214	.214	.214	429	35	-1	0			.929	-0	/3-5	-0.1
1911	Bro-N	122	417	31	77	10	7	3	36	34	37	.185	.249	.264	513	46	-32	9			**.961**	3	*3-122	-2.5
Total	2	127	431	31	80	10	7	3	37	34	37	.186	.248	.262	511	45	-33	9			.960	3	3-127	-2.6

■ JERRY ZIMMERMAN

Zimmerman, Gerald Robert b: 9/21/34, Omaha, Neb. d: 9/9/98, Neskowin, Ore. BR/TR, 6'2", 185 lbs. Deb: 4/14/61 C

YEAR	TM/L	G	AB	R	H	2B	3B	HR	RBI	BB	SO	AVG	OBP	SLG	OPS	OPS+	BR+	SB	CS	SBR	FA	FR	G/POS	TPR
1961	*Cin-N	76	204	8	42	5	0	0	10	11	21	.206	.253	.230	484	29	-20	1	1	-0	.975	3	C-76	-1.5
1962	Min-A	34	62	8	17	4	0	0	7	3	5	.274	.318	.339	657	74	-2	0	0	0	.992	2	C-34	0.1
1963	Min-A	39	56	3	13	1	0	0	3	2	8	.232	.259	.250	509	43	-4	0	0	0	1.000	6	C-39	0.2
1964	Min-A	63	120	6	24	3	0	0	12	10	15	.200	.278	.225	503	42	-9	0	0	0	.993	6	C-63	-0.2
1965	*Min-A	83	154	8	33	1	1	1	11	12	23	.214	.275	.253	529	49	-10	0	0	0	**.997**	12	C-82	0.5
1966	Min-A	60	119	11	30	4	1	1	15	15	23	.252	.341	.328	668	88	-1	0	0	0	.996	9	C-59	1.0
1967	Min-A	104	234	13	39	3	0	1	12	22	49	.167	.244	.192	436	28	-20	0	1	-0	.992	15	*C-104	-0.2
1968	Min-A	24	45	3	5	1	0	0	2	3	10	.111	.184	.133	317	-3	-5	0	0	0	.991	5	C-24	0.0
Total	8	483	994	60	203	22	2	3	72	78	154	.204	.270	.239	509	43	-73	1	2	-0	.991	58	C-481	-0.1

■ HEINIE ZIMMERMAN

Zimmerman, Henry b: 2/9/1887, New York, N.Y. d: 3/14/69, New York, N.Y. BR/TR, 5'11.5", 176 lbs. Deb: 9/8/07 Career OF: (3-LF 8-CF 2-RF)

YEAR	TM/L	G	AB	R	H	2B	3B	HR	RBI	BB	SO	AVG	OBP	SLG	OPS	OPS+	BR+	SB	CS	SBR	FA	FR	G/POS	TPR
1907	*Chi-N	5	9	0	2	1	0	0	1	0		.222	.222	.333	556	70	-0	0			.789	1	/2-4,S-1,O-1(1-0-0)	0.1
1908	Chi-N	46	113	17	33	4	1	0	9	1		.292	.298	.345	643	101	-0	2			.923	-10	2-20/O-8C,S-1,3-1	-1.2
1909	Chi-N	65	183	23	50	9	2	0	21	3		.273	.285	.344	629	93	-3	7			.945	-7	2-31,S-12/3-4	-1.0
1910	*Chi-N	99	335	35	95	16	6	3	38	20	36	.284	.326	.394	720	111	3	7			.948	-10	2-32,S-26,3-23,/O1	-0.6
1911	Chi-N	143	535	80	164	22	17	9	85	25	50	.307	.343	.462	805	124	14	23			.946	-1	*2-108,3-20,1-11	1.5
1912	Chi-N	145	557	95	**207**	**41**	14	**14**	99	38	60	**.372**	.418	**.571**	**989**	**170**	**50**	23			.916	2	*3-121,1-22	5.3
1913	Chi-N	127	447	69	140	28	12	9	95	41	40	.313	.379	.490	868	147	26	18			.912	5	*3-125	3.5
1914	Chi-N	146	564	75	167	36	12	4	87	20	46	.296	.326	.424	750	123	12	17			.897	-21	*3-118,S-15,2-12	-0.4
1915	Chi-N	139	520	65	138	28	11	3	62	21	33	.265	.300	.379	679	105	1	19	13	-0	.943	-9	*2-100,3-36/S-4	-0.6
1916	Chi-N	107	398	54	116	25	5	6	64	16	33	.291	.324	.425	748	116	7	15	12	-1	.932	7	3-85,2-14/S-4	1.9
	NY-N	40	151	22	41	4	0	0	19	7	10	.272	.304	.298	602	90	-2	9	8	-1	.943	-3	3-40/2-1	-0.5
	Yr	147	549	76	157	29	5	6	**83**	23	43	.286	.318	.390	708	110	5	24	20	-2	.935	4	*3-125,2-15/S-4	1.4
1917	*NY-N	150	585	61	174	22	9	5	**102**	16	43	.297	.317	.391	709	121	11	13			.947	13	*3-149/2-5	3.1
1918	NY-N	121	463	43	126	19	10	1	56	13	23	.272	.294	.363	656	102	-1	14			.955	-4	*3-100,1-19	-0.4
1919	NY-N	123	444	56	113	20	6	4	58	21	30	.255	.296	.354	649	96	-3	8			.940	-1	*3-123	-0.1
Total	13	1456	5304	695	1566	275	105	58	796	242	404	.295	.331	.419	750	121	115	175	33		.928	-38	3-945,2-327/S-63,1O	10.6

■ ROY ZIMMERMAN

Zimmerman, Roy Franklin b: 9/13/16, Pine Grove, Pa. d: 11/22/91, Pine Grove, Pa. BL/TL, 6'2", 187 lbs. Deb: 9/2/45

YEAR	TM/L	G	AB	R	H	2B	3B	HR	RBI	BB	SO	AVG	OBP	SLG	OPS	OPS+	BR+	SB	CS	SBR	FA	FR	G/POS	TPR
1945	NY-N	27	98	14	27	1	0	5	15	5	16	.276	.330	.439	769	111	1	1			.988	-2	1-25/O-1(0-0-1)	-0.2

■ BILL ZIMMERMAN

Zimmerman, William H. b: 1/20/1889, Kengen, Germany d: 10/4/52, Newark, N.J. BR/TR, 5'8.5", 172 lbs. Deb: 4/14/15

YEAR	TM/L	G	AB	R	H	2B	3B	HR	RBI	BB	SO	AVG	OBP	SLG	OPS	OPS+	BR+	SB	CS	SBR	FA	FR	G/POS	TPR
1915	Bro-N	22	57	3	16	2	0	0	7	4	8	.281	.328	.316	644	93	-0	1			.864	-4	O-18(0-0-18)	-0.6

■ FRANK ZINN

Zinn, Frank b: 12/21/1865, Phoenixville, Pa. d: 5/12/36, Manayunk, Pa. 5'8", 150 lbs. Deb: 4/18/1888

YEAR	TM/L	G	AB	R	H	2B	3B	HR	RBI	BB	SO	AVG	OBP	SLG	OPS	OPS+	BR+	SB	CS	SBR	FA	FR	G/POS	TPR
1888	Phi-a	2	7	0	0	0	0	0	0	1		.000	.125	.000	125	-59	-1	0			.938	-1	/C-2	-0.1

■ GUY ZINN

Zinn, Guy b: 2/13/1887, Holbrook, W.Va. d: 10/6/49, Clarksburg, W.Va. BL/TR, 5'10.5", 170 lbs. Deb: 9/11/11

YEAR	TM/L	G	AB	R	H	2B	3B	HR	RBI	BB	SO	AVG	OBP	SLG	OPS	OPS+	BR+	SB	CS	SBR	FA	FR	G/POS	TPR
1911	NY-A	9	27	5	4	0	2	0	1	4		.148	.281	.296	578	57	-2	0			.923	-0	/O-8(2-4-2)	-0.2
1912	NY-A	106	401	56	105	15	10	6	55	50		.262	.345	.394	739	105	2	17			.893	-12	*O-106(13-31-61)	-1.6
1913	Bos-N	36	138	15	41	8	2	1	15	4	23	.297	.322	.406	727	105	0	3			.948	4	O-35(1-34-0)	0.2
1914	Bal-F	61	225	30	63	10	6	3	25	16	26	.280	.336	.418	754	101	-3	6			.935	-5	O-57(31-12-14)	-1.2
1915	Bal-F	102	312	30	84	18	3	5	43	35	28	.269	.343	.394	737	104	-3	2			.949	-5	O-88(63-17-8)	-1.2
Total	5	314	1103	136	297	51	23	15	139	109	77	.269	.338	.398	736	103	-6	28			.927	-17	O-294(110-98-85)	-4.0

■ BUD ZIPFEL

Zipfel, Marion Sylvester b: 11/18/38, Belleville, Ill. BL/TR, 6'3", 200 lbs. Deb: 7/26/61

YEAR	TM/L	G	AB	R	H	2B	3B	HR	RBI	BB	SO	AVG	OBP	SLG	OPS	OPS+	BR+	SB	CS	SBR	FA	FR	G/POS	TPR
1961	Was-A	50	170	17	34	7	5	4	18	15	49	.200	.265	.371	635	69	-8	1	1	-0	.983	-4	1-44	-1.5
1962	Was-A	68	184	21	44	4	1	6	21	17	43	.239	.307	.370	676	82	-5	1	2	-0	.976	-2	1-26,O-23(23-0-0)	-1.1
Total	2	118	354	38	78	11	6	10	39	32	92	.220	.287	.370	657	76	-13	2	3	-1	.981	-7	/1-70,O-23(23-0-0)	-2.6

■ RICHIE ZISK

Zisk, Richard Walter b: 2/6/49, Brooklyn, N.Y. BR/TR, 6'1", 208 lbs. Deb: 9/8/71 Career OF: (413-LF 0-CF 507-RF)

YEAR	TM/L	G	AB	R	H	2B	3B	HR	RBI	BB	SO	AVG	OBP	SLG	OPS	OPS+	BR+	SB	CS	SBR	FA	FR	G/POS	TPR
1971	Pit-N	7	15	2	3	1	0	1	2	4	7	.200	.368	.467	835	136	1	0	0	0	1.000	-1	/O-6(3-0-3)	0.0
1972	Pit-N	17	37	4	7	3	0	0	4	7	10	.189	.318	.270	588	70	-1	0	0	0	.938	-2	O-12(12-0-1)	-0.4
1973	Pit-N	103	333	44	108	23	7	10	54	21	63	.324	.364	.526	890	148	20	0	0	0	.987	2	O-84(22-0-65)	1.8
1974	*Pit-N	149	536	75	168	30	3	17	100	65	91	.313	.388	.476	863	146	33	1	1	-0	.985	9	*O-141(9-0-135)	3.5
1975	*Pit-N	147	504	69	146	27	3	20	75	68	109	.290	.376	.474	851	136	25	0	1	-0	.975	1	*O-140(140-0-0)	1.7
1976	Pit-N	155	581	91	168	35	2	21	89	52	96	.289	.348	.465	812	128	20	1	0	0	.987	9	*O-152(152-0-0)	2.1
1977	Chi-A★	141	531	78	154	17	6	30	101	55	98	.290	.360	.514	874	135	25	0	4	-1	.982	6	*O-109(10-0-100),D-28	2.3
1978	Tex-A★	140	511	68	134	19	1	22	85	58	76	.262	.341	.432	773	116	11	3	3	-0	.988	-2	O-90(48-0-42),D-49	0.2
1979	Tex-A	144	503	69	132	21	1	18	64	57	75	.262	.338	.416	753	103	2	1	1	-0	.972	-4	*O-134(15-0-126)/D-3	-0.9
1980	Tex-A	135	448	48	130	17	1	19	77	39	72	.290	.347	.460	807	123	13	0	2	-1	.980	-3	D-86,O-37(2-0-35)	0.5
1981	Sea-A	94	357	42	111	12	1	16	43	28	63	.311	.366	.485	851	138	17	0	2	-1	.000	0	D-93	1.4
1982	Sea-A	131	503	61	147	28	1	21	62	49	89	.292	.356	.477	833	123	16	2	1	0	.000	0	*D-130	1.2
1983	Sea-A	90	285	30	69	12	0	12	36	30	61	.242	.314	.411	725	94	-3	0	0	0	.000	0	D-84	-0.5
Total	13	1453	5144	681	1477	245	26	207	792	533	910	.287	.355	.466	821	126	177	8	15	-3	.981	14	O-905R,D-473	12.9

■ BILLY ZITZMANN

Zitzmann, William Arthur b: 11/19/1895, Long Island City, N.Y.
d: 5/29/85, Passaic, N.J. BR/TR, 5'10.5", 175 lbs. Deb: 4/17/19 Career OF: (189-LF 57-CF 46-RF)

YEAR	TM/L	G	AB	R	H	2B	3B	HR	RBI	BB	SO	AVG	OBP	SLG	OPS	OPS+	BR+	SB	CS	SBR	FA	FR	G/POS	TPR
1919	Pit-N	11	26	5	5	1	0	0	2	0	6	.192	.192	.231	423	26	-2	2			.917	-2	/O-8(8-0-0)	-0.5
	Cin-N	2	1	0	0	0	0	0	0	0	0	.000	.000	.000	0	-99	-0	0			.000	-1	/O-1(1-0-0)	-0.1
	Yr	13	27	5	5	1	0	0	2	0	6	.185	.185	.222	407	22	-3	2			.917	-2	/O-9(9-0-0)	-0.6
1925	Cin-N	104	301	53	76	13	3	0	21	35	22	.252	.342	.316	658	71	-12	11	11	-1	.959	-14	O-89(80-4-7)/S-1	-3.2
1926	Cin-N	53	94	21	23	2	1	0	3	6	7	.245	.304	.287	591	61	-5	3			.965	-3	O-31(22-5-2)	-1.0
1927	Cin-N	88	232	47	66	10	4	0	24	20	18	.284	.352	.362	714	94	-1	9			.958	-9	O-60(17-36-7)/S-8,3-3	-1.2
1928	Cin-N	101	266	53	79	9	3	3	33	13	22	.297	.337	.387	724	90	-4	13			.958	-6	O-78(46-12-23)/3-1	-1.5
1929	Cin-N	47	84	18	19	3	0	0	6	9	10	.226	.309	.262	570	45	-7	4			.940	-3	O-22(15-0-7)/1-5	-1.0
Total	6	406	1004	197	268	38	11	3	89	83	85	.267	.333	.336	668	77	-32	42	11		.956	-37	O-289L/S-9,1-5,3-4	-8.5

■ EDDIE ZOSKY

Zosky, Edward James b: 2/10/68, Whittier, Cal. BR/TR, 6', 175 lbs. Deb: 9/2/91

YEAR	TM/L	G	AB	R	H	2B	3B	HR	RBI	BB	SO	AVG	OBP	SLG	OPS	OPS+	BR+	SB	CS	SBR	FA	FR	G/POS	TPR
1991	Tor-A	18	27	2	4	1	1	0	2	0	8	.148	.148	.259	407	10	-3	0	0	0	1.000	1	S-18	-0.1
1992	Tor-A	8	7	1	2	0	1	0	1	0	2	.286	.286	.571	857	129	0	0	0	0	.923	1	/S-8	0.1
1995	Fla-N	6	5	0	1	0	0	0	0	0	0	.200	.200	.200	400	6	-1	0	0	0	.667	-0	/S-4,2-1	-0.1
1999	Mil-N	8	7	1	1	0	0	0	0	1	2	.143	.250	.143	393	3	-1	0	0	0	1.000	0	/3-4,2-2	-0.1
2000	Hou-N	4	4	0	0	0	0	0	0	0	1	.000	.000	.000	0	-95	-1	0	0	0	.000	0	/H	-0.1
Total	5	44	50	4	8	1	2	0	3	1	13	.160	.176	.260	436	16	-6	0	0	0	.963	2	/S-30,3-4,2-3	-0.3

YEAR	TM/L	G	AB	R	H	2B	3B	HR	RBI	BB	SO	AVG	OBP	SLG	OPS	OPS+	BR+	SB	CS	SBR	FA	FR	G/POS	TPR
■ **JON ZUBER**	Zuber, Jon Edward b: 12/10/69, Encino, Cal. BL/TL, 6', 190 lbs. Deb: 4/19/96																							
1996	Phi-N	30	91	7	23	4	0	1	10	6	11	.253	.299	.330	629	65	-5	1	0	0	.987	-2	1-22	-0.8
1998	Phi-N	38	45	6	11	3	1	2	6	6	9	.244	.346	.489	835	115	1	0	0	0	1.000	-1	/O-5(5-0-0),1-4	0.0
Total	2	68	136	13	34	7	1	3	16	12	20	.250	.315	.382	698	82	-4	1	0	0	.989	-2	/1-26,O-5(5-0-0)	-0.8
■ **JULIO ZULETA**	Zuleta, Julio Ernesto (Tapia) b: 3/28/75, Panama City, Pan. BR/TR, 6'6", 230 lbs. Deb: 4/6/2000																							
2000	Chi-N	30	68	13	20	8	0	3	12	2	19	.294	.342	.544	887	122	2	0	1	-0	.966	-1	1-14/O-6(6-0-0)	0.0
■ **BOB ZUPCIC**	Zupcic, Robert b: 8/18/66, Pittsburgh, Pa. BR/TR, 6'4", 220 lbs. Deb: 9/7/91 Career OF: (100-LF 112-CF 96-RF)																							
1991	Bos-A	18	25	3	4	0	0	1	3	1	6	.160	.192	.280	472	28	-3	0	0	0	.875	-5	O-16(3-7-6)	-0.7
1992	Bos-A	124	392	46	108	19	1	3	43	25	60	.276	.325	.352	677	84	-8	2	2	-0	.977	-2	*O-114(32-68-22)/D-5	-1.2
1993	Bos-A	141	286	40	69	24	2	2	26	27	54	.241	.311	.360	671	75	-10	5	2	0	.979	-19	*O-122(48-37-54)/D-5	-3.1
1994	Bos-A	4	4	0	0	0	0	0	0	0	1	.000	.000	.000	0	-96	-1	0	1	-0	1.000	-0	/O-2(2-0-0),D-1	-0.2
	Chi-A	32	88	10	18	4	1	1	8	4	16	.205	.239	.307	546	40	-8	0	0	0	1.000	-1	O-28(15-0-14)/3-2,1-1	-0.9
	Yr	36	92	10	18	4	1	1	8	4	17	.196	.229	.293	523	34	-9	0	1	-0	1.000	-1	O-30L/3-2,D-1,1-1	-1.1
Total	4	319	795	99	199	47	4	7	80	57	137	.250	.305	.346	651	73	-30	7	5	-0	.977	-27	O-282C/D-11,3-2,1-1	-6.1
■ **FRANK ZUPO**	Zupo, Frank Joseph "Noodles" b: 8/29/39, San Francisco, Cal BL/TR, 5'11", 182 lbs. Deb: 7/1/57																							
1957	Bal-A	10	12	2	1	0	0	0	0	1	4	.083	.154	.083	237	-36	-2	0	0	0	.913	0	/C-8	-0.2
1958	Bal-A	1	2	0	0	0	0	0	0	0	1	.000	.000	.000	0	-99	-1	0	0	0	1.000	0	/C-1	0.0
1961	Bal-A	5	4	1	2	1	0	0	0	1	1	.500	.600	.750	1350	268	1	0	0	0	1.000	0	/C-4	0.1
Total	3	16	18	3	3	1	0	0	0	2	6	.167	.250	.222	472	31	-2	0	0	0	.941	1	/C-13	-0.1
■ **PAUL ZUVELLA**	Zuvella, Paul b: 10/31/58, San Mateo, Cal. BR/TR, 6', 178 lbs. Deb: 9/4/82 C																							
1982	Atl-N	2	1	0	0	0	0	0	0	0	0	.000	.000	.000	0	-96	-0	0	0	0	.800	1	/S-1	0.1
1983	Atl-N	3	5	0	0	0	0	0	0	2	1	.000	.375	.000	375	11	-0	0	0	0	.750	-2	/S-2	-0.2
1984	Atl-N	11	25	2	5	1	0	0	1	2	3	.200	.259	.240	499	38	-2	0	0	0	1.000	1	/2-6,S-6	-0.1
1985	Atl-N	81	190	16	48	8	1	0	4	16	14	.253	.311	.305	616	69	-8	2	0	0	.986	9	2-42,S-33/3-5	0.6
1986	NY-A	21	48	2	4	1	0	0	2	5	4	.083	.170	.104	274	-24	-8	0	0	0	.966	4	S-21	-0.2
1987	NY-A	14	34	2	6	0	0	0	0	0	4	.176	.176	.176	353	-6	-5	0	0	0	1.000	-1	/2-7,S-6,3-1	-0.6
1988	Cle-A	51	130	9	30	5	1	0	7	8	13	.231	.275	.285	560	56	-8	0	0	0	.959	-3	S-49	-0.8
1989	Cle-A	24	58	10	16	2	0	2	6	1	11	.276	.300	.414	714	98	-0	0	0	0	.963	-3	S-15/3-5,D-3	-0.3
1991	KC-A	2	0	0	0	0	0	0	0	0	0	—	—	—	—	—	0	0	0	0	.000	0	/3-2	0.0
Total	9	209	491	41	109	17	2	2	20	34	50	.222	.275	.277	552	52	-32	2	0	0	.959	5	S-133/2-55,3-13,D-3	-1.5
■ **DUTCH ZWILLING**	Zwilling, Edward Harrison b: 11/2/1888, St.Louis, Mo. d: 3/27/78, LaCrescenta, Cal. BL/TL, 5'6.5", 160 lbs. Deb: 8/14/10 C																							
1910	Chi-A	27	87	7	16	5	0	0	5	11		.184	.283	.241	524	67	-3	1			.940	-2	O-27(0-27-0)	-0.7
1914	Chi-F	154	592	91	185	38	8	**16**	95	46	68	.313	.363	.485	848	138	19	21			.962	2	*O-154(0-153-1)	1.0
1915	Chi-F	150	548	65	157	32	7	13	**94**	67	65	.286	.366	.442	808	135	16	24			.979	8	*O-148(0-148-0)/1-3	1.5
1916	Chi-N	35	53	4	6	1	0	1	8	4	6	.113	.175	.189	364	11	-6	0			1.000	-2	O-10(0-5-4)	-0.9
Total	4	366	1280	167	364	76	15	30	202	128	139	.284	.351	.438	789	127	26	46			.969	6	O-339(0-333-5)/1-3	0.9

The Pitcher Register

The Pitcher Register consists of the central pitching statistics of every man who has pitched in major league play since 1871, *without exception.* Pitcher batting is expressed in Batting Runs in the Pitcher Batting column, and in the newly added columns for base hits and batting average. Pitcher defense is expressed in Fielding Runs in the Pitcher Defense column.

The pitchers are listed alphabetically by surname and, when more than one pitcher bears the name, alphabetically by *given* name—not by "use name," by which we mean the name he may have had applied to him during his playing career. This is the standard method of alphabetizing used in other biographical reference works, and in the case of baseball it makes it easier to find a lesser-known player with a common surname like Smith or Johnson. This method also jibes with that employed in the Team Roster and Annual Record where, for example, Charles "Old Hoss" Radbourn is shown not as the puzzling O. Radbourn or H. Radbourn, as some reference books have it, but as C. Radbourn. On the whole, we have been conservative in ascribing nicknames, doing so only when the player was in fact known by that name during his playing days.

Pitcher batting and pitcher defense, because the win-denominated numbers they produce are so small, are not sorted for single-season leaders (although the all-time leaders in these categories, single season and lifetime, will be found in the separate section called "All-Time Leaders"). Symbols denoting All-Star Game selection and/or play appear to the right of the team/league column. An additional finding aid is an asterisk alongside the team for which a player appeared in postseason competition, thus making for easy cross-reference to the other sections on postseason play.

The record of a man who pitched in more than one season is given in one line for each season, plus a career total line. If he pitched for more than one team in a given year, his totals for each team are given on separate lines; and if the teams for which he pitched in his "traded year" are in the same league, then his full record is stated in both separate and combined fashion. (In the odd case of a man playing for three or more clubs in one year, with some of these clubs being in the same league, the combined total line will reflect only his play in that one league.) A man who pitched in only one year has no additional career total line since it would be identical to his seasonal listing.

In *Total Baseball 1*, fractional innings were calculated for teams in the Annual Record but were rounded off to the nearest whole inning for individuals, in accordance with baseball scoring practice.

Pitching records for the National Association are included in the Pitcher Register because the editors, like most baseball historians, regard it as a major league, inasmuch as it was the only professional league of its day and supplied the National League of 1876 with most of its personnel. Unless Major League Baseball reverses the position it adopted in 1969 and restores the NA to official major league status, we will continue the practice of carrying separate totals for the National Association rather than integrating them into the career marks of those pitchers whose major league tenures began before 1876 and concluded in that year or after it.

Gaps remain elsewhere in the official record of baseball and in the ongoing process of sabermetric reconstruction. The reader will note occasional blank elements in biographical lines; these are not typographical lapses but signs that the information does not exist or has not yet been found. Where official statistics did not exist or the raw data have not survived, as with batters facing pitchers before 1908 in the American League and before 1903 in the National, we have constructed figures from the available raw data. For example, to obtain a pitcher's BFP—Batters Facing Pitchers—for calculating Opponents' On-Base Percentage or Batting Average, we have subtracted league base hits from league at bats, divided by league innings pitched, multiplied by the pitcher's innings and added his hits and walks allowed and hit-by-pitch, if available.

For a key to the team and league abbreviations used in the Pitcher Register go to the last page of the book. For a guide to the other procedures and abbreviations employed in the Pitcher Register, review the comments on the prodigiously extended pitching record on the next page.

Looking at the biographical line for any pitcher, we see first his use name in full capitals, then his given name and nickname (and any other name he may have used or been born with, such as the matronymic of a Latin American player). His date and place of birth follow "b" and his date and place of death follow "d"; years through 1900 are expressed fully, in four digits, and years after 1900 are expressed in only their last two digits. Then comes his manner of batting and throwing, abbreviated for a left-handed batter who throws right as BL/TR (a switch hitter would be shown as BB for "bats both" and a switch thrower as TB for "throws both"; dates are given for pitchers who batted or threw both ways for part of a season or part of a career). Next, and for most pitchers last, is the pitcher's debut date.

Some pitchers continue in major league baseball after their pitching days are through, as managers, coaches, or even umpires. A pitcher whose biographical line concludes with an M can also be located in the Manager Roster; one whose line bears a C will be listed in the Coach Roster; and one with a U occupies a place in the Umpire Roster. (In the last case we have placed a U on the biographical line only for those pitchers who umpired in at least six games in a year, for in the 19th century—and especially in the years of the National Association—there were literally hundreds of players who were pressed into service as umpires for a game or two; it would be misleading to accord such pitchers the same code we give to Bob Emslie or Bill Dinneen.) The select few who have been enshrined in the Baseball Hall of Fame are noted with an H. They are also listed in the Hall of Fame Roster found toward the end of "Awards and Honors." An F in this line denotes family connection—father-son-grandfather-grandson or brother.

YEAR	TM/L	W	L	PCT	G	GS	CG	SH	SV	IP	H	R	HR	HB	BB	SO	RAT	ERA	ERA+	OAV	OOB	BH	AVG	PB	PR	PR+	PD	TPI
● **RIP VAN WINKLE**	Van Winkle, Rip "Half Moon" (Also Played in 1874 as Geoffrey Crayon) b: 4/30/1820, Plattekill, N.Y. d: 12/12/80, Hudson, N.Y. BL/TL, 5'5", 145 lbs. Deb: 5/7/1874 MUCHF ♦																											
1874	Bos-n	27	30	.474	57	57	56	1	0	498	502	288	5	7	18	20	9.4	*3.90*	104	.258	.270	40	.167	-3	5	3	-1	-0.1
1875	Wes-n	29	22	.569	52	51	50	2	1	450	491	261	4	16	25	16	10.3	*4.02*	106	.260	.272	50	.200	1	7	7	0	0.5
1883	Bal-a	5	18	.217	27	23	19	0	1	196	207	97	7	10	76	77	13.0	3.44	101	.274	.340	18	.180	-0	-3	1	0	-0.1
1884	Was-U	0	1	.000	1	1	1	0	0	8	10	4	0	0	2	3	13.5	4.50	110	.309	.349	0	.000	1	-0	-0	0	0.0
	KC-U	5	2	.714	8	6	5	0	0	52	66	37	0	1	9	14	13.0	4.33	104	.312	.340	9	.250	2	3	1	0	0.1
	Yr	5	3	.625	7	7	6	0	0	60	76	41	0	1	11	17	13.0	4.35	104	.311	.341	9	.225	2	3	1	0	0.1
1890	Cin-P	0	0	—	1	1	0	0	0	0	5	10	2	0	2	0	∞	∞	-97	1.000	1.000	1	.250	0	-2	-2	0	-0.2
1907	NY-N	16	13	.552	35	34	18	0	2	251	224	100	19	8	78	170	10.8	2.76	126	.236	.293	30	.250	1	17	20	2	2.2
1908	NY-N	16	12	.571	36	35	14	1	5	278	224	88	15	9	48	205	8.8	2.20	130	.215	.250	25	.200	1	24	20	-3	2.2
1909	NY-N	25	7	.781	36	35	18	0	5	273	202	87	24	9	82	208	9.4	2.21	164	.201	.261	20	.147	-1	42	43	1	4.2
1910	NY-N	18	12	.600	37	36	19	0	2	291	230	118	21	13	83	283	9.4	2.81	135	.211	.267	38	.277	4	40	32	1	3.6
1911	NY-N	20	10	.667	36	35	21	0	4	286	210	71	18	10	61	289	8.6	1.76	188	.202	.246	40	.296	4	54	49	-1	5.5
1912	NY-N	21	12	.636	35	35	13	0	3	262	215	110	23	9	77	249	10.0	2.92	116	.219	.275	34	.281	3	18	14	1	1.7
1913	NY-N	19	10	.655	36	36	18	0	3	290	219	87	23	11	64	251	8.8	2.08	184	.202	.247	31	.263	3	51	56	2	5.9
1914	Ind-F	11	11	.500	32	32	12	0	5	236	199	109	19	7	75	201	10.4	3.20	126	.226	.287	22	.227	-1	11	22	1	2.2
1915	NY-N	22	9	.710	36	36	15	0	5	280	217	96	11	7	88	243	9.8	2.38	155	.211	.274	33	.311	3	39	41	1	4.2
1936	NY-N☆	7	3	.700	13	13	5	0	3	96	79	41	7	1	28	72	10.0	3.00	140	.218	.274	11	.196	1	10	13	3	1.5
	Bos-A	5	7	.417	16	16	1	0	0	104	114	57	8	2	29	72	12.4	3.81	112	.271	.318	20	.189	0	4	5	-2	0.7
1967	*Bos-A★	0	1	.000	1	1	0	0	0	⅓	5	4	2	0	1	1	180.0	108.00	1200	.833	.857	0	.000	0	-2	-2	0	-0.2
Total	2 n	56	52	.519	109	108	106	3	1	948	993	549	9	23	43	36	9.8	3.96	105	.259	.271	90	.184	-2	12	7	7	0.4
Total	14	190	128	.597	384	375	180	1	38	2903	2486	1234	199	97	803	2338	10.2	2.76	134	.226	.285	294	.224	23	304	313	6	33.6

A black diamond appears at the end of the biographical line for pitchers who also appear in the Player Register by virtue of their having played in 100 or more games at another position, including pinch hitter, or having played more than half of their total major league games at another position, or having played more games at a position other than pitcher in at least one year.

The explanations for the statistical column heads follow; for more technical information about formulas and calculations, see the Glossary. The vertical rules in the column-header line separate the stats into six logical groupings: year, team, league; wins and losses; game-related counting stats; inning-related counting stats; basic calculated averages; pitcher batting; sabermetric figures of more complex calculation; and run-denominated Linear Weights stats for pitching, fielding, and Total Pitcher Index.

Note that the TPI (Total Pitcher Index) in this edition differs from those in earlier volumes, because for players who were both batters and pitchers, the method of allocating Wins between TPI and TPR (Total Player Rating) was improved. Previously, if a pitcher pitched in over half his games, all his batting was included with his pitcher rating (TPI); if he pitched in less than half his games, his Batting Wins were thrown over to his batter rating (TPR), with his TPI including only his Pitching Wins and Pitcher Defense. The new method prorates batting proportionally with the number of games pitched. In addition, fielding ratings at nonpitching positions for players who pitched in over half their games, previously omitted, are now part of the Total Baseball Ranking. In any case, the TPR values of batter-pitchers should remain about the same.

Also—and this is a key difference—the formula for Total Pitcher Index has been revised to employ the Relief Ranking formula (see Glossary) for all pitchers, not just relievers. The principal effect will be to calculate Pitcher Wins for relievers instead of Adjusted Pitcher Runs, as was formerly the case. The TPI will still be the sum of pitching, batting, fielding, and baserunning runs, but the Pitcher Runs will be expressed as Ranking Runs rather than Adjusted Pitching Runs. Check the Glossary for the specifics, but the net effect will be to raise the TPIs of relief closers and, to a lesser extent, starters who average a high number of innings per start, and to lower somewhat the TPIs of mop-up relievers (few saves, few decisions) and starters with many no-decision games.

Taken out from the Pitcher Register of earlier editions are the following statistics: Hits Per Game and Bases on Balls Per Game (still available in the Annual Record and Leaders sections, and now stated in combined fashion as Ratio); Strikeouts Per Game (still available in the Annual Record and Leaders sections and, in any event, fairly evident from a glance at the SO and IP columns); Park Factor for pitchers (still available from the Annual Record); Clutch Pitching Index, newly developed for Total Baseball but which we have judged to be of lesser interest and value than the more established sabermetric measures (still, it is present in the Annual Record and Leaders sections); and Wins Above Team, a stat that has so many cautions associated with it that we judged it to be of little value when applied to all pitchers. For the first time, this edition includes Runs Allowed and Hit Batsmen in the Pitcher Register.

Finally, we have made an upward adjustment to overall league performance in the Federal League of 1914–1915 and the Union Association of 1884 (thus lowering individual ratings), because while both leagues are regarded as major leagues, there can be no doubt that their caliber of play was not equivalent to that in the rival leagues of those years. Suffice it to say here that league earned run averages were reduced by 20 percent for the UA and 10 percent for the FL. A full explanantion of the adjustment procedure may be found in the Glossary, under "League Performance."

YEAR Year in which a man pitched (When a space in the column is blank, this indicates that the man pitched for two or more clubs in the last year stated in the column; if those clubs were in the same league, then the man will also have a combined total line, beginning with the abbreviation "Yr" placed in the TM/L column.)

* Denotes postseason play, World Series, League Championship Series, or Division Series.

Yr Year's totals for pitching with two or more clubs in same league (see comments for YEAR)

★ Named to All-Star Game, played

☆ Named to All-Star Game, did not play

† Named to All-Star Game, replaced because of injury

TM/L Team and League (see comments for YEAR)

W Wins

L Losses

PCT Win Percentage (Wins divided by decisions)

G Games pitched

GS Games Started

CG Complete Games

SH Shutouts (Complete-game shutouts only)

SV Saves (Employing definition in force at the time, and 1969 definition for years prior to 1969)

IP Innings Pitched (Fractional innings included, as discussed above)

H Hits allowed (Bases on balls were counted as hits by scorers in 1887.)

R Runs allowed

HR Home Runs allowed

HB Hit Batsmen (Data is available from 1884–1891 in the American Association, from 1887 on for the National League, for the 1890 Players League, and the Federal League in 1914–1915.)

BB Bases on Balls allowed (Bases on balls were counted as outs by scorers in 1876.)

SO Strikeouts

RAT Ratio (Hits allowed plus walks allowed per nine innings)

ERA Earned Run Average (In a handful of cases, a pitcher will have faced one or more batters for his full season's work yet failed to retire any of them [thus having an innings pitched figure of zero]; if any of the men he put on base came around to score earned runs, these runs produced an infinite ERA, expressed in the pitcher's record as ∞. (see Van Winkle's 1890 season)

ERA+ Adjusted Earned Run Average normalized to league average and adjusted for home-park factor. (See comments for PR+.)

OAV Opponents' Batting Average

OOB Opponents' On Base Percentage

BH Base Hits (as a batter)

AVG Batting Average

PB Pitcher Batting (Expressed in Batting Runs. Pitcher Batting is park-adjusted and weighted, for those who played primarily at other positions, by the ratio of games pitched to games played. For more technical data about Runs Per Win and Batting Run formulas, see Glossary.)

PR Pitching Runs (Linear Weights measure of runs saved *beyond* what a league-average pitcher might have saved, defined as zero. New to this edition, the formula used to calculate Relief Ranking is now employed for all pitchers; this creates small differences for starters but large differences for relievers, especially closers [see Glossary for further detail]. Occasionally the curious figure of – 0 will appear in this column, or in the columns of other Linear Weights measures of batting, fielding, and the TPI. This "negative zero" figure signifies a run contribution that falls below the league average, but to so small a degree that it cannot be said to have cost the team a run.

PR+ Adjusted Pitching Runs (It is normalized to league average and adjusted for home-park factor. A mark of 100 is a league-average performance, and superior marks exceed 100. A recent innovation is to use three-year averages for pitching park factors. If a team moved, or the park changed dramatically, then two-year averages are employed; if the park was used for only one year, then of course only that run-scoring data is used.)

PD Pitcher Defense (Expressed in Fielding Runs. See comment above on PB and see Glossary.)

TPI Total Pitcher Index (The sum, expressed in wins beyond league average, of a pitcher's Pitching Runs, [now expressed as Ranking Runs—see Glossary] Batting Runs—in the AL since 1973—and Fielding Runs, all divided by the Runs Per Win factor for that year—which is generally around 10, historically in the 9–11 range; see Glossary.)

Total For players whose careers include play in the National Association as well as other major leagues, two totals are given, as described above and as illustrated in Rip Van Winkle's record, where the record of his years in the National Association is shown alongside the notation "Total 2 n," where *2* stands for the number of years totaled and *n* stands for National Association. For players whose careers began in 1876 or later, the lifetime record is shown alongside the notation "Total x," where *x* stands for the number of post-1875 years totaled.

● DON AASE Aase, Donald William b: 9/8/54, Orange, Cal. BR/TR, 6'3", 210 lbs. Deb: 7/26/77

YEAR	TM/L	W	L	PCT	G	GS	CG	SH	SV	IP	H	R	HR	HB	BB	SO	RAT	ERA	ERA+	OAV	OOB	BH	AVG	PB	PR	PR+	PD	TPI
1977	Bos-A	6	2	.750	13	13	4	2	0	92^1	85	36	6	1	19	49	10.2	3.12	144	.244	.285	0	—	0	10	13	-0	1.0
1978	Cal-A	11	8	.579	29	29	6	1	0	178^2	185	88	14	2	80	93	13.4	4.03	90	.270	.348	0	—	0	-5	-8	0	-0.8
1979	*Cal-A	9	10	.474	37	28	7	1	2	185^1	200	104	19	1	77	96	13.5	4.81	85	.277	.347	0	—	0	-12	-15	-2	-1.6
1980	Cal-A	8	13	.381	40	21	5	1	2	175	193	83	13	1	66	74	13.4	4.06	97	.287	.351	0	—	0	-0	-2	-1	-0.4
1981	Cal-A	4	4	.500	39	0	0	0	11	65^1	56	17	4	0	24	38	11.0	2.34	156	.234	.304	0	—	0	10	10	-0	1.5
1982	Cal-A	3	3	.500	24	0	0	0	4	52	45	20	5	0	23	40	11.8	3.46	117	.243	.327	0	—	0	4	3	-0	0.4
1984	Cal-A	4	1	.800	23	0	0	0	8	39	30	7	1	0	19	28	11.3	1.62	246	.221	.316	0	—	0	10	10	-0	1.7
1985	Bal-A	10	6	.625	54	0	0	0	14	88	83	44	6	1	35	67	12.2	3.78	107	.258	.332	0	—	0	4	3	0	0.5
1986	Bal-A★	6	7	.462	66	0	0	0	34	81^2	71	29	6	0	28	67	10.9	2.98	139	.234	.298	0	—	0	11	11	0	2.2
1987	Bal-A	1	0	1.000	7	0	0	0	2	8	8	2	1	0	4	3	13.5	2.25	196	.276	.364	0	—	0	2	2	-0	0.3
1988	Bal-A	0	0	—	35	0	0	0	0	46^2	40	22	4	0	37	28	14.9	4.05	97	.240	.377	0	—	0	-0	-1	-1	-0.1
1989	NY-N	1	5	.167	49	0	0	0	2	59^1	56	27	5	1	26	34	12.6	3.94	83	.245	.324	0	.000	-1	-3	-5	0	-0.5
1990	LA-N	3	1	.750	32	0	0	0	3	38	33	24	5	0	19	24	12.3	4.97	74	.232	.323	0	—	0	-5	-6	-1	-0.7
Total	13	66	60	.524	448	91	22	5	82	1109^1	1085	503	89	7	457	641	12.6	3.80	103	.259	.333	0	.000	-1	24	16	-5	3.5

● BERT ABBEY Abbey, Bert Wood b: 11/29/1869, Essex, Vt. d: 6/11/62, Essex Junction, Vt. BR/TR, 5'11", 175 lbs. Deb: 6/14/1892

YEAR	TM/L	W	L	PCT	G	GS	CG	SH	SV	IP	H	R	HR	HB	BB	SO	RAT	ERA	ERA+	OAV	OOB	BH	AVG	PB	PR	PR+	PD	TPI
1892	Was-N	5	18	.217	27	22	19	0	1	195^2	207	139	7	6	76	77	13.3	3.45	94	.261	.330	9	.120	-3	-4	-4	2	-0.6
1893	Chi-N	2	4	.333	7	7	5	0	0	56	74	52	1	4	20	6	15.8	5.46	85	.308	.371	6	.231	-0	-5	-5	0	-0.4
1894	Chi-N	2	7	.222	11	11	10	0	0	92	119	74	3	3	37	24	15.6	5.18	108	.310	.375	5	.128	-5	1	4	-1	-0.2
1895	Chi-N	0	1	.000	1	1	1	0	0	8	10	8	0	1	2	3	14.6	4.50	113	.303	.361	1	.333	-0	0	0	0	0.1
	Bro-N	5	2	.714	8	6	5	0	0	52	66	34	0	3	9	14	13.5	4.33	102	.304	.341	5	.263	1	3	0	1	0.2
	Yr	5	3	.625	9	7	6	0	0	60	76	42	0	4	11	17	13.7	4.35	103	.304	.343	6	.273	1	3	1	1	0.3
1896	Bro-N	8	8	.500	25	18	12	0	0	164^1	210	135	7	9	48	37	14.6	5.15	80	.308	.361	12	.190	-1	-14	-20	-2	-1.6
Total	5	22	40	.355	79	65	52	0	1	568	686	442	18	26	192	161	14.3	4.52	92	.292	.352	38	.169	-8	-18	-24	0	-2.5

● CHARLIE ABBEY Abbey, Charles S. b: 10/14/1866, Falls City, Neb. d: 4/27/26, San Francisco, Cal. BL/TL, 5'8.5", 169 lbs. Deb: 8/16/1893 ♦

YEAR	TM/L	W	L	PCT	G	GS	CG	SH	SV	IP	H	R	HR	HB	BB	SO	RAT	ERA	ERA+	OAV	OOB	BH	AVG	PB	PR	PR+	PD	TPI
1896	Was-N	0	0	—	1	0	0	0	0	2	6	3	0	0	0	0	27.0	4.50	98	.500	.500	79	.262	0	-0	-0	-0	0.0

● JIM ABBOTT Abbott, James Anthony b: 9/19/67, Flint, Mich. BL/TL, 6'3", 210 lbs. Deb: 4/8/89

YEAR	TM/L	W	L	PCT	G	GS	CG	SH	SV	IP	H	R	HR	HB	BB	SO	RAT	ERA	ERA+	OAV	OOB	BH	AVG	PB	PR	PR+	PD	TPI
1989	Cal-A	12	12	.500	29	29	4	2	0	181^1	190	95	13	4	74	115	13.3	3.92	97	.274	.347	0	—	0	-1	-2	-1	-0.3
1990	Cal-A	10	14	.417	33	33	4	1	0	211^2	246	116	16	5	72	105	13.7	4.51	85	.295	.355	0	—	0	-14	-16	1	-1.6
1991	Cal-A	18	11	.621	34	34	5	1	0	243	222	85	14	5	73	158	11.1	2.89	142	.244	.304	0	—	0	33	33	3	4.1
1992	Cal-A	7	15	.318	29	29	7	0	0	211	208	73	12	4	68	130	11.9	2.77	144	.263	.325	0	—	0	28	28	2	3.0
1993	NY-A	11	14	.440	32	32	4	1	0	214	221	115	22	3	73	95	12.5	4.37	95	.271	.334	0	—	0	-1	-5	1	-0.4
1994	NY-A	9	8	.529	24	24	2	0	0	160^1	167	88	24	2	64	90	13.1	4.55	101	.273	.344	0	—	0	5	1	0	0.1
1995	Chi-A	6	4	.600	17	17	3	0	0	112^1	116	50	10	1	35	45	12.2	3.36	133	.269	.325	0	—	0	17	14	-0	1.1
	Cal-A	5	4	.556	13	13	1	1	0	84^2	93	43	4	1	29	41	13.1	4.15	113	.280	.340	0	—	0	5	5	1	0.5
	Yr	11	8	.579	30	30	4	1	0	197	209	93	14	2	64	86	12.6	3.70	123	.274	.331	0	—	0	22	20	0	1.6
1996	Cal-A	2	18	.100	27	23	1	0	0	142	171	128	23	4	78	58	16.0	7.48	67	.306	.395	0	—	0	-39	-39	1	-4.1
1998	Chi-A	5	0	1.000	5	5	0	0	0	31^2	35	16	2	1	12	14	13.6	4.55	100	.292	.361	0	—	0	0	0	1	0.1
1999	Mil-N	2	8	.200	20	15	0	0	0	82	110	71	14	2	42	37	16.9	6.91	66	.317	.394	2	.095	-1	-21	-22	2	-2.1
Total	10	87	108	.446	263	254	31	6	0	1674	1779	880	154	32	620	888	13.1	4.25	100	.276	.343	2	.095	-1	12	-2	10	0.4

● KYLE ABBOTT Abbott, Lawrence Kyle b: 2/18/68, Newburyport, Mass. BL/TL, 6'4", 200 lbs. Deb: 9/10/91

YEAR	TM/L	W	L	PCT	G	GS	CG	SH	SV	IP	H	R	HR	HB	BB	SO	RAT	ERA	ERA+	OAV	OOB	BH	AVG	PB	PR	PR+	PD	TPI
1991	Cal-A	1	2	.333	5	3	0	0	0	19^2	22	11	2	1	13	12	16.5	4.58	90	.301	.414	0	—	0	-1	-1	0	-0.1
1992	Phi-N	1	14	.067	31	19	0	0	0	133^1	147	80	20	1	45	88	13.0	5.13	68	.283	.341	2	.069	-1	-24	-24	-1	-2.8
1995	Phi-N	2	0	1.000	18	0	0	0	0	28^1	28	12	3	0	16	21	14.0	3.81	111	.267	.364	1	.500	0	1	1	0	0.1
1996	Cal-A	0	1	.000	3	0	0	0	0	4	10	9	1	0	5	3	33.8	20.25	25	.500	.600	0	—	0	-7	-7	0	-1.0
Total	4	4	17	.190	57	22	0	0	0	185^1	207	112	26	2	79	124	14.0	5.20	71	.288	.360	3	.097	-1	-31	-31	-1	-3.8

● DAN ABBOTT Abbott, Leander Franklin "Big Dan" b: 3/16/1862, Portage, Ohio d: 2/13/30, Ottawa Lake, Mich. BR/TR, 5'11", 190 lbs. Deb: 4/19/1890

YEAR	TM/L	W	L	PCT	G	GS	CG	SH	SV	IP	H	R	HR	HB	BB	SO	RAT	ERA	ERA+	OAV	OOB	BH	AVG	PB	PR	PR+	PD	TPI
1890	Tol-a	0	2	.000	3	1	1	0	1	13	19	14	0	1	8	1	19.4	6.23	63	.328	.418	1	.143	0	-3	-3	1	-0.4

● PAUL ABBOTT Abbott, Paul David b: 9/15/67, Van Nuys, Cal. BR/TR, 6'3", 185 lbs. Deb: 8/21/90

YEAR	TM/L	W	L	PCT	G	GS	CG	SH	SV	IP	H	R	HR	HB	BB	SO	RAT	ERA	ERA+	OAV	OOB	BH	AVG	PB	PR	PR+	PD	TPI
1990	Min-A	0	5	.000	7	7	0	0	0	34^2	37	24	0	1	28	25	17.1	5.97	70	.282	.412	0	—	0	-8	-7	-1	-0.9
1991	Min-A	3	1	.750	15	3	0	0	0	47^1	38	27	5	0	36	43	14.1	4.75	90	.232	.370	0	—	0	-3	-2	-0	-0.2
1992	Min-A	0	0	—	6	0	0	0	0	11	12	4	1	1	5	13	14.7	3.27	124	.279	.367	0	—	0	1	1	1	0.1
1993	Cle-A	0	1	.000	5	5	0	0	0	18^1	19	15	5	0	11	7	14.7	6.38	68	.260	.357	0	—	0	-4	-4	0	-0.2
1998	Sea-A	3	1	.750	4	4	0	0	0	24^2	24	11	2	0	10	22	12.4	4.01	116	.255	.327	0	—	0	2	2	-0	0.2
1999	Sea-A	6	2	.750	25	7	0	0	0	72^2	50	31	9	0	32	68	10.2	3.10	153	.193	.282	0	—	0	14	14	0	1.3
2000	*Sea-A	9	7	.563	35	27	0	0	0	179	164	89	23	5	80	100	12.5	4.22	113	.243	.327	2	.400	1	14	12	-1	0.9
Total	7	21	17	.553	97	53	0	0	0	387^2	344	201	45	7	202	278	12.8	4.29	108	.239	.335	2	.400	1	15	14	-1	1.2

● GLENN ABBOTT Abbott, William Glenn b: 2/16/51, Little Rock, Ark. BR/TR, 6'6", 200 lbs. Deb: 7/29/73

YEAR	TM/L	W	L	PCT	G	GS	CG	SH	SV	IP	H	R	HR	HB	BB	SO	RAT	ERA	ERA+	OAV	OOB	BH	AVG	PB	PR	PR+	PD	TPI
1973	Oak-A	1	0	1.000	5	3	1	0	0	18^2	16	8	3	0	7	6	11.1	3.86	92	.225	.295	0	—	0	-0	-1	-0	-0.1
1974	Oak-A	5	7	.417	19	17	3	0	0	96	89	38	4	3	34	38	11.8	3.00	111	.247	.317	0	—	0	7	4	-0	0.4
1975	*Oak-A	5	5	.500	30	15	3	1	0	114^1	109	61	12	2	50	51	12.7	4.25	86	.253	.333	0	—	0	-6	-8	-1	-0.7
1976	Oak-A	2	4	.333	19	10	0	0	0	62^1	87	41	6	1	16	27	15.0	5.49	61	.333	.374	0	—	0	-14	-15	0	-1.3
1977	Sea-A	12	13	.480	36	34	7	0	0	204^1	212	111	32	12	56	100	12.3	4.45	93	.270	.328	0	—	0	-9	-7	-0	-0.8
1978	Sea-A	7	15	.318	29	28	8	1	0	155^1	191	99	22	2	44	67	13.7	5.27	72	.303	.350	0	—	0	-26	-25	0	-3.0
1979	Sea-A	4	10	.286	23	19	3	0	0	116^2	138	78	19	3	38	25	13.8	5.17	85	.301	.358	0	—	0	-12	-10	-0	-1.1
1980	Sea-A	12	12	.500	31	31	7	2	0	215	228	110	27	3	49	78	11.7	4.10	101	.272	.315	0	—	0	-1	1	2	0.3
1981	Sea-A	4	9	.308	22	20	1	0	0	130^1	127	64	14	0	28	35	10.7	3.94	98	.258	.298	0	—	0	-4	-1	-0	-0.1
1983	Sea-A	5	3	.625	14	14	2	0	0	82^1	103	46	9	4	15	38	13.3	4.59	93	.311	.349	0	—	0	-5	-3	-1	-0.3
	Det-A	2	1	.667	7	7	1	1	0	46^2	43	12	5	0	7	11	9.6	1.93	203	.244	.273	0	—	0	11	11	-1	0.6
	Yr	7	4	.636	21	21	3	1	0	129	146	58	14	4	22	49	12.0	3.63	114	.288	.323	0	—	0	6	7	-1	0.3
1984	Det-A	3	4	.429	13	8	1	0	0	44	62	39	9	2	8	8	14.7	5.93	66	.326	.360	0	—	0	-9	-10	0	-1.3
Total	11	62	83	.428	248	206	37	5	0	1286	1405	707	162	32	352	484	12.5	4.39	90	.280	.331	0	—	0	-68	-65	-0	-7.4

● AL ABER Aber, Albert Julius "Lefty" b: 7/31/27, Cleveland, Ohio d: 5/20/93, Garfield Heights, Ohio BL/TL, 6'2", 195 lbs. Deb: 9/15/50

YEAR	TM/L	W	L	PCT	G	GS	CG	SH	SV	IP	H	R	HR	HB	BB	SO	RAT	ERA	ERA+	OAV	OOB	BH	AVG	PB	PR	PR+	PD	TPI
1950	Cle-A	1	0	1.000	1	1	1	0	0	9	5	2	0	0	4	4	9.0	2.00	217	.167	.265	0	.000	0	3	2	-0	0.3
1953	Cle-A	1	1	.500	6	0	0	0	0	6	6	6	0	0	9	4	22.5	7.50	50	.240	.441	0	—	1	-2	-3	0	-0.4
	Det-A	4	3	.571	17	10	2	0	0	66^2	63	35	3	0	41	34	14.0	4.45	91	.260	.367	3	.130	-1	-3	-3	1	-0.3
	Yr	5	4	.556	23	10	2	0	0	72^2	69	41	3	0	50	38	14.7	4.71	86	.258	.375	3	.130	-1	-6	-5	1	-0.7
1954	Det-A	5	11	.313	32	18	4	0	3	124^2	121	63	8	3	40	54	11.8	3.97	93	.257	.320	5	.128	-1	-3	-4	1	-0.6
1955	Det-A	6	3	.667	39	1	0	0	3	80	86	32	9	0	28	37	12.8	3.37	114	.275	.334	1	.059	-2	5	4	1	0.4
1956	Det-A	4	4	.500	42	0	0	0	7	63	65	30	1	2	25	21	13.1	3.43	120	.270	.343	3	.300	1	5	5	0	0.7
1957	Det-A	3	3	.500	28	0	0	0	1	37	46	33	6	1	11	15	14.1	6.81	57	.315	.367	1	.125	-0	-12	-12	1	-1.8
	KC-A	0	0	—	3	0	0	0	0	3	6	4	2	0	2	0	24.0	12.00	33	.400	.471	1	1.000	1	-3	-3	0	-0.1
	Yr	3	3	.500	31	0	0	0	1	40	52	37	8	1	13	15	14.8	7.20	54	.323	.377	2	.222	0	-15	-15	1	-1.9
Total	6	24	25	.490	168	30	7	0	14	389^1	398	205	29	6	160	169	13.0	4.18	93	.269	.342	14	.140	-3	-11	-13	3	-1.8

● BILL ABERNATHIE Abernathie, William Edward b: 1/30/29, Torrance, Cal. BR/TR, 5'10", 190 lbs. Deb: 9/27/52

YEAR	TM/L	W	L	PCT	G	GS	CG	SH	SV	IP	H	R	HR	HB	BB	SO	RAT	ERA	ERA+	OAV	OOB	BH	AVG	PB	PR	PR+	PD	TPI
1952	Cle-A	0	0	—	1	0	0	0	1	2	4	3	1	0	1	0	22.5	13.50	25	.444	.500	0	.000	-0	-2	-2	-0	-0.3

● TED ABERNATHY Abernathy, Talmadge Lafayette b: 10/30/21, Mebane, N.C. BR/TL, 6'2", 210 lbs. Deb: 9/19/42

YEAR	TM/L	W	L	PCT	G	GS	CG	SH	SV	IP	H	R	HR	HB	BB	SO	RAT	ERA	ERA+	OAV	OOB	BH	AVG	PB	PR	PR+	PD	TPI
1942	Phi-A	0	0	—	1	0	0	0	0	2^2	2	3	0	0	3	1	16.9	10.13	37	.222	.417	0	—	0	-2	-2	0	0.0
1943	Phi-A	0	3	.000	5	2	1	0	0	14^2	24	22	0	0	13	10	22.7	12.89	26	.353	.457	1	.250	0	-16	-15	0	-2.3
1944	Phi-A	0	0	—	1	0	0	0	0	3	5	1	0	0	1	2	18.0	3.00	116	.417	.462	0	.000	-0	0	0	-0	0.0
Total	3	0	3	.000	7	2	1	0	0	20^1	31	26	0	0	17	13	21.2	11.07	31	.348	.453	1	.200	0	-17	-17	0	-2.3

YEAR	TM/L	W	L	PCT	G	GS	CG	SH	SV	IP	H	R	HR	HB	BB	SO	RAT	ERA	ERA+	OAV	OOB	BH	AVG	PB	PR	PR+	PD	TPI
● **TED ABERNATHY**		Abernathy, Theodore Wade b: 3/6/33, Stanley, N.C. BR/TR, 6'4", 215 lbs. Deb: 4/13/55																										
1955	Was-A	5	9	.357	40	14	3	2	0	119^1	136	87	9	7	67	79	15.8	5.96	64	.294	.392	4	.154	-1	-26	-29	1	-2.9
1956	Was-A	1	3	.250	5	4	2	0	0	30^1	35	16	2	1	10	18	13.6	4.15	104	.292	.351	2	.182	-0	0	1	2	0.2
1957	Was-A	2	10	.167	26	16	2	0	0	85	100	65	9	4	65	50	17.9	6.78	57	.314	.437	4	.167	0	-28	-26	1	-3.1
1960	Was-A	0	0	—	2	0	0	0	0	3	4	4	0	0	4	1	24.0	12.00	32	.308	.471	1	1.000	0	-3	-3	0	-0.1
1963	Cle-A	7	2	.778	43	0	0	0	12	59^1	54	25	3	0	29	47	12.6	2.88	126	.251	.340	2	.400	1	5	5	2	1.3
1964	Cle-A	2	6	.250	53	0	0	0	11	72^2	66	40	5	2	46	57	14.1	4.33	83	.247	.362	0	.000	-1	-6	-6	3	-0.6
1965	Chi-N	4	6	.400	**84**	0	0	0	**31**	136^1	113	49	7	5	56	104	11.5	2.57	143	.227	.311	3	.167	0	15	16	4	2.5
1966	Chi-N	1	3	.250	20	0	0	0	4	27^2	26	19	4	2	17	18	14.6	6.18	60	.255	.372	0	.000	-0	-8	-8	2	-1.1
	Atl-N	4	4	.500	38	0	0	0	4	65^1	58	34	5	0	36	42	12.9	3.86	94	.247	.347	2	.250	1	-2	-2	1	-0.1
	Yr	5	7	.417	58	0	0	0	8	93	84	53	9	2	53	60	13.5	4.55	80	.249	.355	2	.167	0	-10	-9	2	-1.2
1967	Cin-N	6	3	.667	**70**	0	0	0	**28**	106^1	63	19	1	5	41	88	9.2	1.27	295	.170	.261	1	.059	-1	**25**	**26**	2	**4.0**
1968	Cin-N	10	7	.588	**78**	0	0	0	13	134^2	111	43	9	4	55	64	11.4	2.47	128	.228	.312	0	.000	-1	8	10	3	1.8
1969	Chi-N	4	3	.571	56	0	0	0	3	85^1	75	38	8	1	42	55	12.4	3.16	127	.234	.325	2	.250	0	4	7	2	0.9
1970	Chi-N	0	0	—	11	0	0	0	1	9	9	2	0	1	5	2	15.0	2.00	225	.281	.395	0	—	0	2	2	0	0.1
	StL-N	1	0	1.000	11	0	0	0	1	18^1	15	6	0	3	12	8	14.7	2.95	140	.246	.395	0	.000	-0	2	2	1	0.2
	Yr	1	0	1.000	22	0	0	0	2	27^1	24	8	0	4	17	10	14.8	2.63	161	.258	.395	0	.000	-0	4	5	1	0.3
	KC-A	9	3	.750	36	0	0	0	12	55^2	41	23	3	1	38	49	12.9	2.59	145	.209	.340	3	.214	0	7	7	0	1.6
1971	KC-A	4	6	.400	63	0	0	0	23	81	60	28	3	6	50	55	12.9	2.56	134	.210	.339	1	.077	-1	8	8	2	1.6
1972	KC-A	3	4	.429	45	0	0	0	5	58^1	44	15	2	3	19	28	10.2	1.70	179	.210	.284	0	.000	-1	9	9	1	1.3
Total	14	63	69	.477	681	34	7	2	148	1147^2	1010	513	70	45	592	765	12.9	3.46	106	.241	.341	25	.138	-4	12	25	27	7.6
● **WOODY ABERNATHY**		Abernathy, Virgil Woodrow b: 2/1/15, Forest City, N.C. d: 12/5/94, Louisville, Ky. BL/TL, 6', 170 lbs. Deb: 7/28/46																										
1946	NY-N	1	1	.500	15	1	0	0	1	40	32	16	5	0	10	6	9.4	3.37	102	.232	.284	0	.000	-1	0	0	-1	-0.2
1947	NY-N	0	0	—	1	0	0	0	0	2	4	3	0	0	1	0	22.5	9.00	45	.400	.455	0	—	0	-1	-1	-0	-0.1
Total	2	1	1	.500	16	1	0	0	1	42	36	19	5	0	11	6	10.1	3.64	95	.243	.296	0	.000	-1	-1	-1	-1	-0.3
● **HARRY ABLES**		Ables, Harry Terrell "Hans" b: 10/4/1884, Terrell, Tex. d: 2/8/51, San Antonio, Tex. BR/TL, 6'2.5", 200 lbs. Deb: 9/4/05																										
1905	StL-A	0	3	.000	6	3	1	0	0	30^2	37	22	0	0	13	11	14.7	3.82	67	.301	.368	0	.000	-1	-4	-5	-1	-0.6
1909	Cle-A	1	1	.500	5	3	3	0	0	29^2	26	14	1	1	10	24	11.2	2.12	120	.226	.294	0	.000	-1	1	1	-1	-0.2
1911	NY-A	0	1	.000	3	2	0	0	0	11	16	15	0	0	7	6	18.8	9.82	37	.333	.418	0	.000	-1	-8	-7	-0	-0.6
Total	3	1	5	.167	14	8	4	0	0	71^1	79	51	1	1	30	41	13.9	4.04	67	.276	.347	0	.000	-4	-11	-10	-2	-1.4
● **GEORGE ABRAMS**		Abrams, George Allen b: 11/9/1899, Seattle, Wash. d: 12/5/86, Clearwater, Fla. BR/TR, 5'9", 170 lbs. Deb: 4/19/23																										
1923	Cin-N	0	0	—	3	0	0	0	0	4^2	10	5	0	1	3	1	27.0	9.64	40	.500	.583	1	1.000	0	-3	-3	-0	-0.1
● **JOHNNY ABREGO**		Abrego, Johnny Ray b: 7/4/62, Corpus Christi, Tex BR/TR, 6', 185 lbs. Deb: 9/4/85																										
1985	Chi-N	1	1	.500	6	5	0	0	0	24	32	18	3	0	12	13	16.5	6.38	63	.352	.427	0	.000	-1	-7	-6	0	-0.5
● **JUAN ACEVEDO**		Acevedo, Juan Carlos b: 5/5/70, Juarez, Mexico BR/TR, 6'2", 195 lbs. Deb: 4/30/95																										
1995	Col-N	4	6	.400	17	11	0	0	0	65^2	82	53	15	6	20	40	14.8	6.44	84	.317	.379	1	.056	-2	-16	-6	-1	-1.0
1997	NY-N	3	1	.750	25	2	0	0	0	47^2	52	24	6	4	22	33	14.7	3.59	113	.286	.375	0	.000	-1	3	2	0	0.2
1998	StL-N	8	3	.727	50	9	0	0	15	98^1	83	30	7	4	29	56	10.6	2.56	164	.236	.301	3	.176	0	18	18	0	2.4
1999	StL-N	6	8	.429	50	12	0	0	4	102^1	115	71	17	4	48	52	14.7	5.89	78	.291	.374	1	.050	-2	-15	-15	-2	-2.1
2000	Mil-N	3	7	.300	62	0	0	0	0	82^2	77	38	11	1	31	51	11.9	3.81	120	.246	.316	0	.000	0	8	7	-1	0.7
Total	5	24	25	.490	204	34	0	0	19	396^2	409	216	56	19	150	232	13.1	4.45	103	.272	.346	5	.081	-3	-2	5	-2	0.2
● **JIM ACKER**		Acker, James Justin b: 9/24/58, Freer, Tex. BR/TR, 6'2", 212 lbs. Deb: 4/7/83																										
1983	Tor-A	5	1	.833	38	5	0	0	1	97^2	103	52	7	8	38	44	13.7	4.33	100	.273	.352	0	—	0	-3	-0	1	0.1
1984	Tor-A	3	5	.375	32	3	0	0	1	72	79	39	3	6	25	33	13.8	4.38	94	.286	.358	0	—	0	-3	-2	-0	-0.2
1985	*Tor-A	7	2	.778	61	0	0	0	10	86^1	86	35	7	3	43	42	13.8	3.23	130	.268	.360	0	—	0	9	9	1	1.2
1986	Tor-A	2	4	.333	23	5	0	0	0	60	63	34	6	2	22	32	13.1	4.35	97	.281	.351	0	—	0	-1	-1	1	0.0
	Atl-N	3	8	.273	21	14	0	0	0	95	100	47	7	1	26	37	12.0	3.79	105	.274	.324	3	.107	-1	-1	2	1	0.2
1987	Atl-N	4	9	.308	68	0	0	0	14	114^2	109	57	11	4	51	68	12.9	4.16	105	.253	.338	3	.214	0	-1	2	1	0.4
1988	Atl-N	0	4	.000	21	1	0	0	0	42	45	26	6	1	14	25	12.9	4.71	78	.280	.341	2	.400	1	-6	-5	0	-0.3
1989	Atl-N	0	6	.000	59	0	0	0	2	97^2	84	29	5	1	20	68	9.7	2.67	137	.237	.280	1	.143	-0	9	10	1	0.7
	*Tor-A	2	1	.667	14	0	0	0	0	28^1	24	7	1	1	12	24	11.8	1.59	238	.235	.322	0	—	0	7	7	1	0.8
1990	Tor-A	4	4	.500	59	0	0	0	1	91^2	103	49	9	3	30	54	13.4	3.83	103	.281	.341	0	—	0	1	1	1	0.2
1991	*Tor-A	3	5	.375	54	4	0	0	1	88^1	77	53	16	2	36	44	11.7	5.20	81	.238	.318	0	—	0	-11	-9	0	-0.8
1992	Sea-A	0	0	—	17	0	0	0	0	30^2	45	19	4	0	12	11	16.7	5.28	75	.338	.393	0	—	0	-5	-4	-0	-0.2
Total	10	33	49	.402	467	32	0	0	30	904^1	918	447	82	32	329	482	12.7	3.97	103	.267	.337	9	.167	0	-4	10	8	2.1
● **TOM ACKER**		Acker, Thomas James b: 3/7/30, Paterson, N.J. BR/TR, 6'4", 215 lbs. Deb: 4/20/56																										
1956	Cin-N	4	3	.571	29	7	1	1	1	83^2	60	23	7	2	29	54	9.8	2.37	168	.201	.277	1	.053	-1	13	14	1	1.1
1957	Cin-N	10	5	.667	49	6	1	0	4	108^2	122	63	16	8	41	67	14.2	4.97	83	.293	.368	1	.053	-1	-13	-10	-0	-1.4
1958	Cin-N	4	3	.571	38	10	3	0	1	124^2	126	64	10	3	43	90	12.4	4.55	91	.266	.331	2	.067	-1	-8	-5	-2	-0.6
1959	Cin-N	1	2	.333	37	0	0	0	2	63^1	57	31	10	4	37	45	13.9	4.12	98	.246	.359	1	.111	-0	-1	-0	-1	-0.2
Total	4	19	13	.594	153	23	5	1	8	380^1	365	181	43	17	150	256	12.6	4.12	99	.257	.335	5	.065	-3	-10	-1	-2	-1.1
● **FRITZ ACKLEY**		Ackley, Florian Frederick b: 4/10/37, Hayward, Wis. BL/TR, 6'1.5", 202 lbs. Deb: 9/21/63																										
1963	Chi-A	1	0	1.000	2	2	0	0	0	13	7	4	2	0	7	11	9.7	2.08	169	.167	.286	1	.200	0	2	2	0	0.2
1964	Chi-A	0	0	—	3	2	0	0	0	6^1	10	6	2	0	4	6	19.9	8.53	41	.345	.424	1	1.000	1	-3	-4	0	-0.1
Total	2	1	0	1.000	5	4	0	0	0	19^1	17	10	4	0	11	17	13.0	4.19	83	.239	.341	2	.333	1	-1	-2	1	0.1
● **CY ACOSTA**		Acosta, Cecilio (Miranda) b: 11/22/46, Sabino, Mexico BR/TR, 5'10", 165 lbs. Deb: 6/4/72																										
1972	Chi-A	3	0	1.000	26	0	0	0	5	34^2	25	6	2	0	17	28	10.9	1.56	201	.210	.309	0	.000	-0	6	6	-1	0.7
1973	Chi-A	10	6	.625	48	0	0	0	18	97	66	30	8	7	39	60	10.4	2.23	178	.193	.289	0	.000	-0	17	18	-1	3.5
1974	Chi-A	0	3	.000	27	0	0	0	3	45^2	43	22	3	5	18	19	13.0	3.74	100	.256	.346	0	.000	-0	-1	-0	0	0.0
1975	Phi-N	0	0	—	6	0	0	0	1	8^2	9	7	2	0	3	2	12.5	6.23	60	.273	.333	0	—	0	-3	-2	-0	-0.2
Total	4	13	9	.591	107	0	0	0	27	186	143	65	15	12	77	109	11.2	2.66	141	.216	.309	0	.000	-1	20	22	-2	4.0
● **ED ACOSTA**		Acosta, Eduardo Elixbet b: 3/9/44, Boquete, Panama BB/TR, 6'5", 215 lbs. Deb: 9/7/70																										
1970	Pit-N	0	0	—	3	0	0	0	1	2^2	5	4	1	1	2	1	27.0	13.50	29	.417	.533	0	—	0	-3	-3	-0	-0.2
1971	SD-N	3	3	.500	8	6	3	1	0	46	43	18	4	0	7	16	9.8	2.74	121	.246	.275	0	.000	-2	4	3	-1	0.1
1972	SD-N	3	6	.333	46	2	0	0	0	89	105	49	7	3	30	53	14.0	4.45	74	.302	.362	1	.083	-0	-10	-12	-1	-1.3
Total	3	6	9	.400	57	8	3	1	1	137^2	153	71	12	4	39	70	12.8	4.05	82	.286	.339	1	.034	-2	-9	-12	-1	-1.4
● **JOSE ACOSTA**		Acosta, Jose "Acostica" b: 3/4/1891, Havana, Cuba d: 11/16/77, Havana, Cuba BR/TR, 5'6", 134 lbs. Deb: 7/28/20 F																										
1920	Was-A	5	4	.556	17	5	4	1	1	82^2	92	40	1	0	26	9	12.8	4.03	93	.290	.344	6	.240	1	-2	-3	-3	-0.4
1921	Was-A	5	4	.556	33	7	2	0	3	115^2	148	65	4	0	36	30	14.3	4.36	94	.317	.366	2	.067	-2	-1	-3	-1	-0.5
1922	Chi-A	0	2	.000	5	1	0	0	0	15	25	14	4	0	6	6	18.6	8.40	48	.417	.470	1	.200	0	-7	-7	-0	-0.8
Total	3	10	10	.500	55	13	6	1	4	213^1	265	119	9	0	68	45	14.0	4.51	88	.314	.365	9	.150	-1	-10	-13	-4	-1.7
● **MARK ACRE**		Acre, Mark Robert b: 9/16/68, Concord, Cal. BR/TR, 6'8", 235 lbs. Deb: 5/13/94																										
1994	Oak-A	5	1	.833	34	0	0	0	0	34^1	24	13	4	1	23	21	12.6	3.41	130	.202	.336	0	—	0	5	4	-1	0.6
1995	Oak-A	1	2	.333	43	0	0	0	0	52	52	35	7	2	28	47	14.2	5.71	78	.256	.352	0	—	0	-6	-8	-1	-0.4
1996	Oak-A	1	3	.250	22	0	0	0	2	25	38	17	4	2	9	18	17.6	6.12	81	.339	.398	0	—	0	-3	-3	-0	-0.5
1997	Oak-A	2	0	1.000	15	0	0	0	0	15^2	21	10	1	0	8	12	16.7	5.74	79	.318	.392	0	—	0	-2	-2	-0	-0.2
Total	4	9	6	.600	114	0	0	0	2	127	135	75	16	5	68	98	14.7	5.17	88	.270	.363	0	—	0	-6	-9	-2	-0.5
● **ACE ADAMS**		Adams, Ace Townsend b: 3/2/12, Willows, Cal. BR/TR, 5'10.5", 182 lbs. Deb: 4/15/41																										
1941	NY-N	4	1	.800	38	0	0	0	1	71	84	43	3	1	35	18	15.2	4.82	77	.304	.385	1	.083	-1	-9	-9	-1	-0.8

YEAR	TM/L	W	L	PCT	G	GS	CG	SH	SV	IP	H	R	HR	HB	BB	SO	RAT	ERA	ERA+	OAV	OOB	BH	AVG	PB	PR	PR+	PD	TPI
1942	NY-N	7	4	.636	**61**	0	0	0	11	88	69	23	1	0	31	33	10.2	1.84	183	.223	.293	1	.100	-1	**14**	**15**	0	2.2
1943	NY-N☆	11	7	.611	**70**	3	1	0	9	140^1	121	50	5	1	55	46	11.4	2.82	122	.236	.311	4	.125	-1	9	10	-1	1.1
1944	NY-N	8	11	.421	**65**	4	1	0	**13**	137^2	149	71	8	4	58	32	13.8	4.25	86	.279	.354	3	.103	-2	-10	-9	-2	-1.6
1945	NY-N	11	9	.550	65	0	0	0	**15**	113	109	55	7	2	44	39	12.3	3.42	114	.252	.324	3	.188	0	5	6	1	1.3
1946	NY-N	0	1	.000	3	0	0	0	0	2^2	9	5	2	0	1	3	33.8	16.88	20	.500	.526	0	—	0	-4	-4	0	-0.7
Total	6	41	33	.554	302	7	2	0	49	552^2	541	247	26	8	224	171	12.6	3.47	104	.260	.334	12	.121	-4	5	9	-2	1.5

● BABE ADAMS Adams, Charles Benjamin b: 5/18/1882, Tipton, Ind. d: 7/27/68, Silver Spring, Md BL/TR, 5'11.5", 185 lbs. Deb: 4/18/06

YEAR	TM/L	W	L	PCT	G	GS	CG	SH	SV	IP	H	R	HR	HB	BB	SO	RAT	ERA	ERA+	OAV	OOB	BH	AVG	PB	PR	PR+	PD	TPI
1906	StL-N	0	1	.000	1	1	0	0	0	4	9	8	0	0	2	0	24.8	13.50	19	.474	.524	0	.000	-0	-5	-5	0	-0.7
1907	Pit-N	0	2	.000	4	3	1	0	0	22	40	25	1	3	3	11	18.8	6.95	35	.408	.442	2	.286	0	-11	-11	0	-0.8
1909	*Pit-N	12	3	.800	25	12	7	3	2	130	88	25	0	3	23	65	7.9	1.11	246	.196	.240	2	.051	-3	22	22	-1	2.4
1910	Pit-N	18	9	.667	34	30	16	3	0	245	217	95	4	6	60	101	10.4	2.24	138	.240	.291	16	.193	1	22	23	-5	2.0
1911	Pit-N	22	12	.647	40	37	24	6	0	293^1	253	97	5	8	42	133	**9.3**	2.33	147	.237	**.271**	26	.252	4	35	36	-8	3.5
1912	Pit-N	11	8	.579	28	20	11	2	0	170^1	169	73	4	3	35	63	10.9	2.91	112	.262	.303	12	.226	4	10	7	-2	0.9
1913	Pit-N	21	10	.677	43	37	24	4	0	313^2	271	94	8	0	49	144	9.2	2.15	140	.235	.267	33	.289	9	37	32	-1	3.9
1914	Pit-N	13	16	.448	40	35	19	3	1	283	253	97	5	7	39	91	9.5	2.51	105	.244	**.276**	16	.165	1	9	5	-2	0.3
1915	Pit-N	14	14	.500	40	30	17	2	2	245	229	90	6	2	34	62	9.7	2.87	95	.252	.280	12	.141	-2	-3	-4	-0	-0.7
1916	Pit-N	2	9	.182	16	10	4	1	0	72^1	91	51	2	3	12	22	13.2	5.72	47	.320	.355	6	.273	2	-25	-24	0	-3.1
1918	Pit-N	1	1	.500	3	3	2	0	0	22^2	15	4	0	0	4	6	7.5	1.19	241	.197	.237	3	.333	1	4	4	-1	0.4
1919	Pit-N	17	10	.630	34	29	23	6	1	263^1	213	66	1	3	23	92	**8.2**	1.98	152	.220	**.241**	17	.185	-0	27	29	-4	2.6
1920	Pit-N	17	13	.567	35	33	19	**8**	2	263	240	83	6	1	18	84	**8.9**	2.16	149	.244	**.259**	13	.146	-5	29	30	-2	2.7
1921	Pit-N	14	5	.737	25	20	11	2	0	160	155	57	4	0	18	55	**9.7**	2.64	**145**	.251	**.272**	16	.254	3	20	21	-2	2.5
1922	Pit-N	8	11	.421	27	19	12	4	0	171^1	191	77	1	4	15	39	11.0	3.57	114	.287	.307	16	.286	4	10	10	1	1.4
1923	Pit-N	13	7	.650	26	22	11	0	1	158^2	196	83	8	1	25	38	12.6	4.42	91	.309	.336	15	.273	5	-7	-7	-2	-0.7
1924	Pit-N	3	1	.750	9	3	2	0	0	39^2	31	9	1	0	3	5	7.7	1.13	338	.209	.225	2	.182	-0	12	12	-1	1.0
1925	*Pit-N	6	5	.545	33	10	3	0	3	101^1	129	67	7	3	17	18	13.2	5.42	82	.306	.338	7	.226	0	-13	-10	-2	-1.1
1926	Pit-N	2	3	.400	19	0	0	0	3	36^2	51	32	5	0	8	7	14.5	6.14	64	.347	.381	2	.222	-0	-9	-9	-1	-1.3
Total	19	194	140	.581	482	354	206	44	15	2995^1	2841	1133	68	47	430	1036	10.0	2.76	118	.253	.284	216	.212	24	161	161	-33	15.2

● RED ADAMS Adams, Charles Dwight b: 10/7/21, Parlier, Cal. BR/TR, 6', 185 lbs. Deb: 5/5/46 C

YEAR	TM/L	W	L	PCT	G	GS	CG	SH	SV	IP	H	R	HR	HB	BB	SO	RAT	ERA	ERA+	OAV	OOB	BH	AVG	PB	PR	PR+	PD	TPI
1946	Chi-N	0	1	.000	8	0	0	0	0	12	18	12	1	0	7	8	18.8	8.25	40	.353	.431	0	.000	-0	-6	-7	1	-0.5

● DAN ADAMS Adams, Daniel Leslie "Rube" b: 6/19/1887, St.Louis, Mo. d: 10/6/64, St.Louis, Mo. BR/TR, 5'11.5", 165 lbs. Deb: 5/22/14

YEAR	TM/L	W	L	PCT	G	GS	CG	SH	SV	IP	H	R	HR	HB	BB	SO	RAT	ERA	ERA+	OAV	OOB	BH	AVG	PB	PR	PR+	PD	TPI
1914	KC-F	4	9	.308	36	14	6	0	3	136	141	67	3	7	52	38	13.2	3.51	79	.273	.347	7	.152	-2	-9	-11	-1	-1.3
1915	KC-F	0	2	.000	11	2	0	0	0	35	41	20	2	1	13	16	14.1	4.63	57	.301	.367	1	.111	-1	-7	-8	0	-0.5
Total	2	4	11	.267	47	16	6	0	3	171	182	87	5	8	65	54	13.4	3.74	74	.279	.351	8	.145	-2	-17	-20	-1	-1.8

● WILLIE ADAMS Adams, James Irvin b: 9/27/1890, Clearfield, Pa. d: 6/18/37, Albany, N.Y. BR/TR, 6'4", 180 lbs. Deb: 6/30/12

YEAR	TM/L	W	L	PCT	G	GS	CG	SH	SV	IP	H	R	HR	HB	BB	SO	RAT	ERA	ERA+	OAV	OOB	BH	AVG	PB	PR	PR+	PD	TPI
1912	StL-A	2	3	.400	13	5	0	0	0	46^1	50	32	0	2	19	16	13.8	3.88	85	.284	.360	0	.000	-2	-3	-3	-1	-0.6
1913	StL-A	0	0	—	4	0	0	0	0	9	12	14	1	3	4	5	19.0	10.00	29	.286	.388	0	.000	-0	-7	-7	-0	-0.4
1914	Pit-F	1	1	.500	15	2	1	0	2	55^1	70	29	4	1	22	14	15.1	3.74	77	.326	.391	1	.067	-1	-5	-5	-1	-0.5
1918	Phi-A	5	12	.294	32	14	7	0	0	169	164	95	2	12	97	39	14.5	4.42	66	.272	.383	8	.140	-3	-31	-26	1	-2.8
1919	Phi-A	0	0	—	1	0	0	0	0	4^2	7	2	1	1	2	0	19.3	3.86	89	.389	.476	0	.000	-0	-0	-0	-0	-0.1
Total	5	8	16	.333	65	21	8	0	2	284^1	303	172	8	19	144	74	14.8	4.37	69	.287	.383	9	.102	-6	-46	-42	-2	-4.4

● JOE ADAMS Adams, Joseph Edward b: 10/28/1877, Cowden, Ill. d: 10/8/52, Montgomery City, Mo BR/TL, 6', 190 lbs. Deb: 4/26/02

YEAR	TM/L	W	L	PCT	G	GS	CG	SH	SV	IP	H	R	HR	HB	BB	SO	RAT	ERA	ERA+	OAV	OOB	BH	AVG	PB	PR	PR+	PD	TPI
1902	StL-N	0	0	—	1	0	0	0	0	4	9	6	0	1	2	0	27.0	9.00	30	.450	.522	0	.000	-0	-3	-3	1	-0.1

● KARL ADAMS Adams, Karl Tutwiler "Rebel" b: 8/11/1891, Columbus, Ga. d: 9/17/67, Everett, Wash. BR/TR, 6'2", 170 lbs. Deb: 4/19/14

YEAR	TM/L	W	L	PCT	G	GS	CG	SH	SV	IP	H	R	HR	HB	BB	SO	RAT	ERA	ERA+	OAV	OOB	BH	AVG	PB	PR	PR+	PD	TPI
1914	Cin-N	0	0	—	4	0	0	0	0	8	14	10	0	0	5	5	21.4	9.00	33	.424	.500	1	.500	0	-6	-5	0	-0.2
1915	Chi-N	1	9	.100	26	12	3	0	0	107	105	62	5	2	43	57	12.6	4.71	59	.267	.342	0	.000	-4	-23	-23	0	-2.4
Total	2	1	9	.100	30	12	3	0	0	115	119	72	5	2	48	62	13.2	5.01	56	.279	.355	1	.031	-4	-29	-28	0	-2.6

● RICK ADAMS Adams, Reuben Alexander b: 12/23/1878, Paris, Tex. d: 3/10/55, Paris, Tex. BL/TL, 6', 165 lbs. Deb: 7/13/05

YEAR	TM/L	W	L	PCT	G	GS	CG	SH	SV	IP	H	R	HR	HB	BB	SO	RAT	ERA	ERA+	OAV	OOB	BH	AVG	PB	PR	PR+	PD	TPI
1905	Was-A	2	5	.286	11	6	3	1	0	62^2	63	30	1	8	24	25	13.6	3.59	74	.264	.351	4	.174	0	-7	-7	0	-0.6

● BOB ADAMS Adams, Robert Andrew b: 1/20/07, Birmingham, Ala. d: 3/6/70, Jacksonville, Fla. BR/TR, 6'0.5", 165 lbs. Deb: 9/27/31

YEAR	TM/L	W	L	PCT	G	GS	CG	SH	SV	IP	H	R	HR	HB	BB	SO	RAT	ERA	ERA+	OAV	OOB	BH	AVG	PB	PR	PR+	PD	TPI
1931	Phi-N	0	1	.000	1	1	0	0	0	6	14	10	0	0	1	3	22.5	9.00	47	.424	.441	0	.000	-0	-3	-3	-0	-0.4
1932	Phi-N	0	0	—	4	0	0	0	0	6	7	1	0	0	2	2	13.5	1.50	294	.318	.375	0	—	0	2	2	0	0.1
Total	2	0	1	.000	5	1	0	0	0	12	21	11	0	0	3	5	18.0	5.25	82	.382	.414	0	.000	-0	-2	-1	0	-0.3

● BOB ADAMS Adams, Robert Burdette b: 7/24/01, Holyoke, Mass. d: 10/17/96, Lemoyne, Pa. BR/TR, 5'11", 168 lbs. Deb: 9/22/25

YEAR	TM/L	W	L	PCT	G	GS	CG	SH	SV	IP	H	R	HR	HB	BB	SO	RAT	ERA	ERA+	OAV	OOB	BH	AVG	PB	PR	PR+	PD	TPI
1925	Bos-A	0	0	—	2	0	0	0	0	5^2	10	5	1	0	3	1	20.6	7.94	57	.417	.481	1	.333	0	-2	-2	1	0.0

● TERRY ADAMS Adams, Terry Wayne b: 3/6/73, Mobile, Ala. BR/TR, 6'3", 205 lbs. Deb: 8/10/95

YEAR	TM/L	W	L	PCT	G	GS	CG	SH	SV	IP	H	R	HR	HB	BB	SO	RAT	ERA	ERA+	OAV	OOB	BH	AVG	PB	PR	PR+	PD	TPI
1995	Chi-N	1	1	.500	18	0	0	0	1	18	22	15	0	0	10	15	16.0	6.50	63	.289	.372	0	—	0	-5	-5	-0	-0.5
1996	Chi-N	3	6	.333	69	0	0	0	4	101	84	36	6	1	49	78	11.9	2.94	148	.231	.324	0	.000	-0	14	15	-0	1.3
1997	Chi-N	2	9	.182	74	0	0	0	18	74	91	43	3	1	40	64	16.1	4.62	93	.306	.391	0	.000	-0	-3	-3	-0	-0.5
1998	Chi-N	7	7	.500	63	0	0	0	1	72^2	72	39	7	1	41	73	14.1	4.33	102	.255	.352	0	.000	0	-1	1	0	0.1
1999	Chi-N	6	3	.667	52	0	0	0	13	65	60	33	9	0	28	57	12.2	4.02	112	.245	.322	0	.000	-0	4	4	0	0.5
2000	LA-N	6	9	.400	66	0	0	0	2	84^1	80	42	6	0	39	56	12.7	3.52	125	.245	.325	0	.000	-0	10	9	3	1.6
Total	6	25	35	.417	342	0	0	0	39	415	409	208	31	3	207	343	13.4	3.93	112	.257	.344	0	.000	-1	20	21	3	2.5

● WILLIE ADAMS Adams, William Edward b: 10/8/72, Gallup, N.Mex. BR/TR, 6'7", 215 lbs. Deb: 6/11/96

YEAR	TM/L	W	L	PCT	G	GS	CG	SH	SV	IP	H	R	HR	HB	BB	SO	RAT	ERA	ERA+	OAV	OOB	BH	AVG	PB	PR	PR+	PD	TPI
1996	Oak-A	3	4	.429	12	12	1	1	0	76^1	76	39	11	5	23	68	12.3	4.01	123	.257	.321	0	—	0	8	8	-1	0.6
1997	Oak-A	3	5	.375	13	12	0	0	0	58^1	73	53	9	4	32	37	16.8	8.18	55	.307	.398	0	—	0	-23	-24	0	-2.5
Total	2	6	9	.400	25	24	1	1	0	134^2	149	92	20	9	55	105	14.2	5.81	82	.279	.356	0	—	0	-15	-16	-0	-1.9

● JOEL ADAMSON Adamson, Joel Lee b: 7/2/71, Lakewood, Cal. BL/TL, 6'4", 185 lbs. Deb: 4/10/96

YEAR	TM/L	W	L	PCT	G	GS	CG	SH	SV	IP	H	R	HR	HB	BB	SO	RAT	ERA	ERA+	OAV	OOB	BH	AVG	PB	PR	PR+	PD	TPI
1996	Fla-N	0	0	—	9	0	0	0	0	11	18	9	1	1	7	7	21.3	7.36	55	.400	.491	0	—	0	-4	-4	0	-0.2
1997	Mil-A	5	3	.625	30	6	0	0	0	76^1	78	36	13	5	19	56	12.0	3.54	131	.265	.321	0	.000	-0	9	9	0	0.8
1998	Ari-N	0	3	.000	5	5	0	0	0	23	25	21	5	3	11	14	15.3	8.22	51	.284	.382	3	.429	1	-10	-10	-0	-1.0
Total	3	5	6	.455	44	11	0	0	0	110^1	121	66	19	9	37	77	13.6	4.89	92	.283	.353	3	.300	1	-5	-5	0	-0.4

● MIKE ADAMSON Adamson, John Michael b: 9/13/47, San Diego, Cal. BR/TR, 6'2", 185 lbs. Deb: 7/1/67

YEAR	TM/L	W	L	PCT	G	GS	CG	SH	SV	IP	H	R	HR	HB	BB	SO	RAT	ERA	ERA+	OAV	OOB	BH	AVG	PB	PR	PR+	PD	TPI
1967	Bal-A	0	1	.000	3	2	0	0	0	9^2	9	9	1	0	12	8	19.6	8.38	38	.257	.447	1	.500	1	-6	-6	-0	-0.5
1968	Bal-A	0	2	.000	2	2	0	0	0	7^2	9	9	2	0	4	4	15.3	9.39	31	.281	.361	1	.333	0	-5	-6	-0	-1.0
1969	Bal-A	0	1	.000	6	0	0	0	0	8	10	4	0	0	6	2	18.0	4.50	79	.357	.471	0	.000	-0	-1	-1	1	-0.1
Total	3	0	4	.000	11	4	0	0	0	25^1	28	22	3	0	22	14	17.8	7.46	43	.295	.427	2	.333	1	-12	-12	-0	-1.6

● GRADY ADKINS Adkins, Grady Emmett "Butcher Boy" b: 6/29/1897, Jacksonville, Ark d: 3/31/66, Little Rock, Ark. BR/TR, 5'11", 175 lbs. Deb: 4/13/28

YEAR	TM/L	W	L	PCT	G	GS	CG	SH	SV	IP	H	R	HR	HB	BB	SO	RAT	ERA	ERA+	OAV	OOB	BH	AVG	PB	PR	PR+	PD	TPI
1928	Chi-A	10	16	.385	36	27	14	0	1	224^2	235	113	12	6	89	54	13.2	3.73	109	.278	.351	10	.143	-3	8	8	-1	0.4
1929	Chi-A	2	11	.154	31	15	5	0	0	138^1	168	98	12	1	67	24	15.4	5.33	80	.303	.379	11	.239	3	-17	-16	2	-0.8
Total	2	12	27	.308	67	42	19	0	1	363	403	211	24	7	156	78	14.0	4.34	95	.288	.363	21	.181	-1	-9	-8	1	-0.4

● DEWEY ADKINS Adkins, John Dewey b: 5/11/18, Norcatur, Kan. d: 12/26/98, Santa Monica, Cal. BR/TR, 6'2", 195 lbs. Deb: 9/19/42

YEAR	TM/L	W	L	PCT	G	GS	CG	SH	SV	IP	H	R	HR	HB	BB	SO	RAT	ERA	ERA+	OAV	OOB	BH	AVG	PB	PR	PR+	PD	TPI
1942	Was-A	0	0	—	1	1	0	0	0	6^1	7	8	0	0	6	3	18.5	9.95	37	.259	.394	1	.500	0	-4	-4	-0	-0.2
1943	Was-A	0	0	—	7	0	0	0	0	10^1	9	3	0	0	5	1	12.2	2.61	123	.250	.341	0	—	0	1	1	-1	0.0
1949	Chi-N	2	4	.333	30	5	1	0	0	82^1	98	58	10	0	39	43	15.0	5.68	71	.298	.372	4	.200	1	-15	-15	1	-0.7
Total	3	2	4	.333	38	6	1	0	0	99	114	69	10	0	50	47	14.9	5.64	70	.291	.371	5	.227	1	-19	-19	0	-0.9

● DOC ADKINS Adkins, Merle Theron b: 8/5/1872, Troy, Wis. d: 2/21/34, Durham, N.C. BR/TR, 5'10.5", 220 lbs. Deb: 6/24/02

YEAR	TM/L	W	L	PCT	G	GS	CG	SH	SV	IP	H	R	HR	HB	BB	SO	RAT	ERA	ERA+	OAV	OOB	BH	AVG	PB	PR	PR+	PD	TPI
1902	Bos-A	1	1	.500	4	2	1	0	0	20	30	20	2	0	7	3	16.6	4.05	88	.345	.394	2	.222	-0	-1	-1	0	-0.1

YEAR TM/L		W	L	PCT	G	GS	CG	SH	SV	IP	H	R	HR	HB	BB	SO	RAT	ERA	ERA+	OAV	OOB	BH	AVG	PB	PR	PR+	PD	TPI
1903	NY-A	0	0	—	2	1	0	0	1	7	10	8	0	1	5	0	20.6	7.71	40	.333	.444	0	.000	-0	-4	-3	-1	-0.3
Total	2	1	1	.500	6	3	1	0	1	27	40	28	2	1	12	3	17.7	5.00	69	.342	.408	2	.167	-1	-5	-5	-0	-0.4
● STEVE ADKINS	Adkins, Steven Thomas b: 10/26/64, Chicago, Ill. BR/TL, 6'6", 210 lbs. Deb: 9/12/90																											
1990	NY-A	1	2	.333	5	5	0	0	0	24	19	18	4	0	29	14	18.0	6.38	62	.226	.425	0	—	0	-7	-6	-0	-0.7
● JUAN AGOSTO	Agosto, Juan Roberto (Gonzalez) b: 2/23/58, Rio Piedras, P.R. BL/TL, 6'2", 190 lbs. Deb: 9/7/81																											
1981	Chi-A	0	0	—	2	0	0	0	0	5^2	5	3	1	1	0	3	9.5	4.76	75	.238	.273	0	—	0	-1	-1	0	0.0
1982	Chi-A	0	0	—	1	0	0	0	0	2	7	4	0	0	0	1	31.5	18.00	22	.538	.538	0	—	0	-3	-3	0	-0.1
1983	*Chi-A	2	2	.500	39	0	0	0	7	41^2	41	20	2	1	11	29	11.4	4.10	102	.283	.338	0	—	0	-0	0	0	0.1
1984	Chi-A	2	1	.667	49	0	0	0	7	55^1	54	20	2	3	34	26	14.8	3.09	135	.270	.384	0	—	0	6	6	2	0.7
1985	Chi-A	4	3	.571	54	0	0	0	1	60^1	45	27	3	3	23	39	10.6	3.58	121	.210	.296	0	—	0	4	5	2	0.7
1986	Chi-A	0	2	.000	9	0	0	0	0	4^2	6	5	0	0	4	3	19.3	7.71	56	.300	.417	0	—	0	-2	-2	-0	-0.3
	Min-A	1	2	.333	17	1	0	0	1	20^1	43	25	1	2	14	9	26.1	8.85	49	.443	.522	0	—	0	-11	-10	0	-1.3
	Yr	1	4	.200	26	1	0	0	1	25	49	30	1	2	18	12	24.8	8.64	50	.419	.504	0	—	0	-12	-12	0	-1.6
1987	Hou-N	1	1	.500	27	0	0	0	2	27^1	26	12	1	0	10	6	11.9	2.63	149	.248	.313	0	.000	-0	4	4	1	0.4
1988	Hou-N	10	2	.833	75	0	0	0	4	91^2	74	27	6	0	30	33	10.2	2.26	147	.226	.291	0	.000	-0	12	11	4	1.9
1989	Hou-N	4	5	.444	71	0	0	0	1	83	81	32	3	2	32	46	12.5	2.93	116	.256	.329	1	.200	0	5	4	1	0.6
1990	Hou-N	9	8	.529	**82**	0	0	0	4	92^1	91	46	4	7	39	50	13.4	4.29	87	.261	.347	0	.000	-0	-5	-6	2	-0.9
1991	StL-N	5	3	.625	72	0	0	0	2	86	92	52	4	8	39	34	14.5	4.81	77	.291	.383	1	.333	1	-11	-10	1	-0.8
1992	StL-N	2	4	.333	22	0	0	0	0	31^2	39	24	2	3	9	13	14.5	6.25	54	.312	.372	0	.000	-0	-10	-10	1	-1.7
	Sea-A	0	0	—	17	1	0	0	0	18^1	27	12	0	0	3	12	14.7	5.89	68	.346	.370	0	—	0	-4	-4	0	-0.2
1993	Hou-N	0	0	—	6	0	0	0	0	6	8	4	1	0	0	3	12.0	6.00	65	.308	.308	0	—	0	-1	-1	-0	-0.1
Total	13	40	33	.548	543	2	0	0	29	626^1	639	313	30	30	248	307	13.2	4.01	94	.272	.349	2	.100	-1	-16	-17	14	-1.0
● RICK AGUILERA	Aguilera, Richard Warren b: 12/31/61, San Gabriel, Cal. BR/TR, 6'5", 205 lbs. Deb: 6/12/85																											
1985	NY-N	10	7	.588	21	19	2	0	0	122^1	118	49	8	2	37	74	11.6	3.24	107	.258	.317	10	.278	3	5	3	-0	0.7
1986	*NY-N	10	7	.588	28	20	2	0	0	141^2	145	70	15	7	36	104	11.9	3.88	91	.263	.316	8	.157	2	-2	-5	2	-0.2
1987	NY-N	11	3	.786	18	17	1	0	0	115	124	53	12	3	33	77	12.5	3.60	105	.276	.330	9	.225	3	6	3	2	0.8
1988	*NY-N	0	4	.000	11	3	0	0	0	24^2	29	20	2	1	10	16	14.6	6.93	47	.296	.367	1	.250	0	-10	-11	0	-1.5
1989	NY-N	6	6	.500	36	0	0	0	7	69^1	59	19	3	2	21	80	10.6	2.34	140	.231	.295	0	.000	-0	9	8	-0	1.4
	Min-A	3	5	.375	11	11	3	0	0	75^2	71	32	5	1	17	57	10.6	3.21	129	.245	.289	0	—	0	6	7	1	0.8
1990	Min-A	5	3	.625	56	0	0	0	32	65^1	55	27	5	4	19	61	10.7	2.76	151	.224	.291	0	—	0	8	10	-1	1.8
1991	*Min-A★	4	5	.444	63	0	0	0	42	69	44	20	3	1	30	61	9.8	2.35	182	.183	.277	0	—	0	13	14	-0	2.9
1992	Min-A★	2	6	.250	64	0	0	0	41	66^2	60	28	7	1	17	52	10.5	2.84	143	.238	.289	0	—	0	8	9	-1	1.8
1993	Min-A★	4	3	.571	65	0	0	0	34	72^1	60	25	9	1	14	59	9.3	3.11	140	.223	.264	0	—	0	10	10	1	1.7
1994	Min-A	1	4	.200	44	0	0	0	23	44^2	57	23	7	0	10	46	13.5	3.63	134	.306	.342	0	—	0	6	6	1	1.2
1995	Min-A	1	1	.500	22	0	0	0	12	25	20	7	2	1	6	29	9.7	2.52	190	.222	.278	0	—	0	6	6	-0	0.9
	*Bos-A	2	2	.500	30	0	0	0	20	30^1	26	9	4	0	7	23	9.8	2.67	183	.228	.273	0	—	0	7	7	0	1.4
	Yr	3	3	.500	52	0	0	0	32	55^1	46	16	6	1	13	52	9.8	2.60	186	.225	.275	0	—	0	13	13	0	2.3
1996	Min-A	8	6	.571	19	19	2	0	0	111^1	124	69	20	3	27	83	12.4	5.42	94	.276	.321	0	—	0	-5	-4	-2	-0.5
1997	Min-A	5	4	.556	61	0	0	0	26	68^1	65	29	9	2	22	68	11.7	3.82	122	.257	.321	0	—	0	6	6	1	1.2
1998	Min-A	4	9	.308	68	0	0	0	38	74^1	75	35	8	1	15	57	11.0	4.24	113	.262	.301	0	—	0	3	4	-0	0.8
1999	Min-A	3	1	.750	17	0	0	0	6	21^1	10	3	2	0	2	13	5.1	1.27	403	.135	.158	0	—	0	9	9	-0	1.7
	Chi-N	6	3	.667	44	0	0	0	8	46^1	44	22	6	2	10	32	10.9	3.69	122	.254	.303	0	.000	-0	5	4	0	0.8
2000	Chi-N	1	2	.333	54	0	0	0	29	47^2	47	28	11	4	18	38	13.0	4.91	93	.251	.330	0	—	0	-1	-2	0	-0.2
Total	16	86	81	.515	732	89	10	0	318	1291^1	1233	568	138	36	351	1030	11.3	3.57	117	.251	.305	28	.201	8	88	87	4	17.5
● HANK AGUIRRE	Aguirre, Henry John b: 1/31/31, Azusa, Cal. d: 9/5/94, Bloomfield Hills, Mich. BR/TL, 6'4", 205 lbs. Deb: 9/10/55 C																											
1955	Cle-A	2	0	1.000	4	1	1	1	0	12^2	6	3	0	0	12	6	12.8	1.42	281	.143	.333	0	.000	-1	4	4	-0	0.4
1956	Cle-A	3	5	.375	16	9	2	1	1	65^1	63	35	7	1	27	31	12.5	3.72	113	.253	.329	2	.111	-2	3	3	-1	0.2
1957	Cle-A	1	1	.500	10	1	0	0	0	20^1	26	15	0	0	13	9	17.3	5.75	65	.317	.411	0	.000	-1	-4	-5	-0	-0.5
1958	Det-A	3	4	.429	44	3	0	0	5	69^2	67	31	5	1	27	38	12.3	3.75	108	.255	.326	3	.214	0	0	2	1	0.3
1959	Det-A	0	0	—	3	0	0	0	0	2^2	4	1	0	0	3	3	23.6	3.38	120	.364	.500	0	—	0	0	0	0	0.0
1960	Det-A	5	3	.625	37	6	1	0	10	94^2	75	31	7	3	30	80	10.3	2.85	139	.217	.286	1	.036	-3	11	11	-2	0.7
1961	Det-A	4	4	.500	45	0	0	0	8	55^1	44	22	5	2	38	32	13.7	3.25	126	.224	.356	0	.000	-1	5	5	-1	0.6
1962	Det-A★	16	8	.667	42	22	11	2	3	216	162	67	14	5	65	156	9.7	**2.21**	**184**	**.205**	**.269**	2	.027	-8	**42**	**44**	-3	3.6
1963	Det-A	14	15	.483	38	33	14	3	0	225^2	222	96	25	8	68	134	11.9	3.67	102	.256	.316	10	.132	-2	-1	2	-3	-0.3
1964	Det-A	5	10	.333	32	27	3	0	1	161^2	134	76	15	8	59	88	11.2	3.79	97	.223	.301	3	.057	-4	-3	-2	-3	-0.9
1965	Det-A	14	10	.583	32	32	10	2	0	208^1	185	89	24	10	60	141	11.0	3.59	97	.236	.298	6	.086	-2	-3	-3	-1	-0.7
1966	Det-A	3	9	.250	30	14	2	0	0	103^2	104	50	14	3	26	50	11.5	3.82	91	.260	.310	3	.120	0	-4	-4	-2	-0.6
1967	Det-A	0	1	.000	31	1	0	0	0	41^1	34	15	2	0	17	33	11.1	2.40	136	.219	.297	1	.500	1	4	4	0	0.3
1968	LA-N	1	2	.333	25	0	0	0	3	39^1	32	8	0	3	13	25	11.0	0.69	403	.227	.306	0	.000	-0	10	10	-1	0.8
1969	Chi-N	1	0	1.000	41	0	0	0	1	45	45	13	2	2	12	19	11.8	2.60	155	.269	.326	2	.400	0	5	6	1	0.5
1970	Chi-N	3	0	1.000	17	0	0	0	1	14	13	10	3	1	9	11	14.8	4.50	100	.250	.371	0	.000	-0	-1	0	-0	-0.1
Total	16	75	72	.510	447	149	44	9	33	1375^2	1216	562	123	47	479	856	11.4	3.24	116	.236	.307	33	.085	-21	67	78	-16	4.3
● PAT AHEARNE	Ahearne, Patrick Howard b: 12/10/69, San Francisco, Cal. BR/TR, 6'3", 195 lbs. Deb: 6/14/95																											
1995	Det-A	0	2	.000	4	3	0	0	0	10	20	13	2	0	5	4	22.5	11.70	41	.400	.455	0	—	0	-8	-8	0	-1.1
● EDDIE AINSMITH	Ainsmith, Edward Wilbur "Dorf" b: 2/4/1892, Cambridge, Mass. d: 9/6/81, Ft.Lauderdale, Fla BR/TR, 5'11", 180 lbs. Deb: 8/9/10 ♦																											
1913	Was-A	0	0	—	1	0	0	0	0	0^1	2	2	0	0	0	0	54.0	54.00	5	.667	.667	49	.214	0	-2	-2	0	-0.1
● RALEIGH AITCHISON	Aitchison, Raleigh Leonidas b: 12/5/1887, Tyndall, S.D. d: 9/26/58, Columbus, Kan. BR/TL, 5'11.5", 175 lbs. Deb: 4/19/11																											
1911	Bro-N	0	1	.000	1	0	0	0	0	1^1	1	2	0	0	1	0	13.5	0.00	—	.200	.333	0	—	0	1	1	-0	0.1
1914	Bro-N	12	7	.632	26	17	8	3	0	172^1	156	71	4	3	60	87	11.4	2.66	107	.244	.312	10	.196	1	2	4	-3	0.2
1915	Bro-N	0	4	.000	7	5	2	0	0	32^2	36	25	3	2	6	14	12.1	4.96	56	.267	.308	0	.000	-0	-8	-8	0	-0.9
Total	3	12	12	.500	34	22	10	3	0	206^1	193	98	7	5	67	101	11.6	3.01	95	.247	.311	10	.169	1	-5	-4	-3	-0.6
● JACK AKER	Aker, Jackie Delane b: 7/13/40, Tulare, Cal. BR/TR, 6'2", 190 lbs. Deb: 5/3/64 C																											
1964	KC-A	0	1	.000	9	0	0	0	0	16^1	17	18	6	6	10	7	18.2	8.82	43	.266	.412	0	.000	-0	-9	-9	1	-0.5
1965	KC-A	4	3	.571	34	0	0	0	3	51^1	45	18	3	3	18	26	11.6	3.16	111	.242	.319	0	.000	-1	2	2	1	0.3
1966	KC-A	8	4	.667	66	0	0	0	**32**	113	81	27	6	3	28	68	8.9	1.99	171	.201	.258	2	.095	-1	**18**	**18**	3	3.2
1967	KC-A	3	8	.273	57	0	0	0	12	88	87	44	9	3	32	65	12.5	4.30	74	.264	.334	1	.125	-0	-10	-11	2	-1.5
1968	Oak-A	4	4	.500	54	0	0	0	11	74^2	72	39	6	6	33	44	13.4	4.10	69	.258	.349	1	.143	-0	-9	-11	0	-1.6
1969	Sea-A	0	2	.000	15	0	0	0	3	16^2	25	15	4	1	13	7	21.1	7.56	48	.357	.464	0	.000	-0	-7	-7	1	-1.0
	NY-A	8	4	.667	38	0	0	0	11	65^2	51	17	4	4	22	40	10.6	2.06	169	.217	.295	1	.111	-0	11	11	2	2.5
	Yr	8	6	.571	53	0	0	0	14	82^1	76	32	8	5	35	47	12.7	3.17	111	.249	.336	1	.100	-0	4	3	2	1.5
1970	NY-A	4	2	.667	41	0	0	0	16	70	57	19	3	4	20	36	10.4	2.06	171	.226	.293	1	.063	-1	13	12	-0	1.4
1971	NY-A	4	4	.500	41	0	0	0	4	55^2	48	20	3	0	26	24	12.0	2.59	125	.238	.325	0	.000	-0	4	4	1	0.7
1972	NY-A	0	0	—	4	0	0	0	0	6	5	2	0	1	3	1	13.5	3.00	99	.238	.360	0	—	0	-0	-0	1	0.1
	Chi-N	6	6	.500	48	0	0	0	17	67	65	31	4	5	23	36	12.5	2.96	129	.259	.333	0	.000	-0	4	6	2	1.4
1973	Chi-N	4	5	.444	47	0	0	0	12	63^2	76	33	8	2	23	25	14.3	4.10	96	.308	.371	0	.000	-1	-3	-1	2	-0.1
1974	Atl-N	0	1	.000	17	0	0	0	0	16^2	17	11	3	0	9	7	14.0	3.78	100	.298	.394	0	.000	-0	-0	0	0	0.0
	NY-N	2	1	.667	24	0	0	0	2	41^1	33	18	4	2	14	18	10.7	3.48	103	.213	.287	1	.500	1	0	0	-1	0.0
	Yr	2	2	.500	41	0	0	0	2	58	50	29	7	2	23	25	11.6	3.57	102	.236	.316	1	.333	1	0	0	-1	0.0
Total	11	47	45	.511	495	0	0	0	123	746	679	312	63	40	274	404	12.0	3.28	105	.247	.324	7	.076	-5	14	13	13	4.9
● DARREL AKERFELDS	Akerfelds, Darrel Wayne b: 6/12/62, Denver, Colo. BR/TR, 6'2", 210 lbs. Deb: 8/1/86																											
1986	Oak-A	0	0	—	2	0	0	0	0	5^1	7	5	2	0	3	5	16.9	6.75	57	.304	.385	0	—	0	-2	-2	0	-0.1
1987	Cle-A	2	6	.250	16	13	1	0	0	74^2	84	60	18	7	38	42	15.5	6.75	67	.284	.378	0	—	0	-19	-18	-0	-1.6

YEAR	TM/L	W	L	PCT	G	GS	CG	SH	SV	IP	H	R	HR	HB	BB	SO	RAT	ERA	ERA+	OAV	OOB	BH	AVG	PB	PR	PR+	PD	TPI
1989	Tex-A	0	1	.000	6	0	0	0	0	11	11	6	1	0	5	9	13.1	3.27	121	.250	.327	0	—	0	1	1	0	0.1
1990	Phi-N	5	2	.714	71	0	0	0	3	93	65	45	10	3	54	42	11.8	3.77	101	.201	.320	1	.167	-0	0	1	-1	0.0
1991	Phi-N	2	1	.667	30	0	0	0	0	49^2	49	30	5	3	27	31	14.3	5.26	70	.257	.357	0	.000	-0	-9	-9	1	-0.5
Total	5	9	10	.474	125	13	1	0	3	233^2	216	146	36	13	127	129	13.7	5.08	79	.246	.350	1	.111	-0	-28	-27	0	-2.1
● JERRY AKERS Akers, Albert Earl b: 11/1/1887, Shelbyville, Ind. d: 5/15/79, Bay Pines, Fla. BR/TR, 5'11", 175 lbs. Deb: 5/4/12																												
1912	Was-A	1	1	.500	5	1	0	0	0	20^1	24	17	1	2	15	11	18.1	4.87	68	.300	.423	2	.333	0	-4	-3	-1	-0.4
● GIBSON ALBA Alba, Gibson Alberto (Rosado) b: 1/18/60, Santiago, D.R. BL/TL, 6'2", 160 lbs. Deb: 5/3/88																												
1988	StL-N	0	0	—	3	0	0	0	0	3^1	1	2	0	0	2	3	8.1	2.70	129	.091	.231	0	—	0	0	0	-0	0.0
● JOE ALBANESE Albanese, Joseph Peter b: 6/26/33, New York, N.Y. BR/TR, 6'3", 215 lbs. Deb: 7/18/58																												
1958	Was-A	0	0	—	6	0	0	0	0	6	8	3	1	0	2	3	15.0	4.50	85	.348	.400	0	—	0	-0	-0	0	0.0
● JOSE ALBERRO Alberro, Jose Edgardo b: 6/29/69, San Juan, P.R. BR/TR, 6'2", 190 lbs. Deb: 4/27/95																												
1995	Tex-A	0	0	—	12	0	0	0	0	20^2	26	18	2	1	12	10	17.0	7.40	65	.299	.390	0	—	0	-6	-6	0	-0.2
1996	Tex-A	0	1	.000	5	1	0	0	0	9^1	14	6	1	0	7	2	20.3	5.79	91	.368	.467	0	—	0	-1	-1	0	0.0
1997	Tex-A	0	3	.000	10	4	0	0	0	28^1	37	33	4	1	17	11	17.5	7.94	60	.303	.393	0	—	0	-11	-9	0	-0.8
Total	3	0	4	.000	27	5	0	0	0	58^1	77	57	7	2	36	23	17.7	7.41	66	.312	.404	0	—	0	-18	-16	1	-1.0
● CY ALBERTS Alberts, Frederick Joseph b: 1/14/1882, Grand Rapids, Mich d: 8/27/17, Fort Wayne, Ind. BR/TR, 6', 230 lbs. Deb: 9/17/10																												
1910	StL-N	1	2	.333	4	3	2	0	0	27^2	35	22	1	0	20	10	17.9	6.18	48	.330	.437	0	.000	-0	-10	-10	-1	-1.0
● ED ALBOSTA Albosta, Edward John "Rube" b: 10/27/18, Saginaw, Mich. BR/TR, 6'1", 175 lbs. Deb: 9/3/41																												
1941	Bro-N	0	2	.000	2	2	0	0	0	13	11	9	1	0	8	5	13.2	6.23	59	.239	.352	0	.000	-1	-4	-4	0	-0.5
1946	Pit-N	0	6	.000	17	6	0	0	0	39^2	41	34	3	1	35	19	17.5	6.13	58	.266	.405	1	.125	-0	-12	-11	0	-1.6
Total	2	0	8	.000	19	8	0	0	0	52^2	52	43	4	1	43	24	16.4	6.15	58	.260	.393	1	.083	-1	-16	-15	0	-2.1
● ED ALBRECHT Albrecht, Edward Arthur b: 2/28/29, Affton, Mo. d: 12/29/79, Cahokia, Ill. BR/TR, 5'10.5", 165 lbs. Deb: 10/2/49																												
1949	StL-A	1	0	1.000	1	1	1	0	0	5	1	3	0	0	4	1	9.0	5.40	84	.063	.250	0	.000	-0	-1	-0	0	-0.1
1950	StL-A	0	1	.000	2	1	0	0	0	6^2	6	7	0	0	7	1	17.6	5.40	92	.250	.419	0	.000	-0	-1	-0	-0	-0.1
Total	2	1	1	.500	3	2	1	0	0	11^2	7	10	0	0	11	2	13.9	5.40	88	.175	.353	0	.000	-0	-1	-1	-0	-0.2
● VIC ALBURY Albury, Victor b: 5/12/47, Key West, Fla. BL/TL, 6', 190 lbs. Deb: 8/7/73																												
1973	Min-A	1	0	1.000	14	0	0	0	0	23^1	13	7	1	0	19	13	12.3	2.70	147	.169	.333	0	—	0	3	3	-1	0.1
1974	Min-A	8	9	.471	32	22	4	1	0	164	159	83	19	6	80	85	13.4	4.12	91	.259	.350	0	—	0	-9	-7	-1	-0.7
1975	Min-A	6	7	.462	32	15	2	0	1	135	115	82	16	4	97	72	14.4	4.53	85	.237	.368	0	.000	-0	-11	-10	1	-0.9
1976	Min-A	3	1	.750	23	0	0	0	0	50^1	51	22	0	2	24	23	13.8	3.58	100	.271	.360	0	—	0	-0	0	-0	0.0
Total	4	18	17	.514	101	37	6	1	1	372^2	338	194	36	12	220	193	13.8	4.11	92	.247	.357	0	.000	-0	-18	-14	-1	-1.5
● SANTO ALCALA Alcala, Santo (b: Santo Anibal (Alcala)) b: 12/23/52, San Pedro De Macoris, D.R. BR/TR, 6'5", 195 lbs. Deb: 4/10/76																												
1976	Cin-N	11	4	.733	30	21	3	1	0	132	131	72	12	3	67	67	13.7	4.70	75	.261	.352	6	.140	-0	-18	-17	-1	-2.0
1977	Cin-N	1	1	.500	7	2	0	0	0	15^2	22	11	1	1	7	9	17.2	5.74	68	.349	.423	0	.000	-0	-3	-3	0	-0.4
	Mon-N	2	6	.250	31	10	0	0	2	101^2	104	55	12	2	47	64	13.5	4.69	81	.263	.344	2	.080	-1	-9	-10	-1	-1.0
	Yr	3	7	.300	38	12	0	0	2	117^1	126	66	13	3	54	73	14.0	4.83	79	.275	.355	2	.071	-1	-12	-13	-1	-1.4
Total	2	14	11	.560	68	33	3	1	2	249^1	257	138	25	6	121	140	13.9	4.76	77	.268	.353	8	.113	-2	-30	-31	-2	-3.4
● DALE ALDERSON Alderson, Dale Leonard b: 3/9/18, Belden, Neb. d: 2/12/82, Garden Grove, Cal. BR/TR, 5'10", 190 lbs. Deb: 9/18/43																												
1943	Chi-N	0	1	.000	4	2	0	0	0	14	21	12	2	0	3	4	15.4	6.43	52	.356	.387	0	.000	-0	-5	-5	0	-0.3
1944	Chi-N	0	0	—	12	1	0	0	0	21^2	31	18	2	0	9	7	16.6	6.65	53	.344	.404	0	.000	-1	-7	-8	1	-0.4
Total	2	0	1	.000	16	3	0	0	0	35^2	52	30	4	0	12	11	16.1	6.56	53	.349	.398	0	.000	-1	-12	-13	1	-0.7
● SCOTT ALDRED Aldred, Scott Phillip b: 6/12/68, Flint, Mich. BL/TL, 6'4", 195 lbs. Deb: 9/9/90																												
1990	Det-A	1	2	.333	4	3	0	0	0	14^1	13	6	0	1	10	7	15.1	3.77	105	.265	.400	0	—	0	0	0	-0	0.1
1991	Det-A	2	4	.333	11	11	1	0	0	57^1	58	37	9	0	30	35	13.8	5.18	80	.266	.355	0	—	0	-7	-6	0	-0.6
1992	Det-A	3	8	.273	16	13	0	0	0	65	80	51	12	3	33	34	16.1	6.78	58	.307	.391	0	—	0	-20	-20	1	-2.8
1993	Col-N	0	0	—	5	0	0	0	0	6^2	10	10	1	1	9	5	27.0	10.80	44	.357	.526	0	—	0	-5	-4	0	-0.2
	Mon-N	1	0	1.000	3	0	0	0	0	5^1	9	4	1	0	1	4	16.9	6.75	62	.375	.400	0	—	0	-2	-1	0	-0.2
	Yr	1	0	1.000	8	0	0	0	0	12	19	14	2	1	10	9	22.5	9.00	50	.365	.476	0	—	0	-7	-5	0	-0.4
1996	Det-A	0	4	.000	11	8	0	0	0	43^1	60	52	9	3	26	36	18.5	9.35	54	.328	.420	0	—	0	-21	-20	-1	-1.5
	Min-A	6	5	.545	25	17	0	0	0	122	134	73	20	3	42	75	13.2	5.09	101	.281	.343	0	—	0	-1	0	-1	-0.1
	Yr	6	9	.400	36	25	0	0	0	165^1	194	125	29	6	68	111	14.6	6.21	82	.294	.365	0	—	0	-22	-20	-2	-1.6
1997	Min-A	2	10	.167	17	15	0	0	0	77^1	102	66	20	3	28	33	15.5	7.68	61	.323	.383	0	—	0	-27	-25	-1	-3.1
1998	TB-A	0	0	—	48	0	0	0	0	31^1	33	13	1	2	12	21	13.5	3.73	128	.280	.356	0	—	0	3	4	1	0.3
1999	TB-A	3	2	.600	37	0	0	0	0	24^1	26	15	1	2	14	22	15.5	5.18	96	.274	.378	0	—	0	-1	-1	-0	-0.1
	Phi-N	1	1	.500	29	0	0	0	1	32^1	33	15	1	0	15	19	13.4	3.90	121	.277	.358	0	.000	-0	2	3	0	0.2
2000	Phi-N	1	3	.250	23	0	0	0	0	20^1	23	14	3	1	10	21	15.0	5.75	82	.284	.370	0	—	0	-3	-2	-0	-0.4
Total	9	20	39	.339	229	67	1	0	1	499^2	581	356	78	19	230	312	14.9	6.02	78	.295	.374	0	.000	-0	-80	-74	-1	-8.4
● MIKE ALDRETE Aldrete, Michael Peter b: 1/29/61, Carmel, Cal. BL/TL, 5'11", 185 lbs. Deb: 5/28/86 ◆																												
1996	*NY-A	0	0	—	1	0	0	0	0	1	1	0	0	0	0	0	9.0	0.00	—	.333	.333	17	.250	0	1	1	0	0.0
● JAY ALDRICH Aldrich, Jay Robert b: 4/14/61, Alexandria, La. BR/TR, 6'3", 210 lbs. Deb: 6/5/87																												
1987	Mil-A	3	1	.750	31	0	0	0	0	58^1	71	33	8	2	13	22	13.3	4.94	93	.306	.348	0	—	0	-3	-2	-1	-0.2
1989	Mil-A	1	0	1.000	16	0	0	0	1	26	24	11	3	1	13	12	13.2	3.81	101	.253	.349	0	—	0	0	0	0	0.0
	Atl-N	1	2	.333	8	0	0	0	0	12^1	7	5	0	0	6	7	9.5	2.19	167	.167	.271	0	.000	-0	2	2	-0	0.4
1990	Bal-A	1	2	.333	7	0	0	0	1	12	17	13	1	0	7	5	18.0	8.25	46	.327	.407	0	—	0	-6	-6	0	-1.1
Total	3	6	5	.545	62	0	0	0	2	108^2	119	62	12	3	39	46	13.3	4.72	89	.283	.348	0	.000	-0	-7	-6	-1	-0.9
● VIC ALDRIDGE Aldridge, Victor Eddington b: 10/25/1893, Indian Springs, Ind. d: 4/17/73, Terre Haute, Ind. BR/TR, 5'9.5", 175 lbs. Deb: 4/15/17																												
1917	Chi-N	6	6	.500	30	6	1	1	2	106^2	100	52	1	2	37	44	11.7	3.12	93	.252	.319	4	.138	-2	-5	-2	3	-0.2
1918	Chi-N	0	1	.000	3	0	0	0	0	12^1	11	3	0	0	6	10	12.4	1.46	191	.275	.370	1	.333	0	2	2	-0	0.2
1922	Chi-N	16	15	.516	36	34	20	2	0	258^1	287	129	14	12	56	66	12.4	3.52	119	.286	.332	26	.260	3	17	19	1	2.4
1923	Chi-N	16	9	.640	30	30	15	2	0	217	209	101	17	1	67	64	11.5	3.48	115	.251	.307	19	.268	3	12	12	-1	1.5
1924	Chi-N	15	12	.556	32	32	20	0	0	244^1	261	110	10	7	80	74	12.8	3.50	112	.279	.341	15	.176	-3	10	11	-0	0.7
1925	*Pit-N	15	7	.682	30	26	14	1	0	213^1	218	99	15	5	74	88	12.5	3.63	123	.269	.334	20	.233	-1	15	19	-3	1.3
1926	Pit-N	10	13	.435	30	26	12	1	1	190	204	100	7	4	73	61	13.3	4.07	97	.279	.348	16	.225	-1	-5	-3	-2	-0.5
1927	*Pit-N	15	10	.600	35	34	17	1	1	239^1	248	123	16	5	74	86	12.3	4.25	97	.270	.328	21	.219	-0	-9	-4	-3	-0.7
1928	NY-N	4	7	.364	22	16	3	0	2	119^1	133	68	7	3	45	33	13.7	4.83	81	.285	.352	11	.275	2	-11	-12	-1	-0.9
Total	9	97	80	.548	248	204	102	8	6	1600^2	1671	785	87	39	512	526	12.5	3.76	107	.273	.333	133	.229	2	26	43	-7	3.8
● DOYLE ALEXANDER Alexander, Doyle Lafayette b: 9/4/50, Cordova, Ala. BR/TR, 6'3", 205 lbs. Deb: 6/26/71																												
1971	LA-N	6	6	.500	17	12	4	0	0	92^1	105	45	6	1	18	30	12.1	3.80	85	.282	.317	9	.273	3	-3	-6	-1	-0.6
1972	Bal-A	6	8	.429	35	9	2	2	2	106^1	78	36	5	1	30	49	9.2	2.45	126	.203	.262	2	.080	-1	7	7	2	1.1
1973	*Bal-A	12	8	.600	29	26	10	0	0	174^2	169	85	19	7	52	63	11.7	3.86	97	.258	.319	0	—	0	-1	-3	1	-0.1
1974	Bal-A	6	9	.400	30	12	2	0	0	114^1	127	65	7	4	43	40	13.7	4.01	86	.290	.359	0	—	0	-5	-7	3	-0.6
1975	Bal-A	8	8	.500	32	11	3	1	1	133^1	127	47	7	1	47	46	11.8	3.04	116	.251	.316	0	—	0	11	8	2	1.1
1976	Bal-A	3	4	.429	11	6	2	1	0	64^1	58	27	3	0	24	17	11.5	3.50	94	.247	.317	0	—	0	0	-2	1	0.0
	*NY-A	10	5	.667	19	19	5	2	0	136^2	114	54	9	3	39	41	10.3	3.29	104	.229	.289	0	—	0	3	2	-2	0.0
	Yr	13	9	.591	30	25	7	3	0	201	172	81	12	3	63	58	10.7	3.36	100	.235	.298	0	—	0	4	0	-1	0.0
1977	Tex-A	17	11	.607	34	34	12	1	0	237	221	103	24	2	82	82	11.6	3.65	112	.246	.311	0	—	0	11	12	1	1.4
1978	Tex-A	9	10	.474	31	28	7	1	0	191	198	84	18	1	71	81	12.7	3.86	97	.270	.336	0	—	0	-2	-2	2	0.0
1979	Tex-A	5	7	.417	23	18	0	0	0	113^1	114	65	3	1	69	50	14.6	4.45	94	.268	.371	0	—	0	-3	-4	2	-0.2

YEAR	TM/L	W	L	PCT	G	GS	CG	SH	SV	IP	H	R	HR	HB	BB	SO	RAT	ERA	ERA+	OAV	OOB	BH	AVG	PB	PR	PR+	PD	TPI
1980	Atl-N	14	11	.560	35	35	7	1	0	231^2	227	120	20	4	74	114	11.8	4.20	89	.256	.316	15	.181	0	-15	-11	3	-0.8
1981	SF-N	11	7	.611	24	24	1	1	0	152^1	156	51	11	2	44	77	11.9	2.89	119	.263	.316	9	.176	1	10	9	-2	1.1
1982	NY-A	1	7	.125	16	11	0	0	0	66^2	81	52	14	0	14	26	12.8	6.08	66	.298	.332	0	—	0	-15	-16	-0	-1.6
1983	NY-A	0	2	.000	8	5	0	0	0	28^1	31	21	6	0	7	17	12.1	6.35	61	.277	.319	0	—	0	-7	-8	-0	-0.5
	Tor-A	7	6	.538	17	15	5	0	0	116^2	126	55	14	1	26	46	11.8	3.93	110	.279	.319	0	—	0	2	5	0	0.5
	Yr	7	8	.467	25	20	5	0	0	145	157	76	20	1	33	63	11.9	4.41	96	.278	.319	0	—	0	-5	-3	0	0.0
1984	Tor-A	17	6	**.739**	36	35	11	2	0	261^2	238	99	21	3	59	139	10.3	3.13	131	.242	.287	0	—	0	25	28	-0	2.2
1985	*Tor-A	17	10	.630	36	36	6	1	0	260^2	268	105	28	6	67	142	11.8	3.45	122	.266	.315	0	—	0	20	22	0	2.1
1986	Tor-A	5	4	.556	17	17	3	0	0	111	120	56	18	4	20	65	11.7	4.46	95	.273	.310	0	—	0	-3	-3	-1	-0.3
	Atl-N	6	6	.500	17	17	2	0	0	117^1	135	58	9	0	17	74	11.7	3.84	104	.287	.312	8	.211	1	-1	2	-1	0.2
1987	Atl-N	5	10	.333	16	16	3	0	0	117^2	115	57	21	2	27	64	11.0	4.13	105	.257	.302	1	.029	-3	-1	3	-2	-0.1
	*Det-A	9	0	1.000	11	11	3	3	0	88^1	63	16	3	0	26	44	9.1	1.53	277	.201	.263	0	—	0	29	28	0	2.8
1988	Det-A☆	14	11	.560	34	34	5	1	0	229	260	122	30	5	46	126	12.2	4.32	88	.282	.320	0	—	0	-9	-13	-3	-1.5
1989	Det-A	6	18	.250	33	33	5	1	0	223	245	118	28	5	76	95	13.2	4.44	86	.280	.341	0	—	0	-14	-15	0	-1.4
Total	19	194	174	.527	561	464	98	18	3	3367^2	3376	1541	324	53	978	1528	11.8	3.76	103	.261	.316	44	.166	1	41	35	7	4.8

● GERALD ALEXANDER

Alexander, Gerald Paul b: 3/26/68, Baton Rouge, La. BR/TR, 5′11″, 190 lbs. Deb: 9/9/90

YEAR	TM/L	W	L	PCT	G	GS	CG	SH	SV	IP	H	R	HR	HB	BB	SO	RAT	ERA	ERA+	OAV	OOB	BH	AVG	PB	PR	PR+	PD	TPI
1990	Tex-A	0	0	—	3	2	0	0	0	7	14	6	0	1	5	8	25.7	7.71	51	.438	.526	0	—	0	-3	-3	0	-0.1
1991	Tex-A	5	3	.625	30	9	0	0	0	89^1	93	56	11	3	48	50	14.5	5.24	77	.272	.366	0	—	0	-11	-12	0	-0.9
1992	Tex-A	1	0	1.000	3	0	0	0	0	1^2	5	5	1	0	1	1	32.4	27.00	14	.500	.545	0	—	0	-4	-4	0	-0.8
Total	3	6	3	.667	36	11	0	0	0	98	112	67	12	4	54	59	15.6	5.79	70	.292	.385	0	—	0	-19	-19	0	-1.8

● GROVER ALEXANDER

Alexander, Grover Cleveland "Pete" b: 2/26/1887, Elba, Neb. d: 11/4/50, St.Paul, Neb. BR/TR, 6′1″, 185 lbs. Deb: 4/15/11 H

YEAR	TM/L	W	L	PCT	G	GS	CG	SH	SV	IP	H	R	HR	HB	BB	SO	RAT	ERA	ERA+	OAV	OOB	BH	AVG	PB	PR	PR+	PD	TPI
1911	Phi-N	**28**	13	.683	48	37	**31**	**7**	3	**367**	285	133	5	8	129	227	10.3	2.57	134	**.219**	.293	24	.174	-2	34	35	1	3.5
1912	Phi-N	19	17	.528	46	34	25	3	3	**310**^{1}	289	133	11	6	105	**195**	11.6	2.81	129	.251	.317	19	.186	0	21	26	1	2.9
1913	Phi-N	22	8	.733	47	36	23	**9**	2	306^1	288	106	9	3	75	159	10.8	2.79	120	.254	.302	13	.126	-4	14	18	2	1.4
1914	Phi-N	**27**	15	.643	46	39	**32**	6	1	**355**	327	133	8	11	76	**214**	10.5	2.38	123	.244	.290	32	.234	2	16	21	4	3.2
1915	*Phi-N	**31**	10	**.756**	49	42	**36**	**12**	3	**376**^{1}	253	86	3	10	64	**241**	**7.8**	**1.22**	**225**	**.191**	**.234**	22	.169	0	**64**	**64**	7	**8.7**
1916	Phi-N	**33**	12	.733	48	45	**38**	**16**	3	**389**	323	90	6	10	50	**167**	8.9	**1.55**	**171**	.230	.262	33	.239	8	**46**	**47**	1	**7.3**
1917	Phi-N	**30**	13	.698	45	44	**34**	**8**	0	**388**	336	107	4	6	56	**200**	9.2	**1.83**	153	.234	.266	30	.216	4	**38**	**41**	2	**5.7**
1918	Chi-N	2	1	.667	3	3	3	0	0	26	19	7	0	1	3	15	8.0	1.73	161	.207	.240	1	.100	-1	3	3	0	0.3
1919	Chi-N	16	11	.593	30	27	20	**9**	1	235	180	51	3	0	38	121	8.3	**1.72**	**167**	**.211**	.245	12	.171	1	31	31	5	**4.5**
1920	Chi-N	**27**	14	.659	46	40	**33**	7	5	**363**^{1}	335	96	8	1	69	**173**	10.0	**1.91**	**168**	.248	.285	27	.229	4	**50**	**51**	2	**7.0**
1921	Chi-N	15	13	.536	31	30	21	**3**	1	252	286	110	10	1	33	77	11.4	3.39	113	.296	.320	29	.305	6	11	12	-1	1.8
1922	Chi-N	16	13	.552	33	31	20	1	1	245^2	283	111	8	3	34	48	11.7	3.63	116	.295	.321	15	.176	-2	13	15	3	1.7
1923	Chi-N	22	12	.647	39	36	26	3	2	305	308	128	17	0	30	72	**10.0**	3.19	126	.259	**.277**	24	.216	0	28	28	4	3.2
1924	Chi-N	12	5	.706	21	20	12	0	0	169^1	183	82	9	1	25	33	11.1	3.03	129	.272	.299	15	.231	1	16	16	2	1.7
1925	Chi-N	15	11	.577	32	30	20	1	0	236	270	106	14	3	29	63	11.5	3.39	127	.288	.312	19	.241	3	23	24	-2	2.4
1926	Chi-N	3	3	.500	7	7	4	0	0	52	55	26	0	0	7	12	10.7	3.46	111	.270	.294	7	.467	3	2	2	1	0.6
	*StL-N	9	7	.563	23	16	11	2	2	148^1	136	57	8	2	24	35	9.8	2.91	134	.242	.276	6	.120	-4	15	16	-0	1.3
	Yr	12	10	.545	30	23	15	2	2	200^1	191	83	8	2	31	47	**10.1**	3.05	127	.250	**.281**	13	.200	-1	17	18	1	1.9
1927	StL-N	21	10	.677	37	30	22	2	3	268	261	94	11	1	38	48	**10.1**	2.52	157	.258	**.286**	23	.245	3	**42**	**42**	1	**5.2**
1928	*StL-N	16	9	.640	34	31	18	1	2	243^2	262	107	15	2	37	59	11.1	3.36	119	.277	.306	25	.291	6	17	17	-1	2.1
1929	StL-N	9	8	.529	22	19	8	0	0	132	149	65	10	1	23	33	11.8	3.89	120	.285	.317	2	.049	-4	12	12	2	1.0
1930	Phi-N	0	3	.000	9	3	0	0	0	21^2	40	24	5	0	6	6	19.1	9.14	60	.396	.430	0	.000	-0	-10	-8	-1	-0.9
Total	20	373	208	.642	696	600	437	90	32	5190	4868	1852	164	70	951	2198	10.2	2.56	135	.250	.288	378	.209	24	484	512	31	64.6

● MANNY ALEXANDER

Alexander, Manuel De Jesus (b: Manuel De Jesus (Alexander))
b: 3/20/71, San Pedro De Macoris, D.R. BR/TR, 5′10″, 165 lbs. Deb: 9/18/92 ◆

YEAR	TM/L	W	L	PCT	G	GS	CG	SH	SV	IP	H	R	HR	HB	BB	SO	RAT	ERA	ERA+	OAV	OOB	BH	AVG	PB	PR	PR+	PD	TPI
1996	*Bal-A	0	0	—	1	0	0	0	0	0^2	1	5	1	0	4	0	67.5	67.50	7	.500	.833	7	.103	-0	-5	-5	0	-0.2

● BOB ALEXANDER

Alexander, Robert Somerville b: 8/7/22, Vancouver, B.C., Can d: 4/7/93, Oceanside, Cal. BR/TR, 6′2.5″, 205 lbs. Deb: 4/11/55

YEAR	TM/L	W	L	PCT	G	GS	CG	SH	SV	IP	H	R	HR	HB	BB	SO	RAT	ERA	ERA+	OAV	OOB	BH	AVG	PB	PR	PR+	PD	TPI
1955	Bal-A	1	0	1.000	4	0	0	0	0	4	8	6	0	1	2	1	24.8	13.50	28	.444	.524	0	—	0	-4	-4	-0	-0.8
1957	Cle-A	0	1	.000	5	0	0	0	0	7	10	7	0	1	5	1	20.6	9.00	41	.357	.471	0	.000	-0	-4	-4	-0	-0.6
Total	2	1	1	.500	9	0	0	0	0	11	18	13	0	2	7	2	22.1	10.64	35	.391	.491	0	.000	-0	-8	-9	-1	-1.4

● ANTONIO ALFONSECA

Alfonseca, Antonio b: 4/16/72, LaRomana, D.R. BR/TR, 6′5″, 235 lbs. Deb: 6/17/97

YEAR	TM/L	W	L	PCT	G	GS	CG	SH	SV	IP	H	R	HR	HB	BB	SO	RAT	ERA	ERA+	OAV	OOB	BH	AVG	PB	PR	PR+	PD	TPI
1997	*Fla-N	1	3	.250	17	0	0	0	0	25^2	36	16	3	1	10	19	16.5	4.91	82	.324	.385	0	.000	-0	-2	-3	-0	-0.4
1998	Fla-N	4	6	.400	58	0	0	0	8	70^2	75	36	10	3	33	46	14.1	4.08	100	.281	.366	0	.000	-0	1	-0	-1	-0.2
1999	Fla-N	4	5	.444	73	0	0	0	21	77^2	79	28	4	4	29	46	13.0	3.24	134	.274	.349	0	.000	-0	11	10	1	1.5
2000	Fla-N	5	6	.455	68	0	0	0	**45**	70	82	35	7	1	24	47	13.8	4.24	104	.291	.349	0	—	0	3	1	1	0.3
Total	4	14	20	.412	216	0	0	0	74	244	272	115	24	9	96	158	13.9	3.95	108	.287	.358	0	.000	-1	14	9	0	1.2

● BRIAN ALLARD

Allard, Brian Marshall b: 1/3/58, Spring Valley, Ill. BR/TR, 6′1″, 175 lbs. Deb: 8/8/79

YEAR	TM/L	W	L	PCT	G	GS	CG	SH	SV	IP	H	R	HR	HB	BB	SO	RAT	ERA	ERA+	OAV	OOB	BH	AVG	PB	PR	PR+	PD	TPI
1979	Tex-A	1	3	.250	7	4	2	0	0	33^1	36	17	4	0	13	14	13.2	4.32	96	.283	.350	0	—	0	-0	-1	0	-0.1
1980	Tex-A	0	1	.000	5	2	0	0	0	14^1	13	13	0	1	10	10	15.1	5.65	69	.236	.364	0	—	0	-3	-3	-0	-0.2
1981	Sea-A	3	2	.600	7	7	1	0	0	48	48	22	5	0	8	20	10.5	3.75	103	.265	.296	0	—	0	-0	1	-0	0.0
Total	3	4	6	.400	19	13	3	0	0	95^2	97	52	9	1	31	44	12.1	4.23	94	.267	.327	0	—	0	-3	-3	-1	-0.3

● FRANK ALLEN

Allen, Frank Leon b: 8/26/1889, Newbern, Ala. d: 7/30/33, Gainesville, Ala. BR/TL, 5′9″, 175 lbs. Deb: 4/24/12

YEAR	TM/L	W	L	PCT	G	GS	CG	SH	SV	IP	H	R	HR	HB	BB	SO	RAT	ERA	ERA+	OAV	OOB	BH	AVG	PB	PR	PR+	PD	TPI
1912	Bro-N	3	9	.250	20	15	5	1	0	109	119	70	1	1	57	58	14.6	3.63	92	.285	.373	6	.167	2	-3	-3	0	-0.2
1913	Bro-N	4	18	.182	34	25	11	0	2	174^2	144	75	6	10	81	82	12.1	2.83	116	.231	.329	7	.137	-1	7	9	-3	0.6
1914	Bro-N	8	14	.364	36	21	10	1	0	171^1	165	79	6	3	57	68	11.8	3.10	92	.265	.330	6	.128	0	-6	-4	-1	-0.7
	Pit-F	1	0	1.000	1	1	1	0	0	7	9	4	0	0	0	3	11.6	5.14	56	.321	.321	1	.500	1	-2	-2	-0	-0.1
1915	Pit-F	23	13	.639	41	37	24	6	0	283^1	230	90	9	11	100	127	10.8	2.51	108	.227	.304	7	.079	-6	7	6	-1	0.1
1916	Bos-N	8	2	.800	19	14	7	2	1	113	102	32	1	4	31	63	10.9	2.07	120	.244	.302	7	.206	3	7	5	-1	0.8
1917	Bos-N	3	10	.231	29	14	2	0	0	112	124	61	3	6	47	56	14.2	3.94	65	.297	.376	5	.172	2	-15	-18	-2	-2.1
Total	6	50	66	.431	180	127	60	10	3	970^1	893	411	26	35	373	457	12.1	2.93	98	.252	.330	39	.135	1	-5	-7	-8	-1.6

● JOHN ALLEN

Allen, John Marshall b: 10/27/1890, Berkeley Springs, W.Va. d: 9/24/67, Hagerstown, Md. BR/TR, 6′1″, 170 lbs. Deb: 6/2/14

YEAR	TM/L	W	L	PCT	G	GS	CG	SH	SV	IP	H	R	HR	HB	BB	SO	RAT	ERA	ERA+	OAV	OOB	BH	AVG	PB	PR	PR+	PD	TPI
1914	Bal-F	0	0	—	1	0	0	0	0	2	2	4	0	1	2	2	22.5	18.00	17	.286	.500	0	—	0	-3	-3	0	-0.1

● JOHNNY ALLEN

Allen, John Thomas b: 9/30/05, Lenoir, N.C. d: 3/29/59, St.Petersburg, Fla BR/TR, 6′, 180 lbs. Deb: 4/19/32

YEAR	TM/L	W	L	PCT	G	GS	CG	SH	SV	IP	H	R	HR	HB	BB	SO	RAT	ERA	ERA+	OAV	OOB	BH	AVG	PB	PR	PR+	PD	TPI
1932	*NY-A	17	4	**.810**	33	21	13	3	4	192	162	86	10	5	76	109	11.4	3.70	110	.228	.306	9	.123	-2	17	9	-1	0.5
1933	NY-A	15	7	.682	25	24	10	1	1	184^2	171	96	9	4	87	119	12.8	4.39	89	.242	.328	13	.181	0	-2	-11	-1	-1.2
1934	NY-A	5	2	.714	13	10	4	0	0	71^2	62	30	3	2	32	54	12.1	2.89	141	.227	.313	5	.192	1	13	10	0	1.0
1935	NY-A	13	6	.684	23	23	12	2	0	167	149	76	11	4	58	113	11.4	3.61	112	**.238**	.307	15	.224	1	16	9	1	1.1
1936	Cle-A	20	10	.667	36	31	19	4	1	243	234	108	5	1	97	165	12.3	3.44	146	.256	.328	14	.161	-3	43	43	2	4.5
1937	Cle-A	15	1	**.938**	24	20	14	0	0	173	157	55	4	5	60	87	11.5	2.55	181	.244	.313	6	.090	-7	40	40	1	2.7
1938	Cle-A★	14	8	.636	30	27	13	0	0	200	189	107	15	3	81	112	12.3	4.18	111	.246	.321	20	.253	4	13	10	2	1.6
1939	Cle-A	9	7	.563	28	26	9	2	0	175	199	96	9	3	56	79	13.3	4.58	96	.291	.347	16	.225	1	1	-4	3	0.0
1940	Cle-A	9	8	.529	32	17	5	3	5	138^2	126	61	3	3	48	62	11.5	3.44	123	.243	.311	10	.208	0	15	12	-0	1.4
1941	StL-A	2	5	.286	20	9	2	0	1	67	89	53	4	2	29	27	16.1	6.58	65	.319	.387	3	.136	0	-18	-16	-0	-1.5
	*Bro-N	3	0	1.000	11	4	1	0	0	57^1	38	18	6	0	12	21	7.8	2.51	146	.188	.234	1	.050	-2	7	7	-0	0.1
1942	Bro-N	10	6	.625	27	15	5	1	3	118	106	53	11	2	39	50	11.2	3.20	102	.238	.302	7	.179	-0	1	1	0	0.0
1943	Bro-N	5	1	.833	17	1	0	0	1	38	42	21	3	2	25	15	16.3	4.26	79	.280	.390	3	.429	2	-4	-4	-0	-0.4
	NY-N	1	3	.250	15	0	0	0	2	41	37	16	4	0	14	24	11.2	3.07	112	.245	.309	0	.000	-2	1	2	1	0.1
	Yr	6	4	.600	32	1	0	0	3	79	79	37	7	2	39	39	13.7	3.65	93	.262	.351	3	.143	-0	-2	-2	1	-0.3
1944	NY-N	4	7	.364	18	13	2	1	0	84	88	48	7	2	24	33	12.2	4.07	90	.260	.313	2	.083	-2	-4	-4	-1	-0.8
Total	13	142	75	.654	352	241	109	17	18	1950^1	1849	924	104	38	738	1070	12.1	3.75	113	.249	.321	124	.173	-8	138	106	6	9.1

● LLOYD ALLEN Allen, Lloyd Cecil b: 5/8/50, Merced, Cal. BR/TR, 6'1", 185 lbs. Deb: 9/1/69

YEAR	TM/L	W	L	PCT	G	GS	CG	SH	SV	IP	H	R	HR	HB	BB	SO	RAT	ERA	ERA+	OAV	OOB	BH	AVG	PB	PR	PR+	PD	TPI
1969	Cal-A	0	1	.000	4	1	0	0	0	10	5	7	1	0	10	5	13.5	5.40	65	.147	.341	1	.500	1	-2	-2	1	-0.1
1970	Cal-A	1	1	.500	8	2	0	0	0	24	23	7	0	1	11	12	13.1	2.63	138	.261	.350	0	.000	-0	3	3	-0	0.1
1971	Cal-A	4	6	.400	54	1	0	0	15	94	75	29	4	0	40	72	11.0	2.49	130	.221	.303	5	.294	2	10	8	0	1.5
1972	Cal-A	3	7	.300	42	6	0	0	5	85^1	76	38	7	3	55	53	14.1	3.48	84	.240	.357	2	.118	-1	-4	-6	-1	-0.9
1973	Cal-A	0	0	—	5	0	0	0	1	8^2	15	10	0	0	5	4	20.8	10.38	34	.417	.488	0	—	0	-6	-7	-0	-0.4
	Tex-A	0	6	.000	23	5	0	0	1	41	58	59	3	5	39	25	22.4	9.22	40	.326	.459	0	—	0	-25	-26	1	-3.2
	Yr	0	6	.000	28	5	0	0	2	49^2	73	69	3	5	44	29	22.1	9.42	39	.341	.464	0	—	0	-31	-33	1	-3.6
1974	Tex-A	0	1	.000	14	0	0	0	0	22	24	17	2	1	18	18	17.6	6.55	55	.276	.406	0	—	0	-7	-7	-1	-0.4
	Chi-A	0	1	.000	6	2	0	0	0	7	7	9	0	1	12	3	25.7	10.29	36	.259	.500	0	—	0	-5	-5	-0	-0.6
	Yr	0	2	.000	20	2	0	0	0	29	31	26	2	2	30	21	19.6	7.45	48	.272	.432	0	—	0	-12	-12	-1	-1.0
1975	Chi-A	0	2	.000	3	2	0	0	0	5^1	8	7	2	0	6	2	23.6	11.81	33	.348	.483	0	—	0	-5	-5	0	-0.8
Total	7	8	25	.242	159	19	0	0	22	297^1	291	183	19	11	196	194	15.1	4.69	71	.258	.373	8	.200	2	-41	-48	0	-4.8

● MYRON ALLEN Allen, Myron Smith "Zeke" b: 3/22/1854, Kingston, N.Y. d: 3/8/24, Kingston, N.Y. BR/TR, 5'8", 150 lbs. Deb: 7/19/1883 ♦

YEAR	TM/L	W	L	PCT	G	GS	CG	SH	SV	IP	H	R	HR	HB	BB	SO	RAT	ERA	ERA+	OAV	OOB	BH	AVG	PB	PR	PR+	PD	TPI
1883	NY-N	0	1	.000	1	1	1	0	0	8	8	5	0		3	0	12.4	1.13	275	.276	.344	0	.000	-1	2	2	-0	0.1
1887	Cle-a	1	0	1.000	2	0	0	0	0	9^2	12	4	0	1	3	1	12.1	0.93	466	.300	.317	164	.329	0	4	4	-0	0.3
1888	KC-a	0	2	.000	2	2	2	0	0	18	17	7	0	2	1	2	10.0	2.50	137	.239	.270	29	.213	0	1	2	1	0.2
Total	3	1	3	.250	5	3	3	0	0	35^2	37	16	0	3	7	3	11.1	1.77	205	.264	.299	193	.301	-0	7	7	0	0.6

● NEIL ALLEN Allen, Neil Patrick b: 1/24/58, Kansas City, Kan. BR/TR, 6'2", 190 lbs. Deb: 4/15/79

YEAR	TM/L	W	L	PCT	G	GS	CG	SH	SV	IP	H	R	HR	HB	BB	SO	RAT	ERA	ERA+	OAV	OOB	BH	AVG	PB	PR	PR+	PD	TPI
1979	NY-N	6	10	.375	50	5	0	0	8	99	100	46	4	0	47	65	13.4	3.55	103	.268	.350	0	.000	-2	2	1	0	0.1
1980	NY-N	7	10	.412	59	0	0	0	22	97^1	87	43	7	0	40	79	11.7	3.70	96	.244	.320	2	.143	-0	-1	-2	-1	-0.4
1981	NY-N	7	6	.538	43	0	0	0	18	66^2	64	26	4	0	26	50	12.2	2.97	117	.259	.330	1	.200	1	4	4	1	1.0
1982	NY-N	3	7	.300	50	0	0	0	19	64^2	65	22	5	1	30	59	13.4	3.06	119	.266	.349	1	.167	1	4	4	-0	0.9
1983	NY-N	2	7	.222	21	4	1	1	2	54	57	29	6	0	36	32	15.5	4.50	81	.278	.386	0	.000	-1	-5	-5	-0	-1.0
	StL-N	10	6	.625	25	18	4	2	0	121^2	122	55	6	1	48	74	12.6	3.70	98	.265	.335	5	.128	-1	-1	-1	-0	-0.2
	Yr	12	13	.480	46	22	5	3	2	175^2	179	84	12	1	84	106	13.5	3.94	92	.269	.352	5	.102	-2	-6	-6	-1	-1.2
1984	StL-N	9	6	.600	57	1	0	0	3	119	105	54	6	0	49	66	11.6	3.55	98	.239	.315	6	.240	2	1	-1	1	0.1
1985	StL-N	1	4	.200	23	1	0	0	2	29	32	22	3	1	17	10	15.5	5.59	63	.283	.382	0	.000	-0	-6	-7	0	-1.2
	NY-A	1	0	1.000	17	0	0	0	1	29^1	26	9	1	0	13	16	12.0	2.76	145	.234	.315	0	—	0	5	4	-0	0.2
1986	Chi-A	7	2	.778	22	17	2	2	0	113	101	50	8	2	38	57	11.2	3.82	113	.244	.311	0	—	0	5	6	-0	0.4
1987	Chi-A	0	7	.000	15	10	0	0	0	49^2	74	40	6	2	26	26	18.5	7.07	65	.365	.442	0	—	0	-14	-13	-0	-1.5
	NY-A	0	1	.000	8	1	0	0	0	24^2	23	12	2	0	10	16	12.0	3.65	121	.242	.314	0	—	0	2	2	-0	0.1
	Yr	0	8	.000	23	11	0	0	0	74^1	97	52	8	2	36	42	16.3	5.93	76	.326	.402	0	—	0	-12	-11	-1	-1.4
1988	NY-A	5	3	.625	41	2	0	1	0	117^1	121	51	14	2	37	61	12.3	3.84	103	.268	.326	0	—	0	2	1	-2	-0.1
1989	Cle-A	0	1	.000	3	0	0	0	0	3	8	5	1	0	0	0	24.0	15.00	26	.500	.500	0	—	0	-4	-4	0	-0.6
Total	11	58	70	.453	434	59	7	6	75	988^1	985	464	73	9	417	611	12.8	3.88	98	.264	.339	15	.130	-1	-8	-10	-3	-2.2

● BOB ALLEN Allen, Robert Earl "Thin Man" b: 7/2/14, Smithville, Tenn. BR/TR, 6'1", 165 lbs. Deb: 9/19/37

YEAR	TM/L	W	L	PCT	G	GS	CG	SH	SV	IP	H	R	HR	HB	BB	SO	RAT	ERA	ERA+	OAV	OOB	BH	AVG	PB	PR	PR+	PD	TPI
1937	Phi-N	0	1	.000	3	1	0	0	0	12	18	12	2	0	8	8	19.5	6.75	64	.321	.406	1	.333	0	-4	-3	-1	-0.3

● BOB ALLEN Allen, Robert Gray b: 10/23/37, Tatum, Tex. BL/TL, 6'2", 185 lbs. Deb: 4/14/61

YEAR	TM/L	W	L	PCT	G	GS	CG	SH	SV	IP	H	R	HR	HB	BB	SO	RAT	ERA	ERA+	OAV	OOB	BH	AVG	PB	PR	PR+	PD	TPI
1961	Cle-A	3	2	.600	48	0	0	0	3	81^2	96	42	7	1	40	42	15.1	3.75	105	.294	.373	2	.167	0	3	2	-0	0.1
1962	Cle-A	1	1	.500	30	0	0	0	4	30^2	29	24	5	0	25	23	15.8	5.87	66	.250	.383	0	.000	-1	-6	-7	0	-0.6
1963	Cle-A	1	2	.333	43	0	0	0	2	56	58	37	5	1	29	51	14.1	4.66	78	.266	.355	1	.200	-0	-6	-7	0	-0.4
1966	Cle-A	2	2	.500	36	0	0	0	5	51^1	56	27	2	2	13	33	12.4	4.21	82	.273	.323	1	.111	-0	-4	-4	1	-0.4
1967	Cle-A	0	5	.000	47	0	0	0	5	54^1	49	22	4	1	25	50	12.4	2.98	110	.243	.329	0	—	0	2	2	1	0.3
Total	5	7	12	.368	204	0	0	0	19	274	288	152	23	5	132	199	14.0	4.11	89	.270	.353	4	.129	-1	-13	-14	2	-1.0

● DANA ALLISON Allison, Dana Eric b: 8/14/66, Front Royal, Va. BR/TL, 6'3", 215 lbs. Deb: 4/9/91

YEAR	TM/L	W	L	PCT	G	GS	CG	SH	SV	IP	H	R	HR	HB	BB	SO	RAT	ERA	ERA+	OAV	OOB	BH	AVG	PB	PR	PR+	PD	TPI
1991	Oak-A	1	1	.500	11	0	0	0	0	11	16	9	0	0	5	4	17.2	7.36	52	.381	.447	0	—	0	-4	-5	-0	-0.8

● DOUG ALLISON Allison, Douglas L. b: 7/1845, Philadelphia, Pa. d: 12/19/16, Washington, D.C. BR/TR, 5'10.5", 160 lbs. Deb: 5/5/1871 FM♦

YEAR	TM/L	W	L	PCT	G	GS	CG	SH	SV	IP	H	R	HR	HB	BB	SO	RAT	ERA	ERA+	OAV	OOB	BH	AVG	PB	PR	PR+	PD	TPI
1878	Pro-N	0	0	—	1	0	0	0	0	5	11	5	0		1	0	21.6	1.80	123	.440	.462	22	.289	0	0	0	-0	0.0

● MACK ALLISON Allison, Mack Pendleton b: 1/23/1887, Owensboro, Ky. d: 3/13/64, Mount Vernon, Mo. BR/TR, 6'1", 185 lbs. Deb: 9/13/11

YEAR	TM/L	W	L	PCT	G	GS	CG	SH	SV	IP	H	R	HR	HB	BB	SO	RAT	ERA	ERA+	OAV	OOB	BH	AVG	PB	PR	PR+	PD	TPI
1911	StL-A	2	1	.667	3	3	3	0	0	26^1	24	9	0	2	5	2	10.6	2.05	165	.253	.304	2	.200	-0	4	4	-1	0.3
1912	StL-A	6	17	.261	31	20	11	1	1	169	171	102	4	6	49	43	12.0	3.62	92	.269	.327	7	.135	-3	-6	-6	-1	-1.1
1913	StL-A	1	3	.250	11	4	3	0	0	51^1	52	24	0	3	13	12	11.9	2.28	129	.287	.345	0	.000	-2	4	4	-2	-0.1
Total	3	9	21	.300	45	27	17	1	1	246^2	247	135	4	11	67	57	11.9	3.17	102	.271	.328	9	.118	-6	2	2	-4	-0.9

● ARMANDO ALMANZA Almanza, Armando N. b: 10/26/72, ElPaso, Tex. BL/TL, 6'3", 205 lbs. Deb: 7/29/99

YEAR	TM/L	W	L	PCT	G	GS	CG	SH	SV	IP	H	R	HR	HB	BB	SO	RAT	ERA	ERA+	OAV	OOB	BH	AVG	PB	PR	PR+	PD	TPI
1999	Fla-N	0	1	.000	14	0	0	0	0	15^2	8	4	1	1	9	20	10.3	1.72	253	.154	.290	0	.000	-0	5	5	0	0.2
2000	Fla-N	4	2	.667	67	0	0	0	0	46^1	38	27	3	2	43	46	16.1	4.86	91	.228	.392	0	.000	-0	-1	-2	-1	-0.3
Total	2	4	3	.571	81	0	0	0	0	62	46	31	4	3	52	66	14.7	4.06	108	.210	.369	0	.000	-0	4	2	-1	-0.1

● CARLOS ALMANZAR Almanzar, Carlos Manuel (Giron) b: 11/6/73, Santiago, D.R. BR/TR, 6'2", 166 lbs. Deb: 9/4/97

YEAR	TM/L	W	L	PCT	G	GS	CG	SH	SV	IP	H	R	HR	HB	BB	SO	RAT	ERA	ERA+	OAV	OOB	BH	AVG	PB	PR	PR+	PD	TPI
1997	Tor-A	0	1	.000	4	0	0	0	0	3^1	1	1	1	0	1	4	5.4	2.70	170	.091	.167	0	—	0	1	1	-0	0.1
1998	Tor-A	2	2	.500	25	0	0	0	0	28^2	34	18	4	1	8	20	13.5	5.34	87	.286	.336	0	—	0	-2	-2	-0	-0.3
1999	SD-N	0	0	—	28	0	0	0	0	37^1	48	32	6	3	15	30	15.9	7.47	56	.316	.388	0	.000	-0	-12	-15	-0	-0.7
2000	SD-N	4	5	.444	62	0	0	0	0	69^2	73	35	12	4	25	56	13.2	4.39	100	.266	.337	0	.000	-0	2	-0	0	0.0
Total	4	6	8	.429	119	0	0	0	0	139	156	86	23	8	49	110	13.8	5.37	82	.281	.347	0	.000	-0	-12	-16	-1	-0.9

● HECTOR ALMONTE Almonte, Hector Radhames (Moreta) b: 10/17/75, Santo Domingo, D.R. BR/TR, 6'2", 190 lbs. Deb: 7/26/99

YEAR	TM/L	W	L	PCT	G	GS	CG	SH	SV	IP	H	R	HR	HB	BB	SO	RAT	ERA	ERA+	OAV	OOB	BH	AVG	PB	PR	PR+	PD	TPI
1999	Fla-N	0	2	.000	15	0	0	0	0	15	20	7	1	0	6	8	15.6	4.20	104	.339	.400	0	—	0	1	0	0	0.1

● LUIS ALOMA Aloma, Luis (Barba) "Witto" b: 6/19/23, Havana, Cuba d: 4/7/97, Park Ridge, Ill. BR/TR, 6'2", 195 lbs. Deb: 4/19/50

YEAR	TM/L	W	L	PCT	G	GS	CG	SH	SV	IP	H	R	HR	HB	BB	SO	RAT	ERA	ERA+	OAV	OOB	BH	AVG	PB	PR	PR+	PD	TPI
1950	Chi-A	7	2	.778	42	0	0	0	4	87^2	77	44	6	1	53	49	13.4	3.80	118	.234	.342	1	.067	-2	8	7	-0	0.5
1951	Chi-A	6	0	1.000	25	1	1	1	3	69^1	52	14	3	2	24	25	10.1	1.82	222	.215	.291	7	.350	2	18	17	-2	1.6
1952	Chi-A	3	1	.750	25	0	0	0	6	40	42	20	5	1	11	18	12.1	4.27	85	.278	.331	0	.000	-1	-3	-3	-0	-0.5
1953	Chi-A	2	0	1.000	24	0	0	0	2	38^1	41	20	7	0	23	23	15.0	4.70	86	.283	.381	0	.000	-1	-3	-3	0	-0.2
Total	4	18	3	.857	116	1	1	1	15	235^1	212	98	21	4	111	115	12.5	3.44	120	.245	.333	8	.167	-2	20	18	-2	1.4

● MATTY ALOU Alou, Mateo Rojas (b: Mateo Rojas (Alou)) b: 12/22/38, Haina, D.R. BL/TL, 5'9", 160 lbs. Deb: 9/26/60 F♦

YEAR	TM/L	W	L	PCT	G	GS	CG	SH	SV	IP	H	R	HR	HB	BB	SO	RAT	ERA	ERA+	OAV	OOB	BH	AVG	PB	PR	PR+	PD	TPI
1965	SF-N	0	0	—	1	0	0	0	0	2	3	0	0	0	1	3	18.0	0.00	—	.333	.400	75	.231	0	1	1	-0	0.0

● GARVIN ALSTON Alston, Garvin James b: 12/8/71, Mt.Vernon, N.Y. BR/TR, 6'2", 185 lbs. Deb: 6/6/96

YEAR	TM/L	W	L	PCT	G	GS	CG	SH	SV	IP	H	R	HR	HB	BB	SO	RAT	ERA	ERA+	OAV	OOB	BH	AVG	PB	PR	PR+	PD	TPI
1996	Col-N	1	0	1.000	6	0	0	0	0	6	9	6	1	1	3	5	19.5	9.00	58	.375	.464	0	.000	-0	-3	-2	0	-0.3

● PORFI ALTAMIRANO Altamirano, Porfirio (Ramirez) b: 5/17/52, Darillo, Nic. BR/TR, 6', 175 lbs. Deb: 5/9/82

YEAR	TM/L	W	L	PCT	G	GS	CG	SH	SV	IP	H	R	HR	HB	BB	SO	RAT	ERA	ERA+	OAV	OOB	BH	AVG	PB	PR	PR+	PD	TPI
1982	Phi-N	5	1	.833	29	0	0	0	2	39	41	19	2	1	14	26	12.9	4.15	88	.281	.348	1	.250	0	-2	-2	0	-0.3
1983	Phi-N	2	3	.400	31	0	0	0	0	41^1	38	18	9	2	15	24	12.0	3.70	97	.255	.331	0	.000	-0	-0	-1	0	-0.1
1984	Chi-N	0	0	—	5	0	0	0	0	11^1	8	6	2	0	1	7	7.1	4.76	82	.195	.214	0	.000	-0	-1	-1	0	0.0
Total	3	7	4	.636	65	0	0	0	2	91^2	87	43	13	3	30	57	11.8	4.03	91	.259	.325	1	.125	-0	-4	-4	1	-0.4

● ERNIE ALTEN Alten, Ernest Matthias "Lefty" b: 12/1/1894, Avon, Ohio d: 9/9/81, Napa, Cal. BR/TL, 6', 175 lbs. Deb: 4/17/20

YEAR	TM/L	W	L	PCT	G	GS	CG	SH	SV	IP	H	R	HR	HB	BB	SO	RAT	ERA	ERA+	OAV	OOB	BH	AVG	PB	PR	PR+	PD	TPI
1920	Det-A	0	1	.000	14	1	0	0	0	23	40	27	2	1	9	4	19.6	9.00	41	.392	.446	0	.000	-1	-13	-14	0	-0.7

● NICK ALTROCK Altrock, Nicholas b: 9/15/1876, Cincinnati, Ohio d: 1/20/65, Washington, D.C. BB/TL, 5'10", 197 lbs. Deb: 7/14/1898 C♦

YEAR	TM/L	W	L	PCT	G	GS	CG	SH	SV	IP	H	R	HR	HB	BB	SO	RAT	ERA	ERA+	OAV	OOB	BH	AVG	PB	PR	PR+	PD	TPI
1898	Lou-N	3	3	.500	11	7	6	0	0	70	89	54	2	3	21	13	14.5	4.50	79	.307	.360	7	.241	0	-7	-7	2	-0.3
1902	Bos-A	0	2	.000	3	2	1	0	1	18	19	13	0	1	7	5	13.5	2.00	179	.271	.346	0	.000	-1	3	3	1	0.3
1903	Bos-A	0	1	.000	1	1	1	0	0	8	13	10	0	0	4	3	19.1	9.00	34	.361	.425	2	.667	1	-5	-5	1	-0.3

YEAR	TM/L	W	L	PCT	G	GS	CG	SH	SV	IP	H	R	HR	HB	BB	SO	RAT	ERA	ERA+	OAV	OOB	BH	AVG	PB	PR	PR+	PD	TPI
	Chi-A	4	3	.571	12	8	6	1	0	71	59	35	3	3	19	19	10.3	2.15	130	.226	.286	9	.300	2	6	5	3	1.1
	Yr	4	4	.500	13	9	7	1	0	79	72	45	3	3	23	22	11.2	2.85	99	.242	.303	11	.333	4	1	-0	4	0.8
1904	Chi-A	19	14	.576	38	36	31	6	1	307	274	117	2	3	48	87	9.5	2.96	83	.240	.272	22	.198	1	-12	-18	4	-1.4
1905	Chi-A	23	12	.657	38	34	31	3	0	315^2	274	89	3	2	63	97	9.7	1.88	131	.236	.276	14	.125	-3	27	22	8	3.0
1906	*Chi-A	20	13	.606	38	30	25	4	0	287^2	269	95	0	3	42	99	9.8	2.06	123	.250	.281	16	.160	-1	20	16	4	2.2
1907	Chi-A	7	13	.350	30	21	15	1	2	213^2	210	76	3	2	31	61	10.2	2.57	93	.259	.288	13	.181	1	-1	-4	5	0.2
1908	Chi-A	5	7	.417	23	13	8	1	2	136	127	55	2	2	18	21	9.7	2.71	85	.248	.276	10	.204	1	-5	-6	5	0.1
1909	Chi-A	0	1	.000	1	1	1	0	0	9	16	6	0	0	1	2	17.0	5.00	47	.485	.500	0	.000	-0	-3	-3	0	-0.3
	Was-A	1	3	.250	9	5	2	0	0	38	55	23	0	1	5	9	14.4	5.45	45	.333	.357	1	.053	-1	-13	-13	0	-1.3
	Yr	1	4	.200	10	6	3	0	0	47	71	29	0	1	6	11	14.9	5.36	45	.359	.380	1	.045	-1	-15	-16	1	-1.6
1912	Was-A	0	1	.000	1	0	0	0	0	1	1	2	0	0	2	0	27.0	18.00	19	.200	.429	0	.000	-0	-2	-2	-0	-0.3
1913	Was-A	0	0	—	4	0	0	0	0	9	7	5	0	1	4	2	12.0	5.00	59	.184	.279	0	.000	-0	-2	-2	0	-0.1
1914	Was-A	0	0	—	1	0	0	0	0	1	3	0	0	0	0	0	27.0	0.00	—	.750	.750	0	—	0	0	0	-0	0.0
1915	Was-A	0	0	—	1	0	0	0	1	3	7	4	0	0	1	2	24.0	9.00	33	.438	.471	0	.000	-0	-2	-2	-0	-0.2
1918	Was-A	1	2	.333	5	3	1	0	0	24	24	11	1	1	6	5	11.6	3.00	91	.279	.333	1	.125	0	-1	-1	0	0.0
1919	Was-A	0	0	—	1	0	0	0	0	0	4	0	0	0	—	—	∞	—	1.000	1.000	99	—	0	-4	-4		0	-0.3
1924	Was-A	0	0	—	1	0	0	0	0	2	4	1	0	0	0	0	18.0	0.00	—	.500	.500	1	1.000	1	1	1	0	0.2
Total	16	83	75	.525	218	161	128	16	7	1514	1455	600	16	22	272	425	10.4	2.67	95	.254	.291	97	.176	1	2	-22	34	2.6
● TAVO ALVAREZ	Alvarez, Cesar Octavio b: 11/25/71, Ciudad Obregon, Mexico BR/TR, 6'3", 245 lbs. Deb: 8/21/95																											
1995	Mon-N	1	5	.167	8	8	0	0	0	37^1	46	30	2	3	14	17	15.2	6.75	64	.297	.366	0	.000	-1	-11	-10	-0	-1.4
1996	Mon-N	2	1	.667	11	5	0	0	0	21	19	10	0	1	12	9	13.7	3.00	144	.235	.340	2	.500	1	3	3	0	0.5
Total	2	3	6	.333	19	13	0	0	0	58^1	65	40	2	4	26	26	14.7	5.40	80	.275	.357	2	.125	-1	-8	-7	-0	-0.9
● JOSE ALVAREZ	Alvarez, Jose Lino b: 4/12/56, Tampa, Fla. BR/TR, 5'10", 170 lbs. Deb: 10/1/81																											
1981	Atl-N	0	0	—	1	0	0	0	0	2	0	0	0	0	0	2	0.0	0.00	—	.000	.000	0	—	0	1	1	-0	0.0
1982	Atl-N	0	0	—	7	0	0	0	0	7^2	8	4	1	0	2	6	11.7	4.70	80	.308	.357	0	—	0	-1	-1	0	0.0
1988	Atl-N	5	6	.455	60	0	0	0	3	102^1	88	34	7	6	53	81	12.9	2.99	123	.240	.346	3	.375	1	5	7	1	1.1
1989	Atl-N	3	3	.500	30	0	0	0	2	50^1	44	18	4	1	24	45	12.3	2.86	128	.237	.327	0	.000	-0	4	4	1	0.6
Total	4	8	9	.471	98	0	0	0	5	162^1	140	56	12	7	79	134	12.5	2.99	123	.240	.337	3	.273	1	9	12	2	1.7
● JUAN ALVAREZ	Alvarez, Juan M. b: 8/9/73, Coral Gables, Fla. BL/TL, 6'1", 175 lbs. Deb: 9/1/99																											
1999	Ana-A	0	1	.000	8	0	0	0	0	3	1	1	0	0	4	4	15.0	3.00	162	.111	.385	0	—	0	1	1	0	0.1
2000	Ana-A	0	0	—	11	0	0	0	0	6	14	9	3	0	7	2	31.5	13.50	37	.467	.568	0	—	0	-6	-6	0	-0.2
Total	2	0	1	.000	19	0	0	0	0	9	15	10	3	0	11	6	26.0	10.00	49	.385	.520	0	—	0	-5	-5	0	-0.1
● WILSON ALVAREZ	Alvarez, Wilson Eduardo (Fuenmayor) b: 3/24/70, Maracaibo, Venez. BL/TL, 6'1", 235 lbs. Deb: 7/24/89																											
1989	Tex-A	0	1	.000	1	1	0	0	0	0	3	2	0	2	—	—	∞	—	1.000	1.000	102	—	0	-3	-3	0	-0.3	
1991	Chi-A	3	2	.600	10	9	2	1	0	56^1	47	26	9	0	29	32	12.1	3.51	113	.230	.326	0	—	0	4	3	-0	0.2
1992	Chi-A	5	3	.625	34	9	0	0	1	100^1	103	64	12	4	65	66	15.4	5.20	74	.272	.384	0	—	0	-14	-15	-0	-1.1
1993	*Chi-A	15	8	.652	31	31	1	1	0	207^2	168	78	14	7	122	155	12.9	2.95	142	.230	.346	0	—	0	32	30	-0	3.0
1994	Chi-A★	12	8	.600	24	24	2	1	0	161^2	147	72	16	0	62	108	11.6	3.45	135	.241	.311	0	—	0	24	23	-2	2.2
1995	Chi-A	8	11	.421	29	29	3	0	0	175	171	96	21	2	93	118	13.7	4.32	103	.258	.351	0	—	0	8	3	1	0.4
1996	Chi-A	15	10	.600	35	35	0	0	0	217^1	216	106	21	4	97	181	13.1	4.22	112	.258	.338	0	—	0	19	13	0	1.3
1997	Chi-A	9	8	.529	22	22	2	1	0	145^2	126	61	9	3	55	110	11.4	3.03	145	.232	.306	0	.000	-0	25	23	-1	2.3
	*SF-N	4	3	.571	11	11	0	0	0	66^1	54	36	9	1	36	69	12.3	4.48	91	.224	.327	3	.130	-0	-2	-3	-1	-0.3
1998	TB-A	6	14	.300	25	25	0	0	0	142^2	130	78	18	9	68	107	13.1	4.73	101	.239	.333	0	—	0	-1	1	-3	-0.2
1999	TB-A	9	9	.500	28	28	1	0	0	160	159	92	22	6	79	128	13.7	4.22	118	.260	.350	0	.000	-0	12	13	0	1.2
Total	10	86	77	.528	250	224	11	4	1	1433	1324	712	153	36	708	1074	13.0	3.96	113	.247	.338	3	.103	-1	103	87	-5	8.7
● RED AMES	Ames, Leon Kessling b: 8/2/1882, Warren, Ohio d: 10/8/36, Warren, Ohio BB/TR, 5'10.5", 185 lbs. Deb: 9/14/03																											
1903	NY-N	2	0	1.000	2	2	2	1	0	14	5	2	0	0	8	14	8.4	1.29	260	.114	.250	0	.000	-1	3	3	-1	0.3
1904	NY-N	4	6	.400	16	13	11	1	3	115	94	44	2	3	38	93	10.6	2.27	120	.222	.291	5	.125	-1	6	6	-0	0.3
1905	*NY-N	22	8	.733	34	31	21	2	0	262^2	220	113	2	3	105	198	11.2	2.74	107	.230	.308	14	.144	-1	8	6	1	0.6
1906	NY-N	12	10	.545	31	25	15	1	1	203^1	166	79	1	3	93	156	11.6	2.66	98	.223	.312	4	.066	-3	-0	-1	3	-0.1
1907	NY-N	10	12	.455	39	26	17	2	1	233^1	184	93	4	10	108	146	11.6	2.16	115	.219	.315	12	.174	2	8	8	3	1.3
1908	NY-N	7	4	.636	18	15	5	0	1	114^1	96	35	0	1	27	81	9.8	1.81	133	.232	.281	7	.194	-0	7	8	1	0.9
1909	NY-N	15	10	.600	34	26	20	2	1	244	217	109	2	4	81	156	11.1	2.69	95	.241	.306	6	.074	-5	-3	-4	7	-0.2
1910	NY-N	12	11	.522	33	23	13	3	0	190^1	161	78	3	6	63	94	10.9	2.22	133	.237	.308	11	.177	-1	17	16	4	2.2
1911	*NY-N	11	10	.524	34	23	13	1	2	205	170	80	0	4	54	118	10.0	2.68	126	.223	.277	6	.094	-3	16	16	3	1.5
1912	*NY-N	11	5	.688	33	22	9	2	2	179	194	82	3	4	35	83	11.7	2.46	137	.281	.320	13	.224	1	19	18	2	1.9
1913	NY-N	2	1	.667	8	5	2	0	1	41^2	35	11	0	1	8	30	9.5	2.16	144	.241	.286	2	.154	-1	5	5	2	0.5
	Cin-N	11	13	.458	31	24	12	1	2	187^1	185	82	7	5	70	80	12.5	2.88	113	.265	.336	6	.102	-4	7	8	0	0.5
	Yr	13	14	.481	39	29	14	1	3	229	220	93	7	6	78	110	11.9	2.75	117	.261	.328	8	.111	-5	12	12	2	1.0
1914	Cin-N	15	23	.395	47	37	18	4	**6**	297	274	125	8	6	94	128	11.3	2.64	111	.248	.311	12	.128	-4	5	9	4	1.2
1915	Cin-N	2	4	.333	17	7	4	1	1	68	82	39	2	0	24	26	14.0	4.50	64	.311	.368	1	.050	-1	-13	-12	1	-1.1
	StL-N	9	3	.750	15	14	8	2	1	113^1	93	35	1	0	32	48	9.9	2.46	113	.226	.282	4	.114	-2	4	4	2	0.4
	Yr	11	7	.611	32	21	12	3	2	181^1	175	74	3	0	56	74	11.5	3.23	87	.259	.316	5	.091	-3	-10	-8	2	-0.7
1916	StL-N	11	16	.407	45	25	10	2	**8**	228	225	100	3	5	57	98	11.3	2.64	100	.263	.313	12	.176	-0	-1	0	-2	-0.2
1917	StL-N	15	10	.600	43	19	10	2	3	209	189	75	2	3	57	62	10.7	2.71	99	.249	.304	12	.188	2	-0	-0	4	0.7
1918	StL-N	9	14	.391	27	25	17	0	1	206^2	192	75	1	5	52	68	10.8	2.31	117	.252	.304	10	.156	-1	10	9	-1	0.9
1919	StL-N	3	5	.375	23	6	1	0	1	70	88	44	1	1	25	19	14.7	4.89	57	.314	.373	4	.222	-0	-15	-17	-2	-2.1
	Phi-N	0	2	.000	3	2	1	0	1	16	26	12	0	0	3	4	16.3	6.19	52	.400	.426	2	.400	1	-6	-5	0	-0.5
	Yr	3	7	.300	26	8	2	0	2	86	114	56	1	1	28	23	15.0	5.13	56	.330	.382	6	.261	1	-21	-22	-2	-2.6
Total	17	183	167	.523	533	370	209	27	36	3198	2896	1313	42	64	1034	1702	11.2	2.63	108	.245	.310	143	.141	-21	77	77	32	9.0
● DOC AMOLE	Amole, Morris George b: 7/5/1878, Coatesville, Pa. d: 3/7/12, Wilmington, Del. BR/TL, 5'9", 165 lbs. Deb: 8/19/1897																											
1897	Bal-N	4	4	.500	11	7	6	0	0	70	67	34	0	6	17	19	11.6	2.57	162	.250	.309	3	.107	-3	14	13	0	1.0
1898	Was-N	0	6	.000	7	5	4	0	0	49^1	83	57	0	6	22	11	20.3	7.84	47	.369	.439	2	.100	-2	-23	-23	1	-2.1
Total	2	4	10	.286	18	12	10	0	0	119^1	150	91	0	12	39	30	15.2	4.75	83	.304	.369	5	.104	-4	-10	-11	1	-1.1
● VICENTE AMOR	Amor, Vicente (Alvarez) b: 8/8/32, Havana, Cuba BR/TR, 6'3", 182 lbs. Deb: 4/16/55																											
1955	Chi-N	0	1	.000	4	0	0	0	0	6	11	3	0	0	3	3	21.0	4.50	91	.407	.467	0	—	0	-0	-0	1	0.0
1957	Cin-N	1	2	.333	9	4	1	0	0	27^1	39	19	2	2	10	9	16.8	5.93	69	.345	.408	1	.167	-0	-6	-5	-0	-0.6
Total	2	1	3	.250	13	4	1	0	0	33^1	50	22	2	2	13	12	17.6	5.67	72	.357	.419	1	.167	-0	-7	-6	0	-0.6
● WALTER ANCKER	Ancker, Walter b: 4/10/1894, New York, N.Y. d: 2/13/54, Englewood, N.J. BR/TR, 6'1", 190 lbs. Deb: 9/3/15																											
1915	Phi-A	0	0	—	4	1	0	0	0	17^2	19	10	1	3	17	4	19.9	3.57	82	.279	.443	0	.000	-1	-1	-1	0	-0.2
● LARRY ANDERSEN	Andersen, Larry Eugene b: 5/6/53, Portland, Ore. BR/TR, 6'3", 205 lbs. Deb: 9/5/75																											
1975	Cle-A	0	0	—	3	0	0	0	0	5^2	4	3	0	0	2	4	9.5	4.76	80	.200	.273	0	—	0	-1	-1	0	0.0
1977	Cle-A	0	1	.000	11	0	0	0	0	14^1	10	7	1	0	9	8	11.9	3.14	126	.200	.322	0	—	0	1	1	1	0.2
1979	Cle-A	0	0	—	8	0	0	0	0	16^2	25	14	3	0	4	7	15.7	7.56	56	.357	.392	0	—	0	-6	-6	0	-0.3
1981	Sea-A	3	3	.500	41	0	0	0	5	67^2	57	27	4	2	18	40	10.2	2.66	145	.228	.285	0	—	0	8	9	-0	0.9
1982	Sea-A	0	0	—	40	1	0	0	1	79^2	100	56	16	4	23	32	14.3	5.99	71	.311	.364	0	—	0	-17	-15	1	-0.6
1983	*Phi-N	1	0	1.000	17	0	0	0	0	26^1	19	7	0	0	9	14	9.6	2.39	149	.200	.269	0	.000	-0	4	4	0	0.2
1984	Phi-N	3	7	.300	64	0	0	0	4	90^2	85	32	5	0	25	54	10.9	2.38	153	.248	.299	0	.000	-0	12	12	0	1.4
1985	Phi-N	3	3	.500	57	0	0	0	3	73	78	41	5	3	26	50	13.2	4.32	86	.274	.341	0	.000	-0	-6	-5	2	-0.2
1986	Phi-N	0	0	—	10	0	0	0	0	12^2	19	8	0	0	3	9	15.6	4.26	91	.388	.423	0	—	0	-1	-1	0	0.0
	*Hou-N	2	1	.667	38	0	0	0	1	64^2	64	22	2	1	23	33	12.2	2.78	130	.276	.344	0	.000	-1	7	6	0	0.3
	Yr	2	1	.667	48	0	0	0	1	77^1	83	30	2	1	26	42	12.8	3.03	121	.295	.357	0	.000	-1	6	5	0	0.3

YEAR	TM/L	W	L	PCT	G	GS	CG	SH	SV	IP	H	R	HR	HB	BB	SO	RAT	ERA	ERA+	OAV	OOB	BH	AVG	PB	PR	PR+	PD	TPI
1987	Hou-N	9	5	.643	67	0	0	0	5	101^{2}	95	46	7	2	41	94	12.2	3.45	114	.246	.322	1	.167	0	7	6	-0	0.7
1988	Hou-N	2	4	.333	53	0	0	0	5	82^{2}	82	29	3	1	20	66	11.2	2.94	113	.254	.299	2	.333	1	5	4	-0	0.3
1989	Hou-N	4	4	.500	60	0	0	0	3	87^{2}	63	19	2	0	24	85	8.9	1.54	220	.198	.254	1	.333	0	**19**	**19**	1	1.9
1990	Hou-N	5	2	.714	50	0	0	0	6	73^{2}	61	19	2	1	24	68	10.5	1.95	190	.229	.296	0	.000	-0	15	15	1	1.7
	*Bos-A	0	0	—	15	0	0	0	1	22	18	3	0	1	3	25	9.0	1.23	333	.220	.256	0	—	0	7	7	-1	0.3
1991	SD-N	3	4	.429	38	0	0	0	13	47	39	13	0	0	13	40	10.0	2.30	165	.231	.286	0	.000	-0	7	8	0	1.5
1992	SD-N	1	1	.500	34	0	0	0	2	35	26	14	2	1	8	35	9.0	3.34	107	.202	.254	0	.000	0	1	1	0	0.1
1993	*Phi-N	3	2	.600	64	0	0	0	0	61^{2}	54	22	4	1	21	67	11.1	2.92	136	.233	.299	1	1.000	0	8	7	-1	0.5
1994	Phi-N	1	2	.333	29	0	0	0	0	32^{2}	33	20	2	0	15	27	13.2	4.41	97	.256	.333	0	—	0	-1	-0	-0	0.0
Total	17	40	39	.506	699	1	0	0	49	995^{1}	932	402	58	17	311	758	11.4	3.15	120	.249	.309	5	.132	-0	69	69	5	8.9
● ALLAN ANDERSON Anderson, Allan Lee b: 1/7/64, Lancaster, Ohio BL/TL, 6′, 186 lbs. Deb: 6/11/86																												
1986	Min-A	3	6	.333	21	10	1	0	0	84^{1}	106	54	11	1	30	51	14.6	5.55	78	.316	.374	0	—	0	-13	-11	0	-1.0
1987	Min-A	1	0	1.000	4	2	0	0	0	12^{1}	20	15	3	0	10	3	21.9	10.95	42	.392	.492	0	—	0	-9	-8	-0	-0.6
1988	Min-A	16	9	.640	30	30	3	1	0	202^{1}	199	70	14	7	37	83	10.8	**2.45**	**167**	.261	.301	0	—	0	34	36	1	4.5
1989	Min-A	17	10	.630	33	33	4	1	0	196^{2}	214	97	15	7	53	69	12.5	3.80	109	.275	.327	0	.000	-0	2	7	-1	0.9
1990	Min-A	7	18	.280	31	31	5	1	0	188^{2}	214	106	20	5	39	82	12.3	4.53	92	.289	.329	0	—	0	-13	-7	2	-0.7
1991	Min-A	5	11	.313	29	22	2	0	0	134^{1}	148	82	24	5	42	51	13.1	4.96	86	.281	.340	0	—	0	-13	-10	-0	-1.0
Total	6	49	54	.476	148	128	15	3	0	818^{2}	901	424	87	25	211	339	12.5	4.11	102	.282	.331	0	.000	-0	-11	6	2	2.1
● RED ANDERSON Anderson, Arnold Revola b: 6/19/12, Lawton, Iowa d: 8/7/72, Sioux City, Iowa BR/TR, 6′3″, 210 lbs. Deb: 9/19/37																												
1937	Was-A	0	1	.000	2	1	0	0	0	10^{2}	11	9	0	1	11	3	19.4	6.75	66	.282	.451	0	.000	-0	-3	-3	0	-0.2
1940	Was-A	1	1	.500	2	2	2	0	0	14	12	6	0	0	5	3	10.9	3.86	108	.245	.315	3	.600	1	1	1	0	0.2
1941	Was-A	4	6	.400	32	6	1	0	0	112	127	69	7	3	53	34	14.7	4.18	97	.296	.377	8	.258	2	-0	-2	-1	0.0
Total	3	5	8	.385	36	9	3	0	0	136^{2}	150	84	7	4	69	40	14.7	4.35	94	.290	.378	11	.282	3	-2	-4	-1	0.0
● BRIAN ANDERSON Anderson, Brian James b: 4/26/72, Portsmouth, Va. BL/TL, 6′1″, 190 lbs. Deb: 9/10/93																												
1993	Cal-A	0	0	—	4	1	0	0	0	11^{1}	11	5	1	0	2	4	10.3	3.97	114	.256	.289	0	—	0	0	1	-0	0.0
1994	Cal-A	7	5	.583	18	18	0	0	0	101^{2}	120	63	13	5	27	47	13.5	5.22	94	.300	.352	0	—	0	-5	-4	-1	-0.5
1995	Cal-A	6	8	.429	18	17	1	0	0	99^{2}	110	66	24	3	30	45	12.9	5.87	80	.282	.338	0	—	0	-13	-13	-0	-1.5
1996	Cle-A	3	1	.750	10	9	0	0	0	51^{1}	58	29	9	0	14	21	12.6	4.91	100	.296	.343	0	—	0	1	-0	1	0.1
1997	*Cle-A	4	2	.667	8	8	0	0	0	48	55	28	7	0	11	22	12.4	4.69	100	.301	.340	0	—	0	-1	0	1	0.1
1998	Ari-N	12	13	.480	32	32	2	1	0	208	221	109	39	4	24	95	10.8	4.33	97	.274	.299	7	.106	-2	-2	-3	3	-0.2
1999	*Ari-N	8	2	.800	31	19	2	1	1	130	144	69	18	1	28	75	12.0	4.57	100	.279	.317	5	.132	1	-0	0	4	0.4
2000	Ari-N	11	7	.611	33	32	2	0	0	213^{1}	226	101	38	3	39	104	11.3	4.05	114	.275	.310	13	.188	1	14	13	3	1.4
Total	8	51	38	.573	154	136	7	2	1	863^{1}	945	470	149	16	175	413	11.8	4.63	99	.282	.320	25	.145	-1	-5	-5	9	-0.2
● DAVE ANDERSON Anderson, David S. b: 10/10/1868, Chester, Pa. d: 3/22/1897, Chester, Pa. TL, Deb: 8/24/1889																												
1889	Phi-N	0	1	.000	5	2	1	0	0	23	30	21	2	0	14	8	17.2	7.43	59	.306	.393	2	.182	-0	-9	-7	0	-0.3
1890	Phi-N	1	1	.500	3	2	1	0	0	19^{1}	31	25	0	1	11	7	20.0	7.45	49	.352	.430	1	.111	-1	-8	-8	0	-0.6
	Pit-N	2	11	.154	13	13	13	0	0	108	116	84	2	7	49	41	14.3	4.67	71	.266	.350	3	.071	-5	-13	-18	4	-1.7
	Yr	3	12	.200	16	15	14	0	0	127^{1}	147	109	2	8	60	48	15.2	5.09	66	.281	.363	4	.078	-6	-21	-26	4	-2.3
Total	2	3	13	.188	21	17	15	0	0	150^{1}	177	130	4	8	74	56	15.5	5.45	64	.285	.368	6	.097	-6	-30	-34	4	-2.6
● JIMMY ANDERSON Anderson, James Drew b: 1/22/76, Portsmouth, Va. BL/TL, 6′1″, 195 lbs. Deb: 7/4/99																												
1999	Pit-N	2	1	.667	13	4	0	0	0	29^{1}	25	15	2	1	16	13	12.9	3.99	115	.234	.339	3	.333	1	2	2	0	0.3
2000	Pit-N	5	11	.313	27	26	1	0	0	144	169	94	13	7	58	73	14.6	5.25	88	.294	.366	7	.140	-1	-10	-10	2	-0.9
Total	2	7	12	.368	40	30	1	0	0	173^{1}	194	109	15	8	74	86	14.3	5.04	91	.284	.361	10	.169	-0	-8	-9	2	-0.6
● JOHN ANDERSON Anderson, John Charles b: 11/23/32, St.Paul, Minn. BR/TR, 6′1″, 190 lbs. Deb: 8/17/58																												
1958	Phi-N	0	0	—	5	1	0	0	0	16	26	17	5	1	4	9	17.4	7.88	50	.361	.403	0	.000	-0	-7	-7	-0	-0.4
1960	Bal-A	0	0	—	4	0	0	0	0	4^{2}	8	7	0	0	4	1	23.1	13.50	28	.444	.545	0	—	0	-5	-5	0	-0.2
1962	StL-N	0	0	—	5	0	0	0	1	6^{1}	4	1	0	0	3	3	9.9	1.42	300	.182	.280	0	—	0	2	2	-0	0.1
	Hou-N	0	0	—	10	0	0	0	0	17^{2}	26	12	1	0	3	6	14.8	5.09	73	.338	.363	0	.000	-0	-2	-3	1	-0.1
	Yr	0	0	—	15	0	0	0	1	24	30	13	1	0	6	9	13.5	4.13	94	.303	.343	0	.000	-0	-0	-1	0	0.0
Total	3	0	0	—	24	1	0	0	1	44^{2}	64	37	6	1	14	19	15.9	6.45	60	.339	.387	0	.000	-0	-12	-13	0	-0.6
● FRED ANDERSON Anderson, John Frederick b: 12/11/1885, Calahaln, N.C. d: 11/8/57, Winston-Salem, N.C. BR/TR, 6′2″, 180 lbs. Deb: 9/25/09																												
1909	Bos-A	0	0	—	1	1	0	0	0	8	3	3	0	0	1	5	4.5	1.13	222	.115	.148	0	.000	-0	1	1	0	0.1
1913	Bos-A	0	6	.000	10	8	4	0	0	57^{1}	84	51	0	1	21	32	16.6	5.97	49	.350	.405	1	.050	-2	-19	-19	-0	-2.0
1914	Buf-F	13	15	.464	37	28	21	2	0	260^{1}	243	115	8	2	64	144	10.7	3.08	96	.249	.297	17	.189	-3	-6	-3	-1	-0.7
1915	Buf-F	19	13	.594	36	28	14	5	0	240	192	80	5	3	72	142	10.0	2.51	111	.222	.285	12	.150	-5	6	7	-1	0.4
1916	NY-N	9	13	.409	38	27	13	2	2	188	206	99	7	5	38	98	11.9	3.40	72	.277	.316	8	.138	-0	-16	-22	-2	-2.9
1917	*NY-N	8	8	.500	38	18	8	1	3	162	122	40	1	2	34	69	**8.8**	1.44	**177**	.209	**.255**	3	.071	-3	23	21	-1	1.9
1918	NY-N	4	2	.667	18	4	2	1	**3**	70^{2}	62	27	1	2	17	24	10.3	2.67	98	.246	.299	0	.000	-3	1	-0	3	0.0
Total	7	53	57	.482	178	114	62	11	8	986^{1}	912	415	22	15	247	514	10.7	2.86	95	.248	.298	41	.131	-16	-11	-15	-2	-3.2
● BUD ANDERSON Anderson, Karl Adam b: 5/27/56, Westbury, N.Y. BR/TR, 6′3″, 210 lbs. Deb: 6/11/82																												
1982	Cle-A	3	4	.429	25	5	1	0	0	80^{2}	84	37	4	1	30	44	12.8	3.35	122	.268	.334	0	—	0	7	7	-0	0.5
1983	Cle-A	1	6	.143	39	1	0	0	7	68^{1}	64	34	8	0	32	32	12.6	4.08	104	.255	.339	0	—	0	-0	1	-1	0.0
Total	2	4	10	.286	64	6	1	0	7	149	148	71	12	1	62	76	12.7	3.68	113	.262	.337	0	—	0	7	8	-1	0.5
● LARRY ANDERSON Anderson, Lawrence Dennis b: 12/3/52, Maywood, Cal. BR/TR, 6′3″, 190 lbs. Deb: 9/25/74																												
1974	Mil-A	0	0	—	2	0	0	0	0	2^{1}	2	0	0	0	1	3	11.6	0.00	—	.250	.333	0	—	0	1	1	0	0.1
1975	Mil-A	1	0	1.000	8	1	1	1	0	30^{1}	36	18	3	0	6	13	12.5	5.04	76	.298	.331	0	—	0	-4	-4	0	-0.2
1977	Chi-A	1	3	.250	6	0	0	0	0	8^{2}	10	10	1	0	15	7	26.0	9.35	44	.286	.500	0	—	0	-5	-5	-0	-0.9
Total	3	2	3	.400	16	1	1	1	0	41^{1}	48	28	4	0	22	23	15.2	5.66	69	.293	.376	0	—	0	-8	-8	0	-1.0
● MATT ANDERSON Anderson, Matthew Jason b: 8/17/76, Louisville, Ky. BR/TR, 6′4″, 200 lbs. Deb: 6/25/98																												
1998	Det-A	5	1	.833	42	0	0	0	0	44	38	16	3	2	31	44	14.5	3.27	144	.250	.384	0	—	0	7	7	0	0.8
1999	Det-A	2	1	.667	37	0	0	0	0	38	33	27	8	1	35	32	16.3	5.68	86	.232	.388	0	—	0	-3	-3	-1	-0.3
2000	Det-A	3	2	.600	69	0	0	0	1	74^{1}	61	44	8	3	45	71	13.2	4.72	101	.228	.345	0	—	0	2	0	-0	0.0
Total	3	10	4	.714	148	0	0	0	1	156^{1}	132	87	19	6	111	147	14.3	4.55	105	.235	.367	0	—	0	5	4	-1	0.5
● MIKE ANDERSON Anderson, Michael Allen b: 6/22/51, Florence, S.C. BR/TR, 6′2″, 200 lbs. Deb: 9/2/71 F◆																												
1979	Phi-N	0	0	—	1	0	0	0	0	1	2	0	0	0	0	2	18.0	0.00	—	.400	.400	18	.231	0	0	0	0	0.0
● MIKE ANDERSON Anderson, Michael James b: 7/30/66, Austin, Tex. BR/TR, 6′3″, 200 lbs. Deb: 9/7/93																												
1993	Cin-N	0	0	—	3	0	0	0	0	5^{1}	12	11	3	0	3	4	25.3	18.56	22	.444	.500	0	.000	-0	-9	-9	0	-0.4
● CRAIG ANDERSON Anderson, Norman Craig b: 7/1/38, Washington, D.C. BR/TR, 6′2″, 205 lbs. Deb: 6/23/61																												
1961	StL-N	4	3	.571	25	0	0	0	1	38^{2}	38	15	3	1	12	21	11.9	3.26	135	.255	.315	3	.333	1	3	4	0	0.8
1962	NY-N	3	17	.150	50	14	2	0	4	131^{1}	150	108	18	5	63	62	14.9	5.35	78	.278	.359	3	.094	-2	-20	-16	3	-2.2
1963	NY-N	0	2	.000	3	2	0	0	0	9^{1}	17	15	0	0	3	6	19.3	8.68	40	.362	.400	1	.333	0	-6	-5	0	-0.9
1964	NY-N	0	1	.000	4	1	0	0	0	13	21	9	0	0	3	5	16.6	5.54	65	.382	.414	0	.000	-0	-3	-3	0	-0.2
Total	4	7	23	.233	82	17	2	0	5	192^{1}	226	147	21	6	81	94	14.6	5.10	81	.286	.357	7	.149	-1	-26	-19	3	-2.5
● RICK ANDERSON Anderson, Richard Arlen b: 11/29/56, Everett, Wash. BR/TR, 6′, 175 lbs. Deb: 6/9/86																												
1986	NY-N	2	1	.667	15	5	0	0	1	49^{2}	45	17	3	0	11	21	10.1	2.72	130	.245	.287	1	.091	-1	6	5	-1	0.2
1987	KC-A	0	2	.000	6	2	0	0	0	13	26	22	3	2	9	12	25.6	13.85	33	.394	.481	0	—	0	-14	-13	0	-1.5
1988	KC-A	2	1	.667	7	3	0	0	0	34	41	17	3	1	9	9	13.5	4.24	94	.308	.357	0	—	0	-1	-1	-1	-0.1
Total	3	4	4	.500	28	10	0	0	1	96^{2}	112	56	9	3	29	42	13.4	4.75	81	.292	.347	1	.091	-1	-9	-10	-1	-1.4

● RICK ANDERSON Anderson, Richard Lee b: 12/25/53, Inglewood, Cal. d: 6/23/89, Wilmington, Cal. BR/TR, 6′2″, 210 lbs. Deb: 9/18/79

YEAR	TM/L	W	L	PCT	G	GS	CG	SH	SV	IP	H	R	HR	HB	BB	SO	RAT	ERA	ERA+	OAV	OOB	BH	AVG	PB	PR	PR+	PD	TPI
1979	NY-A	0	0	—	1	0	0	0	0	2^1	1	1	0	0	4	0	19.3	3.86	106	.167	.500	0	—	0	0	0	1	0.1
1980	Sea-A	0	0	—	5	2	0	0	0	9^2	8	5	1	0	10	7	16.8	3.72	111	.229	.400	0	—	0	0	0	-0	0.0
Total	2	0	0	—	6	2	0	0	0	12	9	6	1	0	14	7	17.3	3.75	110	.220	.418	0	—	0	0	1	0	0.1

● BOB ANDERSON Anderson, Robert Carl b: 9/29/35, E.Chicago, Ind. BR/TR, 6′4.5″, 210 lbs. Deb: 7/31/57

YEAR	TM/L	W	L	PCT	G	GS	CG	SH	SV	IP	H	R	HR	HB	BB	SO	RAT	ERA	ERA+	OAV	OOB	BH	AVG	PB	PR	PR+	PD	TPI
1957	Chi-N	0	1	.000	8	0	0	0	0	16^1	20	16	2	1	8	7	16.0	7.71	50	.317	.403	0	.000	-1	-7	-7	0	-0.4
1958	Chi-N	3	3	.500	17	8	2	0	0	65^2	61	29	3	1	29	51	12.5	3.97	99	.255	.338	2	.118	-1	-0	-0	0	-0.1
1959	Chi-N	12	13	.480	37	36	7	1	0	235^1	245	117	21	5	77	113	12.5	4.13	96	.272	.333	6	.075	-4	-5	-5	1	-0.8
1960	Chi-N	9	11	.450	38	30	5	0	1	203^2	201	105	26	7	68	115	12.2	4.11	92	.255	.320	12	.169	0	-8	-7	1	-0.6
1961	Chi-N	7	10	.412	57	12	1	0	8	152	162	85	14	2	56	96	13.0	4.26	98	.275	.340	6	.143	0	-4	-1	4	0.2
1962	Chi-N	2	7	.222	57	4	0	0	4	107^2	111	70	9	5	60	82	14.7	5.02	83	.266	.364	3	.130	0	-13	-10	-0	-0.8
1963	Det-A	3	1	.750	32	3	0	0	0	60	58	28	5	6	21	38	12.8	3.30	113	.258	.337	4	.444	2	2	3	-0	0.3
Total	7	36	46	.439	246	93	15	1	13	840^2	858	450	80	27	319	502	12.9	4.26	93	.266	.337	33	.134	-4	-34	-28	5	-2.2

● SCOTT ANDERSON Anderson, Scott Richard b: 8/1/62, Corvallis, Ore. BR/TR, 6′6″, 190 lbs. Deb: 4/8/87

YEAR	TM/L	W	L	PCT	G	GS	CG	SH	SV	IP	H	R	HR	HB	BB	SO	RAT	ERA	ERA+	OAV	OOB	BH	AVG	PB	PR	PR+	PD	TPI
1987	Tex-A	0	1	.000	8	0	0	0	0	11^1	17	12	0	1	8	6	20.6	9.53	47	.347	.448	0	—	0	-6	-6	1	-0.4
1990	Mon-N	0	1	.000	4	3	0	0	0	18	12	6	1	0	5	16	8.5	3.00	122	.188	.246	0	.000	-0	2	1	-0	0.0
1995	KC-A	1	0	1.000	6	4	0	0	0	25^1	29	15	3	1	8	6	13.5	5.33	90	.290	.349	0	—	0	-2	-1	-0	-0.1
Total	3	1	2	.333	18	7	0	0	0	54^2	58	33	4	2	21	28	13.3	5.43	80	.272	.343	0	.000	-0	-6	-7	0	-0.5

● VARNEY ANDERSON Anderson, Varney Samuel "Varn" b: 6/18/1866, Geneva, Ill. d: 11/5/41, Rockford, Ill. BR/TR, 5′10″, 165 lbs. Deb: 8/1/1889

YEAR	TM/L	W	L	PCT	G	GS	CG	SH	SV	IP	H	R	HR	HB	BB	SO	RAT	ERA	ERA+	OAV	OOB	BH	AVG	PB	PR	PR+	PD	TPI
1889	Ind-N	0	1	.000	2	1	1	0	0	12	13	10	0	3	9	3	18.8	4.50	93	.265	.410	0	.000	-1	-1	-0	0	-0.1
1894	Was-N	0	2	.000	2	2	2	0	0	14	15	12	0	1	6	3	14.1	7.07	75	.273	.355	3	.429	0	-3	-3	-0	-0.2
1895	Was-N	9	16	.360	29	25	18	0	0	204^2	288	199	13	10	97	35	17.4	5.89	81	.327	.400	28	.289	3	-25	-25	1	-1.8
1896	Was-N	0	1	.000	2	2	1	0	0	9	23	16	0	0	3	0	26.0	13.00	34	.469	.500	3	.600	1	-9	-9	-1	-0.6
Total	4	9	20	.310	35	30	22	0	0	239^2	339	237	13	14	115	41	17.6	6.16	78	.328	.402	34	.298	4	-37	-36	0	-2.7

● WALTER ANDERSON Anderson, Walter Carl "Lefty" b: 9/25/1897, Grand Rapids, Mich. d: 1/6/90, Battle Creek, Mich. BL/TL, 6′2″, 160 lbs. Deb: 5/14/17

YEAR	TM/L	W	L	PCT	G	GS	CG	SH	SV	IP	H	R	HR	HB	BB	SO	RAT	ERA	ERA+	OAV	OOB	BH	AVG	PB	PR	PR+	PD	TPI
1917	Phi-A	0	0	—	14	2	0	0	0	38^2	32	16	0	1	21	10	12.6	3.03	91	.246	.355	3	.429	1	-2	-1	-0	0.0
1919	Phi-A	1	0	1.000	3	0	0	0	0	14	13	8	0	1	8	10	14.1	3.86	89	.245	.355	0	.000	-1	-1	-1	0	-0.1
Total	2	1	0	1.000	17	2	0	0	0	52^2	45	24	0	2	29	20	13.0	3.25	90	.246	.355	3	.273	0	-3	-2	-0	-0.1

● BILL ANDERSON Anderson, William Edward "Lefty" b: 11/28/1895, Boston, Mass. d: 3/13/83, Medford, Mass. BR/TL, 6′1″, 165 lbs. Deb: 9/10/25

YEAR	TM/L	W	L	PCT	G	GS	CG	SH	SV	IP	H	R	HR	HB	BB	SO	RAT	ERA	ERA+	OAV	OOB	BH	AVG	PB	PR	PR+	PD	TPI
1925	Bos-N	0	0	—	2	0	0	0	0	2^2	5	3	0	0	2	1	23.6	10.13	40	.500	.583	0	.000	-0	-2	-2	-0	-0.1

● WINGO ANDERSON Anderson, Wingo Charlie b: 8/13/1886, Alvarado, Tex. d: 12/19/50, Fort Worth, Tex. BL/TL, 5′10.5″, 150 lbs. Deb: 4/16/10

YEAR	TM/L	W	L	PCT	G	GS	CG	SH	SV	IP	H	R	HR	HB	BB	SO	RAT	ERA	ERA+	OAV	OOB	BH	AVG	PB	PR	PR+	PD	TPI
1910	Cin-N	0	0	—	7	2	0	0	0	17^1	16	15	0	1	17	11	17.7	4.67	62	.258	.425	1	.200	-0	-3	-4	-1	-0.3

● JOHN ANDRE Andre, John Edward b: 1/3/23, Barnstable, Mass. d: 11/25/76, Centerville, Mass. BL/TR, 6′4″, 200 lbs. Deb: 4/16/55

YEAR	TM/L	W	L	PCT	G	GS	CG	SH	SV	IP	H	R	HR	HB	BB	SO	RAT	ERA	ERA+	OAV	OOB	BH	AVG	PB	PR	PR+	PD	TPI
1955	Chi-N	0	1	.000	22	3	0	0	1	45	45	34	7	1	28	19	14.8	5.80	70	.259	.365	1	.111	-1	-9	-8	-0	-0.5

● CLAYTON ANDREWS Andrews, Clayton John b: 5/15/78, Dunedin, Fla. BR/TL, 6′, 175 lbs. Deb: 4/16/2000

YEAR	TM/L	W	L	PCT	G	GS	CG	SH	SV	IP	H	R	HR	HB	BB	SO	RAT	ERA	ERA+	OAV	OOB	BH	AVG	PB	PR	PR+	PD	TPI
2000	Tor-A	1	2	.333	8	2	0	0	0	20^2	34	23	6	0	9	12	18.7	10.02	50	.374	.430	0	.000	-0	-12	-11	-1	-1.3

● ELBERT ANDREWS Andrews, Elbert De Vore b: 12/11/01, Greenwood, S.C. d: 11/25/79, Greenwood, S.C. BL/TR, 6′, 175 lbs. Deb: 5/1/25

YEAR	TM/L	W	L	PCT	G	GS	CG	SH	SV	IP	H	R	HR	HB	BB	SO	RAT	ERA	ERA+	OAV	OOB	BH	AVG	PB	PR	PR+	PD	TPI
1925	Phi-A	0	0	—	6	0	0	0	0	8	12	12	0	0	11	0	25.9	10.13	46	.375	.535	0	—	0	-5	-5	-0	-0.2

● HUB ANDREWS Andrews, Herbert Carl b: 8/31/22, Burbank, Okla. BR/TR, 6′, 170 lbs. Deb: 4/20/47

YEAR	TM/L	W	L	PCT	G	GS	CG	SH	SV	IP	H	R	HR	HB	BB	SO	RAT	ERA	ERA+	OAV	OOB	BH	AVG	PB	PR	PR+	PD	TPI
1947	NY-N	0	0	—	7	0	0	0	0	8^2	14	7	1	0	4	2	18.7	6.23	65	.368	.429	0	—	0	-2	-2	0	-0.1
1948	NY-N	0	0	—	1	0	0	0	0	3	3	1	0	0	0	0	9.0	0.00	—	.300	.300	0	—	0	1	1	0	0.1
Total	2	0	0	—	8	0	0	0	0	11^2	17	8	1	0	4	2	16.2	4.63	87	.354	.404	0	—	0	-1	-1	0	0.0

● IVY ANDREWS Andrews, Ivy Paul "Poison" b: 5/6/07, Dora, Ala. d: 11/24/70, Birmingham, Ala. BR/TR, 6′1″, 200 lbs. Deb: 8/15/31

YEAR	TM/L	W	L	PCT	G	GS	CG	SH	SV	IP	H	R	HR	HB	BB	SO	RAT	ERA	ERA+	OAV	OOB	BH	AVG	PB	PR	PR+	PD	TPI
1931	NY-A	2	0	1.000	7	3	1	0	0	34^1	36	17	3	0	8	10	11.5	4.19	95	.273	.314	2	.182	0	1	-1	-0	0.0
1932	NY-A	2	1	.667	4	1	1	0	0	24^2	20	8	0	0	9	7	10.6	1.82	223	.215	.284	2	.222	1	7	7	0	0.9
	Bos-A	8	6	.571	25	19	8	0	0	141^2	144	76	4	2	53	30	12.6	3.81	118	.262	.329	7	.137	-3	11	11	-1	0.5
	Yr	10	7	.588	29	20	9	0	0	166^1	164	84	4	2	62	37	12.3	3.52	126	.255	.322	9	.150	-2	18	17	-0	1.4
1933	Bos-A	7	13	.350	34	17	5	0	1	140	157	96	8	1	61	37	14.1	4.95	88	.279	.350	9	.214	-0	-10	-9	-1	-1.1
1934	StL-A	4	11	.267	43	13	2	0	3	139	166	84	7	0	65	51	15.0	4.66	107	.301	.375	14	.350	3	-3	5	-2	0.6
1935	StL-A	13	7	.650	50	20	10	0	1	213^1	231	95	10	1	53	43	12.0	3.54	135	.273	.317	9	.132	-5	22	28	-2	1.5
1936	StL-A	7	12	.368	36	25	11	0	1	191^1	221	109	19	0	50	33	12.7	4.84	111	.286	.330	10	.169	-1	4	11	-2	0.6
1937	Cle-A	3	4	.429	20	4	1	1	0	59^2	76	33	3	0	9	16	12.8	4.37	105	.311	.336	3	.250	1	2	2	-1	0.1
	*NY-A	3	2	.600	11	5	3	1	1	49	49	19	2	0	17	17	12.1	3.12	142	.259	.320	1	.067	-1	8	7	0	0.6
	Yr	6	6	.500	31	9	4	2	1	108^2	125	52	5	0	26	33	12.5	3.81	119	.289	.329	4	.148	-1	10	9	-0	0.7
1938	NY-A	1	3	.250	19	1	1	0	1	48	51	25	3	0	17	13	12.8	3.00	151	.268	.329	2	.167	-0	10	9	0	0.6
Total	8	50	59	.459	249	108	43	2	8	1041	1151	562	59	4	342	257	12.9	4.14	115	.279	.335	59	.185	-6	51	67	-9	4.3

● JOHN ANDREWS Andrews, John Richard b: 2/9/49, Monterey Park, Cal. BL/TL, 5′10″, 175 lbs. Deb: 4/8/73

YEAR	TM/L	W	L	PCT	G	GS	CG	SH	SV	IP	H	R	HR	HB	BB	SO	RAT	ERA	ERA+	OAV	OOB	BH	AVG	PB	PR	PR+	PD	TPI
1973	StL-N	1	1	.500	16	0	0	0	0	18^1	16	10	3	0	11	5	13.3	4.42	83	.235	.342	1	.500	0	-2	-2	-0	-0.2

● NATE ANDREWS Andrews, Nathan Hardy b: 9/30/13, Pembroke, N.C. d: 4/26/91, Winston-Salem, N.C. BR/TR, 6′, 195 lbs. Deb: 5/1/37

YEAR	TM/L	W	L	PCT	G	GS	CG	SH	SV	IP	H	R	HR	HB	BB	SO	RAT	ERA	ERA+	OAV	OOB	BH	AVG	PB	PR	PR+	PD	TPI
1937	StL-N	0	0	—	4	0	0	0	0	9	12	4	1	0	3	6	15.0	4.00	100	.324	.375	0	—	0	-0	-0	0	0.1
1939	StL-N	1	2	.333	11	1	0	0	0	16	24	14	0	0	12	6	20.3	6.75	61	.343	.439	0	.000	-0	-5	-4	0	-0.7
1940	Cle-A	0	1	.000	6	0	0	0	0	12	16	9	1	0	6	3	16.5	6.00	70	.327	.400	0	—	0	-2	-2	1	-0.1
1941	Cle-A	0	0	—	2	0	0	0	0	2^1	3	4	0	0	2	1	19.3	11.57	34	.300	.417	0	.000	-0	-2	-2	-0	-0.1
1943	Bos-N	14	20	.412	36	34	23	3	0	283^2	253	100	11	6	75	80	10.6	2.57	133	.238	.291	14	.156	-0	26	26	2	3.4
1944	Bos-N☆	16	15	.516	37	34	16	2	2	257^1	263	106	14	2	74	76	11.9	3.22	119	.261	.312	10	.114	-4	11	16	1	1.7
1945	Bos-N	7	12	.368	21	19	8	0	0	137^2	160	75	9	0	52	26	13.9	4.58	84	.295	.356	9	.209	0	-12	-11	-0	-1.4
1946	Cin-N	2	4	.333	7	7	3	0	0	43^1	50	29	2	1	8	13	12.3	3.95	85	.281	.316	1	.071	-1	-3	-3	-0	-0.5
	NY-N	1	0	1.000	3	2	0	0	0	12	17	9	2	0	4	5	15.8	6.00	57	.362	.412	1	.500	1	-3	-3	-0	-0.2
	Yr	3	4	.429	10	9	3	0	0	55^1	67	38	4	1	12	18	13.0	4.39	77	.298	.336	2	.125	-0	-6	-6	-0	-0.7
Total	8	41	54	.432	127	97	50	5	2	773^1	798	350	40	9	236	216	12.1	3.46	106	.265	.321	35	.146	-4	10	17	4	2.2

● FRED ANDRUS Andrus, Frederick Hotham b: 8/23/1850, Washington, Mich. d: 11/10/37, Detroit, Mich. BR/TR, 6′2″, 185 lbs. Deb: 7/25/1876 ♦

YEAR	TM/L	W	L	PCT	G	GS	CG	SH	SV	IP	H	R	HR	HB	BB	SO	RAT	ERA	ERA+	OAV	OOB	BH	AVG	PB	PR	PR+	PD	TPI
1884	Chi-N	1	0	1.000	1	1	1	0	0	9	11	3	1		2	2	13.0	2.00	157	.297	.333	1	.200	0	1	1	0	0.1

● JOAQUIN ANDUJAR Andujar, Joaquin b: 12/21/52, San Pedro De Macoris, D.R. BB/TR, 6′, 180 lbs. Deb: 4/8/76

YEAR	TM/L	W	L	PCT	G	GS	CG	SH	SV	IP	H	R	HR	HB	BB	SO	RAT	ERA	ERA+	OAV	OOB	BH	AVG	PB	PR	PR+	PD	TPI
1976	Hou-N	9	10	.474	28	25	9	4	0	172^1	163	74	8	1	75	59	12.5	3.60	89	.255	.334	8	.140	-0	-2	-9	-1	-1.0
1977	Hou-N☆	11	8	.579	26	25	4	1	0	158^2	149	80	11	4	64	69	12.3	3.69	97	.251	.328	10	.189	2	4	-2	2	0.1
1978	Hou-N	5	7	.417	35	13	2	0	1	110^2	88	45	3	4	58	55	12.2	3.42	97	.224	.330	3	.130	-0	2	-1	2	0.1
1979	Hou-N★	12	12	.500	46	23	8	0	4	194	168	86	7	2	88	77	12.0	3.43	103	.233	.319	5	.088	-0	7	2	4	0.6
1980	*Hou-N	3	8	.273	35	14	0	0	2	122	132	59	8	0	43	75	12.9	3.91	84	.277	.337	5	.172	2	-4	-9	1	-0.4
1981	Hou-N	2	3	.400	9	3	0	0	0	23^2	29	17	2	0	12	18	15.6	4.94	67	.296	.373	0	.000	-0	-4	-5	-1	-1.0
	StL-N	6	1	.857	11	8	1	0	0	55^1	56	24	4	0	11	19	10.9	3.74	95	.265	.302	0	.000	-2	-2	-1	0	-0.3
	Yr	8	4	.667	20	11	1	0	0	79	85	41	6	0	23	37	12.3	4.10	85	.275	.325	0	.000	-2	-5	-5	-0	-1.3
1982	*StL-N	15	10	.600	38	37	9	5	0	265^2	237	85	11	7	50	137	10.0	2.47	147	.240	.282	15	.158	-1	34	34	2	3.2
1983	StL-N	6	16	.273	39	34	5	2	1	225	215	112	23	3	75	125	11.7	4.16	87	.253	.316	6	.082	-3	-13	-13	5	-1.0
1984	StL-N†	**20**	14	.588	36	36	12	**4**	0	**261^1**	218	104	20	7	70	147	10.2	3.34	104	.229	.286	11	.131	3	7	4	3	1.0
1985	*StL-N†	21	12	.636	38	38	10	2	0	269^2	265	113	15	11	82	112	11.9	3.40	104	.260	.322	10	.106	-2	6	4	-1	0.2
1986	Oak-A	12	7	.632	28	26	7	1	1	155^1	139	70	23	4	56	72	11.5	3.82	101	.239	.310	0	—	0	6	1	0	0.1
1987	Oak-A	3	5	.375	13	13	1	0	0	60^2	63	43	11	3	26	32	13.6	6.08	68	.269	.350	0	—	0	-11	-14	0	-1.5

YEAR	TM/L	W	L	PCT	G	GS	CG	SH	SV	IP	H	R	HR	HB	BB	SO	RAT	ERA	ERA+	OAV	OOB	BH	AVG	PB	PR	PR+	PD	TPI
1988	Hou-N	2	5	.286	23	10	0	0	0	78^2	94	43	9	5	21	35	13.7	4.00	83	.297	.350	4	.211	2	-5	-6	0	-0.3
Total	13	127	118	.518	405	305	68	19	9	2153	2016	955	155	51	731	1032	11.7	3.58	99	.250	.316	77	.127	-1	26	-12	18	-0.2

● **LUIS ANDUJAR** Andujar, Luis (Sanchez) b: 11/22/72, Bani, D.R. BR/TR, 6'2", 175 lbs. Deb: 9/8/95

YEAR	TM/L	W	L	PCT	G	GS	CG	SH	SV	IP	H	R	HR	HB	BB	SO	RAT	ERA	ERA+	OAV	OOB	BH	AVG	PB	PR	PR+	PD	TPI
1995	Chi-A	2	1	.667	5	5	0	0	0	30^1	26	12	4	1	14	9	12.2	3.26	137	.230	.320	0	—	0	5	4	-1	0.3
1996	Chi-A	0	2	.000	5	5	0	0	0	23	32	22	4	0	15	6	18.4	8.22	58	.337	.427	0	—	0	-8	-9	-0	-0.7
	Tor-A	1	1	.500	3	2	0	0	0	14^1	14	8	4	1	1	5	10.0	5.02	100	.264	.291	0	—	0	-0	-0	-1	-0.1
	Yr	1	3	.250	8	7	0	0	0	37^1	46	30	8	1	16	11	15.2	6.99	69	.311	.382	0	—	0	-8	-9	-1	-0.8
1997	Tor-A	0	6	.000	17	8	0	0	0	50	76	45	9	0	21	28	17.5	6.48	71	.352	.409	0	—	0	-11	-10	-0	-1.1
1998	Tor-A	0	0	—	5	0	0	0	0	5^2	12	6	0	0	2	1	22.2	9.53	49	.429	.467	0	—	0	-3	-3	-0	-0.1
Total	4	3	10	.231	35	20	0	0	0	123^1	160	93	21	2	53	49	15.7	5.98	78	.317	.384	0	—	0	-17	-19	-2	-1.7

● **NORM ANGELINI** Angelini, Norman Stanley b: 9/24/47, San Francisco, Cal. BL/TL, 5'11", 175 lbs. Deb: 7/22/72

YEAR	TM/L	W	L	PCT	G	GS	CG	SH	SV	IP	H	R	HR	HB	BB	SO	RAT	ERA	ERA+	OAV	OOB	BH	AVG	PB	PR	PR+	PD	TPI
1972	KC-A	2	1	.667	21	0	0	0	2	16	13	4	1	1	12	16	14.6	2.25	135	.228	.371	0	.000	-0	1	1	-0	0.3
1973	KC-A	0	0	—	7	0	0	0	1	3^2	2	2	0	0	7	3	22.1	4.91	84	.200	.529	0	—	0	-0	-0	-0	0.0
Total	2	2	1	.667	28	0	0	0	3	19^2	15	6	1	1	19	19	16.0	2.75	118	.224	.402	0	.000	-0	1	1	-0	0.3

● **RICK ANKIEL** Ankiel, Richard Alexander b: 7/19/79, Fort Pierce, Fla. BL/TL, 6'1", 210 lbs. Deb: 8/23/99

YEAR	TM/L	W	L	PCT	G	GS	CG	SH	SV	IP	H	R	HR	HB	BB	SO	RAT	ERA	ERA+	OAV	OOB	BH	AVG	PB	PR	PR+	PD	TPI
1999	StL-N	0	1	.000	9	5	0	0	1	33	26	12	2	1	14	39	11.2	3.27	140	.215	.301	1	.100	-1	5	5	-1	0.1
2000	*StL-N	11	7	.611	31	30	0	0	0	175	137	80	21	6	90	194	12.0	3.50	132	.219	.323	17	.250	6	22	22	-2	2.4
Total	2	11	8	.579	40	35	0	0	1	208	163	92	23	7	104	233	11.9	3.46	133	.218	.320	18	.231	6	27	27	-2	2.5

● **CAP ANSON** Anson, Adrian Constantine b: 4/11/1852, Marshalltown, Iowa d: 4/14/22, Chicago, Ill. BR/TR, 6', 227 lbs. Deb: 5/6/1871 MH♦

YEAR	TM/L	W	L	PCT	G	GS	CG	SH	SV	IP	H	R	HR	HB	BB	SO	RAT	ERA	ERA+	OAV	OOB	BH	AVG	PB	PR	PR+	PD	TPI
1883	Chi-N	0	0	—	2	0	0	0	1	3	1	1	0		1	0	6.0	0.00	—	.091	.167	127	.308	1	1	1	0	0.1
1884	Chi-N	0	1	.000	1	0	0	0	0	1	3	4	2		1	1	36.0	18.00	17	.375	.444	159	.335	0	-2	-2	0	-0.2
Total	2	0	1	.000	3	0	0	0	1	4	4	5	2		2	1	13.5	4.50	72	.211	.286	3056	.333	1	-1	-1	0	-0.1

● **JOHNNY ANTONELLI** Antonelli, John August b: 4/12/30, Rochester, N.Y. BL/TL, 6', 190 lbs. Deb: 7/4/48

YEAR	TM/L	W	L	PCT	G	GS	CG	SH	SV	IP	H	R	HR	HB	BB	SO	RAT	ERA	ERA+	OAV	OOB	BH	AVG	PB	PR	PR+	PD	TPI
1948	Bos-N	0	0	—	4	0	0	0	1	4	2	1	0	0	3	0	11.3	2.25	170	.143	.294	0	—	0	1	1	0	0.1
1949	Bos-N	3	7	.300	22	10	3	1	0	96	99	49	6	2	42	48	13.4	3.56	106	.273	.351	3	.120	-1	5	2	-1	0.0
1950	Bos-N	2	3	.400	20	6	2	1	0	57^2	81	46	3	4	22	33	16.7	5.93	65	.335	.399	2	.125	-1	-11	-14	0	-1.1
1953	Mil-N	12	12	.500	31	26	11	2	1	175^1	167	83	15	1	71	131	12.3	3.18	123	.242	.314	11	.177	0	22	16	1	2.1
1954	*NY-N★	21	7	**.750**	39	37	18	**6**	2	258^2	209	78	22	5	94	152	10.7	**2.30**	**176**	**.219**	.293	16	.163	0	**51**	**50**	2	**5.5**
1955	NY-N	14	16	.467	38	34	14	2	1	235^1	206	105	24	11	82	143	11.4	3.33	121	.234	.307	17	.207	3	19	18	1	2.6
1956	NY-N★	20	13	.606	41	36	15	5	1	258^1	225	93	20	3	75	145	10.6	2.86	132	.234	.292	14	.157	1	26	**26**	1	3.6
1957	NY-N☆	12	18	.400	40	30	8	3	0	212^1	228	98	19	3	67	114	12.6	3.77	104	.276	.333	11	.153	3	3	4	-2	0.6
1958	SF-N☆	16	13	.552	41	34	13	0	3	241^2	216	101	31	3	87	143	11.4	3.28	116	.239	.308	19	.226	4	18	15	-3	1.8
1959	SF-N★	19	10	.655	40	38	17	**4**	1	282	247	107	29	3	76	165	10.4	3.10	123	.233	.286	16	.158	1	27	23	-1	2.3
1960	SF-N	6	7	.462	41	10	1	1	11	112^1	106	51	7	2	47	57	12.4	3.77	92	.253	.331	8	.235	2	-0	-4	-1	-0.3
1961	Cle-A	0	4	.000	11	7	0	0	0	48	68	39	8	1	18	23	16.3	6.56	60	.338	.395	4	.267	1	-14	-14	1	-0.9
	Mil-N	1	0	1.000	9	0	0	0	0	10^2	16	9	2	0	3	8	16.0	7.59	49	.340	.380	0	.000	-0	-4	-5	-0	-0.4
Total	12	126	110	.534	377	268	102	25	21	1992^1	1870	860	186	38	687	1162	11.7	3.34	116	.247	.313	121	.178	15	141	121	-1	15.9

● **BOB APODACA** Apodaca, Robert John b: 1/31/50, Los Angeles, Cal. BR/TR, 5'11", 170 lbs. Deb: 9/18/73 C

YEAR	TM/L	W	L	PCT	G	GS	CG	SH	SV	IP	H	R	HR	HB	BB	SO	RAT	ERA	ERA+	OAV	OOB	BH	AVG	PB	PR	PR+	PD	TPI
1973	NY-N	0	0	—	1	0	0	0	0	0	0	0	0	2	—	—	∞	—	—	1.000	99	—	0	-1	-1	0	-0.1	
1974	NY-N	6	6	.500	35	8	1	0	3	103	92	47	7	2	42	54	11.9	3.50	102	.241	.319	3	.120	0	2	1	-1	0.1
1975	NY-N	3	4	.429	46	0	0	0	13	84^2	66	18	4	0	28	45	10.0	1.49	233	.222	.289	4	.364	2	20	19	2	2.7
1976	NY-N	3	7	.300	43	3	0	0	5	89^2	71	34	4	3	29	45	10.3	2.81	117	.223	.293	2	.125	0	7	5	1	0.7
1977	NY-N	4	8	.333	59	0	0	0	5	84	83	38	7	1	30	53	12.2	3.43	109	.255	.319	1	.167	-0	5	3	1	0.5
Total	5	16	25	.390	184	11	1	0	26	361^1	312	138	22	6	131	197	11.2	2.86	123	.236	.307	10	.172	2	32	27	4	3.9

● **LUIS APONTE** Aponte, Luis Eduardo (Yuripe) b: 6/14/53, ElTigre, Venez. BR/TR, 6', 185 lbs. Deb: 9/4/80

YEAR	TM/L	W	L	PCT	G	GS	CG	SH	SV	IP	H	R	HR	HB	BB	SO	RAT	ERA	ERA+	OAV	OOB	BH	AVG	PB	PR	PR+	PD	TPI
1980	Bos-A	0	0	—	4	0	0	0	0	7	6	1	0	0	2	1	10.3	1.29	329	.250	.308	0	—	0	2	2	0	0.1
1981	Bos-A	1	0	1.000	7	0	0	0	1	15^2	11	1	0	0	3	11	8.0	0.57	675	.208	.250	0	—	0	5	5	1	0.5
1982	Bos-A	2	2	.500	40	0	0	0	3	85	78	31	5	0	25	44	10.9	3.18	136	.246	.301	0	—	0	9	10	2	0.7
1983	Bos-A	5	4	.556	34	0	0	0	3	62	74	28	7	2	23	32	14.4	3.63	120	.301	.365	0	—	0	3	5	1	0.7
1984	Cle-A	1	0	1.000	25	0	0	0	0	50^1	53	25	5	1	15	25	12.3	4.11	100	.269	.324	0	—	0	-1	-0	-1	-0.1
Total	5	9	6	.600	110	0	0	0	7	220	222	86	17	3	68	113	12.0	3.27	130	.265	.323	0	—	0	19	23	3	1.9

● **KEVIN APPIER** Appier, Robert Kevin b: 12/6/67, Lancaster, Cal. BR/TR, 6'2", 195 lbs. Deb: 6/14/89

YEAR	TM/L	W	L	PCT	G	GS	CG	SH	SV	IP	H	R	HR	HB	BB	SO	RAT	ERA	ERA+	OAV	OOB	BH	AVG	PB	PR	PR+	PD	TPI
1989	KC-A	1	4	.200	6	5	0	0	0	21^2	34	22	3	0	12	10	19.1	9.14	42	.374	.447	0	—	0	-13	-13	-1	-2.2
1990	KC-A	12	8	.600	32	24	3	3	0	185^2	179	67	13	6	54	127	11.6	2.76	139	.252	.310	0	—	0	24	23	-0	2.3
1991	KC-A	13	10	.565	34	31	6	3	0	207^2	205	97	13	2	61	158	11.6	3.42	120	.255	.309	0	—	0	16	16	0	1.7
1992	KC-A	15	8	.652	30	30	3	0	0	208^1	167	59	10	2	68	150	10.2	2.46	165	.217	.282	0	—	0	34	36	0	4.0
1993	KC-A	18	8	.692	34	34	5	1	0	238^2	183	74	8	1	81	186	10.0	**2.56**	**179**	.212	.280	0	—	0	**47**	**51**	-2	**5.1**
1994	KC-A	7	6	.538	23	23	1	0	0	155	137	68	11	4	63	145	11.8	3.83	131	.240	.320	0	—	0	17	19	-1	1.3
1995	KC-A★	15	10	.600	31	31	4	1	0	201^1	163	90	14	8	80	185	11.2	3.89	123	.221	.304	0	—	0	19	20	-0	2.2
1996	KC-A	14	11	.560	32	32	5	1	0	211^1	192	87	17	5	75	207	11.6	3.62	138	.245	.315	0	—	0	32	33	-1	3.2
1997	KC-A	9	13	.409	34	34	4	1	0	235^2	215	96	24	4	74	196	11.2	3.40	139	.243	.304	0	.000	-1	31	33	-1	2.6
1998	KC-A	1	2	.333	3	3	0	0	0	15	21	13	3	1	5	9	16.2	7.80	62	.339	.397	0	—	0	-5	-5	-0	-0.7
1999	KC-A	9	9	.500	22	22	1	0	0	140^1	153	81	18	6	51	78	13.5	4.87	103	.279	.347	0	.000	-0	-0	2	-1	0.1
	Oak-A	7	5	.583	12	12	0	0	0	68^2	77	50	9	1	33	53	14.5	5.77	81	.280	.359	0	—	0	-7	-9	-0	-1.2
	Yr	16	14	.533	34	34	1	0	0	209	230	131	27	7	84	131	13.8	5.17	95	.279	.351	0	.000	-0	-7	-6	-1	-1.1
2000	*Oak-A	15	11	.577	31	31	1	1	0	195^1	200	109	23	9	102	129	14.3	4.52	106	.262	.356	1	.167	-0	9	6	-2	0.4
Total	12	136	105	.564	324	312	33	11	0	2084^2	1926	913	166	49	759	1633	11.8	3.63	126	.245	.315	1	.071	-1	203	216	-9	18.8

● **FRED APPLEGATE** Applegate, Frederick Romaine b: 5/9/1879, Williamsport, Pa. d: 4/21/68, Williamsport, Pa. BR/TR, 6'2", 180 lbs. Deb: 9/30/04

YEAR	TM/L	W	L	PCT	G	GS	CG	SH	SV	IP	H	R	HR	HB	BB	SO	RAT	ERA	ERA+	OAV	OOB	BH	AVG	PB	PR	PR+	PD	TPI
1904	Phi-A	1	2	.333	3	3	3	0	0	21	29	18	0	1	8	12	16.3	6.43	42	.330	.392	2	.286	0	-9	-8	0	-1.0

● **ED APPLETON** Appleton, Edward Samuel "Whitey" b: 2/29/1892, Arlington, Tex. d: 1/27/32, Arlington, Tex. BR/TR, 6'0.5", 173 lbs. Deb: 4/16/15

YEAR	TM/L	W	L	PCT	G	GS	CG	SH	SV	IP	H	R	HR	HB	BB	SO	RAT	ERA	ERA+	OAV	OOB	BH	AVG	PB	PR	PR+	PD	TPI
1915	Bro-N	4	10	.286	34	10	5	0	0	138^1	133	71	3	8	66	50	13.5	3.32	84	.263	.357	7	.159	-0	-9	-8	-1	-0.9
1916	Bro-N	1	2	.333	14	3	1	0	1	47	49	25	1	1	18	14	13.0	3.06	88	.278	.349	2	.167	-0	-2	-2	-1	-0.3
Total	2	5	12	.294	48	13	6	0	1	185^1	182	96	4	9	84	64	13.4	3.25	85	.267	.355	9	.161	-1	-11	-10	-2	-1.2

● **PETE APPLETON** Appleton, Peter William "Jake" (a.k.a. Jablonowski In 1927-33)
b: 5/20/04, Terryville, Conn. d: 1/18/74, Trenton, N.J. BR/TR, 5'11", 180 lbs. Deb: 9/14/27

YEAR	TM/L	W	L	PCT	G	GS	CG	SH	SV	IP	H	R	HR	HB	BB	SO	RAT	ERA	ERA+	OAV	OOB	BH	AVG	PB	PR	PR+	PD	TPI
1927	Cin-N	2	1	.667	6	2	2	1	0	29^2	29	7	0	0	17	3	14.0	1.82	208	.261	.359	6	.545	2	7	7	1	1.0
1928	Cin-N	3	4	.429	31	3	0	0	0	82^2	101	50	7	2	22	20	13.6	4.68	85	.311	.358	10	.323	3	-6	-7	2	0.0
1930	Cle-A	8	7	.533	39	7	2	0	1	118^2	122	71	8	5	53	45	13.7	4.02	120	.274	.357	8	.200	-1	8	10	2	1.1
1931	Cle-A	4	4	.500	29	4	3	0	0	79^2	100	51	2	1	29	25	14.7	4.63	100	.293	.350	5	.208	0	-2	-0	-0	0.0
1932	Cle-A	0	0	—	4	0	0	0	0	5	11	11	1	0	3	1	25.2	16.20	29	.407	.467	0	—	0	-7	-6	0	-0.3
	Bos-A	0	3	.000	11	3	0	0	0	46	49	35	2	2	26	15	15.1	4.11	109	.265	.362	3	.176	-0	2	2	2	0.3
	Yr	0	3	.000	15	3	0	0	0	51	60	46	3	2	29	16	16.1	5.29	85	.283	.374	3	.176	-0	-5	-4	2	0.0
1933	NY-A	0	0	—	1	0	0	0	0	2	3	0	0	0	1	0	18.0	0.00	—	.375	.444	0	—	0	1	1	0	0.1
1936	Was-A	14	9	.609	38	20	12	1	3	201^2	199	94	7	3	77	77	12.5	3.53	135	.254	.324	19	.250	2	34	30	1	3.2
1937	Was-A	8	15	.348	35	18	7	4	2	168	167	103	16	5	72	62	13.1	4.39	101	.260	.339	11	.186	-2	4	1	3	0.2
1938	Was-A	7	9	.438	43	10	5	0	5	164^1	175	99	12	1	61	62	13.0	4.60	98	.270	.333	15	.254	3	3	-2	-0	0.1
1939	Was-A	5	10	.333	40	4	2	0	6	102^2	104	62	7	4	48	50	13.7	4.56	95	.265	.351	4	.160	-1	1	-3	0	-0.4
1940	Chi-A	4	0	1.000	25	0	0	0	5	57^2	54	39	8	1	28	21	13.0	5.62	79	.248	.336	3	.176	-0	-8	-8	-0	-0.7
1941	Chi-A	0	3	.000	13	0	0	0	1	27^1	27	21	4	2	17	12	15.1	5.27	78	.257	.371	1	.250	0	-3	-4	0	-0.3
1942	Chi-A	0	0	—	4	0	0	0	0	4^2	2	2	0	0	3	2	9.6	3.86	93	.133	.278	0	—	0	-0	-0	0	0.0
	StL-A	1	1	.500	14	0	0	0	2	27^1	25	9	1	0	11	12	11.9	2.96	125	.243	.316	1	.167	1	2	2	1	0.4

YEAR	TM/L	W	L	PCT	G	GS	CG	SH	SV	IP	H	R	HR	HB	BB	SO	RAT	ERA	ERA+	OAV	OOB	BH	AVG	PB	PR	PR+	PD	TPI
	Yr	1	1	.500	18	0	0	0	2	32	27	11	1	0	14	14	11.5	3.09	119	.229	.311	1	.167	1	2	2	1	0.4
1945	StL-A	0	0	—	2	0	0	0	0	2^1	3	5	0	0	7	1	38.6	15.43	23	.273	.556	0	—	0	-3	-3	0	-0.1
	Was-A	1	0	1.000	6	2	1	0	1	21^1	16	8	1	0	11	12	11.4	3.38	92	.211	.310	1	.200	-0	-0	-1	-0	-0.1
	Yr	1	0	1.000	8	2	1	0	1	23^2	19	13	1	0	18	13	14.1	4.56	69	.218	.352	1	.200	-0	-3	-4	0	-0.2
Total	14	57	66	.463	341	73	34	6	26	1141	1187	667	76	26	486	420	13.4	4.30	104	.268	.343	87	.233	7	33	20	12	4.5
● LUIS AQUINO	Aquino, Luis Antonio (Colon) b: 5/19/64, Santurce, P.R. BR/TR, 6'1", 195 lbs. Deb: 8/8/86																											
1986	Tor-A	1	1	.500	7	0	0	0	0	11^1	14	8	2	0	3	5	13.5	6.35	67	.304	.347	0	—	0	-3	-3	-0	-0.4
1988	KC-A	1	0	1.000	7	5	1	1	0	29	33	15	1	1	17	11	15.8	2.79	143	.282	.378	0	—	0	4	4	-0	0.2
1989	KC-A	6	8	.429	34	16	2	1	0	141^1	148	62	6	4	35	68	11.9	3.50	110	.271	.320	0	—	0	6	6	1	0.6
1990	KC-A	4	1	.800	20	3	1	0	0	68^1	59	25	6	4	27	28	11.9	3.16	122	.237	.321	0	—	0	6	5	0	0.4
1991	KC-A	8	4	.667	38	18	1	1	3	157	152	67	10	4	47	80	11.6	3.44	120	.253	.311	0	—	0	12	12	0	0.9
1992	KC-A	3	6	.333	15	13	0	0	0	67^2	81	35	5	1	20	11	13.6	4.52	90	.303	.354	0	—	0	-4	-3	1	-0.3
1993	Fla-N	6	8	.429	38	13	0	0	0	110^2	115	43	6	5	40	67	13.0	3.42	127	.276	.346	2	.080	-2	8	10	4	1.4
1994	Fla-N	2	1	.667	29	1	0	0	0	50^2	39	22	3	3	22	22	11.4	3.73	117	.210	.303	1	.167	-0	3	3	1	0.2
1995	Mon-N	0	2	.000	29	0	0	0	2	37^1	47	24	4	3	11	22	14.7	3.86	111	.301	.359	1	.333	1	1	2	-0	0.1
	SF-N	0	1	.000	5	0	0	0	0	5	10	10	2	0	2	4	21.6	14.40	28	.400	.444	0	.000	-0	-6	-6	0	-0.9
	Yr	0	3	.000	34	0	0	0	2	42^1	57	34	6	3	13	26	15.5	5.10	84	.315	.371	1	.250	0	-4	-4	-0	-0.8
Total	9	31	32	.492	222	69	5	3	5	678^1	698	311	45	25	224	318	12.6	3.68	111	.267	.331	4	.114	-1	26	31	6	2.2
● FRED ARCHER	Archer, Frederick Marvin "Lefty" b: 3/7/10, Johnson City, Tenn. d: 10/31/81, Charlotte, N.C. BL/TL, 6', 193 lbs. Deb: 9/5/36																											
1936	Phi-A	2	3	.400	6	5	2	0	0	36^2	41	28	3	3	15	9	14.5	6.38	80	.289	.369	4	.267	0	-5	-5	-0	-0.5
1937	Phi-A	0	0	—	1	0	0	0	0	3	4	2	0	0	0	2	12.0	6.00	79	.333	.333	0	—	0	-0	-0	0	0.0
Total	2	2	3	.400	7	5	2	0	0	39^2	45	30	3	3	15	11	14.3	6.35	80	.292	.366	4	.267	1	-6	-6	0	-0.5
● JIM ARCHER	Archer, James William b: 5/25/32, Max Meadows, Va. BR/TL, 6', 190 lbs. Deb: 4/30/61																											
1961	KC-A	9	15	.375	39	27	9	2	5	205^1	204	99	11	5	60	110	11.8	3.20	131	.257	.313	4	.063	-5	19	22	-0	1.9
1962	KC-A	0	1	.000	18	1	0	0	0	27^2	40	30	8	0	10	12	16.3	9.43	45	.342	.394	1	1.000	0	-17	-15	-0	-0.7
Total	2	9	16	.360	57	28	9	2	5	233	244	129	19	5	70	122	12.3	3.94	106	.268	.323	5	.078	-4	2	6	-1	1.2
● RUGGER ARDIZOIA	Ardizoia, Rinaldo Joseph b: 11/20/19, Oleggio, Italy BR/TR, 5'11", 180 lbs. Deb: 4/30/47																											
1947	NY-A	0	0	—	1	0	0	0	0	2	4	2	1	0	1	0	22.5	9.00	39	.500	.556	0	—	0	-1	-1	0	-0.1
● FRANK ARELLANES	Arellanes, Frank Julian b: 1/28/1882, Santa Cruz, Cal. d: 12/13/18, San Jose, Cal. BR/TR, 6', 180 lbs. Deb: 7/28/08																											
1908	Bos-A	4	3	.571	11	8	6	1	0	79	60	26	1	3	18	33	9.2	1.82	135	.205	.259	5	.167	0	5	5	-1	0.4
1909	Bos-A	16	12	.571	45	28	17	1	**8**	230^2	192	80	3	5	43	82	9.4	2.18	114	.229	.270	13	.167	-1	8	8	0	0.9
1910	Bos-A	4	7	.364	18	13	2	0	0	100	106	41	1	3	24	33	12.0	2.88	89	.283	.332	6	.176	0	-4	-4	0	-0.4
Total	3	24	22	.522	74	49	25	2	8	409^2	358	147	5	11	85	148	10.0	2.28	110	.238	.283	24	.169	-1	9	10	-1	0.9
● RUDY ARIAS	Arias, Rodolfo (Martinez) b: 6/6/31, Las Villas, Cuba BL/TL, 5'10", 165 lbs. Deb: 4/10/59																											
1959	Chi-A	2	0	1.000	34	0	0	0	2	44	49	23	7	1	20	28	14.3	4.09	92	.277	.354	0	.000	-1	-1	-2	1	-0.1
● DON ARLICH	Arlich, Donald Louis b: 2/15/43, Wayne, Mich. BL/TL, 6'2", 185 lbs. Deb: 10/2/65																											
1965	Hou-N	0	0	—	1	1	0	0	0	6	5	2	0	0	1	0	9.0	3.00	112	.227	.261	0	.000	-0	0	0	-0	0.0
1966	Hou-N	0	1	.000	7	0	0	0	0	4	11	9	0	1	4	1	36.0	15.75	22	.478	.571	0	.000	-0	-5	-6	-0	-1.1
Total	2	0	1	.000	8	1	0	0	0	10	16	11	0	1	5	1	19.8	8.10	42	.356	.431	0	.000	-0	-5	-6	-0	-1.1
● STEVE ARLIN	Arlin, Stephen Ralph b: 9/25/45, Seattle, Wash. BR/TR, 6'3.5", 195 lbs. Deb: 6/17/69																											
1969	SD-N	0	1	.000	4	1	0	0	0	10^2	13	11	2	0	9	9	18.6	9.28	38	.289	.407	0	.000	-0	-7	-7	-0	-0.6
1970	SD-N	1	0	1.000	2	2	1	1	0	12^2	11	4	0	0	8	3	13.5	2.84	140	.244	.358	0	.000	-1	2	2	0	0.1
1971	SD-N	9	19	.321	36	34	10	4	0	227^2	211	114	8	6	103	156	12.7	3.48	95	.244	.329	9	.123	-1	-0	-5	-1	-0.8
1972	SD-N	10	21	.323	38	37	12	3	0	250	217	115	19	9	122	159	12.5	3.60	91	.237	.332	11	.153	3	-4	-9	-0	-0.8
1973	SD-N	11	14	.440	34	27	7	3	0	180	196	107	26	1	72	98	13.4	5.10	68	.278	.346	10	.167	1	-29	-34	-1	-4.1
1974	SD-N	1	7	.125	16	12	1	0	1	64	85	46	5	2	37	18	17.4	5.91	60	.326	.413	2	.111	-1	-16	-17	-0	-2.0
	Cle-A	2	5	.286	11	10	1	0	0	43^2	59	34	1	0	22	20	16.7	6.60	55	.333	.407	0	—	0	-14	-14	-1	-2.0
Total	6	34	67	.337	141	123	32	11	1	788^2	792	431	61	18	373	463	13.5	4.33	78	.263	.348	32	.139	1	-68	-86	-3	-10.2
● TONY ARMAS	Armas, Antonio Jose b: 4/29/78, Puerto Piritu, Venez. BR/TR, 6'4", 205 lbs. Deb: 8/16/99 F																											
1999	Mon-N	0	1	.000	1	1	0	0	0	6	8	4	0	0	2	2	15.0	1.50	299	.320	.370	0	.000	-0	2	2	-0	0.3
2000	Mon-N	7	9	.438	17	17	0	0	0	95	74	49	10	3	50	59	12.0	4.36	108	.218	.323	1	.038	-2	3	4	0	0.3
Total	2	7	10	.412	18	18	0	0	0	101	82	53	10	3	52	61	12.2	4.19	112	.225	.326	1	.036	-2	5	6	-0	0.6
● ORVILLE ARMBRUST	Armbrust, Orville Martin b: 3/2/10, Beirne, Ark. d: 10/2/67, Mobile, Ala. BR/TR, 5'10", 195 lbs. Deb: 9/18/34																											
1934	Was-A	1	0	1.000	3	2	0	0	0	12^2	10	3	1	0	3	3	9.2	2.13	203	.208	.255	0	.000	-1	3	3	1	0.2
● HOWARD ARMSTRONG	Armstrong, Howard Elmer b: 12/2/1889, E.Claridon, Ohio d: 3/8/26, Canisteo, N.Y. BR/TR, 5'9", 165 lbs. Deb: 9/30/11																											
1911	Phi-A	0	1	.000	1	0	0	0	0	3	3	2	0	0	1	0	12.0	0.00	—	.273	.333	0	.000	-0	1	1	0	0.3
● JACK ARMSTRONG	Armstrong, Jack William b: 3/7/65, Englewood, N.J. BR/TR, 6'5", 215 lbs. Deb: 6/21/88																											
1988	Cin-N	4	7	.364	14	13	0	0	0	65^1	63	44	8	0	38	45	13.9	5.79	62	.256	.356	2	.095	-1	-17	-15	1	-2.3
1989	Cin-N	2	3	.400	9	8	0	0	0	42^2	40	24	5	0	21	23	12.9	4.64	78	.245	.332	0	.000	-1	-5	-5	0	-0.5
1990	*Cin-N★	12	9	.571	29	27	2	1	0	166	151	72	9	6	59	110	11.7	3.42	116	.241	.313	5	.106	-2	7	9	0	1.0
1991	Cin-N	7	13	.350	27	24	1	0	0	139^2	158	90	25	2	54	93	13.8	5.48	69	.293	.359	4	.093	-2	-28	-25	-0	-3.3
1992	Cle-A	6	15	.286	35	23	1	0	0	166^2	176	100	23	3	67	114	13.3	4.64	84	.269	.340	0	—	0	-13	-14	1	-1.4
1993	Fla-N	9	17	.346	36	33	0	0	0	196^1	210	105	29	7	78	118	13.5	4.49	96	.271	.343	10	.152	-2	-10	-3	-0	-0.6
1994	Tex-A	0	1	.000	2	2	0	0	0	10	9	4	3	0	2	7	9.9	3.60	134	.231	.268	0	—	0	1	1	-0	0.1
Total	7	40	65	.381	152	130	4	1	0	786^2	807	439	102	18	319	510	13.1	4.58	87	.265	.338	21	.114	-6	-64	-51	2	-7.0
● MIKE ARMSTRONG	Armstrong, Michael Dennis b: 3/7/54, Glen Cove, N.Y. BR/TR, 6'3", 206 lbs. Deb: 8/12/80																											
1980	SD-N	0	0	—	11	0	0	0	0	14^1	16	10	3	0	13	14	18.2	5.65	61	.296	.433	0	.000	-0	-3	-4	-0	-0.3
1981	SD-N	0	2	.000	10	0	0	0	0	12	14	9	1	0	11	9	18.8	6.00	54	.311	.446	0	—	0	-3	-4	-0	-0.7
1982	KC-A	5	5	.500	52	0	0	0	6	112^2	88	45	9	3	43	75	10.7	3.20	128	.215	.295	0	—	0	11	11	-1	0.9
1983	KC-A	10	7	.588	58	0	0	0	3	102^2	86	53	11	3	45	52	11.7	3.86	106	.228	.315	0	—	0	3	3	-0	0.4
1984	NY-A	3	2	.600	36	0	0	0	1	54^1	47	21	6	0	26	43	12.1	3.48	109	.239	.327	0	—	0	3	2	-0	0.2
1985	NY-A	0	0	—	9	0	0	0	0	14^2	9	5	4	0	2	11	6.8	3.07	130	.173	.204	0	—	0	2	2	-0	0.1
1986	NY-A	0	1	.000	7	1	0	0	0	8^2	13	9	4	0	5	8	18.7	9.35	44	.351	.429	0	—	0	-5	-5	-0	-0.5
1987	Cle-A	1	0	1.000	14	0	0	0	1	18^2	27	18	4	0	10	9	17.8	8.68	52	.333	.407	0	—	0	-9	-8	-0	-0.5
Total	8	19	17	.528	197	1	0	0	11	338	300	170	42	6	155	221	12.3	4.10	98	.240	.326	0	.000	-0	-2	-4	-3	-0.4
● JAMIE ARNOLD	Arnold, James Lee b: 3/24/74, Dearborn, Mich. BR/TR, 6'2", 190 lbs. Deb: 4/20/99																											
1999	LA-N	2	4	.333	36	3	0	0	1	69	81	50	6	6	34	26	15.8	5.48	78	.300	.390	2	.200	0	-7	-10	2	-0.6
2000	Chi-N	0	3	.000	12	4	0	0	1	32^2	34	28	1	3	19	13	15.4	6.61	69	.274	.384	1	.111	0	-7	-8	-1	-0.7
	LA-N	0	0	—	2	0	0	0	0	6^2	4	3	0	1	5	3	13.5	4.05	108	.174	.345	0	—	0	0	0	0	0.0
	Yr	0	3	.000	14	4	0	0	1	39^1	38	31	1	4	24	16	15.1	6.18	73	.259	.377	1	.111	0	-7	-7	-1	-0.7
Total	2	2	7	.222	50	7	0	0	2	108^1	119	81	7	10	58	42	15.5	5.73	76	.285	.386	3	.158	0	-14	-17	1	-1.3
● SCOTT ARNOLD	Arnold, Scott Gentry b: 8/18/62, Lexington, Ky. BR/TR, 6'2", 210 lbs. Deb: 4/7/88																											
1988	StL-N	0	0	—	6	0	0	0	0	6^2	9	4	0	0	4	8	17.6	5.40	64	.321	.406	0	—	0	-1	-1	0	-0.1
● TONY ARNOLD	Arnold, Tony Dale b: 5/3/59, ElPaso, Tex. BR/TR, 5'11", 170 lbs. Deb: 8/9/86																											
1986	Bal-A	0	2	.000	11	0	0	0	0	25^1	25	15	0	0	11	7	12.8	3.55	117	.278	.356	0	—	0	2	2	1	0.2
1987	Bal-A	0	0	—	27	0	0	0	0	53	71	35	8	2	17	18	15.3	5.77	76	.330	.385	0	—	0	-8	-8	2	-0.2
Total	2	0	2	.000	38	0	0	0	0	78^1	96	50	8	2	28	25	14.5	5.06	86	.315	.376	0	—	0	-6	-6	3	0.0

YEAR	TM/L	W	L	PCT	G	GS	CG	SH	SV	IP	H	R	HR	HB	BB	SO	RAT	ERA	ERA+	OAV	OOB	BH	AVG	PB	PR	PR+	PD	TPI
● BRAD ARNSBERG	Arnsberg, Bradley James b: 8/20/63, Seattle, Wash. BR/TR, 6'4", 215 lbs. Deb: 9/6/86 C																											
1986	NY-A	0	0	—	2	1	0	0	0	8	13	3	1	0	1	3	15.8	3.38	121	.342	.359	0	—	0	1	1	-0	0.0
1987	NY-A	1	3	.250	6	2	0	0	0	19^1	22	12	5	0	13	14	16.3	5.59	79	.289	.393	0	—	0	-2	-3	1	-0.4
1989	Tex-A	2	1	.667	16	1	0	0	1	48	45	27	6	3	22	26	13.1	4.13	96	.247	.338	0	—	0	-1	-1	1	0.1
1990	Tex-A	6	1	.857	53	0	0	0	5	62^2	56	20	4	2	33	44	13.1	2.15	182	.235	.333	0	—	0	12	12	1	1.5
1991	Tex-A	0	1	.000	9	0	0	0	0	9^2	10	9	5	0	5	8	14.0	8.38	48	.256	.341	0	—	0	-5	-5	-0	-0.5
1992	Cle-A	0	0	—	8	0	0	0	0	10^2	13	14	6	2	11	5	21.9	11.81	33	.317	.481	0	—	0	-9	-9	-0	-0.5
Total	6	9	6	.600	94	4	0	0	6	158^1	159	85	27	7	85	100	14.3	4.26	94	.259	.356	0	—	0	-5	-4	2	0.2
● ORIE ARNTZEN	Arntzen, Orie Edgar "Old Folks" b: 10/18/09, Beverly, Ill. d: 1/28/70, Cedar Rapids, Iowa BR/TR, 6'1", 200 lbs. Deb: 4/20/43																											
1943	Phi-A	4	13	.235	32	20	9	0	0	164^1	172	85	5	5	69	66	13.5	4.22	81	.277	.354	8	.160	-1	-17	-15	-3	-1.8
● RENE AROCHA	Arocha, Rene (Magaly) b: 2/24/66, Havana, Cuba BR/TR, 6', 180 lbs. Deb: 4/9/93																											
1993	StL-N	11	8	.579	32	29	1	0	0	188	197	89	20	3	31	96	11.1	3.78	105	.271	.304	6	.103	-2	6	4	-1	0.1
1994	StL-N	4	4	.500	45	7	1	1	11	83	94	42	9	4	21	62	12.9	4.01	104	.286	.336	1	.111	0	2	1	-0	0.1
1995	StL-N	3	5	.375	41	0	0	0	0	49^2	55	24	6	3	18	25	13.8	3.99	105	.297	.369	0	.000	-0	1	1	0	0.2
1997	SF-N	0	0	—	6	0	0	0	0	10^1	17	14	2	1	5	7	20.0	11.32	36	.370	.442	0	.000	-0	-8	-9	1	-0.4
Total	4	18	17	.514	124	36	2	1	11	331	363	169	37	11	75	190	12.2	4.11	99	.282	.327	7	.101	-2	0	-2	-0	0.0
● GERRY ARRIGO	Arrigo, Gerald William b: 6/12/41, Chicago, Ill. BL/TL, 6'1", 195 lbs. Deb: 6/12/61																											
1961	Min-A	0	1	.000	7	2	0	0	0	9^2	9	12	0	2	10	6	19.6	10.24	41	.265	.457	1	.500	0	-7	-6	0	-0.5
1962	Min-A	0	0	—	1	0	0	0	0	1	3	3	0	0	1	1	36.0	18.00	23	.600	.667	0	—	0	-2	-2	0	-0.1
1963	Min-A	1	2	.333	5	1	0	0	0	15^2	12	5	2	0	4	13	9.2	2.87	127	.211	.262	0	.000	-0	1	1	0	0.2
1964	Min-A	7	4	.636	41	12	2	1	1	105^1	97	48	11	2	45	96	12.3	3.84	93	.244	.324	5	.172	1	-3	-3	0	-0.2
1965	Cin-N	2	4	.333	27	5	0	0	2	54	75	38	4	2	30	43	17.8	6.17	61	.342	.426	2	.167	1	-16	-14	-1	-1.6
1966	Cin-N	0	0	—	3	0	0	0	0	7^1	7	4	2	0	3	3	12.3	4.91	79	.250	.323	0	.000	-0	-1	-1	-0	-0.1
	NY-N	3	3	.500	17	5	0	0	0	43^1	47	20	5	0	16	28	13.1	3.74	97	.276	.339	5	.500	3	-1	-0	1	0.3
	Yr	3	3	.500	20	5	0	0	0	50^2	54	24	7	0	19	31	13.0	3.91	94	.273	.336	5	.455	3	-2	-1	0	0.2
1967	Cin-N	6	6	.500	32	5	1	1	1	74	61	31	6	4	35	56	12.2	3.16	119	.232	.331	4	.211	1	2	4	-2	0.6
1968	Cin-N	12	10	.545	36	31	5	1	0	205^1	181	84	13	4	77	140	11.5	3.33	95	.237	.310	5	.075	-2	-8	-4	1	-0.5
1969	Cin-N	4	7	.364	20	16	1	0	0	91	89	50	9	8	61	35	15.6	4.15	91	.256	.379	5	.161	-0	-6	-4	-2	-0.7
1970	Chi-A	0	3	.000	5	3	0	0	0	13^1	24	20	4	0	9	12	22.3	12.83	30	.393	.471	0	.000	-0	-13	-13	-0	-2.1
Total	10	35	40	.467	194	80	9	3	4	620	605	315	56	22	291	433	13.3	4.14	85	.258	.345	27	.151	2	-52	-40	-3	-4.7
● ROLANDO ARROJO	Arrojo, Luis Rolando b: 7/18/68, Santa Clara, Cuba BR/TR, 6'4", 215 lbs. Deb: 4/1/98																											
1998	TB-A★	14	12	.538	32	32	2	2	0	202	195	84	21	19	65	152	12.4	3.56	135	.256	.330	0	.000	-0	25	27	3	3.4
1999	TB-A	7	12	.368	24	24	2	0	0	140^2	162	84	23	14	60	107	15.1	5.18	96	.296	.379	0	—	0	-5	-3	1	-0.2
2000	Col-N	5	9	.357	19	19	0	0	0	101^1	120	77	14	12	46	80	15.8	6.04	98	.299	.387	3	.107	-2	-16	-1	1	-0.1
	Bos-A	5	2	.714	13	13	0	0	0	71^1	67	41	10	4	22	44	11.7	5.05	101	.245	.310	0	—	0	-1	0	1	0.1
Total	3	31	35	.470	88	88	4	2	0	515^1	544	286	68	49	193	383	13.7	4.70	109	.274	.353	3	.097	-2	3	22	6	3.2
● BRONSON ARROYO	Arroyo, Bronson Anthony b: 2/24/77, Key West, Fla. BR/TR, 6'5", 180 lbs. Deb: 6/12/2000																											
2000	Pit-N	2	6	.250	20	12	0	0	0	71^2	88	61	10	4	36	50	16.1	6.40	72	.302	.387	3	.143	-0	-14	-14	-1	-1.4
● FERNANDO ARROYO	Arroyo, Fernando b: 3/21/52, Sacramento, Cal. BR/TR, 6'3", 195 lbs. Deb: 6/28/75																											
1975	Det-A	2	1	.667	14	2	1	0	0	53^1	56	28	5	1	22	25	13.3	4.56	88	.272	.345	0	—	0	-5	-3	1	0.0
1977	Det-A	8	18	.308	38	28	8	1	0	209^1	227	102	23	1	52	60	12.0	4.17	103	.278	.321	0	—	0	-2	3	6	0.9
1978	Det-A	0	0	—	2	0	0	0	0	4^1	8	4	1	1	0	1	18.7	8.31	47	.400	.429	0	—	0	-2	-2	0	-0.1
1979	Det-A	1	1	.500	6	0	0	0	0	12	17	11	3	0	4	7	15.8	8.25	53	.340	.389	0	—	0	-5	-5	0	-0.7
1980	Min-A	6	6	.500	21	11	1	1	0	92^1	97	55	7	2	32	27	12.8	4.68	93	.273	.337	0	—	0	-7	-3	-1	-0.5
1981	Min-A	7	10	.412	23	19	2	0	0	128^1	144	66	11	5	34	39	12.8	3.93	101	.290	.342	0	—	0	-4	0	0	0.1
1982	Min-A	0	1	.000	6	0	0	0	0	13^2	17	8	2	0	6	4	15.1	5.27	81	.321	.390	0	—	0	-2	-1	1	0.0
	Oak-A	0	0	—	10	0	0	0	0	22^1	23	14	4	1	7	9	12.5	5.24	75	.271	.333	0	—	0	-3	-3	0	-0.2
	Yr	0	1	.000	16	0	0	0	0	36	40	22	6	1	13	13	13.5	5.25	77	.290	.355	0	—	0	-5	-5	1	-0.2
1986	Oak-A	0	0	—	1	0	0	0	0	0	0	0	0	3	—	—	—	—	—	1.000	93	—	0	0	0	0	0.0	
Total	8	24	37	.393	121	60	12	2	0	535^2	589	288	56	11	160	172	12.8	4.44	94	.283	.337	0	—	0	-29	-14	7	-0.5
● LUIS ARROYO	Arroyo, Luis Enrique b: 2/18/27, Penuelas, P.R. BL/TL, 5'8", 190 lbs. Deb: 4/20/55																											
1955	StL-N☆	11	8	.579	35	24	9	1	0	159	162	80	22	2	63	68	12.8	4.19	97	.261	.331	13	.232	1	-3	-2	-2	-0.4
1956	Pit-N	3	3	.500	18	2	1	0	0	28^2	36	17	5	0	12	17	15.1	4.71	80	.298	.361	2	.500	1	-3	-3	0	-0.5
1957	Pit-N	3	11	.214	54	10	0	0	1	130^2	151	76	19	7	31	101	13.0	4.68	81	.282	.329	5	.156	-1	-12	-13	-2	-1.6
1959	Cin-N	1	0	1.000	10	0	0	0	0	13^2	17	11	0	0	11	8	18.4	3.95	103	.321	.438	0	.000	-0	-0	0	0	0.0
1960	*NY-A	5	1	.833	29	0	0	0	7	40^2	30	14	2	0	22	29	11.5	2.88	125	.207	.311	0	.000	-0	5	3	0	0.6
1961	*NY-A☆	15	5	.750	**65**	0	0	0	**29**	119	83	34	5	3	49	87	10.2	2.19	169	.199	.288	7	.280	2	**24**	**22**	-1	**4.6**
1962	NY-A	1	3	.250	27	0	0	0	7	33^2	33	20	5	1	17	21	13.6	4.81	78	.262	.354	2	.500	1	-3	-4	-1	-0.6
1963	NY-A	1	1	.500	6	0	0	0	0	6	12	9	0	0	3	5	22.5	13.50	26	.444	.500	0	—	0	-7	-7	-0	-1.3
Total	8	40	32	.556	244	36	10	1	44	531^1	524	261	58	13	208	336	12.6	3.93	98	.256	.329	29	.227	3	2	-6	-5	0.8
● RUDY ARROYO	Arroyo, Rudolph b: 6/19/50, New York, N.Y. BL/TL, 6'2", 195 lbs. Deb: 6/1/71																											
1971	StL-N	0	1	.000	9	0	0	0	0	11^2	18	8	2	0	5	5	17.7	5.40	67	.375	.434	0	.000	-0	-3	-2	-0	-0.2
● HARRY ARUNDEL	Arundel, Harry b: 2/1855, Philadelphia, Pa. d: 3/25/04, Cleveland, Ohio TR, 5'6", 145 lbs. Deb: 7/19/1875																											
1875	Atl-n	0	1	.000	1	1	0	0	0	2^1	6	6	0		0	0	23.1	7.71	27	.400	.400	0	.000	-1	-1	-2		-0.3
1882	Pit-a	4	10	.286	14	14	13	0	0	120	155	112	3		23	47	13.4	4.65	56	.294	.323	10	.189	0	-26	-28	5	-2.1
1884	Pro-N	1	0	1.000	1	1	1	0	0	9	8	2	0		4	4	12.0	1.00	285	.250	.333	1	.333	0	2	2	-0	0.2
Total	2	5	10	.333	15	15	14	0	0	129	163	114	3		27	51	13.3	4.40	60	.291	.324	11	.196	0	-24	-26	5	-1.9
● KEN ASH	Ash, Kenneth Lowther b: 9/16/01, Anmoore, W.Va. d: 11/15/79, Clarksburg, W.Va. BR/TR, 5'11", 165 lbs. Deb: 4/17/25																											
1925	Chi-A	0	0	—	2	0	0	0	0	4	7	4	2	0	0	0	15.8	9.00	46	.389	.389	0	—	0	-2	-2	-0	-0.1
1928	Cin-N	3	3	.500	8	5	2	0	0	36	43	26	1	1	13	6	14.3	6.50	61	.314	.377	1	.071	-1	-10	-10	0	-1.5
1929	Cin-N	1	5	.167	29	7	2	0	2	82	91	57	2	5	30	26	13.8	4.83	95	.292	.363	3	.143	-1	-1	-2	-0	-0.3
1930	Cin-N	2	0	1.000	16	1	1	0	0	39^1	37	22	1	0	16	15	12.1	3.43	141	.268	.344	2	.182	-1	7	6	1	0.4
Total	4	6	8	.429	55	13	5	0	2	161^1	178	109	6	6	59	47	13.6	4.96	90	.294	.363	6	.130	-3	-6	-9	1	-1.5
● ANDY ASHBY	Ashby, Andrew Jason b: 7/11/67, Kansas City, Mo. BR/TR, 6'5", 190 lbs. Deb: 6/10/91																											
1991	Phi-N	1	5	.167	8	8	0	0	0	42	41	28	5	3	19	26	13.5	6.00	61	.256	.346	1	.083	-1	-11	-11	0	-1.4
1992	Phi-N	1	3	.250	10	8	0	0	0	37	42	31	6	1	21	24	15.6	7.54	46	.290	.383	1	.091	-0	-17	-17	0	-1.6
1993	Col-N	0	4	.000	20	9	0	0	1	54	89	54	5	3	32	33	20.7	8.50	56	.377	.458	4	.267	0	-27	-19	1	-1.1
	SD-N	3	6	.333	12	12	0	0	0	69	79	46	14	1	24	44	13.6	5.48	76	.295	.355	1	.048	-1	-11	-10	0	-1.2
	Yr	3	10	.231	32	21	0	0	1	123	168	100	19	4	56	77	16.7	6.80	65	.333	.404	5	.139	-1	-38	-30	1	-2.3
1994	SD-N	6	11	.353	24	24	4	0	0	164^1	145	75	16	3	43	121	10.5	3.40	121	.233	.286	8	.163	-0	15	13	0	1.3
1995	SD-N	12	10	.545	31	31	2	2	0	192^2	180	79	17	11	62	150	11.8	2.94	137	.252	.322	8	.163	-0	27	24	-2	2.4
1996	*SD-N	9	5	.643	24	24	1	0	0	150^2	147	60	17	3	34	85	11.0	3.23	123	.259	.305	11	.244	3	17	13	1	1.6
1997	SD-N	9	11	.450	30	30	2	0	0	200^2	207	108	17	5	49	144	11.7	4.13	94	.266	.314	4	.067	-3	2	-6	1	-0.7
1998	*SD-N★	17	9	.654	33	33	5	1	0	226^2	223	90	23	7	58	151	11.4	3.34	117	.259	.311	8	.111	-2	23	16	1	1.5
1999	SD-N★	14	10	.583	31	31	4	**3**	0	206	204	95	26	7	54	132	11.6	3.80	111	.258	.311	8	.129	-0	18	10	2	1.2
2000	Phi-N	4	7	.364	16	16	1	0	0	101^1	113	75	17	5	38	51	13.9	5.68	83	.288	.359	5	.179	0	-12	-11	-0	-0.9
	*Atl-N	8	6	.571	15	15	2	1	0	98	103	49	12	1	23	55	11.7	4.13	110	.271	.314	4	.121	-1	6	4	0	0.4
	Yr	12	13	.480	31	31	3	1	0	199^1	216	124	29	6	61	106	12.8	4.92	94	.280	.337	9	.148	-1	-6	-7	0	-0.5
Total	10	84	87	.491	254	241	21	7	1	1542^1	1573	790	175	50	457	1016	12.1	4.10	100	.266	.324	63	.138	-5	29	1	4	1.5

● PAUL ASSENMACHER Assenmacher, Paul Andre b: 12/10/60, Detroit, Mich. BL/TL, 6'3", 200 lbs. Deb: 4/12/86

YEAR	TM/L	W	L	PCT	G	GS	CG	SH	SV	IP	H	R	HR	HB	BB	SO	RAT	ERA	ERA+	OAV	OOB	BH	AVG	PB	PR	PR+	PD	TPI
1986	Atl-N	7	3	.700	61	0	0	0	7	68^1	61	23	5	0	26	56	11.5	2.50	159	.241	.312	0	.000	-0	9	11	1	1.8
1987	Atl-N	1	1	.500	52	0	0	0	2	54^2	58	41	8	1	24	39	13.7	5.10	85	.260	.335	0	.000	-0	-6	-4	-1	-0.3
1988	Atl-N	8	7	.533	64	0	0	0	5	79^1	72	28	4	1	32	71	11.9	3.06	120	.251	.328	1	.333	1	3	5	0	1.1
1989	Atl-N	1	3	.250	49	0	0	0	0	57^2	55	26	2	1	16	64	11.2	3.59	102	.249	.303	0	.000	-0	-1	0	0	0.0
	*Chi-N	2	1	.667	14	0	0	0	0	19	19	11	1	0	12	15	14.7	5.21	72	.275	.383	0	.000	-0	-4	-3	0	-0.4
	Yr	3	4	.429	63	0	0	0	0	76^2	74	37	3	1	28	79	12.1	3.99	92	.255	.323	0	.000	-1	-4	-3	1	-0.4
1990	Chi-N	7	2	.778	74	1	0	0	10	103	90	33	10	1	36	95	11.1	2.80	146	.239	.308	0	.000	-1	11	14	1	1.4
1991	Chi-N	7	8	.467	75	0	0	0	15	102^2	85	41	10	3	31	117	10.4	3.24	120	.223	.287	1	.250	0	5	7	-1	1.1
1992	Chi-N	4	4	.500	70	0	0	0	8	68	72	32	6	3	26	67	13.4	4.10	88	.271	.342	0	.000	-0	-4	-4	-1	-0.6
1993	Chi-N	2	1	.667	46	0	0	0	0	38^2	44	15	5	0	13	34	13.3	3.49	114	.288	.343	1	.500	0	2	2	-0	0.1
	NY-A	2	2	.500	26	0	0	0	0	17^1	10	6	0	1	9	11	10.4	3.12	134	.175	.299	0	—	0	2	2	-0	0.4
1994	Chi-A	1	2	.333	44	0	0	0	1	33	26	13	2	1	13	29	10.9	3.55	132	.224	.308	0	—	0	5	4	0	0.4
1995	*Cle-A	6	2	.750	47	0	0	0	0	38^1	32	13	3	3	12	40	11.0	2.82	167	.225	.299	0	—	0	8	8	0	1.4
1996	*Cle-A	4	2	.667	63	0	0	0	1	46^2	46	18	1	4	14	44	12.3	3.09	159	.260	.328	0	—	0	10	10	-0	1.0
1997	*Cle-A	5	0	1.000	75	0	0	0	4	49	43	17	5	1	15	53	10.8	2.94	160	.231	.292	0	—	0	9	9	0	1.0
1998	*Cle-A	2	5	.286	69	0	0	0	3	47	54	22	5	1	19	43	14.2	3.26	147	.286	.354	0	—	0	7	8	-0	1.0
1999	*Cle-A	2	1	.667	55	0	0	0	0	33	50	32	6	1	17	29	18.5	8.18	62	.347	.420	0	—	0	-12	-11	0	-0.8
Total	14	61	44	.581	884	1	0	0	56	855^2	817	371	73	22	315	807	12.1	3.53	118	.252	.323	3	.083	-0	46	58	0	8.6

● PEDRO ASTACIO Astacio, Pedro Julio (Pura) b: 11/28/69, Hato Mayor, D.R. BR/TR, 6'2", 190 lbs. Deb: 7/3/92

YEAR	TM/L	W	L	PCT	G	GS	CG	SH	SV	IP	H	R	HR	HB	BB	SO	RAT	ERA	ERA+	OAV	OOB	BH	AVG	PB	PR	PR+	PD	TPI
1992	LA-N	5	5	.500	11	11	4	4	0	82	80	23	1	2	20	43	11.2	1.98	175	.255	.304	3	.125	-1	14	14	-0	1.7
1993	LA-N	14	9	.609	31	31	3	2	0	186^1	165	80	14	5	68	122	11.5	3.57	107	.239	.312	10	.161	-1	10	5	-1	0.4
1994	LA-N	6	8	.429	23	23	3	1	0	149	142	77	18	4	47	108	11.7	4.29	92	.252	.314	3	.064	-3	-1	-6	-1	-0.9
1995	*LA-N	7	8	.467	48	11	1	1	0	104	103	53	12	4	29	80	11.8	4.24	90	.261	.318	3	.125	-0	-1	-6	0	-0.7
1996	*LA-N	9	8	.529	35	32	0	0	0	211^2	207	86	18	9	67	130	12.0	3.44	112	.261	.326	6	.088	-4	18	11	1	0.5
1997	LA-N	7	9	.438	26	24	2	1	0	153^2	151	75	15	4	47	115	11.8	4.10	94	.256	.316	6	.146	-0	2	-5	2	-0.2
	Col-N	5	1	.833	7	7	0	0	0	48^2	49	23	9	5	14	51	12.6	4.25	122	.262	.330	1	.077	-1	-0	4	1	0.5
	Yr	12	10	.545	33	31	2	1	0	202^1	200	98	24	9	61	166	12.0	4.14	101	.258	.319	7	.130	-1	2	1	3	0.3
1998	Col-N	13	14	.481	35	34	0	0	0	209^1	245	160	39	17	74	170	14.4	6.23	83	.294	.364	8	.129	-3	-46	-20	2	-2.3
1999	Col-N	17	11	.607	34	34	7	0	0	232	258	140	38	11	75	210	13.3	5.04	115	.285	.347	20	.233	-0	-12	16	-0	1.6
2000	Col-N	12	9	.571	32	32	3	0	0	196^1	217	119	32	15	77	193	14.2	5.27	113	.281	.358	8	.098	-6	-14	11	1	0.6
Total	9	95	82	.537	282	239	23	9	0	1573	1617	836	196	76	518	1222	12.7	4.44	103	.268	.333	68	.134	-19	-31	21	4	1.2

● KEITH ATHERTON Atherton, Keith Rowe b: 2/19/59, Newport News, Va. BR/TR, 6'4", 200 lbs. Deb: 7/14/83

YEAR	TM/L	W	L	PCT	G	GS	CG	SH	SV	IP	H	R	HR	HB	BB	SO	RAT	ERA	ERA+	OAV	OOB	BH	AVG	PB	PR	PR+	PD	TPI
1983	Oak-A	2	5	.286	29	0	0	0	4	68^1	53	22	7	1	23	40	10.1	2.77	140	.215	.285	0	.000	-0	10	9	-1	0.8
1984	Oak-A	7	6	.538	57	0	0	0	2	104	110	51	13	2	39	58	13.1	4.33	87	.274	.341	0	—	0	-4	-7	-2	-1.0
1985	Oak-A	4	7	.364	56	0	0	0	3	104^2	89	51	17	0	42	77	11.3	4.30	90	.231	.306	0	—	0	-2	-6	-2	-0.7
1986	Oak-A	1	2	.333	13	0	0	0	0	15^1	18	10	2	0	11	8	17.0	5.87	66	.295	.403	0	—	0	-3	-4	-0	-0.6
	Min-A	5	8	.385	47	0	0	0	10	81^2	82	37	9	1	35	59	13.0	3.75	115	.264	.340	0	—	0	4	5	-0	0.8
	Yr	6	10	.375	60	0	0	0	10	97	100	47	11	1	46	67	13.6	4.08	104	.269	.351	0	—	0	1	2	-0	0.2
1987	*Min-A	7	5	.583	59	0	0	0	2	79^1	81	46	10	4	30	51	13.0	4.54	102	.262	.335	0	—	0	-1	1	-0	0.1
1988	Min-A	7	5	.583	49	0	0	0	3	74	65	29	10	2	22	43	10.8	3.41	120	.235	.296	0	—	0	5	5	-0	0.8
1989	Cle-A	0	3	.000	32	0	0	0	2	39	48	22	7	0	13	13	14.1	4.15	96	.293	.345	0	—	0	-1	-1	-1	-0.2
Total	7	33	41	.446	342	0	0	0	26	566^1	546	268	75	10	215	349	12.3	3.99	102	.253	.324	0	.000	-0	8	4	-6	0.0

● TOMMY ATKINS Atkins, Francis Montgomery b: 12/9/1887, Ponca, Neb. d: 5/7/56, Cleveland, Ohio BL/TL, 5'10.5", 165 lbs. Deb: 10/2/09

YEAR	TM/L	W	L	PCT	G	GS	CG	SH	SV	IP	H	R	HR	HB	BB	SO	RAT	ERA	ERA+	OAV	OOB	BH	AVG	PB	PR	PR+	PD	TPI
1909	Phi-A	0	0	—	1	1	0	0	0	6	6	4	0	0	5	4	16.5	4.50	53	.261	.393	0	.000	-0	-1	-1	0	-0.1
1910	Phi-A	3	2	.600	15	3	2	0	2	57	53	33	0	1	23	29	12.2	2.68	88	.254	.330	2	.118	-1	-1	-2	0	-0.3
Total	2	3	2	.600	16	4	2	0	2	63	59	37	0	1	28	33	12.6	2.86	83	.254	.337	2	.105	-1	-2	-4	0	-0.4

● JAMES ATKINS Atkins, James Curtis b: 3/10/21, Birmingham, Ala. BL/TR, 6'3", 205 lbs. Deb: 9/29/50

YEAR	TM/L	W	L	PCT	G	GS	CG	SH	SV	IP	H	R	HR	HB	BB	SO	RAT	ERA	ERA+	OAV	OOB	BH	AVG	PB	PR	PR+	PD	TPI
1950	Bos-A	0	0	—	1	0	0	0	0	4^2	4	2	1	1	4	0	17.4	3.86	127	.235	.409	0	.000	-0	0	1	-0	0.0
1952	Bos-A	0	1	.000	3	1	0	0	0	10^1	11	6	0	0	7	2	15.7	3.48	113	.275	.383	2	.667	1	0	0	0	0.1
Total	2	0	1	.000	4	1	0	0	0	15	15	8	1	1	11	2	16.2	3.60	118	.263	.391	2	.400	0	1	1	0	0.1

● AL ATKINSON Atkinson, Albert Wright b: 3/9/1861, Clinton, Ill. d: 6/17/52, Elkhorn Township, Mo. BR/TR, 5'11.5", 165 lbs. Deb: 5/1/1884

YEAR	TM/L	W	L	PCT	G	GS	CG	SH	SV	IP	H	R	HR	HB	BB	SO	RAT	ERA	ERA+	OAV	OOB	BH	AVG	PB	PR	PR+	PD	TPI
1884	Phi-a	11	11	.500	22	22	20	1	0	184	186	130	3	10	21	93	10.6	4.21	80	.244	.274	16	.193	-1	-20	-16	0	-1.6
	CP-U	6	10	.375	16	16	16	1	0	140	127	83	1		21	104	9.5	2.76	88	.226	.253	14	.206	-5	-5	-5	1	-0.9
	Bal-U	3	5	.375	8	8	8	0	0	69^2	60	34	4		12	50	9.3	2.33	115	.217	.249	4	.138	-4	1	3	0	-0.1
	Yr	9	15	.375	24	24	24	1	0	209^2	187	117	5		33	154	9.4	2.62	96	.223	.252	18	.186	-9	-4	-2	1	-1.0
1886	Phi-a	25	17	.595	45	45	44	1	0	396^2	414	288	11	22	101	154	12.2	3.95	89	.256	.308	18	.122	-6	-22	-19	-2	-2.3
1887	Phi-a	6	8	.429	15	15	11	0	0	124^2	210	121	2	6	54	34	15.6	5.92	72	.357	.364	17	.266	-1	-22	-23	1	-1.8
Total	3	51	51	.500	106	106	99	3	0	915	997	656	21	38	209	435	11.7	3.96	85	.262	.297	69	.176	-16	-68	-59	-1	-6.7

● BILL ATKINSON Atkinson, William Cecil Glenn b: 10/4/54, Chatham, Ont., Can. BL/TR, 5'7", 165 lbs. Deb: 9/18/76

YEAR	TM/L	W	L	PCT	G	GS	CG	SH	SV	IP	H	R	HR	HB	BB	SO	RAT	ERA	ERA+	OAV	OOB	BH	AVG	PB	PR	PR+	PD	TPI
1976	Mon-N	0	0	—	4	0	0	0	0	5	3	0	0	0	1	4	7.2	0.00	—	.176	.222	0	—	0	2	2	0	0.1
1977	Mon-N	7	2	.778	55	0	0	0	7	83^1	72	33	12	0	29	56	10.9	3.35	114	.234	.300	1	.200	-0	5	4	1	0.6
1978	Mon-N	2	2	.500	29	0	0	0	3	45^1	45	23	5	1	28	32	14.7	4.37	81	.268	.376	2	.500	1	-4	-4	0	-0.3
1979	Mon-N	2	0	1.000	10	0	0	0	1	13^2	9	4	0	0	4	7	8.6	1.98	186	.170	.228	0	.000	-0	3	3	-0	0.4
Total	4	11	4	.733	98	0	0	0	11	147^1	129	60	17	1	62	99	11.7	3.42	108	.236	.315	3	.300	1	6	5	1	0.8

● DEREK AUCOIN Aucoin, Derek Alfred b: 3/27/70, Lachine, Que., Can. BR/TR, 6'7", 235 lbs. Deb: 5/21/96

YEAR	TM/L	W	L	PCT	G	GS	CG	SH	SV	IP	H	R	HR	HB	BB	SO	RAT	ERA	ERA+	OAV	OOB	BH	AVG	PB	PR	PR+	PD	TPI
1996	Mon-N	0	1	.000	2	0	0	0	0	2^2	3	1	0	0	1	1	13.5	3.38	128	.300	.364	0	—	0	0	0	0	0.1

● DON AUGUST August, Donald Glenn b: 7/3/63, Inglewood, Cal. BR/TR, 6'3", 190 lbs. Deb: 6/2/88

YEAR	TM/L	W	L	PCT	G	GS	CG	SH	SV	IP	H	R	HR	HB	BB	SO	RAT	ERA	ERA+	OAV	OOB	BH	AVG	PB	PR	PR+	PD	TPI
1988	Mil-A	13	7	.650	24	22	6	1	0	148^1	137	55	12	0	48	66	11.2	3.09	129	.245	.305	0	—	0	15	15	2	2.1
1989	Mil-A	12	12	.500	31	25	2	1	0	142^1	175	93	17	2	58	51	14.9	5.31	72	.302	.368	0	—	0	-22	-23	1	-3.3
1990	Mil-A	0	3	.000	5	0	0	0	0	11	13	10	0	0	5	2	14.7	6.55	59	.295	.367	0	—	0	-3	-3	0	-0.6
1991	Mil-A	9	8	.529	28	23	1	1	0	138^1	166	87	18	3	47	62	14.1	5.47	73	.301	.359	0	—	0	-21	-24	0	-2.4
Total	4	34	30	.531	88	70	9	3	0	440	491	245	47	5	158	181	13.4	4.64	85	.283	.345	0	—	0	-32	-35	4	-4.2

● JERRY AUGUSTINE Augustine, Gerald Lee b: 7/24/52, Kewaunee, Wis. BL/TL, 6', 185 lbs. Deb: 9/9/75

YEAR	TM/L	W	L	PCT	G	GS	CG	SH	SV	IP	H	R	HR	HB	BB	SO	RAT	ERA	ERA+	OAV	OOB	BH	AVG	PB	PR	PR+	PD	TPI
1975	Mil-A	2	0	1.000	5	3	1	0	0	26^2	26	9	2	1	12	8	13.2	3.04	126	.274	.361	0	—	0	2	2	-0	0.1
1976	Mil-A	9	12	.429	39	24	5	3	0	171^2	167	69	9	4	56	59	11.9	3.30	106	.261	.324	0	—	0	4	4	-2	0.2
1977	Mil-A	12	18	.400	33	33	10	1	0	209	222	119	23	3	72	68	12.8	4.48	91	.277	.339	0	—	0	-9	-9	0	-1.1
1978	Mil-A	13	12	.520	35	30	9	2	0	188^1	204	100	14	4	61	59	12.9	4.54	83	.280	.339	0	—	0	-16	-16	2	-1.7
1979	Mil-A	9	6	.600	43	2	0	0	5	85^2	95	38	6	1	30	41	13.2	3.47	121	.284	.344	0	—	0	7	7	-2	1.0
1980	Mil-A	4	3	.571	39	1	0	0	2	69^2	83	37	5	2	36	22	15.6	4.52	86	.301	.385	0	—	0	-4	-5	0	-0.5
1981	Mil-A	2	2	.500	27	2	0	0	2	61^1	75	30	4	1	18	26	13.8	4.26	81	.300	.349	0	—	0	-4	-6	0	-0.4
1982	Mil-A	1	3	.250	20	2	1	0	0	62	63	43	13	2	26	22	13.2	5.08	75	.267	.345	0	—	0	-7	-10	-1	-0.7
1983	Mil-A	3	3	.500	34	7	1	0	2	64^1	89	45	11	1	25	40	16.1	5.74	65	.328	.387	0	—	0	-12	-15	-0	-1.4
1984	Mil-A	0	0	—	4	0	0	0	0	5^1	4	1	0	1	4	3	15.2	0.00	—	.211	.375	0	—	0	2	2	0	0.1
Total	10	55	59	.482	279	104	27	6	11	944	1028	491	87	20	340	348	13.2	4.23	90	.281	.346	0	—	0	-36	-44	-3	-4.4

● ELDEN AUKER Auker, Elden Le Roy "Submarine" b: 9/21/10, Norcatur, Kan. BR/TR, 6'2", 194 lbs. Deb: 8/10/33

YEAR	TM/L	W	L	PCT	G	GS	CG	SH	SV	IP	H	R	HR	HB	BB	SO	RAT	ERA	ERA+	OAV	OOB	BH	AVG	PB	PR	PR+	PD	TPI
1933	Det-A	3	3	.500	15	6	2	1	0	55	63	34	3	2	25	17	14.7	5.24	82	.285	.363	2	.118	-1	-6	-6	-1	-0.7
1934	*Det-A	15	7	.682	43	18	10	2	1	205	234	103	9	3	56	86	12.9	3.42	128	.288	.336	11	.149	-2	24	23	3	2.2
1935	*Det-A	18	7	**.720**	36	25	13	2	0	195	213	86	13	9	61	63	13.1	3.83	109	.279	.340	16	.216	1	14	8	1	1.1
1936	Det-A	13	16	.448	35	31	14	2	0	215^1	263	140	11	3	83	66	14.6	4.89	101	.302	.365	24	.308	7	4	1	5	1.2
1937	Det-A	17	9	.654	39	32	19	1	1	252^2	250	127	13	6	97	73	12.6	3.88	120	.260	.331	18	.198	4	21	22	5	2.9

YEAR	TM/L	W	L	PCT	G	GS	CG	SH	SV	IP	H	R	HR	HB	BB	SO	RAT	ERA	ERA+	OAV	OOB	BH	AVG	PB	PR	PR+	PD	TPI
1938	Det-A	11	10	.524	27	24	12	1	0	160^2	184	97	14	5	56	46	13.7	5.27	95	.284	.346	5	.088	-4	-9	-5	3	-0.6
1939	Bos-A	9	10	.474	31	25	6	1	0	151	183	108	13	1	61	43	14.6	5.36	88	.294	.358	12	.226	2	-12	-10	2	-0.8
1940	StL-A	16	11	.593	38	35	20	2	0	263^2	299	129	17	3	96	78	13.6	3.96	116	.281	.342	19	.213	3	12	18	2	2.0
1941	StL-A	14	15	.483	34	31	13	0	0	216	268	150	20	1	85	60	14.8	5.50	78	.303	.365	10	.125	-3	-32	-28	1	-3.2
1942	StL-A	14	13	.519	35	34	17	2	0	249	273	132	16	3	86	62	13.1	4.08	91	.277	.337	14	.161	-1	-12	-10	1	-1.1
Total	10	130	101	.563	333	261	126	14	2	1963^1	2230	1106	129	36	706	594	13.6	4.42	101	.285	.347	131	.187	6	3	11	21	3.0

● JOE AUSANIO Ausanio, Joseph John b: 12/9/65, Kingston, N.Y. BR/TR, 6'1", 205 lbs. Deb: 7/14/94

YEAR	TM/L	W	L	PCT	G	GS	CG	SH	SV	IP	H	R	HR	HB	BB	SO	RAT	ERA	ERA+	OAV	OOB	BH	AVG	PB	PR	PR+	PD	TPI
1994	NY-A	2	1	.667	13	0	0	0	0	15^2	16	9	3	0	6	15	12.6	5.17	89	.254	.319	0	—	0	-1	-1	0	-0.2
1995	NY-A	2	0	1.000	28	0	0	0	1	37^2	42	24	9	0	23	36	15.5	5.73	81	.286	.382	0	—	0	-4	-5	-0	-0.3
Total	2	4	1	.800	41	0	0	0	1	53^1	58	33	12	0	29	51	14.7	5.57	83	.276	.364	0	—	0	-5	-6	-0	-0.5

● DENNIS AUST Aust, Dennis Kay b: 11/25/40, Tecumseh, Neb. BR/TR, 5'11", 180 lbs. Deb: 9/6/65

YEAR	TM/L	W	L	PCT	G	GS	CG	SH	SV	IP	H	R	HR	HB	BB	SO	RAT	ERA	ERA+	OAV	OOB	BH	AVG	PB	PR	PR+	PD	TPI
1965	StL-N	0	0	—	6	0	0	0	1	7^1	6	4	0	0	2	7	9.8	4.91	78	.214	.267	0	.000	-0	-1	-1	0	0.0
1966	StL-N	0	1	.000	9	0	0	0	1	9^2	12	7	1	0	6	7	16.8	6.52	55	.308	.400	0	.000	-0	-3	-3	-0	-0.4
Total	2	0	1	.000	15	0	0	0	2	17	18	11	1	0	8	14	13.8	5.82	64	.269	.347	0	.000	-0	-4	-4	-0	-0.4

● JIM AUSTIN Austin, James Parker b: 12/7/63, Farmville, Va. BR/TR, 6'2", 200 lbs. Deb: 7/4/91

YEAR	TM/L	W	L	PCT	G	GS	CG	SH	SV	IP	H	R	HR	HB	BB	SO	RAT	ERA	ERA+	OAV	OOB	BH	AVG	PB	PR	PR+	PD	TPI
1991	Mil-A	0	0	—	5	0	0	0	0	8^2	8	8	1	3	11	3	22.8	8.31	48	.276	.512	0	—	0	-4	-4	0	-0.2
1992	Mil-A	5	2	.714	47	0	0	0	0	58^1	38	13	2	2	32	30	11.1	1.85	208	.191	.309	0	—	0	14	13	-1	1.4
1993	Mil-A	1	2	.333	31	0	0	0	0	33	28	15	3	1	13	15	11.5	3.82	112	.230	.309	0	—	0	2	2	-0	0.1
Total	3	6	4	.600	83	0	0	0	0	100	74	36	6	6	56	48	12.2	3.06	131	.211	.330	0	—	0	11	11	-1	1.3

● RICK AUSTIN Austin, Rick Gerald b: 10/27/46, Seattle, Wash. BR/TL, 6'4", 190 lbs. Deb: 6/21/70

YEAR	TM/L	W	L	PCT	G	GS	CG	SH	SV	IP	H	R	HR	HB	BB	SO	RAT	ERA	ERA+	OAV	OOB	BH	AVG	PB	PR	PR+	PD	TPI
1970	Cle-A	2	5	.286	31	8	1	1	3	67^2	74	36	10	3	26	53	13.7	4.79	83	.281	.353	2	.111	0	-8	-6	1	-0.5
1971	Cle-A	0	0	—	23	0	0	0	1	23	25	15	3	3	20	20	18.8	5.09	75	.291	.440	0	.000	-0	-4	-3	0	-0.1
1975	Mil-A	2	3	.400	32	0	0	0	2	40	32	19	3	1	32	30	14.6	4.05	95	.222	.367	0	—	0	-1	-1	-1	-0.2
1976	Mil-A	0	0	—	3	0	0	0	0	5^1	10	3	1	1	0	3	18.6	5.06	69	.435	.458	0	—	0	-1	-1	0	0.0
Total	4	4	8	.333	89	8	1	1	6	136	141	73	17	8	78	106	15.0	4.63	84	.273	.377	2	.105	0	-14	-11	1	-0.8

● AL AUTRY Autry, Albert b: 2/29/52, Modesto, Cal. BR/TR, 6'5", 225 lbs. Deb: 9/14/76

YEAR	TM/L	W	L	PCT	G	GS	CG	SH	SV	IP	H	R	HR	HB	BB	SO	RAT	ERA	ERA+	OAV	OOB	BH	AVG	PB	PR	PR+	PD	TPI
1976	Atl-N	1	0	1.000	1	1	0	0	0	5	4	3	2	0	3	3	12.6	5.40	70	.222	.333	0	.000	-0	-1	-1	-0	-0.2

● STEVE AVERY Avery, Steven Thomas b: 4/14/70, Trenton, Mich. BL/TL, 6'4", 190 lbs. Deb: 6/13/90

YEAR	TM/L	W	L	PCT	G	GS	CG	SH	SV	IP	H	R	HR	HB	BB	SO	RAT	ERA	ERA+	OAV	OOB	BH	AVG	PB	PR	PR+	PD	TPI
1990	Atl-N	3	11	.214	21	20	1	1	0	99	121	79	7	2	45	75	15.3	5.64	72	.302	.375	4	.133	-1	-20	-16	2	-2.0
1991	*Atl-N	18	8	.692	35	35	3	1	0	210^1	189	89	21	3	65	137	11.0	3.38	115	.240	.300	17	.215	3	7	11	-0	1.7
1992	*Atl-N	11	11	.500	35	35	2	2	0	233^2	216	95	14	0	71	129	11.1	3.20	115	.246	.302	13	.171	2	8	12	-0	1.2
1993	*Atl-N★	18	6	.750	35	35	3	1	0	223^1	216	81	14	0	43	125	10.4	2.94	137	.261	.297	12	.160	1	27	27	2	3.0
1994	Atl-N	8	3	.727	24	24	1	0	0	151^2	127	71	15	4	55	122	11.0	4.04	105	.227	.301	5	.102	-2	3	4	0	0.1
1995	*Atl-N	7	13	.350	29	29	3	1	0	173^1	165	92	22	6	52	141	11.6	4.67	91	.252	.312	11	.208	3	-9	-8	2	-0.3
1996	*Atl-N	7	10	.412	24	23	1	0	0	131	146	70	10	4	40	86	13.1	4.47	99	.285	.341	11	.239	5	-4	-1	1	0.5
1997	Bos-A	6	7	.462	22	18	0	0	0	96^2	127	76	15	2	49	51	16.6	6.42	72	.320	.397	0	.000	-0	-20	-19	1	-2.0
1998	Bos-A	10	7	.588	34	23	0	0	0	123^2	128	74	14	4	64	57	14.3	5.02	94	.269	.361	0	.000	-0	-5	-4	4	-0.1
1999	Cin-N	6	7	.462	19	19	0	0	0	96	75	62	11	1	78	51	14.4	5.16	90	.222	.369	2	.077	-2	-6	-5	0	-0.7
Total	10	94	83	.531	278	261	14	6	0	1538^2	1510	789	143	26	562	974	12.3	4.17	100	.259	.327	75	.172	9	-19	0	12	1.4

● JAY AVREA Avrea, James Epherium b: 7/6/20, Cleburne, Tex. d: 6/26/87, Dallas, Tex. BR/TR, 6'1.5", 175 lbs. Deb: 4/22/50

YEAR	TM/L	W	L	PCT	G	GS	CG	SH	SV	IP	H	R	HR	HB	BB	SO	RAT	ERA	ERA+	OAV	OOB	BH	AVG	PB	PR	PR+	PD	TPI
1950	Cin-N	0	0	—	2	0	0	0	0	5^1	6	2	0	0	3	2	15.2	3.38	125	.273	.360	0	.000	-0	0	0	-0	0.0

● BOBBY AYALA Ayala, Robert Joseph b: 7/8/69, Ventura, Cal. BR/TR, 6'3", 200 lbs. Deb: 9/5/92

YEAR	TM/L	W	L	PCT	G	GS	CG	SH	SV	IP	H	R	HR	HB	BB	SO	RAT	ERA	ERA+	OAV	OOB	BH	AVG	PB	PR	PR+	PD	TPI
1992	Cin-N	2	1	.667	5	5	0	0	0	29	33	15	1	1	13	23	14.6	4.34	83	.297	.376	0	.000	-1	-3	-2	1	-0.2
1993	Cin-N	7	10	.412	43	9	0	0	3	98	106	72	16	7	45	65	14.5	5.60	72	.274	.360	2	.095	-1	-17	-17	-1	-2.8
1994	Sea-A	4	3	.571	46	0	0	0	18	56^2	42	25	2	0	26	76	10.8	2.86	171	.203	.292	0	—	0	12	13	-0	2.0
1995	*Sea-A	6	5	.545	63	0	0	0	19	71	73	42	9	6	30	77	13.8	4.44	107	.262	.346	0	—	0	2	2	-0	0.4
1996	Sea-A	6	3	.667	50	0	0	0	3	67^1	65	45	10	2	25	61	12.3	5.88	84	.256	.327	0	—	0	-7	-7	-0	-0.8
1997	*Sea-A	10	5	.667	71	0	0	0	8	96^2	91	45	14	3	41	92	12.6	3.82	118	.260	.343	0	—	0	8	7	-0	1.1
1998	Sea-A	1	10	.091	62	0	0	0	8	75^1	100	66	9	1	26	68	15.2	7.29	64	.323	.377	0	—	0	-22	-22	-0	-3.1
1999	Mon-N	1	6	.143	53	0	0	0	0	66	60	36	6	4	34	64	13.4	3.68	122	.235	.334	0	.000	-0	6	6	1	0.6
	Chi-N	0	1	.000	13	0	0	0	0	16	11	7	4	2	5	15	10.1	2.81	161	.193	.281	0	—	0	3	3	0	0.2
	Yr	1	7	.125	66	0	0	0	0	82	71	43	10	6	39	79	12.7	3.51	128	.228	.325	0	.000	-0	10	9	1	0.8
Total	8	37	44	.457	406	14	0	0	59	576	581	353	71	26	245	541	13.3	4.78	94	.263	.343	2	.065	-2	-16	-17	0	-2.6

● MANNY AYBAR Aybar, Manuel Antonio b: 10/5/74, Bani, D.R. BR/TR, 6'1", 165 lbs. Deb: 8/4/97

YEAR	TM/L	W	L	PCT	G	GS	CG	SH	SV	IP	H	R	HR	HB	BB	SO	RAT	ERA	ERA+	OAV	OOB	BH	AVG	PB	PR	PR+	PD	TPI
1997	StL-N	2	4	.333	12	12	0	0	0	68	66	33	8	4	29	41	13.1	4.24	98	.263	.349	3	.143	-0	-0	-1	-0	-0.1
1998	StL-N	6	6	.500	20	14	0	0	0	81^1	90	58	6	2	42	57	14.8	5.98	70	.281	.368	6	.222	1	-16	-16	-1	-1.9
1999	StL-N	4	5	.444	65	1	0	0	3	97	104	67	13	4	36	74	13.4	5.47	84	.272	.340	1	.083	-1	-10	-10	-0	-0.9
2000	Col-N	0	1	.000	1	0	0	0	0	1^2	5	3	1	0	0	0	27.0	16.20	37	.500	.500	0	—	0	-2	-1	-0	-0.2
	Cin-N	1	1	.500	32	0	0	0	0	50^1	51	31	7	2	22	31	13.4	4.83	99	.262	.342	0	.000	-0	-1	-0	0	0.0
	Fla-N	1	0	1.000	21	0	0	0	0	27^1	18	8	3	0	13	14	10.2	2.63	168	.184	.279	0	—	0	6	6	1	0.3
	Yr	2	2	.500	54	0	0	0	0	79^1	74	42	11	2	35	45	12.6	4.31	108	.244	.326	0	.000	-0	3	3	1	0.0
Total	4	14	17	.452	151	27	0	0	3	325^2	334	200	38	12	142	217	13.5	5.06	87	.266	.346	10	.152	0	-23	-23	-0	-2.9

● JAKE AYDELOTT Aydelott, Jacob Stuart b: 7/6/1861, N.Manchester, Ind. d: 10/22/26, Detroit, Mich. 6', 180 lbs. Deb: 5/15/1884

YEAR	TM/L	W	L	PCT	G	GS	CG	SH	SV	IP	H	R	HR	HB	BB	SO	RAT	ERA	ERA+	OAV	OOB	BH	AVG	PB	PR	PR+	PD	TPI
1884	Ind-a	5	7	.417	12	12	11	0	0	106	129	100	0	0	29	30	13.4	4.92	67	.282	.324	5	.114	-3	-20	-19	-2	-2.0
1886	Phi-a	0	2	.000	2	2	2	0	0	18	21	11	0	0	12	5	16.5	4.00	88	.304	.407	0	.000	-1	-1	-1	-0	-0.2
Total	2	5	9	.357	14	14	13	0	0	124	150	111	0	0	41	35	13.9	4.79	69	.285	.336	5	.100	-4	-21	-20	-2	-2.2

● BILL AYERS Ayers, William Oscar b: 9/27/19, Newnan, Ga. d: 9/24/80, Newnan, Ga. BR/TR, 6'3", 185 lbs. Deb: 4/17/47

YEAR	TM/L	W	L	PCT	G	GS	CG	SH	SV	IP	H	R	HR	HB	BB	SO	RAT	ERA	ERA+	OAV	OOB	BH	AVG	PB	PR	PR+	PD	TPI
1947	NY-N	0	3	.000	13	4	0	0	1	35^1	46	35	7	1	14	22	15.5	8.15	50	.322	.386	2	.250	0	-16	-16	1	-1.2

● DOC AYERS Ayers, Yancy Wyatt b: 5/20/1890, Fancy Gap, Va. d: 5/26/68, Pulaski, Va. BR/TR, 6'1", 185 lbs. Deb: 9/9/13

YEAR	TM/L	W	L	PCT	G	GS	CG	SH	SV	IP	H	R	HR	HB	BB	SO	RAT	ERA	ERA+	OAV	OOB	BH	AVG	PB	PR	PR+	PD	TPI
1913	Was-A	1	1	.500	4	2	1	1	1	17^2	12	7	0	1	4	17	8.7	1.53	193	.182	.239	0	.000	-1	3	3	1	0.3
1914	Was-A	11	15	.423	49	32	8	3	3	265^1	221	106	5	8	54	148	9.6	2.54	111	.238	.286	14	.169	-0	6	8	-2	0.5
1915	Was-A	14	9	.609	40	16	8	2	3	211^1	178	66	1	7	38	96	9.5	2.21	134	.234	.276	12	.190	-1	17	18	-4	1.2
1916	Was-A	5	8	.385	43	17	7	0	2	157	173	89	4	4	52	69	13.1	3.78	74	.285	.346	6	.140	-2	-17	-18	-4	-2.1
1917	Was-A	11	10	.524	40	15	12	3	1	207^2	192	67	3	8	59	78	11.2	2.17	121	.256	.317	13	.206	-0	11	11	-1	1.0
1918	Was-A	10	12	.455	40	24	11	4	3	219^2	215	91	2	7	63	67	11.7	2.83	96	.261	.319	10	.152	-2	-1	-2	-0	-0.5
1919	Was-A	0	6	.000	11	5	0	0	1	43^2	52	27	0	4	17	12	15.0	2.89	111	.317	.395	5	.417	2	2	2	1	0.4
	Det-A	5	3	.625	24	5	3	1	0	93^2	88	34	2	3	31	32	11.7	2.69	119	.254	.320	3	.125	-1	6	5	-0	0.3
	Yr	5	9	.357	35	10	3	1	1	137^1	140	61	2	7	48	44	12.8	2.75	116	.274	.345	8	.222	0	7	7	0	0.7
1920	Det-A	7	14	.333	46	23	8	3	1	208^2	217	115	6	8	62	103	12.4	3.88	96	.280	.340	9	.153	-2	-2	-4	-0	-0.6
1921	Det-A	0	0	—	2	1	0	0	0	4	9	6	0	0	2	0	24.8	9.00	47	.450	.500	0	—	0	-2	-2	-0	-0.1
Total	9	64	78	.451	299	140	58	17	15	1428^2	1357	608	23	50	382	622	11.3	2.84	105	.259	.315	72	.171	-8	22	21	-10	0.4

● BOB AYRAULT Ayrault, Robert Cunningham b: 4/27/66, South Lake Tahoe, Cal. BR/TR, 6'4", 230 lbs. Deb: 6/7/92

YEAR	TM/L	W	L	PCT	G	GS	CG	SH	SV	IP	H	R	HR	HB	BB	SO	RAT	ERA	ERA+	OAV	OOB	BH	AVG	PB	PR	PR+	PD	TPI
1992	Phi-N	2	2	.500	30	0	0	0	0	43^1	32	16	0	1	17	27	10.4	3.12	112	.209	.292	0	—	0	2	2	0	0.2
1993	Phi-N	2	0	1.000	10	0	0	0	0	10^1	18	11	1	1	10	8	25.3	9.58	41	.375	.492	0	.000	-0	-6	-7	-0	-1.1
	Sea-A	1	1	.500	14	0	0	0	0	19^2	18	8	1	0	6	7	11.0	3.20	138	.254	.312	0	—	0	2	3	-0	0.2
Total	2	5	3	.625	54	0	0	0	0	73^1	68	35	2	2	33	42	12.6	4.05	94	.250	.336	0	.000	-0	-2	-2	-0	-0.7

● BOB BABCOCK Babcock, Robert Ernest b: 8/25/49, New Castle, Pa. BR/TR, 6'5", 210 lbs. Deb: 7/22/79

YEAR	TM/L	W	L	PCT	G	GS	CG	SH	SV	IP	H	R	HR	HB	BB	SO	RAT	ERA	ERA+	OAV	OOB	BH	AVG	PB	PR	PR+	PD	TPI
1979	Tex-A	0	0	—	4	0	0	0	0	5^1	7	7	1	0	7	6	23.6	10.13	41	.318	.483	0	—	0	-3	-4	0	-0.2

YEAR	TM/L	W	L	PCT	G	GS	CG	SH	SV	IP	H	R	HR	HB	BB	SO	RAT	ERA	ERA+	OAV	OOB	BH	AVG	PB	PR	PR+	PD	TPI
1980	Tex-A	1	2	.333	19	0	0	0	0	23^1	20	13	3	2	8	15	11.6	4.63	84	.238	.319	0	—	0	-2	-2	-0	-0.2
1981	Tex-A	1	1	.500	16	0	0	0	0	28^2	21	7	2	1	16	18	11.9	2.20	158	.219	.336	0	—	0	5	4	-0	0.3
Total	3	2	3	.400	39	0	0	0	0	57^1	48	27	6	3	31	39	12.9	3.92	95	.238	.347	0	—	0	-0	-1	-0	-0.1
● **JOHNNY BABICH**	Babich, John Charles b: 5/14/13, Albion, Cal. BR/TR, 6′1.5″, 185 lbs. Deb: 6/19/34																											
1934	Bro-N	7	11	.389	25	18	7	0	1	135	148	76	5	2	51	62	13.4	4.20	93	.281	.347	7	.140	-3	-2	-5	2	-0.7
1935	Bro-N	7	14	.333	37	24	7	2	0	143^1	191	124	7	2	52	55	15.4	6.66	60	.317	.373	9	.184	-0	-42	-43	0	-5.2
1936	Bos-N	0	0	—	3	0	0	0	0	6	11	8	1	1	6	1	27.0	10.50	37	.440	.563	0	.000	-0	-4	-5	0	-0.2
1940	Phi-A	14	13	.519	31	30	16	1	0	229^1	222	111	16	1	80	94	11.9	3.73	119	.248	.310	10	.116	-6	17	18	0	1.4
1941	Phi-A	2	7	.222	16	14	4	0	0	78^1	85	57	9	3	31	19	13.7	6.09	69	.281	.353	10	.400	4	-17	-16	1	-1.1
Total	5	30	45	.400	112	86	34	3	1	592	657	376	38	9	220	231	13.5	4.93	85	.279	.343	36	.171	-5	-49	-50	3	-5.8
● **LES BACKMAN**	Backman, Lester John b: 3/20/1888, Cleves, Ohio d: 11/8/75, Cincinnati, Ohio BR/TR, 6′0.5″, 195 lbs. Deb: 7/3/09																											
1909	StL-N	3	11	.214	21	15	8	0	0	128^1	146	69	1	3	39	35	13.2	4.14	61	.302	.357	4	.103	-1	-22	-24	-0	-2.6
1910	StL-N	6	7	.462	26	11	4	0	2	116	117	55	4	2	53	41	13.3	3.03	98	.265	.346	4	.114	0	0	-1	-0	-0.1
Total	2	9	18	.333	47	26	12	0	2	244^1	263	124	5	5	92	76	13.3	3.61	76	.284	.352	8	.108	-1	-22	-24	-1	-2.7
● **EDDIE BACON**	Bacon, Edgar Suter b: 4/8/1895, Franklin Co., Ky. d: 10/2/63, Louisville, Ky. Deb: 8/13/17 ♦																											
1917	Phi-A	0	0	—	1	0	0	0	0	6	5	7	0	0	7	0	18.0	6.00	46	.238	.429	3	.500	1	-2	-2	1	0.2
● **MIKE BACSIK**	Bacsik, Michael James b: 4/1/52, Dallas, Tex. BR/TR, 6′1″, 185 lbs. Deb: 6/15/75																											
1975	Tex-A	1	2	.333	7	3	0	0	0	26^2	28	17	1	1	9	13	12.8	3.71	101	.275	.339	0	—	0	0	0	-0	0.0
1976	Tex-A	3	2	.600	23	0	0	0	0	55	66	31	3	2	26	21	15.4	4.25	84	.308	.388	0	—	0	-4	-4	-1	-0.4
1977	Tex-A	0	0	—	2	0	0	0	0	2^1	9	5	1	0	0	1	34.7	19.29	21	.563	.563	0	—	0	-4	-4	0	-0.2
1979	Min-A	4	2	.667	31	0	0	0	0	65^2	61	39	6	0	29	33	12.3	4.39	100	.249	.328	0	—	0	-1	0	-0	0.0
1980	Min-A	0	0	—	10	0	0	0	0	23	26	12	1	0	11	9	14.5	4.30	101	.286	.363	0	—	0	-1	0	0	0.0
Total	5	8	6	.571	73	3	0	0	0	172^2	190	104	12	3	75	77	14.0	4.43	91	.284	.359	0	—	0	-10	-7	-1	-0.6
● **FRED BACZEWSKI**	Baczewski, Frederic John "Lefty" b: 5/15/26, St.Paul, Minn. d: 11/14/76, Culver City, Cal. BL/TL, 6′2.5″, 185 lbs. Deb: 4/26/53																											
1953	Chi-N	0	0	—	9	0	0	0	0	10	20	9	1	1	6	3	24.3	6.30	71	.435	.509	1	.500	0	-2	-2	-0	-0.1
	Cin-N	11	4	.733	24	18	10	1	1	138^1	125	56	13	1	52	58	11.6	3.45	126	.244	.315	8	.178	-0	13	14	-3	1.0
	Yr	11	4	.733	33	18	10	1	1	148^1	145	65	14	2	58	61	12.4	3.64	120	.260	.332	9	.191	0	11	12	-3	0.9
1954	Cin-N	6	6	.500	29	22	4	1	0	130	159	82	22	1	53	43	14.7	5.26	80	.305	.370	3	.071	-3	-17	-15	-1	-1.6
1955	Cin-N	0	0	—	1	0	0	0	0	1	2	2	2	0	0	0	18.0	18.00	24	.400	.400	0	—	0	-2	-1	-0	-0.1
Total	3	17	10	.630	63	40	14	2	1	279^1	306	149	38	3	111	104	13.5	4.45	96	.282	.351	12	.135	-3	-8	-5	-4	-0.8
● **LORE BADER**	Bader, Lore Verne "King" b: 4/27/1888, Bader, Ill. d: 6/2/73, LeRoy, Kan. BL/TR, 6′, 175 lbs. Deb: 9/30/12 C																											
1912	NY-N	2	0	1.000	2	1	1	0	0	10	9	2	0	1	6	3	14.4	0.90	376	.250	.372	0	.000	-0	3	3	0	0.5
1917	Bos-A	2	0	1.000	15	1	0	0	1	38^1	48	15	1	1	18	14	15.7	2.35	110	.306	.381	3	.300	1	1	1	-1	0.2
1918	Bos-A	1	3	.250	5	4	2	1	0	27	26	13	1	3	12	10	13.7	3.33	81	.271	.369	1	.111	-1	-2	-2	-1	-0.5
Total	3	5	3	.625	22	6	3	1	1	75^1	83	30	2	5	36	27	14.8	2.51	109	.287	.376	4	.182	-0	2	2	-0	0.2
● **ED BAECHT**	Baecht, Edward Joseph b: 5/15/07, Paden, Okla. d: 8/15/57, Grafton, Ill. BR/TR, 6′3″, 195 lbs. Deb: 4/24/26																											
1926	Phi-N	2	0	1.000	28	1	1	0	0	56	73	43	4	1	28	14	16.4	6.11	68	.324	.402	2	.143	-1	-14	-11	2	-0.5
1927	Phi-N	0	1	.000	1	1	0	0	0	6	12	8	0	0	2	0	21.0	12.00	34	.429	.467	0	.000	-0	-5	-5	0	-0.6
1928	Phi-N	1	1	.500	9	1	0	0	0	24	37	16	1	0	9	10	17.3	6.00	71	.385	.438	1	.143	-0	-5	-4	0	-0.3
1931	Chi-N	2	4	.333	22	6	2	0	0	67	64	34	1	8	32	34	14.0	3.76	103	.250	.351	5	.278	1	1	1	1	0.2
1932	Chi-N	0	0	—	1	0	0	0	0	1	1	0	0	0	1	0	18.0	0.00	—	.333	.500	0	—	0	0	0	-0	0.0
1937	StL-A	0	0	—	3	0	0	0	0	6^1	13	15	3	2	6	3	29.8	12.79	38	.419	.538	0	.000	-0	-6	-5	0	-0.3
Total	6	5	6	.455	64	9	3	0	0	160^1	200	116	9	11	78	61	16.2	5.56	73	.313	.397	8	.190	-1	-29	-25	3	-1.5
● **JIM BAGBY**	Bagby, James Charles Jacob Jr. b: 9/8/16, Cleveland, Ohio d: 9/2/88, Marietta, Ga. BR/TR, 6′2″, 170 lbs. Deb: 4/18/38 F																											
1938	Bos-A	15	11	.577	43	25	10	1	2	198^2	218	110	9	3	90	73	14.1	4.21	117	.283	.360	13	.191	-1	13	15	2	1.8
1939	Bos-A	5	5	.500	21	11	3	0	0	80	119	66	7	2	36	35	17.7	7.09	67	.347	.412	10	.294	3	-22	-21	-0	-1.8
1940	Bos-A	10	16	.385	36	21	6	1	2	182^2	217	104	15	1	83	57	14.8	4.73	95	.296	.368	15	.203	-0	-7	-5	0	-0.6
1941	Cle-A	9	15	.375	33	27	12	0	2	200^2	214	104	10	6	76	53	13.3	4.04	98	.273	.341	18	.243	2	2	-2	2	0.1
1942	Cle-A☆	17	9	.654	38	35	16	4	1	270^2	267	105	19	1	64	54	11.0	2.96	117	.258	.302	18	.189	1	21	16	0	1.6
1943	Cle-A☆	17	14	.548	36	33	16	3	1	**273**	248	112	15	3	80	70	10.9	3.10	100	.240	.296	30	.268	4	6	0	2	0.9
1944	Cle-A	4	5	.444	13	10	2	0	0	79	101	48	2	4	34	12	15.8	4.33	76	.312	.384	7	.226	1	-8	-9	0	-0.8
1945	Cle-A	8	11	.421	25	19	11	3	1	159^1	171	70	3	2	59	38	13.1	3.73	87	.279	.344	17	.293	3	-6	-9	3	-0.4
1946	*Bos-A	7	6	.538	21	11	6	1	0	106^2	117	55	4	1	49	16	14.1	3.71	99	.279	.356	5	.119	-2	-2	-1	-0	-0.3
1947	Pit-N	5	4	.556	37	6	2	0	0	115^2	143	75	14	5	37	23	14.4	4.67	90	.304	.361	7	.219	1	-8	-6	1	-0.2
Total	10	97	96	.503	303	198	84	13	9	1666^1	1815	849	98	28	608	431	13.2	3.96	97	.278	.342	140	.226	12	-11	-24	10	0.3
● **JIM BAGBY**	Bagby, James Charles Jacob Sr. "Sarge" b: 10/5/1889, Barnett, Ga. d: 7/28/54, Marietta, Ga. BB/TR, 6′, 170 lbs. Deb: 4/22/12 F																											
1912	Cin-N	2	1	.667	5	1	0	0	0	17^1	17	6	2	0	9	10	13.5	3.12	108	.270	.361	0	.000	-1	1	0	0	0.0
1916	Cle-A	16	17	.485	48	27	14	3	5	272^2	253	109	2	8	67	88	10.8	2.61	115	.251	.303	15	.167	-1	7	11	-3	1.1
1917	Cle-A	23	13	.639	49	37	26	8	7	320^2	277	91	6	6	73	83	10.0	1.99	142	.235	.283	25	.231	2	24	28	-3	3.4
1918	Cle-A	17	16	.515	**45**	31	23	2	6	271^1	274	107	0	2	78	57	11.7	2.69	112	.276	.330	21	.212	-0	3	9	-2	0.9
1919	Cle-A	17	11	.607	35	32	21	0	3	241^1	258	96	3	4	44	61	11.4	2.80	120	.275	.310	23	.258	5	12	14	-0	2.1
1920	*Cle-A	**31**	12	**.721**	**48**	38	**30**	3	0	**339^2**	338	122	9	5	79	73	11.2	2.89	132	.266	.311	33	.252	6	34	34	-7	3.8
1921	Cle-A	14	12	.538	40	26	13	0	4	191^2	238	112	14	4	44	37	13.4	4.70	91	.308	.348	15	.197	-1	-9	-9	-2	-1.4
1922	Cle-A	4	5	.444	25	10	4	0	1	98^1	134	77	5	3	39	25	16.1	6.32	63	.340	.404	11	.262	3	-25	-25	1	-1.7
1923	Pit-N	3	2	.600	21	6	2	0	3	68^2	95	49	6	1	25	16	15.9	5.24	76	.336	.392	1	.050	-2	-9	-9	-1	-0.9
Total	9	127	89	.588	316	208	133	16	29	1821^2	1884	769	47	33	458	450	11.7	3.11	110	.273	.321	144	.218	11	37	59	-15	7.3
● **STAN BAHNSEN**	Bahnsen, Stanley Raymond b: 12/15/44, Council Bluffs, Ia. BR/TR, 6′2″, 203 lbs. Deb: 9/9/66																											
1966	NY-A	1	1	.500	4	3	1	0	1	23	15	9	3	0	7	16	8.6	3.52	94	.181	.244	1	.143	-0	-0	-1	-0	-0.1
1968	NY-A	17	12	.586	37	34	10	1	0	267^1	216	72	14	2	68	162	9.6	2.05	141	.221	.273	4	.049	-4	27	26	-2	2.3
1969	NY-A	9	16	.360	40	33	5	2	1	220^2	222	102	28	0	90	130	12.7	3.83	91	.260	.331	5	.083	-3	-5	-9	1	-1.2
1970	NY-A	14	11	.560	36	35	6	2	0	232^2	227	100	23	2	75	116	11.8	3.33	106	.256	.316	11	.149	-0	10	5	1	0.6
1971	NY-A	14	12	.538	36	34	14	3	0	242	221	99	20	5	72	110	11.1	3.35	97	.248	.308	12	.152	0	3	-3	3	0.0
1972	Chi-A	21	16	.568	43	41	5	1	0	252^1	263	107	22	6	73	157	12.2	3.60	87	.268	.323	14	.152	-1	-15	-13	2	-1.7
1973	Chi-A	18	21	.462	42	42	14	4	0	282^1	290	128	20	5	117	120	13.1	3.57	111	.269	.343	0	—	0	8	12	2	1.8
1974	Chi-A	12	15	.444	38	35	10	1	0	216^1	230	128	17	4	110	102	14.3	4.70	79	.277	.364	0	—	0	-26	-23	1	-2.5
1975	Chi-A	4	6	.400	12	12	2	0	0	67^1	78	49	9	3	40	31	16.2	6.01	65	.291	.389	0	—	0	-17	-16	-0	-1.9
	Oak-A	6	7	.462	21	16	2	0	0	100	88	42	2	3	37	49	11.5	3.24	112	.238	.313	0	.000	-0	6	5	0	0.6
	Yr	10	13	.435	33	28	4	0	0	167^1	166	91	11	6	77	80	13.4	4.36	86	.261	.346	0	.000	-0	-11	-12	0	-1.3
1976	Oak-A	8	7	.533	35	14	1	1	0	143	124	55	13	2	43	82	10.6	3.34	101	.232	.292	0	—	0	3	0	1	0.1
1977	Oak-A	1	2	.333	11	2	0	0	1	22	24	16	5	1	13	21	15.5	6.14	66	.286	.388	0	—	0	-5	-5	-1	-0.7
	Mon-N	8	9	.471	23	22	3	1	0	127^1	142	76	14	0	38	58	12.7	4.81	79	.283	.333	5	.119	-1	-13	-14	-0	-1.8
1978	Mon-N	1	5	.167	44	1	0	0	7	75	74	35	9	0	31	44	12.6	3.84	92	.261	.334	1	.091	-1	-2	-3	-0	-0.4
1979	Mon-N	3	1	.750	55	0	0	0	5	94^1	80	34	10	0	42	71	11.6	3.15	117	.236	.320	1	.071	-0	6	6	-0	0.3
1980	Mon-N	7	6	.538	57	0	0	0	4	91^1	80	40	7	0	33	48	11.1	3.05	117	.235	.302	1	.111	1	6	5	-0	0.9
1981	*Mon-N	2	1	.667	25	3	0	0	1	49	45	27	7	1	24	28	12.9	4.96	70	.247	.338	1	.111	-0	-8	-8	-1	-0.7
1982	Cal-A	0	1	.000	7	0	0	0	0	9^2	13	6	0	0	8	5	19.6	4.66	87	.310	.420	0	—	0	-1	-1	-0	-0.1
	Phi-N	0	0	—	8	0	0	0	0	13^1	8	2	0	0	3	9	7.4	1.35	272	.182	.234	0	—	0	3	3	-0	0.2
Total	16	146	149	.495	574	327	73	16	20	2529	2440	1127	223	34	924	1359	12.1	3.60	97	.255	.323	56	.117	-9	-18	-34	4	-4.3
● **ED BAHR**	Bahr, Edson Garfield b: 10/16/19, Rouleau, Sask., Canada BR/TR, 6′1.5″, 172 lbs. Deb: 5/1/46																											
1946	Pit-N	8	6	.571	27	14	7	0	0	136^2	128	57	8	5	52	44	12.2	2.63	134	.254	.330	8	.178	-1	12	13	-0	1.2

YEAR	TM/L	W	L	PCT	G	GS	CG	SH	SV	IP	H	R	HR	HB	BB	SO	RAT	ERA	ERA+	OAV	OOB	BH	AVG	PB	PR	PR+	PD	TPI
1947	Pit-N	3	5	.375	19	11	1	0	0	82^1	82	45	5	3	43	25	14.0	4.59	92	.263	.358	2	.087	-2	-5	-3	-1	-0.5
Total	2	11	11	.500	46	25	8	0	0	219	210	102	13	8	95	69	12.9	3.37	112	.257	.341	10	.147	-3	7	10	-1	0.7
● **GROVER BAICHLEY** Baichley, Grover Cleveland b: 1/7/1890, Toledo, Ill. d: 6/28/56, San Jose, Cal. BR/TR, 5′8″, 165 lbs. Deb: 8/24/14																												
1914	StL-A	0	0	—	4	0	0	0	0	7	9	5	0	0	3	3	15.4	5.14	53	.346	.414	0	.000	-0	-2	-2	0	-0.1
● **SCOTT BAILES** Bailes, Scott Alan b: 12/18/61, Chillicothe, Ohio BL/TL, 6′2″, 184 lbs. Deb: 4/9/86																												
1986	Cle-A	10	10	.500	62	10	0	0	7	112^2	123	70	12	1	43	60	13.3	4.95	84	.276	.342	0	—	0	-10	-10	-1	-1.8
1987	Cle-A	7	8	.467	39	17	0	0	6	120^1	145	75	21	4	47	65	14.7	4.64	98	.296	.362	0	—	0	-2	-1	0	-0.2
1988	Cle-A	9	14	.391	37	21	5	2	0	145	149	89	22	2	46	53	12.2	4.90	84	.266	.324	0	—	0	-15	-12	-0	-1.7
1989	Cle-A	5	9	.357	34	11	0	0	0	113^2	116	57	7	3	29	47	11.7	4.28	93	.269	.320	0	—	0	-5	-4	0	-0.4
1990	Cal-A	2	0	1.000	27	0	0	0	0	35^1	46	30	8	1	20	16	17.1	6.37	60	.315	.401	0	—	0	-10	-10	1	-0.4
1991	Cal-A	1	2	.333	42	0	0	0	0	51^2	41	26	5	4	22	41	11.7	4.18	98	.218	.313	0	—	0	-0	-0	-0	0.0
1992	Cal-A	3	1	.750	32	0	0	0	0	38^2	59	34	7	1	28	25	20.5	7.45	54	.351	.447	0	—	0	-15	-15	-0	-1.4
1997	Tex-A	1	0	1.000	24	0	0	0	0	22	18	9	2	0	10	14	11.5	2.86	167	.231	.318	0	—	0	4	5	1	0.3
1998	Tex-A	1	0	1.000	46	0	0	0	0	40^1	61	33	5	0	11	30	16.1	6.47	75	.351	.389	0	—	0	-8	-7	-1	-0.4
Total	9	39	44	.470	343	59	5	2	13	679^2	758	423	89	16	256	351	13.6	4.95	85	.283	.349	0	—	0	-61	-55	0	-6.0
● **SWEETBREADS BAILEY** Bailey, Abraham Lincoln b: 2/12/1895, Joliet, Ill. d: 9/27/39, Joliet, Ill. BR/TR, 6′, 184 lbs. Deb: 5/23/19																												
1919	Chi-N	3	5	.375	21	5	0	0	0	71^1	75	30	2	3	20	19	12.4	3.15	91	.288	.346	7	.389	3	-2	-2	2	0.2
1920	Chi-N	1	2	.333	21	1	0	0	0	36^2	55	38	1	2	11	8	16.7	7.12	45	.359	.410	1	.143	-0	-16	-16	1	-1.2
1921	Chi-N	0	0	—	3	0	0	0	0	5	6	2	0	1	2	2	16.2	3.60	106	.300	.391	0	—	0	0	0	0	0.0
	Bro-N	0	0	—	7	0	0	0	0	24^1	35	15	1	1	7	6	15.9	5.18	75	.368	.417	0	.000	-0	-4	-3	-0	-0.2
	Yr	0	0	—	10	0	0	0	0	29^1	41	17	1	2	9	8	16.0	4.91	79	.357	.413	0	.000	-0	-4	-3	-0	-0.2
Total	3	4	7	.364	52	6	0	0	0	137^1	171	85	4	7	40	35	14.3	4.59	69	.324	.379	8	.267	2	-22	-21	2	-1.2
● **ROGER BAILEY** Bailey, Charles Roger b: 10/3/70, Chattahoochee, Fla. BR/TR, 6′1″, 180 lbs. Deb: 4/27/95																												
1995	Col-N	7	6	.538	39	6	0	0	0	81^1	88	49	9	1	39	33	14.2	4.98	108	.283	.365	2	.125	-1	-7	3	-0	0.3
1996	Col-N	2	3	.400	24	11	0	0	1	83^2	94	64	7	1	52	45	15.8	6.24	84	.288	.388	5	.263	2	-19	-8	3	0.1
1997	Col-N	9	10	.474	29	29	5	2	0	191	210	103	27	13	70	84	13.8	4.29	121	.283	.356	13	.210	-0	-2	15	5	1.9
Total	3	18	19	.486	92	46	5	2	1	356	392	216	43	15	161	162	14.4	4.90	107	.284	.366	20	.206	1	-28	11	8	2.3
● **HARVEY BAILEY** Bailey, Harvey Francis b: 11/24/1876, Adrian, Mich. d: 7/10/22, Toledo, Ohio TL, 6′, 160 lbs. Deb: 6/30/1899																												
1899	Bos-N	6	4	.600	12	11	8	0	0	86^2	83	42	7	6	35	26	12.9	3.95	105	.252	.335	8	.235	0	-1	2	-1	0.1
1900	Bos-N	0	0	—	4	1	0	0	0	20	24	16	0	2	11	9	16.6	4.95	83	.296	.394	2	.222	0	-3	-2	1	0.0
Total	2	6	4	.600	16	12	8	0	0	106^2	107	58	7	8	46	35	13.6	4.13	100	.261	.347	10	.233	0	-4	0	-0	0.1
● **HOWARD BAILEY** Bailey, Howard L b: 7/31/57, Grand Haven, Mich. BR/TL, 6′, 195 lbs. Deb: 4/12/81																												
1981	Det-A	1	4	.200	9	5	0	0	0	36^2	45	31	4	3	13	17	15.0	7.36	51	.308	.377	0	—	0	-15	-14	1	-1.6
1982	Det-A	0	0	—	8	0	0	0	1	10	6	0	0	0	2	3	7.2	0.00	—	.182	.229	0	—	0	5	5	0	0.2
1983	Det-A	5	5	.500	33	3	0	0	0	72	69	45	11	2	25	21	12.0	4.88	80	.255	.322	0	—	0	-6	-8	0	-1.0
Total	3	6	9	.400	50	8	0	0	1	118^2	120	76	15	5	40	41	12.5	5.23	74	.267	.333	0	—	0	-17	-18	1	-2.4
● **JIM BAILEY** Bailey, James Hopkins b: 12/16/34, Strawberry Plains, Tenn. BB/TL, 6′2.5″, 210 lbs. Deb: 9/10/59 F																												
1959	Cin-N	0	1	.000	3	1	0	0	0	11^2	17	8	1	1	6	7	18.5	6.17	66	.333	.414	0	.000	-0	-3	-3	-0	-0.3
● **KING BAILEY** Bailey, Linwood C. b: 11/1870, Virginia d: 11/19/17, Macon, Ga. BL/TL, 6′ ″, 185 lbs. Deb: 9/21/1895																												
1895	Cin-N	1	0	1.000	1	1	1	0	0	8	13	8	0	1	0	0	15.8	5.63	88	.361	.378	2	.500	1	-1	-1	0	0.0
● **CORY BAILEY** Bailey, Phillip Cory b: 1/24/71, Marion, Ill. BR/TR, 6′1″, 202 lbs. Deb: 9/1/93																												
1993	Bos-A	0	1	.000	11	0	0	0	0	15^2	12	7	0	0	12	11	13.8	3.45	134	.231	.375	0	—	0	2	2	1	0.2
1994	Bos-A	0	1	.000	5	0	0	0	0	4^1	10	6	2	0	3	4	27.0	12.46	40	.476	.542	0	—	0	-4	-3	-0	-0.6
1995	StL-N	0	0	—	3	0	0	0	0	3^2	2	3	0	0	2	5	9.8	7.36	57	.154	.267	0	—	0	-1	-1	0	-0.1
1996	StL-N	5	2	.714	51	0	0	0	0	57	57	21	1	1	30	38	13.9	3.00	140	.263	.355	0	.000	1	8	8	-0	0.8
1997	SF-N	0	1	.000	7	0	0	0	0	9^2	15	9	1	0	4	5	17.7	8.38	49	.375	.432	1	1.000	0	-4	-5	-0	-0.4
1998	SF-N	0	0	—	5	0	0	0	0	3^1	2	1	1	0	1	2	8.1	2.70	147	.167	.231	0	—	0	1	1	-0	0.0
Total	6	5	5	.500	82	0	0	0	0	93^2	98	47	5	1	52	65	14.5	4.23	101	.276	.370	1	.500	1	0	1	-0	-0.1
● **STEVE BAILEY** Bailey, Steven John b: 2/12/42, Bronx, N.Y. BR/TR, 6′1″, 194 lbs. Deb: 4/14/67																												
1967	Cle-A	2	5	.286	32	1	0	0	2	64^2	62	31	5	3	42	46	14.9	3.90	84	.259	.377	0	.000	-1	-5	-4	0	-0.6
1968	Cle-A	0	1	.000	2	1	0	0	0	5	4	3	1	0	2	1	10.8	3.60	82	.235	.316	0	—	0	-0	-0	-0	-0.1
Total	2	2	6	.250	34	2	0	0	2	69^2	66	34	6	3	44	47	14.6	3.88	84	.258	.373	0	.000	-1	-5	-5	-0	-0.7
● **BILL BAILEY** Bailey, William F. b: 4/12/1889, Ft.Smith, Ark. d: 11/2/26, Houston, Tex. BL/TL, 5′11″, 165 lbs. Deb: 9/17/07																												
1907	StL-A	4	1	.800	6	5	3	0	0	48^1	39	16	0	4	15	17	10.8	2.42	104	.223	.299	3	.150	-1	1	1	-1	-0.2
1908	StL-A	3	5	.375	22	12	7	0	0	106^2	85	53	2	3	50	42	11.6	3.04	79	.220	.314	3	.088	-2	-8	-8	-2	-1.1
1909	StL-A	9	10	.474	32	20	17	1	0	199	174	71	2	6	75	114	11.5	2.44	99	.248	.325	22	.286	5	1	-1	-1	0.5
1910	StL-A	3	18	.143	34	20	13	0	0	192^1	186	133	2	10	97	90	13.7	3.32	74	.262	.359	13	.206	0	-17	-18	-1	-2.0
1911	StL-A	0	3	.000	7	2	2	0	0	31^2	42	26	1	2	16	8	17.1	4.55	74	.339	.423	0	.000	-2	-4	-4	0	-0.5
1912	StL-A	0	1	.000	3	2	0	0	0	10^2	15	12	0	0	10	2	21.1	9.28	36	.341	.463	1	.500	1	-7	-7	-1	-0.5
1914	Bal-F	7	9	.438	19	18	10	1	0	128^2	106	58	2	7	68	131	12.7	3.08	99	.230	.338	7	.163	-1	-3	-1	3	0.2
1915	Bal-F	6	19	.240	36	23	11	2	0	190^1	179	118	8	9	115	98	14.3	4.63	62	.255	.366	15	.231	-0	-40	-36	-1	-4.4
	Chi-F	3	1	.750	5	5	3	3	0	33^1	23	9	1	0	10	24	8.9	2.16	116	.202	.266	2	.222	0	2	1	1	0.3
	Yr	9	20	.310	41	28	14	5	0	223^2	202	127	9	9	125	122	13.5	4.27	66	.247	.353	17	.230	-0	-38	-35	-1	-4.1
1918	Det-A	1	2	.333	8	4	1	0	0	37^2	53	34	0	1	26	13	19.1	5.97	45	.368	.468	1	.077	-1	-13	-14	1	-1.1
1921	StL-N	2	5	.286	19	6	3	1	0	74	95	41	1	2	22	20	14.5	4.26	86	.330	.381	2	.091	-2	-4	-5	1	-0.5
1922	StL-N	0	2	.000	12	0	0	0	0	31^2	38	22	1	0	23	11	17.3	5.40	72	.325	.436	2	.286	0	-5	-6	1	-0.2
Total	11	38	76	.333	203	117	70	8	0	1084^1	1035	593	20	44	527	570	13.3	3.57	77	.261	.354	71	.194	-3	-97	-98	-1	-9.5
● **BOB BAILOR** Bailor, Robert Michael b: 7/10/51, Connellsville, Pa. BR/TR, 5′11″, 170 lbs. Deb: 9/6/75 C♦																												
1980	Tor-A	0	0	—	3	0	0	0	0	2^1	4	2	0	0	1	0	19.3	7.71	56	.364	.417	82	.236	1	-1	-1	-0	0.0
● **LOREN BAIN** Bain, Herbert Loren b: 7/4/22, Staples, Minn. d: 11/24/96, Chetek, Wis. BR/TR, 6′, 190 lbs. Deb: 6/23/45																												
1945	NY-N	0	0	—	3	0	0	0	0	8	10	7	1	1	4	1	16.9	7.88	50	.323	.417	1	.333	0	-4	-3	-0	-0.2
● **DOUG BAIR** Bair, Charles Douglas b: 8/22/49, Defiance, Ohio BR/TR, 6′, 180 lbs. Deb: 9/13/76																												
1976	Pit-N	0	0	—	4	0	0	0	0	6^1	4	4	0	0	5	4	12.8	5.68	61	.174	.321	0	—	0	-2	-2	-0	-0.1
1977	Oak-A	4	6	.400	45	0	0	0	8	83^1	78	39	11	0	57	68	14.6	3.46	117	.253	.370	0	—	0	6	5	1	0.8
1978	Cin-N	7	6	.538	70	0	0	0	28	100^1	87	23	6	0	38	91	11.2	1.97	180	.236	.307	2	.143	-0	18	18	-1	3.3
1979	*Cin-N	11	7	.611	65	0	0	0	16	94^1	93	47	7	3	51	86	14.0	4.29	87	.256	.353	0	.000	-1	-6	-6	-1	-1.3
1980	Cin-N	3	6	.333	61	0	0	0	6	85	91	42	7	1	39	62	13.9	4.24	85	.277	.355	0	.000	-0	-6	-6	2	-0.6
1981	Cin-N	2	2	.500	24	0	0	0	0	39	42	28	5	0	17	16	13.6	5.77	62	.271	.343	1	.333	1	-10	-9	-1	-0.9
	StL-N	2	0	1.000	11	0	0	0	1	15^2	13	6	0	0	2	14	8.6	3.45	103	.224	.250	0	.000	-0	0	0	-0	0.0
	Yr	4	2	.667	35	0	0	0	1	54^2	55	34	5	0	19	30	12.2	5.10	70	.258	.319	1	.167	1	-10	-9	-1	-0.9
1982	*StL-N	5	3	.625	63	0	0	0	8	91^2	69	27	7	1	36	68	10.4	2.55	142	.211	.291	1	.077	-1	11	11	0	1.0
1983	StL-N	1	1	.500	26	0	0	0	1	29^2	24	11	4	0	13	21	11.2	3.03	120	.224	.308	0	.000	-0	2	2	-0	0.1
	Det-A	7	3	.700	27	1	0	0	4	55^2	51	27	8	1	19	39	11.5	3.88	101	.242	.307	0	—	0	1	0	-0	0.0
1984	*Det-A	5	3	.625	47	1	0	0	4	93^2	82	42	10	0	36	57	11.3	3.75	105	.238	.310	0	—	0	3	2	1	0.2
1985	Det-A	2	0	1.000	21	3	0	0	0	49	54	38	3	1	25	30	14.7	6.24	65	.281	.367	0	—	0	-11	-12	1	-0.5
	StL-N	0	0	—	2	0	0	0	0	2	1	0	0	0	2	0	13.5	0.00	—	.167	.375	0	—	0	1	1	-0	0.0
1986	Oak-A	2	3	.400	31	0	0	0	4	45	37	15	5	0	18	40	11.0	3.00	129	.224	.301	0	—	0	6	5	0	0.6
1987	Phi-N	2	0	1.000	11	0	0	0	0	13^2	17	9	4	0	5	10	14.5	5.93	72	.309	.367	0	.000	-0	-3	-2	-0	-0.4

YEAR	TM/L	W	L	PCT	G	GS	CG	SH	SV	IP	H	R	HR	HB	BB	SO	RAT	ERA	ERA+	OAV	OOB	BH	AVG	PB	PR	PR+	PD	TPI
1988	Tor-A	0	0	—	10	0	0	0	0	13^1	14	6	2	0	3	8	11.5	4.05	97	.280	.321	0	—	0	-0	-0	0	0.0
1989	Pit-N	2	3	.400	44	0	0	0	1	67^1	52	19	4	0	28	56	10.7	2.27	148	.211	.292	1	.200	0	9	8	1	0.7
1990	Pit-N	0	0	—	22	0	0	0	0	24^1	30	15	3	0	11	19	15.2	4.81	75	.306	.376	0	.000	-0	-3	-3	0	-0.2
Total	15	55	43	.561	584	5	0	0	81	909^1	839	398	86	7	405	689	12.4	3.63	103	.246	.328	5	.096	-2	16	11	2	2.7
● **BOB BAIRD** Baird, Robert Allen b: 1/16/40, Knoxville, Tenn. d: 4/11/74, Chattanooga, Tenn. BL/TL, 6'4", 195 lbs. Deb: 9/3/62																												
1962	Was-A	0	1	.000	3	3	0	0	0	10^2	13	8	0	0	8	3	17.7	6.75	60	.310	.420	0	.000	-0	-3	-3	-0	-0.3
1963	Was-A	0	3	.000	5	3	0	0	0	11^2	12	15	1	1	7	7	15.4	7.71	48	.261	.370	1	.333	0	-5	-5	-0	-1.0
Total	2	0	4	.000	8	6	0	0	0	22^1	25	23	1	1	15	10	16.5	7.25	53	.284	.394	1	.167	-0	-9	-8	-1	-1.3
● **JERSEY BAKELY** Bakely, Edward Enoch (b: Edward Enoch Bakley) b: 4/17/1864, Blackwood, N.J. d: 2/17/15, Philadelphia, Pa. BR/TR, Deb: 5/11/1883																												
1883	Phi-a	5	3	.625	8	8	7	0	0	61^1	65	47	0		12	14	11.3	3.23	110	.255	.288	5	.192	1	1	2	-0	0.2
1884	Phi-U	14	25	.359	39	38	38	1	0	344^2	390	305	0		76	204	12.2	4.47	52	.267	.303	22	.132	-16	-77	-86	-3	-8.5
	Wil-U	0	2	.000	2	2	2	0	0	17	24	17	0		1	9	13.2	4.24	63	.312	.321	0	.000	-1	-3	-3	0	-0.3
	KC-U	2	3	.400	5	5	3	0	0	33	29	16	0		4	13	9.0	2.45	91	.220	.243	3	.150	-2	-0	-1	-1	-0.3
	Yr	16	30	.348	46	45	43	1	0	394^2	443	338	0		81	226	11.9	4.29	54	.265	.299	25	.130	-18	-81	-90	-4	-9.1
1888	Cle-a	25	33	.431	61	61	60	4	0	532^2	518	321	14	15	128	212	11.2	2.97	104	.246	.294	26	.134	-6	5	7	-1	0.1
1889	Cle-N	12	22	.353	36	34	33	2	0	304^1	296	169	9	8	106	105	12.1	2.96	136	.247	.313	15	.135	-1	36	36	2	3.4
1890	Cle-P	12	25	.324	43	38	32	0	0	326^1	412	307	13	7	147	67	15.6	4.47	89	.295	.365	28	.203	-2	-9	-19	-3	-1.9
1891	Was-a	2	10	.167	13	12	11	0	0	104^1	127	107	6	6	60	32	16.6	5.35	70	.291	.384	10	.222	-0	-19	-19	-2	-1.7
	Bal-a	4	2	.667	8	6	5	0	0	59	48	32	1	1	30	13	12.1	2.29	163	.214	.310	2	.095	0	9	9	-1	0.8
	Yr	6	12	.333	21	18	16	0	0	163^1	175	139	7	7	90	45	15.0	4.24	88	.265	.359	12	.182	-0	-10	-9	-3	-0.9
Total	6	76	125	.378	215	204	191	7	0	1782^2	1909	1321	43	37	564	669	12.7	3.66	91	.262	.318	111	.153	-26	-57	-68	-9	-8.2
● **DAVE BAKENHASTER** Bakenhaster, David Lee b: 3/5/45, Columbus, O. BR/TR, 5'10", 168 lbs. Deb: 6/20/64																												
1964	StL-N	0	0	—	2	0	0	0	0	3	9	6	1	0	1	0	30.0	6.00	63	.474	.500	0	—	0	-1	-1	0	0.0
● **AL BAKER** Baker, Albert Jones b: 2/28/06, Batesville, Miss. d: 11/6/82, Kenedy, Tex. BR/TR, 5'11", 170 lbs. Deb: 8/20/38																												
1938	Bos-A	0	0	—	3	0	0	0	0	7^2	13	8	2	1	2	2	18.8	9.39	53	.371	.421	0	.000	-1	-4	-4	-0	-0.2
● **BOCK BAKER** Baker, Charles "Smiling Bock" b: 7/17/1878, Troy, N.Y. d: 8/17/40, New York, N.Y. TL, 5'9", 181 lbs. Deb: 4/28/01																												
1901	Cle-A	0	1	.000	1	1	1	0	0	8	23	13	0	1	6	0	33.8	5.63	63	.500	.566	0	.000	-1	-2	-2	0	-0.2
	Phi-A	0	1	.000	1	1	0	0	0	6	6	11	0	0	6	1	18.0	10.50	36	.261	.414	1	.333	0	-5	-4	-0	-0.5
	Yr	0	2	.000	2	2	1	0	0	14	29	24	0	1	12	1	27.0	7.71	47	.420	.512	1	.143	-1	-6	-6	-0	-0.7
● **ERNIE BAKER** Baker, Earnest Gould b: 8/8/1875, Concord, Mich. d: 10/25/45, Homer, Mich. BR/TR, 5'10", 160 lbs. Deb: 8/18/05																												
1905	Cin-N	0	0	—	1	0	0	0	0	4	7	4	1	1	0	1	18.0	4.50	73	.412	.444	0	.000	-0	-1	-0	-0	-0.1
● **JESSE BAKER** Baker, Jesse Ormond b: 6/3/1888, Anderson Island, Wash. d: 9/26/72, Tacoma, Wash. BL/TL, 5'11", 188 lbs. Deb: 4/23/11																												
1911	Chi-A	2	7	.222	22	8	3	0	1	94	101	52	3	4	30	51	12.9	3.93	82	.288	.351	3	.103	-2	-6	-8	1	-0.7
● **KIRTLEY BAKER** Baker, Kirtley "Whitey" b: 6/24/1869, Aurora, Ind. d: 4/15/27, Covington, Ky. BR/TR, 5'9", 160 lbs. Deb: 5/7/1890 ♦																												
1890	Pit-N	3	19	.136	25	21	19	2	0	178^1	209	176	11	20	86	76	15.9	5.60	59	.284	.374	10	.147	-1	-40	-50	-0	-4.6
1893	Bal-N	3	8	.273	15	12	8	0	0	91^2	138	111	5	5	58	26	19.7	8.44	56	.337	.426	17	.298	2	-38	-37	3	-2.6
1894	Bal-N	0	1	.000	1	0	0	0	0	0	1	0	0	2	—	—	∞	—	1.000	1.000	103	.000	-0	-5	-5	-0	-0.3	
1898	Was-N	2	3	.400	6	5	4	0	0	47	56	31	1	0	18	7	14.2	3.06	120	.293	.354	5	.278	2	3	3	-1	0.4
1899	Was-N	1	7	.125	11	6	3	0	0	54	79	65	3	6	22	6	17.8	6.83	57	.339	.410	3	.158	-1	-18	-17	2	-1.9
Total	5	9	38	.191	58	44	34	2	0	371	483	388	20	31	186	115	17.0	6.28	60	.307	.391	35	.211	1	-99	-106	4	-9.0
● **NEAL BAKER** Baker, Neal Vernon b: 4/30/04, Harlingen, Tex. d: 1/5/82, Houston, Tex. BR/TR, 6'1", 175 lbs. Deb: 6/26/27																												
1927	Phi-A	0	0	—	5	2	0	0	0	17^1	27	17	2	0	7	3	17.7	5.71	75	.365	.420	1	.167	-0	-3	-3	0	-0.1
● **NORM BAKER** Baker, Norman Leslie b: 10/14/1863, Philadelphia, Pa. d: 2/20/49, Hurffville, N.J. Deb: 5/21/1883																												
1883	Pit-a	0	2	.000	3	3	2	0	0	19	24	16	0		11	5	16.6	3.32	98	.289	.372	0	.000	-2	-0	-0	-1	-0.2
1885	Lou-a	13	12	.520	25	24	24	1	0	217	210	142	3	10	69	79	12.0	3.40	95	.241	.304	18	.207	-1	-4	-4	-2	-0.6
1886	Bal-a	1	1	.500	2	2	2	0	0	17	16	9	0	0	6	10	11.6	3.71	109	.242	.306	0	.000	-1	0	1	0	0.0
Total	3	14	15	.483	30	29	28	1	0	253	250	167	3	10	86	94	12.3	3.42	96	.245	.309	18	.170	-3	-3	-4	-2	-0.8
● **SCOTT BAKER** Baker, Scott b: 5/18/70, San Jose, Cal. BL/TL, 6'2", 175 lbs. Deb: 7/17/95																												
1995	Oak-A	0	0	—	1	0	0	0	0	3^2	5	4	0	1	5	3	27.0	9.82	46	.333	.524	0	—	0	-2	-2	-0	-0.1
● **STEVE BAKER** Baker, Steven Byrne b: 8/30/56, Eugene, Ore. BR/TR, 6', 185 lbs. Deb: 5/25/78																												
1978	Det-A	2	4	.333	15	10	0	0	0	63^1	66	37	6	0	42	39	15.3	4.55	85	.276	.384	0	—	0	-5	-5	-1	-0.5
1979	Det-A	1	7	.125	21	12	0	0	1	84	97	63	13	6	51	54	16.5	6.64	65	.296	.400	0	—	0	-23	-21	-1	-1.8
1982	Oak-A	1	1	.500	5	3	0	0	0	25^2	30	14	3	0	4	14	11.9	4.56	86	.288	.315	0	—	0	-1	-2	-0	-0.2
1983	Oak-A	3	3	.500	35	1	0	0	5	54	59	32	4	2	26	23	14.5	4.33	89	.282	.367	0	—	0	-2	-3	-1	-0.4
	StL-N	0	1	.000	8	0	0	0	0	10	10	4	0	1	4	1	13.5	1.80	202	.286	.375	0	—	0	2	2	0	0.2
Total	4	7	16	.304	84	26	0	0	6	237	262	150	26	9	127	131	15.1	5.13	79	.286	.379	0	—	0	-29	-29	-3	-2.7
● **TOM BAKER** Baker, Thomas Calvin "Rattlesnake" b: 6/11/13, Nursery, Tex. d: 1/3/91, Fort Worth, Tex. BR/TR, 6'1.5", 180 lbs. Deb: 8/15/35																												
1935	Bro-N	1	0	1.000	11	1	1	0	0	42	48	25	2	0	20	10	14.6	4.29	93	.277	.352	9	.474	4	-1	-1	-1	0.2
1936	Bro-N	1	8	.111	35	8	2	0	2	87^2	98	56	3	2	48	35	15.2	4.72	88	.288	.379	7	.233	1	-7	-6	0	-0.4
1937	Bro-N	0	1	.000	7	0	0	0	0	8^1	14	10	1	1	5	2	21.6	8.64	47	.378	.465	0	—	0	-4	-4	0	-0.4
	NY-N	1	0	1.000	13	0	0	0	0	31	30	15	0	0	16	11	13.4	4.06	96	.268	.359	2	.222	0	-1	-1	-0	-0.1
	Yr	1	1	.500	20	0	0	0	0	39^1	44	25	1	1	21	13	15.1	5.03	78	.295	.386	2	.222	-0	-5	-5	-0	-0.5
1938	NY-N	0	0	—	2	0	0	0	0	4	5	3	0	0	3	0	18.0	6.75	56	.313	.421	0	—	0	-1	-1	0	0.0
Total	4	3	9	.250	68	9	3	0	2	173	195	109	6	3	92	58	15.1	4.73	85	.288	.375	18	.310	5	-14	-13	-1	-0.9
● **TOM BAKER** Baker, Thomas Henry b: 5/6/34, Port Townsend, Wash. d: 3/9/80, Port Townsend, Wash BL/TL, 6', 195 lbs. Deb: 8/2/63																												
1963	Chi-N	0	1	.000	10	1	0	0	0	18	20	12	2	1	7	14	14.0	3.00	117	.282	.354	0	.000	-0	1	1	0	0.0
● **MIKE BALAS** Balas, Mitchell Francis (b: Mitchell Francis Balaski) b: 5/17/10, Lowell, Mass. BR/TR, 6', 195 lbs. Deb: 4/27/38																												
1938	Bos-N	0	0	—	1	0	0	0	0	1^1	3	3	0	0	0	0	20.3	6.75	51	.375	.375	0	—	0	-0	-1	-0	0.0
● **JACK BALDSCHUN** Baldschun, Jack Edward b: 10/16/36, Greenville, O. BR/TR, 6', 190 lbs. Deb: 4/28/61																												
1961	Phi-N	5	3	.625	**65**	0	0	0	3	99^2	90	53	7	5	49	59	13.0	3.88	105	.243	.339	0	.000	-1	2	2	0	0.1
1962	Phi-N	12	7	.632	67	0	0	0	13	112^2	95	41	6	2	58	95	12.4	2.96	131	.231	.328	1	.063	-1	12	12	1	2.1
1963	Phi-N	11	7	.611	65	0	0	0	16	113^2	99	37	7	3	42	89	11.4	2.30	141	.232	.306	0	.000	-2	13	12	1	2.3
1964	Phi-N	6	9	.400	71	0	0	0	21	118^1	111	50	8	3	40	96	11.7	3.12	111	.246	.312	4	.250	1	6	5	1	1.1
1965	Phi-N	5	8	.385	65	0	0	0	6	99	102	53	4	4	42	81	13.5	3.82	91	.273	.352	0	.000	-1	-3	-4	1	-0.6
1966	Cin-N	1	5	.167	42	0	0	0	0	57^1	71	35	4	4	25	44	15.7	5.49	71	.318	.397	1	.333	0	-12	-9	0	-0.9
1967	Cin-N	0	0	—	9	0	0	0	0	13	15	6	0	0	9	12	16.6	4.15	90	.283	.387	0	.000	-0	-1	-1	-0	0.0
1969	SD-N	7	2	.778	61	0	0	0	1	77	80	45	7	2	29	67	13.0	4.79	74	.264	.332	1	.250	0	-10	-11	-0	-1.2
1970	SD-N	1	0	1.000	12	0	0	0	0	13^1	24	15	2	0	4	12	18.9	10.13	39	.375	.412	0	—	0	-9	-9	-0	-0.6
Total	9	48	41	.539	457	0	0	0	60	704	687	335	45	23	298	555	12.9	3.69	98	.257	.336	7	.090	-3	-3	-5	4	2.3
● **LADY BALDWIN** Baldwin, Charles Busted b: 4/8/1859, Oramel, N.Y. d: 3/7/37, Hastings, Mich. BR/TL, 5'11", 160 lbs. Deb: 9/30/1884 ♦																												
1884	Mil-U	1	1	.500	2	2	2	0	0	17	7	5	0		1	21	4.2	2.65	50	.117	.131	6	.222	-0	-0	-5	-0	-0.4
1885	Det-N	11	9	.550	21	20	19	1	1	179^1	137	84	2		28	135	**8.3**	1.86	153	**.197**	**.228**	30	.242	3	19	20	2	2.4
1886	Det-N	**42**	13	.764	56	56	55	**7**	0	487	371	194	11		100	**323**	**8.7**	2.24	148	**.202**	**.243**	41	.201	3	58	58	4	6.1
1887	*Det-N	13	10	.565	24	24	24	1	0	211	286	136	8	5	61	60	12.4	3.84	105	.319	.323	33	.347	3	6	5	1	0.6
1888	Det-N	3	3	.500	6	6	5	0	0	53	76	50	5	1	15	26	15.6	5.43	51	.322	.365	6	.261	2	-15	-16	-1	-1.4
1890	Bro-N	1	0	1.000	2	1	0	0	0	7^2	15	6	0	0	4	4	22.3	7.04	49	.395	.452	0	.000	-0	-3	-3	0	-0.3

YEAR	TM/L	W	L	PCT	G	GS	CG	SH	SV	IP	H	R	HR	HB	BB	SO	RAT	ERA	ERA+	OAV	OOB	BH	AVG	PB	PR	PR+	PD	TPI
	Buf-P	2	5	.286	7	7	7	0	0	62	90	72	5	3	24	13	17.0	4.50	91	.325	.385	8	.286	1	-2	-3	-0	-0.1
Total	6	73	41	.640	118	116	112	9	1	1017	982	547	31	9	233	582	10.3	2.85	118	.243	.276	124	.246	12	63	59	6	6.9
● **KID BALDWIN**	Baldwin, Clarence Geoghan b: 11/1/1864, Newport, Ky. d: 7/10/1897, Cincinnati, Ohio BR/TR, 5′6″, 147 lbs. Deb: 7/27/1884 ♦																											
1885	Cin-a	0	0	—	2	1	0	0	0	4	5	6	0	0	6	1	24.8	9.00	36	.294	.478	17	.135	-0	-3	-3	0	-0.1
● **DAVE BALDWIN**	Baldwin, David George b: 3/30/38, Tucson, Ariz. BR/TR, 6′2″, 200 lbs. Deb: 9/6/66																											
1966	Was-A	0	0	—	4	0	0	0	0	7	8	3	0	0	1	4	11.6	3.86	90	.267	.290	0	—	0	-0	-0	-0	0.0
1967	Was-A	2	4	.333	58	0	0	0	12	68^2	53	19	2	4	20	52	10.1	1.70	186	.215	.285	0	.000	-0	12	11	1	1.6
1968	Was-A	0	2	.000	40	0	0	0	5	42	40	19	7	0	12	30	11.1	4.07	72	.260	.313	0	.000	0	-5	-6	1	-0.4
1969	Was-A	2	4	.333	43	0	0	0	4	66^2	57	31	4	5	34	51	13.0	4.05	86	.236	.342	0	.000	-1	-3	-4	-0	-0.6
1970	Mil-A	2	1	.667	28	0	0	0	1	35^1	25	11	4	0	18	26	11.0	2.55	149	.205	.307	1	.500	0	5	5	2	0.7
1973	Chi-A	0	0	—	3	0	0	0	0	5	7	2	0	0	4	1	19.8	3.60	110	.368	.478	0	—	0	0	0	0	0.0
Total	6	6	11	.353	176	0	0	0	22	224^2	190	85	17	9	89	164	11.5	3.08	108	.234	.316	1	.067	-1	8	6	4	1.3
● **HARRY BALDWIN**	Baldwin, Howard Edward b: 6/3/1900, Baltimore, Md. d: 1/23/58, Baltimore, Md. BR/TR, 5′11″, 160 lbs. Deb: 5/4/24																											
1924	*NY-N	3	1	.750	10	2	1	0	0	33^2	42	18	5	0	11	5	14.2	4.28	86	.309	.361	4	.364	1	-2	-2	-0	-0.2
1925	NY-N	0	0	—	1	0	0	0	0	1	3	2	0	0	1	0	36.0	9.00	45	.500	.571	0	—	0	-1	-1	-0	0.0
Total	2	3	1	.750	11	2	1	0	0	34^2	45	20	5	0	12	5	14.8	4.41	83	.317	.370	4	.364	1	-2	-3	-0	-0.2
● **JAMES BALDWIN**	Baldwin, James J. b: 7/15/71, Southern Pines, N.C. BR/TR, 6′3″, 210 lbs. Deb: 4/30/95																											
1995	Chi-A	0	1	.000	6	4	0	0	0	14^2	32	22	6	0	9	10	25.2	12.89	35	.444	.506	0	—	0	-13	-15	0	-0.8
1996	Chi-A	11	6	.647	28	28	0	0	0	169	168	88	24	4	57	127	12.2	4.42	107	.257	.320	0	—	0	11	6	-1	0.4
1997	Chi-A	12	15	.444	32	32	1	0	0	200	205	128	19	5	83	140	13.2	5.27	83	.262	.337	0	.000	-0	-15	-20	-1	-2.3
1998	Chi-A	13	6	.684	37	24	1	0	0	159	176	103	18	10	60	108	13.9	5.32	86	.278	.349	0	.000	-0	-12	-14	-2	-1.6
1999	Chi-A	12	13	.480	35	33	1	0	0	199^1	219	119	34	7	81	123	13.9	5.10	96	.278	.351	1	.500	1	-5	-5	-1	-0.5
2000	*Chi-A★	14	7	.667	29	28	2	1	0	178	185	96	34	8	59	116	12.7	4.65	107	.272	.337	0	.000	-0	5	6	1	0.7
Total	6	62	48	.564	167	149	5	1	0	920	985	556	135	34	349	624	13.4	5.09	92	.273	.343	1	.091	0	-29	-40	-4	-4.1
● **MARK BALDWIN**	Baldwin, Marcus Elmore "Fido" b: 10/29/1863, Pittsburgh, Pa. d: 11/10/29, Pittsburgh, Pa. BR/TR, 6′, 190 lbs. Deb: 5/2/1887																											
1887	Chi-N	18	17	.514	40	39	35	1	**1**	334	451	218	23	17	122	164	12.6	3.40	132	.311	.319	36	.242	-4	25	37	-3	2.4
1888	Chi-N	13	15	.464	30	30	27	2	0	251	241	137	13	13	99	157	12.7	2.76	110	.249	.327	16	.151	-1	2	7	2	0.7
1889	Col-a	27	34	.443	**63**	59	54	6	1	**513^2**	458	358	9	20	274	**368**	13.2	3.61	100	.231	.331	39	.188	1	14	1	1	0.2
1890	Chi-P	**33**	24	.579	**58**	56	**53**	1	0	**492**	494	321	10	16	249	**206**	13.9	3.35	130	.250	.339	45	.212	-1	48	53	3	4.7
1891	Pit-N	21	28	.429	53	51	48	2	1	437^2	385	278	10	23	227	197	13.1	2.76	119	.227	.327	27	.153	-3	29	26	1	2.1
1892	Pit-N	26	27	.491	56	53	45	0	0	440^1	447	272	11	22	194	157	13.6	3.47	95	.253	.334	18	.101	-12	-9	-9	-2	-2.1
1893	Pit-N	0	0	—	1	1	0	0	0	2^1	6	4	0	0	1	0	27.0	11.57	39	.462	.500	0	.000	-0	-2	-2	0	-0.1
	NY-N	16	20	.444	45	39	33	2	2	331^1	335	228	6	12	141	100	13.3	4.10	114	.255	.332	17	.127	-11	21	20	-3	0.5
	Yr	16	20	.444	46	40	33	2	**2**	333^2	341	232	6	12	142	100	13.4	4.15	112	.257	.334	17	.126	-11	19	19	-3	0.4
Total	7	154	165	.483	346	328	295	14	5	2802^1	2817	1816	82	123	1307	1349	13.2	3.37	113	.252	.331	198	.170	-31	128	137	-1	8.4
● **O. F. BALDWIN**	Baldwin, Orson F. b: 11/3/1881, Carson City, Mich. d: 2/16/42, Los Angeles, Cal. TR, 185 lbs. Deb: 9/6/08																											
1908	StL-N	1	3	.250	4	4	0	0	0	14^2	16	10	0	3	11	5	18.4	6.14	38	.302	.448	0	.000	-1	-6	-6	-0	-1.3
● **RICK BALDWIN**	Baldwin, Rickey Alan b: 6/1/53, Fresno, Cal. BL/TR, 6′3″, 180 lbs. Deb: 4/10/75																											
1975	NY-N	3	5	.375	54	0	0	0	6	97^1	97	39	4	4	34	54	12.5	3.33	104	.263	.332	3	.200	0	3	2	1	0.2
1976	NY-N	0	0	—	11	0	0	0	0	22^2	14	6	0	2	10	9	10.3	2.38	139	.189	.302	1	.333	0	3	2	0	0.2
1977	NY-N	1	2	.333	40	0	0	0	1	62^2	62	32	6	5	31	23	14.1	4.45	84	.265	.363	2	.500	1	-4	-5	1	-0.1
Total	3	4	7	.364	105	0	0	0	7	182^2	173	77	10	11	75	86	12.8	3.60	98	.256	.339	6	.273	1	2	-1	1	0.3
● **JOHN BALE**	Bale, John Robert b: 5/22/74, Cheverly, Md. BL/TL, 6′4″, 195 lbs. Deb: 9/30/99																											
1999	Tor-A	0	0	—	1	0	0	0	0	2	2	3	1	0	2	4	18.0	13.50	37	.250	.400	0	—	0	-2	-2	0	-0.1
2000	Tor-A	0	0	—	2	0	0	0	0	3^2	5	7	1	2	3	6	24.5	14.73	34	.313	.476	0	—	0	-4	-4	-0	-0.2
Total	2	0	0	—	3	0	0	0	0	5^2	7	10	2	2	5	10	22.2	14.29	35	.292	.452	0	—	0	-6	-6	-0	-0.3
● **JEFF BALLARD**	Ballard, Jeffrey Scott b: 8/13/63, Billings, Mont. BL/TL, 6′2″, 198 lbs. Deb: 5/9/87																											
1987	Bal-A	2	8	.200	14	14	0	0	0	69^2	100	60	15	0	35	27	17.4	6.59	67	.344	.414	0	—	0	-16	-17	0	-2.0
1988	Bal-A	8	12	.400	25	25	6	1	0	153^1	167	83	15	6	42	41	12.6	4.40	89	.278	.332	0	—	0	-7	-8	-2	-1.2
1989	Bal-A	18	8	.692	35	35	4	1	0	215^1	240	95	16	4	57	62	12.6	3.43	111	.287	.336	0	—	0	11	9	4	1.5
1990	Bal-A	2	11	.154	44	17	0	0	0	133^1	152	79	22	3	42	50	13.3	4.93	77	.289	.345	0	—	0	-15	-17	0	-1.5
1991	Bal-A	6	12	.333	26	22	0	0	0	123^2	153	91	16	2	28	37	13.3	5.60	71	.302	.341	0	—	0	-21	-23	-1	-3.0
1993	Pit-N	4	1	.800	25	5	0	0	0	53^2	70	31	3	2	15	16	14.6	4.86	83	.332	.382	4	.364	1	-5	-5	1	-0.2
1994	Pit-N	1	1	.500	28	0	0	0	2	24^1	32	19	5	1	10	11	15.9	6.66	65	.323	.391	1	.500	0	-7	-6	-0	-0.5
Total	7	41	53	.436	197	118	10	2	2	773^1	914	458	92	18	229	244	13.5	4.71	84	.298	.350	5	.385	2	-60	-68	2	-6.9
● **JAY BALLER**	Baller, Jay Scot b: 10/6/60, Stayton, Ore. BR/TR, 6′7″, 225 lbs. Deb: 9/19/82																											
1982	Phi-N	0	0	—	4	1	0	0	0	8	7	4	1	1	2	7	11.3	3.38	109	.226	.294	0	—	0	0	0	-0	0.0
1985	Chi-N	2	3	.400	20	4	0	0	1	52	52	21	8	1	17	31	12.1	3.46	116	.260	.321	0	.000	-1	1	3	-0	0.1
1986	Chi-N	2	4	.333	36	0	0	0	5	53^2	58	37	7	2	28	42	14.8	5.37	75	.275	.365	0	.000	-1	-10	-7	-1	-1.0
1987	Chi-N	0	1	.000	23	0	0	0	0	29^1	38	22	4	0	20	27	17.8	6.75	63	.325	.423	1	1.000	0	-9	-8	-0	-0.4
1990	KC-A	0	1	.000	3	0	0	0	0	2^1	4	4	1	1	2	1	27.0	15.43	25	.364	.500	0	—	0	-3	-3	-0	-0.6
1992	Phi-N	0	0	—	8	0	0	0	0	11	10	10	5	0	10	9	16.4	8.18	43	.250	.400	0	—	0	-6	-6	-0	-0.3
Total	6	4	9	.308	94	5	0	0	6	156^1	169	98	26	5	79	117	14.6	5.24	77	.277	.365	1	.071	-1	-26	-20	-2	-2.2
● **MARK BALLINGER**	Ballinger, Mark Alan b: 1/31/49, Glendale, Cal. BR/TR, 6′6″, 205 lbs. Deb: 8/6/71																											
1971	Cle-A	1	2	.333	18	0	0	0	0	34^2	30	21	3	1	13	25	11.4	4.67	82	.233	.308	1	.200	-0	-5	-3	-0	-0.3
● **WIN BALLOU**	Ballou, Noble Winfield b: 11/30/1897, Mount Morgan, Ky. d: 1/30/63, San Francisco, Cal BR/TL, 5′10.5″, 170 lbs. Deb: 8/24/25																											
1925	*Was-A	1	1	.500	10	1	1	0	0	27^2	38	17	1	0	13	13	16.6	4.55	93	.342	.411	1	.143	-0	-0	-1	0	-0.1
1926	StL-A	11	10	.524	43	14	5	0	2	154	186	99	12	4	71	59	15.3	4.79	90	.311	.387	2	.048	-3	-13	-8	3	-1.0
1927	StL-A	5	6	.455	21	11	4	0	0	90^1	105	56	4	1	46	17	15.1	4.78	91	.309	.393	1	.036	-4	-6	-4	-0	-0.8
1929	Bro-N	2	3	.400	25	2	0	0	0	57^2	69	52	5	0	38	20	16.7	6.71	69	.304	.404	1	.063	-2	-13	-14	2	-1.0
Total	4	19	20	.487	99	28	10	0	2	329^2	398	224	22	5	168	109	15.6	5.11	86	.312	.394	5	.054	-9	-33	-26	5	-2.9
● **TONY BALSAMO**	Balsamo, Anthony Fred b: 11/21/37, Brooklyn, N.Y. BR/TR, 6′2″, 185 lbs. Deb: 4/14/62																											
1962	Chi-N	0	1	.000	18	0	0	0	0	29^1	34	22	1	1	20	27	16.9	6.44	64	.293	.401	1	.200	0	-8	-7	1	-0.3
● **GEORGE BAMBERGER**	Bamberger, George Irvin b: 8/1/25, Staten Island, N.Y. BR/TR, 6′, 175 lbs. Deb: 4/19/51 MC																											
1951	NY-N	0	0	—	2	0	0	0	0	2	4	4	2	0	2	1	27.0	18.00	22	.444	.545	0	—	0	-3	-3	-0	-0.2
1952	NY-N	0	0	—	5	0	0	0	0	4	6	4	1	0	6	0	27.0	9.00	41	.353	.522	0	—	0	-2	-2	0	-0.1
1959	Bal-A	0	0	—	3	1	0	0	1	8^1	15	7	1	0	2	2	18.4	7.56	50	.405	.436	0	.000	-0	-3	-4	0	-0.2
Total	3	0	0	—	10	1	0	0	1	14^1	25	15	4	0	10	3	22.0	9.42	40	.397	.479	0	.000	-0	-9	-9	0	-0.5
● **SAL BANDO**	Bando, Salvatore Leonard b: 2/13/44, Cleveland, O. BR/TR, 6′, 205 lbs. Deb: 9/3/66 FC♦																											
1979	Mil-A	0	0	—	1	0	0	0	0	3	3	2	0	0	0	0	9.0	6.00	70	.231	.231	117	.246	0	-1	-1	-0	0.0
● **EDDIE BANE**	Bane, Edward Norman b: 3/22/52, Chicago, Ill. BR/TL, 5′9″, 160 lbs. Deb: 7/4/73																											
1973	Min-A	0	5	.000	23	6	0	0	2	60^1	62	40	5	2	30	42	14.0	4.92	81	.270	.359	0	—	0	-7	-6	1	-0.4
1975	Min-A	3	1	.750	4	4	0	0	0	28^1	28	11	2	1	15	14	14.0	2.86	134	.262	.358	0	—	0	3	3	-1	0.3
1976	Min-A	4	7	.364	17	15	1	0	0	79^1	92	52	6	0	39	24	14.9	5.11	70	.290	.368	0	—	0	-14	-13	-2	-1.8
Total	3	7	13	.350	44	25	1	0	2	168	182	103	13	3	84	80	14.4	4.66	81	.278	.363	0	—	0	-18	-16	-1	-1.9

● DICK BANEY Baney, Richard Lee b: 11/1/46, Fullerton, Cal. BR/TR, 6', 185 lbs. Deb: 7/11/69

YEAR	TM/L	W	L	PCT	G	GS	CG	SH	SV	IP	H	R	HR	HB	BB	SO	RAT	ERA	ERA+	OAV	OOB	BH	AVG	PB	PR	PR+	PD	TPI
1969	Sea-A	1	0	1.000	9	1	0	0	0	18^2	21	8	2	0	7	9	13.5	3.86	94	.292	.354	0	.000	-0	-0	-0	-0	-0.1
1973	Cin-N	2	1	.667	11	1	0	0	2	30^2	26	10	1	4	6	17	10.6	2.93	116	.234	.298	2	.222	1	3	2	-1	0.1
1974	Cin-N	1	0	1.000	22	1	0	0	1	41	51	27	4	0	17	12	14.9	5.49	64	.305	.370	0	.000	-1	-8	-9	-1	-0.7
Total	3	4	1	.800	42	3	0	0	3	90^1	98	45	7	4	30	38	13.2	4.28	82	.280	.344	2	.125	-0	-6	-8	-3	-0.7

● DAN BANKHEAD Bankhead, Daniel Robert b: 5/3/20, Empire, Ala. d: 5/2/76, Houston, Tex. BR/TR, 6'1", 184 lbs. Deb: 8/26/47

YEAR	TM/L	W	L	PCT	G	GS	CG	SH	SV	IP	H	R	HR	HB	BB	SO	RAT	ERA	ERA+	OAV	OOB	BH	AVG	PB	PR	PR+	PD	TPI
1947	*Bro-N	0	0	—	4	0	0	0	1	10	15	8	1	1	8	6	21.6	7.20	57	.341	.453	1	.250	1	-3	-3	-0	-0.1
1950	Bro-N	9	4	.692	41	12	2	1	3	129^1	119	84	16	2	88	96	14.5	5.50	75	.252	.371	9	.231	1	-19	-20	-1	-1.8
1951	Bro-N	0	1	.000	7	1	0	0	0	14	27	24	5	0	14	9	26.4	15.43	25	.422	.526	0	.000	-0	-18	-18	0	-1.1
Total	3	9	5	.643	52	13	2	1	4	153^1	161	116	22	3	110	111	16.1	6.52	63	.277	.395	10	.222	2	-41	-42	-1	-3.0

● SCOTT BANKHEAD Bankhead, Michael Scott b: 7/31/63, Raleigh, N.C. BR/TR, 5'10", 185 lbs. Deb: 5/25/86

YEAR	TM/L	W	L	PCT	G	GS	CG	SH	SV	IP	H	R	HR	HB	BB	SO	RAT	ERA	ERA+	OAV	OOB	BH	AVG	PB	PR	PR+	PD	TPI
1986	KC-A	8	9	.471	24	17	0	0	0	121	121	66	14	3	37	94	12.0	4.61	92	.259	.318	0	—	0	-6	-5	-0	-0.6
1987	Sea-A	9	8	.529	27	25	2	0	0	149^1	168	96	35	3	37	95	12.5	5.42	87	.283	.329	0	—	0	-16	-11	-2	-1.2
1988	Sea-A	7	9	.438	21	21	2	1	0	135	115	53	8	1	38	102	10.3	3.07	136	.224	.278	0	—	0	14	16	-1	1.7
1989	Sea-A	14	6	.700	33	33	3	2	0	210^1	187	84	19	3	63	140	10.8	3.34	121	.239	.298	0	—	0	13	16	-2	1.2
1990	Sea-A	0	2	.000	4	4	0	0	0	13	18	16	2	0	7	10	17.3	11.08	36	.333	.410	0	—	0	-10	-10	-0	-1.2
1991	Sea-A	3	6	.333	17	9	0	0	0	60^2	73	35	8	2	21	28	14.2	4.90	84	.297	.357	0	—	0	-5	-5	-0	-0.7
1992	Cin-N	10	4	.714	54	0	0	0	1	70^2	57	26	4	3	29	53	11.3	2.93	123	.218	.304	2	.222	0	5	5	-2	0.8
1993	Bos-A	2	1	.667	40	0	0	0	0	64^1	59	28	7	0	29	47	12.3	3.50	132	.250	.332	0	—	0	6	8	-1	0.3
1994	Bos-A	3	2	.600	27	0	0	0	0	37^2	34	21	5	0	12	25	11.0	4.54	111	.239	.299	0	—	0	1	2	-1	0.1
1995	NY-A	1	1	.500	20	1	0	0	0	39	44	26	9	0	16	20	13.8	6.00	77	.278	.345	0	—	0	-6	-6	-1	-0.4
Total	10	57	48	.543	267	110	7	3	1	901	876	451	111	15	289	614	11.8	4.18	103	.254	.314	2	.222	0	-5	10	-11	0.0

● BILL BANKS Banks, William John (b: William John Yerrick) b: 2/26/1874, Danville, Pa. d: 9/8/36, Danville, Pa. BR/TR, 5'11", 150 lbs. Deb: 9/27/1895

YEAR	TM/L	W	L	PCT	G	GS	CG	SH	SV	IP	H	R	HR	HB	BB	SO	RAT	ERA	ERA+	OAV	OOB	BH	AVG	PB	PR	PR+	PD	TPI
1895	Bos-N	1	0	1.000	1	1	1	0	0	7	7	2	0	0	4	4	14.1	0.00	—	.259	.355	0	.000	-1	4	4	0	0.4
1896	Bos-N	0	3	.000	4	3	2	0	0	23	42	31	2	2	13	6	22.3	10.57	43	.389	.463	3	.273	0	-16	-15	-1	-1.3
Total	2	1	3	.250	5	4	3	0	0	30	49	33	2	2	17	10	20.4	8.10	58	.363	.442	3	.214	-1	-12	-11	-1	-0.9

● WILLIE BANKS Banks, Willie Anthony b: 2/27/69, Jersey City, N.J. BR/TR, 6'1", 202 lbs. Deb: 7/31/91

YEAR	TM/L	W	L	PCT	G	GS	CG	SH	SV	IP	H	R	HR	HB	BB	SO	RAT	ERA	ERA+	OAV	OOB	BH	AVG	PB	PR	PR+	PD	TPI
1991	Min-A	1	1	.500	5	3	0	0	0	17^1	21	15	1	0	12	16	17.1	5.71	75	.288	.388	0	—	0	-3	-3	-1	-0.3
1992	Min-A	4	4	.500	16	12	0	0	0	71	80	46	6	2	37	37	15.1	5.70	71	.288	.375	0	—	0	-14	-13	-0	-1.3
1993	Min-A	11	12	.478	31	30	0	0	0	171^1	186	91	17	3	78	138	14.0	4.04	108	.280	.358	0	—	0	6	6	-1	0.6
1994	Chi-N	8	12	.400	23	23	1	1	0	138^1	139	88	16	2	56	91	12.8	5.40	77	.261	.333	5	.122	-1	-18	-19	-2	-2.6
1995	Chi-N	0	1	.000	10	0	0	0	0	11^2	27	23	5	0	12	9	30.1	15.43	27	.458	.549	0	.000	-0	-15	-15	0	-1.1
	LA-N	0	2	.000	6	6	0	0	0	29	36	21	2	1	16	23	16.4	4.03	94	.303	.390	1	.125	0	0	-1	0	0.0
	Fla-N	2	3	.400	9	9	0	0	0	50	43	27	7	1	30	30	13.3	4.32	98	.235	.346	6	.353	2	-1	-1	-0	0.1
	Yr	2	6	.250	25	15	0	0	0	90^2	106	71	14	2	58	62	16.5	5.66	72	.294	.394	7	.269	2	-15	-16	0	-1.0
1997	NY-A	3	0	1.000	5	1	0	0	0	14	9	3	0	0	6	8	10.3	1.93	231	.188	.291	0	—	0	4	4	0	0.9
1998	NY-A	1	1	.500	9	0	0	0	0	14^1	20	16	4	1	12	8	20.7	10.05	44	.323	.440	0	—	0	-9	-10	1	-1.0
	Ari-N	1	2	.333	33	0	0	0	1	43^2	34	21	2	1	25	32	12.4	3.09	136	.217	.328	0	.000	-0	6	5	0	0.4
Total	7	31	38	.449	147	84	1	1	1	560^2	595	351	60	12	284	392	14.3	4.93	86	.273	.360	12	.176	1	-43	-44	-2	-4.3

● FLOYD BANNISTER Bannister, Floyd Franklin b: 6/10/55, Pierre, S.D. BL/TL, 6'1", 195 lbs. Deb: 4/19/77

YEAR	TM/L	W	L	PCT	G	GS	CG	SH	SV	IP	H	R	HR	HB	BB	SO	RAT	ERA	ERA+	OAV	OOB	BH	AVG	PB	PR	PR+	PD	TPI
1977	Hou-N	8	9	.471	24	23	4	1	0	142^2	138	70	11	4	68	112	13.2	4.04	88	.254	.341	9	.188	0	-2	-8	-1	-1.0
1978	Hou-N	3	9	.250	28	16	2	2	0	110^1	120	59	13	1	63	94	15.0	4.81	69	.280	.374	5	.161	0	-15	-20	-2	-2.1
1979	Sea-A	10	15	.400	30	30	6	2	0	182^1	185	92	25	4	68	115	12.7	4.05	108	.260	.328	0	—	0	4	6	-2	0.6
1980	Sea-A	9	13	.409	32	32	8	0	0	217^2	200	96	24	2	66	155	11.1	3.47	119	.239	.296	0	—	0	14	16	-1	1.4
1981	Sea-A	9	9	.500	21	20	5	2	0	121^1	128	62	14	3	39	85	12.6	4.45	87	.268	.327	0	—	0	-11	-8	-1	-1.1
1982	Sea-A★	12	13	.480	35	35	5	3	0	247	225	112	32	3	77	**209**	11.1	3.43	124	.243	.303	0	—	0	18	22	-1	2.0
1983	*Chi-A	16	10	.615	34	34	5	2	0	217^1	191	88	19	2	71	193	10.9	3.35	125	.233	.295	0	—	0	17	20	-1	2.1
1984	Chi-A	14	11	.560	34	33	4	0	0	218	211	127	30	6	80	152	12.3	4.83	86	.252	.322	0	.000	-0	-20	-15	-2	-1.8
1985	Chi-A	10	14	.417	34	34	4	1	0	210^2	211	121	30	4	100	198	13.5	4.87	89	.261	.346	0	—	0	-17	-12	-1	-1.4
1986	Chi-A	10	14	.417	28	27	6	1	0	165^1	162	81	17	2	48	92	11.5	3.54	122	.259	.314	0	—	0	12	14	-1	1.8
1987	Chi-A	16	11	.593	34	34	11	2	0	228^2	216	100	38	0	49	124	10.4	3.58	128	.246	.286	0	—	0	23	25	-3	2.4
1988	KC-A	12	13	.480	31	31	2	0	0	189^1	182	102	22	5	68	113	12.1	4.33	92	.248	.316	0	—	0	-7	-7	-0	-0.9
1989	KC-A	4	1	.800	14	14	0	0	0	75^1	87	40	8	1	18	35	12.7	4.66	83	.290	.332	0	—	0	-6	-7	1	-0.3
1991	Cal-A	0	0	—	16	0	0	0	0	25	25	12	5	0	10	16	12.6	3.96	104	.266	.337	0	—	0	0	0	-1	0.0
1992	Tex-A	1	1	.500	36	0	0	0	0	37	39	27	3	3	21	30	15.3	6.32	60	.281	.387	0	—	0	-10	-11	0	-0.5
Total	15	134	143	.484	431	363	62	16	0	2388	2320	1189	291	40	846	1723	12.1	4.06	102	.253	.319	14	.175	0	-0	18	-15	1.2

● JIMMY BANNON Bannon, James Henry "Foxy Grandpa" b: 5/5/1871, Amesbury, Mass. d: 3/24/48, Glen Rock, N.J. BR/TR, 5'5", 160 lbs. Deb: 6/15/1893 F◆

YEAR	TM/L	W	L	PCT	G	GS	CG	SH	SV	IP	H	R	HR	HB	BB	SO	RAT	ERA	ERA+	OAV	OOB	BH	AVG	PB	PR	PR+	PD	TPI
1893	StL-N	0	1	.000	1	1	0	0	0	4	10	18	1	2	5	1	38.3	22.50	21	.455	.586	36	.336	0	-8	-8	-0	-0.9
1894	Bos-N	0	0	—	1	0	0	0	0	2	4	3	1	0	1	0	22.5	0.00	—	.400	.455	166	.336	0	1	1	0	0.1
1895	Bos-N	0	0	—	1	0	0	0	0	3	4	2	0	0	2	1	18.0	6.00	85	.308	.400	171	.347	0	-0	-0	0	0.0
Total	3	0	1	.000	3	1	0	0	0	9	18	23	2	2	8	2	28.0	12.00	42	.400	.509	460	.320	1	-7	-7	-0	-0.8

● JACK BANTA Banta, Jackie Kay b: 6/24/25, Hutchinson, Kan. BL/TR, 6'2.5", 175 lbs. Deb: 9/18/47

YEAR	TM/L	W	L	PCT	G	GS	CG	SH	SV	IP	H	R	HR	HB	BB	SO	RAT	ERA	ERA+	OAV	OOB	BH	AVG	PB	PR	PR+	PD	TPI
1947	Bro-N	0	1	.000	3	1	0	0	0	7^2	7	6	1	1	4	3	14.1	7.04	59	.226	.333	0	.000	-0	-3	-2	1	-0.2
1948	Bro-N	0	1	.000	2	1	0	0	0	3^1	5	6	0	0	5	1	27.0	8.10	49	.385	.556	0	.000	-0	-2	-2	-0	-0.3
1949	*Bro-N	10	6	.625	48	12	2	1	3	152^1	125	63	12	6	68	97	11.8	3.37	122	.223	.314	5	.109	-2	11	12	1	1.1
1950	Bro-N	4	4	.500	16	5	1	0	2	41^1	39	22	2	3	36	15	17.0	4.35	94	.252	.402	2	.167	-0	-1	-1	-1	-0.3
Total	4	14	12	.538	69	19	3	1	5	204^2	176	97	15	10	113	116	13.1	3.78	108	.232	.339	7	.115	-2	6	7	0	0.3

● TRAVIS BAPTIST Baptist, Travis Steven b: 12/30/71, Forest Grove, Ore. BL/TL, 6', 195 lbs. Deb: 8/1/98

YEAR	TM/L	W	L	PCT	G	GS	CG	SH	SV	IP	H	R	HR	HB	BB	SO	RAT	ERA	ERA+	OAV	OOB	BH	AVG	PB	PR	PR+	PD	TPI
1998	Min-A	0	1	.000	13	0	0	0	0	27	34	18	5	0	11	11	15.0	5.67	84	.321	.385	0	—	0	-3	-3	0	-0.1

● BRIAN BARBER Barber, Brian Scott b: 3/4/73, Hamilton, Ohio BR/TR, 6'1", 170 lbs. Deb: 8/12/95

YEAR	TM/L	W	L	PCT	G	GS	CG	SH	SV	IP	H	R	HR	HB	BB	SO	RAT	ERA	ERA+	OAV	OOB	BH	AVG	PB	PR	PR+	PD	TPI
1995	StL-N	2	1	.667	9	4	0	0	0	29^1	31	17	4	0	16	27	14.4	5.22	80	.279	.370	1	.125	-0	-3	-3	-1	-0.4
1996	StL-N	0	0	—	1	1	0	0	0	3	4	5	0	1	6	1	33.0	15.00	28	.364	.611	0	—	0	-4	-4	-0	-0.2
1998	KC-A	2	4	.333	8	8	0	0	0	42	45	28	5	1	13	24	12.6	6.00	80	.276	.333	0	—	0	-6	-5	-1	-0.7
1999	KC-A	1	3	.250	8	3	0	0	1	18^2	31	20	6	2	10	7	20.7	9.64	52	.383	.462	0	—	0	-10	-9	0	-1.6
Total	4	5	8	.385	26	16	0	0	1	93	111	70	15	4	45	59	15.5	6.77	69	.303	.386	1	.125	-0	-23	-22	-2	-2.9

● STEVE BARBER Barber, Stephen David b: 2/22/39, Takoma Park, Md. BL/TL, 6', 200 lbs. Deb: 4/21/60

YEAR	TM/L	W	L	PCT	G	GS	CG	SH	SV	IP	H	R	HR	HB	BB	SO	RAT	ERA	ERA+	OAV	OOB	BH	AVG	PB	PR	PR+	PD	TPI
1960	Bal-A	10	7	.588	36	27	6	1	2	181^2	148	78	10	3	113	112	13.1	3.22	118	.226	.343	3	.056	-4	13	12	0	0.7
1961	Bal-A	18	12	.600	37	34	14	**8**	1	248^1	194	102	13	2	130	150	11.8	3.33	115	.218	.319	13	.162	2	19	15	4	2.3
1962	Bal-A	9	6	.600	28	19	5	2	0	140^1	145	66	9	1	61	89	13.3	3.46	107	.262	.337	3	.071	-2	8	4	1	0.3
1963	Bal-A†	20	13	.606	39	36	11	2	0	258^2	253	99	12	4	92	180	12.1	2.75	126	.258	.324	12	.138	-0	25	22	2	2.9
1964	Bal-A	9	13	.409	36	26	4	0	1	157	144	72	15	7	81	118	13.3	3.84	93	.248	.347	7	.149	1	-4	-5	3	-0.3
1965	Bal-A	15	10	.600	37	32	7	2	0	220^2	177	79	16	2	81	130	10.6	2.69	129	.224	.297	5	.077	-2	19	19	1	2.1
1966	Bal-A☆	10	5	.667	25	22	5	3	0	133^1	104	38	6	3	49	91	10.5	2.30	145	.218	.294	3	.068	-3	17	16	1	1.6
1967	Bal-A	4	9	.308	15	15	1	1	0	74^2	47	39	5	5	61	48	13.6	4.10	77	.185	.353	2	.091	-1	-7	-8	0	-1.4
	NY-A	6	9	.400	17	17	3	1	0	97^2	103	47	4	3	54	70	14.7	4.05	77	.278	.375	5	.172	1	-9	-10	-1	-1.5
	Yr	10	18	.357	32	32	4	2	0	172^1	150	86	9	8	115	118	14.3	4.07	77	.240	.365	7	.137	1	-16	-18	-1	-2.9
1968	NY-A	6	5	.545	20	19	3	1	0	128^1	127	63	7	3	64	87	13.6	3.23	90	.256	.345	2	.051	-1	-4	-5	0	-0.5
1969	Sea-A	4	7	.364	25	16	0	0	0	86^1	99	51	9	1	48	69	15.4	4.80	76	.292	.381	5	.200	1	-11	-11	0	-1.2
1970	Chi-N	0	1	.000	5	0	0	0	0	5^2	10	6	0	0	6	3	25.4	9.53	47	.417	.533	0	—	0	-3	-3	-0	-0.4
	Atl-N	0	1	.000	5	2	0	0	0	14^2	17	10	3	1	5	11	14.1	4.91	88	.288	.354	1	.250	0	-1	-1	-0	-0.1
	Yr	0	2	.000	10	2	0	0	0	20^1	27	16	3	1	11	14	17.3	6.20	70	.325	.411	1	.250	0	-5	-4	-0	-0.5

YEAR	TM/L	W	L	PCT	G	GS	CG	SH	SV	IP	H	R	HR	HB	BB	SO	RAT	ERA	ERA+	OAV	OOB	BH	AVG	PB	PR	PR+	PD	TPI
1971	Atl-N	3	1	.750	39	3	0	0	2	75	92	42	6	2	25	40	14.3	4.80	77	.301	.357	2	.154	-0	-11	-8	0	-0.5
1972	Atl-N	0	0	—	5	0	0	0	0	15^2	18	10	1	1	6	6	14.4	5.74	66	.290	.362	1	.200	-0	-4	-3	1	-0.1
	Cal-A	4	4	.500	34	3	0	0	2	58	37	16	4	1	30	34	10.6	2.02	145	.188	.298	1	.143	1	7	6	-1	0.9
1973	Cal-A	3	2	.600	50	1	0	0	4	89^1	90	40	5	3	32	58	12.6	3.53	101	.265	.333	0	—	0	3	0	-1	-0.1
1974	SF-N	0	1	.000	13	0	0	0	1	13^2	13	12	0	0	12	13	16.5	5.27	72	.255	.397	0	—	0	-2	-2	-1	-0.2
Total	15	121	106	.533	466	272	59	21	13	1999	1818	870	125	42	950	1309	12.7	3.36	105	.245	.334	65	.115	-6	54	35	10	4.5

● STEVE BARBER Barber, Steven Lee b: 3/13/48, Grand Rapids, Mich. BR/TR, 6'1", 190 lbs. Deb: 4/9/70

YEAR	TM/L	W	L	PCT	G	GS	CG	SH	SV	IP	H	R	HR	HB	BB	SO	RAT	ERA	ERA+	OAV	OOB	BH	AVG	PB	PR	PR+	PD	TPI
1970	Min-A	0	0	—	18	0	0	0	2	27^1	26	14	1	2	18	14	15.1	4.61	81	.263	.387	0	.000	-0	-3	-3	-0	-0.2
1971	Min-A	1	0	1.000	4	2	0	0	0	11^2	8	9	2	0	13	4	16.2	6.17	58	.190	.382	0	.000	-1	-4	-3	-0	-0.3
Total	2	1	0	1.000	22	2	0	0	2	39	34	23	3	2	31	18	15.5	5.08	72	.241	.385	0	.000	-1	-6	-6	-1	-0.5

● FRANK BARBERICH Barberich, Frank Frederick b: 2/3/1882, Newtown, N.Y. d: 5/1/65, Ocala, Fla. BB/TR, 5'10.5", 175 lbs. Deb: 9/17/07

YEAR	TM/L	W	L	PCT	G	GS	CG	SH	SV	IP	H	R	HR	HB	BB	SO	RAT	ERA	ERA+	OAV	OOB	BH	AVG	PB	PR	PR+	PD	TPI
1907	Bos-N	1	1	.500	2	2	1	0	0	12^1	19	10	0	0	5	1	17.5	5.84	44	.358	.414	0	.000	-0	-5	-4	0	-0.6
1910	Bos-A	0	0	—	2	0	0	0	0	5	7	6	0	0	2	0	16.2	7.20	35	.350	.409	0	.000	-0	-3	-3	0	-0.1
Total	2	1	1	.500	4	2	1	0	0	17^1	26	16	0	0	7	1	17.1	6.23	41	.356	.412	0	.000	-1	-7	-7	0	-0.7

● LORENZO BARCELO Barcelo, Lorenzo Antonio b: 8/10/77, San Pedro De Macoris, D.R. BR/TR, 6'4", 220 lbs. Deb: 7/22/2000

YEAR	TM/L	W	L	PCT	G	GS	CG	SH	SV	IP	H	R	HR	HB	BB	SO	RAT	ERA	ERA+	OAV	OOB	BH	AVG	PB	PR	PR+	PD	TPI
2000	*Chi-A	4	2	.667	22	1	0	0	0	39	34	17	5	0	9	26	9.9	3.69	135	.231	.276	0	—	0	5	5	-1	0.6

● CURT BARCLAY Barclay, Curtis Cordell b: 8/22/31, Chicago, Ill. d: 3/25/85, Missoula, Montana BR/TR, 6'3", 210 lbs. Deb: 4/21/57

YEAR	TM/L	W	L	PCT	G	GS	CG	SH	SV	IP	H	R	HR	HB	BB	SO	RAT	ERA	ERA+	OAV	OOB	BH	AVG	PB	PR	PR+	PD	TPI
1957	NY-N	9	9	.500	37	28	5	2	0	183	196	85	21	2	48	67	12.1	3.44	114	.274	.321	11	.190	0	9	10	3	1.2
1958	SF-N	1	0	1.000	6	1	0	0	0	16	16	5	3	3	5	6	13.5	2.81	136	.258	.343	4	.667	2	2	2	0	0.4
1959	SF-N	0	0	—	1	0	0	0	0	0^1	2	5	0	0	2	0	108.0	54.00	7	.500	.667	0	—	0	-2	-2	-0	-0.1
Total	3	10	9	.526	44	29	5	2	0	199^1	214	95	24	5	55	73	12.4	3.48	113	.274	.325	15	.234	2	9	10	3	1.5

● RAY BARE Bare, Raymond Douglas b: 4/15/49, Miami, Fla. d: 3/29/94, Miami, Fla. BR/TR, 6'2", 195 lbs. Deb: 7/30/72

YEAR	TM/L	W	L	PCT	G	GS	CG	SH	SV	IP	H	R	HR	HB	BB	SO	RAT	ERA	ERA+	OAV	OOB	BH	AVG	PB	PR	PR+	PD	TPI
1972	StL-N	0	1	.000	14	0	0	0	1	16^2	18	2	0	0	6	5	13.0	0.54	630	.281	.343	0	—	0	5	5	-0	0.4
1974	StL-N	1	2	.333	10	3	0	0	0	24^1	25	17	2	0	9	6	12.6	5.92	61	.281	.347	1	.200	-0	-6	-6	1	-0.6
1975	Det-A	8	13	.381	29	21	6	1	0	150^2	174	81	10	1	47	71	13.3	4.48	90	.293	.346	0	—	0	-12	-7	2	-0.7
1976	Det-A	7	8	.467	30	21	3	2	0	134	157	85	13	0	51	59	14.0	4.63	80	.293	.354	0	—	0	-17	-13	1	-1.3
1977	Det-A	0	2	.000	5	4	0	0	0	14^1	24	21	3	0	7	4	19.5	12.56	34	.381	.443	0	—	0	-14	-12	1	-1.2
Total	5	16	26	.381	88	49	9	3	1	340	398	206	28	1	120	145	13.7	4.79	80	.296	.354	1	.200	-0	-42	-34	4	-3.4

● JOHN BARFIELD Barfield, John David b: 10/15/64, Pine Bluff, Ark. BL/TL, 6'1", 185 lbs. Deb: 9/7/89

YEAR	TM/L	W	L	PCT	G	GS	CG	SH	SV	IP	H	R	HR	HB	BB	SO	RAT	ERA	ERA+	OAV	OOB	BH	AVG	PB	PR	PR+	PD	TPI
1989	Tex-A	0	1	.000	4	2	0	0	0	11^2	15	10	0	0	4	9	14.7	6.17	64	.319	.373	0	—	0	-3	-3	-0	-0.2
1990	Tex-A	4	3	.571	33	0	0	0	1	44^1	42	25	2	1	13	17	11.4	4.67	84	.268	.327	0	—	0	-4	-4	0	-0.5
1991	Tex-A	4	4	.500	28	9	0	0	1	83^1	96	51	11	0	22	27	12.7	4.54	89	.289	.333	0	—	0	-4	-5	-0	-0.4
Total	3	8	8	.500	65	11	0	0	2	139^1	153	86	13	1	39	53	12.5	4.72	85	.285	.335	0	—	0	-11	-11	-0	-1.1

● CLYDE BARFOOT Barfoot, Clyde Raymond "Foots" b: 7/8/1891, Richmond, Va. d: 3/11/71, Highland Park, Cal BR/TR, 6', 170 lbs. Deb: 4/13/22

YEAR	TM/L	W	L	PCT	G	GS	CG	SH	SV	IP	H	R	HR	HB	BB	SO	RAT	ERA	ERA+	OAV	OOB	BH	AVG	PB	PR	PR+	PD	TPI
1922	StL-N	4	5	.444	42	2	1	0	2	117^2	139	75	2	10	30	19	13.7	4.21	92	.307	.363	12	.353	5	-1	-5	1	0.2
1923	StL-N	3	3	.500	33	2	1	1	1	101^1	112	49	7	1	27	23	12.4	3.73	105	.289	.337	7	.189	-1	3	2	0	0.0
1926	Det-A	1	2	.333	11	1	0	0	2	31^1	42	27	4	0	9	7	14.6	4.88	83	.318	.362	1	.200	0	-3	-3	1	-0.2
Total	3	8	10	.444	86	5	2	1	5	250^1	293	151	13	11	66	49	13.3	4.10	95	.301	.353	20	.263	4	-1	-6	1	0.0

● GREG BARGAR Bargar, Greg Robert b: 1/27/59, Inglewood, Cal. BR/TR, 6'2", 185 lbs. Deb: 7/17/83

YEAR	TM/L	W	L	PCT	G	GS	CG	SH	SV	IP	H	R	HR	HB	BB	SO	RAT	ERA	ERA+	OAV	OOB	BH	AVG	PB	PR	PR+	PD	TPI
1983	Mon-N	2	0	1.000	8	3	0	0	0	20	23	15	6	1	8	9	14.4	6.75	53	.271	.340	1	.167	-0	-7	-7	-1	-0.7
1984	Mon-N	0	1	.000	3	1	0	0	0	8	8	7	1	0	7	2	16.9	7.88	44	.286	.429	0	.000	-0	-4	-4	0	-0.5
1986	StL-N	0	2	.000	22	0	0	0	0	27^1	36	19	3	3	10	12	16.1	5.60	65	.330	.402	0	.000	-0	-6	-6	1	-0.4
Total	3	2	3	.400	33	4	0	0	0	55^1	67	41	10	4	25	23	15.6	6.34	57	.302	.382	1	.111	-0	-16	-17	0	-1.6

● CY BARGER Barger, Eros Bolivar b: 5/18/1885, Jamestown, Ky. d: 9/23/64, Columbia, Ky. BL/TR, 6', 160 lbs. Deb: 8/30/06

YEAR	TM/L	W	L	PCT	G	GS	CG	SH	SV	IP	H	R	HR	HB	BB	SO	RAT	ERA	ERA+	OAV	OOB	BH	AVG	PB	PR	PR+	PD	TPI
1906	NY-A	0	0	—	2	1	0	0	1	5^1	7	8	0	0	3	3	16.9	10.13	29	.318	.400	1	.333	0	-4	-4	-0	-0.2
1907	NY-A	0	0	—	1	0	0	0	0	6	10	2	0	1	1	0	18.0	3.00	93	.370	.414	0	.000	-0	-0	-0	-1	-0.1
1910	Bro-N	15	15	.500	35	30	25	2	1	271^2	267	105	2	6	107	87	12.6	2.88	105	.275	.351	24	.231	3	5	5	2	1.0
1911	Bro-N	11	15	.423	30	30	21	1	0	217^1	224	112	4	7	71	60	12.5	3.52	95	.279	.342	33	.228	1	-3	-5	1	-0.2
1912	Bro-N	1	9	.100	16	11	6	0	0	94	120	78	4	4	42	30	15.9	5.46	61	.326	.401	7	.189	-0	-21	-22	1	-1.9
1914	Pit-F	10	16	.385	33	26	18	1	1	228^1	252	125	7	6	63	70	12.7	4.34	66	.290	.342	17	.205	-1	-37	-38	-2	-4.1
1915	Pit-F	9	8	.529	34	13	8	1	6	153	130	49	1	4	47	47	10.6	2.29	118	.238	.303	15	.278	2	7	7	-1	0.9
Total	7	46	63	.422	151	111	78	5	9	975^2	1010	479	18	28	334	297	12.7	3.56	85	.280	.346	97	.227	5	-54	-57	-0	-4.6

● BRIAN BARK Bark, Brian Stuart b: 8/26/68, Baltimore, Md. BL/TL, 5'9", 170 lbs. Deb: 7/6/95

YEAR	TM/L	W	L	PCT	G	GS	CG	SH	SV	IP	H	R	HR	HB	BB	SO	RAT	ERA	ERA+	OAV	OOB	BH	AVG	PB	PR	PR+	PD	TPI
1995	Bos-A	0	0	—	3	0	0	0	0	2^1	2	0	0	0	1	0	11.6	0.00	—	.286	.375	0	—	0	1	1	-0	0.0

● LEN BARKER Barker, Leonard Harold b: 7/7/55, Fort Knox, Ky. BR/TR, 6'5", 225 lbs. Deb: 9/14/76

YEAR	TM/L	W	L	PCT	G	GS	CG	SH	SV	IP	H	R	HR	HB	BB	SO	RAT	ERA	ERA+	OAV	OOB	BH	AVG	PB	PR	PR+	PD	TPI
1976	Tex-A	1	0	1.000	2	2	1	1	0	15	7	4	0	2	6	7	9.0	2.40	150	.149	.273	0	—	0	2	2	-0	0.1
1977	Tex-A	4	1	.800	15	3	0	0	1	47^1	36	15	1	1	24	51	11.6	2.66	154	.217	.319	0	—	0	7	7	1	0.8
1978	Tex-A	1	5	.167	29	0	0	0	4	52^1	63	31	6	2	29	33	16.2	4.82	78	.304	.395	0	—	0	-6	-6	0	-0.7
1979	Cle-A	6	6	.500	29	19	2	0	0	137^1	146	79	6	2	70	93	14.3	4.92	87	.277	.364	0	—	0	-10	-10	-1	-0.9
1980	Cle-A	19	12	.613	36	36	8	1	0	246^1	237	127	17	3	92	**187**	12.1	4.17	98	.252	.320	0	—	0	-3	-2	-2	-0.4
1981	Cle-A★	8	7	.533	22	22	9	3	0	154^1	150	72	7	1	46	**127**	11.5	3.91	93	.249	.303	0	—	0	-4	-5	-0	-0.5
1982	Cle-A	15	11	.577	33	33	10	1	0	244^2	211	117	17	3	88	187	11.1	3.90	105	.232	.301	0	—	0	5	5	-0	0.5
1983	Cle-A	8	13	.381	24	24	4	1	0	149^2	150	92	16	2	52	105	12.3	5.11	83	.266	.330	0	—	0	-17	-14	-1	-1.7
	Atl-N	1	3	.250	6	6	0	0	0	33	31	17	0	0	14	21	12.3	3.82	102	.248	.324	1	.125	-0	-1	0	1	0.1
1984	Atl-N	7	8	.467	21	20	1	0	0	126^1	120	59	10	2	38	95	11.4	3.85	100	.254	.312	2	.053	-1	-4	0	3	0.2
1985	Atl-N	2	9	.182	20	18	0	0	0	73^2	84	55	10	1	37	47	14.9	6.35	61	.288	.370	0	.000	-2	-23	-19	-1	-2.8
1987	Mil-A	2	1	.667	11	11	0	0	0	43^2	54	27	6	2	17	22	15.0	5.36	86	.303	.371	0	—	0	-4	-4	-0	-0.2
Total	11	74	76	.493	248	194	35	7	5	1323^2	1289	695	96	21	513	975	12.4	4.34	93	.256	.327	3	.048	-3	-58	-45	-1	-5.5

● RICHARD BARKER Barker, Richard Frank b: 10/29/72, Revere, Mass. BR/TR, 6'2", 210 lbs. Deb: 4/25/99

YEAR	TM/L	W	L	PCT	G	GS	CG	SH	SV	IP	H	R	HR	HB	BB	SO	RAT	ERA	ERA+	OAV	OOB	BH	AVG	PB	PR	PR+	PD	TPI
1999	Chi-N	0	0	—	5	0	0	0	0	5	6	4	0	0	4	3	18.0	7.20	63	.300	.417	0	—	0	-1	-2	-0	-0.1

● BRIAN BARKLEY Barkley, Brian Edward b: 12/8/75, Conroe, Tex. BL/TL, 6'2", 180 lbs. Deb: 5/28/98 F

YEAR	TM/L	W	L	PCT	G	GS	CG	SH	SV	IP	H	R	HR	HB	BB	SO	RAT	ERA	ERA+	OAV	OOB	BH	AVG	PB	PR	PR+	PD	TPI
1998	Bos-A	0	0	—	6	0	0	0	0	11	16	13	2	1	9	2	21.3	9.82	48	.340	.456	0	—	0	-6	-6	-0	-0.3

● JEFF BARKLEY Barkley, Jeffrey Carver b: 11/21/59, Hickory, N.C. BB/TR, 6'3", 185 lbs. Deb: 9/16/84 F

YEAR	TM/L	W	L	PCT	G	GS	CG	SH	SV	IP	H	R	HR	HB	BB	SO	RAT	ERA	ERA+	OAV	OOB	BH	AVG	PB	PR	PR+	PD	TPI
1984	Cle-A	0	0	—	3	0	0	0	0	4	6	3	0	0	1	4	15.8	6.75	61	.353	.389	0	—	0	-1	-1	0	0.0
1985	Cle-A	0	3	.000	21	0	0	0	1	41	37	26	5	0	15	30	11.4	5.27	79	.243	.311	0	—	0	-5	-5	0	-0.4
Total	2	0	3	.000	24	0	0	0	1	45	43	29	5	0	16	34	11.8	5.40	77	.254	.319	0	—	0	-6	-6	0	-0.4

● MIKE BARLOW Barlow, Michael Roswell b: 4/30/48, Stamford, N.Y. BL/TR, 6'6", 215 lbs. Deb: 6/18/75

YEAR	TM/L	W	L	PCT	G	GS	CG	SH	SV	IP	H	R	HR	HB	BB	SO	RAT	ERA	ERA+	OAV	OOB	BH	AVG	PB	PR	PR+	PD	TPI
1975	StL-N	0	0	—	9	0	0	0	0	7^2	11	6	0	1	3	2	17.6	4.70	80	.355	.429	0	—	0	-1	-1	-0	-0.1
1976	Hou-N	2	2	.500	16	0	0	0	0	22	27	13	0	0	17	11	18.0	4.50	71	.318	.431	0	.000	-0	-2	-3	1	-0.6
1977	Cal-A	4	2	.667	20	1	0	0	1	59	53	33	3	4	27	25	12.8	4.58	86	.249	.344	0	—	0	-3	-4	0	-0.4
1978	Cal-A	0	0	—	1	0	0	0	0	2	3	1	0	0	0	1	13.5	4.50	80	.375	.375	0	—	0	-0	-0	-0	0.0
1979	*Cal-A	1	1	.500	35	0	0	0	0	86	106	54	8	4	30	33	14.7	5.13	80	.314	.376	0	—	0	-9	-10	-0	-0.5
1980	Tor-A	3	1	.750	40	1	0	0	5	55	57	29	4	2	21	19	13.1	4.09	105	.273	.345	0	—	0	-0	1	-0	0.1
1981	Tor-A	0	0	—	12	0	0	0	0	15	22	11	1	4	6	5	19.2	4.20	94	.338	.427	0	—	0	-1	-0	0	0.0
Total	7	10	6	.625	133	2	0	0	6	246^2	279	147	16	15	104	96	14.5	4.63	86	.294	.373	0	.000	-0	-17	-18	0	-1.5

● CHARLIE BARNABE Barnabe, Charles Edward b: 6/12/1900, Russell Gulch, Colo. d: 8/16/77, Waco, Tex. BL/TL, 5'11.5", 164 lbs. Deb: 4/14/27

YEAR	TM/L	W	L	PCT	G	GS	CG	SH	SV	IP	H	R	HR	HB	BB	SO	RAT	ERA	ERA+	OAV	OOB	BH	AVG	PB	PR	PR+	PD	TPI
1927	Chi-A	0	5	.000	17	4	1	0	0	61	86	46	2	5	20	5	16.4	5.31	76	.351	.411	3	.158	1	-8	-9	1	-0.5

YEAR	TM/L	W	L	PCT	G	GS	CG	SH	SV	IP	H	R	HR	HB	BB	SO	RAT	ERA	ERA+	OAV	OOB	BH	AVG	PB	PR	PR+	PD	TPI
1928	Chi-A	0	2	.000	7	2	0	0	0	9^2	17	9	0	1	0	3	16.8	6.52	62	.395	.409	4	.500	2	-3	-3	1	-0.2
Total	2	0	7	.000	24	6	1	0	0	70^2	103	55	2	6	20	8	16.4	5.48	74	.358	.411	7	.259	3	-11	-11	1	-0.7

● **BRIAN BARNES** Barnes, Brian Keith b: 3/25/67, Roanoke Rapids, N.C. BL/TL, 5'9", 170 lbs. Deb: 9/14/90

YEAR	TM/L	W	L	PCT	G	GS	CG	SH	SV	IP	H	R	HR	HB	BB	SO	RAT	ERA	ERA+	OAV	OOB	BH	AVG	PB	PR	PR+	PD	TPI
1990	Mon-N	1	1	.500	4	4	1	0	0	28	25	10	2	0	7	23	10.3	2.89	126	.236	.283	0	.000	-1	3	2	0	0.1
1991	Mon-N	5	8	.385	28	27	1	0	0	160	135	82	16	6	84	117	12.7	4.22	86	.233	.336	4	.082	-1	-9	-11	1	-0.7
1992	Mon-N	6	6	.500	21	17	0	0	0	100	77	34	9	3	46	65	11.3	2.97	117	.213	.307	8	.276	2	6	6	0	0.9
1993	Mon-N	2	6	.250	52	8	0	0	3	100	105	53	9	0	48	60	13.8	4.41	95	.274	.355	3	.150	-0	-4	-3	-0	-0.2
1994	Cle-A	0	1	.000	6	0	0	0	0	13^1	12	10	2	0	15	5	18.2	5.40	87	.235	.409	0	.000	0	-1	-1	-0	-0.1
	LA-N	0	0	—	5	0	0	0	0	5	10	4	1	0	4	5	25.2	7.20	55	.400	.483	0	—	0	-2	-2	-0	-0.1
Total	5	14	22	.389	116	56	2	0	3	406^1	364	193	39	9	204	275	12.8	3.94	95	.242	.335	15	.140	1	-7	-8	1	-0.1

● **FRANK BARNES** Barnes, Frank b: 8/26/26, Longwood, Miss. BR/TR, 6', 170 lbs. Deb: 9/22/57

YEAR	TM/L	W	L	PCT	G	GS	CG	SH	SV	IP	H	R	HR	HB	BB	SO	RAT	ERA	ERA+	OAV	OOB	BH	AVG	PB	PR	PR+	PD	TPI
1957	StL-N	0	1	.000	3	1	0	0	0	10	13	5	0	0	9	5	19.8	4.50	88	.317	.440	0	.000	-0	-1	-1	-0	-0.1
1958	StL-N	1	1	.500	8	1	0	0	0	19	19	16	3	2	16	17	17.5	7.58	54	.260	.407	1	.167	-0	-8	-7	-0	-0.7
1960	StL-N	0	1	.000	4	1	0	0	1	7^2	8	5	1	1	9	8	21.1	3.52	116	.267	.450	0	.000	-0	0	0	-0	0.0
Total	3	1	3	.250	15	3	0	0	1	36^2	40	26	4	3	34	30	18.9	5.89	69	.278	.425	1	.100	-1	-8	-7	-1	-0.8

● **FRANK BARNES** Barnes, Frank Samuel "Lefty" b: 1/9/1900, Dallas, Tex. d: 9/27/67, Houston, Tex. BL/TL, 6'2.5", 195 lbs. Deb: 4/18/29

YEAR	TM/L	W	L	PCT	G	GS	CG	SH	SV	IP	H	R	HR	HB	BB	SO	RAT	ERA	ERA+	OAV	OOB	BH	AVG	PB	PR	PR+	PD	TPI
1929	Det-A	0	1	.000	4	1	0	0	0	5	10	8	0	1	3	0	25.2	7.20	60	.400	.483	0	.000	-0	-2	-2	-0	-0.3
1930	NY-A	0	1	.000	2	2	0	0	0	12^1	13	11	0	1	13	2	19.7	8.03	54	.283	.450	2	.333	1	-5	-6	1	-0.1
Total	2	0	2	.000	6	3	0	0	0	17^1	23	19	0	2	16	2	21.3	7.79	55	.324	.461	2	.286	1	-6	-7	2	-0.4

● **JESSE BARNES** Barnes, Jesse Lawrence "Nubby" b: 8/26/1892, Perkins, Okla. d: 9/9/61, Santa Rosa, N.Mex. BL/TR, 6', 170 lbs. Deb: 7/30/15 F

YEAR	TM/L	W	L	PCT	G	GS	CG	SH	SV	IP	H	R	HR	HB	BB	SO	RAT	ERA	ERA+	OAV	OOB	BH	AVG	PB	PR	PR+	PD	TPI
1915	Bos-N	3	0	1.000	9	3	2	0	0	45^1	41	14	1	4	10	16	10.9	1.39	186	.244	.302	3	.176	0	7	6	-1	0.4
1916	Bos-N	6	15	.286	33	18	9	3	1	163	154	63	3	5	37	55	10.8	2.37	105	.254	.302	9	.188	0	4	2	4	0.7
1917	Bos-N	13	21	.382	50	33	26	2	1	295	261	115	3	3	50	107	9.6	2.68	95	.241	.277	24	.238	4	1	-5	3	0.3
1918	NY-N	6	1	.857	9	9	4	2	0	54^2	53	15	0	0	13	12	10.9	1.81	145	.255	.299	4	.222	-0	6	5	2	0.9
1919	NY-N	**25**	9	.735	38	34	23	4	1	295^2	263	98	8	2	35	92	9.1	2.40	117	.236	.260	32	.267	5	17	14	3	2.5
1920	NY-N	20	15	.571	43	34	23	2	0	292^2	271	108	9	2	56	63	10.1	2.64	113	.250	.288	22	.204	-2	16	12	3	1.4
1921	*NY-N	15	9	.625	42	31	15	1	6	258^2	298	108	13	3	44	56	12.0	3.10	118	.299	.331	19	.207	-1	20	17	1	1.5
1922	*NY-N	13	8	.619	37	29	14	2	0	212^2	236	108	10	3	38	52	11.7	3.51	114	.278	.311	14	.182	-1	14	12	3	1.2
1923	NY-N	3	1	.750	12	4	1	0	1	36	48	25	1	0	13	12	15.3	6.25	61	.329	.384	3	.273	0	-9	-10	1	-0.9
	Bos-N	10	14	.417	31	23	12	5	2	195^1	204	86	8	0	43	41	11.4	2.76	144	.270	.310	10	.147	-4	27	27	3	3.0
	Yr	13	15	.464	43	27	13	5	3	231^1	252	111	9	0	56	53	12.0	3.31	120	.280	.322	13	.165	-4	18	17	4	2.1
1924	Bos-N	15	20	.429	37	32	21	**4**	0	267^2	292	115	7	0	53	49	11.6	3.23	118	.284	.319	20	.222	-1	19	18	1	2.1
1925	Bos-N	11	16	.407	32	28	17	0	0	216^1	255	127	14	1	63	55	13.3	4.53	88	.297	.346	16	.198	-1	-6	-13	-2	-1.6
1926	Bro-N	10	11	.476	31	24	10	1	1	158	204	104	6	2	35	29	13.7	5.24	73	.321	.358	14	.237	-0	-25	-25	-1	-2.9
1927	Bro-N	2	10	.167	18	10	2	0	0	78^2	106	64	5	0	25	14	15.0	5.72	69	.331	.380	5	.217	-0	-16	-15	-0	-2.0
Total	13	152	150	.503	422	312	179	26	13	2569^2	2686	1150	88	25	515	653	11.3	3.22	104	.273	.310	195	.214	1	74	42	20	6.6

● **JUNIE BARNES** Barnes, Junie Shoaf "Lefty" b: 12/1/11, Linwood, N.C. d: 12/31/63, Jacksonville, N.C. BL/TL, 5'11.5", 170 lbs. Deb: 9/12/34

YEAR	TM/L	W	L	PCT	G	GS	CG	SH	SV	IP	H	R	HR	HB	BB	SO	RAT	ERA	ERA+	OAV	OOB	BH	AVG	PB	PR	PR+	PD	TPI
1934	Cin-N	0	0	—	2	0	0	0	0	0^1	0	0	0	0	1	0	27.0	0.00	—	.000	.500	0	—	0	0	0	0	0.0

● **RICH BARNES** Barnes, Richard Monroe b: 7/21/59, Palm Beach, Fla. BR/TL, 6'4", 186 lbs. Deb: 7/18/82

YEAR	TM/L	W	L	PCT	G	GS	CG	SH	SV	IP	H	R	HR	HB	BB	SO	RAT	ERA	ERA+	OAV	OOB	BH	AVG	PB	PR	PR+	PD	TPI
1982	Chi-A	0	2	.000	6	2	0	0	1	17	21	15	1	2	4	6	14.3	4.76	85	.292	.346	0	—	0	-1	-1	0	-0.1
1983	Cle-A	1	1	.500	4	2	0	0	0	11^2	18	10	0	0	10	2	21.6	6.94	61	.375	.483	0	—	0	-4	-3	-0	-0.5
Total	2	1	3	.250	10	4	0	0	1	28^2	39	25	1	2	14	8	17.3	5.65	73	.325	.404	0	—	0	-5	-5	0	-0.6

● **BOB BARNES** Barnes, Robert Avery "Lefty" b: 1/6/02, Washburn, Ill. d: 12/8/93, Peoria, Ill. BL/TL, 5'11.5", 150 lbs. Deb: 7/8/24

YEAR	TM/L	W	L	PCT	G	GS	CG	SH	SV	IP	H	R	HR	HB	BB	SO	RAT	ERA	ERA+	OAV	OOB	BH	AVG	PB	PR	PR+	PD	TPI
1924	Chi-A	0	0	—	2	0	0	0	0	4^2	14	11	1	0	0	1	27.0	19.29	21	.519	.519	0	.000	-0	-8	-8	0	-0.4

● **ROSS BARNES** Barnes, Roscoe Charles b: 5/8/1850, Mount Morris, N.Y. d: 2/5/15, Chicago, Ill. BR/TR, 5'8.5", 145 lbs. Deb: 5/5/1871 U◆

YEAR	TM/L	W	L	PCT	G	GS	CG	SH	SV	IP	H	R	HR	HB	BB	SO	RAT	ERA	ERA+	OAV	OOB	BH	AVG	PB	PR	PR+	PD	TPI
1876	Chi-N	0	0	—	1	0	0	0	0	1^1	7	8	0	0	0	0	47.3	20.25	12	.538	.538	138	.404	1	-3	-2	0	-0.1

● **VIRGIL BARNES** Barnes, Virgil Jennings "Zeke" b: 3/5/1897, Ontario, Kan. d: 7/24/58, Wichita, Kan. BR/TR, 6', 165 lbs. Deb: 9/25/19 F

YEAR	TM/L	W	L	PCT	G	GS	CG	SH	SV	IP	H	R	HR	HB	BB	SO	RAT	ERA	ERA+	OAV	OOB	BH	AVG	PB	PR	PR+	PD	TPI
1919	NY-N	0	0	—	1	0	0	0	0	2	6	4	0	0	1	1	31.5	18.00	16	.545	.583	0	—	0	-3	-4	-0	-0.2
1920	NY-N	0	1	.000	1	1	0	0	0	7	9	3	0	0	1	2	12.9	3.86	78	.310	.333	0	.000	-0	-1	-1	-0	-0.1
1922	NY-N	1	0	1.000	22	2	1	0	2	51^2	46	27	1	0	11	16	9.9	3.48	115	.243	.285	2	.167	-1	4	3	0	0.1
1923	*NY-N	2	3	.400	22	2	0	0	1	53	59	31	2	0	19	6	13.2	3.91	98	.285	.345	0	.000	-2	1	-1	0	-0.2
1924	*NY-N	16	10	.615	35	29	15	1	3	229^1	239	87	10	0	57	59	11.6	3.06	120	.270	.314	14	.182	-2	21	16	2	1.7
1925	NY-N	15	11	.577	32	27	17	1	2	221^2	242	110	9	1	53	53	12.0	3.53	114	.281	.323	9	.101	-9	18	13	0	0.5
1926	NY-N	8	13	.381	31	25	9	2	1	185	183	73	4	3	56	54	11.8	2.87	131	.261	.318	3	.054	-7	20	18	-1	1.1
1927	NY-N	14	11	.560	35	29	12	2	2	228^2	251	116	14	4	51	66	12.0	3.98	97	.283	.325	9	.108	-7	-1	-3	-1	-1.1
1928	NY-N	3	3	.500	10	9	3	1	0	55^1	71	32	3	0	18	11	14.5	5.04	78	.330	.382	2	.091	-2	-6	-7	-1	-0.9
	Bos-N	2	7	.222	16	10	1	0	0	60^1	86	42	3	3	26	7	16.7	5.82	67	.344	.406	1	.059	-2	-12	-13	-1	-1.8
	Yr	5	10	.333	26	19	4	1	0	115^2	157	74	6	0	44	18	15.6	5.45	72	.338	.395	3	.077	-3	-19	-20	-1	-2.7
Total	9	61	59	.508	205	134	58	7	11	1094	1192	525	46	8	293	275	12.3	3.66	105	.282	.329	40	.108	-31	38	23	1	-0.9

● **REX BARNEY** Barney, Rex Edward b: 12/19/24, Omaha, Neb. d: 8/12/97, Baltimore, Md. BR/TR, 6'3", 185 lbs. Deb: 8/18/43

YEAR	TM/L	W	L	PCT	G	GS	CG	SH	SV	IP	H	R	HR	HB	BB	SO	RAT	ERA	ERA+	OAV	OOB	BH	AVG	PB	PR	PR+	PD	TPI
1943	Bro-N	2	2	.500	9	8	1	0	0	45^1	36	32	4	2	41	23	15.7	6.35	53	.217	.378	1	.056	-2	-15	-15	-0	-1.4
1946	Bro-N	2	5	.286	16	9	1	0	0	53^2	46	42	2	0	51	36	16.3	5.87	58	.240	.399	4	.235	1	-15	-15	-0	-1.7
1947	*Bro-N	5	2	.714	28	9	0	0	0	77^2	66	52	4	2	59	36	14.7	4.75	87	.240	.378	3	.111	-1	-6	-5	-1	-0.6
1948	Bro-N	15	13	.536	44	34	12	4	0	246^2	193	101	17	6	122	138	11.7	3.10	129	.217	.315	14	.167	-2	23	24	-4	1.9
1949	*Bro-N	9	8	.529	38	20	6	2	1	140^2	108	75	15	3	89	80	12.8	4.41	93	.216	.338	10	.213	0	-6	-5	-3	-0.8
1950	Bro-N	2	1	.667	20	1	0	0	0	33^2	25	26	6	2	48	23	20.0	6.42	64	.214	.449	1	.125	0	-9	-9	-1	-0.7
Total	6	35	31	.530	155	81	20	6	1	597^2	474	328	48	15	410	336	13.5	4.31	91	.221	.350	33	.164	-4	-26	-24	-9	-3.3

● **EDGAR BARNHART** Barnhart, Edgar Vernon b: 9/16/04, Providence, Mo. d: 9/14/84, Columbia, Mo. BL/TR, 5'10", 160 lbs. Deb: 9/23/24

YEAR	TM/L	W	L	PCT	G	GS	CG	SH	SV	IP	H	R	HR	HB	BB	SO	RAT	ERA	ERA+	OAV	OOB	BH	AVG	PB	PR	PR+	PD	TPI
1924	StL-A	0	0	—	1	0	0	0	0	1	0	0	0	0	2	0	18.0	0.00	—	.000	.400	0	—	0	0	0	0	0.0

● **LES BARNHART** Barnhart, Leslie Earl "Barney" b: 2/23/05, Hoxie, Kan. d: 10/7/71, Scottsdale, Ariz. BR/TR, 6', 180 lbs. Deb: 9/22/28

YEAR	TM/L	W	L	PCT	G	GS	CG	SH	SV	IP	H	R	HR	HB	BB	SO	RAT	ERA	ERA+	OAV	OOB	BH	AVG	PB	PR	PR+	PD	TPI
1928	Cle-A	0	1	.000	2	1	1	0	0	9	13	7	1	0	4	1	17.0	7.00	59	.325	.386	1	.500	0	-3	-3	-1	-0.3
1930	Cle-A	1	0	1.000	1	1	0	0	0	8^1	12	7	0	0	4	1	17.3	6.48	74	.364	.432	0	.000	-1	-2	-1	0	-0.2
Total	2	1	1	.500	3	2	0	0	0	17^1	25	14	1	0	8	2	17.1	6.75	66	.342	.407	1	.200	-0	-5	-4	-0	-0.5

● **GEORGE BARNICLE** Barnicle, George Bernard "Barney" b: 8/26/17, Fitchburg, Mass. d: 10/10/90, Largo, Fla. BR/TR, 6'2", 175 lbs. Deb: 9/6/39

YEAR	TM/L	W	L	PCT	G	GS	CG	SH	SV	IP	H	R	HR	HB	BB	SO	RAT	ERA	ERA+	OAV	OOB	BH	AVG	PB	PR	PR+	PD	TPI
1939	Bos-N	2	2	.500	6	1	0	0	0	18^1	16	11	1	0	8	15	11.8	4.91	75	.235	.316	0	.000	-1	-2	-3	0	-0.5
1940	Bos-N	1	0	1.000	13	2	1	0	0	32^2	28	28	1	6	31	11	17.9	7.44	50	.233	.414	0	.000	-1	-13	-14	1	-0.8
1941	Bos-N	0	1	.000	1	1	0	0	0	6^2	5	5	0	1	4	2	13.5	6.75	53	.238	.385	0	.000	-0	-2	-2	0	-0.3
Total	3	3	3	.500	20	4	1	0	0	57^2	49	44	2	7	43	28	15.5	6.55	56	.234	.382	0	.000	-2	-17	-19	1	-1.6

● **ED BARNOWSKI** Barnowski, Edward Anthony b: 8/23/43, Scranton, Pa. BR/TR, 6'2", 195 lbs. Deb: 9/8/65

YEAR	TM/L	W	L	PCT	G	GS	CG	SH	SV	IP	H	R	HR	HB	BB	SO	RAT	ERA	ERA+	OAV	OOB	BH	AVG	PB	PR	PR+	PD	TPI
1965	Bal-A	0	0	—	4	0	0	0	0	4^1	3	1	0	0	7	6	20.8	2.08	167	.200	.455	0	—	0	1	1	-0	0.0
1966	Bal-A	0	0	—	2	0	0	0	0	3	4	1	0	0	1	2	15.0	3.00	111	.364	.417	0	—	0	0	0	0	0.0
Total	2	0	0	—	6	0	0	0	0	7^1	7	2	0	0	8	8	18.4	2.45	139	.269	.441	0	—	0	1	1	0	0.0

● **SALOME BAROJAS** Barojas, Salome (Romero) b: 6/16/57, Cordoba, Mex. BR/TR, 5'9", 188 lbs. Deb: 4/11/82

YEAR	TM/L	W	L	PCT	G	GS	CG	SH	SV	IP	H	R	HR	HB	BB	SO	RAT	ERA	ERA+	OAV	OOB	BH	AVG	PB	PR	PR+	PD	TPI
1982	Chi-A	6	6	.500	61	0	0	0	21	106^2	96	43	9	1	46	56	12.1	3.54	114	.244	.324	0	—	0	6	6	3	1.2
1983	*Chi-A	3	3	.500	52	0	0	0	12	87^1	70	24	2	5	32	38	11.0	2.47	170	.224	.306	0	—	0	16	16	0	1.5
1984	Chi-A	3	2	.600	24	0	0	0	1	39^1	48	24	3	0	19	18	15.3	4.58	91	.310	.385	0	—	0	-3	-2	1	-0.1
	Sea-A	6	5	.545	19	14	0	0	1	95^1	88	46	12	1	41	37	12.5	3.97	101	.249	.332	0	—	0	0	0	1	0.1
	Yr	9	7	.563	43	14	0	0	2	134^2	136	70	15	3	60	55	13.3	4.14	98	.268	.349	0	—	0	-2	-1	2	0.0

YEAR	TM/L	W	L	PCT	G	GS	CG	SH	SV	IP	H	R	HR	HB	BB	SO	RAT	ERA	ERA+	OAV	OOB	BH	AVG	PB	PR	PR+	PD	TPI
1985	Sea-A	0	5	.000	17	4	0	0	0	52^2	65	40	6	0	33	27	16.7	5.98	70	.305	.398	0	—	0	-11	-10	0	-0.8
1988	Phi-N	0	0	—	6	0	0	0	0	8^2	7	9	1	0	8	1	15.6	8.31	43	.250	.417	0	—	0	-5	-4	-0	-0.2
Total	5	18	21	.462	179	18	0	0	35	390	374	186	33	9	179	177	13.0	3.95	104	.257	.342	0	—	0	4	6	5	1.7
● **JIM BARR**	Barr, James Leland b: 2/10/48, Lynwood, Cal. BR/TR, 6'3", 205 lbs. Deb: 7/31/71																											
1971	*SF-N	1	1	.500	17	0	0	0	0	35^1	33	15	3	1	5	16	9.9	3.57	95	.254	.287	0	.000	-0	-0	-1	1	0.0
1972	SF-N	8	10	.444	44	18	8	2	2	179	166	66	16	3	41	86	10.6	2.87	122	.246	.292	9	.184	1	12	12	1	1.4
1973	SF-N	11	17	.393	41	33	8	3	2	231^1	240	105	24	5	49	88	11.4	3.81	100	.268	.310	10	.152	-1	-4	0	-1	-0.1
1974	SF-N	13	9	.591	44	27	11	5	2	239^2	223	81	17	2	47	84	10.2	2.74	139	.251	.290	18	.254	4	24	27	1	3.0
1975	SF-N	13	14	.481	35	33	12	2	0	244	244	94	17	3	58	77	11.3	3.06	124	.265	.310	9	.118	-3	15	19	3	2.1
1976	SF-N	15	12	.556	37	37	8	3	0	252^1	260	104	9	2	60	75	11.5	2.89	126	.266	.310	12	.162	2	17	20	3	2.7
1977	SF-N	12	16	.429	38	38	6	2	0	234^1	286	130	18	3	56	97	13.3	4.76	82	.306	.347	10	.132	-2	-22	-22	3	-2.3
1978	SF-N	8	11	.421	32	25	5	2	1	163	180	69	7	0	35	44	11.9	3.53	98	.281	.319	5	.100	-3	1	-2	1	-0.4
1979	Cal-A	10	12	.455	36	25	5	0	0	197	217	100	22	3	55	69	12.6	4.20	97	.287	.338	0	—	0	1	-3	2	-0.1
1980	Cal-A	1	4	.200	24	7	0	0	1	68	90	43	12	3	23	22	15.4	5.56	71	.323	.380	0	—	0	-11	-13	-1	-0.9
1982	SF-N	4	3	.571	53	9	1	1	2	128^2	125	54	9	4	20	36	10.4	3.29	110	.262	.297	8	.250	1	5	5	0	0.4
1983	SF-N	5	3	.625	53	0	0	0	2	92^2	106	47	7	1	20	47	12.3	3.98	89	.294	.332	2	.133	-0	-4	-5	0	-0.4
Total	12	101	112	.474	454	252	64	20	12	2065^1	2170	908	161	30	469	741	11.6	3.56	105	.273	.316	83	.162	-0	33	44	12	5.4
● **BOB BARR**	Barr, Robert Alexander b: 3/12/08, Newton, Mass. BR/TR, 6', 175 lbs. Deb: 9/11/35																											
1935	Bro-N	0	0	—	2	0	0	0	0	2^1	5	3	0	0	2	0	27.0	3.86	103	.385	.467	0	—	0	0	0	-0	0.0
● **BOB BARR**	Barr, Robert McClelland b: 12/1856, Washington, D.C. d: 3/11/30, Washington, D.C. BR/TR, 6'1", 192 lbs. Deb: 6/23/1883																											
1883	Pit-a	6	18	.250	26	23	19	0	**1**	203^1	263	166	5		28	81	12.9	4.38	74	.294	.316	35	.246	3	-24	-26	1	-2.0
1884	Was-a	9	23	.281	32	32	32	2	0	281	311	210	9	13	31	138	11.4	3.46	88	.258	.284	20	.148	-2	-7	-14	-1	-1.5
	Ind-a	3	11	.214	16	16	15	0	0	132	160	117	2	5	19	69	12.5	4.98	66	.275	.304	12	.185	0	-25	-24	-1	-2.1
	Yr	12	34	.261	48	48	47	2	0	413	471	327	11	18	50	207	11.7	3.94	79	.264	.291	32	.160	-2	-32	-40	-2	-3.6
1886	Was-N	3	18	.143	23	23	21	1	0	191^2	221	153	7		54	80	12.9	4.41	74	.280	.326	13	.165	-2	-23	-24	-1	-2.4
1890	Roc-a	28	24	.538	57	54	52	3	0	493^1	458	267	7	14	219	209	12.6	3.25	110	.239	.321	36	.179	-1	34	19	3	1.7
1891	NY-N	0	4	.000	5	4	2	0	0	27	47	25	1	3	12	11	20.7	5.33	60	.367	.434	1	.091	-0	-6	-7	0	-0.8
Total	5	49	98	.333	159	152	141	6	1	1328^1	1460	938	31	35	363	588	12.6	3.85	87	.265	.314	117	.185	-3	-52	-79	1	-7.1
● **STEVE BARR**	Barr, Steven Charles b: 9/8/51, St.Louis, Mo. BL/TL, 6'4", 200 lbs. Deb: 10/1/74																											
1974	Bos-A	1	0	1.000	1	1	1	0	0	9	7	4	0	0	6	3	13.0	4.00	96	.212	.333	0	—	0	-0	-0	0	0.0
1975	Bos-A	0	1	.000	3	2	0	0	0	7	11	9	1	0	7	2	23.1	2.57	159	.367	.486	0	—	0	1	1	-0	0.1
1976	Tex-A	2	6	.250	20	10	3	0	0	67^2	70	51	10	0	44	27	15.2	5.59	64	.269	.375	0	—	0	-16	-15	0	-1.6
Total	3	3	7	.300	24	13	4	0	0	83^2	88	64	11	0	57	32	15.6	5.16	71	.272	.382	0	—	0	-15	-14	0	-1.5
● **RED BARRETT**	Barrett, Charles Henry b: 2/14/15, Santa Barbara, Cal d: 7/28/90, Wilson, N.C. BR/TR, 5'11", 183 lbs. Deb: 9/15/37																											
1937	Cin-N	0	0	—	1	0	0	0	0	6^1	5	1	0	0	2	1	9.9	1.42	263	.227	.292	0	.000	-0	2	2	-0	0.0
1938	Cin-N	2	0	1.000	6	2	2	0	0	28^2	28	13	2	0	15	5	13.5	3.14	116	.257	.347	1	.143	-0	2	2	-0	0.0
1939	Cin-N	0	0	—	2	0	0	0	0	5^1	5	1	0	0	1	1	10.1	1.69	227	.263	.300	0	.000	-0	1	1	0	0.0
1940	Cin-N	1	0	1.000	3	0	0	0	0	2^2	5	2	0	0	1	0	20.3	6.75	56	.455	.500	0	—	0	-1	-1	0	-0.1
1943	Bos-N	12	18	.400	38	31	14	3	0	255	240	107	11	2	63	64	10.8	3.18	107	.250	.298	11	.136	-4	6	7	1	0.4
1944	Bos-N	9	16	.360	42	30	11	1	2	230^1	257	124	13	2	63	54	12.6	4.06	94	.279	.327	13	.173	-1	-12	-6	2	-0.5
1945	Bos-N	2	3	.400	9	5	2	0	2	38	43	22	6	1	16	13	14.2	4.74	81	.281	.353	2	.222	-0	-4	-4	1	-0.4
	StL-N†	21	9	.700	36	29	22	3	0	246^2	244	84	12	1	38	63	10.3	2.74	137	.256	.285	10	.112	-5	29	28	-1	2.5
	Yr	**23**	12	.657	45	34	**24**	3	2	**284^2**	287	106	18	2	54	76	10.8	3.00	125	.259	.295	12	.122	-5	25	24	0	2.1
1946	StL-N	3	2	.600	23	9	1	1	2	67	75	35	5	2	24	22	13.6	4.03	86	.282	.346	1	.059	-1	-5	-4	1	-0.4
1947	Bos-N	11	12	.478	36	30	12	3	1	210^2	200	102	16	2	53	53	10.9	3.55	110	.244	.292	8	.111	-2	12	8	-0	0.6
1948	*Bos-N	7	8	.467	34	13	3	0	0	128^1	132	56	9	0	26	40	11.1	3.65	105	.268	.305	7	.179	-1	4	3	1	0.3
1949	Bos-N	1	1	.500	23	0	0	0	0	44^1	58	32	4	2	10	17	14.2	5.68	66	.326	.368	1	.200	-0	-8	-10	1	-0.4
Total	11	69	69	.500	253	149	67	11	7	1263^1	1292	579	78	12	312	333	11.5	3.53	105	.264	.309	54	.136	-16	28	26	5	2.0
● **FRANK BARRETT**	Barrett, Francis Joseph "Red" b: 7/1/13, Ft.Lauderdale, Fla d: 3/6/98, Leesburg, Fla. BR/TR, 6'2", 173 lbs. Deb: 10/1/39																											
1939	StL-N	0	1	.000	1	0	0	0	0	1^2	1	1	0	0	1	3	10.8	5.40	76	.167	.286	0	—	0	-0	-0	0	0.0
1944	Bos-A	8	7	.533	38	2	0	0	8	90^1	93	45	5	1	42	40	13.5	3.69	92	.271	.352	4	.143	-1	-3	-3	-0	-0.6
1945	Bos-A	4	3	.571	37	0	0	0	3	86	77	30	0	0	29	35	11.1	2.62	130	.249	.314	5	.250	1	7	7	-1	0.7
1946	Bos-N	2	4	.333	23	0	0	0	1	35^1	35	21	2	1	17	12	13.5	5.09	67	.252	.338	0	.000	-1	-7	-7	1	-1.0
1950	Pit-N	1	2	.333	5	0	0	0	0	4^1	5	3	1	0	1	0	12.5	4.15	106	.357	.400	0	—	0	-0	0	0	0.1
Total	5	15	17	.469	104	2	0	0	12	217^2	211	100	8	2	90	90	12.5	3.51	98	.260	.336	9	.167	-1	-2	-2	1	-0.8
● **TIM BARRETT**	Barrett, Timothy Wayne b: 1/24/61, Huntingburg, Ind. BL/TR, 6'1", 185 lbs. Deb: 7/18/88																											
1988	Mon-N	0	0	—	4	0	0	0	1	9^1	10	6	2	0	2	5	11.6	5.79	62	.270	.308	0	.000	-0	-2	-2	0	-0.1
● **DICK BARRETT**	Barrett, Tracy Souter "Kewpie Dick" (a.k.a. Richard Oliver 1933 And Richard Oliver Barrett 1934-43) b: 9/28/06, Montoursville, Pa d: 10/30/66, Seattle, Wash. BR/TR, 5'9", 175 lbs. Deb: 6/27/33																											
1933	Phi-A	4	4	.500	15	7	3	0	0	70^1	74	51	2	1	49	26	15.9	5.76	74	.272	.385	6	.286	2	-12	-11	0	-0.9
1934	Bos-N	1	3	.250	15	3	0	0	0	32^1	50	27	2	0	12	14	17.3	6.68	57	.365	.416	1	.143	-0	-9	-11	1	-1.1
1943	Chi-N	0	4	.000	15	4	0	0	0	45	52	28	2	1	28	20	16.2	4.80	70	.291	.389	1	.111	-1	-7	-7	-0	-0.7
	Phi-N	10	9	.526	23	20	10	2	1	169^1	137	53	5	2	51	65	10.1	2.39	141	.221	.282	7	.143	-0	19	19	0	2.2
	Yr	10	13	.435	38	24	10	2	1	214^1	189	81	7	3	79	85	11.4	2.90	116	.237	.308	8	.138	-1	12	11	0	1.5
1944	Phi-N	12	18	.400	37	28	11	1	0	221^1	223	110	7	3	88	74	12.8	3.86	94	.262	.333	16	.216	2	-6	-6	2	-0.3
1945	Phi-N	8	20	.286	36	30	8	0	1	190^2	217	129	11	7	92	72	14.9	5.38	71	.281	.363	9	.145	-1	-33	-33	1	-4.1
Total	5	35	58	.376	141	92	32	3	2	729	753	398	29	14	320	271	13.4	4.28	86	.266	.343	40	.180	1	-49	-50	4	-4.9
● **BILL BARRETT**	Barrett, William Joseph "Whispering Bill" b: 5/28/1900, Cambridge, Mass. d: 1/26/51, Cambridge, Mass. BR/TR, 6', 175 lbs. Deb: 5/13/21 ♦																											
1921	Phi-A	1	0	1.000	4	0	0	0	0	5	2	4	0	0	9	2	19.8	7.20	62	.133	.458	7	.233	0	-2	-1	0	-0.2
● **FRANCISCO BARRIOS**	Barrios, Francisco Javier (Jimenez) b: 6/10/53, Hermosillo, Mex. d: 4/9/82, Hermosillo, Mexico BR/TR, 6'3", 195 lbs. Deb: 8/18/74																											
1974	Chi-A	0	0	—	2	0	0	0	0	2	7	6	0	0	2	2	40.5	27.00	14	.538	.600	0	—	0	-5	-5	-0	-0.2
1976	Chi-A	5	9	.357	35	14	6	0	3	141^2	136	72	13	4	46	81	11.8	4.32	83	.255	.318	0	—	0	-13	-12	-1	-1.2
1977	Chi-A	14	7	.667	33	31	9	0	0	231^1	241	117	22	5	58	119	11.8	4.12	99	.267	.315	0	—	0	-1	-1	-1	-0.1
1978	Chi-A	9	15	.375	33	32	9	2	0	195^2	180	93	13	7	85	79	12.5	4.05	94	.246	.330	0	—	0	-6	-5	2	-0.3
1979	Chi-A	8	3	.727	15	15	2	0	0	94^2	88	49	9	5	33	28	12.0	3.61	118	.242	.314	0	—	0	6	7	-1	0.6
1980	Chi-A	1	1	.500	3	3	0	0	0	16^1	21	9	4	1	8	2	16.5	4.96	81	.323	.405	0	—	0	-2	-2	-0	-0.2
1981	Chi-A	1	3	.250	8	7	1	0	0	36^1	45	23	3	1	14	12	14.9	3.96	90	.292	.355	0	—	0	-1	-2	-0	-0.2
Total	7	38	38	.500	129	102	27	2	3	718	718	369	64	23	246	323	12.4	4.15	94	.260	.326	0	—	0	-21	-19	-1	-1.6
● **MANUEL BARRIOS**	Barrios, Manuel Antonio b: 9/21/74, Cabecera, Panama BR/TR, 6', 170 lbs. Deb: 9/16/97																											
1997	Hou-N	0	0	—	2	0	0	0	0	3	6	4	0	0	3	3	27.0	12.00	33	.400	.500	0	—	0	-3	-3	-0	-0.1
1998	Fla-N	0	0	—	2	0	0	0	0	2^2	4	1	1	0	2	1	20.3	3.38	120	.364	.462	0	—	0	0	0	-0	0.0
	LA-N	0	0	—	1	0	0	0	0	1	0	0	0	0	2	0	18.0	0.00	—	.000	.500	0	—	0	0	0	-0	0.0
	Yr	0	0	—	3	0	0	0	0	3^2	4	1	1	0	4	1	19.6	2.45	164	.308	.471	0	—	0	1	1	-0	0.0
Total	2	0	0	—	5	0	0	0	0	6^2	10	5	1	0	7	4	23.0	6.75	60	.357	.486	0	—	0	-2	-2	-0	-0.1
● **FRANK BARRON**	Barron, Frank John b: 8/6/1890, St.Marys, W.Va. d: 9/18/64, St.Marys, W.Va. BL/TL, 6'1", 175 lbs. Deb: 8/19/14																											
1914	Was-A	0	0	—	1	0	0	0	0	1	1	0	0	0	0	1	9.0	0.00	—	.333	.333	0	—	0	0	0	0	0.0
● **ED BARRY**	Barry, Edward "Jumbo" b: 10/2/1882, Madison, Wis. d: 6/19/20, Montague, Mass. TL, 6'3", 185 lbs. Deb: 8/21/05																											
1905	Bos-A	1	2	.333	7	5	2	0	0	40^2	38	19	2	4	15	18	12.6	2.88	94	.248	.331	1	.091	-0	-1	-1	-2	-0.3

YEAR	TM/L	W	L	PCT	G	GS	CG	SH	SV	IP	H	R	HR	HB	BB	SO	RAT	ERA	ERA+	OAV	OOB	BH	AVG	PB	PR	PR+	PD	TPI
1906	Bos-A	0	3	.000	3	3	3	0	0	21	23	22	2	3	5	10	13.3	6.00	46	.280	.344	1	.111	-0	-8	-7	0	-0.9
1907	Bos-A	0	1	.000	2	2	1	0	0	17^{1}	13	6	1	1	5	6	9.9	2.08	124	.210	.279	0	.000	-0	1	1	-0	0.0
Total	3	1	6	.143	12	10	6	0	0	79	74	47	5	8	25	34	12.2	3.53	76	.249	.324	2	.087	-1	-8	-7	-2	-1.2
● HARDIN BARRY Barry, Hardin "Finn" b: 3/26/1891, Susanville, Cal. d: 11/5/69, Carson City, Nev. BR/TR, 6′, 185 lbs. Deb: 6/21/12																												
1912	Phi-A	0	0	—	3	0	0	0	0	13	18	11	0	1	4	3	15.9	7.62	40	.360	.418	0	.000	-0	-6	-7	-0	-0.4
● TOM BARRY Barry, Thomas Arthur b: 4/10/1879, St.Louis, Mo. d: 6/4/46, St.Louis, Mo. TR, 5′9″, 155 lbs. Deb: 4/15/04																												
1904	Phi-N	0	1	.000	1	1	0	0	0	0^{2}	6	5	0	0	1	1	94.5	40.50	7	.667	.700	0	—	0	-3	-3	0	-0.5
● BOB BARTHELSON Barthelson, Robert Edward b: 7/15/24, New Haven, Conn. d: 4/14/2000, Branford, Conn. BR/TR, 6′, 185 lbs. Deb: 7/4/44																												
1944	NY-N	1	1	.500	7	1	0	0	0	9^{2}	13	9	2	0	5	4	16.8	4.66	79	.310	.383	0	—	0	-1	-1	-0	-0.2
● JOHN BARTHOLD Barthold, John Francis "Hans" b: 4/14/1882, Philadelphia, Pa. d: 11/4/46, Fairview Village, Pa. BB/TR, 5′11″, 180 lbs. Deb: 5/17/04																												
1904	Phi-A	0	0	—	4	0	0	0	0	10^{2}	12	9	0	1	8	5	17.7	5.06	53	.286	.412	1	.333	1	-3	-3	0	0.0
● LES BARTHOLOMEW Bartholomew, Lester Justin b: 4/4/03, Madison, Wis. d: 9/19/72, Barrington, Ill. BR/TL, 5′11.5″, 195 lbs. Deb: 4/11/28																												
1928	Pit-N	0	0	—	6	0	0	0	0	22^{2}	31	18	2	0	9	6	15.9	7.15	57	.356	.417	1	.143	-0	-8	-8	-0	-0.4
1932	Chi-A	0	0	—	3	0	0	0	0	5^{1}	5	3	0	0	6	1	18.6	5.06	85	.250	.423	0	.000	-0	-0	-0	0	0.0
Total	2	0	0	—	9	0	0	0	0	28	36	21	2	0	15	7	16.4	6.75	61	.336	.418	1	.125	-0	-8	-8	-0	-0.4
● BILL BARTLEY Bartley, William Jackson b: 1/8/1885, Cincinnati, Ohio d: 5/17/65, Cincinnati, Ohio BR/TR, 5′11.5″, 190 lbs. Deb: 9/15/03																												
1903	NY-N	0	0	—	1	0	0	0	0	3	3	4	0	0	4	2	21.0	0.00	—	.273	.467	0	.000	-0	1	1	0	0.0
1906	Phi-A	0	0	—	3	0	0	0	1	8^{2}	10	9	0	0	6	6	16.6	9.35	29	.294	.400	1	.333	1	-6	-6	1	-0.2
1907	Phi-A	0	1	.000	15	3	2	0	0	56^{1}	44	22	0	0	19	16	10.1	2.24	116	.218	.285	2	.095	-2	2	2	-0	-0.1
Total	3	0	1	.000	19	3	2	0	1	68	57	35	0	0	29	24	11.4	3.04	87	.231	.312	3	.120	-1	-3	-3	0	-0.3
● SHAWN BARTON Barton, Shawn Edward b: 5/14/63, Los Angeles, Cal. BR/TL, 6′3″, 195 lbs. Deb: 8/6/92																												
1992	Sea-A	0	1	.000	14	0	0	0	0	12^{1}	10	5	1	0	7	4	12.4	2.92	136	.238	.347	0	—	0	1	1	0	0.1
1995	SF-N	4	1	.800	52	0	0	0	1	44^{1}	37	22	3	2	19	22	11.8	4.26	96	.237	.328	0	—	0	-0	-1	1	0.0
1996	SF-N	0	0	—	7	0	0	0	0	8^{1}	19	12	2	0	1	3	21.6	9.72	42	.442	.455	0	—	0	-5	-5	0	-0.2
Total	3	4	2	.667	73	0	0	0	1	65	66	39	6	2	27	29	13.2	4.71	86	.274	.352	0	—	0	-4	-5	1	-0.1
● CHARLIE BARTSON Bartson, Charles Franklin b: 3/13/1865, Peoria, Ill. d: 6/9/36, Peoria, Ill. 6′, 170 lbs. Deb: 5/14/1890																												
1890	Chi-P	9	10	.474	26	20	17	0	1	197	226	145	8	13	66	52	13.9	4.11	106	.276	.339	13	.167	-3	3	5	5	0.6
● JIM BASKETTE Baskette, James Blaine "Big Jim" b: 12/10/1887, Athens, Tenn. d: 7/30/42, Athens, Tenn. BR/TR, 6′2″, 185 lbs. Deb: 9/22/11																												
1911	Cle-A	1	2	.333	4	2	2	0	0	21^{1}	21	8	0	1	9	8	13.1	3.38	101	.273	.356	2	.333	1	-0	0	-0	0.0
1912	Cle-A	8	4	.667	29	11	7	1	1	116	109	50	2	7	46	51	12.6	3.18	107	.252	.334	5	.125	-1	2	3	-3	-0.1
1913	Cle-A	0	0	—	2	1	0	0	0	4^{2}	8	3	1	0	2	0	19.3	5.79	52	.400	.455	1	1.000	1	-1	-1	0	0.1
Total	3	9	6	.600	35	14	9	1	1	142	138	61	3	8	57	59	12.9	3.30	103	.261	.342	8	.170	1	0	2	-3	0.0
● NORM BASS Bass, Norman Delaney b: 1/21/39, Laurel, Miss. BR/TR, 6′3″, 205 lbs. Deb: 4/23/61																												
1961	KC-A	11	11	.500	40	23	6	2	0	170^{2}	164	98	17	4	82	74	13.2	4.69	89	.255	.343	7	.119	-2	-13	-9	-3	-1.5
1962	KC-A	2	6	.250	22	10	0	0	0	75^{1}	96	55	7	0	46	33	17.0	6.09	69	.317	.407	1	.045	-2	-18	-15	1	-1.4
1963	KC-A	0	0	—	3	1	0	0	0	7^{2}	11	11	2	0	9	4	23.5	11.74	33	.333	.476	0	.000	-0	-7	-6	-0	-0.3
Total	3	13	17	.433	65	34	6	2	0	253^{2}	271	164	26	4	137	111	14.6	5.32	79	.277	.368	8	.098	-4	-37	-31	-2	-3.2
● DICK BASS Bass, Richard William b: 7/7/06, Rogersville, Tenn. d: 2/3/89, Graceville, Fla. BR/TR, 6′2″, 175 lbs. Deb: 9/21/39																												
1939	Was-A	0	1	.000	1	1	0	0	0	8	7	6	0	1	6	1	15.8	6.75	64	.241	.389	0	.000	-0	-2	-2	-0	-0.2
● CHARLIE BASTIAN Bastian, Charles J. b: 7/4/1860, Philadelphia, Pa. d: 1/18/32, Pennsauken, N.J. BR/TR, 5′6.5″, 145 lbs. Deb: 8/18/1884 ♦																												
1884	Wil-U	0	0	—	1	0	0	0	0	6	6	5	0	1	0	2	9.0	3.00	89	.240	.240	12	.200	-0	-0	-0	-0	0.0
● JOE BATCHELDER Batchelder, Joseph Edmund "Win" b: 7/11/1898, Wenham, Mass. d: 5/5/89, Beverly, Mass. BR/TL, 5′7″, 165 lbs. Deb: 9/29/23																												
1923	Bos-N	1	0	1.000	4	1	1	0	0	9	12	7	2	1	1	2	14.0	7.00	57	.353	.389	0	.000	0	-3	-3	-0	-0.3
1924	Bos-N	0	0	—	3	0	0	0	0	4^{2}	4	2	0	0	2	2	11.6	3.86	99	.235	.316	0	.000	-0	0	-0	0	0.0
1925	Bos-N	0	0	—	4	0	0	0	0	7	10	5	0	0	1	2	14.1	5.14	78	.357	.379	0	.000	-0	-1	-1	0	0.0
Total	3	1	0	1.000	11	1	1	0	0	20^{2}	26	14	2	1	4	6	13.5	5.66	70	.329	.369	0	.000	-0	-4	-4	0	-0.3
● RICH BATCHELOR Batchelor, Richard Anthony b: 4/8/67, Florence, S.C. BR/TR, 6′1″, 195 lbs. Deb: 9/3/93																												
1993	StL-N	0	0	—	9	0	0	0	0	10	14	12	1	0	3	4	15.3	8.10	49	.359	.405	0	.000	-0	-5	-5	-0	-0.2
1996	StL-N	2	0	1.000	11	0	0	0	0	15	9	2	0	0	1	11	6.0	1.20	349	.173	.189	0	.000	-0	5	5	-0	0.6
1997	StL-N	1	1	.500	10	0	0	0	0	16	21	12	0	2	7	8	16.9	4.50	92	.323	.405	0	—	0	-1	-1	-1	-0.1
	SD-N	2	0	1.000	13	0	0	0	0	12^{2}	19	11	2	1	7	10	19.2	7.82	50	.358	.443	0	—	0	-5	-6	0	-0.8
	Yr	3	1	.750	23	0	0	0	0	28^{2}	40	23	2	3	14	18	17.9	5.97	68	.339	.422	0	—	0	-6	-6	-1	-0.9
Total	3	5	1	.833	43	0	0	0	0	53^{2}	63	37	3	3	18	33	14.1	5.03	81	.301	.365	0	.000	-0	-5	-6	-1	-0.5
● DICK BATES Bates, Charles Richard b: 10/7/45, McArthur, Ohio BL/TR, 6′, 190 lbs. Deb: 4/27/69																												
1969	Sea-A	0	0	—	1	0	0	0	0	1^{2}	3	5	1	0	3	3	32.4	27.00	13	.375	.545	0	—	0	-4	-4	0	-0.2
● FRANK BATES Bates, Creed Frank b: Chattanooga, Tenn. Deb: 10/7/1898																												
1898	Cle-N	2	1	.667	4	4	4	0	0	29	30	15	0	1	11	5	13.0	3.10	117	.265	.336	1	.111	0	2	2	-0	0.1
1899	StL-N	0	0	—	2	0	0	0	0	8^{2}	7	2	0	0	5	0	12.5	1.04	383	.219	.324	1	.333	1	3	3	-0	0.2
	Cle-N	1	18	.053	20	19	17	0	0	153	239	181	6	23	105	13	21.6	7.24	51	.355	.458	14	.215	1	-58	-63	0	-5.5
	Yr	1	18	.053	22	19	17	0	0	161^{2}	246	183	6	23	110	13	21.1	6.90	54	.348	.452	15	.221	2	-55	-60	-0	-5.3
Total	2	3	19	.136	26	23	21	0	0	190^{2}	276	198	6	24	121	18	19.9	6.33	58	.337	.437	16	.208	2	-53	-58	-0	-5.2
● JOHN BATES Bates, John William b: 5/28/1868, Ohio d: 3/24/19, Oakland, Cal. Deb: 8/25/1889																												
1889	KC-a	0	1	.000	1	1	1	0	0	8	15	14	0	0	5	3	22.5	13.50	31	.385	.455	0	.000	-1	-9	-8	-0	-0.6
● MIGUEL BATISTA Batista, Miguel Jerez (Decartes) b: 2/19/71, Santo Domingo, D.R. BR/TR, 6′, 160 lbs. Deb: 4/11/92																												
1992	Pit-N	0	0	—	1	0	0	0	0	2	4	2	1	0	3	1	31.5	9.00	38	.400	.538	0	—	0	-1	-1	-0	-0.1
1996	Fla-N	0	0	—	9	0	0	0	0	11^{1}	9	8	0	0	7	6	12.7	5.56	73	.231	.348	0	—	0	-2	-2	-0	-0.1
1997	Chi-N	0	5	.000	11	6	0	0	0	36^{1}	36	24	4	1	24	27	15.1	5.70	76	.267	.381	0	.000	-1	-6	-5	0	-0.7
1998	Mon-N	3	5	.375	56	13	0	0	0	135	141	66	12	6	65	92	14.1	3.80	111	.274	.362	0	.000	-4	7	6	1	0.0
1999	Mon-N	8	7	.533	39	17	2	1	1	134^{2}	146	88	10	7	58	95	14.1	4.88	92	.280	.359	7	.200	2	-5	-6	0	-0.4
2000	Mon-N	0	1	.000	4	0	0	0	0	8^{1}	19	14	2	2	3	7	25.9	14.04	34	.452	.511	0	.000	0	-9	-8	-0	-0.8
	KC-A	2	6	.250	14	9	0	0	0	57	66	54	17	0	34	30	15.8	7.74	65	.292	.385	0	.000	-0	-18	-17	-1	-1.9
Total	6	13	24	.351	134	45	2	1	1	384^{2}	421	256	46	16	194	258	14.8	5.24	85	.283	.371	7	.089	-3	-34	-35	-1	-4.0
● JOE BATTIN Battin, Joseph V. b: 11/11/1851, Philadelphia, Pa. d: 12/10/37, Akron, Ohio BR/TR, Deb: 8/11/1871 MU♦																												
1877	StL-N	0	0	—	1	0	0	0	0	3^{2}	3	2	0		1	1	9.8	4.91	53	.200	.250	45	.199	0	-1	-1	-0	-0.1
1883	Pit-a	0	0	—	2	0	0	0	0	4	9	4	0		1	0	22.5	2.25	145	.429	.455	83	.214	-0	0	0	-0	0.0
Total	2	0	0	—	3	0	0	0	0	7^{2}	12	6	0		2	1	16.4	3.52	83	.333	.368	313	.217	-0	-0	-1	-0	-0.1
● CHRIS BATTON Batton, Christopher Sean b: 8/24/54, Los Angeles, Cal. BR/TR, 6′4″, 195 lbs. Deb: 9/19/76																												
1976	Oak-A	0	0	—	2	1	0	0	0	4	5	4	1	0	3	4	18.0	9.00	37	.313	.421	0	—	0	-2	-3	-0	-0.1
● LOU BAUER Bauer, Louis Walter b: 11/30/1898, Egg Harbor City, N.J. d: 2/4/79, Pomona, N.J. BR/TR, 6′, 175 lbs. Deb: 8/13/18																												
1918	Phi-A	0	0	—	1	0	0	0	0	0	0	0	0	2	—	—	∞	—	—	1.000	106	—	0	-1	-1	0	-0.1	
● BAUERS Bauers TL, Deb: 9/22/1884																												
1884	Col-a	1	2	.333	3	3	3	0	0	25	22	21	1	0	14	13	13.0	4.68	65	.224	.321	3	.273	0	-4	-5	0	-0.4

YEAR	TM/L	W	L	PCT	G	GS	CG	SH	SV	IP	H	R	HR	HB	BB	SO	RAT	ERA	ERA+	OAV	OOB	BH	AVG	PB	PR	PR+	PD	TPI
1886	StL-N	0	4	.000	4	4	3	0	0	28^2	31	27	1		27	13	18.2	5.97	54	.267	.406	2	.167	-1	-8	-9	-1	-1.0
Total	2	1	6	.143	7	7	6	0	0	53^2	53	48	2		41	26	15.8	5.37	58	.248	.369	5	.217	-0	-12	-14	-1	-1.4

● RUSS BAUERS Bauers, Russell Lee b: 5/10/14, Townsend, Wis. d: 1/1/95, Hines, Ill. BL/TR, 6'3", 195 lbs. Deb: 8/20/36

YEAR	TM/L	W	L	PCT	G	GS	CG	SH	SV	IP	H	R	HR	HB	BB	SO	RAT	ERA	ERA+	OAV	OOB	BH	AVG	PB	PR	PR+	PD	TPI
1936	Pit-N	0	0	—	1	1	0	0	0	1^1	2	5	0	1	4	0	47.3	33.75	12	.500	.778	0	—	0	-4	-4	-0	-0.2
1937	Pit-N	13	6	.684	34	19	11	2	1	187^2	174	70	2	4	80	118	12.4	2.88	134	.245	.325	15	.217	1	22	21	3	2.4
1938	Pit-N	13	14	.481	40	34	12	2	3	243	207	102	7	6	99	117	11.6	3.07	124	.233	.314	21	.239	4	19	19	-3	2.1
1939	Pit-N	2	4	.333	15	8	1	0	1	53^2	46	27	4	1	25	12	12.1	3.35	114	.240	.330	4	.211	-0	3	3	-1	0.2
1940	Pit-N	0	2	.000	15	2	0	0	0	30^2	42	29	2	2	18	11	18.2	7.63	50	.323	.413	2	.286	0	-13	-13	0	-0.7
1941	Pit-N	1	3	.250	8	5	1	0	0	37^1	40	28	1	0	25	20	15.7	5.54	65	.267	.371	5	.357	1	-8	-8	-1	-0.8
1946	Chi-N	2	1	.667	15	2	2	0	1	43^1	45	17	1	1	19	22	13.5	3.53	94	.273	.351	3	.300	1	-1	-1	-0	0.1
1950	StL-A	0	0	—	1	0	0	0	0	2	6	4	0	0	1	0	31.5	4.50	110	.600	.636	0	—	0	0	0	0	0.0
Total	8	31	30	.508	129	71	27	4	6	599	562	282	17	15	271	300	12.7	3.53	107	.250	.334	50	.242	7	19	17	-2	3.1

● FRANK BAUMANN Baumann, Frank Matt "The Beau" b: 7/1/33, St.Louis, Mo. BL/TL, 6'1", 210 lbs. Deb: 7/31/55

YEAR	TM/L	W	L	PCT	G	GS	CG	SH	SV	IP	H	R	HR	HB	BB	SO	RAT	ERA	ERA+	OAV	OOB	BH	AVG	PB	PR	PR+	PD	TPI
1955	Bos-A	2	1	.667	7	5	0	0	0	34	38	28	2	1	17	27	14.8	5.82	74	.281	.366	3	.231	-0	-7	-5	0	-0.4
1956	Bos-A	2	1	.667	7	1	0	0	0	24^2	22	11	3	0	14	18	13.1	3.28	141	.234	.333	3	.333	1	2	3	-1	0.4
1957	Bos-A	1	0	1.000	4	1	0	0	0	12	13	5	1	1	3	7	12.8	3.75	106	.277	.333	1	.500	0	0	0	-0	0.0
1958	Bos-A	2	2	.500	10	7	2	0	0	52^1	56	27	4	4	27	31	15.0	4.47	90	.276	.372	3	.214	1	-4	-3	-1	-0.1
1959	Bos-A	6	4	.600	26	10	2	0	1	95^2	96	47	11	1	55	48	14.3	4.05	100	.259	.357	6	.207	1	-2	0	1	0.1
1960	Chi-A	13	6	.684	47	20	7	2	3	185^1	169	67	11	1	53	71	10.8	**2.67**	142	.247	.302	8	.154	1	25	23	-2	2.2
1961	Chi-A	10	13	.435	53	23	5	1	3	187^2	249	128	22	2	59	75	14.9	5.61	70	.318	.368	16	.262	6	-33	-36	1	-3.3
1962	Chi-A	7	6	.538	40	10	3	1	4	119^2	117	46	10	2	36	55	11.7	3.38	115	.258	.316	8	.267	4	8	7	0	1.2
1963	Chi-A	2	1	.667	24	1	0	0	1	50^1	52	22	2	0	17	31	12.3	3.04	115	.265	.324	1	.091	-0	3	3	0	0.1
1964	Chi-A	0	3	.000	22	0	0	0	1	32	40	22	4	0	16	19	15.8	6.19	56	.320	.397	0	.000	-0	-9	-10	-0	-1.0
1965	Chi-N	0	1	.000	4	0	0	0	0	3^2	4	3	0	0	3	2	17.2	7.36	50	.286	.412	0	—	0	-2	-1	0	-0.3
Total	11	45	38	.542	244	78	19	4	13	797^1	856	406	70	12	300	384	13.2	4.11	95	.276	.342	49	.218	14	-19	-19	-2	-1.1

● GEORGE BAUMGARDNER Baumgardner, George Washington b: 7/22/1891, Barboursville, W.Va. d: 12/13/70, Barboursville, W.Va. BL/TR, 5'11", 178 lbs. Deb: 4/14/12

YEAR	TM/L	W	L	PCT	G	GS	CG	SH	SV	IP	H	R	HR	HB	BB	SO	RAT	ERA	ERA+	OAV	OOB	BH	AVG	PB	PR	PR+	PD	TPI
1912	StL-A	11	13	.458	30	27	18	2	0	218^1	222	101	1	11	79	102	12.9	3.38	98	.274	.346	11	.145	-0	-2	-2	-0	-0.1
1913	StL-A	10	20	.333	38	31	23	2	1	253^1	267	119	6	10	84	78	12.8	3.13	94	.283	.348	13	.167	2	-5	-6	-2	-0.5
1914	StL-A	16	14	.533	45	18	9	3	1	183^2	152	72	3	8	84	93	12.0	2.79	97	.229	.323	7	.132	-1	-1	-2	-1	-0.6
1915	StL-A	0	2	.000	7	1	1	0	0	22^1	29	15	0	0	11	6	16.1	4.43	65	.358	.435	0	.000	-1	-4	-4	1	-0.4
1916	StL-A	1	0	1.000	4	2	0	0	0	8	12	8	0	0	5	4	19.1	7.88	35	.364	.447	0	.000	0	-4	-5	-1	-0.6
Total	5	38	49	.437	124	79	51	7	2	685^2	682	315	10	29	263	283	12.8	3.22	93	.269	.345	31	.144	-0	-16	-17	-2	-2.2

● ROSS BAUMGARTEN Baumgarten, Ross b: 5/27/55, Highland Park, Ill. BL/TL, 6'1", 180 lbs. Deb: 8/16/78

YEAR	TM/L	W	L	PCT	G	GS	CG	SH	SV	IP	H	R	HR	HB	BB	SO	RAT	ERA	ERA+	OAV	OOB	BH	AVG	PB	PR	PR+	PD	TPI
1978	Chi-A	2	2	.500	7	4	1	1	0	23	29	15	3	1	9	15	15.3	5.87	65	.315	.382	0	—	0	-5	-5	-0	-0.8
1979	Chi-A	13	8	.619	28	28	4	3	0	190^2	175	82	18	1	83	72	12.2	3.54	120	.243	.322	0	—	0	15	15	-0	1.5
1980	Chi-A	2	12	.143	24	23	3	1	0	136	127	60	10	1	52	66	11.9	3.44	117	.256	.327	0	—	0	9	9	2	1.1
1981	Chi-A	5	9	.357	19	19	2	1	0	101^2	101	56	9	1	40	52	12.6	4.07	88	.260	.331	0	—	0	-5	-6	0	-0.7
1982	Pit-N	0	5	.000	12	10	0	0	0	44	60	33	3	0	27	17	17.8	6.55	57	.347	.435	1	.083	-1	-14	-13	0	-1.4
Total	5	22	36	.379	90	84	10	6	0	495^1	492	246	43	4	211	222	12.8	4.00	100	.263	.339	1	.083	-1	-1	-0	2	-0.3

● HARRY BAUMGARTNER Baumgartner, Harry E. b: 10/8/1892, S.Pittsburg, Tenn. d: 12/3/30, Augusta, Ga. BR/TR, 5'11", 175 lbs. Deb: 9/6/20

YEAR	TM/L	W	L	PCT	G	GS	CG	SH	SV	IP	H	R	HR	HB	BB	SO	RAT	ERA	ERA+	OAV	OOB	BH	AVG	PB	PR	PR+	PD	TPI
1920	Det-A	0	1	.000	9	0	0	0	0	18	18	10	1	0	6	7	12.0	4.00	93	.273	.333	1	.250	0	-0	-1	0	0.0

● STAN BAUMGARTNER Baumgartner, Stanwood Fulton b: 12/14/1894, Houston, Tex. d: 10/4/55, Philadelphia, Pa. BL/TL, 6', 175 lbs. Deb: 6/26/14

YEAR	TM/L	W	L	PCT	G	GS	CG	SH	SV	IP	H	R	HR	HB	BB	SO	RAT	ERA	ERA+	OAV	OOB	BH	AVG	PB	PR	PR+	PD	TPI
1914	Phi-N	2	2	.500	15	4	2	1	0	60^1	60	29	0	2	16	24	11.6	3.28	90	.270	.325	1	.053	-1	-3	-2	-1	-0.4
1915	Phi-N	0	2	.000	16	1	0	0	0	48^1	38	22	2	1	23	27	11.5	2.42	113	.226	.323	1	.083	-1	2	2	1	0.1
1916	Phi-N	0	0	—	1	0	0	0	0	4	5	2	0	0	1	0	13.5	2.25	118	.333	.375	0	.000	-0	0	0	-0	0.0
1921	Phi-N	3	6	.333	22	7	2	0	0	66^2	103	72	8	2	22	13	17.1	7.02	60	.355	.404	6	.200	0	-24	-18	-1	-2.1
1922	Phi-N	1	1	.500	6	1	0	0	0	9^2	18	9	1	0	5	2	21.4	6.52	72	.409	.469	1	.333	0	-3	-2	0	-0.2
1924	Phi-A	13	6	.684	36	16	12	1	4	181	181	72	6	4	73	45	12.8	2.88	**149**	.271	.347	13	.217	-0	27	28	-2	2.5
1925	Phi-A	6	3	.667	37	12	2	1	3	113^1	120	55	2	7	35	18	12.9	3.57	130	.275	.338	7	.233	-0	10	13	-1	0.9
1926	Phi-A	1	1	.500	10	1	0	0	0	22^1	28	10	0	0	10	0	15.3	4.03	103	.326	.396	1	.333	0	-0	0	1	0.1
Total	8	26	21	.553	143	42	18	3	7	505^2	553	271	19	16	185	129	13.4	3.70	109	.287	.354	30	.190	-2	9	18	-3	0.9

● GEORGE BAUSEWINE Bausewine, George W. b: 3/22/1869, Philadelphia, Pa. d: 7/29/47, Norristown, Pa. 6'2", 207 lbs. Deb: 9/14/1889 U

YEAR	TM/L	W	L	PCT	G	GS	CG	SH	SV	IP	H	R	HR	HB	BB	SO	RAT	ERA	ERA+	OAV	OOB	BH	AVG	PB	PR	PR+	PD	TPI
1889	Phi-a	1	4	.200	7	6	6	0	0	55^1	64	46	1	9	33	18	17.2	3.90	97	.281	.393	1	.048	-2	-0	-1	0	-0.2

● ED BAUTA Bauta, Eduardo (Galvez) b: 1/6/35, Florida, Cuba BR/TR, 6'3", 200 lbs. Deb: 7/6/60

YEAR	TM/L	W	L	PCT	G	GS	CG	SH	SV	IP	H	R	HR	HB	BB	SO	RAT	ERA	ERA+	OAV	OOB	BH	AVG	PB	PR	PR+	PD	TPI
1960	StL-N	0	0	—	9	0	0	0	1	15^2	14	11	4	1	11	6	14.9	6.32	65	.237	.366	0	.000	-0	-4	-4	-0	-0.2
1961	StL-N	2	0	1.000	13	0	0	0	5	19^1	12	5	2	0	5	12	7.9	1.40	315	.171	.227	2	.500	1	6	6	-0	1.0
1962	StL-N	1	0	1.000	20	0	0	0	1	32^1	28	18	5	1	21	25	13.9	5.01	85	.239	.360	1	.250	0	-4	-2	0	-0.1
1963	StL-N	3	4	.429	38	0	0	0	3	52^2	55	26	2	2	21	30	13.3	3.93	90	.279	.355	0	.000	-1	-4	-2	-1	-0.5
	NY-N	0	0	—	9	0	0	0	0	19	22	11	0	0	9	13	14.7	5.21	67	.289	.365	0	.000	-0	-4	-3	-0	-0.2
	Yr	3	4	.429	47	0	0	0	3	71^2	77	37	2	2	30	43	13.7	4.27	83	.282	.357	0	.000	-1	-8	-5	-1	-0.7
1964	NY-N	0	2	.000	8	0	0	0	1	10	17	6	1	0	3	3	18.0	5.40	66	.395	.435	0	—	0	-2	-2	0	-0.4
Total	5	6	6	.500	97	0	0	0	11	149	148	77	14	4	70	89	13.4	4.35	89	.263	.349	3	.176	-0	-13	-7	-1	-0.4

● JOSE BAUTISTA Bautista, Jose Joaquin (Arias) b: 7/25/64, Bani, D.R. BR/TR, 6'2", 205 lbs. Deb: 4/9/88

YEAR	TM/L	W	L	PCT	G	GS	CG	SH	SV	IP	H	R	HR	HB	BB	SO	RAT	ERA	ERA+	OAV	OOB	BH	AVG	PB	PR	PR+	PD	TPI
1988	Bal-A	6	15	.286	33	25	3	0	0	171^2	171	86	21	7	45	76	11.7	4.30	91	.258	.311	0	—	0	-6	-8	-1	-0.9
1989	Bal-A	3	4	.429	15	10	0	0	0	78	84	46	17	1	15	30	11.5	5.31	72	.274	.310	0	—	0	-12	-13	-1	-1.1
1990	Bal-A	1	0	1.000	22	0	0	0	0	26^2	28	15	4	0	7	15	11.8	4.05	94	.272	.318	0	—	0	-0	-1	-0	-0.1
1991	Bal-A	0	1	.000	5	0	0	0	0	5^1	13	10	1	1	5	3	32.1	16.88	23	.464	.559	0	—	0	-8	-8	0	-1.2
1993	Chi-N	10	3	.769	58	7	1	0	2	111^2	105	38	11	5	27	63	11.0	2.82	142	.250	.303	4	.190	0	15	15	1	1.7
1994	Chi-N	4	5	.444	58	0	0	0	1	69^1	75	30	10	3	17	45	12.3	3.89	107	.284	.335	0	.000	-0	2	2	-0	0.2
1995	SF-N	3	8	.273	52	6	0	0	0	100^2	120	77	24	5	26	45	13.5	6.44	64	.295	.345	0	.000	-2	-25	-27	-1	-2.8
1996	SF-N	3	4	.429	37	1	0	0	0	69^2	66	32	10	2	15	28	10.7	3.36	122	.249	.294	1	.111	-0	7	6	0	0.5
1997	Det-A	2	2	.500	21	0	0	0	0	40^1	55	32	6	2	12	19	15.4	6.69	69	.324	.375	0	—	0	-10	-9	-0	-0.8
	StL-N	0	0	—	11	0	0	0	0	12^1	15	10	2	1	2	4	13.1	6.57	63	.300	.340	0	—	0	-3	-3	-0	-0.2
Total	9	32	42	.432	312	49	4	0	3	685^2	732	376	106	27	171	328	12.2	4.62	87	.273	.323	5	.100	-2	-40	-46	-3	-4.7

● BILL BAYNE Bayne, William Lear "Beverly" b: 4/18/1899, Pittsburgh, Pa. d: 5/22/81, St.Louis, Mo. BL/TL, 5'9", 160 lbs. Deb: 9/20/19

YEAR	TM/L	W	L	PCT	G	GS	CG	SH	SV	IP	H	R	HR	HB	BB	SO	RAT	ERA	ERA+	OAV	OOB	BH	AVG	PB	PR	PR+	PD	TPI
1919	StL-A	1	1	.500	2	2	1	0	0	12	16	8	0	0	6	0	16.5	5.25	63	.320	.393	2	.400	0	-3	-3	0	-0.3
1920	StL-A	5	6	.455	18	13	6	1	0	99^2	102	51	3	7	41	38	13.5	3.70	106	.279	.363	6	.171	-2	1	2	-2	-0.2
1921	StL-A	11	5	.688	47	14	6	1	3	164	167	103	8	5	80	82	13.8	4.72	95	.270	.358	18	.300	5	-8	-4	-1	0.0
1922	StL-A	4	5	.444	26	9	3	0	2	92^2	86	49	5	9	37	38	12.8	4.56	91	.249	.338	7	.233	-1	-5	-4	-2	-0.6
1923	StL-A	2	2	.500	19	2	0	0	0	46	49	25	4	3	31	15	16.2	4.50	93	.287	.405	3	.231	-0	-3	-2	-1	-0.2
1924	StL-A	1	3	.250	22	3	0	0	0	50^2	47	31	4	8	29	20	14.9	4.44	102	.250	.373	6	.429	2	-1	0	-1	0.2
1928	Cle-A	2	5	.286	37	6	3	0	3	108^2	128	68	3	10	43	39	15.0	5.13	81	.309	.388	11	.367	3	-13	-12	2	-0.3
1929	Bos-A	5	5	.500	27	6	2	0	0	84^1	111	72	9	8	29	26	15.8	6.72	64	.326	.392	8	.320	2	-23	-23	1	-1.9
1930	Bos-A	0	0	—	1	0	0	0	0	4	5	2	1	0	1	1	13.5	4.50	102	.294	.333	1	.500	0	0	0	0	0.0
Total	9	31	32	.492	199	55	21	2	8	662	711	409	37	50	297	259	14.4	4.84	87	.283	.370	62	.290	10	-55	-44	-3	-3.3

● WALTER BEALL Beall, Walter Esau b: 7/29/1899, Washington, D.C. d: 1/28/59, Suitland, Md. BR/TR, 5'10", 178 lbs. Deb: 9/3/24

YEAR	TM/L	W	L	PCT	G	GS	CG	SH	SV	IP	H	R	HR	HB	BB	SO	RAT	ERA	ERA+	OAV	OOB	BH	AVG	PB	PR	PR+	PD	TPI
1924	NY-A	2	0	1.000	4	2	0	0	0	23	19	11	2	0	17	18	14.1	3.52	118	.237	.371	1	.143	-1	2	2	-1	0.0
1925	NY-A	0	1	.000	8	1	0	0	0	11^1	11	17	0	3	19	8	26.2	12.71	34	.282	.541	0	.000	-1	-10	-11	0	-0.8
1926	NY-A	2	4	.333	20	9	1	0	1	81^2	71	46	2	6	68	56	16.0	3.53	109	.240	.392	3	.136	0	4	3	1	0.3
1927	NY-A	0	0	—	1	0	0	0	0	1	1	1	0	0	0	0	9.0	9.00	43	.333	.333	0	—	0	-1	-1	-0	0.0

YEAR	TM/L	W	L	PCT	G	GS	CG	SH	SV	IP	H	R	HR	HB	BB	SO	RAT	ERA	ERA+	OAV	OOB	BH	AVG	PB	PR	PR+	PD	TPI
1929	Was-A	1	0	1.000	3	0	0	0	0	7	8	4	0	0	7	3	19.3	3.86	110	.348	.500	0	.000	-1	0	0	0	0.0
Total	5	5	5	.500	36	12	1	0	1	124	110	79	4	9	111	85	16.7	4.43	90	.249	.410	4	.114	-1	-4	-7	0	-0.5

● ALEX BEAM
Beam, Alexander Rodger b: 11/21/1870, Johnstown, Pa. d: 4/17/38, Nogales, Ariz. Deb: 5/25/1889

YEAR	TM/L	W	L	PCT	G	GS	CG	SH	SV	IP	H	R	HR	HB	BB	SO	RAT	ERA	ERA+	OAV	OOB	BH	AVG	PB	PR	PR+	PD	TPI
1889	Pit-N	1	1	.500	2	2	2	0	0	18	11	16	0	0	15	1	13.0	6.50	58	.172	.329	1	.167	0	-5	-6	-0	-0.5

● ERNIE BEAM
Beam, Ernest Joseph b: 3/17/1867, Mansfield, Ohio d: 9/12/18, Mansfield, Ohio TR, 6'0.5", 185 lbs. Deb: 5/2/1895

YEAR	TM/L	W	L	PCT	G	GS	CG	SH	SV	IP	H	R	HR	HB	BB	SO	RAT	ERA	ERA+	OAV	OOB	BH	AVG	PB	PR	PR+	PD	TPI
1895	Phi-N	0	2	.000	9	1	1	0	**3**	24^{2}	33	33	1	1	25	3	21.5	11.31	42	.317	.454	2	.182	-1	-18	-18	-0	-1.4

● CHARLIE BEAMON
Beamon, Charles Alfonzo Sr. b: 12/25/34, Oakland, Cal. BR/TR, 5'11", 195 lbs. Deb: 9/26/56 F

YEAR	TM/L	W	L	PCT	G	GS	CG	SH	SV	IP	H	R	HR	HB	BB	SO	RAT	ERA	ERA+	OAV	OOB	BH	AVG	PB	PR	PR+	PD	TPI
1956	Bal-A	2	0	1.000	2	1	1	1	0	13	9	2	0	0	8	14	11.8	1.38	283	.191	.309	0	.000	-1	4	4	0	0.5
1957	Bal-A	0	0	—	4	1	0	0	0	8^{2}	8	6	1	1	7	5	16.6	5.19	69	.229	.372	0	.000	-0	-1	-2	-0	-0.1
1958	Bal-A	1	3	.250	21	3	0	0	0	49^{2}	47	27	3	6	21	26	13.4	4.35	83	.266	.363	0	.000	-1	-3	-4	2	-0.2
Total	3	3	3	.500	27	5	1	1	0	71^{1}	64	35	4	7	36	45	13.5	3.91	93	.247	.354	0	.000	-2	-1	-2	2	0.2

● BELVE BEAN
Bean, Beveric Benton "Bill" b: 4/23/05, Mullin, Tex. d: 6/1/88, Comanche, Tex. BR/TR, 6'1.5", 197 lbs. Deb: 5/30/30

YEAR	TM/L	W	L	PCT	G	GS	CG	SH	SV	IP	H	R	HR	HB	BB	SO	RAT	ERA	ERA+	OAV	OOB	BH	AVG	PB	PR	PR+	PD	TPI
1930	Cle-A	3	3	.500	23	3	1	0	2	74^{1}	99	58	7	0	32	19	15.9	5.45	89	.331	.396	9	.346	2	-7	-5	0	-0.2
1931	Cle-A	0	1	.000	4	0	0	0	0	7	11	5	0	1	4	3	20.6	6.43	72	.379	.471	0	.000	-0	-2	-1	0	-0.1
1933	Cle-A	1	2	.333	27	2	0	0	0	70^{1}	80	43	6	1	20	41	12.9	5.25	85	.300	.351	4	.182	-1	-8	-6	1	-0.3
1934	Cle-A	5	1	.833	21	1	0	0	0	51^{1}	53	25	2	3	21	20	13.5	3.86	118	.265	.344	3	.200	0	4	4	1	0.5
1935	Cle-A	0	0	—	1	0	0	0	0	1	2	1	1	0	0	0	18.0	9.00	50	.400	.400	0	—	0	-1	-0	-0	0.0
	Was-A	2	0	1.000	10	2	0	0	0	31	43	28	5	0	19	6	18.0	7.26	60	.339	.425	3	.375	3	-10	-10	-1	-0.4
	Yr	2	0	1.000	11	2	0	0	0	32	45	29	6	0	19	6	18.0	7.31	59	.341	.424	3	.375	3	-10	-11	-1	-0.4
Total	5	11	7	.611	86	8	1	0	2	235	288	160	21	5	96	89	14.9	5.32	86	.311	.378	19	.264	4	-22	-19	1	-0.5

● DAVE BEARD
Beard, Charles David b: 10/2/59, Atlanta, Ga. BL/TR, 6'5", 215 lbs. Deb: 7/16/80

YEAR	TM/L	W	L	PCT	G	GS	CG	SH	SV	IP	H	R	HR	HB	BB	SO	RAT	ERA	ERA+	OAV	OOB	BH	AVG	PB	PR	PR+	PD	TPI
1980	Oak-A	0	1	.000	13	0	0	0	1	16	12	6	0	1	7	12	11.3	3.38	112	.218	.317	0	—	0	1	1	-0	0.0
1981	*Oak-A	1	1	.500	8	0	0	0	3	13	9	5	1	1	4	15	9.7	2.77	126	.191	.269	0	—	0	1	1	0	0.2
1982	Oak-A	10	9	.526	54	2	0	0	11	91^{2}	85	41	9	1	35	73	11.9	3.44	114	.244	.315	0	—	0	7	5	-0	1.0
1983	Oak-A	5	5	.500	43	0	0	0	10	61	55	39	8	2	36	40	13.7	5.61	69	.246	.355	0	—	0	-10	-12	-1	-2.3
1984	Sea-A	3	2	.600	43	0	0	0	5	76	88	56	15	4	33	40	14.8	5.80	69	.291	.369	0	—	0	-15	-15	-0	-1.1
1985	Chi-N	0	0	—	9	0	0	0	0	12^{2}	16	9	2	0	7	4	16.3	6.39	63	.314	.397	0	—	0	-4	-3	-0	-0.2
1989	Det-A	0	2	.000	2	1	0	0	0	5^{1}	9	7	2	1	2	1	20.3	5.06	76	.375	.444	0	—	0	-1	-1	0	-0.1
Total	7	19	20	.487	172	3	0	0	30	275^{2}	274	163	37	10	124	185	13.3	4.70	83	.261	.344	0	—	0	-21	-25	-2	-2.5

● MIKE BEARD
Beard, Michael Richard b: 6/21/50, Little Rock, Ark. BL/TL, 6'1", 185 lbs. Deb: 9/7/74

YEAR	TM/L	W	L	PCT	G	GS	CG	SH	SV	IP	H	R	HR	HB	BB	SO	RAT	ERA	ERA+	OAV	OOB	BH	AVG	PB	PR	PR+	PD	TPI
1974	Atl-N	0	0	—	6	0	0	0	0	9^{1}	5	3	1	1	1	7	6.8	2.89	131	.156	.206	0	—	0	1	1	0	0.1
1975	Atl-N	4	0	1.000	34	2	0	0	0	70^{1}	71	31	4	2	28	27	12.9	3.20	118	.265	.339	1	.111	-0	3	4	0	0.2
1976	Atl-N	0	2	.000	30	0	0	0	1	33^{2}	38	18	1	0	14	8	13.9	4.28	89	.299	.369	0	.000	-0	-3	-2	1	0.0
1977	Atl-N	0	0	—	4	0	0	0	0	4^{2}	14	11	3	0	2	1	30.9	9.64	46	.452	.485	0	—	0	-3	-2	0	-0.1
Total	4	4	2	.667	74	2	0	0	1	118	128	63	9	3	45	43	13.4	3.74	102	.279	.348	1	.100	-0	-2	1	1	0.2

● RALPH BEARD
Beard, Ralph William b: 2/11/29, Cincinnati, Ohio BR/TR, 6'5", 200 lbs. Deb: 6/29/54

YEAR	TM/L	W	L	PCT	G	GS	CG	SH	SV	IP	H	R	HR	HB	BB	SO	RAT	ERA	ERA+	OAV	OOB	BH	AVG	PB	PR	PR+	PD	TPI
1954	StL-N	0	4	.000	13	10	0	0	0	58	62	32	2	2	28	17	14.3	3.72	110	.278	.364	1	.059	-1	2	2	-1	-0.1

● GENE BEARDEN
Bearden, Henry Eugene b: 9/5/20, Lexa, Ark. BL/TL, 6'3", 204 lbs. Deb: 5/10/47

YEAR	TM/L	W	L	PCT	G	GS	CG	SH	SV	IP	H	R	HR	HB	BB	SO	RAT	ERA	ERA+	OAV	OOB	BH	AVG	PB	PR	PR+	PD	TPI
1947	Cle-A	0	0	—	1	0	0	0	0	0^{1}	2	3	0	0	1	0	81.0	81.00	4	.667	.750	0	—	0	-3	-3	0	-0.1
1948	*Cle-A	20	7	.741	37	29	15	6	1	229^{2}	187	72	9	3	106	80	11.6	**2.43**	**167**	.229	.320	23	.256	5	47	**44**	3	5.8
1949	Cle-A	8	8	.500	32	19	5	0	0	127	140	77	6	2	92	41	16.6	5.10	78	.286	.401	5	.111	-3	-13	-16	4	-1.7
1950	Cle-A	1	3	.250	14	3	0	0	0	45^{1}	57	32	5	0	32	10	17.7	6.15	70	.328	.432	2	.154	1	-8	-10	-1	-0.7
	Was-A	3	5	.375	12	9	4	0	0	68^{1}	81	35	1	2	33	20	15.3	4.21	107	.297	.377	5	.227	1	3	2	0	0.3
	Yr	4	8	.333	26	12	4	0	0	113^{2}	138	67	6	2	65	30	16.2	4.99	89	.309	.399	7	.200	2	-5	-7	-0	-0.4
1951	Was-A	0	0	—	1	1	0	0	0	2^{2}	6	5	0	0	2	1	27.0	16.88	24	.429	.500	0	—	0	-4	-4	-0	-0.2
	Det-A	3	4	.429	37	4	2	1	0	106	112	58	6	1	58	38	14.5	4.33	96	.275	.366	6	.188	1	-2	-2	0	0.0
	Yr	3	4	.429	38	5	2	1	0	108^{2}	118	63	6	1	60	39	14.8	4.64	90	.280	.371	6	.188	1	-6	-6	-0	-0.2
1952	StL-A	7	8	.467	34	16	3	0	0	150^{2}	158	89	13	1	78	45	14.2	4.30	91	.270	.357	23	.354	6	-10	-6	1	0.2
1953	Chi-A	3	3	.500	25	3	0	0	0	58^{1}	48	27	8	0	33	24	12.5	2.93	137	.223	.327	4	.190	-1	7	7	-0	0.6
Total	7	45	38	.542	193	84	29	7	1	788^{1}	791	398	48	9	435	259	14.1	3.96	103	.266	.361	68	.236	10	17	12	7	4.2

● GARY BEARE
Beare, Gary Ray b: 8/22/52, San Diego, Cal. BR/TR, 6'4", 205 lbs. Deb: 9/7/76

YEAR	TM/L	W	L	PCT	G	GS	CG	SH	SV	IP	H	R	HR	HB	BB	SO	RAT	ERA	ERA+	OAV	OOB	BH	AVG	PB	PR	PR+	PD	TPI
1976	Mil-A	2	3	.400	6	5	2	0	0	41	43	16	4	0	15	32	12.7	3.29	106	.274	.337	0	—	0	1	1	-0	0.1
1977	Mil-A	3	3	.500	17	6	0	0	0	58^{2}	63	46	6	1	38	32	15.6	6.44	63	.276	.382	0	—	0	-15	-15	2	-1.2
Total	2	5	6	.455	23	11	2	0	0	99^{2}	106	62	10	1	53	64	14.4	5.15	75	.275	.364	0	—	0	-14	-14	1	-1.1

● LARRY BEARNARTH
Bearnarth, Lawrence Donald b: 9/11/41, New York, N.Y. d: 12/31/99, Seminole, Fla. BR/TR, 6'2", 203 lbs. Deb: 4/16/63 C

YEAR	TM/L	W	L	PCT	G	GS	CG	SH	SV	IP	H	R	HR	HB	BB	SO	RAT	ERA	ERA+	OAV	OOB	BH	AVG	PB	PR	PR+	PD	TPI
1963	NY-N	3	8	.273	58	2	0	0	4	126^{1}	127	61	7	5	47	48	12.8	3.42	102	.268	.340	6	.200	1	-2	1	2	0.5
1964	NY-N	5	5	.500	44	1	0	0	3	78	79	38	6	2	38	31	13.7	4.15	86	.271	.360	2	.143	-0	-5	-5	3	-0.4
1965	NY-N	3	5	.375	40	3	0	0	1	60^{2}	75	43	6	4	28	16	15.9	4.60	77	.304	.384	1	.111	0	-7	-7	0	-0.9
1966	NY-N	2	3	.400	29	1	0	0	0	54^{2}	59	31	11	1	20	27	13.2	4.45	82	.281	.346	1	.111	-0	-5	-5	1	-0.3
1971	Mil-A	0	0	—	2	0	0	0	0	3	10	6	1	0	2	2	36.0	18.00	19	.556	.600	0	—	0	-5	-5	0	-0.2
Total	5	13	21	.382	173	7	0	0	8	322^{2}	350	179	31	12	135	124	13.9	4.13	86	.282	.358	10	.161	1	-24	-20	7	-1.3

● KEVIN BEARSE
Bearse, Kevin Gerard b: 11/7/65, Jersey City, N.J. BL/TL, 6'2", 195 lbs. Deb: 4/15/90

YEAR	TM/L	W	L	PCT	G	GS	CG	SH	SV	IP	H	R	HR	HB	BB	SO	RAT	ERA	ERA+	OAV	OOB	BH	AVG	PB	PR	PR+	PD	TPI
1990	Cle-A	0	2	.000	3	3	0	0	0	7^{2}	16	11	2	2	5	2	27.0	12.91	30	.421	.511	0	—	0	-8	-8	-0	-1.2

● CHRIS BEASLEY
Beasley, Christopher Charles b: 6/23/62, Jackson, Tenn. BR/TR, 6'2", 190 lbs. Deb: 7/20/91

YEAR	TM/L	W	L	PCT	G	GS	CG	SH	SV	IP	H	R	HR	HB	BB	SO	RAT	ERA	ERA+	OAV	OOB	BH	AVG	PB	PR	PR+	PD	TPI
1991	Cal-A	0	1	.000	22	0	0	0	0	26^{2}	26	14	2	1	10	14	12.5	3.38	122	.257	.330	0	—	0	2	2	0	0.1

● ED BEATIN
Beatin, Ebenezer Ambrose b: 8/10/1866, Baltimore, Md. d: 5/9/25, Baltimore, Md. BR/TL, 5'9", 162 lbs. Deb: 8/2/1887

YEAR	TM/L	W	L	PCT	G	GS	CG	SH	SV	IP	H	R	HR	HB	BB	SO	RAT	ERA	ERA+	OAV	OOB	BH	AVG	PB	PR	PR+	PD	TPI
1887	Det-N	1	1	.500	2	2	2	0	0	18	21	11	2	1	8	6	11.0	4.00	101	.292	.301	0	.000	-1	0	0	-0	-0.1
1888	Det-N	5	7	.417	12	12	12	1	0	107	111	60	6	2	16	44	10.9	2.86	97	.251	.280	14	.250	5	-0	-1	0	0.4
1889	Cle-N	20	15	.571	36	36	35	3	0	317^{2}	316	179	12	6	141	126	13.1	3.57	113	.251	.330	14	.116	-5	16	16	-1	0.9
1890	Cle-N	22	30	.423	54	54	53	1	0	474^{1}	518	300	11	15	186	155	13.6	3.83	93	.269	.339	27	.141	-9	-14	-13	3	-1.7
1891	Cle-N	0	3	.000	5	4	2	0	0	29	39	44	1	6	21	4	20.5	5.28	66	.310	.431	1	.077	-1	-6	-6	-0	-0.6
Total	5	48	56	.462	109	108	104	5	0	946	1005	594	32	30	372	335	13.3	3.68	99	.263	.332	56	.144	-12	-4	-4	1	-1.1

● JIM BEATTIE
Beattie, James Louis b: 7/4/54, Hampton, Va. BR/TR, 6'6", 220 lbs. Deb: 4/25/78

YEAR	TM/L	W	L	PCT	G	GS	CG	SH	SV	IP	H	R	HR	HB	BB	SO	RAT	ERA	ERA+	OAV	OOB	BH	AVG	PB	PR	PR+	PD	TPI
1978	*NY-A	6	9	.400	25	22	0	0	0	128	123	60	8	8	51	65	12.8	3.73	98	.255	.336	0	—	0	1	-1	1	-0.1
1979	NY-A	3	6	.333	15	13	1	1	0	76	85	45	5	0	41	32	14.9	5.21	78	.294	.382	0	—	0	-8	-10	1	-0.9
1980	Sea-A	5	15	.250	33	29	3	0	0	187^{1}	205	115	19	4	98	67	14.7	4.85	85	.286	.375	0	—	0	-17	-14	0	-1.3
1981	Sea-A	3	2	.600	13	9	0	0	1	66^{2}	59	24	2	2	18	36	10.7	2.97	130	.232	.288	0	—	0	5	6	0	0.5
1982	Sea-A	8	12	.400	28	26	6	1	0	172^{1}	149	73	13	1	65	140	11.2	3.34	127	.233	.305	0	—	0	14	17	1	1.9
1983	Sea-A	10	15	.400	30	29	8	2	0	196^{2}	197	89	12	3	66	132	12.2	3.84	111	.259	.321	0	—	0	5	9	3	1.4
1984	Sea-A	12	16	.429	32	32	12	2	0	211	206	86	13	5	75	119	12.2	3.41	117	.260	.328	0	—	0	14	14	1	1.8
1985	Sea-A	5	6	.455	18	15	1	1	0	70^{1}	93	61	9	3	33	45	16.5	7.29	58	.316	.391	0	—	0	-25	-24	-1	-3.1
1986	Sea-A	0	6	.000	9	7	0	0	0	40^{1}	57	28	7	3	14	24	16.5	6.02	71	.341	.402	0	—	0	-8	-8	1	-0.9
Total	9	52	87	.374	203	182	31	7	1	1148^{2}	1174	581	88	29	461	660	13.0	4.17	98	.267	.341	0	—	0	-19	-11	7	-0.7

● BLAINE BEATTY
Beatty, Gordon Blaine b: 4/25/64, Victoria, Tex. BL/TL, 6'2", 185 lbs. Deb: 9/16/89

YEAR	TM/L	W	L	PCT	G	GS	CG	SH	SV	IP	H	R	HR	HB	BB	SO	RAT	ERA	ERA+	OAV	OOB	BH	AVG	PB	PR	PR+	PD	TPI
1989	NY-N	0	0	—	2	1	0	0	0	6	5	1	1	0	2	3	10.5	1.50	218	.217	.280	1	.500	0	1	1	0	0.1
1991	NY-N	0	0	—	5	0	0	0	0	9^{2}	9	3	0	0	4	7	12.1	2.79	130	.250	.325	0	—	0	1	1	0	0.0
Total	2	0	0	—	7	1	0	0	0	15^{2}	14	4	1	0	6	10	11.5	2.30	152	.237	.308	1	.500	0	2	2	0	0.1

YEAR	TM/L	W	L	PCT	G	GS	CG	SH	SV	IP	H	R	HR	HB	BB	SO	RAT	ERA	ERA+	OAV	OOB	BH	AVG	PB	PR	PR+	PD	TPI
● JOHNNY BEAZLEY	Beazley, John Andrew "Nig" b: 5/25/18, Nashville, Tenn. d: 4/21/90, Nashville, Tenn. BR/TR, 6'1.5", 190 lbs. Deb: 9/28/41																											
1941	StL-N	1	0	1.000	1	1	1	0	0	9	10	1	0	0	3	4	13.0	1.00	376	.294	.351	0	.000	-0	3	3	-0	0.2
1942	*StL-N	21	6	.778	43	23	13	3	3	215^1	181	67	4	3	73	91	10.7	2.13	161	.226	.293	10	.137	-1	28	30	0	3.8
1946	*StL-N	7	5	.583	19	18	5	0	0	103	109	55	6	4	55	36	14.7	4.46	77	.275	.368	8	.242	1	-12	-11	-1	-1.2
1947	Bos-N	2	0	1.000	9	2	2	0	0	28^2	30	15	1	0	19	12	15.4	4.40	89	.273	.380	0	.000	-1	-1	-2	-0	-0.2
1948	Bos-N	0	1	.000	3	2	0	0	0	16	19	13	2	0	7	4	14.6	4.50	85	.284	.351	0	.000	-1	-1	-1	-0	-0.1
1949	Bos-N	0	0	—	1	0	0	0	0	2	0	0	0	0	0	0	0.0	0.00	—	.000	.000	0	—	0	1	1	-0	0.0
Total	6	31	12	.721	76	46	21	3	3	374	349	151	13	7	157	147	12.3	3.01	116	.247	.325	18	.150	-1	18	20	-1	2.5
● BUCK BECANNON	Becannon, James Melvin b: 8/22/1859, New York, N.Y. d: 11/5/23, New York, N.Y. 5'10", 165 lbs. Deb: 10/15/1884 ♦																											
1884	*NY-a	1	0	1.000	1	1	1	0	0	6	2	2	0	0	2	2	6.0	1.50	208	.091	.167	0	.000	-0	1	1	0	0.1
1885	NY-a	2	8	.200	10	10	10	0	0	85	108	84	5	5	24	13	14.5	6.25	47	.296	.348	10	.303	2	-28	-34	0	-2.7
Total	2	3	8	.273	11	11	11	0	0	91	110	86	5	5	26	15	13.9	5.93	50	.284	.337	10	.244	2	-27	-33	0	-2.6
● GEORGE BECHTEL	Bechtel, George A. b: 1848, Philadelphia, Pa. 5'11", 165 lbs. Deb: 5/20/1871 ♦																											
1871	Ath-n	1	2	.333	3	3	2	0	0	26	43	42	0		11	1	18.7	7.96	51	.319	.370	33	.351	1	-11	-12		-0.6
1873	Phi-n	0	2	.000	3	2	1	0	0	16	27	24	0		2	0	16.3	4.50	73	.318	.333	63	.244	0	-2	-2		-0.2
1874	Phi-n	1	3	.250	6	4	4	0	0	39	57	42	0		1	0	13.4	1.62	137	.297	.301	42	.278	1	2	3		0.2
1875	Cen-n	2	12	.143	14	14	14	0	0	126	169	138	0		5	6	12.4	2.71	80	.274	.280	17	.279	3	-7	-8		-0.4
	Ath-n	3	1	.750	4	4	4	0	0	36	41	19	0		3	3	11.0	2.50	96	.279	.293	46	.280	0	-1	-0		0.0
	Yr	5	13	.278	18	18	18	0	0	162	210	157	0		8	9	12.1	2.67	83	.275	.283	63	.280	4	-8	-8		-0.4
Total	4 n	7	20	.259	30	27	25	0	0	243	337	265	0		22	10	13.3	3.19	70	.287	.300	275	.282	6	-26	-26		-1.0
● GEORGE BECK	Beck, Ernest George B. b: 2/21/1890, South Bend, Ind. d: 10/29/73, South Bend, Ind. BR/TR, 5'11", 165 lbs. Deb: 5/15/14																											
1914	Cle-A	0	0	—	1	0	0	0	0	1	1	0	0	1	0	0	18.0	0.00	—	.250	.400	0	—	0	0	0	-0	0.0
● FRANK BECK	Beck, Frank J. (b: Frank J. Hengstebeck) b: 4/29/1860, Poughkeepsie, N.Y. d: 2/8/41, Detroit, Mich. TR, 5'9", 141 lbs. Deb: 5/2/1884 ♦																											
1884	Pit-a	0	3	.000	3	3	3	0	0	25	33	29	0	5	6	11	15.8	6.12	54	.306	.370	4	.333	1	-8	-8	0	-0.6
	Bal-U	0	2	.000	2	2	1	0	0	9	17	13	0		4	7	21.0	8.00	34	.378	.429	2	.100	-1	-6	-5	0	-0.8
Total	1	0	5	.000	5	5	4	0	0	34	50	42	0	5	10	18	17.2	6.62	48	.327	.387	6	.188	-0	-14	-13	0	-1.4
● RICH BECK	Beck, Richard Henry b: 1/21/41, Pasco, Wash. BB/TR, 6'3", 190 lbs. Deb: 9/14/65																											
1965	NY-A	2	1	.667	3	3	1	1	0	21	22	6	1	0	7	10	12.4	2.14	159	.275	.333	0	.000	-0	3	3	0	0.4
● ROD BECK	Beck, Rodney Roy b: 8/3/68, Burbank, Cal. BR/TR, 6'1", 236 lbs. Deb: 5/6/91																											
1991	SF-N	1	1	.500	31	0	0	0	1	52^1	53	22	4	1	13	38	11.5	3.78	95	.273	.322	1	.500	0	-1	-1	0	0.0
1992	SF-N	3	3	.500	65	0	0	0	17	92	62	20	4	2	15	87	7.7	1.76	188	.190	.230	1	.500	0	18	17	-0	1.7
1993	SF-N★	3	1	.750	76	0	0	0	48	79^1	57	20	11	3	13	86	8.3	2.16	182	.201	.243	0	.000	-0	17	16	-1	2.3
1994	SF-N★	2	4	.333	48	0	0	0	28	48^2	49	17	10	0	13	39	11.5	2.77	145	.261	.308	0	.000	-0	8	7	-0	1.3
1995	SF-N	5	6	.455	60	0	0	0	33	58^2	60	31	7	2	21	42	12.7	4.45	92	.267	.335	1	.333	0	-2	-2	-0	-0.5
1996	SF-N	0	9	.000	63	0	0	0	35	62	56	23	9	1	10	48	9.7	3.34	123	.238	.272	1	.333	0	6	5	-1	1.0
1997	*SF-N☆	7	4	.636	73	0	0	0	37	70	67	31	7	2	8	53	9.9	3.47	118	.248	.275	0	—	0	6	5	-1	0.9
1998	*Chi-N	3	4	.429	**81**	0	0	0	51	80^1	86	33	11	2	20	81	12.1	3.02	146	.269	.316	0	.000	-0	11	12	1	2.3
1999	Chi-N	2	4	.333	31	0	0	0	7	30	41	26	5	0	13	13	16.2	7.80	58	.331	.394	0	—	0	-11	-11	0	-2.0
	*Bos-A	0	1	.000	12	0	0	0	3	14	9	3	0	1	5	12	9.6	1.93	258	.184	.273	0	—	0	5	5	0	0.5
2000	Bos-A	3	0	1.000	34	0	0	0	0	40^2	34	15	2	2	12	35	10.6	3.10	164	.222	.287	0	—	0	8	9	-1	0.5
Total	10	29	37	.439	574	0	0	0	260	628	574	241	70	16	143	534	10.5	3.20	127	.242	.290	4	.222	0	65	60	-2	8.0
● BOOM-BOOM BECK	Beck, Walter William b: 10/16/04, Decatur, Ill. d: 5/7/87, Champaign, Ill. BR/TR, 6'2", 200 lbs. Deb: 9/22/24 C																											
1924	StL-A	0	0	—	1	0	0	0	0	1	2	0	0	0	1	0	27.0	0.00	—	.667	.750	0	—	0	0	0	0	0.0
1927	StL-A	1	0	1.000	3	1	1	0	0	11^1	15	8	0	1	5	6	16.7	5.56	78	.333	.412	1	.250	-0	-2	-1	-0	-0.1
1928	StL-A	2	3	.400	16	4	2	0	0	49	52	29	4	4	20	17	14.0	4.41	95	.289	.373	6	.429	1	-2	-1	-0	0.0
1933	Bro-N	12	20	.375	43	35	15	3	1	257	270	128	9	11	69	89	12.3	3.54	91	.267	.321	18	.189	0	-6	-9	-0	-1.1
1934	Bro-N	2	6	.250	22	9	2	0	0	57	72	50	6	5	32	24	17.2	7.42	53	.301	.395	4	.235	1	-21	-23	1	-2.5
1939	Phi-N	7	14	.333	34	16	12	0	3	182^2	203	104	11	3	64	77	13.3	4.73	85	.284	.345	9	.132	-3	-16	-14	-0	-1.8
1940	Phi-N	4	9	.308	29	15	4	0	0	129^1	147	69	13	9	41	38	13.7	4.31	90	.286	.349	2	.056	-3	-7	-6	1	-0.7
1941	Phi-N	1	9	.100	34	7	2	0	0	95^1	104	52	8	2	35	34	13.3	4.63	80	.276	.341	3	.120	-2	-11	-10	-3	-1.4
1942	Phi-N	0	1	.000	26	1	0	0	0	53	69	30	4	1	17	10	14.8	4.75	70	.325	.378	4	.333	1	-8	-9	-1	-0.4
1943	Phi-N	0	0	—	4	0	0	0	0	13^2	24	15	1	2	5	3	20.4	9.88	34	.393	.456	2	.500	1	-10	-10	-0	-0.5
1944	Det-A	1	2	.333	28	2	0	0	1	74	67	36	5	3	27	25	11.8	3.89	92	.243	.317	7	.318	2	-4	-3	-2	-0.1
1945	Cin-N	2	4	.333	11	6	2	0	1	47^2	42	21	0	1	12	9	10.4	3.40	111	.236	.288	3	.214	-0	2	2	0	0.2
	Pit-N	6	1	.857	14	5	4	0	0	63	54	19	2	0	14	20	9.7	2.14	184	.234	.278	2	.125	-1	12	12	-0	1.2
	Yr	8	5	.615	25	11	6	0	1	110^2	96	40	2	1	26	29	10.0	2.68	144	.235	.282	5	.167	-1	14	14	-0	1.4
Total	12	38	69	.355	265	101	44	3	6	1034	1121	561	63	42	342	352	13.1	4.30	86	.277	.340	61	.187	-2	-72	-71	-5	-7.2
● CHARLIE BECKER	Becker, Charles S. "Buck" b: 10/14/1888, Washington, D.C. d: 7/30/28, Washington, D.C. BL/TL, 6'2", 180 lbs. Deb: 8/2/11																											
1911	Was-A	3	5	.375	11	5	5	1	0	71^1	80	44	2	7	23	31	13.9	4.04	81	.268	.335	5	.227	-0	-5	-6	-0	-0.6
1912	Was-A	0	0	—	4	0	0	0	0	9	8	6	0	0	6	5	14.0	3.00	111	.258	.378	1	.500	0	0	0	-0	0.0
Total	2	3	5	.375	15	5	5	1	0	80^1	88	50	2	7	29	36	13.9	3.92	84	.267	.340	6	.250	0	-5	-6	-1	-0.6
● BOB BECKER	Becker, Robert Charles b: 8/15/1875, Syracuse, N.Y. d: 10/11/51, Syracuse, N.Y. TL, Deb: 9/6/1897																											
1897	Phi-N	0	2	.000	5	2	2	0	0	24	32	18	0	1	7	10	15.0	5.63	75	.317	.367	1	.111	-0	-4	-4	-0	-0.3
1898	Phi-N	0	0	—	1	0	0	0	0	5	6	6	0	0	5	0	19.8	10.80	32	.300	.440	0	.000	0	-4	-4	0	-0.2
Total	2	0	2	.000	6	2	2	0	0	29	38	24	0	1	12	10	15.8	6.52	62	.314	.381	1	.100	-0	-8	-8	-0	-0.5
● ROBBIE BECKETT	Beckett, Robert Joseph b: 7/16/72, Austin, Tex. BR/TL, 6'5", 235 lbs. Deb: 9/12/96																											
1996	Col-N	0	0	—	5	0	0	0	0	5^1	6	8	3	0	9	6	25.3	13.50	39	.286	.500	0	—	0	-5	-4	-0	-0.2
1997	Col-N	0	0	—	2	0	0	0	0	1^2	1	1	0	0	1	2	10.8	5.40	96	.167	.286	0	—	0	-0	-0	-0	0.0
Total	2	0	0	—	7	0	0	0	0	7	7	9	3	0	10	8	21.9	11.57	45	.259	.459	0	—	0	-6	-4	-0	-0.2
● JAKE BECKLEY	Beckley, Jacob Peter "Eagle Eye" b: 8/4/1867, Hannibal, Mo. d: 6/25/18, Kansas City, Mo. BL/TL, 5'10", 200 lbs. Deb: 6/20/1888 H♦																											
1902	Cin-N	0	1	.000	1	1	0	0	0	4	9	8	0	0	1	2	22.5	6.75	44	.450	.476	175	.330	0	-2	-2	1	-0.2
● JIM BECKMAN	Beckman, James Joseph (b: Reinhardt Boeckman) b: 3/1/05, Cincinnati, Ohio d: 12/5/74, Montgomery, Ohio BR/TR, 5'10", 172 lbs. Deb: 7/27/27																											
1927	Cin-N	0	1	.000	4	1	0	0	0	12^1	18	10	2	1	6	0	18.2	5.84	65	.340	.417	0	.000	0	-3	-3	-1	-0.3
1928	Cin-N	0	1	.000	6	0	0	0	0	15^1	19	12	1	0	9	4	16.4	5.87	67	.306	.394	0	.000	-0	-3	-3	-0	-0.3
Total	2	0	2	.000	10	1	0	0	0	27^2	37	22	3	1	15	4	17.2	5.86	66	.322	.405	0	.000	-0	-6	-6	-1	-0.6
● BILL BECKMANN	Beckmann, William Aloysius b: 12/8/07, Clayton, Mo. d: 1/2/90, Florissant, Mo. BR/TR, 6', 175 lbs. Deb: 5/2/39																											
1939	Phi-A	7	11	.389	27	19	7	2	0	155^1	198	104	15	1	41	20	13.9	5.39	87	.312	.355	13	.250	0	-13	-12	-2	-1.2
1940	Phi-A	8	4	.667	34	9	6	2	1	127^1	132	68	11	1	35	47	11.9	4.17	107	.265	.314	8	.205	-1	3	4	-2	0.1
1941	Phi-A	5	9	.357	22	15	4	0	1	130	141	76	11	2	33	28	12.2	4.57	92	.270	.315	9	.191	0	-6	-5	-3	-0.8
1942	Phi-A	0	1	.000	5	1	0	0	0	20^1	24	17	1	0	9	10	14.6	7.08	53	.289	.359	2	.500	1	-8	-7	-1	-0.3
	StL-N	1	0	1.000	2	0	0	0	0	7	4	0	0	0	1	3	6.4	0.00	—	.200	.238	0	.000	-0	3	3	0	0.4
Total	4	21	25	.457	90	44	17	4	2	440	499	265	38	4	119	108	12.7	4.79	92	.284	.330	32	.224	1	-22	-18	-7	-1.8
● JOE BECKWITH	Beckwith, Thomas Joseph b: 1/28/55, Opelika, Ala. BL/TR, 6'3", 200 lbs. Deb: 7/21/79																											
1979	LA-N	1	2	.333	17	0	0	0	2	37^1	42	18	4	0	15	28	13.7	4.34	84	.284	.350	0	.000	-1	-2	-3	0	-0.3
1980	LA-N	3	3	.500	38	0	0	0	0	59^2	60	17	1	1	23	40	12.7	1.96	179	.263	.333	0	.000	0	11	11	-1	0.9
1982	LA-N	2	1	.667	19	1	0	0	1	40	38	14	2	0	14	33	11.7	2.70	129	.252	.315	0	.000	-1	4	4	-1	0.1
1983	*LA-N	3	4	.429	42	3	0	0	1	71	73	40	5	1	35	50	13.8	3.55	101	.264	.348	1	.200	0	1	0	1	0.2
1984	KC-A	8	4	.667	49	1	0	0	2	100^2	92	39	13	2	25	75	10.6	3.40	119	.247	.298	0	—	0	7	7	0	0.8

YEAR TM/L	W	L	PCT	G	GS	CG	SH	SV	IP	H	R	HR	HB	BB	SO	RAT	ERA	ERA+	OAV	OOB	BH	AVG	PB	PR	PR+	PD	TPI
1985 *KC-A	1	5	.167	49	0	0	0	1	95	99	45	9	3	32	80	12.7	4.07	102	.269	.333	0	—	0	1	1	0	0.1
1986 LA-N	0	0	—	15	0	0	0	0	18^1	28	16	5	0	6	13	16.7	6.87	50	.350	.395	0	—	0	-6	-7	-1	-0.4
Total 7	18	19	.486	229	5	0	0	7	422	432	189	39	7	150	319	12.6	3.54	107	.266	.331	1	.053	-1	14	12	-0	1.4
● JULIO BECQUER Becquer, Julio (Villegas) b: 12/20/31, Havana, Cuba BL/TL, 5'11.5", 178 lbs. Deb: 9/13/55 ◆																											
1960 Was-A	0	0	—	1	0	0	0	0	1	1	1	1	0	0	0	9.0	9.00	43	.250	.250	75	.252	0	-1	-1	-0	0.0
1961 Min-A	0	0	—	1	0	0	0	0	1^1	4	3	0	0	1	0	33.8	20.25	21	.500	.556	20	.238	0	-2	-2	-0	-0.1
Total 2	0	0	—	2	0	0	0	0	2^1	5	4	1	0	1	0	23.1	15.43	26	.417	.462	238	.244	0	-3	-3	-0	-0.1
● PHIL BEDGOOD Bedgood, Phillip Burlette b: 3/8/1898, Harrison, Ga. d: 11/8/27, Fort Pierce, Fla. BR/TR, 6'3", 218 lbs. Deb: 9/20/22																											
1922 Cle-A	1	0	1.000	1	1	1	0	0	9	7	4	0	3	4	5	14.0	4.00	100	.233	.378	0	.000	-0	0	0	-0	0.0
1923 Cle-A	0	2	.000	9	2	0	0	0	18^2	16	13	0	2	14	7	15.4	5.30	75	.246	.395	1	.250	0	-3	-3	-0	-0.2
Total 2	1	2	.333	10	3	1	0	0	27^2	23	17	0	5	18	12	15.0	4.88	82	.242	.390	1	.167	0	-3	-3	-0	-0.2
● HUGH BEDIENT Bedient, Hugh Carpenter b: 10/23/1889, Gerry, N.Y. d: 7/21/65, Jamestown, N.Y. BR/TR, 6', 185 lbs. Deb: 4/26/12																											
1912 *Bos-A	20	9	.690	41	28	19	0	2	231	206	93	6	3	55	122	10.3	2.92	116	.240	.288	14	.192	1	10	12	1	1.5
1913 Bos-A	15	14	.517	43	28	15	1	5	259	255	104	0	6	67	122	11.4	2.78	106	.261	.312	10	.125	-3	4	5	-4	-0.2
1914 Bos-A	8	12	.400	42	16	7	1	2	177^1	187	97	4	5	45	70	12.0	3.60	75	.281	.331	5	.100	-2	-17	-18	-1	-2.3
1915 Buf-F	16	18	.471	53	30	16	2	**10**	269^1	284	131	5	3	69	106	11.9	3.17	88	.274	.321	9	.108	-5	-13	-11	-2	-2.2
Total 4	59	53	.527	179	102	57	4	19	936^2	932	425	15	17	236	420	11.4	3.08	96	.263	.312	38	.133	-9	-16	-12	-7	-3.2
● ANDY BEDNAR Bednar, Andrew Jackson b: 8/16/08, Streator, Ill. d: 11/26/37, Graham, Tex. BR/TR, 5'10.5", 180 lbs. Deb: 9/6/30																											
1930 Pit-N	0	0	—	2	0	0	0	0	1^1	4	4	0	0	1	1	33.8	27.00	18	.500	.556	0	—	0	-3	-3	0	-0.1
1931 Pit-N	0	0	—	3	0	0	0	0	4	10	5	1	0	0	2	22.5	11.25	34	.476	.476	0	—	0	-3	-3	0	-0.2
Total 2	0	0	—	5	0	0	0	0	5^1	14	9	1	0	1	3	25.3	15.19	27	.483	.500	0	—	0	-7	-7	0	-0.3
● STEVE BEDROSIAN Bedrosian, Stephen Wayne b: 12/6/57, Methuen, Mass. BR/TR, 6'3", 200 lbs. Deb: 8/14/81																											
1981 Atl-N	1	2	.333	15	1	0	0	0	24^1	15	14	2	1	15	9	11.5	4.44	81	.169	.295	0	.000	-0	-3	-2	-0	-0.3
1982 *Atl-N	8	6	.571	64	3	0	0	11	137^2	102	39	7	4	57	123	10.7	2.42	155	.206	.293	1	.038	-2	18	19	-0	2.0
1983 Atl-N	9	10	.474	70	1	0	0	19	120	100	50	11	4	51	114	11.6	3.60	108	.229	.315	2	.105	-1	0	4	0	0.6
1984 Atl-N	9	6	.600	40	4	0	0	11	83^2	65	23	5	1	33	81	10.6	2.37	163	.210	.289	2	.118	-1	11	13	-1	2.4
1985 Atl-N	7	15	.318	37	37	0	0	0	206^2	198	101	17	5	111	134	13.7	3.83	101	.254	.351	5	.078	-4	-5	1	-2	-0.5
1986 Phi-N	8	6	.571	68	0	0	0	29	90^1	79	39	12	0	34	82	11.3	3.39	114	.232	.301	1	.200	0	3	5	-1	0.9
1987 Phi-N★	5	3	.625	65	0	0	0	**40**	89	79	31	11	1	28	74	10.9	2.83	150	.237	.298	0	.000	-0	12	13	-1	2.0
1988 Phi-N	6	6	.500	57	0	0	0	28	74^1	75	34	6	0	27	61	12.3	3.75	95	.257	.320	0	.000	-0	-2	-1	-0	-0.4
1989 Phi-N	2	3	.400	28	0	0	0	6	33^2	21	13	7	1	17	24	10.4	3.21	111	.183	.293	0	—	0	1	1	-0	0.2
*SF-N	1	4	.200	40	0	0	0	17	51	35	18	5	0	22	34	10.1	2.65	128	.192	.279	1	.167	-0	5	4	-1	0.5
Yr	3	7	.300	68	0	0	0	23	84^2	56	31	12	1	39	58	10.2	2.87	120	.189	.285	1	.167	-0	6	6	-2	0.7
1990 SF-N	9	9	.500	68	0	0	0	17	79^1	72	40	6	2	44	43	13.4	4.20	87	.241	.342	2	.500	1	-4	-5	0	-0.9
1991 *Min-A	5	3	.625	56	0	0	0	6	77^1	70	42	11	3	35	44	12.6	4.42	97	.243	.331	0	—	0	-3	-1	-1	-0.2
1993 Atl-N	5	2	.714	49	0	0	0	0	49^2	34	11	4	2	14	33	9.1	1.63	246	.194	.262	0	.000	-0	13	13	-0	1.6
1994 Atl-N	0	2	.000	46	0	0	0	0	46	41	20	4	2	18	43	11.9	3.33	128	.243	.323	1	.500	0	5	5	-0	0.2
1995 Atl-N	1	2	.333	29	0	0	0	0	28	40	21	6	1	12	22	17.0	6.11	70	.354	.421	0	—	0	-6	-6	-0	-0.6
Total 14	76	79	.490	732	46	0	0	184	1191	1026	496	114	27	518	921	11.9	3.38	115	.232	.317	15	.098	-7	47	63	-9	7.5
● FRED BEEBE Beebe, Frederick Leonard b: 12/31/1880, Lincoln, Neb. d: 10/30/57, Elgin, Ill. BR/TR, 6'1", 190 lbs. Deb: 4/17/06																											
1906 Chi-N	6	1	.857	14	6	4	0	1	70	56	27	1	5	32	55	12.0	2.70	98	.210	.306	3	.103	-1	-1	-0	-1	-0.3
StL-N	9	9	.500	20	19	16	1	0	160^2	115	65	1	9	68	116	10.8	3.02	87	.208	.305	10	.172	0	-7	-7	-0	-0.8
Yr	15	10	.600	34	25	20	1	1	230^2	171	92	2	14	100	**171**	11.1	2.93	90	.209	.305	13	.149	-1	-7	-8	-1	-1.1
1907 StL-N	7	19	.269	31	29	24	4	0	238^1	192	95	1	10	109	141	11.7	2.72	92	.230	.326	11	.128	-3	-7	-6	1	-0.8
1908 StL-N	5	13	.278	29	19	12	0	0	174^1	134	88	3	4	66	72	10.5	2.63	90	**.193**	.267	7	.125	-2	-5	-5	2	-0.6
1909 StL-N	15	21	.417	44	34	18	1	1	287^2	256	142	5	7	104	105	11.5	2.82	90	.229	.299	18	.167	-2	-7	-9	1	-1.3
1910 Cin-N	12	14	.462	35	26	11	2	0	214^1	193	101	3	7	94	93	12.3	3.07	95	.246	.333	12	.164	-2	-1	-4	3	-0.3
1911 Phi-N	3	3	.500	9	8	3	0	0	48^1	52	26	2	3	24	20	14.7	4.47	77	.297	.391	5	.263	2	-6	-5	1	-0.3
1916 Cle-A	5	3	.625	20	12	5	1	2	100^2	92	43	1	1	37	32	11.6	2.41	125	.251	.321	6	.214	1	5	6	-0	0.5
Total 7	62	83	.428	202	153	93	9	4	1294^1	1090	587	17	46	534	634	11.6	2.86	93	.227	.311	72	.158	-8	-28	-30	6	-3.9
● MATT BEECH Beech, Lucas Matthew b: 1/20/72, Oakland, Cal. BL/TL, 6'2", 190 lbs. Deb: 8/8/96																											
1996 Phi-N	1	4	.200	8	8	0	0	0	41^1	49	32	8	3	11	33	13.7	6.97	62	.306	.362	1	.071	-1	-13	-12	-0	-1.3
1997 Phi-N	4	9	.308	24	24	0	0	0	136^2	147	81	25	5	57	120	13.8	5.07	84	.279	.355	5	.167	-0	-13	-12	0	-1.0
1998 Phi-N	3	9	.250	21	21	0	0	0	117	126	78	19	4	63	113	14.8	5.15	84	.275	.368	5	.152	-1	-12	-10	-1	-1.1
Total 3	8	22	.267	53	53	0	0	0	295	322	191	52	12	131	266	14.2	5.37	80	.281	.361	11	.143	-2	-38	-35	-1	-3.4
● ED BEECHER Beecher, Edward Harry b: 7/2/1860, Guilford, Conn. d: 9/12/35, Hartford, Conn. BL/TL, 5'10", 185 lbs. Deb: 6/28/1887 ◆																											
1890 Buf-P	0	0	—	1	0	0	0	0	6	10	8	0	0	3	0	19.5	12.00	34	.357	.419	159	.297	0	-5	-5	-0	-0.2
● ROY BEECHER Beecher, Leroy "Colonel" b: 5/10/1884, Swanton, Ohio d: 10/11/52, Toledo, Ohio BL/TR, 6'2", 180 lbs. Deb: 9/29/07																											
1907 NY-N	0	2	.000	2	2	2	0	0	14	17	8	0	0	6	5	14.8	2.57	96	.293	.359	0	.000	-1	-0	-0	-0	-0.1
1908 NY-N	0	0	—	2	0	0	0	1	5^2	11	5	0	0	3	0	22.2	7.94	30	.440	.500	1	.333	1	-4	-3	0	-0.1
Total 2	0	2	.000	4	2	2	0	1	19^2	28	13	0	0	9	5	16.9	4.12	60	.337	.402	1	.125	-0	-4	-4	0	-0.2
● FRED BEENE Beene, Freddy Ray b: 11/24/42, Angleton, Tex. BB/TR, 5'9", 160 lbs. Deb: 9/18/68																											
1968 Bal-A	0	0	—	1	0	0	0	0	1	2	1	0	0	1	1	27.0	9.00	33	.500	.600	0	—	0	-1	-1	0	0.0
1969 Bal-A	0	0	—	2	0	0	0	0	2^2	2	0	0	0	1	0	10.1	0.00	—	.200	.273	0	—	0	1	1	0	0.1
1970 Bal-A	0	0	—	4	0	0	0	0	6	8	5	1	0	5	4	19.5	6.00	61	.320	.433	0	—	0	-2	-2	-0	-0.1
1972 NY-A	1	3	.250	29	1	0	0	3	57^2	55	21	3	1	24	37	12.5	2.34	126	.256	.333	0	.000	-1	5	4	0	0.2
1973 NY-A	6	0	1.000	19	4	0	0	1	91	67	21	5	1	27	49	9.4	1.68	218	.209	.273	0	—	0	22	21	1	1.5
1974 NY-A	0	0	—	6	0	0	0	1	10	9	4	1	1	2	10	10.8	2.70	131	.231	.286	0	—	0	1	1	0	0.1
Cle-A	4	4	.500	32	0	0	0	2	73	68	44	7	1	26	35	11.7	4.93	73	.246	.314	0	—	0	-11	-11	1	-1.0
Yr	4	4	.500	38	0	0	0	3	83	77	48	8	2	28	45	11.6	4.66	77	.244	.310	0	—	0	-10	-10	1	-0.9
1975 Cle-A	1	0	1.000	19	1	0	0	1	46^2	63	42	4	3	25	20	17.6	6.94	55	.323	.408	0	—	0	-16	-16	0	-0.8
Total 7	12	7	.632	112	6	0	0	8	288	274	138	21	7	111	156	12.3	3.63	97	.253	.326	0	.000	-1	-1	-3	2	0.0
● ANDY BEENE Beene, Ramon Andrew b: 10/13/56, Freeport, Tex. BR/TR, 6'3", 205 lbs. Deb: 9/22/83																											
1983 Mil-A	0	0	—	1	0	0	0	0	2	3	3	0	0	1	0	18.0	4.50	83	.333	.400	0	—	0	-0	-0	-0	0.0
1984 Mil-A	0	2	.000	5	3	0	0	0	18^2	28	23	1	2	9	11	18.8	11.09	35	.350	.429	0	—	0	-15	-16	0	-1.3
Total 2	0	2	.000	6	3	0	0	0	20^2	31	26	1	2	10	11	18.7	10.45	37	.348	.426	0	—	0	-15	-16	0	-1.3
● CLARENCE BEERS Beers, Clarence Scott b: 12/9/18, ElDorado, Kan. BR/TR, 6', 175 lbs. Deb: 5/2/48																											
1948 StL-N	0	0	—	1	0	0	0	0	0^2	3	4	0	0	1	0	54.0	13.50	30	.500	.571	0	—	0	-1	-1	-0	0.0
● JOE BEGGS Beggs, Joseph Stanley "Fireman" b: 11/4/10, Rankin, Pa. d: 7/19/83, Indianapolis, Ind BR/TR, 6'1", 182 lbs. Deb: 4/19/38																											
1938 NY-A	3	2	.600	14	9	4	0	0	58^1	69	41	7	0	20	8	13.7	5.40	84	.299	.355	5	.250	1	-4	-6	2	-0.2
1940 *Cin-N	12	3	.800	37	1	0	0	**7**	76^2	68	19	1	1	21	25	10.6	2.00	190	.243	.298	4	.190	-0	**16**	**16**	1	3.3
1941 Cin-N	4	3	.571	37	0	0	0	5	57	57	29	2	0	27	19	13.3	3.79	95	.313	.402	3	.300	1	-1	-1	0	-0.1
1942 Cin-N	6	5	.545	38	0	0	0	8	88^2	65	28	4	1	33	24	10.0	2.13	154	.206	.283	0	.000	-3	12	11	3	1.6
1943 Cin-N	7	6	.538	39	4	4	2	6	115^1	121	38	0	0	25	28	11.4	2.34	142	.276	.315	5	.143	-1	**13**	**13**	1	1.6
1944 Cin-N	1	0	1.000	1	1	1	0	0	9	8	2	0	0	0	2	8.0	2.00	174	.222	.222	0	.000	-1	2	2	0	0.1
1946 Cin-N	12	10	.545	28	22	14	2	1	190	175	63	15	1	39	38	10.2	2.32	144	.247	.287	14	.222	2	23	22	1	3.0
1947 Cin-N	0	3	.000	11	4	0	0	0	32^1	42	26	4	0	6	11	13.4	5.29	78	.316	.345	1	.091	-1	-4	-4	1	-0.4
NY-N	3	3	.500	32	0	0	0	2	66	81	38	6	1	18	23	13.6	4.23	96	.300	.346	1	.077	-1	-1	-1	-0	-0.2
Yr	3	6	.333	43	4	0	0	2	98^1	123	64	10	1	24	34	13.5	4.58	89	.305	.346	2	.083	-2	-6	-5	0	-0.6

YEAR TM/L	W	L	PCT	G	GS	CG	SH	SV	IP	H	R	HR	HB	BB	SO	RAT	ERA	ERA+	OAV	OOB	BH	AVG	PB	PR	PR+	PD	TPI
1948 NY-N	0	0	—	1	0	0	0	0	0^{1}	2	0	0	0	0	0	54.0	0.00	—	.667	.667	0	—	0	0	0	0	0.0
Total 9	48	35	.578	238	41	23	4	29	693^{2}	688	284	39	4	189	178	11.4	2.96	122	.265	.316	33	.167	-3	55	51	8	8.7

● ED BEGLEY

Begley, Edward N. (b: Edward N. Bagley) b: 1863, New York, N.Y. d: 7/24/19, Waterbury, Conn. Deb: 5/3/1884

YEAR TM/L	W	L	PCT	G	GS	CG	SH	SV	IP	H	R	HR	HB	BB	SO	RAT	ERA	ERA+	OAV	OOB	BH	AVG	PB	PR	PR+	PD	TPI
1884 NY-N	12	18	.400	31	30	30	0	0	266	296	209	9		99	104	13.4	4.16	72	.263	.323	22	.182	-3	-35	-35	-2	-3.4
1885 NY-a	4	9	.308	15	14	10	0	0	115	131	102	5	8	48	44	14.6	4.93	60	.278	.355	9	.173	-0	-21	-28	1	-2.3
Total 2	16	27	.372	46	44	40	0	0	381	427	311	14	8	147	148	13.7	4.39	68	.268	.333	31	.179	-3	-56	-62	-1	-5.7

● PETIE BEHAN

Behan, Charles Frederick b: 12/11/1887, Dallas City, Pa. d: 1/22/57, Bradford, Pa. BR/TR, 5'10", 160 lbs. Deb: 9/16/21

YEAR TM/L	W	L	PCT	G	GS	CG	SH	SV	IP	H	R	HR	HB	BB	SO	RAT	ERA	ERA+	OAV	OOB	BH	AVG	PB	PR	PR+	PD	TPI
1921 Phi-N	0	1	.000	2	2	1	0	0	10^{2}	17	8	0	0	1	3	15.2	5.91	72	.354	.367	0	.000	-1	-3	-2	-0	-0.2
1922 Phi-N	4	2	.667	7	5	3	1	0	47^{1}	49	27	3	1	14	13	12.2	2.47	189	.259	.314	5	.250	-0	9	10	-1	1.1
1923 Phi-N	3	12	.200	31	17	5	0	2	131	182	102	11	1	57	27	16.5	5.50	84	.336	.401	8	.186	-2	-22	-11	-1	-1.4
Total 3	7	15	.318	40	24	9	1	2	189	248	137	14	2	72	43	15.3	4.76	97	.319	.378	13	.194	-3	-16	-3	-2	-0.5

● RICK BEHENNA

Behenna, Richard Kipp b: 3/6/60, Miami, Fla. BR/TR, 6'2", 170 lbs. Deb: 4/12/83

YEAR TM/L	W	L	PCT	G	GS	CG	SH	SV	IP	H	R	HR	HB	BB	SO	RAT	ERA	ERA+	OAV	OOB	BH	AVG	PB	PR	PR+	PD	TPI
1983 Atl-N	3	3	.500	14	6	0	0	0	37^{1}	37	20	7	1	12	17	12.1	4.58	85	.255	.316	4	.333	2	-4	-3	-0	-0.3
Cle-A	0	2	.000	5	4	0	0	0	26	22	13	0	1	14	9	12.8	4.15	102	.232	.336	0	—	0	-0	0	0	0.0
1984 Cle-A	0	3	.000	3	3	0	0	0	9^{2}	17	15	5	1	8	6	24.2	13.97	29	.386	.491	0	—	0	-11	-10	0	-1.6
1985 Cle-A	0	2	.000	4	4	0	0	0	19^{2}	29	17	3	0	8	4	16.9	7.78	53	.354	.411	0	—	0	-8	-8	-1	-0.7
Total 3	3	10	.231	26	17	0	0	0	92^{2}	105	65	15	3	42	36	14.6	6.12	67	.287	.365	4	.333	2	-23	-20	-1	-2.6

● MEL BEHNEY

Behney, Melvin Brian b: 9/2/47, Newark, N.J. BL/TL, 6'2", 180 lbs. Deb: 8/14/70

YEAR TM/L	W	L	PCT	G	GS	CG	SH	SV	IP	H	R	HR	HB	BB	SO	RAT	ERA	ERA+	OAV	OOB	BH	AVG	PB	PR	PR+	PD	TPI
1970 Cin-N	0	2	.000	5	1	0	0	0	10	15	11	1	0	8	2	20.7	4.50	90	.341	.442	0	.000	-0	-0	-1	-0	-0.1

● HANK BEHRMAN

Behrman, Henry Bernard b: 6/27/21, Brooklyn, N.Y. d: 1/20/87, New York, N.Y. BR/TR, 5'11", 174 lbs. Deb: 4/17/46

YEAR TM/L	W	L	PCT	G	GS	CG	SH	SV	IP	H	R	HR	HB	BB	SO	RAT	ERA	ERA+	OAV	OOB	BH	AVG	PB	PR	PR+	PD	TPI
1946 Bro-N	11	5	.688	47	11	2	0	4	150^{2}	138	63	3	2	69	78	12.5	2.93	115	.241	.325	4	.095	-3	8	8	-2	0.3
1947 *Bro-N	0	0	—	2	0	0	0	0	3^{2}	3	4	1	0	4	2	17.2	9.82	42	.231	.412	0	—	0	-2	-2	-0	-0.1
Pit-N	0	2	.000	10	2	0	0	0	24^{2}	33	26	6	2	17	11	19.0	9.12	46	.347	.456	0	.000	-1	-14	-13	-1	-1.0
*Bro-N	5	3	.625	38	6	0	0	8	88^{1}	94	60	9	0	44	31	14.1	5.30	78	.274	.357	6	.231	1	-12	-11	-1	-1.2
Yr	5	5	.500	50	8	0	0	8	116^{2}	130	90	16	2	65	44	15.2	6.25	66	.288	.380	6	.188	-0	-28	-27	-2	-2.3
1948 Bro-N	5	4	.556	34	4	2	1	7	91	95	51	7	3	42	42	13.8	4.05	99	.268	.350	3	.107	-2	-1	-1	-0	-0.3
1949 NY-N	3	3	.500	43	4	1	1	0	71^{1}	64	46	5	0	52	25	14.6	4.92	81	.239	.363	1	.077	-1	-7	-8	-0	-0.6
Total 4	24	17	.585	174	27	5	2	19	429^{2}	427	250	31	7	228	189	13.9	4.40	87	.259	.352	14	.122	-5	-28	-28	-5	-2.9

● KEVIN BEIRNE

Beirne, Kevin Patrick b: 1/1/74, Houston, Tex. BL/TR, 6'4", 210 lbs. Deb: 5/17/2000

YEAR TM/L	W	L	PCT	G	GS	CG	SH	SV	IP	H	R	HR	HB	BB	SO	RAT	ERA	ERA+	OAV	OOB	BH	AVG	PB	PR	PR+	PD	TPI
2000 Chi-A	1	3	.250	29	1	0	0	0	49^{2}	50	41	9	4	20	41	13.4	6.70	74	.263	.346	0	—	0	-10	-10	-1	-0.7

● TIM BELCHER

Belcher, Timothy Wayne b: 10/19/61, Mount Gilead, Ohio BR/TR, 6'3", 220 lbs. Deb: 9/6/87

YEAR TM/L	W	L	PCT	G	GS	CG	SH	SV	IP	H	R	HR	HB	BB	SO	RAT	ERA	ERA+	OAV	OOB	BH	AVG	PB	PR	PR+	PD	TPI
1987 LA-N	4	2	.667	6	5	0	0	0	34	30	11	2	0	7	23	9.8	2.38	167	.240	.280	2	.200	0	6	6	-0	1.1
1988 *LA-N	12	6	.667	36	27	4	1	4	179^{2}	143	65	8	2	51	152	9.8	2.91	115	.217	.275	4	.071	-2	11	9	-1	0.7
1989 LA-N	15	12	.556	39	30	**10**	**8**	1	230	182	81	20	7	80	200	10.5	2.82	121	.217	.291	7	.100	-2	17	16	-2	1.4
1990 LA-N	9	9	.500	24	24	5	2	0	153	136	76	17	2	48	102	10.9	4.00	92	.240	.302	7	.163	1	-3	-6	-2	-0.7
1991 LA-N	10	9	.526	33	33	2	1	0	209^{1}	189	76	10	2	75	156	11.4	2.62	137	.240	.307	8	.119	-2	25	23	-2	1.7
1992 Cin-N	15	14	.517	35	34	2	1	0	227^{2}	201	104	17	3	80	149	11.2	3.91	92	.238	.307	8	.105	-2	-10	-8	-0	-1.2
1993 Cin-N	9	6	.600	22	22	4	2	0	137	134	72	11	7	47	101	12.4	4.47	90	.254	.324	10	.200	1	-6	-7	-1	-0.7
*Chi-A	3	5	.375	12	11	1	1	0	71^{2}	64	36	8	1	27	34	11.6	4.40	95	.242	.314	0	—	0	-0	-2	-1	-0.2
1994 Det-A	7	15	.318	25	25	3	0	0	162	192	124	21	4	78	76	15.2	5.89	82	.290	.368	0	—	0	-19	-19	-1	-1.9
1995 *Sea-A	10	12	.455	28	28	1	0	0	179^{1}	188	101	19	5	88	96	14.1	4.52	105	.269	.354	0	—	0	4	4	-1	0.4
1996 KC-A	15	11	.577	35	35	4	1	0	238^{2}	262	117	28	6	68	113	12.7	3.92	128	.281	.334	0	—	0	29	29	-0	2.7
1997 KC-A	13	12	.520	32	32	3	1	0	213^{1}	242	128	31	5	70	113	13.4	5.02	94	.288	.346	0	.000	-1	-11	-7	-1	-0.8
1998 KC-A	14	14	.500	34	34	2	0	0	234	247	127	37	7	73	130	12.6	4.27	113	.272	.331	1	.200	0	10	14	-3	1.2
1999 Ana-A	6	8	.429	24	24	0	0	0	132^{1}	168	104	27	5	46	52	14.9	6.73	72	.315	.374	1	.200	0	-27	-28	-1	-2.3
2000 Ana-A	4	5	.444	9	9	1	0	0	40^{2}	45	31	8	2	22	22	15.3	6.86	72	.281	.375	0	—	0	-9	-8	-0	-1.4
Total 14	146	140	.510	394	373	42	18	5	2442^{2}	2423	1253	264	58	860	1519	12.3	4.16	101	.259	.325	48	.124	-6	15	15	-12	-0.0

● STAN BELINDA

Belinda, Stanley Peter b: 8/6/66, Huntingdon, Pa. BR/TR, 6'3", 187 lbs. Deb: 9/8/89

YEAR TM/L	W	L	PCT	G	GS	CG	SH	SV	IP	H	R	HR	HB	BB	SO	RAT	ERA	ERA+	OAV	OOB	BH	AVG	PB	PR	PR+	PD	TPI
1989 Pit-N	0	1	.000	8	0	0	0	0	10^{1}	13	8	0	0	2	10	13.1	6.10	55	.295	.326	0	—	0	-3	-3	-0	-0.3
1990 *Pit-N	3	4	.429	55	0	0	0	8	58^{1}	48	23	4	1	29	55	12.0	3.55	102	.227	.324	0	.000	-1	2	-1	-1	-0.1
1991 *Pit-N	7	5	.583	60	0	0	0	16	78^{1}	50	30	10	4	35	71	10.2	3.45	104	.184	.286	0	.000	-0	2	1	-1	0.1
1992 *Pit-N	6	4	.600	59	0	0	0	18	71^{1}	58	26	8	0	29	57	11.0	3.15	109	.223	.301	2	.667	1	3	2	-1	0.4
1993 Pit-N	3	1	.750	40	0	0	0	19	42^{1}	35	18	4	1	11	30	10.0	3.61	112	.224	.280	0	.000	-0	2	2	-0	0.3
KC-A	1	1	.500	23	0	0	0	0	27^{1}	30	13	2	1	6	25	12.2	4.28	107	.280	.325	0	—	0	0	1	-1	0.0
1994 KC-A	2	2	.500	37	0	0	0	1	49	47	36	6	5	24	37	14.0	5.14	97	.250	.350	0	—	0	-2	-1	-1	-0.1
1995 *Bos-A	8	1	.889	63	0	0	0	10	69^{2}	51	25	5	4	28	57	10.7	3.10	157	.205	.295	0	—	0	13	13	-1	1.7
1996 Bos-A	2	1	.667	31	0	0	0	2	28^{2}	31	22	3	4	20	18	17.3	6.59	77	.272	.399	0	—	0	-5	-5	-0	-0.5
1997 Cin-N	1	5	.167	84	0	0	0	1	99^{1}	84	42	11	9	33	114	11.4	3.71	115	.229	.308	1	.333	0	5	6	-2	0.2
1998 Cin-N	4	8	.333	40	0	0	0	1	61^{1}	46	23	7	1	28	57	11.0	3.23	133	.212	.305	0	.000	-0	7	7	0	1.3
1999 Cin-N	3	1	.750	29	0	0	0	2	42^{2}	42	26	11	1	18	40	12.9	5.27	88	.258	.335	1	.250	0	-3	-3	-0	-0.3
2000 Col-N	1	3	.250	46	0	0	0	1	35^{2}	39	32	10	2	17	40	14.6	7.07	84	.277	.363	0	.000	-0	-10	-3	-0	-0.4
Atl-N	0	0	—	10	0	0	0	0	11	16	12	4	1	5	11	18.0	9.82	46	.348	.423	0	—	0	-6	-7	-0	-0.3
Yr	1	3	.250	56	0	0	0	1	46^{2}	55	44	14	3	22	51	15.4	7.71	73	.294	.377	0	.000	-0	-16	-9	-1	-0.7
Total 12	41	37	.526	585	0	0	0	79	685^{1}	590	336	85	34	285	622	11.9	4.15	103	.233	.319	4	.160	1	4	10	-8	2.0

● BO BELINSKY

Belinsky, Robert b: 12/7/36, New York, N.Y. BL/TL, 6'2", 191 lbs. Deb: 4/18/62

YEAR TM/L	W	L	PCT	G	GS	CG	SH	SV	IP	H	R	HR	HB	BB	SO	RAT	ERA	ERA+	OAV	OOB	BH	AVG	PB	PR	PR+	PD	TPI
1962 LA-A	10	11	.476	33	31	5	3	1	187^{1}	149	86	12	13	122	145	13.6	3.56	109	.216	.344	10	.167	1	9	6	-0	0.7
1963 LA-A	2	9	.182	13	13	2	0	0	76^{2}	78	54	12	4	35	60	13.7	5.75	60	.262	.347	2	.074	-2	-18	-21	1	-2.6
1964 LA-A	9	8	.529	23	22	4	1	0	135^{1}	120	45	8	6	49	91	11.6	2.86	115	.240	.315	4	.095	-1	11	7	-1	0.6
1965 Phi-N	4	9	.308	30	14	3	0	1	109^{2}	103	72	13	6	48	71	12.9	4.84	71	.248	.334	6	.188	-0	-16	-17	-1	-2.0
1966 Phi-N	0	2	.000	9	1	0	0	0	15^{1}	14	5	3	3	5	8	12.9	2.93	123	.250	.344	1	.333	0	1	1	0	0.2
1967 Hou-N	3	9	.250	27	18	0	0	0	115^{1}	112	74	12	8	54	80	13.6	4.68	71	.255	.347	3	.077	-2	-17	-18	-2	-2.1
1969 Pit-N	0	3	.000	8	3	0	0	0	17^{2}	17	10	1	2	14	15	16.8	4.76	76	.266	.412	0	.000	-0	-2	-2	-0	-0.4
1970 Cin-N	0	0	—	3	0	0	0	0	8	10	6	0	0	6	6	18.0	4.50	90	.294	.400	1	1.000	1	-0	-0	-0	0.0
Total 8	28	51	.354	146	102	14	4	2	665^{1}	603	352	61	42	333	476	13.2	4.10	86	.241	.340	27	.131	-2	-32	-45	-4	-5.6

● TODD BELITZ

Belitz, Todd Stephen b: 10/23/75, Des Moines, Ia. BL/TL, 6'1", 220 lbs. Deb: 9/4/2000

YEAR TM/L	W	L	PCT	G	GS	CG	SH	SV	IP	H	R	HR	HB	BB	SO	RAT	ERA	ERA+	OAV	OOB	BH	AVG	PB	PR	PR+	PD	TPI
2000 Oak-A	0	0	—	5	0	0	0	0	3^{1}	4	2	0	0	4	3	21.6	2.70	176	.267	.421	0	—	0	1	1	-0	0.0

● CHARLIE BELL

Bell, Charles C. b: 8/12/1868, Cincinnati, Ohio d: 2/7/37, Cincinnati, Ohio TR, Deb: 10/13/1889 F♦

YEAR TM/L	W	L	PCT	G	GS	CG	SH	SV	IP	H	R	HR	HB	BB	SO	RAT	ERA	ERA+	OAV	OOB	BH	AVG	PB	PR	PR+	PD	TPI
1889 KC-a	1	0	1.000	1	1	1	0	0	9	4	5	0	1	3	3	8.0	1.00	418	.129	.229	1	.167	0	3	3	1	0.4
1891 Lou-a	2	6	.250	10	9	8	0	0	77	93	65	4	8	20	16	14.1	4.68	78	.289	.346	1	.036	-2	-8	-9	-2	-1.0
Cin-a	1	0	1.000	1	1	1	0	0	9	2	2	0	1	3	1	6.0	0.00	—	.069	.182	2	.500	0	4	4	0	0.5
Yr	3	6	.333	11	10	9	0	0	86	95	67	4	9	23	17	13.3	4.19	88	.271	.332	3	.094	-2	-5	-5	-1	-0.5
Total 2	4	6	.400	12	11	10	0	0	95	99	72	4	10	26	20	12.8	3.88	96	.259	.323	4	.105	-2	-2	-2	-1	-0.1

● DEREK BELL

Bell, Derek Nathaniel b: 12/11/68, Tampa, Fla. BR/TR, 6'2", 215 lbs. Deb: 6/28/91 ♦

YEAR TM/L	W	L	PCT	G	GS	CG	SH	SV	IP	H	R	HR	HB	BB	SO	RAT	ERA	ERA+	OAV	OOB	BH	AVG	PB	PR	PR+	PD	TPI
2000 *NY-N	0	0	—	1	0	0	0	0	1	3	5	0	0	3	0	54.0	36.00	12	.429	.600	145	.266	1	-3	-4	0	-0.2

● ERIC BELL

Bell, Eric Alvin b: 10/27/63, Modesto, Cal. BL/TL, 6'3", 195 lbs. Deb: 9/24/85

YEAR TM/L	W	L	PCT	G	GS	CG	SH	SV	IP	H	R	HR	HB	BB	SO	RAT	ERA	ERA+	OAV	OOB	BH	AVG	PB	PR	PR+	PD	TPI
1985 Bal-A	0	0	—	4	0	0	0	0	5^{2}	4	3	1	0	4	4	12.7	4.76	85	.200	.333	0	—	0	-0	-0	0	0.0
1986 Bal-A	1	2	.333	4	4	0	0	0	23^{1}	23	14	4	0	14	18	14.3	5.01	83	.258	.359	0	—	0	-2	-2	-1	-0.3
1987 Bal-A	10	13	.435	33	29	2	0	0	165	174	113	32	2	78	111	13.9	5.45	81	.271	.351	0	—	0	-18	-19	-1	-2.3
1991 Cle-A	4	0	1.000	10	0	0	0	0	18	5	2	0	1	5	7	5.5	0.50	832	.091	.180	0	—	0	7	7	-0	1.5

YEAR	TM/L	W	L	PCT	G	GS	CG	SH	SV	IP	H	R	HR	HB	BB	SO	RAT	ERA	ERA+	OAV	OOB	BH	AVG	PB	PR	PR+	PD	TPI
1992	Cle-A	0	2	.000	7	1	0	0	0	15^1	22	13	1	1	9	10	18.8	7.63	51	.349	.438	0	—	0	-6	-6	1	-0.7
1993	Hou-N	0	1	.000	10	0	0	0	0	7^1	10	5	0	0	2	2	14.7	6.14	63	.313	.353	0	—	0	-2	-2	-0	-0.3
Total	6	15	18	.455	68	34	2	0	0	234^2	238	150	38	4	112	152	13.6	5.18	83	.264	.348	0	—	0	-21	-23	-2	-2.1
● GARY BELL	Bell, Gary b: 11/17/36, San Antonio, Tex. BR/TR, 6'1", 198 lbs. Deb: 6/1/58																											
1958	Cle-A	12	10	.545	33	23	10	0	1	182	141	70	18	5	73	110	10.8	3.31	110	.213	.296	11	.196	2	9	7	-2	0.8
1959	Cle-A	16	11	.593	44	28	12	1	5	234	208	107	28	5	105	136	12.2	4.04	91	.238	.323	18	.240	3	-5	-10	-2	-1.0
1960	Cle-A★	9	10	.474	28	23	6	2	1	154^2	139	78	15	7	82	109	13.3	4.13	90	.242	.344	7	.149	-0	-4	-7	1	-0.7
1961	Cle-A	12	16	.429	34	34	11	2	0	228^1	214	125	32	6	100	163	12.6	4.10	96	.245	.326	16	.198	1	-2	-4	-1	-0.4
1962	Cle-A	10	9	.526	57	6	1	0	12	107^2	104	56	14	3	52	80	13.3	4.26	91	.264	.354	5	.208	1	-4	-5	-1	-0.8
1963	Cle-A	8	5	.615	58	7	0	0	5	119	91	48	13	4	52	98	11.1	2.95	123	.208	.298	3	.115	-1	9	9	1	1.0
1964	Cle-A	8	6	.571	56	2	0	0	4	106	106	56	15	4	53	89	13.8	4.33	83	.260	.351	6	.375	2	-8	-9	-1	-1.0
1965	Cle-A	6	5	.545	60	0	0	0	17	103^2	86	43	7	2	50	86	12.0	3.04	115	.226	.319	1	.063	-0	5	5	-1	0.6
1966	Cle-A☆	14	15	.483	40	37	12	0	0	254^1	211	102	19	4	79	194	10.4	3.22	107	.228	.291	10	.132	-1	6	6	2	0.8
1967	Cle-A	1	5	.167	9	9	1	0	0	60^2	50	28	7	1	24	39	11.1	3.71	88	.234	.314	0	.000	-2	-3	-3	1	-0.4
	*Bos-A	12	8	.600	29	24	8	0	3	165^1	143	70	16	4	47	115	10.6	3.16	110	.231	.290	12	.203	1	1	6	-1	0.8
	Yr	13	13	.500	38	33	9	0	3	226	193	98	23	5	71	154	10.7	3.31	104	.232	.296	12	.162	-1	-2	3	0	0.4
1968	Bos-A☆	11	11	.500	35	27	9	3	1	199^1	177	82	7	5	68	103	11.3	3.12	101	.239	.308	13	.220	2	-3	1	0	0.3
1969	Sea-A	2	6	.250	13	11	1	1	2	61^1	76	40	8	2	34	30	16.4	4.70	77	.305	.393	3	.214	1	-7	-7	0	-0.7
	Chi-A	0	0	—	23	2	0	0	0	38^2	48	27	8	2	23	26	17.0	6.28	61	.308	.403	0	.000	-0	-11	-10	0	-0.5
	Yr	2	6	.250	36	13	1	1	2	100	124	67	16	4	57	56	16.7	5.31	70	.306	.397	3	.158	1	-19	-17	0	-1.2
Total	12	121	117	.508	519	233	71	9	51	2015	1794	932	207	54	842	1378	12.0	3.68	98	.239	.320	105	.185	9	-17	-18	-3	-1.2
● GEORGE BELL	Bell, George Glenn "Farmer" b: 11/2/1874, Greenwood, N.Y. d: 12/25/41, New York, N.Y. BR/TR, 6', 195 lbs. Deb: 4/17/07																											
1907	Bro-N	8	16	.333	35	27	20	3	1	263^2	222	102	1	6	77	88	10.4	2.25	104	.238	.300	8	.095	-2	6	3	2	0.3
1908	Bro-N	4	15	.211	29	19	12	2	1	155^1	162	80	3	2	45	63	12.1	3.59	65	.270	.324	8	.170	1	-21	-22	1	-2.4
1909	Bro-N	16	15	.516	33	30	29	6	1	256	236	103	5	4	73	95	11.0	2.71	96	.251	.307	15	.167	1	-3	-3	2	-0.1
1910	Bro-N	10	27	.270	44	36	25	4	1	310	267	127	4	4	82	102	10.2	2.64	115	.241	.296	13	.134	-4	13	13	-3	0.7
1911	Bro-N	5	6	.455	19	12	6	2	0	101	123	59	2	2	28	28	13.6	4.28	78	.315	.364	4	.121	-1	-10	-11	2	-1.0
Total	5	43	79	.352	160	124	92	17	4	1086	1010	471	15	18	305	376	11.0	2.85	94	.254	.310	48	.137	-6	-14	-20	4	-2.5
● HI BELL	Bell, Herman S b: 7/16/1897, Mt.Sherman, Ky. d: 6/7/49, Glendale, Cal. BR/TR, 6', 185 lbs. Deb: 4/16/24																											
1924	StL-N	3	8	.273	28	10	5	0	1	113^1	124	68	5	5	29	29	12.5	4.92	77	.292	.344	2	.065	-2	-13	-15	0	-1.5
1926	*StL-N	6	6	.500	27	8	3	0	2	85	82	41	1	2	17	27	10.7	3.18	123	.255	.296	3	.120	-1	6	7	-1	0.6
1927	StL-N	1	3	.250	25	1	0	0	0	57^1	71	37	5	1	22	31	14.8	3.92	101	.317	.381	1	.091	-1	-0	0	0	-0.1
1929	StL-N	0	2	.000	7	0	0	0	0	13	19	15	1	0	4	4	15.9	6.92	67	.339	.383	0	.000	-0	-3	-3	-0	-0.5
1930	*StL-N	4	3	.571	39	9	2	0	**8**	115^1	143	65	4	2	23	42	13.1	3.90	129	.299	.334	2	.077	-3	**14**	**14**	1	0.7
1932	NY-N	8	4	.667	35	10	3	0	2	120	132	58	12	2	16	25	11.3	3.68	101	.280	.307	3	.088	-2	1	1	-1	-0.3
1933	*NY-N	6	5	.545	38	7	1	1	5	105^1	100	31	4	2	20	24	10.4	2.05	157	.246	.285	4	.138	-1	**15**	**14**	-1	1.4
1934	NY-N	4	3	.571	22	2	0	0	6	54	72	25	2	2	12	9	14.3	3.67	105	.319	.358	2	.105	-1	2	1	-1	0.0
Total	8	32	34	.485	221	47	14	1	24	663^1	743	340	34	16	143	191	12.2	3.69	107	.285	.326	17	.096	-12	23	19	-4	0.3
● JERRY BELL	Bell, Jerry Houston b: 10/6/47, Madison, Tenn. BB/TR, 6'4", 190 lbs. Deb: 9/6/71																											
1971	Mil-A	2	1	.667	8	0	0	0	0	14^2	10	5	0	0	6	8	9.8	3.07	113	.200	.286	0	—	0	1	1	-0	0.1
1972	Mil-A	5	1	.833	25	3	0	0	0	70^2	50	15	1	3	33	20	11.0	1.66	184	.209	.313	1	.071	-1	11	11	1	0.9
1973	Mil-A	9	9	.500	31	25	8	0	1	183^2	185	95	14	5	70	57	12.7	3.97	95	.263	.334	0	—	0	-3	-4	1	-0.3
1974	Mil-A	1	0	1.000	5	0	0	0	0	14	17	6	2	0	5	4	14.1	2.57	141	.315	.373	0	—	0	2	2	-0	0.1
Total	4	17	11	.607	69	28	8	0	1	283	262	121	17	8	114	89	12.2	3.28	109	.250	.329	1	.071	-1	10	9	1	0.8
● RALPH BELL	Bell, Ralph Albert "Lefty" b: 11/6/1890, Kahoka, Mo. d: 10/18/59, Burlington, Iowa BL/TL, 5'11.5", 170 lbs. Deb: 7/16/12																											
1912	Chi-A	0	0	—	3	0	0	0	0	6	8	7	1	0	8	5	24.0	9.00	36	.333	.500	0	.000	-0	-4	-4	0	-0.2
● ROB BELL	Bell, Robert Allen b: 1/17/77, Newburgh, N.Y. BR/TR, 6'5", 225 lbs. Deb: 4/8/2000																											
2000	Cin-N	7	8	.467	26	26	1	0	0	140^1	130	84	32	1	73	112	13.1	5.00	95	.243	.336	3	.067	-3	-6	-3	-1	-0.7
● BILL BELL	Bell, William Samuel "Ding Dong" b: 10/24/33, Goldsboro, N.C. d: 10/11/62, Durham, N.C. BR/TR, 6'3", 200 lbs. Deb: 9/5/52																											
1952	Pit-N	0	1	.000	4	1	0	0	0	15^2	16	11	3	0	13	4	16.7	4.60	87	.254	.382	0	.000	-0	-2	-1	0	-0.1
1955	Pit-N	0	0	—	1	0	0	0	0	1	0	0	0	0	1	0	9.0	0.00	—	.000	.250	0	—	0	0	0	-0	0.0
Total	2	0	1	.000	5	1	0	0	0	16^2	16	11	3	0	14	4	16.2	4.32	93	.242	.375	0	.000	-0	-1	-1	0	-0.1
● RIGO BELTRAN	Beltran, Rigoberto b: 11/13/69, Tijuana, Mex. BL/TL, 5'11", 185 lbs. Deb: 6/2/97																											
1997	StL-N	1	2	.333	35	4	0	0	1	54^1	47	25	3	0	17	50	10.6	3.48	119	.237	.298	1	.143	0	4	4	1	0.3
1998	NY-N	0	0	—	7	0	0	0	0	8	6	3	1	0	4	5	11.3	3.38	123	.214	.313	0	.000	-0	1	1	-0	0.0
1999	NY-N	1	1	.500	21	0	0	0	0	31	30	15	5	0	12	35	12.2	3.48	126	.250	.318	0	.000	-0	4	3	1	0.2
	Col-N	0	0	—	12	0	0	0	0	11	20	9	2	1	7	15	22.9	7.36	79	.385	.467	1	.500	0	-3	-1	0	0.0
	Yr	1	1	.500	33	0	0	0	0	42	50	24	7	1	19	50	15.0	4.50	106	.291	.365	1	.333	0	0	1	1	0.2
2000	Col-N	0	0	—	1	1	0	0	0	1^1	6	6	2	0	3	1	60.8	40.50	15	.600	.692	0	—	0	-5	-4	0	-0.2
Total	4	2	3	.400	76	5	0	0	1	105^2	109	58	13	1	43	106	13.0	4.34	101	.267	.338	2	.182	0	0	1	1	0.3
● CHIEF BENDER	Bender, Charles Albert b: 5/5/1884, Crow Wing Co., Minn d: 5/22/54, Philadelphia, Pa. BR/TR, 6'2", 185 lbs. Deb: 4/20/03 CH																											
1903	Phi-A	17	14	.548	36	33	29	2	0	270	239	115	6	25	65	127	11.0	3.07	100	.237	.299	22	.183	-1	-3	-0	-1	-0.2
1904	Phi-A	10	11	.476	29	20	18	4	0	203^2	167	90	1	4	59	149	10.2	2.87	93	.225	.285	18	.228	3	-6	-4	-2	-0.4
1905	*Phi-A	18	11	.621	35	23	18	4	0	229	193	103	5	11	90	142	11.6	2.83	94	.230	.313	20	.217	2	-4	-4	3	-0.1
1906	Phi-A	15	10	.600	36	27	24	0	**3**	238^1	208	98	5	8	48	159	10.0	2.53	108	.238	.284	25	.253	7	4	5	-1	1.3
1907	Phi-A	16	8	.667	33	24	20	4	3	219^1	185	67	1	3	34	112	9.1	2.05	127	.231	.265	23	.230	3	12	13	-2	1.7
1908	Phi-A	8	9	.471	18	17	14	2	1	138^2	121	48	1	3	21	85	9.4	1.75	146	.236	.270	11	.220	2	10	12	-2	1.6
1909	Phi-A	18	8	.692	34	29	24	5	1	250	196	68	1	5	45	161	8.9	1.66	145	.214	.254	20	.215	4	23	21	2	3.0
1910	*Phi-A	23	5	**.821**	30	28	25	3	0	250	182	63	1	10	47	155	8.6	1.58	150	.207	.255	25	.269	8	26	23	2	3.9
1911	*Phi-A	17	5	**.773**	31	24	16	2	3	216^1	198	66	2	4	58	114	10.8	2.16	146	.252	.307	13	.165	-3	28	25	1	2.2
1912	Phi-A	13	8	.619	27	19	12	1	2	171	169	63	1	1	33	90	10.7	2.74	113	.277	.315	9	.150	-1	11	7	-2	0.5
1913	*Phi-A	21	10	.677	48	21	14	2	**13**	236^2	208	78	2	3	59	135	10.3	2.21	125	.228	.277	12	.154	0	19	16	-2	2.0
1914	*Phi-A	17	3	**.850**	28	23	14	7	2	179	159	49	4	1	55	107	10.8	2.26	115	.240	.299	9	.145	0	10	7	-0	0.9
1915	Bal-F	4	16	.200	26	23	15	0	1	178^1	198	103	5	7	37	89	12.2	3.99	72	.298	.342	16	.267	3	-25	-21	-1	-2.0
1916	Phi-N	7	7	.500	27	13	4	0	3	122^2	137	71	3	10	34	43	13.3	3.74	71	.287	.347	12	.279	4	-15	-15	2	-1.2
1917	Phi-N	8	2	.800	20	10	8	4	2	113	84	24	1	7	26	43	9.3	1.67	168	.215	.277	8	.205	1	13	14	-2	1.3
1925	Chi-A	0	0	—	1	0	0	0	0	1	1	2	1	0	1	0	18.0	18.00	23	.333	.500	0	—	0	-2	-2	-0	-0.1
Total	16	212	127	.625	459	334	255	40	34	3017	2645	1108	40	102	712	1711	10.3	2.46	111	.239	.291	243	.212	33	101	95	-5	14.4
● ALAN BENES	Benes, Alan Paul b: 1/21/72, Evansville, Ind. BR/TR, 6'5", 215 lbs. Deb: 9/19/95 F																											
1995	StL-N	1	2	.333	3	3	0	0	0	16	24	15	2	1	4	20	16.3	8.44	50	.343	.387	0	.000	-1	-8	-8	-0	-1.1
1996	*StL-N	13	10	.565	34	32	3	1	0	191	192	120	27	7	87	131	13.5	4.90	86	.266	.350	9	.148	-0	-14	-15	-2	-1.8
1997	StL-N	9	9	.500	23	23	2	0	0	161^2	128	60	13	4	68	160	11.1	2.89	143	.219	.304	9	.173	0	24	23	-1	2.3
1999	StL-N	0	0	—	2	0	0	0	0	2	2	0	0	0	0	2	9.0	0.00	—	.286	.286	0	—	0	1	1	0	0.1
2000	StL-N	2	2	.500	30	0	0	0	0	46	54	33	7	2	23	26	15.5	5.67	82	.290	.374	2	.500	1	-5	-5	-1	-0.4
Total	5	25	23	.521	92	58	5	1	0	416^2	400	228	49	14	182	339	12.9	4.32	98	.255	.337	20	.163	1	-3	-4	-4	-0.9
● ANDY BENES	Benes, Andrew Charles b: 8/20/67, Evansville, Ind. BR/TR, 6'6", 240 lbs. Deb: 8/11/89 F																											
1989	SD-N	6	3	.667	10	10	0	0	0	66^2	51	28	7	1	31	66	11.2	3.51	100	.213	.305	6	.250	2	-0	-0	0	0.2
1990	SD-N	10	11	.476	32	31	2	0	0	192^1	177	87	18	1	69	140	11.6	3.60	106	.242	.309	6	.100	-2	4	5	-3	0.0
1991	SD-N	15	11	.577	33	33	4	1	0	223	194	76	23	4	59	167	10.4	3.03	126	.232	.286	2	.032	-2	16	19	-1	1.8
1992	SD-N	13	14	.481	34	34	2	2	0	231^1	230	90	14	5	61	169	11.5	3.35	107	.264	.316	10	.149	2	4	6	0	0.9
1993	SD-N★	15	15	.500	34	34	4	2	0	230^2	200	111	23	4	86	179	11.3	3.78	109	.232	.305	9	.125	-0	7	9	-3	0.7

YEAR TM/L	W	L	PCT	G	GS	CG	SH	SV	IP	H	R	HR	HB	BB	SO	RAT	ERA	ERA+	OAV	OOB	BH	AVG	PB	PR	PR+	PD	TPI
1994 SD-N	6	14	.300	25	25	2	2	0	172^1	155	82	20	1	51	**189**	10.8	3.86	106	.237	.294	8	.163	-0	7	5	1	0.6
1995 SD-N	4	7	.364	19	19	1	1	0	118^2	121	65	10	4	45	126	12.9	4.17	97	.262	.333	6	.150	-0	0	-2	-1	-0.3
*Sea-A	7	2	.778	12	12	0	0	0	63	72	42	8	2	33	45	15.3	5.86	81	.287	.374	0	—	0	-8	-8	-0	-0.9
1996 *StL-N	18	10	.643	36	34	3	1	1	230^1	215	107	28	6	77	160	11.6	3.83	109	.247	.312	11	.151	-0	10	9	-3	0.7
1997 StL-N	10	7	.588	26	26	0	0	0	177	149	64	9	5	61	175	10.9	3.10	134	.230	.301	12	.218	2	22	21	-2	1.9
1998 Ari-N	14	13	.519	34	34	1	0	0	231^1	221	111	25	6	74	164	11.7	3.97	106	.251	.314	11	.169	3	7	6	-1	0.9
1999 Ari-N	13	12	.520	33	32	0	0	0	198^1	216	117	34	4	82	141	13.7	4.81	95	.273	.344	9	.155	1	-5	-5	-2	-0.7
2000 *StL-N	12	9	.571	30	27	1	0	0	166	174	95	30	1	68	137	13.2	4.88	95	.275	.346	4	.080	-1	-4	-5	-1	-0.7
Total 12	143	128	.528	358	351	20	9	1	2301	2175	1075	249	44	797	1858	11.8	3.86	106	.249	.315	94	.139	4	59	61	-15	5.1
● RAY BENGE Benge, Raymond Adelphia b: 4/22/02, Jacksonville, Tex. d: 6/27/97, Centerville, Tex. BR/TR, 5'9.5", 160 lbs. Deb: 9/26/25																											
1925 Cle-A	1	0	1.000	2	2	1	1	0	11^2	9	2	0	0	3	3	9.3	1.54	286	.205	.255	2	.400	0	4	4	-1	0.3
1926 Cle-A	1	0	1.000	8	0	0	0	0	11^2	15	11	0	0	4	3	14.7	3.86	105	.313	.365	1	.333	0	0	0	0	0.1
1928 Phi-N	8	18	.308	40	28	12	1	1	201^2	219	117	15	5	88	68	13.9	4.55	94	.286	.363	12	.207	-0	-13	-6	-2	-0.8
1929 Phi-N	11	15	.423	38	26	9	2	4	199	255	147	24	4	77	78	15.2	6.29	83	.322	.385	15	.203	-3	-35	-22	-3	-2.8
1930 Phi-N	11	15	.423	38	29	14	0	1	225^2	305	178	22	1	81	70	15.4	5.70	96	.328	.382	18	.205	-3	-18	-5	-1	-0.9
1931 Phi-N	14	18	.438	38	31	16	2	2	247	251	107	12	5	61	117	11.6	3.17	134	.262	.310	18	.205	-2	19	27	-2	2.9
1932 Phi-N	13	12	.520	41	28	13	2	6	222^1	247	119	15	4	58	89	12.5	4.05	109	.281	.329	13	.173	-3	-4	8	-1	0.5
1933 Bro-N	10	17	.370	37	30	16	2	1	228^2	238	104	11	6	55	74	11.8	3.42	94	.268	.315	14	.184	0	-2	-5	-3	-0.9
1934 Bro-N	14	12	.538	36	32	14	1	0	227	252	124	11	3	61	64	12.5	4.32	90	.272	.319	15	.169	-2	-7	-11	-1	-1.3
1935 Bro-N	9	9	.500	23	17	5	1	1	124^2	142	77	12	1	47	39	13.7	4.48	89	.289	.353	9	.191	-1	-6	-7	-2	-1.1
1936 Bos-N	7	9	.438	21	19	2	0	0	115	161	79	6	1	38	32	15.7	5.79	66	.333	.382	6	.140	-3	-23	-26	-2	-3.4
Phi-N	1	4	.200	15	6	0	0	1	45^2	70	35	3	0	19	13	17.5	4.73	96	.350	.406	0	.000	-1	-4	-1	-2	-0.4
Yr	8	13	.381	36	25	2	0	1	160^2	231	114	9	1	57	45	16.2	5.49	73	.338	.389	6	.113	-4	-26	-26	-4	-3.8
1938 Cin-N	1	1	.500	9	0	0	0	2	15^1	13	8	1	0	6	5	11.2	4.11	89	.228	.302	1	.333	0	-1	-1	-0	-0.1
Total 12	101	130	.437	346	248	102	12	19	1875^1	2177	1108	132	30	598	655	13.5	4.52	95	.292	.347	124	.188	-17	-89	-44	-18	-7.9
● ARMANDO BENITEZ Benitez, Armando German b: 11/3/72, Ramon Santana, D.R. BR/TR, 6'4", 180 lbs. Deb: 7/28/94																											
1994 Bal-A	0	0	—	3	0	0	0	0	10	8	1	0	1	4	14	11.7	0.90	557	.216	.310	0	—	0	4	4	0	0.2
1995 Bal-A	1	5	.167	44	0	0	0	2	47^2	37	33	8	5	37	56	14.9	5.66	84	.213	.366	0	—	0	-5	-5	-1	-0.6
1996 *Bal-A	1	0	1.000	18	0	0	0	4	14^1	7	6	2	0	6	20	8.2	3.77	131	.143	.236	0	—	0	2	2	-0	0.2
1997 *Bal-A	4	5	.444	71	0	0	0	9	73^1	49	22	7	1	43	106	11.4	2.45	180	.191	.309	0	—	0	17	17	-1	2.0
1998 Bal-A	5	6	.455	71	0	0	0	22	68^1	48	29	10	4	39	87	12.0	3.82	119	.199	.320	0	—	0	6	6	-0	1.1
1999 *NY-N	4	3	.571	77	0	0	0	22	78	40	17	4	0	41	128	9.3	1.85	237	.148	.260	0	.000	-1	24	23	-0	2.8
2000 *NY-N	4	4	.500	76	0	0	0	41	76	39	24	10	0	38	106	9.1	2.61	169	.148	.256	0	—	0	17	16	-1	2.9
Total 7	19	23	.452	360	0	0	0	100	367^2	228	132	41	11	208	517	10.9	3.04	149	.176	.296	0	.000	-1	66	62	-4	8.6
● MIKE BENJAMIN Benjamin, Michael Paul b: 11/22/65, Euclid, Ohio BR/TR, 6', 169 lbs. Deb: 7/7/89 ◆																											
1997 Bos-A	0	0	—	1	0	0	0	0	1	0	0	0	0	0	0	0.0	0.00	—	.000	.000	27	.233	0	1	1	0	0.0
● HENRY BENN Benn, Henry Omer b: 1/25/1890, Viola, Wis. d: 6/4/67, Madison, Wis. BR/TR, 6', 190 lbs. Deb: 9/24/14																											
1914 Cle-A	0	0	—	1	0	0	0	0	1	0	0	0	0	0	1	0.0	0.00	—	.000	.000	0	—	0	0	0	-0	0.0
● DAVE BENNETT Bennett, David Hans b: 11/7/45, Berkeley, Cal. BR/TR, 6'5", 195 lbs. Deb: 6/12/64 F																											
1964 Phi-N	0	0	—	1	0	0	0	0	1	2	1	0	0	0	1	18.0	9.00	39	.400	.400	0	—	0	-1	-1	0	0.0
● DENNIS BENNETT Bennett, Dennis John b: 10/5/39, Oakland, Cal. BL/TL, 6'5", 205 lbs. Deb: 5/12/62 F																											
1962 Phi-N	9	9	.500	31	24	7	2	3	174^2	144	78	17	6	68	149	11.2	3.81	102	.224	.304	8	.127	-1	3	1	-1	0.0
1963 Phi-N	9	5	.643	23	16	6	1	1	119^1	102	44	12	4	33	82	10.5	2.64	122	.231	.290	9	.225	3	9	8	0	1.3
1964 Phi-N	12	14	.462	41	32	7	2	1	208	222	92	23	5	58	125	12.3	3.68	94	.280	.333	13	.197	3	-3	-5	-1	-0.3
1965 Bos-A	5	7	.417	34	18	3	0	0	141^2	152	76	15	6	53	85	13.4	4.38	85	.279	.350	7	.179	2	-15	-10	-1	-0.6
1966 Bos-A	3	3	.500	16	13	0	0	0	75	75	30	9	1	23	47	11.9	3.24	117	.261	.318	3	.130	1	2	4	-1	0.3
1967 Bos-A	4	3	.571	13	11	4	1	0	69^2	72	32	12	2	22	34	12.4	3.88	90	.268	.328	3	.120	-0	-5	-3	-0	-0.3
NY-N	1	1	.500	8	6	0	0	0	26^1	37	15	4	1	7	14	15.4	5.13	66	.336	.381	2	.250	0	-5	-5	-0	-0.3
1968 Cal-A	0	5	.000	16	7	1	0	1	48^1	46	22	6	4	17	36	12.5	3.54	82	.250	.327	1	.077	-1	-3	-3	1	-0.4
Total 7	43	47	.478	182	127	28	6	6	863	850	389	98	29	281	572	12.1	3.69	96	.260	.324	46	.166	7	-18	-12	-2	-0.3
● ERIK BENNETT Bennett, Erik Hans b: 9/13/68, Yreka, Cal. BR/TR, 6'2", 205 lbs. Deb: 5/15/95																											
1995 Cal-A	0	0	—	1	0	0	0	0	0^1	0	0	0	0	0	0	0.0	0.00	—	.000	.000	0	—	0	0	0	0	0.0
1996 Min-A	2	0	1.000	24	0	0	0	1	27^1	33	24	7	2	16	13	16.8	7.90	65	.306	.405	0	—	0	-9	-8	0	-0.5
Total 2	2	0	1.000	25	0	0	0	1	27^2	33	24	7	2	16	13	16.6	7.81	65	.303	.402	0	—	0	-9	-8	0	-0.5
● FRANK BENNETT Bennett, Francis Allen "Chip" b: 10/27/04, Mardela Springs, Md. d: 3/18/66, Wilmington, Del. BR/TR, 5'10.5", 163 lbs. Deb: 9/17/27																											
1927 Bos-A	0	1	.000	4	1	0	0	0	12^1	15	4	0	0	6	1	15.3	2.92	145	.333	.412	0	.000	-1	2	2	0	0.1
1928 Bos-A	0	0	—	1	0	0	0	0	1	1	0	0	0	0	0	9.0	0.00	—	.250	.250	0	—	0	0	0	0	0.0
Total 2	0	1	.000	5	1	0	0	0	13^1	16	4	0	0	6	1	14.9	2.70	156	.327	.400	0	.000	-1	2	2	0	0.1
● JOEL BENNETT Bennett, Joel Todd b: 1/31/70, Binghamton, N.Y. BR/TR, 6'1", 160 lbs. Deb: 7/15/98																											
1998 Bal-A	0	0	—	2	0	0	0	0	2	2	1	0	0	3	0	22.5	4.50	101	.250	.455	0	—	0	0	0	-0	0.0
1999 Phi-N	2	1	.667	5	3	0	0	0	17	26	17	10	0	7	13	17.5	9.00	52	.351	.407	0	.000	-0	-8	-8	0	-1.0
Total 2	2	1	.667	7	3	0	0	0	19	28	18	10	0	10	13	18.0	8.53	55	.341	.413	0	.000	-0	-8	-8	0	-1.0
● SHAYNE BENNETT Bennett, Shayne Anthony b: 4/10/72, Adelaide, South Australia BR/TR, 6'5", 200 lbs. Deb: 8/22/97																											
1997 Mon-N	0	1	.000	16	0	0	0	0	22^2	21	9	2	0	9	8	11.9	3.18	132	.247	.319	0	.000	0	3	3	-1	0.1
1998 Mon-N	5	5	.500	62	0	0	0	1	91^2	97	61	8	6	45	59	14.5	5.50	77	.276	.368	0	.000	-0	-13	-13	-0	-1.3
1999 Mon-N	0	1	.000	5	1	0	0	0	11^1	24	18	4	1	3	4	22.2	14.29	31	.444	.483	0	.000	-0	-12	-13	-0	-0.9
Total 3	5	7	.417	83	1	0	0	1	125^2	142	88	14	7	57	71	14.8	5.87	72	.290	.372	0	.000	-0	-23	-23	-1	-2.1
● ALLEN BENSON Benson, Allen Wilbert "Bullet Ben" b: 7/12/08, Hurley, S.Dak. d: 11/16/99, Viborg, S.Dak. BR/TR, 6'1", 185 lbs. Deb: 8/19/34																											
1934 Was-A	0	1	.000	2	2	0	0	0	9^2	19	14	0	2	5	4	24.2	12.10	36	.413	.491	0	.000	-0	-8	-9	-0	-0.7
● KRIS BENSON Benson, Kristen James b: 11/7/74, Kennesaw, Ga. BR/TR, 6'4", 190 lbs. Deb: 4/9/99																											
1999 Pit-N	11	14	.440	31	31	2	0	0	196^2	184	105	16	6	83	139	12.5	4.07	112	.249	.330	10	.154	0	11	11	1	1.3
2000 Pit-N	10	12	.455	32	32	2	1	0	217^2	206	104	24	10	86	184	12.5	3.85	120	.249	.327	6	.092	-2	19	18	-1	1.4
Total 2	21	26	.447	63	63	4	1	0	414^1	390	209	40	16	169	323	12.5	3.95	116	.249	.329	16	.123	-2	30	29	0	2.7
● CY BENTLEY Bentley, Clytus G. b: 11/23/1850, East Haven, Conn. d: 2/26/1873, Middletown, Conn. Deb: 4/26/1872																											
1872 Man-n	2	15	.118	18	17	14	0	0	144	268	252	4		12	5	17.5	6.19	58	.343	.353	27	.235	-2	-41	-42		-3.0
● JACK BENTLEY Bentley, John Needles b: 3/8/1895, Sandy Spring, Md. d: 10/24/69, Olney, Md. BL/TL, 5'11.5", 200 lbs. Deb: 9/6/13 ◆																											
1913 Was-A	1	0	1.000	3	1	0	0	1	11	5	0	0	0	2	5	5.7	0.00	—	.147	.194	0	.000	-0	4	4	0	0.4
1914 Was-A	5	7	.417	30	11	3	2	**4**	125^1	110	49	3	3	53	55	11.9	2.37	119	.249	.334	11	.275	2	5	6	-1	0.8
1915 Was-A	0	2	.000	4	2	0	0	0	11^1	8	4	0	0	3	0	8.7	0.79	374	.200	.256	0	.000	-0	3	3	-0	0.4
1916 Was-A	0	0	—	2	0	0	0	0	1^1	0	0	0	0	1	1	6.8	0.00	—	.000	.250	0	—	0	0	0	0	0.0
1923 *NY-N	13	8	.619	31	26	12	1	3	183	198	102	10	5	67	80	13.3	4.48	85	.277	.343	38	.427	16	-10	-14	-1	-0.1
1924 *NY-N	16	5	.762	28	24	13	1	1	188	196	85	11	4	56	60	12.3	3.78	97	.273	.329	26	.265	4	2	-3	-1	0.0
1925 NY-N	11	9	.550	28	22	11	0	0	157	200	90	10	1	59	47	14.9	5.04	80	.323	.383	30	.303	6	-14	-19	-1	-1.0
1926 Phi-N	0	2	.000	7	3	0	0	0	25^1	37	28	2	0	10	7	16.7	8.17	51	.327	.382	62	.258	1	-12	-10	-0	-0.7
NY-N	0	0	—	1	0	0	0	0	2	0	0	0	0	2	1	9.0	0.00	—	.000	.250	1	.250	-0	1	1	-0	0.0
Yr	0	2	.000	8	3	0	0	0	27^1	37	28	2	0	12	8	16.1	7.57	54	.311	.374	63	.258	1	-11	-10	-0	-0.7
1927 NY-N	0	0	—	4	0	0	0	0	9^2	7	7	1	1	10	3	16.8	2.79	138	.206	.400	2	.222	1	1	1	-0	0.1
Total 9	46	33	.582	138	89	39	4	9	714	761	365	37	14	263	259	13.1	4.01	91	.280	.346	170	.291	28	-20	-29	-3	-0.1

● AL BENTON
Benton, John Alton b: 3/18/11, Noble, Okla. d: 4/14/68, Lynwood, Cal. BR/TR, 6'4", 215 lbs. Deb: 4/18/34

YEAR	TM/L	W	L	PCT	G	GS	CG	SH	SV	IP	H	R	HR	HB	BB	SO	RAT	ERA	ERA+	OAV	OOB	BH	AVG	PB	PR	PR+	PD	TPI
1934	Phi-A	7	9	.438	32	21	7	0	1	155	145	98	7	2	88	58	13.6	4.88	90	.249	.349	6	.109	-4	-7	-9	0	-1.1
1935	Phi-A	3	4	.429	27	9	0	0	0	78^1	110	81	7	1	47	42	18.2	7.70	59	.328	.413	1	.040	-3	-28	-27	-1	-2.3
1938	Det-A	5	3	.625	19	10	6	0	0	95^1	93	40	10	1	39	33	12.6	3.30	151	.259	.333	4	.121	-3	16	17	1	1.1
1939	Det-A	6	8	.429	37	16	3	0	5	150	182	94	11	1	58	67	14.5	4.56	107	.294	.355	4	.091	-4	1	5	0	0.1
1940	Det-A	6	10	.375	42	0	0	0	**17**	79^1	93	44	5	0	36	50	14.6	4.42	107	.294	.366	0	.000	-3	-0	3	-0	0.2
1941	Det-A☆	15	6	.714	38	14	7	1	7	157^2	130	63	11	3	65	63	11.3	2.97	153	**.221**	.302	3	.060	-5	21	25	-0	2.8
1942	Det-A★	7	13	.350	35	30	9	1	2	226^2	210	87	9	0	84	110	11.7	2.90	136	.246	.314	5	.075	-5	19	25	-1	1.4
1945	*Det-A	13	8	.619	31	27	12	5	3	191^2	175	68	7	2	63	76	11.3	2.02	174	.241	.303	4	.063	-6	29	31	2	3.0
1946	Det-A	11	7	.611	28	15	6	1	1	140^2	132	69	9	1	58	60	12.2	3.65	100	.245	.319	9	.184	-1	-2	0	1	0.0
1947	Det-A	6	7	.462	36	14	4	0	7	133	147	77	11	1	61	33	14.1	4.40	86	.288	.365	6	.154	-2	-10	-9	-0	-1.1
1948	Det-A	2	2	.500	30	0	0	0	3	44^1	45	34	4	1	36	18	16.6	5.68	77	.273	.406	2	.182	-0	-7	-6	0	-0.6
1949	Cle-A	9	6	.600	40	11	4	2	10	135^2	116	33	7	1	51	41	11.1	2.12	188	.238	.312	5	.132	-2	31	30	-2	3.1
1950	Cle-A	4	2	.667	36	0	0	0	4	63	57	32	7	1	30	26	12.6	3.57	121	.243	.331	1	.083	-1	7	6	-1	0.4
1952	Bos-A	4	3	.571	24	0	0	0	6	37^2	37	11	1	0	17	20	12.9	2.39	165	.268	.348	0	.000	-1	5	6	-0	1.1
Total	14	98	88	.527	455	167	58	10	66	1688^1	1672	831	106	15	733	697	12.9	3.66	115	.259	.336	50	.098	-39	74	98	-1	8.1

● RUBE BENTON
Benton, John Clebon b: 6/27/1887, Clinton, N.C. d: 12/12/37, Dothan, Ala. BL/TL, 6'1", 190 lbs. Deb: 6/28/10

YEAR	TM/L	W	L	PCT	G	GS	CG	SH	SV	IP	H	R	HR	HB	BB	SO	RAT	ERA	ERA+	OAV	OOB	BH	AVG	PB	PR	PR+	PD	TPI
1910	Cin-N	0	1	.000	12	2	0	0	0	38	44	34	1	1	23	15	16.1	4.74	62	.282	.378	1	.091	-1	-7	-8	1	-0.5
1911	Cin-N	3	3	.500	6	6	5	0	0	44^2	44	18	0	3	23	28	14.1	2.01	164	.270	.370	2	.143	-0	7	7	-1	0.7
1912	Cin-N	18	20	.474	**50**	39	22	2	2	302	316	143	2	18	118	162	13.5	3.10	108	.278	.356	14	.135	-6	10	9	2	0.6
1913	Cin-N	11	7	.611	23	22	9	1	0	144^1	140	76	4	9	60	68	13.0	3.49	93	.265	.350	10	.208	1	-5	-4	-1	-0.4
1914	Cin-N	16	18	.471	41	35	16	4	2	271	223	124	3	11	95	121	10.9	2.96	99	.228	.303	13	.143	-3	-5	-1	0	-0.4
1915	Cin-N	6	13	.316	35	21	6	2	4	176^1	165	79	2	14	67	83	12.6	3.32	86	.257	.340	11	.208	-0	-11	-9	2	-0.8
	NY-N	3	5	.375	10	6	3	0	1	60^2	57	26	0	5	9	26	10.5	2.82	91	.253	.297	5	.217	1	-0	-2	-0	-0.2
	Yr	9	18	.333	45	27	9	2	5	237	222	105	2	19	76	109	12.0	3.19	87	.256	.329	16	.211	1	-12	-11	2	-1.0
1916	NY-N	16	8	.667	38	29	15	3	2	238^2	210	84	5	10	58	115	10.5	2.87	85	.241	.296	7	.090	-4	-7	-12	-1	-1.9
1917	*NY-N	15	9	.625	35	25	14	3	3	215	190	78	5	7	41	70	10.0	2.72	94	.238	.281	12	.167	-1	-0	-4	-2	-0.8
1918	NY-N	1	2	.333	3	3	2	0	0	24	17	8	0	0	3	9	7.5	1.88	140	.202	.230	1	.143	1	2	2	0	0.4
1919	NY-N	17	11	.607	35	28	11	1	2	209	181	71	5	4	52	53	10.2	2.63	107	.237	.289	13	.194	-1	7	4	-1	0.4
1920	NY-N	9	16	.360	33	25	12	4	2	193^1	222	82	8	3	31	52	11.9	3.03	99	.291	.321	6	.092	-7	2	-1	4	-0.3
1921	NY-N	5	2	.714	18	9	3	1	0	72	72	28	2	0	17	11	11.1	2.88	128	.266	.309	3	.143	-1	7	7	-1	0.4
1923	Cin-N	14	10	.583	33	26	15	0	1	219	243	106	10	5	57	59	12.5	3.66	106	.284	.333	23	.287	4	8	5	1	0.9
1924	Cin-N	7	9	.438	32	19	6	1	1	162^2	166	70	2	4	24	42	10.7	2.77	136	.266	.297	12	.261	2	20	19	1	2.0
1925	Cin-N	9	10	.474	33	16	6	1	1	146^2	182	88	3	1	34	36	13.3	4.05	102	.301	.340	9	.200	1	4	1	-1	0.1
Total	15	150	144	.510	437	311	145	23	21	2517^1	2472	1115	52	95	712	950	11.7	3.09	102	.261	.319	142	.172	-14	33	13	4	0.2

● LARRY BENTON
Benton, Lawrence James b: 11/20/1897, St.Louis, Mo. d: 4/3/53, Amberley, Ohio BR/TR, 5'11", 165 lbs. Deb: 4/25/23

YEAR	TM/L	W	L	PCT	G	GS	CG	SH	SV	IP	H	R	HR	HB	BB	SO	RAT	ERA	ERA+	OAV	OOB	BH	AVG	PB	PR	PR+	PD	TPI
1923	Bos-N	5	9	.357	35	9	2	0	0	128	141	78	4	4	57	42	14.2	4.99	80	.293	.373	5	.161	-1	-14	-14	1	-1.3
1924	Bos-N	5	7	.417	30	13	4	0	1	128	129	63	4	3	64	41	13.8	4.15	92	.274	.365	3	.091	-3	-4	-5	-0	-0.7
1925	Bos-N	14	7	.667	31	21	16	2	1	183^1	170	72	6	2	70	49	11.9	3.09	130	.249	.320	14	.241	2	24	20	-1	2.1
1926	Bos-N	14	14	.500	43	27	12	1	1	231^2	244	113	10	7	81	103	12.9	3.85	92	.280	.346	12	.154	-4	-1	-8	-3	-1.5
1927	Bos-N	4	2	.667	11	10	3	0	0	60^1	72	33	3	2	27	25	15.1	4.48	83	.310	.387	4	.222	1	-4	-5	-1	-0.5
	NY-N	13	5	.722	29	23	8	1	2	173	183	83	9	2	54	65	12.4	3.95	98	.275	.331	8	.160	-2	-1	-2	-0	-0.4
	Yr	17	7	**.708**	40	33	11	1	2	233^1	255	116	12	4	81	90	13.1	4.09	93	.284	.346	12	.176	-1	-4	-7	-1	-0.9
1928	NY-N	**25**	9	**.735**	42	36	**28**	2	4	310^1	299	106	14	0	71	90	10.7	2.73	144	.258	.300	16	.143	-3	44	42	-0	4.0
1929	NY-N	11	17	.393	39	31	14	3	3	237	276	129	16	0	61	63	12.8	4.14	111	.297	.340	9	.105	-6	15	12	1	0.7
1930	NY-N	1	3	.250	8	4	1	0	1	30	42	31	8	0	14	16	16.8	7.80	61	.323	.389	3	.300	2	-9	-11	-0	-1.0
	Cin-N	7	12	.368	35	22	9	0	1	177^2	246	124	7	0	45	47	14.7	5.12	94	.337	.375	11	.177	-2	-3	-6	-3	-0.9
	Yr	8	15	.348	43	26	10	0	2	207^2	288	155	15	0	59	63	15.0	5.50	87	.334	.377	14	.194	-0	-12	-16	-3	-1.9
1931	Cin-N	10	15	.400	38	23	12	2	2	204^1	240	98	6	1	53	35	12.9	3.35	112	.299	.343	11	.167	-1	12	9	1	1.1
1932	Cin-N	6	13	.316	35	22	7	0	2	179^2	201	104	10	0	27	35	11.4	4.31	90	.285	.311	11	.204	0	-9	-9	-1	-0.9
1933	Cin-N	10	11	.476	34	19	7	2	2	152^2	160	70	5	3	36	33	11.7	3.71	91	.271	.316	9	.170	-1	-6	-5	-2	-1.0
1934	Cin-N	0	1	.000	16	1	0	0	2	29	53	25	1	0	7	5	18.6	6.52	63	.393	.423	2	.286	0	-8	-8	-0	-0.4
1935	Bos-N	2	3	.400	29	0	0	0	0	72	103	61	6	1	24	21	16.0	6.88	55	.338	.388	4	.200	0	-23	-26	-1	-1.6
Total	13	127	128	.498	455	261	123	13	22	2297	2559	1190	109	25	691	670	12.8	4.03	98	.288	.341	122	.165	-17	14	-16	-8	-2.3

● SID BENTON
Benton, Sidney Wright b: 8/4/1895, Buckner, Ark. d: 3/8/77, Fayetteville, Ark. BR/TR, 6'1", 170 lbs. Deb: 4/18/22

YEAR	TM/L	W	L	PCT	G	GS	CG	SH	SV	IP	H	R	HR	HB	BB	SO	RAT	ERA	ERA+	OAV	OOB	BH	AVG	PB	PR	PR+	PD	TPI
1922	StL-N	0	0	—	1	0	0	0	0	0	0	0	0	2	—	—	—	—	—	1.000	94	—	0	0	0	0	0.0	

● JOE BENZ
Benz, Joseph Louis "Blitzen" or "Butcher Boy" b: 1/21/1886, New Alsace, Ind. d: 4/22/57, Chicago, Ill. BR/TR, 6'1.5", 196 lbs. Deb: 8/16/11

YEAR	TM/L	W	L	PCT	G	GS	CG	SH	SV	IP	H	R	HR	HB	BB	SO	RAT	ERA	ERA+	OAV	OOB	BH	AVG	PB	PR	PR+	PD	TPI
1911	Chi-A	3	2	.600	12	6	1	0	0	55^2	52	23	0	2	13	28	10.8	2.26	142	.251	.302	1	.059	-2	7	6	1	0.4
1912	Chi-A	13	17	.433	42	31	12	3	0	238^2	231	107	5	8	70	97	11.7	2.90	110	.259	.319	10	.132	-5	11	8	1	0.5
1913	Chi-A	7	10	.412	33	17	6	1	1	151	146	64	1	2	59	79	12.3	2.74	107	.254	.325	9	.180	-1	3	3	4	0.7
1914	Chi-A	15	19	.441	48	35	16	4	2	283^1	245	103	4	2	66	142	9.9	2.26	119	.236	.282	12	.130	-3	15	14	6	2.1
1915	Chi-A	15	11	.577	39	28	17	2	0	238^1	209	78	4	3	43	81	9.6	2.11	141	.238	.276	10	.127	-5	22	23	3	2.2
1916	Chi-A	9	5	.643	28	16	6	4	0	142	108	40	0	3	32	57	9.1	2.03	136	.214	.265	3	.065	-4	13	12	1	0.8
1917	Chi-A	7	3	.700	19	13	7	2	0	94^2	76	36	1	2	23	25	9.6	2.47	108	.220	.272	5	.167	-1	2	2	0	0.1
1918	Chi-A	8	8	.500	29	17	10	1	0	154	156	57	1	2	28	30	10.9	2.63	104	.269	.304	11	.216	-1	3	2	3	0.5
1919	Chi-A	0	0	—	1	0	0	0	0	2	2	1	0	0	0	0	9.0	0.00	—	.250	.250	0	—	0	1	1	0	0.0
Total	9	77	75	.507	251	163	75	17	3	1359^2	1225	509	16	24	334	539	10.5	2.43	119	.243	.294	61	.138	-21	76	71	19	7.3

● JASON BERE
Bere, Jason Phillip b: 5/26/71, Cambridge, Mass. BR/TR, 6'3", 185 lbs. Deb: 5/27/93

YEAR	TM/L	W	L	PCT	G	GS	CG	SH	SV	IP	H	R	HR	HB	BB	SO	RAT	ERA	ERA+	OAV	OOB	BH	AVG	PB	PR	PR+	PD	TPI
1993	*Chi-A	12	5	.706	24	24	1	0	0	142^2	109	60	12	5	81	129	12.3	3.47	121	.210	.323	0	—	0	14	12	-0	1.2
1994	Chi-A★	12	2	**.857**	24	24	0	0	0	141^2	119	65	17	1	80	127	12.7	3.81	123	.229	.333	0	—	0	16	14	-1	1.1
1995	Chi-A	8	15	.348	27	27	1	0	0	137^2	151	120	21	6	106	110	17.2	7.19	62	.277	.400	0	—	0	-38	-44	1	-5.5
1996	Chi-A	0	1	.000	5	5	0	0	0	16^2	26	19	3	0	18	19	23.8	10.26	46	.356	.484	0	—	0	-10	-11	0	-0.5
1997	Chi-A	4	2	.667	6	6	0	0	0	28^2	20	15	4	3	17	21	12.6	4.71	93	.198	.331	0	—	0	-0	-1	-0	-0.2
1998	Chi-A	3	7	.300	18	15	0	0	0	83^2	98	71	14	2	58	53	17.0	6.45	71	.293	.400	0	—	0	-17	-18	-1	-1.8
	Cin-N	3	2	.600	9	7	0	0	0	43^2	39	20	3	1	20	31	12.4	4.12	104	.242	.330	0	.000	-1	1	1	-0	-0.1
1999	Cin-N	3	0	1.000	12	10	0	0	0	43^1	56	37	6	2	40	28	20.4	6.85	68	.326	.458	4	.286	1	-11	-10	0	-0.5
	Mil-N	2	0	1.000	5	4	0	0	0	23^1	23	15	3	0	10	19	12.7	4.63	98	.256	.330	3	.375	1	-0	-0	-1	0.1
	Yr	5	0	1.000	17	14	0	0	0	66^2	79	52	9	2	50	47	17.7	6.08	76	.302	.417	7	.318	2	-11	-11	-0	-0.4
2000	Mil-N	6	7	.462	20	20	0	0	0	115	115	66	19	1	63	98	14.0	4.93	92	.264	.358	8	.205	1	-4	-5	1	-0.3
	Cle-A	6	3	.667	11	11	0	0	0	54^1	65	41	6	4	26	44	15.7	6.63	75	.297	.382	0	—	0	-10	-10	-0	-1.3
Total	8	59	44	.573	161	153	2	0	0	830^2	821	529	108	25	519	679	14.8	5.28	86	.259	.368	15	.200	2	-60	-72	-2	-7.8

● JUAN BERENGUER
Berenguer, Juan Bautista b: 11/30/54, Aguadulce, Pan. BR/TR, 5'11", 215 lbs. Deb: 8/17/78

YEAR	TM/L	W	L	PCT	G	GS	CG	SH	SV	IP	H	R	HR	HB	BB	SO	RAT	ERA	ERA+	OAV	OOB	BH	AVG	PB	PR	PR+	PD	TPI
1978	NY-N	0	2	.000	5	3	0	0	0	13	17	12	1	1	11	8	20.1	8.31	42	.327	.453	0	.000	-0	-7	-7	-0	-1.0
1979	NY-N	1	1	.500	5	5	0	0	0	30^2	28	13	2	1	12	25	12.0	2.93	124	.252	.331	1	.143	0	3	2	-1	0.1
1980	NY-N	0	1	.000	6	0	0	0	0	9^1	9	9	1	0	10	7	18.3	5.79	62	.250	.413	0	—	0	-2	-2	0	-0.2
1981	KC-A	0	4	.000	8	3	0	0	0	19^2	22	21	4	2	16	20	18.3	8.69	42	.289	.426	0	—	0	-11	-11	-1	-1.9
	Tor-A	2	9	.182	12	11	1	0	0	71	62	41	7	3	35	29	12.7	4.31	92	.235	.331	0	—	0	-5	-3	-1	-0.5
	Yr	2	13	.133	20	14	1	0	0	90^2	84	62	11	5	51	49	13.9	5.26	74	.247	.354	0	—	0	-16	-13	-2	-2.4
1982	Det-A	0	0	—	2	1	0	0	0	6^2	5	5	0	0	9	8	18.9	6.75	60	.200	.412	0	—	0	-2	-2	-0	-0.1
1983	Det-A	9	5	.643	37	19	2	1	1	157^2	110	58	19	6	71	129	10.7	3.14	125	.193	.289	0	—	0	16	14	-2	1.0
1984	Det-A	11	10	.524	31	27	2	1	0	168^1	146	75	14	5	79	118	12.3	3.48	113	.232	.323	0	—	0	10	9	-1	0.8
1985	Det-A	5	6	.455	31	13	0	0	0	95	96	67	12	1	48	82	13.7	5.59	73	.259	.346	0	—	0	-15	-16	1	-1.6
1986	SF-N	2	3	.400	46	4	0	0	4	73^1	64	23	4	2	44	72	13.5	2.70	131	.242	.354	1	.143	-0	8	7	-1	0.4
1987	*Min-A	8	1	.889	47	6	0	0	4	112	100	51	10	0	47	110	11.8	3.94	118	.238	.315	0	—	0	7	8	-1	0.5

YEAR	TM/L	W	L	PCT	G	GS	CG	SH	SV	IP	H	R	HR	HB	BB	SO	RAT	ERA	ERA+	OAV	OOB	BH	AVG	PB	PR	PR+	PD	TPI
1988	Min-A	8	4	.667	57	1	0	0	2	100	74	44	7	1	61	99	12.2	3.96	103	.207	.325	0	—	0	0	1	0	0.2
1989	Min-A	9	3	.750	56	0	0	0	3	106	96	44	11	2	47	93	12.3	3.48	119	.246	.330	0	—	0	5	7	-1	0.7
1990	Min-A	8	5	.615	51	0	0	0	0	100^1	85	43	9	2	58	77	13.0	3.41	122	.232	.340	0	—	0	6	8	-2	0.8
1991	Atl-N	0	3	.000	49	0	0	0	17	64^1	43	18	5	3	20	53	9.2	2.24	174	.189	.263	0	.000	-1	10	11	-0	0.9
1992	Atl-N	3	1	.750	28	0	0	0	1	33^1	35	22	7	1	16	19	14.0	5.13	71	.269	.354	0	.000	-0	-6	-5	-0	-0.7
	KC-A	1	4	.200	19	2	0	0	0	44^2	42	30	3	1	20	26	12.7	5.64	72	.247	.330	0	—	0	-8	-8	-0	-0.8
Total	15	67	62	.519	490	95	5	2	32	1205^1	1034	576	116	31	604	975	12.5	3.90	103	.232	.328	2	.083	-1	8	15	-11	-1.4
● **BRUCE BERENYI** Berenyi, Bruce Michael b: 8/21/54, Bryan, Ohio BR/TR, 6'3", 215 lbs. Deb: 7/5/80																												
1980	Cin-N	2	2	.500	6	6	0	0	0	27^2	34	26	1	0	23	19	18.5	7.81	46	.318	.438	0	.000	-1	-13	-13	-0	-1.6
1981	Cin-N	9	6	.600	21	20	5	3	0	126	97	55	3	0	77	106	12.4	3.50	102	.211	.324	8	.190	1	-0	1	-1	0.1
1982	Cin-N	9	18	.333	34	34	4	1	0	222^1	208	90	8	2	96	157	12.4	3.36	110	.255	.335	15	.242	3	6	8	2	1.5
1983	Cin-N	9	14	.391	32	31	4	1	0	186^1	173	92	9	2	102	151	13.4	3.86	99	.247	.345	12	.218	2	-5	-1	3	0.3
1984	Cin-N	3	7	.300	13	11	0	0	0	51	63	35	0	0	42	53	18.5	6.00	63	.306	.423	1	.063	-1	-14	-12	0	-2.1
	NY-N	9	6	.600	19	19	0	0	0	115	100	58	6	1	53	81	12.1	3.76	94	.238	.325	9	.243	2	-2	-3	-1	-0.3
	Yr	12	13	.480	32	30	0	0	0	166	163	93	6	1	95	134	14.0	4.45	81	.260	.359	10	.189	0	-16	-15	-1	-2.4
1985	NY-N	1	0	1.000	3	3	0	0	0	13^2	8	6	0	1	10	10	12.5	2.63	131	.170	.328	1	.250	0	1	1	1	0.2
1986	NY-N	2	2	.500	14	7	0	0	0	39^2	47	30	5	1	22	30	15.9	6.35	56	.299	.389	0	.000	-1	-12	-13	-0	-1.3
Total	7	44	55	.444	142	131	13	5	0	781^2	730	392	32	7	425	607	13.4	4.03	91	.251	.347	46	.197	4	-37	-31	3	-3.2
● **HEINIE BERGER** Berger, Charles b: 1/7/1882, LaSalle, Ill. d: 2/10/54, Lakewood, Ohio TR, 5'9", Deb: 5/6/07																												
1907	Cle-A	3	3	.500	14	7	5	1	0	87^1	74	35	0	1	20	50	9.8	2.99	84	.232	.279	5	.179	0	-4	-5	-1	-0.5
1908	Cle-A	13	8	.619	29	24	16	0	0	199^1	152	60	1	4	66	101	10.0	2.12	113	.219	.290	8	.108	-4	6	6	-0	0.1
1909	Cle-A	13	14	.481	34	29	19	4	1	247	221	95	2	12	58	162	10.6	2.73	94	.256	.312	11	.133	-1	-7	-5	0	-0.7
1910	Cle-A	3	4	.429	13	8	2	0	0	65^1	57	25	0	3	32	24	12.7	3.03	85	.243	.341	3	.143	-1	-4	-3	-1	-0.5
Total	4	32	29	.525	90	68	42	5	1	599	504	215	3	20	176	337	10.5	2.60	96	.239	.303	27	.131	-6	-9	-7	-2	-1.6
● **SEAN BERGMAN** Bergman, Sean Frederick b: 4/11/70, Joliet, Ill. BR/TR, 6'4", 205 lbs. Deb: 7/7/93																												
1993	Det-A	1	4	.200	9	6	1	0	0	39^2	47	29	6	1	23	19	16.1	5.67	76	.294	.386	0	—	0	-6	-6	0	-0.6
1994	Det-A	2	1	.667	3	3	0	0	0	17^2	22	11	2	1	7	12	15.3	5.60	87	.301	.370	0	—	0	-2	-1	-0	-0.2
1995	Det-A	7	10	.412	28	28	1	1	0	135^1	169	95	19	4	67	86	16.0	5.12	93	.307	.386	0	—	0	-6	-5	-1	-0.6
1996	SD-N	6	8	.429	41	14	0	0	0	113^1	119	63	14	2	33	85	12.2	4.37	91	.274	.328	3	.100	-1	-2	-5	1	-0.5
1997	SD-N	2	4	.333	44	9	0	0	0	99	126	72	11	3	38	74	15.2	6.09	64	.316	.380	3	.231	1	-21	-26	1	-1.2
1998	Hou-N	12	9	.571	31	27	1	0	0	172	183	81	20	5	42	100	12.0	3.72	109	.268	.316	5	.083	-3	10	7	-2	0.2
1999	Hou-N	4	6	.400	19	16	2	1	0	99	130	60	9	3	26	38	14.5	5.36	82	.332	.378	3	.107	1	-9	-11	-2	-1.0
	Atl-N	1	0	1.000	6	0	0	0	0	6^1	5	2	0	0	3	6	11.4	2.84	158	.217	.308	0	—	0	1	1	0	0.2
	Yr	5	6	.455	25	16	2	1	0	105^1	135	62	9	3	29	44	14.3	5.21	85	.325	.374	3	.107	1	-8	-10	-1	-0.8
2000	Min-A	4	5	.444	15	14	0	0	0	68	111	76	18	2	33	35	19.3	9.66	54	.374	.440	1	.500	1	-36	-31	1	-2.9
Total	8	39	47	.453	196	117	5	2	0	750^1	912	489	99	21	272	455	14.5	5.28	82	.303	.365	15	.113	-2	-69	-81	-2	-6.6
● **JACK BERLY** Berly, John Chambers b: 5/24/03, Natchitoches, La. d: 6/26/77, Houston, Tex. BR/TR, 5'11.5", 190 lbs. Deb: 4/22/24																												
1924	StL-N	0	0	—	4	0	0	0	0	8	8	5	2	0	4	2	13.5	5.63	67	.267	.353	0	.000	-0	-2	-2	0	-0.1
1931	NY-N	7	8	.467	27	11	4	1	0	111^1	114	55	6	4	51	45	13.7	3.88	95	.270	.354	6	.171	-1	-0	-2	1	-0.2
1932	Phi-N	1	2	.333	21	1	1	0	2	46	61	42	4	1	21	15	16.2	7.63	58	.333	.405	0	.000	-1	-19	-14	1	-1.0
1933	Phi-N	2	3	.400	13	6	1	1	0	50	62	30	5	2	22	4	15.5	5.04	76	.307	.381	4	.308	0	-9	-6	1	-0.4
Total	4	10	13	.435	65	18	6	2	2	215^1	245	132	17	7	98	66	14.6	5.02	78	.292	.371	10	.167	-2	-30	-26	3	-1.7
● **VICTOR BERNAL** Bernal, Victor Hugo b: 10/6/53, Los Angeles, Cal. BR/TR, 6'1", 175 lbs. Deb: 4/6/77																												
1977	SD-N	1	1	.500	15	0	0	0	0	20^1	23	13	4	0	9	6	14.2	5.31	67	.287	.360	0	.000	-0	-3	-4	-0	-0.4
● **DWIGHT BERNARD** Bernard, Dwight Vern b: 5/31/52, Mt.Vernon, Ill. BR/TR, 6'2", 170 lbs. Deb: 6/29/78																												
1978	NY-N	1	4	.200	30	1	0	0	0	48	54	25	4	0	27	26	15.2	4.31	81	.297	.388	1	.200	0	-4	-4	0	-0.4
1979	NY-N	0	3	.000	32	1	0	0	0	44	59	26	2	0	26	20	17.4	4.70	78	.331	.417	0	—	0	-5	-5	0	-0.3
1981	*Mil-A	0	0	—	6	0	0	0	0	5	5	3	0	0	6	1	19.8	3.60	95	.263	.440	0	—	0	0	-0	-0	0.0
1982	*Mil-A	3	1	.750	47	0	0	0	6	79	78	39	4	1	27	45	12.1	3.76	101	.263	.326	0	—	0	3	0	-1	-0.1
Total	4	4	8	.333	115	2	0	0	6	176	196	93	10	1	86	92	14.5	4.14	89	.290	.371	1	.200	1	-6	-10	-1	-0.8
● **JOE BERNARD** Bernard, Joseph Carl "J.C." b: 3/24/1882, Brighton, Ill. d: 9/22/60, Springfield, Ill BR/TR, 6'1", 175 lbs. Deb: 9/23/09																												
1909	StL-N	0	0	—	1	0	0	0	0	1	1	0	0	0	2	2	27.0	0.00	—	.250	.500	0	—	0	0	0	0	0.0
● **ADAM BERNERO** Bernero, Adam G. b: 11/28/76, San Jose, Cal. BR/TR, 6'4", 205 lbs. Deb: 8/1/2000																												
2000	Det-A	0	1	.000	12	4	0	0	0	34^1	33	18	3	1	13	20	12.3	4.19	114	.270	.346	0	—	0	3	2	1	0.2
● **BILL BERNHARD** Bernhard, William Henry "Strawberry Bill" b: 3/16/1871, Clarence, N.Y. d: 3/30/49, San Diego, Cal. BB/TR, 6'1", 205 lbs. Deb: 4/24/1899																												
1899	Phi-N	6	6	.500	21	12	10	1	0	132^1	120	66	3	6	36	23	11.0	2.65	139	.242	.301	13	.241	0	18	16	-0	1.2
1900	Phi-N	15	10	.600	32	27	20	0	2	218^2	284	151	3	5	74	49	14.9	4.77	76	.313	.368	14	.154	-5	-26	-29	1	-3.0
1901	Phi-A	17	10	.630	31	27	26	1	0	257	328	169	6	2	50	58	13.3	4.52	84	.307	.339	20	.187	-1	-24	-21	4	-1.6
1902	Phi-A	1	0	1.000	1	1	1	0	0	9	7	1	0	0	3	1	10.0	1.00	367	.212	.278	0	.000	-1	3	3	-1	0.1
	Cle-A	17	5	.773	27	24	22	3	1	217	169	78	4	5	34	57	8.6	2.20	157	.216	.253	18	.200	-1	33	31	1	2.9
	Yr	18	5	**.783**	28	25	23	3	1	226	176	79	4	5	37	58	**8.7**	2.15	161	**.215**	**.254**	18	.191	-2	36	34	1	3.0
1903	Cle-A	14	5	.737	20	19	18	3	0	165^2	151	62	1	0	21	60	9.3	2.12	135	.242	.267	12	.185	-1	16	14	1	1.6
1904	Cle-A	23	13	.639	38	37	35	4	0	320^2	323	107	3	4	55	137	10.7	2.13	119	.263	.296	22	.177	-1	17	15	-1	1.4
1905	Cle-A	7	13	.350	22	19	17	0	0	174^1	185	93	5	1	34	56	11.4	3.36	78	.274	.309	6	.087	-6	-14	-14	-0	-2.1
1906	Cle-A	16	15	.516	31	30	23	2	0	255^1	235	99	1	5	47	85	10.1	2.54	103	.248	.287	21	.212	2	4	2	2	0.7
1907	Cle-A	0	4	.000	8	4	3	0	0	42	58	32	0	0	11	19	14.8	3.21	78	.330	.369	3	.200	0	-3	-3	0	-0.3
Total	9	116	81	.589	231	200	175	14	3	1792	1860	858	26	28	365	545	11.3	3.04	102	.268	.307	129	.180	-13	23	11	6	0.9
● **WALTER BERNHARDT** Bernhardt, Walter Jacob b: 5/20/1893, Pleasant Village, Pa. d: 7/26/58, Watertown, N.Y. BR/TR, 6'2", 175 lbs. Deb: 7/16/18																												
1918	NY-A	0	0	—	1	0	0	0	0	0^2	0	0	0	0	0	1	0.0	0.00	—	.000	.000	0	—	0	0	0	0	0.0
● **JOE BERRY** Berry, Jonas Arthur "Jittery Joe" b: 12/16/04, Huntsville, Ark. d: 9/27/58, Anaheim, Cal. BL/TR, 5'10.5", 145 lbs. Deb: 9/6/42																												
1942	Chi-N	0	0	—	2	0	0	0	0	2	7	4	0	0	2	1	40.5	18.00	18	.538	.600	0	—	0	-3	-3	0	-0.2
1944	Phi-A	10	8	.556	53	0	0	0	**12**	111^1	78	32	4	2	23	44	8.3	1.94	179	.192	.238	3	.120	-1	18	**19**	2	3.6
1945	Phi-A	8	7	.533	**52**	0	0	0	5	130^1	114	40	5	0	38	51	10.5	2.35	146	.232	.287	5	.143	-1	**15**	**15**	1	1.9
1946	Phi-A	0	1	.000	5	0	0	0	0	13	15	5	1	1	3	5	13.2	2.77	128	.288	.339	1	.333	0	1	1	0	0.1
	Cle-A	3	6	.333	21	0	0	0	1	37^1	32	18	4	0	21	16	12.8	3.38	98	.235	.338	2	.286	0	1	-0	-1	-0.1
	Yr	3	7	.300	26	0	0	0	1	50^1	47	23	5	1	24	21	12.9	3.22	105	.250	.338	3	.300	1	2	1	-0	0.0
Total	4	21	22	.488	133	0	0	0	18	294	246	99	14	3	87	117	10.3	2.45	140	.224	.282	11	.157	-2	31	32	3	5.3
● **FRANK BERTAINA** Bertaina, Frank Louis b: 4/14/44, San Francisco, Cal. BL/TL, 5'11", 180 lbs. Deb: 8/1/64																												
1964	Bal-A	1	0	1.000	6	4	1	1	0	26	18	8	3	0	13	18	10.7	2.77	129	.198	.298	0	.000	-1	2	2	0	0.1
1965	Bal-A	0	0	—	2	1	0	0	0	6	9	4	0	0	4	5	19.5	6.00	58	.360	.448	0	.000	-0	-2	-2	0	-0.1
1966	Bal-A	2	5	.286	16	9	0	0	0	63^1	52	29	3	4	36	46	13.1	3.13	107	.226	.341	2	.105	-1	2	1	-2	-0.1
1967	Bal-A	1	1	.500	5	2	0	0	0	21^2	17	9	4	0	14	19	12.9	3.32	95	.224	.344	1	.111	-0	-0	-0	-0	-0.1
	Was-A	6	5	.545	18	17	4	4	0	95^2	90	36	8	0	37	67	11.9	2.92	108	.251	.322	2	.057	-3	3	3	-1	0.0
	Yr	7	6	.538	23	19	4	4	0	117^1	107	45	12	0	51	86	12.1	2.99	106	.247	.326	3	.068	-3	3	2	-1	-0.1
1968	Was-A	7	13	.350	27	23	1	0	0	127^1	133	76	15	6	69	81	14.7	4.66	63	.273	.369	5	.132	-0	-24	-25	-0	-3.8
1969	Was-A	1	3	.250	14	5	0	0	0	35^2	43	30	8	0	23	25	16.7	6.56	53	.291	.386	4	.364	2	-12	-13	0	-1.0
	Bal-A	0	0	—	3	0	0	0	0	6	1	0	0	0	3	5	6.0	0.00	—	.063	.211	1	1.000	1	2	2	-0	0.2
	Yr	1	3	.250	17	5	0	0	0	41^2	44	30	8	0	26	30	15.1	5.62	62	.268	.368	5	.417	3	-9	-10	0	-0.8

YEAR	TM/L	W	L	PCT	G	GS	CG	SH	SV	IP	H	R	HR	HB	BB	SO	RAT	ERA	ERA+	OAV	OOB	BH	AVG	PB	PR	PR+	PD	TPI
1970	StL-N	1	2	.333	8	5	0	0	0	31^1	36	16	1	0	15	14	14.6	3.16	130	.293	.370	1	.143	0	3	3	-0	0.3
Total	7	19	29	.396	99	66	6	5	0	413	399	208	42	10	214	280	13.6	3.84	85	.257	.350	16	.127	-1	-24	-28	-2	-4.5
● MIKE BERTOTTI	Bertotti, Michael David b: 1/18/70, Jersey City, N.J. BL/TL, 6'1", 185 lbs. Deb: 7/29/95																											
1995	Chi-A	1	1	.500	4	4	0	0	0	14^1	23	20	6	3	11	15	23.2	12.56	36	.365	.481	0	—	0	-12	-14	-0	-1.4
1996	Chi-A	2	0	1.000	15	2	0	0	0	28	28	18	5	0	20	19	15.4	5.14	92	.257	.372	0	—	0	-0	-1	0	-0.1
1997	Chi-A	0	0	—	9	0	0	0	0	3^2	9	3	0	0	2	4	27.0	7.36	60	.450	.500	0	—	0	-1	-1	-0	-0.1
Total	3	3	1	.750	28	6	0	0	0	46	60	41	11	3	33	38	18.8	7.63	61	.313	.421	0	—	0	-14	-16	-0	-1.6
● LEFTY BERTRAND	Bertrand, Roman Mathias b: 2/28/09, Cobden, Minn. BR/TL, 6', 180 lbs. Deb: 4/15/36																											
1936	Phi-N	0	0	—	1	0	0	0	0	2	3	2	1	0	2	1	22.5	9.00	50	.333	.455	0	—	0	-1	-1	-0	-0.1
● ANDRES BERUMEN	Berumen, Andres b: 4/5/71, Tijuana, Mexico BR/TR, 6'2", 210 lbs. Deb: 4/27/95																											
1995	SD-N	2	3	.400	37	0	0	0	1	44^1	37	29	3	3	36	42	15.4	5.68	71	.226	.374	0	.000	-0	-7	-8	-1	-1.0
1996	SD-N	0	0	—	3	0	0	0	0	3^1	3	2	1	1	2	4	16.2	5.40	74	.231	.375	0	—	0	-0	-1	-0	0.0
Total	2	2	3	.400	40	0	0	0	1	47^2	40	31	4	4	38	46	15.5	5.66	71	.226	.374	0	.000	-0	-8	-9	-1	-1.0
● FRED BESANA	Besana, Frederick Cyril b: 4/5/31, Lincoln, Cal. BR/TL, 6'3.5", 200 lbs. Deb: 4/18/56																											
1956	Bal-A	1	0	1.000	7	2	0	0	0	17^2	22	12	0	2	14	7	19.4	5.60	70	.310	.437	0	.000	-0	-3	-4	1	-0.2
● HERMAN BESSE	Besse, Herman A. b: 8/16/11, St.Louis, Mo. d: 8/13/72, Los Angeles, Cal. BL/TL, 6'2", 190 lbs. Deb: 4/19/40																											
1940	Phi-A	0	3	.000	17	5	0	0	0	53	70	56	10	3	34	19	18.2	8.83	50	.315	.413	5	.263	2	-26	-25	-1	-1.1
1941	Phi-A	2	0	1.000	6	2	1	0	0	19^2	28	22	4	0	12	8	18.3	10.07	42	.329	.412	1	.200	-0	-13	-13	0	-1.0
1942	Phi-A	2	9	.182	30	14	4	0	1	133	163	99	7	4	69	78	16.0	6.16	61	.300	.383	12	.226	2	-37	-34	-2	-2.5
1943	Phi-A	1	1	.500	5	1	0	0	0	16^1	18	6	2	1	4	3	12.7	3.31	103	.295	.348	0	.000	-1	-0	0	0	-0.1
1946	Phi-A	0	2	.000	7	3	0	0	1	20^2	19	12	1	0	9	10	12.2	5.23	68	.247	.326	0	.000	-0	-4	-4	-0	-0.4
Total	5	5	15	.250	65	25	5	0	2	242^2	298	195	24	8	128	118	16.1	6.79	58	.302	.386	18	.200	2	-80	-76	-3	-5.1
● DON BESSENT	Bessent, Fred Donald b: 3/13/31, Jacksonville, Fla. d: 7/7/90, Jacksonville, Fla. BR/TR, 6', 175 lbs. Deb: 7/17/55																											
1955	*Bro-N	8	1	.889	24	2	1	0	3	63^1	51	19	7	0	21	29	10.2	2.70	150	.220	.285	2	.100	-2	9	10	-0	1.1
1956	*Bro-N	4	3	.571	38	0	0	0	9	79^1	63	23	5	0	31	52	10.7	2.50	159	.221	.297	2	.111	-1	11	12	-1	1.1
1957	Bro-N	1	3	.250	27	0	0	0	0	44	58	28	5	0	19	24	15.8	5.73	73	.328	.393	1	.250	0	-9	-7	-0	-0.6
1958	LA-N	1	0	1.000	19	0	0	0	0	24^1	24	14	3	1	17	13	15.5	3.33	123	.270	.393	0	.000	-0	2	2	1	0.1
Total	4	14	7	.667	108	2	1	0	12	211	196	84	20	1	88	118	12.2	3.33	122	.250	.327	5	.114	-3	13	16	-1	1.7
● KARL BEST	Best, Karl Jon b: 3/6/59, Aberdeen, Wash. BR/TR, 6'4", 210 lbs. Deb: 8/19/83																											
1983	Sea-A	0	1	.000	4	0	0	0	0	5^1	14	9	2	2	5	3	35.4	13.50	32	.483	.583	0	—	0	-6	-5	-0	-0.8
1984	Sea-A	1	1	.500	5	0	0	0	0	6	7	2	0	0	0	6	10.5	3.00	133	.292	.292	0	—	0	1	1	-0	0.1
1985	Sea-A	2	1	.667	15	0	0	0	4	32^1	25	9	1	1	6	32	8.9	1.95	216	.207	.250	0	—	0	8	8	-0	0.8
1986	Sea-A	2	3	.400	26	0	0	0	1	35^2	35	19	3	1	21	23	14.4	4.04	105	.255	.358	0	—	0	1	1	-1	0.1
1988	Min-A	0	0	—	11	0	0	0	0	12	15	9	1	0	7	9	16.5	6.00	68	.306	.393	0	—	0	-3	-2	-0	-0.1
Total	5	5	6	.455	61	0	0	0	5	91^1	96	48	7	4	39	73	13.7	4.04	104	.267	.345	0	—	0	1	2	-2	0.1
● JIM BETHKE	Bethke, James Charles b: 11/5/46, Falls City, Neb. BR/TR, 6'3", 185 lbs. Deb: 4/12/65																											
1965	NY-N	2	0	1.000	25	0	0	0	0	40	41	24	3	6	22	19	15.5	4.27	83	.266	.379	0	.000	-0	-3	-3	1	-0.1
● JEFF BETTENDORF	Bettendorf, Jeffrey Allen b: 12/10/60, Lompoc, Cal. BR/TR, 6'3", 180 lbs. Deb: 4/8/84																											
1984	Oak-A	0	0	—	3	0	0	0	1	9^2	9	5	3	0	5	5	13.0	4.66	81	.243	.333	0	—	0	-1	-1	-0	-0.1
● HARRY BETTS	Betts, Harold Matthew "Chubby" or "Ginger" b: 6/19/1881, Alliance, Ohio d: 5/22/46, San Antonio, Tex. BR/TR, 5'10", 200 lbs. Deb: 9/22/03																											
1903	StL-N	0	1	.000	1	1	1	0	0	9	11	10	0	2	5	2	18.0	10.00	33	.297	.409	0	.000	-0	-7	-7	-0	-0.5
1913	Cin-N	0	0	—	1	0	0	0	0	3^1	1	1	0	1	3	0	13.5	2.70	120	.143	.455	0	.000	-0	0	0	-0	0.0
Total	2	0	1	.000	2	1	1	0	0	12^1	12	11	0	3	8	2	16.8	8.03	41	.273	.418	0	.000	-1	-7	-7	-0	-0.5
● HUCK BETTS	Betts, Walter Martin b: 2/18/1897, Millsboro, Del. d: 6/13/87, Millsboro, Del. BR/TR, 5'11", 170 lbs. Deb: 4/26/20																											
1920	Phi-N	1	1	.500	27	4	1	0	0	88^1	86	48	3	2	33	18	12.3	3.57	96	.261	.332	2	.080	-2	-4	-1	-1	-0.4
1921	Phi-N	3	7	.300	32	2	1	0	4	100^2	141	65	8	4	14	28	14.2	4.47	95	.337	.365	8	.267	0	-8	-2	0	-0.2
1922	Phi-N	1	0	1.000	7	0	0	0	0	15	23	17	3	0	8	4	18.6	9.60	49	.348	.419	0	.000	-0	-9	-7	-0	-0.5
1923	Phi-N	2	4	.333	19	4	3	0	1	84^1	100	38	7	4	14	18	12.6	3.09	149	.314	.351	3	.097	-3	9	12	0	0.5
1924	Phi-N	7	10	.412	37	9	2	0	2	144^1	160	76	8	5	42	46	12.9	4.30	104	.286	.341	7	.156	-2	-7	2	-2	-0.2
1925	Phi-N	4	5	.444	35	7	1	0	1	97^1	146	86	10	3	38	28	17.3	5.55	86	.342	.400	10	.294	2	-14	-7	1	-0.3
1932	Bos-N	13	11	.542	31	27	16	3	1	221^2	229	84	9	0	35	32	10.7	2.80	134	.267	.295	19	.241	2	27	24	-2	2.4
1933	Bos-N	11	11	.500	35	26	17	2	4	242	225	79	9	0	55	40	10.4	2.79	110	.248	.290	17	.224	2	15	8	4	1.5
1934	Bos-N	17	10	.630	40	27	10	2	3	213	258	105	17	3	42	69	12.8	4.06	94	.296	.330	13	.188	1	0	-6	-2	-0.8
1935	Bos-N	2	9	.182	44	19	2	1	0	159^2	213	118	9	2	40	40	14.4	5.47	69	.321	.362	7	.159	-0	-26	-32	1	-1.8
Total	10	61	68	.473	307	125	53	8	16	1366^1	1581	716	83	23	321	323	12.7	3.93	98	.292	.334	86	.197	-2	-18	-9	-0	0.2
● BILL BEVENS	Bevens, Floyd Clifford b: 10/21/16, Hubbard, Ore. d: 10/26/91, Salem, Ore. BR/TR, 6'3.5", 210 lbs. Deb: 5/12/44																											
1944	NY-A	4	1	.800	8	5	3	0	0	43^2	44	18	4	1	13	16	12.0	2.68	130	.273	.331	1	.063	-2	4	4	-0	0.2
1945	NY-A	13	9	.591	29	25	14	2	0	184	174	83	12	1	68	76	11.9	3.67	94	.254	.322	7	.111	-4	-6	-4	1	-0.8
1946	NY-A	16	13	.552	31	31	18	3	0	249^2	213	73	11	1	78	120	10.5	2.23	154	.232	.293	7	.083	-4	35	34	-4	3.1
1947	*NY-A	7	13	.350	28	23	11	1	0	165	167	79	13	1	77	77	13.4	3.82	93	.264	.345	7	.121	-3	-2	-5	-0	-0.9
Total	4	40	36	.526	96	84	46	6	0	642^1	598	253	40	4	236	289	11.7	3.08	113	.250	.318	22	.100	-13	31	29	-4	1.6
● BRIAN BEVIL	Bevil, Brian Scott b: 9/5/71, Houston, Tex. BR/TR, 6'3", 190 lbs. Deb: 6/17/96																											
1996	KC-A	1	0	1.000	3	1	0	0	0	11	9	7	2	0	5	7	11.5	5.73	88	.237	.326	0	—	0	-1	-1	0	-0.1
1997	KC-A	1	2	.333	18	0	0	0	1	16^1	16	13	1	1	9	13	14.3	6.61	71	.267	.371	0	—	0	-4	-3	-0	-0.6
1998	KC-A	3	1	.750	39	0	0	0	0	40	47	29	4	3	22	47	16.2	6.30	77	.283	.377	0	—	0	-7	-6	-1	-0.6
Total	3	5	3	.625	60	1	0	0	1	67^1	72	49	7	4	36	67	15.0	6.28	77	.273	.368	0	—	0	-12	-11	-1	-1.3
● LOU BEVIL	Bevil, Louis Eugene (b: Louis Eugene Bevilacqua) b: 11/27/22, Nelson, Ill. d: 2/1/73, Dixon, Ill. BB/TR, 5'11.5", 190 lbs. Deb: 9/2/42																											
1942	Was-A	0	1	.000	4	1	0	0	0	9^2	9	7	0	1	11	2	19.6	6.52	56	.265	.457	0	.000	-0	-3	-3	-0	-0.3
● BEN BEVILLE	Beville, Clarence Benjamin b: 8/28/1877, Colusa, Cal. d: 1/5/37, Yountville, Cal. BR/TR, 5'9", 190 lbs. Deb: 5/24/01																											
1901	Bos-A	0	2	.000	2	2	1	0	0	9	8	7	0	1	9	1	18.0	4.00	88	.235	.409	2	.286	0	-0	-0	-0	-0.1
● JIM BIBBY	Bibby, James Blair b: 10/29/44, Franklinton, N.C. BR/TR, 6'5", 235 lbs. Deb: 9/4/72																											
1972	StL-N	1	3	.250	6	6	0	0	0	40^1	29	18	4	1	19	28	10.9	3.35	102	.206	.304	1	.125	0	0	0	0	0.1
1973	StL-N	0	2	.000	6	3	0	0	0	16	19	17	2	2	17	12	21.4	9.56	38	.306	.469	0	.000	0	-10	-11	0	-1.1
	Tex-A	9	10	.474	26	23	11	2	1	180^1	121	73	14	6	106	155	11.6	3.24	115	**.192**	.314	0	—	0	12	10	-2	0.8
1974	Tex-A	19	19	.500	41	41	11	5	0	264	255	146	25	9	113	149	12.9	4.74	75	.255	.336	0	—	0	-33	-35	1	-4.4
1975	Tex-A	2	6	.250	12	12	4	1	0	68^1	73	41	2	2	28	31	13.6	5.00	75	.274	.348	0	—	0	-9	-9	-1	-1.0
	Cle-A	5	9	.357	24	12	2	0	1	112^2	99	48	7	0	50	62	11.9	3.20	119	.235	.316	0	—	0	7	7	1	0.9
	Yr	7	15	.318	36	24	6	1	1	181	172	89	9	2	78	93	12.5	3.88	98	.250	.329	0	—	0	-2	-2	0	-0.1
1976	Cle-A	13	7	.650	34	21	4	3	1	163^1	162	61	6	1	56	84	12.1	3.20	109	.266	.329	0	—	0	6	5	-1	0.5
1977	Cle-A	12	13	.480	37	30	9	2	2	206^2	197	100	17	4	73	141	11.9	3.57	111	.250	.317	0	—	0	12	9	-2	0.8
1978	Pit-N	8	7	.533	34	14	3	2	1	107	100	52	10	2	39	72	11.9	3.53	105	.246	.315	4	.129	1	1	2	0	0.4
1979	*Pit-N	12	4	.750	34	17	4	1	0	137^2	110	51	9	4	47	103	10.5	2.81	138	.218	.290	8	.178	2	14	16	-2	1.8
1980	Pit-N★	19	6	**.760**	35	34	6	1	0	238^1	210	95	20	6	88	144	11.5	3.32	110	.238	.312	12	.156	2	8	9	-2	0.9
1981	Pit-N	6	3	.667	14	14	2	2	0	93^2	79	30	4	2	26	48	10.3	2.50	144	.225	.282	4	.143	1	10	11	-1	1.1
1983	Pit-N	5	12	.294	29	12	0	0	2	78	92	60	10	1	51	44	16.6	6.69	55	.297	.398	2	.111	-1	-26	-25	-0	-4.9
1984	Tex-A	0	0	—	8	0	0	0	0	16^1	19	8	1	0	10	6	16.0	4.41	94	.297	.392	0	—	0	-1	-0	-0	0.0
Total	12	111	101	.524	340	239	56	19	8	1722^2	1565	800	131	40	723	1079	12.2	3.76	99	.243	.323	31	.148	5	-10	-10	-8	-4.1

● VERN BICKFORD Bickford, Vernon Edgell b: 8/17/20, Hellier, Ky. d: 5/6/60, Concord, Va. BR/TR, 6', 185 lbs. Deb: 4/24/48

YEAR TM/L	W	L	PCT	G	GS	CG	SH	SV	IP	H	R	HR	HB	BB	SO	RAT	ERA	ERA+	OAV	OOB	BH	AVG	PB	PR	PR+	PD	TPI
1948 *Bos-N	11	5	.688	33	22	10	1	1	146	125	59	9	3	63	60	11.8	3.27	117	.226	.309	10	.204	1	11	9	-1	0.9
1949 Bos-N★	16	11	.593	37	36	15	2	0	230^{2}	246	125	20	6	106	101	14.0	4.25	89	.273	.354	15	.185	-1	-5	-13	2	-1.2
1950 Bos-N	19	14	.576	40	39	**27**	2	0	**311^{2}**	293	135	25	6	122	126	12.2	3.47	111	.248	.321	16	.138	-4	23	14	-1	0.8
1951 Bos-N	11	9	.550	25	20	12	3	0	164^{2}	146	68	7	6	76	76	12.5	3.12	118	.240	.330	6	.115	-2	15	11	3	1.3
1952 Bos-N	7	12	.368	26	22	7	1	0	161^{1}	165	73	7	2	64	62	12.9	3.74	97	.269	.340	9	.176	-0	-0	-2	1	-0.2
1953 Mil-N	2	5	.286	20	9	2	0	1	58	60	35	8	2	35	25	15.1	5.28	74	.279	.385	1	.067	-1	-6	-10	1	-1.0
1954 Bal-A	0	1	.000	1	1	0	0	0	4	5	5	0	0	1	0	13.5	9.00	40	.333	.375	0	.000	-0	-2	-3	0	-0.4
Total 7	66	57	.537	182	149	73	9	2	1076^{1}	1040	500	76	25	467	450	12.8	3.71	102	.254	.335	57	.156	-7	36	8	3	0.2

● DAN BICKHAM Bickham, Daniel Denison b: 10/31/1864, Dayton, Ohio d: 3/3/51, Dayton, Ohio BR/TR, 5'10", 160 lbs. Deb: 8/13/1886

YEAR TM/L	W	L	PCT	G	GS	CG	SH	SV	IP	H	R	HR	HB	BB	SO	RAT	ERA	ERA+	OAV	OOB	BH	AVG	PB	PR	PR+	PD	TPI
1886 Cin-a	1	0	1.000	1	1	1	0	0	9	13	11	0	0	3	6	16.0	3.00	117	.351	.400	1	.333	0	0	1	0	0.1

● CHARLIE BICKNELL Bicknell, Charles Stephen "Bud" b: 7/27/28, Plainfield, N.J. BR/TR, 5'11", 170 lbs. Deb: 4/22/48

YEAR TM/L	W	L	PCT	G	GS	CG	SH	SV	IP	H	R	HR	HB	BB	SO	RAT	ERA	ERA+	OAV	OOB	BH	AVG	PB	PR	PR+	PD	TPI
1948 Phi-N	0	1	.000	17	1	0	0	0	25^{2}	29	20	5	0	17	5	16.1	5.96	66	.287	.390	0	.000	-1	-6	-6	-1	-0.4
1949 Phi-N	0	0	—	13	0	0	0	0	28^{1}	32	24	3	2	17	4	16.2	7.62	52	.291	.395	0	.000	1	-11	-12	-0	-0.5
Total 2	0	1	.000	30	1	0	0	0	54	61	44	8	2	34	9	16.2	6.83	58	.289	.393	0	.000	-0	-17	-18	-1	-0.9

● ROCKY BIDDLE Biddle, Lee F. b: 5/21/76, Las Vegas, Nev. BR/TR, 6'3", 230 lbs. Deb: 8/10/2000

YEAR TM/L	W	L	PCT	G	GS	CG	SH	SV	IP	H	R	HR	HB	BB	SO	RAT	ERA	ERA+	OAV	OOB	BH	AVG	PB	PR	PR+	PD	TPI
2000 Chi-A	1	2	.333	4	4	0	0	0	22^{2}	31	25	5	0	8	7	15.5	8.34	60	.326	.379	0	—	0	-9	-8	-0	-0.8

● MIKE BIELECKI Bielecki, Michael Joseph b: 7/31/59, Baltimore, Md. BR/TR, 6'3", 195 lbs. Deb: 9/14/84

YEAR TM/L	W	L	PCT	G	GS	CG	SH	SV	IP	H	R	HR	HB	BB	SO	RAT	ERA	ERA+	OAV	OOB	BH	AVG	PB	PR	PR+	PD	TPI
1984 Pit-N	0	0	—	4	0	0	0	0	4^{1}	4	0	0	0	0	1	8.3	0.00	—	.250	.250	0	—	0	2	2	0	0.1
1985 Pit-N	2	3	.400	12	7	0	0	0	45^{2}	45	26	5	1	31	22	15.2	4.53	79	.257	.372	0	.000	-1	-5	-5	1	-0.5
1986 Pit-N	6	11	.353	31	27	0	0	0	148^{2}	149	87	10	2	83	83	14.2	4.66	82	.262	.358	3	.063	-3	-15	-13	-1	-1.7
1987 Pit-N	2	3	.400	8	8	2	0	0	45^{2}	43	25	6	1	12	25	11.0	4.73	87	.250	.303	1	.063	-1	-3	-3	-0	-0.4
1988 Chi-N	2	2	.500	19	5	0	0	0	48^{1}	55	22	4	0	16	33	13.2	3.35	108	.284	.338	1	.100	-0	1	1	-0	0.0
1989 *Chi-N	18	7	**.720**	33	33	4	3	0	212^{1}	187	82	16	0	81	147	11.4	3.14	120	.237	.308	3	.043	-5	9	14	-1	0.9
1990 Chi-N	8	11	.421	36	29	0	0	1	168	188	101	13	5	70	103	14.1	4.93	83	.287	.361	7	.163	-0	-21	-15	3	-1.3
1991 Chi-N	13	11	.542	39	25	0	0	0	172	169	91	18	2	54	72	11.8	4.50	86	.262	.321	3	.065	-2	-16	-11	1	-1.6
Atl-N	0	0	—	2	0	0	0	0	1^{2}	2	0	0	0	2	3	21.6	0.00	—	.286	.444	0	—	0	1	1	0	0.0
Yr	13	11	.542	41	25	0	0	0	173^{2}	171	91	18	2	56	75	11.9	4.46	87	.262	.322	3	.065	-2	-15	-10	1	-1.6
1992 Atl-N	2	4	.333	19	14	1	1	0	80^{2}	77	27	2	1	27	62	11.7	2.57	143	.254	.317	3	.125	-1	8	9	1	0.7
1993 Cle-A	4	5	.444	13	13	0	0	0	68^{2}	90	47	8	2	23	38	15.1	5.90	74	.310	.365	0	—	0	-12	-12	0	-1.3
1994 Atl-N	2	0	1.000	19	1	0	0	0	27	28	12	2	1	12	18	13.7	4.00	106	.277	.360	0	.000	-0	1	1	0	0.0
1995 Cal-A	4	6	.400	22	11	0	0	0	75^{1}	80	56	15	3	31	45	13.6	5.97	79	.273	.349	0	—	0	-11	-11	-1	-1.2
1996 *Atl-N	4	3	.571	40	5	0	0	2	75^{1}	63	24	8	0	33	71	11.5	2.63	168	.224	.306	1	.100	0	13	14	1	1.3
1997 Atl-N	3	7	.300	50	0	0	0	2	57^{1}	56	33	9	1	21	60	12.2	4.08	103	.250	.317	0	.000	0	1	1	0	0.1
Total 14	70	73	.490	347	178	7	4	5	1231	1236	633	116	19	496	783	12.8	4.18	96	.262	.335	22	.078	-14	-48	-25	3	-4.9

● HARRY BIEMILLER Biemiller, Harry Lee b: 10/9/1897, Baltimore, Md. d: 5/25/65, Orlando, Fla. BR/TR, 6'1", 171 lbs. Deb: 8/26/20

YEAR TM/L	W	L	PCT	G	GS	CG	SH	SV	IP	H	R	HR	HB	BB	SO	RAT	ERA	ERA+	OAV	OOB	BH	AVG	PB	PR	PR+	PD	TPI
1920 Was-A	1	0	1.000	5	2	1	0	0	17	21	13	1	0	13	10	18.0	4.76	78	.318	.430	0	.000	-1	-2	-2	1	-0.1
1925 Cin-N	0	1	.000	23	1	0	0	2	47	45	28	2	7	21	9	14.0	4.02	102	.280	.386	0	.000	-0	1	0	2	0.1
Total 2	1	1	.500	28	3	1	0	2	64	66	41	3	7	34	19	15.0	4.22	95	.291	.399	0	.000	-1	-1	-2	2	0.0

● LOU BIERBAUER Bierbauer, Louis W. b: 9/28/1865, Erie, Pa. d: 1/31/26, Erie, Pa. BL/TR, 5'8", 140 lbs. Deb: 4/17/1886 ◆

YEAR TM/L	W	L	PCT	G	GS	CG	SH	SV	IP	H	R	HR	HB	BB	SO	RAT	ERA	ERA+	OAV	OOB	BH	AVG	PB	PR	PR+	PD	TPI
1886 Phi-a	0	0	—	2	0	0	0	0	10^{2}	8	9	0	0	5	1	11.0	4.22	83	.178	.260	118	.226	-0	-1	-1	-1	-0.1
1887 Phi-a	0	0	—	1	0	0	0	1	1	0	0	0	0	0	1	0.0	0.00	—	.000	.000	157	.289	0	0	0	0	0.1
1888 Phi-a	0	0	—	1	0	0	0	0	3	5	1	0	0	0	3	15.0	0.00	—	.357	.357	143	.267	0	1	1	-0	0.0
Total 3	0	0	—	4	0	0	0	1	14^{2}	13	10	0	0	5	5	11.0	3.07	112	.210	.269	1537	.268	0	1	1	-1	0.0

● LYLE BIGBEE Bigbee, Lyle Randolph "Al" b: 8/22/1893, Sweet Home, Ore. d: 8/5/42, Portland, Ore. BL/TR, 6', 180 lbs. Deb: 4/15/20 F◆

YEAR TM/L	W	L	PCT	G	GS	CG	SH	SV	IP	H	R	HR	HB	BB	SO	RAT	ERA	ERA+	OAV	OOB	BH	AVG	PB	PR	PR+	PD	TPI
1920 Phi-A	0	3	.000	12	2	0	0	0	45	66	42	5	0	25	12	18.2	8.00	50	.369	.446	14	.187	0	-21	-19	0	-1.0
1921 Pit-N	0	0	—	5	0	0	0	0	8	4	1	0	0	4	1	9.0	1.13	341	.154	.267	0	.000	-0	2	2	-0	0.1
Total 2	0	3	.000	17	2	0	0	0	53	70	43	5	0	29	13	16.8	6.96	57	.341	.423	14	.182	-0	-19	-17	0	-0.9

● CHARLIE BIGGS Biggs, Charles Orval b: 9/15/06, French Lick, Ind. d: 5/24/54, French Lick, Ind. BR/TR, 6'1", 185 lbs. Deb: 9/3/32

YEAR TM/L	W	L	PCT	G	GS	CG	SH	SV	IP	H	R	HR	HB	BB	SO	RAT	ERA	ERA+	OAV	OOB	BH	AVG	PB	PR	PR+	PD	TPI
1932 Chi-A	1	1	.500	6	4	0	0	0	24^{2}	32	22	2	3	12	1	17.1	6.93	62	.314	.402	1	.111	-0	-7	-7	-0	-0.5

● LARRY BIITTNER Biittner, Lawrence David b: 7/27/45, Pocahontas, Ia. BL/TL, 6'2", 205 lbs. Deb: 7/17/70 ◆

YEAR TM/L	W	L	PCT	G	GS	CG	SH	SV	IP	H	R	HR	HB	BB	SO	RAT	ERA	ERA+	OAV	OOB	BH	AVG	PB	PR	PR+	PD	TPI
1977 Chi-N	0	0	—	1	0	0	0	0	1^{1}	5	6	3	0	1	3	40.5	40.50	11	.556	.600	147	.298	0	-5	-5	0	-0.2

● JIM BILBREY Bilbrey, James Melvin b: 4/20/24, Rickman, Tenn. d: 12/26/85, Toledo, Ohio BR/TR, 6'2.5", 205 lbs. Deb: 5/17/49

YEAR TM/L	W	L	PCT	G	GS	CG	SH	SV	IP	H	R	HR	HB	BB	SO	RAT	ERA	ERA+	OAV	OOB	BH	AVG	PB	PR	PR+	PD	TPI
1949 StL-A	0	0	—	1	0	0	0	0	1	1	2	0	0	3	0	36.0	18.00	25	.250	.571	0	—	0	-2	-1	0	-0.1

● EMIL BILDILLI Bildilli, Emil "Hill Billy" b: 9/16/12, Diamond, Ind. d: 9/16/46, Hartford City, Ind. BR/TL, 5'10", 170 lbs. Deb: 8/24/37

YEAR TM/L	W	L	PCT	G	GS	CG	SH	SV	IP	H	R	HR	HB	BB	SO	RAT	ERA	ERA+	OAV	OOB	BH	AVG	PB	PR	PR+	PD	TPI
1937 StL-A	0	1	.000	4	1	0	0	0	8	12	9	1	0	3	2	16.9	10.13	48	.353	.405	0	.000	-0	-5	-5	1	-0.4
1938 StL-A	1	2	.333	5	3	2	0	0	21^{2}	33	18	3	0	11	11	18.3	7.06	70	.359	.427	2	.250	-0	-5	-5	-0	-0.5
1939 StL-A	1	1	.500	2	2	2	0	0	19	21	8	0	0	6	8	12.8	3.32	147	.266	.318	0	.000	-0	3	3	0	0.3
1940 StL-A	2	4	.333	28	11	3	0	1	97	113	68	12	2	52	32	15.5	5.57	82	.298	.386	6	.200	-1	-13	-10	3	-0.3
1941 StL-A	0	0	—	2	0	0	0	0	2^{1}	5	3	0	0	3	2	30.9	11.57	37	.417	.533	0	—	0	-2	-2	0	-0.1
Total 5	4	8	.333	41	17	7	0	1	148	184	106	16	2	75	55	15.9	5.84	80	.309	.388	8	.178	-2	-22	-18	4	-1.0

● HARRY BILLIARD Billiard, Harry Pree "Pree" b: 11/11/1883, Monroe, Ind. d: 6/3/23, Wooster, Ohio BR/TR, 6', 190 lbs. Deb: 7/31/08

YEAR TM/L	W	L	PCT	G	GS	CG	SH	SV	IP	H	R	HR	HB	BB	SO	RAT	ERA	ERA+	OAV	OOB	BH	AVG	PB	PR	PR+	PD	TPI
1908 NY-A	0	0	—	6	0	0	0	0	17	15	15	1	5	14	10	18.0	2.65	94	.234	.410	1	.167	-0	-0	-0	-1	-0.1
1914 Ind-F	8	7	.533	32	16	5	0	2	125^{2}	117	71	4	7	63	45	13.4	3.72	84	.257	.356	7	.184	-1	-12	-8	-2	-1.2
1915 New-F	0	1	.000	14	2	0	0	1	28^{1}	32	23	0	3	28	7	20.0	5.72	45	.291	.447	2	.333	0	-9	-11	1	-0.5
Total 3	8	8	.500	52	18	5	0	3	171	164	109	5	15	105	62	14.9	3.95	75	.260	.379	10	.200	-1	-22	-18	-2	-1.8

● JACK BILLINGHAM Billingham, John Eugene b: 2/21/43, Orlando, Fla. BR/TR, 6'4", 215 lbs. Deb: 4/11/68

YEAR TM/L	W	L	PCT	G	GS	CG	SH	SV	IP	H	R	HR	HB	BB	SO	RAT	ERA	ERA+	OAV	OOB	BH	AVG	PB	PR	PR+	PD	TPI
1968 LA-N	3	0	1.000	50	1	0	0	8	70^{2}	54	18	0	2	30	46	11.0	2.17	128	.215	.304	0	.000	0	6	5	1	0.5
1969 Hou-N	6	7	.462	52	4	1	0	2	82^{2}	92	45	12	5	29	71	13.7	4.25	83	.290	.359	1	.071	0	-6	-7	-0	-1.0
1970 Hou-N	13	9	.591	46	24	8	2	0	187^{2}	190	102	10	10	63	134	12.6	3.98	98	.259	.326	6	.103	-2	2	-2	1	-0.3
1971 Hou-N	10	16	.385	33	33	8	3	0	228^{1}	205	98	9	16	68	139	11.4	3.39	99	.243	.311	9	.123	-3	2	-1	0	-0.3
1972 *Cin-N	12	12	.500	36	31	8	4	1	217^{2}	197	83	18	7	64	137	11.1	3.18	101	.241	.301	5	.070	-4	7	1	-1	-0.4
1973 *Cin-N☆	19	10	.655	40	40	16	**7**	0	**293^{1}**	257	112	20	10	95	155	11.1	3.04	112	.236	.303	6	.065	-5	21	13	2	0.9
1974 Cin-N	19	11	.633	36	35	8	3	0	212^{1}	233	105	16	6	64	103	12.8	3.94	89	.288	.345	5	.075	-5	-7	-11	-1	-1.9
1975 *Cin-N	15	10	.600	33	32	5	0	0	208	222	100	22	9	76	79	13.3	4.11	88	.279	.348	7	.108	-1	-11	-12	-2	-1.6
1976 *Cin-N	12	10	.545	34	29	5	2	1	177	190	96	17	4	62	76	13.0	4.32	81	.279	.343	14	.237	3	-16	-16	-1	-1.6
1977 Cin-N	10	10	.500	36	23	3	2	0	161^{2}	195	105	16	10	56	76	14.5	5.23	75	.306	.371	9	.161	-1	-24	-23	2	-2.4
1978 Det-A	15	8	.652	30	30	10	4	0	201^{2}	218	95	16	8	65	59	13.0	3.88	100	.284	.346	0	—	0	-2	-0	-1	-0.1
1979 Det-A	10	7	.588	35	19	2	0	3	158	163	74	13	7	60	59	13.1	3.30	131	.275	.348	0	—	0	16	18	-1	1.7
1980 Det-A	0	0	—	8	0	0	0	0	7^{1}	11	6	1	0	6	3	20.9	7.36	56	.355	.459	0	—	0	-3	-3	0	-0.1
Bos-A	1	3	.250	7	4	0	0	0	24^{1}	45	30	6	4	12	4	22.6	11.10	38	.413	.488	0	—	0	-19	-18	-0	-2.2
Yr	1	3	.250	15	4	0	0	0	31^{2}	56	36	7	4	18	7	22.2	10.23	41	.400	.481	0	—	0	-22	-20	-0	-2.3
Total 13	145	113	.562	476	305	74	27	15	2230^{2}	2272	1069	176	98	750	1141	12.6	3.83	94	.268	.335	62	.111	-17	-35	-58	0	-8.8

● JOSH BILLINGS Billings, Haskell Clark b: 9/27/07, New York, N.Y. d: 12/26/83, Greenbrae, Cal. BR/TR, 5'11", 180 lbs. Deb: 8/17/27

YEAR TM/L	W	L	PCT	G	GS	CG	SH	SV	IP	H	R	HR	HB	BB	SO	RAT	ERA	ERA+	OAV	OOB	BH	AVG	PB	PR	PR+	PD	TPI
1927 Det-A	5	4	.556	10	9	5	0	0	67	64	36	3	6	39	18	14.6	4.84	87	.259	.373	7	.259	0	-5	-5	-1	-0.5
1928 Det-A	5	10	.333	21	16	3	1	0	110^{2}	118	83	4	5	59	48	14.8	5.12	80	.276	.371	10	.286	3	-13	-12	-0	-1.2
1929 Det-A	0	1	.000	8	0	0	0	0	19^{1}	27	14	0	1	9	1	17.2	5.12	84	.365	.440	0	.000	-1	-2	-2	1	-0.1
Total 3	10	15	.400	39	25	8	1	0	197	209	133	7	12	107	67	15.0	5.03	83	.279	.378	17	.250	2	-20	-19	0	-1.8

● **BRENT BILLINGSLEY** Billingsley, Brent Aaron b: 4/19/75, Downey, Cal. BL/TL, 6'2", 200 lbs. Deb: 5/20/99

YEAR	TM/L	W	L	PCT	G	GS	CG	SH	SV	IP	H	R	HR	HB	BB	SO	RAT	ERA	ERA+	OAV	OOB	BH	AVG	PB	PR	PR+	PD	TPI
1999	Fla-N	0	0	—	8	0	0	0	0	7^2	11	14	3	2	10	3	27.0	16.43	27	.379	.561	0	—	0	-10	-11	-0	-0.5

● **DOUG BIRD** Bird, James Douglas b: 3/5/50, Corona, Cal. BR/TR, 6'4", 180 lbs. Deb: 4/29/73

YEAR	TM/L	W	L	PCT	G	GS	CG	SH	SV	IP	H	R	HR	HB	BB	SO	RAT	ERA	ERA+	OAV	OOB	BH	AVG	PB	PR	PR+	PD	TPI
1973	KC-A	4	4	.500	54	0	0	0	20	102^1	81	37	10	2	30	83	9.9	2.99	138	.217	.279	0	—	0	9	12	-2	1.2
1974	KC-A	7	6	.538	55	1	1	0	10	92^1	100	31	6	1	27	62	12.5	2.73	140	.286	.339	0	—	0	9	11	1	1.8
1975	KC-A	9	6	.600	51	4	0	0	11	105^1	100	42	7	2	40	81	12.1	3.25	119	.258	.331	0	—	0	6	7	-1	1.0
1976	*KC-A	12	10	.545	39	27	2	1	2	197^2	191	90	17	3	31	107	10.2	3.37	104	.251	.283	0	—	0	3	3	-2	0.2
1977	*KC-A	11	4	.733	53	5	0	0	14	118^1	120	52	14	3	29	83	11.6	3.88	104	.270	.319	0	—	0	3	2	-1	0.2
1978	*KC-A	6	6	.500	40	6	0	0	1	98^2	110	63	8	2	31	48	13.0	5.29	73	.284	.340	0	—	0	-17	-16	-0	-1.8
1979	Phi-N	2	0	1.000	32	1	1	0	0	61	73	35	7	2	16	33	13.4	5.16	74	.305	.354	1	.167	0	-10	-9	-1	-0.6
1980	NY-A	3	0	1.000	22	1	0	0	1	50^2	47	16	3	1	14	17	11.0	2.66	148	.257	.313	0	—	0	8	7	1	0.5
1981	NY-A	5	1	.833	17	4	0	0	0	53^1	58	19	5	0	16	28	12.5	2.70	133	.280	.332	0	—	0	6	5	0	0.6
	Chi-N	4	5	.444	12	12	2	1	0	75^1	72	34	5	1	16	34	10.6	3.58	103	.254	.297	2	.100	-1	-1	1	-1	-0.1
1982	Chi-N	9	14	.391	35	33	2	1	0	191	230	119	26	3	30	71	12.4	5.14	73	.297	.325	8	.143	-2	-32	-29	-2	-3.4
1983	Bos-A	1	4	.200	22	6	0	0	1	67^2	91	52	14	2	16	33	14.5	6.65	66	.324	.365	0	—	0	-19	-16	-0	-1.1
Total	11	73	60	.549	432	100	8	3	60	1213^2	1273	590	122	22	296	680	11.8	3.99	96	.272	.319	11	.134	-2	-34	-21	-8	-1.5

● **RED BIRD** Bird, James Edward b: 4/25/1890, Stephenville, Tex. d: 3/23/72, Murfreesboro, Ark. BL/TL, 5'11", 170 lbs. Deb: 9/17/21

YEAR	TM/L	W	L	PCT	G	GS	CG	SH	SV	IP	H	R	HR	HB	BB	SO	RAT	ERA	ERA+	OAV	OOB	BH	AVG	PB	PR	PR+	PD	TPI
1921	Was-A	0	0	—	1	0	0	0	0	5	5	3	0	1	1	2	12.6	5.40	76	.294	.368	0	.000	-0	-1	-1	0	0.0

● **MIKE BIRKBECK** Birkbeck, Michael Lawrence b: 3/10/61, Orrville, Ohio BR/TR, 6'1", 190 lbs. Deb: 8/17/86

YEAR	TM/L	W	L	PCT	G	GS	CG	SH	SV	IP	H	R	HR	HB	BB	SO	RAT	ERA	ERA+	OAV	OOB	BH	AVG	PB	PR	PR+	PD	TPI
1986	Mil-A	1	1	.500	7	4	0	0	0	22	24	12	0	0	12	13	14.7	4.50	96	.282	.371	0	—	0	-1	-0	-0	-0.1
1987	Mil-A	1	4	.200	10	10	1	0	0	45	63	33	8	0	19	25	16.4	6.20	74	.335	.396	0	—	0	-9	-8	1	-0.6
1988	Mil-A	10	8	.556	23	23	0	0	0	124	141	69	10	1	37	64	13.0	4.72	85	.285	.336	0	—	0	-10	-10	2	-1.1
1989	Mil-A	0	4	.000	9	9	1	0	0	44^2	57	32	4	3	22	31	16.5	5.44	71	.310	.392	0	—	0	-8	-8	-0	-0.7
1992	NY-N	0	1	.000	1	1	0	0	0	7	12	7	3	0	1	2	16.7	9.00	39	.387	.406	0	.000	-0	-4	-4	0	-0.5
1995	NY-N	0	1	.000	4	4	0	0	0	27^2	22	5	2	0	2	14	7.8	1.63	249	.220	.235	2	.333	1	8	8	-0	0.5
Total	6	12	19	.387	54	51	2	0	0	270^1	319	158	27	4	93	149	13.8	4.86	84	.295	.353	2	.250	1	-24	-23	2	-2.5

● **RALPH BIRKOFER** Birkofer, Ralph Joseph "Lefty" b: 11/5/08, Cincinnati, Ohio d: 3/16/71, Cincinnati, Ohio BL/TL, 5'11", 213 lbs. Deb: 4/25/33

YEAR	TM/L	W	L	PCT	G	GS	CG	SH	SV	IP	H	R	HR	HB	BB	SO	RAT	ERA	ERA+	OAV	OOB	BH	AVG	PB	PR	PR+	PD	TPI
1933	Pit-N	4	2	.667	9	8	3	1	0	50^2	43	22	1	1	17	20	10.8	2.31	144	.229	.296	7	.318	1	6	6	-0	0.8
1934	Pit-N	11	12	.478	41	23	11	0	1	204	227	106	11	5	66	71	13.1	4.10	100	.277	.335	17	.227	1	-1	0	-2	-0.1
1935	Pit-N	9	7	.563	37	18	8	1	1	150^1	173	87	5	6	42	80	13.2	4.07	101	.283	.335	14	.241	2	-1	1	-3	0.0
1936	Pit-N	7	5	.583	34	13	2	0	0	109^1	130	73	4	5	41	44	14.5	4.69	86	.295	.362	9	.220	-0	-8	-8	-3	-1.0
1937	Bro-N	0	2	.000	11	1	0	0	0	29^2	45	28	3	0	9	9	16.4	6.67	60	.341	.383	3	.273	1	-9	-8	-1	-0.5
Total	5	31	28	.525	132	63	24	2	2	544	618	316	24	17	175	224	13.4	4.19	96	.282	.340	50	.242	5	-13	-10	-8	-0.8

● **BABE BIRRER** Birrer, Werner Joseph b: 7/4/29, Buffalo, N.Y. BR/TR, 6', 195 lbs. Deb: 6/5/55

YEAR	TM/L	W	L	PCT	G	GS	CG	SH	SV	IP	H	R	HR	HB	BB	SO	RAT	ERA	ERA+	OAV	OOB	BH	AVG	PB	PR	PR+	PD	TPI
1955	Det-A	4	3	.571	36	3	1	0	3	80^1	77	39	9	0	29	28	11.9	4.15	93	.248	.313	3	.158	2	-2	-3	-1	-0.1
1956	Bal-A	0	0	—	4	0	0	0	0	5^1	9	5	0	0	1	1	16.9	6.75	58	.360	.385	0	.000	-0	-2	-2	-0	-0.1
1958	LA-N	0	0	—	16	0	0	0	1	34	43	20	4	1	7	16	13.5	4.50	91	.309	.347	4	.571	2	-2	-1	-1	0.0
Total	3	4	3	.571	56	3	1	0	4	119^2	129	64	13	1	37	45	12.6	4.36	90	.272	.326	7	.259	4	-5	-6	-2	-0.2

● **TIM BIRTSAS** Birtsas, Timothy Dean b: 9/5/60, Pontiac, Mich. BL/TL, 6'7", 240 lbs. Deb: 5/3/85

YEAR	TM/L	W	L	PCT	G	GS	CG	SH	SV	IP	H	R	HR	HB	BB	SO	RAT	ERA	ERA+	OAV	OOB	BH	AVG	PB	PR	PR+	PD	TPI
1985	Oak-A	10	6	.625	29	25	2	0	0	141^1	124	72	18	3	91	94	13.9	4.01	96	.238	.354	0	—	0	2	-3	-3	-0.5
1986	Oak-A	0	0	—	2	0	0	0	0	2	2	5	1	0	4	1	27.0	22.50	17	.286	.545	0	—	0	-4	-4	-0	-0.2
1988	Cin-N	1	3	.250	36	4	0	0	0	64^1	61	34	6	3	24	38	12.3	4.20	85	.250	.325	0	.000	-1	-5	-4	-1	-0.4
1989	Cin-N	2	2	.500	42	1	0	0	1	69^2	68	33	5	3	27	57	12.7	3.75	96	.261	.337	1	.250	1	-2	-1	-1	0.0
1990	Cin-N	1	3	.250	29	0	0	0	0	51^1	69	24	7	1	24	41	16.5	3.86	102	.325	.397	0	.000	-0	-0	1	0	0.0
Total	5	14	14	.500	138	30	2	0	1	328^2	324	168	37	10	170	231	13.8	4.08	93	.260	.354	1	.056	-0	-9	-11	-4	-1.1

● **FRANK BISCAN** Biscan, Frank Stephen "Porky" b: 3/13/20, Mt.Olive, Ill. d: 5/22/59, St.Louis, Mo. BL/TL, 5'11", 190 lbs. Deb: 5/3/42

YEAR	TM/L	W	L	PCT	G	GS	CG	SH	SV	IP	H	R	HR	HB	BB	SO	RAT	ERA	ERA+	OAV	OOB	BH	AVG	PB	PR	PR+	PD	TPI
1942	StL-A	0	1	.000	11	0	0	0	1	27	13	8	1	0	11	10	8.0	2.33	159	.143	.235	0	.000	-0	4	4	0	0.2
1946	StL-A	1	1	.500	16	0	0	0	1	22^2	28	13	0	0	22	9	19.9	5.16	72	.318	.455	0	.000	-0	-4	-3	-0	-0.4
1948	StL-A	6	7	.462	47	4	1	0	2	98^2	129	78	3	9	71	45	19.1	6.11	75	.322	.435	5	.192	1	-20	-16	0	-1.8
Total	3	7	9	.438	74	4	1	0	4	148^1	170	99	4	9	104	64	17.2	5.28	81	.294	.409	5	.143	-0	-20	-16	0	-2.0

● **CHARLIE BISHOP** Bishop, Charles Tuller b: 1/1/24, Atlanta, Ga. d: 7/5/93, Lawrenceville, Ga. BR/TR, 6'2", 195 lbs. Deb: 8/22/52

YEAR	TM/L	W	L	PCT	G	GS	CG	SH	SV	IP	H	R	HR	HB	BB	SO	RAT	ERA	ERA+	OAV	OOB	BH	AVG	PB	PR	PR+	PD	TPI
1952	Phi-A	2	2	.500	6	5	1	0	0	30^2	29	24	2	0	24	17	15.6	6.46	61	.238	.363	1	.111	-0	-9	-8	0	-0.9
1953	Phi-A	3	14	.176	39	20	1	1	2	160^2	174	106	15	5	86	66	14.8	5.66	76	.282	.375	5	.089	-4	-30	-23	2	-2.4
1954	Phi-A	4	6	.400	20	12	4	0	1	96	98	49	10	5	50	34	14.3	4.41	89	.275	.372	4	.121	-2	-7	-5	-2	-0.8
1955	KC-A	1	0	1.000	4	0	0	0	0	6^2	6	7	1	3	8	4	23.0	5.40	77	.261	.500	1	.500	0	-1	-1	0	-0.1
Total	4	10	22	.313	69	37	6	1	3	294	307	186	28	13	168	121	14.9	5.33	77	.275	.376	11	.110	-6	-47	-37	1	-4.2

● **JIM BISHOP** Bishop, James Morton b: 1/28/1898, Montgomery City, Mo. d: 9/20/73, Montgomery City, Mo. BR/TR, 6', 195 lbs. Deb: 4/26/23

YEAR	TM/L	W	L	PCT	G	GS	CG	SH	SV	IP	H	R	HR	HB	BB	SO	RAT	ERA	ERA+	OAV	OOB	BH	AVG	PB	PR	PR+	PD	TPI
1923	Phi-N	0	3	.000	15	0	0	0	1	32^2	48	31	2	3	11	5	17.1	6.34	73	.353	.413	0	.000	-2	-8	-5	1	-0.5
1924	Phi-N	0	1	.000	7	1	0	0	0	16^2	24	14	3	0	7	3	16.7	6.48	69	.348	.408	1	.200	0	-5	-3	0	-0.2
Total	2	0	4	.000	22	1	0	0	1	49^1	72	45	5	3	18	8	17.0	6.39	71	.351	.412	1	.067	-2	-13	-9	1	-0.7

● **LLOYD BISHOP** Bishop, Lloyd Clifton b: 4/25/1890, Conway Springs, Kan. d: 6/18/68, Wichita, Kan. BR/TR, 6', 180 lbs. Deb: 9/5/14

YEAR	TM/L	W	L	PCT	G	GS	CG	SH	SV	IP	H	R	HR	HB	BB	SO	RAT	ERA	ERA+	OAV	OOB	BH	AVG	PB	PR	PR+	PD	TPI
1914	Cle-A	0	1	.000	3	1	0	0	0	8	14	5	0	0	3	1	19.1	5.63	51	.389	.436	0	.000	-0	-3	-2	-0	-0.3

● **BILL BISHOP** Bishop, William Henry "Lefty" b: 10/22/1900, Houtzdale, Pa. d: 2/14/56, St.Joseph, Mo. BR/TR, 5'8", 170 lbs. Deb: 9/15/21

YEAR	TM/L	W	L	PCT	G	GS	CG	SH	SV	IP	H	R	HR	HB	BB	SO	RAT	ERA	ERA+	OAV	OOB	BH	AVG	PB	PR	PR+	PD	TPI
1921	Phi-A	0	0	—	2	0	0	0	0	7	8	9	0	0	10	4	23.1	9.00	50	.267	.450	0	.000	-1	-4	-3	0	-0.2

● **BILL BISHOP** Bishop, William Robinson b: 12/27/1869, Adamsburg, Pa. d: 12/15/32, Pittsburgh, Pa. 5'8", 187 lbs. Deb: 9/13/1886

YEAR	TM/L	W	L	PCT	G	GS	CG	SH	SV	IP	H	R	HR	HB	BB	SO	RAT	ERA	ERA+	OAV	OOB	BH	AVG	PB	PR	PR+	PD	TPI
1886	Pit-a	0	1	.000	2	2	2	0	0	17	17	14	0	1	11	4	15.4	3.18	107	.221	.326	1	.143	-1	1	0	-1	-0.1
1887	Pit-N	0	3	.000	3	3	3	0	0	27	67	46	2	2	22	4	23.0	13.33	29	.450	.457	1	.100	-1	-28	-30	-0	-2.0
1889	Chi-N	0	0	—	2	0	0	0	2	3	6	13	0	0	6	1	36.0	18.00	23	.400	.571	0	.000	0	-5	-4	-0	-0.5
Total	3	0	4	.000	7	5	5	0	2	47	90	73	2	3	39	9	21.1	9.96	37	.373	.421	2	.111	-2	-32	-34	-1	-2.6

● **HI BITHORN** Bithorn, Hiram Gabriel (Sosa) b: 3/18/16, Santurce, P.R. d: 1/1/52, ElMante, Mex. BR/TR, 6'1", 200 lbs. Deb: 4/15/42

YEAR	TM/L	W	L	PCT	G	GS	CG	SH	SV	IP	H	R	HR	HB	BB	SO	RAT	ERA	ERA+	OAV	OOB	BH	AVG	PB	PR	PR+	PD	TPI
1942	Chi-N	9	14	.391	38	16	9	0	2	171^1	191	93	8	0	81	65	14.3	3.68	87	.296	.374	7	.123	-1	-7	-9	-1	-1.4
1943	Chi-N	18	12	.600	39	30	19	**7**	2	249^2	227	79	8	2	65	86	10.6	2.60	129	.244	.294	16	.174	-0	22	21	1	2.6
1946	Chi-N	6	5	.545	26	7	2	1	1	86^2	97	42	5	0	25	34	12.7	3.84	86	.283	.332	5	.179	-0	-4	-5	-0	-0.7
1947	Chi-A	1	0	1.000	2	0	0	0	0	2	2	0	0	0	0	0	9.0	0.00	—	.286	.286	0	—	0	1	1	-0	0.2
Total	4	34	31	.523	105	53	30	8	5	509^2	517	214	21	2	171	185	12.2	3.16	104	.268	.328	28	.158	-2	12	7	-0	0.7

● **JOE BITKER** Bitker, Joseph Anthony b: 2/12/64, Glendale, Cal. BR/TR, 6'1", 175 lbs. Deb: 7/31/90

YEAR	TM/L	W	L	PCT	G	GS	CG	SH	SV	IP	H	R	HR	HB	BB	SO	RAT	ERA	ERA+	OAV	OOB	BH	AVG	PB	PR	PR+	PD	TPI
1990	Oak-A	0	0	—	1	0	0	0	0	3	1	0	0	0	1	2	6.0	0.00	—	.111	.200	0	—	0	1	1	0	0.1
	Tex-A	0	0	—	5	0	0	0	0	9	7	3	0	1	3	6	11.0	3.00	131	.212	.297	0	—	0	1	1	0	0.0
	Yr	0	0	—	6	0	0	0	0	12	8	3	0	1	4	8	9.8	2.25	172	.190	.277	0	—	0	2	2	0	0.1
1991	Tex-A	1	0	1.000	9	0	0	0	0	14^2	17	11	4	0	8	16	15.3	6.75	60	.274	.357	0	—	0	-4	-4	-0	-0.3
Total	2	1	0	1.000	15	0	0	0	0	26^2	25	14	4	1	12	24	12.8	4.73	84	.240	.325	0	—	0	-2	-2	-0	-0.2

● **JEFF BITTIGER** Bittiger, Jeffrey Scott b: 4/13/62, Jersey City, N.J. BR/TR, 5'10", 175 lbs. Deb: 9/2/86

YEAR	TM/L	W	L	PCT	G	GS	CG	SH	SV	IP	H	R	HR	HB	BB	SO	RAT	ERA	ERA+	OAV	OOB	BH	AVG	PB	PR	PR+	PD	TPI
1986	Phi-N	1	1	.500	3	3	0	0	0	14^2	16	10	2	1	7	8	14.7	5.52	70	.271	.358	1	.333	1	-3	-3	0	-0.2
1987	Min-A	1	0	1.000	3	1	0	0	0	8^1	11	5	2	1	0	5	13.0	5.40	86	.314	.333	0	—	0	-1	-1	-0	-0.1
1988	Chi-A	2	4	.333	25	7	0	0	0	61^2	59	31	11	0	29	33	12.8	4.23	94	.255	.338	0	—	0	-2	-2	-1	-0.2
1989	Chi-A	0	1	.000	2	1	0	0	0	9^2	9	7	2	0	6	7	14.0	6.52	59	.257	.366	0	—	0	-3	-3	-0	-0.3
Total	4	4	6	.400	33	12	0	0	0	94^1	95	53	17	2	42	53	13.3	4.77	84	.264	.344	1	.333	1	-8	-8	-1	-0.8

YEAR	TM/L	W	L	PCT	G	GS	CG	SH	SV	IP	H	R	HR	HB	BB	SO	RAT	ERA	ERA+	OAV	OOB	BH	AVG	PB	PR	PR+	PD	TPI
● JIM BIVIN	Bivin, James Nathaniel b: 12/11/09, Jackson, Miss. d: 11/7/82, Pueblo, Colo. BR/TR, 6′, 155 lbs. Deb: 4/16/35																											
1935	Phi-N	2	9	.182	47	14	0	0	1	161^{2}	220	129	20	3	65	54	16.0	5.79	78	.316	.377	7	.146	-1	-32	-20	-1	-1.4
● DAVE BLACK	Black, David b: 4/19/1892, Chicago, Ill. d: 10/27/36, Pittsburgh, Pa. BL/TR, 6′2″, 175 lbs. Deb: 5/2/14																											
1914	Chi-F	1	0	1.000	8	1	1	0	0	25	28	19	1	0	4	19	11.5	6.12	43	.311	.340	2	.333	1	-9	-10	0	-0.5
1915	Chi-F	6	7	.462	25	10	2	0	0	121^{1}	104	46	3	6	33	43	10.6	2.45	103	.241	.304	4	.108	-3	4	1	2	0.0
	Bal-F	1	3	.250	8	4	1	0	0	34	32	18	2	2	15	10	13.0	3.71	77	.260	.350	3	.250	0	-4	-3	1	-0.3
	Yr	7	10	.412	33	14	3	0	0	155^{1}	136	64	5	8	48	53	11.1	2.72	95	.245	.315	7	.143	-3	0	-2	2	-0.3
1923	Bos-A	0	0	—	2	0	0	0	0	1	2	0	0	0	0	0	18.0	0.00	—	.500	.500	0	—	0	0	0	-0	0.0
Total	3	8	10	.444	43	15	4	0	0	181^{1}	166	83	6	8	52	72	11.2	3.18	82	.256	.319	9	.164	-2	-8	-12	2	-0.8
● DON BLACK	Black, Donald Paul b: 7/20/16, Salix, Iowa d: 4/21/59, Cuyahoga Falls, O. BR/TR, 6′, 185 lbs. Deb: 4/24/43																											
1943	Phi-A	6	16	.273	33	26	12	1	1	208	193	105	8	6	110	65	13.4	4.20	81	.247	.344	13	.188	-1	-21	-18	0	-1.9
1944	Phi-A	10	12	.455	29	27	8	0	0	177^{1}	177	94	6	4	75	78	13.0	4.06	86	.259	.336	11	.186	-1	-12	-11	-0	-1.3
1945	Phi-A	5	11	.313	26	18	8	0	0	125^{1}	154	77	5	0	69	47	16.0	5.17	66	.307	.391	6	.162	-2	-25	-24	-1	-3.0
1946	Cle-A	1	2	.333	18	4	0	0	0	43^{2}	45	26	5	1	21	15	13.8	4.53	73	.273	.358	2	.200	0	-5	-6	1	-0.3
1947	Cle-A	10	12	.455	30	28	8	3	0	190^{2}	177	90	17	1	85	72	12.4	3.92	89	.249	.330	12	.182	-1	-5	-10	1	-1.1
1948	Cle-A	2	2	.500	18	10	1	0	0	52	57	33	5	1	40	16	17.0	5.37	76	.282	.403	3	.200	-0	-6	-8	0	-0.5
Total	6	34	55	.382	154	113	37	4	1	797	803	425	46	13	400	293	13.7	4.35	80	.264	.352	47	.184	-4	-74	-77	0	-8.1
● BUD BLACK	Black, Harry Ralston b: 6/30/57, San Mateo, Cal. BL/TL, 6′2″, 180 lbs. Deb: 9/5/81																											
1981	Sea-A	0	0	—	2	0	0	0	0	1	2	0	0	0	3	0	45.0	0.00	—	.500	.714	0	—	0	0	0	0	0.0
1982	KC-A	4	6	.400	22	14	0	0	0	88^{1}	92	48	10	3	34	40	13.1	4.58	89	.269	.340	0	—	0	-5	-5	-0	-0.5
1983	KC-A	10	7	.588	24	24	3	0	0	161^{1}	159	75	19	2	43	58	11.4	3.79	108	.257	.308	0	—	0	5	5	2	0.7
1984	*KC-A	17	12	.586	35	35	8	1	0	257	226	99	22	4	64	140	**10.3**	3.12	129	.233	**.283**	0	—	0	25	26	3	3.1
1985	*KC-A	10	15	.400	33	33	5	2	0	205^{2}	216	111	17	8	59	122	12.4	4.33	96	.268	.324	0	—	0	-4	-4	-1	-0.5
1986	KC-A	5	10	.333	56	4	0	0	9	121	100	49	14	7	43	68	11.2	3.20	133	.225	.303	0	—	0	13	14	1	1.8
1987	KC-A	8	6	.571	29	18	0	0	1	122^{1}	126	63	16	5	35	61	12.2	3.60	127	.265	.322	0	—	0	12	13	-0	1.3
1988	KC-A	2	1	.667	17	0	0	0	0	22	23	12	2	0	11	19	13.9	4.91	81	.267	.351	0	—	0	-2	-2	-0	-0.3
	Cle-A	2	3	.400	16	7	0	0	1	59	59	35	6	4	23	44	13.1	5.03	82	.262	.341	0	—	0	-7	-6	1	-0.4
	Yr	4	4	.500	33	7	0	0	1	81	82	47	8	4	34	63	13.3	5.00	82	.264	.344	0	—	0	-9	-8	0	-0.7
1989	Cle-A	12	11	.522	33	32	6	3	0	222^{1}	213	95	14	1	52	88	10.8	3.36	118	.252	.296	0	—	0	13	15	-1	1.4
1990	Cle-A	11	10	.524	29	29	5	2	0	191	171	79	17	4	58	103	11.0	3.53	111	.236	.296	0	—	0	8	8	-0	0.8
	Tor-A	2	1	.667	3	2	0	0	0	15^{2}	10	7	2	1	3	3	8.0	4.02	98	.189	.246	0	—	0	-0	-0	1	0.0
	Yr	13	11	.542	32	31	5	2	0	206^{2}	181	86	19	5	61	106	10.8	3.57	110	.233	.293	0	—	0	8	8	0	0.8
1991	SF-N	12	16	.429	34	34	3	3	0	214^{1}	201	104	25	4	71	104	11.6	3.99	90	.251	.315	13	.183	1	-7	-10	2	-0.9
1992	SF-N	10	12	.455	28	28	2	1	0	177	178	88	23	1	59	82	12.1	3.97	83	.263	.323	3	.056	-3	-9	-14	1	-1.7
1993	SF-N	8	2	.800	16	16	0	0	0	93^{2}	89	44	13	2	33	45	11.9	3.56	110	.256	.325	9	.243	2	5	4	1	0.7
1994	SF-N	4	2	.667	10	10	0	0	0	54^{1}	50	31	9	3	16	28	11.4	4.47	90	.245	.309	1	.059	-1	-2	-3	-0	-0.4
1995	Cle-A	4	2	.667	11	10	0	0	0	47^{1}	63	42	8	0	16	34	15.0	6.85	69	.317	.367	0	—	0	-11	-11	0	-1.1
Total	15	121	116	.511	398	296	32	12	11	2053^{1}	1978	982	217	49	623	1039	11.6	3.84	104	.253	.312	26	.145	-1	35	32	9	4.0
● JOE BLACK	Black, Joseph b: 2/8/24, Plainfield, N.J. BR/TR, 6′2″, 220 lbs. Deb: 5/1/52																											
1952	*Bro-N	15	4	.789	56	2	1	0	15	142^{1}	102	40	9	1	41	85	9.1	2.15	169	.201	.262	5	.139	-1	**25**	**24**	-2	3.4
1953	*Bro-N	6	3	.667	34	3	0	0	5	72^{2}	74	46	12	1	27	42	12.6	5.33	80	**.259**	.325	4	.235	0	-8	-9	-0	-1.1
1954	Bro-N	0	0	—	5	0	0	0	0	7	11	9	3	0	5	3	20.6	11.57	35	.355	.444	0	—	0	-6	-6	-0	-0.3
1955	Bro-N	1	0	1.000	6	0	0	0	0	15^{1}	15	5	1	0	5	9	11.7	2.93	138	.273	.333	1	.333	0	2	2	-0	0.1
	Cin-N	5	2	.714	32	11	1	0	3	102^{1}	106	58	13	0	25	54	11.5	4.22	100	.263	.306	3	.100	-2	-2	0	-0	-0.3
	Yr	6	2	.750	38	11	1	0	3	117^{2}	121	63	14	0	30	63	11.5	4.05	104	.264	.309	4	.121	-2	-0	2	-1	-0.2
1956	Cin-N	3	2	.600	32	0	0	0	2	61^{2}	61	31	11	0	25	27	12.6	4.52	88	.256	.327	0	.000	-1	-5	-4	-1	-0.5
1957	Was-A	0	1	.000	7	0	0	0	0	12^{2}	22	11	4	0	1	2	16.3	7.11	55	.393	.404	0	—	0	-5	-4	0	-0.3
Total	6	30	12	.714	172	16	2	0	25	414	391	200	53	2	129	222	11.3	3.91	102	.248	.306	13	.135	-5	1	3	-3	1.0
● BOB BLACK	Black, Robert Benjamin b: 12/10/1862, Cincinnati, Ohio d: 3/21/33, Sioux City, Iowa 5′5.5″, 155 lbs. Deb: 8/19/1884 ♦																											
1884	KC-U	4	9	.308	16	15	13	0	0	123	127	79	1		17	93	10.5	3.22	69	.249	.273	36	.247	1	-11	-15	2	-0.9
● BUD BLACK	Black, William Carroll b: 7/9/32, St.Louis, Mo. BR/TR, 6′3″, 197 lbs. Deb: 9/13/52 C																											
1952	Det-A	0	1	.000	2	2	0	0	0	8	14	11	0	0	5	0	21.4	10.13	38	.389	.463	0	.000	-0	-6	-5	-0	-0.6
1955	Det-A	1	1	.500	3	2	1	1	0	14	12	5	0	2	8	7	14.1	1.29	299	.231	.355	1	.250	0	4	4	0	0.6
1956	Det-A	1	1	.500	5	1	0	0	0	10	10	4	2	0	5	7	13.5	3.60	114	.256	.341	0	.000	-0	1	1	0	0.1
Total	3	2	3	.400	10	5	1	1	0	32	36	20	2	2	18	14	15.8	4.22	93	.283	.381	1	.111	-1	-1	-1	0	0.1
● CHARLIE BLACKBURN	Blackburn, Foster Edwin b: 1/6/1895, Chicago, Ill. d: 3/9/84, New Port Richey, Fla. BR/TR, 6′1″, 165 lbs. Deb: 4/17/15																											
1915	KC-F	0	1	.000	7	2	0	0	0	15^{2}	19	15	2	0	13	7	18.4	8.62	31	.306	.427	0	.000	-1	-10	-11	0	-0.7
1921	Chi-A	0	0	—	1	0	0	0	0	1	0	0	0	0	1	0	9.0	0.00	—	.000	.333	0	—	0	0	0	-0	0.0
Total	2	0	1	.000	8	2	0	0	0	16^{2}	19	15	2	0	14	7	17.8	8.10	34	.297	.423	0	.000	-1	-10	-10	0	-0.7
● GEORGE BLACKBURN	Blackburn, George W. "Smiling George" b: 9/21/1871, Ozark, Mo. TR, 5′11″, 184 lbs. Deb: 7/6/1897																											
1897	Bal-N	2	2	.500	5	4	3	0	0	33	34	30	2	1	12	1	12.8	6.82	61	.264	.331	1	.077	-2	-9	-10	-0	-1.0
● JIM BLACKBURN	Blackburn, James Ray "Bones" b: 6/19/24, Warsaw, Ky. d: 10/26/69, Cincinnati, Ohio BR/TR, 6′4″, 175 lbs. Deb: 7/24/48																											
1948	Cin-N	0	2	.000	16	0	0	0	0	32^{1}	38	18	1	0	14	10	14.5	4.18	94	.302	.371	0	.000	-0	-1	-1	-0	-0.1
1951	Cin-N	0	0	—	2	0	0	0	0	3^{2}	8	7	3	2	2	1	29.5	17.18	24	.444	.545	0	—	0	-5	-5	0	-0.2
Total	2	0	2	.000	18	0	0	0	0	36	46	25	4	2	16	11	16.0	5.50	71	.319	.395	0	.000	-0	-6	-6	-0	-0.3
● RON BLACKBURN	Blackburn, Ronald Hamilton b: 4/23/35, Mt.Airy, N.C. d: 4/29/98, Morganton, N.C. BR/TR, 6′0.5″, 160 lbs. Deb: 4/15/58																											
1958	Pit-N	2	1	.667	38	2	0	0	3	63^{2}	61	33	7	3	27	31	12.9	3.39	114	.261	.345	2	.286	1	4	3	1	0.4
1959	Pit-N	1	1	.500	26	0	0	0	1	44^{1}	50	21	5	2	15	19	13.6	3.65	106	.286	.349	1	.200	1	1	1	-1	0.1
Total	2	3	2	.600	64	2	0	0	4	108	111	54	12	5	42	50	13.2	3.50	110	.271	.346	3	.250	2	5	4	0	0.5
● LENA BLACKBURNE	Blackburne, Russell Aubrey "Slats" b: 10/23/1886, Clifton Heights, Pa. d: 2/29/68, Riverside, N.J. BR/TR, 5′11″, 160 lbs. Deb: 4/14/10 MC ♦																											
1929	Chi-A	0	0	—	1	0	0	0	0	0^{1}	1	0	0	0	0	0	27.0	0.00	—	1.000	1.000	0	—	0	0	0	0	0.0
● EWELL BLACKWELL	Blackwell, Ewell "The Whip" b: 10/23/22, Fresno, Cal. d: 10/29/96, Hendersonville, N.C. BR/TR, 6′6″, 195 lbs. Deb: 4/21/42																											
1942	Cin-N	0	0	—	2	0	0	0	0	3	3	4	0	0	3	1	18.0	6.00	55	.231	.375	0	.000	-0	-1	-1	0	0.0
1946	Cin-N★	9	13	.409	33	25	10	**5**	0	194^{1}	160	62	1	4	79	100	11.3	2.45	136	.226	.307	6	.107	-3	21	20	4	2.3
1947	Cin-N★	**22**	8	.733	33	33	**23**	6	0	273	227	91	10	4	95	**193**	10.7	2.47	166	.234	.304	13	.123	-5	48	49	5	5.2
1948	Cin-N★	7	9	.438	22	20	4	1	1	138^{2}	134	73	12	4	52	114	12.3	4.54	86	.251	.323	11	.229	1	-9	-10	4	-0.5
1949	Cin-N★	5	5	.500	30	4	0	0	1	76^{2}	80	36	7	3	34	55	13.7	4.23	99	.271	.352	4	.211	-0	-2	-0	1	0.1
1950	Cin-N★	17	15	.531	40	32	18	1	4	261	203	105	12	13	112	188	11.3	2.97	143	**.210**	.301	13	.146	-2	34	**36**	2	**4.2**
1951	Cin-N★	16	15	.516	38	32	11	2	2	232^{2}	204	110	16	9	97	120	12.0	3.44	118	.233	.315	24	.293	7	13	16	0	2.9
1952	Cin-N	3	12	.200	23	17	3	0	0	102	107	66	6	5	60	48	15.2	5.38	70	.275	.379	5	.156	-0	-19	-18	-0	-2.4
	*NY-A	1	0	1.000	5	2	0	0	1	16	12	2	0	0	12	7	13.5	0.56	591	.203	.338	1	.200	-0	6	5	-0	0.4
1953	NY-A	2	0	1.000	8	4	0	0	1	19^{2}	17	10	2	1	13	11	14.2	3.66	101	.233	.356	0	.000	-1	1	0	-0	-0.1
1955	KC-A	0	1	.000	2	0	0	0	1	4	3	3	1	1	5	2	20.3	6.75	62	.250	.500	0	—	0	-1	-1	-0	-0.2
Total	10	82	78	.512	236	169	69	15	11	1321	1150	562	67	44	562	839	12.0	3.30	120	.235	.319	77	.174	-3	91	95	16	11.9
● GEORGE BLAEHOLDER	Blaeholder, George Franklin b: 1/26/04, Orange, Cal. d: 12/29/47, Garden Grove, Cal. BR/TR, 5′11″, 175 lbs. Deb: 4/20/25																											
1925	StL-A	0	0	—	2	0	0	0	0	2	6	7	3	1	1	1	36.0	31.50	15	.600	.667	0	—	0	-6	-6	-0	-0.3
1927	StL-A	0	1	.000	1	1	1	0	0	9	8	5	1	1	4	2	13.0	5.00	87	.258	.361	1	.333	0	-1	-1	0	0.0
1928	StL-A	10	15	.400	38	26	9	1	3	214^{1}	235	123	23	2	52	87	12.1	4.37	96	.280	.324	15	.211	2	-8	-4	5	0.2

YEAR	TM/L	W	L	PCT	G	GS	CG	SH	SV	IP	H	R	HR	HB	BB	SO	RAT	ERA	ERA+	OAV	OOB	BH	AVG	PB	PR	PR+	PD	TPI
1929	StL-A	14	15	.483	42	24	13	**4**	2	222	237	113	18	0	61	72	12.1	4.18	106	.275	.323	9	.122	-4	2	6	6	0.9
1930	StL-A	11	13	.458	37	23	10	1	4	191^1	235	119	20	2	46	70	13.3	4.61	106	.303	.343	12	.185	-1	1	5	-1	0.3
1931	StL-A	11	15	.423	35	32	13	1	0	226^1	280	137	15	1	56	79	13.4	4.53	102	.295	.335	11	.143	-3	-4	2	3	0.3
1932	StL-A	14	14	.500	42	36	16	1	0	258^1	304	163	19	3	76	80	13.3	4.70	103	.290	.340	12	.136	-4	-6	4	0	0.1
1933	StL-A	15	19	.441	38	36	14	3	0	255^2	283	146	24	0	69	63	12.4	4.72	99	.280	.326	14	.182	-1	-12	-2	3	0.1
1934	StL-A	14	18	.438	39	33	14	1	3	234^1	276	130	16	0	68	66	13.2	4.22	118	.296	.343	7	.093	-5	7	18	0	1.7
1935	StL-A	1	1	.500	6	2	0	0	0	17^2	25	15	3	0	6	0	15.8	7.13	67	.342	.392	0	.000	-1	-5	-4	1	-0.4
	Phi-A	6	10	.375	23	22	10	1	0	149	173	78	10	0	49	22	13.4	3.99	114	.289	.343	2	.043	-6	8	9	2	0.4
	Yr	7	11	.389	29	24	10	1	0	166^2	198	93	13	0	55	22	13.7	4.32	106	.295	.348	2	.040	-7	3	5	2	0.0
1936	Cle-A	8	4	.667	35	16	6	1	0	134^1	158	83	21	3	47	30	13.9	5.09	99	.295	.356	6	.130	-3	-1	-1	2	-0.2
Total	11	104	125	.454	338	251	106	14	12	1914^1	2220	1119	173	13	535	572	13.0	4.54	103	.290	.337	89	.142	-25	-26	29	20	3.1
● DENNIS BLAIR Blair, Dennis Herman b: 6/5/54, Middletown, Ohio BR/TR, 6'5", 182 lbs. Deb: 5/26/74																												
1974	Mon-N	11	7	.611	22	22	4	1	0	146	113	61	7	5	72	76	11.7	3.27	118	.210	.308	6	.118	-2	6	9	3	1.1
1975	Mon-N	8	15	.348	30	27	1	0	0	163^1	150	77	14	3	106	82	14.3	3.80	101	.251	.366	7	.143	-1	-3	1	-1	-0.1
1976	Mon-N	0	2	.000	5	4	1	0	0	15^2	21	11	1	2	11	9	19.5	4.02	93	.300	.410	0	.000	-0	-1	-0	-0	-0.1
1980	SD-N	0	1	.000	5	1	0	0	0	14	18	10	3	0	3	11	13.5	6.43	54	.310	.344	1	.200	0	-4	-5	-1	-0.4
Total	4	19	25	.432	62	54	6	1	0	339	302	159	25	10	192	178	13.4	3.69	104	.239	.344	14	.128	-4	-2	5	1	0.5
● WILLIE BLAIR Blair, William Allen b: 12/18/65, Paintsville, Ky. BR/TR, 6'1", 185 lbs. Deb: 4/11/90																												
1990	Tor-A	3	5	.375	27	6	0	0	0	68^2	66	33	4	1	28	43	12.5	4.06	97	.250	.324	0	—	0	-1	-1	-1	-0.2
1991	Cle-A	2	3	.400	11	5	0	0	0	36	58	27	7	1	10	13	17.3	6.75	62	.377	.418	0	—	0	-11	-10	0	-1.2
1992	Hou-N	5	7	.417	29	8	0	0	0	78^2	74	47	5	2	25	48	11.6	4.00	84	.249	.312	1	.059	-1	-4	-6	-1	-1.1
1993	Col-N	6	10	.375	46	18	1	0	0	146	184	90	20	3	42	84	14.1	4.75	101	.306	.354	4	.111	-2	-11	0	-1	-0.2
1994	Col-N	0	5	.000	47	1	0	0	3	77^2	98	57	9	4	39	68	16.3	5.79	86	.308	.391	0	.000	-1	-14	-6	-1	-0.5
1995	SD-N	7	5	.583	40	12	0	0	0	114	112	60	11	2	45	83	12.6	4.34	93	.262	.335	0	.000	-2	-2	-4	-1	-0.7
1996	*SD-N	2	6	.250	60	0	0	0	1	88	80	52	13	7	29	67	11.9	4.60	86	.240	.314	0	.000	-0	-4	-7	-2	-0.7
1997	Det-A	16	8	.667	29	27	2	0	0	175	186	85	18	3	46	90	12.1	4.17	110	.273	.322	0	.000	-0	8	8	-2	0.7
1998	Ari-N	4	15	.211	23	23	0	0	0	146^2	165	91	27	3	51	71	13.4	5.34	79	.292	.353	4	.083	-3	-18	-18	1	-2.1
	NY-N	1	1	.500	11	2	0	0	0	28^2	23	10	4	1	10	21	10.7	3.14	132	.228	.304	1	.250	1	3	3	0	0.3
	Yr	5	16	.238	34	25	0	0	0	175^1	188	101	31	4	61	92	13.0	4.98	84	.282	.346	5	.096	-2	-14	-15	2	-1.8
1999	Det-A	3	11	.214	39	16	0	0	0	134	169	107	29	4	44	82	14.6	6.85	71	.308	.363	0	.000	-0	-29	-29	-1	-2.5
2000	Det-A	10	6	.625	47	17	0	0	0	156^2	185	89	20	2	35	74	12.8	4.88	98	.296	.335	1	.333	0	1	-2	-2	-0.3
Total	11	59	82	.418	409	135	3	0	4	1250	1400	748	167	33	404	744	13.2	4.93	90	.285	.343	11	.075	-8	-82	-69	-10	-8.5
● BILL BLAIR Blair, William Ellsworth b: 9/17/1863, Pittsburgh, Pa. d: 2/22/1890, Pittsburgh, Pa. BL/TL, 5'8.5", 172 lbs. Deb: 7/19/1888																												
1888	Phi-a	1	3	.250	4	4	3	0	0	31	29	21	0	1	8	16	11.0	2.61	114	.238	.290	4	.308	1	2	1	1	0.3
● DICK BLAISDELL Blaisdell, Howard Carleton b: 6/18/1862, Bradford, Mass. d: 8/20/1886, Malden, Mass. Deb: 7/9/1884																												
1884	KC-U	0	3	.000	3	3	3	0	0	26	49	39	0		4	8	18.3	8.65	26	.377	.396	5	.313	0	-18	-20	-1	-1.5
● ED BLAKE Blake, Edward James b: 12/23/25, E.St.Louis, Ill. BR/TR, 5'11", 175 lbs. Deb: 5/1/51																												
1951	Cin-N	0	0	—	3	0	0	0	0	4	10	5	3	0	1	1	24.8	11.25	36	.476	.500	0	—	0	-3	-3	0	-0.1
1952	Cin-N	0	0	—	2	0	0	0	0	3	3	0	0	0	0	0	9.0	0.00	—	.250	.250	0	—	0	1	1	0	0.1
1953	Cin-N	0	0	—	1	0	0	0	0	0	1	0	0	1	—	—	∞	—	1.000	1.000	102	—	0	-2	-2	0	-0.2	
1957	KC-A	0	0	—	2	0	0	0	0	1^2	1	1	1	0	2	0	16.2	5.40	73	.167	.375	0	—	0	-0	-0	-0	0.0
Total	4	0	0	—	8	0	0	0	0	8^2	15	8	4	0	4	1	19.7	8.31	48	.375	.432	0	—	0	-4	-4	1	-0.2
● SHERIFF BLAKE Blake, John Frederick b: 9/17/1899, Ansted, W.Va. d: 10/31/82, Beckley, W.Va. BB/TR, 6', 180 lbs. Deb: 6/29/20																												
1920	Pit-N	0	0	—	6	0	0	0	0	13^1	21	14	0	1	6	7	18.9	8.10	40	.368	.438	1	.250	-0	-7	-7	0	-0.4
1924	Chi-N	6	6	.500	29	11	4	0	1	106^1	123	58	3	2	44	42	14.3	4.57	85	.299	.370	9	.290	1	-8	-8	1	-0.6
1925	Chi-N	10	18	.357	36	31	14	0	2	231^1	260	144	17	5	114	93	14.7	4.86	89	.287	.370	12	.152	-4	-15	-14	0	-1.8
1926	Chi-N	11	12	.478	39	27	11	4	1	197^2	204	91	7	6	92	95	13.8	3.60	107	.280	.366	14	.215	-1	5	5	2	0.7
1927	Chi-N	13	14	.481	32	27	13	2	0	224^1	238	101	3	4	82	64	13.0	3.29	117	.282	.348	16	.193	-2	16	14	3	1.7
1928	Chi-N	17	11	.607	34	29	16	**4**	1	240^2	209	80	4	3	101	78	11.7	2.47	156	.240	.321	19	.216	0	41	38	-2	4.0
1929	*Chi-N	14	13	.519	35	29	13	1	1	218^1	244	122	8	2	103	70	14.4	4.29	108	.291	.370	14	.173	-2	10	8	-2	0.5
1930	Chi-N	10	14	.417	34	24	7	0	0	186^2	213	127	14	3	99	80	15.2	4.82	101	.291	.378	15	.227	-1	3	1	3	0.3
1931	Chi-N	0	4	.000	16	5	0	0	0	50	64	34	4	1	26	29	16.4	5.22	74	.312	.392	8	.500	3	-8	-8	1	-0.2
	Phi-N	4	5	.444	14	9	1	0	1	71	90	49	2	3	35	31	16.2	5.58	76	.305	.384	6	.240	0	-13	-10	2	-0.8
	Yr	4	9	.308	30	14	1	0	1	121	154	83	6	4	61	60	16.3	5.43	75	.308	.388	14	.341	3	-21	-17	3	-1.0
1937	StL-A	2	2	.500	15	1	0	0	1	36^2	55	33	5	0	20	12	18.4	7.61	63	.350	.424	1	.100	-1	-12	-11	0	-1.1
	StL-N	0	3	.000	14	2	2	0	0	43^2	45	23	1	0	18	20	13.0	3.71	107	.271	.342	3	.300	0	1	1	0	0.2
Total	10	87	102	.460	304	195	81	11	8	1620	1766	876	68	30	740	621	14.1	4.13	101	.284	.363	118	.211	-6	12	10	9	2.5
● AL BLANCHE Blanche, Prosper Albert (b: Prosper Bilangio) b: 9/21/09, Somerville, Mass. d: 4/2/97, Melrose, Mass. BR/TR, 6', 178 lbs. Deb: 8/23/35																												
1935	Bos-N	0	0	—	6	0	0	0	0	17^1	14	3	0	0	5	4	9.9	1.56	243	.230	.288	1	.167	-0	5	5	0	0.2
1936	Bos-N	0	1	.000	11	0	0	0	1	16	20	15	1	1	8	4	16.3	6.19	62	.303	.387	1	.250	0	-4	-4	1	-0.2
Total	2	0	1	.000	17	0	0	0	1	33^1	34	18	1	1	13	8	13.0	3.78	101	.268	.340	2	.200	-0	1	0	1	0.0
● GIL BLANCO Blanco, Gilbert Henry b: 12/15/45, Phoenix, Ariz. BL/TL, 6'5", 205 lbs. Deb: 4/24/65																												
1965	NY-A	1	1	.500	17	1	0	0	0	20^1	16	10	1	1	12	14	12.8	3.98	85	.232	.354	0	—	0	-1	-1	-1	-0.2
1966	KC-A	2	4	.333	11	8	0	0	0	38^1	31	26	3	4	36	21	16.7	4.70	72	.237	.415	2	.167	-0	-5	-6	0	-0.8
Total	2	3	5	.375	28	9	0	0	0	58^2	47	36	4	5	48	35	15.3	4.45	76	.235	.395	2	.167	-0	-7	-7	-0	-1.0
● FRED BLANDING Blanding, Frederick James "Fritz" b: 2/8/1886, Redlands, Cal. d: 7/16/50, Salem, Va. BR/TR, 5'11", 185 lbs. Deb: 9/15/10																												
1910	Cle-A	2	2	.500	6	5	4	1	0	45^1	43	19	0	4	12	25	11.7	2.78	93	.254	.319	2	.111	-1	-1	-1	-1	-0.3
1911	Cle-A	7	11	.389	29	16	11	0	2	176	190	95	5	6	60	80	13.1	3.68	93	.283	.347	17	.262	2	-7	-5	0	-0.3
1912	Cle-A	18	14	.563	39	31	23	1	1	262	259	117	4	3	79	75	11.7	2.92	117	.267	.324	21	.226	1	12	14	0	1.8
1913	Cle-A	15	10	.600	41	22	14	3	0	215	234	79	6	3	72	63	12.9	2.55	119	.282	.341	21	.244	4	9	11	-2	1.4
1914	Cle-A	4	9	.308	29	12	5	0	0	116	133	82	0	1	54	35	14.6	3.96	73	.301	.378	4	.103	-2	-16	-13	1	-1.5
Total	5	46	46	.500	144	86	57	5	3	814^1	859	392	15	17	277	278	12.7	3.13	102	.279	.341	65	.216	4	-3	6	-2	1.1
● MATT BLANK Blank, Clarence Matthew b: 4/5/76, Texarkana, Tex. BL/TL, 6'2", 200 lbs. Deb: 4/3/2000																												
2000	Mon-N	0	1	.000	13	0	0	0	0	14	12	8	1	1	5	4	11.6	5.14	92	.222	.300	0	.000	-0	-1	-1	-0	-0.1
● FRED BLANK Blank, Frederick August b: 6/18/1874, DeSoto, Mo. d: 2/5/36, St.Louis, Mo. BL/TL, 6'0.5", 175 lbs. Deb: 6/20/1894																												
1894	Cin-N	0	1	.000	1	1	1	0	0	8	5	4	0	0	9	1	15.8	4.50	124	.179	.378	0	.000	-1	1	1	1	0.1
● HOMER BLANKENSHIP Blankenship, Homer "Si" b: 8/4/02, Bonham, Tex. d: 6/22/74, Longview, Tex. BR/TR, 6', 185 lbs. Deb: 9/6/22 F																												
1922	Chi-A	0	0	—	4	0	0	0	0	13	21	7	1	0	5	3	18.0	4.85	84	.389	.441	0	.000	-1	-1	-1	-0	-0.1
1923	Chi-A	1	1	.500	4	0	0	0	1	5	9	5	0	0	1	1	18.0	3.60	110	.429	.455	0	—	0	0	0	0	0.0
1928	Pit-N	0	2	.000	5	2	1	0	0	21^2	27	15	1	0	9	6	15.0	5.82	70	.321	.387	3	.375	1	-4	-4	1	-0.2
Total	3	1	3	.250	13	2	1	0	1	39^2	57	27	2	0	15	10	16.3	5.22	78	.358	.414	3	.250	0	-5	-5	1	-0.3
● KEVIN BLANKENSHIP Blankenship, Kevin De Wayne b: 1/26/63, Anaheim, Cal. BR/TR, 6', 180 lbs. Deb: 9/20/88																												
1988	Atl-N	0	1	.000	2	2	0	0	0	10^2	7	4	0	1	7	5	12.7	3.38	109	.194	.341	0	.000	-0	0	0	-0	0.0
	Chi-N	1	0	1.000	1	1	0	0	0	5	7	4	2	0	1	4	14.4	7.20	50	.318	.348	0	.000	-0	-2	-2	-0	-0.3
	Yr	1	1	.500	3	3	0	0	0	15^2	14	8	2	1	8	9	13.2	4.60	80	.241	.343	0	.000	-1	-2	-2	-1	-0.3
1989	Chi-N	0	0	—	2	0	0	0	0	5^1	4	1	0	0	2	2	10.1	1.69	223	.200	.273	0	.000	-0	1	1	-0	0.0
1990	Chi-N	0	2	.000	3	2	0	0	0	12^1	13	10	1	0	6	5	13.9	5.84	70	.265	.345	0	.000	-0	-3	-2	0	-0.4
Total	3	1	3	.250	8	5	0	0	0	33^1	31	19	3	1	16	16	13.0	4.59	83	.244	.333	0	.000	-1	-4	-3	-1	-0.7

YEAR	TM/L	W	L	PCT	G	GS	CG	SH	SV	IP	H	R	HR	HB	BB	SO	RAT	ERA	ERA+	OAV	OOB	BH	AVG	PB	PR	PR+	PD	TPI
● **TED BLANKENSHIP** Blankenship, Theodore b: 5/10/01, Bonham, Tex. d: 1/14/45, Atoka, Okla. BR/TR, 6'1", 170 lbs. Deb: 7/2/22 F																												
1922	Chi-A	8	10	.444	24	15	7	0	1	127^{2}	124	58	4	2	47	42	12.2	3.81	107	.266	.335	7	.171	-1	3	4	0	0.4
1923	Chi-A	9	14	.391	44	23	9	1	0	204^{2}	219	115	8	4	100	57	14.2	4.35	91	.287	.372	16	.211	2	-8	-9	-1	-0.8
1924	Chi-A	7	6	.538	25	11	7	0	1	129^{1}	167	79	1	1	38	36	14.3	5.01	82	.317	.364	15	.326	6	-11	-13	-2	-0.8
1925	Chi-A	17	8	.680	40	23	16	3	1	232	218	90	11	0	69	81	11.1	3.03	137	.253	.308	18	.205	2	35	31	-4	2.7
1926	Chi-A	13	10	.565	29	26	15	1	1	209^{1}	217	96	13	1	65	66	12.2	3.61	107	.273	.328	10	.132	-2	10	6	-2	0.2
1927	Chi-A	12	17	.414	37	34	11	3	0	236^{2}	280	156	14	2	74	51	13.5	5.06	80	.299	.352	15	.188	3	-24	-27	-3	-2.7
1928	Chi-A	9	11	.450	27	22	8	0	0	158	186	92	9	2	80	36	15.3	4.61	88	.306	.388	10	.169	-2	-10	-10	-2	-1.4
1929	Chi-A	0	2	.000	8	1	0	0	0	18^{1}	28	18	3	0	9	7	18.2	8.84	48	.359	.425	1	.250	-0	-9	-9	-1	-0.9
1930	Chi-A	2	1	.667	7	1	0	0	0	14^{2}	23	15	0	1	7	2	19.0	9.20	50	.371	.443	1	.200	-0	-7	-8	-1	-1.2
Total	9	77	79	.494	241	156	73	8	4	1330^{2}	1462	719	63	13	489	378	13.3	4.29	94	.287	.351	93	.196	7	-22	-37	-15	-4.5
● **CY BLANTON** Blanton, Darrell Elijah b: 7/6/08, Waurika, Okla. d: 9/13/45, Norman, Okla. BL/TR, 5'11.5", 180 lbs. Deb: 9/23/34																												
1934	Pit-N	0	1	.000	1	1	0	0	0	8	5	3	1	1	4	5	11.3	3.38	122	.161	.278	0	.000	0	1	1	0	0.1
1935	Pit-N	18	13	.581	35	30	23	**4**	1	254^{1}	220	93	3	2	55	142	**9.8**	**2.58**	**159**	**.229**	**.272**	13	.134	-4	**41**	**42**	2	**4.6**
1936	Pit-N	13	15	.464	44	32	15	**4**	3	235^{2}	235	114	9	3	55	127	11.2	3.51	115	.257	.301	13	.155	-3	13	14	1	1.3
1937	Pit-N★	14	12	.538	36	34	14	4	0	242^{2}	250	115	13	5	76	143	12.3	3.30	117	.266	.324	14	.165	-0	17	15	-0	1.4
1938	Pit-N	11	7	.611	29	26	10	1	0	172^{2}	190	84	13	2	46	80	12.4	3.70	103	.281	.329	13	.203	-1	2	2	2	0.3
1939	Pit-N	2	3	.400	10	6	1	0	0	42	45	23	4	0	10	11	11.8	4.29	90	.266	.307	4	.286	1	-2	-2	-0	-0.2
1940	Phi-N	4	3	.571	13	10	5	0	0	77	82	43	7	1	21	24	12.2	4.32	90	.272	.322	2	.083	-1	-4	-4	0	-0.4
1941	Phi-N☆	6	13	.316	28	25	7	1	0	163^{2}	186	98	11	3	57	64	13.5	4.51	82	.284	.344	6	.118	-2	-16	-14	-3	-2.0
1942	Phi-N	0	4	.000	6	3	0	0	0	22^{1}	30	15	3	1	13	15	17.7	5.64	59	.345	.436	1	.125	-0	-6	-6	0	-1.0
Total	9	68	71	.489	202	167	75	14	4	1218^{1}	1243	588	64	18	337	611	11.8	3.55	110	.262	.314	66	.154	-11	45	48	2	4.1
● **WADE BLASINGAME** Blasingame, Wade Allen b: 11/22/43, Deming, N.Mex. BL/TL, 6'1", 185 lbs. Deb: 9/17/63																												
1963	Mil-N	0	0	—	2	0	0	0	0	3	7	4	0	0	2	6	27.0	12.00	27	.467	.529	0	—	0	-3	-3	0	-0.1
1964	Mil-N	9	5	.643	28	13	3	1	2	116^{2}	113	58	15	0	51	70	12.7	4.24	83	.257	.334	7	.175	3	-9	-9	0	-0.7
1965	Mil-N	16	10	.615	38	36	10	1	1	224^{2}	200	103	17	5	116	117	12.9	3.77	94	.244	.341	15	.185	3	-6	-6	1	-0.2
1966	Atl-N	3	7	.300	16	12	0	0	0	67^{2}	71	42	5	2	25	34	13.0	5.32	68	.272	.340	5	.217	1	-13	-13	-0	-1.6
1967	Atl-N	1	0	1.000	10	4	0	0	0	25^{1}	27	13	1	1	21	20	17.4	4.62	72	.287	.422	1	.143	0	-4	-4	0	-0.1
	Hou-N	4	7	.364	15	14	0	0	0	77	91	57	9	2	27	46	14.0	5.96	56	.298	.359	4	.182	2	-22	-23	-0	-2.7
	Yr	5	7	.417	25	18	0	0	0	102^{1}	118	70	10	3	48	66	14.9	5.63	59	.296	.376	5	.172	2	-26	-27	0	-2.8
1968	Hou-N	1	2	.333	22	2	0	0	1	36	45	21	3	0	10	22	13.8	4.75	62	.308	.353	0	.000	0	-7	-7	1	-0.5
1969	Hou-N	0	5	.000	26	5	0	0	1	52	66	47	4	2	33	33	17.5	5.37	66	.306	.402	0	.000	-1	-10	-11	0	-1.1
1970	Hou-N	3	3	.500	13	13	1	0	0	77^{2}	76	34	4	2	23	55	11.7	3.48	112	.261	.320	2	.083	-0	5	4	0	0.3
1971	Hou-N	9	11	.450	30	28	2	0	0	158^{1}	177	90	11	13	45	93	13.4	4.60	73	.285	.346	10	.204	4	-20	-22	1	-2.1
1972	Hou-N	0	0	—	10	0	0	0	0	8^{1}	4	9	1	2	8	9	15.1	8.64	39	.148	.378	0	—	0	-5	-5	0	-0.3
	NY-A	0	1	.000	12	1	0	0	0	17	14	8	5	1	11	7	13.8	4.24	70	.250	.382	0	.000	0	-2	-3	1	0.0
Total	10	46	51	.474	222	128	16	2	5	863^{2}	891	486	75	30	372	512	13.5	4.52	77	.271	.350	44	.166	14	-95	-102	4	-9.1
● **STEVE BLASS** Blass, Stephen Robert b: 4/18/42, Canaan, Conn. BR/TR, 6', 165 lbs. Deb: 5/10/64																												
1964	Pit-N	5	8	.385	24	13	3	1	0	104^{2}	107	52	9	1	45	67	13.2	4.04	87	.266	.341	2	.067	-1	-6	-6	0	-0.8
1966	Pit-N	11	7	.611	34	25	1	0	0	155^{2}	173	80	12	2	46	76	12.8	3.87	92	.284	.336	12	.231	1	-5	-5	-3	-0.7
1967	Pit-N	6	8	.429	32	16	2	0	0	126^{2}	126	65	12	2	47	72	12.4	3.55	95	.261	.329	5	.128	-1	-3	-3	0	-0.3
1968	Pit-N	18	6	**.750**	33	31	12	7	0	220^{1}	191	64	13	4	57	132	10.3	2.12	138	.234	.288	11	.138	-1	21	20	-1	2.1
1969	Pit-N	16	10	.615	38	32	9	0	2	210	207	119	21	6	86	147	12.8	4.46	78	.258	.335	21	.250	6	-20	-23	3	-1.8
1970	Pit-N	10	12	.455	31	31	6	1	0	196^{2}	187	92	14	5	73	120	12.1	3.52	111	.254	.326	8	.114	-2	12	9	0	0.7
1971	*Pit-N	15	8	.652	33	33	12	**5**	0	240	226	81	16	2	68	136	11.1	2.85	119	.249	.303	10	.120	-3	17	15	1	1.2
1972	*Pit-N★	19	8	.704	33	32	11	2	0	249^{2}	227	80	18	4	84	117	11.4	2.49	134	.246	.311	15	.183	1	27	24	2	3.0
1973	Pit-N	3	9	.250	23	18	1	0	0	88^{2}	109	98	11	12	84	27	20.8	9.85	36	.313	.462	10	.417	4	-61	-65	1	-6.5
1974	Pit-N	0	0	—	1	0	0	0	0	5	5	8	2	0	7	2	21.6	9.00	38	.238	.429	0	.000	-0	-3	-3	0	-0.2
Total	10	103	76	.575	282	231	57	16	2	1597^{1}	1558	739	128	38	597	896	12.4	3.63	94	.258	.328	94	.172	4	-21	-37	3	-3.3
● **STEVE BLATERIC** Blateric, Stephen Lawrence b: 3/20/44, Denver, Colo. BR/TR, 6'3", 200 lbs. Deb: 9/17/71																												
1971	Cin-N	0	0	—	2	0	0	0	0	2^{2}	5	4	2	1	0	4	20.3	13.50	25	.385	.429	0	—	0	-3	-3	0	-0.1
1972	NY-A	0	0	—	1	0	0	0	0	4	2	0	0	0	0	4	4.5	0.00	—	.143	.143	0	.000	-0	1	1	0	0.1
1975	Cal-A	0	0	—	2	0	0	0	0	4^{1}	9	5	0	0	1	5	20.8	6.23	57	.429	.455	0	—	0	-1	-1	-0	-0.1
Total	3	0	0	—	5	0	0	0	0	11	16	9	2	1	1	13	14.7	5.73	58	.333	.360	0	.000	-0	-3	-3	0	-0.1
● **HENRY BLAUVELT** Blauvelt, Henry Russell b: 4/8/1873, Nyack, N.Y. d: 12/28/26, Portland, Ore. Deb: 6/22/1890																												
1890	Roc-a	0	0	—	2	0	0	0	0	12^{1}	19	23	0	0	8	5	19.7	10.22	35	.339	.422	3	.500	1	-9	-10	0	-0.3
● **GARY BLAYLOCK** Blaylock, Gary Nelson b: 10/11/31, Clarkton, Mo. BR/TR, 6', 196 lbs. Deb: 4/10/59 C																												
1959	StL-N	4	5	.444	26	12	3	0	0	100	117	61	14	2	43	61	14.6	5.13	83	.298	.371	4	.118	0	-13	-9	1	-0.7
	NY-A	0	1	.000	15	1	0	0	0	25^{2}	30	13	0	1	15	20	16.1	3.51	104	.306	.404	1	.500	1	1	0	-0	0.1
Total	1	4	6	.400	41	13	3	0	0	125^{2}	147	74	14	3	58	81	14.9	4.80	86	.300	.377	5	.139	1	-12	-9	0	-0.6
● **BOB BLAYLOCK** Blaylock, Robert Edward b: 6/28/35, Chattanooga, Okla BR/TR, 6'1", 185 lbs. Deb: 7/22/56																												
1956	StL-N	1	6	.143	14	6	0	0	0	41	45	32	7	0	24	39	15.1	6.37	59	.276	.369	1	.091	-1	-12	-12	0	-1.8
1959	StL-N	0	1	.000	3	1	0	0	0	9	8	5	1	0	3	3	11.0	4.00	106	.229	.289	0	.000	-0	-0	0	0	0.0
Total	2	1	7	.125	17	7	0	0	0	50	53	37	8	0	27	42	14.4	5.94	65	.268	.356	1	.083	-1	-12	-11	0	-1.8
● **RON BLAZIER** Blazier, Ronald Patrick b: 7/30/71, Altoona, Pa. BR/TR, 6'6", 215 lbs. Deb: 5/31/96																												
1996	Phi-N	3	1	.750	27	0	0	0	0	38^{1}	49	30	6	0	10	25	13.9	5.87	74	.310	.351	1	1.000	0	-7	-6	-1	-0.6
1997	Phi-N	1	1	.500	36	0	0	0	0	53^{2}	62	31	8	0	21	42	13.9	5.03	84	.290	.353	2	.400	1	-5	-5	-1	-0.3
Total	2	4	2	.667	63	0	0	0	0	92	111	61	14	0	31	67	13.9	5.38	79	.298	.352	3	.500	1	-12	-11	-2	-0.9
● **RAY BLEMKER** Blemker, Raymond b: 8/9/37, Huntingburg, Ind. d: 2/15/94, Evansville, Ind BR/TL, 5'11", 190 lbs. Deb: 7/3/60																												
1960	KC-A	0	0	—	1	0	0	0	0	1^{2}	3	5	1	1	2	0	32.4	27.00	15	.375	.545	0	—	0	-4	-4	-0	-0.2
● **CLARENCE BLETHEN** Blethen, Clarence Waldo "Climax" b: 7/11/1893, Dover-Foxcroft, Maine d: 4/11/73, Frederick, Md. BL/TR, 5'11", 165 lbs. Deb: 9/17/23																												
1923	Bos-A	0	0	—	5	0	0	0	0	17^{2}	29	15	0	0	7	2	18.3	7.13	58	.382	.434	0	.000	-1	-6	-6	-1	-0.4
1929	Bro-N	0	0	—	2	0	0	0	0	2	4	2	0	0	3	0	31.5	9.00	51	.444	.583	0	—	0	-1	-1	0	0.0
Total	2	0	0	—	7	0	0	0	0	19^{2}	33	17	0	0	10	2	19.7	7.32	57	.388	.453	0	.000	-1	-7	-7	-1	-0.4
● **BOB BLEWETT** Blewett, Robert Lawrence b: 6/28/1877, Fond Du Lac, Wis. d: 3/17/58, Sedro Woolley, Wash. BL/TL, 5'11", 170 lbs. Deb: 6/17/02																												
1902	NY-N	0	2	.000	5	3	2	0	0	28	39	26	0	1	7	8	15.1	4.82	58	.328	.370	0	.000	-1	-6	-6	-1	-0.6
● **ELMER BLISS** Bliss, Elmer Ward b: 3/9/1875, Penfield, Pa. d: 3/18/62, Bradford, Pa. BL/TR, 6', 180 lbs. Deb: 9/28/03 ♦																												
1903	NY-A	1	0	1.000	1	0	0	0	0	7	4	1	0	0	0	3	5.1	0.00	—	.167	.167	0	.000	-0	2	2	-0	0.3
● **TERRY BLOCKER** Blocker, Terry Fennell b: 8/18/59, Columbia, S.C. BL/TL, 6'2", 195 lbs. Deb: 4/11/85 ♦																												
1989	Atl-N	0	0	—	1	0	0	0	0	1	0	0	0	0	2	0	18.0	0.00	—	.000	.500	7	.226	0	0	0	0	0.0
● **BEN BLOMDAHL** Blomdahl, Benjamin Earl b: 12/30/70, Long Beach, Cal. BR/TR, 6'2", 185 lbs. Deb: 4/28/95																												
1995	Det-A	0	0	—	14	0	0	0	1	24^{1}	36	21	5	0	13	15	18.1	7.77	61	.356	.430	0	—	0	-8	-8	1	-0.3
● **JOE BLONG** Blong, Joseph Myles b: 9/17/1853, St.Louis, Mo. d: 9/16/1892, St.Louis, Mo. BR/TR, Deb: 5/4/1875 ♦																												
1875	RS-n	3	12	.200	15	15	12	1	0	129	169	121	0		2	14	11.9	3.07	71	.284	.286	10	.147	-4	-12	-13		-1.1
1876	StL-N	0	0	—	1	0	0	0	0	4	2	0	0		1	0	6.8	0.00	—	.143	.214	62	.233	-0	1	1	0	0.1

YEAR	TM/L	W	L	PCT	G	GS	CG	SH	SV	IP	H	R	HR	HB	BB	SO	RAT	ERA	ERA+	OAV	OOB	BH	AVG	PB	PR	PR+	PD	TPI
1877	StL-N	10	9	.526	25	21	17	0	0	187^1	203	121	0		38	51	11.6	2.74	95	.262	.296	47	.216	0	1	-3	-2	-0.4
Total	2	10	9	.526	26	21	17	0	0	191^1	205	121	0		39	51	11.5	2.68	97	.260	.295	109	.225	0	2	-2	-1	-0.3
● VIDA BLUE	Blue, Vida Rochelle b: 7/28/49, Mansfield, La. BB/TL, 6′, 189 lbs. Deb: 7/20/69																											
1969	Oak-A	1	1	.500	12	4	0	0	1	42	49	34	13	0	18	24	14.4	6.64	52	.290	.358	0	.000	-0	-14	-16	-1	-0.9
1970	Oak-A	2	0	1.000	6	6	2	2	0	38^2	20	12	0	1	12	35	7.7	2.09	169	.152	.228	3	.200	2	7	7	0	0.6
1971	*Oak-A★	24	8	.750	39	39	24	**8**	0	312	209	73	19	4	88	301	**8.7**	**1.82**	184	**.189**	**.252**	12	.118	-2	57	55	-4	5.1
1972	*Oak-A	6	10	.375	25	23	5	4	0	151	117	55	11	1	48	111	9.9	2.80	102	.215	.280	2	.044	-2	5	1	-2	-0.4
1973	*Oak-A	20	9	.690	37	37	13	4	0	263^2	214	108	26	4	105	158	11.0	3.28	108	.224	.303	0	.000	-0	16	9	-2	0.6
1974	*Oak-A	17	15	.531	40	40	12	1	0	282^1	246	118	17	1	98	174	11.0	3.25	102	.236	.303	0	—	0	12	2	-5	-0.3
1975	*Oak-A★	22	11	.667	39	38	13	2	1	278	243	103	21	5	99	189	11.2	3.01	121	.236	.307	0	—	0	24	20	-2	2.1
1976	Oak-A	18	13	.581	37	37	20	6	0	298^1	268	90	9	1	63	166	10.0	2.35	143	.239	.280	0	—	0	**39**	35	-3	3.3
1977	Oak-A†	14	19	.424	38	38	16	1	0	279^2	284	138	23	1	86	157	11.9	3.83	105	.264	.319	0	.000	-0	8	7	-1	0.6
1978	SF-N★	18	10	.643	35	35	9	4	0	258	233	87	12	0	70	171	10.6	2.79	124	.246	.298	6	.076	2	23	20	-2	2.1
1979	SF-N	14	14	.500	34	34	10	0	0	237	246	143	23	1	111	138	13.6	5.01	70	.272	.352	10	.120	0	-33	-43	2	-4.1
1980	SF-N†	14	10	.583	31	31	10	3	0	224	202	79	14	0	61	129	10.6	2.97	119	.242	.294	5	.074	-4	16	14	2	1.3
1981	SF-N★	8	6	.571	18	18	1	0	0	124^2	97	40	7	1	54	63	11.0	2.45	140	.217	.303	7	.200	2	14	14	2	2.0
1982	KC-A	13	12	.520	31	31	6	2	0	181	163	80	20	0	80	103	12.1	3.78	108	.238	.318	0	—	0	6	6	-0	0.7
1983	KC-A	0	5	.000	19	14	1	0	0	85^1	96	62	12	2	35	53	14.0	6.01	68	.286	.357	0	—	0	-18	-18	-0	-1.0
1985	SF-N	8	8	.500	33	20	1	0	0	131	115	70	17	1	80	103	13.5	4.47	77	.240	.350	4	.133	1	-13	-16	0	-1.6
1986	SF-N	10	10	.500	28	28	0	0	0	156^2	137	65	19	0	77	100	12.3	3.27	108	.239	.329	4	.093	1	8	5	-1	0.6
Total	17	209	161	.565	502	473	143	37	2	3343^1	2939	1357	263	23	1185	2175	11.2	3.27	108	.237	.305	53	.104	-2	155	102	-17	10.7
● JIM BLUEJACKET	Bluejacket, James (b: James Smith) b: 7/8/1887, Adair, Okla. d: 3/26/47, Pekin, Ill. BR/TR, 6′2.5″, 200 lbs. Deb: 8/6/14 F																											
1914	Bro-F	4	5	.444	17	7	3	1	1	67	77	34	2	0	19	29	12.9	3.76	76	.302	.350	3	.136	-1	-7	-7	1	-0.8
1915	Bro-F	10	11	.476	24	21	10	2	0	162^2	155	74	2	0	75	48	12.7	3.15	86	.258	.340	8	.131	-5	-8	-8	-4	-1.8
1916	Cin-N	0	1	.000	3	2	0	0	0	7	12	6	0	0	3	1	19.3	7.71	34	.400	.455	0	.000	-0	-4	-4	-0	-0.6
Total	3	14	17	.452	44	30	13	3	1	236^2	244	114	4	0	97	78	13.0	3.46	80	.275	.347	11	.129	-6	-18	-19	-3	-3.2
● JAIME BLUMA	Bluma, James Andrew b: 5/18/72, Beaufort, S.C. BR/TR, 5′11″, 195 lbs. Deb: 8/9/96																											
1996	KC-A	0	0	—	17	0	0	0	5	20	18	9	2	2	4	14	10.8	3.60	139	.247	.304	0	—	0	3	3	1	0.2
● CLINT BLUME	Blume, Clinton Willis b: 10/17/1898, Brooklyn, N.Y. d: 6/12/73, Islip, N.Y. BR/TR, 5′11″, 175 lbs. Deb: 9/30/22																											
1922	NY-N	1	0	1.000	1	1	1	0	0	9	7	3	0	0	1	2	8.0	1.00	400	.212	.235	1	1.000	1	3	3	-1	0.4
1923	NY-N	2	0	1.000	12	1	0	0	0	24	22	11	0	2	20	2	16.5	3.75	102	.265	.419	0	.000	-0	1	0	-1	-0.1
Total	2	3	0	1.000	13	2	1	0	0	33	29	14	0	2	21	4	14.2	3.00	129	.250	.374	1	.167	1	4	3	-1	0.3
● BERT BLYLEVEN	Blyleven, Rik Aalbert b: 4/6/51, Zeist, Netherlands BR/TR, 6′3″, 207 lbs. Deb: 6/5/70																											
1970	*Min-A	10	9	.526	27	25	5	1	0	164	143	66	17	2	47	135	10.5	3.18	117	.232	.289	7	.140	-1	10	10	-2	0.8
1971	Min-A	16	15	.516	38	38	17	5	0	278^1	267	95	21	5	59	224	10.7	2.81	126	.255	.298	12	.132	-3	20	22	-0	2.2
1972	Min-A	17	17	.500	39	38	11	3	0	287^1	247	93	22	10	69	228	10.2	2.73	118	.233	.286	15	.160	-1	11	15	1	1.9
1973	Min-A★	20	17	.541	40	40	25	**9**	0	325	296	109	16	9	67	258	10.3	2.52	**157**	.242	.287	0	—	0	**47**	**50**	-2	5.5
1974	Min-A	17	17	.500	37	37	19	3	0	281	244	99	14	9	77	249	10.6	2.66	140	.233	.292	0	—	0	30	33	0	4.0
1975	Min-A	15	10	.600	35	35	20	3	0	275^2	219	104	24	4	84	233	10.0	3.00	128	.219	.283	0	—	0	24	25	3	2.4
1976	Min-A	4	5	.444	12	12	4	0	0	95^1	101	39	3	4	35	75	13.2	3.12	115	.283	.354	0	—	0	4	5	0	0.5
	Tex-A	9	11	.450	24	24	14	6	0	202^1	182	67	11	8	46	144	10.5	2.76	130	.242	.293	0	—	0	17	18	2	2.0
	Yr	13	16	.448	36	36	18	6	0	297^2	283	106	14	12	81	219	11.4	2.87	125	.255	.313	0	—	0	21	23	2	2.5
1977	Tex-A	14	12	.538	30	30	15	5	0	234^2	181	81	20	7	69	182	**9.9**	2.72	150	.214	.279	0	—	0	35	36	0	3.8
1978	Pit-N	14	10	.583	34	34	11	4	0	243^2	217	94	17	6	66	182	10.7	3.03	122	.235	.290	11	.129	-2	15	18	1	1.6
1979	*Pit-N	12	5	.706	37	37	4	0	0	237^1	238	102	21	6	92	172	12.7	3.60	108	.265	.338	9	.129	-3	4	7	-2	0.0
1980	Pit-N	8	13	.381	34	32	5	2	0	216^2	219	102	20	0	59	168	11.5	3.82	95	.262	.311	5	.082	-4	-5	-4	-0	-0.8
1981	Cle-A	11	7	.611	20	20	9	1	0	159^1	145	52	9	5	40	107	10.7	2.88	126	.245	.298	0	—	0	14	13	-2	1.3
1982	Cle-A	2	2	.500	4	4	0	0	0	20^1	16	14	2	0	11	19	12.0	4.87	84	.211	.310	0	—	0	-2	-2	0	-0.3
1983	Cle-A	7	10	.412	24	24	5	0	0	156^1	160	74	8	10	44	123	12.3	3.91	109	.267	.328	0	—	0	3	6	1	0.7
1984	Cle-A	19	7	.731	33	32	12	4	0	245	204	86	19	6	74	170	10.4	2.87	143	.224	.287	0	—	0	31	33	0	3.4
1985	Cle-A★	9	11	.450	23	23	15	4	0	179^2	163	76	14	7	49	129	11.0	3.26	127	.240	.298	0	—	0	18	18	-1	1.7
	Min-A	8	5	.615	14	14	9	1	0	114	101	45	9	2	26	77	10.2	3.00	147	.237	.284	0	—	0	15	17	-0	1.8
	Yr	17	16	.515	37	37	**24**	**5**	0	**293**^{2}	264	121	23	9	75	**206**	10.7	3.16	134	.239	.292	0	—	0	32	35	-1	3.5
1986	Min-A	17	14	.548	36	36	16	3	0	**271**^{2}	262	134	50	10	58	215	10.9	4.01	108	.250	.295	0	—	0	5	9	-1	0.9
1987	*Min-A	15	12	.556	37	37	8	1	0	267	249	132	46	9	101	196	12.1	4.01	116	.249	.323	0	—	0	14	18	2	1.7
1988	Min-A	10	17	.370	33	33	7	0	0	207^1	240	128	21	16	51	145	13.3	5.43	75	.294	.348	0	—	0	-33	-30	-1	-3.4
1989	Cal-A	17	5	.773	33	33	8	**5**	0	241	225	76	14	8	44	131	10.3	2.73	140	.248	.289	0	—	0	31	30	1	2.7
1990	Cal-A	8	7	.533	23	23	2	0	0	134	163	85	15	7	25	69	13.1	5.24	73	.303	.342	0	—	0	-20	-22	0	-2.1
1992	Cal-A	8	12	.400	25	24	1	0	0	133	150	76	17	5	29	70	12.5	4.74	84	.285	.329	0	—	0	-12	-11	-1	-1.6
Total	22	287	250	.534	692	685	242	60	0	4970	4632	2029	430	155	1322	3701	11.1	3.31	118	.247	.303	59	.131	-13	276	315	1	30.7
● MIKE BLYZKA	Blyzka, Michael John (b: Michael John Bliska) b: 12/25/28, Hamtramck, Mich. BR/TR, 5′11.5″, 190 lbs. Deb: 4/21/53																											
1953	StL-A	2	6	.250	33	9	2	0	0	94^1	110	78	6	0	56	23	15.8	6.39	66	.292	.383	0	.000	-3	-25	-22	-1	-2.0
1954	Bal-A	1	5	.167	37	0	0	0	1	86^1	83	48	2	0	51	35	14.0	4.69	76	.254	.354	2	.133	-1	-9	-11	0	-0.8
Total	2	3	11	.214	70	9	2	0	1	180^2	193	126	8	0	107	58	14.9	5.58	70	.274	.370	2	.053	-4	-34	-33	-0	-2.8
● CHARLIE BOARDMAN	Boardman, Charles Louis b: 4/27/1893, Seneca Falls, N.Y. d: 8/10/68, Sacramento, Cal. BL/TR, 6′2.5″, 194 lbs. Deb: 9/26/13																											
1913	Phi-A	0	2	.000	2	2	1	0	0	9	10	5	0	0	6	4	16.0	2.00	138	.294	.400	0	.000	-0	1	1	-0	0.1
1914	Phi-A	0	0	—	2	0	0	0	0	7^1	10	5	0	0	4	2	17.2	4.91	53	.357	.438	0	.000	-0	-2	-2	-0	-0.1
1915	StL-N	1	0	1.000	3	1	1	0	0	19	12	12	0	0	15	7	12.8	2.84	98	.188	.342	2	.286	0	-0	-0	-0	0.0
Total	3	1	2	.333	7	3	2	0	0	35^1	32	22	0	0	25	13	14.5	3.06	90	.254	.377	2	.167	-0	-1	-1	-1	0.0
● DOUG BOCHTLER	Bochtler, Douglas Eugene b: 7/5/70, W.Palm Beach, Fla. BR/TR, 6′3″, 205 lbs. Deb: 5/5/95																											
1995	SD-N	4	4	.500	34	0	0	0	1	45^1	38	18	5	0	19	45	11.3	3.57	113	.239	.320	0	.000	-0	3	2	0	0.4
1996	*SD-N	2	4	.333	63	0	0	0	3	65^2	45	25	6	1	39	68	11.6	3.02	132	.195	.314	0	—	0	9	7	-1	0.5
1997	SD-N	3	6	.333	54	0	0	0	2	60^1	51	35	3	1	50	46	15.2	4.77	81	.229	.372	0	—	0	-4	-6	-1	-1.0
1998	Det-A	0	2	.000	51	0	0	0	0	67^1	73	48	17	3	42	45	15.8	6.15	77	.279	.384	0	—	0	-11	-11	-1	-0.6
1999	LA-N	0	0	—	12	0	0	0	0	13	11	8	3	1	6	7	12.5	5.54	77	.224	.321	0	—	0	-1	-2	0	-0.1
2000	KC-A	0	2	.000	6	0	0	0	0	8^1	13	6	2	0	10	4	24.8	6.48	77	.371	.511	0	—	0	-1	-1	-0	-0.3
Total	6	9	18	.333	220	0	0	0	6	260	231	140	36	6	166	215	13.9	4.57	92	.241	.356	0	.000	-0	-6	-11	-3	-1.1
● RANDY BOCKUS	Bockus, Randy Walter b: 10/5/60, Canton, Ohio BL/TR, 6′2″, 190 lbs. Deb: 9/10/86																											
1986	SF-N	0	0	—	5	0	0	0	0	7	7	5	1	0	6	4	16.7	2.57	137	.241	.371	0	.000	-0	1	1	1	0.1
1987	SF-N	1	0	1.000	12	0	0	0	0	17^1	17	8	2	0	4	9	10.9	3.63	106	.266	.309	0	.000	-0	1	0	-0	0.0
1988	SF-N	1	1	.500	20	0	0	0	0	32	35	19	2	1	13	18	13.8	4.78	68	.297	.371	1	.167	0	-5	-6	0	-0.3
1989	Det-A	0	0	—	2	0	0	0	0	5^1	7	3	0	0	2	2	15.2	5.06	76	.333	.391	0	—	0	-1	-1	-0	-0.1
Total	4	2	1	.667	39	0	0	0	0	61^2	66	35	5	1	25	33	13.4	4.23	83	.284	.357	1	.125	-0	-4	-5	1	-0.3
● MIKE BODDICKER	Boddicker, Michael James b: 8/23/57, Cedar Rapids, Iowa BR/TR, 5′11″, 172 lbs. Deb: 10/4/80																											
1980	Bal-A	0	1	.000	1	1	0	0	0	7^1	6	6	1	0	5	4	13.5	6.14	65	.207	.324	0	—	0	-2	-2	-0	-0.2
1981	Bal-A	0	0	—	2	0	0	0	0	5^2	6	4	1	0	2	2	12.7	4.76	76	.261	.320	0	—	0	-1	-1	-0	-0.1
1982	Bal-A	1	0	1.000	7	0	0	0	0	25^2	25	10	2	0	12	20	13.0	3.51	115	.258	.339	0	—	0	2	2	0	0.1
1983	*Bal-A	16	8	.667	27	26	10	**5**	0	179	141	65	13	0	52	120	9.7	2.77	143	**.216**	.274	0	—	0	26	25	3	3.5
1984	Bal-A☆	**20**	11	.645	34	34	16	4	0	261^1	218	95	23	5	81	128	10.5	**2.79**	139	.228	.292	0	—	0	**35**	33	6	**4.4**
1985	Bal-A	12	17	.414	32	32	9	2	0	203^1	227	104	13	5	89	135	14.2	4.07	99	.286	.361	0	—	0	2	-1	6	0.4
1986	Bal-A	14	12	.538	33	33	7	0	0	218^1	214	125	30	11	74	175	12.3	4.70	88	.255	.323	0	—	0	-12	-14	3	-1.1
1987	Bal-A	10	12	.455	33	33	7	2	0	226	212	114	29	7	78	152	11.8	4.18	106	.248	.316	0	—	0	7	6	4	0.9

YEAR	TM/L	W	L	PCT	G	GS	CG	SH	SV	IP	H	R	HR	HB	BB	SO	RAT	ERA	ERA+	OAV	OOB	BH	AVG	PB	PR	PR+	PD	TPI
1988	Bal-A	6	12	.333	21	21	4	0	0	147	149	72	14	11	51	100	12.9	3.86	101	.265	.338	0	—	0	2	1	-1	0.0
	*Bos-A	7	3	.700	15	14	1	1	0	89	85	30	3	3	26	56	11.5	2.63	157	.257	.317	0	—	0	13	14	2	1.8
	Yr	13	15	.464	36	35	5	1	0	236	234	102	17	14	77	156	12.4	3.39	118	.262	.330	0	—	0	15	16	1	1.8
1989	Bos-A	15	11	.577	34	34	3	2	0	211^2	217	101	19	10	71	145	12.7	4.00	103	.267	.333	0	—	0	-2	2	1	0.4
1990	*Bos-A	17	8	.680	34	34	4	0	0	228	225	92	16	10	69	143	12.0	3.36	122	.258	.319	0	—	0	14	18	1	2.0
1991	KC-A	12	12	.500	30	29	1	0	0	180^2	188	89	13	13	59	79	13.0	4.08	101	.272	.340	0	—	0	0	1	2	0.3
1992	KC-A	1	4	.200	29	8	0	0	3	86^2	92	50	5	8	37	47	14.2	4.98	82	.269	.354	0	—	0	-10	-9	1	-0.4
1993	Mil-A	3	5	.375	10	10	1	0	0	54	77	35	6	4	15	24	16.0	5.67	75	.338	.389	0	—	0	-8	-9	0	-1.0
Total	14	134	116	.536	342	309	63	16	3	2123^2	2082	992	188	87	721	1330	12.2	3.80	107	.257	.325	0	—	0	66	67	28	11.0
● GEORGE BOEHLER	Boehler, George Henry b: 1/2/1892, Lawrenceburg, Ind. d: 6/23/58, Lawrenceburg, Ind BR/TR, 6′2″, 180 lbs. Deb: 9/13/12																											
1912	Det-A	0	2	.000	5	4	2	0	0	32	50	31	0	2	14	15	18.6	6.47	50	.365	.431	1	.100	-1	-11	-12	1	-0.6
1913	Det-A	0	1	.000	1	1	1	0	0	8	11	9	0	2	6	2	21.4	6.75	43	.355	.487	1	.333	1	-3	-3	1	-0.3
1914	Det-A	2	3	.400	18	6	2	0	0	63	54	39	1	8	48	37	15.7	3.57	79	.242	.394	3	.176	1	-6	-5	-0	-0.4
1915	Det-A	1	1	.500	8	0	0	0	0	15	19	10	0	1	4	7	14.4	1.80	168	.328	.381	3	.750	2	2	2	-0	0.4
1916	Det-A	1	1	.500	5	2	1	0	0	13^1	12	8	0	2	9	8	15.5	4.73	61	.261	.404	0	.000	0	-3	-3	1	-0.3
1920	StL-A	0	1	.000	3	1	0	0	0	7	10	10	1	0	4	2	18.0	7.71	51	.303	.378	0	.000	0	-3	-3	0	-0.3
1921	StL-A	0	0	—	1	0	0	0	0	1	1	0	0	0	0	0	9.0	0.00	—	.500	.500	0	—	0	0	0	-0	0.0
1923	Pit-N	1	3	.250	10	3	1	0	0	28^1	33	26	1	1	26	12	19.1	6.04	66	.314	.455	3	.300	1	-6	-6	-0	-0.7
1926	Bro-N	1	0	1.000	10	1	0	0	0	34^2	42	23	1	3	23	10	17.7	4.41	87	.302	.412	3	.250	0	-2	-2	-1	-0.1
Total	9	6	12	.333	61	18	7	0	0	202^1	232	156	4	19	134	93	17.1	4.71	70	.300	.415	14	.233	3	-33	-32	1	-2.3
● JOE BOEHLING	Boehling, John Joseph b: 3/20/1891, Richmond, Va. d: 9/8/41, Richmond, Va. BL/TL, 5′11″, 168 lbs. Deb: 6/20/12																											
1912	Was-A	0	0	—	3	0	0	0	0	5	4	4	0	2	6	2	21.6	7.20	46	.235	.480	0	—	0	-2	-2	0	-0.1
1913	Was-A	17	7	.708	38	25	18	3	4	235^1	197	82	3	9	82	110	11.0	2.14	138	.229	.303	19	.221	1	21	21	4	2.7
1914	Was-A	13	8	.619	27	24	14	2	0	196	180	76	3	9	76	91	12.2	3.03	93	.258	.339	17	.239	4	-6	-5	2	0.1
1915	Was-A	14	13	.519	40	32	14	2	0	229^1	217	105	5	9	119	108	13.5	3.22	92	.255	.352	13	.173	0	-7	-6	2	-0.4
1916	Was-A	9	11	.450	27	19	7	2	0	139^2	134	62	1	3	54	52	12.3	3.09	90	.260	.333	7	.171	1	-4	-5	4	-0.2
	Cle-A	2	4	.333	12	9	3	0	0	60^2	63	23	0	2	23	18	13.1	2.67	113	.281	.353	5	.263	1	1	2	1	0.4
	Yr	11	15	.423	39	28	10	2	0	200^1	197	85	1	5	77	70	12.5	2.97	96	.266	.339	12	.200	1	-3	-2	4	0.2
1917	Cle-A	1	6	.143	12	7	1	0	0	46^1	50	27	1	3	16	11	13.4	4.66	61	.291	.361	3	.188	-0	-10	-9	-0	-1.3
1920	Cle-A	0	1	.000	3	2	0	0	0	13	16	10	0	0	10	4	18.0	4.85	78	.333	.448	2	.500	1	-2	-2	0	0.0
Total	7	56	50	.528	162	118	57	9	4	925^1	861	389	13	37	386	396	12.5	2.97	98	.254	.337	66	.212	7	-10	-5	12	1.2
● BRIAN BOEHRINGER	Boehringer, Brian Edward b: 1/8/69, St.Louis, Mo. BB/TR, 6′2″, 180 lbs. Deb: 4/30/95																											
1995	NY-A	0	3	.000	7	3	0	0	0	17^2	24	27	5	1	22	10	23.9	13.75	34	.320	.480	0	—	0	-18	-18	-1	-2.3
1996	*NY-A	2	4	.333	15	3	0	0	0	46^1	46	28	6	1	21	37	13.2	5.44	91	.260	.342	0	—	0	-2	-3	-0	-0.3
1997	*NY-A	3	2	.600	34	0	0	0	0	48	39	16	4	0	32	53	13.3	2.63	170	.225	.346	0	—	0	10	10	0	0.9
1998	*SD-N	5	2	.714	56	1	0	0	0	76^1	75	38	10	4	45	67	14.6	4.36	90	.257	.364	0	.000	-0	-1	-4	-0	-0.4
1999	SD-N	6	5	.545	33	11	0	0	0	94^1	97	38	10	1	35	64	12.7	3.24	129	.267	.333	1	.063	-1	14	11	-1	1.0
2000	SD-N	0	3	.000	7	3	0	0	0	15^2	18	15	4	0	10	9	16.1	5.74	76	.286	.384	1	.250	0	-2	-3	-1	-0.4
Total	6	16	19	.457	152	21	0	0	0	298^1	299	162	39	7	165	240	14.2	4.53	95	.262	.358	2	.074	-0	1	-7	-2	-1.5
● LARRY BOERNER	Boerner, Lawrence Hyer b: 1/21/05, Staunton, Va. d: 10/16/69, Staunton, Va. BR/TR, 6′4.5″, 175 lbs. Deb: 6/30/32																											
1932	Bos-A	0	4	.000	21	5	0	0	0	61	71	41	2	3	37	19	16.4	5.02	90	.302	.404	0	.000	-3	-4	-4	0	-0.4
● JOE BOEVER	Boever, Joseph Martin b: 10/4/60, Kirkwood, Mo. BR/TR, 6′1″, 200 lbs. Deb: 7/19/85																											
1985	StL-N	0	0	—	13	0	0	0	0	16^1	17	8	3	0	4	20	11.6	4.41	80	.270	.313	0	—	0	-1	-2	-0	-0.1
1986	StL-N	0	1	.000	11	0	0	0	0	21^2	19	5	2	0	11	8	12.5	1.66	220	.232	.323	1	.500	0	5	5	-0	0.3
1987	Atl-N	1	0	1.000	14	0	0	0	0	18^1	29	15	4	0	12	18	20.1	7.36	59	.367	.451	0	—	0	-7	-6	-0	-0.3
1988	Atl-N	0	2	.000	16	0	0	0	1	20^1	12	4	1	1	1	7	6.2	1.77	208	.182	.206	0	—	0	4	4	0	0.4
1989	Atl-N	4	11	.267	66	0	0	0	21	82^1	78	37	6	1	34	68	12.4	3.94	93	.252	.328	0	.000	-0	-4	-2	1	-0.4
1990	Atl-N	1	3	.250	33	0	0	0	8	42^1	40	23	6	0	35	35	15.9	4.68	86	.252	.387	0	.000	-0	-4	-3	-1	-0.5
	Phi-N	2	3	.400	34	0	0	0	6	46	37	12	0	0	16	40	10.4	2.15	178	.215	.282	0	.000	-0	8	8	0	1.1
	Yr	3	6	.333	67	0	0	0	14	88^1	77	35	6	0	51	75	13.0	3.36	117	.233	.335	0	.000	-0	4	5	-1	0.6
1991	Phi-N	3	5	.375	68	0	0	0	0	98^1	90	45	10	0	54	89	13.2	3.84	95	.245	.341	1	.333	0	-2	-2	-1	-0.2
1992	Hou-N	3	6	.333	**81**	0	0	0	2	111^1	103	38	3	4	45	67	12.3	2.51	134	.248	.327	0	.000	-1	12	11	0	0.8
1993	Oak-A	4	2	.667	42	0	0	0	0	79^1	87	40	8	4	33	49	14.1	3.86	106	.280	.356	0	—	0	4	2	0	0.2
	Det-A	2	1	.667	19	0	0	0	3	23	14	10	1	0	11	14	9.8	2.74	157	.179	.281	0	—	0	4	4	-0	0.5
	Yr	6	3	.667	61	0	0	0	3	102^1	101	50	9	4	44	63	13.1	3.61	115	.260	.341	0	—	0	8	6	-0	0.7
1994	Det-A	9	2	.818	46	0	0	0	3	81^1	80	40	12	2	37	49	13.2	3.98	122	.263	.347	0	—	0	7	8	1	1.0
1995	Det-A	5	7	.417	60	0	0	0	3	98^2	128	74	17	3	44	71	16.0	6.39	75	.319	.391	0	—	0	-18	-18	-1	-2.0
1996	Pit-N	0	2	.000	13	0	0	0	2	15	17	11	2	1	6	6	14.4	5.40	81	.288	.364	0	.000	-0	-2	-2	-0	-0.3
Total	12	34	45	.430	516	0	0	0	49	754^1	751	362	75	16	343	541	13.2	3.93	102	.262	.344	2	.118	-1	7	8	-2	0.5
● TIM BOGAR	Bogar, Timothy Paul b: 10/28/66, Indianapolis, Ind. BR/TR, 6′2″, 198 lbs. Deb: 4/21/93 ♦																											
2000	Hou-N	0	0	—	2	0	0	0	0	2	2	1	1	0	1	1	13.5	4.50	109	.250	.333	63	.207	0	0	0	-0	0.0
● JOHN BOGART	Bogart, John Renzie "Big John" b: 9/21/1900, Bloomsburg, Pa. d: 12/7/86, Clarence, N.Y. BR/TR, 6′2″, 195 lbs. Deb: 9/17/20																											
1920	Det-A	2	1	.667	4	2	0	0	0	23^2	16	12	0	0	18	5	12.9	3.04	122	.195	.340	2	.250	-0	2	2	-1	0.1
● RAY BOGGS	Boggs, Raymond Joseph "Lefty" b: 12/12/04, Reamsville, Kan. d: 11/27/89, Grand Junction, Colo. BL/TL, 6′0.5″, 170 lbs. Deb: 9/1/28																											
1928	Bos-N	0	0	—	4	0	0	0	0	5	2	3	0	3	7	0	21.6	5.40	72	.167	.545	0	—	0	-1	-1	-0	0.0
● TOMMY BOGGS	Boggs, Thomas Winton b: 10/25/55, Poughkeepsie, N.Y. BR/TR, 6′2″, 200 lbs. Deb: 7/19/76																											
1976	Tex-A	1	7	.125	13	13	3	0	0	90^1	87	42	7	1	34	36	12.2	3.49	103	.257	.326	0	—	0	0	1	-1	0.0
1977	Tex-A	0	3	.000	6	6	0	0	0	27^1	40	18	1	1	12	15	17.5	5.93	69	.351	.417	0	—	0	-6	-6	-0	-0.6
1978	Atl-N	2	8	.200	16	12	1	1	0	59	80	46	8	1	26	21	16.3	6.71	60	.323	.389	3	.167	0	-21	-15	-2	-2.4
1979	Atl-N	0	2	.000	3	3	0	0	0	12^2	21	11	0	1	4	1	18.5	6.39	63	.362	.413	1	.250	0	-4	-3	0	-0.4
1980	Atl-N	12	9	.571	32	26	4	3	0	192^1	180	80	14	4	46	84	10.8	3.42	110	.249	.298	10	.159	-2	4	7	-2	0.3
1981	Atl-N	3	13	.188	25	24	2	0	0	142^2	140	72	11	3	54	81	12.4	4.10	87	.265	.336	7	.152	-1	-10	-8	-1	-1.0
1982	Atl-N	2	2	.500	10	10	0	0	0	46^1	43	22	2	2	22	29	13.0	3.30	113	.253	.345	4	.235	0	2	2	-0	0.2
1983	Atl-N	0	0	—	5	0	0	0	0	6^1	8	4	1	0	1	5	12.8	5.68	68	.320	.346	0	—	0	-1	-1	-0	-0.1
1985	Tex-A	0	0	—	4	0	0	0	0	7	13	9	3	0	2	6	19.3	11.57	37	.382	.417	0	—	0	-6	-6	0	-0.2
Total	9	20	44	.313	114	94	10	4	0	584	612	304	47	13	201	278	12.7	4.22	89	.273	.337	25	.169	-2	-41	-30	-5	-4.2
● WADE BOGGS	Boggs, Wade Anthony b: 6/15/58, Omaha, Neb. BL/TR, 6′2″, 197 lbs. Deb: 4/10/82 ♦																											
1997	*NY-A	0	0	—	1	0	0	0	0	1	0	0	0	0	1	1	9.0	0.00	—	.000	.250	103	.292	1	1	1	0	0.0
1999	TB-A	0	0	—	1	0	0	0	0	1^1	3	1	0	0	0	1	20.3	6.75	74	.429	.429	88	.301	0	-0	-0	0	0.0
Total	2	0	0	—	2	0	0	0	0	2^1	3	1	0	0	1	2	15.4	3.86	123	.300	.364	3010	.328	1	0	0	0	0.0
● WARREN BOGLE	Bogle, Warren Frederick b: 10/19/46, Passaic, N.J. BL/TL, 6′4″, 220 lbs. Deb: 7/31/68																											
1968	Oak-A	0	0	—	16	1	0	0	0	23	26	12	3	0	8	26	13.3	4.30	65	.283	.340	0	.000	-1	-3	-4	1	-0.2
● BRIAN BOHANON	Bohanon, Brian Edward b: 8/1/68, Denton, Tex. BL/TL, 6′2″, 220 lbs. Deb: 4/10/90																											
1990	Tex-A	0	3	.000	11	6	0	0	0	34	40	30	6	2	18	15	15.9	6.62	59	.296	.387	0	—	0	-10	-10	1	-0.7
1991	Tex-A	4	3	.571	11	11	1	0	0	61^1	66	35	4	2	23	34	13.4	4.84	83	.274	.342	0	—	0	-5	-6	-1	-0.6
1992	Tex-A	1	1	.500	18	7	0	0	0	45^2	57	38	7	1	25	29	16.4	6.31	60	.297	.381	0	—	0	-12	-13	-0	-0.7
1993	Tex-A	4	4	.500	36	8	0	0	0	92^2	107	54	8	4	46	45	15.2	4.76	87	.296	.382	0	—	0	-4	-6	1	-0.4
1994	Tex-A	2	2	.500	11	5	0	0	0	37^1	51	31	7	1	8	26	14.5	7.23	67	.321	.357	0	—	0	-10	-10	0	-0.8
1995	Det-A	1	1	.500	52	10	0	0	1	105^2	121	68	10	4	41	63	14.1	5.54	86	.285	.354	0	—	0	-10	-9	-0	-0.4
1996	Tor-A	0	1	.000	20	0	0	0	1	22	27	19	4	2	19	17	19.6	7.77	64	.303	.436	0	—	0	-7	-7	-0	-0.3

YEAR	TM/L	W	L	PCT	G	GS	CG	SH	SV	IP	H	R	HR	HB	BB	SO	RAT	ERA	ERA+	OAV	OOB	BH	AVG	PB	PR	PR+	PD	TPI
1997	NY-N	6	4	.600	19	14	0	0	0	94^1	95	49	9	4	34	66	12.7	3.82	106	.258	.328	6	.182	0	4	2	-1	0.2
1998	NY-N	2	4	.333	25	4	0	0	0	54^1	47	21	4	6	21	39	12.3	3.15	131	.234	.325	6	.429	2	7	6	2	1.0
	LA-N	5	7	.417	14	14	2	0	0	97^1	74	35	9	5	36	72	10.6	2.40	165	.213	.296	6	.207	2	20	18	2	2.6
	Yr	7	11	.389	39	18	2	0	0	151^2	121	56	13	11	57	111	11.2	2.67	151	.220	.306	12	.279	4	26	24	3	3.6
1999	Col-N	12	12	.500	33	33	3	1	0	197^1	236	146	30	14	92	120	15.6	6.20	94	.304	.388	14	.197	-0	-36	-7	0	-0.7
2000	Col-N	12	10	.545	34	26	2	1	0	177	181	101	24	6	79	98	13.5	4.68	127	.266	.348	11	.208	1	-1	19	-0	2.2
Total	11	49	52	.485	284	138	8	2	2	1019	1102	627	122	51	442	624	14.1	5.00	96	.277	.357	43	.215	5	-64	-20	4	1.4
● **PAT BOHEN** Bohen, Leo Ignatius b: 9/30/1891, Oakland, Iowa d: 4/8/42, Napa, Cal. BR/TR, 5′10.5″, 155 lbs. Deb: 10/1/13																												
1913	Phi-A	0	1	.000	1	1	1	0	0	8	3	1	0	0	2	5	5.6	1.13	246	.115	.179	0	.000	-0	2	2	-0	0.1
1914	Pit-N	0	0	—	1	0	0	0	0	1	2	2	0	1	2	0	45.0	18.00	15	.500	.714	0	.000	-0	-2	-2	-0	-0.1
Total	2	0	1	.000	2	1	1	0	0	9	5	3	0	1	4	5	10.0	3.00	92	.167	.286	0	.000	-1	-0	-0	-0	0.0
● **CHARLIE BOHN** Bohn, Charles b: 1857, Cleveland, Ohio d: 8/1/03, Cleveland, Ohio BR/TR, 5′9″, 165 lbs. Deb: 6/20/1882 ♦																												
1882	Lou-a	1	1	.500	2	2	2	0	0	18	21	8	0		3	1	12.0	3.00	83	.273	.300	2	.154	-0	-1	-1	0	-0.1
● **JOHN BOHNET** Bohnet, John Kelly b: 1/18/61, Pasadena, Cal. BB/TL, 6′, 175 lbs. Deb: 5/10/82																												
1982	Cle-A	0	0	—	3	3	0	0	0	11^2	11	9	4	1	7	4	14.7	6.94	59	.250	.365	0	—	0	-4	-4	0	-0.2
● **DAN BOITANO** Boitano, Danny Jon b: 3/22/53, Sacramento, Cal. BR/TR, 6′, 185 lbs. Deb: 10/1/78																												
1978	Phi-N	0	0	—	1	0	0	0	0	1	0	0	0	0	1	0	9.0	0.00	—	.000	.250	0	—	0	0	0	0	0.0
1979	Mil-A	0	0	—	5	0	0	0	0	6	6	1	1	0	3	5	13.5	1.50	279	.273	.360	0	—	0	2	2	0	0.1
1980	Mil-A	0	1	.000	11	0	0	0	0	17^2	26	17	7	1	6	11	16.8	8.15	48	.342	.398	0	—	0	-8	-9	0	-0.4
1981	NY-N	2	1	.667	15	0	0	0	0	16^1	21	10	2	2	5	8	15.4	5.51	63	.309	.373	0	—	0	-4	-4	0	-0.6
1982	Tex-A	0	0	—	19	0	0	0	0	30^1	33	19	5	2	13	28	14.2	5.34	73	.280	.361	0	—	0	-4	-5	-0	-0.3
Total	5	2	2	.500	51	0	0	0	0	71^1	86	47	15	5	28	52	15.0	5.68	67	.300	.372	0	—	0	-14	-15	-0	-1.2
● **DICK BOKELMANN** Bokelmann, Richard Werner b: 10/26/26, Arlington Heights, Ill. BR/TR, 6′0.5″, 180 lbs. Deb: 8/3/51																												
1951	StL-N	3	3	.500	20	1	0	0	3	52^1	49	30	2	1	31	22	13.9	3.78	105	.245	.349	0	.000	-2	1	1	-1	-0.1
1952	StL-N	0	1	.000	11	0	0	0	0	12^2	20	17	0	0	7	5	19.2	9.24	40	.357	.429	0	—	0	-8	-8	1	-0.5
1953	StL-N	0	0	—	3	0	0	0	0	3	4	2	0	0	0	0	12.0	6.00	71	.308	.308	0	—	0	-1	-1	0	0.0
Total	3	3	4	.429	34	1	0	0	3	68	73	49	2	1	38	27	14.8	4.90	80	.271	.364	0	.000	-2	-7	-7	0	-0.6
● **JOE BOKINA** Bokina, Joseph b: 4/4/10, Northampton, Mass. d: 10/25/91, Chattanooga, Tenn. BR/TR, 6′, 184 lbs. Deb: 4/16/36																												
1936	Was-A	0	2	.000	5	1	0	0	0	8^1	15	8	0	0	6	5	22.7	8.64	55	.395	.477	0	.000	-0	-3	-4	-0	-0.6
● **BERNIE BOLAND** Boland, Bernard Anthony b: 1/21/1892, Rochester, N.Y. d: 9/12/73, Detroit, Mich. BR/TR, 5′8.5″, 168 lbs. Deb: 4/14/15																												
1915	Det-A	13	7	.650	45	18	8	1	3	202^2	167	86	2	6	75	72	11.0	3.11	98	.230	.307	11	.175	-1	-4	-2	0	-0.2
1916	Det-A	10	3	.769	46	9	5	1	3	130^1	111	69	1	4	73	59	13.0	3.94	73	.240	.349	8	.250	2	-16	-15	-3	-1.7
1917	Det-A	16	11	.593	43	28	13	3	6	238	192	89	0	6	95	89	11.1	2.68	99	.226	.308	4	.056	-5	-1	-1	0	-0.7
1918	Det-A	14	10	.583	29	25	14	4	0	204	176	69	1	6	67	63	11.0	2.65	101	.236	.304	12	.174	0	3	0	-1	-0.1
1919	Det-A	14	16	.467	35	30	18	1	1	242^2	222	93	7	3	80	71	11.3	3.04	105	.253	.318	8	.108	-3	5	4	-2	0.0
1920	Det-A	0	2	.000	4	3	1	0	0	17^1	23	18	0	2	14	4	20.3	7.79	48	.348	.476	1	.143	-0	-8	-8	0	-0.7
1921	StL-A	1	4	.200	7	6	0	0	0	27	34	36	2	1	28	6	21.0	9.33	48	.309	.453	1	.100	-1	-15	-14	-0	-2.0
Total	7	68	53	.562	209	119	59	10	13	1062	925	460	13	28	432	364	11.7	3.25	91	.241	.322	45	.138	-8	-35	-36	-5	-5.4
● **BILL BOLDEN** Bolden, William Horace "Big Bill" b: 5/9/1893, Dandridge, Tenn. d: 12/8/66, Jefferson City, Tenn. BR/TR, 6′4″, 200 lbs. Deb: 6/27/19																												
1919	StL-N	0	1	.000	3	1	0	0	0	12	17	7	0	1	4	4	16.5	5.25	53	.340	.400	1	.333	0	-3	-3	0	-0.2
● **STEW BOLEN** Bolen, Stewart O'Neal b: 10/12/02, Jackson, Ala. d: 8/30/69, Mobile, Ala. BL/TL, 5′11″, 180 lbs. Deb: 4/15/26																												
1926	StL-A	0	0	—	5	0	0	0	0	14^2	21	10	2	0	6	7	16.6	6.14	70	.356	.415	2	.500	1	-3	-3	-0	-0.1
1927	StL-A	0	1	.000	3	1	1	0	0	9^2	14	9	0	0	5	7	17.7	8.38	52	.368	.442	1	.333	0	-5	-4	0	-0.3
1931	Phi-N	3	12	.200	28	16	2	0	0	98^2	117	75	5	4	63	55	16.8	6.39	66	.297	.399	5	.156	-1	-28	-21	0	-2.8
1932	Phi-N	0	0	—	5	0	0	0	0	16	18	8	0	2	10	3	16.9	2.81	157	.281	.395	1	.143	-0	2	2	-0	0.1
Total	4	3	13	.188	41	17	3	0	0	139	170	102	7	6	84	72	16.8	6.09	70	.306	.403	9	.196	-0	-34	-25	-0	-3.1
● **BOBBY BOLIN** Bolin, Bobby Donald b: 1/29/39, Hickory Grove, S.C. BR/TR, 6′4″, 200 lbs. Deb: 4/18/61																												
1961	SF-N	2	2	.500	37	1	0	0	5	48	37	20	6	3	37	48	14.4	3.19	120	.210	.356	2	.286	0	5	4	-1	0.3
1962	*SF-N	7	3	.700	41	5	2	0	5	92	84	41	10	5	35	74	12.1	3.62	105	.243	.321	6	.261	2	3	2	-1	0.3
1963	SF-N	10	6	.625	47	12	2	0	7	137^1	128	73	13	7	57	134	12.6	3.28	98	.242	.324	5	.143	2	0	-1	-2	-0.2
1964	SF-N	6	9	.400	38	23	5	3	1	174^2	143	71	16	10	77	146	11.9	3.25	110	.220	.313	5	.100	0	6	6	-1	0.5
1965	SF-N	14	6	.700	45	13	2	0	2	163	125	51	17	4	56	135	10.2	2.76	130	.214	.288	9	.167	1	14	15	-2	1.8
1966	SF-N	11	10	.524	36	34	10	4	1	224^1	174	85	25	10	70	143	10.2	2.89	127	.211	.281	13	.171	3	18	19	-2	1.9
1967	SF-N	6	8	.429	37	15	0	0	0	120	120	71	16	3	50	69	13.0	4.88	67	.258	.333	8	.242	2	-20	-22	-1	-2.2
1968	SF-N	10	5	.667	34	19	6	3	0	176^2	128	44	9	4	46	126	9.1	1.99	148	.200	.258	5	.091	-1	20	19	-1	1.5
1969	SF-N	7	7	.500	30	22	2	0	0	146^1	149	86	17	7	49	102	12.6	4.43	79	.260	.326	6	.154	3	-14	-15	-1	-1.1
1970	Mil-A	5	11	.313	32	20	3	0	1	132	131	84	20	4	67	81	13.8	4.91	77	.256	.346	7	.194	2	-17	-16	-1	-1.7
	Bos-A	2	0	1.000	6	0	0	0	2	8	2	0	0	1	5	8	9.0	0.00	—	.080	.258	0	.000	-0	3	3	0	0.7
	Yr	7	11	.389	38	20	3	0	3	140	133	84	20	5	72	89	13.5	4.63	82	.248	.342	7	.189	2	-14	-13	-1	-1.0
1971	Bos-A	5	3	.625	52	0	0	0	6	69^2	74	34	7	0	24	51	12.7	4.26	87	.273	.332	3	.250	0	-6	-4	-1	-0.6
1972	Bos-A	0	1	.000	21	0	0	0	5	30^2	24	11	3	1	11	27	10.6	2.93	110	.209	.283	0	.000	-0	0	1	-0	0.0
1973	Bos-A	3	4	.429	39	0	0	0	15	53^1	45	16	5	1	13	31	10.0	2.70	149	.232	.284	0	—	0	7	7	1	1.5
Total	13	88	75	.540	495	164	32	10	50	1576	1364	687	164	60	597	1175	11.5	3.40	103	.231	.308	69	.163	15	18	19	-13	2.7
● **GREG BOLLO** Bollo, Gregory Gene b: 11/16/43, Detroit, Mich. BR/TR, 6′4″, 183 lbs. Deb: 5/9/65																												
1965	Chi-A	0	0	—	15	0	0	0	0	22^2	12	11	5	2	9	16	9.1	3.57	89	.152	.256	0	—	0	-0	-1	0	0.0
1966	Chi-A	0	1	.000	3	1	0	0	0	7	7	2	0	1	3	4	14.1	2.57	123	.269	.367	0	.000	-0	1	1	-0	0.0
Total	2	0	1	.000	18	1	0	0	0	29^2	19	13	5	3	12	20	10.3	3.34	96	.181	.283	0	.000	-0	0	-1	0	0.0
● **RODNEY BOLTON** Bolton, Rodney Earl b: 9/23/68, Chattanooga, Tenn. BR/TR, 6′2″, 190 lbs. Deb: 4/10/93																												
1993	Chi-A	2	6	.250	9	8	0	0	0	42^1	55	40	4	1	16	17	15.3	7.44	56	.314	.375	0	—	0	-15	-16	1	-2.2
1995	Chi-A	0	2	.000	8	3	0	0	0	22	33	23	4	0	14	10	19.2	8.18	55	.351	.435	0	—	0	-8	-10	0	-0.7
Total	2	2	8	.200	17	11	0	0	0	64^1	88	63	8	1	30	27	16.6	7.69	56	.327	.397	0	—	0	-23	-25	1	-2.9
● **TOM BOLTON** Bolton, Thomas Edward b: 5/6/62, Nashville, Tenn. BL/TL, 6′3″, 175 lbs. Deb: 5/17/87																												
1987	Bos-A	1	0	1.000	29	0	0	0	0	61^2	83	33	5	2	27	49	16.3	4.38	104	.329	.399	0	—	0	1	1	0	0.1
1988	Bos-A	1	3	.250	28	0	0	0	1	30^1	35	17	1	0	14	21	14.5	4.75	87	.285	.358	0	—	0	-3	-2	1	-0.1
1989	Bos-A	0	4	.000	4	4	0	0	0	17^1	21	18	1	0	10	9	16.1	8.31	49	.292	.378	0	—	0	-9	-8	-0	-1.3
1990	*Bos-A	10	5	.667	21	16	3	0	0	119^2	111	46	6	3	47	65	12.1	3.38	121	.251	.327	0	—	0	7	9	1	1.1
1991	Bos-A	8	9	.471	25	19	0	0	0	110	136	72	16	1	51	64	15.4	5.24	82	.308	.381	0	—	0	-14	-11	-1	-1.5
1992	Bos-A	1	2	.333	21	1	0	0	0	29	34	11	0	2	14	23	15.5	3.41	124	.286	.370	0	—	0	2	2	0	0.3
	Cin-N	3	3	.500	16	8	0	0	0	46^1	52	28	9	2	23	27	15.0	5.24	69	.284	.370	0	.000	-1	-9	-8	0	-1.1
1993	Det-A	6	6	.500	43	8	0	0	0	102^2	113	57	5	7	45	66	14.5	4.47	96	.282	.364	0	—	0	-2	-2	0	-0.2
1994	Bal-A	1	2	.333	22	0	0	0	0	23^1	29	15	3	0	13	12	16.2	5.40	93	.309	.393	0	—	0	-2	-1	0	-0.1
Total	8	31	34	.477	209	56	3	0	1	540^1	614	297	46	17	244	336	14.6	4.56	93	.289	.366	0	.000	-1	-28	-19	2	-2.8
● **MARK BOMBACK** Bomback, Mark Vincent b: 4/14/53, Portsmouth, Va. BR/TR, 5′11″, 170 lbs. Deb: 9/12/78																												
1978	Mil-A	0	0	—	2	1	0	0	0	1^2	5	3	1	0	1	1	32.4	16.20	23	.500	.545	0	—	0	-2	-2	-0	-0.1
1980	NY-N	10	8	.556	36	25	2	1	0	162^2	191	80	17	4	49	68	13.5	4.09	87	.297	.350	10	.233	3	-9	-10	2	-0.4
1981	Tor-A	5	5	.500	20	11	0	0	0	90^1	84	42	6	1	35	33	12.0	3.89	102	.251	.323	0	—	0	-2	1	0	0.1
1982	Tor-A	1	5	.167	16	8	0	0	0	59^2	87	44	10	3	25	22	17.3	6.03	74	.343	.408	0	—	0	-13	-9	0	-0.8
Total	4	16	18	.471	74	45	2	1	0	314^1	367	169	34	8	110	124	13.9	4.47	86	.295	.356	10	.233	3	-26	-21	3	-1.2

● TOMMY BOND
Bond, Thomas Henry b: 4/2/1856, Granard, Ireland d: 1/24/41, Boston, Mass. BR/TR, 5'7.5", 160 lbs. Deb: 5/5/1874 MU♦

YEAR	TM/L	W	L	PCT	G	GS	CG	SH	SV	IP	H	R	HR	HB	BB	SO	RAT	ERA	ERA+	OAV	OOB	BH	AVG	PB	PR	PR+	PD	TPI
1874	Atl-n	22	32	.407	55	55	55	1	0	497	606	440	15		8	42	11.1	2.03	102	.266	.268	54	.220	-0	9	2		1.0
1875	Har-n	19	16	.543	40	39	37	6	0	352	302	152	3		7	70	7.9	1.41	167	.216	.219	77	.266	3	32	35		3.5
1876	Har-N	31	13	.705	45	45	45	6	0	408	355	164	2		13	88	8.1	1.68	141	.219	.227	50	.275	1	29	31	5	3.1
1877	Bos-N	**40**	17	**.702**	58	58	58	**6**	0	521	530	248	5		36	**170**	**9.8**	**2.11**	133	.249	**.261**	59	.228	-4	**41**	41	3	3.5
1878	Bos-N	**40**	19	**.678**	**59**	59	**57**	**9**	0	**532^{2}**	571	222	5		33	**182**	10.2	2.06	115	.269	.280	50	.212	-4	15	17	2	1.3
1879	Bos-N	43	19	.694	64	64	59	**11**	0	555^{1}	543	206	8		24	155	**9.2**	**1.96**	**126**	.251	.259	62	.241	2	33	**32**	7	**3.8**
1880	Bos-N	26	29	.473	63	57	49	3	0	493	559	298	1		45	118	11.0	2.67	85	.274	.290	62	.220	-2	-16	-23	10	-1.5
1881	Bos-N	0	3	.000	3	3	2	0	0	25^{1}	40	17	3		2	2	14.9	4.26	62	.360	.372	2	.200	-0	-4	-5	1	-0.4
1882	Wor-N	0	1	.000	2	2	0	0	0	12^{1}	12	13	0		7	2	13.9	4.38	71	.218	.306	4	.133	-1	-2	-2	-0	-0.2
1884	Bos-U	13	9	.591	23	21	19	0	0	189	185	120	3		14	128	9.5	3.00	79	.239	.253	48	.296	-0	-12	-13	3	-1.0
	Ind-a	0	5	.000	5	5	5	0	0	43	62	51	5	2	4	15	14.2	5.65	58	.310	.330	3	.130	-1	-11	-11	-1	-1.1
Total	2 n	41	48	.461	95	94	92	7	0	849	908	592	18	0	15	112	9.8	1.77	123	.247	.250	131	.245	2	41	39		4.5
Total	8	193	115	.627	322	314	294	35	0	2779^{2}	2857	1339	32	2	178	860	9.8	2.25	110	.255	.267	340	.236	-9	71	70	30	7.5

● RICKY BONES
Bones, Ricardo Ricky b: 4/7/69, Salinas, P.R. BR/TR, 6', 190 lbs. Deb: 8/11/91

YEAR	TM/L	W	L	PCT	G	GS	CG	SH	SV	IP	H	R	HR	HB	BB	SO	RAT	ERA	ERA+	OAV	OOB	BH	AVG	PB	PR	PR+	PD	TPI
1991	SD-N	4	6	.400	11	11	0	0	0	54	57	33	3	0	18	31	12.5	4.83	79	.269	.326	1	.077	-0	-7	-6	-1	-1.1
1992	Mil-A	9	10	.474	31	28	0	0	0	163^{1}	169	90	27	9	48	65	12.5	4.57	84	.264	.324	0	—	0	-11	-14	-1	-1.5
1993	Mil-A	11	11	.500	32	31	3	0	0	203^{2}	222	122	28	8	63	63	12.9	4.86	88	.278	.336	0	—	0	-12	-14	-1	-1.3
1994	Mil-A☆	10	9	.526	24	24	4	1	0	170^{2}	166	76	17	3	45	57	11.3	3.43	147	.255	.306	0	—	0	26	29	-3	2.6
1995	Mil-A	10	12	.455	32	31	3	0	0	200^{1}	218	108	26	4	83	77	13.7	4.63	108	.281	.353	0	—	0	2	8	2	0.9
1996	Mil-A	7	14	.333	32	23	0	0	0	145	170	104	28	9	62	59	15.0	5.83	89	.294	.371	0	—	0	-13	-10	-2	-1.3
	NY-A	0	0	—	4	1	0	0	0	7	14	11	2	1	6	4	27.0	14.14	35	.438	.538	0	—	0	-7	-7	0	-0.3
	Yr	7	14	.333	36	24	0	0	0	152	184	115	30	10	68	63	15.5	6.22	83	.301	.380	0	—	0	-21	-17	-2	-1.6
1997	Cin-N	0	1	.000	9	2	0	0	0	17^{2}	31	22	2	2	11	8	22.4	10.19	42	.378	.463	0	.000	-0	-12	-11	0	-0.6
	KC-A	4	7	.364	21	11	1	0	0	78^{1}	102	59	10	5	25	36	15.2	5.97	79	.325	.384	0	—	0	-12	-11	0	-1.2
1998	KC-A	2	2	.500	32	0	0	0	1	53^{1}	49	18	4	1	24	38	12.5	3.04	159	.244	.327	0	.000	-0	10	10	2	0.9
1999	Bal-A	0	3	.000	30	2	0	0	0	43^{2}	59	29	7	2	19	26	16.5	5.98	79	.322	.392	0	—	0	-5	-6	-1	-0.4
2000	Fla-N	2	3	.400	56	0	0	0	0	77^{1}	94	43	6	3	27	59	14.4	4.54	97	.303	.365	0	.000	0	1	-1	0	0.0
Total	10	59	78	.431	314	164	11	1	1	1214^{1}	1351	715	160	47	431	523	13.6	4.84	95	.283	.348	1	.056	-0	-41	-31	-5	-3.3

● JULIO BONETTI
Bonetti, Julio Giacomo b: 7/14/11, Genoa, Italy d: 6/17/52, Belmont, Cal. BR/TR, 6', 180 lbs. Deb: 4/22/37

YEAR	TM/L	W	L	PCT	G	GS	CG	SH	SV	IP	H	R	HR	HB	BB	SO	RAT	ERA	ERA+	OAV	OOB	BH	AVG	PB	PR	PR+	PD	TPI
1937	StL-A	4	11	.267	28	16	7	0	1	143^{1}	190	103	13	2	60	43	15.8	5.84	83	.321	.385	7	.149	-2	-19	-15	2	-1.3
1938	StL-A	2	3	.400	17	0	0	0	0	28^{1}	41	21	1	0	13	7	17.2	6.35	78	.350	.415	0	.000	-1	-5	-4	0	-0.7
1940	Chi-N	0	0	—	1	0	0	0	0	1^{1}	3	3	0	0	0	4	47.3	20.25	19	.429	.636	0	—	0	-2	-3	-0	-0.1
Total	3	6	14	.300	46	16	7	0	1	173	234	127	14	2	77	50	16.3	6.03	80	.327	.394	7	.127	-3	-27	-22	2	-2.1

● HANK BONEY
Boney, Henry Tate "Haney" b: 10/28/03, Wallace, N.C. BR/TR, 5'11", 176 lbs. Deb: 6/28/27

YEAR	TM/L	W	L	PCT	G	GS	CG	SH	SV	IP	H	R	HR	HB	BB	SO	RAT	ERA	ERA+	OAV	OOB	BH	AVG	PB	PR	PR+	PD	TPI
1927	NY-N	0	0	—	3	0	0	0	0	4	4	1	0	0	2	0	13.5	2.25	171	.267	.353	0	—	0	1	1	-0	0.0

● TINY BONHAM
Bonham, Ernest Edward b: 8/16/13, Ione, Cal. d: 9/15/49, Pittsburgh, Pa. BR/TR, 6'2", 215 lbs. Deb: 8/5/40

YEAR	TM/L	W	L	PCT	G	GS	CG	SH	SV	IP	H	R	HR	HB	BB	SO	RAT	ERA	ERA+	OAV	OOB	BH	AVG	PB	PR	PR+	PD	TPI
1940	NY-A	9	3	.750	12	12	10	3	0	99^{1}	83	24	4	0	13	37	8.7	1.90	212	.224	.250	7	.189	0	27	26	-2	2.7
1941	*NY-A	9	6	.600	23	14	7	1	2	126^{2}	118	44	12	1	31	43	10.7	2.98	132	.246	.294	8	.160	-1	16	14	-3	1.2
1942	*NY-A☆	21	5	**.808**	28	27	**22**	**6**	0	226	199	65	11	1	24	71	**8.9**	2.27	152	.237	**.259**	9	.122	-2	**35**	31	-4	2.8
1943	*NY-A☆	15	8	.652	28	26	17	4	1	225^{2}	197	63	13	1	52	71	10.0	2.27	142	.236	.282	15	.197	0	26	24	-5	2.0
1944	NY-A	12	9	.571	26	25	17	1	0	213^{2}	228	84	14	0	41	54	11.3	2.99	116	.273	.307	10	.133	-3	10	12	-3	0.5
1945	NY-A	8	11	.421	23	23	12	0	0	180^{2}	186	72	11	1	22	42	10.4	3.29	105	.265	.288	15	.238	3	2	3	-3	0.3
1946	NY-A	5	8	.385	18	14	6	2	3	104^{2}	97	47	6	0	23	30	10.3	3.70	93	.243	.284	4	.129	-0	-2	-3	-2	-0.6
1947	Pit-N	11	8	.579	33	18	7	3	3	149^{2}	167	67	17	2	35	63	12.3	3.85	110	.277	.319	7	.156	-0	3	6	-3	0.3
1948	Pit-N	6	10	.375	22	20	7	0	0	135^{2}	145	71	18	3	23	42	11.3	4.31	94	.276	.310	8	.163	-2	-5	-4	-4	-0.9
1949	Pit-N	7	4	.636	18	14	5	1	0	89	81	43	11	0	23	25	10.5	4.25	99	.246	.295	1	.045	-1	-2	-0	-2	-0.3
Total	10	103	72	.589	231	193	110	21	9	1551	1501	580	117	9	287	478	10.4	3.06	120	.254	.289	84	.161	-7	110	106	-29	8.0

● BILL BONHAM
Bonham, William Gordon b: 10/1/48, Glendale, Cal. BR/TR, 6'3", 195 lbs. Deb: 4/7/71

YEAR	TM/L	W	L	PCT	G	GS	CG	SH	SV	IP	H	R	HR	HB	BB	SO	RAT	ERA	ERA+	OAV	OOB	BH	AVG	PB	PR	PR+	PD	TPI
1971	Chi-N	2	1	.667	33	2	0	0	0	60	63	38	6	5	36	41	15.6	4.65	85	.281	.392	2	.167	-0	-8	-4	1	-0.1
1972	Chi-N	1	1	.500	19	4	0	0	4	57^{2}	56	22	4	1	25	49	12.8	3.12	122	.260	.340	4	.286	1	2	4	0	0.4
1973	Chi-N	7	5	.583	44	15	3	0	6	152	126	55	10	4	64	121	11.5	3.02	131	.230	.315	4	.093	-3	11	15	4	1.4
1974	Chi-N	11	22	.333	44	36	10	2	1	242^{2}	246	133	13	6	109	191	13.4	3.86	99	.263	.343	12	.143	-3	-6	-1	5	0.1
1975	Chi-N	13	15	.464	38	36	7	2	0	229^{1}	254	133	15	5	109	165	14.4	4.71	82	.281	.361	15	.183	-0	-27	-21	1	-2.1
1976	Chi-N	9	13	.409	32	31	3	0	0	196	215	102	11	2	96	110	14.4	4.27	90	.283	.365	13	.200	1	-17	-8	0	-0.7
1977	Chi-N	10	13	.435	34	34	1	0	0	214^{2}	207	111	15	3	82	134	12.2	4.36	101	.254	.324	15	.231	1	-11	1	3	0.5
1978	Cin-N	11	5	.688	23	23	1	0	0	140^{1}	151	59	9	1	50	83	13.0	3.53	101	.276	.337	8	.186	2	1	0	3	0.6
1979	Cin-N	9	7	.563	29	29	2	0	0	175^{2}	173	80	14	8	60	78	12.3	3.79	99	.261	.330	8	.140	-1	-1	-1	0	-0.2
1980	Cin-N	2	1	.667	4	4	0	0	0	19	21	10	1	0	5	13	12.3	4.74	76	.276	.321	0	.000	-0	-2	-2	0	-0.4
Total	10	75	83	.475	300	214	27	4	11	1487^{1}	1512	743	98	35	636	985	13.2	4.01	97	.266	.343	81	.172	-2	-58	-17	18	-0.5

● JOE BONIKOWSKI
Bonikowski, Joseph Peter b: 1/16/41, Philadelphia, Pa. BR/TR, 6', 175 lbs. Deb: 4/12/62

YEAR	TM/L	W	L	PCT	G	GS	CG	SH	SV	IP	H	R	HR	HB	BB	SO	RAT	ERA	ERA+	OAV	OOB	BH	AVG	PB	PR	PR+	PD	TPI
1962	Min-A	5	7	.417	30	13	3	0	2	99^{2}	95	47	6	1	38	45	12.1	3.88	105	.255	.325	4	.148	-1	1	2	1	0.3

● BILL BONNESS
Bonness, William John "Lefty" b: 12/15/23, Cleveland, Ohio d: 12/3/77, Detroit, Mich. BR/TL, 6'4", 200 lbs. Deb: 9/26/44

YEAR	TM/L	W	L	PCT	G	GS	CG	SH	SV	IP	H	R	HR	HB	BB	SO	RAT	ERA	ERA+	OAV	OOB	BH	AVG	PB	PR	PR+	PD	TPI
1944	Cle-A	0	1	.000	2	1	0	0	0	7	11	6	0	2	5	1	23.1	7.71	43	.367	.486	0	.000	-0	-3	-4	0	-0.5

● GUS BONO
Bono, Adlai Wendell b: 8/29/1894, Doe Run, Mo. d: 12/3/48, Dearborn, Mich. BR/TR, 5'11", 175 lbs. Deb: 9/13/20

YEAR	TM/L	W	L	PCT	G	GS	CG	SH	SV	IP	H	R	HR	HB	BB	SO	RAT	ERA	ERA+	OAV	OOB	BH	AVG	PB	PR	PR+	PD	TPI
1920	Was-A	0	2	.000	4	1	0	0	0	12^{1}	17	13	0	0	6	4	16.8	8.76	43	.315	.383	0	.000	-0	-7	-7	0	-0.9

● GREG BOOKER
Booker, Gregory Scott b: 6/22/60, Lynchburg, Va. BR/TR, 6'6", 233 lbs. Deb: 9/11/83 C

YEAR	TM/L	W	L	PCT	G	GS	CG	SH	SV	IP	H	R	HR	HB	BB	SO	RAT	ERA	ERA+	OAV	OOB	BH	AVG	PB	PR	PR+	PD	TPI
1983	SD-N	0	1	.000	6	1	0	0	0	11^{2}	18	10	2	0	9	5	20.8	7.71	45	.375	.474	0	.000	-0	-5	-6	0	-0.4
1984	*SD-N	1	1	.500	32	1	0	0	0	57^{1}	67	27	4	0	27	28	14.8	3.30	108	.295	.370	2	.286	1	2	2	0	0.2
1985	SD-N	0	1	.000	17	0	0	0	0	22^{1}	20	17	3	1	17	7	15.3	6.85	52	.247	.384	0	.000	-0	-8	-8	0	-0.5
1986	SD-N	1	0	1.000	9	0	0	0	0	11	10	5	0	0	4	7	11.5	1.64	224	.233	.298	0	—	0	3	3	0	0.2
1987	SD-N	1	1	.500	44	0	0	0	1	68^{1}	62	29	5	3	30	17	12.5	3.16	125	.246	.333	0	.000	-1	7	6	-0	0.2
1988	SD-N	2	2	.500	34	2	0	0	0	63^{2}	68	31	5	1	19	43	12.4	3.39	100	.278	.332	2	.250	1	0	0	1	0.2
1989	SD-N	0	1	.000	11	0	0	0	0	19	15	10	2	0	10	8	11.8	4.26	82	.224	.325	0	—	0	-2	-2	0	-0.1
	Min-A	0	0	—	6	0	0	0	0	8^{2}	11	4	1	0	2	3	13.5	4.15	100	.306	.342	0	—	0	-0	0	0	0.1
1990	SF-N	0	0	—	2	0	0	0	0	2	7	3	0	0	0	1	31.5	13.50	27	.538	.538	0	—	0	-2	-2	-0	-0.1
Total	8	5	7	.417	161	4	0	0	1	264	278	136	22	5	118	119	13.7	3.89	94	.275	.353	4	.174	1	-5	-7	1	-0.2

● RED BOOLES
Booles, Seabron Jesse b: 7/14/1880, Bernice, La. d: 3/16/55, Monroe, La. BL/TR, 5'10", 150 lbs. Deb: 7/30/09

YEAR	TM/L	W	L	PCT	G	GS	CG	SH	SV	IP	H	R	HR	HB	BB	SO	RAT	ERA	ERA+	OAV	OOB	BH	AVG	PB	PR	PR+	PD	TPI
1909	Cle-A	0	1	.000	4	1	0	0	0	22^{2}	20	12	0	1	8	6	11.5	1.99	129	.235	.309	1	.167	0	1	1	-0	0.1

● DANNY BOONE
Boone, Daniel Hugh b: 1/14/54, Long Beach, Cal. BL/TL, 5'8", 150 lbs. Deb: 4/11/81 F

YEAR	TM/L	W	L	PCT	G	GS	CG	SH	SV	IP	H	R	HR	HB	BB	SO	RAT	ERA	ERA+	OAV	OOB	BH	AVG	PB	PR	PR+	PD	TPI
1981	SD-N	1	0	1.000	37	0	0	0	2	63^{1}	63	23	2	1	21	43	12.1	2.84	115	.267	.329	2	.500	1	5	3	1	0.4
1982	SD-N	1	0	1.000	10	0	0	0	1	16	21	10	2	0	3	8	13.5	5.63	61	.323	.353	1	.200	0	-4	-4	0	-0.2
	Hou-N	0	1	.000	10	0	0	0	1	12^{2}	7	6	1	0	4	4	7.8	3.55	94	.171	.244	0	.000	-0	-0	-0	0	0.0
	Yr	1	1	.500	20	0	0	0	2	28^{2}	28	16	3	0	7	12	11.0	4.71	72	.264	.310	1	.167	0	-4	-5	0	-0.2
1990	Bal-A	0	0	—	4	1	0	0	0	9^{2}	12	3	1	1	3	2	14.9	2.79	136	.308	.372	0	—	0	1	1	0	0.1
Total	3	2	1	.667	61	1	0	0	4	101^{2}	103	42	6	2	31	57	12.0	3.36	99	.270	.329	3	.300	1	2	-0	1	0.3

● GEORGE BOONE
Boone, George Morris b: 3/1/1871, Louisville, Ky. d: 9/24/10, Louisville, Ky. Deb: 4/23/1891

YEAR	TM/L	W	L	PCT	G	GS	CG	SH	SV	IP	H	R	HR	HB	BB	SO	RAT	ERA	ERA+	OAV	OOB	BH	AVG	PB	PR	PR+	PD	TPI
1891	Lou-a	0	0	—	4	1	0	0	1	15	15	15	0	0	9	4	14.4	7.80	47	.250	.348	2	.333	0	-7	-7	-0	-0.3

YEAR	TM/L	W	L	PCT	G	GS	CG	SH	SV	IP	H	R	HR	HB	BB	SO	RAT	ERA	ERA+	OAV	OOB	BH	AVG	PB	PR	PR+	PD	TPI
● **DAN BOONE**	Boone, James Albert b: 1/19/1895, Samantha, Ala. d: 5/11/68, Tuscaloosa, Ala. BR/TR, 6'2", 190 lbs. Deb: 9/10/19																											
1919	Phi-A	0	1	.000	3	2	0	0	0	14^{2}	24	14	0	0	10	1	20.9	6.75	51	.375	.459	0	.000	-1	-6	-5	1	-0.3
1921	Det-A	0	0	—	1	0	0	0	1	2	1	1	0	0	2	0	13.5	0.00	—	.200	.429	0	.000	-0	1	1	0	0.1
1922	Cle-A	4	6	.400	11	10	4	2	0	75^{1}	87	39	3	1	19	9	12.8	4.06	99	.298	.343	5	.192	-1	-0	-0	1	-0.1
1923	Cle-A	4	6	.400	27	4	2	0	0	70^{1}	93	56	3	3	31	15	16.3	6.01	66	.322	.393	4	.211	0	-16	-16	3	-1.7
Total	4	8	13	.381	42	16	6	2	1	162^{1}	205	110	6	4	62	25	15.0	5.10	77	.315	.378	9	.180	-1	-21	-21	4	-2.0
● **AMOS BOOTH**	Booth, Amos Smith "Darling" b: 9/14/1853, Cincinnati, O. d: 7/1/21, Miamisburg, Ohio BR/TR, 5'9", 159 lbs. Deb: 4/25/1876 ♦																											
1876	Cin-N	0	1	.000	3	1	0	0	0	9^{2}	22	18	0		0	0	20.5	9.31	24	.431	.431	71	.253	0	-8	-8	-0	-0.6
1877	Cin-N	1	7	.125	12	8	6	0	0	86	114	75	1		13	18	13.3	3.56	74	.296	.319	27	.172	-1	-7	-9	-1	-0.8
Total	2	1	8	.111	15	9	6	0	0	95^{2}	136	93	1		13	18	14.0	4.14	63	.312	.332	98	.219	-1	-15	-17	-1	-1.4
● **EDDIE BOOTH**	Booth, Edward H. b: Brooklyn, N.Y. Deb: 4/26/1872 ♦																											
1876	NY-N	0	0	—	1	0	0	0	0	5	16	10	0		0	0	28.8	10.80	20	.471	.471	49	.213	-0	-5	-5	-0	-0.2
● **JOHN BOOZER**	Boozer, John Morgan b: 7/6/38, Columbia, S.C. d: 1/24/86, Lexington, S.C. BR/TR, 6'3", 205 lbs. Deb: 7/22/62																											
1962	Phi-N	0	0	—	9	0	0	0	0	20^{1}	22	13	3	0	10	13	14.2	5.75	67	.282	.364	0	.000	-0	-4	-4	-0	-0.2
1963	Phi-N	3	4	.429	26	8	2	0	1	83	67	31	11	1	33	69	11.0	2.93	110	.227	.307	3	.143	-0	3	3	-2	0.0
1964	Phi-N	3	4	.429	22	3	0	0	2	60^{1}	64	37	6	2	18	51	12.5	5.07	68	.271	.328	1	.077	-1	-10	-11	1	-1.3
1966	Phi-N	0	0	—	2	2	0	0	0	5^{1}	8	5	1	0	3	5	18.6	6.75	53	.348	.423	0	.000	-0	-2	-2	0	-0.1
1967	Phi-N	5	4	.556	28	7	1	0	1	74^{2}	86	39	6	1	24	48	13.4	4.10	83	.292	.347	4	.211	1	-6	-6	0	-0.6
1968	Phi-N	2	2	.500	38	0	0	0	5	68^{2}	76	32	3	2	15	49	12.2	3.67	82	.279	.322	1	.111	-0	-5	-5	0	-0.4
1969	Phi-N	1	2	.333	46	2	0	0	6	82	91	46	12	0	36	47	13.9	4.28	83	.283	.356	3	.333	1	-6	-7	-1	-0.3
Total	7	14	16	.467	171	22	3	0	15	394^{1}	414	203	42	6	139	282	12.8	4.09	82	.272	.336	12	.162	-0	-30	-32	-2	-2.9
● **PEDRO BORBON**	Borbon, Pedro (Rodriguez) b: 12/2/46, Valverde, Mao, D.R. BR/TR, 6'2", 185 lbs. Deb: 4/9/69 F																											
1969	Cal-A	2	3	.400	22	0	0	0	0	41	55	31	5	4	11	20	15.4	6.15	57	.324	.378	0	.000	-0	-11	-13	-0	-1.5
1970	Cin-N	0	2	.000	12	1	0	0	0	17^{1}	21	15	2	3	6	6	15.6	6.75	60	.309	.390	0	.000	-0	-5	-5	2	-0.4
1971	Cin-N	0	0	—	3	0	0	0	0	4^{1}	3	3	1	0	1	4	8.3	4.15	81	.200	.250	0	—	0	-0	-0	-0	0.0
1972	*Cin-N	8	3	.727	62	2	0	0	11	122	115	45	5	3	32	48	11.1	3.17	101	.254	.307	1	.048	-1	4	1	-1	-0.1
1973	*Cin-N	11	4	.733	80	0	0	0	14	121	137	33	4	1	35	60	12.9	2.16	158	.298	.349	5	.333	1	**20**	18	-0	2.8
1974	Cin-N	10	7	.588	73	0	0	0	14	139	133	54	11	4	32	53	10.9	3.24	108	.255	.303	5	.192	-0	6	4	-1	0.5
1975	*Cin-N	9	5	.643	67	0	0	0	5	125	145	47	6	3	21	29	12.2	2.95	122	.301	.334	7	.292	2	9	9	-1	1.2
1976	*Cin-N	4	3	.571	69	1	0	0	8	121	135	49	4	4	31	53	12.6	3.35	105	.292	.342	4	.222	0	2	2	-0	0.1
1977	Cin-N	10	5	.667	73	0	0	0	18	127	131	48	7	3	24	48	11.2	3.19	123	.268	.307	4	.182	-0	10	10	-2	1.3
1978	Cin-N	8	2	.800	62	0	0	0	4	99^{1}	102	56	6	3	27	35	12.0	4.98	71	.274	.328	2	.182	-0	-15	-16	-0	-1.7
1979	Cin-N	2	2	.500	30	0	0	0	2	44^{2}	48	17	2	0	8	23	11.3	3.43	109	.277	.309	2	.333	0	2	2	0	0.2
	SF-N	4	3	.571	30	0	0	0	3	46	56	28	7	0	13	26	13.5	4.89	72	.303	.348	1	.333	0	-6	-8	-1	-1.2
	Yr	6	5	.545	60	0	0	0	5	90^{2}	104	45	9	0	21	49	12.4	4.17	87	.291	.330	3	.333	1	-4	-6	-1	-1.0
1980	StL-N	1	0	1.000	10	0	0	0	1	19	17	10	3	0	10	4	12.8	3.79	98	.250	.346	1	.250	0	-0	-0	-0	0.0
Total	12	69	39	.639	593	4	0	0	80	1026^{2}	1098	436	63	28	251	409	12.1	3.52	101	.280	.328	32	.205	2	15	4	-4	1.2
● **PEDRO BORBON**	Borbon, Pedro Felix (Marte) b: 11/15/67, Mao, D.R. BR/TL, 6'1", 205 lbs. Deb: 10/2/92 F																											
1992	Atl-N	0	1	.000	2	0	0	0	0	1^{1}	2	1	0	0	1	1	20.3	6.75	54	.333	.429	0	—	0	-0	-0	0	-0.1
1993	Atl-N	0	0	—	3	0	0	0	0	1^{2}	3	4	0	0	3	2	32.4	21.60	19	.429	.600	0	—	0	-3	-3	-0	-0.2
1995	*Atl-N	2	2	.500	41	0	0	0	2	32	29	12	2	1	17	33	13.2	3.09	138	.240	.338	0	.000	-0	4	4	0	0.5
1996	Atl-N	3	0	1.000	43	0	0	0	1	36	26	12	1	1	7	31	8.5	2.75	160	.203	.250	1	1.000	0	6	6	0	0.6
1999	LA-N	4	3	.571	70	0	0	0	1	50^{2}	39	23	5	1	29	33	12.3	4.09	105	.209	.318	0	.000	-0	3	1	-0	0.1
2000	Tor-A	1	1	.500	59	0	0	0	1	41^{2}	45	37	5	5	38	29	19.0	6.48	77	.280	.431	0	—	0	-7	-7	1	-0.2
Total	6	10	7	.588	218	0	0	0	5	163^{1}	144	89	13	8	95	129	13.6	4.41	102	.236	.346	1	.250	0	2	1	1	0.7
● **GEORGE BORCHERS**	Borchers, George Benard "Chief" b: 4/18/1869, Sacramento, Cal. d: 10/24/38, Sacramento, Cal. BB/TR, 5'10", 180 lbs. Deb: 5/18/1888																											
1888	Chi-N	4	4	.500	10	10	7	1	0	67	67	45	2	6	29	26	13.7	3.49	87	.251	.338	2	.061	-2	-5	-3	0	-0.5
1895	Lou-N	0	1	.000	1	1	0	0	0	0^{2}	1	2	0	0	3	0	54.0	27.00	17	.333	.667	0	—	0	-2	-2	-0	-0.3
Total	2	4	5	.444	11	11	7	1	0	67^{2}	68	47	2	6	32	26	14.1	3.72	82	.252	.344	2	.061	-2	-6	-5	-0	-0.8
● **JOE BORDEN**	Borden, Joseph Emley (a.k.a. Joseph Emley Josephs In 1875) b: 5/9/1854, Jacobstown, N.J. d: 10/14/29, Yeadon, Pa. BR/TR, 5'9", 140 lbs. Deb: 7/24/1875																											
1875	Phi-n	2	4	.333	7	7	7	2	0	66	47	30	0		7	9	**7.4**	1.50	152	**.181**	**.203**	3	.107	-3	5	6		0.1
1876	Bos-N	11	12	.478	29	24	16	2	1	218^{1}	257	155	4		51	34	12.7	2.89	78	.261	.313	25	.202	-3	-14	-16	-2	-1.7
● **RICH BORDI**	Bordi, Richard Albert b: 4/18/59, San Francisco, Cal. BR/TR, 6'7", 220 lbs. Deb: 7/16/80																											
1980	Oak-A	0	0	—	1	0	0	0	0	2	4	1	0	0	0	0	18.0	4.50	84	.400	.400	0	—	0	-0	-0	-0	0.0
1981	Oak-A	0	0	—	2	0	0	0	0	2	1	0	0	0	1	0	9.0	0.00	—	.143	.250	0	—	0	1	1	-0	0.0
1982	Sea-A	0	2	.000	7	2	0	0	0	13	18	12	4	1	1	10	13.8	8.31	51	.310	.333	0	—	0	-6	-6	-0	-0.7
1983	Chi-N	0	2	.000	11	1	0	0	1	25^{1}	34	15	2	0	12	20	16.3	4.97	76	.321	.390	0	.000	-0	-4	-3	0	-0.3
1984	Chi-N	5	2	.714	31	7	0	0	4	83^{1}	78	37	11	0	20	41	10.6	3.46	113	.242	.287	1	.053	-1	1	4	-1	0.1
1985	NY-A	6	8	.429	51	3	0	0	2	98	95	41	5	1	29	64	11.5	3.21	125	.253	.308	0	—	0	10	9	-1	1.1
1986	Bal-A	6	4	.600	52	1	0	0	3	107	105	56	13	4	41	83	12.6	4.46	93	.254	.327	0	—	0	-3	-4	1	-0.3
1987	NY-A	3	1	.750	16	1	0	0	0	33	42	28	7	0	12	23	14.7	7.64	58	.309	.365	0	—	0	-12	-12	-1	-1.3
1988	Oak-A	0	1	.000	2	2	0	0	0	7^{2}	6	6	0	0	5	6	12.9	4.70	81	.214	.333	0	—	0	-1	-1	-0	-0.1
Total	9	20	20	.500	173	17	0	0	10	371^{1}	383	196	42	6	121	247	12.4	4.34	94	.263	.322	1	.043	-2	-13	-11	-2	-1.5
● **BILL BORDLEY**	Bordley, William Clarke b: 1/9/58, Los Angeles, Cal. BR/TL, 6'3", 185 lbs. Deb: 6/30/80																											
1980	SF-N	2	3	.400	8	6	0	0	0	30^{2}	34	19	3	0	21	11	16.1	4.70	75	.288	.396	1	.167	0	-4	-4	1	-0.5
● **PAUL BORIS**	Boris, Paul Stanley b: 12/13/55, Irvington, N.J. BR/TR, 6'2", 200 lbs. Deb: 5/21/82																											
1982	Min-A	1	2	.333	23	0	0	0	0	49^{2}	46	24	8	2	19	30	12.1	3.99	107	.246	.322	0	—	0	1	1	-1	0.0
● **FRANK BORK**	Bork, Frank Bernard b: 7/13/40, Buffalo, N.Y. BR/TL, 6'2", 175 lbs. Deb: 4/15/64																											
1964	Pit-N	2	2	.500	33	2	0	0	2	42	51	22	6	1	11	31	13.5	4.07	86	.295	.341	1	.200	0	-2	-3	0	-0.2
● **DAVE BORKOWSKI**	Borkowski, David Richard b: 2/7/77, Detroit, Mich. BR/TR, 6'1", 200 lbs. Deb: 7/17/99																											
1999	Det-A	2	6	.250	17	12	0	0	0	76^{2}	86	58	10	4	40	50	15.3	6.10	80	.283	.374	0	.000	-0	-10	-10	-0	-0.9
2000	Det-A	0	1	.000	2	1	0	0	0	5^{1}	11	13	2	0	7	1	30.4	21.94	22	.423	.545	0	—	0	-10	-10	-0	-1.2
Total	2	2	7	.222	19	13	0	0	0	82	97	71	12	4	47	51	16.2	7.13	68	.294	.388	0	.000	-0	-21	-21	-0	-2.1
● **TOM BORLAND**	Borland, Thomas Bruce "Spike" b: 2/14/33, ElDorado, Kan. BL/TL, 6'3", 172 lbs. Deb: 5/15/60																											
1960	Bos-A	0	4	.000	26	4	0	0	3	51	67	40	4	0	23	32	15.9	6.53	62	.322	.390	0	.000	-2	-15	-13	0	-1.3
1961	Bos-A	0	0	—	1	0	0	0	0	1	3	2	0	0	0	0	27.0	18.00	23	.500	.500	0	—	0	-2	-1	-0	-0.1
Total	2	0	4	.000	27	4	0	0	3	52	70	42	4	0	23	32	16.1	6.75	60	.327	.392	0	.000	-2	-17	-15	0	-1.4
● **TOBY BORLAND**	Borland, Toby Shawn b: 5/29/69, Ruston, La. BR/TR, 6'6", 186 lbs. Deb: 5/27/94																											
1994	Phi-N	1	0	1.000	24	0	0	0	1	34^{1}	31	10	1	4	14	26	12.8	2.36	182	.248	.343	0	.000	-0	7	7	-0	0.3
1995	Phi-N	1	3	.250	50	0	0	0	6	74	81	37	3	5	37	59	15.0	3.77	112	.277	.368	1	.200	0	3	4	-1	0.2
1996	Phi-N	7	3	.700	69	0	0	0	0	90^{2}	83	51	9	3	43	76	12.8	4.07	106	.239	.327	0	.000	-0	2	2	-1	0.1
1997	NY-N	0	1	.000	13	0	0	0	1	13^{1}	11	9	1	1	14	7	17.6	6.08	66	.220	.400	0	—	0	-3	-3	-0	-0.3
	Bos-A	0	0	—	3	0	0	0	0	3^{1}	6	5	1	2	7	1	40.5	13.50	34	.400	.625	0	—	0	-3	-3	-0	-0.2
1998	Phi-N	0	0	—	6	0	0	0	0	9	8	5	1	0	5	9	13.0	5.00	87	.242	.342	0	—	0	-1	-1	-0	0.0
Total	5	9	7	.563	165	0	0	0	8	224^{2}	220	117	16	15	120	178	14.2	4.01	107	.255	.356	1	.083	-1	5	7	-2	0.1

YEAR TM/L	W	L	PCT	G	GS	CG	SH	SV	IP	H	R	HR	HB	BB	SO	RAT	ERA	ERA+	OAV	OOB	BH	AVG	PB	PR	PR+	PD	TPI
● JOE BOROWSKI Borowski, Joseph Thomas b: 5/4/71, Bayonne, N.J. BR/TR, 6'2", 225 lbs. Deb: 7/9/95																											
1995 Bal-A	0	0	—	6	0	0	0	0	7^1	5	1	0	0	4	3	11.0	1.23	388	.192	.300	0	—	0	3	3	0	0.2
1996 Atl-N	2	4	.333	22	0	0	0	0	26	33	15	4	1	13	15	16.3	4.85	91	.324	.405	0	.000	-0	-2	-1	2	-0.1
1997 Atl-N	2	2	.500	20	0	0	0	0	24	27	11	2	0	16	6	16.1	3.75	112	.287	.391	0	—	0	1	1	0	0.2
NY-A	0	1	.000	1	0	0	0	0	2	2	2	0	0	4	2	27.0	9.00	49	.250	.500	0	—	0	-1	-1	-0	-0.2
1998 NY-A	1	0	1.000	8	0	0	0	0	9^2	11	7	0	0	4	7	14.0	6.52	67	.289	.357	0	—	0	-2	-2	0	-0.2
Total 4	5	7	.417	57	0	0	0	0	69	78	36	6	1	41	33	15.7	4.43	99	.291	.387	0	.000	-0	-1	-0	2	-0.1
● HANK BOROWY Borowy, Henry Ludwig b: 5/12/16, Bloomfield, N.J. BR/TR, 6', 175 lbs. Deb: 4/18/42																											
1942 *NY-A	15	4	.789	25	21	13	4	1	178^1	157	56	6	0	66	85	11.3	2.52	136	.233	.301	11	.157	-1	22	19	1	2.0
1943 *NY-A	14	9	.609	29	27	14	3	0	217^1	195	75	11	2	72	113	11.1	2.82	114	.241	.305	15	.203	3	12	10	1	1.4
1944 NY-A★	17	12	.586	35	30	19	3	2	252^2	224	93	15	0	88	107	11.1	2.64	132	.236	.301	12	.133	-3	22	23	1	2.4
1945 NY-A†	10	5	.667	18	18	7	1	0	132^1	107	61	6	1	58	35	11.3	3.13	111	.221	.305	11	.220	1	3	5	1	0.8
*Chi-N	11	2	.846	15	14	11	1	1	122^1	105	33	2	0	47	47	11.2	**2.13**	171	.231	.303	7	.171	0	23	21	-1	2.2
1946 Chi-N	12	10	.545	32	28	8	1	0	201	220	96	9	1	61	95	12.6	3.76	88	.274	.326	13	.181	1	-8	-10	0	-1.0
1947 Chi-N	8	12	.400	40	25	7	1	2	183	190	99	19	1	63	75	12.5	4.38	90	.267	.328	7	.125	-1	-6	-9	0	-0.9
1948 Chi-N	5	10	.333	39	17	2	1	1	127	156	80	9	0	49	50	14.5	4.89	80	.308	.369	8	.222	2	-13	-14	2	-1.1
1949 Phi-N	12	12	.500	28	28	12	1	0	193^1	188	99	19	0	63	43	11.7	4.19	94	.259	.319	13	.213	3	-3	-5	-2	-0.4
1950 Phi-N	0	0	—	3	0	0	0	0	6^1	5	4	0	0	4	3	12.8	5.68	71	.250	.375	0	—	0	-1	-1	-0	-0.1
Pit-N	1	3	.250	11	3	0	0	0	25^1	32	19	6	1	9	9	14.9	6.39	69	.311	.372	1	.167	-0	-6	-5	0	-0.7
Yr	1	3	.250	14	3	0	0	0	31^2	37	23	6	1	13	12	14.5	6.25	69	.301	.372	1	.167	-0	-7	-7	0	-0.8
Det-A	1	1	.500	13	2	1	0	0	32^2	23	15	3	0	16	12	10.7	3.31	142	.205	.305	1	.143	-0	5	5	-0	0.2
1951 Det-A	2	2	.500	26	1	0	0	0	45^1	58	39	3	1	27	16	17.1	6.95	60	.314	.404	0	.000	-1	-14	-14	1	-1.1
Total 10	108	82	.568	314	214	94	16	7	1717	1660	769	108	7	623	690	12.0	3.50	104	.254	.320	99	.173	3	35	24	5	3.7
● CHRIS BOSIO Bosio, Christopher Louis b: 4/3/63, Carmichael, Cal. BR/TR, 6'3", 225 lbs. Deb: 8/3/86																											
1986 Mil-A	0	4	.000	10	4	0	0	0	34^2	41	27	9	0	13	29	14.0	7.01	62	.293	.353	0	—	0	-11	-10	0	-0.9
1987 Mil-A	11	8	.579	46	19	2	1	2	170	187	102	18	1	50	150	12.6	5.24	88	.276	.327	0	—	0	-15	-12	1	-1.1
1988 Mil-A	7	15	.318	38	22	9	1	6	182	190	80	13	2	38	84	11.4	3.36	119	.268	.307	0	—	0	12	13	3	1.8
1989 Mil-A	15	10	.600	33	33	8	2	0	234^2	225	90	16	6	48	173	10.7	2.95	130	.249	.291	0	—	0	24	24	1	2.5
1990 Mil-A	4	9	.308	20	20	4	1	0	132^2	131	67	15	3	38	76	11.7	4.00	97	.258	.313	0	—	0	-1	-2	2	0.0
1991 Mil-A	14	10	.583	32	32	5	1	0	204^2	187	80	15	8	58	117	11.1	3.25	122	.244	.304	0	—	0	19	17	-1	1.8
1992 Mil-A	16	6	.727	33	33	4	2	0	231^1	223	100	21	4	44	120	10.5	3.62	106	.254	.293	0	—	0	8	6	0	0.5
1993 Sea-A	9	9	.500	29	24	3	1	1	164^1	138	75	14	6	59	119	11.1	3.45	128	.229	.304	0	—	0	16	17	0	1.8
1994 Sea-A	4	10	.286	19	19	4	0	0	125	137	72	15	2	40	67	12.9	4.32	113	.277	.333	0	—	0	7	8	2	0.9
1995 *Sea-A	10	8	.556	31	31	0	0	0	170	211	98	18	5	69	85	15.1	4.92	96	.312	.380	0	—	0	-4	-3	0	-0.3
1996 Sea-A	4	4	.500	18	9	0	0	0	60^2	72	44	8	4	24	39	14.8	5.93	83	.299	.372	0	—	0	-6	-7	0	-0.7
Total 11	94	93	.503	309	246	39	9	9	1710	1742	835	162	41	481	1059	11.9	3.96	106	.264	.318	0	—	0	51	49	9	6.3
● SHAWN BOSKIE Boskie, Shawn Kealoha b: 3/28/67, Hawthorne, Nev. BR/TR, 6'3", 200 lbs. Deb: 5/20/90																											
1990 Chi-N	5	6	.455	15	15	1	0	0	97^2	99	42	8	1	31	49	12.1	3.69	111	.265	.323	8	.222	1	1	4	0	0.6
1991 Chi-N	4	9	.308	28	20	0	0	0	129	150	78	14	5	52	62	14.4	5.23	74	.294	.364	7	.171	2	-22	-18	1	-1.4
1992 Chi-N	5	11	.313	23	18	0	0	0	91^2	96	55	14	4	36	39	13.4	5.01	72	.284	.360	5	.185	1	-15	-14	1	-2.0
1993 Chi-N	5	3	.625	39	2	0	0	0	65^2	63	30	7	7	21	39	12.5	3.43	117	.258	.335	3	.273	1	5	4	-1	0.4
1994 Chi-N	0	0	—	2	0	0	0	0	3^2	3	0	0	0	0	2	7.4	0.00	—	.214	.214	0	—	0	2	2	0	0.1
Phi-N	4	6	.400	18	14	1	0	0	84^1	85	56	14	3	29	59	12.5	5.23	82	.258	.323	3	.115	1	-9	-9	0	-0.8
Yr	4	6	.400	20	14	1	0	0	88	88	56	14	3	29	61	12.3	5.01	86	.256	.319	3	.115	1	-8	-7	1	-0.7
Sea-A	0	1	.000	2	1	0	0	0	2^2	4	2	1	0	1	0	16.9	6.75	72	.333	.385	0	—	0	-1	-1	0	-0.1
1995 Cal-A	7	7	.500	20	20	1	0	0	111^2	127	73	16	7	25	51	12.8	5.64	83	.281	.329	0	—	0	-11	-12	0	-1.2
1996 Cal-A	12	11	.522	37	28	1	0	0	189^1	226	126	40	13	67	133	14.5	5.32	94	.294	.360	0	—	0	-7	-7	0	-0.6
1997 Bal-A	6	6	.500	28	9	0	0	1	77	95	57	14	2	26	50	14.4	6.43	69	.304	.362	0	—	0	-16	-18	0	-2.3
1998 Mon-N	1	3	.250	5	5	0	0	0	17^2	34	21	5	2	4	10	20.4	9.17	46	.415	.455	0	.000	-0	-10	-10	0	-1.6
Total 9	49	63	.438	217	132	4	0	1	870^1	982	540	133	44	292	494	13.6	5.14	85	.286	.349	26	.179	5	-84	-76	3	-8.9
● DICK BOSMAN Bosman, Richard Allen b: 2/17/44, Kenosha, Wis. BR/TR, 6'3", 208 lbs. Deb: 6/1/66 C																											
1966 Was-A	2	6	.250	13	7	0	0	0	39	60	36	4	0	12	20	16.6	7.62	45	.361	.404	3	.250	0	-18	-18	-1	-3.1
1967 Was-A	3	1	.750	7	7	2	1	0	51^1	38	12	3	0	10	25	8.4	1.75	180	.204	.245	3	.200	0	8	8	-1	0.7
1968 Was-A	2	9	.182	46	10	0	0	1	139	139	63	9	4	35	63	11.5	3.69	79	.262	.312	6	.200	1	-11	-12	-0	-0.9
1969 Was-A	14	5	.737	31	26	5	2	1	193	156	59	11	2	39	99	9.2	**2.19**	**158**	.220	.262	6	.094	-1	31	29	1	2.9
1970 Was-A	16	12	.571	36	34	7	3	0	230^2	212	81	16	2	71	134	11.1	3.00	118	.245	.304	11	.138	-2	18	15	0	1.5
1971 Was-A	12	16	.429	35	35	7	1	0	236^2	245	110	29	5	71	113	12.2	3.73	89	.272	.329	7	.093	-1	-7	-11	-2	-1.6
1972 Tex-A	8	10	.444	29	29	1	1	0	173^1	183	87	11	6	48	105	12.3	3.63	83	.273	.327	5	.094	-2	-11	-12	1	-1.3
1973 Tex-A	2	5	.286	7	7	1	0	0	40^1	42	24	6	1	17	14	13.4	4.24	88	.268	.343	0	—	0	-2	-2	-0	-0.4
Cle-A	1	8	.111	22	17	2	1	0	97	130	74	19	6	29	41	15.3	6.22	63	.320	.374	0	—	0	-26	-24	-1	-2.0
Yr	3	13	.188	29	24	3	1	0	137^1	172	98	25	7	46	55	14.7	5.64	69	.306	.365	0	—	0	-28	-27	-1	-2.4
1974 Cle-A	7	5	.583	25	18	2	1	0	127^1	126	69	13	1	29	56	11.0	4.10	88	.255	.298	0	—	0	-7	-7	-2	-0.8
1975 Cle-A	0	2	.000	6	3	0	0	0	28^2	33	17	3	3	8	11	13.8	4.08	93	.292	.355	0	—	0	-1	-1	-0	-0.1
*Oak-A	11	4	.733	22	21	2	0	0	122^2	112	50	12	3	24	42	10.2	3.52	103	.240	.281	0	—	0	4	2	-1	0.1
Yr	11	6	.647	28	24	2	0	0	151^1	145	67	15	6	32	53	10.9	3.63	101	.250	.296	0	—	0	3	1	-1	0.0
1976 Oak-A	4	2	.667	27	15	0	0	0	112	118	54	13	1	19	34	11.1	4.10	82	.274	.306	0	—	0	-7	-10	0	-0.5
Total 11	82	85	.491	306	229	29	10	2	1591	1594	736	149	34	412	757	11.5	3.67	93	.261	.312	41	.125	-5	-28	-47	-5	-5.5
● MEL BOSSER Bosser, Melvin Edward b: 2/8/14, Johnstown, Pa. d: 3/26/86, Crossville, Tenn. BR/TR, 6', 173 lbs. Deb: 4/29/45																											
1945 Cin-N	2	0	1.000	7	1	0	0	0	16	9	6	0	0	17	3	14.6	3.38	111	.158	.351	0	.000	-1	1	1	-0	0.0
● ANDY BOSWELL Boswell, Andrew Cottrell b: 9/5/1874, New Gretna, N.J. d: 2/3/36, Ocean City, N.J. TR, 6'1", 165 lbs. Deb: 5/10/1895																											
1895 NY-N	2	2	.500	5	4	3	0	0	34	41	35	1	3	22	18	17.5	5.82	80	.293	.400	3	.188	-1	-4	-5	-1	-0.5
Was-N	1	2	.333	6	3	3	0	0	30	44	32	1	2	19	12	19.5	6.00	80	.336	.428	4	.286	0	-4	-4	-0	-0.3
Yr	3	4	.429	11	7	6	0	0	64	85	67	2	5	41	30	18.4	5.91	80	.314	.413	7	.233	-1	-8	-9	-1	-0.8
● DAVE BOSWELL Boswell, David Wilson b: 1/20/45, Baltimore, Md. BR/TR, 6'3", 185 lbs. Deb: 9/18/64																											
1964 Min-A	2	0	1.000	4	4	0	0	0	23^1	21	11	4	0	12	25	12.7	4.24	84	.236	.327	2	.222	0	-2	-2	-1	-0.1
1965 *Min-A	6	5	.545	27	12	1	0	0	106	77	43	20	5	46	85	10.9	3.40	105	.204	.298	12	.316	4	1	2	-1	0.5
1966 Min-A	12	5	.706	28	21	8	1	0	169^1	120	66	19	5	65	173	10.1	3.14	115	.197	.280	9	.143	-1	6	8	1	0.8
1967 Min-A	14	12	.538	37	32	11	3	0	222^2	162	84	14	7	107	204	11.2	3.27	106	.202	.302	16	.219	4	-1	4	-1	0.8
1968 Min-A	10	13	.435	34	28	7	2	0	190	148	79	19	7	87	143	11.5	3.32	93	.213	.307	14	.233	5	-7	-5	-2	-0.3
1969 *Min-A	20	12	.625	39	38	10	0	0	256^1	215	105	18	8	99	190	11.3	3.23	113	.226	.304	16	.170	3	11	12	-2	1.5
1970 Min-A	3	7	.300	18	15	0	0	0	68^2	80	55	12	2	44	45	16.5	6.42	58	.292	.394	4	.160	-0	-21	-21	-1	-2.7
1971 Det-A	0	0	—	3	0	0	0	0	4^1	3	3	0	0	6	3	18.7	6.23	58	.200	.429	0	—	0	-1	-1	0	0.0
Bal-A	1	2	.333	15	1	0	0	0	24^2	32	16	4	0	15	14	17.1	4.38	77	.305	.392	1	.200	0	-2	-3	0	-0.3
Yr	1	2	.333	18	1	0	0	0	29	35	19	4	0	21	17	17.4	4.66	73	.292	.397	1	.200	0	-4	-4	0	-0.3
Total 8	68	56	.548	205	151	37	6	0	1065^1	858	462	110	34	481	882	11.6	3.52	99	.219	.310	74	.202	13	-17	-3	-4	0.2
● DEREK BOTELHO Botelho, Derek Wayne b: 8/2/56, Long Beach, Cal. BR/TR, 6'2", 180 lbs. Deb: 7/18/82																											
1982 KC-A	2	1	.667	8	4	0	0	0	24	25	11	4	0	8	12	12.4	4.13	99	.275	.333	0	—	0	-0	-0	-0	0.0
1985 Chi-N	1	3	.250	11	7	1	0	0	44	52	27	8	2	23	23	15.8	5.32	75	.299	.387	2	.143	-0	-8	-6	-0	-0.5
Total 2	3	4	.429	19	11	1	0	0	68	77	38	12	2	31	35	14.6	4.90	83	.291	.369	2	.143	-0	-9	-6	-1	-0.5
● RICKY BOTTALICO Bottalico, Ricky Paul b: 8/26/69, New Britain, Conn. BL/TR, 6'1", 200 lbs. Deb: 7/29/94																											
1994 Phi-N	0	0	—	3	0	0	0	0	3	3	0	0	0	1	3	12.0	0.00	—	.250	.308	0	—	0	1	1	-0	0.1
1995 Phi-N	5	3	.625	62	0	0	0	1	87^2	50	25	7	4	42	87	9.9	2.46	172	.167	.277	0	.000	-1	17	17	-1	1.3

YEAR	TM/L	W	L	PCT	G	GS	CG	SH	SV	IP	H	R	HR	HB	BB	SO	RAT	ERA	ERA+	OAV	OOB	BH	AVG	PB	PR	PR+	PD	TPI
1996	Phi-N★	4	5	.444	61	0	0	0	34	67^2	47	24	6	2	23	74	9.6	3.19	135	.197	.274	1	.333	1	8	8	-1	1.6
1997	Phi-N	2	5	.286	69	0	0	0	34	74	68	31	7	2	42	89	13.6	3.65	116	.245	.349	0	.000	-0	5	5	-1	0.8
1998	Phi-N	1	5	.167	39	0	0	0	6	43^1	54	31	7	1	25	27	16.6	6.44	67	.305	.394	0	—	0	-11	-10	0	-1.4
1999	StL-N	3	7	.300	68	0	0	0	20	73^1	83	45	8	3	49	66	16.6	4.91	93	.284	.392	0	.000	-0	-3	-3	0	-0.5
2000	KC-A	9	6	.600	62	0	0	0	16	72^2	65	40	12	2	41	56	13.4	4.83	104	.239	.343	0	—	0	1	1	-0	0.2
Total	7	24	31	.436	364	0	0	0	111	421^2	370	196	47	14	223	402	13.0	4.01	111	.236	.336	1	.083	-0	18	20	-2	2.1
● **KENT BOTTENFIELD**	Bottenfield, Kent Dennis b: 11/14/68, Portland, Ore. BB/TR, 6'3", 237 lbs. Deb: 7/6/92																											
1992	Mon-N	1	2	.333	10	4	0	0	1	32^1	26	9	1	1	11	14	10.6	2.23	156	.217	.288	3	.375	1	5	5	-1	0.5
1993	Mon-N	2	5	.286	23	11	0	0	0	83	93	49	11	5	33	33	14.2	4.12	101	.288	.363	4	.167	-0	-1	1	-0	0.0
	Col-N	3	5	.375	14	14	1	0	0	76^2	86	53	13	1	38	30	14.7	6.10	78	.302	.386	7	.269	1	-18	-10	2	-0.6
	Yr	5	10	.333	37	25	1	0	0	159^2	179	102	24	6	71	63	14.4	5.07	88	.294	.374	11	.220	1	-18	-10	2	-0.6
1994	Col-N	3	1	.750	15	1	0	0	1	24^2	28	16	1	2	10	15	14.6	5.84	85	.283	.360	0	.000	-0	-4	-2	-1	-0.4
	SF-N	0	0	—	1	0	0	0	0	1^2	5	2	1	0	0	0	27.0	10.80	37	.556	.556	0	—	0	-1	-1	-0	-0.1
	Yr	3	1	.750	16	1	0	0	1	26^1	33	18	2	2	10	15	15.4	6.15	80	.306	.375	0	.000	-0	-6	-3	-1	-0.5
1996	Chi-N	3	5	.375	48	0	0	0	1	61^2	59	25	3	3	19	33	11.8	2.63	165	.255	.320	1	.500	0	11	11	1	1.5
1997	Chi-N	2	3	.400	64	0	0	0	2	84	82	39	13	2	35	74	12.8	3.86	112	.259	.337	0	.000	-0	3	4	-1	0.1
1998	StL-N	4	6	.400	44	17	0	0	4	133^2	128	72	13	4	57	98	12.7	4.44	94	.254	.335	3	.088	-2	-3	-4	1	-0.4
1999	StL-N★	18	7	.720	31	31	0	0	0	190^1	197	91	21	5	89	124	13.8	3.97	115	.270	.354	9	.148	-1	13	13	1	1.5
2000	Ana-A	7	8	.467	21	21	0	0	0	127^2	144	82	25	3	56	75	14.3	5.71	87	.285	.360	2	.667	1	-11	-10	0	-0.9
	Phi-N	1	2	.333	8	8	1	1	0	44	41	24	5	0	21	31	12.7	4.50	105	.240	.323	0	.000	-2	1	1	0	-0.1
Total	8	44	44	.500	279	107	2	1	9	859^2	889	462	107	26	369	527	13.4	4.43	101	.270	.348	29	.164	-2	-6	6	2	1.1
● **RALPH BOTTING**	Botting, Ralph Wayne b: 5/12/55, Houlton, Maine BL/TL, 6', 195 lbs. Deb: 6/28/79																											
1979	Cal-A	2	0	1.000	12	1	0	0	0	29^2	46	30	6	1	15	22	18.8	8.80	46	.362	.434	0	—	0	-15	-16	-0	-0.9
1980	Cal-A	0	3	.000	6	6	0	0	0	26^1	40	20	1	0	13	12	18.1	5.81	68	.348	.414	0	—	0	-5	-6	-0	-0.6
Total	2	2	3	.400	18	7	0	0	0	56	86	50	7	1	28	34	18.5	7.39	54	.355	.424	0	—	0	-20	-22	-0	-1.5
● **BOB BOTZ**	Botz, Robert Allen b: 4/28/35, Milwaukee, Wis. BR/TR, 5'11", 170 lbs. Deb: 5/8/62																											
1962	LA-A	2	1	.667	35	0	0	0	2	63	71	30	7	2	11	24	12.0	3.43	113	.285	.321	0	.000	-1	4	3	-1	-0.1
● **DENIS BOUCHER**	Boucher, Denis b: 3/7/68, Montreal, Que., Can. BR/TL, 6'1", 195 lbs. Deb: 4/12/91																											
1991	Tor-A	0	3	.000	7	7	0	0	0	35^1	39	20	6	2	16	16	14.5	4.58	92	.279	.361	0	—	0	-2	-1	1	-0.1
	Cle-A	1	4	.200	5	5	0	0	0	22^2	35	21	6	0	8	13	17.1	8.34	50	.350	.398	0	—	0	-11	-10	0	-1.7
	Yr	1	7	.125	12	12	0	0	0	58	74	41	12	2	24	29	15.5	6.05	69	.308	.376	0	—	0	-13	-12	1	-1.8
1992	Cle-A	2	2	.500	8	7	0	0	0	41	48	29	9	1	20	17	15.1	6.37	61	.302	.383	0	—	0	-11	-11	-1	-1.0
1993	Mon-N	3	1	.750	5	5	0	0	0	28^1	24	7	1	0	3	14	8.6	1.91	219	.229	.250	1	.167	0	7	7	-0	1.0
1994	Mon-N	0	1	.000	10	2	0	0	0	18^2	24	16	6	0	7	17	14.9	6.75	63	.324	.383	1	.333	1	-5	-5	0	-0.2
Total	4	6	11	.353	35	26	0	0	0	146	170	93	28	3	54	77	14.0	5.42	76	.294	.357	2	.222	1	-22	-21	0	-2.0
● **CARL BOULDIN**	Bouldin, Carl Edward b: 9/17/39, Germantown, Ky. BB/TR, 6'2", 180 lbs. Deb: 9/2/61																											
1961	Was-A	0	1	.000	2	1	0	0	0	3^1	9	6	0	0	2	2	29.7	16.20	25	.500	.550	0	.000	-0	-5	-5	0	-0.7
1962	Was-A	1	2	.333	6	3	1	0	0	20	26	13	0	1	9	12	16.2	5.85	69	.321	.396	0	.000	-1	-4	-4	-0	-0.6
1963	Was-A	2	2	.500	10	3	0	0	0	23^1	31	18	3	0	8	10	15.0	5.79	64	.307	.358	0	.000	-1	-6	-5	0	-0.9
1964	Was-A	0	3	.000	9	3	0	0	0	25	30	20	2	2	11	12	15.5	5.40	69	.294	.374	0	.000	-0	-5	-5	-0	-0.6
Total	4	3	8	.273	27	10	1	0	0	71^2	96	57	5	3	30	36	16.2	6.15	62	.318	.385	0	.000	-2	-19	-18	0	-2.8
● **JAKE BOULTES**	Boultes, Jacob John b: 8/6/1884, St.Louis, Mo. d: 12/24/55, St.Louis, Mo. TR, 6'3", Deb: 4/18/07																											
1907	Bos-N	5	9	.357	24	12	11	0	0	139^2	140	75	1	8	50	49	12.8	2.71	94	.266	.338	9	.132	-2	-4	-2	4	0.0
1908	Bos-N	3	5	.375	17	5	1	0	0	74^2	80	40	7	1	8	28	10.7	3.01	80	.274	.296	3	.143	-0	-5	-5	-0	-0.7
1909	Bos-N	0	0	—	1	0	0	0	0	8	9	7	2	1	0	1	11.3	6.75	42	.290	.313	1	.333	0	-4	-3	-0	-0.1
Total	3	8	14	.364	42	17	12	0	0	222^1	229	122	10	10	58	78	12.0	2.96	85	.269	.324	13	.141	-2	-13	-11	4	-0.8
● **STEVE BOURGEOIS**	Bourgeois, Steven James b: 8/4/72, Lutcher, La. BR/TR, 6'1", 220 lbs. Deb: 4/3/96																											
1996	SF-N	1	3	.250	15	5	0	0	0	40	60	35	4	4	21	17	19.1	6.30	65	.355	.438	3	.273	2	-9	-10	0	-0.6
● **JIM BOUTON**	Bouton, James Alan b: 3/8/39, Newark, N.J. BR/TR, 6', 185 lbs. Deb: 4/22/62																											
1962	NY-A	7	7	.500	36	16	3	1	2	133	124	63	9	0	59	71	12.4	3.99	94	.254	.334	2	.063	-2	-0	-4	0	-0.5
1963	*NY-A★	21	7	.750	40	30	12	6	1	249^1	191	79	18	3	87	148	10.1	2.53	139	.212	.284	6	.072	-6	31	28	-1	2.4
1964	*NY-A	18	13	.581	38	37	11	4	0	271^1	227	100	32	6	60	125	9.7	3.02	120	.225	.273	13	.130	-3	18	18	-3	1.3
1965	NY-A	4	15	.211	30	25	2	0	0	151^1	158	89	23	5	60	97	13.3	4.82	71	.269	.342	4	.093	-0	-23	-24	-0	-2.8
1966	NY-A	3	8	.273	24	19	3	0	1	120^1	117	49	13	1	38	65	11.7	2.69	123	.257	.315	4	.105	-2	10	9	1	0.7
1967	NY-A	1	0	1.000	17	1	0	0	0	44^1	47	31	5	1	18	31	13.4	4.67	67	.275	.347	0	.000	-0	-7	-8	0	-0.5
1968	NY-A	1	1	.500	12	3	1	0	0	44	49	20	5	2	9	24	12.3	3.68	79	.287	.330	0	.000	-0	-3	-4	1	-0.1
1969	Sea-A	2	1	.667	57	1	0	0	1	92	77	48	12	2	38	68	11.4	3.91	93	.219	.299	0	.000	-1	-3	-3	1	-0.2
	Hou-N	0	2	.000	16	1	1	0	1	30^2	32	16	1	2	12	32	13.5	4.11	86	.267	.343	0	.000	-0	-2	-2	0	-0.2
1970	Hou-N	4	6	.400	29	6	1	0	0	73^1	84	53	5	1	33	49	14.5	5.40	72	.285	.359	6	.353	2	-11	-13	-0	-1.3
1978	Atl-N	1	3	.250	5	5	0	0	0	29	25	18	4	0	21	10	14.3	4.97	82	.234	.359	0	.000	-1	-4	-3	-0	-0.4
Total	10	62	63	.496	304	144	34	11	6	1238^2	1131	566	127	23	435	720	11.5	3.57	99	.243	.311	35	.101	-13	5	-5	-1	-1.6
● **MIKE BOVEE**	Bovee, Michael Craig b: 8/21/73, San Diego, Cal. BR/TR, 5'10", 200 lbs. Deb: 9/13/97																											
1997	Ana-A	0	0	—	3	0	0	0	0	3^1	3	2	1	0	1	5	10.8	5.40	85	.231	.286	0	—	0	-0	-0	-0	0.0
● **RYAN BOWEN**	Bowen, Ryan Eugene b: 2/10/68, Hanford, Cal. BR/TR, 6', 185 lbs. Deb: 7/22/91																											
1991	Hou-N	6	4	.600	14	13	0	0	0	71^2	73	43	4	3	36	49	14.1	5.15	68	.268	.360	4	.182	1	-12	-14	-2	-1.7
1992	Hou-N	0	7	.000	11	9	0	0	0	33^2	48	43	8	2	30	22	21.4	10.96	31	.333	.455	1	.111	-0	-28	-30	-1	-4.7
1993	Fla-N	8	12	.400	27	27	2	1	0	156^2	156	83	11	3	87	98	14.1	4.42	98	.263	.360	6	.118	-1	-7	-2	-0	-0.3
1994	Fla-N	1	5	.167	8	8	1	0	0	47^1	50	28	9	2	19	32	13.5	4.94	88	.273	.348	5	.357	2	-4	-3	-1	-0.2
1995	Fla-N	2	0	1.000	4	3	0	0	0	16^2	23	11	3	0	12	15	18.9	3.78	112	.329	.427	2	.333	0	1	1	-0	0.1
Total	5	17	28	.378	64	60	3	1	0	326	350	208	35	10	184	216	15.0	5.30	76	.277	.373	18	.176	2	-49	-45	-4	-6.8
● **CY BOWEN**	Bowen, Sutherland McCoy b: 2/17/1871, Kingston, Ind. d: 1/25/25, Greensburg, Ind. BR/TR, 6', 175 lbs. Deb: 4/28/1896																											
1896	NY-N	0	1	.000	2	1	1	0	0	12	12	13	0	3	9	3	18.0	6.00	70	.261	.414	1	.333	0	-2	-2	0	-0.1
● **FRANK BOWERMAN**	Bowerman, Frank Eugene "Mike" b: 12/5/1868, Romeo, Mich. d: 11/30/48, Romeo, Mich. BR/TR, 6'2", 190 lbs. Deb: 8/24/1895 M♦																											
1904	NY-N	0	0	—	1	0	0	0	0	1	3	4	0	0	1	0	36.0	9.00	30	.429	.500	67	.232	0	-1	-1	-0	0.0
● **SHANE BOWERS**	Bowers, Shane Patrick b: 7/27/71, Glendora, Cal. BR/TR, 6'4", 215 lbs. Deb: 7/26/97																											
1997	Min-A	0	3	.000	5	5	0	0	0	19	27	20	2	1	8	7	17.1	8.05	58	.329	.396	0	—	0	-7	-7	-0	-0.9
● **STEW BOWERS**	Bowers, Stewart Cole "Doc" b: 2/26/15, New Freedom, Pa. BB/TR, 6', 170 lbs. Deb: 8/5/35 ♦																											
1935	Bos-A	2	1	.667	10	2	1	0	0	23^2	26	14	1	0	17	5	16.4	3.42	139	.283	.394	1	.200	0	3	3	0	0.4
1936	Bos-A	0	0	—	5	0	0	0	0	5^2	10	7	1	0	2	0	19.1	9.53	56	.370	.414	0	—	0	-3	-3	-0	-0.1
Total	2	2	1	.667	15	2	1	0	0	29^1	36	21	2	0	19	5	16.9	4.60	106	.303	.399	1	.200	0	-0	1	-0	0.3
● **MICAH BOWIE**	Bowie, Micah Andrew b: 11/10/74, Humble, Tex. BL/TL, 6'4", 185 lbs. Deb: 7/24/99																											
1999	Atl-N	0	1	.000	3	0	0	0	0	4	8	6	1	0	4	2	27.0	13.50	33	.421	.522	0	—	0	-4	-4	-0	-0.7
	Chi-N	2	6	.250	11	11	0	0	0	47	73	54	8	2	30	39	20.1	9.96	45	.358	.445	3	.214	0	-28	-29	-0	-3.5
	Yr	2	7	.222	14	11	0	0	0	51	81	60	9	2	34	41	20.6	10.24	44	.363	.452	3	.214	0	-32	-33	-0	-4.2
● **GRANT BOWLER**	Bowler, Grant Tierney "Moose" b: 10/24/07, Denver, Col. d: 6/25/68, Denver, Colo. BR/TR, 6', 190 lbs. Deb: 8/21/31																											
1931	Chi-A	0	1	.000	13	3	1	0	0	35^1	40	26	1	0	24	15	16.3	5.35	80	.288	.393	1	.100	-0	-4	-4	-1	-0.3

YEAR TM/L	W	L	PCT	G	GS	CG	SH	SV	IP	H	R	HR	HB	BB	SO	RAT	ERA	ERA+	OAV	OOB	BH	AVG	PB	PR	PR+	PD	TPI
1932 Chi-A	0	0	—	4	0	0	0	0	6^{1}	15	12	1	0	3	2	25.6	15.63	28	.484	.529	0	.000	-0	-8	-8	0	-0.4
Total 2	0	1	.000	17	3	1	0	0	41^{2}	55	38	2	0	27	17	17.7	6.91	62	.324	.416	1	.083	-1	-12	-13	-1	-0.7

● CHARLIE BOWLES Bowles, Charles James b: 3/15/17, Norwood, Mass. BR/TR, 6'3", 180 lbs. Deb: 9/25/43

YEAR TM/L	W	L	PCT	G	GS	CG	SH	SV	IP	H	R	HR	HB	BB	SO	RAT	ERA	ERA+	OAV	OOB	BH	AVG	PB	PR	PR+	PD	TPI
1943 Phi-A	1	1	.500	2	2	2	0	0	18	17	10	0	0	4	6	10.5	3.00	113	.258	.300	1	.125	-1	1	1	0	0.0
1945 Phi-A	0	3	.000	8	4	1	0	0	33^{1}	35	19	3	0	23	11	15.7	5.13	67	.273	.384	5	.238	0	-7	-6	0	-0.5
Total 2	1	4	.200	10	6	3	0	0	51^{1}	52	29	3	0	27	17	13.9	4.38	78	.268	.357	6	.207	-0	-6	-5	0	-0.5

● EMMETT BOWLES Bowles, Emmett Jerome "Chief" b: 8/2/1898, Wanette, Okla. d: 9/3/59, Flagstaff, Ariz. BR/TR, 6', 180 lbs. Deb: 9/12/22

YEAR TM/L	W	L	PCT	G	GS	CG	SH	SV	IP	H	R	HR	HB	BB	SO	RAT	ERA	ERA+	OAV	OOB	BH	AVG	PB	PR	PR+	PD	TPI
1922 Chi-A	0	0	—	1	0	0	0	0	1	2	3	0	0	1	0	27.0	27.00	15	.500	.600	0	—	0	-3	-3	-0	-0.1

● ABE BOWMAN Bowman, Alvah Edson b: 1/25/1893, Greenup, Ill. d: 10/11/79, Longview, Tex. BR/TR, 6'1", 190 lbs. Deb: 5/19/14

YEAR TM/L	W	L	PCT	G	GS	CG	SH	SV	IP	H	R	HR	HB	BB	SO	RAT	ERA	ERA+	OAV	OOB	BH	AVG	PB	PR	PR+	PD	TPI
1914 Cle-A	2	7	.222	22	10	2	1	0	72^{2}	74	45	0	4	45	27	15.2	4.46	65	.277	.389	1	.048	-2	-14	-12	-0	-1.7
1915 Cle-A	0	1	.000	2	1	0	0	0	1^{1}	1	4	0	0	3	0	27.0	20.25	15	.250	.571	0	—	0	-3	-2	1	-0.4
Total 2	2	8	.200	24	11	2	1	0	74	75	49	0	4	48	27	15.4	4.74	61	.277	.393	1	.048	-2	-16	-14	0	-2.1

● JOE BOWMAN Bowman, Joseph Emil b: 6/17/10, Kansas City, Kan. d: 11/22/90, Kansas City, Mo. BL/TR, 6'2", 190 lbs. Deb: 4/18/32 ♦

YEAR TM/L	W	L	PCT	G	GS	CG	SH	SV	IP	H	R	HR	HB	BB	SO	RAT	ERA	ERA+	OAV	OOB	BH	AVG	PB	PR	PR+	PD	TPI
1932 Phi-A	0	1	.000	7	0	0	0	0	11	14	10	2	3	6	4	18.8	8.18	55	.318	.434	1	1.000	0	-5	-4	1	-0.2
1934 NY-N	5	4	.556	30	10	3	0	3	107^{1}	119	52	9	2	36	36	13.2	3.61	107	.279	.338	5	.172	0	5	3	-0	0.2
1935 Phi-N	7	10	.412	33	17	6	1	1	148^{1}	157	86	13	4	56	58	13.2	4.25	107	.269	.337	13	.194	0	-4	4	-0	0.5
1936 Phi-N	9	20	.310	40	28	12	0	1	203^{2}	243	140	14	7	53	80	13.4	5.04	90	.289	.336	15	.195	-1	-23	-10	-2	-1.6
1937 Pit-N	8	8	.500	30	19	7	0	1	128	161	78	11	1	35	38	13.9	4.57	85	.306	.351	10	.213	2	-9	-10	0	-1.0
1938 Pit-N	3	4	.429	17	1	0	0	1	60	68	33	2	0	20	25	13.2	4.65	82	.285	.340	7	.333	2	-6	-6	-1	-0.5
1939 Pit-N	10	14	.417	37	27	10	1	1	184^{2}	217	105	15	7	43	58	13.0	4.48	86	.292	.336	33	.344	12	-12	-13	0	-0.4
1940 Pit-N	9	10	.474	32	24	10	0	2	187^{2}	209	113	10	7	66	57	13.5	4.46	85	.274	.337	22	.244	9	-13	-14	0	-0.3
1941 Pit-N	3	2	.600	18	7	1	1	1	69^{1}	77	24	3	1	28	22	13.8	2.99	121	.278	.346	8	.258	1	5	5	-0	0.5
1944 Bos-A	12	8	.600	26	24	10	1	0	168^{1}	175	95	14	2	64	53	12.9	4.81	71	.269	.336	20	.200	3	-26	-27	-2	-2.7
1945 Bos-A	0	2	.000	3	3	0	0	0	11^{2}	18	12	1	0	9	0	20.8	9.26	37	.360	.458	2	.222	0	-8	-7	-0	-1.0
Cin-N	11	13	.458	25	24	15	1	0	185^{2}	198	89	8	7	68	71	13.2	3.59	105	.270	.338	5	.070	-5	4	4	-2	-0.2
Total 11	77	96	.445	298	184	74	5	11	1465^{2}	1656	837	102	41	484	502	13.4	4.40	89	.282	.341	141	.221	24	-89	-75	-7	-6.7

● BOB BOWMAN Bowman, Robert James b: 10/3/10, Keystone, W.Va. d: 9/4/72, Bluefield, W.Va. BR/TR, 5'10.5", 160 lbs. Deb: 4/21/39

YEAR TM/L	W	L	PCT	G	GS	CG	SH	SV	IP	H	R	HR	HB	BB	SO	RAT	ERA	ERA+	OAV	OOB	BH	AVG	PB	PR	PR+	PD	TPI
1939 StL-N	13	5	.722	51	15	4	2	**9**	169^{1}	141	54	8	1	60	78	10.7	2.60	158	.232	.302	4	.085	-3	25	27	-1	2.6
1940 StL-N	7	5	.583	28	17	7	0	0	114^{1}	118	66	9	4	43	43	13.0	4.33	92	.267	.337	2	.061	-2	-6	-4	-0	-0.6
1941 NY-N	6	7	.462	29	6	2	0	1	80^{1}	100	55	10	1	36	25	15.3	5.71	65	.302	.372	1	.048	-1	-19	-18	1	-2.6
1942 Chi-N	0	0	—	1	0	0	0	0	1	1	0	0	0	0	0	9.0	0.00	—	.250	.250	0	—	0	0	0	-0	0.0
Total 4	26	17	.605	109	38	13	2	10	365	360	175	27	6	139	146	12.5	3.82	104	.260	.330	7	.069	-5	0	6	-1	-0.6

● BOB BOWMAN Bowman, Robert Leroy b: 5/10/31, Laytonville, Cal. BR/TR, 6'1", 195 lbs. Deb: 4/16/55 ♦

YEAR TM/L	W	L	PCT	G	GS	CG	SH	SV	IP	H	R	HR	HB	BB	SO	RAT	ERA	ERA+	OAV	OOB	BH	AVG	PB	PR	PR+	PD	TPI
1959 Phi-N	0	1	.000	5	0	0	0	0	6	5	5	1	0	5	0	15.0	6.00	68	.227	.370	10	.127	-0	-1	-1	0	-0.2

● ROGER BOWMAN Bowman, Roger Clinton b: 8/18/27, Amsterdam, N.Y. d: 7/21/97, Los Angeles, Cal. BR/TL, 6', 175 lbs. Deb: 9/22/49

YEAR TM/L	W	L	PCT	G	GS	CG	SH	SV	IP	H	R	HR	HB	BB	SO	RAT	ERA	ERA+	OAV	OOB	BH	AVG	PB	PR	PR+	PD	TPI
1949 NY-N	0	0	—	2	2	0	0	0	6^{1}	6	3	1	0	7	4	18.5	4.26	93	.261	.433	0	.000	-0	-0	-0	1	0.0
1951 NY-N	2	4	.333	9	5	0	0	0	26^{1}	35	18	2	1	22	24	19.8	6.15	64	.297	.411	0	.000	-0	-6	-7	-1	-1.3
1952 NY-N	0	0	—	2	1	0	0	0	3	6	4	0	1	3	3	30.0	12.00	31	.429	.556	0	.000	-0	-3	-3	-0	-0.2
1953 Pit-N	0	4	.000	30	2	0	0	0	65^{1}	65	42	9	1	29	36	13.1	4.82	93	.261	.341	2	.286	0	-4	-2	0	0.0
1955 Pit-N	0	3	.000	7	2	0	0	0	16^{2}	25	18	2	1	10	8	19.4	8.64	48	.347	.434	1	.500	0	-9	-8	0	-1.1
Total 5	2	11	.154	50	12	0	0	0	117^{2}	137	85	14	4	71	75	16.2	5.81	73	.288	.385	3	.167	-0	-22	-20	1	-2.6

● SUMNER BOWMAN Bowman, Sumner Sallade b: 2/9/1867, Millersburg, Pa. d: 1/11/54, Millersburg, Pa. BL/TL, 6', 160 lbs. Deb: 6/11/1890

YEAR TM/L	W	L	PCT	G	GS	CG	SH	SV	IP	H	R	HR	HB	BB	SO	RAT	ERA	ERA+	OAV	OOB	BH	AVG	PB	PR	PR+	PD	TPI
1890 Phi-N	0	0	—	1	1	0	0	0	8	11	7	0	1	2	2	15.8	7.88	46	.314	.368	2	.500	1	-4	-4	-0	-0.1
Pit-N	2	5	.286	9	7	6	0	0	70^{2}	100	90	1	11	50	22	20.5	6.62	50	.324	.435	10	.278	2	-24	-28	-0	-1.9
Yr	2	5	.286	10	8	6	0	0	78^{2}	111	97	1	12	52	24	20.0	6.75	49	.323	.429	12	.300	2	-28	-32	-0	-2.0
1891 Phi-a	2	5	.286	8	8	8	0	0	68	73	54	0	5	37	22	15.2	3.44	110	.265	.363	13	.241	0	2	3	-1	0.2
Total 2	4	10	.286	18	16	14	0	0	146^{2}	184	151	1	17	89	46	17.8	5.22	68	.297	.400	25	.266	3	-26	-28	-1	-1.8

● TED BOWSFIELD Bowsfield, Edward Oliver b: 1/10/35, Vernon, B.C., Canada BR/TL, 6'1", 190 lbs. Deb: 7/20/58

YEAR TM/L	W	L	PCT	G	GS	CG	SH	SV	IP	H	R	HR	HB	BB	SO	RAT	ERA	ERA+	OAV	OOB	BH	AVG	PB	PR	PR+	PD	TPI
1958 Bos-A	4	2	.667	16	10	2	0	0	65^{2}	58	32	3	1	36	38	13.0	3.84	104	.233	.332	4	.154	-1	-1	1	1	0.1
1959 Bos-A	0	1	.000	5	2	0	0	0	9	16	15	2	0	9	4	25.0	15.00	27	.390	.500	0	.000	-0	-11	-10	-0	-1.0
1960 Bos-A	1	2	.333	17	2	0	0	2	21	20	12	1	1	13	18	14.6	5.14	79	.260	.374	1	.250	0	-3	-2	1	-0.3
Cle-A	3	4	.429	11	6	1	1	0	40^{2}	47	30	1	0	20	14	14.8	5.09	73	.296	.374	1	.100	-0	-5	-6	1	-0.9
Yr	4	6	.400	28	8	1	1	2	61^{2}	67	42	2	1	33	32	14.7	5.11	75	.284	.374	2	.143	-0	-8	-9	1	-1.2
1961 LA-A	11	8	.579	41	21	4	1	0	157	154	75	18	1	63	88	12.5	3.73	121	.255	.327	7	.137	-1	5	12	-1	1.1
1962 LA-A	9	8	.529	34	25	1	0	1	139	154	82	12	2	40	52	12.7	4.40	88	.277	.328	6	.162	1	-7	-9	-3	-1.1
1963 KC-A	5	7	.417	41	11	2	1	3	111^{1}	115	60	14	3	47	67	13.3	4.45	88	.269	.345	1	.043	-1	-10	-6	2	-0.6
1964 KC-A	4	7	.364	50	9	2	1	0	118^{2}	135	63	12	4	31	45	12.9	4.10	93	.285	.334	2	.095	-1	-6	-3	0	-0.4
Total 7	37	39	.487	215	86	12	4	6	662^{1}	699	369	63	12	259	326	13.2	4.35	93	.270	.339	22	.127	-3	-38	-22	1	-3.1

● OIL CAN BOYD Boyd, Dennis Ray b: 10/6/59, Meridian, Miss. BR/TR, 6'1", 155 lbs. Deb: 9/13/82

YEAR TM/L	W	L	PCT	G	GS	CG	SH	SV	IP	H	R	HR	HB	BB	SO	RAT	ERA	ERA+	OAV	OOB	BH	AVG	PB	PR	PR+	PD	TPI
1982 Bos-A	0	1	.000	3	1	0	0	0	8^{1}	11	5	2	0	2	2	14.0	5.40	80	.314	.351	0	—	0	-1	-1	-0	-0.1
1983 Bos-A	4	8	.333	15	13	5	0	0	98^{2}	103	46	9	1	23	43	11.6	3.28	133	.269	.312	0	—	0	9	11	-1	1.2
1984 Bos-A	12	12	.500	29	26	10	3	0	197^{2}	207	109	18	1	53	134	11.9	4.37	95	.269	.317	0	—	0	-8	-4	2	-0.3
1985 Bos-A	15	13	.536	35	35	13	3	0	272^{1}	273	117	26	4	67	154	11.4	3.70	116	.261	.308	0	—	0	14	17	3	1.9
1986 *Bos-A	16	10	.615	30	30	10	0	0	214^{1}	222	99	32	2	45	129	11.3	3.78	110	.265	.304	0	—	0	10	9	1	1.1
1987 Bos-A	1	3	.250	7	7	0	0	0	36^{2}	47	31	6	2	9	12	14.2	5.89	77	.315	.363	0	—	0	-6	-5	1	-0.4
1988 Bos-A	9	7	.563	23	23	1	0	0	129^{2}	147	82	25	2	41	71	13.2	5.34	77	.289	.344	0	—	0	-20	-17	-1	-1.9
1989 Bos-A	3	2	.600	10	10	0	0	0	59	57	31	8	0	19	26	11.6	4.42	93	.253	.311	0	—	0	-3	-2	1	-0.1
1990 Mon-N	10	6	.625	31	31	3	3	0	190^{2}	164	64	19	3	52	113	10.3	2.93	125	.233	.289	3	.051	-4	18	16	-1	0.7
1991 Mon-N	6	8	.429	19	19	1	1	0	120^{1}	115	49	9	0	40	82	11.6	3.52	103	.256	.316	3	.083	-1	2	1	-1	-0.1
Tex-A	2	7	.222	12	12	0	0	0	62	81	47	12	0	17	33	14.2	6.68	60	.314	.356	0	—	0	-18	-18	-1	-2.2
Total 10	78	77	.503	214	207	43	10	0	1389^{2}	1427	680	166	15	368	799	11.7	4.04	101	.266	.315	6	.063	-5	-3	7	3	-0.2

● GARY BOYD Boyd, Gary Lee b: 8/22/46, Pasadena, Cal. BR/TR, 6'4", 200 lbs. Deb: 8/1/69

YEAR TM/L	W	L	PCT	G	GS	CG	SH	SV	IP	H	R	HR	HB	BB	SO	RAT	ERA	ERA+	OAV	OOB	BH	AVG	PB	PR	PR+	PD	TPI
1969 Cle-A	0	2	.000	8	3	0	0	0	11	8	11	1	0	14	9	18.0	9.00	42	.205	.415	0	.000	-0	-7	-6	-0	-1.0

● JAKE BOYD Boyd, Jacob Henry b: 1/19/1874, Martinsburg, W.Va. d: 8/12/32, Gettysburg, Pa. TL, 160 lbs. Deb: 9/20/1894 ♦

YEAR TM/L	W	L	PCT	G	GS	CG	SH	SV	IP	H	R	HR	HB	BB	SO	RAT	ERA	ERA+	OAV	OOB	BH	AVG	PB	PR	PR+	PD	TPI
1894 Was-N	0	3	.000	3	3	3	0	0	19	37	35	1	1	14	3	24.6	8.53	62	.402	.486	3	.143	-1	-7	-7	0	-0.7
1895 Was-N	2	11	.154	15	13	8	0	0	92^{2}	132	95	1	11	40	18	17.8	6.80	71	.329	.405	43	.270	2	-21	-21	1	-1.8
1896 Was-N	1	2	.333	4	2	2	0	0	32	45	34	0	6	15	6	18.6	6.75	65	.328	.418	1	.077	-1	-8	-8	0	-0.6
Total 3	3	16	.158	22	18	13	0	0	143^{2}	214	164	2	18	69	27	18.9	7.02	68	.340	.420	47	.244	-1	-36	-36	2	-3.1

● JASON BOYD Boyd, Jason Pernell b: 2/23/73, St.Clair, Ill. BR/TR, 6'3", 170 lbs. Deb: 9/10/99

YEAR TM/L	W	L	PCT	G	GS	CG	SH	SV	IP	H	R	HR	HB	BB	SO	RAT	ERA	ERA+	OAV	OOB	BH	AVG	PB	PR	PR+	PD	TPI
1999 Pit-N	0	0	—	4	0	0	0	0	5^{1}	5	2	0	1	2	4	13.5	3.38	135	.250	.348	0	.000	-0	1	1	-0	0.0
2000 Phi-N	0	1	.000	30	0	0	0	0	34^{1}	39	28	2	1	24	32	16.8	6.55	72	.293	.405	0	—	0	-7	-7	0	-0.3
Total 2	0	1	.000	34	0	0	0	0	39^{2}	44	30	2	2	26	36	16.3	6.13	77	.288	.398	0	.000	-0	-7	-6	0	-0.3

● RAY BOYD Boyd, Raymond C. b: 2/11/1887, Hortonville, Ind. d: 2/11/20, Hortonville, Ind. BR/TR, 5'10", 160 lbs. Deb: 9/24/10

YEAR TM/L	W	L	PCT	G	GS	CG	SH	SV	IP	H	R	HR	HB	BB	SO	RAT	ERA	ERA+	OAV	OOB	BH	AVG	PB	PR	PR+	PD	TPI
1910 StL-A	0	2	.000	3	2	1	0	0	14^{1}	16	10	0	1	5	6	13.8	4.40	56	.286	.355	1	.200	-0	-3	-3	-1	-0.5
1911 Cin-N	2	2	.500	7	4	3	0	1	44	34	22	0	2	19	20	11.3	2.66	124	.206	.296	1	.083	-0	4	3	-0	0.3
Total 2	2	4	.333	10	6	4	0	1	58^{1}	50	32	0	3	24	26	11.9	3.09	101	.226	.310	2	.118	-0	1	0	-1	-0.2

● BILL BOYD Boyd, William J. b: 12/22/1852, New York, N.Y. d: 9/30/12, Jamaica, N.Y. Deb: 4/22/1872 MU♦

YEAR TM/L	W	L	PCT	G	GS	CG	SH	SV	IP	H	R	HR	HB	BB	SO	RAT	ERA	ERA+	OAV	OOB	BH	AVG	PB	PR	PR+	PD	TPI
1875 Atl-n	0	0	—	1	0	0	0	0	1^{2}	4	3	0		0	0	21.6	0.00	—	.444	.444	44	.291	0	0	0		0.0

YEAR	TM/L	W	L	PCT	G	GS	CG	SH	SV	IP	H	R	HR	HB	BB	SO	RAT	ERA	ERA+	OAV	OOB	BH	AVG	PB	PR	PR+	PD	TPI
● **CLOYD BOYER**	Boyer, Cloyd Victor "Junior" b: 9/1/27, Alba, Mo. BR/TR, 6'1", 188 lbs. Deb: 4/23/49 FC																											
1949	StL-N	0	0	—	4	1	0	0	0	3^1	5	4	0	0	7	0	32.4	10.80	39	.357	.571	0	—	0	-3	-2	0	-0.1
1950	StL-N	7	7	.500	36	14	6	1	1	120^1	105	52	15	3	49	82	11.7	3.52	122	.233	.312	6	.182	0	8	10	0	1.1
1951	StL-N	2	5	.286	19	8	1	0	1	63^1	68	42	9	3	46	40	16.6	5.26	75	.286	.408	4	.200	0	-9	-9	-2	-1.1
1952	StL-N	6	6	.500	23	14	4	2	0	110^1	108	56	11	4	47	44	13.0	4.24	88	.258	.338	8	.211	2	-6	-7	-2	-0.6
1955	KC-A	5	5	.500	30	11	2	0	0	98^1	107	81	21	7	69	32	16.7	6.22	67	.282	.402	2	.069	-2	-25	-21	-1	-2.1
Total	5	20	23	.465	112	48	13	3	2	395^2	393	235	56	17	218	198	14.3	4.73	86	.262	.362	20	.167	1	-34	-29	-4	-2.8
● **HENRY BOYLE**	Boyle, Henry J. "Handsome Henry" b: 9/20/1860, Philadelphia, Pa. d: 5/25/32, Philadelphia, Pa. TR, Deb: 7/9/1884 ♦																											
1884	StL-U	15	3	.833	19	16	16	2	1	150	118	63	3		10	88	7.7	1.74	138	.202	.215	68	.260	-1	12	11	-1	0.9
1885	StL-N	16	24	.400	42	39	39	1	0	366^2	346	207	2		100	133	10.9	2.75	100	.239	.288	52	.202	1	3	0	-1	0.0
1886	StL-N	9	15	.375	25	24	23	2	0	210	183	106	5		46	101	9.8	**1.76**	**184**	.220	.261	27	.250	4	36	35	1	4.1
1887	Ind-N	13	24	.351	38	38	37	0	0	328	425	204	11	12	69	85	12.0	3.65	114	.301	.307	36	.240	-1	15	18	-4	1.2
1888	Ind-N	15	22	.405	37	37	36	3	0	323	315	179	11	10	58	98	10.7	3.26	91	.245	.283	18	.144	-3	-15	-10	3	-1.1
1889	Ind-N	21	23	.477	46	45	38	2	0	378^2	422	224	14	14	95	97	12.6	3.92	106	.273	.321	38	.245	5	4	10	-5	1.0
Total	6	89	111	.445	207	199	189	10	1	1756^1	1809	983	46	36	378	602	11.0	3.06	110	.255	.289	239	.226	5	56	61	-7	6.1
● **HARRY BOYLES**	Boyles, Harry "Stretch" b: 11/29/13, Granite City, Ill. BR/TR, 6'5", 185 lbs. Deb: 8/3/38																											
1938	Chi-A	0	4	.000	9	2	1	0	1	29^1	31	27	2	2	25	18	17.8	5.22	94	.263	.400	1	.125	-1	-1	-1	1	-0.1
1939	Chi-A	0	0	—	2	0	0	0	0	3^1	4	4	0	0	6	1	27.0	10.80	44	.308	.526	0	.000	-0	-2	-2	-0	-0.1
Total	2	0	4	.000	11	2	1	0	1	32^2	35	31	2	2	31	19	18.7	5.79	84	.267	.415	1	.111	-1	-4	-3	1	-0.2
● **MARSHALL BOZE**	Boze, Marshall Wayne b: 5/23/71, San Manuel, Ariz. BR/TR, 6'1", 214 lbs. Deb: 4/28/96																											
1996	Mil-A	0	2	.000	25	0	0	0	1	32^1	47	29	5	6	25	19	21.7	7.79	67	.362	.484	0	—	0	-10	-9	1	-0.4
● **GENE BRABENDER**	Brabender, Eugene Mathew b: 8/16/41, Madison, Wis. d: 12/27/96, Madison, Wis. BR/TR, 6'5.5", 225 lbs. Deb: 5/11/66																											
1966	Bal-A	4	3	.571	31	1	0	0	2	71	57	30	4	1	29	62	11.0	3.55	94	.229	.312	1	.077	-1	-1	-2	0	-0.2
1967	Bal-A	6	4	.600	14	14	3	1	0	94	77	38	6	1	23	71	9.7	3.35	94	.220	.270	2	.071	-1	-1	-2	-0	-0.4
1968	Bal-A	6	7	.462	37	15	3	2	3	124^2	116	52	9	3	48	92	12.1	3.32	88	.248	.322	3	.086	-0	-5	-6	-1	-0.8
1969	Sea-A	13	14	.481	40	29	7	1	0	202^1	193	111	26	13	103	139	13.7	4.36	83	.254	.353	9	.129	-1	-16	-16	-3	-2.3
1970	Mil-A	6	15	.286	29	21	2	0	1	128^2	127	94	9	2	79	76	14.5	6.02	63	.255	.359	4	.098	-2	-33	-31	-0	-4.6
Total	5	35	43	.449	151	80	15	4	6	620^2	570	325	54	20	282	440	12.6	4.25	80	.245	.332	19	.102	-5	-56	-58	-3	-8.3
● **JACK BRACKEN**	Bracken, John James b: 4/14/1881, Cleveland, Ohio d: 7/16/54, Highland Park, Mich. BR/TR, 5'11", 175 lbs. Deb: 8/7/01																											
1901	Cle-A	4	8	.333	12	12	12	0	0	100	137	94	4	10	31	18	16.0	6.21	57	.322	.381	10	.227	0	-28	-30	-1	-2.7
● **JOHN BRACKENRIDGE**	Brackenridge, John Givler b: 12/24/1880, Harrisburg, Pa. d: 3/20/53, Harrisburg, Pa. BR/TR, 6', Deb: 4/15/04																											
1904	Phi-N	0	1	.000	7	1	0	0	0	34	37	32	4	4	16	11	15.1	5.56	48	.298	.396	2	.154	-0	-11	-11	2	-0.4
● **DON BRADEY**	Bradey, Donald Eugene b: 10/4/34, Charlotte, N.C. BR/TR, 5'9", 180 lbs. Deb: 9/25/64																											
1964	Hou-N	0	2	.000	3	1	0	0	0	2^1	6	7	0	0	3	2	34.7	19.29	18	.429	.529	0	—	0	-4	-4	-0	-0.8
● **CHAD BRADFORD**	Bradford, Chadwick L. b: 9/14/74, Jackson, Miss. BR/TR, 6'5", 205 lbs. Deb: 8/1/98																											
1998	Chi-A	2	1	.667	29	0	0	0	1	30^2	27	16	0	0	7	11	10.0	3.23	141	.229	.272	0	—	0	5	5	0	0.5
1999	Chi-A	0	0	—	3	0	0	0	0	3^2	9	8	1	0	5	0	34.4	19.64	25	.474	.583	0	—	0	-6	-6	1	-0.2
2000	*Chi-A	1	0	1.000	12	0	0	0	0	13^2	13	4	0	0	1	9	9.2	1.98	251	.255	.269	0	—	0	4	5	0	0.3
Total	3	3	1	.750	44	0	0	0	1	48	49	28	1	0	13	20	11.6	4.13	114	.261	.308	0	—	0	3	3	1	0.6
● **LARRY BRADFORD**	Bradford, Larry b: 12/21/49, Chicago, Ill. d: 9/11/98, Atlanta, Ga. BR/TL, 6'1", 200 lbs. Deb: 9/24/77																											
1977	Atl-N	0	0	—	2	0	0	0	0	2^2	3	1	1	0	0	1	10.1	3.38	132	.273	.273	0	—	0	0	0	0	0.0
1979	Atl-N	1	0	1.000	21	0	0	0	2	19	11	5	0	1	10	11	10.4	0.95	428	.172	.293	0	.000	-0	6	6	0	0.5
1980	Atl-N	3	4	.429	56	0	0	0	4	55^1	49	20	3	1	22	32	11.7	2.44	154	.243	.320	0	.000	-0	7	8	-0	1.0
1981	Atl-N	2	0	1.000	25	0	0	0	1	26^2	26	13	1	0	12	14	12.8	3.71	97	.268	.349	1	1.000	0	-1	-0	0	0.0
Total	4	6	4	.600	104	0	0	0	7	103^2	89	39	5	2	44	58	11.7	2.52	150	.238	.321	1	.200	-0	13	14	1	1.5
● **BILL BRADFORD**	Bradford, William D b: 8/28/21, Choctaw, Ark. BR/TR, 6'2", 180 lbs. Deb: 4/24/56																											
1956	KC-A	0	0	—	1	0	0	0	0	2	2	2	2	0	1	0	13.5	9.00	48	.250	.333	0	—	0	-1	-1	0	0.0
● **FRED BRADLEY**	Bradley, Fred Langdon b: 7/31/20, Parsons, Kan. BR/TR, 6'1", 180 lbs. Deb: 5/1/48																											
1948	Chi-A	0	0	—	8	0	0	0	0	15^2	11	12	2	1	4	2	9.2	4.60	93	.190	.254	0	.000	-0	-1	-1	0	0.0
1949	Chi-A	0	0	—	1	1	0	0	0	2	4	3	0	0	3	0	31.5	13.50	31	.444	.583	0	.000	-0	-2	-2	0	-0.1
Total	2	0	0	—	9	1	0	0	0	17^2	15	15	2	1	7	2	11.7	5.60	76	.224	.307	0	.000	-0	-3	-3	0	-0.1
● **FOGHORN BRADLEY**	Bradley, George H. b: 7/1/1855, Milford, Mass. d: 3/31/1900, Philadelphia, Pa. BR/TR, Deb: 8/23/1876 U																											
1876	Bos-N	9	10	.474	22	21	16	1	1	173^1	201	116	1		16	16	11.3	2.49	91	.258	.279	19	.226	-1	-4	-5	-1	-0.5
● **GEORGE BRADLEY**	Bradley, George Washington "Grin" b: 7/13/1852, Reading, Pa. d: 10/2/31, Philadelphia, Pa. BR/TR, 5'10.5", 175 lbs. Deb: 5/4/1875 ♦																											
1875	StL-n	33	26	.559	60	60	57	5	0	535^2	540	304	3		17	60	9.4	2.13	94	.241	.247	62	.244	7	5	-8		0.1
1876	StL-N	45	19	.703	64	64	63	**16**	0	573	470	229	3		38	103	**8.0**	**1.23**	**174**	**.207**	**.224**	66	.246	4	**69**	63	1	6.2
1877	Chi-N	18	23	.439	50	44	35	2	0	394	452	266	4		39	59	11.2	3.31	90	.269	.286	52	.243	0	-22	-14	1	-1.2
1879	Tro-N	13	40	.245	54	54	53	3	0	487	590	361	12		26	133	11.4	2.85	88	.275	.284	62	.247	4	-19	-19	4	-0.6
1880	Pro-N	13	8	.619	28	20	16	4	2	196	158	66	2		6	54	7.5	1.38	160	.210	.217	70	.227	1	22	19	1	2.1
1881	Cle-N	2	4	.333	6	6	5	0	0	51	70	36	2		3	6	12.9	3.88	67	.320	.329	60	.249	0	-6	-8	-1	-0.7
1882	Cle-N	6	9	.400	18	16	15	0	0	147	164	102	5		22	32	11.4	3.73	75	.264	.289	21	.183	-3	-14	-16	3	-1.3
1883	Phi-a	16	7	.696	26	23	22	0	0	214^1	215	129	7		22	56	10.0	3.15	112	.244	.263	73	.234	-0	4	9	-1	0.6
1884	Cin-U	25	15	.625	41	38	36	3	0	342	350	203	7		23	168	9.8	2.71	95	.248	.260	43	.190	-12	-10	-5	2	-1.3
Total	8	138	125	.525	287	265	245	28	2	2404^1	2469	1392	42		179	611	9.9	2.50	103	.247	.262	456	.227	-5	23	20	11	3.8
● **HERB BRADLEY**	Bradley, Herbert Theodore b: 1/3/03, Agenda, Kan. d: 10/16/59, Clay Center, Kan. BR/TR, 6', 170 lbs. Deb: 5/9/27																											
1927	Bos-A	1	1	.500	6	2	2	0	0	23	16	9	0	2	7	6	9.8	3.13	135	.198	.278	3	.429	1	3	3	-0	0.3
1928	Bos-A	0	3	.000	15	5	1	1	0	47^1	64	41	2	2	16	14	15.6	7.23	57	.339	.396	2	.154	-1	-17	-16	1	-0.8
1929	Bos-A	0	0	—	3	0	0	0	0	4	7	3	1	0	2	0	20.3	6.75	63	.438	.500	0	.000	-0	-1	-1	0	0.0
Total	3	1	4	.200	24	7	3	1	0	74^1	87	53	3	4	25	20	14.0	5.93	70	.304	.368	5	.238	-0	-15	-14	1	-0.5
● **RYAN BRADLEY**	Bradley, Ryan J. b: 10/26/75, Covina, Cal. BR/TR, 6'4", 220 lbs. Deb: 8/22/98																											
1998	NY-A	2	1	.667	5	1	0	0	0	12^2	12	9	2	1	9	13	15.6	5.68	77	.250	.379	0	—	0	-1	-2	-0	-0.4
● **BERT BRADLEY**	Bradley, Steven Bert b: 12/23/56, Athens, Ga. BB/TR, 6'1", 190 lbs. Deb: 9/3/83																											
1983	Oak-A	0	0	—	6	0	0	0	0	8^1	14	7	1	0	4	3	19.4	6.48	60	.400	.462	0	—	0	-2	-3	1	-0.1
● **TOM BRADLEY**	Bradley, Thomas William b: 3/16/47, Asheville, N.C. BR/TR, 6'3", 185 lbs. Deb: 9/9/69																											
1969	Cal-A	0	1	.000	3	0	0	0	0	2	9	9	1	0	0	2	40.5	27.00	13	.600	.600	0	—	0	-5	-5	0	-0.9
1970	Cal-A	2	5	.286	17	11	1	1	0	69^2	71	38	3	1	33	53	13.6	4.13	87	.270	.354	3	.167	0	-3	-4	-0	-0.4
1971	Chi-A	15	15	.500	45	39	7	6	2	285^2	273	111	16	2	74	206	11.0	2.96	121	.248	.297	15	.156	-1	16	19	-2	1.7
1972	Chi-A	15	14	.517	40	40	11	2	0	260	225	94	19	2	65	209	10.1	2.98	105	.231	.280	12	.132	-2	3	5	-0	0.2
1973	SF-N	13	12	.520	35	34	6	1	0	224	212	109	26	3	69	136	11.4	3.90	98	.246	.304	15	.195	1	-6	-2	-2	-0.3
1974	SF-N	8	11	.421	30	21	2	0	0	134^1	152	90	15	1	52	72	13.7	5.16	74	.282	.346	3	.075	-2	-23	-19	-1	-2.8
1975	SF-N	2	3	.400	13	6	0	0	0	42	57	33	6	1	18	13	16.3	6.21	61	.326	.392	0	.000	-1	-12	-11	0	-1.2
Total	7	55	61	.474	183	151	27	10	2	1017^2	999	484	86	10	311	691	11.7	3.72	96	.254	.311	48	.145	-5	-30	-17	-5	-3.7
● **BILL BRADLEY**	Bradley, William Joseph b: 2/13/1878, Cleveland, Ohio d: 3/11/54, Cleveland, Ohio BR/TR, 6', 185 lbs. Deb: 8/26/1899 M♦																											
1901	Cle-A	0	0	—	1	0	0	0	0	1	4	3	0	0	0	0	36.0	0.00	—	.571	.571	151	.293	0	0	0	-0	0.0

● JOE BRADSHAW Bradshaw, Joe Siah b: 8/17/1897, RoEllen, Tenn. d: 1/30/85, Tavares, Fla. BR/TR, 6'2.5", 200 lbs. Deb: 5/9/29

YEAR TM/L	W	L	PCT	G	GS	CG	SH	SV	IP	H	R	HR	HB	BB	SO	RAT	ERA	ERA+	OAV	OOB	BH	AVG	PB	PR	PR+	PD	TPI
1929 Bro-N	0	0	—	2	0	0	0	0	4	3	3	0	2	4	1	20.3	4.50	103	.231	.474	0	—	0	0	0	0	0.0

● NEAL BRADY Brady, Cornelius Joseph b: 3/4/1897, Covington, Ky. d: 6/19/47, Fort Mitchell, Ky BR/TR, 6'0.5", 197 lbs. Deb: 9/25/15

YEAR TM/L	W	L	PCT	G	GS	CG	SH	SV	IP	H	R	HR	HB	BB	SO	RAT	ERA	ERA+	OAV	OOB	BH	AVG	PB	PR	PR+	PD	TPI
1915 NY-A	0	0	—	2	1	0	0	0	8^{2}	9	3	0	0	7	6	16.6	3.12	94	.281	.410	0	.000	-1	-0	-0	-0	-0.1
1917 NY-A	1	0	1.000	2	1	0	0	0	9	6	2	0	0	5	4	11.0	2.00	134	.188	.297	1	.500	0	1	1	0	0.2
1925 Cin-N	1	3	.250	20	3	2	0	1	63^{2}	73	44	4	4	20	12	13.7	4.66	88	.289	.350	6	.240	1	-3	-4	0	-0.1
Total 3	2	3	.400	24	5	2	0	1	81^{1}	88	49	4	4	32	22	13.7	4.20	91	.278	.351	7	.226	1	-2	-3	1	0.0

● JIM BRADY Brady, James Joseph "Diamond Jim" b: 3/2/36, Jersey City, N.J. BL/TL, 6'2", 185 lbs. Deb: 5/12/56

YEAR TM/L	W	L	PCT	G	GS	CG	SH	SV	IP	H	R	HR	HB	BB	SO	RAT	ERA	ERA+	OAV	OOB	BH	AVG	PB	PR	PR+	PD	TPI
1956 Det-A	0	0	—	6	0	0	0	0	6^{1}	15	21	3	0	11	3	36.9	28.42	14	.484	.619	0	—	0	-17	-17	0	-0.8

● KING BRADY Brady, James Ward b: 5/28/1881, Elmer, N.J. d: 8/21/47, Albany, N.Y. BR/TR, 6', 190 lbs. Deb: 9/21/05

YEAR TM/L	W	L	PCT	G	GS	CG	SH	SV	IP	H	R	HR	HB	BB	SO	RAT	ERA	ERA+	OAV	OOB	BH	AVG	PB	PR	PR+	PD	TPI
1905 Phi-N	1	1	.500	2	2	2	0	0	13	19	7	0	0	2	3	14.5	3.46	84	.333	.356	1	.200	-0	-1	-1	-0	-0.1
1906 Pit-N	1	1	.500	3	2	1	0	0	23	30	7	0	0	4	14	13.3	2.35	114	.313	.340	1	.100	-1	1	1	-1	-0.1
1907 Pit-N	0	0	—	1	0	0	0	0	2	2	1	0	0	1	0	13.5	0.00	—	.286	.375	0	—	0	1	1	-0	0.0
1908 Bos-A	1	0	1.000	1	1	1	1	0	9	8	0	0	0	0	3	8.0	0.00	—	.242	.242	0	.000	-0	2	2	-0	0.2
1912 Bos-N	0	0	—	1	0	0	0	0	2^{2}	5	6	0	0	3	0	27.0	20.25	18	.313	.421	0	.000	-0	-5	-5	-0	-0.2
Total 5	3	2	.600	8	5	4	1	0	49^{2}	64	21	0	0	10	20	13.4	3.08	89	.306	.338	2	.111	-1	-2	-2	-1	-0.2

● BILL BRADY Brady, William Aloysius "King" b: 8/18/1889, New York, N.Y. TR, 6'2", Deb: 7/9/12

YEAR TM/L	W	L	PCT	G	GS	CG	SH	SV	IP	H	R	HR	HB	BB	SO	RAT	ERA	ERA+	OAV	OOB	BH	AVG	PB	PR	PR+	PD	TPI
1912 Bos-N	0	0	—	1	0	0	0	0	1	2	0	0	0	0	0	18.0	0.00	—	.500	.500	0	—	0	0	0	-0	0.0

● DICK BRAGGINS Braggins, Richard Realf b: 12/25/1879, Mercer, Pa. d: 8/16/63, Lake Wales, Fla. BR/TR, 5'11", 170 lbs. Deb: 5/16/01

YEAR TM/L	W	L	PCT	G	GS	CG	SH	SV	IP	H	R	HR	HB	BB	SO	RAT	ERA	ERA+	OAV	OOB	BH	AVG	PB	PR	PR+	PD	TPI
1901 Cle-A	1	2	.333	4	3	2	0	0	32	44	28	1	1	15	1	16.9	4.78	74	.324	.395	2	.154	-1	-4	-5	0	-0.4

● ASA BRAINARD Brainard, Asa "Count" b: 1841, Albany, N.Y. d: 12/29/1888, Denver, Colo. TR, 5'8.5", 150 lbs. Deb: 5/5/1871 ◆

YEAR TM/L	W	L	PCT	G	GS	CG	SH	SV	IP	H	R	HR	HB	BB	SO	RAT	ERA	ERA+	OAV	OOB	BH	AVG	PB	PR	PR+	PD	TPI
1871 Oly-n	12	15	.444	30	30	30	0	0	264	361	292	4		37	13	13.6	4.50	93	.288	.308	30	.224	-6	-8	-10		-1.0
1872 Oly-n	2	7	.222	9	9	9	0	0	79	148	140	0		5	1	17.4	6.38	56	.333	.341	16	.372	4	-24	-25		-1.4
Man-n	0	2	.000	2	2	1	0	0	8	13	17	1		0	0	14.6	5.63	64	.260	.260	5	.200	-0	-2	-2		-0.3
Yr	2	9	.182	11	11	10	0	0	87	161	157	1		5	1	17.2	6.31	57	.326	.333	21	.309	3	-26	-27		-1.7
1873 Bal-n	5	7	.417	14	14	12	0	0	108^{2}	182	139	0		9	3	15.8	4.14	79	.323	.334	18	.261	0	-11	-11		-0.8
1874 Bal-n	5	22	.185	30	27	25	0	0	240	405	329	1		27	8	16.2	3.71	60	.327	.341	47	.240	-1	-41	-39		-3.2
Total 4 n	24	53	.312	85	82	77	0	0	699^{2}	1109	917	6		78	25	15.3	4.40	51	.312	.327	116	.248	-4	-172	-166		-6.7

● AL BRAITHWOOD Braithwood, Alfred b: 2/15/1892, Braceville, Ill. d: 11/24/60, Rowlesburg, W.Va. BR/TL, 6'1.5", 145 lbs. Deb: 9/1/15

YEAR TM/L	W	L	PCT	G	GS	CG	SH	SV	IP	H	R	HR	HB	BB	SO	RAT	ERA	ERA+	OAV	OOB	BH	AVG	PB	PR	PR+	PD	TPI
1915 Pit-F	0	0	—	2	0	0	0	0	3	0	0	0	0	0	2	0.0	0.00	—	.000	.000	0	—	0	1	1	0	0.0

● ERV BRAME Brame, Ervin Beckham b: 10/12/01, Big Rock, Tenn. d: 11/22/49, Hopkinsville, Ky. BL/TR, 6'2", 190 lbs. Deb: 4/14/28

YEAR TM/L	W	L	PCT	G	GS	CG	SH	SV	IP	H	R	HR	HB	BB	SO	RAT	ERA	ERA+	OAV	OOB	BH	AVG	PB	PR	PR+	PD	TPI
1928 Pit-N	7	4	.636	24	11	6	0	0	95^{2}	110	62	5	1	44	22	14.6	5.08	80	.291	.366	13	.265	4	-12	-11	-1	-0.8
1929 Pit-N	16	11	.593	37	28	19	1	0	229^{2}	250	123	17	0	71	68	12.6	4.55	105	.278	.331	36	.310	12	4	6	-4	1.2
1930 Pit-N	17	8	.680	32	28	**22**	0	1	235^{2}	291	153	21	5	56	55	13.4	4.70	106	.305	.346	41	.353	11	7	7	-3	1.3
1931 Pit-N	9	13	.409	26	21	15	2	0	179^{2}	211	102	14	0	45	33	12.8	4.21	91	.295	.336	26	.274	6	-7	-7	-2	-0.4
1932 Pit-N	3	1	.750	23	3	0	0	0	51	84	52	6	0	16	10	17.6	7.41	51	.365	.407	5	.250	1	-20	-21	-1	-1.4
Total 5	52	37	.584	142	91	62	3	1	791^{2}	946	492	63	6	232	188	13.5	4.76	94	.298	.347	121	.306	33	-27	-25	-11	-0.1

● RALPH BRANCA Branca, Ralph Theodore Joseph "Hawk" b: 1/6/26, Mt.Vernon, N.Y. BR/TR, 6'3", 220 lbs. Deb: 6/12/44

YEAR TM/L	W	L	PCT	G	GS	CG	SH	SV	IP	H	R	HR	HB	BB	SO	RAT	ERA	ERA+	OAV	OOB	BH	AVG	PB	PR	PR+	PD	TPI
1944 Bro-N	0	2	.000	21	1	0	0	1	44^{2}	46	36	2	5	32	16	16.7	7.05	50	.274	.405	0	.000	-1	-17	-18	-0	-1.0
1945 Bro-N	5	6	.455	16	15	7	0	1	109^{2}	73	44	4	0	79	69	12.5	3.04	124	.189	.327	4	.100	-3	9	9	0	0.6
1946 Bro-N	3	1	.750	24	10	2	2	3	67^{1}	62	34	4	0	41	42	13.8	3.88	87	.246	.352	2	.111	0	-3	-4	-1	-0.4
1947 *Bro-N☆	21	12	.636	43	36	15	4	1	280	251	100	22	6	98	148	11.4	2.67	155	.240	.309	12	.124	-3	43	45	-4	4.3
1948 Bro-N★	14	9	.609	36	28	11	1	1	215^{2}	189	93	24	4	80	122	11.4	3.51	114	.232	.304	15	.203	1	11	12	-4	0.8
1949 *Bro-N☆	13	5	.722	34	27	9	2	1	186^{2}	181	100	21	2	91	109	13.2	4.39	93	.253	.339	5	.081	-2	-7	-6	-4	-1.1
1950 Bro-N	7	9	.438	43	15	5	0	7	142	152	80	24	0	55	100	13.1	4.69	87	.271	.336	4	.118	1	-9	-9	-1	-1.0
1951 Bro-N	13	12	.520	42	27	13	3	3	204	180	81	19	3	85	118	11.8	3.26	120	.237	.316	11	.175	-1	16	15	-3	1.4
1952 Bro-N	4	2	.667	16	7	2	0	0	61	52	29	8	4	21	26	11.4	3.84	95	.232	.309	3	.158	-0	-1	-1	-1	-0.3
1953 Bro-N	0	0	—	7	0	0	0	0	11	15	12	4	2	5	5	18.0	9.82	43	.341	.431	0	—	0	-7	-7	-0	-0.3
Det-A	4	7	.364	17	14	7	0	1	102	98	55	7	2	31	50	11.6	4.15	98	.253	.311	4	.118	-1	-2	-1	-1	-0.3
1954 Det-A	3	3	.500	17	5	0	0	0	45^{1}	63	33	10	2	30	15	18.9	5.76	64	.330	.426	4	.308	2	-10	-10	-0	-1.1
NY-A	1	0	1.000	5	3	0	0	0	12^{2}	9	5	0	1	13	7	16.3	2.84	121	.209	.404	2	.500	1	1	1	0	0.2
Yr	4	3	.571	22	8	0	0	0	58	72	38	10	3	43	22	18.3	5.12	71	.308	.421	6	.353	2	-9	-10	-0	-0.9
1956 Bro-N	0	0	—	1	0	0	0	0	2	1	0	0	0	2	2	13.5	0.00	—	.143	.333	0	—	0	1	1	0	0.1
Total 12	88	68	.564	322	188	71	12	19	1484	1372	702	149	31	663	829	12.5	3.79	104	.245	.328	66	.142	-6	25	27	-18	1.9

● HARVEY BRANCH Branch, Harvey Alfred b: 2/8/39, Memphis, Tenn. BR/TL, 6', 175 lbs. Deb: 9/18/62

YEAR TM/L	W	L	PCT	G	GS	CG	SH	SV	IP	H	R	HR	HB	BB	SO	RAT	ERA	ERA+	OAV	OOB	BH	AVG	PB	PR	PR+	PD	TPI
1962 StL-N	0	1	.000	1	1	0	0	0	5	5	3	1	0	5	2	18.0	5.40	79	.263	.417	0	.000	-0	-1	-1	-0	-0.1

● NORM BRANCH Branch, Norman Downs "Red" b: 3/22/15, Spokane, Wash. d: 11/21/71, Navasota, Tex. BR/TR, 6'3", 200 lbs. Deb: 5/5/41

YEAR TM/L	W	L	PCT	G	GS	CG	SH	SV	IP	H	R	HR	HB	BB	SO	RAT	ERA	ERA+	OAV	OOB	BH	AVG	PB	PR	PR+	PD	TPI
1941 NY-A	5	1	.833	27	0	0	0	2	47	37	16	2	0	26	28	12.1	2.87	137	.224	.330	0	.000	-1	7	6	1	0.7
1942 NY-A	0	1	.000	10	0	0	0	2	15^{2}	18	15	3	0	16	13	19.5	6.32	54	.290	.436	1	.333	0	-5	-5	0	-0.4
Total 2	5	2	.714	37	0	0	0	4	62^{2}	55	31	5	0	42	41	13.9	3.73	102	.242	.361	1	.077	-1	2	1	1	0.3

● ROY BRANCH Branch, Roy b: 7/12/53, St.Louis, Mo. BR/TR, 6', 175 lbs. Deb: 9/11/79

YEAR TM/L	W	L	PCT	G	GS	CG	SH	SV	IP	H	R	HR	HB	BB	SO	RAT	ERA	ERA+	OAV	OOB	BH	AVG	PB	PR	PR+	PD	TPI
1979 Sea-A	0	1	.000	2	2	0	0	0	11^{1}	12	11	2	0	7	6	15.1	7.94	55	.273	.373	0	—	0	-5	-4	-0	-0.3

● MARK BRANDENBURG Brandenburg, Mark Clay b: 7/14/70, Houston, Tex. BR/TR, 6', 180 lbs. Deb: 7/20/95

YEAR TM/L	W	L	PCT	G	GS	CG	SH	SV	IP	H	R	HR	HB	BB	SO	RAT	ERA	ERA+	OAV	OOB	BH	AVG	PB	PR	PR+	PD	TPI
1995 Tex-A	0	1	.000	11	0	0	0	0	27^{1}	36	18	5	1	7	21	14.5	5.93	82	.316	.361	0	—	0	-4	-3	-0	-0.2
1996 Tex-A	1	3	.250	26	0	0	0	0	47^{2}	48	22	3	2	25	37	14.2	3.21	163	.262	.357	0	—	0	9	10	-1	0.6
Bos-A	4	2	.667	29	0	0	0	0	28^{1}	28	13	5	1	8	29	11.8	3.81	133	.250	.306	0	—	0	4	4	0	0.7
Yr	5	5	.500	55	0	0	0	0	76	76	35	8	3	33	66	13.3	3.43	151	.258	.338	0	—	0	13	14	-1	1.3
1997 Bos-A	0	2	.000	31	0	0	0	0	41	49	25	3	2	16	34	14.7	5.49	85	.299	.368	0	—	0	-4	-4	0	-0.2
Total 3	5	8	.385	97	0	0	0	0	144^{1}	161	78	16	6	56	121	13.9	4.49	110	.281	.351	0	—	0	5	7	-1	0.9

● CHICK BRANDOM Brandom, Chester Milton b: 3/31/1887, Coldwater, Kan. d: 10/7/58, Santa Ana, Cal. BR/TR, 5'8", 161 lbs. Deb: 9/3/08

YEAR TM/L	W	L	PCT	G	GS	CG	SH	SV	IP	H	R	HR	HB	BB	SO	RAT	ERA	ERA+	OAV	OOB	BH	AVG	PB	PR	PR+	PD	TPI
1908 Pit-N	1	0	1.000	3	1	0	1	1	17	13	5	0	1	4	8	9.5	0.53	435	.228	.290	1	.143	-0	3	3	0	0.3
1909 Pit-N	1	0	1.000	13	2	1	0	2	40^{2}	33	12	0	1	10	21	9.7	1.11	246	.239	.295	1	.100	-1	7	7	1	0.4
1915 New-F	1	1	.500	16	1	1	0	0	50^{1}	55	36	0	1	15	15	12.7	3.40	75	.293	.348	2	.200	1	-4	-5	1	-0.1
Total 3	3	1	.750	32	4	2	0	3	108	101	53	0	3	29	44	11.1	2.08	124	.264	.320	4	.148	-0	6	6	2	0.6

● BUCKY BRANDON Brandon, Darrell G b: 7/8/40, Nacogdoches, Tex. BR/TR, 6'2", 200 lbs. Deb: 4/19/66

YEAR TM/L	W	L	PCT	G	GS	CG	SH	SV	IP	H	R	HR	HB	BB	SO	RAT	ERA	ERA+	OAV	OOB	BH	AVG	PB	PR	PR+	PD	TPI
1966 Bos-A	8	8	.500	40	17	5	2	2	157^{2}	129	70	13	4	70	101	11.6	3.31	115	.222	.310	8	.182	1	2	8	0	1.0
1967 Bos-A	5	11	.313	39	19	2	0	3	157^{2}	147	86	21	7	59	96	12.2	4.17	84	.245	.320	8	.186	1	-16	-11	-0	-1.1
1968 Bos-A	0	0	—	8	0	0	0	0	12^{2}	19	11	1	1	9	10	20.6	6.39	49	.333	.433	0	.000	-0	-5	-4	0	-0.3
1969 Sea-A	0	1	.000	8	1	0	0	0	15	15	15	4	2	16	10	19.8	8.40	43	.250	.423	0	—	0	-8	-8	-0	-0.5
Min-A	0	0	—	3	0	0	0	0	3^{1}	5	3	1	0	3	1	21.6	2.70	135	.357	.471	0	.000	0	0	0	-0	0.0
Yr	0	1	.000	11	1	0	0	0	18^{1}	20	18	5	2	19	11	20.1	7.36	49	.270	.432	0	.000	0	-8	-8	-0	-0.5
1971 Phi-N	6	6	.500	52	0	0	0	4	83	81	42	5	0	47	44	13.9	3.90	90	.264	.362	2	.154	-0	-4	-3	-1	-0.6
1972 Phi-N	7	7	.500	42	6	0	0	2	104^{1}	106	49	9	6	46	67	13.6	3.45	104	.268	.353	1	.067	-1	0	2	-2	-0.1
1973 Phi-N	2	4	.333	36	0	0	0	2	56^{1}	54	35	5	3	25	25	13.1	5.43	70	.261	.349	1	.200	0	-11	-10	0	-1.0
Total 7	28	37	.431	228	43	7	2	13	590	556	311	59	23	275	354	13.0	4.04	90	.250	.339	20	.164	1	-42	-26	-2	-2.6

● ED BRANDT Brandt, Edward Arthur "Big Ed" b: 2/17/05, Spokane, Wash. d: 11/1/44, Spokane, Wash. BL/TL, 6'1", 190 lbs. Deb: 4/26/28

YEAR TM/L	W	L	PCT	G	GS	CG	SH	SV	IP	H	R	HR	HB	BB	SO	RAT	ERA	ERA+	OAV	OOB	BH	AVG	PB	PR	PR+	PD	TPI
1928 Bos-N	9	21	.300	38	32	12	1	0	225^{1}	234	141	22	7	109	84	14.0	5.07	77	.273	.359	17	.243	5	-27	-30	2	-2.7

YEAR	TM/L	W	L	PCT	G	GS	CG	SH	SV	IP	H	R	HR	HB	BB	SO	RAT	ERA	ERA+	OAV	OOB	BH	AVG	PB	PR	PR+	PD	TPI
1929	Bos-N	8	13	.381	26	21	13	0	0	167^2	196	111	12	5	83	50	15.2	5.53	85	.302	.385	15	.234	2	-15	-16	2	-1.2
1930	Bos-N	4	11	.267	41	13	4	1	1	147^1	168	88	15	0	59	65	13.9	5.01	99	.291	.356	12	.240	1	-1	-1	2	0.1
1931	Bos-N	18	11	.621	33	29	23	3	2	250	228	94	11	4	77	112	11.1	2.92	130	.244	.304	21	.256	5	26	25	3	3.6
1932	Bos-N	16	16	.500	35	31	19	2	1	254	271	122	11	5	57	79	11.8	3.97	95	.275	.318	19	.207	-0	-3	-6	1	-0.6
1933	Bos-N	18	14	.563	41	32	23	4	4	287^2	256	85	10	3	77	104	10.5	2.60	118	.245	.298	30	.309	9	24	16	-0	2.9
1934	Bos-N	16	14	.533	40	29	20	3	5	255	249	111	13	4	83	106	11.9	3.53	108	.254	.315	23	.240	4	15	9	-3	1.2
1935	Bos-N	5	19	.208	29	25	12	0	0	174^2	224	110	12	1	66	61	15.0	5.00	76	.319	.378	13	.210	-0	-19	-25	1	-2.8
1936	Bro-N	11	13	.458	38	29	12	1	2	234	246	105	14	4	65	104	12.1	3.50	118	.268	.319	16	.190	0	14	16	-2	1.3
1937	Pit-N	11	10	.524	33	25	7	2	2	176^1	177	73	11	2	67	74	12.6	3.11	124	.263	.332	10	.169	1	16	15	1	1.8
1938	Pit-N	5	4	.556	24	13	5	1	0	96^1	93	44	3	0	35	38	12.0	3.46	110	.250	.314	11	.297	2	4	4	-1	0.5
Total	11	121	146	.453	378	279	150	18	17	2268^1	2342	1084	134	35	778	877	12.5	3.86	101	.269	.332	187	.236	30	34	5	6	4.1

● BILL BRANDT

Brandt, William George b: 3/21/15, Aurora, Ind. d: 5/16/68, Fort Wayne, Ind. BR/TR, 5'8.5", 170 lbs. Deb: 9/20/41

YEAR	TM/L	W	L	PCT	G	GS	CG	SH	SV	IP	H	R	HR	HB	BB	SO	RAT	ERA	ERA+	OAV	OOB	BH	AVG	PB	PR	PR+	PD	TPI
1941	Pit-N	0	1	.000	2	1	0	0	0	7	5	3	0	0	3	0	10.3	3.86	94	.200	.286	0	.000	-0	-0	-0	-0	-0.1
1942	Pit-N	1	1	.500	3	3	1	0	0	16^1	23	10	1	0	5	4	15.4	4.96	68	.343	.389	1	.143	-0	-3	-3	-0	-0.4
1943	Pit-N	4	1	.800	29	3	0	0	0	57^1	57	25	3	1	19	17	12.1	3.14	111	.248	.308	1	.143	-0	2	2	-0	0.1
Total	3	5	3	.625	34	7	1	0	0	80^2	85	38	4	1	27	21	12.6	3.57	97	.264	.323	2	.133	-1	-2	-1	-1	-0.4

● CLIFF BRANTLEY

Brantley, Clifford b: 4/12/68, Staten Island, N.Y. BR/TR, 6'1", 190 lbs. Deb: 9/3/91

YEAR	TM/L	W	L	PCT	G	GS	CG	SH	SV	IP	H	R	HR	HB	BB	SO	RAT	ERA	ERA+	OAV	OOB	BH	AVG	PB	PR	PR+	PD	TPI
1991	Phi-N	2	2	.500	6	5	0	0	0	31^2	26	12	0	2	19	25	13.4	3.41	108	.228	.348	0	.000	-1	1	1	0	0.0
1992	Phi-N	2	6	.250	28	9	0	0	0	76^1	71	45	6	4	58	32	15.7	4.60	76	.251	.386	3	.214	1	-9	-9	0	-0.8
Total	2	4	8	.333	34	14	0	0	0	108	97	57	6	6	77	57	15.0	4.25	83	.244	.375	3	.136	0	-8	-8	0	-0.8

● JEFF BRANTLEY

Brantley, Jeffrey Hoke b: 9/5/63, Florence, Ala. BR/TR, 5'11", 190 lbs. Deb: 8/5/88

YEAR	TM/L	W	L	PCT	G	GS	CG	SH	SV	IP	H	R	HR	HB	BB	SO	RAT	ERA	ERA+	OAV	OOB	BH	AVG	PB	PR	PR+	PD	TPI
1988	SF-N	0	1	.000	9	1	0	0	1	20^2	22	13	2	1	6	11	12.6	5.66	58	.275	.333	1	.500	0	-5	-6	1	-0.2
1989	*SF-N	7	1	.875	59	1	0	0	0	97^1	101	50	10	2	37	69	12.9	4.07	83	.271	.340	1	.083	-1	-6	-8	0	-0.7
1990	SF-N★	5	3	.625	55	0	0	0	19	86^2	77	18	3	3	33	61	11.7	1.56	234	.240	.317	2	.286	1	22	21	0	2.8
1991	SF-N	5	2	.714	67	0	0	0	15	95^1	78	27	8	5	52	81	12.7	2.45	146	.225	.335	0	.000	-0	13	12	-1	1.1
1992	SF-N	7	7	.500	56	4	0	0	7	91^2	67	32	8	3	45	86	11.3	2.95	112	.207	.310	1	.111	0	6	4	-1	0.6
1993	SF-N	5	6	.455	53	12	0	0	0	113^2	112	60	19	7	46	76	13.1	4.28	92	.259	.340	3	.107	-1	-3	-5	-2	-0.7
1994	Cin-N	6	6	.500	50	0	0	0	15	65^1	46	20	6	0	28	63	10.2	2.48	167	.202	.289	0	.000	-0	13	12	0	2.5
1995	*Cin-N	3	2	.600	56	0	0	0	28	70^1	53	22	11	1	20	62	9.5	2.82	146	.206	.266	0	.000	-0	11	10	-1	1.3
1996	Cin-N	1	2	.333	66	0	0	0	**44**	71	54	21	7	0	28	76	10.4	2.41	176	.215	.294	0	.000	-0	14	14	-1	2.0
1997	Cin-N	1	1	.500	13	0	0	0	1	11^2	9	5	2	2	7	16	13.9	3.86	111	.205	.340	0	—	0	0	1	-0	0.1
1998	StL-N	0	5	.000	48	0	0	0	14	50^2	40	26	12	1	18	48	10.5	4.44	95	.220	.294	0	—	0	-1	-1	-1	-0.3
1999	Phi-N	1	2	.333	10	0	0	0	5	8^2	5	6	0	0	8	11	13.5	5.19	91	.161	.333	0	—	0	-1	-0	0	-0.1
2000	Phi-N	2	7	.222	55	0	0	0	23	55^1	64	36	12	2	29	57	15.5	5.86	81	.288	.375	0	—	0	-7	-7	-1	-1.4
Total	13	43	45	.489	597	18	0	0	172	838^1	728	336	100	27	357	717	11.9	3.35	115	.236	.320	8	.118	-2	55	47	-6	7.0

● KITTY BRASHEAR

Brashear, Norman C. b: 8/27/1877, Mansfield, Ohio d: 12/22/34, Los Angeles, Cal. BR/TR, Deb: 6/25/1899 F

YEAR	TM/L	W	L	PCT	G	GS	CG	SH	SV	IP	H	R	HR	HB	BB	SO	RAT	ERA	ERA+	OAV	OOB	BH	AVG	PB	PR	PR+	PD	TPI
1899	Lou-N	1	0	1.000	3	0	0	0	0	8	8	7	0	1	2	5	12.4	4.50	86	.258	.324	1	.500	0	-1	-1	0	0.0

● JOHN BRAUN

Braun, John Paul b: 12/26/39, Madison, Wis. BR/TR, 6'5", 218 lbs. Deb: 10/2/64

YEAR	TM/L	W	L	PCT	G	GS	CG	SH	SV	IP	H	R	HR	HB	BB	SO	RAT	ERA	ERA+	OAV	OOB	BH	AVG	PB	PR	PR+	PD	TPI
1964	Mil-N	0	0	—	1	0	0	0	0	2	2	0	0	0	1	1	13.5	0.00	—	.286	.375	0	—	0	1	1	-0	0.0

● GARLAND BRAXTON

Braxton, Edgar Garland b: 6/10/1900, Snow Camp, N.C. d: 2/25/66, Norfolk, Va. BB/TL, 5'11", 152 lbs. Deb: 5/27/21

YEAR	TM/L	W	L	PCT	G	GS	CG	SH	SV	IP	H	R	HR	HB	BB	SO	RAT	ERA	ERA+	OAV	OOB	BH	AVG	PB	PR	PR+	PD	TPI
1921	Bos-N	1	3	.250	17	2	0	0	0	37^1	44	26	0	2	17	16	15.2	4.82	76	.310	.391	0	.000	-1	-4	-5	1	-0.5
1922	Bos-N	1	2	.333	25	5	2	0	0	66^2	75	37	3	4	24	15	13.9	3.38	118	.286	.355	1	.063	-2	5	5	-1	0.0
1925	NY-A	1	1	.500	3	2	0	0	0	19^1	26	14	1	1	5	11	14.9	6.52	65	.338	.386	2	.333	0	-5	-5	0	-0.4
1926	NY-A	5	1	.833	37	1	0	0	2	67^1	71	28	1	0	19	30	12.0	2.67	144	.275	.325	6	.300	1	10	9	0	0.9
1927	Was-A	10	9	.526	**58**	2	0	0	**13**	155^1	144	62	5	2	33	96	10.4	2.95	138	.246	.289	9	.231	0	**20**	**20**	-2	2.2
1928	Was-A	13	11	.542	38	24	15	2	6	218^1	177	78	7	5	44	94	**9.3**	**2.51**	**160**	**.222**	**.267**	9	.125	-4	37	37	0	3.5
1929	Was-A	12	10	.545	37	20	9	0	4	182	219	116	6	2	51	59	13.5	4.85	88	.299	.346	8	.148	-1	-12	-12	-1	-1.5
1930	Was-A	3	2	.600	15	0	0	0	5	27^1	22	11	3	0	9	7	10.2	3.29	140	.222	.287	0	.000	-1	4	4	-1	0.6
	Chi-A	4	10	.286	19	10	2	0	1	90^2	127	80	9	1	33	44	16.0	6.45	72	.333	.388	2	.087	-2	-18	-19	-1	-2.5
	Yr	7	12	.368	34	10	2	0	6	118	149	91	12	1	42	51	14.6	5.72	81	.310	.367	2	.071	-2	-14	-15	-2	-1.9
1931	Chi-A	0	3	.000	17	3	0	0	1	47^1	71	43	1	2	23	28	18.3	6.85	62	.338	.409	1	.091	-1	-13	-14	1	-0.8
	StL-A	0	0	—	11	1	0	0	0	18	27	24	2	1	10	7	19.0	10.50	44	.370	.452	2	.667	-1	-12	-11	-0	-0.4
	Yr	0	3	.000	28	4	0	0	1	65^1	98	67	3	3	33	35	18.5	7.85	56	.346	.420	3	.214	0	-25	-25	0	-1.2
1933	StL-A	0	1	.000	5	1	0	0	0	8^1	11	10	0	1	8	5	21.6	9.72	48	.289	.426	0	.000	-0	-5	-4	-0	-0.4
Total	10	50	53	.485	282	71	28	2	32	938	1014	529	38	21	276	412	12.6	4.13	101	.278	.332	40	.156	-8	8	2	-5	0.7

● AL BRAZLE

Brazle, Alpha Eugene "Cotton" b: 10/19/13, Loyal, Okla. d: 10/24/73, Grand Junction, Colo. BL/TL, 6'2", 185 lbs. Deb: 7/25/43

YEAR	TM/L	W	L	PCT	G	GS	CG	SH	SV	IP	H	R	HR	HB	BB	SO	RAT	ERA	ERA+	OAV	OOB	BH	AVG	PB	PR	PR+	PD	TPI
1943	*StL-N	8	2	.800	13	9	8	1	0	88	74	18	0	0	29	26	10.5	1.53	219	.231	.295	9	.281	2	18	18	0	2.4
1946	*StL-N	11	10	.524	37	15	6	2	0	153^1	152	69	1	2	55	58	12.3	3.29	105	.261	.327	11	.212	-0	2	3	0	0.3
1947	StL-N	14	8	.636	44	19	7	0	4	168	186	65	7	2	48	85	12.6	2.84	146	.284	.335	14	.219	1	23	24	3	3.3
1948	StL-N	10	6	.625	42	23	6	2	1	156^1	171	77	8	0	50	55	12.7	3.80	108	.281	.335	8	.145	-2	3	5	3	0.6
1949	StL-N	14	8	.636	39	25	9	1	0	206^1	208	85	18	6	61	75	12.0	3.18	131	.263	.321	11	.134	-4	20	22	-0	1.6
1950	StL-N	11	9	.550	46	12	3	0	6	164^2	188	81	12	4	80	47	14.9	4.10	105	.296	.378	13	.213	-1	1	3	-1	0.3
1951	StL-N	6	5	.545	56	8	5	0	7	154^1	139	61	13	5	60	66	11.9	3.09	128	.245	.322	5	.109	-3	**15**	**15**	-2	0.6
1952	StL-N	12	5	.706	46	6	3	1	**16**	109^1	75	38	6	1	42	55	9.7	2.72	137	.198	.280	4	.125	-1	12	12	-2	2.0
1953	StL-N	6	7	.462	60	0	0	0	**18**	92	101	47	8	2	43	57	14.3	4.21	101	.280	.360	5	.333	1	1	1	2	0.4
1954	StL-N	5	4	.556	58	0	0	0	8	84^1	93	48	10	3	24	30	12.8	4.16	99	.288	.343	0	.000	-2	-1	-0	-1	-0.3
Total	10	97	64	.602	441	117	47	7	60	1376^2	1387	589	83	25	492	554	12.4	3.31	120	.266	.332	80	.177	-9	93	101	3	11.2

● LESLIE BREA

Brea, Leslie Guillermo b: 10/12/73, San Pedro De Macoris, D.R. BR/TR, 5'10", 170 lbs. Deb: 8/13/2000

YEAR	TM/L	W	L	PCT	G	GS	CG	SH	SV	IP	H	R	HR	HB	BB	SO	RAT	ERA	ERA+	OAV	OOB	BH	AVG	PB	PR	PR+	PD	TPI
2000	Bal-A	0	1	.000	6	1	0	0	0	9	12	11	1	1	10	5	23.0	11.00	44	.324	.479	0	—	0	-6	-6	-0	-0.6

● HARRY BRECHEEN

Brecheen, Harry David "Harry The Cat" b: 10/14/14, Broken Bow, Okla. BL/TL, 5'10", 160 lbs. Deb: 4/22/40 C

YEAR	TM/L	W	L	PCT	G	GS	CG	SH	SV	IP	H	R	HR	HB	BB	SO	RAT	ERA	ERA+	OAV	OOB	BH	AVG	PB	PR	PR+	PD	TPI
1940	StL-N	0	0	—	3	0	0	0	0	3^1	2	1	0	0	2	4	10.8	0.00	—	.167	.286	0	—	0	1	1	0	0.1
1943	*StL-N	9	6	.600	29	13	8	1	4	135^1	98	41	4	3	39	68	9.3	2.26	149	.206	.270	8	.190	1	17	17	1	2.1
1944	*StL-N	16	5	.762	30	22	13	3	0	189^1	174	67	8	3	46	88	10.6	2.85	124	.242	.290	11	.162	1	16	15	-0	1.6
1945	StL-N	15	4	**.789**	24	18	13	3	2	157^1	136	48	5	5	44	63	10.6	2.52	149	.238	.298	7	.123	-1	22	22	-1	2.3
1946	*StL-N	15	15	.500	36	30	14	**5**	3	231^1	212	73	8	4	67	117	11.0	2.49	139	.244	.301	11	.133	-3	24	24	2	3.1
1947	StL-N★	16	11	.593	29	28	18	1	1	223^1	220	92	20	3	66	89	11.6	3.30	125	.260	.316	20	.241	5	19	20	1	2.8
1948	StL-N☆	20	7	**.741**	33	30	21	**7**	1	233^1	193	62	6	2	49	**149**	**9.4**	**2.24**	**183**	.222	**.265**	12	.146	-1	45	**46**	1	5.3
1949	StL-N	14	11	.560	32	31	14	2	1	214^2	207	96	18	7	65	88	11.7	3.35	124	.252	.312	21	.273	5	16	19	-1	2.4
1950	StL-N	8	11	.421	27	23	12	2	1	163^1	151	77	18	3	45	80	11.0	3.80	113	.244	.298	14	.241	3	6	9	-0	1.2
1951	StL-N	8	4	.667	24	16	5	0	2	138^2	134	54	11	1	54	57	12.3	3.25	122	.256	.327	12	.218	2	11	11	-0	1.1
1952	StL-N	7	5	.583	25	13	4	1	2	100^1	82	39	12	3	28	54	10.1	3.32	112	.223	.283	6	.207	1	5	4	2	0.9
1953	StL-A	5	13	.278	26	16	3	0	1	117^1	122	51	7	3	31	44	12.0	3.07	137	.269	.320	7	.179	-1	12	14	2	2.1
Total	12	133	92	.591	318	240	125	25	18	1907^2	1731	701	117	37	536	901	10.9	2.92	133	.242	.298	129	.192	11	194	202	6	25.0

● BILL BRECKINRIDGE

Breckinridge, William Robertson b: 10/16/07, Tulsa, Okla. d: 8/23/58, Tulsa, Okla. BR/TR, 5'11", 175 lbs. Deb: 6/30/29

YEAR	TM/L	W	L	PCT	G	GS	CG	SH	SV	IP	H	R	HR	HB	BB	SO	RAT	ERA	ERA+	OAV	OOB	BH	AVG	PB	PR	PR+	PD	TPI
1929	Phi-A	0	0	—	3	1	0	0	0	10	10	10	0	0	16	2	23.4	8.10	52	.270	.491	0	.000	-1	-4	-4	-1	-0.3

● FRED BREINING

Breining, Fred Lawrence b: 11/15/55, San Francisco, Cal. BR/TR, 6'4", 185 lbs. Deb: 9/4/80

YEAR	TM/L	W	L	PCT	G	GS	CG	SH	SV	IP	H	R	HR	HB	BB	SO	RAT	ERA	ERA+	OAV	OOB	BH	AVG	PB	PR	PR+	PD	TPI
1980	SF-N	0	0	—	5	0	0	0	0	6^2	8	4	0	1	4	3	17.6	5.40	66	.333	.448	0	—	0	-1	-1	-0	-0.1
1981	SF-N	5	2	.714	45	1	0	0	1	77^2	66	28	4	2	38	37	12.3	2.55	135	.243	.340	0	.000	-1	8	8	-0	0.6
1982	SF-N	11	6	.647	54	9	2	0	0	143^1	146	61	6	1	52	98	12.5	3.08	117	.269	.334	6	.207	1	8	8	1	1.2
1983	SF-N	11	12	.478	32	32	6	0	0	202^2	202	97	15	5	60	117	11.9	3.82	93	.259	.316	10	.149	1	-4	-6	-1	-0.6

YEAR	TM/L	W	L	PCT	G	GS	CG	SH	SV	IP	H	R	HR	HB	BB	SO	RAT	ERA	ERA+	OAV	OOB	BH	AVG	PB	PR	PR+	PD	TPI
1984	Mon-N	0	0	—	4	0	0	0	0	6^{2}	4	1	0	0	5	5	12.2	1.35	254	.190	.346	0	.000	-0	2	2	-0	0.0
Total	5	27	20	.574	140	42	8	0	1	437	426	191	25	9	159	260	12.2	3.34	106	.260	.329	16	.148	1	13	10	-0	1.1
● ALONZO BREITENSTEIN	Breitenstein, Alonzo b: 11/9/1857, Utica, N.Y. d: 6/19/32, Utica, N.Y. Deb: 7/7/1883																											
1883	Phi-N	0	1	.000	1	1	0	0	0	5	8	9	0	2	0		18.0	9.00	34	.320	.370	0	.000	-0	-3	-3	-0	-0.5
● TED BREITENSTEIN	Breitenstein, Theodore P. "Theo" b: 6/1/1869, St.Louis, Mo. d: 5/3/35, St.Louis, Mo. BL/TL, 5'9", 167 lbs. Deb: 4/28/1891																											
1891	StL-a	2	0	1.000	6	1	1	1	1	28^{2}	15	14	2	0	14	13	9.1	2.20	191	.150	.254	0	.000	-2	5	6	-1	0.2
1892	StL-N	9	19	.321	39	32	28	1	0	282^{1}	280	192	8	6	148	126	13.8	4.69	68	.248	.339	16	.122	-3	-44	-48	3	-3.8
1893	StL-N	19	24	.442	48	42	38	1	1	382^{2}	359	197	8	8	156	102	12.3	**3.18**	**149**	.241	.316	29	.181	-5	63	65	2	5.5
1894	StL-N	27	23	.540	**56**	50	**46**	1	0	**447^{1}**	497	320	21	11	191	140	14.1	4.79	113	.278	.352	40	.220	-1	27	31	3	2.6
1895	StL-N	19	30	.388	55	51	**47**	1	1	438^{2}	468	299	16	14	182	131	13.6	4.37	111	.269	.343	42	.190	-7	20	22	4	1.5
1896	StL-N	18	26	.409	44	43	37	1	0	339^{2}	376	236	12	5	138	114	13.8	4.48	97	.278	.347	42	.259	3	-4	-5	4	0.2
1897	Cin-N	23	12	.657	40	39	32	2	0	320^{1}	345	172	3	9	91	98	12.5	3.62	126	.273	.326	33	.266	3	24	31	-0	2.9
1898	Cin-N	20	14	.588	39	37	32	3	0	315^{2}	313	170	2	11	123	68	12.7	3.42	112	.257	.330	26	.215	1	7	14	3	1.6
1899	Cin-N	13	9	.591	26	24	21	0	0	210^{2}	219	111	2	9	71	59	12.8	3.59	109	.268	.333	37	.352	9	6	8	-0	1.5
1900	Cin-N	10	10	.500	24	20	18	1	0	192^{1}	205	111	4	14	79	39	13.9	3.65	101	.272	.352	24	.190	-0	1	0	2	0.2
1901	StL-N	0	3	.000	3	3	1	0	0	15	24	26	1	0	14	3	22.8	6.60	48	.358	.469	2	.333	0	-5	-6	1	-0.8
Total	11	160	170	.485	380	342	301	12	3	2973^{1}	3101	1848	79	87	1207	893	13.3	4.03	109	.265	.338	291	.216	-4	99	123	20	11.6
● AD BRENNAN	Brennan, Addison Foster b: 7/18/1881, LaHarpe, Kan. d: 1/7/62, Kansas City, Mo. BL/TL, 5'11", 170 lbs. Deb: 5/19/10																											
1910	Phi-N	2	0	1.000	19	5	2	0	0	73^{1}	72	36	2	3	28	28	12.6	2.33	134	.264	.339	7	.280	1	6	6	-2	0.3
1911	Phi-N	2	1	.667	5	3	1	0	0	22^{2}	22	12	0	1	12	12	13.9	3.57	96	.259	.357	2	.222	-0	-0	-0	0	0.0
1912	Phi-N	11	9	.550	27	19	13	1	2	174	185	88	4	3	49	78	12.3	3.57	102	.274	.326	15	.254	4	-3	1	2	0.7
1913	Phi-N	14	12	.538	40	24	12	1	1	207	204	76	5	6	46	94	11.1	2.39	139	.268	.314	11	.164	-2	19	21	0	2.3
1914	Chi-F	5	5	.500	16	11	5	1	0	85^{2}	84	44	6	2	21	31	11.2	3.57	74	.256	.305	8	.250	1	-7	-9	-1	-1.0
1915	Chi-F	3	9	.250	19	13	7	2	0	106	117	55	4	7	30	40	13.1	3.74	67	.287	.346	5	.185	0	-12	-16	-2	-1.8
1918	Was-A	0	0	—	2	1	0	0	0	5^{1}	7	4	0	1	5	0	21.9	5.06	54	.241	.371	0	.000	-0	-1	-1	0	-0.1
	Cle-A	0	0	—	1	0	0	0	0	3	3	1	0	0	3	0	18.0	3.00	100	.333	.500	0	—	0	-0	0	-0	0.0
	Yr	0	0	—	3	1	0	0	0	8^{1}	10	5	0	1	8	0	20.5	4.32	65	.263	.404	0	.000	-0	-1	-1	-0	-0.1
Total	7	37	36	.507	129	76	40	5	3	677	694	316	21	23	194	283	12.1	3.11	102	.270	.327	48	.218	4	1	4	-2	0.4
● DON BRENNAN	Brennan, James Donald b: 12/2/03, Augusta, Maine d: 4/26/53, Boston, Mass. BR/TR, 6', 210 lbs. Deb: 4/16/33																											
1933	NY-A	5	1	.833	18	10	3	0	3	85	92	56	4	0	47	46	14.7	4.98	78	.275	.365	7	.259	2	-7	-11	1	-0.5
1934	Cin-N	4	3	.571	28	7	2	0	2	78	89	51	3	1	35	31	14.4	3.81	107	.290	.364	5	.227	0	2	2	-1	0.2
1935	Cin-N	5	5	.500	38	5	2	1	5	114^{1}	101	43	4	4	44	48	11.7	3.15	126	.242	.320	3	.100	-1	11	11	-2	0.6
1936	Cin-N	5	2	.714	41	4	0	0	9	94^{1}	117	60	2	1	35	40	14.6	4.39	87	.305	.364	2	.080	-3	-4	-6	-0	-0.8
1937	Cin-N	1	1	.500	10	0	0	0	0	16	25	14	1	0	10	6	19.7	6.75	55	.347	.427	0	.000	-1	-5	-6	0	-0.7
	*NY-N	1	0	1.000	6	0	0	0	0	9^{1}	12	8	0	1	9	1	21.2	6.75	58	.316	.458	0	.000	0	-3	-3	-0	-0.3
	Yr	2	1	.667	16	0	0	0	0	25^{1}	37	22	1	1	19	7	20.3	6.75	56	.336	.438	0	.000	-1	-8	-9	-0	-1.0
Total	5	21	12	.636	141	26	7	1	19	397	436	232	14	7	180	172	14.1	4.19	94	.281	.358	17	.155	-2	-5	-12	-2	-1.5
● TOM BRENNAN	Brennan, Thomas Martin b: 10/30/52, Chicago, Ill. BR/TR, 6'1", 180 lbs. Deb: 9/5/81																											
1981	Cle-A	2	2	.500	7	6	1	0	0	48^{1}	49	20	5	0	14	15	11.7	3.17	115	.259	.310	0	—	0	3	3	1	0.3
1982	Cle-A	4	2	.667	30	4	0	0	2	92^{2}	112	51	9	2	10	46	12.0	4.27	96	.300	.322	0	—	0	-2	-2	0	-0.1
1983	Cle-A	2	2	.500	11	5	1	1	0	39^{2}	45	22	3	1	8	21	12.3	3.86	110	.288	.327	0	—	0	1	2	-0	0.1
1984	Chi-A	0	1	.000	4	1	0	0	0	6^{2}	8	5	1	0	3	3	14.9	4.05	103	.308	.379	0	—	0	-0	0	0	0.0
1985	LA-N	1	3	.250	12	4	0	0	0	31^{2}	41	26	2	0	11	17	14.8	7.39	47	.333	.388	1	.125	-0	-13	-14	1	-1.5
Total	5	9	10	.474	64	20	2	1	2	219	255	124	20	3	46	102	12.5	4.40	89	.294	.332	1	.125	-0	-12	-11	3	-1.2
● WILLIAM BRENNAN	Brennan, William Raymond b: 1/15/63, Tampa, Fla. BR/TR, 6'3", 200 lbs. Deb: 7/19/88																											
1988	LA-N	0	1	.000	4	2	0	0	0	9^{1}	13	7	0	0	6	7	18.3	6.75	49	.342	.432	0	.000	-0	-3	-4	0	-0.4
1993	Chi-N	2	1	.667	8	1	0	0	0	15	16	8	2	1	8	11	15.0	4.20	95	.291	.391	0	.000	0	-0	-0	0	0.0
Total	2	2	2	.500	12	3	0	0	0	24^{1}	29	15	2	1	14	18	16.3	5.18	72	.312	.407	0	.000	0	-4	-4	0	-0.4
● JIM BRENNEMAN	Brenneman, James Leroy b: 2/13/41, San Diego, Cal. BR/TR, 6'2", 180 lbs. Deb: 7/9/65																											
1965	NY-A	0	0	—	3	0	0	0	0	2	5	5	1	0	3	2	36.0	18.00	19	.455	.571	0	—	0	-3	-3	-0	-0.2
● BERT BRENNER	Brenner, Delbert Henry "Dutch" b: 7/18/1887, Minneapolis, Minn d: 4/11/71, St.Louis Park, Minn. BR/TR, 6', 175 lbs. Deb: 9/21/12																											
1912	Cle-A	1	0	1.000	2	1	1	0	0	13	14	8	0	0	4	3	12.5	2.77	123	.286	.340	0	.000	-1	1	1	0	0.0
● LYNN BRENTON	Brenton, Lynn Davis "Buck" or "Herb" b: 10/7/1890, Peoria, Ill. d: 10/14/68, Los Angeles, Cal. BR/TR, 5'10", 165 lbs. Deb: 8/10/13																											
1913	Cle-A	0	0	—	1	0	0	0	0	2	4	2	0	0	0	2	18.0	9.00	34	.400	.400	0	—	0	-1	-1	-0	-0.1
1915	Cle-A	2	3	.400	11	5	1	1	0	51	60	31	1	2	20	18	14.5	3.35	91	.308	.378	2	.118	-1	-2	-2	-1	-0.4
1920	Cin-N	2	1	.667	5	1	1	0	1	18^{1}	17	14	0	0	4	13	10.3	4.91	62	.236	.276	2	.250	0	-4	-4	2	-0.5
1921	Cin-N	1	8	.111	17	8	2	0	1	60	80	35	0	1	17	19	14.7	4.05	88	.342	.389	2	.133	-0	-2	-3	2	-0.3
Total	4	5	12	.294	34	14	4	1	2	131^{1}	161	82	1	3	41	52	14.0	3.97	83	.315	.369	6	.150	-1	-9	-10	3	-1.3
● ROGER BRESNAHAN	Bresnahan, Roger Philip "The Duke Of Tralee" b: 6/11/1879, Toledo, Ohio d: 12/4/44, Toledo, Ohio BR/TR, 5'9", 200 lbs. Deb: 8/27/1897 MCH♦																											
1897	Was-N	4	0	1.000	6	5	3	1	0	41	52	21	1	3	10	12	14.3	3.95	110	.306	.355	6	.375	1	2	2	-0	0.2
1901	Bal-A	0	1	.000	2	1	0	0	0	6	10	8	0	0	4	3	21.0	6.00	64	.370	.452	79	.268	0	-2	-1	0	-0.2
1910	StL-N	0	0	—	1	0	0	0	0	3^{1}	6	1	0	0	1	0	18.9	0.00	—	.400	.438	65	.278	0	1	1	1	0.1
Total	3	4	1	.800	9	6	3	1	0	50^{1}	68	30	1	3	15	15	15.4	3.93	107	.321	.374	1252	.279	2	1	1	0	0.1
● RUBE BRESSLER	Bressler, Raymond Bloom b: 10/23/1894, Coder, Pa. d: 11/7/66, Cincinnati, Ohio BR/TL, 6', 187 lbs. Deb: 4/24/14 ♦																											
1914	Phi-A	10	4	.714	29	10	8	1	2	147^{2}	112	37	1	4	56	96	10.5	1.77	148	.220	.302	11	.216	4	16	15	-2	1.6
1915	Phi-A	4	17	.190	32	20	7	1	0	178^{1}	183	133	3	7	118	69	15.5	5.20	56	.283	.399	8	.145	1	-45	-45	0	-4.5
1916	Phi-A	0	2	.000	4	2	0	0	0	15	16	11	0	2	14	8	19.2	6.60	43	.296	.457	1	.200	1	-6	-6	-0	-0.7
1917	Cin-N	0	0	—	2	1	0	0	0	9	15	11	0	0	5	2	20.0	6.00	44	.429	.500	1	.200	-0	-3	-4	0	-0.2
1918	Cin-N	8	5	.615	17	13	10	0	0	128	124	48	3	1	39	37	11.5	2.46	108	.261	.318	17	.274	4	4	3	3	1.1
1919	Cin-N	2	4	.333	13	4	1	0	0	41^{2}	37	19	1	0	8	13	9.7	3.46	80	.248	.287	34	.206	2	-3	-3	1	-0.3
1920	Cin-N	2	0	1.000	10	2	1	1	0	20^{1}	24	8	0	0	2	4	11.5	1.77	172	.300	.317	8	.267	0	3	3	0	0.3
Total	7	26	32	.448	107	52	27	3	2	540	511	267	8	14	242	229	12.8	3.40	81	.262	.348	1170	.301	12	-34	-39	1	-2.7
● HERB BRETT	Brett, Herbert James "Duke" b: 5/23/1900, Lawrenceville, Va. d: 11/25/74, St.Petersburg, Fla BR/TR, 6', 175 lbs. Deb: 8/8/24																											
1924	Chi-N	0	0	—	1	1	0	0	0	5^{1}	6	4	0	0	7	1	21.9	5.06	77	.300	.481	0	.000	-0	-1	-1	-0	-0.1
1925	Chi-N	1	1	.500	10	1	0	0	0	17^{1}	12	7	0	1	3	6	8.3	3.63	119	.194	.242	0	.000	-0	1	1	1	0.2
Total	2	1	1	.500	11	2	0	0	0	22^{2}	18	11	0	1	10	7	11.5	3.97	106	.220	.312	0	.000	-0	1	1	0	0.1
● KEN BRETT	Brett, Kenneth Alven b: 9/18/48, Brooklyn, N.Y. BL/TL, 5'11", 195 lbs. Deb: 9/27/67 F																											
1967	*Bos-A	0	0	—	1	0	0	0	0	2	3	1	0	0	0	2	13.5	4.50	77	.375	.375	0	—	0	-0	-0	-0	0.0
1969	Bos-A	2	3	.400	8	8	0	0	0	39^{1}	41	24	6	3	22	23	15.1	5.26	72	.275	.379	3	.300	2	-7	-6	0	-0.5
1970	Bos-A	8	9	.471	41	14	1	0	2	139^{1}	118	71	17	3	79	155	12.9	4.07	97	.223	.327	13	.317	6	-5	-2	1	0.5
1971	Bos-A	0	3	.000	29	2	0	0	1	59	57	38	7	1	35	57	14.2	5.34	69	.253	.356	2	.200	-0	-12	-10	-0	-0.6
1972	Mil-A	7	12	.368	26	22	2	1	0	133	121	76	13	1	49	74	11.6	4.53	67	.242	.311	10	.227	2	-22	-22	-2	-3.0
1973	Phi-N	13	9	.591	31	25	10	1	0	211^{2}	206	91	19	0	74	111	11.9	3.44	110	.259	.322	20	.250	8	5	8	2	1.9
1974	*Pit-N★	13	9	.591	27	27	10	3	0	191	192	81	9	2	52	96	11.6	3.30	105	.257	.308	27	.310	11	7	4	-0	1.5
1975	*Pit-N	9	5	.643	23	16	4	1	0	118	110	47	10	2	43	47	11.8	3.36	106	.250	.320	12	.231	4	4	3	0	0.7
1976	NY-A	0	0	—	2	0	0	0	1	2^{1}	2	0	0	0	0	1	7.7	0.00	—	.222	.222	0	—	0	1	1	-0	0.1
	Chi-A	10	12	.455	27	26	16	1	1	200^{2}	171	82	5	3	76	91	11.2	3.32	107	.234	.308	1	.083	-1	5	5	1	0.6
	Yr	10	12	.455	29	26	16	1	2	203	173	82	5	3	76	92	11.2	3.28	109	.233	.307	1	.083	-1	5	6	0	0.7

YEAR TM/L	W	L	PCT	G	GS	CG	SH	SV	IP	H	R	HR	HB	BB	SO	RAT	ERA	ERA+	OAV	OOB	BH	AVG	PB	PR	PR+	PD	TPI
1977 Chi-A	6	4	.600	13	13	2	0	0	82^2	101	47	10	1	15	39	12.7	5.01	82	.305	.337	0	—	0	-9	-8	-0	-0.9
Cal-A	7	10	.412	21	21	5	0	0	142	157	73	15	3	38	41	12.5	4.25	92	.287	.337	0	—	0	-3	-5	2	-0.3
Yr	13	14	.481	34	34	7	0	0	224^2	258	120	25	4	53	80	12.6	4.53	88	.294	.337	0	—	0	-11	-14	2	-1.2
1978 Cal-A	3	5	.375	31	10	1	1	1	100	100	60	12	1	42	43	12.9	4.95	73	.262	.336	0	—	0	-13	-15	2	-1.0
1979 Min-A	0	0	—	9	0	0	0	0	12^2	16	7	1	0	6	3	15.6	4.97	88	.320	.393	0	—	0	-1	-1	0	0.0
LA-N	4	3	.571	30	0	0	0	2	47	52	20	1	1	12	13	12.4	3.45	106	.277	.323	3	.273	1	2	1	2	0.4
1980 KC-A	0	0	—	8	0	0	0	1	13^1	8	0	0	1	5	4	9.5	0.00	—	.174	.269	0	—	0	6	6	0	0.3
1981 KC-A	1	1	.500	22	0	0	0	2	32^1	35	16	2	1	14	7	13.9	4.18	87	.282	.360	0	—	0	-2	-2	0	-0.1
Total 14	83	85	.494	349	184	51	8	11	1526^1	1490	734	127	23	562	807	12.2	3.93	93	.257	.325	91	.262	33	-45	-44	8	-0.4

● MARV BREUER
Breuer, Marvin Howard "Baby Face" b: 4/29/14, Rolla, Mo. d: 1/17/91, Rolla, Mo. BR/TR, 6'2", 185 lbs. Deb: 5/4/39

YEAR TM/L	W	L	PCT	G	GS	CG	SH	SV	IP	H	R	HR	HB	BB	SO	RAT	ERA	ERA+	OAV	OOB	BH	AVG	PB	PR	PR+	PD	TPI
1939 NY-A	0	0	—	1	0	0	0	0	1^1	2	1	0	0	1	0	27.0	9.00	48	.667	.750	0	—	0	-0	-1	0	0.0
1940 NY-A	8	9	.471	27	22	10	0	0	164	175	89	20	0	61	71	13.0	4.55	89	.267	.329	2	.037	-5	-3	-10	-1	-1.4
1941 *NY-A	9	7	.563	26	18	7	1	2	141	131	73	10	2	49	77	11.6	4.09	96	.243	.308	4	.087	-3	1	-3	-1	-0.6
1942 *NY-A	8	9	.471	27	19	6	0	1	164^1	157	67	11	1	37	72	10.7	3.07	112	.252	.295	3	.056	-3	11	7	-2	0.2
1943 NY-A	0	1	.000	5	1	0	0	0	14	22	16	0	0	6	6	18.0	8.36	39	.349	.406	1	.333	0	-8	-8	0	-0.5
Total 5	25	26	.490	86	60	23	1	3	484^1	487	246	41	3	154	226	12.0	4.03	94	.258	.315	10	.064	-11	0	-14	-3	-2.3

● JIM BREWER
Brewer, James Thomas b: 11/17/37, Merced, Cal. d: 11/16/87, Tyler, Tex. BL/TL, 6'2", 195 lbs. Deb: 7/17/60 C

YEAR TM/L	W	L	PCT	G	GS	CG	SH	SV	IP	H	R	HR	HB	BB	SO	RAT	ERA	ERA+	OAV	OOB	BH	AVG	PB	PR	PR+	PD	TPI
1960 Chi-N	0	3	.000	5	4	0	0	0	21^2	25	14	2	1	6	7	13.3	5.82	65	.272	.323	1	.167	0	-5	-5	0	-0.6
1961 Chi-N	1	7	.125	36	11	0	0	0	86^2	116	65	17	1	21	57	14.3	5.82	72	.321	.360	4	.182	0	-17	-15	-2	-1.4
1962 Chi-N	0	1	.000	6	1	0	0	0	5^2	10	6	2	0	3	1	20.6	9.53	44	.435	.500	0	—	0	-4	-3	0	-0.5
1963 Chi-N	3	2	.600	29	1	0	0	0	49^2	59	32	10	0	15	35	13.4	4.89	72	.294	.343	0	.000	0	-9	-7	-1	-0.8
1964 LA-N	4	3	.571	34	5	1	1	1	93	79	33	5	0	25	63	10.1	3.00	108	.232	.284	6	.273	2	6	3	-1	0.3
1965 *LA-N	3	2	.600	19	2	0	0	2	49^1	33	13	1	0	28	31	11.1	1.82	179	.196	.311	0	.000	-1	9	9	0	0.9
1966 *LA-N	0	2	.000	13	0	0	0	2	22	17	9	0	0	11	8	11.5	3.68	90	.221	.318	0	—	0	-0	-1	0	-0.1
1967 LA-N	5	4	.556	30	11	0	0	1	100^2	78	32	8	1	31	74	9.8	2.68	116	.218	.283	1	.045	-1	8	5	-1	0.2
1968 LA-N	8	3	.727	54	0	0	0	14	76^1	59	22	5	0	33	75	10.8	2.48	112	.219	.304	2	.222	0	4	3	0	0.6
1969 LA-N	7	6	.538	59	0	0	0	20	88^1	71	30	5	4	41	92	11.8	2.55	131	.221	.317	1	.091	0	10	8	0	1.7
1970 LA-N	7	6	.538	58	0	0	0	24	89	66	36	10	0	33	91	10.0	3.13	122	.207	.281	1	.083	-0	9	7	0	1.4
1971 LA-N	6	5	.545	55	0	0	0	22	81^1	55	17	4	0	24	66	8.7	1.88	172	.194	.257	3	.333	1	14	13	1	2.8
1972 LA-N	8	7	.533	51	0	0	0	17	78^1	41	16	6	2	25	69	7.8	1.26	264	.157	.236	0	.000	0	19	19	-0	4.2
1973 LA-N★	6	8	.429	56	0	0	0	20	71^2	58	26	8	0	25	56	10.4	3.01	114	.229	.299	2	.400	1	5	4	0	0.8
1974 *LA-N	4	4	.500	24	0	0	0	0	39^1	29	14	5	0	10	26	8.9	2.52	136	.207	.260	0	.000	-0	5	4	-1	0.7
1975 LA-N	3	1	.750	21	0	0	0	2	33	44	20	2	1	12	21	15.5	5.18	66	.333	.393	0	.000	-0	-6	-7	-0	-0.9
Cal-A	1	0	1.000	21	0	0	0	5	34^2	38	9	2	0	11	22	12.7	1.82	196	.279	.333	0	—	0	8	7	-1	0.4
1976 Cal-A	3	1	.750	13	0	0	0	2	20	20	7	0	0	6	16	11.7	2.70	123	.256	.310	0	—	0	2	1	0	0.3
Total 17	69	65	.515	584	35	1	1	132	1040^2	898	401	92	10	360	810	11.0	3.07	111	.236	.303	21	.150	1	59	40	-4	10.0

● JACK BREWER
Brewer, John Herndon "Buddy" b: 7/21/19, Los Angeles, Cal. BR/TR, 6'2", 170 lbs. Deb: 7/15/44

YEAR TM/L	W	L	PCT	G	GS	CG	SH	SV	IP	H	R	HR	HB	BB	SO	RAT	ERA	ERA+	OAV	OOB	BH	AVG	PB	PR	PR+	PD	TPI
1944 NY-N	1	4	.200	14	7	2	0	0	55	66	40	8	3	16	21	13.9	5.56	66	.288	.343	4	.211	0	-12	-11	-1	-1.0
1945 NY-N	8	6	.571	28	21	8	0	0	159^2	162	77	14	3	58	49	12.6	3.83	102	.260	.326	10	.179	-1	-1	1	-3	-0.3
1946 NY-N	0	0	—	1	0	0	0	0	2	3	3	0	0	2	3	22.5	13.50	25	.333	.455	0	—	0	-2	-2	-0	-0.1
Total 3	9	10	.474	43	28	10	0	0	216^2	231	120	22	6	76	73	13.0	4.36	88	.268	.332	14	.187	-1	-15	-12	-3	-1.4

● ROD BREWER
Brewer, Rodney Lee b: 2/24/66, Eustis, Fla. BL/TL, 6'3", 210 lbs. Deb: 9/5/90 ◆

YEAR TM/L	W	L	PCT	G	GS	CG	SH	SV	IP	H	R	HR	HB	BB	SO	RAT	ERA	ERA+	OAV	OOB	BH	AVG	PB	PR	PR+	PD	TPI
1993 StL-N	0	0	—	1	0	0	0	0	1	3	5	1	0	2	1	45.0	45.00	9	.500	.625	42	.286	0	-5	-5	0	-0.2

● TOM BREWER
Brewer, Thomas Austin b: 9/3/31, Wadesboro, N.C. BR/TR, 6'1", 175 lbs. Deb: 4/18/54

YEAR TM/L	W	L	PCT	G	GS	CG	SH	SV	IP	H	R	HR	HB	BB	SO	RAT	ERA	ERA+	OAV	OOB	BH	AVG	PB	PR	PR+	PD	TPI
1954 Bos-A	10	9	.526	33	23	7	0	0	162^2	152	90	15	7	95	69	14.1	4.65	88	.249	.356	16	.267	3	-17	-9	-2	-0.9
1955 Bos-A	11	10	.524	31	28	9	2	0	192^2	198	101	21	8	87	91	13.7	4.20	102	.263	.346	11	.151	-2	-5	2	3	0.3
1956 Bos-A★	19	9	.679	32	32	15	4	0	244^1	200	103	14	1	112	127	11.7	3.50	132	.220	.309	28	.298	4	18	27	4	3.8
1957 Bos-A	16	13	.552	32	32	15	2	0	238^1	225	113	24	7	93	128	12.3	3.85	103	.250	.325	19	.202	-1	-2	3	6	0.9
1958 Bos-A	12	12	.500	33	32	10	1	0	227^1	227	122	21	8	93	124	13.0	3.72	108	.259	.335	16	.195	-0	1	7	4	1.1
1959 Bos-A	10	12	.455	36	32	11	3	2	215^1	219	96	14	2	88	121	12.9	3.76	108	.265	.338	8	.111	-4	2	7	4	0.7
1960 Bos-A	10	15	.400	34	29	8	1	1	186^2	220	115	13	6	72	60	14.4	4.82	84	.301	.368	12	.194	0	-20	-15	3	-1.5
1961 Bos-A	3	2	.600	10	9	0	0	0	42	37	21	4	0	29	13	14.1	3.43	122	.242	.363	4	.286	1	3	3	1	0.6
Total 8	91	82	.526	241	217	75	13	3	1509^1	1478	761	126	43	669	733	13.1	4.00	104	.257	.338	114	.207	1	-19	26	22	5.0

● BILLY BREWER
Brewer, William Robert b: 4/15/68, Fort Worth, Tex. BL/TL, 6'1", 175 lbs. Deb: 4/8/93

YEAR TM/L	W	L	PCT	G	GS	CG	SH	SV	IP	H	R	HR	HB	BB	SO	RAT	ERA	ERA+	OAV	OOB	BH	AVG	PB	PR	PR+	PD	TPI
1993 KC-A	2	2	.500	46	0	0	0	0	39	31	16	6	0	20	28	11.8	3.46	133	.230	.329	0	—	0	4	5	-1	0.4
1994 KC-A	4	1	.800	50	0	0	0	3	38^2	28	11	4	2	16	25	10.7	2.56	196	.207	.301	0	—	0	10	10	0	1.2
1995 KC-A	2	4	.333	48	0	0	0	0	45^1	54	28	9	2	20	31	15.1	5.56	86	.290	.365	0	—	0	-4	-4	-0	-0.4
1996 NY-A	1	0	1.000	4	0	0	0	0	5^2	7	6	0	0	8	8	23.8	9.53	52	.292	.469	0	—	0	-3	-3	-0	-0.4
1997 Oak-A	0	0	—	3	0	0	0	0	2	4	3	1	0	2	1	27.0	13.50	34	.444	.545	0	—	0	-2	-2	-0	-0.1
Phi-N	1	2	.333	25	0	0	0	0	22	15	8	2	0	11	16	10.6	3.27	130	.188	.286	0	.000	-0	2	2	0	0.3
1998 Phi-N	0	1	.000	2	0	0	0	0	0^1	3	4	0	0	2	0	135.0	108.00	4	.750	.833	0	—	0	-4	-4	0	-0.6
1999 Phi-N	1	1	.500	25	0	0	0	2	25^2	30	20	4	0	14	28	15.4	7.01	67	.294	.379	0	—	0	-7	-6	-1	-0.5
Total 7	11	11	.500	203	0	0	0	5	178^2	172	96	26	4	93	137	13.6	4.79	99	.255	.348	0	.000	-0	-4	-1	-1	-0.1

● JAMIE BREWINGTON
Brewington, Jamie Chancellor b: 9/28/71, Greenville, N.C. BR/TR, 6'4", 180 lbs. Deb: 7/24/95

YEAR TM/L	W	L	PCT	G	GS	CG	SH	SV	IP	H	R	HR	HB	BB	SO	RAT	ERA	ERA+	OAV	OOB	BH	AVG	PB	PR	PR+	PD	TPI
1995 SF-N	6	4	.600	13	13	0	0	0	75^1	68	38	8	4	45	45	14.0	4.54	90	.245	.359	5	.217	0	-3	-4	-0	-0.4
2000 Cle-A	3	0	1.000	26	0	0	0	0	45^1	56	28	3	2	19	34	15.3	5.36	93	.311	.383	0	.000	0	-2	-2	0	-0.1
Total 2	9	4	.692	39	13	0	0	0	120^2	124	66	11	6	64	79	14.5	4.85	91	.271	.368	5	.208	1	-5	-6	-0	-0.5

● ALAN BRICE
Brice, Alan Healey b: 10/1/37, New York, N.Y. BR/TR, 6'5", 215 lbs. Deb: 9/22/61

YEAR TM/L	W	L	PCT	G	GS	CG	SH	SV	IP	H	R	HR	HB	BB	SO	RAT	ERA	ERA+	OAV	OOB	BH	AVG	PB	PR	PR+	PD	TPI
1961 Chi-A	0	1	.000	3	0	0	0	0	3^1	4	2	0	0	3	3	18.9	0.00	—	.308	.438	0	—	0	1	1	-0	0.3

● RALPH BRICKNER
Brickner, Ralph Harold "Brick" b: 5/2/25, Cincinnati, Ohio d: 5/9/94, Port Jefferson, N.Y. BR/TR, 6'3.5", 215 lbs. Deb: 5/4/52

YEAR TM/L	W	L	PCT	G	GS	CG	SH	SV	IP	H	R	HR	HB	BB	SO	RAT	ERA	ERA+	OAV	OOB	BH	AVG	PB	PR	PR+	PD	TPI
1952 Bos-A	3	1	.750	14	1	0	0	1	33	32	8	1	0	11	9	11.7	2.18	181	.264	.326	2	.250	0	5	6	-1	0.7

● MARSHALL BRIDGES
Bridges, Marshall "Sheriff" b: 6/2/31, Jackson, Miss. d: 9/3/90, Jackson, Miss. BB/TL, 6'1", 180 lbs. Deb: 6/17/59

YEAR TM/L	W	L	PCT	G	GS	CG	SH	SV	IP	H	R	HR	HB	BB	SO	RAT	ERA	ERA+	OAV	OOB	BH	AVG	PB	PR	PR+	PD	TPI
1959 StL-N	6	3	.667	27	4	1	0	1	76	67	38	10	0	37	76	12.3	4.26	99	.240	.329	5	.217	2	-3	-0	-2	0.0
1960 StL-N	2	2	.500	20	1	0	0	1	31^1	33	15	2	1	16	27	14.4	3.45	119	.266	.355	0	.000	-0	1	2	0	0.2
Cin-N	4	0	1.000	14	0	0	0	2	25^1	14	3	1	0	7	26	7.5	1.07	359	.161	.223	1	.250	0	8	8	-0	1.3
Yr	6	2	.750	34	1	0	0	3	56^2	47	18	3	1	23	53	11.3	2.38	167	.223	.302	1	.100	-0	9	9	1	1.5
1961 Cin-N	0	1	.000	13	0	0	0	0	20^2	26	19	4	1	11	17	16.5	7.84	52	.317	.404	0	.000	-0	-9	-9	-0	-0.5
1962 *NY-A	8	4	.667	52	0	0	0	18	71^2	49	30	4	0	48	66	12.2	3.14	119	.194	.323	0	.000	-2	7	5	2	1.1
1963 NY-A	2	0	1.000	23	0	0	0	1	33	27	18	2	1	30	35	15.8	3.82	92	.237	.400	0	—	0	-1	-1	2	0.1
1964 Was-A	0	3	.000	17	0	0	0	2	30	37	22	3	0	17	16	16.2	5.70	65	.303	.388	0	.000	-0	-7	-7	-0	-0.7
1965 Was-A	1	2	.333	40	0	0	0	0	57^1	62	26	3	0	25	39	13.7	2.67	130	.268	.340	1	.143	0	5	5	-0	0.3
Total 7	23	15	.605	206	5	1	0	25	345^1	315	171	29	3	191	302	13.3	3.75	102	.244	.343	7	.119	-0	1	3	1	1.8

● TOMMY BRIDGES
Bridges, Thomas Jefferson Davis b: 12/28/06, Gordonsville, Tenn d: 4/19/68, Nashville, Tenn. BR/TR, 5'10.5", 155 lbs. Deb: 8/13/30 C

YEAR TM/L	W	L	PCT	G	GS	CG	SH	SV	IP	H	R	HR	HB	BB	SO	RAT	ERA	ERA+	OAV	OOB	BH	AVG	PB	PR	PR+	PD	TPI
1930 Det-A	3	2	.600	8	5	2	0	0	37^2	28	18	4	0	23	17	12.2	4.06	118	.215	.333	3	.300	1	2	3	-0	0.4
1931 Det-A	8	16	.333	35	23	8	2	0	173	182	120	13	0	108	105	15.1	4.99	92	.263	.363	8	.148	-2	-12	-7	-1	-1.2
1932 Det-A	14	12	.538	34	26	10	**4**	1	201	174	95	14	1	119	108	13.2	3.36	140	.233	.339	11	.164	-1	25	29	-1	3.1
1933 Det-A	14	12	.538	33	28	17	2	2	233	192	102	8	6	110	120	11.9	3.09	140	**.226**	.319	16	.205	2	31	31	1	3.5
1934 *Det-A☆	22	11	.667	36	35	23	3	1	275	249	117	16	3	104	151	11.7	3.67	120	.241	.312	12	.122	-4	25	23	-2	1.8
1935 *Det-A☆	21	10	.677	36	34	23	4	1	274^1	277	129	22	3	113	**163**	12.9	3.51	119	.259	.332	26	.239	3	29	21	-1	2.3
1936 Det-A†	**23**	11	.676	39	38	26	5	0	294^2	289	141	21	5	115	**175**	12.5	3.60	137	.255	.326	25	.212	0	47	45	2	4.5
1937 Det-A★	15	12	.556	34	31	18	3	0	245^1	267	129	15	3	91	138	13.2	4.07	115	.274	.338	23	.240	2	15	16	1	1.8

YEAR	TM/L	W	L	PCT	G	GS	CG	SH	SV	IP	H	R	HR	HB	BB	SO	RAT	ERA	ERA+	OAV	OOB	BH	AVG	PB	PR	PR+	PD	TPI
1938	Det-A	13	9	.591	25	20	13	0	1	151	171	83	14	2	58	101	13.8	4.59	109	.287	.353	7	.130	-1	3	7	-1	0.6
1939	Det-A★	17	7	.708	29	26	16	2	2	198	186	87	11	6	61	129	11.5	3.50	140	.243	.304	14	.197	0	25	29	-0	3.1
1940	*Det-A☆	12	9	.571	29	28	12	2	0	197^2	171	89	11	0	88	133	11.8	3.37	141	.229	.311	12	.176	-2	22	28	-1	2.4
1941	Det-A	9	12	.429	25	22	10	1	0	147^2	128	66	10	1	70	90	12.1	3.41	133	.233	.320	4	.085	-3	12	17	2	2.1
1942	Det-A	9	7	.563	23	22	11	2	1	174	164	66	6	4	61	97	11.8	2.74	144	.246	.313	6	.095	-2	18	22	1	1.7
1943	Det-A	12	7	.632	25	22	11	3	0	191^2	159	57	9	0	61	124	10.3	2.39	147	.226	.287	14	.219	2	19	22	-1	2.4
1945	*Det-A	1	0	1.000	4	1	0	0	0	11	14	6	2	0	2	6	13.1	3.27	107	.311	.340	0	.000	-0	0	0	1	0.0
1946	Det-A	1	1	.500	9	1	0	0	1	21^1	24	16	5	1	8	17	13.9	5.91	62	.279	.347	0	.000	0	-6	-5	0	-0.5
Total	16	194	138	.584	424	362	200	33	10	2826^1	2675	1321	181	35	1192	1674	12.4	3.57	126	.248	.325	181	.180	-5	256	284	-3	28.0

● BUTTONS BRIGGS Briggs, Herbert Theodore b: 7/8/1875, Poughkeepsie, N.Y. d: 2/18/11, Cleveland, Ohio BR/TR, 6'1", 180 lbs. Deb: 4/23/1896

YEAR	TM/L	W	L	PCT	G	GS	CG	SH	SV	IP	H	R	HR	HB	BB	SO	RAT	ERA	ERA+	OAV	OOB	BH	AVG	PB	PR	PR+	PD	TPI
1896	Chi-N	12	8	.600	26	21	19	0	1	194	202	129	6	15	108	84	15.1	4.31	105	.266	.368	10	.128	-6	1	5	-3	-0.4
1897	Chi-N	4	17	.190	22	22	21	0	0	186^2	246	166	6	9	85	60	16.4	5.26	85	.315	.388	13	.160	-6	-20	-16	-1	-1.9
1898	Chi-N	1	3	.250	4	4	3	0	0	30	38	22	0	1	10	14	14.7	5.70	63	.306	.363	6	.429	2	-7	-7	-0	-0.6
1904	Chi-N	19	11	.633	34	30	28	3	3	277	252	102	3	8	77	112	10.9	2.05	130	.246	.304	16	.170	-0	21	20	-4	1.6
1905	Chi-N	8	8	.500	20	20	13	5	0	168	141	58	1	6	52	68	10.7	2.14	139	.237	.304	3	.053	-4	16	16	-2	0.7
Total	5	44	47	.484	106	97	84	8	4	855^2	879	477	16	39	332	338	13.1	3.41	104	.268	.342	48	.148	-15	12	14	-10	-0.6

● JOHN BRIGGS Briggs, Jonathan Tift b: 1/24/34, Natoma, Cal. BR/TR, 5'10", 175 lbs. Deb: 4/17/56

YEAR	TM/L	W	L	PCT	G	GS	CG	SH	SV	IP	H	R	HR	HB	BB	SO	RAT	ERA	ERA+	OAV	OOB	BH	AVG	PB	PR	PR+	PD	TPI
1956	Chi-N	0	0	—	3	0	0	0	0	5^1	5	1	1	3	4	1	20.3	1.69	223	.238	.429	0	—	0	1	1	0	0.1
1957	Chi-N	0	1	.000	3	0	0	0	0	4^1	7	6	2	0	3	1	20.8	12.46	31	.368	.455	0	—	0	-4	-4	-0	-0.7
1958	Chi-N	5	5	.500	20	17	3	1	0	95^2	99	52	12	1	45	46	13.6	4.52	87	.270	.352	9	.257	2	-6	-6	-1	-0.5
1959	Cle-A	0	1	.000	4	1	0	0	0	12^2	12	5	1	0	3	5	10.7	2.13	173	.245	.288	0	.000	-0	2	2	-0	0.1
1960	Cle-A	4	2	.667	21	2	0	0	1	36^1	32	20	4	1	15	19	11.9	4.46	84	.250	.333	1	.125	-0	-2	-3	-1	-0.6
	KC-A	0	2	.000	8	1	0	0	0	11^1	19	17	3	0	12	8	24.6	12.71	31	.380	.500	0	.000	-0	-11	-11	-0	-1.6
	Yr	4	4	.500	29	3	0	0	1	47^2	51	37	7	1	27	27	14.9	6.42	59	.287	.383	1	.091	-1	-13	-14	-1	-2.2
Total	5	9	11	.450	59	21	3	1	1	165^2	174	101	23	5	82	80	14.2	5.00	77	.275	.363	10	.208	1	-20	-21	-2	-3.2

● NELSON BRILES Briles, Nelson Kelley b: 8/5/43, Dorris, Cal. BR/TR, 5'11", 200 lbs. Deb: 4/19/65

YEAR	TM/L	W	L	PCT	G	GS	CG	SH	SV	IP	H	R	HR	HB	BB	SO	RAT	ERA	ERA+	OAV	OOB	BH	AVG	PB	PR	PR+	PD	TPI
1965	StL-N	3	3	.500	37	2	0	0	4	82^1	79	33	4	6	26	52	12.1	3.50	110	.258	.328	2	.133	-0	0	3	-1	0.1
1966	StL-N	4	15	.211	49	17	0	0	6	154	162	65	14	7	54	100	13.0	3.21	112	.279	.348	3	.079	-2	7	6	1	0.7
1967	*StL-N	14	5	.737	49	14	4	2	6	155^1	139	45	8	5	40	94	10.7	2.43	135	.236	.290	6	.150	0	16	15	-2	1.8
1968	*StL-N	19	11	.633	33	33	13	4	0	243^2	251	90	18	7	55	141	11.6	2.81	103	.266	.311	11	.138	1	5	2	-2	0.1
1969	StL-N	15	13	.536	36	33	10	3	0	227^2	218	104	17	2	63	126	11.2	3.52	102	.251	.303	8	.105	-1	2	1	-1	-0.1
1970	StL-N	6	7	.462	30	19	1	1	0	106^2	129	84	14	2	36	59	14.1	6.24	66	.297	.353	7	.179	1	-26	-25	-2	-2.6
1971	*Pit-N	8	4	.667	37	14	4	2	1	136	131	51	12	3	35	76	11.2	3.04	111	.250	.301	10	.256	4	6	5	-1	0.8
1972	*Pit-N	14	11	.560	28	27	9	2	0	195^2	185	83	14	1	43	120	10.5	3.08	108	.249	.291	11	.157	-0	8	5	-1	0.6
1973	Pit-N	14	13	.519	33	33	7	1	0	218^2	201	87	19	1	51	94	10.4	2.84	124	.244	.288	14	.194	3	20	17	0	2.4
1974	KC-A	5	7	.417	18	17	3	0	0	103	118	48	9	2	21	41	12.3	4.02	95	.293	.331	0	—	0	-5	-2	-1	-0.3
1975	KC-A	6	6	.500	24	16	3	0	2	112	127	60	19	5	25	73	12.6	4.26	91	.285	.330	0	—	0	-6	-5	0	-0.5
1976	Tex-A	11	9	.550	32	31	7	1	1	210	224	87	17	2	47	98	11.7	3.26	110	.273	.314	0	—	0	6	8	-3	0.4
1977	Tex-A	6	4	.600	28	15	2	1	1	108^1	114	58	13	6	30	57	12.5	4.24	97	.275	.333	0	—	0	-2	-2	-1	-0.2
	Bal-A	0	0	—	2	0	0	0	1	4	5	3	2	0	0	2	11.3	6.75	56	.294	.294	0	—	0	-1	-1	-0	-0.1
	Yr	6	4	.600	30	15	2	1	2	112^1	119	61	15	6	30	59	12.4	4.33	94	.276	.332	0	—	0	-3	-3	-1	-0.3
1978	Bal-A	4	4	.500	16	8	1	0	0	54^1	58	31	6	2	21	30	13.4	4.64	76	.279	.351	0	—	0	-5	-7	-1	-1.1
Total	14	129	112	.535	452	279	64	17	22	2111^2	2141	929	186	51	547	1163	11.7	3.44	103	.264	.314	72	.154	5	26	20	-14	2.0

● FRANK BRILL Brill, Francis Hasbrouck (b: Francis Hasbrouck Briell)
b: 3/30/1864, Astoria, N.Y. d: 11/19/44, Flushing, N.Y. BR/TR, 5'8", 155 lbs. Deb: 6/23/1884

YEAR	TM/L	W	L	PCT	G	GS	CG	SH	SV	IP	H	R	HR	HB	BB	SO	RAT	ERA	ERA+	OAV	OOB	BH	AVG	PB	PR	PR+	PD	TPI
1884	Det-N	2	10	.167	12	12	12	1	0	103	148	98	7		26	18	15.2	5.50	53	.312	.348	6	.136	-3	-29	-31	-2	-2.9

● JIM BRILLHEART Brillheart, James Benson b: 9/28/03, Dublin, Va. d: 9/2/72, Radford, Va. BR/TL, 5'11", 170 lbs. Deb: 4/17/22

YEAR	TM/L	W	L	PCT	G	GS	CG	SH	SV	IP	H	R	HR	HB	BB	SO	RAT	ERA	ERA+	OAV	OOB	BH	AVG	PB	PR	PR+	PD	TPI
1922	Was-A	4	6	.400	31	10	3	0	1	119^2	120	58	3	8	72	47	15.0	3.61	107	.275	.388	3	.083	-4	6	4	-2	-0.3
1923	Was-A	0	1	.000	12	0	0	0	0	18	27	15	1	1	12	8	20.0	7.00	54	.360	.455	0	.000	-0	-6	-7	0	-0.3
1927	Chi-N	4	2	.667	32	12	4	0	0	128^2	140	67	4	4	38	36	12.7	4.13	94	.286	.343	1	.023	-5	-3	-4	-1	-0.8
1931	Bos-A	0	0	—	11	1	0	0	0	19^2	27	16	2	0	15	7	19.2	5.49	78	.325	.429	2	.500	2	-2	-3	1	0.1
Total	4	8	9	.471	86	23	7	0	1	286	314	156	10	13	137	98	14.6	4.19	93	.290	.376	6	.070	-8	-6	-10	-2	-1.3

● BRAD BRINK Brink, Bradford Albert b: 1/20/65, Roseville, Cal. BR/TR, 6'2", 195 lbs. Deb: 5/17/92

YEAR	TM/L	W	L	PCT	G	GS	CG	SH	SV	IP	H	R	HR	HB	BB	SO	RAT	ERA	ERA+	OAV	OOB	BH	AVG	PB	PR	PR+	PD	TPI
1992	Phi-N	0	4	.000	8	7	0	0	0	41^1	53	27	2	1	13	16	14.6	4.14	85	.308	.360	1	.083	-0	-3	-3	-0	-0.3
1993	Phi-N	0	0	—	2	0	0	0	0	6	3	2	1	0	3	8	9.0	3.00	132	.143	.250	0	.000	-0	1	1	-0	0.0
1994	SF-N	0	0	—	4	0	0	0	0	8^1	4	1	1	0	4	3	8.6	1.08	371	.143	.250	0	.000	-0	3	3	0	0.1
Total	3	0	4	.000	14	7	0	0	0	55^2	60	30	4	1	20	27	13.1	3.56	102	.271	.335	1	.071	-1	1	0	-0	-0.2

● JOHN BRISCOE Briscoe, John Eric b: 9/22/67, LaGrange, Ill. BR/TR, 6'3", 185 lbs. Deb: 4/18/91

YEAR	TM/L	W	L	PCT	G	GS	CG	SH	SV	IP	H	R	HR	HB	BB	SO	RAT	ERA	ERA+	OAV	OOB	BH	AVG	PB	PR	PR+	PD	TPI
1991	Oak-A	0	0	—	11	0	0	0	0	14	12	11	3	0	10	9	14.1	7.07	54	.235	.361	0	—	0	-5	-5	-0	-0.3
1992	Oak-A	0	1	.000	2	2	0	0	0	7	12	6	0	0	9	4	27.0	6.43	58	.400	.538	0	—	0	-2	-2	-0	-0.3
1993	Oak-A	1	0	1.000	17	0	0	0	0	24^2	26	25	2	0	26	24	19.0	8.03	51	.277	.433	0	—	0	-10	-11	0	-0.5
1994	Oak-A	4	2	.667	37	0	0	0	1	49^1	31	24	7	1	39	45	13.0	4.01	110	.185	.341	0	—	0	4	2	-1	0.2
1995	Oak-A	0	1	.000	16	0	0	0	0	18^1	25	17	4	2	21	19	23.6	8.35	54	.347	.505	0	—	0	-7	-8	0	-0.4
1996	Oak-A	0	1	.000	17	0	0	0	1	26^1	18	11	2	0	24	14	14.4	3.76	131	.205	.375	0	—	0	4	3	-0	0.1
Total	6	5	5	.500	100	2	0	0	2	139^2	124	94	18	3	129	115	16.5	5.67	77	.247	.403	0	—	0	-16	-21	-1	-1.2

● LOU BRISSIE Brissie, Leland Victor b: 6/5/24, Anderson, S.C. BL/TL, 6'4", 215 lbs. Deb: 9/28/47

YEAR	TM/L	W	L	PCT	G	GS	CG	SH	SV	IP	H	R	HR	HB	BB	SO	RAT	ERA	ERA+	OAV	OOB	BH	AVG	PB	PR	PR+	PD	TPI
1947	Phi-A	0	1	.000	1	1	0	0	0	7	9	5	1	0	5	4	18.0	6.43	59	.310	.412	0	.000	-0	-2	-2	0	-0.2
1948	Phi-A	14	10	.583	39	25	11	0	5	194	202	100	6	2	95	127	13.9	4.13	104	.269	.352	18	.237	0	3	3	-2	0.2
1949	Phi-A★	16	11	.593	34	29	18	0	3	229^1	220	113	20	5	118	118	13.5	4.28	96	.251	.344	24	.267	3	-2	-4	-4	-0.5
1950	Phi-A	7	19	.269	46	31	15	2	8	246	237	127	22	4	117	101	13.1	4.02	113	.253	.338	15	.172	-3	15	14	-0	1.1
1951	Phi-A	0	2	.000	2	2	0	0	0	13^1	20	10	0	0	8	3	18.9	6.75	63	.357	.438	1	.200	-0	-4	-4	-0	-0.5
	Cle-A	4	3	.571	54	4	1	0	9	112^1	90	44	5	3	61	50	12.3	3.20	118	.223	.329	6	.261	0	11	8	-2	0.4
	Yr	4	5	.444	56	6	1	0	9	125^2	110	54	5	3	69	53	13.0	3.58	107	.239	.342	7	.250	0	8	4	-2	-0.1
1952	Cle-A	3	2	.600	42	1	0	0	2	82^2	68	41	5	0	34	28	11.1	3.48	96	.221	.299	3	.250	1	2	-1	1	0.1
1953	Cle-A	0	0	—	16	0	0	0	2	13	21	11	2	0	13	5	23.5	7.62	49	.389	.507	0	—	0	-5	-6	-0	-0.3
Total	7	44	48	.478	234	93	45	2	29	897^2	867	451	61	14	451	436	13.4	4.07	102	.254	.343	67	.227	1	19	8	-7	0.3

● JIM BRITT Britt, James Edward b: 2/25/1856, Brooklyn, N.Y. d: 2/28/23, San Francisco, Cal Deb: 5/2/1872

YEAR	TM/L	W	L	PCT	G	GS	CG	SH	SV	IP	H	R	HR	HB	BB	SO	RAT	ERA	ERA+	OAV	OOB	BH	AVG	PB	PR	PR+	PD	TPI
1872	Atl-n	9	28	.243	37	37	37	0	0	336	570	473	6		19	13	15.8	4.34	104	.328	.335	40	.256	-8	-26	5		0.0
1873	Atl-n	17	36	.321	54	54	**51**	1	0	480^2	696	519	6		40	15	13.8	3.89	78	.300	.312	47	.196	-3	-34	-49		-3.7
Total	2 n	26	64	.289	91	91	88	1	0	816^2	1266	992	12		59	28	14.6	4.08	74	.312	.322	87	.220	-11	-75	-101		-3.7

● JACK BRITTIN Brittin, John Albert b: 3/4/24, Athens, Ill. d: 1/5/94, Springfield, Ill. BR/TR, 5'11", 175 lbs. Deb: 9/15/50

YEAR	TM/L	W	L	PCT	G	GS	CG	SH	SV	IP	H	R	HR	HB	BB	SO	RAT	ERA	ERA+	OAV	OOB	BH	AVG	PB	PR	PR+	PD	TPI
1950	Phi-N	0	0	—	3	0	0	0	0	4	2	2	0	0	3	3	11.3	4.50	90	.143	.294	0	—	0	-0	-0	0	0.0
1951	Phi-N	0	0	—	3	0	0	0	0	4	5	5	0	0	6	3	24.8	9.00	43	.294	.478	0	—	0	-2	-2	0	-0.1
Total	2	0	0	—	6	0	0	0	0	8	7	7	0	0	9	6	18.0	6.75	58	.226	.400	0	—	0	-2	-3	0	-0.1

● JIM BRITTON Britton, James Allan b: 3/25/44, N.Tonawanda, N.Y. BR/TR, 6'5", 225 lbs. Deb: 9/20/67

YEAR	TM/L	W	L	PCT	G	GS	CG	SH	SV	IP	H	R	HR	HB	BB	SO	RAT	ERA	ERA+	OAV	OOB	BH	AVG	PB	PR	PR+	PD	TPI
1967	Atl-N	0	2	.000	2	2	0	0	0	13^1	15	9	2	0	2	4	11.5	6.08	55	.278	.304	0	.000	-0	-4	-4	-0	-0.6
1968	Atl-N	4	6	.400	34	9	2	2	3	90	81	35	1	2	34	61	11.7	3.10	97	.245	.320	3	.143	-0	-1	-1	0	-0.2
1969	*Atl-N	7	5	.583	24	13	2	1	1	88	69	38	10	0	49	60	12.1	3.78	95	.218	.323	4	.190	0	-2	-2	-1	-0.3
1971	Mon-N	2	3	.400	16	6	0	0	0	45^2	49	33	10	2	27	23	15.4	5.72	62	.274	.375	0	.000	-1	-11	-11	-1	-1.3
Total	4	13	16	.448	76	30	4	3	4	237	214	115	23	4	112	148	12.5	4.03	83	.243	.332	7	.127	-2	-18	-18	-2	-2.4

● TONY BRIZZOLARA Brizzolara, Anthony John b: 1/14/57, Santa Monica, Cal. BR/TR, 6'5", 215 lbs. Deb: 5/19/79

YEAR	TM/L	W	L	PCT	G	GS	CG	SH	SV	IP	H	R	HR	HB	BB	SO	RAT	ERA	ERA+	OAV	OOB	BH	AVG	PB	PR	PR+	PD	TPI
1979	Atl-N	6	9	.400	20	19	2	0	0	107^{1}	133	70	6	3	33	64	14.2	5.28	77	.303	.356	1	.029	-3	-18	-13	0	-1.9
1983	Atl-N	1	0	1.000	14	0	0	0	1	20^{1}	22	8	2	0	6	17	12.4	3.54	110	.278	.329	0	—	0	0	1	-0	0.0
1984	Atl-N	1	2	.333	10	4	0	0	0	29	33	22	4	0	13	17	14.3	5.28	73	.284	.357	0	.000	-1	-5	-4	0	-0.5
Total	3	8	11	.421	44	23	2	0	1	156^{2}	188	100	12	3	52	98	14.0	5.06	79	.297	.353	1	.024	-4	-24	-17	-0	-2.4

● JOHNNY BROACA Broaca, John Joseph b: 10/3/09, Lawrence, Mass. d: 5/16/85, Lawrence, Mass. BR/TR, 5'11", 190 lbs. Deb: 6/2/34

YEAR	TM/L	W	L	PCT	G	GS	CG	SH	SV	IP	H	R	HR	HB	BB	SO	RAT	ERA	ERA+	OAV	OOB	BH	AVG	PB	PR	PR+	PD	TPI
1934	NY-A	12	9	.571	26	24	13	1	0	177^{1}	203	94	9	1	65	74	13.7	4.16	98	.284	.344	2	.030	-7	7	-2	-2	-1.1
1935	NY-A	15	7	.682	29	27	14	2	0	201	199	96	16	0	79	78	12.4	3.58	113	.254	.323	12	.150	-4	19	11	-3	0.4
1936	NY-A	12	7	.632	37	27	12	1	3	206	235	110	16	0	66	84	13.2	4.24	110	.284	.337	9	.110	-6	18	10	-2	0.0
1937	NY-A	1	4	.200	7	6	3	0	0	44	58	27	5	0	17	9	15.3	4.70	94	.324	.383	0	.000	-2	-0	-1	-1	-0.4
1939	Cle-A	4	2	.667	22	2	0	0	0	46	53	39	5	0	28	13	15.8	4.70	94	.288	.382	0	.000	-2	-0	-2	-0	-0.3
Total	5	44	29	.603	121	86	42	4	3	674^{1}	748	366	51	1	255	258	13.4	4.08	105	.278	.341	23	.091	-21	44	17	-8	-1.4

● PETE BROBERG Broberg, Peter Sven b: 3/2/50, W.Palm Beach, Fla. BR/TR, 6'3", 205 lbs. Deb: 6/20/71

YEAR	TM/L	W	L	PCT	G	GS	CG	SH	SV	IP	H	R	HR	HB	BB	SO	RAT	ERA	ERA+	OAV	OOB	BH	AVG	PB	PR	PR+	PD	TPI
1971	Was-A	5	9	.357	18	18	7	1	0	124^{2}	104	57	10	10	53	89	12.1	3.47	96	.228	.322	5	.114	0	0	-2	-1	-0.3
1972	Tex-A	5	12	.294	39	25	3	2	1	176^{1}	153	93	14	13	85	133	12.8	4.29	70	.237	.338	4	.078	-2	-24	-25	1	-2.5
1973	Tex-A	5	9	.357	22	20	6	1	0	118^{2}	130	77	8	5	66	57	15.2	5.61	66	.283	.379	0	—	0	-24	-26	-0	-2.6
1974	Tex-A	0	4	.000	12	2	0	0	0	29	29	29	7	1	13	15	13.3	8.07	44	.264	.347	0	—	0	-14	-15	-0	-1.8
1975	Mil-A	14	16	.467	38	32	7	2	0	220^{1}	219	114	18	16	106	100	13.9	4.13	93	.263	.357	0	—	0	-8	-7	-0	-0.9
1976	Mil-A	1	7	.125	20	11	1	0	0	92^{1}	99	59	5	4	72	28	17.1	4.97	70	.281	.409	0	—	0	-15	-15	-1	-1.3
1977	Chi-N	1	2	.333	22	0	0	0	0	36	34	22	8	0	18	20	13.0	4.75	92	.256	.344	0	.000	-1	-3	-1	0	-0.2
1978	Oak-A	10	12	.455	35	26	2	0	0	165^{2}	174	101	16	3	65	94	13.1	4.62	79	.269	.338	0	—	0	-15	-18	1	-2.1
Total	8	41	71	.366	206	134	26	6	1	963	942	552	86	52	478	536	13.8	4.56	78	.259	.353	9	.089	-3	-104	-109	-0	-11.7

● DOUG BROCAIL Brocail, Douglas Keith b: 5/16/67, Clearfield, Pa. BL/TR, 6'5", 235 lbs. Deb: 9/8/92

YEAR	TM/L	W	L	PCT	G	GS	CG	SH	SV	IP	H	R	HR	HB	BB	SO	RAT	ERA	ERA+	OAV	OOB	BH	AVG	PB	PR	PR+	PD	TPI
1992	SD-N	0	0	—	3	3	0	0	0	14	17	10	2	0	5	15	14.1	6.43	56	.298	.355	1	.200	0	-5	-4	-0	-0.2
1993	SD-N	4	13	.235	24	24	0	0	0	128^{1}	143	75	16	4	42	70	13.3	4.56	91	.282	.342	6	.182	-0	-7	-6	0	-0.7
1994	SD-N	0	0	—	12	0	0	0	0	17	21	13	1	2	5	11	14.8	5.82	71	.304	.368	0	.000	-0	-3	-3	-0	-0.2
1995	Hou-N	6	4	.600	36	7	0	0	1	77^{1}	87	40	10	4	22	39	13.2	4.19	92	.280	.335	4	.250	1	-0	-3	-0	-0.2
1996	Hou-N	1	5	.167	23	4	0	0	0	53	58	31	7	2	23	34	14.1	4.58	84	.289	.367	0	.000	-1	-2	-5	-0	-0.6
1997	Det-A	3	4	.429	61	4	0	0	2	78	74	31	10	3	36	60	13.0	3.23	142	.256	.345	0	—	0	12	12	1	1.0
1998	Det-A	5	2	.714	60	0	0	0	0	62^{2}	47	23	2	1	18	55	9.5	2.73	173	.211	.273	0	—	0	13	14	0	1.3
1999	Det-A	4	4	.500	70	0	0	0	2	82	60	23	7	4	25	78	9.8	2.52	193	.206	.278	0	—	0	21	21	0	1.9
2000	Det-A	5	4	.556	49	0	0	0	0	50^{2}	57	25	5	1	14	41	12.8	4.09	117	.285	.335	0	—	0	5	4	1	0.6
Total	9	28	36	.438	338	42	0	0	5	563	564	271	60	21	190	403	12.4	3.87	113	.263	.329	11	.164	-0	34	31	1	2.9

● CHRIS BROCK Brock, Terrence Christopher b: 2/5/70, Orlando, Fla. BR/TR, 6', 175 lbs. Deb: 6/11/97

YEAR	TM/L	W	L	PCT	G	GS	CG	SH	SV	IP	H	R	HR	HB	BB	SO	RAT	ERA	ERA+	OAV	OOB	BH	AVG	PB	PR	PR+	PD	TPI
1997	Atl-N	0	0	—	7	6	0	0	0	30^{2}	34	23	2	0	19	16	15.6	5.58	75	.288	.387	1	.100	-0	-5	-5	1	-0.2
1998	SF-N	0	0	—	13	0	0	0	0	27^{2}	31	13	3	0	7	19	12.4	3.90	102	.279	.322	1	.250	0	1	0	-1	0.0
1999	SF-N	6	8	.429	19	19	0	0	0	106^{2}	124	69	18	4	41	76	14.3	5.48	77	.291	.359	7	.200	1	-11	-16	-1	-1.7
2000	Phi-N	7	8	.467	63	5	0	0	1	93^{1}	85	48	21	3	41	69	12.4	4.34	109	.239	.322	2	.222	1	3	4	1	0.6
Total	4	13	16	.448	102	30	0	0	1	258^{1}	274	153	44	7	108	180	13.6	4.91	89	.271	.345	11	.190	2	-11	-16	-1	-1.3

● LEW BROCKETT Brockett, Lewis Albert "King" b: 7/23/1880, Brownsville, Ill. d: 9/19/60, Norris City, Ill. BR/TR, 5'10.5", 168 lbs. Deb: 4/25/07

YEAR	TM/L	W	L	PCT	G	GS	CG	SH	SV	IP	H	R	HR	HB	BB	SO	RAT	ERA	ERA+	OAV	OOB	BH	AVG	PB	PR	PR+	PD	TPI
1907	NY-A	1	2	.333	8	4	1	0	0	46^{1}	58	36	1	2	26	13	16.7	6.22	45	.309	.398	4	.182	-0	-19	-16	-1	-1.1
1909	NY-A	10	8	.556	26	18	10	3	1	170	148	68	3	6	59	70	11.3	2.12	119	.245	.318	17	.283	3	7	8	4	1.7
1911	NY-A	2	4	.333	16	8	2	0	0	75^{1}	73	45	3	5	39	25	14.0	4.66	77	.256	.356	12	.308	2	-11	-8	1	-0.4
Total	3	13	14	.481	50	30	13	3	1	291^{2}	279	149	7	13	124	108	12.8	3.43	83	.259	.343	33	.273	5	-23	-18	3	0.2

● DICK BRODOWSKI Brodowski, Richard Stanley b: 7/26/32, Bayonne, N.J. BR/TR, 6'2", 190 lbs. Deb: 6/15/52

YEAR	TM/L	W	L	PCT	G	GS	CG	SH	SV	IP	H	R	HR	HB	BB	SO	RAT	ERA	ERA+	OAV	OOB	BH	AVG	PB	PR	PR+	PD	TPI
1952	Bos-A	5	5	.500	20	12	4	0	0	114^{2}	111	66	12	3	50	42	12.9	4.40	90	.252	.333	8	.205	1	-9	-5	0	-0.3
1955	Bos-A	1	0	1.000	16	0	0	0	0	32	36	25	5	1	25	10	17.4	5.63	76	.295	.419	5	.500	3	-6	-4	1	0.1
1956	Was-A	0	3	.000	7	3	1	0	0	17^{2}	31	18	5	0	12	8	21.9	9.17	47	.397	.478	0	.000	-1	-10	-9	0	-1.3
1957	Was-A	0	1	.000	6	0	0	0	0	11^{1}	12	15	2	1	10	4	18.3	11.12	35	.261	.404	0	.000	-0	-9	-9	0	-0.7
1958	Cle-A	1	0	1.000	5	0	0	0	0	10	3	0	0	0	6	12	8.1	0.00	—	.100	.250	0	.000	-0	4	4	-0	0.4
1959	Cle-A	2	2	.500	18	0	0	0	5	30	19	13	3	3	21	9	12.9	1.80	205	.181	.333	2	.333	0	7	7	-1	1.1
Total	6	9	11	.450	72	15	5	0	5	215^{2}	212	137	27	8	124	85	14.4	4.76	84	.258	.361	15	.242	3	-23	-18	0	-0.7

● ERNIE BROGLIO Broglio, Ernest Gilbert b: 8/27/35, Berkeley, Cal. BR/TR, 6'2", 200 lbs. Deb: 4/11/59

YEAR	TM/L	W	L	PCT	G	GS	CG	SH	SV	IP	H	R	HR	HB	BB	SO	RAT	ERA	ERA+	OAV	OOB	BH	AVG	PB	PR	PR+	PD	TPI
1959	StL-N	7	12	.368	35	25	6	3	0	181^{1}	174	104	20	0	89	133	13.1	4.72	90	.250	.335	6	.098	-3	-15	-9	1	-1.0
1960	StL-N	**21**	9	**.700**	52	24	9	3	0	226^{1}	172	76	18	2	100	188	10.9	2.74	**149**	.213	.301	14	.206	2	26	31	1	4.4
1961	StL-N	9	12	.429	29	26	7	2	0	174^{2}	166	97	19	1	75	113	12.5	4.12	107	.248	.325	9	.145	-2	-2	5	-1	0.3
1962	StL-N	12	9	.571	34	30	11	4	0	222^{1}	193	80	22	2	93	132	11.7	3.00	143	.237	.316	10	.139	-2	23	29	1	2.4
1963	StL-N	18	8	.692	39	35	11	5	0	250	202	97	24	4	90	145	10.7	2.99	119	.216	.287	10	.112	-3	8	14	0	1.2
1964	StL-N	3	5	.375	11	11	3	1	0	69^{1}	65	33	7	1	26	36	11.9	3.50	109	.247	.317	2	.095	-0	0	2	-0	0.2
	Chi-N	4	7	.364	18	16	3	0	1	100^{1}	111	51	12	0	30	46	12.6	4.04	92	.281	.332	10	.286	3	-6	-3	-1	-0.2
	Yr	7	12	.368	29	27	6	1	1	169^{2}	176	84	19	1	56	82	12.4	3.82	98	.267	.326	12	.214	2	-5	-1	-2	0.0
1965	Chi-N	1	6	.143	26	6	0	0	0	50^{2}	63	44	7	0	46	22	19.4	6.93	53	.313	.441	0	.000	-0	-19	-18	-1	-2.3
1966	Chi-N	2	6	.250	15	11	2	0	1	62^{1}	70	46	14	0	38	34	15.6	6.35	58	.290	.387	7	.368	3	-19	-18	2	-1.7
Total	8	77	74	.510	259	184	52	18	2	1337^{1}	1216	628	143	10	587	849	12.2	3.74	107	.242	.322	68	.158	-2	-3	36	1	3.3

● KEN BRONDELL Brondell, Kenneth Leroy b: 10/17/21, Bradshaw, Neb. BR/TR, 6'1", 195 lbs. Deb: 5/3/44

YEAR	TM/L	W	L	PCT	G	GS	CG	SH	SV	IP	H	R	HR	HB	BB	SO	RAT	ERA	ERA+	OAV	OOB	BH	AVG	PB	PR	PR+	PD	TPI
1944	NY-N	0	1	.000	7	2	1	0	0	19^{1}	27	18	3	0	8	1	16.3	8.38	44	.329	.389	0	.000	-1	-10	-10	-1	-0.6

● JEFF BRONKEY Bronkey, Jacob Jeffrey b: 9/18/65, Kabul, Afghanistan BR/TR, 6'3", 215 lbs. Deb: 5/2/93

YEAR	TM/L	W	L	PCT	G	GS	CG	SH	SV	IP	H	R	HR	HB	BB	SO	RAT	ERA	ERA+	OAV	OOB	BH	AVG	PB	PR	PR+	PD	TPI
1993	Tex-A	1	1	.500	21	0	0	0	1	36	39	20	4	1	11	18	12.8	4.00	104	.285	.342	0	.000	-0	1	1	1	0.1
1994	Mil-A	1	1	.500	16	0	0	0	1	20^{2}	20	10	3	0	12	13	13.9	4.35	116	.247	.344	0	—	0	1	1	0	0.2
1995	Mil-A	0	0	—	8	0	0	0	0	12^{1}	15	6	0	0	6	5	15.3	3.65	137	.313	.389	0	—	0	1	2	-0	0.1
Total	3	2	2	.500	45	0	0	0	2	69	74	36	7	1	29	36	13.6	4.04	113	.278	.351	0	.000	-0	4	4	1	0.4

● JIM BRONSTAD Bronstad, James Warren b: 6/22/36, Ft.Worth, Tex. BR/TR, 6'3", 196 lbs. Deb: 6/7/59

YEAR	TM/L	W	L	PCT	G	GS	CG	SH	SV	IP	H	R	HR	HB	BB	SO	RAT	ERA	ERA+	OAV	OOB	BH	AVG	PB	PR	PR+	PD	TPI
1959	NY-A	0	3	.000	16	3	0	0	2	29^{1}	34	19	2	1	13	14	14.7	5.22	70	.288	.364	0	.000	-0	-4	-5	0	-0.6
1963	Was-A	1	3	.250	25	0	0	0	1	57^{1}	66	38	9	1	22	22	14.0	5.65	66	.297	.363	0	.000	-1	-13	-12	1	-0.8
1964	Was-A	0	1	.000	4	0	0	0	0	7	10	4	0	0	2	9	15.4	5.14	72	.345	.387	0	—	0	-1	-1	-0	-0.2
Total	3	1	7	.125	45	3	0	0	3	93^{2}	110	61	11	2	37	45	14.3	5.48	67	.298	.365	0	.000	-2	-18	-19	2	-1.6

● IKE BROOKENS Brookens, Edward Dwain b: 1/3/49, Chambersburg, Pa. BR/TR, 6'5", 170 lbs. Deb: 6/17/75

YEAR	TM/L	W	L	PCT	G	GS	CG	SH	SV	IP	H	R	HR	HB	BB	SO	RAT	ERA	ERA+	OAV	OOB	BH	AVG	PB	PR	PR+	PD	TPI
1975	Det-A	0	0	—	3	0	0	0	0	10^{1}	11	6	3	1	5	8	14.8	5.23	77	.282	.378	0	—	0	-2	-1	0	-0.1

● HARRY BROOKS Brooks, Harry Frank b: 11/30/1865, Philadelphia, Pa. d: 12/5/45, Philadelphia, Pa. Deb: 7/24/1886 ♦

YEAR	TM/L	W	L	PCT	G	GS	CG	SH	SV	IP	H	R	HR	HB	BB	SO	RAT	ERA	ERA+	OAV	OOB	BH	AVG	PB	PR	PR+	PD	TPI
1886	NY-a	0	1	.000	1	1	0	0	0	2	9	13	0	0	2	0	49.5	36.00	9	.429	.478	0	.000	-0	-7	-7	-0	-0.9

● JIM BROSNAN Brosnan, James Patrick b: 10/24/29, Cincinnati, O. BR/TR, 6'4", 210 lbs. Deb: 4/15/54

YEAR	TM/L	W	L	PCT	G	GS	CG	SH	SV	IP	H	R	HR	HB	BB	SO	RAT	ERA	ERA+	OAV	OOB	BH	AVG	PB	PR	PR+	PD	TPI
1954	Chi-N	1	0	1.000	18	0	0	0	0	33^{1}	44	35	9	1	18	17	17.0	9.45	44	.331	.414	1	.125	-0	-20	-19	1	-0.8
1956	Chi-N	5	9	.357	30	10	1	1	1	95	95	44	9	0	45	51	13.3	3.79	100	.270	.353	4	.182	-0	-0	-0	-1	-0.1
1957	Chi-N	5	5	.500	41	5	1	0	0	98^{2}	79	38	11	1	46	73	11.5	3.38	115	.219	.310	5	.250	2	6	5	1	0.8
1958	Chi-N	3	4	.429	8	8	2	0	0	51^{2}	41	20	3	0	29	24	12.2	3.14	125	.225	.332	2	.105	-1	5	5	1	0.6
	StL-N	8	4	.667	33	12	2	0	7	115	107	46	10	1	50	65	12.4	3.44	120	.250	.330	3	.097	-1	6	8	0	0.8
	Yr	11	8	.579	41	20	4	0	7	166^{2}	148	66	13	1	79	89	12.3	3.35	121	.243	.330	5	.100	-2	11	13	1	1.4
1959	StL-N	1	3	.250	20	1	0	0	2	33	34	18	5	1	15	18	13.6	4.91	86	.276	.360	2	.286	1	-4	-2	1	-0.1
	Cin-N	8	3	.727	26	9	1	1	2	83^{1}	79	35	7	5	26	56	11.9	3.35	121	.248	.314	1	.043	-2	6	6	1	0.7

YEAR	TM/L	W	L	PCT	G	GS	CG	SH	SV	IP	H	R	HR	HB	BB	SO	RAT	ERA	ERA+	OAV	OOB	BH	AVG	PB	PR	PR+	PD	TPI
	Yr	9	6	.600	46	10	1	1	4	116^{1}	113	53	12	6	41	74	12.4	3.79	108	.256	.327	3	.100	-1	2	4	1	0.6
1960	Cin-N	7	2	.778	57	2	0	0	12	99	79	31	5	0	22	62	9.2	2.36	162	.225	.271	3	.200	2	15	16	-0	2.0
1961	*Cin-N	10	4	.714	53	0	0	0	16	80	77	34	7	0	18	40	10.7	3.04	134	.249	.291	2	.154	-0	9	9	1	1.9
1962	Cin-N	4	4	.500	48	0	0	0	13	64^{2}	76	27	6	0	18	51	13.1	3.34	120	.292	.338	0	.000	-1	4	5	-1	0.6
1963	Cin-N	0	1	.000	6	0	0	0	0	4^{2}	8	4	2	0	3	4	21.2	7.71	43	.421	.500	0	—	0	-2	-2	0	-0.4
	Chi-A	3	8	.273	45	0	0	0	14	73	71	24	7	0	22	46	11.5	2.84	124	.263	.318	4	.308	1	6	6	-0	1.1
Total	9	55	47	.539	385	47	7	2	67	831^{1}	790	356	81	9	312	507	12.0	3.54	111	.254	.324	27	.153	1	31	36	3	7.1

● TERRY BROSS

Bross, Terrence Paul b: 3/30/66, ElPaso, Tex. BR/TR, 6'9", 234 lbs. Deb: 9/4/91

YEAR	TM/L	W	L	PCT	G	GS	CG	SH	SV	IP	H	R	HR	HB	BB	SO	RAT	ERA	ERA+	OAV	OOB	BH	AVG	PB	PR	PR+	PD	TPI
1991	NY-N	0	0	—	8	0	0	0	0	10	7	2	1	0	3	5	9.0	1.80	202	.200	.263	0	—	0	2	2	-0	0.1
1993	SF-N	0	0	—	2	0	0	0	0	2	3	2	1	0	1	1	18.0	9.00	43	.333	.400	0	—	0	-1	-1	-0	-0.1
Total	2	0	0	—	10	0	0	0	0	12	10	4	2	0	4	6	10.5	3.00	123	.227	.292	0	—	0	1	1	-1	0.0

● FRANK BROSSEAU

Brosseau, Franklin Lee b: 7/31/44, Drayton, N.D. BR/TR, 6'1", 180 lbs. Deb: 9/10/69

YEAR	TM/L	W	L	PCT	G	GS	CG	SH	SV	IP	H	R	HR	HB	BB	SO	RAT	ERA	ERA+	OAV	OOB	BH	AVG	PB	PR	PR+	PD	TPI
1969	Pit-N	0	0	—	2	0	0	0	0	1^{2}	2	2	0	0	2	2	21.6	10.80	32	.286	.444	0	—	0	-1	-1	-0	-0.1
1971	Pit-N	0	0	—	1	0	0	0	0	2	1	0	0	0	0	0	4.5	0.00	—	.200	.200	0	—	0	1	1	0	0.1
Total	2	0	0	—	3	0	0	0	0	3^{2}	3	2	0	0	2	2	12.3	4.91	70	.250	.357	0	—	0	-1	-1	0	0.0

● DAN BROUTHERS

Brouthers, Dennis Joseph "Big Dan"
b: 5/8/1858, Sylvan Lake, N.Y. d: 8/2/32, E.Orange, N.J. BL/TL (BR 1882 (1 game)), 6'2", 207 lbs. Deb: 6/23/1879 H♦

YEAR	TM/L	W	L	PCT	G	GS	CG	SH	SV	IP	H	R	HR	HB	BB	SO	RAT	ERA	ERA+	OAV	OOB	BH	AVG	PB	PR	PR+	PD	TPI
1879	Tro-N	0	2	.000	3	2	2	0	0	21	35	30	0		8	6	18.4	5.57	45	.343	.391	46	.274	1	-7	-7	-1	-0.5
1883	Buf-N	0	0	—	1	0	0	0	0	2	9	7	0		3	2	54.0	31.50	10	.643	.706	159	.374	1	-6	-6	-0	-0.2
Total	2	0	2	.000	4	2	2	0	0	23	44	37	0		11	8	21.5	7.83	33	.379	.433	2367	.349	1	-13	-13	-1	-0.7

● SCOTT BROW

Brow, Scott John b: 3/17/69, Butte, Mont. BR/TR, 6'3", 200 lbs. Deb: 4/28/93

YEAR	TM/L	W	L	PCT	G	GS	CG	SH	SV	IP	H	R	HR	HB	BB	SO	RAT	ERA	ERA+	OAV	OOB	BH	AVG	PB	PR	PR+	PD	TPI
1993	Tor-A	1	1	.500	6	3	0	0	0	18	19	15	2	1	10	7	15.0	6.00	72	.275	.375	0	—	0	-3	-3	1	-0.2
1994	Tor-A	0	3	.000	18	0	0	0	2	29	34	27	4	1	19	15	16.8	5.90	82	.288	.391	0	—	0	-4	-3	0	-0.3
1996	Tor-A	1	0	1.000	18	1	0	0	0	38^{2}	45	25	5	0	25	23	16.3	5.59	90	.294	.393	0	—	0	-3	-2	-0	-0.1
1998	Ari-N	1	0	1.000	17	0	0	0	0	21^{1}	22	17	2	0	14	13	15.2	7.17	59	.272	.379	0	.000	-0	-7	-7	-0	-0.4
Total	4	3	4	.429	59	4	0	0	2	107	120	84	13	2	68	58	16.0	6.06	77	.285	.387	0	.000	-0	-16	-16	1	-1.0

● FRANK BROWER

Brower, Frank Willard "Turkeyfoot" b: 3/26/1893, Gainesville, Va. d: 11/20/60, Baltimore, Md. BL/TR, 6'2", 180 lbs. Deb: 8/14/20 ♦

YEAR	TM/L	W	L	PCT	G	GS	CG	SH	SV	IP	H	R	HR	HB	BB	SO	RAT	ERA	ERA+	OAV	OOB	BH	AVG	PB	PR	PR+	PD	TPI
1924	Cle-A	0	0	—	4	0	0	0	0	9^{2}	7	2	0	1	4	0	11.2	0.93	459	.212	.316	30	.280	1	4	4	-0	0.2

● JIM BROWER

Brower, James Robert b: 12/29/72, Edina, Minn. BR/TR, 6'2", 205 lbs. Deb: 9/5/99

YEAR	TM/L	W	L	PCT	G	GS	CG	SH	SV	IP	H	R	HR	HB	BB	SO	RAT	ERA	ERA+	OAV	OOB	BH	AVG	PB	PR	PR+	PD	TPI
1999	Cle-A	3	1	.750	9	2	0	0	0	25^{2}	27	13	8	1	10	18	13.3	4.56	111	.270	.342	0	—	0	1	1	-0	0.1
2000	Cle-A	2	3	.400	17	11	0	0	0	62	80	45	11	2	31	32	16.4	6.24	80	.309	.387	0	.000	-0	-9	-8	1	-0.5
Total	2	5	4	.556	26	13	0	0	0	87^{2}	107	58	19	3	41	50	15.5	5.75	87	.298	.375	0	.000	-0	-8	-7	1	-0.4

● ALTON BROWN

Brown, Alton Leo "Deacon" b: 4/16/25, Norfolk, Va. BR/TR, 6'2", 195 lbs. Deb: 4/21/51

YEAR	TM/L	W	L	PCT	G	GS	CG	SH	SV	IP	H	R	HR	HB	BB	SO	RAT	ERA	ERA+	OAV	OOB	BH	AVG	PB	PR	PR+	PD	TPI
1951	Was-A	0	0	—	7	0	0	0	0	11^{2}	14	12	1	1	12	7	20.8	9.26	44	.298	.450	0	.000	-0	-7	-7	-0	-0.4

● BOARDWALK BROWN

Brown, Carroll William b: 2/20/1887, Woodbury, N.J. d: 2/8/77, Burlington, N.J. BR/TR, 6'1.5", 178 lbs. Deb: 9/27/11

YEAR	TM/L	W	L	PCT	G	GS	CG	SH	SV	IP	H	R	HR	HB	BB	SO	RAT	ERA	ERA+	OAV	OOB	BH	AVG	PB	PR	PR+	PD	TPI
1911	Phi-A	0	1	.000	2	1	1	0	0	12	12	7	0	0	2	6	10.5	4.50	70	.267	.298	0	.000	-1	-2	-2	0	-0.2
1912	Phi-A	13	11	.542	34	24	15	3	0	199	204	115	2	9	87	64	13.6	3.66	84	.283	.367	11	.145	-3	-8	-14	3	-1.5
1913	Phi-A	17	11	.607	43	35	11	3	1	235^{1}	200	94	6	10	87	70	11.4	2.94	94	.219	.294	13	.159	-1	-0	-5	-2	-0.9
1914	Phi-A	1	5	.167	15	7	2	0	0	66	64	34	1	0	26	20	12.3	4.09	64	.268	.340	0	.000	-2	-10	-11	0	-1.2
	NY-A	6	5	.545	20	14	8	0	0	122^{1}	123	57	2	1	42	57	12.2	3.24	85	.271	.334	8	.182	1	-7	-6	3	-0.1
	Yr	7	10	.412	35	21	10	0	0	188^{1}	187	91	3	1	68	77	12.2	3.54	77	.270	.336	8	.125	-0	-17	-18	3	-1.3
1915	NY-A	3	6	.333	19	11	5	0	0	96^{2}	95	49	4	5	47	34	13.7	4.10	72	.275	.370	6	.188	-1	-12	-12	-0	-1.2
Total	5	40	39	.506	133	92	42	6	1	731^{1}	698	356	15	25	291	251	12.5	3.47	83	.257	.334	38	.147	-6	-39	-51	4	-5.1

● CHARLIE BROWN

Brown, Charles E. b: 1878, Baltimore, Md. TL, 6', 180 lbs. Deb: 8/4/1897

YEAR	TM/L	W	L	PCT	G	GS	CG	SH	SV	IP	H	R	HR	HB	BB	SO	RAT	ERA	ERA+	OAV	OOB	BH	AVG	PB	PR	PR+	PD	TPI
1897	Cle-N	1	2	.333	4	4	2	0	0	24^{1}	30	25	2	5	17	8	19.2	7.77	58	.300	.426	3	.273	0	-9	-9	-0	-0.7

● BUSTER BROWN

Brown, Charles Edward "Yank" b: 8/31/1881, Boone, Iowa d: 2/9/14, Sioux City, Iowa BR/TR, 6', 180 lbs. Deb: 6/22/05

YEAR	TM/L	W	L	PCT	G	GS	CG	SH	SV	IP	H	R	HR	HB	BB	SO	RAT	ERA	ERA+	OAV	OOB	BH	AVG	PB	PR	PR+	PD	TPI
1905	StL-N	8	11	.421	23	21	17	3	0	178^{2}	172	80	5	10	62	57	12.3	2.97	100	.260	.332	6	.092	-3	1	0	3	0.0
1906	StL-N	8	16	.333	32	27	21	0	0	238^{1}	208	98	2	11	112	109	12.5	2.64	99	.234	.327	14	.165	0	-0	-0	2	0.2
1907	StL-N	1	6	.143	9	8	6	0	0	63^{2}	57	38	2	5	45	17	15.1	3.39	74	.263	.401	7	.269	2	-7	-6	2	-0.3
	Phi-N	9	6	.600	21	16	13	4	0	130	118	47	3	6	56	38	12.5	2.42	100	.246	.333	10	.189	2	1	-0	-1	0.1
	Yr	10	12	.455	30	24	19	4	0	193^{2}	175	85	5	11	101	55	13.3	2.74	89	.251	.355	17	.215	3	-6	-6	1	-0.2
1908	Phi-N	0	0	—	3	0	0	0	0	7	9	6	0	1	5	3	19.3	2.57	94	.346	.469	1	.200	-0	-0	-0	1	0.1
1909	Phi-N	0	0	—	7	1	0	0	0	25	22	10	1	1	16	10	14.0	3.24	80	.259	.382	0	.000	-1	-2	-2	0	-0.2
	Bos-N	4	8	.333	18	17	8	2	0	123^{1}	108	45	1	7	56	32	12.5	3.14	90	.244	.339	7	.146	-2	-7	-4	1	-0.5
	Yr	4	8	.333	25	18	8	2	0	148^{1}	130	55	2	8	72	42	12.7	3.16	88	.247	.346	7	.123	-3	-9	-6	1	-0.7
1910	Bos-N	9	23	.281	46	29	16	1	2	263	251	113	4	4	94	88	11.9	2.67	125	.268	.337	16	.198	0	11	18	1	2.3
1911	Bos-N	8	18	.308	42	25	13	0	2	241	258	161	11	10	116	76	14.3	4.29	89	.284	.371	21	.250	3	-24	-11	0	-0.7
1912	Bos-N	4	15	.211	31	21	12	0	0	168^{1}	146	107	7	2	66	68	11.4	4.01	89	.239	.315	13	.213	1	-11	-8	0	-0.6
1913	Bos-N	0	0	—	2	0	0	0	0	13^{1}	19	10	0	2	3	3	16.2	4.73	70	.396	.453	0	.000	-0	-2	-2	-0	-0.1
Total	9	51	103	.331	234	165	106	10	4	1451^{2}	1368	715	36	59	631	501	12.8	3.21	96	.258	.343	95	.182	3	-42	-17	9	0.3

● CURLY BROWN

Brown, Charles Roy "Lefty" b: 12/9/1888, Spring Hill, Kan. d: 6/10/68, Spring Hill, Kan. BL/TL, 5'10.5", 165 lbs. Deb: 9/8/11

YEAR	TM/L	W	L	PCT	G	GS	CG	SH	SV	IP	H	R	HR	HB	BB	SO	RAT	ERA	ERA+	OAV	OOB	BH	AVG	PB	PR	PR+	PD	TPI
1911	StL-A	1	2	.333	3	2	2	0	0	23	22	9	0	1	5	8	11.0	2.74	123	.247	.295	0	.000	-1	2	2	0	0.0
1912	StL-A	1	3	.250	16	4	2	1	0	64^{2}	69	56	0	3	35	28	14.9	4.87	68	.277	.373	5	.208	-0	-11	-11	-3	-0.9
1913	StL-A	1	1	.500	2	2	2	0	0	14	12	5	0	0	4	3	10.3	2.57	114	.245	.302	2	.400	1	1	1	-0	0.1
1915	Cin-N	0	2	.000	7	3	0	0	0	27	26	20	2	2	6	13	11.3	4.67	61	.245	.298	4	.364	1	-6	-5	-1	-0.4
Total	4	3	8	.273	28	11	6	1	0	128^{2}	129	90	2	6	50	52	12.9	4.20	76	.262	.337	11	.224	0	-15	-14	-4	-1.2

● CLINT BROWN

Brown, Clinton Harold b: 7/8/03, Blackash, Pa. d: 12/31/55, Rocky River, Ohio BL/TR, 6'1", 190 lbs. Deb: 9/27/28

YEAR	TM/L	W	L	PCT	G	GS	CG	SH	SV	IP	H	R	HR	HB	BB	SO	RAT	ERA	ERA+	OAV	OOB	BH	AVG	PB	PR	PR+	PD	TPI
1928	Cle-A	0	1	.000	2	1	1	0	0	11	14	6	0	0	2	2	13.1	4.91	84	.304	.333	1	.200	-0	-1	-1	0	-0.1
1929	Cle-A	0	2	.000	3	1	1	0	0	16^{1}	18	8	0	0	6	1	13.2	3.31	134	.286	.348	0	.000	-1	2	2	1	0.2
1930	Cle-A	11	13	.458	35	31	16	**3**	1	213^{2}	271	138	14	4	51	54	13.7	4.97	97	.314	.356	18	.247	2	-8	-3	2	0.1
1931	Cle-A	11	15	.423	39	33	12	2	0	233^{1}	284	143	10	1	55	50	13.1	4.71	98	.295	.333	15	.172	-2	-8	-2	4	0.0
1932	Cle-A	15	12	.556	37	32	21	1	1	262^{2}	298	143	14	4	50	59	12.1	4.08	116	.279	.314	25	.250	6	12	18	2	2.3
1933	Cle-A	11	12	.478	33	23	10	2	1	185	202	83	10	2	34	47	11.6	3.41	130	.276	.310	9	.145	-3	18	21	3	2.3
1934	Cle-A	4	3	.571	17	2	0	0	1	50^{1}	83	42	3	0	14	15	17.3	5.90	77	.359	.396	5	.294	1	-8	-7	-0	-0.8
1935	Cle-A	4	3	.571	23	5	1	0	2	49	61	34	3	1	14	20	14.0	5.14	88	.300	.349	2	.200	0	-4	-3	1	-0.3
1936	Chi-A	6	2	.750	38	2	0	0	5	83	106	50	5	3	24	19	14.4	4.99	104	.315	.366	4	.160	-0	0	2	0	0.2
1937	Chi-A	7	7	.500	**53**	0	0	0	**18**	100	92	47	7	1	36	51	11.6	3.42	135	.242	.309	4	.222	1	**13**	**13**	1	2.3
1938	Chi-A	1	3	.250	8	0	0	0	2	13^{2}	16	8	0	0	9	2	16.5	4.61	106	.333	.439	1	.500	1	0	0	1	0.3
1939	Chi-A	11	10	.524	**61**	0	0	0	18	118^{1}	127	58	8	0	27	41	11.7	3.88	122	.281	.322	4	.211	1	10	11	2	2.2
1940	Chi-A	4	6	.400	37	0	0	0	10	66	75	30	5	2	16	23	12.7	3.68	120	.284	.330	1	.071	-1	5	5	0	0.8
1941	Cle-A	3	3	.500	41	0	0	0	5	74^{1}	77	30	3	1	28	22	12.8	3.27	120	.279	.348	2	.118	0	7	6	3	0.8
1942	Cle-A	1	1	.500	7	0	0	0	0	9	16	10	2	1	2	4	19.0	6.00	57	.356	.396	0	.000	-0	-2	-3	-0	-0.6
Total	15	89	93	.489	434	130	62	8	64	1485^{2}	1740	830	84	20	368	410	12.9	4.26	109	.291	.335	91	.199	5	37	58	19	9.7

● CURT BROWN

Brown, Curtis Steven b: 1/15/60, Ft.Lauderdale, Fla. BR/TR, 6'5", 200 lbs. Deb: 6/10/83

YEAR	TM/L	W	L	PCT	G	GS	CG	SH	SV	IP	H	R	HR	HB	BB	SO	RAT	ERA	ERA+	OAV	OOB	BH	AVG	PB	PR	PR+	PD	TPI
1983	Cal-A	1	1	.500	10	0	0	0	0	16	25	13	1	0	4	7	16.3	7.31	55	.368	.403	0	—	0	-6	-6	-0	-0.7
1984	NY-A	1	1	.500	13	0	0	0	0	16^{2}	18	5	1	0	4	10	11.9	2.70	141	.281	.324	0	—	0	2	2	0	0.2
1986	Mon-N	0	1	.000	6	0	0	0	0	12	15	6	0	0	2	4	12.8	3.00	123	.319	.347	0	.000	-0	1	1	0	0.1
1987	Mon-N	0	1	.000	5	0	0	0	0	7	10	7	2	0	4	6	18.0	7.71	55	.333	.412	0	—	0	-3	-3	0	-0.3
Total	4	2	4	.333	34	0	0	0	0	51^{2}	68	31	4	0	14	27	14.3	4.88	80	.325	.368	0	.000	-0	-5	-6	-0	-0.7

● ED BROWN Brown, Edward P. b: Chicago, Ill. TR, 178 lbs. Deb: 8/19/1882 ♦

YEAR	TM/L	W	L	PCT	G	GS	CG	SH	SV	IP	H	R	HR	HB	BB	SO	RAT	ERA	ERA+	OAV	OOB	BH	AVG	PB	PR	PR+	PD	TPI
1882	StL-a	0	0	—	1	0	0	0	0	2	2	1	0		0	1	9.0	0.00	—	.250	.250	11	.183	-0	1	1	-0	0.0
1884	Tol-a	0	1	.000	1	1	1	0	0	9	19	16	0	1	4	1	24.0	9.00	38	.396	.453	27	.176	-0	-6	-5	-0	-0.4
Total	2	0	1	.000	2	1	1	0	0	11	21	17	0	1	4	2	21.3	7.36	45	.375	.426	38	.178	-0	-5	-5	-0	-0.4

● ELMER BROWN Brown, Elmer Young "Shook" b: 3/25/1883, Southport, Ind. d: 1/23/55, Indianapolis, Ind. BL/TR, 5'11.5", 172 lbs. Deb: 9/16/11

YEAR	TM/L	W	L	PCT	G	GS	CG	SH	SV	IP	H	R	HR	HB	BB	SO	RAT	ERA	ERA+	OAV	OOB	BH	AVG	PB	PR	PR+	PD	TPI
1911	StL-A	1	1	.500	5	3	1	1	0	16^2	16	17	0	0	14	5	16.2	6.48	52	.242	.375	1	.125	-1	-6	-6	1	-0.6
1912	StL-A	5	8	.385	23	13	2	1	0	120^1	122	56	2	12	42	45	13.2	2.99	111	.280	.359	6	.167	-1	4	4	-1	0.3
1913	Bro-N	0	0	—	3	1	0	0	0	13	6	3	0	1	10	6	11.8	2.08	159	.158	.347	0	.000	-1	2	2	-0	0.0
1914	Bro-N	1	2	.333	11	5	1	0	0	36^2	33	28	2	7	23	22	15.5	3.93	73	.402	.563	1	.083	-1	-5	-4	1	-0.4
1915	Bro-N	0	0	—	1	0	0	0	0	2	4	4	0	0	3	1	31.5	9.00	31	.500	.636	0	—	0	-1	-1	0	0.0
Total	5	7	11	.389	43	22	4	2	0	188^2	181	108	4	20	92	79	14.0	3.48	93	.287	.395	8	.133	-3	-6	-5	0	-0.7

● HAL BROWN Brown, Hector Harold "Skinny" b: 12/11/24, Greensboro, N.C. BR/TR, 6'2", 182 lbs. Deb: 4/19/51 C

YEAR	TM/L	W	L	PCT	G	GS	CG	SH	SV	IP	H	R	HR	HB	BB	SO	RAT	ERA	ERA+	OAV	OOB	BH	AVG	PB	PR	PR+	PD	TPI
1951	Chi-A	0	0	—	3	0	0	0	1	8^2	15	9	3	0	4	4	19.7	9.35	43	.385	.442	2	1.000	1	-5	-5	0	-0.1
1952	Chi-A	2	3	.400	24	8	1	0	0	72^1	82	39	8	0	21	31	12.8	4.23	86	.284	.332	3	.158	1	-4	-5	-0	-0.2
1953	Bos-A	11	6	.647	30	25	6	1	0	166^1	177	94	16	0	57	62	12.7	4.65	90	.269	.327	17	.293	5	-12	-8	-0	-0.3
1954	Bos-A	1	8	.111	40	5	1	0	0	118	126	64	6	3	41	66	13.0	4.12	100	.269	.331	3	.125	-0	-5	-0	1	0.0
1955	Bos-A	1	0	1.000	2	0	0	0	0	4	2	1	0	0	2	2	9.0	2.25	191	.143	.250	1	1.000	0	1	1	-0	0.2
	Bal-A	0	4	.000	15	5	1	0	0	57	51	30	5	0	26	26	12.2	4.11	93	.241	.324	0	.000	-1	-1	-2	-1	-0.3
	Yr	1	4	.200	17	5	1	0	0	61	53	31	5	0	28	28	12.0	3.98	97	.235	.319	1	.059	-1	-0	-1	-1	-0.1
1956	Bal-A	9	7	.563	35	14	4	1	2	151^2	142	72	18	1	37	57	10.7	4.04	97	.247	.294	8	.190	1	2	-2	0	0.0
1957	Bal-A	7	8	.467	25	20	7	2	1	150	132	68	17	2	37	62	10.3	3.90	92	.236	.285	10	.208	2	-2	-5	-1	-0.4
1958	Bal-A	7	5	.583	19	17	4	2	1	96^2	96	35	9	0	20	44	10.8	3.07	117	.259	.297	4	.148	-0	7	6	-0	0.7
1959	Bal-A	11	9	.550	31	21	2	0	3	164	158	73	16	1	32	81	10.5	3.79	100	.252	.290	2	.048	-3	1	-0	-1	-0.3
1960	Bal-A	12	5	.706	30	20	6	1	0	159	155	61	14	1	22	66	**10.1**	3.06	125	.258	**.286**	8	.182	3	14	13	-1	1.5
1961	Bal-A	10	6	.625	27	23	6	3	1	166^2	153	62	14	1	33	61	10.1	3.19	121	.247	.286	7	.140	-0	16	13	-0	1.1
1962	Bal-A	6	4	.600	22	11	0	0	1	85^2	88	41	12	3	21	25	11.8	4.10	90	.268	.318	8	.286	2	-1	-4	-1	-0.4
	NY-A	0	1	.000	2	1	0	0	0	6^2	9	10	3	0	2	2	14.9	6.75	56	.333	.379	0	.000	-0	-2	-2	-0	-0.3
	Yr	6	5	.545	24	12	0	0	1	92^1	97	51	15	3	23	27	12.0	4.29	86	.273	.323	8	.276	1	-3	-6	-1	-0.7
1963	Hou-N	5	11	.313	26	20	6	3	0	141^1	137	54	14	0	8	68	9.2	3.31	95	.255	.266	4	.093	-2	-0	-3	-3	-0.7
1964	Hou-N	3	15	.167	27	21	3	0	1	132	154	68	18	2	26	53	12.4	3.95	86	.292	.327	5	.128	-1	-6	-8	-2	-1.3
Total	14	85	92	.480	358	211	47	13	11	1680	1677	781	173	14	389	710	11.1	3.81	98	.260	.303	82	.169	8	2	-12	-10	-0.8

● JACKIE BROWN Brown, Jackie Gene b: 5/31/43, Holdenville, Okla. BR/TR, 6'1", 195 lbs. Deb: 7/2/70 FC

YEAR	TM/L	W	L	PCT	G	GS	CG	SH	SV	IP	H	R	HR	HB	BB	SO	RAT	ERA	ERA+	OAV	OOB	BH	AVG	PB	PR	PR+	PD	TPI
1970	Was-A	2	2	.500	24	5	1	0	0	57	49	28	8	0	37	47	13.6	3.95	90	.231	.345	2	.154	-0	-1	-3	-1	-0.3
1971	Was-A	3	4	.429	14	9	0	0	0	47	60	34	9	1	27	21	16.9	5.94	56	.316	.404	2	.133	-0	-13	-14	1	-1.9
1973	Tex-A	5	5	.500	25	3	2	1	2	66^2	82	31	7	2	25	45	14.7	3.92	95	.309	.373	0	—	0	-1	-1	-0	-0.3
1974	Tex-A	13	12	.520	35	26	9	2	0	216^2	219	97	13	4	74	134	12.3	3.57	100	.265	.329	0	—	0	1	-0	-1	-0.1
1975	Tex-A	5	5	.500	17	7	2	1	0	70^1	70	37	7	2	35	35	13.7	4.22	89	.266	.357	0	—	0	-3	-4	-2	-0.6
	Cle-A	1	2	.333	25	3	1	0	1	69^1	72	40	9	0	29	41	13.1	4.28	89	.276	.348	0	—	0	-4	-4	-0	-0.2
	Yr	6	7	.462	42	10	3	1	1	139^2	142	77	16	2	64	76	13.4	4.25	89	.271	.353	0	—	0	-7	-7	-2	-0.8
1976	Cle-A	9	11	.450	32	27	5	2	0	180	193	94	14	7	55	104	12.8	4.25	82	.276	.335	0	—	0	-15	-15	-1	-1.6
1977	Mon-N	9	12	.429	42	25	6	2	0	185^2	189	99	15	4	71	89	12.8	4.51	85	.264	.334	7	.125	-2	-12	-15	-2	-1.9
Total	7	47	53	.470	214	105	26	8	3	892^2	934	460	82	20	353	516	13.2	4.18	87	.272	.343	11	.131	-3	-48	-55	-7	-6.9

● KEVIN BROWN Brown, James Kevin b: 3/14/65, Milledgeville, Ga. BR/TR, 6'4", 195 lbs. Deb: 9/30/86

YEAR	TM/L	W	L	PCT	G	GS	CG	SH	SV	IP	H	R	HR	HB	BB	SO	RAT	ERA	ERA+	OAV	OOB	BH	AVG	PB	PR	PR+	PD	TPI
1986	Tex-A	1	0	1.000	1	1	0	0	0	5	6	2	0	0	0	4	10.8	3.60	120	.316	.316	0	—	0	0	0	0	0.1
1988	Tex-A	1	1	.500	4	4	1	0	0	23^1	33	15	2	1	8	12	16.2	4.24	96	.330	.385	0	—	0	-1	-0	-0	-0.1
1989	Tex-A	12	9	.571	28	28	7	0	0	191	167	81	10	4	70	104	11.4	3.35	119	.234	.305	0	—	0	12	13	3	1.7
1990	Tex-A	12	10	.545	26	26	6	2	0	180	175	84	13	3	60	88	11.9	3.60	109	.255	.318	0	.000	-0	6	7	-0	0.7
1991	Tex-A	9	12	.429	33	33	0	0	0	210^2	233	116	17	13	90	96	14.4	4.40	92	.284	.364	0	—	0	-7	-9	1	-0.7
1992	Tex-A★	**21**	11	.656	35	35	11	1	0	**265^2**	262	117	11	10	76	173	11.8	3.32	115	.260	.318	0	—	0	19	15	2	1.9
1993	Tex-A	15	12	.556	34	34	12	3	0	233	228	105	14	15	74	142	12.2	3.59	116	.252	.319	0	—	0	19	15	4	2.0
1994	Tex-A	7	9	.438	26	25	3	0	0	170	218	109	18	6	50	123	14.5	4.82	100	.314	.365	0	—	0	-0	0	3	0.3
1995	Bal-A	10	9	.526	26	26	3	1	0	172^1	155	73	10	9	48	117	11.1	3.60	132	.241	.303	0	—	0	21	22	7	2.8
1996	Fla-N★	17	11	.607	32	32	5	**3**	0	233	187	60	8	16	33	159	9.1	**1.89**	**215**	.220	.263	9	.120	-1	**60**	**59**	6	**7.6**
1997	*Fla-N★	16	8	.667	33	33	6	2	0	237^1	214	77	10	14	66	205	11.1	2.69	150	.240	.303	9	.125	-0	40	37	5	4.0
1998	*SD-N★	18	7	.720	36	35	7	3	0	257	225	77	8	10	49	257	9.9	2.38	164	.235	.280	17	.207	4	53	47	3	5.2
1999	LA-N	18	9	.667	35	35	5	1	0	252^1	210	99	19	7	59	221	9.8	3.00	143	.222	.273	5	.064	-5	44	39	5	3.7
2000	LA-N★	13	6	.684	33	33	5	1	0	230	181	76	21	9	47	216	**9.3**	**2.58**	170	**.213**	**.262**	5	.076	-3	53	49	3	3.6
Total	14	170	114	.599	382	380	71	17	0	2660^2	2494	1091	161	117	730	1917	11.3	3.21	130	.248	.306	45	.120	-6	319	290	41	32.8

● JIM BROWN Brown, James W. H. b: 12/12/1860, Clinton Co., Pa. d: 4/6/08, Williamsport, Pa. Deb: 4/17/1884 ♦

YEAR	TM/L	W	L	PCT	G	GS	CG	SH	SV	IP	H	R	HR	HB	BB	SO	RAT	ERA	ERA+	OAV	OOB	BH	AVG	PB	PR	PR+	PD	TPI
1884	Alt-U	1	9	.100	11	11	7	0	0	74	99	80	0		36	39	16.4	5.35	50	.301	.370	22	.250	-2	-24	-20	0	-2.0
	NY-N	0	1	.000	1	1	1	0	0	9	10	9	0		8	2	18.0	5.00	60	.263	.391	0	.000	-1	-2	-2	-0	-0.2
	StP-U	1	4	.200	6	6	4	1	0	36	43	34	1		14	20	14.3	3.75	35	.277	.337	5	.313	4	-5	-18	0	-1.5
1886	Phi-a	0	1	.000	1	1	1	0	0	8^1	9	5	0	0	3	4	13.0	3.24	108	.265	.324	0	.000	-1	0	-0	-0	0.0
Total	2	2	15	.118	19	19	13	1	0	127^1	161	128	1	0	61	65	15.7	4.74	50	.290	.360	27	.245	1	-31	-37	0	-3.7

● JOHN BROWN Brown, John J. "Ad" b: Trenton, N.J. Deb: 8/11/1897

YEAR	TM/L	W	L	PCT	G	GS	CG	SH	SV	IP	H	R	HR	HB	BB	SO	RAT	ERA	ERA+	OAV	OOB	BH	AVG	PB	PR	PR+	PD	TPI
1897	Bro-N	0	1	.000	1	1	0	0	0	5	7	8	0	3	4	0	25.2	7.20	57	.333	.500	1	.500	0	-2	-2	0	-0.2

● JOPHERY BROWN Brown, Jophery Clifford b: 1/22/45, Grambling, La. BL/TR, 6'2", 190 lbs. Deb: 9/21/68

YEAR	TM/L	W	L	PCT	G	GS	CG	SH	SV	IP	H	R	HR	HB	BB	SO	RAT	ERA	ERA+	OAV	OOB	BH	AVG	PB	PR	PR+	PD	TPI
1968	Chi-N	0	0	—	1	0	0	0	0	2	2	1	0	0	1	0	13.5	4.50	70	.286	.375	0	—	0	-0	-0	0	0.0

● JOE BROWN Brown, Joseph E. b: 4/4/1859, Warren, Pa. d: 6/28/1888, Warren, Pa. 5'10", 162 lbs. Deb: 8/16/1884 ♦

YEAR	TM/L	W	L	PCT	G	GS	CG	SH	SV	IP	H	R	HR	HB	BB	SO	RAT	ERA	ERA+	OAV	OOB	BH	AVG	PB	PR	PR+	PD	TPI
1884	Chi-N	4	2	.667	7	6	5	0	0	50	56	36	4		7	27	11.3	4.68	67	.258	.281	13	.213	-1	-9	-8	-0	-0.8
1885	Bal-a	0	4	.000	4	4	4	0	0	38	52	33	0	0	4	9	13.3	5.68	57	.306	.322	3	.158	-1	-10	-10	-0	-0.9
Total	2	4	6	.400	11	10	9	0	0	88	108	69	4	0	11	36	12.2	5.11	62	.279	.299	16	.200	-2	-20	-18	-1	-1.7

● JOE BROWN Brown, Joseph Henry b: 7/3/1900, Little Rock, Ark. d: 3/7/50, Los Angeles, Cal. BR/TR, 6', 176 lbs. Deb: 5/17/27

YEAR	TM/L	W	L	PCT	G	GS	CG	SH	SV	IP	H	R	HR	HB	BB	SO	RAT	ERA	ERA+	OAV	OOB	BH	AVG	PB	PR	PR+	PD	TPI
1927	Chi-A	0	0	—	1	1	0	0	0	0	2	0	0	1	—	—	∞	—	1.000	1.000	98	—	0	-3	-3	0	-0.3	

● KEITH BROWN Brown, Keith Edward b: 2/14/64, Flagstaff, Ariz. BB/TR, 6'4", 215 lbs. Deb: 8/25/88

YEAR	TM/L	W	L	PCT	G	GS	CG	SH	SV	IP	H	R	HR	HB	BB	SO	RAT	ERA	ERA+	OAV	OOB	BH	AVG	PB	PR	PR+	PD	TPI
1988	Cin-N	2	1	.667	4	3	0	0	0	16^1	14	5	1	0	4	6	9.9	2.76	130	.237	.286	0	.000	-0	1	1	0	0.2
1990	Cin-N	0	0	—	8	0	0	0	0	11^1	12	6	2	0	3	8	11.9	4.76	83	.286	.333	0	—	0	-1	-1	0	0.0
1991	Cin-N	0	0	—	11	0	0	0	0	12	15	4	0	0	6	4	15.8	2.25	169	.306	.382	0	—	0	2	2	0	0.1
1992	Cin-N	0	1	.000	2	2	0	0	0	8	10	5	2	0	5	5	16.9	4.50	80	.313	.405	0	.000	-0	-1	-1	-0	-0.1
Total	4	2	2	.500	25	5	0	0	0	47^2	51	20	5	0	18	23	13.0	3.40	110	.280	.345	0	.000	-1	1	2	0	0.2

● KEVIN BROWN Brown, Kevin Dewayne b: 3/5/66, Oroville, Cal. BL/TL, 6'1", 185 lbs. Deb: 7/27/90

YEAR	TM/L	W	L	PCT	G	GS	CG	SH	SV	IP	H	R	HR	HB	BB	SO	RAT	ERA	ERA+	OAV	OOB	BH	AVG	PB	PR	PR+	PD	TPI
1990	NY-N	0	0	—	2	0	0	0	0	2	2	0	0	0	1	0	13.5	0.00	—	.250	.333	0	—	0	1	1	0	0.1
	Mil-A	1	1	.500	5	3	0	0	0	21	14	7	1	1	7	12	9.4	2.57	151	.182	.259	0	—	0	3	3	1	0.3
1991	Mil-A	2	4	.333	15	10	0	0	0	63^2	66	39	6	1	34	30	14.3	5.51	72	.270	.362	0	—	0	-10	-11	-0	-0.9
1992	Sea-A	0	0	—	2	0	0	0	0	3	4	3	1	0	3	2	21.0	9.00	44	.333	.467	0	—	0	-2	-2	0	-0.1
Total	3	3	5	.375	24	13	0	0	0	89^2	86	49	8	2	45	44	13.3	4.82	82	.252	.343	0	—	0	-8	-9	1	-0.6

● LEW BROWN Brown, Lewis J. "Blower" b: 2/1/1858, Leominster, Mass. d: 1/15/1889, Boston, Mass. BR/TR, 5'10.5", 185 lbs. Deb: 6/17/1876 ♦

YEAR	TM/L	W	L	PCT	G	GS	CG	SH	SV	IP	H	R	HR	HB	BB	SO	RAT	ERA	ERA+	OAV	OOB	BH	AVG	PB	PR	PR+	PD	TPI
1878	Pro-N	0	0	—	1	0	0	0	0	1	0	4	0		4	0	36.0	18.00	12	.000	.500	74	.305	0	-2	-2	-0	-0.1
1884	Bos-U	0	0	—	1	0	0	0	1	1	6	7	0		1	0	63.0	36.00	7	.667	.700	75	.231	-0	-4	-4	-0	-0.5
Total	2	0	0	—	2	0	0	0	1	2	6	11	0		5	0	49.5	27.00	8	.462	.611	379	.247	0	-5	-6	0	-0.6

● LLOYD BROWN Brown, Lloyd Andrew "Gimpy" b: 12/25/04, Beeville, Tex. d: 1/14/74, Opa-Locka, Fla. BL/TL, 5'9", 170 lbs. Deb: 7/17/25

YEAR	TM/L	W	L	PCT	G	GS	CG	SH	SV	IP	H	R	HR	HB	BB	SO	RAT	ERA	ERA+	OAV	OOB	BH	AVG	PB	PR	PR+	PD	TPI
1925	Bro-N	0	3	.000	17	5	1	0	0	63^1	79	39	1	2	25	23	15.1	4.12	101	.319	.385	2	.087	-2	1	0	0	-0.2
1928	Was-A	4	4	.500	27	10	2	0	1	107	112	62	7	2	40	38	13.0	4.04	99	.273	.341	5	.161	0	0	-0	3	0.3
1929	Was-A	8	7	.533	40	15	7	1	0	168	186	92	7	1	69	48	13.7	4.18	101	.297	.368	11	.220	3	1	1	2	0.5
1930	Was-A	16	12	.571	38	22	10	1	0	197	220	99	6	5	65	59	13.2	4.25	108	.293	.354	14	.215	2	9	8	3	1.4
1931	Was-A	15	14	.517	42	32	15	1	0	258^2	256	120	13	0	79	79	11.7	3.20	134	.257	.311	22	.229	3	34	32	1	3.5
1932	Was-A	15	12	.556	46	24	10	2	5	202^2	239	115	11	1	55	53	13.1	4.44	97	.296	.342	7	.100	-5	1	-3	1	-0.7
1933	StL-A	1	6	.143	8	6	0	0	0	39	57	35	1	0	17	7	17.1	7.15	65	.350	.411	3	.273	1	-12	-10	1	-1.3
	Bos-A	8	11	.421	33	21	9	2	1	163^1	180	93	4	0	64	37	13.4	4.02	109	.281	.347	16	.281	6	5	6	4	1.7
	Yr	9	17	.346	41	27	9	2	1	202^1	237	128	5	0	81	44	14.1	4.63	96	.295	.360	19	.279	7	-8	-4	5	0.4
1934	Cle-A	5	10	.333	38	15	5	0	6	117	116	67	7	2	51	39	13.0	3.85	118	.263	.342	7	.233	1	8	9	0	1.2
1935	Cle-A	8	7	.533	42	8	4	2	4	122	123	52	6	3	37	45	12.0	3.61	125	.265	.323	4	.108	-2	**11**	**12**	1	1.2
1936	Cle-A	8	10	.444	24	16	12	1	1	140^1	166	78	13	3	45	34	13.7	4.17	121	.294	.349	10	.222	2	14	14	1	1.7
1937	Cle-A	2	6	.250	31	5	2	0	0	77	107	59	4	3	27	32	16.0	6.55	70	.329	.386	4	.167	-1	-16	-17	1	-1.4
1940	Phi-N	1	3	.250	18	2	0	0	3	37^2	58	26	3	0	16	16	17.7	6.21	63	.354	.411	1	.077	-1	-10	-10	0	-1.2
Total	12	91	105	.464	404	181	77	10	21	1693	1899	937	83	22	590	510	13.3	4.20	105	.288	.348	106	.192	6	45	42	19	6.7

● MACE BROWN Brown, Mace Stanley b: 5/21/09, North English, Ia. BR/TR, 6'1", 190 lbs. Deb: 5/21/35 C

YEAR	TM/L	W	L	PCT	G	GS	CG	SH	SV	IP	H	R	HR	HB	BB	SO	RAT	ERA	ERA+	OAV	OOB	BH	AVG	PB	PR	PR+	PD	TPI
1935	Pit-N	4	1	.800	18	5	2	0	0	72^2	84	41	5	0	22	28	13.1	3.59	114	.287	.337	4	.167	-0	3	4	2	0.4
1936	Pit-N	10	11	.476	47	10	3	0	3	165	178	89	8	1	55	56	12.8	3.87	105	.275	.332	10	.167	-2	3	3	1	0.3
1937	Pit-N	7	2	.778	50	2	0	0	**7**	107^2	109	59	2	1	45	60	13.0	4.18	92	.261	.334	9	.300	2	-3	-4	-1	-0.2
1938	Pit-N★	15	9	.625	**51**	2	0	0	5	132^2	155	68	5	0	44	55	13.5	3.80	100	.294	.349	5	.132	-2	-0	-0	-0	-0.2
1939	Pit-N	9	13	.409	47	19	8	1	7	200^1	232	90	8	2	52	71	12.8	3.37	114	.293	.338	7	.109	-4	12	11	1	0.8
1940	Pit-N	10	9	.526	48	17	5	1	**7**	173	181	78	5	2	49	73	12.1	3.49	109	.267	.318	6	.115	-1	7	6	1	0.7
1941	Pit-N	0	0	—	1	0	0	0	0	1^1	2	0	0	0	0	0	13.5	0.00	—	.333	.333	0	—	0	1	1	0	0.1
	Bro-N	3	2	.600	24	0	0	0	3	42^2	31	17	3	1	26	22	12.2	3.16	116	.208	.330	0	.000	-1	2	2	1	0.3
	Yr	3	2	.600	25	0	0	0	3	44	33	17	3	1	26	22	12.3	3.07	119	.213	.330	0	.000	-1	3	3	1	0.4
1942	Bos-A	9	3	.750	34	0	0	0	6	60^1	56	27	4	0	28	20	12.5	3.43	109	.255	.339	1	.067	-1	2	2	1	0.4
1943	Bos-A	6	6	.500	**49**	0	0	0	9	93^1	71	26	2	0	51	40	11.8	2.12	156	.222	.329	1	.059	-1	**12**	**12**	0	1.7
1946	*Bos-A	3	1	.750	18	0	0	0	1	26^1	26	7	2	0	16	10	14.4	2.05	179	.268	.372	0	.000	-1	4	5	1	0.7
Total	10	76	57	.571	387	55	18	2	48	1075^1	1125	502	44	7	388	435	12.7	3.46	110	.271	.335	43	.137	-11	43	43	6	5.0

● MARK BROWN Brown, Mark Anthony b: 7/13/59, Bellows Falls, Vt. BB/TR, 6'2", 190 lbs. Deb: 8/9/84

YEAR	TM/L	W	L	PCT	G	GS	CG	SH	SV	IP	H	R	HR	HB	BB	SO	RAT	ERA	ERA+	OAV	OOB	BH	AVG	PB	PR	PR+	PD	TPI
1984	Bal-A	1	2	.333	9	0	0	0	0	23	22	11	2	1	7	10	11.7	3.91	99	.256	.319	0	—	0	0	-0	-0	-0.1
1985	Min-A	0	0	—	6	0	0	0	0	15^2	21	13	1	0	7	5	16.1	6.89	64	.333	.400	0	—	0	-5	-4	-0	-0.2
Total	2	1	2	.333	15	0	0	0	0	38^2	43	24	3	1	14	15	13.5	5.12	80	.289	.354	0	—	0	-5	-4	-1	-0.3

● MIKE BROWN Brown, Michael Gary b: 3/4/59, Camden County, N.J. BR/TR, 6'2", 195 lbs. Deb: 9/16/82

YEAR	TM/L	W	L	PCT	G	GS	CG	SH	SV	IP	H	R	HR	HB	BB	SO	RAT	ERA	ERA+	OAV	OOB	BH	AVG	PB	PR	PR+	PD	TPI
1982	Bos-A	1	0	1.000	3	0	0	0	0	6	7	0	0	0	1	4	12.0	0.00	—	.304	.333	0	—	0	3	3	-0	0.4
1983	Bos-A	6	6	.500	19	18	3	1	0	104	110	62	12	2	43	35	13.4	4.67	93	.276	.350	0	—	0	-7	-3	-1	-0.4
1984	Bos-A	1	8	.111	15	11	0	0	0	67	104	63	9	3	19	32	16.9	6.85	61	.347	.391	0	—	0	-21	-19	0	-2.1
1985	Bos-A	0	0	—	2	1	0	0	0	3^1	9	8	0	0	3	3	32.4	21.60	20	.500	.571	0	—	0	-6	-6	-0	-0.3
1986	Bos-A	4	4	.500	15	10	0	0	0	57^1	72	35	10	1	25	32	15.4	5.34	78	.316	.386	0	—	0	-7	-7	0	-0.9
	Sea-A	0	2	.000	6	2	0	0	0	15^2	19	14	4	0	11	9	17.2	7.47	57	.302	.405	0	—	0	-6	-6	0	-0.6
	Yr	4	6	.400	21	12	0	0	0	73	91	49	14	1	36	41	15.8	5.79	72	.313	.390	0	—	0	-13	-13	1	-1.5
1987	Sea-A	0	0	—	1	0	0	0	0	0^1	3	2	0	0	0	0	81.0	54.00	9	.750	.750	0	—	0	-2	-2	0	-0.1
Total	6	12	20	.375	61	42	3	1	0	253^2	324	184	35	6	102	115	15.3	5.75	74	.313	.378	0	—	0	-47	-40	0	-4.0

● MORDECAI BROWN Brown, Mordecai Peter Centennial "Three Finger" or "Miner"
b: 10/19/1876, Nyesville, Ind. d: 2/14/48, Terre Haute, Ind. BB/TR, 5'10", 175 lbs. Deb: 4/19/03 MH

YEAR	TM/L	W	L	PCT	G	GS	CG	SH	SV	IP	H	R	HR	HB	BB	SO	RAT	ERA	ERA+	OAV	OOB	BH	AVG	PB	PR	PR+	PD	TPI
1903	StL-N	9	13	.409	26	24	19	1	0	201	231	105	7	6	59	83	13.3	2.60	126	.293	.347	15	.195	-0	15	15	2	1.6
1904	Chi-N	15	10	.600	26	23	21	4	1	212^1	155	74	1	6	50	81	**8.9**	1.86	143	**.199**	**.253**	19	.213	1	21	19	-1	2.3
1905	Chi-N	18	12	.600	30	24	24	4	0	249	219	89	3	1	44	89	9.5	2.17	138	.235	.271	13	.140	-1	23	23	-0	2.4
1906	*Chi-N	26	6	.813	36	32	27	**9**	3	277^1	198	56	1	4	61	144	**8.5**	**1.04**	**254**	.202	**.252**	20	.204	1	**49**	**49**	2	**6.8**
1907	*Chi-N	20	6	.769	34	27	20	6	3	233	180	51	2	6	40	107	8.7	1.39	179	.221	.262	13	.153	-0	28	28	4	**3.9**
1908	*Chi-N	29	9	.763	44	31	27	9	**5**	312^1	214	64	1	5	49	123	7.7	1.47	160	.195	.232	25	.207	1	31	31	-1	4.2
1909	Chi-N	**27**	9	.750	**50**	34	**32**	8	**7**	**342^2**	246	78	1	7	53	172	8.0	1.31	193	.202	.239	22	.176	1	**49**	**48**	-1	5.5
1910	*Chi-N	25	14	.641	46	31	**27**	**6**	**7**	295^1	256	95	3	4	64	143	**9.9**	1.86	155	.232	**.277**	18	.175	-0	39	35	3	5.1
1911	Chi-N	21	11	.656	**53**	27	21	0	**13**	270	267	110	5	6	55	129	10.9	2.80	118	.262	.303	23	.253	5	18	16	-4	2.0
1912	Chi-N	5	6	.455	15	8	5	2	0	88^2	92	35	2	1	20	34	11.5	2.64	126	.274	.317	9	.290	2	8	7	-2	0.8
1913	Cin-N	11	12	.478	39	16	11	1	6	173^1	174	79	7	1	44	41	11.4	2.91	112	.277	.325	11	.204	-0	6	6	-1	0.7
1914	StL-F	12	6	.667	26	18	13	2	0	175	172	73	7	3	43	81	11.2	3.29	92	.254	.302	15	.254	1	-8	-5	-2	-0.6
	Bro-F	2	5	.286	9	8	5	0	0	57^2	63	33	1	0	18	32	12.6	4.21	68	.276	.329	4	.211	-1	-9	-9	-0	-1.0
	Yr	14	11	.560	35	26	18	2	0	232^2	235	106	8	3	61	113	11.6	3.52	85	.260	.309	19	.244	0	-16	-13	-3	-1.6
1915	Chi-F	17	8	.680	35	25	17	3	4	236^1	189	75	2	7	64	95	9.9	2.09	120	.220	.279	24	.293	5	17	12	3	2.1
1916	Chi-N	2	3	.400	12	4	2	0	0	48^1	52	27	0	4	9	21	12.1	3.91	74	.289	.337	4	.250	0	-7	-5	-0	-0.5
Total	14	239	130	.648	481	332	271	55	49	3172^1	2708	1044	43	61	673	1375	9.8	2.06	137	.233	.278	235	.206	15	279	270	1	35.3

● MYRL BROWN Brown, Myrl Lincoln b: 10/10/1894, Waynesboro, Pa. d: 2/23/81, Harrisburg, Pa. BR/TR, 5'11", 172 lbs. Deb: 8/19/22

YEAR	TM/L	W	L	PCT	G	GS	CG	SH	SV	IP	H	R	HR	HB	BB	SO	RAT	ERA	ERA+	OAV	OOB	BH	AVG	PB	PR	PR+	PD	TPI
1922	Pit-N	3	1	.750	7	5	2	0	0	34^2	42	25	2	0	13	9	14.3	5.97	68	.296	.355	3	.273	1	-7	-7	0	-0.6

● NORM BROWN Brown, Norman Ladelle b: 2/1/19, Evergreen, N.C. d: 5/31/95, Bennettsville, S.C. BB/TR, 6'3", 180 lbs. Deb: 10/3/43

YEAR	TM/L	W	L	PCT	G	GS	CG	SH	SV	IP	H	R	HR	HB	BB	SO	RAT	ERA	ERA+	OAV	OOB	BH	AVG	PB	PR	PR+	PD	TPI
1943	Phi-A	0	0	—	1	1	0	0	0	7	5	4	0	0	0	1	6.4	0.00	—	.185	.185	0	.000	-0	3	3	0	0.1
1946	Phi-A	0	1	.000	4	0	0	0	0	7^1	8	8	2	0	6	3	17.2	6.14	58	.267	.389	0	—	0	-2	-2	-0	-0.3
Total	2	0	1	.000	5	1	0	0	0	14^1	13	12	2	0	6	4	11.9	3.14	111	.228	.302	0	.000	-0	0	1	0	-0.2

● PAUL BROWN Brown, Paul Dwayne b: 6/18/41, Ft.Smith, Ark. BR/TR, 6'1", 190 lbs. Deb: 7/23/61 F

YEAR	TM/L	W	L	PCT	G	GS	CG	SH	SV	IP	H	R	HR	HB	BB	SO	RAT	ERA	ERA+	OAV	OOB	BH	AVG	PB	PR	PR+	PD	TPI
1961	Phi-N	0	1	.000	5	1	0	0	0	10	13	9	3	1	8	1	19.8	8.10	50	.325	.449	1	.500	0	-5	-4	-0	-0.4
1962	Phi-N	0	6	.000	23	9	0	0	1	63^2	74	45	9	3	33	29	15.5	5.94	65	.298	.387	2	.154	0	-14	-15	-1	-1.3
1963	Phi-N	0	1	.000	6	2	0	0	0	15^1	15	10	2	2	5	11	12.9	4.11	79	.238	.314	1	.500	0	-1	-2	0	0.0
1968	Phi-N	0	0	—	2	0	0	0	0	4	6	4	0	0	1	4	15.8	9.00	33	.353	.389	0	—	0	-3	-3	-0	-0.2
Total	4	0	8	.000	36	12	0	0	1	93	108	68	14	6	47	45	15.6	6.00	63	.293	.382	4	.235	1	-23	-24	-0	-1.9

● RAY BROWN Brown, Paul Percival b: 1/31/1889, Chicago, Ill. d: 5/29/55, Los Angeles, Cal. BR/TR, 6'1", 172 lbs. Deb: 9/29/09

YEAR	TM/L	W	L	PCT	G	GS	CG	SH	SV	IP	H	R	HR	HB	BB	SO	RAT	ERA	ERA+	OAV	OOB	BH	AVG	PB	PR	PR+	PD	TPI
1909	Chi-N	1	0	1.000	1	1	1	0	0	9	5	3	0	0	4	2	9.0	2.00	127	.172	.273	0	.000	-0	1	1	-0	0.0

● STUB BROWN Brown, Richard P. b: 8/3/1870, Baltimore, Md. d: 3/11/48, Baltimore, Md. TL, 6'2", 220 lbs. Deb: 8/15/1893

YEAR	TM/L	W	L	PCT	G	GS	CG	SH	SV	IP	H	R	HR	HB	BB	SO	RAT	ERA	ERA+	OAV	OOB	BH	AVG	PB	PR	PR+	PD	TPI
1893	Bal-N	0	0	—	2	0	0	0	0	9	13	8	0	1	5	0	19.0	6.00	79	.325	.413	1	.200	-0	-1	-1	-0	-0.1
1894	Bal-N	4	0	1.000	9	6	3	0	0	49^2	59	39	3	1	24	8	15.2	4.89	112	.292	.370	2	.087	-4	2	3	-1	-0.2
1897	Cin-N	0	1	.000	2	1	1	0	0	13	17	8	1	0	8	2	17.3	4.15	110	.315	.403	0	.000	-1	0	1	0	-0.1
Total	3	4	1	.800	13	7	4	0	0	71^2	89	55	4	2	37	10	16.1	4.90	106	.301	.382	3	.091	-5	1	2	-1	-0.4

● BOB BROWN Brown, Robert Murray b: 4/1/11, Dorchester, Mass. d: 8/3/90, Pembroke, Mass. BR/TR, 6'0.5", 190 lbs. Deb: 4/21/30

YEAR	TM/L	W	L	PCT	G	GS	CG	SH	SV	IP	H	R	HR	HB	BB	SO	RAT	ERA	ERA+	OAV	OOB	BH	AVG	PB	PR	PR+	PD	TPI
1930	Bos-N	0	0	—	3	0	0	0	0	6	10	7	0	0	8	1	27.0	10.50	47	.417	.563	0	.000	-0	-4	-4	0	-0.2
1931	Bos-N	0	1	.000	3	1	0	0	0	6^1	9	7	0	0	3	2	17.1	8.53	44	.375	.444	1	.500	0	-3	-3	0	-0.4
1932	Bos-N	14	7	.667	35	28	9	0	1	213	187	89	6	2	104	110	12.4	3.30	114	.238	.329	13	.194	-0	14	11	-1	0.9
1933	Bos-N	0	0	—	5	0	0	0	0	6^2	6	4	0	0	3	3	12.2	2.70	114	.250	.333	0	.000	-0	0	0	-0	0.0
1934	Bos-N	1	3	.250	16	8	2	1	0	58^1	59	40	2	3	36	21	15.1	5.71	67	.262	.371	5	.238	0	-11	-13	-1	-0.8
1935	Bos-N	1	8	.111	15	10	2	1	0	65	79	55	2	0	36	17	15.9	6.37	59	.302	.386	2	.105	-1	-17	-20	-1	-2.4
1936	Bos-N	0	2	.000	2	2	0	0	0	8^1	10	6	1	0	3	5	14.0	5.40	71	.278	.333	0	.000	-0	-1	-2	0	-0.3
Total	7	16	21	.432	79	49	13	2	1	363^2	360	208	11	5	193	159	13.8	4.48	84	.261	.354	21	.183	-2	-22	-29	-3	-3.2

YEAR TM/L	W	L	PCT	G	GS	CG	SH	SV	IP	H	R	HR	HB	BB	SO	RAT	ERA	ERA+	OAV	OOB	BH	AVG	PB	PR	PR+	PD	TPI
● SCOTT BROWN	Brown, Scott Edward b: 8/30/56, DeQuincy, La. BR/TR, 6'2", 220 lbs. Deb: 8/11/81																										
1981 Cin-N	1	0	1.000	10	0	0	0	0	13	16	4	0	0	1	7	11.8	2.77	128	.314	.327	0	.000	-0	1	1	-0	0.1
● STEVE BROWN	Brown, Steven Elbert b: 2/12/57, San Francisco, Cal. BR/TR, 6'5", 200 lbs. Deb: 8/1/83																										
1983 Cal-A	2	3	.400	12	4	2	1	0	46	45	19	4	0	16	23	11.9	3.52	114	.256	.318	0	—	0	3	3	-0	0.2
1984 Cal-A	0	1	.000	3	3	0	0	0	11	16	13	0	0	9	5	20.5	9.00	44	.340	.446	0	—	0	-6	-6	-0	-0.5
Total 2	2	4	.333	15	7	2	1	0	57	61	32	4	0	25	28	13.6	4.58	88	.274	.347	0	—	0	-3	-4	-0	-0.3
● TOM BROWN	Brown, Thomas Dale b: 8/10/49, Lafayette, La. BR/TR, 6'1", 170 lbs. Deb: 9/14/78																										
1978 Sea-A	0	0	—	6	0	0	0	0	13	14	6	2	0	4	8	12.5	4.15	92	.286	.340	0	—	0	-1	-0	0	0.0
● TOM BROWN	Brown, Thomas Tarlton b: 9/21/1860, Liverpool, England d: 10/25/27, Washington, D.C. BL/TR, 5'10", 168 lbs. Deb: 7/6/1882 MU♦																										
1882 Bal-a	0	0	—	2	0	0	0	0	8^1	13	7	0		6	2	20.5	1.08	255	.333	.422	55	.304	1	1	2	-1	0.0
1883 Col-a	0	1	.000	3	1	1	0	0	14	14	17	0		10	6	15.4	5.79	53	.246	.358	115	.274	1	-4	-5	-1	-0.3
1884 Col-a	2	1	.667	4	0	0	0	0	19	27	24	0	0	7	5	16.1	7.11	43	.281	.330	123	.273	1	-8	-9	-1	-1.1
1885 Pit-a	0	0	—	2	0	0	0	0	6	0	3	0	3	3	2	9.0	3.00	107	.000	.207	134	.307	1	0	0	-0	0.0
1886 Pit-a	0	0	—	1	0	0	0	0	2	2	4	0	0	5	1	31.5	9.00	38	.125	.333	131	.285	0	-1	-1	0	0.0
Total 5	2	2	.500	12	1	1	0	0	49^1	56	55	0	3	31	16	16.4	5.29	57	.242	.340	1973	.267	4	-12	-13	-2	-1.4
● JUMBO BROWN	Brown, Walter George b: 4/30/07, Greene, R.I. d: 10/2/66, Freeport, N.Y. BR/TR, 6'4", 295 lbs. Deb: 8/26/25																										
1925 Chi-N	0	0	—	2	0	0	0	0	6	5	5	0	0	4	0	13.5	3.00	144	.217	.333	0	.000	-0	1	1	0	0.0
1927 Cle-A	0	2	.000	8	0	0	0	0	18^2	19	14	3	1	26	8	22.2	6.27	67	.284	.489	2	.667	1	-4	-4	0	-0.2
1928 Cle-A	0	1	.000	5	0	0	0	0	14^2	19	15	0	0	15	12	20.9	6.75	61	.365	.507	2	.667	1	-4	-4	-0	-0.1
1932 NY-A	5	2	.714	19	3	3	1	1	55^2	58	30	1	2	30	31	14.6	4.53	90	.270	.364	4	.174	-1	-0	-3	1	-0.3
1933 NY-A	7	5	.583	21	8	1	0	0	74	78	48	3	0	52	55	15.8	5.23	74	.269	.380	5	.179	-1	-8	-12	-0	-1.7
1935 NY-A	6	5	.545	20	8	3	1	0	87^1	94	41	2	0	37	41	13.5	3.61	112	.279	.350	10	.313	3	8	5	0	0.8
1936 NY-A	1	4	.200	20	3	0	0	1	64	93	47	4	0	29	19	17.2	5.91	79	.352	.416	0	.000	-3	-6	-10	1	-0.8
1937 Cin-N	1	0	1.000	4	1	0	0	0	9^2	16	10	0	0	3	4	17.7	8.38	45	.390	.432	0	.000	0	-5	-5	-0	-0.5
NY-N	1	0	1.000	4	0	0	0	0	8^2	5	2	0	0	5	4	10.4	1.04	374	.172	.294	0	—	0	3	3	1	0.4
Yr	2	0	1.000	8	1	0	0	0	18^1	21	12	0	0	8	8	14.2	4.91	78	.300	.372	0	.000	0	-2	-2	0	-0.1
1938 NY-N	5	3	.625	43	0	0	0	5	90	65	26	5	1	28	42	9.4	1.80	209	.204	.271	3	.188	1	**20**	**20**	-1	1.8
1939 NY-N	4	0	1.000	31	0	0	0	7	56^1	69	30	1	1	25	24	15.2	4.15	95	.304	.375	4	.364	1	-1	-1	0	0.0
1940 NY-N	2	4	.333	41	0	0	0	**7**	55^1	49	25	5	0	25	31	12.0	3.42	114	.232	.314	1	.100	-1	3	3	-1	0.2
1941 NY-N	1	5	.167	31	0	0	0	**8**	57	49	23	2	0	21	30	11.1	3.32	111	.238	.308	1	.111	-1	2	2	-1	0.2
Total 12	33	31	.516	249	23	7	2	29	597^1	619	316	26	5	300	301	13.9	4.07	99	.271	.357	32	.204	2	7	-4	-0	-0.2
● WALTER BROWN	Brown, Walter Irving b: 4/23/15, Jamestown, N.Y. d: 2/3/91, Westfield, N.Y. BR/TR, 5'11", 175 lbs. Deb: 5/16/47																										
1947 StL-A	1	0	1.000	19	0	0	0	0	46	50	27	3	0	28	10	15.3	4.89	79	.294	.394	0	.000	-1	-6	-5	0	-0.4
● CAL BROWNING	Browning, Calvin Duane b: 3/16/38, Burns Flat, Okla. BL/TL, 5'11", 190 lbs. Deb: 6/12/60																										
1960 StL-N	0	0	—	1	0	0	0	0	0^2	5	3	1	0	1	0	81.0	40.50	10	.714	.750	0	—	0	-3	-2	-0	-0.1
● FRANK BROWNING	Browning, Frank "Dutch" b: 10/29/1882, Falmouth, Ky. d: 5/20/48, San Antonio, Tex. BR/TR, 5'6", 155 lbs. Deb: 4/16/10																										
1910 Det-A	2	2	.500	11	6	2	0	3	49	51	22	0	0	10	16	11.2	2.57	102	.262	.298	0	.000	-2	-0	0	1	0.0
● PETE BROWNING	Browning, Louis Rogers "The Gladiator" b: 6/17/1861, Louisville, Ky. d: 9/10/05, Louisville, Ky. BR/TR, 6', 180 lbs. Deb: 5/2/1882 ♦																										
1884 Lou-a	0	1	.000	1	1	0	0	0	0^1	2	3	0	1	2	0	135.0	54.00	6	1.000	1.000	150	.336	1	-2	-2	0	-0.3
● TOM BROWNING	Browning, Thomas Leo b: 4/28/60, Casper, Wyoming BL/TL, 6'1", 190 lbs. Deb: 9/9/84																										
1984 Cin-N	1	0	1.000	3	3	0	0	0	23^1	27	4	0	0	5	14	12.3	1.54	245	.303	.340	1	.143	-0	5	6	-0	0.3
1985 Cin-N	20	9	.690	38	38	6	4	0	261^1	242	111	29	3	73	155	11.0	3.55	107	.245	.299	17	.193	2	2	7	-2	0.8
1986 Cin-N	14	13	.519	39	39	4	2	0	243^1	225	123	26	1	70	147	10.9	3.81	102	.245	.299	14	.163	-1	-2	2	-3	-0.2
1987 Cin-N	10	13	.435	32	31	2	0	0	183	201	107	27	5	61	117	13.1	5.02	85	.284	.345	8	.154	0	-19	-15	-2	-1.7
1988 Cin-N	18	5	.783	36	36	5	2	0	250^2	205	98	36	7	64	124	9.9	3.41	105	.224	.280	12	.145	0	1	5	-3	0.2
1989 Cin-N	15	12	.556	37	37	9	2	0	249^2	241	109	31	3	64	118	11.1	3.39	106	.255	.304	7	.090	-3	3	6	-1	0.1
1990 *Cin-N	15	9	.625	35	35	2	1	0	227^2	235	98	24	5	52	99	11.5	3.80	104	.266	.311	7	.093	-3	0	4	-2	-0.2
1991 Cin-N☆	14	14	.500	36	36	1	0	0	230^1	241	124	32	4	56	115	11.8	4.18	91	.266	.312	12	.171	2	-13	-9	-3	-1.2
1992 Cin-N	6	5	.545	16	16	0	0	0	87	108	49	6	2	28	33	14.3	5.07	71	.311	.366	7	.226	1	-15	-14	0	-1.5
1993 Cin-N	7	7	.500	21	20	0	0	0	114	159	61	15	1	20	53	14.2	4.74	85	.333	.361	8	.216	2	-9	-9	1	-0.6
1994 Cin-N	3	1	.750	7	7	2	1	0	40^2	34	20	8	1	13	22	10.6	4.20	98	.222	.287	2	.143	-0	0	-0	-0	-0.1
1995 KC-A	0	2	.000	2	2	0	0	0	10	13	9	2	0	5	3	16.2	8.10	59	.302	.375	0	—	0	-4	-4	0	-0.5
Total 12	123	90	.577	302	300	31	12	0	1921	1931	913	236	32	511	1000	11.6	3.94	97	.262	.312	95	.153	2	-50	-21	-15	-4.6
● MARK BROWNSON	Brownson, Mark Phillip b: 6/17/75, Lake Worth, Fla. BL/TR, 6'2", 185 lbs. Deb: 7/21/98																										
1998 Col-N	1	0	1.000	2	2	1	1	0	13^1	16	7	2	1	2	8	12.8	4.73	109	.296	.333	0	.000	-1	-1	1	-0	-0.1
1999 Col-N	0	2	.000	7	7	0	0	0	29^2	42	26	8	1	8	21	15.5	7.89	74	.333	.378	1	.111	-1	-11	-5	0	-0.4
2000 Phi-N	1	0	1.000	2	0	0	0	0	5	7	4	1	0	3	3	18.0	7.20	66	.333	.417	0	—	0	-1	-1	0	-0.2
Total 3	2	2	.500	11	9	1	1	0	48	65	37	11	2	13	32	15.0	6.94	80	.323	.370	1	.071	-1	-13	-6	-0	-0.7
● BRUCE BRUBAKER	Brubaker, Bruce Ellsworth b: 12/29/41, Harrisburg, Pa. BR/TR, 6'1", 198 lbs. Deb: 4/15/67																										
1967 LA-N	0	0	—	1	0	0	0	0	1^1	3	3	1	0	0	2	20.3	20.25	15	.429	.429	0	—	0	-3	-3	0	-0.1
1970 Mil-A	0	0	—	1	0	0	0	0	2	2	2	1	0	1	0	13.5	9.00	42	.250	.333	0	—	0	-1	-1	-0	-0.1
Total 2	0	0	—	2	0	0	0	0	3^1	5	5	2	0	1	2	16.2	13.50	26	.333	.375	0	—	0	-4	-4	0	-0.2
● LOU BRUCE	Bruce, Louis R. b: 1/16/1877, St.Regis, N.Y. d: 2/9/68, Ilion, N.Y. BL/TR, 5'5", 145 lbs. Deb: 6/22/04 ♦																										
1904 Phi-A	0	0	—	2	0	0	0	0	11	11	7	1	0	2	2	10.6	4.91	55	.262	.295	27	.267	0	-3	-3	0	-0.1
● BOB BRUCE	Bruce, Robert James b: 5/16/33, Detroit, Mich. BR/TR, 6'3", 210 lbs. Deb: 9/14/59																										
1959 Det-A	0	1	.000	2	1	0	0	0	2	2	5	1	0	3	1	22.5	9.00	45	.250	.455	0	—	0	-1	-1	-0	-0.2
1960 Det-A	4	7	.364	34	15	1	0	0	130	127	68	16	5	56	76	13.0	3.74	106	.250	.331	7	.179	0	2	3	1	0.3
1961 Det-A	1	2	.333	14	6	0	0	0	44^2	57	28	6	2	24	25	16.7	4.43	92	.320	.407	1	.111	0	-2	-2	-1	-0.2
1962 Hou-N	10	9	.526	32	27	6	0	0	175	164	92	16	12	82	135	13.3	4.06	92	.248	.342	11	.200	5	-2	-7	0	-0.1
1963 Hou-N	5	9	.357	30	25	1	1	0	170^1	162	73	7	8	60	123	12.2	3.59	88	.250	.321	7	.127	2	-6	-9	-1	-0.6
1964 Hou-N	15	9	.625	35	29	9	4	0	202^1	191	70	8	3	33	135	10.1	2.76	124	.246	.279	12	.190	2	18	15	-0	2.1
1965 Hou-N	9	18	.333	35	34	7	1	0	229^2	241	107	22	9	38	145	11.3	3.72	90	.270	.307	9	.122	-1	-5	-10	0	-1.2
1966 Hou-N	3	13	.188	25	23	1	0	0	129^2	160	83	16	8	29	71	13.7	5.34	64	.301	.346	3	.077	-2	-25	-29	0	-3.3
1967 Atl-N	2	3	.400	12	7	1	0	1	38^2	42	25	3	1	15	22	13.5	4.89	68	.269	.337	2	.167	0	-7	-7	-1	-0.9
Total 9	49	71	.408	219	167	26	6	1	1122^1	1146	551	95	48	340	733	12.3	3.85	91	.263	.323	52	.150	6	-28	-45	-2	-4.1
● FRED BRUCKBAUER	Bruckbauer, Frederick John b: 5/27/38, New Ulm, Minn. BR/TR, 6'1", 185 lbs. Deb: 4/25/61																										
1961 Min-A	0	0	—	1	0	0	0	0	0	3	0	0	1	—	—	∞	—	1.000	1.000	105	—	0	-3	-3	0	-0.2	
● ANDY BRUCKMILLER	Bruckmiller, Andrew b: 1/1/1882, McKeesport, Pa. d: 1/12/70, McKeesport, Pa. BR/TR, 5'11", 175 lbs. Deb: 6/26/05																										
1905 Det-A	0	0	—	1	0	0	0	0	1	4	3	0	0	1	1	45.0	27.00	10	.571	.625	0	.000	-0	-3	-3	-0	-0.2
● MIKE BRUHERT	Bruhert, Michael Edwin b: 6/24/51, Jamaica, N.Y. BR/TR, 6'6", 220 lbs. Deb: 4/9/78																										
1978 NY-N	4	11	.267	27	22	1	1	0	133^2	171	83	6	1	34	56	13.9	4.78	73	.317	.359	3	.075	-3	-18	-20	-0	-2.3
● DUFF BRUMLEY	Brumley, Duff Lechaun b: 8/25/70, Cleveland, Tenn. BR/TR, 6'4", 195 lbs. Deb: 6/1/94																										
1994 Tex-A	0	0	—	2	0	0	0	0	3^1	6	6	1	0	5	4	29.7	16.20	30	.400	.550	0	—	0	-4	-4	-0	-0.2
● GREG BRUMMETT	Brummett, Gregory Scott b: 4/20/67, Wichita, Kan. BR/TR, 6', 180 lbs. Deb: 5/29/93																										
1993 SF-N	2	3	.400	8	8	0	0	0	46	53	25	9	0	13	20	12.9	4.70	83	.294	.342	0	.000	-1	-3	-4	-0	-0.5

YEAR	TM/L	W	L	PCT	G	GS	CG	SH	SV	IP	H	R	HR	HB	BB	SO	RAT	ERA	ERA+	OAV	OOB	BH	AVG	PB	PR	PR+	PD	TPI
	Min-A	2	1	.667	5	5	0	0	0	26^2	29	17	3	0	15	10	14.9	5.74	76	.299	.393	0	—	0	-4	-4	-1	-0.4
Total	1	4	4	.500	13	13	0	0	0	72^2	82	42	12	0	28	30	13.6	5.08	80	.296	.361	0	.000	-1	-7	-8	-1	-0.9

● **JACK BRUNER** Bruner, Jack Raymond b: 7/1/24, Waterloo, Iowa BL/TL, 6'1", 185 lbs. Deb: 9/16/49

YEAR	TM/L	W	L	PCT	G	GS	CG	SH	SV	IP	H	R	HR	HB	BB	SO	RAT	ERA	ERA+	OAV	OOB	BH	AVG	PB	PR	PR+	PD	TPI
1949	Chi-A	1	2	.333	4	2	0	0	0	7^2	10	7	0	0	8	4	21.1	8.22	51	.357	.500	0	.000	-0	-3	-3	-0	-0.7
1950	Chi-A	0	0	—	9	0	0	0	0	12^1	7	6	0	1	14	8	16.1	3.65	123	.184	.415	0	—	0	1	1	-0	0.0
	StL-A	1	2	.333	13	1	0	0	1	35	36	21	4	2	23	16	15.7	4.63	107	.267	.381	0	.000	-1	-0	1	-1	-0.1
	Yr	1	2	.333	22	1	0	0	1	47^1	43	27	4	3	37	24	15.8	4.37	110	.249	.390	0	.000	-1	1	2	-1	-0.1
Total	2	2	4	.333	26	3	0	0	1	55	53	34	4	3	45	28	16.5	4.91	96	.264	.406	0	.000	-1	-2	-1	-1	-0.8

● **ROY BRUNER** Bruner, Walter Roy b: 2/10/17, Cecilia, Ky. d: 11/30/86, St.Matthews, Ky. BR/TR, 6', 165 lbs. Deb: 9/14/39

YEAR	TM/L	W	L	PCT	G	GS	CG	SH	SV	IP	H	R	HR	HB	BB	SO	RAT	ERA	ERA+	OAV	OOB	BH	AVG	PB	PR	PR+	PD	TPI
1939	Phi-N	0	4	.000	4	4	2	0	0	27	38	22	3	0	13	11	17.0	6.67	60	.339	.408	1	.111	-1	-8	-8	-1	-1.0
1940	Phi-N	0	0	—	2	0	0	0	0	6^1	5	4	2	0	6	4	15.6	5.68	69	.227	.393	1	.500	0	-1	-1	0	0.0
1941	Phi-N	0	3	.000	13	1	0	0	0	29^1	37	17	1	0	25	13	19.0	4.91	75	.336	.459	0	.000	-0	-4	-4	-1	-0.5
Total	3	0	7	.000	19	5	2	0	0	62^2	80	43	6	0	44	28	17.8	5.74	67	.328	.431	2	.118	-1	-14	-13	-1	-1.5

● **GEORGE BRUNET** Brunet, George Stuart "Lefty" b: 6/8/35, Houghton, Mich. d: 10/25/91, Poza Rica, Mex. BR/TL, 6'1", 210 lbs. Deb: 9/14/56

YEAR	TM/L	W	L	PCT	G	GS	CG	SH	SV	IP	H	R	HR	HB	BB	SO	RAT	ERA	ERA+	OAV	OOB	BH	AVG	PB	PR	PR+	PD	TPI
1956	KC-A	0	0	—	6	1	0	0	0	9	10	8	1	0	11	5	21.0	7.00	62	.286	.457	0	.000	-0	-3	-3	0	-0.1
1957	KC-A	0	1	.000	4	2	0	0	0	11^1	13	7	2	0	4	3	13.5	5.56	71	.277	.333	0	.000	-0	-2	-2	-0	-0.2
1959	KC-A	0	0	—	2	0	0	0	0	4^2	10	9	2	1	7	7	34.7	11.57	35	.435	.581	0	—	0	-4	-4	1	-0.1
1960	KC-A	0	2	.000	3	2	0	0	0	10^1	12	6	0	1	10	4	20.0	4.35	91	.308	.460	0	.000	-0	-1	-0	1	0.0
	Mil-N	2	0	1.000	17	6	0	0	0	49^2	53	31	6	1	22	39	13.8	5.07	68	.275	.352	1	.091	-1	-7	-10	0	-0.6
1961	Mil-N	0	0	—	5	0	0	0	0	5	7	3	1	0	2	0	16.2	5.40	69	.412	.474	0	—	0	-1	-1	0	0.0
1962	Hou-N	2	4	.333	17	11	2	0	0	54	62	31	2	0	21	36	13.8	4.50	83	.291	.355	1	.059	-1	-3	-5	1	-0.5
1963	Hou-N	0	3	.000	5	2	0	0	0	12^2	24	11	2	0	6	11	21.3	7.11	44	.393	.448	0	.000	-0	-5	-6	0	-1.1
	Bal-A	0	1	.000	16	0	0	0	1	20	25	15	3	1	9	13	15.7	5.40	64	.301	.376	0	.000	-0	-4	-4	0	-0.3
1964	LA-A	2	2	.500	10	7	0	0	0	42^1	38	17	2	0	25	36	13.4	3.61	91	.237	.341	2	.182	0	0	-2	-0	-0.1
1965	Cal-A	9	11	.450	41	26	8	3	2	197	149	64	9	3	69	141	10.1	2.56	133	.209	.282	3	.054	-2	20	19	-1	1.5
1966	Cal-A	13	13	.500	41	32	8	2	0	212	183	88	21	5	106	148	12.5	3.31	101	.234	.329	7	.103	-2	3	1	-0	0.0
1967	Cal-A	11	19	.367	40	37	7	2	1	250	203	99	19	4	90	165	10.7	3.31	95	.223	.295	6	.077	-4	-2	-5	-2	-1.2
1968	Cal-A	13	17	.433	39	36	8	5	0	245^1	191	83	23	2	68	132	9.6	2.86	102	.215	.273	6	.081	-3	3	1	-2	-0.5
1969	Cal-A	6	7	.462	23	19	2	2	0	100^2	98	51	15	1	39	56	12.3	3.84	91	.255	.325	1	.037	-1	-2	-4	-1	-0.7
	Sea-A	2	5	.286	12	11	2	0	0	63^2	70	41	11	0	28	37	13.9	5.37	68	.280	.353	3	.150	1	-12	-12	1	-1.1
	Yr	8	12	.400	35	30	4	2	0	164^1	168	92	26	1	67	93	12.9	4.44	80	.265	.336	4	.085	-0	-15	-17	-0	-1.8
1970	Was-A	8	6	.571	24	20	2	1	0	118	124	64	10	1	48	67	13.2	4.42	80	.275	.346	6	.158	1	-9	-12	-1	-1.2
	Pit-N	1	1	.500	12	1	0	0	0	16^2	19	5	1	1	9	17	15.7	2.70	145	.311	.408	0	.000	-0	3	2	0	0.2
1971	StL-N	0	1	.000	7	0	0	0	0	9^1	12	6	3	0	7	4	18.3	5.79	62	.316	.422	1	.333	0	-2	-2	-0	-0.2
Total	15	69	93	.426	324	213	39	15	4	1431^2	1303	639	133	21	581	921	12.0	3.62	92	.244	.320	37	.089	-14	-31	-48	-4	-6.2

● **JUSTIN BRUNETTE** Brunette, Justin Thomas b: 10/7/75, Los Alamitos, Cal. BL/TL, 6'1", 200 lbs. Deb: 4/13/2000

YEAR	TM/L	W	L	PCT	G	GS	CG	SH	SV	IP	H	R	HR	HB	BB	SO	RAT	ERA	ERA+	OAV	OOB	BH	AVG	PB	PR	PR+	PD	TPI
2000	StL-N	0	0	—	4	0	0	0	0	4^2	8	3	0	0	5	2	25.1	5.79	80	.364	.481	1	1.000	0	-1	-1	0	0.0

● **TOM BRUNO** Bruno, Thomas Michael b: 1/26/53, Chicago, Ill. BR/TR, 6'5", 210 lbs. Deb: 8/1/76

YEAR	TM/L	W	L	PCT	G	GS	CG	SH	SV	IP	H	R	HR	HB	BB	SO	RAT	ERA	ERA+	OAV	OOB	BH	AVG	PB	PR	PR+	PD	TPI
1976	KC-A	1	0	1.000	12	0	0	0	0	17^1	20	13	3	0	9	11	15.1	6.75	52	.290	.372	0	—	0	-6	-6	-0	-0.4
1977	Tor-A	0	1	.000	12	0	0	0	0	18^1	30	18	4	1	13	9	21.6	7.85	54	.366	.458	0	—	0	-8	-7	-0	-0.3
1978	StL-N	4	3	.571	18	3	0	0	1	49^2	38	12	3	0	17	33	10.0	1.99	177	.209	.276	1	.083	-1	9	9	-1	1.1
1979	StL-N	2	3	.400	27	1	0	0	0	38^1	37	18	1	2	22	27	14.3	4.23	89	.253	.359	1	.200	0	-2	-2	-0	-0.2
Total	4	7	7	.500	69	4	0	0	1	123^2	125	61	11	3	61	80	13.8	4.22	88	.261	.348	2	.118	-1	-7	-7	-1	0.2

● **WILL BRUNSON** Brunson, William Donald b: 3/20/70, Irving, Tex. BL/TL, 6'4", 185 lbs. Deb: 6/21/98

YEAR	TM/L	W	L	PCT	G	GS	CG	SH	SV	IP	H	R	HR	HB	BB	SO	RAT	ERA	ERA+	OAV	OOB	BH	AVG	PB	PR	PR+	PD	TPI
1998	LA-N	0	1	.000	2	0	0	0	0	2^1	3	3	0	0	2	1	19.3	11.57	34	.333	.455	0	—	0	-2	-2	-0	-0.4
	Det-A	0	0	—	8	0	0	0	0	3	2	0	0	0	1	1	9.0	0.00	—	.200	.273	0	—	0	2	2	0	0.1
1999	Det-A	1	0	1.000	17	0	0	0	0	12	18	9	3	0	6	9	18.0	6.00	81	.367	.436	0	—	0	-2	-1	0	-0.1
Total	2	1	1	.500	27	0	0	0	0	17^1	23	12	3	0	9	11	16.6	5.71	83	.338	.416	0	—	0	-2	-2	0	-0.4

● **JIM BRUSKE** Bruske, James Scott b: 10/7/64, E.St.Louis, Ill. BR/TR, 6'1", 185 lbs. Deb: 8/25/95

YEAR	TM/L	W	L	PCT	G	GS	CG	SH	SV	IP	H	R	HR	HB	BB	SO	RAT	ERA	ERA+	OAV	OOB	BH	AVG	PB	PR	PR+	PD	TPI
1995	LA-N	0	0	—	9	0	0	0	1	10	12	7	0	1	4	5	15.3	4.50	84	.300	.378	0	—	0	-0	-1	-0	-0.1
1996	LA-N	0	0	—	11	0	0	0	0	12^2	17	8	2	1	3	12	14.9	5.68	68	.315	.362	0	—	0	-2	-3	0	-0.1
1997	SD-N	4	1	.800	28	0	0	0	0	44^2	37	22	4	1	25	32	12.7	3.63	107	.228	.335	1	.167	0	3	1	-1	0.1
1998	LA-N	3	0	1.000	35	0	0	0	1	44	47	18	2	3	19	31	14.1	3.48	114	.272	.354	0	.000	-0	4	3	-1	0.1
	SD-N	0	0	—	4	0	0	0	0	7	10	4	1	0	4	4	18.0	3.86	101	.333	.412	0	—	0	0	0	-0	0.0
	Yr	3	0	1.000	39	0	0	0	1	51	57	22	3	3	23	35	14.6	3.53	112	.281	.362	0	.000	-0	4	3	-1	0.1
	NY-A	1	0	1.000	3	1	0	0	0	9	9	3	2	0	1	3	10.0	3.00	146	.257	.278	0	—	0	2	1	0	0.1
2000	Mil-N	1	0	1.000	15	0	0	0	0	16^2	22	15	5	2	12	8	19.4	6.48	70	.314	.429	0	.000	-0	-3	-4	-0	-0.2
Total	5	9	1	.900	105	1	0	0	2	144	154	77	16	8	68	95	14.4	4.13	97	.273	.359	1	.100	-0	3	-2	-2	-0.1

● **WARREN BRUSSTAR** Brusstar, Warren Scott b: 2/2/52, Oakland, Cal. BR/TR, 6'3", 200 lbs. Deb: 5/6/77

YEAR	TM/L	W	L	PCT	G	GS	CG	SH	SV	IP	H	R	HR	HB	BB	SO	RAT	ERA	ERA+	OAV	OOB	BH	AVG	PB	PR	PR+	PD	TPI
1977	*Phi-N	7	2	.778	46	0	0	0	3	71^1	64	26	7	1	24	46	11.2	2.65	151	.250	.317	0	.000	-1	10	11	1	1.4
1978	*Phi-N	6	3	.667	58	0	0	0	0	88^2	74	25	0	3	30	60	10.9	2.33	153	.239	.312	1	.143	0	12	12	2	1.4
1979	Phi-N	1	0	1.000	13	0	0	0	1	14^1	23	12	1	0	4	3	17.0	6.91	56	.383	.422	0	—	0	-5	-5	0	-0.4
1980	*Phi-N	2	2	.500	26	0	0	0	0	38^2	42	16	3	0	13	21	12.8	3.72	102	.286	.344	0	.000	-0	-0	0	0	0.0
1981	*Phi-N	0	1	.000	14	0	0	0	0	12^1	12	6	0	1	10	8	16.8	4.38	83	.250	.390	0	—	0	-1	-1	0	-0.1
1982	Phi-N	2	3	.400	22	0	0	0	2	22^2	31	12	2	1	5	11	14.7	4.76	77	.348	.389	0	.000	-0	-3	-3	0	-0.6
	Chi-A	2	0	1.000	10	0	0	0	0	18^1	19	7	2	1	3	8	11.3	3.44	118	.257	.295	0	—	0	1	1	1	0.2
1983	Chi-N	3	1	.750	59	0	0	0	1	80^1	67	21	1	2	37	46	11.9	2.35	162	.234	.326	0	.000	-0	11	12	0	0.6
1984	*Chi-N	1	1	.500	41	0	0	0	3	63^2	57	23	4	1	21	36	11.2	3.11	126	.247	.312	1	.200	1	3	5	-0	0.3
1985	Chi-N	4	3	.571	51	0	0	0	4	74^1	87	55	8	3	36	34	15.3	6.05	66	.292	.374	1	.143	0	-20	-15	-2	-1.7
Total	9	28	16	.636	340	0	0	0	14	484^2	476	203	28	13	183	273	12.5	3.51	109	.265	.337	3	.094	-1	9	17	2	1.1

● **CLAY BRYANT** Bryant, Claiborne Henry b: 11/16/11, Madison Heights, Va. d: 4/9/99, Boca Raton, Fla. BR/TR, 6'2.5", 195 lbs. Deb: 4/19/35 C

YEAR	TM/L	W	L	PCT	G	GS	CG	SH	SV	IP	H	R	HR	HB	BB	SO	RAT	ERA	ERA+	OAV	OOB	BH	AVG	PB	PR	PR+	PD	TPI
1935	Chi-N	1	2	.333	9	1	0	0	2	22^2	34	15	1	0	7	13	16.3	5.16	76	.358	.402	2	.333	2	-3	-3	-0	-0.3
1936	Chi-N	1	2	.333	26	0	0	0	0	57^1	57	25	0	2	24	35	13.0	3.30	121	.259	.337	5	.417	1	**5**	**4**	1	0.4
1937	Chi-N	9	3	.750	38	9	4	1	3	135^1	117	69	1	1	78	75	13.0	4.26	94	.232	.336	14	.311	5	-5	-4	-3	-0.2
1938	*Chi-N	19	11	.633	44	30	17	3	2	270^1	235	105	6	1	125	**135**	12.0	3.10	124	.235	.321	24	.226	4	21	22	-3	2.4
1939	Chi-N	2	1	.667	4	4	2	0	0	31^1	42	23	3	1	14	9	16.4	5.74	69	.307	.375	3	.214	0	-6	-6	-1	-0.5
1940	Chi-N	0	1	.000	8	0	0	0	0	26^1	26	17	2	0	14	5	13.7	4.78	78	.265	.357	3	.333	1	-3	-3	0	-0.1
Total	6	32	20	.615	129	44	23	4	7	543^1	511	254	13	5	262	272	12.9	3.73	104	.249	.335	51	.266	13	8	10	-6	1.7

● **RON BRYANT** Bryant, Ronald Raymond b: 11/12/47, Redlands, Cal. BB/TL, 6', 190 lbs. Deb: 9/29/67

YEAR	TM/L	W	L	PCT	G	GS	CG	SH	SV	IP	H	R	HR	HB	BB	SO	RAT	ERA	ERA+	OAV	OOB	BH	AVG	PB	PR	PR+	PD	TPI
1967	SF-N	0	0	—	1	0	0	0	0	4	3	2	0	1	0	2	9.0	4.50	73	.200	.250	0	.000	-0	-1	-1	-0	-0.1
1969	SF-N	4	3	.571	16	8	0	0	1	57^2	60	29	8	2	25	30	13.6	4.37	80	.271	.351	3	.188	1	-5	-6	-0	-0.6
1970	SF-N	5	8	.385	34	11	1	0	0	96	103	58	7	2	38	66	13.4	4.78	83	.274	.344	3	.111	1	-8	-9	1	-1.0
1971	*SF-N	7	10	.412	27	22	3	2	0	140	146	69	9	3	49	79	12.7	3.79	90	.272	.336	10	.200	1	-5	-6	0	-0.6
1972	SF-N	14	7	.667	35	28	11	4	0	214	176	81	20	2	77	107	10.7	2.90	120	.224	.295	12	.171	1	13	14	-4	0.9
1973	SF-N	**24**	12	.667	41	39	8	0	0	270	240	125	23	9	115	143	12.1	3.53	108	.234	.316	16	.168	1	4	8	0	1.2
1974	SF-N	3	15	.167	41	23	0	0	0	126^2	142	92	11	4	68	75	15.2	5.61	68	.286	.376	4	.129	-1	-28	-24	-0	-3.2
1975	StL-N	0	1	.000	10	1	0	0	0	8^2	20	17	2	0	7	7	28.0	16.62	23	.444	.519	0	.000	-0	-13	-12	0	-1.2
Total	8	57	56	.504	205	132	23	6	1	917	890	473	80	23	379	509	12.7	4.02	91	.254	.331	48	.165	0	-41	-35	-4	-4.6

● **T.R. BRYDEN** Bryden, Thomas Ray b: 1/17/59, Moses Lake, Wash. BR/TR, 6'4", 190 lbs. Deb: 4/10/86

YEAR	TM/L	W	L	PCT	G	GS	CG	SH	SV	IP	H	R	HR	HB	BB	SO	RAT	ERA	ERA+	OAV	OOB	BH	AVG	PB	PR	PR+	PD	TPI
1986	Cal-A	2	1	.667	16	0	0	0	0	34^1	38	25	4	2	21	25	16.0	6.55	63	.290	.396	0	—	0	-9	-9	0	-0.7

● TOD BRYNAN
Brynan, Charles Ruley b: 7/1863, Philadelphia, Pa. d: 5/10/25, Philadelphia, Pa. BR/TR, Deb: 6/22/1888

YEAR	TM/L	W	L	PCT	G	GS	CG	SH	SV	IP	H	R	HR	HB	BB	SO	RAT	ERA	ERA+	OAV	OOB	BH	AVG	PB	PR	PR+	PD	TPI
1888	Chi-N	2	1	.667	3	3	2	0	0	25	29	26	2	2	7	11	13.7	6.48	47	.271	.328	2	.182	0	-10	-9	-1	-0.9
1891	Bos-N	0	1	.000	1	1	0	0	0	1	4	6	0	0	3	0	63.0	54.00	7	.571	.700	0	—	0	-6	-5	-0	-0.7
Total	2	2	2	.500	4	4	2	0	0	26	33	32	2	2	10	11	15.6	8.31	37	.289	.357	2	.182	0	-16	-14	-1	-1.6

● JIM BUCHANAN
Buchanan, James Forrest b: 7/1/1876, Chatham Hill, Va. d: 6/15/49, Norfolk, Neb. BL/TR, 5′10″, 165 lbs. Deb: 4/16/05

YEAR	TM/L	W	L	PCT	G	GS	CG	SH	SV	IP	H	R	HR	HB	BB	SO	RAT	ERA	ERA+	OAV	OOB	BH	AVG	PB	PR	PR+	PD	TPI
1905	StL-A	5	9	.357	22	15	12	1	**2**	141^{1}	149	76	2	2	27	54	11.3	3.50	73	.272	.309	7	.152	-0	-13	-16	0	-1.5

● BOB BUCHANAN
Buchanan, Robert Gordon b: 5/3/61, Ridley Park, Pa. BL/TL, 6′1″, 185 lbs. Deb: 7/13/85

YEAR	TM/L	W	L	PCT	G	GS	CG	SH	SV	IP	H	R	HR	HB	BB	SO	RAT	ERA	ERA+	OAV	OOB	BH	AVG	PB	PR	PR+	PD	TPI
1985	Cin-N	1	0	1.000	14	0	0	0	0	16	25	15	4	0	9	3	19.1	8.44	45	.368	.442	0	.000	-0	-9	-8	0	-0.5
1989	KC-A	0	0	—	2	0	0	0	0	3^{1}	5	6	1	0	3	3	21.6	16.20	24	.333	.444	0	—	0	-5	-5	-0	-0.2
Total	2	1	0	1.000	16	0	0	0	0	19^{1}	30	21	5	0	12	6	19.6	9.78	39	.361	.442	0	.000	-0	-13	-12	-0	-0.7

● GARY BUCKELS
Buckels, Gary Scott b: 7/22/65, LaMirada, Cal. BR/TR, 6′, 185 lbs. Deb: 7/23/94

YEAR	TM/L	W	L	PCT	G	GS	CG	SH	SV	IP	H	R	HR	HB	BB	SO	RAT	ERA	ERA+	OAV	OOB	BH	AVG	PB	PR	PR+	PD	TPI
1994	StL-N	0	1	.000	10	0	0	0	0	12	8	5	2	0	7	9	11.3	2.25	185	.186	.300	0	.000	-0	3	3	0	0.2

● GARLAND BUCKEYE
Buckeye, Garland Maiers "Gob" b: 10/16/1897, Heron Lake, Minn. d: 11/14/75, Stone Lake, Wis. BB/TL, 6′, 260 lbs. Deb: 6/19/18

YEAR	TM/L	W	L	PCT	G	GS	CG	SH	SV	IP	H	R	HR	HB	BB	SO	RAT	ERA	ERA+	OAV	OOB	BH	AVG	PB	PR	PR+	PD	TPI
1918	Was-A	0	0	—	1	0	0	0	0	2	3	4	0	0	6	2	40.5	18.00	15	.333	.600	0	—	0	-3	-3	0	-0.2
1925	Cle-A	13	8	.619	30	18	11	1	0	153	161	74	3	6	58	49	13.2	3.65	121	.267	.338	14	.226	2	13	13	-1	1.7
1926	Cle-A	6	9	.400	32	18	5	1	0	165^{2}	160	79	3	6	69	36	12.8	3.10	131	.264	.345	12	.200	2	17	18	-2	1.4
1927	Cle-A	10	17	.370	35	25	13	2	1	204^{2}	231	106	6	5	74	38	13.6	3.96	106	.296	.360	19	.268	3	4	5	-1	0.8
1928	Cle-A	1	5	.167	9	6	0	0	0	35	58	32	2	2	5	6	16.7	6.69	62	.389	.417	1	.111	-1	-10	-10	-0	-1.4
	NY-N	0	0	—	1	0	0	0	0	3^{2}	9	6	1	0	2	3	27.0	14.73	27	.409	.458	1	.500	1	-4	-4	0	-0.1
Total	5	30	39	.435	108	67	29	4	1	564	622	301	15	19	214	134	13.6	3.91	108	.287	.356	47	.230	7	16	18	-3	2.2

● ED BUCKINGHAM
Buckingham, Edward Taylor b: 5/12/1874, Metuchen, N.J. d: 7/30/42, Bridgeport, Conn. Deb: 8/30/1895

YEAR	TM/L	W	L	PCT	G	GS	CG	SH	SV	IP	H	R	HR	HB	BB	SO	RAT	ERA	ERA+	OAV	OOB	BH	AVG	PB	PR	PR+	PD	TPI
1895	Was-N	0	0	—	1	1	0	0	0	3	6	5	0	0	2	1	24.0	6.00	80	.400	.471	0	.000	-0	-0	-0	0	0.0

● JESS BUCKLES
Buckles, Jesse Robert "Jim" b: 5/20/1890, LaVerne, Cal. d: 8/2/75, Westminster, Cal. BL/TL, 6′2.5″, 205 lbs. Deb: 9/17/16

YEAR	TM/L	W	L	PCT	G	GS	CG	SH	SV	IP	H	R	HR	HB	BB	SO	RAT	ERA	ERA+	OAV	OOB	BH	AVG	PB	PR	PR+	PD	TPI
1916	NY-A	0	0	—	2	0	0	0	0	4	3	2	0	0	1	2	9.0	2.25	128	.188	.235	0	.000	-0	0	0	-0	0.0

● JOHN BUCKLEY
Buckley, John Edward b: 3/20/1869, Marlborough, Mass. d: 5/3/42, Westborough, Mass. BL/TR, 6′1″, 200 lbs. Deb: 7/15/1890

YEAR	TM/L	W	L	PCT	G	GS	CG	SH	SV	IP	H	R	HR	HB	BB	SO	RAT	ERA	ERA+	OAV	OOB	BH	AVG	PB	PR	PR+	PD	TPI
1890	Buf-P	1	3	.250	4	4	4	0	0	34	49	32	5	0	16	4	17.2	7.68	53	.325	.389	0	.000	-2	-13	-14	0	-1.2

● MIKE BUDDIE
Buddie, Michael J. b: 12/12/70, Berea, Ohio BR/TR, 6′3″, 210 lbs. Deb: 4/6/98

YEAR	TM/L	W	L	PCT	G	GS	CG	SH	SV	IP	H	R	HR	HB	BB	SO	RAT	ERA	ERA+	OAV	OOB	BH	AVG	PB	PR	PR+	PD	TPI
1998	NY-A	4	1	.800	24	2	0	0	0	41^{2}	46	29	5	3	13	20	13.4	5.62	78	.284	.348	0	—	0	-4	-6	-1	-0.7
1999	NY-A	0	0	—	2	0	0	0	0	2	3	1	1	0	0	1	13.5	4.50	105	.333	.333	0	—	0	0	0	0	0.0
2000	Mil-N	0	0	—	5	0	0	0	0	6	8	3	0	0	1	5	13.5	4.50	101	.320	.346	0	—	0	0	0	-0	0.0
Total	3	4	1	.800	31	2	0	0	0	49^{2}	57	33	6	3	14	26	13.4	5.44	81	.291	.347	0	—	0	-4	-6	-1	-0.7

● MIKE BUDNICK
Budnick, Michael Joe b: 9/15/19, Astoria, Ore. d: 12/2/99, Seattle, Wash. BR/TR, 6′1″, 200 lbs. Deb: 4/18/46

YEAR	TM/L	W	L	PCT	G	GS	CG	SH	SV	IP	H	R	HR	HB	BB	SO	RAT	ERA	ERA+	OAV	OOB	BH	AVG	PB	PR	PR+	PD	TPI
1946	NY-N	2	3	.400	35	7	1	1	3	88^{1}	75	40	13	0	48	36	12.5	3.16	109	.231	.330	6	.300	3	2	3	1	0.5
1947	NY-N	0	0	—	7	1	0	0	0	12	16	16	0	0	10	6	19.5	10.50	39	.314	.426	1	.250	0	-9	-9	0	-0.4
Total	2	2	3	.400	42	8	1	1	3	100^{1}	91	56	13	0	58	42	13.4	4.04	87	.242	.343	7	.292	3	-6	-6	1	0.1

● MARK BUEHRLE
Buehrle, Mark A. b: 3/23/79, St.Charles, Mo. BL/TL, 6′2″, 200 lbs. Deb: 7/16/2000

YEAR	TM/L	W	L	PCT	G	GS	CG	SH	SV	IP	H	R	HR	HB	BB	SO	RAT	ERA	ERA+	OAV	OOB	BH	AVG	PB	PR	PR+	PD	TPI
2000	*Chi-A	4	1	.800	28	3	0	0	0	51^{1}	55	27	5	3	19	37	13.5	4.21	118	.272	.344	0	—	0	4	4	1	0.4

● CHARLIE BUFFINTON
Buffinton, Charles G. b: 6/14/1861, Fall River, Mass. d: 9/23/07, Fall River, Mass. BR/TR, 6′1″, 180 lbs. Deb: 5/17/1882 M◆

YEAR	TM/L	W	L	PCT	G	GS	CG	SH	SV	IP	H	R	HR	HB	BB	SO	RAT	ERA	ERA+	OAV	OOB	BH	AVG	PB	PR	PR+	PD	TPI
1882	Bos-N	2	3	.400	5	5	4	1	0	42	53	34	2		14	17	14.4	4.07	70	.296	.347	13	.260	0	-5	-6	1	-0.5
1883	Bos-N	25	14	.641	43	41	34	4	1	333	346	187	4		51	188	10.7	3.03	102	.254	.281	81	.238	0	4	3	-1	0.1
1884	Bos-N	48	16	.750	67	67	63	8	0	587	506	225	15		76	417	8.9	2.15	135	.219	.244	94	.267	12	54	50	3	5.8
1885	Bos-N	22	27	.449	51	50	49	6	0	434^{1}	425	238	10		112	242	11.1	2.88	93	.246	.292	81	.240	5	-3	-10	6	0.0
1886	Bos-N	7	10	.412	18	17	16	0	0	151	203	129	4		39	47	14.4	4.59	70	.308	.346	51	.290	4	-21	-24	-1	-1.9
1887	Phi-N	21	17	.553	40	38	35	1	0	332^{1}	444	224	16	4	92	160	12.1	3.66	116	.311	.313	83	.296	2	15	21	7	2.5
1888	Phi-N	28	17	.622	46	46	43	6	0	400^{1}	324	139	6	4	59	199	8.7	1.91	155	.213	.244	29	.181	-1	42	45	10	**5.6**
1889	Phi-N	28	16	.636	47	43	37	2	0	380	390	196	10	6	121	153	12.2	3.24	134	.257	.315	32	.208	-3	33	43	2	4.0
1890	Phi-P	19	15	.559	36	33	28	0	1	283^{1}	312	211	8	7	126	89	14.1	3.81	112	.268	.343	41	.273	4	13	14	1	1.6
1891	Bos-a	29	9	**.763**	48	43	33	2	1	363^{2}	303	153	8	7	120	158	**10.6**	2.55	137	.219	**.284**	34	.188	-0	47	40	6	3.8
1892	Bal-N	4	8	.333	13	13	9	0	0	97	130	88	4	3	46	30	16.6	4.92	70	.309	.381	15	.349	4	-18	-15	2	-1.0
Total	11	233	152	.605	414	396	351	30	3	3404	3436	1824	87	31	856	1700	11.2	2.96	114	.251	.292	554	.249	27	162	161	35	20.0

● BOB BUHL
Buhl, Robert Ray b: 8/12/28, Saginaw, Mich. BR/TR, 6′2″, 190 lbs. Deb: 4/17/53

YEAR	TM/L	W	L	PCT	G	GS	CG	SH	SV	IP	H	R	HR	HB	BB	SO	RAT	ERA	ERA+	OAV	OOB	BH	AVG	PB	PR	PR+	PD	TPI
1953	Mil-N	13	8	.619	30	18	8	3	0	154^{1}	133	59	9	3	73	83	12.2	2.97	132	.235	.326	6	.113	-3	23	18	1	2.0
1954	Mil-N	2	7	.222	31	14	2	1	3	110^{1}	117	54	5	2	65	57	15.0	4.00	93	.277	.376	1	.032	-3	1	-4	-0	-0.6
1955	Mil-N	13	11	.542	38	27	11	1	1	201^{2}	168	85	13	1	109	117	12.4	3.21	117	.227	.327	6	.105	-4	18	13	-1	1.0
1956	Mil-N	18	8	.692	38	33	13	2	0	216^{2}	190	96	18	2	105	86	12.3	3.32	104	.236	.326	7	.096	-4	11	4	0	0.0
1957	*Mil-N	18	7	**.720**	34	31	14	2	0	216^{2}	191	77	15	0	121	117	13.0	2.74	128	.241	.341	6	.082	-3	27	20	-2	1.6
1958	Mil-N	5	2	.714	11	10	3	0	1	73	74	33	5	1	30	27	12.9	3.45	102	.260	.332	5	.200	0	4	1	1	0.2
1959	Mil-N	15	9	.625	31	25	12	**4**	0	198	181	76	19	2	74	105	11.7	2.86	124	.243	.313	4	.057	-5	24	17	3	1.7
1960	Mil-N★	16	9	.640	36	33	11	2	0	238^{2}	202	89	23	3	103	121	11.6	3.09	111	.229	.312	14	.157	-2	18	10	3	1.1
1961	Mil-N	9	10	.474	32	28	9	1	0	188^{1}	180	99	23	5	98	77	13.5	4.11	91	.256	.351	4	.067	-4	-2	-8	1	-1.1
1962	Mil-N	0	1	.000	1	1	0	0	0	2	6	5	0	0	4	1	45.0	22.50	17	.545	.667	0	.000	-0	-4	-4	-0	-0.6
	Chi-N	12	13	.480	34	30	8	1	0	212	204	108	23	6	94	109	12.9	3.69	112	.255	.338	0	.000	-6	6	10	-2	0.3
	Yr	12	14	.462	35	31	8	1	0	214	210	113	23	6	98	110	13.2	3.87	107	.259	.343	0	.000	-6	2	6	-2	-0.3
1963	Chi-N	11	14	.440	37	34	6	0	0	226	219	96	24	3	62	108	11.3	3.38	104	.259	.312	8	.108	-3	-2	3	1	0.1
1964	Chi-N	15	14	.517	36	35	11	3	0	227^{2}	208	103	22	5	68	107	11.1	3.83	97	.244	.303	7	.096	-2	-8	-3	2	-0.3
1965	Chi-N	13	11	.542	32	31	2	0	0	184^{1}	207	100	26	0	57	92	12.9	4.39	84	.284	.335	4	.060	-4	-17	-14	0	-2.1
1966	Chi-N	0	0	—	1	1	0	0	0	2^{1}	4	4	1	0	1	1	19.3	15.43	24	.400	.455	0	.000	-0	-3	-3	0	-0.1
	Phi-N	6	8	.429	32	18	1	0	1	132	156	74	10	4	39	59	13.6	4.77	75	.298	.351	4	.098	-2	-17	-17	1	-1.8
	Yr	6	8	.429	33	19	1	0	1	134^{1}	160	78	11	4	40	60	13.7	4.96	73	.300	.353	4	.095	-2	-20	-20	1	-1.9
1967	Phi-N	0	0	—	3	0	0	0	0	3	6	4	2	0	2	1	24.0	12.00	28	.462	.533	0	—	0	-3	-3	0	-0.1
Total	15	166	132	.557	457	369	111	20	6	2587	2446	1162	238	37	1105	1268	12.5	3.55	103	.251	.330	76	.089	-43	75	37	8	1.3

● DE WAYNE BUICE
Buice, De Wayne Allison b: 8/20/57, Lynwood, Cal. BR/TR, 6′, 170 lbs. Deb: 4/25/87

YEAR	TM/L	W	L	PCT	G	GS	CG	SH	SV	IP	H	R	HR	HB	BB	SO	RAT	ERA	ERA+	OAV	OOB	BH	AVG	PB	PR	PR+	PD	TPI
1987	Cal-A	6	7	.462	57	0	0	0	17	114	87	45	12	2	40	109	10.2	3.39	127	.213	.287	0	—	0	14	12	0	1.6
1988	Cal-A	2	4	.333	32	0	0	0	3	41^{1}	45	29	5	0	19	38	13.9	5.88	66	.287	.364	0	—	0	-9	-9	0	-1.3
1989	Tor-A	1	0	1.000	7	0	0	0	0	17	13	12	2	0	13	10	13.8	5.82	65	.220	.361	0	—	0	-4	-4	0	-0.2
Total	3	9	11	.450	96	0	0	0	20	172^{1}	145	86	19	2	72	157	11.4	4.23	98	.232	.314	0	—	0	1	-1	0	0.1

● CY BUKER
Buker, Cyril Owen b: 2/5/19, Greenwood, Wis. BL/TR, 5′11″, 190 lbs. Deb: 5/17/45

YEAR	TM/L	W	L	PCT	G	GS	CG	SH	SV	IP	H	R	HR	HB	BB	SO	RAT	ERA	ERA+	OAV	OOB	BH	AVG	PB	PR	PR+	PD	TPI
1945	Bro-N	7	2	.778	42	4	0	0	5	87^{1}	90	41	2	1	45	48	14.0	3.30	114	.268	.356	3	.188	-0	5	4	-1	0.4

● JIM BULLINGER
Bullinger, James Eric b: 8/21/65, New Orleans, La. BR/TR, 6′2″, 185 lbs. Deb: 5/27/92 F

YEAR	TM/L	W	L	PCT	G	GS	CG	SH	SV	IP	H	R	HR	HB	BB	SO	RAT	ERA	ERA+	OAV	OOB	BH	AVG	PB	PR	PR+	PD	TPI
1992	Chi-N	2	8	.200	39	9	1	0	7	85	72	49	9	4	54	36	13.8	4.66	77	.233	.354	5	.250	2	-11	-10	2	-0.8
1993	Chi-N	1	0	1.000	15	0	0	0	1	16^{2}	18	9	1	0	9	10	14.6	4.32	92	.277	.365	0	.000	-0	-1	-1	-0	-0.1
1994	Chi-N	6	2	.750	33	10	1	0	2	100	87	43	6	1	34	72	11.0	3.60	116	.235	.300	3	.136	1	7	6	-1	0.5
1995	Chi-N	12	8	.600	24	24	1	1	0	150	152	80	14	9	65	93	13.6	4.14	99	.265	.349	6	.128	1	1	-1	1	0.1
1996	Chi-N	6	10	.375	37	20	1	1	1	129^{1}	144	101	15	8	68	90	15.3	6.54	66	.283	.376	8	.250	5	-33	-31	1	-2.7
1997	Mon-N	7	12	.368	36	25	2	2	0	155^{1}	165	106	17	12	74	87	14.5	5.56	75	.276	.367	9	.209	2	-23	-24	2	-2.1
1998	Sea-A	0	1	.000	2	1	0	0	0	5^{2}	13	10	3	0	2	4	23.8	15.88	29	.433	.469	0	—	0	-7	-7	-0	-0.9
Total	7	34	41	.453	186	89	6	4	11	642	651	398	65	34	306	392	13.9	5.06	81	.265	.355	31	.188	10	-68	-67	4	-6.0

YEAR	TM/L	W	L	PCT	G	GS	CG	SH	SV	IP	H	R	HR	HB	BB	SO	RAT	ERA	ERA+	OAV	OOB	BH	AVG	PB	PR	PR+	PD	TPI
● **KIRK BULLINGER** Bullinger, Kirk Matthew b: 10/28/69, New Orleans, La. BR/TR, 6'2", 170 lbs. Deb: 8/30/98 F																												
1998	Mon-N	1	0	1.000	8	0	0	0	0	7	14	8	1	0	0	2	18.0	9.00	47	.400	.400	0	.000	-0	-4	-4	0	-0.4
1999	Bos-A	0	0	—	4	0	0	0	0	2	2	1	0	0	2	0	18.0	4.50	111	.286	.444	0	—	0	0	0	1	0.1
2000	Phi-N	0	0	—	3	0	0	0	0	3^1	4	2	0	0	0	4	10.8	5.40	88	.308	.308	0	—	0	-0	-0	0	0.0
Total	3	1	0	1.000	15	0	0	0	0	12^1	20	11	1	0	2	6	16.1	7.30	61	.364	.386	0	.000	-0	-4	-4	1	-0.3
● **RED BULLOCK** Bullock, Malton Joseph b: 10/12/11, Biloxi, Miss. d: 6/27/88, Pascagoula, Miss. BL/TL, 6'1", 192 lbs. Deb: 5/19/36																												
1936	Phi-A	0	2	.000	12	2	0	0	0	16^2	19	32	0	0	37	7	30.2	14.04	36	.271	.523	0	.000	-1	-17	-16	0	-1.5
● **MELVIN BUNCH** Bunch, Melvin Lynn b: 11/4/71, Texarkana, Tex. BR/TR, 6'1", 165 lbs. Deb: 5/6/95																												
1995	KC-A	1	3	.250	13	5	0	0	0	40	42	25	11	0	14	19	12.6	5.62	85	.261	.320	0	—	0	-4	-4	-1	-0.4
1999	Sea-A	0	0	—	5	1	0	0	0	10	20	13	3	0	7	4	24.3	11.70	41	.426	.500	0	—	0	-8	-8	0	-0.4
Total	2	1	3	.250	18	6	0	0	0	50	62	38	14	0	21	23	14.9	6.84	70	.298	.362	0	—	0	-12	-11	-1	-0.8
● **WALLY BUNKER** Bunker, Wallace Edward b: 1/25/45, Seattle, Wash. BR/TR, 6'2", 197 lbs. Deb: 9/29/63																												
1963	Bal-A	0	1	.000	1	1	0	0	0	4	10	6	1	0	3	1	29.3	13.50	26	.476	.542	1	.500	0	-4	-5	-0	-0.7
1964	Bal-A	19	5	**.792**	29	29	12	1	0	214	161	72	17	3	62	96	9.5	2.69	133	.207	.269	5	.069	-2	22	21	1	2.2
1965	Bal-A	10	8	.556	34	27	4	1	2	189	170	79	16	4	58	84	11.0	3.38	103	.242	.303	4	.073	-1	2	2	-1	-0.1
1966	*Bal-A	10	6	.625	29	24	3	0	0	142^2	151	74	16	2	48	89	12.7	4.29	78	.269	.329	5	.104	-0	-14	-16	-1	-1.7
1967	Bal-A	3	7	.300	29	9	1	0	1	88	83	46	7	2	31	51	11.9	4.09	77	.254	.322	2	.077	-2	-8	-9	1	-1.1
1968	Bal-A	2	0	1.000	18	10	2	1	0	71	59	25	4	1	14	44	9.4	2.41	121	.225	.267	2	.111	-0	5	4	-0	0.2
1969	KC-A	12	11	.522	35	31	10	1	2	222^2	198	89	29	4	62	130	10.7	3.23	114	.238	.294	10	.143	0	10	11	3	1.5
1970	KC-A	2	11	.154	24	15	2	1	0	121^2	109	63	16	0	50	59	11.8	4.22	89	.238	.313	2	.065	-0	-7	-6	-1	-0.7
1971	KC-A	2	3	.400	7	6	0	0	0	32^1	35	19	7	0	6	15	11.4	5.01	69	.271	.304	0	.000	-1	-6	-6	-0	-0.9
Total	9	60	52	.536	206	152	34	5	5	1085^1	976	473	113	16	334	569	11.0	3.51	99	.240	.300	31	.094	-5	-1	-3	1	-1.3
● **JIM BUNNING** Bunning, James Paul David b: 10/23/31, Southgate, Ky. BR/TR, 6'3", 195 lbs. Deb: 7/20/55 H																												
1955	Det-A	3	5	.375	15	8	0	0	1	51	59	38	8	3	32	37	16.6	6.35	60	.291	.395	3	.200	-0	-14	-15	0	-2.0
1956	Det-A	5	1	.833	15	3	0	0	1	53^1	55	24	6	0	28	34	14.0	3.71	111	.257	.343	6	.333	2	3	2	-1	0.4
1957	Det-A★	**20**	8	.714	45	30	14	1	1	**267^1**	214	91	33	11	72	182	10.0	2.69	143	.218	.279	20	.213	3	**33**	**34**	-5	3.2
1958	Det-A	14	12	.538	35	34	10	3	0	219^2	188	96	28	10	79	177	11.3	3.52	115	.228	.304	14	.187	-1	6	12	-3	0.9
1959	Det-A★	17	13	.567	40	35	14	1	1	249^2	220	111	37	11	75	**201**	11.0	3.89	104	.234	.298	17	.191	1	-1	4	-5	0.1
1960	Det-A	11	14	.440	36	34	10	3	0	252	217	92	20	11	64	**201**	10.4	2.79	**142**	.236	.293	13	.160	-2	**30**	**32**	-1	2.6
1961	Det-A★	17	11	.607	38	37	12	4	1	268	232	113	25	9	71	194	10.5	3.19	128	.229	.285	13	.130	-4	25	27	-2	2.0
1962	Det-A★	19	10	.655	41	35	12	2	6	258	262	112	28	13	74	184	12.2	3.59	113	.261	.320	23	.242	4	11	13	-5	1.4
1963	Det-A★	12	13	.480	39	35	6	2	1	248^1	245	119	38	5	69	196	11.6	3.88	97	.254	.307	13	.155	-1	-7	-4	-2	-0.6
1964	Phi-N★	19	8	.704	41	39	13	5	2	284^1	248	99	23	14	46	219	9.7	2.63	132	.233	.274	12	.121	-2	29	27	-4	1.9
1965	Phi-N	19	9	.679	39	39	15	7	0	291	253	92	23	12	62	268	10.1	2.60	133	.232	.281	22	.214	4	30	28	0	3.2
1966	Phi-N★	19	14	.576	43	41	16	**5**	1	314	260	91	26	19	55	252	9.6	2.41	149	.223	.270	19	.179	1	42	42	-3	4.1
1967	Phi-N	17	15	.531	40	40	16	**6**	0	**302^1**	241	94	18	13	73	**253**	9.7	2.29	149	.217	.273	17	.163	2	**36**	**37**	-3	4.0
1968	Pit-N	4	14	.222	27	26	3	1	0	160	168	75	14	8	48	95	12.6	3.88	75	.272	.333	5	.098	-2	-16	-17	-3	-2.4
1969	Pit-N	10	9	.526	25	25	4	0	0	156	147	74	10	6	49	124	11.7	3.81	92	.249	.313	2	.043	-3	-4	-6	-3	-1.3
	LA-N	3	1	.750	9	9	1	0	0	56^1	65	23	5	1	10	33	12.1	3.36	99	.288	.321	2	.111	-1	2	-0	-1	-0.2
	Yr	13	10	.565	34	34	5	0	0	212^1	212	97	15	7	59	157	11.8	3.69	93	.259	.315	4	.062	-4	-2	-6	-4	-1.5
1970	Phi-N	10	15	.400	34	33	4	0	0	219	233	111	19	8	56	147	12.2	4.11	97	.274	.325	9	.127	-2	-1	-3	-1	-0.6
1971	Phi-N	5	12	.294	29	16	1	0	1	110	126	72	11	6	37	58	13.8	5.48	64	.297	.362	3	.120	0	-25	-23	-0	-3.3
Total	17	224	184	.549	591	519	151	40	16	3760^1	3433	1527	372	160	1000	2855	11.0	3.27	114	.242	.299	213	.167	-1	179	191	-41	13.4
● **DAVE BURBA** Burba, David Allen b: 7/7/66, Dayton, Ohio BR/TR, 6'4", 240 lbs. Deb: 9/8/90																												
1990	Sea-A	0	0	—	6	0	0	0	0	8	8	6	0	1	2	4	12.4	4.50	88	.267	.333	0	—	0	-1	-0	0	0.0
1991	Sea-A	2	2	.500	22	2	0	0	1	36^2	34	16	6	0	14	16	11.8	3.68	112	.245	.314	0	—	0	2	2	-0	0.2
1992	SF-N	2	7	.222	23	11	0	0	0	70^2	80	43	4	2	31	47	14.4	4.97	67	.287	.362	1	.067	-1	-11	-14	-1	-1.8
1993	SF-N	10	3	.769	54	5	0	0	0	95^1	95	49	14	3	37	88	12.7	4.25	92	.265	.338	5	.294	2	-2	-4	0	-0.3
1994	SF-N	3	6	.333	57	0	0	0	0	74	59	39	5	6	45	84	13.4	4.38	92	.221	.346	0	.000	-0	-1	-3	-1	-0.4
1995	SF-N	4	2	.667	37	0	0	0	0	43^1	38	26	5	0	25	46	13.1	4.98	82	.235	.337	0	—	0	-4	-4	-0	-0.6
	*Cin-N	6	2	.750	15	9	1	1	0	63^1	52	24	4	0	26	50	11.1	3.27	126	.223	.301	1	.067	-0	6	6	-1	0.6
	Yr	10	4	.714	52	9	1	1	0	106^2	90	50	9	0	51	96	11.9	3.97	104	.228	.316	1	.067	-0	3	2	-1	0.0
1996	Cin-N	11	13	.458	34	33	0	0	0	195	179	96	18	2	97	148	12.8	3.83	111	.244	.334	7	.104	-1	9	9	-2	0.7
1997	Cin-N	11	10	.524	30	27	2	0	0	160	157	88	22	9	73	131	13.4	4.72	90	.255	.343	9	.196	1	-9	-8	1	-0.7
1998	*Cle-A	15	10	.600	32	31	0	0	0	203^2	210	100	30	7	69	132	12.6	4.11	116	.269	.334	1	.167	1	12	15	-0	1.6
1999	*Cle-A	15	9	.625	34	34	1	0	0	220	211	113	30	8	96	174	12.9	4.25	119	.254	.337	1	.333	1	15	19	1	1.9
2000	Cle-A	16	6	.727	32	32	0	0	0	191^1	199	99	19	2	91	180	13.7	4.47	112	.267	.348	0	.000	-0	10	11	1	1.2
Total	11	95	70	.576	376	184	4	1	1	1361^1	1322	699	157	40	606	1100	13.0	4.26	104	.256	.338	25	.145	2	25	28	-2	2.4
● **BILL BURBACH** Burbach, William David b: 8/22/47, Dickeyville, Wis. BR/TR, 6'4", 215 lbs. Deb: 4/11/69																												
1969	NY-A	6	8	.429	31	24	2	1	0	140^2	112	68	15	2	102	82	13.8	3.65	95	.219	.351	4	.100	-1	-0	-3	-1	-0.4
1970	NY-A	0	2	.000	4	4	0	0	0	16^2	23	19	2	1	9	10	17.8	10.26	34	.324	.407	0	.000	-1	-12	-13	-0	-1.3
1971	NY-A	0	1	.000	2	0	0	0	0	3^1	6	6	0	0	5	3	29.7	10.80	30	.400	.550	0	.000	-0	-3	-3	-0	-0.6
Total	3	6	11	.353	37	28	2	1	0	160^2	141	93	17	3	116	95	14.6	4.48	78	.236	.363	4	.085	-2	-15	-19	-1	-2.3
● **LARRY BURCHART** Burchart, Larry Wayne b: 2/8/46, Tulsa, Okla. BR/TR, 6'3", 205 lbs. Deb: 4/10/69																												
1969	Cle-A	0	2	.000	29	0	0	0	0	42^1	42	28	2	1	24	26	14.2	4.25	89	.266	.366	0	—	0	-3	-2	-1	-0.2
● **FRED BURCHELL** Burchell, Frederick Duff b: 7/14/1879, Perth Amboy, N.J. d: 11/20/51, Jordan, N.Y. BL/TL, 5'11", 175 lbs. Deb: 4/17/03																												
1903	Phi-N	0	3	.000	6	3	2	0	0	44	48	28	0	2	14	12	13.1	2.86	114	.293	.356	3	.188	-1	2	2	-0	0.0
1907	Bos-A	0	1	.000	2	1	0	0	0	10	8	5	0	1	2	6	9.9	2.70	95	.222	.282	1	.200	-0	-0	-0	-0	0.0
1908	Bos-A	10	8	.556	31	19	9	0	0	179^2	161	84	2	11	65	94	11.9	2.96	83	.247	.326	17	.246	1	-11	-10	-2	-1.1
1909	Bos-A	3	3	.500	10	5	1	0	0	52	51	22	1	2	11	12	11.1	2.94	85	.271	.318	3	.158	-0	-3	-3	1	-0.3
Total	4	13	15	.464	49	28	12	0	0	285^2	268	139	3	16	92	124	11.8	2.93	89	.258	.328	24	.220	-0	-12	-10	-2	-1.4
● **FREDDIE BURDETTE** Burdette, Freddie Thomason b: 9/15/36, Moultrie, Ga. BR/TR, 6'1", 170 lbs. Deb: 9/5/62																												
1962	Chi-N	0	0	—	8	0	0	0	1	9^2	5	4	2	0	8	5	12.1	3.72	111	.161	.333	0	.000	-0	0	0	-0	0.0
1963	Chi-N	0	0	—	4	0	0	0	0	4^2	5	2	1	0	2	1	13.5	3.86	91	.313	.389	0	—	0	-0	-0	0	0.0
1964	Chi-N	1	0	1.000	18	0	0	0	0	20	17	7	2	1	10	4	12.6	3.15	118	.243	.346	1	1.000	0	1	1	-0	0.1
Total	3	1	0	1.000	30	0	0	0	1	34^1	27	13	5	1	20	10	12.6	3.41	112	.231	.348	1	.500	0	1	1	-0	0.1
● **LEW BURDETTE** Burdette, Selva Lewis b: 11/22/26, Nitro, W.Va. BR/TR, 6'2", 190 lbs. Deb: 9/26/50 C																												
1950	NY-A	0	0	—	2	0	0	0	0	1^1	3	1	0	0	0	0	20.3	6.75	64	.500	.500	0	—	0	-0	-0	0	0.0
1951	Bos-N	0	0	—	3	0	0	0	0	4^1	6	4	0	1	5	1	24.9	6.23	59	.375	.545	0	.000	-0	-1	-1	0	-0.1
1952	Bos-N	6	11	.353	45	9	5	0	7	137	138	58	8	2	47	47	12.3	3.61	100	.265	.328	4	.114	-0	2	-0	1	0.0
1953	Mil-N	15	5	.750	46	13	6	1	8	175	177	73	7	5	56	58	12.2	3.24	121	.264	.326	9	.170	-1	20	15	2	1.6
1954	Mil-N	15	14	.517	38	32	13	4	0	238	224	87	17	4	62	79	11.0	2.76	135	.251	.302	7	.089	-5	35	28	1	2.8
1955	Mil-N	13	8	.619	42	33	11	2	0	230	253	114	25	6	73	70	13.0	4.03	93	.280	.337	20	.233	3	0	-8	2	-0.2
1956	Mil-N	19	10	.655	39	35	16	**6**	1	256^1	234	92	22	3	52	110	10.1	**2.70**	128	.241	.282	16	.186	1	30	24	1	2.8
1957	*Mil-N★	17	9	.654	37	33	14	1	0	256^2	260	117	25	2	59	78	11.3	3.72	94	.264	.307	13	.148	1	5	-7	2	-0.4
1958	*Mil-N	20	10	**.667**	40	36	19	3	0	275^1	279	102	18	5	50	113	10.9	2.91	121	.264	.301	24	.242	9	**32**	21	3	3.3
1959	Mil-N★	**21**	15	.583	41	39	20	**4**	1	289^2	312	144	38	1	38	105	10.9	4.07	87	.273	.297	21	.202	6	-4	-19	0	-1.5
1960	Mil-N	19	13	.594	45	32	**18**	4	4	275^2	277	116	19	5	35	83	10.3	3.36	102	.260	.287	16	.176	5	12	2	5	1.2
1961	Mil-N	18	11	.621	40	36	14	3	0	**272^1**	295	131	31	3	33	92	10.9	4.00	94	.273	.296	21	.204	5	1	-8	2	-0.1
1962	Mil-N	10	9	.526	37	19	6	1	2	143^2	172	85	26	2	23	59	12.3	4.89	78	.298	.327	9	.176	0	-15	-18	1	-2.0
1963	Mil-N	6	5	.545	15	13	4	1	0	84	71	40	15	1	24	28	10.3	3.64	88	.228	.285	1	.038	-0	-3	-4	-0	-0.6

YEAR	TM/L	W	L	PCT	G	GS	CG	SH	SV	IP	H	R	HR	HB	BB	SO	RAT	ERA	ERA+	OAV	OOB	BH	AVG	PB	PR	PR+	PD	TPI
	StL-N	3	8	.273	21	14	3	0	2	98	106	50	6	7	16	45	11.8	3.77	94	.278	.319	3	.097	-1	-5	-2	-2	-0.5
	Yr	9	13	.409	36	27	7	1	2	182	177	90	21	8	40	73	11.1	3.71	92	.255	.304	4	.070	-2	-9	-6	-2	-1.1
1964	StL-N	1	0	1.000	8	0	0	0	0	10	10	3	1	0	3	3	11.7	1.80	211	.256	.310	0	.000	-0	2	2	-0	0.2
	Chi-N	9	9	.500	28	17	8	2	0	131	152	74	15	1	19	40	11.8	4.88	76	.292	.319	12	.279	6	-20	-16	2	-1.3
	Yr	10	9	.526	36	17	8	2	0	141	162	77	16	1	22	43	11.8	4.66	80	.290	.318	12	.273	6	-18	-14	2	-1.1
1965	Chi-N	0	2	.000	7	3	0	0	0	20^{1}	26	17	3	1	4	5	13.7	5.31	69	.299	.337	2	.333	1	-4	-4	-0	-0.2
	Phi-N	3	3	.500	19	9	1	1	0	70^{2}	95	50	5	5	17	23	14.9	5.48	63	.329	.376	6	.300	1	-15	-16	0	-1.1
	Yr	3	5	.375	26	12	1	1	0	91	121	67	8	6	21	28	14.6	5.44	65	.322	.367	8	.308	2	-19	-20	0	-1.3
1966	Cal-A	7	2	.778	54	0	0	0	5	79^{2}	80	32	4	1	12	27	10.5	3.39	99	.268	.298	1	.125	-0	0	-0	-1	-0.1
1967	Cal-A	1	0	1.000	19	0	0	0	1	18^{1}	16	10	4	1	0	8	8.3	4.91	64	.232	.243	0	—	0	-3	-4	0	-0.2
Total	18	203	144	.585	626	373	158	33	31	3067^{1}	3186	1400	289	56	628	1074	11.4	3.66	99	.268	.308	185	.183	30	68	-19	19	3.6
● BILL BURDICK	Burdick, William Byron b: 10/11/1859, Austin, Minn. d: 10/23/49, Spokane, Wash. BR/TR, Deb: 7/23/1888																											
1888	Ind-N	10	10	.500	20	20	20	0	0	176	168	88	12	6	43	55	11.1	2.81	105	.242	.292	10	.147	-2	1	3	-0	0.0
1889	Ind-N	2	4	.333	10	4	2	0	1	45^{2}	58	42	7	0	13	16	14.0	4.53	92	.301	.345	2	.118	-0	-3	-2	-0	-0.2
Total	2	12	14	.462	30	24	22	0	1	221^{2}	226	130	19	6	56	71	11.7	3.17	101	.255	.304	12	.141	-3	-2	1	-0	-0.2
● TOM BURGMEIER	Burgmeier, Thomas Henry b: 8/2/43, St.Paul, Minn. BL/TL, 5'11", 185 lbs. Deb: 4/10/68 C																											
1968	Cal-A	1	4	.200	56	2	0	0	5	72^{2}	65	41	5	0	24	33	11.0	4.33	67	.250	.313	0	.000	0	-11	-12	4	-0.6
1969	KC-A	3	1	.750	31	0	0	0	0	54	67	31	5	1	21	23	14.8	4.17	89	.316	.380	3	.167	-0	-3	-3	2	0.0
1970	KC-A	6	6	.500	41	0	0	0	1	68^{1}	59	31	6	0	23	43	10.8	3.16	118	.236	.300	2	.143	-0	4	4	2	0.9
1971	KC-A	9	7	.563	67	0	0	0	17	88^{1}	71	23	3	7	30	44	11.0	1.73	198	.223	.303	5	.250	2	17	17	3	4.3
1972	KC-A	6	2	.750	51	0	0	0	9	55^{1}	67	32	0	1	33	18	16.4	4.23	72	.313	.407	4	.333	1	-7	-7	1	-1.2
1973	KC-A	0	0	—	6	0	0	0	1	10	13	6	2	1	4	4	16.2	5.40	76	.310	.383	0	—	0	-2	-1	-0	-0.1
1974	Min-A	5	3	.625	50	0	0	0	4	91^{2}	92	46	7	2	26	34	11.8	4.52	83	.270	.325	0	—	0	-9	-8	3	-0.4
1975	Min-A	5	8	.385	46	0	0	0	11	75^{2}	76	32	7	1	23	41	11.9	3.09	124	.264	.321	0	—	0	6	6	0	1.2
1976	Min-A	8	1	.889	57	0	0	0	1	115^{1}	95	36	11	2	29	45	9.8	2.50	143	.226	.279	0	—	0	13	14	2	1.3
1977	Min-A	6	4	.600	61	0	0	0	7	97^{1}	113	56	15	2	33	35	13.7	5.09	79	.299	.358	0	—	0	-11	-12	1	-1.2
1978	Bos-A	2	1	.667	35	1	0	0	4	61^{1}	74	33	7	3	23	24	14.7	4.40	94	.302	.369	0	—	0	-4	-2	1	0.0
1979	Bos-A	3	2	.600	44	0	0	0	4	88^{2}	89	32	8	4	16	60	11.1	2.74	162	.263	.304	0	—	0	15	16	1	1.0
1980	Bos-A☆	5	4	.556	62	0	0	0	24	99	87	30	3	2	20	54	9.9	2.00	211	.241	.285	0	—	0	22	23	3	3.6
1981	Bos-A	4	5	.444	32	0	0	0	6	59^{2}	61	23	5	4	17	35	12.4	2.87	135	.268	.329	0	—	0	5	6	1	1.2
1982	Bos-A	7	0	1.000	40	0	0	0	2	102^{1}	98	30	6	2	22	44	10.7	2.29	189	.259	.303	0	—	0	20	22	2	1.7
1983	Oak-A	6	7	.462	49	0	0	0	4	96	89	33	2	0	32	39	11.3	2.81	138	.244	.305	0	—	0	13	12	2	1.8
1984	Oak-A	3	0	1.000	17	0	0	0	2	23	15	6	2	0	8	8	9.0	2.35	160	.190	.264	0	—	0	4	4	0	0.5
Total	17	79	55	.590	745	3	0	0	102	1258^{2}	1231	521	94	32	384	584	11.8	3.23	118	.261	.321	14	.212	2	73	81	27	14.0
● ENRIQUE BURGOS	Burgos, Enrique (Calles) b: 10/7/65, Chorrera, Panama BL/TL, 6'4", 195 lbs. Deb: 7/15/93																											
1993	KC-A	0	1	.000	5	0	0	0	0	5	5	5	0	1	6	6	21.6	9.00	51	.238	.429	0	—	0	-3	-2	0	-0.4
1995	SF-N	0	0	—	5	0	0	0	0	8^{1}	14	8	1	1	6	12	22.7	8.64	47	.378	.477	0	—	0	-4	-4	-0	-0.2
Total	2	0	1	.000	10	0	0	0	0	13^{1}	19	13	1	2	12	18	22.3	8.78	49	.328	.458	0	—	0	-7	-7	-0	-0.6
● SANDY BURK	Burk, Charles Sanford b: 4/22/1887, Columbus, Ohio d: 10/11/34, Brooklyn, N.Y. BR/TR, 5'8", 155 lbs. Deb: 9/12/10																											
1910	Bro-N	0	3	.000	4	3	1	0	0	19^{1}	17	16	0	2	27	14	21.4	6.05	50	.258	.484	0	.000	-1	-6	-6	0	-0.9
1911	Bro-N	1	3	.250	13	7	1	0	0	58	54	36	1	3	47	15	16.1	5.12	65	.261	.405	2	.105	-1	-11	-12	0	-0.8
1912	Bro-N	0	0	—	2	0	0	0	0	8^{1}	9	3	0	0	3	2	13.0	3.24	103	.273	.333	1	.250	0	0	0	0	0.0
	StL-N	1	3	.250	12	4	2	0	1	44^{2}	37	19	0	1	12	17	10.1	2.42	142	.236	.294	0	.000	-2	5	5	-1	0.2
	Yr	1	3	.250	14	4	2	0	1	53	46	22	0	1	15	19	10.5	2.55	134	.242	.301	1	.067	-1	5	5	-1	0.2
1913	StL-N	0	2	.000	19	7	0	0	1	70	81	45	1	6	33	29	15.4	5.14	63	.290	.377	2	.091	-2	-15	-15	-0	-1.0
1915	Pit-F	2	0	1.000	2	2	1	0	0	18	8	3	0	0	11	9	9.5	1.00	271	.140	.279	1	.167	-0	3	3	-1	0.3
Total	5	4	11	.267	52	23	5	0	2	218^{1}	206	122	2	12	133	86	14.5	4.25	76	.258	.372	6	.090	-6	-24	-24	-2	-2.2
● ELMER BURKART	Burkart, Elmer Robert "Swede" b: 2/1/17, Torresdale, Pa. d: 2/6/95, Baltimore, Md. BR/TR, 6'2", 190 lbs. Deb: 9/14/36																											
1936	Phi-N	0	0	—	2	2	0	0	0	7^{2}	4	3	0	0	12	2	18.8	3.52	129	.160	.432	0	.000	-0	1	1	0	0.0
1937	Phi-N	0	0	—	7	0	0	0	0	16	20	11	0	0	9	4	16.3	6.19	70	.323	.408	0	.000	-1	-4	-3	0	-0.2
1938	Phi-N	0	1	.000	2	1	1	0	0	10	12	5	0	1	3	1	14.4	4.50	86	.286	.348	0	.000	-0	-1	-1	-0	-0.1
1939	Phi-N	1	0	1.000	5	0	0	0	0	8^{1}	11	4	0	0	2	2	14.0	4.32	93	.344	.382	1	1.000	1	-0	-0	-0	0.0
Total	4	1	1	.500	16	3	1	0	0	42	47	23	0	1	26	9	15.9	4.93	85	.292	.394	1	.083	-1	-5	-3	-0	-0.3
● JAMES BURKE	Burke, James b: Attleboro, Mass. Deb: 6/10/1882																											
1882	Buf-N	0	1	.000	1	1	0	0	0	4	10	9	0		0	0	22.5	11.25	26	.435	.435	0	.000	-1	-4	-4	1	-0.5
1883	Buf-N	0	0	—	1	1	0	0	0	8	9	8	0		1	3	13.5	5.63	56	.243	.300	1	.200	-0	-2	-2	-0	-0.1
1884	Bos-U	19	15	.559	38	36	34	0	0	322	326	201	10		31	255	10.0	2.85	84	.245	.263	41	.223	-7	-15	-17	-4	-2.3
Total	3	19	16	.543	40	38	34	0	0	334	345	218	10		34	256	10.2	3.02	80	.249	.267	42	.218	-8	-21	-23	-4	-2.9
● JOHN BURKE	Burke, John C. b: 2/9/70, Durango, Colo. BB/TR, 6'4", 220 lbs. Deb: 8/13/96																											
1996	Col-N	2	1	.667	11	0	0	0	0	15^{2}	21	13	3	1	7	19	16.7	7.47	70	.318	.392	1	.500	0	-6	-3	0	-0.5
1997	Col-N	2	5	.286	17	9	0	0	0	59	83	46	13	6	26	39	17.5	6.56	79	.329	.405	3	.158	-1	-15	-7	-1	-0.9
Total	2	4	6	.400	28	9	0	0	0	74^{2}	104	59	16	7	33	58	17.4	6.75	77	.327	.402	4	.190	-1	-21	-11	-1	-1.4
● JOHN BURKE	Burke, John Patrick b: 1/27/1877, Hazleton, Pa. d: 8/4/50, Jersey City, N.J. BR/TR, Deb: 6/27/02 ♦																											
1902	NY-N	0	1	.000	2	1	1	0	0	14	21	11	0	0	3	3	15.4	5.79	49	.344	.375	2	.154	-0	-5	-5	0	-0.3
● BOBBY BURKE	Burke, Robert James "Lefty" b: 1/23/07, Joliet, Ill. d: 2/8/71, Joliet, Ill. BL/TL, 6'0.5", 150 lbs. Deb: 4/16/27																											
1927	Was-A	3	2	.600	36	6	1	0	0	100	91	48	6	7	32	20	11.7	3.96	103	.245	.316	3	.125	-2	2	1	0	-0.2
1928	Was-A	2	4	.333	26	7	2	1	0	85^{1}	87	44	1	2	18	27	11.3	3.90	103	.277	.320	5	.250	1	1	1	0	0.2
1929	Was-A	6	8	.429	37	17	4	0	0	141	154	91	6	4	55	51	13.6	4.79	89	.279	.349	6	.140	-3	-8	-9	-2	-1.2
1930	Was-A	3	4	.429	24	4	2	0	3	74^{1}	62	41	2	3	29	35	11.4	3.63	127	.229	.310	4	.174	-1	8	8	-1	0.5
1931	Was-A	8	3	.727	30	13	3	1	2	128^{2}	124	67	6	2	50	38	12.3	4.27	101	.255	.327	10	.213	-0	2	0	0	0.0
1932	Was-A	3	6	.333	22	10	2	0	0	91	98	55	4	1	44	32	14.1	5.14	84	.272	.353	5	.200	0	-7	-9	-1	-0.8
1933	Was-A	4	3	.571	25	6	4	1	0	64	64	29	1	2	31	28	13.6	3.23	129	.256	.343	4	.235	0	7	7	0	0.7
1934	Was-A	8	8	.500	37	15	7	1	0	168	155	67	2	1	72	52	12.2	3.21	134	.245	.323	13	.228	2	24	21	0	2.0
1935	Was-A	1	8	.111	15	10	2	0	0	66^{1}	90	63	7	2	27	16	16.1	7.46	58	.327	.391	4	.182	-0	-22	-24	1	-2.5
1937	Phi-N	0	0	—	2	0	0	0	0	0	1	0	0	2	—	—	∞	—	.500	.750	111	—	0	-1	-1	0		-0.1
Total	10	38	46	.452	254	88	27	4	5	918^{2}	926	506	35	24	360	299	12.8	4.29	99	.263	.336	54	.194	-3	6	-3	-3	-1.4
● STEVE BURKE	Burke, Steven Michael b: 3/5/55, Stockton, Cal. BB/TR, 6'2", 200 lbs. Deb: 9/10/77																											
1977	Sea-A	0	1	.000	6	0	0	0	0	15^{2}	12	6	0	0	7	6	10.9	2.87	144	.226	.317	0	—	0	2	2	0	0.1
1978	Sea-A	0	1	.000	18	0	0	0	0	49	46	22	2	1	24	16	13.0	3.49	110	.258	.350	0	—	0	2	2	0	0.1
Total	2	0	2	.000	24	0	0	0	0	64^{2}	58	28	2	1	31	22	12.5	3.34	117	.251	.342	0	—	0	4	4	0	0.2
● TIM BURKE	Burke, Timothy Philip b: 2/19/59, Omaha, Neb. BR/TR, 6'3", 205 lbs. Deb: 4/8/85																											
1985	Mon-N	9	4	.692	**78**	0	0	0	8	120^{1}	86	32	9	7	44	87	10.2	2.39	142	.204	.290	1	.100	-0	**16**	14	1	1.7
1986	Mon-N	9	7	.563	68	2	0	0	4	101^{1}	103	37	7	4	46	82	13.6	2.93	126	.262	.345	0	.000	-0	9	9	1	1.5
1987	Mon-N	7	0	1.000	55	0	0	0	18	91	64	18	3	0	17	58	8.0	1.19	355	.196	.235	0	.000	-1	**29**	**30**	1	3.1
1988	Mon-N	3	5	.375	61	0	0	0	18	82	84	36	7	3	25	42	12.3	3.40	106	.272	.332	0	.000	-0	0	2	0	0.3
1989	Mon-N★	9	3	.750	68	0	0	0	28	84^{2}	68	24	6	0	22	54	9.6	2.55	139	.225	.278	0	.000	-0	9	9	1	1.9
1990	Mon-N	3	3	.500	58	0	0	0	20	75	71	29	6	2	21	47	11.3	2.52	145	.247	.303	1	.167	0	11	10	2	1.5
1991	Mon-N	3	4	.429	37	0	0	0	5	46	41	24	3	4	14	25	11.5	4.11	88	.243	.316	0	.000	-0	-2	-3	0	-0.4
	NY-N	3	3	.500	35	0	0	0	1	55^{2}	55	22	5	0	12	34	10.8	2.75	133	.255	.294	0	.000	-1	6	6	1	0.6
	Yr	6	7	.462	72	0	0	0	6	101^{2}	96	46	8	4	26	59	11.2	3.36	108	.249	.304	0	.000	-1	4	3	1	0.2
1992	NY-N	1	2	.333	15	0	0	0	0	15^{2}	26	15	1	0	3	7	16.7	5.74	61	.366	.392	0	—	0	-4	-4	0	-0.7

YEAR	TM/L	W	L	PCT	G	GS	CG	SH	SV	IP	H	R	HR	HB	BB	SO	RAT	ERA	ERA+	OAV	OOB	BH	AVG	PB	PR	PR+	PD	TPI
	NY-A	2	2	.500	23	0	0	0	0	27^2	26	14	2	1	15	8	13.7	3.25	121	.250	.350	0	—	0	2	2	1	0.4
Total	8	49	33	.598	498	2	0	0	102	699^1	624	251	49	21	219	444	11.1	2.72	135	.240	.304	2	.045	-2	76	75	7	9.9
● **BILLY BURKE** Burke, William Ignatius b: 7/11/1889, Clinton, Mass. d: 2/9/67, Worcester, Mass. BL/TL, 5′10″, 165 lbs. Deb: 4/30/10																												
1910	Bos-N	1	0	1.000	19	1	1	0	0	64	68	32	1	2	29	22	13.9	4.08	82	.302	.387	4	.190	-1	-7	-5	-1	-0.4
1911	Bos-N	0	1	.000	2	1	0	0	0	3^1	6	7	0	0	5	1	29.7	18.90	20	.429	.579	1	1.000	0	-6	-5	-0	-0.8
Total	2	1	1	.500	21	2	1	0	0	67^1	74	39	1	2	34	23	14.7	4.81	70	.310	.400	5	.227	-0	-13	-10	-2	-1.2
● **BILL BURKE** Burke, William R. b: 11/1865, Cincinnati, Ohio d: 3/17/39, Atchison, Kan. 6′, 200 lbs. Deb: 7/20/1887																												
1887	Det-N	0	1	.000	2	2	1	0	0	15	26	14	0	2	5	3	16.8	6.00	67	.366	.384	2	.250	-0	-3	-3	-0	-0.2
● **JESSE BURKETT** Burkett, Jesse Cail "Crab" b: 12/4/1868, Wheeling, W.Va. d: 5/27/53, Worcester, Mass. BL/TL, 5′8″, 155 lbs. Deb: 4/22/1890 CH♦																												
1890	NY-N	3	10	.231	21	14	6	0	0	118	134	123	3	14	92	82	18.3	5.57	63	.277	.407	124	.309	8	-26	-28	2	-1.8
1894	Cle-N	0	0	—	1	0	0	0	0	4	6	2	0	0	1	0	15.8	4.50	121	.333	.368	187	.358	0	0	0	-0	0.0
1902	StL-A	0	1	.000	1	0	0	0	0	1	4	4	0	0	1	2	45.0	9.00	39	.571	.625	169	.306	0	-1	-1	0	-0.1
Total	3	3	11	.214	23	14	6	0	0	123	144	129	3	14	94	84	18.4	5.56	64	.283	.408	2850	.338	9	-26	-28	2	-1.9
● **JOHN BURKETT** Burkett, John David b: 11/28/64, New Brighton, Pa. BR/TR, 6′2″, 211 lbs. Deb: 9/15/87																												
1987	SF-N	0	0	—	3	0	0	0	0	6	7	4	2	1	3	5	16.5	4.50	86	.304	.407	0	.000	-0	-0	-0	0	0.0
1990	SF-N	14	7	.667	33	32	2	0	1	204	201	92	18	4	61	118	11.7	3.79	96	.257	.314	3	.048	-3	0	-3	-1	-0.7
1991	SF-N	12	11	.522	36	34	3	1	0	206^2	223	103	19	10	60	131	12.8	4.18	86	.277	.335	5	.091	-1	-11	-14	-1	-1.7
1992	SF-N	13	9	.591	32	32	3	1	0	189^2	194	96	13	4	45	107	11.5	3.84	86	.264	.310	1	.018	-3	-7	-12	-3	-1.9
1993	SF-N★	**22**	7	.759	34	34	2	1	0	231^2	224	100	18	11	40	145	10.7	3.65	107	.255	.296	9	.118	-1	10	7	1	0.8
1994	SF-N	6	8	.429	25	25	0	0	0	159^1	176	72	14	7	36	85	12.4	3.62	111	.286	.332	3	.059	-4	11	7	0	0.3
1995	Fla-N	14	14	.500	30	30	4	0	0	188^1	208	95	22	6	57	126	13.0	4.30	98	.282	.339	7	.106	-2	-2	-2	0	-0.4
1996	Fla-N	6	10	.375	24	24	1	0	0	154	154	84	15	3	42	108	11.6	4.32	94	.263	.316	9	.173	0	-2	-4	0	-0.4
	*Tex-A	5	2	.714	10	10	1	1	0	68^2	75	33	4	2	16	47	12.2	4.06	129	.280	.325	0	—	0	7	9	-1	0.7
1997	Tex-A	9	12	.429	30	30	2	0	0	189^1	240	106	20	4	30	139	13.0	4.56	105	.307	.335	1	.200	0	0	5	1	0.5
1998	Tex-A	9	13	.409	32	32	0	0	0	195	230	131	19	8	46	131	13.1	5.68	85	.292	.337	0	.000	-0	-22	-18	-2	-1.8
1999	Tex-A	9	8	.529	30	25	0	0	0	147^1	184	95	18	3	46	96	14.2	5.62	91	.307	.360	0	.000	-0	-12	-8	-0	-0.8
2000	*Atl-N	10	6	.625	31	22	0	0	0	134^1	162	79	13	4	51	110	14.5	4.89	93	.303	.368	6	.143	0	-4	-6	-0	-0.6
Total	12	129	107	.547	350	330	18	4	1	2074^1	2278	1090	195	67	533	1348	12.5	4.35	96	.280	.330	44	.093	-15	-33	-43	-4	-6.0
● **KEN BURKHART** Burkhart, Kenneth William (b: Kenneth William Burkhardt) b: 11/18/16, Knoxville, Tenn. BR/TR, 6′1″, 190 lbs. Deb: 4/21/45 U																												
1945	StL-N	18	8	.692	42	22	12	4	2	217^1	206	76	9	3	66	67	11.4	2.90	129	.251	.309	13	.181	1	22	21	-1	2.3
1946	StL-N	6	3	.667	25	13	5	2	2	100	111	34	4	2	36	32	13.4	2.88	120	.282	.346	5	.147	-0	6	6	-2	0.4
1947	StL-N	3	6	.333	34	6	1	0	1	95	108	55	13	4	23	44	12.8	5.21	79	.292	.340	3	.125	-1	-12	-11	1	-1.0
1948	StL-N	0	0	—	20	0	0	0	1	37^1	50	24	4	2	14	16	15.9	5.54	74	.331	.395	1	.250	0	-7	-6	1	-0.2
	Cin-N	0	3	.000	16	0	0	0	0	41^2	42	34	3	1	16	14	12.7	6.91	57	.255	.324	3	.333	2	-14	-14	-0	-0.7
	Yr	0	3	.000	36	0	0	0	1	79	92	58	7	3	30	30	14.2	6.27	64	.291	.358	4	.308	2	-20	-20	0	-0.9
1949	Cin-N	0	0	—	11	0	0	0	1	28^1	29	10	2	0	10	8	12.4	3.18	132	.282	.345	2	.286	0	3	3	0	0.2
Total	5	27	20	.574	148	41	18	6	7	519^2	546	233	35	12	165	181	12.5	3.84	99	.273	.332	27	.180	2	-2	-1	-2	1.0
● **A.J. BURNETT** Burnett, Allan James b: 1/3/77, North Little Rock, Ark. BR/TR, 6′5″, 205 lbs. Deb: 8/17/99																												
1999	Fla-N	4	2	.667	7	7	0	0	0	41^1	37	23	3	0	25	33	13.5	3.48	125	.242	.348	2	.118	-1	5	4	-0	0.5
2000	Fla-N	3	7	.300	13	13	0	0	0	82^2	80	46	8	2	44	57	13.7	4.79	92	.259	.355	7	.280	4	-1	-4	-1	0.0
Total	2	7	9	.438	20	20	0	0	0	124	117	69	11	2	69	90	13.6	4.35	101	.253	.353	9	.214	4	4	1	-1	0.5
● **WALLY BURNETTE** Burnette, Wallace Harper b: 6/20/29, Blairs, Va. BR/TR, 6′0.5″, 178 lbs. Deb: 7/15/56																												
1956	KC-A	6	8	.429	18	14	4	1	0	121^1	115	48	13	2	39	54	11.6	2.89	150	.252	.314	2	.051	-4	17	19	-1	1.4
1957	KC-A	7	12	.368	38	9	1	0	1	113	115	62	8	1	44	57	12.7	4.30	92	.268	.338	8	.250	1	-6	-4	2	-0.4
1958	KC-A	1	1	.500	12	4	0	0	0	28^1	29	14	2	0	14	11	13.7	3.49	112	.264	.347	1	.167	0	1	1	-1	0.0
Total	3	14	21	.400	68	27	5	1	1	262^2	259	124	23	3	97	122	12.3	3.56	116	.260	.328	11	.143	-4	11	16	1	1.0
● **DENNIS BURNS** Burns, Dennis b: 5/24/1898, Tiff City, Mo. d: 5/21/69, Tulsa, Okla. BR/TR, 5′10″, 180 lbs. Deb: 9/22/23																												
1923	Phi-A	2	1	.667	4	3	2	0	0	27	21	9	1	0	7	8	9.3	2.00	205	.210	.262	1	.111	-1	6	6	-0	0.5
1924	Phi-A	6	8	.429	37	17	7	0	1	154	191	101	3	1	68	26	15.2	5.08	84	.314	.384	6	.143	-2	-15	-14	-0	-1.2
Total	2	8	9	.471	41	20	9	0	1	181	212	110	4	1	75	34	14.3	4.62	92	.299	.367	7	.137	-3	-9	-7	-0	-0.7
● **FARMER BURNS** Burns, James "Slab" b: Ashtabula, Ohio TR, 5′7″, 168 lbs. Deb: 7/6/01																												
1901	StL-N	0	0	—	1	0	0	0	0	1	2	1	0	1	1	0	36.0	9.00	35	.400	.571	0	—	0	-1	-1	-0	0.0
● **DICK BURNS** Burns, Richard Simon b: 12/26/1863, Holyoke, Mass. d: 11/16/37, Holyoke, Mass. BL/TL, 5′7″, 140 lbs. Deb: 5/3/1883 ♦																												
1883	Det-N	2	12	.143	17	13	13	0	0	127^2	172	122	8		33	30	14.5	4.51	69	.301	.339	26	.186	-2	-19	-20	-0	-1.8
1884	Cin-U	23	15	.605	40	40	34	1	0	329^2	298	179	7		47	167	9.4	2.46	104	.225	.252	107	.306	3	-1	4	0	0.6
1885	StL-N	0	0	—	1	0	0	0	0	3	3	3	0		0	2	9.0	9.00	31	.250	.250	12	.222	0	-2	-2	1	-0.1
Total	3	25	27	.481	58	53	47	1	0	460^1	473	304	15		80	199	10.8	3.07	89	.248	.278	145	.267	2	-22	-17	1	-1.3
● **BRITT BURNS** Burns, Robert Britt b: 6/8/59, Houston, Tex. BL/TL, 6′5″, 218 lbs. Deb: 8/5/78																												
1978	Chi-A	0	2	.000	2	2	0	0	0	7^2	14	12	2	0	3	3	20.0	12.91	30	.378	.425	0	—	0	-8	-8	0	-1.1
1979	Chi-A	0	0	—	6	0	0	0	0	5	10	5	1	0	1	2	19.8	5.40	79	.435	.458	0	—	0	-1	-1	-0	0.0
1980	Chi-A	15	13	.536	34	32	11	1	0	238	213	83	17	4	63	133	10.6	2.84	142	.241	.295	0	—	0	32	32	-1	3.5
1981	Chi-A☆	10	6	.625	24	23	5	1	0	156^2	139	52	14	6	49	108	11.1	2.64	136	.238	.303	0	—	0	18	17	-4	1.2
1982	Chi-A	13	5	.722	28	28	5	1	0	169^1	168	89	12	3	67	116	12.6	4.04	100	.257	.329	0	—	0	1	0	-3	-0.3
1983	*Chi-A	10	11	.476	29	26	8	4	0	173^2	165	79	14	5	55	115	11.7	3.58	118	.249	.311	0	—	0	10	12	-2	1.1
1984	Chi-A	4	12	.250	34	16	2	0	3	117	130	74	7	4	45	85	13.8	5.00	83	.280	.349	0	—	0	-13	-10	-0	-1.3
1985	Chi-A	18	11	.621	36	34	8	4	0	227	206	105	26	2	79	172	11.4	3.96	109	.242	.308	0	—	0	5	9	-1	0.9
Total	8	70	60	.538	193	161	39	11	3	1094^1	1045	499	93	24	362	734	11.8	3.66	111	.251	.315	0	—	0	43	49	-11	4.0
● **TOM BURNS** Burns, Thomas Everett b: 3/30/1857, Honesdale, Pa. d: 3/19/02, Jersey City, N.J. BR/TR, 5′7″, 152 lbs. Deb: 5/1/1880 MU♦																												
1880	Chi-N	0	0	—	1	0	0	0	0	1^1	2	4	0		2	1	27.0	0.00	—	.250	.400	103	.309	0	0	0	0	0.0
● **OYSTER BURNS** Burns, Thomas P. b: 9/6/1864, Philadelphia, Pa. d: 11/11/28, Brooklyn, N.Y. BL/TR, 5′8″, 183 lbs. Deb: 8/18/1884 ♦																												
1884	Bal-a	0	0	—	2	0	0	0	**1**	9	12	5	0	0	2	6	14.0	3.00	116	.343	.378	39	.298	1	0	0	-0	0.1
1885	Bal-a	7	4	.636	15	11	10	1	**3**	105^2	112	76	2	13	21	30	12.4	3.58	91	.266	.321	74	.231	3	-4	-4	-1	-0.2
1887	Bal-a	1	0	1.000	3	0	0	0	0	11^1	20	16	0	3	4	2	18.3	9.53	43	.339	.371	251	.409	2	-7	-7	-1	-0.4
1888	Bal-a	0	1	.000	5	0	0	0	0	12^2	12	8	0	0	3	2	10.7	4.26	70	.240	.283	97	.298	2	-2	-2	-0	-0.1
Total	4	8	5	.615	25	11	10	1	4	138^2	156	105	2	16	30	40	12.9	4.09	81	.276	.326	1453	.309	7	-12	-12	-2	-0.6
● **TODD BURNS** Burns, Todd Edward b: 7/6/63, Maywood, Cal. BR/TR, 6′2″, 190 lbs. Deb: 5/31/88																												
1988	*Oak-A	8	2	.800	17	14	2	0	1	102^2	93	38	8	1	34	57	11.2	3.16	120	.241	.304	0	—	0	9	8	-1	0.6
1989	*Oak-A	6	5	.545	50	2	0	0	8	96^1	66	27	3	1	28	49	8.9	2.24	165	.196	.260	0	—	0	18	16	-1	1.9
1990	*Oak-A	3	3	.500	43	2	0	0	3	78^2	78	28	8	0	32	43	12.6	2.97	125	.263	.334	0	—	0	8	7	-1	0.4
1991	Oak-A	1	0	1.000	9	0	0	0	0	13^1	10	5	2	0	8	3	12.2	3.38	114	.217	.333	0	—	0	1	1	0	0.1
1992	Tex-A	3	5	.375	35	10	0	0	1	103	97	54	8	4	32	55	11.6	3.84	99	.248	.311	0	—	0	1	-1	-1	-0.2
1993	Tex-A	0	4	.000	25	5	0	0	0	65	63	36	6	2	32	35	13.4	4.57	91	.253	.343	0	—	0	-2	-3	-1	-0.3
	StL-N	0	4	.000	24	0	0	0	0	30^2	32	21	8	0	9	10	12.0	6.16	64	.274	.325	0	.000	-0	-7	-8	-1	-1.0
Total	6	21	23	.477	203	33	2	0	13	489^2	439	209	43	8	175	252	11.4	3.47	110	.241	.310	0	.000	-0	29	20	-6	1.5
● **BILL BURNS** Burns, William Thomas "Sleepy Bill" b: 1/29/1880, San Saba, Tex. d: 6/6/53, Ramona, Cal. BB/TL, 6′2″, 195 lbs. Deb: 4/18/08																												
1908	Was-A	6	11	.353	23	19	11	2	0	164	135	58	3	4	18	55	8.6	1.70	134	.229	.257	8	.148	-1	13	11	3	1.4
1909	Was-A	1	1	.500	6	4	1	0	0	29^1	25	7	0	3	7	13	10.7	1.23	198	.229	.294	3	.273	0	4	4	0	0.4
	Chi-A	7	13	.350	23	19	10	3	0	168	161	64	2	8	34	50	10.9	2.04	115	.264	.312	9	.153	1	8	6	1	1.0

YEAR	TM/L	W	L	PCT	G	GS	CG	SH	SV	IP	H	R	HR	HB	BB	SO	RAT	ERA	ERA+	OAV	OOB	BH	AVG	PB	PR	PR+	PD	TPI
	Yr	8	14	.364	29	23	11	3	0	197^1	186	71	2	11	41	63	10.9	1.92	123	.259	.309	12	.171	1	12	10	1	1.4
1910	Chi-A	0	0	—	1	0	0	0	0	0^1	0	0	0	0	1	0	27.0	0.00	—	.000	.500	0	—	0	0	0	0	0.0
	Cin-N	8	13	.381	31	21	13	2	0	178^2	183	103	3	12	49	57	12.3	3.48	84	.273	.333	16	.262	2	-9	-12	1	-1.0
1911	Cin-N	1	0	1.000	6	3	0	0	1	17^2	17	11	1	3	3	5	11.7	3.06	108	.254	.315	3	.429	2	1	1	1	0.3
	Phi-N	6	10	.375	21	14	8	3	1	121	132	59	5	6	26	47	12.2	3.42	101	.287	.333	6	.150	-1	-0	0	2	0.0
	Yr	7	10	.412	27	17	8	3	2	138^2	149	70	6	9	29	52	12.1	3.38	102	.283	.331	9	.191	0	0	1	3	0.3
1912	Det-A	1	4	.200	6	5	2	0	0	38^2	52	29	0	2	9	6	14.7	5.35	61	.338	.382	3	.231	1	-9	-9	-0	-0.9
Total	5	30	52	.366	117	85	45	10	2	717^2	705	331	14	38	147	233	11.2	2.72	100	.265	.313	48	.196	4	8	0	7	1.2

● PETE BURNSIDE Burnside, Peter Willits b: 7/2/30, Evanston, Ill. BR/TL, 6'2", 190 lbs. Deb: 9/20/55

YEAR	TM/L	W	L	PCT	G	GS	CG	SH	SV	IP	H	R	HR	HB	BB	SO	RAT	ERA	ERA+	OAV	OOB	BH	AVG	PB	PR	PR+	PD	TPI
1955	NY-N	1	0	1.000	2	2	1	0	0	12^2	10	9	1	0	9	2	13.5	2.84	142	.204	.328	1	.200	0	2	2	-0	0.1
1957	NY-N	1	4	.200	10	9	1	1	0	30^2	47	30	5	1	13	18	17.9	8.80	45	.356	.418	0	.000	-1	-17	-16	-0	-2.3
1958	SF-N	0	0	—	6	1	0	0	0	10^2	20	10	3	0	5	4	21.1	6.75	56	.400	.455	0	—	0	-3	-4	-0	-0.2
1959	Det-A	1	3	.250	30	0	0	0	1	62	55	31	7	2	25	49	11.9	3.77	108	.237	.317	0	.000	-1	1	2	0	0.1
1960	Det-A	7	7	.500	31	15	2	0	2	113^2	122	56	14	4	50	71	13.9	4.28	93	.277	.356	4	.148	-1	-5	-4	-1	-0.6
1961	Was-A	4	9	.308	33	16	4	2	2	113^1	106	66	11	3	51	56	12.7	4.53	89	.251	.335	2	.059	-3	-6	-6	-1	-1.0
1962	Was-A	5	11	.313	40	20	6	0	2	149^2	152	82	20	2	51	74	12.3	4.45	91	.263	.325	2	.057	-3	-8	-7	-2	-1.1
1963	Bal-A	0	1	.000	6	0	0	0	0	7^1	11	4	0	1	2	6	17.2	4.91	71	.344	.400	0	.000	-0	-1	-1	-0	-0.2
	Was-A	0	1	.000	38	1	0	0	0	67^1	84	49	12	0	24	23	14.4	6.15	60	.308	.364	1	.091	-0	-19	-18	-1	-1.1
	Yr	0	2	.000	44	1	0	0	0	74^2	95	53	12	1	26	29	14.7	6.03	61	.311	.367	1	.083	-1	-20	-19	-2	-1.3
Total	8	19	36	.345	196	64	14	3	7	567^1	607	337	73	13	230	303	13.5	4.81	82	.275	.347	10	.076	-8	-57	-52	-6	-6.3

● SHELDON BURNSIDE Burnside, Sheldon John b: 12/22/54, South Bend, Ind. BR/TL, 6'5", 200 lbs. Deb: 9/4/78

YEAR	TM/L	W	L	PCT	G	GS	CG	SH	SV	IP	H	R	HR	HB	BB	SO	RAT	ERA	ERA+	OAV	OOB	BH	AVG	PB	PR	PR+	PD	TPI
1978	Det-A	0	0	—	2	0	0	0	0	4	4	4	0	0	2	3	13.5	9.00	43	.250	.333	0	—	0	-2	-2	-0	-0.1
1979	Det-A	1	1	.500	10	0	0	0	0	21^1	28	16	2	1	8	13	15.6	6.33	69	.333	.398	0	—	0	-5	-5	0	-0.4
1980	Cin-N	1	0	1.000	7	0	0	0	0	4^2	6	1	1	0	1	2	13.5	1.93	186	.333	.368	0	.000	-0	1	1	1	0.2
Total	3	2	1	.667	19	0	0	0	0	30	38	21	3	1	11	18	15.0	6.00	69	.322	.385	0	.000	-0	-6	-6	1	-0.3

● GEORGE BURPO Burpo, George Harvie b: 6/19/22, Jenkins, Ky. BR/TL, 6', 195 lbs. Deb: 6/9/46

YEAR	TM/L	W	L	PCT	G	GS	CG	SH	SV	IP	H	R	HR	HB	BB	SO	RAT	ERA	ERA+	OAV	OOB	BH	AVG	PB	PR	PR+	PD	TPI
1946	Cin-N	0	0	—	2	0	0	0	0	2^1	4	4	0	0	5	1	34.7	15.43	22	.400	.600	0	—	0	-3	-3	-0	-0.2

● HARRY BURRELL Burrell, Harry J. b: 5/26/1869, Bethel, Vt. d: 12/11/14, Omaha, Neb. BR/TL, Deb: 9/13/1891

YEAR	TM/L	W	L	PCT	G	GS	CG	SH	SV	IP	H	R	HR	HB	BB	SO	RAT	ERA	ERA+	OAV	OOB	BH	AVG	PB	PR	PR+	PD	TPI
1891	StL-a	4	2	.667	7	4	3	0	0	43	51	36	4	2	21	19	15.5	4.81	87	.285	.366	4	.200	-1	-5	-3	-1	-0.4

● AL BURRIS Burris, Alva Burton b: 1/28/1874, Warwick, Md. d: 3/25/38, Salisbury, Md. BR/TR, Deb: 6/22/1894

YEAR	TM/L	W	L	PCT	G	GS	CG	SH	SV	IP	H	R	HR	HB	BB	SO	RAT	ERA	ERA+	OAV	OOB	BH	AVG	PB	PR	PR+	PD	TPI
1894	Phi-N	0	0	—	1	0	0	0	0	5	14	10	0	0	2	0	28.8	18.00	28	.500	.533	2	.500	1	-7	-7	0	-0.2

● RAY BURRIS Burris, Bertram Ray b: 8/22/50, Idabel, Okla. BR/TR, 6'5", 200 lbs. Deb: 4/8/73 C

YEAR	TM/L	W	L	PCT	G	GS	CG	SH	SV	IP	H	R	HR	HB	BB	SO	RAT	ERA	ERA+	OAV	OOB	BH	AVG	PB	PR	PR+	PD	TPI
1973	Chi-N	1	1	.500	31	1	0	0	0	64^2	65	22	2	0	27	57	12.8	2.92	135	.261	.333	1	.143	0	5	7	1	0.5
1974	Chi-N	3	5	.375	40	5	0	0	1	75	91	61	8	4	26	40	14.5	6.60	58	.300	.363	1	.077	-1	-25	-22	-1	-2.3
1975	Chi-N	15	10	.600	36	35	8	2	0	238^1	259	121	25	4	73	108	12.7	4.12	94	.281	.337	15	.183	1	-13	-7	-4	-0.9
1976	Chi-N	15	13	.536	37	36	10	4	0	249	251	102	22	5	70	112	11.8	3.11	124	.263	.317	9	.111	-4	11	19	0	1.7
1977	Chi-N	14	16	.467	39	39	5	1	0	221	270	132	29	3	67	105	13.8	4.72	93	.305	.356	12	.174	1	-20	-7	3	-0.5
1978	Chi-N	7	13	.350	40	32	4	1	1	199	210	112	15	10	79	94	13.5	4.75	85	.274	.349	7	.115	-1	-26	-14	2	-1.3
1979	Chi-N	0	0	—	14	0	0	0	0	21^2	23	17	0	1	15	14	16.2	6.23	66	.284	.402	0	.000	0	-6	-5	0	-0.2
	NY-A	1	3	.250	15	0	0	0	0	27^2	40	22	5	0	10	19	16.3	6.18	66	.342	.394	0	—	0	-6	-7	-0	-0.8
	NY-N	0	2	.000	4	4	0	0	0	21^2	21	10	2	1	6	10	11.6	3.32	110	.247	.304	1	.167	-0	1	1	0	0.1
1980	NY-N	7	13	.350	29	29	1	0	0	170^1	181	86	20	4	54	83	12.6	4.02	89	.277	.336	5	.098	-2	-8	-9	-1	-1.3
1981	*Mon-N	9	7	.563	22	21	4	0	0	135^2	117	56	9	3	41	52	10.7	3.05	115	.235	.297	7	.189	1	7	7	-1	0.7
1982	Mon-N	4	14	.222	37	15	2	0	2	123^2	143	77	14	2	53	55	14.4	4.73	77	.297	.369	5	.179	1	-15	-15	-1	-2.0
1983	Mon-N	4	7	.364	40	17	2	1	0	154	139	68	13	2	56	100	11.5	3.68	98	.244	.314	9	.231	3	-1	-1	0	0.3
1984	Oak-A	13	10	.565	34	28	5	1	0	211^2	193	84	15	8	90	93	12.4	3.15	119	.244	.327	0	—	0	20	15	-3	1.2
1985	Mil-A	9	13	.409	29	28	6	0	0	170^1	182	95	25	3	53	81	12.6	4.81	87	.272	.328	0	—	0	-12	-12	-1	-1.4
1986	StL-N	4	5	.444	23	10	0	0	0	82	92	52	13	4	32	34	14.0	5.60	65	.287	.359	4	.148	0	-17	-18	-1	-1.8
1987	Mil-A	2	2	.500	10	2	0	0	0	23	33	16	4	0	12	8	17.6	5.87	78	.351	.425	0	—	0	-4	-3	0	-0.5
Total	15	108	134	.446	480	302	47	10	4	2188^2	2310	1133	221	54	764	1065	12.9	4.17	93	.274	.338	76	.151	-1	-108	-70	-6	-8.5

● JOHN BURROWS Burrows, John b: 10/30/13, Winnfield, La. d: 4/27/87, Coal Run, Ohio BR/TL, 5'10", 200 lbs. Deb: 4/25/43

YEAR	TM/L	W	L	PCT	G	GS	CG	SH	SV	IP	H	R	HR	HB	BB	SO	RAT	ERA	ERA+	OAV	OOB	BH	AVG	PB	PR	PR+	PD	TPI
1943	Phi-A	0	1	.000	4	1	0	0	0	7^2	8	7	0	1	9	3	21.1	8.22	41	.276	.462	0	.000	-0	-4	-4	-0	-0.5
	Chi-N	0	2	.000	23	1	0	0	2	32^2	25	17	0	2	16	18	11.8	3.86	87	.205	.307	2	.667	1	-2	-2	0	0.0
1944	Chi-N	0	0	—	3	0	0	0	0	3	7	7	0	0	3	1	30.0	18.00	20	.467	.556	0	—	0	-5	-5	0	-0.2
Total	2	0	3	.000	30	2	0	0	2	43^1	40	31	0	3	28	22	14.7	5.61	60	.241	.360	2	.500	1	-11	-11	0	-0.7

● TERRY BURROWS Burrows, Terry Dale b: 11/28/68, Lake Charles, La. BL/TL, 6'1", 185 lbs. Deb: 6/12/94

YEAR	TM/L	W	L	PCT	G	GS	CG	SH	SV	IP	H	R	HR	HB	BB	SO	RAT	ERA	ERA+	OAV	OOB	BH	AVG	PB	PR	PR+	PD	TPI
1994	Tex-A	0	0	—	1	0	0	0	0	1	1	1	1	0	1	0	18.0	9.00	54	.250	.400	0	—	0	-0	-0	0	0.0
1995	Tex-A	2	2	.500	28	3	0	0	1	44^2	60	37	11	2	19	22	16.3	6.45	75	.323	.391	0	—	0	-9	-8	-1	-0.7
1996	Mil-A	2	0	1.000	8	0	0	0	0	12^2	12	4	2	1	10	5	16.3	2.84	183	.261	.404	0	—	0	3	3	-0	0.4
1997	SD-N	0	2	.000	13	0	0	0	0	10^1	12	13	1	1	8	8	18.3	10.45	37	.286	.412	0	—	0	-7	-8	-0	-1.3
Total	4	4	4	.500	50	3	0	0	1	68^2	85	55	15	4	38	35	16.6	6.42	74	.306	.397	0	—	0	-13	-13	-1	-1.6

● JIM BURTON Burton, Jim Scott b: 10/27/49, Royal Oak, Mich. BR/TL, 6'3", 195 lbs. Deb: 6/10/75

YEAR	TM/L	W	L	PCT	G	GS	CG	SH	SV	IP	H	R	HR	HB	BB	SO	RAT	ERA	ERA+	OAV	OOB	BH	AVG	PB	PR	PR+	PD	TPI
1975	*Bos-A	1	2	.333	29	4	0	0	1	53	58	30	6	0	19	39	13.1	2.89	141	.276	.336	0	—	0	5	7	0	0.4
1977	Bos-A	0	0	—	1	0	0	0	0	2^2	2	0	0	0	1	3	10.1	0.00	—	.200	.273	0	—	0	1	1	-0	0.1
Total	2	1	2	.333	30	4	0	0	1	55^2	60	30	6	0	20	42	12.9	2.75	149	.273	.333	0	—	0	7	8	-0	0.5

● MOE BURTSCHY Burtschy, Edward Frank b: 4/18/22, Cincinnati, Ohio BR/TR, 6'3", 208 lbs. Deb: 6/17/50

YEAR	TM/L	W	L	PCT	G	GS	CG	SH	SV	IP	H	R	HR	HB	BB	SO	RAT	ERA	ERA+	OAV	OOB	BH	AVG	PB	PR	PR+	PD	TPI
1950	Phi-A	0	1	.000	9	1	0	0	0	19	22	16	2	1	21	12	20.8	7.11	64	.289	.449	0	.000	-0	-5	-5	0	-0.3
1951	Phi-A	0	0	—	7	0	0	0	0	17	18	11	0	1	12	4	16.4	5.29	81	.277	.397	1	.333	0	-2	-2	0	-0.1
1954	Phi-A	5	4	.556	46	0	0	0	4	94^2	80	45	7	8	53	54	13.4	3.80	103	.234	.350	2	.118	-1	-1	1	0	0.0
1955	KC-A	2	0	1.000	7	0	0	0	0	11^1	17	13	0	1	10	9	22.2	10.32	40	.354	.475	1	.333	0	-8	-7	-0	-1.1
1956	KC-A	3	1	.750	21	0	0	0	0	43^1	41	22	6	3	30	18	15.4	3.95	110	.263	.392	1	.125	-1	1	2	2	0.3
Total	5	10	6	.625	90	1	0	0	4	185^1	178	107	15	14	126	97	15.4	4.71	88	.259	.385	5	.139	-1	-15	-12	1	-1.2

● DENNIS BURTT Burtt, Dennis Allen b: 11/29/57, San Diego, Cal. BB/TR, 6', 180 lbs. Deb: 9/4/85

YEAR	TM/L	W	L	PCT	G	GS	CG	SH	SV	IP	H	R	HR	HB	BB	SO	RAT	ERA	ERA+	OAV	OOB	BH	AVG	PB	PR	PR+	PD	TPI
1985	Min-A	2	2	.500	5	2	0	0	0	28^1	20	13	2	0	7	9	8.6	3.81	116	.200	.252	0	—	0	1	2	0	0.2
1986	Min-A	0	0	—	3	0	0	0	0	2	7	7	1	0	3	1	45.0	31.50	14	.538	.625	0	—	0	-6	-6	-0	-0.3
Total	2	2	2	.500	8	2	0	0	0	30^1	27	20	3	0	10	10	11.0	5.64	78	.239	.301	0	—	0	-5	-4	0	-0.1

● DICK BURWELL Burwell, Richard Matthew b: 1/23/40, Alton, Ill. BR/TR, 6'1", 190 lbs. Deb: 9/13/60

YEAR	TM/L	W	L	PCT	G	GS	CG	SH	SV	IP	H	R	HR	HB	BB	SO	RAT	ERA	ERA+	OAV	OOB	BH	AVG	PB	PR	PR+	PD	TPI
1960	Chi-N	0	0	—	3	1	0	0	0	9^2	11	6	2	1	7	1	17.7	5.59	68	.306	.432	1	.333	0	-2	-2	-0	-0.1
1961	Chi-N	0	0	—	2	0	0	0	0	4	6	4	0	0	4	0	22.5	9.00	46	.375	.500	0	.000	-0	-2	-2	0	-0.1
Total	2	0	0	—	5	1	0	0	0	13^2	17	10	2	1	11	1	19.1	6.59	59	.327	.453	1	.250	0	-4	-4	0	-0.2

● BILL BURWELL Burwell, William Edwin b: 3/27/1895, Jarbalo, Kan. d: 6/11/73, Ormond Beach, Fla BL/TR, 5'11", 175 lbs. Deb: 5/1/20 MC

YEAR	TM/L	W	L	PCT	G	GS	CG	SH	SV	IP	H	R	HR	HB	BB	SO	RAT	ERA	ERA+	OAV	OOB	BH	AVG	PB	PR	PR+	PD	TPI
1920	StL-A	6	4	.600	33	2	0	0	4	113^1	133	55	5	4	42	30	14.2	3.65	107	.303	.369	7	.167	-2	2	3	-0	0.1
1921	StL-A	2	4	.333	33	3	1	0	2	84^1	102	62	2	2	29	17	14.2	5.12	87	.309	.368	6	.240	-0	-8	-6	-1	-0.5
1928	Pit-N	1	0	1.000	4	1	0	0	0	20^2	18	12	2	0	8	2	11.3	5.23	78	.234	.306	2	.222	-0	-3	-3	1	-0.1
Total	3	9	8	.529	70	6	1	0	6	218^1	253	129	9	6	79	49	13.9	4.37	95	.299	.363	15	.197	-2	-9	-5	-1	-0.5

● MIKE BUSBY Busby, Michael James b: 12/27/72, Lomita, Cal. BR/TR, 6'4", 210 lbs. Deb: 4/7/96

YEAR	TM/L	W	L	PCT	G	GS	CG	SH	SV	IP	H	R	HR	HB	BB	SO	RAT	ERA	ERA+	OAV	OOB	BH	AVG	PB	PR	PR+	PD	TPI
1996	StL-N	0	1	.000	1	1	0	0	0	4	9	13	4	1	4	4	31.5	18.00	23	.409	.519	1	.500	0	-6	-6	0	-0.8
1997	StL-N	0	2	.000	3	3	0	0	0	14^1	24	14	2	0	4	6	17.6	8.79	47	.393	.431	2	.500	1	-7	-7	-0	-0.8

YEAR	TM/L	W	L	PCT	G	GS	CG	SH	SV	IP	H	R	HR	HB	BB	SO	RAT	ERA	ERA+	OAV	OOB	BH	AVG	PB	PR	PR+	PD	TPI
1998	StL-N	5	2	.714	26	2	0	0	0	46	45	23	3	5	15	33	12.7	4.50	93	.254	.330	0	.000	-0	-1	-2	-0	-0.3
1999	StL-N	0	1	.000	15	0	0	0	0	17^2	21	15	2	2	14	7	18.8	7.13	64	.300	.430	0	—	0	-5	-5	-0	-0.2
Total	4	5	6	.455	45	6	0	0	0	82	99	65	11	8	37	50	15.8	6.48	66	.300	.384	3	.333	1	-20	-20	-1	-2.1
● STEVE BUSBY	Busby, Steven Lee b: 9/29/49, Burbank, Cal. BR/TR, 6'2", 205 lbs. Deb: 9/8/72																											
1972	KC-A	3	1	.750	5	5	3	0	0	40	28	9	1	0	8	31	8.1	1.57	193	.200	.243	3	.200	0	7	7	-1	0.7
1973	KC-A	16	15	.516	37	37	7	1	0	238^1	246	125	18	6	105	174	13.5	4.23	97	.271	.350	0	—	0	-11	-3	2	-0.1
1974	KC-A☆	22	14	.611	38	38	20	3	0	292^1	284	118	14	9	92	198	11.9	3.39	113	.258	.320	0	—	0	8	13	3	1.9
1975	KC-A★	18	12	.600	34	34	18	3	0	260^1	233	96	18	3	81	160	11.0	3.08	125	.242	.303	0	—	0	21	22	4	2.8
1976	KC-A	3	3	.500	13	13	1	0	0	71^2	58	42	7	3	49	29	13.8	4.40	80	.218	.346	0	—	0	-7	-7	-0	-0.6
1978	KC-A	1	0	1.000	7	5	0	0	0	21^1	24	18	2	2	15	10	17.3	7.59	51	.282	.402	0	—	0	-9	-9	0	-0.4
1979	KC-A	6	6	.500	22	12	4	0	0	94^1	71	45	10	0	64	45	12.9	3.63	118	.220	.349	0	—	0	6	7	2	1.0
1980	KC-A	1	3	.250	11	6	0	0	0	42^1	59	30	3	2	19	12	17.0	6.17	66	.335	.406	0	—	0	-10	-10	-0	-0.8
Total	8	70	54	.565	167	150	53	7	0	1060^2	1003	483	73	25	433	659	12.4	3.72	105	.253	.330	3	.200	0	5	21	10	4.5
● DON BUSCHHORN	Buschhorn, Donald Lee b: 4/29/46, Independence, Mo. BR/TR, 6', 170 lbs. Deb: 5/15/65																											
1965	KC-A	0	1	.000	12	3	0	0	0	31	36	17	7	1	8	9	13.1	4.35	80	.295	.344	2	.500	1	-3	-3	-0	-0.1
● GUY BUSH	Bush, Guy Terrell "The Mississippi Mudcat" b: 8/23/01, Aberdeen, Miss. d: 7/2/85, Shannon, Miss. BR/TR, 6', 175 lbs. Deb: 9/17/23																											
1923	Chi-N	0	0	—	1	0	0	0	0	1	1	0	0	0	0	2	9.0	0.00	—	.250	.250	0	—	0	0	0	0	0.0
1924	Chi-N	2	5	.286	16	8	4	0	0	80^2	91	51	7	2	24	36	13.1	4.02	97	.285	.339	4	.154	-1	-1	-1	-2	-0.4
1925	Chi-N	6	13	.316	42	15	5	0	**4**	182	213	102	15	3	52	76	13.3	4.30	101	.300	.350	11	.193	-2	-1	0	4	0.2
1926	Chi-N	13	9	.591	35	15	7	2	2	157^1	149	58	3	3	42	32	11.1	2.86	134	.258	.311	8	.167	-2	17	17	1	1.9
1927	Chi-N	10	10	.500	36	22	9	1	2	193^1	177	76	3	6	79	62	12.2	3.03	128	.250	.330	8	.123	-4	19	18	0	1.3
1928	Chi-N	15	6	.714	42	24	9	2	2	204^1	229	104	10	5	86	61	14.1	3.83	100	.293	.367	6	.082	-6	4	0	-1	-0.6
1929	*Chi-N	18	7	.720	**50**	30	18	2	**8**	270^2	277	135	16	4	107	82	12.9	3.66	126	.265	.335	15	.165	-4	32	29	0	2.1
1930	Chi-N	15	10	.600	46	25	11	0	3	225	291	174	22	2	86	75	15.2	6.20	79	.316	.376	22	.282	3	-31	-33	1	-2.6
1931	Chi-N	16	8	.667	39	24	14	1	2	180^1	190	104	9	2	66	54	12.9	4.49	86	.268	.332	7	.123	-2	-13	-13	4	-1.3
1932	*Chi-N	19	11	.633	40	30	15	1	0	238^2	262	106	13	7	70	73	12.8	3.21	118	.278	.332	15	.179	0	18	15	1	1.8
1933	Chi-N	20	12	.625	41	32	20	4	2	259	261	95	9	1	68	84	11.5	2.75	119	.257	.304	11	.125	-1	17	15	4	2.2
1934	Chi-N	18	10	.643	40	27	15	1	2	209^1	213	96	15	1	54	75	11.5	3.83	101	.262	.309	16	.229	1	5	1	1	0.3
1935	Pit-N	11	11	.500	41	25	8	1	2	204^1	237	115	16	5	40	42	12.4	4.32	95	.285	.321	8	.127	-1	-7	-5	-1	-0.6
1936	Pit-N	1	3	.250	16	0	0	0	2	34^2	49	28	3	0	11	10	15.6	5.97	68	.336	.382	3	.333	0	-8	-7	1	-0.7
	Bos-N	4	5	.444	15	11	5	0	0	90^1	98	38	2	0	20	28	11.8	3.39	113	.281	.320	3	.120	-1	6	5	1	0.4
	Yr	5	8	.385	31	11	5	0	2	125	147	66	5	0	31	38	12.8	4.10	95	.297	.338	6	.176	-0	-1	-3	1	-0.3
1937	Bos-N	8	15	.348	32	20	11	1	1	180^2	201	77	8	0	48	56	12.4	3.54	101	.282	.328	6	.111	-2	8	1	1	0.0
1938	StL-N	0	1	.000	6	0	0	0	1	6	6	3	1	0	3	1	13.5	4.50	88	.286	.375	0	—	0	-0	-0	-0	-0.1
1945	Cin-N	0	0	—	4	0	0	0	1	4^1	5	4	0	0	3	1	16.6	8.31	45	.278	.381	0	—	0	-2	-2	-0	-0.1
Total	17	176	136	.564	542	308	151	16	34	2722	2950	1366	152	41	859	850	12.7	3.86	103	.277	.334	143	.161	-22	64	41	12	3.8
● JOE BUSH	Bush, Leslie Ambrose "Bullet Joe" b: 11/27/1892, Brainerd, Minn. d: 11/1/74, Ft.Lauderdale, Fla. BR/TR, 5'9", 173 lbs. Deb: 9/30/12																											
1912	Phi-A	0	0	—	1	1	0	0	0	8	14	10	0	0	4	3	20.3	7.88	39	.368	.429	2	.500	1	-4	-5	-0	-0.1
1913	*Phi-A	15	6	.714	39	16	6	1	3	200^1	199	95	3	5	66	81	12.1	3.82	72	.248	.310	11	.157	-0	-20	-25	4	-2.2
1914	*Phi-A	17	13	.567	38	23	14	2	2	206	184	84	2	8	81	109	11.9	3.06	85	.242	.322	14	.189	2	-7	-11	-0	-1.4
1915	Phi-A	5	15	.250	25	18	8	0	0	145^2	137	86	3	4	89	89	14.2	4.14	71	.263	.375	7	.143	-3	-19	-20	0	-2.7
1916	Phi-A	15	24	.385	40	33	25	8	0	286^2	222	109	3	3	130	157	11.1	2.57	111	.219	.310	14	.140	-4	8	9	5	1.4
1917	Phi-A	11	17	.393	37	31	17	4	2	233^1	207	101	3	1	111	121	12.3	2.47	111	.241	.328	16	.200	1	5	7	0	1.0
1918	*Bos-A	15	15	.500	36	31	26	7	2	272^2	241	88	3	3	91	125	11.1	2.11	127	.242	.307	27	.276	6	20	18	3	3.2
1919	Bos-A	0	0	—	3	2	0	0	0	9	11	5	0	0	4	3	15.0	5.00	60	.324	.395	2	.400	1	-2	-2	0	-0.1
1920	Bos-A	15	15	.500	35	32	18	0	1	243^2	287	138	3	10	94	88	14.4	4.25	86	.300	.369	25	.245	2	-12	-17	3	-1.4
1921	Bos-A	16	9	.640	37	32	21	3	1	254^1	244	111	10	6	93	96	12.1	3.50	121	.260	.330	39	.325	6	22	21	1	2.7
1922	*NY-A	26	7	**.788**	39	30	20	0	3	255^1	240	109	16	1	85	92	11.5	3.31	121	.252	.314	31	.326	8	21	20	1	3.2
1923	*NY-A	19	15	.559	37	30	22	3	0	275^2	263	115	7	5	117	125	12.6	3.43	115	.260	.340	31	.274	7	17	16	1	2.6
1924	NY-A	17	16	.515	39	31	19	3	1	252	262	117	9	7	109	80	13.5	3.57	116	.273	.352	42	.339	14	18	17	2	3.5
1925	StL-A	14	14	.500	33	30	15	2	0	208^2	230	129	18	2	91	63	13.9	5.09	92	.284	.357	26	.255	3	-16	-9	2	-0.3
1926	Was-A	1	8	.111	12	11	3	0	0	71^1	83	54	6	5	35	27	15.5	6.69	58	.292	.380	7	.233	1	-21	-23	0	-2.3
	Pit-N	6	6	.500	19	12	9	2	3	110^2	97	45	7	2	45	38	10.9	3.01	131	.236	.299	13	.265	2	10	11	1	1.3
1927	Pit-N	1	2	.333	5	3	0	0	0	6^2	14	14	1	0	5	1	25.7	13.50	30	.412	.487	3	.600	1	-7	-7	0	-1.1
	NY-N	1	1	.500	3	2	1	0	0	12	18	10	1	0	5	6	17.3	7.50	51	.340	.397	2	.500	1	-5	-5	-0	-0.6
	Yr	2	3	.400	8	5	1	0	0	18^2	32	24	2	0	10	7	20.3	9.64	41	.368	.433	5	.556	2	-12	-12	0	-1.7
1928	Phi-A	2	1	.667	11	2	1	0	1	35^1	39	21	1	1	18	15	14.8	5.09	79	.300	.389	1	.067	-1	-4	-4	1	-0.4
Total	17	196	184	.516	489	370	225	35	19	3087^1	2992	1441	96	63	1263	1319	12.6	3.51	99	.259	.335	313	.253	49	4	-8	21	6.3
● JACK BUSHELMAN	Bushelman, John Francis b: 8/29/1885, Cincinnati, Ohio d: 10/26/55, Roanoke, Va. BR/TR, 6'2", 175 lbs. Deb: 10/5/09																											
1909	Cin-N	0	1	.000	1	1	1	0	0	7	7	7	1	0	4	3	14.1	2.57	101	.241	.333	0	.000	-0	0	0	-0	-0.1
1911	Bos-A	0	1	.000	3	1	1	0	0	12	8	9	0	1	10	5	14.3	3.00	109	.186	.352	0	.000	-0	0	0	-0	0.0
1912	Bos-A☆	1	0	1.000	3	0	0	0	0	7^2	9	4	0	0	5	5	16.4	4.70	72	.310	.412	0	.000	-0	-1	-1	0	-0.1
Total	3	1	2	.333	7	2	2	0	0	26^2	24	20	1	1	19	13	14.9	3.38	93	.238	.364	0	.000	-1	-1	-1	-0	-0.2
● FRANK BUSHEY	Bushey, Francis Clyde b: 8/1/06, Wheaton, Kan. d: 3/18/72, Topeka, Kan. BR/TR, 6', 180 lbs. Deb: 9/17/27																											
1927	Bos-A	0	0	—	1	0	0	0	0	1^1	2	1	0	0	2	0	27.0	6.75	63	.500	.667	0	—	0	-0	-0	-0	0.0
1930	Bos-A	0	1	.000	11	0	0	0	0	30	34	22	1	2	15	4	15.3	6.30	73	.306	.398	1	.111	-1	-6	-6	0	-0.3
Total	2	0	1	.000	12	0	0	0	0	31^1	36	23	1	2	17	4	15.8	6.32	73	.313	.410	1	.111	-1	-6	-6	0	-0.3
● CHRIS BUSHING	Bushing, Christopher Shaun b: 11/4/67, Rockville Centre, N.Y. BR/TR, 6', 190 lbs. Deb: 9/3/93																											
1993	Cin-N	0	0	—	6	0	0	0	0	4^1	9	7	1	0	4	3	27.0	12.46	32	.450	.542	0	—	0	-4	-4	-0	-0.2
● TOM BUSKEY	Buskey, Thomas William b: 2/20/47, Harrisburg, Pa. d: 6/7/98, Harrisburg, Pa. BR/TR, 6'3", 220 lbs. Deb: 8/5/73																											
1973	NY-A	0	1	.000	8	0	0	0	1	16^2	18	12	2	1	4	8	12.4	5.40	68	.286	.338	0	—	0	-3	-3	-0	-0.2
1974	NY-A	0	1	.000	4	0	0	0	1	5^2	10	4	1	1	3	3	22.2	6.35	56	.400	.483	0	—	0	-2	-2	-0	-0.4
	Cle-A	2	6	.250	51	0	0	0	17	93	93	36	10	1	33	40	12.3	3.19	113	.263	.327	0	—	0	4	4	1	0.6
	Yr	2	7	.222	55	0	0	0	18	98^2	103	40	11	2	36	43	12.9	3.38	107	.272	.338	0	—	0	3	3	1	0.2
1975	Cle-A	5	3	.625	50	0	0	0	7	77	69	27	7	1	29	29	11.6	2.57	147	.252	.326	0	—	0	10	10	2	1.4
1976	Cle-A	5	4	.556	39	0	0	0	1	94^1	88	42	9	3	34	32	11.9	3.63	96	.256	.328	0	—	0	-1	-1	1	-0.1
1977	Cle-A	0	0	—	21	0	0	0	0	34	45	24	6	1	8	15	14.3	5.29	75	.313	.353	0	—	0	-5	-5	-0	-0.3
1978	Tor-A	0	1	.000	8	0	0	0	0	13^1	14	5	1	0	5	7	12.8	3.38	117	.275	.339	0	—	0	1	1	0	0.1
1979	Tor-A	6	10	.375	44	0	0	0	7	78^2	74	33	10	1	25	44	11.4	3.43	127	.249	.310	0	—	0	7	8	2	1.7
1980	Tor-A	3	1	.750	33	0	0	0	0	66^2	68	35	11	0	26	34	12.7	4.45	97	.278	.347	0	—	0	-3	-1	0	0.0
Total	8	21	27	.438	258	0	0	0	34	479^1	479	218	57	9	167	212	12.3	3.66	106	.267	.332	0	—	0	9	11	5	2.8
● MAX BUTCHER	Butcher, Albert Maxwell b: 9/21/10, Holden, W.Va. d: 9/15/57, Man, W.Va. BR/TR, 6'2", 220 lbs. Deb: 4/20/36																											
1936	Bro-N	6	6	.500	38	15	5	0	2	147^2	154	85	11	1	59	55	13.0	3.96	104	.268	.337	6	.125	-3	1	3	-2	-0.2
1937	Bro-N	11	15	.423	39	24	8	1	0	191^2	203	106	12	7	75	57	13.4	4.27	94	.280	.354	10	.161	-1	-8	-5	-3	-0.5
1938	Bro-N	5	4	.556	24	8	3	0	2	72^2	104	66	9	1	39	21	17.8	6.56	59	.334	.410	4	.160	0	-22	-21	1	-2.2
	Phi-N	4	8	.333	12	12	11	0	0	98^1	94	40	6	2	31	29	11.6	2.93	133	.253	.314	9	.257	1	9	10	0	1.3
	Yr	9	12	.429	36	20	14	0	2	171	198	106	15	3	70	50	14.3	4.47	87	.290	.359	13	.217	1	-13	-11	2	-0.9
1939	Phi-N	2	13	.133	19	16	3	0	0	104^1	131	72	10	1	51	27	15.8	5.61	71	.308	.383	7	.184	-1	-20	-18	-2	-2.5
	Pit-N	4	4	.500	14	12	5	2	0	86^2	104	37	2	0	23	21	13.2	3.43	112	.297	.340	3	.097	-2	5	4	2	0.3
	Yr	6	17	.261	33	28	8	2	0	191	235	109	12	1	74	48	14.6	4.62	85	.303	.364	10	.145	-3	-15	-15	-0	-2.2
1940	Pit-N	8	9	.471	35	24	6	2	2	136^1	161	99	13	1	46	40	13.7	6.01	63	.290	.346	15	.300	4	-33	-34	1	-3.2
1941	Pit-N	17	12	.586	33	32	19	0	0	236	249	98	11	1	66	61	12.1	3.05	118	.265	.314	15	.183	-1	15	15	0	1.7

YEAR	TM/L	W	L	PCT	G	GS	CG	SH	SV	IP	H	R	HR	HB	BB	SO	RAT	ERA	ERA+	OAV	OOB	BH	AVG	PB	PR	PR+	PD	TPI
1942	Pit-N	5	8	.385	24	18	9	0	1	150^2	144	59	7	2	44	49	11.3	2.93	116	.247	.303	7	.143	-2	6	8	0	0.4
1943	Pit-N	10	8	.556	33	21	10	2	1	193^2	191	65	4	2	57	45	11.6	2.60	134	.262	.317	10	.164	-1	17	18	0	1.6
1944	Pit-N	13	11	.542	35	27	13	5	1	199	216	83	8	1	46	43	11.9	3.12	119	.273	.314	12	.190	-0	11	13	3	1.7
1945	Pit-N	10	8	.556	28	20	12	2	0	169^1	184	76	7	4	46	37	12.4	3.03	130	.277	.328	12	.222	0	15	17	1	1.7
Total	10	95	106	.473	334	229	104	14	9	1786^1	1935	886	100	23	583	485	12.8	3.73	101	.276	.333	110	.184	-6	-3	10	8	0.2
● JOHN BUTCHER	Butcher, John Daniel b: 3/8/57, Glendale, Cal. BR/TR, 6′4″, 190 lbs. Deb: 9/8/80																											
1980	Tex-A	3	3	.500	6	6	1	0	0	35^1	34	19	2	0	13	27	12.0	4.08	96	.248	.313	0	—	0	-0	-1	0	-0.1
1981	Tex-A	1	2	.333	5	3	1	1	0	27^2	18	6	0	0	8	19	8.5	1.63	213	.186	.248	0	—	0	6	6	0	0.7
1982	Tex-A	1	5	.167	18	13	2	0	1	94^1	102	53	10	2	34	39	13.2	4.87	80	.280	.345	0	—	0	-8	-11	2	-0.5
1983	Tex-A	6	6	.500	38	6	1	1	5	123	128	50	8	1	41	58	12.4	3.51	114	.270	.329	0	—	0	8	7	0	0.7
1984	Min-A	13	11	.542	34	34	8	1	0	225	242	98	18	4	53	83	12.0	3.44	122	.276	.320	0	—	0	14	18	-1	1.7
1985	Min-A	11	14	.440	34	33	8	2	0	207^2	239	125	24	6	43	92	12.5	4.98	88	.289	.328	0	—	0	-19	-12	0	-1.3
1986	Min-A	0	3	.000	16	10	1	0	0	70	82	50	11	1	24	29	13.8	6.30	68	.294	.352	0	—	0	-16	-15	0	-0.7
	Cle-A	1	5	.167	13	8	1	1	0	50^2	86	43	6	3	13	16	18.1	6.93	60	.381	.421	0	—	0	-15	-16	-1	-1.6
	Yr	1	8	.111	29	18	2	1	0	120^2	168	93	17	4	37	45	15.6	6.56	65	.333	.383	0	—	0	-32	-31	-1	-2.3
Total	7	36	49	.424	164	113	23	6	6	833^2	931	444	79	17	229	363	12.7	4.42	94	.284	.334	0	—	0	-32	-23	1	-1.1
● MIKE BUTCHER	Butcher, Michael Dana b: 5/10/65, Davenport, Iowa BR/TR, 6′1″, 200 lbs. Deb: 7/6/92																											
1992	Cal-A	2	2	.500	19	0	0	0	0	27^2	29	11	3	2	13	24	14.3	3.25	123	.264	.352	0	—	0	2	2	-0	0.3
1993	Cal-A	1	0	1.000	23	0	0	0	8	28^1	21	12	2	2	15	24	12.1	2.86	158	.204	.317	0	—	0	5	5	-1	0.3
1994	Cal-A	2	1	.667	33	0	0	0	1	29^2	31	24	2	2	23	19	17.0	6.67	73	.274	.406	0	—	0	-6	-6	1	-0.4
1995	Cal-A	6	1	.857	40	0	0	0	0	51^1	49	28	7	1	31	29	14.2	4.73	99	.257	.363	0	—	0	-0	-0	-1	-0.1
Total	4	11	4	.733	115	0	0	0	9	137	130	75	14	7	82	96	14.4	4.47	102	.251	.361	0	—	0	1	1	-0	0.1
● SAL BUTERA	Butera, Salvatore Philip b: 9/25/52, Richmond Hill, N.Y BR/TR, 6′, 190 lbs. Deb: 4/10/80 C♦																											
1985	Mon-N	0	0	—	1	0	0	0	0	1	0	0	0	0	0	0	0.0	0.00	—	.000	.000	24	.200	0	0	0	-0	0.0
1986	Cin-N	0	0	—	1	0	0	0	0	1	0	0	0	0	1	1	9.0	0.00	—	.000	.250	27	.239	0	0	0	0	0.0
Total	2	0	0	—	2	0	0	0	0	2	0	0	0	0	1	1	4.5	0.00	—	.000	.143	182	.227	0	1	1	-0	0.0
● BILL BUTLAND	Butland, Wilburn Rue b: 3/22/18, Terre Haute, Ind. d: 9/19/97, Terre Haute, Ind. BR/TL, 6′5″, 185 lbs. Deb: 5/29/40																											
1940	Bos-A	1	2	.333	3	3	1	0	0	21	27	13	0	0	10	5	15.9	5.57	81	.307	.378	0	.000	-1	-3	-2	1	-0.3
1942	Bos-A	7	1	.875	23	10	6	2	1	111^1	85	35	8	3	33	46	9.8	2.51	149	.206	.270	1	.036	-1	14	15	0	1.0
1946	Bos-A	1	0	1.000	5	2	0	0	0	16^1	23	20	3	0	13	10	19.8	11.02	33	.343	.450	1	.250	0	-14	-13	0	-0.7
1947	Bos-A	0	0	—	1	0	0	0	0	2	3	1	0	0	0	1	13.5	4.50	86	.333	.333	0	—	0	-0	-0	-0	0.0
Total	4	9	3	.750	32	15	7	2	1	150^2	138	69	11	3	56	62	11.8	3.88	99	.240	.310	2	.051	-2	-2	-1	1	0.0
● ADAM BUTLER	Butler, Adam Christopher b: 8/17/73, Fairfax, Va. BL/TL, 6′2″, 225 lbs. Deb: 3/31/98																											
1998	Atl-N	0	1	.000	8	0	0	0	0	5	5	7	1	1	6	7	21.6	10.80	39	.278	.480	0	—	0	-4	-4	-0	-0.7
● CECIL BUTLER	Butler, Cecil Dean "Slewfoot" b: 10/23/37, Dallas, Ga. BR/TR, 6′4″, 195 lbs. Deb: 4/23/62																											
1962	Mil-N	2	0	1.000	9	2	1	0	0	31	26	13	4	0	9	22	10.2	2.61	145	.217	.271	0	.000	-1	5	4	0	0.2
1964	Mil-N	0	0	—	2	0	0	0	0	4^1	7	4	2	0	0	2	14.5	8.31	42	.368	.368	0	—	0	-2	-2	0	-0.1
Total	2	2	0	1.000	11	2	1	0	0	35^1	33	17	6	0	9	24	10.7	3.31	114	.237	.284	0	.000	-1	2	2	0	0.1
● CHARLIE BUTLER	Butler, Charles Thomas b: 5/12/06, Green Cove Springs, Fla. d: 5/10/64, Brunswick, Ga. BR/TL, 6′1.5″, 210 lbs. Deb: 5/1/33																											
1933	Phi-N	0	0	—	1	0	0	0	0	1	1	1	0	0	2	0	27.0	9.00	42	.250	.500	0	—	0	-1	-1	-0	0.0
● IKE BUTLER	Butler, Isaac Burr b: 8/22/1873, Langston, Mich. d: 3/17/48, Oakland, Cal. TR, 6′, 175 lbs. Deb: 8/5/02																											
1902	Bal-A	1	10	.091	16	14	12	0	0	116^1	168	103	1	2	45	13	16.6	5.34	71	.337	.394	6	.113	-3	-23	-19	-1	-1.8
● BILL BUTLER	Butler, William Franklin b: 3/12/47, Hyattsville, Md. BL/TL, 6′2″, 210 lbs. Deb: 4/9/69																											
1969	KC-A	9	10	.474	34	29	5	4	0	193^2	174	91	15	3	91	156	12.5	3.90	95	.240	.328	3	.050	-4	-6	-4	-3	-1.1
1970	KC-A	4	12	.250	25	25	2	1	0	140^2	117	66	17	1	87	75	13.1	3.77	99	.229	.342	2	.045	-3	-1	-1	-2	-0.6
1971	KC-A	1	2	.333	14	6	0	0	0	44^1	45	19	6	0	18	32	12.8	3.45	100	.268	.339	1	.083	-1	0	-0	-0	-0.1
1972	Cle-A	0	0	—	6	2	0	0	0	11^2	9	3	1	0	10	6	14.7	1.54	209	.220	.373	0	.000	-0	2	2	-0	0.1
1974	Min-A	4	6	.400	26	12	2	0	1	98^2	91	47	9	1	56	79	13.5	4.10	91	.251	.353	0	—	0	-5	-4	-2	-0.6
1975	Min-A	5	4	.556	23	8	1	0	0	81^2	100	61	12	0	35	55	14.9	5.95	64	.301	.368	0	—	0	-20	-19	-0	-1.9
1977	Min-A	0	1	.000	6	4	0	0	0	21	19	17	5	1	15	5	15.0	6.86	58	.244	.372	0	—	0	-6	-7	-1	-0.4
Total	7	23	35	.397	134	86	10	5	1	591^2	555	304	65	6	312	408	13.3	4.21	88	.250	.345	6	.051	-7	-36	-32	-9	-4.6
● TOM BUTTERS	Butters, Thomas Arden b: 4/8/38, Delaware, O. BR/TR, 6′2″, 195 lbs. Deb: 9/8/62																											
1962	Pit-N	0	0	—	4	0	0	0	0	6	5	1	0	1	6	10	18.0	1.50	262	.238	.429	0	—	0	2	2	0	0.1
1963	Pit-N	0	0	—	6	1	0	0	0	16^1	15	8	1	2	8	11	13.8	4.41	75	.259	.368	1	.333	0	-2	-2	-0	-0.1
1964	Pit-N	2	2	.500	28	4	0	0	0	64^1	52	21	3	0	37	58	12.5	2.38	148	.221	.327	2	.182	0	8	8	-1	0.4
1965	Pit-N	0	1	.000	5	0	0	0	0	9	9	8	2	0	5	6	14.0	7.00	50	.250	.341	0	.000	-0	-3	-4	0	-0.4
Total	4	2	3	.400	43	5	0	0	0	95^2	81	38	6	3	56	85	13.2	3.10	113	.231	.342	3	.200	0	4	4	-1	0.0
● FRANK BUTTERY	Buttery, Frank b: 5/13/1851, Silvermine, Conn. d: 12/16/02, Silvermine, Conn. Deb: 4/26/1872 ♦																											
1872	Man-n	3	2	.600	8	5	5	0	0	59	93	78	1		2	0	14.5	4.42	81	.318	.323	24	.258	-1	-5	-6		-0.3
● RALPH BUXTON	Buxton, Ralph Stanley "Buck" b: 6/7/14, Rainton, Sask., Canada d: 1/6/88, San Leandro, Cal. BR/TR, 5′11.5″, 163 lbs. Deb: 9/11/38																											
1938	Phi-A	0	1	.000	5	0	0	0	0	9^1	12	7	1	0	5	9	16.4	4.82	100	.324	.405	0	.000	-0	0	0	-0	0.0
1949	NY-A	0	1	.000	14	0	0	0	2	26^2	22	13	3	0	16	14	12.8	4.05	100	.229	.339	0	.000	-0	0	-0	-0	-0.1
Total	2	0	2	.000	19	0	0	0	2	36	34	20	4	0	21	23	13.8	4.25	100	.256	.357	0	.000	-1	0	-0	-0	-0.1
● JOHN BUZHARDT	Buzhardt, John William b: 8/17/36, Prosperity, S.C. BR/TR, 6′2″, 198 lbs. Deb: 9/10/58																											
1958	Chi-N	3	0	1.000	6	2	1	0	0	24^1	16	5	2	0	7	9	8.5	1.85	212	.184	.245	1	.125	-0	6	6	1	0.7
1959	Chi-N	4	5	.444	31	10	1	1	0	101^1	107	64	12	1	29	33	12.2	4.97	79	.271	.322	2	.069	-1	-12	-12	1	-1.0
1960	Phi-N	5	16	.238	30	29	5	0	0	200^1	198	101	14	2	68	73	12.0	3.86	100	.259	.321	10	.161	-1	-2	0	-1	-0.1
1961	Phi-N	6	18	.250	41	27	6	1	0	202^1	200	107	28	6	65	92	12.1	4.49	91	.263	.326	6	.105	-2	-10	-9	0	-1.2
1962	Chi-A	8	12	.400	28	25	8	2	0	152^1	156	75	16	4	59	64	12.9	4.19	93	.264	.335	6	.118	-2	-4	-5	2	-0.6
1963	Chi-A	9	4	.692	19	18	6	3	0	126^1	100	35	8	5	31	59	9.7	2.42	145	.216	.273	4	.083	-3	17	16	1	1.4
1964	Chi-A	10	8	.556	31	25	8	3	0	160	150	60	13	4	35	97	10.6	2.98	116	.250	.295	11	.204	2	11	9	0	1.2
1965	Chi-A	13	8	.619	32	30	4	1	1	188^2	167	69	12	7	56	108	11.0	3.01	106	.242	.305	7	.125	0	10	4	-1	0.4
1966	Chi-A	6	11	.353	33	22	5	4	1	150^1	144	74	13	4	30	66	10.7	3.83	83	.248	.289	5	.116	-1	-7	-12	3	-1.1
1967	Chi-A	3	9	.250	28	7	0	0	0	88^2	100	44	11	6	37	33	14.5	3.96	78	.294	.373	4	.200	0	-7	-9	0	-1.1
	Bal-A	0	1	.000	7	1	0	0	0	11^2	14	6	1	0	5	7	14.7	4.63	68	.298	.365	0	.000	-0	-2	-2	0	-0.1
	Yr	3	10	.231	35	8	0	0	0	100^1	114	50	12	6	42	40	14.5	4.04	77	.295	.372	4	.190	0	-9	-11	1	-1.2
	Hou-N	0	0	—	1	0	0	0	0	0^2	0	0	0	0	0	0	0.0	0.00	—	.000	.000	0	—	0	0	0	0	0.0
1968	Hou-N	4	4	.500	39	4	0	0	5	83^2	73	35	0	4	35	37	12.0	3.12	95	.239	.325	4	.250	1	-1	-2	1	0.0
Total	11	71	96	.425	326	200	44	15	7	1490^2	1425	675	130	43	457	678	11.6	3.66	97	.253	.314	60	.135	-7	-1	-16	7	-1.5
● BUD BYERLY	Byerly, Eldred William b: 10/26/20, Webster Groves, Mo BR/TR, 6′2.5″, 185 lbs. Deb: 9/26/43																											
1943	StL-N	1	0	1.000	2	2	0	0	0	13	14	6	0	0	5	6	13.2	3.46	97	.280	.345	0	.000	-0	-0	-0	-0	-0.1
1944	*StL-N	2	2	.500	9	4	2	0	0	42^1	37	18	2	0	20	13	12.1	3.40	104	.228	.313	2	.167	-0	1	1	1	0.1
1945	StL-N	4	5	.444	33	8	2	0	0	95	111	61	3	1	41	39	14.5	4.74	79	.288	.358	5	.217	1	-10	-11	2	-0.6
1950	Cin-N	0	1	.000	4	1	0	0	0	14^2	12	4	1	0	4	5	9.8	2.45	173	.218	.271	0	.000	-0	3	3	-0	0.1
1951	Cin-N	2	1	.667	40	0	0	0	0	66	69	33	6	2	25	28	13.1	3.27	125	.267	.337	0	.000	-0	5	6	1	0.3
1952	Cin-N	0	1	.000	12	2	0	0	1	24^2	29	15	0	0	7	14	13.1	5.11	74	.309	.356	1	.200	0	-4	-4	0	-0.2
1956	Was-A	2	4	.333	25	0	0	0	4	51^2	45	19	6	2	14	19	10.6	2.96	146	.243	.303	1	.091	-1	7	8	0	0.8
1957	Was-A	6	6	.500	47	0	0	0	6	95	94	38	6	1	22	39	11.1	3.13	125	.264	.309	1	.067	-1	7	8	1	1.1

YEAR	TM/L	W	L	PCT	G	GS	CG	SH	SV	IP	H	R	HR	HB	BB	SO	RAT	ERA	ERA+	OAV	OOB	BH	AVG	PB	PR	PR+	PD	TPI
1958	Was-A	2	0	1.000	17	0	0	0	1	24	34	20	4	1	11	13	17.3	6.75	56	.347	.418	0	.000	-0	-8	-8	-0	-0.7
	Bos-A	1	2	.333	18	0	0	0	0	30^1	31	12	1	1	7	16	11.6	1.78	225	.272	.320	0	.000	-1	7	7	-0	0.6
	Yr	3	2	.600	35	0	0	0	1	54^1	65	32	5	2	18	29	14.1	3.98	99	.307	.366	0	.000	-1	-1	-0	-0	-0.1
1959	SF-N	1	0	1.000	11	0	0	0	0	13	11	2	2	0	5	4	11.1	1.38	275	.234	.308	0	—	0	4	4	1	0.3
1960	SF-N	1	0	1.000	19	0	0	0	2	22	32	14	3	1	6	13	16.0	5.32	65	.340	.386	0	.000	-0	-4	-5	-0	-0.3
Total	11	22	22	.500	237	17	4	0	14	491^2	519	242	34	9	167	209	12.7	3.70	105	.273	.335	10	.118	-4	8	10	4	1.4

● HARRY BYRD

Byrd, Harry Gladwin b: 2/3/25, Darlington, S.C. d: 5/14/85, Darlington, S.C. BR/TR (BB 1955), 6'1", 188 lbs. Deb: 4/21/50

YEAR	TM/L	W	L	PCT	G	GS	CG	SH	SV	IP	H	R	HR	HB	BB	SO	RAT	ERA	ERA+	OAV	OOB	BH	AVG	PB	PR	PR+	PD	TPI
1950	Phi-A	0	0	—	6	0	0	0	0	10^2	25	20	3	2	9	2	30.4	16.88	27	.481	.571	0	.000	-0	-15	-15	-0	-0.7
1952	Phi-A	15	15	.500	37	28	15	3	2	228^1	244	100	12	7	98	116	13.8	3.31	120	.274	.351	10	.133	-3	9	15	0	1.6
1953	Phi-A	11	20	.355	40	37	11	2	0	236^2	279	155	23	14	115	122	15.5	5.51	78	.294	.379	18	.222	-1	-40	-30	-1	-3.6
1954	NY-A	9	7	.563	25	21	5	1	0	132^1	131	56	10	7	43	52	12.3	2.99	115	.258	.324	9	.196	1	11	7	-1	0.8
1955	Bal-A	3	2	.600	14	8	1	1	1	65^1	64	33	7	7	28	25	13.6	4.55	84	.261	.354	3	.158	-0	-4	-6	-1	-0.5
	Chi-A	4	6	.400	25	12	1	1	1	91	85	49	10	2	30	44	11.6	4.65	85	.251	.315	2	.067	-3	-7	-7	0	-1.0
	Yr	7	8	.467	39	20	2	2	2	156^1	149	82	17	9	58	69	12.4	4.61	85	.255	.332	5	.102	-3	-11	-13	-1	-1.5
1956	Chi-A	0	1	.000	3	1	0	0	0	4^1	9	6	0	0	4	0	27.0	10.38	39	.474	.565	0	.000	-0	-3	-3	0	-0.5
1957	Det-A	4	3	.571	37	1	0	0	5	59	53	23	6	2	28	20	12.7	3.36	115	.249	.342	0	.000	-1	3	3	-1	0.3
Total	7	46	54	.460	187	108	33	8	9	827^2	890	442	71	41	355	381	14.0	4.35	91	.277	.356	42	.160	-8	-46	-35	-3	-3.6

● JEFF BYRD

Byrd, Jeffrey Alan b: 11/11/56, LaMesa, Cal. BR/TR, 6'3", 195 lbs. Deb: 6/20/77

YEAR	TM/L	W	L	PCT	G	GS	CG	SH	SV	IP	H	R	HR	HB	BB	SO	RAT	ERA	ERA+	OAV	OOB	BH	AVG	PB	PR	PR+	PD	TPI
1977	Tor-A	2	13	.133	17	17	1	0	0	87^1	98	68	5	0	68	40	17.1	6.18	68	.286	.404	0	—	0	-20	-18	1	-2.6

● PAUL BYRD

Byrd, Paul Gregory b: 12/3/70, Louisville, Ky. BR/TR, 6'1", 185 lbs. Deb: 7/28/95

YEAR	TM/L	W	L	PCT	G	GS	CG	SH	SV	IP	H	R	HR	HB	BB	SO	RAT	ERA	ERA+	OAV	OOB	BH	AVG	PB	PR	PR+	PD	TPI
1995	NY-N	2	0	1.000	17	0	0	0	0	22	18	6	1	1	7	26	10.6	2.05	198	.222	.292	1	1.000	0	5	5	0	0.5
1996	NY-N	1	2	.333	38	0	0	0	0	46^2	48	22	7	0	21	31	13.3	4.24	95	.265	.342	0	.000	-0	-0	-1	-0	-0.1
1997	Atl-N	4	4	.500	31	4	0	0	0	53	47	34	6	4	28	37	13.4	5.26	80	.235	.341	1	.143	-0	-6	-6	-1	-0.9
1998	Atl-N	0	0	—	1	0	0	0	0	2	4	3	0	0	1	1	22.5	13.50	31	.400	.455	0	—	0	-2	-2	-0	-0.1
	Phi-N	5	2	.714	8	8	2	1	0	55	41	16	6	0	17	38	9.5	2.29	189	.203	.265	3	.167	0	12	12	-0	1.5
	Yr	5	2	.714	9	8	2	1	0	57	45	19	6	0	18	39	9.9	2.68	161	.212	.274	3	.167	0	10	10	-0	1.4
1999	Phi-N☆	15	11	.577	32	32	1	0	0	199^2	205	119	34	17	70	106	13.2	4.60	103	.265	.339	7	.127	-1	-1	3	-1	0.1
2000	Phi-N	2	9	.182	17	15	0	0	0	83	89	67	17	3	35	53	13.8	6.51	73	.271	.346	3	.150	0	-17	-16	-0	-1.8
Total	6	29	28	.509	144	59	3	1	0	461^1	452	267	71	25	179	292	12.8	4.62	97	.254	.331	15	.146	-1	-9	-6	-3	-0.8

● TIM BYRDAK

Byrdak, Timothy Christopher b: 10/31/73, Oak Lawn, Ill. BL/TL, 5'11", 170 lbs. Deb: 8/7/98

YEAR	TM/L	W	L	PCT	G	GS	CG	SH	SV	IP	H	R	HR	HB	BB	SO	RAT	ERA	ERA+	OAV	OOB	BH	AVG	PB	PR	PR+	PD	TPI
1998	KC-A	0	0	—	3	0	0	0	0	1^2	5	1	1	0	0	1	27.0	5.40	89	.556	.556	0	—	0	-0	-0	-0	0.0
1999	KC-A	0	3	.000	33	0	0	0	1	24^2	32	24	5	1	20	17	19.3	7.66	65	.308	.424	1	.500	1	-8	-7	1	-0.6
2000	KC-A	0	1	.000	12	0	0	0	0	6^1	11	8	3	0	4	8	21.3	11.37	44	.367	.441	0	—	0	-5	-4	0	-0.6
Total	3	0	4	.000	48	0	0	0	1	32^2	48	33	9	1	24	26	20.1	8.27	61	.336	.435	1	.500	1	-12	-12	1	-1.2

● JERRY BYRNE

Byrne, Gerald Wilfred b: 2/2/07, Parnell, Mich. d: 8/11/55, Lansing, Mich. BR/TR, 6', 170 lbs. Deb: 8/31/29

YEAR	TM/L	W	L	PCT	G	GS	CG	SH	SV	IP	H	R	HR	HB	BB	SO	RAT	ERA	ERA+	OAV	OOB	BH	AVG	PB	PR	PR+	PD	TPI
1929	Chi-A	0	1	.000	3	1	0	0	0	7^1	11	6	0	0	6	1	20.9	7.36	58	.379	.486	0	.000	-0	-3	-2	-0	-0.3

● TOMMY BYRNE

Byrne, Thomas Joseph b: 12/31/19, Baltimore, Md. BL/TL, 6'1", 182 lbs. Deb: 4/27/43

YEAR	TM/L	W	L	PCT	G	GS	CG	SH	SV	IP	H	R	HR	HB	BB	SO	RAT	ERA	ERA+	OAV	OOB	BH	AVG	PB	PR	PR+	PD	TPI
1943	NY-A	2	1	.667	11	2	0	0	0	31^2	28	26	1	3	35	22	18.8	6.54	49	.248	.437	1	.091	-0	-11	-12	0	-1.0
1946	NY-A	0	1	.000	4	1	0	0	0	9^1	7	8	1	1	8	5	15.4	5.79	60	.194	.356	2	.222	0	-2	-2	0	-0.2
1947	NY-A	0	0	—	4	1	0	0	0	4^1	5	2	0	0	6	2	22.8	4.15	85	.294	.478	0	—	0	-0	-0	0	0.0
1948	NY-A	8	5	.615	31	11	5	1	2	133^2	79	55	8	9	101	93	12.7	3.30	124	.172	.332	15	.326	6	15	12	-1	1.5
1949	*NY-A	15	7	.682	32	30	12	3	0	196	125	84	11	13	179	129	14.6	3.72	109	**.183**	.362	16	.193	1	10	7	-3	0.5
1950	NY-A☆	15	9	.625	31	31	10	2	0	203^1	188	115	23	17	160	118	16.2	4.74	91	.245	.387	22	.272	7	-4	-11	-2	-0.6
1951	NY-A	2	1	.667	9	3	0	0	0	21	16	17	0	3	36	14	23.6	6.86	56	.213	.482	2	.222	1	-6	-8	-0	-0.9
	StL-A	4	10	.286	19	17	7	2	0	122^2	104	56	5	12	114	57	16.9	3.82	115	.235	.404	16	.281	3	4	7	-1	1.0
	Yr	6	11	.353	28	20	7	2	0	143^2	120	73	5	15	150	71	17.9	4.26	101	.232	.417	18	.273	4	-2	1	-1	0.1
1952	StL-A	7	14	.333	29	24	14	0	0	196	182	117	16	10	112	91	14.0	4.68	84	.247	.354	21	.250	5	-22	-16	-4	-1.4
1953	Chi-A	2	0	1.000	6	6	0	0	0	16	18	18	0	0	26	4	24.8	10.13	40	.295	.506	3	.167	1	-11	-11	0	-1.0
	Was-A	0	5	.000	6	5	2	0	0	33^2	35	17	3	1	22	22	15.5	4.28	91	.276	.387	1	.059	-1	-1	-1	0	-0.2
	Yr	2	5	.286	12	11	2	0	0	49^2	53	35	3	1	48	26	18.5	6.16	64	.282	.430	4	.114	-0	-12	-12	1	-1.2
1954	NY-A	3	2	.600	5	5	4	1	0	40	36	13	1	0	19	24	12.4	2.70	127	.240	.325	7	.368	4	5	4	0	0.9
1955	*NY-A	16	5	**.762**	27	22	9	3	2	160	137	69	12	7	87	76	13.0	3.15	119	.237	.344	16	.205	4	14	11	-1	1.7
1956	*NY-A	7	3	.700	37	8	1	0	6	109^2	108	50	9	2	72	52	14.9	3.36	115	.262	.374	14	.269	6	10	7	1	1.2
1957	*NY-A	4	6	.400	30	4	1	0	2	84^2	70	41	8	7	60	57	14.6	4.36	82	.227	.364	7	.189	4	-5	-8	-1	-0.6
Total	13	85	69	.552	281	170	65	12	12	1362	1138	688	98	85	1037	766	14.9	4.11	97	.229	.371	143	.238	41	-5	-21	-11	0.9

● MARTY BYSTROM

Bystrom, Martin Eugene b: 7/26/58, Coral Gables, Fla. BR/TR, 6'5", 200 lbs. Deb: 9/7/80

YEAR	TM/L	W	L	PCT	G	GS	CG	SH	SV	IP	H	R	HR	HB	BB	SO	RAT	ERA	ERA+	OAV	OOB	BH	AVG	PB	PR	PR+	PD	TPI
1980	*Phi-N	5	0	1.000	6	5	1	1	0	36	26	6	1	0	9	21	8.8	1.50	253	.195	.246	1	.071	-1	8	9	1	1.4
1981	Phi-N	4	3	.571	9	9	1	0	0	53^2	55	21	3	1	16	24	12.1	3.35	108	.264	.320	2	.118	-1	1	2	1	0.1
1982	Phi-N	5	6	.455	19	16	1	0	0	89	93	53	2	5	35	50	13.4	4.85	76	.277	.354	3	.125	-0	-12	-11	-1	-1.4
1983	*Phi-N	6	9	.400	24	23	1	1	0	119^1	136	75	6	7	44	87	14.1	4.60	78	.285	.353	9	.237	2	-13	-14	-1	-1.5
1984	Phi-N	4	4	.500	11	11	0	0	0	56^2	66	36	5	0	22	36	14.0	5.08	72	.283	.345	3	.158	-0	-9	-9	-0	-1.2
	NY-A	2	2	.500	7	7	0	0	0	39^1	34	16	3	1	13	24	11.0	2.97	128	.230	.296	0	—	0	4	4	-1	0.3
1985	NY-A	3	2	.600	8	8	0	0	0	41	44	29	8	1	19	16	14.0	5.71	70	.280	.362	0	—	0	-7	-8	0	-0.8
Total	6	29	26	.527	84	79	4	2	0	435	454	236	28	15	158	258	13.0	4.26	87	.268	.336	18	.161	0	-28	-27	-1	-3.1

● JOSE CABRERA

Cabrera, Jose Alberto b: 3/24/72, Santiago, D.R. BR/TR, 6', 200 lbs. Deb: 7/15/97

YEAR	TM/L	W	L	PCT	G	GS	CG	SH	SV	IP	H	R	HR	HB	BB	SO	RAT	ERA	ERA+	OAV	OOB	BH	AVG	PB	PR	PR+	PD	TPI
1997	Hou-N	0	0	—	12	0	0	0	0	15^1	6	2	1	0	6	18	7.0	1.17	341	.125	.222	0	.000	-0	5	5	0	0.2
1998	Hou-N	0	0	—	3	0	0	0	0	4^1	7	4	0	0	1	1	16.6	8.31	49	.389	.421	0	—	0	-2	-2	0	-0.1
1999	*Hou-N	4	0	1.000	26	0	0	0	0	29^1	21	7	3	0	9	28	9.2	2.15	206	.196	.259	0	—	0	8	8	-0	0.9
2000	Hou-N	2	3	.400	52	0	0	0	2	59^1	74	40	10	3	17	41	14.3	5.92	83	.308	.362	0	.000	-0	-8	-6	-1	-0.6
Total	4	6	3	.667	93	0	0	0	2	108^1	108	53	14	3	33	88	12.0	4.32	106	.262	.321	0	.000	-0	3	3	-1	0.4

● GREG CADARET

Cadaret, Gregory James b: 2/27/62, Detroit, Mich. BL/TL, 6'3", 214 lbs. Deb: 7/5/87

YEAR	TM/L	W	L	PCT	G	GS	CG	SH	SV	IP	H	R	HR	HB	BB	SO	RAT	ERA	ERA+	OAV	OOB	BH	AVG	PB	PR	PR+	PD	TPI
1987	Oak-A	6	2	.750	29	0	0	0	0	39^2	37	22	6	1	24	30	14.1	4.54	91	.252	.360	0	—	0	-0	-2	1	-0.3
1988	*Oak-A	5	2	.714	58	0	0	0	3	71^2	60	26	2	1	36	64	12.2	2.89	131	.226	.320	0	—	0	9	8	0	0.7
1989	Oak-A	0	0	—	26	0	0	0	0	27^2	21	9	0	0	19	14	13.0	2.28	162	.214	.342	0	—	0	5	5	1	0.3
	NY-A	5	5	.500	20	13	3	1	0	92^1	109	53	7	2	38	66	14.5	4.58	85	.298	.367	0	—	0	-7	-7	0	-0.7
	Yr	5	5	.500	46	13	3	1	0	120	130	62	7	2	57	80	14.2	4.05	95	.280	.361	0	—	0	-2	-3	1	-0.4
1990	NY-A	5	4	.556	54	6	0	0	3	121^1	120	62	8	1	64	80	13.7	4.15	96	.268	.361	0	—	0	-3	-2	2	0.1
1991	NY-A	8	6	.571	68	5	0	0	3	121^2	110	52	8	2	59	105	12.6	3.62	114	.246	.337	0	—	0	6	7	1	0.8
1992	NY-A	4	8	.333	46	11	1	1	1	103^2	104	53	12	2	74	73	15.6	4.25	92	.267	.387	0	—	0	-4	-4	1	-0.3
1993	Cin-N	2	1	.667	34	0	0	0	1	32^2	40	19	3	1	23	23	17.6	4.96	81	.305	.413	0	.000	-0	-3	-3	-0	-0.3
	KC-A	1	1	.500	13	0	0	0	0	15^1	14	5	0	1	7	2	12.9	2.93	157	.264	.361	0	—	0	2	3	0	0.3
1994	Tor-A	0	1	.000	21	0	0	0	0	20	24	15	4	0	17	15	18.4	5.85	82	.289	.410	0	—	0	-2	-2	-0	-0.1
	Det-A	1	0	1.000	17	0	0	0	2	20	17	9	0	0	16	14	14.8	3.60	135	.227	.363	0	—	0	3	3	1	0.2
	Yr	1	1	.500	38	0	0	0	2	40	41	24	4	0	33	29	16.6	4.72	102	.259	.387	0	—	0	0	0	1	0.1
1997	Ana-A	0	0	—	15	0	0	0	0	13^2	11	5	1	2	8	11	13.8	3.29	139	.220	.350	0	—	0	2	2	-0	0.1
1998	Ana-A	1	2	.333	39	0	0	0	1	37	38	17	6	3	15	37	13.6	4.14	113	.257	.337	0	—	0	2	2	-0	0.1
	Tex-A	0	0	—	11	0	0	0	0	7^2	11	4	1	0	3	5	16.4	4.70	103	.355	.412	0	—	0	-0	0	-0	0.0
	Yr	1	2	.333	50	0	0	0	1	44^2	49	21	7	3	18	42	14.1	4.23	111	.274	.350	0	—	0	2	2	-0	0.1
Total	10	38	32	.543	451	35	4	2	14	724^1	716	351	58	16	403	539	14.1	3.99	102	.262	.360	0	.000	-0	9	8	6	0.9

● LEON CADORE

Cadore, Leon Joseph "Caddy" b: 11/20/1890, Chicago, Ill. d: 3/16/58, Spokane, Wash. BR/TR, 6'1", 190 lbs. Deb: 4/28/15

YEAR	TM/L	W	L	PCT	G	GS	CG	SH	SV	IP	H	R	HR	HB	BB	SO	RAT	ERA	ERA+	OAV	OOB	BH	AVG	PB	PR	PR+	PD	TPI
1915	Bro-N	0	2	.000	7	2	1	0	0	21	28	15	0	2	8	12	16.3	5.57	50	.337	.409	0	.000	-1	-7	-6	0	-0.7
1916	Bro-N	0	0	—	1	0	0	0	0	6	10	4	0	0	2	2	15.0	4.50	60	.370	.370	0	.000	-0	-1	-1	0	-0.1

YEAR TM/L	W	L	PCT	G	GS	CG	SH	SV	IP	H	R	HR	HB	BB	SO	RAT	ERA	ERA+	OAV	OOB	BH	AVG	PB	PR	PR+	PD	TPI
1917 Bro-N	13	13	.500	37	30	21	1	3	264	231	86	3	7	63	115	10.3	2.45	114	.241	.292	24	.261	5	8	10	-2	1.4
1918 Bro-N	1	0	1.000	2	2	1	1	0	17	6	1	0	1	2	5	4.8	0.53	526	.115	.164	0	.000	-0	4	4	0	0.2
1919 Bro-N	14	12	.538	35	27	16	3	0	250^2	228	80	5	6	39	94	9.8	2.37	125	.245	.280	14	.161	-3	15	16	-3	1.0
1920 *Bro-N	15	14	.517	35	30	16	4	0	254^1	256	91	4	3	56	79	11.1	2.62	122	.270	.313	20	.220	2	15	16	1	2.2
1921 Bro-N	13	14	.481	35	30	12	1	0	211^2	243	112	17	6	46	79	12.5	4.17	93	.292	.334	14	.187	-1	-9	-6	-1	-1.0
1922 Bro-N	8	15	.348	29	21	13	0	0	190^1	224	115	13	1	57	49	13.3	4.35	94	.299	.349	19	.268	4	-5	-6	-3	-0.5
1923 Bro-N	4	1	.800	8	4	3	0	0	36	39	14	2	0	13	5	13.0	3.25	119	.291	.354	1	.077	-1	3	3	-1	0.1
Chi-A	0	1	.000	1	1	0	0	0	2^1	6	7	0	0	2	3	30.9	23.14	17	.500	.571	0	—	0	-5	-5	-0	-0.7
1924 NY-N	0	0	—	2	0	0	0	0	4	2	0	0	0	3	2	11.3	0.00	—	.154	.313	0	—	0	2	2	0	0.1
Total 10	68	72	.486	192	147	83	10	3	1257^1	1273	525	44	26	289	445	11.4	3.14	106	.269	.314	92	.208	5	19	27	-8	2.0

● CHARLIE CADY

Cady, Charles B. b: 12/1865, Chicago, Ill. d: 6/7/09, Kankakee, Ill. 5'11", 180 lbs. Deb: 9/5/1883 ♦

YEAR TM/L	W	L	PCT	G	GS	CG	SH	SV	IP	H	R	HR	HB	BB	SO	RAT	ERA	ERA+	OAV	OOB	BH	AVG	PB	PR	PR+	PD	TPI
1883 Cle-N	0	1	.000	1	1	1	0	0	8	13	13	0		4	5	19.1	7.88	40	.361	.425	0	.000	-1	-4	-4	-0	-0.4
1884 CP-U	3	1	.750	4	4	4	0	0	35	37	25	0		13	15	12.9	2.83	86	.253	.314	2	.100	-1	-2	-2	-0	-0.3
Total 2	3	2	.600	5	5	5	0	0	43	50	38	0		17	20	14.0	3.77	68	.275	.337	2	.059	-2	-6	-6	-0	-0.7

● JOHN CAHILL

Cahill, John Patrick Parnell "Patsy"
b: 4/30/1865, San Francisco, Cal d: 10/31/01, Pleasanton, Cal. BR/TR, 5'7.5", 168 lbs. Deb: 5/31/1884 ♦

YEAR TM/L	W	L	PCT	G	GS	CG	SH	SV	IP	H	R	HR	HB	BB	SO	RAT	ERA	ERA+	OAV	OOB	BH	AVG	PB	PR	PR+	PD	TPI
1884 Col-a	1	0	1.000	2	1	1	0	0	16	15	15	0	3	4	1	12.4	5.06	60	.211	.282	46	.219	0	-3	-4	-0	-0.2
1886 StL-N	1	0	1.000	2	0	0	0	0	12	11	5	0		3	2	10.5	3.00	108	.268	.318	92	.199	-0	0	0	0	0.0
1887 Ind-N	0	2	.000	6	1	1	0	0	22	59	38	2	2	19	5	25.0	14.32	29	.527	.535	63	.232	-1	-25	-24	-1	-1.6
Total 3	2	2	.500	10	2	2	0	0	50	85	58	2	5	26	8	17.5	8.64	41	.379	.411	201	.213	-1	-28	-29	-1	-1.8

● LES CAIN

Cain, Leslie b: 1/13/48, San Luis Obispo, Cal. BL/TL, 6'1", 200 lbs. Deb: 4/28/68

YEAR TM/L	W	L	PCT	G	GS	CG	SH	SV	IP	H	R	HR	HB	BB	SO	RAT	ERA	ERA+	OAV	OOB	BH	AVG	PB	PR	PR+	PD	TPI
1968 Det-A	1	0	1.000	8	4	0	0	0	24	25	9	1	0	20	13	16.9	3.00	100	.269	.398	1	.143	0	-0	0	0	0.1
1970 Det-A	12	7	.632	29	29	5	0	0	180^2	167	92	15	7	98	156	13.5	3.84	97	.247	.349	11	.162	0	-2	-2	-0	-0.2
1971 Det-A	10	9	.526	26	26	3	1	0	144^2	121	77	14	6	91	118	13.6	4.35	83	.228	.348	8	.145	-0	-14	-12	-1	-1.5
1972 Det-A	0	3	.000	5	5	0	0	0	23^2	18	12	2	0	16	16	12.9	3.80	83	.209	.333	1	.143	-0	-2	-2	-0	-0.3
Total 4	23	19	.548	68	64	8	1	0	373	331	190	32	13	225	303	13.7	3.98	90	.239	.351	21	.153	-0	-19	-16	-1	-1.9

● SUGAR CAIN

Cain, Merritt Patrick b: 4/5/07, Macon, Ga. d: 4/3/75, Atlanta, Ga. BL/TR (BB 1932-33), 5'11", 190 lbs. Deb: 4/15/32

YEAR TM/L	W	L	PCT	G	GS	CG	SH	SV	IP	H	R	HR	HB	BB	SO	RAT	ERA	ERA+	OAV	OOB	BH	AVG	PB	PR	PR+	PD	TPI
1932 Phi-A	3	4	.429	10	6	3	0	0	45	42	27	1	0	28	24	14.0	5.00	90	.256	.365	3	.250	1	-3	-2	-0	-0.3
1933 Phi-A	13	12	.520	38	32	16	1	1	218	244	132	18	3	137	43	15.9	4.25	101	.280	.379	16	.200	-1	1	1	-1	-0.1
1934 Phi-A	9	17	.346	36	32	15	0	1	230^2	235	128	15	3	128	66	14.3	4.41	99	.266	.360	13	.159	-3	2	-1	-1	-0.4
1935 Phi-A	0	5	.000	6	5	0	0	0	26	39	22	1	0	19	5	20.1	6.58	69	.382	.479	0	.000	-1	-6	-6	-0	-1.0
StL-A	9	8	.529	31	24	8	0	0	167^2	197	112	7	4	104	68	16.4	5.26	91	.290	.388	11	.193	-2	-15	-8	-3	-1.2
Yr	9	13	.409	37	29	8	0	0	193^2	236	134	8	4	123	73	16.9	5.44	88	.302	.400	11	.169	-4	-21	-14	-3	-2.2
1936 StL-A	1	1	.500	4	3	1	0	0	16^1	20	13	0	0	9	8	16.0	6.61	81	.286	.367	2	.286	0	-3	-2	-0	-0.2
Chi-A	14	10	.583	30	26	14	1	0	195^1	228	112	18	5	75	42	14.2	4.75	110	.293	.359	7	.103	-4	6	10	-3	0.3
Yr	15	11	.577	34	29	15	1	0	211^2	248	125	18	5	84	50	14.3	4.89	107	.292	.360	9	.120	-4	3	7	-3	0.1
1937 Chi-A	4	2	.667	18	6	1	0	0	68^2	88	48	7	0	51	17	18.2	6.16	75	.325	.432	4	.182	-1	-12	-12	-0	-0.9
1938 Chi-A	0	1	.000	5	3	0	0	0	19^2	26	17	0	0	18	6	20.1	4.58	107	.321	.444	0	.000	-1	0	1	-1	-0.2
Total 7	53	60	.469	178	137	58	2	1	987^1	1119	611	67	15	569	279	15.5	4.83	96	.287	.380	56	.163	-13	-29	-20	-9	-4.0

● BOB CAIN

Cain, Robert Max "Sugar" b: 10/16/24, Longford, Kan. d: 4/8/97, Cleveland, Ohio BL/TL, 6', 165 lbs. Deb: 9/18/49 ♦

YEAR TM/L	W	L	PCT	G	GS	CG	SH	SV	IP	H	R	HR	HB	BB	SO	RAT	ERA	ERA+	OAV	OOB	BH	AVG	PB	PR	PR+	PD	TPI
1949 Chi-A	0	0	—	6	0	0	0	1	11	7	3	0	0	5	5	9.8	2.45	170	.179	.273	0	.000	-0	2	2	-0	0.0
1950 Chi-A	9	12	.429	34	23	11	1	2	171^2	153	80	12	5	109	77	14.0	3.93	114	.244	.361	12	.197	-0	12	11	0	1.1
1951 Chi-A	1	2	.333	4	4	1	0	0	26^1	25	14	3	3	13	3	14.0	3.76	107	.248	.350	3	.333	1	1	1	-0	0.1
Det-A	11	10	.524	35	22	6	1	2	149^1	135	88	13	11	82	58	13.7	4.70	89	.239	.347	13	.245	2	-10	-9	0	-0.9
Yr	12	12	.500	39	26	7	1	2	175^2	160	102	16	14	95	61	13.8	4.56	91	.241	.348	16	.258	3	-9	-8	-0	-0.8
1952 StL-A	12	10	.545	29	27	8	1	2	170	169	79	15	2	62	70	12.3	4.13	95	.264	.331	8	.138	-1	-9	-4	-2	-0.8
1953 StL-A	4	10	.286	32	13	1	0	1	99^2	129	74	8	1	45	36	15.8	6.23	67	.310	.379	6	.200	0	-25	-21	-2	-2.8
Total 5	37	44	.457	140	89	27	3	8	628	618	338	51	22	316	249	13.7	4.50	93	.259	.351	42	.196	0	-27	-21	-4	-3.3

● CAMERON CAIRNCROSS

Cairncross, Cameron b: 5/11/72, Cairns, Queensland, Australia BL/TL, 6', 195 lbs. Deb: 7/20/2000

YEAR TM/L	W	L	PCT	G	GS	CG	SH	SV	IP	H	R	HR	HB	BB	SO	RAT	ERA	ERA+	OAV	OOB	BH	AVG	PB	PR	PR+	PD	TPI
2000 Cle-A	1	0	1.000	15	0	0	0	0	9^1	11	4	1	0	3	8	13.5	3.86	130	.306	.359	0	—	0	1	1	-0	0.1

● CHARLIE CALDWELL

Caldwell, Charles William "Chuck" b: 8/2/01, Bristol, Va. d: 11/1/57, Princeton, N.J. BR/TR, 5'10", 180 lbs. Deb: 7/7/25

YEAR TM/L	W	L	PCT	G	GS	CG	SH	SV	IP	H	R	HR	HB	BB	SO	RAT	ERA	ERA+	OAV	OOB	BH	AVG	PB	PR	PR+	PD	TPI
1925 NY-A	0	0	—	3	0	0	0	0	2^2	7	6	0	0	3	1	33.8	16.88	25	.467	.556	0	.000	-0	-4	-4	-0	-0.2

● EARL CALDWELL

Caldwell, Earl Welton "Teach" b: 4/9/05, Sparks, Tex. d: 9/15/81, Mission, Tex. BR/TR, 6'1", 178 lbs. Deb: 9/8/28

YEAR TM/L	W	L	PCT	G	GS	CG	SH	SV	IP	H	R	HR	HB	BB	SO	RAT	ERA	ERA+	OAV	OOB	BH	AVG	PB	PR	PR+	PD	TPI
1928 Phi-N	1	4	.200	5	5	1	1	0	34^2	46	23	5	0	17	6	16.4	5.71	75	.348	.423	1	.111	-0	-7	-5	0	-0.6
1935 StL-A	3	2	.600	6	5	2	1	0	36^2	34	16	2	0	17	5	12.5	3.68	130	.245	.327	2	.182	-0	3	4	1	0.6
1936 StL-A	7	16	.304	41	25	10	2	2	189	252	146	15	15	83	59	16.7	6.00	90	.319	.394	11	.190	-1	-20	-12	-1	-1.4
1937 StL-A	0	0	—	9	2	0	0	0	29	39	22	3	2	13	8	16.8	6.83	71	.317	.391	2	.222	0	-7	-6	0	-0.3
1945 Chi-A	6	7	.462	27	11	5	1	4	105^1	108	50	8	3	37	45	12.6	3.59	92	.265	.331	8	.216	-0	-3	-3	3	-0.1
1946 Chi-A	13	4	.765	39	0	0	0	8	90^2	60	28	2	1	29	42	8.9	2.08	164	.186	.255	3	.167	1	**14**	**14**	1	3.0
1947 Chi-A	1	4	.200	40	0	0	0	8	54^1	53	23	4	1	30	22	13.9	3.64	100	.261	.359	0	.000	-1	0	0	-1	-0.2
1948 Chi-A	1	5	.167	25	1	0	0	3	39	53	25	3	2	22	10	17.8	5.31	80	.335	.423	0	.000	-0	-4	-5	-0	-0.7
Bos-A	1	1	.500	8	0	0	0	0	9	11	14	2	1	11	5	23.0	13.00	34	.333	.511	1	.333	0	-9	-8	-0	-1.5
Yr	2	6	.250	33	1	0	0	3	48	64	39	5	3	33	15	18.8	6.75	63	.335	.441	1	.125	-0	-13	-13	-1	-2.2
Total 8	33	43	.434	200	49	18	5	25	587^2	656	347	44	25	259	202	14.4	4.69	92	.284	.363	28	.178	-2	-32	-24	3	-1.2

● RALPH CALDWELL

Caldwell, Ralph Grant "Lefty" b: 1/18/1884, Philadelphia, Pa. d: 8/5/69, W.Trenton, N.J. BL/TL, 5'9", 155 lbs. Deb: 9/10/04

YEAR TM/L	W	L	PCT	G	GS	CG	SH	SV	IP	H	R	HR	HB	BB	SO	RAT	ERA	ERA+	OAV	OOB	BH	AVG	PB	PR	PR+	PD	TPI
1904 Phi-N	2	2	.500	6	5	5	0	0	41	40	29	1	2	15	30	12.5	4.17	64	.242	.313	8	.444	3	-7	-7	0	-0.3
1905 Phi-N	1	3	.250	7	2	1	0	1	34	44	25	1	3	7	29	14.3	4.24	69	.321	.367	0	.000	-2	-5	-5	-1	-0.8
Total 2	3	5	.375	13	7	6	0	1	75	84	54	2	5	22	59	13.3	4.20	66	.278	.337	8	.242	1	-11	-12	-1	-1.1

● MIKE CALDWELL

Caldwell, Ralph Michael b: 1/22/49, Tarboro, N.C. BR/TL, 6', 185 lbs. Deb: 9/4/71

YEAR TM/L	W	L	PCT	G	GS	CG	SH	SV	IP	H	R	HR	HB	BB	SO	RAT	ERA	ERA+	OAV	OOB	BH	AVG	PB	PR	PR+	PD	TPI
1971 SD-N	1	0	1.000	6	0	0	0	0	6^2	4	0	0	0	3	5	9.5	0.00	—	.174	.269	1	1.000	1	3	3	0	0.5
1972 SD-N	7	11	.389	42	20	4	2	2	163^2	183	92	10	4	49	102	13.0	4.01	82	.282	.337	7	.140	-1	-10	-14	5	-1.1
1973 SD-N	5	14	.263	55	13	3	1	10	149	146	77	8	2	53	86	12.1	3.74	93	.260	.326	5	.143	-1	-1	-5	2	-0.5
1974 SF-N	14	5	.737	31	27	6	2	0	189^1	176	80	17	4	63	83	11.6	2.95	129	.249	.314	9	.143	-2	14	17	4	1.9
1975 SF-N	7	13	.350	38	21	4	0	1	163^1	194	102	16	5	48	57	13.6	4.79	79	.296	.348	7	.159	-0	-21	-17	2	-1.8
1976 SF-N	1	7	.125	50	9	0	0	2	107^1	145	74	5	2	20	55	14.0	4.86	75	.324	.356	3	.158	-0	-16	-14	1	-0.9
1977 Cin-N	0	0	—	14	0	0	0	1	24^2	25	11	1	0	8	11	12.0	4.01	98	.260	.317	2	.500	2	-0	-0	-0	0.1
Mil-A	5	8	.385	21	12	2	0	0	94^1	101	58	6	2	36	38	13.3	4.58	89	.271	.338	0	—	0	-5	-5	3	-0.4
1978 Mil-A	22	9	.710	37	34	**23**	6	1	293^1	258	90	14	7	54	131	9.8	2.36	160	.234	.274	0	—	0	46	46	1	5.0
1979 Mil-A	16	6	**.727**	30	30	16	4	0	235	252	96	18	4	39	89	11.3	3.29	127	.278	.311	0	—	0	24	23	5	2.5
1980 Mil-A	13	11	.542	34	33	11	2	1	225^1	248	112	29	2	56	74	12.2	4.03	96	.285	.330	0	—	0	0	-4	0	-0.4
1981 *Mil-A	11	9	.550	24	23	3	0	0	144^1	151	70	18	1	38	41	11.8	3.93	87	.272	.319	0	—	0	-4	-9	-0	-1.1
1982 *Mil-A	17	13	.567	35	34	12	3	0	258	269	119	30	0	58	75	11.4	3.91	97	.271	.311	0	—	0	5	-4	2	-0.2
1983 Mil-A	12	11	.522	32	32	10	2	0	228^1	269	125	35	1	51	58	12.7	4.53	83	.296	.334	0	—	0	-12	-22	-0	-1.9
1984 Mil-A	6	13	.316	26	19	4	1	0	126	160	76	11	1	21	34	13.0	4.64	83	.314	.343	0	—	0	-9	-11	1	-1.4
Total 14	137	130	.513	475	307	98	23	18	2408^2	2581	1182	218	35	597	939	12.0	3.81	99	.276	.322	34	.157	-2	14	-11	24	0.3

● RAY CALDWELL

Caldwell, Raymond Benjamin "Rube" or "Sum" b: 4/26/1888, Corydon, Pa. d: 8/17/67, Salamanca, N.Y. BL/TR, 6'2", 190 lbs. Deb: 9/9/10 ♦

YEAR TM/L	W	L	PCT	G	GS	CG	SH	SV	IP	H	R	HR	HB	BB	SO	RAT	ERA	ERA+	OAV	OOB	BH	AVG	PB	PR	PR+	PD	TPI
1910 NY-A	1	0	1.000	6	2	1	0	1	19^1	19	8	1	0	9	17	13.0	3.72	71	.260	.341	0	.000	-1	-3	-2	-0	-0.2
1911 NY-A	14	14	.500	41	26	19	1	1	255	240	115	7	13	79	145	11.7	3.35	107	.260	.327	40	.272	3	-0	6	-3	0.7
1912 NY-A	8	16	.333	30	26	13	3	0	183^1	196	111	1	6	67	95	13.2	4.47	80	.277	.344	18	.237	1	-23	-16	1	-1.6
1913 NY-A	9	8	.529	27	16	15	2	1	164^1	131	59	5	9	60	87	11.0	2.41	124	.219	.299	28	.289	3	10	10	-1	1.7
1914 NY-A	18	9	.667	31	23	22	5	0	213	153	53	5	4	51	92	8.8	1.94	142	.205	.260	22	.195	1	19	19	-2	2.5

YEAR	TM/L	W	L	PCT	G	GS	CG	SH	SV	IP	H	R	HR	HB	BB	SO	RAT	ERA	ERA+	OAV	OOB	BH	AVG	PB	PR	PR+	PD	TPI
1915	NY-A	19	16	.543	36	35	31	3	0	305	266	115	6	5	107	130	11.2	2.89	101	.244	.315	35	.243	8	2	1	-3	0.7
1916	NY-A	5	12	.294	21	18	14	1	0	165^{2}	142	62	6	8	65	76	11.7	2.99	97	.243	.327	19	.204	-0	-3	-2	-1	-0.3
1917	NY-A	13	16	.448	32	29	21	1	0	236	199	92	8	6	76	102	10.7	2.86	94	.234	.302	32	.258	6	-5	-5	-1	0.3
1918	NY-A	9	8	.529	24	21	14	1	1	176^{2}	173	69	2	1	62	59	12.0	3.06	93	.261	.325	44	.291	4	-5	-4	-3	-0.1
1919	Bos-A	7	4	.636	18	12	6	1	0	86^{1}	92	49	1	3	31	23	13.1	3.96	76	.279	.346	13	.271	1	-7	-10	-2	-1.1
	Cle-A	5	1	.833	6	6	4	1	0	52^{2}	33	13	1	2	19	24	9.2	1.71	196	.181	.266	8	.348	2	9	9	-1	1.2
	Yr	12	5	.706	24	18	10	2	0	139	125	62	2	5	50	47	11.7	3.11	101	.244	.317	21	.296	4	2	1	-3	0.1
1920	*Cle-A	20	10	.667	34	33	20	1	0	237^{2}	286	135	9	4	63	80	13.4	3.86	98	.303	.350	19	.213	1	-2	-2	-3	-0.5
1921	Cle-A	6	6	.500	37	12	4	1	4	147	159	91	7	2	49	76	12.9	4.90	87	.275	.333	11	.208	0	-10	-10	-0	-0.8
Total	12	134	120	.528	343	259	184	21	8	2242	2089	972	59	63	738	1006	11.6	3.22	99	.253	.319	289	.248	31	-20	-4	-19	2.5

● JEFF CALHOUN Calhoun, Jeffrey Wilton b: 4/11/58, LaGrange, Ga. BL/TL, 6'2", 190 lbs. Deb: 9/2/84

YEAR	TM/L	W	L	PCT	G	GS	CG	SH	SV	IP	H	R	HR	HB	BB	SO	RAT	ERA	ERA+	OAV	OOB	BH	AVG	PB	PR	PR+	PD	TPI
1984	Hou-N	0	1	.000	9	0	0	0	0	15^{1}	5	3	0	0	2	11	4.1	1.17	283	.100	.135	0	—	0	4	4	-0	0.2
1985	Hou-N	2	5	.286	44	0	0	0	4	63^{2}	56	21	2	0	24	47	11.3	2.54	136	.243	.315	0	.000	-0	7	7	0	0.8
1986	*Hou-N	1	0	1.000	20	0	0	0	0	26^{2}	28	16	3	0	12	14	13.5	3.71	97	.264	.339	0	—	0	0	-0	-1	-0.1
1987	Phi-N	3	1	.750	42	0	0	0	1	42^{2}	25	13	1	1	26	31	11.0	1.48	288	.168	.295	0	.000	-0	12	13	1	1.2
1988	Phi-N	0	0	—	3	0	0	0	0	2^{1}	6	4	2	0	1	1	27.0	15.43	23	.462	.500	0	—	0	-3	-3	-0	-0.2
Total	5	6	7	.462	118	0	0	0	5	150^{2}	120	57	8	1	65	104	11.1	2.51	147	.219	.303	0	.000	-0	21	20	-0	1.9

● FRED CALIGIURI Caligiuri, Frederick John b: 10/22/18, W.Hickory, Pa. BR/TR, 6', 190 lbs. Deb: 9/3/41

YEAR	TM/L	W	L	PCT	G	GS	CG	SH	SV	IP	H	R	HR	HB	BB	SO	RAT	ERA	ERA+	OAV	OOB	BH	AVG	PB	PR	PR+	PD	TPI
1941	Phi-A	2	2	.500	5	5	4	0	0	43	45	22	2	0	14	7	12.3	2.93	143	.257	.312	4	.200	1	6	6	-1	0.5
1942	Phi-A	0	3	.000	13	2	0	0	1	36^{2}	45	27	2	2	18	20	16.0	6.38	59	.300	.382	1	.083	-0	-11	-10	-0	-0.8
Total	2	2	5	.286	18	7	4	0	1	79^{2}	90	49	4	2	32	27	14.0	4.52	89	.277	.345	5	.156	1	-5	-4	-1	-0.3

● WILL CALIHAN Calihan, William T. (b: William T. Callahan) b: 1869, Oswego, N.Y. d: 12/20/17, Rochester, N.Y. 5'8", 150 lbs. Deb: 4/17/1890

YEAR	TM/L	W	L	PCT	G	GS	CG	SH	SV	IP	H	R	HR	HB	BB	SO	RAT	ERA	ERA+	OAV	OOB	BH	AVG	PB	PR	PR+	PD	TPI
1890	Roc-a	18	15	.545	37	36	31	0	0	296^{1}	276	170	4	16	125	127	12.7	3.28	109	.239	.322	23	.145	-3	19	10	3	0.8
1891	Phi-a	6	6	.500	13	11	11	0	0	112	151	103	7	12	47	28	16.9	6.43	59	.312	.387	11	.196	-1	-34	-32	2	-2.4
Total	2	24	21	.533	50	47	42	0	0	408^{1}	427	273	11	28	172	155	13.8	4.14	88	.261	.341	34	.158	-4	-14	-25	4	-1.6

● BEN CALLAHAN Callahan, Benjamin Franklin b: 5/19/57, Mt.Airy, N.C. BR/TR, 6'7", 230 lbs. Deb: 6/22/83

YEAR	TM/L	W	L	PCT	G	GS	CG	SH	SV	IP	H	R	HR	HB	BB	SO	RAT	ERA	ERA+	OAV	OOB	BH	AVG	PB	PR	PR+	PD	TPI
1983	Oak-A	1	2	.333	4	2	0	0	0	9^{1}	18	16	0	0	5	2	22.2	12.54	31	.400	.460	0	—	0	-9	-9	0	-1.5

● NIXEY CALLAHAN Callahan, James Joseph b: 3/18/1874, Fitchburg, Mass. d: 10/4/34, Boston, Mass. BR/TR, 5'10.5", 180 lbs. Deb: 5/12/1894 M♦

YEAR	TM/L	W	L	PCT	G	GS	CG	SH	SV	IP	H	R	HR	HB	BB	SO	RAT	ERA	ERA+	OAV	OOB	BH	AVG	PB	PR	PR+	PD	TPI
1894	Phi-N	1	2	.333	9	2	1	0	2	33^{2}	64	52	3	5	17	9	23.0	9.89	52	.398	.470	5	.238	-1	-17	-19	1	-1.3
1897	Chi-N	12	9	.571	23	22	21	1	0	189^{2}	221	111	6	8	55	52	13.5	4.03	111	.289	.343	105	.292	3	6	9	1	1.1
1898	Chi-N	20	10	.667	31	31	30	2	0	274^{1}	267	137	2	10	71	73	11.4	2.46	146	.253	.307	43	.262	4	35	34	1	3.9
1899	Chi-N	21	12	.636	35	34	33	3	0	294^{1}	327	155	5	24	76	77	13.1	3.06	122	.281	.338	39	.260	4	26	23	5	3.1
1900	Chi-N	13	16	.448	32	32	32	2	0	285^{1}	347	195	5	22	74	77	14.0	3.82	94	.299	.353	27	.235	2	-4	-7	6	0.2
1901	Chi-A	15	8	.652	27	22	20	1	0	215^{1}	195	94	4	9	50	70	10.6	2.42	144	.239	.290	39	.331	8	30	27	6	4.1
1902	Chi-A	16	14	.533	35	31	29	2	0	282^{1}	287	150	8	11	89	75	12.3	3.60	94	.264	.326	51	.234	3	-1	-7	6	0.2
1903	Chi-A	1	2	.333	3	3	3	0	0	28	40	24	0	1	5	12	14.8	4.50	62	.333	.365	128	.292	1	-5	-6	1	-0.3
Total	8	99	73	.576	195	177	169	11	2	1603	1748	918	33	90	437	445	12.8	3.39	109	.276	.332	901	.273	25	70	55	26	11.0

● JOHN CALLAHAN Callahan, John W. b: Moberly, Mo. Deb: 9/3/1898

YEAR	TM/L	W	L	PCT	G	GS	CG	SH	SV	IP	H	R	HR	HB	BB	SO	RAT	ERA	ERA+	OAV	OOB	BH	AVG	PB	PR	PR+	PD	TPI
1898	StL-N	0	2	.000	2	2	1	0	0	8^{1}	18	20	2	2	7	2	29.2	16.20	23	.429	.529	0	.000	-1	-12	-11	0	-1.5

● JOE CALLAHAN Callahan, Joseph Thomas b: 10/8/16, E.Boston, Mass. d: 5/24/49, S.Boston, Mass. BR/TR, 6'2", 170 lbs. Deb: 9/13/39

YEAR	TM/L	W	L	PCT	G	GS	CG	SH	SV	IP	H	R	HR	HB	BB	SO	RAT	ERA	ERA+	OAV	OOB	BH	AVG	PB	PR	PR+	PD	TPI
1939	Bos-N	1	0	1.000	4	1	1	0	0	17^{1}	17	6	0	1	3	8	10.9	3.12	119	.250	.292	0	.000	-0	2	1	0	0.1
1940	Bos-N	0	2	.000	6	2	0	0	0	15	20	17	1	0	13	3	19.8	10.20	36	.351	.471	0	.000	-1	-11	-11	1	-1.2
Total	2	1	2	.333	10	3	1	0	0	32^{1}	37	23	1	1	16	11	15.0	6.40	58	.296	.380	0	.000	-1	-9	-10	1	-1.1

● RAY CALLAHAN Callahan, Raymond James "Pat" b: 8/29/1891, Ashland, Wis. d: 1/23/73, Olympia, Wash. BL/TL, 5'10.5", 170 lbs. Deb: 9/12/15

YEAR	TM/L	W	L	PCT	G	GS	CG	SH	SV	IP	H	R	HR	HB	BB	SO	RAT	ERA	ERA+	OAV	OOB	BH	AVG	PB	PR	PR+	PD	TPI
1915	Cin-N	0	0	—	3	0	0	0	0	6^{1}	12	7	1	0	1	4	18.5	8.53	34	.364	.382	1	.333	0	-4	-4	-0	-0.2

● MICKEY CALLAWAY Callaway, Michael Christopher b: 5/13/75, Memphis, Tenn. BR/TR, 6'2", 190 lbs. Deb: 6/12/99

YEAR	TM/L	W	L	PCT	G	GS	CG	SH	SV	IP	H	R	HR	HB	BB	SO	RAT	ERA	ERA+	OAV	OOB	BH	AVG	PB	PR	PR+	PD	TPI
1999	TB-A	1	2	.333	5	4	0	0	0	19^{1}	30	20	2	0	14	11	20.5	7.45	67	.357	.449	2	.667	1	-6	-5	0	-0.5

● DICK CALMUS Calmus, Richard Lee b: 1/7/44, Los Angeles, Cal. BR/TR, 6'4", 187 lbs. Deb: 4/22/63

YEAR	TM/L	W	L	PCT	G	GS	CG	SH	SV	IP	H	R	HR	HB	BB	SO	RAT	ERA	ERA+	OAV	OOB	BH	AVG	PB	PR	PR+	PD	TPI
1963	LA-N	3	1	.750	21	1	0	0	0	44	32	14	3	0	16	25	9.8	2.66	114	.204	.277	0	.000	-1	3	2	-1	0.0
1967	Chi-N	0	0	—	1	1	0	0	0	4^{1}	5	4	2	0	0	1	10.4	8.31	43	.278	.278	1	.500	0	-2	-2	0	-0.1
Total	2	3	1	.750	22	2	0	0	0	48^{1}	37	18	5	0	16	26	9.9	3.17	97	.211	.277	1	.125	-0	1	-1	-1	-0.1

● MARK CALVERT Calvert, Mark b: 9/29/56, Tulsa, Okla. BR/TR, 6'1", 195 lbs. Deb: 4/17/83

YEAR	TM/L	W	L	PCT	G	GS	CG	SH	SV	IP	H	R	HR	HB	BB	SO	RAT	ERA	ERA+	OAV	OOB	BH	AVG	PB	PR	PR+	PD	TPI
1983	SF-N	1	4	.200	18	4	0	0	0	37^{1}	46	33	2	3	34	14	20.0	6.27	57	.307	.444	0	.000	-1	-11	-12	1	-1.4
1984	SF-N	2	4	.333	10	5	1	0	0	32	40	21	4	1	9	5	14.1	5.06	69	.303	.352	0	.000	-1	-5	-6	0	-1.0
Total	2	3	8	.273	28	9	1	0	0	69^{1}	86	54	6	4	43	19	17.3	5.71	62	.305	.404	0	.000	-1	-16	-17	1	-2.4

● PAUL CALVERT Calvert, Paul Leo Emile b: 10/6/17, Montreal, Que., Can. d: 2/1/99, Sherbrooke, Que., Can. BR/TR, 6', 185 lbs. Deb: 9/24/42

YEAR	TM/L	W	L	PCT	G	GS	CG	SH	SV	IP	H	R	HR	HB	BB	SO	RAT	ERA	ERA+	OAV	OOB	BH	AVG	PB	PR	PR+	PD	TPI
1942	Cle-A	0	0	—	1	0	0	0	0	2	0	0	0	0	2	2	9.0	0.00	—	.000	.286	0	—	0	1	1	-0	0.0
1943	Cle-A	0	0	—	5	0	0	0	0	8^{1}	6	4	0	1	6	2	14.0	4.32	72	.200	.351	0	.000	-0	-1	-1	0	-0.1
1944	Cle-A	1	3	.250	35	4	0	0	0	77	89	48	4	0	38	31	14.8	4.56	72	.289	.367	4	.267	1	-10	-11	2	-0.3
1945	Cle-A	0	0	—	1	0	0	0	0	1^{1}	3	2	0	0	1	1	27.0	13.50	24	.429	.500	0	—	0	-2	-2	0	-0.1
1949	Was-A	6	17	.261	34	23	5	0	1	160^{2}	175	111	11	2	86	52	14.7	5.43	78	.279	.368	7	.137	-2	-22	-21	3	-2.5
1950	Det-A	2	2	.500	32	0	0	0	4	51^{1}	71	42	7	2	25	14	17.2	6.31	74	.324	.398	0	.000	-1	-10	-9	1	-0.7
1951	Det-A	0	0	—	1	0	0	0	0	1	1	0	0	0	0	0	9.0	0.00	—	.250	.250	0	—	0	0	0	0	0.0
Total	7	9	22	.290	109	27	5	0	5	301^{2}	345	207	22	5	158	102	15.2	5.31	76	.287	.373	11	.149	-2	-43	-43	5	-3.7

● ERNIE CAMACHO Camacho, Ernest Carlos b: 2/1/55, Salinas, Cal. BR/TR, 6'1", 180 lbs. Deb: 5/22/80

YEAR	TM/L	W	L	PCT	G	GS	CG	SH	SV	IP	H	R	HR	HB	BB	SO	RAT	ERA	ERA+	OAV	OOB	BH	AVG	PB	PR	PR+	PD	TPI
1980	Oak-A	0	0	—	5	0	0	0	0	11^{2}	20	9	2	1	5	9	20.1	6.94	54	.364	.426	0	—	0	-4	-4	-0	-0.3
1981	Pit-N	0	1	.000	7	3	0	0	0	21^{2}	23	13	0	0	15	11	15.8	4.98	72	.295	.409	0	.000	-0	-4	-3	-0	-0.2
1983	Cle-A	0	1	.000	4	0	0	0	0	5^{1}	5	3	1	1	2	2	13.5	5.06	84	.250	.348	0	—	0	-1	-0	-0	-0.1
1984	Cle-A	5	9	.357	69	0	0	0	23	100	83	31	6	1	37	48	10.9	2.43	169	.229	.303	0	—	0	17	18	-0	3.2
1985	Cle-A	0	1	.000	2	0	0	0	0	3^{1}	4	3	0	0	1	2	13.5	8.10	51	.333	.385	0	—	0	-1	-1	0	-0.3
1986	Cle-A	2	4	.333	51	0	0	0	20	57^{1}	60	26	1	2	31	36	14.6	4.08	102	.269	.363	0	—	0	1	0	1	0.1
1987	Cle-A	0	1	.000	15	0	0	0	1	13^{2}	21	14	1	3	5	9	19.1	9.22	49	.350	.426	0	—	0	-7	-7	1	-0.5
1988	Hou-N	0	3	.000	13	0	0	0	1	17^{2}	25	15	1	0	12	13	18.8	7.64	44	.352	.446	0	.000	-0	-8	-9	0	-1.5
1989	SF-N	3	0	1.000	13	0	0	0	0	16^{1}	10	5	1	0	11	14	11.6	2.76	123	.175	.309	0	.000	-0	1	1	1	0.3
1990	SF-N	0	0	—	8	0	0	0	0	10	10	4	1	0	3	8	11.7	3.60	101	.256	.310	0	—	0	0	0	-0	0.0
	StL-N	0	0	—	6	0	0	0	0	5^{2}	7	6	2	0	6	7	20.6	7.94	48	.318	.464	0	—	0	-3	-3	0	-0.1
	Yr	0	0	—	14	0	0	0	0	15^{2}	17	10	3	0	9	15	14.9	5.17	72	.279	.371	0	—	0	-2	-3	-0	-0.1
Total	10	10	20	.333	193	3	0	0	45	262^{2}	268	129	16	8	128	159	13.8	4.21	94	.268	.356	0	.000	-1	-8	-7	1	0.6

● FRED CAMBRIA Cambria, Frederick Dennis b: 1/22/48, Cambria Heights, N.Y. BR/TR, 6'2", 195 lbs. Deb: 8/26/70

YEAR	TM/L	W	L	PCT	G	GS	CG	SH	SV	IP	H	R	HR	HB	BB	SO	RAT	ERA	ERA+	OAV	OOB	BH	AVG	PB	PR	PR+	PD	TPI
1970	Pit-N	1	2	.333	6	5	0	0	0	33^{1}	37	15	2	1	12	14	13.5	3.51	111	.272	.336	2	.200	1	2	2	0	0.2

● JACK CAMERON Cameron, John William "Happy Jack" b: 9/1884, Nova Scotia, Can. d: 8/17/51, Boston, Mass. Deb: 9/13/06 ♦

YEAR	TM/L	W	L	PCT	G	GS	CG	SH	SV	IP	H	R	HR	HB	BB	SO	RAT	ERA	ERA+	OAV	OOB	BH	AVG	PB	PR	PR+	PD	TPI
1906	Bos-N	0	0	—	2	1	0	0	0	6	4	0	0	0	6	2	15.0	0.00	—	.211	.400	11	.180	-0	2	2	0	0.1

● ERIC CAMMACK Cammack, Eric Wade b: 8/14/75, Nederland, Tex. BR/TR, 6'1", 175 lbs. Deb: 4/28/2000

YEAR	TM/L	W	L	PCT	G	GS	CG	SH	SV	IP	H	R	HR	HB	BB	SO	RAT	ERA	ERA+	OAV	OOB	BH	AVG	PB	PR	PR+	PD	TPI
2000	NY-N	0	0	—	8	0	0	0	0	10	7	7	1	1	10	9	16.2	6.30	70	.194	.383	1	1.000	1	-2	-2	0	0.0

● HARRY CAMNITZ Camnitz, Henry Richardson b: 10/26/1884, McKinney, Ky. d: 1/6/51, Louisville, Ky. BR/TR, 6'1", 168 lbs. Deb: 9/29/09 F

YEAR	TM/L	W	L	PCT	G	GS	CG	SH	SV	IP	H	R	HR	HB	BB	SO	RAT	ERA	ERA+	OAV	OOB	BH	AVG	PB	PR	PR+	PD	TPI
1909	Pit-N	0	0	—	1	0	0	0	0	4	6	2	0	0	1	1	15.8	4.50	60	.353	.389	0	.000	-0	-1	-1	0	-0.1

YEAR	TM/L	W	L	PCT	G	GS	CG	SH	SV	IP	H	R	HR	HB	BB	SO	RAT	ERA	ERA+	OAV	OOB	BH	AVG	PB	PR	PR+	PD	TPI
1911	StL-N	1	0	1.000	2	0	0	0	0	2	0	0	0	0	1	2	4.5	0.00	—	.000	.143	0	—	0	1	1	-0	0.1
Total	2	1	0	1.000	3	0	0	0	0	6	6	2	0	0	2	3	12.0	3.00	98	.261	.320	0	.000	-0	-0	-0	0	0.0
● **HOWIE CAMNITZ**	Camnitz, Samuel Howard "Red" b: 8/22/1881, Covington, Ky. d: 3/2/60, Louisville, Ky. BR/TR, 5'9", 169 lbs. Deb: 4/22/04 F																											
1904	Pit-N	1	4	.200	10	2	2	0	0	49	48	39	0	3	20	21	13.0	4.22	65	.259	.341	1	.063	-1	-8	-8	-1	-1.0
1906	Pit-N	1	0	1.000	2	1	1	1	0	9	6	2	0	0	5	5	11.0	2.00	134	.188	.297	0	.000	-0	1	1	-0	0.0
1907	Pit-N	13	8	.619	31	19	15	4	1	180	135	65	0	3	59	85	9.9	2.15	113	.211	.281	3	.050	-5	6	6	-0	0.1
1908	Pit-N	16	9	.640	38	26	17	3	2	236^2	182	76	6	5	69	118	9.7	1.56	148	.210	.272	6	.083	-3	21	20	-1	1.8
1909	*Pit-N	25	6	**.806**	41	30	20	6	3	283	207	75	1	7	68	133	9.0	1.62	168	.211	.267	12	.138	-0	31	33	-3	3.5
1910	Pit-N	12	13	.480	38	31	16	1	2	260	246	110	1	12	61	120	11.0	3.22	96	.256	.308	11	.125	-3	-5	-3	-2	-0.9
1911	Pit-N	20	15	.571	40	33	18	1	1	267^2	245	112	8	4	84	139	11.2	3.13	110	.248	.309	12	.143	-3	8	9	-3	0.4
1912	Pit-N	22	12	.647	41	32	22	2	2	276^2	256	104	8	13	82	121	11.4	2.83	115	.251	.315	23	.235	1	18	14	-3	1.3
1913	Pit-N	6	17	.261	36	22	5	1	2	192^1	203	106	7	8	84	64	13.8	3.74	81	.282	.363	9	.153	-1	-12	-16	1	-1.9
	Phi-N	3	3	.500	9	5	1	0	1	49	49	25	1	2	23	21	13.6	3.67	91	.268	.356	1	.063	-1	-3	-2	-1	-0.4
	Yr	9	20	.310	45	27	6	1	3	241^1	252	131	8	10	107	85	13.8	3.73	83	.279	.362	10	.133	-3	-14	-18	-0	-2.3
1914	Pit-F	14	19	.424	36	34	20	1	1	262	256	132	8	8	90	82	12.2	3.23	89	.258	.324	14	.161	-5	-10	-11	-5	-2.1
1915	Pit-F	0	0	—	4	2	0	0	0	20	19	11	1	0	11	6	13.5	4.50	60	.257	.353	0	.000	-1	-4	-4	-1	-0.4
Total	11	133	106	.556	326	237	137	20	15	2085^1	1852	857	41	65	656	915	11.1	2.75	106	.242	.307	92	.136	-24	43	40	-18	0.4
● **RICK CAMP**	Camp, Rick Lamar b: 6/10/53, Trion, Ga. BR/TR, 6', 198 lbs. Deb: 9/15/76																											
1976	Atl-N	0	1	.000	5	1	0	0	0	11^1	13	9	0	0	2	6	11.9	6.35	60	.302	.333	0	.000	-0	-4	-3	1	-0.2
1977	Atl-N	6	3	.667	54	0	0	0	10	78^2	89	47	6	1	47	51	15.7	4.00	111	.283	.377	0	.000	-1	-1	3	-0	0.3
1978	Atl-N	2	4	.333	42	4	0	0	0	74^1	99	42	5	3	32	23	16.2	3.75	108	.329	.399	0	.000	-1	-1	2	-0	0.1
1980	Atl-N	6	4	.600	77	0	0	0	22	108^1	92	26	3	4	29	33	10.4	1.91	196	.235	.294	1	.111	-0	20	21	4	3.2
1981	Atl-N	9	3	.750	48	0	0	0	17	76	68	17	5	1	12	47	9.6	1.78	202	.239	.272	0	.000	-1	14	**15**	0	2.9
1982	*Atl-N	11	13	.458	51	21	3	0	5	177^1	199	84	18	1	52	68	12.8	3.65	102	.291	.342	1	.024	-3	-1	2	1	-0.1
1983	Atl-N	10	9	.526	40	16	1	0	0	140	146	64	16	4	38	61	12.1	3.79	102	.270	.323	3	.077	-2	-2	1	0	0.0
1984	Atl-N	8	6	.571	31	21	1	0	0	148^2	134	59	11	2	63	69	12.0	3.27	118	.245	.325	5	.111	-2	5	9	0	0.7
1985	Atl-N	4	6	.400	66	2	0	0	3	127^2	130	72	8	5	61	49	13.8	3.95	98	.263	.349	3	.231	1	-5	-1	-2	-0.2
Total	9	56	49	.533	414	65	5	0	57	942^1	970	420	72	21	336	407	12.7	3.37	115	.269	.335	13	.074	-8	26	49	3	6.7
● **KID CAMP**	Camp, Winfield Scott b: 1870, Columbus, Ohio d: 3/2/1895, Omaha, Neb. TR, 6', 160 lbs. Deb: 5/3/1892 F																											
1892	Pit-N	0	1	.000	4	1	1	0	0	23	31	23	4	1	9	6	16.0	6.26	53	.310	.373	1	.091	-1	-8	-8	-1	-0.5
1894	Chi-N	0	1	.000	3	2	2	0	0	22	34	24	0	1	12	6	19.2	6.55	86	.351	.427	0	.000	-3	-3	-2	0	-0.2
Total	2	0	2	.000	7	3	3	0	0	45	65	47	4	2	21	12	17.6	6.40	69	.330	.400	1	.045	-4	-11	-10	-1	-0.7
● **BERT CAMPANERIS**	Campaneris, Dagoberto (Blanco) "Campy" (b: Dagoberto Campaneria (Blanco)) b: 3/9/42, Pueblo Nuevo, Cuba BR/TR, 5'10", 160 lbs. Deb: 7/23/64 ♦																											
1965	KC-A	0	0	—	1	0	0	0	0	1	1	1	0	0	2	1	27.0	9.00	39	.333	.600	156	.270	0	-1	-1	0	0.0
● **ARCHIE CAMPBELL**	Campbell, Archibald Stewart "Iron Man" b: 10/20/03, Maplewood, N.J. d: 12/22/89, Sparks, Nevada BR/TR, 6', 180 lbs. Deb: 4/21/28																											
1928	NY-A	0	1	.000	13	1	0	0	2	24	30	22	0	0	11	9	15.4	5.25	72	.288	.357	1	.250	0	-3	-4	-1	-0.3
1929	Was-A	0	1	.000	4	0	0	0	0	4	10	7	1	0	5	1	33.8	15.75	27	.500	.600	0	—	0	-5	-5	0	-0.8
1930	Cin-N	2	4	.333	23	3	1	0	4	58	71	38	2	1	31	19	16.0	5.43	89	.311	.396	4	.267	0	-3	-4	2	-0.2
Total	3	2	6	.250	40	4	1	0	6	86	111	67	3	1	47	29	16.6	5.86	77	.315	.398	5	.263	0	-11	-14	2	-1.3
● **DAVE CAMPBELL**	Campbell, David Alan b: 9/3/51, Princeton, Ind. BR/TR, 6'3", 210 lbs. Deb: 5/6/77																											
1977	Atl-N	0	6	.000	65	0	0	0	13	88^2	78	32	7	3	33	42	11.6	3.05	146	.239	.315	1	.083	-1	9	12	-2	0.9
1978	Atl-N	4	4	.500	53	0	0	0	1	69^1	67	39	10	5	49	45	15.7	4.80	84	.258	.385	0	—	0	-9	-5	0	-0.6
Total	2	4	10	.286	118	0	0	0	14	158	145	71	17	8	82	87	13.4	3.82	112	.247	.348	1	.083	-1	-1	7	-2	0.3
● **HUGH CAMPBELL**	Campbell, Hugh F. b: 1846, Ireland d: 3/1/1881, Elizabeth, N.J. Deb: 4/28/1873 F																											
1873	Res-n	2	16	.111	19	18	18	0	0	165	250	213	6		7	5	14.0	2.84	118	.296	.302	13	.149	-5	8	9		0.5
● **JIM CAMPBELL**	Campbell, James Marcus b: 5/19/66, Santa Maria, Cal. BL/TL, 5'11", 175 lbs. Deb: 8/21/90																											
1990	KC-A	1	0	1.000	2	2	0	0	0	9^2	15	9	1	0	1	2	14.9	8.38	46	.349	.364	0	—	0	-5	-5	-0	-0.4
● **JOHN CAMPBELL**	Campbell, John Millard b: 9/13/07, Washington, D.C. d: 4/24/95, Daytona Beach, Fla. BR/TR, 6'1.5", 184 lbs. Deb: 7/23/33																											
1933	Was-A	0	0	—	1	0	0	0	0	1	1	1	0	0	1	0	18.0	0.00	—	.200	.333	0	—	0	0	0	-0	0.0
● **KEVIN CAMPBELL**	Campbell, Kevin Wade b: 12/6/64, Marianna, Ark. BR/TR, 6'2", 225 lbs. Deb: 7/19/91																											
1991	Oak-A	1	0	1.000	14	0	0	0	0	23	13	7	4	1	14	16	11.0	2.74	140	.167	.301	0	—	0	3	3	0	0.1
1992	Oak-A	2	3	.400	32	5	0	0	1	65	66	39	4	0	45	38	15.4	5.12	73	.267	.380	0	—	0	-8	-10	-1	-0.8
1993	Oak-A	0	0	—	11	0	0	0	0	16	20	13	1	1	11	9	18.0	7.31	56	.313	.421	0	—	0	-5	-6	-0	-0.3
1994	Min-A	1	0	1.000	14	0	0	0	0	24^2	20	8	2	1	5	15	9.5	2.92	167	.233	.283	0	—	0	5	5	1	0.3
1995	Min-A	0	0	—	6	0	0	0	0	9^2	8	5	0	0	5	5	12.1	4.66	103	.235	.333	0	—	0	0	0	-0	0.0
Total	5	4	3	.571	77	5	0	0	1	138^1	127	72	11	3	80	83	13.7	4.55	89	.250	.355	0	—	0	-5	-8	-1	-0.7
● **MIKE CAMPBELL**	Campbell, Michael Thomas b: 2/17/64, Seattle, Wash. BR/TR, 6'3", 210 lbs. Deb: 7/4/87																											
1987	Sea-A	1	4	.200	9	9	1	0	0	49^1	41	29	9	2	25	35	12.4	4.74	100	.224	.324	0	—	0	-1	-0	0	0.0
1988	Sea-A	6	10	.375	20	20	2	0	0	114^2	128	81	18	0	43	63	13.4	5.89	71	.280	.342	0	—	0	-24	-21	-1	-2.5
1989	Sea-A	1	2	.333	5	5	0	0	0	21	28	22	4	0	10	6	16.3	7.29	55	.301	.369	0	—	0	-8	-7	-0	-0.9
1992	Tex-A	0	1	.000	1	0	0	0	0	3^2	3	4	1	0	2	2	12.3	9.82	39	.231	.333	0	—	0	-2	-3	-0	-0.4
1994	SD-N	1	1	.500	3	2	0	0	0	8^1	13	12	5	0	5	10	19.4	12.96	32	.351	.429	1	.333	0	-8	-8	-0	-1.3
1996	Chi-N	3	1	.750	13	5	0	0	0	36^1	29	19	7	0	10	19	9.7	4.46	97	.216	.271	4	.364	2	-1	-0	-1	0.0
Total	6	12	19	.387	51	41	3	0	0	233^1	242	167	44	2	95	135	13.1	5.86	73	.264	.334	5	.357	2	-45	-39	-2	-5.1
● **BILLY CAMPBELL**	Campbell, William James b: 11/5/1873, Pittsburgh, Pa. d: 10/6/57, Cincinnati, Ohio BL/TL, 5'10", 165 lbs. Deb: 4/17/05																											
1905	StL-N	1	1	.500	2	2	2	0	0	17	27	17	0	0	7	2	18.0	7.41	40	.365	.420	1	.143	-0	-8	-8	1	-0.7
1907	Cin-N	3	0	1.000	3	3	3	0	0	21	19	5	0	0	3	4	9.4	2.14	121	.244	.272	2	.250	0	1	1	1	0.2
1908	Cin-N	12	13	.480	35	24	19	2	2	221^1	203	99	3	10	44	73	10.5	2.60	89	.252	.299	6	.083	-3	-6	-7	4	-0.8
1909	Cin-N	7	11	.389	30	15	7	0	2	148^1	162	65	0	9	39	37	12.7	2.67	97	.288	.344	6	.140	-1	-1	-1	2	0.0
Total	4	23	25	.479	70	44	31	2	4	407^2	411	186	3	19	93	116	11.5	2.80	88	.270	.320	15	.115	-4	-15	-16	8	-1.3
● **BILL CAMPBELL**	Campbell, William Richard b: 8/9/48, Highland Park, Mich. BR/TR, 6'3", 190 lbs. Deb: 7/14/73 C																											
1973	Min-A	3	3	.500	28	2	0	0	7	51^2	44	20	5	1	20	42	11.3	3.14	126	.226	.301	0	—	0	4	5	0	0.6
1974	Min-A	8	7	.533	63	0	0	0	19	120^1	109	37	4	2	55	89	12.4	2.62	143	.242	.327	0	—	0	13	14	1	2.3
1975	Min-A	4	6	.400	47	7	2	1	5	121	119	58	13	2	46	76	12.4	3.79	101	.262	.333	0	.000	-0	-0	1	1	0.1
1976	Min-A	17	5	**.773**	**78**	0	0	0	20	167^2	145	63	9	5	62	115	11.4	3.01	119	.234	.309	0	—	0	10	10	-0	1.6
1977	Bos-A★	13	9	.591	69	0	0	0	**31**	140	112	48	13	5	60	114	11.4	2.96	152	.224	.313	0	—	0	17	22	2	4.4
1978	Bos-A	7	5	.583	29	0	0	0	4	50^2	62	25	3	0	17	47	14.0	3.91	106	.308	.362	0	—	0	-1	1	1	0.3
1979	Bos-A	3	4	.429	41	0	0	0	9	54^2	55	28	5	1	23	25	13.0	4.28	103	.262	.338	0	—	0	-0	1	1	0.3
1980	Bos-A	4	0	1.000	23	0	0	0	0	41^1	44	26	1	0	22	17	14.4	4.79	88	.284	.373	0	—	0	-3	-2	-1	-0.3
1981	Bos-A	1	1	.500	30	0	0	0	7	48^1	45	23	5	0	20	37	12.1	3.17	122	.245	.319	0	—	0	3	4	0	0.3
1982	Chi-N	3	6	.333	62	0	0	0	8	100	89	44	6	0	40	71	11.6	3.69	101	.245	.319	1	.143	-0	-1	1	2	0.3
1983	Chi-N	6	8	.429	**82**	0	0	0	8	122^1	128	65	4	1	49	97	13.1	4.49	85	.275	.346	1	.100	-1	-12	-9	2	-0.9
1984	Phi-N	6	5	.545	57	0	0	0	1	81^1	68	43	2	0	35	52	11.4	3.43	106	.222	.302	0	.000	-0	1	2	-1	0.1
1985	*StL-N	5	3	.625	50	0	0	0	4	64^1	55	32	5	2	21	41	10.9	3.50	101	.230	.298	2	.333	1	1	0	-1	0.0
1986	Det-A	3	6	.333	34	0	0	0	3	55^2	46	26	5	1	21	37	11.0	3.88	106	.230	.306	0	—	0	2	2	-1	0.2
1987	Mon-N	0	0	—	7	0	0	0	0	10	18	12	2	0	4	4	19.8	8.10	52	.360	.407	0	.000	0	-4	-4	0	-0.2
Total	15	83	68	.550	700	9	2	1	126	1229^1	1139	550	82	20	495	864	12.1	3.54	110	.248	.324	4	.154	1	30	47	5	9.1

● CARDELL CAMPER

Camper, Cardell b: 7/6/52, Boley, Okla. BR/TR, 6'3", 208 lbs. Deb: 9/11/77

YEAR	TM/L	W	L	PCT	G	GS	CG	SH	SV	IP	H	R	HR	HB	BB	SO	RAT	ERA	ERA+	OAV	OOB	BH	AVG	PB	PR	PR+	PD	TPI
1977	Cle-A	1	0	1.000	3	1	0	0	0	9^1	7	4	0	0	4	9	10.6	3.86	103	.200	.282	0	—	0	0	0	-0	0.0

● SAL CAMPFIELD

Campfield, William Holton b: 2/19/1868, Meadville, Pa. d: 5/16/52, Meadville, Pa. BR/TR, 6'0.5", Deb: 5/15/1896

YEAR	TM/L	W	L	PCT	G	GS	CG	SH	SV	IP	H	R	HR	HB	BB	SO	RAT	ERA	ERA+	OAV	OOB	BH	AVG	PB	PR	PR+	PD	TPI
1896	NY-N	1	1	.500	6	2	2	0	0	27	31	15	1	2	6	6	13.0	4.00	105	.284	.333	2	.167	-0	1	1	-1	0.0

● SAL CAMPISI

Campisi, Salvatore John b: 8/11/42, Brooklyn, N.Y. BR/TR, 6'2", 210 lbs. Deb: 8/15/69

YEAR	TM/L	W	L	PCT	G	GS	CG	SH	SV	IP	H	R	HR	HB	BB	SO	RAT	ERA	ERA+	OAV	OOB	BH	AVG	PB	PR	PR+	PD	TPI
1969	StL-N	1	0	1.000	7	0	0	0	0	9^2	4	1	0	0	6	7	9.3	0.93	384	.121	.256	0	—	0	3	3	0	0.3
1970	StL-N	2	2	.500	37	0	0	0	4	49^1	53	19	2	3	37	26	17.0	2.92	141	.282	.408	0	.000	-0	6	6	-0	0.6
1971	Min-A	0	0	—	6	0	0	0	0	4^1	5	2	1	0	4	2	18.7	4.15	86	.294	.429	0	—	0	-0	-0	0	0.0
Total	3	3	2	.600	50	0	0	0	4	63^1	62	22	3	3	47	35	15.9	2.70	148	.261	.389	0	.000	-0	9	9	0	0.9

● HUGH CANAVAN

Canavan, Hugh Edward "Hugo" b: 5/13/1897, Worcester, Mass. d: 9/4/67, Boston, Mass. BL/TL, 5'8", 160 lbs. Deb: 4/23/18

YEAR	TM/L	W	L	PCT	G	GS	CG	SH	SV	IP	H	R	HR	HB	BB	SO	RAT	ERA	ERA+	OAV	OOB	BH	AVG	PB	PR	PR+	PD	TPI
1918	Bos-N	0	4	.000	11	3	3	0	0	46^2	70	42	0	5	15	18	17.4	6.36	42	.366	.427	2	.095	-0	-19	-20	1	-1.5

● JOHN CANDELARIA

Candelaria, John Robert "Candy Man" b: 11/6/53, New York, N.Y. BL/TL, 6'7", 232 lbs. Deb: 6/8/75

YEAR	TM/L	W	L	PCT	G	GS	CG	SH	SV	IP	H	R	HR	HB	BB	SO	RAT	ERA	ERA+	OAV	OOB	BH	AVG	PB	PR	PR+	PD	TPI
1975	*Pit-N	8	6	.571	18	18	4	1	0	120^2	95	47	8	2	36	95	9.9	2.76	129	.212	.273	6	.140	-0	12	11	-1	1.0
1976	Pit-N	16	7	.696	32	31	11	4	1	220	173	87	22	2	60	138	9.6	3.15	111	.216	.273	14	.184	3	9	8	-1	1.1
1977	Pit-N☆	20	5	**.800**	33	33	6	1	0	230^2	197	64	29	2	50	133	9.7	**2.34**	**170**	.232	.276	18	.225	4	**40**	41	-2	4.6
1978	Pit-N	12	11	.522	30	29	3	1	1	189	191	73	15	5	49	94	11.7	3.24	114	.261	.312	9	.173	3	7	10	-2	1.3
1979	*Pit-N	14	9	.609	33	30	8	0	0	207	201	83	25	3	41	101	10.7	3.22	121	.253	.292	9	.132	-1	12	15	0	1.5
1980	Pit-N	11	14	.440	35	34	7	0	1	233^1	246	114	14	3	50	97	11.5	4.01	91	.276	.317	15	.195	2	-10	-9	-1	-0.8
1981	Pit-N	2	2	.500	6	6	0	0	0	40^2	42	17	3	0	11	14	11.7	3.54	102	.271	.319	3	.231	0	-0	0	-0	0.0
1982	Pit-N	12	7	.632	31	30	1	1	1	174^2	166	62	13	4	37	133	10.7	2.94	126	.255	.299	12	.222	3	13	15	-1	1.8
1983	Pit-N	15	8	.652	33	32	2	0	0	197^2	191	73	15	2	45	157	10.8	3.23	115	.257	.302	9	.138	-0	9	10	-2	0.9
1984	Pit-N	12	11	.522	33	28	3	1	2	185^1	179	69	19	1	34	133	10.4	2.72	133	.256	.291	8	.129	1	18	18	-2	2.1
1985	Pit-N	2	4	.333	37	0	0	0	9	54^1	57	23	7	1	14	47	11.9	3.64	98	.275	.324	0	.000	-0	-0	-0	-0	-0.1
	Cal-A	7	3	.700	13	13	1	1	0	71	70	33	7	3	24	53	12.3	3.80	108	.262	.330	0	—	0	3	2	-1	0.3
1986	*Cal-A	10	2	.833	16	16	1	1	0	91^2	68	30	4	3	26	81	9.5	2.55	161	.206	.270	0	—	0	17	16	-1	2.0
1987	Cal-A	8	6	.571	20	20	0	0	0	116^2	127	70	17	1	20	74	11.4	4.71	92	.279	.311	0	—	0	-3	-5	1	-0.4
	NY-N	2	0	1.000	3	3	0	0	0	12^1	17	8	1	0	3	10	14.6	5.84	65	.333	.370	1	.200	0	-2	-3	0	-0.4
1988	NY-A	13	7	.650	25	24	6	2	1	157	150	69	18	2	23	121	10.0	3.38	117	.248	.278	0	—	0	10	10	0	1.2
1989	NY-A	3	3	.500	10	6	1	0	0	49	49	28	8	0	12	37	11.2	5.14	75	.258	.302	0	—	0	-7	-7	-0	-0.8
	Mon-N	0	2	.000	12	0	0	0	0	16^1	17	8	3	0	4	14	11.6	3.31	107	.283	.328	0	—	0	0	0	-0	0.0
1990	Min-A	7	3	.700	34	1	0	0	4	58^1	55	23	9	0	9	44	9.9	3.39	123	.244	.274	0	—	0	3	5	-1	0.7
	Tor-A	0	3	.000	13	2	0	0	1	21^1	32	13	2	2	11	19	19.0	5.48	72	.356	.437	0	—	0	-4	-4	1	-0.4
	Yr	7	6	.538	47	3	0	0	5	79^2	87	36	11	2	20	63	12.3	3.95	104	.276	.323	0	—	0	-0	1	-0	0.3
1991	LA-N	1	1	.500	59	0	0	0	2	33^2	31	16	3	0	11	38	11.2	3.74	96	.252	.313	0	—	0	-0	-1	-1	-0.1
1992	LA-N	2	5	.286	50	0	0	0	5	25^1	20	9	1	0	13	23	11.7	2.84	121	.220	.317	0	—	0	2	2	0	0.4
1993	Pit-N	0	3	.000	24	0	0	0	1	19^2	25	19	2	1	9	17	16.0	8.24	49	.313	.389	0	—	0	-9	-9	-1	-1.3
Total	19	177	122	.592	600	356	54	13	29	2525^2	2399	1038	245	37	592	1673	10.8	3.33	114	.251	.298	104	.174	15	119	128	-13	14.6

● MILO CANDINI

Candini, Mario Cain b: 8/3/17, Manteca, Cal. d: 3/17/98, Manteca, Cal. BR/TR, 6', 187 lbs. Deb: 5/1/43

YEAR	TM/L	W	L	PCT	G	GS	CG	SH	SV	IP	H	R	HR	HB	BB	SO	RAT	ERA	ERA+	OAV	OOB	BH	AVG	PB	PR	PR+	PD	TPI
1943	Was-A	11	7	.611	28	21	8	3	1	166	144	55	3	1	65	67	11.4	2.49	128	.238	.313	9	.161	-1	15	13	1	1.5
1944	Was-A	6	7	.462	28	10	4	2	1	103	110	53	3	1	49	31	14.0	4.11	79	.276	.357	10	.313	3	-8	-10	-0	-0.9
1946	Was-A	2	0	1.000	9	0	0	0	1	21^2	15	5	1	0	4	6	7.9	2.08	161	.192	.232	2	.333	1	3	3	-0	0.4
1947	Was-A	3	4	.429	38	2	0	0	1	87	96	53	5	0	35	31	13.6	5.17	72	.273	.339	3	.167	-0	-14	-14	0	-1.0
1948	Was-A	2	3	.400	35	4	1	0	3	94^1	96	56	1	1	63	23	15.3	5.15	84	.267	.378	8	.364	3	-9	-8	0	-0.2
1949	Was-A	0	0	—	3	0	0	0	1	5^2	4	3	0	0	1	1	7.9	4.76	89	.200	.238	1	1.000	0	-0	-0	-0	0.0
1950	Phi-N	1	0	1.000	18	0	0	0	0	30	32	11	2	0	15	10	14.1	2.70	150	.281	.364	1	.167	-0	5	5	1	0.3
1951	Phi-N	1	0	1.000	15	0	0	0	0	30	33	22	3	0	18	14	15.3	6.00	64	.275	.370	1	.333	1	-7	-7	0	-0.3
Total	8	26	21	.553	174	37	13	5	8	537^2	530	258	18	3	250	183	13.1	3.92	92	.259	.341	35	.243	7	-15	-20	1	-0.2

● TOM CANDIOTTI

Candiotti, Thomas Caesar b: 8/31/57, Walnut Creek, Cal. BR/TR, 6'2", 200 lbs. Deb: 8/8/83

YEAR	TM/L	W	L	PCT	G	GS	CG	SH	SV	IP	H	R	HR	HB	BB	SO	RAT	ERA	ERA+	OAV	OOB	BH	AVG	PB	PR	PR+	PD	TPI
1983	Mil-A	4	4	.500	10	8	2	1	0	55^2	62	21	4	2	16	21	12.9	3.23	116	.291	.346	0	—	0	5	3	-1	0.4
1984	Mil-A	2	2	.500	8	6	0	0	0	32^1	38	21	5	0	10	23	13.4	5.29	73	.277	.327	0	—	0	-5	-5	-1	-0.6
1986	Cle-A	16	12	.571	36	34	**17**	3	0	252^1	234	112	18	8	106	167	12.4	3.57	116	.246	.326	0	—	0	17	17	3	2.0
1987	Cle-A	7	18	.280	32	32	7	2	0	201^2	193	132	28	4	93	111	12.9	4.78	95	.250	.333	0	—	0	-7	-5	0	-0.5
1988	Cle-A	14	8	.636	31	31	11	1	0	216^2	225	86	15	6	53	137	11.8	3.28	126	.272	.321	0	—	0	17	20	2	2.1
1989	Cle-A	13	10	.565	31	31	4	0	0	206	188	80	10	4	55	124	10.8	3.10	128	.242	.295	0	—	0	18	19	4	2.5
1990	Cle-A	15	11	.577	31	29	3	1	0	202	207	92	23	6	55	128	11.9	3.65	108	.263	.316	0	—	0	6	6	3	1.1
1991	Cle-A	7	6	.538	15	15	3	0	0	108^1	88	35	6	2	28	86	9.8	2.24	185	.218	.272	0	—	0	22	23	-0	2.7
	*Tor-A	6	7	.462	19	19	3	0	0	129^2	114	47	6	4	45	81	11.3	2.98	141	.236	.306	0	—	0	16	17	0	1.7
	Yr	13	13	.500	34	34	6	0	0	238	202	82	12	6	73	167	10.6	2.65	158	.228	.291	0	—	0	38	40	-0	4.4
1992	LA-N	11	15	.423	32	30	6	2	0	203^2	177	78	13	3	63	152	10.7	3.00	115	.237	.299	6	.107	-1	11	10	1	1.3
1993	LA-N	8	10	.444	33	32	2	0	0	213^2	192	86	12	6	71	155	11.3	3.12	123	.241	.308	8	.133	-1	22	18	-0	1.3
1994	LA-N	7	7	.500	23	22	5	0	0	153	149	77	9	5	54	102	12.2	4.12	95	.259	.328	7	.140	-1	2	-3	1	-0.3
1995	LA-N	7	14	.333	30	30	1	1	0	190^1	187	93	18	9	58	141	12.0	3.50	108	.255	.318	6	.109	-1	15	7	-0	0.5
1996	*LA-N	9	11	.450	28	27	1	0	0	152^1	172	91	18	3	43	79	12.9	4.49	86	.288	.339	4	.089	-2	-5	-12	3	-1.2
1997	LA-N	10	7	.588	41	18	0	0	0	135	128	60	21	11	40	89	11.9	3.60	107	.248	.315	3	.094	-1	9	4	1	0.4
1998	Oak-A	11	16	.407	33	33	3	0	0	201	222	124	30	9	63	98	13.2	4.84	95	.281	.341	1	1.000	1	-4	-6	2	-0.4
1999	Oak-A	3	5	.375	11	11	0	0	0	56^2	67	46	11	2	23	30	14.6	6.35	73	.298	.368	0	—	0	-9	-11	-0	-1.3
	Cle-A	1	1	.500	7	2	0	0	0	14^2	19	18	3	1	7	11	16.6	11.05	46	.306	.386	0	—	0	-10	-9	1	-1.0
	Yr	4	6	.400	18	13	0	0	0	71^1	86	64	14	3	30	41	15.0	7.32	65	.300	.372	0	—	0	-19	-21	0	-2.3
Total	16	151	164	.479	451	410	68	11	0	2725	2662	1299	250	85	883	1735	12.0	3.73	108	.256	.319	35	.117	-7	121	96	19	10.7

● JOHN CANEIRA

Caneira, John Cascaes b: 10/7/52, Waterbury, Conn. BR/TR, 6'3", 180 lbs. Deb: 9/10/77

YEAR	TM/L	W	L	PCT	G	GS	CG	SH	SV	IP	H	R	HR	HB	BB	SO	RAT	ERA	ERA+	OAV	OOB	BH	AVG	PB	PR	PR+	PD	TPI
1977	Cal-A	2	2	.500	6	4	0	0	0	28^2	27	15	5	0	16	17	13.5	4.08	96	.252	.350	0	—	0	-0	-1	-1	-0.1
1978	Cal-A	0	0	—	2	2	0	0	0	7^2	8	6	2	0	3	0	12.9	7.04	51	.286	.355	0	—	0	-3	-3	-0	-0.2
Total	2	2	2	.500	8	6	0	0	0	36^1	35	21	7	0	19	17	13.4	4.71	82	.259	.351	0	—	0	-3	-4	-1	-0.3

● JOHN CANGELOSI

Cangelosi, John Anthony b: 3/10/63, Brooklyn, N.Y. BB/TL, 5'8", 160 lbs. Deb: 6/3/85 ♦

YEAR	TM/L	W	L	PCT	G	GS	CG	SH	SV	IP	H	R	HR	HB	BB	SO	RAT	ERA	ERA+	OAV	OOB	BH	AVG	PB	PR	PR+	PD	TPI
1988	Pit-N	0	0	—	1	0	0	0	0	2	1	0	0	0	0	0	4.5	0.00	—	.143	.143	30	.254	0	1	1	-0	0.0
1995	Hou-N	0	0	—	1	0	0	0	0	1	0	0	0	0	1	0	9.0	0.00	—	.000	.250	64	.318	0	0	0	0	0.0
1997	*Fla-N	0	0	—	1	0	0	0	0	1	0	0	0	0	1	0	9.0	0.00	—	.000	.250	47	.245	0	0	0	-0	0.0
Total	3	0	0	—	3	0	0	0	0	4	1	0	0	0	2	0	6.8	0.00	—	.077	.200	501	.250	1	2	2	0	0.0

● JOSE CANO

Cano, Joselito (Soriano) b: 3/7/62, Boca Del Soco, D.R. BR/TR, 6'3", 175 lbs. Deb: 8/28/89

YEAR	TM/L	W	L	PCT	G	GS	CG	SH	SV	IP	H	R	HR	HB	BB	SO	RAT	ERA	ERA+	OAV	OOB	BH	AVG	PB	PR	PR+	PD	TPI
1989	Hou-N	1	1	.500	6	3	1	0	0	23	24	13	2	0	7	8	12.1	5.09	67	.267	.320	0	.000	-1	-4	-4	-0	-0.5

● JOSE CANSECO

Canseco, Jose (Capas) b: 7/2/64, Havana, Cuba BR/TR, 6'4", 240 lbs. Deb: 9/2/85 F♦

YEAR	TM/L	W	L	PCT	G	GS	CG	SH	SV	IP	H	R	HR	HB	BB	SO	RAT	ERA	ERA+	OAV	OOB	BH	AVG	PB	PR	PR+	PD	TPI
1993	Tex-A	0	0	—	1	0	0	0	0	1	2	3	0	0	3	0	45.0	27.00	15	.500	.714	59	.255	1	-3	-3	0	-0.1

● GUY CANTRELL

Cantrell, Guy Dewey "Gunner" b: 4/9/04, Clarita, Okla. d: 1/31/61, McAlester, Okla. BR/TR, 6', 190 lbs. Deb: 8/18/25

YEAR	TM/L	W	L	PCT	G	GS	CG	SH	SV	IP	H	R	HR	HB	BB	SO	RAT	ERA	ERA+	OAV	OOB	BH	AVG	PB	PR	PR+	PD	TPI
1925	Bro-N	1	0	1.000	14	3	1	0	0	36	42	27	0	1	14	13	14.3	3.00	139	.294	.361	0	.000	-1	5	5	1	0.2
1927	Bro-N	0	0	—	6	0	0	0	0	10	10	3	0	0	6	5	14.4	2.70	147	.250	.348	1	.333	0	1	1	0	0.1
	Phi-A	0	2	.000	2	2	2	0	0	18	25	10	0	0	7	7	16.0	5.00	85	.338	.395	1	.167	-0	-2	-1	0	-0.2
1930	Det-A	1	5	.167	16	2	1	0	0	35	38	30	5	1	20	20	15.2	5.66	85	.271	.366	0	.000	-2	-4	-3	1	-0.5
Total	3	2	7	.222	38	7	4	0	0	99	115	70	5	2	47	45	14.9	4.27	103	.290	.368	2	.074	-3	1	1	2	-0.4

● BEN CANTWELL

Cantwell, Benjamin Caldwell b: 4/13/02, Milan, Tenn. d: 12/4/62, Salem, Mo. BR/TR, 6'1", 168 lbs. Deb: 8/19/27

YEAR	TM/L	W	L	PCT	G	GS	CG	SH	SV	IP	H	R	HR	HB	BB	SO	RAT	ERA	ERA+	OAV	OOB	BH	AVG	PB	PR	PR+	PD	TPI
1927	NY-N	1	1	.500	5	2	1	0	0	19^2	26	9	1	1	2	6	13.3	4.12	94	.313	.337	2	.250	0	-0	-1	-0	-0.1

YEAR	TM/L	W	L	PCT	G	GS	CG	SH	SV	IP	H	R	HR	HB	BB	SO	RAT	ERA	ERA+	OAV	OOB	BH	AVG	PB	PR	PR+	PD	TPI
1928	NY-N	1	0	1.000	7	1	0	0	1	18^1	20	10	1	1	4	0	12.3	4.42	89	.282	.329	2	.500	1	-1	-1	1	0.1
	Bos-N	3	3	.500	22	10	3	0	0	90	112	63	7	2	36	18	15.0	5.10	77	.304	.369	5	.172	-1	-11	-12	1	-0.7
	Yr	4	3	.571	29	11	3	0	1	108^1	132	73	8	3	40	18	14.5	4.98	79	.301	.363	7	.212	-0	-12	-13	2	-0.6
1929	Bos-N	4	13	.235	27	20	8	0	2	157	171	98	11	2	52	25	12.9	4.47	105	.280	.338	9	.180	0	4	4	4	0.7
1930	Bos-N	9	15	.375	31	21	10	0	2	173^1	213	99	15	1	45	43	13.4	4.88	101	.312	.355	19	.302	2	2	1	4	0.7
1931	Bos-N	7	9	.438	33	16	9	2	2	156^1	160	73	4	0	34	32	11.2	3.63	104	.262	.301	13	.228	0	4	3	3	0.6
1932	Bos-N	13	11	.542	37	9	3	1	5	146	133	56	6	5	33	33	10.5	2.96	127	.247	.296	14	.280	2	15	13	3	2.7
1933	Bos-N	20	10	**.667**	40	29	18	2	2	254^2	242	89	12	3	54	57	10.6	2.62	117	.249	.291	12	.141	-1	20	14	4	2.0
1934	Bos-N	5	11	.313	27	19	6	1	5	143^1	163	88	8	2	34	45	12.5	4.33	88	.285	.327	12	.279	1	-4	-9	2	-0.6
1935	Bos-N	4	25	.138	39	24	13	0	0	210^2	235	117	15	2	44	34	12.0	4.61	82	.282	.320	19	.284	4	-14	-21	2	-1.8
1936	Bos-N	9	9	.500	34	12	4	0	2	133^1	127	55	8	4	35	42	11.2	3.04	126	.252	.306	8	.195	-1	15	12	3	1.8
1937	NY-N	0	1	.000	1	1	0	0	0	4	6	4	1	0	1	1	15.8	9.00	43	.375	.412	0	—	0	-2	-2	0	-0.3
	Bro-N	0	0	—	13	0	0	0	0	27^1	32	17	1	0	8	12	13.2	4.61	88	.288	.336	1	.167	-0	-2	-2	2	0.1
	Yr	0	1	.000	14	1	0	0	0	31^1	38	21	2	0	9	13	13.5	5.17	78	.299	.346	1	.167	0	-4	-4	2	-0.2
Total	11	76	108	.413	316	164	75	6	21	1534	1640	778	90	23	382	348	12.0	3.91	100	.275	.321	116	.231	8	25	-2	28	5.2

● MIKE CANTWELL Cantwell, Michael Joseph b: 1/15/1896, Washington, D.C. d: 1/5/53, Oteen, N.C. BL/TL, 5'10", 155 lbs. Deb: 8/17/16 F

YEAR	TM/L	W	L	PCT	G	GS	CG	SH	SV	IP	H	R	HR	HB	BB	SO	RAT	ERA	ERA+	OAV	OOB	BH	AVG	PB	PR	PR+	PD	TPI
1916	NY-A	0	0	—	1	0	0	0	0	2	0	2	0	0	2	0	9.0	0.00	—	.000	.333	0	—	0	1	1	-0	0.0
1919	Phi-N	1	3	.250	5	3	2	0	0	27^1	36	19	2	2	9	6	15.5	5.60	58	.343	.405	2	.222	-0	-8	-7	-1	-0.9
1920	Phi-N	0	3	.000	5	1	0	0	0	23^1	25	18	1	3	15	8	16.6	3.86	89	.284	.406	1	.143	-1	-2	-1	0	-0.1
Total	3	1	6	.143	11	4	2	0	0	52^2	61	39	2	5	26	14	15.7	4.61	71	.310	.404	3	.188	-1	-9	-7	-1	-1.0

● TOM CANTWELL Cantwell, Thomas Aloysius b: 12/23/1888, Washington, D.C. d: 4/1/68, Washington, D.C. BR/TR, 6', 170 lbs. Deb: 5/19/09 F

YEAR	TM/L	W	L	PCT	G	GS	CG	SH	SV	IP	H	R	HR	HB	BB	SO	RAT	ERA	ERA+	OAV	OOB	BH	AVG	PB	PR	PR+	PD	TPI
1909	Cin-N	1	0	1.000	6	1	1	0	0	21^2	16	10	0	1	7	7	10.0	1.66	156	.205	.279	3	.600	1	2	2	-0	0.3
1910	Cin-N	0	0	—	2	0	0	0	0	1^1	2	2	0	0	3	0	33.8	13.50	22	.400	.625	0	—	0	-2	-2	-0	-0.1
Total	2	1	0	1.000	8	1	1	0	0	23	18	12	0	1	10	7	11.3	2.35	111	.217	.309	3	.600	1	1	1	-0	0.2

● MIKE CAPEL Capel, Michael Lee b: 10/13/61, Marshall, Tex. BR/TR, 6'1", 175 lbs. Deb: 5/7/88

YEAR	TM/L	W	L	PCT	G	GS	CG	SH	SV	IP	H	R	HR	HB	BB	SO	RAT	ERA	ERA+	OAV	OOB	BH	AVG	PB	PR	PR+	PD	TPI
1988	Chi-N	2	1	.667	22	0	0	0	0	29^1	34	19	5	3	13	19	15.3	4.91	74	.293	.379	0	.000	-0	-5	-4	-0	-0.4
1990	Mil-A	0	0	—	2	0	0	0	0	0^1	6	6	0	1	1	1	216.0	135.00	3	.857	.889	0	—	0	-5	-5	0	-0.2
1991	Hou-N	1	3	.250	25	0	0	0	3	32^2	33	14	3	0	15	23	13.2	3.03	116	.266	.345	0	—	0	2	2	0	0.3
Total	3	3	4	.429	49	0	0	0	3	62^1	73	39	8	4	29	43	15.3	4.62	77	.296	.379	0	.000	-0	-7	-7	-0	-0.3

● DOUG CAPILLA Capilla, Douglas Edmund b: 1/7/52, Honolulu, Hawaii BL/TL, 5'8", 175 lbs. Deb: 9/12/76

YEAR	TM/L	W	L	PCT	G	GS	CG	SH	SV	IP	H	R	HR	HB	BB	SO	RAT	ERA	ERA+	OAV	OOB	BH	AVG	PB	PR	PR+	PD	TPI
1976	StL-N	1	0	1.000	7	0	0	0	0	8^1	8	5	0	0	4	5	13.0	5.40	66	.242	.324	0	—	0	-2	-2	0	-0.2
1977	StL-N	0	0	—	2	0	0	0	0	2^1	2	4	0	0	2	1	15.4	15.43	25	.222	.364	0	—	0	-3	-3	0	-0.1
	Cin-N	7	8	.467	22	16	1	0	0	106^1	94	53	10	2	59	74	13.1	4.23	93	.237	.338	2	.059	-3	-4	-3	-1	-0.8
	Yr	7	8	.467	24	16	1	0	0	108^2	96	57	10	2	61	75	13.2	4.47	88	.236	.339	2	.059	-3	-7	-6	-1	-0.9
1978	Cin-N	0	1	.000	6	3	0	0	0	11	14	12	1	0	11	9	20.5	9.82	36	.318	.455	0	.000	-0	-8	-8	-0	-0.7
1979	Cin-N	1	0	1.000	5	0	0	0	0	6^1	7	6	1	1	5	0	18.5	8.53	44	.269	.406	1	1.000	0	-3	-3	0	-0.4
	Chi-N	0	1	.000	13	1	0	0	0	17^1	14	6	1	0	7	10	10.9	2.60	159	.206	.280	0	—	0	2	3	0	0.2
	Yr	1	1	.500	18	1	0	0	0	23^2	21	12	2	1	12	10	12.9	4.18	96	.223	.318	1	1.000	0	-1	-0	1	-0.2
1980	Chi-N	2	8	.200	39	11	0	0	0	89^2	82	46	7	3	51	51	13.7	4.12	95	.253	.360	4	.190	0	-5	-2	1	-0.1
1981	Chi-N	1	0	1.000	42	0	0	0	0	51	52	20	1	2	34	28	15.5	3.18	116	.284	.402	0	.000	-0	2	3	0	0.1
Total	6	12	18	.400	136	31	1	0	0	292^1	273	152	21	8	173	178	14.0	4.34	89	.252	.359	7	.115	-3	-21	-14	0	-2.0

● GEORGE CAPPUZZELLO Cappuzzello, George Angelo b: 1/15/54, Youngstown, Ohio BR/TL, 6', 175 lbs. Deb: 5/31/81

YEAR	TM/L	W	L	PCT	G	GS	CG	SH	SV	IP	H	R	HR	HB	BB	SO	RAT	ERA	ERA+	OAV	OOB	BH	AVG	PB	PR	PR+	PD	TPI
1981	Det-A	1	1	.500	18	3	0	0	1	33^2	28	14	2	2	18	19	12.8	3.48	109	.222	.329	0	—	0	1	1	-0	0.1
1982	Hou-N	0	1	.000	17	0	0	0	0	19^1	16	6	2	3	7	13	12.1	2.79	119	.232	.329	0	.000	-0	2	1	0	0.1
Total	2	1	2	.333	35	3	0	0	1	53	44	20	4	5	25	32	12.6	3.23	112	.226	.329	0	.000	-0	2	2	0	0.2

● BUZZ CAPRA Capra, Lee William b: 10/1/47, Chicago, Ill. BR/TR, 5'10", 168 lbs. Deb: 9/15/71

YEAR	TM/L	W	L	PCT	G	GS	CG	SH	SV	IP	H	R	HR	HB	BB	SO	RAT	ERA	ERA+	OAV	OOB	BH	AVG	PB	PR	PR+	PD	TPI
1971	NY-N	0	1	.000	3	0	0	0	0	5^1	3	6	0	0	5	6	13.5	8.44	40	.167	.348	0	.000	-0	-3	-3	0	-0.5
1972	NY-N	3	2	.600	14	6	0	0	0	53	50	27	7	0	27	45	13.1	4.58	73	.253	.342	3	.250	1	-7	-7	0	-0.4
1973	NY-N	2	7	.222	24	0	0	0	4	42	35	18	4	2	28	35	13.9	3.86	94	.233	.361	0	.000	0	-1	-1	0	-0.2
1974	Atl-N☆	16	8	.667	39	27	11	5	1	217	163	67	13	3	84	137	10.4	**2.28**	**166**	**.208**	.287	11	.164	0	33	35	-3	3.6
1975	Atl-N	4	7	.364	12	12	5	0	0	78^1	77	41	8	1	28	35	12.2	4.25	89	.257	.322	1	.043	-2	-5	-4	1	-0.6
1976	Atl-N	0	1	.000	5	0	0	0	0	9^1	9	9	0	0	6	4	14.5	8.68	44	.265	.375	0	—	0	-5	-5	0	-0.4
1977	Atl-N	6	11	.353	45	16	0	0	0	139^1	142	88	28	4	80	100	14.6	5.36	83	.263	.362	4	.111	-2	-22	-12	-1	-1.5
Total	7	31	37	.456	142	61	16	5	5	544^1	479	256	60	10	258	362	12.4	3.87	101	.237	.326	19	.135	-2	-11	1	-0	0.0

● PAT CARAWAY Caraway, Cecil Bradford Patrick b: 9/26/05, Erath Co., Tex. d: 6/9/74, ElPaso, Tex. BL/TL, 6'4", 175 lbs. Deb: 4/19/30

YEAR	TM/L	W	L	PCT	G	GS	CG	SH	SV	IP	H	R	HR	HB	BB	SO	RAT	ERA	ERA+	OAV	OOB	BH	AVG	PB	PR	PR+	PD	TPI
1930	Chi-A	10	10	.500	38	21	9	1	1	193^1	194	96	11	3	57	83	11.8	3.86	120	.267	.323	11	.172	-1	17	16	3	1.6
1931	Chi-A	10	24	.294	51	32	11	1	2	220	268	177	17	7	101	55	15.4	6.22	68	.295	.370	14	.194	-1	-45	-49	-1	-6.2
1932	Chi-A	2	6	.250	19	9	1	0	0	64^2	80	55	6	3	37	13	16.7	6.82	63	.304	.396	3	.143	-1	-17	-19	0	-1.9
Total	3	22	40	.355	108	62	21	2	3	478	542	328	34	13	195	151	14.1	5.35	83	.286	.356	28	.178	-3	-45	-51	2	-6.5

● JOHN CARDEN Carden, John Bruton b: 5/19/21, Killeen, Tex. d: 2/8/49, Mexia, Tex. BR/TR, 6'5", 210 lbs. Deb: 5/18/46

YEAR	TM/L	W	L	PCT	G	GS	CG	SH	SV	IP	H	R	HR	HB	BB	SO	RAT	ERA	ERA+	OAV	OOB	BH	AVG	PB	PR	PR+	PD	TPI
1946	NY-N	0	0	—	1	0	0	0	0	2	4	7	0	1	4	1	40.5	22.50	15	.400	.600	0	—	0	-4	-4	-0	-0.2

● CONRAD CARDINAL Cardinal, Conrad Seth b: 3/30/42, Brooklyn, N.Y. BR/TR, 6'1", 190 lbs. Deb: 4/11/63

YEAR	TM/L	W	L	PCT	G	GS	CG	SH	SV	IP	H	R	HR	HB	BB	SO	RAT	ERA	ERA+	OAV	OOB	BH	AVG	PB	PR	PR+	PD	TPI
1963	Hou-N	0	1	.000	6	1	0	0	0	13^1	15	14	0	0	7	7	14.9	6.08	52	.283	.367	0	.000	-0	-4	-5	0	-0.3

● BEN CARDONI Cardoni, Armand Joseph "Big Ben" b: 8/21/20, Jessup, Pa. d: 4/2/69, Jessup, Pa. BR/TR, 6'3", 195 lbs. Deb: 8/22/43

YEAR	TM/L	W	L	PCT	G	GS	CG	SH	SV	IP	H	R	HR	HB	BB	SO	RAT	ERA	ERA+	OAV	OOB	BH	AVG	PB	PR	PR+	PD	TPI
1943	Bos-N	0	0	—	11	0	0	0	1	28	38	20	1	1	14	5	17.0	6.43	53	.336	.414	0	.000	-1	-9	-9	0	-0.6
1944	Bos-N	0	6	.000	22	5	1	0	0	75^2	83	40	5	1	37	24	14.4	3.93	97	.284	.367	4	.235	-0	-3	-1	-1	-0.1
1945	Bos-N	0	0	—	3	0	0	0	0	4	6	5	0	1	3	5	22.5	9.00	43	.300	.417	0	—	0	-2	-2	-0	-0.1
Total	3	0	6	.000	36	5	1	0	1	107^2	127	65	6	3	54	34	15.4	4.76	78	.299	.382	4	.167	-1	-14	-12	-1	-0.8

● DON CARDWELL Cardwell, Donald Eugene b: 12/7/35, Winston-Salem, N.C. BR/TR, 6'4", 210 lbs. Deb: 4/21/57

YEAR	TM/L	W	L	PCT	G	GS	CG	SH	SV	IP	H	R	HR	HB	BB	SO	RAT	ERA	ERA+	OAV	OOB	BH	AVG	PB	PR	PR+	PD	TPI
1957	Phi-N	4	8	.333	30	19	5	1	1	128^1	122	71	17	4	42	92	11.8	4.91	78	.251	.316	7	.200	1	-15	-16	-0	-1.2
1958	Phi-N	3	6	.333	16	14	3	0	0	107^2	99	55	16	2	37	77	11.5	4.51	88	.241	.307	8	.211	1	-7	-7	0	-0.4
1959	Phi-N	9	10	.474	25	22	5	1	0	153	135	77	22	4	65	106	12.0	4.06	101	.238	.320	3	.055	-3	-2	1	-3	-0.5
1960	Phi-N	1	2	.333	5	4	0	0	0	28^1	28	14	4	1	11	21	12.7	4.45	87	.262	.336	2	.250	2	-2	-2	-0	0.0
	Chi-N	8	14	.364	31	26	6	1	0	177	166	101	19	5	68	129	12.2	4.37	86	.249	.323	14	.203	3	-12	-12	-2	-1.1
	Yr	9	16	.360	36	30	6	1	0	205^1	194	115	23	6	79	150	12.2	4.38	87	.251	.325	16	.208	5	-14	-13	-2	-1.1
1961	Chi-N	15	14	.517	39	38	13	3	0	259^1	243	121	22	10	88	156	11.8	3.82	110	.246	.314	10	.105	-1	6	10	2	1.1
1962	Chi-N	7	16	.304	41	29	6	1	4	195^2	205	116	27	9	60	104	12.6	4.92	84	.267	.327	9	.148	-0	-21	-16	1	-1.7
1963	Pit-N	13	15	.464	33	32	7	2	0	213^2	195	92	21	16	52	112	11.1	3.07	107	.245	.305	6	.085	-2	5	5	-1	0.4
1964	Pit-N	1	2	.333	4	4	1	1	0	19^1	15	9	1	3	7	10	11.6	2.79	126	.217	.316	1	.143	-0	2	2	0	0.3
1965	Pit-N	13	10	.565	37	34	12	2	0	240^1	214	101	21	12	59	107	10.7	3.18	110	.239	.295	12	.162	3	10	9	2	1.4
1966	Pit-N	6	6	.500	32	14	1	0	1	101^2	112	58	15	6	27	60	12.8	4.60	78	.282	.337	3	.103	-1	-11	-12	2	-1.2
1967	NY-N	5	9	.357	26	16	3	3	0	118^1	112	55	8	7	39	71	12.0	3.57	95	.249	.319	6	.158	2	-3	-2	2	0.2
1968	NY-N	7	13	.350	29	25	5	1	1	179^2	156	69	9	10	50	82	10.8	2.96	102	.233	.296	3	.049	-3	1	1	2	0.0
1969	*NY-N	8	10	.444	30	21	4	0	0	152^1	145	63	15	5	47	60	11.6	3.01	121	.252	.314	8	.170	1	10	11	2	1.6
1970	NY-N	0	2	.000	16	1	0	0	0	25	31	19	3	3	6	8	14.4	6.48	62	.316	.374	0	.000	-1	-7	-7	0	-0.5
	Atl-N	2	1	.667	16	2	1	1	0	23	31	23	5	1	13	16	17.6	9.00	48	.326	.413	2	.400	1	-13	-11	1	-1.2
	Yr	2	3	.400	32	3	1	1	0	48	62	42	8	4	19	24	15.9	7.69	54	.321	.394	2	.200	-0	-19	-18	1	-1.7
Total	14	102	138	.425	410	301	72	17	7	2122^2	2009	1044	225	98	671	1211	11.8	3.92	95	.250	.315	94	.135	2	-59	-47	10	-2.8

● TEX CARLETON Carleton, James Otto b: 8/19/06, Comanche, Tex. d: 1/11/77, Fort Worth, Tex. BB/TR, 6'1.5", 180 lbs. Deb: 4/17/32

YEAR	TM/L	W	L	PCT	G	GS	CG	SH	SV	IP	H	R	HR	HB	BB	SO	RAT	ERA	ERA+	OAV	OOB	BH	AVG	PB	PR	PR+	PD	TPI
1932	StL-N	10	13	.435	44	22	9	3	0	196^1	198	94	12	3	70	113	12.4	4.08	96	.261	.326	9	.150	-2	-4	-3	2	-0.3

YEAR	TM/L	W	L	PCT	G	GS	CG	SH	SV	IP	H	R	HR	HB	BB	SO	RAT	ERA	ERA+	OAV	OOB	BH	AVG	PB	PR	PR+	PD	TPI
1933	StL-N	17	11	.607	44	33	15	4	3	277	263	117	15	4	97	147	11.8	3.38	103	.249	.315	17	.187	1	-1	3	-1	0.3
1934	*StL-N	16	11	.593	40	31	16	0	2	240^{2}	260	126	14	7	52	103	11.9	4.26	99	.271	.314	17	.193	1	-5	-1	0	0.0
1935	*Chi-N	11	8	.579	31	22	8	0	1	171	169	82	17	3	60	84	12.2	3.89	101	.257	.322	8	.129	-3	2	1	2	0.0
1936	Chi-N	14	10	.583	35	26	12	**4**	1	197^{1}	204	85	14	6	67	88	12.6	3.65	109	.268	.332	14	.233	6	8	7	2	1.6
1937	Chi-N	16	8	.667	32	27	18	4	0	208^{1}	183	80	10	4	94	105	12.1	3.15	126	.236	.321	12	.169	1	18	19	1	2.2
1938	*Chi-N	10	9	.526	33	24	9	0	0	167^{2}	213	118	11	8	74	80	15.8	5.42	71	.307	.381	15	.231	3	-30	-29	-0	-2.7
1940	Bro-N	6	6	.500	34	17	4	1	2	149	140	68	12	3	47	88	11.5	3.81	105	.245	.305	8	.186	-0	1	3	-1	0.1
Total	8	100	76	.568	293	202	91	16	9	1607^{1}	1630	770	105	38	561	808	12.5	3.91	100	.261	.326	100	.185	6	-13	-0	6	1.2

● CISCO CARLOS Carlos, Francisco Manuel b: 9/17/40, Monrovia, Cal. BR/TR, 6'3", 205 lbs. Deb: 8/25/67

YEAR	TM/L	W	L	PCT	G	GS	CG	SH	SV	IP	H	R	HR	HB	BB	SO	RAT	ERA	ERA+	OAV	OOB	BH	AVG	PB	PR	PR+	PD	TPI
1967	Chi-A	2	0	1.000	8	7	1	1	0	41^{2}	23	5	0	1	9	27	7.1	0.86	359	.161	.216	1	.063	-1	11	11	0	0.5
1968	Chi-A	4	14	.222	29	21	0	0	0	122^{1}	121	64	13	10	37	57	12.4	3.90	78	.258	.326	2	.065	-1	-13	-12	2	-1.6
1969	Chi-A	4	3	.571	25	4	0	0	0	49^{1}	52	33	4	5	23	28	14.6	5.66	68	.274	.367	0	.000	-1	-11	-9	1	-1.2
	Was-A	1	1	.500	6	4	0	0	0	17^{2}	23	9	2	0	6	5	14.8	4.58	76	.348	.403	1	.200	1	-2	-2	0	-0.1
	Yr	5	4	.556	31	8	0	0	0	67	75	42	6	5	29	33	14.6	5.37	70	.293	.376	1	.067	-0	-13	-12	1	-1.3
1970	Was-A	0	0	—	5	0	0	0	0	6	3	1	0	0	4	2	10.5	1.50	237	.150	.292	0	—	0	1	1	0	0.1
Total	4	11	18	.379	73	36	1	1	0	237	222	112	19	16	79	119	12.0	3.72	88	.250	.322	4	.065	-3	-13	-12	3	-2.3

● DON CARLSEN Carlsen, Donald Herbert b: 10/15/26, Chicago, Ill. BR/TR, 6'1", 175 lbs. Deb: 4/28/48

YEAR	TM/L	W	L	PCT	G	GS	CG	SH	SV	IP	H	R	HR	HB	BB	SO	RAT	ERA	ERA+	OAV	OOB	BH	AVG	PB	PR	PR+	PD	TPI
1948	Chi-N	0	0	—	1	0	0	0	0	1	5	4	0	0	2	1	63.0	36.00	11	.625	.700	0	—	0	-4	-4	0	-0.2
1951	Pit-N	2	3	.400	7	6	2	0	0	43	50	22	4	1	14	20	13.6	4.19	101	.292	.349	4	.250	0	-1	0	-1	0.0
1952	Pit-N	0	1	.000	5	1	0	0	0	10	20	13	1	0	5	2	22.5	10.80	37	.417	.472	1	.333	0	-8	-7	1	-0.5
Total	3	2	4	.333	13	7	2	0	0	54	75	39	5	1	21	23	16.2	6.00	70	.330	.390	5	.263	0	-12	-10	0	-0.7

● DAN CARLSON Carlson, Daniel Steven b: 1/26/70, Portland, Ore. BR/TR, 6'1", 185 lbs. Deb: 9/13/96

YEAR	TM/L	W	L	PCT	G	GS	CG	SH	SV	IP	H	R	HR	HB	BB	SO	RAT	ERA	ERA+	OAV	OOB	BH	AVG	PB	PR	PR+	PD	TPI
1996	SF-N	1	0	1.000	5	0	0	0	0	10	13	6	2	0	2	4	13.5	2.70	152	.310	.341	0	.000	-0	2	2	-0	0.1
1997	SF-N	0	0	—	6	0	0	0	0	15^{1}	20	14	5	0	8	14	16.4	7.63	54	.317	.394	0	.000	-0	-6	-6	-0	-0.3
1998	TB-A	0	0	—	10	0	0	0	0	17^{2}	25	15	3	3	8	16	18.3	7.64	63	.347	.434	0	—	0	-6	-5	-0	-0.3
1999	Ari-N	0	0	—	2	0	0	0	0	4	5	4	0	0	0	3	11.3	9.00	51	.278	.278	0	—	0	-2	-2	-0	-0.1
Total	4	1	0	1.000	23	0	0	0	0	47	63	39	10	3	18	37	16.1	6.70	66	.323	.389	0	.000	-0	-12	-12	-1	-0.6

● HAL CARLSON Carlson, Harold Gust b: 5/17/1892, Rockford, Ill. d: 5/28/30, Chicago, Ill. BR/TR, 6', 180 lbs. Deb: 4/13/17

YEAR	TM/L	W	L	PCT	G	GS	CG	SH	SV	IP	H	R	HR	HB	BB	SO	RAT	ERA	ERA+	OAV	OOB	BH	AVG	PB	PR	PR+	PD	TPI
1917	Pit-N	7	11	.389	34	17	9	1	1	161^{1}	140	64	0	4	49	68	10.8	2.90	98	.241	.304	6	.122	-2	-3	-1	2	-0.2
1918	Pit-N	0	1	.000	3	2	0	0	0	12	12	5	1	0	5	5	12.8	3.75	77	.286	.362	1	.200	-0	-1	-1	-0	-0.1
1919	Pit-N	8	10	.444	22	14	7	1	0	141	114	41	0	2	39	49	9.9	2.23	135	.243	.303	7	.163	-1	11	12	1	1.6
1920	Pit-N	14	13	.519	39	31	16	3	3	246^{2}	262	102	4	8	63	62	12.1	3.36	96	.281	.331	23	.271	3	-6	-4	-5	-0.6
1921	Pit-N	4	8	.333	31	10	3	0	4	109^{2}	121	59	6	2	23	37	12.0	4.27	90	.290	.330	10	.294	1	-6	-5	1	-0.3
1922	Pit-N	9	12	.429	39	18	6	0	2	145^{1}	193	106	10	4	58	64	15.8	5.70	72	.323	.386	15	.268	3	-26	-26	2	-2.7
1923	Pit-N	0	0	—	4	0	0	0	0	13^{1}	19	9	2	1	2	4	14.9	4.73	85	.358	.393	0	.000	-0	-1	-1	0	-0.1
1924	Phi-N	8	17	.320	38	23	12	1	2	203^{2}	267	122	9	3	55	66	14.4	4.86	92	.329	.374	21	.276	2	-22	-8	1	-0.6
1925	Phi-N	13	14	.481	35	32	18	**4**	0	234	281	131	19	6	52	80	13.0	4.23	113	.298	.338	17	.183	-2	1	13	-1	1.0
1926	Phi-N	17	12	.586	35	34	20	3	0	267^{1}	293	116	9	2	47	55	11.5	3.23	128	.281	.313	23	.240	2	18	25	-4	2.4
1927	Phi-N	4	5	.444	11	9	4	0	1	63^{2}	80	41	7	0	18	13	13.9	5.23	79	.316	.362	6	.240	0	-9	-7	-1	-0.9
	Chi-N	12	8	.600	27	22	15	2	0	184^{1}	201	73	9	2	27	27	11.2	3.17	122	.280	.307	11	.164	-3	15	14	-0	1.1
	Yr	16	13	.552	38	31	19	2	1	248	281	114	16	2	45	40	11.9	3.70	106	.289	.322	17	.185	-3	6	6	-1	0.2
1928	Chi-N	3	2	.600	20	4	2	0	4	56^{1}	74	42	4	0	15	11	14.2	5.91	65	.329	.371	5	.263	0	-12	-13	0	-1.2
1929	*Chi-N	11	5	.688	31	13	6	2	2	111^{2}	131	71	8	1	31	35	13.1	5.16	90	.292	.340	9	.231	1	-5	-7	2	-0.6
1930	Chi-N	4	2	.667	8	6	3	0	0	51^{2}	68	31	5	1	14	14	14.5	5.05	97	.313	.358	5	.250	0	-0	-1	1	0.0
Total	14	114	120	.487	377	235	121	17	19	2002	2256	1013	93	36	498	590	12.5	3.97	99	.291	.337	159	.223	4	-49	-8	-0	-1.2

● LEON CARLSON Carlson, Leon Alton "Swede" b: 2/17/1895, Jamestown, N.Y. d: 9/15/61, Jamestown, N.Y. BR/TR, 6'3", 195 lbs. Deb: 5/31/20

YEAR	TM/L	W	L	PCT	G	GS	CG	SH	SV	IP	H	R	HR	HB	BB	SO	RAT	ERA	ERA+	OAV	OOB	BH	AVG	PB	PR	PR+	PD	TPI
1920	Was-A	0	0	—	3	0	0	0	0	12^{1}	14	7	1	0	2	3	11.7	3.65	102	.292	.320	1	.167	-0	0	0	-0	-0.1

● STEVE CARLTON Carlton, Steven Norman "Lefty" b: 12/22/44, Miami, Fla. BL/TL, 6'4", 210 lbs. Deb: 4/12/65 H

YEAR	TM/L	W	L	PCT	G	GS	CG	SH	SV	IP	H	R	HR	HB	BB	SO	RAT	ERA	ERA+	OAV	OOB	BH	AVG	PB	PR	PR+	PD	TPI
1965	StL-N	0	0	—	15	2	0	0	0	25	27	7	3	1	8	21	13.0	2.52	153	.287	.350	0	.000	-0	3	3	1	0.2
1966	StL-N	3	3	.500	9	9	2	1	0	52	56	22	2	0	18	25	12.8	3.12	115	.280	.339	4	.267	1	3	3	0	0.4
1967	*StL-N	14	9	.609	30	28	11	2	1	193	173	71	10	2	62	168	11.1	2.98	110	.238	.300	11	.153	1	8	7	0	0.9
1968	*StL-N★	13	11	.542	34	33	10	5	0	231^{2}	214	87	11	3	61	162	10.8	2.99	97	.246	.298	12	.164	2	-0	-3	-1	-0.1
1969	StL-N★	17	11	.607	31	31	12	2	0	236^{1}	185	66	15	4	93	210	10.7	2.17	165	.216	.295	17	.213	5	37	37	-1	5.0
1970	StL-N	10	19	.345	34	33	13	2	0	253^{2}	239	123	25	2	109	193	12.4	3.73	111	.251	.329	16	.200	2	9	11	-1	1.3
1971	StL-N☆	20	9	.690	37	36	18	4	0	273^{1}	275	120	23	5	98	172	12.4	3.56	101	.262	.328	17	.177	1	-3	1	-0	0.2
1972	Phi-N★	**27**	10	.730	41	41	**30**	8	0	**346**^{1}	257	84	17	1	87	**310**	9.0	**1.97**	**182**	.206	.259	23	.197	4	**57**	**60**	-2	**7.1**
1973	Phi-N	13	20	.394	40	40	**18**	3	0	**293**^{1}	293	146	29	3	113	223	12.5	3.90	98	.260	.329	16	.160	0	-7	-3	-1	-0.4
1974	Phi-N☆	16	13	.552	39	39	17	1	0	291	249	118	21	5	136	**240**	12.1	3.22	118	.234	.323	25	.245	2	13	18	-1	1.8
1975	Phi-N	15	14	.517	37	37	14	3	0	255^{1}	217	116	24	2	104	192	11.4	3.56	105	.233	.312	14	.156	-0	2	5	-1	0.4
1976	*Phi-N	20	7	**.741**	35	35	13	2	0	252^{2}	224	94	19	1	72	195	10.6	3.13	113	.237	.291	20	.217	2	10	12	-4	1.0
1977	*Phi-N☆	**23**	10	.697	36	36	17	2	0	283	229	99	25	4	89	198	10.2	2.64	152	.223	.287	26	.268	8	40	**42**	1	5.9
1978	*Phi-N	16	13	.552	34	34	12	3	0	247^{1}	228	91	30	3	63	161	10.7	2.84	126	.246	.297	25	.291	7	20	20	1	3.3
1979	Phi-N★	18	11	.621	35	35	13	4	0	251	202	112	25	5	89	213	10.6	3.62	106	.219	.292	21	.223	3	3	6	-1	0.9
1980	*Phi-N☆	**24**	9	.727	38	38	13	3	0	**304**	243	87	15	2	90	**286**	9.9	2.34	**162**	.218	.278	19	.188	-1	**43**	**47**	-1	**5.0**
1981	*Phi-N☆	13	4	.765	24	24	10	1	0	190	152	59	9	1	62	179	10.2	2.42	150	.222	.288	9	.134	-0	23	25	-1	2.1
1982	Phi-N★	**23**	11	.676	38	38	**19**	**6**	0	**295**^{2}	253	114	17	1	86	**286**	10.3	3.10	118	.232	.289	22	.218	4	17	18	-1	2.4
1983	*Phi-N	15	16	.484	37	37	8	3	0	**283**^{2}	277	117	20	3	84	**275**	11.5	3.11	115	.258	.314	19	.196	3	17	15	-1	1.8
1984	Phi-N	13	7	.650	33	33	1	0	0	229	214	104	14	0	79	163	11.5	3.58	102	.246	.309	16	.190	2	0	2	-3	0.1
1985	Phi-N	1	8	.111	16	16	0	0	0	92	84	43	6	0	53	48	13.4	3.33	111	.249	.350	5	.179	0	3	4	1	0.4
1986	Phi-N	4	8	.333	16	16	0	0	0	83	102	70	15	0	45	62	15.9	6.18	62	.297	.379	7	.206	1	-23	-21	-1	-2.6
	SF-N	1	3	.250	6	6	0	0	0	30	36	20	4	1	16	18	15.9	5.10	69	.303	.390	2	.182	1	-5	-6	1	-0.5
	Yr	5	11	.313	22	22	0	0	0	113	138	90	19	1	61	80	15.9	5.89	64	.299	.382	9	.200	2	-27	-26	-0	-3.1
	Chi-A	4	3	.571	10	10	0	0	0	63^{1}	58	30	6	0	25	40	11.8	3.69	117	.252	.325	0	—	0	3	4	-1	0.4
1987	Cle-A	5	9	.357	23	14	3	0	1	109	111	76	17	2	63	71	14.5	5.37	85	.266	.364	0	—	0	-11	-10	-0	-1.1
	Min-A	1	5	.167	9	7	0	0	0	43	54	35	7	2	23	20	16.5	6.70	69	.310	.397	0	—	0	-11	-10	0	-1.1
	Yr	6	14	.300	32	21	3	0	1	152	165	111	24	4	86	91	15.1	5.74	80	.279	.374	0	—	0	-21	-19	-0	-2.2
1988	Min-A	0	1	.000	4	1	0	0	0	9^{2}	20	19	5	0	5	5	23.3	16.76	24	.408	.463	0	—	0	-14	-13	-0	-1.1
Total	24	329	244	.574	741	709	254	55	2	5217^{1}	4672	2130	414	53	1833	4136	11.3	3.22	115	.240	.308	346	.201	49	240	275	-18	33.7

● BUDDY CARLYLE Carlyle, Earl L. b: 12/21/77, Omaha, Neb. BL/TR, 6'3", 175 lbs. Deb: 8/29/99

YEAR	TM/L	W	L	PCT	G	GS	CG	SH	SV	IP	H	R	HR	HB	BB	SO	RAT	ERA	ERA+	OAV	OOB	BH	AVG	PB	PR	PR+	PD	TPI
1999	SD-N	1	3	.250	7	7	0	0	0	37^{2}	36	28	7	2	17	29	13.1	5.97	70	.257	.346	2	.222	1	-6	-8	-1	-0.7
2000	SD-N	0	0	—	4	0	0	0	0	3	6	7	0	0	3	2	27.0	21.00	21	.400	.500	0	—	0	-5	-6	0	-0.3
Total	2	1	3	.250	11	7	0	0	0	40^{2}	42	35	7	2	20	31	14.2	7.08	59	.271	.362	2	.222	1	-11	-14	-1	-1.0

● DON CARMAN Carman, Donald Wayne b: 8/14/59, Oklahoma City, Okla BL/TL, 6'3", 195 lbs. Deb: 10/1/83

YEAR	TM/L	W	L	PCT	G	GS	CG	SH	SV	IP	H	R	HR	HB	BB	SO	RAT	ERA	ERA+	OAV	OOB	BH	AVG	PB	PR	PR+	PD	TPI
1983	Phi-N	0	0	—	1	0	0	0	1	1	0	0	0	0	0	0	0.0	0.00	—	.000	.000	0	—	0	0	0	0	0.1
1984	Phi-N	0	1	.000	11	0	0	0	0	13^{1}	14	9	2	0	6	16	13.5	5.40	67	.255	.328	0	.000	-0	-3	-3	-0	-0.2
1985	Phi-N	9	4	.692	71	0	0	0	7	86^{1}	52	25	6	2	38	87	9.6	2.08	177	.178	.277	0	.000	-0	15	15	0	2.4
1986	Phi-N	10	5	.667	50	14	2	1	1	134^{1}	113	50	11	3	52	98	11.3	3.22	120	.234	.313	0	.000	-3	8	9	2	0.8
1987	Phi-N	13	11	.542	35	35	3	2	0	211	194	110	34	5	69	125	11.4	4.22	101	.244	.308	5	.082	-3	-3	1	-3	-0.6
1988	Phi-N	10	14	.417	36	32	2	0	0	201^{1}	211	101	20	4	70	116	12.7	4.29	83	.270	.333	3	.048	-5	-19	-16	-3	-2.5
1989	Phi-N	5	15	.250	49	20	0	0	0	149^{1}	152	98	21	3	86	81	14.5	5.24	68	.260	.358	1	.029	-3	-29	-28	-1	-3.8
1990	Phi-N	6	2	.750	59	1	0	0	1	86^{2}	69	43	13	4	38	58	11.5	4.15	92	.218	.310	3	.273	1	-3	-3	0	-0.2
1991	Cin-N	0	2	.000	28	0	0	0	1	36	40	23	8	1	19	15	15.0	5.25	72	.286	.375	0	.000	-1	-6	-6	0	-0.3

YEAR	TM/L	W	L	PCT	G	GS	CG	SH	SV	IP	H	R	HR	HB	BB	SO	RAT	ERA	ERA+	OAV	OOB	BH	AVG	PB	PR	PR+	PD	TPI
1992	Tex-A	0	0	—	2	0	0	0	0	2^1	4	3	0	0	0	2	15.4	7.71	49	.364	.364	0	—	0	-1	-1	-0	-0.1
Total	10	53	54	.495	342	102	7	3	11	921^2	849	462	115	22	378	598	12.2	4.11	93	.245	.323	12	.057	-14	-42	-30	-5	-4.4
● **CHET CARMICHAEL**	Carmichael, Chester Keller b: 1/9/1888, Muncie, Ind. d: 8/22/60, Rochester, N.Y. BR/TR, 5′11.5″, 200 lbs. Deb: 9/5/09																											
1909	Cin-N	0	0	—	2	0	0	0	0	7	9	6	0	2	3	2	18.0	0.00	—	.321	.424	0	.000	-0	2	2	-0	0.0
● **RAFAEL CARMONA**	Carmona, Rafael b: 10/2/72, Rio Piedras, P.R. BL/TR, 6′2″, 185 lbs. Deb: 5/18/95																											
1995	Sea-A	2	4	.333	15	3	0	0	1	47^2	55	31	9	2	34	28	17.2	5.66	84	.293	.406	0	—	0	-5	-5	0	-0.5
1996	Sea-A	8	3	.727	53	1	0	0	1	90^1	95	47	11	3	55	62	15.2	4.28	116	.273	.377	0	—	0	7	7	-0	0.7
1997	Sea-A	0	0	—	4	0	0	0	0	5^2	3	3	1	0	2	6	7.9	3.18	142	.150	.227	0	—	0	1	1	-0	0.0
1999	Sea-A	1	0	1.000	9	0	0	0	0	11^1	18	11	3	0	9	0	21.4	7.94	60	.409	.509	0	—	0	-4	-4	-0	-0.3
Total	4	11	7	.611	81	4	0	0	2	155	171	92	24	5	100	96	16.0	4.94	98	.285	.391	0	—	0	-1	-1	-0	-0.1
● **EDDIE CARNETT**	Carnett, Edwin Elliott "Lefty" b: 10/21/16, Springfield, Mo. BL/TL, 6′, 185 lbs. Deb: 4/19/41 ♦																											
1941	Bos-N	0	0	—	2	0	0	0	0	1^1	4	3	0	0	3	2	47.3	20.25	18	.500	.636	0	—	0	-2	-3	0	-0.1
1944	Chi-A	0	0	—	2	0	0	0	0	2	3	2	1	0	0	1	13.5	9.00	38	.333	.333	126	.276	1	-1	-1	0	0.0
1945	Cle-A	0	0	—	2	0	0	0	0	2	0	0	0	0	0	1	0.0	0.00	—	.000	.000	16	.219	0	1	1	-0	0.0
Total	3	0	0	—	6	0	0	0	0	5^1	7	5	1	0	3	4	16.9	8.44	40	.304	.385	142	.268	1	-3	-3	0	-0.1
● **PAT CARNEY**	Carney, Patrick Joseph "Doc" b: 8/7/1876, Holyoke, Mass. d: 1/9/53, Worcester, Mass. BL/TL, 6′, 200 lbs. Deb: 9/20/01 ♦																											
1902	Bos-N	0	1	.000	2	1	0	0	0	5	6	5	1	1	3	3	18.0	9.00	31	.300	.417	141	.270	0	-3	-3	-0	-0.6
1903	Bos-N	4	5	.444	10	9	9	0	0	78	93	52	2	2	31	29	14.5	4.04	79	.284	.349	94	.240	2	-7	-7	-0	-0.6
1904	Bos-N	0	4	.000	4	3	1	0	0	26^1	40	27	1	1	12	5	18.1	5.81	47	.364	.431	57	.204	0	-9	-9	-0	-1.1
Total	3	4	10	.286	16	13	10	0	0	109^1	139	84	4	4	46	37	15.6	4.69	66	.303	.372	308	.247	2	-19	-20	-1	-2.3
● **CHRIS CARPENTER**	Carpenter, Christopher John b: 4/27/75, Exeter, N.H. BR/TR, 6′6″, 215 lbs. Deb: 5/12/97																											
1997	Tor-A	3	7	.300	14	13	1	1	0	81^1	108	55	7	2	37	55	16.3	5.09	90	.325	.396	0	—	0	-5	-4	-1	-0.5
1998	Tor-A	12	7	.632	33	24	1	1	0	175	177	97	18	5	61	136	12.5	4.37	107	.265	.332	0	.000	-0	6	6	-1	0.4
1999	Tor-A	9	8	.529	24	24	4	1	0	150	177	81	16	3	48	106	13.7	4.38	113	.294	.349	0	.000	0	8	9	-1	0.9
2000	Tor-A	10	12	.455	34	27	2	0	0	175^1	204	130	30	5	83	113	15.0	6.26	80	.290	.369	0	.000	-0	-26	-25	-2	-2.6
Total	4	34	34	.500	105	88	8	3	0	581^2	666	363	71	15	229	410	14.1	5.04	96	.289	.357	0	.000	-0	-17	-14	-5	-1.8
● **CRIS CARPENTER**	Carpenter, Cris Howell b: 4/5/65, St.Augustine, Fla. BR/TR, 6′1″, 185 lbs. Deb: 5/14/88																											
1988	StL-N	2	3	.400	8	8	1	0	0	47^2	56	27	3	1	9	24	12.5	4.72	74	.298	.333	2	.143	-0	-7	-7	-0	-0.7
1989	StL-N	4	4	.500	36	5	0	0	0	68	70	30	4	2	26	35	13.0	3.18	114	.262	.332	4	.444	1	2	3	-0	0.5
1990	StL-N	0	0	—	4	0	0	0	0	8	5	4	2	0	2	6	7.9	4.50	85	.167	.219	0	.000	-0	-1	-1	-0	-0.1
1991	StL-N	10	4	.714	59	0	0	0	0	66	53	31	6	0	20	47	10.0	4.23	88	.220	.280	1	.333	0	-4	-4	-0	-0.7
1992	StL-N	5	4	.556	73	0	0	0	1	88	69	29	10	4	27	46	10.2	2.97	114	.220	.291	1	.333	0	5	4	-1	0.4
1993	Fla-N	0	1	.000	29	0	0	0	0	37^1	29	15	1	2	13	26	10.6	2.89	150	.212	.289	0	—	0	5	6	1	0.3
	Tex-A	4	1	.800	27	0	0	0	1	32	35	15	4	2	12	27	13.8	4.22	99	.289	.363	0	—	0	0	-0	-0	0.0
1994	Tex-A	2	5	.286	47	0	0	0	5	59	69	35	7	0	20	39	13.6	5.03	96	.291	.346	0	—	0	-1	-1	-0	-0.2
1996	Mil-A	0	0	—	8	0	0	0	0	8^1	12	8	1	0	2	2	15.1	7.56	69	.333	.368	0	—	0	-2	-2	-0	-0.1
Total	8	27	22	.551	291	13	1	0	7	414^1	398	194	38	11	131	252	11.7	3.91	99	.254	.315	8	.267	1	-2	-1	-1	-0.6
● **LEW CARPENTER**	Carpenter, Lewis Emmett b: 8/16/13, Woodstock, Ga. d: 4/25/79, Marietta, Ga. BR/TR, 6′2″, 195 lbs. Deb: 5/1/43																											
1943	Was-A	0	0	—	4	0	0	0	0	3^1	1	0	0	1	4	1	16.2	0.00	—	.125	.462	0	—	0	1	1	-0	0.1
● **PAUL CARPENTER**	Carpenter, Paul Calvin b: 8/12/1894, Granville, Ohio d: 3/14/68, Newark, Ohio BR/TR, 5′11″, 165 lbs. Deb: 7/26/16																											
1916	Pit-N	0	0	—	5	0	0	0	0	7^2	8	3	0	0	4	5	14.1	1.17	229	.258	.343	0	.000	-0	1	1	0	0.0
● **BOB CARPENTER**	Carpenter, Robert Louis b: 12/12/17, Chicago, Ill. BR/TR, 6′3″, 195 lbs. Deb: 9/12/40																											
1940	NY-N	2	0	1.000	5	3	2	0	0	33	29	11	2	0	14	25	11.7	2.73	142	.238	.316	1	.100	-0	4	4	-0	0.2
1941	NY-N	11	6	.647	29	19	8	1	2	131^2	138	71	15	2	42	42	12.4	3.83	97	.265	.323	7	.156	-0	-3	-2	-3	-0.5
1942	NY-N	11	10	.524	28	25	12	2	0	185^2	192	73	13	1	51	53	11.8	3.15	107	.263	.312	12	.185	-1	3	4	-3	0.1
1946	NY-N	1	3	.250	12	6	1	1	0	39	37	22	7	0	18	13	12.7	4.85	71	.245	.325	1	.100	-0	-6	-6	-1	-0.7
1947	NY-N	0	0	—	2	0	0	0	0	3	5	5	0	0	3	0	24.0	12.00	34	.385	.500	0	—	0	-3	-3	0	-0.1
	Chi-N	0	1	.000	4	1	0	0	0	7^1	10	5	1	0	4	1	17.2	4.91	80	.323	.400	1	1.000	0	-1	-1	0	0.0
	Yr	0	1	.000	6	1	0	0	0	10^1	15	10	1	0	7	1	19.2	6.97	57	.341	.431	1	1.000	0	-3	-3	0	-0.1
Total	5	25	20	.556	80	54	23	4	2	399^2	411	187	38	3	132	134	12.3	3.60	98	.262	.321	22	.168	-1	-5	-3	-6	-1.0
● **FRANK CARPIN**	Carpin, Frank Dominic b: 9/14/38, Brooklyn, N.Y. BL/TL, 5′10″, 172 lbs. Deb: 5/25/65																											
1965	Pit-N	3	1	.750	39	0	0	0	4	39^2	35	16	0	3	24	27	14.1	3.18	111	.243	.363	0	.000	-0	2	1	1	0.3
1966	Hou-N	1	0	1.000	10	0	0	0	0	6	9	7	0	0	6	2	22.5	7.50	46	.346	.469	0	—	0	-3	-3	-0	-0.5
Total	2	4	1	.800	49	0	0	0	4	45^2	44	23	0	3	30	29	15.2	3.74	93	.259	.379	0	.000	-0	-1	-1	1	-0.2
● **GIOVANNI CARRARA**	Carrara, Giovanni (Jimenez) b: 3/4/68, Edo Anzoategui, Venez. BR/TR, 6′2″, 210 lbs. Deb: 7/29/95																											
1995	Tor-A	2	4	.333	12	7	1	0	0	48^2	64	46	10	1	25	27	16.6	7.21	65	.320	.398	0	—	0	-13	-14	-1	-1.4
1996	Tor-A	0	1	.000	11	0	0	0	0	15	23	19	5	0	12	10	21.0	11.40	44	.359	.461	0	—	0	-11	-11	-0	-0.6
	Cin-N	1	0	1.000	8	5	0	0	0	23	31	17	6	2	13	13	18.0	5.87	72	.323	.414	0	.000	-1	-4	-4	-0	-0.3
1997	Cin-N	0	1	.000	2	2	0	0	0	10^1	14	9	4	0	6	5	17.4	7.84	54	.333	.417	0	.000	-0	-4	-4	0	-0.3
2000	Col-N	0	1	.000	8	0	0	0	0	13^1	21	19	5	1	11	15	22.3	12.83	46	.356	.465	0	.000	-0	-12	-8	0	-0.5
Total	4	3	7	.300	41	14	1	0	0	110^1	153	110	30	4	67	70	18.3	8.24	58	.332	.421	0	.000	-1	-45	-41	-1	-3.1
● **HECTOR CARRASCO**	Carrasco, Hector (Pacheco) b: 10/22/69, San Pedro De Macoris, D.R. BR/TR, 6′2″, 175 lbs. Deb: 4/4/94																											
1994	Cin-N	5	6	.455	45	0	0	0	6	56^1	42	17	3	2	30	41	11.8	2.24	185	.210	.319	0	.000	-1	12	12	-0	2.3
1995	*Cin-N	2	7	.222	64	0	0	0	5	87^1	86	45	1	2	46	64	13.8	4.12	100	.257	.350	0	.000	-1	1	0	-1	-0.2
1996	Cin-N	4	3	.571	56	0	0	0	0	74^1	58	37	6	1	45	59	12.6	3.75	113	.214	.328	1	.200	0	4	4	0	0.3
1997	Cin-N	1	2	.333	38	0	0	0	0	51^1	51	25	3	4	25	46	14.0	3.68	116	.250	.343	0	—	0	3	3	-1	0.1
	KC-A	1	6	.143	28	0	0	0	0	34^2	29	21	4	4	16	30	12.7	5.45	87	.227	.331	0	—	0	-3	-3	0	-0.4
1998	Min-A	4	2	.667	63	0	0	0	1	61^2	75	30	4	1	31	46	15.6	4.38	109	.304	.384	0	—	0	2	3	0	0.2
1999	Min-A	2	3	.400	39	0	0	0	1	49	48	29	3	1	18	35	12.3	4.96	103	.261	.330	0	—	0	-0	1	-1	0.0
2000	Min-A	4	3	.571	61	0	0	0	1	72	75	38	6	3	33	57	13.9	4.25	124	.270	.354	0	—	0	5	8	1	0.7
	Bos-A	1	1	.500	8	1	0	0	0	6^2	15	8	2	1	5	7	28.4	9.45	54	.469	.553	0	—	0	-3	-3	-0	-0.6
	Yr	5	4	.556	69	1	0	0	1	78^2	90	46	8	4	38	64	15.1	4.69	112	.290	.375	0	—	0	2	5	0	0.1
Total	7	24	33	.421	402	1	0	0	14	493^1	479	250	32	19	249	385	13.6	4.10	111	.255	.348	1	.056	-1	20	24	-2	2.4
● **ALEX CARRASQUEL**	Carrasquel, Alejandro Eloy (Aparicio) b: 7/24/12, Caracas, Venez. d: 8/19/69, Caracas, Venez. BR/TR, 6′1″, 182 lbs. Deb: 4/23/39																											
1939	Was-A	5	9	.357	40	17	7	0	2	159^1	165	89	7	1	68	41	13.2	4.69	93	.266	.340	7	.167	1	-1	-6	0	-0.4
1940	Was-A	6	2	.750	28	0	0	0	0	48	42	26	4	0	29	19	13.3	4.88	86	.240	.348	0	.000	-1	-3	-4	0	-0.6
1941	Was-A	6	2	.750	35	5	4	0	2	96^2	103	44	7	1	49	30	14.2	3.44	117	.278	.364	2	.095	0	8	7	4	0.9
1942	Was-A	7	7	.500	35	15	7	1	4	152^1	161	74	7	1	53	40	12.7	3.43	107	.267	.327	6	.136	-0	4	4	1	0.5
1943	Was-A	11	7	.611	39	13	4	1	5	144^1	160	76	3	1	54	48	13.4	3.68	87	.279	.342	8	.186	1	-6	-8	1	-0.9
1944	Was-A	8	7	.533	43	7	3	0	2	134	143	68	8	2	50	35	13.1	3.43	95	.273	.339	7	.194	1	0	-3	1	-0.1
1945	Was-A	7	5	.583	35	7	5	2	1	122^2	105	43	5	0	40	38	10.6	2.71	114	.228	.289	3	.083	-2	9	6	-0	0.4
1949	Chi-A	0	0	—	3	0	0	0	0	3^2	8	6	1	0	4	1	29.5	14.73	28	.421	.522	0	—	0	-4	-4	0	-0.2
Total	8	50	39	.562	258	64	30	4	16	861	887	426	42	6	347	252	13.0	3.73	98	.265	.335	33	.144	0	6	-9	8	-0.4
● **AMALIO CARRENO**	Carreno, Amalio Rafael (Adrian) b: 4/11/64, Chacachacare, Ven. BR/TR, 6′, 170 lbs. Deb: 7/7/91																											
1991	Phi-N	0	0	—	3	0	0	0	0	3^1	5	6	1	2	3	2	27.0	16.20	23	.333	.500	0	.000	-0	-5	-5	-0	-0.3
● **BILL CARRICK**	Carrick, William Martin "Doughnut Bill" b: 9/5/1873, Erie, Pa. d: 3/7/32, Philadelphia, Pa. TR, Deb: 7/30/1898																											
1898	NY-N	3	1	.750	5	4	4	0	0	39^2	39	23	0	5	21	10	14.7	3.40	102	.255	.363	3	.167	-1	1	0	1	0.0
1899	NY-N	16	27	.372	44	43	**40**	3	0	361^2	485	250	4	18	122	60	15.6	4.65	81	.320	.378	18	.138	-6	-32	-37	2	-3.8

YEAR	TM/L	W	L	PCT	G	GS	CG	SH	SV	IP	H	R	HR	HB	BB	SO	RAT	ERA	ERA+	OAV	OOB	BH	AVG	PB	PR	PR+	PD	TPI
1900	NY-N	19	22	.463	**45**	41	32	1	0	341^2	415	224	7	13	92	63	13.7	3.53	102	.299	.348	20	.174	-3	6	3	-0	0.1
1901	Was-A	14	22	.389	42	37	34	0	0	324	367	198	12	20	93	70	13.3	3.75	98	.282	.339	20	.159	-5	-3	-3	0	-0.7
1902	Was-A	11	17	.393	31	30	28	0	0	257^2	344	194	10	9	72	36	14.8	4.86	76	.320	.368	20	.185	-2	-37	-32	-3	-3.2
Total	5	63	89	.414	167	155	138	4	0	1324^2	1650	889	33	65	400	239	14.4	4.14	89	.304	.359	81	.163	-16	-65	-69	-0	-7.6
● **DON CARRITHERS** Carrithers, Donald George b: 9/15/49, Lynwood, Cal. BR/TR, 6'2", 180 lbs. Deb: 8/1/70																												
1970	SF-N	2	1	.667	11	2	0	0	0	22	31	19	5	0	14	14	18.4	7.36	54	.333	.421	0	.000	-0	-8	-8	-0	-1.0
1971	*SF-N	5	3	.625	22	12	2	1	1	80^1	77	48	6	2	37	41	13.0	4.03	84	.254	.339	3	.176	0	-5	-6	-1	-0.5
1972	SF-N	4	8	.333	25	14	2	0	1	90	108	66	10	5	42	42	15.5	5.80	60	.296	.376	6	.207	1	-23	-23	0	-2.8
1973	SF-N	1	2	.333	25	3	0	0	0	58	64	40	2	4	35	36	16.0	4.81	80	.278	.383	4	.250	0	-7	-6	1	-0.1
1974	Mon-N	5	2	.714	22	3	0	0	1	60	56	22	6	3	17	31	11.4	3.00	128	.249	.310	4	.286	0	4	5	1	0.8
1975	Mon-N	5	3	.625	19	14	5	2	0	101	90	39	7	4	38	37	11.8	3.30	116	.240	.317	6	.176	0	4	6	2	0.7
1976	Mon-N	6	12	.333	34	19	2	0	0	140^1	153	84	9	7	78	71	15.3	4.43	84	.286	.384	4	.108	-1	-14	-10	1	-1.2
1977	Min-A	0	1	.000	7	0	0	0	0	14^1	16	13	2	1	6	3	14.4	6.91	58	.271	.348	0	—	0	-5	-5	0	-0.3
Total	8	28	32	.467	165	67	11	3	3	566	595	331	47	26	267	275	14.1	4.45	83	.272	.358	27	.176	0	-55	-46	5	-4.4
● **CLAY CARROLL** Carroll, Clay Palmer "Hawk" b: 5/2/41, Clanton, Ala. BR/TR, 6'1", 200 lbs. Deb: 9/2/64																												
1964	Mil-N	2	0	1.000	11	1	0	0	1	20^1	15	4	1	0	3	17	8.0	1.77	199	.200	.231	0	.000	-0	4	4	1	0.5
1965	Mil-N	0	1	.000	19	1	0	0	1	34^2	35	18	3	1	13	16	12.7	4.41	80	.269	.340	0	.000	-1	-3	-3	-0	-0.3
1966	Atl-N	8	7	.533	**73**	3	0	0	11	144^1	127	45	8	4	29	67	10.0	2.37	154	.236	.280	3	.100	-2	20	20	1	2.3
1967	Atl-N	6	12	.333	42	7	1	0	0	93	111	62	6	3	29	35	13.8	5.52	60	.304	.360	1	.063	-1	-22	-23	1	-4.1
1968	Atl-N	0	1	.000	10	0	0	0	0	22^1	26	15	1	0	6	10	12.9	4.84	62	.310	.356	0	.000	-0	-5	-5	0	-0.3
	Cin-N	7	7	.500	58	1	0	0	17	121^2	102	35	3	6	32	61	10.4	2.29	138	.230	.290	6	.250	1	9	11	1	2.1
	Yr	7	8	.467	68	1	0	0	17	144	128	50	4	6	38	71	10.8	2.69	117	.242	.301	6	.207	1	5	7	2	1.8
1969	Cin-N	12	6	.667	71	4	0	0	7	150^2	149	70	9	7	78	90	14.0	3.52	107	.262	.358	6	.207	2	1	4	3	1.0
1970	*Cin-N	9	4	.692	65	0	0	0	16	104^1	104	38	4	2	27	63	11.5	2.59	156	.259	.309	1	.071	-1	17	17	1	2.6
1971	Cin-N☆	10	4	.714	61	0	0	0	15	93^2	78	26	5	2	42	64	11.7	2.50	134	.234	.324	1	.100	-1	10	9	4	2.1
1972	*Cin-N☆	6	4	.600	**65**	0	0	0	**37**	96	89	27	5	1	32	51	11.4	2.25	143	.256	.321	2	.182	0	13	11	1	2.3
1973	*Cin-N	8	8	.500	53	5	0	0	14	92^2	111	47	5	5	34	41	14.6	3.69	92	.307	.374	3	.214	0	-0	-3	1	-0.5
1974	Cin-N	12	5	.706	57	3	0	0	6	100^2	96	27	3	0	30	46	11.3	2.15	163	.256	.311	3	.167	-0	17	16	2	2.9
1975	*Cin-N	7	5	.583	56	2	0	0	7	96^1	93	30	2	3	32	44	12.0	2.62	138	.255	.320	0	.000	-2	11	11	-1	1.2
1976	Chi-A	4	4	.500	29	0	0	0	6	77^1	67	26	1	2	24	38	10.8	2.56	139	.242	.307	0	—	0	8	9	0	1.1
1977	StL-N	4	2	.667	51	1	0	0	4	90	77	28	8	1	24	34	10.2	2.50	154	.238	.293	1	.091	-1	14	14	1	1.0
	Chi-A	1	3	.250	8	0	0	0	1	11^1	14	7	3	0	4	4	14.3	4.76	86	.311	.367	0	—	0	-1	-1	0	-0.1
1978	Pit-N	0	0	—	2	0	0	0	0	4	2	1	0	0	3	0	11.3	2.25	165	.143	.294	0	—	0	1	1	0	0.1
Total	15	96	73	.568	731	28	1	0	143	1353^1	1296	506	67	37	442	681	11.8	2.94	121	.257	.321	27	.130	-5	94	91	17	13.9
● **ED CARROLL** Carroll, Edgar Fleischer b: 7/27/07, Baltimore, Md. d: 10/13/84, Rossville, Md. BR/TR, 6'3", 185 lbs. Deb: 5/1/29																												
1929	Bos-A	1	0	1.000	24	2	0	0	0	67^1	77	46	6	4	20	13	13.5	5.61	76	.291	.349	1	.063	-2	-10	-10	0	-0.6
● **OWNIE CARROLL** Carroll, Owen Thomas b: 11/11/02, Kearny, N.J. d: 6/8/75, Orange, N.J. BR/TR, 5'10.5", 165 lbs. Deb: 6/20/25																												
1925	Det-A	2	2	.500	10	4	1	0	0	40^2	46	30	1	2	28	12	16.8	3.76	114	.293	.406	6	.375	1	3	3	-2	0.2
1927	Det-A	10	6	.625	31	15	8	0	0	172	186	99	5	6	73	41	13.9	3.98	106	.281	.358	12	.174	-2	3	4	2	0.3
1928	Det-A	16	12	.571	34	28	19	2	2	231	219	100	6	7	87	51	12.2	3.27	126	.262	.337	19	.194	-0	20	21	1	2.4
1929	Det-A	9	17	.346	34	26	12	0	1	202	249	133	10	8	86	54	15.3	4.63	93	.310	.383	17	.230	2	-9	-8	2	-0.5
1930	Det-A	0	5	.000	6	3	0	0	0	20^1	30	24	3	0	9	4	17.3	10.62	45	.333	.394	1	.143	-1	-13	-13	0	-2.0
	NY-A	0	1	.000	10	1	0	0	0	32^2	49	32	2	4	18	8	19.6	6.61	65	.374	.464	2	.200	0	-7	-9	1	-0.3
	Yr	0	6	.000	16	4	0	0	0	53	79	56	5	4	27	12	18.7	8.15	55	.357	.437	3	.176	-0	-21	-22	1	-2.3
	Cin-N	0	1	.000	3	2	1	0	0	14	17	9	3	0	3	0	12.9	4.50	107	.309	.345	1	.200	-0	1	1	0	0.0
1931	Cin-N	3	9	.250	29	12	4	0	0	107^1	135	76	6	4	51	24	15.9	5.53	67	.314	.392	7	.206	0	-20	-22	1	-2.0
1932	Cin-N	10	19	.345	32	26	15	0	1	210	245	124	7	9	44	55	12.8	4.50	86	.286	.328	16	.208	2	-14	-15	-1	-1.7
1933	Bro-N	13	15	.464	33	31	11	0	0	226^1	248	117	9	7	54	45	12.3	3.78	85	.281	.327	11	.149	-1	-11	-15	3	-1.4
1934	Bro-N	1	3	.250	26	5	0	0	1	74^1	108	64	9	1	33	17	17.2	6.42	61	.342	.406	6	.240	1	-19	-22	3	-0.7
Total	9	64	90	.416	248	153	71	2	5	1330^2	1532	808	61	48	486	311	14.0	4.43	89	.294	.359	98	.200	2	-68	-73	11	-5.7
● **DICK CARROLL** Carroll, Richard Thomas "Shadow" b: 7/21/1884, Cleveland, Ohio d: 11/22/45, Cleveland, Ohio BR/TR, 6'2", Deb: 9/25/09																												
1909	NY-A	0	0	—	2	1	0	0	0	5	7	6	1	0	1	1	14.4	3.60	70	.292	.320	1	.500	0	-1	-1	-0	0.0
● **TOM CARROLL** Carroll, Thomas Michael b: 11/5/52, Utica, N.Y. BL/TR, 6'3", 190 lbs. Deb: 7/7/74																												
1974	Cin-N	4	3	.571	16	13	0	0	0	78^1	68	44	11	0	44	37	12.9	3.68	95	.231	.331	4	.154	-1	-0	-2	-1	-0.3
1975	Cin-N	4	1	.800	12	7	0	0	0	47	52	28	1	2	26	14	15.3	4.98	72	.284	.379	0	.000	-2	-7	-7	-1	-0.9
Total	2	8	4	.667	28	20	0	0	0	125^1	120	72	12	2	70	51	13.8	4.16	85	.252	.350	4	.100	-2	-7	-9	-2	-1.2
● **KID CARSEY** Carsey, Wilfred b: 10/22/1870, New York, N.Y. d: 3/29/60, Miami, Fla. BL/TR, 5'7", 168 lbs. Deb: 4/8/1891 ♦																												
1891	Was-a	14	37	.275	54	53	46	1	0	415	513	358	17	28	161	174	15.2	4.99	75	.293	.362	28	.150	-5	-59	-58	6	-5.2
1892	Phi-N	19	16	.543	43	36	30	1	1	317^2	317	160	6	12	104	76	12.3	3.12	104	.250	.312	20	.153	-3	6	5	2	0.3
1893	Phi-N	20	15	.571	39	35	30	1	0	318^1	375	229	7	19	124	50	14.6	4.81	95	.285	.355	27	.186	-7	-5	-8	2	-1.2
1894	Phi-N	18	12	.600	37	32	26	0	0	288^1	366	241	22	18	106	43	15.3	5.52	92	.306	.371	36	.279	4	-6	-14	2	-0.6
1895	Phi-N	24	16	.600	44	40	35	0	1	342^1	460	274	14	21	118	64	15.7	4.92	97	.317	.376	41	.291	3	-5	-5	-1	-0.3
1896	Phi-N	11	11	.500	27	21	18	1	1	187^1	273	164	4	9	72	36	17.0	5.62	77	.337	.397	18	.222	1	-26	-28	1	-2.2
1897	Phi-N	2	1	.667	4	4	2	0	0	28	35	20	0	1	16	1	16.7	5.14	82	.304	.394	3	.231	-1	-3	-3	-0	-0.3
	StL-N	3	8	.273	12	11	11	0	0	99	133	81	5	4	31	14	15.3	6.00	73	.319	.372	13	.302	2	-19	-17	1	-1.1
	Yr	5	9	.357	16	15	13	0	0	127	168	101	5	5	47	15	15.6	5.81	75	.316	.377	16	.286	2	-21	-20	1	-1.4
1898	StL-N	2	12	.143	20	13	10	0	0	123^2	177	112	2	10	37	10	16.3	6.33	60	.333	.387	21	.200	-0	-37	-33	2	-2.8
1899	Cle-N	1	8	.111	10	9	8	0	0	77^2	109	66	2	2	24	11	15.6	5.68	65	.330	.379	10	.278	1	-16	-18	1	-1.4
	Was-N	1	2	.333	4	3	2	0	0	29	27	14	0	1	4	3	9.9	3.72	105	.248	.281	0	.000	-2	0	1	1	-0.1
	Yr	2	10	.167	14	12	10	0	0	106^2	136	80	2	3	28	14	14.1	5.15	73	.310	.355	10	.213	-1	-15	-17	2	-1.5
1901	Bro-N	1	0	1.000	2	0	0	0	0	7	9	9	1	1	3	4	16.7	10.29	33	.310	.394	0	.000	-0	-5	-5	-0	-0.6
Total	10	116	138	.457	296	257	218	4	3	2233^1	2794	1728	80	126	800	486	15.0	4.95	85	.300	.363	223	.214	-7	-175	-184	15	-15.5
● **AL CARSON** Carson, Albert James "Soldier" b: 8/22/1882, Chicago, Ill. d: 11/26/62, San Diego, Cal. TR, Deb: 5/6/10																												
1910	Chi-N	0	0	—	2	0	0	0	0	6^2	6	5	0	0	1	2	9.5	4.05	71	.240	.269	0	.000	0	-1	-1	0	0.0
● **ANDY CARTER** Carter, Andrew Godfrey b: 11/9/68, Philadelphia, Pa. BL/TL, 6'5", 200 lbs. Deb: 5/3/94																												
1994	Phi-N	0	2	.000	20	0	0	0	0	34^1	34	18	5	6	12	18	13.6	4.46	96	.268	.359	0	.000	-1	-1	-1	-1	-0.2
1995	Phi-N	0	0	—	4	0	0	0	0	7^1	4	5	3	1	2	6	8.6	6.14	69	.167	.259	1	1.000	0	-2	-2	-0	-0.1
Total	2	0	2	.000	24	0	0	0	0	41^2	38	23	8	7	14	24	12.7	4.75	90	.252	.343	1	.143	-0	-2	-2	-1	-0.3
● **ARNOLD CARTER** Carter, Arnold Lee "Hook" or "Lefty" b: 3/14/18, Rainelle, W.Va. d: 4/12/89, Louisville, Ky. BL/TL, 5'10", 170 lbs. Deb: 4/29/44																												
1944	Cin-N	11	7	.611	33	18	9	3	3	148^2	143	54	1	3	40	33	11.3	2.60	134	.256	.309	12	.250	5	17	15	1	2.5
1945	Cin-N	2	4	.333	13	6	2	1	0	46^2	54	21	2	2	13	4	13.3	3.09	122	.286	.338	3	.176	0	4	4	0	0.5
Total	2	13	11	.542	46	24	11	4	3	195^1	197	75	3	5	53	37	11.7	2.72	131	.264	.317	15	.231	5	20	19	1	3.0
● **NICK CARTER** Carter, Conrad Powell b: 5/19/1879, Oatlands, Va. d: 11/23/61, Grasonville, Md. BR/TR, 5'8", 140 lbs. Deb: 4/14/08																												
1908	Phi-A	2	5	.286	14	4	2	0	0	60^2	58	26	1	2	17	17	11.4	2.97	86	.270	.329	2	.100	-2	-4	-3	1	-0.4
● **JEFF CARTER** Carter, Jeffrey Allen b: 12/3/64, Tampa, Fla. BR/TR, 6'3", 195 lbs. Deb: 7/31/91																												
1991	Chi-A	0	1	.000	5	2	0	0	0	12	8	8	1	0	5	2	9.8	5.25	76	.182	.265	0	—	0	-2	-2	-0	-0.2
● **LANCE CARTER** Carter, Lance David b: 12/18/74, Bradenton, Fla. BR/TR, 6'1", 190 lbs. Deb: 9/15/99																												
1999	KC-A	0	1	.000	6	0	0	0	0	5^1	3	3	2	0	3	3	10.1	5.06	99	.167	.286	0	—	0	-0	-0	0	0.0

YEAR	TM/L	W	L	PCT	G	GS	CG	SH	SV	IP	H	R	HR	HB	BB	SO	RAT	ERA	ERA+	OAV	OOB	BH	AVG	PB	PR	PR+	PD	TPI
● LARRY CARTER	Carter, Larry Gene b: 5/22/65, Charleston, W.Va. BR/TR, 6'5", 195 lbs. Deb: 9/6/92																											
1992	SF-N	1	5	.167	6	6	0	0	0	33	34	17	6	0	18	21	14.2	4.64	71	.270	.361	2	.200	1	-4	-5	-1	-0.8
● PAUL CARTER	Carter, Paul Warren "Nick" b: 5/1/1894, Lake Park, Ga. d: 9/11/84, Lake Park, Ga. BL/TR, 6'3", 175 lbs. Deb: 9/15/14																											
1914	Cle-A	1	3	.250	5	4	1	0	0	24^2	35	15	0	0	5	9	14.6	2.92	99	.340	.370	0	.000	-1	-0	-0	-0	-0.1
1915	Cle-A	1	1	.500	11	2	2	0	0	42	44	22	1	0	18	14	13.3	3.21	95	.272	.344	3	.214	1	-1	-1	1	0.1
1916	Chi-N	2	2	.500	8	5	2	0	0	36	26	16	1	0	17	14	10.8	2.75	106	.203	.297	2	.167	-0	-1	1	1	0.2
1917	Chi-N	5	8	.385	23	13	6	0	2	113^1	115	47	2	3	19	34	10.9	3.26	89	.276	.313	6	.171	-0	-7	-4	-1	-0.7
1918	Chi-N	3	2	.600	21	4	1	0	2	73	78	29	2	1	19	13	12.1	2.71	103	.290	.339	6	.240	0	0	1	2	0.2
1919	Chi-N	5	4	.556	28	7	2	0	1	85	81	36	1	2	28	17	11.8	2.65	109	.252	.316	7	.269	1	3	2	-0	0.3
1920	Chi-N	3	6	.333	31	8	2	0	2	106	131	68	3	5	36	14	14.6	4.67	69	.324	.387	6	.171	-1	-18	-17	-2	-1.7
Total	7	20	26	.435	127	43	16	0	7	480	510	233	10	11	142	115	12.4	3.32	89	.283	.339	30	.195	-1	-24	-18	1	-1.7
● SOL CARTER	Carter, Solomon Mobley "Buck" b: 12/23/08, Picayune, Miss. BR/TR, 6', 178 lbs. Deb: 4/15/31																											
1931	Phi-A	0	0	—	2	0	0	0	0	2^1	1	5	0	0	4	1	19.3	19.29	23	.143	.455	0	—	0	-4	-4	1	-0.1
● BOB CARUTHERS	Caruthers, Robert Lee "Parisian Bob" b: 1/5/1864, Memphis, Tenn. d: 8/5/11, Peoria, Ill. BL/TR, 5'7", 138 lbs. Deb: 9/7/1884 MU♦																											
1884	StL-a	7	2	.778	13	7	7	0	0	82^2	61	34	1	3	15	58	8.6	2.61	125	.189	.232	22	.268	2	6	6	-1	0.6
1885	*StL-a	**40**	13	**.755**	53	53	53	6	0	482^1	430	196	3	19	57	190	9.4	**2.07**	**158**	.230	.260	50	.225	6	**63**	**64**	0	6.5
1886	*StL-a	30	14	.682	44	43	42	2	0	387^1	323	164	3	7	86	166	9.7	2.32	148	.217	.263	106	.334	26	48	48	-2	6.8
1887	*StL-a	29	9	**.763**	39	39	39	2	0	341	398	185	6	16	61	74	10.9	3.30	138	**.279**	.287	196	.456	20	38	44	7	6.0
1888	Bro-a	29	15	.659	44	43	42	4	0	391^2	337	176	4	10	53	140	9.2	2.39	125	.224	.255	77	.230	10	29	27	1	3.6
1889	*Bro-a	**40**	11	**.784**	56	50	46	**7**	1	445	444	215	16	13	104	118	11.3	3.13	119	.252	.298	43	.250	17	35	30	2	4.3
1890	*Bro-N	23	11	.676	37	33	30	1	0	300	292	163	9	12	87	64	11.7	3.09	111	.247	.305	63	.265	11	16	12	3	2.3
1891	Bro-N	18	14	.563	38	32	29	2	1	297	323	185	7	13	107	69	13.4	3.12	106	.267	.333	48	.281	11	7	6	1	1.7
1892	StL-N	2	10	.167	16	10	10	0	1	101^2	131	75	10	6	27	21	14.5	5.84	55	.300	.350	142	.277	6	-29	-31	0	-2.5
Total	9	218	99	.688	340	310	298	24	3	2828^2	2739	1393	59	99	597	900	10.7	2.83	123	.244	.285	761	.301	111	214	208	11	29.3
● CHUCK CARY	Cary, Charles Douglas b: 3/3/60, Whittier, Cal. BL/TL, 6'4", 210 lbs. Deb: 8/22/85																											
1985	Det-A	0	1	.000	16	0	0	0	2	23^2	16	9	2	2	8	22	9.9	3.42	119	.190	.277	0	—	0	2	2	-0	0.1
1986	Det-A	1	2	.333	22	0	0	0	0	31^2	33	18	3	0	15	21	13.6	3.41	121	.273	.353	0	—	0	3	3	-0	0.2
1987	Atl-N	1	1	.500	13	0	0	0	1	16^2	17	7	3	1	4	15	11.9	3.78	115	.266	.319	0	.000	-0	1	1	0	0.1
1988	Atl-N	0	0	—	7	0	0	0	0	8^1	8	6	1	1	4	7	14.0	6.48	57	.250	.351	0	—	0	-3	-2	-0	-0.1
1989	NY-A	4	4	.500	22	11	2	0	0	99^1	78	42	13	0	29	79	9.7	3.26	119	.209	.266	0	—	0	7	7	-2	0.3
1990	NY-A	6	12	.333	28	27	2	0	0	156^2	155	77	21	1	55	134	12.1	4.19	95	.260	.323	0	—	0	-5	-4	-1	-0.5
1991	NY-A	1	6	.143	10	9	0	0	0	53^1	61	35	6	0	32	34	15.7	5.91	70	.285	.378	0	—	0	-11	-10	-0	-1.2
1993	Chi-A	1	0	1.000	16	0	0	0	0	20^2	22	12	1	3	11	10	15.7	5.23	80	.286	.396	0	—	0	-2	-2	0	-0.1
Total	8	14	26	.350	134	47	4	0	3	410^1	390	206	50	8	158	322	12.2	4.17	96	.250	.322	0	.000	-0	-8	-7	-4	-1.2
● SCOTT CARY	Cary, Scott Russell "Red" b: 4/11/23, Kendallville, Ind. BL/TL, 5'11.5", 168 lbs. Deb: 5/1/47																											
1947	Was-A	3	1	.750	23	3	1	0	0	54^2	73	38	5	1	20	25	15.5	5.93	63	.312	.369	1	.077	-1	-13	-13	-1	-1.0
● JERRY CASALE	Casale, Jerry Joseph b: 9/27/33, Brooklyn, N.Y. BR/TR, 6'2", 200 lbs. Deb: 9/14/58																											
1958	Bos-A	0	0	—	2	0	0	0	0	3	1	0	0	0	2	3	9.0	0.00	—	.111	.273	0	—	0	1	1	0	0.1
1959	Bos-A	13	8	.619	31	26	9	3	0	179^2	162	89	20	5	89	93	12.8	4.31	94	.238	.331	10	.169	3	-9	-5	-4	-0.7
1960	Bos-A	2	9	.182	29	14	1	0	0	96^1	113	78	14	1	67	54	16.9	6.17	66	.294	.400	9	.273	3	-25	-22	-0	-2.0
1961	LA-A	1	5	.167	13	7	0	0	1	42^2	52	34	9	1	25	35	16.5	6.54	69	.297	.388	6	.462	3	-12	-9	-0	-0.8
	Det-A	0	0	—	3	1	0	0	0	12	15	8	3	0	3	6	13.5	5.25	78	.313	.353	0	.000	-0	-2	-2	0	-0.1
	Yr	1	5	.167	16	8	0	0	1	54^2	67	42	12	1	28	41	15.8	6.26	71	.300	.381	6	.375	3	-14	-10	-0	-0.9
1962	Det-A	1	2	.333	18	1	0	0	0	36^2	33	19	5	0	18	16	12.5	4.66	87	.236	.323	0	.000	-1	-3	-2	0	-0.2
Total	5	17	24	.415	96	49	10	3	1	370^1	376	228	51	7	204	207	14.3	5.08	81	.262	.356	25	.216	7	-49	-38	-5	-3.7
● JOE CASCARELLA	Cascarella, Joseph Thomas "Crooning Joe" b: 6/28/07, Philadelphia, Pa. BR/TR, 5'10.5", 175 lbs. Deb: 4/17/34																											
1934	Phi-A	12	15	.444	42	22	9	2	1	194^1	214	111	8	3	104	71	14.9	4.68	94	.288	.377	6	.094	-4	-4	-7	2	-1.0
1935	Phi-A	1	6	.143	9	3	1	0	0	32^1	29	21	1	0	22	15	14.2	5.29	86	.252	.372	1	.125	-1	-3	-3	2	-0.4
	Bos-A	0	3	.000	6	4	0	0	0	17	25	17	3	0	11	9	19.1	6.88	69	.329	.414	0	.000	-0	-5	-4	0	-0.6
	Yr	1	9	.100	15	7	1	0	0	49^1	54	38	4	0	33	24	15.9	5.84	79	.283	.388	1	.100	-1	-8	-6	2	-1.0
1936	Bos-A	0	2	.000	10	1	0	0	0	20^2	27	16	0	0	9	7	15.7	6.97	76	.329	.396	0	.000	-1	-4	-4	0	-0.3
	Was-A	9	8	.529	22	16	7	1	1	139^1	147	66	7	6	54	34	13.4	4.07	117	.276	.349	7	.143	-2	15	12	-2	0.8
	Yr	9	10	.474	32	17	7	1	1	160	174	82	7	6	63	41	13.7	4.44	109	.283	.355	7	.132	-3	11	7	-2	0.5
1937	Was-A	0	5	.000	10	4	1	0	1	32^1	50	41	3	1	23	10	20.6	8.07	55	.347	.440	2	.222	-0	-12	-14	0	-1.7
	Cin-N	1	2	.333	11	3	2	0	1	43^2	44	24	1	0	22	16	13.6	3.92	95	.263	.349	1	.091	-1	-0	-1	-0	-0.1
1938	Cin-N	4	7	.364	33	1	0	0	4	61	66	33	2	0	22	30	13.0	4.57	80	.275	.336	3	.167	-1	-5	-7	-0	-1.2
Total	5	27	48	.360	143	54	20	3	8	540^2	602	329	25	10	267	192	14.6	4.84	91	.287	.370	20	.121	-9	-19	-27	1	-4.5
● CHARLIE CASE	Case, Charles Emmett b: 9/7/1879, Smith Landing, O. d: 4/16/64, Batavia, Ohio BR/TR, 6', 170 lbs. Deb: 7/5/01																											
1901	Cin-N	1	2	.333	3	3	3	0	0	27	34	21	0	0	6	5	13.3	4.67	69	.306	.342	1	.100	-1	-4	-5	-0	-0.5
1904	Pit-N	10	5	.667	18	17	14	3	0	141	129	56	0	4	31	49	10.5	2.94	93	.243	.290	9	.170	1	-3	-3	1	-0.2
1905	Pit-N	11	11	.500	31	24	18	3	1	217	202	81	2	15	66	57	11.7	2.57	117	.251	.319	7	.103	-2	10	10	-3	0.5
1906	Pit-N	1	1	.500	2	2	1	0	0	11	8	9	0	1	5	3	11.5	5.73	47	.190	.292	1	.500	1	-4	-4	0	-0.5
Total	4	23	19	.548	54	46	36	6	1	396	373	167	2	20	108	114	11.4	2.93	99	.251	.310	18	.135	-1	-0	-1	-3	-0.7
● DAN CASEY	Casey, Daniel Maurice b: 11/20/1862, Binghamton, N.Y. d: 2/8/43, Washington, D.C. BR/TL, 6', 180 lbs. Deb: 8/18/1884 F																											
1884	Wil-U	1	1	.500	2	2	2	0	0	18	23	17	0		4	10	13.5	1.00	266	.291	.325	1	.167	-1	3	3	-0	0.2
1885	Det-N	4	8	.333	12	12	12	1	0	104	105	61	1		35	79	12.1	3.29	86	.256	.315	5	.116	-3	-5	-5	1	-0.7
1886	Phi-N	24	18	.571	44	44	39	4	0	369	326	169	8		104	193	10.5	2.41	137	.223	.275	23	.152	-5	37	36	-1	2.9
1887	Phi-N	28	13	.683	45	45	43	**4**	0	390^1	492	199	15	14	115	119	11.7	**2.86**	**148**	.299	.305	33	.194	-11	53	57	-2	3.6
1888	Phi-N	14	18	.438	33	33	31	2	0	285^2	298	156	6	5	48	108	11.1	3.15	94	.259	.291	18	.153	-4	-10	-6	1	-0.9
1889	Phi-N	6	10	.375	20	20	15	1	0	152^2	170	92	4	8	72	65	14.7	3.77	115	.273	.356	15	.221	-2	4	9	0	0.6
1890	Syr-a	19	22	.463	45	42	40	2	0	360^2	365	249	8	14	165	169	13.6	4.14	85	.255	.337	26	.162	-4	-11	-27	2	-2.5
Total	7	96	90	.516	201	198	182	14	0	1680^1	1779	943	42	41	543	743	12.0	3.18	113	.261	.309	121	.169	-27	71	74	1	3.2
● HUGH CASEY	Casey, Hugh Thomas b: 10/14/13, Atlanta, Ga. d: 7/3/51, Atlanta, Ga. BR/TR, 6'1", 207 lbs. Deb: 4/29/35																											
1935	Chi-N	0	0	—	13	0	0	0	0	25^2	29	13	2	0	14	10	15.1	3.86	102	.279	.364	1	.167	-0	0	0	0	0.0
1939	Bro-N	15	10	.600	40	25	15	0	1	227^1	228	88	13	11	54	79	11.6	2.93	137	.260	.311	15	.203	0	25	27	2	3.1
1940	Bro-N	11	8	.579	44	10	5	2	2	154	136	63	13	6	51	53	11.3	3.62	110	.237	.306	9	.250	2	4	6	1	1.0
1941	*Bro-N	14	11	.560	45	18	4	1	7	162	155	81	8	1	57	61	11.8	3.89	94	.251	.316	6	.120	-1	-5	-4	2	-0.6
1942	Bro-N	6	3	.667	50	2	0	0	**13**	112	91	32	3	2	44	54	11.0	2.25	145	.221	.300	4	.148	-0	13	13	-1	1.3
1946	Bro-N	11	5	.688	46	1	0	0	5	99^2	101	31	2	2	33	31	12.3	1.99	170	.267	.329	3	.136	-1	**16**	**16**	3	2.9
1947	*Bro-N	10	4	.714	46	0	0	0	**18**	76^2	75	36	7	2	29	40	12.4	3.99	104	.260	.331	1	.056	-1	1	1	0	0.1
1948	Bro-N	3	0	1.000	22	0	0	0	4	36	59	36	6	2	17	7	19.5	8.00	50	.391	.459	0	.000	-1	-16	-16	-0	-1.6
1949	Pit-N	4	1	.800	33	0	0	0	5	38^2	50	24	4	1	14	9	15.1	4.66	90	.314	.374	1	.333	0	-3	-2	-2	-0.4
	NY-A	1	0	1.000	4	0	0	0	0	7^2	11	10	0	0	8	5	22.3	8.22	49	.324	.452	0	.000	-0	-3	-4	-0	-0.4
Total	9	75	42	.641	343	56	24	3	55	939^2	935	414	58	27	321	349	12.3	3.45	110	.260	.325	40	.164	-2	32	37	6	5.4
● BILL CASEY	Casey, William B. b: St.Louis, Mo. Deb: 8/17/1887																											
1887	Phi-a	0	0	—	1	0	0	0	0	1	5	3	0	0	1	0	45.0	18.00	24	.714	.714	0	—	0	-2	-2	-0	-0.1
● CARL CASHION	Cashion, Jay Carl b: 6/6/1891, Mecklenburg Co, N.C. d: 11/17/35, Lake Millicent, Wis. BL/TR, 6'2", 200 lbs. Deb: 8/4/11																											
1911	Was-A	1	5	.167	11	9	5	0	0	71^1	67	45	4	7	47	26	15.3	4.16	79	.220	.338	12	.324	2	-6	-7	1	-0.2
1912	Was-A	10	6	.625	26	17	13	1	1	170^1	150	84	4	5	103	84	13.6	3.17	105	.250	.365	22	.214	2	3	3	-1	0.5
1913	Was-A	1	1	.500	4	3	0	0	0	9	7	11	0	3	14	3	24.0	6.00	49	.269	.558	3	.250	0	-3	-3	0	-0.5

YEAR	TM/L	W	L	PCT	G	GS	CG	SH	SV	IP	H	R	HR	HB	BB	SO	RAT	ERA	ERA+	OAV	OOB	BH	AVG	PB	PR	PR+	PD	TPI
1914	Was-A	0	1	.000	2	1	0	0	0	5	4	7	0	1	6	1	19.8	10.80	26	.250	.478	0	.000	-0	-4	-4	0	-0.7
Total	4	12	13	.480	43	30	18	1	1	255^2	228	147	8	16	170	114	14.6	3.70	89	.241	.366	37	.242	5	-11	-11	1	-0.9

● LARRY CASIAN Casian, Lawrence Paul b: 10/28/65, Lynwood, Cal. BR/TL, 6', 170 lbs. Deb: 9/9/90

YEAR	TM/L	W	L	PCT	G	GS	CG	SH	SV	IP	H	R	HR	HB	BB	SO	RAT	ERA	ERA+	OAV	OOB	BH	AVG	PB	PR	PR+	PD	TPI
1990	Min-A	2	1	.667	5	3	0	0	0	22^1	26	9	2	0	4	11	12.1	3.22	129	.306	.337	0	—	0	2	2	-0	0.3
1991	Min-A	0	0	—	15	0	0	0	0	18^1	28	16	4	1	7	6	17.7	7.36	58	.354	.414	0	—	0	-7	-6	0	-0.3
1992	Min-A	1	0	1.000	6	0	0	0	0	6^2	7	2	0	0	1	2	10.8	2.70	150	.259	.286	0	—	0	1	1	0	0.2
1993	Min-A	5	3	.625	54	0	0	0	1	56^2	59	23	1	1	14	31	11.8	3.02	145	.268	.315	0	—	0	8	8	-1	1.0
1994	Min-A	1	3	.250	33	0	0	0	1	40^2	57	34	11	2	12	18	15.7	7.08	69	.343	.394	0	—	0	-10	-10	1	-0.8
	Cle-A	0	2	.000	7	0	0	0	0	8^1	16	9	1	0	4	2	21.6	8.64	55	.421	.476	0	—	0	-4	-4	0	-0.6
	Yr	1	5	.167	40	0	0	0	1	49	73	43	12	2	16	20	16.7	7.35	66	.358	.410	0	—	0	-14	-13	1	-1.4
1995	Chi-N	1	0	1.000	42	0	0	0	0	23^1	23	6	1	0	15	11	14.7	1.93	213	.258	.365	0	.000	-0	6	6	0	0.3
1996	Chi-N	1	1	.500	35	0	0	0	0	24	14	5	2	1	11	15	9.8	1.88	231	.187	.299	0	—	0	6	6	0	0.5
1997	Chi-N	0	1	.000	12	0	0	0	0	9^2	16	9	3	1	2	7	17.7	7.45	58	.364	.404	0	.000	-0	-3	-3	-0	-0.3
	KC-A	0	2	.000	32	0	0	0	0	26^2	32	15	5	0	6	16	12.8	5.06	93	.299	.336	0	—	0	-1	-1	0	0.0
1998	Chi-A	0	0	—	4	0	0	0	0	4	8	5	0	2	1	6	24.8	11.25	40	.400	.478	0	—	0	-3	-3	0	-0.1
Total	9	11	13	.458	245	3	0	0	2	240^2	286	133	30	8	77	125	13.9	4.56	97	.301	.358	0	.000	-0	-5	-3	2	0.2

● CRAIG CASKEY Caskey, Craig Douglas b: 12/11/49, Visalia, Cal. BB/TL, 5'11", 185 lbs. Deb: 7/19/73

YEAR	TM/L	W	L	PCT	G	GS	CG	SH	SV	IP	H	R	HR	HB	BB	SO	RAT	ERA	ERA+	OAV	OOB	BH	AVG	PB	PR	PR+	PD	TPI
1973	Mon-N	0	0	—	9	1	0	0	0	14^1	15	11	3	1	4	6	12.6	5.65	68	.278	.339	0	.000	-0	-3	-3	0	-0.1

● ED CASSIAN Cassian, Edward T. b: 11/8/1867, Wilbraham, Mass. d: 9/10/18, Meriden, Conn. TR, 5'8", 160 lbs. Deb: 6/26/1891

YEAR	TM/L	W	L	PCT	G	GS	CG	SH	SV	IP	H	R	HR	HB	BB	SO	RAT	ERA	ERA+	OAV	OOB	BH	AVG	PB	PR	PR+	PD	TPI
1891	Phi-N	1	3	.250	6	4	3	0	0	38	40	20	0	3	16	10	14.0	2.84	120	.260	.341	2	.118	-1	2	2	1	0.1
	Was-a	2	4	.333	7	5	5	0	0	53	73	63	4	5	35	14	19.2	5.60	67	.316	.417	9	.346	2	-11	-11	0	-0.7
Total	1	3	7	.300	13	9	8	0	0	91	113	83	4	8	51	24	17.0	4.45	81	.294	.387	11	.256	1	-9	-9	1	-0.6

● JOHN CASSIDY Cassidy, John P. b: 1857, Brooklyn, N.Y. d: 7/2/1891, Brooklyn, N.Y. BR/TL, 5'8", 168 lbs. Deb: 4/24/1875 ♦

YEAR	TM/L	W	L	PCT	G	GS	CG	SH	SV	IP	H	R	HR	HB	BB	SO	RAT	ERA	ERA+	OAV	OOB	BH	AVG	PB	PR	PR+	PD	TPI
1875	Atl-n	1	21	.045	30	22	18	0	0	213^2	284	242	3		11	9	12.4	3.03	69	.277	.285	29	.175	-3	-19	-24		-2.0
1877	Har-N	1	1	.500	2	2	2	0	0	18	24	11	0		1	2	12.5	5.00	49	.320	.329	95	.378	1	-4	-6	-0	-0.4

● GEORGE CASTER Caster, George Jasper "Ug" b: 8/4/07, Colton, Cal. d: 12/18/55, Lakewood, Cal. BR/TR, 6'1.5", 180 lbs. Deb: 9/10/34

YEAR	TM/L	W	L	PCT	G	GS	CG	SH	SV	IP	H	R	HR	HB	BB	SO	RAT	ERA	ERA+	OAV	OOB	BH	AVG	PB	PR	PR+	PD	TPI
1934	Phi-A	3	2	.600	5	3	2	0	0	37	32	16	3	3	14	15	11.9	3.41	129	.235	.320	4	.267	0	4	4	1	0.6
1935	Phi-A	1	4	.200	25	1	0	0	1	63^1	86	59	8	2	37	24	17.8	6.25	73	.322	.408	5	.227	0	-13	-12	2	-0.7
1937	Phi-A	12	19	.387	34	33	19	3	0	231^2	227	141	23	2	107	100	13.1	4.43	106	.258	.339	19	.211	-1	5	7	0	0.8
1938	Phi-A	16	20	.444	42	40	20	2	1	281^1	310	156	25	3	117	112	13.8	4.35	111	.277	.347	20	.198	1	14	15	-2	1.6
1939	Phi-A	9	9	.500	28	17	7	1	0	136	144	82	16	3	45	59	12.7	4.90	96	.276	.337	9	.209	-1	-4	-3	0	-0.4
1940	Phi-A	4	19	.174	36	24	11	0	2	178^1	234	160	18	3	69	75	15.4	6.56	68	.312	.372	8	.129	-3	-43	-41	-1	-4.7
1941	StL-A	3	7	.300	32	9	3	0	3	104^1	105	66	12	2	37	36	12.4	5.00	86	.259	.324	3	.103	-2	-10	-8	1	-0.8
1942	StL-A	8	2	.800	39	0	0	0	5	80	62	30	3	3	39	34	11.7	2.81	132	.217	.317	1	.067	-1	8	8	1	1.0
1943	StL-A	6	8	.429	35	0	0	0	8	76^1	69	22	4	1	41	43	13.1	2.12	157	.246	.345	3	.136	-1	10	10	0	2.1
1944	StL-A	6	6	.500	42	0	0	0	**12**	81	91	37	5	0	33	46	13.8	2.44	147	.284	.351	5	.250	0	9	10	-0	1.8
1945	StL-A	1	2	.333	10	0	0	0	1	15^2	20	13	0	0	7	9	15.5	6.89	51	.308	.375	1	.333	0	-6	-6	-0	-1.1
	*Det-A	5	1	.833	22	0	0	0	2	51^1	47	25	3	2	27	23	13.3	3.86	91	.250	.350	2	.182	0	-3	-2	-0	-0.2
	Yr	6	3	.667	32	0	0	0	3	67	67	38	3	2	34	32	13.8	4.57	77	.265	.356	3	.214	0	-9	-7	-0	-1.3
1946	Det-A	2	1	.667	26	0	0	0	4	41^1	42	26	1	1	24	19	14.6	5.66	65	.264	.364	1	.143	-0	-10	-9	1	-0.8
Total	12	76	100	.432	376	127	62	6	39	1377^2	1469	833	121	25	597	595	13.7	4.54	96	.273	.349	81	.184	-7	-39	-26	2	-0.8

● TONY CASTILLO Castillo, Antonio Jose (Jimenez) b: 3/1/63, Quibor, Venez. BL/TL, 5'10", 188 lbs. Deb: 8/14/88

YEAR	TM/L	W	L	PCT	G	GS	CG	SH	SV	IP	H	R	HR	HB	BB	SO	RAT	ERA	ERA+	OAV	OOB	BH	AVG	PB	PR	PR+	PD	TPI
1988	Tor-A	1	0	1.000	14	0	0	0	0	15	10	5	2	0	2	14	7.2	3.00	131	.200	.231	0	—	0	2	2	0	0.1
1989	Tor-A	1	1	.500	17	0	0	0	1	17^2	23	14	0	1	10	10	17.3	6.11	62	.333	.425	0	—	0	-4	-5	-0	-0.6
	Atl-N	0	1	.000	12	0	0	0	0	9^1	8	5	0	0	4	5	11.6	4.82	76	.222	.300	0	.000	-0	-1	-1	0	-0.1
1990	Atl-N	5	1	.833	52	3	0	0	1	76^2	93	41	5	1	20	64	13.4	4.23	96	.302	.347	1	.143	0	-4	-1	1	0.0
1991	Atl-N	1	1	.500	7	0	0	0	0	8^2	13	9	3	0	5	8	18.7	7.27	54	.342	.419	0	—	0	-3	-3	-0	-0.6
	NY-N	1	0	1.000	10	3	0	0	0	23^2	27	7	1	0	6	10	12.5	1.90	192	.281	.324	0	.000	-0	5	5	1	0.3
	Yr	2	1	.667	17	3	0	0	0	32^1	40	16	4	0	11	18	14.2	3.34	111	.299	.352	0	.000	-0	1	1	0	-0.3
1993	*Tor-A	3	2	.600	51	0	0	0	0	50^2	44	19	4	0	22	28	11.7	3.38	128	.242	.324	0	—	0	5	5	0	0.5
1994	Tor-A	5	2	.714	41	0	0	0	1	68	66	22	7	3	28	43	12.8	2.51	192	.260	.340	0	—	0	17	17	1	1.7
1995	Tor-A	1	5	.167	55	0	0	0	13	72^2	64	27	7	3	24	38	11.3	3.22	146	.243	.314	0	—	0	12	12	-0	1.2
1996	Tor-A	2	3	.400	40	0	0	0	1	72^1	72	38	9	2	20	48	11.7	4.23	118	.260	.314	0	—	0	6	6	1	0.5
	Chi-A	3	1	.750	15	0	0	0	1	22^2	23	7	1	1	4	9	11.1	1.59	299	.267	.308	0	—	0	9	8	-0	1.3
	Yr	5	4	.556	55	0	0	0	2	95	95	45	10	3	24	57	11.6	3.60	137	.262	.313	0	—	0	15	14	1	1.8
1997	Chi-A	4	4	.500	64	0	0	0	4	62^1	74	48	6	1	23	42	14.1	4.91	89	.296	.358	0	.000	-0	-2	-4	2	-0.3
1998	Chi-A	1	2	.333	25	0	0	0	0	27	38	25	7	2	11	14	17.0	8.00	57	.328	.395	0	—	0	-10	-11	1	-0.9
Total	10	28	23	.549	403	6	0	0	22	526^2	555	267	52	14	179	333	12.8	3.93	114	.274	.337	1	.077	-1	31	31	6	3.1

● CARLOS CASTILLO Castillo, Carlos b: 4/21/75, Boston, Mass. BR/TR, 6'2", 240 lbs. Deb: 4/2/97

YEAR	TM/L	W	L	PCT	G	GS	CG	SH	SV	IP	H	R	HR	HB	BB	SO	RAT	ERA	ERA+	OAV	OOB	BH	AVG	PB	PR	PR+	PD	TPI
1997	Chi-A	2	1	.667	37	2	0	0	1	66^1	68	35	9	1	33	43	13.8	4.48	98	.265	.351	1	1.000	0	1	-1	-1	-0.1
1998	Chi-A	6	4	.600	54	2	0	0	0	100^1	94	61	17	5	35	64	12.0	5.11	89	.246	.318	0	.000	0	-5	-6	0	-0.5
1999	Chi-A	2	2	.500	18	2	0	0	0	41	45	26	10	0	14	23	13.0	5.71	86	.274	.331	0	—	0	-4	-4	-0	-0.3
Total	3	10	7	.588	109	6	0	0	1	207^2	207	122	36	6	82	130	12.8	5.03	91	.258	.331	1	.500	0	-8	-11	-1	-0.9

● MANNY CASTILLO Castillo, Esteban Manuel Antonio (Cabrera) b: 4/1/57, Santo Domingo, D.R. BB/TR, 5'9", 160 lbs. Deb: 9/1/80 ♦

YEAR	TM/L	W	L	PCT	G	GS	CG	SH	SV	IP	H	R	HR	HB	BB	SO	RAT	ERA	ERA+	OAV	OOB	BH	AVG	PB	PR	PR+	PD	TPI
1983	Sea-A	0	0	—	1	0	0	0	0	2^2	8	7	3	1	3	2	40.5	23.63	18	.533	.632	42	.207	0	-6	-5	-0	-0.2

● FRANK CASTILLO Castillo, Frank Anthony b: 4/1/69, ElPaso, Tex. BR/TR, 6'1", 190 lbs. Deb: 6/27/91

YEAR	TM/L	W	L	PCT	G	GS	CG	SH	SV	IP	H	R	HR	HB	BB	SO	RAT	ERA	ERA+	OAV	OOB	BH	AVG	PB	PR	PR+	PD	TPI
1991	Chi-N	6	7	.462	18	18	4	0	0	111^2	107	56	5	0	33	73	11.3	4.35	89	.252	.306	5	.143	-0	-8	-5	-0	-0.7
1992	Chi-N	10	11	.476	33	33	0	0	0	205^1	179	91	19	6	63	135	10.9	3.46	104	.232	.295	6	.092	-2	1	3	-1	0.0
1993	Chi-N	5	8	.385	29	25	2	0	0	141^1	162	83	20	9	39	84	13.4	4.84	83	.293	.349	7	.163	-0	-12	-13	3	-0.9
1994	Chi-N	2	1	.667	4	4	1	0	0	23	25	13	3	0	5	19	11.7	4.30	97	.278	.316	0	.000	-1	-0	-0	-0	-0.1
1995	Chi-N	11	10	.524	29	29	2	2	0	188	179	75	22	6	52	135	11.3	3.21	128	.248	.303	6	.102	-2	20	19	-1	1.6
1996	Chi-N	7	16	.304	33	33	1	1	0	182^1	209	112	28	8	46	139	13.0	5.28	82	.288	.337	5	.088	-3	-21	-19	0	-2.3
1997	Chi-N	6	9	.400	20	19	0	0	0	98	113	64	9	4	44	67	14.8	5.42	79	.292	.370	5	.152	-1	-13	-12	-0	-1.6
	Col-N	6	3	.667	14	14	0	0	0	86^1	107	57	16	4	25	59	14.2	5.42	96	.308	.362	2	.080	-2	-12	-2	1	-0.4
	Yr	12	12	.500	34	33	0	0	0	184^1	220	121	25	8	69	126	14.5	5.42	87	.300	.366	7	.121	-2	-25	-13	-1	-2.0
1998	Det-A	3	9	.250	27	19	0	0	1	116	150	91	17	5	44	81	15.4	6.83	69	.316	.380	0	.000	-0	-28	-27	-0	-2.3
2000	Tor-A	10	5	.667	25	24	0	0	0	138	112	58	18	5	56	104	11.3	3.59	139	.220	.304	1	.143	-0	20	21	1	2.1
Total	9	66	79	.455	232	218	10	3	1	1290	1343	700	157	47	407	896	12.5	4.52	94	.268	.329	37	.111	-12	-53	-35	-0	-4.6

● JUAN CASTILLO Castillo, Juan Francisco (Azdura) b: 6/23/70, Caracas, Venez. BR/TR, 6'5", 205 lbs. Deb: 7/26/94

YEAR	TM/L	W	L	PCT	G	GS	CG	SH	SV	IP	H	R	HR	HB	BB	SO	RAT	ERA	ERA+	OAV	OOB	BH	AVG	PB	PR	PR+	PD	TPI
1994	NY-N	0	0	—	2	2	0	0	0	11^2	17	9	2	0	5	1	17.0	6.94	60	.362	.423	1	.200	0	-4	-4	1	-0.1

● BOBBY CASTILLO Castillo, Robert Ernie b: 4/18/55, Los Angeles, Cal. BR/TR, 5'10", 170 lbs. Deb: 9/10/77

YEAR	TM/L	W	L	PCT	G	GS	CG	SH	SV	IP	H	R	HR	HB	BB	SO	RAT	ERA	ERA+	OAV	OOB	BH	AVG	PB	PR	PR+	PD	TPI
1977	LA-N	1	0	1.000	6	1	0	0	0	11^1	12	5	2	0	2	7	11.1	3.97	96	.279	.311	0	.000	-0	-0	-0	0	0.0
1978	LA-N	0	4	.000	18	0	0	0	1	34	28	19	2	0	33	30	16.1	3.97	88	.239	.407	0	.000	-1	-1	-2	0	-0.3
1979	LA-N	2	0	1.000	19	0	0	0	7	24^1	26	5	0	1	13	25	14.8	1.11	328	.277	.370	0	.000	-0	7	7	0	1.0
1980	LA-N	8	6	.571	61	0	0	0	5	98^1	70	31	4	1	45	60	10.6	2.75	128	.206	.301	1	.111	-0	9	9	1	1.3
1981	*LA-N	2	4	.333	34	1	0	0	5	50^2	50	31	5	0	24	35	13.1	5.33	62	.262	.344	4	.444	2	-10	-12	-1	-1.4
1982	Min-A	13	11	.542	40	25	6	1	0	218^2	194	96	26	0	85	123	11.5	3.66	116	.241	.313	0	—	0	10	14	-2	1.2
1983	Min-A	8	12	.400	27	25	3	0	0	158^1	170	91	17	1	65	90	13.4	4.77	89	.278	.348	0	—	0	-12	-9	1	-0.9
1984	Min-A	2	1	.667	10	2	0	0	0	25^1	14	7	2	0	19	7	11.7	1.78	237	.177	.337	0	—	0	6	7	-0	0.7
1985	*LA-N	2	2	.500	35	5	0	0	0	68	59	42	9	1	41	57	13.4	5.43	64	.230	.339	1	.100	-0	-14	-15	0	-0.8
Total	9	38	40	.487	250	59	9	1	18	689	623	327	67	4	327	434	12.5	3.94	100	.246	.333	6	.154	0	-5	-1	-1	0.8

YEAR	TM/L	W	L	PCT	G	GS	CG	SH	SV	IP	H	R	HR	HB	BB	SO	RAT	ERA	ERA+	OAV	OOB	BH	AVG	PB	PR	PR+	PD	TPI
● **SLICK CASTLEMAN** Castleman, Clydell b: 9/8/13, Donelson, Tenn. d: 3/2/98, Nashville, Tenn. BR/TR, 6', 185 lbs. Deb: 5/9/34																												
1934	NY-N	1	0	1.000	7	0	0	0	0	16^2	18	11	1	0	10	5	15.1	5.40	72	.277	.373	1	.250	1	-2	-3	1	0.0
1935	NY-N	15	6	.714	29	25	9	1	0	173^2	186	93	14	1	64	64	13.0	4.09	94	.268	.330	12	.179	-0	-1	-5	1	-0.4
1936	*NY-N	4	7	.364	29	12	2	1	1	111^2	148	80	6	5	56	54	16.8	5.64	69	.323	.403	5	.128	-1	-20	-22	1	-2.0
1937	NY-N	11	6	.647	23	23	10	2	0	160^1	148	66	19	0	33	78	10.2	3.31	117	.247	.287	4	.070	-5	11	10	-3	0.3
1938	NY-N	4	5	.444	21	14	4	0	0	90^2	108	55	4	3	37	18	14.7	4.17	90	.296	.365	3	.097	-2	-4	-4	-1	-0.6
1939	NY-N	1	2	.333	12	4	0	0	0	33^2	36	18	1	0	23	6	15.8	4.54	86	.286	.396	3	.333	1	-2	-2	-1	-0.2
Total	6	36	26	.581	121	78	25	4	1	586^2	644	323	45	9	223	225	13.4	4.25	91	.279	.345	28	.135	-6	-19	-26	-2	-2.9
● **ROY CASTLETON** Castleton, Royal Eugene b: 7/26/1885, Salt Lake City, Utah d: 6/24/67, Los Angeles, Cal. BR/TL, 5'11", 167 lbs. Deb: 4/16/07																												
1907	NY-A	1	1	.500	3	2	1	0	0	16	11	6	1	0	3	3	7.9	2.81	99	.196	.237	0	.000	-1	-0	-0	-0	-0.1
1909	Cin-N	1	1	.500	4	1	1	0	0	14	14	6	0	2	6	5	14.1	1.93	135	.275	.373	2	.667	1	1	1	0	0.3
1910	Cin-N	1	2	.333	4	2	1	0	0	13^2	15	5	0	1	6	5	14.5	3.29	89	.288	.373	0	.000	-1	-0	-1	0	-0.2
Total	3	3	4	.429	11	5	3	0	0	43^2	40	17	1	3	15	13	12.0	2.68	104	.252	.328	2	.154	-0	0	0	0	0.0
● **PAUL CASTNER** Castner, Paul Henry "Lefty" b: 2/16/1897, St.Paul, Minn. d: 3/3/86, St.Paul, Minn. BL/TL, 5'11", 187 lbs. Deb: 8/6/23																												
1923	Chi-A	0	0	—	6	0	0	0	0	10	14	9	0	0	5	0	17.1	6.30	63	.326	.396	0	.000	-0	-3	-3	0	-0.2
● **BILL CASTRO** Castro, William Radhames (Checo) b: 12/13/53, Santiago, D.R. BR/TR, 5'11", 170 lbs. Deb: 8/20/74 C																												
1974	Mil-A	0	0	—	8	0	0	0	0	18	19	10	2	0	5	10	12.0	4.50	81	.264	.312	0	—	0	-2	-2	0	-0.1
1975	Mil-A	3	2	.600	18	5	0	0	1	75	78	28	3	2	17	25	11.6	2.52	152	.271	.316	0	—	0	11	11	0	0.7
1976	Mil-A	4	6	.400	39	0	0	0	8	70^1	70	29	4	3	19	23	11.8	3.45	101	.265	.322	0	—	0	1	0	-0	0.0
1977	Mil-A	8	6	.571	51	0	0	0	13	69^1	76	34	7	2	23	28	13.1	4.15	98	.293	.356	0	—	0	-1	-1	1	0.0
1978	Mil-A	5	4	.556	42	0	0	0	8	49^2	43	14	2	6	14	17	11.4	1.81	208	.234	.309	0	—	0	11	11	0	2.3
1979	Mil-A	3	1	.750	39	0	0	0	6	44^1	40	14	2	0	13	10	10.8	2.03	206	.244	.299	0	—	0	11	11	-0	1.2
1980	Mil-A	2	4	.333	56	0	0	0	8	84^1	89	35	2	2	17	32	11.5	2.77	140	.274	.314	0	—	0	12	11	1	1.0
1981	NY-A	1	1	.500	11	0	0	0	0	19	26	13	2	0	5	4	14.7	3.79	94	.329	.369	0	—	0	-0	-0	-0	-0.1
1982	KC-A	3	2	.600	21	4	0	0	1	75^2	72	34	8	2	20	37	11.2	3.45	119	.243	.296	0	—	0	5	5	-1	0.2
1983	KC-A	2	0	1.000	18	0	0	0	0	40^2	51	34	4	5	12	17	15.0	6.64	62	.300	.364	0	—	0	-12	-11	0	-0.5
Total	10	31	26	.544	303	9	0	0	45	546^1	564	245	36	22	145	203	12.0	3.33	117	.268	.322	0	—	0	36	34	0	4.7
● **ELI CATES** Cates, Eli Eldo b: 1/26/1877, Greens Fork, Ind. d: 5/29/64, Anderson, Ind. BR/TR, 5'9.5", 175 lbs. Deb: 4/20/08 ♦																												
1908	Was-A	4	8	.333	19	10	7	0	0	113^2	112	46	3	1	32	33	11.5	2.53	90	.261	.314	11	.186	1	-2	-3	1	0.0
● **MIKE CATHER** Cather, Michael Peter b: 12/17/70, San Diego, Cal. BR/TR, 6'2", 195 lbs. Deb: 7/13/97																												
1997	*Atl-N	2	4	.333	35	0	0	0	0	37^2	23	12	1	2	19	29	10.5	2.39	176	.174	.288	0	.000	-0	8	8	0	1.1
1998	Atl-N	2	2	.500	36	0	0	0	0	41^1	39	21	7	2	12	33	11.5	3.92	106	.255	.317	0	—	0	1	1	-0	0.1
1999	Atl-N	1	0	1.000	4	0	0	0	0	2^2	5	3	2	0	1	0	20.3	10.13	44	.417	.462	0	—	0	-2	-2	0	-0.3
Total	3	5	6	.455	75	0	0	0	0	81^2	67	36	10	4	32	62	11.4	3.42	123	.226	.309	0	.000	-0	7	7	0	0.9
● **TED CATHER** Cather, Theodore Physick b: 5/20/1889, Chester, Pa. d: 4/9/45, Elkton, Md. BR/TR, 5'10.5", 178 lbs. Deb: 9/23/12 ♦																												
1913	StL-N	0	0	—	1	0	0	0	0	0^1	1	2	0	1	2	0	108.0	54.00	6	.500	.800	39	.213	0	-2	-2	0	-0.1
● **HARDIN CATHEY** Cathey, Hardin Abner "Lil Abner" b: 7/6/19, Burns, Tenn. d: 7/27/97, Nashville, Tenn. BR/TR, 6'4", 190 lbs. Deb: 4/16/42																												
1942	Was-A	1	1	.500	12	2	0	0	0	30^1	44	26	1	0	16	8	17.8	7.42	49	.341	.414	3	.375	1	-13	-13	-0	-0.7
● **KEEFE CATO** Cato, John Keefe b: 5/6/58, Yonkers, N.Y. BR/TR, 6'1", 185 lbs. Deb: 6/13/83																												
1983	Cin-N	1	0	1.000	4	0	0	0	0	3^2	2	1	0	0	1	3	7.4	2.45	155	.154	.214	0	—	0	0	1	-0	0.1
1984	Cin-N	0	1	.000	8	0	0	0	1	15^2	22	14	5	0	4	12	14.9	8.04	47	.344	.382	2	.500	1	-8	-7	0	-0.4
Total	2	1	1	.500	12	0	0	0	1	19^1	24	15	5	0	5	15	13.5	6.98	54	.312	.354	2	.500	1	-7	-7	0	-0.3
● **JOHN CATTANACH** Cattanach, John Leckie b: 5/10/1863, Providence, R.I. d: 11/10/26, Providence, R.I. 5'10", 190 lbs. Deb: 6/5/1884																												
1884	Pro-N	0	0	—	1	1	0	0	0	5	2	7	0		4	2	10.8	9.00	32	.100	.250	0	.000	-1	-3	-4	-0	-0.2
	StL-U	1	1	.500	2	2	2	0	0	17	12	10	0		4	13	8.5	2.12	113	.185	.232	0	.000	-2	1	1	0	-0.1
Total	1	1	1	.500	3	3	2	0	0	22	14	17	0		8	15	9.0	3.68	68	.165	.237	0	.000	-2	-3	-3	-0	-0.3
● **BILL CAUDILL** Caudill, William Holland b: 7/13/56, Santa Monica, Cal. BR/TR, 6'1", 210 lbs. Deb: 5/12/79																												
1979	Chi-N	1	7	.125	29	12	0	0	0	90	89	57	16	4	41	104	13.4	4.80	86	.255	.340	1	.059	-1	-11	-6	1	-0.6
1980	Chi-N	4	6	.400	72	2	0	0	1	127^2	100	37	10	1	59	112	11.3	2.19	180	.223	.314	2	.222	0	20	23	-1	1.7
1981	Chi-N	1	5	.167	30	10	0	0	0	71	87	50	9	2	31	45	15.2	5.83	63	.301	.373	2	.143	0	-18	-16	-1	-1.3
1982	Sea-A	12	9	.571	70	0	0	0	26	95^2	65	25	9	1	35	111	9.5	2.35	181	.192	.270	0	—	0	18	19	-1	3.9
1983	Sea-A	2	8	.200	63	0	0	0	26	72^2	70	39	10	2	38	73	13.6	4.71	91	.257	.353	0	—	0	-5	-3	-1	-0.7
1984	Oak-A★	9	7	.563	68	0	0	0	36	96^1	77	30	9	0	31	89	10.1	2.71	138	.218	.281	0	.000	-0	14	12	-2	2.3
1985	Tor-A	4	6	.400	67	0	0	0	14	69^1	53	26	9	2	35	46	11.7	2.99	141	.209	.310	0	—	0	9	9	-1	1.5
1986	Tor-A	2	4	.333	40	0	0	0	2	36^1	36	25	6	2	17	32	13.6	6.19	68	.254	.342	0	—	0	-8	-8	-1	-1.3
1987	Oak-A	0	0	—	6	0	0	0	1	8	10	8	3	0	1	8	12.4	9.00	46	.294	.314	0	—	0	-4	-5	-0	-0.2
Total	9	35	52	.402	445	24	0	0	106	667	587	297	81	14	288	620	12.0	3.68	110	.237	.320	5	.122	-1	15	26	-7	5.3
● **RED CAUSEY** Causey, Cecil Algernon b: 8/11/1893, Georgetown, Fla. d: 11/11/60, Avon Park, Fla. BR/TR, 6'1", 160 lbs. Deb: 4/26/18																												
1918	NY-N	11	6	.647	29	18	10	2	2	158^1	143	58	2	7	42	48	10.9	2.79	94	.245	.304	6	.125	-3	-0	-3	-1	-0.7
1919	NY-N	9	3	.750	19	16	6	0	0	105	99	52	5	2	38	25	11.9	3.69	76	.251	.320	5	.132	-1	-9	-11	-1	-1.4
	Bos-N	4	5	.444	10	10	3	0	0	69	81	38	1	1	20	14	13.3	4.57	63	.308	.359	2	.095	-2	-13	-13	0	-1.8
	Yr	13	8	.619	29	26	9	0	0	174	180	90	6	3	58	39	12.5	4.03	70	.274	.336	7	.119	-3	-22	-24	-1	-3.2
1920	Phi-N	7	14	.333	35	26	11	1	3	181^1	203	109	4	5	79	30	14.2	4.32	79	.299	.376	11	.186	-2	-24	-17	-2	-2.2
1921	Phi-N	3	3	.500	7	7	4	0	0	50^2	58	22	4	1	11	8	12.4	2.84	149	.294	.335	3	.150	-1	5	7	-0	0.7
	NY-N	1	1	.500	7	1	0	0	0	14^2	13	8	0	0	6	1	11.7	2.45	149	.228	.302	1	.333	0	2	2	-0	0.2
	Yr	4	4	.500	14	8	4	0	0	65^1	71	30	4	1	17	9	12.3	2.76	149	.280	.327	4	.174	-1	7	9	-0	0.9
1922	NY-N	4	3	.571	24	2	1	0	1	70^2	69	34	2	0	34	13	13.1	3.18	126	.262	.347	5	.238	-0	7	7	1	0.6
Total	5	39	35	.527	131	80	35	3	6	649^2	666	321	18	16	230	139	12.6	3.59	89	.273	.340	33	.157	-9	-31	-28	-3	-4.6
● **PUG CAVET** Cavet, Tiller H. b: 12/26/1889, McGregor, Tex. d: 8/4/66, San Luis Obispo, Cal. BL/TL, 6'3", 176 lbs. Deb: 4/25/11																												
1911	Det-A	0	0	—	1	1	0	0	0	4	6	5	0	0	1	1	15.8	4.50	77	.316	.350	0	.000	-0	-1	-0	-0	0.0
1914	Det-A	7	7	.500	31	14	6	1	2	151^1	129	61	2	9	44	51	10.8	2.44	115	.238	.306	5	.106	-2	5	6	1	0.5
1915	Det-A	4	2	.667	17	7	2	0	1	71	83	39	1	2	22	26	13.6	4.06	75	.300	.355	6	.250	1	-9	-8	-0	-0.5
Total	3	11	9	.550	49	22	8	1	3	226^1	218	105	3	11	67	78	11.8	2.98	97	.260	.323	11	.153	-0	-4	-2	1	0.0
● **ART CECCARELLI** Ceccarelli, Arthur Edward "Chic" b: 4/2/30, New Haven, Conn. BR/TL (BB 1957), 6', 190 lbs. Deb: 5/3/55																												
1955	KC-A	4	7	.364	31	16	3	1	0	123^2	123	81	20	0	71	68	14.1	5.31	79	.258	.354	3	.079	-3	-19	-15	-2	-1.6
1956	KC-A	0	1	.000	3	2	0	0	0	10	13	13	3	1	4	2	16.2	7.20	60	.317	.391	0	.000	-0	-3	-3	1	-0.2
1957	Bal-A	0	5	.000	20	8	1	0	0	58	62	34	3	2	31	30	14.7	4.50	80	.278	.371	0	.000	-2	-5	-6	-1	-0.7
1959	Chi-N	5	5	.500	18	15	4	2	0	102	95	58	19	1	37	56	11.7	4.76	83	.245	.312	3	.091	-1	-9	-9	-1	-1.0
1960	Chi-N	0	0	—	7	1	0	0	0	13	16	12	1	0	4	10	13.8	5.54	68	.296	.345	0	—	0	-3	-3	-0	-0.1
Total	5	9	18	.333	79	42	8	3	0	306^2	309	198	46	4	147	166	13.5	5.05	79	.261	.345	6	.068	-6	-38	-36	-3	-3.6
● **JOSE CECENA** Cecena, Jose Isabel (Lugo) b: 8/20/63, Ciudad Obregon, Mexico BR/TR, 5'11", 180 lbs. Deb: 4/6/88																												
1988	Tex-A	0	0	—	22	0	0	0	1	26^1	20	16	2	2	23	27	15.4	4.78	85	.213	.378	0	—	0	-2	-2	-0	-0.1
● **REX CECIL** Cecil, Rex Rolston b: 10/8/16, Lindsay, Okla. d: 10/30/66, Long Beach, Cal. BL/TR, 6'3", 195 lbs. Deb: 8/13/44																												
1944	Bos-A	4	5	.444	11	9	4	0	0	61	72	44	5	1	33	33	15.6	5.16	66	.286	.371	5	.278	2	-12	-12	-0	-1.4
1945	Bos-A	2	5	.286	7	7	1	0	0	45	46	37	4	0	27	30	14.6	5.20	66	.261	.360	6	.300	1	-9	-9	1	-1.1
Total	2	6	10	.375	18	16	5	0	0	106	118	81	9	1	60	63	15.2	5.18	66	.276	.366	11	.289	2	-21	-21	1	-2.5

YEAR	TM/L	W	L	PCT	G	GS	CG	SH	SV	IP	H	R	HR	HB	BB	SO	RAT	ERA	ERA+	OAV	OOB	BH	AVG	PB	PR	PR+	PD	TPI
● **PETE CENTER**	Center, Marvin Earl b: 4/22/12, Hazel Green, Ky. BR/TR, 6'4", 190 lbs. Deb: 9/11/42																											
1942	Cle-A	0	0	—	1	0	0	0	0	3^1	7	6	0	1	4	0	32.4	16.20	21	.438	.571	0	.000	-0	-5	-5	-0	-0.2
1943	Cle-A	1	2	.333	24	1	0	0	1	42^1	29	18	3	0	18	10	10.0	2.76	112	.201	.290	0	.000	-1	3	2	-1	0.0
1945	Cle-A	6	3	.667	31	8	2	0	1	85^2	89	42	2	1	28	34	12.4	3.99	81	.270	.329	2	.091	-2	-6	-7	-2	-1.1
1946	Cle-A	0	2	.000	21	0	0	0	1	29	29	16	2	1	20	6	15.5	4.97	67	.269	.388	0	.000	-0	-5	-6	-0	-0.5
Total	4	7	7	.500	77	9	2	0	3	160^1	154	82	7	3	70	50	12.7	4.10	79	.258	.338	2	.065	-3	-13	-16	-3	-1.8
● **RICK CERONE**	Cerone, Richard Aldo b: 5/19/54, Newark, N.J. BR/TR, 5'11", 192 lbs. Deb: 8/17/75 ♦																											
1987	NY-A	0	0	—	2	0	0	0	0	2	0	0	0	0	1	1	4.5	0.00	—	.000	.143	69	.243	1	1	1	-0	0.0
● **JOHN CERUTTI**	Cerutti, John Joseph b: 4/28/60, Albany, N.Y. BL/TL, 6'2", 200 lbs. Deb: 9/1/85																											
1985	Tor-A	0	2	.000	4	1	0	0	0	6^2	10	7	1	1	4	5	20.3	5.40	78	.323	.417	0	—	0	-1	-1	0	-0.2
1986	Tor-A	9	4	.692	34	20	2	1	1	145^1	150	73	25	1	47	89	12.3	4.15	102	.268	.326	0	—	0	1	1	0	0.1
1987	Tor-A	11	4	.733	44	21	2	0	0	151^1	144	75	30	1	59	92	12.1	4.40	102	.251	.322	0	—	0	1	2	-2	0.0
1988	Tor-A	6	7	.462	46	12	0	0	1	123^2	120	56	12	3	42	65	12.0	3.13	126	.256	.322	0	—	0	12	11	3	1.4
1989	*Tor-A	11	11	.500	33	31	3	1	0	205^1	214	90	19	6	53	69	12.0	3.07	123	.273	.323	0	—	0	19	17	3	2.0
1990	Tor-A	9	9	.500	30	23	0	0	0	140	162	77	23	4	49	49	13.8	4.76	83	.297	.359	0	—	0	-13	-12	-0	-1.4
1991	Det-A	3	6	.333	38	8	1	0	2	88^2	94	49	9	2	37	29	13.5	4.57	91	.276	.351	0	—	0	-5	-4	1	-0.3
Total	7	49	43	.533	229	116	8	2	4	861	894	427	119	18	291	398	12.6	3.94	103	.271	.333	0	—	0	14	13	4	1.6
● **RAY CHADWICK**	Chadwick, Ray Charles b: 11/17/62, Durham, N.C. BB/TR, 6'2", 180 lbs. Deb: 7/29/86																											
1986	Cal-A	0	5	.000	7	7	0	0	0	27^1	39	26	5	1	15	9	18.1	7.24	57	.336	.417	0	—	0	-9	-10	0	-1.4
● **LEON CHAGNON**	Chagnon, Leon Wilbur "Shag" b: 9/28/02, Pittsfield, N.H. d: 7/30/53, Amesbury, Mass. BR/TR, 6', 182 lbs. Deb: 10/5/29																											
1929	Pit-N	0	0	—	1	1	0	0	0	7	11	7	1	0	1	4	15.4	9.00	53	.333	.353	0	.000	-0	-3	-3	0	-0.1
1930	Pit-N	0	3	.000	18	4	3	0	0	62	92	52	9	5	23	27	17.4	6.82	73	.355	.418	4	.200	-1	-13	-13	0	-0.6
1932	Pit-N	9	6	.600	30	10	4	1	0	128	140	62	10	2	34	52	12.4	3.94	97	.276	.324	9	.225	2	-1	-2	-2	-0.2
1933	Pit-N	6	4	.600	39	5	1	0	1	100	100	48	2	3	17	35	10.8	3.69	90	.259	.296	1	.048	-2	-4	-4	-1	-0.7
1934	Pit-N	4	1	.800	33	0	0	0	1	58	68	32	5	1	24	19	14.4	4.81	86	.288	.356	3	.231	0	-5	-4	1	-0.2
1935	NY-N	0	2	.000	14	1	0	0	1	38^1	32	17	7	0	5	16	8.7	3.52	109	.232	.259	0	.000	-1	2	1	0	0.0
Total	6	19	16	.543	135	21	8	1	3	393^1	443	218	34	11	104	153	12.8	4.51	87	.284	.333	17	.162	-2	-24	-25	-1	-1.8
● **BOB CHAKALES**	Chakales, Robert Edward "Chick" b: 8/10/27, Asheville, N.C. BR/TR, 6'1", 185 lbs. Deb: 4/21/51																											
1951	Cle-A	3	4	.429	17	10	2	1	0	68^1	80	40	3	0	43	32	16.2	4.74	80	.292	.388	7	.350	2	-5	-8	-0	-0.5
1952	Cle-A	1	2	.333	5	1	0	0	0	12	19	13	2	0	8	7	20.3	9.75	34	.388	.474	2	.500	1	-8	-9	-1	-1.6
1953	Cle-A	0	2	.000	7	3	1	0	0	27	28	13	2	1	10	6	13.0	2.67	141	.283	.355	2	.286	0	4	3	0	0.3
1954	Cle-A	2	0	1.000	3	0	0	0	0	10^1	4	1	0	0	12	3	13.9	0.87	422	.114	.340	1	.333	1	3	3	-0	0.7
	Bal-A	3	7	.300	38	6	0	0	3	89^1	81	43	8	1	43	44	12.6	3.73	96	.245	.333	8	.364	2	-0	-2	0	0.1
	Yr	5	7	.417	41	6	0	0	3	99^2	85	44	8	1	55	47	12.7	3.43	105	.232	.334	9	.360	3	3	2	-0	0.8
1955	Chi-A	0	0	—	7	0	0	0	0	12^1	11	2	2	0	6	6	12.4	1.46	271	.256	.347	0	.000	-0	3	3	0	0.2
	Was-A	2	3	.400	29	0	0	0	0	54^2	55	38	4	1	25	28	13.3	5.27	73	.263	.345	0	.000	-1	-8	-9	1	-0.8
	Yr	2	3	.400	36	0	0	0	0	67	66	40	6	1	31	34	13.2	4.57	84	.262	.345	0	.000	-1	-5	-5	1	-0.6
1956	Was-A	4	4	.500	43	1	0	0	4	96	94	53	3	3	57	33	14.4	4.03	107	.268	.375	3	.150	-1	1	3	1	0.3
1957	Was-A	0	1	.000	4	2	0	0	0	18^1	20	13	2	0	10	12	14.7	5.40	72	.274	.361	1	.143	0	-3	-3	0	-0.1
	Bos-A	0	2	.000	18	0	0	0	3	32	53	30	5	1	11	16	18.3	8.16	49	.379	.428	2	.667	1	-16	-14	-1	-1.1
	Yr	0	3	.000	22	2	0	0	3	50^1	73	43	7	1	21	28	17.0	7.15	55	.343	.404	3	.300	1	-19	-17	-0	-1.2
Total	7	15	25	.375	171	23	3	1	10	420^1	445	246	31	7	225	187	14.5	4.54	85	.277	.369	26	.271	5	-28	-31	1	-2.5
● **GEORGE CHALMERS**	Chalmers, George W. "Dut" b: 6/7/1888, Edinburgh, Scot. d: 8/5/60, Bronx, N.Y. BR/TR, 6'1", 189 lbs. Deb: 9/21/10																											
1910	Phi-N	1	1	.500	4	3	2	0	0	22	21	17	0	1	11	12	13.5	5.32	59	.280	.379	1	.143	-0	-6	-5	1	-0.3
1911	Phi-N	13	10	.565	38	22	11	3	4	208^2	196	107	5	4	101	101	13.0	3.11	111	.256	.346	13	.178	-1	7	8	-1	0.6
1912	Phi-N	3	4	.429	12	8	3	0	0	57^2	64	34	4	2	37	22	16.1	3.28	111	.296	.404	3	.188	-0	1	2	-2	0.0
1913	Phi-N	3	10	.231	26	15	4	0	1	116	133	75	3	5	51	46	14.7	4.81	69	.296	.374	7	.212	-1	-21	-18	1	-1.9
1914	Phi-N	0	3	.000	3	2	1	0	0	18	23	17	0	1	15	6	19.5	5.50	53	.324	.448	0	.000	-1	-5	-5	0	-0.8
1915	*Phi-N	8	9	.471	26	20	13	1	1	170^1	159	58	3	0	45	82	10.8	2.48	110	.255	.305	10	.169	-0	5	5	1	0.5
1916	Phi-N	1	4	.200	12	8	2	0	0	53^2	49	31	2	2	19	21	11.7	3.19	83	.244	.315	0	.000	-2	-3	-3	0	-0.5
Total	7	29	41	.414	121	78	36	4	6	646^1	645	339	17	15	279	290	13.1	3.41	93	.269	.348	34	.163	-5	-22	-18	1	-2.4
● **CRAIG CHAMBERLAIN**	Chamberlain, Craig Philip b: 2/2/57, Hollywood, Cal. BR/TR, 6'1", 190 lbs. Deb: 8/12/79																											
1979	KC-A	4	4	.500	10	10	4	0	0	69^2	68	31	7	1	18	30	11.2	3.75	114	.261	.311	0	—	0	4	4	-2	0.2
1980	KC-A	0	1	.000	5	0	0	0	0	9^1	10	8	3	0	5	3	14.5	6.75	60	.270	.357	0	—	0	-3	-3	0	-0.3
Total	2	4	5	.444	15	10	4	0	0	79	78	39	10	1	23	33	11.6	4.10	104	.262	.317	0	—	0	1	1	-2	-0.1
● **ELTON CHAMBERLAIN**	Chamberlain, Elton P. "Icebox" b: 11/5/1867, Buffalo, N.Y. d: 9/22/29, Baltimore, Md. BR/TR (TB 1888 (part)), 5'9", 168 lbs. Deb: 9/13/1886																											
1886	Lou-a	0	3	.000	4	4	4	0	0	31^1	39	43	0	0	17	18	16.1	6.61	55	.287	.366	3	.158	-0	-11	-10	-0	-0.7
1887	Lou-a	18	16	.529	36	36	35	1	0	309	457	226	8	14	117	118	13.7	3.79	116	.336	.343	38	.266	-3	17	20	1	1.4
1888	Lou-a	14	9	.609	24	24	21	1	0	196	177	123	2	11	59	119	11.3	2.53	122	.232	.297	18	.191	0	12	12	1	1.4
	*StL-a	11	2	.846	14	14	13	1	0	112	61	34	1	6	27	57	7.6	1.61	203	.154	.220	5	.100	-3	18	19	-1	1.6
	Yr	25	11	.694	38	38	34	2	0	308	238	157	3	17	86	176	10.0	2.19	143	.206	.271	23	.160	-3	30	32	0	3.0
1889	StL-a	32	15	.681	53	51	44	3	1	421^2	376	220	18	17	165	202	11.9	2.97	142	.231	.309	34	.199	-2	41	54	-3	4.3
1890	StL-a	3	1	.750	5	5	3	0	0	35	47	37	1	0	26	14	18.8	5.91	73	.311	.412	2	.133	-1	-8	-6	0	-0.6
	Col-a	12	6	.667	25	21	19	6	0	175	128	69	2	8	70	114	10.6	2.21	162	.198	.285	15	.231	3	32	29	-2	2.6
	Yr	15	7	.682	30	26	22	**6**	0	210	175	106	3	8	96	128	12.0	2.83	131	.220	.310	17	.213	1	24	21	-2	2.0
1891	Phi-a	22	23	.489	49	46	44	0	0	405^2	397	263	10	12	206	204	13.6	4.22	90	.248	.338	33	.188	2	-23	-19	0	-1.4
1892	Cin-N	19	23	.452	52	49	43	2	0	406^1	391	230	8	17	170	169	12.8	3.39	96	.243	.322	36	.225	2	-5	-5	-4	-0.6
1893	Cin-N	16	12	.571	34	27	19	1	0	241	248	148	3	15	112	59	14.0	3.73	128	.258	.345	19	.196	-3	25	27	-2	2.0
1894	Cin-N	10	9	.526	23	22	18	1	0	177^2	220	155	10	12	91	57	16.4	5.77	96	.301	.387	22	.314	4	-9	-4	-1	0.0
1896	Cle-N	0	1	.000	2	2	1	0	0	11	21	12	0	1	5	2	22.1	7.36	62	.396	.458	0	.000	-0	-4	-3	-0	-0.3
Total	10	157	120	.567	321	301	264	16	1	2521^2	2562	1560	63	113	1065	1133	12.9	3.57	112	.255	.327	225	.212	-2	87	114	-11	9.7
● **BILL CHAMBERLAIN**	Chamberlain, William Vincent b: 4/21/09, Stoughton, Mass. d: 2/6/94, Brockton, Mass. BR/TL, 5'10.5", 173 lbs. Deb: 8/2/32																											
1932	Chi-A	0	5	.000	12	5	0	0	0	41^1	39	30	3	0	25	11	13.9	4.57	95	.250	.354	1	.100	-1	-0	-1	-1	-0.2
● **CLIFF CHAMBERS**	Chambers, Clifford Day "Lefty" b: 1/10/22, Portland, Ore. BL/TL, 6'3", 208 lbs. Deb: 4/24/48																											
1948	Chi-N	2	9	.182	29	12	3	1	0	103^2	100	57	4	3	48	51	13.1	4.43	88	.254	.339	4	.133	-1	-5	-6	0	-0.6
1949	Pit-N	13	7	.650	34	21	10	1	0	177^1	186	89	15	5	58	93	12.6	3.96	106	.268	.329	13	.236	3	2	5	1	0.8
1950	Pit-N	12	15	.444	37	33	11	2	0	249^1	262	138	18	6	92	93	13.0	4.30	102	.265	.332	26	.289	7	-4	2	-2	0.7
1951	Pit-N	3	6	.333	10	10	2	1	0	59^2	64	38	5	4	31	19	14.9	5.58	76	.276	.371	7	.333	2	-11	-8	-2	-1.0
	StL-N	11	6	.647	21	16	9	1	0	129^1	120	59	13	0	56	45	12.2	3.83	104	.251	.329	8	.163	0	2	2	-2	0.1
	Yr	14	12	.538	31	26	11	2	0	189	184	97	18	4	87	64	13.1	4.38	92	.259	.343	15	.214	2	-9	-7	-3	-0.9
1952	StL-N	4	4	.500	26	13	2	1	1	98^1	110	51	8	2	33	47	13.3	4.12	90	.285	.344	9	.281	3	-4	-4	0	0.0
1953	StL-N	3	6	.333	32	8	0	0	0	79^2	82	50	7	1	43	26	14.2	4.86	88	.266	.358	2	.118	-1	-5	-5	0	-0.6
Total	6	48	53	.475	189	113	37	7	1	897^1	924	482	70	21	361	374	13.1	4.29	96	.266	.338	69	.235	13	-26	-15	-4	-0.6
● **JOHNNIE CHAMBERS**	Chambers, Johnnie Monroe b: 9/10/11, Copperhill, Tenn d: 5/11/77, Palatka, Fla. BL/TR, 6', 185 lbs. Deb: 5/4/37																											
1937	StL-N	0	0	—	2	0	0	0	0	2	5	4	0	0	2	1	31.5	18.00	22	.455	.538	0	—	0	-3	-3	-0	-0.2
● **ROME CHAMBERS**	Chambers, Richard Jerome b: 8/31/1875, Weaverville, N.C. d: 8/30/02, Weaverville, N.C. BL/TL, 6'2", 173 lbs. Deb: 5/7/00																											
1900	Bos-N	0	0	—	1	0	0	0	1	4	5	6	0	0	5	2	22.5	11.25	37	.313	.476	0	.000	-0	-3	-3	-0	-0.2

YEAR	TM/L	W	L	PCT	G	GS	CG	SH	SV	IP	H	R	HR	HB	BB	SO	RAT	ERA	ERA+	OAV	OOB	BH	AVG	PB	PR	PR+	PD	TPI
● **BILL CHAMBERS**	Chambers, William Christopher b: 9/13/1889, Cameron, W.Va. d: 3/27/62, Fort Wayne, Ind. BR/TR, 5'9", 185 lbs. Deb: 7/11/10																											
1910	StL-N	0	0	—	1	0	0	0	0	1	1	1	0	0	0	0	9.0	0.00	—	.250	.250	0		0	0	0	-0	0.0
● **BILL CHAMPION**	Champion, Buford Billy b: 9/18/47, Shelby, N.C. BR/TR, 6'4", 188 lbs. Deb: 6/4/69																											
1969	Phi-N	5	10	.333	23	20	4	2	1	116^2	130	68	7	3	63	70	15.1	5.01	71	.286	.376	6	.171	0	-18	-19	1	-2.1
1970	Phi-N	0	2	.000	7	1	0	0	0	14	21	14	3	1	10	12	20.6	9.00	44	.375	.478	0	.000	-0	-8	-8	0	-1.0
1971	Phi-N	3	5	.375	37	9	0	0	0	108^2	100	61	10	3	48	49	12.5	4.39	80	.249	.334	3	.111	-1	-11	-10	1	-0.7
1972	Phi-N	4	14	.222	30	22	2	0	0	132^2	155	80	11	1	54	54	14.2	5.09	71	.301	.368	5	.147	0	-24	-21	1	-2.6
1973	Mil-A	5	8	.385	37	11	2	0	1	136^1	139	58	10	4	62	67	13.5	3.70	102	.267	.350	0	—	0	2	1	2	0.3
1974	Mil-A	11	4	.733	31	23	2	0	0	161^2	168	72	12	0	49	60	12.1	3.62	100	.270	.323	0	—	0	0	0	-1	-0.1
1975	Mil-A	6	6	.500	27	13	3	1	0	110	125	77	11	0	55	40	14.7	5.89	65	.290	.370	0	—	0	-26	-25	1	-2.3
1976	Mil-A	0	1	.000	10	3	0	0	0	24^1	35	20	0	1	13	8	18.1	7.03	50	.361	.441	0	—	0	-9	-10	1	-0.4
Total	8	34	50	.405	202	102	13	3	2	804^1	873	450	64	13	354	360	13.9	4.69	78	.282	.358	14	.141	-1	-94	-92	4	-8.9
● **DEAN CHANCE**	Chance, Wilmer Dean b: 6/1/41, Plain Twsp., Ohio BR/TR, 6'3", 200 lbs. Deb: 9/11/61																											
1961	LA-A	0	2	.000	5	4	0	0	0	18^1	33	15	0	1	5	11	19.1	6.87	66	.412	.453	0	.000	-1	-6	-4	1	-0.4
1962	LA-A	14	10	.583	50	24	6	2	8	206^2	195	83	14	5	66	127	11.6	2.96	130	.250	.313	4	.062	-5	23	21	1	2.1
1963	LA-A	13	18	.419	45	35	6	2	3	248	229	109	10	10	90	168	11.9	3.19	107	.243	.316	12	.150	-1	12	7	1	0.8
1964	LA-A★	**20**	9	.690	46	35	**15**	**11**	4	**278^1**	194	56	7	2	86	207	9.1	**1.65**	**199**	.195	.261	7	.079	-5	**61**	**56**	-2	**5.3**
1965	Cal-A	15	10	.600	36	33	10	4	0	225^2	197	86	12	9	101	164	12.2	3.15	108	.238	.328	7	.093	-2	8	6	3	0.8
1966	Cal-A	12	17	.414	41	37	11	2	1	259^2	206	113	18	7	114	180	11.3	3.08	109	.222	.312	2	.026	-6	10	8	2	0.4
1967	Min-A★	20	14	.588	41	39	**18**	5	1	**283^2**	244	109	17	7	68	220	10.1	2.73	127	.229	.279	3	.033	-6	16	22	2	2.2
1968	Min-A	16	16	.500	43	39	15	6	1	292	224	96	15	10	63	234	9.2	2.53	122	.211	.261	5	.054	-6	15	18	3	1.8
1969	*Min-A	5	4	.556	20	15	1	0	0	88^1	76	39	6	4	35	50	11.7	2.95	124	.233	.315	1	.042	-1	7	7	1	0.4
1970	Cle-A	9	8	.529	45	19	1	1	4	155	172	80	18	6	59	109	13.8	4.24	93	.287	.357	3	.071	-3	-9	-4	1	-0.8
	NY-N	0	1	.000	3	0	0	0	1	2	3	3	0	0	2	0	22.5	13.50	30	.500	.625	0	—	0	-2	-2	0	-0.4
1971	Det-A	4	6	.400	31	14	0	0	0	89^2	91	43	5	4	50	64	14.6	3.51	102	.265	.364	0	.000	-2	-0	1	-0	-0.2
Total	11	128	115	.527	406	294	83	33	23	2147^1	1864	832	122	65	739	1534	11.2	2.92	119	.234	.305	44	.066	-37	134	131	8	12.0
● **ED CHANDLER**	Chandler, Edward Oliver b: 2/17/22, Pinson, Ala. BR/TR, 6'2", 190 lbs. Deb: 4/18/47																											
1947	Bro-N	0	1	.000	15	1	0	0	1	29^2	31	23	7	0	12	8	13.0	6.37	65	.263	.331	0	.000	0	-8	-7	0	-0.3
● **SPUD CHANDLER**	Chandler, Spurgeon Ferdinand b: 9/12/07, Commerce, Ga. d: 1/9/90, S.Pasadena, Fla. BR/TR, 6', 181 lbs. Deb: 5/6/37 C																											
1937	NY-A	7	4	.636	12	10	6	2	0	82^1	79	31	8	1	20	31	10.9	2.84	156	.253	.300	4	.133	-2	16	15	2	1.8
1938	NY-A	14	5	.737	23	23	14	2	0	172	183	86	7	2	47	36	12.1	4.03	113	.271	.320	14	.203	2	15	10	4	1.5
1939	NY-A	3	0	1.000	11	0	0	0	0	19	26	7	0	0	9	4	16.6	2.84	153	.329	.398	2	.400	1	4	3	1	0.6
1940	NY-A	8	7	.533	27	24	6	1	0	172	184	100	12	6	60	56	13.1	4.60	88	.275	.341	9	.150	-0	-4	-12	3	-0.5
1941	*NY-A	10	4	.714	28	20	11	4	4	163^2	146	68	5	0	60	60	11.3	3.19	123	.239	.307	11	.183	-1	17	14	3	1.4
1942	*NY-A★	16	5	.762	24	24	17	3	0	200^2	176	64	13	4	74	74	11.4	2.38	145	.237	.309	15	.211	4	29	25	3	3.3
1943	*NY-A☆	**20**	4	**.833**	30	30	**20**	**5**	0	253	197	62	5	4	54	134	**9.1**	**1.64**	**197**	.215	**.261**	25	.258	7	**47**	**46**	3	**5.8**
1944	NY-A	0	0	—	1	1	0	0	0	6	6	3	1	1	1	1	12.0	4.50	77	.300	.364	0	.000	-0	-1	-1	0	0.0
1945	NY-A	2	1	.667	4	4	2	1	0	31	30	16	2	0	7	12	10.7	4.65	75	.250	.291	4	.333	1	-4	-4	0	-0.3
1946	NY-A☆	20	8	.714	34	32	20	6	2	257^1	200	71	7	1	90	138	10.2	2.10	164	.218	.288	14	.149	-0	40	39	4	4.9
1947	*NY-A☆	9	5	.643	17	16	13	2	0	128	100	41	4	0	41	68	9.9	2.46	144	.214	.277	12	.245	4	18	16	3	2.5
Total	11	109	43	.717	211	184	109	26	6	1485	1327	549	64	19	463	614	11.0	2.84	132	.240	.301	110	.201	17	176	155	27	21.0
● **ESTY CHANEY**	Chaney, Esty Clyon b: 1/29/1891, Hadley, Pa. d: 2/5/52, Cleveland, Ohio BR/TR, 5'11", 170 lbs. Deb: 8/2/13																											
1913	Bos-A	0	0	—	1	1	0	0	0	1	1	1	0	0	2	0	27.0	9.00	33	.200	.429	0	—	0	-1	-1	-0	0.0
1914	Bro-F	0	0	—	1	0	0	0	0	4	7	3	0	0	2	1	20.3	6.75	43	.389	.450	0	.000	-0	-2	-2	-0	-0.1
Total	2	0	0	—	2	0	0	0	0	5	8	4	0	0	4	1	21.6	7.20	40	.348	.444	0	.000	-0	-2	-2	-0	-0.1
● **DARRIN CHAPIN**	Chapin, Darrin John b: 2/1/66, Warren, Ohio BR/TR, 6', 170 lbs. Deb: 9/21/91																											
1991	NY-A	0	1	.000	3	0	0	0	0	5^1	3	3	0	0	6	5	15.2	5.06	82	.158	.360	0	—	0	-1	-1	0	-0.1
1992	Phi-N	0	0	—	1	0	0	0	0	2	2	2	1	0	0	1	9.0	9.00	39	.250	.250	0	—	0	-1	-1	0	-0.1
Total	2	0	1	.000	4	0	0	0	0	7^1	5	5	1	0	6	6	13.5	6.14	65	.185	.333	0	—	0	-2	-2	0	-0.2
● **TINY CHAPLIN**	Chaplin, James Bailey b: 7/13/05, Los Angeles, Cal. d: 3/25/39, National City, Cal BR/TR, 6'1", 195 lbs. Deb: 4/13/28																											
1928	NY-N	0	2	.000	12	1	0	0	0	24	27	15	0	0	8	5	13.1	4.50	87	.284	.340	0	.000	-1	-1	-2	1	-0.2
1930	NY-N	2	6	.250	19	8	3	0	1	73	89	45	8	4	16	20	13.4	5.18	91	.305	.349	2	.105	-0	-2	-4	0	-0.4
1931	NY-N	3	0	1.000	16	3	1	0	1	42^1	39	17	2	2	16	7	12.1	3.19	116	.242	.318	2	.182	0	3	2	1	0.1
1936	Bos-N	10	15	.400	40	31	14	0	2	231^2	273	131	21	3	62	86	13.1	4.12	93	.294	.340	17	.202	-0	-3	-8	2	-0.6
Total	4	15	23	.395	87	43	18	0	4	371	428	208	31	9	102	118	13.1	4.25	94	.290	.340	21	.176	-1	-2	-11	1	-1.1
● **ED CHAPMAN**	Chapman, Edwin Volney b: 11/28/05, Courtland, Miss. d: 5/3/2000, Clarksdale, Miss. BB/TR, 6'1", 185 lbs. Deb: 8/6/33																											
1933	Was-A	0	0	—	6	1	0	0	0	9	10	9	2	0	2	4	12.0	8.00	52	.270	.308	0	.000	-0	-4	-4	-0	-0.2
● **FRED CHAPMAN**	Chapman, Frederick Joseph b: 11/24/1872, Little Cooley, Pa. d: 12/14/57, Union City, Pa. BR/TR, 5'8", 165 lbs. Deb: 7/22/1887																											
1887	Phi-a	0	0	—	1	1	1	0	0	5	10	6	0	0	2	4	18.0	7.20	60	.417	.417	0	.000	-0	-2	-2	-0	-0.1
● **BEN CHAPMAN**	Chapman, William Benjamin b: 12/25/08, Nashville, Tenn. d: 7/7/93, Hoover, Ala. BR/TR, 6', 190 lbs. Deb: 4/15/30 MC♦																											
1944	Bro-N	5	3	.625	11	9	6	0	0	79^1	75	36	4	3	33	37	12.6	3.40	104	.242	.321	14	.368	6	2	1	-2	0.6
1945	Bro-N	3	3	.500	10	7	2	0	0	53^2	64	33	3	3	32	23	16.6	5.53	68	.296	.394	3	.136	-1	-10	-11	1	-1.0
	Phi-N	0	0	—	3	0	0	0	0	7	7	8	0	0	6	4	16.7	7.71	50	.259	.394	16	.314	0	-3	-3	-0	-0.1
	Yr	3	3	.500	13	7	2	0	0	60^2	71	41	3	3	38	27	16.6	5.79	65	.292	.394	19	.260	-0	-13	-14	0	-1.1
1946	Phi-N	0	0	—	1	0	0	0	0	1	1	0	0	0	0	1	9.0	0.00	—	.200	.200	0	.000	-0	0	0	0	0.0
Total	3	8	6	.571	25	16	8	0	0	141	147	77	7	6	71	65	14.3	4.40	83	.263	.353	1958	.302	6	-11	-12	-1	-0.5
● **BILL CHAPPELLE**	Chappelle, William Hogan "Big Bill" b: 3/22/1884, Waterloo, N.Y. d: 12/31/44, Mineola, N.Y. BR/TR, 6'2", 206 lbs. Deb: 8/20/08																											
1908	Bos-N	2	4	.333	13	6	3	1	0	70^1	60	28	0	4	17	23	10.4	1.79	135	.233	.290	1	.048	-1	4	5	1	0.4
1909	Bos-N	1	1	.500	5	3	2	0	0	29	31	13	0	1	11	8	13.3	1.86	151	.279	.350	4	.364	2	2	3	1	0.6
	Cin-N	0	0	—	1	0	0	0	1	4	5	2	0	1	2	0	18.0	2.25	115	.278	.381	0	.000	-0	0	0	-0	0.0
	Yr	1	1	.500	6	3	2	0	1	33	36	15	0	2	13	8	13.9	1.91	146	.279	.354	4	.333	2	3	3	1	0.6
1914	Bro-F	4	2	.667	16	6	4	0	0	74^1	71	43	1	3	29	31	12.5	3.15	91	.255	.332	0	.000	-4	-2	-2	1	-0.7
Total	3	7	7	.500	35	15	9	1	1	177^2	167	86	1	9	59	62	11.9	2.38	113	.251	.321	5	.089	-3	5	6	1	0.3
● **NORM CHARLTON**	Charlton, Norman Wood b: 1/6/63, Fort Polk, La. BB/TL, 6'3", 205 lbs. Deb: 8/19/88																											
1988	Cin-N	4	5	.444	10	10	0	0	0	61^1	60	27	6	2	20	39	12.0	3.96	91	.256	.320	0	.000	-1	-3	-2	-0	-0.5
1989	Cin-N	8	3	.727	69	0	0	0	0	95^1	67	38	5	2	40	98	10.3	2.93	123	.197	.285	0	.000	-1	6	7	-0	0.7
1990	*Cin-N	12	9	.571	56	16	1	1	2	154^1	131	53	10	4	70	117	12.0	2.74	144	.231	.320	5	.135	0	18	20	1	2.7
1991	Cin-N	3	5	.375	39	11	0	0	1	108^1	92	37	6	6	34	77	11.0	2.91	131	.236	.307	1	.043	-2	9	10	1	0.7
1992	Cin-N★	4	2	.667	64	0	0	0	26	81^1	79	39	7	3	26	90	12.0	2.99	121	.262	.326	1	.200	0	5	5	-1	0.7
1993	Sea-A	1	3	.250	34	0	0	0	18	34^2	22	12	4	0	17	48	10.1	2.34	189	.179	.279	0	—	0	8	8	-0	1.5
1995	Phi-N	2	5	.286	25	0	0	0	0	22	23	19	2	3	15	12	16.8	7.36	57	.280	.410	1	1.000	1	-8	-8	-1	-1.4
	*Sea-A	2	1	.667	30	0	0	0	14	47^2	23	12	2	1	16	58	7.6	1.51	314	.143	.225	0	—	0	17	17	0	1.8
1996	Sea-A	4	7	.364	70	0	0	0	20	75^2	68	37	7	1	38	73	12.7	4.04	122	.244	.336	0	—	0	8	8	0	1.3
1997	*Sea-A	3	8	.273	71	0	0	0	14	69^1	89	59	7	4	47	55	18.2	7.27	62	.312	.417	0	—	0	-21	-22	1	-3.5
1998	Bal-A	2	1	.667	36	0	0	0	0	35	46	27	5	0	25	41	18.3	6.94	66	.305	.403	0	—	0	-9	-9	1	-0.6
	Atl-N	0	0	—	13	0	0	0	1	13	7	2	0	1	8	6	11.1	1.38	300	.167	.314	0	.000	-0	4	4	0	0.2
1999	TB-A	2	3	.400	42	0	0	0	0	50^2	49	29	4	1	36	45	15.3	4.44	112	.257	.377	0	—	0	2	3	-0	0.2
2000	Cin-N	0	0	—	2	0	0	0	0	3	6	9	1	0	6	1	36.0	27.00	18	.429	.600	0	—	0	-7	-7	0	-0.3
Total	12	47	52	.475	561	37	1	1	96	851^2	762	400	66	28	398	760	12.6	3.75	110	.241	.331	8	.092	-2	29	36	1	3.5

● **PETE CHARTON** Charton, Frank Lane b: 12/21/42, Jackson, Tenn. BL/TR, 6'2", 190 lbs. Deb: 4/19/64

YEAR	TM/L	W	L	PCT	G	GS	CG	SH	SV	IP	H	R	HR	HB	BB	SO	RAT	ERA	ERA+	OAV	OOB	BH	AVG	PB	PR	PR+	PD	TPI
1964	Bos-A	0	2	.000	25	5	0	0	0	65	67	39	12	1	24	37	12.7	5.26	73	.275	.342	1	.100	-0	-12	-10	2	-0.4

● **HAL CHASE** Chase, Harold Homer "Prince Hal" b: 2/13/1883, Los Gatos, Cal. d: 5/18/47, Colusa, Cal. BR/TL (BL 1909 (1 game)), 6', 175 lbs. Deb: 4/14/05 M♦

YEAR	TM/L	W	L	PCT	G	GS	CG	SH	SV	IP	H	R	HR	HB	BB	SO	RAT	ERA	ERA+	OAV	OOB	BH	AVG	PB	PR	PR+	PD	TPI
1908	NY-A	0	0	—	1	0	0	0	0	0^1	0	0	0	0	0	0	0.0	0.00	—	.000	.000	104	.257	0	0	0	0	0.0

● **KEN CHASE** Chase, Kendall Fay "Lefty" b: 10/6/13, Oneonta, N.Y. d: 1/16/85, Oneonta, N.Y. BL/TL, 6'2", 210 lbs. Deb: 4/23/36

YEAR	TM/L	W	L	PCT	G	GS	CG	SH	SV	IP	H	R	HR	HB	BB	SO	RAT	ERA	ERA+	OAV	OOB	BH	AVG	PB	PR	PR+	PD	TPI
1936	Was-A	0	0	—	1	0	0	0	0	2^1	2	3	0	0	4	1	23.1	11.57	41	.250	.500	1	1.000	1	-2	-2	-0	0.0
1937	Was-A	4	3	.571	14	9	4	0	0	76^1	74	41	4	0	60	43	15.8	4.13	107	.257	.385	1	.034	-4	4	3	-0	-0.2
1938	Was-A	9	10	.474	32	21	7	0	1	150	151	99	4	4	113	64	16.1	5.58	81	.268	.394	10	.208	1	-13	-19	1	-1.8
1939	Was-A	10	19	.345	32	31	15	1	0	232	215	116	10	1	114	118	12.8	3.80	114	.243	.330	15	.169	-3	21	15	0	1.4
1940	Was-A	15	17	.469	35	34	20	1	0	261^2	260	120	14	5	143	129	14.0	3.23	129	.261	.357	15	.163	-1	33	29	-1	3.0
1941	Was-A	6	18	.250	33	30	8	1	0	205^2	228	136	11	3	115	98	15.1	5.08	80	.280	.371	11	.149	-2	-21	-24	1	-2.4
1942	Bos-A	5	1	.833	13	10	4	0	0	80^1	82	37	5	0	41	34	13.8	3.81	98	.263	.348	6	.182	1	-1	-1	-1	-0.1
1943	Bos-A	0	4	.000	7	5	0	0	0	27^1	36	25	0	0	30	9	21.7	6.91	48	.316	.458	1	.091	-1	-11	-11	0	-1.4
	NY-N	4	12	.250	21	20	4	1	0	129^1	140	70	7	2	74	86	15.0	4.11	84	.275	.369	9	.214	0	-10	-9	-1	-1.1
Total	8	53	84	.387	188	160	62	4	1	1165	1188	647	55	15	694	582	14.7	4.27	97	.265	.365	69	.165	-8	-0	-20	-0	-2.6

● **JIM CHATTERTON** Chatterton, James M. b: 10/14/1864, Brooklyn, N.Y. d: 12/15/44, Tewksbury, Mass. Deb: 6/7/1884 ♦

YEAR	TM/L	W	L	PCT	G	GS	CG	SH	SV	IP	H	R	HR	HB	BB	SO	RAT	ERA	ERA+	OAV	OOB	BH	AVG	PB	PR	PR+	PD	TPI
1884	KC-U	0	1	.000	1	1	0	0	0	5	11	7	0		2	2	23.4	3.60	62	.407	.448	2	.133	-0	-1	-1	0	-0.1

● **ANTHONY CHAVEZ** Chavez, Anthony Francisco b: 10/22/70, Turlock, Cal. BR/TR, 5'11", 180 lbs. Deb: 9/2/97

YEAR	TM/L	W	L	PCT	G	GS	CG	SH	SV	IP	H	R	HR	HB	BB	SO	RAT	ERA	ERA+	OAV	OOB	BH	AVG	PB	PR	PR+	PD	TPI
1997	Ana-A	0	0	—	7	0	0	0	0	9^2	7	1	1	0	5	10	11.2	0.93	492	.206	.308	0	—	0	4	4	1	0.2

● **NESTOR CHAVEZ** Chavez, Nestor Isais (Silva) b: 7/6/47, Chacao, Venez. d: 3/16/69, Maracaibo, Venez. BR/TR, 6', 170 lbs. Deb: 9/9/67

YEAR	TM/L	W	L	PCT	G	GS	CG	SH	SV	IP	H	R	HR	HB	BB	SO	RAT	ERA	ERA+	OAV	OOB	BH	AVG	PB	PR	PR+	PD	TPI
1967	SF-N	1	0	1.000	2	0	0	0	0	5	4	2	0	0	3	3	12.6	0.00	—	.211	.318	0	.000	-0	2	2	0	0.4

● **DAVE CHEADLE** Cheadle, David Baird b: 2/19/52, Greensboro, N.C. BL/TL, 6'2", 203 lbs. Deb: 9/16/73

YEAR	TM/L	W	L	PCT	G	GS	CG	SH	SV	IP	H	R	HR	HB	BB	SO	RAT	ERA	ERA+	OAV	OOB	BH	AVG	PB	PR	PR+	PD	TPI
1973	Atl-N	0	1	.000	2	0	0	0	0	2	2	4	1	0	3	2	22.5	18.00	22	.250	.455	0	—	0	-3	-3	-0	-0.5

● **CHARLIE CHECH** Chech, Charles William b: 4/27/1878, Madison, Wis. d: 1/31/38, Los Angeles, Cal. BR/TR, 5'11.5", 190 lbs. Deb: 4/14/05

YEAR	TM/L	W	L	PCT	G	GS	CG	SH	SV	IP	H	R	HR	HB	BB	SO	RAT	ERA	ERA+	OAV	OOB	BH	AVG	PB	PR	PR+	PD	TPI
1905	Cin-N	14	14	.500	39	25	20	1	0	267^2	300	139	4	11	77	79	13.0	2.89	114	.288	.344	17	.191	1	3	11	-0	1.1
1906	Cin-N	1	4	.200	11	5	5	0	3	66	59	32	1	6	24	17	12.1	2.32	119	.243	.326	5	.200	1	2	3	0	0.4
1908	Cle-A	11	7	.611	27	20	14	4	0	165^2	136	51	2	7	34	51	9.6	1.74	137	.229	.279	5	.104	-1	12	12	1	1.4
1909	Bos-A	7	5	.583	17	13	6	1	0	106^2	107	51	3	5	27	40	11.7	2.95	85	.260	.314	3	.083	-2	-6	-5	-0	-0.9
Total	4	33	30	.524	94	63	45	6	3	606	602	273	10	29	162	187	11.8	2.52	113	.263	.320	30	.152	-1	12	20	1	2.0

● **ROBINSON CHECO** Checo, Robinson (Perez) b: 9/9/71, Santo Domingo, D.R. BR/TR, 6'1", 185 lbs. Deb: 9/16/97

YEAR	TM/L	W	L	PCT	G	GS	CG	SH	SV	IP	H	R	HR	HB	BB	SO	RAT	ERA	ERA+	OAV	OOB	BH	AVG	PB	PR	PR+	PD	TPI
1997	Bos-A	1	1	.500	5	2	0	0	0	13^1	12	5	0	0	3	14	10.1	3.38	137	.235	.278	0	—	0	2	2	-0	0.2
1998	Bos-A	0	2	.000	2	2	0	0	0	7^2	11	8	3	0	5	5	18.8	9.39	50	.379	.471	0	—	0	-4	-4	-0	-0.6
1999	LA-N	2	2	.500	9	2	0	0	0	15^2	24	20	5	0	13	11	21.3	10.34	41	.333	.435	1	.333	0	-10	-11	-1	-1.9
Total	3	3	5	.375	16	6	0	0	0	36^2	47	33	8	0	21	30	16.7	7.61	59	.309	.393	1	.333	0	-12	-13	-1	-2.3

● **VIRGIL CHEEVES** Cheeves, Virgil Earl "Chief" b: 2/12/01, Oklahoma City, Okla. d: 5/5/79, Dallas, Tex. BR/TR, 6', 195 lbs. Deb: 9/7/20

YEAR	TM/L	W	L	PCT	G	GS	CG	SH	SV	IP	H	R	HR	HB	BB	SO	RAT	ERA	ERA+	OAV	OOB	BH	AVG	PB	PR	PR+	PD	TPI
1920	Chi-N	0	0	—	5	2	0	0	0	18	16	7	0	0	7	3	11.5	3.50	92	.250	.324	0	.000	-0	-1	-1	-1	-0.1
1921	Chi-N	11	12	.478	37	22	9	1	0	163	192	97	8	9	47	39	13.7	4.64	82	.309	.366	8	.167	-2	-15	-15	-3	-2.2
1922	Chi-N	12	11	.522	39	22	9	1	2	182^2	195	99	9	10	76	40	13.8	4.09	103	.281	.360	13	.210	1	0	2	-1	0.2
1923	Chi-N	3	4	.429	19	8	0	0	0	71^1	89	54	8	3	37	13	16.3	6.18	65	.314	.399	4	.174	-1	-17	-17	-1	-1.6
1924	Cle-A	0	0	—	8	1	0	0	0	17^1	26	17	2	1	17	2	22.8	7.79	55	.388	.518	1	.250	0	-7	-7	0	-0.3
1927	NY-N	0	0	—	3	0	0	0	0	6^1	8	3	1	0	4	1	17.1	4.26	90	.333	.429	0	—	0	-0	-0	0	0.0
Total	6	26	27	.491	111	55	18	2	2	458^2	526	277	28	23	188	98	14.5	4.73	84	.300	.375	26	.184	-1	-40	-37	-5	-4.0

● **ITALO CHELINI** Chelini, Italo Vincent "Chilly" or "Lefty"
b: 10/10/14, San Francisco, Cal d: 8/25/72, San Francisco, Cal BL/TL, 5'10.5", 175 lbs. Deb: 9/12/35

YEAR	TM/L	W	L	PCT	G	GS	CG	SH	SV	IP	H	R	HR	HB	BB	SO	RAT	ERA	ERA+	OAV	OOB	BH	AVG	PB	PR	PR+	PD	TPI
1935	Chi-A	0	0	—	2	0	0	0	0	5	7	7	1	1	4	1	21.6	12.60	37	.350	.480	1	.500	0	-5	-4	0	-0.2
1936	Chi-A	4	3	.571	18	6	5	0	0	83^2	100	51	8	0	30	16	14.0	4.95	105	.291	.348	5	.156	-1	1	2	-1	-0.1
1937	Chi-A	0	1	.000	4	0	0	0	0	8^2	15	10	2	1	0	3	16.6	10.38	44	.405	.421	0	.000	0	-6	-6	-0	-0.5
Total	3	4	4	.500	24	6	5	0	0	97^1	122	68	11	2	34	20	14.6	5.83	88	.304	.362	6	.171	-1	-9	-7	-1	-0.8

● **BRUCE CHEN** Chen, Bruce Kastulo b: 6/19/77, Panama City, Panama BL/TL, 6'1", 150 lbs. Deb: 9/7/98

YEAR	TM/L	W	L	PCT	G	GS	CG	SH	SV	IP	H	R	HR	HB	BB	SO	RAT	ERA	ERA+	OAV	OOB	BH	AVG	PB	PR	PR+	PD	TPI
1998	Atl-N	2	0	1.000	4	4	0	0	0	20^1	23	9	3	1	9	17	14.6	3.98	104	.287	.367	1	.143	-0	1	0	-1	0.0
1999	Atl-N	2	2	.500	16	7	0	0	0	51	38	32	11	2	27	45	11.8	5.47	82	.208	.316	0	.000	-1	-5	-6	-1	-0.6
2000	Atl-N	4	0	1.000	22	0	0	0	0	39^2	35	15	4	1	19	32	12.5	2.50	181	.232	.322	0	.000	-1	9	9	-1	0.7
	Phi-N	3	4	.429	15	15	0	0	0	94^1	81	39	14	1	27	80	10.4	3.63	130	.232	.289	1	.040	-2	11	11	-1	0.5
	Yr	7	4	.636	37	15	0	0	0	134	116	54	18	2	46	112	11.0	3.29	142	.232	.299	1	.033	-3	20	20	-1	1.2
Total	3	11	6	.647	57	26	0	0	0	205^1	177	95	32	5	82	174	11.6	3.90	117	.232	.311	2	.042	-4	15	15	-3	0.6

● **LARRY CHENEY** Cheney, Laurance Russell b: 5/2/1886, Belleville, Kan. d: 1/6/69, Daytona Beach, Fla. BR/TR, 6'1.5", 185 lbs. Deb: 9/9/11

YEAR	TM/L	W	L	PCT	G	GS	CG	SH	SV	IP	H	R	HR	HB	BB	SO	RAT	ERA	ERA+	OAV	OOB	BH	AVG	PB	PR	PR+	PD	TPI
1911	Chi-N	1	0	1.000	3	1	0	0	0	10	8	0	0	0	3	11	9.9	0.00	—	.229	.289	1	.250	0	4	4	1	0.5
1912	Chi-N	**26**	10	.722	42	37	**28**	4	0	303^1	262	122	5	7	111	140	11.3	2.85	117	.234	.307	24	.226	5	19	17	-2	2.0
1913	Chi-N	21	14	.600	**54**	36	25	2	**11**	305	271	117	7	8	98	136	11.1	2.57	124	.241	.306	20	.192	2	22	21	-0	2.6
1914	Chi-N	20	18	.526	**50**	40	21	6	5	311^1	239	136	9	10	140	157	11.2	2.54	109	.215	.308	18	.180	3	9	8	1	1.4
1915	Chi-N	8	9	.471	25	18	6	2	0	131^1	120	69	1	4	55	68	12.3	3.56	78	.246	.327	6	.150	-1	-12	-11	2	-1.4
	Bro-N	0	2	.000	5	4	1	0	0	27	16	10	0	2	17	11	11.7	1.67	167	.174	.315	1	.143	0	3	3	0	0.3
	Yr	8	11	.421	30	22	7	2	0	158^1	136	79	1	6	72	79	12.2	3.24	86	.234	.325	7	.149	-1	-9	-8	2	-1.1
1916	*Bro-N	18	12	.600	41	32	15	5	0	253	178	91	5	10	105	166	10.4	1.92	140	**.198**	.289	9	.114	-3	20	21	-1	2.2
1917	Bro-N	8	12	.400	35	24	14	1	2	210^1	185	80	4	5	73	102	11.3	2.35	119	.239	.309	14	.206	2	8	10	-1	1.1
1918	Bro-N	11	13	.458	32	21	15	0	1	200^2	177	84	2	10	74	83	11.7	3.00	93	.241	.319	16	.242	2	-5	-5	1	-0.2
1919	Bro-N	1	3	.250	9	4	2	0	0	39	45	21	1	2	14	14	14.1	4.15	72	.300	.367	2	.182	-0	-5	-5	-0	-0.6
	Bos-N	0	2	.000	8	2	0	0	0	33	35	20	0	0	15	13	13.6	3.55	81	.294	.373	2	.182	0	-2	-3	0	-0.1
	Phi-N	2	5	.286	9	6	5	0	0	57^1	69	34	2	1	28	25	15.4	4.55	71	.315	.395	2	.095	-2	-10	-8	-1	-1.2
	Yr	3	10	.231	26	12	7	0	0	129^1	149	75	3	3	57	52	14.5	4.18	73	.305	.381	6	.140	-2	-18	-15	-1	-1.9
Total	9	116	100	.537	313	225	132	20	19	1881^1	1605	784	36	59	733	926	11.5	2.70	109	.234	.313	115	.186	9	49	52	0	6.6

● **TOM CHENEY** Cheney, Thomas Edgar b: 10/14/34, Morgan, Ga. BR/TR, 6', 180 lbs. Deb: 4/21/57

YEAR	TM/L	W	L	PCT	G	GS	CG	SH	SV	IP	H	R	HR	HB	BB	SO	RAT	ERA	ERA+	OAV	OOB	BH	AVG	PB	PR	PR+	PD	TPI
1957	StL-N	0	1	.000	4	3	0	0	0	9	6	6	0	0	15	10	21.0	5.00	79	.207	.477	0	.000	-0	-1	-1	0	-0.1
1959	StL-N	0	1	.000	11	2	0	0	0	11^2	17	9	2	2	11	8	23.1	6.94	61	.354	.492	0	—	0	-4	-3	0	-0.3
1960	*Pit-N	2	2	.500	11	8	1	1	0	52	44	25	5	0	33	35	13.3	3.98	94	.238	.353	3	.176	0	-1	-1	-2	-0.2
1961	Pit-N	0	0	—	1	0	0	0	0	0	1	1	0	4	—	—	∞	—	.500	.833	99	—	0	-4	-4	0	-0.3	
	Was-A	1	3	.250	10	7	0	0	0	29^2	32	30	8	0	26	20	17.6	8.80	46	.283	.417	4	.500	2	-16	-16	-1	-1.6
1962	Was-A	7	9	.438	37	23	4	3	1	173^1	134	68	12	2	97	147	12.1	3.17	127	.213	.320	3	.063	-3	15	16	0	1.1
1963	Was-A	8	9	.471	23	21	7	4	0	136^1	99	51	14	1	40	97	9.2	2.71	137	.202	.264	5	.109	-3	14	15	-2	1.3
1964	Was-A	1	3	.250	15	6	1	0	1	48^2	45	26	10	0	13	25	10.7	3.70	100	.245	.294	3	.250	0	-0	0	-0	0.0
1966	Was-A	0	1	.000	3	1	0	0	0	5^1	4	4	1	1	6	3	18.6	5.06	68	.222	.440	0	—	0	-1	-1	0	-0.1
Total	8	19	29	.396	115	71	13	8	2	466	382	224	53	6	245	345	12.2	3.77	103	.225	.325	18	.135	-3	2	5	-4	-0.2

● **JACK CHESBRO** Chesbro, John Dwight "Happy Jack" b: 6/5/1874, N.Adams, Mass. d: 11/6/31, Conway, Mass. BR/TR, 5'9", 180 lbs. Deb: 7/12/1899 CH

YEAR	TM/L	W	L	PCT	G	GS	CG	SH	SV	IP	H	R	HR	HB	BB	SO	RAT	ERA	ERA+	OAV	OOB	BH	AVG	PB	PR	PR+	PD	TPI
1899	Pit-N	6	9	.400	19	17	15	0	0	149	165	99	3	11	59	28	14.2	4.11	93	.280	.357	9	.155	-3	-4	-5	-3	-0.9
1900	Pit-N	15	13	.536	32	26	20	3	1	215^2	220	123	4	12	79	56	13.0	3.67	99	.264	.336	15	.176	-1	1	-1	-2	-0.4
1901	Pit-N	21	10	**.677**	36	28	26	**6**	1	287^2	261	104	4	14	52	129	10.2	2.38	137	.240	.284	25	.216	3	30	29	-3	2.7
1902	Pit-N	**28**	6	**.824**	35	33	31	**8**	1	286^1	242	81	1	21	62	136	10.2	2.17	126	.229	.285	20	.179	-2	20	18	-2	1.7
1903	NY-A	21	15	.583	40	36	33	1	0	324^2	300	140	7	9	74	147	10.6	2.77	113	.245	.293	23	.185	-1	7	12	2	1.3

YEAR	TM/L	W	L	PCT	G	GS	CG	SH	SV	IP	H	R	HR	HB	BB	SO	RAT	ERA	ERA+	OAV	OOB	BH	AVG	PB	PR	PR+	PD	TPI
1904	NY-A	**41**	12	**.774**	**55**	51	**48**	6	0	**454^2**	338	128	4	7	88	239	8.6	1.82	149	**.208**	.252	41	.236	6	39	43	5	**6.7**
1905	NY-A	19	15	.559	41	38	24	3	0	303^1	262	125	5	6	71	156	10.1	2.20	134	.235	.284	21	.188	0	15	23	1	2.7
1906	NY-A	23	17	.575	**49**	42	24	4	1	325	314	138	2	10	75	152	11.0	2.96	100	.257	.305	26	.208	-1	-10	0	-0	-0.1
1907	NY-A	10	10	.500	30	25	17	1	0	206	192	83	0	6	46	78	10.7	2.53	110	.249	.297	15	.197	-1	0	5	1	0.5
1908	NY-A	14	20	.412	45	31	20	3	1	288^2	276	134	6	14	67	124	11.1	2.93	85	.256	.307	18	.176	-2	-17	-14	1	-1.7
1909	NY-A	0	4	.000	9	4	2	0	0	49^2	70	47	2	3	13	17	15.6	6.34	40	.347	.394	3	.176	-0	-21	-21	1	-1.4
	Bos-A	0	1	.000	1	1	0	0	0	6	7	4	1	0	4	3	16.5	4.50	56	.318	.423	1	.500	0	-1	-1	-0	-0.2
	Yr	0	5	.000	10	5	2	0	0	55^2	77	51	3	3	17	20	15.7	6.14	41	.344	.398	4	.211	0	-23	-22	1	-1.6
Total	11	198	132	.600	392	332	260	35	5	2896^2	2647	1206	39	113	690	1265	10.7	2.68	111	.244	.297	217	.197	-2	58	92	-1	10.9

● BOB CHESNES Chesnes, Robert Vincent b: 5/6/21, Oakland, Cal. d: 5/23/79, Everett, Wash. BB/TR, 6', 180 lbs. Deb: 5/6/48

YEAR	TM/L	W	L	PCT	G	GS	CG	SH	SV	IP	H	R	HR	HB	BB	SO	RAT	ERA	ERA+	OAV	OOB	BH	AVG	PB	PR	PR+	PD	TPI
1948	Pit-N	14	6	.700	25	23	15	0	0	194^1	180	92	13	4	90	69	12.7	3.57	114	.247	.333	25	.275	7	8	11	3	2.1
1949	Pit-N	7	13	.350	27	25	8	1	1	145^1	153	104	15	5	82	49	14.9	5.88	71	.276	.374	17	.250	6	-30	-26	3	-2.3
1950	Pit-N	3	3	.500	9	7	2	0	0	39	44	26	7	3	17	12	14.8	5.54	79	.293	.376	2	.154	-0	-6	-5	2	-0.5
Total	3	24	22	.522	61	55	25	1	1	378^2	377	222	35	12	189	130	13.7	4.66	89	.263	.354	44	.256	12	-27	-21	8	-0.7

● MITCH CHETKOVICH Chetkovich, Mitchell b: 7/21/17, Fairpoint, Ohio d: 8/24/71, Grass Valley, Cal. BR/TR, 6'3.5", 208 lbs. Deb: 4/19/45

YEAR	TM/L	W	L	PCT	G	GS	CG	SH	SV	IP	H	R	HR	HB	BB	SO	RAT	ERA	ERA+	OAV	OOB	BH	AVG	PB	PR	PR+	PD	TPI
1945	Phi-N	0	0	—	4	0	0	0	0	3	2	2	0	0	3	0	15.0	0.00	—	.182	.357	0	—	0	1	1	-0	0.0

● TONY CHEVEZ Chevez, Silvio Antonio (b: Silvio Antonio Aguilera (Chevez)) b: 6/20/54, Telica, Nicaragua BR/TR, 5'11", 177 lbs. Deb: 5/31/77

YEAR	TM/L	W	L	PCT	G	GS	CG	SH	SV	IP	H	R	HR	HB	BB	SO	RAT	ERA	ERA+	OAV	OOB	BH	AVG	PB	PR	PR+	PD	TPI
1977	Bal-A	0	0	—	4	0	0	0	0	8	10	13	3	2	8	7	22.5	12.38	31	.294	.455	0	—	0	-7	-8	-0	-0.4

● SCOTT CHIAMPARINO Chiamparino, Scott Michael b: 8/22/66, San Mateo, Cal. BR/TR, 6'2", 190 lbs. Deb: 9/5/90

YEAR	TM/L	W	L	PCT	G	GS	CG	SH	SV	IP	H	R	HR	HB	BB	SO	RAT	ERA	ERA+	OAV	OOB	BH	AVG	PB	PR	PR+	PD	TPI
1990	Tex-A	1	2	.333	6	6	0	0	0	37^2	36	14	1	2	12	19	11.9	2.63	150	.250	.316	0	—	0	5	5	-1	0.3
1991	Tex-A	1	0	1.000	5	5	0	0	0	22^1	26	11	1	0	12	8	15.3	4.03	100	.295	.380	0	—	0	0	0	-1	-0.1
1992	Tex-A	0	4	.000	4	4	0	0	0	25^1	25	11	2	0	5	13	10.7	3.55	107	.260	.297	0	—	0	1	1	-1	0.1
Total	3	2	6	.250	15	15	0	0	0	85^1	87	36	4	2	29	40	12.4	3.27	120	.265	.329	0	—	0	7	6	-2	0.3

● FLOYD CHIFFER Chiffer, Floyd John b: 4/20/56, Glen Cove, N.Y. BR/TR, 6'2", 185 lbs. Deb: 4/7/82

YEAR	TM/L	W	L	PCT	G	GS	CG	SH	SV	IP	H	R	HR	HB	BB	SO	RAT	ERA	ERA+	OAV	OOB	BH	AVG	PB	PR	PR+	PD	TPI
1982	SD-N	4	3	.571	51	0	0	0	4	79^1	73	33	9	4	34	48	12.6	2.95	116	.247	.333	0	.000	-1	6	4	-0	0.3
1983	SD-N	0	2	.000	15	0	0	0	1	22^2	17	10	0	0	10	15	10.7	3.18	110	.210	.297	0	.000	-0	1	1	-0	0.1
1984	SD-N	1	0	1.000	15	1	0	0	0	28	42	24	1	0	16	20	18.6	7.71	46	.347	.423	0	.000	-0	-13	-13	-1	-0.8
Total	3	5	5	.500	81	1	0	0	5	130	132	67	10	4	60	83	13.6	4.02	86	.266	.349	0	.000	-1	-6	-8	-1	-0.4

● HARRY CHILD Child, Harry Stephen Patrick (b: Harry Stephen Patrick Chesley)
b: 5/23/05, Baltimore, Md. d: 11/8/72, Alexandria, Va. BB/TR, 5'11", 187 lbs. Deb: 7/16/30

YEAR	TM/L	W	L	PCT	G	GS	CG	SH	SV	IP	H	R	HR	HB	BB	SO	RAT	ERA	ERA+	OAV	OOB	BH	AVG	PB	PR	PR+	PD	TPI
1930	Was-A	0	0	—	5	0	0	0	0	10	10	7	1	0	5	5	13.5	6.30	73	.263	.349	1	.250	-0	-2	-2	0	-0.1

● BILL CHILDERS Childers, William b: St.Louis, Mo. Deb: 7/27/1895

YEAR	TM/L	W	L	PCT	G	GS	CG	SH	SV	IP	H	R	HR	HB	BB	SO	RAT	ERA	ERA+	OAV	OOB	BH	AVG	PB	PR	PR+	PD	TPI
1895	Lou-N	0	0	—	1	0	0	0	0	0	2	0	0	5	—	—	∞	—	1.000	1.000	97	—	0	-6	-6	0	-0.4	

● ROCKY CHILDRESS Childress, Rodney Osborne b: 2/18/62, Santa Rosa, Cal. BR/TR, 6'2", 195 lbs. Deb: 5/17/85

YEAR	TM/L	W	L	PCT	G	GS	CG	SH	SV	IP	H	R	HR	HB	BB	SO	RAT	ERA	ERA+	OAV	OOB	BH	AVG	PB	PR	PR+	PD	TPI
1985	Phi-N	0	1	.000	16	1	0	0	0	33^1	45	23	3	0	9	14	14.6	6.21	59	.326	.367	1	.167	-0	-10	-9	-0	-0.5
1986	Phi-N	0	0	—	2	0	0	0	0	2^2	4	3	0	0	1	1	16.9	6.75	57	.364	.417	0	—	0	-1	-1	-0	-0.1
1987	Hou-N	1	2	.333	32	0	0	0	0	48^1	46	17	4	0	18	26	11.9	2.98	132	.260	.328	0	.000	-0	6	5	-0	0.2
1988	Hou-N	1	0	1.000	11	0	0	0	0	23^1	26	17	3	1	9	24	13.9	6.17	54	.280	.350	1	.250	0	-7	-8	-1	-0.4
Total	4	2	3	.400	61	1	0	0	0	107^2	121	60	10	1	37	65	13.3	4.76	78	.289	.348	2	.167	-0	-12	-13	-1	-0.8

● BOB CHIPMAN Chipman, Robert Howard "Mr. Chips" b: 10/11/18, Brooklyn, N.Y. d: 11/8/73, Huntington, N.Y. BL/TL, 6'2", 190 lbs. Deb: 9/28/41

YEAR	TM/L	W	L	PCT	G	GS	CG	SH	SV	IP	H	R	HR	HB	BB	SO	RAT	ERA	ERA+	OAV	OOB	BH	AVG	PB	PR	PR+	PD	TPI
1941	Bro-N	1	0	1.000	1	0	0	0	0	5	3	0	0	0	1	3	7.2	0.00	—	.150	.190	0	.000	-0	2	2	-0	0.4
1942	Bro-N	0	0	—	2	0	0	0	0	1^1	1	0	0	0	2	1	20.3	0.00	—	.250	.500	0	—	0	0	0	0	0.0
1943	Bro-N	0	0	—	1	0	0	0	0	1^2	2	0	0	0	2	0	21.6	0.00	—	.400	.571	0	—	0	1	1	-0	0.0
1944	Bro-N	3	1	.750	11	3	1	0	0	36^1	38	19	1	0	24	20	15.4	4.21	84	.270	.376	2	.182	-0	-2	-3	0	-0.3
	Chi-N	9	9	.500	26	21	8	1	2	129	147	62	9	0	40	41	13.0	3.49	101	.288	.340	5	.104	-3	2	1	-0	-0.2
	Yr	12	10	.545	37	24	9	1	2	165^1	185	81	10	0	64	61	13.6	3.65	97	.284	.348	7	.119	-3	-1	-2	-0	-0.5
1945	*Chi-N	4	5	.444	25	10	3	1	0	72	63	37	4	1	34	29	12.3	3.50	104	.230	.317	3	.176	1	2	1	1	0.2
1946	Chi-N	6	5	.545	34	10	5	3	2	109^1	103	44	8	1	54	42	13.0	3.13	106	.255	.344	2	.061	-3	3	2	-1	-0.1
1947	Chi-N	7	6	.538	32	17	5	1	0	134^2	135	58	6	0	66	51	13.4	3.68	107	.264	.348	4	.091	-3	6	4	1	0.2
1948	Chi-N	2	1	.667	34	3	0	0	4	60^1	73	34	5	0	24	16	14.5	3.58	109	.293	.355	4	.250	1	3	2	1	0.4
1949	Chi-N	7	8	.467	38	11	3	1	1	113^1	110	65	7	2	63	46	13.9	3.97	102	.248	.344	3	.125	-0	1	1	-1	-0.1
1950	Bos-N	7	7	.500	27	12	4	0	1	124^2	127	75	10	4	37	40	12.2	4.43	87	.262	.319	6	.154	-1	-4	-9	-3	-1.2
1951	Bos-N	4	3	.571	33	0	0	0	4	52	59	29	5	2	19	17	13.8	4.85	76	.284	.349	1	.100	-1	-5	-7	-0	-1.1
1952	Bos-N	1	1	.500	29	0	0	0	0	41^2	28	15	5	0	20	16	10.4	2.81	129	.188	.284	2	.400	1	4	4	0	0.3
Total	12	51	46	.526	293	87	29	7	14	880^2	889	438	60	10	386	322	13.1	3.72	100	.261	.338	32	.128	-8	13	1	-2	-1.5

● STEVE CHITREN Chitren, Stephen Vincent b: 6/8/67, Tokyo, Japan BR/TR, 6', 180 lbs. Deb: 9/15/90

YEAR	TM/L	W	L	PCT	G	GS	CG	SH	SV	IP	H	R	HR	HB	BB	SO	RAT	ERA	ERA+	OAV	OOB	BH	AVG	PB	PR	PR+	PD	TPI
1990	Oak-A	1	0	1.000	8	0	0	0	0	17^2	7	2	0	0	4	19	5.6	1.02	366	.117	.172	0	—	0	6	6	0	0.3
1991	Oak-A	1	4	.200	56	0	0	0	4	60^1	59	31	8	4	32	47	14.2	4.33	89	.258	.358	0	—	0	-2	-3	-0	-0.3
Total	2	2	4	.333	64	0	0	0	4	78	66	33	8	4	36	66	12.2	3.58	107	.228	.322	0	—	0	4	2	-0	0.0

● NELSON CHITTUM Chittum, Nelson Boyd b: 3/25/33, Harrisonburg, Va. BR/TR, 6'1", 180 lbs. Deb: 8/17/58

YEAR	TM/L	W	L	PCT	G	GS	CG	SH	SV	IP	H	R	HR	HB	BB	SO	RAT	ERA	ERA+	OAV	OOB	BH	AVG	PB	PR	PR+	PD	TPI
1958	StL-N	0	1	.000	13	2	0	0	0	29^1	31	21	5	1	7	13	12.0	6.44	64	.265	.312	1	.250	0	-8	-7	0	-0.3
1959	Bos-A	3	0	1.000	21	0	0	0	0	30^1	29	9	0	0	11	12	11.9	1.19	342	.266	.333	1	.200	0	9	9	1	0.9
1960	Bos-A	0	0	—	6	0	0	0	0	8^1	8	4	0	0	6	5	15.1	4.32	94	.242	.359	0	.000	-0	-0	-0	0	0.0
Total	3	3	1	.750	40	2	0	0	0	68	68	34	5	1	24	30	12.3	3.84	106	.263	.327	2	.200	0	0	2	1	0.6

● BOB CHLUPSA Chlupsa, Robert Joseph b: 9/16/45, New York, N.Y. BR/TR, 6'7", 215 lbs. Deb: 7/16/70

YEAR	TM/L	W	L	PCT	G	GS	CG	SH	SV	IP	H	R	HR	HB	BB	SO	RAT	ERA	ERA+	OAV	OOB	BH	AVG	PB	PR	PR+	PD	TPI
1970	StL-N	0	2	.000	14	0	0	0	0	16^1	26	16	2	0	9	10	19.3	8.82	47	.366	.438	0	—	0	-9	-8	1	-0.8
1971	StL-N	0	0	—	1	0	0	0	0	2	3	2	0	0	0	1	13.5	9.00	40	.333	.333	0	—	0	-1	-1	0	0.0
Total	2	0	2	.000	15	0	0	0	0	18^1	29	18	2	0	9	11	18.7	8.84	46	.363	.427	0	—	0	-10	-10	1	-0.8

● JIN HO CHO Cho, Jin Ho b: 8/16/75, Jun Ju City, South Korea BR/TR, 6', 175 lbs. Deb: 7/4/98

YEAR	TM/L	W	L	PCT	G	GS	CG	SH	SV	IP	H	R	HR	HB	BB	SO	RAT	ERA	ERA+	OAV	OOB	BH	AVG	PB	PR	PR+	PD	TPI
1998	Bos-A	0	3	.000	4	4	0	0	0	18^2	28	17	4	1	3	15	15.4	8.20	58	.341	.372	0	—	0	-7	-7	-0	-0.9
1999	Bos-A	2	3	.400	9	7	0	0	0	39^1	45	26	7	2	8	16	12.6	5.72	87	.287	.329	0	.000	-0	-4	-3	-0	-0.4
Total	2	2	6	.250	13	11	0	0	0	58	73	43	11	3	11	31	13.5	6.52	75	.305	.344	0	.000	-0	-11	-10	-1	-1.3

● DON CHOATE Choate, Donald Leon b: 7/2/38, Potosi, Mo. BR/TR, 6', 185 lbs. Deb: 9/12/60

YEAR	TM/L	W	L	PCT	G	GS	CG	SH	SV	IP	H	R	HR	HB	BB	SO	RAT	ERA	ERA+	OAV	OOB	BH	AVG	PB	PR	PR+	PD	TPI
1960	SF-N	0	0	—	4	0	0	0	0	8	7	4	0	0	4	7	12.4	2.25	155	.233	.324	0	—	0	1	1	0	0.1

● RANDY CHOATE Choate, Randol Doyle b: 9/5/75, San Antonio, Tex. BL/TL, 6'3", 180 lbs. Deb: 7/1/2000

YEAR	TM/L	W	L	PCT	G	GS	CG	SH	SV	IP	H	R	HR	HB	BB	SO	RAT	ERA	ERA+	OAV	OOB	BH	AVG	PB	PR	PR+	PD	TPI
2000	*NY-A	0	1	.000	22	0	0	0	0	17	14	10	3	1	8	12	12.2	4.76	101	.215	.311	0	—	0	0	0	0	0.0

● BOBBY CHOUINARD Chouinard, Robert William b: 5/1/72, Manila, Philippines BR/TR, 6'1", 188 lbs. Deb: 5/26/96

YEAR	TM/L	W	L	PCT	G	GS	CG	SH	SV	IP	H	R	HR	HB	BB	SO	RAT	ERA	ERA+	OAV	OOB	BH	AVG	PB	PR	PR+	PD	TPI
1996	Oak-A	4	2	.667	13	11	0	0	0	59	75	41	10	3	32	32	16.8	6.10	81	.316	.404	0	—	0	-7	-8	1	-0.5
1998	Mil-N	0	0	—	1	0	0	0	0	3	5	1	0	0	0	1	15.0	3.00	142	.455	.455	0	—	0	0	0	0	0.0
	Ari-N	0	2	.000	26	2	0	0	0	38^1	41	23	5	0	11	26	12.2	4.23	100	.268	.317	0	.000	-0	0	-0	-0	-0.1
	Yr	0	2	.000	27	2	0	0	0	41^1	46	24	5	0	11	27	12.4	4.14	102	.280	.326	0	.000	-0	0	0	-0	-0.1
1999	*Ari-N	5	2	.714	32	0	0	0	1	40^1	31	16	3	0	12	23	9.6	2.68	171	.220	.281	0	.000	-0	8	8	0	1.3
2000	Col-N	2	2	.500	31	0	0	0	0	32^2	35	17	4	1	9	23	12.4	3.86	154	.273	.326	1	.333	0	3	6	-1	0.6
Total	4	11	8	.579	103	13	0	0	1	173^1	187	98	22	4	64	105	13.2	4.41	110	.279	.346	1	.125	-0	5	8	0	1.3

● CHIEF CHOUNEAU Chouneau, William (b: William Cadreau) b: 9/2/1889, Cloquet, Minn. d: 9/17/48, Cloquet, Minn. BR/TR, 5'9", 150 lbs. Deb: 10/9/10

YEAR	TM/L	W	L	PCT	G	GS	CG	SH	SV	IP	H	R	HR	HB	BB	SO	RAT	ERA	ERA+	OAV	OOB	BH	AVG	PB	PR	PR+	PD	TPI
1910	Chi-A	0	1	.000	1	1	0	0	0	5^1	7	2	0	0	0	1	11.8	3.38	71	.292	.292	0	.000	1	-1	-1	-0	-0.1

● MIKE CHRIS

Chris, Michael b: 10/8/57, Santa Monica, Cal. BL/TL, 6'3", 180 lbs. Deb: 7/31/79

YEAR	TM/L	W	L	PCT	G	GS	CG	SH	SV	IP	H	R	HR	HB	BB	SO	RAT	ERA	ERA+	OAV	OOB	BH	AVG	PB	PR	PR+	PD	TPI
1979	Det-A	3	3	.500	13	8	0	0	0	39	46	30	3	0	21	31	15.5	6.92	63	.297	.381	0	—	0	-12	-11	1	-1.4
1982	SF-N	0	2	.000	9	6	0	0	0	26	23	16	2	1	26	10	17.3	4.85	74	.245	.413	1	.143	-0	-4	-4	1	-0.2
1983	SF-N	0	0	—	7	0	0	0	0	13^1	16	14	1	2	16	5	23.0	8.10	44	.308	.486	0	.000	-0	-7	-7	-0	-0.4
Total	3	3	5	.375	29	14	0	0	0	78^1	85	60	6	3	63	46	17.3	6.43	61	.282	.411	1	.111	-0	-22	-21	1	-2.0

● GARY CHRISTENSON

Christenson, Gary Richard b: 5/5/53, Mineola, N.Y. BL/TL, 6'5", 200 lbs. Deb: 9/1/79

YEAR	TM/L	W	L	PCT	G	GS	CG	SH	SV	IP	H	R	HR	HB	BB	SO	RAT	ERA	ERA+	OAV	OOB	BH	AVG	PB	PR	PR+	PD	TPI
1979	KC-A	0	0	—	6	0	0	0	0	10^2	10	5	1	0	2	4	10.1	3.38	127	.250	.286	0	—	0	1	1	0	0.1
1980	KC-A	3	0	1.000	24	0	0	0	1	31^1	35	23	4	2	18	16	15.8	5.17	79	.278	.377	0	—	0	-4	-4	1	-0.3
Total	2	3	0	1.000	30	0	0	0	1	42	45	28	5	2	20	20	14.4	4.71	87	.271	.356	0	—	0	-3	-3	1	-0.2

● LARRY CHRISTENSON

Christenson, Larry Richard b: 11/10/53, Everett, Wash. BR/TR, 6'4", 215 lbs. Deb: 4/13/73

YEAR	TM/L	W	L	PCT	G	GS	CG	SH	SV	IP	H	R	HR	HB	BB	SO	RAT	ERA	ERA+	OAV	OOB	BH	AVG	PB	PR	PR+	PD	TPI
1973	Phi-N	1	4	.200	10	9	1	0	0	34^1	53	25	3	1	20	11	19.4	6.55	58	.366	.446	0	.000	-1	-11	-10	-0	-1.3
1974	Phi-N	1	1	.500	10	1	0	0	2	23	20	11	2	0	15	18	13.7	4.30	88	.241	.357	0	.000	-1	-2	-1	-0	-0.2
1975	Phi-N	11	6	.647	29	26	5	2	1	171^2	149	73	12	1	45	88	10.2	3.67	102	.236	.288	14	.246	5	-1	1	-3	0.4
1976	Phi-N	13	8	.619	32	29	2	0	0	168^2	199	77	8	1	42	54	12.9	3.68	96	.297	.339	10	.196	4	-3	-2	-3	-0.2
1977	*Phi-N	19	6	.760	34	34	5	1	0	219^1	229	113	21	7	69	118	12.5	4.06	99	.268	.327	10	.135	1	-4	-1	-2	-0.3
1978	*Phi-N	13	14	.481	33	33	9	3	0	228	209	90	16	1	47	131	10.1	3.24	110	.244	.284	5	.075	-2	9	9	-0	0.7
1979	Phi-N	5	10	.333	19	17	2	0	0	106	118	56	9	2	30	53	12.7	4.50	85	.291	.342	9	.290	5	-9	-8	-0	-0.5
1980	*Phi-N	5	1	.833	14	14	0	0	0	73^2	62	35	4	3	27	49	11.2	4.03	94	.227	.304	7	.368	3	-3	-2	1	0.3
1981	*Phi-N	4	7	.364	20	15	0	0	1	106^2	108	48	8	1	30	70	11.7	3.54	102	.267	.319	3	.100	-1	-1	1	-1	-0.1
1982	Phi-N	9	10	.474	33	33	3	0	0	223	212	95	15	3	53	145	10.8	3.47	106	.253	.300	5	.075	-3	3	5	-1	0.0
1983	Phi-N	2	4	.333	9	9	0	0	0	48^1	42	25	2	1	17	44	11.2	3.91	91	.233	.303	1	.059	-1	-1	-2	1	-0.2
Total	11	83	71	.539	243	220	27	6	4	1402^2	1401	648	100	21	395	781	11.7	3.79	98	.262	.315	64	.150	10	-23	-11	-8	-1.4

● CLAY CHRISTIANSEN

Christiansen, Clay C. b: 6/28/58, Wichita, Kan. BR/TR, 6'5", 205 lbs. Deb: 5/10/84

YEAR	TM/L	W	L	PCT	G	GS	CG	SH	SV	IP	H	R	HR	HB	BB	SO	RAT	ERA	ERA+	OAV	OOB	BH	AVG	PB	PR	PR+	PD	TPI
1984	NY-A	2	4	.333	24	1	0	0	2	38^2	50	28	4	1	12	27	14.7	6.05	63	.309	.360	0	—	0	-9	-10	-0	-1.5

● JASON CHRISTIANSEN

Christiansen, Jason Samuel b: 9/21/69, Omaha, Neb. BR/TL, 6'5", 230 lbs. Deb: 4/26/95

YEAR	TM/L	W	L	PCT	G	GS	CG	SH	SV	IP	H	R	HR	HB	BB	SO	RAT	ERA	ERA+	OAV	OOB	BH	AVG	PB	PR	PR+	PD	TPI
1995	Pit-N	1	3	.250	63	0	0	0	0	56^1	49	28	5	3	34	53	13.7	4.15	104	.234	.350	0	.000	-0	0	1	-0	0.0
1996	Pit-N	3	3	.500	33	0	0	0	0	44^1	56	34	7	1	19	38	15.4	6.70	65	.311	.380	0	.000	-0	-12	-11	0	-1.3
1997	Pit-N	3	0	1.000	39	0	0	0	0	33^2	37	11	2	2	17	37	15.0	2.94	146	.274	.364	0	—	0	5	5	-0	0.4
1998	Pit-N	3	3	.500	60	0	0	0	6	64^2	51	22	2	0	27	71	10.9	2.51	172	.216	.297	1	.250	0	12	13	-1	1.2
1999	Pit-N	2	3	.400	39	0	0	0	3	37^2	26	17	2	2	22	35	11.9	4.06	113	.198	.323	0	.000	-0	2	2	0	0.3
2000	Pit-N	2	8	.200	44	0	0	0	1	38	28	22	2	0	25	41	12.6	4.97	93	.207	.331	0	—	0	-1	-2	1	-0.2
	*StL-N	1	0	1.000	21	0	0	0	0	10	13	7	1	2	2	12	15.3	5.40	86	.317	.378	0	—	0	-1	-1	-0	-0.1
	Yr	3	8	.273	65	0	0	0	1	48	41	29	3	2	27	53	13.1	5.06	91	.233	.341	0	—	0	-2	-2	1	-0.3
Total	6	15	20	.429	299	0	0	0	10	284^2	260	141	21	10	146	287	13.2	4.17	105	.244	.340	1	.100	-1	5	7	-0	0.3

● MIKE CHRISTOPHER

Christopher, Michael Wayne b: 11/3/63, Petersburg, Va. BR/TR, 6'5", 206 lbs. Deb: 9/10/91

YEAR	TM/L	W	L	PCT	G	GS	CG	SH	SV	IP	H	R	HR	HB	BB	SO	RAT	ERA	ERA+	OAV	OOB	BH	AVG	PB	PR	PR+	PD	TPI
1991	LA-N	0	0	—	3	0	0	0	0	4	2	0	0	0	3	2	11.3	0.00	—	.167	.333	0	—	0	2	2	0	0.1
1992	Cle-A	0	0	—	10	0	0	0	0	18	17	8	2	0	10	13	13.5	3.00	130	.254	.351	0	—	0	2	2	0	0.1
1993	Cle-A	0	0	—	9	0	0	0	0	11^2	14	6	3	0	2	8	12.3	3.86	113	.286	.314	0	—	0	1	1	-0	0.0
1995	Det-A	4	0	1.000	36	0	0	0	1	61^1	71	28	8	2	14	34	12.8	3.82	125	.292	.336	0	—	0	6	6	-0	0.4
1996	Det-A	1	1	.500	13	0	0	0	0	30	47	36	12	0	11	19	17.4	9.30	54	.351	.400	0	—	0	-14	-14	-0	-0.8
Total	5	5	1	.833	71	0	0	0	1	125	151	78	25	2	40	76	13.9	4.90	95	.299	.353	0	—	0	-4	-4	-1	-0.2

● RUSS CHRISTOPHER

Christopher, Russell Ormand b: 9/12/17, Richmond, Cal. d: 12/5/54, Richmond, Cal. BR/TR, 6'3", 180 lbs. Deb: 4/14/42 F

YEAR	TM/L	W	L	PCT	G	GS	CG	SH	SV	IP	H	R	HR	HB	BB	SO	RAT	ERA	ERA+	OAV	OOB	BH	AVG	PB	PR	PR+	PD	TPI
1942	Phi-A	4	13	.235	30	18	10	0	1	165	154	78	8	3	99	58	14.0	3.82	99	.254	.362	5	.089	-3	-3	-1	6	0.2
1943	Phi-A	5	8	.385	24	15	5	0	2	133	120	58	3	3	58	56	12.2	3.45	98	.242	.325	7	.156	-1	-2	-1	8	0.7
1944	Phi-A	14	14	.500	35	24	13	1	1	215^1	200	91	6	9	63	84	11.4	2.97	117	.245	.306	18	.222	3	11	12	5	2.6
1945	Phi-A†	13	13	.500	33	27	17	2	2	227^1	213	92	9	9	75	100	11.8	3.17	108	.251	.319	13	.171	-1	5	7	7	1.5
1946	Phi-A	5	7	.417	30	13	1	0	0	119^1	119	71	5	3	44	79	12.5	4.30	82	.254	.322	5	.139	-0	-11	-10	4	-0.5
1947	Phi-A	10	7	.588	44	0	0	0	12	80^2	70	30	4	0	33	33	11.5	2.90	131	.236	.313	2	.125	-0	7	8	1	1.7
1948	*Cle-A	3	2	.600	45	0	0	0	**17**	59	55	21	3	0	27	14	12.5	2.90	140	.247	.328	0	.000	-0	9	8	0	1.1
Total	7	54	64	.458	241	97	46	3	35	999^2	931	441	38	27	399	424	12.2	3.37	106	.248	.325	50	.158	-3	17	23	31	7.3

● BUBBA CHURCH

Church, Emory Nicholas b: 9/12/24, Birmingham, Ala. BR/TR, 6', 180 lbs. Deb: 4/30/50

YEAR	TM/L	W	L	PCT	G	GS	CG	SH	SV	IP	H	R	HR	HB	BB	SO	RAT	ERA	ERA+	OAV	OOB	BH	AVG	PB	PR	PR+	PD	TPI
1950	Phi-N	8	6	.571	31	18	8	2	1	142	113	50	12	0	56	50	10.7	2.73	149	.225	.303	8	.182	0	22	21	-0	1.9
1951	Phi-N	15	11	.577	38	33	15	4	1	247	246	107	17	1	90	104	12.3	3.53	109	.261	.326	22	.256	5	12	9	-2	1.1
1952	Phi-N	0	0	—	2	1	0	0	0	5	11	6	0	1	1	3	23.4	10.80	34	.440	.481	0	.000	-0	-4	-4	0	-0.2
	Cin-N	5	9	.357	29	22	5	1	0	153^1	173	85	21	3	48	47	13.1	4.34	87	.301	.358	12	.240	3	-10	-10	-1	-0.6
	Yr	5	9	.357	31	23	5	1	0	158^1	184	91	21	4	49	50	13.5	4.55	83	.307	.363	12	.235	3	-14	-14	-1	-0.8
1953	Cin-N	3	3	.500	11	7	2	0	0	43^2	55	32	9	2	19	12	15.7	5.98	73	.318	.392	4	.267	1	-8	-8	-0	-0.8
	Chi-N	4	5	.444	27	11	1	0	1	104^1	115	67	16	2	49	47	14.3	5.00	89	.276	.355	7	.212	1	-8	-6	-1	-0.5
	Yr	7	8	.467	38	18	3	0	1	148	170	99	25	4	68	59	14.7	5.29	84	.289	.366	11	.229	2	-17	-14	-1	-1.3
1954	Chi-N	1	3	.250	7	3	1	0	0	14^2	21	18	8	0	13	8	20.9	9.82	43	.350	.466	0	.000	-1	-9	-9	0	-1.6
1955	Chi-N	0	0	—	2	0	0	0	1	3^1	4	2	1	0	1	3	13.5	5.40	76	.286	.333	0	.000	-0	-1	-0	-0	-0.1
Total	6	36	37	.493	147	95	32	7	4	713^1	738	367	84	9	277	274	12.9	4.10	97	.272	.342	53	.226	9	-7	-8	-4	-0.8

● LEN CHURCH

Church, Leonard b: 3/21/42, Chicago, Ill. d: 4/22/88, Richardson, Tex. BB/TR, 6', 190 lbs. Deb: 8/27/66

YEAR	TM/L	W	L	PCT	G	GS	CG	SH	SV	IP	H	R	HR	HB	BB	SO	RAT	ERA	ERA+	OAV	OOB	BH	AVG	PB	PR	PR+	PD	TPI
1966	Chi-N	0	1	.000	4	0	0	0	0	6	10	6	1	0	7	3	25.5	7.50	49	.400	.531	0	.000	-0	-3	-2	0	-0.4

● CHUCK CHURN

Churn, Clarence Nottingham b: 2/1/30, Bridgetown, Va. BR/TR, 6'3", 205 lbs. Deb: 4/18/57

YEAR	TM/L	W	L	PCT	G	GS	CG	SH	SV	IP	H	R	HR	HB	BB	SO	RAT	ERA	ERA+	OAV	OOB	BH	AVG	PB	PR	PR+	PD	TPI
1957	Pit-N	0	0	—	5	0	0	0	0	8^1	9	4	1	0	4	4	14.0	4.32	88	.333	.419	0	.000	-0	-0	-1	1	0.0
1958	Cle-A	0	0	—	6	0	0	0	0	8^2	12	7	1	0	5	4	17.7	6.23	59	.343	.425	0	—	0	-2	-3	-0	-0.1
1959	*LA-N	3	2	.600	14	0	0	0	1	30^2	28	17	2	1	10	24	11.4	4.99	85	.255	.322	1	.167	0	-4	-2	0	-0.3
Total	3	3	2	.600	25	0	0	0	1	47^2	49	28	4	1	19	32	13.0	5.10	79	.285	.359	1	.143	0	-6	-5	1	-0.4

● MARK CIARDI

Ciardi, Mark Thomas b: 8/19/61, New Brunswick, N.J. BR/TR, 6' ", 180 lbs. Deb: 4/9/87

YEAR	TM/L	W	L	PCT	G	GS	CG	SH	SV	IP	H	R	HR	HB	BB	SO	RAT	ERA	ERA+	OAV	OOB	BH	AVG	PB	PR	PR+	PD	TPI
1987	Mil-A	1	1	.500	4	3	0	0	0	16^1	26	17	5	0	9	8	19.3	9.37	49	.361	.432	0	—	0	-9	-8	0	-0.8

● AL CICOTTE

Cicotte, Alva Warren "Bozo" b: 12/23/29, Melvindale, Mich. d: 11/29/82, Westland, Mich. BR/TR, 6'3", 185 lbs. Deb: 4/22/57

YEAR	TM/L	W	L	PCT	G	GS	CG	SH	SV	IP	H	R	HR	HB	BB	SO	RAT	ERA	ERA+	OAV	OOB	BH	AVG	PB	PR	PR+	PD	TPI
1957	NY-A	2	2	.500	20	2	0	0	2	65^1	57	25	5	1	30	36	12.1	3.03	118	.237	.325	3	.150	-0	6	4	0	0.2
1958	Was-A	0	3	.000	8	4	0	0	0	28	36	18	3	0	14	14	16.1	4.82	79	.316	.391	2	.200	-0	-3	-3	-1	-0.4
	Det-A	3	1	.750	14	2	0	0	0	43	50	19	1	0	15	21	13.6	3.56	113	.307	.365	3	.176	-1	1	2	1	0.3
	Yr	3	4	.429	22	6	0	0	0	71	86	37	4	0	29	35	14.6	4.06	97	.310	.376	5	.185	-1	-2	-1	1	-0.1
1959	Cle-A	3	1	.750	26	1	0	0	1	44	46	29	4	2	25	23	14.9	5.32	69	.299	.403	1	.333	1	-7	-8	0	-0.7
1961	StL-N	2	6	.250	29	7	0	0	1	75	83	47	16	2	34	51	14.3	5.28	83	.283	.362	6	.286	1	-10	-7	0	-0.6
1962	Hou-N	0	0	—	5	0	0	0	0	4^2	8	4	1	0	1	4	17.4	3.86	97	.381	.409	0	—	0	0	-0	-0	0.0
Total	5	10	13	.435	102	16	0	0	4	260	280	142	30	5	119	149	14.0	4.36	90	.284	.364	15	.211	0	-14	-12	1	-1.2

● EDDIE CICOTTE

Cicotte, Edward Victor "Knuckles" b: 6/19/1884, Springwells, Mich. d: 5/5/69, Detroit, Mich. BB/TR, 5'9", 175 lbs. Deb: 9/3/05

YEAR	TM/L	W	L	PCT	G	GS	CG	SH	SV	IP	H	R	HR	HB	BB	SO	RAT	ERA	ERA+	OAV	OOB	BH	AVG	PB	PR	PR+	PD	TPI
1905	Det-A	1	1	.500	3	1	1	0	0	18	25	8	0	0	5	6	15.0	3.50	78	.329	.370	3	.429	1	-2	-1	-1	-0.1
1908	Bos-A	11	12	.478	39	24	17	2	2	207^1	198	77	0	11	59	95	11.6	2.43	101	.256	.318	17	.236	2	-1	1	0	0.4
1909	Bos-A	14	5	.737	27	17	10	1	1	162^1	117	63	3	1	56	82	9.6	1.94	129	.207	.280	12	.235	3	10	10	-0	1.5
1910	Bos-A	15	11	.577	36	30	20	3	0	250	213	94	4	13	86	104	11.2	2.74	93	.233	.308	12	.141	-1	-6	-5	3	-0.4
1911	Bos-A	11	15	.423	35	25	16	1	0	220	236	121	2	4	73	106	12.8	2.82	116	.282	.342	10	.141	-2	13	11	1	1.0
1912	Bos-A	1	3	.250	9	6	2	0	0	46	58	34	0	1	15	20	14.5	5.67	60	.319	.374	2	.154	0	-12	-11	1	-0.7
	Chi-A	9	7	.563	20	18	13	1	0	152	159	63	3	0	37	70	11.6	2.84	113	.277	.320	13	.245	1	8	6	2	1.0
	Yr	10	10	.500	29	24	15	1	0	198	217	97	3	1	52	90	12.3	3.50	93	.287	.333	15	.227	1	-4	-6	3	0.3
1913	Chi-A	18	11	.621	41	30	18	3	1	268	224	77	2	3	73	121	10.1	1.58	185	.226	.281	13	.143	-3	40	40	7	5.0

YEAR	TM/L	W	L	PCT	G	GS	CG	SH	SV	IP	H	R	HR	HB	BB	SO	RAT	ERA	ERA+	OAV	OOB	BH	AVG	PB	PR	PR+	PD	TPI
1914	Chi-A	11	16	.407	45	30	15	4	3	269^{1}	220	96	0	3	72	122	9.9	2.04	132	.232	.288	14	.163	-1	21	20	7	2.7
1915	Chi-A	13	12	.520	39	26	15	1	3	223^{1}	216	89	2	6	48	106	10.9	3.02	99	.261	.306	14	.209	1	-2	-1	0	0.0
1916	Chi-A	15	7	**.682**	44	19	11	2	5	187	138	56	1	1	70	91	10.1	1.78	155	.218	.296	12	.211	2	22	21	1	2.9
1917	*Chi-A	**28**	12	.700	49	35	29	7	4	**346^{2}**	246	76	2	3	70	150	**8.3**	**1.53**	**174**	.203	**.248**	20	.179	1	**44**	**43**	-1	**5.4**
1918	Chi-A	12	19	.387	38	30	24	1	2	266	275	102	2	2	40	104	10.7	2.77	99	.271	.300	14	.163	2	0	-1	-0	0.0
1919	*Chi-A	**29**	7	**.806**	40	35	**30**	5	1	**306^{2}**	256	77	5	2	49	110	**9.0**	1.82	175	.228	.261	20	.202	1	48	47	-4	5.3
1920	Chi-A	21	10	.677	37	35	28	4	2	303^{1}	316	128	6	2	74	87	11.6	3.26	115	.275	.320	22	.196	-3	18	17	0	1.4
Total	14	209	148	.585	502	361	249	35	24	3226	2897	1161	32	52	827	1374	10.5	2.38	123	.245	.297	198	.186	4	201	196	15	25.4
● PETE CIMINO Cimino, Peter William b: 10/17/42, Philadelphia, Pa. BR/TR, 6'2", 195 lbs. Deb: 9/22/65																												
1965	Min-A	0	0	—	1	0	0	0	0	1	0	0	0	0	0	0	0.0	0.00	—	.000	.000	0	—	0	0	0	-0	0.0
1966	Min-A	2	5	.286	35	0	0	0	4	64^{2}	53	27	4	1	30	57	11.7	2.92	123	.222	.311	0	.000	-0	4	5	-1	0.4
1967	Cal-A	3	3	.500	46	1	0	0	1	88^{1}	73	38	12	2	31	80	10.8	3.26	96	.229	.301	5	.417	2	-0	-1	-1	-0.1
1968	Cal-A	0	0	—	4	0	0	0	0	7	7	5	0	0	4	2	14.1	2.57	113	.259	.355	0	—	0	0	0	-0	0.0
Total	4	5	8	.385	86	1	0	0	5	161	133	70	16	3	65	139	11.2	3.07	108	.226	.306	5	.278	1	4	4	-2	0.3
● FRANK CIMORELLI Cimorelli, Frank Thomas b: 8/2/68, Poughkeepsie, N.Y. BR/TR, 6', 175 lbs. Deb: 4/30/94																												
1994	StL-N	0	0	—	11	0	0	0	1	13^{1}	20	14	0	2	10	1	21.6	8.78	47	.345	.457	0	.000	-0	-7	-7	-1	-0.4
● LOU CIOLA Ciola, Louis Alexander b: 9/6/22, Norfolk, Va. d: 10/18/81, Austin, Minn. BR/TR, 5'9", 165 lbs. Deb: 7/25/43																												
1943	Phi-A	1	3	.250	12	3	2	0	0	43^{2}	48	33	2	1	22	7	14.6	5.56	61	.273	.357	3	.167	-1	-11	-10	-0	-1.0
● GALEN CISCO Cisco, Galen Bernard b: 3/7/36, St.Marys, Ohio BR/TR, 5'11", 215 lbs. Deb: 6/11/61 C																												
1961	Bos-A	2	4	.333	17	8	0	0	0	52^{1}	67	40	5	0	28	26	16.3	6.71	62	.325	.406	1	.100	-0	-16	-14	-0	-1.4
1962	Bos-A	4	7	.364	23	9	1	0	0	83	95	66	11	3	50	43	16.0	6.72	61	.292	.392	2	.080	-1	-25	-23	1	-2.5
	NY-N	1	1	.500	4	2	1	0	0	19^{1}	15	7	0	3	11	13	13.5	3.26	128	.208	.337	0	.000	-1	1	2	-0	0.1
1963	NY-N	7	15	.318	51	17	1	0	0	155^{2}	165	88	15	7	64	81	13.6	4.34	80	.273	.349	5	.132	0	-18	-14	-0	-1.9
1964	NY-N	6	19	.240	36	25	5	2	0	191^{2}	182	85	17	6	54	78	11.4	3.62	99	.256	.313	6	.111	-0	-2	-1	2	0.1
1965	NY-N	4	8	.333	35	17	1	1	0	112^{1}	119	63	12	1	51	58	13.7	4.49	79	.272	.349	7	.259	2	-12	-12	-2	-1.1
1967	Bos-A	0	1	.000	11	0	0	0	1	22^{1}	21	10	4	0	8	8	11.7	3.63	96	.266	.333	0	.000	-0	-1	-0	0	-0.1
1969	KC-A	1	1	.500	15	0	0	0	1	22^{1}	17	11	4	0	15	18	12.9	3.63	102	.215	.340	0	—	0	0	0	0	0.1
Total	7	25	56	.309	192	78	9	3	2	659	681	370	68	20	281	325	13.4	4.56	81	.271	.349	21	.128	0	-72	-62	1	-6.7
● RALPH CITARELLA Citarella, Ralph Alexander b: 2/7/58, East Orange, N.J. BR/TR, 6', 180 lbs. Deb: 9/13/83																												
1983	StL-N	0	0	—	6	0	0	0	0	11	8	2	0	0	3	4	9.0	1.64	222	.205	.262	0	.000	-0	2	2	-0	0.1
1984	StL-N	0	1	.000	10	2	0	0	0	22^{1}	20	9	0	3	7	15	12.1	3.63	96	.238	.319	1	.250	0	-0	-0	0	0.0
1987	Chi-A	0	0	—	5	0	0	0	0	11	13	9	4	2	4	9	15.5	7.36	62	.302	.388	0	—	0	-4	-3	-0	-0.2
Total	3	0	1	.000	21	2	0	0	0	44^{1}	41	20	4	5	14	28	12.2	4.06	93	.247	.324	1	.200	0	-1	-1	0	-0.1
● BOBBY CLACK Clack, Robert S. "Gentlemanly Bob" (b: Robert S. Clark) b: 6/1850, England d: 10/22/33, Danvers, Mass. BR/TR, 5'9", 153 lbs. Deb: 5/13/1874 ♦																												
1876	Cin-N	0	0	—	1	0	0	0	0	2	2	1	0		0	0	9.0	4.50	49	.250	.250	19	.154	-0	-0	-1	0	0.0
● JIM CLANCY Clancy, James b: 12/18/55, Chicago, Ill. BR/TR, 6'4", 220 lbs. Deb: 7/26/77																												
1977	Tor-A	4	9	.308	13	13	4	1	0	76^{2}	80	47	7	0	47	44	14.9	5.05	83	.280	.381	0	—	0	-8	-7	1	-0.9
1978	Tor-A	10	12	.455	31	30	7	0	0	193^{2}	199	96	10	1	91	106	13.5	4.09	96	.270	.351	0	—	0	-7	-3	1	-0.3
1979	Tor-A	2	7	.222	12	11	2	0	0	63^{2}	65	44	8	0	31	33	13.6	5.51	79	.272	.356	0	—	0	-9	-8	0	-0.9
1980	Tor-A	13	16	.448	34	34	15	2	0	250^{2}	217	108	19	2	128	152	12.5	3.30	131	.233	.327	0	—	0	21	26	-0	2.8
1981	Tor-A	6	12	.333	22	22	2	0	0	125	126	77	12	5	64	56	14.0	4.90	81	.262	.355	0	—	0	-17	-12	-3	-1.9
1982	Tor-A★	16	14	.533	40	40	11	3	0	266^{2}	251	122	26	2	77	139	11.1	3.71	121	.248	.302	0	—	0	11	21	-2	1.9
1983	Tor-A	15	11	.577	34	34	11	1	0	223	238	115	23	1	61	99	12.1	3.91	110	.271	.319	0	—	0	4	9	-2	0.8
1984	Tor-A	13	15	.464	36	36	5	0	0	219^{2}	249	132	25	3	88	118	13.9	5.12	80	.287	.355	0	—	0	-27	-24	0	-2.6
1985	*Tor-A	9	6	.600	23	23	1	0	0	128^{2}	117	54	15	0	37	66	10.8	3.78	111	.241	.295	0	—	0	5	6	-1	0.5
1986	Tor-A	14	14	.500	34	34	6	3	0	219^{1}	202	100	24	4	63	126	11.0	3.94	107	.243	.299	0	—	0	6	7	1	0.9
1987	Tor-A	15	11	.577	37	37	5	1	0	241^{1}	234	103	24	1	80	180	11.7	3.54	127	.255	.315	0	—	0	25	26	2	2.7
1988	Tor-A	11	13	.458	36	31	4	0	1	196^{1}	207	106	26	9	47	118	12.1	4.49	88	.272	.322	0	—	0	-11	-12	-1	-1.4
1989	Hou-N	7	14	.333	33	26	1	0	0	147	155	100	13	0	66	91	13.5	5.08	67	.269	.344	6	.146	-0	-26	-28	-3	-3.9
1990	Hou-N	2	8	.200	33	10	0	0	1	76	100	58	4	3	33	44	16.1	6.51	57	.322	.392	3	.214	0	-23	-24	1	-2.8
1991	Hou-N	0	3	.000	30	0	0	0	5	55	37	19	5	0	20	33	9.3	2.78	126	.193	.269	0	.000	-0	6	5	-1	0.2
	*Atl-N	3	2	.600	24	0	0	0	3	34^{2}	36	23	3	1	14	17	13.2	5.71	68	.267	.340	0	.000	-0	-8	-7	0	-1.0
	Yr	3	5	.375	54	0	0	0	8	89^{2}	73	42	8	1	34	50	10.8	3.91	93	.223	.298	0	.000	-1	-2	-3	-1	-0.8
Total	15	140	167	.456	472	381	74	11	10	2517^{1}	2513	1304	244	32	947	1422	12.5	4.23	98	.261	.329	9	.148	-0	-59	-22	-8	-5.9
● BRYAN CLARK Clark, Bryan Donald b: 7/12/56, Madera, Cal. BL/TL, 6'2", 185 lbs. Deb: 4/11/81																												
1981	Sea-A	2	5	.286	29	9	1	0	2	93^{1}	92	54	3	1	55	52	14.3	4.34	89	.261	.363	0	—	0	-7	-5	1	-0.3
1982	Sea-A	5	2	.714	37	5	1	1	0	114^{2}	104	44	6	0	58	70	12.7	2.75	155	.241	.331	0	—	0	17	18	1	1.1
1983	Sea-A	7	10	.412	41	17	2	0	0	162^{1}	160	82	14	3	72	76	13.0	3.94	109	.261	.342	0	—	0	3	6	3	0.9
1984	Tor-A	1	2	.333	20	3	0	0	0	45^{2}	66	33	6	1	22	21	17.5	5.91	69	.342	.412	0	—	0	-10	-9	1	-0.4
1985	Cle-A	3	4	.429	31	3	0	0	2	62^{2}	78	47	8	0	34	24	16.1	6.32	65	.311	.393	0	—	0	-15	-15	1	-1.5
1986	Chi-A	0	0	—	5	0	0	0	0	8	8	4	0	0	2	5	11.3	4.50	96	.276	.323	0	—	0	-0	-0	-0	0.0
1987	Chi-A	0	0	—	11	0	0	0	0	18^{2}	19	5	1	0	8	8	13.0	2.41	191	.297	.375	0	—	0	4	4	-1	0.2
1990	Sea-A	2	0	1.000	12	0	0	0	0	11	9	4	0	0	10	3	15.5	3.27	121	.237	.396	0	—	0	1	1	0	0.2
Total	8	20	23	.465	186	37	4	1	4	516^{1}	536	273	38	5	261	259	14.0	4.15	100	.272	.359	0	—	0	-7	1	7	0.2
● ED CLARK Clark, Edward C. b: Cincinnati, Ohio Deb: 7/4/1886																												
1886	Phi-a	0	1	.000	1	1	1	0	0	8	10	8	2	2	2	2	15.8	6.75	52	.294	.368	0	.000	-0	-3	-3	-0	-0.3
1891	Col-a	0	0	—	1	0	0	0	0	2	2	0	0	0	0	1	9.0	0.00	—	.250	.250	0	.000	-0	1	1	0	0.0
Total	2	0	1	.000	2	1	1	0	0	10	12	8	2	2	2	3	14.4	5.40	65	.286	.348	0	.000	-0	-2	-2	-0	-0.3
● GEORGE CLARK Clark, George Myron b: 5/19/1891, Smithland, Iowa d: 11/14/40, Sioux City, Iowa BR/TL, 6', 190 lbs. Deb: 5/16/13																												
1913	NY-A	0	1	.000	11	1	0	0	0	19	22	23	1	3	19	5	20.8	9.00	33	.272	.427	2	.500	1	-13	-12	-0	-0.6
● GINGER CLARK Clark, Harvey Daniel b: 3/7/1879, Wooster, Ohio d: 5/10/43, Lake Charles, La. BR/TR, 5'11", 165 lbs. Deb: 8/11/02																												
1902	Cle-A	1	0	1.000	1	0	0	0	0	6	10	6	0	1	3	1	21.0	6.00	57	.370	.452	2	.500	1	-2	-2	0	-0.2
● MARK CLARK Clark, Mark Willard b: 5/12/68, Bath, Ill. BR/TR, 6'5", 225 lbs. Deb: 9/6/91																												
1991	StL-N	1	1	.500	7	2	0	0	0	22^{1}	17	10	3	0	11	13	11.3	4.03	92	.215	.311	0	.000	-1	-1	-1	-0	-0.2
1992	StL-N	3	10	.231	20	20	1	1	0	113^{1}	117	59	12	0	36	44	12.2	4.45	76	.265	.321	5	.139	-1	-12	-14	-2	-1.7
1993	Cle-A	7	5	.583	26	15	1	0	0	109^{1}	119	55	18	1	25	57	11.9	4.28	101	.279	.321	0	—	0	1	1	-2	-0.1
1994	Cle-A	11	3	.786	20	20	4	1	0	127^{1}	133	61	14	4	40	60	12.5	3.82	124	.273	.333	0	—	0	14	13	1	1.3
1995	Cle-A	9	7	.563	22	21	2	0	0	124^{2}	143	77	13	4	42	68	13.6	5.27	89	.288	.348	0	—	0	-8	-8	-0	-0.9
1996	NY-N	14	11	.560	32	32	2	0	0	212^{1}	217	98	20	3	48	142	11.4	3.43	117	.265	.308	3	.043	-5	19	14	-2	0.9
1997	NY-N	8	7	.533	23	22	1	0	0	142	158	74	18	3	47	72	13.2	4.25	95	.289	.348	2	.047	-2	-1	-3	-1	-0.5
	Chi-N	6	1	.857	9	9	2	0	0	63	55	22	6	1	12	51	9.7	2.86	151	.226	.266	0	.000	-2	9	10	0	0.9
	Yr	14	8	.636	32	31	3	0	0	205	213	96	24	4	59	123	12.1	3.82	108	.270	.324	2	.030	-4	9	7	-0	0.4
1998	*Chi-N	9	14	.391	33	33	2	1	0	213^{2}	236	116	23	4	48	161	12.1	4.84	91	.278	.320	4	.065	-3	-14	-10	-2	-1.4
1999	Tex-A	3	7	.300	15	15	0	0	0	74^{1}	103	73	17	1	34	44	16.7	8.60	59	.329	.397	0	.000	-0	-31	-28	-1	-2.9
2000	Tex-A	3	5	.375	12	8	0	0	0	44	66	42	10	3	24	16	19.0	7.98	64	.347	.429	0	—	0	-15	-14	0	-1.9
Total	10	74	71	.510	219	197	15	3	0	1246^{1}	1364	687	154	24	367	728	12.7	4.61	93	.279	.332	14	.058	-14	-38	-42	-8	-6.5
● MIKE CLARK Clark, Michael John b: 2/12/22, Camden, N.J. d: 1/25/96, Camden, N.J. BR/TR, 6'4", 190 lbs. Deb: 7/27/52																												
1952	StL-N	2	0	1.000	12	4	0	0	0	25^{1}	32	18	2	0	14	10	16.3	6.04	61	.311	.393	0	.000	-1	-6	-7	0	-0.5

YEAR	TM/L	W	L	PCT	G	GS	CG	SH	SV	IP	H	R	HR	HB	BB	SO	RAT	ERA	ERA+	OAV	OOB	BH	AVG	PB	PR	PR+	PD	TPI
1953	StL-N	1	0	1.000	23	2	0	0	1	35^2	46	21	2	2	21	17	17.4	4.79	89	.315	.408	0	.000	-1	-2	-2	1	-0.1
Total	2	3	0	1.000	35	6	0	0	1	61	78	39	4	2	35	27	17.0	5.31	76	.313	.402	0	.000	-1	-9	-9	1	-0.6
● SPIDER CLARK	Clark, Owen F. b: 9/16/1867, Brooklyn, N.Y. d: 2/8/1892, Brooklyn, N.Y. TR, 5'10", 150 lbs. Deb: 5/2/1889 ♦																											
1890	Buf-P	0	0	—	1	0	0	0	0	4	8	4	0	0	2	2	22.5	6.75	61	.400	.455	69	.265	0	-1	-1	-0	-0.1
● PHIL CLARK	Clark, Philip James b: 10/3/32, Albany, Ga. BR/TR, 6'3", 210 lbs. Deb: 4/15/58																											
1958	StL-N	0	1	.000	7	0	0	0	1	7^2	11	5	2	0	3	1	16.4	3.52	117	.355	.412	0	.000	-0	0	0	-0	0.0
1959	StL-N	0	1	.000	7	0	0	0	0	7	8	11	0	0	8	5	20.6	12.86	33	.286	.444	0	—	0	-7	-6	0	-0.7
Total	2	0	2	.000	14	0	0	0	1	14^2	19	16	2	0	11	6	18.4	7.98	52	.322	.429	0	.000	-0	-7	-6	-0	-0.7
● RICKEY CLARK	Clark, Rickey Charles b: 3/21/46, Mt.Clemens, Mich. BR/TR, 6'2", 170 lbs. Deb: 4/22/67																											
1967	Cal-A	12	11	.522	32	30	1	1	0	174	144	69	15	6	69	81	11.3	2.59	121	.224	.305	2	.040	-4	12	11	1	1.2
1968	Cal-A	1	11	.083	21	17	0	0	0	94^1	74	51	4	1	54	60	12.3	3.53	82	.217	.326	3	.107	-1	-6	-7	1	-0.9
1969	Cal-A	0	0	—	6	1	0	0	0	9^2	12	6	2	0	7	6	17.7	5.59	62	.300	.404	1	.500	0	-2	-2	-1	-0.1
1971	Cal-A	2	1	.667	11	7	1	1	1	44	36	15	6	2	28	28	13.5	2.86	113	.220	.340	4	.267	1	3	2	-1	0.2
1972	Cal-A	4	9	.308	26	15	2	0	1	109^2	105	59	10	2	55	61	13.3	4.51	65	.261	.352	3	.097	-1	-18	-20	1	-2.4
Total	5	19	32	.373	96	70	4	2	2	431^2	371	200	37	11	213	236	12.4	3.38	90	.233	.328	13	.103	-5	-10	-16	1	-2.0
● BOB CLARK	Clark, Robert William b: 8/22/1897, Newport, Pa. d: 5/18/44, Carlsbad, N.Mex. BR/TR, 6'3", 188 lbs. Deb: 5/26/20																											
1920	Cle-A	1	2	.333	11	2	2	1	0	42	59	19	0	1	13	8	15.6	3.43	111	.383	.435	2	.200	-0	2	2	-0	0.0
1921	Cle-A	0	0	—	5	0	0	0	0	9^1	23	17	2	1	6	2	28.9	14.46	29	.511	.577	0	.000	-1	-11	-11	-0	-0.5
Total	2	1	2	.333	16	2	2	1	0	51^1	82	36	2	2	19	10	18.1	5.44	71	.412	.468	2	.154	-1	-9	-9	-1	-0.5
● TERRY CLARK	Clark, Terry Lee b: 10/18/60, Los Angeles, Cal. BR/TR, 6'2", 196 lbs. Deb: 7/7/88																											
1988	Cal-A	6	6	.500	15	15	2	1	0	94	120	54	8	0	31	39	14.5	5.07	76	.323	.375	0	—	0	-11	-13	0	-1.4
1989	Cal-A	0	2	.000	4	2	0	0	0	11	13	8	0	0	3	7	13.1	4.91	78	.310	.356	0	—	0	-1	-1	0	-0.2
1990	Hou-N	0	0	—	1	1	0	0	0	4	9	7	0	0	3	2	27.0	13.50	28	.429	.500	1	.500	0	-4	-4	-0	-0.2
1995	Atl-N	0	0	—	3	0	0	0	0	3^2	3	2	0	0	5	2	19.6	4.91	87	.231	.444	0	—	0	-0	-0	0	0.0
	Bal-A	2	5	.286	38	0	0	0	1	39	40	15	3	1	15	18	12.9	3.46	137	.276	.348	0	—	0	5	6	-1	0.8
1996	KC-A	1	1	.500	12	0	0	0	0	17^1	28	15	3	0	7	12	18.2	7.79	64	.350	.402	0	—	0	-5	-5	-0	-0.5
	Hou-N	0	2	.000	5	0	0	0	0	6^1	16	10	1	1	2	5	27.0	11.37	34	.471	.514	0	—	0	-5	-6	1	-1.0
1997	Cle-A	0	3	.000	4	4	0	0	0	26^1	29	21	3	0	13	13	14.4	6.15	76	.284	.365	0	—	0	-5	-4	0	-0.4
	Tex-A	1	4	.200	9	5	0	0	0	30^2	41	20	3	2	10	11	15.6	5.87	82	.325	.384	1	1.000	0	-4	-3	-0	-0.3
	Yr	1	7	.125	13	9	0	0	0	57	70	41	6	2	23	24	15.0	6.00	79	.307	.375	1	1.000	0	-9	-8	1	-0.7
Total	6	10	23	.303	91	27	2	1	1	232^1	299	152	21	4	89	109	15.2	5.54	78	.320	.381	2	.667	1	-31	-32	1	-3.2
● OTIE CLARK	Clark, William Otis b: 5/22/18, Boscobel, Wis. BR/TR, 6'1.5", 190 lbs. Deb: 4/17/45																											
1945	Bos-A	4	4	.500	12	9	4	1	0	82	86	33	6	1	19	20	11.6	3.07	111	.268	.311	5	.208	0	3	3	-2	0.1
● WATTY CLARK	Clark, William Watson "Lefty" b: 5/16/02, St.Joseph, La. d: 3/4/72, Clearwater, Fla. BL/TL, 6'0.5", 175 lbs. Deb: 5/28/24																											
1924	Cle-A	1	3	.250	12	1	0	0	0	25^2	38	27	0	2	14	6	18.9	7.01	61	.345	.429	2	.222	1	-8	-8	-0	-1.0
1927	Bro-N	7	2	.778	27	3	1	0	2	73^2	74	23	2	0	19	32	11.4	2.32	171	.265	.312	3	.143	-1	**13**	**13**	0	1.5
1928	Bro-N	12	9	.571	40	19	10	2	3	194^2	193	75	4	1	50	85	11.3	2.68	148	.259	.306	10	.152	-2	28	28	1	2.7
1929	Bro-N	16	19	.457	41	39	19	3	1	**279**	295	136	14	3	71	140	11.9	3.74	123	.270	.316	16	.165	-3	30	28	-0	2.6
1930	Bro-N	13	13	.500	44	24	9	1	6	200	209	110	20	0	38	81	11.1	4.18	117	.271	.306	14	.206	0	17	16	0	1.9
1931	Bro-N	14	10	.583	34	28	16	3	1	233^1	243	86	4	1	52	96	11.4	3.20	119	.267	.308	21	.250	4	17	16	-3	1.7
1932	Bro-N	20	12	.625	40	36	19	2	0	273	282	122	10	4	49	99	11.0	3.49	109	.264	.299	21	.216	1	12	10	1	1.3
1933	Bro-N	2	4	.333	11	8	4	1	1	50^2	61	29	2	3	6	14	12.4	4.80	67	.303	.333	2	.154	-0	-8	-9	-0	-1.1
	NY-N	3	4	.429	16	5	0	0	0	44	58	25	3	1	11	11	14.3	4.70	68	.317	.359	3	.273	1	-7	-8	1	-1.0
	Yr	5	8	.385	27	13	4	1	1	94^2	119	54	5	4	17	25	13.3	4.75	68	.310	.346	5	.208	1	-15	-17	0	-2.1
1934	NY-N	1	2	.333	5	4	1	0	0	18^2	23	15	5	0	5	6	13.5	6.75	57	.295	.337	1	.167	0	-6	-6	0	-0.8
	Bro-N	2	0	1.000	17	1	0	0	0	25^1	40	19	0	1	9	10	17.8	5.33	73	.345	.397	1	.125	-1	-4	-4	-0	-0.4
	Yr	3	2	.600	22	5	1	0	0	44	63	34	5	1	14	16	16.0	5.93	66	.325	.373	2	.143	-0	-9	-10	-0	-1.2
1935	Bro-N	13	8	.619	33	25	11	1	0	207	215	93	11	1	28	35	10.6	3.30	120	.264	.289	14	.177	-0	16	16	2	1.6
1936	Bro-N	7	11	.389	33	16	1	1	2	120	162	73	11	0	28	28	14.3	4.43	93	.316	.351	9	.231	0	-5	-4	0	-0.5
1937	Bro-N	0	0	—	2	0	0	0	0	2^1	4	3	0	0	3	0	27.0	7.71	52	.308	.438	0	—	0	-1	-1	0	0.0
Total	12	111	97	.534	355	209	91	14	16	1747^1	1897	836	86	17	383	643	11.8	3.66	112	.275	.315	117	.196	1	96	88	1	8.5
● LEFTY CLARKE	Clarke, Alan Thomas b: 3/8/1896, Clarksville, Md. d: 3/11/75, Cheverly, Md. BB/TL, 5'11", 180 lbs. Deb: 10/2/21																											
1921	Cin-N	0	1	.000	1	1	1	0	0	5	7	7	0	0	2	1	16.2	5.40	66	.304	.360	0	.000	-0	-1	-1	-0	-0.2
● HENRY CLARKE	Clarke, Henry Tefft b: 8/28/1875, Bellevue, Neb. d: 3/28/50, Colorado Springs, Colo. BR/TR, Deb: 6/26/1897 ♦																											
1897	Cle-N	0	4	.000	5	4	3	0	0	30^2	32	29	4	3	12	3	13.8	5.87	76	.267	.348	7	.280	0	-5	-5	-1	-0.5
1898	Chi-N	1	0	1.000	1	1	1	0	0	9	8	4	0	1	5	1	14.0	2.00	179	.235	.350	1	.250	0	2	2	-0	0.2
Total	2	1	4	.200	6	5	4	0	0	39^2	40	33	4	4	17	4	13.8	4.99	86	.260	.349	8	.276	0	-4	-3	-1	-0.3
● RUFE CLARKE	Clarke, Rufus Rivers b: 4/13/1900, Estill, S.C. d: 2/8/83, Columbia, S.C. BR/TR, 6'1", 203 lbs. Deb: 9/3/23 F																											
1923	Det-A	1	1	.500	5	0	0	0	0	6	6	3	0	1	6	2	19.5	4.50	86	.300	.481	0	—	0	-0	-0	0	-0.1
1924	Det-A	0	0	—	2	0	0	0	0	5^1	3	2	0	1	5	1	15.2	3.38	122	.158	.360	0	.000	-0	1	0	-0	0.0
Total	2	1	1	.500	7	0	0	0	0	11^1	9	5	0	2	11	3	17.5	3.97	100	.231	.423	0	.000	-0	0	0	0	-0.1
● STAN CLARKE	Clarke, Stanley Martin b: 8/9/60, Toledo, Ohio BL/TL, 6'1", 180 lbs. Deb: 6/7/83																											
1983	Tor-A	1	1	.500	10	0	0	0	0	11	10	4	2	0	5	7	12.3	3.27	132	.256	.341	0	—	0	1	1	0	0.2
1985	Tor-A	0	0	—	4	0	0	0	0	4	3	2	1	0	2	2	11.3	4.50	94	.214	.313	0	—	0	-0	-0	0	0.0
1986	Tor-A	0	1	.000	10	0	0	0	0	12^2	18	13	4	0	10	9	19.9	9.24	46	.375	.483	0	—	0	-7	-7	0	-0.5
1987	Sea-A	2	2	.500	22	0	0	0	0	23	31	14	7	0	10	13	16.0	5.48	86	.333	.398	0	—	0	-3	-2	-0	-0.3
1989	KC-A	0	2	.000	2	2	0	0	0	7	14	12	2	0	4	2	23.1	15.43	25	.438	.500	0	—	0	-9	-9	-0	-1.3
1990	StL-N	0	0	—	2	0	0	0	0	3^1	2	1	0	0	0	3	5.4	2.70	142	.167	.167	0	—	0	0	0	-0	0.0
Total	6	3	6	.333	50	2	0	0	0	61	78	46	16	0	31	36	16.1	6.79	64	.328	.405	0	—	0	-17	-16	-0	-1.9
● WEBBO CLARKE	Clarke, Vibert Ernesto b: 6/8/28, Colon, Panama d: 6/14/70, Cristobal, C.Z. BL/TL, 6', 165 lbs. Deb: 9/4/55																											
1955	Was-A	0	0	—	7	2	0	0	0	21^1	17	11	2	0	14	9	13.1	4.64	83	.221	.341	1	.167	-0	-2	-2	0	-0.1
● DAD CLARKE	Clarke, William H. b: 1/7/1865, Oswego, N.Y. d: 6/3/11, Lorain, Ohio BB/TR, 5'7", 160 lbs. Deb: 4/23/1888																											
1888	Chi-N	1	0	1.000	2	2	1	0	0	16	23	17	2	2	6	6	17.4	5.06	60	.315	.383	2	.286	2	-4	-3	0	0.0
1891	Col-a	1	2	.333	4	3	2	0	0	21	30	21	0	1	16	2	20.1	6.86	50	.326	.431	1	.111	0	-7	-9	-0	-0.9
1894	NY-N	3	4	.429	15	6	5	0	1	84	114	76	3	3	26	15	15.3	4.93	106	.320	.371	8	.216	-0	4	3	0	0.1
1895	NY-N	18	15	.545	37	30	27	1	1	281^2	336	174	5	11	60	67	13.0	3.39	137	.292	.333	29	.240	-2	44	40	-2	3.2
1896	NY-N	17	24	.415	48	40	33	1	1	351	431	246	9	11	60	66	12.9	4.26	99	.300	.332	30	.204	-4	4	-2	-3	-0.8
1897	NY-N	2	1	.667	6	4	2	0	0	31	43	34	1	2	11	10	16.3	6.10	68	.326	.386	3	.167	-1	-6	-7	-0	-0.6
	Lou-N	2	4	.333	7	6	6	0	0	54^2	74	33	3	2	10	7	14.2	3.95	108	.320	.354	5	.227	-1	2	2	-0	0.1
	Yr	4	5	.444	13	10	8	0	0	85^2	117	67	4	4	21	17	14.9	4.73	89	.322	.366	8	.200	-2	-4	-5	-0	-0.5
1898	Lou-N	0	1	.000	1	1	1	0	0	9	10	7	1	2	2	1	14.0	5.00	72	.278	.350	0	.000	-1	-1	-1	-0	-0.2
Total	7	44	51	.463	120	92	77	2	3	848^1	1061	608	24	34	191	174	13.6	4.17	106	.302	.344	78	.214	-6	35	23	-6	0.9
● DAD CLARKSON	Clarkson, Arthur Hamilton b: 8/31/1866, Cambridge, Mass. d: 2/5/11, Somerville, Mass. BR/TR, 5'10", 165 lbs. Deb: 8/20/1891 F																											
1891	NY-N	1	2	.333	5	2	1	0	0	28	24	23	0	3	18	11	14.5	2.89	111	.222	.349	4	.444	2	1	1	0	0.3
1892	Bos-N	1	0	1.000	1	1	1	0	0	7	5	1	0	0	3	0	10.3	1.29	273	.192	.276	0	.000	-0	2	2	-0	0.2
1893	StL-N	12	9	.571	24	21	17	1	0	186^1	194	116	4	14	79	37	13.9	3.48	136	.260	.342	10	.133	-5	25	26	1	1.8
1894	StL-N	8	17	.320	32	32	24	1	0	233^1	318	236	9	11	117	46	17.2	6.36	85	.321	.399	16	.182	-4	-27	-24	1	-1.9
1895	StL-N	1	6	.143	7	7	7	0	0	61	91	66	7	2	26	9	17.6	7.38	66	.340	.402	1	.043	-3	-18	-17	-1	-1.6

YEAR	TM/L	W	L	PCT	G	GS	CG	SH	SV	IP	H	R	HR	HB	BB	SO	RAT	ERA	ERA+	OAV	OOB	BH	AVG	PB	PR	PR+	PD	TPI
	Bal-N	12	3	.800	20	14	10	0	0	142	169	84	5	4	64	23	15.0	3.87	123	.291	.365	8	.140	-4	14	14	2	0.9
	Yr	13	9	.591	27	21	17	0	0	203	260	150	12	6	90	32	15.8	4.92	97	.306	.377	9	.112	-7	-3	-3	1	-0.7
1896	Bal-N	4	2	.667	7	4	3	0	0	47	72	40	1	2	18	7	17.6	4.98	86	.348	.405	5	.278	0	-3	-4	-0	-0.4
Total	6	39	39	.500	96	81	63	2	0	704^2	873	566	26	36	325	133	15.8	4.90	99	.298	.376	44	.161	-14	-6	-3	2	-0.7

● JOHN CLARKSON

Clarkson, John Gibson b: 7/1/1861, Cambridge, Mass. d: 2/4/09, Belmont, Mass. BR/TR, 5′10″, 155 lbs. Deb: 5/2/1882 FH

YEAR	TM/L	W	L	PCT	G	GS	CG	SH	SV	IP	H	R	HR	HB	BB	SO	RAT	ERA	ERA+	OAV	OOB	BH	AVG	PB	PR	PR+	PD	TPI
1882	Wor-N	1	2	.333	3	3	2	0	0	24	49	31	0		2	3	19.1	4.50	69	.392	.402	4	.364	1	-4	-3	0	-0.2
1884	Chi-N	10	3	.769	14	13	12	0	0	118	94	64	10		25	102	9.1	2.14	147	.208	.249	22	.262	4	11	12	3	1.8
1885	*Chi-N	**53**	16	.768	**70**	70	**68**	**10**	0	**623**	497	255	21		97	**308**	8.6	1.85	163	.208	.239	61	.216	2	**67**	**75**	8	**8.2**
1886	*Chi-N	36	17	.679	55	55	50	3	0	466^2	419	248	20		86	313	9.7	2.41	150	.229	.264	49	.233	1	47	57	4	5.9
1887	Chi-N	**38**	21	.644	**60**	59	**56**	2	0	**523**	605	283	20	8	92	**237**	10.5	3.08	146	.278	.281	63	.279	2	**58**	**74**	9	**7.6**
1888	Bos-N	33	20	.623	54	54	53	3	0	**483^1**	448	247	17	10	119	223	10.7	2.76	103	.236	.284	40	.195	3	5	5	3	0.9
1889	Bos-N	**49**	19	**.721**	**73**	72	**68**	**8**	1	**620**	589	280	16	17	203	**284**	**11.7**	**2.73**	**153**	.243	**.306**	54	.206	0	**89**	**95**	11	**9.8**
1890	Bos-N	26	18	.591	44	44	43	2	0	383	370	186	14	16	140	138	12.4	3.27	115	.246	.317	43	.249	3	13	20	-1	2.0
1891	Bos-N	33	19	.635	55	51	47	3	**3**	460^2	435	244	18	15	154	141	11.8	2.79	131	.240	.305	42	.225	3	28	40	4	4.5
1892	Bos-N	8	6	.571	16	16	15	4	0	145^2	115	65	4	5	60	48	11.1	2.35	150	.208	.292	13	.228	1	15	18	0	1.6
	*Cle-N	17	10	.630	29	28	27	1	1	243^1	235	132	4	4	72	91	11.5	2.55	133	.244	.299	14	.139	-5	20	22	-1	1.5
	Yr	25	16	.610	45	44	42	5	1	389	350	197	8	9	132	139	11.4	2.48	139	.231	.296	27	.171	-4	35	40	-1	3.1
1893	Cle-N	16	17	.485	36	35	31	0	0	295	358	240	11	5	95	62	14.0	4.45	110	.291	.344	27	.206	-4	7	13	3	1.0
1894	Cle-N	8	10	.444	22	18	13	1	0	150^2	173	109	6	0	46	28	13.1	4.42	124	.285	.335	11	.200	-3	15	17	2	1.4
Total	12	328	178	.648	531	518	485	37	5	4536^1	4387	2384	161	80	1191	1978	11.0	2.81	134	.244	.291	443	.223	9	371	450	45	46.0

● WALTER CLARKSON

Clarkson, Walter Hamilton b: 11/3/1878, Cambridge, Mass. d: 10/10/46, Cambridge, Mass. BR/TR, 5′10″, 150 lbs. Deb: 7/2/04 F

YEAR	TM/L	W	L	PCT	G	GS	CG	SH	SV	IP	H	R	HR	HB	BB	SO	RAT	ERA	ERA+	OAV	OOB	BH	AVG	PB	PR	PR+	PD	TPI
1904	NY-A	1	2	.333	13	4	2	0	1	66^1	63	42	3	10	25	43	13.3	5.02	54	.251	.343	7	.269	2	-18	-16	-1	-0.8
1905	NY-A	3	3	.500	9	4	3	0	0	46	40	26	1	2	13	35	10.8	3.91	75	.235	.297	1	.053	-2	-6	-5	-1	-0.8
1906	NY-A	9	4	.692	32	16	9	3	0	151	135	59	6	5	55	64	11.6	2.32	128	.242	.316	8	.157	-1	6	10	-1	0.6
1907	NY-A	1	1	.500	5	2	0	0	1	17^1	19	12	1	2	8	3	15.1	6.23	45	.279	.372	2	.286	0	-7	-6	0	-0.7
	Cle-A	4	6	.400	17	10	9	1	0	90^2	77	40	1	3	29	32	10.8	1.99	126	.232	.299	1	.036	-3	6	5	-0	0.2
	Yr	5	7	.417	22	12	9	1	1	108	96	52	2	5	37	35	11.5	2.67	96	.240	.312	3	.086	-3	-1	-1	-0	-0.5
1908	Cle-A	0	0	—	2	1	0	0	0	3^1	6	4	0	2	2	1	27.0	10.80	22	.400	.526	1	1.000	0	-3	-3	-0	-0.1
Total	5	18	16	.529	78	37	23	4	2	374^2	340	183	12	24	132	178	11.9	3.17	88	.244	.320	20	.152	-4	-23	-15	-4	-1.6

● BILL CLARKSON

Clarkson, William Henry "Blackie" b: 9/27/1898, Portsmouth, Va. d: 8/27/71, Raleigh, N.C. BR/TR, 5′11″, 160 lbs. Deb: 5/2/27

YEAR	TM/L	W	L	PCT	G	GS	CG	SH	SV	IP	H	R	HR	HB	BB	SO	RAT	ERA	ERA+	OAV	OOB	BH	AVG	PB	PR	PR+	PD	TPI
1927	NY-N	3	9	.250	26	7	2	0	2	86^2	92	50	3	1	52	28	15.1	4.36	88	.280	.380	1	.050	-1	-4	-5	0	-0.7
1928	NY-N	0	0	—	4	0	0	0	0	5^2	10	6	0	0	1	3	17.5	7.94	49	.455	.478	0	—	0	-2	-3	-0	-0.1
	Bos-N	0	2	.000	19	2	0	0	0	34^2	53	29	2	1	22	8	19.7	6.75	58	.349	.434	0	.000	-0	-11	-11	1	-0.5
	Yr	0	2	.000	23	2	0	0	0	40^1	63	35	2	1	23	11	19.4	6.92	57	.362	.439	0	.000	-0	-13	-14	1	-0.6
1929	Bos-N	0	1	.000	2	1	0	0	0	7	16	10	0	0	4	0	25.7	10.29	45	.485	.541	1	.500	0	-4	-4	0	-0.4
Total	3	3	12	.200	51	10	2	0	2	134	171	95	5	2	79	39	16.9	5.44	72	.319	.408	2	.080	-1	-22	-23	1	-1.7

● MARTY CLARY

Clary, Martin Keith b: 4/3/62, Detroit, Mich. BR/TR, 6′4″, 190 lbs. Deb: 9/5/87

YEAR	TM/L	W	L	PCT	G	GS	CG	SH	SV	IP	H	R	HR	HB	BB	SO	RAT	ERA	ERA+	OAV	OOB	BH	AVG	PB	PR	PR+	PD	TPI
1987	Atl-N	0	1	.000	7	1	0	0	0	14^2	20	13	2	1	4	7	15.3	6.14	71	.328	.379	0	.000	-0	-3	-3	-0	-0.2
1989	Atl-N	4	3	.571	18	17	2	1	0	108^2	103	47	6	1	31	30	11.2	3.15	116	.249	.303	5	.161	0	4	6	0	0.4
1990	Atl-N	1	10	.091	33	14	0	0	0	101^2	128	72	9	1	39	44	14.9	5.67	71	.308	.368	0	.000	-3	-21	-17	1	-1.9
Total	3	5	14	.263	58	32	2	1	0	225	251	132	17	3	74	81	13.1	4.48	86	.282	.339	5	.083	-2	-20	-14	1	-1.7

● GOWELL CLASET

Claset, Gowell Sylvester "Lefty" b: 11/26/07, Battle Creek, Mich d: 3/8/81, St.Petersburg, Fla. BB/TL, 6′3.5″, 210 lbs. Deb: 4/12/33

YEAR	TM/L	W	L	PCT	G	GS	CG	SH	SV	IP	H	R	HR	HB	BB	SO	RAT	ERA	ERA+	OAV	OOB	BH	AVG	PB	PR	PR+	PD	TPI
1933	Phi-A	2	0	1.000	8	1	0	0	0	11^1	23	15	1	0	11	1	27.0	9.53	45	.426	.523	1	.500	1	-7	-7	0	-0.8

● FRITZ CLAUSEN

Clausen, Frederick William b: 4/26/1869, New York, N.Y. d: 2/11/60, Memphis, Tenn. BR/TL, 5′11″, 190 lbs. Deb: 7/23/1892

YEAR	TM/L	W	L	PCT	G	GS	CG	SH	SV	IP	H	R	HR	HB	BB	SO	RAT	ERA	ERA+	OAV	OOB	BH	AVG	PB	PR	PR+	PD	TPI
1892	Lou-N	9	13	.409	24	24	24	2	0	200	181	120	3	3	87	94	12.2	3.06	100	.232	.311	13	.155	-3	5	0	-1	-0.3
1893	Lou-N	1	4	.200	5	5	3	0	0	33	41	25	2	1	22	4	17.5	6.00	73	.295	.395	3	.214	-1	-5	-6	0	-0.7
	Chi-N	6	2	.750	10	9	8	0	1	76	71	46	1	5	39	31	13.6	3.08	150	.240	.338	4	.121	-3	13	13	0	0.8
	Yr	7	6	.538	15	14	11	0	1	109	112	71	3	6	61	35	14.8	3.96	115	.257	.357	7	.149	-4	8	7	0	0.1
1894	Chi-N	0	1	.000	2	2	0	0	0	4^1	5	7	0	0	5	1	20.8	14.54	39	.294	.455	0	.000	-0	-4	-4	0	-0.6
1896	Lou-N	0	2	.000	2	2	1	0	0	11	17	13	1	3	6	4	21.3	6.55	66	.347	.448	0	.000	-1	-3	-3	0	-0.4
Total	4	16	22	.421	43	42	36	2	1	324^1	315	211	7	12	159	134	13.5	3.64	100	.246	.334	20	.147	-8	6	-0	-0	-1.2

● AL CLAUSS

Clauss, Albert Stanley "Lefty" b: 6/24/1891, New Haven, Conn. d: 9/13/52, New Haven, Conn. BR/TL, 5′10.5″, 178 lbs. Deb: 4/22/13

YEAR	TM/L	W	L	PCT	G	GS	CG	SH	SV	IP	H	R	HR	HB	BB	SO	RAT	ERA	ERA+	OAV	OOB	BH	AVG	PB	PR	PR+	PD	TPI
1913	Det-A	0	1	.000	5	1	0	0	0	13^1	11	9	0	2	12	1	16.9	4.73	62	.220	.391	0	.000	-1	-3	-3	-0	-0.3

● DANNY CLAY

Clay, Danny Bruce b: 10/24/61, Sun Valley, Cal. BR/TR, 6′1″, 190 lbs. Deb: 5/1/88

YEAR	TM/L	W	L	PCT	G	GS	CG	SH	SV	IP	H	R	HR	HB	BB	SO	RAT	ERA	ERA+	OAV	OOB	BH	AVG	PB	PR	PR+	PD	TPI
1988	Phi-N	0	1	.000	17	0	0	0	0	24	27	17	5	0	21	12	18.0	6.00	59	.303	.436	0	.000	-0	-7	-6	-1	-0.4

● KEN CLAY

Clay, Kenneth Earl b: 4/6/54, Lynchburg, Va. BR/TR, 6′3″, 195 lbs. Deb: 6/7/77

YEAR	TM/L	W	L	PCT	G	GS	CG	SH	SV	IP	H	R	HR	HB	BB	SO	RAT	ERA	ERA+	OAV	OOB	BH	AVG	PB	PR	PR+	PD	TPI
1977	*NY-A	2	3	.400	21	3	0	0	1	55^2	53	32	6	1	24	20	12.6	4.37	91	.251	.331	0	—	0	-2	-3	0	-0.2
1978	*NY-A	3	4	.429	28	6	0	0	0	75^2	89	41	3	2	21	32	13.3	4.28	85	.291	.340	0	—	0	-4	-6	-1	-0.5
1979	NY-A	1	7	.125	32	5	0	0	2	78^1	88	49	12	2	25	28	13.2	5.40	76	.291	.350	0	—	0	-10	-12	0	-1.1
1980	Tex-A	2	3	.400	8	8	0	0	0	43	43	24	4	3	29	17	15.7	4.60	85	.256	.375	0	—	0	-3	-3	-1	-0.4
1981	Sea-A	2	7	.222	22	14	0	0	0	101	116	62	10	3	42	32	14.3	4.63	83	.294	.366	0	—	0	-11	-8	-2	-0.8
Total	5	10	24	.294	111	36	0	0	3	353^2	389	208	35	11	141	129	13.8	4.68	83	.281	.353	0	—	0	-30	-32	-3	-3.0

● MARK CLEAR

Clear, Mark Alan b: 5/27/56, Los Angeles, Cal. BR/TR, 6′4″, 215 lbs. Deb: 4/4/79

YEAR	TM/L	W	L	PCT	G	GS	CG	SH	SV	IP	H	R	HR	HB	BB	SO	RAT	ERA	ERA+	OAV	OOB	BH	AVG	PB	PR	PR+	PD	TPI
1979	*Cal-A★	11	5	.688	52	0	0	0	14	109	87	48	6	3	68	98	13.0	3.63	112	.219	.337	0	—	0	7	6	-1	0.8
1980	Cal-A	11	11	.500	58	0	0	0	9	106^1	82	51	2	5	65	105	12.9	3.30	119	.216	.338	0	—	0	9	8	-1	1.5
1981	Bos-A	8	3	.727	34	0	0	0	9	76^2	69	36	11	2	51	82	14.3	4.11	94	.239	.357	0	—	0	-4	-2	-1	-0.4
1982	Bos-A☆	14	9	.609	55	0	0	0	14	105	92	39	11	7	61	109	13.7	3.00	144	.238	.352	0	—	0	13	15	-0	3.0
1983	Bos-A	4	5	.444	48	0	0	0	4	96	101	71	10	3	68	81	16.1	6.28	70	.273	.390	0	—	0	-24	-19	-1	-1.8
1984	Bos-A	8	3	.727	47	0	0	0	8	67	47	38	2	2	70	76	16.0	4.03	104	.198	.385	0	—	0	-0	1	0	0.2
1985	Bos-A	1	3	.250	41	0	0	0	3	55^2	45	26	1	5	50	55	16.2	3.72	115	.225	.392	0	—	0	3	3	1	0.4
1986	Mil-A	5	5	.500	59	0	0	0	16	73^2	53	23	4	1	36	85	11.0	2.20	197	.201	.299	0	—	0	16	17	-0	2.8
1987	Mil-A	8	5	.615	58	1	0	0	6	78^1	70	46	9	5	55	81	14.9	4.48	102	.239	.368	0	—	0	-0	1	1	0.2
1988	Mil-A	1	0	1.000	25	0	0	0	0	29	23	12	4	0	21	26	13.7	2.79	143	.215	.344	0	—	0	4	4	-0	0.2
1990	Cal-A	0	0	—	4	0	0	0	0	7^2	5	7	0	2	9	6	18.8	5.87	65	.200	.444	0	—	0	-2	-2	-0	-0.1
Total	11	71	49	.592	481	1	0	0	83	804^1	674	397	60	35	554	804	14.1	3.85	109	.228	.357	0	—	0	22	30	-3	6.8

● JOE CLEARY

Cleary, Joseph Christopher "Fire" b: 12/3/18, Cork, Ireland BR/TR, 5′9″, 150 lbs. Deb: 8/4/45

YEAR	TM/L	W	L	PCT	G	GS	CG	SH	SV	IP	H	R	HR	HB	BB	SO	RAT	ERA	ERA+	OAV	OOB	BH	AVG	PB	PR	PR+	PD	TPI
1945	Was-A	0	0	—	1	0	0	0	0	0^1	5	7	0	0	3	1	216.0	189.00	2	.833	.889	0	—	0	-7	-7	0	-0.3

● ROGER CLEMENS

Clemens, William Roger "Rocket" b: 8/4/62, Dayton, Ohio BR/TR, 6′4″, 220 lbs. Deb: 5/15/84

YEAR	TM/L	W	L	PCT	G	GS	CG	SH	SV	IP	H	R	HR	HB	BB	SO	RAT	ERA	ERA+	OAV	OOB	BH	AVG	PB	PR	PR+	PD	TPI
1984	Bos-A	9	4	.692	21	20	5	1	0	133^1	146	67	13	2	29	126	11.9	4.32	97	.271	.311	0	—	0	-5	-2	0	-0.2
1985	Bos-A	7	5	.583	15	15	3	1	0	98^1	83	38	5	3	37	74	11.3	3.29	130	.228	.304	0	—	0	9	10	0	1.2
1986	*Bos-A★	**24**	4	**.857**	33	33	10	1	0	254	179	77	21	4	67	238	**8.9**	**2.48**	**168**	**.195**	**.253**	0	—	0	**48**	**48**	-1	5.0
1987	Bos-A	**20**	9	**.690**	36	36	**18**	**7**	0	281^2	248	100	19	9	83	256	10.9	2.97	153	.235	.296	0	—	0	47	49	-2	4.4
1988	*Bos-A★	18	12	.600	35	35	**14**	**8**	0	264	217	93	17	6	62	**291**	9.7	2.93	141	.220	.270	0	—	0	31	34	-2	3.5
1989	Bos-A	17	11	.607	35	35	8	3	0	253^1	215	101	20	8	93	230	11.2	3.13	131	.231	.307	0	—	0	22	26	-1	2.7
1990	*Bos-A☆	21	6	.778	31	31	7	**4**	0	228^1	193	59	7	7	54	209	10.0	**1.93**	**212**	.228	.280	0	—	0	**50**	**52**	1	**6.5**
1991	Bos-A★	18	10	.643	35	35	13	**4**	0	**271^1**	219	93	15	5	65	**241**	9.6	**2.62**	**164**	.221	.272	0	—	0	**45**	**48**	1	**5.0**
1992	Bos-A★	18	11	.621	32	32	11	**5**	0	246^2	203	80	11	9	62	208	10.0	**2.41**	**175**	.224	.280	0	—	0	**42**	**46**	-0	**5.5**
1993	Bos-A	11	14	.440	29	29	2	1	0	191^2	175	99	17	11	67	160	11.9	4.46	104	.244	.318	0	—	0	-3	3	-1	0.3
1994	Bos-A	9	7	.563	24	24	3	1	0	170^2	124	62	15	4	71	168	10.5	2.85	**177**	**.203**	.291	0	—	0	**37**	**40**	-0	3.3
1995	*Bos-A	10	5	.667	23	23	0	0	0	140	141	70	15	14	60	132	13.8	4.18	117	.259	.348	0	—	0	8	10	1	1.1

YEAR	TM/L	W	L	PCT	G	GS	CG	SH	SV	IP	H	R	HR	HB	BB	SO	RAT	ERA	ERA+	OAV	OOB	BH	AVG	PB	PR	PR+	PD	TPI
1996	Bos-A	10	13	.435	34	34	6	2	0	242^2	216	106	19	4	106	**257**	12.1	3.63	140	.237	.319	1	1.000	0	37	38	-1	3.0
1997	Tor-A★	**21**	7	.750	34	34	**9**	**3**	0	**264**	204	65	9	12	68	**292**	**9.7**	**2.05**	**225**	.213	**.274**	1	.500	1	**74**	**74**	2	**8.0**
1998	Tor-A★	**20**	6	.769	33	33	5	3	0	234^2	169	78	11	7	88	**271**	10.1	**2.65**	**176**	**.197**	.278	0	.000	-0	**52**	**53**	-0	**5.3**
1999	*NY-A	14	10	.583	30	30	1	1	0	187^2	185	101	20	9	90	163	13.6	4.60	103	.261	.352	0	.000	-0	6	3	2	0.5
2000	*NY-A	13	8	.619	32	32	1	0	0	204^1	184	96	26	10	84	188	12.2	3.70	130	.236	.318	0	.000	-0	28	26	2	2.4
Total	17	260	142	.647	512	511	116	45	0	3666^2	3101	1385	260	124	1186	3504	10.8	3.07	146	.228	.295	2	.143	1	529	561	2	57.5

● BILL CLEMENSEN Clemensen, William Melville b: 6/20/19, New Brunswick, N.J. d: 2/18/94, Alta, Cal. BR/TR, 6'1", 193 lbs. Deb: 5/22/39

YEAR	TM/L	W	L	PCT	G	GS	CG	SH	SV	IP	H	R	HR	HB	BB	SO	RAT	ERA	ERA+	OAV	OOB	BH	AVG	PB	PR	PR+	PD	TPI
1939	Pit-N	0	1	.000	12	1	0	0	0	27	32	26	0	3	20	13	18.3	7.33	52	.311	.437	2	.333	1	-10	-11	1	-0.3
1941	Pit-N	1	0	1.000	2	1	1	0	0	13	7	5	0	0	7	4	9.7	2.77	130	.159	.275	0	.000	-1	1	1	-0	0.0
1946	Pit-N	0	0	—	1	0	0	0	0	2	0	0	0	0	0	2	0.0	0.00	—	.000	.000	0	—	0	1	1	-0	0.0
Total	3	1	1	.500	15	2	1	0	0	42	39	31	0	3	27	19	14.8	5.57	67	.255	.377	2	.200	0	-8	-9	1	-0.3

● MATT CLEMENT Clement, Matthew Paul b: 8/12/74, McCandless Twsp., Pa. BR/TR, 6'3", 190 lbs. Deb: 9/6/98

YEAR	TM/L	W	L	PCT	G	GS	CG	SH	SV	IP	H	R	HR	HB	BB	SO	RAT	ERA	ERA+	OAV	OOB	BH	AVG	PB	PR	PR+	PD	TPI
1998	SD-N	2	0	1.000	4	2	0	0	0	13^2	15	8	0	0	7	13	14.5	4.61	85	.283	.367	0	.000	-0	-1	-1	-0	-0.2
1999	SD-N	10	12	.455	31	31	0	0	0	180^2	190	106	18	9	86	135	14.2	4.48	94	.273	.361	4	.077	-2	2	-6	-2	-1.0
2000	SD-N	13	17	.433	34	34	0	0	0	205	194	131	22	16	125	170	14.7	5.14	85	.248	.363	4	.067	-2	-11	-18	1	-2.3
Total	3	25	29	.463	69	67	0	0	0	399^1	399	245	40	25	218	318	14.5	4.82	89	.261	.362	8	.070	-5	-10	-26	-2	-3.5

● PAT CLEMENTS Clements, Patrick Brian b: 2/2/62, McCloud, Cal. BR/TL, 6', 180 lbs. Deb: 4/9/85

YEAR	TM/L	W	L	PCT	G	GS	CG	SH	SV	IP	H	R	HR	HB	BB	SO	RAT	ERA	ERA+	OAV	OOB	BH	AVG	PB	PR	PR+	PD	TPI
1985	Cal-A	5	0	1.000	41	0	0	0	1	62	47	23	4	2	25	19	10.7	3.34	123	.218	.305	0	—	0	6	5	1	0.5
	Pit-N	0	2	.000	27	0	0	0	2	34^1	39	14	2	0	15	17	14.2	3.67	98	.289	.360	1	.333	0	-0	-0	-1	-0.1
1986	Pit-N	0	4	.000	65	0	0	0	2	61	53	20	1	2	32	31	12.8	2.80	137	.251	.355	0	.000	-1	6	7	1	0.5
1987	NY-A	3	3	.500	55	0	0	0	7	80	91	45	4	3	30	36	13.9	4.95	89	.299	.368	0	—	0	-4	-5	1	-0.3
1988	NY-A	0	0	—	6	1	0	0	0	8^1	12	8	1	0	4	3	17.3	6.48	61	.343	.410	0	—	0	-2	-2	0	-0.1
1989	SD-N	4	1	.800	23	1	0	0	0	39	39	17	4	0	15	18	12.5	3.92	89	.267	.335	0	.000	-1	-2	-2	0	-0.3
1990	SD-N	0	0	—	9	0	0	0	0	13	20	9	1	0	7	6	18.7	4.15	92	.357	.429	0	—	0	-1	-0	0	0.0
1991	SD-N	1	0	1.000	12	0	0	0	0	14^1	13	8	0	0	9	8	13.8	3.77	101	.255	.367	0	.000	-0	-0	0	0	0.0
1992	SD-N	2	1	.667	27	0	0	0	0	23^2	25	9	0	2	12	11	14.8	2.66	135	.281	.379	0	.000	-0	2	2	1	0.3
	Bal-A	2	0	1.000	23	0	0	0	0	24^2	23	10	0	2	11	9	13.1	3.28	123	.258	.353	0	—	0	2	2	1	0.2
Total	8	17	11	.607	288	2	0	0	12	360^1	362	163	17	11	160	158	13.3	3.77	105	.272	.355	1	.059	-1	7	7	4	0.7

● CHRIS CLEMONS Clemons, Christopher Hale b: 10/31/72, Baytown, Tex. BR/TR, 6'4", 220 lbs. Deb: 7/23/97

YEAR	TM/L	W	L	PCT	G	GS	CG	SH	SV	IP	H	R	HR	HB	BB	SO	RAT	ERA	ERA+	OAV	OOB	BH	AVG	PB	PR	PR+	PD	TPI
1997	Chi-A	0	2	.000	5	2	0	0	0	12^2	19	13	4	1	11	8	22.0	8.53	51	.345	.463	0	—	0	-6	-6	-0	-0.8

● LANCE CLEMONS Clemons, Lance Levis b: 7/6/47, Philadelphia, Pa. BL/TL, 6'2", 205 lbs. Deb: 8/12/71

YEAR	TM/L	W	L	PCT	G	GS	CG	SH	SV	IP	H	R	HR	HB	BB	SO	RAT	ERA	ERA+	OAV	OOB	BH	AVG	PB	PR	PR+	PD	TPI
1971	KC-A	1	0	1.000	10	3	0	0	0	24	26	16	2	1	12	20	14.6	4.13	83	.263	.348	2	.286	2	-2	-2	0	0.1
1972	StL-N	0	1	.000	3	1	0	0	0	5^1	8	7	1	1	5	2	23.6	10.13	34	.364	.500	0	.000	-0	-4	-4	0	-0.7
1974	Bos-A	1	0	1.000	6	0	0	0	0	6^1	8	8	1	1	4	1	18.5	9.95	39	.296	.406	0	—	0	-4	-4	0	-0.6
Total	3	2	1	.667	19	4	0	0	0	35^2	42	31	4	3	21	23	16.7	6.06	58	.284	.384	2	.250	2	-10	-10	0	-1.2

● REGGIE CLEVELAND Cleveland, Reginald Leslie b: 5/23/48, Swift Current, Sask., Canada BR/TR, 6'1", 195 lbs. Deb: 10/1/69

YEAR	TM/L	W	L	PCT	G	GS	CG	SH	SV	IP	H	R	HR	HB	BB	SO	RAT	ERA	ERA+	OAV	OOB	BH	AVG	PB	PR	PR+	PD	TPI
1969	StL-N	0	0	—	1	1	0	0	0	4	7	4	0	0	1	3	18.0	9.00	40	.368	.400	0	.000	-0	-2	-2	-0	-0.1
1970	StL-N	0	4	.000	16	1	0	0	0	26	31	27	3	0	18	22	17.0	7.62	54	.298	.402	1	.250	0	-10	-10	-1	-1.4
1971	StL-N	12	12	.500	34	34	10	2	0	222	238	107	20	6	53	148	12.0	4.01	90	.271	.317	14	.171	-1	-13	-10	-0	-1.1
1972	StL-N	14	15	.483	33	33	11	3	0	230^2	229	120	21	5	60	153	11.5	3.94	86	.258	.308	17	.239	3	-12	-14	-1	-1.5
1973	StL-N	14	10	.583	32	32	6	3	0	224	211	88	13	4	61	122	11.1	3.01	121	.246	.300	17	.230	4	16	16	-2	1.8
1974	Bos-A	12	14	.462	41	27	10	0	0	221^1	234	121	25	9	69	103	12.7	4.31	89	.271	.332	0	—	0	-17	-11	1	-1.1
1975	*Bos-A	13	9	.591	31	20	3	1	0	170^2	173	90	19	3	52	78	12.0	4.43	92	.263	.320	0	—	0	-12	-6	-0	-0.7
1976	Bos-A	10	9	.526	41	14	3	0	2	170	159	73	3	4	61	76	11.9	3.07	127	.246	.315	0	—	0	9	14	-0	1.6
1977	Bos-A	11	8	.579	36	27	9	1	2	190^1	211	97	20	4	43	85	12.2	4.26	106	.281	.323	0	—	0	-4	5	-1	0.3
1978	Bos-A	0	1	.000	1	0	0	0	0	0^1	1	1	0	0	0	0	27.0	0.00	—	.333	.333	0	—	0	0	0	0	0.0
	Tex-A	5	7	.417	53	0	0	0	12	75^2	65	33	5	3	23	46	10.8	3.09	122	.236	.301	0	—	0	6	6	0	1.1
	Yr	5	8	.385	54	0	0	0	12	76	66	34	5	3	23	46	10.9	3.08	122	.237	.302	0	—	0	6	6	0	1.1
1979	Mil-A	1	5	.167	29	1	0	0	4	55	77	44	9	0	23	22	16.4	6.71	62	.344	.405	0	—	0	-15	-16	-1	-1.8
1980	Mil-A	11	9	.550	45	13	5	2	4	154^1	150	73	9	5	49	54	11.9	3.73	104	.254	.317	0	—	0	5	3	-1	0.2
1981	Mil-A	2	3	.400	35	0	0	0	1	64^2	57	41	5	1	30	18	12.2	5.15	67	.239	.327	0	—	0	-11	-13	-1	-1.1
Total	13	105	106	.498	428	203	57	12	25	1809	1843	919	152	44	543	930	12.1	4.01	95	.264	.321	49	.211	6	-61	-36	-9	-3.8

● TEX CLEVENGER Clevenger, Truman Eugene b: 7/9/32, Visalia, Cal. BR/TR, 6'1", 180 lbs. Deb: 4/18/54

YEAR	TM/L	W	L	PCT	G	GS	CG	SH	SV	IP	H	R	HR	HB	BB	SO	RAT	ERA	ERA+	OAV	OOB	BH	AVG	PB	PR	PR+	PD	TPI
1954	Bos-A	2	4	.333	23	8	1	0	0	67^2	67	42	9	2	29	43	13.0	4.79	86	.262	.341	3	.214	0	-8	-5	0	-0.4
1956	Was-A	0	0	—	20	1	0	0	0	31^2	33	22	4	0	21	17	15.3	5.40	80	.264	.370	0	.000	-0	-4	-4	-0	-0.2
1957	Was-A	7	6	.538	52	9	2	0	8	139^2	139	69	11	4	47	75	12.2	4.19	93	.261	.326	7	.212	1	-6	-4	1	-0.2
1958	Was-A	9	9	.500	**55**	4	0	0	6	124	119	65	12	1	50	70	12.3	4.35	88	.251	.324	3	.136	0	-8	-7	3	-0.8
1959	Was-A	8	5	.615	50	7	2	2	8	117^1	114	56	8	2	51	71	12.8	3.91	100	.256	.335	4	.174	1	-1	0	4	0.5
1960	Was-A	5	11	.313	53	11	1	0	7	128^2	150	77	10	3	49	49	14.1	4.20	93	.298	.363	2	.091	-1	-5	-4	-1	-0.7
1961	LA-A	2	1	.667	12	0	0	0	1	16	13	5	1	0	13	11	14.6	1.69	267	.220	.361	0	.000	-0	4	4	1	0.9
	NY-A	1	1	.500	21	0	0	0	0	31^2	35	20	3	1	21	14	16.2	4.83	77	.287	.396	1	.250	0	-3	-4	1	-0.1
	Yr	3	2	.600	33	0	0	0	1	47^2	48	25	4	1	34	25	15.7	3.78	105	.265	.384	1	.143	0	1	1	1	0.8
1962	NY-A	2	0	1.000	21	0	0	0	0	38	36	14	3	1	17	11	12.8	2.84	132	.248	.331	0	.000	-0	5	4	0	0.2
Total	8	36	37	.493	307	40	6	2	30	694^2	706	370	61	14	298	361	13.2	4.18	94	.265	.342	20	.157	1	-26	-20	8	-0.8

● STEW CLIBURN Cliburn, Stewart Walker b: 12/19/56, Jackson, Miss. BR/TR, 6', 195 lbs. Deb: 9/17/84 F

YEAR	TM/L	W	L	PCT	G	GS	CG	SH	SV	IP	H	R	HR	HB	BB	SO	RAT	ERA	ERA+	OAV	OOB	BH	AVG	PB	PR	PR+	PD	TPI
1984	Cal-A	0	0	—	1	0	0	0	0	2	3	3	0	0	1	1	18.0	13.50	29	.333	.400	0	—	0	-2	-2	0	-0.1
1985	Cal-A	9	3	.750	44	0	0	0	6	99	87	25	5	1	26	48	10.4	2.09	197	.241	.294	0	—	0	23	22	1	2.9
1988	Cal-A	4	2	.667	40	1	0	0	0	84	83	45	11	6	32	42	13.0	4.07	95	.266	.346	0	—	0	-1	-2	0	-0.1
Total	3	13	5	.722	85	1	0	0	6	185	173	73	16	7	59	91	11.6	3.11	128	.254	.320	0	—	0	20	19	2	2.7

● JIM CLINTON Clinton, James Lawrence "Big Jim" b: 8/10/1850, New York, N.Y. d: 9/3/21, Brooklyn, N.Y. BR/TR, 5'8.5", 174 lbs. Deb: 5/18/1872 U♦

YEAR	TM/L	W	L	PCT	G	GS	CG	SH	SV	IP	H	R	HR	HB	BB	SO	RAT	ERA	ERA+	OAV	OOB	BH	AVG	PB	PR	PR+	PD	TPI
1875	Atl-n	1	13	.071	17	14	9	0	0	123	141	104	0		5	7	10.7	2.41	86	.262	.268	10	.123	-5	-3	-5		-0.7
1876	Lou-N	0	1	.000	1	1	1	0	0	9	12	11	0		0	1	12.0	6.00	45	.279	.279	22	.338	0	-4	-3	0	-0.2

● TONY CLONINGER Cloninger, Tony Lee b: 8/13/40, Lincoln Co., N.C. BR/TR, 6', 210 lbs. Deb: 6/15/61 C

YEAR	TM/L	W	L	PCT	G	GS	CG	SH	SV	IP	H	R	HR	HB	BB	SO	RAT	ERA	ERA+	OAV	OOB	BH	AVG	PB	PR	PR+	PD	TPI
1961	Mil-N	7	2	.778	19	10	3	0	0	84	84	49	16	1	33	51	12.6	5.25	71	.258	.328	5	.167	-0	-11	-15	1	-1.4
1962	Mil-N	8	3	.727	24	15	4	1	0	111	113	61	10	1	46	69	13.0	4.30	88	.264	.337	4	.103	-2	-4	-6	0	-0.7
1963	Mil-N	9	11	.450	41	18	4	2	1	145^1	131	68	17	2	63	100	12.1	3.78	85	.239	.320	5	.135	-0	-8	-9	-2	-1.5
1964	Mil-N	19	14	.576	38	34	15	3	2	242^2	206	112	20	3	82	163	10.8	3.56	99	.231	.298	21	.241	3	-1	-1	-0	0.2
1965	Mil-N	24	11	.686	40	38	16	1	1	279	247	115	20	3	119	211	11.9	3.29	107	.236	.316	17	.162	2	8	7	-1	0.9
1966	Atl-N	14	11	.560	39	38	11	1	1	257^2	253	134	29	6	116	178	13.1	4.12	88	.258	.340	26	.234	10	-15	-14	-0	-0.3
1967	Atl-N	4	7	.364	16	16	1	0	0	76^2	85	50	13	0	31	55	13.6	5.17	64	.285	.353	5	.200	1	-15	-16	-0	-2.0
1968	Atl-N	1	3	.250	8	1	0	0	0	19	15	9	0	0	11	7	12.3	4.26	70	.227	.338	0	.000	-0	-3	-3	0	-0.6
	Cin-N	4	3	.571	17	17	2	2	0	91^1	81	49	7	3	48	65	13.0	4.04	78	.233	.331	7	.206	3	-11	-8	-0	-0.4
	Yr	5	6	.455	25	18	2	2	0	110^1	96	58	7	3	59	72	12.9	4.08	77	.232	.332	7	.184	3	-13	-11	-0	-1.0
1969	Cin-N	11	17	.393	35	34	6	2	0	189^2	184	123	24	5	103	103	13.9	5.03	75	.250	.346	12	.167	1	-30	-25	-2	-3.4
1970	*Cin-N	9	7	.563	30	18	0	0	1	148	136	69	10	4	78	56	13.3	3.83	105	.249	.347	10	.213	3	4	3	2	0.8
1971	Cin-N	3	6	.333	28	8	1	1	0	97^1	79	42	12	4	49	51	12.2	3.88	87	.230	.332	7	.259	1	-4	-6	0	-0.4
1972	StL-N	0	2	.000	17	0	0	0	0	26	29	17	2	1	19	11	17.0	5.19	66	.293	.412	0	.000	-0	-5	-5	1	-0.4
Total	12	113	97	.538	352	247	63	13	6	1767^2	1643	898	180	33	798	1120	12.6	4.07	88	.247	.330	119	.192	21	-96	-98	-2	-9.2

● BRAD CLONTZ Clontz, John Bradley b: 4/25/71, Stuart, Va. BR/TR, 6'1", 180 lbs. Deb: 4/26/95

YEAR	TM/L	W	L	PCT	G	GS	CG	SH	SV	IP	H	R	HR	HB	BB	SO	RAT	ERA	ERA+	OAV	OOB	BH	AVG	PB	PR	PR+	PD	TPI
1995	*Atl-N	8	1	.889	59	0	0	0	4	69	71	29	5	4	22	55	12.7	3.65	117	.269	.334	0	.000	-0	4	5	0	0.6
1996	*Atl-N	6	3	.667	**81**	0	0	0	1	80^2	78	53	11	2	33	49	12.6	5.69	78	.255	.331	0	.000	0	-13	-11	1	-1.0

YEAR	TM/L	W	L	PCT	G	GS	CG	SH	SV	IP	H	R	HR	HB	BB	SO	RAT	ERA	ERA+	OAV	OOB	BH	AVG	PB	PR	PR+	PD	TPI
1997	Atl-N	5	1	.833	51	0	0	0	1	48	52	24	3	1	18	42	13.3	3.75	112	.286	.353	0	.000	-0	2	2	-1	0.2
1998	LA-N	2	0	1.000	18	0	0	0	0	20^2	15	13	3	2	10	14	11.8	5.66	70	.200	.310	0	.000	-0	-3	-4	-1	-0.4
	NY-N	0	0	—	2	0	0	0	0	3	4	3	1	0	2	2	18.0	9.00	46	.333	.429	0	—	0	-2	-2	0	-0.1
	Yr	2	0	1.000	20	0	0	0	0	23^2	19	16	4	2	12	16	12.5	6.08	66	.218	.327	0	.000	-0	-5	-6	-1	-0.5
1999	Pit-N	1	3	.250	56	0	0	0	2	49^1	49	21	6	3	24	40	13.9	2.74	167	.254	.345	0	.000	-0	10	10	0	0.7
2000	Pit-N	0	0	—	5	0	0	0	0	7	7	4	1	0	11	8	23.1	5.14	89	.269	.486	0	—	0	-0	-0	0	0.0
Total	6	22	8	.733	272	0	0	0	8	277^2	276	147	30	12	120	210	13.2	4.34	100	.261	.343	0	.000	-0	-2	-0	-1	0.0

● AL CLOSTER Closter, Alan Edward b: 6/15/43, Creighton, Neb. BL/TL, 6'2", 190 lbs. Deb: 4/19/66

YEAR	TM/L	W	L	PCT	G	GS	CG	SH	SV	IP	H	R	HR	HB	BB	SO	RAT	ERA	ERA+	OAV	OOB	BH	AVG	PB	PR	PR+	PD	TPI
1966	Was-A	0	0	—	1	0	0	0	0	0^1	1	0	0	0	2	0	81.0	0.00	—	.500	.750	0	—	0	0	0	0	0.0
1971	NY-A	2	2	.500	14	1	0	0	0	28^1	33	22	4	2	13	22	15.2	5.08	64	.289	.372	0	.000	-1	-5	-6	1	-0.8
1972	NY-A	0	0	—	2	0	0	0	0	2^1	2	3	1	0	4	2	23.1	11.57	26	.250	.500	0	.000	-0	-2	-2	0	-0.1
1973	Atl-N	0	0	—	4	0	0	0	0	4^1	7	7	1	0	4	2	22.8	14.54	27	.389	.500	0	—	0	-5	-5	0	-0.2
Total	4	2	2	.500	21	1	0	0	0	35^1	43	32	6	2	23	26	17.3	6.62	50	.303	.407	0	.000	-1	-12	-14	1	-1.1

● KEN CLOUDE Cloude, Kenneth Brian b: 1/9/75, Baltimore, Md. BR/TR, 6'1", 200 lbs. Deb: 8/9/97

YEAR	TM/L	W	L	PCT	G	GS	CG	SH	SV	IP	H	R	HR	HB	BB	SO	RAT	ERA	ERA+	OAV	OOB	BH	AVG	PB	PR	PR+	PD	TPI
1997	Sea-A	4	2	.667	10	9	0	0	0	51	41	32	8	3	26	46	12.4	5.12	88	.218	.323	0	.000	-0	-3	-4	-0	-0.4
1998	Sea-A	8	10	.444	30	30	0	0	0	155^1	187	116	29	3	80	114	15.6	6.37	73	.296	.378	0	.000	-0	-30	-30	-1	-2.9
1999	Sea-A	4	4	.500	31	6	0	0	1	72^1	106	67	10	5	46	35	19.5	7.96	60	.346	.440	0	.000	-0	-25	-27	-0	-2.5
Total	3	16	16	.500	71	45	0	0	1	278^2	334	215	47	11	152	195	16.1	6.56	71	.297	.386	0	.000	-1	-58	-60	-2	-5.8

● ED CLOUGH Clough, Edgar George "Big Ed" or "Spec" b: 10/28/06, Wiconisco, Pa. d: 1/30/44, Harrisburg, Pa. BL/TL, 6', 188 lbs. Deb: 8/28/24 ♦

YEAR	TM/L	W	L	PCT	G	GS	CG	SH	SV	IP	H	R	HR	HB	BB	SO	RAT	ERA	ERA+	OAV	OOB	BH	AVG	PB	PR	PR+	PD	TPI
1925	StL-N	0	1	.000	3	1	0	0	0	10	11	9	1	1	5	3	15.3	8.10	53	.289	.386	1	.250	-0	-4	-4	-0	-0.3
1926	StL-N	0	0	—	1	0	0	0	0	2	5	6	0	1	3	0	40.5	22.50	17	.556	.692	0	.000	-0	-4	-4	-0	-0.2
Total	2	0	1	.000	4	1	0	0	0	12	16	15	1	2	8	3	19.5	10.50	40	.340	.456	2	.105	-0	-8	-8	-0	-0.5

● BILL CLOWERS Clowers, William Perry b: 8/14/1898, San Marcos, Tex. d: 1/13/78, Sweeny, Tex. BL/TL, 5'11", 175 lbs. Deb: 7/20/26

YEAR	TM/L	W	L	PCT	G	GS	CG	SH	SV	IP	H	R	HR	HB	BB	SO	RAT	ERA	ERA+	OAV	OOB	BH	AVG	PB	PR	PR+	PD	TPI
1926	Bos-A	0	0	—	2	0	0	0	0	1^2	2	1	0	0	0	0	10.8	0.00	—	.333	.333	0	—	0	1	1	0	0.0

● BRYAN CLUTTERBUCK Clutterbuck, Bryan Richard b: 12/17/59, Detroit, Mich. BR/TR, 6'4", 223 lbs. Deb: 7/18/86

YEAR	TM/L	W	L	PCT	G	GS	CG	SH	SV	IP	H	R	HR	HB	BB	SO	RAT	ERA	ERA+	OAV	OOB	BH	AVG	PB	PR	PR+	PD	TPI
1986	Mil-A	0	1	.000	20	0	0	0	0	56^2	68	32	8	2	16	38	13.7	4.29	101	.296	.347	0	—	0	-1	0	-0	0.0
1989	Mil-A	2	5	.286	14	11	1	0	0	67^1	73	39	11	0	16	29	11.9	4.14	93	.269	.310	0	—	0	-2	-2	-2	-0.4
Total	2	2	6	.250	34	11	1	0	0	124	141	71	19	2	32	67	12.7	4.21	97	.281	.327	0	—	0	-3	-2	-2	-0.4

● DAVID CLYDE Clyde, David Eugene b: 4/22/55, Kansas City, Kan. BL/TL, 6'1", 185 lbs. Deb: 6/27/73

YEAR	TM/L	W	L	PCT	G	GS	CG	SH	SV	IP	H	R	HR	HB	BB	SO	RAT	ERA	ERA+	OAV	OOB	BH	AVG	PB	PR	PR+	PD	TPI
1973	Tex-A	4	8	.333	18	18	0	0	0	93^1	106	63	8	4	54	74	15.8	5.01	74	.293	.390	0	—	0	-12	-14	-0	-1.6
1974	Tex-A	3	9	.250	28	21	4	0	0	117	129	64	14	4	47	52	13.8	4.38	81	.286	.359	0	—	0	-10	-11	-2	-1.2
1975	Tex-A	0	1	.000	1	1	0	0	0	7	6	3	0	0	6	2	15.4	2.57	146	.273	.429	0	—	0	1	1	-0	0.1
1978	Cle-A	8	11	.421	28	25	5	0	0	153^1	166	80	4	3	60	83	13.4	4.28	88	.280	.350	0	—	0	-9	-9	-1	-1.1
1979	Cle-A	3	4	.429	9	8	1	0	0	45^2	50	33	7	1	13	17	12.6	5.91	72	.279	.332	0	—	0	-9	-8	-0	-1.1
Total	5	18	33	.353	84	73	10	0	0	416^1	457	243	33	12	180	228	14.0	4.63	81	.285	.361	0	—	0	-38	-41	-4	-4.9

● TOM CLYDE Clyde, Thomas Knox b: 8/17/23, Wachapreague, Va. BR/TR, 6'3", 195 lbs. Deb: 5/31/43

YEAR	TM/L	W	L	PCT	G	GS	CG	SH	SV	IP	H	R	HR	HB	BB	SO	RAT	ERA	ERA+	OAV	OOB	BH	AVG	PB	PR	PR+	PD	TPI
1943	Phi-A	0	0	—	4	0	0	0	0	6	7	8	1	1	4	0	18.0	9.00	38	.304	.429	0	.000	-0	-4	-4	-0	-0.3

● ANDY COAKLEY Coakley, Andrew James (a.k.a. Jack McAllister In 1902)
b: 11/20/1882, Providence, R.I. d: 9/27/63, New York, N.Y. BL/TR, 6', 165 lbs. Deb: 9/17/02

YEAR	TM/L	W	L	PCT	G	GS	CG	SH	SV	IP	H	R	HR	HB	BB	SO	RAT	ERA	ERA+	OAV	OOB	BH	AVG	PB	PR	PR+	PD	TPI
1902	Phi-A	2	1	.667	3	3	3	0	0	27	25	15	0	2	9	9	12.0	2.67	138	.245	.319	3	.375	1	3	3	0	0.5
1903	Phi-A	0	3	.000	6	3	2	0	0	37^2	48	31	2	2	11	20	14.6	5.50	56	.310	.363	3	.200	-0	-11	-10	-0	-0.7
1904	Phi-A	4	3	.571	8	8	7	2	0	62	48	19	1	2	23	33	10.6	1.89	142	.215	.294	2	.087	-2	5	5	-0	0.3
1905	*Phi-A	18	8	.692	35	31	21	3	0	255	227	93	2	6	73	145	10.8	1.84	145	.240	.299	13	.138	-3	23	23	-1	1.9
1906	Phi-A	7	8	.467	22	16	10	0	0	149	144	78	0	3	44	59	11.5	3.14	87	.257	.314	7	.143	-2	-7	-7	-3	-1.1
1907	Cin-N	17	16	.515	37	30	21	1	1	265^1	269	97	1	7	79	89	12.0	2.34	111	.274	.332	6	.071	-6	4	7	-3	-0.1
1908	Cin-N	8	18	.308	32	28	20	4	2	242^1	219	79	3	4	64	61	10.7	1.86	124	.249	.303	7	.092	-4	14	12	-4	0.4
	Chi-N	2	0	1.000	4	3	2	1	0	20^1	14	4	0	0	6	7	8.9	0.89	266	.192	.253	0	.000	-1	3	3	-0	0.2
	Yr	10	18	.357	36	31	22	5	2	262^2	233	83	3	4	70	68	10.5	1.78	130	.245	.299	7	.085	-5	17	16	-5	0.6
1909	Chi-N	0	1	.000	1	1	0	0	0	2	7	7	0	0	3	1	45.0	18.00	14	.583	.667	0	—	0	-3	-4	0	-0.6
1911	NY-A	0	1	.000	2	1	1	0	0	11^2	20	13	0	0	2	4	17.0	5.40	67	.377	.400	1	.250	0	-3	-2	0	-0.1
Total	9	58	59	.496	150	124	87	11	3	1072^1	1021	436	9	26	314	428	11.4	2.35	111	.256	.315	42	.117	-16	28	31	-12	0.7

● JIM COATES Coates, James Alton b: 8/4/32, Farnham, Va. BR/TR, 6'4", 192 lbs. Deb: 9/21/56

YEAR	TM/L	W	L	PCT	G	GS	CG	SH	SV	IP	H	R	HR	HB	BB	SO	RAT	ERA	ERA+	OAV	OOB	BH	AVG	PB	PR	PR+	PD	TPI
1956	NY-A	0	0	—	2	0	0	0	0	2	1	3	0	1	4	0	27.0	13.50	29	.167	.545	0	—	0	-2	-2	0	-0.1
1959	NY-A	6	1	.857	37	4	2	0	3	100^1	89	39	10	3	36	64	11.5	2.87	127	.234	.305	2	.095	-1	11	9	0	0.5
1960	*NY-A★	13	3	.813	35	18	6	2	1	149^1	139	78	16	2	66	73	12.5	4.28	84	.248	.330	12	.250	4	-7	-12	-2	-1.1
1961	*NY-A	11	5	.688	43	11	4	1	5	141^1	128	60	15	7	53	80	12.0	3.44	108	.243	.321	1	.029	-3	9	5	-0	0.2
1962	*NY-A	7	6	.538	50	6	0	0	6	117^2	119	62	9	5	50	67	13.3	4.44	84	.263	.343	4	.125	-1	-6	-10	-2	-1.3
1963	Was-A	2	4	.333	20	2	0	0	0	44^1	51	29	4	3	21	31	15.2	5.28	70	.297	.383	0	.000	-1	-8	-8	0	-1.0
	Cin-N	0	0	—	9	0	0	0	0	16^1	21	10	2	0	7	11	15.4	5.51	61	.313	.378	0	.000	-0	-4	-4	0	-0.2
1965	Cal-A	2	0	1.000	17	0	0	0	3	28	23	13	1	0	16	15	12.5	3.54	96	.228	.333	0	.000	-0	-0	-0	-0	-0.1
1966	Cal-A	1	1	.500	9	4	1	1	0	31^2	32	16	3	0	10	16	11.9	3.98	84	.258	.313	1	.091	-1	-2	-2	-0	-0.2
1967	Cal-A	1	2	.333	25	1	0	0	0	52^1	47	26	5	4	23	39	12.7	4.30	73	.244	.336	1	.333	1	-6	-7	0	-0.3
Total	9	43	22	.662	247	46	13	4	18	683^1	650	336	65	25	286	396	12.7	4.00	90	.252	.332	21	.131	-3	-15	-32	-4	-3.6

● GEORGE COBB Cobb, George Woodworth b: 9/25/1865, Independence, Ia. d: 8/19/26, Pomona, Cal. 6', 168 lbs. Deb: 4/15/1892

YEAR	TM/L	W	L	PCT	G	GS	CG	SH	SV	IP	H	R	HR	HB	BB	SO	RAT	ERA	ERA+	OAV	OOB	BH	AVG	PB	PR	PR+	PD	TPI
1892	Bal-N	10	37	.213	53	47	42	0	0	394^1	495	333	21	19	140	159	14.9	4.86	71	.295	.356	36	.209	5	-69	-60	2	-5.0

● HERB COBB Cobb, Herbert Edward b: 8/6/04, Pinetops, N.C. d: 1/8/80, Tarboro, N.C. BR/TR, 5'11", 150 lbs. Deb: 4/21/29

YEAR	TM/L	W	L	PCT	G	GS	CG	SH	SV	IP	H	R	HR	HB	BB	SO	RAT	ERA	ERA+	OAV	OOB	BH	AVG	PB	PR	PR+	PD	TPI
1929	StL-A	0	0	—	1	0	0	0	0	1	3	4	1	0	1	0	36.0	36.00	12	.600	.667	0	—	0	-4	-3	-0	-0.2

● TY COBB Cobb, Tyrus Raymond "The Georgia Peach" b: 12/18/1886, Narrows, Ga. d: 7/17/61, Atlanta, Ga. BL/TR, 6'1", 175 lbs. Deb: 8/30/05 MH♦

YEAR	TM/L	W	L	PCT	G	GS	CG	SH	SV	IP	H	R	HR	HB	BB	SO	RAT	ERA	ERA+	OAV	OOB	BH	AVG	PB	PR	PR+	PD	TPI
1918	Det-A	0	0	—	2	0	0	0	0	4	6	2	0	0	2	0	18.0	4.50	59	.400	.471	161	.382	1	-1	-1	-0	0.0
1925	Det-A	0	0	—	1	0	0	0	1	1	0	0	0	0	0	0	0.0	0.00	—	.000	.000	157	.378	1	0	0	0	0.1
Total	2	0	0	—	3	0	0	0	1	5	6	2	0	0	2	0	14.4	3.60	83	.333	.400	4189	.366	2	-0	-0	0	0.1

● JAIME COCANOWER Cocanower, James Stanley b: 2/14/57, San Juan, P.R. BR/TR, 6'4", 200 lbs. Deb: 9/7/83

YEAR	TM/L	W	L	PCT	G	GS	CG	SH	SV	IP	H	R	HR	HB	BB	SO	RAT	ERA	ERA+	OAV	OOB	BH	AVG	PB	PR	PR+	PD	TPI
1983	Mil-A	2	0	1.000	5	3	1	0	0	30	21	8	1	1	12	8	10.2	1.80	208	.200	.288	0	—	0	8	7	0	0.5
1984	Mil-A	8	16	.333	33	27	1	0	0	174^2	188	99	13	9	78	65	14.2	4.02	96	.279	.362	0	—	0	-0	-3	1	-0.3
1985	Mil-A	6	8	.429	24	15	3	1	0	116^1	122	72	6	8	73	44	15.7	4.33	96	.274	.386	0	—	0	-2	-2	0	-0.2
1986	Mil-A	0	1	.000	17	2	0	0	0	44^2	40	29	1	2	38	22	16.1	4.43	98	.248	.398	0	—	0	-1	-0	1	0.1
Total	4	16	25	.390	79	47	5	1	0	365^2	371	208	21	20	201	139	14.6	3.99	100	.268	.369	0	—	0	4	1	3	0.1

● GOAT COCHRAN Cochran, Alvah Jackson "Al" or "Goat" b: 1/31/1891, Concord, Ga. d: 5/23/47, Atlanta, Ga. BR/TR, 5'10", 175 lbs. Deb: 8/25/15

YEAR	TM/L	W	L	PCT	G	GS	CG	SH	SV	IP	H	R	HR	HB	BB	SO	RAT	ERA	ERA+	OAV	OOB	BH	AVG	PB	PR	PR+	PD	TPI
1915	Cin-N	0	0	—	1	0	0	0	0	2	5	3	0	0	0	1	22.5	9.00	32	.455	.455	0	—	0	-1	-1	-0	-0.1

● PASCUAL COCO Coco, Pascual (Reynoso) b: 9/8/77, Santo Domingo, D.R. BR/TR, 6'1", 185 lbs. Deb: 7/17/2000

YEAR	TM/L	W	L	PCT	G	GS	CG	SH	SV	IP	H	R	HR	HB	BB	SO	RAT	ERA	ERA+	OAV	OOB	BH	AVG	PB	PR	PR+	PD	TPI
2000	Tor-A	0	0	—	1	1	0	0	0	4	5	4	1	1	5	2	24.8	9.00	55	.294	.478	0	—	0	-2	-2	-0	-0.1

● GENE COCREHAM Cocreham, Eugene b: 11/14/1884, Luling, Tex. d: 12/27/45, Luling, Tex. BR/TR, 6'3.5", 192 lbs. Deb: 9/25/13

YEAR	TM/L	W	L	PCT	G	GS	CG	SH	SV	IP	H	R	HR	HB	BB	SO	RAT	ERA	ERA+	OAV	OOB	BH	AVG	PB	PR	PR+	PD	TPI
1913	Bos-N	0	1	.000	1	1	0	0	0	8^1	13	7	0	1	4	3	19.4	7.56	43	.371	.450	0	.000	-1	-4	-4	0	-0.4
1914	Bos-N	3	4	.429	15	3	1	0	0	44^2	48	30	2	0	27	15	15.1	4.84	57	.296	.397	1	.100	-0	-10	-10	-1	-1.7
1915	Bos-N	0	0	—	1	0	0	0	0	1^2	3	2	0	0	0	0	16.2	5.40	48	.429	.429	0	—	0	-0	-1	-0	0.0
Total	3	3	5	.375	17	4	1	0	0	54^2	64	39	2	1	31	18	15.8	5.27	54	.314	.407	1	.071	-1	-15	-15	-2	-2.1

YEAR	TM/L	W	L	PCT	G	GS	CG	SH	SV	IP	H	R	HR	HB	BB	SO	RAT	ERA	ERA+	OAV	OOB	BH	AVG	PB	PR	PR+	PD	TPI
● **CHRIS CODIROLI**	Codiroli, Christopher Allen b: 3/26/58, Oxnard, Cal. BR/TR, 6'1", 160 lbs. Deb: 9/11/82																											
1982	Oak-A	1	2	.333	3	3	0	0	0	16^2	16	8	1	0	4	5	10.8	4.32	91	.246	.290	0	—	0	-0	-1	0	-0.1
1983	Oak-A	12	12	.500	37	31	7	2	1	205^2	208	115	17	7	72	85	12.6	4.46	87	.264	.331	0	—	0	-9	-14	-2	-1.7
1984	Oak-A	6	4	.600	28	14	1	0	1	89^1	111	67	16	3	34	44	14.9	5.84	64	.304	.368	0	—	0	-18	-22	-0	-2.2
1985	Oak-A	14	14	.500	37	37	4	0	0	226	228	125	23	3	78	111	12.3	4.46	87	.259	.321	0	—	0	-8	-16	-1	-1.8
1986	Oak-A	5	8	.385	16	16	1	0	0	91^2	91	54	15	2	38	43	12.9	4.03	96	.250	.324	0	—	0	2	-2	1	-0.1
1987	Oak-A	0	2	.000	3	3	0	0	0	11^1	12	11	1	1	8	4	16.7	8.74	47	.273	.396	0	—	0	-5	-6	-0	-0.8
1988	Cle-A	0	4	.000	14	2	0	0	1	19^1	32	22	2	3	10	12	20.9	9.31	44	.372	.455	0	—	0	-11	-11	0	-1.9
1990	KC-A	0	1	.000	6	2	0	0	0	10^1	13	11	1	4	17	8	29.6	9.58	40	.325	.557	0	—	0	-7	-7	-0	-0.6
Total	8	38	47	.447	144	108	13	2	3	670^1	711	413	76	23	261	312	13.4	4.87	79	.270	.341	0	—	0	-57	-80	-2	-9.2
● **SLICK COFFMAN**	Coffman, George David b: 12/11/10, Veto, Ala. BR/TR, 6', 155 lbs. Deb: 5/21/37 F																											
1937	Det-A	7	5	.583	28	5	1	0	0	101	121	61	8	3	39	22	14.5	4.37	107	.295	.361	5	.172	0	3	3	-1	0.3
1938	Det-A	4	4	.500	39	6	1	0	2	95^2	120	70	6	0	48	31	15.8	6.02	83	.310	.386	4	.167	-0	-13	-10	-1	-0.8
1939	Det-A	2	1	.667	23	1	0	0	0	42^1	51	36	4	1	22	10	15.7	6.38	77	.295	.378	0	.000	-0	-8	-7	0	-0.4
1940	StL-A	2	2	.500	31	4	1	0	1	74^2	108	62	5	0	23	26	15.8	6.27	73	.334	.379	3	.200	-0	-16	-13	1	-0.6
Total	4	15	12	.556	121	16	3	0	3	313^2	400	229	23	4	132	89	15.4	5.60	85	.309	.375	12	.164	-0	-34	-27	-1	-1.5
● **KEVIN COFFMAN**	Coffman, Kevin Reese b: 1/19/65, Austin, Tex. BR/TR, 6'2", 175 lbs. Deb: 9/5/87																											
1987	Atl-N	2	3	.400	5	5	0	0	0	25^1	31	14	2	3	22	14	19.9	4.62	94	.313	.452	1	.100	-0	-1	-1	1	0.0
1988	Atl-N	2	6	.250	18	11	0	0	0	67	62	52	3	4	54	24	16.1	5.78	64	.251	.393	5	.227	2	-17	-15	0	-1.4
1990	Chi-N	0	2	.000	8	2	0	0	0	18^1	26	24	0	0	19	9	22.1	11.29	36	.333	.464	1	.200	0	-15	-14	1	-1.2
Total	3	4	11	.267	31	18	0	0	0	110^2	119	90	5	7	95	47	18.0	6.42	61	.281	.420	7	.189	1	-34	-29	2	-2.6
● **DICK COFFMAN**	Coffman, Samuel Richard b: 12/18/06, Veto, Ala. d: 3/24/72, Athens, Ala. BR/TR, 6'2", 195 lbs. Deb: 4/28/27 F																											
1927	Was-A	0	1	.000	5	2	0	0	0	16	20	9	0	2	2	5	13.5	3.38	120	.313	.353	1	.333	0	1	1	0	0.1
1928	StL-A	4	5	.444	29	7	3	0	1	85^2	122	68	7	1	37	25	16.8	6.09	69	.359	.423	1	.043	-3	-20	-17	0	-1.8
1929	StL-A	1	1	.500	27	3	1	1	1	52^2	61	40	3	3	14	11	13.3	5.98	74	.295	.348	0	.000	-1	-10	-9	0	-0.5
1930	StL-A	8	18	.308	38	30	12	1	1	196	250	134	14	5	69	54	14.9	5.14	95	.311	.369	9	.136	-5	-11	-6	0	-1.0
1931	StL-A	9	13	.409	32	17	11	2	1	169^1	159	81	10	2	51	39	11.3	3.88	119	.241	.298	4	.078	-5	9	13	-2	0.9
1932	StL-A	5	3	.625	9	6	3	1	0	61	66	24	3	2	21	14	13.1	3.10	157	.277	.341	1	.045	-2	9	11	-1	1.0
	Was-A	1	6	.143	22	9	2	0	0	76^1	92	45	2	1	31	17	14.6	4.83	89	.307	.373	2	.091	-1	-3	-5	-1	-0.5
	Yr	6	9	.400	31	15	5	1	0	137^1	158	69	5	3	52	31	14.0	4.06	112	.294	.359	3	.068	-3	6	7	-2	0.5
1933	StL-A	3	7	.300	21	13	3	1	1	81	114	57	9	2	39	19	17.2	5.89	79	.329	.399	1	.037	-3	-14	-10	-1	-1.3
1934	StL-A	9	10	.474	40	21	6	1	3	173	212	112	11	1	59	55	14.2	4.53	110	.303	.358	11	.216	-1	-1	8	0	0.7
1935	StL-A	5	11	.313	41	18	5	0	2	143^2	206	116	14	2	46	34	15.9	6.14	78	.335	.383	6	.146	-1	-27	-20	-1	-2.1
1936	*NY-N	7	5	.583	42	2	0	0	7	101^2	119	53	7	2	23	26	12.7	3.90	100	.296	.337	4	.200	-0	1	0	1	0.1
1937	*NY-N	8	3	.727	42	1	0	0	3	80	93	36	4	4	31	30	14.4	3.04	128	.289	.359	7	.368	2	**8**	**8**	0	1.3
1938	NY-N	8	4	.667	**51**	3	1	1	**12**	111^1	116	50	3	3	21	21	11.3	3.48	108	.268	.306	2	.071	-3	4	4	-2	0.0
1939	NY-N	1	2	.333	28	0	0	0	3	38	50	18	1	3	6	9	14.0	3.08	128	.316	.353	0	.000	-1	4	4	-0	0.2
1940	Bos-N	1	5	.167	31	0	0	0	3	48^1	63	33	4	2	11	11	14.2	5.40	69	.323	.365	1	.083	-1	-8	-9	-1	-1.3
1945	Phi-N	2	1	.667	14	0	0	0	0	26^1	39	18	0	0	2	2	14.0	5.13	75	.351	.363	1	.250	0	-4	-4	1	-0.2
Total	15	72	95	.431	472	132	47	8	38	1460^1	1782	894	92	35	463	372	14.1	4.65	96	.302	.357	51	.127	-22	-61	-32	-2	-4.4
● **DICK COGAN**	Cogan, Richard Henry b: 12/5/1871, Paterson, N.J. d: 5/2/48, Paterson, N.J. BR/TR, 5'7", 150 lbs. Deb: 5/10/1897																											
1897	Bal-N	0	0	—	1	0	0	0	0	2	4	3	0	1	2	0	31.5	13.50	31	.400	.538	0	.000	-0	-2	-2	-0	-0.1
1899	Chi-N	2	3	.400	5	5	5	0	0	44	54	32	1	4	24	9	16.8	4.30	87	.302	.396	5	.200	1	-2	-3	-1	-0.2
1900	NY-N	0	0	—	2	0	0	0	0	8	10	6	0	0	6	1	18.0	6.75	54	.303	.410	1	.125	-0	-3	-3	-0	-0.2
Total	3	2	3	.400	8	5	5	0	0	54	68	41	1	5	32	10	17.5	5.00	75	.306	.405	6	.176	0	-7	-8	-1	-0.5
● **DAVID COGGIN**	Coggin, David Raymond b: 10/30/76, Covina, Cal. BR/TR, 6'4", 195 lbs. Deb: 6/23/2000																											
2000	Phi-N	2	0	1.000	5	5	0	0	0	27	35	20	2	1	12	17	16.0	5.33	89	.315	.387	0	.000	-1	-2	-2	-0	-0.2
● **HY COHEN**	Cohen, Hyman b: 1/29/31, Brooklyn, N.Y. BR/TR, 6'5", 220 lbs. Deb: 4/17/55																											
1955	Chi-N	0	0	—	7	1	0	0	0	17	28	17	2	1	10	4	20.6	7.94	51	.378	.459	0	.000	-0	-7	-7	-0	-0.4
● **SYD COHEN**	Cohen, Sydney Harry b: 5/7/06, Baltimore, Md. d: 4/9/88, ElPaso, Tex. BB/TL, 5'11", 180 lbs. Deb: 9/18/34 F																											
1934	Was-A	1	1	.500	3	2	2	0	0	18	25	15	2	0	6	6	15.5	7.50	58	.333	.383	3	.273	0	-6	-7	1	-0.5
1936	Was-A	0	2	.000	19	1	0	0	1	36	44	27	4	3	14	21	15.3	5.25	91	.303	.377	0	.000	-1	-1	-2	2	0.0
1937	Was-A	2	4	.333	33	0	0	0	4	55	64	30	1	0	17	22	13.3	3.11	142	.299	.351	2	.143	-1	9	8	2	1.0
Total	3	3	7	.300	55	3	2	0	5	109	133	72	7	3	37	49	14.3	4.54	100	.306	.365	5	.152	-2	2	-0	5	0.5
● **ROCKY COLAVITO**	Colavito, Rocco Domenico b: 8/10/33, New York, N.Y. BR/TR, 6'3", 190 lbs. Deb: 9/10/55 C♦																											
1958	Cle-A	0	0	—	1	0	0	0	0	3	0	0	0	0	3	1	9.0	0.00	—	.000	.273	148	.303	1	1	1	0	0.1
1968	NY-A	1	0	1.000	1	0	0	0	0	2^2	1	0	0	0	2	1	10.1	0.00	—	.111	.273	20	.220	0	1	1	-0	0.2
Total	2	1	0	1.000	2	0	0	0	0	5^2	1	0	0	0	5	2	9.5	0.00	—	.059	.273	1730	.266	1	2	2	0	0.3
● **VINCE COLBERT**	Colbert, Vincent Norman b: 12/20/45, Washington, D.C. BR/TR, 6'4", 200 lbs. Deb: 5/19/70																											
1970	Cle-A	1	1	.500	23	0	0	0	2	31	37	25	4	1	16	17	15.7	7.26	55	.298	.383	0	.000	-0	-12	-11	0	-0.8
1971	Cle-A	7	6	.538	50	10	2	0	2	142^2	140	71	11	6	71	74	13.7	3.97	96	.265	.358	4	.138	-0	-8	-2	0	-0.2
1972	Cle-A	1	7	.125	22	11	1	1	0	74^2	74	42	8	7	38	36	14.3	4.58	70	.267	.370	4	.200	1	-13	-11	0	-1.0
Total	3	9	14	.391	95	21	3	1	4	248^1	251	138	23	14	125	127	14.1	4.57	80	.270	.365	8	.157	0	-33	-23	1	-2.0
● **JIM COLBORN**	Colborn, James William b: 5/22/46, Santa Paula, Cal. BR/TR, 6', 191 lbs. Deb: 7/13/69																											
1969	Chi-N	1	0	1.000	6	2	0	0	0	14^2	15	6	2	1	9	4	15.3	3.07	131	.283	.397	0	.000	-0	1	1	0	0.1
1970	Chi-N	3	1	.750	34	5	0	0	4	72^2	88	37	3	1	23	50	13.9	3.59	125	.298	.351	1	.067	-1	4	7	1	0.4
1971	Chi-N	0	1	.000	14	0	0	0	0	10^1	18	8	1	0	3	2	18.3	6.97	57	.383	.420	0	—	0	-4	-3	0	-0.2
1972	Mil-A	7	7	.500	39	12	4	1	0	147^2	135	53	14	2	43	97	11.0	3.11	98	.245	.302	3	.081	-1	-1	-1	-1	-0.4
1973	Mil-A☆	20	12	.625	43	36	22	4	1	314^1	297	133	21	3	87	135	11.1	3.18	118	.251	.304	0	—	0	22	21	2	2.2
1974	Mil-A	10	13	.435	33	31	10	1	0	224	230	104	27	6	60	83	11.9	4.06	89	.268	.320	0	—	0	-11	-11	0	-1.0
1975	Mil-A	11	13	.458	36	29	8	1	2	206^1	215	111	18	5	65	79	12.4	4.27	90	.270	.329	0	—	0	-11	-10	1	-0.9
1976	Mil-A	9	15	.375	32	32	7	0	0	225^2	232	97	20	2	54	101	11.5	3.71	94	.268	.312	0	—	0	-5	-5	-0	-0.6
1977	KC-A	18	14	.563	36	35	6	1	0	239	233	106	22	13	81	103	12.3	3.62	112	.255	.324	0	—	0	12	12	1	1.5
1978	KC-A	1	2	.333	8	3	0	0	0	28^1	31	18	4	2	12	8	14.3	4.76	81	.282	.363	0	—	0	-3	-3	1	-0.2
	Sea-A	3	10	.231	20	19	3	0	0	114^1	125	77	21	6	38	26	13.3	5.35	71	.279	.343	0	—	0	-20	-19	3	-1.7
	Yr	4	12	.250	28	22	3	0	0	142^2	156	95	25	8	50	34	13.5	5.24	73	.280	.347	0	—	0	-23	-22	3	-1.9
Total	10	83	88	.485	301	204	60	8	7	1597^1	1619	750	153	41	475	688	12.0	3.80	98	.265	.322	4	.073	-3	-15	-12	7	-0.8
● **TOM COLCOLOUGH**	Colcolough, Thomas Bernard b: 10/8/1870, Charleston, S.C. d: 12/10/19, Charleston, S.C. BR/TR, 5'10.5", 180 lbs. Deb: 8/1/1893																											
1893	Pit-N	1	0	1.000	8	3	1	0	**2**	43^2	45	30	1	0	32	7	15.9	4.12	110	.259	.374	2	.143	0	3	2	-1	0.1
1894	Pit-N	8	5	.615	23	14	11	0	0	150^2	213	147	5	5	72	29	17.3	7.23	73	.329	.401	14	.200	-3	-32	-34	0	-2.1
1895	Pit-N	1	1	.500	7	6	3	0	0	43^1	54	49	3	5	21	16	16.6	6.65	68	.300	.388	5	.294	3	-9	-11	-0	-0.3
1899	NY-N	4	5	.444	11	8	7	0	0	81^2	85	49	1	3	41	14	14.2	3.97	95	.268	.357	10	.270	1	-1	-2	1	0.0
Total	4	14	11	.560	49	31	22	0	2	319^1	397	275	10	13	166	66	16.2	5.89	79	.301	.385	31	.225	1	-39	-45	0	-2.3
● **BERT COLE**	Cole, Albert George b: 7/1/1896, San Francisco, Cal. d: 5/30/75, San Mateo, Cal. BL/TL, 6'1", 180 lbs. Deb: 4/19/21																											
1921	Det-A	7	4	.636	20	11	7	1	1	109^2	134	66	3	4	36	22	14.3	4.27	100	.305	.363	13	.283	3	0	0	-1	0.2
1922	Det-A	1	6	.143	23	5	2	1	0	79^1	105	60	4	1	39	21	16.4	4.88	80	.313	.387	4	.160	-1	-7	-9	0	-0.7
1923	Det-A	13	5	.722	52	13	6	1	5	163	183	95	9	5	61	32	13.7	4.14	93	.284	.351	14	.255	2	-3	-5	-1	-0.4
1924	Det-A	3	9	.250	28	12	2	1	2	109^1	135	69	4	4	35	16	14.3	4.69	88	.314	.371	10	.270	1	-6	-7	1	-0.5
1925	Det-A	2	3	.400	14	2	1	0	1	33^2	44	27	2	1	15	7	16.0	5.88	73	.336	.408	3	.273	0	-6	-6	1	-0.7
	Cle-A	1	1	.500	13	2	0	0	1	44	55	33	1	1	25	9	16.6	6.14	72	.322	.411	2	.154	-0	-9	-8	-0	-0.4

YEAR	TM/L	W	L	PCT	G	GS	CG	SH	SV	IP	H	R	HR	HB	BB	SO	RAT	ERA	ERA+	OAV	OOB	BH	AVG	PB	PR	PR+	PD	TPI
	Yr	3	4	.429	27	4	1	0	2	77^2	99	60	3	2	40	16	16.3	6.03	73	.328	.410	5	.208	0	-14	-14	0	-1.1
1927	Chi-A	1	4	.200	27	2	0	0	0	66^2	79	43	3	3	19	12	13.6	4.72	86	.309	.363	3	.167	-1	-4	-5	2	-0.3
Total	6	28	32	.467	177	47	18	4	10	605^2	735	393	26	19	230	119	14.6	4.67	87	.305	.370	49	.239	5	-34	-41	2	-2.8
● **DAVE COLE**	Cole, David Bruce b: 8/29/30, Williamsport, Md. BR/TR, 6'2", 175 lbs. Deb: 9/9/50																											
1950	Bos-N	0	1	.000	4	0	0	0	0	8	7	2	0	1	3	8	12.4	1.13	342	.259	.355	0	.000	-0	3	3	-0	0.3
1951	Bos-N	2	4	.333	23	7	1	0	0	67^2	64	43	3	2	64	33	17.3	4.26	86	.254	.409	6	.353	4	-2	-5	0	0.0
1952	Bos-N	1	1	.500	22	3	0	0	0	44^2	38	21	2	3	42	22	16.7	4.03	90	.241	.409	0	.000	-1	-1	-2	0	-0.2
1953	Mil-N	0	1	.000	10	0	0	0	0	14^2	17	14	1	0	14	13	19.0	8.59	46	.279	.413	1	.500	1	-7	-8	0	-0.3
1954	Chi-N	3	8	.273	18	14	2	1	0	84	74	56	7	1	62	37	14.7	5.36	78	.241	.370	6	.214	1	-12	-10	-0	-1.1
1955	Phi-N	0	3	.000	7	3	0	0	0	18^1	21	15	3	0	14	6	17.2	6.38	62	.304	.422	1	.200	-0	-5	-5	0	-0.7
Total	6	6	18	.250	84	27	3	1	0	237^1	221	151	16	7	199	119	16.2	4.93	79	.253	.395	14	.230	5	-25	-28	1	-2.0
● **ED COLE**	Cole, Edward William (b: Edward William Kisleauskas) b: 3/22/09, Wilkes-Barre, Pa. d: 7/28/99, Nashville, Tenn. BR/TR, 5'11", 170 lbs. Deb: 4/22/38																											
1938	StL-A	1	5	.167	36	6	1	0	3	88^2	116	69	8	5	48	26	17.2	5.18	96	.313	.399	3	.143	-1	-4	-2	-1	-0.3
1939	StL-A	0	2	.000	6	0	0	0	0	6^1	8	7	1	0	6	5	19.9	7.11	68	.308	.438	0	.000	-0	-2	-1	0	-0.3
Total	2	1	7	.125	42	6	1	0	3	95	124	76	9	5	54	31	17.3	5.31	94	.312	.401	3	.136	-2	-6	-3	-1	-0.6
● **KING COLE**	Cole, Leonard Leslie b: 4/15/1886, Toledo, Iowa d: 1/6/16, Bay City, Mich. BR/TR, 6'1", 170 lbs. Deb: 10/6/09																											
1909	Chi-N	1	0	1.000	1	1	1	1	0	9	6	0	0	0	3	1	9.0	0.00	—	.194	.265	3	.750	2	3	3	-0	0.7
1910	*Chi-N	20	4	**.833**	33	29	21	4	1	239^2	174	64	2	9	130	114	11.8	1.80	**160**	**.211**	.325	21	.231	2	33	30	-1	3.2
1911	Chi-N	18	7	.720	32	27	13	2	0	221^1	188	87	3	9	99	101	12.0	3.13	106	.236	.328	12	.152	-2	7	5	-2	0.1
1912	Chi-N	1	2	.333	8	3	0	0	0	19	36	26	2	2	8	9	21.8	10.89	31	.409	.469	2	.400	1	-16	-16	0	-1.9
	Pit-N	2	2	.500	12	5	2	0	0	49	61	42	1	2	18	11	14.9	6.43	51	.330	.395	2	.133	-1	-16	-18	-0	-1.3
	Yr	3	4	.429	20	8	2	0	0	68	97	68	3	4	26	20	16.8	7.68	43	.355	.419	4	.200	0	-32	-35	0	-3.2
1914	NY-A	10	9	.526	33	15	8	2	0	141^2	151	63	3	1	51	43	12.9	3.30	84	.288	.352	2	.048	-3	-9	-8	-3	-1.8
1915	NY-A	2	3	.400	10	6	2	0	1	51	41	27	2	3	22	19	11.6	3.18	92	.224	.317	1	.077	-1	-1	-1	-0	-0.3
Total	6	54	27	.667	129	86	47	9	2	730^2	657	309	13	26	331	298	12.5	3.12	97	.250	.340	43	.173	-2	-0	-7	-6	-1.3
● **VICTOR COLE**	Cole, Victor Alexander b: 1/23/68, Leningrad, Ussr BB/TR, 5'10", 160 lbs. Deb: 6/6/92																											
1992	Pit-N	0	2	.000	8	4	0	0	0	23	23	14	1	0	14	12	14.5	5.48	63	.261	.363	0	.000	-0	-5	-5	0	-0.5
● **JOHN COLEMAN**	Coleman, John b: Bristol, Pa. TR, Deb: 6/23/1890																											
1890	Phi-N	0	1	.000	1	1	0	0	0	1^2	4	8	0	0	3	2	37.8	21.60	17	.444	.583	0	—	0	-3	-3	-0	-0.5
● **JOHN COLEMAN**	Coleman, John b: 1874, Lees Summit, Mo. TL, 5'10", 174 lbs. Deb: 9/25/1895																											
1895	StL-N	0	1	.000	1	1	1	0	0	8	12	15	1	1	8	5	23.6	13.50	36	.343	.477	1	.200	-0	-8	-8	0	-0.6
● **JOHN COLEMAN**	Coleman, John Francis b: 3/6/1863, Saratoga Springs, N.Y d: 5/31/22, Detroit, Mich. BL/TR (BB 1887), 5'9.5", 170 lbs. Deb: 5/1/1883 ♦																											
1883	Phi-N	12	48	.200	65	61	59	3	0	538^1	772	510	17		48	159	13.7	4.87	63	.309	.322	83	.234	4	-103	-108	1	-8.2
1884	Phi-N	5	15	.250	21	19	14	1	0	154^1	216	147	9		22	37	13.9	4.90	61	.308	.329	42	.246	2	-33	-33	1	-2.9
	Phi-a	0	2	.000	3	2	2	0	0	21	28	14	0	4	2	5	14.6	3.43	99	.304	.347	22	.206	0	-0	-0	0	0.0
1885	Phi-a	2	2	.500	8	3	3	0	0	60^1	82	46	0	0	5	12	13.0	3.43	100	.366	.380	119	.299	2	-1	0	-0	0.2
1886	Phi-a	1	1	.500	3	1	1	0	0	20^2	18	9	1	1	5	2	10.5	2.61	134	.225	.279	121	.246	0	2	2	-0	0.2
1889	Phi-a	3	2	.600	5	5	4	0	0	34	38	23	2	1	14	6	14.0	2.91	130	.273	.344	1	.053	-2	4	3	1	0.2
1890	Pit-N	0	2	.000	2	2	1	0	0	14	28	23	1	0	6	3	21.9	9.64	34	.406	.453	2	.182	0	-9	-11	-0	-1.0
Total	6	23	72	.242	107	93	84	4	0	842^2	1182	772	30	6	102	224	13.8	4.68	67	.311	.330	676	.266	7	-142	-145	3	-11.5
● **JOE COLEMAN**	Coleman, Joseph Howard b: 2/3/47, Boston, Mass. BR/TR, 6'3", 195 lbs. Deb: 9/28/65 FC																											
1965	Was-A	2	0	1.000	2	2	2	0	0	18	9	3	0	0	8	7	8.5	1.50	232	.153	.254	0	.000	-1	4	4	1	0.5
1966	Was-A	1	0	1.000	1	1	1	0	0	9	6	2	0	0	2	4	8.0	2.00	173	.188	.235	0	.000	-0	1	1	0	0.2
1967	Was-A	8	9	.471	28	22	3	0	0	134	154	78	6	9	47	77	14.1	4.63	68	.291	.359	2	.056	-1	-21	-22	-2	-3.0
1968	Was-A	12	16	.429	33	33	12	2	0	223	212	98	18	12	51	139	11.1	3.27	89	.250	.302	9	.129	-1	-7	-9	-1	-1.3
1969	Was-A	12	13	.480	40	36	12	4	1	247^2	222	102	26	6	100	182	11.9	3.27	106	.243	.322	9	.107	-2	10	6	1	0.4
1970	Was-A	8	12	.400	39	29	6	1	0	218^2	190	98	25	4	89	152	11.6	3.58	99	.233	.311	8	.119	2	3	-1	0	0.2
1971	Det-A	20	9	.690	39	38	16	3	0	286	241	106	17	7	96	236	10.8	3.15	114	.229	.298	9	.094	-3	10	14	-2	0.8
1972	*Det-A†	19	14	.576	40	39	9	3	0	280	216	99	23	9	110	222	10.8	2.80	113	.214	.297	9	.110	-2	9	11	-1	0.9
1973	Det-A	23	15	.605	40	40	13	2	0	288^1	283	125	32	10	93	202	12.0	3.53	116	.258	.322	0	—	0	9	17	-0	2.1
1974	Det-A	14	12	.538	41	41	11	2	0	285^2	272	160	30	12	158	177	13.9	4.32	88	.254	.356	0	—	0	-22	-15	2	-1.1
1975	Det-A	10	18	.357	31	31	6	1	0	201	234	137	27	9	85	125	14.7	5.55	73	.291	.366	0	—	0	-39	-32	0	-3.8
1976	Det-A	2	5	.286	12	12	1	0	0	66^2	80	44	1	5	34	38	16.1	4.86	76	.308	.398	0	—	0	-10	-8	2	-0.6
	Chi-N	2	8	.200	39	4	0	0	4	79	72	43	9	2	35	66	12.4	4.10	94	.246	.330	2	.154	-0	-5	-2	0	-0.3
1977	Oak-A	4	4	.500	43	12	2	0	2	127^2	114	51	11	2	49	55	11.6	2.96	136	.241	.314	0	—	0	16	15	-0	0.9
1978	Oak-A	3	0	1.000	10	0	0	0	0	19^2	12	3	1	0	5	4	7.8	1.37	266	.185	.243	0	—	0	5	5	0	0.8
	Tor-A	2	0	1.000	31	0	0	0	0	60^2	67	34	6	1	30	28	14.5	4.60	86	.286	.370	0	—	0	-6	-4	-1	-0.3
	Yr	5	0	1.000	41	0	0	0	0	80^1	79	37	7	1	35	32	12.9	3.81	102	.264	.343	0	—	0	-0	0	-1	0.5
1979	SF-N	0	0	—	5	0	0	0	0	3^2	3	2	0	1	2	0	14.7	0.00	—	.231	.375	0	—	0	2	2	-0	0.1
	Pit-N	0	0	—	10	0	0	0	0	20^2	29	17	1	1	9	14	17.0	6.10	64	.326	.394	1	.200	0	-5	-5	-1	-0.3
	Yr	0	0	—	15	0	0	0	0	24^1	32	19	1	2	11	14	16.6	5.18	74	.314	.391	1	.200	0	-4	-4	-1	-0.2
Total	15	142	135	.513	484	340	94	18	7	2569^1	2416	1202	233	90	1003	1728	12.3	3.70	98	.250	.327	49	.106	-10	-46	-25	-2	-3.8
● **JOE COLEMAN**	Coleman, Joseph Patrick b: 7/30/22, Medford, Mass. d: 4/9/97, Ft.Myers, Fla. BR/TR, 6'2.5", 200 lbs. Deb: 9/19/42 F																											
1942	Phi-A	0	1	.000	1	0	0	0	0	6	8	5	0	0	1	0	13.5	3.00	126	.308	.333	0	.000	-1	0	1	-0	0.0
1946	Phi-A	0	2	.000	4	2	0	0	0	13	19	8	1	0	8	8	18.7	5.54	64	.345	.429	2	.400	1	-3	-3	-0	-0.4
1947	Phi-A	6	12	.333	32	21	9	2	1	160^1	171	84	17	0	62	65	13.1	4.32	88	.275	.341	7	.146	-1	-11	-9	-2	-1.2
1948	Phi-A★	14	13	.519	33	29	13	3	0	215^2	224	105	11	1	90	86	13.1	4.09	105	.269	.341	9	.122	-4	5	5	-1	0.0
1949	Phi-A	13	14	.481	33	30	18	1	1	240^1	249	119	12	3	127	109	14.2	3.86	107	.271	.361	14	.177	0	9	7	-5	0.3
1950	Phi-A	0	5	.000	15	6	2	0	0	54	74	54	9	0	50	12	20.7	8.50	54	.332	.454	1	.059	-1	-24	-24	-2	-1.9
1951	Phi-A	1	6	.143	28	9	1	0	1	96^1	117	69	12	3	59	34	16.7	5.98	72	.305	.402	7	.259	1	-20	-18	-1	-1.2
1953	Phi-A	3	4	.429	21	9	2	1	0	90	85	46	8	1	49	18	13.5	4.00	107	.254	.352	8	.286	1	-0	3	-2	0.2
1954	Bal-A	13	17	.433	33	32	15	4	0	221^1	184	102	16	3	96	103	11.5	3.50	102	.232	.317	13	.176	2	6	2	1	0.7
1955	Bal-A	0	1	.000	6	2	0	0	0	11^2	19	15	5	1	10	4	23.1	10.80	35	.373	.484	2	.667	1	-9	-9	-0	-0.6
	Det-A	2	1	.667	17	0	0	0	3	25^1	22	9	1	1	14	5	13.1	3.20	120	.239	.346	3	.750	1	2	2	0	0.4
	Yr	2	2	.500	23	2	0	0	3	37	41	24	6	2	24	9	16.3	5.59	69	.287	.396	5	.714	3	-7	-7	0	-0.2
Total	10	52	76	.406	223	140	60	11	6	1134	1172	616	92	13	566	444	13.9	4.38	92	.271	.357	66	.182	2	-44	-44	-12	-3.7
● **PERCY COLEMAN**	Coleman, Pierce D. b: 10/15/1876, Mason, Ohio d: 2/16/48, Van Nuys, Cal. TR, Deb: 7/2/1897																											
1897	StL-N	1	2	.333	13	5	3	0	0	66^1	108	76	0	8	33	10	20.2	7.19	61	.362	.440	7	.226	-1	-21	-20	1	-0.8
1898	Cin-N	0	1	.000	1	1	1	0	0	9	13	7	0	1	3	2	17.0	3.00	128	.333	.395	0	.000	-1	1	1	-0	0.0
Total	2	1	3	.250	14	6	4	0	0	75^1	121	83	0	9	36	12	19.8	6.69	65	.359	.435	7	.206	-1	-21	-19	0	-0.8
● **RIP COLEMAN**	Coleman, Walter Gary b: 7/31/31, Troy, N.Y. BL/TL, 6'2", 185 lbs. Deb: 8/15/55																											
1955	*NY-A	2	1	.667	10	6	0	0	1	29	40	19	2	1	16	15	17.7	5.28	71	.331	.413	2	.200	1	-4	-5	0	-0.5
1956	NY-A	3	5	.375	29	9	0	0	2	88^1	97	42	6	1	42	42	14.3	3.67	105	.285	.366	1	.042	-3	5	2	0	-0.1
1957	KC-A	0	7	.000	19	6	1	1	0	41	53	32	5	0	25	15	17.1	5.93	67	.325	.415	0	.000	-1	-10	-9	0	-1.4
1959	KC-A	2	10	.167	29	11	2	0	2	81	85	46	8	1	34	54	13.3	4.56	88	.273	.347	2	.080	-2	-6	-5	-0	-0.9
	Bal-A	0	0	—	3	0	0	0	0	4	4	0	0	0	2	4	13.5	0.00	—	.267	.353	0	—	0	2	2	1	0.2
	Yr	2	10	.167	32	11	2	0	2	85	89	46	8	1	36	58	13.3	4.34	92	.273	.347	2	.080	-2	-5	-3	1	-0.7
1960	Bal-A	0	2	.000	5	1	0	0	0	4	8	5	0	1	5	0	31.5	11.25	34	.444	.583	0	.000	-0	-3	-3	0	-0.6
Total	5	7	25	.219	95	33	3	1	5	247^1	287	144	21	4	124	130	15.1	4.58	85	.296	.379	5	.072	-5	-17	-19	2	-3.3

YEAR	TM/L	W	L	PCT	G	GS	CG	SH	SV	IP	H	R	HR	HB	BB	SO	RAT	ERA	ERA+	OAV	OOB	BH	AVG	PB	PR	PR+	PD	TPI
● ALLAN COLLAMORE	Collamore, Allan Edward b: 6/5/1887, Worcester, Mass. d: 8/8/80, Battle Creek, Mich. BR/TR, 6', 170 lbs. Deb: 4/15/11																											
1911	Phi-A	0	1	.000	2	0	0	0	0	2	6	9	0	2	3	1	49.5	36.00	9	.600	.733	0	—	0	-7	-8	-0	-1.1
1914	Cle-A	3	7	.300	27	8	3	0	0	105^{1}	100	52	3	6	49	32	13.2	3.25	89	.264	.357	3	.094	-2	-6	-4	-1	-0.7
1915	Cle-A	2	5	.286	11	6	5	2	0	64^{1}	52	22	1	0	22	15	10.4	2.38	128	.235	.305	4	.174	0	4	5	1	0.6
Total	3	5	13	.278	40	14	8	2	0	171^{2}	158	83	4	8	74	48	12.6	3.30	89	.259	.347	7	.127	-2	-9	-6	-0	-1.2
● HAP COLLARD	Collard, Earl Clinton b: 8/29/1898, Williams, Ariz. d: 7/9/68, Jamestown, Cal. BR/TR, 6', 170 lbs. Deb: 4/23/27																											
1927	Cle-A	0	0	—	4	0	0	0	0	5^{1}	8	7	0	0	3	2	18.6	5.06	83	.333	.407	0	—	0	-1	-1	0	0.0
1928	Cle-A	0	0	—	1	0	0	0	0	4	4	3	0	0	4	1	18.0	2.25	184	.250	.400	1	1.000	0	1	1	-0	0.1
1930	Phi-N	6	12	.333	30	15	4	0	0	127	188	106	15	3	39	25	16.3	6.80	80	.350	.397	9	.205	-2	-26	-17	1	-1.9
Total	3	6	12	.333	35	15	4	0	0	136^{1}	200	116	15	3	46	28	16.4	6.60	81	.347	.398	10	.222	-1	-26	-17	1	-1.8
● ORLIN COLLIER	Collier, Orlin Edward b: 2/17/07, E.Prairie, Mo. d: 9/9/44, Memphis, Tenn. BR/TR, 5'11.5", 180 lbs. Deb: 9/11/31																											
1931	Det-A	0	1	.000	2	2	0	0	0	10^{1}	17	12	0	0	7	3	20.9	7.84	59	.362	.444	0	.000	-0	-4	-4	-0	-0.3
● HARRY COLLIFLOWER	Colliflower, James Harry "Collie" b: 3/11/1869, Petersville, Md. d: 8/12/61, Washington, D.C. BL/TL, 5'11.5", 175 lbs. Deb: 7/21/1899 U																											
1899	Cle-N	1	11	.083	14	12	11	0	0	98	152	122	6	11	41	8	18.7	8.17	45	.353	.422	23	.303	2	-47	-51	0	-4.2
● DAN COLLINS	Collins, Daniel Thomas b: 7/12/1854, St.Louis, Mo. d: 9/21/1883, New Orleans, La. Deb: 6/8/1874 ♦																											
1874	Chi-n	1	1	.500	2	2	1	0	0	11	22	17	0		2	0	19.6	4.91	45	.386	.407	1	.083	-1	-3	-3		-0.4
● DON COLLINS	Collins, Donald Edward b: 9/15/52, Lyons, Ga. BR/TL, 6'2", 195 lbs. Deb: 5/4/77																											
1977	Atl-N	3	9	.250	40	6	0	0	2	70^{2}	82	43	8	1	41	27	15.8	5.09	87	.299	.392	0	.000	-1	-9	-4	-1	-1.0
1980	Cle-A	0	0	—	4	0	0	0	0	6	9	5	0	0	7	0	24.0	7.50	54	.346	.485	0	—	0	-2	-2	-0	-0.1
Total	2	3	9	.250	44	6	0	0	2	76^{2}	91	48	8	1	48	27	16.4	5.28	84	.303	.401	0	.000	-1	-12	-6	-1	-1.1
● RIP COLLINS	Collins, Harry Warren b: 2/26/1896, Weatherford, Tex. d: 5/27/68, Bryan, Tex. BR/TR (BB 1920-23), 6'1", 205 lbs. Deb: 4/19/20																											
1920	NY-A	14	8	.636	36	18	10	2	1	187^{1}	171	83	6	14	79	66	12.7	3.22	119	.247	.337	8	.129	-4	12	12	-1	0.8
1921	*NY-A	11	5	.688	28	16	7	2	0	137^{1}	158	103	6	10	78	64	16.1	5.44	78	.293	.392	11	.196	-1	-18	-19	-1	-2.0
1922	Bos-A	14	11	.560	32	29	15	3	0	210^{2}	219	101	4	10	103	69	14.2	3.76	109	.274	.364	12	.158	-3	7	8	-1	0.5
1923	Det-A	3	7	.300	17	14	3	1	0	92^{1}	104	61	3	10	22	25	13.3	4.87	79	.284	.342	3	.111	-2	-9	-11	0	-1.1
1924	Det-A	14	7	.667	34	30	11	1	0	216	199	99	6	4	63	75	11.1	3.21	128	.249	.307	11	.145	-5	25	22	0	1.4
1925	Det-A	6	11	.353	26	20	5	0	0	140	149	86	7	6	52	33	13.3	4.56	94	.281	.352	5	.119	-4	-3	-4	0	-0.4
1926	Det-A	8	8	.500	30	13	5	3	1	122	128	53	4	7	44	44	13.2	2.73	149	.278	.350	6	.154	-1	17	18	1	2.1
1927	Det-A	13	7	.650	30	25	10	1	0	172^{2}	207	116	5	8	59	37	14.3	4.69	90	.312	.375	11	.204	0	-11	-9	5	-0.4
1929	StL-A	11	6	.647	26	20	10	1	1	155^{1}	162	79	16	6	73	47	14.0	4.00	111	.270	.355	17	.274	4	4	7	0	1.1
1930	StL-A	9	7	.563	35	20	6	1	2	171^{2}	168	90	11	5	63	75	12.4	4.35	112	.259	.330	7	.130	-2	6	9	-0	0.5
1931	StL-A	5	5	.500	17	14	2	0	0	107	130	55	5	1	38	34	14.2	3.79	122	.307	.366	5	.147	-1	7	10	1	0.8
Total	11	108	82	.568	311	219	84	15	5	1712^{1}	1795	926	73	81	674	569	13.4	3.99	106	.275	.351	96	.165	-18	38	45	9	3.3
● ORTH COLLINS	Collins, Orth Stein "Buck" b: 4/27/1880, Lafayette, Ind. d: 12/13/49, Ft.Lauderdale, Fla BL/TR, 6', 150 lbs. Deb: 6/1/04 ♦																											
1909	Was-A	0	0	—	1	0	0	0	0	1	0	0	0	0	0	1	0.0	0.00	—	.000	.000	0	.000	-0	0	0	-0	0.0
● PHIL COLLINS	Collins, Philip Eugene "Fidgety Phil" b: 8/27/01, Chicago, Ill. d: 8/14/48, Chicago, Ill. BR/TR, 5'11", 175 lbs. Deb: 10/7/23																											
1923	Chi-N	1	0	1.000	1	1	0	0	0	5	8	2	0	0	1	2	16.2	3.60	111	.400	.429	0	.000	-0	0	0	1	0.1
1929	Phi-N	9	7	.563	43	11	3	0	5	153^{1}	172	106	18	4	83	61	15.2	5.75	90	.284	.374	11	.190	-0	-18	-9	-1	-0.9
1930	Phi-N	16	11	.593	47	25	17	1	3	239	287	148	22	10	86	87	14.4	4.78	114	.299	.363	22	.253	3	5	16	-2	1.7
1931	Phi-N	12	16	.429	42	27	16	2	4	240^{1}	268	126	14	5	83	73	13.3	3.86	110	.283	.344	16	.168	-4	0	9	1	0.8
1932	Phi-N	14	12	.538	43	21	6	0	3	184^{1}	231	117	21	6	65	66	14.7	5.27	84	.314	.375	18	.265	2	-29	-16	-0	-1.7
1933	Phi-N	8	13	.381	42	13	5	1	**6**	151	178	79	9	6	57	40	14.4	4.11	93	.293	.360	7	.132	-2	-13	-4	-1	-1.0
1934	Phi-N	13	18	.419	45	32	15	0	1	254	277	138	30	3	87	72	13.0	4.18	113	.273	.333	15	.170	-5	-3	13	-3	0.7
1935	Phi-N	0	2	.000	3	3	0	0	0	14^{2}	24	20	5	0	9	4	20.3	11.66	39	.348	.423	0	.000	-1	-12	-10	0	-1.1
	StL-N	7	6	.538	26	9	2	0	2	82^{2}	96	48	6	3	26	18	13.6	4.57	90	.290	.347	4	.160	-1	-5	-4	-1	-0.8
	Yr	7	8	.467	29	12	2	0	2	97^{1}	120	68	11	3	35	22	14.6	5.64	74	.300	.361	4	.129	-2	-18	-15	-1	-1.9
Total	8	80	85	.485	292	142	64	4	24	1324^{1}	1541	784	125	37	497	423	14.1	4.66	100	.291	.356	93	.193	-8	-75	-3	-7	-2.2
● RAY COLLINS	Collins, Ray Williston b: 2/11/1887, Colchester, Vt. d: 1/9/70, Burlington, Vt. BL/TL, 6'1", 185 lbs. Deb: 7/19/09																											
1909	Bos-A	4	3	.571	12	8	4	2	0	73^{2}	70	29	2	0	18	31	10.8	2.81	89	.269	.317	3	.130	-0	-3	-3	1	-0.2
1910	Bos-A	13	11	.542	35	26	18	4	1	244^{2}	205	73	1	1	41	109	9.1	1.62	158	.229	.264	15	.179	-1	25	25	-4	2.1
1911	Bos-A	11	12	.478	31	24	14	0	1	194^{2}	184	81	1	4	44	86	10.7	2.40	136	.256	.302	9	.150	0	20	19	-3	1.8
1912	*Bos-A	13	8	.619	27	24	17	4	0	199^{1}	192	65	4	2	42	82	10.7	2.53	135	.256	.297	11	.169	0	17	19	-3	1.6
1913	Bos-A	19	8	.704	30	30	19	3	0	246^{2}	242	88	3	2	37	88	10.3	2.63	112	.263	.293	12	.150	2	8	9	-4	0.6
1914	Bos-A	20	13	.606	39	30	16	6	0	272^{1}	252	95	3	0	56	72	10.2	2.51	107	.258	.298	11	.139	-0	7	6	-6	0.0
1915	Bos-A	4	7	.364	25	9	2	0	2	104^{2}	101	62	1	1	31	43	11.4	4.30	65	.261	.317	8	.286	5	-16	-19	-3	-1.8
Total	7	84	62	.575	199	151	90	19	4	1336	1246	493	15	10	269	511	10.3	2.51	115	.254	.294	69	.165	6	59	58	-22	4.1
● JACKIE COLLUM	Collum, Jack Dean b: 6/21/27, Victor, Ia. BL/TL, 5'7", 163 lbs. Deb: 9/21/51																											
1951	StL-N	2	1	.667	3	2	1	1	0	17	11	3	0	0	10	5	11.1	1.59	250	.204	.328	3	.429	1	4	4	0	1.0
1952	StL-N	0	0	—	2	0	0	0	0	3	2	1	0	0	1	0	9.0	0.00	—	.200	.273	0	—	0	1	1	0	0.1
1953	StL-N	0	0	—	7	0	0	0	0	11^{1}	15	10	1	0	4	5	15.1	6.35	67	.326	.380	0	.000	-0	-3	-3	1	0.0
	Cin-N	7	11	.389	30	12	4	1	3	124^{2}	123	57	8	6	39	51	12.1	3.75	116	.263	.328	10	.278	3	7	8	1	1.4
	Yr	7	11	.389	37	12	4	1	3	136	138	67	9	6	43	56	12.4	3.97	109	.269	.333	10	.256	2	5	6	2	1.4
1954	Cin-N	7	3	.700	36	2	1	0	0	79	86	43	8	5	32	28	14.0	3.76	112	.283	.361	3	.231	2	3	4	3	0.9
1955	Cin-N	9	8	.529	32	17	5	0	1	134	128	65	17	2	37	49	11.2	3.63	117	.254	.308	10	.250	2	6	9	-0	1.2
1956	StL-N	6	2	.750	38	1	0	0	7	60	63	29	6	2	27	17	13.8	4.20	90	.281	.364	3	.214	1	-3	-3	-1	-0.3
1957	Chi-N	1	1	.500	9	0	0	0	1	10^{2}	8	8	0	1	9	7	15.2	6.75	57	.211	.375	0	—	0	-3	-3	0	-0.6
	Bro-N	0	0	—	3	0	0	0	0	4^{1}	7	4	1	0	1	3	16.6	8.31	50	.368	.400	0	—	0	-2	-2	-0	-0.1
	Yr	1	1	.500	12	0	0	0	1	15	15	12	1	1	10	10	15.6	7.20	55	.263	.382	0	—	0	-6	-5	-0	-0.7
1958	LA-N	0	0	—	2	0	0	0	0	3^{1}	4	3	2	0	2	0	16.2	8.10	51	.308	.400	0	.000	-0	-2	-1	0	-0.1
1962	Min-A	0	2	.000	8	3	0	0	0	15^{1}	29	22	1	0	11	5	23.5	11.15	37	.414	.494	0	.000	-0	-12	-12	0	-1.3
	Cle-A	0	0	—	1	0	0	0	0	1^{1}	4	2	0	0	0	1	27.0	13.50	29	.571	.571	0	—	0	-1	-1	0	-0.1
	Yr	0	2	.000	9	3	0	0	0	16^{2}	33	24	1	0	11	6	23.8	11.34	36	.429	.500	0	.000	-0	-14	-13	0	-1.4
Total	9	32	28	.533	171	37	11	2	12	464	480	247	44	16	173	171	13.0	4.15	101	.273	.344	29	.246	8	-4	1	6	2.1
● BARTOLO COLON	Colon, Bartolo b: 5/24/75, Altamira, D.R. BR/TR, 6', 185 lbs. Deb: 4/4/97																											
1997	Cle-A	4	7	.364	19	17	1	0	0	94	107	66	12	3	45	66	14.8	5.65	83	.286	.367	0	.000	-0	-11	-10	1	-0.9
1998	*Cle-A★	14	9	.609	31	31	6	2	0	204	205	91	15	3	79	158	12.7	3.71	129	.260	.330	1	.500	0	22	24	2	2.5
1999	*Cle-A	18	5	.783	32	32	1	1	0	205	185	97	24	7	76	161	11.8	3.95	128	.242	.316	1	.143	-0	21	24	2	2.5
2000	Cle-A	15	8	.652	30	30	2	1	0	188	163	86	21	4	98	212	12.7	3.88	129	.233	.330	0	.000	-1	22	23	1	2.4
Total	4	51	29	.637	112	110	10	4	0	691	660	340	72	17	298	597	12.7	4.09	120	.251	.331	2	.133	-0	53	61	5	6.5
● DICK COLPAERT	Colpaert, Richard Charles b: 1/3/44, Fraser, Mich. BR/TR, 5'10", 182 lbs. Deb: 7/21/70																											
1970	Pit-N	1	0	1.000	8	0	0	0	0	10^{2}	9	7	3	0	8	6	14.3	5.91	66	.237	.370	0	—	0	-2	-2	-0	-0.2
● LOYD COLSON	Colson, Loyd Albert b: 11/4/47, Wellington, Tex. BR/TR, 6'1", 190 lbs. Deb: 9/25/70																											
1970	NY-A	0	0	—	1	0	0	0	0	2	3	1	0	0	0	3	13.5	4.50	78	.333	.333	0	—	0	-0	-0	0	0.0
● LARRY COLTON	Colton, Lawrence Robert b: 6/8/42, Los Angeles, Cal. BL/TR, 6'3", 200 lbs. Deb: 5/6/68																											
1968	Phi-N	0	0	—	1	0	0	0	0	2	3	1	0	0	0	2	13.5	4.50	67	.333	.333	0	—	0	-0	-0	-0	0.0

YEAR	TM/L	W	L	PCT	G	GS	CG	SH	SV	IP	H	R	HR	HB	BB	SO	RAT	ERA	ERA+	OAV	OOB	BH	AVG	PB	PR	PR+	PD	TPI
● **GEOFF COMBE**	Combe, Geoffrey Wade b: 2/1/56, Melrose, Mass. BR/TR, 6'2", 185 lbs. Deb: 9/2/80																											
1980	Cin-N	0	0	—	4	0	0	0	0	6^2	9	8	0	0	4	10	17.6	10.80	33	.346	.433	0	—	0	-5	-5	0	-0.3
1981	Cin-N	1	0	1.000	14	0	0	0	0	17^2	27	15	3	0	10	9	18.8	7.64	47	.370	.446	0	—	0	-8	-8	-0	-0.5
Total	2	1	0	1.000	18	0	0	0	0	24^1	36	23	3	0	14	19	18.5	8.51	42	.364	.442	0	—	0	-13	-13	-0	-0.8
● **PAT COMBS**	Combs, Patrick Dennis b: 10/29/66, Newport, R.I. BL/TL, 6'3", 200 lbs. Deb: 9/5/89																											
1989	Phi-N	4	0	1.000	6	6	1	1	0	38^2	36	10	2	0	6	30	9.8	2.09	169	.248	.278	2	.167	0	6	6	-1	0.6
1990	Phi-N	10	10	.500	32	31	3	2	0	183^1	179	90	12	4	86	108	13.2	4.07	94	.257	.342	9	.150	0	-6	-5	-0	-0.5
1991	Phi-N	2	6	.250	14	13	1	0	0	64^1	64	41	7	2	43	41	15.2	4.90	75	.254	.367	2	.133	1	-9	-9	-0	-1.0
1992	Phi-N	1	1	.500	4	4	0	0	0	18^2	20	16	0	0	12	11	15.4	7.71	45	.278	.381	1	.125	0	-9	-9	1	-0.7
Total	4	17	17	.500	56	54	5	3	0	305	299	157	21	6	147	190	13.3	4.22	89	.257	.343	14	.147	2	-17	-16	-1	-1.6
● **JORGE COMELLAS**	Comellas, Jorge (Pous) "Pancho" b: 12/7/16, Havana, Cuba BR/TR, 6', 190 lbs. Deb: 4/19/45																											
1945	Chi-N	0	2	.000	7	1	0	0	0	12	11	7	1	0	6	6	12.8	4.50	81	.244	.333	0	.000	-0	-1	-1	1	-0.1
● **STEVE COMER**	Comer, Steven Michael b: 1/13/54, Minneapolis, Minn. BB/TR, 6'3", 205 lbs. Deb: 4/15/78 C																											
1978	Tex-A	11	5	.688	30	11	3	2	1	117^1	107	36	5	1	37	65	11.1	2.30	163	.249	.310	0	—	0	19	19	1	2.6
1979	Tex-A	17	12	.586	36	36	6	1	0	242^1	230	114	24	8	84	86	12.0	3.68	113	.252	.320	0	—	0	15	13	-0	1.4
1980	Tex-A	2	4	.333	12	11	0	0	0	41^2	65	41	5	2	22	9	19.2	7.99	49	.367	.443	0	—	0	-18	-20	-0	-2.3
1981	Tex-A	8	2	.800	36	1	0	0	6	77^1	70	25	1	1	31	22	11.9	2.56	136	.241	.317	0	—	0	9	8	1	1.3
1982	Tex-A	1	6	.143	37	3	1	0	6	97	133	64	11	2	36	23	15.9	5.10	76	.342	.400	0	—	0	-11	-14	-0	-1.1
1983	Phi-N	1	0	1.000	3	1	0	0	0	8^2	11	6	0	0	3	1	14.5	5.19	69	.314	.368	0	.000	-0	-1	-2	-0	-0.2
1984	Cle-A	4	8	.333	22	20	1	0	0	117^1	146	80	11	4	39	39	14.5	5.68	72	.309	.366	0	—	0	-22	-20	0	-1.7
Total	7	44	37	.543	176	83	11	3	13	701^2	762	366	57	18	252	245	13.2	4.13	96	.281	.347	0	.000	-0	-9	-15	1	-0.0
● **CHARLIE COMISKEY**	Comiskey, Charles Albert "Commy" or "The Old Roman" b: 8/15/1859, Chicago, Ill. d: 10/26/31, Eagle River, Wis. BR/TR, 6', 180 lbs. Deb: 5/2/1882 MH◆																											
1882	StL-a	0	1	.000	2	1	1	0	0	8	12	8	0		3	2	16.9	0.00	—	.324	.375	80	.243	0	2	2	0	0.3
1884	StL-a	0	0	—	1	0	0	0	0	4	1	1	0	0	0	4	2.3	2.25	145	.059	.059	109	.237	0	0	0	-0	0.0
1889	StL-a	0	0	—	1	0	0	0	0	0^1	0	0	0	0	0	0	0.0	0.00	—	.000	.000	168	.286	0	0	0	0	0.0
Total	3	0	1	.000	4	1	1	0	0	12^1	13	9	0	0	3	6	11.7	0.73	410	.236	.276	1556	.267	0	3	3	-0	0.3
● **JACK COMPTON**	Compton, Harry Leroy b: 3/9/1882, Lancaster, Ohio d: 7/4/74, Lancaster, Ohio BR/TR, 5'9", 157 lbs. Deb: 9/7/11																											
1911	Cin-N	0	1	.000	8	3	0	0	1	25^1	19	11	0	1	15	6	12.4	3.91	85	.204	.321	2	.333	0	-1	-2	-0	-0.1
● **CLINT COMPTON**	Compton, Robert Clinton b: 11/1/50, Montgomery, Ala. BL/TL, 5'11", 185 lbs. Deb: 10/3/72																											
1972	Chi-N	0	0	—	1	0	0	0	0	2	2	2	0	0	2	0	18.0	9.00	42	.286	.444	0	—	0	-1	-1	-0	-0.1
● **KEITH COMSTOCK**	Comstock, Keith Martin b: 12/23/55, San Francisco, Cal. BL/TL, 6', 175 lbs. Deb: 4/3/84																											
1984	Min-A	0	0	—	4	0	0	0	0	6^1	6	6	2	0	4	2	14.2	8.53	49	.261	.370	0	—	0	-3	-3	0	-0.1
1987	SF-N	2	0	1.000	15	0	0	0	1	20^2	19	8	1	0	10	21	12.6	3.05	126	.253	.341	0	.000	-0	2	2	0	0.2
	SD-N	0	1	.000	26	0	0	0	0	36	33	22	4	0	21	38	13.5	5.50	72	.252	.355	0	.000	-0	-6	-6	-1	-0.4
	Yr	2	1	.667	41	0	0	0	1	56^2	52	30	5	0	31	59	13.2	4.61	85	.252	.350	0	.000	-0	-3	-5	-1	-0.2
1988	SD-N	0	0	—	7	0	0	0	0	8	8	6	1	0	3	9	12.4	6.75	50	.250	.314	0	—	0	-3	-3	0	-0.2
1989	Sea-A	1	2	.333	31	0	0	0	0	25^2	26	8	2	0	10	22	12.6	2.81	144	.268	.336	0	—	0	3	3	-0	0.4
1990	Sea-A	7	4	.636	60	0	0	0	2	56	40	22	4	0	26	50	10.6	2.89	137	.206	.300	0	—	0	6	7	1	1.3
1991	Sea-A	0	0	—	1	0	0	0	0	0^1	2	2	0	0	1	0	81.0	54.00	8	.667	.750	0	—	0	-2	-2	0	-0.1
Total	6	10	7	.588	144	0	0	0	3	153	134	74	14	0	75	142	12.3	4.06	97	.241	.332	0	.000	-0	-2	-2	0	1.1
● **RALPH COMSTOCK**	Comstock, Ralph Remick "Commy" b: 11/24/1890, Sylvania, Ohio d: 9/13/66, Toledo, Ohio BR/TR, 5'10", 168 lbs. Deb: 8/26/13																											
1913	Det-A	2	5	.286	10	7	1	0	1	60^1	90	55	0	1	16	37	16.0	5.37	54	.344	.384	5	.227	1	-16	-17	0	-1.6
1915	Bos-A	1	0	1.000	3	0	0	0	0	9	10	3	2	0	2	1	12.0	2.00	139	.294	.333	0	.000	0	1	1	0	0.1
	Pit-F	3	3	.500	12	7	3	0	2	52^2	44	25	3	1	7	18	8.9	3.25	83	.237	.268	0	.000	-2	-3	-3	-0	-0.6
1918	Pit-N	5	6	.455	15	8	6	0	1	81	78	33	0	2	14	44	10.4	3.00	96	.259	.297	5	.192	-0	-2	-1	0	-0.2
Total	3	11	14	.440	40	22	10	0	4	203	222	116	5	4	39	100	11.7	3.72	76	.284	.321	10	.152	-2	-21	-20	-0	-2.3
● **DAVE CONCEPCION**	Concepcion, David Ismael (Benitez) b: 6/17/48, Aragua, Venez. BR/TR, 6'1", 180 lbs. Deb: 4/6/70 ◆																											
1988	Cin-N	0	0	—	1	0	0	0	0	1^1	2	0	0	0	0	1	13.5	0.00	—	.333	.333	39	.198	0	1	1	0	0.0
● **DAVID CONE**	Cone, David Brian b: 1/2/63, Kansas City, Mo. BL/TR, 6'1", 190 lbs. Deb: 6/8/86																											
1986	KC-A	0	0	—	11	0	0	0	0	22^2	29	14	2	1	13	21	17.1	5.56	77	.309	.398	0	—	0	-3	-3	-0	-0.2
1987	NY-N	5	6	.455	21	13	1	0	1	99^1	87	46	11	5	44	68	12.3	3.71	102	.239	.329	2	.065	-1	4	1	-0	-0.1
1988	*NY-N★	20	3	**.870**	35	28	8	4	0	231^1	178	67	10	4	80	213	10.2	2.22	145	.213	.285	12	.150	1	32	28	-1	2.8
1989	NY-N	14	8	.636	34	33	7	2	0	219^2	183	92	20	4	74	190	10.7	3.52	93	.223	.290	18	.234	4	-1	-7	-2	-0.4
1990	NY-N	14	10	.583	31	30	6	2	0	211^2	177	84	21	1	65	**233**	10.3	3.23	116	.226	.286	14	.200	3	13	12	-0	1.6
1991	NY-N	14	14	.500	34	34	5	2	0	232^2	204	95	13	5	73	**241**	10.9	3.29	111	.235	.298	9	.125	-1	10	9	0	1.0
1992	NY-N★	13	7	.650	27	27	7	**5**	0	196^2	162	75	12	9	82	214	11.6	2.88	121	.223	.309	6	.092	-2	14	13	-0	1.1
	*Tor-A	4	3	.571	8	7	0	0	0	53	39	16	3	3	29	47	12.1	2.55	161	.206	.321	0	—	0	8	9	-1	1.1
1993	KC-A	11	14	.440	34	34	6	1	0	254	205	102	20	10	114	191	11.7	3.33	138	.223	.315	0	—	0	28	34	-1	3.0
1994	KC-A★	16	5	.762	23	23	4	3	0	171^2	130	60	15	7	54	132	10.0	2.94	171	.209	.279	0	—	0	36	38	0	**4.3**
1995	Tor-A	9	6	.600	17	17	5	2	0	130^1	113	53	12	5	41	102	11.0	3.38	139	.232	.298	0	—	0	19	19	0	2.0
	*NY-A	9	2	.818	13	13	1	0	0	99	82	42	12	1	47	89	11.8	3.82	121	.223	.313	0	—	0	10	9	-1	0.8
	Yr	18	8	.692	30	30	6	2	0	**229^1**	195	95	24	6	88	191	11.3	3.57	131	.228	.305	0	—	0	29	28	-1	2.8
1996	*NY-A	7	2	.778	11	11	1	0	0	72	50	25	3	2	34	71	10.8	2.88	172	.198	.298	0	—	0	17	17	-1	1.8
1997	*NY-A★	12	6	.667	29	29	1	0	0	195	155	67	17	4	86	222	11.3	2.82	158	.218	.306	0	.000	-0	38	36	-2	2.8
1998	*NY-A	**20**	7	.741	31	31	3	0	0	207^2	186	89	20	15	59	209	11.3	3.55	123	.237	.303	0	.000	-0	25	20	0	2.3
1999	*NY-A★	12	9	.571	31	31	1	1	0	193^1	164	84	21	11	90	177	12.3	3.44	138	.229	.325	1	.333	1	31	29	-2	2.5
2000	*NY-A	4	14	.222	30	29	0	0	0	155	192	124	25	9	82	120	16.4	6.91	69	.306	.394	1	.333	0	-34	-37	0	-3.3
Total	15	184	116	.613	420	390	56	22	1	2745	2336	1135	237	96	1067	2540	11.5	3.40	122	.230	.309	63	.155	5	248	229	-10	23.1
● **BOB CONE**	Cone, Robert Earl b: 2/27/1894, Galveston, Tex. d: 5/24/55, Galveston, Tex. BR/TR, 6'2", 172 lbs. Deb: 7/25/15																											
1915	Phi-A	0	0	—	1	1	0	0	0	0^2	5	3	0	0	0	0	67.5	40.50	7	.714	.714	0	—	0	-3	-3	-0	-0.1
● **DICK CONGER**	Conger, Richard b: 4/3/21, Los Angeles, Cal. d: 2/16/70, Los Angeles, Cal. BR/TR, 6', 185 lbs. Deb: 4/22/40																											
1940	Det-A	1	0	1.000	2	0	0	0	0	3	2	1	0	0	3	1	15.0	3.00	159	.200	.385	0	—	0	0	1	-0	0.1
1941	Pit-N	0	0	—	2	1	0	0	0	4	3	0	0	0	3	2	13.5	0.00	—	.214	.353	0	—	0	2	2	-0	0.1
1942	Pit-N	0	0	—	2	1	0	0	0	8^1	9	3	0	0	5	3	15.1	2.16	157	.290	.389	0	.000	-0	1	1	1	0.1
1943	Phi-N	2	7	.222	13	10	2	0	0	54^2	72	46	3	5	24	18	16.6	6.09	55	.327	.406	1	.063	-1	-16	-17	-0	-2.4
Total	4	3	7	.300	19	12	2	0	0	70	86	50	3	5	35	24	16.2	5.14	67	.313	.400	1	.053	-1	-13	-13	0	-2.1
● **ALLEN CONKWRIGHT**	Conkwright, Allen Howard "Red" b: 12/4/1896, Sedalia, Mo. d: 7/30/91, LaMesa, Cal. BR/TR, 5'10", 170 lbs. Deb: 9/16/20																											
1920	Det-A	2	1	.667	5	3	0	0	1	19^1	29	16	0	0	16	4	20.9	6.98	53	.397	.506	1	.200	1	-7	-7	0	-0.9
● **GENE CONLEY**	Conley, Donald Eugene b: 11/10/30, Muskogee, Okla. BR/TR, 6'8", 225 lbs. Deb: 4/17/52																											
1952	Bos-N	0	3	.000	4	3	0	0	0	12^2	23	16	4	2	9	6	24.2	7.82	46	.397	.493	2	.400	1	-6	-6	-0	-1.0
1954	Mil-N★	14	9	.609	28	27	12	2	0	194^1	171	73	17	7	79	113	11.9	2.96	126	.240	.322	12	.156	-2	24	18	-1	1.7
1955	Mil-N★	11	7	.611	22	21	10	0	0	158	152	81	23	1	52	107	11.7	4.16	90	.254	.315	11	.204	-1	-2	-8	-0	-0.8
1956	Mil-N	8	9	.471	31	19	5	1	3	158^1	169	74	13	2	52	68	12.7	3.13	111	.276	.335	7	.156	-1	11	6	-1	0.6
1957	*Mil-N	9	9	.500	35	18	6	1	1	148	133	63	9	2	64	61	12.1	3.16	111	.244	.325	9	.196	1	12	6	-0	0.8
1958	Mil-N	0	6	.000	26	7	0	0	2	72	89	44	8	4	17	53	13.8	4.88	72	.309	.356	3	.188	1	-7	-12	0	-0.9
1959	Phi-N★	12	7	.632	25	22	12	3	1	180	159	68	13	2	42	102	10.1	3.00	**137**	.235	.281	16	.239	2	19	21	-0	2.4
1960	Phi-N	8	14	.364	29	25	9	2	0	183^1	192	85	10	2	42	117	11.6	3.68	105	.272	.314	8	.127	-1	2	4	-2	0.2

YEAR TM/L	W	L	PCT	G	GS	CG	SH	SV	IP	H	R	HR	HB	BB	SO	RAT	ERA	ERA+	OAV	OOB	BH	AVG	PB	PR	PR+	PD	TPI
1961 Bos-A	11	14	.440	33	30	6	2	1	199^2	229	116	33	3	65	113	13.4	4.91	85	.287	.343	16	.219	4	-20	-16	-1	-1.5
1962 Bos-A	15	14	.517	34	33	9	2	1	241^2	238	116	28	5	68	134	11.6	3.95	105	.256	.310	18	.207	3	1	5	-1	0.8
1963 Bos-A	3	4	.429	9	9	0	0	0	40^2	51	31	4	1	21	14	16.2	6.64	57	.305	.386	3	.200	0	-14	-12	-1	-1.8
Total 11	91	96	.487	276	214	69	13	9	1588^2	1606	767	162	31	511	888	12.2	3.82	101	.264	.324	105	.192	8	20	6	-6	0.5
● ED CONLEY Conley, Edward J. b: 7/10/1864, Sandwich, Mass. d: 10/16/1894, Cumberland, R.I. 5'8", 142 lbs. Deb: 7/20/1884																											
1884 Pro-N	4	4	.500	8	8	8	1	0	71	63	47	4		22	33	10.8	2.15	132	.223	.280	4	.143	-2	7	6	-1	0.2
● SNIPE CONLEY Conley, James Patrick b: 4/25/1894, Cressona, Pa. d: 1/7/78, DeSoto, Tex. BR/TR, 5'11.5", 179 lbs. Deb: 5/20/14																											
1914 Bal-F	4	6	.400	35	11	4	2	1	125	112	49	2	6	47	86	11.9	2.52	120	.259	.340	4	.114	-3	5	7	-1	0.1
1915 Bal-F	1	4	.200	25	6	4	0	0	86	97	48	5	4	32	40	13.9	4.29	67	.314	.386	6	.250	1	-15	-13	-1	-0.6
1918 Cin-N	2	0	1.000	5	0	0	0	0	13^2	17	10	2	0	5	2	14.5	5.27	51	.321	.379	1	.250	0	-4	-4	0	-0.6
Total 3	7	10	.412	65	17	8	2	2	224^2	226	107	9	10	84	128	12.8	3.36	88	.284	.360	11	.175	-1	-14	-10	-1	-1.1
● BOB CONLEY Conley, Robert Burns b: 2/1/34, Mousie, Ky. BR/TR, 6'1", 188 lbs. Deb: 9/11/58																											
1958 Phi-N	0	0	—	2	2	0	0	0	8^1	9	7	0	0	1	0	10.8	7.56	52	.273	.294	0	.000	-0	-3	-3	-0	-0.2
● BERT CONN Conn, Albert Thomas b: 9/22/1879, Philadelphia, Pa. d: 11/2/44, Philadelphia, Pa. TR, 6', 178 lbs. Deb: 9/16/1898 ◆																											
1898 Phi-N	0	1	.000	1	1	0	0	0	7	13	9	1	0	2	3	19.3	6.43	53	.394	.429	1	.333	1	-2	-2	-0	-0.2
1900 Phi-N	0	2	.000	4	1	1	0	0	17^1	29	29	0	6	16	2	26.5	8.31	44	.372	.510	3	.333	1	-9	-9	-1	-0.8
Total 2	0	3	.000	5	2	1	0	0	24^1	42	38	1	6	18	5	24.4	7.77	46	.378	.489	8	.267	2	-11	-12	-1	-1.0
● SARGE CONNALLY Connally, George Walter b: 8/31/1898, McGregor, Tex. d: 1/27/78, Temple, Tex. BR/TR, 5'11", 170 lbs. Deb: 9/10/21																											
1921 Chi-A	0	1	.000	5	2	0	0	0	22^1	29	16	0	1	10	6	16.1	6.45	66	.330	.404	4	.500	2	-5	-6	0	-0.1
1923 Chi-A	0	0	—	3	0	0	0	0	8^2	7	6	0	1	12	3	20.8	6.23	64	.241	.476	1	.333	0	-2	-2	-0	-0.1
1924 Chi-A	7	13	.350	44	13	6	0	6	160	177	95	4	9	68	55	14.3	4.05	102	.290	.369	11	.220	-1	3	1	3	0.4
1925 Chi-A	6	7	.462	40	2	0	0	8	104^2	122	66	2	2	58	45	15.6	4.64	89	.310	.402	7	.250	1	-3	-6	3	-0.3
1926 Chi-A	6	5	.545	31	8	5	0	3	108^1	128	51	0	2	35	47	13.7	3.16	122	.300	.356	5	.156	-1	10	9	2	0.9
1927 Chi-A	10	15	.400	43	18	11	1	5	198^1	217	108	8	9	83	58	14.0	4.08	99	.292	.370	22	.328	4	1	-1	1	0.3
1928 Chi-A	2	5	.286	28	5	1	0	2	74^1	89	52	1	4	29	28	14.8	4.84	84	.313	.385	2	.105	-1	-7	-7	-0	-0.7
1929 Chi-A	0	0	—	11	0	0	0	1	11^1	13	6	0	0	8	3	16.7	4.76	90	.317	.429	0	—	0	-1	-1	-0	-0.1
1931 Cle-A	5	5	.500	17	9	5	0	1	85^2	87	56	7	6	50	37	15.0	4.20	110	.256	.361	5	.185	0	2	4	-0	0.4
1932 Cle-A	8	6	.571	35	7	4	1	3	112^1	119	59	6	3	42	32	13.1	4.33	110	.266	.333	7	.175	-0	2	5	0	0.5
1933 Cle-A	5	3	.625	41	3	1	0	1	103	112	60	4	3	49	30	14.3	4.89	91	.271	.353	6	.231	1	-7	-5	-2	-0.5
1934 Cle-A	0	0	—	5	0	0	0	1	5^1	4	3	0	0	5	1	15.2	5.06	90	.222	.391	0	.000	-0	-0	-0	0	0.0
Total 12	49	60	.450	303	67	33	2	31	994^1	1104	578	32	40	449	345	14.4	4.30	98	.288	.368	70	.233	5	-7	-8	5	0.7
● STEVE CONNELLY Connelly, Steven Lee b: 4/27/74, Long Beach, Cal. BR/TR, 6'4", 210 lbs. Deb: 6/28/98																											
1998 Oak-A	0	0	—	3	0	0	0	0	4^2	10	1	0	1	4	1	28.9	1.93	237	.435	.536	0	—	0	1	1	0	0.1
● BILL CONNELLY Connelly, William Wirt "Wild Bill" b: 6/29/25, Alberta, Va. d: 11/27/80, Richmond, Va. BL/TR, 6', 175 lbs. Deb: 8/22/45																											
1945 Phi-A	1	1	.500	2	1	0	0	0	8	7	4	0	0	8	0	16.9	4.50	76	.259	.429	0	.000	0	-1	-1	-0	-0.2
1950 Chi-A	0	0	—	2	0	0	0	0	2^1	5	3	1	0	1	0	23.1	11.57	39	.455	.500	0	—	0	-2	-2	-0	-0.1
Det-A	0	0	—	2	0	0	0	0	4	4	3	1	0	2	1	13.5	6.75	69	.250	.333	0	.000	0	-1	-1	0	0.0
Yr	0	0	—	4	0	0	0	0	6^1	9	6	2	0	3	1	17.1	8.53	54	.333	.400	0	.000	0	-3	-3	0	-0.1
1952 NY-N	5	0	1.000	11	4	0	0	0	31^2	22	18	4	0	25	22	13.4	4.55	81	.208	.359	4	.364	3	-3	-3	1	-0.1
1953 NY-N	0	1	.000	8	2	0	0	0	20^1	33	26	4	0	17	11	22.1	11.07	39	.371	.472	0	.000	-1	-15	-15	-0	-0.8
Total 4	6	2	.750	25	7	0	0	0	66^1	71	54	10	0	53	34	16.8	6.92	57	.285	.411	4	.211	3	-22	-22	-0	-1.2
● ED CONNOLLY Connolly, Edward Joseph Jr. b: 12/3/39, Brooklyn, N.Y. d: 7/1/98, New Canaan, Conn. BL/TL, 6'1", 190 lbs. Deb: 4/19/64 F																											
1964 Bos-A	4	11	.267	27	15	1	1	0	80^2	80	50	3	6	64	73	16.7	4.91	79	.261	.398	3	.167	0	-12	-9	-1	-1.6
1967 Cle-A	2	1	.667	15	4	0	0	0	49^1	63	46	6	1	34	45	17.9	7.48	44	.315	.417	2	.182	0	-23	-23	-0	-1.3
Total 2	6	12	.333	42	19	1	1	0	130	143	96	9	7	98	118	17.2	5.88	62	.282	.405	5	.172	0	-35	-31	-2	-2.9
● JOHN CONNOR Connor, John b: 8/1854, Glasgow, Scotland d: 10/13/32, Boston, Mass. Deb: 7/26/1884																											
1884 Bos-N	1	4	.200	7	7	7	0	0	60	70	44	1		18	29	13.2	3.15	92	.275	.322	2	.080	-3	-1	-2	0	-0.3
1885 Buf-N	0	1	.000	1	1	1	0	0	9	14	9	0		2	0	16.0	4.00	75	.378	.410	0	.000	-0	-1	-1	-1	-0.2
Lou-a	1	3	.250	4	4	4	0	0	35	43	27	0	2	12	19	14.7	4.89	66	.295	.356	2	.143	-1	-6	-6	-1	-0.7
Total 2	2	8	.200	12	12	12	0	0	104	127	80	1	2	32	48	13.9	3.81	79	.290	.341	4	.095	-4	-9	-9	-1	-1.2
● JOE CONNORS Connors, Joseph P. b: Paterson, N.J. Deb: 5/3/1884 ◆																											
1884 Alt-U	0	1	.000	1	1	1	0	0	9	18	14	0		5	0	23.0	7.00	38	.391	.451	1	.091	-1	-5	-4	0	-0.3
KC-U	0	1	.000	2	1	1	0	0	12	24	14	1		0	1	18.0	4.50	50	.393	.393	1	.091	-1	-3	-3	-1	-0.3
Yr	0	2	.000	3	2	2	0	0	21	42	28	1		5	1	20.1	5.57	43	.393	.420	2	.091	-2	-7	-7	-0	-0.6
● BILL CONNORS Connors, William Joseph b: 11/2/41, Schenectady, N.Y. BR/TR, 6'1", 180 lbs. Deb: 5/3/66 C																											
1966 Chi-N	0	1	.000	11	0	0	0	0	16	20	13	4	0	7	3	15.2	7.31	50	.308	.375	0	—	0	-7	-6	-0	-0.3
1967 NY-N	0	0	—	6	1	0	0	0	13	8	9	3	1	5	13	9.7	6.23	54	.170	.264	0	.000	-0	-4	-4	-0	-0.3
1968 NY-N	0	1	.000	9	0	0	0	0	14	21	14	0	1	7	8	18.6	9.00	34	.339	.414	1	1.000	1	-9	-9	0	-0.6
Total 3	0	2	.000	26	1	0	0	0	43	49	36	7	2	19	24	14.7	7.53	45	.282	.359	1	.500	1	-20	-20	-0	-1.2
● TED CONOVAR Conovar, Theodore "Huck" b: 3/10/1868, Lexington, Ky. d: 7/27/10, Paris, Ky. BR/TR, 5'10.5", 165 lbs. Deb: 5/26/1889																											
1889 Cin-a	0	0	—	1	0	0	0	1	2	4	4	0	0	2	1	27.0	13.50	29	.400	.500	0	—	0	-2	-2	-0	-0.2
● TIM CONROY Conroy, Timothy James b: 4/3/60, McKeesport, Pa. BL/TL, 5'11", 185 lbs. Deb: 6/23/78																											
1978 Oak-A	0	0	—	2	2	0	0	0	4^2	3	6	0	1	9	0	25.1	7.71	47	.188	.500	0	—	0	-2	-2	-0	-0.1
1982 Oak-A	2	2	.500	5	5	1	0	0	25^1	20	13	1	0	18	17	13.5	3.55	110	.222	.352	0	—	0	1	1	-0	0.1
1983 Oak-A	7	10	.412	39	18	3	1	0	162^1	141	89	17	2	98	112	13.4	3.94	98	.232	.340	0	—	0	3	-1	-2	-0.4
1984 Oak-A	1	6	.143	38	14	0	0	0	93	82	58	11	2	63	69	14.2	5.23	72	.236	.356	0	—	0	-13	-16	-1	-1.2
1985 Oak-A	0	1	.000	16	2	0	0	0	25^1	22	15	3	1	15	8	13.5	4.26	91	.237	.349	0	—	0	-0	-1	-0	-0.1
1986 StL-N	5	11	.313	25	21	1	0	0	115^1	122	72	15	3	56	79	14.1	5.23	70	.275	.360	4	.138	1	-19	-21	-1	-2.6
1987 StL-N	3	2	.600	10	9	0	0	0	40^2	48	26	0	1	25	22	16.4	5.53	75	.306	.404	0	.000	-2	-7	-6	-0	-0.8
Total 7	18	32	.360	135	71	5	1	0	466^2	438	279	47	10	284	307	14.1	4.69	81	.249	.357	4	.091	-1	-37	-47	-6	-5.1
● JIM CONSTABLE Constable, Jimmy Lee "Sheriff" b: 6/14/33, Jonesborough, Tenn. BB/TL, 6'1", 185 lbs. Deb: 6/24/56																											
1956 NY-N	0	0	—	3	0	0	0	0	4^1	9	7	0	1	7	1	35.3	14.54	26	.429	.586	0	—	0	-5	-5	-0	-0.3
1957 NY-N	1	1	.500	16	0	0	0	0	28^1	27	10	2	4	7	13	12.1	2.86	138	.262	.333	0	.000	-0	3	3	-0	0.1
1958 SF-N	1	0	1.000	9	0	0	0	1	8	10	6	1	0	3	4	14.6	5.63	68	.323	.382	1	1.000	1	-1	-2	1	-0.1
Cle-A	0	1	.000	6	2	0	0	0	9^1	17	13	2	1	4	3	21.2	11.57	32	.415	.478	2	1.000	1	-8	-8	-0	-0.7
Was-A	0	1	.000	15	2	0	0	0	27^2	29	15	3	1	15	25	14.6	4.88	78	.271	.366	1	.250	0	-3	-3	-0	-0.2
Yr	0	2	.000	21	4	0	0	0	37	46	28	5	2	19	28	16.3	6.57	57	.311	.396	3	.500	1	-12	-11	-1	-0.9
1962 Mil-N	1	1	.500	3	2	1	1	1	18	14	4	1	0	4	12	9.0	2.00	190	.222	.269	0	.000	-0	4	4	-1	0.4
1963 SF-N	0	0	—	4	0	0	0	0	2^1	3	1	0	0	1	1	15.4	3.86	83	.333	.400	0	—	0	-0	-0	-0	0.0
Total 5	3	4	.429	56	6	1	1	2	98	109	56	9	7	41	59	14.4	4.87	78	.291	.371	4	.235	2	-11	-12	-1	-0.8
● SANDY CONSUEGRA Consuegra, Sandalio Simeon (Castello) b: 9/3/20, Potrerillos, Cuba BR/TR, 5'10", 165 lbs. Deb: 6/10/50																											
1950 Was-A	7	8	.467	21	18	8	2	2	124^2	132	71	6	1	57	38	13.7	4.40	102	.270	.347	7	.175	-1	2	1	0	0.1
1951 Was-A	7	8	.467	40	12	5	0	3	146	140	71	10	0	63	31	12.5	4.01	102	.251	.327	10	.233	-0	2	1	1	0.2
1952 Was-A	6	0	1.000	30	2	0	0	5	73^2	80	30	2	0	27	19	13.1	3.05	116	.276	.338	3	.176	-0	5	4	-1	0.3
1953 Was-A	0	0	—	4	0	0	0	0	5	9	6	0	0	4	0	23.4	10.80	36	.391	.481	0	—	0	-4	-4	0	-0.2
Chi-A	7	5	.583	29	13	5	1	3	124	122	39	9	2	28	30	11.0	2.54	158	.258	.302	2	.057	-4	20	20	3	1.9
Yr	7	5	.583	33	13	5	1	3	129	131	45	9	2	32	30	11.5	2.86	141	.264	.311	2	.057	-4	16	17	3	1.7
1954 Chi-A★	16	3	**.842**	39	17	3	2	3	154	142	52	9	0	35	31	10.3	2.69	139	.248	.292	11	.229	1	18	18	1	2.4

YEAR	TM/L	W	L	PCT	G	GS	CG	SH	SV	IP	H	R	HR	HB	BB	SO	RAT	ERA	ERA+	OAV	OOB	BH	AVG	PB	PR	PR+	PD	TPI
1955	Chi-A	6	5	.545	44	7	3	0	7	126^1	120	42	4	2	18	35	10.0	2.64	150	.256	.286	3	.103	-2	**19**	**18**	-0	1.5
1956	Chi-A	1	2	.333	28	1	0	0	3	38^1	45	25	0	1	11	7	13.4	5.17	79	.296	.348	0	.000	-1	-4	-5	0	-0.5
	Bal-A	1	1	.500	4	1	0	0	0	8^2	10	4	2	0	2	1	12.5	4.15	94	.294	.333	1	.500	0	0	-0	-0	0.0
	Yr	2	3	.400	32	2	0	0	3	47	55	29	2	1	13	8	13.2	4.98	82	.296	.345	1	.167	-0	-4	-5	-0	-0.5
1957	Bal-A	0	0	—	5	0	0	0	0	5	4	1	0	0	0	0	7.2	1.80	200	.211	.211	0	—	0	1	1	0	0.1
	NY-N	0	0	—	4	0	0	0	0	3^2	7	5	1	0	1	1	19.6	2.45	160	.389	.421	0	—	0	1	1	0	0.1
Total	8	51	32	.614	248	71	24	5	26	809^1	811	346	43	6	246	193	11.8	3.37	119	.262	.318	37	.170	-5	59	57	4	5.9
● NARDI CONTRERAS	Contreras, Arnaldo Juan b: 9/19/51, Tampa, Fla. BB/TR, 6′2″, 193 lbs. Deb: 5/23/80 C																											
1980	Chi-A	0	0	—	8	0	0	0	0	13^2	18	10	1	2	7	8	17.8	5.93	68	.333	.429	0	—	0	-3	-3	0	-0.1
● JIM CONVERSE	Converse, James Daniel b: 8/17/71, San Francisco, Cal. BL/TR, 5′9″, 180 lbs. Deb: 5/22/93																											
1993	Sea-A	1	3	.250	4	4	0	0	0	20^1	23	12	0	0	14	10	16.4	5.31	83	.295	.402	0	—	0	-2	-2	1	-0.3
1994	Sea-A	0	5	.000	13	8	0	0	0	48^2	73	49	5	1	40	39	21.1	8.69	56	.353	.460	0	—	0	-21	-20	-0	-1.6
1995	Sea-A	0	3	.000	6	1	0	0	1	11	16	9	2	0	8	9	19.6	7.36	64	.348	.444	0	—	0	-3	-3	-0	-0.6
	KC-A	1	0	1.000	9	0	0	0	0	12^1	12	8	0	0	8	5	14.6	5.84	82	.267	.377	0	—	0	-2	-1	0	-0.1
	Yr	1	3	.250	15	1	0	0	1	23^1	28	17	2	0	16	14	17.0	6.56	73	.308	.411	0	—	0	-5	-5	0	-0.7
1997	KC-A	0	0	—	3	0	0	0	0	5	4	2	2	0	5	3	16.2	3.60	131	.222	.391	0	—	0	1	1	-0	0.0
Total	4	2	11	.154	35	13	0	0	1	97^1	128	80	9	1	75	66	18.9	7.21	66	.325	.434	0	—	0	-27	-26	1	-2.6
● JIM CONWAY	Conway, James P. b: 10/8/1858, Clifton, Pa. TR, Deb: 5/5/1884 F																											
1884	Bro-a	3	9	.250	13	13	10	0	0	105^1	132	84	4	3	15	25	12.8	4.44	75	.289	.316	6	.128	-4	-14	-13	-2	-1.6
1885	Phi-a	0	1	.000	2	2	1	0	0	12^1	19	16	0	0	2	0	15.3	7.30	47	.358	.382	0	.000	-0	-6	-5	-0	-0.3
1889	KC-a	19	19	.500	41	37	33	0	0	335	334	232	12	14	90	115	11.8	3.25	129	.252	.306	31	.208	-6	22	32	1	2.4
Total	3	22	29	.431	56	52	44	0	0	452^2	485	332	16	17	107	140	12.1	3.64	109	.264	.311	37	.183	-10	3	15	-1	0.5
● JERRY CONWAY	Conway, Jerome Patrick b: 6/7/01, Holyoke, Mass. d: 4/16/80, Holyoke, Mass. BL/TL, 6′2″, 190 lbs. Deb: 8/31/20																											
1920	Was-A	0	0	—	1	0	0	0	0	2	1	0	0	0	1	0	9.0	0.00	—	.167	.286	0	—	0	1	1	-0	0.0
● PETE CONWAY	Conway, Peter J. b: 10/30/1866, Burmont, Pa. d: 1/13/03, Clifton Heights, Pa. BR/TR, 5′10.5″, 162 lbs. Deb: 8/10/1885 F♦																											
1885	Buf-N	10	17	.370	27	27	26	1	0	210	256	173	10		44	94	12.9	4.67	64	.287	.320	10	.111	-4	-43	-37	1	-4.0
1886	KC-N	5	15	.250	23	20	19	0	0	180	236	185	6		61	81	14.9	5.75	66	.294	.343	47	.242	0	-49	-35	-2	-3.0
	Det-N	6	5	.545	11	11	11	0	0	91	93	55	1		25	35	11.7	3.36	99	.255	.303	8	.186	1	-1	-0	-0	-0.1
	Yr	11	20	.355	34	31	30	0	0	271	329	240	7		86	116	13.8	4.95	73	.282	.331	55	.232	1	-49	-37	-2	-3.1
1887	*Det-N	8	9	.471	17	17	16	0	0	146	179	95	3	5	47	40	11.3	2.90	140	.294	.300	24	.247	0	19	19	3	1.9
1888	Det-N	30	14	.682	45	45	43	4	0	391	315	170	11	13	57	176	8.9	2.26	123	.208	**.243**	46	.275	15	26	23	3	4.0
1889	Pit-N	2	1	.667	3	3	2	0	0	22	26	16	1	0	16	2	17.2	4.91	76	.286	.393	1	.100	0	-2	-3	0	-0.3
Total	5	61	61	.500	126	123	117	5	0	1040	1105	694	32	18	250	428	11.5	3.59	90	.258	.295	136	.226	12	-50	-41	4	-1.5
● DICK CONWAY	Conway, Richard Butler b: 4/25/1865, Lowell, Mass. d: 9/9/26, Lowell, Mass. BL/TR, 5′7.5″, 140 lbs. Deb: 7/22/1886 F																											
1886	Bal-a	2	7	.222	9	9	8	0	0	76^2	106	91	6	3	43	64	17.8	6.81	50	.312	.394	7	.206	0	-29	-29	2	-2.2
1887	Bos-N	9	15	.375	26	26	25	0	0	222^1	335	161	10	7	86	45	13.8	4.66	87	.339	.343	52	.323	2	-14	-15	1	-1.0
1888	Bos-N	4	2	.667	6	6	6	0	0	53	49	31	2	4	8	12	10.4	2.38	120	.240	.282	4	.160	-1	3	3	-0	0.2
Total	3	15	24	.385	41	41	39	0	0	352	490	283	18	14	137	121	14.2	4.78	78	.320	.347	63	.286	1	-40	-41	2	-3.0
● JOE CONZELMAN	Conzelman, Joseph Harrison b: 7/14/1885, Bristol, Conn. d: 4/17/79, Mountain Brook, Ala. BR/TR, 6′, 170 lbs. Deb: 5/1/13																											
1913	Pit-N	0	1	.000	3	2	1	0	0	15	13	4	0	1	5	9	11.4	1.20	252	.245	.322	0	.000	-1	3	3	0	0.1
1914	Pit-N	5	6	.455	33	9	4	1	2	101	88	39	2	3	40	39	11.7	2.94	90	.254	.337	3	.111	-2	-2	-3	2	-0.4
1915	Pit-N	1	1	.500	18	1	0	0	0	47^1	41	18	0	3	20	22	12.2	3.42	80	.248	.340	1	.091	-1	-4	-4	1	-0.2
Total	3	6	8	.429	54	12	5	1	2	163^1	142	61	2	7	65	70	11.8	2.92	93	.252	.336	4	.095	-3	-2	-4	2	-0.5
● ANDY COOK	Cook, Andrew Bernard b: 8/30/67, Memphis, Tenn. BR/TR, 6′5″, 215 lbs. Deb: 5/9/93																											
1993	NY-A	0	1	.000	4	0	0	0	0	5^1	4	3	1	0	7	4	18.6	5.06	82	.200	.407	0	—	0	-0	-1	0	-0.1
● DENNIS COOK	Cook, Dennis Bryan b: 10/4/62, LaMarque, Tex. BL/TL, 6′3″, 185 lbs. Deb: 9/12/88																											
1988	SF-N	2	1	.667	4	4	1	1	0	22	9	8	1	0	11	13	8.2	2.86	114	.125	.241	0	.000	1	1	1	-1	0.1
1989	SF-N	1	0	1.000	2	2	1	0	0	15	13	3	1	0	5	9	10.8	1.80	188	.245	.310	1	.167	1	3	3	0	0.3
	Phi-N	6	8	.429	21	16	1	1	0	106	97	56	17	2	33	58	11.2	3.99	89	.243	.304	8	.222	1	-6	-5	-1	-0.6
	Yr	7	8	.467	23	18	2	1	0	121	110	59	18	2	38	67	11.2	3.72	95	.243	.305	9	.214	2	-3	-3	-1	-0.3
1990	Phi-N	8	3	.727	42	13	2	1	1	141^2	132	61	13	2	54	58	11.9	3.56	108	.250	.322	13	.310	4	4	4	-0	0.7
	LA-N	1	1	.500	5	3	0	0	0	14^1	23	13	7	0	2	6	15.7	7.53	49	.365	.385	2	.286	1	-6	-6	0	-0.7
	Yr	9	4	.692	47	16	2	1	1	156	155	74	20	2	56	64	12.3	3.92	97	.262	.328	15	.306	5	-2	-2	-0	0.0
1991	LA-N	1	0	1.000	20	1	0	0	0	17^2	12	3	0	0	7	8	9.7	0.51	706	.203	.288	0	.000	-0	6	6	0	0.3
1992	Cle-A	5	7	.417	32	25	1	0	0	158	156	79	29	2	50	96	11.8	3.82	103	.255	.314	0	—	0	2	2	-2	-0.1
1993	Cle-A	5	5	.500	25	6	0	0	0	54	62	36	9	2	16	34	13.3	5.67	77	.295	.351	0	—	0	-8	-8	-1	-1.3
1994	Chi-A	3	1	.750	38	0	0	0	0	33	29	17	4	0	14	26	11.7	3.55	132	.230	.307	0	—	0	5	4	-0	0.4
1995	Cle-A	0	0	—	11	0	0	0	0	12^2	16	9	3	1	10	13	19.2	6.39	73	.320	.443	0	—	0	-2	-2	0	-0.1
	Tex-A	0	2	.000	35	1	0	0	2	45	47	23	6	1	16	40	12.8	4.00	121	.280	.346	0	—	0	4	4	-1	0.1
	Yr	0	2	.000	46	1	0	0	2	57^2	63	32	9	2	26	53	14.2	4.53	106	.289	.370	0	—	0	1	2	-1	0.0
1996	*Tex-A	5	2	.714	60	0	0	0	0	70^1	53	34	2	7	35	64	12.2	4.09	128	.214	.328	0	—	0	7	9	-1	0.6
1997	*Fla-N	1	2	.333	59	0	0	0	0	62^1	64	28	4	2	28	63	13.6	3.90	103	.267	.348	5	.556	3	2	1	0	0.4
1998	NY-N	8	4	.667	73	0	0	0	1	68	60	21	5	3	27	79	11.9	2.38	174	.240	.321	0	.000	-0	14	14	0	2.2
1999	*NY-N	10	5	.667	71	0	0	0	3	63	50	27	11	1	27	68	11.1	3.86	114	.216	.301	0	.000	-0	5	4	0	0.7
2000	*NY-N	6	3	.667	68	0	0	0	2	59	63	35	8	5	31	53	15.1	5.34	83	.270	.368	0	—	0	-5	-6	1	-0.8
Total	13	62	44	.585	566	71	6	3	9	942	886	453	120	28	366	688	12.2	3.90	106	.250	.325	29	.266	9	26	23	-4	2.2
● EARL COOK	Cook, Earl Davis b: 12/10/08, Stouffville, Ont., Canada d: 11/21/96, Markham, Ont., Canada BR/TR, 6′, 195 lbs. Deb: 9/12/41																											
1941	Det-A	0	0	—	1	0	0	0	0	2	4	1	0	0	0	1	18.0	4.50	101	.400	.400	0	—	0	-0	0	-0	0.0
● GLEN COOK	Cook, Glen Patrick b: 9/8/59, Buffalo, N.Y. BR/TR, 5′11″, 180 lbs. Deb: 6/23/85																											
1985	Tex-A	2	3	.400	9	7	0	0	0	40	53	42	12	3	18	19	16.6	9.45	45	.327	.404	0	—	0	-24	-23	-1	-2.3
● MIKE COOK	Cook, Michael Horace b: 8/14/63, Charleston, S.C. BR/TR, 6′3″, 200 lbs. Deb: 7/1/86																											
1986	Cal-A	0	2	.000	5	1	0	0	0	9	13	12	3	0	7	6	20.0	9.00	46	.333	.435	0	—	0	-5	-5	0	-0.9
1987	Cal-A	1	2	.333	16	1	0	0	0	34^1	34	21	7	0	18	27	13.6	5.50	78	.264	.354	0	—	0	-4	-5	1	-0.3
1988	Cal-A	0	1	.000	3	0	0	0	0	3^2	4	2	0	1	1	2	14.7	4.91	79	.308	.400	0	—	0	-0	-0	-0	-0.1
1989	Min-A	0	1	.000	15	0	0	0	0	21^1	22	12	1	1	17	15	16.9	5.06	82	.268	.400	0	—	0	-3	-2	-1	-0.2
1993	Bal-A	0	0	—	2	0	0	0	0	3	1	0	0	0	2	3	9.0	0.00	—	.091	.231	0	—	0	1	1	-0	0.1
Total	5	1	6	.143	41	2	0	0	0	71^1	74	47	11	2	45	53	15.3	5.55	76	.270	.377	0	—	0	-10	-10	0	-1.4
● ROLLIN COOK	Cook, Rollin Edward b: 10/5/1890, Toledo, Ohio d: 8/11/75, Toledo, Ohio BR/TR, 5′9″, 152 lbs. Deb: 7/6/15																											
1915	StL-A	0	0	—	5	0	0	0	0	13^2	16	14	0	1	9	7	17.1	7.24	40	.276	.382	1	.250	0	-7	-7	0	-0.3
● RON COOK	Cook, Ronald Wayne b: 7/11/47, Jefferson, Tex. BL/TL, 6′1″, 175 lbs. Deb: 4/10/70																											
1970	Hou-N	4	4	.500	41	7	0	0	2	82^1	80	37	4	3	42	50	13.7	3.72	104	.274	.371	4	.235	2	3	2	-0	0.3
1971	Hou-N	0	4	.000	5	4	0	0	0	25^2	23	14	2	1	8	10	11.2	4.91	69	.237	.302	2	.250	0	-4	-5	0	-0.6
Total	2	4	8	.333	46	11	0	0	2	108	103	51	6	4	50	60	13.1	4.00	94	.265	.354	6	.240	2	-1	-3	-0	-0.3
● STEVE COOKE	Cooke, Steven Montague b: 1/14/70, Lihue, Hawaii BR/TL, 6′6″, 229 lbs. Deb: 7/28/92																											
1992	Pit-N	2	0	1.000	11	0	0	0	1	23	22	9	2	0	4	10	10.2	3.52	98	.253	.286	1	.333	0	-0	-0	-0	0.0
1993	Pit-N	10	10	.500	32	32	3	1	0	210^2	207	101	22	3	59	132	11.5	3.89	104	.258	.312	11	.155	-1	4	4	-2	0.1
1994	Pit-N	4	11	.267	25	23	2	0	0	134^1	157	79	21	5	46	74	13.9	5.02	86	.298	.360	8	.190	0	-12	-10	-1	-1.1
1996	Pit-N	0	0	—	3	0	0	0	0	8^1	11	7	1	0	5	7	17.3	7.56	58	.314	.400	0	.000	-0	-3	-3	-0	-0.2

YEAR TM/L	W	L	PCT	G	GS	CG	SH	SV	IP	H	R	HR	HB	BB	SO	RAT	ERA	ERA+	OAV	OOB	BH	AVG	PB	PR	PR+	PD	TPI
1997 Pit-N	9	15	.375	32	32	0	0	0	167^1	184	95	15	9	77	109	14.5	4.30	100	.284	.368	3	.058	-4	-2	-0	1	-0.3
1998 Cin-N	1	0	1.000	1	1	0	0	0	6	4	1	0	1	0	3	7.5	1.50	286	.182	.217	1	.500	0	2	2	0	0.4
Total 6	26	36	.419	104	88	5	1	1	549^2	585	292	61	18	191	335	13.0	4.31	97	.276	.341	24	.140	-3	-11	-8	-4	-1.1
● DANNY COOMBS	Coombs, Daniel Bernard b: 3/23/42, Lincoln, Me. BR/TL, 6'5", 210 lbs. Deb: 9/27/63																										
1963 Hou-N	0	0	—	1	0	0	0	0	0^1	3	1	0	0	0	0	81.0	27.00	12	.750	.750	0	—	0	-1	-1	0	0.0
1964 Hou-N	1	1	.500	7	1	0	0	0	18	21	10	1	1	10	14	16.0	5.00	68	.300	.395	0	.000	-0	-3	-3	-0	-0.4
1965 Hou-N	0	2	.000	26	3	0	0	0	47	54	26	3	3	23	35	15.3	4.79	70	.292	.379	1	.111	0	-7	-8	1	-0.3
1966 Hou-N	0	0	—	2	0	0	0	0	2^2	4	1	0	0	0	3	13.5	3.38	101	.333	.333	0	.000	-0	0	-0	-0	0.0
1967 Hou-N	3	0	1.000	6	2	0	0	0	24^1	21	9	0	0	9	23	11.1	3.33	99	.233	.303	1	.125	0	0	-0	0	0.0
1968 Hou-N	4	3	.571	40	2	0	0	2	46^2	52	21	0	1	17	29	13.5	3.28	90	.286	.350	4	.400	1	-2	-2	1	-0.1
1969 Hou-N	0	1	.000	8	0	0	0	0	8	12	6	0	1	2	3	16.9	6.75	52	.364	.417	0	.000	-0	-3	-3	-0	-0.4
1970 SD-N	10	14	.417	35	27	5	1	0	188^1	185	83	12	2	76	105	12.6	3.30	121	.256	.329	5	.096	-2	16	15	-2	1.3
1971 SD-N	1	6	.143	19	7	0	0	0	57^2	81	52	10	0	25	37	16.5	6.24	53	.327	.388	3	.214	1	-18	-20	1	-2.0
Total 9	19	27	.413	144	42	5	1	2	393	433	209	26	8	162	249	13.8	4.08	88	.280	.351	14	.140	-0	-16	-21	0	-1.9
● JACK COOMBS	Coombs, John Wesley "Colby Jack" b: 11/18/1882, LeGrand, Iowa d: 4/15/57, Palestine, Tex. BB/TR, 6', 185 lbs. Deb: 7/5/06 MC◆																										
1906 Phi-A	10	10	.500	23	18	13	1	0	173	144	65	0	7	68	90	11.4	2.50	109	.229	.312	16	.239	1	4	4	-0	0.6
1907 Phi-A	6	9	.400	23	17	10	2	2	132^2	109	58	2	9	64	73	12.3	3.12	83	.227	.329	8	.167	-1	-8	-7	0	-1.0
1908 Phi-A	7	5	.583	26	18	10	4	0	153	130	63	1	3	64	80	11.6	2.00	128	.233	.316	56	.255	4	7	9	0	1.1
1909 Phi-A	12	11	.522	30	24	18	6	1	205^2	156	63	1	6	73	97	10.3	2.32	104	.213	.289	14	.169	1	4	2	-0	0.3
1910 *Phi-A	**31**	9	.775	**45**	38	35	**13**	1	353	248	74	0	7	115	224	9.4	1.30	183	.201	.273	29	.220	4	48	45	-5	5.2
1911 *Phi-A	**28**	12	.700	47	40	26	1	2	336^2	360	166	8	16	119	185	13.2	3.53	89	.280	.348	45	.319	14	-7	-15	-3	-0.6
1912 Phi-A	21	10	.677	40	32	23	1	2	262^1	227	120	5	10	94	120	11.4	3.29	93	.241	.316	28	.255	6	1	-7	-1	-0.1
1913 Phi-A	0	0	—	2	2	0	0	0	5^1	5	9	0	1	6	0	20.3	10.13	27	.250	.444	1	.333	1	-4	-5	-0	-0.2
1914 Phi-A	0	1	.000	2	2	0	0	0	8	8	4	0	1	3	1	13.5	4.50	58	.267	.353	3	.273	0	-2	-2	-0	-0.2
1915 Bro-N	15	10	.600	29	24	17	2	0	195^2	166	71	1	16	91	56	12.6	2.58	108	.236	.337	21	.280	4	4	4	-4	0.6
1916 *Bro-N	13	8	.619	27	20	10	3	0	159	136	54	3	2	44	47	10.3	2.66	101	.239	.296	11	.180	-0	-1	0	-6	-0.6
1917 Bro-N	7	11	.389	31	14	9	0	0	141	147	76	7	8	49	34	13.0	3.96	71	.284	.355	10	.227	2	-20	-18	-3	-2.3
1918 Bro-N	8	14	.364	27	20	16	2	0	189	191	97	10	2	49	44	11.5	3.81	73	.266	.315	19	.168	-0	-22	-21	-3	-2.7
1920 Det-A	0	0	—	2	0	0	0	0	5^2	7	5	0	0	2	1	14.3	3.18	117	.318	.375	0	.000	-0	0	0	-0	0.0
Total 14	158	110	.590	354	269	187	35	8	2320	2034	925	38	88	841	1052	11.5	2.78	99	.241	.316	261	.235	36	3	-8	-25	0.1
● BOBBY COOMBS	Coombs, Raymond Franklin b: 2/2/08, Goodwins Mills, Me. d: 10/21/91, Ogunquit, Me. BR/TR, 5'9.5", 160 lbs. Deb: 6/8/33																										
1933 Phi-A	0	1	.000	21	0	0	0	2	31^1	47	30	4	0	20	8	19.2	7.47	57	.348	.432	2	.400	1	-11	-11	-0	-0.4
1943 NY-N	0	1	.000	9	0	0	0	0	16	33	26	1	0	8	5	23.1	12.94	27	.423	.477	0	.000	0	-17	-17	0	-0.9
Total 2	0	2	.000	30	0	0	0	2	47^1	80	56	5	0	28	13	20.5	9.32	43	.376	.448	2	.286	1	-28	-28	-0	-1.3
● WILLIAM COON	Coon, William K. b: 3/21/1855, Pennsylvania d: 8/30/15, Burlington, N.J. Deb: 9/4/1875 ◆																										
1876 Phi-N	0	0	—	2	0	0	0	0	7	9	8	0		0	0	11.6	5.14	47	.257	.257	50	.225	-0	-2	-2	-0	-0.1
● JOHNNY COONEY	Cooney, John Walter b: 3/18/01, Cranston, R.I. d: 7/8/86, Sarasota, Fla. BR/TL, 5'10", 165 lbs. Deb: 4/19/21 FMC◆																										
1921 Bos-N	0	1	.000	8	1	0	0	0	20^2	19	12	3	0	10	9	12.6	3.92	93	.241	.326	1	.200	-0	-0	-1	0	0.0
1922 Bos-N	1	2	.333	4	3	1	0	0	25	19	10	0	1	6	7	9.4	2.16	185	.224	.283	0	.000	-1	5	5	0	0.5
1923 Bos-N	3	5	.375	23	8	5	2	0	98	92	43	3	3	22	23	10.7	3.31	121	.246	.293	25	.379	4	8	7	-2	0.8
1924 Bos-N	8	9	.471	34	19	12	2	2	181	176	79	4	4	50	67	11.4	3.18	120	.260	.314	33	.254	2	14	13	-1	1.2
1925 Bos-N	14	14	.500	31	29	20	2	0	245^2	267	123	18	3	50	65	11.7	3.48	115	.274	.312	33	.320	5	22	15	1	2.5
1926 Bos-N	3	3	.500	19	8	3	1	0	83^1	106	52	0	7	29	23	15.3	4.00	89	.320	.387	38	.302	3	-2	-4	0	0.1
1928 Bos-N	3	7	.300	24	5	2	0	1	89^2	106	47	7	0	31	18	13.8	4.32	91	.303	.360	7	.171	-0	-3	-4	3	-0.1
1929 Bos-N	2	3	.400	14	2	1	0	3	45	57	29	4	0	22	11	15.8	5.00	94	.315	.389	23	.319	2	-1	-2	1	0.1
1930 Bos-N	0	0	—	2	0	0	0	0	7	16	14	2	1	3	1	25.7	18.00	27	.471	.526	0	.000	-1	-10	-10	-1	-0.4
Total 9	34	44	.436	159	75	44	7	6	795^1	858	409	41	19	223	224	12.4	3.72	106	.278	.331	965	.286	15	32	20	4	4.7
● BOB COONEY	Cooney, Robert Daniel b: 7/12/07, Glens Falls, N.Y. d: 5/4/76, Glens Falls, N.Y. BR/TR, 5'11", 160 lbs. Deb: 9/6/31																										
1931 StL-A	0	3	.000	5	4	1	0	0	39^1	46	21	1	1	20	13	15.3	4.12	113	.291	.374	5	.385	1	1	2	-0	0.2
1932 StL-A	1	2	.333	23	3	1	0	1	71	94	61	8	2	36	23	16.7	6.97	70	.324	.402	0	.000	-3	-20	-15	-2	-1.1
Total 2	1	5	.167	28	7	2	0	1	110^1	140	82	9	3	56	36	16.2	5.95	80	.313	.393	5	.143	-2	-19	-13	-2	-0.9
● BILL COONEY	Cooney, William A. "Cush" b: 4/7/1883, Boston, Mass. d: 11/6/28, Roxbury, Mass. TR, Deb: 9/22/09 ◆																										
1909 Bos-N	0	0	—	3	0	0	0	0	6^1	4	2	0	0	2	3	8.5	1.42	198	.182	.250	3	.300	0	1	1	-0	0.0
● WILBUR COOPER	Cooper, Arley Wilbur b: 2/24/1892, Bearsville, W.Va. d: 8/7/73, Encino, Cal. BR/TL, 5'11", 175 lbs. Deb: 8/29/12																										
1912 Pit-N	3	0	1.000	6	4	3	2	0	38	32	7	1	0	15	30	11.1	1.66	197	.227	.301	2	.154	-0	7	7	-0	0.5
1913 Pit-N	5	3	.625	30	9	3	1	0	93	98	52	0	2	45	39	14.0	3.29	92	.276	.361	2	.077	-1	-1	-3	-2	-0.6
1914 Pit-N	16	15	.516	40	34	19	0	0	266^2	246	99	4	5	79	102	11.1	2.13	125	.254	.313	19	.207	1	20	16	0	2.1
1915 Pit-N	5	16	.238	38	20	11	1	4	185^2	180	92	4	9	52	71	11.7	3.30	83	.262	.323	7	.117	-3	-11	-12	1	-1.6
1916 Pit-N	12	11	.522	42	23	16	2	2	246	189	72	4	4	74	111	9.8	1.87	144	.215	.279	17	.215	0	21	22	-1	2.2
1917 Pit-N	17	11	.607	40	34	23	7	1	297^2	276	96	4	4	54	99	10.1	2.36	120	.258	.297	21	.204	2	12	15	-3	1.4
1918 Pit-N	19	14	.576	38	29	26	2	**3**	273^1	219	86	2	10	65	117	9.7	2.11	136	.223	.279	23	.242	3	20	22	-2	3.0
1919 Pit-N	19	13	.594	35	32	**27**	4	1	286^2	229	97	10	15	74	106	10.0	2.67	113	.225	.287	29	.287	6	8	11	-5	1.3
1920 Pit-N	24	15	.615	44	37	28	3	2	327	307	113	4	11	52	114	10.2	2.39	134	.253	.290	25	.221	1	27	29	-3	3.2
1921 Pit-N	**22**	14	.611	38	38	29	2	0	**327**	341	145	9	10	80	134	11.9	3.25	118	.272	.320	31	.254	4	19	21	-3	2.2
1922 Pit-N	23	14	.622	41	36	**27**	4	0	294^2	330	130	13	7	61	129	12.2	3.18	128	.286	.326	29	.269	9	**30**	**30**	-2	**4.1**
1923 Pit-N	17	19	.472	39	38	26	1	0	294^2	331	136	11	11	71	77	12.6	3.57	112	.288	.335	28	.262	4	14	14	-1	1.7
1924 Pit-N	20	14	.588	38	35	25	**4**	1	268^2	296	116	13	5	40	62	11.4	3.28	117	.283	.313	36	.346	10	17	17	-4	2.5
1925 Chi-N	12	14	.462	32	26	13	0	0	212^1	249	115	18	4	61	41	13.3	4.28	101	.291	.341	17	.207	1	-0	1	-2	-0.1
1926 Chi-N	2	1	.667	8	8	3	2	0	55	65	32	6	0	21	18	14.1	4.42	87	.311	.374	7	.389	3	-4	-3	-1	0.0
Det-A	0	4	.000	8	3	0	0	0	13^2	27	18	0	3	9	2	25.7	11.20	36	.443	.534	0	.000	-1	-11	-11	0	-1.9
Total 15	216	178	.548	517	406	279	35	14	3480	3415	1406	103	100	853	1252	11.3	2.89	116	.262	.312	293	.239	39	168	178	-27	20.0
● BRIAN COOPER	Cooper, Brian John b: 8/19/74, Hollywood, Cal. BR/TR, 6'1", 175 lbs. Deb: 9/7/99																										
1999 Ana-A	1	1	.500	5	5	0	0	0	27^2	23	15	3	4	18	15	14.6	4.88	100	.228	.366	0	—	0	-0	-0	1	0.0
2000 Ana-A	4	8	.333	15	15	1	1	0	87	105	66	18	2	35	36	14.7	5.90	84	.299	.366	0	.000	-0	-9	-9	-0	-1.0
Total 2	5	9	.357	20	20	1	1	0	114^2	128	81	21	6	53	51	14.7	5.65	87	.283	.366	0	.000	-0	-9	-9	0	-1.0
● CAL COOPER	Cooper, Calvin Asa b: 8/11/22, Great Falls, S.C. d: 7/4/94, Clinton, S.C. BR/TR, 6'2.5", 180 lbs. Deb: 9/14/48																										
1948 Was-A	0	0	—	1	0	0	0	0	1	5	5	1	0	1	0	54.0	45.00	10	.625	.667	0	—	0	-5	-4	-0	-0.2
● DON COOPER	Cooper, Donald James b: 1/15/57, New York, N.Y. BR/TR, 6'1", 185 lbs. Deb: 4/9/81																										
1981 Min-A	1	5	.167	27	2	0	0	0	58^2	61	33	9	1	32	33	14.4	4.30	92	.274	.367	0	—	0	-4	-2	-1	-0.3
1982 Min-A	0	1	.000	6	1	0	0	0	11^1	14	12	0	0	11	5	19.9	9.53	45	.311	.446	0	—	0	-7	-6	-0	-0.5
1983 Tor-A	0	0	—	4	0	0	0	0	5^1	8	4	3	0	0	5	13.5	6.75	64	.348	.348	0	—	0	-2	-1	-0	-0.1
1985 NY-A	0	0	—	7	0	0	0	0	10	12	6	2	0	3	4	13.5	5.40	74	.300	.349	0	—	0	-1	-2	-0	-0.1
Total 4	1	6	.143	44	3	0	0	0	85^1	95	55	14	1	46	47	15.0	5.27	76	.287	.376	0	—	0	-14	-11	-2	-1.0
● GUY COOPER	Cooper, Guy Evans "Rebel" b: 1/28/1893, Rome, Ga. d: 8/2/51, Santa Monica, Cal. BB/TR, 6'1", 185 lbs. Deb: 5/2/14																										
1914 NY-A	0	0	—	1	0	0	0	0	3	3	3	0	0	2	3	15.0	9.00	31	.273	.385	0	.000	-0	-2	-2	-0	-0.1
Bos-A	1	0	1.000	9	1	0	0	0	22	23	15	1	3	9	5	14.3	5.32	51	.299	.393	0	.000	-1	-6	-7	-1	-0.6
Yr	1	0	1.000	10	1	0	0	0	25	26	18	1	3	11	8	14.4	5.76	47	.295	.392	0	.000	-1	-8	-9	-1	-0.7
1915 Bos-A	0	0	—	1	0	0	0	0	2	0	0	0	0	2	0	9.0	0.00	—	.000	.286	0	—	0	1	1	-0	0.0
Total 2	1	0	1.000	11	1	0	0	0	27	26	18	1	3	13	8	14.0	5.33	51	.280	.385	0	.000	-1	-8	-8	-1	-0.7

● **MORT COOPER** Cooper, Morton Cecil b: 3/2/13, Atherton, Mo. d: 11/17/58, Little Rock, Ark. BR/TR, 6'2", 210 lbs. Deb: 9/14/38 F

YEAR	TM/L	W	L	PCT	G	GS	CG	SH	SV	IP	H	R	HR	HB	BB	SO	RAT	ERA	ERA+	OAV	OOB	BH	AVG	PB	PR	PR+	PD	TPI
1938	StL-N	2	1	.667	4	3	1	0	1	23^2	17	11	1	1	12	11	11.4	3.04	130	.195	.300	2	.222	0	2	2	1	0.4
1939	StL-N	12	6	.667	45	26	7	2	4	210^2	208	94	6	2	97	130	13.1	3.25	127	.260	.342	16	.232	3	16	19	-3	1.6
1940	StL-N	11	12	.478	38	29	16	3	3	230^2	225	103	12	3	86	95	12.3	3.63	110	.253	.321	13	.157	-2	6	9	-2	0.3
1941	StL-N	13	9	.591	29	25	12	0	0	186^2	175	88	15	3	69	118	11.9	3.91	96	.244	.313	13	.186	-0	-6	-3	-1	-0.5
1942	*StL-N★	**22**	7	.759	37	35	22	**10**	0	278^2	207	73	9	5	68	152	**9.0**	**1.78**	**193**	**.204**	**.258**	19	.184	-1	**48**	**49**	-3	**4.9**
1943	*StL-N★	**21**	8	**.724**	37	32	24	6	3	274	228	81	5	5	79	141	10.2	2.30	146	.226	.286	17	.170	-1	33	33	-2	3.2
1944	*StL-N	22	7	.759	34	33	22	**7**	1	252^1	227	74	6	5	60	97	10.4	2.46	143	.239	.288	19	.202	2	32	31	-5	3.1
1945	StL-N	2	0	1.000	4	3	1	0	1	23^2	20	7	1	1	7	14	10.6	1.52	246	.227	.292	2	.333	1	6	6	-1	0.5
	Bos-N†	7	4	.636	20	11	4	1	1	78	77	35	4	1	27	45	12.1	3.35	115	.257	.320	6	.231	1	4	4	0	0.7
	Yr	9	4	.692	24	14	5	1	1	101^2	97	42	5	2	34	59	11.8	2.92	130	.250	.314	8	.250	2	10	10	-0	1.2
1946	Bos-N☆	13	11	.542	28	27	15	4	1	199	181	76	16	0	39	83	**9.9**	3.12	110	.239	**.276**	14	.209	1	6	7	-3	0.6
1947	Bos-N	2	5	.286	10	7	2	0	0	46^2	48	26	2	2	13	15	12.2	4.05	96	.271	.328	0	.000	-1	0	-1	-1	-0.3
	NY-N	1	5	.167	8	8	2	0	0	36^2	51	32	7	0	13	12	15.7	7.12	57	.323	.374	6	.429	4	-12	-12	-1	-1.4
	Yr	3	10	.231	18	15	4	0	0	83^1	99	58	9	2	26	27	13.7	5.40	74	.296	.350	6	.222	2	-12	-14	-2	-1.7
1949	Chi-N	0	0	—	1	0	0	0	0	0	2	1	0	1	—	—	∞	—	1.000	1.000	100	—	0	-3	-3	0		-0.3
Total	11	128	75	.631	295	239	128	33	14	1840^2	1666	703	85	28	571	913	11.1	2.97	123	.240	.300	127	.194	6	132	141	-20	12.8

● **PAT COOPER** Cooper, Orge Patterson b: 11/26/17, Albemarle, N.C. d: 3/15/93, Charlotte, N.C. BR/TR, 6'3", 180 lbs. Deb: 5/11/46 ♦

YEAR	TM/L	W	L	PCT	G	GS	CG	SH	SV	IP	H	R	HR	HB	BB	SO	RAT	ERA	ERA+	OAV	OOB	BH	AVG	PB	PR	PR+	PD	TPI
1946	Phi-A	0	0	—	1	0	0	0	0	1	1	0	0	0	1	0	18.0	0.00	—	.250	.400	0	—	0	0	0	-0	0.0

● **MAYS COPELAND** Copeland, Mays b: 8/31/13, Mountain View, Ark d: 11/29/82, Indio, Cal. BR/TR, 6', 180 lbs. Deb: 4/27/35

YEAR	TM/L	W	L	PCT	G	GS	CG	SH	SV	IP	H	R	HR	HB	BB	SO	RAT	ERA	ERA+	OAV	OOB	BH	AVG	PB	PR	PR+	PD	TPI
1935	StL-N	0	0	—	1	0	0	0	0	0^2	2	1	0	0	0	0	27.0	13.50	30	.667	.667	0	—	0	-1	-1	0	0.0

● **ROCKY COPPINGER** Coppinger, John Thomas b: 3/19/74, ElPaso, Tex. BR/TR, 6'5", 245 lbs. Deb: 6/11/96

YEAR	TM/L	W	L	PCT	G	GS	CG	SH	SV	IP	H	R	HR	HB	BB	SO	RAT	ERA	ERA+	OAV	OOB	BH	AVG	PB	PR	PR+	PD	TPI
1996	*Bal-A†	10	6	.625	23	22	0	0	0	125	126	76	25	2	60	104	13.5	5.18	95	.263	.348	0	—	0	-3	-4	-2	-0.5
1997	Bal-A	1	1	.500	5	4	0	0	0	20	21	14	2	1	16	22	17.1	6.30	70	.273	.404	0	—	0	-4	-4	-0	-0.4
1998	Bal-A	0	0	—	6	1	0	0	0	15^2	16	9	3	0	7	13	13.2	5.17	88	.246	.319	0	—	0	-1	-1	-0	-0.1
1999	Bal-A	0	1	.000	11	2	0	0	0	21^2	25	21	8	0	19	17	18.3	8.31	57	.294	.423	1	1.000	0	-8	-9	-0	-0.4
	Mil-N	5	3	.625	29	0	0	0	0	36^2	35	16	5	0	23	39	14.2	3.68	123	.250	.356	0	.000	-0	4	4	-1	0.5
Total	4	16	11	.593	74	29	0	0	0	219	223	136	43	3	125	195	14.4	5.34	89	.264	.360	1	.333	0	-12	-14	-3	-0.9

● **HENRY COPPOLA** Coppola, Henry Peter b: 8/4/12, E.Douglas, Mass. d: 7/10/90, Norfolk, Mass. BR/TR, 5'11", 175 lbs. Deb: 4/19/35

YEAR	TM/L	W	L	PCT	G	GS	CG	SH	SV	IP	H	R	HR	HB	BB	SO	RAT	ERA	ERA+	OAV	OOB	BH	AVG	PB	PR	PR+	PD	TPI
1935	Was-A	3	4	.429	19	5	2	1	0	59^1	72	40	6	1	29	19	15.5	5.92	73	.300	.378	1	.071	-0	-10	-11	-0	-1.1
1936	Was-A	0	0	—	6	0	0	0	1	14	17	9	1	0	12	2	18.6	4.50	106	.315	.439	1	.333	1	1	0	0	0.1
Total	2	3	4	.429	25	5	2	1	1	73^1	89	49	7	1	41	21	16.1	5.65	78	.303	.390	2	.118	0	-9	-10	0	-1.0

● **DOUG CORBETT** Corbett, Douglas Mitchell b: 11/4/52, Sarasota, Fla. BR/TR, 6'1", 185 lbs. Deb: 4/10/80

YEAR	TM/L	W	L	PCT	G	GS	CG	SH	SV	IP	H	R	HR	HB	BB	SO	RAT	ERA	ERA+	OAV	OOB	BH	AVG	PB	PR	PR+	PD	TPI
1980	Min-A	8	6	.571	73	0	0	0	23	136^1	102	31	7	1	42	89	9.6	1.98	221	.213	.278	0	—	0	**31**	**33**	3	4.8
1981	Min-A☆	2	6	.250	**54**	0	0	0	17	87^2	80	29	5	0	34	60	11.7	2.57	154	.239	.309	0	—	0	11	13	2	1.9
1982	Min-A	0	2	.000	10	0	0	0	3	22	27	13	3	0	10	15	15.1	5.32	80	.300	.370	0	—	0	-3	-3	1	-0.2
	Cal-A	1	7	.125	33	0	0	0	8	57	46	32	8	0	25	37	11.2	5.05	80	.223	.307	0	—	0	-6	-6	0	-0.9
	Yr	1	9	.100	43	0	0	0	11	79	73	45	11	0	35	52	12.3	5.13	80	.247	.326	0	—	0	-9	-9	1	-1.1
1983	Cal-A	1	1	.500	11	0	0	0	0	17^1	26	10	1	1	4	18	16.1	3.63	111	.351	.392	0	—	0	1	1	-0	0.1
1984	Cal-A	5	1	.833	45	1	0	0	4	85	76	22	2	2	30	48	11.4	2.12	188	.244	.314	0	—	0	18	18	0	1.3
1985	Cal-A	3	3	.500	30	0	0	0	0	46	49	33	7	1	20	24	13.7	4.89	84	.274	.350	0	—	0	-4	-4	0	-0.4
1986	*Cal-A	4	2	.667	46	0	0	0	10	78^2	66	36	11	1	22	36	10.2	3.66	112	.231	.288	0	—	0	5	4	1	0.5
1987	Bal-A	0	2	.000	11	0	0	0	1	23	25	20	5	0	13	16	14.9	7.83	56	.281	.373	0	—	0	-9	-9	1	-0.7
Total	8	24	30	.444	313	1	0	0	66	553	497	226	49	6	200	343	11.4	3.32	125	.242	.312	0	—	0	44	49	8	6.4

● **JOE CORBETT** Corbett, Joseph A. b: 12/4/1875, San Francisco, Cal. d: 5/2/45, San Francisco, Cal. BR/TR, 5'10", Deb: 8/23/1895

YEAR	TM/L	W	L	PCT	G	GS	CG	SH	SV	IP	H	R	HR	HB	BB	SO	RAT	ERA	ERA+	OAV	OOB	BH	AVG	PB	PR	PR+	PD	TPI
1895	Was-N	0	2	.000	3	3	3	0	0	19	26	22	3	2	9	3	17.5	5.68	84	.321	.402	2	.133	-1	-2	-2	0	-0.2
1896	*Bal-N	3	0	1.000	8	3	3	0	1	41	31	17	0	5	17	28	11.6	2.20	195	.208	.310	6	.273	1	10	10	-1	0.6
1897	*Bal-N	24	8	.750	37	37	34	1	0	313	330	173	2	21	115	149	13.4	3.11	134	.269	.341	37	.247	-0	42	38	2	3.2
1904	StL-N	5	8	.385	14	14	12	0	0	108^2	110	75	2	8	51	68	14.0	4.39	61	.240	.327	9	.209	1	-20	-21	0	-2.0
Total	4	32	18	.640	62	57	52	1	1	481^2	497	287	7	36	192	248	13.5	3.42	113	.259	.338	54	.235	1	30	25	2	1.6

● **SHERMAN CORBETT** Corbett, Sherman Stanley b: 11/3/62, New Braunfels, Tex. BL/TL, 6'4", 205 lbs. Deb: 5/29/88

YEAR	TM/L	W	L	PCT	G	GS	CG	SH	SV	IP	H	R	HR	HB	BB	SO	RAT	ERA	ERA+	OAV	OOB	BH	AVG	PB	PR	PR+	PD	TPI
1988	Cal-A	2	1	.667	34	0	0	0	1	45^2	47	23	2	0	23	28	13.8	4.14	93	.273	.359	0	—	0	-1	-1	-0	-0.1
1989	Cal-A	0	0	—	4	0	0	0	0	5^1	3	2	1	0	1	3	6.8	3.38	113	.158	.200	0	—	0	0	0	-0	0.0
1990	Cal-A	0	0	—	4	0	0	0	0	5	8	5	0	0	3	2	19.8	9.00	43	.364	.440	0	—	0	-3	-3	-0	-0.2
Total	3	2	1	.667	42	0	0	0	1	56	58	30	3	0	27	33	13.7	4.50	86	.272	.354	0	—	0	-3	-4	-1	-0.3

● **RAY CORBIN** Corbin, Alton Ray b: 2/12/49, Live Oak, Fla. BR/TR, 6'2", 200 lbs. Deb: 4/6/71

YEAR	TM/L	W	L	PCT	G	GS	CG	SH	SV	IP	H	R	HR	HB	BB	SO	RAT	ERA	ERA+	OAV	OOB	BH	AVG	PB	PR	PR+	PD	TPI
1971	Min-A	8	11	.421	52	11	2	0	3	140^1	141	74	19	3	70	83	13.7	4.10	87	.265	.353	7	.206	1	-10	-8	1	-0.9
1972	Min-A	8	9	.471	31	19	5	3	0	161^2	135	56	12	6	53	83	10.8	2.62	123	.230	.300	4	.082	-2	8	10	-2	0.6
1973	Min-A	8	5	.615	51	7	1	0	14	148^1	124	58	7	5	60	83	11.5	3.03	131	.229	.311	0	—	0	13	15	-1	1.4
1974	Min-A	7	6	.538	29	15	1	0	0	112^1	133	78	8	3	40	50	14.1	5.29	71	.294	.356	0	—	0	-21	-19	1	-1.9
1975	Min-A	5	7	.417	18	11	3	0	0	89^2	105	59	13	2	38	49	14.6	5.12	75	.295	.366	0	—	0	-13	-13	1	-1.4
Total	5	36	38	.486	181	63	12	3	17	652^1	638	325	59	19	261	348	12.7	3.84	95	.258	.334	11	.133	-2	-23	-14	-0	-2.2

● **ARCHIE CORBIN** Corbin, Archie Ray b: 12/30/67, Beaumont, Tex. BR/TR, 6'4", 190 lbs. Deb: 9/10/91

YEAR	TM/L	W	L	PCT	G	GS	CG	SH	SV	IP	H	R	HR	HB	BB	SO	RAT	ERA	ERA+	OAV	OOB	BH	AVG	PB	PR	PR+	PD	TPI
1991	KC-A	0	0	—	2	0	0	0	0	2^1	3	1	0	0	2	1	19.3	3.86	107	.300	.417	0	—	0	0	0	-0	0.0
1996	Bal-A	2	0	1.000	18	0	0	0	0	27^1	22	7	2	1	22	20	14.8	2.30	214	.222	.369	0	—	0	8	8	-1	0.4
1999	Fla-N	0	1	.000	17	0	0	0	0	21	25	20	2	1	15	30	17.6	7.29	60	.291	.402	0	.000	-0	-6	-7	-0	-0.4
Total	3	2	1	.667	37	0	0	0	0	50^2	50	28	4	2	39	51	16.2	4.44	105	.256	.386	0	.000	-0	2	1	-1	0.0

● **JACK CORCORAN** Corcoran, John H. b: 1860, Lowell, Mass. Deb: 5/1/1884 ♦

YEAR	TM/L	W	L	PCT	G	GS	CG	SH	SV	IP	H	R	HR	HB	BB	SO	RAT	ERA	ERA+	OAV	OOB	BH	AVG	PB	PR	PR+	PD	TPI
1884	Bro-a	0	0	—	1	0	0	0	0	1	0	0	0	0	1	0	9.0	0.00	—	.000	.091	39	.211	0	0	0	-0	0.0

● **LARRY CORCORAN** Corcoran, Lawrence J. b: 8/10/1859, Brooklyn, N.Y. d: 10/14/1891, Newark, N.J. BL/TR (TB 1884 (part)), 120 lbs. Deb: 5/1/1880 F♦

YEAR	TM/L	W	L	PCT	G	GS	CG	SH	SV	IP	H	R	HR	HB	BB	SO	RAT	ERA	ERA+	OAV	OOB	BH	AVG	PB	PR	PR+	PD	TPI
1880	Chi-N	43	14	.754	63	60	57	4	2	536^1	404	218	6		99	**268**	8.4	1.95	124	.199	.236	66	.231	-0	25	28	6	3.1
1881	Chi-N	**31**	14	.689	45	44	43	4	0	396^2	380	204	10		78	150	10.4	2.31	118	.242	.278	42	.222	-1	20	19	-2	1.4
1882	Chi-N	27	12	**.692**	39	39	38	3	0	355^2	281	153	5		63	170	**8.7**	**1.95**	**147**	**.200**	**.234**	35	.207	-2	38	37	1	3.2
1883	Chi-N	34	20	.630	56	53	51	3	0	473^2	483	281	7		82	216	10.7	2.49	132	.247	.277	55	.209	-2	34	41	1	3.6
1884	Chi-N	35	23	.603	60	59	57	7	0	516^2	473	286	35		116	272	10.3	2.40	130	.229	.270	61	.243	2	33	40	7	4.4
1885	Chi-N	5	2	.714	7	7	6	1	0	59^1	63	38	2		24	10	13.2	3.64	83	.259	.326	6	.273	2	-5	-4	-0	-0.2
	NY-N	2	1	.667	3	3	2	0	0	25	24	12	1		11	10	12.6	2.88	93	.245	.321	5	.357	1	-0	-1	1	0.1
	Yr	7	3	.700	10	10	8	1	0	84^1	87	50	3		35	20	13.0	3.42	85	.255	.324	11	.306	3	-6	-5	1	-0.1
1886	Was-N	0	1	.000	2	1	1	0	0	14	16	11	0		4	3	12.9	5.79	57	.271	.317	15	.185	0	-4	-4	-0	-0.2
1887	Ind-N	0	2	.000	2	2	1	0	0	15	42	31	3	2	19	4	26.4	12.60	33	.483	.494	4	.333	-0	-14	-14	0	-1.1
Total	8	177	89	.665	277	268	256	22	2	2392^1	2166	1234	69	2	496	1103	10.0	2.36	123	.227	.264	289	.224	-0	127	141	14	14.3

● **MIKE CORCORAN** Corcoran, Michael b: Brooklyn, N.Y. Deb: 7/15/1884 F

YEAR	TM/L	W	L	PCT	G	GS	CG	SH	SV	IP	H	R	HR	HB	BB	SO	RAT	ERA	ERA+	OAV	OOB	BH	AVG	PB	PR	PR+	PD	TPI
1884	Chi-N	0	1	.000	1	1	1	0	0	9	16	14	1		7	2	23.0	4.00	78	.372	.460	0	.000	-0	-1	-1	-0	-0.1

● **FRANCISCO CORDERO** Cordero, Francisco Javier b: 8/11/77, Santo Domingo, D.R. BR/TR, 6'2", 200 lbs. Deb: 8/2/99

YEAR	TM/L	W	L	PCT	G	GS	CG	SH	SV	IP	H	R	HR	HB	BB	SO	RAT	ERA	ERA+	OAV	OOB	BH	AVG	PB	PR	PR+	PD	TPI
1999	Det-A	2	2	.500	20	0	0	0	0	19	19	7	2	0	18	19	17.5	3.32	147	.284	.435	0	—	0	3	3	1	0.7
2000	Tex-A	1	2	.333	56	0	0	0	0	77^1	87	51	11	4	48	49	16.2	5.35	95	.285	.389	0	—	0	-4	-2	-1	-0.2
Total	2	3	4	.429	76	0	0	0	0	96^1	106	58	13	4	66	68	16.4	4.95	102	.285	.398	0	—	0	-0	1	-0	0.5

YEAR TM/L	W	L	PCT	G	GS	CG	SH	SV	IP	H	R	HR	HB	BB	SO	RAT	ERA	ERA+	OAV	OOB	BH	AVG	PB	PR	PR+	PD	TPI
● FRANCISCO CORDOVA Cordova, Francisco b: 4/26/72, Veracruz, Mex. BR/TR, 5'11", 165 lbs. Deb: 4/2/96																											
1996 Pit-N	4	7	.364	59	6	0	0	12	99	103	49	11	2	20	95	11.4	4.09	107	.263	.303	2	.125	-1	1	3	1	0.3
1997 Pit-N	11	8	.579	29	29	2	2	0	178^2	175	80	14	9	49	121	11.7	3.63	118	.259	.317	5	.089	-2	11	13	2	1.2
1998 Pit-N	13	14	.481	33	33	3	2	0	220^1	204	91	22	3	69	157	11.3	3.31	130	.245	.305	9	.120	-2	23	24	-1	2.5
1999 Pit-N	8	10	.444	27	27	2	0	0	160^2	166	83	16	4	59	98	12.8	4.43	103	.273	.341	8	.163	-0	3	3	1	0.3
2000 Pit-N	6	8	.429	18	17	0	0	0	95	107	63	12	2	38	66	13.9	5.21	88	.285	.354	4	.114	-1	-6	-6	1	-0.8
Total 5	42	47	.472	166	112	7	4	12	753^2	755	366	75	20	235	537	12.1	3.96	111	.262	.322	28	.121	-6	32	36	4	3.5
● BRYAN COREY Corey, Bryan Scott b: 10/21/73, Thousand Oaks, Cal. BR/TR, 6'1", 170 lbs. Deb: 5/13/98																											
1998 Ari-N	0	0	—	3	0	0	0	0	4	6	4	1	1	2	1	20.3	9.00	47	.375	.474	0	—	0	-2	-2	0	-0.1
● ED COREY Corey, Edward Norman "Ike" (b: Abraham Simon Cohen) b: 7/13/1899, Chicago, Ill. d: 9/17/70, Kenosha, Wis. BR/TR, 6', 170 lbs. Deb: 7/2/18																											
1918 Chi-A	0	0	—	1	0	0	0	0	2	2	1	0	0	1	0	13.5	4.50	61	.333	.429	0	.000	-0	-0	-0	0	0.0
● FRED COREY Corey, Frederick Harrison b: 1857, S.Kingston, R.I. d: 11/27/12, Providence, R.I. BR/TR, Deb: 5/1/1878 ◆																											
1878 Pro-N	1	2	.333	5	5	2	0	0	23	22	10	0		7	7	11.3	2.35	94	.250	.305	3	.143	-1	-0	-0	-1	-0.2
1880 Wor-N	8	9	.471	25	17	9	2	2	148^1	131	72	6		16	47	8.9	2.43	107	.219	.239	24	.174	-3	-1	3	-3	-0.3
1881 Wor-N	6	15	.286	23	21	20	1	0	188^2	231	127	3		31	33	12.5	3.72	81	.299	.326	45	.222	-1	-20	-14	-1	-1.4
1882 Wor-N	1	13	.071	21	14	12	0	0	139	180	132	5		19	36	12.9	3.56	87	.286	.307	63	.247	0	-10	-6	1	-0.4
1883 Phi-a	10	7	.588	18	16	15	0	0	148^1	182	106	3		24	42	12.5	3.40	104	.283	.309	77	.258	2	-2	2	1	0.4
1885 Phi-a	1	0	1.000	1	1	1	0	0	9	18	9	2	0	1	3	19.0	7.00	49	.419	.432	94	.245	0	-4	-3	0	-0.2
Total 6	27	46	.370	93	74	59	3	2	656^1	764	456	19	0	98	168	11.8	3.32	92	.276	.300	427	.246	-3	-36	-19	-2	-2.1
● POP CORKHILL Corkhill, John Stewart b: 4/11/1858, Parkesburg, Pa. d: 4/3/21, Pennsauken, N.J. BL/TR, 5'10", 180 lbs. Deb: 5/1/1883 ◆																											
1884 Cin-a	1	0	1.000	1	0	0	0	0	5	1	1	0	0	2	4	5.4	1.80	185	.063	.167	124	.274	0	1	1	-0	0.1
1885 Cin-a	1	4	.200	8	1	0	0	1	37	36	25	2	1	10	12	11.4	3.65	89	.243	.296	111	.252	1	-2	-2	0	-0.1
1886 Cin-a	0	0	—	1	0	0	0	0	0^2	1	1	0	0	0	1	13.5	13.50	26	.125	.125	143	.265	0	-1	-1	0	0.0
1887 Cin-a	1	0	1.000	5	0	0	0	0	14^2	27	15	0	0	5	3	16.6	5.52	79	.370	.370	182	.328	1	-2	-2	-0	-0.1
1888 Cin-a	0	0	—	2	0	0	0	1	5	8	6	1	0	0	1	14.4	10.80	29	.348	.348	133	.271	0	-4	-4	-0	-0.2
Total 5	3	4	.429	17	1	0	0	2	62^1	73	48	3	1	17	21	12.4	4.62	76	.272	.306	1134	.257	3	-8	-8	-1	-0.3
● MIKE CORKINS Corkins, Michael Patrick b: 5/25/46, Riverside, Cal. BR/TR, 6'1", 200 lbs. Deb: 9/8/69																											
1969 SD-N	1	3	.250	6	4	0	0	0	17	27	17	3	0	8	13	18.5	8.47	42	.370	.432	0	.000	0	-9	-9	0	-1.7
1970 SD-N	5	6	.455	24	18	1	0	0	111	109	62	11	4	79	75	15.6	4.62	86	.258	.379	8	.216	2	-7	-8	-1	-0.6
1971 SD-N	0	0	—	8	0	0	0	0	13	14	6	1	0	6	16	13.8	3.46	95	.280	.357	0	—	0	0	-0	-0	0.0
1972 SD-N	6	9	.400	47	9	2	1	6	140	125	61	14	4	62	108	12.3	3.54	93	.240	.325	9	.237	3	-1	-4	0	-0.1
1973 SD-N	5	8	.385	47	11	2	0	3	122	130	79	12	11	61	82	14.9	4.50	77	.274	.370	7	.212	4	-11	-15	-2	-1.2
1974 SD-N	2	2	.500	25	2	0	0	0	56^1	53	32	5	1	32	41	13.7	4.79	74	.255	.357	0	.000	-0	-7	-8	-0	-0.6
Total 6	19	28	.404	157	44	5	1	9	459^1	458	257	46	20	248	335	14.2	4.39	81	.262	.360	24	.202	10	-36	-45	-4	-4.2
● RHEAL CORMIER Cormier, Rheal Paul b: 4/23/67, Moncton, N.B., Can. BL/TL, 5'10", 185 lbs. Deb: 8/15/91																											
1991 StL-N	4	5	.444	11	10	2	0	0	67^2	74	35	5	2	8	38	11.2	4.12	90	.277	.303	5	.238	1	-3	-3	-1	-0.4
1992 StL-N	10	10	.500	31	30	3	0	0	186	194	83	15	5	33	117	11.2	3.68	92	.269	.306	6	.102	-2	-3	-6	1	-0.7
1993 StL-N	7	6	.538	38	21	1	0	0	145^1	163	80	18	4	27	75	12.0	4.33	92	.284	.321	11	.234	2	-5	-6	1	-0.2
1994 StL-N	3	2	.600	7	7	0	0	0	39^2	40	24	6	3	7	26	11.3	5.45	76	.256	.301	4	.286	1	-5	-6	-1	-0.6
1995 *Bos-A	7	5	.583	48	12	0	0	0	115	131	60	12	3	31	69	12.9	4.07	120	.294	.344	0	—	0	8	10	1	1.0
1996 Mon-N	7	10	.412	33	27	1	1	0	159^2	165	80	16	9	41	100	12.1	4.17	104	.270	.325	8	.186	1	1	3	3	0.6
1997 Mon-N	0	1	.000	1	1	0	0	0	1^1	4	5	1	0	1	0	33.8	33.75	12	.500	.556	0	—	0	-4	-4	-0	-0.6
1999 *Bos-A	2	0	1.000	60	0	0	0	0	63^1	61	34	4	5	18	39	11.9	3.69	135	.246	.310	0	—	0	8	9	-1	0.4
2000 Bos-A	3	3	.500	64	0	0	0	0	68^1	74	40	7	0	17	43	12.0	4.61	110	.275	.318	0	—	0	2	4	1	0.3
Total 9	43	42	.506	293	108	7	1	0	846^1	906	441	84	31	183	507	11.9	4.18	100	.275	.319	34	.185	3	-1	-0	4	-0.2
● MARDIE CORNEJO Cornejo, Nieves Mardie b: 8/5/51, Wellington, Kan. BR/TR, 6'3", 200 lbs. Deb: 4/8/78																											
1978 NY-N	4	2	.667	25	0	0	0	3	36^2	37	12	1	3	14	17	13.3	2.45	142	.285	.367	0	—	0	5	4	-0	0.7
● REID CORNELIUS Cornelius, Jonathan Reid b: 6/2/70, Thomasville, Ala. BR/TR, 6', 200 lbs. Deb: 4/29/95																											
1995 Mon-N	0	0	—	8	0	0	0	0	9	11	8	3	2	5	4	18.0	8.00	54	.306	.419	0	—	0	-4	-4	-0	-0.2
NY-N	3	7	.300	10	10	0	0	0	57^2	64	36	8	1	25	35	14.0	5.15	79	.284	.359	2	.100	-1	-6	-7	1	-1.1
Yr	3	7	.300	18	10	0	0	0	66^2	75	44	11	3	30	39	14.6	5.54	74	.287	.367	2	.100	-1	-10	-11	1	-1.3
1999 Fla-N	1	0	1.000	5	2	0	0	0	19^1	16	7	0	0	5	12	9.8	3.26	134	.229	.280	1	.200	0	3	2	0	0.2
2000 Fla-N	4	10	.286	22	21	0	0	0	125	135	74	19	4	50	50	13.6	4.82	92	.282	.355	5	.135	-1	-3	-6	2	-0.4
Total 3	8	17	.320	45	33	0	0	0	211	226	125	30	7	85	101	13.6	4.91	88	.279	.353	8	.129	-2	-10	-14	3	-1.5
● JEFF CORNELL Cornell, Jeffery Ray b: 2/10/57, Kansas City, Mo. BB/TR, 5'11", 170 lbs. Deb: 6/2/84																											
1984 SF-N	1	3	.250	23	0	0	0	0	38^1	51	30	4	1	22	19	17.4	6.10	58	.340	.428	0	.000	-0	-11	-11	-1	-1.2
● BRAD CORNETT Cornett, Brad Byron b: 2/4/69, Lamesa, Tex. BR/TR, 6'3", 190 lbs. Deb: 6/8/94																											
1994 Tor-A	1	3	.250	9	4	0	0	0	31	40	25	1	3	11	22	15.7	6.68	72	.331	.400	0	—	0	-6	-6	0	-0.7
1995 Tor-A	0	0	—	5	0	0	0	0	5	9	6	1	1	3	4	23.4	9.00	52	.429	.520	0	—	0	-2	-2	0	-0.1
Total 2	1	3	.250	14	4	0	0	0	36	49	31	2	4	14	26	16.8	7.00	69	.345	.419	0	—	0	-9	-9	0	-0.8
● TERRY CORNUTT Cornutt, Terry Stanton b: 10/2/52, Roseburg, Ore. BR/TR, 6'2", 195 lbs. Deb: 4/9/77																											
1977 SF-N	1	2	.333	28	1	0	0	0	44^1	38	24	4	0	22	23	12.2	3.86	102	.229	.319	0	.000	-0	0	0	-1	-0.1
1978 SF-N	0	0	—	1	0	0	0	0	3	1	0	0	0	0	0	3.0	0.00	—	.100	.100	0	—	0	1	1	-0	0.0
Total 2	1	2	.333	29	1	0	0	0	47^1	39	24	4	0	22	23	11.6	3.61	108	.222	.308	0	.000	-0	1	1	-1	-0.1
● ED CORREA Correa, Edwin Josue (Andino) b: 4/29/66, Hato Rey, P.R. BR/TR, 6'2", 192 lbs. Deb: 9/18/85																											
1985 Chi-A	1	0	1.000	5	1	0	0	0	10^1	11	9	2	0	11	10	19.2	6.97	62	.275	.431	0	—	0	-3	-3	-0	-0.3
1986 Tex-A	12	14	.462	32	32	4	2	0	202^1	167	102	15	3	126	189	13.2	4.23	102	.223	.337	0	—	0	-1	2	3	0.5
1987 Tex-A	3	5	.375	15	15	0	0	0	70	83	63	17	4	52	61	17.9	7.59	59	.296	.414	0	—	0	-24	-24	-0	-2.2
Total 3	16	19	.457	52	48	4	2	0	282^2	261	174	34	7	189	260	14.6	5.16	84	.244	.361	0	—	0	-28	-25	2	-2.0
● FRANK CORRIDON Corridon, Frank J. "Fiddler" b: 11/25/1880, Newport, R.I. d: 2/21/41, Syracuse, N.Y. BR/TR, 6', 170 lbs. Deb: 4/15/04																											
1904 Chi-N	5	5	.500	12	10	9	0	0	100^1	88	43	2	7	37	34	11.8	3.05	87	.240	.321	13	.224	0	-3	-4	3	-0.1
Phi-N	6	5	.545	12	11	11	1	0	94^1	88	33	2	8	28	44	11.8	2.19	122	.250	.320	6	.171	-0	6	5	3	0.9
Yr	11	10	.524	24	21	20	1	0	194^2	176	76	4	15	65	78	11.8	2.64	101	.245	.320	19	.204	0	2	1	6	0.8
1905 Phi-N	10	12	.455	35	26	18	1	1	212	203	109	2	16	57	79	11.7	3.48	84	.257	.319	15	.208	4	-11	-14	2	-0.6
1907 Phi-N	18	14	.563	37	32	23	3	2	274	228	107	0	9	89	131	10.7	2.46	98	.230	.299	16	.165	0	0	-1	5	0.4
1908 Phi-N	14	10	.583	27	24	18	2	1	208^1	178	69	0	6	48	50	10.0	2.51	97	.239	.290	9	.123	-2	-3	-2	3	-0.1
1909 Phi-N	11	7	.611	27	19	11	3	0	171	147	61	0	6	61	69	11.3	2.11	123	.242	.318	11	.186	0	9	9	5	1.5
1910 StL-N	6	14	.300	30	18	9	0	3	156	168	88	1	9	55	51	13.4	3.81	78	.283	.353	10	.196	-0	-13	-15	3	-1.5
Total 6	70	67	.511	180	140	99	10	7	1216	1100	510	7	61	375	458	11.4	2.80	95	.247	.315	80	.180	3	-16	-20	24	0.5
● JIM CORSI Corsi, James Bernard b: 9/9/61, Newton, Mass. BR/TR, 6'1", 220 lbs. Deb: 6/28/88																											
1988 Oak-A	0	1	.000	11	1	0	0	0	21^1	20	10	1	0	6	10	11.0	3.80	100	.260	.313	0	—	0	0	-0	-0	0.0
1989 Oak-A	1	2	.333	22	0	0	0	0	38^1	26	8	2	1	10	21	8.7	1.88	196	.194	.255	0	—	0	9	8	-0	0.6
1991 Hou-N	0	5	.000	47	0	0	0	0	77^2	76	37	6	0	23	53	11.5	3.71	95	.259	.312	0	.000	-0	-0	-2	1	0.0
1992 *Oak-A	4	2	.667	32	0	0	0	0	44	44	12	2	0	18	19	12.7	1.43	262	.273	.346	0	—	0	12	12	1	1.7
1993 Fla-N	0	2	.000	15	0	0	0	0	20^1	28	15	1	0	10	7	16.8	6.64	65	.337	.409	0	—	0	-6	-5	0	-0.4
1995 Oak-A	2	4	.333	38	0	0	0	2	45	31	14	2	2	26	26	11.8	2.20	203	.203	.326	0	—	0	13	12	1	1.6
1996 Oak-A	6	0	1.000	56	0	0	0	3	73^2	71	33	6	3	34	43	13.2	4.03	122	.269	.359	0	—	0	8	7	2	0.7
1997 Bos-A	5	3	.625	52	0	0	0	2	57^2	56	26	1	4	21	40	12.6	3.43	135	.255	.331	0	—	0	7	8	0	1.0

YEAR	TM/L	W	L	PCT	G	GS	CG	SH	SV	IP	H	R	HR	HB	BB	SO	RAT	ERA	ERA+	OAV	OOB	BH	AVG	PB	PR	PR+	PD	TPI
1998	*Bos-A	3	2	.600	59	0	0	0	0	66	58	23	6	1	23	49	11.2	2.59	182	.235	.303	0	.000	-0	15	15	1	1.1
1999	Bos-A	1	2	.333	23	0	0	0	0	24	25	15	4	2	19	14	17.3	5.25	95	.284	.422	0	—	0	-1	-1	0	-0.1
	Bal-A	0	1	.000	13	0	0	0	0	13^1	15	4	2	0	1	8	10.8	2.70	174	.294	.308	0	—	0	3	3	1	0.3
	Yr	1	3	.250	36	0	0	0	0	37^1	40	19	6	2	20	22	14.9	4.34	112	.288	.385	0	—	0	2	2	1	0.2
Total	10	22	24	.478	368	1	0	0	7	481^1	450	197	33	13	191	290	12.2	3.25	132	.254	.331	0	.000	-0	60	57	7	6.5
● BARRY CORT	Cort, Barry Lee b: 4/15/56, Toronto, Ont., Can. BR/TR, 6'5", 210 lbs. Deb: 4/22/77																											
1977	Mil-A	1	1	.500	7	3	1	0	0	24^1	25	9	1	1	9	17	12.9	3.33	123	.281	.354	0	—	0	2	2	0	0.2
● DAVID CORTES	Cortes, David C. b: 10/15/73, Mexicali, Mexico BR/TR, 5'11", 195 lbs. Deb: 8/30/99																											
1999	Atl-N	0	0	—	4	0	0	0	0	3^2	3	3	0	0	4	2	17.2	4.91	92	.214	.389	0	—	0	-0	-0	0	0.0
● AL CORWIN	Corwin, Elmer Nathan b: 12/3/26, Newburgh, N.Y. BR/TR, 6'1", 170 lbs. Deb: 7/25/51																											
1951	*NY-N	5	1	.833	15	8	3	1	1	59	49	27	7	0	21	30	10.7	3.66	107	.222	.289	1	.050	-2	2	2	-2	-0.2
1952	NY-N	6	1	.857	21	7	1	0	2	67^2	58	23	5	0	36	36	12.5	2.66	139	.237	.335	2	.095	-1	8	8	-1	0.6
1953	NY-N	6	4	.600	48	7	2	1	2	106^2	122	65	17	3	68	49	16.3	4.98	86	.290	.393	9	.281	4	-8	-8	-1	-0.4
1954	NY-N	1	3	.250	20	0	0	0	0	31^1	35	19	4	0	14	14	14.1	4.02	100	.297	.371	0	.000	-0	0	0	-1	-0.1
1955	NY-N	0	1	.000	13	0	0	0	0	24^2	25	11	3	0	17	13	15.3	4.01	100	.263	.375	0	.000	-0	0	0	-0	-0.1
Total	5	18	10	.643	117	22	6	2	5	289^1	289	145	36	3	156	142	13.9	3.98	101	.263	.356	12	.152	0	2	1	-6	-0.2
● MIKE COSGROVE	Cosgrove, Michael John b: 2/17/51, Phoenix, Ariz. BL/TL, 6'1", 180 lbs. Deb: 9/10/72																											
1972	Hou-N	0	1	.000	7	1	0	0	1	13^2	16	8	2	0	3	7	12.5	4.61	73	.286	.322	0	.000	-0	-2	-2	-1	-0.2
1973	Hou-N	1	1	.500	13	0	0	0	0	10	11	2	1	0	8	2	17.1	1.80	202	.282	.404	0	—	0	2	2	-0	0.3
1974	Hou-N	7	3	.700	45	0	0	0	2	90	76	35	2	1	39	47	11.6	3.50	99	.232	.316	1	.056	-1	1	-0	-1	-0.2
1975	Hou-N	1	2	.333	32	3	1	0	5	71^1	62	24	2	0	37	32	12.5	3.03	112	.245	.341	2	.154	0	5	3	0	0.2
1976	Hou-N	3	4	.429	22	16	1	1	0	89^2	106	63	6	2	58	34	16.7	5.52	58	.303	.405	2	.087	-1	-20	-25	-0	-1.9
Total	5	12	11	.522	119	20	2	1	8	274^2	271	132	13	3	145	122	13.7	4.03	83	.264	.357	5	.089	-2	-14	-22	-2	-1.8
● JIM COSMAN	Cosman, James Henry b: 2/19/43, Brockport, N.Y. BR/TR, 6'4.5", 211 lbs. Deb: 10/2/66																											
1966	StL-N	1	0	1.000	1	1	1	1	0	9	2	0	0	1	2	5	5.0	0.00	—	.074	.167	0	.000	-0	4	4	-0	0.4
1967	StL-N	1	0	1.000	10	5	0	0	0	31^1	21	12	2	5	24	11	14.4	3.16	104	.198	.370	1	.125	-0	1	0	-1	-0.1
1970	Chi-N	0	0	—	1	0	0	0	0	1	3	3	1	0	1	0	36.0	27.00	17	.600	.667	0	—	0	-3	-2	0	-0.1
Total	3	2	0	1.000	12	6	1	1	0	41^1	26	15	3	6	27	16	12.8	3.05	111	.188	.345	1	.091	-1	2	2	-1	0.2
● JOHN COSTELLO	Costello, John Reilly b: 12/24/60, Bronx, N.Y. BR/TR, 6'1", 190 lbs. Deb: 6/2/88																											
1988	StL-N	5	2	.714	36	0	0	0	1	49^2	44	15	3	0	25	38	12.5	1.81	192	.235	.325	0	.000	-0	9	9	-1	1.2
1989	StL-N	5	4	.556	48	0	0	0	3	62^1	48	24	5	2	20	40	10.1	3.32	109	.213	.283	2	.000	-1	1	2	-1	0.1
1990	StL-N	0	0	—	4	0	0	0	0	4^1	7	3	1	1	1	1	18.7	6.23	61	.368	.429	0	—	0	-1	-1	-0	-0.1
	Mon-N	0	0	—	4	0	0	0	0	6^1	5	5	2	0	1	1	8.5	5.68	64	.208	.240	0	—	0	-1	-1	-0	-0.1
	Yr	0	0	—	8	0	0	0	0	10^2	12	8	3	1	2	2	12.7	5.91	63	.279	.326	0	—	0	-2	-3	-0	-0.2
1991	SD-N	1	0	1.000	27	0	0	0	0	35	37	15	2	0	17	24	13.9	3.09	123	.276	.358	0	.000	-0	2	3	-0	0.1
Total	4	11	6	.647	119	0	0	0	4	157^2	141	62	13	3	64	104	11.9	2.97	122	.239	.317	0	.000	-1	10	11	-3	1.2
● DAN COTTER	Cotter, Daniel Joseph b: 4/14/1867, Boston, Mass. d: 9/4/35, Boston, Mass. BR/TR, Deb: 7/16/1890																											
1890	Buf-P	0	1	.000	1	1	1	0	0	9	18	19	1	0	7	0	25.0	14.00	29	.400	.481	0	.000	-1	-10	-10	-0	-0.7
● ENSIGN COTTRELL	Cottrell, Ensign Stover b: 8/29/1888, Hoosick Falls, N.Y d: 2/27/47, Syracuse, N.Y. BL/TL, 5'9.5", 173 lbs. Deb: 6/21/11																											
1911	Pit-N	0	0	—	1	0	0	0	0	1	4	4	0	0	1	0	45.0	9.00	38	.667	.714	0	—	0	-1	-1	-0	0.0
1912	Chi-N	0	0	—	1	0	0	0	0	4	8	4	0	0	1	1	20.3	9.00	37	.444	.474	0	.000	-0	-2	-3	-0	-0.2
1913	Phi-A	1	0	1.000	2	1	1	0	0	10	15	7	0	0	2	3	15.3	5.40	51	.326	.354	1	.250	1	-3	-3	-0	-0.2
1914	Bos-N	0	1	.000	1	1	0	0	0	1	2	2	0	0	3	1	45.0	9.00	31	.333	.556	0	—	0	-1	-1	0	-0.1
1915	NY-A	0	1	.000	7	0	0	0	0	21^1	29	12	2	1	7	7	15.6	3.38	87	.330	.385	0	.000	-1	-1	-1	0	-0.1
Total	5	1	2	.333	12	2	1	0	0	37^1	58	29	2	1	14	12	17.6	4.82	61	.354	.408	1	.083	-0	-8	-8	-0	-0.6
● JOHNNY COUCH	Couch, John Daniel b: 3/31/1891, Vaughn, Mont. d: 12/8/75, San Mateo, Cal. BL/TR, 6', 180 lbs. Deb: 4/11/17																											
1917	Det-A	0	0	—	3	0	0	0	0	13^1	13	6	0	0	1	1	9.5	2.70	98	.255	.269	0	.000	-0	-0	-0	0	0.0
1922	Cin-N	16	9	.640	43	33	18	2	1	264	301	132	13	5	56	45	12.3	3.89	103	.289	.328	12	.132	-3	6	3	1	0.0
1923	Cin-N	2	7	.222	19	8	1	0	0	69^1	98	60	2	0	15	14	14.7	5.97	65	.344	.377	4	.174	-1	-15	-17	-1	-1.9
	Phi-N	2	4	.333	11	7	2	0	0	65	91	45	4	3	21	18	15.9	5.26	87	.335	.389	6	.250	0	-9	-4	-0	-0.4
	Yr	4	11	.267	30	15	3	0	0	134^1	189	105	6	3	36	32	15.3	5.63	75	.339	.383	10	.213	-1	-24	-20	-1	-2.3
1924	Phi-N	4	8	.333	37	7	3	0	3	137	170	97	13	1	39	23	13.8	4.73	94	.306	.352	10	.204	-1	-13	-4	1	-0.3
1925	Phi-N	5	6	.455	34	7	2	1	2	94^1	112	71	9	1	39	11	14.5	5.44	88	.298	.365	5	.161	-1	-12	-6	1	-0.6
Total	5	29	34	.460	147	62	26	3	6	643	785	411	41	10	171	112	13.5	4.63	91	.304	.350	37	.167	-6	-43	-28	2	-3.2
● MIKE COUCHEE	Couchee, Michael Eugene b: 12/4/57, San Jose, Cal. BR/TR, 6', 190 lbs. Deb: 4/5/83 C																											
1983	SD-N	0	1	.000	8	0	0	0	0	14	12	8	1	0	6	5	11.6	5.14	68	.214	.290	1	.500	0	-2	-3	-0	-0.2
● ED COUGHLIN	Coughlin, Edward E. b: 8/5/1861, Hartford, Conn. d: 12/25/52, Hartford, Conn. Deb: 5/15/1884 ♦																											
1884	Buf-N	0	0	—	1	0	0	0	0	0	3	0		0	—	—	∞	—	.600	.600	106	.250	-0	-3	-3	0	-0.2	
● ROSCOE COUGHLIN	Coughlin, William Edward b: 3/15/1868, Walpole, Mass. d: 3/20/51, Chelsea, Mass. TR, 5'10", 160 lbs. Deb: 4/22/1890																											
1890	Chi-N	4	6	.400	11	10	10	0	0	95	102	60	3	4	40	29	13.8	4.26	86	.266	.342	10	.256	1	-7	-6	1	-0.4
1891	NY-N	3	4	.429	8	7	6	0	0	61	74	50	5	3	23	22	14.8	3.84	83	.289	.355	3	.130	1	-3	-5	1	-0.3
Total	2	7	10	.412	19	17	16	0	0	156	176	110	8	7	63	51	14.2	4.10	85	.275	.347	13	.210	2	-11	-11	2	-0.7
● FRITZ COUMBE	Coumbe, Frederick Nicholas b: 12/13/1889, Antrim, Pa. d: 3/21/78, Paradise, Cal. BL/TL, 6', 152 lbs. Deb: 4/22/14																											
1914	Bos-A	1	2	.333	17	5	1	0	1	62^1	49	20	0	0	16	17	9.4	1.44	186	.222	.274	2	.111	-1	9	9	0	0.4
	Cle-A	1	5	.167	14	5	2	0	0	55^1	59	31	0	4	16	22	12.8	3.25	89	.288	.351	6	.261	1	-3	-2	1	0.0
	Yr	2	7	.222	31	10	3	0	1	117^2	108	51	0	4	32	39	11.0	2.29	121	.254	.312	8	.195	0	6	6	1	0.4
1915	Cle-A	4	7	.364	30	12	4	1	2	114	123	63	1	3	37	37	12.9	3.47	88	.294	.355	10	.270	1	-7	-5	3	-0.1
1916	Cle-A	7	5	.583	29	13	7	2	0	120^1	121	36	1	1	27	39	11.1	2.02	149	.279	.323	2	.057	-3	11	12	5	1.5
1917	Cle-A	8	6	.571	34	10	4	1	5	134^1	119	54	0	3	35	30	10.5	2.14	132	.251	.307	6	.154	-1	8	10	3	1.3
1918	Cle-A	13	7	.650	30	17	9	0	3	150	164	61	4	1	52	41	13.0	3.06	98	.286	.347	12	.214	-1	-5	-1	5	0.3
1919	Cle-A	1	1	.500	8	2	0	0	1	23^2	32	15	2	0	9	7	15.6	5.32	63	.348	.406	3	.500	1	-6	-5	0	-0.3
1920	Cin-N	0	1	.000	3	0	0	0	0	14^2	17	13	0	0	4	7	12.9	4.91	62	.304	.350	3	.231	1	-3	-3	0	-0.1
1921	Cin-N	3	4	.429	28	6	3	0	1	86^2	89	42	2	1	21	12	11.5	3.22	111	.280	.326	8	.320	1	5	4	2	0.7
Total	8	38	38	.500	193	70	30	4	13	761^1	773	335	10	13	217	212	11.9	2.80	108	.277	.332	52	.206	-1	10	19	20	3.7
● HARRY COURTNEY	Courtney, Henry Seymour b: 11/19/1898, Asheville, N.C. d: 12/11/54, Lyme, Conn. BL/TL, 6'4", 185 lbs. Deb: 9/13/19																											
1919	Was-A	3	0	1.000	4	3	2	1	0	26^1	21	9	0	0	19	6	15.0	2.73	117	.269	.393	2	.200	-0	1	1	-1	0.0
1920	Was-A	8	11	.421	37	24	10	1	0	188	223	128	6	9	77	48	14.8	4.74	79	.298	.371	16	.232	4	-20	-21	-3	-1.8
1921	Was-A	6	9	.400	30	15	3	0	1	132^2	159	103	7	8	71	26	16.1	5.63	73	.305	.397	14	.298	2	-20	-23	-0	-2.0
1922	Was-A	0	1	.000	5	0	0	0	0	10	11	4	0	0	9	4	18.0	3.60	107	.306	.444	0	.000	-1	0	0	-0	0.0
	Chi-A	5	6	.455	18	11	5	0	0	86^2	100	52	5	1	37	28	14.3	4.98	82	.299	.371	9	.273	3	-9	-9	-1	-0.7
	Yr	5	7	.417	23	11	5	0	0	96^2	111	56	5	1	46	32	14.7	4.84	84	.300	.379	9	.243	2	-9	-8	-1	-0.7
Total	4	22	27	.449	94	53	20	2	1	443^2	518	296	18	18	213	112	15.2	4.91	79	.299	.382	41	.252	7	-47	-51	-5	-4.5
● JOHN COURTRIGHT	Courtright, John Charles b: 5/30/70, Marion, Ohio BL/TL, 6'2", 185 lbs. Deb: 5/6/95																											
1995	Cin-N	0	0	—	1	0	0	0	0	1	2	1	0	0	0	0	18.0	9.00	46	.500	.500	0	—	0	-1	-1	-0	0.0
● HARRY COVELESKI	Coveleski, Harry Frank "The Giant Killer" (b: Harry Frank Kowalewski) b: 4/23/1886, Shamokin, Pa. d: 8/4/50, Shamokin, Pa. BB/TL, 6', 180 lbs. Deb: 9/10/07 F																											
1907	Phi-N	1	0	1.000	4	0	0	0	0	20	10	2	0	1	3	6	6.3	0.00	—	.147	.194	0	.000	-0	5	5	-0	0.3

YEAR	TM/L	W	L	PCT	G	GS	CG	SH	SV	IP	H	R	HR	HB	BB	SO	RAT	ERA	ERA+	OAV	OOB	BH	AVG	PB	PR	PR+	PD	TPI
1908	Phi-N	4	1	.800	6	5	5	2	0	43^2	29	7	0	2	12	22	8.9	1.24	196	.196	.265	2	.133	-0	5	6	1	0.8
1909	Phi-N	6	10	.375	24	17	8	2	1	121^2	109	51	0	5	49	56	12.1	2.74	95	.247	.329	4	.108	-2	-2	-2	1	-0.4
1910	Cin-N	1	1	.500	7	4	2	0	0	39^1	35	41	1	4	42	27	18.5	5.26	55	.246	.431	1	.063	-1	-10	-11	1	-0.6
1914	Det-A	22	12	.647	44	36	23	5	2	303^1	251	109	4	12	100	124	10.8	2.49	113	.227	.298	23	.242	5	8	10	7	2.4
1915	Det-A	22	13	.629	**50**	38	20	1	4	312^2	271	123	2	20	87	150	10.9	2.45	124	.233	.298	18	.175	-2	17	20	4	2.4
1916	Det-A	21	11	.656	44	39	22	3	2	324^1	278	105	6	11	63	108	9.8	1.97	145	.237	.282	25	.212	1	31	32	4	3.9
1917	Det-A	4	6	.400	16	11	2	0	0	69	70	39	0	2	14	15	11.2	2.61	101	.265	.307	5	.227	-0	0	0	2	0.2
1918	Det-A	0	1	.000	3	1	1	0	0	14	17	9	0	0	6	3	14.8	3.86	69	.315	.383	1	.250	0	-2	-2	1	-0.1
Total	9	81	55	.596	198	151	83	13	9	1248	1070	486	13	57	376	511	10.8	2.39	118	.235	.301	79	.189	-0	54	60	20	8.9
● STAN COVELESKI	Coveleski, Stanley Anthony (b: Stanislaus Kowalewski) b: 7/13/1889, Shamokin, Pa. d: 3/20/84, South Bend, Ind. BR/TR, 5'11", 166 lbs. Deb: 9/10/12 FH																											
1912	Phi-A	2	1	.667	5	2	2	1	0	21	18	9	0	1	4	9	9.9	3.43	90	.231	.277	1	.143	-0	-0	-1	-1	-0.2
1916	Cle-A	15	13	.536	45	27	11	1	3	232	247	100	6	1	58	76	11.9	3.41	88	.278	.323	13	.173	-0	-15	-10	2	-1.0
1917	Cle-A	19	14	.576	45	36	24	**9**	4	298^1	202	78	3	1	94	133	9.0	1.81	157	**.194**	.261	13	.134	-4	28	32	-4	2.9
1918	Cle-A	22	13	.629	38	33	25	2	1	311	261	90	2	4	76	87	9.9	1.82	165	.229	.279	21	.191	-3	33	38	-0	4.2
1919	Cle-A	24	12	.667	43	34	24	4	4	286	286	99	2	5	60	118	11.0	2.61	128	.267	.308	20	.213	4	20	23	3	3.5
1920	*Cle-A	24	14	.632	41	38	26	3	2	315	284	110	6	4	65	**133**	**10.1**	2.49	153	**.243**	**.285**	25	.225	3	**46**	**46**	3	**5.9**
1921	Cle-A	23	13	.639	43	40	28	2	2	315	341	137	6	4	84	99	12.3	3.37	126	.280	.329	18	.155	-6	32	31	7	3.2
1922	Cle-A	17	14	.548	35	33	21	3	2	276^2	292	120	14	2	64	98	11.6	3.32	121	.274	.316	10	.101	-7	22	21	1	1.5
1923	Cle-A	13	14	.481	33	31	17	**5**	2	228	251	98	8	2	42	54	11.6	**2.76**	**143**	.282	.316	7	.089	-8	**31**	31	3	2.9
1924	Cle-A	15	16	.484	37	33	18	2	0	240^1	286	140	6	4	73	58	13.6	4.04	106	.294	.346	11	.134	-5	5	6	-0	0.2
1925	*Was-A	20	5	**.800**	32	32	15	3	0	241	230	86	7	2	73	58	11.4	**2.84**	**149**	.255	.312	9	.111	-8	42	39	0	2.7
1926	Was-A	14	11	.560	36	34	11	3	1	245^1	272	112	1	0	81	50	12.9	3.12	124	.286	.342	17	.207	1	25	21	1	2.2
1927	Was-A	2	1	.667	5	4	0	0	0	14^1	13	7	0	0	8	3	13.2	3.14	129	.250	.350	2	.333	0	2	2	-0	0.3
1928	NY-A	5	1	.833	12	8	2	0	0	58	72	41	5	0	20	5	14.3	5.74	66	.323	.379	1	.053	-2	-11	-14	1	-1.3
Total	14	215	142	.602	450	385	224	38	21	3082	3055	1227	66	30	802	981	11.4	2.89	128	.262	.311	168	.159	-34	259	272	16	27.0
● CHET COVINGTON	Covington, Chester Rogers "Chesty" b: 11/6/10, Cairo, Ill. d: 6/11/76, Pembroke Park, Fla. BB/TL, 6'2", 195 lbs. Deb: 4/23/44																											
1944	Phi-N	1	1	.500	19	0	0	0	0	38^2	46	22	2	0	8	13	12.6	4.66	78	.297	.331	0	.000	-1	-4	-4	-0	-0.3
● TEX COVINGTON	Covington, William Wilkes b: 3/19/1887, Henryville, Tenn. d: 12/10/31, Denison, Tex. BL/TR, 6'1", 175 lbs. Deb: 4/25/11 F																											
1911	Det-A	7	1	.875	17	6	5	0	0	83^2	94	43	2	10	33	29	14.7	4.09	85	.297	.381	6	.188	-1	-7	-6	-1	-0.7
1912	Det-A	3	4	.429	14	9	2	1	0	63^1	58	33	0	3	30	19	12.9	4.12	79	.253	.347	2	.133	0	-6	-6	-1	-0.6
Total	2	10	5	.667	31	15	7	1	0	147	152	76	2	13	63	48	14.0	4.10	82	.278	.367	8	.170	-1	-13	-12	-2	-1.3
● JOE COWLEY	Cowley, Joseph Alan b: 8/15/58, Lexington, Ky. BR/TR, 6'5", 210 lbs. Deb: 4/13/82																											
1982	Atl-N	1	2	.333	17	8	0	0	0	52^1	53	27	6	1	16	27	12.0	4.47	84	.265	.323	3	.200	-0	-5	-4	-0	-0.2
1984	NY-A	9	2	.818	16	11	3	1	0	83^1	75	34	12	2	31	71	11.7	3.56	107	.234	.305	0	—	0	4	2	0	0.3
1985	NY-A	12	6	.667	30	26	1	0	0	159^2	132	75	29	6	85	97	12.6	3.95	101	.224	.328	0	—	0	4	1	-1	0.0
1986	Chi-A	11	11	.500	27	27	4	0	0	162^1	133	81	20	3	83	132	12.1	3.88	111	.223	.321	0	—	0	5	8	-1	0.9
1987	Phi-N	0	4	.000	5	4	0	0	0	11^2	21	26	2	2	17	5	30.9	15.43	28	.389	.548	1	.333	1	-15	-14	-1	-2.2
Total	5	33	25	.569	95	76	8	1	0	469^1	414	243	69	14	232	332	12.7	4.20	97	.235	.329	4	.222	1	-7	-8	-1	-1.2
● DANNY COX	Cox, Danny Bradford b: 9/21/59, Northampton, England BR/TR, 6'4", 235 lbs. Deb: 8/6/83																											
1983	StL-N	3	6	.333	12	12	0	0	0	83	92	38	6	0	23	36	12.5	3.25	112	.286	.333	2	.074	-2	4	3	1	0.3
1984	StL-N	9	11	.450	29	27	1	1	0	156^1	171	81	9	7	54	70	13.4	4.03	86	.289	.355	7	.132	0	-8	-10	1	-1.1
1985	*StL-N	18	9	.667	35	35	10	4	0	241	226	91	19	3	64	131	10.9	2.88	123	.251	.303	12	.152	1	19	18	-1	2.0
1986	StL-N	12	13	.480	32	32	8	0	0	220	189	85	14	2	60	108	10.3	2.90	126	.234	.289	5	.077	-3	20	19	-5	1.2
1987	*StL-N	11	9	.550	31	31	2	0	0	199^1	224	99	17	3	71	101	13.5	3.88	107	.290	.352	8	.116	-2	4	6	-1	0.3
1988	StL-N	3	8	.273	13	13	0	0	0	86	89	40	6	1	25	47	12.0	3.98	88	.272	.326	1	.043	-2	-5	-5	0	-0.7
1991	Phi-N	4	6	.400	23	17	0	0	0	102^1	98	57	14	1	39	46	12.1	4.57	80	.258	.329	3	.103	-1	-10	-10	-1	-1.0
1992	Phi-N	2	2	.500	9	7	0	0	0	38^1	46	28	3	0	19	30	15.3	5.40	65	.299	.376	1	.091	-1	-8	-8	1	-0.8
	*Pit-N	3	1	.750	16	0	0	0	3	24^1	20	9	2	0	8	18	10.4	3.33	104	.225	.289	0	.000	-0	0	0	-0	0.0
	Yr	5	3	.625	25	7	0	0	3	62^2	66	37	5	0	27	48	13.4	4.60	76	.272	.344	1	.071	-1	-8	-8	0	-0.8
1993	*Tor-A	7	6	.538	44	0	0	0	2	83^2	73	31	8	0	29	84	11.0	3.12	139	.230	.294	0	—	0	11	11	-1	1.5
1994	Tor-A	1	1	.500	10	0	0	0	3	18^2	7	3	0	1	7	14	7.2	1.45	334	.113	.214	0	—	0	7	7	-0	0.8
1995	Tor-A	1	3	.250	24	0	0	0	0	45	57	40	4	1	33	38	18.2	7.40	64	.317	.425	0	—	0	-13	-13	-0	-1.0
Total	11	74	75	.497	278	174	21	5	8	1298	1292	602	102	19	432	723	12.1	3.64	103	.263	.325	39	.109	-9	22	18	-6	1.5
● ERNIE COX	Cox, Ernest Thompson b: 2/19/1894, Birmingham, Ala. d: 4/29/74, Birmingham, Ala. BL/TR, 6'1", 180 lbs. Deb: 5/5/22																											
1922	Chi-A	0	0	—	1	0	0	0	0	1	1	2	0	0	2	0	27.0	18.00	23	.250	.500	0	—	0	-2	-2	-0	-0.1
● GEORGE COX	Cox, George Melvin b: 11/15/04, Sherman, Tex. d: 12/17/95, Bedford, Tex. BR/TR, 6'1", 170 lbs. Deb: 4/12/28																											
1928	Chi-A	1	2	.333	26	2	0	0	0	89	110	58	6	2	39	22	15.3	5.26	77	.313	.385	2	.077	-2	-12	-12	2	-0.6
● GLENN COX	Cox, Glenn Melvin b: 2/3/31, Montebello, Cal. BR/TR, 6'2", 210 lbs. Deb: 9/20/55																											
1955	KC-A	0	2	.000	2	2	0	0	0	2^1	11	8	0	0	1	2	46.3	30.86	14	.611	.632	0	.000	-0	-7	-7	0	-1.0
1956	KC-A	0	2	.000	3	3	1	0	0	23^1	15	11	2	0	22	6	14.3	4.24	102	.203	.385	0	.000	-1	-0	0	-1	-0.2
1957	KC-A	1	0	1.000	10	0	0	0	0	14^1	18	9	1	0	9	8	17.0	5.02	79	.321	.415	0	.000	0	-2	-2	0	-0.1
1958	KC-A	0	0	—	2	0	0	0	0	3^2	6	4	1	0	3	1	22.1	9.82	40	.400	.500	0	—	0	-2	-2	-0	-0.1
Total	4	1	4	.200	17	5	1	0	0	43^2	50	32	4	0	35	17	17.5	6.39	65	.307	.429	0	.000	-1	-12	-10	-1	-1.4
● CASEY COX	Cox, Joseph Casey b: 7/3/41, Long Beach, Cal. BR/TR, 6'5", 200 lbs. Deb: 4/15/66																											
1966	Was-A	4	5	.444	66	0	0	0	7	113	104	53	6	4	35	46	11.4	3.50	99	.250	.314	0	.000	-1	-1	-1	0	-0.1
1967	Was-A	7	4	.636	54	0	0	0	1	73	67	33	2	4	21	32	11.3	2.96	107	.250	.314	0	.000	-0	2	2	0	0.2
1968	Was-A	0	1	.000	4	0	0	0	0	7^2	7	2	0	0	0	4	8.2	2.35	124	.250	.250	0	—	0	1	0	-0	0.0
1969	Was-A	12	7	.632	52	13	4	0	0	171^2	161	62	15	1	64	73	11.8	2.78	125	.251	.320	5	.106	-2	16	14	-1	1.2
1970	Was-A	8	12	.400	37	30	1	0	1	192^1	211	108	27	4	44	68	12.1	4.45	80	.285	.329	7	.121	-2	-16	-20	-2	-2.2
1971	Was-A	5	7	.417	54	11	0	0	7	124^1	131	69	9	7	40	43	12.9	3.98	83	.273	.338	2	.077	-1	-7	-10	-1	-1.2
1972	Tex-A	3	5	.375	35	4	0	0	4	65^1	73	41	7	1	26	27	13.8	4.41	69	.277	.344	1	.111	1	-10	-10	0	-1.3
	NY-A	0	1	.000	5	1	0	0	0	11^2	13	6	0	2	3	4	13.9	4.63	64	.289	.360	0	—	0	-2	-2	-0	-0.2
	Yr	3	6	.333	40	5	0	0	4	77	86	47	7	3	29	31	13.8	4.44	68	.278	.346	1	.111	1	-12	-12	-0	-1.5
1973	NY-A	0	0	—	1	0	0	0	0	3	5	3	0	2	1	0	24.0	6.00	61	.357	.471	0	—	0	-1	-1	0	0.0
Total	8	39	42	.481	308	59	5	0	20	762	772	377	66	25	234	297	12.2	3.70	92	.266	.327	15	.099	-6	-17	-27	-3	-3.6
● LES COX	Cox, Leslie Warren b: 8/14/05, Junction, Tex. d: 10/14/34, San Angelo, Tex. BR/TR, 6', 164 lbs. Deb: 9/11/26																											
1926	Chi-A	0	1	.000	2	0	0	0	0	5	6	10	2	0	5	3	19.8	5.40	72	.261	.393	1	.500	0	-1	-1	0	-0.2
● RED COX	Cox, Plateau Rex b: 2/16/1895, Laurel Springs, N.C. d: 10/15/84, Roanoke, Va. BL/TR, 6'2", 190 lbs. Deb: 4/17/20																											
1920	Det-A	0	0	—	3	0	0	0	0	5	9	4	0	0	3	1	21.6	5.40	69	.375	.444	0	.000	-0	-1	-1	-0	-0.1
● TERRY COX	Cox, Terry Lee b: 3/30/49, Odessa, Tex. BR/TR, 6'5", 215 lbs. Deb: 9/7/70																											
1970	Cal-A	0	0	—	3	0	0	0	0	2^1	4	1	0	0	0	3	15.4	3.86	94	.400	.400	0	—	0	-0	-0	0	0.0
● BILL COX	Cox, William Donald b: 6/23/13, Ashmore, Ill. d: 2/16/88, Charleston, Ill. BR/TR, 6'1", 185 lbs. Deb: 6/6/36																											
1936	StL-N	0	0	—	2	0	0	0	0	2^2	4	5	0	0	1	1	16.9	6.75	58	.333	.385	0	—	0	-1	-1	-0	-0.1
1937	Chi-A	1	0	1.000	3	2	1	1	0	12^2	9	1	0	0	5	8	9.9	0.71	648	.200	.280	1	.250	0	6	5	-0	0.4
1938	Chi-A	0	2	.000	7	1	0	0	0	11^2	11	14	0	0	13	5	18.5	6.94	70	.244	.414	0	.000	-0	-3	-3	-0	-0.4
	StL-A	1	4	.200	22	7	1	0	0	63	81	53	8	0	35	16	16.6	7.00	71	.315	.397	1	.059	-1	-15	-14	0	-1.0
	Yr	1	6	.143	29	8	1	0	0	74^2	92	67	8	0	48	21	16.9	6.99	71	.305	.400	1	.053	-2	-18	-16	0	-1.4
1939	StL-A	0	2	.000	4	2	1	0	0	9^1	10	10	0	0	8	8	17.4	9.64	50	.256	.383	0	.000	-0	-5	-5	1	-0.7

YEAR	TM/L	W	L	PCT	G	GS	CG	SH	SV	IP	H	R	HR	HB	BB	SO	RAT	ERA	ERA+	OAV	OOB	BH	AVG	PB	PR	PR+	PD	TPI
1940	StL-A	0	1	.000	12	0	0	0	0	17^1	23	17	3	0	12	7	18.2	7.27	63	.333	.432	0	.000	-0	-6	-5	0	-0.2
Total	5	2	9	.182	50	12	3	1	0	116^2	138	100	11	0	74	45	16.4	6.56	74	.296	.392	2	.080	-2	-24	-22	1	-2.0
● **BILL COYLE** Coyle, William Claude b: 9/20/1871, Kentucky d: 6/4/41, San Francisco, Cal. TR, Deb: 7/7/1893																												
1893	Bos-N	0	1	.000	2	1	0	0	0	8	14	10	1	0	3	2	19.1	9.00	55	.368	.415	0	.000	-1	-4	-3	0	-0.3
● **CHARLIE COZART** Cozart, Charles Rhubin b: 10/17/19, Lenoir, N.C. BR/TL, 6′, 190 lbs. Deb: 4/17/45																												
1945	Bos-N	1	0	1.000	5	0	0	0	0	8	10	11	2	0	15	4	28.1	10.13	38	.303	.521	0	.000	-0	-6	-6	1	-0.5
● **ROY CRABB** Crabb, James Roy b: 8/23/1890, Monticello, Iowa d: 3/30/40, Lewistown, Mont. BR/TR, 5′11″, 160 lbs. Deb: 8/10/12																												
1912	Chi-A	0	1	.000	2	1	0	0	0	8^2	6	2	0	0	4	3	10.4	1.04	308	.214	.313	0	.000	-0	2	2	0	0.2
	Phi-A	2	4	.333	7	7	3	0	0	43^1	48	22	0	4	17	12	14.3	3.74	82	.287	.367	0	.000	-3	-2	-3	0	-0.6
	Yr	2	5	.286	9	8	3	0	0	52	54	24	0	4	21	15	13.7	3.29	94	.277	.359	0	.000	-3	0	-1	0	-0.4
● **GEORGE CRABLE** Crable, George E. b: 12/1885, Nebraska BL/TL, 6′1″, 190 lbs. Deb: 8/3/10																												
1910	Bro-N	0	0	—	2	1	1	0	0	7^1	5	4	0	2	5	3	14.7	4.91	62	.217	.400	0	.000	0	-2	-2	0	-0.1
● **TIM CRABTREE** Crabtree, Timothy Lyle b: 10/13/69, Jackson, Mich. BR/TR, 6′4″, 205 lbs. Deb: 6/23/95																												
1995	Tor-A	0	2	.000	31	0	0	0	0	32	30	16	1	2	13	21	12.7	3.09	152	.240	.321	0	—	0	6	6	1	0.4
1996	Tor-A	5	3	.625	53	0	0	0	1	67^1	59	26	4	3	22	57	11.2	2.54	197	.231	.300	0	—	0	18	18	0	1.9
1997	Tor-A	3	3	.500	37	0	0	0	2	40^2	65	32	7	2	17	26	18.6	7.08	65	.374	.435	0	—	0	-11	-11	1	-1.4
1998	*Tex-A	6	1	.857	64	0	0	0	0	85^1	86	40	3	3	35	60	13.1	3.59	135	.264	.341	0	.000	-0	10	11	-1	0.7
1999	*Tex-A	5	1	.833	68	0	0	0	0	65	71	26	4	1	18	54	12.5	3.46	147	.280	.330	0	—	0	10	11	-1	0.8
2000	Tex-A	2	7	.222	68	0	0	0	2	80^1	86	52	7	2	31	54	13.3	5.15	99	.274	.343	0	—	0	-2	-0	1	0.0
Total	6	21	17	.553	321	0	0	0	5	370^2	397	192	26	13	136	272	13.3	4.05	122	.274	.342	0	.000	-0	31	35	1	2.4
● **WALT CRADDOCK** Craddock, Walter Anderson b: 3/25/32, Pax, W.Va. d: 7/6/80, Parma Heights, O. BR/TL, 5′11.5″, 176 lbs. Deb: 9/3/55																												
1955	KC-A	0	2	.000	4	2	0	0	0	15	18	14	3	0	10	9	16.8	7.80	54	.300	.400	0	.000	-1	-6	-6	-0	-0.7
1956	KC-A	0	2	.000	2	2	0	0	0	9^1	9	7	1	0	10	8	18.3	6.75	64	.265	.432	0	.000	-0	-3	-2	-0	-0.4
1958	KC-A	0	3	.000	23	1	0	0	0	36^2	41	25	4	1	20	22	15.2	5.89	66	.289	.380	0	.000	-0	-9	-8	0	-0.6
Total	3	0	7	.000	29	5	0	0	0	61	68	46	8	1	40	39	16.1	6.49	62	.288	.394	0	.000	-1	-18	-16	0	-1.7
● **MOLLY CRAFT** Craft, Maurice Montague b: 11/28/1895, Portsmouth, Va. d: 10/25/78, Los Angeles, Cal. BR/TR, 6′2″, 165 lbs. Deb: 8/8/16																												
1916	Was-A	0	1	.000	2	1	1	0	0	11	12	5	0	0	6	9	14.7	3.27	85	.316	.409	0	.000	-0	-1	-1	0	0.0
1917	Was-A	0	0	—	8	0	0	0	1	14	17	10	0	0	8	2	16.1	3.86	68	.315	.403	1	.500	0	-2	-2	0	0.0
1918	Was-A	0	0	—	3	0	0	0	0	7	5	1	0	0	1	5	7.7	1.29	212	.208	.240	0	.000	-0	1	1	0	0.0
1919	Was-A	0	3	.000	16	2	0	0	1	48^2	59	28	2	2	18	17	14.6	3.88	83	.309	.374	2	.111	-2	-4	-4	-0	-0.4
Total	4	0	4	.000	29	3	1	0	2	80^2	93	44	2	2	33	33	14.3	3.57	84	.303	.374	3	.115	-2	-5	-5	1	-0.4
● **HOWARD CRAGHEAD** Craghead, Howard Oliver "Judge" b: 5/25/08, Selma, Cal. d: 7/15/62, San Diego, Cal. BR/TR, 6′2″, 200 lbs. Deb: 4/30/31																												
1931	Cle-A	0	0	—	4	0	0	0	0	5^2	8	4	0	0	2	2	15.9	6.35	73	.320	.370	0	—	0	-1	-1	0	0.0
1933	Cle-A	0	0	—	11	0	0	0	0	17^1	19	13	1	1	10	2	15.6	6.23	71	.292	.395	0	.000	-0	-4	-3	0	-0.2
Total	2	0	0	—	15	0	0	0	0	23	27	17	1	1	12	4	15.7	6.26	72	.300	.388	0	.000	-0	-5	-4	0	-0.2
● **GEORGE CRAIG** Craig, George McCarthy "Lefty" b: 11/15/1887, Philadelphia, Pa. d: 4/23/11, Indianapolis, Ind. TL, Deb: 7/19/07																												
1907	Phi-A	0	0	—	2	0	0	0	0	1^2	2	3	0	2	3	0	37.8	10.80	24	.286	.583	0	.000	-0	-2	-1	-0	-0.1
● **PETE CRAIG** Craig, Peter Joel b: 7/10/40, LaSalle, Ontario, Canada BL/TR, 6′5″, 220 lbs. Deb: 9/6/64																												
1964	Was-A	0	0	—	2	1	0	0	0	1^2	8	9	1	0	4	0	64.8	48.60	8	.667	.750	0	—	0	-8	-8	-0	-0.4
1965	Was-A	0	3	.000	3	3	0	0	0	14^1	18	15	1	0	8	2	16.3	8.16	43	.321	.406	2	.667	1	-7	-7	1	-1.1
1966	Was-A	0	0	—	1	0	0	0	0	2	2	2	0	0	1	1	13.5	4.50	77	.250	.333	0	—	0	-0	-0	-0	0.0
Total	3	0	3	.000	6	4	0	0	0	18	28	26	2	0	13	3	20.5	11.50	30	.368	.461	2	.667	1	-16	-16	0	-1.5
● **ROGER CRAIG** Craig, Roger Lee b: 2/17/30, Durham, N.C. BR/TR, 6′4″, 191 lbs. Deb: 7/17/55 MC																												
1955	*Bro-N	5	3	.625	21	10	3	0	2	90^2	81	37	8	1	43	48	12.4	2.78	146	.238	.325	2	.077	-2	13	13	-1	0.8
1956	*Bro-N	12	11	.522	35	32	8	2	1	199	169	90	25	4	87	109	11.8	3.71	107	.231	.316	1	.016	-5	1	5	-2	-0.2
1957	Bro-N	6	9	.400	32	13	1	0	0	111^1	102	58	18	2	47	69	12.2	4.61	90	.249	.329	4	.138	-1	-9	-5	1	-0.6
1958	LA-N	2	1	.667	9	2	1	0	0	32	30	20	3	0	12	16	11.8	4.50	91	.242	.309	0	.000	-1	-2	-1	-1	-0.3
1959	*LA-N	11	5	.688	29	17	7	**4**	0	152^2	122	49	13	1	45	76	9.9	2.06	205	.217	.276	3	.058	-4	32	**34**	-1	3.0
1960	LA-N	8	3	.727	21	15	6	1	0	115^2	99	48	8	3	43	69	11.3	3.27	121	.230	.305	2	.056	-2	6	9	-0	0.5
1961	LA-N	5	6	.455	40	14	2	0	2	112^2	130	87	22	4	52	63	14.9	6.15	71	.288	.367	4	.148	-0	-27	-21	-1	-2.0
1962	NY-N	10	24	.294	42	33	13	0	3	233^1	261	133	35	7	70	118	13.0	4.51	93	.288	.343	4	.053	-5	-15	-8	4	-1.2
1963	NY-N	5	22	.185	46	31	14	0	2	236	249	117	28	6	58	108	11.9	3.78	92	.267	.314	6	.087	-2	-13	-7	3	-0.7
1964	*StL-N	7	9	.438	39	19	3	0	5	166	180	76	16	4	35	84	11.9	3.25	117	.276	.317	10	.208	2	5	9	2	1.3
1965	Cin-N	1	4	.200	40	0	0	0	3	64^1	74	33	6	3	25	30	14.3	3.64	103	.289	.359	2	.182	-0	-1	1	-0	0.0
1966	Phi-N	2	1	.667	14	0	0	0	1	22^2	31	15	4	0	5	13	14.3	5.56	65	.326	.360	0	.000	-0	-5	-5	1	-0.6
Total	12	74	98	.430	368	186	58	7	19	1536^1	1528	763	186	35	522	803	12.2	3.83	104	.259	.323	38	.085	-22	-13	24	4	-0.0
● **JERRY CRAM** Cram, Gerald Allen b: 12/9/47, Los Angeles, Cal. BR/TR, 6′, 180 lbs. Deb: 9/3/69																												
1969	KC-A	0	1	.000	5	2	0	0	0	16^2	15	8	0	0	6	10	11.3	3.24	114	.231	.296	0	.000	-0	1	1	-0	0.0
1974	NY-N	0	1	.000	10	0	0	0	0	22^1	22	4	1	0	4	8	10.5	1.61	222	.275	.310	1	.333	0	5	5	0	0.3
1975	NY-N	0	1	.000	4	0	0	0	0	5	7	3	2	0	2	2	16.2	5.40	64	.333	.391	0	—	0	-1	-1	0	-0.2
1976	KC-A	0	0	—	4	0	0	0	0	4^1	8	3	0	0	1	2	18.7	6.23	56	.421	.450	0	—	0	-1	-1	0	-0.1
Total	4	0	3	.000	23	2	0	0	0	48^1	52	18	3	0	13	22	12.1	2.98	121	.281	.328	1	.167	-0	3	3	0	0.0
● **DOC CRAMER** Cramer, Roger Maxwell "Flit" b: 7/22/05, Beach Haven, N.J. d: 9/9/90, Manahawkin, N.J. BL/TR, 6′2″, 185 lbs. Deb: 9/18/29 C♦																												
1938	Bos-A★	0	0	—	1	0	0	0	0	4	3	2	0	0	3	1	13.5	4.50	110	.214	.353	198	.301	0	0	0	0	0.0
● **BILL CRAMER** Cramer, William Wendell b: 5/21/1891, Bedford, Ind. d: 9/11/66, Fort Wayne, Ind. BR/TR, 6′, 175 lbs. Deb: 6/25/12																												
1912	Cin-N	0	0	—	1	0	0	0	0	2^1	6	6	0	0	0	2	23.1	0.00	—	.500	.500	0	.000	-0	1	1	-0	0.0
● **DOC CRANDALL** Crandall, James Otis b: 10/8/1887, Wadena, Ind. d: 8/17/51, Bell, Cal. BR/TR, 5′10.5″, 180 lbs. Deb: 4/24/08 ♦																												
1908	NY-N	12	12	.500	32	24	13	0	0	214^2	198	83	3	9	59	77	11.2	2.93	82	.248	.307	16	.222	5	-14	-12	-1	-1.0
1909	NY-N	6	4	.600	30	8	4	0	6	122	117	58	5	3	33	55	11.3	2.88	89	.252	.305	10	.244	3	-4	-4	2	0.0
1910	NY-N	17	4	.810	42	18	13	2	5	207^2	194	86	10	4	43	73	10.4	2.56	116	.246	.289	25	.342	10	11	10	-1	1.9
1911	*NY-N	15	5	.750	41	15	9	2	5	198^2	199	82	10	6	51	94	11.6	2.63	128	.256	.307	27	.239	5	17	16	2	2.4
1912	*NY-N	13	7	.650	37	10	7	0	2	162	181	85	7	2	35	60	12.1	3.61	94	.286	.326	25	.313	6	-4	-4	-0	0.2
1913	*NY-N	2	4	.333	24	1	1	0	5	55^1	61	28	2	1	13	28	12.2	3.09	101	.293	.338	7	.280	2	1	0	1	0.3
	*NY-N	2	0	1.000	11	1	1	0	1	42^1	41	17	1	0	11	14	11.1	2.55	122	.248	.295	8	.364	3	3	3	1	0.5
	Yr	4	4	.500	35	2	2	0	6	97^2	102	45	3	1	24	42	11.7	2.86	109	.273	.319	15	.319	5	**4**	**3**	1	0.8
1914	StL-F	13	9	.591	27	21	18	1	0	196	194	94	8	2	52	84	11.4	3.54	86	.256	.305	86	.309	7	-14	-10	-1	-0.3
1915	StL-F	21	15	.583	51	33	22	4	1	312^2	307	116	5	10	77	117	11.3	2.59	111	.263	.314	40	.284	12	5	9	1	2.5
1916	StL-A	0	0	—	2	0	0	0	0	1^1	7	9	0	1	1	0	60.8	27.00	10	.636	.692	1	.083	-0	-4	-4	-0	-0.2
1918	Bos-N	1	2	.333	5	3	3	0	0	34	39	11	1	1	4	4	11.6	2.38	113	.307	.333	8	.286	1	1	1	0	0.3
Total	10	102	62	.622	302	134	91	9	25	1546^2	1538	669	52	39	379	606	11.4	2.92	101	.261	.310	253	.285	54	-1	5	1	6.6
● **ED CRANE** Crane, Edward Nicholas "Cannon-Ball" b: 5/27/1862, Boston, Mass. d: 9/20/1896, Rochester, N.Y. BR/TR, 5′10.5″, 204 lbs. Deb: 4/17/1884 ♦																												
1884	Bos-U	0	2	.000	4	2	1	0	0	18	17	14	1		6	13	11.5	4.00	60	.233	.291	122	.285	0	-3	-3	1	-0.2
1886	Was-N	1	7	.125	10	8	7	1	0	70	91	85	5		53	39	18.5	7.20	46	.313	.419	50	.171	-1	-30	-31	0	-2.5
1888	*NY-N	5	6	.455	12	11	11	2	1	92^2	70	51	3	2	40	58	10.9	2.43	113	.193	.277	6	.162	1	4	3	1	0.5
1889	*NY-N	14	10	.583	29	25	23	0	0	230	221	161	10	10	136	130	14.4	3.68	107	.245	.350	21	.204	3	9	7	-4	0.5
1890	NY-P	16	19	.457	43	35	28	0	0	330^1	323	280	12	10	208	116	14.7	4.63	98	.245	.352	46	.315	7	-15	-3	-3	0.1
1891	Cin-a	14	14	.500	32	31	25	1	0	250	216	151	3	14	139	122	13.3	**2.45**	**168**	.225	.332	17	.155	-6	35	42	-2	3.1

YEAR	TM/L	W	L	PCT	G	GS	CG	SH	SV	IP	H	R	HR	HB	BB	SO	RAT	ERA	ERA+	OAV	OOB	BH	AVG	PB	PR	PR+	PD	TPI
	Cin-N	4	8	.333	15	13	11	1	0	116^{2}	134	91	3	3	64	51	15.5	4.09	83	.277	.365	5	.109	-3	-10	-9	0	-1.0
1892	NY-N	16	24	.400	47	42	35	2	1	364^{1}	350	276	10	12	189	174	13.6	3.80	85	.243	.335	40	.245	4	-21	-24	-1	-1.9
1893	NY-N	2	4	.333	10	7	4	0	0	68^{1}	84	62	2	6	41	11	17.3	5.93	79	.294	.393	12	.462	4	-10	-10	-1	-0.3
	Bro-N	0	2	.000	2	2	1	0	0	10	19	19	2	1	9	5	26.1	13.50	33	.388	.492	2	.400	0	-10	-11	-0	-1.2
	Yr	2	6	.250	12	9	5	0	0	78^{1}	103	81	4	7	50	16	18.4	6.89	67	.307	.408	14	.452	5	-19	-20	-1	-1.5
Total	8	72	96	.429	204	176	146	7	2	1550^{1}	1525	1190	51	58	885	719	14.3	3.99	95	.247	.347	335	.238	11	-50	-35	-9	-2.9

● CARLOS CRAWFORD

Crawford, Carlos Lamonte b: 10/4/71, Charlotte, N.C. BR/TR, 6′1″, 185 lbs. Deb: 6/7/96

YEAR	TM/L	W	L	PCT	G	GS	CG	SH	SV	IP	H	R	HR	HB	BB	SO	RAT	ERA	ERA+	OAV	OOB	BH	AVG	PB	PR	PR+	PD	TPI
1996	Phi-N	0	1	.000	1	1	0	0	0	3^{2}	7	10	1	1	2	4	24.5	4.91	88	.389	.476	0	.000	-0	-0	-0	-0	-0.1

● LARRY CRAWFORD

Crawford, Charles Lowrie b: 4/27/14, Swissvale, Pa. d: 12/20/94, Hanover, Pa. BL/TL, 6′1″, 165 lbs. Deb: 7/21/37

YEAR	TM/L	W	L	PCT	G	GS	CG	SH	SV	IP	H	R	HR	HB	BB	SO	RAT	ERA	ERA+	OAV	OOB	BH	AVG	PB	PR	PR+	PD	TPI
1937	Phi-N	0	0	—	6	0	0	0	0	6	12	10	2	0	1	2	19.5	15.00	29	.387	.406	0	—	0	-7	-6	-0	-0.3

● JIM CRAWFORD

Crawford, James Frederick "Catfish" b: 9/29/50, Chicago, Ill. BL/TL, 6′3″, 200 lbs. Deb: 4/6/73

YEAR	TM/L	W	L	PCT	G	GS	CG	SH	SV	IP	H	R	HR	HB	BB	SO	RAT	ERA	ERA+	OAV	OOB	BH	AVG	PB	PR	PR+	PD	TPI
1973	Hou-N	2	4	.333	48	0	0	0	6	70	69	41	7	2	33	56	13.4	4.50	81	.256	.341	3	.231	1	-6	-7	1	-0.5
1975	Hou-N	3	5	.375	44	2	0	0	4	86^{2}	92	40	0	2	37	37	13.6	3.63	93	.280	.356	5	.294	2	-0	-3	0	0.0
1976	Det-A	1	8	.111	32	5	1	0	2	109^{1}	115	65	4	0	43	68	13.0	4.53	82	.275	.343	0	—	0	-12	-9	5	-0.3
1977	Det-A	7	8	.467	37	7	0	0	1	126	156	82	13	1	50	91	14.8	4.79	90	.310	.373	0	—	0	-10	-6	1	-0.6
1978	Det-A	2	3	.400	20	0	0	0	0	39^{1}	45	24	3	2	19	24	15.1	4.35	89	.292	.377	0	—	0	-2	-2	-0	-0.3
Total	5	15	28	.349	181	14	1	0	13	431^{1}	477	252	27	7	182	276	13.9	4.40	87	.285	.357	8	.267	3	-31	-28	6	-1.7

● JOE CRAWFORD

Crawford, Joseph Randal b: 5/2/70, Gainesville, Fla. BL/TL, 6′3″, 225 lbs. Deb: 4/7/97

YEAR	TM/L	W	L	PCT	G	GS	CG	SH	SV	IP	H	R	HR	HB	BB	SO	RAT	ERA	ERA+	OAV	OOB	BH	AVG	PB	PR	PR+	PD	TPI
1997	NY-N	4	3	.571	19	2	0	0	0	46^{1}	36	18	7	0	13	25	9.5	3.30	122	.216	.272	0	.000	-1	5	4	0	0.4

● PAXTON CRAWFORD

Crawford, Paxton Keith b: 8/4/77, Little Rock, Ark. BR/TR, 6′3″, 205 lbs. Deb: 7/1/2000

YEAR	TM/L	W	L	PCT	G	GS	CG	SH	SV	IP	H	R	HR	HB	BB	SO	RAT	ERA	ERA+	OAV	OOB	BH	AVG	PB	PR	PR+	PD	TPI
2000	Bos-A	2	1	.667	7	4	0	0	0	29	25	15	0	2	13	17	12.4	3.41	149	.240	.336	0	—	0	5	5	-1	0.4

● STEVE CRAWFORD

Crawford, Steven Ray b: 4/29/58, Pryor, Okla. BR/TR, 6′5″, 225 lbs. Deb: 9/2/80

YEAR	TM/L	W	L	PCT	G	GS	CG	SH	SV	IP	H	R	HR	HB	BB	SO	RAT	ERA	ERA+	OAV	OOB	BH	AVG	PB	PR	PR+	PD	TPI
1980	Bos-A	2	0	1.000	6	4	2	0	0	32^{1}	41	14	3	0	8	10	13.6	3.62	117	.306	.345	0	—	0	2	2	-0	0.1
1981	Bos-A	0	5	.000	14	11	0	0	0	57^{2}	69	38	10	3	18	29	14.0	4.99	78	.301	.360	0	—	0	-9	-7	0	-0.5
1982	Bos-A	1	0	1.000	5	0	0	0	0	9	14	3	0	0	0	2	14.0	2.00	216	.341	.341	0	—	0	2	2	-0	0.2
1984	Bos-A	5	0	1.000	35	0	0	0	1	62	69	31	6	1	21	21	13.2	3.34	125	.286	.346	0	—	0	5	5	-0	0.4
1985	Bos-A	6	5	.545	44	1	0	0	12	91	103	47	5	0	28	58	13.0	3.76	114	.289	.340	0	—	0	4	5	1	0.8
1986	*Bos-A	0	2	.000	40	0	0	0	4	57^{1}	69	29	5	0	19	32	13.8	3.92	106	.308	.362	0	—	0	2	2	0	0.1
1987	Bos-A	5	4	.556	29	0	0	0	0	72^{2}	91	48	13	2	32	43	15.5	5.33	86	.314	.386	0	—	0	-7	-6	1	-0.6
1989	KC-A	3	1	.750	25	0	0	0	0	54	48	19	2	3	19	33	11.7	2.83	136	.242	.318	0	—	0	6	6	2	0.6
1990	KC-A	5	4	.556	46	0	0	0	1	80	79	38	7	3	23	54	11.8	4.16	92	.254	.312	0	—	0	-2	-3	1	-0.2
1991	KC-A	3	2	.600	33	0	0	0	1	46^{2}	60	31	3	1	18	38	15.2	5.98	69	.311	.373	0	—	0	-10	-10	-0	-0.9
Total	10	30	23	.566	277	16	2	0	19	562^{2}	643	298	54	13	186	320	13.5	4.17	99	.290	.348	0	—	0	-7	-2	3	0.0

● DOUG CREEK

Creek, Paul Douglas b: 3/1/69, Winchester, Va. BL/TL, 5′10″, 205 lbs. Deb: 9/17/95

YEAR	TM/L	W	L	PCT	G	GS	CG	SH	SV	IP	H	R	HR	HB	BB	SO	RAT	ERA	ERA+	OAV	OOB	BH	AVG	PB	PR	PR+	PD	TPI
1995	StL-N	0	0	—	6	0	0	0	0	6^{2}	2	0	0	0	3	10	6.8	0.00	—	.095	.208	0	—	0	3	3	-0	0.1
1996	SF-N	0	2	.000	63	0	0	0	0	48^{1}	45	41	11	2	32	38	14.7	6.52	63	.243	.361	0	.000	-0	-12	-13	-1	-0.7
1997	SF-N	1	2	.333	3	3	0	0	0	13^{1}	12	12	1	0	14	14	17.6	6.75	61	.240	.406	1	.333	0	-4	-4	0	-0.7
1999	Chi-N	0	0	—	3	0	0	0	0	6	6	7	1	0	8	6	21.0	10.50	43	.261	.452	0	—	0	-4	-4	-0	-0.2
2000	TB-A	1	3	.250	45	0	0	0	1	60^{2}	49	33	10	2	39	73	13.4	4.60	108	.224	.346	0	—	0	2	2	1	0.2
Total	5	2	7	.222	120	3	0	0	1	135	114	93	23	4	96	141	14.3	5.53	81	.229	.358	1	.250	0	-15	-16	-0	-1.3

● JACK CREEL

Creel, Jack Dalton "Tex" b: 4/23/16, Kyle, Tex. BR/TR, 6′, 165 lbs. Deb: 4/22/45

YEAR	TM/L	W	L	PCT	G	GS	CG	SH	SV	IP	H	R	HR	HB	BB	SO	RAT	ERA	ERA+	OAV	OOB	BH	AVG	PB	PR	PR+	PD	TPI
1945	StL-N	5	4	.556	26	8	2	0	2	87	78	41	5	6	45	34	13.3	4.14	90	.245	.349	2	.077	-2	-3	-4	0	-0.5

● KEITH CREEL

Creel, Steven Keith b: 2/4/59, Dallas, Tex. BR/TR, 6′2″, 180 lbs. Deb: 5/25/82

YEAR	TM/L	W	L	PCT	G	GS	CG	SH	SV	IP	H	R	HR	HB	BB	SO	RAT	ERA	ERA+	OAV	OOB	BH	AVG	PB	PR	PR+	PD	TPI
1982	KC-A	1	4	.200	9	6	0	0	0	41^{2}	43	28	8	0	25	13	14.7	5.40	76	.267	.366	0	—	0	-6	-6	0	-0.6
1983	KC-A	2	5	.286	25	10	1	0	0	89^{1}	116	66	17	2	35	31	15.4	6.35	64	.320	.382	0	—	0	-23	-22	-1	-1.6
1985	Cle-A	2	5	.286	15	8	0	0	0	62	73	35	7	2	23	31	14.2	4.79	86	.296	.360	0	—	0	-4	-5	-1	-0.6
1987	Tex-A	0	0	—	6	0	0	0	0	9^{2}	12	5	2	0	5	5	15.8	4.66	96	.293	.370	0	—	0	-0	-0	0	0.0
Total	4	5	14	.263	55	24	1	0	0	202^{2}	244	134	34	4	88	80	14.9	5.60	74	.300	.372	0	—	0	-33	-33	-2	-2.8

● BOB CREMINS

Cremins, Robert Anthony "Lefty" or "Crooked Arm" b: 2/15/06, Pelham Manor, N.Y. BL/TL, 5′11″, 178 lbs. Deb: 8/17/27

YEAR	TM/L	W	L	PCT	G	GS	CG	SH	SV	IP	H	R	HR	HB	BB	SO	RAT	ERA	ERA+	OAV	OOB	BH	AVG	PB	PR	PR+	PD	TPI
1927	Bos-A	0	0	—	4	0	0	0	0	5^{1}	5	4	0	0	3	0	13.5	5.06	83	.250	.348	0	—	0	-1	-0	0	0.0

● WALKER CRESS

Cress, Walker James "Foots" b: 3/6/17, Ben Hur, Va. d: 4/21/96, Baton Rouge, La. BR/TR, 6′5″, 205 lbs. Deb: 4/27/48

YEAR	TM/L	W	L	PCT	G	GS	CG	SH	SV	IP	H	R	HR	HB	BB	SO	RAT	ERA	ERA+	OAV	OOB	BH	AVG	PB	PR	PR+	PD	TPI
1948	Cin-N	0	1	.000	30	2	1	0	0	60	60	32	2	1	42	33	15.5	4.50	87	.271	.390	4	.500	2	-4	-4	-1	-0.1
1949	Cin-N	0	0	—	3	0	0	0	0	2	2	0	0	0	3	0	22.5	0.00	—	.286	.500	0	—	0	1	1	-0	0.0
Total	2	0	1	.000	33	2	1	0	0	62	62	32	2	1	45	33	15.7	4.35	90	.272	.394	4	.500	2	-3	-3	-1	-0.1

● JACK CRESSEND

Cressend, John Baptiste b: 5/13/75, New Orleans, La. BR/TR, 6′1″, 185 lbs. Deb: 8/26/2000

YEAR	TM/L	W	L	PCT	G	GS	CG	SH	SV	IP	H	R	HR	HB	BB	SO	RAT	ERA	ERA+	OAV	OOB	BH	AVG	PB	PR	PR+	PD	TPI
2000	Min-A	0	0	—	11	0	0	0	0	13^{2}	20	8	0	0	6	6	17.1	5.27	100	.364	.426	0	—	0	-1	-0	-0	0.0

● TIM CREWS

Crews, Stanley Timothy b: 4/3/61, Tampa, Fla. d: 3/23/93, Orlando, Fla. BR/TR, 6′, 192 lbs. Deb: 7/27/87

YEAR	TM/L	W	L	PCT	G	GS	CG	SH	SV	IP	H	R	HR	HB	BB	SO	RAT	ERA	ERA+	OAV	OOB	BH	AVG	PB	PR	PR+	PD	TPI
1987	LA-N	1	1	.500	20	0	0	0	3	29	30	9	2	2	8	20	12.4	2.48	160	.268	.328	0	.000	-0	5	5	0	0.4
1988	LA-N	4	0	1.000	42	0	0	0	0	71^{2}	77	29	3	0	16	45	11.7	3.14	106	.278	.317	1	.200	0	2	2	-1	0.0
1989	LA-N	0	1	.000	44	0	0	0	1	61^{2}	69	27	7	2	23	56	13.7	3.21	107	.284	.351	0	—	0	2	1	-0	0.1
1990	LA-N	4	5	.444	66	2	0	0	5	107^{1}	98	40	9	1	24	76	10.3	2.77	132	.238	.282	0	.000	-1	12	11	-1	0.8
1991	LA-N	2	3	.400	60	0	0	0	6	76	75	30	7	0	19	53	11.1	3.43	105	.256	.301	0	.000	0	2	1	0	0.1
1992	LA-N	0	3	.000	49	2	0	0	0	78	95	46	6	2	20	43	13.5	5.19	66	.310	.357	2	.286	0	-15	-15	-1	-0.8
Total	6	11	13	.458	281	4	0	0	15	423^{2}	444	181	34	7	110	293	11.9	3.44	103	.270	.319	3	.136	-0	9	5	-3	0.6

● JERRY CRIDER

Crider, Jerry Stephen b: 9/2/41, Sioux Falls, S.D. BR/TR, 6′2″, 200 lbs. Deb: 5/21/69

YEAR	TM/L	W	L	PCT	G	GS	CG	SH	SV	IP	H	R	HR	HB	BB	SO	RAT	ERA	ERA+	OAV	OOB	BH	AVG	PB	PR	PR+	PD	TPI
1969	Min-A	1	0	1.000	21	1	0	0	1	28^{2}	31	15	3	2	15	16	15.1	4.71	78	.284	.381	4	.444	2	-3	-3	0	0.0
1970	Chi-A	4	7	.364	32	8	0	0	4	91	101	49	13	2	34	40	13.5	4.45	88	.288	.354	2	.083	-1	-7	-5	-2	-1.0
Total	2	5	7	.417	53	9	0	0	5	119^{2}	132	64	16	4	49	56	13.9	4.51	85	.287	.361	6	.182	1	-11	-9	-2	-1.0

● CHUCK CRIM

Crim, Charles Robert b: 7/23/61, Van Nuys, Cal. BR/TR, 6′, 185 lbs. Deb: 4/8/87

YEAR	TM/L	W	L	PCT	G	GS	CG	SH	SV	IP	H	R	HR	HB	BB	SO	RAT	ERA	ERA+	OAV	OOB	BH	AVG	PB	PR	PR+	PD	TPI
1987	Mil-A	6	8	.429	53	5	0	0	12	130	133	60	15	3	39	56	12.1	3.67	125	.266	.323	0	—	0	12	13	-0	1.4
1988	Mil-A	7	6	.538	**70**	0	0	0	9	105	95	38	11	2	28	58	10.7	2.91	137	.247	.302	0	—	0	12	12	0	1.6
1989	Mil-A	9	7	.563	**76**	0	0	0	7	117^{2}	114	42	7	2	36	59	11.6	2.83	136	.259	.318	0	—	0	14	13	-1	1.7
1990	Mil-A	3	5	.375	67	0	0	0	11	85^{2}	88	39	7	2	23	39	11.9	3.47	112	.261	.312	0	—	0	4	4	0	0.5
1991	Mil-A	8	5	.615	66	0	0	0	3	91^{1}	115	52	9	2	25	39	14.0	4.63	86	.305	.351	0	—	0	-5	-7	0	-0.9
1992	Cal-A	7	6	.538	57	0	0	0	1	87	100	56	11	6	29	30	14.0	5.17	77	.293	.359	0	—	0	-12	-11	0	-1.5
1993	Cal-A	2	2	.500	11	0	0	0	0	15^{1}	17	11	2	2	5	10	14.1	5.87	77	.298	.375	0	—	0	-3	-2	1	-0.4
1994	Chi-N	5	4	.556	49	1	0	0	2	64^{1}	69	36	9	1	24	43	13.2	4.48	93	.271	.336	0	.000	-0	-2	-2	0	-0.3
Total	8	47	43	.522	449	6	0	0	45	696^{1}	731	334	71	20	209	334	12.4	3.83	107	.272	.329	0	.000	-0	20	20	-0	2.1

● JACK CRIMIAN

Crimian, John Melvin b: 2/17/26, Philadelphia, Pa. BR/TR, 5′10″, 180 lbs. Deb: 7/3/51

YEAR	TM/L	W	L	PCT	G	GS	CG	SH	SV	IP	H	R	HR	HB	BB	SO	RAT	ERA	ERA+	OAV	OOB	BH	AVG	PB	PR	PR+	PD	TPI
1951	StL-N	1	0	1.000	11	0	0	0	1	17	24	17	3	0	8	5	16.9	9.00	44	.338	.405	1	.333	0	-10	-10	-0	-0.6
1952	StL-N	0	0	—	5	0	0	0	0	8^{1}	15	9	4	0	4	4	20.5	9.72	38	.417	.475	0	.000	0	-6	-6	-0	-0.3
1956	KC-A	4	8	.333	54	7	0	0	3	129	129	87	19	5	49	59	12.8	5.51	79	.265	.339	5	.227	1	-19	-16	-0	-1.4
1957	Det-A	0	1	.000	4	0	0	0	0	5^{2}	9	8	1	0	4	1	20.6	12.71	30	.375	.464	0	—	0	-6	-5	-0	-0.8
Total	4	5	9	.357	74	7	0	0	4	160	177	121	27	5	65	69	13.9	6.36	67	.287	.360	6	.231	1	-40	-36	-1	-3.1

● DODE CRISS

Criss, Dode b: 3/12/1885, Sherman, Miss. d: 9/8/55, Sherman, Miss. BL/TR, 6′2″, 200 lbs. Deb: 4/20/08 ♦

YEAR	TM/L	W	L	PCT	G	GS	CG	SH	SV	IP	H	R	HR	HB	BB	SO	RAT	ERA	ERA+	OAV	OOB	BH	AVG	PB	PR	PR+	PD	TPI
1908	StL-A	0	1	.000	9	1	0	0	0	18	15	14	1	3	13	9	15.5	6.50	37	.250	.408	28	.341	1	-8	-8	-1	-0.4

YEAR	TM/L	W	L	PCT	G	GS	CG	SH	SV	IP	H	R	HR	HB	BB	SO	RAT	ERA	ERA+	OAV	OOB	BH	AVG	PB	PR	PR+	PD	TPI
1909	StL-A	1	5	.167	11	6	3	0	0	55^1	53	33	0	2	32	43	14.2	3.42	71	.262	.369	14	.292	5	-6	-6	-1	-0.1
1910	StL-A	2	1	.667	6	0	0	0	0	19^1	12	7	0	4	9	9	11.6	1.40	177	.176	.309	21	.231	1	2	2	-0	0.5
1911	StL-A	0	2	.000	4	2	0	0	0	18^1	24	21	0	2	10	9	17.7	8.35	40	.333	.429	21	.253	0	-10	-10	0	-0.8
Total	4	3	9	.250	30	9	3	0	0	111	104	75	1	11	64	70	14.5	4.38	59	.259	.375	84	.276	8	-22	-23	-2	-0.8
● BILL CRISTALL Cristall, William Arthur "Lefty" b: 9/12/1878, Odessa, Russia d: 1/28/39, Buffalo, N.Y. BL/TL, 5'7", 145 lbs. Deb: 9/3/01																												
1901	Cle-A	1	5	.167	6	6	5	1	0	48^1	54	42	1	4	30	12	16.4	4.84	73	.280	.388	7	.350	2	-6	-7	2	-0.4
● LEO CRISTANTE Cristante, Dante Leo b: 12/10/26, Detroit, Mich. d: 8/24/77, Dearborn, Mich. BR/TR, 6'1", 195 lbs. Deb: 4/21/51																												
1951	Phi-N	1	1	.500	10	1	0	0	0	22	28	13	3	1	9	6	15.5	4.91	78	.318	.388	1	.167	-0	-2	-3	0	-0.2
1955	Det-A	0	1	.000	20	1	0	0	0	36^2	37	15	1	0	14	9	12.5	3.19	120	.261	.327	0	.000	-1	3	3	-1	-0.1
Total	2	1	2	.333	30	2	0	0	0	58^2	65	28	4	1	23	15	13.7	3.84	100	.283	.350	1	.077	-1	1	0	-1	-0.3
● MORRIE CRITCHLEY Critchley, Morris Arthur b: 3/26/1850, New London, Conn. d: 3/6/10, Pittsburgh, Pa. 6'1", 190 lbs. Deb: 5/8/1882																												
1882	Pit-a	1	0	1.000	1	1	1	1	0	9	7	0	0		1	3	8.0	0.00	—	.200	.222	0	.000	-1	3	3	0	0.2
	StL-a	0	4	.000	4	4	4	0	0	34	43	31	3		7	2	13.2	4.24	66	.289	.321	3	.214	-0	-6	-5	-1	-0.6
	Yr	1	4	.200	5	5	5	1	0	43	50	31	3		8	5	12.1	3.35	83	.272	.302	3	.158	-1	-3	-3	-1	-0.4
● CLAUDE CROCKER Crocker, Claude Arthur b: 7/20/24, Caroleen, N.C. BR/TR, 6'2", 185 lbs. Deb: 8/1/44																												
1944	Bro-N	0	0	—	2	0	0	0	0	3^1	6	4	0	0	5	1	29.7	10.80	33	.400	.550	1	1.000	0	-3	-3	0	-0.1
1945	Bro-N	0	0	—	1	0	0	0	1	2	2	0	0	0	1	1	13.5	0.00	—	.286	.375	0	—	0	1	1	-0	0.1
Total	2	0	0	—	3	0	0	0	1	5^1	8	4	0	0	6	2	23.6	6.75	54	.364	.500	1	1.000	0	-2	-2	0	0.0
● RAY CRONE Crone, Raymond Hayes b: 8/7/31, Memphis, Tenn. BR/TR, 6'2", 185 lbs. Deb: 4/13/54																												
1954	Mil-N	1	0	1.000	19	2	1	0	1	49	44	11	6	1	19	33	11.8	2.02	184	.247	.323	2	.200	-0	11	10	-0	0.5
1955	Mil-N	10	9	.526	33	15	6	1	0	140^1	117	63	11	0	42	76	10.2	3.46	108	.227	.285	7	.159	-1	9	5	0	0.5
1956	Mil-N	11	10	.524	35	21	6	0	2	169^2	173	92	19	1	44	73	11.6	3.87	89	.263	.311	6	.122	1	-2	-8	-1	-1.0
1957	Mil-N	3	1	.750	11	5	2	0	0	42^1	54	23	8	0	15	15	14.7	4.46	78	.312	.367	2	.182	1	-3	-5	1	-0.3
	NY-N	4	8	.333	25	17	2	0	1	120^2	131	68	11	3	40	56	13.0	4.33	91	.272	.331	1	.025	-4	-6	-5	2	-0.6
	Yr	7	9	.438	36	22	4	0	1	163	185	91	19	3	55	71	13.4	4.36	88	.282	.341	3	.059	-3	-9	-10	3	-0.9
1958	SF-N	1	2	.333	14	1	0	0	0	24	35	18	5	0	13	7	18.0	6.75	56	.354	.429	0	.000	-0	-7	-8	-0	-0.9
Total	5	30	30	.500	137	61	17	1	4	546	554	275	60	5	173	260	12.1	3.87	95	.263	.321	18	.115	-3	2	-12	2	-1.8
● JACK CRONIN Cronin, John J. b: 5/26/1874, Staten Island, N.Y d: 7/12/29, Middletown, N.Y. BR/TR, 6' ", 200 lbs. Deb: 8/24/1895																												
1895	Bro-N	0	0	—	2	0	0	0	2	5	10	8	0	0	3	1	23.4	10.80	41	.417	.481	1	.500	1	-3	-4	-0	-0.2
1898	Pit-N	2	2	.500	4	4	2	1	0	28	35	14	0	0	8	9	13.8	3.54	101	.304	.350	1	.100	-0	0	0	0	0.0
1899	Cin-N	2	2	.500	5	5	5	0	0	41	56	35	2	5	16	9	16.9	5.49	71	.324	.397	2	.118	-1	-7	-7	-1	-0.7
1901	Det-A	13	16	.448	30	28	21	1	0	219^2	261	145	6	11	42	62	12.9	3.89	99	.292	.331	21	.247	2	-6	-1	-3	-0.2
1902	Det-A	0	0	—	4	0	0	0	0	17^1	26	23	1	3	8	5	19.2	9.35	39	.347	.430	0	.000	-1	-11	-11	0	-0.5
	Bal-A	3	5	.375	10	8	8	0	0	75^2	66	29	1	0	24	20	10.7	2.62	144	.236	.296	4	.148	-1	8	9	2	1.0
	Yr	3	5	.375	14	8	8	0	0	93	92	52	2	3	32	25	12.3	3.87	97	.259	.326	4	.118	-2	-3	-1	3	0.5
	NY-N	5	6	.455	13	12	11	0	0	114	105	49	3	0	18	52	9.7	2.45	115	.245	.275	11	.169	-1	4	5	0	0.3
1903	NY-N	6	4	.600	20	11	8	0	1	115^2	130	67	5	6	37	50	13.5	3.81	88	.284	.345	9	.196	0	-7	-6	0	-0.5
1904	Bro-N	12	23	.343	40	34	33	4	0	307	284	132	10	12	79	110	11.0	2.70	102	.245	.300	17	.157	-3	1	2	0	-0.1
Total	7	43	58	.426	128	102	88	6	3	923^1	973	502	28	37	235	318	12.1	3.40	96	.270	.321	66	.180	-5	-20	-13	-1	-0.9
● GEORGE CROSBY Crosby, George Washington b: 1860, Iowa d: 1/9/13, San Francisco, Cal. Deb: 5/22/1884																												
1884	Chi-N	1	2	.333	3	3	3	0	0	28	27	21	3		12	11	12.5	3.54	89	.227	.298	4	.308	1	-2	-1	1	0.0
● KEN CROSBY Crosby, Kenneth Stewart b: 12/15/47, New Denver, B.C., Canada BR/TR, 6'2", 179 lbs. Deb: 8/5/75																												
1975	Chi-N	1	0	1.000	9	0	0	0	0	8^1	10	3	0	0	7	6	18.4	3.24	119	.294	.415	0	—	0	0	1	0	0.1
1976	Chi-N	0	0	—	7	1	0	0	0	12	20	16	3	0	8	5	21.0	12.00	32	.377	.459	1	.500	0	-11	-10	0	-0.5
Total	2	1	0	1.000	16	1	0	0	0	20^1	30	19	3	0	15	11	19.9	8.41	46	.345	.441	1	.500	1	-11	-9	0	-0.4
● LEM CROSS Cross, George Lewis b: 1/9/1872, Sanbornton, N.H. d: 10/9/30, Manchester, N.H. TR, 5'9", 155 lbs. Deb: 8/6/1893																												
1893	Cin-N	0	2	.000	3	3	2	0	0	21	24	16	3	0	9	7	14.1	5.57	86	.279	.347	2	.333	1	-2	-2	0	0.0
1894	Cin-N	3	4	.429	8	7	3	0	0	53	94	73	8	5	21	11	20.4	8.49	66	.381	.440	6	.231	-1	-19	-17	-1	-1.5
Total	2	3	6	.333	11	10	5	0	0	74	118	89	11	5	30	18	18.6	7.66	70	.354	.416	8	.250	-0	-21	-18	-0	-1.5
● DOUG CROTHERS Crothers, Douglas b: 11/16/1859, Natchez, Miss. d: 3/29/07, St.Louis, Mo. BR/TR, Deb: 8/3/1884																												
1884	KC-U	1	2	.333	3	3	3	0	0	25	26	15	0		6	11	11.5	1.80	124	.250	.291	2	.133	-2	2	1	-1	-0.1
1885	NY-a	7	11	.389	18	18	18	1	0	154	192	135	4	2	49	40	14.2	5.08	58	.293	.344	8	.157	0	-31	-40	0	-3.4
Total	2	8	13	.381	21	21	21	1	0	179	218	150	4	2	55	51	13.8	4.63	62	.287	.337	10	.152	-1	-30	-39	-0	-3.5
● BILL CROUCH Crouch, William Henry "Skip" b: 12/3/1886, Marshallton, Del. d: 12/22/45, Highland Park, Mich. BL/TL, 6'1", 210 lbs. Deb: 7/12/10 F																												
1910	StL-A	0	0	—	1	1	1	0	0	8	6	4	0	0	7	2	14.6	3.38	73	.231	.394	0	.000	-0	-1	-1	-0	-0.1
● BILL CROUCH Crouch, Wilmer Elmer b: 8/20/10, Wilmington, Del. d: 12/26/80, Howell, Mich. BB/TR, 6'1", 180 lbs. Deb: 5/9/39 F																												
1939	Bro-N	4	0	1.000	6	3	3	0	0	38^1	37	14	3	0	14	10	12.0	2.58	156	.255	.321	2	.133	-1	6	6	-1	0.4
1941	Phi-N	2	3	.400	20	5	1	0	1	59	65	31	4	0	17	26	12.5	4.42	84	.286	.336	1	.091	-0	-5	-5	2	-0.2
	StL-N	1	2	.333	18	4	0	0	6	45	45	16	2	0	14	15	11.8	3.00	125	.271	.328	0	.000	-1	3	4	-1	0.1
	Yr	3	5	.375	38	9	1	0	7	104	110	47	6	0	31	41	12.2	3.81	98	.280	.333	1	.042	-2	-2	-1	1	-0.1
1945	StL-N	1	0	1.000	6	0	0	0	0	13^1	12	5	1	1	7	4	13.5	3.38	111	.255	.364	0	.000	-0	1	1	0	0.0
Total	3	8	5	.615	50	12	4	0	7	155^2	159	66	10	1	52	55	12.3	3.47	110	.272	.332	3	.073	-3	4	6	0	0.3
● ZACH CROUCH Crouch, Zachary Quinn b: 10/26/65, Folsom, Cal. BL/TL, 6'3", 180 lbs. Deb: 6/4/88																												
1988	Bos-A	0	0	—	3	0	0	0	0	1^1	4	1	0	0	2	0	40.5	6.75	61	.571	.667	0	—	0	-0	-0	0	0.0
● RICK CROUSHORE Croushore, Richard Steven b: 8/7/70, Lakehurst, N.J. BR/TR, 6'4", 210 lbs. Deb: 5/18/98																												
1998	StL-N	0	3	.000	41	0	0	0	8	54^1	44	31	6	4	29	47	12.8	4.97	84	.213	.321	0	—	0	-4	-5	1	-0.2
1999	StL-N	3	7	.300	59	0	0	0	3	71^2	68	42	9	3	43	88	14.3	4.14	110	.247	.355	1	.333	1	3	3	-1	0.4
2000	Col-N	2	0	1.000	6	0	0	0	0	11^1	15	11	1	1	6	11	17.5	8.74	68	.313	.400	1	1.000	0	-5	-3	-0	-0.4
	Bos-A	0	1	.000	5	0	0	0	0	4^2	4	3	0	1	5	3	19.3	5.79	88	.250	.455	0	—	0	-0	-0	0	-0.1
Total	3	5	11	.313	111	0	0	0	11	142	131	87	16	9	83	149	14.1	4.88	93	.240	.350	2	.500	1	-7	-5	-0	-0.3
● DEAN CROW Crow, Paul Dean b: 8/21/72, Garland, Tex. BL/TR, 6'4", 215 lbs. Deb: 5/29/98																												
1998	Det-A	2	2	.500	32	0	0	0	0	45^2	55	22	6	2	16	18	14.4	3.94	120	.313	.376	0	—	0	4	4	-0	0.3
● ALVIN CROWDER Crowder, Alvin Floyd "General" b: 1/11/1899, Winston-Salem, N.C d: 4/3/72, Winston-Salem, N.C. BL/TR, 5'10", 170 lbs. Deb: 7/24/26																												
1926	Was-A	7	4	.636	19	12	6	0	1	100	97	52	3	2	60	26	14.3	3.96	98	.261	.367	9	.237	1	1	-1	1	0.1
1927	Was-A	4	7	.364	15	11	4	2	0	67^1	58	44	3	2	42	22	13.6	4.54	89	.232	.347	3	.136	-1	-3	-4	-1	-0.7
	StL-A	3	5	.375	21	8	2	1	3	73^2	71	44	3	1	42	30	13.9	5.01	87	.260	.361	6	.261	0	-7	-5	-1	-0.6
	Yr	7	12	.368	36	19	6	3	3	141	129	88	6	3	84	52	13.8	4.79	88	.247	.354	9	.200	-1	-10	-9	-2	-1.3
1928	StL-A	21	5	**.808**	41	31	19	1	2	244	238	113	11	1	91	99	12.2	3.69	114	.258	.325	15	.188	-2	10	13	-5	0.6
1929	StL-A	17	15	.531	40	34	19	**4**	4	266^2	272	133	22	0	93	79	12.3	3.92	113	.271	.332	18	.188	-3	10	14	-2	1.0
1930	StL-A	3	7	.300	13	10	5	1	1	77^1	85	43	11	1	27	42	13.2	4.66	105	.283	.345	4	.160	-2	-0	2	1	0.1
	Was-A	15	9	.625	27	25	20	0	1	202^1	191	90	6	1	69	65	11.6	3.60	128	.249	.312	13	.171	-2	24	23	-4	1.7
	Yr	18	16	.529	40	35	25	1	2	279^2	276	133	17	2	96	107	12.0	3.89	120	.259	.321	17	.168	-4	23	24	-3	1.8
1931	Was-A	18	11	.621	44	26	13	1	2	234^1	255	117	13	1	72	85	12.6	3.88	111	.275	.328	19	.216	-1	13	11	-3	0.8
1932	Was-A	**26**	13	.667	50	39	21	3	1	**327**	319	136	17	0	77	103	10.9	3.33	130	.252	.295	27	.221	2	42	37	-2	3.7
1933	*Was-A★	**24**	15	.615	**52**	35	17	0	4	299^1	311	140	14	3	81	110	11.9	3.97	105	.267	.316	19	.186	1	10	7	-3	0.6
1934	Was-A	4	10	.286	29	13	4	0	3	100^2	142	88	9	0	38	39	16.1	6.79	64	.326	.380	7	.219	1	-26	-29	-1	-3.3
	*Det-A	5	1	.833	9	9	3	1	0	66^2	81	35	3	0	20	30	13.6	4.18	105	.295	.342	4	.133	-2	2	2	-1	-0.2

YEAR	TM/L	W	L	PCT	G	GS	CG	SH	SV	IP	H	R	HR	HB	BB	SO	RAT	ERA	ERA+	OAV	OOB	BH	AVG	PB	PR	PR+	PD	TPI
	Yr	9	11	.450	38	22	7	1	3	167^1	223	123	12	0	58	69	15.1	5.75	76	.314	.365	11	.177	-1	-23	-27	-2	-3.5
1935	*Det-A	16	10	.615	33	32	16	2	0	241	269	127	16	4	67	59	12.7	4.26	98	.285	.335	17	.183	-2	5	-2	-3	-0.7
1936	Det-A	4	3	.571	9	7	1	0	0	44	64	42	5	0	21	10	17.4	8.39	59	.342	.409	3	.150	-1	-16	-17	-0	-2.0
Total	11	167	115	.592	402	292	150	16	22	2344^1	2453	1204	136	16	800	799	12.5	4.12	105	.270	.330	164	.194	-12	64	53	-24	1.1

● JIM CROWELL Crowell, James Everette b: 5/14/74, Minneapolis, Minn. BL/TL, 6'4", 220 lbs. Deb: 9/12/97

YEAR	TM/L	W	L	PCT	G	GS	CG	SH	SV	IP	H	R	HR	HB	BB	SO	RAT	ERA	ERA+	OAV	OOB	BH	AVG	PB	PR	PR+	PD	TPI
1997	Cin-N	0	1	.000	2	1	0	0	0	6^1	12	7	2	0	5	3	24.2	9.95	43	.414	.500	0	.000	-0	-4	-4	0	-0.5

● CAP CROWELL Crowell, Minot Joy b: 9/5/1892, Roxbury, Mass. d: 9/30/62, Central Falls, R.I. BR/TR, 6'1", 178 lbs. Deb: 6/23/15

YEAR	TM/L	W	L	PCT	G	GS	CG	SH	SV	IP	H	R	HR	HB	BB	SO	RAT	ERA	ERA+	OAV	OOB	BH	AVG	PB	PR	PR+	PD	TPI
1915	Phi-A	2	6	.250	10	8	4	0	0	54^1	56	53	1	5	47	15	17.9	5.47	54	.292	.443	5	.227	-0	-15	-15	-0	-2.0
1916	Phi-A	0	5	.000	9	6	1	0	0	39^2	43	33	0	2	34	15	17.9	4.99	57	.289	.427	0	.000	-2	-10	-9	-1	-1.3
Total	2	2	11	.154	19	14	5	0	0	94	99	86	1	7	81	30	17.9	5.27	55	.290	.436	5	.147	-2	-25	-25	-1	-3.3

● BILLY CROWELL Crowell, William Theodore b: 11/6/1865, Cincinnati, Ohio d: 7/24/35, Ft.Worth, Tex. BR/TR, 5'8.5", 160 lbs. Deb: 4/20/1887

YEAR	TM/L	W	L	PCT	G	GS	CG	SH	SV	IP	H	R	HR	HB	BB	SO	RAT	ERA	ERA+	OAV	OOB	BH	AVG	PB	PR	PR+	PD	TPI
1887	Cle-a	14	31	.311	45	45	45	1	0	389^1	679	350	9	20	138	72	16.2	4.88	89	.379	.386	32	.193	-13	-25	-23	-3	-3.1
1888	Cle-a	5	13	.278	18	18	16	0	0	150^2	212	148	8	9	61	61	16.8	5.79	53	.320	.385	5	.086	-5	-46	-45	-1	-4.4
	Lou-a	0	1	.000	1	1	1	0	0	9	12	14	1	1	6	5	19.0	6.00	51	.308	.413	0	.000	-0	-3	-3	0	-0.2
	Yr	5	14	.263	19	19	17	0	0	159^2	224	162	9	10	67	66	17.0	5.81	53	.320	.387	5	.082	-5	-49	-48	-0	-4.6
Total	2	19	45	.297	64	64	62	1	0	549	903	512	18	30	205	138	16.4	5.15	77	.362	.386	37	.163	-18	-74	-71	-4	-7.7

● WOODY CROWSON Crowson, Thomas Woodrow b: 9/9/18, Fuquay Sprgs., N.C d: 8/14/47, Mayodan, N.C. BR/TR, 6'2", 185 lbs. Deb: 4/17/45

YEAR	TM/L	W	L	PCT	G	GS	CG	SH	SV	IP	H	R	HR	HB	BB	SO	RAT	ERA	ERA+	OAV	OOB	BH	AVG	PB	PR	PR+	PD	TPI
1945	Phi-A	0	0	—	1	0	0	0	0	3	2	2	0	0	3	2	15.0	6.00	57	.200	.385	0	.000	-0	-1	-1	0	0.0

● CAL CRUM Crum, Calvin N. b: 7/27/1890, Cooks Mills, Ill. d: 12/7/45, Tulsa, Okla. BR/TR, 6'1", 175 lbs. Deb: 4/17/17

YEAR	TM/L	W	L	PCT	G	GS	CG	SH	SV	IP	H	R	HR	HB	BB	SO	RAT	ERA	ERA+	OAV	OOB	BH	AVG	PB	PR	PR+	PD	TPI
1917	Bos-N	0	0	—	1	0	0	0	0	1	1	0	0	0	1	0	18.0	0.00	—	.250	.400	0	—	0	0	0	0	0.1
1918	Bos-N	0	1	.000	1	1	0	0	0	2^1	6	4	0	1	3	0	38.6	15.43	17	.600	.714	0	.000	-0	-3	-3	0	-0.5
Total	2	0	1	.000	2	1	0	0	0	3^1	7	4	0	1	4	0	32.4	10.80	24	.500	.632	0	.000	-0	-3	-3	1	-0.4

● ROY CRUMPLER Crumpler, Roy Maxton b: 7/8/1896, Clinton, N.C. d: 10/6/69, Fayetteville, N.C. BL/TL, 6'1", 195 lbs. Deb: 9/16/20

YEAR	TM/L	W	L	PCT	G	GS	CG	SH	SV	IP	H	R	HR	HB	BB	SO	RAT	ERA	ERA+	OAV	OOB	BH	AVG	PB	PR	PR+	PD	TPI
1920	Det-A	1	0	1.000	2	2	1	0	0	13	17	13	2	1	11	2	20.1	5.54	67	.315	.439	3	.333	1	-3	-3	-0	-0.1
1925	Phi-N	0	0	—	3	1	0	0	0	4^2	8	4	0	0	2	1	19.3	7.71	62	.381	.435	0	.000	-0	-2	-1	0	-0.1
Total	2	1	0	1.000	5	3	1	0	0	17^2	25	17	2	1	13	3	19.9	6.11	65	.333	.438	3	.273	1	-4	-4	-0	-0.2

● DICK CRUTCHER Crutcher, Richard Louis b: 11/25/1889, Frankfort, Ky. d: 6/19/52, Frankfort, Ky. BR/TR, 5'9", 148 lbs. Deb: 4/14/14

YEAR	TM/L	W	L	PCT	G	GS	CG	SH	SV	IP	H	R	HR	HB	BB	SO	RAT	ERA	ERA+	OAV	OOB	BH	AVG	PB	PR	PR+	PD	TPI
1914	Bos-N	5	7	.417	33	15	5	1	0	158^2	169	73	4	6	66	48	13.7	3.46	80	.293	.371	8	.148	-1	-12	-13	1	-0.9
1915	Bos-N	2	2	.500	14	4	1	0	2	43^2	50	28	1	2	16	17	14.0	4.33	60	.309	.378	3	.231	1	-8	-9	0	-0.8
Total	2	7	9	.438	47	19	6	1	2	202^1	219	101	5	8	82	65	13.7	3.65	75	.296	.373	11	.164	-0	-19	-21	1	-1.7

● NELSON CRUZ Cruz, Nelson b: 9/13/72, Puerto Plata, D.R. BR/TR, 6'1", 160 lbs. Deb: 8/1/97

YEAR	TM/L	W	L	PCT	G	GS	CG	SH	SV	IP	H	R	HR	HB	BB	SO	RAT	ERA	ERA+	OAV	OOB	BH	AVG	PB	PR	PR+	PD	TPI
1997	Chi-A	0	2	.000	19	0	0	0	0	26^1	29	19	6	0	9	23	13.0	6.49	68	.274	.330	0	—	0	-6	-6	-0	-0.4
1999	Det-A	2	5	.286	29	6	0	0	0	66^2	74	44	11	3	23	46	13.5	5.67	86	.281	.346	0	—	0	-6	-6	2	-0.3
2000	Det-A	5	2	.714	27	0	0	0	0	41	39	14	4	3	13	34	12.1	3.07	156	.253	.324	0	.000	-0	8	8	0	1.2
Total	3	7	9	.438	75	6	0	0	0	134	142	77	21	6	45	103	13.0	5.04	94	.272	.336	0	.000	-0	-3	-4	2	0.5

● TODD CRUZ Cruz, Todd Ruben b: 11/23/55, Highland Park, Mich BR/TR, 6', 175 lbs. Deb: 9/4/78 ♦

YEAR	TM/L	W	L	PCT	G	GS	CG	SH	SV	IP	H	R	HR	HB	BB	SO	RAT	ERA	ERA+	OAV	OOB	BH	AVG	PB	PR	PR+	PD	TPI
1984	Bal-A	0	0	—	1	0	0	0	0	1	0	0	0	0	0	0	0.0	0.00	—	.000	.000	31	.218	0	0	0	0	0.0

● VICTOR CRUZ Cruz, Victor Manuel (b: Victor Manuel De La Cruz (Gil)) b: 12/24/57, Rancho Viejo La Vega, D.R. BR/TR, 5'9", 200 lbs. Deb: 6/24/78

YEAR	TM/L	W	L	PCT	G	GS	CG	SH	SV	IP	H	R	HR	HB	BB	SO	RAT	ERA	ERA+	OAV	OOB	BH	AVG	PB	PR	PR+	PD	TPI
1978	Tor-A	7	3	.700	32	0	0	0	9	47^1	28	10	0	1	35	51	12.2	1.71	230	.179	.333	0	—	0	11	11	-0	2.4
1979	Cle-A	3	9	.250	61	0	0	0	10	78^2	70	41	10	1	44	63	13.2	4.23	101	.244	.346	0	—	0	-0	0	-2	-0.1
1980	Cle-A	6	7	.462	55	0	0	0	12	86	71	36	10	3	27	88	10.6	3.45	118	.229	.297	0	—	0	6	6	-1	0.9
1981	Pit-N	1	1	.500	22	0	0	0	1	34	33	10	6	1	15	28	13.0	2.65	136	.264	.348	0	.000	-0	3	3	0	0.2
1983	Tex-A	1	3	.250	17	0	0	0	5	25	16	7	2	1	10	18	9.7	1.44	279	.184	.276	0	—	0	7	7	-0	1.4
Total	5	18	23	.439	187	0	0	0	37	271	218	104	28	7	131	248	11.8	3.09	131	.226	.323	0	.000	-0	27	28	-4	4.8

● DARWIN CUBILLAN Cubillan, Darwin Harrikson (Salom) b: 11/15/74, Bobure, Venez. BR/TR, 6'2", 170 lbs. Deb: 5/20/2000

YEAR	TM/L	W	L	PCT	G	GS	CG	SH	SV	IP	H	R	HR	HB	BB	SO	RAT	ERA	ERA+	OAV	OOB	BH	AVG	PB	PR	PR+	PD	TPI
2000	Tor-A	1	0	1.000	7	0	0	0	0	15^2	20	14	5	1	11	14	18.4	8.04	62	.317	.427	0	.000	-0	-5	-5	0	-0.3
	Tex-A	0	0	—	13	0	0	0	0	17^2	32	22	4	0	14	13	23.4	10.70	48	.400	.489	0	—	0	-11	-11	0	-0.5
	Yr	1	0	1.000	20	0	0	0	0	33^1	52	36	9	1	25	27	21.1	9.45	53	.364	.462	0	.000	-0	-17	-16	0	-0.8

● COOKIE CUCCURULLO Cuccurullo, Arthur Joseph b: 2/8/18, Asbury Park, N.J. d: 1/23/83, W.Orange, N.J. BL/TL, 5'10", 168 lbs. Deb: 10/3/43

YEAR	TM/L	W	L	PCT	G	GS	CG	SH	SV	IP	H	R	HR	HB	BB	SO	RAT	ERA	ERA+	OAV	OOB	BH	AVG	PB	PR	PR+	PD	TPI
1943	Pit-N	0	1	.000	1	1	0	0	0	7	10	7	0	0	3	3	16.7	6.43	54	.357	.419	0	—	1	-2	-2	0	-0.2
1944	Pit-N	2	1	.667	32	4	0	0	4	106^1	110	65	5	3	44	31	13.3	4.06	91	.270	.346	14	.368	5	-5	-4	1	0.4
1945	Pit-N	1	3	.250	29	4	0	0	1	56^2	68	41	2	1	34	17	16.4	5.24	75	.305	.399	3	.214	-0	-9	-8	0	-0.5
Total	3	3	5	.375	62	9	0	0	5	170	188	113	7	4	81	51	14.5	4.55	83	.286	.367	17	.327	5	-17	-14	1	-0.3

● JIM CUDWORTH Cudworth, James Alaric "Cuddy" b: 8/22/1858, Fairhaven, Mass. d: 12/21/43, Middleboro, Mass. BR/TR, 6', 165 lbs. Deb: 7/27/1884 ♦

YEAR	TM/L	W	L	PCT	G	GS	CG	SH	SV	IP	H	R	HR	HB	BB	SO	RAT	ERA	ERA+	OAV	OOB	BH	AVG	PB	PR	PR+	PD	TPI
1884	KC-U	0	0	—	2	1	1	0	0	17	19	16	1		3	6	11.6	4.24	53	.264	.293	17	.147	-1	-3	-4	-1	-0.3

● CHARLIE CUELLAR Cuellar, Jesus Patracis b: 8/23/17, Ybor City, Fla. d: 10/11/94, Tampa, Fla. BR/TR, 5'11", 183 lbs. Deb: 7/2/50

YEAR	TM/L	W	L	PCT	G	GS	CG	SH	SV	IP	H	R	HR	HB	BB	SO	RAT	ERA	ERA+	OAV	OOB	BH	AVG	PB	PR	PR+	PD	TPI
1950	Chi-A	0	0	—	2	0	0	0	0	1^1	6	6	0	0	3	1	60.8	33.75	13	.600	.692	0	—	0	-4	-4	0	-0.2

● MIKE CUELLAR Cuellar, Miguel Angel (Santana) b: 5/8/37, Santa Clara, Cuba BL/TL, 5'11", 175 lbs. Deb: 4/18/59

YEAR	TM/L	W	L	PCT	G	GS	CG	SH	SV	IP	H	R	HR	HB	BB	SO	RAT	ERA	ERA+	OAV	OOB	BH	AVG	PB	PR	PR+	PD	TPI
1959	Cin-N	0	0	—	2	0	0	0	0	4	7	8	1	0	4	5	24.8	15.75	26	.368	.478	0	.000	-0	-5	-5	-0	-0.3
1964	StL-N	5	5	.500	32	7	1	0	4	72	80	43	8	1	33	56	14.3	4.50	85	.288	.365	0	.000	-2	-8	-5	1	-0.8
1965	Hou-N	1	4	.200	25	4	0	0	2	56	55	24	3	1	21	46	12.4	3.54	95	.262	.332	0	.000	-1	0	-1	0	-0.2
1966	Hou-N	12	10	.545	38	28	11	1	2	227^1	193	79	10	0	52	175	9.7	2.22	154	.229	.274	8	.113	-1	35	32	0	3.0
1967	Hou-N★	16	11	.593	36	32	16	3	1	246^1	233	99	16	1	63	203	10.9	3.03	109	.248	.296	13	.140	1	9	8	0	0.9
1968	Hou-N	8	11	.421	28	24	11	2	1	170^2	152	60	8	1	45	133	10.4	2.74	108	.237	.289	11	.193	2	5	4	-0	0.7
1969	*Bal-A	23	11	.676	39	39	18	5	0	290^2	213	94	18	1	79	182	9.1	2.38	150	.204	**.261**	12	.117	-3	**40**	**39**	-0	4.2
1970	*Bal-A☆	**24**	8	**.750**	40	40	**21**	4	0	297^2	273	126	34	1	69	190	10.4	3.48	105	.242	.286	10	.089	-4	8	6	-3	-0.2
1971	*Bal-A★	20	9	.690	38	38	21	4	0	292^1	250	111	30	1	78	124	10.1	3.08	109	.234	.287	11	.103	-4	13	9	1	0.5
1972	Bal-A	18	12	.600	35	35	17	4	0	248^1	197	78	21	0	71	132	9.7	2.57	120	.220	.277	11	.126	-1	14	14	0	1.6
1973	*Bal-A	18	13	.581	38	38	17	2	0	267	265	120	29	0	84	140	11.8	3.27	114	.258	.314	0	—	0	16	14	0	1.6
1974	*Bal-A☆	22	10	**.688**	38	38	20	5	0	269^1	253	106	17	2	86	106	11.4	3.11	111	.252	.312	0	—	0	15	11	-3	1.0
1975	Bal-A	14	12	.538	36	36	17	5	0	256	229	112	17	1	84	105	11.0	3.66	96	.249	.313	0	—	0	4	-4	2	-0.2
1976	Bal-A	4	13	.235	26	19	2	1	1	107	129	63	8	2	50	32	15.2	4.96	66	.307	.383	0	—	0	-17	-22	-0	-3.1
1977	Cal-A	0	1	.000	2	1	0	0	0	3^1	9	7	2	0	3	3	32.4	18.90	21	.500	.571	0	—	0	-5	-6	-0	-0.9
Total	15	185	130	.587	453	379	172	36	11	2808	2538	1130	222	12	822	1632	10.8	3.14	110	.243	.299	76	.115	-13	124	96	-2	7.8

● BOBBY CUELLAR Cuellar, Robert b: 8/20/52, Alice, Tex. BR/TR, 5'11", 188 lbs. Deb: 9/9/77

YEAR	TM/L	W	L	PCT	G	GS	CG	SH	SV	IP	H	R	HR	HB	BB	SO	RAT	ERA	ERA+	OAV	OOB	BH	AVG	PB	PR	PR+	PD	TPI
1977	Tex-A	0	0	—	4	0	0	0	0	6^2	4	1	1	0	2	3	8.1	1.35	303	.182	.250	0	—	0	2	2	-0	0.1

● BERT CUETO Cueto, Dagoberto (Concepcion) b: 8/14/37, San Luis, Cuba BR/TR, 6'4", 170 lbs. Deb: 6/18/61

YEAR	TM/L	W	L	PCT	G	GS	CG	SH	SV	IP	H	R	HR	HB	BB	SO	RAT	ERA	ERA+	OAV	OOB	BH	AVG	PB	PR	PR+	PD	TPI
1961	Min-A	1	3	.250	7	5	0	0	0	21^1	27	24	7	1	10	5	16.0	7.17	59	.300	.376	0	.000	-0	-7	-7	0	-1.0

● JACK CULLEN Cullen, John Patrick b: 10/6/39, Newark, N.J. BR/TR, 5'11", 170 lbs. Deb: 9/9/62

YEAR	TM/L	W	L	PCT	G	GS	CG	SH	SV	IP	H	R	HR	HB	BB	SO	RAT	ERA	ERA+	OAV	OOB	BH	AVG	PB	PR	PR+	PD	TPI
1962	NY-A	0	0	—	2	0	0	0	1	3	2	0	0	0	2	2	12.0	0.00	—	.182	.308	0	—	0	1	1	-0	0.1
1965	NY-A	3	4	.429	12	9	2	1	0	59	59	22	2	0	21	25	12.2	3.05	112	.262	.325	3	.150	-0	3	2	1	0.3
1966	NY-A	1	0	1.000	5	0	0	0	0	11^1	11	5	0	0	5	7	12.7	3.97	84	.256	.333	0	.000	-0	-1	-1	-0	-0.1
Total	3	4	4	.500	19	9	2	1	1	73^1	72	27	2	0	28	34	12.3	3.07	111	.258	.326	3	.130	-1	3	3	0	0.3

YEAR TM/L	W	L	PCT	G	GS	CG	SH	SV	IP	H	R	HR	HB	BB	SO	RAT	ERA	ERA+	OAV	OOB	BH	AVG	PB	PR	PR+	PD	TPI
● **NICK CULLOP** Cullop, Henry Nicholas "Tomato Face" (b: Heinrich Nicholas Kolop) b: 10/16/1900, St.Louis, Mo. d: 12/8/78, Westerville, Ohio BR/TR, 6', 200 lbs. Deb: 4/14/26 ♦																											
1927 Cle-A	0	0	—	1	0	0	0	0	1	3	1	0	0	0	0	27.0	9.00	47	.600	.600	16	.235	0	-1	-1	-0	0.0
● **NICK CULLOP** Cullop, Norman Andrew b: 9/17/1887, Chilhowie, Va. d: 4/15/61, Tazewell, Va. BL/TL, 5'11.5", 172 lbs. Deb: 5/20/13																											
1913 Cle-A	3	6	.333	23	8	4	0	0	97^2	105	58	3	3	35	30	13.2	4.42	69	.291	.358	4	.129	-1	-16	-15	1	-1.3
1914 Cle-A	0	1	.000	1	0	0	0	0	3^1	4	3	0	0	1	3	13.5	2.70	107	.364	.417	0	.000	-0	0	0	-0	0.0
KC-F	14	19	.424	44	36	22	4	1	295^2	256	116	6	12	87	149	10.8	2.34	119	.235	.299	14	.141	-5	18	15	1	1.1
1915 KC-F	22	11	.667	44	36	22	3	2	302^1	278	105	8	9	67	111	10.5	2.44	108	.249	.297	18	.188	-1	10	7	6	1.3
1916 NY-A	13	6	.684	28	22	9	0	1	167	151	60	4	3	32	77	10.0	2.05	141	.243	.284	6	.109	-3	14	15	-5	0.9
1917 NY-A	5	9	.357	30	18	5	2	1	146^1	161	70	2	2	31	27	11.9	3.32	81	.307	.348	7	.159	-1	-11	-10	-0	-1.1
1921 StL-A	0	2	.000	4	1	0	0	0	11^2	18	12	1	0	6	3	18.5	8.49	53	.340	.407	0	.000	-1	-5	-5	0	-0.7
Total 6	57	54	.514	174	121	62	9	5	1024	973	424	24	29	259	400	11.1	2.73	102	.258	.310	49	.149	-12	10	6	3	0.2
● **BUD CULLOTON** Culloton, Bernard Aloysius b: 5/19/1897, Kingston, N.Y. d: 11/9/76, Kingston, N.Y. BR/TR, 5'11", 180 lbs. Deb: 4/16/25																											
1925 Pit-N	0	1	.000	9	1	0	0	0	21	19	8	1	0	1	3	8.6	2.57	173	.241	.250	0	.000	-0	4	4	-0	0.1
1926 Pit-N	0	0	—	4	0	0	0	0	3^2	3	4	0	0	6	1	22.1	7.36	53	.214	.450	0	—	0	-1	-1	0	-0.1
Total 2	0	1	.000	13	1	0	0	0	24^2	22	12	1	0	7	4	10.6	3.28	133	.237	.290	0	.000	-0	3	3	-0	0.0
● **RAY CULP** Culp, Raymond Leonard b: 8/6/41, Elgin, Tex. BR/TR, 6', 200 lbs. Deb: 4/10/63																											
1963 Phi-N★	14	11	.560	34	30	10	5	0	203^1	148	76	15	6	102	176	11.3	2.97	109	.206	.309	9	.136	-0	7	6	-0	0.7
1964 Phi-N	8	7	.533	30	19	3	1	0	135	139	77	15	5	56	96	13.3	4.13	84	.263	.340	5	.114	-1	-9	-10	-1	-1.2
1965 Phi-N	14	10	.583	33	30	11	2	0	204^1	188	89	14	12	78	134	12.2	3.22	108	.243	.322	6	.088	-2	7	6	-1	0.3
1966 Phi-N	7	4	.636	34	12	1	0	1	110^2	106	66	19	7	53	100	13.5	5.04	71	.246	.338	2	.077	-2	-18	-18	-1	-1.9
1967 Chi-N	8	11	.421	30	22	4	1	0	152^2	138	69	22	2	59	111	11.7	3.89	91	.239	.311	5	.098	-1	-9	-6	-1	-0.9
1968 Bos-A	16	6	.727	35	30	11	6	0	216^1	166	79	18	9	82	190	10.7	2.91	108	.210	.292	8	.114	-1	2	6	-1	0.3
1969 Bos-A★	17	8	.680	32	32	9	2	0	227	195	103	25	6	79	172	11.1	3.81	100	.231	.302	12	.152	1	-5	0	-0	0.0
1970 Bos-A	17	14	.548	33	33	15	1	0	251^1	211	104	22	11	91	197	11.2	3.04	130	.224	.300	12	.124	-3	19	24	-1	2.4
1971 Bos-A	14	16	.467	35	35	12	3	0	242^1	236	108	21	5	67	151	11.4	3.60	103	.253	.307	8	.118	-2	-4	2	-2	-0.1
1972 Bos-A	5	8	.385	16	16	4	1	0	105	104	60	8	3	53	52	13.7	4.46	72	.260	.351	7	.212	1	-16	-14	0	-1.6
1973 Bos-A	2	6	.250	10	9	0	0	0	50^1	46	32	9	4	32	32	14.7	4.47	90	.247	.369	0	—	0	-4	-2	0	-0.3
Total 11	122	101	.547	322	268	80	22	1	1898^1	1677	863	188	70	752	1411	11.8	3.58	99	.235	.314	74	.123	-11	-28	-4	-8	-2.3
● **BILL CULP** Culp, William Edward b: 6/11/1887, Bellaire, Ohio d: 9/3/69, Arnold, Pa. BB/TR, 6'1.5", 165 lbs. Deb: 9/8/10																											
1910 Phi-N	0	0	—	4	0	0	0	1	6^2	8	6	0	0	4	4	16.2	8.10	39	.333	.429	0	.000	-0	-4	-4	1	-0.1
● **GEORGE CULVER** Culver, George Raymond b: 7/8/43, Salinas, Cal. BR/TR, 6'2", 185 lbs. Deb: 9/7/66																											
1966 Cle-A	0	2	.000	5	1	0	0	0	9^2	15	9	1	1	7	6	21.4	8.38	41	.357	.460	0	.000	-0	-5	-5	0	-0.9
1967 Cle-A	7	3	.700	53	1	0	0	3	75	71	40	2	6	31	41	13.0	3.96	82	.258	.346	1	.250	0	-6	-6	1	-0.7
1968 Cin-N	11	16	.407	42	35	5	2	2	226^1	229	95	8	14	84	114	13.0	3.22	98	.264	.339	8	.121	-1	-6	-1	2	-0.1
1969 Cin-N	5	7	.417	32	13	0	0	4	101^1	117	55	8	9	52	58	15.8	4.26	88	.291	.384	3	.097	-2	-8	-5	2	-0.6
1970 StL-N	3	3	.500	11	7	2	0	0	56^2	64	31	6	1	24	23	14.1	4.61	89	.284	.356	3	.176	0	-3	-3	2	-0.1
Hou-N	3	3	.500	32	0	0	0	3	45	44	17	1	3	21	31	13.6	3.20	121	.254	.345	1	.250	0	4	4	-1	0.4
Yr	6	6	.500	43	7	2	0	3	101^2	108	48	7	4	45	54	13.9	3.98	101	.271	.351	4	.190	0	1	0	1	0.3
1971 Hou-N	5	8	.385	59	0	0	0	7	95^1	89	33	4	2	38	57	12.2	2.64	128	.257	.334	1	.091	-1	9	8	1	1.2
1972 Hou-N	6	2	.750	45	0	0	0	2	97^1	73	33	7	5	43	82	11.2	3.05	110	.212	.309	3	.158	0	4	3	-0	0.3
1973 LA-N	4	4	.500	28	0	0	0	2	42	45	15	4	1	21	23	14.4	3.00	115	.292	.381	0	.000	-0	3	2	1	0.5
Phi-N	3	1	.750	14	0	0	0	0	18^2	26	10	0	0	15	7	19.8	4.82	79	.342	.451	0	—	0	-2	-2	1	-0.3
Yr	7	5	.583	42	0	0	0	2	60^2	71	25	4	1	36	30	16.0	3.56	100	.309	.404	0	.000	-0	1	-0	2	0.2
1974 Phi-N	1	0	1.000	14	0	0	0	0	21^2	20	16	1	1	16	9	15.4	6.65	57	.267	.402	0	.000	-0	-7	-7	-0	-0.4
Total 9	48	49	.495	335	57	7	2	23	789	793	354	42	43	352	451	13.6	3.62	96	.266	.352	20	.124	-4	-17	-13	8	-0.7
● **JOHN CUMBERLAND** Cumberland, John Sheldon b: 5/10/47, Westbrook, Me. BR/TL, 6', 190 lbs. Deb: 9/27/68 C																											
1968 NY-A	0	0	—	1	0	0	0	0	2	3	4	1	0	1	1	18.0	9.00	32	.333	.400	0	—	0	-1	-1	0	0.0
1969 NY-A	0	0	—	2	0	0	0	0	4	3	2	0	0	4	0	15.8	4.50	77	.231	.412	0	—	0	-0	-0	0	0.0
1970 NY-A	3	4	.429	15	8	1	0	0	64	62	31	9	0	15	38	10.8	3.94	89	.252	.295	1	.059	-1	-2	-3	-1	-0.5
SF-N	2	0	1.000	7	0	0	0	0	11	6	3	0	0	4	6	8.2	0.82	486	.158	.238	0	.000	-0	4	4	0	0.7
1971 *SF-N	9	6	.600	45	21	5	2	2	185	153	66	22	0	55	65	10.1	2.92	117	.223	.281	7	.119	-2	11	10	-3	0.3
1972 SF-N	0	4	.000	9	6	0	0	0	25	38	29	6	0	7	8	16.2	8.64	40	.336	.375	1	.111	-0	-14	-14	-1	-2.1
StL-N	1	1	.500	14	1	0	0	0	21^2	23	17	6	0	7	7	12.5	6.65	51	.291	.349	0	.000	-1	-8	-8	-1	-0.8
Yr	1	5	.167	23	7	0	0	0	46^2	61	46	12	0	14	15	14.5	7.71	45	.318	.364	1	.071	-1	-22	-22	-2	-2.9
1974 Cal-A	0	1	.000	17	0	0	0	0	21^2	24	9	2	0	10	12	14.1	3.74	92	.289	.366	0	—	0	-0	-1	-0	-0.1
Total 6	15	16	.484	110	36	6	2	2	334^1	312	161	46	0	103	137	11.2	3.82	90	.246	.303	9	.099	-5	-10	-14	-6	-2.5
● **JOHN CUMMINGS** Cummings, John Russell b: 5/10/69, Torrance, Cal. BL/TL, 6'3", 200 lbs. Deb: 4/10/93																											
1993 Sea-A	0	6	.000	10	8	1	0	0	46^1	59	34	6	2	16	19	15.0	6.02	73	.316	.376	0	—	0	-9	-8	-0	-0.9
1994 Sea-A	2	4	.333	17	8	0	0	0	64	66	43	7	0	37	33	14.5	5.63	87	.270	.367	0	—	0	-6	-5	-1	-0.5
1995 Sea-A	0	0	—	4	0	0	0	0	5^1	8	8	0	0	7	4	25.3	11.81	40	.400	.556	0	—	0	-4	-4	0	-0.2
*LA-N	3	1	.750	35	0	0	0	0	39	38	16	3	0	10	21	11.1	3.00	127	.250	.296	0	.000	-0	5	4	-0	0.3
1996 LA-N	0	1	.000	4	0	0	0	0	5^1	12	7	1	0	2	5	23.6	6.75	57	.462	.500	0	—	0	-1	-2	0	-0.3
Det-A	3	3	.500	21	0	0	0	0	31^2	36	20	3	2	20	24	16.5	5.12	99	.283	.389	0	—	0	-0	-0	-0	-0.1
1997 Det-A	2	0	1.000	19	0	0	0	0	24^2	32	22	3	0	14	8	16.8	5.47	84	.311	.393	0	—	0	-2	-2	0	-0.2
Total 5	10	15	.400	110	16	1	0	0	216^1	251	150	23	4	106	114	15.0	5.33	85	.292	.373	0	.000	-0	-18	-19	-1	-1.9
● **STEVE CUMMINGS** Cummings, Steven Brent b: 7/15/64, Houston, Tex. BB/TR, 6'2", 200 lbs. Deb: 6/24/89																											
1989 Tor-A	2	0	1.000	5	2	0	0	0	21	18	9	1	1	11	8	12.9	3.00	126	.231	.333	0	—	0	2	2	-0	0.2
1990 Tor-A	0	0	—	6	2	0	0	0	12^1	22	7	4	1	5	4	20.4	5.11	77	.431	.491	0	—	0	-2	-2	-0	-0.1
Total 2	2	0	1.000	11	4	0	0	0	33^1	40	16	5	2	16	12	15.7	3.78	102	.310	.395	0	—	0	0	0	-0	0.1
● **CANDY CUMMINGS** Cummings, William Arthur b: 10/18/1848, Ware, Mass. d: 5/16/24, Toledo, Ohio BR/TR, 5'9", 120 lbs. Deb: 4/22/1872 H																											
1872 Mut-n	33	20	.623	**55**	55	**53**	**3**	0	**497**	605	347	2		30	43	11.5	2.97	113	.273	.283	52	.208	-4	37	24		1.3
1873 Bal-n	28	14	.667	42	42	42	1	0	382	475	292	4		33	34	12.0	2.66	122	.274	.287	48	.250	2	25	25		1.7
1874 Phi-n	28	26	.519	54	54	52	3	0	483	616	386	4		18	61	11.8	1.96	113	.276	.282	52	.225	-4	13	14		0.4
1875 Har-n	35	12	.745	48	47	46	**7**	0	416	397	184	0		4	**82**	8.7	1.60	146	.235	.236	44	.199	-5	29	33		2.6
1876 Har-N	16	8	.667	24	24	24	5	0	216	215	97	0		14	26	9.5	1.67	142	.235	.251	17	.162	-8	15	16	-2	0.6
1877 Cin-N	5	14	.263	19	19	16	0	0	155^2	219	144	2		13	11	13.4	4.34	61	.315	.327	14	.200	0	-26	-31	0	-2.7
Total 4 n	124	72	.633	199	198	193	14	0	1778	2093	1209	10		85	220	11.0	2.31	122	.266	.274	196	.219	-10	103	101		6.0
Total 2	21	22	.488	43	43	40	5	0	371^2	434	241	2		27	37	11.2	2.78	90	.270	.284	31	.177	-7	-11	-12	-2	-2.1
● **WILL CUNNANE** Cunnane, William Joseph b: 4/24/74, Suffern, N.Y. BR/TR, 6'2", 175 lbs. Deb: 4/3/97																											
1997 SD-N	6	3	.667	54	8	0	0	0	91^1	114	69	11	5	49	79	16.6	5.81	67	.305	.393	5	.357	3	-16	-21	-1	-1.6
1998 SD-N	0	0	—	3	0	0	0	0	3	4	2	1	0	1	1	15.0	6.00	65	.308	.357	0	—	0	-1	-1	0	0.0
1999 SD-N	2	1	.667	24	0	0	0	0	31	34	19	8	0	12	22	13.4	5.23	80	.293	.359	0	.000	-0	-2	-4	-0	-0.4
2000 SD-N	1	1	.500	27	3	0	0	0	38^1	35	21	2	1	21	34	13.4	4.23	103	.241	.341	1	.143	0	2	1	0	0.0
Total 4	9	5	.643	108	11	0	0	0	163^2	187	111	22	6	83	136	15.2	5.33	76	.289	.374	6	.250	3	-17	-25	-1	-2.0
● **BRUCE CUNNINGHAM** Cunningham, Bruce Lee b: 9/29/05, San Francisco, Cal. d: 3/8/84, Hayward, Cal. BR/TR, 5'10.5", 165 lbs. Deb: 5/7/29																											
1929 Bos-N	4	6	.400	17	8	4	0	1	91^2	100	52	7	2	32	22	13.2	4.52	104	.282	.344	4	.148	-0	2	2	1	0.2
1930 Bos-N	5	6	.455	36	6	2	0	0	106^2	121	73	7	0	41	28	13.7	5.48	90	.289	.352	6	.194	0	-6	-7	3	-0.2
1931 Bos-N	3	12	.200	33	16	6	1	1	136^2	157	74	7	2	54	32	14.0	4.48	85	.296	.363	3	.071	-4	-9	-11	4	-1.0
1932 Bos-N	1	0	1.000	18	3	0	0	0	47	50	21	1	4	19	21	14.0	3.45	109	.281	.363	2	.222	2	2	2	1	0.3
Total 4	13	24	.351	104	33	12	1	2	382	428	220	22	8	146	103	13.7	4.64	93	.289	.356	15	.138	-2	-11	-14	9	-0.7

YEAR	TM/L	W	L	PCT	G	GS	CG	SH	SV	IP	H	R	HR	HB	BB	SO	RAT	ERA	ERA+	OAV	OOB	BH	AVG	PB	PR	PR+	PD	TPI
● **BERT CUNNINGHAM**	Cunningham, Ellsworth Elmer b: 11/25/1865, Wilmington, Del. d: 5/14/52, Cragmere, Del. BR/TR, 5'6", 187 lbs. Deb: 9/15/1887 U																											
1887	Bro-a	0	2	.000	3	3	3	0	0	23	39	22	0	4	13	8	16.8	5.09	85	.348	.371	2	.200	-1	-2	-2	-0	-0.2
1888	Bal-a	22	29	.431	51	51	50	0	0	453^1	412	275	8	30	157	186	11.9	3.39	88	.233	.307	33	.186	-2	-17	-22	0	-2.2
1889	Bal-a	16	19	.457	39	33	29	0	1	279^1	306	245	11	15	141	140	14.9	4.87	81	.270	.358	27	.206	-3	-32	-28	-0	-2.8
1890	Phi-P	3	9	.250	14	11	11	0	0	108^2	133	103	0	7	67	33	17.1	5.22	82	.289	.387	6	.115	-4	-12	-11	1	-1.1
	Buf-P	9	15	.375	25	25	24	2	0	211	251	190	8	6	134	78	16.7	5.84	70	.283	.381	23	.228	1	-38	-42	-1	-3.2
	Yr	12	24	.333	39	36	35	2	0	319^2	384	293	8	13	201	111	16.8	5.63	74	.285	.383	29	.190	-4	-50	-53	0	-4.3
1891	Bal-a	11	14	.440	30	25	21	0	0	237^2	241	181	8	11	138	59	14.8	4.01	93	.254	.356	15	.150	-2	-8	-8	2	-0.6
1895	Lou-N	11	16	.407	31	28	24	1	0	231	299	185	6	5	104	49	15.9	4.75	97	.309	.378	30	.300	6	1	-3	2	0.4
1896	Lou-N	7	14	.333	27	20	17	0	1	189^1	242	168	6	17	74	37	15.8	5.09	85	.308	.380	22	.250	3	-15	-16	2	-1.0
1897	Lou-N	14	13	.519	30	28	26	0	0	242^2	294	152	3	14	72	49	14.1	4.15	102	.297	.353	22	.227	-1	4	3	2	0.4
1898	Lou-N	28	15	.651	44	42	41	0	0	362	387	174	8	20	65	34	11.7	3.16	113	.272	.313	32	.229	2	18	17	-1	1.8
1899	Lou-N	17	17	.500	39	37	33	1	0	323^2	385	188	4	15	75	36	13.2	3.84	100	.295	.340	40	.260	3	1	1	6	0.8
1900	Chi-N	4	3	.571	8	7	7	0	0	64	84	53	0	4	21	7	15.3	4.36	83	.316	.375	4	.148	-1	-5	-5	-1	-0.6
1901	Chi-N	0	1	.000	1	1	1	0	0	9	11	6	0	0	3	2	14.0	5.00	65	.297	.350	0	.000	0	-2	-2	1	-0.1
Total	12	142	167	.460	342	311	287	4	2	2734^2	3084	1942	62	148	1064	718	14.1	4.22	91	.278	.349	256	.217	1	-106	-119	12	-8.4
● **GEORGE CUNNINGHAM**	Cunningham, George Harold b: 7/13/1894, Sturgeon Lake, Minn. d: 3/10/72, Chattanooga, Tenn. BR/TR, 5'11", 185 lbs. Deb: 4/14/16 ♦																											
1916	Det-A	7	10	.412	35	14	5	0	2	150^1	146	71	0	3	74	68	13.4	2.75	104	.269	.360	11	.268	5	1	2	1	0.9
1917	Det-A	2	7	.222	44	8	4	0	4	139	113	72	2	4	51	49	10.9	2.91	91	.227	.304	6	.176	1	-4	-4	0	-0.2
1918	Det-A	6	7	.462	27	14	10	0	1	140	131	68	0	5	38	39	11.2	3.15	84	.255	.312	25	.223	3	-6	-8	0	-0.3
1919	Det-A	1	1	.500	17	0	0	0	1	47^2	54	36	0	5	15	11	14.0	4.91	65	.292	.361	5	.217	2	-9	-9	0	-0.2
Total	4	16	25	.390	123	36	19	0	8	477	444	247	2	17	178	167	12.1	3.13	89	.255	.330	47	.224	11	-17	-19	2	0.2
● **MIKE CUNNINGHAM**	Cunningham, Mody b: 6/14/1882, Lancaster, S.C. d: 12/10/69, Lancaster, S.C. BR/TR, 5'10.5", 175 lbs. Deb: 8/31/06																											
1906	Phi-A	1	0	1.000	5	1	1	0	0	28	29	15	1	1	9	15	12.5	3.21	85	.271	.333	4	.333	1	-2	-1	-0	0.0
● **NIG CUPPY**	Cuppy, George Joseph (b: George Koppe) b: 7/3/1869, Logansport, Ind. d: 7/27/22, Elkhart, Ind. BR/TR, 5'7", 160 lbs. Deb: 4/16/1892																											
1892	*Cle-N	28	13	.683	47	42	38	1	1	376	333	175	9	10	121	103	11.1	2.51	135	.228	.292	36	.214	0	32	36	3	3.7
1893	Cle-N	17	10	.630	31	30	24	0	0	243^2	316	200	6	10	75	39	14.8	4.47	109	.305	.357	27	.248	1	5	11	-1	0.8
1894	Cle-N	24	15	.615	43	33	29	**3**	0	316	381	246	11	10	128	65	14.8	4.56	120	.295	.363	35	.259	1	27	31	1	2.9
1895	*Cle-N	26	14	.650	47	40	36	1	2	353	384	210	9	8	95	91	12.4	3.54	141	.273	.323	40	.286	7	48	54	4	5.6
1896	*Cle-N	25	14	.641	46	40	35	1	1	358	388	173	8	7	75	86	11.8	3.12	146	.274	.314	38	.270	6	50	54	4	5.7
1897	Cle-N	10	6	.625	19	17	13	1	0	138	150	69	3	5	26	23	11.8	3.20	140	.275	.314	8	.145	-4	17	19	-1	1.4
1898	Cle-N	9	8	.529	18	15	13	1	0	128	147	62	4	6	25	27	12.5	3.30	110	.286	.327	5	.104	-4	4	4	-2	0.0
1899	StL-N	11	8	.579	21	21	18	1	0	171^2	203	89	3	5	26	25	12.3	3.15	126	.294	.324	13	.186	-3	13	15	0	1.2
1900	Bos-N	8	4	.667	17	13	9	0	1	105^1	107	64	8	6	24	23	11.7	3.08	134	.263	.314	11	.262	1	7	11	-1	1.1
1901	Bos-A	4	6	.400	13	11	9	0	0	93^1	111	58	1	2	14	22	12.2	4.15	85	.292	.321	10	.204	0	-5	-7	-2	-0.7
Total	10	162	98	.623	302	262	224	9	5	2283	2520	1346	62	69	609	504	12.6	3.48	127	.275	.325	223	.233	6	200	230	6	21.7
● **SAMMY CURRAN**	Curran, Simon Francis b: 10/30/1874, Dorchester, Mass. d: 5/19/36, Dorchester, Mass. TL, Deb: 8/1/02																											
1902	Bos-N	0	0	—	1	0	0	0	0	6^2	6	1	0	0	0	3	8.1	1.35	209	.240	.240	0	.000	-0	1	1	-0	0.0
● **LAFAYETTE CURRENCE**	Currence, Delancy Lafayette b: 12/3/51, Rock Hill, S.C. BB/TL, 5'11", 175 lbs. Deb: 7/24/75																											
1975	Mil-A	0	2	.000	8	1	0	0	0	18^2	25	17	5	0	14	7	18.8	7.71	50	.316	.419	0	—	0	-8	-8	-1	-0.8
● **MURPHY CURRIE**	Currie, Archibald Murphy b: 8/31/1893, Fayetteville, N.C. d: 6/22/39, Asheboro, N.C. BR/TR, 5'11.5", 185 lbs. Deb: 8/31/16																											
1916	StL-N	0	0	—	6	0	0	0	0	14^1	7	4	1	0	9	8	10.0	1.88	140	.149	.286	0	.000	-0	1	1	-1	0.0
● **CLARENCE CURRIE**	Currie, Clarence Franklin b: 12/30/1878, Glencoe, Ont., Can. d: 7/15/41, Little Chute, Wis BR/TR, Deb: 4/25/02																											
1902	Cin-N	3	4	.429	10	7	6	1	0	65^1	70	37	1	2	17	20	12.3	3.72	81	.273	.324	2	.083	-2	-7	-5	1	-0.6
	StL-N	7	5	.583	15	12	10	2	0	124^2	125	54	0	6	35	30	12.0	2.60	106	.261	.319	9	.196	-0	3	2	2	0.4
	Yr	10	9	.526	25	19	16	3	0	190	195	91	1	8	52	50	12.1	2.98	95	.265	.321	11	.157	-2	-4	-3	3	-0.2
1903	StL-N	4	12	.250	22	16	13	1	1	148	155	93	7	10	60	52	13.7	4.01	81	.281	.362	4	.085	-3	-12	-12	4	-1.1
	Chi-N	1	2	.333	6	3	2	0	1	33^1	35	25	1	3	9	9	12.7	2.97	106	.254	.313	5	.417	2	1	1	1	0.3
	Yr	5	14	.263	28	19	15	1	2	181^1	190	118	8	13	69	61	13.5	3.82	85	.275	.352	9	.153	-1	-11	-12	5	-0.8
Total	2	15	23	.395	53	38	31	4	2	371^1	385	209	9	21	121	111	12.8	3.39	89	.270	.336	20	.155	-4	-15	-15	8	-1.0
● **BILL CURRIE**	Currie, William Cleveland b: 11/29/28, Leary, Ga. BR/TR, 6', 175 lbs. Deb: 4/13/55																											
1955	Was-A	0	0	—	3	0	0	0	0	4^1	7	7	3	1	2	2	20.8	12.46	31	.350	.435	0	—	0	-4	-4	0	-0.2
● **GEORGE CURRY**	Curry, George James "Soldier Boy" b: 12/21/1888, Bridgeport, Conn. d: 10/5/63, West Haven, Conn. BR/TR, 6', 185 lbs. Deb: 7/16/11																											
1911	StL-A	0	3	.000	3	3	0	0	0	15^2	19	15	0	0	24	2	24.7	7.47	45	.339	.538	0	.000	-1	-7	-7	-0	-1.1
● **STEVE CURRY**	Curry, Stephen Thomas b: 9/13/65, Winter Park, Fla. BR/TR, 6'6", 217 lbs. Deb: 7/10/88																											
1988	Bos-A	0	1	.000	3	3	0	0	0	11	15	10	0	0	14	4	23.7	8.18	50	.357	.518	0	—	0	-5	-5	0	-0.4
● **WES CURRY**	Curry, Wesley b: 4/1/1860, Wilmington, Del. d: 5/19/33, Philadelphia, Pa. Deb: 8/6/1884 U																											
1884	Ric-a	0	2	.000	2	2	2	0	0	16	15	14	2	1	3	1	10.7	5.06	66	.221	.264	2	.250	-0	-3	-3	-0	-0.3
● **CLIFF CURTIS**	Curtis, Clifton Garfield b: 7/3/1883, Delaware, Ohio d: 4/23/43, Utica, Ohio BR/TR, 6'2", 180 lbs. Deb: 8/23/09																											
1909	Bos-N	4	5	.444	10	9	8	2	0	83	53	17	1	2	30	22	9.2	1.41	200	.191	.275	1	.034	-3	11	12	1	1.1
1910	Bos-N	6	24	.200	43	37	12	2	2	251	251	154	9	12	124	75	13.9	3.55	94	.277	.371	12	.146	-4	-14	-6	6	-0.5
1911	Bos-N	1	8	.111	12	9	5	0	1	77	79	50	4	2	34	23	13.4	4.44	86	.265	.344	7	.250	-0	-9	-5	1	-0.4
	Chi-N	1	2	.333	4	1	0	0	0	7	7	4	0	3	5	4	19.3	3.86	86	.241	.405	1	.500	0	-0	-0	0	-0.1
	Phi-N	2	1	.667	8	5	3	1	0	45	45	19	0	1	15	13	12.2	2.60	132	.260	.323	4	.267	0	4	4	-0	0.2
	Yr	4	11	.267	24	15	8	1	1	129	131	73	4	6	54	40	13.3	3.77	97	.262	.341	12	.267	0	-5	-1	0	-0.3
1912	Phi-N	2	5	.286	10	8	2	0	0	50	55	30	3	4	17	20	13.7	3.24	112	.286	.357	0	.000	-2	1	2	1	0.1
	Bro-N	4	7	.364	19	9	3	0	1	80	72	44	4	6	37	22	12.9	3.94	85	.250	.347	8	.308	1	-5	-5	-0	-0.6
	Yr	6	12	.333	29	17	5	0	1	130	127	74	7	10	54	42	13.2	3.67	94	.265	.351	8	.195	-1	-4	-3	1	-0.5
1913	Bro-N	8	9	.471	30	16	6	0	2	151^2	145	75	1	7	55	57	12.3	3.26	101	.255	.328	6	.122	-3	-1	0	2	-0.1
Total	5	28	61	.315	136	94	39	5	6	744^2	707	393	22	37	317	236	12.8	3.31	101	.259	.344	39	.159	-10	-13	3	9	-0.3
● **JACK CURTIS**	Curtis, Jack Patrick b: 1/11/37, Rhodhiss, N.C. BL/TL, 5'10", 175 lbs. Deb: 4/22/61																											
1961	Chi-N	10	13	.435	31	27	6	0	0	180^1	220	117	23	1	51	57	13.6	4.89	85	.303	.350	10	.167	3	-17	-14	0	-1.2
1962	Chi-N	0	2	.000	4	3	0	0	0	18	18	8	2	0	6	8	12.0	3.50	118	.277	.338	1	.250	0	1	1	-0	0.1
	Mil-N	4	4	.500	30	5	0	0	1	75^2	82	39	8	2	27	40	13.2	4.16	91	.282	.347	4	.222	2	-2	-3	-1	-0.2
	Yr	4	6	.400	34	8	0	0	1	93^2	100	47	10	2	33	48	13.0	4.04	96	.281	.345	5	.227	2	-1	-2	-1	-0.1
1963	Cle-A	0	0	—	4	0	0	0	0	5	8	10	0	1	5	3	25.2	18.00	20	.348	.483	0	—	0	-8	-8	0	-0.4
Total	3	14	19	.424	69	35	6	0	1	279	328	174	33	4	89	108	13.6	4.84	84	.297	.352	15	.183	5	-26	-24	-1	-1.7
● **JOHN CURTIS**	Curtis, John Duffield b: 3/9/48, Newton, Mass. BL/TL, 6'2", 185 lbs. Deb: 8/13/70																											
1970	Bos-A	0	0	—	1	0	0	0	0	2^1	4	4	1	0	1	1	19.3	11.57	34	.333	.385	0	—	0	-2	-2	0	-0.1
1971	Bos-A	2	2	.500	5	3	1	0	0	26	30	9	3	0	6	19	12.5	3.12	119	.291	.330	1	.111	-0	1	2	-1	0.1
1972	Bos-A	11	8	.579	26	21	8	3	0	154^1	161	69	8	0	50	106	12.3	3.73	86	.271	.328	5	.094	-2	-11	-8	-0	-1.3
1973	Bos-A	13	13	.500	35	30	10	4	0	221^1	225	103	24	2	83	101	12.6	3.58	112	.264	.331	0	—	0	6	10	-1	1.1
1974	StL-N	10	14	.417	33	29	5	2	1	195	199	91	15	2	83	89	13.1	3.78	95	.267	.342	10	.159	-0	-3	-4	0	-0.6
1975	StL-N	8	9	.471	39	18	4	0	1	146^2	151	70	13	2	65	67	13.4	3.44	110	.268	.346	8	.211	2	3	5	2	0.9
1976	StL-N	6	11	.353	37	15	3	1	1	134	139	68	11	0	65	52	13.7	4.50	79	.276	.359	7	.200	2	-15	-14	0	-1.5
1977	SF-N	3	3	.500	43	9	1	1	1	77	95	48	5	1	48	47	16.8	5.49	71	.314	.409	3	.231	1	-14	-14	1	-0.7
1978	SF-N	4	3	.571	46	0	0	0	1	63	60	31	1	0	29	38	12.7	3.71	93	.262	.345	0	.000	-0	-1	-2	0	-0.2

YEAR	TM/L	W	L	PCT	G	GS	CG	SH	SV	IP	H	R	HR	HB	BB	SO	RAT	ERA	ERA+	OAV	OOB	BH	AVG	PB	PR	PR+	PD	TPI
1979	SF-N	10	9	.526	27	18	3	2	0	120^2	121	62	15	0	42	85	12.2	4.18	84	.257	.318	5	.147	1	-6	-10	-1	-1.4
1980	SD-N	10	8	.556	30	27	6	0	0	187	184	84	9	2	67	71	12.2	3.51	98	.262	.329	12	.194	1	2	-2	1	0.0
1981	SD-N	2	6	.250	28	8	0	0	0	66^2	70	41	11	1	30	31	13.6	5.13	64	.275	.353	1	.077	-1	-12	-15	-0	-1.8
1982	SD-N	8	6	.571	26	18	1	1	0	116^1	121	62	15	1	46	54	13.0	4.10	84	.271	.341	11	.297	3	-6	-9	-1	-0.8
	Cal-A	0	1	.000	8	0	0	0	1	12	16	8	0	0	3	10	14.3	6.00	68	.320	.358	0	—	0	-3	-3	-0	-0.3
1983	Cal-A	1	2	.333	37	3	0	0	5	90	89	44	5	2	40	36	13.1	3.80	106	.258	.339	0	—	0	3	2	-1	0.0
1984	Cal-A	1	2	.333	17	0	0	0	0	28^2	30	16	4	0	11	18	12.9	4.40	90	.263	.328	0	—	0	-1	-1	0	-0.1
Total	15	89	97	.478	438	199	42	14	11	1641	1695	810	140	13	669	825	13.0	3.96	92	.270	.341	63	.175	5	-59	-61	-1	-6.7
● VERN CURTIS Curtis, Vernon Eugene "Turk" b: 5/24/20, Cairo, Ill. d: 6/24/92, Cairo, Ill. BR/TR, 6', 170 lbs. Deb: 9/6/43																												
1943	Was-A	0	0	—	2	0	0	0	0	4	3	3	0	0	6	1	20.3	6.75	47	.200	.429	0	—	0	-2	-2	-0	-0.1
1944	Was-A	0	1	.000	3	1	0	0	0	9^2	8	3	0	0	3	2	10.2	2.79	117	.235	.297	0	.000	-0	1	1	-0	0.0
1946	Was-A	0	0	—	11	0	0	0	0	16^1	19	13	1	0	10	7	16.0	7.16	47	.297	.392	0	.000	-0	-7	-7	0	-0.4
Total	3	0	1	.000	16	1	0	0	0	30	30	19	1	0	19	10	14.7	5.70	58	.265	.371	0	.000	-1	-7	-8	-0	-0.5
● ED CUSHMAN Cushman, Edgar Leander b: 3/27/1852, Eagleville, Ohio d: 9/26/15, Erie, Pa. BR/TL, 6', 177 lbs. Deb: 7/6/1883																												
1883	Buf-N	3	3	.500	7	7	5	0	0	50^1	61	41	0		17	34	13.9	3.93	81	.285	.338	5	.217	-0	-4	-4	-0	-0.4
1884	Mil-U	4	0	1.000	4	4	4	2	0	36	10	4	0		3	47	3.3	1.00	132	.082	.104	1	.091	-2	6	2	-1	0.1
1885	Phi-a	3	7	.300	10	10	10	0	0	87	101	77	1	3	17	37	12.5	3.52	98	.269	.306	7	.189	-1	-3	-1	-1	-0.3
	NY-a	8	14	.364	22	22	22	0	0	191	158	105	2	3	33	133	9.1	2.78	106	.210	.246	10	.145	-1	10	4	-2	0.2
	Yr	11	21	.344	32	32	32	0	0	278	259	182	3	6	50	170	10.2	3.01	103	.229	.266	17	.160	-2	7	3	-3	-0.1
1886	NY-a	17	21	.447	38	38	37	2	0	325^2	278	180	6	1	99	167	10.4	3.12	109	.220	.277	19	.151	-7	12	11	0	0.4
1887	NY-a	10	15	.400	26	26	25	0	0	220	393	232	9	9	83	64	16.4	5.97	71	.379	.384	33	.320	3	-41	-43	-1	-3.1
1890	Tol-a	17	21	.447	40	38	34	0	1	315^2	346	208	5	10	107	125	13.2	4.19	94	.270	.331	13	.100	-9	-11	-8	-5	-2.0
Total	6	62	81	.434	147	145	137	4	1	1225^2	1347	847	23	26	359	607	12.1	3.86	92	.267	.308	88	.176	-17	-32	-44	-10	-5.1
● HARVEY CUSHMAN Cushman, Harvey Barnes b: 7/10/1877, Rockland, Me. d: 12/27/20, Emsworth, Pa. Deb: 8/24/02																												
1902	Pit-N	0	4	.000	4	4	3	0	0	25^2	30	31	0	2	31	12	22.1	7.36	37	.291	.463	2	.200	-0	-13	-13	-1	-1.6
● MIKE CVENGROS Cvengros, Michael John b: 12/1/01, Pana, Ill. d: 8/2/70, Hot Springs, Ark. BL/TL, 5'8", 159 lbs. Deb: 9/30/22																												
1922	NY-N	0	1	.000	1	1	1	0	0	9	6	5	1	1	3	3	10.0	4.00	100	.194	.286	0	.000	-0	0	0	0	0.0
1923	Chi-A	12	13	.480	40	26	14	0	3	214^1	216	110	6	13	107	86	14.1	4.41	90	.269	.364	15	.203	-1	-10	-11	0	-1.2
1924	Chi-A	3	12	.200	26	15	2	0	0	105^2	119	80	5	3	67	36	16.1	5.88	70	.300	.405	6	.200	2	-19	-21	0	-2.3
1925	Chi-A	3	9	.250	22	11	4	0	0	104^2	109	56	7	3	55	32	14.4	4.30	97	.278	.371	5	.152	-1	1	-2	-0	-0.3
1927	*Pit-N	2	1	.667	23	4	0	0	1	53^2	55	25	3	1	24	21	13.4	3.35	123	.271	.351	3	.158	-0	3	4	1	0.3
1929	Chi-N	5	4	.556	32	4	0	0	2	64	82	39	2	1	29	23	15.8	4.64	99	.319	.390	6	.400	2	1	-0	0	0.2
Total	6	25	40	.385	144	61	21	0	6	551^1	587	315	24	22	285	201	14.6	4.59	90	.282	.374	35	.201	1	-24	-29	1	-3.3
● JIM CZAJKOWSKI Czajkowski, James Mark b: 12/18/63, Parma, Ohio BB/TR, 6'4", 215 lbs. Deb: 7/29/94																												
1994	Col-N	0	0	—	5	0	0	0	0	8^2	9	4	2	3	6	2	18.7	4.15	120	.281	.439	0	—	0	0	1	0	0.1
● OMAR DAAL Daal, Omar Jesus (Cordero) b: 3/1/72, Maracaibo, Venez. BL/TL, 6'3", 175 lbs. Deb: 4/24/93																												
1993	LA-N	2	3	.400	47	0	0	0	0	35^1	36	20	5	0	21	19	14.5	5.09	75	.277	.377	0	—	0	-4	-5	0	-0.6
1994	LA-N	0	0	—	24	0	0	0	0	13^2	12	5	1	0	5	9	11.2	3.29	119	.245	.315	0	—	0	1	1	-0	0.0
1995	LA-N	4	0	1.000	28	0	0	0	0	20	29	16	1	1	15	11	20.2	7.20	53	.354	.459	0	—	0	-7	-8	-0	-1.5
1996	Mon-N	4	5	.444	64	6	0	0	0	87^1	74	40	10	1	37	82	11.5	4.02	108	.228	.309	0	.000	-1	2	3	1	0.2
1997	Mon-N	1	2	.333	33	0	0	0	1	30^1	48	35	4	2	15	16	19.3	9.79	43	.378	.451	1	.200	0	-19	-19	1	-1.6
	Tor-A	1	1	.500	9	3	0	0	0	27	34	13	3	0	6	28	13.3	4.00	115	.304	.339	0	—	0	2	2	0	0.1
1998	Ari-N	8	12	.400	33	23	3	1	0	162^2	146	60	12	3	51	132	11.1	2.88	146	.245	.308	5	.109	-1	25	24	2	2.9
1999	*Ari-N	16	9	.640	32	32	2	1	0	214^2	188	92	21	7	79	148	11.5	3.65	125	.236	.310	16	.232	3	22	22	1	2.6
2000	Ari-N	2	10	.167	20	16	0	0	0	96	127	88	17	7	42	45	16.5	7.22	64	.315	.389	7	.259	3	-28	-28	0	-2.5
	Phi-N	2	9	.182	12	12	0	0	0	71	81	40	9	2	30	51	14.3	4.69	101	.290	.363	5	.278	2	-0	0	1	0.3
	Yr	4	19	.174	32	28	0	0	0	167	208	128	26	9	72	96	15.6	6.14	76	.305	.379	12	.267	5	-28	-27	1	-2.2
Total	8	40	51	.440	302	92	5	2	1	758	775	409	83	23	301	541	13.0	4.49	98	.267	.341	34	.193	6	-6	-7	6	-0.1
● JOHN D'ACQUISTO D'Acquisto, John Francis b: 12/24/51, San Diego, Cal. BR/TR, 6'2", 205 lbs. Deb: 9/2/73																												
1973	SF-N	1	1	.500	7	3	1	0	0	27^2	23	14	4	0	19	29	13.7	3.58	107	.219	.339	0	.000	-1	0	1	-0	-0.1
1974	SF-N	12	14	.462	38	36	5	1	0	215	182	101	13	6	124	167	13.1	3.77	101	.227	.334	8	.113	-1	-3	1	-4	-0.4
1975	SF-N	2	4	.333	10	6	0	0	0	28	29	35	5	2	34	22	20.9	10.29	37	.264	.445	0	.000	-0	-21	-19	-1	-3.3
1976	SF-N	3	8	.273	28	19	0	0	0	106	93	69	5	3	102	53	16.8	5.35	68	.243	.406	7	.269	2	-22	-20	-0	-1.7
1977	StL-N	0	0	—	3	2	0	0	0	8^1	5	4	0	1	10	9	17.3	4.32	89	.185	.421	0	.000	-0	-0	-0	-0	-0.1
	SD-N	1	2	.333	17	12	0	0	0	44	49	41	3	1	47	45	19.8	6.95	51	.297	.455	0	.000	-0	-15	-18	0	-1.1
	Yr	1	2	.333	20	14	0	0	0	52^1	54	45	3	2	57	54	19.4	6.54	55	.281	.450	0	.000	-1	-15	-19	0	-1.2
1978	SD-N	4	3	.571	45	3	0	0	10	93	60	24	2	1	56	104	11.3	2.13	156	.185	.307	4	.190	1	15	13	-1	1.3
1979	SD-N	9	13	.409	51	11	1	1	2	133^2	140	83	15	3	86	97	15.4	4.92	72	.275	.383	4	.129	1	-17	-22	-2	-3.4
1980	SD-N	2	3	.400	39	0	0	0	1	67	67	29	2	1	36	44	14.0	3.76	91	.270	.365	0	.000	-1	-1	-3	-0	-0.3
	Mon-N	0	2	.000	11	0	0	0	2	20^2	14	7	0	0	9	15	10.0	2.18	164	.206	.299	0	—	0	3	3	0	0.4
	Yr	2	5	.286	50	0	0	0	3	87^2	81	36	2	1	45	59	13.0	3.39	102	.256	.351	0	.000	-1	2	1	-0	0.1
1981	Cal-A	0	0	—	6	0	0	0	0	19^1	26	24	2	1	12	8	18.2	10.71	34	.338	.433	0	—	0	-15	-15	-0	-0.8
1982	Oak-A	0	1	.000	11	0	0	0	0	17	20	11	1	0	9	7	15.4	5.29	74	.290	.372	0	—	0	-2	-3	0	-0.1
Total	10	34	51	.400	266	92	7	2	15	779^2	708	442	52	19	544	600	14.7	4.56	80	.245	.368	23	.127	0	-78	-81	-9	-9.6
● JOHN DAGENHARD Dagenhard, John Douglas b: 4/25/17, Magnolia, Ohio BR/TR, 6'2", 195 lbs. Deb: 9/28/43																												
1943	Bos-N	1	0	1.000	2	1	1	0	0	11	9	2	0	2	4	2	12.3	0.00	—	.225	.326	0	.000	-0	4	4	1	0.5
● PETE DAGLIA Daglia, Peter George b: 2/28/07, Napa, Cal. d: 3/11/52, Willits, Cal. BR/TR, 6'3", 210 lbs. Deb: 6/8/32																												
1932	Chi-A	2	4	.333	12	5	2	0	0	50	67	35	4	4	20	16	16.4	5.76	75	.324	.394	1	.077	-1	-7	-8	-1	-0.9
● JAY DAHL Dahl, Jay Steven b: 12/6/45, San Bernardino, Cal. d: 6/20/65, Salisbury, N.C. BB/TL, 5'10", 183 lbs. Deb: 9/27/63																												
1963	Hou-N	0	1	.000	1	1	0	0	0	2^2	7	7	0	0	0	0	23.6	16.88	19	.438	.438	0	—	0	-4	-4	-0	-0.6
● JERRY DAHLKE Dahlke, Jerome Alexander "Joe" b: 6/8/30, Marathon, Wis. BR/TR, 6', 180 lbs. Deb: 5/6/56																												
1956	Chi-A	0	0	—	5	0	0	0	0	2^1	5	5	0	0	6	1	42.4	19.29	21	.455	.647	0	—	0	-4	-4	0	-0.2
● SAM DAILEY Dailey, Samuel Laurence b: 3/31/04, Oakford, Ill. d: 12/2/79, Columbia, Mo. BL/TR, 5'11", 168 lbs. Deb: 7/4/29																												
1929	Phi-N	2	2	.500	20	4	0	0	0	51^1	74	48	5	1	23	18	17.2	7.54	69	.349	.415	1	.059	-2	-16	-12	-1	-1.1
● VINCE DAILEY Dailey, Vincent Perry b: 12/25/1864, Osceola, Pa. d: 11/14/19, Hornell, N.Y. 6', 200 lbs. Deb: 4/21/1890 ♦																												
1890	Cle-N	0	1	.000	2	1	0	0	0	7	12	17	0	0	7	0	24.4	7.71	46	.364	.475	71	.289	1	-3	-3	0	-0.3
● BILL DAILEY Dailey, William Garland b: 5/13/35, Arlington, Va. BR/TR, 6'3", 185 lbs. Deb: 8/17/61																												
1961	Cle-A	1	0	1.000	12	0	0	0	0	19	16	4	0	0	6	7	10.4	0.95	415	.232	.293	0	.000	-0	6	6	0	0.3
1962	Cle-A	2	2	.500	27	0	0	0	1	42^2	43	18	0	2	17	24	13.1	3.59	108	.270	.348	0	.000	-0	2	1	-0	0.1
1963	Min-A	6	3	.667	66	0	0	0	21	108^2	80	26	9	0	19	72	8.2	1.99	183	.208	.246	5	.238	2	20	20	2	3.0
1964	Min-A	1	2	.333	14	0	0	0	0	15^1	23	16	3	4	17	6	25.8	8.22	44	.377	.537	0	—	0	-8	-8	0	-1.4
Total	4	10	7	.588	119	0	0	0	22	185^2	162	64	12	6	59	109	11.0	2.76	135	.241	.308	5	.192	1	20	20	3	2.0
● ED DAILY Daily, Edward M. b: 9/7/1862, Providence, R.I. d: 10/21/1891, Washington, D.C. BR/TR, 5'10.5", 174 lbs. Deb: 5/4/1885 F♦																												
1885	Phi-N	26	23	.531	50	50	49	4	0	440	370	212	12		90	140	9.4	2.21	126	.217	.256	38	.207	-0	30	29	-4	2.4
1886	Phi-N	16	9	.640	27	23	22	1	0	218	211	123	7		59	95	11.1	3.06	108	.242	.290	70	.227	3	6	6	2	0.8
1887	Phi-N	0	4	.000	6	5	4	0	0	41^1	77	52	2	0	25	7	16.8	7.19	59	.376	.376	33	.303	1	-14	-13	1	-0.8
	Was-N	0	1	.000	1	1	1	0	0	7	11	6	0	0	6	3	14.1	7.71	53	.200	.367	92	.283	0	-3	-3	0	-0.3
	Yr	0	5	.000	7	6	5	0	0	48^1	88	58	2	0	31	10	16.4	7.26	58	.431	.374	125	.288	1	-17	-16	1	-1.1

YEAR	TM/L	W	L	PCT	G	GS	CG	SH	SV	IP	H	R	HR	HB	BB	SO	RAT	ERA	ERA+	OAV	OOB	BH	AVG	PB	PR	PR+	PD	TPI
1888	Was-N	2	7	.222	9	8	8	0	0	73^2	88	69	7	3	19	20	13.4	4.89	57	.278	.325	102	.225	1	-17	-17	0	-1.6
1889	Col-a	0	0	—	2	0	0	0	1	1^2	1	7	0	0	4	2	27.0	21.60	17	.167	.500	148	.256	0	-3	-4	-0	-0.4
1890	Bro-a	10	15	.400	27	27	27	0	0	235^2	252	161	3	18	93	82	13.9	4.05	96	.265	.342	94	.239	3	-5	-4	2	0.1
	NY-N	2	0	1.000	2	1	1	0	0	16	6	6	0	4	6	0	9.0	2.25	156	.113	.254	2	.133	-1	2	2	1	0.2
	*Lou-a	6	3	.667	12	10	9	1	0	93	83	35	2	4	30	31	11.3	1.94	199	.232	.298	20	.250	2	20	20	2	2.1
1891	Lou-a	4	8	.333	15	14	11	0	0	111^1	149	109	6	8	48	27	16.6	5.74	64	.310	.382	16	.250	2	-25	-26	0	-1.9
Total	7	66	70	.485	151	139	132	6	1	1237^2	1248	780	39	37	380	407	11.9	3.39	98	.251	.305	633	.244	12	-8	-11	5	0.6
● **HUGH DAILY**	Daily, Hugh Ignatius "One Arm" (b: Harry Criss) b: 1857, Baltimore, Md. BR/TR, 6'2", 180 lbs. Deb: 5/1/1882																											
1882	Buf-N	15	14	.517	29	29	29	0	0	255^2	246	165	6		70	116	11.1	2.99	98	.234	.282	18	.164	-6	-3	-2	-5	-1.1
1883	Cle-N	23	19	.548	45	43	40	4	1	378^2	360	193	5		99	171	10.9	2.42	130	.243	.291	18	.127	-10	30	30	-1	1.8
1884	CP-U	27	27	.500	56	56	54	5	0	484^2	430	257	11		71	469	9.3	2.43	100	.222	.249	43	.219	-11	1	1	-0	-0.8
	Was-U	1	1	.500	2	2	2	0	0	16	16	11	0		1	14	9.6	2.25	107	.242	.254	0	.000	-1	0	0	-0	-0.1
	Yr	28	28	.500	58	58	56	5	0	500^2	446	268	11		72	**483**	9.3	2.43	101	.223	.250	43	.214	-12	1	1	1	-0.9
1885	StL-N	3	8	.273	11	11	10	1	0	91^1	92	72	5		44	31	13.4	3.94	70	.252	.333	3	.086	-3	-11	-12	-0	-1.4
1886	Was-N	0	6	.000	6	6	6	0	0	49	69	60	2		40	15	20.0	7.35	45	.332	.440	2	.125	-1	-22	-22	-0	-2.0
1887	Cle-a	4	12	.250	16	16	16	0	0	139^2	225	108	1	3	44	30	14.7	3.67	118	.359	.362	7	.115	-8	10	10	-1	0.1
Total	6	73	87	.456	165	163	157	10	1	1415	1438	866	30	3	369	846	11.2	2.92	101	.251	.291	91	.161	-39	5	6	-6	-3.5
● **BRUCE DalCANTON**	DalCanton, John Bruce b: 6/15/42, California, Pa. BR/TR, 6'2", 205 lbs. Deb: 9/3/67 C																											
1967	Pit-N	2	1	.667	8	2	1	0	0	24	19	5	1	1	10	13	11.3	1.88	179	.211	.297	2	.333	1	4	4	-1	0.5
1968	Pit-N	1	1	.500	7	0	0	0	2	17	7	4	0	2	6	8	7.9	2.12	138	.127	.238	0	.000	-0	2	2	-1	0.1
1969	Pit-N	8	2	.800	57	0	0	0	5	86^1	79	34	3	0	49	56	13.3	3.34	105	.252	.353	3	.300	2	3	2	-0	0.4
1970	Pit-N	9	4	.692	41	6	1	0	1	84^2	94	48	7	1	39	53	14.2	4.57	85	.282	.359	0	.000	-1	-5	-6	-1	-1.0
1971	KC-A	8	6	.571	25	22	2	0	0	141^1	144	63	8	0	44	58	12.0	3.44	100	.262	.317	4	.087	-3	0	-0	-2	-0.4
1972	KC-A	6	6	.500	35	16	1	0	2	132^1	135	54	7	1	29	75	11.2	3.40	89	.265	.306	4	.098	-2	-5	-5	-2	-0.9
1973	KC-A	4	3	.571	32	3	1	0	3	97^1	108	60	8	4	46	38	14.6	4.81	86	.284	.367	0	—	0	-11	-7	0	-0.5
1974	KC-A	8	10	.444	31	22	9	2	0	175^1	135	71	5	5	82	96	11.4	3.13	122	.211	.306	0	—	0	10	13	0	1.3
1975	KC-A	0	2	.000	4	2	0	0	0	8^2	23	18	0	1	7	5	32.2	15.58	25	.479	.554	0	—	0	-11	-11	0	-1.8
	Atl-N	2	7	.222	26	9	0	0	3	67	63	33	2	6	24	38	12.5	3.36	113	.248	.327	2	.105	-1	2	3	1	0.4
1976	Atl-N	3	5	.375	42	1	0	0	1	73^1	67	41	6	2	42	36	13.6	3.56	107	.244	.348	2	.222	0	-0	2	1	0.3
1977	Chi-A	0	2	.000	8	0	0	0	2	24	20	11	1	0	13	9	12.4	3.75	109	.230	.330	0	—	0	1	1	-1	0.0
Total	11	51	49	.510	316	83	15	2	19	931^1	894	442	48	23	391	485	12.6	3.67	99	.253	.331	17	.113	-3	-11	-4	-3	-1.6
● **GENE DALE**	Dale, Emmett Eugene b: 6/16/1889, St.Louis, Mo. d: 3/20/58, St.Louis, Mo. BR/TR, 6'3", 179 lbs. Deb: 9/19/11																											
1911	StL-N	0	2	.000	5	2	0	0	0	14^2	13	12	0	2	16	13	19.0	6.75	50	.250	.443	2	.400	1	-5	-6	0	-0.6
1912	StL-N	0	5	.000	19	3	1	0	0	61^2	76	58	4	3	51	37	19.0	6.57	52	.311	.436	6	.273	1	-22	-21	-1	-1.5
1915	Cin-N	18	17	.514	49	35	20	4	3	296^2	256	115	6	6	107	104	11.2	2.46	116	.243	.316	20	.220	2	10	13	-1	1.6
1916	Cin-N	3	4	.429	17	5	2	0	0	69^2	80	44	3	2	33	23	14.9	5.17	50	.304	.386	3	.143	-0	-20	-20	1	-1.8
Total	4	21	28	.429	90	45	23	4	3	442^2	425	229	13	13	207	177	13.1	3.60	81	.263	.352	31	.223	3	-37	-33	-1	-2.3
● **CARL DALE**	Dale, James Carl b: 12/7/72, Indianapolis, Ind. BR/TR, 6'2", 215 lbs. Deb: 9/7/99																											
1999	Mil-N	0	1	.000	4	0	0	0	0	4	8	9	2	1	6	4	33.8	20.25	22	.400	.556	0	—	0	-7	-7	-0	-1.2
● **BUD DALEY**	Daley, Leavitt Leo b: 10/7/32, Orange, Cal. BL/TL, 6'1", 185 lbs. Deb: 9/10/55																											
1955	Cle-A	0	1	.000	2	1	0	0	0	7	10	5	1	0	1	2	14.1	6.43	62	.333	.355	0	.000	-0	-2	-2	0	-0.2
1956	Cle-A	1	0	1.000	14	0	0	0	0	20^1	21	15	2	5	14	13	17.7	6.20	68	.273	.417	0	.000	-0	-5	-4	1	-0.2
1957	Cle-A	2	8	.200	34	10	1	0	2	87^1	99	59	6	10	40	54	15.4	4.43	84	.279	.368	4	.200	0	-6	-7	1	-0.6
1958	KC-A	3	2	.600	26	5	1	0	0	70^2	67	29	5	6	19	39	11.7	3.31	118	.249	.313	2	.125	-1	4	5	1	0.3
1959	KC-A★	16	13	.552	39	29	12	2	1	216^1	212	90	24	11	62	125	11.9	3.16	127	.257	.317	23	.295	4	17	20	-0	3.0
1960	KC-A★	16	16	.500	37	35	13	1	0	231	234	129	27	10	96	126	13.2	4.56	87	.263	.341	12	.160	1	-18	-14	1	-1.6
1961	KC-A	4	8	.333	16	10	2	0	1	63^2	84	46	6	5	22	36	15.7	4.95	84	.319	.383	2	.111	-1	-7	-5	1	-0.9
	*NY-A	8	9	.471	23	17	7	0	0	129^2	127	63	17	4	51	83	12.6	3.96	94	.257	.331	6	.133	-1	1	-4	-1	-0.6
	Yr	12	17	.414	39	27	9	0	1	193^1	211	109	23	9	73	119	13.6	4.28	90	.278	.349	8	.127	-2	-6	-9	-0	-1.5
1962	*NY-A	7	5	.583	43	6	0	0	4	105^1	105	47	8	5	21	55	11.2	3.59	104	.258	.303	5	.185	-0	4	2	-0	0.2
1963	NY-A	0	0	—	1	0	0	0	1	1	2	0	0	0	0	0	18.0	0.00	—	.667	.667	0	—	0	0	0	-0	0.1
1964	NY-A	3	2	.600	13	3	0	0	1	35	37	19	3	4	25	16	17.0	4.63	78	.274	.402	2	.250	1	-4	-4	1	-0.4
Total	10	60	64	.484	248	116	36	3	10	967^1	998	502	99	60	351	549	13.1	4.03	97	.266	.339	56	.192	3	-15	-14	4	-0.9
● **BILL DALEY**	Daley, William b: 6/27/1868, Poughkeepsie, N.Y d: 5/4/22, Poughkeepsie, N.Y. TL, Deb: 7/17/1889																											
1889	Bos-N	3	3	.500	9	7	4	0	0	48	34	29	1	2	43	40	14.8	4.31	97	.193	.357	3	.150	-1	-2	-1	3	0.1
1890	Bos-P	18	7	**.720**	34	25	19	2	2	235	246	178	7	9	167	110	16.2	3.60	122	.258	.373	17	.155	-5	17	20	-1	1.1
1891	Bos-a	8	6	.571	19	11	10	0	**2**	126^2	119	76	6	7	81	68	14.7	2.98	117	.240	.354	10	.169	-3	10	7	1	0.5
Total	3	29	16	.644	62	43	33	2	4	409^2	399	283	14	18	291	218	15.6	3.49	117	.245	.366	30	.159	-8	25	26	3	1.7
● **MIKE DALTON**	Dalton, Michael Edward b: 3/27/63, Palo Alto, Cal. BR/TL, 6', 215 lbs. Deb: 5/31/91																											
1991	Det-A	0	0	—	4	0	0	0	0	8	12	3	2	0	2	4	15.8	3.38	123	.333	.368	0	—	0	1	1	0	0.0
● **GEORGE DALY**	Daly, George Josephs "Pecks" b: 7/28/1887, Buffalo, N.Y. d: 12/12/57, Buffalo, N.Y. BR/TR, 5'10.5", 175 lbs. Deb: 9/26/09																											
1909	NY-N	0	3	.000	3	3	3	0	0	21	31	19	0	1	8	8	17.1	6.00	43	.341	.400	1	.111	-1	-8	-8	-1	-1.1
● **JEFF D'AMICO**	D'Amico, Jeffrey Charles b: 12/27/75, St.Petersburg, Fla. BR/TR, 6'7", 250 lbs. Deb: 6/28/96																											
1996	Mil-A	6	6	.500	17	17	0	0	0	86	88	53	21	0	31	53	12.5	5.44	95	.267	.330	0	—	0	-4	-2	-1	-0.3
1997	Mil-A	9	7	.563	23	23	1	1	0	135^2	139	81	25	8	43	94	12.6	4.71	98	.264	.329	0	.000	-0	-2	-1	-1	-0.3
1999	Mil-N	0	0	—	1	0	0	0	0	1	1	0	0	0	0	1	9.0	0.00	—	.250	.250	0	—	0	1	1	0	0.0
2000	Mil-N	12	7	.632	23	23	1	1	0	162^1	143	55	14	6	46	101	10.8	2.66	171	.238	.298	4	.091	-0	36	35	-2	3.5
Total	4	27	20	.574	64	63	2	2	0	385	371	189	60	14	120	249	11.8	4.00	118	.254	.316	4	.083	-1	30	31	-4	2.9
● **JEFF D'AMICO**	D'Amico, Jeffrey Michael b: 11/9/74, Inglewood, Cal. BR/TR, 6'3", 200 lbs. Deb: 6/3/2000																											
2000	KC-A	0	1	.000	7	1	0	0	0	13^2	19	14	2	0	15	9	22.4	9.22	54	.345	.486	0	—	0	-7	-6	-0	-0.4
● **BILL DAMMANN**	Dammann, William Henry "Wee Willie" b: 8/9/1872, Chicago, Ill. d: 12/6/48, Lynnhaven, Va. BL/TL, 5'7", 155 lbs. Deb: 4/24/1897																											
1897	Cin-N	6	4	.600	16	11	7	1	0	95	122	65	2	5	37	21	15.5	4.74	96	.309	.375	5	.161	-1	-5	-2	1	-0.1
1898	Cin-N	16	10	.615	35	22	16	2	2	224^2	277	132	3	7	67	51	14.1	3.61	106	.301	.353	16	.195	1	0	5	-3	0.4
1899	Cin-N	2	1	.667	9	5	3	1	1	48	74	30	0	1	11	2	16.1	4.88	80	.351	.386	1	.056	-2	-5	-5	0	-0.4
Total	3	24	15	.615	60	38	26	4	3	367^2	473	227	5	13	115	74	14.7	4.06	99	.310	.363	22	.168	-1	-10	-1	-2	-0.1
● **PAT DANEKER**	Daneker, Patrick Rees b: 1/14/76, Williamsport, Pa. BR/TR, 6'3", 195 lbs. Deb: 7/2/99																											
1999	Chi-A	0	0	—	3	2	0	0	0	15	14	8	1	0	6	5	12.0	4.20	116	.255	.328	0	.000	-0	1	1	0	0.0
● **ART DANEY**	Daney, Arthur Lee b: 7/9/04, Talihina, Okla. d: 3/11/88, Phoenix, Ariz. BR/TR, 5'11", 165 lbs. Deb: 5/25/28																											
1928	Phi-A	0	0	—	1	0	0	0	0	1	1	0	0	0	0	0	9.0	0.00	—	.250	.250	0		0	0	0	0	0.0
● **DAVE DANFORTH**	Danforth, David Charles "Dauntless Dave" b: 3/7/1890, Granger, Tex. d: 9/19/70, Baltimore, Md. BL/TL, 6', 167 lbs. Deb: 8/1/11																											
1911	Phi-A	4	1	.800	14	2	1	0	1	33^2	29	18	1	3	17	21	13.1	3.74	84	.240	.348	1	.167	0	-1	-2	-0	-0.3
1912	Phi-A	0	0	—	3	0	0	0	0	20^1	26	14	0	0	12	8	16.8	3.98	77	.338	.427	2	.250	0	-2	-2	0	-0.1
1916	Chi-A	6	5	.545	28	8	1	0	2	93^2	87	43	1	3	37	49	12.2	3.27	85	.259	.338	2	.087	-1	-5	-5	1	-0.7
1917	*Chi-A	11	6	.647	**50**	9	1	1	**9**	173	155	56	1	3	74	79	12.1	2.65	100	.244	.325	6	.130	0	0	0	-3	-0.3
1918	Chi-A	6	15	.286	39	11	5	0	2	139	148	73	1	5	40	48	12.5	3.43	80	.288	.345	6	.143	-2	-10	-11	0	-1.8
1919	Chi-A	1	2	.333	15	1	0	0	1	41^2	58	44	1	1	20	17	17.1	7.78	41	.333	.405	1	.111	0	-21	-22	-0	-1.5
1922	StL-A	5	2	.714	20	10	3	0	1	79^2	93	37	1	1	38	48	14.9	3.28	127	.304	.383	2	.087	-2	7	8	-1	0.3
1923	StL-A	16	14	.533	38	29	16	0	1	226^1	221	111	4	12	87	96	12.7	3.94	106	.262	.340	15	.211	2	1	6	-0	0.8

YEAR	TM/L	W	L	PCT	G	GS	CG	SH	SV	IP	H	R	HR	HB	BB	SO	RAT	ERA	ERA+	OAV	OOB	BH	AVG	PB	PR	PR+	PD	TPI
1924	StL-A	15	12	.556	41	27	12	1	4	219^{2}	246	126	16	3	69	65	13.0	4.51	100	.292	.348	13	.171	-2	-7	0	-3	-0.4
1925	StL-A	7	9	.438	38	15	5	0	2	159	172	96	19	3	61	53	13.4	4.36	107	.284	.353	8	.174	-2	1	5	4	-0.1
Total	10	71	66	.518	286	112	44	2	23	1186	1235	618	45	34	455	484	13.1	3.89	95	.277	.349	56	.160	-6	-37	-25	-10	-4.1
● CHUCK DANIEL	Daniel, Charles Edward b: 9/17/33, Bluffton, Ark. BR/TR, 6'2", 195 lbs. Deb: 9/21/57																											
1957	Det-A	0	0	—	1	0	0	0	0	2^{1}	3	2	1	0	0	2	11.6	7.71	50	.333	.333	0	—	0	-1	-1	-0	-0.1
● BENNIE DANIELS	Daniels, Bennie b: 6/17/32, Tuscaloosa, Ala. BL/TR, 6'1.5", 193 lbs. Deb: 9/24/57																											
1957	Pit-N	0	1	.000	1	1	0	0	0	7	5	2	0	0	3	2	10.3	1.29	295	.208	.296	0	.000	-0	2	2	1	0.3
1958	Pit-N	0	3	.000	8	5	1	0	0	27^{2}	31	19	3	1	15	7	15.3	5.53	70	.290	.382	1	.125	-0	-5	-5	1	-0.4
1959	Pit-N	7	9	.438	34	12	0	0	1	100^{2}	115	69	9	2	39	67	13.9	5.45	71	.287	.353	9	.310	6	-17	-18	-1	-2.0
1960	Pit-N	1	3	.250	10	6	0	0	0	40^{1}	52	35	4	0	17	16	15.4	7.81	48	.311	.375	3	.188	-0	-18	-18	1	-1.5
1961	Was-A	12	11	.522	32	28	12	1	0	212	184	90	14	3	80	110	11.3	3.44	117	.237	.311	15	.197	3	14	14	1	1.8
1962	Was-A	7	16	.304	44	21	3	1	2	161^{1}	172	98	14	2	68	66	13.5	4.85	83	.280	.354	6	.130	-1	-16	-14	5	-1.5
1963	Was-A	5	10	.333	35	24	6	1	1	168^{2}	163	90	19	1	58	88	11.8	4.38	85	.250	.312	7	.152	1	-14	-12	3	-0.6
1964	Was-A	8	10	.444	33	24	3	2	0	163	147	75	20	0	64	73	11.7	3.70	100	.245	.317	6	.128	0	-1	0	3	0.3
1965	Was-A	5	13	.278	33	18	1	0	1	116^{1}	135	75	16	0	39	42	13.5	4.72	74	.290	.345	4	.133	0	-16	-16	-0	-2.3
Total	9	45	76	.372	230	139	26	5	5	997	1004	553	99	9	383	471	12.6	4.44	86	.264	.332	51	.170	9	-72	-68	12	-5.9
● CHARLIE DANIELS	Daniels, Charles L. b: 7/1/1861, Roxbury, Mass. d: 2/9/38, Boston, Mass. Deb: 4/18/1884																											
1884	Bos-U	0	2	.000	2	2	2	0	0	16^{2}	20	14	0		2	12	11.9	4.32	55	.278	.297	3	.273	0	-3	-4	-0	-0.3
● PETE DANIELS	Daniels, Peter J. "Smiling Pete" b: 4/8/1864, County Cavan, Ireland d: 2/13/28, Indianapolis, Ind. BL/TL, Deb: 4/19/1890																											
1890	Pit-N	1	2	.333	4	4	3	0	0	28	40	29	1	3	12	8	17.7	7.07	47	.325	.399	4	.333	1	-11	-13	-0	-0.9
1898	StL-N	1	6	.143	10	6	3	0	0	54^{2}	62	41	0	3	14	13	13.0	3.62	105	.283	.335	3	.176	0	-0	1	-0	0.1
Total	2	2	8	.200	14	10	6	0	0	82^{2}	102	70	1	6	26	21	14.6	4.79	76	.298	.358	7	.241	1	-11	-11	-0	-0.8
● GEORGE DARBY	Darby, George William "Deacon" b: 2/6/1869, Kansas City, Mo. d: 2/25/37, Sacramento, Cal. BR/TR, 5'10.5", 160 lbs. Deb: 4/28/1893																											
1893	Cin-N	1	1	.500	4	3	2	0	0	29	41	32	2	3	18	6	19.2	7.76	62	.323	.419	3	.300	0	-10	-9	1	-0.3
● PAT DARCY	Darcy, Patrick Leonard b: 5/12/50, Troy, Ohio BL/TR, 6'3", 175 lbs. Deb: 9/12/74																											
1974	Cin-N	1	0	1.000	6	2	0	0	0	17	17	7	2	0	8	14	13.2	3.71	94	.262	.342	1	.333	0	-0	-0	-0	0.0
1975	*Cin-N	11	5	.688	27	22	1	0	1	130^{2}	134	54	4	0	59	46	13.3	3.58	101	.269	.346	4	.085	-3	1	0	-0	-0.3
1976	Cin-N	2	3	.400	11	4	0	0	2	39	41	27	2	0	22	15	14.5	6.23	56	.279	.373	2	.182	1	-12	-12	-1	-1.5
Total	3	14	8	.636	44	28	1	0	3	186^{2}	192	88	8	0	89	75	13.5	4.15	86	.270	.352	7	.115	-2	-11	-12	-1	-1.8
● VIC DARENSBOURG	Darensbourg, Victor Anthony b: 11/13/70, Los Angeles, Cal. BL/TL, 5'10", 165 lbs. Deb: 4/1/98																											
1998	Fla-N	0	7	.000	59	0	0	0	1	71	52	29	5	0	30	74	10.4	3.68	110	.207	.292	0	.000	-1	4	3	-1	0.1
1999	Fla-N	0	1	.000	56	0	0	0	0	34^{2}	50	36	3	5	21	16	19.7	8.83	49	.340	.439	0	—	0	-16	-18	-0	-0.8
2000	Fla-N	5	3	.625	56	0	0	0	0	62	61	32	7	2	28	59	13.2	4.06	109	.260	.343	2	.250	0	4	3	1	0.4
Total	3	5	11	.313	171	0	0	0	1	167^{2}	163	97	15	7	79	149	13.4	4.88	87	.258	.346	2	.125	0	-8	-12	0	-0.3
● ALVIN DARK	Dark, Alvin Ralph "Blackie" b: 1/7/22, Comanche, Okla. BR/TR, 5'11", 185 lbs. Deb: 7/14/46 MC♦																											
1953	NY-N	0	0	—	1	1	0	0	0	1	1	2	1	0	1	0	18.0	18.00	24	.250	.400	194	.300	0	-2	-2	-0	-0.1
● RON DARLING	Darling, Ronald Maurice b: 8/19/60, Honolulu, Hawaii BR/TR, 6'3", 195 lbs. Deb: 9/6/83																											
1983	NY-N	1	3	.250	5	5	1	0	0	35^{1}	31	11	0	3	17	23	13.0	2.80	130	.248	.352	1	.100	-1	3	3	0	0.3
1984	NY-N	12	9	.571	33	33	2	2	0	205^{2}	179	97	17	5	104	136	12.6	3.81	93	.235	.331	10	.149	-1	-5	-6	2	-0.5
1985	NY-N☆	16	6	.727	36	35	4	2	0	248	214	93	21	3	114	167	12.0	2.90	119	.235	.323	13	.171	2	19	16	3	2.0
1986	*NY-N	15	6	.714	34	34	4	2	0	237	203	84	21	3	81	184	10.9	2.81	126	.234	.302	8	.099	-2	24	20	3	1.9
1987	NY-N	12	8	.600	32	32	2	0	0	207^{2}	183	111	24	3	96	167	12.2	4.29	88	.233	.319	8	.123	1	-5	-13	4	-0.7
1988	*NY-N	17	9	.654	34	34	7	4	0	240^{2}	218	97	24	5	60	161	10.6	3.25	99	.245	.297	18	.220	6	5	-1	0	0.5
1989	NY-N	14	14	.500	33	33	4	0	0	217^{1}	214	100	19	3	70	153	11.9	3.52	93	.258	.318	9	.123	1	-0	-6	2	-0.6
1990	NY-N	7	9	.438	33	18	1	0	0	126	135	73	20	5	44	99	13.1	4.50	83	.273	.338	4	.129	0	-10	-11	1	-1.1
1991	NY-N	5	6	.455	17	17	0	0	0	102^{1}	96	50	9	6	28	58	11.4	3.87	94	.251	.313	4	.118	-0	-2	-3	-0	-0.3
	Mon-N	0	2	.000	3	3	0	0	0	17	25	16	6	1	5	11	16.4	7.41	49	.333	.383	1	.167	0	-7	-7	-0	-0.7
	Yr	5	8	.385	20	20	0	0	0	119^{1}	121	66	15	7	33	69	12.1	4.37	83	.265	.324	5	.125	-0	-9	-10	-0	-1.0
	Oak-A	3	7	.300	12	12	0	0	0	75	64	34	7	2	38	60	12.5	4.08	94	.237	.335	0	—	0	0	-2	0	-0.2
1992	*Oak-A	15	10	.600	33	33	4	3	0	206^{1}	198	98	15	4	72	99	12.0	3.66	102	.253	.319	0	—	0	7	2	-1	0.2
1993	Oak-A	5	9	.357	31	29	3	0	0	178	198	107	22	5	72	95	13.9	5.16	79	.281	.352	0	—	0	-16	-22	-2	-1.7
1994	Oak-A	10	11	.476	25	25	4	0	0	160	162	89	18	7	59	108	12.8	4.50	98	.267	.339	0	.000	-0	5	-1	0	-0.1
1995	Oak-A	4	7	.364	21	21	1	0	0	104	124	79	16	4	46	69	15.1	6.23	72	.296	.371	0	—	0	-17	-21	2	-1.7
Total	13	136	116	.540	382	364	37	13	0	2360^{1}	2244	1139	239	59	906	1590	12.2	3.87	95	.252	.325	76	.144	6	1	-51	15	-2.7
● BOB DARNELL	Darnell, Robert Jack b: 11/6/30, Wewoka, Okla. d: 1/1/95, Fredericksburg, Tex. BR/TR, 5'10", 175 lbs. Deb: 8/10/54																											
1954	Bro-N	0	0	—	6	1	0	0	0	14^{1}	15	7	2	0	7	5	13.8	3.14	130	.278	.361	0	.000	-0	1	1	0	0.1
1956	Bro-N	0	0	—	1	0	0	0	0	1^{1}	1	0	0	0	0	0	6.8	0.00	—	.200	.200	0	—	0	1	1	-0	0.0
Total	2	0	0	—	7	1	0	0	0	15^{2}	16	7	2	0	7	5	13.2	2.87	142	.271	.348	0	.000	-0	2	2	0	0.1
● MIKE DARR	Darr, Michael Edward b: 3/23/56, Pomona, Cal. BR/TR, 6'4", 190 lbs. Deb: 9/6/77																											
1977	Tor-A	0	1	.000	1	1	0	0	0	1^{1}	3	5	1	1	4	1	54.0	33.75	12	.429	.667	0	—	0	-4	-4	0	-0.6
● GEORGE DARROW	Darrow, George Oliver b: 7/12/03, Beloit, Kan. d: 3/24/83, Sun City, Ariz. BL/TL, 6', 180 lbs. Deb: 4/22/34																											
1934	Phi-N	2	6	.250	17	8	2	0	1	49	57	37	4	4	28	14	16.3	5.51	86	.302	.403	2	.133	0	-8	-4	0	-0.5
● BOBBY DARWIN	Darwin, Arthur Bobby Lee b: 2/16/43, Los Angeles, Cal. BR/TR, 6'2", 200 lbs. Deb: 9/30/62 ♦																											
1962	LA-A	0	1	.000	1	1	0	0	0	3^{1}	8	6	0	0	4	6	32.4	10.80	36	.421	.522	0	.000	-0	-3	-3	-0	-0.4
1969	LA-N	0	0	—	3	0	0	0	0	3^{2}	4	4	0	2	5	0	27.0	9.82	34	.333	.579	0	—	0	-3	-3	-0	-0.2
Total	2	0	1	.000	4	1	0	0	0	7	12	10	0	2	9	6	29.6	10.29	35	.387	.548	559	.251	-0	-5	-6	-0	-0.6
● DANNY DARWIN	Darwin, Daniel Wayne b: 10/25/55, Bonham, Tex. BR/TR, 6'3", 190 lbs. Deb: 9/8/78 F																											
1978	Tex-A	1	0	1.000	3	1	0	0	0	8^{2}	11	4	0	0	1	8	12.5	4.15	90	.324	.343	0	—	0	-0	-0	-0	-0.1
1979	Tex-A	4	4	.500	20	6	1	0	0	78	50	36	5	5	30	58	9.8	4.04	103	.186	.280	0	—	0	2	1	-1	0.0
1980	Tex-A	13	4	.765	53	2	0	0	8	109^{2}	98	37	4	2	50	104	12.3	2.63	149	.243	.329	0	—	0	17	16	-0	2.6
1981	Tex-A	9	9	.500	22	22	6	2	0	146	115	67	12	6	57	98	11.0	3.64	95	.218	.302	0	—	0	0	-3	-1	-0.4
1982	Tex-A	10	8	.556	56	1	0	0	7	89	95	38	6	2	37	61	13.6	3.44	113	.279	.354	0	—	0	6	5	2	1.1
1983	Tex-A	8	13	.381	28	26	9	2	0	183	175	86	9	3	62	92	11.8	3.49	115	.250	.313	0	—	0	12	11	-1	1.1
1984	Tex-A	8	12	.400	35	32	5	1	0	223^{2}	249	110	19	4	54	123	12.4	3.94	105	.279	.323	0	—	0	1	5	-2	0.2
1985	Mil-A	8	18	.308	39	29	11	1	2	217^{2}	212	112	34	4	65	125	11.6	3.80	110	.254	.311	0	—	0	8	9	-3	0.7
1986	Mil-A	6	8	.429	27	14	5	1	0	130^{1}	120	62	13	3	35	80	10.9	3.52	123	.246	.300	0	—	0	10	11	1	1.2
	Hou-N	5	2	.714	12	8	1	0	0	54^{1}	50	19	3	0	9	40	9.8	2.32	156	.239	.271	1	.063	-1	8	8	-1	0.8
1987	Hou-N	9	10	.474	33	30	3	1	0	195^{2}	184	87	17	5	69	134	11.9	3.59	109	.246	.314	12	.182	2	11	8	-2	0.7
1988	Hou-N	8	13	.381	44	20	3	0	3	192	189	86	20	7	48	129	11.4	3.84	87	.259	.311	4	.071	-1	-8	-11	2	-1.2
1989	Hou-N	11	4	.733	68	0	0	0	7	122	92	34	8	2	33	104	9.4	2.36	144	.212	.271	2	.118	-1	15	14	-1	1.7
1990	Hou-N	11	4	.733	48	17	3	0	2	162^{2}	136	42	11	4	31	109	**9.5**	**2.21**	**168**	.225	**.267**	5	.132	1	29	28	-1	2.4
1991	Bos-A	3	6	.333	12	12	0	0	0	68	71	39	15	4	15	42	11.9	5.16	83	.263	.311	0	—	0	-8	-6	0	-0.7
1992	Bos-A	9	9	.500	51	15	2	0	3	161^{1}	159	76	11	5	53	124	12.1	3.96	107	.257	.321	0	—	0	-0	4	-1	0.4
1993	Bos-A	15	11	.577	34	34	2	1	0	229^{1}	196	93	31	3	49	130	**9.7**	3.26	142	.230	**.274**	0	—	0	27	33	-0	3.4
1994	Bos-A	7	5	.583	13	13	0	0	0	75^{2}	101	54	13	1	24	54	15.0	6.30	80	.317	.366	0	—	0	-13	-10	-0	-1.3
1995	Tor-A	1	8	.111	13	11	1	0	0	65	91	60	13	3	24	36	16.3	7.62	62	.340	.400	0	—	0	-21	-21	-1	-2.3
	Tex-A	2	2	.500	7	4	0	0	0	34	40	27	12	1	7	22	12.7	7.15	68	.292	.331	0	—	0	-9	-9	-0	-0.8
	Yr	3	10	.231	20	15	1	0	0	99	131	87	25	4	31	58	15.1	7.45	64	.323	.377	0	—	0	-30	-29	-2	-3.1

YEAR	TM/L	W	L	PCT	G	GS	CG	SH	SV	IP	H	R	HR	HB	BB	SO	RAT	ERA	ERA+	OAV	OOB	BH	AVG	PB	PR	PR+	PD	TPI
1996	Pit-N	7	9	.438	19	19	0	0	0	122^1	117	48	9	6	16	69	10.2	3.02	145	.253	.287	8	.205	2	16	18	1	2.5
	Hou-N	3	2	.600	15	6	0	0	0	42^1	43	31	7	6	11	27	12.8	5.95	65	.267	.337	1	.100	-0	-8	-11	-1	-1.2
	Yr	10	11	.476	34	25	0	0	0	164^2	160	79	16	12	27	96	10.9	3.77	112	.257	.301	9	.184	2	8	9	0	1.3
1997	Chi-A	4	8	.333	21	17	1	0	0	113^1	130	60	21	1	31	62	12.9	4.13	106	.286	.333	0	.000	-0	6	3	1	0.4
	SF-N	1	3	.250	10	7	0	0	0	44	51	26	5	1	14	30	13.5	4.91	83	.288	.344	2	.133	-0	-3	-4	0	-0.3
1998	SF-N	8	10	.444	33	25	0	0	0	148^2	176	97	23	3	49	81	13.8	5.51	72	.297	.353	4	.089	-2	-21	-27	0	-2.9
Total	21	171	182	.484	716	371	53	9	32	3016^2	2951	1431	321	81	874	1942	11.7	3.84	106	.256	.313	39	.128	-0	78	74	-11	8.0
● JEFF DARWIN Darwin, Jeffrey Scott b: 7/6/69, Sherman, Tex. BR/TR, 6'3", 180 lbs. Deb: 6/13/94 F																												
1994	Sea-A	0	0	—	2	0	0	0	0	4	7	6	1	1	3	1	24.8	13.50	36	.389	.500	0	—	0	-4	-4	-0	-0.2
1996	Chi-A	0	1	.000	22	0	0	0	0	30^2	26	10	5	2	9	15	10.9	2.93	162	.232	.301	0	—	0	7	7	-0	0.3
1997	Chi-A	0	1	.000	14	0	0	0	0	13^2	17	8	1	0	7	9	15.8	5.27	83	.298	.375	0	—	0	-1	-1	-0	-0.1
Total	3	0	2	.000	38	0	0	0	0	48^1	50	24	7	3	19	25	13.4	4.47	104	.267	.344	0	—	0	2	1	-1	0.0
● DOUG DASCENZO Dascenzo, Douglas Craig b: 6/30/64, Cleveland, Ohio BB/TL, 5'8", 160 lbs. Deb: 9/2/88 ♦																												
1990	Chi-N	0	0	—	1	0	0	0	0	1	1	0	0	0	0	0	9.0	0.00	—	.333	.333	61	.253	0	0	0	0	0.0
1991	Chi-N	0	0	—	3	0	0	0	0	4	2	0	0	0	2	2	9.0	0.00	—	.154	.267	61	.255	1	2	2	-0	0.1
Total	2	0	0	—	4	0	0	0	0	5	3	0	0	0	2	2	9.0	0.00	—	.188	.278	287	.234	1	2	2	-0	0.1
● LEE DASHNER Dashner, Lee Claire "Lefty" b: 4/25/1887, Renault, Ill. d: 12/16/59, ElDorado, Kan. BB/TL, 5'11.5", 192 lbs. Deb: 8/4/13																												
1913	Cle-A	0	0	—	1	0	0	0	0	1^2	0	1	0	0	0	2	0.0	5.40	56	.000	.000	0	—	0	-0	-0	-0	0.0
● FRANK DASSO Dasso, Francis Joseph Nicholas b: 8/31/17, Chicago, Ill. BR/TR, 5'11.5", 185 lbs. Deb: 4/22/45																												
1945	Cin-N	4	5	.444	16	12	6	0	0	95^2	89	50	9	0	53	39	13.4	3.67	102	.253	.351	5	.161	-1	1	1	0	0.1
1946	Cin-N	0	0	—	2	0	0	0	0	1	2	3	0	0	2	1	36.0	27.00	12	.400	.571	0	—	0	-3	-3	0	-0.1
Total	2	4	5	.444	18	12	6	0	0	96^2	91	53	9	0	55	40	13.6	3.91	96	.255	.354	5	.161	-1	-1	-2	0	0.0
● DAN DAUB Daub, Daniel William "Mickey" b: 1/12/1868, Middletown, Ohio d: 3/25/51, Bradenton, Fla. BR/TR, 5'10", 160 lbs. Deb: 8/31/1892																												
1892	Cin-N	1	2	.333	4	3	2	0	0	25	23	10	0	2	13	7	13.7	2.88	113	.235	.336	0	.000	-1	1	1	0	0.0
1893	Bro-N	6	6	.500	12	12	12	0	0	103	104	64	3	5	61	25	14.9	3.84	115	.254	.358	8	.190	-2	9	7	3	0.7
1894	Bro-N	10	12	.455	34	27	15	0	0	224	291	209	7	18	91	45	16.1	6.11	81	.311	.383	18	.189	-6	-19	-31	-1	-2.5
1895	Bro-N	10	10	.500	25	21	16	0	0	184^2	212	134	4	11	51	36	13.4	4.29	102	.284	.339	14	.197	-2	10	2	2	0.2
1896	Bro-N	12	11	.522	32	24	18	0	0	225	255	120	4	8	63	53	13.0	3.60	115	.283	.335	19	.226	2	19	14	4	1.6
1897	Bro-N	6	11	.353	19	16	11	0	0	137^2	180	117	8	10	48	19	15.6	6.08	67	.313	.376	11	.224	2	-27	-32	-0	-2.7
Total	6	45	52	.464	126	103	74	0	0	899^1	1065	654	26	54	327	185	14.5	4.75	92	.291	.357	70	.201	-6	-7	-38	8	-2.7
● HOOKS DAUSS Dauss, George August (b: George August Daus) b: 9/22/1889, Indianapolis, Ind d: 7/27/63, St.Louis, Mo. BR/TR, 5'10.5", 168 lbs. Deb: 9/28/12																												
1912	Det-A	1	1	.500	2	2	2	0	0	17	11	7	0	3	9	7	12.2	3.18	103	.186	.324	1	.250	1	0	0	1	0.2
1913	Det-A	13	12	.520	33	29	22	2	1	225	188	96	4	13	82	107	11.3	2.48	118	.228	.308	14	.177	3	11	11	-1	1.5
1914	Det-A	19	15	.559	45	35	22	3	3	302	286	126	3	18	87	150	11.7	2.86	98	.257	.321	21	.216	6	-4	-2	1	0.5
1915	Det-A	24	13	.649	46	35	27	1	2	309^2	261	115	1	11	115	132	11.2	2.50	121	.235	.313	15	.146	0	15	18	9	3.2
1916	Det-A	19	12	.613	39	29	18	1	4	238^2	220	102	2	16	90	95	12.3	3.21	89	.257	.339	16	.222	8	-10	-9	2	-0.1
1917	Det-A	17	14	.548	37	31	22	6	2	270^2	243	105	3	7	87	102	11.2	2.43	109	.245	.311	11	.126	-1	7	7	4	1.1
1918	Det-A	12	16	.429	33	26	21	1	3	249^2	243	105	3	9	58	73	11.2	2.99	89	.263	.313	14	.182	3	-6	-10	2	-0.6
1919	Det-A	21	9	.700	34	32	22	2	0	256^1	262	125	9	5	63	73	11.6	3.55	90	.267	.315	14	.144	-3	-9	-10	6	-0.8
1920	Det-A	13	21	.382	38	32	18	0	0	270^1	308	158	11	8	84	82	13.3	3.56	105	.289	.345	14	.169	1	7	5	8	1.5
1921	Det-A	10	15	.400	32	28	16	0	1	233	275	141	11	13	81	68	14.3	4.33	99	.297	.362	23	.261	2	-1	-1	5	0.6
1922	Det-A	13	13	.500	39	25	12	1	4	218^2	251	123	7	6	59	78	13.0	4.20	92	.289	.339	15	.208	3	-4	-8	1	-0.5
1923	Det-A	21	13	.618	50	39	22	4	3	316	331	140	10	7	78	105	11.8	3.62	107	.272	.319	24	.231	5	13	9	2	1.5
1924	Det-A	12	11	.522	40	10	5	0	6	131^1	155	78	6	1	40	44	13.4	4.59	90	.302	.354	5	.132	-2	-5	-7	0	-1.3
1925	Det-A	16	11	.593	35	30	16	1	1	228	238	110	11	4	85	58	12.9	3.16	136	.272	.339	15	.185	1	31	30	-1	3.1
1926	Det-A	12	6	.667	35	5	0	0	9	124^1	135	63	6	0	49	27	13.3	4.20	97	.287	.354	10	.238	4	-2	-2	-0	0.1
Total	15	223	182	.551	538	388	245	22	39	3390^2	3407	1594	87	121	1067	1201	12.2	3.30	103	.266	.329	212	.189	32	44	34	38	10.0
● VIC DAVALILLO Davalillo, Victor Jose (Romero) b: 7/31/36, Cabimas, Venez. BL/TL, 5'7", 155 lbs. Deb: 4/9/63 F♦																												
1969	StL-N	0	0	—	2	0	0	0	0	0	2	0	0	2	—	—	∞	—	1.000	1.000	99	.265	0	-1	-1	0	-0.1	
● CLAUDE DAVENPORT Davenport, Claude Edwin "Big Dave" b: 5/28/1898, Runge, Tex. d: 6/13/76, Corpus Christi, Tex. BR/TR, 6'6", 193 lbs. Deb: 10/2/20 F																												
1920	NY-N	0	0	—	1	0	0	0	0	2	2	1	1	0	1	0	13.5	4.50	67	.250	.333	0	.000	-0	-0	-0	-0	0.0
● DAVE DAVENPORT Davenport, David W. b: 2/20/1890, DeRidder, La. d: 10/16/54, ElDorado, Ark. BR/TR, 6'6", 220 lbs. Deb: 4/17/14 F																												
1914	Cin-N	2	2	.500	10	6	3	1	2	54	38	18	1	3	30	22	11.8	2.50	117	.202	.321	2	.111	-1	2	2	-0	0.1
	StL-F	8	13	.381	33	26	13	2	4	215^2	204	100	3	7	80	142	12.1	3.46	88	.251	.324	6	.088	-6	-14	-10	1	-1.4
1915	StL-F	22	18	.550	**55**	46	**30**	**10**	1	**392^2**	300	116	5	5	96	**229**	9.2	2.20	131	**.215**	.268	12	.092	-11	23	**28**	-8	0.8
1916	StL-A	12	11	.522	**59**	31	13	1	2	290^2	267	112	4	8	100	129	11.6	2.85	96	.256	.326	10	.137	3	-1	-3	-3	-0.3
1917	StL-A	17	17	.500	47	39	20	2	2	280^2	273	137	5	8	105	100	12.4	3.08	84	.260	.331	9	.098	-6	-13	-15	-1	-2.6
1918	StL-A	10	11	.476	31	22	12	2	1	180	182	84	0	7	69	60	12.9	3.25	84	.273	.347	7	.135	1	-9	-10	2	-0.9
1919	StL-A	2	11	.154	24	16	5	0	0	123^1	135	74	4	2	41	37	13.0	3.94	84	.280	.339	3	.077	-4	-10	-8	1	-1.1
Total	6	73	83	.468	259	186	96	18	12	1537	1399	641	22	40	521	719	11.5	2.93	97	.248	.316	49	.104	-24	-22	-15	-9	-5.4
● JOE DAVENPORT Davenport, Joseph Jonathan b: 3/24/76, Chicago, Ill. BR/TR, 6'5", 225 lbs. Deb: 7/20/99																												
1999	Chi-A	0	0	—	3	0	0	0	0	1^2	1	0	0	0	2	0	16.2	0.00	—	.200	.429	0	—	0	1	1	0	0.1
● LUM DAVENPORT Davenport, Joubert Lum b: 6/27/1900, Tucson, Ariz. d: 4/21/61, Dallas, Tex. BL/TL, 6'1", 165 lbs. Deb: 5/2/21																												
1921	Chi-A	0	3	.000	13	2	0	0	0	35^1	41	35	1	1	32	9	18.8	6.88	62	.318	.457	7	.412	2	-10	-10	-0	-0.6
1922	Chi-A	1	1	.500	9	1	0	0	0	16^2	14	21	2	0	13	9	14.6	10.80	38	.233	.370	0	.000	-0	-13	-12	0	-1.2
1923	Chi-A	0	0	—	2	0	0	0	0	4^1	7	4	0	0	4	1	22.8	6.23	64	.438	.550	1	1.000	0	-1	-1	0	0.0
1924	Chi-A	0	0	—	1	0	0	0	0	2	1	1	0	0	2	1	13.5	0.00	—	.125	.300	0	—	0	1	1	-0	0.0
Total	4	1	4	.200	25	3	0	0	0	58^1	63	61	3	1	51	20	17.7	7.71	54	.296	.434	8	.381	2	-23	-23	-0	-1.8
● MIKE DAVEY Davey, Michael Gerard b: 6/2/52, Spokane, Wash. BR/TL, 6'2", 190 lbs. Deb: 8/13/77																												
1977	Atl-N	0	0	—	16	0	0	0	2	16	19	9	1	0	9	7	15.8	5.06	88	.302	.389	0	.000	-0	-2	-1	-0	-0.1
1978	Atl-N	0	0	—	3	0	0	0	0	2^2	1	0	0	0	1	0	6.8	0.00	—	.125	.222	0	—	0	1	1	-0	0.0
Total	2	0	0	—	19	0	0	0	2	18^2	20	9	1	0	10	7	14.5	4.34	101	.282	.370	0	.000	-0	-1	0	-0	-0.1
● TOM DAVEY Davey, Thomas Joseph b: 9/11/73, Garden City, Mich. BR/TR, 6'7", 215 lbs. Deb: 4/6/99																												
1999	Tor-A	1	1	.500	29	0	0	0	1	44	40	28	5	3	26	42	14.1	4.70	105	.241	.354	0	—	0	1	1	-0	0.0
	Sea-A	1	0	1.000	16	0	0	0	0	21	22	13	0	4	14	17	17.1	4.71	101	.268	.400	0	—	0	0	0	0	0.0
	Yr	2	1	.667	45	0	0	0	1	65	62	41	5	7	40	59	15.1	4.71	104	.250	.369	0	—	0	1	1	-0	0.0
2000	SD-N	2	1	.667	11	0	0	0	0	12^2	12	1	0	0	2	6	9.9	0.71	616	.250	.280	0	—	0	6	5	0	1.1
Total	2	4	2	.667	56	0	0	0	1	77^2	74	42	5	7	42	65	14.3	4.06	118	.250	.357	0	—	0	7	6	0	1.1
● RAY DAVIAULT Daviault, Raymond Joseph Robert b: 5/27/34, Montreal, Que., Can BR/TR, 6'1", 170 lbs. Deb: 4/13/62																												
1962	NY-N	1	5	.167	36	3	0	0	0	81	92	64	14	4	48	51	16.0	6.22	67	.288	.388	1	.067	-1	-21	-17	-1	-1.3
● BOB DAVIDSON Davidson, Robert Banks b: 1/6/63, Bad Kurznach, W.Ger. BR/TR, 6', 185 lbs. Deb: 7/15/89																												
1989	NY-A	0	0	—	1	0	0	0	0	1	1	2	1	0	1	0	18.0	18.00	22	.250	.400	0	—	0	-2	-2	0	-0.1
● TED DAVIDSON Davidson, Thomas Eugene b: 10/4/39, Las Vegas, Nev. BR/TL, 6', 192 lbs. Deb: 7/24/65																												
1965	Cin-N	4	3	.571	24	1	0	0	1	68^2	57	21	5	2	17	54	10.0	2.23	168	.233	.288	0	.000	-2	10	11	0	1.0
1966	Cin-N	5	4	.556	54	0	0	0	4	85^1	82	41	11	1	23	54	11.2	3.90	100	.253	.305	0	.000	-1	-3	-0	-0	-0.2

YEAR	TM/L	W	L	PCT	G	GS	CG	SH	SV	IP	H	R	HR	HB	BB	SO	RAT	ERA	ERA+	OAV	OOB	BH	AVG	PB	PR	PR+	PD	TPI
1967	Cin-N	1	0	1.000	9	0	0	0	0	13	13	6	0	0	3	6	11.1	4.15	90	.250	.291	0	—	0	-1	-1	0	0.0
1968	Cin-N	1	0	1.000	23	0	0	0	0	21^{2}	27	15	3	0	7	7	14.1	6.23	51	.307	.358	0	.000	-0	-8	-7	0	-0.4
	Atl-N	0	0	—	4	0	0	0	0	6^{2}	10	5	2	0	4	3	18.9	6.75	44	.345	.424	0	—	0	-3	-3	0	-0.1
	Yr	1	0	1.000	27	0	0	0	0	28^{1}	37	20	5	0	11	10	15.2	6.35	49	.316	.375	0	.000	0	-11	-10	0	-0.5
Total	4	11	7	.611	114	1	0	0	5	195^{1}	189	88	21	3	54	124	11.3	3.69	101	.256	.309	0	.000	-3	-5	1	1	0.3
● **JERRY DAVIE**	Davie, Gerald Lee b: 2/10/33, Detroit, Mich. BR/TR, 6', 180 lbs. Deb: 4/14/59																											
1959	Det-A	2	2	.500	11	5	1	0	0	36^{2}	40	25	8	4	17	20	15.0	4.17	97	.265	.355	4	.400	2	-1	-0	1	0.2
● **GEORGE DAVIES**	Davies, George Washington b: 2/22/1868, Portage, Wis. d: 9/22/06, Waterloo, Wis. 180 lbs. Deb: 8/18/1891																											
1891	Mil-a	7	5	.583	12	12	12	1	0	102	94	48	2	3	35	61	11.6	2.65	166	.237	.303	9	.243	1	12	17	-1	1.6
1892	Cle-N	10	16	.385	26	26	23	0	0	215^{2}	201	112	4	6	69	95	11.5	2.59	131	.237	.299	12	.138	-5	17	19	3	1.6
1893	Cle-N	0	2	.000	3	3	1	0	0	15	28	25	1	0	10	3	22.8	11.40	43	.389	.463	2	.333	0	-11	-10	0	-0.9
	NY-N	1	1	.500	5	1	1	0	0	36^{1}	41	31	1	0	13	7	13.4	6.19	75	.275	.333	4	.333	2	-6	-6	0	-0.1
	Yr	1	3	.250	8	4	2	0	0	51^{1}	69	56	2	0	23	10	16.1	7.71	61	.312	.377	6	.333	2	-17	-17	1	-1.0
Total	3	18	24	.429	46	42	37	1	0	369	364	216	8	9	127	166	12.2	3.32	116	.248	.312	27	.190	-3	11	20	2	2.2
● **CHICK DAVIES**	Davies, Lloyd Garrison b: 3/6/1892, Peabody, Mass. d: 9/5/73, Middletown, Conn BL/TL, 5'8", 145 lbs. Deb: 7/11/14 ♦																											
1914	Phi-A	1	0	1.000	1	1	1	0	0	9	8	4	0	0	3	4	11.0	1.00	261	.258	.324	11	.239	0	2	2	0	0.3
1915	Phi-A	1	2	.333	4	2	0	0	0	15^{1}	20	16	0	1	12	2	19.4	8.80	33	.339	.458	24	.182	0	-10	-10	1	-1.5
1925	NY-N	0	0	—	2	1	0	0	0	7^{1}	13	8	0	0	4	5	20.9	6.14	66	.361	.425	0	.000	-0	-2	-2	0	-0.1
1926	NY-N	2	4	.333	38	1	0	0	**6**	89	96	60	3	0	35	27	13.2	3.94	95	.277	.344	4	.222	1	-1	-2	1	0.0
Total	4	4	6	.400	45	5	1	0	6	120^{2}	137	88	3	1	54	38	14.3	4.48	80	.290	.364	39	.193	1	-11	-12	2	-1.3
● **CHILI DAVIS**	Davis, Charles Theodore b: 1/17/60, Kingston, Jamaica BB/TR, 6'3", 210 lbs. Deb: 4/10/81 ♦																											
1993	Cal-A	0	0	—	1	0	0	0	0	2	0	0	0	1	0	0	4.5	0.00	—	.000	.143	139	.243	0	1	1	-0	0.1
● **CURT DAVIS**	Davis, Curtis Benton "Coonskin" b: 9/7/03, Greenfield, Mo. d: 10/13/65, Covina, Cal. BR/TR, 6'2", 185 lbs. Deb: 4/21/34																											
1934	Phi-N	19	17	.528	**51**	31	18	3	5	274^{1}	283	114	14	7	60	99	11.5	2.95	160	.269	.313	20	.211	-2	34	46	9	**6.8**
1935	Phi-N	16	14	.533	44	27	19	3	2	231	264	103	14	7	47	74	12.4	3.66	124	.285	.324	13	.173	-1	9	20	2	2.5
1936	Phi-N	2	4	.333	10	8	3	0	0	60^{1}	71	37	6	1	19	18	13.6	4.62	98	.291	.345	4	.154	-1	-4	-1	0	-0.2
	Chi-N★	11	9	.550	24	20	10	0	1	153	146	60	11	1	31	52	10.5	3.00	133	.251	.290	8	.151	-2	17	17	3	2.1
	Yr	13	13	.500	34	28	13	0	1	213^{1}	217	97	17	2	50	70	11.3	3.46	120	.263	.307	12	.152	-3	13	16	3	1.9
1937	Chi-N	10	5	.667	28	14	8	0	1	123^{2}	138	64	7	5	30	32	12.6	4.08	98	.286	.334	12	.300	4	-2	-1	2	0.4
1938	StL-N	12	8	.600	40	21	8	2	3	173^{1}	187	80	9	1	27	36	11.2	3.63	109	.272	.301	13	.228	2	3	6	1	0.9
1939	StL-N☆	22	16	.579	49	31	13	3	7	248	279	121	18	3	48	70	12.0	3.63	113	.280	.315	40	.381	12	8	13	1	3.2
1940	StL-N	0	4	.000	14	7	0	0	1	54	73	34	4	1	19	12	15.5	5.17	77	.327	.383	0	.000	-2	-8	-7	1	-0.6
	Bro-N	8	7	.533	22	18	9	0	2	137	135	62	13	1	19	46	10.2	3.81	105	.256	.283	6	.128	-1	1	3	1	0.3
	Yr	8	11	.421	36	25	9	0	3	191	208	96	17	2	38	58	11.7	4.19	95	.277	.314	6	.091	-3	-7	-4	2	-0.3
1941	*Bro-N	13	7	.650	28	16	10	5	2	154^{1}	141	58	6	2	27	50	9.9	2.97	123	.244	.280	11	.186	2	11	12	4	2.1
1942	Bro-N	15	6	.714	32	26	13	5	2	206	179	62	10	7	51	60	10.4	2.36	138	.233	.287	12	.176	-0	22	21	3	2.5
1943	Bro-N	10	13	.435	31	21	8	2	3	164^{1}	182	85	8	2	39	47	12.2	3.78	89	.281	.324	9	.164	-1	-7	-8	2	-0.9
1944	Bro-N	10	11	.476	31	23	12	1	4	194	207	84	12	5	39	49	11.6	3.34	106	.270	.310	10	.159	-2	6	5	2	0.5
1945	Bro-N	10	10	.500	24	18	10	0	0	149^{2}	171	66	9	3	21	39	11.7	3.25	116	.280	.308	7	.137	-1	9	9	0	1.0
1946	Bro-N	0	0	—	1	0	0	0	0	2	3	3	1	1	2	0	27.0	13.50	25	.375	.545	0	—	0	-2	-2	0	-0.1
Total	13	158	131	.547	429	281	141	24	33	2325	2459	1033	142	47	479	684	11.6	3.42	116	.270	.310	165	.203	7	96	134	31	20.5
● **DOUG DAVIS**	Davis, Douglas P. b: 9/21/75, Sacramento, Cal. BR/TL, 6'3", 185 lbs. Deb: 8/9/99																											
1999	Tex-A	0	0	—	2	0	0	0	0	2^{2}	12	10	3	0	0	3	40.5	33.75	15	.600	.600	0	—	0	-9	-8	0	-0.3
2000	Tex-A	7	6	.538	30	13	1	0	0	98^{2}	109	61	14	3	58	66	15.5	5.38	95	.288	.386	0	—	0	-5	-3	1	-0.3
Total	2	7	6	.538	32	13	1	0	0	101^{1}	121	71	17	3	58	69	16.2	6.13	83	.303	.396	0	—	0	-14	-11	1	-0.6
● **DIXIE DAVIS**	Davis, Frank Talmadge b: 10/12/1890, Wilsons Mills, N.C. d: 2/4/44, Raleigh, N.C. BR/TR, 5'11", 155 lbs. Deb: 7/12/12																											
1912	Cin-N	0	1	.000	7	0	0	0	0	26^{2}	25	17	0	1	16	12	14.2	2.70	124	.258	.368	2	.200	-0	2	2	-1	0.0
1915	Chi-A	0	0	—	2	0	0	0	0	3	2	0	0	1	2	2	15.0	0.00	—	.250	.455	0	—	0	1	1	0	0.1
1918	Phi-N	0	2	.000	17	2	1	0	0	47	43	25	1	0	30	18	14.0	3.06	98	.247	.358	0	.000	-0	-2	-0	-1	-0.2
1920	StL-A	18	12	.600	38	31	22	0	0	269^{1}	250	117	10	7	149	85	13.6	3.17	123	.256	.359	25	.266	3	19	22	-4	2.0
1921	StL-A	16	16	.500	40	36	20	2	0	265^{1}	279	150	12	10	123	100	14.0	4.44	101	.281	.366	20	.211	-3	-5	1	-1	-0.3
1922	StL-A	11	6	.647	25	25	7	2	0	174^{1}	162	91	10	8	87	65	13.3	4.08	102	**.250**	.345	8	.136	-3	-1	1	-0	-0.3
1923	StL-A	4	6	.400	19	17	5	1	0	109^{1}	106	61	4	5	63	36	14.3	3.62	115	.259	.365	10	.250	0	4	6	-2	0.3
1924	StL-A	11	13	.458	29	24	11	5	0	160^{1}	159	84	9	6	72	45	13.3	4.10	110	.263	.347	7	.152	-2	2	7	-1	0.6
1925	StL-A	12	7	.632	35	22	9	0	1	180^{1}	192	121	10	6	106	58	15.2	4.59	102	.279	.380	11	.172	-4	-4	2	1	-0.1
1926	StL-A	3	8	.273	27	7	2	0	1	83	93	56	7	1	40	39	14.5	4.66	92	.292	.372	4	.167	-0	-6	-3	-0	-0.4
Total	10	75	71	.514	239	164	77	10	2	1318^{2}	1311	722	63	45	688	460	14.0	3.97	107	.267	.362	87	.197	-10	12	38	-10	1.7
● **GEORGE DAVIS**	Davis, George Allen "Iron" b: 3/9/1890, Lancaster, N.Y. d: 6/4/61, Buffalo, N.Y. BB/TR, 5'10.5", 175 lbs. Deb: 7/16/12																											
1912	NY-A	1	4	.200	10	7	5	0	0	54	61	43	3	3	28	22	15.3	6.50	55	.293	.385	2	.111	-1	-19	-16	-2	-1.5
1913	Bos-N	0	0	—	2	0	0	0	0	8	7	5	1	0	5	3	13.5	4.50	73	.241	.353	0	.000	-0	-1	-1	-0	-0.1
1914	Bos-N	3	3	.500	9	6	4	1	0	55^{2}	42	25	1	3	26	26	11.5	3.40	81	.215	.317	3	.167	0	-4	-4	-2	-0.6
1915	Bos-N	3	3	.500	15	9	4	0	0	73^{1}	85	45	2	4	19	26	13.3	3.80	68	.304	.356	6	.261	1	-9	-10	0	-0.7
Total	4	7	10	.412	36	22	13	1	0	191	195	118	7	10	78	77	13.3	4.48	66	.274	.354	11	.180	-0	-33	-33	-3	-2.9
● **STORM DAVIS**	Davis, George Earl b: 12/26/61, Dallas, Tex. BR/TR, 6'4", 207 lbs. Deb: 4/29/82																											
1982	Bal-A	8	4	.667	29	8	1	0	0	100^{2}	96	40	8	0	28	67	11.1	3.49	116	.257	.308	0	—	0	7	6	-0	0.6
1983	*Bal-A	13	7	.650	34	29	6	1	0	200^{1}	180	90	14	2	64	125	11.1	3.59	110	.238	.299	0	—	0	11	9	-2	0.6
1984	Bal-A	14	9	.609	35	31	10	2	1	225	205	86	7	5	71	105	11.2	3.12	124	.247	.310	0	—	0	22	20	-3	1.6
1985	Bal-A	10	8	.556	31	28	8	1	0	175	172	92	11	1	70	93	12.5	4.53	89	.256	.327	0	—	0	-7	-10	-1	-0.9
1986	Bal-A	9	12	.429	25	25	2	0	0	154	166	70	16	0	49	96	12.6	3.62	114	.275	.330	0	—	0	10	9	2	1.3
1987	SD-N	2	7	.222	21	10	0	0	0	62^{2}	70	48	5	2	36	37	15.5	6.18	64	.280	.375	1	.063	-1	-15	-16	0	-2.0
	Oak-A	1	1	.500	5	5	0	0	0	30^{1}	28	13	3	0	11	28	11.6	3.26	127	.241	.307	0	—	0	4	3	-1	0.1
1988	*Oak-A	16	7	.696	33	33	1	0	0	201^{2}	211	86	16	1	91	127	13.5	3.70	102	.274	.352	0	—	0	6	2	-2	0.0
1989	*Oak-A	19	7	.731	31	31	1	0	0	169^{1}	187	91	19	3	68	91	13.7	4.36	85	.288	.358	0	—	0	-9	-13	-2	-2.0
1990	KC-A	7	10	.412	21	20	0	0	0	112	129	66	9	0	35	62	13.2	4.74	81	.281	.332	0	—	0	-10	-11	-1	-1.6
1991	KC-A	3	9	.250	51	9	1	1	2	114^{1}	140	69	11	1	46	53	14.7	4.96	83	.306	.370	0	—	0	-11	-11	-1	-1.1
1992	Bal-A	7	3	.700	48	2	0	0	4	89^{1}	79	35	5	2	36	53	11.8	3.43	118	.244	.323	0	—	0	5	6	1	0.7
1993	Oak-A	2	6	.250	19	8	0	0	0	62^{2}	68	45	5	2	33	37	14.8	6.18	66	.276	.367	0	—	0	-13	-15	0	-1.6
	Det-A	0	2	.000	24	0	0	0	4	35^{1}	25	12	4	1	15	36	10.4	3.06	141	.198	.289	0	—	0	5	5	-0	0.3
	Yr	2	8	.200	43	8	0	0	4	98	93	57	9	3	48	73	13.2	5.05	82	.250	.340	0	—	0	-8	-10	0	-1.3
1994	Det-A	2	4	.333	35	0	0	0	0	48	36	23	3	0	34	38	13.1	3.56	136	.207	.337	0	—	0	7	7	1	0.8
Total	13	113	96	.541	442	239	30	5	11	1780^{2}	1792	866	136	20	687	1048	12.6	4.02	99	.263	.332	1	.063	-1	11	-9	-8	-3.2
● **GEORGE DAVIS**	Davis, George Stacey b: 8/23/1870, Cohoes, N.Y. d: 10/17/40, Philadelphia, Pa. BB/TR, 5'9", 180 lbs. Deb: 4/19/1890 MH♦																											
1891	Cle-N	0	1	.000	3	0	0	0	1	4	8	8	0	0	3	4	24.8	15.75	22	.400	.478	165	.289	1	-6	-5	-0	-0.8
● **JIM DAVIS**	Davis, James Bennett b: 9/15/24, Red Bluff, Cal. d: 12/6/95, San Mateo, Cal. BB/TL, 6', 180 lbs. Deb: 4/18/54																											
1954	Chi-N	11	7	.611	46	12	2	0	4	127^{2}	114	57	12	3	51	58	11.8	3.52	119	.247	.326	2	.063	-1	8	9	1	1.3
1955	Chi-N	7	11	.389	42	16	0	0	3	133^{2}	122	79	16	2	58	62	12.3	4.44	92	.246	.327	1	.027	-4	-6	-5	-1	-1.1
1956	Chi-N	5	7	.417	46	11	2	1	2	120^{1}	116	56	11	6	59	66	13.5	3.66	103	.256	.349	5	.179	-0	1	1	1	0.2
1957	StL-N	0	1	.000	10	0	0	0	1	13^{2}	18	8	1	0	6	5	15.8	5.27	75	.340	.407	0	.000	-0	-2	-2	0	-0.2
	NY-N	1	0	1.000	10	0	0	0	0	11	13	9	2	0	5	6	14.7	6.55	60	.283	.353	1	1.000	0	-3	-3	0	-0.2
	Yr	1	1	.500	20	0	0	0	1	24^{2}	31	17	3	0	11	11	15.3	5.84	68	.313	.382	1	.500	0	-5	-5	0	-0.4
Total	4	24	26	.480	154	39	4	1	10	406^{1}	383	209	42	11	179	197	12.7	4.01	100	.253	.337	9	.091	-5	-2	0	1	-0.0

● JOEL DAVIS Davis, Joel Clark b: 1/30/65, Jacksonville, Fla. BL/TR, 6'5", 205 lbs. Deb: 8/11/85

YEAR	TM/L	W	L	PCT	G	GS	CG	SH	SV	IP	H	R	HR	HB	BB	SO	RAT	ERA	ERA+	OAV	OOB	BH	AVG	PB	PR	PR+	PD	TPI
1985	Chi-A	3	3	.500	12	11	1	0	0	71^1	71	34	6	1	26	37	12.4	4.16	104	.256	.322	0	—	0	-0	1	-2	-0.1
1986	Chi-A	4	5	.444	19	19	1	0	0	105^1	115	64	9	1	51	54	14.3	4.70	92	.280	.361	0	—	0	-6	-4	1	-0.3
1987	Chi-A	1	5	.167	13	9	1	0	0	55	56	35	7	0	29	25	13.9	5.73	80	.264	.353	0	—	0	-8	-7	-1	-0.7
1988	Chi-A	0	1	.000	5	2	0	0	0	16	21	12	4	0	5	10	14.6	6.75	59	.328	.377	0	—	0	-5	-5	-0	-0.3
Total	4	8	14	.364	49	41	3	0	0	247^2	263	145	26	2	111	126	13.7	4.91	89	.273	.349	0	—	0	-19	-15	-3	-1.4

● DAISY DAVIS Davis, John Henry Albert b: 11/28/1858, Boston, Mass. d: 11/5/02, Lynn, Mass. TR, Deb: 5/6/1884

YEAR	TM/L	W	L	PCT	G	GS	CG	SH	SV	IP	H	R	HR	HB	BB	SO	RAT	ERA	ERA+	OAV	OOB	BH	AVG	PB	PR	PR+	PD	TPI
1884	StL-a	10	12	.455	25	24	20	1	0	198^1	196	113	1	14	35	143	11.1	2.90	112	.249	.293	15	.172	-2	8	8	-1	0.4
	Bos-N	1	3	.250	4	4	3	0	0	31	50	36	2		8	13	16.8	7.84	37	.355	.389	0	.000	-3	-17	-18	0	-1.7
1885	Bos-N	5	6	.455	11	11	10	1	0	94^1	110	58	2		28	30	13.2	4.29	63	.280	.328	7	.189	-0	-15	-18	-1	-1.7
Total	2	16	21	.432	40	39	33	2	0	323^2	356	207	5	14	71	186	12.3	3.78	81	.269	.313	22	.157	-5	-25	-27	-2	-3.0

● JOHN DAVIS Davis, John Kirk b: 1/5/63, Chicago, Ill. BR/TR, 6'7", 215 lbs. Deb: 7/24/87

YEAR	TM/L	W	L	PCT	G	GS	CG	SH	SV	IP	H	R	HR	HB	BB	SO	RAT	ERA	ERA+	OAV	OOB	BH	AVG	PB	PR	PR+	PD	TPI
1987	KC-A	5	2	.714	27	0	0	0	2	43^2	29	13	0	2	26	24	11.7	2.27	202	.195	.322	0	—	0	11	11	0	1.7
1988	Chi-A	2	5	.286	34	1	0	0	1	63^2	77	58	5	4	50	37	18.5	6.64	60	.297	.419	0	—	0	-19	-19	-0	-1.9
1989	Chi-A	0	1	.000	4	0	0	0	1	6	5	4	2	0	2	5	10.5	4.50	85	.217	.280	0	—	0	-0	-0	0	-0.1
1990	SD-N	0	1	.000	6	0	0	0	0	9^1	9	7	1	0	4	7	12.5	5.79	66	.257	.333	0	.000	-0	-2	-2	-0	-0.2
Total	4	7	9	.438	71	1	0	0	4	122^2	120	82	8	6	82	73	15.3	4.92	85	.258	.375	0	.000	-0	-11	-10	0	-0.5

● BUD DAVIS Davis, John Wilbur "Country" b: 12/7/1896, Merry Point, Va. d: 5/26/67, Williamsburg, Va. BL/TR, 6', 207 lbs. Deb: 4/19/15

YEAR	TM/L	W	L	PCT	G	GS	CG	SH	SV	IP	H	R	HR	HB	BB	SO	RAT	ERA	ERA+	OAV	OOB	BH	AVG	PB	PR	PR+	PD	TPI
1915	Phi-A	0	2	.000	18	2	2	0	0	66^2	65	53	1	6	59	18	17.6	4.05	72	.273	.429	8	.308	2	-8	-8	-1	-0.3

● KANE DAVIS Davis, Kane Thomas b: 6/25/75, Ripley, W.Va. BR/TR, 6'3", 194 lbs. Deb: 6/12/2000

YEAR	TM/L	W	L	PCT	G	GS	CG	SH	SV	IP	H	R	HR	HB	BB	SO	RAT	ERA	ERA+	OAV	OOB	BH	AVG	PB	PR	PR+	PD	TPI
2000	Cle-A	0	3	.000	5	2	0	0	0	11	20	21	3	1	8	2	23.7	14.73	34	.385	.475	0	.000	-0	-12	-12	0	-1.8
	Mil-N	0	0	—	3	0	0	0	0	4	7	3	1	1	5	2	29.3	6.75	68	.389	.542	0	—	0	-1	-1	-0	-0.1
Total	1	0	3	.000	8	2	0	0	0	15	27	24	4	2	13	4	25.2	12.60	39	.386	.494	0	.000	-0	-13	-13	0	-1.9

● MARK DAVIS Davis, Mark William b: 10/19/60, Livermore, Cal. BL/TL, 6'4", 205 lbs. Deb: 9/12/80

YEAR	TM/L	W	L	PCT	G	GS	CG	SH	SV	IP	H	R	HR	HB	BB	SO	RAT	ERA	ERA+	OAV	OOB	BH	AVG	PB	PR	PR+	PD	TPI
1980	Phi-N	0	0	—	2	1	0	0	0	7	4	2	0	0	5	5	11.6	2.57	148	.160	.300	1	.500	0	1	1	-0	0.1
1981	Phi-N	1	4	.200	9	9	0	0	0	43	49	37	7	0	24	29	15.3	7.74	47	.299	.388	1	.091	-0	-20	-19	-0	-1.9
1983	SF-N	6	4	.600	20	20	2	2	0	111	93	51	14	3	50	83	11.8	3.49	102	.227	.315	4	.133	0	2	1	-1	0.0
1984	SF-N	5	17	.227	46	27	1	0	0	174^2	201	113	25	5	54	124	13.4	5.36	66	.293	.349	6	.130	0	-34	-37	-2	-4.3
1985	SF-N	5	12	.294	77	1	0	0	7	114^1	89	49	13	3	41	131	10.5	3.54	97	.219	.295	3	.250	1	1	-1	-1	-0.2
1986	SF-N	5	7	.417	67	2	0	0	4	84^1	63	33	6	1	34	90	10.5	2.99	118	.212	.295	1	.125	0	7	5	-0	0.7
1987	SF-N	4	5	.444	20	11	1	0	0	70^2	72	38	9	4	28	51	13.2	4.71	82	.273	.351	5	.217	2	-5	-7	-1	-0.7
	SD-N	5	3	.625	43	0	0	0	2	62^1	51	26	5	2	31	47	12.1	3.18	125	.224	.322	2	.286	0	6	6	0	0.8
	Yr	9	8	.529	63	11	1	0	2	133	123	64	14	6	59	98	12.7	3.99	98	.250	.338	7	.233	2	1	-1	-0	0.1
1988	SD-N★	5	10	.333	62	0	0	0	28	98^1	70	24	2	0	42	102	10.3	2.01	169	.199	.284	2	.200	1	16	15	2	3.6
1989	SD-N★	4	3	.571	70	0	0	0	**44**	92^2	66	21	6	2	31	92	9.6	1.85	190	.200	.273	0	.000	-1	17	17	-1	2.6
1990	KC-A	2	7	.222	53	3	0	0	6	68^2	71	43	9	4	52	73	16.6	5.11	75	.259	.385	0	—	0	-9	-10	-1	-1.4
1991	KC-A	6	3	.667	29	5	0	0	1	62^2	55	36	6	1	39	47	13.6	4.45	93	.240	.353	0	—	0	-2	-2	-0	-0.3
1992	KC-A	1	3	.250	13	6	0	0	0	36^1	42	31	6	0	28	19	17.3	7.18	57	.294	.409	0	—	0	-13	-12	0	-1.2
	Atl-N	1	0	1.000	14	0	0	0	0	16^2	22	13	3	1	13	15	19.4	7.02	52	.314	.429	0	.000	-0	-7	-6	-1	-0.4
1993	Phi-N	1	2	.333	25	0	0	0	0	31^1	35	22	4	1	24	28	17.2	5.17	77	.273	.392	1	.333	0	-4	-4	-0	-0.4
	SD-N	0	3	.000	35	0	0	0	4	38^1	44	15	6	0	20	42	15.0	3.52	118	.295	.379	0	.000	-0	2	3	0	0.2
	Yr	1	5	.167	60	0	0	0	4	69^2	79	37	10	1	44	70	16.0	4.26	95	.285	.385	1	.250	0	-2	-2	-0	-0.2
1994	SD-N	0	1	.000	20	0	0	0	0	16^1	20	18	4	0	13	15	18.2	8.82	47	.299	.412	0	—	0	-8	-9	0	-0.5
1997	Mil-A	0	0	—	19	0	0	0	0	16^1	21	10	4	1	5	14	14.9	5.51	84	.323	.380	0	—	0	-2	-2	1	0.0
Total	15	51	84	.378	624	85	4	2	96	1145	1068	582	129	28	534	1007	12.8	4.17	88	.249	.336	26	.156	5	-53	-63	-4	-3.3

● BOB DAVIS Davis, Robert Edward b: 9/11/33, New York, N.Y. BR/TR, 6', 170 lbs. Deb: 7/26/58

YEAR	TM/L	W	L	PCT	G	GS	CG	SH	SV	IP	H	R	HR	HB	BB	SO	RAT	ERA	ERA+	OAV	OOB	BH	AVG	PB	PR	PR+	PD	TPI
1958	KC-A	0	4	.000	8	4	0	0	0	31	45	28	5	2	12	22	17.1	7.84	50	.346	.410	1	.167	-0	-14	-13	0	-1.4
1960	KC-A	0	0	—	21	0	0	0	1	32	31	15	1	1	22	28	15.2	3.66	109	.263	.383	1	.250	0	1	1	1	0.2
Total	2	0	4	.000	29	4	0	0	1	63	76	43	6	3	34	50	16.1	5.71	69	.306	.396	2	.200	-0	-13	-12	2	-1.2

● RON DAVIS Davis, Ronald Gene b: 8/6/55, Houston, Tex. BR/TR, 6'4", 207 lbs. Deb: 7/29/78

YEAR	TM/L	W	L	PCT	G	GS	CG	SH	SV	IP	H	R	HR	HB	BB	SO	RAT	ERA	ERA+	OAV	OOB	BH	AVG	PB	PR	PR+	PD	TPI
1978	NY-A	0	0	—	4	0	0	0	0	2^1	3	4	0	0	3	0	23.1	11.57	31	.333	.500	0	—	0	-2	-2	0	-0.1
1979	NY-A	14	2	.875	44	0	0	0	9	85^1	84	29	5	1	28	43	11.9	2.85	143	.262	.323	0	.000	-0	13	12	1	2.4
1980	*NY-A	9	3	.750	53	0	0	0	7	131	121	50	9	5	32	65	10.9	2.95	133	.246	.299	0	.000	-0	16	15	0	1.4
1981	*NY-A★	4	5	.444	43	0	0	0	6	73	47	22	6	0	25	83	8.9	2.71	132	.186	.259	0	—	0	8	7	-1	0.9
1982	Min-A	3	9	.250	63	0	0	0	22	106	106	53	16	1	47	89	13.1	4.42	96	.261	.339	0	—	0	-4	-2	-0	-0.3
1983	Min-A	5	8	.385	66	0	0	0	30	89	89	34	6	3	33	84	12.6	3.34	128	.266	.338	0	—	0	7	9	-2	1.6
1984	Min-A	7	11	.389	64	0	0	0	29	83	79	44	11	2	41	74	13.2	4.55	92	.253	.344	0	—	0	-5	-3	-0	-0.6
1985	Min-A	2	6	.250	57	0	0	0	25	64^2	55	28	7	4	35	72	13.1	3.48	127	.230	.338	0	—	0	5	6	-0	1.1
1986	Min-A	2	6	.250	36	0	0	0	2	38^2	55	42	7	4	29	30	20.5	9.08	48	.340	.451	0	—	0	-21	-20	0	-3.6
	Chi-N	0	2	.000	17	0	0	0	0	20	31	18	3	0	3	10	15.3	7.65	53	.356	.378	0	.000	-0	-9	-7	-1	-0.8
1987	Chi-N	0	0	—	21	0	0	0	0	32^1	43	23	8	0	12	31	15.3	5.85	73	.328	.385	0	—	0	-6	-5	-1	-0.3
	LA-N	0	0	—	4	0	0	0	0	4	7	4	0	1	6	1	31.5	6.75	59	.412	.583	0	—	0	-1	-1	0	0.0
	Yr	0	0	—	25	0	0	0	0	36^1	50	27	8	1	18	32	17.1	5.94	71	.338	.413	0	—	0	-8	-7	-0	-0.3
1988	SF-N	1	1	.500	9	0	0	0	0	17^1	15	10	4	1	6	15	11.4	4.67	70	.234	.310	0	.000	-0	-2	-3	0	-0.3
Total	11	47	53	.470	481	0	0	0	130	746^2	735	361	82	22	300	597	12.7	4.05	101	.260	.336	0	.000	-1	-2	3	-3	1.4

● PEACHES DAVIS Davis, Roy Thomas b: 5/31/05, Glen Rose, Tex. d: 4/28/95, Duncan, Okla. BL/TR, 6'3.5", 190 lbs. Deb: 7/11/36

YEAR	TM/L	W	L	PCT	G	GS	CG	SH	SV	IP	H	R	HR	HB	BB	SO	RAT	ERA	ERA+	OAV	OOB	BH	AVG	PB	PR	PR+	PD	TPI
1936	Cin-N	8	8	.500	26	15	5	0	5	125^2	139	62	7	2	36	32	12.7	3.58	107	.280	.331	7	.163	-1	6	4	0	0.3
1937	Cin-N	11	13	.458	42	24	11	1	3	218	252	105	5	2	51	59	12.6	3.59	104	.295	.337	10	.128	-4	8	4	-3	-0.3
1938	Cin-N	7	12	.368	29	19	11	1	1	167^2	193	86	9	1	40	28	12.6	3.97	92	.290	.331	15	.246	1	-3	-6	-3	-0.9
1939	Cin-N	1	0	1.000	20	0	0	0	2	30^2	43	24	5	1	11	4	16.1	6.46	59	.341	.399	1	.333	0	-9	-9	0	-0.4
Total	4	27	33	.450	117	58	27	2	11	542	627	277	26	6	138	123	12.8	3.87	96	.293	.337	33	.178	-4	2	-9	-6	-1.3

● STEVE DAVIS Davis, Steven Kennon b: 8/4/60, San Antonio, Tex. BL/TL, 6'1", 195 lbs. Deb: 8/25/85

YEAR	TM/L	W	L	PCT	G	GS	CG	SH	SV	IP	H	R	HR	HB	BB	SO	RAT	ERA	ERA+	OAV	OOB	BH	AVG	PB	PR	PR+	PD	TPI
1985	Tor-A	2	1	.667	10	5	0	0	0	28	23	14	5	0	13	22	11.6	3.54	119	.223	.310	0	—	0	2	2	-0	0.2
1986	Tor-A	0	0	—	3	0	0	0	0	3^2	8	7	2	0	5	5	31.9	17.18	25	.471	.591	0	—	0	-5	-5	-0	-0.3
1989	Cle-A	1	1	.500	12	2	0	0	0	25^2	34	24	2	0	14	12	16.8	8.06	49	.318	.397	0	—	0	-12	-11	-0	-0.8
Total	3	3	2	.600	25	7	0	0	0	57^1	65	45	9	0	32	39	15.2	6.44	64	.286	.375	0	—	0	-15	-15	-1	-0.9

● TIM DAVIS Davis, Timothy Howard b: 7/14/70, Marianna, Fla. BL/TL, 5'11", 165 lbs. Deb: 4/4/94

YEAR	TM/L	W	L	PCT	G	GS	CG	SH	SV	IP	H	R	HR	HB	BB	SO	RAT	ERA	ERA+	OAV	OOB	BH	AVG	PB	PR	PR+	PD	TPI
1994	Sea-A	2	2	.500	42	1	0	0	2	49^1	57	25	4	1	25	28	15.1	4.01	122	.295	.379	0	—	0	4	5	0	0.4
1995	Sea-A	2	1	.667	5	5	0	0	0	24	30	21	2	0	18	19	18.0	6.38	74	.306	.414	0	—	0	-4	-4	1	-0.4
1996	Sea-A	2	2	.500	40	0	0	0	0	42^2	43	21	4	2	17	34	13.1	4.01	124	.259	.335	0	—	0	5	5	-0	0.3
1997	Sea-A	0	0	—	2	0	0	0	0	6^2	6	5	1	1	4	10	14.9	6.75	67	.231	.355	0	—	0	-2	-2	0	-0.1
Total	4	6	5	.545	89	6	0	0	2	122^2	136	72	11	4	64	91	15.0	4.62	105	.282	.370	0	—	0	3	3	1	0.2

● WILEY DAVIS Davis, Wiley Anderson b: 8/1/1875, Seymour, Tenn. d: 9/22/42, Detroit, Mich. BR/TR, 5'10", 165 lbs. Deb: 4/18/1896

YEAR	TM/L	W	L	PCT	G	GS	CG	SH	SV	IP	H	R	HR	HB	BB	SO	RAT	ERA	ERA+	OAV	OOB	BH	AVG	PB	PR	PR+	PD	TPI
1896	Cin-N	1	1	.500	2	0	0	0	0	4^1	8	4	0	0	2	1	20.8	8.31	56	.400	.455	0	.000	0	-2	-2	1	-0.2

● WOODY DAVIS Davis, Woodrow Wilson "Babe" b: 4/25/13, Nicholls, Ga. BL/TR, 6'1", 200 lbs. Deb: 5/2/38

YEAR	TM/L	W	L	PCT	G	GS	CG	SH	SV	IP	H	R	HR	HB	BB	SO	RAT	ERA	ERA+	OAV	OOB	BH	AVG	PB	PR	PR+	PD	TPI
1938	Det-A	0	0	—	2	0	0	0	0	6	3	1	0	0	4	1	10.5	1.50	333	.158	.304	0	.000	-0	2	2	-0	0.1

● MIKE DAVISON Davison, Michael Lynn b: 8/4/45, Galesburg, Ill. BL/TL, 6'1", 170 lbs. Deb: 10/1/69

YEAR	TM/L	W	L	PCT	G	GS	CG	SH	SV	IP	H	R	HR	HB	BB	SO	RAT	ERA	ERA+	OAV	OOB	BH	AVG	PB	PR	PR+	PD	TPI
1969	SF-N	0	0	—	1	0	0	0	0	2	2	1	0	0	0	2	9.0	4.50	78	.250	.250	0	—	0	-0	-0	-0	0.0

YEAR	TM/L	W	L	PCT	G	GS	CG	SH	SV	IP	H	R	HR	HB	BB	SO	RAT	ERA	ERA+	OAV	OOB	BH	AVG	PB	PR	PR+	PD	TPI
1970	SF-N	3	5	.375	31	0	0	0	1	36	46	29	4	0	22	21	17.0	6.50	61	.324	.415	0	.000	0	-10	-10	1	-1.9
Total	2	3	5	.375	32	0	0	0	1	38	48	30	4	0	22	23	16.6	6.39	62	.320	.407	0	.000	0	-10	-10	1	-1.9

● SCOTT DAVISON Davison, Scotty Ray b: 10/16/70, Inglewood, Cal. BR/TR, 6', 190 lbs. Deb: 9/4/95

YEAR	TM/L	W	L	PCT	G	GS	CG	SH	SV	IP	H	R	HR	HB	BB	SO	RAT	ERA	ERA+	OAV	OOB	BH	AVG	PB	PR	PR+	PD	TPI
1995	Sea-A	0	0	—	3	0	0	0	0	4^1	7	3	1	0	1	3	16.6	6.23	76	.350	.381	0	—	0	-1	-1	0	0.0
1996	Sea-A	0	0	—	5	0	0	0	0	9	11	9	6	0	3	9	14.0	9.00	55	.297	.350	0	—	0	-4	-4	0	-0.2
Total	2	0	0	—	8	0	0	0	0	13^1	18	12	7	0	4	12	14.9	8.10	60	.316	.361	0	—	0	-5	-5	0	-0.2

● BILL DAWLEY Dawley, William Chester b: 2/6/58, Norwich, Conn. BR/TR, 6'4", 240 lbs. Deb: 4/15/83

YEAR	TM/L	W	L	PCT	G	GS	CG	SH	SV	IP	H	R	HR	HB	BB	SO	RAT	ERA	ERA+	OAV	OOB	BH	AVG	PB	PR	PR+	PD	TPI
1983	Hou-N★	6	6	.500	48	0	0	0	14	79^2	51	26	9	1	22	60	8.4	2.82	121	.185	.247	2	.222	0	7	6	-1	0.9
1984	Hou-N	11	4	.733	60	0	0	0	5	98	82	24	5	0	35	47	10.7	1.93	172	.234	.303	3	.333	2	18	16	-1	2.7
1985	Hou-N	5	3	.625	49	0	0	0	2	81	76	35	7	0	37	48	12.6	3.56	98	.259	.341	2	.200	0	0	-1	0	0.0
1986	Chi-A	0	7	.000	46	0	0	0	2	97^2	91	38	10	1	28	66	11.1	3.32	130	.247	.302	0	.000	-0	9	11	-1	0.6
1987	StL-N	5	8	.385	60	0	0	0	2	96^2	93	51	15	1	38	65	12.3	4.47	93	.259	.332	2	.167	0	-4	-3	1	-0.2
1988	Phi-N	0	2	.000	8	0	0	0	0	8^2	16	13	3	0	4	3	20.8	13.50	26	.381	.435	0	—	0	-10	-9	-0	-1.8
1989	Oak-A	0	0	—	4	0	0	0	0	9	11	5	0	1	2	3	14.0	4.00	92	.297	.350	0	—	0	-0	-0	-0	0.0
Total	7	27	30	.474	275	0	0	0	25	470^2	420	192	49	4	166	292	11.3	3.42	109	.243	.311	9	.214	3	21	17	-2	2.2

● JOE DAWSON Dawson, Ralph Fenton b: 3/9/1897, Bow, Wash. d: 1/4/78, Longview, Tex. BR/TR, 5'11", 182 lbs. Deb: 7/4/24

YEAR	TM/L	W	L	PCT	G	GS	CG	SH	SV	IP	H	R	HR	HB	BB	SO	RAT	ERA	ERA+	OAV	OOB	BH	AVG	PB	PR	PR+	PD	TPI
1924	Cle-A	1	2	.333	4	4	0	0	0	20^1	24	17	0	1	21	7	20.4	6.64	64	.300	.451	2	.286	0	-5	-5	1	-0.6
1927	*Pit-N	3	7	.300	20	7	4	0	0	80^2	80	47	2	0	32	17	12.5	4.46	92	.268	.338	5	.200	-1	-5	-3	-1	-0.5
1928	Pit-N	7	7	.500	31	7	1	0	3	128^2	116	54	6	1	56	36	12.1	3.29	124	.242	.322	12	.279	3	10	11	-3	1.2
1929	Pit-N	0	1	.000	4	0	0	0	0	8^2	13	9	2	0	3	2	16.6	8.31	57	.342	.390	1	.500	1	-3	-3	-0	-0.3
Total	4	11	17	.393	59	18	5	0	3	238^1	233	127	10	2	112	62	13.1	4.15	99	.260	.343	20	.260	3	-4	-1	-3	-0.2

● REX DAWSON Dawson, Rexford Paul b: 2/10/1889, Skagit Co., Wash. d: 10/20/58, Indianapolis, Ind. BL/TR, 6', 185 lbs. Deb: 10/3/13

YEAR	TM/L	W	L	PCT	G	GS	CG	SH	SV	IP	H	R	HR	HB	BB	SO	RAT	ERA	ERA+	OAV	OOB	BH	AVG	PB	PR	PR+	PD	TPI
1913	Was-A	0	0	—	1	0	0	0	0	1	1	0	0	0	0	1	9.0	0.00	—	.250	.250	0	—	0	0	-0	-0	0.0

● PEA RIDGE DAY Day, Clyde Henry b: 8/26/1899, Pea Ridge, Ark. d: 3/21/34, Kansas City, Mo. BR/TR, 6', 190 lbs. Deb: 9/19/24

YEAR	TM/L	W	L	PCT	G	GS	CG	SH	SV	IP	H	R	HR	HB	BB	SO	RAT	ERA	ERA+	OAV	OOB	BH	AVG	PB	PR	PR+	PD	TPI
1924	StL-N	1	1	.500	3	3	1	0	0	17^2	22	11	0	0	6	3	14.3	4.58	82	.306	.359	1	.125	-1	-1	-2	-0	-0.3
1925	StL-N	2	4	.333	17	4	1	0	1	40	53	31	5	3	7	13	14.2	6.30	69	.325	.364	2	.154	-1	-9	-9	-1	-1.2
1926	Cin-N	0	0	—	4	0	0	0	0	7^1	13	13	1	0	2	2	18.4	7.36	50	.406	.441	0	.000	-0	-3	-3	-0	-0.2
1931	Bro-N	2	2	.500	22	2	1	0	1	57^1	75	38	5	0	13	30	13.8	4.55	84	.315	.351	4	.222	0	-4	-5	-1	-0.4
Total	4	5	7	.417	46	9	3	0	2	122^1	163	93	11	3	28	48	14.3	5.30	75	.323	.362	7	.171	-2	-18	-18	-2	-2.1

● BILL DAY Day, William M. b: 7/28/1867, Wilmington, Del. d: 8/16/23, Wilmington, Del. TR, 5'8", 150 lbs. Deb: 8/20/1889

YEAR	TM/L	W	L	PCT	G	GS	CG	SH	SV	IP	H	R	HR	HB	BB	SO	RAT	ERA	ERA+	OAV	OOB	BH	AVG	PB	PR	PR+	PD	TPI
1889	Phi-N	0	3	.000	4	3	2	0	0	19	16	24	0	0	23	20	18.5	5.21	83	.222	.411	0	.000	-2	-3	-2	-0	-0.3
1890	Phi-N	1	1	.500	4	2	2	0	0	23^2	26	16	0	0	12	9	14.5	3.04	120	.271	.352	1	.100	-1	1	2	-1	-0.1
	Pit-N	0	6	.000	6	6	6	0	0	50	66	50	1	1	24	10	16.4	5.22	63	.308	.381	1	.043	-4	-9	-12	1	-1.2
	Yr	1	7	.125	10	8	8	0	0	73^2	92	66	1	1	36	19	15.8	4.52	75	.297	.372	2	.061	-5	-8	-10	1	-1.3
Total	2	1	10	.091	14	11	10	0	0	92^2	108	90	1	1	59	39	16.3	4.66	77	.283	.380	2	.047	-6	-10	-11	0	-1.6

● KEN DAYLEY Dayley, Kenneth Grant b: 2/25/59, Jerome, Idaho BL/TL, 6', 175 lbs. Deb: 5/13/82

YEAR	TM/L	W	L	PCT	G	GS	CG	SH	SV	IP	H	R	HR	HB	BB	SO	RAT	ERA	ERA+	OAV	OOB	BH	AVG	PB	PR	PR+	PD	TPI
1982	Atl-N	5	6	.455	20	11	0	0	0	71^1	79	39	9	0	25	34	13.1	4.54	82	.286	.346	5	.250	1	-7	-6	-2	-0.9
1983	Atl-N	5	8	.385	24	16	0	0	0	104^2	100	59	12	2	39	70	12.1	4.30	90	.257	.328	7	.219	1	-8	-4	-2	-0.6
1984	Atl-N	0	3	.000	4	4	0	0	0	18^2	28	18	5	1	6	10	16.9	5.30	73	.341	.393	2	.500	1	-4	-3	0	-0.3
	StL-N	0	2	.000	3	2	0	0	0	5	16	10	1	0	5	0	37.8	18.00	19	.615	.677	0	—	0	-8	-8	-0	-1.4
	Yr	0	5	.000	7	6	0	0	0	23^2	44	28	6	1	11	10	21.3	7.99	47	.407	.467	2	.500	1	-12	-11	0	-1.7
1985	*StL-N	4	4	.500	57	0	0	0	11	65^1	65	24	2	0	18	62	11.4	2.76	129	.263	.313	2	.400	1	6	6	2	1.1
1986	StL-N	0	3	.000	31	0	0	0	5	38^2	42	19	1	1	11	33	12.6	3.26	112	.275	.327	1	.200	0	2	2	0	0.2
1987	*StL-N	9	5	.643	53	0	0	0	4	61	52	21	2	2	33	63	12.8	2.66	157	.234	.339	0	—	0	10	10	-1	2.0
1988	StL-N	2	7	.222	54	0	0	0	5	55^1	48	20	2	1	19	38	11.1	2.77	126	.239	.308	0	.000	-0	4	4	-0	0.7
1989	StL-N	4	3	.571	71	0	0	0	12	75^1	63	26	3	0	30	40	11.1	2.87	127	.228	.304	0	.000	-1	5	6	-2	0.5
1990	StL-N	4	4	.500	58	0	0	0	2	73^1	63	32	5	0	30	51	11.4	3.56	107	.233	.310	0	.000	-1	2	2	-0	0.1
1991	Tor-A	0	0	—	8	0	0	0	0	4^1	7	3	0	1	5	3	27.0	6.23	68	.368	.520	0	—	0	-1	-1	0	0.0
1993	Tor-A	0	0	—	2	0	0	0	0	0^2	1	2	0	0	4	2	67.5	0.00	—	.333	.714	0	—	0	0	0	0	0.0
Total	11	33	45	.423	385	33	0	0	39	573^2	564	273	42	8	225	406	12.5	3.64	103	.261	.332	17	.210	3	2	8	-5	1.4

● REN DEAGLE Deagle, Lorenzo Burroughs b: 6/26/1858, New York, N.Y. d: 12/24/36, Kansas City, Mo. BR/TR, 5'9", 190 lbs. Deb: 5/17/1883

YEAR	TM/L	W	L	PCT	G	GS	CG	SH	SV	IP	H	R	HR	HB	BB	SO	RAT	ERA	ERA+	OAV	OOB	BH	AVG	PB	PR	PR+	PD	TPI
1883	Cin-a	10	8	.556	18	18	17	1	0	148	136	78	0		34	48	10.3	2.31	141	.229	.270	9	.129	-5	16	16	-1	1.0
1884	Cin-a	3	1	.750	4	4	4	1	0	34	39	26	0	1	9	12	13.0	5.03	66	.322	.374	0	.000	-2	-7	-6	-0	-0.7
	Lou-a	4	6	.400	12	12	8	0	0	87^1	80	43	0	7	13	23	10.3	2.58	120	.238	.281	6	.133	-3	7	5	1	0.3
	Yr	7	7	.500	16	16	12	1	0	121^1	119	69	0	8	22	35	11.1	3.26	97	.260	.306	6	.103	-5	-0	-1	-1	-0.4
Total	2	17	15	.531	34	34	29	2	0	269^1	255	147	0	8	56	83	10.7	2.74	117	.242	.286	15	.117	-9	16	14	-1	0.6

● COT DEAL Deal, Ellis Fergason b: 1/23/23, Arapaho, Okla. BB/TR (BL 1947-48), 5'10.5", 185 lbs. Deb: 9/11/47 C

YEAR	TM/L	W	L	PCT	G	GS	CG	SH	SV	IP	H	R	HR	HB	BB	SO	RAT	ERA	ERA+	OAV	OOB	BH	AVG	PB	PR	PR+	PD	TPI
1947	Bos-A	0	1	.000	5	2	0	0	0	12^2	20	13	0	0	7	6	19.2	9.24	42	.364	.435	2	.500	1	-8	-7	0	-0.4
1948	Bos-A	1	0	1.000	4	0	0	0	0	4	3	0	0	0	3	2	13.5	0.00	—	.200	.333	0	—	0	2	2	0	0.4
1950	StL-N	0	0	—	3	0	0	0	0	1	3	5	0	0	2	1	45.0	18.00	24	.500	.625	0	—	0	-2	-1	-0	-0.1
1954	StL-N	2	3	.400	33	0	0	0	1	71^2	85	56	14	4	36	25	15.7	6.28	65	.297	.383	2	.100	0	-18	-17	-0	-1.1
Total	4	3	4	.429	45	2	0	0	1	89^1	111	74	14	4	48	34	16.4	6.55	63	.307	.394	4	.167	1	-25	-24	-0	-1.2

● CHUBBY DEAN Dean, Alfred Lovill b: 8/24/16, Mt.Airy, N.C. d: 12/21/70, Riverside, Cal. BL/TL, 5'11", 181 lbs. Deb: 4/14/36 ♦

YEAR	TM/L	W	L	PCT	G	GS	CG	SH	SV	IP	H	R	HR	HB	BB	SO	RAT	ERA	ERA+	OAV	OOB	BH	AVG	PB	PR	PR+	PD	TPI
1937	Phi-A	1	0	1.000	2	1	0	0	0	9	7	4	0	0	6	4	13.0	4.00	118	.219	.342	81	.262	0	1	1	0	0.1
1938	Phi-A	2	1	.667	6	1	0	0	0	23	22	10	3	0	15	3	14.5	3.52	137	.250	.359	6	.300	2	3	3	1	0.6
1939	Phi-A	5	8	.385	54	1	0	0	7	116^2	132	93	8	0	80	39	16.4	5.25	90	.289	.395	27	.351	8	-8	-7	1	0.2
1940	Phi-A	6	13	.316	30	19	8	1	1	159^1	220	136	21	0	63	38	16.0	6.61	67	.324	.381	26	.289	4	-39	-38	1	-2.9
1941	Phi-A	2	4	.333	18	7	2	0	0	75^2	90	53	9	0	35	22	14.9	6.19	68	.294	.367	9	.243	2	-17	-17	0	-0.9
	Cle-A	1	4	.200	8	8	2	0	0	53^1	57	31	3	0	24	14	13.7	4.39	90	.282	.358	4	.160	0	-1	-3	1	-0.1
	Yr	3	8	.273	26	15	4	0	0	129	147	84	12	0	59	36	14.4	5.44	75	.289	.363	13	.210	2	-19	-20	1	-1.0
1942	Cle-A	8	11	.421	27	22	8	0	1	172^2	170	83	7	0	66	46	12.3	3.81	91	.261	.329	27	.267	8	-3	-7	-3	-0.2
1943	Cle-A	5	5	.500	17	9	3	0	0	76	83	46	1	1	34	29	14.0	4.50	69	.281	.358	9	.196	1	-10	-12	-1	-1.5
Total	7	30	46	.395	162	68	23	1	9	685^2	781	456	52	1	323	195	14.5	5.08	79	.288	.364	287	.274	25	-75	-82	-1	-4.7

● DORY DEAN Dean, Charles Wilson b: 11/6/1852, Cincinnati, Ohio d: 5/4/35, Nashville, Tenn. BR/TR, Deb: 6/22/1876

YEAR	TM/L	W	L	PCT	G	GS	CG	SH	SV	IP	H	R	HR	HB	BB	SO	RAT	ERA	ERA+	OAV	OOB	BH	AVG	PB	PR	PR+	PD	TPI
1876	Cin-N	4	26	.133	30	30	26	0	0	262^2	397	268	1		24	22	14.4	3.73	59	.316	.335	36	.257	1	-42	-47	-1	-3.8

● HARRY DEAN Dean, James Harry b: 5/12/15, Rockmart, Ga. d: 6/1/60, Rockmart, Ga. BR/TR, 6'4", 185 lbs. Deb: 4/16/41

YEAR	TM/L	W	L	PCT	G	GS	CG	SH	SV	IP	H	R	HR	HB	BB	SO	RAT	ERA	ERA+	OAV	OOB	BH	AVG	PB	PR	PR+	PD	TPI
1941	Was-A	0	0	—	2	0	0	0	0	2	2	3	0	1	3	0	27.0	4.50	90	.250	.500	0	—	0	-0	-0	-0	0.0

● DIZZY DEAN Dean, Jay Hanna b: 1/16/10, Lucas, Ark. d: 7/17/74, Reno, Nevada BR/TR, 6'2", 182 lbs. Deb: 9/28/30 FCH

YEAR	TM/L	W	L	PCT	G	GS	CG	SH	SV	IP	H	R	HR	HB	BB	SO	RAT	ERA	ERA+	OAV	OOB	BH	AVG	PB	PR	PR+	PD	TPI
1930	StL-N	1	0	1.000	1	1	1	0	0	9	3	1	0	0	3	5	6.0	1.00	502	.103	.188	1	.333	0	4	4	1	0.5
1932	StL-N	18	15	.545	46	33	16	**4**	2	**286**	280	122	14	5	102	**191**	12.2	3.30	119	.260	.327	25	.258	5	18	20	-1	2.5
1933	StL-N	20	18	.526	**48**	34	**26**	3	4	293	279	113	11	5	64	**199**	10.7	3.04	114	.250	.293	19	.181	1	10	14	-5	1.3
1934	*StL-N★	**30**	7	**.811**	50	33	24	**7**	7	311^2	288	110	14	6	75	**195**	10.7	2.66	159	.241	.289	29	.246	4	49	52	-2	6.2
1935	StL-N★	**28**	12	.700	50	36	**29**	3	5	**325^1**	326	126	16	4	77	**190**	11.2	3.04	135	.256	.300	30	.234	4	35	37	-5	4.2
1936	StL-N★	24	13	.649	**51**	34	**28**	2	**11**	**315**	310	128	21	3	53	195	10.5	3.17	124	.253	.285	27	.223	1	30	28	-4	2.9
1937	StL-N★	13	10	.565	27	25	17	4	1	197^1	200	76	9	2	33	120	10.7	2.69	148	.259	.291	15	.227	2	27	28	-3	2.9
1938	*Chi-N	7	1	.875	13	10	3	1	0	74^2	63	20	2	1	8	22	8.7	1.81	212	.226	.250	5	.192	-0	16	17	-1	1.6
1939	Chi-N	6	4	.600	19	13	7	2	0	96^1	98	40	4	1	17	27	10.8	3.36	117	.261	.294	5	.147	-1	6	6	-1	0.4
1940	Chi-N	3	3	.500	10	9	3	0	0	54	68	35	4	0	20	18	14.7	5.17	73	.306	.364	4	.222	0	-8	-9	1	-0.7
1941	Chi-N	0	0	—	1	1	0	0	0	1	3	3	0	0	0	1	27.0	18.00	19	.429	.429	0	—	0	-2	-2	0	-0.1

YEAR	TM/L	W	L	PCT	G	GS	CG	SH	SV	IP	H	R	HR	HB	BB	SO	RAT	ERA	ERA+	OAV	OOB	BH	AVG	PB	PR	PR+	PD	TPI
1947	StL-A	0	0	—	1	1	0	0	0	4	3	0	0	0	1	0	9.0	0.00	—	.231	.286	1	1.000	0	2	2	-0	0.1
Total	12	150	83	.644	317	230	154	26	30	1967^1	1919	774	95	27	453	1163	11.0	3.02	130	.253	.298	161	.225	15	187	198	-20	21.8
● PAUL DEAN Dean, Paul Dee "Daffy" b: 8/14/13, Lucas, Ark. d: 3/17/81, Springdale, Ark. BR/TR, 6', 175 lbs. Deb: 4/18/34 F																												
1934	*StL-N	19	11	.633	39	26	16	5	2	233^1	225	96	19	5	52	150	10.9	3.43	123	.248	.292	20	.241	1	16	20	-6	1.8
1935	StL-N	19	12	.613	46	33	19	2	5	269^2	261	109	16	9	55	143	10.8	3.37	122	.249	.292	12	.133	-5	19	21	-6	1.2
1936	StL-N	5	5	.500	17	14	5	0	1	92	113	57	3	1	20	28	13.1	4.60	86	.300	.337	2	.059	-4	-6	-7	-3	-1.3
1937	StL-N	0	0	—	1	0	0	0	0	0	1	0	0	2	—	—	∞	—	1.000	1.000	102	—	0	-3	-3	0	-0.3	
1938	StL-N	3	1	.750	5	4	2	1	0	31	37	12	3	0	5	14	12.2	2.61	151	.298	.326	2	.182	-0	4	4	-1	0.4
1939	StL-N	0	1	.000	16	2	0	0	0	43	54	30	4	1	10	16	13.6	6.07	68	.310	.351	1	.111	-1	-10	-9	-0	-0.5
1940	NY-N	4	4	.500	27	7	2	0	0	99^1	110	50	8	0	29	32	12.6	3.90	100	.281	.330	3	.115	-2	-1	-0	-1	-0.3
1941	NY-N	0	0	—	5	0	0	0	0	5^2	8	2	0	0	3	3	17.5	3.18	116	.320	.393	0	—	0	0	0	-0	0.0
1943	StL-A	0	0	—	3	1	0	0	0	13^1	16	5	0	1	3	1	13.5	3.38	99	.296	.345	0	.000	-0	-0	-0	-0	-0.1
Total	9	50	34	.595	159	87	44	8	8	787^1	825	364	53	17	179	387	11.7	3.75	109	.266	.309	40	.156	-10	20	27	-18	0.9
● WAYLAND DEAN Dean, Wayland Ogden b: 6/20/02, Richwood, W.Va. d: 4/10/30, Huntington, W.Va. BB/TR, 6'1", 178 lbs. Deb: 4/17/24																												
1924	*NY-N	6	12	.333	26	20	6	0	0	125^2	139	80	9	5	45	39	13.5	5.01	73	.280	.346	8	.200	1	-16	-20	3	-2.1
1925	NY-N	10	7	.588	33	14	6	1	1	151^1	169	98	13	4	50	53	13.3	4.64	87	.282	.342	12	.235	3	-6	-11	0	-0.7
1926	Phi-N	8	16	.333	33	26	15	1	0	203^2	245	136	9	3	89	52	14.9	4.91	84	.307	.379	27	.265	5	-24	-16	-1	-1.3
1927	Phi-N	0	1	.000	2	0	0	0	0	3	6	4	0	0	2	1	24.0	12.00	34	.500	.571	2	.667	1	-3	-2	0	-0.3
	Chi-N	0	0	—	2	0	0	0	0	2	0	0	0	1	2	2	13.5	0.00	—	.000	.429	0	—	0	1	1	0	0.1
	Yr	0	1	.000	4	0	0	0	0	5	6	4	0	1	4	3	19.8	7.20	56	.375	.524	2	.667	1	-2	-2	0	-0.2
Total	4	24	36	.400	96	60	27	2	1	485^2	559	318	31	13	188	147	14.1	4.87	82	.293	.360	49	.250	10	-48	-47	2	-4.3
● DENNIS DeBARR DeBarr, Dennis Lee b: 1/16/53, Cheyenne, Wyo. BL/TL, 6'2", 190 lbs. Deb: 5/14/77																												
1977	Tor-A	0	1	.000	14	0	0	0	0	21^1	29	14	1	0	8	10	15.6	5.91	71	.337	.394	0	—	0	-4	-4	-0	-0.2
● JOE DeBERRY DeBerry, Joseph Gaddy b: 11/29/1896, Mt.Gilead, N.C. d: 10/9/44, Southern Pines, N.C BL/TR, 6'1", 175 lbs. Deb: 8/24/20																												
1920	StL-A	2	4	.333	10	7	3	1	0	54^2	65	35	2	2	20	12	14.3	4.94	79	.307	.372	3	.167	-1	-7	-6	0	-0.6
1921	StL-A	0	1	.000	10	1	0	0	0	12^1	15	9	0	0	10	1	18.2	6.57	68	.300	.417	0	.000	-0	-3	-3	0	-0.2
Total	2	2	5	.286	20	8	3	1	0	67	80	44	2	2	30	13	15.0	5.24	77	.305	.381	3	.150	-1	-10	-9	0	-0.8
● DAVE DeBUSSCHERE DeBusschere, David Albert b: 10/16/40, Detroit, Mich. BR/TR, 6'6", 225 lbs. Deb: 4/22/62																												
1962	Chi-A	0	0	—	12	0	0	0	0	18	5	7	1	1	23	8	14.5	2.00	195	.089	.363	0	—	0	4	4	0	0.2
1963	Chi-A	3	4	.429	24	10	1	1	0	84^1	80	35	9	4	34	53	12.6	3.09	113	.249	.329	1	.045	-2	5	4	0	0.2
Total	2	3	4	.429	36	10	1	1	0	102^1	85	42	10	5	57	61	12.9	2.90	123	.225	.335	1	.045	-2	9	8	0	0.4
● ART DECATUR Decatur, Arthur Rue b: 1/14/1894, Cleveland, Ohio d: 4/25/66, Talladega, Ala. BR/TR, 6'1", 190 lbs. Deb: 4/15/22																												
1922	Bro-N	3	4	.429	29	3	1	0	1	87^2	87	31	3	1	29	31	12.0	2.77	147	.265	.327	2	.080	-2	13	13	-2	0.6
1923	Bro-N	3	3	.500	36	5	2	0	3	97^2	101	44	3	2	32	25	12.4	2.58	150	.264	.325	0	.000	-3	**15**	**15**	-2	0.4
1924	Bro-N	10	9	.526	31	10	3	0	1	126^1	156	74	12	4	27	38	13.3	4.13	91	.308	.348	5	.114	-4	-4	-6	-2	-1.3
1925	Bro-N	0	0	—	1	0	0	0	0	1	3	2	0	0	0	0	27.0	18.00	23	.600	.600	0	—	0	-2	-2	-0	-0.1
	Phi-N	4	13	.235	25	15	4	0	2	128	170	87	13	2	35	31	14.6	5.27	91	.316	.360	2	.049	-5	-14	-6	-2	-1.3
	Yr	4	13	.235	26	15	4	0	2	129	173	89	13	2	35	31	14.7	5.37	89	.319	.362	2	.049	-5	-16	-8	-2	-1.4
1926	Phi-N	0	0	—	2	1	0	0	0	3	6	3	0	0	2	0	24.0	6.00	69	.375	.444	0	.000	-0	-1	-1	-0	-0.1
1927	Phi-N	3	5	.375	29	3	0	0	0	94^2	130	78	11	4	20	27	14.6	7.42	56	.334	.373	6	.222	0	-37	-33	-2	-2.5
Total	6	23	34	.404	153	37	10	0	7	538^1	653	319	42	13	145	152	13.6	4.51	92	.302	.349	15	.094	-14	-29	-22	-10	-4.3
● MARTY DECKER Decker, Dee Martin b: 6/7/57, Upland, Cal. BR/TR, 5'10", 168 lbs. Deb: 9/20/83																												
1983	SD-N	0	0	—	4	0	0	0	0	8^2	5	2	1	1	3	9	9.3	2.08	168	.167	.265	0	—	0	2	1	0	0.1
● JOE DECKER Decker, George Henry b: 6/16/47, Storm Lake, Ia. BR/TR, 6', 180 lbs. Deb: 9/18/69																												
1969	Chi-N	1	0	1.000	4	1	0	0	0	12^1	10	4	0	0	6	13	11.7	2.92	138	.222	.314	0	.000	-0	1	1	-0	0.1
1970	Chi-N	2	7	.222	24	17	1	0	0	108^2	108	64	12	4	56	79	13.9	4.64	97	.263	.357	6	.176	1	-7	-1	-1	-0.1
1971	Chi-N	3	2	.600	21	4	0	0	0	45^2	62	24	2	0	25	37	17.1	4.73	83	.343	.422	2	.250	1	-6	-4	1	-0.2
1972	Chi-N	1	0	1.000	5	1	0	0	0	12^2	9	3	1	0	4	7	9.2	2.13	179	.188	.250	0	.000	-0	2	2	-0	0.1
1973	Min-A	10	10	.500	29	24	6	3	0	170^1	167	87	12	4	88	109	13.7	4.17	95	.260	.352	0	—	0	-7	-4	0	-0.4
1974	Min-A	16	14	.533	37	37	11	1	0	248^2	234	105	24	2	97	158	12.1	3.29	113	.252	.324	0	—	0	9	12	-2	1.1
1975	Min-A	1	3	.250	10	7	1	0	0	26^1	25	25	2	0	36	8	20.8	8.54	45	.260	.462	0	—	0	-14	-14	-0	-1.8
1976	Min-A	2	7	.222	13	12	0	0	0	58	60	37	3	1	51	35	17.4	5.28	68	.273	.412	0	—	0	-11	-11	1	-1.4
1979	Sea-A	0	1	.000	9	2	0	0	0	27^1	27	14	2	0	14	12	13.5	4.28	102	.255	.342	0	—	0	-0	0	1	0.1
Total	9	36	44	.450	152	105	19	4	0	710	702	363	58	11	377	458	13.8	4.17	94	.262	.355	8	.174	1	-34	-17	-1	-2.5
● JEFF DEDMON Dedmon, Jeffrey Linden b: 3/4/60, Torrance, Cal. BL/TR, 6'2", 200 lbs. Deb: 9/2/83																												
1983	Atl-N	0	0	—	5	0	0	0	0	4	10	6	1	0	0	3	22.5	13.50	29	.455	.455	0	—	0	-4	-4	0	-0.2
1984	Atl-N	4	3	.571	54	0	0	0	4	81	86	39	5	2	35	51	13.7	3.78	102	.277	.354	0	.000	-1	-2	1	2	0.2
1985	Atl-N	6	3	.667	60	0	0	0	0	86	84	52	5	1	49	41	14.0	4.08	94	.264	.364	1	.111	-0	-5	-2	3	0.1
1986	Atl-N	6	6	.500	57	0	0	0	3	99^2	90	43	8	4	39	58	12.0	2.98	134	.242	.320	2	.125	-1	8	10	2	1.3
1987	Atl-N	3	4	.429	53	3	0	0	4	89^2	82	46	8	1	42	40	12.5	3.91	111	.246	.332	4	.250	1	2	4	1	0.5
1988	Cle-A	1	0	1.000	21	0	0	0	1	33^2	35	20	3	3	21	17	15.8	4.54	91	.276	.391	0	—	0	-2	-2	1	0.0
Total	6	20	16	.556	250	3	0	0	12	394	387	206	30	11	186	210	13.3	3.84	105	.261	.348	7	.149	-0	-3	8	9	1.9
● JIM DEDRICK Dedrick, James Michael b: 4/4/68, Los Angeles, Cal. BB/TR, 6', 185 lbs. Deb: 8/12/95																												
1995	Bal-A	0	0	—	6	0	0	0	0	7^2	8	2	1	1	6	3	17.6	2.35	203	.308	.455	0	—	0	2	2	0	0.1
● DUMMY DEEGAN Deegan, William John b: 11/16/1874, Bronx, N.Y. d: 5/17/57, Bronx, N.Y. Deb: 8/3/01																												
1901	NY-N	0	1	.000	2	1	1	0	0	17	27	17	0	0	6	8	17.5	6.35	52	.355	.402	0	.000	-1	-6	-6	0	-0.3
● JOHN DEERING Deering, John Thomas b: 6/25/1879, Lynn, Mass. d: 2/15/43, Beverly, Mass. BR/TR, 6', 180 lbs. Deb: 5/12/03																												
1903	Det-A	3	4	.429	10	8	5	0	0	60^2	77	38	3	1	24	14	15.1	3.86	75	.308	.371	8	.333	2	-6	-6	-1	-0.5
	NY-A	4	3	.571	9	7	6	1	0	60	59	33	0	1	18	14	11.7	3.75	83	.257	.313	1	.043	-3	-5	-4	-1	-0.8
	Yr	7	7	.500	19	15	11	1	0	120^2	136	71	3	2	42	28	13.4	3.80	79	.283	.344	9	.191	-0	-11	-10	-2	-1.3
● MIKE DEGERICK Degerick, Michael Arthur b: 4/1/43, New York, N.Y. BR/TR, 6'2", 178 lbs. Deb: 9/4/61																												
1961	Chi-A	0	0	—	1	0	0	0	0	1^2	2	1	0	0	1	0	16.2	5.40	72	.400	.500	0	—	0	-0	-0	0	0.0
1962	Chi-A	0	0	—	1	0	0	0	0	1	1	0	0	0	1	0	18.0	0.00	—	.250	.400	0	—	0	0	0	0	0.0
Total	2	0	0	—	2	0	0	0	0	2^2	3	1	0	0	2	0	16.9	3.38	116	.333	.455	0	—	0	0	0	0	0.0
● RICK DeHART DeHart, Rick Allen b: 3/21/70, Topeka, Kan. BL/TL, 6'1", 180 lbs. Deb: 7/16/97																												
1997	Mon-N	2	1	.667	23	0	0	0	0	29^1	33	21	7	0	14	29	14.4	5.52	76	.292	.370	0	.000	-0	-4	-4	0	-0.4
1998	Mon-N	0	0	—	26	0	0	0	1	28	34	22	3	0	13	14	15.1	4.82	87	.291	.362	0	—	0	-2	-2	1	0.0
1999	Mon-N	0	0	—	3	0	0	0	0	1^2	6	4	2	0	3	1	48.6	21.60	21	.545	.643	0	—	0	-3	-3	-0	-0.2
Total	3	2	1	.667	52	0	0	0	1	59	73	47	12	0	30	44	15.7	5.64	75	.303	.380	0	.000	-0	-9	-9	1	-0.6
● PEP DEININGER Deininger, Otto Charles b: 10/10/1877, Wasseralfingen, Germany d: 9/25/50, Boston, Mass. BL/TL, 5'8.5", 180 lbs. Deb: 4/26/02 ♦																												
1902	Bos-A	0	0	—	2	1	0	0	0	12	19	16	3	2	9	2	22.5	9.75	37	.358	.469	2	.333	1	-8	-8	-1	-0.3
● MIKE DeJEAN DeJean, Michel Dwain b: 9/28/70, Baton Rouge, La. BR/TR, 6'2", 205 lbs. Deb: 5/2/97																												
1997	Col-N	5	0	1.000	55	0	0	0	2	67^2	74	34	4	3	24	38	13.4	3.99	130	.280	.347	1	.333	0	2	7	0	0.6
1998	Col-N	3	1	.750	59	1	0	0	2	74^1	78	29	4	1	24	27	12.5	3.03	171	.285	.344	0	.000	-1	10	15	-1	0.6
1999	Col-N	2	4	.333	56	0	0	0	0	61	83	61	13	2	32	31	17.3	8.41	69	.335	.415	0	.000	-0	-26	-14	1	-1.1
2000	Col-N	4	4	.500	54	0	0	0	0	53^1	54	31	9	0	30	34	14.2	4.89	121	.269	.364	0	.000	-0	-2	5	0	0.6
Total	4	14	9	.609	224	1	0	0	4	256^1	289	155	30	6	110	130	14.2	4.95	111	.293	.367	1	.083	-1	-16	12	-0	0.7

YEAR	TM/L	W	L	PCT	G	GS	CG	SH	SV	IP	H	R	HR	HB	BB	SO	RAT	ERA	ERA+	OAV	OOB	BH	AVG	PB	PR	PR+	PD	TPI
● JOSE DeJESUS	DeJesus, Jose Luis b: 1/6/65, Brooklyn, N.Y. BR/TR, 6'5", 195 lbs. Deb: 9/9/88																											
1988	KC-A	0	1	.000	2	1	0	0	0	2^2	6	10	0	0	5	2	37.1	27.00	15	.429	.579	0	—	0	-7	-7	-0	-1.0
1989	KC-A	0	0	—	3	1	0	0	0	8	7	4	1	0	8	2	16.9	4.50	86	.241	.405	0	—	0	-1	-1	-0	0.0
1990	Phi-N	7	8	.467	22	22	3	1	0	130	97	63	10	2	73	87	11.9	3.74	102	.210	.321	3	.079	-1	1	1	-1	0.0
1991	Phi-N	10	9	.526	31	29	3	0	1	181^2	147	74	7	4	128	118	13.8	3.42	107	.224	.355	8	.129	-1	5	5	-3	0.1
1994	KC-A	3	1	.750	5	4	0	0	0	26^2	27	14	2	0	13	12	13.5	4.73	106	.276	.360	0	—	0	0	1	-1	0.1
Total	5	20	19	.513	63	57	6	1	1	349	284	165	20	6	227	221	13.3	3.84	100	.226	.347	11	.110	-2	-1	-0	-4	-0.8
● TOMMY de la CRUZ	de la Cruz, Tomas (Rivero) b: 9/18/11, Marianao, Cuba d: 9/6/58, Havana, Cuba BR/TR, 6'2", 168 lbs. Deb: 4/20/44																											
1944	Cin-N	9	9	.500	34	20	9	0	1	191^1	170	73	9	1	45	65	10.2	3.25	108	.238	.284	9	.155	-0	8	5	-0	0.4
● ROLAND de la MAZA	de la Maza, Roland Robert b: 11/11/71, Granada Hills, Cal. BR/TR, 6'2", 195 lbs. Deb: 9/26/97																											
1997	KC-A	0	0	—	1	0	0	0	0	2	1	1	1	0	1	1	9.0	4.50	105	.125	.222	0	—	0	0	0	-0	0.0
● JIM DELAHANTY	Delahanty, James Christopher b: 6/20/1879, Cleveland, Ohio d: 10/17/53, Cleveland, Ohio BR/TR, 5'10.5", 170 lbs. Deb: 4/19/01 F♦																											
1904	Bos-N	0	0	—	1	0	0	0	0	3^1	5	3	0	0	1	0	16.2	0.00	—	.357	.400	142	.285	0	1	1	0	0.1
1905	Bos-N	0	0	—	1	1	0	0	0	2	5	2	1	0	0	0	22.5	4.50	69	.500	.500	119	.258	0	-0	-0	0	0.0
Total	2	0	0	—	2	1	0	0	0	5^1	10	5	1	0	1	0	18.6	1.69	171	.417	.440	1159	.283	1	1	1	0	0.1
● ART DELANEY	Delaney, Arthur Dewey "Swede" (b: Arthur Dewey Helenius) b: 1/5/1895, Chicago, Ill. d: 5/2/70, Hayward, Cal. BR/TR, 5'10.5", 178 lbs. Deb: 4/16/24																											
1924	StL-N	1	0	1.000	8	1	1	0	0	20	19	4	0	0	6	2	11.2	1.80	210	.250	.305	2	.286	0	5	5	0	0.3
1928	Bos-N	9	17	.346	39	22	8	0	2	192^1	197	100	11	1	56	45	11.9	3.79	103	.267	.319	9	.143	-3	4	3	1	0.2
1929	Bos-N	3	5	.375	20	8	3	1	0	75	103	59	6	1	35	17	16.7	6.12	76	.336	.405	3	.143	0	-12	-12	-1	-1.0
Total	3	13	22	.371	67	31	12	1	2	287^1	319	163	17	2	97	64	13.1	4.26	96	.285	.343	14	.154	-2	-3	-5	0	-0.5
● FRANCISCO de la ROSA	de la Rosa, Francisco (Jimenez) b: 3/3/66, LaRomana, D.R. BB/TR, 5'11", 185 lbs. Deb: 9/7/91																											
1991	Bal-A	0	0	—	2	0	0	0	0	4	6	3	0	0	2	1	18.0	4.50	88	.353	.421	0	—	0	-0	-0	-0	0.0
● JOSE DeLEON	DeLeon, Jose (Chestaro) b: 12/20/60, Rancho Viejo, D.R. BR/TR, 6'3", 215 lbs. Deb: 7/23/83																											
1983	Pit-N	7	3	.700	15	15	3	2	0	108	75	36	5	1	47	118	10.3	2.83	131	.196	.285	2	.059	-1	10	10	-1	0.8
1984	Pit-N	7	13	.350	30	28	5	1	0	192^1	147	86	10	3	92	153	11.3	3.74	96	.214	.310	5	.085	-4	-3	-3	-3	-0.9
1985	Pit-N	2	19	.095	31	25	1	0	3	162^2	138	93	15	3	89	149	12.7	4.70	76	.231	.334	2	.056	-2	-20	-20	-1	-2.7
1986	Pit-N	1	3	.250	9	1	0	0	1	16^1	17	16	2	1	17	11	19.3	8.27	46	.266	.427	0	.000	0	-8	-8	0	-1.4
	Chi-A	4	5	.444	13	13	1	0	0	79	49	30	7	4	42	68	10.8	2.96	146	.179	.297	0	—	0	11	12	0	1.3
1987	Chi-A	11	12	.478	33	31	2	0	0	206	177	106	24	10	97	153	12.4	4.02	114	.230	.324	0	—	0	10	13	-3	0.9
1988	StL-N	13	10	.565	34	34	3	1	0	225^1	198	95	13	2	86	208	11.4	3.67	95	.237	.310	10	.139	-0	-6	-5	-2	-0.8
1989	StL-N	16	12	.571	36	36	5	3	0	244^2	173	96	16	6	80	**201**	9.5	3.05	119	**.197**	.269	8	.096	-4	12	15	-4	0.8
1990	StL-N	7	19	.269	32	32	0	0	0	182^2	168	96	15	5	86	164	12.8	4.43	86	.246	.335	6	.107	-1	-13	-12	-2	-1.9
1991	StL-N	5	9	.357	28	28	1	0	0	162^2	144	57	15	6	61	118	11.7	2.71	137	.239	.315	2	.043	-4	18	18	-2	0.9
1992	StL-N	2	7	.222	29	15	0	0	0	102^1	95	56	7	2	43	72	12.3	4.57	74	.245	.324	1	.048	-1	-12	-14	-1	-1.4
	Phi-N	0	1	.000	3	3	0	0	0	15	16	7	0	0	5	7	12.6	3.00	117	.281	.339	2	.400	1	1	1	-0	0.1
	Yr	2	8	.200	32	18	0	0	0	117^1	111	63	7	2	48	79	12.3	4.37	78	.250	.326	3	.115	-0	-11	-13	-2	-1.3
1993	Phi-N	3	0	1.000	24	3	0	0	0	47	39	25	5	5	27	34	13.6	3.26	122	.229	.351	0	.000	-1	4	4	-1	0.1
	*Chi-A	0	0	—	11	0	0	0	0	10^1	5	2	2	1	3	6	7.8	1.74	241	.152	.243	0	—	0	3	3	-0	0.1
1994	Chi-A	3	2	.600	42	0	0	0	2	67	48	28	5	6	31	67	11.4	3.36	139	.200	.307	0	—	0	11	10	-1	0.6
1995	Chi-A	5	3	.625	38	0	0	0	0	67^2	60	41	10	6	28	53	12.5	5.19	86	.238	.329	0	—	0	-4	-6	-1	-0.7
	Mon-N	0	1	.000	7	0	0	0	0	8^1	7	7	2	1	7	12	16.2	7.56	57	.233	.395	0	—	0	-3	-3	-0	-0.3
Total	13	86	119	.420	415	264	21	7	6	1897^1	1556	877	153	62	841	1594	11.7	3.76	102	.224	.313	38	.091	-16	11	17	-22	-4.5
● LUIS DeLEON	DeLeon, Luis Antonio (Tricoche) b: 8/19/58, Ponce, P.R. BR/TR, 6'1", 153 lbs. Deb: 9/6/81																											
1981	StL-N	0	1	.000	10	0	0	0	0	15^1	11	4	1	0	3	8	8.2	2.35	152	.200	.241	0	.000	-0	2	2	-0	0.1
1982	SD-N	9	5	.643	61	0	0	0	15	102	77	25	10	1	16	60	8.3	2.03	169	.212	.247	1	.091	0	18	17	1	2.8
1983	SD-N	6	6	.500	63	0	0	0	13	111	89	34	8	1	27	90	9.5	2.68	131	.224	.275	2	.143	0	12	11	-2	1.1
1984	SD-N	2	2	.500	32	0	0	0	0	42^2	44	34	12	4	12	44	12.7	5.48	65	.256	.319	0	.000	-0	-9	-9	-0	-0.8
1985	SD-N	0	3	.000	29	0	0	0	3	38^2	39	18	6	3	10	31	12.1	4.19	85	.267	.327	1	.200	0	-3	-3	-0	-0.3
1987	Bal-A	0	2	.000	11	0	0	0	1	20^2	19	15	1	2	8	13	12.6	4.79	92	.253	.341	0	—	0	-1	-1	-1	-0.1
1989	Sea-A	0	0	—	1	1	0	0	0	4	5	1	1	1	1	2	15.8	2.25	179	.313	.389	0	—	0	1	1	-0	0.0
Total	7	17	19	.472	207	1	0	0	32	334^1	284	131	39	12	77	248	10.0	3.12	114	.232	.284	4	.114	-0	20	17	-2	2.8
● FLAME DELHI	Delhi, Lee William b: 11/5/1892, Harqua Hala, Ariz. d: 5/9/66, Greenbrae, Cal. BR/TR, 6'2.5", 198 lbs. Deb: 4/16/12																											
1912	Chi-A	0	0	—	1	0	0	0	0	3	7	6	0	0	3	2	30.0	9.00	36	.412	.500	0	—	0	-2	-2	0	-0.1
● WHEEZER DELL	Dell, William George b: 6/11/1887, Tuscarora, Nev. d: 8/24/66, Independence, Cal. BR/TR, 6'4", 210 lbs. Deb: 4/22/12																											
1912	StL-N	0	0	—	3	0	0	0	0	2^1	3	3	0	0	3	0	23.1	11.57	30	.188	.316	0	—	0	-2	-2	-0	-0.1
1915	Bro-N	11	10	.524	40	24	12	4	1	215	166	80	5	8	100	94	11.5	2.34	119	.218	.315	10	.152	-1	10	10	0	1.0
1916	*Bro-N	8	9	.471	32	16	9	2	1	155	143	52	2	4	43	76	11.0	2.26	118	.256	.314	4	.091	-2	6	7	-1	0.4
1917	Bro-N	0	4	.000	17	4	0	0	1	58	55	35	3	2	25	28	12.7	3.72	75	.263	.347	1	.063	-2	-7	-6	-1	-0.7
Total	4	19	23	.452	92	44	21	6	3	430^1	367	170	10	14	171	198	11.5	2.55	108	.237	.319	15	.119	-5	7	9	-2	0.6
● IKE DELOCK	Delock, Ivan Martin b: 11/11/29, Highland Park, Mich BR/TR, 5'11", 175 lbs. Deb: 4/17/52																											
1952	Bos-A	4	9	.308	39	7	1	1	5	95	88	50	9	2	50	46	13.3	4.26	92	.245	.341	1	.045	-1	-6	-3	-0	-0.6
1953	Bos-A	3	1	.750	23	1	0	0	1	48^2	60	27	2	2	20	22	15.2	4.44	95	.308	.378	1	.100	-1	-2	-1	-1	-0.2
1955	Bos-A	9	7	.563	29	18	6	0	3	143^2	136	67	17	4	61	88	12.6	3.76	114	.247	.326	7	.143	-1	3	8	-1	0.6
1956	Bos-A	13	7	.650	48	8	1	0	9	128^1	122	65	12	5	80	105	14.5	4.21	110	.252	.363	3	.103	-2	-1	5	0	0.6
1957	Bos-A	9	8	.529	49	2	0	0	11	94	80	40	11	3	45	62	12.3	3.83	104	.230	.323	1	.048	-1	-0	2	-1	0.1
1958	Bos-A	14	8	.636	31	19	9	1	2	160	155	66	13	0	56	82	11.9	3.37	119	.252	.315	3	.063	-4	7	11	-1	0.9
1959	Bos-A	11	6	.647	28	17	4	0	0	134^1	120	53	12	2	62	55	12.3	2.95	138	.236	.322	3	.064	-3	14	16	-2	1.4
1960	Bos-A	9	10	.474	24	23	3	1	0	129^1	145	77	21	4	52	49	14.0	4.73	85	.283	.354	5	.116	-3	-12	-9	-1	-1.6
1961	Bos-A	6	9	.400	28	28	3	1	0	156	185	110	24	2	52	80	13.8	4.90	85	.293	.349	5	.104	-2	-15	-12	-2	-1.4
1962	Bos-A	4	5	.444	17	13	4	2	0	86^1	89	39	10	0	24	49	11.8	3.75	110	.268	.317	2	.087	-1	2	3	-1	0.1
1963	Bos-A	1	2	.333	6	6	1	0	0	32	31	18	4	0	12	23	12.1	4.50	84	.246	.312	0	.000	-1	-3	-2	-0	-0.4
	Bal-A	1	3	.250	7	5	0	0	0	30^1	25	17	7	0	16	11	12.2	5.04	69	.236	.336	0	.000	-1	-5	-6	-0	-0.8
	Yr	2	5	.286	13	11	1	0	0	62^1	56	35	11	0	28	34	12.1	4.76	76	.241	.323	0	.000	-3	-8	-8	-0	-1.2
Total	11	84	75	.528	329	147	32	6	31	1238	1236	629	142	24	530	672	13.0	4.03	102	.259	.336	31	.086	-20	-19	11	-9	-1.3
● RAMON de los SANTOS	de los Santos, Ramon (Genero) b: 1/19/49, Santo Domingo, D.R. BL/TL, 6'1", 175 lbs. Deb: 8/21/74																											
1974	Hou-N	1	1	.500	12	0	0	0	0	12^1	11	6	0	0	9	7	14.6	2.19	159	.234	.357	0	—	0	2	2	0	0.3
● VALERIO de los SANTOS	de los Santos, Valerio Lorenzo b: 10/6/75, Las Matas De Farfan, D.R. BL/TL, 6'4", 185 lbs. Deb: 7/31/98																											
1998	Mil-N	0	0	—	13	0	0	0	0	21^2	11	7	4	0	2	18	5.4	2.91	147	.151	.173	0	—	0	3	3	-0	0.1
1999	Mil-N	0	1	.000	7	0	0	0	0	8^1	12	6	1	1	7	5	21.6	6.48	70	.343	.465	0	—	0	-2	-2	0	-0.2
2000	Mil-N	2	3	.400	66	2	0	0	0	73^2	72	43	15	1	33	70	13.0	5.13	89	.254	.334	0	.000	-1	-4	-5	-0	-0.4
Total	3	2	4	.333	86	2	0	0	0	103^2	95	56	20	2	42	93	12.1	4.77	94	.243	.320	0	.000	-1	-3	-3	-0	-0.5
● MIGUEL Del TORO	Del Toro, Miguel b: 6/22/72, Sonora, Mex. BR/TR, 6'1", 160 lbs. Deb: 4/6/99																											
1999	SF-N	0	0	—	14	0	0	0	0	23^2	24	11	5	0	11	20	13.3	4.18	101	.264	.343	0	.000	-0	1	0	0	0.0
2000	*SF-N	2	0	1.000	9	1	0	0	0	17^1	17	10	3	2	6	16	13.0	5.19	82	.250	.329	1	.500	0	-1	-2	0	-0.2
Total	2	2	0	1.000	23	1	0	0	0	41	41	21	8	2	17	36	13.2	4.61	91	.258	.337	1	.167	-0	-0	-2	0	-0.2
● RICH DeLUCIA	DeLucia, Richard Anthony b: 10/7/64, Reading, Pa. BR/TR, 6', 185 lbs. Deb: 9/8/90																											
1990	Sea-A	1	2	.333	5	5	1	0	0	36	30	9	2	0	9	20	9.8	2.00	198	.226	.275	0	—	0	8	8	-1	0.6

YEAR	TM/L	W	L	PCT	G	GS	CG	SH	SV	IP	H	R	HR	HB	BB	SO	RAT	ERA	ERA+	OAV	OOB	BH	AVG	PB	PR	PR+	PD	TPI
1991	Sea-A	12	13	.480	32	31	0	0	0	182	176	107	31	4	78	98	12.8	5.09	81	.260	.339	0	—	0	-20	-19	-2	-2.5
1992	Sea-A	3	6	.333	30	11	0	0	1	83^2	100	55	13	2	35	66	14.7	5.49	73	.293	.362	0	—	0	-14	-14	-1	-1.4
1993	Sea-A	3	6	.333	30	1	0	0	0	42^2	46	24	5	1	23	48	14.8	4.64	95	.272	.363	0	—	0	-1	-1	1	-0.1
1994	Cin-N	0	0	—	8	0	0	0	0	10^2	9	6	4	0	5	15	11.8	4.22	98	.214	.298	0	—	0	-0	-0	-0	0.0
1995	StL-N	8	7	.533	56	1	0	0	0	82^1	63	38	9	3	36	76	11.1	3.39	124	.213	.304	2	.200	0	7	7	0	1.3
1996	SF-N	3	6	.333	56	0	0	0	0	61^2	62	44	8	3	31	55	14.0	5.84	70	.259	.352	1	.250	0	-11	-12	1	-1.4
1997	SF-N	0	0	—	3	0	0	0	0	1^2	6	3	0	0	0	2	32.4	10.80	38	.500	.500	0	—	0	-1	-1	0	0.0
	Ana-A	6	4	.600	33	0	0	0	3	42^1	29	18	5	1	27	42	12.1	3.61	127	.204	.335	0	—	0	5	5	0	0.9
1998	Ana-A	2	6	.250	61	0	0	0	3	71^2	56	36	10	3	46	73	13.2	4.27	110	.221	.348	0	—	0	3	3	-1	0.3
1999	Cle-A	0	1	.000	6	0	0	0	0	9^1	13	7	4	0	9	7	21.2	6.75	75	.317	.440	0	—	0	-2	-2	-0	-0.2
Total	10	38	51	.427	320	49	1	0	7	624	590	347	91	17	299	502	13.1	4.62	92	.251	.340	3	.214	1	-28	-26	-2	-2.5
● **FRED DEMARAIS**	Demarais, Frederick b: 11/1/1866, Canada d: 3/6/19, Stamford, Conn. TR, 5'9", 168 lbs. Deb: 7/26/1890																											
1890	Chi-N	0	0	—	1	0	0	0	0	2	1	0	0	0	1	1	9.0	0.00	—	.143	.250	0	.000	-0	1	1	0	0.0
● **AL DEMAREE**	Demaree, Albert Wentworth b: 9/8/1884, Quincy, Ill. d: 4/30/62, Los Angeles, Cal. BL/TR, 6', 170 lbs. Deb: 9/26/12																											
1912	NY-N	1	0	1.000	2	2	1	1	0	16	17	3	0	0	2	11	10.7	1.69	200	.288	.311	0	.000	-1	3	3	0	0.1
1913	*NY-N	13	4	.765	31	25	11	2	2	199^2	176	65	4	5	38	76	9.9	2.21	141	.243	.286	7	.106	-3	22	21	-3	1.0
1914	NY-N	10	17	.370	38	29	13	2	0	224	219	97	3	8	77	89	12.2	3.09	86	.263	.331	9	.132	-2	-8	-12	-1	-1.7
1915	Phi-N	14	11	.560	32	26	13	3	1	209^2	201	84	4	3	58	69	11.2	3.05	90	.260	.314	12	.176	0	-7	-7	-5	-1.4
1916	Phi-N	19	14	.576	39	35	25	4	1	285	252	99	4	8	48	130	9.7	2.62	101	.242	.281	11	.109	-4	-0	1	-6	-1.1
1917	Chi-N	5	9	.357	24	18	6	1	1	141^1	125	53	5	2	37	43	10.4	2.55	114	.244	.297	5	.122	-1	3	5	1	0.4
	NY-N	4	5	.444	15	11	1	0	0	78^1	70	33	1	1	17	23	10.1	2.64	97	.239	.283	2	.111	-1	1	-1	0	-0.2
	Yr	9	14	.391	39	29	7	1	1	219^2	195	86	6	3	54	66	10.3	2.58	108	.242	.292	7	.119	-2	3	5	1	0.2
1918	NY-N	8	6	.571	26	14	8	2	1	142	143	56	5	2	25	39	10.8	2.47	106	.262	.297	6	.128	-3	5	3	-0	-0.1
1919	Bos-N	6	6	.500	25	13	6	0	3	128	147	66	8	1	35	34	12.9	3.80	75	.300	.348	2	.048	-5	-13	-14	-2	-2.0
Total	8	80	72	.526	232	173	84	15	9	1424	1350	556	34	30	337	514	10.9	2.77	100	.256	.304	54	.118	-20	6	0	-16	-5.0
● **LARRY DEMERY**	Demery, Lawrence Calvin b: 6/4/53, Bakersfield, Cal. BR/TR, 6', 170 lbs. Deb: 6/2/74																											
1974	*Pit-N	6	6	.500	19	15	2	0	0	95^1	95	47	12	0	51	51	13.8	4.25	81	.262	.354	5	.152	1	-7	-9	-1	-1.1
1975	*Pit-N	7	5	.583	45	8	1	0	4	114^2	95	40	7	3	43	59	11.1	2.90	122	.230	.307	3	.125	1	9	8	-1	0.9
1976	Pit-N	10	7	.588	36	15	4	1	2	145	123	56	8	2	58	72	11.4	3.17	110	.234	.313	5	.125	-1	6	5	-0	0.5
1977	Pit-N	6	5	.545	39	8	0	0	1	90^1	100	59	13	0	47	35	14.6	5.08	79	.279	.363	3	.150	-0	-12	-11	-0	-1.3
Total	4	29	23	.558	139	46	7	1	7	445^1	413	202	40	5	199	217	12.5	3.72	97	.249	.331	16	.137	0	-3	-6	-2	-1.0
● **HARRY DeMILLER**	DeMiller, Harry b: 11/12/1867, Wooster, Ohio d: 10/19/28, Santa Ana, Cal. BR/TL, Deb: 8/20/1892																											
1892	Chi-N	1	1	.500	4	2	2	0	0	24	29	22	1	1	16	15	17.3	6.38	52	.287	.390	3	.300	1	-8	-8	0	-0.4
● **DON DeMOLA**	DeMola, Donald John b: 7/5/52, Glen Cove, N.Y. BR/TR, 6'2", 185 lbs. Deb: 4/13/74																											
1974	Mon-N	1	0	1.000	25	1	0	0	0	57^2	46	21	7	0	21	47	10.5	3.12	123	.223	.295	0	.000	-1	3	4	-1	0.1
1975	Mon-N	4	7	.364	60	0	0	0	1	97^2	92	47	8	4	42	63	12.7	4.15	93	.251	.335	0	.000	-1	-6	-3	-3	-0.7
Total	2	5	7	.417	85	1	0	0	1	155^1	138	68	15	4	63	110	11.9	3.77	102	.241	.321	0	.000	-1	-2	1	-3	-0.6
● **BEN DeMOTT**	DeMott, Benyew Harrison b: 4/2/1889, Green Village, N.J. d: 7/5/63, Somerville, N.J. BR/TR, 6', 192 lbs. Deb: 8/12/10																											
1910	Cle-A	0	3	.000	6	4	1	0	0	28^1	45	25	0	1	8	13	17.2	5.40	48	.388	.432	3	.167	-0	-9	-9	0	-0.8
1911	Cle-A	0	1	.000	1	1	0	0	0	3^2	10	5	0	0	2	2	29.5	12.27	28	.588	.632	0	.000	-0	-4	-4	0	-0.5
Total	2	0	4	.000	7	5	1	0	0	32	55	30	0	1	10	15	18.6	6.19	43	.414	.458	3	.136	-0	-13	-12	1	-1.3
● **CON DEMPSEY**	Dempsey, Cornelius Francis b: 9/16/23, San Francisco, Cal. BR/TR, 6'4", 190 lbs. Deb: 4/28/51																											
1951	Pit-N	0	2	.000	3	2	0	0	0	7	11	7	2	0	4	3	19.3	9.00	47	.393	.469	0	.000	-0	-4	-3	0	-0.6
● **RICK DEMPSEY**	Dempsey, John Rikard b: 9/13/49, Fayetteville, Tenn. BR/TR, 6', 190 lbs. Deb: 9/23/69 C◆																											
1991	Mil-A	0	0	—	2	0	0	0	0	2	3	1	0	0	1	0	18.0	4.50	88	.333	.400	34	.231	1	-0	-0	-0	0.0
● **MARK DEMPSEY**	Dempsey, Mark Steven b: 12/17/57, Dayton, Ohio BR/TR, 6'6", 220 lbs. Deb: 9/4/82																											
1982	SF-N	0	0	—	3	1	0	0	0	5^2	11	5	1	0	2	4	20.6	7.94	45	.440	.481	0	.000	-0	-3	-3	0	-0.2
● **RYAN DEMPSTER**	Dempster, Ryan Scott b: 5/3/77, Sechelt, B.C., Canada BR/TR, 6'2", 195 lbs. Deb: 5/23/98																											
1998	Fla-N	1	5	.167	14	11	0	0	0	54^2	72	47	6	9	38	35	19.6	7.08	57	.336	.456	0	.000	-1	-17	-19	1	-1.8
1999	Fla-N	7	8	.467	25	25	0	0	0	147	146	77	21	6	93	126	15.0	4.71	92	.262	.373	5	.102	-2	-2	-6	-0	-0.7
2000	Fla-N☆	14	10	.583	33	33	2	1	0	226^1	210	102	30	5	97	209	12.4	3.66	121	.243	.323	6	.078	-4	25	20	-0	1.5
Total	3	22	23	.489	72	69	2	1	0	428	428	226	57	20	228	370	14.2	4.46	98	.262	.359	11	.079	-8	5	-5	1	-1.0
● **BILL DENEHY**	Denehy, William Francis b: 3/31/46, Middletown, Conn. BB/TR, 6'3", 200 lbs. Deb: 4/16/67																											
1967	NY-N	1	7	.125	15	8	0	0	0	53^2	51	38	8	0	29	35	13.4	4.70	72	.248	.340	0	.000	-1	-8	-8	-1	-1.2
1968	Was-A	0	0	—	3	0	0	0	0	2	4	3	0	0	4	1	36.0	9.00	32	.444	.615	0	—	0	-1	-1	0	-0.1
1971	Det-A	0	3	.000	31	1	0	0	1	49	47	25	4	4	28	27	14.5	4.22	85	.250	.359	0	.000	1	-4	-3	-0	-0.2
Total	3	1	10	.091	49	9	0	0	1	104^2	102	66	12	4	61	63	14.4	4.56	76	.253	.357	0	.000	0	-13	-12	-1	-1.5
● **BRIAN DENMAN**	Denman, Brian John b: 2/12/56, Minneapolis, Minn. BR/TR, 6'4", 205 lbs. Deb: 8/22/82																											
1982	Bos-A	3	4	.429	9	9	2	1	0	49	55	32	6	0	9	9	11.8	4.78	90	.282	.314	0	—	0	-4	-2	-0	-0.3
● **DON DENNIS**	Dennis, Donald Ray b: 3/3/42, Uniontown, Kan. BR/TR, 6'2", 190 lbs. Deb: 6/18/65																											
1965	StL-N	2	3	.400	41	0	0	0	6	55	47	17	3	1	16	29	10.5	2.29	168	.236	.296	2	.400	1	8	9	2	1.2
1966	StL-N	4	2	.667	38	1	0	0	2	59^2	73	36	8	1	17	25	13.7	4.98	72	.302	.350	1	.083	-1	-9	-9	3	-0.7
Total	2	6	5	.545	79	1	0	0	8	114^2	120	53	11	2	33	54	12.2	3.69	101	.272	.326	3	.176	-0	-1	0	4	0.5
● **JERRY DENNY**	Denny, Jeremiah Dennis (b: Jeremiah Dennis Eldridge) b: 3/16/1859, New York, N.Y. d: 8/16/27, Houston, Tex. BR/TR, 5'11.5", 180 lbs. Deb: 5/2/1881 ◆																											
1888	Ind-N	0	0	—	1	0	0	0	0	4	5	5	1	0	4	1	20.3	9.00	33	.278	.409	137	.261	0	-3	-3	0	-0.1
● **JOHN DENNY**	Denny, John Allen b: 11/8/52, Prescott, Ariz. BR/TR, 6'3", 190 lbs. Deb: 9/12/74																											
1974	StL-N	0	0	—	2	0	0	0	0	2	3	2	0	0	0	1	13.5	0.00	—	.273	.273	0	—	0	1	1	-0	0.0
1975	StL-N	10	7	.588	25	24	3	2	0	136	149	73	5	3	51	72	13.4	3.97	95	.280	.346	10	.227	1	-5	-3	2	-0.1
1976	StL-N	11	9	.550	30	30	8	3	0	207	189	71	11	8	74	74	11.8	**2.52**	**140**	.246	.318	15	.224	2	23	**23**	1	2.6
1977	StL-N	8	8	.500	26	26	3	1	0	149^2	165	85	9	5	62	60	14.0	4.51	85	.281	.355	5	.098	-3	-10	-11	3	-1.0
1978	StL-N	14	11	.560	33	33	11	2	0	234	200	81	13	6	74	103	10.8	2.96	119	.238	.304	13	.178	2	16	15	8	2.7
1979	StL-N	8	11	.421	31	31	5	2	0	206	206	116	24	3	100	99	13.5	4.85	78	.264	.350	9	.129	-1	-25	-24	2	-2.0
1980	Cle-A	8	6	.571	16	16	4	1	0	108^2	116	54	4	5	47	59	13.9	4.39	93	.284	.365	0	—	0	-4	-4	1	-0.4
1981	Cle-A	10	6	.625	19	19	6	3	0	145^2	139	62	9	3	66	94	12.9	3.15	115	.254	.338	0	—	0	8	8	5	1.3
1982	Cle-A	6	11	.353	21	21	5	0	0	138^1	126	80	11	6	73	94	13.3	5.01	82	.240	.340	0	—	0	-14	-14	1	-1.4
	Phi-N	0	2	.000	4	4	0	0	0	22^1	18	12	1	0	10	19	11.3	4.03	91	.217	.301	1	.167	0	-1	-1	1	0.1
1983	*Phi-N	**19**	6	**.760**	36	36	7	1	0	242^2	229	77	9	4	53	139	10.6	2.37	151	.250	.294	13	.169	0	**34**	**33**	1	3.6
1984	Phi-N	7	7	.500	22	22	2	0	0	154^1	122	53	11	4	29	94	9.0	2.45	149	.214	.257	9	.191	0	20	20	4	2.3
1985	Phi-N	11	14	.440	33	33	6	2	0	230^2	252	112	15	3	83	123	13.2	3.82	97	.282	.345	10	.123	-2	-6	-3	1	-0.3
1986	Cin-N	11	10	.524	27	27	2	1	0	171^1	179	89	15	4	56	115	12.6	4.20	92	.272	.333	12	.222	2	-9	-6	3	-0.2
Total	13	123	108	.532	325	322	62	18	0	2148^2	2093	967	137	54	778	1146	12.3	3.59	104	.258	.327	97	.170	2	27	32	31	7.2
● **EDDIE DENT**	Dent, Elliott Estill b: 12/8/1887, Baltimore, Md. d: 11/25/74, Birmingham, Ala. BR/TR, 6'1", 190 lbs. Deb: 8/31/09																											
1909	Bro-N	2	4	.333	6	5	4	0	0	42	47	23	2	0	15	17	13.3	4.29	60	.307	.369	1	.067	-1	-8	-8	-1	-1.2
1911	Bro-N	2	1	.667	5	3	1	0	0	31^2	30	15	0	2	10	3	11.9	3.69	90	.256	.326	1	.100	-0	-1	-1	0	-0.1
1912	Bro-N	0	0	—	1	0	0	0	0	1	4	4	0	0	1	1	45.0	36.00	9	.571	.625	0	.000	-0	-4	-4	0	-0.2
Total	3	4	5	.444	12	8	5	0	0	74^2	81	42	2	2	26	21	13.1	4.46	65	.292	.357	2	.077	-2	-13	-13	-0	-1.5

● ROGER DENZER
Denzer, Roger "Peaceful Valley" b: 10/5/1871, LeSueur, Minn. d: 9/18/49, LeSueur, Minn. BL/TR, 6', 180 lbs. Deb: 4/24/1897

YEAR TM/L	W	L	PCT	G	GS	CG	SH	SV	IP	H	R	HR	HB	BB	SO	RAT	ERA	ERA+	OAV	OOB	BH	AVG	PB	PR	PR+	PD	TPI
1897 Chi-N	2	8	.200	12	10	8	0	0	94^2	125	91	4	2	34	17	15.3	5.13	87	.315	.372	6	.154	-3	-9	-7	-1	-0.8
1901 NY-N	2	6	.250	11	9	3	1	0	61^2	69	30	2	2	5	22	11.1	3.36	99	.280	.300	2	.091	-1	-0	-0	-2	-0.3
Total 2	4	14	.222	23	19	11	1	0	156^1	194	121	6	4	39	39	13.6	4.43	90	.302	.345	8	.131	-4	-9	-7	-2	-1.1

● SEAN DePAULA
DePaula, Sean M. b: 11/7/73, Newton, Mass. BR/TR, 6'4", 215 lbs. Deb: 8/31/99

YEAR TM/L	W	L	PCT	G	GS	CG	SH	SV	IP	H	R	HR	HB	BB	SO	RAT	ERA	ERA+	OAV	OOB	BH	AVG	PB	PR	PR+	PD	TPI
1999 *Cle-A	0	0	—	11	0	0	0	0	11^2	8	6	0	0	3	18	8.5	4.63	109	.200	.256	0	—	0	0	1	0	0.0
2000 Cle-A	0	0	—	13	0	0	0	0	16^2	20	11	3	0	14	16	18.4	5.94	84	.294	.415	0	—	0	-2	-2	0	0.0
Total 2	0	0	—	24	0	0	0	0	28^1	28	17	3	0	17	34	14.3	5.40	93	.259	.360	0	—	0	-2	-1	1	0.0

● GEORGE DERBY
Derby, George H. "Jonah" b: 7/6/1857, Webster, Mass. d: 7/4/25, Philadelphia, Pa. BL/TR, 6', 175 lbs. Deb: 5/2/1881

YEAR TM/L	W	L	PCT	G	GS	CG	SH	SV	IP	H	R	HR	HB	BB	SO	RAT	ERA	ERA+	OAV	OOB	BH	AVG	PB	PR	PR+	PD	TPI
1881 Det-N	29	26	.527	56	55	55	**9**	0	494^2	505	252	3		86	**212**	10.8	2.20	132	.251	.281	44	.186	-10	**32**	**37**	2	**2.8**
1882 Det-N	17	20	.459	40	39	38	3	0	362	386	267	8		81	182	11.6	3.26	90	.256	.294	29	.195	-6	-14	-13	1	-1.5
1883 Buf-N	2	10	.167	14	13	12	0	1	107^2	173	120	3		15	34	15.7	5.85	54	.334	.353	14	.237	-1	-32	-32	1	-2.6
Total 3	48	56	.462	110	107	105	12	1	964^1	1064	639	14		182	428	11.6	3.01	98	.263	.295	87	.196	-17	-15	-5	4	-1.3

● PAUL DERRINGER
Derringer, Samuel Paul "Duke" b: 10/17/06, Springfield, Ky. d: 11/17/87, Sarasota, Fla. BR/TR, 6'3.5", 205 lbs. Deb: 4/16/31

YEAR TM/L	W	L	PCT	G	GS	CG	SH	SV	IP	H	R	HR	HB	BB	SO	RAT	ERA	ERA+	OAV	OOB	BH	AVG	PB	PR	PR+	PD	TPI
1931 *StL-N	18	8	**.692**	35	23	15	4	2	211^2	225	88	9	4	65	134	12.5	3.36	117	.274	.330	7	.097	-6	12	13	-0	0.9
1932 StL-N	11	14	.440	39	30	14	1	0	233^1	296	133	6	2	67	78	14.1	4.05	97	.310	.356	13	.178	-0	-4	-3	-2	-0.5
1933 StL-N	0	2	.000	3	2	1	0	0	17	24	11	0	1	9	3	18.0	4.24	82	.353	.436	0	.000	-1	-2	-1	0	-0.2
Cin-N	7	25	.219	33	31	16	2	1	231	240	106	4	5	51	86	11.5	3.23	105	.271	.315	14	.184	-1	3	4	1	0.5
Yr	7	27	.206	36	33	17	2	1	248	264	117	4	6	60	89	12.0	3.30	103	.277	.324	14	.173	-2	1	3	1	0.3
1934 Cin-N	15	21	.417	47	31	18	1	4	261	297	129	8	4	59	122	12.4	3.59	114	.283	.323	18	.196	0	14	14	-2	1.7
1935 Cin-N★	22	13	.629	45	33	20	3	2	276^2	295	132	13	4	49	120	11.3	3.51	113	.271	.305	13	.140	-5	16	14	3	1.5
1936 Cin-N	19	19	.500	**51**	37	13	2	5	282^1	331	147	11	4	42	121	12.0	4.02	95	.289	.316	18	.200	-1	-0	-6	0	-0.8
1937 Cin-N	10	14	.417	43	26	12	1	1	222^2	240	112	7	0	55	94	11.9	4.04	92	.271	.313	16	.200	1	-3	-8	1	-0.6
1938 Cin-N☆	21	14	.600	41	37	**26**	4	3	**307**	315	110	20	0	49	132	10.7	2.93	124	.262	.291	21	.176	-0	29	25	-2	2.5
1939 *Cin-N★	25	7	**.781**	38	35	28	5	0	301	321	115	15	3	35	128	10.7	2.93	131	.272	.295	23	.209	0	33	31	-3	2.7
1940 *Cin-N★	20	12	.625	37	37	26	3	0	296^2	280	110	17	0	48	115	**10.0**	3.06	124	.246	**.276**	18	.167	-2	26	24	-4	1.9
1941 Cin-N★	12	14	.462	29	28	17	2	1	228^1	233	91	16	0	54	76	11.3	3.31	109	.266	.309	13	.155	-3	8	7	-1	0.4
1942 Cin-N†	10	11	.476	29	27	13	1	0	208^2	203	83	4	4	49	68	11.0	3.06	107	.250	.296	9	.132	-2	6	5	-4	-0.1
1943 Chi-N	10	14	.417	32	22	10	2	3	174	184	90	7	0	39	75	11.5	3.57	93	.264	.303	13	.224	1	-4	-5	-4	-0.9
1944 Chi-N	7	13	.350	42	16	7	0	3	180	205	96	13	0	39	69	12.2	4.15	85	.284	.321	9	.158	-2	-11	-13	-1	-1.6
1945 *Chi-N	16	11	.593	35	30	15	1	4	213^2	223	99	8	1	51	86	11.6	3.45	106	.265	.308	15	.200	0	8	5	-2	0.4
Total 15	223	212	.513	579	445	251	32	29	3645	3912	1652	158	32	761	1507	11.6	3.46	108	.272	.310	220	.175	-20	131	109	-17	7.8

● JIM DERRINGTON
Derrington, Charles James "Blackie" b: 11/29/39, Compton, Cal. BL/TL, 6'3", 190 lbs. Deb: 9/30/56

YEAR TM/L	W	L	PCT	G	GS	CG	SH	SV	IP	H	R	HR	HB	BB	SO	RAT	ERA	ERA+	OAV	OOB	BH	AVG	PB	PR	PR+	PD	TPI
1956 Chi-A	0	1	.000	1	1	0	0	0	6	9	6	2	0	6	3	22.5	7.50	55	.375	.500	1	.500	0	-2	-2	-0	-0.3
1957 Chi-A	0	1	.000	20	5	0	0	0	37	29	21	4	1	29	14	14.4	4.86	77	.216	.360	0	.000	-0	-4	-5	-1	-0.4
Total 2	0	2	.000	21	6	0	0	0	43	38	27	6	1	35	17	15.5	5.23	72	.241	.381	1	.167	0	-7	-7	-1	-0.7

● JIM DESHAIES
Deshaies, James Joseph b: 6/23/60, Massena, N.Y. BL/TL, 6'4", 220 lbs. Deb: 8/7/84

YEAR TM/L	W	L	PCT	G	GS	CG	SH	SV	IP	H	R	HR	HB	BB	SO	RAT	ERA	ERA+	OAV	OOB	BH	AVG	PB	PR	PR+	PD	TPI
1984 NY-A	0	1	.000	2	2	0	0	0	7	14	9	1	0	7	5	27.0	11.57	33	.438	.538	0	—	0	-6	-6	0	-0.7
1985 Hou-N	0	0	—	2	0	0	0	0	3	1	0	0	0	0	2	3.0	0.00	—	.100	.100	0	—	0	1	1	-0	0.1
1986 Hou-N	12	5	.706	26	26	1	1	0	144	124	58	16	2	59	128	11.6	3.25	111	.234	.313	2	.047	-1	8	6	-2	0.4
1987 Hou-N	11	6	.647	26	25	1	0	0	152	149	81	22	0	57	104	12.2	4.62	85	.257	.324	5	.094	-0	-9	-12	-1	-1.3
1988 Hou-N	11	14	.440	31	31	3	2	0	207	164	77	20	2	72	127	10.3	3.00	111	.218	.288	3	.048	-4	10	8	-2	0.2
1989 Hou-N	15	10	.600	34	34	6	3	0	225^2	180	80	15	4	79	153	10.5	2.91	117	.217	.288	9	.120	-2	15	12	-1	1.0
1990 Hou-N	7	12	.368	34	34	2	0	0	209^1	186	93	21	8	84	119	12.0	3.78	98	.245	.326	4	.063	-3	0	-2	-1	-0.5
1991 Hou-N	5	12	.294	28	28	1	0	0	161	156	90	19	1	72	98	12.8	4.98	71	.259	.339	4	.098	-1	-23	-28	-2	-2.8
1992 SD-N	4	7	.364	15	15	0	0	0	96	92	40	6	1	33	46	11.8	3.28	109	.258	.323	6	.207	1	2	3	1	0.5
1993 Min-A	11	13	.458	27	27	1	0	0	167^1	159	85	24	6	51	80	11.6	4.41	99	.254	.317	0	—	0	-1	-1	-1	-0.2
SF-N	2	2	.500	5	4	0	0	0	17	24	9	2	1	6	5	16.4	4.24	92	.348	.408	0	.000	-1	-0	-1	-0	-0.2
1994 Min-A	6	12	.333	25	25	0	0	0	130^1	170	109	30	2	54	78	15.6	7.39	66	.321	.386	0	—	0	-37	-36	-1	-3.9
1995 Phi-N	0	1	.000	2	2	0	0	0	5^1	15	12	3	0	1	6	27.0	20.25	21	.484	.500	0	.000	-0	-10	-9	-0	-1.2
Total 12	84	95	.469	257	253	15	6	0	1525	1434	743	179	27	575	951	12.0	4.14	91	.251	.323	33	.088	-12	-50	-65	-9	-8.6

● JIMMIE DeSHONG
DeShong, James Brooklyn b: 11/30/09, Harrisburg, Pa. d: 10/16/93, Lower Paxton Township, Pa. BR/TR, 5'11", 165 lbs. Deb: 4/12/32

YEAR TM/L	W	L	PCT	G	GS	CG	SH	SV	IP	H	R	HR	HB	BB	SO	RAT	ERA	ERA+	OAV	OOB	BH	AVG	PB	PR	PR+	PD	TPI
1932 Phi-A	0	0	—	6	0	0	0	0	10	17	14	3	1	9	5	24.3	11.70	39	.378	.491	0	.000	-0	-8	-8	0	-0.4
1934 NY-A	6	7	.462	31	12	6	0	3	133^2	126	71	6	2	56	40	12.4	4.11	99	.243	.319	8	.190	2	6	-1	-0	0.1
1935 NY-A	4	1	.800	29	3	0	0	3	69	64	30	6	2	33	30	12.9	3.26	124	.242	.331	1	.071	-1	9	7	2	0.5
1936 Was-A	18	10	.643	34	31	16	2	2	223^2	255	135	11	3	96	59	14.2	4.63	103	.285	.356	15	.190	2	10	4	-2	0.5
1937 Was-A	14	15	.483	37	34	20	0	1	264^1	290	161	15	3	124	86	14.2	4.90	90	.280	.359	19	.202	2	-8	-15	1	-1.1
1938 Was-A	5	8	.385	31	14	1	0	0	131^1	160	104	11	1	83	41	16.7	6.58	69	.310	.407	12	.261	3	-26	-32	0	-2.2
1939 Was-A	0	3	.000	7	6	1	0	0	40^2	56	45	7	0	31	12	19.3	8.63	50	.337	.442	3	.200	0	-18	-21	1	-1.0
Total 7	47	44	.516	175	100	44	2	9	872^2	968	560	59	12	432	273	14.6	5.08	87	.281	.363	58	.198	7	-35	-67	3	-3.6

● JOHN DeSILVA
DeSilva, John Reed b: 9/30/67, Fort Bragg, Cal. BR/TR, 6', 193 lbs. Deb: 8/15/93

YEAR TM/L	W	L	PCT	G	GS	CG	SH	SV	IP	H	R	HR	HB	BB	SO	RAT	ERA	ERA+	OAV	OOB	BH	AVG	PB	PR	PR+	PD	TPI
1993 Det-A	0	0	—	1	0	0	0	0	1	2	1	0	0	0	0	18.0	9.00	48	.667	.667	0	—	0	-1	-1	0	0.0
LA-N	0	0	—	3	0	0	0	0	5^1	6	4	0	0	1	6	11.8	6.75	57	.273	.304	0	—	0	-2	-2	-0	-0.1
1995 Bal-A	1	0	1.000	2	2	0	0	0	8^2	8	7	3	1	7	1	16.6	7.27	65	.258	.410	0	—	0	-2	-2	-0	-0.2
Total 2	1	0	1.000	6	2	0	0	0	15	16	12	3	1	8	7	15.0	7.20	61	.286	.385	0	—	0	-5	-5	-0	-0.3

● SHORTY DesJARDIEN
DesJardien, Paul Raymond b: 8/24/1893, Coffeyville, Kan. d: 3/7/56, Monrovia, Cal. BR/TR, 6'4.5", 205 lbs. Deb: 5/20/16

YEAR TM/L	W	L	PCT	G	GS	CG	SH	SV	IP	H	R	HR	HB	BB	SO	RAT	ERA	ERA+	OAV	OOB	BH	AVG	PB	PR	PR+	PD	TPI
1916 Cle-A	0	0	—	1	0	0	0	0	1	1	2	0	0	1	0	18.0	18.00	17	.200	.333	0	—	0	-2	-2	-0	-0.1

● RUBE DESSAU
Dessau, Frank Rolland b: 3/29/1883, New Galilee, Pa. d: 5/6/52, York, Pa. BB/TR, 5'11", 175 lbs. Deb: 9/22/07

YEAR TM/L	W	L	PCT	G	GS	CG	SH	SV	IP	H	R	HR	HB	BB	SO	RAT	ERA	ERA+	OAV	OOB	BH	AVG	PB	PR	PR+	PD	TPI
1907 Bos-N	0	1	.000	2	2	1	0	0	9^1	13	11	0	1	10	1	23.1	10.61	24	.394	.545	0	.000	-0	-8	-8	-0	-0.7
1910 Bro-N	2	3	.400	19	0	0	0	1	51^1	67	48	0	5	29	24	17.7	5.79	52	.328	.424	1	.067	-1	-16	-16	-1	-1.7
Total 2	2	4	.333	21	2	1	0	1	60^2	80	59	0	6	39	25	18.5	6.53	45	.338	.443	1	.053	-1	-24	-24	-2	-2.4

● ELMER DESSENS
Dessens, Elmer b: 1/13/72, Hermosillo, Mex. BR/TR, 6', 190 lbs. Deb: 6/24/96

YEAR TM/L	W	L	PCT	G	GS	CG	SH	SV	IP	H	R	HR	HB	BB	SO	RAT	ERA	ERA+	OAV	OOB	BH	AVG	PB	PR	PR+	PD	TPI
1996 Pit-N	0	2	.000	15	3	0	0	0	25	40	23	2	0	4	13	15.8	8.28	53	.385	.407	2	.400	1	-11	-11	-0	-0.7
1997 Pit-N	0	0	—	3	0	0	0	0	3^1	2	0	0	1	0	2	8.1	0.00	—	.167	.231	0	—	0	2	2	0	0.1
1998 Pit-N	2	6	.250	43	5	0	0	0	74^2	90	50	10	0	25	43	13.9	5.67	76	.300	.354	0	.000	-1	-12	-11	-1	-1.2
2000 Cin-N	11	5	.688	40	16	1	0	1	147^1	170	73	10	3	43	85	13.2	4.28	112	.296	.348	4	.100	-0	6	8	1	0.8
Total 4	13	13	.500	101	24	1	0	1	250^1	302	146	22	4	72	143	13.6	5.03	91	.305	.354	6	.113	-0	-16	-12	0	-1.0

● JOHN DETTMER
Dettmer, John Franklin b: 3/4/70, Centreville, Ill. BR/TR, 6', 185 lbs. Deb: 6/16/94

YEAR TM/L	W	L	PCT	G	GS	CG	SH	SV	IP	H	R	HR	HB	BB	SO	RAT	ERA	ERA+	OAV	OOB	BH	AVG	PB	PR	PR+	PD	TPI
1994 Tex-A	0	6	.000	11	9	0	0	0	54	63	42	10	3	20	27	14.3	4.33	111	.286	.354	0	—	0	3	3	-0	0.3
1995 Tex-A	0	0	—	1	0	0	0	0	0^1	2	1	0	0	0	0	54.0	27.00	18	.667	.667	0	—	0	-1	-1	0	0.0
Total 2	0	6	.000	12	9	0	0	0	54^1	65	43	10	3	20	27	14.6	4.47	108	.291	.358	0	—	0	2	2	-0	0.3

● TOM DETTORE
Dettore, Thomas Anthony b: 11/17/47, Canonsburg, Pa. BL/TR, 6'4", 200 lbs. Deb: 6/11/73

YEAR TM/L	W	L	PCT	G	GS	CG	SH	SV	IP	H	R	HR	HB	BB	SO	RAT	ERA	ERA+	OAV	OOB	BH	AVG	PB	PR	PR+	PD	TPI
1973 Pit-N	0	1	.000	12	1	0	0	0	22^2	33	19	1	3	14	13	19.9	5.96	59	.340	.439	0	.000	-0	-6	-6	-0	-0.4
1974 Chi-N	3	5	.375	16	9	0	0	0	64^2	64	39	4	6	31	43	14.1	4.18	92	.255	.351	5	.250	1	-4	-2	-1	-0.1
1975 Chi-N	5	4	.556	36	5	0	0	0	85^1	88	57	8	9	31	46	13.5	5.38	72	.270	.350	6	.250	1	-17	-14	0	-1.2
1976 Chi-N	0	1	.000	4	0	0	0	0	7	11	8	3	0	2	4	16.7	10.29	38	.355	.394	0	—	0	-5	-5	-0	-0.6
Total 4	8	11	.421	68	15	0	0	0	179^2	196	123	16	18	78	106	14.6	5.21	73	.278	.365	11	.229	2	-32	-27	0	-2.3

● MEL DEUTSCH
Deutsch, Melvin Elliott b: 7/26/15, Caldwell, Tex. BR/TR, 6'4", 215 lbs. Deb: 4/21/46

YEAR TM/L	W	L	PCT	G	GS	CG	SH	SV	IP	H	R	HR	HB	BB	SO	RAT	ERA	ERA+	OAV	OOB	BH	AVG	PB	PR	PR+	PD	TPI
1946 Bos-A	0	0	—	3	0	0	0	0	6^1	7	5	1	0	3	2	14.2	5.68	64	.280	.357	0	.000	-0	-2	-1	-0	-0.1

YEAR	TM/L	W	L	PCT	G	GS	CG	SH	SV	IP	H	R	HR	HB	BB	SO	RAT	ERA	ERA+	OAV	OOB	BH	AVG	PB	PR	PR+	PD	TPI
● CHARLIE DEVENS Devens, Charles b: 1/1/10, Milton, Mass. BR/TR, 6'1", 180 lbs. Deb: 9/24/32																												
1932	NY-A	1	0	1.000	1	1	1	0	0	9	6	2	0	0	7	4	13.0	2.00	204	.200	.351	0	.000	0	2	2	-0	0.2
1933	NY-A	3	3	.500	14	8	2	0	0	62	59	39	1	0	50	23	15.8	4.35	89	.250	.381	2	.095	-1	-1	-4	-1	-0.5
1934	NY-A	1	0	1.000	1	1	1	0	0	11	9	3	0	0	5	4	11.5	1.64	248	.225	.311	1	.500	1	3	3	0	0.5
Total	3	5	3	.625	16	10	4	0	0	82	74	44	1	0	62	31	14.9	3.73	105	.242	.370	3	.120	0	5	2	-1	0.2
● ADRIAN DEVINE Devine, Paul Adrian b: 12/2/51, Galveston, Tex. BR/TR, 6'4", 205 lbs. Deb: 6/27/73																												
1973	Atl-N	2	3	.400	24	1	0	0	4	32^1	45	24	6	2	12	15	16.4	6.40	62	.338	.401	1	.250	0	-10	-8	-1	-1.4
1975	Atl-N	1	0	1.000	5	2	0	0	0	16^1	19	8	2	1	7	8	14.9	4.41	86	.284	.360	0	.000	-1	-1	-1	-0	-0.1
1976	Atl-N	5	6	.455	48	1	0	0	9	73	72	30	3	1	26	48	12.2	3.21	118	.255	.320	0	.000	-2	2	4	-1	0.5
1977	Tex-A	11	6	.647	56	2	0	0	15	105^2	102	43	8	4	31	67	11.7	3.58	114	.259	.319	0	—	0	6	6	2	1.3
1978	Atl-N	5	4	.556	31	6	0	0	3	65^1	84	45	3	0	25	26	15.0	5.92	68	.323	.382	1	.091	-1	-17	-12	0	-1.7
1979	Atl-N	1	2	.333	40	0	0	0	0	66^2	84	28	8	2	25	22	15.0	3.24	125	.311	.374	0	.000	-1	4	6	-0	0.2
1980	Tex-A	1	1	.500	13	0	0	0	0	28	49	22	4	1	9	8	19.0	4.82	81	.377	.421	0	—	0	-2	-3	-0	-0.2
Total	7	26	22	.542	217	12	0	0	31	387^1	455	200	34	11	135	194	14.0	4.21	95	.296	.357	2	.049	-3	-19	-9	0	-1.4
● JIM DEVINE Devine, Walter James b: 10/5/1858, Brooklyn, N.Y. d: 1/11/05, Syracuse, N.Y. TL, Deb: 5/9/1883 ♦																												
1883	Bal-a	1	1	.500	2	2	1	0	0	11	15	15	0		1	3	13.1	7.36	47	.306	.320	2	.222	-0	-5	-5	-1	-0.6
● HAL DEVINEY Deviney, Harold John b: 4/11/1893, Newton, Mass. d: 1/4/33, Westwood, Mass. BR/TR, Deb: 7/30/20																												
1920	Bos-A	0	0	—	1	0	0	0	0	3	7	5	0	0	2	0	27.0	15.00	24	.500	.563	2	1.000	2	-4	-4	-0	0.0
● JIM DEVLIN Devlin, James Alexander b: 1849, Philadelphia, Pa. d: 10/10/1883, Philadelphia, Pa. BR/TR, 5'11", 175 lbs. Deb: 4/21/1873 ♦																												
1875	Chi-n	7	16	.304	28	24	24	0	0	224	254	179	0		12	23	10.7	1.93	118	.256	.265	92	.289	7	7	8		1.3
1876	Lou-N	30	35	.462	**68**	68	**66**	5	0	**622**	566	309	3		37	**122**	8.7	1.56	174	.220	.235	94	.314	2	51	**68**	1	**6.3**
1877	Lou-N	35	25	.583	**61**	61	**61**	4	0	**559**	617	288	4		41	141	10.6	2.25	**147**	.270	.283	72	.269	-2	34	**56**	2	**5.1**
Total	2	65	60	.520	129	129	127	9	0	1181	1183	597	7		78	263	9.6	1.89	159	.244	.258	166	.293	1	86	123	3	11.4
● JIM DEVLIN Devlin, James H. b: 4/16/1866, Troy, N.Y. d: 12/14/1900, Troy, N.Y. TL, 5'7", 135 lbs. Deb: 6/28/1886																												
1886	NY-N	0	0	—	1	0	0	0	1	2	3	5	0		4	2	31.5	18.00	18	.250	.438	0	.000	-0	-3	-3	0	-0.3
1887	Phi-N	0	2	.000	2	2	2	0	0	18	30	19	0	3	10	6	16.5	6.00	71	.353	.375	3	.429	0	-4	-3	0	-0.2
1888	*StL-a	6	5	.545	11	11	10	0	0	90^1	82	54	3	8	20	45	11.0	3.19	102	.233	.289	11	.297	2	-1	1	0	0.2
1889	StL-a	5	3	.625	9	8	5	0	0	60	56	38	0	7	24	37	13.1	2.40	176	.239	.328	5	.192	-2	10	11	1	1.1
Total	4	11	10	.524	23	21	17	0	1	170^1	171	116	3	18	58	90	12.5	3.38	109	.250	.316	19	.268	1	1	6	2	0.8
● CHARLIE DEWALD Dewald, Charles H. b: 9/1867, Newark, N.J. d: 8/22/04, Cleveland, Ohio TL, Deb: 9/2/1890																												
1890	Cle-P	2	0	1.000	2	2	2	0	0	14	13	7	0	0	5	6	11.6	0.64	618	.236	.300	3	.375	1	6	6	-0	0.7
● MARK DEWEY Dewey, Mark Alan b: 1/3/65, Grand Rapids, Mich. BR/TR, 6', 207 lbs. Deb: 8/24/90																												
1990	SF-N	1	1	.500	14	0	0	0	0	22^2	22	7	1	0	5	11	10.7	2.78	131	.259	.300	0	.000	0	3	2	-0	0.2
1992	NY-N	1	0	1.000	20	0	0	0	0	33^1	37	16	2	0	10	24	12.7	4.32	81	.280	.331	0	.000	-0	-3	-3	0	-0.2
1993	Pit-N	1	2	.333	21	0	0	0	7	26^2	14	8	0	3	10	14	9.1	2.36	172	.157	.265	0	—	0	5	5	0	0.8
1994	Pit-N	2	1	.667	45	0	0	0	1	51^1	61	22	4	3	19	30	14.6	3.68	117	.303	.372	1	1.000	0	3	4	-1	0.2
1995	SF-N	1	0	1.000	27	0	0	0	0	31^2	30	12	2	0	17	32	13.4	3.13	131	.254	.348	0	.000	-0	4	3	-0	0.1
1996	SF-N	6	3	.667	78	0	0	0	0	83^1	79	40	9	5	41	57	13.5	4.21	97	.257	.354	0	.000	-0	0	-1	2	0.0
Total	6	12	7	.632	205	0	0	0	8	249	243	105	18	11	102	168	12.9	3.65	110	.261	.341	1	.091	0	11	10	1	1.1
● MATT DeWITT DeWitt, Matthew Brian b: 9/4/77, San Bernardino, Cal. BR/TR, 6'4", 220 lbs. Deb: 6/20/2000																												
2000	Tor-A	1	0	1.000	8	0	0	0	0	13^2	20	13	4	2	9	6	20.4	8.56	58	.351	.456	0	—	0	-6	-5	-0	-0.3
● CARLOS DIAZ Diaz, Carlos Antonio b: 1/7/58, Kaneohe, Hawaii BR/TL, 6', 170 lbs. Deb: 6/30/82																												
1982	Atl-N	3	2	.600	19	0	0	0	1	25^1	31	15	3	0	9	16	14.2	4.62	81	.307	.364	0	.000	-0	-3	-2	0	-0.5
	NY-N	0	0	—	4	0	0	0	0	3^2	6	2	0	0	4	0	24.5	0.00	—	.353	.476	0	—	0	1	1	0	0.1
	Yr	3	2	.600	23	0	0	0	1	29	37	17	3	0	13	16	15.5	4.03	92	.314	.382	0	.000	-0	-1	-1	0	-0.4
1983	NY-N	3	1	.750	54	0	0	0	2	83^1	62	22	1	1	35	64	10.6	2.05	177	.211	.297	0	.000	-0	15	15	1	0.8
1984	LA-N	1	0	1.000	37	0	0	0	1	41	47	26	4	0	24	36	15.6	5.49	64	.285	.376	0	.000	-0	-9	-9	-1	-0.6
1985	*LA-N	6	3	.667	46	0	0	0	0	79^1	70	28	7	0	18	73	10.0	2.61	134	.230	.273	0	.000	-0	9	8	-1	0.7
1986	LA-N	0	0	—	19	0	0	0	0	25^1	33	14	2	0	7	18	14.2	4.26	81	.317	.360	0	.000	-0	-2	-2	0	-0.1
Total	5	13	6	.684	179	0	0	0	4	258	249	107	17	1	97	207	12.1	3.21	111	.253	.320	0	.000	-1	12	10	-0	0.4
● ROB DIBBLE Dibble, Robert Keith b: 1/24/64, Bridgeport, Conn. BL/TR, 6'4", 230 lbs. Deb: 6/29/88																												
1988	Cin-N	1	1	.500	37	0	0	0	0	59^1	43	12	2	1	21	59	9.9	1.82	197	.207	.283	0	.000	-0	11	11	-1	0.5
1989	Cin-N	10	5	.667	74	0	0	0	2	99	62	23	4	3	39	141	9.5	2.09	172	.176	.264	0	.000	-1	16	16	-1	2.3
1990	*Cin-N★	8	3	.727	68	0	0	0	11	98	62	22	3	1	34	136	8.9	1.74	226	.183	.259	0	.000	-1	**22**	**23**	-0	2.9
1991	Cin-N★	3	5	.375	67	0	0	0	31	82^1	67	32	5	0	25	124	10.1	3.17	120	.223	.282	0	.000	-0	5	6	-0	0.9
1992	Cin-N	3	5	.375	63	0	0	0	25	70^1	48	26	3	2	31	110	10.4	3.07	117	.193	.287	2	.400	1	3	4	-1	0.7
1993	Cin-N	1	4	.200	45	0	0	0	19	41^2	34	33	8	2	42	49	16.8	6.48	62	.225	.400	1	1.000	0	-11	-11	0	-2.0
1995	Chi-A	0	1	.000	16	0	0	0	1	14^1	7	10	1	3	27	16	23.2	6.28	71	.156	.493	0	—	0	-2	-3	0	-0.2
	Mil-A	1	1	.500	15	0	0	0	0	12	9	11	1	0	19	10	21.0	8.25	60	.225	.475	0	—	0	-5	-4	-0	-0.6
	Yr	1	2	.333	31	0	0	0	1	26^1	16	21	2	3	46	26	22.2	7.18	65	.188	.485	0	—	0	-7	-7	-0	-0.8
Total	7	27	25	.519	385	0	0	0	89	477	332	169	27	12	238	645	11.0	2.98	128	.197	.301	3	.120	-1	38	43	-3	4.5
● PEDRO DIBUT Dibut, Pedro (Villafana) b: 11/18/1892, Cienfuegos, Cuba d: 12/4/79, Hialeah, Fla. BR/TR, 5'8", 190 lbs. Deb: 5/1/24																												
1924	Cin-N	3	0	1.000	7	2	2	0	0	36^2	24	9	1	0	12	15	8.8	2.21	170	.188	.257	3	.273	1	7	7	1	0.7
1925	Cin-N	0	0	—	1	0	0	0	0	0	3	0	0	0	—	—	∞	—	1.000	1.000	96	—	0	-2	-2	0	-0.2	
Total	2	3	0	1.000	8	2	2	0	0	36^2	27	11	1	0	12	15	9.6	2.70	139	.206	.273	3	.273	1	5	4	1	0.5
● LEO DICKERMAN Dickerman, Leo Louis b: 10/31/1896, DeSoto, Mo. d: 4/30/82, Atkins, Ark. BR/TR, 6'4", 192 lbs. Deb: 4/21/23																												
1923	Bro-N	8	12	.400	35	20	7	1	0	159^2	180	95	4	2	72	58	14.3	3.72	104	.283	.357	13	.250	3	5	3	2	0.8
1924	Bro-N	0	0	—	7	2	0	0	0	19^2	20	16	0	2	16	9	17.4	5.49	68	.263	.404	1	.167	-0	-4	-4	0	-0.2
	StL-N	7	4	.636	18	13	8	1	0	119^2	108	43	6	0	51	28	12.0	2.41	157	.249	.328	9	.231	1	19	19	0	1.7
	Yr	7	4	.636	25	15	8	1	0	139^1	128	59	6	2	67	37	12.7	2.84	133	.251	.340	10	.222	1	16	15	1	1.5
1925	StL-N	4	11	.267	29	18	7	2	1	130^2	135	95	10	2	79	40	14.9	5.58	77	.273	.376	5	.114	-3	-19	-18	4	-1.7
Total	3	19	27	.413	89	53	22	4	1	429^2	443	249	20	6	218	135	14.0	4.00	99	.270	.358	28	.199	1	2	-1	6	0.6
● GEORGE DICKERSON Dickerson, George Clark b: 12/1/1892, Renner, Tex. d: 7/9/38, Los Angeles, Cal. BR/TR, 6'1", 170 lbs. Deb: 8/2/17																												
1917	Cle-A	0	0	—	1	0	0	0	0	1	0	0	0	0	0	0	0.0	0.00	—	.000	.000	0	—	0	0	0	-0	0.0
● EMERSON DICKMAN Dickman, George Emerson b: 11/12/14, Buffalo, N.Y. d: 4/27/81, New York, N.Y. BR/TR, 6'2", 175 lbs. Deb: 6/27/36																												
1936	Bos-A	0	0	—	1	0	0	0	0	1	2	2	0	0	1	2	27.0	9.00	59	.400	.500	0	—	0	-0	-0	0	0.0
1938	Bos-A	5	5	.500	32	11	3	1	0	104	117	74	9	4	54	22	15.1	5.28	93	.288	.377	10	.286	4	-6	-4	-0	0.0
1939	Bos-A	8	3	.727	48	1	0	0	5	113^2	126	70	10	3	43	46	13.6	4.43	107	.282	.349	2	.056	-4	2	4	3	0.2
1940	Bos-A	8	6	.571	35	9	2	0	3	100	121	74	15	4	38	40	14.7	6.03	75	.291	.356	3	.107	-2	-18	-17	2	-2.0
1941	Bos-A	1	1	.500	9	3	1	0	0	31	37	23	4	0	17	16	15.7	6.39	65	.301	.386	1	.091	-1	-8	-8	-1	-0.6
Total	5	22	15	.595	125	24	6	1	8	349^2	403	243	38	11	153	126	14.6	5.33	88	.288	.363	16	.145	-2	-30	-25	4	-2.4
● JIM DICKSON Dickson, James Edward b: 4/20/38, Portland, Ore. BL/TR, 6'1", 185 lbs. Deb: 7/2/63																												
1963	Hou-N	0	1	.000	13	0	0	0	2	14^2	22	13	0	0	2	6	14.7	6.14	51	.344	.364	0	.000	-0	-5	-5	-0	-0.5
1964	Cin-N	1	0	1.000	4	0	0	0	0	5	8	4	0	0	5	6	23.4	7.20	50	.444	.565	0	—	0	-2	-2	0	-0.3
1965	KC-A	3	2	.600	68	0	0	0	0	85^2	68	40	6	2	47	54	12.3	3.47	101	.220	.327	0	.000	-0	-0	0	-1	-0.1
1966	KC-A	1	0	1.000	24	1	0	0	1	37	37	28	4	0	23	20	14.6	5.35	63	.264	.368	1	.250	0	-8	-8	-0	-0.4
Total	4	5	3	.625	109	1	0	0	3	142^1	135	85	10	2	77	86	13.5	4.36	79	.254	.351	1	.143	-0	-15	-15	-1	-1.3

YEAR	TM/L	W	L	PCT	G	GS	CG	SH	SV	IP	H	R	HR	HB	BB	SO	RAT	ERA	ERA+	OAV	OOB	BH	AVG	PB	PR	PR+	PD	TPI
● JASON DICKSON	Dickson, Jason Royce b: 3/30/73, London, Ont., Can. BL/TR, 6′, 190 lbs. Deb: 8/21/96																											
1996	Cal-A	1	4	.200	7	7	0	0	0	43^1	52	22	6	1	18	20	14.7	4.57	110	.306	.376	0	—	0	2	2	-0	0.2
1997	Ana-A☆	13	9	.591	33	32	2	1	0	203^2	236	111	32	7	56	115	13.2	4.29	107	.289	.340	0	.000	-0	6	7	-2	0.4
1998	Ana-A	10	10	.500	27	18	0	0	0	122	147	89	17	6	41	61	14.3	6.05	78	.303	.365	0	.000	-0	-19	-18	-2	-2.6
2000	Ana-A	2	2	.500	6	6	0	0	0	28	39	20	5	1	7	18	15.1	6.11	81	.336	.379	0	—	0	-4	-3	-0	-0.4
Total	4	26	25	.510	73	63	2	1	0	397	474	242	60	15	122	214	13.9	4.99	94	.299	.354	0	.000	-0	-14	-13	-4	-2.4
● LANCE DICKSON	Dickson, Lance Michael b: 10/19/69, Fullerton, Cal. BR/TL, 6′, 185 lbs. Deb: 8/9/90																											
1990	Chi-N	0	3	.000	3	3	0	0	0	13^2	20	12	2	0	4	4	15.8	7.24	56	.370	.414	0	.000	-0	-5	-4	1	-0.7
● MURRY DICKSON	Dickson, Murry Monroe b: 8/21/16, Tracy, Mo. d: 9/21/89, Kansas City, Kan. BR/TR, 5′10.5″, 157 lbs. Deb: 9/30/39																											
1939	StL-N	0	0	—	1	0	0	0	0	3^2	1	0	0	0	1	2	4.9	0.00	—	.091	.167	0	.000	-0	2	2	0	0.1
1940	StL-N	0	0	—	1	1	0	0	0	1^2	5	4	0	0	1	0	32.4	16.20	25	.500	.545	0	—	0	-2	-2	-0	-0.1
1942	StL-N	6	3	.667	36	7	2	0	2	120^2	91	41	1	1	61	66	11.4	2.91	118	.216	.316	8	.190	-0	5	7	1	0.6
1943	*StL-N	8	2	.800	31	7	2	0	0	115^2	119	51	4	1	49	44	13.1	3.58	94	.269	.343	9	.265	1	-3	-3	-0	-0.2
1946	*StL-N	15	6	**.714**	47	19	12	2	1	184^1	160	71	8	4	56	82	10.7	2.88	120	.234	.295	18	.277	4	11	12	4	2.2
1947	StL-N	13	16	.448	47	25	11	4	3	231^2	211	101	16	2	88	111	11.7	3.07	135	.243	.315	17	.213	1	25	27	1	3.3
1948	StL-N	12	16	.429	42	29	11	1	1	252^1	257	121	39	0	85	113	12.2	4.14	99	.265	.325	27	.281	4	-5	-1	1	0.4
1949	Pit-N	12	14	.462	44	20	11	2	0	224^1	216	97	17	6	80	89	12.1	3.29	128	.255	.324	17	.202	0	19	22	5	2.9
1950	Pit-N	10	15	.400	51	22	8	0	3	225	227	104	20	2	83	76	12.5	3.80	115	.260	.326	21	.256	3	9	14	2	1.9
1951	Pit-N	20	16	.556	45	35	19	3	2	288^2	294	151	32	6	101	112	12.5	4.02	105	.262	.327	30	.273	5	-2	6	4	1.7
1952	Pit-N	14	21	.400	43	34	21	2	2	277^2	278	128	26	1	76	112	11.5	3.57	112	.261	.311	24	.224	2	5	12	4	2.2
1953	Pit-N★	10	19	.345	45	26	10	1	4	200^2	240	121	27	3	58	88	13.5	4.53	99	.298	.348	7	.115	-4	-5	-1	-0	-0.5
1954	Phi-N	10	20	.333	40	31	12	4	3	226^1	256	107	31	2	73	64	13.2	3.78	107	.286	.342	15	.190	0	7	7	3	1.1
1955	Phi-N	12	11	.522	36	28	12	4	0	216	190	98	27	4	82	92	11.5	3.50	113	.238	.312	18	.220	1	13	11	1	1.3
1956	Phi-N	0	3	.000	3	3	0	0	0	23	20	15	1	0	12	1	12.5	5.09	73	.241	.337	3	.333	1	-3	-4	0	-0.3
	StL-N	13	8	.619	28	27	12	3	0	196^1	175	75	20	1	57	109	10.7	3.07	123	.240	.296	19	.247	4	15	15	4	2.5
	Yr	13	11	.542	31	30	12	3	0	219^1	195	90	21	1	69	110	10.9	3.28	115	.240	.301	22	.256	4	12	12	4	2.2
1957	StL-N	5	3	.625	14	13	3	1	0	74	87	41	8	1	25	29	13.7	4.14	96	.296	.353	6	.222	1	-2	-1	2	0.1
1958	KC-A	9	5	.643	27	9	3	0	1	99	99	42	12	2	31	46	12.0	3.27	119	.258	.317	9	.257	2	5	7	2	1.4
	*NY-A	1	2	.333	6	2	0	0	1	20^1	18	17	4	1	12	9	13.7	5.75	61	.237	.348	2	.286	0	-4	-5	-0	-0.7
	Yr	10	7	.588	33	11	3	0	2	119^1	117	59	16	3	43	55	12.3	3.70	104	.255	.323	11	.262	2	1	2	2	0.7
1959	KC-A	2	1	.667	38	0	0	0	0	71	85	46	9	0	27	36	14.2	4.94	81	.290	.350	3	.176	-1	-9	-7	-0	-0.4
Total	18	172	181	.487	625	338	149	27	23	3052^1	3029	1431	302	37	1058	1281	12.2	3.66	110	.260	.323	253	.231	25	81	116	32	19.5
● WALT DICKSON	Dickson, Walter R. "Hickory" b: 12/3/1878, New Summerfield, Tex. d: 12/9/18, Ardmore, Okla. BR/TR, 5′11.5″, 175 lbs. Deb: 4/26/10																											
1910	NY-N	1	0	1.000	12	1	0	0	0	29^2	31	19	1	0	9	9	12.1	5.46	54	.272	.325	1	.250	0	-8	-8	-1	-0.5
1912	Bos-N	3	19	.136	36	20	9	1	1	189	233	123	2	3	61	47	14.1	3.86	93	.320	.375	10	.167	-1	-9	-6	2	-0.5
1913	Bos-N	6	7	.462	19	15	8	0	0	128	118	71	4	1	45	47	11.5	3.23	102	.249	.316	8	.178	-1	-0	1	-1	-0.2
1914	Pit-F	9	19	.321	40	32	19	3	1	256^2	262	117	5	2	74	63	11.9	3.16	91	.273	.327	7	.084	-9	-8	-8	-0	-1.8
1915	Pit-F	7	5	.583	27	11	4	0	0	96^2	115	51	5	2	33	36	14.0	4.19	65	.316	.376	4	.129	-1	-16	-16	0	-1.9
Total	5	26	50	.342	134	79	40	4	2	700	759	381	17	8	222	202	12.7	3.60	86	.288	.345	30	.135	-12	-41	-37	0	-4.9
● GEORGE DIEHL	Diehl, George Krause b: 2/25/18, Emmaus, Pa. d: 8/24/86, Kingsport, Tenn. BR/TR, 6′2″, 196 lbs. Deb: 4/19/42																											
1942	Bos-N	0	0	—	1	0	0	0	0	3^2	2	2	0	1	2	0	12.3	2.45	136	.167	.333	0	.000	-0	0	0	0	0.0
1943	Bos-N	0	0	—	1	0	0	0	0	4	4	2	0	0	3	1	15.8	4.50	76	.267	.389	0	.000	-0	-0	-0	1	0.0
Total	2	0	0	—	2	0	0	0	0	7^2	6	4	0	1	5	1	14.1	3.52	96	.222	.364	0	.000	-0	-0	-0	1	0.0
● LARRY DIERKER	Dierker, Lawrence Edward b: 9/22/46, Hollywood, Cal BR/TR, 6′4″, 215 lbs. Deb: 9/22/64 M																											
1964	Hou-N	0	1	.000	3	1	0	0	0	9	7	4	1	0	3	5	10.0	2.00	171	.219	.286	0	.000	-0	2	1	-1	0.1
1965	Hou-N	7	8	.467	26	19	1	0	0	146^2	135	69	16	3	37	109	10.7	3.50	96	.240	.290	5	.100	-1	1	-2	-2	-0.5
1966	Hou-N	10	8	.556	29	28	8	2	0	187	173	73	17	1	45	108	10.5	3.18	108	.240	.285	10	.149	1	9	5	-1	0.5
1967	Hou-N	6	5	.545	15	15	4	0	0	99	95	44	4	1	25	68	11.0	3.36	98	.252	.300	7	.226	2	0	-1	-1	0.0
1968	Hou-N	12	15	.444	32	32	10	1	0	233^2	206	95	14	8	89	161	11.7	3.31	89	.240	.317	5	.068	-3	-9	-9	-2	-1.7
1969	Hou-N★	20	13	.606	39	37	20	4	0	305^1	240	97	18	1	72	232	9.2	2.33	152	.214	**.262**	17	.144	-1	43	42	-1	4.4
1970	Hou-N	16	12	.571	37	36	17	2	1	269^2	263	124	31	6	82	191	11.7	3.87	100	.254	.313	16	.174	-0	5	0	-1	-0.1
1971	Hou-N†	12	6	.667	24	23	6	2	0	159	150	50	8	2	33	91	10.5	2.72	124	.248	.289	4	.074	-3	13	12	0	1.0
1972	Hou-N	15	8	.652	31	31	12	5	0	214^2	209	87	14	5	51	115	11.1	3.40	99	.256	.304	13	.167	-0	1	-1	-2	-0.3
1973	Hou-N	1	1	.500	14	3	0	0	0	27	27	14	3	2	13	18	14.0	4.33	84	.265	.359	0	.000	-0	-2	-2	-0	-0.2
1974	Hou-N	11	10	.524	33	33	7	3	0	223^2	189	76	18	6	82	150	11.1	2.90	120	.232	.307	14	.197	1	18	15	0	1.5
1975	Hou-N	14	16	.467	34	34	14	2	0	232	225	109	24	7	91	127	12.5	4.00	85	.260	.335	7	.092	-4	-9	-17	-1	-2.5
1976	Hou-N	13	14	.481	28	28	7	4	0	187^2	171	85	9	6	72	112	11.9	3.69	87	.243	.319	9	.141	-1	-4	-11	-1	-1.7
1977	StL-N	2	6	.250	11	9	0	0	0	39^1	40	21	7	2	16	6	13.3	4.58	84	.267	.345	0	.000	-1	-3	-3	-0	-0.7
Total	14	139	123	.531	356	329	106	25	1	2333^2	2130	948	184	50	711	1493	11.1	3.31	104	.243	.303	107	.136	-12	66	31	-12	-0.2
● BILL DIETRICH	Dietrich, William John "Bullfrog" b: 3/29/10, Philadelphia, Pa. d: 6/20/78, Philadelphia, Pa. BR/TR, 6′, 185 lbs. Deb: 4/13/33																											
1933	Phi-A	0	1	.000	8	1	0	0	0	17	13	11	1	0	19	4	16.9	5.82	74	.236	.432	1	.333	1	-3	-3	0	0.0
1934	Phi-A	11	12	.478	39	23	14	4	3	207^2	201	121	12	3	114	88	13.8	4.68	94	.255	.351	15	.208	3	-4	-7	-2	-0.5
1935	Phi-A	7	13	.350	43	15	8	1	3	185^1	203	128	7	1	101	59	14.8	5.39	84	.276	.364	5	.083	-6	-19	-17	-1	-2.2
1936	Phi-A	4	6	.400	21	4	0	0	3	71^2	91	55	4	0	40	34	16.5	6.53	78	.305	.388	3	.111	-2	-12	-11	1	-1.3
	Was-A	0	1	.000	5	0	0	0	0	8^1	13	11	0	0	6	4	20.5	9.72	49	.351	.442	0	—	0	-4	-5	0	-0.4
	Chi-A	4	4	.500	14	11	6	1	0	82^2	93	50	8	1	36	39	14.2	4.68	111	.284	.356	8	.267	1	3	5	-0	0.4
	Yr	8	11	.421	40	15	6	1	3	162^2	197	116	12	1	82	77	15.5	5.75	89	.297	.375	11	.193	-1	-13	-11	1	-1.3
1937	Chi-A	8	10	.444	29	20	7	1	1	143^1	162	93	15	0	72	62	14.7	4.90	94	.285	.366	8	.182	1	-4	-5	1	-0.3
1938	Chi-A	2	4	.333	8	7	1	0	0	48	49	33	7	0	31	11	15.0	5.44	90	.259	.364	1	.063	-1	-3	-3	-0	-0.4
1939	Chi-A	7	8	.467	25	19	2	0	0	127^2	134	81	14	2	56	43	13.5	5.22	91	.272	.349	8	.216	2	-8	-7	-1	-0.5
1940	Chi-A	10	6	.625	23	17	6	1	0	149^2	154	78	10	0	65	43	13.2	4.03	110	.266	.340	12	.240	3	6	6	-2	0.8
1941	Chi-A	5	8	.385	19	15	4	1	0	109^1	114	73	7	4	50	26	13.8	5.35	77	.263	.345	3	.088	0	-15	-15	-2	-1.6
1942	Chi-A	6	11	.353	26	23	6	0	0	160	173	92	16	5	70	39	13.9	4.89	74	.277	.355	5	.104	-1	-22	-23	-0	-2.3
1943	Chi-A	12	10	.545	26	26	12	2	0	186^2	180	72	4	2	53	52	11.3	2.80	119	.253	.307	8	.143	0	10	11	1	1.5
1944	Chi-A	16	17	.485	36	36	15	2	0	246	269	132	15	2	68	70	12.4	3.62	95	.279	.328	9	.117	-3	-5	-5	-1	-1.0
1945	Chi-A	7	10	.412	18	16	6	3	0	122^1	136	61	4	0	36	43	12.7	4.19	79	.279	.329	6	.167	0	-11	-12	0	-1.5
1946	Chi-A	3	3	.500	11	9	3	0	1	62	63	21	4	0	24	20	12.6	2.61	131	.267	.335	1	.053	-2	6	6	1	0.5
1947	Phi-A	5	2	.714	11	9	2	1	0	60^2	48	24	0	2	40	18	13.4	3.12	122	.223	.350	1	.063	-2	4	5	-1	0.2
1948	Phi-A	1	2	.333	4	2	0	0	0	15^1	21	10	0	0	9	5	17.6	5.87	73	.356	.441	0	.000	-0	-3	-3	0	-0.4
Total	16	108	128	.458	366	253	92	17	11	2003^2	2117	1146	128	22	890	660	13.6	4.48	92	.271	.348	94	.150	-5	-85	-84	-3	-9.0
● DUTCH DIETZ	Dietz, Lloyd Arthur b: 2/9/12, Cincinnati, Ohio d: 10/29/72, Beaumont, Tex. BR/TR, 5′11.5″, 180 lbs. Deb: 4/26/40																											
1940	Pit-N	0	1	.000	4	2	0	0	0	15^1	22	11	2	0	4	8	15.3	5.87	65	.355	.394	1	.143	-0	-3	-4	-0	-0.3
1941	Pit-N	7	2	.778	33	6	4	1	1	100^1	88	28	6	2	33	22	11.0	2.33	155	.233	.298	4	.160	-1	15	14	0	1.2
1942	Pit-N	6	9	.400	40	13	3	0	3	134^1	139	67	8	1	57	35	13.2	3.95	86	.268	.342	7	.200	1	-10	-8	-2	-1.1
1943	Pit-N	0	3	.000	8	0	0	0	0	9	12	6	0	1	4	4	17.0	6.00	58	.324	.405	0	—	0	-3	-2	1	-0.4
	Phi-N	1	1	.500	21	0	0	0	2	36	42	29	2	0	15	10	14.3	6.50	52	.292	.358	1	.167	0	-12	-13	-0	-0.8
	Yr	1	4	.200	29	0	0	0	2	45	54	35	2	1	19	14	14.8	6.40	53	.298	.368	1	.167	0	-15	-15	0	-1.2
Total	4	14	16	.467	106	21	7	1	6	295	303	141	18	4	113	79	12.8	3.87	90	.266	.334	13	.178	-0	-14	-13	-1	-1.4
● REESE DIGGS	Diggs, Reese Wilson "Diggsy" b: 9/22/15, Mathews, Va. d: 10/30/78, Baltimore, Md. BB/TR, 6′2″, 180 lbs. Deb: 9/15/34																											
1934	Was-A	1	2	.333	4	3	2	0	0	21^1	26	17	3	0	15	2	17.3	6.75	64	.313	.418	2	.250	0	-5	-6	-0	-0.7
● JACK DiLAURO	DiLauro, Jack Edward b: 5/3/43, Akron, Ohio BB/TL, 6′2″, 185 lbs. Deb: 5/15/69																											
1969	NY-N	1	4	.200	23	4	0	0	1	63^2	50	19	4	0	18	27	9.6	2.40	152	.216	.272	0	.000	-1	8	9	-0	0.5

YEAR	TM/L	W	L	PCT	G	GS	CG	SH	SV	IP	H	R	HR	HB	BB	SO	RAT	ERA	ERA+	OAV	OOB	BH	AVG	PB	PR	PR+	PD	TPI
1970	Hou-N	1	3	.250	42	0	0	0	3	33^2	34	23	4	0	17	23	13.6	4.28	91	.262	.347	0	.000	-0	-1	-2	-0	-0.3
Total	2	2	7	.222	65	4	0	0	4	97^1	84	42	8	0	35	50	11.0	3.05	123	.232	.300	0	.000	-2	8	7	-1	0.2

● GORDON DILLARD Dillard, Gordon Lee b: 5/20/64, Salinas, Cal. BL/TL, 6'1", 190 lbs. Deb: 8/12/88

YEAR	TM/L	W	L	PCT	G	GS	CG	SH	SV	IP	H	R	HR	HB	BB	SO	RAT	ERA	ERA+	OAV	OOB	BH	AVG	PB	PR	PR+	PD	TPI
1988	Bal-A	0	0	—	2	1	0	0	0	3	3	2	1	0	4	2	21.0	6.00	65	.273	.467	0	—	0	-1	-1	0	0.0
1989	Phi-N	0	0	—	5	0	0	0	0	4	7	3	0	0	0	2	15.8	6.75	53	.368	.368	0	—	0	-1	-1	0	-0.1
Total	2	0	0	—	7	1	0	0	0	7	10	5	1	0	4	4	18.0	6.43	58	.333	.412	0	—	0	-2	-2	0	-0.1

● HARLEY DILLINGER Dillinger, Harley Hugh "Hoke" or "Lefty" b: 10/30/1894, Pomeroy, Ohio d: 1/8/59, Cleveland, Ohio BR/TL, 5'11", 175 lbs. Deb: 8/16/14

YEAR	TM/L	W	L	PCT	G	GS	CG	SH	SV	IP	H	R	HR	HB	BB	SO	RAT	ERA	ERA+	OAV	OOB	BH	AVG	PB	PR	PR+	PD	TPI
1914	Cle-A	0	1	.000	11	2	1	0	0	33^2	41	28	0	1	25	11	17.9	4.54	64	.325	.441	0	.000	-1	-7	-6	-1	-0.5

● BILL DILLMAN Dillman, William Howard b: 5/25/45, Trenton, N.J. BR/TR, 6'2", 180 lbs. Deb: 4/14/67

YEAR	TM/L	W	L	PCT	G	GS	CG	SH	SV	IP	H	R	HR	HB	BB	SO	RAT	ERA	ERA+	OAV	OOB	BH	AVG	PB	PR	PR+	PD	TPI
1967	Bal-A	5	9	.357	32	15	2	1	3	124	115	61	13	3	33	69	11.0	4.35	72	.249	.303	5	.161	-0	-15	-17	-1	-2.1
1970	Mon-N	2	3	.400	18	0	0	0	0	30^2	28	18	4	1	18	17	13.8	5.28	78	.255	.364	0	.000	-0	-4	-4	0	-0.5
Total	2	7	12	.368	50	15	2	1	3	154^2	143	79	17	4	51	86	11.5	4.54	74	.250	.316	5	.152	-1	-20	-21	-1	-2.6

● STEVE DILLON Dillon, Stephen Edward b: 3/20/43, Yonkers, N.Y. BL/TL, 5'10", 160 lbs. Deb: 9/5/63

YEAR	TM/L	W	L	PCT	G	GS	CG	SH	SV	IP	H	R	HR	HB	BB	SO	RAT	ERA	ERA+	OAV	OOB	BH	AVG	PB	PR	PR+	PD	TPI
1963	NY-N	0	0	—	1	0	0	0	0	1^2	3	2	0	0	0	1	16.2	10.80	32	.429	.429	0	—	0	-1	-1	0	-0.1
1964	NY-N	0	0	—	2	0	0	0	0	3	4	3	1	0	2	2	18.0	9.00	40	.333	.429	0	—	0	-2	-2	-0	-0.1
Total	2	0	0	—	3	0	0	0	0	4^2	7	5	1	0	2	3	17.4	9.64	37	.368	.429	0	—	0	-3	-3	-0	-0.2

● FRANK DiMICHELE DiMichele, Frank Lawrence b: 2/16/65, Philadelphia, Pa. BR/TL, 6'3", 205 lbs. Deb: 4/8/88

YEAR	TM/L	W	L	PCT	G	GS	CG	SH	SV	IP	H	R	HR	HB	BB	SO	RAT	ERA	ERA+	OAV	OOB	BH	AVG	PB	PR	PR+	PD	TPI
1988	Cal-A	0	0	—	4	0	0	0	0	4^2	5	5	2	0	2	1	13.5	9.64	40	.263	.333	0	—	0	-3	-3	-0	-0.2

● CRAIG DINGMAN Dingman, Craig Allen b: 3/12/74, Wichita, Kan. BR/TR, 6'4", 215 lbs. Deb: 6/30/2000

YEAR	TM/L	W	L	PCT	G	GS	CG	SH	SV	IP	H	R	HR	HB	BB	SO	RAT	ERA	ERA+	OAV	OOB	BH	AVG	PB	PR	PR+	PD	TPI
2000	NY-A	0	0	—	10	0	0	0	0	11	18	8	1	0	3	8	17.2	6.55	73	.375	.412	0	—	0	-2	-2	-0	-0.1

● BILL DINNEEN Dinneen, William Henry "Big Bill" b: 4/5/1876, Syracuse, N.Y. d: 1/13/55, Syracuse, N.Y. BR/TR (BL 1904 (1 game)), 6'1", 190 lbs. Deb: 4/22/1898 U

YEAR	TM/L	W	L	PCT	G	GS	CG	SH	SV	IP	H	R	HR	HB	BB	SO	RAT	ERA	ERA+	OAV	OOB	BH	AVG	PB	PR	PR+	PD	TPI
1898	Was-N	9	16	.360	29	27	22	0	0	218^1	238	140	6	16	88	83	14.1	4.00	92	.275	.353	8	.100	-4	-9	-8	0	-1.1
1899	Was-N	14	20	.412	37	35	30	0	0	291	350	191	6	11	106	91	14.4	3.93	100	.297	.361	36	.303	5	-2	-1	4	0.8
1900	Bos-N	20	14	.588	40	37	33	1	0	320^2	304	161	11	9	105	107	11.7	3.12	133	.250	.314	35	.280	2	21	32	2	**3.3**
1901	Bos-N	15	18	.455	37	34	31	0	0	309^1	295	136	8	6	77	141	11.0	2.94	123	.250	.299	31	.211	0	13	21	-1	2.0
1902	Bos-A	21	21	.500	42	42	39	2	0	371^1	348	155	9	8	99	136	11.0	2.93	122	.248	.302	18	.128	-6	27	27	-6	1.3
1903	*Bos-A	21	13	.618	37	34	32	6	**2**	299	255	98	6	4	66	148	9.8	2.26	134	.230	.276	17	.160	-1	23	25	-1	2.6
1904	Bos-A	23	14	.622	37	37	37	5	0	335^2	283	115	8	2	63	153	9.3	2.20	122	.230	.268	25	.208	-0	15	17	-2	1.7
1905	Bos-A	12	14	.462	31	29	23	2	1	243^2	235	117	7	7	50	97	10.8	3.73	72	.255	.299	13	.148	-3	-29	-28	0	-3.1
1906	Bos-A	8	19	.296	28	27	22	1	0	218^2	209	101	4	1	52	60	10.8	2.92	94	.255	.300	7	.111	-1	-6	-4	-3	-0.9
1907	Bos-A	0	4	.000	5	5	3	0	0	32^2	42	25	5	2	8	8	14.3	5.23	49	.313	.361	0	.000	-1	-10	-10	-1	-1.2
	StL-A	7	10	.412	24	16	15	2	4	155^1	153	67	3	5	33	38	11.1	2.43	103	.260	.305	10	.204	2	2	1	-3	0.0
	Yr	7	14	.333	29	21	18	2	**4**	188	195	92	8	7	41	46	11.6	2.92	86	.270	.315	10	.169	1	-8	-8	-4	-1.2
1908	StL-A	14	7	.667	27	16	11	2	0	167	133	52	2	4	53	39	10.2	2.10	114	.231	.300	12	.203	0	5	5	-3	0.4
1909	StL-A	6	7	.462	17	13	8	3	0	112	112	53	3	1	29	26	11.4	3.46	70	.267	.316	7	.194	2	-12	-13	-0	-1.3
Total	12	170	177	.490	391	352	306	24	7	3074^2	2957	1411	78	76	829	1127	11.3	3.01	107	.254	.308	219	.192	-6	38	68	-15	4.5

● RON DIORIO Diorio, Ronald Michael b: 7/15/46, Waterbury, Conn. BR/TR, 6'6", 212 lbs. Deb: 8/9/73

YEAR	TM/L	W	L	PCT	G	GS	CG	SH	SV	IP	H	R	HR	HB	BB	SO	RAT	ERA	ERA+	OAV	OOB	BH	AVG	PB	PR	PR+	PD	TPI
1973	Phi-N	0	0	—	23	0	0	0	1	19^1	18	5	1	0	6	11	11.2	2.33	163	.257	.316	0	—	0	3	3	-0	0.1
1974	Phi-N	0	0	—	2	0	0	0	0	1	2	2	1	0	1	0	27.0	18.00	21	.400	.500	0	—	0	-2	-2	0	-0.1
Total	2	0	0	—	25	0	0	0	1	20^1	20	7	2	0	7	11	12.0	3.10	123	.267	.329	0	—	0	1	2	0	0.0

● FRANK DiPINO DiPino, Frank Michael b: 10/22/56, Syracuse, N.Y. BL/TL, 6', 180 lbs. Deb: 9/14/81

YEAR	TM/L	W	L	PCT	G	GS	CG	SH	SV	IP	H	R	HR	HB	BB	SO	RAT	ERA	ERA+	OAV	OOB	BH	AVG	PB	PR	PR+	PD	TPI
1981	Mil-A	0	0	—	2	0	0	0	0	2^1	0	0	0	0	3	3	11.6	0.00	—	.000	.300	0	—	0	1	1	-0	0.0
1982	Hou-N	2	2	.500	6	6	0	0	0	28^1	32	20	1	0	11	25	13.7	6.04	55	.302	.368	0	.000	-1	-8	-9	-1	-1.2
1983	Hou-N	3	4	.429	53	0	0	0	20	71^1	52	21	2	1	20	67	9.2	2.65	129	.205	.265	1	.167	1	8	6	1	1.1
1984	Hou-N	4	9	.308	57	0	0	0	14	75^1	74	32	3	1	36	65	13.3	3.35	99	.260	.345	0	.000	-1	2	-0	0	-0.1
1985	Hou-N	3	7	.300	54	0	0	0	6	76	69	44	7	2	43	49	13.5	4.03	86	.248	.353	2	.167	-0	-4	-5	-2	-0.8
1986	Hou-N	1	3	.250	31	0	0	0	3	40^1	27	18	5	2	16	27	10.0	3.57	101	.189	.280	1	.200	0	1	0	0	0.1
	Chi-N	2	4	.333	30	0	0	0	0	40	47	27	6	0	14	43	13.7	5.17	78	.297	.355	0	.000	-0	-6	-5	1	-0.5
	Yr	3	7	.300	61	0	0	0	3	80^1	74	45	11	2	30	70	11.9	4.37	88	.246	.318	1	.167	-0	-6	-5	2	-0.4
1987	Chi-N	3	3	.500	69	0	0	0	4	80	75	31	7	1	34	61	12.4	3.15	136	.252	.330	1	.500	0	8	10	1	0.8
1988	Chi-N	2	3	.400	63	0	0	0	6	90^1	102	54	6	0	32	69	13.4	4.98	73	.285	.344	1	.100	-0	-15	-13	-0	-1.0
1989	StL-N	9	0	1.000	67	0	0	0	0	88^1	73	26	6	0	20	44	9.5	2.45	149	.227	.273	1	.077	-1	10	11	0	1.0
1990	StL-N	5	2	.714	62	0	0	0	3	81	92	45	8	1	31	49	13.8	4.56	84	.294	.359	1	.250	0	-7	-7	1	-0.5
1992	StL-N	0	0	—	9	0	0	0	0	11	9	2	0	0	3	8	9.8	1.64	207	.220	.273	1	1.000	0	2	2	0	0.2
1993	KC-A	1	1	.500	11	0	0	0	0	15^2	21	12	2	2	6	5	16.7	6.89	67	.328	.403	0	—	0	-4	-4	0	-0.4
Total	12	35	38	.479	514	6	0	0	56	700	673	332	53	10	269	515	12.2	3.83	96	.256	.328	9	.125	-1	-12	-12	2	-1.3

● JERRY DIPOTO Dipoto, Gerard Peter b: 5/24/68, Jersey City, N.J. BR/TR, 6'2", 200 lbs. Deb: 5/11/93

YEAR	TM/L	W	L	PCT	G	GS	CG	SH	SV	IP	H	R	HR	HB	BB	SO	RAT	ERA	ERA+	OAV	OOB	BH	AVG	PB	PR	PR+	PD	TPI
1993	Cle-A	4	4	.500	46	0	0	0	11	56^1	57	21	0	1	30	41	14.1	2.40	181	.270	.364	0	—	0	12	12	1	2.0
1994	Cle-A	0	0	—	7	0	0	0	0	15^2	26	14	1	1	10	9	21.3	8.04	59	.406	.493	0	—	0	-6	-6	-0	-0.3
1995	NY-N	4	6	.400	58	0	0	0	2	78^2	77	41	2	4	29	49	12.6	3.78	107	.267	.343	0	.000	-1	4	2	1	0.3
1996	NY-N	7	2	.778	57	0	0	0	0	77^1	91	44	5	3	45	52	16.2	4.19	96	.298	.394	0	.000	-0	0	-2	0	-0.2
1997	Col-N	5	3	.625	74	0	0	0	16	95^2	108	56	6	4	33	74	13.6	4.70	110	.288	.352	1	.111	-1	-5	4	-0	0.3
1998	Col-N	3	4	.429	68	0	0	0	19	71^1	61	31	8	3	25	49	11.2	3.53	146	.232	.306	0	.000	0	6	11	-1	1.4
1999	Col-N	4	5	.444	63	0	0	0	1	86^2	91	44	10	3	44	69	14.3	4.26	137	.279	.370	0	.000	-0	3	12	-0	1.0
2000	Col-N	0	0	—	17	0	0	0	0	13^2	16	6	1	0	5	9	13.8	3.95	150	.314	.375	0	.000	-0	1	2	-0	0.1
Total	8	27	24	.529	390	0	0	0	49	495^1	527	257	33	19	221	352	13.9	4.05	119	.280	.361	1	.045	-2	15	38	-0	4.6

● GEORGE DISCH Disch, George Charles b: 3/15/1879, Lincoln, Mo. d: 8/25/50, Rapid City, S.D. 5'11", Deb: 8/8/05

YEAR	TM/L	W	L	PCT	G	GS	CG	SH	SV	IP	H	R	HR	HB	BB	SO	RAT	ERA	ERA+	OAV	OOB	BH	AVG	PB	PR	PR+	PD	TPI
1905	Det-A	0	2	.000	8	3	1	0	0	47^2	43	19	1	2	8	14	10.0	2.64	103	.243	.283	2	.105	-1	0	0	0	-0.1

● GLENN DISHMAN Dishman, Glenelg Edward b: 11/5/70, Baltimore, Md. BR/TL, 6'1", 195 lbs. Deb: 6/22/95

YEAR	TM/L	W	L	PCT	G	GS	CG	SH	SV	IP	H	R	HR	HB	BB	SO	RAT	ERA	ERA+	OAV	OOB	BH	AVG	PB	PR	PR+	PD	TPI
1995	SD-N	4	8	.333	19	16	0	0	0	97	104	60	11	4	34	43	13.2	5.01	81	.278	.345	6	.200	1	-9	-11	-1	-1.2
1996	SD-N	0	0	—	3	0	0	0	0	2^1	3	2	0	0	1	0	15.4	7.71	52	.300	.364	0	—	0	-1	-1	-0	-0.1
	Phi-N	0	0	—	4	1	0	0	0	7	9	6	2	0	2	3	14.1	7.71	56	.321	.367	0	—	0	-3	-3	-0	-0.1
	Yr	0	0	—	7	1	0	0	0	9^1	12	8	2	0	3	3	14.5	7.71	55	.316	.366	0	—	0	-4	-4	-0	-0.2
1997	Det-A	1	2	.333	7	4	0	0	0	29	30	18	4	2	8	20	12.4	5.28	87	.268	.328	0	—	0	-2	-2	-0	-0.1
Total	3	5	10	.333	33	21	0	0	0	135^1	146	86	17	6	45	66	13.1	5.25	79	.279	.343	6	.200	1	-15	-17	-0	-1.5

● ALEC DISTASO Distaso, Alec John b: 12/23/48, Los Angeles, Cal. BR/TR, 6'2", 200 lbs. Deb: 4/20/69

YEAR	TM/L	W	L	PCT	G	GS	CG	SH	SV	IP	H	R	HR	HB	BB	SO	RAT	ERA	ERA+	OAV	OOB	BH	AVG	PB	PR	PR+	PD	TPI
1969	Chi-N	0	0	—	2	0	0	0	0	4^2	6	2	0	0	1	1	13.5	3.86	104	.316	.350	0	—	0	-0	0	0	0.0

● ART DITMAR Ditmar, Arthur John b: 4/3/29, Winthrop, Mass. BR/TR, 6'2", 196 lbs. Deb: 4/19/54

YEAR	TM/L	W	L	PCT	G	GS	CG	SH	SV	IP	H	R	HR	HB	BB	SO	RAT	ERA	ERA+	OAV	OOB	BH	AVG	PB	PR	PR+	PD	TPI
1954	Phi-A	1	4	.200	14	5	0	0	0	39^1	50	35	4	1	36	14	19.9	6.41	61	.314	.444	1	.125	0	-12	-10	-0	-1.2
1955	KC-A	12	12	.500	35	22	7	1	1	175^1	180	109	23	7	86	79	14.0	5.03	83	.270	.360	13	.210	-0	-21	-16	1	-1.9
1956	KC-A	12	22	.353	44	34	14	2	1	254^1	254	141	30	7	108	126	13.1	4.42	98	.262	.340	13	.143	-4	-7	-3	-1	-0.8
1957	*NY-A	8	3	.727	46	11	0	0	6	127^1	128	55	9	2	35	64	11.7	3.25	110	.261	.313	7	.200	-0	8	5	-1	0.3
1958	*NY-A	9	8	.529	38	13	4	0	4	139^2	124	71	14	5	38	52	10.8	3.42	103	.237	.295	11	.250	2	5	2	-2	0.2
1959	NY-A	13	9	.591	38	25	7	1	1	202	156	75	17	8	52	96	**9.6**	2.90	126	.211	**.270**	15	.197	2	22	18	-1	1.9
1960	*NY-A	15	9	.625	34	28	8	1	0	200	195	77	25	1	56	65	11.3	3.06	117	.256	.308	11	.159	0	18	13	-2	1.3
1961	NY-A	2	3	.400	12	8	1	0	0	54^1	59	33	9	2	14	24	12.4	4.64	80	.285	.336	1	.053	-2	-4	-6	1	-0.6
	KC-A	0	5	.000	20	5	0	0	1	54	60	34	6	2	23	19	14.2	5.67	74	.286	.362	2	.167	-0	-10	-9	-0	-0.8

YEAR	TM/L	W	L	PCT	G	GS	CG	SH	SV	IP	H	R	HR	HB	BB	SO	RAT	ERA	ERA+	OAV	OOB	BH	AVG	PB	PR	PR+	PD	TPI
	Yr	2	8	.200	32	13	1	0	1	108^1	119	67	15	4	37	43	13.3	5.15	77	.285	.349	3	.097	-2	-14	-15	0	-1.4
1962	KC-A	0	2	.000	6	5	0	0	0	21^2	31	19	1	2	13	13	19.1	6.65	64	.323	.414	1	.167	-0	-6	-5	-0	-0.5
Total	9	72	77	.483	287	156	41	5	14	1268	1237	649	138	37	461	552	12.3	3.98	97	.256	.326	75	.178	-3	-7	-17	-6	-2.1

● SONNY DIXON Dixon, John Craig b: 11/5/24, Charlotte, N.C. BB/TR, 6'2.5", 205 lbs. Deb: 4/20/53

YEAR	TM/L	W	L	PCT	G	GS	CG	SH	SV	IP	H	R	HR	HB	BB	SO	RAT	ERA	ERA+	OAV	OOB	BH	AVG	PB	PR	PR+	PD	TPI
1953	Was-A	5	8	.385	43	6	3	0	3	120	123	57	13	2	31	40	11.7	3.75	104	.267	.316	4	.154	0	3	2	2	0.4
1954	Was-A	1	2	.333	16	0	0	0	1	29^2	26	15	3	0	12	7	11.5	3.03	117	.236	.311	0	.000	-1	2	2	1	0.2
	Phi-A	5	7	.417	38	6	1	0	4	107^1	136	63	8	3	27	42	13.9	4.86	80	.308	.352	7	.250	2	-14	-11	3	-0.8
	Yr	6	9	.400	**54**	6	1	0	5	137	162	78	11	3	39	49	13.4	4.47	86	.293	.343	7	.206	1	-11	-9	3	-0.6
1955	KC-A	0	0	—	2	0	0	0	0	1^2	6	3	1	0	0	0	32.4	16.20	26	.545	.545	0	—	0	-2	-2	0	-0.1
1956	NY-A	0	1	.000	3	0	0	0	1	4^1	5	3	0	0	5	1	20.8	2.08	186	.294	.455	0	.000	-0	1	1	0	0.2
Total	4	11	18	.379	102	12	4	0	9	263	296	141	25	5	75	90	12.9	4.17	93	.284	.335	11	.180	1	-9	-9	6	-0.1

● KEN DIXON Dixon, Kenneth John b: 10/17/60, Monroe, Va. BB/TR, 5'11", 166 lbs. Deb: 9/22/84

YEAR	TM/L	W	L	PCT	G	GS	CG	SH	SV	IP	H	R	HR	HB	BB	SO	RAT	ERA	ERA+	OAV	OOB	BH	AVG	PB	PR	PR+	PD	TPI
1984	Bal-A	0	1	.000	2	2	0	0	0	13	14	6	1	0	4	8	12.5	4.15	93	.269	.321	0	—	0	-0	-0	0	0.0
1985	Bal-A	8	4	.667	34	18	3	1	1	162	144	68	20	2	64	108	11.7	3.67	110	.237	.312	0	—	0	9	7	-1	0.4
1986	Bal-A	11	13	.458	35	33	2	0	0	202^1	194	111	33	1	83	170	12.4	4.58	90	.249	.322	0	—	0	-9	-10	-1	-1.1
1987	Bal-A	7	10	.412	34	15	0	0	5	105	128	81	31	1	27	91	13.4	6.43	69	.292	.334	0	—	0	-23	-24	-0	-3.4
Total	4	26	28	.481	105	68	5	1	6	482^1	480	266	85	4	178	377	12.4	4.66	89	.256	.322	0	—	0	-23	-28	-2	-4.1

● STEVE DIXON Dixon, Steven Ross b: 8/3/69, Cincinnati, Ohio BL/TL, 6', 190 lbs. Deb: 9/7/93

YEAR	TM/L	W	L	PCT	G	GS	CG	SH	SV	IP	H	R	HR	HB	BB	SO	RAT	ERA	ERA+	OAV	OOB	BH	AVG	PB	PR	PR+	PD	TPI
1993	StL-N	0	0	—	4	0	0	0	0	2^2	7	10	1	0	5	2	40.5	33.75	12	.538	.667	0	—	0	-9	-9	0	-0.4
1994	StL-N	0	0	—	2	0	0	0	0	2^1	3	6	0	0	8	1	42.4	23.14	18	.333	.647	0	—	0	-5	-5	-0	-0.2
Total	2	0	0	—	6	0	0	0	0	5	10	16	1	0	13	3	41.4	28.80	14	.455	.657	0	—	0	-14	-14	0	-0.6

● TOM DIXON Dixon, Thomas Earl b: 4/23/55, Orlando, Fla. BR/TR, 5'11", 175 lbs. Deb: 7/30/77

YEAR	TM/L	W	L	PCT	G	GS	CG	SH	SV	IP	H	R	HR	HB	BB	SO	RAT	ERA	ERA+	OAV	OOB	BH	AVG	PB	PR	PR+	PD	TPI
1977	Hou-N	1	0	1.000	9	4	1	0	0	30^1	40	12	0	1	7	15	14.2	3.26	109	.320	.361	0	.000	-1	2	1	0	0.0
1978	Hou-N	7	11	.389	30	19	3	2	1	140	140	70	8	1	40	66	11.6	3.99	83	.265	.318	4	.100	-2	-6	-11	-1	-1.6
1979	Hou-N	1	2	.333	19	1	0	0	0	25^2	39	23	2	0	15	9	18.9	6.66	53	.348	.425	1	1.000	1	-8	-10	1	-0.9
1983	Mon-N	0	1	.000	4	0	0	0	0	3^2	6	4	1	1	1	4	19.6	9.82	37	.375	.444	0	—	0	-3	-3	-0	-0.5
Total	4	9	14	.391	62	24	4	2	1	199^2	225	109	11	3	63	94	13.1	4.33	78	.288	.343	5	.104	-2	-15	-23	-0	-3.0

● BILL DOAK Doak, William Leopold "Spittin' Bill" b: 1/28/1891, Pittsburgh, Pa. d: 11/26/54, Bradenton, Fla. BR/TR, 6'0.5", 165 lbs. Deb: 9/1/12

YEAR	TM/L	W	L	PCT	G	GS	CG	SH	SV	IP	H	R	HR	HB	BB	SO	RAT	ERA	ERA+	OAV	OOB	BH	AVG	PB	PR	PR+	PD	TPI
1912	Cin-N	0	0	—	1	1	0	0	0	2	4	2	0	0	1	0	22.5	4.50	75	.444	.500	0	—	0	-0	-0	-0	0.0
1913	StL-N	2	8	.200	15	12	5	1	1	93	79	42	4	5	39	51	11.9	3.10	104	.236	.325	1	.032	-3	1	1	1	-0.1
1914	StL-N	19	6	.760	36	33	16	7	1	256	193	79	2	7	87	118	10.1	**1.72**	**162**	.216	.290	10	.118	-3	30	30	5	3.2
1915	StL-N	16	18	.471	38	36	19	3	1	276	263	103	4	8	85	124	11.6	2.64	106	.261	.323	15	.174	1	3	4	7	1.4
1916	StL-N	12	8	.600	29	26	11	2	0	192	177	76	5	3	55	82	11.0	2.63	101	.251	.308	8	.129	-2	-0	0	3	0.1
1917	StL-N	16	20	.444	44	37	16	3	2	281^1	257	123	6	9	85	111	11.2	3.10	87	.250	.312	12	.126	-4	-12	-13	5	-1.7
1918	StL-N	9	15	.375	31	23	16	1	1	211	191	76	3	4	60	74	10.9	2.43	111	.249	.306	12	.182	1	8	7	5	1.5
1919	StL-N	13	14	.481	31	29	13	3	0	202^2	182	87	5	2	55	69	10.6	3.11	90	.246	.299	7	.109	-4	-4	-7	5	-0.9
1920	StL-N	20	12	.625	39	37	20	5	1	270	256	94	7	6	80	90	11.4	2.53	118	.253	.312	10	.114	-6	18	14	0	1.0
1921	StL-N	15	6	**.714**	32	29	13	1	1	208^2	224	85	3	4	37	83	11.4	**2.59**	142	.278	.313	10	.143	-3	28	26	2	2.3
1922	StL-N	11	13	.458	37	29	8	2	2	180^1	222	127	12	3	69	73	14.7	5.54	70	.311	.374	7	.130	-3	-29	-36	0	-4.1
1923	StL-N	8	13	.381	30	26	7	2	0	185	199	85	4	3	69	53	13.2	3.26	120	.279	.346	3	.045	-9	15	14	3	0.8
1924	StL-N	2	1	.667	11	1	0	0	3	22	25	8	0	0	14	7	16.0	3.27	116	.313	.415	1	.200	-0	1	1	1	0.3
	Bro-N	11	5	.688	21	16	8	2	0	149^1	130	58	8	3	35	32	10.1	3.07	122	.239	.289	10	.179	-0	13	12	3	1.4
	Yr	13	6	.684	32	17	8	2	3	171^1	155	66	8	3	49	39	10.9	3.10	121	.249	.307	11	.180	-1	15	13	3	1.7
1927	Bro-N	11	8	.579	27	20	6	1	0	145	153	73	6	3	40	32	12.2	3.48	114	.271	.322	6	.128	-3	7	8	1	0.8
1928	Bro-N	3	8	.273	28	12	4	1	3	99^1	104	51	1	5	35	12	13.0	3.26	122	.271	.340	3	.111	-2	8	8	3	0.9
1929	StL-N	1	2	.333	3	2	0	0	0	9	17	15	1	0	5	3	22.0	12.00	39	.415	.478	0	.000	0	-7	-7	-0	-1.1
Total	16	169	157	.518	453	369	162	34	16	2782^2	2676	1184	71	65	851	1014	11.6	2.98	107	.259	.319	115	.127	-42	80	65	43	5.8

● WALT DOANE Doane, Walter Rudolph b: 3/12/1887, Bellevue, Idaho d: 10/19/35, W.Brandywine Township, Pa. BL/TR, 6', 165 lbs. Deb: 9/20/09 ♦

YEAR	TM/L	W	L	PCT	G	GS	CG	SH	SV	IP	H	R	HR	HB	BB	SO	RAT	ERA	ERA+	OAV	OOB	BH	AVG	PB	PR	PR+	PD	TPI
1909	Cle-A	0	1	.000	1	1	0	0	0	5	10	7	0	0	1	2	19.8	5.40	47	.400	.423	1	.111	-0	-2	-2	-0	-0.3
1910	Cle-A	0	0	—	6	0	0	0	0	17^2	31	21	1	1	8	7	20.4	5.60	46	.413	.476	2	.286	1	-6	-6	-1	-0.3
Total	2	0	1	.000	7	1	0	0	0	22^2	41	28	1	1	9	9	20.3	5.56	46	.410	.464	3	.188	1	-8	-7	-1	-0.6

● JOHN DOBB Dobb, John Kenneth "Lefty" b: 11/15/01, Muskegon, Mich. d: 7/31/91, Muskegon, Mich. BR/TL, 6'2", 180 lbs. Deb: 8/13/24

YEAR	TM/L	W	L	PCT	G	GS	CG	SH	SV	IP	H	R	HR	HB	BB	SO	RAT	ERA	ERA+	OAV	OOB	BH	AVG	PB	PR	PR+	PD	TPI
1924	Chi-A	0	0	—	2	0	0	0	0	2	4	2	0	0	1	2	22.5	9.00	46	.400	.455	0	—	0	-1	-1	-0	-0.1

● RAY DOBENS Dobens, Raymond Joseph "Lefty" b: 7/28/06, Nashua, N.H. d: 4/21/80, Stuart, Fla. BL/TL, 5'8", 175 lbs. Deb: 7/7/29

YEAR	TM/L	W	L	PCT	G	GS	CG	SH	SV	IP	H	R	HR	HB	BB	SO	RAT	ERA	ERA+	OAV	OOB	BH	AVG	PB	PR	PR+	PD	TPI
1929	Bos-A	0	0	—	11	1	0	0	0	28^1	32	12	0	1	9	4	13.3	3.81	112	.302	.362	3	.375	1	1	1	-1	0.0

● JESS DOBERNIC Dobernic, Andrew Joseph b: 11/20/17, Mt.Olive, Ill. d: 7/16/98, St.Louis, Mo. BR/TR, 5'10", 170 lbs. Deb: 7/2/39

YEAR	TM/L	W	L	PCT	G	GS	CG	SH	SV	IP	H	R	HR	HB	BB	SO	RAT	ERA	ERA+	OAV	OOB	BH	AVG	PB	PR	PR+	PD	TPI
1939	Chi-A	0	1	.000	4	0	0	0	0	3^1	3	6	0	1	6	1	27.0	13.50	35	.231	.500	0	.000	-0	-3	-3	0	-0.6
1948	Chi-N	7	2	.778	54	0	0	0	1	85^2	67	33	8	1	40	48	11.3	3.15	124	.213	.303	2	.200	-0	8	7	-2	0.5
1949	Chi-N	0	0	—	4	0	0	0	0	4	9	9	2	0	4	0	29.3	20.25	20	.450	.542	0	—	0	-7	-7	-0	-0.4
	Cin-N	0	0	—	14	0	0	0	0	19^1	28	22	7	0	16	6	20.5	9.78	43	.329	.436	0	.000	0	-12	-12	0	-0.6
	Yr	0	0	—	18	0	0	0	0	23^1	37	31	9	0	20	6	22.0	11.57	36	.352	.456	0	.000	0	-20	-19	-0	-1.0
Total	3	7	3	.700	76	0	0	0	1	112^1	107	70	17	2	66	55	14.0	5.21	76	.247	.349	2	.154	-0	-15	-15	-2	-1.1

● CHUCK DOBSON Dobson, Charles Thomas b: 1/10/44, Kansas City, Mo. BR/TR, 6'4", 200 lbs. Deb: 4/19/66

YEAR	TM/L	W	L	PCT	G	GS	CG	SH	SV	IP	H	R	HR	HB	BB	SO	RAT	ERA	ERA+	OAV	OOB	BH	AVG	PB	PR	PR+	PD	TPI
1966	KC-A	4	6	.400	14	14	1	0	0	83^2	71	41	7	2	50	61	13.2	4.09	83	.234	.346	3	.115	-1	-6	-6	1	-0.7
1967	KC-A	10	10	.500	32	29	4	1	0	197^2	172	83	17	3	75	110	11.4	3.69	86	.233	.306	13	.181	0	-10	-11	-0	-1.1
1968	Oak-A	12	14	.462	35	34	11	3	0	225^1	197	91	20	4	80	168	11.2	3.00	94	.234	.303	15	.200	2	-0	-5	2	-0.1
1969	Oak-A	15	13	.536	35	35	11	1	0	235^1	244	111	16	1	80	137	12.4	3.86	89	.270	.330	8	.101	-3	-6	-12	-2	-1.8
1970	Oak-A	16	15	.516	41	40	13	**5**	0	267	230	122	32	5	92	149	11.0	3.74	95	.229	.297	11	.118	-3	-1	-6	-2	-1.2
1971	Oak-A	15	5	.750	30	30	7	1	0	189	185	84	24	1	71	100	12.2	3.81	88	.259	.327	13	.197	3	-7	-10	0	-0.7
1973	Oak-A	0	1	.000	1	1	0	0	0	2^1	6	4	1	0	2	3	30.9	7.71	46	.429	.500	0	—	0	-1	-1	0	-0.2
1974	Cal-A	2	3	.400	5	5	2	0	0	30	39	19	3	0	13	16	15.6	5.70	60	.315	.380	0	—	0	-7	-8	-0	-1.1
1975	Cal-A	0	2	.000	9	2	0	0	0	28	30	26	5	2	13	14	14.5	6.75	53	.275	.363	0	—	0	-9	-11	-1	-0.7
Total	9	74	69	.517	202	190	49	11	0	1258^1	1174	581	125	18	476	758	11.9	3.78	87	.247	.318	63	.153	-2	-48	-70	-1	-7.6

● JOE DOBSON Dobson, Joseph Gordon "Burrhead" b: 1/20/17, Durant, Okla. d: 6/23/94, Jacksonville, Fla. BR/TR, 6'2", 197 lbs. Deb: 4/26/39

YEAR	TM/L	W	L	PCT	G	GS	CG	SH	SV	IP	H	R	HR	HB	BB	SO	RAT	ERA	ERA+	OAV	OOB	BH	AVG	PB	PR	PR+	PD	TPI
1939	Cle-A	2	3	.400	35	3	0	0	1	78	87	56	3	1	51	27	16.0	5.88	75	.290	.395	1	.056	-2	-11	-13	1	-0.9
1940	Cle-A	3	7	.300	40	7	2	1	3	100	101	60	8	0	48	57	13.4	4.95	85	.268	.351	3	.125	-1	-6	-8	-0	-0.8
1941	Bos-A	12	5	.706	27	18	7	1	0	134^1	136	70	8	2	67	69	13.7	4.49	93	.262	.349	7	.149	0	-5	-5	-2	-0.7
1942	Bos-A	11	9	.550	30	23	10	3	0	182^2	155	73	9	2	68	72	11.1	3.30	113	.231	.303	10	.145	-1	7	9	2	0.9
1943	Bos-A	7	11	.389	25	20	9	3	0	164^1	144	63	4	0	57	63	11.0	3.12	106	.239	.305	5	.096	-3	3	3	-2	-0.2
1946	*Bos-A	13	7	.650	32	24	9	1	0	166^2	148	72	11	1	68	91	11.7	3.24	113	.234	.309	5	.100	-2	5	8	2	0.8
1947	Bos-A	18	8	.692	33	31	15	1	1	228^2	203	84	15	1	73	110	10.9	2.95	132	.238	**.299**	16	.208	1	19	23	-2	2.4
1948	Bos-A☆	16	10	.615	38	32	16	5	2	245^1	237	115	14	1	92	116	12.1	3.56	123	.253	.320	17	.202	1	20	22	-1	2.1
1949	Bos-A	14	12	.538	33	27	12	2	2	212^2	219	103	12	2	97	87	13.5	3.85	113	.269	.348	10	.147	-1	8	12	-1	1.0
1950	Bos-A	15	10	.600	39	27	12	1	4	206^2	217	103	15	0	81	81	13.0	4.18	117	.275	.343	15	.214	1	9	15	1	1.9
1951	Chi-A	7	6	.538	28	21	6	0	3	146^2	136	68	17	0	51	67	11.5	3.62	111	.248	.312	3	.065	-6	8	7	0	0.0
1952	Chi-A	14	10	.583	29	25	11	3	1	200^2	164	66	11	0	60	101	10.0	2.51	145	.222	.280	12	.190	0	26	26	-2	2.8
1953	Chi-A	5	5	.500	23	15	3	1	1	100^2	96	46	10	0	37	50	11.9	3.67	110	.249	.314	2	.069	-2	4	4	-1	0.1
1954	Bos-A	0	0	—	2	0	0	0	0	2^2	5	2	0	0	1	1	20.3	6.75	61	.385	.429	0	—	0	-1	-1	0	0.0
Total	14	137	103	.571	414	273	112	22	18	2170	2048	981	137	10	851	992	12.1	3.62	112	.250	.322	106	.152	-15	86	103	-5	9.4

YEAR TM/L	W	L	PCT	G	GS	CG	SH	SV	IP	H	R	HR	HB	BB	SO	RAT	ERA	ERA+	OAV	OOB	BH	AVG	PB	PR	PR+	PD	TPI
● PAT DOBSON Dobson, Patrick Edward b: 2/12/42, Depew, N.Y. BR/TR, 6'3", 190 lbs. Deb: 5/31/67 C																											
1967 Det-A	1	2	.333	28	1	0	0	0	49^1	38	20	6	2	27	34	12.2	2.92	112	.216	.327	0	.000	-1	2	2	-1	0.0
1968 *Det-A	5	8	.385	47	10	2	1	7	125	89	39	13	2	48	93	10.0	2.66	113	.200	.281	4	.143	0	4	5	1	0.7
1969 Det-A	5	10	.333	49	9	1	0	9	105	100	48	10	1	39	64	12.0	3.60	104	.253	.322	2	.091	-1	0	2	0	0.1
1970 SD-N	14	15	.483	40	34	8	1	1	251	257	126	28	4	78	185	12.2	3.76	106	.265	.322	10	.141	-0	8	6	-0	0.6
1971 *Bal-A	20	8	.714	38	37	18	4	1	282^1	248	104	24	2	63	187	10.0	2.90	116	.235	.279	10	.110	-3	18	15	-1	1.0
1972 Bal-A☆	16	18	.471	38	36	13	3	0	268^1	220	89	13	4	69	161	9.8	2.65	116	.224	.278	12	.141	-2	13	13	-2	1.3
1973 Atl-N	3	7	.300	12	10	1	1	0	57^2	73	33	1	1	19	23	14.5	4.99	79	.315	.369	1	.067	-1	-8	-6	0	-1.1
NY-A	9	8	.529	22	21	6	1	0	142^1	150	72	22	2	34	70	11.8	4.17	88	.266	.311	0	—	0	-6	-8	0	-0.9
1974 NY-A	19	15	.559	39	39	12	2	0	281	282	111	23	4	75	157	11.6	3.07	115	.262	.312	0	—	0	17	15	-1	1.6
1975 NY-A	11	14	.440	33	30	7	1	0	207^2	205	105	21	1	83	129	12.5	4.07	91	.261	.333	0	—	0	-7	-9	-0	-1.0
1976 Cle-A	16	12	.571	35	35	6	0	0	217^1	226	98	13	2	65	117	12.1	3.48	100	.272	.327	0	—	0	1	0	-1	0.0
1977 Cle-A	3	12	.200	33	17	0	0	1	133^1	155	94	23	1	65	81	14.9	6.14	64	.299	.378	0	—	0	-31	-33	0	-3.2
Total 11	122	129	.486	414	279	74	14	19	2120^1	2043	939	197	26	665	1301	11.6	3.54	100	.255	.314	39	.123	-8	12	1	-3	-0.9
● GEORGE DOCKINS Dockins, George Woodrow "Lefty" b: 5/5/17, Clyde, Kan. d: 1/22/97, Clyde, Kan. BL/TL, 6', 175 lbs. Deb: 5/5/45																											
1945 StL-N	8	6	.571	31	12	5	2	0	126^1	132	53	4	0	38	33	12.1	3.21	117	.269	.321	6	.176	1	8	8	-1	0.8
1947 Bro-N	0	0	—	4	0	0	0	0	5^1	10	7	2	0	2	1	20.3	11.81	35	.400	.444	0	.000	-0	-5	-4	0	-0.2
Total 2	8	6	.571	35	12	5	2	0	131^2	142	60	6	0	40	34	12.4	3.55	106	.275	.327	6	.171	1	4	3	-0	0.6
● ROBERT DODD Dodd, Robert Wayne b: 3/14/73, Kansas City, Kan. BL/TL, 6'3", 195 lbs. Deb: 5/28/98																											
1998 Phi-N	1	0	1.000	4	0	0	0	0	5	7	6	1	1	1	4	16.2	7.20	60	.333	.391	0	—	0	-2	-2	-0	-0.3
● SAM DODGE Dodge, Samuel Edward b: 12/9/1889, Neath, Pa. d: 4/5/66, Utica, N.Y. BR/TR, 6'1", 170 lbs. Deb: 9/24/21																											
1921 Bos-A	0	0	—	1	0	0	0	0	1	1	1	0	0	1	0	18.0	9.00	47	.500	.667	0	—	0	-1	-1	-0	0.0
1922 Bos-A	0	0	—	3	0	0	0	0	6	11	6	0	0	3	3	21.0	4.50	91	.379	.438	0	.000	-0	-0	-0	0	0.0
Total 2	0	0	—	4	0	0	0	0	7	12	7	0	0	4	3	20.6	5.14	80	.387	.457	0	.000	-0	-1	-1	0	0.0
● FRED DOE Doe, Alfred George "Count" b: 4/18/1864, Rockport, Mass. d: 10/4/38, Quincy, Mass. BR/TR, 5'10", 165 lbs. Deb: 8/23/1890																											
1890 Buf-P	0	1	.000	1	1	1	0	0	6	10	10	0	0	7	2	25.5	12.00	34	.357	.486	0	.000	-0	-5	-5	0	-0.5
Pit-P	0	0	—	1	0	0	0	0	4	4	2	0	0	2	2	13.5	4.50	87	.250	.333	1	.500	0	-0	-0	-0	0.0
Yr	0	1	.000	2	1	1	0	0	10	14	12	0	0	9	4	20.7	9.00	45	.318	.434	1	.250	-0	-5	-6	-0	-0.5
● ED DOHENY Doheny, Edwin Richard b: 11/24/1873, Northfield, Vt. d: 12/29/16, Medfield, Mass. BL/TL, 5'10.5", 165 lbs. Deb: 9/16/1895																											
1895 NY-N	0	3	.000	3	3	3	0	0	25^2	37	29	2	3	19	9	20.7	6.66	70	.333	.444	1	.100	-1	-5	-6	-0	-0.5
1896 NY-N	6	7	.462	17	15	9	0	0	108^1	112	78	3	6	59	39	14.7	4.49	94	.265	.363	6	.150	-2	-1	-3	-0	-0.5
1897 NY-N	4	4	.500	10	10	10	0	0	85	69	45	0	8	45	37	12.9	2.12	196	.220	.333	7	.200	-1	21	20	3	1.7
1898 NY-N	7	19	.269	28	27	23	0	0	213	238	164	1	20	101	96	15.2	3.68	95	.280	.370	14	.163	-1	-2	-5	3	-0.3
1899 NY-N	14	17	.452	36	34	31	1	0	277^2	291	207	2	37	158	120	15.8	4.38	86	.269	.381	27	.233	-1	-16	-20	5	-1.4
1900 NY-N	4	14	.222	20	18	12	0	0	133^2	148	134	2	22	96	44	17.9	5.45	66	.280	.411	12	.222	-0	-26	-28	2	-2.8
1901 NY-N	2	5	.286	10	6	6	0	0	74	88	53	1	6	17	36	13.5	4.50	73	.293	.344	10	.345	3	-10	-10	0	-0.5
Pit-N	6	2	.750	11	10	6	1	0	76^2	68	36	1	5	22	28	11.2	2.00	164	.236	.302	3	.115	0	11	11	-2	0.9
Yr	8	7	.533	21	16	12	1	0	150^2	156	89	2	11	39	64	12.3	3.23	102	.265	.323	13	.236	4	2	1	-1	0.4
1902 Pit-N	16	4	.800	22	21	19	2	0	188^1	161	68	0	15	61	88	11.3	2.53	108	.231	.307	12	.156	-2	5	4	-1	0.1
1903 Pit-N	16	8	.667	27	25	22	2	2	222^2	209	122	1	19	89	75	12.8	3.19	101	.252	.338	19	.209	-0	2	1	5	0.5
Total 9	75	83	.475	184	169	141	6	2	1405	1421	936	13	141	667	572	14.3	3.73	94	.262	.358	111	.197	-4	-21	-35	15	-2.8
● JOHN DOHERTY Doherty, John Harold b: 6/11/67, New York, N.Y. BR/TR, 6'4", 210 lbs. Deb: 4/8/92																											
1992 Det-A	7	4	.636	47	11	0	0	3	116	131	61	4	4	25	37	12.4	3.88	102	.287	.329	0	—	0	1	1	1	0.2
1993 Det-A	14	11	.560	32	31	3	2	0	184^2	205	104	19	5	48	63	12.6	4.44	97	.286	.335	0	—	0	-2	-3	-2	-0.5
1994 Det-A	6	7	.462	18	17	2	0	0	101^1	139	75	13	3	26	28	14.9	6.48	75	.337	.380	0	—	0	-19	-18	2	-1.7
1995 Det-A	5	9	.357	48	2	0	0	6	113	130	66	10	6	37	46	13.8	5.10	93	.288	.350	0	—	0	-5	-4	1	-0.4
1996 Bos-A	0	0	—	3	0	0	0	0	6^1	8	10	1	1	4	3	18.5	5.68	89	.276	.382	0	—	0	-0	-0	1	0.0
Total 5	32	31	.508	148	61	5	2	9	521^1	613	316	47	19	140	177	13.3	4.87	91	.296	.347	0	—	0	-25	-25	3	-2.4
● JOHN DOLAN Dolan, John b: 9/12/1867, Newport, Ky. d: 5/8/48, Springfield, Ohio TR, 5'10", 170 lbs. Deb: 9/5/1890																											
1890 Cin-N	1	1	.500	2	2	2	0	0	18	17	13	3	1	10	9	14.0	4.50	79	.243	.346	1	.125	-1	-2	-2	-0	-0.2
1891 Col-a	12	11	.522	27	24	19	0	0	203^1	216	131	8	0	84	68	13.3	4.16	83	.263	.331	7	.090	-4	-10	-17	-2	-2.0
1892 Was-N	2	2	.500	5	4	3	0	0	37	39	26	0	1	15	8	13.4	4.38	74	.260	.331	3	.231	0	-4	-5	-1	-0.4
1893 StL-N	0	1	.000	3	1	1	0	1	17^1	26	22	1	1	7	1	17.7	4.15	114	.338	.400	1	.143	0	1	1	-0	0.0
1895 Chi-N	0	1	.000	2	2	1	0	0	11	16	12	0	1	6	1	18.8	6.55	78	.333	.418	0	.000	-0	-2	-2	0	-0.1
Total 5	15	16	.484	39	33	26	0	1	286^2	314	204	12	4	122	87	13.8	4.30	83	.269	.341	12	.110	-5	-18	-25	-3	-2.7
● COZY DOLAN Dolan, Patrick Henry b: 12/3/1872, Cambridge, Mass. d: 3/29/07, Louisville, Ky. BL/TL, 5'10", 160 lbs. Deb: 4/26/1895 ◆																											
1895 Bos-N	11	7	.611	25	21	18	3	1	198^1	215	142	11	14	67	47	13.4	4.27	120	.272	.340	20	.241	-1	11	17	4	1.4
1896 Bos-N	1	4	.200	6	5	3	0	0	41	55	44	1	3	27	14	18.7	4.83	94	.318	.419	2	.143	-1	-2	-1	-0	-0.3
1905 Bos-N	0	1	.000	2	0	0	0	0	4	7	5	2	0	1	1	18.0	9.00	34	.368	.400	119	.275	1	-3	-3	-0	-0.5
1906 Bos-N	0	1	.000	2	0	0	0	0	12	12	6	1	0	6	7	13.5	4.50	60	.300	.391	136	.248	0	-2	-2	-1	-0.2
Total 4	12	13	.480	35	26	21	3	1	255^1	289	197	15	17	101	69	14.3	4.44	109	.283	.357	855	.269	-2	4	11	3	0.4
● TOM DOLAN Dolan, Thomas J. b: 1/10/1859, New York, N.Y. d: 1/16/13, St.Louis, Mo. BR/TR, Deb: 9/30/1879 ◆																											
1883 StL-a	0	0	—	1	0	0	0	0	4	4	3	0		0	0	9.0	4.50	77	.250	.250	63	.214	-0	-1	-0	0	0.0
● ART DOLL Doll, Arthur James "Moose" b: 5/7/13, Chicago, Ill. d: 4/28/78, Calumet City, Ill. BR/TR, 6'1", 190 lbs. Deb: 9/21/35 ◆																											
1936 Bos-N	0	1	.000	1	1	0	0	0	8	11	3	1	1	2	2	15.8	3.38	114	.355	.412	0	.000	-0	1	0	-0	0.0
1938 Bos-N	0	0	—	3	0	0	0	0	4	4	1	0	0	3	1	15.8	2.25	153	.286	.412	1	1.000	1	1	1	0	0.1
Total 2	0	1	.000	4	1	0	0	0	12	15	4	1	1	5	3	15.8	3.00	123	.333	.412	2	.154	0	1	1	0	0.1
● RED DONAHUE Donahue, Francis Rostell b: 1/23/1873, Waterbury, Conn. d: 8/25/13, Philadelphia, Pa. BR/TR, 6', 187 lbs. Deb: 5/6/1893																											
1893 NY-N	0	0	—	2	0	0	0	1	5	8	10	1	2	3	1	23.4	9.00	52	.348	.464	0	.000	-0	-2	-2	0	-0.1
1895 StL-N	0	1	.000	1	1	1	0	0	8	9	6	2	1	3	2	14.6	6.75	72	.281	.361	0	.000	-1	-2	-2	0	-0.2
1896 StL-N	7	24	.226	32	32	28	0	0	267	376	235	6	13	98	70	16.4	5.80	75	.329	.389	17	.159	-8	-43	-43	-1	-4.3
1897 StL-N	10	35	.222	46	42	**38**	1	1	348	485	306	16	22	106	64	15.9	6.13	72	.327	.380	33	.213	-3	-70	-66	5	-6.0
1898 Phi-N	16	17	.485	35	35	33	1	0	284^1	327	165	7	14	80	57	13.3	3.55	97	.286	.340	16	.143	-7	2	-4	4	-0.7
1899 Phi-N	21	8	.724	35	31	27	4	0	279	292	147	6	11	63	51	11.8	3.39	109	.269	.316	20	.180	-5	14	10	1	0.6
1900 Phi-N	15	10	.600	32	24	21	2	0	240	299	144	6	9	50	41	13.4	3.60	100	.304	.344	20	.222	-1	3	0	-1	-0.2
1901 Phi-N	20	13	.606	34	33	33	1	1	295^1	299	111	2	9	59	88	11.2	2.59	131	.261	.302	11	.097	-9	24	26	-2	1.5
1902 StL-A	22	11	.667	35	34	33	2	0	316^1	322	134	7	8	65	63	11.2	2.76	128	.264	.306	11	.093	-9	29	27	7	2.3
1903 StL-A	8	7	.533	16	15	14	0	0	131	145	59	0	0	22	51	11.5	2.75	106	.279	.309	8	.157	-2	3	2	0	0.1
Cle-A	7	9	.438	16	15	14	4	0	136^2	142	61	3	6	12	45	10.5	2.44	117	.267	.291	8	.151	-1	8	7	1	0.7
Yr	15	16	.484	32	30	28	4	0	267^2	287	120	3	6	34	96	11.0	2.59	111	.273	.300	16	.154	-3	11	9	2	0.8
1904 Cle-A	19	14	.576	35	32	30	6	0	277	281	96	2	5	49	127	10.9	2.40	105	.264	.299	17	.168	-1	6	4	2	0.6
1905 Cle-A	6	12	.333	20	18	14	1	0	137^2	132	68	2	5	25	45	10.6	3.40	77	.254	.295	4	.075	-5	-11	-12	1	-1.8
1906 Det-A	13	14	.481	28	28	26	3	0	241	260	96	1	8	54	82	12.0	2.73	101	.278	.323	10	.123	-4	-1	1	-0	-0.3
Total 13	164	175	.484	367	340	312	25	3	2966^1	3377	1638	61	113	689	787	12.7	3.61	96	.286	.331	175	.152	-56	-40	-53	18	-7.8
● DEACON DONAHUE Donahue, John Stephen Michael b: 6/23/20, Chicago, Ill. BR/TR, 6', 180 lbs. Deb: 9/16/43																											
1943 Phi-N	0	0	—	2	0	0	0	0	4	4	3	0	1	1	1	13.5	4.50	75	.235	.316	0	—	0	-0	-1	0	0.0
1944 Phi-N	0	2	.000	6	0	0	0	0	9^1	18	8	0	0	2	2	19.3	7.71	47	.429	.455	0	.000	-0	-4	-4	0	-0.8
Total 2	0	2	.000	8	0	0	0	0	13^1	22	11	0	1	3	3	17.6	6.75	52	.373	.413	0	.000	-0	-5	-5	0	-0.8

YEAR TM/L	W	L	PCT	G	GS	CG	SH	SV	IP	H	R	HR	HB	BB	SO	RAT	ERA	ERA+	OAV	OOB	BH	AVG	PB	PR	PR+	PD	TPI
● ATLEY DONALD	Donald, Richard Atley "Swampy" b: 8/19/10, Morton, Miss. d: 10/19/92, West Monroe, La. BL/TR, 6′1″, 186 lbs. Deb: 4/21/38																										
1938 NY-A	0	1	.000	2	2	0	0	0	12	7	8	0	1	14	6	16.5	5.25	86	.175	.400	1	.167	-0	-1	-1	0	-0.1
1939 NY-A	13	3	.813	24	20	11	2	1	153	144	74	12	0	60	55	12.0	3.71	118	.247	.317	15	.250	3	16	12	-1	1.2
1940 NY-A	8	3	.727	24	11	6	1	0	118^2	113	49	11	2	59	60	13.2	3.03	133	.249	.339	6	.146	-2	18	14	-3	0.7
1941 *NY-A	9	5	.643	22	20	10	0	0	159	141	69	11	3	69	71	12.1	3.57	110	.237	.320	5	.081	-4	10	7	-0	0.1
1942 *NY-A	11	3	.786	20	19	10	1	0	147^2	133	58	6	0	45	53	10.8	3.11	111	.239	.296	9	.148	-1	9	6	-2	0.1
1943 NY-A	6	4	.600	22	15	2	0	0	119^1	134	69	10	0	38	57	13.0	4.60	70	.276	.329	6	.128	-2	-17	-19	-2	-1.9
1944 NY-A	13	10	.565	30	19	9	0	0	159	173	77	13	2	59	48	13.2	3.34	104	.280	.345	10	.182	-0	2	3	-1	0.2
1945 NY-A	5	4	.556	9	9	6	2	0	63^2	62	29	3	0	25	19	12.3	2.97	117	.248	.316	5	.208	0	3	3	-2	0.3
Total 8	65	33	.663	153	115	54	6	1	932^1	907	433	66	8	369	369	12.4	3.52	107	.253	.325	57	.160	-7	39	25	-11	0.6
● ED DONALDS	Donalds, Edward Alexander "Erston" b: 6/22/1885, Bidwell, Ohio d: 7/3/50, Columbus, Ohio BR/TR, 5′11″, 180 lbs. Deb: 9/1/12																										
1912 Cin-N	1	0	1.000	1	0	0	0	0	4	7	2	0	0	0	1	15.8	4.50	75	.438	.438	0	.000	-0	-0	-1	0	-0.1
● MIKE DONLIN	Donlin, Michael Joseph "Turkey Mike" b: 5/30/1878, Peoria, Ill. d: 9/24/33, Hollywood, Cal. BL/TL, 5′9″, 170 lbs. Deb: 7/19/1899 ◆																										
1899 StL-N	0	1	.000	3	1	0	0	0	15^1	15	15	1	1	14	6	17.6	7.63	52	.254	.405	86	.323	1	-6	-6	1	-0.1
1902 Cin-N	0	0	—	1	0	0	0	0	1	1	0	0	0	0	0	9.0	0.00	—	.250	.250	41	.287	0	0	0	-0	0.0
Total 2	0	1	.000	4	1	0	0	0	16^1	16	15	1	1	14	6	17.1	7.16	55	.254	.397	1282	.333	1	-6	-6	1	-0.1
● ED DONNELLY	Donnelly, Edward "Big Ed" or "Ned" (b: Edward O'Donnell) b: 7/29/1880, Hampton, N.Y. d: 11/28/57, Rutland, Vt. BR/TR, 6′1″, 205 lbs. Deb: 9/19/11																										
1911 Bos-N	3	2	.600	5	4	4	1	0	36^2	33	15	0	2	9	16	10.8	2.45	156	.236	.291	1	.071	-1	4	5	-0	0.5
1912 Bos-N	5	10	.333	37	18	10	0	0	184^1	225	127	10	5	72	67	14.7	4.35	82	.304	.370	19	.275	3	-19	-15	1	-0.7
Total 2	8	12	.400	42	22	14	1	0	221	258	142	10	7	81	83	14.1	4.03	90	.293	.357	20	.241	1	-15	-10	1	-0.2
● ED DONNELLY	Donnelly, Edward Vincent b: 12/10/32, Allen, Mich. d: 12/25/97, Houston, Tex. BR/TR, 6′, 175 lbs. Deb: 8/1/59																										
1959 Chi-N	1	1	.500	9	0	0	0	0	14^1	18	7	1	0	9	6	17.0	3.14	126	.305	.397	0	—	0	1	1	0	0.2
● FRANK DONNELLY	Donnelly, Franklin Marion b: 10/7/1869, Tamaroa, Ill. d: 2/3/53, Canton, Ill. 5′6″, 180 lbs. Deb: 8/15/1893																										
1893 Chi-N	3	1	.750	7	5	3	0	**2**	42	51	42	1	4	17	6	15.4	5.36	86	.291	.367	8	.444	4	-3	-3	-0	0.0
1894 Chi-N	0	0	—	1	0	0	0	0	4^2	6	8	0	0	8	1	27.0	15.43	36	.316	.519	0	.000	-0	-5	-5	0	-0.1
Total 2	3	1	.750	8	5	3	0	2	46^2	57	50	1	4	25	7	16.6	6.36	74	.294	.386	8	.421	4	-8	-8	0	-0.1
● BLIX DONNELLY	Donnelly, Sylvester Urban b: 1/21/14, Olivia, Minn. d: 6/20/76, Olivia, Minn. BR/TR, 5′10″, 178 lbs. Deb: 5/6/44																										
1944 *StL-N	2	1	.667	27	4	2	1	2	76^1	61	26	2	2	34	45	11.4	2.12	166	.218	.307	1	.063	-1	13	12	1	0.6
1945 StL-N	8	10	.444	31	23	9	4	2	166^1	157	79	10	6	87	76	13.5	3.52	106	.250	.346	7	.130	-2	5	4	-4	-0.2
1946 StL-N	1	2	.333	13	0	0	0	0	13^2	17	7	1	1	10	11	18.4	3.95	87	.347	.467	0	—	0	-1	-1	-0	-0.2
Phi-N	3	4	.429	12	8	2	0	1	76^1	64	31	7	2	24	38	10.6	2.95	116	.220	.284	7	.280	2	4	4	-1	0.5
Yr	4	6	.400	25	8	2	0	1	90	81	38	8	3	34	49	11.8	3.10	111	.238	.313	7	.280	2	3	3	-1	0.3
1947 Phi-N	4	6	.400	38	10	5	1	5	120^2	113	44	6	3	46	31	12.1	2.98	134	.265	.340	2	.063	-2	14	14	-0	0.9
1948 Phi-N	5	7	.417	26	19	8	1	2	131^2	125	65	13	0	49	46	11.9	3.69	107	.261	.330	10	.222	2	4	4	-3	0.3
1949 Phi-N	2	1	.667	23	10	1	0	0	78^1	84	50	7	1	40	36	14.4	5.06	78	.294	.382	4	.174	-1	-9	-10	-2	-0.7
1950 Phi-N	2	4	.333	14	1	0	0	0	21	30	13	5	0	10	10	17.1	4.29	94	.330	.396	1	.200	-0	-0	-1	0	-0.1
1951 Bos-N	0	1	.000	6	0	0	0	0	7^1	8	6	1	1	6	3	18.4	7.36	50	.286	.429	0	.000	-0	-3	-3	0	-0.4
Total 8	27	36	.429	190	75	27	7	12	691^2	659	321	52	16	306	296	12.8	3.49	109	.257	.340	32	.159	-1	27	24	-8	0.7
● JIM DONOHUE	Donohue, James Thomas b: 10/31/38, St.Louis, Mo. BR/TR, 6′4″, 190 lbs. Deb: 4/11/61																										
1961 Det-A	1	1	.500	14	0	0	0	1	20^1	23	10	2	0	15	20	16.8	3.54	116	.287	.400	0	.000	-0	1	1	-0	0.1
LA-A	4	6	.400	38	7	0	0	5	100^1	93	48	16	0	50	79	12.8	4.31	105	.246	.334	4	.148	-1	-3	2	-0	0.1
Yr	5	7	.417	52	7	0	0	6	120^2	116	58	18	0	65	99	13.5	4.18	106	.253	.346	4	.143	-1	-2	3	-1	0.2
1962 LA-A	1	0	1.000	12	1	0	0	0	24^1	24	14	4	2	11	14	13.7	3.70	104	.258	.349	1	.250	0	1	0	-1	0.0
Min-A	0	1	.000	6	1	0	0	1	10^1	12	8	2	0	6	3	15.7	6.97	59	.324	.419	0	.000	-0	-3	-3	1	-0.3
Yr	1	1	.500	18	2	0	0	1	34^2	36	22	6	2	17	17	14.3	4.67	84	.277	.369	1	.167	0	-3	-3	-0	-0.3
Total 2	6	8	.429	70	9	0	0	7	155^1	152	80	24	2	82	116	13.7	4.29	101	.259	.351	5	.147	-1	-5	1	-1	-0.1
● PETE DONOHUE	Donohue, Peter Joseph b: 11/5/1900, Athens, Tex. d: 2/23/88, Ft.Worth, Tex. BR/TR, 6′2″, 185 lbs. Deb: 7/1/21																										
1921 Cin-N	7	6	.538	21	11	7	0	1	118^1	117	48	5	0	26	44	10.9	3.35	107	.263	.304	8	.211	1	6	3	2	0.6
1922 Cin-N	18	9	**.667**	33	30	18	2	1	242	257	110	7	5	43	66	11.3	3.12	128	.276	.312	16	.182	-3	26	24	1	2.2
1923 Cin-N	21	15	.583	42	36	19	2	3	274^1	304	138	3	10	68	84	12.5	3.38	114	.278	.326	24	.250	3	19	15	1	2.1
1924 Cin-N	16	9	.640	35	31	16	3	0	222^1	248	100	9	9	36	72	11.9	3.60	105	.285	.321	14	.192	-0	7	4	-1	0.2
1925 Cin-N	21	14	.600	42	38	**27**	3	2	**301**	310	122	3	2	49	78	10.8	3.08	133	.268	.299	32	.294	7	40	36	-3	4.2
1926 Cin-N	**20**	14	.588	47	36	17	**5**	2	**285^2**	298	133	6	9	39	73	10.9	3.37	109	.268	.298	33	.311	9	14	11	-3	1.7
1927 Cin-N	6	16	.273	33	24	12	1	1	190^2	253	111	3	1	32	48	13.5	4.11	92	.328	.356	16	.250	1	-4	-7	0	-0.6
1928 Cin-N	7	11	.389	23	18	8	0	0	150	180	84	10	3	32	37	12.9	4.74	83	.309	.348	7	.146	-0	-12	-13	1	-1.3
1929 Cin-N	10	13	.435	32	24	7	0	0	177^2	243	123	12	4	51	30	15.1	5.42	84	.331	.377	20	.333	4	-14	-17	0	-1.4
1930 Cin-N	1	3	.250	8	5	2	0	1	34^1	53	24	0	1	13	4	17.6	6.29	77	.363	.419	1	.100	-1	-5	-6	1	-0.5
NY-N	7	6	.538	18	11	4	0	1	86^2	135	65	6	2	18	26	16.1	6.13	77	.360	.392	9	.273	1	-11	-14	-2	-1.7
Yr	8	9	.471	26	16	6	0	2	121	188	89	6	3	31	30	16.5	6.17	77	.361	.400	10	.233	0	-16	-20	-0	-2.2
1931 NY-N	0	1	.000	4	1	0	0	0	11^1	14	7	1	0	4	4	14.3	5.56	66	.311	.367	0	.000	-0	-2	-2	-0	-0.2
Cle-A	0	0	—	2	0	0	0	0	5^1	9	6	1	0	5	4	23.6	8.44	55	.429	.538	0	.000	-0	-2	-2	-0	-0.1
1932 Bos-A	0	1	.000	4	2	0	0	0	12^2	18	11	2	0	6	1	17.1	7.82	57	.340	.407	0	.000	-0	-5	-5	1	-0.3
Total 12	134	118	.532	344	267	137	16	12	2112^1	2439	1082	68	46	422	571	12.4	3.87	103	.293	.330	180	.246	21	56	26	-1	4.9
● LINO DONOSO	Donoso, Lino (Galeta) b: 9/23/22, Havana, Cuba d: 10/13/90, Veracruz, Mexico BL/TL, 5′11″, 160 lbs. Deb: 6/18/55																										
1955 Pit-N	4	6	.400	25	9	3	0	1	95	106	58	16	1	35	38	13.5	5.31	78	.287	.351	5	.185	-1	-13	-12	0	-1.2
1956 Pit-N	0	0	—	3	0	0	0	0	1^2	2	0	0	0	1	1	16.2	0.00	—	.250	.333	0	—	0	1	1	0	0.0
Total 2	4	6	.400	28	9	3	0	1	96^2	108	58	16	1	36	39	13.5	5.21	79	.286	.350	5	.185	-1	-13	-12	0	-1.2
● DICK DONOVAN	Donovan, Richard Edward b: 12/7/27, Boston, Mass. d: 1/6/97, Weymouth, Mass. BL/TR, 6′3″, 205 lbs. Deb: 4/24/50																										
1950 Bos-N	0	2	.000	10	3	0	0	0	29^2	28	28	4	2	34	9	19.4	8.19	47	.255	.438	1	.167	1	-13	-15	-0	-0.8
1951 Bos-N	0	0	—	8	2	0	0	0	13^2	17	11	0	0	11	4	18.4	5.27	70	.298	.412	1	.333	1	-2	-3	0	0.0
1952 Bos-N	0	2	.000	7	2	0	0	1	13	18	10	1	2	12	6	22.2	5.54	65	.346	.485	0	.000	-0	-3	-3	1	-0.4
1954 Det-A	0	0	—	2	0	0	0	0	6	9	7	1	0	5	2	21.0	10.50	35	.360	.467	0	.000	-0	-5	-5	-0	-0.2
1955 Chi-A☆	15	9	.625	29	24	11	5	0	187	186	77	17	3	48	88	11.4	3.32	119	.261	.311	17	.224	5	13	13	1	2.1
1956 Chi-A	12	10	.545	34	31	14	3	0	234^2	212	99	22	6	59	120	10.6	3.64	113	.240	.292	20	.222	8	13	12	2	1.9
1957 Chi-A	16	6	**.727**	28	28	**16**	2	0	220^2	203	76	17	8	45	88	10.4	2.77	135	.247	.293	12	.145	2	25	24	0	2.5
1958 Chi-A	15	14	.517	34	34	16	4	0	248	240	92	23	7	53	127	10.9	3.01	121	.251	.295	9	.112	-1	21	18	-1	1.7
1959 *Chi-A	9	10	.474	31	29	5	1	0	179^2	171	84	15	5	58	71	11.7	3.66	103	.247	.310	8	.131	1	4	2	-2	0.1
1960 Chi-A	6	1	.857	33	8	0	0	3	78^2	87	49	13	0	25	30	12.8	5.38	70	.283	.337	3	.130	-0	-13	-14	1	-1.2
1961 Was-A★	10	10	.500	23	22	11	2	0	168^2	138	60	10	3	35	62	**9.4**	**2.40**	**167**	.224	**.269**	10	.179	2	30	**30**	-1	3.7
1962 Cle-A★	20	10	.667	34	34	16	**5**	0	250^2	255	109	23	2	47	94	10.9	3.59	108	.263	.299	16	.180	6	11	8	-1	1.4
1963 Cle-A	11	13	.458	30	30	7	3	0	206	211	106	27	5	28	84	10.7	4.24	85	.265	.295	9	.130	-1	-14	-14	-1	-1.7
1964 Cle-A	7	9	.438	30	23	5	0	1	158^1	181	86	19	2	29	83	12.1	4.55	79	.290	.324	7	.146	3	-16	-17	1	-1.2
1965 Cle-A	1	3	.250	12	3	0	0	0	22^2	32	15	6	0	6	12	15.1	5.96	58	.333	.373	0	.000	-1	-6	-6	-0	-1.1
Total 15	122	99	.552	345	273	101	25	5	2017^1	1988	909	198	45	495	880	11.3	3.67	104	.258	.306	113	.163	24	45	31	-0	6.8
● TOM DONOVAN	Donovan, Thomas Joseph b: 1/1/1873, West Troy, N.Y. d: 3/25/33, Watervliet, N.Y. BR/TR, 6′2″, 168 lbs. Deb: 9/10/01 F◆																										
1901 Cle-A	0	0	—	1	0	0	0	0	7	16	11	0	2	3	0	27.0	5.14	69	.444	.512	18	.254	0	-1	-1	0	-0.1
● BILL DONOVAN	Donovan, Willard Earl b: 7/6/16, Maywood, Ill. d: 9/25/97, Maywood, Ill. BB/TL, 6′2″, 198 lbs. Deb: 4/19/42																										
1942 Bos-N	3	6	.333	31	10	2	0	0	89^1	97	43	2	0	32	23	13.0	3.43	97	.283	.344	6	.240	1	-1	-1	2	0.3

YEAR	TM/L	W	L	PCT	G	GS	CG	SH	SV	IP	H	R	HR	HB	BB	SO	RAT	ERA	ERA+	OAV	OOB	BH	AVG	PB	PR	PR+	PD	TPI
1943	Bos-N	1	0	1.000	7	0	0	0	0	14^{2}	17	4	0	0	9	1	16.0	1.84	185	.304	.400	1	.333	0	3	3	1	0.3
Total	2	4	6	.400	38	10	2	0	0	104	114	47	2	0	41	24	13.4	3.20	105	.286	.352	7	.250	1	1	2	3	0.6
● **BILL DONOVAN**	Donovan, William Edward "Wild Bill" b: 10/13/1876, Lawrence, Mass. d: 12/9/23, Forsyth, N.Y. BR/TR, 5'11", 190 lbs. Deb: 4/22/1898 MC♦																											
1898	Was-N	1	6	.143	17	7	6	0	0	88	88	74	0	7	69	36	16.8	4.30	85	.259	.394	17	.165	-1	-7	-6	-0	-0.5
1899	Bro-N	1	2	.333	5	2	2	0	1	25	35	22	0	0	13	11	17.3	4.32	91	.330	.403	3	.231	-0	-1	-1	-0	-0.1
1900	Bro-N	1	2	.333	5	4	2	0	0	31	36	23	0	3	18	13	16.5	6.68	58	.290	.393	0	.000	-2	-10	-9	1	-0.8
1901	Bro-N	**25**	15	.625	**45**	38	36	2	**3**	351	324	151	1	8	152	226	12.4	2.77	121	.244	.325	23	.170	-1	22	23	-1	2.1
1902	Bro-N	17	15	.531	35	33	30	4	1	297^{2}	250	122	1	7	111	170	11.1	2.78	99	.228	.303	28	.174	-0	0	-0	1	0.0
1903	Det-A	17	16	.515	35	34	**34**	4	0	307	247	104	3	5	95	187	10.2	2.29	127	.220	.284	30	.242	4	23	22	-3	2.4
1904	Det-A	16	16	.500	34	34	30	3	0	293	251	111	5	10	94	137	10.9	2.46	104	.232	.300	38	.271	5	5	3	0	1.0
1905	Det-A	18	15	.545	34	32	27	5	0	280^{2}	236	111	2	10	101	135	11.1	2.60	105	.230	.305	25	.192	1	2	4	-3	0.3
1906	Det-A	9	15	.375	25	25	22	0	0	211^{2}	221	92	4	8	72	85	12.8	3.15	88	.272	.337	11	.121	-5	-11	-9	-0	-1.5
1907	*Det-A	25	4	**.862**	32	28	27	3	1	271	222	96	3	8	82	123	10.4	2.19	119	.226	.291	29	.266	7	11	12	-6	1.5
1908	*Det-A	18	7	.720	29	28	25	6	0	242^{2}	210	78	2	6	53	141	10.0	2.08	116	.231	.278	13	.159	0	9	9	-6	0.2
1909	*Det-A	8	7	.533	21	17	13	4	2	140^{1}	121	50	0	6	60	76	12.0	2.31	109	.235	.322	9	.200	1	3	3	-2	0.2
1910	Det-A	17	7	.708	26	23	20	3	0	206^{2}	184	74	4	7	61	107	11.0	2.44	108	.243	.305	10	.145	-2	2	4	-6	-0.4
1911	Det-A	10	9	.526	20	19	15	1	0	168^{1}	160	83	4	3	64	81	12.1	3.31	104	.250	.321	12	.200	3	1	3	-5	0.1
1912	Det-A	1	0	1.000	3	1	0	0	0	10	5	2	0	1	2	6	7.2	0.90	362	.147	.216	1	.077	-1	3	3	-0	0.2
1915	NY-A	0	3	.000	9	1	0	0	0	33^{2}	35	18	1	1	10	17	12.3	4.81	61	.278	.336	1	.083	-1	-7	-7	-1	-0.7
1916	NY-A	0	0	—	1	0	0	0	0	1	1	0	0	0	1	0	18.0	0.00	—	.250	.400	0	—	0	0	0	-0	0.0
1918	Det-A	1	0	1.000	2	1	0	0	0	6	5	1	0	0	1	1	9.0	1.50	177	.227	.261	1	.500	0	1	1	-0	0.2
Total	18	185	139	.571	378	327	289	35	8	2964^{2}	2631	1212	30	90	1059	1552	11.5	2.69	106	.239	.310	251	.193	8	43	53	-31	4.2
● **JOHN DOPSON**	Dopson, John Robert b: 7/14/63, Baltimore, Md. BL/TR, 6'4", 225 lbs. Deb: 9/4/85																											
1985	Mon-N	0	2	.000	4	3	0	0	0	13	25	17	4	0	4	4	20.1	11.08	31	.379	.414	0	.000	0	-11	-12	-0	-1.4
1988	Mon-N	3	11	.214	26	26	1	0	0	168^{2}	150	69	15	1	58	101	11.2	3.04	118	.235	.300	3	.059	-3	8	10	-3	0.2
1989	Bos-A	12	8	.600	29	28	2	0	0	169^{1}	166	84	14	2	69	95	12.6	3.99	103	.257	.330	0	—	0	-2	2	3	0.5
1990	Bos-A	0	0	—	4	4	0	0	0	17^{2}	13	7	2	0	9	9	11.2	2.04	201	.200	.297	0	—	0	4	4	1	0.3
1991	Bos-A	0	0	—	1	0	0	0	0	1	2	2	0	0	1	0	27.0	18.00	24	.500	.600	0	—	0	-2	-1	0	-0.1
1992	Bos-A	7	11	.389	25	25	0	0	0	141^{1}	159	78	17	2	38	55	12.7	4.08	104	.287	.335	0	—	0	-2	2	1	0.3
1993	Bos-A	7	11	.389	34	28	1	1	0	155^{2}	170	93	16	2	59	89	13.4	4.97	93	.281	.347	0	—	0	-11	-6	1	-0.5
1994	Cal-A	1	4	.200	21	5	0	0	1	58^{2}	67	41	6	3	26	33	14.7	6.14	80	.288	.366	0	—	0	-9	-8	0	-0.6
Total	8	30	47	.390	144	119	4	1	1	725^{1}	752	391	74	10	264	386	12.7	4.27	98	.268	.333	3	.055	-3	-24	-7	3	-1.3
● **JOHN DORAN**	Doran, John F. b: 1867, Chicago, Ill. TL, 5'4", 160 lbs. Deb: 4/11/1891																											
1891	Lou-a	5	10	.333	15	14	12	1	0	126	160	111	3	13	75	55	17.7	5.43	67	.299	.398	10	.189	-2	-24	-25	-0	-2.4
● **MIKE DORGAN**	Dorgan, Michael Cornelius b: 10/2/1853, Middletown, Conn. d: 4/26/09, Hartford, Conn. BR/TR, 5'9", 180 lbs. Deb: 5/8/1877 FM♦																											
1879	Syr-N	0	0	—	2	0	0	0	0	12	13	6	0		2	8	11.3	2.25	105	.260	.288	72	.267	0	0	0	0	0.1
1880	Pro-N	0	0	—	1	0	0	0	0	8	4	3	0		0	2	4.5	1.13	196	.138	.138	79	.246	0	1	1	0	0.1
1883	NY-N	0	1	.000	1	1	1	0	0	7	8	7	0		6	3	18.0	3.86	80	.286	.412	61	.234	0	-1	-1	-0	-0.1
1884	NY-N	8	6	.571	14	14	12	0	0	113	98	84	5		51	90	11.9	3.50	85	.215	.294	94	.276	2	-7	-7	1	-0.5
Total	4	8	7	.533	18	15	13	0	0	140	123	100	5		59	103	11.7	3.28	88	.218	.293	817	.278	3	-6	-6	1	-0.4
● **HARRY DORISH**	Dorish, Harry "Fritz" b: 7/13/21, Swoyersville, Pa. BR/TR, 5'11", 206 lbs. Deb: 4/15/47 C																											
1947	Bos-A	7	8	.467	41	9	2	0	2	136	149	80	6	1	54	50	13.5	4.70	83	.283	.351	5	.143	-1	-15	-12	1	-1.3
1948	Bos-A	0	1	.000	9	0	0	0	0	14^{1}	18	13	1	0	6	5	15.1	5.65	78	.281	.343	1	.250	-0	-2	-2	-0	-0.1
1949	Bos-A	0	0	—	5	0	0	0	0	7^{2}	7	2	1	0	1	5	9.4	2.35	186	.241	.267	0	—	0	2	2	0	0.1
1950	StL-A	4	9	.308	29	13	4	0	0	109	162	90	13	9	36	36	17.1	6.44	77	.337	.394	5	.161	0	-23	-17	-1	-1.7
1951	Chi-A	5	6	.455	32	4	2	1	0	96^{2}	101	50	6	0	31	29	12.3	3.54	114	.272	.328	8	.258	0	6	5	0	0.6
1952	Chi-A	8	4	.667	39	1	1	0	**11**	91	66	28	4	1	42	47	10.8	2.47	148	.208	.303	2	.091	-1	**12**	**12**	2	1.9
1953	Chi-A	10	6	.625	55	6	2	0	18	145^{2}	140	59	9	6	52	69	12.2	3.40	118	.254	.325	7	.171	-2	10	10	2	1.3
1954	Chi-A	6	4	.600	37	6	2	1	6	109	88	35	9	1	29	48	9.7	2.72	137	.228	.284	3	.111	-2	12	12	-1	0.9
1955	Chi-A	2	0	1.000	13	0	0	0	1	17	16	4	0	0	9	6	13.2	1.59	249	.258	.352	1	.333	0	4	4	1	0.6
	Bal-A	3	3	.500	35	1	0	0	6	65^{2}	58	25	5	1	28	22	11.9	3.15	121	.238	.319	0	.000	-1	6	5	1	0.5
	Yr	5	3	.625	48	1	0	0	7	82^{2}	74	29	5	1	37	28	12.2	2.83	136	.242	.326	1	.077	-1	10	10	1	1.1
1956	Bal-A	0	0	—	13	0	0	0	0	19^{2}	22	10	3	0	3	4	11.4	4.12	95	.297	.325	0	—	0	0	-0	1	0.1
	Bos-A	0	2	.000	15	0	0	0	0	22^{2}	23	10	1	0	10	11	13.1	3.57	129	.277	.355	0	—	0	1	2	1	0.3
	Yr	0	2	.000	28	0	0	0	0	42^{1}	45	20	4	0	13	15	12.3	3.83	112	.287	.341	0	—	0	2	2	2	0.4
Total	10	45	43	.511	323	40	13	2	44	834^{1}	850	406	58	19	301	332	12.6	3.83	106	.267	.333	32	.157	-6	14	20	6	3.2
● **GUS DORNER**	Dorner, Augustus b: 8/18/1876, Chambersburg, Pa. d: 5/4/56, Chambersburg, Pa. BR/TR, 5'10", 176 lbs. Deb: 9/17/02																											
1902	Cle-A	3	1	.750	4	4	4	1	0	36	33	13	1	1	13	5	11.8	1.25	275	.244	.315	5	.385	2	9	9	-0	1.2
1903	Cle-A	3	5	.375	12	8	4	2	0	73^{2}	83	51	4	1	24	28	13.2	4.52	63	.283	.340	2	.080	-2	-13	-14	0	-1.5
1906	Cin-N	0	1	.000	2	1	1	0	0	15	16	5	0	1	4	5	12.6	1.20	230	.276	.333	0	.000	-1	2	2	-0	0.1
	Bos-N	8	25	.242	34	32	29	0	0	273^{1}	264	152	5	16	103	104	12.6	3.65	74	.260	.338	14	.140	-4	-31	-29	3	-3.4
	Yr	8	26	.235	36	33	30	0	0	288^{1}	280	157	5	17	107	109	12.6	3.53	76	.261	.338	14	.133	-5	-29	-26	2	-3.3
1907	Bos-N	12	16	.429	36	31	24	2	0	271^{1}	253	120	4	15	92	85	11.9	3.12	82	.255	.327	12	.130	-3	-19	-16	-3	-2.3
1908	Bos-N	8	19	.296	38	28	14	3	0	216^{1}	176	120	3	15	77	41	11.1	3.54	68	.224	.305	12	.179	-1	-28	-27	2	-3.2
1909	Bos-N	1	2	.333	5	2	0	0	1	24^{2}	17	11	1	2	17	7	13.1	2.55	110	.198	.343	1	.167	-0	0	1	-0	0.0
Total	6	35	69	.337	131	106	76	8	1	910^{1}	842	472	18	51	330	275	12.1	3.37	78	.250	.326	46	.149	-9	-80	-73	1	-9.1
● **BERT DORR**	Dorr, Charles Albert b: 2/2/1862, New York d: 6/16/14, Dickinson, N.Y. Deb: 8/24/1882																											
1882	StL-a	2	6	.250	8	8	8	0	0	66	53	39	0		1	34	7.4	2.59	108	.205	.208	4	.154	-2	1	2	1	0.1
● **CAL DORSETT**	Dorsett, Calvin Leavelle "Preacher" b: 6/10/13, Lone Oak, Tex. d: 10/22/70, Elk City, Okla. BR/TR, 6', 180 lbs. Deb: 8/19/40																											
1940	Cle-A	0	0	—	1	0	0	0	0	1	1	1	1	0	0	0	9.0	9.00	47	.250	.250	0	—	0	-1	-1	-0	0.0
1941	Cle-A	0	1	.000	5	2	0	0	0	11^{1}	21	15	0	0	10	5	24.6	10.32	38	.382	.477	0	.000	-0	-8	-8	-0	-0.6
1947	Cle-A	0	0	—	2	0	0	0	0	1^{1}	3	4	1	0	3	1	40.5	27.00	13	.500	.667	0	—	0	-3	-4	0	-0.2
Total	3	0	1	.000	8	2	0	0	0	13^{2}	25	20	2	0	13	6	25.0	11.85	33	.385	.487	0	.000	-0	-12	-13	-0	-0.8
● **JIM DORSEY**	Dorsey, James Edward b: 8/2/55, Oak Park, Ill. BR/TR, 6'7", 190 lbs. Deb: 9/2/80																											
1980	Cal-A	1	2	.333	4	4	0	0	0	15^{2}	25	16	2	1	8	8	19.5	9.19	43	.368	.442	0	—	0	-9	-9	-0	-1.3
1984	Bos-A	0	0	—	2	0	0	0	0	2^{2}	6	3	0	0	2	4	27.0	10.13	41	.462	.533	0	—	0	-2	-2	0	-0.1
1985	Bos-A	0	1	.000	2	1	0	0	0	5^{1}	12	12	2	0	10	2	37.1	20.25	21	.444	.595	0	—	0	-10	-9	-0	-1.1
Total	3	1	3	.250	8	5	0	0	0	23^{2}	43	31	4	1	20	14	24.3	11.79	34	.398	.496	0	—	0	-20	-20	-0	-2.5
● **JERRY DORSEY**	Dorsey, Michael Jeremiah b: 1854, Canada d: 11/3/38, Auburn, N.Y. BL, Deb: 7/9/1884 ♦																											
1884	Bal-U	0	1	.000	1	1	0	0	0	4	7	8	1		0	3	15.8	9.00	30	.368	.368	0	.000	-1	-3	-3	0	-0.4
● **JACK DOSCHER**	Doscher, John Henry Jr. b: 7/27/1880, Troy, N.Y. d: 5/27/71, Park Ridge, N.J. BL/TL, 6'1", 205 lbs. Deb: 7/2/03 F																											
1903	Chi-N	0	1	.000	1	1	0	0	0	3	6	5	0	1	2	5	27.0	12.00	26	.429	.529	0	.000	-0	-3	-3	0	-0.5
	Bro-N	0	0	—	3	0	0	0	0	7	8	8	1	1	9	4	23.1	7.71	41	.296	.486	0	.000	-0	-3	-4	-0	-0.2
	Yr	0	1	.000	4	1	0	0	0	10	14	13	1	2	11	9	24.3	9.00	35	.341	.500	0	.000	-1	-6	-7	-0	-0.7
1904	Bro-N	0	0	—	2	0	0	0	0	6^{1}	1	1	0	0	1	2	2.8	0.00	—	.053	.100	1	.500	0	2	2	-0	0.1
1905	Bro-N	1	5	.167	12	7	6	0	0	71	60	34	1	3	30	33	11.8	3.17	91	.232	.318	2	.083	-2	-1	-2	-2	-0.5
1906	Bro-N	0	1	.000	2	1	1	0	0	14	12	3	0	0	4	10	10.3	1.29	196	.250	.308	0	.000	-1	2	2	-0	0.0
1908	Cin-N	1	3	.250	7	4	3	0	0	44^{1}	31	19	1	3	22	7	11.4	1.83	126	.196	.306	2	.133	0	3	2	-0	0.2
Total	5	2	10	.167	27	13	10	0	0	145^{2}	118	70	3	8	68	61	12.0	2.84	95	.225	.323	5	.100	-3	-1	-2	-3	-0.9

YEAR	TM/L	W	L	PCT	G	GS	CG	SH	SV	IP	H	R	HR	HB	BB	SO	RAT	ERA	ERA+	OAV	OOB	BH	AVG	PB	PR	PR+	PD	TPI
● OCTAVIO DOTEL	Dotel, Octavio Eduardo (Diaz) b: 11/25/75, Santo Domingo, D.R. BR/TR, 6', 175 lbs. Deb: 6/26/99																											
1999	*NY-N	8	3	.727	19	14	0	0	0	85^1	69	52	12	6	49	85	13.1	5.38	81	.226	.344	3	.125	1	-8	-10	0	-1.0
2000	Hou-N	3	7	.300	50	16	0	0	16	125	127	80	26	7	61	142	14.0	5.40	91	.265	.356	1	.031	-3	-11	-7	-0	-0.9
Total	2	11	10	.524	69	30	0	0	16	210^1	196	132	38	13	110	227	13.6	5.39	87	.250	.351	4	.071	-2	-18	-16	-0	-1.9
● RICHARD DOTSON	Dotson, Richard Elliott b: 1/10/59, Cincinnati, Ohio BR/TR, 6', 204 lbs. Deb: 9/4/79																											
1979	Chi-A	2	0	1.000	5	5	1	1	0	24^1	28	13	0	0	6	13	12.6	3.70	115	.286	.327	0	—	0	1	2	0	0.1
1980	Chi-A	12	10	.545	33	32	8	0	0	198	185	105	20	6	87	109	12.6	4.27	94	.247	.331	0	—	0	-5	-5	1	-0.4
1981	Chi-A	9	8	.529	24	24	5	**4**	0	141	145	67	13	4	49	73	12.6	3.77	95	.270	.336	0	—	0	-2	-3	-0	-0.4
1982	Chi-A	11	15	.423	34	31	3	1	0	196^2	219	97	19	5	73	109	13.6	3.84	105	.282	.348	0	—	0	5	4	-1	0.5
1983	*Chi-A	22	7	**.759**	35	35	8	1	0	240	209	92	19	8	106	137	12.1	3.23	130	.240	.328	0	—	0	23	25	4	3.4
1984	Chi-A★	14	15	.483	32	32	14	1	0	245^2	216	110	24	7	103	120	11.9	3.59	116	.238	.321	0	—	0	11	15	-0	1.6
1985	Chi-A	3	4	.429	9	9	0	0	0	52^1	53	30	5	3	17	33	12.6	4.47	97	.261	.327	0	—	0	-2	-1	-0	-0.1
1986	Chi-A	10	17	.370	34	34	3	1	0	197	226	125	24	2	69	110	13.6	5.48	79	.289	.348	0	—	0	-28	-25	-1	-3.0
1987	Chi-A	11	12	.478	31	31	7	2	0	211^1	201	109	24	0	86	114	12.2	4.17	110	.249	.321	0	—	0	7	10	2	1.1
1988	NY-A	12	9	.571	32	29	4	0	0	171	178	103	27	4	72	77	13.4	5.00	79	.266	.341	0	—	0	-19	-20	-1	-2.3
1989	NY-A	2	5	.286	11	9	1	0	0	51^2	69	33	8	1	17	14	15.2	5.57	70	.317	.369	0	—	0	-10	-10	-1	-1.2
	Chi-A	3	7	.300	17	17	1	0	0	99^2	112	51	8	0	41	55	13.8	3.88	98	.282	.349	0	—	0	0	-1	0	-0.1
	Yr	5	12	.294	28	26	2	0	0	151^1	181	84	16	1	58	69	14.3	4.46	86	.294	.356	0	—	0	-10	-11	-1	-1.3
1990	KC-A	0	4	.000	8	7	0	0	0	28^2	43	29	3	0	14	9	17.9	8.48	45	.355	.422	0	—	0	-15	-15	-0	-1.7
Total	12	111	113	.496	305	295	55	11	0	1857^1	1884	964	194	40	740	973	12.9	4.23	97	.264	.337	0	—	0	-33	-22	2	-2.5
● GARY DOTTER	Dotter, Gary Richard b: 8/7/42, St.Louis, Mo. BL/TL, 6'1", 180 lbs. Deb: 9/10/61																											
1961	Min-A	0	0	—	2	0	0	0	0	6	6	6	0	0	4	2	15.0	9.00	47	.273	.385	0	.000	-0	-3	-3	0	-0.2
1963	Min-A	0	0	—	2	0	0	0	0	2	0	0	0	0	0	2	0.0	0.00	—	.000	.000	0	—	0	1	1	0	0.1
1964	Min-A	0	0	—	3	0	0	0	0	4^1	3	2	1	0	3	6	12.5	2.08	172	.188	.316	0	—	0	1	1	-0	0.0
Total	3	0	0	—	7	0	0	0	0	12^1	9	8	1	0	7	10	11.7	5.11	76	.205	.314	0	.000	-0	-2	-2	0	-0.1
● BABE DOTY	Doty, Elmer L. b: 12/17/1867, Genoa, Ohio d: 11/20/29, Toledo, Ohio BL/TR, 6', 160 lbs. Deb: 8/18/1890																											
1890	Tol-a	1	0	1.000	1	1	1	0	0	9	9	1	0	0	1	4	10.0	1.00	395	.250	.270	0	.000	-0	3	3	-0	0.2
● JIM DOUGHERTY	Dougherty, James E. b: 3/8/68, Brentwood, N.Y. BR/TR, 6', 210 lbs. Deb: 4/27/95																											
1995	Hou-N	8	4	.667	56	0	0	0	0	67^2	76	37	7	3	25	49	13.8	4.92	79	.292	.361	1	.125	-0	-6	-9	1	-1.2
1996	Hou-N	0	2	.000	12	0	0	0	0	13	14	14	2	1	11	6	18.0	9.00	43	.280	.419	0	—	0	-7	-8	0	-1.0
1998	Oak-A	0	2	.000	9	0	0	0	0	12	17	11	2	1	7	3	18.8	8.25	55	.340	.431	0	—	0	-5	-5	1	-0.6
1999	Pit-N	0	0	—	2	0	0	0	0	2	3	3	0	0	3	1	27.0	9.00	51	.333	.500	0	—	0	-1	-1	-0	0.0
Total	4	8	8	.500	79	0	0	0	0	94^2	110	65	11	5	46	59	15.3	5.99	66	.298	.383	1	.125	0	-18	-23	2	-2.8
● TOM DOUGHERTY	Dougherty, Thomas James "Sugar Boy" b: 5/30/1881, Chicago, Ill. d: 11/6/53, Milwaukee, Wis. BL/TR, 195 lbs. Deb: 4/24/04																											
1904	Chi-A	1	0	1.000	1	0	0	0	0	2	0	0	0	0	0	0	0.0	0.00	—	.000	.000	0	.000	-0	1	1	0	0.1
● WHAMMY DOUGLAS	Douglas, Charles William b: 2/17/35, Carrboro, N.C. BR/TR, 6'2", 185 lbs. Deb: 7/29/57																											
1957	Pit-N	3	3	.500	11	8	0	0	0	47	48	23	5	3	30	28	15.5	3.26	116	.270	.384	1	.063	-1	3	3	-0	0.2
● LARRY DOUGLAS	Douglas, Lawrence Howard b: 6/5/1890, Jellico, Tenn. d: 11/4/49, Jellico, Tenn. 6'3", 175 lbs. Deb: 6/17/15																											
1915	Bal-F	1	0	1.000	2	0	0	0	0	3	3	1	0	0	2	1	15.0	3.00	96	.273	.385	0	—	0	-0	-0	0	0.0
● PHIL DOUGLAS	Douglas, Phillip Brooks "Shufflin' Phil" b: 6/17/1890, Cedartown, Ga. d: 8/1/52, Sequatchie, Tenn. BR/TR, 6'3", 190 lbs. Deb: 8/30/12																											
1912	Chi-A	0	1	.000	3	1	0	0	0	12^1	21	17	0	0	6	7	19.7	7.30	44	.382	.443	0	.000	-0	-5	-6	0	-0.4
1914	Cin-N	11	18	.379	45	25	13	0	1	239^1	186	111	7	11	92	121	10.9	2.56	115	.223	.308	10	.137	-2	6	9	-2	0.7
1915	Cin-N	1	5	.167	8	7	0	0	0	46^2	53	35	0	0	23	29	14.7	5.40	53	.299	.380	2	.118	-1	-14	-13	0	-1.5
	Bro-N	5	5	.500	20	13	5	1	0	116^2	104	45	1	5	17	63	9.7	2.62	106	.241	.278	6	.154	-1	2	2	0	0.1
	Chi-N	1	1	.500	4	4	2	1	0	25	17	9	0	1	7	18	9.0	2.16	129	.187	.253	0	.000	-1	2	2	0	0.0
	Yr	7	11	.389	32	24	7	2	0	188^1	174	89	1	6	47	110	10.8	3.25	86	.249	.301	8	.125	-3	-10	-9	1	-1.4
1917	Chi-N	14	20	.412	**51**	37	20	5	1	293^1	269	123	13	6	50	151	10.0	2.55	114	.250	.287	11	.126	-4	5	11	4	1.3
1918	*Chi-N	10	9	.526	25	19	11	2	2	156^2	145	57	2	1	31	51	10.2	2.13	131	.246	.285	14	.255	1	11	11	3	1.9
1919	Chi-N	10	6	.625	25	19	8	4	0	161^2	133	52	0	2	34	63	9.4	2.00	144	.230	.275	8	.157	-2	16	16	5	2.0
	NY-N	2	4	.333	8	6	4	0	0	51^1	53	22	0	1	6	21	10.5	2.10	133	.264	.288	0	.000	-2	5	4	0	0.2
	Yr	12	10	.545	33	25	12	4	0	213	186	74	0	3	40	84	9.7	2.03	141	.238	.278	8	.121	-4	21	20	5	2.2
1920	NY-N	14	10	.583	46	21	10	3	2	226	225	84	6	2	55	71	11.2	2.71	111	.263	.309	11	.151	-4	11	8	1	0.4
1921	*NY-N	15	10	.600	40	27	13	**3**	2	221^2	266	119	17	2	55	55	13.1	4.22	87	.308	.351	16	.198	0	-11	-14	1	-1.3
1922	NY-N	11	4	.733	24	21	9	1	0	157^2	154	56	6	4	35	33	**11.0**	**2.63**	**152**	**.257**	**.302**	12	.207	1	26	25	0	2.2
Total	9	94	93	.503	299	200	95	20	8	1708^1	1626	730	52	35	411	683	10.9	2.80	111	.256	.305	90	.161	-16	53	57	13	5.6
● KIP DOWD	Dowd, James Joseph b: 2/16/1889, Holyoke, Mass. d: 12/20/60, Holyoke, Mass. BR/TR, 5'10.5", 160 lbs. Deb: 7/5/10																											
1910	Pit-N	0	0	—	1	0	0	0	0	2	4	4	0	1	2	1	31.5	0.00	—	.400	.538	0	—	0	1	1	-0	0.0
● DAVE DOWLING	Dowling, David Barclay b: 8/23/42, Baton Rouge, La. BR/TL, 6'2", 181 lbs. Deb: 10/3/64																											
1964	StL-N	0	0	—	1	0	0	0	0	1	2	0	0	0	0	0	18.0	0.00	—	.400	.400	0	—	0	0	0	-0	0.0
1966	Chi-N	1	0	1.000	1	1	1	0	0	9	10	2	0	0	0	3	10.0	2.00	184	.270	.270	0	.000	-0	2	2	-0	0.1
Total	2	1	0	1.000	2	1	1	0	0	10	12	2	0	0	0	3	10.8	1.80	205	.286	.286	0	.000	-0	2	2	-0	0.1
● PETE DOWLING	Dowling, Henry Peter b: St.Louis, Mo. d: 6/30/05, Hot Lake, Ore. BL/TL, 5'11", 165 lbs. Deb: 7/17/1897																											
1897	Lou-N	1	2	.333	4	4	2	0	0	26	39	30	0	6	8	3	18.3	5.88	72	.342	.414	2	.200	-0	-5	-5	-0	-0.4
1898	Lou-N	13	20	.394	36	32	30	0	0	285^2	284	176	7	22	120	84	13.4	4.16	86	.257	.342	21	.196	1	-17	-19	-1	-1.7
1899	Lou-N	13	17	.433	35	33	30	0	0	298^1	329	166	6	17	95	89	13.3	3.05	127	.280	.342	27	.227	-1	27	27	0	2.1
1901	Mil-A	1	3	.250	10	4	3	0	1	49^2	71	49	1	4	14	25	16.1	5.62	64	.332	.384	4	.211	1	-11	-11	0	-0.7
	Cle-A	11	22	.333	33	30	28	2	0	256^1	269	160	1	15	104	99	13.6	3.86	92	.267	.344	16	.162	-4	-6	-9	0	-1.3
	Yr	12	25	.324	43	34	31	2	1	306	340	209	2	19	118	124	14.0	4.15	86	.278	.351	20	.169	-3	-16	-21	1	-2.0
Total	4	39	64	.379	118	103	93	2	1	916	992	581	15	64	341	300	13.7	3.84	96	.274	.347	70	.198	-3	-12	-17	-0	-2.0
● AL DOWNING	Downing, Alphonso Erwin b: 6/28/41, Trenton, N.J. BR/TL, 5'11", 177 lbs. Deb: 7/19/61																											
1961	NY-A	0	1	.000	5	1	0	0	0	9	7	8	0	1	12	12	20.0	8.00	46	.212	.435	0	.000	-0	-4	-5	0	-0.4
1962	NY-A	0	0	—	1	0	0	0	0	1	0	0	0	0	0	1	0.0	0.00	—	.000	.000	0	—	0	0	0	0	0.0
1963	*NY-A	13	5	.722	24	22	10	4	0	175^2	114	52	7	0	80	171	9.9	2.56	137	**.184**	.277	6	.103	-2	21	19	-1	1.6
1964	*NY-A	13	8	.619	37	35	11	1	2	244	201	104	18	0	120	**217**	11.8	3.47	104	.223	.314	15	.176	1	4	4	0	0.4
1965	NY-A	12	14	.462	35	32	8	2	0	212	185	92	16	2	105	179	12.4	3.40	100	.237	.329	8	.108	-1	1	0	0	0.0
1966	NY-A	10	11	.476	30	30	1	0	0	200	178	90	23	1	79	152	11.6	3.56	94	.235	.309	7	.100	-2	-3	-5	-4	-1.1
1967	NY-A★	14	10	.583	31	28	10	4	0	201^2	158	65	13	6	61	171	10.0	2.63	119	.217	.283	8	.121	1	13	11	-1	1.4
1968	NY-A	3	3	.500	15	12	1	0	0	61^1	54	24	7	1	20	40	11.0	3.52	82	.237	.301	3	.176	0	-4	-4	-0	-0.4
1969	NY-A	7	5	.583	30	15	5	1	0	130^2	117	57	12	0	49	85	11.4	3.38	103	.240	.309	6	.136	-0	4	2	-2	-0.1
1970	Oak-A	3	3	.500	10	6	1	0	0	41	39	19	5	1	22	26	13.6	3.95	90	.252	.348	2	.182	-0	-1	-2	2	-0.1
	Mil-A	2	10	.167	17	16	1	0	0	94^1	79	47	8	3	59	53	13.5	3.34	114	.232	.350	2	.083	-2	4	5	0	0.4
	Yr	5	13	.278	27	22	2	0	0	135^1	118	66	13	4	81	79	13.5	3.52	105	.238	.349	4	.114	-2	3	3	2	0.3
1971	LA-N	20	9	.690	37	36	12	**5**	0	262^1	245	93	16	3	84	136	11.4	2.68	121	.247	.308	16	.174	2	23	17	-1	2.0
1972	LA-N	9	9	.500	31	30	7	4	0	202^2	196	81	13	7	67	117	12.0	2.98	112	.254	.319	8	.121	-1	11	8	5	1.1
1973	LA-N	9	9	.500	30	28	5	2	0	193	155	87	19	1	68	124	10.4	3.31	104	.219	.289	5	.088	-1	8	3	1	0.2
1974	*LA-N	5	6	.455	21	16	1	1	0	98^1	94	52	7	3	45	63	13.0	3.66	93	.255	.341	5	.172	-0	-0	-3	1	-0.2
1975	LA-N	2	1	.667	22	6	0	0	1	74^2	59	31	6	2	28	39	10.7	2.89	118	.215	.293	0	.000	-1	6	5	1	0.2
1976	LA-N	1	2	.333	17	3	0	0	0	46^2	43	21	3	0	18	30	11.8	3.86	88	.250	.321	0	.000	-1	-2	-3	0	-0.2
1977	LA-N	0	1	.000	12	1	0	0	0	20	22	15	4	0	16	23	17.1	6.75	57	.278	.400	0	.000	-0	-6	-7	-0	-0.3
Total	17	123	107	.535	405	317	73	24	3	2268^1	1946	938	177	31	933	1639	11.5	3.22	106	.232	.311	91	.127	-7	76	47	2	4.5

YEAR	TM/L	W	L	PCT	G	GS	CG	SH	SV	IP	H	R	HR	HB	BB	SO	RAT	ERA	ERA+	OAV	OOB	BH	AVG	PB	PR	PR+	PD	TPI
● DAVE DOWNS Downs, David Ralph b: 6/21/52, Logan, Utah BR/TR, 6'5", 220 lbs. Deb: 9/2/72 F																												
1972	Phi-N	1	1	.500	4	4	1	1	0	23	25	7	1	1	3	5	11.3	2.74	131	.294	.326	2	.250	0	2	2	0	0.2
● KELLY DOWNS Downs, Kelly Robert b: 10/25/60, Ogden, Utah BR/TR, 6'4", 200 lbs. Deb: 7/29/86 F																												
1986	SF-N	4	4	.500	14	14	1	0	0	88^1	78	29	5	3	30	64	11.3	2.75	128	.236	.305	5	.172	0	10	8	0	0.7
1987	*SF-N	12	9	.571	41	28	4	3	1	186	185	83	14	4	67	137	12.4	3.63	106	.258	.324	8	.143	-0	9	5	-4	0.1
1988	SF-N	13	9	.591	27	26	6	3	0	168	140	67	11	3	47	118	10.2	3.32	98	.225	.283	9	.167	2	2	-1	0	0.1
1989	*SF-N	4	8	.333	18	15	0	0	0	82^2	82	47	7	1	26	49	11.9	4.79	71	.261	.320	2	.091	-1	-12	-13	-1	-1.9
1990	SF-N	3	2	.600	13	9	0	0	0	63	56	26	2	2	20	31	11.1	3.43	106	.233	.298	0	.000	-1	3	2	1	0.1
1991	SF-N	10	4	.714	45	11	0	0	0	111^2	99	59	12	3	53	62	12.5	4.19	86	.239	.329	2	.087	-1	-6	-8	1	-0.9
1992	SF-N	1	2	.333	19	7	0	0	0	62^1	65	27	4	3	24	33	13.3	3.47	96	.275	.350	0	.000	-1	0	-1	-1	-0.4
	*Oak-A	5	5	.500	18	13	0	0	0	82	72	36	4	4	46	38	13.4	3.29	114	.237	.345	0	—	0	6	4	-1	0.4
1993	Oak-A	5	10	.333	42	12	0	0	0	119^2	135	80	14	2	60	66	14.8	5.64	72	.287	.370	0	—	0	-17	-22	-2	-2.5
Total	8	57	53	.518	237	135	11	6	1	963^2	912	454	73	25	373	598	12.2	3.86	94	.250	.324	26	.123	-2	-5	-27	-7	-4.3
● SCOTT DOWNS Downs, Scott Jeremy b: 3/17/76, Louisville, Ky. BL/TL, 6'2", 180 lbs. Deb: 4/9/2000																												
2000	Chi-N	4	3	.571	18	18	0	0	0	94	117	59	13	5	37	63	15.2	5.17	88	.310	.379	2	.077	-1	-6	-6	-1	-0.6
	Mon-N	0	0	—	1	1	0	0	0	3	5	3	0	0	3	0	24.0	9.00	52	.385	.500	0	.000	-0	-1	-1	-0	-0.1
	Yr	4	3	.571	19	19	0	0	0	97	122	62	13	5	40	63	15.5	5.29	86	.312	.383	2	.071	-1	-7	-8	-1	-0.7
● TOM DOWSE Dowse, Thomas Joseph b: 8/12/1866, Ireland d: 12/14/46, Riverside, Cal. BR/TR, 5'11", 175 lbs. Deb: 4/21/1890 ♦																												
1890	Cle-N	0	0	—	1	0	0	0	0	5	6	3	0	0	1	0	12.6	5.40	66	.286	.318	33	.208	-0	-1	-1	0	0.0
● JESS DOYLE Doyle, Jesse Herbert b: 4/14/1898, Knoxville, Tenn. d: 4/15/61, Belleville, Ill. BR/TR, 5'11", 175 lbs. Deb: 4/14/25																												
1925	Det-A	4	7	.364	45	3	0	0	8	118^1	158	83	6	5	50	31	16.2	5.93	73	.340	.410	8	.242	3	-20	-22	-1	-1.8
1926	Det-A	0	0	—	2	0	0	0	1	4^1	6	3	0	0	1	2	14.5	4.15	98	.316	.350	1	1.000	0	-0	-0	-0	0.0
1927	Det-A	0	0	—	7	0	0	0	0	12^1	16	11	0	0	5	5	15.3	8.03	52	.314	.375	1	.333	0	-5	-5	0	-0.2
1931	StL-A	0	0	—	1	0	0	0	0	1	3	3	0	0	1	0	36.0	27.00	17	.500	.571	0	—	0	-3	-2	-0	-0.1
Total	4	4	7	.364	55	3	0	0	9	136	183	100	6	5	57	38	16.2	6.22	69	.338	.406	10	.270	4	-28	-30	-1	-2.1
● JOHN DOYLE Doyle, John Aloysius b: 1858, Nova Scotia, Canada d: 12/24/15, Providence, R.I. Deb: 7/26/1882																												
1882	StL-a	0	3	.000	3	3	3	0	0	24	41	33	0		3	5	16.5	2.63	107	.353	.370	2	.182	-0	0	0	-1	0.0
● SLOW JOE DOYLE Doyle, Judd Bruce b: 9/15/1881, Clay Center, Kan. d: 11/21/47, Tannersville, N.Y. BR/TR, 5'8", 150 lbs. Deb: 8/25/06																												
1906	NY-A	2	1	.667	9	6	3	2	0	45^1	34	15	1	1	13	28	9.5	2.38	124	.211	.274	3	.214	-0	2	3	0	0.2
1907	NY-A	11	11	.500	29	23	15	1	1	193^2	169	86	2	6	67	94	11.2	2.65	105	.237	.308	8	.138	-1	-2	3	-3	-0.1
1908	NY-A	1	1	.500	12	4	2	1	0	48	42	24	1	2	14	20	10.9	2.63	94	.235	.297	3	.214	0	-1	-1	-2	-0.2
1909	NY-A	8	6	.571	17	15	8	3	0	125^2	103	49	3	2	37	57	10.2	2.58	98	.232	.294	7	.167	0	-1	-1	-4	-0.4
1910	NY-A	0	2	.000	3	2	1	0	0	12^1	19	13	0	1	5	6	18.2	8.03	33	.365	.431	1	.250	0	-8	-7	1	-0.9
	Cin-N	0	0	—	5	0	0	0	0	11^1	16	19	0	0	11	4	21.4	6.35	46	.327	.450	0	.000	-0	-4	-5	-1	-0.3
Total	5	22	21	.512	75	50	29	7	1	436^1	383	206	7	12	147	209	11.2	2.85	95	.240	.308	22	.163	-1	-15	-7	-7	-1.7
● PAUL DOYLE Doyle, Paul Sinnott b: 10/2/39, Philadelphia, Pa. BL/TL, 5'11", 172 lbs. Deb: 5/28/69																												
1969	*Atl-N	2	0	1.000	36	0	0	0	4	39	31	9	4	0	16	25	10.8	2.08	174	.231	.313	0	.000	-0	7	7	1	0.5
1970	Cal-A	3	1	.750	40	0	0	0	5	42	43	25	7	1	21	34	13.9	5.14	70	.267	.355	0	.000	-0	-7	-7	1	-0.8
	SD-N	0	2	.000	9	0	0	0	2	7	9	5	0	0	6	2	19.3	6.43	62	.360	.484	0	.000	-0	-2	-2	1	-0.3
1972	Cal-A	0	0	—	2	0	0	0	0	2^1	2	0	0	0	3	4	19.3	0.00	—	.250	.455	0	—	0	1	1	0	0.1
Total	3	5	3	.625	87	0	0	0	11	90^1	85	39	11	1	46	65	13.2	3.79	96	.259	.352	0	.000	-1	-1	-2	3	-0.5
● CARL DOYLE Doyle, William Carl b: 7/30/12, Knoxville, Tenn. d: 9/4/51, Knoxville, Tenn. BR/TR, 6'1", 185 lbs. Deb: 8/5/35																												
1935	Phi-A	2	7	.222	14	9	3	0	0	79^2	86	63	3	2	72	34	18.1	5.99	76	.282	.422	4	.133	-2	-14	-13	1	-1.3
1936	Phi-A	0	3	.000	8	6	1	0	0	38^2	66	53	4	5	29	12	23.3	10.94	47	.369	.469	4	.267	1	-25	-25	-1	-1.4
1939	Bro-N	1	2	.333	5	1	1	1	1	17^2	8	5	1	0	7	7	7.6	1.02	395	.136	.227	1	.167	0	6	6	0	1.1
1940	Bro-N	0	0	—	3	0	0	0	1	5^2	18	17	3	4	6	4	44.5	27.00	15	.545	.651	1	1.000	1	-15	-14	0	-0.6
	StL-N	3	3	.500	21	5	1	0	0	81	99	57	7	6	41	44	16.2	5.89	68	.294	.380	6	.200	2	-18	-17	-0	-0.9
	Yr	3	3	.500	24	5	1	0	1	86^2	117	74	10	10	47	48	18.1	7.27	55	.316	.407	7	.226	2	-33	-30	0	-1.5
Total	4	6	15	.286	51	21	6	1	2	222^2	277	195	18	17	155	101	18.1	6.95	63	.303	.414	16	.195	1	-66	-62	-0	-3.1
● TOM DOZIER Dozier, Thomas Dean b: 9/5/61, San Pablo, Cal. BR/TR, 6'2", 190 lbs. Deb: 5/17/86																												
1986	Oak-A	0	0	—	4	0	0	0	0	6^1	6	6	1	0	5	4	15.6	5.68	68	.261	.393	0	—	0	-1	-1	-0	-0.1
● BUZZ DOZIER Dozier, William Joseph b: 8/31/27, Waco, Tex. BR/TR, 6'3", 185 lbs. Deb: 9/12/47																												
1947	Was-A	0	0	—	2	0	0	0	0	4^2	2	0	0	0	1	2	5.8	0.00	—	.133	.188	0	.000	-0	2	2	0	0.1
1949	Was-A	0	0	—	2	0	0	0	0	6^1	12	8	0	0	6	1	25.6	11.37	37	.429	.529	0	.000	-0	-5	-5	-0	-0.3
Total	2	0	0	—	4	0	0	0	0	11	14	8	0	0	7	3	17.2	6.55	62	.326	.420	0	.000	-0	-3	-3	-0	-0.2
● DOUG DRABEK Drabek, Douglas Dean b: 7/25/62, Victoria, Tex. BR/TR, 6'1", 185 lbs. Deb: 5/30/86																												
1986	NY-A	7	8	.467	27	21	0	0	0	131^2	126	64	13	3	50	76	12.2	4.10	100	.251	.323	0	—	0	1	-0	-1	-0.1
1987	Pit-N	11	12	.478	29	28	1	1	0	176^1	165	86	22	0	46	120	10.8	3.88	106	.247	.296	7	.119	-1	4	5	1	0.5
1988	Pit-N	15	7	.682	33	32	3	1	0	219^1	194	83	21	6	50	127	10.3	3.08	111	.239	.288	13	.171	3	9	8	-1	1.0
1989	Pit-N	14	12	.538	35	34	8	5	0	244^1	215	83	21	3	69	123	10.6	2.80	120	.238	.295	8	.104	-2	19	16	-0	1.4
1990	*Pit-N	**22**	6	**.786**	33	33	9	3	0	231^1	190	78	15	3	56	131	9.7	2.76	131	.225	.275	18	.214	5	27	23	2	3.5
1991	*Pit-N	15	14	.517	35	35	5	2	0	234^2	245	92	16	3	62	142	11.9	3.07	116	.274	.323	15	.179	1	16	14	2	1.9
1992	*Pit-N	15	11	.577	34	34	10	4	0	256^2	218	84	17	6	54	177	9.7	2.77	124	.231	.277	14	.157	1	21	20	1	2.2
1993	Hou-N	9	18	.333	34	34	7	2	0	237^2	242	108	18	3	60	157	11.5	3.79	102	.267	.315	6	.085	-2	7	2	0	0.1
1994	Hou-N★	12	6	.667	23	23	6	2	0	164^2	132	58	14	2	45	121	9.8	2.84	139	.220	.277	14	.241	3	25	22	2	2.8
1995	Hou-N	10	9	.526	31	31	2	1	0	185	205	104	18	8	54	143	13.0	4.77	81	.282	.338	14	.233	4	-12	-20	0	-1.4
1996	Hou-N	7	9	.438	30	30	1	0	0	175^1	208	102	21	7	60	137	14.1	4.57	85	.298	.359	10	.179	0	-7	-15	0	-1.1
1997	Chi-A	12	11	.522	31	31	0	0	0	169^1	170	109	30	4	69	85	12.9	5.74	76	.261	.335	0	.000	-0	-22	-26	-1	-3.0
1998	Bal-A	6	11	.353	23	21	1	0	0	108^2	138	90	20	5	29	55	14.2	7.29	63	.312	.361	0	.000	-0	-32	-34	-0	-4.1
Total	13	155	134	.536	398	387	53	21	0	2535	2448	1141	246	53	704	1594	11.4	3.73	101	.255	.310	119	.166	13	57	16	5	3.7
● MOE DRABOWSKY Drabowsky, Myron Walter b: 7/21/35, Ozanna, Poland BR/TR, 6'2", 200 lbs. Deb: 8/7/56 C																												
1956	Chi-N	2	4	.333	9	7	3	0	0	51	37	19	1	2	39	36	13.8	2.47	153	.207	.355	4	.250	0	7	7	-0	0.9
1957	Chi-N	13	15	.464	36	33	12	2	0	239^2	214	103	22	10	94	170	11.9	3.53	110	.242	.321	15	.183	2	9	9	0	1.2
1958	Chi-N	9	11	.450	22	20	4	1	0	125^2	118	73	19	5	73	77	14.0	4.51	87	.245	.350	7	.156	-1	-8	-8	-0	-1.3
1959	Chi-N	5	10	.333	31	23	3	1	0	141^2	138	78	21	3	75	70	13.7	4.13	96	.251	.344	5	.111	-1	-3	-3	-0	-0.4
1960	Chi-N	3	1	.750	32	7	0	0	1	50^1	71	44	3	1	23	26	17.0	6.44	59	.338	.406	0	.000	-1	-15	-15	-1	-1.3
1961	Mil-N	0	2	.000	16	0	0	0	2	25^1	26	15	4	1	18	5	16.0	4.62	81	.277	.398	1	.250	0	-2	-3	0	-0.2
1962	Cin-N	2	6	.250	23	10	1	0	1	83	84	49	13	6	31	56	13.1	4.99	81	.267	.344	0	.000	-2	-10	-9	-1	-1.0
	KC-A	1	1	.500	10	3	0	0	0	28	29	20	8	1	10	19	12.9	5.14	82	.266	.333	1	.167	-0	-4	-3	0	-0.2
1963	KC-A	7	13	.350	26	22	9	2	0	174^1	135	62	16	8	64	109	10.7	3.05	128	.214	.295	10	.161	1	11	15	-2	1.6
1964	KC-A	5	13	.278	53	21	1	0	1	168^1	176	103	24	8	72	119	13.7	5.29	72	.273	.353	1	.023	-4	-31	-26	1	-3.0
1965	KC-A	1	5	.167	14	5	0	0	0	38^2	44	22	5	3	18	25	15.1	4.42	79	.291	.378	1	.091	-1	-4	-4	-0	-0.7
1966	*Bal-A	6	0	1.000	44	3	0	0	7	96	62	31	10	1	29	98	8.6	2.81	118	.181	.247	8	.364	4	7	6	-1	0.8
1967	Bal-A	7	5	.583	43	0	0	0	12	95^1	66	21	7	2	25	96	8.8	1.60	196	.194	.253	7	.350	2	17	17	0	3.0
1968	Bal-A	4	4	.500	45	0	0	0	7	61^1	35	17	3	4	25	46	9.4	1.91	153	.166	.267	2	.286	0	7	7	-0	1.2
1969	KC-A	11	9	.550	52	0	0	0	11	98	68	33	10	2	30	76	9.2	2.94	126	.190	.256	4	.235	1	7	8	1	1.9
1970	KC-A	1	2	.333	24	0	0	0	2	35^2	28	13	3	2	12	38	10.6	3.28	114	.217	.294	1	.250	0	2	2	0	0.2
	*Bal-A	4	2	.667	21	0	0	0	1	33^1	30	17	7	1	15	21	12.4	3.78	97	.233	.317	0	.000	-1	-0	-0	-0	-0.2
	Yr	5	4	.556	45	0	0	0	3	69	58	30	10	3	27	59	11.5	3.52	105	.225	.306	1	.111	-0	1	1	-0	0.0
1971	StL-N	6	1	.857	51	0	0	0	8	60^1	45	23	2	2	33	49	11.9	3.43	105	.207	.317	1	.167	-0	0	1	-1	0.1

YEAR	TM/L	W	L	PCT	G	GS	CG	SH	SV	IP	H	R	HR	HB	BB	SO	RAT	ERA	ERA+	OAV	OOB	BH	AVG	PB	PR	PR+	PD	TPI
1972	StL-N	1	1	.500	30	0	0	0	2	27^2	29	13	4	1	14	22	14.3	2.60	131	.259	.346	0	.000	-0	3	3	-1	0.1
	Chi-A	0	0	—	7	0	0	0	0	7^1	6	2	0	0	2	4	9.8	2.45	128	.240	.296	0	.000	-0	1	1	-0	0.0
Total	17	88	105	.456	589	154	33	6	55	1641	1441	758	182	63	702	1162	12.1	3.71	101	.236	.321	68	.162	-0	-4	4	-5	2.7

● DICK DRAGO Drago, Richard Anthony b: 6/25/45, Toledo, Ohio BR/TR, 6'1", 190 lbs. Deb: 4/11/69

YEAR	TM/L	W	L	PCT	G	GS	CG	SH	SV	IP	H	R	HR	HB	BB	SO	RAT	ERA	ERA+	OAV	OOB	BH	AVG	PB	PR	PR+	PD	TPI
1969	KC-A	11	13	.458	41	26	10	2	1	200^2	190	95	19	2	65	108	11.5	3.77	98	.248	.308	3	.058	-3	-3	-2	2	-0.3
1970	KC-A	9	15	.375	35	34	7	1	0	240	239	110	20	7	72	127	11.9	3.75	100	.266	.325	4	.053	-6	-1	-0	-1	-0.7
1971	KC-A	17	11	.607	35	34	15	4	0	241^1	251	84	14	9	46	109	11.4	2.98	115	.276	.318	10	.130	1	13	12	0	1.5
1972	KC-A	12	17	.414	34	33	11	2	0	239^1	230	88	22	6	51	135	10.8	3.01	101	.254	.298	4	.059	-2	2	1	-3	-0.4
1973	KC-A	12	14	.462	37	33	10	1	0	212^2	252	116	16	7	76	98	14.2	4.23	97	.300	.363	0	—	0	-10	-3	-1	-0.2
1974	Bos-A	7	10	.412	33	18	8	0	3	175^2	165	71	17	5	56	90	11.6	3.48	110	.251	.315	0	—	0	3	7	-2	0.5
1975	*Bos-A	2	2	.500	40	2	0	0	15	72^2	69	31	5	0	31	43	12.4	3.84	106	.247	.323	0	—	0	-0	2	0	0.2
1976	Cal-A	7	8	.467	43	0	0	0	6	79^1	80	42	7	5	31	43	13.2	4.42	75	.264	.342	0	—	0	-8	-10	-2	-2.2
1977	Cal-A	0	1	.000	13	0	0	0	2	21	22	8	3	0	3	15	10.7	3.00	131	.272	.298	0	—	0	3	2	-0	0.1
	Bal-A	6	3	.667	36	0	0	0	3	39^2	49	19	2	1	15	20	14.7	3.63	105	.308	.371	0	—	0	2	1	-0	0.1
	Yr	6	4	.600	49	0	0	0	5	60^2	71	27	5	1	18	35	13.4	3.41	113	.296	.347	0	—	0	4	3	-1	0.2
1978	Bos-A	4	4	.500	37	1	0	0	7	77^1	71	30	5	4	32	42	12.5	3.03	136	.246	.329	0	—	0	6	9	-1	1.0
1979	Bos-A	10	6	.625	53	1	0	0	13	89	85	33	6	3	21	67	11.0	3.03	146	.254	.304	0	—	0	12	13	-0	2.6
1980	Bos-A	7	7	.500	43	7	1	0	3	132^2	127	67	17	5	44	63	11.9	4.14	102	.251	.317	0	.000	-0	1	1	-1	0.0
1981	Sea-A	4	6	.400	39	0	0	0	5	53^2	71	33	4	0	15	27	14.4	5.53	70	.324	.368	0	—	0	-11	-9	0	-1.8
Total	13	108	117	.480	519	189	62	10	58	1875	1901	827	157	54	558	987	12.1	3.62	103	.266	.324	21	.077	-11	6	24	-5	0.4

● BRIAN DRAHMAN Drahman, Brian Stacy b: 11/7/66, Kenton, Ky. BR/TR, 6'3", 205 lbs. Deb: 4/16/91

YEAR	TM/L	W	L	PCT	G	GS	CG	SH	SV	IP	H	R	HR	HB	BB	SO	RAT	ERA	ERA+	OAV	OOB	BH	AVG	PB	PR	PR+	PD	TPI
1991	Chi-A	3	2	.600	28	0	0	0	0	30^2	21	12	4	0	13	18	10.0	3.23	123	.193	.279	0	—	0	3	3	-0	0.4
1992	Chi-A	0	0	—	5	0	0	0	0	7	6	3	0	0	2	1	10.3	2.57	150	.222	.276	0	—	0	1	1	-0	0.0
1993	Chi-A	0	0	—	5	0	0	0	1	5^1	7	0	0	0	2	3	15.2	0.00	—	.333	.391	0	—	0	3	3	0	0.1
1994	Fla-N	0	0	—	9	0	0	0	0	13	15	9	2	0	6	7	14.5	6.23	70	.300	.375	0	—	0	-3	-3	0	-0.1
Total	4	3	2	.600	47	0	0	0	1	56	49	24	6	0	23	29	11.6	3.54	115	.237	.313	0	—	0	4	3	-0	0.4

● LOGAN DRAKE Drake, Logan Gaffney "L.G." b: 12/26/1900, Spartanburg, S.C. d: 6/1/40, Columbia, S.C. BR/TR, 5'10.5", 165 lbs. Deb: 9/21/22

YEAR	TM/L	W	L	PCT	G	GS	CG	SH	SV	IP	H	R	HR	HB	BB	SO	RAT	ERA	ERA+	OAV	OOB	BH	AVG	PB	PR	PR+	PD	TPI
1922	Cle-A	0	0	—	1	0	0	0	0	3	4	1	0	0	2	1	18.0	3.00	134	.364	.462	0	.000	-0	0	0	-0	0.0
1923	Cle-A	0	0	—	4	0	0	0	0	4^1	2	2	0	1	4	2	14.5	4.15	95	.133	.350	0	—	0	-0	-0	-0	0.0
1924	Cle-A	0	1	.000	5	1	0	0	0	11^1	18	15	0	1	10	8	23.0	10.32	41	.400	.518	0	.000	-0	-8	-8	-0	-0.6
Total	3	0	1	.000	10	1	0	0	0	18^2	24	18	0	2	16	11	20.3	7.71	54	.338	.472	0	.000	-0	-7	-7	-1	-0.6

● TOM DRAKE Drake, Thomas Kendall b: 8/7/12, Birmingham, Ala. d: 7/2/88, Birmingham, Ala. BR/TR, 6'1", 185 lbs. Deb: 4/24/39

YEAR	TM/L	W	L	PCT	G	GS	CG	SH	SV	IP	H	R	HR	HB	BB	SO	RAT	ERA	ERA+	OAV	OOB	BH	AVG	PB	PR	PR+	PD	TPI
1939	Cle-A	0	1	.000	8	1	0	0	0	15	23	18	2	2	19	1	26.4	9.00	49	.377	.537	0	.000	-0	-7	-8	0	-0.4
1941	Bro-N	1	1	.500	10	2	0	0	0	24^2	26	13	2	0	9	12	12.8	4.38	84	.280	.343	2	.400	0	-2	-2	-0	-0.1
Total	2	1	2	.333	18	3	0	0	0	39^2	49	31	4	2	28	13	17.9	6.13	65	.318	.429	2	.286	0	-9	-10	0	-0.5

● MIKE DRAPER Draper, Michael Anthony b: 9/14/66, Hagerstown, Md. BR/TR, 6'2", 180 lbs. Deb: 4/10/93

YEAR	TM/L	W	L	PCT	G	GS	CG	SH	SV	IP	H	R	HR	HB	BB	SO	RAT	ERA	ERA+	OAV	OOB	BH	AVG	PB	PR	PR+	PD	TPI
1993	NY-N	1	1	.500	29	1	0	0	0	42^1	53	22	2	0	14	16	14.2	4.25	95	.327	.381	2	.667	1	-1	-1	0	0.0

● DAVE DRAVECKY Dravecky, David Francis b: 2/14/56, Youngstown, Ohio BR/TL, 6'1", 195 lbs. Deb: 6/15/82

YEAR	TM/L	W	L	PCT	G	GS	CG	SH	SV	IP	H	R	HR	HB	BB	SO	RAT	ERA	ERA+	OAV	OOB	BH	AVG	PB	PR	PR+	PD	TPI
1982	SD-N	5	3	.625	31	10	0	0	2	105	86	37	8	1	33	59	10.3	2.57	133	.225	.288	3	.130	-0	12	11	2	1.0
1983	SD-N★	14	10	.583	28	28	9	1	0	183^2	181	78	18	3	44	74	11.2	3.58	98	.262	.309	6	.098	-1	1	-2	1	-0.3
1984	*SD-N	9	8	.529	50	14	3	2	8	156^2	125	53	12	4	51	71	10.3	2.93	122	.222	.291	4	.098	-1	12	11	-2	1.0
1985	SD-N	13	11	.542	34	31	7	2	0	214^2	200	79	18	1	57	105	10.8	2.93	121	.249	.300	8	.116	-0	16	15	-1	1.4
1986	SD-N	9	11	.450	26	26	3	1	0	161^1	149	68	17	1	54	87	11.4	3.07	119	.246	.309	7	.140	0	12	11	0	1.3
1987	SD-N	3	7	.300	30	10	1	0	0	79	71	39	10	3	31	60	12.0	3.76	105	.240	.318	3	.167	0	3	2	0	0.2
	*SF-N	7	5	.583	18	18	4	3	0	112^1	115	43	8	2	33	78	12.0	3.20	120	.272	.328	5	.132	0	11	9	1	1.0
	Yr	10	12	.455	48	28	5	3	0	191^1	186	82	18	5	64	138	12.0	3.43	113	.259	.324	8	.143	1	14	10	1	1.2
1988	SF-N	2	2	.500	7	7	1	0	0	37	33	19	4	0	8	19	10.0	3.16	103	.243	.285	1	.100	-0	1	0	0	0.0
1989	SF-N	2	0	1.000	2	2	0	0	0	13	8	5	2	1	4	5	9.0	3.46	98	.182	.265	1	.333	1	0	-0	0	0.1
Total	8	64	57	.529	226	146	28	9	10	1062^2	968	421	97	16	315	558	11.0	3.13	115	.245	.304	38	.121	-2	68	57	1	5.7

● TOM DREES Drees, Thomas Kent b: 6/17/63, Des Moines, Iowa BB/TL, 6'6", 210 lbs. Deb: 9/3/91

YEAR	TM/L	W	L	PCT	G	GS	CG	SH	SV	IP	H	R	HR	HB	BB	SO	RAT	ERA	ERA+	OAV	OOB	BH	AVG	PB	PR	PR+	PD	TPI
1991	Chi-A	0	0	—	4	0	0	0	0	7^1	10	10	4	0	6	2	19.6	12.27	32	.345	.457	0	—	0	-7	-7	-0	-0.3

● DARREN DREIFORT Dreifort, Darren James b: 5/3/72, Wichita, Kan. BR/TR, 6'2", 205 lbs. Deb: 4/7/94

YEAR	TM/L	W	L	PCT	G	GS	CG	SH	SV	IP	H	R	HR	HB	BB	SO	RAT	ERA	ERA+	OAV	OOB	BH	AVG	PB	PR	PR+	PD	TPI
1994	LA-N	0	5	.000	27	0	0	0	6	29	45	21	0	4	15	22	19.9	6.21	63	.357	.441	1	1.000	1	-6	-8	1	-1.3
1996	*LA-N	1	4	.200	19	0	0	0	0	23^2	23	13	2	0	12	24	13.3	4.94	78	.256	.343	0	.000	-0	-2	-3	1	-0.5
1997	LA-N	5	2	.714	48	0	0	0	4	63	45	21	3	1	34	63	11.4	2.86	135	.202	.310	1	.143	-0	9	8	2	1.0
1998	LA-N	8	12	.400	32	26	1	1	0	180	171	84	12	10	57	168	11.9	4.00	99	.256	.324	11	.224	3	5	-1	5	0.7
1999	LA-N	13	13	.500	30	29	1	1	0	178^2	177	105	20	7	76	140	13.1	4.79	90	.260	.341	13	.210	4	-4	-11	1	-0.7
2000	LA-N	12	9	.571	32	32	1	1	0	192^2	175	105	31	12	87	164	12.8	4.16	106	.238	.329	11	.162	4	10	5	3	1.1
Total	6	39	45	.464	188	87	3	3	10	667	636	349	68	34	281	581	12.8	4.28	97	.252	.335	37	.195	11	12	-9	12	0.3

● CLEM DREISEWERD Dreisewerd, Clemens Johann "Steamboat" b: 1/24/16, Old Monroe, Mo. BL/TL, 6'1.5", 195 lbs. Deb: 8/29/44

YEAR	TM/L	W	L	PCT	G	GS	CG	SH	SV	IP	H	R	HR	HB	BB	SO	RAT	ERA	ERA+	OAV	OOB	BH	AVG	PB	PR	PR+	PD	TPI
1944	Bos-A	2	4	.333	7	7	3	0	0	48^2	52	25	2	0	9	9	11.3	4.07	84	.268	.300	3	.188	0	-3	-4	-1	-0.5
1945	Bos-A	0	1	.000	2	2	0	0	0	9^2	13	5	0	1	2	3	14.9	4.66	73	.325	.372	0	.000	-0	-1	-1	-0	-0.2
1946	*Bos-A	4	1	.800	20	1	0	0	0	47^1	50	22	3	0	15	19	12.4	4.18	88	.276	.332	0	.000	-1	-4	-3	-0	-0.2
1948	StL-A	0	2	.000	13	0	0	0	1	22^1	28	15	6	0	8	6	14.5	5.64	81	.318	.375	0	.000	-1	-3	-3	-0	-0.3
	NY-N	0	0	—	4	0	0	0	1	12^2	17	8	3	0	5	2	15.6	5.68	69	.321	.379	1	.250	0	-2	-2	-0	-0.1
Total	4	6	8	.429	46	10	3	0	2	140^2	160	75	14	1	39	39	12.8	4.54	82	.288	.336	4	.105	-1	-14	-13	-1	-1.3

● KIRK DRESSENDORFER Dressendorfer, Kirk Richard b: 4/8/69, Houston, Tex. BR/TR, 5'11", 190 lbs. Deb: 4/13/91

YEAR	TM/L	W	L	PCT	G	GS	CG	SH	SV	IP	H	R	HR	HB	BB	SO	RAT	ERA	ERA+	OAV	OOB	BH	AVG	PB	PR	PR+	PD	TPI
1991	Oak-A	3	3	.500	7	7	0	0	0	34^2	33	28	5	0	21	17	14.0	5.45	70	.244	.346	0	—	0	-5	-7	-0	-1.0

● BOB DRESSER Dresser, Robert Nicholson b: 10/4/1878, Newton, Mass. d: 7/27/24, Duxbury, Mass. BL/TL, Deb: 8/13/02

YEAR	TM/L	W	L	PCT	G	GS	CG	SH	SV	IP	H	R	HR	HB	BB	SO	RAT	ERA	ERA+	OAV	OOB	BH	AVG	PB	PR	PR+	PD	TPI
1902	Bos-N	0	1	.000	1	1	1	0	0	9	12	6	0	0	0	8	12.0	3.00	94	.316	.316	1	.250	0	-0	-0	-0	0.0

● ROB DRESSLER Dressler, Robert Anthony b: 2/2/54, Portland, Ore. BR/TR, 6'3", 180 lbs. Deb: 9/7/75

YEAR	TM/L	W	L	PCT	G	GS	CG	SH	SV	IP	H	R	HR	HB	BB	SO	RAT	ERA	ERA+	OAV	OOB	BH	AVG	PB	PR	PR+	PD	TPI
1975	SF-N	1	0	1.000	3	2	1	0	0	16^1	17	3	0	0	4	6	11.6	1.10	346	.274	.318	0	.000	-0	5	5	0	0.3
1976	SF-N	3	10	.231	25	19	0	0	0	107^2	125	68	8	2	35	33	13.5	4.43	82	.291	.347	4	.129	-1	-11	-9	1	-1.1
1978	StL-N	0	1	.000	3	2	0	0	0	13	12	3	0	0	4	4	11.1	2.08	170	.267	.327	0	.000	-0	2	2	-0	0.1
1979	Sea-A	3	2	.600	21	11	2	0	0	104	134	61	11	0	22	36	13.5	4.93	89	.312	.345	0	—	0	-8	-6	-0	-0.3
1980	Sea-A	4	10	.286	30	14	3	0	0	149^1	161	75	14	3	33	50	11.9	3.98	104	.280	.322	0	—	0	1	3	1	0.3
Total	5	11	23	.324	82	48	6	0	0	390^1	449	210	33	5	98	129	12.7	4.17	97	.291	.335	4	.105	-1	-11	-6	2	-0.7

● DAVE DREW Drew, David Deb: 5/14/1884 ♦

YEAR	TM/L	W	L	PCT	G	GS	CG	SH	SV	IP	H	R	HR	HB	BB	SO	RAT	ERA	ERA+	OAV	OOB	BH	AVG	PB	PR	PR+	PD	TPI
1884	Phi-U	0	1	.000	1	0	0	0	0	7	7	5	0		0	2	9.0	3.86	60	.241	.241	4	.444	0	-1	-1	-0	-0.1

● TIM DREW Drew, Timothy Andrew b: 8/31/78, Valdosta, Ga. BR/TR, 6'1", 195 lbs. Deb: 5/24/2000 F

YEAR	TM/L	W	L	PCT	G	GS	CG	SH	SV	IP	H	R	HR	HB	BB	SO	RAT	ERA	ERA+	OAV	OOB	BH	AVG	PB	PR	PR+	PD	TPI
2000	Cle-A	1	0	1.000	3	3	0	0	0	9	17	12	1	1	8	5	26.0	10.00	50	.425	.531	0	—	0	-5	-5	0	-0.4

● KARL DREWS Drews, Karl August b: 2/22/20, Staten Island, N.Y d: 8/15/63, Dania, Fla. BR/TR, 6'4", 198 lbs. Deb: 9/8/46

YEAR	TM/L	W	L	PCT	G	GS	CG	SH	SV	IP	H	R	HR	HB	BB	SO	RAT	ERA	ERA+	OAV	OOB	BH	AVG	PB	PR	PR+	PD	TPI
1946	NY-A	0	1	.000	3	1	0	0	0	6^1	6	6	0	1	6	4	18.5	8.53	40	.250	.419	0	.000	-0	-4	-4	-0	-0.5
1947	*NY-A	6	6	.500	30	10	0	0	1	91^2	92	57	6	5	55	45	14.9	4.91	72	.264	.373	1	.037	-2	-12	-15	1	-1.9
1948	NY-A	2	3	.400	19	2	0	0	1	38	35	17	3	0	31	11	15.6	3.79	108	.248	.384	0	.000	-1	2	1	1	0.2
	StL-A	3	2	.600	20	2	0	0	2	38	43	35	3	0	38	11	19.2	8.05	57	.289	.433	0	.000	-0	-16	-14	0	-1.7
	Yr	5	5	.500	39	4	0	0	3	76	78	52	6	0	69	22	17.4	5.92	73	.269	.409	0	.000	-1	-14	-13	1	-1.5
1949	StL-A	4	12	.250	31	23	3	1	0	139^2	180	113	11	9	66	35	16.4	6.64	68	.317	.397	0	.000	-5	-38	-30	-1	-3.4

YEAR	TM/L	W	L	PCT	G	GS	CG	SH	SV	IP	H	R	HR	HB	BB	SO	RAT	ERA	ERA+	OAV	OOB	BH	AVG	PB	PR	PR+	PD	TPI
1951	Phi-N	1	0	1.000	5	3	1	0	0	23	29	16	2	4	7	13	15.7	6.26	61	.296	.367	2	.250	1	-6	-6	0	-0.2
1952	Phi-N	14	15	.483	33	30	15	5	0	228^2	213	79	13	4	52	96	10.6	2.72	135	.252	.298	9	.110	-2	26	24	0	2.8
1953	Phi-N	9	10	.474	47	27	6	0	3	185^1	218	116	26	10	50	72	13.5	4.52	93	.293	.346	7	.119	-2	-5	-6	2	-0.7
1954	Phi-N	1	0	1.000	8	0	0	0	0	16	18	10	2	0	8	6	14.6	5.63	72	.300	.382	0	.000	-1	-3	-3	0	-0.2
	Cin-N	4	4	.500	22	9	1	1	0	60	79	44	6	2	19	29	15.0	6.00	70	.326	.380	2	.167	1	-13	-12	0	-1.2
	Yr	5	4	.556	30	9	1	1	0	76	97	54	8	2	27	35	14.9	5.92	70	.321	.381	2	.125	1	-16	-15	0	-1.4
Total	8	44	53	.454	218	107	26	7	7	826^2	913	493	72	35	332	322	13.9	4.76	84	.284	.357	21	.083	-12	-68	-68	3	-6.8

● **STEVE DREYER** Dreyer, Steven William b: 11/19/69, Ames, Iowa BR/TR, 6'3", 180 lbs. Deb: 8/8/93

YEAR	TM/L	W	L	PCT	G	GS	CG	SH	SV	IP	H	R	HR	HB	BB	SO	RAT	ERA	ERA+	OAV	OOB	BH	AVG	PB	PR	PR+	PD	TPI
1993	Tex-A	3	3	.500	10	6	0	0	0	41	48	26	7	1	20	23	15.1	5.71	73	.291	.371	0	—	0	-6	-7	-0	-0.9
1994	Tex-A	1	1	.500	5	3	0	0	0	17^1	19	15	1	1	8	11	14.5	5.71	84	.271	.354	0	—	0	-2	-2	-0	-0.2
Total	2	4	4	.500	15	9	0	0	0	58^1	67	41	8	2	28	34	15.0	5.71	76	.285	.366	0	—	0	-8	-9	-1	-1.1

● **DENNY DRISCOLL** Driscoll, John F. b: 11/19/1855, Lowell, Mass. d: 7/11/1886, Lowell, Mass. BL/TL, 5'10.5", 160 lbs. Deb: 7/1/1880 ♦

YEAR	TM/L	W	L	PCT	G	GS	CG	SH	SV	IP	H	R	HR	HB	BB	SO	RAT	ERA	ERA+	OAV	OOB	BH	AVG	PB	PR	PR+	PD	TPI
1880	Buf-N	1	3	.250	6	4	4	0	0	41^2	48	33	1		9	17	12.3	3.89	63	.270	.305	10	.154	-1	-7	-6	0	-0.6
1882	Pit-a	13	9	.591	23	23	23	0	0	201	162	73	0		12	59	7.8	**1.21**	**216**	.206	.218	11	.138	-2	33	32	-4	2.5
1883	Pit-a	18	21	.462	41	40	35	1	0	336^1	427	239	3		39	79	12.5	3.99	82	.290	.309	27	.182	-5	-26	-28	6	-2.4
1884	Lou-a	6	6	.500	13	13	10	0	0	102	110	69	3	2	7	16	10.5	3.44	90	.252	.267	9	.188	-1	-2	-4	2	-0.3
Total	4	38	39	.494	83	80	72	1	0	681	747	414	7	2	67	171	10.8	3.08	97	.260	.277	57	.167	-9	-2	-7	4	-0.8

● **MICHAEL DRISCOLL** Driscoll, Michael Columbus b: 10/19/1892, Rockland, Mass. d: 3/22/53, Foxboro, Mass. BR/TR, 6'1", 160 lbs. Deb: 7/6/16

YEAR	TM/L	W	L	PCT	G	GS	CG	SH	SV	IP	H	R	HR	HB	BB	SO	RAT	ERA	ERA+	OAV	OOB	BH	AVG	PB	PR	PR+	PD	TPI
1916	Phi-A	0	1	.000	1	0	0	0	0	5	6	5	0	0	2	0	14.4	5.40	53	.273	.333	0	.000	-0	-1	-1	1	-0.2

● **TOM DROHAN** Drohan, Thomas F b: 8/26/1887, Fall River, Mass. d: 9/17/26, Kewanee, Ill. BR/TR, 5'10", 175 lbs. Deb: 5/1/13

YEAR	TM/L	W	L	PCT	G	GS	CG	SH	SV	IP	H	R	HR	HB	BB	SO	RAT	ERA	ERA+	OAV	OOB	BH	AVG	PB	PR	PR+	PD	TPI
1913	Was-A	0	0	—	2	0	0	0	0	2	5	2	1	0	0	2	22.5	9.00	33	.500	.500	0	—	0	-1	-1	0	-0.1

● **DICK DROTT** Drott, Richard Fred "Hummer" b: 7/1/36, Cincinnati, Ohio d: 8/16/85, Glendale Heights, Ill. BR/TR, 6', 185 lbs. Deb: 4/16/57

YEAR	TM/L	W	L	PCT	G	GS	CG	SH	SV	IP	H	R	HR	HB	BB	SO	RAT	ERA	ERA+	OAV	OOB	BH	AVG	PB	PR	PR+	PD	TPI
1957	Chi-N	15	11	.577	38	32	7	3	0	229	200	107	22	7	129	170	13.2	3.58	108	.234	.340	8	.100	-5	8	8	-1	0.2
1958	Chi-N	7	11	.389	39	31	4	0	0	167^1	156	118	23	6	99	127	14.0	5.43	72	.245	.352	15	.273	3	-28	-28	1	-2.3
1959	Chi-N	1	2	.333	8	6	1	1	0	27^1	25	19	5	0	26	15	16.8	5.93	67	.245	.398	1	.125	-0	-6	-6	-0	-0.6
1960	Chi-N	0	6	.000	23	9	0	0	0	55^1	63	49	7	3	42	32	17.6	7.16	53	.296	.419	1	.100	-1	-21	-21	-0	-2.1
1961	Chi-N	1	4	.200	35	8	0	0	0	98	75	54	13	1	51	48	11.7	4.22	99	.215	.317	6	.273	1	-2	-0	-2	-0.1
1962	Hou-N	1	0	1.000	6	1	0	0	0	13	12	12	1	0	9	10	14.5	7.62	49	.240	.356	0	.000	-0	-5	-6	-0	-0.5
1963	Hou-N	2	12	.143	27	14	2	1	0	97^2	95	61	13	6	49	58	13.8	4.98	63	.257	.353	3	.130	-1	-18	-21	-1	-2.9
Total	7	27	46	.370	176	101	14	5	0	687^2	626	420	84	23	405	460	13.8	4.78	80	.243	.351	34	.168	-2	-72	-74	-5	-8.3

● **LOUIS DRUCKE** Drucke, Louis Frank b: 12/3/1888, Waco, Tex. d: 9/22/55, Waco, Tex. BR/TR, 6'1", 188 lbs. Deb: 9/25/09

YEAR	TM/L	W	L	PCT	G	GS	CG	SH	SV	IP	H	R	HR	HB	BB	SO	RAT	ERA	ERA+	OAV	OOB	BH	AVG	PB	PR	PR+	PD	TPI
1909	NY-N	2	1	.667	3	3	2	0	0	24	20	9	0	0	13	8	12.4	2.25	114	.227	.327	1	.125	-0	1	1	-0	0.0
1910	NY-N	12	10	.545	34	27	15	0	0	215^1	174	73	3	11	82	151	11.2	2.47	120	.228	.312	15	.214	4	14	12	2	1.7
1911	NY-N	4	4	.500	15	10	4	0	0	75^2	83	39	1	8	41	42	15.7	4.04	83	.281	.384	2	.087	-1	-5	-6	1	-0.6
1912	NY-N	0	0	—	1	0	0	0	1	2	5	4	0	0	1	0	27.0	13.50	25	.417	.462	0	—	0	-2	-2	-0	-0.2
Total	4	18	15	.545	53	40	21	0	1	317	282	125	4	19	137	201	12.4	2.90	105	.243	.333	18	.178	2	7	5	2	0.9

● **CARL DRUHOT** Druhot, Carl A. "Collie" b: 9/1/1882, Ohio d: 2/11/18, Portland, Ore. BL/TL, 5'7", 150 lbs. Deb: 4/18/06

YEAR	TM/L	W	L	PCT	G	GS	CG	SH	SV	IP	H	R	HR	HB	BB	SO	RAT	ERA	ERA+	OAV	OOB	BH	AVG	PB	PR	PR+	PD	TPI
1906	Cin-N	2	2	.500	4	3	1	0	0	25	27	17	0	2	7	14	13.0	4.32	64	.270	.330	2	.222	0	-5	-4	-1	-0.7
	StL-N	6	7	.462	15	13	12	1	0	130^1	117	55	1	5	46	45	11.6	2.62	100	.238	.310	13	.232	1	0	0	1	0.2
	Yr	8	9	.471	19	16	13	1	0	155^1	144	72	1	7	53	59	11.8	2.90	91	.244	.313	15	.231	1	-5	-4	-1	-0.5
1907	StL-N	0	1	.000	1	1	0	0	0	2^1	3	5	0	1	4	1	30.9	15.43	16	.600	.800	0	—	0	-3	-3	0	-0.5
Total	2	8	10	.444	20	17	13	1	0	157^2	147	77	1	8	57	60	12.1	3.08	86	.247	.321	15	.231	1	-8	-8	-0	-1.0

● **TIM DRUMMOND** Drummond, Timothy Darnell b: 12/24/64, LaPlata, Md. BR/TR, 6'3", 170 lbs. Deb: 9/12/87

YEAR	TM/L	W	L	PCT	G	GS	CG	SH	SV	IP	H	R	HR	HB	BB	SO	RAT	ERA	ERA+	OAV	OOB	BH	AVG	PB	PR	PR+	PD	TPI
1987	Pit-N	0	0	—	6	0	0	0	0	6	5	3	0	0	3	5	12.0	4.50	91	.227	.320	0	.000	-0	-0	-0	0	0.0
1989	Min-A	0	0	—	8	0	0	0	1	16^1	16	7	0	2	8	9	14.3	3.86	108	.246	.347	0	—	0	0	0	-0	0.0
1990	Min-A	3	5	.375	35	4	0	0	1	91	104	46	8	1	36	49	13.9	4.35	96	.295	.362	0	—	0	-4	-2	-1	-0.3
Total	3	3	5	.375	49	4	0	0	2	113^1	125	56	8	3	47	63	13.9	4.29	97	.284	.357	0	.000	-0	-5	-2	-1	-0.3

● **DON DRYSDALE** Drysdale, Donald Scott b: 7/23/36, Van Nuys, Cal. d: 7/3/93, Montreal, Que., Canada BR/TR, 6'6", 216 lbs. Deb: 4/17/56 H

YEAR	TM/L	W	L	PCT	G	GS	CG	SH	SV	IP	H	R	HR	HB	BB	SO	RAT	ERA	ERA+	OAV	OOB	BH	AVG	PB	PR	PR+	PD	TPI
1956	*Bro-N	5	5	.500	25	12	2	0	0	99	95	35	9	3	31	55	11.7	2.64	150	.255	.317	5	.192	1	12	14	1	1.5
1957	Bro-N	17	9	.654	34	29	9	4	0	221	197	76	17	7	61	148	10.8	2.69	155	.236	.294	9	.123	-0	29	**34**	5	**4.4**
1958	LA-N	12	13	.480	44	29	6	1	0	211^2	214	107	21	14	72	131	12.8	4.17	98	.263	.333	15	.227	8	-5	-2	3	1.0
1959	*LA-N★	17	13	.567	44	36	15	**4**	2	270^2	237	113	26	18	93	**242**	11.6	3.46	122	.233	.308	15	.165	3	15	22	2	2.8
1960	LA-N	15	14	.517	41	36	15	5	2	269	214	93	27	10	72	**246**	**9.9**	2.84	140	.215	**.275**	13	.157	2	27	**32**	4	4.1
1961	LA-N☆	13	10	.565	40	37	10	3	0	244	236	111	29	20	83	182	12.5	3.69	118	.254	.329	16	.193	4	9	16	-1	1.7
1962	LA-N★	**25**	9	.735	43	41	19	2	1	**314^1**	272	122	21	11	78	**232**	10.3	2.83	128	.230	.283	22	.198	5	**39**	30	1	3.7
1963	*LA-N★	19	17	.528	42	42	17	3	0	315^1	287	114	25	10	57	251	10.1	2.63	115	.242	.283	16	.167	5	23	15	3	2.6
1964	LA-N★	18	16	.529	40	40	21	5	0	**321^1**	242	91	15	10	68	237	9.0	2.18	148	.207	.256	19	.173	4	**48**	**41**	2	**5.2**
1965	*LA-N★	23	12	.657	44	42	20	7	1	308^1	270	113	30	12	66	210	10.2	2.77	118	.232	.280	39	.300	22	26	18	0	4.6
1966	*LA-N	13	16	.448	40	40	11	3	0	273^2	279	114	21	17	45	177	11.2	3.42	96	.265	.306	20	.189	4	6	-4	-1	-0.1
1967	LA-N★	13	16	.448	38	38	9	3	0	282	269	101	19	8	60	196	10.8	2.74	113	.251	.296	12	.129	-0	20	12	3	1.6
1968	LA-N★	14	12	.538	31	31	12	8	0	239	201	68	11	12	56	155	10.1	2.15	129	.231	.286	14	.177	1	22	18	2	2.5
1969	LA-N	5	4	.556	12	12	1	1	0	62^2	71	34	9	2	13	24	12.4	4.45	75	.291	.332	3	.136	0	-6	-8	0	-1.0
Total	14	209	166	.557	518	465	167	49	6	3432	3084	1292	280	154	855	2486	10.7	2.95	121	.239	.294	218	.186	60	266	237	25	34.6

● **MONK DUBIEL** Dubiel, Walter John b: 2/12/18, Hartford, Conn. d: 10/23/69, Hartford, Conn. BR/TR, 6', 190 lbs. Deb: 4/19/44

YEAR	TM/L	W	L	PCT	G	GS	CG	SH	SV	IP	H	R	HR	HB	BB	SO	RAT	ERA	ERA+	OAV	OOB	BH	AVG	PB	PR	PR+	PD	TPI
1944	NY-A	13	13	.500	30	28	19	3	0	232	217	93	12	1	86	79	11.8	3.38	103	.248	.316	15	.181	-2	1	3	0	0.1
1945	NY-A	10	9	.526	26	20	9	1	0	151^1	157	88	9	0	62	45	13.0	4.64	75	.266	.335	16	.276	4	-21	-19	-2	-2.0
1948	Phi-N	8	10	.444	37	17	6	2	4	150^1	139	84	13	1	58	42	11.9	3.89	101	.248	.320	7	.167	0	1	1	-2	0.0
1949	Chi-N	6	9	.400	32	20	3	1	4	147^2	142	75	16	1	54	52	12.0	4.14	97	.250	.317	10	.286	3	-2	-2	1	0.3
1950	Chi-N	6	10	.375	39	12	4	2	2	142^2	152	79	12	1	67	51	13.9	4.16	101	.270	.348	9	.200	1	-0	1	2	0.3
1951	Chi-N	2	2	.500	22	0	0	0	1	54^2	46	17	3	0	22	19	11.2	2.30	178	.232	.309	0	.000	-1	10	11	0	0.6
1952	Chi-N	0	0	—	1	0	0	0	0	0^2	1	0	0	0	0	1	13.5	0.00	—	.333	.333	0	—	0	0	0	0	0.0
Total	7	45	53	.459	187	97	41	9	11	879^1	854	436	65	4	349	289	12.4	3.87	98	.254	.325	57	.207	5	-11	-6	-0	-0.7

● **BRIAN DuBOIS** DuBois, Brian Andrew b: 4/18/67, Joliet, Ill. BL/TL, 5'10", 195 lbs. Deb: 8/17/89

YEAR	TM/L	W	L	PCT	G	GS	CG	SH	SV	IP	H	R	HR	HB	BB	SO	RAT	ERA	ERA+	OAV	OOB	BH	AVG	PB	PR	PR+	PD	TPI
1989	Det-A	0	4	.000	6	5	0	0	1	36	29	14	2	2	17	13	12.0	1.75	219	.218	.316	0	—	0	9	8	-0	1.0
1990	Det-A	3	5	.375	12	11	0	0	0	58^1	70	37	9	1	22	34	14.3	5.09	78	.310	.373	0	—	0	-8	-7	-1	-1.0
Total	2	3	9	.250	18	16	0	0	1	94^1	99	51	11	3	39	47	13.5	3.82	103	.276	.352	0	—	0	1	1	-1	0.0

● **JEAN DUBUC** Dubuc, Jean Joseph Octave Arthur "Chauncey"
b: 9/15/1888, St.Johnsbury, Vt. d: 8/28/58, Fort Myers, Fla. BR/TR, 5'10.5", 185 lbs. Deb: 6/25/08 C♦

YEAR	TM/L	W	L	PCT	G	GS	CG	SH	SV	IP	H	R	HR	HB	BB	SO	RAT	ERA	ERA+	OAV	OOB	BH	AVG	PB	PR	PR+	PD	TPI
1908	Cin-N	5	6	.455	15	9	7	1	0	85^1	62	34	2	5	41	32	11.4	2.74	84	.205	.309	4	.138	-1	-4	-1	-1	-0.6
1909	Cin-N	2	5	.286	19	5	2	0	1	71^1	72	58	0	4	46	19	15.4	3.66	71	.269	.384	3	.167	0	-8	-8	0	-0.8
1912	Det-A	17	10	.630	37	26	23	2	3	250	217	107	2	7	109	97	12.0	2.77	118	.235	.321	29	.269	6	15	14	4	2.6
1913	Det-A	15	14	.517	36	28	22	1	2	242^2	228	113	1	8	91	73	12.1	2.89	101	.252	.325	36	.267	5	1	1	8	1.9
1914	Det-A	12	14	.462	36	27	15	2	1	224	216	124	3	6	76	70	12.0	3.46	81	.257	.324	28	.226	7	-18	-16	3	-0.6
1915	Det-A	17	12	.586	39	33	22	5	2	258	231	116	6	10	88	74	11.5	3.21	94	.245	.316	23	.205	0	-8	-5	-1	-0.4
1916	Det-A	10	10	.500	36	16	8	1	1	170^1	134	66	1	5	84	40	11.8	2.96	97	.233	.336	20	.256	5	-2	-2	4	0.8
1918	*Bos-A	0	1	.000	2	1	1	0	0	10^2	11	5	1	0	5	1	13.5	4.22	64	.268	.348	1	.167	0	-2	-2	-0	-0.2
1919	NY-N	6	4	.600	36	5	1	0	3	132	119	49	4	2	37	32	10.8	2.66	105	.246	.303	6	.143	-1	4	2	2	0.2
Total	9	84	76	.525	256	150	101	12	13	1444^1	1290	672	20	47	577	438	11.9	3.04	96	.244	.324	150	.230	21	-22	-21	23	2.9

YEAR	TM/L	W	L	PCT	G	GS	CG	SH	SV	IP	H	R	HR	HB	BB	SO	RAT	ERA	ERA+	OAV	OOB	BH	AVG	PB	PR	PR+	PD	TPI
● JIM DUCKWORTH	Duckworth, James Raymond b: 5/24/39, National City, Cal. BR/TR, 6'4", 194 lbs. Deb: 4/13/63																											
1963	Was-A	4	12	.250	37	15	2	0	0	120^2	131	89	13	10	67	66	15.5	6.04	61	.278	.379	0	.000	-3	-32	-31	-1	-4.0
1964	Was-A	1	6	.143	30	2	0	0	3	56	52	37	9	3	25	56	12.9	4.34	85	.244	.332	2	.222	0	-4	-4	0	-0.4
1965	Was-A	2	2	.500	17	8	0	0	0	64	45	30	11	2	36	74	11.7	3.94	88	.202	.318	0	.000	-2	-3	-3	-1	-0.5
1966	Was-A	0	3	.000	5	4	0	0	0	14^1	14	12	2	1	10	14	15.7	5.02	69	.259	.385	0	.000	-0	-3	-2	-0	-0.5
	KC-A	0	2	.000	8	0	0	0	1	12	14	12	2	1	10	10	18.8	9.00	38	.292	.424	0	.000	-0	-7	-8	-0	-1.3
	Yr	0	5	.000	13	4	0	0	1	26^1	28	24	4	2	20	24	17.1	6.84	50	.275	.403	0	.000	-1	-10	-10	-1	-1.8
Total	4	7	25	.219	97	29	2	0	4	267	256	180	37	17	148	220	14.2	5.26	69	.253	.358	2	.034	-5	-50	-48	-2	-6.7
● CLISE DUDLEY	Dudley, Elzie Clise b: 8/8/03, Graham, N.C. d: 1/12/89, Moncks Corner, S.C BL/TR, 6'1", 195 lbs. Deb: 4/18/29																											
1929	Bro-N	6	14	.300	35	20	8	1	0	156^2	202	130	9	10	64	33	15.9	5.69	81	.315	.385	5	.098	-1	-17	-19	2	-1.9
1930	Bro-N	2	4	.333	21	7	2	0	1	66^2	103	62	3	2	27	18	17.8	6.35	77	.371	.430	5	.208	-0	-10	-11	1	-0.7
1931	Phi-N	8	14	.364	30	24	8	0	0	179	206	95	10	6	56	50	13.5	3.52	121	.287	.343	18	.214	-0	7	13	1	1.6
1932	Phi-N	1	1	.500	13	0	0	0	1	17^2	23	14	3	0	8	5	15.8	7.13	62	.329	.397	4	.286	3	-6	-5	0	-0.2
1933	Pit-N	0	0	—	1	0	0	0	0	0^1	6	5	0	0	1	0	189.0	135.00	2	.857	.875	0	—	0	-5	-5	0	-0.2
Total	5	17	33	.340	100	51	18	1	2	420^1	540	306	25	18	156	106	15.3	5.03	90	.315	.378	32	.185	1	-31	-23	4	-1.4
● HAL DUES	Dues, Hal Joseph b: 9/22/54, LaMarque, Tex. BR/TR, 6'3", 180 lbs. Deb: 9/9/77																											
1977	Mon-N	1	1	.500	6	4	0	0	0	23	26	14	2	0	9	9	13.7	4.30	89	.265	.327	0	.000	-1	-1	-1	0	-0.1
1978	Mon-N	5	6	.455	25	12	1	0	1	99	85	29	5	4	42	36	11.9	2.36	149	.240	.327	6	.194	0	13	13	-0	1.4
1980	Mon-N	0	1	.000	6	1	0	0	0	12^1	17	9	1	0	4	2	15.3	6.57	54	.333	.382	0	.000	-0	-4	-4	0	-0.3
Total	3	6	8	.429	37	17	1	0	1	134^1	128	52	8	4	55	47	12.5	3.08	116	.254	.333	6	.154	-1	8	8	0	1.0
● LARRY DUFF	Duff, Cecil Elba b: 11/30/1897, Radersburg, Mont. d: 11/10/69, Bend, Ore. BL/TR, 6'1", 175 lbs. Deb: 9/5/22																											
1922	Chi-A	1	1	.500	3	1	0	0	0	12^2	16	7	1	0	3	7	13.5	4.97	82	.340	.380	2	.400	0	-1	-1	-0	-0.2
● JIM DUFFALO	Duffalo, James Francis b: 11/25/35, Helvetia, Pa. BR/TR, 6'1", 175 lbs. Deb: 4/12/61																											
1961	SF-N	5	1	.833	24	4	1	0	1	61^2	59	31	9	2	32	37	13.6	4.23	90	.257	.352	5	.294	3	-1	-3	-1	-0.1
1962	SF-N	1	2	.333	24	2	0	0	0	42	42	27	3	0	23	29	13.9	3.64	104	.256	.348	0	.000	-0	1	1	-1	0.0
1963	SF-N	4	2	.667	34	5	0	0	2	75^1	56	26	3	2	37	55	11.3	2.87	112	.209	.309	2	.111	-1	4	3	1	0.2
1964	SF-N	5	1	.833	35	3	1	0	3	74	57	25	9	2	31	55	10.9	2.92	122	.209	.294	1	.071	-1	5	5	-1	0.3
1965	SF-N	0	1	.000	2	0	0	0	0	0^1	1	1	0	0	2	0	81.0	27.00	13	.500	.750	0	—	0	-1	-1	0	-0.2
	Cin-N	0	1	.000	22	0	0	0	0	44^1	33	21	3	5	30	34	13.8	3.45	109	.212	.356	0	.000	-1	0	1	1	0.0
	Yr	0	2	.000	24	0	0	0	0	44^2	34	22	3	5	32	34	14.3	3.63	103	.215	.364	0	.000	-1	-0	1	1	-0.2
Total	5	15	8	.652	141	14	2	0	6	297^2	248	131	27	11	155	210	12.5	3.39	106	.227	.329	8	.127	1	8	7	-1	0.2
● JOHN DUFFIE	Duffie, John Brown b: 10/4/45, Greenwood, S.C. BR/TR, 6'7", 210 lbs. Deb: 9/18/67																											
1967	LA-N	0	2	.000	2	2	0	0	0	9^2	11	6	1	0	4	6	14.0	2.79	111	.282	.349	0	.000	-0	1	0	-0	0.0
● BERNIE DUFFY	Duffy, Bernard Allen b: 8/18/1893, Vinson, Okla. d: 2/9/62, Abilene, Tex. BR/TR, 5'11", 180 lbs. Deb: 9/20/13																											
1913	Pit-N	0	0	—	3	2	0	0	0	11^1	18	8	0	0	3	8	16.7	5.56	54	.360	.396	1	.250	0	-3	-3	0	-0.1
● DAN DUGAN	Dugan, Daniel Phillip b: 2/22/07, Plainfield, N.J. d: 6/25/68, Green Brook, N.J. BL/TL, 6'1.5", 187 lbs. Deb: 9/5/28																											
1928	Chi-A	0	0	—	1	0	0	0	0	0^1	0	0	0	0	0	0	0.0	0.00	—	.000	.000	0	—	0	0	0	0	0.0
1929	Chi-A	1	4	.200	19	2	0	0	1	65	77	51	8	2	19	15	13.6	6.65	64	.300	.353	3	.150	-1	-17	-17	-2	-1.4
Total	2	1	4	.200	20	2	0	0	1	65^1	77	51	8	2	19	15	13.5	6.61	65	.298	.351	3	.150	-1	-17	-17	-2	-1.4
● ED DUGAN	Dugan, Edward John b: 1864, Brooklyn, N.Y. Deb: 8/5/1884 F																											
1884	Ric-a	5	14	.263	20	20	20	0	0	166^1	196	137	5	2	15	60	11.5	4.49	74	.267	.284	8	.114	-4	-23	-21	-2	-2.4
● BILL DUGGLEBY	Duggleby, William James "Frosty Bill" b: 3/16/1874, Utica, N.Y. d: 8/30/44, Redfield, N.Y. TR, Deb: 4/21/1898																											
1898	Phi-N	3	3	.500	9	5	4	0	0	54	70	39	4	6	18	12	15.7	5.50	62	.311	.378	5	.238	2	-11	-13	1	-0.9
1901	Phi-N	20	12	.625	35	29	26	5	0	284^2	302	120	9	10	41	95	11.2	2.88	118	.270	.302	19	.165	-3	14	16	5	1.8
1902	Phi-A	1	1	.500	2	2	2	0	0	17	19	9	0	0	4	4	12.2	3.18	116	.284	.324	0	.000	-1	1	1	1	0.1
	Phi-N	11	17	.393	33	27	25	0	1	258^2	282	130	2	12	57	60	12.2	3.38	83	.277	.323	17	.173	-1	-17	-16	2	-1.5
1903	Phi-N	13	16	.448	36	30	28	3	2	264^1	318	162	4	12	79	57	13.9	3.75	87	.303	.358	24	.231	2	-14	-14	1	-1.0
1904	Phi-N	12	13	.480	32	27	22	2	1	223^2	265	138	3	11	53	55	13.2	3.78	71	.292	.338	14	.171	0	-26	-28	0	-2.8
1905	Phi-N	18	17	.514	38	36	27	1	0	289^1	270	116	10	13	83	75	11.4	2.46	119	.253	.315	11	.109	-2	18	15	-2	1.4
1906	Phi-N	13	19	.406	42	30	22	5	2	280^1	241	93	5	12	66	83	10.2	2.25	116	.227	.280	14	.141	-2	12	12	1	1.2
1907	Phi-N	0	2	.000	5	2	2	0	0	29	43	27	2	5	11	8	18.3	7.45	33	.371	.447	1	.111	0	-16	-17	1	-0.9
	Pit-N	2	2	.500	9	3	1	1	0	40^1	34	17	0	2	12	4	10.7	2.68	91	.239	.308	2	.154	-0	-1	-1	1	0.0
	Yr	2	4	.333	14	5	3	1	0	69^1	77	44	2	7	23	12	13.9	4.67	52	.298	.372	3	.136	0	-17	-18	2	-0.9
Total	8	93	102	.477	241	191	159	17	6	1741^1	1844	851	39	83	424	453	12.2	3.18	93	.272	.323	107	.165	-4	-41	-44	11	-2.6
● MARTIN DUKE	Duke, Martin F. "Duck" (b: Martin F. Duck) b: 1867, Zanesville, Ohio d: 12/31/1898, Minneapolis, Minn. TL, Deb: 8/24/1891																											
1891	Was-a	0	3	.000	4	3	2	0	0	23	36	33	0	0	19	5	21.5	7.43	50	.346	.447	1	.111	-1	-10	-9	-0	-0.9
● JAN DUKES	Dukes, Noble Jan b: 8/16/45, Cheyenne, Wyo. BL/TL, 5'11", 175 lbs. Deb: 9/6/69																											
1969	Was-A	0	2	.000	8	0	0	0	0	11	8	3	0	0	4	3	9.8	2.45	141	.216	.293	0	.000	0	1	1	-0	0.2
1970	Was-A	0	0	—	5	0	0	0	0	6^2	6	3	0	1	1	4	10.8	2.70	132	.240	.296	0	.000	-0	1	1	0	0.0
1972	Tex-A	0	0	—	3	0	0	0	0	2^1	1	2	0	0	5	0	23.1	3.86	78	.167	.545	0	—	0	-0	-0	0	0.0
Total	3	0	2	.000	16	0	0	0	0	20	15	8	0	1	10	7	11.7	2.70	128	.221	.329	0	.000	0	2	2	-0	0.2
● TOM DUKES	Dukes, Thomas Earl b: 8/31/42, Knoxville, Tenn. BR/TR, 6'2", 185 lbs. Deb: 8/15/67																											
1967	Hou-N	0	2	.000	17	0	0	0	1	23^2	25	14	2	2	11	23	14.5	5.32	62	.275	.365	1	.500	0	-5	-5	-0	-0.5
1968	Hou-N	2	2	.500	43	0	0	0	4	52^2	62	31	3	2	28	37	15.7	4.27	69	.291	.379	0	.000	-0	-8	-8	0	-0.7
1969	SD-N	1	0	1.000	13	0	0	0	1	22^1	26	18	2	0	10	15	14.5	7.25	49	.295	.367	0	.000	-0	-9	-9	0	-0.5
1970	SD-N	1	6	.143	53	0	0	0	10	69	62	39	7	2	25	56	11.6	4.04	98	.246	.319	0	.000	-1	0	-0	-0	-0.2
1971	*Bal-A	1	5	.167	28	0	0	0	4	38^1	40	15	4	1	8	30	11.5	3.52	95	.263	.304	1	.143	0	-0	-1	-1	-0.2
1972	Cal-A	0	1	.000	7	0	0	0	1	11	11	3	1	1	0	8	9.8	1.64	179	.262	.279	0	—	0	2	2	-1	0.1
Total	6	5	16	.238	161	0	0	0	21	217	226	120	19	8	82	169	13.1	4.35	79	.270	.341	2	.095	-1	-20	-22	-2	-2.0
● BOB DULIBA	Duliba, Robert John b: 1/9/35, Glen Lyon, Pa. BR/TR, 5'10", 185 lbs. Deb: 8/11/59																											
1959	StL-N	0	1	.000	11	0	0	0	1	22^2	19	7	2	0	12	14	12.3	2.78	153	.237	.337	0	.000	-0	3	3	1	0.2
1960	StL-N	4	4	.500	27	0	0	0	0	40^2	49	20	6	0	16	23	14.4	4.20	97	.310	.374	1	.200	-0	-2	-0	-0	-0.1
1962	StL-N	2	0	1.000	28	0	0	0	2	39^1	33	11	3	0	17	22	11.4	2.06	207	.239	.323	0	.000	-0	8	9	0	0.5
1963	LA-A	1	1	.500	6	0	0	0	1	7^2	3	1	0	0	6	4	10.6	1.17	292	.125	.300	0	.000	-0	2	2	-0	0.4
1964	LA-A	6	4	.600	58	0	0	0	9	72^2	80	35	5	1	22	33	12.8	3.59	91	.287	.341	0	.000	-1	0	-3	1	-0.4
1965	Bos-A	4	2	.667	39	0	0	0	1	64^1	60	31	6	0	22	27	11.5	3.78	99	.248	.311	0	.000	-0	-2	-0	-0	-0.1
1967	KC-A	0	0	—	7	0	0	0	0	9^2	13	7	3	0	1	6	13.0	6.52	49	.342	.359	0	—	0	-4	-4	-0	-0.2
Total	7	17	12	.586	176	0	0	0	14	257	257	112	25	1	96	129	12.4	3.47	108	.268	.335	1	.038	-2	6	8	1	0.3
● GEORGE DUMONT	Dumont, George Henry "Pea Soup" b: 11/13/1895, Minneapolis, Minn. d: 10/13/56, Minneapolis, Minn. BR/TR, 5'11", 163 lbs. Deb: 9/14/15																											
1915	Was-A	2	1	.667	6	4	3	2	0	40	23	17	0	2	12	18	8.3	2.02	147	.169	.247	2	.167	-0	4	4	-1	0.2
1916	Was-A	2	3	.400	17	5	2	0	1	53	37	25	0	1	17	21	9.3	3.06	91	.194	.263	1	.071	-0	-1	-2	-1	-0.3
1917	Was-A	5	14	.263	37	23	8	2	2	204^2	171	76	3	6	76	65	11.1	2.55	103	.227	.303	2	.034	-5	3	2	-3	-0.7
1918	Was-A	1	1	.500	4	1	1	0	0	14	18	12	0	0	6	12	15.4	5.14	53	.295	.358	1	.333	1	-4	-4	0	-0.4
1919	Bos-A	0	4	.000	13	2	0	0	0	35^1	45	21	1	1	19	12	16.6	4.33	70	.326	.411	0	.000	-0	-4	-5	0	-0.6
Total	5	10	23	.303	77	35	14	4	3	347	294	151	4	10	130	128	11.3	2.85	96	.230	.306	6	.064	-5	-3	-5	-5	-1.8
● DAN DUMOULIN	Dumoulin, Daniel Lynn b: 8/20/53, Kokomo, Ind. BR/TR, 6', 175 lbs. Deb: 9/5/77																											
1977	Cin-N	0	0	—	5	0	0	0	0	5^1	12	8	0	0	3	5	25.3	13.50	29	.462	.517	0	—	0	-6	-6	0	-0.3

YEAR TM/L	W	L	PCT	G	GS	CG	SH	SV	IP	H	R	HR	HB	BB	SO	RAT	ERA	ERA+	OAV	OOB	BH	AVG	PB	PR	PR+	PD	TPI
1978 Cin-N	1	0	1.000	3	0	0	0	0	5	7	1	0	1	3	2	19.8	1.80	197	.368	.478	0	—	0	1	1	0	0.2
Total 2	1	0	1.000	8	0	0	0	0	10^1	19	9	0	1	6	7	22.6	7.84	48	.422	.500	0	—	0	-5	-5	0	-0.1
● NICK DUMOVICH Dumovich, Nicholas b: 1/2/02, Sacramento, Cal. d: 12/12/78, Laguna Hills, Cal. BL/TL, 6', 170 lbs. Deb: 4/20/23																											
1923 Chi-N	3	5	.375	28	8	1	0	1	94	118	60	4	3	45	23	15.9	4.60	87	.319	.397	7	.241	1	-6	-6	1	-0.2
● MATT DUNBAR Dunbar, Matthew Marshall b: 10/15/68, Tallahassee, Fla. BL/TL, 6', 170 lbs. Deb: 4/25/95																											
1995 Fla-N	0	1	.000	8	0	0	0	0	7	12	9	0	1	11	5	30.9	11.57	36	.387	.558	0	—	0	-6	-6	1	-0.6
● ED DUNDON Dundon, Edward Joseph "Dummy" b: 7/10/1859, Columbus, Ohio d: 8/18/1893, Columbus, Ohio TR, Deb: 6/2/1883 ♦																											
1883 Col-a	3	16	.158	20	19	16	0	0	166^2	213	153	7		38	31	13.6	4.48	69	.292	.327	15	.161	-3	-22	-28	0	-2.6
1884 Col-a	6	4	.600	11	9	7	0	0	81	85	55	9	0	15	37	11.1	3.78	80	.249	.281	12	.140	-1	-5	-7	1	-0.7
Total 2	9	20	.310	31	28	23	0	0	247^2	298	208	16	0	53	68	12.8	4.25	72	.278	.312	27	.151	-4	-27	-35	1	-3.3
● JIM DUNEGAN Dunegan, James William b: 8/6/47, Burlington, Iowa BR/TR, 6'1", 205 lbs. Deb: 5/28/70																											
1970 Chi-N	0	2	.000	7	0	0	0	0	13^1	13	7	2	0	12	3	16.9	4.73	95	.277	.424	1	.250	0	-1	-0	0	0.0
● WILEY DUNHAM Dunham, Henry Huston b: 1/30/1877, Piketon, Ohio d: 1/16/34, Cleveland, Ohio 6'1", 180 lbs. Deb: 5/24/02																											
1902 StL-N	2	3	.400	7	5	3	0	1	38	47	31	1	3	13	15	14.9	5.68	48	.303	.368	1	.083	-1	-12	-13	-0	-1.6
● DAVEY DUNKLE Dunkle, Edward Perks b: 8/30/1872, Philipsburg, Pa. d: 11/19/41, Lock Haven, Pa. BB/TR, 6'2", 220 lbs. Deb: 8/28/1897																											
1897 Phi-N	5	2	.714	7	7	7	0	0	62	72	41	0	1	23	9	13.9	3.48	120	.288	.350	4	.174	-1	6	5	-1	0.3
1898 Phi-N	1	4	.200	12	7	4	0	0	68^1	83	70	1	9	38	21	17.1	6.98	49	.297	.399	6	.214	-0	-26	-28	-1	-1.7
1899 Was-N	0	2	.000	4	2	2	0	0	26	46	34	3	1	14	9	21.1	10.04	39	.383	.452	3	.273	-0	-18	-17	-0	-1.0
1903 Chi-A	4	4	.500	12	7	6	0	1	82	96	58	1	3	31	26	14.3	4.06	69	.291	.357	10	.303	2	-10	-12	-2	-1.1
Was-A	5	9	.357	14	13	10	0	0	108^1	111	60	4	4	33	51	12.3	4.24	74	.264	.324	4	.098	-4	-15	-13	-2	-2.0
Yr	9	13	.409	26	20	16	0	1	190^1	207	118	5	7	64	77	13.1	4.16	72	.276	.339	14	.189	-2	-25	-24	-4	-3.1
1904 Was-A	2	9	.182	12	11	7	0	0	74^1	95	56	1	3	23	23	14.7	4.96	54	.311	.366	4	.143	-2	-20	-19	-0	-2.6
Total 5	17	30	.362	61	47	36	0	1	421	503	319	10	21	162	139	14.7	5.02	65	.295	.364	31	.189	-4	-83	-83	-7	-8.1
● FRED DUNLAP Dunlap, Frederick C. "Sure Shot" b: 5/21/1859, Philadelphia, Pa. d: 12/1/02, Philadelphia, Pa. BR/TR, 5'8", 165 lbs. Deb: 5/1/1880 M♦																											
1884 StL-U	0	0	—	1	0	0	0	1	0^2	2	1	0		0	1	27.0	13.50	18	.500	.500	185	.412	1	-1	-1	0	-0.1
1887 *Det-N	0	0	—	1	0	0	0	0	2	4	2	0	0	0	1	18.0	4.50	90	.500	.500	97	.327	0	-0	-0	-0	0.0
Total 2	0	0	—	2	0	0	0	1	2^2	6	3	0	0	0	2	20.3	6.75	54	.500	.500	1184	.296	1	-1	-1	-0	-0.1
● JACK DUNLEAVY Dunleavy, John Francis b: 9/14/1879, Harrison, N.J. d: 4/11/44, S.Norwalk, Conn. TL, 5'6", 167 lbs. Deb: 5/30/03 ♦																											
1903 StL-N	6	8	.429	14	13	9	0	0	102	101	59	2	8	57	51	14.6	4.06	80	.264	.371	48	.249	2	-9	-9	1	-0.8
1904 StL-N	1	4	.200	7	5	5	0	0	55	63	32	4	1	23	28	14.2	4.42	61	.275	.344	40	.233	2	-10	-11	1	-0.7
Total 2	7	12	.368	21	18	14	0	0	157	164	91	6	9	80	79	14.5	4.18	73	.268	.361	193	.241	4	-19	-20	1	-1.5
● JIM DUNN Dunn, James William "Bill" b: 2/25/31, Valdosta, Ga. d: 1/6/99, Gadsden, Ala. BR/TR, 6'0.5", 185 lbs. Deb: 8/26/52																											
1952 Pit-N	0	0	—	3	0	0	0	0	5^1	4	2	0	0	3	2	11.8	3.38	118	.190	.292	0	.000	-0	0	0	0	0.0
● JACK DUNN Dunn, John Joseph b: 10/6/1872, Meadville, Pa. d: 10/22/28, Towson, Md. BR/TR, 5'9", Deb: 5/6/1897 ♦																											
1897 Bro-N	14	9	.609	25	21	21	0	0	216^2	251	147	6	9	66	26	13.5	4.57	90	.288	.344	29	.221	-2	-6	-12	1	-1.1
1898 Bro-N	16	21	.432	41	37	31	0	0	322^2	352	180	10	15	82	66	12.5	3.60	100	.275	.327	41	.246	0	0	-0	-1	-0.1
1899 Bro-N	23	13	.639	41	34	29	2	2	299^1	323	161	8	18	86	48	12.8	3.70	106	.275	.334	30	.246	0	5	7	3	1.0
1900 Bro-N	3	4	.429	10	7	5	0	0	63	88	48	1	4	28	6	17.1	5.57	69	.330	.401	6	.231	-0	-13	-12	1	-1.0
Phi-N	5	5	.500	10	9	9	1	0	80	87	50	2	5	29	12	13.6	4.84	75	.276	.347	10	.303	1	-10	-11	-1	-1.0
Yr	8	9	.471	20	16	14	1	0	143	175	98	3	9	57	18	15.2	5.16	72	.301	.372	16	.271	1	-23	-23	1	-2.0
1901 Phi-N	0	1	.000	2	2	0	0	0	4^2	11	16	0	2	7	1	38.6	21.21	16	.458	.606	1	1.000	1	-9	-9	-0	-1.2
Bal-A	3	3	.500	9	6	6	0	0	59^2	74	45	2	1	21	5	14.5	3.62	107	.301	.358	90	.249	0	0	2	1	0.2
1902 NY-N	0	3	.000	3	2	2	0	0	26^2	28	14	0	0	12	6	13.5	3.71	76	.269	.345	72	.211	0	-3	-3	1	-0.2
1904 NY-N	0	0	—	1	0	0	0	1	4	3	3	1	0	3	1	13.5	4.50	61	.167	.286	56	.309	0	-1	-1	-0	0.0
Total 7	64	59	.520	142	118	103	3	3	1076^2	1217	664	30	54	334	171	13.4	4.11	92	.283	.342	397	.245	1	-37	-38	5	-3.4
● MIKE DUNNE Dunne, Michael Dennis b: 10/27/62, South Bend, Ind. BR/TR, 6'4", 200 lbs. Deb: 6/5/87																											
1987 Pit-N	13	6	.684	23	23	5	1	0	163^1	143	66	10	1	68	72	11.7	3.03	136	.240	.319	5	.094	-1	19	20	2	2.3
1988 Pit-N	7	11	.389	30	28	1	0	0	170	163	88	15	5	88	70	13.6	3.92	87	.255	.349	5	.109	-1	-9	-10	0	-1.0
1989 Pit-N	1	1	.500	3	3	0	0	0	14^1	21	12	1	1	9	4	19.5	7.53	45	.328	.419	1	.250	0	-6	-7	0	-0.8
Sea-A	2	9	.182	15	15	1	0	0	85^1	104	61	7	2	37	38	15.1	5.27	77	.307	.378	0	—	0	-13	-11	0	-1.2
1990 SD-N	0	3	.000	10	6	0	0	0	28^2	28	21	4	0	17	15	14.1	5.65	68	.241	.338	0	.000	-1	-6	-6	1	-0.6
1992 Chi-A	2	0	1.000	4	1	0	0	0	12^2	12	7	0	1	6	6	13.5	4.26	91	.255	.352	0	—	0	-0	-1	0	-0.1
Total 5	25	30	.455	85	76	7	1	0	474^1	471	255	37	10	225	205	13.4	4.08	93	.261	.347	11	.101	-1	-16	-15	3	-1.4
● ANDY DUNNING Dunning, Andrew Jackson b: 8/12/1871, New York, N.Y. d: 6/21/52, New York, N.Y. BR/TR, 6', 175 lbs. Deb: 5/23/1889																											
1889 Pit-N	0	2	.000	2	2	2	0	0	18	20	19	1	0	16	4	18.0	7.00	54	.274	.404	0	.000	-1	-6	-7	0	-0.6
1891 NY-N	0	1	.000	1	1	0	0	0	2	3	5	1	0	3	1	27.0	4.50	71	.333	.500	0	—	0	-0	-0	-0	-0.1
Total 2	0	3	.000	3	3	2	0	0	20	23	24	2	0	19	5	18.9	6.75	55	.280	.416	0	.000	-1	-6	-7	0	-0.7
● STEVE DUNNING Dunning, Steven John b: 5/15/49, Denver, Colo. BR/TR, 6'2", 205 lbs. Deb: 6/14/70																											
1970 Cle-A	4	9	.308	19	17	0	0	0	94^1	93	55	16	4	54	77	14.4	4.96	80	.261	.364	5	.161	-1	-13	-10	1	-1.2
1971 Cle-A	8	14	.364	31	29	3	1	1	184	173	98	25	5	109	132	14.0	4.50	85	.254	.361	10	.182	1	-21	-12	2	-1.1
1972 Cle-A	6	4	.600	16	16	1	0	0	105	98	39	16	0	43	52	12.1	3.26	99	.248	.322	9	.273	5	-2	-0	-1	0.5
1973 Cle-A	0	2	.000	4	3	0	0	0	18	17	15	2	0	13	10	15.0	6.50	60	.250	.370	0	—	0	-5	-5	-0	-0.5
Tex-A	2	6	.250	23	12	2	0	0	94^1	101	63	11	1	52	38	14.7	5.34	70	.275	.367	0	—	0	-16	-17	-0	-1.3
Yr	2	8	.200	27	15	2	0	0	112^1	118	78	13	1	65	48	14.7	5.53	68	.271	.367	0	—	0	-21	-22	-0	-1.8
1974 Tex-A	0	0	—	1	0	0	0	0	2^1	3	5	2	0	3	1	23.1	19.29	19	.333	.500	0	—	0	-4	-4	0	-0.2
1976 Cal-A	0	0	—	4	0	0	0	0	6	9	9	2	0	6	4	22.5	7.50	44	.310	.429	0	—	0	-3	-3	-0	-0.2
Mon-N	2	6	.250	32	7	1	0	0	91^1	93	50	6	2	33	72	12.6	4.14	90	.274	.342	2	.133	-0	-6	-4	0	-0.3
1977 Oak-A	1	0	1.000	6	0	0	0	0	18^1	17	8	2	0	10	4	13.3	3.93	103	.254	.351	0	—	0	0	0	0	0.0
Total 7	23	41	.359	136	84	7	1	1	613^2	604	342	82	12	323	390	13.8	4.56	82	.261	.355	26	.194	6	-70	-54	3	-4.3
● FRANK DUPEE Dupee, Frank Oliver b: 4/29/1877, Monkton, Vt. d: 8/14/56, Portland, Me. TL, 6'1", 200 lbs. Deb: 8/24/01																											
1901 Chi-A	0	1	.000	1	1	0	0	0	0	0	0	0	3	—	—	∞	—	—	1.000	95	—	0	-3	-3	0	-0.3	
● MIKE DUPREE Dupree, Michael Dennis b: 5/29/53, Kansas City, Kan. BR/TR, 6'1", 185 lbs. Deb: 4/13/76																											
1976 SD-N	0	0	—	12	0	0	0	0	15^2	18	17	4	0	7	5	14.4	9.19	36	.286	.357	1	1.000	1	-10	-11	0	-0.5
● ROBERTO DURAN Duran, Roberto Alejandro b: 3/6/73, Moca, D.R. BL/TL, 6', 167 lbs. Deb: 7/6/97																											
1997 Det-A	0	0	—	13	0	0	0	0	10^2	7	9	0	3	15	11	21.1	7.59	60	.189	.455	0	—	0	-4	-4	-0	-0.2
1998 Det-A	0	1	.000	18	0	0	0	0	15^1	9	10	0	2	17	12	16.4	5.87	80	.170	.389	0	—	0	-2	-2	0	-0.1
Total 2	0	1	.000	31	0	0	0	0	26	16	19	0	5	32	23	18.3	6.58	71	.178	.417	0	—	0	-6	-5	-0	-0.3
● KID DURBIN Durbin, Blaine Alphonsus b: 9/10/1886, Lamar, Mo. d: 9/11/43, Kirkwood, Mo. BL/TL, 5'8", 155 lbs. Deb: 4/24/07 ♦																											
1907 Chi-N	0	1	.000	5	1	1	0	1	16^2	14	13	0	1	10	5	13.5	5.40	46	.233	.352	6	.333	1	-5	-5	0	-0.3
● CHAD DURBIN Durbin, Chad Griffin b: 12/3/77, Spring Valley, Ill. BR/TR, 6'1", 175 lbs. Deb: 9/26/99																											
1999 KC-A	0	0	—	1	0	0	0	0	2^1	1	0	0	0	1	3	7.7	0.00	—	.125	.222	0	—	0	1	1	0	0.1
2000 KC-A	2	5	.286	16	16	0	0	0	72^1	91	71	14	0	43	37	16.7	8.21	61	.301	.388	0	—	0	-26	-25	0	-1.9
Total 2	2	5	.286	17	16	0	0	0	74^2	92	71	14	0	44	40	16.4	7.96	63	.297	.384	0	—	0	-25	-24	0	-1.8

● RYNE DUREN

Duren, Rinold George b: 2/22/29, Cazenovia, Wis. BR/TR, 6'1", 195 lbs. Deb: 9/25/54

YEAR	TM/L	W	L	PCT	G	GS	CG	SH	SV	IP	H	R	HR	HB	BB	SO	RAT	ERA	ERA+	OAV	OOB	BH	AVG	PB	PR	PR+	PD	TPI
1954	Bal-A	0	0	—	1	0	0	0	0	2	3	3	0	0	1	2	18.0	9.00	40	.333	.400	0	—	0	-1	-1	-0	-0.1
1957	KC-A	0	3	.000	14	6	0	0	1	42^2	37	26	4	2	30	37	14.6	5.27	75	.236	.365	1	.071	-1	-7	-6	0	-0.5
1958	*NY-A☆	6	4	.600	44	1	0	0	**20**	75^2	40	20	4	7	43	87	10.7	2.02	175	.157	.296	1	.077	0	15	14	0	2.6
1959	NY-A★	3	6	.333	41	0	0	0	14	76^2	49	18	6	3	43	96	11.2	1.88	194	.181	.301	0	.000	-1	17	16	-0	2.3
1960	*NY-A	3	4	.429	42	1	0	0	9	49	27	29	3	7	49	67	15.2	4.96	72	.160	.369	0	.000	-1	-6	-8	1	-1.4
1961	NY-A	0	1	.000	4	0	0	0	0	5	2	3	2	0	4	7	10.8	5.40	69	.125	.300	0	—	0	-1	-1	-0	-0.2
	LA-A☆	6	12	.333	40	14	1	1	2	99	87	70	13	3	75	108	15.0	5.18	87	.233	.366	1	.040	-2	-13	-7	-1	-1.4
	Yr	6	13	.316	44	14	1	1	2	104	89	73	15	3	79	115	14.8	5.19	86	.229	.363	1	.040	-2	-14	-7	-2	-1.6
1962	LA-A	2	9	.182	42	3	0	0	8	71^1	53	38	1	6	57	74	14.6	4.42	87	.206	.363	1	.067	-1	-4	-5	-1	-0.9
1963	Phi-N	6	2	.750	33	7	1	0	2	87^1	65	33	6	5	52	84	12.6	3.30	98	.210	.332	3	.143	1	-0	-1	-1	-0.1
1964	Phi-N	0	0	—	2	0	0	0	0	3	5	3	0	1	1	5	21.0	6.00	58	.357	.438	0	—	0	-1	-1	-0	-0.1
	Cin-N	0	2	.000	26	0	0	0	1	43^2	41	17	1	3	15	39	12.2	2.89	125	.248	.322	0	.000	-0	3	3	-1	0.1
	Yr	0	2	.000	28	0	0	0	1	46^2	46	20	1	4	16	44	12.7	3.09	117	.257	.332	0	.000	-0	2	3	-1	0.0
1965	Phi-N	0	0	—	6	0	0	0	0	11	10	7	0	1	4	6	12.3	3.27	106	.270	.357	0	.000	-0	0	0	0	0.0
	Was-A	1	1	.500	16	0	0	0	0	23	24	17	0	3	18	18	17.6	6.65	52	.286	.429	0	—	0	-8	-8	-0	-0.7
Total	10	27	44	.380	311	32	2	1	57	589^1	443	284	40	41	392	630	13.4	3.83	98	.209	.344	7	.061	-5	-5	-6	-4	-0.4

● DON DURHAM

Durham, Donald Gary b: 3/21/49, Yosemite, Ky. BR/TR, 6', 170 lbs. Deb: 7/16/72

YEAR	TM/L	W	L	PCT	G	GS	CG	SH	SV	IP	H	R	HR	HB	BB	SO	RAT	ERA	ERA+	OAV	OOB	BH	AVG	PB	PR	PR+	PD	TPI
1972	StL-N	2	7	.222	10	8	1	0	0	47^2	42	28	1	0	22	35	12.1	4.34	78	.240	.325	7	.500	4	-5	-5	-1	-0.5
1973	Tex-A	0	4	.000	15	4	0	0	1	40^1	49	35	7	1	23	23	16.3	7.59	49	.304	.395	0	—	0	-17	-18	-1	-1.7
Total	2	2	11	.154	25	12	1	0	1	88	91	63	8	1	45	58	14.0	5.83	61	.271	.359	7	.500	4	-22	-23	-1	-2.2

● ED DURHAM

Durham, Edward Fant "Bull" b: 8/17/08, Chester, S.C. d: 4/27/76, Chester, S.C. BL/TR, 5'11", 170 lbs. Deb: 4/19/29

YEAR	TM/L	W	L	PCT	G	GS	CG	SH	SV	IP	H	R	HR	HB	BB	SO	RAT	ERA	ERA+	OAV	OOB	BH	AVG	PB	PR	PR+	PD	TPI
1929	Bos-A	1	0	1.000	14	1	0	0	0	22^1	34	24	2	0	14	6	19.3	9.27	46	.374	.457	0	.000	-0	-12	-12	-0	-0.6
1930	Bos-A	4	15	.211	33	12	6	1	1	140	144	81	9	2	43	28	12.2	4.69	98	.270	.326	4	.098	-4	-1	-1	-0	-0.6
1931	Bos-A	8	10	.444	38	15	7	2	0	165^1	175	91	9	4	50	53	12.5	4.25	101	.266	.322	3	.056	-6	2	1	-2	-0.6
1932	Bos-A	6	13	.316	34	22	4	0	0	175^1	187	90	13	4	49	52	12.3	3.80	118	.274	.327	7	.123	-3	13	13	1	1.0
1933	Chi-A	10	6	.625	24	21	6	0	0	138^2	137	74	12	5	46	65	12.2	4.48	95	.256	.320	10	.217	0	-3	-4	-1	-0.5
Total	5	29	44	.397	143	71	23	3	1	641^2	677	360	45	15	202	204	12.5	4.45	99	.271	.329	24	.119	-14	-0	-3	-3	-1.3

● JOHN DURHAM

Durham, John Garfield b: 10/7/1881, Douglass, Kan. d: 5/7/49, Coffeyville, Kan. BR/TR, 6', 175 lbs. Deb: 9/15/02

YEAR	TM/L	W	L	PCT	G	GS	CG	SH	SV	IP	H	R	HR	HB	BB	SO	RAT	ERA	ERA+	OAV	OOB	BH	AVG	PB	PR	PR+	PD	TPI
1902	Chi-A	1	1	.500	3	3	3	0	0	20	21	15	0	0	16	3	16.6	5.85	58	.269	.394	1	.067	-1	-5	-6	0	-0.5

● BULL DURHAM

Durham, Louis Raphael (b: Louis Raphael Staub) b: 6/27/1877, New Oxford, Pa. d: 6/28/60, Bentley, Kan. BR/TR, 5'10", Deb: 9/15/04

YEAR	TM/L	W	L	PCT	G	GS	CG	SH	SV	IP	H	R	HR	HB	BB	SO	RAT	ERA	ERA+	OAV	OOB	BH	AVG	PB	PR	PR+	PD	TPI
1904	Bro-N	2	0	1.000	2	2	1	0	0	11	10	5	0	0	5	1	12.3	3.27	84	.250	.333	1	.250	0	-1	-1	-0	-0.1
1907	Was-A	0	0	—	2	0	0	0	0	5	10	9	0	1	4	1	27.0	12.60	19	.417	.517	0	.000	-0	-6	-6	-0	-0.3
1908	NY-N	0	0	—	1	0	0	0	0	2	2	2	0	0	1	2	13.5	9.00	27	.250	.333	0	—	0	-1	-1	-0	-0.1
1909	NY-N	0	0	—	4	0	0	0	1	11	15	8	0	0	2	2	13.9	3.27	78	.326	.354	0	.000	-0	-1	-1	-0	-0.1
Total	4	2	0	1.000	9	2	1	0	1	29	37	24	0	1	12	6	15.5	5.28	49	.314	.382	1	.143	-0	-9	-9	-1	-0.6

● RICH DURNING

Durning, Richard Knott b: 10/10/1892, Louisville, Ky. d: 9/23/48, Castle Point, N.Y BL/TL, 6'2", 178 lbs. Deb: 4/16/17

YEAR	TM/L	W	L	PCT	G	GS	CG	SH	SV	IP	H	R	HR	HB	BB	SO	RAT	ERA	ERA+	OAV	OOB	BH	AVG	PB	PR	PR+	PD	TPI
1917	Bro-N	0	0	—	1	0	0	0	0	1	0	0	0	0	0	0	0.0	0.00	—	.000	.000	0	—	0	0	0	-0	0.0
1918	Bro-N	0	0	—	1	0	0	0	0	2	3	5	0	0	4	0	31.5	13.50	21	.375	.583	0	—	0	-2	-2	0	-0.1
Total	2	0	0	—	2	0	0	0	0	3	3	5	0	0	4	0	21.0	9.00	31	.273	.467	0	—	0	-2	-2	0	-0.1

● JESSE DURYEA

Duryea, James Newton "Cyclone Jim" b: 9/7/1859, Osage, Iowa d: 8/19/42, Algona, Iowa BR/TR, 5'10", 175 lbs. Deb: 4/20/1889

YEAR	TM/L	W	L	PCT	G	GS	CG	SH	SV	IP	H	R	HR	HB	BB	SO	RAT	ERA	ERA+	OAV	OOB	BH	AVG	PB	PR	PR+	PD	TPI
1889	Cin-a	32	19	.627	53	48	38	2	1	401	372	208	9	16	127	183	11.6	2.56	153	.238	.302	44	.272	6	**57**	**59**	0	6.6
1890	Cin-N	16	12	.571	33	32	29	2	0	274	270	148	11	8	60	108	11.1	2.92	122	.250	.294	15	.152	1	20	19	0	1.7
1891	Cin-N	1	9	.100	10	10	8	0	0	77	101	67	4	7	25	23	15.5	5.38	63	.305	.366	1	.031	-5	-17	-17	-0	-2.0
	StL-a	1	1	.500	3	3	2	0	0	24	19	13	0	0	10	13	10.9	3.38	124	.211	.290	4	.364	1	1	2	0	0.2
1892	Cin-N	2	5	.286	9	7	5	0	0	68	55	37	3	3	26	21	11.1	3.57	91	.212	.292	3	.111	-1	-2	-2	1	-0.2
	Was-N	3	11	.214	18	15	13	1	2	127	102	59	6	9	45	48	11.1	2.41	135	.211	.291	6	.120	-2	12	12	4	1.3
	Yr	5	16	.238	27	22	18	1	2	195	157	96	9	12	71	69	11.1	2.82	116	.212	.291	9	.117	-3	10	10	4	1.1
1893	Was-N	4	10	.286	17	15	9	0	0	117	182	137	8	13	56	20	19.3	7.54	61	.345	.420	13	.277	2	-37	-38	0	-2.9
Total	5	59	67	.468	143	130	104	5	3	1088	1101	669	41	56	349	416	12.5	3.45	109	.254	.318	86	.201	3	34	36	5	4.7

● ERV DUSAK

Dusak, Ervin Frank "Four Sack" b: 7/29/20, Chicago, Ill. d: 11/6/94, Glendale Heights, Ill. BR/TR, 6'2", 185 lbs. Deb: 9/18/41 ◆

YEAR	TM/L	W	L	PCT	G	GS	CG	SH	SV	IP	H	R	HR	HB	BB	SO	RAT	ERA	ERA+	OAV	OOB	BH	AVG	PB	PR	PR+	PD	TPI
1948	StL-N	0	0	—	1	0	0	0	0	1	0	0	0	0	1	0	9.0	0.00	—	.000	.250	65	.209	0	0	0	-0	0.0
1950	StL-N	0	2	.000	14	2	0	0	1	36^1	27	17	2	1	27	16	13.6	3.72	116	.211	.353	1	.083	-0	2	2	0	0.1
1951	StL-N	0	0	—	5	0	0	0	0	10	14	8	0	0	7	8	18.9	7.20	55	.333	.429	1	.500	1	-4	-4	0	0.0
	Pit-N	0	1	.000	3	1	0	0	0	6^2	10	10	2	1	9	2	27.0	12.15	35	.357	.526	12	.308	1	-6	-6	-0	-0.7
	Yr	0	1	.000	8	1	0	0	0	16^2	24	18	2	1	16	10	22.1	9.18	44	.343	.471	13	.317	2	-10	-9	-0	-0.7
Total	3	0	3	.000	23	3	0	0	1	54	51	35	4	2	44	26	16.2	5.33	79	.254	.393	251	.243	2	-8	-6	-0	-0.6

● CARL DUSER

Duser, Carl Robert b: 7/22/32, Hazleton, Pa. BL/TL, 6'1", 175 lbs. Deb: 9/15/56

YEAR	TM/L	W	L	PCT	G	GS	CG	SH	SV	IP	H	R	HR	HB	BB	SO	RAT	ERA	ERA+	OAV	OOB	BH	AVG	PB	PR	PR+	PD	TPI
1956	KC-A	1	1	.500	2	2	0	0	0	6	14	6	0	0	2	5	24.0	9.00	48	.452	.485	0	.000	-0	-3	-3	0	-0.5
1958	KC-A	0	0	—	1	0	0	0	0	2	5	1	0	0	1	0	27.0	4.50	87	.500	.545	0	—	0	-0	-0	0	0.0
Total	2	1	1	.500	3	2	0	0	0	8	19	7	0	0	3	5	24.8	7.88	54	.463	.500	0	.000	-0	-3	-3	0	-0.5

● BOB DUSTAL

Dustal, Robert Andrew b: 9/28/35, Sayreville, N.J. BR/TR, 6', 172 lbs. Deb: 4/9/63

YEAR	TM/L	W	L	PCT	G	GS	CG	SH	SV	IP	H	R	HR	HB	BB	SO	RAT	ERA	ERA+	OAV	OOB	BH	AVG	PB	PR	PR+	PD	TPI
1963	Det-A	0	1	.000	7	0	0	0	0	6	10	9	0	0	5	4	22.5	9.00	42	.357	.455	0	—	0	-4	-3	1	-0.4

● MIKE DUVALL

Duvall, Michael Alan b: 10/11/74, Warrenton, Va. BR/TL, 6', 185 lbs. Deb: 9/22/98

YEAR	TM/L	W	L	PCT	G	GS	CG	SH	SV	IP	H	R	HR	HB	BB	SO	RAT	ERA	ERA+	OAV	OOB	BH	AVG	PB	PR	PR+	PD	TPI
1998	TB-A	0	0	—	3	0	0	0	0	4	4	3	0	0	2	1	13.5	6.75	71	.267	.353	0	—	0	-1	-1	0	0.0
1999	TB-A	1	1	.500	40	0	0	0	0	40	46	21	5	2	27	18	16.9	4.05	123	.293	.403	0	—	0	4	4	0	0.2
2000	TB-A	0	0	—	2	0	0	0	0	2^1	5	2	0	0	1	0	23.1	7.71	64	.455	.500	0	—	0	-1	-1	0	0.0
Total	3	1	1	.500	45	0	0	0	0	46^1	55	26	5	2	30	19	16.9	4.47	111	.301	.405	0	—	0	2	2	0	0.2

● BILL DUZEN

Duzen, William George b: 2/21/1870, Buffalo, N.Y. d: 3/11/44, Buffalo, N.Y. BR/TR, 5'11", 165 lbs. Deb: 9/21/1890

YEAR	TM/L	W	L	PCT	G	GS	CG	SH	SV	IP	H	R	HR	HB	BB	SO	RAT	ERA	ERA+	OAV	OOB	BH	AVG	PB	PR	PR+	PD	TPI
1890	Buf-P	0	2	.000	2	2	2	0	0	13	20	24	2	0	14	5	23.5	13.85	30	.339	.466	1	.250	1	-14	-15	-0	-1.2

● FRANK DWYER

Dwyer, John Francis b: 3/25/1868, Lee, Mass. d: 2/4/43, Pittsfield, Mass. BR/TR, 5'8", 145 lbs. Deb: 9/20/1888 MC

YEAR	TM/L	W	L	PCT	G	GS	CG	SH	SV	IP	H	R	HR	HB	BB	SO	RAT	ERA	ERA+	OAV	OOB	BH	AVG	PB	PR	PR+	PD	TPI
1888	Chi-N	4	1	.800	5	5	5	1	0	42	32	20	1	0	9	17	8.8	1.07	283	.198	.240	4	.190	-0	8	9	0	1.0
1889	Chi-N	16	13	.552	32	30	27	0	0	276	307	177	14	7	72	63	12.6	3.59	116	.273	.321	27	.200	-2	13	17	-2	1.0
1890	Chi-P	3	6	.333	12	6	6	0	0	69^1	98	71	4	0	25	17	16.0	6.23	70	.319	.370	14	.264	-0	-15	-14	1	-1.3
1891	Cin-a	13	19	.406	35	31	29	1	0	289	332	225	10	10	124	101	14.5	4.52	91	.279	.351	40	.284	2	-26	-12	1	-0.7
	Mil-a	6	4	.600	10	10	10	0	0	86	92	41	2	4	21	27	12.2	2.20	199	.264	.314	9	.225	-1	14	18	-0	1.6
	Yr	19	23	.452	45	41	39	1	0	375	424	266	12	14	145	128	14.0	3.98	105	.275	.343	49	.271	1	-11	7	1	0.9
1892	StL-N	2	8	.200	10	10	6	0	0	64	90	58	1	2	24	16	16.3	5.63	57	.319	.377	2	.080	-1	-17	-18	1	-2.1
	Cin-N	20	10	.667	34	28	25	3	1	268^1	262	101	6	5	49	47	10.6	2.31	141	.246	.282	21	.159	-4	29	29	-1	2.2
	Yr	22	18	.550	44	38	31	3	1	332^1	352	159	7	7	73	63	11.7	2.95	110	.261	.302	23	.146	-6	12	11	-0	0.1
1893	Cin-N	18	15	.545	37	30	28	1	**2**	287^1	332	187	17	5	93	53	13.5	4.13	116	.281	.336	24	.200	-3	17	20	3	1.7
1894	Cin-N	19	21	.475	45	39	34	1	1	348	471	282	27	15	106	49	15.3	5.07	110	.320	.371	46	.267	1	10	18	1	1.6
1895	Cin-N	18	15	.545	37	31	23	2	0	280^1	355	191	10	14	74	46	14.2	4.24	117	.304	.353	30	.265	2	17	22	-0	2.0
1896	Cin-N	24	11	.686	36	34	30	3	1	288^2	321	144	8	11	60	57	12.2	3.15	147	.279	.321	29	.264	4	39	44	-2	4.5
1897	Cin-N	18	13	.581	37	31	22	0	0	247^1	315	142	5	11	56	41	13.9	3.78	120	.307	.350	25	.266	0	14	20	-3	1.7
1898	Cin-N	16	10	.615	31	28	24	0	0	240	257	117	3	16	42	29	11.8	3.04	126	.272	.314	12	.141	-4	15	20	-2	1.3
1899	Cin-N	0	5	.000	5	5	2	0	0	32^2	48	26	1	1	9	2	16.0	5.51	71	.340	.384	4	.364	1	-6	-6	0	-0.6
Total	12	177	151	.540	366	318	271	12	6	2819	3312	1782	109	101	764	565	13.3	3.84	115	.286	.336	287	.229	-7	114	169	-4	13.9

YEAR	TM/L	W	L	PCT	G	GS	CG	SH	SV	IP	H	R	HR	HB	BB	SO	RAT	ERA	ERA+	OAV	OOB	BH	AVG	PB	PR	PR+	PD	TPI
● BEN DYER Dyer, Benjamin Franklin b: 2/13/1893, Chicago, Ill. d: 8/7/59, Kenosha, Wis. BR/TR, 5'11", 170 lbs. Deb: 5/23/14 ♦																												
1918	Det-A	0	0	—	2	0	0	0	0	1^2	0	0	0	0	0	0	0.0	0.00	—	.000	.000	5	.278	0	1	1	0	0.0
● EDDIE DYER Dyer, Edwin Hawley b: 10/11/1900, Morgan City, La. d: 4/20/64, Houston, Tex. BL/TL, 5'11.5", 168 lbs. Deb: 7/8/22 M♦																												
1922	StL-N	0	0	—	2	0	0	0	0	3^2	7	2	0	0	0	3	17.2	2.45	157	.412	.412	1	.333	1	1	1	0	0.1
1923	StL-N	2	1	.667	4	3	2	1	0	22	30	10	0	1	5	7	14.7	4.09	95	.333	.375	12	.267	0	-0	-0	-0	0.0
1924	StL-N	8	11	.421	29	15	7	1	0	136^2	174	82	6	4	51	23	15.1	4.61	82	.331	.395	18	.237	1	-11	-13	1	-1.2
1925	StL-N	4	3	.571	27	5	1	0	3	82^1	93	52	4	7	24	25	13.6	4.15	104	.278	.340	3	.097	-2	1	2	0	-0.1
1926	StL-N	1	0	1.000	6	0	0	0	0	9^1	7	14	0	1	14	4	21.2	11.57	34	.219	.468	1	.500	0	-8	-8	0	-0.7
1927	StL-N	0	0	—	1	0	0	0	0	2	5	4	1	0	2	1	31.5	18.00	22	.500	.583	0	—	0	-3	-3	-0	-0.1
Total	6	15	15	.500	69	23	10	2	3	256	316	164	11	13	96	63	14.9	4.75	84	.313	.380	35	.223	1	-21	-22	1	-2.0
● MIKE DYER Dyer, Michael Lawrence b: 9/8/66, Upland, Cal. BR/TR, 6'3", 195 lbs. Deb: 6/29/89																												
1989	Min-A	4	7	.364	16	12	1	0	0	71	74	43	2	2	37	37	14.3	4.82	86	.273	.365	0	—	0	-7	-5	-1	-0.8
1994	Pit-N	1	1	.500	14	0	0	0	4	15^1	15	12	1	3	12	13	17.6	5.87	74	.268	.423	0	.000	-0	-3	-3	-0	-0.4
1995	Pit-N	4	5	.444	55	0	0	0	0	74^2	81	40	9	5	30	53	14.0	4.34	99	.281	.359	4	.571	1	-1	-0	1	0.2
1996	Mon-N	5	5	.500	70	1	0	0	2	75^2	79	40	7	5	34	51	14.0	4.40	98	.277	.364	0	.000	-1	-1	-1	1	-0.1
Total	4	14	18	.438	155	13	1	0	6	236^2	249	135	19	15	113	154	14.3	4.60	93	.277	.367	4	.267	1	-13	-8	0	-1.1
● JIMMY DYGERT Dygert, James Henry "Sunny Jim" b: 7/5/1884, Utica, N.Y. d: 2/8/36, New Orleans, La. BR/TR, 5'10", 185 lbs. Deb: 9/8/05																												
1905	Phi-A	1	4	.200	6	3	2	0	0	35^1	41	20	2	2	11	24	13.8	4.33	61	.291	.351	4	.267	0	-7	-7	2	-0.7
1906	Phi-A	11	13	.458	35	25	15	4	0	213^2	175	88	1	10	91	106	11.6	2.70	101	.226	.316	13	.176	-0	-0	1	1	0.1
1907	Phi-A	21	8	.724	42	28	18	5	1	261^2	200	98	2	18	85	151	10.4	2.34	111	**.214**	.292	12	.128	-4	6	7	-1	0.3
1908	Phi-A	11	15	.423	41	28	15	5	1	238^2	184	95	3	11	97	164	11.0	2.87	89	.220	.309	6	.080	-6	-13	-8	3	-1.3
1909	Phi-A	9	5	.643	32	13	6	1	0	137^1	117	60	1	11	50	79	11.7	2.42	99	.242	.327	9	.205	0	1	-0	-1	-0.1
1910	Phi-A	4	4	.500	19	8	6	1	0	99^1	81	44	0	3	49	59	12.1	2.54	94	.231	.331	3	.083	-2	-0	-2	-2	-0.6
Total	6	57	49	.538	175	105	62	16	2	986	798	405	9	55	383	583	11.3	2.65	97	.227	.312	47	.139	-11	-13	-8	1	-2.3
● JIMMY DYKES Dykes, James Joseph b: 11/10/1896, Philadelphia, Pa. d: 6/15/76, Philadelphia, Pa. BR/TR, 5'9", 185 lbs. Deb: 5/6/18 MC♦																												
1927	Phi-A	0	0	—	2	0	0	0	0	2	2	1	0	0	1	0	13.5	4.50	95	.333	.429	135	.324	1	-0	-0	-0	0.0
● RADHAMES DYKHOFF Dykhoff, Radhames Alviro b: 9/27/74, Paradera, Aruba BL/TL, 6', 205 lbs. Deb: 6/7/98																												
1998	Bal-A	0	0	—	1	0	0	0	0	1	2	2	0	0	1	1	27.0	18.00	25	.400	.500	0	—	0	-1	-2	0	-0.1
● ARNOLD EARLEY Earley, Arnold Carl b: 6/4/33, Lincoln Park, Mich. d: 9/29/99, Flint, Mich. BL/TL, 6'1", 200 lbs. Deb: 9/27/60																												
1960	Bos-A	0	1	.000	2	0	0	0	0	4	9	8	1	0	4	5	29.3	15.75	26	.429	.520	0	.000	0	-5	-5	-0	-0.8
1961	Bos-A	2	4	.333	33	0	0	0	7	49^2	42	31	3	0	34	44	13.8	3.99	105	.226	.345	0	.000	-1	0	1	0	0.1
1962	Bos-A	4	5	.444	38	3	0	0	5	68^1	76	53	8	1	46	59	16.2	5.80	71	.281	.388	2	.200	0	-14	-12	1	-1.5
1963	Bos-A	3	7	.300	53	4	0	0	1	115^2	124	73	13	8	43	97	13.6	4.75	80	.270	.343	5	.278	1	-14	-12	0	-0.9
1964	Bos-A	1	1	.500	25	3	1	0	1	50^1	51	17	3	1	18	45	12.5	2.68	144	.266	.332	1	.111	0	5	6	1	0.4
1965	Bos-A	0	1	.000	57	0	0	0	0	74^1	79	42	5	3	29	47	13.4	3.63	103	.271	.344	0	.000	-0	-1	1	-0	0.0
1966	Chi-N	2	1	.667	13	0	0	0	0	17^2	14	11	1	0	9	12	11.7	3.57	103	.226	.324	0	.000	-0	0	0	-1	-0.1
1967	Hou-N	0	0	—	2	0	0	0	0	1^1	5	5	1	0	1	1	40.5	27.00	12	.625	.667	0	—	0	-4	-4	0	-0.2
Total	8	12	20	.375	223	10	1	0	14	381^1	400	240	35	13	184	310	14.1	4.48	87	.269	.354	8	.157	0	-33	-24	1	-3.0
● TOM EARLEY Earley, Thomas Francis Aloysius b: 2/19/17, Roxbury, Mass. d: 4/5/88, Nantucket, Mass. BR/TR, 6', 180 lbs. Deb: 9/27/38																												
1938	Bos-N	1	0	1.000	2	1	1	0	0	11	8	9	2	1	1	4	8.2	3.27	105	.186	.222	0	.000	-1	1	0	-0	0.0
1939	Bos-N	1	4	.200	14	2	0	0	1	40	49	28	1	2	19	9	15.7	4.72	78	.304	.385	3	.300	1	-4	-5	1	-0.5
1940	Bos-N	2	0	1.000	4	1	1	1	0	16^1	16	7	1	2	3	5	11.6	3.86	96	.267	.323	2	.400	1	-0	-0	-0	0.1
1941	Bos-N	6	8	.429	33	13	6	1	3	138^2	120	52	9	3	46	54	11.0	2.53	141	.233	.300	11	.234	1	17	16	-1	1.7
1942	Bos-N	6	11	.353	27	18	6	0	1	112^2	120	65	10	1	55	28	14.1	4.71	71	.276	.359	4	.118	-1	-18	-17	0	-2.4
1945	Bos-N	2	1	.667	11	2	1	0	0	41	36	22	4	0	19	4	12.1	4.61	83	.235	.320	3	.214	1	-4	-4	0	-0.2
Total	6	18	24	.429	91	37	15	2	5	359^2	349	183	27	9	143	104	12.5	3.78	94	.256	.330	23	.202	2	-7	-9	-0	-1.3
● BILL EARLEY Earley, William Albert b: 1/30/56, Cincinnati, Ohio BR/TL, 6'4", 200 lbs. Deb: 9/22/86																												
1986	StL-N	0	0	—	3	0	0	0	0	3	0	0	0	0	2	2	6.0	0.00	—	.000	.182	0	—	0	1	1	-0	0.1
● GEORGE EARNSHAW Earnshaw, George Livingston "Moose" b: 2/15/1900, New York, N.Y. d: 12/1/76, Little Rock, Ark. BR/TR, 6'4", 210 lbs. Deb: 6/3/28 C																												
1928	Phi-A	7	7	.500	26	22	7	3	1	158^1	143	81	7	1	100	117	13.9	3.81	105	.240	.351	14	.246	1	4	4	-1	0.2
1929	*Phi-A	**24**	8	.750	44	33	13	3	1	254^2	233	110	8	5	125	149	12.8	3.29	129	**.241**	.331	15	.172	-2	27	27	-3	2.4
1930	*Phi-A	22	13	.629	49	39	20	**3**	2	296	299	162	20	1	139	193	13.3	4.44	105	.266	.347	26	.228	1	7	8	-1	0.7
1931	*Phi-A	21	7	.750	43	30	23	3	6	281^2	255	130	16	3	75	152	10.6	3.67	122	.236	.288	30	.263	6	22	25	0	2.8
1932	Phi-A	19	13	.594	36	33	21	1	0	245^1	262	147	28	4	94	109	13.2	4.77	95	.270	.336	26	.286	4	-8	-7	1	-0.3
1933	Phi-A	5	10	.333	21	18	4	0	0	117^2	153	93	8	1	58	37	16.2	5.97	72	.311	.385	8	.182	-0	-22	-22	1	-2.2
1934	Chi-A	14	11	.560	33	30	16	2	0	227	242	128	28	4	104	97	13.9	4.52	105	.270	.349	16	.203	-0	-1	5	-1	0.4
1935	Chi-A	1	2	.333	3	3	0	0	0	18	26	19	2	0	11	8	18.5	9.00	51	.342	.425	2	.286	0	-9	-8	-0	-1.0
	Bro-N	8	12	.400	25	22	6	2	0	166	175	87	14	0	53	72	12.4	4.12	96	.270	.325	13	.217	1	-2	-3	0	-0.2
1936	Bro-N	4	9	.308	19	13	4	1	1	93	113	63	7	3	30	40	14.1	5.32	78	.297	.354	8	.242	0	-13	-12	-0	-1.4
	StL-N	2	1	.667	20	6	1	0	1	57^2	80	43	4	3	20	28	16.1	6.40	62	.333	.392	4	.222	-0	-15	-16	1	-0.7
	Yr	6	10	.375	39	19	5	1	2	150^2	193	106	11	6	50	68	14.9	5.73	71	.311	.368	12	.235	0	-29	-28	1	-2.1
Total	9	127	93	.577	319	249	115	18	12	1915^1	1981	1063	142	25	809	1002	13.2	4.38	100	.265	.339	162	.230	9	-10	0	-2	0.7
● LOGAN EASLEY Easley, Kenneth Logan b: 11/4/61, Salt Lake City, Utah BR/TR, 6'1", 185 lbs. Deb: 4/9/87																												
1987	Pit-N	1	1	.500	17	0	0	0	1	26^1	23	17	5	1	17	21	14.0	5.47	75	.242	.363	0	.000	-0	-4	-4	1	-0.2
1989	Pit-N	1	0	1.000	10	0	0	0	1	12^1	8	6	1	1	7	6	11.7	4.38	77	.190	.320	0	.000	-0	-1	-1	-0	-0.2
Total	2	2	1	.667	27	0	0	0	2	38^2	31	23	6	2	24	27	13.3	5.12	76	.226	.350	0	.000	-0	-5	-5	1	-0.4
● MAL EASON Eason, Malcolm Wayne "Kid" b: 3/13/1879, Brookville, Pa. d: 4/16/70, Douglas, Ariz. BR/TR, 6', 175 lbs. Deb: 10/1/00 U																												
1900	Chi-N	1	0	1.000	1	1	1	0	0	9	9	2	0	0	3	2	12.0	1.00	361	.257	.316	0	.000	-1	3	3	-0	0.2
1901	Chi-N	8	17	.320	27	25	23	1	0	220^2	246	136	9	13	60	68	13.0	3.59	90	.280	.335	12	.138	-5	-7	-9	-2	-1.5
1902	Chi-N	1	1	.500	2	2	2	0	0	18	21	7	0	0	2	4	11.5	1.00	270	.292	.311	1	.200	0	4	4	0	0.5
	Bos-N	9	12	.429	27	27	20	2	0	213^1	249	100	4	12	61	51	13.6	2.91	97	.291	.347	6	.083	-6	-3	-2	-1	-0.9
	Yr	10	13	.435	29	29	22	2	0	231^1	270	107	4	12	63	55	13.4	2.76	102	.291	.344	7	.091	-6	1	1	-0	-0.4
1903	Det-A	2	5	.286	7	6	6	1	0	56^1	60	33	1	3	19	21	13.1	3.36	87	.271	.337	2	.100	-2	-2	-3	1	-0.4
1905	Bro-N	5	21	.192	27	27	20	3	0	207	230	128	5	5	72	64	13.3	4.30	67	.292	.355	14	.173	-1	-30	-34	1	-3.6
1906	Bro-N	10	17	.370	34	26	18	3	1	227	212	109	1	9	74	64	11.7	3.25	78	.256	.323	8	.091	-4	-16	-19	1	-2.6
Total	6	36	73	.330	125	114	90	10	1	951^1	1027	515	20	42	291	274	12.9	3.42	84	.279	.339	43	.121	-19	-51	-60	2	-8.3
● CARL EAST East, Carlton William b: 8/27/1894, Marietta, Ga. d: 1/15/53, Whitesburg, Ga. BL/TR, 6'2", 178 lbs. Deb: 8/24/15 ♦																												
1915	StL-A	0	0	—	1	1	0	0	0	3^1	6	6	0	0	2	1	21.6	16.20	18	.400	.471	0	.000	-0	-5	-5	-0	-0.3
● HUGH EAST East, Gordon Hugh b: 7/7/19, Birmingham, Ala. d: 11/2/81, Charleston, S.C. BR/TR, 6'2", 185 lbs. Deb: 9/13/41																												
1941	NY-N	1	1	.500	2	2	0	0	0	15^2	19	12	0	0	9	4	16.1	3.45	107	.297	.384	2	.222	0	0	0	-0	0.1
1942	NY-N	0	2	.000	4	1	0	0	0	7^1	15	16	1	0	7	2	27.0	9.82	34	.429	.524	1	.500	2	-5	-5	0	-0.8
1943	NY-N	1	3	.250	13	5	1	0	0	40^1	51	27	4	0	25	21	17.0	5.36	64	.298	.388	1	.077	-1	-9	-8	-1	-0.9
Total	3	2	6	.250	19	8	1	0	0	63^1	85	55	5	0	41	27	17.9	5.40	65	.315	.405	4	.167	1	-14	-13	-1	-1.6
● JAMIE EASTERLY Easterly, James Morris b: 2/17/53, Houston, Tex. BL/TL, 5'9", 180 lbs. Deb: 4/6/74																												
1974	Atl-N	0	0	—	3	0	0	0	0	2^2	6	7	0	0	4	0	33.8	16.88	22	.400	.526	0	—	0	-4	-4	0	-0.2
1975	Atl-N	2	9	.182	21	13	0	0	0	68^2	73	47	5	2	42	34	15.3	4.98	76	.275	.379	1	.056	-2	-10	-9	-1	-1.5
1976	Atl-N	1	1	.500	4	4	0	0	0	22	23	12	0	0	13	11	14.7	4.91	77	.280	.379	1	.111	-0	-3	-3	0	-0.2
1977	Atl-N	2	4	.333	22	5	0	0	1	58^2	72	46	5	3	30	37	16.1	6.14	73	.303	.387	4	.267	1	-14	-10	-1	-1.0

YEAR	TM/L	W	L	PCT	G	GS	CG	SH	SV	IP	H	R	HR	HB	BB	SO	RAT	ERA	ERA+	OAV	OOB	BH	AVG	PB	PR	PR+	PD	TPI
1978	Atl-N	3	6	.333	37	6	0	0	1	78	91	52	9	2	45	42	15.9	5.65	72	.299	.393	4	.211	0	-18	-12	0	-1.3
1979	Atl-N	0	0	—	4	0	0	0	0	2^2	7	6	0	0	3	3	33.8	13.50	30	.467	.556	0	—	0	-3	-3	0	-0.1
1981	*Mil-A	3	3	.500	44	0	0	0	4	62	46	23	0	0	34	31	11.6	3.19	107	.219	.328	0	—	0	3	2	0	0.2
1982	Mil-A	0	2	.000	28	0	0	0	2	30^2	39	19	6	0	15	16	15.8	4.70	81	.312	.386	0	—	0	-2	-3	1	-0.2
1983	Mil-A	0	1	.000	12	0	0	0	1	11^2	14	7	0	2	10	6	20.1	3.86	97	.350	.500	0	.000	-0	0	-0	-0	0.0
	Cle-A	4	2	.667	41	0	0	0	3	57	69	25	4	2	22	39	14.7	3.63	117	.309	.377	0	—	0	3	4	0	0.4
	Yr	4	3	.571	53	0	0	0	4	68^2	83	32	4	4	32	45	15.6	3.67	114	.316	.398	0	.000	-0	3	4	0	0.4
1984	Cle-A	3	1	.750	26	1	0	0	2	69^1	74	31	3	1	23	42	12.7	3.38	121	.273	.332	0	—	0	5	5	0	0.4
1985	Cle-A	4	1	.800	50	7	0	0	0	98^2	96	52	9	4	53	58	14.0	3.92	105	.264	.363	0	—	0	2	2	-0	0.1
1986	Cle-A	0	2	.000	13	0	0	0	0	17^2	27	16	3	0	12	9	19.9	7.64	54	.365	.453	0	—	0	-7	-7	-0	-0.7
1987	Cle-A	1	1	.500	16	0	0	0	0	31^2	26	17	4	1	13	22	11.4	4.55	100	.218	.301	0	—	0	-0	-0	0	0.0
Total	13	23	33	.411	321	36	0	0	14	611^1	663	360	48	17	319	350	14.7	4.62	87	.283	.373	10	.161	-1	-48	-38	-0	-4.1

● **JACK EASTON** Easton, John S. b: 2/28/1867, Bridgeport, Ohio d: 11/28/03, Steubenville, Ohio Deb: 9/23/1889

YEAR	TM/L	W	L	PCT	G	GS	CG	SH	SV	IP	H	R	HR	HB	BB	SO	RAT	ERA	ERA+	OAV	OOB	BH	AVG	PB	PR	PR+	PD	TPI
1889	Col-a	1	0	1.000	4	1	1	0	1	18	13	8	0	3	21	7	18.5	3.50	104	.197	.411	0	.000	-1	1	0	-0	-0.1
1890	Col-a	15	14	.517	37	29	23	0	1	255^2	213	148	4	20	125	147	12.6	3.52	102	.220	.321	19	.178	0	10	2	1	0.3
1891	Col-a	5	10	.333	18	16	13	0	0	135^1	145	111	3	15	59	52	14.6	4.52	76	.265	.352	15	.238	2	-12	-17	1	-1.3
	StL-a	3	2	.600	7	6	4	0	0	47^2	48	38	3	4	23	22	14.2	5.10	82	.253	.346	5	.179	-1	-7	-4	-2	-0.5
	Col-a	0	2	.000	2	2	2	0	0	15	15	8	2	2	4	13	12.6	3.60	96	.250	.318	0	.000	-1	0	-0	-1	-0.1
	Yr	8	14	.364	27	24	19	0	0	198	208	157	8	21	86	87	14.3	4.59	79	.261	.348	20	.196	-0	-19	-22	-1	-1.9
1892	StL-N	2	0	1.000	5	2	2	0	0	31	38	31	2	3	26	4	19.5	6.39	50	.290	.419	3	.176	-1	-11	-11	0	-0.6
1894	Pit-N	0	1	.000	3	1	1	0	0	19^2	26	16	0	3	4	1	15.1	4.12	127	.313	.367	0	.000	-1	3	2	-1	-0.1
Total	5	26	29	.473	76	57	46	0	2	522^1	498	360	14	50	262	246	14.0	4.12	89	.243	.343	42	.176	-2	-17	-29	-1	-2.4

● **RAWLY EASTWICK** Eastwick, Rawlins Jackson b: 10/24/50, Camden, N.J. BR/TR, 6'3", 180 lbs. Deb: 9/12/74

YEAR	TM/L	W	L	PCT	G	GS	CG	SH	SV	IP	H	R	HR	HB	BB	SO	RAT	ERA	ERA+	OAV	OOB	BH	AVG	PB	PR	PR+	PD	TPI
1974	Cin-N	0	0	—	8	0	0	0	2	17^2	12	5	1	0	5	14	8.7	2.04	172	.188	.246	0	.000	-0	3	3	-0	0.1
1975	*Cin-N	5	3	.625	58	0	0	0	**22**	90	77	26	6	2	25	61	10.4	2.60	139	.229	.287	1	.067	-1	10	10	-1	1.2
1976	*Cin-N	11	5	.688	71	0	0	0	**26**	107^2	93	30	3	2	27	70	10.2	2.09	168	.232	.284	0	.000	-2	17	17	-2	3.1
1977	Cin-N	2	2	.500	23	0	0	0	7	43^1	40	14	3	0	8	17	10.0	2.91	135	.244	.279	1	.167	-0	5	5	-1	0.5
	StL-N	3	7	.300	41	1	0	0	4	53^2	74	34	6	0	21	30	15.9	4.70	82	.332	.389	2	.400	1	-5	-5	-1	-0.9
	Yr	5	9	.357	64	1	0	0	11	97	114	48	9	0	29	47	13.3	3.90	100	.295	.344	3	.273	1	0	-0	-2	-0.4
1978	NY-A	2	1	.667	8	0	0	0	0	24^2	22	9	2	1	4	13	9.9	3.28	111	.232	.270	0	—	0	1	1	-0	0.1
	*Phi-N	2	1	.667	22	0	0	0	0	40^1	31	21	5	0	18	14	10.9	4.02	89	.209	.295	0	.000	-0	-2	-2	-1	-0.2
1979	Phi-N	3	6	.333	51	0	0	0	6	82^2	90	46	8	1	25	47	12.6	4.90	78	.284	.338	0	.000	-1	-11	-10	-2	-1.3
1980	KC-A	0	1	.000	14	0	0	0	0	22	37	14	2	2	8	5	19.2	5.32	76	.363	.420	0	—	0	-3	-3	1	-0.1
1981	Chi-N	0	1	.000	30	0	0	0	1	43^1	43	16	2	0	15	24	12.0	2.28	162	.264	.326	0	.000	-0	6	6	0	0.4
Total	8	28	27	.509	326	1	0	0	68	525^1	519	215	38	8	156	295	11.7	3.31	112	.258	.314	4	.071	-3	22	23	-7	2.9

● **ADAM EATON** Eaton, Adam Thomas b: 11/23/77, Seattle, Wash. BR/TR, 6'2", 190 lbs. Deb: 5/30/2000

YEAR	TM/L	W	L	PCT	G	GS	CG	SH	SV	IP	H	R	HR	HB	BB	SO	RAT	ERA	ERA+	OAV	OOB	BH	AVG	PB	PR	PR+	PD	TPI
2000	SD-N	7	4	.636	22	22	0	0	0	135	134	63	14	2	61	90	13.1	4.13	106	.260	.340	11	.289	5	8	4	-0	0.8

● **CRAIG EATON** Eaton, Craig b: 9/7/54, Glendale, Ohio BR/TR, 5'11", 175 lbs. Deb: 9/5/79

YEAR	TM/L	W	L	PCT	G	GS	CG	SH	SV	IP	H	R	HR	HB	BB	SO	RAT	ERA	ERA+	OAV	OOB	BH	AVG	PB	PR	PR+	PD	TPI
1979	KC-A	0	0	—	5	0	0	0	0	10	8	3	0	0	3	4	9.9	2.70	158	.222	.282	0	—	0	2	2	0	0.1

● **ZEB EATON** Eaton, Zebulon Vance "Red" b: 2/2/20, Cooleemee, N.C. d: 12/17/89, W.Palm Beach, Fla. BR/TR, 5'10", 185 lbs. Deb: 4/18/44

YEAR	TM/L	W	L	PCT	G	GS	CG	SH	SV	IP	H	R	HR	HB	BB	SO	RAT	ERA	ERA+	OAV	OOB	BH	AVG	PB	PR	PR+	PD	TPI
1944	Det-A	0	0	—	6	0	0	0	0	15^2	19	12	2	0	8	4	15.5	5.74	62	.322	.403	1	.100	-1	-4	-4	-0	-0.3
1945	*Det-A	4	2	.667	17	3	0	0	0	53^1	48	28	0	3	40	15	15.4	4.05	87	.247	.384	8	.250	2	-4	-3	0	-0.1
Total	2	4	2	.667	23	3	0	0	0	69	67	40	2	3	48	19	15.4	4.43	80	.265	.388	9	.214	2	-8	-7	-0	-0.4

● **GARY EAVE** Eave, Gary Louis b: 7/22/63, Monroe, La. BR/TR, 6'4", 200 lbs. Deb: 4/12/88

YEAR	TM/L	W	L	PCT	G	GS	CG	SH	SV	IP	H	R	HR	HB	BB	SO	RAT	ERA	ERA+	OAV	OOB	BH	AVG	PB	PR	PR+	PD	TPI
1988	Atl-N	0	0	—	5	0	0	0	0	5	7	5	0	0	3	0	18.0	9.00	41	.333	.417	0	—	0	-3	-3	-0	-0.2
1989	Atl-N	2	0	1.000	3	3	0	0	0	20^2	15	3	0	1	12	9	12.2	1.31	280	.200	.318	0	.000	-1	5	5	-1	0.4
1990	Sea-A	0	3	.000	8	5	0	0	0	30	27	16	5	2	20	16	14.7	4.20	94	.241	.366	0	—	0	-1	-1	0	-0.1
Total	3	2	3	.400	16	8	0	0	0	55^2	49	24	5	3	35	25	14.1	3.56	108	.236	.354	0	.000	-1	1	2	-1	0.1

● **VALLIE EAVES** Eaves, Vallie Ennis "Chief" b: 9/6/11, Allen, Okla. d: 4/19/60, Norman, Okla. BR/TR, 6'2.5", 180 lbs. Deb: 9/12/35

YEAR	TM/L	W	L	PCT	G	GS	CG	SH	SV	IP	H	R	HR	HB	BB	SO	RAT	ERA	ERA+	OAV	OOB	BH	AVG	PB	PR	PR+	PD	TPI
1935	Phi-A	1	2	.333	3	3	1	0	0	14	12	9	0	0	15	6	17.4	5.14	88	.240	.415	0	.000	-1	-1	-1	-0	-0.2
1939	Chi-A	0	1	.000	2	1	1	0	0	11^2	11	7	1	1	8	5	15.4	4.63	102	.250	.377	2	.333	0	-0	0	-0	0.0
1940	Chi-A	0	2	.000	5	3	0	0	0	18^2	22	16	2	1	24	11	22.7	6.75	66	.301	.480	0	.000	-1	-5	-5	-1	-0.5
1941	Chi-N	3	3	.500	12	7	4	0	0	58^2	56	27	4	3	21	24	12.3	3.53	99	.253	.327	2	.100	-1	1	-0	-1	-0.3
1942	Chi-N	0	0	—	2	0	0	0	0	3	4	3	0	1	2	0	21.0	9.00	36	.308	.438	0	—	0	-2	-2	-0	-0.1
Total	5	4	8	.333	24	14	6	0	0	106	105	62	7	6	70	46	15.4	4.58	86	.262	.379	4	.114	-3	-7	-8	-3	-1.1

● **EDDIE EAYRS** Eayrs, Edwin b: 11/10/1890, Blackstone, Mass. d: 11/30/69, Warwick, R.I. BL/TL, 5'7", 160 lbs. Deb: 6/30/13 ♦

YEAR	TM/L	W	L	PCT	G	GS	CG	SH	SV	IP	H	R	HR	HB	BB	SO	RAT	ERA	ERA+	OAV	OOB	BH	AVG	PB	PR	PR+	PD	TPI
1913	Pit-N	0	0	—	2	0	0	0	0	8	8	6	0	0	6	5	15.8	2.25	134	.267	.389	1	.167	-0	1	1	-0	0.0
1920	Bos-N	1	2	.333	7	3	0	0	0	26^1	36	18	1	2	12	7	17.1	5.47	56	.346	.424	80	.328	2	-7	-7	1	-0.5
1921	Bos-N	0	0	—	2	0	0	0	0	4^2	9	10	0	0	9	1	34.7	17.36	21	.391	.563	1	.067	-2	-7	-7	-0	-0.5
Total	3	1	2	.333	11	3	0	0	0	39	53	34	1	2	27	13	18.9	6.23	50	.338	.441	83	.306	0	-13	-14	0	-1.0

● **DERRIN EBERT** Ebert, Derrin Lee b: 8/21/76, Anaheim, Cal. BR/TL, 6'3", 200 lbs. Deb: 4/6/99

YEAR	TM/L	W	L	PCT	G	GS	CG	SH	SV	IP	H	R	HR	HB	BB	SO	RAT	ERA	ERA+	OAV	OOB	BH	AVG	PB	PR	PR+	PD	TPI
1999	Atl-N	0	1	.000	5	0	0	0	1	8	9	5	2	0	5	4	15.8	5.63	80	.300	.400	0	.000	-0	-1	-1	0	-0.1

● **HARRY ECCLES** Eccles, Harry Josiah "Bugs" b: 7/9/1893, Kennedy, N.Y. d: 6/2/55, Jamestown, N.Y. BL/TL, 6'2", 170 lbs. Deb: 9/13/15

YEAR	TM/L	W	L	PCT	G	GS	CG	SH	SV	IP	H	R	HR	HB	BB	SO	RAT	ERA	ERA+	OAV	OOB	BH	AVG	PB	PR	PR+	PD	TPI
1915	Phi-A	0	1	.000	5	1	0	0	1	21	18	16	2	0	6	13	10.3	4.71	62	.240	.296	1	.167	-0	-4	-4	-1	-0.3

● **DENNIS ECKERSLEY** Eckersley, Dennis Lee b: 10/3/54, Oakland, Cal. BR/TR, 6'2", 190 lbs. Deb: 4/12/75

YEAR	TM/L	W	L	PCT	G	GS	CG	SH	SV	IP	H	R	HR	HB	BB	SO	RAT	ERA	ERA+	OAV	OOB	BH	AVG	PB	PR	PR+	PD	TPI
1975	Cle-A	13	7	.650	34	24	6	2	2	186^2	147	61	16	7	90	152	11.8	2.60	146	.215	.312	0	—	0	25	25	-3	2.3
1976	Cle-A	13	12	.520	36	30	9	3	1	199^1	155	82	13	5	78	200	10.7	3.43	102	.214	.295	0	—	0	2	1	-1	0.1
1977	Cle-A★	14	13	.519	33	33	12	3	0	247^1	214	100	31	7	54	191	10.0	3.53	112	.231	**.278**	0	—	0	15	12	-3	0.8
1978	Bos-A	20	8	.714	35	35	16	3	0	268^1	258	99	30	7	71	162	11.3	2.99	138	.251	.304	0	—	0	24	31	-2	3.0
1979	Bos-A	17	10	.630	33	33	17	2	0	246^2	234	89	29	6	59	150	10.9	2.99	**148**	.250	.298	0	—	0	34	**38**	1	3.9
1980	Bos-A	12	14	.462	30	30	8	0	0	197^2	188	101	25	2	44	121	10.7	4.28	99	.248	.291	0	—	0	-5	-1	-1	-0.3
1981	Bos-A	9	8	.529	23	23	8	2	0	154	160	82	9	3	35	79	11.6	4.27	91	.267	.310	0	—	0	-10	-6	-1	-0.7
1982	Bos-A★	13	13	.500	33	33	11	3	0	224^1	228	101	31	2	43	127	11.0	3.73	116	.261	.297	0	—	0	9	14	-1	1.4
1983	Bos-A	9	13	.409	28	28	2	0	0	176^1	223	119	27	6	39	77	13.7	5.61	78	.303	.343	0	—	0	-30	-23	-1	-2.5
1984	Bos-A	4	4	.500	9	9	2	0	0	64^2	71	38	10	1	13	33	11.8	5.01	83	.284	.322	0	—	0	-7	-6	-1	-0.5
	*Chi-N	10	8	.556	24	24	2	0	0	160^1	152	59	11	4	36	81	10.8	3.03	129	.250	.296	6	.109	-3	10	14	1	1.4
1985	Chi-N	11	7	.611	25	25	6	2	0	169^1	145	61	15	3	19	117	8.9	3.08	130	.229	.255	7	.125	0	10	16	0	1.7
1986	Chi-N	6	11	.353	33	32	1	0	0	201	226	109	21	3	43	137	12.2	4.57	89	.285	.324	11	.159	1	-19	-11	-0	-0.7
1987	Oak-A	6	8	.429	54	2	0	0	16	115^2	99	41	11	3	17	113	9.3	3.03	136	.228	.262	0	—	0	18	15	-1	2.0
1988	*Oak-A★	4	2	.667	60	0	0	0	**45**	72^2	52	20	5	1	11	70	7.9	2.35	161	.198	.233	0	—	0	13	12	-1	2.2
1989	*Oak-A	4	0	1.000	51	0	0	0	33	57^2	32	10	5	1	3	55	5.6	1.56	236	.162	.178	0	—	0	15	14	-0	2.4
1990	*Oak-A★	4	2	.667	63	0	0	0	48	73^1	41	9	2	0	4	73	5.5	0.61	607	.160	.172	0	—	0	27	27	-2	4.9
1991	Oak-A★	5	4	.556	67	0	0	0	43	76	60	26	11	1	9	87	8.3	2.96	130	.208	.235	0	—	0	10	8	0	1.7
1992	*Oak-A★	7	1	.875	69	0	0	0	**51**	80	62	17	5	1	11	93	8.3	1.91	196	.211	.242	0	—	0	18	17	1	3.6
1993	Oak-A	2	4	.333	64	0	0	0	36	67	67	32	7	2	13	80	11.0	4.16	98	.261	.301	0	—	0	1	-1	-1	-0.2
1994	Oak-A	5	4	.556	45	0	0	0	19	44^1	49	26	5	1	13	47	12.8	4.26	104	.275	.328	0	—	0	3	1	-1	0.1
1995	Oak-A	4	6	.400	52	0	0	0	29	50^1	53	29	5	1	11	40	11.6	4.83	93	.269	.311	0	—	0	-1	-2	-0	-0.4
1996	*StL-N	0	6	.000	63	0	0	0	30	60	65	26	8	4	6	49	11.3	3.30	127	.274	.304	0	.000	-0	6	6	-1	1.0
1997	StL-N	1	5	.167	57	0	0	0	36	53	49	24	9	2	8	45	10.0	3.91	106	.238	.273	0	—	0	2	1	-1	0.2
1998	*Bos-A	4	1	.800	50	0	0	0	1	39^2	46	21	6	2	8	22	12.7	4.76	99	.291	.333	0	—	0	-0	-0	-1	-0.1
Total	24	197	171	.535	1071	361	100	20	390	3285^2	3076	1382	347	75	738	2401	10.7	3.50	116	.246	.292	24	.133	-1	168	201	-16	27.3

YEAR TM/L	W	L	PCT	G	GS	CG	SH	SV	IP	H	R	HR	HB	BB	SO	RAT	ERA	ERA+	OAV	OOB	BH	AVG	PB	PR	PR+	PD	TPI
● AL ECKERT Eckert, Albert George "Obbie" b: 5/17/06, Milwaukee, Wis. d: 4/20/74, Milwaukee, Wis. BL/TL, 5'10", 174 lbs. Deb: 4/21/30																											
1930 Cin-N	0	1	.000	2	1	0	0	0	5	7	6	0	0	4	1	19.8	7.20	67	.304	.407	0	.000	-0	-1	-1	0	-0.2
1931 Cin-N	0	1	.000	14	1	0	0	0	18^{2}	26	20	3	0	9	5	16.9	9.16	41	.325	.393	1	.333	0	-11	-12	-0	-0.6
1935 StL-N	0	0	—	2	0	0	0	0	3	7	4	0	0	1	1	24.0	12.00	34	.467	.500	0	—	0	-3	-3	-0	-0.1
Total 3	0	2	.000	18	2	0	0	0	26^{2}	40	30	3	0	14	7	18.2	9.11	44	.339	.409	1	.250	0	-15	-16	0	-0.9
● CHARLIE ECKERT Eckert, Charles William "Buzz" b: 8/8/1897, Philadelphia, Pa. d: 8/22/86, Trevose, Pa. BR/TR, 5'10.5", 165 lbs. Deb: 9/18/19																											
1919 Phi-A	0	1	.000	2	1	1	0	0	16	17	9	1	0	3	6	11.3	3.94	87	.270	.303	1	.167	-0	-1	-1	0	-0.1
1920 Phi-A	0	0	—	2	0	0	0	0	5^{2}	8	3	0	1	1	1	15.9	4.76	84	.421	.476	0	.000	-0	-1	-0	-0	-0.1
1922 Phi-A	0	2	.000	21	0	0	0	0	50	61	33	7	1	23	15	15.3	4.68	91	.319	.395	1	.091	-1	-4	-2	2	-0.1
Total 3	0	3	.000	25	1	1	0	0	71^{2}	86	45	8	2	27	22	14.4	4.52	90	.315	.381	2	.111	-2	-5	-4	1	-0.3
● CHRIS EDDY Eddy, Christopher Mark b: 11/27/69, Dallas, Tex. BL/TL, 6'3", 200 lbs. Deb: 4/26/95																											
1995 Oak-A	0	0	—	6	0	0	0	0	3^{2}	7	3	0	2	2	2	27.0	7.36	61	.438	.550	0	—	0	-1	-1	0	-0.1
● DON EDDY Eddy, Donald Eugene b: 10/25/46, Mason City, Iowa BR/TL, 5'11", 170 lbs. Deb: 9/7/70																											
1970 Chi-A	0	0	—	7	0	0	0	0	11^{2}	10	4	0	0	6	9	12.3	2.31	168	.244	.340	0	—	0	2	2	0	0.1
1971 Chi-A	0	2	.000	22	0	0	0	0	22^{2}	19	6	3	0	19	14	15.1	2.38	151	.232	.376	1	1.000	1	3	3	-1	0.3
Total 2	0	2	.000	29	0	0	0	0	34^{1}	29	10	3	0	25	23	14.2	2.36	157	.236	.365	1	1.000	1	5	5	-1	0.4
● STEVE EDDY Eddy, Steven Allen b: 8/21/57, Sterling, Ill. BR/TR, 6'2", 185 lbs. Deb: 6/13/79																											
1979 Cal-A	1	1	.500	7	4	0	0	0	32^{1}	36	19	1	2	20	7	16.1	4.73	86	.290	.397	0	—	0	-2	-2	0	-0.1
● JOE EDELEN Edelen, Benny Joe b: 9/16/55, Durant, Okla. BR/TR, 6', 165 lbs. Deb: 4/18/81																											
1981 StL-N	1	0	1.000	13	0	0	0	0	17^{1}	29	18	2	1	3	10	17.1	9.35	38	.367	.398	1	.333	0	-11	-11	-0	-0.6
Cin-N	1	0	1.000	5	0	0	0	0	12^{2}	5	1	1	0	0	5	3.6	0.71	500	.128	.128	0	.000	-0	4	4	-1	0.2
Yr	2	0	1.000	18	0	0	0	0	30	34	19	3	1	3	15	11.4	5.70	62	.288	.311	1	.200	0	-7	-7	-1	-0.4
1982 Cin-N	0	0	—	9	0	0	0	0	15^{1}	22	15	2	0	8	11	17.6	8.80	42	.344	.417	1	.500	0	-9	-8	-0	-0.4
Total 2	2	0	1.000	27	0	0	0	0	45^{1}	56	34	5	1	11	26	13.5	6.75	53	.308	.351	2	.286	0	-16	-15	-1	-0.8
● ED EDELEN Edelen, Edward Joseph "Doc" b: 3/16/12, Bryantown, Md. d: 2/1/82, LaPlata, Md. BR/TR, 6', 191 lbs. Deb: 8/20/32																											
1932 Was-A	0	0	—	2	0	0	0	0	1	0	3	0	0	6	0	54.0	27.00	16	.000	.600	0	—	0	-3	-3	-0	-0.1
● JOHN EDELMAN Edelman, John Rogers b: 7/27/35, Philadelphia, Pa. BR/TR, 6'3", 185 lbs. Deb: 6/2/55																											
1955 Mil-N	0	0	—	5	0	0	0	0	5^{2}	7	7	0	0	8	3	23.8	11.12	34	.304	.484	0	—	0	-4	-5	0	-0.2
● CHARLIE EDEN Eden, Charles M. b: 1/18/1855, Lexington, Ky. d: 9/17/20, Cincinnati, Ohio BL/TL, 168 lbs. Deb: 8/17/1877 ♦																											
1884 Pit-a	0	1	.000	2	1	1	0	0	12	12	9	1	1	3	3	12.0	6.00	55	.255	.314	33	.270	1	-4	-4	-1	-0.2
1885 Pit-a	1	2	.333	4	1	0	0	0	15^{2}	22	13	0	0	3	5	14.4	5.17	62	.314	.342	103	.254	1	-3	-3	-1	-0.5
Total 2	1	3	.250	6	2	1	0	0	27^{2}	34	22	1	1	6	8	13.3	5.53	59	.291	.331	244	.261	1	-7	-7	-1	-0.7
● KEN EDENFIELD Edenfield, Kenneth Edward b: 3/18/67, Jesup, Ga. BR/TR, 6'1", 165 lbs. Deb: 5/11/95																											
1995 Cal-A	0	0	—	7	0	0	0	0	12^{2}	15	7	1	0	5	6	14.2	4.26	110	.300	.364	0	—	0	1	1	0	0.0
1996 Cal-A	0	0	—	2	0	0	0	0	4^{1}	10	5	2	1	2	4	27.0	10.38	48	.435	.500	0	—	0	-3	-3	0	-0.1
Total 2	0	0	—	9	0	0	0	0	17	25	12	3	1	7	10	17.5	5.82	82	.342	.407	0	—	0	-2	-2	-0	-0.1
● TOM EDENS Edens, Thomas Patrick b: 6/9/61, Ontario, Ore. BR/TR, 6'2", 188 lbs. Deb: 6/2/87																											
1987 NY-N	0	0	—	2	2	0	0	0	8	15	6	2	0	4	4	21.4	6.75	56	.417	.475	0	.000	-0	-2	-3	0	-0.1
1990 Mil-A	4	5	.444	35	6	0	0	2	89	89	52	8	4	33	40	12.7	4.45	87	.262	.334	0	—	0	-5	-6	-1	-0.6
1991 Min-A	2	2	.500	8	6	0	0	0	33	34	15	2	0	10	19	12.0	4.09	104	.256	.308	0	—	0	0	1	0	0.1
1992 Min-A	6	3	.667	52	0	0	0	3	76^{1}	65	26	1	2	36	57	12.1	2.83	144	.236	.329	0	—	0	9	10	-1	1.1
1993 Hou-N	1	1	.500	38	0	0	0	0	49	47	17	4	0	19	21	12.1	3.12	124	.263	.333	0	.000	-0	5	4	0	0.2
1994 Hou-N	4	1	.800	39	0	0	0	1	50	55	25	3	2	17	38	13.3	4.50	88	.289	.354	0	.000	-0	-2	-3	1	-0.2
Phi-N	1	0	1.000	3	0	0	0	0	4	4	1	0	0	1	1	11.3	2.25	191	.267	.313	0	—	0	1	1	0	0.2
Yr	5	1	.833	42	0	0	0	1	54	59	26	3	2	18	39	13.2	4.33	92	.288	.351	0	.000	-0	-1	-2	1	0.0
1995 Chi-N	1	0	1.000	5	0	0	0	0	3	6	3	0	0	3	2	27.0	6.00	68	.400	.500	0	—	0	-1	-1	-0	-0.1
Total 7	19	12	.613	182	14	0	0	6	312^{1}	315	145	20	8	123	182	12.9	3.86	103	.266	.339	0	.000	-1	6	4	1	0.6
● BUTCH EDGE Edge, Claude Lee b: 7/18/56, Houston, Tex. BR/TR, 6'3", 203 lbs. Deb: 8/13/79																											
1979 Tor-A	3	4	.429	9	9	1	0	0	51^{2}	60	32	6	1	24	19	14.8	5.23	83	.283	.359	0	—	0	-6	-5	-0	-0.6
● BILL EDGERTON Edgerton, William Albert b: 8/16/41, South Bend, Ind. BL/TL, 6'2", 185 lbs. Deb: 9/3/66																											
1966 KC-A	0	1	.000	6	1	0	0	0	8^{1}	10	3	0	0	7	3	18.4	3.24	105	.303	.425	0	—	0	0	0	0	0.0
1967 KC-A	1	0	1.000	7	0	0	0	0	8^{1}	11	4	1	1	3	6	16.2	2.16	147	.324	.395	0	—	0	1	1	0	0.1
1969 Sea-A	0	1	.000	4	0	0	0	0	4	10	7	1	1	0	2	24.8	13.50	27	.455	.478	0	—	0	-4	-4	0	-0.8
Total 3	1	2	.333	17	1	0	0	0	20^{2}	31	14	2	2	10	11	18.7	4.79	70	.348	.426	0	—	0	-3	-3	1	-0.7
● BRIAN EDMONDSON Edmondson, Brian Christopher b: 1/29/73, Fontana, Cal. BR/TR, 6'2", 165 lbs. Deb: 4/2/98																											
1998 Atl-N	0	1	.000	10	0	0	0	0	16^{2}	14	10	2	0	8	8	11.9	4.32	96	.215	.301	0	.000	-0	-0	-0	0	0.0
Fla-N	4	3	.571	43	0	0	0	0	59^{1}	62	28	8	3	29	32	14.3	3.79	107	.281	.372	0	.000	-1	3	2	-1	0.0
Yr	4	4	.500	53	0	0	0	0	76	76	38	10	3	37	40	13.7	3.91	104	.266	.356	0	.000	-1	3	2	-1	0.0
1999 Fla-N	5	8	.385	68	0	0	0	1	94	106	65	11	6	44	58	14.9	5.84	75	.290	.376	4	.364	2	-13	-16	1	-1.7
Total 2	9	12	.429	121	0	0	0	1	170	182	103	21	9	81	98	14.4	4.98	85	.280	.367	4	.174	0	-11	-15	0	-1.7
● GEORGE EDMONDSON Edmondson, George Henderson "Big Ed" b: 5/18/1896, Waxahachie, Tex. d: 7/11/73, Waco, Tex. BR/TR, 6'1", 179 lbs. Deb: 8/15/22																											
1922 Cle-A	0	0	—	2	0	0	0	0	2	4	2	0	0	0	0	18.0	9.00	45	.444	.444	0	—	0	-1	-1	0	0.0
1923 Cle-A	0	0	—	1	0	0	0	0	4	8	5	0	1	3	0	27.0	11.25	35	.444	.545	0	.000	-0	-3	-3	0	-0.1
1924 Cle-A	0	0	—	5	1	0	0	0	8	10	8	1	0	5	3	16.9	9.00	47	.294	.385	1	.333	0	-4	-4	-0	-0.2
Total 3	0	0	—	8	1	0	0	0	14	22	15	1	1	8	3	19.9	9.64	43	.361	.443	1	.250	-0	-9	-9	0	-0.3
● PAUL EDMONDSON Edmondson, Paul Michael b: 2/12/43, Kansas City, Kan. d: 2/13/70, Santa Barbara, Cal. BR/TR, 6'5", 195 lbs. Deb: 6/20/69																											
1969 Chi-A	1	6	.143	14	13	1	0	0	87^{2}	72	36	5	4	39	46	11.8	3.70	105	.227	.319	5	.172	-1	-1	2	3	0.4
● BOB EDMONDSON Edmondson, Robert E. b: 4/30/1879, Paris, Ky. d: 8/14/31, Lawrence, Kan. BR/TR, 5'11", 185 lbs. Deb: 9/15/06 ♦																											
1906 Was-A	0	1	.000	2	1	1	0	0	10	10	8	0	0	2	0	10.8	4.50	59	.263	.300	1	.333	0	-2	-2	0	-0.2
● SAM EDMONSTON Edmonston, Samuel Sherwood "Big Sam" b: 8/30/1883, Washington, D.C. d: 4/12/79, Corpus Christi, Tex. BL/TL, 5'11.5", 185 lbs. Deb: 6/24/07																											
1907 Was-A	0	0	—	1	0	0	0	0	3	8	3	0	0	1	0	27.0	9.00	27	.500	.529	0	.000	-0	-2	-2	0	-0.1
● EDWARDS Edwards Deb: 9/11/1875																											
1875 Atl-n	0	1	.000	1	1	0	0	0	2	4	6	0		0	0	18.0	4.50	46	.308	.308	1	.200	-0	-1	-1		-0.1
● FOSTER EDWARDS Edwards, Foster Hamilton "Eddie" b: 9/1/03, Holstein, Iowa d: 1/4/80, Orleans, Mass. BR/TR, 6'3", 175 lbs. Deb: 7/2/25																											
1925 Bos-N	0	0	—	1	0	0	0	0	2	6	5	0	0	1	1	31.5	9.00	45	.545	.583	0	—	0	-1	-1	-0	-0.1
1926 Bos-N	2	0	1.000	3	3	1	0	0	25	20	4	0	0	13	4	11.9	0.72	492	.230	.330	0	.000	-2	9	8	-0	0.5
1927 Bos-N	2	8	.200	29	11	1	0	0	92	95	59	2	3	45	37	14.0	4.99	74	.274	.362	1	.045	-2	-11	-14	-1	-1.6
1928 Bos-N	2	1	.667	21	3	2	0	0	49^{1}	67	36	2	2	23	17	16.8	5.66	69	.327	.400	1	.091	-1	-9	-10	0	-0.6
1930 NY-A	0	0	—	2	0	0	0	0	1^{2}	5	4	0	0	2	1	37.8	21.60	20	.500	.583	0	—	0	-3	-3	-0	-0.2
Total 5	6	9	.400	56	17	4	0	0	170	193	108	4	5	84	60	14.9	4.76	79	.292	.377	2	.048	-5	-16	-20	-1	-2.0
● JIM JOE EDWARDS Edwards, James Corbette "Little Joe" b: 12/14/1894, Banner, Miss. d: 1/19/65, Sarepta, Miss. BR/TL, 6'2", 185 lbs. Deb: 5/14/22																											
1922 Cle-A	3	8	.273	25	7	0	0	0	92^{2}	113	56	1	5	40	44	15.3	4.47	90	.313	.389	2	.087	-2	-4	-5	-1	-0.8
1923 Cle-A	10	10	.500	38	21	7	1	1	179^{1}	200	101	5	5	75	68	14.1	3.71	107	.286	.359	7	.119	-5	5	5	-1	-0.1

YEAR	TM/L	W	L	PCT	G	GS	CG	SH	SV	IP	H	R	HR	HB	BB	SO	RAT	ERA	ERA+	OAV	OOB	BH	AVG	PB	PR	PR+	PD	TPI
1924	Cle-A	4	3	.571	10	7	5	1	0	57	64	29	3	0	34	15	15.5	2.84	150	.305	.402	3	.150	-1	9	9	0	0.8
1925	Cle-A	0	3	.000	13	3	1	0	0	36	60	44	0	1	23	12	21.0	8.25	54	.382	.464	1	.111	-1	-15	-15	1	-1.0
	Chi-A	1	2	.333	9	4	1	1	0	45^1	46	25	4	1	23	20	13.9	3.97	105	.263	.352	3	.176	-1	2	1	1	0.1
	Yr	1	5	.167	22	7	2	1	0	81^1	106	69	4	2	46	32	17.0	5.86	73	.319	.405	4	.154	-2	-13	-15	2	-0.9
1926	Chi-A	6	9	.400	32	16	8	3	1	142	140	76	4	1	63	41	12.9	4.18	92	.264	.343	5	.109	-3	-3	-5	-1	-0.9
1928	Cin-N	2	2	.500	18	1	0	0	2	32	43	29	1	0	20	11	17.7	7.59	52	.347	.438	3	.300	0	-13	-13	-1	-1.6
Total	6	26	37	.413	145	59	22	6	4	584^1	666	360	18	13	278	211	14.7	4.37	92	.295	.376	24	.130	-13	-19	-23	-1	-3.5
● **SHERMAN EDWARDS**	Edwards, Sherman Stanley b: 7/25/09, Mt.Ida, Ark. d: 3/8/92, ElDorado, Ark. BR/TR, 6', 165 lbs. Deb: 9/21/34																											
1934	Cin-N	0	0	—	1	0	0	0	0	3	4	1	0	0	1	1	15.0	3.00	136	.333	.385	0	.000	-0	0	0	0	0.0
● **WAYNE EDWARDS**	Edwards, Wayne Maurice b: 3/7/64, Burbank, Cal. BL/TL, 6'5", 185 lbs. Deb: 9/11/89																											
1989	Chi-A	0	0	—	7	0	0	0	0	7^1	7	3	1	0	3	9	12.3	3.68	104	.269	.345	0	—	0	0	0	0	0.0
1990	Chi-A	5	3	.625	42	5	0	0	2	95	81	39	6	3	41	63	11.8	3.22	119	.234	.321	0	—	0	7	7	0	0.6
1991	Chi-A	0	2	.000	13	0	0	0	0	23^1	22	14	2	0	17	12	15.0	3.86	103	.259	.382	0	—	0	1	0	-0	0.0
Total	3	5	5	.500	62	5	0	0	2	125^2	110	56	9	3	61	84	12.5	3.37	115	.241	.334	0	—	0	8	7	0	0.6
● **HARRY EELLS**	Eells, Harry Archibald "Slippery" b: 2/14/1881, Ida Grove, Iowa d: 10/15/40, Los Angeles, Cal. BR/TR, 6'1", 195 lbs. Deb: 4/22/06																											
1906	Cle-A	4	5	.444	14	8	6	1	0	86^1	77	39	1	3	48	35	13.3	2.61	100	.242	.347	6	.188	1	1	0	1	0.1
● **WISH EGAN**	Egan, Aloysius Jerome b: 6/16/1881, Evart, Mich. d: 4/13/51, Detroit, Mich. BR/TR, 6'3", 185 lbs. Deb: 9/3/02																											
1902	Det-A	0	2	.000	3	3	2	0	0	22	23	12	0	0	6	0	11.9	2.86	127	.271	.319	2	.250	-0	2	2	1	0.2
1905	StL-N	6	15	.286	23	19	18	0	0	171^1	189	93	2	9	39	29	12.4	3.57	83	.285	.333	6	.102	-3	-11	-11	5	-1.1
1906	StL-N	2	9	.182	16	12	7	0	0	86^1	97	45	3	2	27	23	13.1	4.59	57	.278	.333	2	.069	-2	-19	-19	1	-2.3
Total	3	8	26	.235	42	34	27	0	0	279^2	309	150	5	11	72	52	12.6	3.83	76	.282	.332	10	.104	-5	-28	-28	6	-3.2
● **JIM EGAN**	Egan, James K. "Troy Terrier" b: 1858, Derby, Conn. d: 9/26/1884, New Haven, Conn. TL, Deb: 5/15/1882 ♦																											
1882	Tro-N	4	6	.400	12	10	10	0	0	100	133	79	2		24	20	14.1	4.14	68	.315	.352	23	.200	-2	-14	-15	-2	-1.5
● **RIP EGAN**	Egan, John Joseph b: 7/9/1871, Philadelphia, Pa. d: 12/22/50, Cranston, R.I. TR, 5'11", 168 lbs. Deb: 4/30/1894 U																											
1894	Was-N	0	0	—	1	0	0	0	0	5	8	6	1	0	2	2	18.0	10.80	49	.364	.417	0	.000	-0	-3	-3	0	-0.1
● **DICK EGAN**	Egan, Richard Wallis b: 3/24/37, Berkeley, Cal. BL/TL, 6'4", 193 lbs. Deb: 4/9/63 C																											
1963	Det-A	0	1	.000	20	0	0	0	0	21	25	12	4	0	3	16	12.0	5.14	73	.287	.311	0	—	0	-4	-3	0	-0.2
1964	Det-A	0	0	—	23	0	0	0	2	34^1	33	22	4	1	17	21	13.4	4.46	82	.246	.336	0	.000	-0	-3	-3	1	-0.1
1966	Cal-A	0	0	—	11	0	0	0	0	14^1	17	7	2	0	6	11	14.4	4.40	76	.309	.377	0	.000	-0	-2	-2	-0	-0.1
1967	LA-N	1	1	.500	20	0	0	0	0	31^2	34	25	3	4	15	20	15.1	6.25	50	.272	.368	0	.000	-0	-10	-12	-1	-0.8
Total	4	1	2	.333	74	0	0	0	2	101^1	109	66	13	5	41	68	13.8	5.15	67	.272	.347	0	.000	-1	-18	-19	0	-1.2
● **BRUCE EGLOFF**	Egloff, Bruce Edward b: 4/10/65, Denver, Colo. BR/TR, 6'2", 215 lbs. Deb: 4/13/91																											
1991	Cle-A	0	0	—	6	0	0	0	0	5^2	8	3	0	0	4	8	19.1	4.76	87	.333	.429	0	—	0	-0	-0	0	0.0
● **HOWARD EHMKE**	Ehmke, Howard Jonathan "Bob" b: 4/24/1894, Silver Creek, N.Y. d: 3/17/59, Philadelphia, Pa. BR/TR, 6'3", 190 lbs. Deb: 4/12/15																											
1915	Buf-F	0	2	.000	18	2	0	0	0	53^2	69	46	2	5	25	18	16.6	5.53	51	.325	.409	0	.000	-2	-17	-16	2	-0.9
1916	Det-A	3	1	.750	5	4	4	0	0	37^1	34	16	0	0	15	15	11.8	3.13	91	.252	.327	2	.143	-1	-1	-1	1	-0.1
1917	Det-A	10	15	.400	35	25	13	4	2	206	174	84	3	5	88	90	11.7	2.97	89	.243	.330	17	.246	2	-7	-8	2	-0.4
1919	Det-A	17	10	.630	33	31	20	2	0	248^2	255	114	5	6	107	79	13.3	3.18	100	.274	.353	23	.253	3	1	0	4	0.7
1920	Det-A	15	18	.455	38	33	23	2	3	268^1	250	132	8	13	124	98	13.0	3.25	115	.253	.344	25	.238	2	16	14	6	2.4
1921	Det-A	13	14	.481	30	22	13	1	0	196^1	220	123	15	13	81	68	14.4	4.54	94	.286	.364	21	.284	2	-6	-6	1	-0.4
1922	Det-A	17	17	.500	45	29	16	1	1	279^2	299	146	12	23	101	108	13.6	4.22	92	.281	.356	16	.157	-4	-5	-11	2	-1.4
1923	Bos-A	20	17	.541	43	39	28	2	3	316^2	318	155	12	20	119	121	13.0	3.78	109	.272	.349	25	.223	-2	7	11	5	1.6
1924	Bos-A	19	17	.528	45	36	26	4	4	**315**	324	139	9	11	81	119	11.9	3.46	126	.265	.316	28	.222	-2	27	31	2	3.2
1925	Bos-A	9	20	.310	34	31	**22**	0	1	260^2	285	141	8	11	85	95	13.2	3.73	122	.285	.348	13	.148	-5	19	23	5	2.1
1926	Bos-A	3	10	.231	14	14	7	1	0	97^1	115	69	3	4	45	38	15.2	5.46	75	.303	.382	5	.147	-1	-16	-15	1	-1.6
	Phi-A	12	4	.750	20	18	10	1	0	147^1	125	54	1	4	50	55	10.9	2.81	148	.232	.302	7	.152	-2	20	21	0	2.0
	Yr	15	14	.517	34	32	17	2	0	244^2	240	123	4	8	95	93	12.6	3.86	107	.261	.336	12	.150	-3	4	7	1	0.4
1927	Phi-A	12	10	.545	30	27	10	1	0	189^2	200	103	13	14	60	68	13.0	4.22	101	.281	.349	14	.206	-1	-2	1	3	0.2
1928	Phi-A	9	8	.529	23	18	5	1	0	139^1	135	65	6	4	44	34	11.8	3.62	111	.254	.316	11	.239	1	7	6	0	0.8
1929	*Phi-A	7	2	.778	11	8	2	0	0	54^2	48	24	2	1	15	20	10.5	3.29	129	.233	.288	2	.105	-2	6	6	0	0.7
1930	Phi-A	0	1	.000	3	1	0	0	0	10	22	13	4	3	2	4	24.3	11.70	40	.458	.509	1	.333	0	-8	-8	0	-0.5
Total	15	166	166	.500	427	338	199	20	14	2820^2	2873	1424	103	137	1042	1030	12.9	3.75	104	.271	.343	210	.208	-11	42	51	32	8.4
● **RED EHRET**	Ehret, Philip Sydney b: 8/31/1868, Louisville, Ky. d: 7/28/40, Cincinnati, Ohio BR/TR, 6', 175 lbs. Deb: 7/7/1888 ♦																											
1888	KC-a	3	2	.600	7	6	5	0	0	52	58	30	1	3	22	12	14.4	3.98	86	.272	.349	12	.190	-1	-5	-3	1	-0.2
1889	Lou-a	10	29	.256	45	38	35	1	0	364	441	287	11	18	115	135	14.2	4.80	80	.290	.347	65	.252	2	-38	-38	3	-2.7
1890	*Lou-a	25	14	.641	43	38	35	4	2	359	351	182	5	17	79	174	11.2	2.53	152	.248	.296	31	.212	-3	53	53	-3	4.3
1891	Lou-a	13	13	.500	26	24	23	2	0	220^2	225	150	2	11	70	76	12.5	3.47	105	.255	.318	22	.242	1	6	5	0	0.5
1892	Pit-N	16	20	.444	39	36	32	0	0	316	290	183	7	22	83	101	11.3	2.65	124	.234	.294	34	.258	3	22	23	-4	2.1
1893	Pit-N	18	18	.500	39	35	32	**4**	0	314^1	322	203	3	23	115	70	13.2	3.44	133	.257	.331	24	.176	-6	43	40	1	3.1
1894	Pit-N	19	21	.475	46	38	31	1	0	346^2	441	269	12	10	128	102	15.0	5.14	102	.306	.367	23	.170	-11	7	4	-1	-0.6
1895	StL-N	6	19	.240	37	32	18	0	0	231^2	360	223	11	10	88	55	17.8	6.02	80	.349	.405	21	.219	-3	-32	-30	0	-2.5
1896	Cin-N	18	14	.563	34	33	29	2	0	276^2	298	147	5	9	74	60	12.4	3.42	135	.273	.324	20	.196	-3	29	35	1	3.0
1897	Cin-N	8	10	.444	34	19	11	0	2	184^1	256	135	3	13	47	43	15.4	4.78	95	.326	.374	13	.197	-3	-10	-5	-1	-0.7
1898	Lou-N	3	7	.300	12	10	9	0	0	89	130	72	3	3	20	20	15.5	5.76	62	.338	.375	9	.225	1	-21	-22	-1	-1.9
Total	11	139	167	.454	362	309	260	14	4	2754^1	3172	1881	63	139	841	848	13.6	4.02	105	.282	.339	274	.217	-22	55	62	-4	4.4
● **RUBE EHRHARDT**	Ehrhardt, Welton Claude b: 11/20/1894, Beecher, Ill. d: 4/27/80, Chicago Heights, Ill. BR/TR, 6'2", 190 lbs. Deb: 7/18/24																											
1924	Bro-N	5	3	.625	15	9	6	2	0	83^2	71	27	5	1	17	13	9.6	2.26	166	.232	.275	4	.138	-2	15	14	-2	0.9
1925	Bro-N	10	14	.417	36	25	12	0	1	207^2	239	134	10	3	62	47	13.2	5.03	83	.293	.345	15	.211	2	-17	-20	4	-1.4
1926	Bro-N	2	5	.286	44	1	0	0	4	97	101	52	5	0	35	25	12.6	3.90	98	.275	.338	6	.250	0	-1	-1	-2	-0.2
1927	Bro-N	3	7	.300	46	3	2	0	2	95^2	90	46	3	3	37	22	12.2	3.57	111	.264	.341	6	.250	1	4	4	3	0.7
1928	Bro-N	1	3	.250	28	2	1	0	2	54	74	36	1	1	27	12	17.0	4.67	85	.352	.429	4	.286	0	-4	-4	1	-0.2
1929	Cin-N	1	2	.333	24	1	1	1	1	49^1	58	29	2	1	22	9	14.8	4.74	96	.305	.380	2	.182	-0	-0	-1	1	0.0
Total	6	22	34	.393	193	41	22	3	10	587^1	633	324	26	9	200	128	12.9	4.15	97	.284	.345	37	.214	1	-4	-8	5	-0.2
● **HACK EIBEL**	Eibel, Henry Hack b: 12/6/1893, Brooklyn, N.Y. d: 10/16/45, Macon, Ga. BL/TL, 5'11", 220 lbs. Deb: 6/13/12 ♦																											
1920	Bos-A	0	0	—	3	0	0	0	0	10^1	10	4	0	0	3	5	11.3	3.48	105	.270	.325	8	.186	-0	0	0	-0	0.0
● **JUAN EICHELBERGER**	Eichelberger, Juan Tyrone b: 10/21/53, St.Louis, Mo. BR/TR, 6'3", 205 lbs. Deb: 9/7/78																											
1978	SD-N	0	0	—	3	0	0	0	0	3^1	4	4	0	0	2	2	16.2	10.80	31	.267	.353	0	—	0	-3	-3	0	-0.2
1979	SD-N	1	1	.500	3	3	1	0	0	21	15	10	1	0	11	12	11.1	3.43	103	.211	.317	2	.400	1	1	0	-0	0.1
1980	SD-N	4	2	.667	15	13	0	0	0	88^2	73	41	8	1	55	43	13.1	3.65	94	.233	.350	3	.111	-1	-0	-2	-1	-0.3
1981	SD-N	8	8	.500	25	24	3	1	0	141^1	136	60	5	3	74	81	13.6	3.50	93	.259	.353	4	.087	-3	-0	-4	1	-0.6
1982	SD-N	7	14	.333	31	24	8	0	0	177^2	171	98	23	2	72	74	12.4	4.20	82	.251	.325	5	.091	-2	-12	-16	-1	-2.0
1983	Cle-A	4	11	.267	28	15	2	0	0	134	132	80	10	2	59	56	13.0	4.90	87	.259	.338	0	—	0	-12	-9	-1	-1.0
1988	Atl-N	2	0	1.000	20	0	0	0	0	37^1	44	19	3	0	10	13	13.0	3.86	95	.297	.342	0	.000	-0	-2	-1	1	0.0
Total	7	26	36	.419	125	79	14	1	0	603^1	575	312	50	8	283	281	12.9	4.10	87	.254	.339	14	.103	-4	-28	-36	-2	-4.0
● **MARK EICHHORN**	Eichhorn, Mark Anthony b: 11/21/60, San Jose, Cal. BR/TR, 6'3", 210 lbs. Deb: 8/30/82																											
1982	Tor-A	0	3	.000	7	7	0	0	0	38	40	28	4	0	14	16	12.8	5.45	82	.260	.321	0	—	0	-6	-4	-1	-0.3
1986	Tor-A	14	6	.700	69	0	0	0	10	157	105	32	8	7	45	166	9.0	1.72	246	.191	.261	0	—	0	**43**	**43**	2	**5.8**
1987	Tor-A	10	6	.625	**89**	0	0	0	4	127^2	110	47	14	6	52	96	11.8	3.17	142	.234	.318	0	—	0	18	19	2	2.4

YEAR	TM/L	W	L	PCT	G	GS	CG	SH	SV	IP	H	R	HR	HB	BB	SO	RAT	ERA	ERA+	OAV	OOB	BH	AVG	PB	PR	PR+	PD	TPI
1988	Tor-A	0	3	.000	37	0	0	0	1	66^2	79	32	3	6	27	28	15.1	4.18	94	.304	.382	0	—	0	-2	-2	1	0.0
1989	Atl-N	5	5	.500	45	0	0	0	0	68^1	70	36	6	1	19	49	11.9	4.35	84	.275	.327	0	.000	-0	-6	-5	2	-0.5
1990	Cal-A	2	5	.286	60	0	0	0	13	84^2	98	36	2	6	23	69	13.5	3.08	124	.289	.345	0	—	0	8	7	1	0.9
1991	Cal-A	3	3	.500	70	0	0	0	1	81^2	63	21	2	2	13	49	8.6	1.98	207	.219	.257	0	—	0	19	19	2	1.5
1992	Cal-A	2	4	.333	42	0	0	0	2	56^2	51	19	2	0	18	42	11.0	2.38	168	.238	.297	0	—	0	10	10	1	1.1
	*Tor-A	2	0	1.000	23	0	0	0	0	31	35	15	1	2	7	19	12.8	4.35	94	.285	.333	0	—	0	-1	-1	1	0.0
	Yr	4	4	.500	65	0	0	0	2	87^2	86	34	3	2	25	61	11.6	3.08	131	.255	.310	0	—	0	8	9	2	1.1
1993	*Tor-A	3	1	.750	54	0	0	0	0	72^2	76	26	3	3	22	47	12.5	2.72	159	.272	.332	0	—	0	13	13	2	0.8
1994	Bal-A	6	5	.545	43	0	0	0	1	71	62	19	1	5	19	35	10.9	2.15	233	.240	.305	0	—	0	**21**	**22**	2	3.1
1996	Cal-A	1	2	.333	24	0	0	0	0	30^1	36	17	3	2	11	24	14.5	5.04	99	.308	.377	0	—	0	-0	-0	1	0.0
Total	11	48	43	.527	563	7	0	0	32	885^2	825	328	49	40	270	640	11.5	3.00	142	.249	.314	0	.000	-0	117	121	15	14.8
● **DAVE EILAND**	Eiland, David William b: 7/5/66, Dade City, Fla. BR/TR, 6'3", 205 lbs. Deb: 8/3/88																											
1988	NY-A	0	0	—	3	3	0	0	0	12^2	15	9	6	2	4	7	14.9	6.39	62	.294	.368	0	—	0	-3	-3	0	-0.1
1989	NY-A	1	3	.250	6	6	0	0	0	34^1	44	25	5	2	13	11	15.5	5.77	67	.328	.396	0	—	0	-7	-7	-1	-0.8
1990	NY-A	2	1	.667	5	5	0	0	0	30^1	31	14	2	0	5	16	10.7	3.56	112	.254	.283	0	—	0	1	1	-0	0.1
1991	NY-A	2	5	.286	18	13	0	0	0	72^2	87	51	10	3	23	18	14.0	5.33	78	.302	.360	0	—	0	-10	-9	-2	-1.0
1992	SD-N	0	2	.000	7	7	0	0	0	27	33	21	1	0	5	10	12.7	5.67	63	.287	.317	1	.111	1	-6	-6	0	-0.4
1993	SD-N	0	3	.000	10	9	0	0	0	48^1	58	33	5	1	17	14	14.2	5.21	79	.297	.357	1	.083	-1	-6	-6	0	-0.4
1995	NY-A	1	1	.500	4	1	0	0	0	10	16	10	1	1	3	6	18.0	6.30	73	.348	.400	0	—	0	-2	-2	0	-0.3
1998	TB-A	0	1	.000	1	1	0	0	0	2^2	6	6	0	0	3	1	30.4	20.25	24	.429	.529	0	—	0	-5	-4	-0	-0.6
1999	TB-A	4	8	.333	21	15	0	0	0	80^1	98	59	8	3	27	53	14.3	5.60	89	.294	.353	0	.000	-0	-7	-5	1	-0.6
2000	TB-A	2	3	.400	17	10	0	0	0	54^2	77	46	8	4	18	17	16.3	7.24	68	.326	.384	0	—	0	-14	-14	2	-0.9
Total	10	12	27	.308	92	70	0	0	0	373	465	274	46	16	118	153	14.5	5.74	76	.303	.359	2	.091	-0	-59	-56	1	-5.0
● **DAVE EILERS**	Eilers, David Louis b: 12/3/36, Oldenburg, Tex. BR/TR, 5'11", 188 lbs. Deb: 7/27/64																											
1964	Mil-N	0	0	—	6	0	0	0	0	7^2	11	5	1	1	1	1	15.3	4.70	75	.333	.371	0	—	0	-1	-1	-0	-0.1
1965	Mil-N	0	0	—	6	0	0	0	0	3^2	8	5	1	0	0	1	19.6	12.27	29	.421	.421	0	—	0	-4	-4	0	-0.2
	NY-N	1	1	.500	11	0	0	0	2	18	20	11	2	2	4	9	13.0	4.00	88	.274	.329	1	1.000	0	-1	-1	-0	-0.1
	Yr	1	1	.500	17	0	0	0	2	21^2	28	16	3	2	4	10	14.1	5.40	65	.304	.347	1	1.000	0	-4	-5	-0	-0.3
1966	NY-N	1	1	.500	23	0	0	0	0	34^2	39	18	7	1	7	14	12.2	4.67	78	.287	.326	0	.000	-0	-4	-4	1	-0.2
1967	Hou-N	6	4	.600	35	0	0	0	1	59^1	68	29	3	3	17	27	13.3	3.94	84	.296	.352	0	.000	-1	-4	-4	-0	-0.8
Total	4	8	6	.571	81	0	0	0	3	123^1	146	68	14	7	29	52	13.3	4.45	78	.297	.345	1	.111	-0	-13	-14	-0	-1.4
● **DARRELL EINERTSON**	Einertson, Darrell Lee b: 9/4/72, Rhinelander, Wis. BR/TR, 6'2", 190 lbs. Deb: 4/15/2000																											
2000	NY-A	0	0	—	11	0	0	0	0	12^2	16	9	1	0	4	3	14.2	3.55	135	.302	.351	0	—	0	2	2	-0	0.1
● **JOEY EISCHEN**	Eischen, Joseph Raymond b: 5/25/70, West Covina, Cal. BL/TL, 6'1", 190 lbs. Deb: 6/19/94																											
1994	Mon-N	0	0	—	1	0	0	0	0	0^2	4	4	0	1	0	1	67.5	54.00	8	.667	.714	0	—	0	-4	-4	0	-0.2
1995	LA-N	0	0	—	17	0	0	0	0	20^1	19	9	1	2	11	15	14.2	3.10	123	.232	.337	0	.000	-0	2	2	-0	0.1
1996	LA-N	0	1	.000	28	0	0	0	0	43^1	48	25	4	4	20	36	15.0	4.78	81	.282	.371	0	.000	-1	-3	-5	-1	-0.3
	Det-A	1	1	.500	24	0	0	0	0	25	27	11	3	0	14	15	14.8	3.24	156	.284	.376	0	—	0	5	5	1	0.4
1997	Cin-N	0	0	—	1	0	0	0	0	1^1	2	2	0	0	1	2	20.3	6.75	63	.333	.429	0	.000	-0	-0	-0	0	0.0
Total	4	1	2	.333	71	0	0	0	0	90^2	100	51	8	7	46	69	15.2	4.37	96	.279	.371	0	.000	-1	1	-2	-0	0.0
● **JAKE EISENHART**	Eisenhart, Jacob Henry b: 10/3/22, Perkasie, Pa. d: 12/20/87, Huntingdon, Pa. BL/TL, 6'3.5", 195 lbs. Deb: 6/10/44																											
1944	Cin-N	0	0	—	1	0	0	0	0	0^1	0	0	0	0	1	0	27.0	0.00	—	.000	.500	0	—	0	0	0	0	0.0
● **HARRY EISENSTAT**	Eisenstat, Harry b: 10/10/15, Brooklyn, N.Y. BL/TL, 5'11", 185 lbs. Deb: 5/19/35																											
1935	Bro-N	0	1	.000	2	0	0	0	0	4^2	9	8	0	0	2	2	21.2	13.50	29	.429	.478	0	.000	-0	-5	-5	1	-0.7
1936	Bro-N	1	2	.333	5	2	1	0	0	14^1	22	17	1	0	6	5	17.6	5.65	73	.344	.400	1	.333	0	-3	-2	0	-0.4
1937	Bro-N	3	3	.500	13	5	0	0	0	47^2	61	28	2	1	11	12	13.8	3.97	102	.308	.348	0	.000	-1	-0	0	1	0.0
1938	Det-A	9	6	.600	32	9	5	0	4	125^1	131	60	7	1	29	37	11.6	3.73	134	.266	.308	5	.139	-1	15	17	1	1.7
1939	Det-A	2	2	.500	10	2	1	0	0	29^2	39	24	3	0	9	6	14.6	6.98	70	.315	.361	3	.375	1	-8	-7	1	-0.6
	Cle-A	6	7	.462	26	11	4	1	2	103^2	109	45	8	0	23	38	11.5	3.30	133	.265	.304	8	.250	1	15	13	-1	1.4
	Yr	8	9	.471	36	13	5	1	2	133^1	148	69	11	0	32	44	12.2	4.12	110	.277	.317	11	.275	1	7	6	-0	0.8
1940	Cle-A	1	4	.200	27	3	0	0	4	71^2	78	25	6	0	12	27	11.3	3.14	134	.282	.311	6	.273	1	**10**	**9**	-0	0.7
1941	Cle-A	1	1	.500	21	0	0	0	2	34	43	16	2	2	16	11	16.1	4.24	93	.312	.391	2	.333	1	-0	-1	-1	-0.1
1942	Cle-A	2	1	.667	29	1	0	0	2	47^2	58	19	1	0	6	19	12.1	2.45	140	.304	.325	1	.250	0	6	6	-0	0.4
Total	8	25	27	.481	165	33	11	1	14	478^2	550	242	30	4	114	157	12.6	3.84	114	.287	.328	26	.211	1	30	29	0	2.4
● **ED EITELJORGE**	Eiteljorge, Edward Henry b: 10/14/1871, Berlin, Germany d: 12/5/42, Greencastle, Ind. BR/TR, 6'2", 190 lbs. Deb: 5/2/1890																											
1890	Chi-N	0	1	.000	1	1	0	0	0	2	5	7	0	0	1	1	27.0	22.50	16	.455	.500	0	.000	-0	-4	-4	-0	-0.6
1891	Was-a	1	5	.167	8	7	6	0	0	61^1	79	67	3	9	41	23	18.9	6.16	61	.303	.415	5	.192	-1	-17	-16	2	-1.1
Total	2	1	6	.143	9	8	6	0	0	63^1	84	74	3	9	42	24	19.2	6.68	56	.309	.418	5	.185	-1	-21	-21	1	-1.7
● **SCOTT ELARTON**	Elarton, Vincent Scott b: 2/23/76, Lamar, Colo. BR/TR, 6'7", 240 lbs. Deb: 6/20/98																											
1998	*Hou-N	2	1	.667	28	2	0	0	2	57	40	21	5	1	20	56	9.6	3.32	122	.196	.271	0	.000	-1	6	5	-1	0.1
1999	*Hou-N	9	5	.643	42	15	0	0	1	124	111	55	8	4	43	121	11.5	3.48	127	.238	.308	5	.192	0	15	13	-2	1.2
2000	Hou-N	17	7	.708	30	30	2	0	0	192^2	198	117	29	6	84	131	13.5	4.81	102	.263	.342	10	.159	-0	-4	2	-1	0.1
Total	3	28	13	.683	100	47	2	0	3	373^2	349	193	42	11	147	308	12.2	4.14	111	.245	.321	15	.156	-1	17	19	-3	1.4
● **HEINIE ELDER**	Elder, Henry Knox b: 8/23/1890, Seattle, Wash. d: 11/13/58, Long Beach, Cal. BL/TL, 6'2", 200 lbs. Deb: 7/7/13																											
1913	Det-A	0	0	—	1	0	0	0	0	3^1	4	3	0	0	5	0	24.3	8.10	36	.286	.474	0	.000	-0	-2	-2	-0	-0.1
● **CAL ELDRED**	Eldred, Calvin John b: 11/24/67, Cedar Rapids, Iowa BR/TR, 6'4", 235 lbs. Deb: 9/24/91																											
1991	Mil-A	2	0	1.000	3	3	0	0	0	16	20	9	2	0	6	10	14.6	4.50	88	.299	.356	0	—	0	-1	-1	-0	-0.1
1992	Mil-A	11	2	.846	14	14	2	1	0	100^1	76	21	4	2	23	62	9.1	1.79	214	.207	.257	0	—	0	24	23	-0	3.1
1993	Mil-A	16	16	.500	36	36	8	1	0	**258**	232	120	32	10	91	180	11.6	4.01	106	.239	.311	0	—	0	9	7	-0	0.8
1994	Mil-A	11	11	.500	25	25	6	0	0	179	158	96	23	4	84	98	12.4	4.68	108	.236	.325	0	—	0	3	7	1	0.8
1995	Mil-A	1	1	.500	4	4	0	0	0	23^2	24	10	4	1	10	18	13.3	3.42	146	.261	.340	0	—	0	3	4	-0	0.3
1996	Mil-A	4	4	.500	15	15	0	0	0	84^2	82	43	8	4	38	50	13.2	4.46	116	.259	.345	0	—	0	5	7	-1	0.5
1997	Mil-A	13	15	.464	34	34	1	1	0	202	207	118	31	9	89	122	13.6	4.99	93	.266	.349	0	.000	-0	-9	-8	-3	-1.3
1998	Mil-N	4	8	.333	23	23	0	0	0	133	157	82	14	4	61	86	15.0	4.80	89	.297	.374	4	.125	-0	-8	-8	-1	-0.8
1999	Mil-N	2	8	.200	20	15	0	0	0	82	101	75	19	1	46	60	16.2	7.79	58	.297	.382	2	.083	-1	-29	-30	-2	-3.0
2000	Chi-A	10	2	.833	20	20	2	1	0	112	103	61	12	5	59	97	13.4	4.58	108	.243	.343	1	.250	1	4	5	1	0.5
Total	10	74	67	.525	194	189	19	4	0	1190^2	1160	635	149	40	507	783	12.9	4.52	101	.255	.335	7	.111	-1	1	5	-6	0.8
● **HOD ELLER**	Eller, Horace Owen b: 7/5/1894, Muncie, Ind. d: 7/18/61, Indianapolis, Ind BR/TR, 5'11.5", 185 lbs. Deb: 4/16/17																											
1917	Cin-N	10	5	.667	37	11	7	1	1	152^1	131	60	2	3	37	77	10.1	2.36	111	.239	.290	6	.133	-2	6	4	-2	0.0
1918	Cin-N	16	12	.571	37	22	14	0	1	217^2	205	71	1	6	59	84	11.2	2.36	113	.253	.309	11	.157	-2	10	8	-4	0.3
1919	*Cin-N	19	9	.679	38	30	16	7	2	248^1	216	80	7	4	50	137	9.8	2.39	116	.238	.281	26	.280	7	14	11	-3	1.7
1920	Cin-N	13	12	.520	35	23	15	1	0	210^1	208	79	6	5	52	76	11.3	2.95	103	.266	.315	22	.253	1	4	2	-1	0.2
1921	Cin-N	2	2	.500	13	3	0	0	1	34^1	46	23	3	0	15	7	16.0	4.98	72	.322	.386	3	.231	0	-5	-6	-1	-0.7
Total	5	60	40	.600	160	89	52	9	5	863	806	313	19	18	213	381	10.8	2.62	108	.253	.303	68	.221	5	30	20	-11	1.5
● **JOE ELLICK**	Ellick, Joseph J. b: 4/3/1854, Cincinnati, Ohio d: 4/21/23, Kansas City, Kan. 5'10", 162 lbs. Deb: 5/13/1875 MU♦																											
1878	Mil-N	0	1	.000	1	0	0	0	0	3	1	1	0		1	0	6.0	3.00	88	.100	.182	2	.154	-0	-0	-0	-0	0.0
● **BRUCE ELLINGSEN**	Ellingsen, Harold Bruce b: 4/26/49, Pocatello, Idaho BL/TL, 6', 180 lbs. Deb: 7/4/74																											
1974	Cle-A	1	1	.500	16	2	0	0	0	42	45	21	5	0	17	16	13.3	3.21	113	.278	.346	0	—	0	2	2	-0	0.1

YEAR	TM/L	W	L	PCT	G	GS	CG	SH	SV	IP	H	R	HR	HB	BB	SO	RAT	ERA	ERA+	OAV	OOB	BH	AVG	PB	PR	PR+	PD	TPI
● CLAUD ELLIOTT	Elliott, Claud Judson "Chaucer" or "Old Pardee" b: 11/17/1876, Pardeeville, Wis. d: 6/21/23, Pardeeville, Wis. BR/TR, 6', 190 lbs. Deb: 4/16/04																											
1904	Cin-N	3	1	.750	9	6	4	1	0	57^2	53	25	1	4	23	19	12.5	2.97	99	.247	.331	5	.208	1	-1	-0	0	0.1
	NY-N	0	1	.000	3	1	1	0	0	15	21	14	2	0	3	8	14.4	3.00	91	.328	.358	1	.200	0	-0	-0	-1	-0.1
	Yr	3	2	.600	12	7	5	1	0	72^2	74	39	3	4	26	27	12.9	2.97	97	.265	.337	6	.207	1	-2	-1	-1	0.0
1905	NY-N	0	1	.000	10	2	2	0	**6**	38	41	20	3	1	12	20	12.8	4.03	73	.270	.327	3	.188	-0	-4	-5	1	-0.3
Total	2	3	3	.500	22	9	7	1	6	110^2	115	59	6	5	38	47	12.8	3.33	87	.267	.333	9	.200	1	-6	-5	0	-0.3
● DONNIE ELLIOTT	Elliott, Donald Glenn b: 9/20/68, Pasadena, Tex. BR/TR, 6'4", 190 lbs. Deb: 4/23/94																											
1994	SD-N	0	1	.000	30	1	0	0	0	33	31	12	3	1	21	24	14.5	3.27	126	.250	.363	0	.000	-0	3	3	-0	0.1
1995	SD-N	0	0	—	1	0	0	0	0	2	2	0	0	0	1	3	13.5	0.00	—	.250	.333	0	—	0	1	1	-0	0.0
Total	2	0	1	.000	31	1	0	0	0	35	33	12	3	1	22	27	14.4	3.09	133	.250	.361	0	.000	-0	4	4	-0	0.1
● HAL ELLIOTT	Elliott, Harold William b: 5/29/1899, Mt.Clemens, Mich. d: 4/25/63, Honolulu, Hawaii BR/TR, 6'1.5", 170 lbs. Deb: 4/19/29																											
1929	Phi-N	3	7	.300	40	8	2	0	2	114^1	146	94	5	0	59	32	16.1	6.06	86	.313	.390	5	.167	-1	-17	-10	1	-0.7
1930	Phi-N	6	11	.353	**48**	11	2	0	0	117^1	191	120	7	1	58	37	19.2	7.67	71	.382	.447	3	.094	-3	-35	-26	2	-3.0
1931	Phi-N	0	2	.000	16	4	0	0	2	33	46	36	5	1	19	8	18.0	9.55	44	.338	.423	1	.111	-0	-21	-18	0	-1.2
1932	Phi-N	2	4	.333	16	7	0	0	0	57^2	70	45	5	0	38	13	16.9	5.77	76	.297	.394	3	.167	-0	-12	-8	-1	-0.8
Total	4	11	24	.314	120	30	4	0	4	322^1	453	295	22	2	174	90	17.6	6.95	73	.338	.415	12	.135	-5	-85	-61	2	-5.7
● GLENN ELLIOTT	Elliott, Herbert Glenn "Lefty" b: 11/11/19, Sapulpa, Okla d: 7/27/69, Portland, Ore. BB/TL, 5'10", 170 lbs. Deb: 4/17/47																											
1947	Bos-N	0	1	.000	11	0	0	0	1	19	18	10	4	0	11	8	13.7	4.74	82	.269	.372	1	.500	0	-1	-2	0	0.0
1948	Bos-N	1	0	1.000	1	1	0	0	0	3	5	1	0	0	1	2	18.0	3.00	128	.357	.400	0	.000	-0	0	0	-0	0.0
1949	Bos-N	3	4	.429	22	6	1	0	0	68^1	70	35	7	0	27	15	12.8	3.95	96	.269	.338	1	.059	-1	1	-1	1	-0.2
Total	3	4	5	.444	34	7	1	0	1	90^1	93	46	11	0	39	25	13.2	4.08	93	.273	.347	2	.095	-1	-0	-3	1	-0.2
● JUMBO ELLIOTT	Elliott, James Thomas b: 10/22/1900, St.Louis, Mo. d: 1/7/70, Terre Haute, Ind. BR/TL, 6'3", 235 lbs. Deb: 4/21/23																											
1923	StL-A	0	0	—	1	0	0	0	0	1	1	3	0	0	3	0	36.0	27.00	15	.333	.667	0	—	0	-3	-2	-0	-0.1
1925	Bro-N	0	2	.000	3	1	0	0	0	10^2	17	14	0	1	9	3	22.8	8.44	50	.362	.474	0	.000	-1	-5	-5	-0	-0.8
1927	Bro-N	6	13	.316	30	21	12	2	3	188^1	188	82	5	1	60	99	11.9	3.30	120	.269	.327	9	.141	-1	13	14	-4	0.8
1928	Bro-N	9	14	.391	41	21	7	2	1	192	194	106	8	6	64	74	12.4	3.89	102	.268	.332	12	.176	2	2	2	-3	0.1
1929	Bro-N	1	2	.333	6	3	0	0	0	19	21	17	2	1	16	7	18.0	6.63	70	.280	.413	1	.250	0	-4	-4	-0	-0.5
1930	Bro-N	10	7	.588	35	21	6	2	1	198^1	204	100	16	5	70	59	12.7	3.95	124	.271	.337	10	.147	-2	23	21	-3	1.1
1931	Phi-N	**19**	14	.576	**52**	30	12	2	5	249	288	138	15	4	83	99	13.6	4.27	100	.287	.344	11	.122	-6	-11	-0	-5	-1.2
1932	Phi-N	11	10	.524	39	22	8	0	0	166	210	115	14	2	47	62	14.0	5.42	81	.300	.346	12	.197	-1	-28	-16	-2	-2.1
1933	Phi-N	6	10	.375	35	21	6	0	2	161^2	188	89	8	3	49	43	13.4	3.84	99	.295	.348	12	.231	0	-9	-0	-4	-0.4
1934	Phi-N	0	1	.000	3	1	0	0	0	5^1	8	7	0	1	4	1	21.9	10.13	47	.333	.448	0	.000	-0	-4	-3	-0	-0.5
	Bos-N	1	1	.500	7	3	0	0	0	15^1	19	16	2	1	9	6	17.0	5.87	65	.284	.377	1	.250	0	-3	-4	-0	-0.4
	Yr	1	2	.333	10	4	0	0	0	20^2	27	23	2	2	13	7	18.3	6.97	58	.297	.396	1	.200	0	-7	-7	-0	-0.9
Total	10	63	74	.460	252	144	51	8	12	1206^2	1338	687	70	25	414	453	13.3	4.24	100	.283	.344	68	.163	-8	-29	2	-21	-4.0
● DOCK ELLIS	Ellis, Dock Phillip b: 3/11/45, Los Angeles, Cal. BB/TR, 6'3", 210 lbs. Deb: 6/18/68																											
1968	Pit-N	6	5	.545	26	10	2	0	0	104	82	35	4	1	38	52	10.5	2.51	117	.213	.285	2	.069	-1	5	5	0	0.4
1969	Pit-N	11	17	.393	35	33	8	2	0	218^2	206	101	14	4	76	173	11.8	3.58	97	.250	.316	6	.088	-3	0	-2	1	-0.5
1970	*Pit-N	13	10	.565	30	30	9	4	0	201^2	194	81	9	10	87	128	13.0	3.21	122	.257	.342	7	.100	-3	19	16	2	1.6
1971	*Pit-N★	19	9	.679	31	31	11	2	0	226^2	207	93	15	2	63	137	10.8	3.06	111	.239	.292	16	.203	2	10	9	0	1.4
1972	*Pit-N	15	7	.682	25	25	4	1	0	163^1	156	60	6	3	33	96	10.6	2.70	123	.253	.294	9	.153	-1	14	12	-1	1.4
1973	Pit-N	12	14	.462	28	28	3	1	0	192	176	86	7	6	55	122	11.1	3.05	116	.240	.299	7	.108	-3	13	11	1	1.2
1974	Pit-N	12	9	.571	26	26	9	0	0	176^2	163	71	13	7	41	91	10.7	3.16	109	.242	.292	12	.214	3	9	6	-1	0.9
1975	*Pit-N	8	9	.471	27	24	5	2	0	140	163	69	9	3	43	69	13.4	3.79	94	.292	.345	4	.111	0	-2	-4	-1	-0.5
1976	*NY-A	17	8	.680	32	32	8	1	0	211^2	195	83	14	4	76	65	11.7	3.19	107	.247	.316	0	—	0	8	6	-3	0.3
1977	NY-A	1	1	.500	3	3	1	0	0	19^2	18	9	1	0	8	5	11.9	1.83	216	.237	.310	0	—	0	5	5	-0	0.4
	Oak-A	1	5	.167	7	7	0	0	0	26	35	33	5	1	14	11	17.3	9.69	42	.315	.397	0	—	0	-16	-16	-0	-2.7
	Tex-A	10	6	.625	23	22	7	1	1	167^1	158	60	13	0	42	90	10.8	2.90	141	.254	.301	0	—	0	22	22	-2	1.8
	Yr	12	12	.500	33	32	8	1	1	213	211	102	19	1	64	106	11.7	3.63	112	.260	.315	0	—	0	10	10	-2	-0.5
1978	Tex-A	9	7	.563	22	22	3	0	0	141^1	131	81	15	2	46	45	11.4	4.20	89	.245	.307	0	—	0	-7	-7	-0	-0.7
1979	Tex-A	1	5	.167	10	9	0	0	0	46^2	64	34	5	0	16	10	15.4	5.98	70	.323	.374	0	—	0	-9	-10	-0	-1.0
	NY-N	3	7	.300	17	14	1	0	0	85	110	60	9	1	34	41	15.4	6.04	60	.320	.383	2	.077	-1	-22	-23	0	-2.4
	Pit-N	0	0	—	3	1	0	0	0	7	9	2	1	0	2	1	14.1	2.57	151	.346	.393	0	.000	-0	1	1	-0	0.0
	Yr	3	7	.300	20	15	1	0	0	92	119	62	10	1	36	42	15.3	5.77	64	.322	.383	2	.074	-2	-21	-22	0	-2.4
Total	12	138	119	.537	345	317	71	14	1	2127^2	2067	958	140	44	674	1136	11.8	3.46	103	.255	.315	65	.133	-7	51	29	-3	1.6
● JIM ELLIS	Ellis, James Russell b: 3/25/45, Tulare, Cal. BR/TL, 6'2", 185 lbs. Deb: 8/11/67																											
1967	Chi-N	1	1	.500	8	1	0	0	0	16^2	20	7	1	0	9	8	15.7	3.24	109	.313	.397	1	.200	0	0	1	-0	0.1
1969	StL-N	0	0	—	2	1	0	0	0	5^1	7	1	0	0	3	0	16.9	1.69	212	.318	.400	0	—	0	1	1	-0	0.0
Total	2	1	1	.500	10	2	0	0	0	22	27	8	1	0	12	8	16.0	2.86	124	.314	.398	1	.200	0	1	2	-1	0.1
● ROBERT ELLIS	Ellis, Robert Randolph b: 12/15/70, Baton Rouge, La. BR/TR, 6'5", 220 lbs. Deb: 9/12/96																											
1996	Cal-A	0	0	—	3	0	0	0	0	5	0	0	0	0	4	5	7.2	0.00	—	.000	.211	0	—	0	3	3	-0	0.1
● SAMMY ELLIS	Ellis, Samuel Joseph b: 2/11/41, Youngstown, Ohio BL/TR, 6'1", 180 lbs. Deb: 4/14/62 C																											
1962	Cin-N	2	2	.500	8	4	0	0	0	28	29	25	6	1	29	27	19.0	6.75	60	.269	.428	2	.200	-0	-9	-8	-0	-1.0
1964	Cin-N	10	3	.769	52	5	2	0	14	122^1	101	38	9	1	28	125	9.6	2.57	140	.223	.270	2	.083	-0	13	14	0	1.8
1965	Cin-N☆	22	10	.688	44	39	15	2	2	263^2	222	119	22	6	104	183	11.3	3.79	99	.226	.304	12	.125	-1	-7	-1	-3	-0.6
1966	Cin-N	12	19	.387	41	36	7	0	0	221	226	135	35	3	78	154	12.5	5.29	74	.264	.328	8	.114	-2	-41	-32	-3	-4.4
1967	Cin-N	8	11	.421	32	27	8	1	0	175^2	197	86	18	4	67	80	13.7	3.84	98	.286	.353	4	.082	-2	-9	-2	-1	-0.5
1968	Cal-A	9	10	.474	42	24	3	0	2	164	150	80	22	6	56	93	11.6	3.95	74	.244	.313	2	.045	-3	-18	-19	-2	-2.8
1969	Chi-A	0	3	.000	10	5	0	0	0	29^1	42	20	6	1	16	15	18.1	5.83	66	.336	.415	1	.167	0	-7	-6	0	-0.5
Total	7	63	58	.521	229	140	35	3	18	1004	967	503	118	22	378	677	12.3	4.15	88	.253	.323	31	.104	-8	-78	-55	-9	-8.0
● GEORGE ELLISON	Ellison, George Russell b: 1/24/1895, California d: 1/20/78, San Francisco, Cal. BR/TR, 6'3", 185 lbs. Deb: 8/21/20																											
1920	Cle-A	0	0	—	1	0	0	0	0	1	0	0	0	0	2	1	18.0	0.00	—	.000	.400	0	—	0	0	0	0	0.0
● DICK ELLSWORTH	Ellsworth, Richard Clark b: 3/22/40, Lusk, Wyo. BL/TL, 6'4", 195 lbs. Deb: 6/22/58 F																											
1958	Chi-N	0	1	.000	1	1	0	0	0	2^1	4	4	0	1	3	0	30.9	15.43	25	.364	.533	0	.000	-0	-3	-3	-0	-0.5
1960	Chi-N	7	13	.350	31	27	6	0	0	176^2	170	83	12	2	72	94	12.4	3.72	102	.257	.332	2	.042	-3	1	1	-0	-0.2
1961	Chi-N	10	11	.476	37	31	7	1	0	186^2	213	90	23	3	48	91	12.7	3.86	108	.292	.338	2	.036	-5	4	6	3	0.5
1962	Chi-N	9	20	.310	37	33	6	0	1	208^2	241	131	23	5	77	113	13.9	5.09	81	.291	.355	7	.113	1	-27	-21	0	-2.4
1963	Chi-N	22	10	.688	37	37	19	4	0	290^2	223	75	14	2	75	185	9.3	2.11	**167**	.210	.263	9	.096	-2	38	42	2	**4.9**
1964	Chi-N☆	14	18	.438	37	36	16	1	0	256^2	267	129	34	3	71	148	12.0	3.75	99	.266	.317	4	.046	-5	-6	-1	2	-0.5
1965	Chi-N	14	15	.483	36	34	8	0	1	222^1	227	108	22	4	57	130	11.7	3.81	97	.265	.313	7	.096	-2	-7	-3	2	-0.4
1966	Chi-N	8	22	.267	38	37	9	0	0	269^1	321	150	28	5	51	144	12.6	3.98	92	.294	.328	14	.156	-0	-11	-9	2	-0.8
1967	Phi-N	6	7	.462	32	21	3	1	0	125^1	152	75	6	5	36	45	13.9	4.38	78	.306	.359	4	.108	-1	-14	-13	2	-1.3
1968	Bos-A	16	7	.696	31	28	10	1	0	196	196	74	16	7	37	106	11.0	3.03	104	.260	.301	4	.056	-5	-1	3	-0	-0.2
1969	Bos-A	0	0	—	2	2	0	0	0	12	16	5	1	0	4	4	15.0	3.75	102	.320	.370	0	.000	-0	-0	0	-0	0.0
	Cle-A	6	9	.400	34	22	3	1	0	135	162	73	10	5	40	48	13.8	4.13	91	.301	.354	6	.133	-1	-8	-5	0	-0.6
	Yr	6	9	.400	36	24	3	1	0	147	178	78	11	5	44	52	13.9	4.10	92	.302	.356	6	.125	-2	-8	-5	0	-0.6
1970	Cle-A	3	3	.500	29	1	0	0	2	43^2	49	23	4	1	14	13	13.2	4.53	87	.299	.358	0	.000	-0	-4	-3	1	-0.3
	Mil-A	0	0	—	14	0	0	0	1	15^2	11	3	0	1	3	9	8.6	1.72	220	.196	.250	0	—	0	3	4	-0	0.2
	Yr	3	3	.500	43	1	0	0	3	59^1	60	26	4	2	17	22	12.0	3.79	103	.273	.331	0	.000	-0	-0	1	1	-0.1

YEAR TM/L	W	L	PCT	G	GS	CG	SH	SV	IP	H	R	HR	HB	BB	SO	RAT	ERA	ERA+	OAV	OOB	BH	AVG	PB	PR	PR+	PD	TPI
1971 Mil-A	0	1	.000	11	0	0	0	0	14^2	22	10	1	1	7	10	18.4	4.91	71	.361	.435	0	.000	-0	-2	-2	-0	-0.2
Total 13	115	137	.456	407	310	87	9	5	2155^2	2274	1033	194	45	595	1140	12.2	3.72	100	.272	.324	59	.088	-25	-36	-2	12	-1.8
● STEVE ELLSWORTH Ellsworth, Steven Clark b: 7/30/60, Chicago, Ill. BR/TR, 6'8", 220 lbs. Deb: 4/7/88 F																											
1988 Bos-A	1	6	.143	8	7	0	0	0	36	47	29	7	1	16	16	16.0	6.75	61	.315	.386	0	—	0	-11	-10	-0	-1.6
● DON ELSTON Elston, Donald Ray b: 4/6/29, Campbellstown, Ohio d: 1/2/95, Evanston, Ill. BR/TR, 6', 170 lbs. Deb: 9/17/53																											
1953 Chi-N	0	1	.000	2	1	0	0	0	5	11	8	1	0	0	2	19.8	14.40	31	.458	.458	0	.000	-0	-6	-5	-0	-0.8
1957 Bro-N	0	0	—	1	0	0	0	0	1	1	0	0	0	0	1	9.0	0.00	—	.250	.250	0	—	0	0	0	0	0.0
Chi-N	6	7	.462	39	14	2	0	8	144	139	61	15	5	55	102	12.4	3.56	109	.259	.334	4	.108	-2	5	5	0	0.3
Yr	6	7	.462	40	14	2	0	8	145	140	61	15	5	55	103	12.4	3.54	109	.259	.333	4	.108	-2	5	5	0	0.3
1958 Chi-N	9	8	.529	**69**	0	0	0	10	97	75	35	9	1	39	84	10.7	2.88	136	.214	.294	5	.357	1	**12**	**11**	1	2.4
1959 Chi-N★	10	8	.556	**65**	0	0	0	13	97^2	77	40	11	3	46	82	11.6	3.32	119	.218	.313	4	.211	0	7	7	-0	1.3
1960 Chi-N	8	9	.471	60	0	0	0	11	127	109	57	17	4	55	85	11.9	3.40	111	.231	.316	3	.125	-1	5	5	-2	0.5
1961 Chi-N	6	7	.462	58	0	0	0	8	93^1	108	64	11	6	45	59	15.3	5.59	75	.297	.383	2	.182	-0	-16	-14	0	-2.0
1962 Chi-N	4	8	.333	57	0	0	0	8	66^1	57	25	6	1	32	37	12.2	2.44	170	.247	.341	0	.000	-1	11	12	1	2.3
1963 Chi-N	4	1	.800	51	0	0	0	4	70	57	26	6	2	21	41	10.3	2.83	124	.226	.291	0	.000	-0	4	5	-1	0.3
1964 Chi-N	2	5	.286	48	0	0	0	1	54^1	68	38	4	3	34	26	17.4	5.30	70	.330	.432	1	.167	-0	-11	-9	1	-1.0
Total 9	49	54	.476	450	15	2	0	63	755^2	702	354	80	25	327	519	12.6	3.69	106	.251	.335	19	.153	-3	11	17	1	3.3
● NARCISO ELVIRA Elvira, Narciso Chicho (Delgado) b: 10/29/67, Veracruz, Mex. BL/TL, 5'10", 160 lbs. Deb: 9/9/90																											
1990 Mil-A	0	0	—	4	0	0	0	0	5	6	3	0	0	5	6	19.8	5.40	72	.300	.440	0	—	0	-1	-1	0	0.0
● HARRY ELY Ely, Harry Deb: 9/24/1892																											
1892 Bal-N	0	1	.000	1	1	1	0	0	7	14	9	0	2	7	0	29.6	7.71	44	.400	.523	0	.000	-0	-3	-3	-0	-0.4
● BONES ELY Ely, William Frederick b: 6/7/1863, N.Girard, Pa. d: 1/10/52, Berkeley, Cal. BR/TR, 6'1", 155 lbs. Deb: 6/19/1884 ♦																											
1884 Buf-N	0	1	.000	1	1	0	0	0	5	17	15	1		5	4	39.6	14.40	22	.500	.564	0	.000	-1	-6	-6	-0	-0.7
1886 Lou-a	0	4	.000	6	4	4	0	**1**	44	53	47	0	0	26	28	16.2	5.32	68	.280	.367	5	.156	-1	-9	-8	0	-0.6
1890 Syr-a	0	0	—	1	0	0	0	0	2	7	5	0	0	0	0	31.5	22.50	16	.538	.538	130	.262	0	-4	-5	0	-0.2
1894 StL-N	0	0	—	1	0	0	0	0	1	0	0	0	0	3	0	27.0	0.00	—	.000	.500	156	.306	0	1	1	0	0.0
Total 4	0	5	.000	9	5	4	0	1	52	77	67	1	0	34	32	19.2	6.75	54	.322	.407	1333	.258	-1	-19	-17	0	-1.5
● ALAN EMBREE Embree, Alan Duane b: 1/23/70, Vancouver, Wash. BL/TL, 6'2", 185 lbs. Deb: 9/15/92																											
1992 Cle-A	0	2	.000	4	4	0	0	0	18	19	14	3	1	8	12	14.0	7.00	56	.271	.354	0	—	0	-6	-6	-1	-0.6
1995 *Cle-A	3	2	.600	23	0	0	0	1	24^2	23	16	2	0	16	23	14.2	5.11	92	.253	.364	0	—	0	-1	-1	-0	-0.2
1996 *Cle-A	1	1	.500	24	0	0	0	0	31	30	26	10	0	21	33	14.8	6.39	77	.259	.372	0	—	0	-5	-5	-0	-0.3
1997 *Atl-N	3	1	.750	66	0	0	0	0	46	36	13	1	2	20	45	11.3	2.54	165	.221	.314	0	—	0	8	8	0	0.7
1998 Atl-N	1	0	1.000	20	0	0	0	0	18^2	23	14	2	0	10	19	15.9	4.34	96	.307	.388	0	.000	-0	-0	-0	0	0.0
Ari-N	3	2	.600	35	0	0	0	1	35	33	18	5	1	13	24	12.1	4.11	102	.248	.320	0	—	0	0	0	-1	0.0
Yr	4	2	.667	55	0	0	0	1	53^2	56	32	7	1	23	43	13.4	4.19	100	.269	.345	0	.000	0	0	0	-0	0.0
1999 SF-N	3	2	.600	68	0	0	0	0	58^2	42	22	6	3	26	53	10.9	3.38	125	.200	.297	0	—	0	8	6	-1	0.3
2000 *SF-N	3	5	.375	63	0	0	0	2	60	62	34	4	3	25	49	13.5	4.95	86	.274	.354	0	—	0	-2	-5	0	-0.6
Total 7	17	15	.531	303	4	0	0	4	292	268	157	33	10	139	258	12.9	4.41	98	.247	.338	0	.000	0	2	-3	-2	-0.7
● RED EMBREE Embree, Charles Willard b: 8/30/17, ElMonte, Cal. d: 9/24/96, Eugene, Ore. BR/TR, 6', 165 lbs. Deb: 9/10/41																											
1941 Cle-A	0	1	.000	1	1	0	0	0	4	7	3	0	1	3	4	24.8	6.75	58	.438	.550	0	.000	-0	-1	-1	-0	-0.2
1942 Cle-A	3	4	.429	19	6	2	0	0	63	58	31	0	2	31	44	13.0	3.86	89	.242	.333	2	.133	-0	-1	-3	-0	-0.4
1944 Cle-A	0	1	.000	3	1	0	0	0	3^1	2	5	0	0	5	4	18.9	13.50	24	.167	.412	0	—	0	-4	-4	0	-0.7
1945 Cle-A	4	4	.500	8	8	5	1	0	70	56	17	3	0	26	42	10.5	1.93	168	.215	.287	3	.143	-1	11	11	1	1.3
1946 Cle-A	8	12	.400	28	26	8	0	0	200	170	86	15	2	79	87	11.3	3.47	95	.227	.302	13	.186	1	1	-4	-1	-0.4
1947 Cle-A	8	10	.444	27	21	6	0	0	162^2	137	65	13	1	67	56	11.3	3.15	110	.233	.313	9	.173	-1	10	6	1	0.6
1948 NY-A	5	3	.625	20	8	4	0	0	76^2	77	37	6	1	30	25	12.7	3.76	109	.261	.331	4	.148	-1	5	3	-1	0.0
1949 StL-A	3	13	.188	35	19	4	0	1	127^1	146	90	13	3	89	24	16.8	5.37	84	.294	.405	6	.162	-1	-17	-11	-0	-1.4
Total 8	31	48	.392	141	90	29	1	1	707	653	334	50	10	330	286	12.6	3.72	98	.246	.331	37	.166	-4	4	-5	-2	-1.2
● SLIM EMBREY Embrey, Charles Akin b: 8/17/01, Columbia, Tenn. d: 10/10/47, Nashville, Tenn. BR/TR, 6'2", 184 lbs. Deb: 10/1/23																											
1923 Chi-A	0	0	—	1	0	0	0	0	2^2	7	6	0	0	2	1	30.4	10.13	39	.500	.563	0	—	0	-2	-2	0	0.0
● CHARLIE EMIG Emig, Charles Henry b: 4/5/1875, Cincinnati, Ohio d: 10/2/75, Oklahoma City, Okla. TL, Deb: 9/4/1896																											
1896 Lou-N	0	1	.000	1	1	1	0	0	8	12	17	1	3	7	1	24.8	7.88	55	.343	.489	0	.000	-1	-3	-3	1	-0.3
● SLIM EMMERICH Emmerich, William Peter b: 9/29/19, Allentown, Pa. d: 9/17/98, Allentown, Pa. BR/TR, 6'1", 170 lbs. Deb: 5/14/45																											
1945 NY-N	4	4	.500	31	7	1	0	0	100	111	55	8	1	33	27	13.1	4.86	80	.278	.334	3	.120	-2	-12	-10	-0	-0.9
1946 NY-N	0	0	—	2	0	0	0	0	4	6	2	1	0	0	1	13.5	4.50	76	.400	.400	0	—	0	-0	-0	0	0.0
Total 2	4	4	.500	33	7	1	0	0	104	117	57	9	1	33	28	13.1	4.85	80	.282	.336	3	.120	-2	-12	-11	-0	-0.9
● BOB EMSLIE Emslie, Robert Daniel b: 1/27/1859, Guelph, Ont., Can. d: 4/26/43, St.Thomas, Ont., Canada BR/TR, 5'11", Deb: 7/25/1883 U																											
1883 Bal-a	9	13	.409	24	23	21	1	0	201^1	188	149	3		41	62	10.2	3.17	110	.231	.268	16	.165	-3	3	7	2	0.5
1884 Bal-a	32	17	.653	50	50	50	4	0	455^1	419	241	5	14	88	264	10.3	2.75	126	.224	.264	37	.190	-5	25	34	-1	2.6
1885 Bal-a	3	10	.231	13	13	11	0	0	107	131	87	0	5	30	27	14.0	4.29	76	.298	.350	12	.235	0	-12	-12	-1	-1.2
Phi-a	0	4	.000	4	4	3	0	0	28^2	37	30	1	0	6	9	13.5	6.28	55	.291	.323	1	.083	-1	-10	-9	1	-0.9
Yr	3	14	.176	17	17	14	0	0	135^2	168	117	1	5	36	36	13.9	4.71	70	.297	.344	13	.206	-1	-22	-21	-1	-2.1
Total 3	44	44	.500	91	90	85	5	0	792^1	775	507	9	19	165	362	10.9	3.19	108	.239	.279	66	.186	-9	6	21	0	1.0
● LUIS ENCARNACION Encarnacion, Luis Martin Lora (b: Luis Martin Lora (Encarcnacion)) b: 10/20/63, Santo Domingo, D.R. BR/TR, 5'10", 178 lbs. Deb: 7/27/90																											
1990 KC-A	0	0	—	4	0	0	0	0	10^1	14	10	1	0	4	8	15.7	7.84	49	.311	.367	0	—	0	-5	-5	-0	-0.2
● TREVOR ENDERS Enders, Trevor Hale b: 12/22/74, Milwaukee, Wis. BR/TL, 6'1", 205 lbs. Deb: 9/2/2000																											
2000 TB-A	0	1	.000	9	0	0	0	0	9^1	14	13	2	0	5	5	18.3	10.61	47	.359	.432	0	—	0	-6	-6	0	-0.5
● JOE ENGEL Engel, Joseph William b: 3/12/1893, Washington, D.C. d: 6/12/69, Chattanooga, Tenn BR/TL, 6'1.5", 183 lbs. Deb: 5/30/12																											
1912 Was-A	2	5	.286	17	10	2	0	1	75	70	41	2	4	50	29	14.9	3.96	84	.253	.375	1	.059	-1	-5	-5	1	-0.4
1913 Was-A	8	9	.471	36	24	6	2	0	164^2	124	75	2	11	85	70	12.0	3.06	97	.207	.317	3	.061	-5	-2	-2	-0	-0.7
1914 Was-A	7	5	.583	35	15	1	0	3	124^1	108	53	2	5	75	41	13.6	2.97	95	.254	.372	3	.107	1	-3	-2	-0	-0.2
1915 Was-A	0	3	.000	11	3	0	0	0	33^2	30	15	0	3	19	9	13.9	3.21	93	.261	.380	0	.000	-1	-1	-1	0	-0.1
1917 Cin-N	0	1	.000	1	1	1	0	0	8	12	8	0	0	6	2	20.3	5.63	47	.353	.450	0	.000	-0	-3	-3	0	-0.3
1919 Cle-A	0	0	—	1	0	0	0	0	0	0	0	0	3	—	—	∞		—	1.000	104	—	0	-2	-2		0	-0.2
1920 Was-A	0	0	—	1	0	0	0	0	1^2	0	4	0	1	4	0	27.0	21.60	17	.000	.556	0	.000	-0	-3	-3	-0	-0.2
Total 7	17	23	.425	102	53	10	2	4	407^1	344	199	6	24	242	151	13.5	3.38	88	.237	.355	7	.067	-6	-20	-18	1	-2.1
● STEVE ENGEL Engel, Steven Michael b: 12/31/61, Cincinnati, Ohio BR/TL, 6'3", 216 lbs. Deb: 7/30/85																											
1985 Chi-N	1	5	.167	11	8	1	0	1	51^2	61	-36	10	0	26	29	15.2	5.57	72	.298	.377	3	.188	1	-11	-8	-0	-0.8
● RICK ENGLE Engle, Richard Douglas b: 4/7/57, Corbin, Ky. BR/TL, 5'11.5", 181 lbs. Deb: 9/2/81																											
1981 Mon-N	0	0	—	1	0	0	0	0	2	6	4	0	0	1	2	31.5	18.00	19	.500	.538	0	—	0	-3	-3	-0	-0.2
● JACK ENRIGHT Enright, Jackson Percy b: 11/29/1895, Fort Worth, Tex. d: 8/18/75, Pompano Beach, Fla BR/TR, 5'11", 177 lbs. Deb: 9/26/17																											
1917 NY-A	0	1	.000	1	1	0	0	0	5	5	5	0	0	3	1	14.4	5.40	50	.294	.400	0	.000	-0	-2	-1	1	-0.2
● TERRY ENYART Enyart, Terry Gene b: 10/10/50, Ironton, Ohio BR/TL, 6'2", 190 lbs. Deb: 6/17/74																											
1974 Mon-N	0	0	—	2	0	0	0	0	1^2	4	6	0	0	4	2	43.2	16.20	24	.444	.615	0	—	0	-2	-2	-0	-0.1

YEAR	TM/L	W	L	PCT	G	GS	CG	SH	SV	IP	H	R	HR	HB	BB	SO	RAT	ERA	ERA+	OAV	OOB	BH	AVG	PB	PR	PR+	PD	TPI
● JOHNNY ENZMANN	Enzmann, John "Gentleman John" b: 3/4/1890, Brooklyn, N.Y. d: 3/14/84, Riverhead, N.Y. BR/TR, 5'10", 165 lbs. Deb: 7/10/14																											
1914	Bro-N	1	0	1.000	7	1	0	0	0	19	21	16	1	3	8	5	15.2	4.74	60	.300	.395	0	.000	-1	-4	-4	1	-0.2
1918	Cle-A	5	7	.417	30	14	8	0	2	136^2	130	44	2	5	29	38	10.8	2.37	127	.263	.310	7	.149	-2	6	9	0	0.6
1919	Cle-A	3	2	.600	14	4	2	0	0	55^1	67	29	0	2	8	13	12.5	2.28	147	.312	.342	2	.133	-0	6	6	-1	0.4
1920	Phi-N	2	3	.400	16	2	1	0	0	58^2	79	40	1	5	16	35	15.3	3.84	89	.320	.373	4	.167	1	-5	-2	-0	-0.1
Total	4	11	12	.478	67	21	11	0	2	269^2	297	129	4	15	61	91	12.4	2.84	111	.289	.338	13	.141	-3	3	9	-0	0.7
● AL EPPERLY	Epperly, Albert Paul "Tub" or "Pard" b: 5/7/18, Glidden, Iowa BL/TR, 6'2", 194 lbs. Deb: 4/25/38																											
1938	Chi-N	2	0	1.000	9	4	1	0	0	27	28	11	1	0	15	10	14.3	3.67	104	.264	.355	2	.250	1	0	0	0	0.1
1950	Bro-N	0	0	—	5	0	0	0	0	9	14	8	1	0	5	3	19.0	5.00	82	.378	.452	0	—	0	-1	-1	-0	-0.1
Total	2	2	0	1.000	14	4	1	0	0	36	42	19	2	0	20	13	15.5	4.00	97	.294	.380	2	.250	1	-0	-0	-0	0.0
● GREG ERARDI	Erardi, Joseph Gregory b: 5/31/54, Syracuse, N.Y. BR/TR, 6'1", 190 lbs. Deb: 9/6/77																											
1977	Sea-A	0	1	.000	5	0	0	0	0	9	12	8	3	0	6	5	18.0	6.00	69	.300	.391	0	—	0	-2	-2	-0	-0.2
● EDDIE ERAUTT	Erautt, Edward Lorenz Sebastian b: 9/26/24, Portland, Ore. BR/TR, 6', 186 lbs. Deb: 4/16/47 F																											
1947	Cin-N	4	9	.308	36	10	2	0	0	119	146	78	5	2	53	43	15.2	5.07	81	.307	.379	2	.069	-1	-13	-13	1	-1.2
1948	Cin-N	0	0	—	2	0	0	0	0	3	3	2	0	0	1	0	12.0	6.00	65	.250	.308	0	—	0	-1	-1	-0	0.0
1949	Cin-N	4	11	.267	39	9	1	0	1	112^2	99	53	9	3	61	43	13.0	3.36	125	.247	.351	4	.174	0	**9**	**10**	-1	1.2
1950	Cin-N	4	2	.667	33	2	1	0	1	65^1	82	48	9	6	22	35	15.2	5.65	75	.307	.373	2	.154	0	-11	-10	-0	-0.9
1951	Cin-N	0	0	—	30	0	0	0	0	39^1	50	31	4	3	23	20	17.4	5.72	71	.314	.411	0	.000	-0	-8	-7	1	-0.3
1953	Cin-N	0	0	—	4	0	0	0	0	4^2	11	3	1	0	3	1	27.0	5.79	75	.500	.560	0	.000	-0	-1	-1	0	0.0
	StL-N	3	1	.750	20	1	0	0	0	35^2	43	25	6	2	16	15	15.4	6.31	67	.299	.377	1	.167	-0	-8	-8	0	-0.8
	Yr	3	1	.750	24	1	0	0	0	40^1	54	28	7	2	19	16	16.7	6.25	68	.325	.401	1	.143	-0	-9	-9	0	-0.8
Total	6	15	23	.395	164	22	4	0	2	379^2	434	240	34	16	179	157	14.9	4.86	86	.293	.376	9	.120	-2	-33	-29	0	-2.0
● TODD ERDOS	Erdos, Todd Michael b: 11/21/73, Washington, Pa. BR/TR, 6'1", 205 lbs. Deb: 6/8/97																											
1997	SD-N	2	0	1.000	11	0	0	0	0	13^2	17	9	1	2	4	13	15.1	5.27	74	.293	.359	0	.000	-0	-2	-2	0	-0.3
1998	NY-A	0	0	—	2	0	0	0	0	2	5	2	0	0	1	0	27.0	9.00	49	.500	.545	0	—	0	-1	-1	-0	-0.1
1999	NY-A	0	0	—	4	0	0	0	0	7	5	4	2	0	4	4	11.6	3.86	123	.192	.300	0	—	0	1	1	0	0.0
2000	NY-A	0	0	—	14	0	0	0	1	25	31	14	2	1	11	18	15.5	5.04	95	.304	.377	0	.000	-0	-0	-1	-0	-0.1
	SD-N	0	0	—	22	0	0	0	1	29^2	32	24	5	6	17	16	16.7	6.67	66	.271	.390	0	.000	-0	-7	-8	-0	-0.4
Total	4	2	0	1.000	53	0	0	0	2	77^1	90	53	10	9	37	51	15.8	5.70	78	.287	.378	0	.000	-0	-9	-11	-1	-0.9
● JOHN ERICKS	Ericks, John Edward b: 6/16/67, Tinley Park, Ill. BR/TR, 6'7", 220 lbs. Deb: 6/24/95																											
1995	Pit-N	3	9	.250	19	18	1	0	0	106	108	59	7	2	50	80	13.6	4.58	94	.263	.346	3	.097	-2	-5	-3	-1	-0.6
1996	Pit-N	4	5	.444	28	4	0	0	8	46^2	56	35	11	0	19	46	14.5	5.79	75	.292	.355	0	.000	-1	-8	-7	-1	-1.5
1997	Pit-N	1	0	1.000	10	0	0	0	6	9^1	7	3	1	0	4	6	10.6	1.93	222	.200	.282	0	—	0	2	2	0	0.5
Total	3	8	14	.364	57	22	1	0	14	162	171	97	19	2	73	132	13.7	4.78	90	.268	.346	3	.083	-2	-10	-8	-2	-1.6
● DON ERICKSON	Erickson, Don Lee b: 12/13/31, Springfield, Ill. BR/TR, 6', 175 lbs. Deb: 9/1/58																											
1958	Phi-N	0	1	.000	9	0	0	0	1	11^2	11	7	3	0	9	9	15.4	4.63	86	.244	.370	0	.000	-0	-1	-1	-0	-0.1
● ERIC ERICKSON	Erickson, Eric George Adolph b: 3/13/1895, Goteborg, Sweden d: 5/19/65, Jamestown, N.Y. BR/TR, 6'2", 190 lbs. Deb: 10/6/14																											
1914	NY-N	0	1	.000	1	1	0	0	0	5	8	7	0	0	3	3	19.8	0.00	—	.364	.440	0	.000	-0	2	2	-0	0.3
1916	Det-A	0	0	—	8	0	0	0	0	16	13	6	0	1	8	7	12.4	2.81	102	.220	.324	0	.000	-1	0	0	-1	-0.1
1918	Det-A	4	5	.444	12	9	8	0	1	94^1	81	32	2	3	29	48	10.8	2.48	107	.240	.306	4	.121	-3	3	2	-3	-0.4
1919	Det-A	0	2	.000	3	2	0	0	0	14^2	17	17	0	1	10	4	17.2	6.75	47	.293	.406	1	.200	-0	-6	-6	0	-0.7
	Was-A	6	11	.353	20	15	7	1	0	132	130	69	7	7	63	86	13.6	3.95	81	.254	.344	7	.146	-1	-11	-11	-3	-1.7
	Yr	6	13	.316	23	17	7	1	0	146^2	147	86	7	8	73	90	14.0	4.23	76	.258	.351	8	.151	-2	-16	-17	-3	-2.4
1920	Was-A	12	16	.429	39	27	12	0	1	239^1	231	142	13	11	128	87	13.9	3.84	97	.264	.365	23	.277	4	-1	-3	-4	-0.3
1921	Was-A	8	10	.444	32	22	9	3	0	179	181	90	7	9	65	71	12.8	3.62	114	.269	.341	9	.150	-3	13	10	-3	0.3
1922	Was-A	4	12	.250	30	17	6	2	2	141^2	144	95	8	3	73	61	14.0	4.96	78	.279	.372	6	.133	-2	-14	-18	-2	-2.2
Total	7	34	57	.374	145	93	42	6	4	822	805	458	37	35	379	367	13.3	3.85	93	.264	.352	50	.179	-6	-14	-24	-15	-4.8
● HAL ERICKSON	Erickson, Harold James b: 7/17/19, Portland, Ore. BR/TR, 6'5", 230 lbs. Deb: 4/14/53																											
1953	Det-A	0	1	.000	18	0	0	0	1	32^1	43	23	4	2	10	19	15.3	4.73	86	.323	.379	0	.000	-1	-3	-2	-0	-0.2
● PAUL ERICKSON	Erickson, Paul Walford "Li'L Abner" b: 12/14/15, Zion, Ill. BR/TR, 6'2", 200 lbs. Deb: 6/29/41																											
1941	Chi-N	5	7	.417	32	15	7	1	1	141	126	70	2	2	64	85	12.3	3.70	95	.234	.318	7	.152	0	-1	-3	-1	-0.3
1942	Chi-N	1	6	.143	18	7	1	0	0	63	70	40	4	0	41	26	15.9	5.43	59	.288	.391	3	.143	-1	-15	-16	0	-1.7
1943	Chi-N	1	3	.250	15	4	0	0	0	42^2	47	32	4	2	22	24	15.0	6.12	55	.280	.370	3	.200	0	-13	-13	-1	-1.2
1944	Chi-N	5	9	.357	33	15	5	3	1	124^1	113	59	5	0	67	82	13.0	3.55	100	.243	.338	2	.056	-1	1	-0	2	0.0
1945	*Chi-N	7	4	.636	28	9	3	0	3	108^1	94	41	5	7	48	53	12.4	3.32	110	.233	.325	5	.156	0	6	4	-0	0.4
1946	Chi-N	9	7	.563	32	14	5	1	0	137	119	46	2	3	65	70	12.3	2.43	137	.232	.321	2	.050	-4	15	14	-1	1.1
1947	Chi-N	7	12	.368	40	20	6	0	1	174	179	90	17	5	93	82	14.3	4.34	91	.268	.362	15	.250	3	-6	-8	1	-0.4
1948	Chi-N	0	0	—	3	0	0	0	0	5^2	7	5	0	0	6	4	20.6	6.35	61	.292	.433	0	.000	-0	-2	-2	0	-0.1
	Phi-N	2	0	1.000	4	2	0	0	0	17^1	19	10	2	0	17	5	18.7	5.19	76	.292	.439	1	.143	-0	-2	-2	0	-0.2
	NY-N	0	0	—	2	0	0	0	0	1	0	0	0	0	2	1	18.0	0.00	—	.000	.400	0	—	0	0	0	0	0.0
	Yr	2	0	1.000	9	2	0	0	0	24	26	15	2	0	25	10	19.1	5.25	75	.283	.436	1	.125	-0	-3	-4	0	-0.3
Total	8	37	48	.435	207	86	27	5	6	814^1	774	393	41	19	425	432	13.5	3.86	93	.250	.345	38	.147	-2	-16	-26	-0	-2.4
● RALPH ERICKSON	Erickson, Ralph Lief b: 6/25/02, Dubois, Idaho BL/TL, 6'1", 175 lbs. Deb: 9/11/29																											
1929	Pit-N	0	0	—	1	0	0	0	0	1	2	3	0	0	2	0	36.0	27.00	18	.500	.667	0	—	0	-2	-2	-0	-0.1
1930	Pit-N	1	0	1.000	7	0	0	0	0	14	21	12	1	0	10	2	19.9	7.07	70	.375	.470	1	.250	-0	-3	-3	0	-0.2
Total	2	1	0	1.000	8	0	0	0	0	15	23	15	1	0	12	2	21.0	8.40	59	.383	.486	1	.250	-0	-6	-6	-0	-0.3
● ROGER ERICKSON	Erickson, Roger Farrell b: 8/30/56, Springfield, Ill. BR/TR, 6'3", 190 lbs. Deb: 4/6/78																											
1978	Min-A	14	13	.519	37	37	14	0	0	265^2	268	129	19	8	79	121	12.0	3.96	97	.263	.321	0	—	0	-6	-4	0	-0.3
1979	Min-A	3	10	.231	24	21	0	0	0	123	154	86	17	1	48	47	14.9	5.63	78	.310	.372	0	—	0	-19	-16	-0	-1.5
1980	Min-A	7	13	.350	32	27	7	0	0	191^1	198	83	13	4	56	97	12.1	3.25	135	.268	.322	0	—	0	17	22	-0	2.1
1981	Min-A	3	8	.273	14	14	1	0	0	91^1	93	48	7	0	31	44	12.2	3.84	103	.262	.321	0	—	0	-2	1	-0	0.1
1982	Min-A	4	3	.571	7	7	2	0	0	40^2	56	29	6	1	12	12	15.3	4.87	87	.326	.373	0	—	0	-4	-3	1	-0.4
	NY-A	4	5	.444	16	11	0	0	1	70^2	86	36	5	0	17	37	13.1	4.46	90	.301	.340	0	—	0	-3	-4	-1	-0.5
	Yr	8	8	.500	23	18	2	0	1	111^1	142	65	11	1	29	49	13.9	4.61	89	.310	.352	0	—	0	-6	-6	-1	-0.9
1983	NY-A	0	1	.000	5	0	0	0	0	16^2	13	8	1	0	8	7	11.3	4.32	90	.213	.304	0	—	0	-0	-1	0	0.0
Total	6	35	53	.398	135	117	24	0	1	799^1	868	419	68	14	251	365	12.8	4.13	99	.277	.334	0	—	0	-16	-3	-1	-0.5
● SCOTT ERICKSON	Erickson, Scott Gavin b: 2/2/68, Long Beach, Cal. BR/TR, 6'4", 224 lbs. Deb: 6/25/90																											
1990	Min-A	8	4	.667	19	17	1	0	0	113	108	49	9	5	51	53	13.1	2.87	145	.256	.343	0	—	0	13	15	-0	1.5
1991	*Min-A	**20**	8	**.714**	32	32	5	3	0	204	189	80	13	6	71	108	11.7	3.18	135	.248	.317	0	—	0	21	24	1	3.3
1992	Min-A	13	12	.520	32	32	5	3	0	212	197	86	18	8	83	101	12.2	3.40	120	.252	.330	0	—	0	13	15	2	1.9
1993	Min-A	8	19	.296	34	34	1	0	0	218^2	266	138	17	10	71	116	14.3	5.19	84	.305	.364	0	—	0	-21	-20	1	-2.0
1994	Min-A	8	11	.421	23	23	2	1	0	144	173	95	15	9	59	104	15.1	5.44	90	.299	.372	0	—	0	-10	-9	1	-0.9
1995	Min-A	4	6	.400	15	15	0	0	0	87^2	102	61	11	4	32	45	14.2	5.95	80	.291	.357	0	—	0	-12	-11	2	-0.9
	Bal-A	9	4	.692	17	16	7	2	0	108^2	111	47	7	1	35	61	12.2	3.89	122	.273	.332	0	—	0	10	10	3	1.4
	Yr	13	10	.565	32	31	7	2	0	196^1	213	108	18	5	67	106	13.1	4.81	99	.281	.343	0	—	0	-2	-1	4	0.5
1996	*Bal-A	13	12	.520	34	34	6	0	0	222^1	262	137	21	11	66	100	13.7	5.02	98	.297	.354	0	—	0	-1	-2	4	0.1
1997	*Bal-A	16	7	.696	34	33	3	2	0	221^2	218	100	16	5	61	131	11.5	3.69	119	.257	.310	0	.000	0	22	18	3	2.0
1998	Bal-A	16	13	.552	36	36	**11**	2	0	**251^1**	284	125	23	13	69	186	13.1	4.01	114	.281	.335	0	.000	1	18	16	5	2.1
1999	Bal-A	15	12	.556	34	34	6	**3**	0	230^1	244	127	27	11	99	106	13.8	4.81	98	.280	.360	0	.000	-1	2	-3	3	-0.1

YEAR	TM/L	W	L	PCT	G	GS	CG	SH	SV	IP	H	R	HR	HB	BB	SO	RAT	ERA	ERA+	OAV	OOB	BH	AVG	PB	PR	PR+	PD	TPI
2000	Bal-A	5	8	.385	16	16	1	0	0	92^2	127	81	14	5	48	41	17.5	7.87	61	.330	.411	2	.400	1	-30	-33	-2	-3.4
Total	11	135	116	.538	326	322	48	16	0	2106^1	2281	1126	191	88	745	1152	13.3	4.43	102	.279	.346	2	.133	1	25	25	22	5.0

● DICK ERRICKSON Errickson, Richard Merriwell "Lief" b: 3/5/12, Vineland, N.J. d: 11/28/99, Vineland, N.J. BL/TR, 6'1", 175 lbs. Deb: 4/27/38

YEAR	TM/L	W	L	PCT	G	GS	CG	SH	SV	IP	H	R	HR	HB	BB	SO	RAT	ERA	ERA+	OAV	OOB	BH	AVG	PB	PR	PR+	PD	TPI
1938	Bos-N	9	7	.563	34	10	6	1	6	122^2	113	53	1	2	56	40	12.5	3.15	109	.246	.330	4	.114	-1	9	4	2	0.6
1939	Bos-N	6	9	.400	28	11	3	0	1	128^1	143	63	6	1	54	33	13.9	4.00	92	.293	.365	10	.227	1	-1	-5	2	-0.3
1940	Bos-N	12	13	.480	34	29	17	3	4	236^1	241	91	8	1	90	34	12.6	3.16	118	.270	.338	13	.157	-2	18	15	1	1.5
1941	Bos-N	6	12	.333	38	23	5	2	1	165^2	192	100	12	4	62	45	14.0	4.78	75	.287	.351	8	.178	-0	-21	-23	1	-2.2
1942	Bos-N	2	5	.286	21	4	0	0	1	59^1	76	34	8	0	20	15	14.6	5.01	67	.309	.361	2	.125	-1	-11	-11	-1	-1.4
	Chi-N	1	1	.500	13	0	0	0	0	24	39	12	1	1	8	9	18.0	4.13	78	.411	.462	0	.000	-1	-2	-3	1	-0.2
	Yr	3	6	.333	34	4	0	0	1	83^1	115	46	9	1	28	24	15.6	4.75	69	.337	.389	2	.095	-1	-13	-14	-0	-1.6
Total	5	36	47	.434	168	77	31	6	13	736^1	804	353	36	9	290	176	13.5	3.85	93	.282	.350	37	.162	-5	-9	-22	5	-2.0

● CARL ERSKINE Erskine, Carl Daniel "Oisk" b: 12/13/26, Anderson, Ind. BR/TR, 5'10", 165 lbs. Deb: 7/25/48

YEAR	TM/L	W	L	PCT	G	GS	CG	SH	SV	IP	H	R	HR	HB	BB	SO	RAT	ERA	ERA+	OAV	OOB	BH	AVG	PB	PR	PR+	PD	TPI
1948	Bro-N	6	3	.667	17	9	3	0	0	64	51	28	5	1	35	29	12.2	3.23	124	.231	.339	2	.095	-2	5	5	-1	0.4
1949	*Bro-N	8	1	.889	22	3	2	0	0	79^2	68	44	6	2	51	49	13.7	4.63	89	.235	.354	3	.115	-2	-5	-5	0	-0.6
1950	Bro-N	7	6	.538	22	13	3	0	1	103	109	56	15	1	35	50	12.7	4.72	87	.273	.333	9	.243	2	-7	-7	-1	-0.8
1951	Bro-N	16	12	.571	46	19	7	0	4	189^2	206	105	23	2	78	95	13.6	4.46	88	.280	.351	8	.131	-2	-11	-11	-0	-1.8
1952	*Bro-N	14	6	.700	33	26	10	4	2	206^2	167	72	17	2	71	131	10.5	2.70	135	.220	.289	10	.152	-0	24	22	2	2.3
1953	*Bro-N	20	6	**.769**	39	33	16	4	3	246^2	213	106	21	3	95	187	11.3	3.54	120	.230	.304	20	.215	0	20	20	-2	1.8
1954	Bro-N★	18	15	.545	38	37	12	2	1	260^1	239	128	31	4	92	166	11.6	4.15	98	.243	.311	14	.159	-1	-2	-2	-0	-0.4
1955	*Bro-N	11	8	.579	31	29	7	2	1	194^2	185	89	29	0	64	84	11.5	3.79	107	.253	.313	15	.203	-0	5	6	-2	0.3
1956	*Bro-N	13	11	.542	31	28	8	1	0	186^1	189	92	25	1	57	95	11.9	4.25	93	.264	.320	8	.121	-3	-10	-6	-1	-1.0
1957	Bro-N	5	3	.625	15	7	1	0	0	66	62	27	8	0	20	26	11.2	3.55	118	.248	.304	2	.091	-2	2	4	-1	0.2
1958	LA-N	4	4	.500	31	9	2	1	0	98^1	115	61	14	0	35	54	13.7	5.13	80	.297	.355	1	.037	-3	-13	-11	1	-1.0
1959	LA-N	0	3	.000	10	3	0	0	1	23^1	33	22	5	0	13	15	17.7	7.71	55	.320	.397	0	.000	-1	-10	-8	-0	-1.1
Total	12	122	78	.610	335	216	71	14	13	1718^2	1637	830	199	16	646	981	12.0	4.00	101	.252	.321	92	.156	-13	-0	6	-4	-1.7

● CHICO ESCARREGA Escarrega, Ernesto (Acosta) b: 12/27/49, Los Mochis, Mex. BR/TR, 5'11", 185 lbs. Deb: 4/26/82

YEAR	TM/L	W	L	PCT	G	GS	CG	SH	SV	IP	H	R	HR	HB	BB	SO	RAT	ERA	ERA+	OAV	OOB	BH	AVG	PB	PR	PR+	PD	TPI
1982	Chi-A	1	3	.250	38	2	0	0	1	73^2	73	33	3	0	16	33	10.9	3.67	110	.263	.303	0	—	0	3	3	-1	0.1

● KELVIM ESCOBAR Escobar, Kelvim Jose (Bolivar) b: 4/11/76, LaGuaira, Venez. BR/TR, 6'1", 205 lbs. Deb: 6/29/97

YEAR	TM/L	W	L	PCT	G	GS	CG	SH	SV	IP	H	R	HR	HB	BB	SO	RAT	ERA	ERA+	OAV	OOB	BH	AVG	PB	PR	PR+	PD	TPI
1997	Tor-A	3	2	.600	27	0	0	0	14	31	28	12	1	0	19	36	13.6	2.90	158	.237	.343	0	—	0	6	6	-0	1.1
1998	Tor-A	7	3	.700	22	10	0	0	0	79^2	72	37	5	0	35	72	12.1	3.73	125	.237	.316	0	—	0	8	8	-2	0.8
1999	Tor-A	14	11	.560	33	30	1	0	0	174	203	118	19	10	81	129	15.2	5.69	87	.293	.375	0	.000	-0	-16	-14	-3	-1.9
2000	Tor-A	10	15	.400	43	24	3	1	2	180	186	118	26	3	85	142	13.7	5.35	93	.267	.349	0	.000	-1	-9	-7	-1	-1.0
Total	4	34	31	.523	125	64	4	1	16	464^2	489	285	51	13	220	379	14.0	5.04	97	.270	.353	0	.000	-1	-10	-8	-5	-1.0

● VAUGHN ESHELMAN Eshelman, Vaughn Michael b: 5/22/69, Philadelphia, Pa. BL/TL, 6'3", 205 lbs. Deb: 5/2/95

YEAR	TM/L	W	L	PCT	G	GS	CG	SH	SV	IP	H	R	HR	HB	BB	SO	RAT	ERA	ERA+	OAV	OOB	BH	AVG	PB	PR	PR+	PD	TPI
1995	Bos-A	6	3	.667	23	14	0	0	0	81^2	86	47	3	1	36	41	13.6	4.85	101	.272	.348	0	—	0	-1	0	-1	0.0
1996	Bos-A	6	3	.667	39	10	0	0	0	87^2	112	79	13	2	58	59	17.7	7.08	72	.311	.410	0	—	0	-20	-19	0	-1.5
1997	Bos-A	3	3	.500	21	6	0	0	0	42^2	58	32	3	2	17	18	16.2	6.33	73	.330	.395	1	.250	0	-8	-8	-0	-1.0
Total	3	15	9	.625	83	30	0	0	0	212	256	158	19	5	111	118	15.8	6.07	81	.300	.384	1	.250	0	-30	-27	-1	-2.5

● DUKE ESPER Esper, Charles H. (b: Charles Esbacher) b: 7/28/1868, Salem, N.J. d: 8/31/10, Philadelphia, Pa. TL, 5'11.5", 185 lbs. Deb: 4/18/1890

YEAR	TM/L	W	L	PCT	G	GS	CG	SH	SV	IP	H	R	HR	HB	BB	SO	RAT	ERA	ERA+	OAV	OOB	BH	AVG	PB	PR	PR+	PD	TPI
1890	Phi-a	8	9	.471	18	16	14	1	0	143^2	176	99	1	5	67	61	15.5	4.89	79	.292	.368	18	.295	4	-16	-16	1	-1.0
	Pit-N	0	2	.000	2	2	2	0	0	17	18	16	0	1	10	9	15.4	5.29	62	.265	.367	1	.143	-1	-3	-4	0	-0.4
	Phi-N	5	0	1.000	5	5	4	0	0	41	40	22	1	0	16	18	12.3	3.07	119	.248	.316	3	.158	-1	2	3	0	0.2
	Yr	5	2	.714	7	7	6	0	0	58	58	38	1	1	26	27	13.2	3.72	95	.253	.332	4	.154	-2	-1	-1	1	-0.2
1891	Phi-N	20	15	.571	39	36	25	1	1	296	302	185	8	7	121	108	13.1	3.56	96	.254	.327	27	.220	1	-7	-5	1	-0.4
1892	Phi-N	11	6	.647	21	18	14	0	1	160^1	171	84	2	1	60	45	13.0	3.42	95	.262	.325	17	.243	2	-2	-3	-1	-0.2
	Pit-N	2	0	1.000	3	3	1	0	0	18^1	18	13	0	0	12	5	14.7	5.40	61	.247	.353	0	.000	-1	-4	-4	-0	-0.5
	Yr	13	6	.684	24	21	15	0	1	178^2	189	97	2	1	72	50	13.2	3.63	90	.261	.328	17	.215	0	-7	-8	-1	-0.7
1893	Was-N	12	28	.300	42	36	34	0	0	334^1	442	277	14	12	156	78	16.4	4.71	98	.309	.381	41	.287	7	-2	-3	1	0.4
1894	Was-N	5	10	.333	18	14	7	0	0	116	177	132	8	2	39	24	16.9	7.45	71	.346	.395	14	.259	1	-27	-28	0	-2.3
	*Bal-N	10	2	.833	16	9	8	0	2	101	107	56	1	1	36	25	12.8	3.92	139	.269	.331	10	.222	-1	16	17	1	1.5
	Yr	15	12	.556	34	23	15	0	2	217	284	188	9	3	75	49	15.0	5.81	92	.312	.367	24	.242	0	-12	-11	1	-0.8
1895	*Bal-N	10	12	.455	34	25	16	1	1	218^1	248	132	2	0	79	39	13.5	3.92	121	.281	.341	16	.178	-6	21	20	-2	0.8
1896	Bal-N	14	5	.737	20	18	14	1	0	155^2	168	80	3	2	39	19	12.1	3.58	119	.273	.319	13	.197	-2	13	12	-2	0.8
1897	StL-N	1	6	.143	8	8	7	0	0	61^1	95	51	5	1	12	8	15.8	5.28	83	.351	.380	8	.320	1	-7	-6	1	-0.3
1898	StL-N	3	5	.375	10	8	6	0	0	64^2	86	49	1	0	22	14	15.0	5.98	63	.316	.367	10	.370	2	-17	-15	0	-1.3
Total	9	101	100	.502	236	198	152	4	5	1727^2	2048	1196	46	32	669	453	14.3	4.39	96	.288	.351	178	.241	5	-33	-32	1	-2.7

● NINO ESPINOSA Espinosa, Arnulfo Acevedo (b: Arnulfo Acevedo (Espinosa)) b: 8/15/53, Villa Altagracia, D.R. d: 12/24/87, Villa Altagracia, D.R. BR/TR, 6'1", 192 lbs. Deb: 9/13/74

YEAR	TM/L	W	L	PCT	G	GS	CG	SH	SV	IP	H	R	HR	HB	BB	SO	RAT	ERA	ERA+	OAV	OOB	BH	AVG	PB	PR	PR+	PD	TPI
1974	NY-N	0	0	—	2	1	0	0	0	9	12	5	1	0	0	2	12.0	5.00	72	.324	.324	1	.500	0	-1	-1	0	0.0
1975	NY-N	0	1	.000	2	0	0	0	0	3	8	6	0	0	1	2	27.0	18.00	19	.471	.500	0	—	0	-5	-5	-0	-0.8
1976	NY-N	4	4	.500	12	5	0	0	0	41^2	41	21	3	0	13	30	11.7	3.67	90	.265	.321	0	.000	-1	-1	-2	-1	-0.5
1977	NY-N	10	13	.435	32	29	7	1	0	200	188	82	17	5	55	105	11.2	3.42	109	.249	.304	8	.129	-1	11	8	-0	0.6
1978	NY-N	11	15	.423	32	32	6	1	0	203^2	230	117	24	3	75	76	13.6	4.73	74	.292	.355	14	.209	2	-26	-29	2	-2.8
1979	Phi-N	14	12	.538	33	33	8	3	0	212	211	94	20	3	65	88	11.8	3.65	105	.262	.319	14	.194	2	2	4	0	0.6
1980	Phi-N	3	5	.375	12	12	1	0	0	76^1	73	36	9	2	19	13	11.1	3.77	101	.250	.300	3	.115	-1	-1	0	-1	-0.2
1981	Phi-N	2	5	.286	14	14	2	0	0	73^2	98	52	11	1	24	22	15.0	6.11	59	.333	.386	4	.200	-0	-21	-20	-1	-1.8
	Tor-A	0	0	—	1	0	0	0	0	1	4	1	0	0	0	0	36.0	9.00	44	.667	.667	0	—	0	-1	-1	-0	0.0
Total	8	44	55	.444	140	126	24	5	0	820^1	865	414	85	14	252	338	12.4	4.17	88	.275	.331	44	.171	1	-43	-45	0	-4.9

● ALVARO ESPINOZA Espinoza, Alvaro Alberto b: 2/19/62, Valencia, Venez. BR/TR, 6', 181 lbs. Deb: 9/14/84 ♦

YEAR	TM/L	W	L	PCT	G	GS	CG	SH	SV	IP	H	R	HR	HB	BB	SO	RAT	ERA	ERA+	OAV	OOB	BH	AVG	PB	PR	PR+	PD	TPI
1991	NY-A	0	0	—	1	0	0	0	0	0^2	0	0	0	0	0	0	0.0	0.00	—	.000	.000	123	.256	0	0	0	0	0.0

● MARK ESSER Esser, Mark Gerald b: 4/1/56, Erie, Pa. BR/TL, 6'1", 190 lbs. Deb: 4/22/79

YEAR	TM/L	W	L	PCT	G	GS	CG	SH	SV	IP	H	R	HR	HB	BB	SO	RAT	ERA	ERA+	OAV	OOB	BH	AVG	PB	PR	PR+	PD	TPI
1979	Chi-A	0	0	—	2	0	0	0	0	1^2	2	3	0	0	4	1	32.4	16.20	26	.286	.545	0	—	0	-2	-2	-0	-0.1

● BILL ESSICK Essick, William Earl "Vinegar Bill" b: 12/18/1881, Grand Ridge, Ill. d: 10/12/51, Los Angeles, Cal. TR, 5'10", 175 lbs. Deb: 9/12/06

YEAR	TM/L	W	L	PCT	G	GS	CG	SH	SV	IP	H	R	HR	HB	BB	SO	RAT	ERA	ERA+	OAV	OOB	BH	AVG	PB	PR	PR+	PD	TPI
1906	Cin-N	2	2	.500	6	4	3	0	0	39^1	39	18	1	2	16	16	13.0	2.97	93	.273	.354	1	.077	-1	-1	-1	-1	-0.3
1907	Cin-N	0	2	.000	3	2	2	0	0	21^2	23	15	0	1	8	7	13.3	2.91	89	.274	.344	0	.000	-1	-1	-1	1	-0.1
Total	2	2	4	.333	9	6	5	0	0	61	62	33	1	3	24	23	13.1	2.95	91	.273	.350	1	.048	-2	-3	-2	-0	-0.4

● DICK ESTELLE Estelle, Richard Henry b: 1/18/42, Lakewood, N.J. BB/TL, 6'2", 170 lbs. Deb: 9/4/64

YEAR	TM/L	W	L	PCT	G	GS	CG	SH	SV	IP	H	R	HR	HB	BB	SO	RAT	ERA	ERA+	OAV	OOB	BH	AVG	PB	PR	PR+	PD	TPI
1964	SF-N	1	2	.333	6	6	0	0	0	41^2	39	15	3	0	23	23	13.4	3.02	118	.247	.343	1	.067	-1	2	2	-1	0.0
1965	SF-N	0	0	—	6	1	0	0	0	11^1	12	6	0	1	8	6	16.7	3.97	91	.261	.382	0	.000	0	-1	-0	0	0.0
Total	2	1	2	.333	12	7	0	0	0	53	51	21	3	1	31	29	14.1	3.23	111	.250	.352	1	.063	-0	2	2	-1	0.0

● SHAWN ESTES Estes, Aaron Shawn b: 2/18/73, San Bernardino, Cal. BR/TL, 6'2", 185 lbs. Deb: 9/16/95

YEAR	TM/L	W	L	PCT	G	GS	CG	SH	SV	IP	H	R	HR	HB	BB	SO	RAT	ERA	ERA+	OAV	OOB	BH	AVG	PB	PR	PR+	PD	TPI
1995	SF-N	0	3	.000	3	3	0	0	0	17^1	16	14	2	1	5	14	11.4	6.75	61	.229	.289	0	.000	-1	-5	-5	-0	-0.8
1996	SF-N	3	5	.375	11	11	0	0	0	70	63	30	3	2	39	60	13.4	3.60	114	.243	.347	3	.158	-0	5	4	0	0.4
1997	*SF-N★	19	5	.792	32	32	3	2	0	201	162	80	12	8	100	181	12.1	3.18	129	.223	.324	10	.147	1	23	21	1	2.5
1998	SF-N	7	12	.368	25	25	1	1	0	149^1	150	89	14	5	80	136	14.2	5.06	78	.269	.366	8	.190	1	-14	-19	1	-1.9
1999	SF-N	11	11	.500	32	32	1	1	0	203	209	121	21	5	112	159	14.5	4.92	85	.268	.363	10	.164	2	-8	-18	2	-1.3
2000	*SF-N	15	6	.714	30	30	4	2	0	190^1	194	99	11	3	108	136	14.4	4.26	100	.275	.374	14	.206	4	8	-0	4	0.7
Total	6	55	42	.567	133	133	9	6	0	831	794	433	63	24	444	686	13.7	4.30	96	.256	.354	45	.171	7	9	-16	8	-0.4

YEAR TM/L	W	L	PCT	G	GS	CG	SH	SV	IP	H	R	HR	HB	BB	SO	RAT	ERA	ERA+	OAV	OOB	BH	AVG	PB	PR	PR+	PD	TPI
● GEORGE ESTOCK Estock, George John b: 11/2/24, Stirling, N.J. BR/TR, 6', 185 lbs. Deb: 4/21/51																											
1951 Bos-N	0	1	.000	37	1	0	0	3	60^1	56	33	2	0	37	11	13.9	4.33	85	.258	.366	2	.286	1	-2	-5	0	-0.1
● CHUCK ESTRADA Estrada, Charles Leonard b: 2/15/38, San Luis Obispo, Cal. BR/TR, 6'1", 185 lbs. Deb: 4/21/60 C																											
1960 Bal-A★	**18**	11	.621	36	25	12	1	2	208^2	162	87	18	15	101	144	12.0	3.58	106	**.218**	.323	9	.141	-0	7	5	-0	0.7
1961 Bal-A	15	9	.625	33	31	6	1	0	212	159	91	19	10	132	160	12.8	3.69	104	**.207**	.331	8	.114	-3	8	4	-2	-0.1
1962 Bal-A	9	17	.346	34	33	6	0	0	223^1	199	112	24	10	121	165	13.3	3.83	97	.240	.343	10	.152	-0	3	-3	-3	-0.6
1963 Bal-A	3	2	.600	8	7	0	0	0	31^1	26	17	2	1	19	16	13.2	4.60	76	.226	.341	1	.100	-1	-3	-4	-1	-0.7
1964 Bal-A	3	2	.600	17	6	0	0	0	54^2	62	34	8	2	21	32	14.0	5.27	68	.282	.350	2	.143	-0	-10	-10	-1	-1.1
1966 Chi-N	1	1	.500	9	1	0	0	0	12^1	16	12	2	1	5	3	16.1	7.30	50	.314	.386	0	.000	-0	-5	-5	-0	-0.8
1967 NY-N	1	2	.333	9	2	0	0	0	22	28	24	5	1	17	15	18.8	9.41	36	.326	.442	0	.000	-1	-15	-15	-0	-1.8
Total 7	50	44	.532	146	105	24	2	2	764^1	652	377	78	40	416	535	13.0	4.07	92	.232	.339	30	.129	-5	-15	-29	-8	-4.4
● HORACIO ESTRADA Estrada, Horacio (Jimenez) b: 10/19/75, San Joaquin, Venez. BL/TL, 6'1", 185 lbs. Deb: 5/4/99																											
1999 Mil-N	0	0	—	4	0	0	0	0	7^1	10	6	4	0	4	5	17.2	7.36	62	.313	.389	0	.000	-0	-2	-2	0	-0.1
2000 Mil-N	3	0	1.000	7	4	0	0	0	24^1	30	18	5	2	20	13	19.2	6.29	73	.300	.426	1	.143	-0	-4	-5	0	-0.5
Total 2	3	0	1.000	11	4	0	0	0	31^2	40	24	9	2	24	18	18.8	6.54	70	.303	.418	1	.111	-0	-7	-7	0	-0.6
● OSCAR ESTRADA Estrada, Oscar b: 2/15/04, Havana, Cuba d: 1/2/78, Havana, Cuba BL/TL, 5'8", 160 lbs. Deb: 4/21/29																											
1929 StL-A	0	0	—	1	0	0	0	0	1	1	0	0	0	1	0	18.0	0.00	—	.250	.400	0	—	0	0	0	0	0.0
● LEO ESTRELLA Estrella, Leoncio (Ramirez) b: 2/20/75, Puerto Plata, D.R. BR/TR, 6'1", 185 lbs. Deb: 7/18/2000																											
2000 Tor-A	0	0	—	2	0	0	0	0	4^2	9	3	1	0	0	3	17.4	5.79	86	.450	.450	0	—	0	-0	-0	0	0.0
● SETH ETHERTON Etherton, Seth Michael b: 10/17/76, Laguna Beach, Cal. BR/TR, 6'1", 200 lbs. Deb: 5/26/2000																											
2000 Ana-A	5	1	.833	11	11	0	0	0	60^1	68	38	16	1	22	32	13.6	5.52	90	.278	.340	0	.000	0	-4	-4	1	-0.2
● MARK ETTLES Ettles, Mark Edward b: 10/30/66, Perth, Australia BR/TR, 6', 178 lbs. Deb: 6/5/93																											
1993 SD-N	1	0	1.000	14	0	0	0	0	18	23	16	4	0	4	9	13.5	6.50	64	.307	.342	0	.000	-0	-5	-5	0	-0.2
● JOHN EUBANK Eubank, John Franklin "Honest John" b: 9/9/1872, Servia, Ind. d: 11/3/58, Bellevue, Mich. BR/TR, 6'2", 215 lbs. Deb: 9/19/05																											
1905 Det-A	1	0	1.000	3	2	0	0	0	17^1	13	12	0	1	3	1	8.8	2.08	132	.210	.258	5	.357	1	1	1	-1	0.2
1906 Det-A	4	10	.286	24	12	7	1	2	135	147	69	0	8	35	38	12.7	3.53	78	.280	.335	13	.206	0	-13	-11	1	-1.0
1907 Det-A	3	3	.500	15	8	4	1	0	81	88	40	0	0	20	17	12.0	2.67	98	.279	.322	4	.129	-1	-1	-1	1	-0.1
Total 3	8	13	.381	42	22	11	2	2	233^1	248	121	0	9	58	56	12.1	3.12	87	.275	.325	22	.204	-1	-13	-11	1	-0.9
● UEL EUBANKS Eubanks, Uel Melvin "Poss" b: 2/14/03, Quinlan, Tex. d: 11/21/54, Dallas, Tex. BR/TR, 6'3", 175 lbs. Deb: 7/20/22																											
1922 Chi-N	0	0	—	2	0	0	0	0	1^2	5	9	0	0	4	1	48.6	27.00	16	.556	.692	1	1.000	1	-4	-4	0	-0.1
● FRANK EUFEMIA Eufemia, Frank Anthony b: 12/23/59, Bronx, N.Y. BR/TR, 5'11", 185 lbs. Deb: 5/21/85																											
1985 Min-A	4	2	.667	39	0	0	0	2	61^2	56	27	7	0	21	30	11.2	3.79	116	.250	.314	0	—	0	2	4	1	0.4
● BART EVANS Evans, Bart Steven b: 12/30/70, Springfield, Mo. BR/TR, 6'2", 210 lbs. Deb: 6/16/98																											
1998 KC-A	0	0	—	8	0	0	0	0	9	7	3	1	0	0	7	7.0	2.00	241	.206	.206	0	—	0	3	3	0	0.1
● CHICK EVANS Evans, Charles Franklin b: 10/15/1889, Arlington, Vt. d: 9/2/16, Schenectady, N.Y. BR/TR, Deb: 9/19/09																											
1909 Bos-N	0	3	.000	4	3	1	0	0	21^2	25	16	0	0	14	11	16.2	4.57	62	.305	.406	0	.000	-1	-5	-4	-0	-0.6
1910 Bos-N	1	1	.500	13	1	0	0	2	31	28	20	1	3	27	12	16.8	5.23	64	.275	.439	1	.100	-1	-8	-6	0	-0.5
Total 2	1	4	.200	17	4	1	0	2	52^2	53	36	1	3	41	23	16.6	4.96	63	.288	.425	1	.053	-2	-12	-10	0	-1.1
● ROY EVANS Evans, Roy b: 3/19/1874, Knoxville, Tenn. d: 8/15/15, Galveston, Tex. BR/TR, 6', 180 lbs. Deb: 5/15/1897																											
1897 StL-N	0	0	—	3	0	0	0	0	13	33	27	1	0	13	4	31.8	9.69	45	.471	.554	0	.000	0	-8	-7	-0	-0.3
Lou-N	5	4	.556	9	8	6	0	0	59^1	66	40	4	8	24	20	14.9	4.10	104	.280	.366	3	.130	-2	1	1	-1	-0.1
Yr	5	4	.556	12	8	6	0	0	72^1	99	67	5	8	37	24	17.9	5.10	84	.324	.410	3	.115	-2	-6	-7	-1	-0.4
1898 Was-N	3	3	.500	7	6	4	0	0	50^2	50	27	0	7	25	11	14.6	3.38	109	.256	.361	1	.053	-2	1	2	-1	-0.1
1899 Was-N	3	4	.429	7	7	6	0	0	54	60	40	1	0	25	27	14.2	5.67	69	.280	.356	4	.200	-1	-11	-10	0	-1.1
1902 NY-N	8	13	.381	23	17	17	0	0	176	186	87	2	9	58	48	12.9	3.17	89	.271	.336	8	.148	-1	-8	-7	2	-0.7
Bro-N	5	6	.455	13	11	11	2	0	97^1	91	42	0	2	33	35	11.7	2.68	103	.247	.313	9	.265	2	1	1	-3	0.0
Yr	13	19	.406	36	28	28	2	0	273^1	277	129	2	11	91	83	12.5	3.00	93	.263	.328	17	.193	1	-6	-6	-1	-0.7
1903 Bro-N	5	9	.357	15	12	9	0	0	110	121	75	1	7	41	42	13.8	3.27	98	.297	.371	5	.172	0	-0	-1	-1	-0.2
StL-A	0	4	.000	7	7	4	0	0	54	66	30	1	3	14	24	13.8	4.17	70	.300	.350	2	.105	-1	-7	-8	0	-0.6
Total 5	29	43	.403	84	68	57	2	0	614^1	673	368	10	36	233	211	13.8	3.66	88	.281	.353	32	.159	-4	-30	-30	-5	-3.1
● RED EVANS Evans, Russell Edison b: 11/12/06, Chicago, Ill. d: 6/14/82, Lakeview, Ark. BR/TR, 5'11", 168 lbs. Deb: 4/24/36																											
1936 Chi-A	0	3	.000	17	0	0	0	1	47^1	70	46	4	0	22	19	17.5	7.61	68	.338	.402	2	.133	-1	-14	-12	1	-0.6
1939 Bro-N	1	8	.111	24	6	0	0	1	64^1	74	43	4	0	26	28	14.0	5.18	78	.284	.348	4	.308	1	-9	-8	1	-0.8
Total 2	1	11	.083	41	6	0	0	2	111^2	144	89	8	0	48	47	15.5	6.21	73	.308	.372	6	.214	-0	-23	-20	3	-1.4
● JAKE EVANS Evans, Uriah L. P. "Bloody Jake" b: 9/1856, Baltimore, Md. d: 1/16/07, Baltimore, Md. TR, 5'8", 154 lbs. Deb: 5/1/1879 ◆																											
1880 Tro-N	0	0	—	1	0	0	0	0	4	11	8	0		0	0	24.8	13.50	19	.524	.524	46	.256	0	-5	-5	0	-0.2
1882 Wor-N	0	1	.000	1	1	1	0	0	8	13	10	1		0	2	14.6	5.63	55	.317	.317	71	.213	-0	-2	-2	-0	-0.2
1883 Cle-N	0	0	—	1	0	0	0	0	3	0	0	0		0	1	0.0	0.00	—	.000	.000	79	.238	0	1	1	1	0.1
Total 3	0	1	.000	3	1	1	0	0	15	24	18	1		0	3	14.4	6.60	45	.338	.338	435	.238	-0	-6	-6	1	-0.3
● ART EVANS Evans, William Arthur b: 8/3/11, Elvins, Mo. d: 1/8/52, Wichita, Kan. BB/TL, 6'1.5", 181 lbs. Deb: 6/20/32																											
1932 Chi-A	0	0	—	7	0	0	0	0	18	19	9	1	0	10	6	14.5	3.00	144	.257	.345	0	.000	-0	3	3	1	0.2
● BILL EVANS Evans, William James b: 2/10/1894, Reidsville, N.C. d: 12/21/46, Burlington, N.C. BR/TR, 6', 175 lbs. Deb: 8/13/16																											
1916 Pit-N	2	5	.286	13	7	3	0	0	63	57	27	2	3	16	21	10.9	3.00	89	.249	.306	3	.150	-1	-3	-2	2	-0.1
1917 Pit-N	0	4	.000	8	2	1	0	0	26^2	24	14	0	1	14	5	13.2	3.38	84	.231	.328	1	.111	-0	-2	-2	-0	-0.3
1919 Pit-N	0	4	.000	7	3	2	0	0	36^2	41	25	1	0	18	15	14.5	5.65	53	.297	.378	0	.000	-1	-11	-10	1	-1.1
Total 3	2	13	.133	28	12	6	0	0	126^1	122	66	3	4	48	41	12.4	3.85	73	.259	.333	4	.100	-2	-16	-14	2	-1.5
● BILL EVANS Evans, William Lawrence b: 3/25/19, Quanah, Texas d: 11/30/83, Grand Junction, Colo. BR/TR, 6'2", 180 lbs. Deb: 4/21/49																											
1949 Chi-A	0	1	.000	4	0	0	0	0	6^1	6	6	0	0	8	1	19.9	7.11	59	.261	.452	0	.000	-0	-2	-2	-0	-0.3
1951 Bos-A	0	0	—	9	0	0	0	0	15^1	15	8	0	0	8	3	13.5	4.11	109	.268	.359	0	.000	-1	0	1	-0	-0.1
Total 2	0	1	.000	13	0	0	0	0	21^2	21	14	0	0	16	4	15.4	4.98	88	.266	.389	0	.000	-1	-2	-1	-1	-0.4
● LEON EVERITT Everitt, Edward Leon b: 1/12/47, Marshall, Tex. BL/TR, 6'1.5", 195 lbs. Deb: 4/21/69																											
1969 SD-N	0	1	.000	5	0	0	0	0	15^2	18	14	4	1	12	11	17.8	8.04	44	.300	.425	0	.000	-0	-8	-8	0	-0.4
● BRYAN EVERSGERD Eversgerd, Bryan David b: 2/11/69, Centralia, Ill. BR/TL, 6'1", 190 lbs. Deb: 4/30/94																											
1994 StL-N	2	3	.400	40	1	0	0	0	67^2	75	36	8	2	20	47	12.9	4.52	92	.295	.351	0	.000	-1	-2	-3	1	-0.2
1995 Mon-N	0	0	—	25	0	0	0	0	21	22	13	2	1	9	8	13.7	5.14	84	.268	.348	0	.000	-0	-2	-2	-0	-0.1
1997 Tex-A	0	2	.000	3	0	0	0	0	1^1	5	3	0	0	3	2	54.0	20.25	24	.556	.667	0	—	0	-2	-2	0	-0.4
1998 StL-N	0	0	—	8	0	0	0	0	6	9	7	1	1	2	4	18.0	9.00	47	.346	.414	0	—	0	-3	-3	0	-0.1
Total 4	2	5	.286	76	1	0	0	0	96	111	59	11	4	34	61	14.0	5.16	81	.299	.364	0	.000	-1	-10	-10	1	-0.8
● BOB EWING Ewing, George Lemuel "Long Bob" b: 4/24/1873, New Hampshire, O. d: 6/20/47, Wapakoneta, Ohio BR/TR, 6'1.5", 170 lbs. Deb: 4/19/02																											
1902 Cin-N	5	6	.455	15	12	10	0	0	117^2	126	67	1	3	47	44	13.5	2.98	101	.274	.345	12	.169	-1	-3	0	-1	-0.2
1903 Cin-N	14	13	.519	29	28	27	1	1	246^2	254	127	3	10	64	104	12.0	2.77	128	.265	.317	24	.253	4	14	20	4	2.7
1904 Cin-N	11	13	.458	26	24	22	0	0	212	198	85	3	4	58	99	11.0	2.46	119	.253	.308	25	.258	5	7	10	-1	1.6
1905 Cin-N	20	11	.645	40	34	30	4	0	311^2	284	125	5	11	79	164	10.8	2.51	132	.246	.301	32	.262	4	17	25	-3	2.5

YEAR	TM/L	W	L	PCT	G	GS	CG	SH	SV	IP	H	R	HR	HB	BB	SO	RAT	ERA	ERA+	OAV	OOB	BH	AVG	PB	PR	PR+	PD	TPI
1906	Cin-N	13	14	.481	33	32	26	2	0	287^2	248	98	4	2	60	145	9.7	2.38	116	.238	.281	14	.139	-3	8	12	1	0.8
1907	Cin-N	17	19	.472	41	37	32	2	0	332^2	279	104	2	7	85	147	10.0	1.73	150	.231	.286	19	.154	-1	27	**30**	-6	2.7
1908	Cin-N	17	15	.531	37	32	23	4	3	293^2	247	105	5	5	57	95	9.5	2.21	105	.241	.284	14	.149	-0	5	3	-3	-0.1
1909	Cin-N	11	12	.478	31	29	14	2	0	218^1	195	94	1	6	63	86	10.9	2.43	107	.238	.298	8	.110	-4	4	4	-4	-0.5
1910	Phi-N	16	14	.533	34	32	20	4	0	255^1	235	110	5	7	86	102	11.6	3.00	104	.251	.318	20	.222	2	1	4	-2	0.4
1911	Phi-N	0	1	.000	4	3	1	0	0	24	29	25	2	0	14	12	16.1	7.88	44	.309	.398	2	.333	0	-12	-12	-0	-0.5
1912	StL-N	0	0	—	1	1	0	0	0	1^1	2	0	0	0	1	0	20.3	0.00	—	.333	.429	0	—	0	1	1	0	0.0
Total	11	124	118	.512	291	264	205	19	4	2301	2097	940	31	55	614	998	10.8	2.49	116	.247	.302	170	.195	7	69	98	-16	9.4

● JOHN EWING Ewing, John "Long Jong" b: 6/1/1863, Cincinnati, Ohio d: 4/23/1895, Denver, Colo. TR, Deb: 6/18/1883 F♦

YEAR	TM/L	W	L	PCT	G	GS	CG	SH	SV	IP	H	R	HR	HB	BB	SO	RAT	ERA	ERA+	OAV	OOB	BH	AVG	PB	PR	PR+	PD	TPI
1888	Lou-a	8	13	.381	21	21	21	2	0	191	175	105	3	8	34	87	10.2	2.83	109	.235	.276	16	.203	-2	5	5	0	0.4
1889	Lou-a	6	30	.167	40	39	37	1	0	331	407	296	6	14	147	155	15.4	4.87	79	.293	.367	23	.172	-6	-37	-37	2	-3.3
1890	NY-P	18	12	.600	35	31	27	1	2	267^1	294	196	6	16	104	145	13.9	4.24	107	.267	.339	24	.211	-3	-0	8	0	0.5
1891	NY-N	21	8	**.724**	33	30	28	5	0	269^1	237	118	2	11	105	138	11.8	**2.27**	141	.227	.305	23	.204	-2	32	29	0	2.4
Total	4	53	63	.457	129	121	113	9	2	1058^2	1113	715	17	49	390	525	13.2	3.68	101	.260	.329	87	.192	-12	-1	3	3	0.0

● BUCK EWING Ewing, William b: 10/17/1859, Hoagland, Ohio d: 10/20/06, Cincinnati, Ohio BR/TR, 5'10", 188 lbs. Deb: 9/9/1880 FMH♦

YEAR	TM/L	W	L	PCT	G	GS	CG	SH	SV	IP	H	R	HR	HB	BB	SO	RAT	ERA	ERA+	OAV	OOB	BH	AVG	PB	PR	PR+	PD	TPI
1882	Tro-N	0	0	—	1	0	0	0	0	1	2	1	0		1	0	27.0	9.00	31	.400	.500	89	.271	0	-1	-1	0	0.0
1884	NY-N	0	1	.000	1	1	1	0	0	8	7	3	0		4	3	12.4	1.13	265	.241	.333	106	.277	-0	2	2	-0	0.2
1885	NY-N	0	1	.000	1	0	0	0	0	2	4	4	0		3	0	31.5	4.50	59	.444	.583	104	.304	0	-0	-0	-0	-0.1
1888	*NY-N	0	0	—	2	0	0	0	0	7	8	9	1	1	4	6	16.7	2.57	107	.174	.255	127	.306	1	0	0	-0	0.0
1889	*NY-N	2	0	1.000	3	2	2	0	0	20	23	14	0	0	8	12	13.9	4.05	97	.280	.344	133	.327	2	-0	-0	-0	0.0
1890	NY-P	0	1	.000	1	1	1	0	0	9	11	5	1	0	3	2	14.0	4.00	114	.289	.341	119	.338	0	0	1	-0	0.1
Total	6	2	3	.400	9	4	4	0	0	47	55	36	2	1	23	23	15.1	3.45	105	.263	.339	1655	.307	4	1	1	-1	0.2

● SCOTT EYRE Eyre, Scott Alan b: 5/30/72, Inglewood, Cal. BL/TL, 6'1", 160 lbs. Deb: 8/1/97

YEAR	TM/L	W	L	PCT	G	GS	CG	SH	SV	IP	H	R	HR	HB	BB	SO	RAT	ERA	ERA+	OAV	OOB	BH	AVG	PB	PR	PR+	PD	TPI
1997	Chi-A	4	4	.500	11	11	0	0	0	60^2	62	36	11	1	31	36	13.9	5.04	87	.267	.356	1	.500	0	-3	-5	-1	-0.5
1998	Chi-A	3	8	.273	33	17	0	0	0	107	114	78	24	2	64	73	15.1	5.38	85	.271	.370	0	.000	-0	-9	-10	0	-0.9
1999	Chi-A	1	1	.500	21	0	0	0	0	25	38	22	6	1	15	17	19.4	7.56	65	.339	.422	0	—	0	-7	-7	-1	-0.5
2000	Chi-A	1	1	.500	13	1	0	0	0	19	29	15	3	1	12	16	19.9	6.63	75	.372	.462	0	—	0	-4	-3	0	-0.3
Total	4	9	14	.391	78	29	0	0	0	211^2	243	151	44	5	122	142	15.7	5.66	81	.289	.382	1	.200	0	-23	-26	-1	-2.2

● GEORGE EYRICH Eyrich, George Lincoln b: 3/3/25, Reading, Pa. BR/TR, 5'11", 175 lbs. Deb: 6/13/43

YEAR	TM/L	W	L	PCT	G	GS	CG	SH	SV	IP	H	R	HR	HB	BB	SO	RAT	ERA	ERA+	OAV	OOB	BH	AVG	PB	PR	PR+	PD	TPI
1943	Phi-N	0	0	—	9	0	0	0	0	18^2	27	8	1	0	9	5	17.4	3.38	100	.342	.409	0	.000	-0	0	-0	-0	-0.1

● RED FABER Faber, Urban Charles b: 9/6/1888, Cascade, Iowa d: 9/25/76, Chicago, Ill. BB/TR (BL 1928 (1 game)), 6'2", 180 lbs. Deb: 4/17/14 CH

YEAR	TM/L	W	L	PCT	G	GS	CG	SH	SV	IP	H	R	HR	HB	BB	SO	RAT	ERA	ERA+	OAV	OOB	BH	AVG	PB	PR	PR+	PD	TPI
1914	Chi-A	10	9	.526	40	19	11	2	**4**	181^1	154	77	3	12	64	88	11.4	2.68	100	.239	.319	8	.145	2	1	0	2	0.3
1915	Chi-A	24	14	.632	**50**	32	21	2	2	299^2	264	118	3	11	99	182	11.2	2.55	117	.240	.309	11	.131	2	13	14	-0	2.0
1916	Chi-A	17	9	.654	35	25	15	3	1	205^1	167	67	1	5	61	87	10.2	2.02	137	.228	.292	6	.095	-3	19	17	2	2.1
1917	*Chi-A	16	13	.552	41	29	16	3	3	248	224	92	1	10	85	84	11.6	1.92	138	.247	.319	4	.058	-4	20	20	2	2.2
1918	Chi-A	4	1	.800	11	9	5	1	1	80^2	70	23	3	0	23	26	10.4	1.23	223	.245	.301	1	.042	-2	14	14	1	0.8
1919	Chi-A	11	9	.550	25	20	9	0	0	162^1	185	92	7	8	45	45	13.2	3.83	83	.287	.341	10	.185	-0	-11	-12	0	-1.3
1920	Chi-A	23	13	.639	40	39	28	2	1	319	332	136	8	4	88	108	12.0	2.99	126	.277	.328	11	.106	-4	29	28	-1	2.3
1921	Chi-A	25	15	.625	43	39	**32**	4	1	330^2	293	107	10	7	87	124	**10.5**	**2.48**	**171**	**.242**	**.297**	16	.148	-4	**66**	**65**	1	**7.1**
1922	Chi-A	21	17	.553	43	38	**31**	4	2	**352**	334	128	10	6	83	148	**10.8**	**2.81**	**145**	.252	**.299**	25	.200	-2	**48**	**49**	1	**4.9**
1923	Chi-A	14	11	.560	32	31	15	2	0	232^1	233	114	6	6	62	91	11.7	3.41	116	.259	.311	15	.217	3	15	14	2	1.9
1924	Chi-A	9	11	.450	21	20	9	0	0	161^1	173	78	5	2	58	47	13.0	3.85	107	.282	.346	8	.148	-2	7	5	-2	0.2
1925	Chi-A	12	11	.522	34	32	16	1	0	238	266	117	8	2	59	71	12.4	3.78	110	.289	.333	8	.104	-4	16	10	1	0.6
1926	Chi-A	15	9	.625	27	25	13	1	0	184^2	203	84	3	2	57	65	12.8	3.56	109	.281	.335	9	.150	-0	9	7	-3	0.4
1927	Chi-A	4	7	.364	18	15	6	0	0	110^2	131	64	2	5	41	39	14.4	4.55	89	.312	.380	10	.270	2	-5	-6	2	-0.2
1928	Chi-A	13	9	.591	27	27	16	2	0	201^1	223	98	11	4	68	43	13.2	3.75	108	.286	.347	8	.114	-3	6	7	1	0.4
1929	Chi-A	13	13	.500	31	31	15	1	0	234	241	119	10	9	61	68	12.0	3.88	110	.273	.327	10	.128	-3	9	10	2	0.9
1930	Chi-A	8	13	.381	29	26	10	0	1	169	188	101	7	5	49	62	12.9	4.21	110	.283	.337	2	.041	-5	8	8	2	0.6
1931	Chi-A	10	14	.417	44	19	5	1	1	184	210	96	11	3	57	49	13.2	3.82	112	.285	.339	4	.075	-3	12	9	-2	0.6
1932	Chi-A	2	11	.154	42	5	0	0	6	106	123	61	0	1	38	26	13.8	3.74	116	.290	.350	4	.222	3	**9**	7	-0	1.1
1933	Chi-A	3	4	.429	36	2	0	0	5	86^1	92	41	2	1	28	18	12.6	3.44	123	.275	.332	0	.000	-3	8	8	-1	0.3
Total	20	254	213	.544	669	483	273	29	28	4086^2	4106	1813	111	103	1213	1471	11.9	3.15	119	.266	.323	170	.134	-31	294	277	11	27.2

● ROY FACE Face, Elroy Leon b: 2/20/28, Stephentown, N.Y. BR/TR, 5'8", 155 lbs. Deb: 4/16/53

YEAR	TM/L	W	L	PCT	G	GS	CG	SH	SV	IP	H	R	HR	HB	BB	SO	RAT	ERA	ERA+	OAV	OOB	BH	AVG	PB	PR	PR+	PD	TPI
1953	Pit-N	6	8	.429	41	13	2	0	0	119	145	90	19	2	30	56	13.4	6.58	68	.297	.340	4	.133	-1	-30	-27	-1	-2.9
1955	Pit-N	5	7	.417	42	10	4	0	5	125^2	128	58	10	0	40	84	12.0	3.58	115	.268	.325	3	.115	-1	6	7	-1	0.5
1956	Pit-N	12	13	.480	**68**	3	0	0	6	135^1	131	57	16	1	42	96	11.6	3.52	107	.256	.314	5	.192	-0	4	4	1	0.8
1957	Pit-N	4	6	.400	59	1	0	0	10	93^2	97	41	9	1	24	53	11.7	3.07	123	.270	.318	2	.125	-1	8	8	-2	0.7
1958	Pit-N	5	2	.714	57	0	0	0	**20**	84	77	30	6	0	22	47	10.6	2.89	134	.244	.293	0	.000	-1	10	9	1	1.2
1959	Pit-N★	18	1	**.947**	57	0	0	0	10	93^1	91	29	5	1	25	69	11.3	2.70	143	.266	.318	3	.231	0	13	12	-0	2.5
1960	*Pit-N★	10	8	.556	**68**	0	0	0	24	114^2	93	39	11	0	29	72	9.6	2.90	129	.226	.277	7	.412	2	11	11	1	2.5
1961	Pit-N★	6	12	.333	62	0	0	0	**17**	92	94	44	12	1	10	55	10.3	3.82	105	.267	.289	3	.273	0	2	2	2	0.6
1962	Pit-N	8	7	.533	63	0	0	0	**28**	91	74	23	7	1	18	45	9.2	1.88	209	.231	.274	1	.083	-1	**21**	**21**	-1	4.1
1963	Pit-N	3	9	.250	56	0	0	0	16	69^2	75	33	6	3	19	41	12.5	3.23	102	.285	.340	2	.250	0	0	1	1	0.3
1964	Pit-N	3	3	.500	55	0	0	0	4	79^2	82	48	11	1	27	63	12.4	5.20	68	.269	.330	0	.000	-0	-15	-15	0	-1.2
1965	Pit-N	5	2	.714	16	0	0	0	0	20^1	20	6	1	0	7	19	12.0	2.66	132	.263	.325	0	.000	-0	2	2	-1	0.4
1966	Pit-N	6	6	.500	54	0	0	0	18	70	68	24	9	1	24	67	12.0	2.70	132	.262	.326	0	.000	-1	7	7	1	1.4
1967	Pit-N	7	5	.583	61	0	0	0	17	74^1	62	23	5	0	22	41	10.2	2.42	139	.230	.288	0	.000	-1	8	8	-1	1.5
1968	Pit-N	2	4	.333	43	0	0	0	13	52	46	17	3	2	7	34	9.5	2.60	113	.238	.272	0	.000	-0	2	2	-0	0.3
	Det-A	0	0	—	2	0	0	0	0	1	2	0	0	0	1	1	27.0	0.00	—	.500	.600	0	—	0	0	0	0	0.0
1969	Mon-N	4	2	.667	44	0	0	0	5	59^1	62	29	11	0	15	34	11.7	3.94	93	.263	.307	1	.500	0	-2	-2	-1	-0.2
Total	16	104	95	.523	848	27	6	0	193	1375	1347	591	141	14	362	877	11.3	3.48	109	.260	.310	31	.160	-4	48	48	0	12.5

● TONY FAETH Faeth, Anthony Joseph b: 7/9/1893, Aberdeen, S.D. d: 12/22/82, St.Paul, Minn. BR/TR, 6', 180 lbs. Deb: 8/10/19

YEAR	TM/L	W	L	PCT	G	GS	CG	SH	SV	IP	H	R	HR	HB	BB	SO	RAT	ERA	ERA+	OAV	OOB	BH	AVG	PB	PR	PR+	PD	TPI
1919	Cle-A	0	0	—	6	0	0	0	0	18^1	13	4	0	0	10	7	11.3	0.49	682	.224	.338	0	.000	-1	6	6	-0	0.2
1920	Cle-A	0	0	—	13	0	0	0	0	25	31	19	0	1	20	14	18.7	4.32	88	.333	.456	0	.000	-1	-1	-1	-0	-0.1
Total	2	0	0	—	19	0	0	0	0	43^1	44	23	0	1	30	21	15.6	2.70	134	.291	.412	0	.000	-1	4	4	-0	0.1

● EVERETT FAGAN Fagan, Everett Joseph b: 1/13/18, Pottersville, N.J. d: 2/16/83, Morristown, N.J. BR/TR, 6', 195 lbs. Deb: 4/24/43

YEAR	TM/L	W	L	PCT	G	GS	CG	SH	SV	IP	H	R	HR	HB	BB	SO	RAT	ERA	ERA+	OAV	OOB	BH	AVG	PB	PR	PR+	PD	TPI
1943	Phi-A	2	6	.250	18	2	0	0	3	37^1	41	28	4	2	14	9	13.7	6.27	54	.283	.354	0	.000	-0	-12	-12	0	-2.3
1946	Phi-A	0	1	.000	20	0	0	0	0	45	47	27	2	3	24	12	14.8	4.80	74	.264	.361	4	.286	1	-6	-6	-0	-0.3
Total	2	2	7	.222	38	2	0	0	3	82^1	88	55	6	5	38	21	14.3	5.47	64	.272	.358	4	.190	1	-19	-18	0	-2.6

● BILL FAGAN Fagan, William A. "Clinkers" b: 2/15/1869, Troy, N.Y. d: 3/21/30, Troy, N.Y. TL, 5'11", 165 lbs. Deb: 9/15/1887

YEAR	TM/L	W	L	PCT	G	GS	CG	SH	SV	IP	H	R	HR	HB	BB	SO	RAT	ERA	ERA+	OAV	OOB	BH	AVG	PB	PR	PR+	PD	TPI
1887	NY-a	1	4	.200	6	6	6	0	0	45	79	34	1	2	24	12	16.2	4.00	106	.387	.393	3	.143	-2	1	1	0	-0.1
1888	KC-a	5	11	.313	17	17	15	0	0	142^1	179	148	4	1	75	49	16.1	5.69	60	.296	.375	14	.215	-1	-42	-32	1	-2.7
Total	2	6	15	.286	23	23	21	0	0	187^1	258	182	5	3	99	61	16.1	5.28	69	.319	.379	17	.198	-3	-40	-31	1	-2.8

● FRANK FAHEY Fahey, Francis Raymond b: 1/22/1896, Milford, Mass. d: 3/19/54, Boston, Mass. BB/TR, 6'1", 190 lbs. Deb: 4/25/18 ♦

YEAR	TM/L	W	L	PCT	G	GS	CG	SH	SV	IP	H	R	HR	HB	BB	SO	RAT	ERA	ERA+	OAV	OOB	BH	AVG	PB	PR	PR+	PD	TPI
1918	Phi-A	0	0	—	3	0	0	0	0	9	5	7	0	1	14	1	20.0	6.00	49	.200	.500	3	.176	-0	-3	-3	-1	-0.2

● JERRY FAHR Fahr, Gerald Warren b: 12/9/24, Marmaduke, Ark. BR/TR, 6'5", 185 lbs. Deb: 4/29/51

YEAR	TM/L	W	L	PCT	G	GS	CG	SH	SV	IP	H	R	HR	HB	BB	SO	RAT	ERA	ERA+	OAV	OOB	BH	AVG	PB	PR	PR+	PD	TPI
1951	Cle-A	0	0	—	5	0	0	0	0	5^2	11	3	0	0	2	0	20.6	4.76	80	.500	.542	0	—	0	-0	-1	-0	0.0

● PETE FAHRER Fahrer, Clarence Willie b: 3/10/1890, Holgate, Ohio d: 6/10/67, Fremont, Mich. BL/TR, 6', 190 lbs. Deb: 8/17/14

YEAR	TM/L	W	L	PCT	G	GS	CG	SH	SV	IP	H	R	HR	HB	BB	SO	RAT	ERA	ERA+	OAV	OOB	BH	AVG	PB	PR	PR+	PD	TPI
1914	Cin-N	0	0	—	5	0	0	0	0	8	8	3	0	0	4	2	13.5	1.13	260	.308	.400	0	.000	-0	1	2	0	0.1

YEAR	TM/L	W	L	PCT	G	GS	CG	SH	SV	IP	H	R	HR	HB	BB	SO	RAT	ERA	ERA+	OAV	OOB	BH	AVG	PB	PR	PR+	PD	TPI
● JIM FAIRBANK	Fairbank, James Lee "Lee" or "Smoky" b: 3/17/1881, Deansboro, N.Y. d: 12/27/55, Utica, N.Y. BR/TR, 5'9.5", 175 lbs. Deb: 9/18/03																											
1903	Phi-A	1	1	.500	4	1	1	0	0	24	33	14	1	0	12	10	16.9	4.88	63	.327	.398	1	.100	-1	-5	-5	1	-0.3
1904	Phi-A	0	1	.000	3	1	1	0	0	17	19	14	0	2	13	6	18.0	6.35	42	.284	.415	0	.000	-1	-7	-7	1	-0.4
Total	2	1	2	.333	7	2	2	0	0	41	52	28	1	2	25	16	17.3	5.49	53	.310	.405	1	.063	-1	-12	-11	2	-0.7
● RAGS FAIRCLOTH	Faircloth, James Lamar b: 8/19/1892, Kenton, Tenn. d: 10/5/53, Tucson, Ariz. BR/TR, 5'11", 160 lbs. Deb: 5/6/19																											
1919	Phi-N	0	0	—	2	0	0	0	0	2	5	2	0	0	0	0	22.5	9.00	36	.625	.625	0	—	0	-1	-1	0	-0.1
● HECTOR FAJARDO	Fajardo, Hector (Nabaratte) b: 11/16/70, Sahuayo, Mexico BR/TR, 6'4", 185 lbs. Deb: 8/10/91																											
1991	Pit-N	0	0	—	2	2	0	0	0	6^1	10	7	0	0	7	8	24.2	9.95	36	.357	.486	0	.000	-0	-4	-5	-0	-0.3
	Tex-A	0	2	.000	4	3	0	0	0	19	25	13	2	1	4	15	14.2	5.68	71	.329	.370	0	—	0	-3	-4	-0	-0.3
1993	Tex-A	0	0	—	1	0	0	0	0	0^2	0	0	0	0	0	1	0.0	0.00	—	.000	.000	0	—	0	0	0	0	0.0
1994	Tex-A	5	7	.417	18	12	0	0	0	83^1	95	67	15	2	26	45	13.3	6.91	70	.284	.340	0	—	0	-20	-19	-0	-2.2
1995	Tex-A	0	0	—	5	0	0	0	0	15	19	13	2	1	5	9	15.0	7.80	62	.311	.373	0	—	0	-5	-5	0	-0.2
Total	4	5	9	.357	30	17	0	0	0	124^1	149	100	19	4	42	78	14.1	6.95	67	.297	.356	0	.000	-0	-32	-32	-1	-3.0
● PETE FALCONE	Falcone, Peter Frank b: 10/1/53, Brooklyn, N.Y. BL/TL, 6'2", 185 lbs. Deb: 4/13/75																											
1975	SF-N	12	11	.522	34	32	3	1	0	190	171	97	16	4	111	131	13.5	4.17	91	.244	.350	4	.062	-5	-11	-7	-1	-1.3
1976	StL-N	12	16	.429	32	32	9	2	0	212	173	87	12	2	93	138	11.4	3.23	110	.222	.306	8	.129	-1	7	7	-4	0.3
1977	StL-N	4	8	.333	27	22	1	1	1	124	130	79	19	3	61	75	14.1	5.44	71	.273	.359	10	.244	2	-21	-22	-1	-1.8
1978	StL-N	2	7	.222	19	14	0	0	0	75	94	52	9	2	48	28	17.3	5.76	61	.319	.417	5	.238	1	-18	-19	-2	-2.1
1979	NY-N	6	14	.300	33	31	1	1	0	184	194	91	24	1	76	113	13.3	4.16	88	.276	.347	9	.173	0	-9	-11	-3	-1.4
1980	NY-N	7	10	.412	37	23	1	0	1	157^1	163	89	16	2	58	109	12.8	4.52	79	.269	.335	6	.146	-1	-16	-17	-3	-2.1
1981	NY-N	5	3	.625	35	9	3	1	1	95^1	84	32	3	0	36	56	11.3	2.55	137	.241	.312	4	.182	1	10	10	-2	0.8
1982	NY-N	8	10	.444	40	23	3	0	2	171	159	82	24	1	71	101	12.2	3.84	95	.252	.329	6	.113	-2	-4	-4	-3	-0.9
1983	Atl-N	9	4	.692	33	15	2	0	0	106^2	102	47	14	1	60	59	13.8	3.63	107	.256	.355	3	.115	-1	0	3	-2	0.0
1984	Atl-N	5	7	.417	35	16	2	1	2	120	115	61	15	0	57	55	12.9	4.13	94	.252	.335	7	.212	1	-7	-3	-1	-0.4
Total	10	70	90	.438	325	217	25	7	7	1435^1	1385	717	152	16	671	865	13.0	4.07	90	.257	.341	62	.149	-6	-70	-61	-20	-8.9
● CHET FALK	Falk, Chester Emanuel "Spot" b: 5/15/05, Austin, Tex. d: 1/7/82, Austin, Tex. BL/TL, 6'2", 170 lbs. Deb: 4/20/25 F																											
1925	StL-A	0	0	—	13	0	0	0	0	25	38	26	2	0	17	7	19.8	8.28	56	.362	.451	5	.625	2	-11	-9	0	-0.2
1926	StL-A	4	4	.500	18	8	3	0	0	74	95	53	1	6	27	7	15.6	5.35	80	.338	.408	6	.194	-1	-11	-8	-1	-0.9
1927	StL-A	1	0	1.000	9	0	0	0	0	15^2	25	18	1	0	10	2	20.1	5.74	76	.352	.432	1	.200	-0	-3	-2	0	-0.1
Total	3	5	4	.556	40	8	3	0	0	114^2	158	97	4	6	54	16	17.1	6.04	73	.346	.422	12	.273	1	-25	-20	0	-1.2
● CY FALKENBERG	Falkenberg, Frederick Peter b: 12/17/1880, Chicago, Ill. d: 4/14/61, San Francisco, Cal BR/TR, 6'5", 180 lbs. Deb: 4/21/03																											
1903	Pit-N	1	5	.167	10	6	3	0	0	56	65	43	0	2	32	24	15.9	3.86	84	.295	.390	4	.190	-0	-4	-4	2	-0.2
1905	Was-A	7	2	.778	12	10	6	2	0	75^1	71	41	1	5	31	35	12.8	3.82	69	.251	.335	4	.125	-2	-10	-10	-1	-1.4
1906	Was-A	14	20	.412	40	36	30	2	1	298^2	277	136	1	13	108	178	12.0	2.86	92	.249	.323	18	.170	1	-6	-8	2	-0.5
1907	Was-A	6	17	.261	32	24	17	1	1	233^2	195	105	0	8	77	108	10.8	2.35	103	.229	.299	12	.140	-3	5	2	2	0.1
1908	Was-A	6	2	.750	17	8	5	1	0	82^2	70	29	2	2	21	34	10.1	1.96	117	.236	.291	6	.222	0	4	3	1	0.4
	Cle-A	2	4	.333	8	7	2	0	0	46^1	52	25	1	2	10	17	12.4	3.88	62	.284	.328	2	.118	-1	-8	-8	-1	-1.1
	Yr	8	6	.571	25	15	7	1	0	129	122	54	3	4	31	51	11.0	2.65	88	.254	.305	8	.182	-1	-4	-5	0	-0.7
1909	Cle-A	10	9	.526	24	18	13	2	0	165	135	56	0	5	50	82	10.4	2.40	107	.231	.297	9	.173	-1	1	3	3	0.5
1910	Cle-A	14	13	.519	37	29	18	3	1	256^2	246	114	3	8	75	107	11.5	2.95	88	.261	.320	15	.183	-0	-12	-10	3	-0.8
1911	Cle-A	8	5	.615	15	13	7	0	1	106^2	117	56	0	3	24	46	12.2	3.29	104	.282	.326	7	.175	-1	1	1	1	0.1
1913	Cle-A	23	10	.697	39	36	23	6	0	276	238	85	2	5	88	166	10.8	2.22	137	.235	.299	10	.119	-2	22	24	-2	2.4
1914	Ind-F	25	16	.610	**49**	43	33	**9**	3	**377^1**	332	127	5	5	89	**236**	10.2	2.22	141	.236	.284	21	.168	-4	28	35	3	3.5
1915	New-F	9	11	.450	25	21	14	0	1	172	175	78	6	9	47	76	12.1	3.24	79	.268	.326	3	.053	-7	-10	-14	1	-2.2
	Bro-F	3	3	.500	7	7	5	1	0	48	31	15	1	1	12	20	8.3	1.50	181	.189	.249	1	.067	-2	7	7	-0	0.6
	Yr	12	14	.462	32	28	19	1	1	220	206	93	7	10	59	96	11.3	2.86	91	.252	.311	4	.056	-9	-3	-7	1	-1.6
1917	Phi-A	2	6	.250	15	8	4	0	0	80^2	86	53	1	0	26	35	12.5	3.35	82	.293	.350	5	.185	0	-6	-5	1	-0.3
Total	12	130	123	.514	330	266	180	27	8	2275	2090	963	23	68	690	1164	11.3	2.68	103	.248	.310	117	.152	-23	13	20	14	1.1
● BRIAN FALKENBORG	Falkenborg, Brian Thomas b: 1/18/78, Newport Beach, Cal. BR/TR, 6'6", 187 lbs. Deb: 10/1/99																											
1999	Bal-A	0	0	—	2	0	0	0	0	3	2	0	0	0	2	1	12.0	0.00	—	.200	.333	0	—	0	2	2	0	0.1
● ED FALLENSTEIN	Fallenstein, Edward Joseph "Jack" (b: Edward Joseph Valestin) b: 12/22/08, Newark, N.J. d: 11/24/71, Orange, N.J. BR/TR, 6'3", 180 lbs. Deb: 4/16/31																											
1931	Phi-N	0	0	—	24	0	0	0	0	41^2	56	37	2	0	26	15	17.7	7.13	60	.333	.423	1	.200	0	-15	-12	0	-0.6
1933	Bos-N	2	1	.667	9	4	1	1	0	35	43	23	1	1	13	5	14.7	3.60	85	.305	.368	3	.375	1	-1	-2	-0	-0.1
Total	2	2	1	.667	33	4	1	1	0	76^2	99	60	3	1	39	20	16.3	5.52	67	.320	.398	4	.308	1	-16	-15	-0	-0.7
● BOB FALLON	Fallon, Robert Joseph b: 2/18/60, Bronx, N.Y. BL/TL, 6'3", 200 lbs. Deb: 4/26/84																											
1984	Chi-A	0	0	—	3	3	0	0	0	14^2	12	7	0	0	11	10	14.1	3.68	113	.235	.371	0	—	0	1	1	0	0.1
1985	Chi-A	0	0	—	10	0	0	0	0	16	25	11	5	0	9	17	19.1	6.19	70	.362	.436	0	—	0	-4	-3	1	-0.1
Total	2	0	0	—	13	3	0	0	0	30^2	37	18	5	0	20	27	16.7	4.99	85	.308	.407	0	—	0	-3	-2	1	0.0
● STEVE FALTEISEK	Falteisek, Steven James b: 1/28/72, Mineola, N.Y. BR/TR, 6'2", 200 lbs. Deb: 7/21/97																											
1997	Mon-N	0	0	—	5	0	0	0	0	8	8	4	0	1	3	2	13.5	3.38	124	.286	.375	0	.000	-0	1	1	0	0.0
1999	Mil-N	0	0	—	10	0	0	0	0	12	18	10	3	0	3	5	15.8	7.50	61	.375	.412	0	.000	-0	-4	-4	-0	-0.2
Total	2	0	0	—	15	0	0	0	0	20	26	14	3	1	6	7	14.8	5.85	75	.342	.398	0	.000	-0	-3	-3	-0	-0.2
● CLIFF FANNIN	Fannin, Clifford Bryson "Mule" b: 5/13/24, Louisa, Ky. d: 12/11/66, Sandusky, Ohio BL/TR, 6', 170 lbs. Deb: 9/2/45																											
1945	StL-A	0	0	—	5	0	0	0	0	10^1	8	3	0	0	5	5	11.3	2.61	135	.222	.317	0	.000	-0	1	1	-0	0.0
1946	StL-A	5	2	.714	27	7	4	1	2	86^2	76	37	4	1	42	52	12.4	3.01	124	.236	.326	5	.161	-1	5	7	-0	0.4
1947	StL-A	6	8	.429	26	18	6	2	1	145^2	134	70	10	1	77	77	13.1	3.58	108	.245	.340	9	.196	-0	2	5	0	0.4
1948	StL-A	10	14	.417	34	29	10	3	1	213^2	198	106	14	1	104	102	12.8	4.17	109	.245	.332	11	.169	-0	3	9	-2	0.6
1949	StL-A	8	14	.364	30	25	5	0	1	143	177	106	15	0	93	57	17.0	6.17	73	.308	.404	9	.164	-2	-31	-24	-3	-3.5
1950	StL-A	5	9	.357	25	16	3	0	1	102	116	82	18	0	58	42	15.4	6.53	76	.280	.369	6	.176	-2	-22	-17	-0	-2.0
1951	StL-A	0	2	.000	7	1	0	0	0	15^1	20	16	7	0	5	11	14.7	6.46	68	.317	.368	1	.250	-0	-4	-3	0	-0.4
1952	StL-A	0	2	.000	10	2	0	0	0	16^1	34	25	5	0	9	6	23.7	12.67	31	.453	.512	0	.000	0	-16	-15	-1	-1.6
Total	8	34	51	.400	164	98	28	6	6	733	763	445	73	3	393	352	14.2	4.85	89	.269	.358	41	.173	-5	-63	-39	-6	-6.1
● JACK FANNING	Fanning, John Jacob b: 1863, S.Orange, N.J. d: 6/10/17, Aberdeen, Wash. TR, 5'9", 163 lbs. Deb: 9/20/1889																											
1889	Ind-N	0	1	.000	1	1	0	0	0	1	3	3	0	0	2	0	45.0	18.00	23	.500	.625	0	.000	-0	-2	-1	0	-0.2
1894	Phi-N	1	3	.250	6	4	2	0	0	34^1	54	52	4	2	22	7	20.4	8.91	57	.353	.441	2	.143	-1	-14	-15	-0	-1.2
Total	2	1	4	.200	7	5	2	0	0	35^1	57	55	4	2	24	7	21.1	9.17	55	.358	.449	2	.133	-1	-15	-17	0	-1.4
● HARRY FANOK	Fanok, Harry Michael "The Flame Thrower" b: 5/11/40, Whippany, N.J. BB/TR, 6', 180 lbs. Deb: 4/16/63																											
1963	StL-N	2	1	.667	12	0	0	0	1	25^2	24	16	3	1	21	25	16.1	5.26	67	.255	.397	2	.400	1	-6	-5	-0	-0.5
1964	StL-N	0	0	—	4	0	0	0	0	7^2	5	6	0	0	3	10	9.4	5.87	65	.179	.258	0	.000	-0	-2	-2	-0	-0.1
Total	2	2	1	.667	16	0	0	0	1	33^1	29	22	3	1	24	35	14.6	5.40	67	.238	.367	2	.333	1	-8	-6	-0	-0.6
● FRANK FANOVICH	Fanovich, Frank Joseph "Lefty" b: 1/11/22, New York, N.Y. BL/TL, 5'11", 180 lbs. Deb: 4/25/49																											
1949	Cin-N	0	2	.000	29	1	0	0	0	43^1	44	31	2	2	28	27	15.4	5.40	77	.257	.368	0	.000	-0	-7	-6	0	-0.3
1953	Phi-A	0	3	.000	26	3	0	0	0	61^2	62	41	5	6	37	37	15.3	5.55	77	.273	.389	2	.182	-0	-11	-8	-1	-0.5
Total	2	0	5	.000	55	4	0	0	0	105	106	72	7	8	65	64	15.3	5.49	77	.266	.380	2	.133	-1	-17	-14	-0	-0.8
● STAN FANSLER	Fansler, Stanley Robert b: 2/12/65, Elkins, W.Va. BR/TR, 5'11", 180 lbs. Deb: 9/6/86																											
1986	Pit-N	0	3	.000	5	5	0	0	0	24	20	12	2	0	15	13	13.1	3.75	102	.247	.365	1	.167	-0	-0	0	-0	0.0

YEAR	TM/L	W	L	PCT	G	GS	CG	SH	SV	IP	H	R	HR	HB	BB	SO	RAT	ERA	ERA+	OAV	OOB	BH	AVG	PB	PR	PR+	PD	TPI
● HARRY FANWELL	Fanwell, Harry Clayton b: 10/16/1886, Patapsco, Md. d: 7/15/65, Baltimore, Md. BR/TR, 6', 175 lbs. Deb: 7/23/10																											
1910	Cle-A	2	9	.182	17	11	5	1	0	92	87	52	0	6	38	30	12.8	3.62	71	.260	.347	1	.033	-3	-11	-10	1	-1.4
● ED FARMER	Farmer, Edward Joseph b: 10/18/49, Evergreen Park, Ill BR/TR, 6'5", 210 lbs. Deb: 6/9/71																											
1971	Cle-A	5	4	.556	43	4	0	0	4	78^2	77	42	9	3	41	48	13.8	4.35	88	.263	.359	1	.071	-1	-8	-4	-0	-0.6
1972	Cle-A	2	5	.286	46	1	0	0	7	61^1	51	32	10	1	27	33	11.6	4.40	73	.231	.317	1	.143	-0	-9	-8	0	-1.1
1973	Cle-A	0	2	.000	16	0	0	0	1	17^1	25	12	4	0	5	10	15.6	4.67	84	.325	.366	0	—	0	-2	-1	-0	-0.2
	Det-A	3	0	1.000	24	0	0	0	2	45	52	26	3	2	27	28	16.2	5.00	82	.292	.391	0	—	0	-6	-4	-1	-0.4
	Yr	3	2	.600	40	0	0	0	3	62^1	77	38	7	2	32	38	16.0	4.91	82	.302	.384	0	—	0	-8	-6	-1	-0.6
1974	Phi-N	2	1	.667	14	3	0	0	0	31	41	32	5	0	27	20	19.7	8.42	45	.323	.442	1	.111	-1	-16	-15	-0	-1.4
1977	Bal-A	0	0	—	1	0	0	0	0	0	1	0	0	1	—	—	∞	—	1.000	1.000	93	—	0	-1	-1	0		-0.1
1978	Mil-A	1	0	1.000	3	0	0	0	1	11	7	1	1	0	4	6	9.0	0.82	461	.175	.250	0	—	0	4	4	-0	0.4
1979	Tex-A	2	0	1.000	11	2	0	0	0	33	30	21	2	2	19	25	13.9	4.36	95	.252	.364	0	—	0	-0	-1	-0	0.0
	Chi-A	3	7	.300	42	3	0	0	14	81^1	66	36	2	1	34	48	11.2	2.43	175	.219	.301	0	—	0	16	16	0	2.5
	Yr	5	7	.417	53	5	0	0	14	114^1	96	57	4	3	53	73	12.0	2.99	142	.229	.319	0	—	0	16	16	0	2.5
1980	Chi-A★	7	9	.438	64	0	0	0	30	99^2	92	37	6	1	56	54	13.5	3.34	121	.244	.343	0	—	0	8	8	1	1.6
1981	Chi-A	3	3	.500	42	0	0	0	10	52^2	53	33	5	1	34	42	15.0	4.61	78	.262	.371	0	—	0	-6	-6	1	-0.9
1982	Phi-N	2	6	.250	47	4	0	0	6	76	66	44	2	0	50	58	13.7	4.86	76	.234	.349	0	.000	-1	-11	-10	0	-1.2
1983	Phi-N	0	6	.000	12	3	0	0	0	26^2	35	22	2	1	20	16	18.9	6.08	59	.307	.415	1	.167	-0	-7	-8	0	-1.5
	Oak-A	0	0	—	5	1	0	0	0	10^1	15	4	1	0	0	7	13.1	3.48	111	.366	.366	0	—	0	1	0	-0	0.0
Total	11	30	43	.411	370	21	0	0	75	624	611	343	52	12	345	395	14.0	4.30	90	.257	.355	4	.085	-3	-37	-30	0	-2.9
● HOWARD FARMER	Farmer, Howard Earl b: 11/18/66, Gary, Ind. BR/TR, 6'3", 185 lbs. Deb: 7/2/90 F																											
1990	Mon-N	0	3	.000	6	4	0	0	0	23	26	18	9	0	10	14	14.1	7.04	52	.302	.375	2	.400	1	-8	-9	1	-0.9
● MIKE FARMER	Farmer, Michael Anthony b: 7/3/68, Gary, Ind. BB/TL, 6'1", 193 lbs. Deb: 5/4/96 F																											
1996	Col-N	0	1	.000	7	4	0	0	0	28	32	25	8	0	13	16	14.5	7.71	68	.286	.360	4	.400	1	-11	-6	-0	-0.3
● KYLE FARNSWORTH	Farnsworth, Kyle Lynn b: 4/14/76, Wichita, Kan. BR/TR, 6'4", 205 lbs. Deb: 4/29/99																											
1999	Chi-N	5	9	.357	27	21	1	1	0	130	140	80	28	3	52	70	13.5	5.05	89	.271	.342	3	.086	-1	-7	-8	-1	-0.9
2000	Chi-N	2	9	.182	46	5	0	0	1	77	90	58	14	4	50	74	16.8	6.43	71	.291	.397	1	.071	-1	-15	-16	-1	-2.1
Total	2	7	18	.280	73	26	1	1	1	207	230	138	42	7	102	144	14.7	5.57	81	.279	.363	4	.082	-2	-22	-24	-2	-3.0
● JIM FARR	Farr, James Alfred b: 5/18/56, Waverly, N.Y. BR/TR, 6'1", 195 lbs. Deb: 9/7/82																											
1982	Tex-A	0	0	—	5	0	0	0	0	18	20	8	0	0	7	6	13.5	2.50	155	.278	.342	0	—	0	3	3	-0	0.1
● STEVE FARR	Farr, Steven Michael b: 12/12/56, LaPlata, Md. BR/TR, 5'11", 200 lbs. Deb: 5/16/84																											
1984	Cle-A	3	11	.214	31	16	0	0	1	116	106	61	14	5	46	83	12.2	4.58	89	.245	.325	0	—	0	-7	-6	1	-0.6
1985	*KC-A	2	1	.667	16	3	0	0	1	37^2	34	15	2	2	20	36	13.4	3.11	134	.245	.348	0	—	0	4	4	0	0.4
1986	KC-A	8	4	.667	56	0	0	0	8	109^1	90	39	10	4	39	83	10.9	3.13	136	.228	.304	0	—	0	13	14	1	1.6
1987	KC-A	4	3	.571	47	0	0	0	1	91	97	47	9	2	44	88	14.1	4.15	110	.270	.353	0	—	0	3	4	-1	0.2
1988	KC-A	5	4	.556	62	1	0	0	20	82^2	74	25	5	2	30	72	11.5	2.50	160	.240	.312	0	—	0	14	14	-1	1.9
1989	KC-A	2	5	.286	51	2	0	0	18	63^1	75	35	5	1	22	56	13.9	4.12	94	.296	.355	0	—	0	-2	-2	-0	-0.3
1990	KC-A	13	7	.650	57	6	1	1	1	127	99	32	6	5	48	94	10.8	1.98	194	.220	.302	0	—	0	**27**	**27**	0	4.1
1991	NY-A	5	5	.500	60	0	0	0	23	70	57	19	4	5	20	60	10.5	2.19	190	.219	.288	0	—	0	15	15	1	2.9
1992	NY-A	2	2	.500	50	0	0	0	30	52	34	10	2	2	19	37	9.5	1.56	252	.186	.270	0	—	0	14	14	-1	2.3
1993	NY-A	2	2	.500	49	0	0	0	25	47	44	22	8	2	28	39	14.2	4.21	99	.253	.363	0	—	0	1	-0	1	0.1
1994	Cle-A	1	1	.500	19	0	0	0	4	15^1	17	12	3	2	15	12	20.0	5.28	89	.279	.436	0	—	0	-1	-1	-0	-0.2
	Bos-A	1	0	1.000	11	0	0	0	0	13	24	9	2	0	3	8	18.7	6.23	81	.407	.435	0	—	0	-2	-2	-0	-0.1
	Yr	2	1	.667	30	0	0	0	4	28^1	41	21	5	2	18	20	19.4	5.72	85	.342	.436	0	—	0	-3	-3	-0	-0.3
Total	11	48	45	.516	509	28	1	1	132	824^1	751	326	70	32	334	668	12.2	3.25	127	.244	.325	0	—	0	79	80	1	12.3
● JOHN FARRELL	Farrell, John Edward b: 8/4/62, Monmouth Beach, N.J. BR/TR, 6'4", 210 lbs. Deb: 8/18/87																											
1987	Cle-A	5	1	.833	10	9	1	0	0	69	68	29	7	5	22	28	12.4	3.39	134	.256	.324	0	—	0	8	9	-0	0.6
1988	Cle-A	14	10	.583	31	30	4	0	0	210^1	216	106	15	9	67	92	12.5	4.24	97	.269	.332	0	—	0	-6	-3	-0	-0.3
1989	Cle-A	9	14	.391	31	31	7	2	0	208	196	97	14	7	71	132	11.9	3.63	109	.244	.311	0	—	0	6	8	-2	0.6
1990	Cle-A	4	5	.444	17	17	1	0	0	96^2	108	49	10	1	33	44	13.2	4.28	92	.286	.345	0	—	0	-4	-4	-0	-0.3
1993	Cal-A	3	12	.200	21	17	0	0	0	90^2	110	74	22	7	44	45	16.0	7.35	62	.301	.387	0	—	0	-30	-27	-0	-3.6
1994	Cal-A	1	2	.333	3	3	0	0	0	13	16	14	2	1	8	10	17.3	9.00	54	.308	.410	0	—	0	-6	-6	1	-0.9
1995	Cle-A	0	0	—	1	0	0	0	0	4^2	7	4	0	0	0	4	13.5	3.86	122	.368	.368	0	—	0	0	0	-0	0.0
1996	Det-A	0	2	.000	2	2	0	0	0	6^1	11	10	2	1	5	0	24.2	14.21	36	.407	.515	0	—	0	-6	-6	-0	-0.9
Total	8	36	46	.439	116	109	13	2	0	698^2	732	383	72	31	250	355	13.0	4.56	91	.270	.338	0	—	0	-38	-30	-2	-4.8
● KERBY FARRELL	Farrell, Major Kerby b: 9/3/13, Leapwood, Tenn. d: 12/17/75, Nashville, Tenn. BL/TL, 5'11", 172 lbs. Deb: 4/24/43 MC♦																											
1943	Bos-N	0	1	.000	5	0	0	0	0	23	24	11	1	0	9	4	12.9	4.30	79	.276	.344	75	.268	1	-2	-2	-0	-0.1
● TURK FARRELL	Farrell, Richard Joseph b: 4/8/34, Boston, Mass. d: 6/10/77, Great Yarmouth, England BR/TR, 6'4", 220 lbs. Deb: 9/21/56																											
1956	Phi-N	0	1	.000	1	1	0	0	0	4^1	6	6	0	1	3	0	20.8	12.46	30	.353	.476	0	.000	-0	-4	-4	0	-0.6
1957	Phi-N	10	2	.833	52	0	0	0	10	83^1	74	29	2	2	36	54	12.1	2.38	160	.242	.326	1	.111	0	**14**	13	0	2.3
1958	Phi-N★	8	9	.471	54	0	0	0	11	94	84	41	7	0	40	73	11.9	3.35	118	.244	.323	5	.208	0	6	6	-2	1.1
1959	Phi-N	1	6	.143	38	0	0	0	6	57	61	30	9	0	25	31	13.6	4.74	87	.288	.363	1	.167	-0	-5	-4	-0	-0.6
1960	Phi-N	10	6	.625	59	0	0	0	11	103^1	88	36	3	4	29	70	10.5	2.70	144	.239	.302	3	.200	1	12	13	-1	2.2
1961	Phi-N	2	1	.667	5	0	0	0	0	9^2	10	8	3	1	6	10	15.8	6.52	63	.270	.386	1	.500	0	-3	-3	-0	-0.5
	LA-N	6	6	.500	50	0	0	0	10	89	107	56	12	1	43	80	15.3	5.06	86	.296	.373	0	.000	-2	-10	-7	-2	-1.3
	Yr	8	7	.533	55	0	0	0	10	98^2	117	64	15	2	49	90	15.3	5.20	83	.294	.374	1	.050	-2	-13	-9	-2	-1.8
1962	Hou-N★	10	20	.333	43	29	11	2	4	241^2	210	91	21	5	55	203	10.1	3.02	124	.233	.280	14	.179	2	25	20	-2	2.5
1963	Hou-N	14	13	.519	34	26	12	0	1	202^1	161	76	12	2	35	141	8.8	3.02	104	.219	.256	9	.143	1	6	3	-2	0.4
1964	Hou-N★	11	10	.524	32	27	7	0	0	198^1	196	80	21	3	52	117	11.4	3.27	105	.261	.311	5	.072	-3	6	3	-1	-0.1
1965	Hou-N★	11	11	.500	33	29	8	3	1	208^1	202	94	18	3	35	122	10.4	3.50	96	.252	.286	10	.135	-1	1	-3	-2	-0.6
1966	Hou-N	6	10	.375	32	21	3	0	2	152^2	167	84	23	0	28	101	11.5	4.60	74	.278	.310	7	.146	-0	-17	-21	-2	-2.3
1967	Hou-N	1	0	1.000	7	0	0	0	0	11^2	11	7	0	1	7	10	14.7	4.63	72	.244	.358	0	.000	-0	-2	-2	0	-0.2
	Phi-N	9	6	.600	50	1	0	0	12	92	76	26	6	1	15	68	9.0	2.05	166	.228	.263	2	.105	-0	14	14	-1	2.5
	Yr	10	6	.625	57	1	0	0	12	103^2	87	33	6	2	22	78	9.6	2.34	145	.230	.275	2	.100	-0	12	12	-1	2.3
1968	Phi-N	4	6	.400	54	0	0	0	12	83	83	40	7	2	32	57	12.7	3.47	87	.271	.344	1	.167	-0	-4	-4	-0	-0.7
1969	Phi-N	3	4	.429	46	0	0	0	3	74^1	92	33	8	1	27	40	14.5	4.00	89	.307	.366	0	.000	-0	-3	-4	-2	-0.6
Total	14	106	111	.488	590	134	41	5	83	1705	1628	737	152	27	468	1177	11.2	3.45	103	.254	.307	59	.135	-3	35	22	-17	3.5
● JEFF FASSERO	Fassero, Jeffrey Joseph b: 1/5/63, Springfield, Ill. BL/TL, 6'1", 195 lbs. Deb: 5/4/91																											
1991	Mon-N	2	5	.286	51	0	0	0	8	55^1	39	17	1	1	17	42	9.3	2.44	148	.196	.263	0	.000	0	8	7	1	1.2
1992	Mon-N	8	7	.533	70	0	0	0	1	85^2	81	35	1	2	34	63	12.3	2.84	122	.249	.324	1	.143	0	6	6	0	1.1
1993	Mon-N	12	5	.706	56	15	1	0	1	149^2	119	50	7	0	54	140	10.4	2.29	183	.216	.286	2	.063	-2	**29**	**30**	0	3.1
1994	Mon-N	8	6	.571	21	21	1	0	0	138^2	119	54	13	1	40	119	10.4	2.99	142	.229	.286	3	.068	-2	19	19	3	1.9
1995	Mon-N	13	14	.481	30	30	1	0	0	189	207	102	15	2	74	164	13.5	4.33	99	.283	.351	4	.070	-3	-3	-1	1	-0.2
1996	Mon-N	15	11	.577	34	34	5	1	0	231^2	217	95	20	3	55	222	10.7	3.30	131	.244	.291	6	.094	-1	24	26	3	2.8
1997	*Sea-A	16	9	.640	35	35	2	1	0	234^1	226	108	21	3	84	189	12.0	3.61	125	.249	.315	1	.200	0	25	24	1	2.4
1998	Sea-A	13	12	.520	32	32	7	0	0	224^2	223	115	33	10	66	176	12.0	3.97	117	.259	.319	0	.000	-0	17	17	-0	1.6
1999	Sea-A	4	14	.222	30	24	0	0	0	139	188	123	34	4	73	101	17.2	7.38	64	.321	.400	0	.000	-1	-39	-42	2	-4.1
	*Tex-A	1	0	1.000	7	3	0	0	0	17^1	20	12	1	0	10	13	15.6	5.71	89	.286	.375	0	—	0	-2	-1	-0	-0.1
	Yr	5	14	.263	37	27	0	0	0	156^1	208	135	35	4	83	114	17.0	7.20	66	.318	.398	0	.000	-1	-40	-43	2	-4.2
2000	Bos-A	8	8	.500	38	23	0	0	0	130	153	72	16	1	50	97	14.1	4.78	107	.296	.359	0	.000	-0	2	4	1	0.5
Total	10	100	91	.524	404	217	17	2	10	1595^1	1592	783	162	27	557	1326	12.3	3.89	113	.259	.323	17	.076	-9	87	92	12	10.2

YEAR TM/L	W	L	PCT	G	GS	CG	SH	SV	IP	H	R	HR	HB	BB	SO	RAT	ERA	ERA+	OAV	OOB	BH	AVG	PB	PR	PR+	PD	TPI
● **FAST** Fast b: Milwaukee, Wis. Deb: 7/11/1887																											
1887 Ind-N	0	1	.000	4	2	1	0	**1**	15^2	33	22	1	2	8	0	20.1	10.34	40	.412	.427	2	.182	-1	-11	-11	0	-0.6
● **DARCY FAST** Fast, Darcy Rae b: 3/10/47, Dallas, Ore. BL/TL, 6'3", 195 lbs. Deb: 6/15/68																											
1968 Chi-N	0	1	.000	8	1	0	0	0	10	8	6	1	0	8	10	14.4	5.40	59	.216	.356	0	.000	-0	-3	-2	0	-0.3
● **JACK FASZHOLZ** Faszholz, John Edward "Preacher" b: 4/11/27, St.Louis, Mo. BR/TR, 6'3", 205 lbs. Deb: 4/25/53																											
1953 StL-N	0	0	—	4	1	0	0	0	11^2	16	9	3	1	1	7	13.9	6.94	61	.327	.353	0	.000	-0	-3	-4	-1	-0.2
● **BILL FAUL** Faul, William Alvan b: 4/21/40, Cincinnati, Ohio BR/TR, 5'10", 190 lbs. Deb: 9/19/62																											
1962 Det-A	0	0	—	1	0	0	0	0	1^2	4	6	1	1	3	2	43.2	32.40	13	.444	.615	0	—	0	-5	-5	-0	-0.2
1963 Det-A	5	6	.455	28	10	2	0	1	97	93	55	14	4	48	64	13.5	4.64	81	.251	.343	4	.148	0	-11	-9	-2	-1.2
1964 Det-A	0	0	—	1	1	0	0	0	5	5	6	2	0	2	1	12.6	10.80	34	.250	.318	0	.000	-0	-4	-4	-0	-0.2
1965 Chi-N	6	6	.500	17	16	5	3	0	96^2	83	43	12	3	18	59	9.7	3.54	104	.232	.275	3	.100	-1	0	2	-2	-0.1
1966 Chi-N	1	4	.200	17	6	1	0	0	51^1	47	31	12	4	18	32	12.1	5.08	72	.242	.319	0	.000	-2	-8	-8	-1	-0.9
1970 SF-N	0	0	—	7	0	0	0	1	9^2	15	9	1	0	6	6	19.6	7.45	53	.357	.438	0	—	0	-4	-4	-0	-0.2
Total 6	12	16	.429	71	33	8	3	2	261^1	247	150	42	12	95	164	12.2	4.72	79	.249	.322	7	.097	-2	-32	-28	-5	-2.8
● **JIM FAULKNER** Faulkner, James Leroy "Lefty" b: 7/27/1899, Beatrice, Neb. d: 6/1/62, W.Palm Beach, Fla. BB/TL (BL 1927), 6'3", 190 lbs. Deb: 9/15/27																											
1927 NY-N	1	0	1.000	3	1	0	0	0	9^2	13	4	0	1	5	2	17.7	3.72	104	.317	.404	1	.500	1	0	0	-0	0.1
1928 NY-N	9	8	.529	38	8	3	0	2	117^1	131	61	5	3	41	32	13.4	3.53	111	.289	.351	9	.231	1	6	5	1	0.8
1930 Bro-N	0	0	—	2	1	0	0	1	0^1	2	3	1	0	1	0	81.0	81.00	6	.667	.750	0	—	0	-3	-3	0	-0.4
Total 3	10	8	.556	43	10	3	0	3	127^1	146	68	6	4	47	34	13.9	3.75	104	.293	.359	10	.244	2	3	2	1	0.5
● **BUCK FAUSETT** Fausett, Robert Shaw "Leaky" b: 4/8/08, Sheridan, Ark. d: 5/2/94, College Station, Tex. BL/TR, 5'10", 170 lbs. Deb: 4/18/44 ◆																											
1944 Cin-N	0	0	—	2	0	0	0	0	10^2	13	8	0	2	7	3	18.6	5.91	59	.295	.415	3	.097	-0	-3	-3	0	-0.2
● **CHARLIE FAUST** Faust, Charles Victor "Victory" b: 10/9/1880, Marion, Kan. d: 6/18/15, Fort Steilacoom, Wash. BR/TR, 6'2", Deb: 10/7/11																											
1911 NY-N	0	0	—	2	0	0	0	0	2	2	1	0	0	0	0	9.0	4.50	75	.250	.250	0	—	0	-0	-0	0	0.0
● **CLAY FAUVER** Fauver, Clayton King "Cayt" b: 8/1/1872, N.Eaton, Ohio d: 3/3/42, Chatsworth, Ga. BB/TR, 5'10", Deb: 9/7/1899																											
1899 Lou-N	1	0	1.000	1	1	1	0	0	9	11	4	0	0	2	1	13.0	0.00	—	.297	.333	0	.000	-1	4	4	-0	0.3
● **VERN FEAR** Fear, Luvern Carl b: 8/21/24, Everly, Iowa d: 9/6/76, Spencer, Iowa BB/TR, 6', 170 lbs. Deb: 8/3/52																											
1952 Chi-N	0	0	—	4	0	0	0	0	8	9	7	1	1	3	4	14.6	7.88	49	.290	.371	0	.000	-0	-4	-3	-0	-0.2
● **JACK FEE** Fee, John b: 12/23/1867, Carbondale, Pa. d: 3/3/13, Carbondale, Pa. Deb: 9/14/1889																											
1889 Ind-N	2	2	.500	7	3	2	0	0	40	39	29	2	6	31	10	17.1	4.27	98	.248	.392	3	.143	-2	-1	-0	1	-0.1
● **HARRY FELDMAN** Feldman, Harry b: 11/10/19, New York, N.Y. d: 3/16/62, Fort Smith, Ark. BR/TR, 6', 175 lbs. Deb: 9/10/41																											
1941 NY-N	1	1	.500	3	3	1	1	0	20^1	21	10	0	0	6	9	12.0	3.98	93	.280	.333	1	.167	0	-1	-1	-0	-0.1
1942 NY-N	7	1	.875	31	6	2	1	0	114	100	46	5	1	73	49	13.7	3.16	106	.236	.350	11	.282	3	2	3	-0	0.5
1943 NY-N	4	5	.444	31	10	1	0	0	104^2	114	59	7	4	58	49	15.1	4.30	80	.279	.374	4	.133	-1	-11	-10	0	-0.9
1944 NY-N	11	13	.458	40	27	8	1	2	205^1	214	120	18	2	91	70	13.5	4.16	88	.266	.342	15	.205	0	-13	-11	-2	-1.4
1945 NY-N	12	13	.480	35	30	10	3	1	217^2	213	92	14	1	69	74	11.7	3.27	120	.251	.308	7	.097	-3	13	15	-2	1.1
1946 NY-N	0	2	.000	3	2	0	0	0	4	9	8	1	0	3	3	27.0	18.00	19	.474	.545	0	.000	-0	-6	-6	-0	-1.1
Total 6	35	35	.500	143	78	22	6	3	666	671	335	45	8	300	254	13.2	3.80	96	.260	.339	38	.172	-1	-16	-10	-5	-1.9
● **HARRY FELIX** Felix, Harry b: 1870, Brooklyn, N.Y. d: 10/17/61, Miami, Fla. BR/TR, 5'7.5", 160 lbs. Deb: 10/5/01																											
1901 NY-N	0	0	—	1	0	0	0	0	2	3	0	0	0	0	0	13.5	0.00	—	.333	.333	0	.000	-0	1	1	-0	0.0
1902 Phi-N	1	3	.250	9	5	3	0	0	45	61	37	1	0	11	10	14.4	5.60	50	.323	.360	5	.135	-1	-14	-14	-1	-1.2
Total 2	1	3	.250	10	5	3	0	0	47	64	37	1	0	11	10	14.4	5.36	53	.323	.359	5	.132	-1	-13	-13	-1	-1.2
● **BOB FELLER** Feller, Robert William Andrew "Rapid Robert" (b: Robert William Feller) b: 11/3/18, Van Meter, Iowa BR/TR, 6', 185 lbs. Deb: 7/19/36 H																											
1936 Cle-A	5	3	.625	14	8	5	0	1	62	52	29	1	4	47	76	15.0	3.34	151	.229	.371	3	.136	-2	12	12	-1	1.1
1937 Cle-A	9	7	.563	26	19	9	0	1	148^2	116	68	4	2	106	150	13.6	3.39	136	.218	.351	9	.170	-1	20	20	1	1.9
1938 Cle-A☆	17	11	.607	39	36	20	2	1	277^2	225	136	13	7	208	**240**	14.3	4.08	114	**.220**	.356	17	.181	2	22	18	-2	1.5
1939 Cle-A★	**24**	9	.727	39	35	**24**	4	1	**296^2**	227	105	13	3	142	**246**	11.3	2.85	154	**.210**	.303	21	.212	5	**58**	**54**	0	**5.9**
1940 Cle-A★	**27**	11	.711	**43**	37	**31**	**4**	4	**320^1**	245	102	13	5	118	**261**	**10.3**	**2.61**	161	**.210**	**.285**	18	.157	1	**63**	**59**	-4	**6.4**
1941 Cle-A★	**25**	13	.658	**44**	40	28	**6**	2	**343**	284	129	15	5	194	**260**	12.7	3.15	125	.226	.332	18	.150	2	38	32	-1	3.3
1945 Cle-A	5	3	.625	9	9	7	1	0	72	50	21	1	2	35	59	10.9	2.50	130	.192	.293	4	.160	-0	7	6	-1	0.5
1946 Cle-A★	**26**	15	.634	**48**	42	**36**	**10**	4	**371^1**	277	101	11	3	153	**348**	10.5	2.18	152	.208	.291	16	.129	-2	**55**	49	-1	5.3
1947 Cle-A†	**20**	11	.645	42	37	20	**5**	3	**299**	230	97	17	4	127	**196**	**10.9**	2.68	130	.215	.300	18	.184	3	**34**	**28**	2	3.3
1948 *Cle-A†	19	15	.559	44	38	18	2	3	280^1	255	123	20	2	116	**164**	12.0	3.56	114	.241	.317	9	.095	-8	23	16	-1	0.8
1949 Cle-A	15	14	.517	36	28	15	0	0	211	198	104	18	1	84	108	12.1	3.75	106	.248	.320	17	.236	4	10	6	-4	0.7
1950 Cle-A★	16	11	.593	35	34	16	3	0	247	230	105	20	5	103	119	12.3	3.43	126	.247	.325	10	.120	-2	32	26	-4	1.9
1951 Cle-A	**22**	8	**.733**	33	32	16	4	0	249^2	239	105	22	7	95	111	12.3	3.50	108	.253	.325	10	.123	-4	17	9	-3	0.2
1952 Cle-A	9	13	.409	30	30	11	0	0	191^2	219	124	13	3	83	81	14.3	4.74	71	.288	.360	7	.117	1	-23	-33	-0	-3.2
1953 Cle-A	10	7	.588	25	25	10	1	0	175^2	163	78	16	3	60	60	11.6	3.59	105	.251	.317	6	.107	-2	8	3	1	0.2
1954 Cle-A	13	3	.813	19	19	9	1	0	140	127	53	13	3	39	59	10.9	3.09	119	.239	.294	9	.188	1	10	9	-2	0.9
1955 Cle-A	4	4	.500	25	11	2	1	0	83	71	43	7	4	31	25	11.2	3.47	115	.235	.308	1	.048	-2	5	5	-1	0.1
1956 Cle-A	0	4	.000	19	4	2	0	1	58	63	34	7	0	23	18	13.3	4.97	85	.280	.347	0	.000	-2	-5	-5	-1	-0.6
Total 18	266	162	.621	570	484	279	44	21	3827	3271	1557	224	60	1764	2581	12.0	3.25	122	.231	.319	193	.151	-7	385	316	-22	30.2
● **TERRY FELTON** Felton, Terry Lane b: 10/29/57, Texarkana, Ark. BR/TR, 6'1", 180 lbs. Deb: 9/28/79																											
1979 Min-A	0	0	—	1	0	0	0	0	2	0	0	0	0	0	1	0.0	0.00	—	.000	.000	0	—	0	1	1	-0	0.0
1980 Min-A	0	3	.000	5	4	0	0	0	17^2	20	18	2	1	9	14	15.3	7.13	61	.286	.375	0	—	0	-6	-5	-0	-0.7
1981 Min-A	0	0	—	1	0	0	0	0	1^1	4	6	1	0	2	1	40.5	40.50	10	.500	.600	0	—	0	-5	-5	0	-0.2
1982 Min-A	0	13	.000	48	6	0	0	3	117^1	99	71	18	4	76	92	13.7	4.99	85	.230	.351	0	—	0	-12	-9	-2	-1.2
Total 4	0	16	.000	55	10	0	0	3	138^1	123	95	21	5	87	108	14.0	5.53	77	.240	.355	0	—	0	-22	-19	-3	-2.1
● **HOD FENNER** Fenner, Horace Alfred b: 7/12/1897, Martin, Mich. d: 11/20/54, Detroit, Mich. BR/TR, 5'10.5", 165 lbs. Deb: 9/9/21																											
1921 Chi-A	0	0	—	2	1	0	0	0	7	14	6	0	0	3	1	21.9	7.71	55	.452	.500	0	.000	-0	-3	-3	-0	-0.2
● **STAN FERENS** Ferens, Stanley "Lefty" b: 3/5/15, Wendel, Pa. d: 10/7/94, Hempfield Township, Pa. BB/TL, 5'11", 170 lbs. Deb: 6/10/42																											
1942 StL-A	3	4	.429	19	3	1	0	0	69	76	31	2	0	21	23	12.7	3.78	98	.279	.331	3	.143	-1	-1	-1	-0	-0.1
1946 StL-A	2	9	.182	34	6	1	0	0	88	100	60	3	3	38	28	14.4	4.50	83	.293	.369	4	.167	-1	-10	-7	-1	-0.9
Total 2	5	13	.278	53	9	2	0	0	157	176	91	5	3	59	51	13.6	4.18	89	.287	.353	7	.156	-1	-11	-8	-1	-1.0
● **CHARLIE FERGUSON** Ferguson, Charles Augustus b: 5/10/1875, Okemos, Mich. d: 5/17/31, Sault Ste.Marie, Mich. TR, 5'11", Deb: 9/20/01																											
1901 Chi-N	0	0	—	1	0	0	0	0	2	1	0	0	0	2	0	13.5	0.00	—	.143	.333	0	.000	-0	1	1	-0	0.0
● **CHARLIE FERGUSON** Ferguson, Charles J. b: 4/17/1863, Charlottesville, Va. d: 4/29/1888, Philadelphia, Pa. BB/TR, 6', 165 lbs. Deb: 5/1/1884																											
1884 Phi-N	21	25	.457	50	47	46	2	1	416^2	443	297	13		93	194	11.6	3.54	84	.253	.291	50	.246	7	-26	-26	-2	-1.7
1885 Phi-N	26	20	.565	48	45	45	5	0	405	345	197	5		81	197	9.5	2.22	126	.219	.257	72	.306	17	27	26	1	4.3
1886 Phi-N	30	9	.769	48	45	43	4	**2**	395^2	317	145	11		69	212	8.8	1.98	167	.210	.244	66	.253	12	**59**	**58**	5	**6.5**
1887 Phi-N	22	10	.688	37	33	31	2	**1**	297^1	344	154	13	11	47	125	10.7	3.00	141	.283	.289	123	.413	14	36	39	1	4.6
Total 4	99	64	.607	183	170	165	13	4	1514^2	1449	793	42	11	290	728	10.1	2.67	122	.239	.270	311	.312	49	95	97	6	13.7
● **GEORGE FERGUSON** Ferguson, George Cecil "Cecil" b: 8/19/1886, Ellsworth, Ind. d: 9/5/43, Orlando, Fla. BR/TR, 5'10", 165 lbs. Deb: 4/19/06																											
1906 NY-N	2	0	1.000	22	1	1	1	**7**	52^1	43	22	1	2	24	32	11.9	2.58	101	.229	.322	5	.333	2	**0**	**0**	1	0.3
1907 NY-N	3	2	.600	15	5	4	0	1	64	63	32	2	5	20	37	12.4	2.11	118	.266	.336	1	.056	-1	3	3	-0	0.0
1908 Bos-N	11	11	.500	37	21	13	3	0	208	168	72	1	8	84	98	11.3	2.47	98	.230	.316	11	.169	-1	-2	-1	-3	-0.4

YEAR	TM/L	W	L	PCT	G	GS	CG	SH	SV	IP	H	R	HR	HB	BB	SO	RAT	ERA	ERA+	OAV	OOB	BH	AVG	PB	PR	PR+	PD	TPI
1909	Bos-N	5	23	.179	36	30	19	3	0	226^{2}	235	121	2	12	83	87	13.1	3.73	76	.282	.355	15	.205	1	-29	-21	0	-2.3
1910	Bos-N	7	7	.500	26	14	10	1	0	123	110	56	3	7	58	40	12.8	3.80	87	.254	.351	7	.175	-1	-11	-6	-0	-0.7
1911	Bos-N	1	3	.250	6	3	0	0	0	24	40	29	3	0	12	4	19.5	9.75	39	.388	.452	2	.286	1	-17	-14	-0	-1.7
Total	6	29	46	.387	142	74	47	8	8	698	659	332	12	34	281	298	12.6	3.34	83	.261	.343	41	.188	3	-56	-42	-2	-4.8
● **ALEX FERGUSON**	Ferguson, James Alexander b: 2/16/1897, Montclair, N.J. d: 4/26/76, Sepulveda, Cal. BR/TR, 6', 180 lbs. Deb: 8/16/18																											
1918	NY-A	0	0	—	1	0	0	0	0	1^{2}	2	0	0	0	2	1	21.6	0.00	—	.333	.500	0	.000	-0	1	1	-0	0.0
1921	NY-A	3	1	.750	17	4	1	0	1	56^{1}	64	40	4	4	27	9	15.2	5.91	72	.296	.385	4	.211	-1	-10	-11	-0	-0.8
1922	Bos-A	9	16	.360	39	27	10	1	2	198^{1}	201	108	5	6	62	44	12.2	4.31	95	.265	.326	6	.092	-6	-6	-4	-1	-1.2
1923	Bos-A	9	13	.409	34	27	11	0	0	198^{1}	229	115	5	9	67	72	13.8	4.04	102	.297	.360	6	.097	-5	-1	2	-1	-0.5
1924	Bos-A	14	17	.452	41	32	15	0	2	237^{2}	259	115	6	6	108	78	14.1	3.79	115	.286	.366	12	.140	-6	12	15	1	1.2
1925	Bos-A	0	2	.000	5	4	0	0	1	15^{2}	22	22	6	1	5	5	16.1	10.91	42	.314	.368	0	.000	-0	-11	-11	-0	-1.2
	NY-A	4	2	.667	21	6	0	0	1	54^{1}	83	57	3	2	42	20	21.0	7.79	55	.358	.460	2	.133	-1	-20	-22	1	-2.0
	*Was-A	5	1	.833	7	6	3	0	0	55^{1}	52	22	2	2	23	24	12.5	3.25	130	.256	.338	1	.050	-3	7	6	-1	0.2
	Yr	9	5	.643	33	16	3	0	2	125^{1}	157	101	11	5	70	49	16.7	6.18	69	.311	.400	3	.077	-4	-25	-27	-1	-3.0
1926	Was-A	3	4	.429	19	4	0	0	1	47^{2}	69	51	4	3	18	16	17.0	7.74	50	.343	.405	2	.182	-0	-20	-21	0	-2.6
1927	Phi-N	8	16	.333	31	31	16	0	0	227	280	132	15	6	65	73	13.9	4.84	85	.313	.363	7	.100	-5	-23	-17	0	-2.0
1928	Phi-N	5	10	.333	34	19	5	1	2	134^{2}	168	91	14	6	52	51	15.1	5.88	73	.315	.382	1	.026	-4	-28	-22	2	-2.5
1929	Phi-N	1	2	.333	5	4	1	0	0	12^{2}	19	18	2	0	10	3	20.6	12.08	43	.345	.446	0	.000	-1	-10	-9	0	-1.4
	Bro-N	0	1	.000	3	2	0	0	0	2	7	7	2	0	1	1	36.0	22.50	21	.583	.615	1	1.000	0	-4	-4	0	-0.6
	Yr	1	3	.250	8	6	1	0	0	14^{2}	26	25	4	0	11	4	22.7	13.50	38	.388	.474	1	.200	-0	-14	-13	1	-2.0
Total	10	61	85	.418	257	166	62	2	10	1241^{2}	1455	778	68	45	482	397	14.4	4.93	85	.299	.368	42	.106	-33	-115	-97	1	-13.4
● **BOB FERGUSON**	Ferguson, Robert Lester b: 4/18/19, Birmingham, Ala. BR/TR, 6'1.5", 180 lbs. Deb: 4/29/44																											
1944	Cin-N	0	3	.000	9	2	0	0	1	16	24	17	3	2	10	9	20.3	9.00	39	.358	.456	1	.333	0	-10	-10	0	-1.7
● **BOB FERGUSON**	Ferguson, Robert Vavasour b: 1/31/1845, Brooklyn, N.Y. d: 5/3/1894, Brooklyn, N.Y. BB/TR, 5'9.5", 149 lbs. Deb: 5/18/1871 MU♦																											
1871	Mut-n	0	0	—	1	0	0	0	0	1	8	9	0		0	0	72.0	27.00	14	.571	.571	38	.241	-0	-3	-3		-0.1
1873	Atl-n	0	1	.000	4	1	1	0	0	19^{1}	41	30	2		2	0	20.0	6.05	50	.380	.391	59	.259	1	-6	-7		-0.2
1874	Atl-n	0	1	.000	1	1	1	0	0	9	12	10	0		3	0	15.0	4.00	51	.273	.319	64	.261	0	-2	-2		-0.1
1875	Har-n	0	0	—	1	0	0	0	0	2	9	7	1		0	0	40.5	22.50	10	.600	.600	88	.240	0	-5	-4		-0.2
1877	Har-N	1	1	.500	3	2	2	0	0	25	38	15	0		2	1	14.4	3.96	61	.352	.364	65	.256	0	-3	-5	0	-0.3
1883	Phi-N	0	0	—	1	0	0	0	0	1	2	2	0		0	0	18.0	9.00	34	.286	.286	85	.258	0	-1	-1	0	0.0
Total	4 n	0	2	.000	7	2	2	0	0	31^{1}	70	56	3		5	0	21.5	7.18	38	.387	.403	295	.254	1	-15	-16		-0.6
Total	2	1	1	.500	4	2	2	0	0	26	40	17	0		2	1	14.5	4.15	59	.348	.359	625	.271	0	-4	-6	0	-0.3
● **RAMON FERMIN**	Fermin, Ramon Antonio (Ventura) b: 11/25/72, San Francisco De Macoris, D.R. BR/TR, 6'3", 180 lbs. Deb: 8/6/95																											
1995	Oak-A	0	0	—	1	0	0	0	0	1^{1}	4	2	0	0	1	0	33.8	13.50	33	.500	.556	0	—	0	-1	-1	0	-0.1
● **ALEX FERNANDEZ**	Fernandez, Alexander b: 8/13/69, Miami Beach, Fla. BR/TR, 6'1", 215 lbs. Deb: 8/2/90																											
1990	Chi-A	5	5	.500	13	13	3	0	0	87^{2}	89	40	6	3	34	61	12.9	3.80	101	.265	.338	0	—	0	1	0	-0	0.0
1991	Chi-A	9	13	.409	34	32	2	0	0	191^{2}	186	100	16	2	88	145	13.0	4.51	88	.259	.341	0	—	0	-9	-12	1	-1.1
1992	Chi-A	8	11	.421	29	29	4	2	0	187^{2}	199	100	21	8	50	95	12.3	4.27	91	.270	.324	0	—	0	-7	-8	2	-0.6
1993	*Chi-A	18	9	.667	34	34	3	1	0	247^{1}	221	95	27	6	67	169	10.7	3.13	134	.240	.296	0	—	0	33	30	2	3.2
1994	Chi-A	11	7	.611	24	24	4	3	0	170^{1}	163	83	25	1	50	122	11.3	3.86	121	.250	.305	0	—	0	18	16	4	1.9
1995	Chi-A	12	8	.600	30	30	5	2	0	203^{2}	200	98	19	0	65	159	11.7	3.80	117	.255	.313	0	—	0	21	16	0	1.4
1996	Chi-A	16	10	.615	35	35	6	1	0	258	248	110	34	7	72	200	11.4	3.45	137	.253	.309	0	—	0	44	39	3	3.7
1997	*Fla-N	17	12	.586	32	32	5	1	0	220^{2}	193	93	25	4	69	183	10.8	3.59	112	.238	.301	10	.152	3	15	11	3	2.0
1999	Fla-N	7	8	.467	24	24	1	0	0	141	135	60	10	4	41	91	11.5	3.38	129	.252	.310	10	.233	4	19	16	2	2.1
2000	Fla-N	4	4	.500	8	8	0	0	0	52^{1}	59	25	7	0	16	27	12.9	4.13	107	.292	.344	2	.118	1	3	2	0	0.3
Total	10	107	87	.552	263	261	33	10	0	1760^{1}	1693	804	190	35	552	1252	11.7	3.74	114	.254	.314	22	.175	8	139	110	16	12.9
● **SID FERNANDEZ**	Fernandez, Charles Sidney b: 10/12/62, Honolulu, Hawaii BL/TL, 6'1", 230 lbs. Deb: 9/20/83																											
1983	LA-N	0	1	.000	2	1	0	0	0	6	7	4	0	1	7	9	22.5	6.00	60	.280	.455	1	1.000	0	-2	-2	0	-0.2
1984	NY-N	6	6	.500	15	15	0	0	0	90	74	40	8	0	34	62	10.8	3.50	101	.226	.299	5	.179	-0	1	0	-2	-0.2
1985	NY-N	9	9	.500	26	26	3	0	0	170^{1}	108	56	14	2	80	180	10.0	2.80	124	**.181**	.280	11	.212	2	15	13	-0	1.5
1986	*NY-N★	16	6	.727	32	31	2	1	1	204^{1}	161	82	13	2	91	200	11.2	3.52	101	.216	.303	11	.162	1	5	0	-3	-0.1
1987	NY-N★	12	8	.600	28	27	3	1	0	156	130	75	16	8	67	134	11.8	3.81	99	.224	.313	7	.163	1	5	-0	-3	-0.2
1988	*NY-N	12	10	.545	31	31	1	1	0	187	127	69	15	6	70	189	9.8	3.03	106	**.191**	.274	14	.250	6	9	4	-3	0.8
1989	NY-N	14	5	.737	35	32	6	2	0	219^{1}	157	73	21	6	75	198	9.8	2.83	115	.198	.272	15	.211	4	16	11	-4	1.0
1990	NY-N	9	14	.391	30	30	2	1	0	179^{1}	130	79	18	5	67	181	10.1	3.46	108	**.200**	.280	11	.190	1	7	6	-2	0.6
1991	NY-N	1	3	.250	8	8	0	0	0	44	36	18	4	0	9	31	9.2	2.86	127	.222	.263	2	.154	0	4	4	1	0.4
1992	NY-N	14	11	.560	32	32	5	2	0	214^{2}	162	67	12	4	67	193	9.8	2.73	128	.210	.277	15	.203	2	19	18	-2	2.1
1993	NY-N	5	6	.455	18	18	1	1	0	119^{2}	82	42	17	3	36	81	9.1	2.93	137	.192	.260	3	.094	-1	15	15	-2	0.9
1994	Bal-A	6	6	.500	19	19	2	0	0	115^{1}	109	66	27	2	46	95	12.3	5.15	97	.248	.322	0	—	0	-4	-2	-2	-0.3
1995	Bal-A	0	4	.000	8	7	0	0	0	28	36	26	9	0	17	31	17.0	7.39	64	.305	.393	0	—	0	-8	-8	-1	-1.0
	Phi-N	6	1	.857	11	11	0	0	0	64^{2}	48	25	11	1	21	79	9.7	3.34	127	.200	.267	1	.043	-2	6	6	-2	0.3
1996	Phi-N	3	6	.333	11	11	0	0	0	63	50	25	5	1	26	77	11.0	3.43	126	.215	.296	2	.105	0	6	6	-1	0.7
1997	Hou-N	1	0	1.000	1	1	0	0	0	5	4	2	1	0	2	3	10.8	3.60	111	.211	.286	0	.000	-0	0	0	0	0.0
Total	15	114	96	.543	307	300	25	9	1	1866^{2}	1421	749	191	41	715	1743	10.5	3.36	110	.209	.288	98	.182	15	92	71	-24	6.3
● **OSVALDO FERNANDEZ**	Fernandez, Osvaldo b: 11/4/68, Holguin, Cuba BR/TR, 6'2", 190 lbs. Deb: 4/5/96																											
1996	SF-N	7	13	.350	30	28	2	0	0	171^{2}	193	95	20	10	57	106	13.6	4.61	89	.286	.350	5	.088	-3	-7	-10	1	-1.2
1997	SF-N	3	4	.429	11	11	0	0	0	56^{1}	74	39	9	0	15	31	14.2	4.95	83	.314	.355	0	.000	-1	-5	-6	-1	-0.8
2000	Cin-N	4	3	.571	15	14	1	0	0	79^{2}	69	33	6	2	31	36	11.5	3.62	132	.238	.316	2	.091	-1	9	10	-0	0.7
Total	3	14	20	.412	56	53	3	0	0	307^{2}	336	167	35	12	103	173	13.2	4.42	97	.280	.342	7	.073	-5	-3	-5	-0	-1.3
● **DON FERRARESE**	Ferrarese, Donald Hugh b: 6/19/29, Oakland, Cal. BR/TL, 5'9", 170 lbs. Deb: 4/11/55																											
1955	Bal-A	0	0	—	6	0	0	0	0	9	8	3	0	0	11	5	19.0	3.00	127	.276	.475	0	.000	-0	1	1	-0	0.0
1956	Bal-A	4	10	.286	36	14	3	1	2	102	86	60	8	3	64	81	13.5	5.03	78	.229	.345	1	.036	-3	-10	-13	1	-1.9
1957	Bal-A	1	1	.500	8	2	0	0	0	19	14	13	1	0	12	13	12.3	4.74	76	.200	.317	0	.000	-0	-2	-3	0	-0.3
1958	Cle-A	3	4	.429	28	10	2	0	1	94^{2}	91	45	4	1	46	62	13.1	3.71	98	.254	.341	3	.115	-1	1	-1	-1	-0.3
1959	Cle-A	5	3	.625	15	10	4	0	0	76	58	29	6	1	51	45	13.0	3.20	115	.219	.347	7	.259	2	6	4	0	0.7
1960	Chi-A	0	1	.000	5	0	0	0	0	4	8	8	2	0	9	4	38.3	18.00	21	.400	.586	1	.500	0	-6	-6	-0	-1.1
1961	Phi-N	5	12	.294	42	14	3	1	1	138^{2}	120	64	14	1	68	89	12.3	3.76	108	.234	.325	6	.171	-1	4	5	-3	0.2
1962	Phi-N	0	1	.000	5	0	0	0	0	6^{2}	9	8	1	0	3	6	16.2	8.10	48	.310	.375	1	1.000	0	-3	-3	0	-0.3
	StL-N	1	4	.200	38	0	0	0	1	56^{2}	55	19	2	1	31	45	13.8	2.70	158	.270	.369	1	.200	1	8	9	1	1.0
	Yr	1	5	.167	43	0	0	0	1	63^{1}	64	27	3	1	34	51	14.1	3.27	129	.275	.369	2	.333	1	5	6	1	0.7
Total	8	19	36	.345	183	50	12	2	5	506^{2}	449	249	38	7	295	350	13.3	4.00	98	.241	.347	20	.156	-2	-2	-6	-1	-2.0
● **BILL FERRAZZI**	Ferrazzi, William Joseph b: 4/19/07, W.Quincy, Mass. d: 8/10/93, Gainesville, Fla. BR/TR, 6'2.5", 200 lbs. Deb: 9/7/35																											
1935	Phi-A	1	2	.333	3	2	0	0	0	7	7	5	0	0	5	0	15.4	5.14	88	.269	.387	0	.000	0	-1	-0	0	-0.1
● **TONY FERREIRA**	Ferreira, Anthony Ross b: 10/4/62, Riverside, Cal. BL/TL, 6'1", 160 lbs. Deb: 9/17/85																											
1985	KC-A	0	0	—	2	0	0	0	0	5^{2}	6	5	0	0	2	5	12.7	7.94	52	.273	.333	0	—	0	-2	-2	0	-0.1
● **WES FERRELL**	Ferrell, Wesley Cheek b: 2/2/08, Greensboro, N.C. d: 12/9/76, Sarasota, Fla. BR/TR, 6'2", 195 lbs. Deb: 9/9/27 F♦																											
1927	Cle-A	0	0	—	1	0	0	0	0	1	3	3	0	0	2	0	45.0	27.00	16	.600	.714	0	—	0	-3	-2	-0	-0.1
1928	Cle-A	0	2	.000	2	2	1	0	0	16	15	5	0	0	5	4	11.3	2.25	184	.242	.299	1	.250	1	3	3	0	0.5
1929	Cle-A	21	10	.677	43	25	18	1	5	242^{2}	256	112	7	3	109	100	13.6	3.60	124	.279	.358	22	.237	4	17	22	3	3.2
1930	Cle-A	25	13	.658	43	35	25	1	3	296^{2}	299	141	14	0	106	143	12.3	3.31	146	.262	.325	35	.297	8	44	48	-3	6.0
1931	Cle-A	22	12	.647	40	35	**27**	2	3	276^{1}	276	134	9	3	130	123	13.3	3.75	123	.255	.336	37	.319	17	19	25	5	5.0

YEAR	TM/L	W	L	PCT	G	GS	CG	SH	SV	IP	H	R	HR	HB	BB	SO	RAT	ERA	ERA+	OAV	OOB	BH	AVG	PB	PR	PR+	PD	TPI
1932	Cle-A	23	13	.639	38	34	26	3	1	287^2	299	141	17	0	104	105	12.6	3.66	130	.264	.326	31	.242	5	26	33	1	4.1
1933	Cle-A☆	11	12	.478	28	26	16	1	0	201	225	108	8	2	70	41	13.3	4.21	106	.282	.341	38	.271	7	2	5	1	1.6
1934	Bos-A	14	5	.737	26	23	17	3	1	181	205	87	4	0	49	67	12.6	3.63	132	.282	.327	22	.282	8	17	22	-2	2.6
1935	Bos-A	**25**	14	.641	41	38	**31**	3	0	**322^1**	336	149	16	3	108	110	12.5	3.52	135	.267	.326	52	.347	20	34	41	2	**6.8**
1936	Bos-A	20	15	.571	39	38	**28**	3	0	**301**	330	160	11	6	119	106	13.6	4.19	127	.274	.343	36	.267	11	28	36	-3	4.3
1937	Bos-A	3	6	.333	12	11	5	0	0	73^1	111	66	14	1	34	31	17.9	7.61	62	.348	.412	12	.364	6	-24	-23	2	-1.5
	Was-A☆	11	13	.458	25	24	21	0	0	207^2	214	111	11	2	88	92	13.2	3.94	112	.265	.339	27	.255	5	16	12	-1	1.6
	Yr	14	19	.424	37	35	**26**	0	0	**281**	325	177	25	3	122	123	14.4	4.90	92	.289	.360	39	.281	11	-9	-13	1	0.1
1938	Was-A	13	8	.619	23	22	9	0	0	149	193	111	12	1	68	36	15.8	5.92	76	.311	.380	11	.224	7	-19	-25	1	-2.1
	NY-A	2	2	.500	5	4	1	0	0	30	52	33	6	0	18	7	21.0	8.10	56	.388	.461	2	.167	0	-11	-13	1	-1.1
	Yr	15	10	.600	28	26	10	0	0	179	245	144	18	1	86	43	16.7	6.28	72	.325	.394	13	.213	7	-30	-37	2	-3.2
1939	NY-A	1	2	.333	3	3	1	0	0	19^1	14	10	2	0	17	6	14.4	4.66	94	.219	.383	1	.125	-0	-0	-1	0	-0.1
1940	Bro-N	0	0	—	1	0	0	0	0	4	4	3	0	1	4	0	20.3	6.75	59	.250	.429	0	.000	-0	-1	-1	1	0.0
1941	Bos-N	2	1	.667	4	3	1	0	0	14	13	8	1	1	9	10	14.8	5.14	69	.241	.359	2	.500	2	-2	-2	-0	-0.3
Total	15	193	128	.601	374	323	227	17	13	2623	2845	1382	132	23	1040	985	13.4	4.04	117	.275	.343	329	.280	100	147	188	6	30.5

● **TOM FERRICK** Ferrick, Thomas Jerome b: 1/6/15, New York, N.Y. d: 10/15/96, Lima, Pa. BR/TR, 6'2.5", 220 lbs. Deb: 4/19/41 C

YEAR	TM/L	W	L	PCT	G	GS	CG	SH	SV	IP	H	R	HR	HB	BB	SO	RAT	ERA	ERA+	OAV	OOB	BH	AVG	PB	PR	PR+	PD	TPI
1941	Phi-A	8	10	.444	36	4	2	1	7	119^1	130	61	8	0	33	30	12.3	3.77	111	.275	.322	9	.205	1	5	5	3	1.2
1942	Cle-A	3	2	.600	31	2	2	0	3	81^1	56	20	3	0	32	28	9.7	1.99	173	.200	.282	4	.211	0	**15**	**14**	2	1.2
1946	Cle-A	0	0	—	9	0	0	0	1	18	25	12	3	0	4	9	14.5	5.00	66	.321	.354	2	.667	1	-3	-4	0	-0.1
	StL-A	4	1	.800	25	1	0	0	5	32^1	26	13	1	0	5	13	8.6	2.78	134	.224	.256	0	.000	-1	3	3	0	0.6
	Yr	4	1	.800	34	1	0	0	6	50^1	51	25	4	0	9	22	10.7	3.58	100	.263	.296	2	.286	1	-0	0	0	0.5
1947	Was-A	1	7	.125	31	0	0	0	9	60	57	24	1	0	20	23	11.6	3.15	118	.256	.317	1	.100	-1	4	4	2	0.7
1948	Was-A	2	5	.286	37	0	0	0	10	73^2	75	37	3	0	38	34	13.8	4.15	105	.261	.348	1	.067	-1	1	2	1	0.2
1949	StL-A	6	4	.600	50	0	0	0	6	104^1	102	51	9	1	41	34	12.4	3.88	117	.258	.329	3	.143	-1	4	7	2	0.8
1950	StL-A	1	3	.250	16	0	0	0	2	24	24	15	2	0	7	6	11.6	4.13	120	.267	.320	1	.250	-0	1	2	1	0.4
	*NY-A	8	4	.667	30	0	0	0	9	56^2	49	26	5	0	22	20	11.3	3.65	118	.233	.306	2	.143	0	6	4	0	0.9
	Yr	9	7	.563	46	0	0	0	11	80^2	73	41	7	0	29	26	11.4	3.79	118	.243	.310	3	.167	0	7	6	1	1.3
1951	NY-A	1	1	.500	9	0	0	0	1	12	21	12	4	0	7	3	21.0	7.50	51	.389	.459	1	1.000	1	-5	-5	-0	-0.8
	Was-A	2	0	1.000	22	0	0	0	2	41^2	36	16	3	0	7	17	9.3	2.38	172	.234	.267	2	.286	0	8	8	0	0.5
	Yr	3	1	.750	31	0	0	0	3	53^2	57	28	7	0	14	20	11.9	3.52	115	.274	.320	3	.375	1	4	3	0	-0.3
1952	Was-A	4	3	.571	27	0	0	0	1	50^2	53	19	2	0	11	28	11.4	3.02	118	.273	.312	1	.200	0	4	3	1	0.6
Total	9	40	40	.500	323	7	4	1	56	674	654	306	44	1	227	245	11.8	3.47	117	.256	.317	27	.184	1	42	43	11	6.2

● **BOB FERRIS** Ferris, Robert Eugene b: 5/7/55, Arlington, Va. BR/TR, 6'6", 225 lbs. Deb: 9/12/79

YEAR	TM/L	W	L	PCT	G	GS	CG	SH	SV	IP	H	R	HR	HB	BB	SO	RAT	ERA	ERA+	OAV	OOB	BH	AVG	PB	PR	PR+	PD	TPI
1979	Cal-A	0	0	—	2	0	0	0	0	6	5	2	1	0	3	2	12.0	1.50	272	.217	.308	0	—	0	2	2	0	0.1
1980	Cal-A	0	2	.000	5	3	0	0	0	15^1	23	13	2	0	9	4	18.8	5.87	67	.354	.432	0	—	0	-3	-3	0	-0.4
Total	2	0	2	.000	7	3	0	0	0	21^1	28	15	3	0	12	6	16.9	4.64	86	.318	.400	0	—	0	-1	-2	0	-0.3

● **DAVE FERRISS** Ferriss, David Meadow "Boo" b: 12/5/21, Shaw, Miss. BL/TR, 6'2", 208 lbs. Deb: 4/29/45 C

YEAR	TM/L	W	L	PCT	G	GS	CG	SH	SV	IP	H	R	HR	HB	BB	SO	RAT	ERA	ERA+	OAV	OOB	BH	AVG	PB	PR	PR+	PD	TPI
1945	Bos-A†	21	10	.677	35	31	26	5	2	264^2	263	101	6	7	85	94	12.1	2.96	115	.264	.327	32	.267	11	12	13	5	3.3
1946	*Bos-A☆	25	6	**.806**	40	35	26	6	3	274	274	109	14	3	71	106	11.4	3.25	113	.259	.308	24	.209	2	8	12	0	1.6
1947	Bos-A	12	11	.522	33	28	14	1	0	218^1	241	106	14	7	92	64	14.0	4.04	96	.287	.362	27	.273	7	-8	-4	-1	0.3
1948	Bos-A	7	3	.700	31	9	1	0	3	115^1	127	71	7	7	61	30	15.2	5.23	84	.286	.381	9	.243	2	-12	-10	1	-0.6
1949	Bos-A	0	0	—	4	0	0	0	0	6^2	7	3	1	1	4	1	16.2	4.05	108	.292	.414	1	1.000	1	0	0	-0	0.1
1950	Bos-A	0	0	—	1	0	0	0	0	1	2	2	0	0	1	1	27.0	18.00	27	.500	.600	0	—	0	-1	-1	0	-0.1
Total	6	65	30	.684	144	103	67	12	8	880	914	392	42	25	314	296	12.8	3.64	103	.272	.338	93	.250	23	-2	10	5	4.6

● **CY FERRY** Ferry, Alfred Joseph b: 9/27/1878, Hudson, N.Y. d: 9/27/38, Pittsfield, Mass. BR/TR, 6'1", 170 lbs. Deb: 5/12/04 F

YEAR	TM/L	W	L	PCT	G	GS	CG	SH	SV	IP	H	R	HR	HB	BB	SO	RAT	ERA	ERA+	OAV	OOB	BH	AVG	PB	PR	PR+	PD	TPI
1904	Det-A	0	1	.000	3	1	1	0	0	13	12	9	0	1	11	4	16.6	6.23	41	.245	.393	2	.333	1	-5	-5	0	-0.3
1905	Cle-A	0	0	—	1	1	0	0	0	2	3	3	1	2	0	2	22.5	13.50	19	.333	.455	0	.000	-0	-2	-2	0	-0.1
Total	2	0	1	.000	4	2	1	0	0	15	15	12	1	3	11	6	17.4	7.20	36	.259	.403	2	.286	1	-8	-8	0	-0.4

● **JACK FERRY** Ferry, John Francis b: 4/7/1887, Pittsfield, Mass. d: 8/29/54, Pittsfield, Mass. BR/TR, 5'11", 175 lbs. Deb: 9/4/10 F

YEAR	TM/L	W	L	PCT	G	GS	CG	SH	SV	IP	H	R	HR	HB	BB	SO	RAT	ERA	ERA+	OAV	OOB	BH	AVG	PB	PR	PR+	PD	TPI
1910	Pit-N	1	2	.333	6	3	2	0	0	31	26	10	0	1	8	12	10.2	2.32	133	.230	.287	3	.333	1	2	3	0	0.4
1911	Pit-N	6	4	.600	26	8	4	1	3	85^2	83	35	3	2	27	32	11.8	3.15	109	.260	.322	9	.310	3	2	3	-2	0.4
1912	Pit-N	2	0	1.000	11	3	1	1	1	39	33	21	1	1	23	10	13.2	3.00	109	.234	.345	1	.077	-1	2	1	1	0.0
1913	Pit-N	1	0	1.000	4	0	0	0	0	5	4	3	0	0	2	2	10.8	5.40	56	.286	.375	0	—	0	-1	-1	0	-0.2
Total	4	10	6	.625	47	14	7	2	4	160^2	146	69	4	4	60	56	11.8	3.02	110	.249	.323	13	.255	3	5	5	-1	0.6

● **ALEX FERSON** Ferson, Alexander "Colonel" b: 7/14/1866, Philadelphia, Pa. d: 12/5/57, Boston, Mass. BR/TR, 5'9", 165 lbs. Deb: 5/4/1889

YEAR	TM/L	W	L	PCT	G	GS	CG	SH	SV	IP	H	R	HR	HB	BB	SO	RAT	ERA	ERA+	OAV	OOB	BH	AVG	PB	PR	PR+	PD	TPI
1889	Was-N	17	17	.500	36	34	28	1	0	288^1	319	199	9	12	105	85	13.6	3.90	101	.272	.338	13	.114	-5	4	1	-2	-0.5
1890	Buf-P	1	7	.125	10	10	7	0	0	71	88	66	5	1	40	13	16.4	5.45	75	.291	.376	7	.219	1	-10	-11	0	-0.8
1892	Bal-N	0	1	.000	2	1	1	0	0	9	17	13	1	0	6	8	23.0	11.00	31	.386	.460	0	.000	-1	-8	-7	-0	-0.6
Total	3	18	25	.419	48	45	36	1	0	368^1	424	278	15	13	151	106	14.4	4.37	91	.279	.349	20	.133	-5	-14	-17	-3	-1.9

● **LOU FETTE** Fette, Louis Henry William b: 3/15/07, Alma, Mo. d: 1/3/81, Warrensburg, Mo. BR/TR, 6'1.5", 200 lbs. Deb: 4/26/37

YEAR	TM/L	W	L	PCT	G	GS	CG	SH	SV	IP	H	R	HR	HB	BB	SO	RAT	ERA	ERA+	OAV	OOB	BH	AVG	PB	PR	PR+	PD	TPI
1937	Bos-N	20	10	.667	35	33	23	**5**	0	259	243	93	5	4	81	70	11.4	2.88	124	.251	.311	22	.239	3	30	22	0	2.8
1938	Bos-N	11	13	.458	33	32	17	3	1	239^2	235	95	11	4	79	83	11.9	3.15	109	.258	.320	16	.188	0	17	8	2	0.9
1939	Bos-N★	10	10	.500	27	26	11	**6**	0	146	123	62	7	1	61	35	11.4	2.96	125	.229	.309	3	.061	-4	16	13	3	1.4
1940	Bos-N	0	5	.000	7	5	0	0	0	32^1	38	23	0	1	18	2	15.9	5.57	67	.302	.393	3	.375	1	-6	-7	-1	-0.9
	Bro-N	0	0	—	2	0	0	0	0	3	3	0	0	0	2	0	15.0	0.00	—	.300	.417	0	—	0	1	1	-0	0.0
	Yr	0	5	.000	9	5	0	0	0	35^1	41	23	0	1	20	2	15.8	5.09	73	.301	.395	3	.375	1	-5	-5	-1	-0.9
1945	Bos-N	0	2	.000	5	1	0	0	0	11	16	10	1	1	7	4	19.6	5.73	67	.356	.453	0	.000	-0	-2	-2	0	-0.4
Total	5	41	40	.506	109	97	51	14	1	691	658	283	24	11	248	194	11.9	3.15	113	.253	.321	44	.186	-0	55	35	4	3.8

● **MIKE FETTERS** Fetters, Michael Lee b: 12/19/64, Van Nuys, Cal. BR/TR, 6'4", 212 lbs. Deb: 9/1/89

YEAR	TM/L	W	L	PCT	G	GS	CG	SH	SV	IP	H	R	HR	HB	BB	SO	RAT	ERA	ERA+	OAV	OOB	BH	AVG	PB	PR	PR+	PD	TPI
1989	Cal-A	0	0	—	1	0	0	0	0	3^1	5	4	1	0	1	4	16.2	8.10	47	.333	.375	0	—	0	-2	-2	0	-0.1
1990	Cal-A	1	1	.500	26	2	0	0	1	67^2	77	33	9	2	20	35	13.2	4.12	93	.287	.341	0	—	0	-2	-2	1	0.0
1991	Cal-A	2	5	.286	19	4	0	0	0	44^2	53	29	4	3	28	24	16.9	4.84	85	.305	.410	0	—	0	-4	-4	-1	-0.6
1992	Mil-A	5	1	.833	50	0	0	0	2	62^2	38	15	3	7	24	43	9.9	1.87	206	.185	.292	0	—	0	14	14	1	1.4
1993	Mil-A	3	3	.500	45	0	0	0	0	59^1	59	29	4	2	22	23	12.6	3.34	128	.278	.352	0	—	0	7	6	0	0.6
1994	Mil-A	1	4	.200	42	0	0	0	17	46	41	16	0	1	27	31	13.5	2.54	198	.243	.350	0	—	0	12	12	-0	1.9
1995	Mil-A	0	3	.000	40	0	0	0	22	34^2	40	16	3	0	20	33	15.6	3.38	148	.286	.375	0	—	0	5	6	-1	1.0
1996	Mil-A	3	3	.500	61	0	0	0	32	61^1	65	28	4	1	26	53	13.5	3.38	154	.274	.348	0	—	0	11	12	-0	2.1
1997	Mil-A	1	5	.167	51	0	0	0	6	70^1	62	30	4	1	33	62	12.3	3.45	134	.244	.333	0	—	0	9	9	1	0.8
1998	Oak-A	1	6	.143	48	0	0	0	5	47^1	48	26	3	1	21	34	13.3	3.99	115	.258	.337	0	—	0	3	3	1	0.5
	Ana-A	1	2	.333	12	0	0	0	0	11^1	14	8	2	0	4	9	14.3	5.56	84	.304	.360	0	—	0	-1	-1	-1	-0.2
	Yr	2	8	.200	60	0	0	0	5	58^2	62	34	5	1	25	43	13.5	4.30	107	.267	.341	0	—	0	2	2	1	0.3
1999	Bal-A	1	0	1.000	27	0	0	0	0	31	35	23	5	2	22	22	17.1	5.81	81	.278	.393	0	—	0	-3	-4	-0	-0.2
2000	LA-N	6	2	.750	51	0	0	0	5	50	35	18	7	2	25	40	11.2	3.24	136	.205	.313	0	—	0	8	7	1	1.1
Total	12	25	35	.417	473	6	0	0	90	589^2	572	275	49	22	273	413	13.2	3.59	124	.260	.347	0	—	0	58	57	2	8.3

● **JOHN FICK** Fick, John Ralph b: 5/18/21, Baltimore, Md. d: 6/9/58, Somers Point, N.J. BL/TL, 5'10", 150 lbs. Deb: 7/29/44

YEAR	TM/L	W	L	PCT	G	GS	CG	SH	SV	IP	H	R	HR	HB	BB	SO	RAT	ERA	ERA+	OAV	OOB	BH	AVG	PB	PR	PR+	PD	TPI
1944	Phi-N	0	0	—	4	0	0	0	0	5^1	3	2	0	1	3	2	11.8	3.38	107	.150	.292	0	—	0	0	0	-0	0.0

● **MARK FIDRYCH** Fidrych, Mark Steven "The Bird" b: 8/14/54, Worcester, Mass. BR/TR, 6'3", 175 lbs. Deb: 4/20/76

YEAR	TM/L	W	L	PCT	G	GS	CG	SH	SV	IP	H	R	HR	HB	BB	SO	RAT	ERA	ERA+	OAV	OOB	BH	AVG	PB	PR	PR+	PD	TPI
1976	Det-A★	19	9	.679	31	29	**24**	4	0	250^1	217	76	12	3	53	97	9.8	**2.34**	**159**	.235	.279	0	—	0	33	**36**	5	**4.8**
1977	Det-A†	6	4	.600	11	11	7	1	0	81	82	29	2	1	12	42	10.6	2.89	149	.269	.299	0	—	0	11	12	-1	1.3
1978	Det-A	2	0	1.000	3	3	2	0	0	22	17	6	1	0	5	10	9.0	2.45	158	.213	.259	0	—	0	3	3	1	0.4
1979	Det-A	0	3	.000	4	4	0	0	0	14^2	23	17	3	1	9	5	20.3	10.43	42	.371	.458	0	—	0	-10	-10	-0	-1.4

YEAR	TM/L	W	L	PCT	G	GS	CG	SH	SV	IP	H	R	HR	HB	BB	SO	RAT	ERA	ERA+	OAV	OOB	BH	AVG	PB	PR	PR+	PD	TPI
1980	Det-A	2	3	.400	9	9	1	0	0	44^{1}	58	35	5	1	20	16	16.0	5.68	72	.309	.378	0	—	0	-8	-8	1	-0.7
Total	5	29	19	.604	58	56	34	5	0	412^{1}	397	163	23	6	99	170	11.0	3.10	126	.255	.302	0	—	0	29	35	5	4.4
● **CLARENCE FIEBER** Fieber, Clarence Thomas "Lefty" b: 9/4/13, San Francisco, Cal d: 8/20/85, Redwood City, Cal BL/TL, 6'4", 187 lbs. Deb: 5/18/32																												
1932	Chi-A	1	0	1.000	3	0	0	0	0	5^{1}	6	1	0	0	3	1	15.2	1.69	256	.273	.360	0	—	0	2	2	0	0.3
● **JIM FIELD** Field, James C. b: 4/24/1863, Philadelphia, Pa. d: 5/13/53, Atlantic City, N.J 6'1", 170 lbs. Deb: 6/2/1883 ♦																												
1890	Roc-a	1	0	1.000	2	1	1	0	1	9^{2}	7	4	0	1	4	2	11.2	2.79	128	.194	.293	38	.202	1	1	1	-0	0.1
● **JOCKO FIELDS** Fields, John Joseph b: 10/20/1864, Cork, Ireland d: 10/14/50, Jersey City, N.J. BR/TR, 5'10", 160 lbs. Deb: 5/31/1887 ♦																												
1887	Pit-N	0	0	—	1	0	0	0	0	1	2	3	0	0	2	0	18.0	0.00	—	.286	.286	51	.298	0	0	0	-0	0.0
● **LOU FIENE** Fiene, Louis Henry "Big Finn" b: 12/29/1884, Ft.Dodge, Iowa d: 12/22/64, Chicago, Ill. BR/TR, 6', 175 lbs. Deb: 5/7/06																												
1906	Chi-A	1	1	.500	6	2	1	0	0	31	35	17	0	4	9	12	13.9	2.90	87	.287	.356	2	.200	0	-1	-1	0	-0.1
1907	Chi-A	0	1	.000	6	1	1	0	1	26	30	17	0	2	7	15	13.5	4.15	58	.291	.348	2	.182	-0	-5	-5	0	-0.3
1908	Chi-A	0	1	.000	1	1	1	0	0	9	9	7	0	0	1	3	10.0	4.00	58	.257	.278	0	.000	-0	-2	-2	0	-0.2
1909	Chi-A	2	5	.286	13	6	4	0	0	72	75	37	1	5	18	24	12.3	4.13	57	.284	.341	2	.069	-2	-13	-15	1	-1.5
Total	4	3	8	.273	26	10	7	0	1	138	149	78	1	11	35	54	12.7	3.85	62	.284	.342	6	.113	-2	-20	-24	2	-2.1
● **DANNY FIFE** Fife, Danny Wayne b: 10/5/49, Harrisburg, Ill. BR/TR, 6'3", 175 lbs. Deb: 8/18/73																												
1973	Min-A	3	2	.600	10	7	1	0	0	51^{2}	54	26	2	3	29	18	15.0	4.35	91	.270	.371	0	—	0	-3	-2	-0	-0.2
1974	Min-A	0	0	—	4	0	0	0	0	4^{2}	10	11	0	1	4	3	28.9	17.36	22	.417	.517	0	—	0	-7	-7	-0	-0.4
Total	2	3	2	.600	14	7	1	0	0	56^{1}	64	37	2	4	33	21	16.1	5.43	73	.286	.387	0	—	0	-10	-9	-0	-0.6
● **JACK FIFIELD** Fifield, John Proctor b: 10/5/1871, Enfield, N.H. d: 11/27/39, Syracuse, N.Y. BR/TR, 5'11", 160 lbs. Deb: 4/28/1897																												
1897	Phi-N	5	18	.217	27	26	21	0	0	210^{2}	263	163	8	9	80	38	15.0	5.51	76	.303	.368	18	.234	3	-28	-32	1	-2.3
1898	Phi-N	11	9	.550	21	21	18	2	0	171^{1}	170	91	2	18	60	31	13.0	3.31	104	.257	.336	7	.109	-4	6	3	-3	-0.4
1899	Phi-N	3	8	.273	14	11	9	1	1	92^{2}	110	64	0	4	36	8	14.6	4.08	90	.294	.362	9	.257	1	-2	-4	1	-0.3
	Was-N	2	4	.333	6	6	6	0	0	47	73	44	1	2	17	12	17.6	6.13	64	.353	.407	4	.200	-0	-12	-11	-1	-1.1
	Yr	5	12	.294	20	17	15	1	1	139^{2}	183	108	1	6	53	20	15.6	4.77	79	.315	.378	13	.236	1	-14	-16	-0	-1.4
Total	3	21	39	.350	68	64	54	3	1	521^{2}	616	362	11	33	193	89	14.5	4.59	83	.292	.360	38	.194	-0	-37	-46	-2	-4.1
● **FRANK FIGGEMEIER** Figgemeier, Frank Y. b: 4/22/1874, St.Louis, Mo. d: 4/15/15, St.Louis, Mo. Deb: 9/25/1894																												
1894	Phi-N	0	1	.000	1	1	1	0	0	8	12	14	1	3	4	2	21.4	11.25	45	.343	.452	1	.333	0	-5	-6	0	-0.4
● **ED FIGUEROA** Figueroa, Eduardo (Padilla) b: 10/14/48, Ciales, P.R. BR/TR, 6'1", 190 lbs. Deb: 4/9/74																												
1974	Cal-A	2	8	.200	25	12	5	1	0	105^{1}	119	46	3	4	36	49	13.6	3.67	94	.294	.357	0	—	0	-1	-3	0	-0.2
1975	Cal-A	16	13	.552	33	32	16	2	0	244^{2}	213	96	14	5	84	139	11.1	2.91	122	.233	.301	0	—	0	24	19	1	2.2
1976	*NY-A	19	10	.655	34	34	14	4	0	256^{2}	237	101	13	3	94	119	11.7	3.02	113	.246	.315	0	—	0	14	12	-3	0.9
1977	*NY-A	16	11	.593	32	32	12	2	0	239^{1}	228	102	19	3	75	104	11.5	3.57	111	.252	.312	0	—	0	13	11	-2	0.9
1978	*NY-A	20	9	.690	35	35	12	2	0	253	233	96	22	3	77	92	11.1	2.99	122	.248	.307	0	—	0	22	19	-0	2.0
1979	NY-A	4	6	.400	16	16	4	1	0	104^{2}	109	49	6	0	35	42	12.4	4.13	99	.275	.333	0	—	0	1	-0	0	0.0
1980	NY-A	3	3	.500	15	9	0	0	1	58	90	47	3	1	24	16	17.8	6.98	56	.363	.421	0	—	0	-19	-20	0	-1.8
	Tex-A	0	7	.000	8	8	0	0	0	39^{2}	62	29	9	0	12	9	16.8	5.90	66	.365	.407	0	—	0	-8	-9	1	-1.3
	Yr	3	10	.231	23	17	0	0	1	97^{2}	152	76	12	1	36	25	17.4	6.54	60	.364	.415	0	—	0	-27	-29	1	-3.1
1981	Oak-A	0	0	—	2	1	0	0	0	8^{1}	8	5	1	0	6	1	15.1	5.40	65	.258	.378	0	—	0	-2	-2	-0	-0.1
Total	8	80	67	.544	200	179	63	12	1	1309^{2}	1299	571	90	19	443	571	12.1	3.51	105	.261	.324	0	—	0	46	25	-4	2.6
● **NELSON FIGUEROA** Figueroa, Nelson Walter b: 5/18/74, Brooklyn, N.Y. BB/TR, 6'1", 155 lbs. Deb: 6/3/2000																												
2000	Ari-N	0	1	.000	3	3	0	0	0	15^{2}	17	13	4	0	5	7	12.6	7.47	62	.283	.338	1	.333	0	-5	-5	-0	-0.2
● **TOM FILER** Filer, Thomas Carson b: 12/1/56, Philadelphia, Pa. BR/TR, 6'1", 198 lbs. Deb: 6/8/82																												
1982	Chi-N	1	2	.333	8	8	0	0	0	40^{2}	50	25	5	0	18	15	15.0	5.53	68	.301	.370	1	.083	-0	-9	-8	2	-0.4
1985	Tor-A	7	0	1.000	11	9	0	0	0	48^{2}	38	21	6	0	18	24	10.4	3.88	108	.222	.296	0	—	0	1	2	-1	0.2
1988	Mil-A	5	8	.385	19	16	2	1	0	101^{2}	108	54	8	1	33	39	12.6	4.43	90	.281	.339	0	—	0	-5	-5	3	-0.3
1989	Mil-A	7	3	.700	13	13	0	0	0	72^{1}	74	30	6	4	23	20	12.6	3.61	107	.271	.337	0	—	0	2	2	0	0.3
1990	Mil-A	2	3	.400	7	4	0	0	0	22	26	17	2	0	9	8	14.3	6.14	63	.289	.354	0	—	0	-5	-6	-1	-1.1
1992	NY-N	0	1	.000	9	1	0	0	0	22	18	8	2	0	6	9	9.8	2.05	170	.222	.276	0	.000	-0	4	4	0	0.2
Total	6	22	17	.564	67	51	2	1	0	307^{1}	314	155	29	5	107	115	12.5	4.25	92	.269	.333	1	.067	-1	-12	-11	5	-1.1
● **EDDIE FILES** Files, Charles Edward b: 5/19/1883, Portland, Me. d: 5/10/54, Cornish, Maine BR/TR, Deb: 10/3/08																												
1908	Phi-A	0	0	—	2	0	0	0	0	9	8	7	0	2	3	6	13.0	6.00	43	.286	.394	0	.000	-0	-4	-3	-0	-0.2
● **MARC FILLEY** Filley, Marcus Lucius b: 2/28/12, Lansingburgh, N.Y. d: 1/20/95, Yarmouth, Maine BR/TR, 5'11", 172 lbs. Deb: 4/19/34																												
1934	Was-A	0	0	—	1	0	0	0	0	0^{1}	2	1	0	0	0	0	54.0	27.00	16	.667	.667	0	—	0	-1	-1	0	0.0
● **DANA FILLINGIM** Fillingim, Dana b: 11/6/1893, Columbus, Ga. d: 2/3/61, Tuskegee, Ala. BL/TR, 5'10", 175 lbs. Deb: 8/2/15																												
1915	Phi-A	0	5	.000	8	4	1	0	0	39^{1}	42	25	0	1	32	17	17.2	3.43	85	.313	.449	2	.167	-0	-2	-2	-0	-0.3
1918	Bos-N	7	6	.538	14	13	10	4	0	113	99	37	0	5	28	29	10.5	2.23	120	.243	.300	9	.214	0	7	6	-0	0.7
1919	Bos-N	6	13	.316	32	18	9	0	2	186^{1}	185	80	2	2	39	50	10.9	3.38	85	.270	.312	16	.246	1	-10	-11	2	-0.7
1920	Bos-N	12	21	.364	37	31	22	2	0	272	292	123	8	3	79	66	12.4	3.11	98	.287	.340	16	.174	-2	1	-2	5	0.2
1921	Bos-N	15	10	.600	44	23	11	**3**	1	239^{2}	249	108	10	2	56	54	11.5	3.45	106	.272	.316	21	.247	5	9	5	-1	0.9
1922	Bos-N	5	9	.357	25	12	5	1	2	117	143	74	6	1	37	25	13.9	4.54	88	.311	.363	6	.158	-2	-6	-7	-1	-1.0
1923	Bos-N	1	9	.100	35	12	1	0	0	100^{1}	141	74	6	1	36	27	16.0	5.20	77	.345	.399	7	.226	1	-13	-14	-0	-1.1
1925	Phi-N	1	0	1.000	5	1	0	0	0	8^{2}	19	12	0	0	6	2	26.0	10.38	46	.432	.500	0	.000	0	-6	-5	0	-0.4
Total	8	47	73	.392	200	114	59	10	5	1076^{1}	1170	533	32	15	313	270	12.5	3.56	93	.287	.340	77	.209	4	-21	-31	5	-1.7
● **PETE FILSON** Filson, William Peter b: 9/28/58, Darby, Pa. BB/TL, 6'2", 195 lbs. Deb: 5/15/82																												
1982	Min-A	0	2	.000	5	3	0	0	0	12^{1}	17	12	2	0	8	10	18.2	8.76	49	.321	.410	0	—	0	-6	-6	-0	-0.8
1983	Min-A	4	1	.800	26	8	0	0	1	90	87	34	9	1	29	49	11.7	3.40	125	.252	.312	0	—	0	7	8	-2	0.3
1984	Min-A	6	5	.545	55	7	0	0	1	118^{2}	106	56	14	3	54	59	12.4	4.10	103	.238	.325	0	—	0	-1	1	-1	0.0
1985	Min-A	4	5	.444	40	6	1	0	2	95^{2}	93	42	13	0	30	42	11.6	3.67	120	.251	.307	0	—	0	5	7	-1	0.6
1986	Min-A	0	0	—	4	0	0	0	0	6^{1}	13	4	1	1	2	4	22.7	5.68	76	.406	.457	0	—	0	-1	-1	-0	-0.1
	Chi-A	0	1	.000	3	1	0	0	0	11^{2}	14	9	4	0	5	4	14.7	6.17	70	.286	.352	0	—	0	-3	-2	-0	-0.2
	Yr	0	1	.000	7	1	0	0	0	18	27	13	5	1	7	8	17.5	6.00	72	.333	.393	0	—	0	-4	-3	-1	-0.3
1987	NY-A	1	0	1.000	7	2	0	0	0	22	26	10	2	1	9	10	14.7	3.27	134	.299	.371	0	—	0	3	3	1	0.2
1990	KC-A	0	4	.000	8	7	0	0	0	35	42	31	6	2	13	9	14.7	5.91	65	.282	.348	0	—	0	-8	-8	-1	-0.9
Total	7	15	18	.455	148	34	1	0	4	391^{2}	398	198	51	8	150	187	12.8	4.18	102	.260	.329	0	—	0	-4	3	-4	-0.9
● **JOEL FINCH** Finch, Joel D b: 8/20/56, South Bend, Ind. BR/TR, 6'2", 175 lbs. Deb: 6/12/79																												
1979	Bos-A	0	3	.000	15	7	0	0	0	57^{1}	65	31	5	1	25	25	14.3	4.87	91	.289	.363	0	.000	-0	-4	-3	1	-0.1
● **BILL FINCHER** Fincher, William Allen b: 5/26/1894, Atlanta, Ga. d: 5/7/46, Shreveport, La. BR/TR, 6'1", 180 lbs. Deb: 4/23/16																												
1916	StL-A	0	1	.000	12	1	0	0	0	21	22	11	0	0	7	5	12.4	2.14	128	.282	.341	1	.250	0	2	1	1	0.3
● **TOMMY FINE** Fine, Thomas Morgan b: 10/10/14, Cleburne, Tex. BB/TR, 6', 180 lbs. Deb: 4/26/47																												
1947	Bos-A	1	2	.333	9	7	1	0	0	36	41	24	0	1	19	10	15.3	5.50	71	.285	.372	3	.333	1	-7	-6	2	-0.2
1950	StL-A	0	1	.000	14	0	0	0	0	36^{2}	53	38	6	0	25	6	19.1	8.10	61	.342	.433	4	.333	1	-14	-12	-0	-0.4
Total	2	1	3	.250	23	7	1	0	0	72^{2}	94	62	6	1	44	16	17.2	6.81	65	.314	.404	7	.333	2	-22	-18	1	-0.6
● **ROLLIE FINGERS** Fingers, Roland Glen b: 8/25/46, Steubenville, Ohio BR/TR, 6'4", 195 lbs. Deb: 9/15/68 H																												
1968	Oak-A	0	0	—	1	0	0	0	0	1^{1}	4	4	1	1	1	0	40.5	27.00	10	.571	.667	0	—	0	-4	-4	-0	-0.2
1969	Oak-A	6	7	.462	60	8	1	1	12	119	116	60	13	4	41	61	12.2	3.71	93	.257	.325	5	.200	0	-1	-4	2	-0.2

YEAR	TM/L	W	L	PCT	G	GS	CG	SH	SV	IP	H	R	HR	HB	BB	SO	RAT	ERA	ERA+	OAV	OOB	BH	AVG	PB	PR	PR+	PD	TPI
1970	Oak-A	7	9	.438	45	19	1	0	2	148	137	65	13	2	48	79	11.4	3.65	97	.250	.312	4	.103	-0	1	-2	1	-0.2
1971	*Oak-A	4	6	.400	48	8	2	1	17	129^1	94	46	14	8	30	98	9.2	2.99	112	.207	.268	7	.212	1	7	5	2	0.9
1972	*Oak-A	11	9	.550	65	0	0	0	21	111^1	85	35	8	1	32	113	9.5	2.51	114	.212	.272	6	.316	3	7	5	-0	1.3
1973	*Oak-A★	7	8	.467	62	2	0	0	22	126^2	107	41	5	4	39	110	10.7	1.92	185	.226	.290	0	.000	-0	27	25	-1	3.7
1974	*Oak-A★	9	5	.643	**76**	0	0	0	18	119	104	41	5	1	29	95	10.1	2.65	126	.240	.289	0	—	0	13	10	2	1.6
1975	*Oak-A☆	10	6	.625	**75**	0	0	0	24	126^2	95	43	13	6	33	115	9.5	2.98	122	.213	.276	0	.000	-0	11	10	0	1.5
1976	Oak-A☆	13	11	.542	70	0	0	0	20	134^2	118	40	3	7	40	113	11.0	2.47	136	.243	.310	0	—	0	16	14	2	3.1
1977	SD-N	8	9	.471	**78**	0	0	0	**35**	132^1	123	47	12	1	36	113	10.9	2.99	118	.248	.300	1	.050	-2	14	9	-0	1.3
1978	SD-N★	6	13	.316	67	0	0	0	**37**	107^1	84	33	4	1	29	72	9.6	2.52	132	.212	.267	2	.167	-0	13	10	0	2.3
1979	SD-N	9	9	.500	54	0	0	0	13	83^2	91	47	7	1	37	65	13.9	4.52	78	.281	.356	1	.083	-1	-7	-10	-1	-2.1
1980	SD-N	11	9	.550	66	0	0	0	23	103	101	35	3	0	32	69	11.6	2.80	123	.263	.320	5	.278	2	9	8	-1	1.8
1981	*Mil-A★	6	3	.667	47	0	0	0	**28**	78	55	9	3	1	13	61	8.0	1.04	330	.198	.236	0	—	0	**23**	**22**	0	**4.5**
1982	Mil-A★	5	6	.455	50	0	0	0	29	79^2	63	23	5	1	20	71	9.5	2.60	146	.220	.273	0	—	0	13	11	0	2.4
1984	Mil-A	1	2	.333	33	0	0	0	23	46	38	13	5	0	13	40	10.0	1.96	197	.213	.267	0	—	0	10	10	-0	1.6
1985	Mil-A	1	6	.143	47	0	0	0	17	55^1	59	33	9	0	19	24	12.7	5.04	83	.272	.331	0	—	0	-5	-5	1	-0.8
Total	17	114	118	.491	944	37	4	2	341	1701^1	1474	615	123	39	492	1299	10.6	2.90	119	.235	.295	31	.172	2	146	113	6	22.5
● **HERMAN FINK**	Fink, Herman Adam b: 8/22/11, Concord, N.C. d: 8/24/80, Salisbury, N.C. BR/TR, 6'2", 198 lbs. Deb: 9/16/35																											
1935	Phi-A	0	3	.000	5	3	0	0	0	15^2	18	19	0	1	10	2	16.7	9.19	49	.290	.397	1	.200	-0	-8	-8	0	-1.1
1936	Phi-A	8	16	.333	34	24	9	0	3	188^2	222	126	18	0	78	53	14.3	5.39	95	.294	.360	8	.125	-4	-7	-6	-2	-1.1
1937	Phi-A	2	1	.667	28	3	1	0	1	80	82	43	6	1	35	18	13.3	4.05	116	.263	.339	5	.208	-1	5	6	-0	0.2
Total	3	10	20	.333	67	30	10	0	4	284^1	322	188	24	2	123	73	14.1	5.22	95	.285	.356	14	.151	-5	-11	-8	-2	-2.0
● **PEMBROKE FINLAYSON**	Finlayson, Pembroke b: 7/31/1888, Cheraw, S.C. d: 3/6/12, Brooklyn, N.Y. BR/TR, Deb: 6/6/08																											
1908	Bro-N	0	0	—	1	0	0	0	0	0^1	0	5	0	0	4	0	108.0	135.00	2	.000	.800	0	—	0	-5	-5	0	-0.2
1909	Bro-N	0	0	—	1	0	0	0	0	7	7	4	0	0	4	2	14.1	5.14	50	.212	.297	0	.000	-0	-2	-2	-0	-0.2
Total	2	0	0	—	2	0	0	0	0	7^1	7	9	0	0	8	2	18.4	11.05	23	.206	.357	0	.000	-0	-7	-7	-0	-0.4
● **CHUCK FINLEY**	Finley, Charles Edward b: 11/26/62, Monroe, La. BL/TL, 6'6", 214 lbs. Deb: 5/29/86																											
1986	*Cal-A	3	1	.750	25	0	0	0	0	46^1	40	17	2	1	23	37	12.4	3.30	125	.235	.330	0	—	0	5	4	1	0.4
1987	Cal-A	2	7	.222	35	3	0	0	0	90^2	102	54	7	3	43	63	14.7	4.67	93	.287	.369	0	—	0	-2	-4	-0	-0.3
1988	Cal-A	9	15	.375	31	31	2	0	0	194^1	191	95	15	6	82	111	12.9	4.17	93	.263	.343	0	—	0	-4	-7	-1	-0.9
1989	Cal-A☆	16	9	.640	29	29	9	1	0	199^2	171	64	13	2	82	156	11.5	2.57	149	.233	.312	0	—	0	29	28	-3	3.1
1990	Cal-A★	18	9	.667	32	32	7	2	0	236	210	77	17	2	81	177	11.2	2.40	159	.243	.309	0	—	0	40	38	-2	4.1
1991	Cal-A	18	9	.667	34	34	4	2	0	227^1	205	102	23	8	101	171	12.4	3.80	108	.244	.331	0	—	0	8	8	-3	0.6
1992	Cal-A	7	12	.368	31	31	4	1	0	204^1	212	99	24	3	98	124	13.8	3.96	101	.277	.362	0	—	0	-0	1	-3	-0.2
1993	Cal-A	16	14	.533	35	35	**13**	2	0	251^1	243	108	22	6	82	187	11.9	3.15	143	.253	.316	0	—	0	33	37	-2	3.9
1994	Cal-A	10	10	.500	25	25	7	2	0	**183^1**	178	95	21	3	71	148	12.4	4.32	113	.260	.332	0	—	0	10	11	-2	0.9
1995	Cal-A☆	15	12	.556	32	32	2	1	0	203	192	106	20	7	93	195	12.9	4.21	112	.249	.335	0	—	0	11	11	-2	1.1
1996	*Cal-A★	15	16	.484	35	35	4	1	0	238	241	124	27	11	94	215	13.1	4.16	120	.263	.339	0	—	0	22	22	-1	2.4
1997	Ana-A	13	6	.684	25	25	3	1	0	164	152	79	20	5	65	155	12.2	4.23	108	.248	.325	0	.000	-1	6	6	-1	0.5
1998	Ana-A	11	9	.550	34	34	1	1	0	223^1	210	97	20	6	109	212	13.1	3.39	139	.246	.336	0	.000	-0	32	32	-0	2.5
1999	Ana-A	12	11	.522	33	33	1	0	0	213^1	197	117	23	8	94	200	12.6	4.43	110	.246	.331	0	.000	-0	10	10	0	0.9
2000	Cle-A☆	16	11	.593	34	34	3	0	0	218	211	108	23	2	101	189	13.0	4.17	120	.256	.339	0	.000	-1	18	20	1	1.9
Total	15	181	151	.545	470	413	60	14	0	2893	2755	1342	277	73	1219	2340	12.6	3.76	118	.253	.333	0	.000	-2	218	219	-20	20.9
● **HAPPY FINNERAN**	Finneran, Joseph Ignatius "Smokey Joe" b: 10/29/1891, E.Orange, N.J. d: 2/3/42, Orange, N.J. BR/TR, 5'10.5", 169 lbs. Deb: 8/20/12																											
1912	Phi-N	0	2	.000	14	4	0	0	1	46^1	50	27	2	1	10	10	11.8	2.53	144	.282	.324	2	.200	0	5	5	-0	0.3
1913	Phi-N	0	0	—	3	0	0	0	0	5	12	7	0	0	2	0	25.2	7.20	46	.462	.500	2	.667	1	-2	-2	-0	0.0
1914	Bro-F	12	11	.522	27	23	13	2	1	175^1	153	77	6	6	60	54	11.2	3.18	90	.237	.308	7	.127	-5	-6	-6	-1	-1.3
1915	Bro-F	10	12	.455	37	24	12	1	2	215^1	197	90	2	9	87	68	12.2	2.80	97	.249	.331	11	.149	-5	-2	-2	-1	-0.7
1918	Det-A	0	2	.000	5	2	0	0	1	13^2	22	17	0	0	8	2	19.8	9.88	27	.393	.469	0	.000	-0	-11	-11	1	-1.5
	NY-A	3	6	.333	23	13	4	0	0	114^1	134	52	7	2	35	34	13.5	3.78	75	.305	.359	9	.231	1	-13	-12	-1	-0.9
	Yr	3	8	.273	28	15	4	0	1	128	156	69	7	2	43	36	14.1	4.43	63	.315	.372	9	.214	0	-23	-23	-0	-2.4
Total	5	25	33	.431	109	66	29	3	5	570	568	270	17	18	202	168	12.4	3.30	87	.266	.335	31	.168	-7	-29	-27	-2	-4.1
● **GAR FINNVOLD**	Finnvold, Anders Gar b: 3/11/68, Boynton Beach, Fla. BR/TR, 6'5", 195 lbs. Deb: 5/10/94																											
1994	Bos-A	0	4	.000	8	8	0	0	0	36^1	45	27	4	3	15	17	15.6	5.94	85	.304	.380	0	—	0	-5	-3	-1	-0.4
● **TONY FIORE**	Fiore, Anthony James b: 10/12/71, Oak Park, Ill. BR/TR, 6'4", 210 lbs. Deb: 8/27/2000																											
2000	TB-A	1	1	.500	11	0	0	0	0	15	21	16	3	2	9	8	19.2	8.40	59	.333	.432	0	—	0	-6	-6	-0	-0.6
● **STEVE FIREOVID**	Fireovid, Stephen John b: 6/6/57, Bryan, Ohio BB/TR, 6'2", 195 lbs. Deb: 9/6/81																											
1981	SD-N	0	1	.000	5	4	0	0	0	26^1	30	8	2	0	7	11	12.6	2.73	119	.294	.339	1	.143	-0	2	2	0	0.1
1983	SD-N	0	0	—	3	0	0	0	0	5	4	2	0	0	2	1	10.8	1.80	194	.235	.316	0	—	0	1	1	0	0.1
1984	Phi-N	0	0	—	5	0	0	0	0	5^2	4	1	0	0	0	3	6.4	1.59	229	.200	.200	0	—	0	1	1	0	0.1
1985	Chi-A	0	0	—	4	0	0	0	0	7	17	4	0	0	2	2	24.4	5.14	84	.472	.500	0	—	0	-1	-1	-0	-0.1
1986	Sea-A	2	0	1.000	10	1	0	0	0	21	28	11	1	1	4	10	14.1	4.29	99	.333	.371	0	—	0	-0	-0	0	0.0
1992	Tex-A	1	0	1.000	3	0	0	0	0	6^2	10	5	0	0	4	0	18.9	4.05	94	.370	.452	0	—	0	-0	-0	0	0.0
Total	6	3	1	.750	31	5	0	0	0	71^2	93	31	3	1	19	27	14.2	3.39	110	.325	.369	1	.143	-0	3	3	0	0.2
● **TED FIRTH**	Firth, John E. b: 5/6/1855, Lowell, Mass. d: 6/23/02, Tewksbury, Mass. Deb: 8/15/1884																											
1884	Ric-a	0	1	.000	1	1	1	0	0	9	14	13	0	0	5	0	19.0	8.00	41	.326	.396	1	.333	0	-5	-5	-0	-0.3
● **CARL FISCHER**	Fischer, Charles William b: 11/5/05, Medina, N.Y. d: 12/10/63, Medina, N.Y. BR/TL, 6', 180 lbs. Deb: 7/19/30																											
1930	Was-A	1	1	.500	8	4	1	0	1	33^1	37	22	0	2	18	21	15.4	4.86	95	.285	.380	0	.000	-1	-1	-1	1	-0.1
1931	Was-A	13	9	.591	46	23	7	0	3	191	207	98	12	2	80	96	13.6	4.38	98	.273	.344	8	.121	-5	-0	-2	-4	-1.0
1932	Was-A	3	2	.600	12	7	1	1	1	50^2	57	30	4	0	31	23	15.6	4.97	87	.282	.378	3	.200	1	-3	-4	-2	-0.4
	StL-A	3	7	.300	24	11	4	0	0	97	122	65	12	0	45	35	15.5	5.57	87	.310	.380	9	.265	0	-12	-7	-1	-0.7
	Yr	6	9	.400	36	18	5	1	1	147^2	179	95	16	0	76	58	15.5	5.36	87	.300	.379	12	.245	1	-15	-11	-3	-1.1
1933	Det-A	11	15	.423	35	22	9	0	3	182^2	176	86	5	3	84	93	13.0	3.55	122	.251	.334	9	.145	-3	15	15	-2	1.4
1934	Det-A	6	4	.600	20	15	4	1	1	95	107	50	5	1	38	39	13.8	4.36	101	.288	.356	2	.065	-3	1	0	-2	-0.4
1935	Det-A	0	1	.000	3	1	0	0	0	12	16	8	2	1	5	7	16.5	6.00	69	.320	.393	0	.000	-0	-2	-3	-0	-0.2
	Chi-A	5	5	.500	24	11	3	1	0	88^2	102	67	7	2	39	31	14.5	6.19	75	.283	.356	4	.190	-0	-17	-15	-1	-1.5
	Yr	5	6	.455	27	12	3	1	0	100^2	118	75	9	3	44	38	14.8	6.17	74	.287	.360	4	.174	-1	-19	-17	-1	-1.7
1937	Cle-A	0	1	.000	2	0	0	0	0	0^2	2	2	0	0	1	1	40.5	27.00	17	.667	.750	0	—	0	-2	-2	0	-0.3
	Was-A	4	5	.444	17	11	2	0	2	72	74	43	6	0	31	30	13.1	4.38	101	.270	.344	3	.136	-1	2	0	-2	-0.2
	Yr	4	6	.400	19	11	2	0	2	72^2	76	45	6	0	32	31	13.4	4.58	97	.274	.350	3	.136	-1	0	-1	-2	-0.5
Total	7	46	50	.479	191	105	31	3	11	823	900	471	53	11	372	376	14.0	4.63	96	.277	.354	38	.145	-12	-18	-18	-14	-3.4
● **HANK FISCHER**	Fischer, Henry William "Bulldog" b: 1/11/40, Yonkers, N.Y. BR/TR, 6', 190 lbs. Deb: 4/16/62																											
1962	Mil-N	2	3	.400	29	0	0	0	4	37^1	43	27	4	0	20	29	15.2	5.30	72	.291	.375	0	.000	-0	-6	-6	-0	-0.9
1963	Mil-N	4	3	.571	31	6	1	0	0	74^1	74	46	8	5	28	72	13.0	4.96	65	.262	.340	2	.105	-0	-14	-15	-1	-1.4
1964	Mil-N	11	10	.524	37	28	9	5	2	168^1	177	95	17	3	39	99	11.7	4.01	88	.265	.309	8	.154	1	-9	-9	-1	-1.1
1965	Mil-N	8	9	.471	31	19	2	0	0	122^2	126	61	18	3	39	79	12.3	3.89	91	.270	.331	4	.108	-1	-5	-5	-2	-1.0
1966	Atl-N	2	3	.400	14	8	0	0	0	48^1	55	23	3	1	14	22	13.0	3.91	93	.296	.348	0	.000	-2	-2	-1	-1	-0.4
	Cin-N	0	6	.000	11	9	0	0	0	38	53	31	3	3	15	24	16.8	6.63	59	.331	.399	1	.091	-1	-13	-11	-0	-1.6
	Yr	2	9	.182	25	17	0	0	0	86^1	108	54	6	4	29	46	14.7	5.11	73	.312	.372	1	.042	-2	-14	-12	-2	-2.0
	Bos-A	2	3	.400	6	5	1	0	0	31	35	12	4	1	11	26	13.6	2.90	131	.287	.351	2	.222	0	2	3	0	0.5
1967	Bos-A	1	2	.333	9	2	1	0	1	26^2	24	15	3	1	8	18	11.1	2.36	148	.229	.289	1	.143	-0	3	3	-0	0.3
Total	6	30	39	.435	168	77	14	5	7	546^2	587	310	60	17	174	369	12.8	4.23	84	.275	.334	18	.118	-3	-43	-41	-5	-5.6

YEAR	TM/L	W	L	PCT	G	GS	CG	SH	SV	IP	H	R	HR	HB	BB	SO	RAT	ERA	ERA+	OAV	OOB	BH	AVG	PB	PR	PR+	PD	TPI
● JEFF FISCHER	Fischer, Jeffrey Thomas b: 8/17/63, W.Palm Beach, Fla. BR/TR, 6'3", 185 lbs. Deb: 6/19/87																											
1987	Mon-N	0	1	.000	4	2	0	0	0	13^2	21	14	3	0	5	6	17.1	8.56	49	.362	.413	1	.200	0	-7	-6	-0	-0.4
1989	LA-N	0	0	—	2	0	0	0	0	3^1	7	5	1	0	0	2	18.9	13.50	25	.438	.438	0	—	0	-4	-4	-0	-0.2
Total	2	0	1	.000	6	2	0	0	0	17	28	19	4	0	5	8	17.5	9.53	42	.378	.418	1	.200	0	-10	-10	-0	-0.6
● RUBE FISCHER	Fischer, Reuben Walter b: 9/19/16, Carlock, S.D. d: 7/16/97, Green Bay, Wis. BR/TR, 6'4", 190 lbs. Deb: 9/12/41																											
1941	NY-N	1	0	1.000	2	1	1	0	0	11	10	3	0	0	6	9	13.1	2.45	151	.238	.333	1	.333	0	1	1	-0	0.1
1943	NY-N	5	10	.333	22	17	4	0	1	130^2	140	69	4	2	59	47	13.8	4.61	75	.281	.360	11	.256	3	-18	-17	-2	-1.6
1944	NY-N	6	14	.300	38	18	2	1	2	128^2	128	83	7	6	87	39	15.5	5.18	71	.266	.384	5	.125	-2	-22	-21	-2	-3.4
1945	NY-N	3	8	.273	31	4	0	0	1	76^2	90	55	6	1	49	27	16.4	5.63	69	.288	.387	4	.211	2	-16	-14	-1	-1.8
1946	NY-N	1	2	.333	15	1	0	0	0	35^2	48	32	3	0	21	14	17.4	6.31	55	.316	.399	1	.111	-1	-11	-11	0	-0.9
Total	5	16	34	.320	108	41	7	1	4	382^2	416	242	20	9	222	136	15.2	5.10	71	.280	.377	22	.193	2	-66	-62	-5	-7.6
● TODD FISCHER	Fischer, Todd Richard b: 9/15/60, Columbus, Ohio BR/TR, 5'10", 170 lbs. Deb: 5/29/86																											
1986	Cal-A	0	0	—	9	0	0	0	0	17	18	8	4	0	8	7	13.8	4.24	97	.286	.366	0	—	0	-0	-0	-0	0.0
● BILL FISCHER	Fischer, William Charles b: 10/11/30, Wausau, Wis. BR/TR, 6', 190 lbs. Deb: 4/21/56 C																											
1956	Chi-A	0	0	—	3	0	0	0	0	1^2	6	4	0	0	1	2	37.8	21.60	19	.545	.583	0	—	0	-3	-3	0	-0.2
1957	Chi-A	7	8	.467	33	11	3	1	1	124	139	50	1	3	35	48	12.8	3.48	107	.291	.344	6	.150	-2	4	4	-1	0.1
1958	Chi-A	2	3	.400	17	3	0	0	0	36^1	43	28	6	0	13	16	13.9	6.69	54	.301	.359	1	.143	-0	-12	-13	1	-1.5
	Det-A	2	4	.333	22	0	0	0	2	30^2	46	34	6	0	13	16	17.3	7.63	53	.362	.421	0	.000	0	-13	-11	0	-2.1
	Was-A	0	3	.000	3	3	0	0	0	21	24	9	1	1	5	10	12.9	3.86	99	.320	.370	1	.200	0	-0	-0	0	0.1
	Yr	4	10	.286	42	6	0	0	2	88	113	71	13	1	31	42	14.8	6.34	60	.328	.385	2	.154	0	-25	-24	2	-3.5
1959	Was-A	9	11	.450	34	29	6	1	0	187^1	211	98	16	4	43	62	12.4	4.28	92	.281	.324	7	.130	-2	-9	-7	4	-0.5
1960	Was-A	3	5	.375	20	7	1	0	0	77	85	45	7	0	17	31	11.9	4.91	79	.281	.320	3	.158	1	-9	-9	1	-0.6
	Det-A	5	3	.625	20	6	1	0	0	55	50	23	6	0	18	24	11.1	3.44	115	.244	.305	4	.364	2	3	3	0	0.7
	Yr	8	8	.500	40	13	2	0	0	132	135	68	13	0	35	55	11.6	4.30	91	.266	.314	7	.233	3	-6	-5	2	0.1
1961	Det-A	3	2	.600	26	1	0	0	3	46^2	54	28	10	0	17	18	13.7	5.01	82	.292	.351	0	.000	-1	-5	-5	-0	-0.6
	KC-A	1	0	1.000	15	0	0	0	2	21	26	9	1	0	6	12	13.7	3.86	108	.321	.368	0	.000	-0	0	1	0	0.0
	Yr	4	2	.667	41	1	0	0	5	67^2	80	37	11	0	23	30	13.7	4.66	89	.301	.356	0	.000	-1	-5	-4	-0	-0.6
1962	KC-A	4	12	.250	34	16	5	0	2	127^2	150	61	16	1	8	38	11.2	3.95	107	.293	.305	4	.105	-2	0	4	-1	0.1
1963	KC-A	9	6	.600	45	2	0	0	3	95^2	86	44	13	3	29	34	11.1	3.57	109	.242	.305	1	.067	-0	1	3	-1	0.4
1964	Min-A	0	1	.000	9	0	0	0	0	7^1	16	6	2	0	5	2	25.8	7.36	49	.471	.538	0	—	0	-3	-3	0	-0.4
Total	9	45	58	.437	281	78	16	2	13	831^1	936	439	85	12	210	313	12.5	4.34	91	.287	.333	27	.136	-4	-46	-36	5	-4.5
● LEO FISHEL	Fishel, Leo b: 12/13/1877, Babylon, N.Y. d: 5/19/60, Hempstead, N.Y. BR/TR, 6', 175 lbs. Deb: 5/3/1899																											
1899	NY-N	0	1	.000	1	1	1	0	0	9	9	7	0	2	6	6	17.0	6.00	63	.257	.395	1	.250	-0	-2	-2	0	-0.2
● FISHER	Fisher b: Johnstown, Pa. Deb: 7/17/1884																											
1884	Phi-U	1	7	.125	8	8	8	0	0	70^2	76	49	0		13	42	11.3	3.57	65	.257	.288	8	.222	-1	-9	-10	-1	-1.0
● FISHER	Fisher b: Philadelphia, Pa. Deb: 8/6/1885																											
1885	Buf-N	0	1	.000	1	1	1	0	0	9	10	9	0		2	4	12.0	5.00	60	.256	.293	0	.000	-1	-2	-2	0	-0.2
● BRIAN FISHER	Fisher, Brian Kevin b: 3/18/62, Honolulu, Hawaii BR/TR, 6'4", 210 lbs. Deb: 5/7/85																											
1985	NY-A	4	4	.500	55	0	0	0	14	98^1	77	32	4	0	29	85	9.7	2.38	168	.216	.275	0	—	0	19	18	0	1.9
1986	NY-A	9	5	.643	62	0	0	0	6	96^2	105	61	14	1	37	67	13.3	4.93	83	.277	.343	0	—	0	-8	-9	-1	-1.4
1987	Pit-N	11	9	.550	37	26	6	3	0	185^1	185	99	27	4	72	117	12.7	4.52	91	.262	.334	11	.190	5	-9	-8	-1	-0.5
1988	Pit-N	8	10	.444	33	22	1	1	1	146^1	157	78	13	5	57	66	13.5	4.61	74	.277	.348	2	.048	-2	-19	-20	-2	-2.7
1989	Pit-N	0	3	.000	9	3	0	0	1	17	25	17	2	0	10	8	18.5	7.94	42	.329	.407	0	.000	-1	-8	-9	-0	-1.5
1990	Hou-N	0	0	—	4	0	0	0	0	5	9	5	1	0	0	1	16.2	7.20	52	.409	.409	0	—	0	-2	-2	-0	-0.1
1992	Sea-A	4	3	.571	22	14	0	0	1	91^1	80	49	9	1	47	26	12.6	4.53	88	.234	.328	0	—	0	-6	-6	-0	-0.4
Total	7	36	34	.514	222	65	7	4	23	640	638	341	70	11	252	370	12.7	4.39	89	.261	.332	13	.124	2	-33	-36	-5	-4.7
● CHAUNCEY FISHER	Fisher, Chauncey Burr "Peach" or "Whoa Bill" b: 1/8/1872, Anderson, Ind. d: 4/27/39, Los Angeles, Cal. BR/TR, 5'11", 175 lbs. Deb: 9/20/1893 F																											
1893	Cle-N	0	2	.000	2	2	2	0	0	18	26	18	0	0	9	9	17.5	5.50	89	.329	.398	2	.250	-0	-2	-1	0	-0.1
1894	Cle-N	0	2	.000	3	2	0	0	0	11	22	17	0	1	5	0	22.9	11.45	48	.407	.467	0	.000	-1	-7	-7	1	-0.8
	Cin-N	2	8	.200	12	12	11	0	0	100^1	153	123	4	1	46	17	17.9	7.45	75	.346	.409	10	.213	-2	-24	-20	-1	-1.5
	Yr	2	10	.167	15	14	11	0	0	111^1	175	140	4	2	51	17	18.4	7.84	71	.353	.415	10	.196	-3	-31	-27	-0	-2.3
1896	Cin-N	10	7	.588	27	15	13	2	2	159^2	199	111	9	5	36	25	13.5	4.45	104	.303	.344	14	.246	0	-2	3	-0	0.2
1897	Bro-N	9	7	.563	20	13	11	1	1	149	184	96	5	2	43	31	13.8	4.23	97	.301	.349	12	.203	-1	1	-2	-2	-0.4
1901	NY-N	0	0	—	1	1	0	0	0	4	11	9	0	0	2	1	29.3	15.75	21	.500	.542	0	.000	-0	-6	-6	-0	-0.3
	StL-N	0	0	—	1	0	0	0	0	3	7	5	0	0	1	0	24.0	15.00	21	.438	.471	0	.000	-0	-4	-4	0	-0.2
	Yr	0	0	—	2	1	0	0	0	7	18	14	0	0	3	1	27.0	15.43	21	.474	.512	0	.000	-0	-9	-10	0	-0.5
Total	5	21	26	.447	66	45	37	3	3	445	602	379	18	9	142	83	15.2	5.44	86	.320	.370	38	.213	-4	-42	-38	-2	-3.1
● CLARENCE FISHER	Fisher, Clarence Henry b: 8/27/1898, Letart, W.Va. d: 11/2/65, Point Pleasant, W.Va. BR/TR, 6', 174 lbs. Deb: 9/14/19																											
1919	Was-A	0	0	—	2	0	0	0	0	4	8	6	0	0	3	1	24.8	13.50	24	.421	.500	0	—	0	-5	-5	0	-0.2
1920	Was-A	0	1	.000	2	0	0	0	0	3^2	5	4	0	0	5	0	24.5	9.82	38	.714	.833	0	.000	-0	-2	-3	1	-0.4
Total	2	0	1	.000	4	0	0	0	0	7^2	13	10	0	0	8	1	24.7	11.74	29	.500	.618	0	.000	-0	-7	-7	1	-0.6
● DON FISHER	Fisher, Donald Raymond b: 2/6/16, Cleveland, Ohio d: 7/29/73, Mayfield Heights, Ohio BR/TR, 6', 210 lbs. Deb: 8/25/45																											
1945	NY-N	1	0	1.000	2	1	1	1	0	18	12	4	0	2	7	4	10.5	2.00	196	.190	.292	1	.143	-0	4	4	-0	0.2
● EDDIE FISHER	Fisher, Eddie Gene b: 7/16/36, Shreveport, La. BR/TR, 6'2.5", 200 lbs. Deb: 6/22/59																											
1959	SF-N	2	6	.250	17	5	0	0	1	40	57	37	8	1	8	15	14.8	7.87	48	.339	.373	0	.000	-1	-17	-19	-1	-3.2
1960	SF-N	1	0	1.000	3	1	1	0	0	12^2	11	5	2	0	2	7	9.2	3.55	98	.244	.277	3	.600	1	0	-0	0	0.1
1961	SF-N	0	2	.000	15	1	0	0	1	33^2	36	23	7	0	9	16	12.0	5.35	71	.267	.313	1	.143	0	-5	-6	-0	-0.4
1962	Chi-A	9	5	.643	57	12	2	1	5	182^2	169	74	17	1	45	88	10.6	3.10	126	.245	.293	6	.130	-0	18	17	0	1.3
1963	Chi-A	9	8	.529	33	15	2	1	0	120^2	114	57	14	2	28	67	10.7	3.95	89	.244	.290	5	.139	-1	-4	-6	1	-0.8
1964	Chi-A	6	3	.667	59	2	0	0	9	125	86	43	13	3	32	74	8.7	3.02	114	.192	.250	3	.167	-0	8	6	0	0.5
1965	Chi-A★	15	7	.682	**82**	0	0	0	24	165^1	118	51	13	2	43	90	**8.9**	2.40	133	.205	.262	4	.138	0	20	16	1	2.7
1966	Chi-A	1	3	.250	23	0	0	0	6	35^1	27	11	1	1	17	18	11.5	2.29	138	.214	.313	0	.000	-0	4	4	0	0.5
	Bal-A	5	3	.625	44	0	0	0	13	71^2	60	26	4	2	19	39	10.2	2.64	126	.226	.282	2	.154	0	6	6	-0	0.8
	Yr	6	6	.500	**67**	0	0	0	19	107	87	37	5	3	36	57	10.6	2.52	130	.222	.292	2	.133	-0	11	9	-0	1.3
1967	Bal-A	4	3	.571	46	0	0	0	1	89^2	82	40	7	4	26	53	11.2	3.61	87	.245	.307	1	.200	0	-4	-5	-1	-0.4
1968	Cle-A	4	2	.667	54	0	0	0	4	94^2	87	36	8	2	17	42	10.1	2.85	104	.248	.286	0	.000	-1	1	1	1	0.1
1969	Cal-A	3	2	.600	52	1	0	0	2	96^2	100	46	9	1	28	47	12.0	3.63	96	.272	.326	0	.000	-1	-0	-2	0	-0.2
1970	Cal-A	4	4	.500	67	2	0	0	8	130^1	117	51	15	2	35	74	10.6	3.04	119	.239	.292	1	.091	-1	10	9	1	0.7
1971	Cal-A	10	8	.556	57	3	0	0	3	119	92	46	11	2	50	82	10.9	2.72	119	.211	.295	1	.063	-1	10	7	-0	1.0
1972	Cal-A	4	5	.444	43	1	0	0	4	81^1	73	35	6	0	31	32	11.5	3.76	78	.247	.319	2	.118	-1	-6	-8	-0	-1.1
	Chi-A	0	1	.000	6	4	0	0	0	22^1	31	13	1	0	9	10	16.1	4.43	71	.348	.408	0	.000	-1	-3	-3	0	-0.2
	Yr	4	6	.400	49	5	0	0	4	103^2	104	48	7	0	40	42	12.5	3.91	76	.271	.340	2	.083	-1	-10	-11	-0	-1.3
1973	Chi-A	6	7	.462	26	16	2	0	0	110^2	135	64	12	3	38	57	14.3	4.88	81	.301	.360	0	—	0	-13	-11	0	-1.1
	StL-N	2	1	.667	6	0	0	0	0	7	3	1	1	1	1	1	6.4	1.29	284	.125	.192	1	1.000	0	2	2	-0	0.4
Total	15	85	70	.548	690	63	7	2	81	1538^2	1398	659	149	27	438	812	10.9	3.41	101	.243	.299	30	.122	-5	26	6	3	0.7
● ED FISHER	Fisher, Edward Fredrick b: 10/31/1876, Wayne, Mich. d: 7/24/51, Spokane, Wash. BR/TR, 6'2", 200 lbs. Deb: 9/5/02																											
1902	Det-A	0	0	—	1	0	0	0	0	4	4	0	0	0	1	0	11.3	0.00	—	.267	.313	0	.000	-0	2	2	-0	0.0

YEAR	TM/L	W	L	PCT	G	GS	CG	SH	SV	IP	H	R	HR	HB	BB	SO	RAT	ERA	ERA+	OAV	OOB	BH	AVG	PB	PR	PR+	PD	TPI
● FRITZ FISHER	Fisher, Frederick Brown b: 11/28/41, Adrian, Mich. BL/TL, 6'1", 180 lbs. Deb: 4/19/64																											
1964	Det-A	0	0	—	1	0	0	0	0	0^1	2	4	0	0	2	1	108.0	108.00	3	.667	.800	0	—	0	-4	-4	0	-0.2
● HARRY FISHER	Fisher, Harry Devereux b: 1/3/26, Newbury, Ont., Can. d: 9/20/81, Waterloo, Ont., Canada BL/TR, 6', 180 lbs. Deb: 9/16/51 ♦																											
1952	Pit-N	1	2	.333	8	3	0	0	0	18^1	17	14	4	2	13	5	15.7	6.87	58	.266	.405	5	.333	1	-6	-5	-1	-0.7
● JACK FISHER	Fisher, John Howard "Fat Jack" b: 3/4/39, Frostburg, Md. BR/TR, 6'2", 215 lbs. Deb: 4/14/59																											
1959	Bal-A	1	6	.143	27	7	1	1	2	88^2	76	36	7	1	38	52	11.7	3.05	124	.230	.311	3	.130	-1	8	7	-1	0.4
1960	Bal-A	12	11	.522	40	20	8	3	2	197^2	174	87	13	2	78	99	11.6	3.41	111	.241	.317	11	.183	2	10	9	0	1.2
1961	Bal-A	10	13	.435	36	25	10	1	1	196	205	104	17	4	75	118	13.0	3.90	99	.270	.339	5	.089	-2	3	-1	-3	-0.6
1962	Bal-A	7	9	.438	32	25	4	0	1	152	173	101	23	2	56	81	13.7	5.09	73	.284	.346	5	.102	-1	-19	-25	-1	-2.5
1963	SF-N	6	10	.375	36	12	2	0	1	116	132	77	12	5	38	57	13.6	4.58	70	.284	.344	3	.103	1	-17	-18	-0	-2.3
1964	NY-N	10	17	.370	40	34	8	1	0	227^2	256	124	23	10	56	115	12.7	4.23	85	.283	.331	12	.158	1	-18	-16	-1	-1.8
1965	NY-N	8	24	.250	43	36	10	0	1	253^2	252	121	22	4	68	116	11.5	3.94	90	.259	.310	12	.154	0	-11	-12	2	-1.1
1966	NY-N	11	14	.440	38	33	10	2	0	230	229	108	26	8	54	127	11.4	3.68	99	.260	.309	6	.090	-2	-2	-1	3	0.0
1967	NY-N	9	18	.333	39	30	7	1	0	220^1	251	121	21	4	64	117	13.0	4.70	72	.287	.339	7	.100	-2	-32	-32	1	-3.7
1968	Chi-A	8	13	.381	35	28	2	0	0	180^2	176	68	14	7	48	80	11.5	2.99	101	.257	.312	6	.113	-1	-0	1	-0	-0.1
1969	Cin-N	4	4	.500	34	15	0	0	1	113	137	77	15	5	30	55	13.7	5.50	69	.295	.345	4	.121	-1	-24	-21	-2	-1.7
Total	11	86	139	.382	400	265	62	9	9	1975^2	2061	1024	193	52	605	1017	12.4	4.06	88	.269	.326	74	.125	-6	-102	-108	-1	-12.2
● MAURICE FISHER	Fisher, Maurice Wayne b: 2/16/31, Uniondale, Ind. BR/TR, 6'5", 210 lbs. Deb: 4/16/55																											
1955	Cin-N	0	0	—	1	0	0	0	0	2^2	5	2	1	0	2	1	23.6	6.75	63	.385	.467	0	.000	-0	-1	-1	-0	-0.1
● RAY FISHER	Fisher, Ray Lyle "Pick" b: 10/4/1887, Middlebury, Vt. d: 11/3/82, Ann Arbor, Mich. BR/TR, 5'11.5", 180 lbs. Deb: 7/2/10																											
1910	NY-A	5	3	.625	17	7	3	0	1	92^1	95	41	0	3	18	42	11.3	2.92	91	.274	.315	3	.103	-2	-4	-3	1	-0.3
1911	NY-A	10	11	.476	29	22	8	2	0	171^2	178	85	3	5	55	99	12.5	3.25	111	.269	.330	7	.119	-3	2	6	4	0.8
1912	NY-A	2	8	.200	17	13	5	0	0	90^1	107	70	2	2	32	47	14.0	5.88	61	.312	.374	2	.065	-4	-26	-21	3	-2.1
1913	NY-A	12	16	.429	43	31	14	1	1	246^1	244	113	3	9	71	92	11.8	3.18	94	.261	.319	22	.278	3	-7	-5	2	0.0
1914	NY-A	10	12	.455	29	26	17	2	1	209	177	65	2	4	61	86	10.4	2.28	121	.241	.303	9	.138	-2	11	11	4	1.3
1915	NY-A	18	11	.621	30	28	20	4	0	247^2	219	82	7	5	62	97	10.4	2.11	139	.243	.295	9	.108	-5	23	23	-0	2.1
1916	NY-A	11	8	.579	31	21	9	1	2	179	191	81	4	4	51	56	12.4	3.17	91	.285	.339	11	.177	1	-7	-5	-1	-0.6
1917	NY-A	8	9	.471	23	18	12	3	0	144	126	49	3	2	43	64	10.7	2.19	123	.243	.304	9	.180	-0	8	8	1	1.1
1919	*Cin-N	14	5	.737	26	20	12	5	1	174^1	141	55	5	1	38	41	9.3	2.17	128	.226	.271	16	.271	3	14	12	3	2.1
1920	Cin-N	10	11	.476	33	21	10	1	1	201	189	86	5	8	50	56	11.1	2.73	111	.249	.302	17	.243	1	9	7	2	1.1
Total	10	100	94	.515	278	207	110	19	7	1755^2	1667	727	34	43	481	680	11.2	2.82	106	.257	.312	105	.179	-8	23	30	19	5.5
● TOM FISHER	Fisher, Thomas Chalmers "Red" b: 11/1/1880, Anderson, Ind. d: 9/3/72, Anderson, Ind. BR/TR, 5'10.5", 185 lbs. Deb: 4/17/04 F																											
1904	Bos-N	6	16	.273	31	21	19	2	0	214	257	165	5	10	82	84	14.7	4.25	65	.302	.370	21	.212	3	-36	-35	-5	-3.4
● TOM FISHER	Fisher, Thomas Gene b: 4/4/42, Cleveland, Ohio BR/TR, 6', 180 lbs. Deb: 9/20/67																											
1967	Bal-A	0	0	—	2	0	0	0	0	3^1	2	0	0	0	2	1	10.8	0.00	—	.182	.308	0	—	0	1	1	-0	0.1
● CHEROKEE FISHER	Fisher, William Charles b: 12/1845, Philadelphia, Pa. d: 9/26/12, New York, N.Y. BR/TR, 5'9", 164 lbs. Deb: 5/6/1871 ♦																											
1871	Rok-n	4	16	.200	24	24	22	**1**	0	213	295	257	3		31	15	13.8	4.35	94	.281	.302	28	.228	-3	-3	-7		-0.2
1872	Bal-n	10	1	.909	19	11	9	1	1	110	93	78	0		11	20	**8.5**	**1.80**	**204**	**.197**	**.216**	52	.231	-1	22	23		1.4
1873	Ath-n	3	4	.429	13	5	5	0	2	84^1	90	73	1		10	14	**10.7**	**1.81**	**188**	**.227**	**.246**	66	.261	1	13	14		0.8
1874	Har-n	13	23	.361	39	35	31	0	0	322^1	416	277	1		13	25	12.0	2.32	100	.277	.284	54	.224	-4	-5	-0		-0.5
1875	Phi-n	22	19	.537	41	41	36	2	0	358	345	189	6		9	18	8.9	1.99	115	.229	.233	41	.232	-1	10	11		0.5
1876	Cin-N	4	20	.167	28	24	22	0	0	229^1	294	206	6		6	29	11.8	3.02	73	.283	.289	32	.248	-1	-18	-22	-2	-1.9
1878	Pro-N	0	1	.000	1	1	1	0	0	9	14	12	0		0	2	14.0	4.00	55	.304	.304	0	.000	-0	-2	-2	0	-0.2
Total	5 n	52	63	.452	136	116	103	4	3	1087^2	1239	874	11		74	92	10.9	2.52	115	.252	.263	241	.237	-8	38	44		2.0
Total	2	4	21	.160	29	25	23	0	0	238^1	308	218	6		6	31	11.9	3.06	72	.284	.289	32	.235	-2	-20	-24	-2	-2.1
● MAX FISKE	Fiske, Maximilian Patrick "Ski" b: 10/12/1888, Chicago, Ill. d: 5/15/28, Chicago, Ill. BR/TR, 5'11", 185 lbs. Deb: 4/19/14																											
1914	Chi-F	12	12	.500	38	22	7	0	0	198	161	84	7	7	59	87	10.3	3.14	85	.231	.298	16	.235	0	-6	-12	-0	-1.3
● PAUL FITTERY	Fittery, Paul Clarence b: 10/10/1887, Lebanon, Pa. d: 1/28/74, Cartersville, Ga. BR/TL, 5'8.5", 156 lbs. Deb: 9/5/14																											
1914	Cin-N	0	2	.000	8	4	2	0	0	43^2	41	20	0	1	12	21	11.1	3.09	95	.246	.300	1	.059	-1	-1	-1	0	-0.2
1917	Phi-N	1	1	.500	17	2	1	0	0	55^2	69	36	1	5	27	13	16.3	4.53	62	.317	.404	2	.091	-1	-11	-10	1	-0.5
Total	2	1	3	.250	25	6	3	0	0	99^1	110	56	1	6	39	34	14.0	3.90	73	.286	.360	3	.077	-2	-13	-11	2	-0.7
● JOHN FITZGERALD	Fitzgerald, John Francis b: 9/15/33, Brooklyn, N.Y. BL/TL, 6'3", 190 lbs. Deb: 9/28/58																											
1958	SF-N	0	0	—	1	1	0	0	0	3	1	1	1	0	1	3	6.0	3.00	127	.111	.200	0	.000	-0	0	0	0	0.0
● JOHN FITZGERALD	Fitzgerald, John H. b: 5/30/1870, Natick, Mass. d: 3/31/21, Boston, Mass. Deb: 7/18/1891																											
1891	Bos-a	1	1	.500	6	3	2	0	1	32	49	32	2	2	11	16	17.4	5.63	62	.340	.395	1	.071	-2	-7	-8	0	-0.6
● JOHN FITZGERALD	Fitzgerald, John J. Deb: 4/18/1890																											
1890	Roc-a	3	8	.273	11	11	8	1	0	78	77	51	0	6	45	35	14.8	4.04	88	.250	.357	6	.194	-0	-1	-4	1	-0.4
● WARREN FITZGERALD	Fitzgerald, Warren B. b: 4/1872, Pennsylvania d: 11/7/30, Phoenix, Ariz. TL, 5'9", 162 lbs. Deb: 6/4/1891																											
1891	Lou-a	14	17	.452	32	31	28	3	0	267^1	265	157	5	12	89	110	12.3	3.33	109	.250	.315	19	.176	1	11	10	-4	0.6
1892	Lou-N	1	3	.250	4	4	4	0	0	34	45	27	2	1	11	3	15.1	4.24	72	.306	.358	2	.133	-0	-4	-5	-1	-0.5
Total	2	15	20	.429	36	35	32	3	0	301^1	310	184	7	13	100	113	12.6	3.43	104	.257	.320	21	.171	0	8	5	-4	0.1
● PAUL FITZKE	Fitzke, Paul Frederick Herman "Bob" b: 7/30/1900, LaCrosse, Wis. d: 6/30/50, Sacramento, Cal. BR/TR, 5'11.5", 185 lbs. Deb: 9/1/24																											
1924	Cle-A	0	0	—	1	0	0	0	0	4	5	2	0	0	3	1	18.0	4.50	95	.313	.421	0	.000	-0	-0	-0	-0	0.0
● AL FITZMORRIS	Fitzmorris, Alan James b: 3/21/46, Buffalo, N.Y. BB/TR, 6'2", 190 lbs. Deb: 9/8/69																											
1969	KC-A	1	1	.500	7	0	0	0	2	10^2	9	5	1	0	4	3	11.0	4.22	88	.237	.310	0	.000	-0	-1	-1	-0	-0.2
1970	KC-A	8	5	.615	43	11	2	0	1	117^2	112	60	14	0	52	47	12.5	4.44	84	.254	.333	9	.290	4	-9	-9	1	-0.5
1971	KC-A	7	5	.583	36	15	2	1	0	127^1	112	61	6	1	55	53	11.9	4.17	82	.245	.327	11	.250	2	-10	-10	2	-0.6
1972	KC-A	2	5	.286	38	2	0	0	3	101	99	46	10	1	28	51	11.4	3.74	81	.252	.303	4	.174	1	-8	-8	2	-0.3
1973	KC-A	8	3	.727	15	13	3	1	0	89	88	29	5	0	25	26	11.4	2.83	145	.259	.310	0	—	0	10	12	2	1.6
1974	KC-A	13	6	.684	34	27	9	4	1	190	189	73	8	0	63	53	11.9	2.79	137	.260	.319	0	—	0	18	21	3	2.4
1975	KC-A	16	12	.571	35	35	11	3	0	242	239	104	16	5	76	78	11.9	3.57	108	.262	.322	0	—	0	6	8	1	0.9
1976	KC-A	15	11	.577	35	33	8	2	0	220^1	227	89	6	2	56	80	11.6	3.06	114	.273	.320	0	—	0	11	11	3	1.6
1977	Cle-A	6	10	.375	29	21	1	0	0	133	164	87	12	1	53	54	14.8	5.41	73	.306	.369	0	—	0	-20	-22	-0	-2.3
1978	Cle-A	0	1	.000	7	0	0	0	0	14^1	19	10	3	1	7	5	17.0	6.28	60	.333	.415	0	—	0	-4	-4	-0	-0.3
	Cal-A	1	0	1.000	9	2	0	0	0	31^2	26	9	2	0	14	8	11.4	1.71	212	.236	.323	0	—	0	7	7	-0	0.3
	Yr	1	1	.500	16	2	0	0	0	46	45	19	5	1	21	13	13.1	3.13	117	.269	.354	0	—	0	3	3	-0	0.0
Total	10	77	59	.566	288	159	36	11	7	1277	1284	573	83	11	433	458	12.2	3.65	101	.265	.327	24	.242	7	0	6	12	2.6
● FREDDIE FITZSIMMONS	Fitzsimmons, Frederick Landis "Fat Freddie" b: 7/28/01, Mishawaka, Ind. d: 11/18/79, Yucca Valley, Cal. BR/TR, 5'11", 185 lbs. Deb: 8/12/25 MC																											
1925	NY-N	6	3	.667	10	8	6	1	0	74^2	70	25	4	0	18	17	10.6	2.65	152	.248	.293	9	.310	2	13	12	2	1.7
1926	NY-N	14	10	.583	37	26	12	0	0	219	224	90	7	4	58	48	11.8	2.88	130	.272	.322	11	.128	-6	23	22	3	1.8
1927	NY-N	17	10	.630	42	31	14	1	3	244^2	260	127	15	4	67	78	12.2	3.72	104	.275	.325	18	.207	-0	6	4	2	0.6
1928	NY-N	20	9	.690	40	32	16	1	1	261^1	264	119	13	4	65	67	11.5	3.68	106	.268	.316	18	.191	1	9	7	2	0.9
1929	NY-N	15	11	.577	37	30	14	4	1	221^2	242	122	14	2	66	55	12.6	4.10	112	.285	.338	15	.183	-2	15	12	4	1.4
1930	NY-N	19	7	**.731**	41	29	17	1	1	224^1	230	125	26	1	59	76	11.6	4.25	111	.266	.314	22	.265	5	18	13	7	2.2
1931	NY-N	18	11	.621	35	33	19	4	0	253^2	242	111	16	0	62	78	10.8	3.05	121	.251	.296	21	.228	9	23	19	8	**3.8**
1932	NY-N	11	11	.500	35	31	11	0	0	237^2	287	132	18	3	83	65	14.1	4.43	84	.299	.356	19	.221	4	-15	-20	7	-0.6

YEAR	TM/L	W	L	PCT	G	GS	CG	SH	SV	IP	H	R	HR	HB	BB	SO	RAT	ERA	ERA+	OAV	OOB	BH	AVG	PB	PR	PR+	PD	TPI
1933	*NY-N	16	11	.593	36	35	13	1	0	251^2	243	106	14	2	72	65	11.3	2.90	111	.251	.305	19	.200	3	12	9	6	1.9
1934	NY-N	18	14	.563	38	37	14	3	1	263^1	266	114	12	1	51	73	10.9	3.04	127	.261	.297	22	.232	5	30	25	5	3.8
1935	NY-N	4	8	.333	18	15	6	**4**	0	94	104	43	7	1	22	23	12.2	4.02	96	.281	.323	8	.258	1	-0	-2	1	0.0
1936	*NY-N	10	7	.588	28	17	7	1	2	141	147	58	6	0	39	35	11.9	3.32	117	.274	.323	7	.149	-2	11	9	1	0.9
1937	NY-N	2	2	.500	6	4	1	1	0	27^1	28	14	3	0	8	13	11.9	4.61	84	.272	.324	3	.300	2	-2	-2	-0	-0.2
	Bro-N	4	8	.333	13	13	4	0	0	90^2	91	47	2	1	32	29	12.3	4.27	95	.263	.327	5	.167	-1	-4	-2	1	-0.3
	Yr	6	10	.375	19	17	5	1	0	118	119	61	5	1	40	42	12.2	4.35	92	.265	.327	8	.200	1	-6	-4	1	-0.5
1938	Bro-N	11	8	.579	27	26	12	3	0	202^2	205	83	8	3	43	38	11.1	3.02	129	.261	.302	12	.171	-1	17	19	6	2.2
1939	Bro-N	7	9	.438	27	20	5	0	3	151^1	178	79	6	3	28	44	12.4	3.87	104	.293	.327	11	.234	3	1	3	5	1.0
1940	Bro-N	16	2	**.889**	20	18	11	4	1	134^1	120	43	5	1	25	35	9.8	2.81	142	.233	.269	5	.106	-2	15	17	1	2.1
1941	*Bro-N	6	1	.857	13	12	3	1	0	82^2	78	33	3	2	26	19	11.5	2.07	177	.245	.305	4	.143	-0	14	15	2	1.4
1942	Bro-N	0	0	—	1	1	0	0	0	3	6	5	1	0	1	0	21.0	15.00	22	.400	.438	1	.500	0	-4	-4	0	-0.2
1943	Bro-N	3	4	.429	9	7	1	0	0	44^2	50	29	6	1	21	12	14.5	5.44	62	.281	.360	1	.071	-1	-10	-10	0	-1.5
Total	19	217	146	.598	513	425	186	30	13	3223^2	3335	1505	186	33	846	870	11.8	3.51	111	.268	.316	231	.200	21	174	147	60	22.9

● PATSY FLAHERTY Flaherty, Patrick Joseph b: 6/29/1876, Mansfield, Pa. d: 1/23/68, Alexandria, La. BL/TL, 5'8", 165 lbs. Deb: 9/8/1899 ♦

YEAR	TM/L	W	L	PCT	G	GS	CG	SH	SV	IP	H	R	HR	HB	BB	SO	RAT	ERA	ERA+	OAV	OOB	BH	AVG	PB	PR	PR+	PD	TPI
1899	Lou-N	2	3	.400	5	4	4	0	0	39	41	21	0	1	5	5	10.8	2.31	167	.270	.297	5	.208	1	7	7	-1	0.7
1900	Pit-N	0	0	—	4	1	0	0	0	22	30	16	0	5	9	5	18.0	6.14	59	.323	.411	1	.111	-1	-6	-6	1	-0.3
1903	Chi-A	11	25	.306	40	34	29	2	1	293^2	338	173	9	14	50	65	12.3	3.74	75	.288	.324	14	.137	-3	-25	-32	3	-3.6
1904	Chi-A	1	2	.333	5	5	4	0	0	43	36	19	1	1	10	14	9.8	2.09	117	.228	.278	4	.333	2	2	2	1	0.5
	Pit-N	19	9	.679	29	28	28	5	0	242	210	81	3	11	59	54	10.4	2.05	134	.232	.287	22	.212	5	19	19	5	3.4
1905	Pit-N	10	10	.500	27	20	15	0	1	187^2	197	87	2	6	49	44	12.1	3.50	86	.272	.324	15	.197	2	-10	-10	2	-0.6
1907	Bos-N	12	15	.444	27	25	23	0	0	217	197	90	4	7	59	34	10.9	2.70	95	.248	.306	22	.191	2	-5	-3	2	0.1
1908	Bos-N	12	18	.400	31	31	21	0	0	244	221	109	6	8	81	50	11.4	3.25	74	.236	.303	12	.140	-0	-24	-22	2	-2.6
1910	Phi-N	0	0	—	1	0	0	0	0	0^1	1	4	0	0	1	0	54.0	0.00	—	.333	.500	1	.500	0	0	0	0	0.0
1911	Bos-N	0	2	.000	4	2	1	0	0	14	21	15	0	3	8	0	20.6	7.07	54	.350	.451	27	.287	1	-6	-4	-0	-0.5
Total	9	67	84	.444	173	150	125	7	2	1302^2	1292	615	25	56	331	271	11.6	3.10	89	.259	.312	123	.197	10	-49	-50	14	-2.9

● MIKE FLANAGAN Flanagan, Michael Kendall b: 12/16/51, Manchester, N.H. BL/TL, 6', 195 lbs. Deb: 9/5/75

YEAR	TM/L	W	L	PCT	G	GS	CG	SH	SV	IP	H	R	HR	HB	BB	SO	RAT	ERA	ERA+	OAV	OOB	BH	AVG	PB	PR	PR+	PD	TPI
1975	Bal-A	0	1	.000	2	1	0	0	0	9^2	9	4	0	0	6	7	14.0	2.79	126	.250	.357	0	—	0	1	1	0	0.1
1976	Bal-A	3	5	.375	20	10	4	0	0	85	83	41	7	0	33	56	12.3	4.13	79	.260	.330	0	—	0	-6	-9	0	-0.7
1977	Bal-A	15	10	.600	36	33	15	2	1	235	235	100	17	2	70	149	11.8	3.64	105	.266	.321	0	—	0	11	5	-0	0.4
1978	Bal-A☆	19	15	.559	40	40	17	2	0	281^1	271	128	22	3	87	167	11.5	4.03	87	.257	.315	0	—	0	-8	-18	-2	-2.1
1979	*Bal-A	**23**	9	.719	39	38	16	**5**	0	265^2	245	107	23	3	70	190	10.8	3.08	130	.245	.297	0	—	0	34	29	-0	3.2
1980	Bal-A	16	13	.552	37	37	12	2	0	251^1	278	121	27	2	71	128	12.6	4.12	96	.287	.337	0	—	0	-2	-4	0	-0.4
1981	Bal-A	9	6	.600	20	20	3	2	0	116	108	55	11	2	37	72	11.4	4.19	87	.244	.305	0	—	0	-7	-7	1	-0.8
1982	Bal-A	15	11	.577	36	35	11	1	0	236	233	110	24	4	76	103	11.9	3.97	102	.259	.319	0	—	0	3	2	0	0.2
1983	*Bal-A	12	4	.750	20	20	3	1	0	125^1	135	53	10	2	31	50	12.1	3.30	120	.278	.324	0	—	0	11	9	-1	1.0
1984	Bal-A	13	13	.500	34	34	10	2	0	226^2	213	103	24	1	81	115	11.7	3.53	110	.250	.316	0	—	0	12	9	-1	0.9
1985	Bal-A	4	5	.444	15	15	1	0	0	86	101	49	14	2	28	42	13.7	5.13	79	.297	.354	0	—	0	-9	-11	-0	-1.0
1986	Bal-A	7	11	.389	29	28	2	0	0	172	179	95	15	1	66	96	12.9	4.24	98	.270	.337	0	—	0	-1	-2	-2	-0.4
1987	Bal-A	3	6	.333	16	16	4	0	0	94^2	102	57	9	0	36	50	13.1	4.94	89	.278	.342	0	—	0	-5	-6	-0	-0.5
	Tor-A	3	2	.600	7	7	0	0	0	49^1	46	15	3	0	15	43	11.1	2.37	190	.237	.292	0	—	0	12	12	-0	1.1
	Yr	6	8	.429	23	23	4	0	0	144	148	72	12	0	51	93	12.4	4.06	109	.264	.325	0	—	0	7	6	-1	0.6
1988	Tor-A	13	13	.500	34	34	2	1	0	211	220	106	23	6	80	99	13.1	4.18	94	.271	.341	0	—	0	-5	-6	1	-0.6
1989	*Tor-A	8	10	.444	30	30	1	1	0	171^2	186	82	10	5	47	47	12.5	3.93	96	.283	.335	0	—	0	-1	-3	1	-0.2
1990	Tor-A	2	2	.500	5	5	0	0	0	20^1	28	14	3	0	8	5	15.9	5.31	74	.329	.387	0	—	0	-3	-3	0	-0.5
1991	Bal-A	2	7	.222	64	1	0	0	3	98^1	84	27	6	3	25	55	10.3	2.38	166	.236	.292	0	—	0	19	18	2	1.8
1992	Bal-A	0	0	—	42	0	0	0	0	34^2	50	34	3	5	23	17	20.3	8.05	50	.338	.443	0	—	0	-16	-15	1	-0.7
Total	18	167	143	.539	526	404	101	19	4	2770	2806	1301	251	41	890	1491	12.1	3.90	100	.266	.325	0	—	0	40	0	-1	0.8

● RAY FLANIGAN Flanigan, Raymond Arthur b: 1/8/23, Morgantown, W.Va. d: 3/28/93, Baltimore, Md. BR/TR, 6', 190 lbs. Deb: 9/20/46

YEAR	TM/L	W	L	PCT	G	GS	CG	SH	SV	IP	H	R	HR	HB	BB	SO	RAT	ERA	ERA+	OAV	OOB	BH	AVG	PB	PR	PR+	PD	TPI
1946	Cle-A	0	1	.000	3	1	0	0	0	9	11	12	1	0	8	2	19.0	11.00	30	.289	.413	1	.500	1	-7	-8	0	-0.7

● TOM FLANIGAN Flanigan, Thomas Anthony b: 9/6/34, Cincinnati, Ohio BR/TL, 6'3", 175 lbs. Deb: 4/14/54

YEAR	TM/L	W	L	PCT	G	GS	CG	SH	SV	IP	H	R	HR	HB	BB	SO	RAT	ERA	ERA+	OAV	OOB	BH	AVG	PB	PR	PR+	PD	TPI
1954	Chi-A	0	0	—	2	0	0	0	0	1^2	1	0	0	0	1	0	10.8	0.00	—	.200	.333	0	—	0	1	1	0	0.0
1958	StL-N	0	0	—	1	0	0	0	0	1	2	1	1	0	1	0	27.0	9.00	46	.500	.600	0	—	0	-1	-1	-0	0.0
Total	2	0	0	—	3	0	0	0	0	2^2	3	1	1	0	2	0	16.9	3.38	115	.333	.455	0	—	0	0	0	0	0.0

● JACK FLATER Flater, John William b: 9/22/1880, Sandymount, Md. d: 3/20/70, Westminster, Md. BR/TR, 5'10", 175 lbs. Deb: 9/18/08

YEAR	TM/L	W	L	PCT	G	GS	CG	SH	SV	IP	H	R	HR	HB	BB	SO	RAT	ERA	ERA+	OAV	OOB	BH	AVG	PB	PR	PR+	PD	TPI
1908	Phi-A	1	3	.250	5	3	3	0	0	39^1	35	15	0	2	12	8	11.2	2.06	124	.252	.320	2	.133	-0	1	2	2	0.4

● JOHN FLAVIN Flavin, John Thomas b: 5/7/42, Albany, Cal. BL/TL, 6'2", 208 lbs. Deb: 8/25/64

YEAR	TM/L	W	L	PCT	G	GS	CG	SH	SV	IP	H	R	HR	HB	BB	SO	RAT	ERA	ERA+	OAV	OOB	BH	AVG	PB	PR	PR+	PD	TPI
1964	Chi-N	0	1	.000	5	1	0	0	0	4^2	11	7	0	0	3	5	27.0	13.50	28	.500	.560	0	.000	-0	-5	-5	-0	-0.9

● FRANK FLEET Fleet, Frank H. b: 1848, New York, N.Y. d: 6/13/1900, New York, N.Y. Deb: 10/18/1871 ♦

YEAR	TM/L	W	L	PCT	G	GS	CG	SH	SV	IP	H	R	HR	HB	BB	SO	RAT	ERA	ERA+	OAV	OOB	BH	AVG	PB	PR	PR+	PD	TPI
1871	Mut-n	0	1	.000	1	1	1	0	0	9	20	21	0		3	0	23.0	10.00	38	.370	.404	2	.333	0	-6	-7		-0.3
1873	Res-n	0	3	.000	3	3	2	0	0	24	57	47	0		0	1	21.4	5.63	60	.399	.399	23	.256	0	-6	-6		-0.4
1875	StL-n	2	1	.667	3	3	3	0	0	27	33	17	0		3	3	12.0	3.33	60	.277	.295	1	.063	-1	-3	-4		-0.4
	Atl-n	0	1	.000	2	1	1	0	0	15^1	26	20	0		0	0	15.3	4.70	44	.333	.333	25	.225	-0	-4	-5		-0.2
	Yr	2	2	.500	5	4	4	0	0	42^1	59	37	0		3	3	13.2	3.83	53	.299	.310	26	.205	-1	-8	-9		-0.6
Total	3 n	2	6	.250	9	8	7	0	0	75^1	136	105	0		6	4	17.0	5.14	40	.345	.355	86	.231	-1	-24	-28		-1.3

● DAVE FLEMING Fleming, David Anthony b: 11/7/69, Jackson Heights, N.Y. BL/TL, 6'3", 200 lbs. Deb: 8/6/91

YEAR	TM/L	W	L	PCT	G	GS	CG	SH	SV	IP	H	R	HR	HB	BB	SO	RAT	ERA	ERA+	OAV	OOB	BH	AVG	PB	PR	PR+	PD	TPI
1991	Sea-A	1	0	1.000	9	3	0	0	0	17^2	19	13	3	3	3	11	12.7	6.62	62	.284	.342	0	—	0	-5	-5	1	-0.1
1992	Sea-A	17	10	.630	33	33	7	4	0	228^1	225	95	13	4	60	112	11.4	3.39	117	.257	.307	0	—	0	14	15	-0	1.6
1993	Sea-A	12	5	.706	26	26	1	1	0	167^1	189	84	15	6	67	75	14.1	4.36	101	.290	.361	0	—	0	-0	1	1	0.2
1994	Sea-A	7	11	.389	23	23	0	0	0	117	152	93	17	1	65	65	16.8	6.46	76	.311	.394	0	—	0	-22	-20	-0	-2.4
1995	Sea-A	1	5	.167	16	7	1	0	0	48	57	44	15	0	34	26	17.1	7.50	63	.294	.399	0	—	0	-15	-15	-0	-1.5
	KC-A	0	1	.000	9	5	0	0	0	32	27	17	4	2	19	14	13.5	3.66	131	.229	.345	0	—	0	4	4	0	0.2
	Yr	1	6	.143	25	12	1	0	0	80	84	61	19	2	53	40	15.6	5.96	80	.269	.379	0	—	0	-11	-11	0	-1.3
Total	5	38	32	.543	116	97	9	5	0	610^1	669	346	67	16	248	303	13.8	4.67	94	.279	.351	0	—	0	-24	-20	2	-2.0

● BILL FLEMING Fleming, Leslie Fletchard b: 7/31/13, Rowland, Cal. BR/TR, 6', 190 lbs. Deb: 8/21/40

YEAR	TM/L	W	L	PCT	G	GS	CG	SH	SV	IP	H	R	HR	HB	BB	SO	RAT	ERA	ERA+	OAV	OOB	BH	AVG	PB	PR	PR+	PD	TPI
1940	Bos-A	1	2	.333	10	6	1	0	0	46^1	53	27	4	2	20	24	14.6	4.86	93	.290	.366	0	.000	-2	-2	-2	-1	-0.3
1941	Bos-A	1	1	.500	16	1	0	0	1	41^1	32	21	4	0	24	20	12.2	3.92	106	.212	.320	2	.222	1	1	1	1	0.2
1942	Chi-N	5	6	.455	33	14	4	2	2	134^1	117	51	9	3	63	59	12.3	3.01	106	.230	.318	2	.051	-4	4	3	-1	-0.3
1943	Chi-N	0	1	.000	11	0	0	0	0	32^1	41	24	2	3	12	12	15.6	6.40	52	.311	.381	0	.000	-1	-11	-11	1	-0.6
1944	Chi-N	9	10	.474	39	18	9	1	0	158^1	163	74	6	1	62	42	12.8	3.13	113	.269	.337	9	.170	-1	9	7	1	0.9
1946	Chi-N	0	1	.000	14	1	0	0	0	29^1	37	23	2	1	12	10	15.3	6.14	54	.301	.368	0	.000	-0	-9	-9	0	-0.5
Total	6	16	21	.432	123	40	14	3	3	442	443	220	27	10	193	167	13.2	3.79	94	.260	.339	13	.104	-7	-8	-12	1	-0.6

● HUCK FLENER Flener, Gregory Alan b: 2/25/69, Austin, Tex. BB/TL, 5'11", 185 lbs. Deb: 9/14/93

YEAR	TM/L	W	L	PCT	G	GS	CG	SH	SV	IP	H	R	HR	HB	BB	SO	RAT	ERA	ERA+	OAV	OOB	BH	AVG	PB	PR	PR+	PD	TPI
1993	Tor-A	0	0	—	6	0	0	0	0	6^2	7	3	0	0	4	2	14.9	4.05	107	.269	.367	0	—	0	0	0	0	0.0
1996	Tor-A	3	2	.600	15	11	0	0	0	70^2	68	40	9	1	33	44	13.0	4.58	109	.251	.334	0	—	0	3	3	1	0.2
1997	Tor-A	0	1	.000	8	1	0	0	0	17^1	40	19	3	0	6	9	23.9	9.87	47	.444	.479	0	—	0	-10	-10	-1	-0.5
Total	3	3	3	.500	29	12	0	0	0	94^2	115	62	12	1	43	55	15.1	5.51	89	.297	.369	0	—	0	-7	-7	0	-0.3

● VAN FLETCHER Fletcher, Alfred Vanoide b: 8/6/24, East Bend, N.C. BR/TR, 6'2", 185 lbs. Deb: 4/12/55

YEAR	TM/L	W	L	PCT	G	GS	CG	SH	SV	IP	H	R	HR	HB	BB	SO	RAT	ERA	ERA+	OAV	OOB	BH	AVG	PB	PR	PR+	PD	TPI
1955	Det-A	0	0	—	9	0	0	0	0	12	13	10	1	0	2	4	11.3	3.00	128	.260	.288	0	—	0	1	1	-0	0.1

YEAR	TM/L	W	L	PCT	G	GS	CG	SH	SV	IP	H	R	HR	HB	BB	SO	RAT	ERA	ERA+	OAV	OOB	BH	AVG	PB	PR	PR+	PD	TPI
● PAUL FLETCHER	Fletcher, Edward Paul b: 1/14/67, Gallipolis, Ohio BR/TR, 6'1", 185 lbs. Deb: 7/11/93																											
1993	Phi-N	0	0	—	1	0	0	0	0	0^{1}	0	0	0	0	0	0	0.0	0.00	—	.000	.000	0	—	0	0	0	-0	0.0
1995	Phi-N	1	0	1.000	10	0	0	0	0	13^{1}	15	8	2	1	9	10	16.9	5.40	78	.288	.403	0	—	0	-2	-2	-0	-0.1
1996	Oak-A	0	0	—	1	0	0	0	0	1^{1}	6	3	0	0	1	0	47.3	20.25	24	.667	.700	0	—	0	-2	-2	-0	-0.1
Total	3	1	0	1.000	12	0	0	0	0	15	21	11	2	1	10	10	19.2	6.60	65	.339	.438	0	—	0	-4	-4	-0	-0.2
● SAM FLETCHER	Fletcher, Samuel S. b: Altoona, Pa. TR, 6'2", 210 lbs. Deb: 10/6/09																											
1909	Bro-N	0	1	.000	1	1	1	0	0	9	13	8	0	0	2	5	15.0	8.00	32	.351	.385	0	.000	-0	-5	-5	-0	-0.5
1912	Cin-N	0	0	—	2	0	0	0	0	9^{2}	15	15	1	0	11	3	24.2	12.10	28	.366	.500	2	.500	1	-9	-10	0	-0.4
Total	2	0	1	.000	3	1	1	0	0	18^{2}	28	23	1	0	13	8	19.8	10.13	30	.359	.451	2	.286	0	-15	-15	0	-0.9
● TOM FLETCHER	Fletcher, Thomas Wayne b: 6/28/42, Elmira, N.Y. BB/TL, 6', 170 lbs. Deb: 9/12/62 F																											
1962	Det-A	0	0	—	1	0	0	0	0	2	2	0	0	0	2	1	18.0	0.00	—	.250	.400	0		0	1	1	0	0.0
● JOHN FLINN	Flinn, John Richard b: 9/2/54, Merced, Cal. BR/TR, 6', 175 lbs. Deb: 5/6/78																											
1978	Bal-A	1	1	.500	13	0	0	0	0	15^{2}	24	18	3	0	13	8	21.3	8.04	44	.348	.451	0	—	0	-7	-8	0	-1.0
1979	Bal-A	0	0	—	4	0	0	0	0	2^{2}	2	0	0	0	1	0	10.1	0.00	—	.222	.300	0	—	0	1	1	0	0.1
1980	Mil-A	2	1	.667	20	1	0	0	2	37	31	20	3	0	20	15	12.4	3.89	100	.220	.317	0	—	0	1	-0	-0	0.0
1982	Bal-A	2	0	1.000	5	0	0	0	0	13^{2}	13	3	1	0	3	13	10.5	1.32	307	.260	.302	0	—	0	4	4	-0	0.6
Total	4	5	2	.714	42	1	0	0	2	69	70	41	7	0	37	36	14.0	4.17	92	.260	.350	0	—	0	-1	-3	-0	-0.3
● HILLY FLITCRAFT	Flitcraft, Hildreth Milton b: 8/21/23, Woodstown, N.J. BL/TL, 6'2", 180 lbs. Deb: 8/31/42																											
1942	Phi-N	0	0	—	3	0	0	0	0	3^{1}	6	4	0	0	2	1	21.6	8.10	41	.429	.500	0	—	0	-2	-2	0	-0.1
● MORT FLOHR	Flohr, Moritz Herman "Dutch" b: 8/15/11, Canisteo, N.Y. d: 6/2/94, Hornell, N.Y. BL/TL, 6', 173 lbs. Deb: 6/8/34																											
1934	Phi-A	0	2	.000	14	3	0	0	0	30^{2}	34	21	3	1	33	6	20.0	5.87	75	.296	.456	4	.333	1	-5	-5	1	-0.1
● DON FLORENCE	Florence, Donald Emery b: 3/16/67, Manchester, N.H. BR/TL, 6', 195 lbs. Deb: 8/8/95																											
1995	NY-N	3	0	1.000	14	0	0	0	0	12	17	3	0	0	6	5	17.3	1.50	270	.340	.411	0	.000	-0	4	4	0	0.7
● JESSE FLORES	Flores, Jesse (Sandoval) b: 11/2/14, Guadalajara, Mexico d: 12/17/91, Orange, Cal. BR/TR, 5'10", 175 lbs. Deb: 4/16/42																											
1942	Chi-N	0	1	.000	4	0	0	0	0	5^{1}	5	5	1	0	2	6	11.8	3.38	95	.227	.292	0	—	0	-0	-0	0	0.0
1943	Phi-A	12	14	.462	31	27	13	0	0	231^{1}	208	88	13	5	70	113	11.0	3.11	109	.240	.301	14	.175	-0	5	7	1	0.9
1944	Phi-A	9	11	.450	27	25	11	2	0	185^{2}	172	75	8	4	49	65	10.9	3.39	103	.245	.298	11	.172	-0	1	2	-1	0.1
1945	Phi-A	7	10	.412	29	24	9	4	1	191^{1}	180	79	6	4	63	52	11.6	3.43	100	.250	.314	9	.148	-2	-1	-0	-3	-0.5
1946	Phi-A	9	7	.563	29	15	8	4	1	155	147	51	8	1	38	48	10.8	2.32	153	.249	.295	11	.250	3	20	21	-2	2.3
1947	Phi-A	4	13	.235	28	20	4	0	0	151^{1}	139	72	10	0	59	41	11.8	3.39	112	.244	.315	10	.227	1	5	7	-1	0.7
1950	Cle-A	3	3	.500	28	2	1	1	4	53	53	24	3	1	25	27	13.4	3.74	116	.261	.345	0	.000	-2	5	4	-2	0.1
Total	7	44	59	.427	176	113	46	11	6	973	904	394	49	15	306	352	11.3	3.18	112	.246	.307	55	.181	-0	35	40	-7	3.6
● BRYCE FLORIE	Florie, Bryce Bettencourt b: 5/21/70, Charleston, S.C. BR/TR, 6', 185 lbs. Deb: 7/17/94																											
1994	SD-N	0	0	—	9	0	0	0	0	9^{1}	8	1	0	0	3	8	10.6	0.96	426	.242	.306	0	—	0	3	3	0	0.2
1995	SD-N	2	2	.500	47	0	0	0	1	68^{2}	49	30	8	4	38	68	11.9	3.01	134	.202	.320	0	.000	-0	9	8	0	0.4
1996	SD-N	2	2	.500	39	0	0	0	0	49^{1}	45	24	1	6	27	51	14.2	4.01	99	.239	.353	0	.000	-0	1	-0	0	0.0
	Mil-A	0	1	.000	15	0	0	0	0	19	20	16	3	0	13	12	15.6	6.63	78	.270	.379	0	—	0	-3	-3	-0	-0.2
1997	Mil-A	4	4	.500	32	8	0	0	0	75	74	43	4	3	42	53	14.3	4.32	107	.262	.364	0	—	0	2	2	-1	0.1
1998	Det-A	8	9	.471	42	16	0	0	0	133	141	80	16	4	59	97	13.8	4.80	98	.275	.355	1	.333	1	-2	-1	2	0.1
1999	Det-A	2	1	.667	27	3	0	0	0	51^{1}	61	31	6	1	20	40	14.4	4.56	107	.292	.357	0	.000	-0	2	2	-1	0.0
	Bos-A	2	0	1.000	14	2	0	0	0	30	33	19	2	1	15	25	14.7	4.80	104	.282	.368	0	—	0	0	1	1	0.1
	Yr	4	1	.800	41	5	0	0	0	81^{1}	94	50	8	2	35	65	14.5	4.65	106	.288	.361	0	.000	-0	2	2	0	0.1
2000	Bos-A	0	4	.000	29	0	0	0	1	49^{1}	57	30	5	1	19	34	14.0	4.56	112	.294	.360	0	—	0	2	3	2	0.4
Total	7	20	23	.465	254	29	0	0	2	485	488	274	45	20	236	388	13.8	4.34	106	.264	.353	1	.111	0	14	14	3	1.1
● BEN FLOWERS	Flowers, Bennett b: 6/15/27, Wilson, N.C. BR/TR, 6'4", 195 lbs. Deb: 9/29/51																											
1951	Bos-A	0	0	—	1	0	0	0	0	3	2	0	0	0	1	2	9.0	0.00	—	.200	.273	0	.000	-0	1	1	-0	0.0
1953	Bos-A	1	4	.200	32	6	1	1	3	79^{1}	87	39	6	1	24	36	12.7	3.86	109	.280	.333	3	.158	-0	1	3	1	0.2
1955	Det-A	0	0	—	4	0	0	0	0	6	5	4	1	0	2	2	10.5	6.00	64	.238	.304	0	.000	-0	-1	-1	0	-0.1
	StL-N	1	0	1.000	4	4	0	0	0	27^{1}	27	12	1	0	12	19	12.8	3.62	112	.255	.331	1	.100	-1	1	1	-0	-0.1
1956	StL-N	1	1	.500	3	3	0	0	0	11^{2}	15	9	1	0	5	5	15.4	6.94	54	.341	.408	0	.000	-0	-4	-4	0	-0.6
	Phi-N	0	2	.000	32	0	0	0	0	41	54	29	9	1	10	22	14.3	5.71	65	.331	.374	0	.000	0	-9	-9	1	-0.4
	Yr	1	3	.250	35	3	0	0	0	52^{2}	69	38	10	1	15	27	14.5	5.98	62	.333	.381	0	.000	-0	-13	-13	1	-1.0
Total	4	3	7	.300	76	13	1	1	3	168^{1}	190	93	18	2	54	86	13.2	4.49	90	.290	.346	4	.111	-2	-10	-9	1	-1.0
● DICKIE FLOWERS	Flowers, Charles Richard b: 1850, Philadelphia, Pa. d: 10/5/1892, Philadelphia, Pa. Deb: 6/3/1871 ♦																											
1871	Tro-n	0	0	—	1	0	0	0	0	1	1	0	0	0	0	0	9.0	0.00	—	.333	.333	33	.314	0	0	0		0.0
● WES FLOWERS	Flowers, Charles Wesley b: 8/13/13, Vanndale, Ark. d: 12/31/88, Wynne, Ark. BL/TL, 6'1.5", 190 lbs. Deb: 8/8/40																											
1940	Bro-N	1	1	.500	5	2	0	0	0	21	23	10	2	3	10	8	15.4	3.43	117	.299	.400	1	.200	-0	1	1	0	0.1
1944	Bro-N	1	1	.500	9	1	0	0	0	17^{1}	26	17	3	1	13	3	20.8	7.79	46	.333	.435	3	.600	1	-8	-8	-0	-0.7
Total	2	2	2	.500	14	3	0	0	0	38^{1}	49	27	5	4	23	11	17.8	5.40	70	.316	.418	4	.400	1	-7	-7	-0	-0.6
● CARNEY FLYNN	Flynn, Cornelius Francis Xavier b: 1/23/1875, Cincinnati, Ohio d: 2/10/47, Cincinnati, Ohio BL/TL, 5'11", 165 lbs. Deb: 7/17/1894																											
1894	Cin-N	0	2	.000	2	1	0	0	0	7^{2}	16	15	4	1	10	4	31.7	17.61	32	.421	.551	0	.000	-1	-10	-10	-0	-1.2
1896	NY-N	0	2	.000	3	2	1	0	0	10^{2}	18	22	0	5	8	4	26.2	11.81	36	.367	.500	2	.500	2	-9	-9	0	-1.0
	Was-N	0	1	.000	4	1	1	0	0	20	43	31	0	2	10	3	24.7	8.55	52	.430	.491	2	.250	-0	-9	-9	-1	-0.5
	Yr	0	3	.000	7	3	2	0	0	30^{2}	61	53	0	7	18	7	25.2	9.68	45	.409	.494	4	.333	1	-18	-18	-1	-1.5
Total	2	0	5	.000	9	4	2	0	0	38^{1}	77	68	4	8	28	11	26.5	11.27	41	.412	.507	4	.267	1	-29	-28	-1	-2.7
● JOCKO FLYNN	Flynn, John A. b: 6/30/1864, Lawrence, Mass. d: 12/30/07, Lawrence, Mass. TR, 5'6.5", 143 lbs. Deb: 5/1/1886 ♦																											
1886	Chi-N	23	6	**.793**	32	29	28	2	1	257	207	127	9		63	146	9.5	2.24	162	.210	.257	41	.200	1	31	36	2	3.7
● STU FLYTHE	Flythe, Stuart McGuire b: 12/5/11, Conway, N.C. d: 10/18/63, Durham, N.C. BR/TR, 6'2", 175 lbs. Deb: 5/31/36																											
1936	Phi-A	0	0	—	17	3	0	0	0	39^{1}	49	63	4	3	61	14	25.9	13.04	39	.302	.500	4	.267	0	-35	-34	-0	-1.4
● GENE FODGE	Fodge, Gene Arlan "Suds" b: 7/9/31, South Bend, Ind. BR/TR, 6', 175 lbs. Deb: 4/20/58																											
1958	Chi-N	1	1	.500	16	4	1	0	0	39^{2}	47	22	5	0	11	15	13.2	4.76	82	.296	.341	0	.000	-1	-4	-4	0	-0.2
● JIM FOGARTY	Fogarty, James G. b: 2/12/1864, San Francisco, Cal d: 5/20/1891, Philadelphia, Pa. BR/TR, 5'10.5", 180 lbs. Deb: 5/1/1884 FM♦																											
1884	Phi-N	0	0	—	1	0	0	0	0	1	2	2	0		0	1	18.0	0.00	—	.333	.333	80	.212	0	0	0	0	0.0
1886	Phi-N	0	1	.000	1	0	0	0	0	6	7	6	1		0	4	10.5	0.00	—	.250	.250	82	.293	0	2	2	0	0.4
1887	Phi-N	0	0	—	1	0	0	0	0	3	4	4	0	0	1	0	12.0	9.00	47	.250	.250	211	.366	0	-2	-2	-0	-0.1
1889	Phi-N	0	0	—	4	0	0	0	0	4	4	4	0	0	2	0	13.5	9.00	48	.250	.333	129	.259	1	-2	-2	-0	-0.1
Total	4	0	1	.000	7	0	0	0	0	14	17	16	1	0	3	5	12.2	4.50	84	.258	.279	791	.267	2	-1	-1	0	0.2
● CURRY FOLEY	Foley, Charles Joseph b: 1/14/1856, Milltown, Ireland d: 10/20/1898, Boston, Mass. TL, 5'10", 160 lbs. Deb: 5/13/1879 ♦																											
1879	Bos-N	9	9	.500	21	16	16	1	0	161^{2}	175	111	1		15	57	10.6	2.51	99	.252	.268	46	.315	5	-0	-0	-2	0.2
1880	Bos-N	14	14	.500	36	28	21	1	0	238	264	150	1		40	68	11.5	3.89	58	.274	.303	97	.292	8	-40	-45	1	-3.8
1881	Buf-N	3	4	.429	10	6	2	0	0	41	70	48	1		5	2	16.5	5.27	53	.337	.352	96	.256	1	-11	-11	-0	-1.5
1882	Buf-N	0	0	—	1	0	0	0	0	1	2	2	0		0	0	18.0	18.00	16	.333	.333	104	.305	0	-2	-2	-0	-0.1
1883	Buf-N	1	0	1.000	1	0	0	0	0	1	0	0	0		4	0	36.0	0.00	—	.000	.667	30	.270	0	0	0	-0	0.1
Total	5	27	27	.500	69	50	39	2	0	442^{2}	511	311	3		64	127	11.7	3.54	68	.273	.297	373	.286	14	-53	-58	-2	-5.1

YEAR	TM/L	W	L	PCT	G	GS	CG	SH	SV	IP	H	R	HR	HB	BB	SO	RAT	ERA	ERA+	OAV	OOB	BH	AVG	PB	PR	PR+	PD	TPI
● JOHN FOLEY	Foley, John J b: Hannibal, Mo. TL, Deb: 9/18/1885																											
1885	Pro-N	0	1	.000	1	1	1	0	0	8	6	7	0		5	2	12.4	4.50	60	.188	.297	0	.000	0	-1	-2	0	-0.2
● TOM FOLEY	Foley, Thomas Michael b: 9/9/59, Columbus, Ga. BL/TR, 6'1", 180 lbs. Deb: 4/9/83 ♦																											
1989	Mon-N	0	0	—	1	0	0	0	0	0^{1}	1	1	1	0	0	0	27.0	27.00	13	.500	.500	86	.229	0	-1	-1	0	0.0
● RICH FOLKERS	Folkers, Richard Nevin b: 10/17/46, Waterloo, Iowa BL/TL, 6'2", 180 lbs. Deb: 6/10/70																											
1970	NY-N	0	2	.000	16	1	0	0	2	29^{1}	36	21	6	0	25	15	18.7	6.44	63	.313	.436	2	.333	0	-8	-8	1	-0.4
1972	StL-N	1	0	1.000	9	0	0	0	0	13^{1}	12	5	0	0	5	7	11.5	3.38	101	.240	.309	0	.000	-0	0	0	-0	0.0
1973	StL-N	4	4	.500	34	9	1	0	3	82^{1}	74	34	10	3	34	44	12.1	3.61	101	.239	.321	2	.100	-1	1	0	-0	-0.1
1974	StL-N	6	2	.750	55	0	0	0	2	90	65	31	4	2	38	57	10.5	3.00	120	.207	.297	1	.100	-1	6	6	-1	0.3
1975	SD-N	6	11	.353	45	15	4	0	0	142	155	70	8	1	39	87	12.4	4.18	83	.278	.327	6	.167	1	-9	-12	-0	-1.2
1976	SD-N	2	3	.400	33	3	0	0	0	59^{2}	67	39	10	2	25	26	14.2	5.28	62	.279	.352	0	.000	-0	-12	-14	-0	-1.2
1977	Mil-A	0	1	.000	3	0	0	0	0	6^{1}	7	7	2	0	4	6	15.6	4.26	96	.269	.367	0	—	0	-0	-0	0	0.0
Total	7	19	23	.452	195	28	5	0	7	423	416	207	40	8	170	242	12.6	4.11	86	.258	.332	11	.143	-1	-21	-27	-1	-2.6
● LEW FONSECA	Fonseca, Lewis Albert b: 1/21/1899, Oakland, Cal. d: 11/26/89, Ely, Iowa BR/TR, 5'10.5", 180 lbs. Deb: 4/13/21 M♦																											
1932	Chi-A	0	0	—	1	0	0	0	0	1	0	0	0	0	0	0	0.0	0.00	—	.000	.000	5	.135	-0	0	0	-0	0.0
● JOE FONTENOT	Fontenot, Joseph Daniel b: 3/20/77, Scott, La. BR/TR, 6'2", 185 lbs. Deb: 5/23/98																											
1998	Fla-N	0	7	.000	8	8	0	0	0	42^{2}	56	34	5	5	20	24	17.1	6.33	64	.320	.405	0	.000	-1	-10	-11	1	-1.5
● RAY FONTENOT	Fontenot, Silton Ray b: 8/8/57, Lake Charles, La. BL/TL, 6', 175 lbs. Deb: 6/30/83																											
1983	NY-A	8	2	.800	15	15	3	1	0	97^{1}	101	41	3	1	25	27	11.7	3.33	117	.266	.314	0	—	0	8	7	1	0.7
1984	NY-A	8	9	.471	35	24	0	0	0	169^{1}	189	77	8	3	58	85	13.3	3.61	105	.290	.351	0	—	0	7	4	0	0.4
1985	Chi-N	6	10	.375	38	23	0	0	0	154^{2}	177	86	23	0	45	70	12.9	4.36	92	.294	.343	2	.049	-3	-13	-6	2	-0.7
1986	Chi-N	3	5	.375	42	0	0	0	2	56	57	30	5	0	21	24	12.5	3.86	105	.266	.332	1	.167	-0	-1	1	-1	0.1
	Min-A	0	0	—	15	0	0	0	0	16^{1}	27	19	3	2	4	10	18.2	9.92	44	.360	.407	0	.000	-0	-10	-10	0	-0.5
Total	4	25	26	.490	145	62	3	1	2	493^{2}	551	253	42	6	153	216	12.9	4.03	98	.287	.341	3	.063	-4	-9	-5	2	0.0
● JIM FOOR	Foor, James Emerson b: 1/13/49, St.Louis, Mo. BL/TL, 6'2", 170 lbs. Deb: 4/9/71																											
1971	Det-A	0	0	—	3	0	0	0	0	1	2	2	0	0	4	2	54.0	18.00	20	.400	.667	0	—	0	-2	-2	0	-0.1
1972	Det-A	1	0	1.000	7	0	0	0	0	3^{2}	6	6	1	0	6	2	29.5	14.73	21	.353	.522	0	—	0	-5	-5	0	-1.0
1973	Pit-N	0	0	—	3	0	0	0	0	1^{1}	2	0	0	0	1	1	20.3	0.00	—	.286	.375	0	—	0	1	1	0	0.0
Total	3	1	0	1.000	13	0	0	0	0	6	10	8	1	0	11	5	31.5	12.00	28	.345	.525	0	—	0	-6	-6	0	-1.1
● DAVY FORCE	Force, David W. "Wee Davy" or "Tom Thumb" b: 7/27/1849, New York, N.Y. d: 6/21/18, Englewood, N.J. BR/TR, 5'4", 130 lbs. Deb: 5/5/1871 ♦																											
1873	Bal-n	1	1	.500	3	1	1	0	0	18	23	20	0		0	0	11.5	3.50	93	.264	.264	86	.368	1	-0	-0		0.0
1874	Chi-n	0	0	—	1	0	0	0	0	7	22	24	4		0	0	28.3	15.43	14	.431	.431	92	.313	0	-10	-10		-0.3
Total	2 n	1	1	.500	4	1	1	0	0	25	45	44	4		0	0	16.2	6.84	33	.326	.326	437	.336	2	-13	-13		-0.3
● BEN FORD	Ford, Benjamin Cooper b: 8/15/75, Cedar Rapids, Iowa BR/TR, 6'7", 200 lbs. Deb: 8/20/98																											
1998	Ari-N	0	0	—	8	0	0	0	0	10	13	12	2	2	3	5	16.2	9.90	43	.295	.367	0	—	0	-6	-6	-0	-0.3
2000	NY-A	0	1	.000	4	2	0	0	0	11	14	11	1	3	7	5	19.6	9.00	53	.333	.462	0	—	0	-5	-5	-0	-0.4
Total	2	0	1	.000	12	2	0	0	0	21	27	23	3	5	10	10	18.0	9.43	48	.314	.416	0	—	0	-11	-12	-1	-0.7
● DAVE FORD	Ford, David Alan b: 12/29/56, Cleveland, Ohio BR/TR, 6'4", 190 lbs. Deb: 9/2/78																											
1978	Bal-A	1	0	1.000	2	1	0	0	0	15	10	0	0	0	2	5	7.2	0.00	—	.196	.226	0	—	0	6	6	-0	0.4
1979	Bal-A	2	1	.667	9	2	0	0	2	30	23	7	2	0	7	7	9.0	2.10	192	.219	.268	0	—	0	7	7	0	0.7
1980	Bal-A	1	3	.250	25	3	1	0	1	69^{2}	66	34	11	2	13	22	10.5	4.26	93	.251	.291	0	—	0	-2	-2	-1	-0.2
1981	Bal-A	1	2	.333	15	2	0	0	0	40	61	33	2	0	10	12	16.0	6.52	56	.359	.394	0	—	0	-13	-13	-0	-0.9
Total	4	5	6	.455	51	8	1	0	3	154^{2}	160	74	15	2	32	46	11.3	4.02	96	.272	.311	0	—	0	-1	-3	-1	0.0
● WHITEY FORD	Ford, Edward Charles "Chairman Of The Board" b: 10/21/28, New York, N.Y. BL/TL, 5'10", 181 lbs. Deb: 7/1/50 CH																											
1950	*NY-A	9	1	.900	20	12	7	2	1	112	87	39	7	2	52	59	11.3	2.81	153	.216	.309	7	.194	0	22	20	-0	1.6
1953	*NY-A	18	6	.750	32	30	11	3	0	207	187	77	13	4	110	110	13.1	3.00	123	.245	.344	20	.267	6	23	17	0	2.5
1954	NY-A★	16	8	.667	34	28	11	3	1	210^{2}	170	72	10	1	101	125	11.6	2.82	122	.227	.319	10	.161	2	21	16	1	2.0
1955	*NY-A★	**18**	7	.720	39	33	**18**	5	2	253^{2}	188	83	20	1	113	137	10.7	2.63	143	.208	.297	14	.163	2	38	33	-0	3.3
1956	*NY-A★	19	6	**.760**	31	30	18	2	1	225^{2}	187	70	13	4	84	141	11.0	**2.47**	156	.228	.303	17	.218	3	42	38	5	4.8
1957	*NY-A	11	5	.688	24	17	5	0	0	129^{1}	114	46	10	1	53	84	11.7	2.57	139	.237	.313	6	.143	-1	17	15	2	1.9
1958	*NY-A☆	14	7	.667	30	29	15	**7**	1	219^{1}	174	62	14	3	62	145	**9.8**	**2.01**	**176**	.217	**.276**	15	.205	2	**43**	**40**	1	**4.2**
1959	NY-A★	16	10	.615	35	29	9	2	1	204	194	82	13	1	89	114	12.5	3.04	120	.250	.328	15	.231	7	19	14	4	2.9
1960	*NY-A★	12	9	.571	33	29	8	**4**	0	192^{2}	168	76	15	1	65	85	10.9	3.08	116	.235	.299	8	.151	2	17	12	1	1.5
1961	*NY-A★	**25**	4	**.862**	39	39	11	3	0	**283**	242	108	23	1	92	209	10.7	3.21	116	.229	.292	17	.177	3	26	17	1	1.9
1962	*NY-A	17	8	.680	38	37	7	0	0	257^{2}	243	90	22	4	69	160	11.0	2.90	129	.246	.298	10	.118	-1	31	26	4	2.7
1963	*NY-A	**24**	7	**.774**	38	37	13	3	1	**269^{1}**	240	94	26	2	56	189	10.0	2.74	128	.241	.283	13	.141	0	27	24	-0	2.7
1964	*NY-A☆	17	6	.739	39	36	12	8	1	244^{2}	212	67	10	2	57	172	10.0	2.13	170	.230	.276	8	.119	1	41	40	2	4.2
1965	NY-A	16	13	.552	37	36	9	2	1	244^{1}	241	97	22	1	50	162	10.8	3.24	105	.258	.297	15	.183	2	6	4	2	0.9
1966	NY-A	2	5	.286	22	9	0	0	0	73	79	33	8	0	24	43	12.7	2.47	135	.277	.333	0	.000	-2	8	7	3	0.8
1967	NY-A	2	4	.333	7	7	2	1	0	44	40	11	2	0	9	21	10.0	1.64	191	.247	.287	2	.154	-0	8	8	2	1.3
Total	16	236	106	.690	498	438	156	45	10	3170^{1}	2766	1107	228	28	1086	1956	11.0	2.75	133	.235	.301	177	.173	27	386	332	26	39.2
● GENE FORD	Ford, Eugene Matthew b: 6/23/12, Ft.Dodge, Iowa d: 9/7/70, Emmetsburg, Iowa BR/TR, 6'2", 195 lbs. Deb: 6/17/36																											
1936	Bos-N	0	0	—	2	1	0	0	0	2	2	3	0	0	3	0	22.5	13.50	28	.250	.455	0	—	0	-2	-2	0	-0.1
1938	Chi-A	0	0	—	4	0	0	0	0	14	21	16	1	0	12	2	21.2	10.29	48	.350	.458	1	.167	-0	-9	-8	0	-0.4
Total	2	0	0	—	6	1	0	0	0	16	23	19	1	0	15	2	21.4	10.69	44	.338	.458	1	.167	-0	-11	-10	0	-0.5
● GENE FORD	Ford, Eugene Wyman b: 4/16/1881, Milton, N.S., Can. d: 8/23/73, Dunedin, Fla. BR/TR, 6', 170 lbs. Deb: 5/5/05 F																											
1905	Det-A	0	1	.000	7	1	1	0	0	35	51	30	0	2	14	20	17.2	5.66	48	.340	.404	0	.000	-1	-12	-11	0	-0.6
● WENTY FORD	Ford, Percival Edmund Wentworth b: 11/25/46, Nassau, Bahamas d: 7/8/80, Nassau, Bahamas BR/TR, 5'11", 165 lbs. Deb: 9/10/73																											
1973	Atl-N	1	2	.333	4	2	1	0	0	16^{1}	17	10	3	1	8	4	14.3	5.51	72	.279	.371	2	.400	1	-3	-3	0	-0.4
● RUSS FORD	Ford, Russell William b: 4/25/1883, Brandon, Man., Can. d: 1/24/60, Rockingham, N.C. BR/TR, 5'11", 175 lbs. Deb: 4/28/09 F																											
1909	NY-A	0	0	—	1	0	0	0	0	3	4	4	0	3	4	2	33.0	9.00	28	.333	.579	0	.000	-0	-2	-2	0	-0.1
1910	NY-A	26	6	.813	36	33	29	8	1	299^{2}	194	69	4	8	70	209	8.2	1.65	161	.188	.245	20	.208	4	29	32	-3	3.8
1911	NY-A	22	11	.667	37	33	26	1	0	281^{1}	251	119	3	4	76	158	10.6	2.27	158	.237	.291	20	.196	-2	34	39	-1	3.9
1912	NY-A	13	21	.382	36	35	30	0	0	291^{2}	317	165	10	5	79	112	12.4	3.55	101	.280	.329	32	.286	5	-7	1	1	0.9
1913	NY-A	12	18	.400	33	28	15	1	2	237	244	101	9	4	58	72	11.6	2.66	113	.275	.322	12	.162	0	7	9	-4	0.7
1914	Buf-F	21	6	**.778**	35	26	19	5	**6**	247^{1}	190	63	11	7	41	123	8.7	1.82	**163**	.214	.254	10	.128	-4	29	31	0	3.0
1915	Buf-F	5	9	.357	21	15	7	0	0	127^{1}	140	74	7	3	48	34	13.5	4.52	62	.285	.352	12	.279	3	-25	-24	-0	-2.1
Total	7	99	71	.582	199	170	126	15	9	1487^{1}	1340	595	44	34	376	710	10.6	2.59	121	.243	.296	106	.209	5	64	85	-5	10.1
● TOM FORD	Ford, Thomas Walter b: 1866, Chattanooga, Tenn. d: 5/27/17, Chattanooga, Tenn. 5'10.5", 155 lbs. Deb: 5/6/1890																											
1890	Col-a	0	0	—	1	0	0	0	0	2	0	0	0	0	3	0	13.5	0.00	—	.000	.333	0	.000	-0	1	1	0	0.0
	Bro-a	0	6	.000	7	6	6	0	0	49	70	60	2	0	32	12	18.7	5.14	76	.326	.413	1	.033	-3	-7	-7	0	-0.8
	Yr	0	6	.000	8	6	6	0	0	51	70	60	2	0	35	12	18.5	4.94	79	.317	.410	1	.032	-3	-6	-6	1	-0.8
● TOM FORDHAM	Fordham, Thomas James b: 2/20/74, San Diego, Cal. BL/TL, 6'2", 210 lbs. Deb: 8/19/97																											
1997	Chi-A	0	1	.000	7	1	0	0	0	17^{1}	17	13	2	1	10	10	14.5	6.23	70	.266	.373	0	—	0	-3	-4	-0	-0.2
1998	Chi-A	1	2	.333	29	5	0	0	0	48	51	36	7	1	42	23	17.6	6.75	67	.279	.416	0	.000	-0	-11	-12	1	-0.6
Total	2	1	3	.250	36	6	0	0	0	65^{1}	68	49	9	2	52	33	16.8	6.61	68	.275	.405	0	.000	-0	-14	-16	1	-0.8

YEAR	TM/L	W	L	PCT	G	GS	CG	SH	SV	IP	H	R	HR	HB	BB	SO	RAT	ERA	ERA+	OAV	OOB	BH	AVG	PB	PR	PR+	PD	TPI
● HAPPY FOREMAN	Foreman, August G. b: 7/20/1897, Memphis, Tenn. d: 2/13/53, New York, N.Y. BL/TL, 5'7", 160 lbs. Deb: 9/3/24																											
1924	Chi-A	0	0	—	3	0	0	0	0	4	7	3	0	0	4	1	24.8	2.25	183	.467	.579	0	.000	-0	1	1	-0	0.0
1926	Bos-A	0	0	—	3	0	0	0	0	7^1	3	3	0	0	5	3	9.8	3.68	111	.130	.286	0	.000	-0	0	0	1	0.0
Total	2	0	0	—	6	0	0	0	0	11^1	10	6	0	0	9	4	15.1	3.18	129	.263	.404	0	.000	-1	1	1	0	0.0
● FRANK FOREMAN	Foreman, Francis Isaiah "Monkey" b: 5/1/1863, Baltimore, Md. d: 11/19/57, Baltimore, Md. BL/TL, 6', 160 lbs. Deb: 5/15/1884 F◆																											
1884	CP-U	1	2	.333	3	3	1	0	0	18	23	17	0		2	10	12.5	4.00	61	.291	.309	1	.091	-2	-3	-3	-0	-0.5
	KC-U	0	1	.000	1	1	1	0	0	8	17	12	0		2	5	21.4	5.63	40	.405	.432	0	.000	-1	-3	-3	1	-0.3
	Yr	1	3	.250	4	4	2	0	0	26	40	29	0		4	15	15.2	4.50	53	.331	.352	1	.071	-3	-6	-6	1	-0.8
1885	Bal-a	2	1	.667	3	3	2	0	0	27	33	32	0	1	9	11	14.3	6.00	54	.284	.341	4	.286	1	-8	-8	-0	-0.6
1889	Bal-a	23	21	.523	51	48	43	5	0	414	364	257	8	40	137	180	11.8	3.52	112	.229	.306	26	.144	-10	15	19	-2	0.4
1890	Cin-N	13	10	.565	25	24	20	0	0	198^1	201	139	6	20	89	57	14.1	3.95	90	.255	.345	10	.133	-0	-8	-9	-3	-1.1
1891	Was-a	18	20	.474	43	41	39	1	1	345^1	381	245	9	43	142	170	14.8	3.73	100	.271	.355	34	.222	9	-0	0	-1	0.8
1892	Was-N	2	4	.333	11	7	4	0	0	60	53	39	3	5	37	16	14.3	3.30	99	.227	.345	13	.464	8	-0	-0	-1	0.6
	Bal-N	0	3	.000	4	3	2	0	0	25	40	29	4	1	11	5	18.7	6.84	50	.348	.409	4	.174	0	-10	-9	0	-0.8
	Yr	2	7	.222	15	10	6	0	0	85	93	68	7	6	48	21	15.6	4.34	76	.267	.366	17	.333	8	-10	-10	-1	-0.2
1893	NY-N	0	1	.000	2	1	0	0	0	5^2	19	17	1	1	10	0	47.6	27.00	17	.528	.638	0	.000	-1	-14	-14	-0	-1.4
1895	Cin-N	11	14	.440	32	27	19	0	1	219	253	142	11	15	92	55	14.8	4.11	121	.285	.362	29	.309	4	16	20	-3	1.8
1896	Cin-N	14	7	.667	27	22	17	0	1	185^2	212	110	2	8	62	33	13.7	3.97	116	.285	.346	18	.243	-1	8	12	-1	0.9
1901	Bos-A	0	1	.000	1	1	1	0	0	8	8	9	1	2	2	1	13.5	9.00	39	.258	.343	0	.000	-1	-5	-5	-0	-0.5
	Bal-A	12	6	.667	24	22	18	1	1	191^1	225	120	2	6	58	41	13.6	3.67	105	.290	.344	26	.325	5	-0	4	-3	0.5
	Yr	12	7	.632	25	23	19	1	1	199^1	233	129	3	8	60	42	13.6	3.88	99	.288	.344	26	.310	4	-5	-1	-3	0.0
1902	Bal-A	0	2	.000	2	2	2	0	0	16^1	28	18	0	0	6	2	18.7	6.06	62	.378	.425	3	.429	1	-5	-4	1	-0.2
Total	11	96	93	.508	229	205	169	7	4	1721^2	1857	1186	47	142	659	586	13.9	3.97	100	.268	.344	169	.224	12	-17	1	-14	-0.4
● BROWNIE FOREMAN	Foreman, John Davis b: 8/6/1875, Baltimore, Md. d: 10/10/26, Baltimore, Md. BL/TL, 5'8", 150 lbs. Deb: 7/18/1895 F																											
1895	Pit-N	8	6	.571	19	16	12	0	2	139^2	131	83	0	19	64	54	13.8	3.22	140	**.244**	.346	3	.065	-6	24	21	2	1.4
1896	Pit-N	3	3	.500	9	9	5	0	0	61^2	73	55	4	8	35	18	16.9	6.57	64	.292	.396	3	.150	0	-15	-17	1	-1.1
	Cin-N	1	3	.250	4	4	3	1	0	23	41	30	2	2	16	9	23.1	11.35	41	.383	.472	2	.200	-0	-18	-16	-0	-1.8
	Yr	4	6	.400	13	13	8	1	0	84^2	114	85	6	10	51	27	18.6	7.87	55	.319	.419	5	.167	-0	-33	-34	1	-2.9
Total	2	12	12	.500	32	29	20	1	2	224^1	245	168	6	29	115	81	15.6	4.97	89	.274	.375	8	.105	-6	-9	-14	3	-1.5
● BILL FORMAN	Forman, William Orange b: 10/10/1886, Venango, Pa. d: 10/2/58, Uniontown, Pa. BB/TR, 5'11", 180 lbs. Deb: 9/20/09																											
1909	Was-A	0	2	.000	2	2	1	0	0	11	8	8	0	2	7	2	13.9	4.91	50	.211	.362	1	.333	0	-3	-3	1	-0.4
1910	Was-A	0	0	—	1	0	0	0	0	0^2	1	1	0	0	0	0	13.5	13.50	18	.333	.333	0	—	0	-1	-1	-0	0.0
Total	2	0	2	.000	3	2	1	0	0	11^2	9	9	0	2	7	2	13.9	5.40	45	.220	.360	1	.333	1	-4	-4	1	-0.4
● MIKE FORNIELES	Fornieles, Jose Miguel (Torres) b: 1/18/32, Havana, Cuba d: 2/11/98, St.Petersburg, Fla. BR/TR, 5'11", 172 lbs. Deb: 9/2/52																											
1952	Was-A	2	2	.500	4	2	2	1	0	26^1	13	4	1	0	11	12	8.2	1.37	260	.143	.235	0	.000	-1	7	7	-0	0.9
1953	Chi-A	8	7	.533	39	16	5	0	3	153	160	68	8	2	61	72	13.1	3.59	112	.270	.340	4	.098	-3	7	7	2	0.6
1954	Chi-A	1	2	.333	15	6	0	0	1	42	41	24	4	0	14	18	11.8	4.29	87	.252	.311	3	.273	0	-3	-3	1	-0.1
1955	Chi-A	6	3	.667	26	9	2	0	2	86^1	84	37	12	2	29	23	12.0	3.86	102	.255	.319	3	.103	-2	1	1	0	-0.1
1956	Chi-A	0	1	.000	6	0	0	0	0	15^2	22	9	1	0	6	6	16.1	4.60	89	.306	.359	1	.200	0	-1	-1	-0	0.0
	Bal-A	4	7	.364	30	11	1	1	1	111	109	59	7	0	25	53	10.9	3.97	99	.266	.308	5	.167	-1	2	-1	2	0.1
	Yr	4	8	.333	36	11	1	1	1	126^2	131	68	8	0	31	59	11.5	4.05	97	.272	.316	6	.171	-1	2	-2	2	0.1
1957	Bal-A	2	6	.250	15	4	1	1	0	57	57	30	4	0	17	43	11.7	4.26	84	.257	.310	5	.278	1	-3	-4	1	-0.4
	Bos-A	8	7	.533	25	18	7	1	2	125^1	136	61	7	3	38	64	12.7	3.52	113	.271	.327	6	.136	-2	4	6	-1	0.4
	Yr	10	13	.435	40	22	8	2	2	182^1	193	91	11	3	55	107	12.4	3.75	103	.267	.321	11	.177	-1	1	2	-1	0.0
1958	Bos-A	4	6	.400	37	7	1	0	1	110^2	123	62	10	6	33	49	13.2	4.96	81	.284	.343	6	.207	-0	-15	-11	-0	-1.0
1959	Bos-A	5	3	.625	46	0	0	0	11	82	77	29	6	1	29	54	11.7	3.07	132	.254	.321	3	.158	-1	7	9	-0	1.0
1960	Bos-A	10	5	.667	**70**	0	0	0	**14**	109	86	38	6	6	49	64	11.6	2.64	153	.219	.315	6	.400	2	15	16	1	2.8
1961	Bos-A★	9	8	.529	57	2	1	0	15	119^1	121	65	18	2	54	70	13.3	4.68	89	.265	.345	5	.156	0	-9	-7	2	-0.8
1962	Bos-A	3	6	.333	42	1	0	0	5	82^1	96	57	14	8	37	36	15.4	5.36	77	.303	.390	3	.188	-0	-13	-11	-0	-1.2
1963	Bos-A	0	0	—	9	0	0	0	0	14	16	10	0	0	5	5	13.5	6.43	59	.286	.344	1	.333	1	-4	-4	-0	-0.2
	Min-A	1	1	.500	11	0	0	0	0	22^2	24	14	0	2	13	7	15.5	4.76	76	.273	.379	1	.167	0	-3	-3	-1	-0.3
	Yr	1	1	.500	20	0	0	0	0	36^2	40	24	0	2	18	12	14.7	5.40	68	.278	.366	2	.222	1	-7	-7	-1	-0.5
Total	12	63	64	.496	432	76	20	4	55	1156^2	1165	567	98	32	421	576	12.6	3.96	100	.263	.332	52	.169	-6	-7	2	4	1.7
● KEN FORSCH	Forsch, Kenneth Roth b: 9/8/46, Sacramento, Cal. BR/TR, 6'4", 210 lbs. Deb: 9/7/70 F																											
1970	Hou-N	1	2	.333	4	4	1	0	0	24	28	15	1	0	5	13	12.4	5.63	69	.298	.333	0	.000	-1	-4	-5	-0	-0.6
1971	Hou-N	8	8	.500	33	23	7	2	0	188^1	162	60	8	4	53	131	10.5	2.53	133	.230	.288	8	.136	-1	20	18	-2	1.1
1972	Hou-N	6	8	.429	30	24	1	0	0	156^1	163	75	19	0	62	113	13.0	3.91	86	.273	.341	6	.146	-1	-8	-10	-3	-1.2
1973	Hou-N	9	12	.429	46	26	5	0	4	201^1	197	101	18	4	74	149	12.3	4.20	87	.257	.325	4	.065	-4	-12	-13	-2	-1.9
1974	Hou-N	8	7	.533	70	0	0	0	10	103^1	98	38	3	4	37	48	12.1	2.79	125	.255	.326	0	.000	-1	10	8	-0	1.2
1975	Hou-N	4	8	.333	34	9	2	0	2	109	114	42	9	2	30	54	12.1	3.22	105	.277	.330	1	.045	-1	5	2	-0	0.1
1976	Hou-N★	4	3	.571	52	0	0	0	19	92	76	23	5	2	26	49	10.2	2.15	149	.226	.286	1	.091	-0	14	12	1	1.5
1977	Hou-N	5	8	.385	42	5	0	0	8	86	80	32	2	2	28	45	11.5	2.72	131	.246	.310	1	.077	-1	11	9	1	1.4
1978	Hou-N	10	6	.625	52	6	4	2	7	133^1	136	44	2	1	37	71	11.7	2.70	123	.268	.319	5	.185	0	13	10	1	1.3
1979	Hou-N	11	6	.647	26	24	10	2	0	177^2	155	67	14	0	35	58	**9.6**	3.04	116	.236	**.275**	8	.138	0	14	10	2	1.2
1980	*Hou-N	12	13	.480	32	32	6	3	0	222^1	230	90	15	7	41	84	11.3	3.20	103	.266	.304	18	.234	4	10	3	1	0.8
1981	Cal-A★	11	7	.611	20	20	10	**4**	0	153	143	54	7	4	27	55	10.2	2.88	127	.250	.289	0	—	0	13	13	1	1.6
1982	Cal-A	13	11	.542	37	35	12	4	0	228	225	108	25	11	57	73	11.6	3.87	105	.258	.311	0	—	0	5	5	-2	0.3
1983	Cal-A	11	12	.478	31	31	11	1	0	219^1	226	107	21	4	61	81	11.9	4.06	99	.266	.318	0	—	0	0	-1	-1	-0.2
1984	Cal-A	1	1	.500	2	2	1	0	0	16^1	14	4	2	0	3	10	9.4	2.20	180	.237	.274	0	—	0	3	3	1	0.5
1986	Cal-A	0	1	.000	10	0	0	0	1	17	24	21	4	2	10	13	19.1	9.53	43	.343	.439	0	—	0	-10	-10	0	-0.6
Total	16	114	113	.502	521	241	70	18	51	2127^1	2071	881	155	47	586	1047	11.4	3.37	106	.257	.311	52	.136	-5	85	52	-3	6.5
● BOB FORSCH	Forsch, Robert Herbert b: 1/13/50, Sacramento, Cal. BR/TR, 6'4", 200 lbs. Deb: 7/7/74 F																											
1974	StL-N	7	4	.636	19	14	5	2	0	100	84	38	5	1	34	39	10.7	2.97	121	.230	.298	7	.241	1	7	7	-0	0.9
1975	StL-N	15	10	.600	34	34	7	4	0	230	213	89	14	3	70	108	11.2	2.86	132	.244	.303	24	.308	9	20	22	2	3.6
1976	StL-N	8	10	.444	33	32	2	0	0	194	209	112	17	3	71	76	13.1	3.94	90	.277	.341	11	.177	1	-9	-9	1	-0.6
1977	StL-N	20	7	.741	35	35	8	2	0	217^1	210	97	20	3	69	95	11.7	3.48	111	.251	.311	12	.167	0	11	9	-1	1.0
1978	StL-N	11	17	.393	34	34	7	3	0	233^2	205	110	15	5	97	114	11.8	3.70	95	.238	.318	15	.181	3	-3	-5	1	-0.1
1979	StL-N	11	11	.500	33	32	7	1	0	218^2	215	102	16	3	52	92	11.1	3.83	99	.262	.309	8	.110	-0	-2	-1	1	-0.1
1980	StL-N	11	10	.524	31	31	8	0	0	214^2	225	102	12	4	33	87	11.0	3.77	98	.273	.304	23	.295	9	-4	-2	2	1.0
1981	StL-N	10	5	.667	20	20	1	0	0	124^1	106	47	7	4	29	41	10.1	3.18	112	.232	.284	5	.122	-1	4	5	0	0.5
1982	*StL-N	15	9	.625	36	34	6	2	1	233	238	95	16	4	54	69	11.4	3.48	104	.268	.313	15	.205	3	3	4	-2	0.5
1983	StL-N	10	12	.455	34	30	6	2	0	187	190	104	23	3	54	56	11.9	4.28	85	.266	.320	13	.241	4	-13	-14	-0	-1.1
1984	StL-N	2	5	.286	16	11	1	0	0	52^1	64	38	6	0	19	21	14.3	6.02	58	.303	.361	4	.250	1	-14	-15	0	-1.7
1985	*StL-N	9	6	.600	34	19	3	1	2	136	132	63	11	2	47	48	12.0	3.90	91	.258	.323	11	.244	4	-5	-6	-0	-0.2
1986	StL-N	14	10	.583	33	33	3	0	0	230	211	91	19	2	68	104	11.0	3.25	112	.247	.304	13	.171	3	12	10	1	1.3
1987	*StL-N	11	7	.611	33	30	2	1	0	179	189	90	15	4	45	89	12.0	4.32	96	.273	.321	17	.298	8	-5	-3	-1	0.4
1988	StL-N	9	4	.692	30	12	1	1	0	108^2	111	51	8	1	38	40	12.4	3.73	93	.270	.333	7	.280	2	-3	-3	-2	-0.3
	Hou-N	1	4	.200	6	6	0	0	0	27^2	42	22	2	2	6	14	16.3	6.51	51	.359	.400	1	.143	0	-9	-10	-0	-1.5
	Yr	10	8	.556	36	18	1	1	0	136^1	153	73	10	3	44	54	13.2	4.29	80	.290	.348	8	.250	2	-13	-13	-2	-1.8
1989	Hou-N	4	5	.444	37	15	0	0	0	108^1	133	68	10	1	46	40	15.0	5.32	64	.303	.370	4	.167	-0	-22	-24	-1	-2.0
Total	16	168	136	.553	498	422	67	19	3	2794^2	2777	1319	216	45	832	1133	11.8	3.76	97	.261	.318	190	.213	48	-32	-31	-3	1.6
● SCOTT FORSTER	Forster, Scott Christian b: 10/27/71, Philadelphia, Pa. BR/TL, 6'1", 194 lbs. Deb: 6/18/2000																											
2000	Mon-N	0	1	.000	42	0	0	0	0	32	28	31	5	2	25	23	15.5	7.88	60	.230	.369	0	—	0	-12	-11	0	-0.5

YEAR	TM/L	W	L	PCT	G	GS	CG	SH	SV	IP	H	R	HR	HB	BB	SO	RAT	ERA	ERA+	OAV	OOB	BH	AVG	PB	PR	PR+	PD	TPI
● **TERRY FORSTER**	Forster, Terry Jay b: 1/14/52, Sioux Falls, S.D. BL/TL, 6'3", 210 lbs. Deb: 4/11/71																											
1971	Chi-A	2	3	.400	45	3	0	0	1	49^2	46	23	5	1	23	48	12.7	3.99	90	.241	.326	2	.400	1	-3	-2	0	-0.1
1972	Chi-A	6	5	.545	62	0	0	0	29	100	75	31	0	3	44	104	11.0	2.25	139	.208	.300	10	.526	4	9	10	1	2.5
1973	Chi-A	6	11	.353	51	12	4	0	16	172^2	174	69	7	0	78	120	13.1	3.23	123	.266	.344	0	.000	-0	11	14	5	2.0
1974	Chi-A	7	8	.467	59	1	0	0	**24**	134^1	120	57	6	8	48	105	11.8	3.62	103	.245	.322	0	—	0	0	2	3	0.6
1975	Chi-A	3	3	.500	17	1	0	0	4	37	30	12	0	0	24	32	13.1	2.19	177	.236	.358	0	—	0	7	7	2	1.4
1976	Chi-A	2	12	.143	29	16	1	0	1	111^1	126	61	7	1	41	70	13.6	4.37	82	.288	.351	0	—	0	-10	-10	2	-1.0
1977	Pit-N	6	4	.600	33	6	0	0	1	87^1	90	47	7	2	32	58	12.8	4.43	90	.269	.337	9	.346	3	-5	-4	-0	-0.2
1978	*LA-N	5	4	.556	47	0	0	0	22	65^1	56	19	2	0	23	46	10.9	1.93	182	.233	.300	4	.500	2	12	12	-0	2.7
1979	LA-N	1	2	.333	17	0	0	0	2	16^1	18	11	0	0	11	8	16.0	5.51	66	.295	.403	0	—	0	-3	-3	1	-0.6
1980	LA-N	0	0	—	9	0	0	0	0	11^2	10	4	0	0	4	2	10.8	3.09	114	.222	.286	0	—	0	1	1	0	0.1
1981	*LA-N	0	1	.000	21	0	0	0	0	30^2	37	14	1	0	15	17	15.3	4.11	81	.308	.385	0	.000	-0	-2	-3	1	-0.1
1982	LA-N	5	6	.455	56	0	0	0	3	83	66	38	3	4	31	52	11.0	3.04	114	.221	.302	0	.000	-0	5	4	1	0.6
1983	Atl-N	3	2	.600	56	0	0	0	13	79^1	60	19	3	2	31	54	10.6	2.16	180	.217	.301	4	.500	2	13	14	1	1.5
1984	Atl-N	2	0	1.000	25	0	0	0	5	26^2	30	9	1	0	7	10	12.5	2.70	143	.297	.343	2	.667	1	3	3	0	0.4
1985	Atl-N	2	3	.400	46	0	0	0	1	59^1	49	22	7	0	28	37	11.7	2.28	169	.222	.309	0	.000	-0	9	10	-1	0.7
1986	Cal-A	4	1	.800	41	0	0	0	5	41	47	18	2	3	17	28	14.7	3.51	117	.297	.376	0	—	0	3	3	1	0.5
Total	16	54	65	.454	614	39	5	0	127	1105^2	1034	454	51	24	457	791	12.3	3.23	115	.251	.330	31	.397	11	49	57	16	11.0
● **TIM FORTUGNO**	Fortugno, Timothy Shawn b: 4/11/62, Clinton, Mass. BL/TL, 6'1", 195 lbs. Deb: 7/20/92																											
1992	Cal-A	1	1	.500	14	5	1	1	1	41^2	37	24	5	0	19	31	12.1	5.18	77	.236	.318	0	—	0	-6	-5	-0	-0.3
1994	Cin-N	1	0	1.000	25	0	0	0	0	30	32	14	2	3	14	29	14.7	4.20	99	.288	.383	1	.333	0	-0	-0	1	0.1
1995	Chi-A	1	3	.250	37	0	0	0	0	38^2	30	24	7	0	19	24	11.4	5.59	80	.213	.306	0	—	0	-4	-5	0	-0.4
Total	3	3	4	.429	76	5	1	1	1	110^1	99	62	14	3	52	84	12.6	5.06	83	.242	.332	1	.333	0	-9	-11	0	-0.6
● **GARY FORTUNE**	Fortune, Garrett Reese b: 10/11/1894, High Point, N.C. d: 9/23/55, Washington, D.C. BB/TR, 5'11.5", 176 lbs. Deb: 10/5/16																											
1916	Phi-N	0	1	.000	1	1	0	0	0	5	2	2	0	0	4	3	10.8	3.60	74	.118	.286	0	.000	-0	-1	-1	-0	-0.2
1918	Phi-N	0	2	.000	5	2	1	0	0	31	41	30	2	1	19	10	17.7	8.13	37	.333	.427	2	.200	0	-18	-16	-0	-0.9
1920	Bos-A	0	2	.000	14	3	1	0	0	41^2	46	32	0	0	23	10	14.9	5.83	63	.282	.371	2	.167	-0	-9	-11	-1	-0.6
Total	3	0	5	.000	20	6	2	0	0	77^2	89	64	2	1	46	23	15.8	6.61	51	.294	.389	4	.167	-0	-28	-28	-1	-1.7
● **JERRY FOSNOW**	Fosnow, Gerald Eugene b: 9/21/40, Deshler, Ohio BR/TL, 6'4", 195 lbs. Deb: 6/29/64																											
1964	Min-A	0	1	.000	7	0	0	0	0	10^2	13	13	3	0	8	9	17.7	10.97	33	.302	.412	0	—	0	-9	-9	-0	-0.8
1965	Min-A	3	3	.500	29	0	0	0	2	46^2	33	29	7	1	25	35	11.4	4.44	80	.193	.299	0	.000	-1	-5	-4	0	-0.6
Total	2	3	4	.429	36	0	0	0	2	57^1	46	42	10	1	33	44	12.6	5.65	63	.215	.323	0	.000	-1	-14	-13	0	-1.4
● **LARRY FOSS**	Foss, Larry Curtis b: 4/18/36, Castleton, Kan. BR/TR, 6'2", 187 lbs. Deb: 9/18/61																											
1961	Pit-N	1	1	.500	3	3	0	0	0	15^1	15	11	3	2	11	9	16.4	5.87	68	.273	.412	1	.167	-0	-3	-3	-0	-0.4
1962	NY-N	0	1	.000	5	1	0	0	0	11^2	17	6	2	1	7	3	19.3	4.63	90	.362	.455	0	.000	-0	-1	-1	-0	-0.1
Total	2	1	2	.333	8	4	0	0	0	27	32	17	5	3	18	12	17.7	5.33	76	.314	.431	1	.143	-0	-4	-4	-0	-0.5
● **TONY FOSSAS**	Fossas, Emilio Antonio (Morejon) b: 9/23/57, Havana, Cuba BL/TL, 6', 187 lbs. Deb: 5/15/88																											
1988	Tex-A	0	0	—	5	0	0	0	0	5^2	11	3	0	0	2	0	20.6	4.76	86	.423	.464	0	—	0	-0	-0	0	0.0
1989	Mil-A	2	2	.500	51	0	0	0	1	61	57	27	3	1	22	42	11.8	3.54	109	.256	.325	0	—	0	2	2	0	0.2
1990	Mil-A	2	3	.400	32	0	0	0	0	29^1	44	23	5	0	10	24	16.6	6.44	60	.331	.378	0	—	0	-8	-8	-0	-1.3
1991	Bos-A	3	2	.600	64	0	0	0	1	57	49	27	3	3	28	29	12.6	3.47	124	.236	.335	0	—	0	4	5	1	0.5
1992	Bos-A	1	2	.333	60	0	0	0	2	29^2	31	9	1	1	14	19	14.0	2.43	174	.279	.365	0	—	0	5	6	1	0.6
1993	Bos-A	1	1	.500	71	0	0	0	0	40	38	28	4	2	15	39	12.4	5.17	89	.242	.316	0	—	0	-4	-2	0	-0.1
1994	Bos-A	2	0	1.000	44	0	0	0	1	34	35	18	6	1	15	31	13.5	4.76	106	.263	.342	0	—	0	0	1	-0	0.0
1995	StL-N	3	0	1.000	58	0	0	0	0	36^2	28	6	1	1	10	40	9.6	1.47	285	.214	.275	0	—	0	11	11	-0	0.8
1996	*StL-N	0	4	.000	65	0	0	0	2	47	43	19	7	0	21	36	12.3	2.68	156	.231	.309	0	.000	-0	8	8	0	0.7
1997	StL-N	2	7	.222	71	0	0	0	0	51^2	62	32	7	1	26	41	15.5	3.83	108	.298	.379	0	—	0	2	2	2	0.5
1998	Sea-A	0	3	.000	23	0	0	0	0	11^1	19	11	1	0	6	10	19.9	8.74	53	.404	.472	0	—	0	-5	-5	0	-0.9
	Chi-N	0	0	—	8	0	0	0	0	4	8	4	0	0	6	6	31.5	9.00	49	.421	.560	0	—	0	-2	-2	0	-0.1
	Tex-A	1	0	1.000	10	0	0	0	0	7^1	3	0	0	0	4	7	8.6	0.00	—	.120	.241	0	—	0	4	4	-0	0.4
1999	NY-A	0	0	—	5	0	0	0	0	1	6	4	1	0	1	0	63.0	36.00	13	.667	.700	0	—	0	-3	-4	0	-0.2
Total	12	17	24	.415	567	0	0	0	7	415^2	434	211	39	10	180	324	13.5	3.90	109	.269	.346	0	.000	-0	13	17	3	1.1
● **ALAN FOSTER**	Foster, Alan Benton b: 12/8/46, Pasadena, Cal. BR/TR, 6', 180 lbs. Deb: 4/25/67																											
1967	LA-N	0	1	.000	4	2	0	0	0	16^2	10	4	0	0	3	15	7.0	2.16	143	.169	.210	0	.000	-0	2	2	0	0.1
1968	LA-N	1	1	.500	3	3	0	0	0	15^2	11	4	1	0	2	10	7.5	1.72	160	.200	.228	1	.250	0	2	2	-0	0.3
1969	LA-N	3	9	.250	24	15	2	2	0	102^2	119	55	11	4	29	59	13.3	4.38	76	.290	.342	2	.074	-1	-9	-13	-0	-1.5
1970	LA-N	10	13	.435	33	33	7	1	0	198^2	200	104	22	2	81	83	12.8	4.26	90	.264	.337	7	.109	-2	-5	-10	-1	-1.3
1971	Cle-A	8	12	.400	36	26	3	0	0	181^2	158	93	19	4	82	97	12.1	4.16	92	.232	.318	2	.039	-4	-14	-6	-4	-1.5
1972	Cal-A	0	1	.000	8	0	0	0	0	12^2	12	8	3	2	6	11	14.2	4.97	59	.245	.351	0	—	0	-3	-3	0	-0.2
1973	StL-N	13	9	.591	35	29	6	2	0	203^2	195	82	17	5	63	106	11.6	3.14	116	.254	.315	13	.191	1	12	12	-2	1.1
1974	StL-N	7	10	.412	31	25	5	1	0	162^1	167	81	16	3	61	78	12.8	3.88	92	.268	.336	8	.167	-1	-5	-5	-1	-0.7
1975	SD-N	3	1	.750	17	4	1	0	0	44^2	41	14	1	0	21	20	12.5	2.42	144	.244	.328	1	.091	-1	6	6	0	0.4
1976	SD-N	3	6	.333	26	11	2	0	0	86^2	75	36	9	1	35	22	11.5	3.22	102	.235	.313	1	.056	-0	3	1	-1	0.0
Total	10	48	63	.432	217	148	26	6	0	1025^1	988	481	99	21	383	501	12.2	3.74	97	.254	.324	35	.119	-8	-9	-15	-9	-3.3
● **ED FOSTER**	Foster, Eddy Lee "Slim" b: Georgia d: 3/1/29, Montgomery, Ala. BR/TR, 6'1", Deb: 7/31/08																											
1908	Cle-A	1	0	1.000	6	1	1	0	2	21	16	5	1	2	12	11	12.9	2.14	111	.229	.357	0	.000	-0	1	1	-1	-0.1
● **RUBE FOSTER**	Foster, George b: 1/5/1888, Lehigh, Okla d: 3/1/76, Bokoshe, Okla. BR/TR, 5'7.5", 170 lbs. Deb: 4/10/13																											
1913	Bos-A	3	3	.500	19	8	4	1	0	68^1	64	35	1	4	28	36	12.6	3.16	93	.249	.332	2	.095	-1	-2	-2	1	-0.2
1914	Bos-A	14	8	.636	32	27	17	5	0	211^2	164	68	2	7	52	89	9.5	1.70	158	.218	.274	11	.175	0	24	24	-0	2.6
1915	*Bos-A	19	8	.704	37	33	21	5	1	255^1	217	83	3	10	86	82	11.0	2.11	131	.237	.310	23	.277	7	23	20	1	3.0
1916	*Bos-A	14	7	.667	33	19	9	3	2	182^1	173	73	0	4	86	53	13.0	3.06	90	.263	.352	11	.177	0	-5	-6	2	-0.5
1917	Bos-A	8	7	.533	17	16	9	1	0	124^2	108	43	0	4	53	34	11.9	2.53	102	.243	.329	11	.268	2	2	1	1	0.4
Total	5	58	33	.637	138	103	60	15	3	842^1	726	302	6	29	305	294	11.3	2.36	116	.240	.315	58	.215	9	43	37	3	5.3
● **KEVIN FOSTER**	Foster, Kevin Christopher b: 1/13/69, Evanston, Ill. BR/TR, 6'1", 170 lbs. Deb: 9/12/93																											
1993	Phi-N	0	1	.000	2	1	0	0	0	6^2	13	11	3	0	7	6	27.0	14.85	27	.394	.500	0	.000	-0	-8	-8	-0	-0.9
1994	Chi-N	3	4	.429	13	13	0	0	0	81	70	31	7	1	35	75	11.8	2.89	144	.234	.316	2	.074	-2	12	12	-1	0.6
1995	Chi-N	12	11	.522	30	28	0	0	0	167^2	149	90	32	6	65	146	11.8	4.51	91	.240	.317	15	.250	5	-6	-8	-2	-0.6
1996	Chi-N	7	6	.538	17	16	1	0	0	87	98	63	16	2	35	53	14.0	6.21	70	.288	.358	8	.296	5	-19	-18	1	-1.7
1997	Chi-N	10	7	.588	26	25	1	0	0	146^1	141	79	27	2	66	118	12.9	4.61	93	.255	.337	6	.128	-1	-7	-5	-2	-0.7
1998	Chi-N	0	0	—	3	0	0	0	0	3^1	8	6	1	0	2	3	27.0	16.20	27	.500	.556	0	—	0	-4	-4	-0	-0.2
Total	6	32	29	.525	91	83	2	0	0	492	479	280	86	11	210	401	12.8	4.79	88	.257	.336	31	.190	7	-32	-31	-4	-3.5
● **LARRY FOSTER**	Foster, Larry Lynn b: 12/24/37, Lansing, Mich. BL/TR, 6', 185 lbs. Deb: 9/18/63																											
1963	Det-A	0	0	—	1	0	0	0	0	2	4	3	0	0	1	1	22.5	13.50	28	.364	.417	0	—	0	-2	-2	0	-0.1
● **STEVE FOSTER**	Foster, Stephen Eugene b: 8/16/66, Dallas, Tex. BR/TR, 6', 180 lbs. Deb: 8/22/91																											
1991	Cin-N	0	0	—	11	0	0	0	0	14	7	5	1	0	4	11	7.1	1.93	197	.143	.208	0	—	0	3	3	-0	0.1
1992	Cin-N	1	1	.500	31	1	0	0	2	50	52	16	4	0	13	34	11.7	2.88	125	.275	.322	1	.200	0	4	4	1	0.3
1993	Cin-N	2	2	.500	17	0	0	0	0	25^2	23	8	1	1	5	16	10.2	1.75	230	.235	.279	0	—	0	7	7	-1	0.9
Total	3	3	3	.500	59	1	0	0	2	89^2	82	29	6	1	22	61	10.5	2.41	156	.244	.292	1	.200	0	13	13	0	1.3
● **STEVE FOUCAULT**	Foucault, Steven Raymond b: 10/3/49, Duluth, Minn. BL/TR, 6', 205 lbs. Deb: 4/7/73																											
1973	Tex-A	2	4	.333	32	0	0	0	8	55^2	54	26	6	3	31	28	14.2	3.88	96	.262	.367	0	—	0	-0	-1	1	-0.1

YEAR	TM/L	W	L	PCT	G	GS	CG	SH	SV	IP	H	R	HR	HB	BB	SO	RAT	ERA	ERA+	OAV	OOB	BH	AVG	PB	PR	PR+	PD	TPI
1974	Tex-A	8	9	.471	69	0	0	0	12	144^1	123	51	8	5	40	106	10.5	2.24	159	.234	.295	0	—	0	22	22	1	2.9
1975	Tex-A	8	4	.667	59	0	0	0	10	107	96	57	10	4	55	56	13.0	4.12	91	.249	.349	0	—	0	-4	-4	-1	-0.6
1976	Tex-A	8	8	.500	46	0	0	0	5	75^2	68	31	9	4	25	41	11.5	3.33	108	.249	.321	0	—	0	2	2	2	0.7
1977	Det-A	7	7	.500	44	0	0	0	13	74^1	64	29	7	0	17	58	9.8	3.15	137	.226	.270	0	—	0	8	9	-1	1.8
1978	Det-A	2	4	.333	24	0	0	0	4	37^1	48	18	1	1	21	18	16.9	3.13	124	.324	.412	0	—	0	3	3	-1	0.5
	KC-A	0	0	—	3	0	0	0	0	2^1	5	1	0	0	1	0	23.1	3.86	99	.417	.462	0	—	0	-0	-0	0	0.0
	Yr	2	4	.333	27	0	0	0	4	39^2	53	19	1	1	22	18	17.2	3.18	122	.331	.415	0	—	0	3	3	-0	0.5
Total	6	35	36	.493	277	0	0	0	52	496^2	458	213	41	17	190	307	12.1	3.21	117	.250	.326	0	—	0	30	31	1	5.2

● KEITH FOULKE

Foulke, Keith Charles b: 10/19/72, San Diego, Cal. BR/TR, 6', 195 lbs. Deb: 5/21/97

YEAR	TM/L	W	L	PCT	G	GS	CG	SH	SV	IP	H	R	HR	HB	BB	SO	RAT	ERA	ERA+	OAV	OOB	BH	AVG	PB	PR	PR+	PD	TPI
1997	SF-N	1	5	.167	11	8	0	0	0	44^2	60	41	9	4	18	33	16.5	8.26	49	.324	.396	2	.154	-0	-20	-21	0	-2.3
	Chi-A	3	0	1.000	16	0	0	0	3	28^2	28	11	4	0	5	21	10.4	3.45	127	.255	.287	0	—	0	4	3	0	0.3
1998	Chi-A	3	2	.600	54	0	0	0	1	65^1	51	31	9	4	20	57	10.3	4.13	110	.213	.285	0	—	0	4	3	-1	0.2
1999	Chi-A	3	3	.500	67	0	0	0	9	105^1	72	28	11	3	21	123	8.2	2.22	220	.188	.235	0	.000	-0	**31**	**31**	0	2.0
2000	*Chi-A	3	1	.750	72	0	0	0	34	88	66	31	9	2	22	91	9.2	2.97	167	.207	.262	0	—	0	19	19	-1	2.0
Total	4	13	11	.542	220	8	0	0	47	332	277	142	42	13	86	325	10.2	3.71	126	.224	.281	2	.133	-0	37	36	-1	2.2

● JACK FOURNIER

Fournier, John Frank b: 9/28/1889, AuSable, Mich. d: 9/5/73, Tacoma, Wash. BL/TR, 6', 195 lbs. Deb: 4/13/12 ♦

YEAR	TM/L	W	L	PCT	G	GS	CG	SH	SV	IP	H	R	HR	HB	BB	SO	RAT	ERA	ERA+	OAV	OOB	BH	AVG	PB	PR	PR+	PD	TPI
1922	StL-N	0	0	—	1	0	0	0	0	1	0	0	0	0	0	0	0.0	0.00	—	.000	.000	119	.295	0	0	0	0	0.0

● HENRY FOURNIER

Fournier, Julius Henry "Frenchy" b: 8/8/1865, Syracuse, N.Y. d: 12/8/45, Detroit, Mich. TL, Deb: 8/22/1894

YEAR	TM/L	W	L	PCT	G	GS	CG	SH	SV	IP	H	R	HR	HB	BB	SO	RAT	ERA	ERA+	OAV	OOB	BH	AVG	PB	PR	PR+	PD	TPI
1894	Cin-N	1	3	.250	6	4	4	0	0	45	71	51	4	2	20	5	18.6	5.40	103	.353	.417	2	.105	-3	-0	1	0	-0.1

● DAVE FOUTZ

Foutz, David Luther "Scissors" b: 9/7/1856, Carroll Co., Md. d: 3/5/1897, Waverly, Md. BR/TR, 6'2", 161 lbs. Deb: 7/29/1884 FM♦

YEAR	TM/L	W	L	PCT	G	GS	CG	SH	SV	IP	H	R	HR	HB	BB	SO	RAT	ERA	ERA+	OAV	OOB	BH	AVG	PB	PR	PR+	PD	TPI
1884	StL-a	15	6	.714	25	25	19	2	0	206^2	167	100	7	9	36	95	9.2	2.18	150	.212	.255	27	.227	1	25	25	3	2.5
1885	*StL-a	33	14	.702	47	46	46	2	0	407^2	351	200	8	18	92	147	10.2	2.63	125	.227	.278	59	.248	5	28	29	7	3.8
1886	*StL-a	**41**	16	**.719**	59	57	55	11	**1**	504	418	216	5	10	144	283	10.2	**2.11**	**163**	.216	.274	116	.280	11	**75**	**75**	2	**8.1**
1887	*StL-a	25	12	.676	40	38	36	1	0	339^1	459	244	7	10	90	94	12.4	3.87	117	.301	.306	174	.390	15	16	24	0	3.0
1888	Bro-a	12	7	.632	23	19	19	0	0	176	146	85	3	5	35	73	9.5	2.51	119	.218	.262	156	.277	6	11	10	3	1.6
1889	*Bro-a	3	0	1.000	12	4	3	0	0	59^2	70	50	2	0	19	21	13.4	4.37	85	.283	.335	152	.275	3	-3	-4	1	0.0
1890	*Bro-N	2	1	.667	5	2	2	0	**2**	29	29	10	0	1	6	4	11.2	1.86	185	.252	.295	154	.303	2	6	5	-1	0.6
1891	Bro-N	3	2	.600	6	5	5	0	0	52	51	24	1	1	16	14	11.8	3.29	100	.246	.304	134	.257	1	0	0	-0	0.1
1892	Bro-N	13	8	.619	27	20	17	0	1	203	210	119	3	4	63	56	12.3	3.41	93	.256	.313	41	.186	0	-3	-6	3	-0.3
1893	Bro-N	0	0	—	6	0	0	0	0	18	28	17	2	0	8	3	18.0	7.50	59	.346	.404	137	.246	1	-6	-6	1	-0.2
1894	Bro-N	0	0	—	1	0	0	0	0	2	4	3	0	0	1	0	22.5	13.50	37	.400	.455	90	.303	0	-2	-2	-0	-0.1
Total	11	147	66	.690	251	216	202	16	4	1997^1	1933	1068	38	58	510	790	10.9	2.84	124	.243	.286	1276	.280	45	147	148	18	19.1

● JESSE FOWLER

Fowler, Jesse Peter "Pete" b: 10/30/1898, Spartanburg, S.C. d: 9/23/73, Columbia, S.C. BR/TL, 5'10.5", 158 lbs. Deb: 7/29/24 F

YEAR	TM/L	W	L	PCT	G	GS	CG	SH	SV	IP	H	R	HR	HB	BB	SO	RAT	ERA	ERA+	OAV	OOB	BH	AVG	PB	PR	PR+	PD	TPI
1924	StL-N	1	1	.500	13	3	0	0	0	32^2	28	21	0	2	18	5	13.2	4.41	86	.226	.333	2	.222	0	-2	-2	-1	-0.2

● ART FOWLER

Fowler, John Arthur b: 7/3/22, Converse, S.C. BR/TR, 5'11", 180 lbs. Deb: 4/17/54 FC

YEAR	TM/L	W	L	PCT	G	GS	CG	SH	SV	IP	H	R	HR	HB	BB	SO	RAT	ERA	ERA+	OAV	OOB	BH	AVG	PB	PR	PR+	PD	TPI
1954	Cin-N	12	10	.545	40	29	8	1	0	227^2	256	112	20	4	85	93	13.6	3.83	109	.286	.351	6	.100	-1	6	9	-1	0.5
1955	Cin-N	11	10	.524	46	28	8	3	2	207^2	198	96	20	1	63	94	11.4	3.90	109	.250	.306	12	.200	-0	3	7	-1	0.5
1956	Cin-N	11	11	.500	45	23	8	0	1	177^2	191	92	15	0	35	86	11.4	4.05	98	.278	.313	7	.146	-0	-6	-1	1	-0.1
1957	Cin-N	3	0	1.000	33	7	1	0	0	87^2	111	65	11	2	24	45	14.1	6.47	64	.310	.357	3	.176	0	-25	-22	0	-1.1
1959	LA-N	3	4	.429	36	0	0	0	2	61	70	39	8	0	23	47	13.7	5.31	80	.294	.356	1	.083	-1	-9	-7	0	-0.8
1961	LA-A	5	8	.385	53	3	0	0	11	89	68	42	12	0	29	78	9.8	3.64	124	.209	.274	1	.077	-1	4	8	-1	1.0
1962	LA-A	4	3	.571	48	0	0	0	5	77	67	25	6	1	25	38	10.9	2.81	138	.234	.298	3	.273	1	10	9	-0	1.0
1963	LA-A	5	3	.625	57	0	0	0	10	89^1	70	26	5	0	19	53	9.0	2.42	142	.219	.263	2	.222	0	12	11	-1	1.1
1964	LA-A	0	2	.000	4	0	0	0	1	7	8	8	2	1	5	5	18.0	10.29	32	.296	.424	0	.000	-0	-5	-6	0	-1.1
Total	9	54	51	.514	362	90	25	4	32	1024	1039	505	99	9	308	539	11.9	4.03	102	.265	.320	35	.152	-2	-10	7	-3	1.0

● DICK FOWLER

Fowler, Richard John b: 3/30/21, Toronto, Ont., Can. d: 5/22/72, Oneonta, N.Y. BR/TR, 6'4.5", 215 lbs. Deb: 9/13/41

YEAR	TM/L	W	L	PCT	G	GS	CG	SH	SV	IP	H	R	HR	HB	BB	SO	RAT	ERA	ERA+	OAV	OOB	BH	AVG	PB	PR	PR+	PD	TPI
1941	Phi-A	1	2	.333	4	3	1	0	0	24	26	11	4	0	8	8	12.8	3.38	124	.289	.347	0	.000	-1	2	2	-0	0.1
1942	Phi-A	6	11	.353	31	17	4	0	1	140	159	90	13	0	45	38	13.1	4.95	76	.287	.341	8	.160	-1	-20	-18	-2	-2.3
1945	Phi-A	1	2	.333	7	3	2	1	0	37^1	41	21	1	0	18	21	14.2	4.82	71	.283	.362	8	.444	3	-6	-6	-1	-0.1
1946	Phi-A	9	16	.360	32	28	14	1	0	205^2	213	101	16	2	75	89	12.7	3.28	108	.263	.327	13	.183	-1	5	6	-1	0.5
1947	Phi-A	12	11	.522	36	31	16	3	0	227^1	210	77	12	3	85	75	11.8	2.81	136	.249	.319	14	.171	-3	23	25	-2	1.9
1948	Phi-A	15	8	.652	29	26	16	2	2	204^2	221	93	15	4	76	50	13.2	3.78	113	.281	.348	14	.171	-2	12	12	-1	0.8
1949	Phi-A	15	11	.577	31	28	15	4	1	213^2	210	108	13	2	115	43	13.8	3.75	110	.262	.357	18	.234	3	11	9	1	1.4
1950	Phi-A	1	5	.167	11	9	2	0	0	66^2	75	52	7	3	56	15	18.1	6.48	70	.300	.434	5	.192	-1	-14	-14	0	-1.1
1951	Phi-A	5	11	.313	22	22	4	0	0	125	141	89	11	1	72	29	15.4	5.62	76	.291	.384	8	.190	-0	-21	-18	-1	-2.0
1952	Phi-A	1	2	.333	18	3	1	0	0	58^2	71	43	4	4	28	14	15.8	6.44	61	.302	.386	0	.000	-2	-18	-15	1	-0.9
Total	10	66	79	.455	221	170	75	11	4	1303	1367	685	96	19	578	382	13.6	4.11	97	.273	.351	88	.186	-6	-27	-19	-6	-1.7

● ALAN FOWLKES

Fowlkes, Alan Kim b: 8/8/58, Brawley, Cal. BR/TR, 6'2", 190 lbs. Deb: 4/7/82

YEAR	TM/L	W	L	PCT	G	GS	CG	SH	SV	IP	H	R	HR	HB	BB	SO	RAT	ERA	ERA+	OAV	OOB	BH	AVG	PB	PR	PR+	PD	TPI
1982	SF-N	4	2	.667	21	15	1	0	0	85	111	55	12	5	24	50	14.8	5.19	69	.321	.373	3	.115	-1	-15	-15	-0	-1.1
1985	Cal-A	0	0	—	2	0	0	0	0	7	8	7	4	0	4	5	15.4	9.00	46	.276	.364	0	—	0	-4	-4	0	-0.2
Total	2	4	2	.667	23	15	1	0	0	92	119	62	16	5	28	55	14.9	5.48	66	.317	.373	3	.115	-1	-19	-19	-0	-1.3

● CHAD FOX

Fox, Chad Douglas b: 9/3/70, Coronado, Cal. BR/TR, 6'3", 175 lbs. Deb: 7/13/97

YEAR	TM/L	W	L	PCT	G	GS	CG	SH	SV	IP	H	R	HR	HB	BB	SO	RAT	ERA	ERA+	OAV	OOB	BH	AVG	PB	PR	PR+	PD	TPI
1997	Atl-N	0	1	.000	30	0	0	0	0	27^1	24	12	4	0	16	28	13.2	3.29	128	.231	.333	0	—	0	3	3	-1	0.1
1998	Mil-N	1	4	.200	49	0	0	0	0	57	56	27	4	1	20	64	12.2	3.95	108	.260	.326	0	.000	-0	2	2	-0	0.1
1999	Mil-N	0	0	—	6	0	0	0	0	6^2	11	8	1	1	4	12	21.6	10.80	42	.355	.444	0	.000	-0	-5	-5	0	-0.2
Total	3	1	5	.167	85	0	0	0	0	91	91	47	9	2	40	104	13.2	4.25	100	.260	.339	0	.000	-0	-0	0	-1	0.0

● HENRY FOX

Fox, Henry (b: Henry Fuchs) b: 11/18/1874, Scranton, Pa. d: 6/6/27, Scranton, Pa. Deb: 9/4/02

YEAR	TM/L	W	L	PCT	G	GS	CG	SH	SV	IP	H	R	HR	HB	BB	SO	RAT	ERA	ERA+	OAV	OOB	BH	AVG	PB	PR	PR+	PD	TPI
1902	Phi-N	0	0	—	1	0	0	0	1	1	2	3	0	0	1	1	27.0	18.00	16	.400	.500	0	—	0	-2	-2	0	-0.3

● HOWIE FOX

Fox, Howard Francis b: 3/1/21, Coburg, Ore. d: 10/9/55, San Antonio, Tex. BR/TR, 6'3", 210 lbs. Deb: 9/28/44

YEAR	TM/L	W	L	PCT	G	GS	CG	SH	SV	IP	H	R	HR	HB	BB	SO	RAT	ERA	ERA+	OAV	OOB	BH	AVG	PB	PR	PR+	PD	TPI
1944	Cin-N	0	0	—	2	0	0	0	0	2^1	2	0	0	0	0	0	7.7	0.00	—	.222	.222	0	.000	-0	1	1	-0	0.0
1945	Cin-N	8	13	.381	45	15	7	0	0	164^1	169	102	6	6	77	54	13.8	4.93	76	.268	.353	13	.283	3	-21	-22	4	-1.8
1946	Cin-N	0	0	—	4	0	0	0	0	5	12	13	2	0	5	1	30.6	18.00	19	.462	.548	0	—	0	-8	-8	0	-0.4
1948	Cin-N	6	9	.400	34	24	5	0	1	171	185	100	11	1	62	63	13.1	4.53	86	.280	.343	12	.200	1	-11	-12	1	-0.7
1949	Cin-N	6	19	.240	38	30	9	0	0	215	221	120	13	4	77	60	12.6	3.98	105	.265	.330	17	.236	2	2	5	6	1.2
1950	Cin-N	11	8	.579	34	22	10	1	1	187	196	97	14	2	85	64	13.6	4.33	98	.269	.347	11	.175	-0	-4	-2	3	0.1
1951	Cin-N	9	14	.391	40	30	9	4	2	228	239	105	16	2	69	57	12.2	3.83	107	.272	.326	8	.114	-2	3	6	1	0.4
1952	Phi-N	2	7	.222	13	11	2	0	0	62	70	41	8	0	26	16	13.9	5.08	72	.287	.356	1	.048	-2	-9	-10	1	-1.3
1954	Bal-A	1	2	.333	38	0	0	0	2	73^2	80	33	2	2	34	27	14.2	3.67	98	.289	.371	4	.250	1	0	-1	1	0.2
Total	9	43	72	.374	248	132	42	5	6	1108^1	1174	611	72	17	435	342	13.2	4.33	92	.274	.343	66	.189	2	-46	-42	17	-2.3

● JOHN FOX

Fox, John Joseph b: 2/7/1859, Roxbury, Mass. d: 4/18/1893, Boston, Mass. Deb: 6/2/1881

YEAR	TM/L	W	L	PCT	G	GS	CG	SH	SV	IP	H	R	HR	HB	BB	SO	RAT	ERA	ERA+	OAV	OOB	BH	AVG	PB	PR	PR+	PD	TPI
1881	Bos-N	6	8	.429	17	16	12	0	0	124^1	144	90	0		39	30	13.2	3.33	80	.279	.329	21	.178	-4	-8	-10	1	-1.1
1883	Bal-a	6	13	.316	20	19	18	0	0	165^1	209	140	2		32	49	13.1	4.03	86	.289	.320	14	.152	-4	-13	-10	-1	-1.2
1884	Pit-a	1	6	.143	7	7	7	0	0	59	76	59	2	3	16	22	14.5	5.64	59	.291	.339	6	.240	0	-16	-15	1	-1.3
1886	Was-N	0	1	.000	1	1	1	0	0	8	11	13	0		11	3	24.8	9.00	37	.314	.478	1	.333	0	-5	-5	0	-0.4
Total	4	13	28	.317	45	43	38	0	0	356^2	440	302	4	3	98	104	13.7	4.16	76	.287	.331	42	.176	-7	-42	-40	0	-4.0

● TERRY FOX

Fox, Terrence Edward b: 7/31/35, Chicago, Ill. BR/TR, 6', 175 lbs. Deb: 9/4/60

YEAR	TM/L	W	L	PCT	G	GS	CG	SH	SV	IP	H	R	HR	HB	BB	SO	RAT	ERA	ERA+	OAV	OOB	BH	AVG	PB	PR	PR+	PD	TPI
1960	Mil-N	0	0	—	5	0	0	0	0	8^1	6	5	0	0	6	5	13.0	4.32	79	.200	.333	0	.000	-0	-1	-1	-0	-0.1
1961	Det-A	5	2	.714	39	0	0	0	12	57^1	42	12	6	3	16	32	9.6	1.41	290	.200	.266	2	.167	-0	17	17	1	2.8
1962	Det-A	3	1	.750	44	0	0	0	16	58	48	13	2	1	16	23	10.1	1.71	238	.227	.285	2	.250	2	15	15	0	2.1

YEAR	TM/L	W	L	PCT	G	GS	CG	SH	SV	IP	H	R	HR	HB	BB	SO	RAT	ERA	ERA+	OAV	OOB	BH	AVG	PB	PR	PR+	PD	TPI
1963	Det-A	8	6	.571	46	0	0	0	11	80^1	81	37	9	2	20	35	11.5	3.59	104	.263	.312	1	.091	-0	0	1	0	0.3
1964	Det-A	4	3	.571	32	0	0	0	5	61	77	26	4	1	16	28	13.9	3.39	108	.316	.360	3	.250	1	2	2	1	0.4
1965	Det-A	6	4	.600	42	0	0	0	10	77^2	59	26	7	3	31	34	10.8	2.78	125	.214	.300	0	.000	-1	6	6	2	1.0
1966	Det-A	0	1	.000	4	0	0	0	1	10	9	8	3	0	2	6	9.9	6.30	55	.243	.282	0	.000	-0	-3	-3	0	-0.3
	Phi-N	3	2	.600	36	0	0	0	4	44^1	57	22	3	2	17	22	15.4	4.47	80	.322	.388	0	.000	-0	-4	-4	-0	-0.6
Total	7	29	19	.604	248	0	0	0	59	397	379	149	34	12	124	185	11.7	2.99	125	.254	.316	8	.123	1	31	33	4	5.6

● BILL FOXEN Foxen, William Aloysius b: 5/31/1884, Tenafly, N.J. d: 4/17/37, Brooklyn, N.Y. BL/TL, 5'11.5", 165 lbs. Deb: 5/5/08

YEAR	TM/L	W	L	PCT	G	GS	CG	SH	SV	IP	H	R	HR	HB	BB	SO	RAT	ERA	ERA+	OAV	OOB	BH	AVG	PB	PR	PR+	PD	TPI
1908	Phi-N	7	7	.500	22	16	10	2	0	147^1	126	45	2	8	53	52	11.4	1.95	124	.240	.319	5	.094	-3	7	8	2	0.6
1909	Phi-N	3	7	.300	18	7	5	1	0	83^1	65	40	0	4	32	37	10.9	3.35	78	.219	.303	5	.208	3	-7	-7	4	0.0
1910	Phi-N	5	5	.500	16	9	5	0	0	77^2	73	30	2	3	40	33	13.4	2.55	123	.268	.368	4	.174	-1	4	5	2	0.7
	Chi-N	0	0	—	2	0	0	0	0	5	7	5	0	0	3	2	18.0	9.00	32	.350	.435	0	.000	-0	-3	-4	-0	-0.2
	Yr	5	5	.500	18	9	5	0	0	82^2	80	35	2	3	43	35	13.7	2.94	106	.274	.373	4	.160	-1	1	2	1	0.5
1911	Chi-N	1	1	.500	3	1	0	0	0	13	12	6	0	0	12	6	16.6	2.08	159	.255	.407	1	.250	1	2	2	1	0.4
Total	4	16	20	.444	61	33	20	3	0	326^1	283	126	4	15	140	130	12.1	2.56	104	.244	.333	15	.142	0	3	4	8	1.5

● JIMMIE FOXX Foxx, James Emory "Beast" or "Double X" b: 10/22/07, Sudlersville, Md. d: 7/21/67, Miami, Fla. BR/TR, 6', 195 lbs. Deb: 5/1/25 CH♦

YEAR	TM/L	W	L	PCT	G	GS	CG	SH	SV	IP	H	R	HR	HB	BB	SO	RAT	ERA	ERA+	OAV	OOB	BH	AVG	PB	PR	PR+	PD	TPI
1939	Bos-A☆	0	0	—	1	0	0	0	0	1	0	0	0	0	0	1	0.0	0.00	—	.000	.000	168	.360	1	1	1	0	0.0
1945	Phi-N	1	0	1.000	9	2	0	0	0	22^2	13	4	0	1	14	10	11.1	1.59	241	.171	.308	60	.268	2	6	6	-1	0.4
Total	2	1	0	1.000	10	2	0	0	0	23^2	13	4	0	1	14	11	10.6	1.52	254	.165	.298	2646	.325	3	6	6	-1	0.4

● PAUL FOYTACK Foytack, Paul Eugene b: 11/16/30, Scranton, Pa. BR/TR, 5'11", 180 lbs. Deb: 4/21/53

YEAR	TM/L	W	L	PCT	G	GS	CG	SH	SV	IP	H	R	HR	HB	BB	SO	RAT	ERA	ERA+	OAV	OOB	BH	AVG	PB	PR	PR+	PD	TPI
1953	Det-A	0	0	—	6	0	0	0	0	9^2	15	12	1	1	9	7	23.3	11.17	36	.375	.500	0	.000	-0	-8	-7	-0	-0.4
1955	Det-A	0	1	.000	22	1	0	0	0	49^2	48	29	4	0	36	38	15.2	5.26	73	.259	.380	1	.091	-1	-7	-8	-0	-0.5
1956	Det-A	15	13	.536	43	33	16	1	1	256	211	114	24	2	142	184	12.5	3.59	115	.226	.330	11	.122	-6	16	15	-1	0.8
1957	Det-A	14	11	.560	38	27	8	1	1	212	175	79	19	4	104	118	12.0	3.14	123	.226	.321	14	.222	1	15	17	-2	1.7
1958	Det-A	15	13	.536	39	33	16	2	1	230	198	98	23	3	77	135	10.9	3.44	117	.233	.299	18	.240	2	8	14	-2	1.7
1959	Det-A	14	14	.500	39	37	11	2	1	240^1	239	137	34	2	64	110	11.4	4.64	87	.259	.308	9	.111	-4	-21	-15	-2	-2.1
1960	Det-A	2	11	.154	28	13	1	0	2	96^2	108	70	11	0	49	38	14.6	6.14	64	.286	.369	7	.280	2	-24	-23	-2	-2.7
1961	Det-A	11	10	.524	32	20	6	0	0	169^2	152	81	27	2	56	89	11.1	3.93	104	.238	.301	12	.222	2	2	3	-3	0.2
1962	Det-A	10	7	.588	29	21	5	1	0	143^2	145	80	18	1	86	63	14.5	4.39	93	.259	.359	6	.143	-1	-7	-5	0	-0.6
1963	Det-A	0	1	.000	9	0	0	0	1	17^2	18	18	4	0	8	7	13.2	8.66	43	.265	.342	0	.000	-0	-10	-9	0	-0.7
	LA-A	5	5	.500	25	8	0	0	0	70^1	68	35	9	0	29	37	12.4	3.71	92	.255	.328	4	.267	1	-1	-2	-1	-0.3
	Yr	5	6	.455	34	8	0	0	1	88	86	53	13	0	37	44	12.6	4.70	74	.257	.331	4	.211	1	-11	-12	-1	-1.0
1964	LA-A	0	1	.000	2	0	0	0	0	2^1	4	4	2	0	2	1	23.1	15.43	21	.364	.462	0	—	0	-3	-3	-0	-0.6
Total	11	86	87	.497	312	193	63	7	7	1498	1381	757	176	15	662	827	12.4	4.14	97	.246	.327	82	.178	-3	-39	-23	-13	-3.5

● KEN FRAILING Frailing, Kenneth Douglas b: 1/19/48, Marion, Wis. BL/TL, 6', 190 lbs. Deb: 9/1/72

YEAR	TM/L	W	L	PCT	G	GS	CG	SH	SV	IP	H	R	HR	HB	BB	SO	RAT	ERA	ERA+	OAV	OOB	BH	AVG	PB	PR	PR+	PD	TPI
1972	Chi-A	1	0	1.000	4	0	0	0	0	3	3	1	1	0	1	1	12.0	3.00	105	.250	.308	0	—	0	0	0	0	0.0
1973	Chi-A	0	0	—	10	0	0	0	0	18^1	18	6	1	1	7	15	12.8	1.96	202	.254	.329	0	—	0	4	4	-0	0.2
1974	Chi-N	6	9	.400	55	16	1	0	1	125^1	150	65	11	1	43	71	13.9	3.88	99	.296	.353	8	.258	1	-3	-1	0	0.0
1975	Chi-N	2	5	.286	41	0	0	0	1	53	61	37	6	2	26	39	15.1	5.43	71	.293	.377	1	.143	0	-11	-9	2	-0.9
1976	Chi-N	1	2	.333	6	3	0	0	0	18^2	20	7	0	0	5	10	12.1	2.41	160	.274	.321	0	.000	-0	2	3	0	0.4
Total	5	10	16	.385	116	19	1	0	2	218^1	252	116	19	4	82	136	13.9	3.96	97	.290	.354	9	.220	1	-8	-3	2	-0.3

● OSSIE FRANCE France, Osman Beverly "O. B." b: 10/4/1858, Greensburg, Ohio d: 5/2/47, Akron, Ohio BL/TL, 5'8", 155 lbs. Deb: 7/14/1890

YEAR	TM/L	W	L	PCT	G	GS	CG	SH	SV	IP	H	R	HR	HB	BB	SO	RAT	ERA	ERA+	OAV	OOB	BH	AVG	PB	PR	PR+	PD	TPI
1890	Chi-N	0	0	—	1	0	0	0	0	2	3	3	0	0	2	0	22.5	13.50	27	.333	.455	0	.000	-0	-2	-2	-0	-0.1

● EARL FRANCIS Francis, Earl Coleman b: 7/14/35, Slab Fork, W.Va. BR/TR, 6'2", 215 lbs. Deb: 6/30/60

YEAR	TM/L	W	L	PCT	G	GS	CG	SH	SV	IP	H	R	HR	HB	BB	SO	RAT	ERA	ERA+	OAV	OOB	BH	AVG	PB	PR	PR+	PD	TPI
1960	Pit-N	1	0	1.000	7	0	0	0	0	18	14	5	0	1	4	8	9.5	2.00	188	.222	.279	0	.000	-1	4	4	-0	0.1
1961	Pit-N	2	8	.200	23	15	0	0	0	102^2	110	60	4	1	47	53	13.9	4.21	95	.274	.351	3	.107	-1	-2	-3	0	-0.3
1962	Pit-N	9	8	.529	36	23	5	1	0	176	153	68	8	2	83	121	12.2	3.07	128	.235	.323	10	.164	1	17	17	1	1.7
1963	Pit-N	4	6	.400	33	13	0	0	0	97^1	107	59	6	4	43	72	14.2	4.53	73	.284	.363	8	.308	3	-13	-13	0	-1.0
1964	Pit-N	0	1	.000	2	1	0	0	0	6^1	7	7	2	1	1	6	12.8	8.53	41	.269	.321	0	.000	-0	-4	-4	-0	-0.5
1965	StL-N	0	0	—	2	0	0	0	0	5^1	7	4	1	0	3	3	16.9	5.06	76	.318	.400	0	.000	-0	-1	-1	-0	-0.1
Total	6	16	23	.410	103	52	5	1	0	405^2	398	203	21	9	181	263	13.0	3.77	100	.258	.340	21	.172	2	1	0	1	-0.1

● RAY FRANCIS Francis, Ray James b: 3/8/1893, Sherman, Tex. d: 7/6/34, Atlanta, Ga. BL/TL, 6'1.5", 182 lbs. Deb: 4/18/22

YEAR	TM/L	W	L	PCT	G	GS	CG	SH	SV	IP	H	R	HR	HB	BB	SO	RAT	ERA	ERA+	OAV	OOB	BH	AVG	PB	PR	PR+	PD	TPI
1922	Was-A	7	18	.280	39	26	15	2	2	225	265	136	7	6	66	64	13.5	4.28	90	.303	.356	13	.167	-2	-6	-11	-1	-1.3
1923	Det-A	5	8	.385	33	6	0	0	1	79^1	95	51	2	4	28	27	14.4	4.42	87	.308	.374	3	.143	-2	-4	-5	-0	-0.9
1925	NY-A	0	0	—	4	0	0	0	0	4^2	5	4	0	1	3	1	17.4	7.71	55	.278	.409	0	—	0	-2	-2	-0	-0.1
	Bos-A	0	2	.000	6	4	0	0	0	28	44	29	3	1	13	4	18.6	7.71	59	.373	.439	1	.125	-0	-10	-10	0	-0.5
	Yr	0	2	.000	10	4	0	0	0	32^2	49	33	3	2	16	5	18.5	7.71	58	.360	.435	1	.125	-0	-12	-11	-0	-0.6
Total	3	12	28	.300	82	36	15	2	3	337	409	220	12	12	110	96	14.2	4.65	84	.310	.368	17	.159	-4	-22	-28	-1	-2.8

● JOHN FRANCO Franco, John Anthony b: 9/17/60, Brooklyn, N.Y. BL/TL, 5'10", 185 lbs. Deb: 4/24/84

YEAR	TM/L	W	L	PCT	G	GS	CG	SH	SV	IP	H	R	HR	HB	BB	SO	RAT	ERA	ERA+	OAV	OOB	BH	AVG	PB	PR	PR+	PD	TPI
1984	Cin-N	6	2	.750	54	0	0	0	4	79^1	74	28	3	2	36	55	12.7	2.61	145	.256	.343	0	.000	-0	9	10	1	1.1
1985	Cin-N	12	3	.800	67	0	0	0	12	99	83	27	5	1	40	61	11.3	2.18	174	.234	.314	2	.333	0	16	**17**	2	3.1
1986	Cin-N☆	6	6	.500	74	0	0	0	29	101	90	40	7	2	44	84	12.1	2.94	132	.242	.325	0	.000	-0	9	10	1	1.8
1987	Cin-N★	8	5	.615	68	0	0	0	32	82	76	26	6	0	27	61	11.3	2.52	168	.245	.306	0	.000	-0	14	15	-1	3.0
1988	Cin-N	6	6	.500	70	0	0	0	**39**	86	60	18	3	0	27	46	9.1	1.57	229	.198	.264	0	.000	-0	**18**	**19**	1	4.2
1989	Cin-N☆	4	8	.333	60	0	0	0	32	80^2	77	35	3	0	36	60	12.6	3.12	115	.258	.337	1	.333	0	3	4	1	1.1
1990	NY-N★	5	3	.625	55	0	0	0	**33**	67^2	66	22	4	0	21	56	11.6	2.53	148	.252	.307	0	.000	-1	10	9	1	2.0
1991	NY-N	5	9	.357	52	0	0	0	30	55^1	61	27	2	1	18	45	13.0	2.93	124	.271	.328	0	.000	-0	5	4	1	1.0
1992	NY-N	6	2	.750	31	0	0	0	15	33	24	6	1	0	11	20	9.5	1.64	213	.209	.278	0	.000	-0	7	7	2	1.7
1993	NY-N	4	3	.571	35	0	0	0	10	36^1	46	24	6	1	19	29	16.3	5.20	77	.313	.395	0	.000	-0	-5	-5	1	-0.9
1994	NY-N	1	4	.200	47	0	0	0	**30**	50	47	20	2	1	19	42	12.1	2.70	155	.244	.315	0	.000	-0	8	8	0	1.6
1995	NY-N	5	3	.625	48	0	0	0	29	51^2	48	17	4	0	17	41	11.3	2.44	166	.251	.313	0	—	0	10	10	0	2.0
1996	NY-N	4	3	.571	51	0	0	0	28	54	54	15	2	0	21	48	12.5	1.83	219	.260	.328	0	.000	-0	14	14	0	2.8
1997	NY-N	5	3	.625	59	0	0	0	36	60	49	18	3	1	20	53	10.5	2.55	158	.226	.294	0	—	0	11	10	1	2.2
1998	NY-N	0	8	.000	61	0	0	0	38	64^2	66	28	4	4	29	59	13.8	3.62	114	.267	.354	0	.000	-0	4	4	2	0.9
1999	*NY-N	0	2	.000	46	0	0	0	19	40^2	40	14	1	2	19	41	13.5	2.88	152	.255	.343	0	—	0	8	7	0	0.9
2000	*NY-N	5	4	.556	62	0	0	0	4	55^2	46	24	6	2	26	56	12.0	3.40	130	.221	.314	0	.000	-0	8	7	0	1.0
Total	17	82	74	.526	940	0	0	0	420	1097	1007	389	62	17	430	857	11.9	2.68	147	.246	.320	3	.088	-2	149	151	12	29.5

● MATT FRANCO Franco, Matthew Neil b: 8/19/69, Santa Monica, Cal. BL/TR, 6'2", 200 lbs. Deb: 9/6/95 ♦

YEAR	TM/L	W	L	PCT	G	GS	CG	SH	SV	IP	H	R	HR	HB	BB	SO	RAT	ERA	ERA+	OAV	OOB	BH	AVG	PB	PR	PR+	PD	TPI
1999	*NY-N	0	0	—	2	0	0	0	0	1^1	3	2	1	0	3	2	40.5	13.50	32	.429	.600	31	.235	0	-1	-1	0	-0.1

● TERRY FRANCONA Francona, Terry Jon b: 4/22/59, Aberdeen, S.D. BL/TL, 6'1", 190 lbs. Deb: 8/19/81 FMC♦

YEAR	TM/L	W	L	PCT	G	GS	CG	SH	SV	IP	H	R	HR	HB	BB	SO	RAT	ERA	ERA+	OAV	OOB	BH	AVG	PB	PR	PR+	PD	TPI
1989	Mil-A	0	0	—	1	0	0	0	0	1	0	0	0	0	0	1	0.0	0.00	—	.000	.000	54	.232	0	0	0	0	0.0

● CHARLIE FRANK Frank, Charles b: 5/30/1870, Mobile, Ala. d: 5/24/22, Memphis, Tenn. TL, 5'10", 170 lbs. Deb: 8/18/1893 ♦

YEAR	TM/L	W	L	PCT	G	GS	CG	SH	SV	IP	H	R	HR	HB	BB	SO	RAT	ERA	ERA+	OAV	OOB	BH	AVG	PB	PR	PR+	PD	TPI
1894	StL-N	0	0	—	2	0	0	0	0	3	6	5	1	0	7	1	39.0	15.00	36	.400	.591	89	.279	0	-3	-3	-0	-0.1

● FRED FRANKHOUSE Frankhouse, Frederick Meloy b: 4/9/04, Port Royal, Pa. d: 8/17/89, Port Royal, Pa. BR/TR, 5'11", 175 lbs. Deb: 9/11/27

YEAR	TM/L	W	L	PCT	G	GS	CG	SH	SV	IP	H	R	HR	HB	BB	SO	RAT	ERA	ERA+	OAV	OOB	BH	AVG	PB	PR	PR+	PD	TPI
1927	StL-N	5	1	.833	6	6	5	1	0	50	41	18	2	1	16	20	10.4	2.70	146	.218	.283	5	.250	0	7	7	-1	0.7
1928	StL-N	3	2	.600	21	10	1	0	1	84	91	47	6	5	36	29	14.1	3.96	101	.277	.358	5	.185	1	0	0	1	0.2
1929	StL-N	7	2	.778	30	10	6	0	1	133^1	149	70	9	4	43	37	13.2	4.12	113	.289	.349	15	.288	4	9	8	3	1.0
1930	StL-N	2	3	.400	8	1	0	0	0	19^2	31	16	1	0	11	4	19.2	7.32	69	.373	.447	0	.000	-1	-5	-5	0	-0.9
	Bos-N	7	6	.538	27	11	3	1	0	110^2	138	72	13	2	43	30	14.9	5.61	88	.313	.377	14	.359	4	-8	-8	-0	-0.4
	Yr	9	9	.500	35	12	3	1	0	130^1	169	88	14	2	54	34	15.5	5.87	84	.323	.388	14	.318	3	-13	-13	0	-1.3
1931	Bos-N	8	8	.500	26	15	6	0	1	127^1	125	64	4	3	43	50	12.1	4.03	94	.252	.315	6	.150	-0	-2	-3	1	-0.3

YEAR	TM/L	W	L	PCT	G	GS	CG	SH	SV	IP	H	R	HR	HB	BB	SO	RAT	ERA	ERA+	OAV	OOB	BH	AVG	PB	PR	PR+	PD	TPI
1932	Bos-N	4	6	.400	37	6	3	0	0	108^2	113	56	7	3	45	35	13.3	3.56	106	.278	.355	3	.100	-1	4	2	3	0.4
1933	Bos-N	16	15	.516	43	30	14	2	2	244^2	249	97	12	3	77	83	12.1	3.16	97	.267	.324	19	.237	4	5	-3	4	0.5
1934	Bos-N★	17	9	.654	37	30	13	2	1	233^2	239	102	10	4	77	78	12.3	3.20	120	.262	.322	17	.200	2	22	17	-0	1.9
1935	Bos-N	11	15	.423	40	29	10	1	0	230^2	278	147	12	6	81	64	14.2	4.76	80	.293	.352	20	.263	6	-19	-26	3	-1.6
1936	Bro-N	13	10	.565	41	31	9	1	2	234^1	236	112	18	3	89	84	12.6	3.65	113	.257	.325	13	.143	-4	10	12	1	0.8
1937	Bro-N	10	13	.435	33	25	9	1	0	179^1	214	104	8	4	78	64	14.9	4.27	95	.297	.369	11	.190	-0	-7	-4	3	-0.2
1938	Bro-N	3	5	.375	30	8	2	1	0	93^2	92	48	6	4	44	32	13.5	4.04	97	.256	.344	4	.154	-1	-3	-1	1	-0.1
1939	Bos-N	0	2	.000	23	0	0	0	4	38	37	16	3	1	18	12	13.3	2.61	142	.253	.339	0	.000	-1	6	5	-1	0.2
Total	13	106	97	.522	402	212	81	10	12	1888	2033	969	111	43	701	622	13.2	3.92	100	.275	.341	132	.208	12	18	-0	18	2.2
● WAYNE FRANKLIN	Franklin, Gary Wayne b: 3/9/74, Wilmington, Del. BL/TL, 6'2", 195 lbs. Deb: 7/24/2000																											
2000	Hou-N	0	0	—	25	0	0	0	0	21^1	24	14	2	4	12	21	16.9	5.48	89	.282	.396	0	.000	-0	-2	-1	-0	-0.1
● JACK FRANKLIN	Franklin, Jack Wilford b: 10/20/19, Paris, Ill. d: 11/15/91, Panama City, Fla. BR/TR, 5'11.5", 170 lbs. Deb: 6/12/44																											
1944	Bro-N	0	0	—	1	0	0	0	0	2	2	3	1	2	4	0	36.0	13.50	26	.250	.571	0	—	0	-2	-2	-0	-0.1
● JAY FRANKLIN	Franklin, John William b: 3/16/53, Arlington, Va. BR/TR, 6'2", 180 lbs. Deb: 9/4/71																											
1971	SD-N	0	1	.000	3	1	0	0	0	5^2	5	5	3	0	4	4	14.3	6.35	52	.250	.375	0	.000	-0	-2	-2	0	-0.3
● RYAN FRANKLIN	Franklin, Ryan Ray b: 3/5/73, Fort Smith, Ark. BR/TR, 6'3", 165 lbs. Deb: 5/15/99																											
1999	Sea-A	0	0	—	6	0	0	0	0	11^1	10	6	2	1	8	6	15.1	4.76	99	.238	.373	0	—	0	0	-0	0	0.0
● JOHN FRASCATORE	Frascatore, John Vincent b: 2/4/70, Ozone Park, N.Y. BR/TR, 6'1", 200 lbs. Deb: 7/21/94																											
1994	StL-N	0	1	.000	1	1	0	0	0	3^1	7	6	2	0	2	2	24.3	16.20	26	.438	.500	0	.000	-0	-4	-5	0	-0.6
1995	StL-N	1	1	.500	14	4	0	0	0	32^2	39	19	3	2	16	21	15.7	4.41	95	.298	.383	0	.000	-0	-1	-1	-1	-0.1
1997	StL-N	5	2	.714	59	0	0	0	0	80	74	25	5	6	33	58	12.7	2.47	168	.247	.334	0	.000	-0	15	15	-1	1.0
1998	StL-N	3	4	.429	69	0	0	0	0	95^2	95	48	11	3	36	49	12.6	4.14	101	.256	.327	1	.167	-0	1	1	-1	0.0
1999	Ari-N	1	4	.200	26	0	0	0	0	33	31	16	6	1	12	15	12.0	4.09	112	.256	.328	0	—	0	2	2	-1	0.2
	Tor-A	7	1	.875	33	0	0	0	1	37	42	16	5	1	9	22	12.6	3.41	145	.292	.338	0	—	0	6	6	0	1.2
2000	Tor-A	2	4	.333	60	0	0	0	0	73	87	51	14	7	33	30	15.7	5.42	92	.301	.386	0	—	0	-4	-4	-1	-0.3
Total	6	19	17	.528	262	5	0	0	1	354^2	375	181	46	20	141	197	13.6	4.09	109	.274	.350	1	.059	-1	15	15	-3	1.4
● CHICK FRASER	Fraser, Charles Carrolton b: 3/17/1871, Chicago, Ill. d: 5/8/40, Wendell, Idaho BR/TR, 5'10.5", 188 lbs. Deb: 4/19/1896 C																											
1896	Lou-N	12	27	.308	43	38	36	0	1	349^1	396	282	9	29	166	91	15.2	4.87	89	.283	.371	22	.151	-9	-20	-21	3	-2.2
1897	Lou-N	15	19	.441	36	34	32	0	0	294^1	334	226	11	22	139	70	15.1	4.04	105	.283	.369	18	.157	-5	9	7	6	0.8
1898	Lou-N	7	17	.292	26	26	20	1	0	203	230	157	4	23	100	58	15.7	5.32	67	.283	.378	13	.167	-2	-39	-40	4	-3.5
	Cle-N	2	3	.400	6	6	6	0	0	42	49	34	2	6	12	19	14.4	5.57	65	.290	.358	4	.250	0	-9	-9	0	-0.8
	Yr	9	20	.310	32	32	26	1	0	245	279	191	6	29	112	77	15.4	5.36	67	.284	.374	17	.181	-2	-48	-49	4	-4.3
1899	Phi-N	21	12	.636	35	33	29	4	0	270^2	278	146	1	22	85	68	12.8	3.36	110	.265	.333	21	.179	-2	15	10	2	1.0
1900	Phi-N	15	9	.625	29	26	22	1	0	223^1	250	117	7	11	93	58	14.3	3.14	115	.282	.358	22	.259	4	14	12	3	1.7
1901	Phi-A	22	16	.579	40	37	35	2	0	331	344	210	6	32	132	110	13.8	3.81	99	.265	.347	26	.187	-3	-5	-1	2	-0.2
1902	Phi-N	12	13	.480	27	26	24	3	0	224	238	115	2	15	74	97	13.1	3.42	82	.272	.339	15	.174	0	-16	-15	-0	-1.5
1903	Phi-N	12	17	.414	31	29	26	1	1	250	260	160	8	16	97	104	13.4	4.50	73	.267	.344	19	.204	4	-34	-34	2	-2.7
1904	Phi-N	14	24	.368	42	36	32	2	1	302	287	164	5	11	100	127	11.9	3.25	82	.246	.311	17	.155	-1	-17	-20	2	-2.1
1905	Bos-N	14	21	.400	39	37	35	2	0	334^1	320	174	8	15	149	130	13.0	3.28	94	.254	.340	35	.224	3	-10	-7	-1	-0.3
1906	Cin-N	10	20	.333	31	28	25	2	0	236	221	92	1	8	80	58	11.8	2.67	103	.259	.329	14	.171	-1	-1	2	1	0.2
1907	Chi-N	8	5	.615	22	15	9	2	0	138^1	112	51	1	3	46	41	10.5	2.28	110	.229	.299	3	.067	-3	3	3	0	0.0
1908	Chi-N	11	9	.550	26	17	11	2	2	162^2	141	71	4	6	61	66	11.5	2.27	104	.244	.323	6	.120	-2	2	2	4	0.4
1909	Chi-N	0	0	—	1	0	0	0	0	3	2	1	0	0	4	1	18.0	0.00	—	.222	.462	0	.000	-0	1	1	-0	0.0
Total	14	175	212	.452	434	388	342	22	6	3364	3462	2000	69	219	1338	1098	13.4	3.67	92	.266	.345	235	.178	-15	-108	-106	30	-9.2
● WILLIE FRASER	Fraser, William Patrick b: 5/26/64, New York, N.Y. BR/TR, 6'1", 206 lbs. Deb: 9/10/86																											
1986	Cal-A	0	0	—	1	1	0	0	0	4^1	6	4	0	0	1	2	14.5	8.31	50	.353	.389	0	—	0	-2	-2	-0	-0.1
1987	Cal-A	10	10	.500	36	23	5	1	1	176^2	160	85	26	6	63	106	11.7	3.92	110	.240	.312	0	—	0	11	8	-3	0.5
1988	Cal-A	12	13	.480	34	32	2	0	0	194^2	203	129	33	9	80	86	13.5	5.41	72	.267	.344	0	—	0	-31	-34	-1	-3.8
1989	Cal-A	4	7	.364	44	0	0	0	2	91^2	80	33	6	5	23	46	10.6	3.24	118	.235	.293	0	—	0	7	6	0	0.7
1990	Cal-A	5	4	.556	45	0	0	0	2	76	69	29	4	0	24	32	11.0	3.08	124	.241	.300	0	—	0	7	6	-1	0.6
1991	Tor-A	0	2	.000	13	1	0	0	0	26^1	33	20	4	3	11	12	16.1	6.15	68	.303	.382	0	—	0	-6	-6	-0	-0.4
	StL-N	3	3	.500	35	0	0	0	0	49^1	44	28	9	3	21	25	12.4	4.93	76	.242	.330	0	.000	-0	-7	-7	-1	-0.9
1994	Fla-N	2	0	1.000	9	0	0	0	0	12^1	20	9	1	0	6	7	19.0	5.84	75	.370	.433	0	—	0	-2	-2	-0	-0.3
1995	Mon-N	2	1	.667	22	0	0	0	2	25^2	25	17	6	3	9	12	13.0	5.61	77	.248	.327	0	.000	-0	-4	-4	-0	-0.5
Total	8	38	40	.487	239	57	7	1	7	657	640	354	89	29	238	328	12.4	4.47	90	.254	.326	0	.000	-0	-28	-34	-6	-4.2
● VIC FRASIER	Frasier, Victor Patrick b: 8/5/04, Ruston, La. d: 1/10/77, Jacksonville, Tex. BR/TR, 6', 182 lbs. Deb: 4/18/31																											
1931	Chi-A	13	15	.464	46	29	13	2	4	254	258	156	11	5	127	87	13.8	4.46	95	.259	.345	18	.209	1	-2	-6	-1	-0.6
1932	Chi-A	3	13	.188	29	21	4	0	0	146	180	121	14	4	70	33	15.7	6.23	69	.297	.374	4	.091	-3	-28	-32	2	-2.8
1933	Chi-A	1	1	.500	10	1	0	0	0	20^1	32	22	2	0	11	4	19.0	8.85	48	.368	.439	0	.000	-1	-10	-11	1	-0.8
	Det-A	5	5	.500	20	14	4	0	0	104^1	129	85	9	1	59	26	16.3	6.64	65	.312	.399	7	.189	-0	-27	-27	0	-2.1
	Yr	6	6	.500	30	15	4	0	0	124^2	161	107	11	1	70	30	16.7	7.00	61	.321	.406	7	.171	-1	-38	-37	2	-2.9
1934	Det-A	1	3	.250	8	2	0	0	0	22^2	30	19	0	1	12	11	17.1	5.96	74	.313	.394	2	.286	0	-4	-4	2	-0.4
1937	Bos-N	0	0	—	3	0	0	0	0	8	12	7	1	0	1	2	14.6	5.63	64	.364	.382	0	.000	-0	-2	-2	0	-0.1
1939	Chi-A	0	1	.000	10	1	0	0	0	23^2	45	27	0	0	11	7	21.5	10.27	46	.405	.459	2	.286	0	-15	-14	0	-0.6
Total	6	23	38	.377	126	68	21	2	4	579	686	437	37	11	291	170	15.4	5.77	75	.293	.373	33	.177	-3	-88	-96	4	-7.4
● GEORGE FRAZIER	Frazier, George Allen b: 10/13/54, Oklahoma City, Okla BR/TR, 6'5", 205 lbs. Deb: 5/25/78																											
1978	StL-N	0	3	.000	14	0	0	0	0	22	22	14	2	0	6	8	11.5	4.09	86	.250	.298	1	.333	0	-1	-1	0	-0.2
1979	StL-N	2	4	.333	25	0	0	0	0	32^1	35	19	3	1	12	14	13.4	4.45	85	.278	.345	0	.000	-0	-3	-2	-0	-0.4
1980	StL-N	1	4	.200	22	0	0	0	3	23	24	10	2	0	7	11	12.1	2.74	135	.273	.326	0	—	0	2	2	0	0.5
1981	*NY-A	0	1	.000	16	0	0	0	3	27^2	26	7	1	0	11	17	12.0	1.63	220	.245	.316	0	—	0	6	6	-0	0.3
1982	NY-A	4	4	.500	63	0	0	0	1	111^2	103	51	7	5	39	69	11.8	3.47	115	.252	.325	0	—	0	8	7	0	0.5
1983	NY-A	4	4	.500	61	0	0	0	8	115^1	94	44	5	3	45	78	11.1	3.43	114	.227	.307	0	—	0	8	6	0	0.5
1984	Cle-A	3	2	.600	22	0	0	0	1	44^1	45	19	3	0	14	24	12.0	3.65	112	.259	.314	0	—	0	2	2	-1	0.2
	*Chi-N	6	3	.667	37	0	0	0	3	63^2	53	30	4	1	26	58	11.3	4.10	95	.221	.300	2	.286	0	-4	-1	-1	-0.2
1985	Chi-N	7	8	.467	51	0	0	0	2	76	88	57	11	3	52	46	16.9	6.39	63	.299	.410	0	.000	-1	-24	-18	-0	-3.5
1986	Chi-N	2	4	.333	35	0	0	0	0	51^2	63	36	5	1	34	41	17.1	5.40	75	.310	.412	0	.000	-0	-10	-7	-1	-0.9
	Min-A	1	1	.500	15	0	0	0	6	26^2	23	13	2	0	16	25	13.2	4.39	98	.232	.339	0	—	0	-1	-0	0	0.0
1987	*Min-A	5	5	.500	54	0	0	0	2	81^1	77	49	9	2	51	58	14.4	4.98	93	.258	.369	0	—	0	-5	-3	-1	-0.4
Total	10	35	43	.449	415	0	0	0	29	675^2	653	349	54	16	313	449	13.1	4.20	96	.257	.342	3	.143	-1	-20	-12	-4	-3.6
● SCOTT FREDRICKSON	Fredrickson, Scott Eric b: 8/19/67, Manchester, N.H. BR/TR, 6'3", 215 lbs. Deb: 4/30/93																											
1993	Col-N	0	1	.000	25	0	0	0	0	29	33	25	3	1	17	20	15.8	6.21	77	.287	.383	0	.000	-0	-7	-4	-0	-0.3
● BUCK FREEMAN	Freeman, Alexander Vernon b: 7/5/1893, Mart, Tex. d: 2/21/53, Fort Sam Houston, Tex. BB/TR, 5'10", 167 lbs. Deb: 4/13/21																											
1921	Chi-N	9	10	.474	38	20	6	0	3	177^1	189	96	12	8	70	42	13.6	4.11	93	.281	.356	11	.208	0	-6	-6	-1	-0.7
1922	Chi-N	0	1	.000	11	1	0	0	1	25^2	47	28	0	2	10	10	20.7	8.77	48	.412	.468	1	.125	-0	-13	-13	1	-0.5
Total	2	9	11	.450	49	21	6	0	4	203	236	124	12	10	80	52	14.5	4.70	82	.300	.372	12	.197	-0	-20	-19	-0	-1.2
● HARVEY FREEMAN	Freeman, Harvey Bayard "Buck" b: 12/22/1897, Mottville, Mich. d: 1/10/70, Kalamazoo, Mich. BR/TR, 5'10", 160 lbs. Deb: 7/10/21																											
1921	Phi-A	1	4	.200	18	4	2	0	0	48	65	50	2	5	35	5	19.7	7.69	58	.346	.461	1	.083	-2	-18	-17	1	-1.4
● HERSH FREEMAN	Freeman, Hershell Baskin "Buster" b: 7/1/28, Gadsden, Ala. BR/TR, 6'3", 220 lbs. Deb: 9/10/52																											
1952	Bos-A	1	0	1.000	4	1	1	0	0	13^2	13	5	1	1	5	5	12.5	3.29	120	.260	.339	2	.500	1	1	1	0	0.2

YEAR	TM/L	W	L	PCT	G	GS	CG	SH	SV	IP	H	R	HR	HB	BB	SO	RAT	ERA	ERA+	OAV	OOB	BH	AVG	PB	PR	PR+	PD	TPI
1953	Bos-A	1	4	.200	18	2	0	0	0	39	50	31	2	0	17	15	15.5	5.54	76	.316	.383	1	.091	-1	-7	-5	-0	-0.7
1955	Bos-A	0	0	—	2	0	0	0	0	1^2	1	0	0	0	1	1	10.8	0.00	—	.200	.333	0	—	0	1	1	-0	0.0
	Cin-N	7	4	.636	52	0	0	0	11	91^2	94	31	3	2	30	37	12.4	2.16	196	.276	.338	3	.167	1	**19**	**20**	1	3.0
1956	Cin-N	14	5	.737	64	0	0	0	18	108^2	112	44	2	1	34	50	12.2	3.40	117	.274	.331	1	.056	-1	5	7	-0	1.2
1957	Cin-N	7	2	.778	52	0	0	0	8	83^2	90	49	14	3	14	36	11.5	4.52	91	.277	.313	2	.200	0	-6	-4	-1	-0.5
1958	Cin-N	0	0	—	3	0	0	0	0	7^2	4	3	0	0	5	7	10.6	3.52	118	.154	.290	0	.000	-0	0	1	0	0.0
	Chi-N	0	1	.000	9	0	0	0	0	13	23	13	3	0	3	7	18.0	8.31	47	.354	.382	0	.000	-0	-6	-6	0	-0.4
	Yr	0	1	.000	12	0	0	0	0	20^2	27	16	3	0	8	14	15.2	6.53	61	.297	.354	0	.000	-0	-6	-6	0	-0.4
Total	6	30	16	.652	204	3	1	0	37	359	387	176	25	7	109	158	12.6	3.74	110	.281	.336	9	.143	-0	6	14	1	2.8

● JIMMY FREEMAN

Freeman, Jimmy Lee b: 6/29/51, Carlsbad, N.Mex. BL/TL, 6'4", 180 lbs. Deb: 9/1/72

YEAR	TM/L	W	L	PCT	G	GS	CG	SH	SV	IP	H	R	HR	HB	BB	SO	RAT	ERA	ERA+	OAV	OOB	BH	AVG	PB	PR	PR+	PD	TPI
1972	Atl-N	2	2	.500	6	6	1	0	0	36	40	26	5	0	22	18	15.5	6.00	63	.278	.373	1	.077	-0	-10	-8	-1	-0.9
1973	Atl-N	0	2	.000	13	5	0	0	1	37^1	50	33	7	0	25	20	18.1	7.71	51	.327	.421	2	.154	-0	-17	-15	-1	-0.9
Total	2	2	4	.333	19	11	1	0	1	73^1	90	59	12	0	47	38	16.8	6.87	56	.303	.398	3	.115	-1	-27	-23	-2	-1.8

● BUCK FREEMAN

Freeman, John Frank b: 10/30/1871, Catasauqua, Pa. d: 6/25/49, Wilkes-Barre, Pa. BL/TL, 5'9", 169 lbs. Deb: 6/27/1891 ♦

YEAR	TM/L	W	L	PCT	G	GS	CG	SH	SV	IP	H	R	HR	HB	BB	SO	RAT	ERA	ERA+	OAV	OOB	BH	AVG	PB	PR	PR+	PD	TPI
1891	Was-a	3	2	.600	5	4	4	0	0	44	35	32	0	4	33	28	14.7	3.89	96	.211	.355	4	.222	0	-1	-1	-0	0.0
1899	Was-N	0	0	—	2	0	0	0	0	7	15	13	3	3	3	0	27.0	7.71	51	.429	.512	187	.318	1	-3	-3	0	-0.1
Total	2	3	2	.600	7	4	4	0	0	51	50	45	3	7	36	28	16.4	4.41	85	.249	.381	1235	.293	1	-4	-4	-0	-0.1

● JULIE FREEMAN

Freeman, Julius Benjamin b: 11/7/1868, Missouri d: 6/10/21, St.Louis, Mo. BR, Deb: 10/10/1888

YEAR	TM/L	W	L	PCT	G	GS	CG	SH	SV	IP	H	R	HR	HB	BB	SO	RAT	ERA	ERA+	OAV	OOB	BH	AVG	PB	PR	PR+	PD	TPI
1888	StL-a	0	1	.000	1	1	0	0	0	6^1	7	5	0	1	4	1	17.1	4.26	77	.269	.387	1	.333	0	-1	-1	-0	-0.1

● MARK FREEMAN

Freeman, Mark Price b: 12/7/30, Memphis, Tenn. BR/TR, 6'4", 220 lbs. Deb: 4/18/59

YEAR	TM/L	W	L	PCT	G	GS	CG	SH	SV	IP	H	R	HR	HB	BB	SO	RAT	ERA	ERA+	OAV	OOB	BH	AVG	PB	PR	PR+	PD	TPI
1959	KC-A	0	0	—	3	0	0	0	0	3^2	6	6	0	0	3	1	22.1	9.82	41	.375	.474	0	—	0	-2	-2	-0	-0.1
	NY-A	0	0	—	1	1	0	0	0	7	6	2	0	1	2	4	11.6	2.57	142	.240	.321	0	.000	-0	1	1	-0	0.0
	Yr	0	0	—	4	1	0	0	0	10^2	12	8	0	1	5	5	15.2	5.06	74	.293	.383	0	.000	-0	-1	-2	-0	-0.1
1960	Chi-N	3	3	.500	30	8	1	0	1	76^2	70	51	10	5	33	50	12.7	5.63	67	.240	.327	3	.150	-0	-16	-16	-2	-1.4
Total	2	3	3	.500	34	9	1	0	1	87^1	82	59	10	6	38	55	13.0	5.56	68	.246	.334	3	.136	-1	-17	-17	-2	-1.5

● MARVIN FREEMAN

Freeman, Marvin b: 4/10/63, Chicago, Ill. BR/TR, 6'7", 222 lbs. Deb: 9/16/86

YEAR	TM/L	W	L	PCT	G	GS	CG	SH	SV	IP	H	R	HR	HB	BB	SO	RAT	ERA	ERA+	OAV	OOB	BH	AVG	PB	PR	PR+	PD	TPI
1986	Phi-N	2	0	1.000	3	3	0	0	0	16	6	4	0	0	10	8	9.0	2.25	172	.120	.267	0	.000	-1	3	3	-0	0.2
1988	Phi-N	2	3	.400	11	11	0	0	0	51^2	55	36	2	1	43	37	17.2	6.10	59	.276	.407	3	.214	0	-15	-14	0	-1.2
1989	Phi-N	0	0	—	1	1	0	0	0	3	2	2	0	0	5	0	21.0	6.00	59	.182	.438	0	.000	-0	-1	-1	-0	-0.1
1990	Phi-N	0	2	.000	16	3	0	0	1	32^1	34	21	5	3	14	26	14.2	5.57	69	.264	.349	0	.000	-1	-6	-6	-0	-0.5
	Atl-N	1	0	1.000	9	0	0	0	0	15^2	7	3	0	2	3	12	6.9	1.72	234	.130	.203	0	—	0	4	4	-0	0.2
	Yr	1	2	.333	25	3	0	0	1	48	41	24	5	5	17	38	11.8	4.31	90	.224	.307	0	.000	-1	-3	-2	-0	-0.3
1991	Atl-N	1	0	1.000	34	0	0	0	1	48	37	19	2	2	13	34	9.8	3.00	130	.214	.277	0	.000	-1	4	4	-1	0.1
1992	*Atl-N	7	5	.583	58	0	0	0	3	64^1	61	26	7	1	29	41	12.7	3.22	114	.251	.333	2	.500	1	2	3	-1	0.5
1993	Atl-N	2	0	1.000	21	0	0	0	0	23^2	24	16	1	1	10	25	13.3	6.08	66	.261	.340	0	—	0	-5	-5	-1	-0.5
1994	Col-N	10	2	.833	19	18	0	0	0	112^2	113	39	10	5	23	67	11.3	2.80	178	.262	.307	4	.111	-0	18	23	1	2.4
1995	Col-N	3	7	.300	22	18	0	0	0	94^2	122	64	15	2	41	61	15.7	5.89	92	.318	.386	2	.087	-1	-18	-4	-1	-0.5
1996	Col-N	7	9	.438	26	23	0	0	0	129^2	151	100	21	6	57	71	14.9	6.04	87	.294	.372	5	.122	-2	-26	-9	1	-1.1
	Chi-A	0	0	—	1	1	0	0	0	2	4	3	0	0	1	1	22.5	13.50	35	.364	.417	0	—	0	-2	-2	-0	-0.1
Total	10	35	28	.556	221	78	0	0	5	593^2	616	333	63	23	249	383	13.5	4.64	98	.269	.346	16	.114	-5	-44	-5	-2	-0.6

● JAKE FREEZE

Freeze, Carl Alexander b: 4/25/1900, Huntington, Ark. d: 4/9/83, San Angelo, Tex. BR/TR, 5'8", 150 lbs. Deb: 7/1/25

YEAR	TM/L	W	L	PCT	G	GS	CG	SH	SV	IP	H	R	HR	HB	BB	SO	RAT	ERA	ERA+	OAV	OOB	BH	AVG	PB	PR	PR+	PD	TPI
1925	Chi-A	0	0	—	2	0	0	0	0	3^2	5	7	1	0	3	1	19.6	2.45	169	.333	.444	0	.000	-0	1	1	-0	0.0

● DAVE FREISLEBEN

Freisleben, David James b: 10/31/51, Coraopolis, Pa. BR/TR, 5'11", 200 lbs. Deb: 4/26/74

YEAR	TM/L	W	L	PCT	G	GS	CG	SH	SV	IP	H	R	HR	HB	BB	SO	RAT	ERA	ERA+	OAV	OOB	BH	AVG	PB	PR	PR+	PD	TPI
1974	SD-N	9	14	.391	33	31	6	2	0	211^2	194	100	13	7	112	130	13.3	3.66	98	.241	.339	11	.172	2	-1	-2	-0	0.0
1975	SD-N	5	14	.263	36	27	4	1	0	181	206	102	11	7	82	77	14.7	4.28	81	.289	.368	4	.083	-1	-13	-17	0	-1.7
1976	SD-N	10	13	.435	34	24	6	3	1	172	163	73	10	5	66	81	12.2	3.51	93	.248	.321	7	.189	1	0	-5	2	-0.2
1977	SD-N	7	9	.438	33	23	1	0	0	138^2	140	86	21	2	71	72	13.8	4.61	77	.266	.356	5	.135	0	-11	-18	-2	-2.0
1978	SD-N	0	3	.000	12	4	0	0	0	26^2	41	22	3	0	15	16	18.9	6.08	55	.363	.438	0	.000	-1	-7	-9	-0	-1.0
	Cle-A	1	4	.200	12	10	0	0	0	44^1	52	37	4	2	31	19	17.3	7.11	53	.299	.411	0	—	0	-16	-17	-0	-1.6
1979	Tor-A	2	3	.400	42	2	0	0	3	91	101	57	5	2	53	35	15.4	4.95	88	.294	.391	0	—	0	-7	-6	-1	-0.4
Total	6	34	60	.362	202	121	17	6	4	865^1	897	477	67	25	430	430	14.1	4.30	83	.269	.357	27	.141	2	-55	-73	-2	-6.9

● TONY FREITAS

Freitas, Antonio b: 5/5/08, Mill Valley, Cal. d: 3/13/94, Orangevale, Cal. BR/TL, 5'8", 161 lbs. Deb: 5/31/32

YEAR	TM/L	W	L	PCT	G	GS	CG	SH	SV	IP	H	R	HR	HB	BB	SO	RAT	ERA	ERA+	OAV	OOB	BH	AVG	PB	PR	PR+	PD	TPI
1932	Phi-A	12	5	.706	23	18	10	1	0	150^1	150	68	11	4	48	31	12.1	3.83	118	.263	.325	8	.148	-1	11	11	1	1.1
1933	Phi-A	2	4	.333	19	9	2	0	1	64^1	90	56	8	2	24	15	16.2	7.27	59	.337	.396	1	.063	-1	-21	-21	0	-1.8
1934	Cin-N	6	12	.333	30	18	5	0	1	152^2	194	80	6	3	25	37	13.1	4.01	102	.311	.341	9	.191	0	1	1	2	0.4
1935	Cin-N	5	10	.333	31	18	5	0	2	143^2	174	95	6	2	38	51	13.4	4.57	87	.295	.340	6	.130	-0	-9	-10	1	-0.8
1936	Cin-N	0	2	.000	4	0	0	0	0	7	6	2	0	0	2	1	10.3	1.29	297	.240	.296	0	.000	-0	2	2	-0	0.4
Total	5	25	33	.431	107	63	22	1	4	518	614	301	31	11	137	135	13.2	4.48	94	.296	.343	24	.145	-2	-16	-16	4	-0.7

● LARRY FRENCH

French, Lawrence Herbert b: 11/1/07, Visalia, Cal. d: 2/9/87, San Diego, Cal. BR/TL (BB 1934, 1940–42), 6'1", 195 lbs. Deb: 4/18/29

YEAR	TM/L	W	L	PCT	G	GS	CG	SH	SV	IP	H	R	HR	HB	BB	SO	RAT	ERA	ERA+	OAV	OOB	BH	AVG	PB	PR	PR+	PD	TPI
1929	Pit-N	7	5	.583	30	13	6	0	1	123	130	78	10	3	62	49	14.3	4.90	97	.276	.364	8	.190	-1	-3	-2	1	-0.1
1930	Pit-N	17	18	.486	42	35	21	3	1	274^2	325	163	20	6	89	90	13.8	4.36	114	.295	.351	22	.242	1	19	19	-1	1.9
1931	Pit-N	15	13	.536	39	33	20	1	1	275^2	301	127	9	1	70	73	12.1	3.26	118	.278	.322	17	.179	-1	18	18	-1	1.5
1932	Pit-N	18	16	.529	**47**	33	19	3	4	274^1	301	127	17	1	62	72	11.9	3.02	126	.276	.316	19	.207	1	26	25	-4	2.6
1933	Pit-N	18	13	.581	47	35	21	5	1	291^1	290	106	9	5	55	88	10.8	2.72	122	.257	.294	15	.149	-2	20	20	-4	1.4
1934	Pit-N	12	18	.400	49	34	16	3	1	263^2	299	135	8	3	59	103	12.3	3.58	115	.281	.321	16	.190	-0	14	15	-3	1.2
1935	*Chi-N	17	10	.630	42	30	16	**4**	2	246^1	279	94	10	2	44	90	11.9	2.96	133	.286	.318	12	.141	-4	29	27	1	2.5
1936	Chi-N	18	9	.667	43	28	16	**4**	3	252^1	262	103	16	6	54	104	11.5	3.39	118	.266	.308	18	.212	0	18	17	-3	1.4
1937	Chi-N	16	10	.615	42	28	11	4	0	208	229	106	17	1	65	100	12.8	3.98	100	.274	.327	9	.127	-4	-2	0	2	-0.2
1938	*Chi-N	10	19	.345	43	27	10	3	0	201^1	210	95	17	1	62	83	12.2	3.80	101	.271	.326	13	.210	2	-0	1	1	0.4
1939	Chi-N	15	8	.652	36	21	10	2	1	194	205	80	7	1	50	98	11.9	3.29	120	.269	.314	14	.192	1	13	14	2	1.8
1940	Chi-N★	14	14	.500	40	33	18	3	2	246	240	93	12	4	64	107	11.3	3.29	114	.256	.306	14	.165	1	15	13	2	1.7
1941	Chi-N	5	14	.263	26	18	6	1	0	138	161	88	10	2	43	60	13.4	4.63	76	.285	.338	9	.191	1	-15	-18	-1	-2.2
	*Bro-N	0	0	—	6	1	0	0	0	15^2	16	6	1	1	4	8	12.1	3.45	106	.267	.323	1	.250	0	0	0	-0	0.0
	Yr	5	14	.263	32	19	6	1	0	153^2	177	94	11	3	47	68	13.3	4.51	78	.283	.336	10	.196	1	-15	-17	-1	-2.2
1942	Bro-N	15	4	**.789**	38	14	8	4	0	147^2	127	39	1	5	36	62	10.2	1.83	178	.233	.287	12	.300	4	24	24	-1	3.4
Total	14	197	171	.535	570	383	198	40	17	3152	3375	1440	164	42	819	1187	12.1	3.44	114	.272	.320	199	.188	0	178	172	-7	17.3

● BILL FRENCH

French, William b: Baltimore, Md. Deb: 4/14/1873 ♦

YEAR	TM/L	W	L	PCT	G	GS	CG	SH	SV	IP	H	R	HR	HB	BB	SO	RAT	ERA	ERA+	OAV	OOB	BH	AVG	PB	PR	PR+	PD	TPI
1873	Mar-n	0	1	.000	1	1	1	0	0	9	30	27	0		0	0	30.0	12.00	27	.462	.462	4	.222	-0	-9	-9		-0.5

● BENNY FREY

Frey, Benjamin Rudolph b: 4/6/06, Dexter, Mich. d: 11/1/37, Spring Arbor Township, Mich. BR/TR, 5'10", 165 lbs. Deb: 9/18/29

YEAR	TM/L	W	L	PCT	G	GS	CG	SH	SV	IP	H	R	HR	HB	BB	SO	RAT	ERA	ERA+	OAV	OOB	BH	AVG	PB	PR	PR+	PD	TPI
1929	Cin-N	1	2	.333	3	3	2	0	0	24	29	12	2	0	8	1	13.9	4.13	111	.302	.356	3	.375	1	2	1	1	0.3
1930	Cin-N	11	18	.379	44	28	14	2	1	245	295	145	15	3	62	43	13.2	4.70	103	.305	.349	25	.284	4	7	3	6	1.3
1931	Cin-N	8	12	.400	34	17	7	1	2	133^2	166	76	2	2	36	19	13.7	4.92	76	.319	.365	14	.318	4	-16	-18	4	-1.6
1932	StL-N	0	2	.000	2	0	0	0	0	3	6	5	0	0	2	0	24.0	12.00	33	.600	.667	0	.000	-0	-3	-3	-0	-0.5
	Cin-N	4	10	.286	28	15	5	0	0	131^1	159	72	10	1	30	27	13.0	4.32	89	.299	.338	9	.205	-0	-6	-7	3	-0.4
	Yr	4	12	.250	30	15	5	0	0	134^1	165	77	10	1	32	27	13.3	4.49	86	.305	.345	9	.200	-0	-9	-9	2	-0.9
1933	Cin-N	6	4	.600	37	9	1	1	0	132	144	67	4	0	21	12	11.3	3.82	89	.281	.309	11	.262	3	-7	-6	2	0.1
1934	Cin-N	11	16	.407	39	30	12	2	2	245^1	288	118	10	2	42	33	12.2	3.52	116	.289	.319	14	.171	-0	15	15	4	1.9
1935	Cin-N	6	10	.375	38	13	3	1	2	114^1	164	100	6	4	32	24	15.7	6.85	58	.335	.381	11	.344	4	-36	-37	2	-3.9
1936	Cin-N	10	8	.556	31	12	5	0	0	131^1	164	73	5	0	30	20	13.3	4.25	90	.296	.332	11	.250	2	-3	-7	0	-0.6
Total	8	57	82	.410	256	127	49	7	7	1160	1415	668	54	12	263	179	13.1	4.50	90	.303	.341	98	.255	17	-47	-56	21	-3.4

YEAR	TM/L	W	L	PCT	G	GS	CG	SH	SV	IP	H	R	HR	HB	BB	SO	RAT	ERA	ERA+	OAV	OOB	BH	AVG	PB	PR	PR+	PD	TPI
● STEVE FREY	Frey, Steven Francis b: 7/29/63, Meadowbrook, Pa. BR/TL, 5'9", 170 lbs. Deb: 5/10/89																											
1989	Mon-N	3	2	.600	20	0	0	0	0	21^1	29	15	4	1	11	15	17.3	5.48	64	.326	.406	0	—	0	-5	-5	-0	-1.0
1990	Mon-N	8	2	.800	51	0	0	0	9	55^2	44	15	4	1	29	29	12.0	2.10	174	.219	.320	0	.000	-0	10	10	-0	2.0
1991	Mon-N	0	1	.000	31	0	0	0	1	39^2	43	31	3	1	23	21	15.2	4.99	73	.281	.379	0	.000	0	-6	-6	-1	-0.4
1992	Cal-A	4	2	.667	51	0	0	0	4	45^1	39	18	6	2	22	24	12.5	3.57	112	.238	.335	0	—	0	2	2	0	0.3
1993	Cal-A	2	3	.400	55	0	0	0	13	48^1	41	20	1	3	26	22	13.0	2.98	152	.230	.338	0	—	0	7	8	-0	1.1
1994	SF-N	1	0	1.000	44	0	0	0	0	31	37	17	6	2	15	20	15.7	4.94	81	.322	.409	0	—	0	-2	-3	-0	-0.2
1995	SF-N	0	1	.000	9	0	0	0	0	6^1	7	6	1	0	2	5	12.8	4.26	96	.280	.333	0	—	0	-0	-0	-0	0.0
	Sea-A	0	3	.000	13	0	0	0	0	11^1	16	7	0	1	6	7	18.3	4.76	100	.356	.442	0	—	0	-0	-0	1	0.0
	Phi-N	0	0	—	9	0	0	0	1	10^2	3	1	1	0	2	2	4.2	0.84	501	.091	.143	0	.000	-0	4	4	-0	0.2
1996	Phi-N	0	1	.000	31	0	0	0	0	34^1	38	19	4	0	18	12	14.7	4.72	91	.295	.381	0	—	0	-2	-1	1	0.0
Total	8	18	15	.545	314	0	0	0	28	304	297	149	30	11	154	157	13.7	3.76	107	.262	.356	0	.000	-0	9	8	-1	2.0
● BERNIE FRIBERG	Friberg, Bernard Albert (b: Gustaf Bernhard Friberg) b: 8/18/1899, Manchester, N.H. d: 12/8/58, Lynn, Mass. BR/TR, 5'11", 178 lbs. Deb: 8/20/19 ◆																											
1925	Phi-N	0	0	—	1	0	0	0	0	4	4	2	0	0	3	1	15.8	4.50	106	.286	.412	82	.270	0	-0	0	-0	0.0
● MARION FRICANO	Fricano, Marion John b: 7/15/23, Brant, N.Y. d: 5/18/76, Tijuana, Mex. BR/TR, 6', 170 lbs. Deb: 9/6/52																											
1952	Phi-A	1	0	1.000	2	0	0	0	0	5	5	1	0	0	1	0	10.8	1.80	220	.238	.273	0	—	0	1	1	0	0.2
1953	Phi-A	9	12	.429	39	23	10	0	0	211	206	105	21	6	90	67	12.9	3.88	110	.257	.337	10	.145	-3	3	9	-2	0.4
1954	Phi-A	5	11	.313	37	20	4	0	1	151^2	163	98	17	4	64	43	13.7	5.16	76	.275	.349	4	.098	-3	-24	-20	-2	-2.4
1955	KC-A	0	0	—	10	0	0	0	0	20	19	9	2	0	9	5	12.6	3.15	133	.253	.333	2	.667	1	2	2	0	0.2
Total	4	15	23	.395	88	43	14	0	1	387^2	393	213	40	10	164	115	13.2	4.32	96	.264	.341	16	.142	-5	-19	-8	-3	-1.6
● SKIPPER FRIDAY	Friday, Grier William b: 10/26/1897, Gastonia, N.C. d: 8/25/62, Gastonia, N.C. BR/TR, 5'11", 170 lbs. Deb: 6/17/23																											
1923	Was-A	0	1	.000	7	2	1	0	0	30	35	27	2	2	22	9	17.7	6.90	55	.313	.434	2	.222	0	-10	-11	1	-0.4
● CY FRIED	Fried, Arthur Edwin b: 7/23/1897, San Antonio, Tex. d: 10/10/70, San Antonio, Tex. BL/TL, 5'11.5", 150 lbs. Deb: 9/17/20																											
1920	Det-A	0	0	—	2	0	0	0	0	1^2	3	4	0	0	4	0	37.8	16.20	23	.500	.700	0	—	0	-2	-2	0	-0.1
● BOB FRIEDRICHS	Friedrichs, Robert George b: 8/30/06, Cincinnati, Ohio d: 4/15/97, Jasper, Ind. BR/TR, 5'11.5", 165 lbs. Deb: 5/17/32																											
1932	Was-A	0	0	—	2	0	0	0	0	4	4	5	0	1	7	2	27.0	11.25	38	.250	.500	0	.000	-0	-3	-3	-0	-0.2
● BILL FRIEL	Friel, William Edward b: 4/1/1876, Renovo, Pa. d: 12/24/59, St.Louis, Mo. BL/TR, 5'10", 165 lbs. Deb: 5/3/01 FUC◆																											
1902	StL-A	0	0	—	1	0	0	0	0	4	4	4	0	0	0	0	9.0	4.50	78	.267	.267	64	.240	0	-0	-0	-0	0.0
● DANNY FRIEND	Friend, Daniel Sebastian b: 4/18/1873, Cincinnati, Ohio d: 6/1/42, Chillicothe, Ohio TL, 5'9", 175 lbs. Deb: 9/10/1895																											
1895	Chi-N	2	2	.500	5	5	5	0	0	41	50	27	5	3	14	10	14.7	5.27	97	.296	.360	4	.235	-1	-2	-1	0	-0.1
1896	Chi-N	18	14	.563	36	33	28	1	0	290^2	298	196	11	39	139	86	14.7	4.74	96	.263	.363	30	.238	-1	-12	-6	-2	-0.8
1897	Chi-N	12	11	.522	24	24	23	0	0	203	244	144	5	17	86	58	15.4	4.52	99	.295	.373	25	.284	2	-5	-1	-2	-0.1
1898	Chi-N	0	2	.000	2	2	2	0	0	17	20	15	1	1	10	4	16.4	5.29	68	.290	.387	2	.286	0	-3	-3	2	-0.1
Total	4	32	29	.525	67	64	58	1	0	551^2	612	382	22	60	249	158	15.0	4.71	96	.279	.368	61	.256	0	-22	-12	-2	-1.1
● BOB FRIEND	Friend, Robert Bartmess "Warrior" b: 11/24/30, Lafayette, Ind. BR/TR, 6', 190 lbs. Deb: 4/28/51																											
1951	Pit-N	6	10	.375	34	22	3	1	0	149^2	173	94	12	0	68	41	14.5	4.27	99	.293	.366	4	.091	-2	-5	-1	0	-0.3
1952	Pit-N	7	17	.292	35	23	6	1	0	185	186	96	15	3	84	75	13.3	4.18	95	.258	.338	3	.058	-4	-9	-4	1	-0.8
1953	Pit-N	8	11	.421	32	24	8	0	0	170^2	193	103	18	3	57	66	13.3	4.90	91	.286	.344	7	.135	-2	-12	-8	1	-0.9
1954	Pit-N	7	12	.368	35	20	4	2	2	170^1	204	106	16	1	58	73	13.9	5.07	83	.302	.358	14	.275	5	-19	-16	-1	-1.2
1955	Pit-N	14	9	.609	44	20	9	2	2	200^1	178	80	18	2	52	98	10.4	**2.83**	**145**	.242	.294	10	.164	-2	**27**	**28**	3	3.2
1956	Pit-N★	17	17	.500	49	42	19	4	3	**314^1**	310	137	25	2	85	166	11.4	3.46	109	.258	.308	16	.165	-1	11	11	-1	0.9
1957	Pit-N	14	18	.438	40	38	17	3	0	**277**	273	121	28	1	68	143	11.1	3.38	112	.257	.303	16	.184	1	15	13	-1	1.4
1958	Pit-N★	**22**	14	.611	38	38	16	1	0	274	299	120	25	4	61	135	12.0	3.68	105	.281	.322	10	.106	-4	8	6	-0	0.3
1959	Pit-N	8	19	.296	35	35	7	2	0	234^2	267	129	19	7	52	104	12.5	4.03	96	.283	.325	12	.164	0	-2	-4	0	-0.4
1960	*Pit-N★	18	12	.600	38	37	16	4	1	275^2	266	97	18	0	45	183	10.2	3.00	125	.251	.281	6	.068	-5	23	23	0	1.9
1961	Pit-N	14	19	.424	41	35	10	1	1	236	271	119	16	3	45	108	12.2	3.85	104	.289	.324	11	.139	-3	5	4	-1	0.1
1962	Pit-N	18	14	.563	39	36	13	**5**	1	261^2	280	99	23	2	53	144	11.5	3.06	129	.273	.310	11	.121	-3	26	25	0	2.6
1963	Pit-N	17	16	.515	39	38	12	4	0	268^2	236	87	13	5	44	144	9.5	2.34	141	.233	.269	9	.105	-3	28	28	-1	3.1
1964	Pit-N	13	18	.419	35	35	13	3	0	240^1	253	98	10	4	50	128	11.5	3.33	105	.271	.310	5	.070	-3	5	5	2	0.4
1965	Pit-N	8	12	.400	34	34	8	2	0	222	221	89	17	8	47	74	11.2	3.24	108	.260	.305	3	.042	-5	7	7	0	0.0
1966	NY-A	1	4	.200	12	8	0	0	0	44^2	61	25	2	0	9	22	14.1	4.84	69	.330	.361	0	.000	-1	-7	-8	1	-0.8
	NY-N	5	8	.385	22	12	2	1	1	86	101	52	11	1	16	30	12.3	4.40	83	.289	.322	1	.034	-3	-8	-7	-2	-1.5
Total	16	197	230	.461	602	497	163	36	11	3611	3772	1652	286	46	894	1734	11.7	3.58	107	.269	.315	138	.121	-36	94	100	2	8.0
● PETE FRIES	Fries, Peter Martin b: 10/30/1857, Scranton, Pa. d: 7/30/37, Chicago, Ill. BL/TL, 5'8", 160 lbs. Deb: 8/10/1883 ◆																											
1883	Col-a	0	3	.000	3	3	3	0	0	25	34	31	1	14	7	17.3	6.48	48	.304	.381	3	.300	1	-9	-10	0	-0.8	
● JOHN FRILL	Frill, John Edmond b: 4/3/1879, Reading, Pa. d: 9/28/18, Westerly, R.I. BR/TL, 5'10.5", 170 lbs. Deb: 4/16/10																											
1910	NY-A	2	2	.500	10	5	3	1	1	48^1	55	33	1	1	5	27	11.4	4.47	59	.289	.311	2	.111	-1	-10	-9	0	-0.9
1912	StL-A	0	1	.000	3	3	0	0	0	4^1	16	11	1	1	1	2	37.4	20.77	16	.571	.600	1	.500	0	-8	-8	0	-1.3
	Cin-N	1	0	1.000	3	2	0	0	0	15	19	11	0	2	1	4	13.2	6.00	56	.345	.379	1	.250	0	-4	-4	0	-0.2
Total	2	3	3	.500	16	10	3	1	1	67^2	90	55	2	4	7	33	13.4	5.85	49	.330	.356	4	.167	-1	-23	-22	0	-2.4
● DANNY FRISELLA	Frisella, Daniel Vincent "Bear" b: 3/4/46, San Francisco, Cal. d: 1/1/77, Phoenix, Ariz. BL/TR, 6', 195 lbs. Deb: 7/27/67																											
1967	NY-N	1	6	.143	14	11	0	0	0	74	68	32	6	0	33	51	12.3	3.41	100	.249	.330	2	.087	-1	-0	-0	-0	-0.1
1968	NY-N	2	4	.333	19	4	0	0	2	50^2	53	23	5	0	17	47	12.4	3.91	77	.270	.329	1	.083	-1	-5	-5	0	-0.7
1969	NY-N	0	0	—	3	0	0	0	0	4^2	8	4	1	0	3	5	21.2	7.71	47	.381	.458	0	.000	-0	-2	-2	-0	-0.1
1970	NY-N	8	3	.727	30	1	0	0	1	65^2	49	23	4	0	34	54	11.4	3.02	134	.204	.303	4	.308	1	8	7	-0	1.3
1971	NY-N	8	5	.615	53	0	0	0	12	90^2	76	28	6	3	30	93	10.8	1.99	172	.227	.296	3	.231	1	15	15	1	2.7
1972	NY-N	5	8	.385	39	0	0	0	9	67^1	63	31	8	0	20	46	11.1	3.34	101	.243	.297	2	.286	0	1	0	1	0.2
1973	Atl-N	1	2	.333	42	0	0	0	8	45	40	27	5	1	23	27	12.8	4.20	94	.241	.337	1	.500	0	-3	-1	-0	-0.1
1974	Atl-N	3	4	.429	36	1	0	0	6	41^2	37	26	4	0	28	27	14.0	5.18	73	.240	.357	0	.000	0	-7	-6	-0	-1.2
1975	SD-N	1	6	.143	65	0	0	0	9	97^2	86	36	7	2	51	67	12.8	3.13	111	.242	.340	1	.200	0	5	4	-0	0.3
1976	StL-N	0	0	—	18	0	0	0	1	22^2	19	10	3	0	13	11	12.7	3.97	89	.232	.337	0	.000	-0	-1	-1	0	-0.1
	Mil-A	5	2	.714	32	0	0	0	9	49^1	30	16	4	1	34	43	11.9	2.74	128	.175	.316	0	—	0	4	4	0	0.8
Total	10	34	40	.459	351	17	0	0	57	609^1	529	256	53	7	286	471	12.1	3.32	106	.235	.323	14	.179	1	15	14	0	3.0
● EMIL FRISK	Frisk, John Emil b: 10/15/1874, Kalkaska, Mich. d: 1/27/22, Seattle, Wash. BL/TR, 6'1", 190 lbs. Deb: 9/2/1899 ◆																											
1899	Cin-N	3	6	.333	9	9	9	0	0	68^1	81	52	1	6	17	17	13.7	3.95	99	.295	.349	7	.280	1	-1	-0	-0	0.1
1901	Det-A	5	4	.556	11	7	6	0	0	74^2	94	60	1	2	26	22	14.7	4.34	89	.304	.362	15	.313	2	-6	-4	3	0.1
Total	2	8	10	.444	20	16	15	0	0	143	175	112	2	8	43	39	14.2	4.15	93	.300	.356	135	.267	3	-6	-4	2	0.2
● CHARLIE FRITZ	Fritz, Charles Cornelius b: 6/18/1882, Mobile, Ala. d: 7/30/43, Mobile, Ala. TL, Deb: 10/5/07																											
1907	Phi-A	0	0	—	1	1	0	0	0	3	0	1	0	1	3	1	12.0	3.00	87	.000	.333	0	.000	-0	-0	-0	-0	0.0
● BILL FROATS	Froats, William John b: 10/20/30, New York, N.Y. d: 2/9/98, Minneapolis, Minn. BL/TL, 6', 180 lbs. Deb: 4/22/55																											
1955	Det-A	0	0	—	1	0	0	0	0	2	0	0	0	0	2	0	9.0	0.00	—	.000	.333	0	—	0	1	1	0	0.1
● SAM FROCK	Frock, Samuel William b: 12/23/1882, Baltimore, Md. d: 11/3/25, Baltimore, Md. BR/TR, 6', 168 lbs. Deb: 9/21/07																											
1907	Bos-N	1	2	.333	5	3	3	1	0	33^1	28	17	1	2	11	12	11.1	2.97	86	.243	.320	1	.071	-1	-2	-1	-2	-0.4
1909	Pit-N	2	1	.667	8	4	3	0	1	36^1	44	19	0	3	4	11	12.6	2.48	110	.299	.331	2	.143	-1	0	1	0	0.0
1910	Pit-N	0	0	—	1	0	0	0	0	2	2	4	0	1	2	1	22.5	4.50	69	.400	.625	0	—	0	-0	-0	0	0.0
	Bos-N	12	19	.387	45	29	13	2	2	255^1	245	133	8	4	91	170	12.0	3.21	104	.262	.330	16	.190	-3	-5	3	1	0.2

YEAR	TM/L	W	L	PCT	G	GS	CG	SH	SV	IP	H	R	HR	HB	BB	SO	RAT	ERA	ERA+	OAV	OOB	BH	AVG	PB	PR	PR+	PD	TPI
	Yr	12	19	.387	46	29	13	2	2	257^1	247	137	8	5	93	171	12.1	3.22	103	.263	.333	16	.190	-3	-5	3	2	0.2
1911	Bos-N	0	1	.000	4	1	1	0	0	16	29	18	0	1	5	8	19.7	5.63	68	.426	.473	1	.200	-0	-4	-3	0	-0.2
Total	4	15	23	.395	63	37	20	3	3	343	348	191	9	11	113	202	12.4	3.23	99	.274	.339	20	.171	-5	-11	-1	0	-0.4

● TODD FROHWIRTH Frohwirth, Todd Gerard b: 9/28/62, Milwaukee, Wis. BR/TR, 6'4", 205 lbs. Deb: 8/10/87

YEAR	TM/L	W	L	PCT	G	GS	CG	SH	SV	IP	H	R	HR	HB	BB	SO	RAT	ERA	ERA+	OAV	OOB	BH	AVG	PB	PR	PR+	PD	TPI
1987	Phi-N	1	0	1.000	10	0	0	0	0	11	12	0	0	0	2	9	11.5	0.00	—	.293	.326	0	.000	-0	5	5	0	0.4
1988	Phi-N	1	2	.333	12	0	0	0	0	12	16	11	2	0	11	11	20.3	8.25	43	.327	.450	0	—	0	-6	-6	1	-1.2
1989	Phi-N	1	0	1.000	45	0	0	0	0	62^2	56	26	4	3	18	39	11.1	3.59	99	.240	.303	0	.000	-0	-1	-0	-0	0.0
1990	Phi-N	0	1	.000	5	0	0	0	0	1	3	2	0	0	6	1	81.0	18.00	21	.500	.750	0	—	0	-2	-2	0	-0.3
1991	Bal-A	7	3	.700	51	0	0	0	3	96^1	64	24	2	1	29	77	8.8	1.87	212	.190	.256	0	—	0	**24**	**23**	3	2.7
1992	Bal-A	4	3	.571	65	0	0	0	4	106	97	33	4	3	41	58	12.0	2.46	164	.247	.323	0	—	0	17	18	3	1.5
1993	Bal-A	6	7	.462	70	0	0	0	3	96^1	91	47	7	3	44	50	12.9	3.83	117	.256	.343	0	—	0	5	7	2	1.0
1994	Bos-A	0	3	.000	22	0	0	0	1	26^2	40	36	3	2	17	13	19.9	10.80	47	.339	.431	0	—	0	-18	-16	1	-1.5
1996	Cal-A	0	0	—	4	0	0	0	0	5^2	10	11	1	1	4	1	23.8	11.12	45	.370	.469	0	—	0	-4	-4	-0	-0.2
Total	9	20	19	.513	284	0	0	0	11	417^2	389	190	23	13	172	259	12.4	3.60	114	.250	.329	0	.000	-0	22	24	9	2.4

● ART FROMME Fromme, Arthur Henry b: 9/3/1883, Quincy, Ill. d: 8/24/56, Los Angeles, Cal. BR/TR, 6', 178 lbs. Deb: 9/14/06

YEAR	TM/L	W	L	PCT	G	GS	CG	SH	SV	IP	H	R	HR	HB	BB	SO	RAT	ERA	ERA+	OAV	OOB	BH	AVG	PB	PR	PR+	PD	TPI
1906	StL-N	1	2	.333	3	3	3	1	0	25	19	6	0	1	10	11	10.8	1.44	183	.221	.309	2	.222	0	3	3	1	0.5
1907	StL-N	5	13	.278	23	16	13	2	0	145^2	138	73	3	4	67	67	12.9	2.90	86	.256	.343	10	.182	1	-7	-6	0	-0.7
1908	StL-N	5	13	.278	20	14	9	2	0	116	102	59	1	2	50	62	11.9	2.72	87	.218	.296	5	.139	-1	-5	-5	-0	-0.9
1909	Cin-N	19	13	.594	37	34	22	4	2	279^1	195	84	2	3	101	126	9.6	1.90	137	.201	.278	18	.191	2	22	22	2	3.1
1910	Cin-N	3	4	.429	11	5	1	0	0	49^1	44	22	2	1	39	10	15.3	2.92	100	.260	.402	2	.133	-1	1	-0	0	-0.1
1911	Cin-N	10	11	.476	38	26	11	1	0	208	190	111	8	16	79	107	12.3	3.46	96	.248	.331	14	.189	-1	-1	-4	1	-0.4
1912	Cin-N	16	18	.471	43	37	23	3	0	296	285	126	7	11	88	120	11.7	2.74	123	.260	.321	9	.087	-9	22	21	-0	1.2
1913	Cin-N	1	4	.200	9	7	2	0	0	56	55	30	1	3	21	24	12.7	4.18	78	.274	.351	3	.143	-0	-6	-6	-1	-0.6
	NY-N	11	6	.647	26	12	3	0	0	112^1	112	58	5	2	29	50	11.5	4.01	78	.260	.310	6	.171	-0	-10	-11	1	-1.5
	Yr	12	10	.545	35	19	5	0	0	168^1	167	88	6	5	50	74	11.9	4.06	78	.264	.323	9	.161	-1	-16	-17	1	-2.1
1914	NY-N	9	5	.643	38	12	3	1	2	138	142	57	7	7	44	57	12.6	3.20	83	.283	.349	7	.226	1	-6	-9	3	-0.4
1915	NY-N	0	1	.000	4	1	0	0	0	12^1	15	11	1	0	2	4	12.4	5.84	44	.306	.333	1	.333	1	-4	-5	0	-0.3
Total	10	80	90	.471	252	167	90	14	4	1438	1297	637	37	50	530	638	11.7	2.90	100	.246	.320	77	.162	-8	8	2	8	-0.1

● DAVE FROST Frost, Carl David b: 11/17/52, Long Beach, Cal. BR/TR, 6'6", 235 lbs. Deb: 9/11/77

YEAR	TM/L	W	L	PCT	G	GS	CG	SH	SV	IP	H	R	HR	HB	BB	SO	RAT	ERA	ERA+	OAV	OOB	BH	AVG	PB	PR	PR+	PD	TPI
1977	Chi-A	1	1	.500	4	3	0	0	0	23^2	30	9	0	1	3	15	12.9	3.04	135	.323	.351	0	—	0	3	3	-0	0.2
1978	Cal-A	5	4	.556	11	10	2	1	0	80^1	71	24	6	2	24	30	10.9	2.58	141	.240	.301	0	—	0	11	10	1	1.2
1979	*Cal-A	16	10	.615	36	33	12	2	1	239^1	226	108	17	5	77	107	11.6	3.57	114	.251	.314	0	—	0	17	14	-1	1.3
1980	Cal-A	4	8	.333	15	15	2	0	0	78^1	97	53	8	2	21	28	13.8	5.29	75	.308	.355	0	—	0	-11	-12	-1	-1.7
1981	Cal-A	1	8	.111	12	9	0	0	0	47^1	44	30	3	1	19	16	12.2	5.51	66	.250	.327	0	—	0	-10	-10	0	-1.6
1982	KC-A	6	6	.500	21	14	0	0	0	81^2	103	53	7	3	30	26	15.0	5.51	74	.313	.376	0	—	0	-13	-13	-1	-1.7
Total	6	33	37	.471	99	84	16	3	1	550^2	571	277	41	14	174	222	12.4	4.10	97	.271	.330	0	—	0	-3	-9	-3	-2.3

● JOHNSON FRY Fry, Johnson "Jay" b: 11/21/01, Huntington, W.Va. d: 4/7/59, Carmi, Ill. BR/TR, 6'1", 150 lbs. Deb: 8/24/23

YEAR	TM/L	W	L	PCT	G	GS	CG	SH	SV	IP	H	R	HR	HB	BB	SO	RAT	ERA	ERA+	OAV	OOB	BH	AVG	PB	PR	PR+	PD	TPI
1923	Cle-A	0	0	—	1	0	0	0	0	3^2	6	5	0	0	4	0	24.5	12.27	32	.353	.476	1	1.000	1	-3	-3	-0	-0.1

● CHARLIE FRYE Frye, Charles Andrew b: 7/17/14, Hickory, N.C. d: 5/25/45, Hickory, N.C. BR/TR, 6'1", 175 lbs. Deb: 7/28/40

YEAR	TM/L	W	L	PCT	G	GS	CG	SH	SV	IP	H	R	HR	HB	BB	SO	RAT	ERA	ERA+	OAV	OOB	BH	AVG	PB	PR	PR+	PD	TPI
1940	Phi-N	0	6	.000	15	5	1	0	0	50^1	58	32	3	0	26	18	15.0	4.65	84	.291	.373	5	.263	1	-4	-4	-1	-0.4

● WOODIE FRYMAN Fryman, Woodrow Thompson b: 4/15/40, Ewing, Ky. BR/TL, 6'2", 205 lbs. Deb: 4/15/66

YEAR	TM/L	W	L	PCT	G	GS	CG	SH	SV	IP	H	R	HR	HB	BB	SO	RAT	ERA	ERA+	OAV	OOB	BH	AVG	PB	PR	PR+	PD	TPI
1966	Pit-N	12	9	.571	36	28	9	3	1	181^2	182	86	13	1	47	105	11.4	3.81	94	.261	.309	10	.159	-1	-4	-5	-2	-0.8
1967	Pit-N	3	8	.273	28	18	3	1	1	113^1	121	67	12	4	44	74	13.4	4.05	83	.276	.348	4	.118	-1	-9	-9	2	-0.7
1968	Phi-N☆	12	14	.462	34	32	10	5	0	213^2	198	78	12	6	64	151	11.3	2.78	108	.246	.306	6	.085	-2	5	5	-1	0.2
1969	Phi-N	12	15	.444	36	35	10	3	0	228^1	243	123	15	11	89	150	13.5	4.41	80	.270	.343	9	.118	-2	-21	-22	-1	-2.6
1970	Phi-N	8	6	.571	27	20	4	3	0	127^2	122	61	11	1	43	97	11.7	4.09	98	.253	.315	5	.128	-2	-1	-1	-0	-0.3
1971	Phi-N	10	7	.588	37	17	3	2	2	149^1	133	61	7	3	46	104	11.0	3.38	105	.242	.304	7	.189	0	2	3	2	0.6
1972	Phi-N	4	10	.286	23	17	3	2	1	119^2	131	64	15	2	39	69	12.9	4.36	82	.279	.337	5	.152	1	-12	-10	1	-1.0
	*Det-A	10	3	.769	16	14	6	1	0	113^2	93	31	6	7	31	72	10.4	2.06	153	.220	.285	5	.125	-2	13	14	-1	1.3
1973	Det-A	6	13	.316	34	29	1	0	0	169^2	200	106	23	3	64	119	14.2	5.36	76	.294	.357	0	—	0	-29	-22	1	-2.1
1974	Det-A	6	9	.400	27	22	4	1	0	141^2	120	73	16	4	67	92	12.1	4.32	88	.233	.326	0	—	0	-11	-8	-1	-0.8
1975	Mon-N	9	12	.429	38	20	7	3	3	157	141	69	10	5	68	118	12.3	3.32	115	.239	.323	10	.204	1	5	8	1	1.4
1976	Mon-N☆	13	13	.500	34	32	4	2	2	216^1	218	89	14	9	76	123	12.6	3.37	111	.263	.332	7	.109	-3	3	8	-0	0.6
1977	Cin-N	5	5	.500	17	12	0	0	1	75^1	83	45	13	2	45	57	15.5	5.38	73	.292	.393	7	.318	2	-12	-12	1	-1.2
1978	Chi-N	2	4	.333	13	9	0	0	0	55^2	64	37	6	0	37	28	16.3	5.17	78	.309	.414	1	.063	-1	-10	-6	1	-0.6
	Mon-N	5	7	.417	19	17	4	3	1	94^2	93	39	4	3	37	53	12.6	3.61	98	.260	.334	2	.059	-2	-0	-1	-0	-0.4
	Yr	7	11	.389	32	26	4	3	1	150^1	157	76	10	3	74	81	14.0	4.19	89	.278	.364	3	.060	-3	-10	-8	1	-1.0
1979	Mon-N	3	6	.333	44	0	0	0	10	58	52	25	4	3	22	44	11.9	2.79	132	.248	.328	0	.000	-1	6	6	1	1.1
1980	Mon-N	7	4	.636	61	0	0	0	17	80	61	23	1	2	30	59	10.5	2.25	159	.209	.287	2	.167	-0	12	12	1	2.0
1981	*Mon-N	5	3	.625	35	0	0	0	7	43	38	16	1	1	14	25	11.1	1.88	186	.247	.314	2	.667	1	8	8	0	1.8
1982	Mon-N	9	4	.692	60	0	0	0	12	69^2	66	36	3	2	26	46	12.0	3.75	97	.259	.330	2	.222	0	-1	-1	1	0.0
1983	Mon-N	0	3	.000	6	0	0	0	0	3	8	7	1	0	1	1	27.0	21.00	17	.571	.600	0	—	0	-6	-6	0	-1.1
Total	18	141	155	.476	625	322	68	27	58	2411^1	2367	1136	187	68	890	1587	12.4	3.77	96	.259	.329	84	.138	-12	-61	-40	4	-2.6

● CHARLIE FUCHS Fuchs, Charles Thomas b: 11/18/12, Union Hill, N.J. d: 6/10/69, Weehawken, N.J. BB/TR, 5'8", 168 lbs. Deb: 4/17/42

YEAR	TM/L	W	L	PCT	G	GS	CG	SH	SV	IP	H	R	HR	HB	BB	SO	RAT	ERA	ERA+	OAV	OOB	BH	AVG	PB	PR	PR+	PD	TPI
1942	Det-A	3	3	.500	9	4	1	1	0	36^2	43	27	5	1	19	15	15.5	6.63	60	.285	.368	1	.077	-1	-12	-10	1	-1.4
1943	Phi-N	2	7	.222	17	9	4	1	1	77^2	76	40	4	3	34	12	13.1	4.29	79	.266	.350	2	.091	-2	-8	-8	-1	-1.1
	StL-N	0	0	—	13	0	0	0	0	35^2	42	22	4	1	11	9	13.6	4.04	82	.294	.348	0	.000	-1	-3	-3	-0	-0.3
1944	Bro-N	1	0	1.000	8	0	0	0	0	15^2	25	16	2	1	9	5	20.1	5.74	62	.347	.427	0	.000	0	-4	-4	1	-0.2
Total	3	6	10	.375	47	13	5	2	1	165^2	186	105	15	6	73	41	14.4	4.89	72	.285	.363	3	.070	-4	-27	-25	0	-3.0

● MIGUEL FUENTES Fuentes, Miguel (Pinet) b: 5/10/46, Loiza Aldea, P.R. d: 1/29/70, Loiza Aldea, P.R. BR/TR, 6', 160 lbs. Deb: 9/1/69

YEAR	TM/L	W	L	PCT	G	GS	CG	SH	SV	IP	H	R	HR	HB	BB	SO	RAT	ERA	ERA+	OAV	OOB	BH	AVG	PB	PR	PR+	PD	TPI
1969	Sea-A	1	3	.250	8	4	1	0	0	26	29	15	1	0	16	14	15.6	5.19	70	.284	.381	2	.333	0	-5	-4	-1	-0.6

● OSCAR FUHR Fuhr, Oscar Lawrence b: 8/22/1893, Defiance, Mo. d: 3/27/75, Dallas, Tex. BL/TL, 6'0.5", 176 lbs. Deb: 4/19/21

YEAR	TM/L	W	L	PCT	G	GS	CG	SH	SV	IP	H	R	HR	HB	BB	SO	RAT	ERA	ERA+	OAV	OOB	BH	AVG	PB	PR	PR+	PD	TPI
1921	Chi-N	0	0	—	1	0	0	0	0	4	11	9	1	0	0	2	24.8	9.00	42	.500	.500	0	.000	-0	-2	-2	0	-0.1
1924	Bos-A	3	6	.333	23	10	4	1	0	80^1	100	71	1	5	39	30	16.1	5.94	74	.310	.392	4	.182	-1	-15	-14	1	-1.3
1925	Bos-A	0	6	.000	39	5	0	0	0	91^1	138	83	7	3	30	27	16.9	6.60	69	.364	.415	5	.250	0	-22	-20	1	-1.0
Total	3	3	12	.200	63	15	4	1	0	175^2	249	163	9	8	69	59	16.7	6.35	70	.344	.407	9	.209	-1	-40	-36	2	-2.4

● JOHN FULGHAM Fulgham, John Thomas b: 6/9/56, St.Louis, Mo. BR/TR, 6'2", 205 lbs. Deb: 6/19/79

YEAR	TM/L	W	L	PCT	G	GS	CG	SH	SV	IP	H	R	HR	HB	BB	SO	RAT	ERA	ERA+	OAV	OOB	BH	AVG	PB	PR	PR+	PD	TPI
1979	StL-N	10	6	.625	20	19	10	2	0	146	123	47	10	3	26	75	9.4	2.53	149	.227	.267	6	.143	1	20	20	-2	2.0
1980	StL-N	4	6	.400	15	14	4	1	0	85^1	66	33	7	1	32	48	10.4	3.38	110	.219	.296	0	.000	-3	2	3	-0	0.0
Total	2	14	12	.538	35	33	14	3	0	231^1	189	80	17	4	58	123	9.8	2.84	132	.224	.277	6	.087	-2	22	23	-2	2.0

● ED FULLER Fuller, Edward Ashton b: 3/22/1868, Washington, D.C. d: 3/16/35, Hyattsville, Md. BR/TR, 6', 158 lbs. Deb: 7/17/1886

YEAR	TM/L	W	L	PCT	G	GS	CG	SH	SV	IP	H	R	HR	HB	BB	SO	RAT	ERA	ERA+	OAV	OOB	BH	AVG	PB	PR	PR+	PD	TPI
1886	Was-N	0	1	.000	2	1	1	0	0	13	15	12	0		5	3	13.8	6.92	47	.375	.444	1	.143	-0	-5	-5	-0	-0.3

● CURT FULLERTON Fullerton, Curtis Hooper b: 9/13/1898, Ellsworth, Me. d: 1/2/75, Winthrop, Mass. BL/TR, 6', 162 lbs. Deb: 4/14/21

YEAR	TM/L	W	L	PCT	G	GS	CG	SH	SV	IP	H	R	HR	HB	BB	SO	RAT	ERA	ERA+	OAV	OOB	BH	AVG	PB	PR	PR+	PD	TPI
1921	Bos-A	0	1	.000	4	1	1	0	0	15^1	22	17	3	1	10	4	19.4	8.80	48	.355	.452	0	.000	-0	-8	-8	-1	-0.5
1922	Bos-A	1	4	.200	31	3	0	0	0	64^1	70	40	4	5	35	17	15.4	5.46	75	.290	.391	2	.250	1	-10	-9	1	-0.4
1923	Bos-A	2	15	.118	37	15	6	0	1	143^1	167	108	9	6	71	37	15.3	5.09	81	.300	.385	11	.297	2	-18	-15	-2	-1.5
1924	Bos-A	7	12	.368	33	20	9	0	2	152	166	93	1	6	73	33	14.5	4.32	101	.283	.368	3	.071	-3	-2	1	-0	-0.3
1925	Bos-A	0	3	.000	4	2	0	0	0	22^2	22	11	1	2	9	3	13.1	3.18	143	.259	.344	2	.200	-0	3	3	1	0.4
1933	Bos-A	0	2	.000	6	2	0	0	0	25^1	36	24	1	1	13	10	17.8	8.53	51	.364	.442	2	.222	0	-12	-11	-1	-0.7
Total	6	10	37	.213	115	43	18	0	3	423	483	293	19	21	211	104	15.2	5.11	83	.296	.384	20	.182	-1	-46	-39	-1	-3.0

YEAR	TM/L	W	L	PCT	G	GS	CG	SH	SV	IP	H	R	HR	HB	BB	SO	RAT	ERA	ERA+	OAV	OOB	BH	AVG	PB	PR	PR+	PD	TPI
● CHICK FULMER Fulmer, Charles John b: 2/12/1851, Philadelphia, Pa. d: 2/15/40, Philadelphia, Pa. BR/TR, 6', 158 lbs. Deb: 8/23/1871 FU♦																												
1873	Phi-n	0	0	—	2	0	0	0	0	5	7	4	0		1	0	14.4	3.60	92	.304	.333	66	.280	0	-0	-0		0.0
● CHRIS FULMER Fulmer, Christopher b: 7/4/1858, Tamaqua, Pa. d: 11/9/31, Tamaqua, Pa. BR/TR, 5'8", 165 lbs. Deb: 8/4/1884 ♦																												
1886	Bal-a	0	0	—	1	0	0	0	0	2	2	2	0	0	1	0	13.5	4.50	76	.250	.333	66	.244	0	-0	-0	-0	0.0
● BILL FULTON Fulton, William David b: 10/22/63, Pittsburgh, Pa. BR/TR, 6'3", 195 lbs. Deb: 9/12/87																												
1987	NY-A	1	0	1.000	3	0	0	0	0	4^2	9	6	4	1	1	2	21.2	11.57	38	.409	.458	0	—	0	-4	-4	0	-0.6
● AARON FULTZ Fultz, Richard Aaron b: 9/4/73, Memphis, Tenn. BL/TL, 6', 196 lbs. Deb: 4/5/2000																												
2000	*SF-N	5	2	.714	58	0	0	0	1	69^1	67	38	8	3	28	62	12.7	4.67	91	.263	.343	2	.333	1	-0	-4	2	-0.1
● FRANK FUNK Funk, Franklin Ray b: 8/30/35, Washington, D.C. BR/TR, 6', 175 lbs. Deb: 9/3/60 C																												
1960	Cle-A	4	2	.667	9	0	0	0	1	31^2	27	8	3	0	9	18	10.2	1.99	188	.248	.305	1	.111	-0	7	6	0	1.2
1961	Cle-A	11	11	.500	56	0	0	0	11	92^1	79	35	9	4	31	64	11.1	3.31	119	.234	.306	1	.059	-1	7	7	0	1.2
1962	Cle-A	2	1	.667	47	0	0	0	6	80^2	62	35	11	4	32	49	10.9	3.24	120	.212	.298	1	.067	-1	7	6	-0	0.1
1963	Mil-N	3	3	.500	25	0	0	0	0	43^2	42	14	3	1	13	19	11.5	2.68	120	.258	.316	0	.000	-0	3	3	-1	0.2
Total	4	20	17	.541	137	0	0	0	18	248^1	210	92	26	9	85	150	11.0	3.01	125	.233	.305	3	.067	-3	23	21	-1	2.7
● TOM FUNK Funk, Thomas James b: 3/13/62, Kansas City, Mo. BL/TL, 6'2", 210 lbs. Deb: 7/24/86																												
1986	Hou-N	0	0	—	8	0	0	0	0	8^1	10	6	1	0	6	2	17.3	6.48	56	.286	.390	0	.000	-0	-3	-3	0	-0.2
● EDDIE FUSSELBACK Fusselback, Edward L. b: 7/17/1856, Philadelphia, Pa. d: 4/14/26, Philadelphia, Pa. 5'6", 156 lbs. Deb: 5/3/1882 ♦																												
1882	StL-a	1	2	.333	4	2	2	0	**1**	23	34	24	0		2	3	14.1	4.70	60	.321	.333	31	.228	0	-5	-5	-1	-0.6
● CHRIS FUSSELL Fussell, Christopher Wren b: 5/19/76, Oregon, Ohio BR/TR, 6'2", 200 lbs. Deb: 9/15/98																												
1998	Bal-A	0	1	.000	3	2	0	0	0	9^2	11	9	1	0	9	8	18.6	8.38	54	.306	.444	0	—	0	-4	-4	0	-0.3
1999	KC-A	0	5	.000	17	8	0	0	2	56	72	51	9	5	36	37	18.2	7.39	68	.329	.435	0	—	0	-16	-14	-0	-1.1
2000	KC-A	5	3	.625	20	9	0	0	0	70	76	52	18	2	44	46	15.7	6.30	79	.286	.391	0	.000	-0	-11	-10	-1	-1.0
Total	3	5	9	.357	40	19	0	0	2	135^2	159	112	28	7	89	91	16.9	6.90	72	.305	.413	0	.000	-0	-30	-28	-1	-2.4
● FRED FUSSELL Fussell, Frederick Morris "Moonlight Ace" b: 10/7/1895, Sheridan, Mo. d: 10/23/66, Syracuse, N.Y. BL/TL, 5'10", 155 lbs. Deb: 9/23/22																												
1922	Chi-N	1	1	.500	3	2	1	0	0	19	24	11	0	0	8	4	15.2	4.74	89	.333	.400	0	.000	-1	-1	-1	0	-0.1
1923	Chi-N	3	5	.375	28	2	1	0	3	76^1	90	51	2	3	31	38	14.6	5.54	72	.298	.369	4	.200	-0	-13	-13	0	-1.2
1928	Pit-N	8	9	.471	28	20	9	2	1	159^2	183	79	6	1	41	43	12.7	3.61	113	.295	.340	7	.121	-3	7	8	-3	0.1
1929	Pit-N	2	2	.500	21	3	0	0	1	39^2	68	42	8	1	8	18	17.5	8.62	55	.389	.418	4	.250	2	-17	-17	-0	-1.3
Total	4	14	17	.452	80	27	11	2	5	294^2	365	183	16	5	88	103	14.0	4.86	85	.312	.363	15	.150	-2	-25	-23	-2	-2.5
● MIKE FYHRIE Fyhrie, Michael Edwin b: 12/9/69, Long Beach, Cal. BR/TR, 6'2", 190 lbs. Deb: 9/14/96																												
1996	NY-N	0	1	.000	2	0	0	0	0	2^1	4	4	0	0	3	0	27.0	15.43	26	.364	.500	0	—	0	-3	-3	0	-0.5
1999	Ana-A	0	4	.000	16	7	0	0	0	51^2	61	32	8	0	21	26	14.3	5.05	96	.286	.350	0	—	0	-1	-1	-1	-0.2
2000	Ana-A	0	0	—	32	0	0	0	0	52^2	54	14	4	0	15	43	11.8	2.39	208	.269	.319	0	—	0	15	15	-0	0.7
Total	3	0	5	.000	50	7	0	0	0	106^2	119	50	12	0	39	69	13.3	3.97	123	.280	.341	0	—	0	11	11	-1	0.0
● FRANK GABLER Gabler, Frank Harold "The Great Gabbo" b: 11/6/11, E.Highlands, Cal. d: 11/1/67, Long Beach, Cal. BR/TR, 6'1", 175 lbs. Deb: 4/19/35																												
1935	NY-N	2	1	.667	26	1	0	0	0	60	79	43	6	0	20	24	14.9	5.70	68	.315	.365	2	.125	-1	-11	-13	0	-0.7
1936	*NY-N	9	8	.529	43	14	5	0	6	161^2	170	62	11	3	34	46	11.5	3.12	125	.274	.315	10	.208	2	16	14	-1	1.5
1937	NY-N	0	0	—	6	0	0	0	0	9	20	14	1	0	2	3	22.0	10.00	39	.455	.478	0	—	0	-6	-6	-0	-0.3
	Bos-N	4	7	.364	19	9	2	1	2	76	84	45	7	0	16	19	11.8	5.09	70	.283	.319	4	.182	0	-10	-14	-0	-1.8
	Yr	4	7	.364	25	9	2	1	2	85	104	59	8	0	18	22	12.9	5.61	64	.305	.340	4	.182	0	-16	-20	-0	-2.1
1938	Bos-N	0	0	—	1	0	0	0	0	0^1	3	3	0	0	1	0	108.0	81.00	4	1.000	1.000	0	—	0	-3	-3	0	-0.1
	Chi-A	1	7	.125	18	7	3	0	0	69^1	101	74	12	1	34	17	17.7	9.09	54	.348	.418	5	.238	0	-33	-32	-1	-2.8
Total	4	16	23	.410	113	31	10	1	8	376^1	457	241	37	4	107	109	13.6	5.26	76	.303	.351	21	.196	1	-47	-54	-2	-4.2
● GABE GABLER Gabler, John Richard b: 10/2/30, Kansas City, Mo. BB/TR, 6'2", 165 lbs. Deb: 9/18/59																												
1959	NY-A	1	1	.500	3	1	0	0	0	19^1	21	6	1	1	10	11	14.9	2.79	130	.284	.376	0	.000	-1	2	2	0	0.1
1960	NY-A	3	3	.500	21	4	0	0	1	52	46	27	2	0	32	19	13.5	4.15	86	.242	.351	1	.091	-0	-2	-4	0	-0.4
1961	Was-A	3	8	.273	29	9	0	0	4	92^2	104	61	5	1	37	33	13.8	4.86	83	.283	.351	5	.200	1	-9	-9	1	-0.8
Total	3	7	12	.368	53	14	0	0	5	164	171	94	8	2	79	63	13.8	4.39	87	.271	.354	6	.143	-0	-8	-11	1	-1.1
● KEN GABLES Gables, Kenneth Harlin "Coral" b: 1/31/19, Walnut Grove, Mo. d: 1/2/60, Walnut Grove, Mo. BR/TR, 5'11", 210 lbs. Deb: 4/18/45																												
1945	Pit-N	11	7	.611	29	16	6	0	1	138^2	139	69	5	4	46	49	12.3	4.15	95	.256	.319	4	.103	-3	-5	-3	-2	-0.8
1946	Pit-N	2	4	.333	32	7	0	0	1	100^2	113	64	3	1	52	39	14.8	5.27	67	.281	.365	6	.250	1	-21	-19	-2	-1.1
1947	Pit-N	0	0	—	1	0	0	0	0	0^1	3	2	1	0	0	0	81.0	54.00	8	.750	.750	0	—	0	-2	-2	0	-0.1
Total	3	13	11	.542	62	23	6	0	2	239^2	255	135	9	5	98	88	13.4	4.69	80	.269	.340	10	.159	-1	-28	-24	-4	-2.0
● JOHN GADDY Gaddy, John Wilson "Sheriff" b: 2/5/14, Wadesboro, N.C. d: 5/3/66, Albemarle, N.C. BR/TR, 6'0.5", 182 lbs. Deb: 9/27/38																												
1938	Bro-N	2	0	1.000	2	2	1	0	0	13	13	3	0	1	4	3	12.5	0.69	564	.255	.321	0	.000	-1	4	5	-0	0.7
● GARY GAETTI Gaetti, Gary Joseph b: 8/19/58, Centralia, Ill. BR/TR, 6', 200 lbs. Deb: 9/20/81 ♦																												
1997	StL-N	0	0	—	1	0	0	0	0	0^1	1	0	0	1	0	0	54.0	0.00	—	.500	.667	126	.251	0	0	0	0	0.0
1998	StL-N	0	0	—	1	0	0	0	0	1	2	0	0	0	0	0	18.0	0.00	—	.400	.400	81	.265	0	0	0	-0	0.0
1999	Chi-N	0	0	—	1	0	0	0	0	1	2	2	1	0	1	1	27.0	18.00	25	.400	.500	57	.204	0	-1	-2	0	-0.1
Total	3	0	0	—	3	0	0	0	0	2^1	5	2	1	1	1	1	27.0	7.71	56	.417	.500	2280	.255	1	-1	-1	-0	-0.1
● BRENT GAFF Gaff, Brent Allen b: 10/5/58, Fort Wayne, Ind. BR/TR, 6'2", 200 lbs. Deb: 7/7/82																												
1982	NY-N	0	3	.000	7	5	0	0	0	31^2	41	22	3	1	10	14	14.8	4.55	80	.323	.377	0	.000	-0	-3	-3	-0	-0.3
1983	NY-N	1	0	1.000	4	0	0	0	0	10^1	18	9	0	0	1	4	16.5	6.10	60	.360	.373	0	.000	-0	-3	-3	-0	-0.3
1984	NY-N	3	2	.600	47	0	0	0	1	84^1	77	39	4	1	36	42	12.2	3.63	98	.247	.327	0	.000	-1	-0	-1	0	-0.1
Total	3	4	5	.444	58	5	0	0	1	126^1	136	70	7	2	47	60	13.2	4.06	88	.278	.344	0	.000	-1	-6	-7	0	-0.7
● ERIC GAGNE Gagne, Eric Serge b: 1/7/76, Montreal, Que., Can. BR/TR, 6'2", 195 lbs. Deb: 9/7/99																												
1999	LA-N	1	1	.500	5	5	0	0	0	30	18	8	3	0	15	30	9.9	2.10	204	.175	.280	2	.200	0	8	8	-1	0.4
2000	LA-N	4	6	.400	20	19	0	0	0	101^1	106	62	20	3	60	79	15.0	5.15	85	.270	.371	4	.143	-1	-6	-9	-1	-0.9
Total	2	5	7	.417	25	24	0	0	0	131^1	124	70	23	3	75	109	13.8	4.45	98	.250	.352	6	.158	-1	2	-1	-2	-0.5
● CHARLIE GAGUS Gagus, Charles Frederick (b: Charles Frederick Geggus) b: 3/25/1862, San Francisco, Cal d: 1/16/17, San Francisco, Cal Deb: 8/7/1884																												
1884	Was-U	10	9	.526	23	21	19	0	0	177^1	143	100	2		38	156	9.2	2.54	95	.206	.247	38	.247	-3	-2	-3	1	-0.4
● EDDIE GAILLARD Gaillard, Julian Edward b: 8/13/70, Camden, N.J. BR/TR, 6'1", 180 lbs. Deb: 8/11/97																												
1997	Det-A	1	0	1.000	16	0	0	0	1	20^1	16	12	2	0	10	12	11.5	5.31	86	.211	.302	0	—	0	-2	-2	-1	-0.1
1998	TB-A	0	0	—	6	0	0	0	0	7^2	4	5	3	0	3	5	8.2	5.87	82	.148	.233	0	—	0	-1	-1	-0	0.0
1999	TB-A	1	0	1.000	8	0	0	0	0	8^2	12	9	1	1	4	7	17.7	2.08	240	.324	.405	0	—	0	3	3	0	0.3
Total	3	2	0	1.000	30	0	0	0	1	36^2	32	26	6	1	17	24	12.3	4.66	101	.229	.316	0	—	0	-0	0	-1	0.2
● NEMO GAINES Gaines, Willard Roland b: 12/23/1897, Alexandria, Va. d: 1/26/79, Warrenton, Va. BL/TL, 6', 180 lbs. Deb: 6/26/21																												
1921	Was-A	0	0	—	4	0	0	0	0	4^2	5	0	0	0	2	1	13.5	0.00	—	.294	.368	0	.000	-0	2	2	-0	0.1
● FRED GAISER Gaiser, Frederick Jacob b: 8/31/1885, Stuttgart, Germany d: 10/9/18, Trenton, N.J. Deb: 9/3/08																												
1908	StL-N	0	0	—	1	0	0	0	0	2^1	4	2	0	0	3	2	27.0	7.71	31	.444	.583	0	.000	-0	-1	-1	0	-0.1
● STEVE GAJKOWSKI Gajkowski, Stephen Robert b: 12/30/69, Seattle, Wash. BR/TR, 6'2", 200 lbs. Deb: 5/25/98																												
1998	Sea-A	0	0	—	9	0	0	0	0	8^2	14	8	3	2	4	3	20.8	7.27	64	.389	.476	0	—	0	-3	-3	-0	-0.2

● DAN GAKELER
Gakeler, Daniel Michael b: 5/1/64, Mt.Holly, N.J. BR/TR, 6'6", 215 lbs. Deb: 6/9/91

YEAR	TM/L	W	L	PCT	G	GS	CG	SH	SV	IP	H	R	HR	HB	BB	SO	RAT	ERA	ERA+	OAV	OOB	BH	AVG	PB	PR	PR+	PD	TPI
1991	Det-A	1	4	.200	31	7	0	0	2	73^2	73	52	5	1	39	43	13.8	5.74	72	.256	.348	0	—	0	-13	-13	0	-0.8

● BOB GALASSO
Galasso, Robert Joseph b: 1/13/52, Connellsville, Pa. BL/TR, 6'1", 205 lbs. Deb: 7/24/77

YEAR	TM/L	W	L	PCT	G	GS	CG	SH	SV	IP	H	R	HR	HB	BB	SO	RAT	ERA	ERA+	OAV	OOB	BH	AVG	PB	PR	PR+	PD	TPI
1977	Sea-A	0	6	.000	11	7	0	0	0	35	57	36	8	3	8	21	17.5	9.00	46	.365	.407	0	—	0	-19	-19	-0	-2.6
1979	Mil-A	3	1	.750	31	0	0	0	3	51^1	64	30	5	0	26	28	15.8	4.38	95	.299	.375	0	—	0	-1	-1	-0	-0.1
1981	Sea-A	1	1	.500	13	1	0	0	1	31^2	32	19	2	0	13	14	12.8	4.83	80	.264	.336	0	—	0	-4	-3	-0	-0.2
Total	3	4	8	.333	55	8	0	0	4	118	153	85	15	3	47	63	15.5	5.87	70	.312	.375	0	—	0	-24	-23	-1	-2.9

● MILT GALATZER
Galatzer, Milton b: 5/4/07, Chicago, Ill. d: 1/29/76, San Francisco, Cal BL/TL, 5'10", 168 lbs. Deb: 6/25/33 ♦

YEAR	TM/L	W	L	PCT	G	GS	CG	SH	SV	IP	H	R	HR	HB	BB	SO	RAT	ERA	ERA+	OAV	OOB	BH	AVG	PB	PR	PR+	PD	TPI
1936	Cle-A	0	0	—	1	0	0	0	0	6	7	3	0	0	5	3	18.0	4.50	112	.292	.414	23	.237	0	0	0	0	0.0

● RICH GALE
Gale, Richard Blackwell b: 1/19/54, Littleton, N.H. BR/TR, 6'7", 225 lbs. Deb: 4/30/78 C

YEAR	TM/L	W	L	PCT	G	GS	CG	SH	SV	IP	H	R	HR	HB	BB	SO	RAT	ERA	ERA+	OAV	OOB	BH	AVG	PB	PR	PR+	PD	TPI
1978	KC-A	14	8	.636	31	30	9	3	0	192^1	171	78	10	3	100	88	12.8	3.09	124	.244	.340	0	—	0	15	16	-2	1.5
1979	KC-A	9	10	.474	34	31	2	1	0	181^2	197	131	19	4	99	103	14.9	5.65	76	.278	.369	0	—	0	-29	-27	-1	-2.5
1980	*KC-A	13	9	.591	32	28	6	1	1	190^2	169	90	16	2	78	97	11.8	3.92	104	.239	.316	0	—	0	3	3	-1	0.3
1981	KC-A	6	6	.500	19	15	2	0	0	101^2	107	63	14	2	38	47	13.0	5.40	67	.270	.336	0	—	0	-20	-20	-2	-2.3
1982	SF-N	7	14	.333	33	29	2	0	0	170^1	193	91	9	5	81	102	14.7	4.23	85	.294	.376	6	.125	1	-12	-12	1	-1.2
1983	Cin-N	4	6	.400	33	7	0	0	1	89^2	103	64	8	1	43	53	14.8	5.82	66	.286	.364	3	.150	1	-22	-19	-1	-1.9
1984	Bos-A	2	3	.400	13	4	0	0	0	43^2	57	27	6	1	18	28	15.7	5.56	75	.315	.380	0	—	0	-8	-6	-0	-0.7
Total	7	55	56	.495	195	144	21	5	2	970	997	544	82	18	457	518	13.7	4.54	86	.269	.351	9	.132	2	-72	-67	-5	-6.8

● DENNY GALEHOUSE
Galehouse, Dennis Ward b: 12/7/11, Marshallville, Ohio d: 10/12/98, Doylestown, Pa. BR/TR, 6'1", 195 lbs. Deb: 4/30/34

YEAR	TM/L	W	L	PCT	G	GS	CG	SH	SV	IP	H	R	HR	HB	BB	SO	RAT	ERA	ERA+	OAV	OOB	BH	AVG	PB	PR	PR+	PD	TPI
1934	Cle-A	0	0	—	1	0	0	0	0	1	2	3	0	0	1	0	27.0	18.00	25	.500	.600	0	—	0	-2	-1	-0	-0.1
1935	Cle-A	1	0	1.000	5	1	1	0	0	13	16	14	1	1	9	8	18.0	9.00	50	.314	.426	1	.250	-0	-7	-6	0	-0.4
1936	Cle-A	8	7	.533	36	15	5	0	1	148^1	161	86	5	2	68	71	14.0	4.85	104	.280	.358	8	.170	-0	3	3	-2	0.0
1937	Cle-A	9	14	.391	36	29	7	0	3	200^2	238	114	11	1	83	78	14.4	4.57	101	.302	.369	15	.208	-1	1	1	1	0.0
1938	Cle-A	7	8	.467	36	12	5	1	3	114	119	62	12	1	65	66	14.6	4.34	107	.275	.371	6	.154	-1	6	4	0	0.3
1939	Bos-A	9	10	.474	30	18	6	1	0	146^2	160	84	6	1	52	68	13.1	4.54	104	.276	.337	3	.064	-3	1	3	0	0.1
1940	Bos-A	6	6	.500	25	20	5	0	0	120	155	77	10	0	41	53	14.7	5.18	87	.313	.366	3	.077	-4	-11	-9	1	-1.0
1941	StL-A	9	10	.474	30	24	11	2	0	190^1	183	85	10	4	68	61	12.1	3.64	118	.253	.320	13	.191	-0	11	13	1	1.2
1942	StL-A	12	12	.500	32	28	12	3	1	192^1	193	91	5	4	79	75	12.9	3.60	103	.262	.337	14	.194	1	1	2	1	0.4
1943	StL-A	11	11	.500	31	28	14	2	1	224	217	80	8	1	74	114	11.7	2.77	120	.255	.315	9	.125	-3	13	14	-3	0.7
1944	*StL-A	9	10	.474	24	19	6	2	0	153	162	64	6	1	44	80	12.2	3.12	115	.266	.316	3	.063	-4	5	8	-2	0.3
1946	StL-A	8	12	.400	30	24	11	2	0	180	194	82	9	0	52	90	12.3	3.65	102	.273	.322	5	.091	-3	-3	2	-2	-0.4
1947	StL-A	1	3	.250	9	4	0	0	1	32^1	42	26	3	0	16	11	16.1	6.12	63	.311	.384	0	.000	-1	-9	-8	0	-1.0
	Bos-A	11	7	.611	21	21	11	3	0	149	150	60	7	0	34	38	11.1	3.32	117	.260	.301	5	.096	-4	6	9	-1	0.5
	Yr	12	10	.545	30	25	11	3	1	181^1	192	86	10	0	50	49	12.0	3.82	102	.269	.317	5	.083	-5	-2	1	-0	-0.5
1948	Bos-A	8	8	.500	27	15	6	1	3	137^1	152	68	10	2	46	38	13.1	4.00	110	.282	.341	7	.167	-0	4	6	-2	0.4
1949	Bos-A	0	0	—	2	0	0	0	0	2	4	3	1	0	3	0	31.5	13.50	32	.400	.538	0	—	0	-2	-2	0	-0.1
Total	15	109	118	.480	375	258	100	17	13	2004	2148	999	104	18	735	851	13.0	3.97	105	.275	.338	92	.138	-25	20	39	-8	0.9

● DOUG GALLAGHER
Gallagher, Douglas Eugene b: 2/21/40, Fremont, Ohio BR/TL, 6'3.5", 195 lbs. Deb: 4/9/62

YEAR	TM/L	W	L	PCT	G	GS	CG	SH	SV	IP	H	R	HR	HB	BB	SO	RAT	ERA	ERA+	OAV	OOB	BH	AVG	PB	PR	PR+	PD	TPI
1962	Det-A	0	4	.000	9	2	0	0	1	25	31	18	2	0	15	14	16.6	4.68	87	.290	.377	2	.333	1	-2	-2	0	-0.1

● ED GALLAGHER
Gallagher, Edward Michael "Lefty" b: 11/28/10, Dorchester, Mass. d: 12/22/81, Hyannis, Mass. BB/TL, 6'2", 197 lbs. Deb: 7/8/32

YEAR	TM/L	W	L	PCT	G	GS	CG	SH	SV	IP	H	R	HR	HB	BB	SO	RAT	ERA	ERA+	OAV	OOB	BH	AVG	PB	PR	PR+	PD	TPI
1932	Bos-A	0	3	.000	9	3	0	0	0	23^2	30	36	3	0	28	6	22.1	12.55	36	.323	.479	0	.000	-1	-21	-21	0	-2.0

● BILL GALLAGHER
Gallagher, William John b: Philadelphia, Pa. TL, Deb: 5/2/1883 ♦

YEAR	TM/L	W	L	PCT	G	GS	CG	SH	SV	IP	H	R	HR	HB	BB	SO	RAT	ERA	ERA+	OAV	OOB	BH	AVG	PB	PR	PR+	PD	TPI
1883	Bal-a	0	5	.000	7	5	4	0	0	51^2	79	57	0		6	19	14.8	5.40	64	.331	.347	10	.164	-1	-12	-10	-1	-0.9
1884	Phi-U	1	2	.333	3	3	3	0	0	25	32	29	3		4	12	13.0	3.24	72	.291	.316	1	.091	-2	-2	-3	0	-0.4
Total	2	1	7	.125	10	8	7	0	0	76^2	111	86	3		10	31	14.2	4.70	66	.318	.337	11	.138	-3	-14	-13	-1	-1.3

● BERT GALLIA
Gallia, Melvin Allys b: 10/14/1891, Beeville, Tex. d: 3/19/76, Devine, Tex. BR/TR, 6', 165 lbs. Deb: 9/4/12

YEAR	TM/L	W	L	PCT	G	GS	CG	SH	SV	IP	H	R	HR	HB	BB	SO	RAT	ERA	ERA+	OAV	OOB	BH	AVG	PB	PR	PR+	PD	TPI
1912	Was-A	0	0	—	2	0	0	0	0	2	0	0	0	0	3	0	13.5	0.00	—	.000	.333	0	—	0	1	1	-0	0.0
1913	Was-A	1	5	.167	31	4	0	0	3	96	85	66	2	7	46	46	12.9	4.13	72	.222	.317	2	.087	-2	-13	-12	2	-0.8
1914	Was-A	0	0	—	2	0	0	0	0	6	3	4	0	0	4	4	10.5	4.50	63	.120	.241	0	.000	-0	-1	-1	-0	-0.1
1915	Was-A	17	11	.607	43	29	14	3	1	259^2	220	90	2	4	64	130	10.0	2.29	130	.234	.286	14	.165	-2	19	19	-2	1.7
1916	Was-A	17	13	.567	49	31	13	1	2	283^2	278	109	3	8	99	120	12.2	2.76	101	.266	.334	18	.194	1	2	1	-3	-0.2
1917	Was-A	9	13	.409	42	23	9	1	1	207^2	191	92	1	4	93	84	12.5	2.99	88	.258	.344	14	.209	2	-8	-9	-0	-0.8
1918	StL-A	8	6	.571	19	17	10	1	0	124	126	63	1	6	61	48	14.0	3.48	79	.268	.359	6	.130	-3	-10	-10	0	-1.4
1919	StL-A	12	14	.462	34	25	14	1	1	222^1	220	109	10	8	92	83	13.0	3.60	92	.264	.343	11	.153	-2	-9	-7	2	-0.7
1920	StL-A	0	1	.000	2	1	0	0	0	3^2	8	7	0	0	3	0	27.0	7.36	53	.400	.478	0	.000	-0	-1	-1	-0	-0.3
	Phi-N	2	6	.250	18	5	1	0	2	72	79	48	2	3	29	35	13.9	4.50	76	.287	.362	4	.174	-1	-11	-8	-1	-1.0
Total	9	66	69	.489	242	135	61	7	10	1277	1210	588	21	40	494	550	12.3	3.14	94	.256	.331	69	.167	-7	-31	-28	-3	-3.6

● PHIL GALLIVAN
Gallivan, Philip Joseph b: 5/29/07, Seattle, Wash. d: 11/24/69, St.Paul, Minn. BR/TR, 6', 170 lbs. Deb: 4/21/31

YEAR	TM/L	W	L	PCT	G	GS	CG	SH	SV	IP	H	R	HR	HB	BB	SO	RAT	ERA	ERA+	OAV	OOB	BH	AVG	PB	PR	PR+	PD	TPI
1931	Bro-N	0	1	.000	6	1	0	0	0	15^1	23	11	2	0	7	1	17.6	5.28	72	.354	.417	0	.000	-0	-2	-3	-1	-0.1
1932	Chi-A	1	3	.250	13	3	1	0	0	33^1	49	32	4	1	24	12	20.0	7.56	57	.338	.435	3	.375	1	-11	-12	-0	-1.1
1934	Chi-A	4	7	.364	35	7	3	0	1	126^2	155	97	14	1	64	55	15.6	5.61	84	.295	.373	9	.225	1	-16	-12	1	-0.9
Total	3	5	11	.313	54	11	4	0	1	175^1	227	140	20	2	95	68	16.6	5.95	77	.309	.389	12	.235	1	-30	-26	-1	-2.1

● BALVINO GALVEZ
Galvez, Balvino (Jerez) b: 3/31/64, San Pedro De Macoris, D.R. BR/TR, 6', 170 lbs. Deb: 5/7/86

YEAR	TM/L	W	L	PCT	G	GS	CG	SH	SV	IP	H	R	HR	HB	BB	SO	RAT	ERA	ERA+	OAV	OOB	BH	AVG	PB	PR	PR+	PD	TPI
1986	LA-N	0	1	.000	10	0	0	0	0	20^2	19	10	3	0	12	11	13.5	3.92	88	.241	.341	0	.000	-0	-0	-1	0	-0.1

● JIM GALVIN
Galvin, James Francis "Pud', "Gentle Jeems" or "The Little Steam Engine"
b: 12/25/1856, St.Louis, Mo. d: 3/7/02, Pittsburgh, Pa. BR/TR (BL 1884 (1 game)), 5'8", 190 lbs. Deb: 5/22/1875 MUH

YEAR	TM/L	W	L	PCT	G	GS	CG	SH	SV	IP	H	R	HR	HB	BB	SO	RAT	ERA	ERA+	OAV	OOB	BH	AVG	PB	PR	PR+	PD	TPI
1875	StL-n	4	2	.667	8	7	7	0	1	62	53	37	0		1	8	7.8	**1.16**	**173**	.209	.212	6	.130	-1	7	6		0.6
1879	Buf-N	37	27	.578	66	66	65	6	0	593	585	299	3		31	136	9.3	2.28	115	.243	.253	66	.249	5	14	21	3	2.7
1880	Buf-N	20	35	.364	58	54	46	5	0	458^2	528	281	5		32	128	11.0	2.71	91	.273	.284	51	.212	-4	-17	-12	1	-1.4
1881	Buf-N	28	24	.538	56	53	48	5	0	474	546	250	4		46	136	11.2	2.37	117	.274	.291	50	.212	-1	21	21	7	2.6
1882	Buf-N	28	23	.549	52	51	48	3	0	445^1	476	255	8		40	162	10.4	3.17	93	.256	.272	44	.214	-5	-13	-12	1	-1.5
1883	Buf-N	46	29	.613	**76**	75	**72**	**5**	0	**656^1**	676	367	9		50	279	10.0	2.72	117	.251	.265	71	.220	-4	31	33	-0	2.6
1884	Buf-N	46	22	.676	72	72	71	**12**	0	636^1	566	254	23		63	369	8.9	1.99	158	.227	.246	49	.179	-14	70	77	7	6.4
1885	Buf-N	13	19	.406	33	32	31	3	1	284	356	204	8		37	93	12.5	4.09	73	.292	.313	23	.189	-2	-40	-33	4	-2.8
	Pit-a	3	7	.300	11	11	9	0	0	88^1	97	64	2	0	7	27	10.6	3.67	88	.266	.280	4	.105	-4	-4	-4	-1	-0.7
1886	Pit-a	29	21	.580	50	50	49	2	0	434^2	457	229	3	7	75	72	11.2	2.67	127	.263	.296	49	.253	2	38	35	3	3.7
1887	Pit-N	28	21	.571	49	48	47	3	0	440^2	557	259	12	11	67	76	11.6	3.29	118	.295	.299	43	.221	-2	38	31	8	3.1
1888	Pit-N	23	25	.479	50	50	49	6	0	437^1	446	190	9	8	53	107	10.4	2.63	101	.255	.280	25	.143	-6	10	2	4	-0.1
1889	Pit-N	23	16	.590	41	40	38	4	0	341	392	230	19	10	78	77	12.7	4.17	90	.280	.322	28	.187	-1	-6	-17	1	-1.4
1890	Pit-P	12	13	.480	26	25	23	1	0	217	275	192	3	9	49	35	13.8	4.35	90	.296	.337	20	.206	-1	-3	-12	4	-0.7
1891	Pit-N	15	14	.517	33	30	23	2	0	246^2	256	143	10	13	62	46	12.1	2.88	114	.258	.310	18	.165	-4	13	11	0	0.7
1892	Pit-N	5	6	.455	12	12	10	0	0	96	104	51	0	0	28	29	12.4	2.63	126	.265	.314	5	.122	-3	7	7	-0	0.4
	StL-N	5	6	.455	12	12	10	0	0	92	102	47	4	3	26	27	12.8	3.23	99	.270	.322	2	.051	-5	1	-0	-2	-0.6
	Yr	10	12	.455	24	24	20	0	0	188	206	98	4	3	54	56	12.6	2.92	111	.268	.318	7	.087	-7	8	7	-2	-0.2
Total	14	361	308	.540	697	681	639	57	1	5941^1	6419	3315	122	61	744	1799	10.8	2.87	109	.263	.284	548	.203	-48	160	162	39	13.0

● LOU GALVIN
Galvin, Louis J. b: 4/1862, St.Paul, Minn. d: 6/17/1895, Deb: 10/1/1884

YEAR	TM/L	W	L	PCT	G	GS	CG	SH	SV	IP	H	R	HR	HB	BB	SO	RAT	ERA	ERA+	OAV	OOB	BH	AVG	PB	PR	PR+	PD	TPI
1884	StP-U	0	2	.000	3	3	3	0	0	25	21	18	0		10	17	11.2	2.88	46	.212	.284	2	.222	-1	-1	-8	-1	-0.5

● BOB GAMBLE
Gamble, Robert J. b: 2/1867, Hazleton, Pa. TR, 5'10", 155 lbs. Deb: 5/2/1888

YEAR	TM/L	W	L	PCT	G	GS	CG	SH	SV	IP	H	R	HR	HB	BB	SO	RAT	ERA	ERA+	OAV	OOB	BH	AVG	PB	PR	PR+	PD	TPI
1888	Phi-a	0	1	.000	1	1	1	0	0	9	10	10	0	0	3	2	13.0	8.00	37	.270	.325	1	.333	0	-5	-5	-0	-0.4

YEAR	TM/L	W	L	PCT	G	GS	CG	SH	SV	IP	H	R	HR	HB	BB	SO	RAT	ERA	ERA+	OAV	OOB	BH	AVG	PB	PR	PR+	PD	TPI
● **GUSSIE GANNON**	Gannon, James Edward b: 11/26/1873, Erie, Pa. d: 4/12/66, Erie, Pa. BL/TL, 5'11", 154 lbs. Deb: 6/15/1895																											
1895	Pit-N	0	0	—	1	0	0	0	0	5	7	4	0	0	2	0	16.2	1.80	251	.333	.391	0	.000	-0	2	2	-0	0.0
● **JOE GANNON**	Gannon, Joseph b: St.Louis, Mo. Deb: 8/28/1898																											
1898	StL-N	0	1	.000	1	1	1	0	0	9	13	13	0	1	5	2	19.0	11.00	34	.333	.422	0	.000	-1	-7	-7	-0	-0.5
● **JIM GANTNER**	Gantner, James Elmer b: 1/5/53, Fond Du Lac, Wis. BL/TR, 6', 180 lbs. Deb: 9/3/76 C♦																											
1979	Mil-A	0	0	—	1	0	0	0	0	1	2	0	0	0	0	0	18.0	0.00	—	.400	.400	59	.284	0	0	0	0	0.0
● **KEITH GARAGOZZO**	Garagozzo, Keith John b: 10/25/69, Camden, N.J. BL/TL, 6', 170 lbs. Deb: 4/5/94																											
1994	Min-A	0	0	—	7	0	0	0	0	9^1	9	10	3	0	13	3	21.2	9.64	51	.273	.478	0	—	0	-5	-5	0	-0.2
● **GENE GARBER**	Garber, Henry Eugene b: 11/13/47, Lancaster, Pa. BR/TR, 5'10", 175 lbs. Deb: 6/17/69																											
1969	Pit-N	0	0	—	2	1	0	0	0	5	6	3	3	0	1	3	12.6	5.40	65	.333	.368	0	.000	-0	-1	-1	-0	-0.1
1970	Pit-N	0	3	.000	14	0	0	0	0	22^1	22	13	4	2	10	7	13.7	5.24	75	.275	.370	2	.667	1	-3	-3	1	-0.2
1972	Pit-N	0	0	—	4	0	0	0	0	6^1	7	5	3	0	3	3	14.2	7.11	47	.269	.345	0	.000	-0	-3	-3	0	-0.1
1973	KC-A	9	9	.500	48	8	4	0	11	152^2	164	78	14	2	49	60	12.7	4.24	97	.283	.341	0	—	0	-7	-2	1	-0.2
1974	KC-A	1	2	.333	17	0	0	0	1	28	35	21	3	1	13	14	15.8	4.82	79	.313	.389	0	—	0	-4	-3	-0	-0.3
	Phi-N	4	0	1.000	34	0	0	0	4	48	39	15	1	1	31	27	13.3	2.06	184	.236	.360	0	.000	-0	8	9	0	0.9
1975	Phi-N	10	12	.455	**71**	0	0	0	14	110	104	48	13	2	27	69	10.9	3.60	104	.254	.304	2	.167	-0	0	2	-0	0.3
1976	*Phi-N	9	3	.750	59	0	0	0	11	92^2	78	33	4	4	30	92	10.9	2.82	126	.228	.298	2	.286	1	7	7	1	1.4
1977	*Phi-N	8	6	.571	64	0	0	0	19	103^1	82	30	6	2	23	78	9.3	2.35	170	.220	.270	0	.000	-1	18	19	2	3.2
1978	Phi-N	2	1	.667	22	0	0	0	3	38^2	26	6	1	3	11	24	9.3	1.40	256	.191	.267	0	.000	-0	9	9	-0	0.8
	Atl-N	4	4	.500	43	0	0	0	22	78^1	58	26	11	2	13	61	8.4	2.53	160	.204	.244	1	.091	-0	9	12	1	2.0
	Yr	6	5	.545	65	0	0	0	25	117	84	32	12	5	24	85	8.7	2.15	181	.200	.252	1	.071	-1	19	**21**	1	2.8
1979	Atl-N	6	16	.273	68	0	0	0	25	106	121	66	10	5	24	56	12.7	4.33	94	.283	.328	3	.300	1	-7	-3	1	-0.4
1980	Atl-N	5	5	.500	68	0	0	0	7	82^1	95	42	6	0	24	51	13.0	3.83	98	.288	.336	1	.500	0	-2	-1	2	0.1
1981	Atl-N	4	6	.400	35	0	0	0	2	58^2	49	23	2	0	20	34	10.6	2.61	137	.214	.277	0	.000	-1	6	6	2	1.2
1982	*Atl-N	8	10	.444	69	0	0	0	30	119^1	100	40	4	2	32	68	10.1	2.34	160	.231	.288	2	.133	0	17	18	2	3.8
1983	Atl-N	4	5	.444	43	0	0	0	9	60^2	72	37	8	2	23	45	14.4	4.60	85	.300	.366	0	.000	0	-6	-4	2	-0.5
1984	Atl-N	3	6	.333	62	0	0	0	11	106	103	45	7	2	24	55	11.0	3.06	126	.254	.299	2	.143	-0	6	9	1	0.9
1985	Atl-N	6	6	.500	59	0	0	0	1	97^1	98	41	8	2	25	66	11.6	3.61	107	.263	.313	1	.200	0	-0	3	1	0.4
1986	Atl-N	5	5	.500	61	0	0	0	24	78	76	23	3	1	20	56	11.2	2.54	157	.260	.310	1	.167	0	10	12	1	2.2
1987	Atl-N	8	10	.444	49	0	0	0	10	69^1	87	39	7	1	28	48	15.1	4.41	99	.311	.375	0	.000	-0	-3	-0	2	0.1
	KC-A	0	0	—	13	0	0	0	8	14^1	13	5	1	1	1	3	9.4	2.51	182	.245	.273	0	—	0	3	3	0	0.4
1988	KC-A	0	4	.000	26	0	0	0	6	32^2	29	15	4	2	13	20	12.1	3.58	112	.238	.321	0	—	0	1	1	0	0.3
Total	19	96	113	.459	931	9	4	0	218	1510	1464	654	123	37	445	940	11.6	3.34	117	.257	.314	17	.148	-0	61	89	20	16.2
● **BOB GARBER**	Garber, Robert Mitchell b: 9/10/28, Hunker, Pa. d: 6/7/99, Redwood City, Cal. BR/TR, 6'1", 190 lbs. Deb: 5/13/56																											
1956	Pit-N	0	0	—	2	0	0	0	0	4	3	1	1	0	3	3	13.5	2.25	168	.200	.333	0	—	0	1	1	-0	0.0
● **RICH GARCES**	Garces, Richard Aron (Mendoza) b: 5/18/71, Maracay, Venez. BR/TR, 6', 215 lbs. Deb: 9/18/90																											
1990	Min-A	0	0	—	5	0	0	0	2	5^2	4	2	0	0	4	1	12.7	1.59	262	.200	.333	0	—	0	1	2	0	0.1
1993	Min-A	0	0	—	3	0	0	0	0	4	4	2	0	0	2	3	13.5	0.00	—	.250	.333	0	—	0	2	2	-0	0.1
1995	Chi-N	0	0	—	7	0	0	0	0	11	11	6	0	0	3	6	11.5	3.27	126	.256	.304	0	.000	-0	1	1	-0	0.0
	Fla-N	0	2	.000	11	0	0	0	0	13^1	14	9	1	0	8	16	14.9	5.40	78	.264	.361	0	—	0	-2	-2	-0	-0.3
	Yr	0	2	.000	18	0	0	0	0	24^1	25	15	1	0	11	22	13.3	4.44	94	.260	.336	0	.000	-0	-1	-1	-0	-0.3
1996	Bos-A	3	2	.600	37	0	0	0	0	44	42	26	5	0	33	55	15.3	4.91	103	.251	.375	0	—	0	0	1	1	0.1
1997	Bos-A	0	1	.000	12	0	0	0	0	13^2	14	9	2	1	9	12	15.8	4.61	101	.255	.369	0	—	0	-0	0	0	0.0
1998	Bos-A	1	1	.500	30	0	0	0	1	46	36	19	6	2	27	34	12.7	3.33	142	.213	.328	0	—	0	7	7	-0	0.3
1999	*Bos-A	5	1	.833	30	0	0	0	2	40^2	25	9	1	0	18	33	9.5	1.55	321	.171	.262	0	—	0	15	15	1	2.1
2000	Bos-A	8	1	.889	64	0	0	0	1	74^2	64	28	7	1	23	69	10.6	3.25	156	.229	.289	0	—	0	14	15	-0	1.5
Total	8	17	8	.680	199	0	0	0	6	253	214	110	22	4	127	229	12.3	3.38	144	.226	.319	0	.000	-0	39	41	0	3.9
● **MIKE GARCIA**	Garcia, Edward Miguel "The Big Bear" b: 11/17/23, San Gabriel, Cal. d: 1/13/86, Fairview Park, O. BR/TR, 6'1", 200 lbs. Deb: 10/3/48																											
1948	Cle-A	0	0	—	1	0	0	0	0	2	3	0	0	0	0	1	13.5	0.00	—	.333	.333	0	—	0	1	1	0	0.1
1949	Cle-A	14	5	.737	41	20	8	5	2	175^2	154	51	6	2	60	94	11.1	**2.36**	**169**	.241	.308	12	.235	3	36	34	1	3.8
1950	Cle-A	11	11	.500	33	29	11	0	0	184	191	88	15	0	74	76	13.0	3.86	112	.266	.334	13	.200	-1	15	10	2	1.2
1951	Cle-A	20	13	.606	47	30	15	1	6	254	239	101	10	3	82	118	11.5	3.15	120	.246	.307	18	.212	2	27	19	1	2.6
1952	Cle-A☆	22	11	.667	46	36	19	**6**	4	292^1	284	93	9	7	87	143	11.6	2.37	141	.253	.310	13	.137	-2	42	35	2	4.0
1953	Cle-A★	18	9	.667	38	35	21	3	0	271^2	260	106	18	3	81	134	11.4	3.25	116	.250	.307	24	.250	4	23	16	-0	1.8
1954	*Cle-A†	19	8	.704	45	34	13	**5**	5	258^2	220	85	6	2	71	129	**10.2**	**2.64**	**139**	.229	**.284**	11	.136	-2	**31**	**30**	0	2.9
1955	Cle-A	11	13	.458	38	31	6	2	3	210^2	230	101	17	3	56	120	12.3	4.02	99	.278	.327	15	.217	2	-1	-1	-1	0.0
1956	Cle-A	11	12	.478	35	30	8	4	0	197^2	213	93	18	5	74	119	13.3	3.78	111	.272	.339	7	.115	-3	8	9	-0	0.6
1957	Cle-A	12	8	.600	38	27	9	1	0	211^1	221	98	14	6	73	110	12.8	3.75	99	.269	.333	12	.160	-1	1	-1	-2	-0.4
1958	Cle-A	1	0	1.000	6	1	0	0	0	8	15	10	2	1	7	2	25.9	9.00	41	.395	.500	0	.000	-0	-5	-5	0	-0.6
1959	Cle-A	3	6	.333	29	8	1	0	1	72	72	39	4	0	31	49	12.9	4.00	92	.265	.340	1	.071	-1	-1	-3	0	-0.4
1960	Chi-A	0	0	—	15	0	0	0	2	17^2	23	9	2	0	10	8	16.8	4.58	82	.338	.423	1	.333	0	-1	-2	0	0.0
1961	Was-A	0	1	.000	16	0	0	0	0	19	23	14	1	1	13	14	17.5	4.74	85	.287	.394	0	—	0	-2	-2	-1	-0.2
Total	14	142	97	.594	428	281	111	27	23	2174^2	2148	888	122	33	719	1117	12.0	3.27	117	.257	.319	127	.182	1	174	140	2	15.4
● **FREDDY GARCIA**	Garcia, Freddy Antonio b: 10/6/76, Caracas, Venez. BR/TR, 6'4", 235 lbs. Deb: 4/7/99																											
1999	Sea-A	17	8	.680	33	33	2	1	0	201^1	205	96	18	10	90	170	13.6	4.07	117	.263	.347	1	.250	0	18	15	1	1.7
2000	*Sea-A	9	5	.643	21	20	0	0	0	124^1	112	62	16	2	64	79	12.9	3.91	123	.241	.335	2	.667	1	14	13	0	1.3
Total	2	26	13	.667	54	53	2	1	0	325^2	317	158	34	12	154	249	13.3	4.01	119	.255	.343	3	.429	1	32	28	1	3.0
● **MIKE GARCIA**	Garcia, Michael R. b: 5/11/68, Riverside, Cal. BR/TR, 6'2", 220 lbs. Deb: 9/10/99																											
1999	Pit-N	1	0	1.000	7	0	0	0	0	7	2	1	1	0	3	9	6.4	1.29	355	.091	.200	0	—	0	3	3	-0	0.3
2000	Pit-N	0	2	.000	13	0	0	0	0	11^1	21	15	1	0	7	9	22.2	11.12	41	.429	.500	1	.333	0	-8	-8	-0	-1.2
Total	2	1	2	.333	20	0	0	0	0	18^1	23	16	2	0	10	18	16.2	7.36	62	.324	.407	1	.333	0	-6	-6	-0	-0.9
● **MIGUEL GARCIA**	Garcia, Miguel Angel (Silfontes) b: 4/3/67, Caracas, Venez. BL/TL, 5'11", 173 lbs. Deb: 4/30/87																											
1987	Cal-A	0	0	—	1	0	0	0	0	1^2	3	4	0	0	3	0	32.4	16.20	27	.375	.545	0	—	0	-2	-2	0	-0.1
	Pit-N	0	0	—	1	0	0	0	0	0^2	0	0	0	0	0	0	0.0	0.00	—	.000	.000	0	—	0	0	0	-0	0.0
1988	Pit-N	0	0	—	1	0	0	0	0	2	3	2	1	1	2	2	27.0	4.50	76	.375	.545	0	—	0	-0	-0	-0	0.0
1989	Pit-N	0	2	.000	11	0	0	0	0	16	25	15	2	0	7	9	18.0	8.44	40	.357	.416	1	1.000	0	-9	-9	0	-1.0
Total	3	0	2	.000	14	0	0	0	0	20^1	31	21	3	1	12	11	19.5	8.41	41	.352	.436	1	1.000	0	-11	-12	0	-1.1
● **RALPH GARCIA**	Garcia, Ralph b: 12/14/48, Los Angeles, Cal. BR/TR, 6', 195 lbs. Deb: 9/26/72																											
1972	SD-N	0	0	—	3	0	0	0	0	5	4	1	0	0	3	3	12.6	1.80	183	.211	.318	0	—	0	1	1	0	0.1
1974	SD-N	0	0	—	8	0	0	0	0	10^1	15	8	1	0	7	9	19.2	6.10	59	.357	.449	0	—	0	-3	-3	0	-0.1
Total	2	0	0	—	11	0	0	0	0	15^1	19	9	1	0	10	12	17.0	4.70	74	.311	.408	0	—	0	-2	-2	0	0.0
● **RAMON GARCIA**	Garcia, Ramon (Garcia) b: 3/5/24, LaEsperanza, Cuba BR/TR, 5'10", 170 lbs. Deb: 4/19/48																											
1948	Was-A	0	0	—	4	0	0	0	0	3^2	11	7	0	1	4	2	39.3	17.18	25	.524	.615	1	1.000	0	-5	-5	0	-0.2
● **RAMON GARCIA**	Garcia, Ramon Antonio (Fortunato) b: 12/9/69, Guanare, Venez. BR/TR, 6'2", 200 lbs. Deb: 5/31/91																											
1991	Chi-A	4	4	.500	16	15	0	0	0	78^1	79	50	13	2	31	40	12.9	5.40	74	.269	.343	0	—	0	-11	-13	1	-1.1
1996	Mil-A	4	4	.500	37	2	0	0	4	75^2	84	58	17	6	21	40	13.2	6.66	78	.287	.347	0	—	0	-14	-12	0	-1.1
1997	*Hou-N	9	8	.529	42	20	1	1	1	158^2	155	71	20	9	52	120	12.3	3.69	108	.262	.331	4	.111	-0	9	6	1	0.6
Total	3	17	16	.515	95	37	1	1	5	312^2	318	179	50	17	104	200	12.6	4.84	88	.270	.338	4	.111	-0	-16	-20	2	-1.6

YEAR	TM/L	W	L	PCT	G	GS	CG	SH	SV	IP	H	R	HR	HB	BB	SO	RAT	ERA	ERA+	OAV	OOB	BH	AVG	PB	PR	PR+	PD	TPI
● **ART GARDINER** Gardiner, Arthur Cecil b: 12/26/1899, Brooklyn, N.Y. d: 10/21/54, Copiague, N.Y. BR/TR, Deb: 9/25/23																												
1923	Phi-N	0	0	—	1	0	0	0	0	0	1	0	0	1	—	—	—	—	1.000	1.000	115	—	0	0	0	0	0.0	
● **MIKE GARDINER** Gardiner, Michael James b: 10/19/65, Sarnia, Ont., Can. BB/TR, 6', 200 lbs. Deb: 9/8/90																												
1990	Sea-A	0	2	.000	5	3	0	0	0	12^2	22	17	1	2	5	6	20.6	10.66	37	.379	.446	0	—	0	-9	-9	0	-1.2
1991	Bos-A	9	10	.474	22	22	0	0	0	130	140	79	18	0	47	91	12.9	4.85	89	.274	.335	0	—	0	-11	-7	-0	-1.0
1992	Bos-A	4	10	.286	28	18	0	0	0	130^2	126	78	12	2	58	79	12.8	4.75	89	.253	.333	0	—	0	-12	-7	0	-0.7
1993	Mon-N	2	3	.400	24	2	0	0	0	38	40	28	3	1	19	21	14.2	5.21	80	.268	.355	0	.000	-0	-5	-4	-0	-0.5
	Det-A	0	0	—	10	0	0	0	0	11^1	12	5	0	0	7	4	15.1	3.97	108	.279	.380	0	—	0	0	0	0	0.0
1994	Det-A	2	2	.500	38	1	0	0	5	58^2	53	35	10	0	23	31	11.7	4.14	117	.233	.304	0	—	0	4	5	-1	0.2
1995	Det-A	0	0	—	9	0	0	0	0	12^1	27	20	5	0	2	7	21.2	14.59	33	.458	.475	0	—	0	-14	-13	0	-0.6
Total	6	17	27	.386	136	46	0	0	5	393^2	420	262	49	5	161	239	13.4	5.21	84	.272	.342	0	.000	-0	-46	-36	-1	-3.8
● **CHRIS GARDNER** Gardner, Christopher John b: 3/30/69, Long Beach, Cal. BR/TR, 6', 175 lbs. Deb: 9/10/91																												
1991	Hou-N	1	2	.333	5	4	0	0	0	24^2	19	12	5	0	14	12	12.0	4.01	87	.218	.327	0	.000	-0	-1	-1	1	-0.1
● **GID GARDNER** Gardner, Frank Washington b: 6/9/1859, Attleboro, Mass. d: 8/1/14, Cambridge, Mass. 165 lbs. Deb: 8/23/1879 ◆																												
1879	Tro-N	0	2	.000	2	2	2	0	0	14	27	21	0		0	3	17.4	5.79	43	.365	.365	1	.167	-0	-5	-5	-1	-0.6
1880	Cle-N	1	8	.111	9	9	9	0	0	77	80	53	2		20	21	11.7	2.57	91	.254	.299	6	.188	-0	-2	-2	-0	-0.2
1883	Bal-a	1	0	1.000	2	0	0	0	0	7	9	7	1		1	2	12.9	5.14	68	.290	.313	44	.273	1	-1	-1	-0	-0.1
1884	CP-U	0	1	.000	1	1	0	0	0	6	10	8	0		1	4	16.5	6.00	41	.345	.367	38	.255	-0	-2	-2	0	-0.2
1885	Bal-a	0	1	.000	1	1	1	0	0	9	16	13	2	1	6	3	23.0	10.00	33	.372	.460	37	.218	0	-7	-7	0	-0.5
Total	5	2	12	.143	15	13	12	0	0	113	142	102	5	1	28	33	13.6	3.90	64	.289	.328	190	.245	0	-17	-18	-1	-1.6
● **HARRY GARDNER** Gardner, Harry Ray b: 6/1/1887, Quincy, Mich. d: 8/2/61, Canby, Ore. BR/TR, 6'2", 180 lbs. Deb: 4/17/11																												
1911	Pit-N	1	1	.500	13	3	2	0	2	42	39	25	2	2	20	24	13.1	4.50	76	.244	.335	3	.214	0	-5	-5	-1	-0.3
1912	Pit-N	0	0	—	1	0	0	0	0	0^1	3	6	0	0	1	0	108.0	0.00	—	.500	.571	0	—	0	0	0	0	0.0
Total	2	1	1	.500	14	3	2	0	2	42^1	42	31	2	2	21	24	13.8	4.46	77	.253	.344	3	.214	0	-5	-5	-1	-0.3
● **JIM GARDNER** Gardner, James Anderson b: 10/4/1874, Pittsburgh, Pa. d: 4/24/05, Pittsburgh, Pa. TR, Deb: 6/20/1895																												
1895	Pit-N	8	2	.800	11	10	8	0	0	85^1	99	53	1	6	27	31	13.9	2.64	171	.286	.348	9	.265	1	20	19	-1	1.7
1897	Pit-N	5	5	.500	14	11	8	0	0	95^1	115	72	4	9	32	35	14.7	5.19	80	.296	.363	12	.158	-1	-9	-11	-0	-0.9
1898	Pit-N	10	13	.435	25	22	19	1	0	185^1	179	96	3	8	48	41	11.4	3.21	111	.252	.306	14	.154	-2	8	7	-2	0.4
1899	Pit-N	1	0	1.000	6	3	0	0	0	32^1	52	37	1	0	13	2	18.1	7.52	51	.361	.414	3	.231	1	-13	-13	-2	-0.7
1902	Chi-N	1	2	.333	3	3	2	0	0	25	23	12	0	0	10	6	11.9	2.88	94	.245	.317	2	.200	0	-0	-1	0	0.0
Total	5	25	22	.532	59	49	37	1	0	423^1	468	270	9	23	130	115	13.2	3.85	100	.278	.338	40	.179	-1	6	1	-4	0.5
● **MARK GARDNER** Gardner, Mark Allan b: 3/1/62, Los Angeles, Cal. BR/TR, 6'1", 205 lbs. Deb: 5/16/89																												
1989	Mon-N	0	3	.000	7	4	0	0	0	26^1	26	16	2	2	11	21	13.3	5.13	69	.250	.333	1	.167	-0	-5	-5	-0	-0.5
1990	Mon-N	7	9	.438	27	26	3	3	0	152^2	129	62	13	9	61	135	11.7	3.42	107	.230	.315	5	.114	-1	6	4	2	0.5
1991	Mon-N	9	11	.450	27	27	0	0	0	168^1	139	78	17	4	75	107	11.7	3.85	94	.230	.319	5	.091	-2	-3	-4	-2	-0.9
1992	Mon-N	12	10	.545	33	30	0	0	0	179^2	179	91	15	9	60	132	12.4	4.36	80	.259	.327	7	.140	1	-17	-18	-1	-2.1
1993	KC-A	4	6	.400	17	16	0	0	0	91^2	92	65	17	4	36	54	13.0	6.19	74	.271	.348	0	—	0	-19	-15	-2	-1.5
1994	Fla-N	4	4	.500	20	14	0	0	0	92^1	97	53	14	1	30	57	12.5	4.87	90	.276	.335	1	.040	-2	-7	-5	-1	-0.6
1995	Fla-N	5	5	.500	39	11	1	1	1	102^1	109	60	14	5	43	87	13.8	4.49	94	.272	.350	4	.190	-0	-3	-3	-1	-0.4
1996	SF-N	12	7	.632	30	28	4	1	0	179^1	200	105	28	8	57	145	13.3	4.42	93	.283	.344	11	.162	0	-4	-7	-2	-0.8
1997	SF-N	12	9	.571	30	30	2	1	0	180^1	188	92	28	1	57	136	12.3	4.29	95	.272	.329	7	.115	-2	-2	-4	1	-0.5
1998	SF-N	13	6	.684	33	33	4	2	0	212	203	106	29	6	65	151	11.6	4.33	92	.253	.314	12	.164	2	-2	-9	1	-0.5
1999	SF-N	5	11	.313	29	21	1	0	0	139	142	103	27	8	57	86	13.4	6.47	65	.267	.347	4	.103	0	-29	-38	-0	-3.5
2000	*SF-N	11	7	.611	30	20	0	0	0	149	155	72	16	5	42	92	12.2	4.05	105	.270	.325	5	.116	-2	10	3	-3	-0.1
Total	12	94	88	.516	322	260	15	8	1	1673	1659	903	220	62	594	1203	12.5	4.51	88	.261	.330	62	.128	-6	-75	-100	-8	-10.9
● **GLENN GARDNER** Gardner, Miles Glenn b: 1/25/16, Burnsville, N.C. d: 7/7/64, Rochester, N.Y. BR/TR, 5'11", 180 lbs. Deb: 7/21/45																												
1945	StL-N	3	1	.750	17	4	2	1	1	54^2	50	21	2	0	27	20	12.7	3.29	114	.242	.329	7	.333	2	3	3	-1	0.3
● **ROB GARDNER** Gardner, Richard Frank b: 12/19/44, Binghamton, N.Y. BR/TL, 6'1", 176 lbs. Deb: 9/1/65																												
1965	NY-N	0	2	.000	5	4	0	0	0	28	23	13	4	0	7	19	9.6	3.21	110	.217	.265	0	.000	-1	1	1	0	0.0
1966	NY-N	4	8	.333	41	17	3	0	1	133^2	147	82	15	3	64	74	14.4	5.12	71	.285	.367	7	.171	-0	-22	-22	0	-1.9
1967	Chi-N	0	2	.000	18	5	0	0	0	31^2	33	14	2	0	6	16	11.1	3.98	89	.260	.293	0	.000	-0	-2	-1	0	-0.1
1968	Cle-A	0	0	—	5	0	0	0	0	2^2	5	3	0	0	2	6	23.6	6.75	44	.417	.500	0	—	0	-1	-1	-0	-0.1
1970	NY-A	1	0	1.000	1	1	0	0	0	7^1	8	4	2	0	4	6	14.7	4.91	72	.276	.364	1	.333	1	-1	-1	0	-0.1
1971	Oak-A	0	0	—	4	1	0	0	0	7^2	8	2	1	0	3	5	12.9	2.35	142	.267	.333	1	.500	0	1	1	0	0.1
	NY-A	0	0	—	2	0	0	0	0	3	3	1	0	0	2	2	15.0	3.00	108	.273	.385	0	—	0	0	0	-0	0.0
	Yr	0	0	—	6	1	0	0	0	10^2	11	3	1	0	5	7	13.5	2.53	131	.268	.348	1	.500	0	1	1	0	0.1
1972	NY-A	8	5	.615	20	14	1	0	0	97	91	43	9	0	28	58	11.0	3.06	97	.243	.296	3	.107	-1	0	-1	-1	-0.4
1973	Oak-A	0	0	—	3	0	0	0	0	7^1	10	4	2	0	4	2	17.2	4.91	72	.370	.452	0	—	0	-1	-1	-0	-0.1
	Mil-A	1	1	.500	10	0	0	0	1	12^2	17	14	0	1	13	5	22.0	9.95	38	.327	.470	0	—	0	-9	-9	0	-1.3
	Yr	1	1	.500	13	0	0	0	1	20	27	18	2	1	17	7	20.2	8.10	46	.342	.464	0	—	0	-10	-10	0	-1.4
Total	8	14	18	.438	109	42	4	0	2	331	345	180	35	4	133	193	13.1	4.35	78	.269	.339	12	.138	-2	-34	-35	-0	-3.9
● **WES GARDNER** Gardner, Wesley Brian b: 4/29/61, Benton, Ark. BR/TR, 6'4", 197 lbs. Deb: 7/29/84																												
1984	NY-N	1	1	.500	21	0	0	0	1	25^1	34	19	0	0	8	19	14.9	6.39	55	.321	.368	0	.000	-0	-8	-8	0	-0.7
1985	NY-N	0	2	.000	9	0	0	0	0	12	18	14	1	0	8	11	19.5	5.25	66	.375	.464	0	—	0	-2	-2	0	-0.3
1986	Bos-A	0	0	—	1	0	0	0	0	1	1	1	0	0	0	1	9.0	9.00	46	.333	.333	0	—	0	-1	-1	0	0.0
1987	Bos-A	3	6	.333	49	1	0	0	10	89^2	98	55	17	2	42	70	14.3	5.42	84	.279	.359	0	—	0	-9	-8	-1	-1.0
1988	*Bos-A	8	6	.571	36	18	1	0	2	149	119	61	17	3	64	106	11.2	3.50	118	.220	.305	0	—	0	8	10	-0	0.9
1989	Bos-A	3	7	.300	22	16	0	0	0	86	97	64	10	1	47	81	15.2	5.97	69	.287	.376	0	—	0	-20	-17	-1	-1.8
1990	Bos-A	3	7	.300	34	9	0	0	0	77^1	77	43	6	2	35	58	13.3	4.89	84	.259	.341	0	—	0	-8	-7	-0	-0.8
1991	SD-N	0	1	.000	14	0	0	0	1	20^1	27	16	1	0	12	9	17.3	7.08	54	.310	.394	0	.000	-0	-8	-7	0	-0.4
	KC-A	0	0	—	3	0	0	0	0	5^2	5	4	0	0	2	3	11.1	1.59	260	.208	.269	0	—	0	2	2	0	0.1
Total	8	18	30	.375	189	44	1	0	14	466^1	476	277	52	8	218	358	13.5	4.90	84	.265	.347	0	.000	-0	-46	-39	-2	-4.0
● **BILL GARDNER** Gardner, William A. b: 9/1868, Baltimore, Md. Deb: 8/9/1887																												
1887	Bal-a	0	1	.000	3	2	1	0	0	13	33	20	0	1	10	3	23.5	11.08	37	.516	.523	4	.333	0	-10	-11	-0	-0.6
● **BILL GARFIELD** Garfield, William Milton b: 10/26/1867, Sheffield, Ohio d: 12/16/41, Danville, Ill. BR/TR, 5'11.5", 160 lbs. Deb: 7/10/1889																												
1889	Pit-N	0	2	.000	4	2	2	0	0	29	45	35	2	1	17	4	19.6	7.76	48	.344	.423	0	.000	-2	-12	-14	0	-0.8
1890	Cle-N	1	7	.125	9	8	7	0	0	70	91	64	3	8	35	16	17.2	4.89	73	.305	.393	4	.154	-1	-10	-10	-0	-1.0
Total	2	1	9	.100	13	10	9	0	0	99	136	99	5	9	52	20	17.9	5.73	63	.317	.402	4	.103	-3	-22	-23	-0	-1.8
● **BOB GARIBALDI** Garibaldi, Robert Roy b: 3/3/42, Stockton, Cal. BL/TR, 6'4", 210 lbs. Deb: 7/15/62																												
1962	SF-N	0	0	—	9	0	0	0	1	12^1	13	7	1	0	5	9	13.1	5.11	74	.265	.333	0	.000	-0	-2	-2	0	-0.1
1963	SF-N	0	1	.000	4	0	0	0	1	8	8	2	0	1	4	4	14.6	1.13	284	.276	.382	0	.000	-0	2	2	0	0.3
1966	SF-N	0	0	—	1	0	0	0	0	1	1	0	0	0	0	0	9.0	0.00	—	.250	.250	0	—	0	0	0	-0	0.0
1969	SF-N	0	1	.000	1	1	0	0	0	5	6	4	0	0	2	1	14.4	1.80	195	.316	.381	0	.000	-0	1	1	0	0.2
Total	4	0	2	.000	15	1	0	0	2	26^1	28	13	1	1	11	14	13.7	3.08	116	.277	.354	0	.000	-0	2	1	0	0.4
● **DANIEL GARIBAY** Garibay, Daniel (Bravo) b: 2/14/73, Maneadero, Mex. BL/TL, 5'8", 154 lbs. Deb: 4/9/2000																												
2000	Chi-N	2	8	.200	30	8	0	0	0	74^2	88	54	9	1	39	46	15.4	6.03	76	.299	.383	2	.133	-1	-12	-12	2	-1.2
● **JON GARLAND** Garland, Jon Steven b: 9/27/79, Valencia, Cal. BR/TR, 6'6", 205 lbs. Deb: 7/4/2000																												
2000	Chi-A	4	8	.333	15	13	0	0	0	69^2	82	55	10	1	40	42	15.9	6.46	77	.292	.382	0	—	0	-12	-11	-0	-1.6

● LOU GARLAND
Garland, Louis Lyman b: 7/16/05, Archie, Mo. d: 8/30/90, Idaho Falls, Idaho BR/TR, 6'2.5", 200 lbs. Deb: 8/31/31

YEAR TM/L	W	L	PCT	G	GS	CG	SH	SV	IP	H	R	HR	HB	BB	SO	RAT	ERA	ERA+	OAV	OOB	BH	AVG	PB	PR	PR+	PD	TPI
1931 Chi-A	0	2	.000	7	2	0	0	0	16^{2}	30	24	2	1	14	4	24.3	10.26	41	.400	.500	0	.000	-0	-11	-11	1	-1.1

● WAYNE GARLAND
Garland, Marcus Wayne b: 10/26/50, Nashville, Tenn. BR/TR, 6', 195 lbs. Deb: 9/13/73

YEAR TM/L	W	L	PCT	G	GS	CG	SH	SV	IP	H	R	HR	HB	BB	SO	RAT	ERA	ERA+	OAV	OOB	BH	AVG	PB	PR	PR+	PD	TPI
1973 Bal-A	0	1	.000	4	1	0	0	0	16	14	8	1	0	7	10	11.8	3.94	95	.233	.313	0	—	0	-0	-0	-0	0.0
1974 *Bal-A	5	5	.500	20	6	0	0	1	91	68	37	5	3	26	40	9.6	2.97	117	.211	.276	0	—	0	7	5	-1	0.5
1975 Bal-A	2	5	.286	29	1	0	0	4	87^{1}	80	37	7	1	31	46	11.5	3.71	95	.252	.321	0	—	0	1	-2	-0	-0.2
1976 Bal-A	20	7	.741	38	25	14	4	1	232^{1}	224	81	10	6	64	113	11.4	2.67	123	.255	.309	0	—	0	22	17	2	2.1
1977 Cle-A	13	19	.406	38	38	21	1	0	282^{2}	281	130	23	2	88	118	11.8	3.60	110	.261	.318	0	—	0	15	12	-0	1.2
1978 Cle-A	2	3	.400	6	6	0	0	0	29^{2}	43	27	6	1	16	13	18.2	7.89	48	.347	.426	0	—	0	-14	-14	0	-1.8
1979 Cle-A	4	10	.286	18	14	2	0	0	94^{2}	120	70	11	3	34	40	14.9	5.23	82	.318	.379	0	—	0	-11	-10	-1	-1.4
1980 Cle-A	6	9	.400	25	20	4	1	0	150^{1}	163	85	18	6	48	55	13.0	4.61	89	.276	.337	0	—	0	-9	-9	-1	-0.9
1981 Cle-A	3	7	.300	12	10	2	1	0	56	89	40	8	0	14	15	16.6	5.79	63	.374	.409	0	—	0	-13	-14	0	-2.0
Total 9	55	66	.455	190	121	43	7	6	1040	1082	515	89	22	328	450	12.4	3.89	96	.272	.330	0	—	0	-3	-18	-2	-2.5

● MIKE GARMAN
Garman, Michael Douglas b: 9/16/49, Caldwell, Idaho BR/TR, 6'3", 215 lbs. Deb: 9/22/69

YEAR TM/L	W	L	PCT	G	GS	CG	SH	SV	IP	H	R	HR	HB	BB	SO	RAT	ERA	ERA+	OAV	OOB	BH	AVG	PB	PR	PR+	PD	TPI
1969 Bos-A	1	0	1.000	2	2	0	0	0	12^{1}	13	6	0	0	10	10	16.8	4.38	87	.277	.404	2	.400	1	-1	-1	0	0.0
1971 Bos-A	1	1	.500	3	3	0	0	0	18^{2}	15	8	3	1	9	6	12.1	3.86	96	.217	.316	2	.333	0	-1	-0	-1	-0.1
1972 Bos-A	0	1	.000	3	1	0	0	0	3	4	4	1	0	2	1	16.2	10.80	30	.286	.375	0	—	0	-3	-3	-0	-0.6
1973 Bos-A	0	0	—	12	0	0	0	0	22	32	15	1	0	15	9	19.2	5.32	76	.352	.443	0	—	0	-4	-3	-0	-0.2
1974 StL-N	7	2	.778	64	0	0	0	6	81^{2}	66	26	4	2	27	45	10.5	2.64	136	.227	.297	1	.100	-1	9	9	0	1.0
1975 StL-N	3	8	.273	66	0	0	0	10	79	73	31	3	1	48	48	13.9	2.39	157	.245	.352	0	.000	-0	11	12	-1	1.8
1976 Chi-N	2	4	.333	47	2	0	0	1	76^{1}	79	48	7	3	35	37	13.8	4.95	78	.273	.358	0	.000	-1	-12	-8	0	-0.7
1977 *LA-N	4	4	.500	49	0	0	0	12	62^{2}	60	20	7	2	22	29	12.1	2.73	140	.254	.323	0	.000	-1	8	8	-1	1.1
1978 LA-N	0	1	.000	10	0	0	0	0	16^{1}	15	8	3	0	3	5	9.9	4.41	80	.259	.295	0	—	0	-1	-2	-0	-0.1
Mon-N	4	6	.400	47	0	0	0	13	61^{1}	54	32	5	0	31	23	12.5	4.40	80	.238	.329	0	.000	-1	-6	-6	-0	-1.3
Yr	4	7	.364	57	0	0	0	13	77^{2}	69	40	8	0	34	28	11.9	4.40	80	.242	.323	0	.000	-1	-7	-8	-1	-1.4
Total 9	22	27	.449	303	8	0	0	42	433^{2}	411	198	34	9	202	213	12.9	3.63	103	.254	.340	5	.119	-2	0	4	-3	0.9

● WILLIE GARONI
Garoni, William b: 7/28/1877, Ft.Lee, N.J. d: 9/9/14, Ft.Lee, N.J. BR/TR, 6'1", 165 lbs. Deb: 9/7/1899

YEAR TM/L	W	L	PCT	G	GS	CG	SH	SV	IP	H	R	HR	HB	BB	SO	RAT	ERA	ERA+	OAV	OOB	BH	AVG	PB	PR	PR+	PD	TPI
1899 NY-N	0	1	.000	3	1	1	0	0	10	12	7	0	0	2	2	12.6	4.50	83	.300	.333	0	.000	-1	-1	-1	0	-0.1

● SCOTT GARRELTS
Garrelts, Scott William b: 10/30/61, Urbana, Ill. BR/TR, 6'4", 195 lbs. Deb: 10/2/82

YEAR TM/L	W	L	PCT	G	GS	CG	SH	SV	IP	H	R	HR	HB	BB	SO	RAT	ERA	ERA+	OAV	OOB	BH	AVG	PB	PR	PR+	PD	TPI
1982 SF-N	0	0	—	1	0	0	0	0	2	3	3	0	0	2	4	22.5	13.50	27	.333	.455	0	—	0	-2	-2	0	-0.1
1983 SF-N	2	2	.500	5	5	1	0	0	35^{2}	33	11	4	2	19	16	13.6	2.52	140	.254	.358	2	.222	0	4	4	0	0.5
1984 SF-N	2	3	.400	21	3	0	0	0	43	45	33	6	1	34	32	16.7	5.65	62	.274	.402	1	.100	-0	-10	-10	-1	-1.2
1985 SF-N☆	9	6	.600	74	0	0	0	13	105^{2}	76	37	2	3	58	106	11.7	2.30	150	.198	.308	2	.222	1	15	14	2	2.6
1986 SF-N	13	9	.591	53	18	2	0	10	173^{2}	144	65	17	2	74	125	11.4	3.11	113	.231	.314	8	.178	2	12	9	2	1.6
1987 *SF-N	11	7	.611	64	0	0	0	12	106^{1}	70	41	10	0	55	127	10.6	3.22	120	.192	.298	2	.200	1	10	8	-1	1.4
1988 SF-N	5	9	.357	65	0	0	0	13	98	80	42	3	2	46	86	11.8	3.58	91	.226	.318	1	.077	-1	-1	-4	-1	-0.7
1989 *SF-N	14	5	.737	30	29	2	1	0	193^{1}	149	58	11	0	46	119	**9.1**	**2.28**	**148**	.212	**.260**	9	.136	1	26	24	-0	2.4
1990 SF-N	12	11	.522	31	31	4	2	0	182	190	91	16	3	70	80	13.0	4.15	88	.272	.341	4	.061	-3	-7	-11	-1	-1.6
1991 SF-N	1	1	.500	8	3	0	0	0	19^{2}	25	14	5	0	9	8	15.6	6.41	56	.313	.382	0	.000	-0	-6	-6	-0	-0.6
Total 10	69	53	.566	352	89	9	4	48	959^{1}	815	395	74	13	413	703	11.6	3.29	107	.232	.315	29	.125	-1	41	26	1	4.3

● CLARENCE GARRETT
Garrett, Clarence Raymond "Laz" b: 3/6/1891, Reader, W.Va. d: 2/11/77, Moundsville, W.Va. BR/TR, 6'5.5", 185 lbs. Deb: 9/13/15

YEAR TM/L	W	L	PCT	G	GS	CG	SH	SV	IP	H	R	HR	HB	BB	SO	RAT	ERA	ERA+	OAV	OOB	BH	AVG	PB	PR	PR+	PD	TPI
1915 Cle-A	2	2	.500	4	4	2	0	0	23^{1}	19	13	1	1	6	5	10.0	2.31	132	.224	.283	0	.000	-0	2	2	1	0.4

● GREG GARRETT
Garrett, Gregory b: 3/12/48, Atascadero, Cal. BB/TL, 6', 200 lbs. Deb: 4/24/70

YEAR TM/L	W	L	PCT	G	GS	CG	SH	SV	IP	H	R	HR	HB	BB	SO	RAT	ERA	ERA+	OAV	OOB	BH	AVG	PB	PR	PR+	PD	TPI
1970 Cal-A	5	6	.455	32	7	0	0	0	74^{2}	48	23	6	1	44	53	11.2	2.65	136	.190	.312	1	.067	-1	9	8	-0	1.1
1971 Cin-N	0	1	.000	2	1	0	0	0	8^{2}	7	1	0	0	10	2	17.7	1.04	324	.250	.447	1	.333	0	2	2	-0	0.3
Total 2	5	7	.417	34	8	0	0	0	83^{1}	55	24	6	1	54	55	11.9	2.48	145	.196	.327	2	.111	-1	11	11	-0	1.4

● CLIFF GARRISON
Garrison, Clifford William b: 8/13/06, Bellemont, Okla. d: 8/25/94, Woodland, Cal. BR/TR, 6', 180 lbs. Deb: 4/16/28

YEAR TM/L	W	L	PCT	G	GS	CG	SH	SV	IP	H	R	HR	HB	BB	SO	RAT	ERA	ERA+	OAV	OOB	BH	AVG	PB	PR	PR+	PD	TPI
1928 Bos-A	0	0	—	6	0	0	0	0	16	22	15	2	0	6	0	15.8	7.88	52	.361	.418	0	.000	-0	-7	-7	1	-0.3

● JIM GARRY
Garry, James Thomas b: 9/21/1869, Great Barrington, Mass. d: 1/15/17, Pittsfield, Mass. TL, 5'10", 165 lbs. Deb: 5/2/1893

YEAR TM/L	W	L	PCT	G	GS	CG	SH	SV	IP	H	R	HR	HB	BB	SO	RAT	ERA	ERA+	OAV	OOB	BH	AVG	PB	PR	PR+	PD	TPI
1893 Bos-N	0	1	.000	1	1	0	0	0	1	5	8	0	0	4	2	81.0	63.00	8	.625	.750	0	.000	-0	-6	-6	0	-0.7

● NED GARVER
Garver, Ned Franklin b: 12/25/25, Ney, Ohio BR/TR, 5'10.5", 180 lbs. Deb: 4/28/48

YEAR TM/L	W	L	PCT	G	GS	CG	SH	SV	IP	H	R	HR	HB	BB	SO	RAT	ERA	ERA+	OAV	OOB	BH	AVG	PB	PR	PR+	PD	TPI
1948 StL-A	7	11	.389	38	24	7	0	5	198	200	92	14	1	95	75	13.5	3.41	134	.268	.352	19	.288	4	19	24	1	2.6
1949 StL-A	12	17	.414	41	32	16	1	3	223^{2}	245	126	14	3	102	70	14.1	3.98	114	.277	.354	14	.187	1	5	13	0	1.7
1950 StL-A	13	18	.419	37	31	**22**	2	0	260	264	120	18	4	108	85	13.0	3.39	**146**	.264	.338	26	.286	4	**34**	**42**	2	**5.3**
1951 StL-A★	20	12	.625	33	30	**24**	1	0	246	237	114	17	5	96	84	12.4	3.73	118	.255	.328	29	.305	7	11	17	1	3.0
1952 StL-A	7	10	.412	21	21	7	2	0	148^{2}	130	67	14	4	55	60	11.4	3.69	106	.235	.309	9	.184	0	-0	3	-0	0.4
Det-A	1	0	1.000	1	1	1	0	0	9	9	2	1	0	3	3	12.0	2.00	190	.265	.324	0	.000	0	2	2	0	0.3
Yr	8	10	.444	22	22	8	2	0	157^{2}	139	69	15	4	58	63	11.5	3.60	109	.237	.310	9	.176	0	1	5	0	0.7
1953 Det-A	11	11	.500	30	26	13	0	1	198^{1}	228	107	16	2	66	69	13.4	4.45	91	.290	.347	11	.153	-1	-10	-8	1	-0.8
1954 Det-A	14	11	.560	35	32	16	3	1	246^{1}	216	93	20	4	62	93	10.3	2.81	131	.236	.287	13	.165	-0	25	24	2	2.6
1955 Det-A	12	16	.429	33	32	16	1	0	230^{2}	251	115	21	5	67	83	12.6	3.98	97	.279	.333	17	.224	5	-1	-4	0	0.1
1956 Det-A	0	2	.000	6	3	1	0	0	17^{2}	15	10	2	1	13	6	14.8	4.08	101	.234	.372	0	.000	-0	0	0	1	0.0
1957 KC-A	6	13	.316	24	23	6	1	0	145^{1}	120	72	13	5	55	61	11.1	3.84	103	.223	.301	8	.182	0	-1	2	-0	0.2
1958 KC-A	12	11	.522	31	28	10	3	1	201	192	97	24	2	66	72	11.6	4.03	97	.244	.304	12	.174	0	-6	-3	5	0.3
1959 KC-A	10	13	.435	32	30	9	2	1	201^{1}	214	94	22	3	42	61	11.6	3.71	108	.270	.309	20	.282	6	3	6	-0	1.3
1960 KC-A	4	9	.308	28	15	5	2	0	122^{1}	110	57	15	2	35	50	10.8	3.83	104	.240	.296	2	.074	-1	1	2	-0	0.1
1961 LA-A	0	3	.000	12	2	0	0	0	29	40	18	2	0	16	9	17.4	5.59	81	.348	.427	0	.000	-1	-5	-3	1	-0.3
Total 14	129	157	.451	402	330	153	18	12	2477^{1}	2471	1184	213	41	881	881	12.3	3.73	112	.260	.325	180	.218	24	78	118	14	16.8

● JERRY GARVIN
Garvin, Theodore Jared b: 10/21/55, Oakland, Cal. BL/TL, 6'3", 195 lbs. Deb: 4/10/77

YEAR TM/L	W	L	PCT	G	GS	CG	SH	SV	IP	H	R	HR	HB	BB	SO	RAT	ERA	ERA+	OAV	OOB	BH	AVG	PB	PR	PR+	PD	TPI
1977 Tor-A	10	18	.357	34	34	12	1	0	244^{2}	247	127	33	4	85	127	12.4	4.19	100	.264	.328	0	—	0	-3	1	5	0.6
1978 Tor-A	4	12	.250	26	22	3	0	0	144^{2}	189	92	20	4	48	67	15.0	5.54	71	.319	.374	0	—	0	-28	-25	1	-2.3
1979 Tor-A	0	1	.000	8	1	0	0	0	22^{2}	15	9	2	2	10	14	10.7	2.78	157	.197	.307	0	—	0	4	4	-0	0.2
1980 Tor-A	4	7	.364	61	0	0	0	8	82^{2}	70	23	6	0	27	52	10.6	2.29	189	.233	.296	0	—	0	16	17	1	2.6
1981 Tor-A	1	2	.333	35	4	0	0	0	53	46	20	3	0	23	25	11.7	3.40	116	.240	.321	0	—	0	2	3	0	0.2
1982 Tor-A	1	1	.500	32	4	0	0	0	58^{1}	81	48	10	1	26	35	16.7	7.25	62	.335	.401	0	—	0	-21	-16	2	-0.6
Total 6	20	41	.328	196	65	15	1	8	606	648	319	74	11	219	320	13.0	4.43	94	.277	.342	0	—	0	-31	-16	9	0.7

● NED GARVIN
Garvin, Virgil Lee b: 1/1/1874, Navasota, Tex. d: 6/16/08, Fresno, Cal. BR/TR, 6'3.5", 160 lbs. Deb: 7/13/1896

YEAR TM/L	W	L	PCT	G	GS	CG	SH	SV	IP	H	R	HR	HB	BB	SO	RAT	ERA	ERA+	OAV	OOB	BH	AVG	PB	PR	PR+	PD	TPI
1896 Phi-N	0	1	.000	2	1	1	0	0	13	19	13	0	0	7	4	18.0	7.62	57	.339	.413	0	.000	-1	-5	-5	-0	-0.4
1899 Chi-N	9	13	.409	24	23	22	4	0	199	202	101	1	12	42	69	11.6	2.85	131	.263	.311	11	.155	-5	22	20	1	1.5
1900 Chi-N	10	18	.357	30	28	25	1	0	246^{1}	225	126	4	18	63	107	11.2	2.41	150	.243	.304	14	.154	-5	**35**	**34**	4	3.2
1901 Mil-A	8	20	.286	37	27	22	1	1	257^{1}	258	155	4	14	90	122	12.7	3.46	104	.258	.328	14	.108	-9	6	4	4	-0.2
1902 Chi-A	10	10	.500	23	19	16	2	0	175^{1}	169	68	3	8	43	55	11.3	2.21	153	.254	.307	9	.153	-2	27	24	3	2.5
Bro-N	1	1	.500	2	2	2	1	0	18	15	3	0	0	4	7	9.5	1.00	277	.227	.271	1	.143	-0	4	4	0	0.4
1903 Bro-N	15	18	.455	38	34	30	2	2	298	277	163	2	13	84	154	11.3	3.08	104	.248	.308	8	.075	-8	6	4	8	0.3
1904 Bro-N	5	15	.250	23	22	16	2	0	181^{2}	141	81	6	6	78	86	11.1	1.68	163	.218	.308	8	.127	-4	21	21	4	2.4
NY-A	0	1	.000	2	1	1	0	0	12	14	4	0	0	2	8	12.0	2.25	121	.292	.320	0	.000	-1	0	1	1	0.1
Total 7	58	97	.374	181	158	134	13	3	1400^{2}	1320	714	20	71	413	612	11.6	2.72	125	.249	.312	61	.122	-35	117	107	24	9.8

● HARRY GASPAR
Gaspar, Harry Lambert b: 4/28/1883, Kingsley, Iowa d: 5/14/40, Orange, Cal. BR/TR, 6', 180 lbs. Deb: 4/21/09

YEAR TM/L	W	L	PCT	G	GS	CG	SH	SV	IP	H	R	HR	HB	BB	SO	RAT	ERA	ERA+	OAV	OOB	BH	AVG	PB	PR	PR+	PD	TPI
1909 Cin-N	19	11	.633	44	29	19	4	2	260	228	97	0	9	57	65	10.2	2.01	129	.242	.291	10	.122	-3	17	17	-5	1.1
1910 Cin-N	15	17	.469	48	31	16	4	**7**	275	257	103	6	15	75	74	11.4	2.59	113	.255	.317	10	.115	-3	14	10	-2	0.7

YEAR	TM/L	W	L	PCT	G	GS	CG	SH	SV	IP	H	R	HR	HB	BB	SO	RAT	ERA	ERA+	OAV	OOB	BH	AVG	PB	PR	PR+	PD	TPI
1911	Cin-N	11	17	.393	44	32	11	2	4	253^{2}	272	112	9	14	69	76	12.6	3.30	100	.283	.340	13	.153	-2	3	0	-1	-0.4
1912	Cin-N	1	3	.250	7	6	2	1	0	36^{2}	38	21	0	1	16	13	13.5	4.17	81	.277	.357	3	.250	0	-3	-3	0	-0.3
Total	4	46	48	.489	143	98	48	11	13	825^{1}	795	333	15	39	217	228	11.5	2.69	110	.261	.318	36	.135	-9	31	25	-8	1.1
● **CHARLIE GASSAWAY**	Gassaway, Charles Cason "Sheriff" b: 8/12/18, Gassaway, Tenn. d: 1/15/92, Miami, Fla. BL/TL, 6'2.5", 210 lbs. Deb: 9/25/44																											
1944	Chi-N	0	1	.000	2	2	0	0	0	11^{2}	20	11	3	0	10	7	23.1	7.71	46	.385	.484	1	.250	0	-5	-6	-0	-0.4
1945	Phi-A	4	7	.364	24	11	4	0	0	118	114	59	4	2	55	50	13.0	3.74	92	.252	.336	6	.154	-2	-5	-4	-1	-0.7
1946	Cle-A	1	1	.500	13	6	0	0	0	50^{2}	54	25	2	4	26	23	14.9	3.91	85	.273	.368	1	.067	-1	-2	-4	0	-0.3
Total	3	5	9	.357	39	19	4	0	0	180^{1}	188	95	9	6	91	80	14.2	4.04	84	.268	.357	8	.138	-3	-12	-13	-2	-1.4
● **MILT GASTON**	Gaston, Nathaniel Milton b: 1/27/1896, Ridgefield Park, N.J. d: 4/26/96, Barnstable, Mass. BR/TR (BB 1933), 6'1", 185 lbs. Deb: 4/20/24 F																											
1924	NY-A	5	3	.625	29	2	0	0	1	86	92	48	3	6	44	24	14.9	4.50	92	.286	.382	6	.222	-1	-3	-3	-1	-0.5
1925	StL-A	15	14	.517	42	29	16	0	1	238^{2}	284	146	8	5	101	84	14.7	4.41	106	.305	.376	21	.262	2	-0	6	-2	0.7
1926	StL-A	10	18	.357	32	28	14	1	0	214^{1}	227	116	13	4	101	39	13.9	4.33	99	.283	.366	13	.167	-2	-7	-1	-1	-0.3
1927	StL-A	13	17	.433	37	30	21	0	1	254	275	177	18	3	100	77	13.4	5.00	87	.281	.350	25	.260	5	-24	-17	1	-1.1
1928	Was-A	6	12	.333	28	22	8	3	0	148^{2}	179	102	3	0	53	45	14.0	5.51	73	.302	.360	7	.143	-3	-24	-25	1	-2.7
1929	Bos-A	12	19	.387	39	28	20	1	2	243^{2}	265	121	15	3	81	83	12.9	3.73	115	.289	.348	15	.192	0	14	15	-1	1.6
1930	Bos-A	13	20	.394	38	34	20	2	2	273	272	138	15	0	98	99	12.2	3.92	117	.259	.323	20	.204	-4	22	21	1	1.9
1931	Bos-A	2	13	.133	23	18	4	0	0	119	137	76	4	0	41	33	13.5	4.46	96	.291	.348	6	.158	-2	-1	-2	-0	-0.4
1932	Chi-A	7	17	.292	28	25	7	1	1	166^{2}	183	101	10	1	73	44	13.9	4.00	108	.279	.352	14	.233	2	9	6	2	1.1
1933	Chi-A	8	12	.400	30	25	7	1	0	167	177	106	9	1	60	39	12.8	4.85	87	.272	.334	8	.154	-0	-11	-11	-1	-1.2
1934	Chi-A	6	19	.240	29	28	10	1	0	194	247	146	16	1	84	48	15.4	5.85	81	.313	.379	10	.147	-3	-29	-23	3	-2.4
Total	11	97	164	.372	355	269	127	10	8	2105	2338	1277	114	24	836	615	13.7	4.55	97	.287	.355	145	.200	-5	-54	-35	0	-3.3
● **WELCOME GASTON**	Gaston, Welcome Thornburg b: 12/19/1872, Guernsey Co., Ohio d: 12/13/44, Columbus, Ohio TL, Deb: 10/6/1898																											
1898	Bro-N	1	1	.500	2	2	2	0	0	16	17	9	0	0	9	0	14.6	2.81	128	.270	.361	1	.125	-0	1	1	-0	0.1
1899	Bro-N	0	0	—	1	0	0	0	0	3	3	1	0	1	4	0	24.0	3.00	130	.250	.471	1	1.000	1	0	0	0	0.1
Total	2	1	1	.500	3	2	2	0	0	19	20	10	0	1	13	0	16.1	2.84	128	.267	.382	2	.222	1	2	2	-0	0.2
● **HANK GASTRIGHT**	Gastright, Henry Carl (b: Henry Carl Gastreich) b: 3/29/1865, Covington, Ky. d: 10/9/37, Cold Spring, Ky. BR/TR, 6'2", 190 lbs. Deb: 4/19/1889																											
1889	Col-a	10	16	.385	32	26	21	0	0	222^{2}	255	175	8	5	104	115	14.7	4.57	79	.279	.355	17	.181	-4	-18	-25	-0	-2.5
1890	Col-a	30	14	.682	48	45	41	4	0	401^{1}	312	204	8	18	135	199	10.4	2.94	122	.208	.281	36	.213	3	42	31	-4	2.6
1891	Col-a	12	19	.387	35	33	28	1	0	283^{2}	280	196	7	11	136	109	13.5	3.78	91	.249	.336	23	.197	2	-2	-11	1	-0.6
1892	Was-N	3	3	.500	11	8	6	0	0	79^{2}	94	54	3	3	38	32	15.3	5.08	64	.282	.361	4	.138	0	-16	-16	-1	-1.1
1893	Pit-N	3	1	.750	9	5	3	0	0	59	74	54	3	3	39	12	17.7	6.25	73	.297	.399	1	.042	-4	-10	-11	1	-0.8
	Bos-N	12	4	.750	19	18	16	0	0	156	179	117	9	9	76	27	15.2	5.13	96	.279	.364	13	.191	-3	-8	-3	-2	-0.6
	Yr	15	5	**.750**	28	23	19	0	0	215	253	171	12	12	115	39	15.9	5.44	89	.284	.374	14	.152	-6	-19	-14	-1	-1.4
1894	Bro-N	2	6	.250	16	8	6	1	2	93	135	85	1	6	55	20	19.0	6.39	77	.335	.422	7	.171	-3	-11	-16	-1	-1.2
1896	Cin-N	0	0	—	1	0	0	0	0	6	8	6	0	0	1	0	13.5	4.50	103	.320	.346	0	.000	-0	-0	0	-0	0.0
Total	7	72	63	.533	171	143	121	6	2	1301^{1}	1337	891	39	55	584	514	13.7	4.20	92	.258	.339	101	.186	-8	-24	-54	-7	-4.2
● **AUBREY GATEWOOD**	Gatewood, Aubrey Lee b: 11/17/38, Little Rock, Ark. BR/TR, 6'1", 170 lbs. Deb: 9/11/63																											
1963	LA-A	1	1	.500	4	3	1	0	0	24	12	5	0	0	16	13	10.5	1.50	228	.148	.289	0	.000	-1	6	5	-0	0.3
1964	LA-A	3	3	.500	15	7	0	0	0	60^{1}	59	18	4	1	12	25	10.7	2.24	147	.258	.298	2	.100	-1	9	8	-0	0.6
1965	Cal-A	4	5	.444	46	3	0	0	0	92	91	41	5	1	37	37	12.6	3.42	99	.266	.339	3	.214	1	0	-0	-1	0.0
1970	Atl-N	0	0	—	3	0	0	0	0	2	4	6	0	1	2	0	31.5	4.50	95	.364	.500	0	—	0	-0	-0	0	0.0
Total	4	8	9	.471	68	13	1	0	0	178^{1}	166	70	9	3	67	75	11.9	2.78	122	.250	.322	5	.119	-1	15	12	-1	0.9
● **CHIPPY GAW**	Gaw, George Joseph b: 3/13/1892, W.Newton, Mass. d: 5/26/68, Boston, Mass. BR/TR, 5'11", 180 lbs. Deb: 4/20/20																											
1920	Chi-N	1	1	.500	6	1	0	0	0	13	16	9	1	1	3	4	13.8	4.85	66	.320	.370	1	.250	-0	-2	-2	-0	-0.3
● **DALE GEAR**	Gear, Dale Dudley b: 2/2/1872, Lone Elm, Kan. d: 9/23/51, Topeka, Kan. BR/TR, 5'11", 165 lbs. Deb: 8/15/1896 ◆																											
1896	Cle-N	0	2	.000	3	2	2	0	0	23	35	23	1	2	6	6	16.8	5.48	83	.347	.394	6	.400	2	-3	-2	-0	0.0
1901	Was-A	4	11	.267	24	16	14	1	1	163	199	100	9	4	22	35	12.4	4.03	91	.297	.324	47	.236	0	-7	-7	2	-0.3
Total	2	4	13	.235	27	18	16	1	1	186	234	123	10	6	28	41	13.0	4.21	90	.304	.333	57	.239	2	-9	-9	2	-0.3
● **DINTY GEARIN**	Gearin, Dennis John b: 10/15/1897, Providence, R.I. d: 3/11/59, Providence, R.I. BL/TL, 5'4", 148 lbs. Deb: 8/6/23																											
1923	*NY-N	1	1	.500	6	2	1	0	0	24	23	11	1	0	10	9	12.4	3.38	113	.264	.340	2	.286	0	2	1	-0	0.1
1924	NY-N	1	2	.333	6	3	2	0	0	29	30	9	3	0	16	4	14.3	2.48	148	.275	.368	3	.333	0	4	4	-0	0.4
	Bos-N	0	1	.000	1	1	0	0	0	0	3	0	0	2	—	—	∞	—	1.000	1.000	99	—	0	-5	-5	0	-0.4	
	Yr	1	3	.250	7	4	2	0	0	29	33	14	3	0	18	4	15.8	4.03	91	.295	.392	3	.333	0	-1	-1	-0	0.0
Total	2	2	4	.333	13	6	3	0	0	53	56	25	4	0	28	13	14.3	3.74	100	.281	.370	5	.313	1	1	0	-1	0.1
● **BOB GEARY**	Geary, Robert Norton "Speed" b: 5/10/1891, Cincinnati, Ohio d: 1/3/80, Cincinnati, Ohio BR/TR, 5'11", 168 lbs. Deb: 4/25/18																											
1918	Phi-A	2	5	.286	16	7	6	2	4	87	94	37	0	3	31	22	13.2	2.69	109	.289	.357	4	.148	-1	1	2	-1	0.1
1919	Phi-A	0	3	.000	9	2	1	0	0	32^{1}	32	22	1	0	18	9	13.9	4.73	72	.264	.360	5	.500	2	-5	-4	0	-0.2
1921	Cin-N	1	1	.500	10	1	0	0	0	29	38	17	1	0	2	10	12.4	4.34	82	.333	.345	2	.250	0	-2	-3	-0	-0.2
Total	3	3	9	.250	35	10	7	2	4	148^{1}	164	76	2	3	51	41	13.2	3.46	92	.293	.355	11	.244	1	-6	-4	-1	-0.3
● **BOB GEBHARD**	Gebhard, Robert Henry b: 1/3/43, Lamberton, Minn. BR/TR, 6'2", 210 lbs. Deb: 8/2/71 C																											
1971	Min-A	1	2	.333	17	0	0	0	0	18	17	6	0	1	11	13	14.5	3.00	119	.243	.354	0	—	0	1	1	1	0.3
1972	Min-A	0	1	.000	13	0	0	0	1	21	36	29	3	2	13	13	21.9	8.57	38	.371	.455	0	—	0	-13	-12	1	-0.6
1974	Mon-N	0	0	—	1	0	0	0	0	2	5	1	1	0	0	0	22.5	4.50	86	.500	.500	0	—	0	-0	-0	0	0.0
Total	3	1	3	.250	31	0	0	0	1	41	58	36	4	3	24	26	18.7	5.93	57	.328	.417	0	—	0	-12	-11	1	-0.3
● **PETE GEBRIAN**	Gebrian, Peter "Gabe" b: 8/10/23, Bayonne, N.J. BR/TR, 6', 170 lbs. Deb: 5/6/47																											
1947	Chi-A	2	3	.400	27	4	0	0	5	66^{1}	61	40	7	2	33	17	13.0	4.48	82	.247	.340	0	.000	-2	-6	-6	-1	-0.8
● **JIM GEDDES**	Geddes, James Lee b: 3/23/49, Columbus, Ohio BR/TR, 6'2", 200 lbs. Deb: 4/28/72																											
1972	Chi-A	0	0	—	5	1	0	0	0	10^{1}	12	9	1	1	10	3	20.0	6.97	45	.293	.442	0	.000	-0	-4	-4	-0	-0.3
1973	Chi-A	0	0	—	6	1	0	0	0	15^{2}	14	6	0	3	14	7	17.8	2.87	138	.255	.431	0	—	0	2	2	0	0.1
Total	2	0	0	—	11	2	0	0	0	26	26	15	1	4	24	10	18.7	4.50	81	.271	.435	0	.000	-0	-3	-2	0	-0.2
● **JOE GEDEON**	Gedeon, Elmer Joseph b: 12/5/1893, Sacramento, Cal. d: 5/19/41, San Francisco, Cal BR/TR, 6', 167 lbs. Deb: 5/13/13 ◆																											
1913	Was-A	0	0	—	1	0	0	0	1	0^{1}	0	0	0	0	0	0	0.0	0.00	—	.000	.000	13	.183	0	0	0	0	0.0
● **COUNT GEDNEY**	Gedney, Alfred W. b: 5/10/1849, Brooklyn, N.Y. d: 3/26/22, Hackensack, N.J. 5'9", 140 lbs. Deb: 4/27/1872 ◆																											
1875	Mut-n	1	0	1.000	2	1	1	0	0	11	7	4	0		1	2	6.5	0.82	285	.167	.186	55	.206	-0	2	2		0.1
● **JOHNNY GEE**	Gee, John Alexander "Whiz" b: 12/7/15, Syracuse, N.Y. d: 1/23/88, Cortland, N.Y. BL/TL, 6'9", 225 lbs. Deb: 9/17/39																											
1939	Pit-N	1	2	.333	3	3	1	0	0	19^{2}	20	17	0	0	10	16	13.7	4.12	93	.253	.337	0	.000	-1	-0	-1	1	-0.1
1941	Pit-N	0	2	.000	3	2	0	0	0	7^{1}	10	10	0	0	5	2	18.4	6.14	59	.294	.385	1	.333	0	-2	-2	-0	-0.4
1943	Pit-N	4	4	.500	15	10	2	0	0	82	89	42	5	0	27	18	12.7	4.28	81	.280	.336	3	.115	-1	-8	-7	-3	-1.0
1944	Pit-N	0	0	—	4	0	0	0	0	11^{1}	20	10	0	0	5	3	19.9	7.15	52	.377	.431	1	.500	0	-4	-4	-0	-0.2
	NY-N	0	0	—	4	0	0	0	0	4^{2}	5	1	0	0	0	3	9.6	0.00	—	.263	.263	0	—	0	2	2	0	0.1
	Yr	0	0	—	8	0	0	0	0	16	25	11	0	0	5	6	16.9	5.06	73	.347	.390	1	.500	0	-3	-2	0	-0.1
1945	NY-N	0	0	—	2	0	0	0	1	3	5	3	0	0	2	1	21.0	9.00	43	.385	.467	0	.000	-0	-2	-2	0	-0.1
1946	NY-N	2	4	.333	13	6	1	0	0	47^{1}	60	27	3	2	15	22	14.6	3.99	86	.308	.363	3	.231	0	-3	-3	-1	-0.4
Total	6	7	12	.368	44	21	4	0	1	175^{1}	209	110	8	2	64	65	14.1	4.41	80	.294	.354	8	.157	-1	-18	-17	-3	-2.1

YEAR	TM/L	W	L	PCT	G	GS	CG	SH	SV	IP	H	R	HR	HB	BB	SO	RAT	ERA	ERA+	OAV	OOB	BH	AVG	PB	PR	PR+	PD	TPI
● BILLY GEER	Geer, William Henry Harrison (b: George Harrison Geer) b: 8/13/1859, Syracuse, N.Y. d: 1/3/22, Syracuse, N.Y. TR, 5′8″, 160 lbs. Deb: 10/15/1874 ♦																											
1884	Bro-a	0	0	—	2	0	0	0	0	5	14	12	0	0	3	1	30.6	12.60	26	.609	.654	82	.210	0	-5	-5	-0	-0.2
● HENRY GEHRING	Gehring, Henry b: 1/24/1881, St.Paul, Minn. d: 4/18/12, Kansas City, Mo. BR/TR, Deb: 7/16/07																											
1907	Was-A	3	7	.300	15	9	8	2	0	87	92	44	1	1	14	31	11.1	3.31	73	.274	.305	9	.205	3	-7	-9	-2	-0.9
1908	Was-A	0	1	.000	3	1	0	0	0	5	9	8	0	2	2	0	23.4	14.40	16	.450	.542	3	.600	2	-7	-7	0	-1.0
Total	2	3	8	.273	18	10	8	2	0	92	101	52	1	3	16	31	11.7	3.91	62	.284	.320	12	.245	5	-14	-16	-2	-1.9
● PAUL GEHRMAN	Gehrman, Paul Arthur "Dutch" b: 5/3/12, Marquam, Ore. d: 10/23/86, Bend, Ore. BR/TR, 6′, 195 lbs. Deb: 9/15/37																											
1937	Cin-N	0	1	.000	2	1	0	0	0	9^1	11	8	0	0	5	1	15.4	2.89	129	.282	.364	0	.000	-0	1	1	0	0.1
● GARY GEIGER	Geiger, Gary Merle b: 4/4/37, Sand Ridge, Ill. d: 4/24/96, Murphysboro, Ill. BL/TR, 6′, 168 lbs. Deb: 4/15/58 ♦																											
1958	Cle-A	0	0	—	1	0	0	0	0	2	2	2	0	0	1	2	13.5	9.00	41	.286	.375	45	.231	0	-1	-1	0	0.0
● EMIL GEIS	Geis, Emil Michael b: 3/1861, Villmar, Germany BR/TR, 5′11″, 170 lbs. Deb: 7/19/1882																											
1882	Bal-a	4	9	.308	13	13	10	1	0	95^2	84	73	2		22	10	10.0	4.80	57	.220	.263	6	.146	-2	-22	-21	-3	-2.5
● BILL GEIS	Geis, William J. (b: William J. Geiss) b: 7/15/1858, Chicago, Ill. d: 9/18/24, Chicago, Ill. 5′10″, 164 lbs. Deb: 5/1/1884 F♦																											
1884	Det-N	0	0	—	1	0	0	0	0	5	14	16	0		2	1	28.8	14.40	20	.424	.457	50	.177	-0	-6	-7	0	-0.3
● DAVE GEISEL	Geisel, John David b: 1/18/55, Windber, Pa. BL/TL, 6′3″, 210 lbs. Deb: 6/13/78																											
1978	Chi-N	1	0	1.000	18	1	0	0	0	23^1	27	12	0	0	11	15	14.7	4.24	95	.278	.352	0	.000	-0	-2	-0	-0	-0.1
1979	Chi-N	0	0	—	7	0	0	0	0	15	10	1	0	1	4	5	9.0	0.60	688	.189	.259	0	.000	-0	5	5	-0	0.2
1981	Chi-N	2	0	1.000	11	2	0	0	0	16	11	3	0	0	10	7	11.8	0.56	657	.204	.328	0	.000	-0	5	5	-0	0.6
1982	Tor-A	1	1	.500	16	2	0	0	0	31^2	32	15	6	2	17	22	14.5	3.98	113	.260	.359	0	—	0	0	2	-0	0.1
1983	Tor-A	0	3	.000	47	0	0	0	5	52^1	47	28	4	2	31	50	13.8	4.64	93	.240	.349	0	—	0	-3	-2	-1	-0.2
1984	Sea-A	1	1	.500	20	3	0	0	3	43^1	47	22	2	2	9	28	12.0	4.15	96	.273	.317	0	—	0	-1	-1	-1	-0.1
1985	Sea-A	0	0	—	12	0	0	0	0	27	35	21	3	0	15	17	16.7	6.33	67	.310	.391	0	—	0	-7	-6	-0	-0.3
Total	7	5	5	.500	131	8	0	0	8	208^2	209	102	15	7	97	144	13.5	4.01	104	.259	.343	0	.000	-1	-1	4	-3	0.2
● VERN GEISHERT	Geishert, Vernon William b: 1/10/46, Madison, Wis. BR/TR, 6′1″, 215 lbs. Deb: 8/26/69																											
1969	Cal-A	1	1	.500	11	3	0	0	1	31	32	18	4	1	7	18	11.6	4.65	75	.267	.313	0	.000	-1	-4	-4	0	-0.3
● EMIL GEISS	Geiss, Emil August b: 3/20/1867, Chicago, Ill. d: 10/4/11, Chicago, Ill. BR/TR, 5′11″, 170 lbs. Deb: 5/18/1887 F♦																											
1887	Chi-N	0	1	.000	1	1	1	0	0	9	20	11	0	0	3	4	20.0	8.00	56	.435	.435	1	.083	-1	-4	-3	0	-0.3
● CHARLIE GELBERT	Gelbert, Charles Magnus b: 1/26/06, Scranton, Pa. d: 1/13/67, Easton, Pa. BR/TR, 5′11″, 170 lbs. Deb: 4/16/29 ♦																											
1940	Was-A	0	0	—	2	0	0	0	0	4	5	4	2	0	3	1	18.0	9.00	46	.278	.381	20	.370	1	-2	-2	0	-0.1
● JOHN GELNAR	Gelnar, John Richard b: 6/25/43, Granite, Okla BR/TR, 6′1.5″, 190 lbs. Deb: 8/4/64																											
1964	Pit-N	0	0	—	7	0	0	0	0	9	11	5	2	0	1	4	12.0	5.00	70	.314	.333	0	—	0	-1	-1	-0	-0.1
1967	Pit-N	0	1	.000	10	1	0	0	0	19	30	18	4	2	11	5	20.4	8.05	42	.375	.462	1	.167	0	-10	-10	0	-0.5
1969	Sea-A	3	10	.231	39	10	0	0	3	108^2	103	49	7	5	26	69	11.1	3.31	110	.250	.302	1	.053	-2	4	4	-0	0.3
1970	Mil-A	4	3	.571	53	0	0	0	4	92^1	98	46	7	5	23	48	12.3	4.19	90	.277	.330	1	.083	-1	-5	-4	1	-0.2
1971	Mil-A	0	0	—	2	0	0	0	0	1^1	3	2	0	0	1	0	27.0	13.50	26	.429	.500	0	—	0	-1	-1	0	-0.1
Total	5	7	14	.333	111	11	0	0	7	230^1	245	120	20	12	62	126	12.5	4.18	88	.276	.332	3	.081	-2	-14	-13	1	-0.6
● JOE GENEWICH	Genewich, Joseph Edward b: 1/15/1897, Elmira, N.Y. d: 12/21/85, Lockport, N.Y. BR/TR, 6′, 174 lbs. Deb: 9/3/22																											
1922	Bos-N	0	2	.000	6	2	1	0	0	23	29	19	2	0	11	4	15.7	7.04	57	.319	.392	1	.167	-0	-8	-8	-0	-0.6
1923	Bos-N	13	14	.481	43	24	12	1	1	227^1	272	110	15	7	46	54	12.9	3.72	107	.303	.341	19	.247	2	7	7	2	1.1
1924	Bos-N	10	19	.345	34	27	11	2	1	200^1	258	136	4	8	65	43	14.9	5.21	73	.329	.386	10	.167	-2	-30	-31	-0	-4.0
1925	Bos-N	12	10	.545	34	21	10	0	0	169	185	87	4	6	41	34	12.4	3.99	100	.279	.327	15	.273	1	5	0	-1	0.1
1926	Bos-N	8	16	.333	37	26	12	2	2	216	239	114	6	6	63	59	12.8	3.88	92	.288	.342	11	.164	-1	-1	-9	1	-0.9
1927	Bos-N	11	8	.579	40	19	7	0	1	181	199	93	7	2	54	38	12.7	3.83	97	.279	.332	11	.193	-1	2	-2	0	-0.3
1928	Bos-N	3	7	.300	13	11	4	0	0	80^2	88	43	14	3	18	15	12.2	4.13	95	.280	.325	1	.038	-3	-1	-2	1	-0.4
	NY-N	11	4	.733	26	18	10	2	3	158^1	136	62	10	1	54	37	10.9	3.18	123	.232	.298	13	.203	-1	14	13	1	1.1
	Yr	14	11	.560	39	29	14	2	3	239	224	105	24	4	72	52	11.3	3.50	112	.249	.307	14	.156	-4	13	11	2	0.7
1929	NY-N	3	7	.300	21	9	1	0	1	85	133	70	9	1	30	19	17.4	6.78	68	.359	.409	12	.375	3	-19	-21	0	-1.8
1930	NY-N	2	5	.286	18	9	3	0	3	61	71	44	6	1	20	13	13.6	5.61	84	.297	.354	3	.150	-1	-4	-6	2	-0.5
Total	9	73	92	.442	272	166	71	7	12	1401^2	1610	778	77	35	402	316	13.1	4.29	91	.293	.345	96	.207	-4	-35	-60	5	-6.2
● GARY GENTRY	Gentry, Gary Edward b: 10/6/46, Phoenix, Ariz. BR/TR, 6′, 183 lbs. Deb: 4/10/69																											
1969	*NY-N	13	12	.520	35	35	6	3	0	233^2	192	94	24	5	81	154	10.7	3.43	107	.222	.293	6	.081	-4	4	6	1	0.3
1970	NY-N	9	9	.500	32	29	5	2	1	188^1	155	88	19	9	86	134	11.9	3.68	109	.224	.318	4	.068	-2	8	7	-2	0.2
1971	NY-N	12	11	.522	32	31	8	3	0	203^1	167	84	16	6	82	155	11.3	3.23	106	.224	.305	5	.074	-5	5	4	-1	-0.2
1972	NY-N	7	10	.412	32	26	3	0	0	164	153	82	20	6	75	120	12.8	4.01	84	.250	.338	5	.104	-1	-10	-12	2	-1.1
1973	Atl-N	4	6	.400	16	14	3	0	1	86^2	74	37	7	1	35	42	11.4	3.43	115	.231	.308	7	.233	1	2	5	-1	0.5
1974	Atl-N	0	0	—	3	1	0	0	0	6^2	4	1	1	1	2	0	9.5	1.35	281	.167	.259	0	.000	-0	2	2	-0	0.1
1975	Atl-N	1	1	.500	7	2	0	0	0	20	25	14	3	0	8	10	14.8	4.95	76	.313	.375	0	.000	-1	-3	-2	0	-0.3
Total	7	46	49	.484	157	138	25	8	2	902^2	770	400	90	28	369	615	11.6	3.56	103	.231	.312	27	.095	-12	9	10	-1	-0.5
● RUFE GENTRY	Gentry, James Ruffus b: 5/18/18, Daisy Station, N.C. d: 7/3/97, Winston-Salem, N.C BR/TR, 6′1″, 180 lbs. Deb: 9/10/43 F																											
1943	Det-A	1	3	.250	4	4	2	0	0	29^1	30	12	2	2	12	8	13.5	3.68	96	.268	.349	0	.000	-1	-1	-0	-0	-0.2
1944	Det-A	12	14	.462	37	30	10	3	0	203^2	211	104	9	4	108	68	14.3	4.24	84	.273	.365	15	.197	-1	-18	-15	1	-1.7
1946	Det-A	0	0	—	2	0	0	0	0	3	4	5	0	0	7	1	33.0	15.00	24	.333	.579	0	—	0	-4	-4	-0	-0.2
1947	Det-A	0	0	—	1	0	0	0	0	0^1	1	3	0	0	2	0	81.0	81.00	5	.500	.750	0	—	0	-3	-3	0	-0.1
1948	Det-A	0	0	—	4	0	0	0	0	6^2	5	2	0	1	5	1	14.9	2.70	162	.208	.367	1	1.000	0	1	1	-0	0.1
Total	5	13	17	.433	48	34	12	3	0	243	251	126	11	7	134	78	14.5	4.37	82	.272	.368	16	.184	-1	-25	-20	0	-2.1
● CHRIS GEORGE	George, Christopher Sean b: 9/24/66, Pittsburgh, Pa. BR/TR, 6′2″, 200 lbs. Deb: 10/1/91																											
1991	Mil-A	0	0	—	2	1	0	0	0	6	8	2	0	0	0	2	12.0	3.00	133	.333	.333	0	—	0	1	1	-0	0.0
● LEFTY GEORGE	George, Thomas Edward b: 8/13/1886, Pittsburgh, Pa. d: 5/13/55, York, Pa. BL/TL, 6′, 155 lbs. Deb: 4/14/11																											
1911	StL-A	4	9	.308	27	13	6	1	0	116^1	136	81	3	9	51	23	15.2	4.18	81	.256	.332	5	.114	-3	-11	-10	-1	-1.4
1912	Cle-A	0	5	.000	11	5	2	0	0	44^1	69	38	1	2	18	18	18.1	4.87	70	.373	.434	3	.214	1	-8	-7	0	-0.6
1915	Cin-N	2	2	.500	5	3	2	1	0	28	24	12	1	5	8	11	11.9	3.86	74	.242	.330	4	.333	2	-3	-3	1	-0.1
1918	Bos-N	1	5	.167	9	5	4	0	0	54^1	56	23	0	3	21	22	13.3	2.32	116	.281	.359	2	.091	-2	3	2	2	0.3
Total	4	7	21	.250	52	26	14	2	0	243	285	154	5	19	98	74	14.9	3.85	82	.281	.355	14	.152	-2	-19	-18	1	-1.8
● BILL GEORGE	George, William M. b: 1/27/1865, Bellaire, Ohio d: 8/23/16, Wheeling, W.Va. BR/TL, 5′8″, 165 lbs. Deb: 5/11/1887 ♦																											
1887	NY-N	3	9	.250	13	13	10	0	0	108	215	112	1	14	89	49	19.1	5.25	72	.413	.429	10	.185	-4	-14	-19	2	-1.7
1888	*NY-N	2	1	.667	4	3	3	1	0	33^2	18	9	0	1	11	26	8.0	1.34	205	.149	.226	9	.231	1	6	5	-0	0.5
1889	Col-a	0	0	—	2	0	0	0	0	8	11	13	1	0	3	3	15.8	7.88	46	.314	.368	4	.235	-0	-4	-4	0	-0.2
Total	3	5	10	.333	19	16	13	1	0	149^2	244	134	2	15	103	78	16.4	4.51	78	.361	.387	27	.216	-3	-12	-17	2	-1.4
● OSCAR GEORGY	Georgy, Oscar John b: 11/25/16, New Orleans, La. d: 1/15/99, New Orleans, La. BR/TR, 6′3.5″, 180 lbs. Deb: 6/4/38																											
1938	NY-N	0	0	—	1	0	0	0	0	1	2	2	0	0	1	0	27.0	18.00	21	.400	.500	0	—	0	-2	-2	-0	-0.1
● DAVE GERARD	Gerard, David Frederick b: 8/6/36, New York, N.Y. BR/TR, 6′2″, 205 lbs. Deb: 4/10/62																											
1962	Chi-N	2	3	.400	39	0	0	0	3	58^2	67	40	10	1	28	30	14.7	4.91	84	.289	.368	3	.375	1	-6	-5	-0	-0.4

YEAR	TM/L	W	L	PCT	G	GS	CG	SH	SV	IP	H	R	HR	HB	BB	SO	RAT	ERA	ERA+	OAV	OOB	BH	AVG	PB	PR	PR+	PD	TPI
● GEORGE GERBERMAN Gerberman, George Alois b: 3/8/42, ElCampo, Tex. BR/TR, 6', 180 lbs. Deb: 9/23/62																												
1962	Chi-N	0	0	—	1	1	0	0	0	5^1	3	1	1	0	5	1	13.5	1.69	246	.158	.333	0	.000	0	1	1	-0	0.1
● RUSTY GERHARDT Gerhardt, Allen Russell b: 8/13/50, Baltimore, Md. BB/TL, 5'9", 175 lbs. Deb: 7/27/74																												
1974	SD-N	2	1	.667	23	1	0	0	1	35^2	44	28	1	2	17	22	15.9	7.07	51	.308	.389	1	.167	-0	-14	-14	-0	-1.2
● AL GERHEAUSER Gerheauser, Albert "Lefty" b: 6/24/17, St.Louis, Mo. d: 5/28/72, Springfield, Mo. BL/TL, 6'3", 190 lbs. Deb: 4/24/43																												
1943	Phi-N	10	19	.345	38	31	11	2	0	215	222	108	10	2	70	92	12.3	3.60	94	.263	.321	8	.113	-3	-5	-5	-1	-1.1
1944	Phi-N	8	16	.333	30	29	10	2	0	182^2	210	102	8	1	65	66	13.6	4.58	79	.285	.344	15	.231	3	-20	-20	-2	-2.1
1945	Pit-N	5	10	.333	32	14	5	0	1	140^1	170	72	5	1	54	55	14.4	3.91	101	.304	.366	12	.250	3	-2	1	2	0.5
1946	Pit-N	2	2	.500	35	3	1	0	0	81^2	92	42	2	1	25	32	13.0	3.97	89	.286	.339	7	.333	2	-5	-4	1	0.1
1948	StL-A	0	3	.000	14	2	0	0	0	23^1	32	23	0	1	10	10	16.6	7.33	62	.317	.384	2	.333	0	-8	-7	-0	-0.7
Total	5	25	50	.333	149	79	27	4	1	643	726	347	25	6	224	255	13.4	4.13	88	.283	.342	44	.209	5	-40	-35	-0	-3.3
● STEVE GERKIN Gerkin, Stephen Paul "Splinter" b: 11/19/12, Grafton, W.Va. d: 11/9/78, Bay Pines, Fla. BR/TR, 6'1", 162 lbs. Deb: 5/13/45																												
1945	Phi-A	0	12	.000	21	12	3	0	0	102	112	49	4	3	27	25	12.5	3.62	95	.285	.336	2	.059	-4	-3	-2	0	-0.6
● LES GERMAN German, Lester Stanley b: 6/1/1869, Baltimore, Md. d: 6/10/34, Germantown, Md. BR/TR, 5'8", 165 lbs. Deb: 8/27/1890																												
1890	Bal-a	5	11	.313	17	16	15	0	0	132^1	147	95	2	13	54	37	14.6	4.83	84	.273	.353	6	.118	-2	-14	-11	-2	-1.3
1893	NY-N	8	8	.500	20	18	14	0	0	152	162	109	6	9	70	35	14.3	4.14	112	.265	.349	23	.311	2	9	9	-1	0.8
1894	NY-N	9	8	.529	24	16	11	0	1	143^1	186	139	7	12	68	21	16.7	5.53	95	.311	.392	18	.300	0	-3	-4	2	-0.2
1895	NY-N	7	11	.389	25	18	16	0	0	178^1	243	159	7	9	78	36	16.7	5.96	78	.320	.390	29	.261	3	-23	-27	-0	-1.7
1896	NY-N	0	0	—	1	0	0	0	0	2^2	9	6	0	0	1	0	33.8	13.50	31	.529	.556	0	.000	-0	-3	-3	-0	-0.1
	Was-N	2	20	.091	28	20	14	0	1	166^2	240	174	6	5	74	20	17.2	6.32	70	.334	.400	16	.229	0	-36	-35	1	-3.3
	Yr	2	20	.091	29	20	14	0	1	169^1	249	180	6	5	75	20	17.5	6.43	69	.339	.404	16	.225	-0	-39	-38	1	-3.4
1897	Was-N	3	5	.375	15	5	4	0	0	83^2	117	74	2	7	33	2	16.9	5.59	78	.328	.395	15	.341	2	-12	-12	-1	-0.7
Total	6	34	63	.351	130	93	74	0	2	859	1104	756	30	55	378	151	16.1	5.45	84	.306	.381	107	.260	5	-83	-82	-0	-6.5
● ED GERNER Gerner, Edwin Frederick "Lefty" b: 7/22/1897, Philadelphia, Pa. d: 5/15/70, Philadelphia, Pa. BL/TL, 5'8.5", 175 lbs. Deb: 5/14/19																												
1919	Cin-N	1	0	1.000	5	1	0	0	0	17	22	10	0	2	3	2	14.3	3.18	87	.333	.380	1	.167	0	-0	-1	1	0.0
● LEFTY GERVAIS Gervais, Lucien Edward b: 7/6/1890, Grover, Wis. d: 10/19/50, Los Angeles, Cal. BL/TL, 5'10", 165 lbs. Deb: 4/17/13																												
1913	Bos-N	0	1	.000	5	2	1	0	0	15^2	18	11	0	0	4	1	12.6	5.74	57	.383	.431	0	.000	-0	-4	-4	-0	-0.3
● CHARLIE GESSNER Gessner, Charles J. b: Philadelphia, Pa. Deb: 7/19/1886																												
1886	Phi-a	0	1	.000	1	1	1	0	0	8	13	14	0	2	5	0	22.5	9.00	39	.351	.455	1	.250	-0	-5	-5	-0	-0.4
● AL GETTEL Gettel, Allen Jones b: 9/17/17, Norfolk, Va. BR/TR, 6'3.5", 200 lbs. Deb: 4/20/45																												
1945	NY-A	9	8	.529	27	17	9	0	3	154^2	141	70	11	7	53	67	11.7	3.90	89	.243	.314	16	.281	2	-9	-7	-1	-0.7
1946	NY-A	6	7	.462	26	11	5	2	0	103	89	40	6	2	40	54	11.4	2.97	116	.229	.305	4	.125	-2	6	6	0	0.5
1947	Cle-A	11	10	.524	31	21	9	2	0	149	122	54	12	3	62	64	11.3	3.20	109	.229	.313	15	.294	4	8	5	1	1.2
1948	Cle-A	0	1	.000	5	2	0	0	0	7^2	15	15	2	1	10	4	30.5	17.61	23	.385	.520	0	.000	-0	-11	-12	-0	-1.3
	Chi-A	8	10	.444	22	19	7	0	1	148	154	76	7	4	60	49	13.3	4.01	106	.268	.342	13	.241	0	5	4	-1	0.4
	Yr	8	11	.421	27	21	7	0	1	155^2	169	91	9	5	70	53	14.1	4.68	91	.276	.355	13	.228	-0	-7	-8	-1	-0.9
1949	Chi-A	2	5	.286	19	7	1	1	1	63	69	48	12	2	26	22	13.9	6.43	65	.283	.357	3	.167	-0	-16	-16	-1	-1.6
	Was-A	0	2	.000	16	1	0	0	1	34^2	43	24	4	0	24	7	17.4	5.45	78	.314	.416	0	.000	-1	-5	-5	1	-0.3
	Yr	2	7	.222	35	8	1	1	2	97^2	112	72	16	2	50	29	15.1	6.08	69	.294	.379	3	.115	-1	-20	-20	-0	-1.9
1951	NY-N	1	2	.333	30	1	0	0	0	57^1	52	37	12	0	25	36	12.1	4.87	80	.240	.318	1	.083	-1	-6	-6	1	-0.3
1955	StL-N	1	0	1.000	8	0	0	0	0	17	26	18	6	0	10	7	19.1	9.00	45	.361	.439	3	.500	1	-9	-9	-1	-0.4
Total	7	38	45	.458	184	79	31	5	6	734^1	711	382	72	19	310	310	12.7	4.28	88	.255	.334	55	.228	3	-37	-41	-1	-2.5
● CHARLIE GETTIG Gettig, Charles Henry b: 12/1870, Baltimore, Md. d: 4/11/35, Baltimore, Md. BR, 5'10", 172 lbs. Deb: 8/5/1896 ◆																												
1896	NY-N	1	0	1.000	4	1	1	0	1	14	20	17	0	2	8	5	19.3	9.64	44	.333	.429	3	.333	1	-8	-9	0	-0.5
1897	NY-N	1	1	.500	3	2	2	0	0	19	23	23	0	2	9	7	16.1	5.21	80	.295	.382	15	.200	0	-2	-2	0	-0.2
1898	NY-N	6	3	.667	17	8	7	0	0	115	141	72	1	8	39	14	14.7	3.83	91	.299	.363	49	.250	2	-3	-5	1	0.0
1899	NY-N	7	8	.467	18	15	12	0	0	128	161	102	3	4	54	25	15.4	4.43	85	.307	.376	24	.247	1	-8	-10	-1	-0.9
Total	4	15	12	.556	42	26	22	0	1	276	345	214	4	16	110	51	15.4	4.50	82	.304	.374	91	.241	4	-21	-26	1	-1.6
● TOM GETTINGER Gettinger, Lewis Thomas Leyton (b: Lewis Thomas Leyton Gittinger) b: 12/11/1868, Frederick, Md. d: 7/26/43, Pensacola, Fla. BL/TL, 5'10", 180 lbs. Deb: 9/21/1889 ◆																												
1895	Lou-N	0	0	—	2	0	0	0	0	6^1	13	7	1	0	1	0	19.9	7.11	65	.419	.438	70	.269	0	-2	-2	0	-0.1
● CHARLIE GETZIEN Getzien, Charles H. "Pretzels" b: 2/14/1864, Germany d: 6/19/32, Chicago, Ill. BR/TR, 5'10", 172 lbs. Deb: 8/13/1884																												
1884	Det-N	5	12	.294	17	17	17	1	0	147^1	118	73	2		25	107	8.7	1.95	148	.204	.237	6	.109	-4	17	16	-2	1.0
1885	Det-N	12	25	.324	37	37	37	1	0	330	360	222	8		92	110	12.3	3.03	94	.264	.311	29	.212	-1	-7	-7	-2	-0.9
1886	Det-N	30	11	.732	43	43	42	1	0	386^2	388	203	6		85	172	11.0	3.03	110	.250	.288	29	.176	-3	12	12	-2	0.4
1887	*Det-N	29	13	**.690**	43	42	41	2	0	366^2	479	217	24	2	106	135	11.8	3.73	109	.304	.305	39	.235	-2	14	13	0	0.8
1888	Det-N	19	25	.432	46	46	45	2	0	404	411	225	13	8	54	202	10.5	3.05	91	.251	.279	41	.246	10	-9	-13	-2	-0.7
1889	Ind-N	18	22	.450	45	44	36	0	1	349	395	256	27	9	100	139	13.0	4.54	92	.277	.328	25	.180	2	-20	-14	-3	-1.2
1890	Bos-N	23	17	.575	40	40	39	4	0	350	342	201	5	3	82	140	11.0	3.19	118	.248	.292	34	.231	5	15	21	-2	2.1
1891	Bos-N	4	5	.444	11	9	7	0	0	89	112	62	4	0	23	29	13.7	3.84	95	.296	.337	7	.171	1	-5	-2	1	0.0
	Cle-N	0	1	.000	1	1	1	0	0	9	12	9	1	0	4	4	16.0	8.00	43	.308	.372	0	.000	-1	-5	-4	-1	-0.4
	Yr	4	6	.400	12	10	8	0	0	98	124	71	5	0	27	33	13.9	4.22	86	.297	.340	7	.156	0	-10	-6	0	-0.4
1892	StL-N	5	8	.385	13	13	12	0	0	108	159	87	5	6	31	32	16.3	5.67	56	.329	.377	9	.200	0	-29	-31	-1	-2.8
Total	9	145	139	.511	296	292	277	11	1	2539^2	2776	1555	95	28	602	1070	11.7	3.46	99	.267	.302	219	.205	8	-17	-9	-13	-1.7
● RUBE GEYER Geyer, Jacob Bowman b: 3/26/1884, Allegheny, Pa. d: 10/12/62, Ford Township, Minn. BR/TR, 5'10", 170 lbs. Deb: 4/24/10																												
1910	StL-N	0	1	.000	4	0	0	0	0	4	5	3	0	0	3	5	18.0	4.50	66	.294	.400	0	.000	-0	-1	-1	-0	-0.2
1911	StL-N	9	6	.600	29	11	7	1	0	148^2	141	80	7	6	56	46	12.3	3.27	103	.259	.335	13	.228	1	2	2	-1	0.1
1912	StL-N	7	14	.333	41	18	5	0	0	181	191	110	4	4	84	61	13.9	3.28	104	.288	.371	11	.208	-0	3	3	0	0.3
1913	StL-N	1	5	.167	30	4	2	0	1	78^2	83	57	6	2	38	21	14.1	5.26	61	.282	.368	2	.091	-2	-18	-18	-1	-1.5
Total	4	17	26	.395	104	33	14	1	1	412^1	420	250	17	12	181	133	13.4	3.67	92	.276	.358	26	.195	-1	-14	-14	-2	-1.3
● TONY GHELFI Ghelfi, Anthony Paul b: 8/23/61, LaCrosse, Wis. BR/TR, 6'3", 185 lbs. Deb: 9/1/83																												
1983	Phi-N	1	1	.500	3	3	0	0	0	14^1	15	5	2	0	6	14	13.2	3.14	114	.268	.339	1	.250	0	1	1	1	0.2
● BOB GIALLOMBARDO Giallombardo, Robert Paul b: 5/20/37, Brooklyn, N.Y. BL/TL, 6', 175 lbs. Deb: 6/21/58																												
1958	LA-N	1	1	.500	6	5	0	0	0	26^1	29	14	3	0	15	14	15.0	3.76	109	.284	.376	1	.167	-0	1	1	0	0.1
● JOE GIARD Giard, Joseph Oscar "Peco" b: 10/7/1898, Ware, Mass. d: 7/10/56, Worcester, Mass. BL/TL, 5'10.5", 170 lbs. Deb: 4/18/25																												
1925	StL-A	10	5	.667	30	21	9	4	0	160^2	179	96	13	5	87	43	15.2	5.04	93	.295	.388	3	.057	-6	-12	-6	2	-0.9
1926	StL-A	3	10	.231	22	15	2	0	0	90	113	81	7	1	67	18	18.1	7.00	61	.318	.428	8	.276	0	-30	-25	-1	-3.0
1927	NY-A	0	0	—	16	0	0	0	0	27	38	25	1	0	19	10	19.0	8.00	48	.352	.449	2	.286	0	-12	-13	-0	-0.6
Total	3	13	15	.464	68	36	11	4	0	277^2	330	202	21	6	173	71	16.5	5.96	75	.309	.408	13	.146	-6	-53	-44	1	-4.5
● JOE GIBBON Gibbon, Joseph Charles b: 4/10/35, Hickory, Miss. BR/TL, 6'4", 210 lbs. Deb: 4/17/60																												
1960	*Pit-N	4	2	.667	27	9	0	0	0	80^1	87	40	5	0	31	60	13.2	4.03	93	.277	.342	4	.211	1	-2	-3	0	-0.1
1961	Pit-N	13	10	.565	30	29	7	3	0	195^1	185	85	16	4	57	145	11.3	3.32	120	.251	.309	8	.136	-2	16	15	-0	1.4
1962	Pit-N	3	4	.429	19	8	0	0	0	57	53	29	4	0	24	26	12.2	3.63	108	.250	.326	3	.176	-0	2	2	1	0.3
1963	Pit-N	5	12	.294	37	22	5	0	1	147^1	147	61	7	5	54	110	12.6	3.30	100	.258	.328	4	.093	-2	-0	-0	1	-0.1
1964	Pit-N	10	7	.588	28	24	3	0	0	146^2	145	66	10	6	54	97	12.6	3.68	95	.262	.334	12	.255	3	-2	-3	1	0.1
1965	Pit-N	4	9	.308	31	15	1	0	1	105^2	85	57	7	4	34	63	10.5	4.51	78	.221	.291	3	.115	-0	-11	-12	0	-1.4
1966	SF-N	4	6	.400	37	10	1	0	1	81	86	41	4	2	16	48	11.6	3.67	100	.275	.314	3	.200	0	-1	0	1	0.2

YEAR	TM/L	W	L	PCT	G	GS	CG	SH	SV	IP	H	R	HR	HB	BB	SO	RAT	ERA	ERA+	OAV	OOB	BH	AVG	PB	PR	PR+	PD	TPI
1967	SF-N	6	2	.750	28	10	3	1	1	82	65	31	4	3	33	63	11.1	3.07	107	.220	.305	1	.042	-1	3	2	2	0.3
1968	SF-N	1	2	.333	29	0	0	0	1	40	33	10	3	2	19	22	12.1	1.57	187	.234	.333	0	.000	-0	6	6	0	0.5
1969	SF-N	1	3	.250	16	0	0	0	2	20	15	10	1	1	13	9	13.0	3.60	97	.211	.341	0	.000	-0	-0	-0	1	0.0
	Pit-N	5	1	.833	35	0	0	0	9	51^1	38	14	5	2	17	35	10.0	1.93	181	.208	.282	0	.000	-1	10	9	1	1.4
	Yr	6	4	.600	51	0	0	0	11	71^1	53	24	6	3	30	44	10.9	2.40	146	.209	.300	0	.000	-1	10	9	2	1.4
1970	*Pit-N	0	1	.000	41	0	0	0	5	41	44	25	2	2	24	26	15.4	4.83	81	.280	.383	0	.000	-0	-4	-4	0	-0.2
1971	Cin-N	5	6	.455	50	0	0	0	11	64^1	54	25	3	1	32	34	12.2	2.94	114	.239	.336	0	.000	-0	4	3	1	0.8
1972	Cin-N	0	0	—	2	0	0	0	0	0^1	3	2	1	0	1	1	108.0	54.00	6	.750	.800	0	—	0	-2	-2	0	-0.1
	Hou-N	0	0	—	9	0	0	0	0	7^1	13	9	2	1	5	4	23.3	9.82	34	.394	.487	0	—	0	-5	-5	1	-0.2
	Yr	0	0	—	11	0	0	0	0	7^2	16	11	3	1	6	5	27.0	11.74	29	.432	.523	0	—	0	-7	-7	1	-0.3
Total	13	61	65	.484	419	127	20	4	32	1119^2	1053	505	74	33	414	743	12.1	3.52	102	.251	.323	38	.144	-3	12	8	11	2.9

● NORWOOD GIBSON

Gibson, Norwood Ringold "Gibby" b: 3/11/1877, Peoria, Ill. d: 7/7/59, Peoria, Ill. BR/TR, 5'10", 165 lbs. Deb: 4/29/03

YEAR	TM/L	W	L	PCT	G	GS	CG	SH	SV	IP	H	R	HR	HB	BB	SO	RAT	ERA	ERA+	OAV	OOB	BH	AVG	PB	PR	PR+	PD	TPI
1903	Bos-A	13	9	.591	24	21	17	2	0	183^1	166	95	2	7	65	76	11.7	3.19	95	.241	.313	17	.266	5	-5	-3	0	0.1
1904	Bos-A	17	14	.548	33	32	29	1	0	273	216	111	8	4	81	112	9.9	2.21	121	.219	.281	6	.065	-6	12	14	-3	0.5
1905	Bos-A	4	7	.364	23	17	9	0	0	134	118	77	9	5	55	67	12.0	3.69	73	.238	.321	4	.095	-2	-15	-15	-2	-1.6
1906	Bos-A	0	2	.000	5	2	1	0	0	18^2	25	21	2	0	7	3	15.4	5.30	52	.325	.381	1	.200	0	-5	-5	-0	-0.5
Total	4	34	32	.515	85	72	56	3	0	609	525	304	21	16	208	258	11.1	2.93	95	.233	.303	28	.138	-4	-14	-9	-5	-1.5

● PAUL GIBSON

Gibson, Paul Marshall b: 1/4/60, Southampton, N.Y. BR/TL, 6', 185 lbs. Deb: 4/8/88

YEAR	TM/L	W	L	PCT	G	GS	CG	SH	SV	IP	H	R	HR	HB	BB	SO	RAT	ERA	ERA+	OAV	OOB	BH	AVG	PB	PR	PR+	PD	TPI
1988	Det-A	4	2	.667	40	1	0	0	0	92	83	33	6	2	34	50	11.6	2.93	130	.240	.312	0	—	0	11	9	0	0.6
1989	Det-A	4	8	.333	45	13	0	0	0	132	129	71	11	6	57	77	13.1	4.64	82	.259	.342	0	—	0	-11	-12	-0	-1.0
1990	Det-A	5	4	.556	61	0	0	0	3	97^1	99	36	10	1	44	56	13.3	3.05	130	.269	.349	0	—	0	9	10	0	0.9
1991	Det-A	5	7	.417	68	0	0	0	8	96	112	51	10	3	48	52	15.3	4.59	91	.297	.381	0	—	0	-5	-5	-0	-0.6
1992	NY-N	0	1	.000	43	1	0	0	0	62	70	37	7	0	25	49	13.8	5.23	67	.287	.353	0	.000	-0	-12	-12	-1	-0.8
1993	NY-N	1	1	.500	8	0	0	0	0	8^2	14	6	1	0	2	12	16.6	5.19	77	.350	.381	0	—	0	-1	-1	0	-0.2
	NY-A	2	0	1.000	20	0	0	0	0	35^1	31	15	4	0	9	25	10.2	3.06	136	.238	.288	0	—	0	5	5	0	0.2
1994	NY-A	1	1	.500	30	0	0	0	0	29	26	17	5	1	17	21	13.7	4.97	92	.236	.344	0	—	0	-1	-1	0	-0.1
1996	NY-A	0	0	—	4	0	0	0	0	4^1	6	3	1	0	0	3	12.5	6.23	79	.316	.316	0	—	0	-1	-1	0	0.0
Total	8	22	24	.478	319	15	0	0	11	556^2	570	269	55	13	236	345	13.2	4.07	97	.267	.344	0	.000	-0	-5	-8	-1	-1.0

● BOB GIBSON

Gibson, Robert (b: Pack Robert Gibson) b: 11/9/35, Omaha, Neb. BR/TR, 6'1.5", 195 lbs. Deb: 4/15/59 CH

YEAR	TM/L	W	L	PCT	G	GS	CG	SH	SV	IP	H	R	HR	HB	BB	SO	RAT	ERA	ERA+	OAV	OOB	BH	AVG	PB	PR	PR+	PD	TPI
1959	StL-N	3	5	.375	13	9	2	1	0	75^2	77	35	4	1	39	48	13.9	3.33	127	.273	.363	3	.115	-1	5	7	-0	0.6
1960	StL-N	3	6	.333	27	12	2	0	0	86^2	97	61	7	1	48	69	15.2	5.61	73	.284	.374	5	.179	-0	-18	-13	1	-1.2
1961	StL-N	13	12	.520	35	27	10	2	1	211^1	186	91	13	6	119	166	13.2	3.24	136	.239	.344	13	.197	2	19	25	1	3.0
1962	StL-N★	15	13	.536	32	30	15	**5**	1	233^2	174	84	15	10	95	208	10.7	2.85	**150**	.204	.291	20	.263	6	28	34	1	**4.7**
1963	StL-N	18	9	.667	36	33	14	2	0	254^2	224	110	19	13	96	204	11.8	3.39	105	.233	.311	18	.207	7	-3	4	-2	1.0
1964	*StL-N	19	12	.613	40	36	17	2	1	287^1	250	106	25	9	86	245	10.8	3.01	127	.232	.294	15	.156	1	17	24	-1	2.5
1965	StL-N★	20	12	.625	38	36	20	6	1	299	243	110	34	11	103	270	10.7	3.07	125	.222	.295	25	.240	8	16	24	-2	3.3
1966	StL-N†	21	12	.636	35	35	20	**5**	0	280^1	210	90	20	5	78	225	9.4	2.44	147	.207	.267	20	.200	3	36	36	-1	4.5
1967	*StL-N★	13	7	.650	24	24	10	2	0	175^1	151	62	10	3	40	147	10.0	2.98	110	.231	.278	8	.133	1	8	6	0	0.8
1968	*StL-N☆	22	9	.710	34	34	28	**13**	0	304^2	198	49	11	7	62	**268**	**7.9**	**1.12**	**258**	**.184**	**.233**	16	.170	4	**63**	**62**	-3	**7.6**
1969	StL-N★	20	13	.606	35	35	**28**	4	0	314	251	84	12	10	95	269	10.2	2.18	164	.219	.285	29	.246	8	49	**49**	-2	**6.1**
1970	StL-N★	**23**	7	**.767**	34	34	23	3	0	294	262	111	13	4	88	274	10.8	3.12	132	.237	.296	33	.303	12	30	32	-1	4.3
1971	StL-N	16	13	.552	31	31	20	**5**	0	245^2	215	96	14	7	76	185	10.9	3.04	119	.232	.296	15	.172	2	12	15	0	2.0
1972	StL-N★	19	11	.633	34	34	23	4	0	278	226	83	14	3	88	208	10.3	2.46	138	.224	.288	20	.194	7	31	30	2	4.3
1973	StL-N	12	10	.545	25	25	13	1	0	195	159	71	12	3	57	142	10.1	2.77	132	.224	.284	12	.185	2	19	19	-1	2.3
1974	StL-N	11	13	.458	33	33	9	1	0	240	236	111	24	5	104	129	12.9	3.83	94	.259	.338	17	.210	3	-5	-6	-1	-0.5
1975	StL-N	3	10	.231	22	14	1	0	2	109	120	66	10	4	62	60	15.4	5.04	75	.287	.384	5	.179	0	-17	-15	-0	-1.6
Total	17	251	174	.591	528	482	255	56	6	3884^1	3279	1420	257	102	1336	3117	10.9	2.91	127	.228	.299	274	.206	65	291	326	-10	43.7

● BOB GIBSON

Gibson, Robert Louis b: 6/19/57, Philadelphia, Pa. BR/TR, 6', 195 lbs. Deb: 4/13/83

YEAR	TM/L	W	L	PCT	G	GS	CG	SH	SV	IP	H	R	HR	HB	BB	SO	RAT	ERA	ERA+	OAV	OOB	BH	AVG	PB	PR	PR+	PD	TPI
1983	Mil-A	3	4	.429	27	7	0	0	2	80^2	71	40	6	1	46	46	13.2	3.90	96	.237	.340	0	—	0	2	-2	-1	-0.2
1984	Mil-A	2	5	.286	18	9	1	1	0	69	61	43	10	0	47	54	14.1	4.96	78	.236	.354	0	—	0	-7	-9	0	-0.7
1985	Mil-A	6	7	.462	41	1	0	0	11	92^1	86	44	10	1	49	53	13.3	3.90	107	.260	.357	0	—	0	3	3	-0	0.4
1986	Mil-A	1	2	.333	11	1	0	0	0	26^2	23	18	3	0	23	11	15.5	4.73	92	.232	.377	0	—	0	-2	-1	-0	-0.1
1987	NY-N	0	0	—	1	0	0	0	0	1	0	0	0	0	1	2	9.0	0.00	—	.000	.250	0	—	0	0	0	0	0.0
Total	5	12	18	.400	98	18	1	1	13	269^2	241	145	29	2	166	166	13.7	4.24	94	.243	.353	0	—	0	-4	-8	-1	-0.6

● ROBERT GIBSON

Gibson, Robert Murray b: 8/20/1869, Duncansville, Pa. d: 12/19/49, Pittsburgh, Pa. BR/TR, 6'3", 185 lbs. Deb: 6/4/1890

YEAR	TM/L	W	L	PCT	G	GS	CG	SH	SV	IP	H	R	HR	HB	BB	SO	RAT	ERA	ERA+	OAV	OOB	BH	AVG	PB	PR	PR+	PD	TPI
1890	Chi-N	1	0	1.000	1	1	1	0	0	9	6	1	0	0	2	1	8.0	0.00	—	.182	.229	0	.000	-0	4	4	0	0.3
	Pit-N	0	3	.000	3	3	2	0	0	12	24	38	0	3	23	3	37.5	17.25	19	.400	.581	3	.231	-0	-18	-20	-1	-2.5
	Yr	1	3	.250	4	4	3	0	0	21	30	39	0	3	25	4	24.9	9.86	35	.323	.479	3	.176	-1	-15	-15	-0	-2.2

● SAM GIBSON

Gibson, Samuel Braxton b: 8/5/1899, King, N.C. d: 1/31/83, High Point, N.C. BL/TR, 6'2", 198 lbs. Deb: 4/19/26

YEAR	TM/L	W	L	PCT	G	GS	CG	SH	SV	IP	H	R	HR	HB	BB	SO	RAT	ERA	ERA+	OAV	OOB	BH	AVG	PB	PR	PR+	PD	TPI
1926	Det-A	12	9	.571	35	24	16	2	2	196^1	199	94	6	6	75	61	12.8	3.48	117	.269	.341	18	.250	2	12	12	0	1.4
1927	Det-A	11	12	.478	33	26	11	0	0	184^2	201	113	9	8	86	76	14.4	3.80	111	.285	.369	14	.212	-1	7	8	-1	0.6
1928	Det-A	5	8	.385	20	18	5	1	0	119^2	155	83	4	7	52	29	16.1	5.42	76	.322	.396	12	.286	2	-18	-17	-1	-1.5
1930	NY-A	0	1	.000	2	2	0	0	0	6	14	11	1	0	6	3	30.0	15.00	29	.424	.513	1	.333	0	-7	-8	0	-0.8
1932	NY-N	4	8	.333	41	5	1	1	3	81^2	107	51	7	2	30	39	15.3	4.85	77	.322	.382	5	.263	0	-9	-11	-1	-1.5
Total	5	32	38	.457	131	75	33	4	5	588^1	676	352	27	23	249	208	14.5	4.28	95	.295	.370	50	.248	3	-15	-14	-3	-1.8

● GEORGE GICK

Gick, George Edward b: 10/18/15, Dunnington, Ind. BB/TR, 6', 190 lbs. Deb: 10/3/37

YEAR	TM/L	W	L	PCT	G	GS	CG	SH	SV	IP	H	R	HR	HB	BB	SO	RAT	ERA	ERA+	OAV	OOB	BH	AVG	PB	PR	PR+	PD	TPI
1937	Chi-A	0	0	—	1	0	0	0	1	2	0	0	0	0	0	1	0.0	0.00	—	.000	.000	0	—	0	1	1	-0	0.1
1938	Chi-A	0	0	—	1	0	0	0	0	1	0	0	0	1	0	1	9.0	0.00	—	.000	.250	0	—	0	1	1	0	0.0
Total	2	0	0	—	2	0	0	0	1	3	0	0	0	1	0	2	3.0	0.00	—	.000	.100	0	—	0	2	2	-0	0.1

● BRETT GIDEON

Gideon, Byron Brett b: 8/8/63, Ozona, Tex. BR/TR, 6'2", 200 lbs. Deb: 7/5/87

YEAR	TM/L	W	L	PCT	G	GS	CG	SH	SV	IP	H	R	HR	HB	BB	SO	RAT	ERA	ERA+	OAV	OOB	BH	AVG	PB	PR	PR+	PD	TPI
1987	Pit-N	1	5	.167	29	0	0	0	3	36^2	34	22	6	1	10	31	11.0	4.66	88	.243	.298	1	1.000	1	-2	-2	-0	-0.3
1989	Mon-N	0	0	—	4	0	0	0	0	4^2	5	1	1	0	5	2	19.3	1.93	183	.294	.455	0	—	0	1	1	-0	0.0
1990	Mon-N	0	0	—	1	0	0	0	0	1	2	1	0	0	4	0	54.0	9.00	41	.500	.750	0	—	0	-1	-1	0	0.0
Total	3	1	5	.167	34	0	0	0	3	42^1	41	24	7	1	19	33	13.0	4.46	90	.255	.337	1	1.000	1	-2	-2	-0	-0.3

● JIM GIDEON

Gideon, James Leslie b: 9/26/53, Taylor, Tex. BR/TR, 6'3", 190 lbs. Deb: 9/14/75

YEAR	TM/L	W	L	PCT	G	GS	CG	SH	SV	IP	H	R	HR	HB	BB	SO	RAT	ERA	ERA+	OAV	OOB	BH	AVG	PB	PR	PR+	PD	TPI
1975	Tex-A	0	0	—	1	1	0	0	0	5^2	7	6	1	0	5	2	19.1	7.94	47	.292	.414	0	—	0	-3	-3	-0	-0.1

● FLOYD GIEBELL

Giebell, Floyd George b: 12/10/09, Pennsboro, W.Va. BL/TR, 6'2.5", 172 lbs. Deb: 4/21/39

YEAR	TM/L	W	L	PCT	G	GS	CG	SH	SV	IP	H	R	HR	HB	BB	SO	RAT	ERA	ERA+	OAV	OOB	BH	AVG	PB	PR	PR+	PD	TPI
1939	Det-A	1	1	.500	9	0	0	0	0	15^1	19	7	1	0	12	9	18.2	2.93	167	.317	.431	0	.000	-0	3	3	-0	0.3
1940	Det-A	2	0	1.000	2	2	2	1	0	18	14	2	2	0	4	11	9.0	1.00	476	.206	.250	0	.000	-1	7	7	-0	0.7
1941	Det-A	0	0	—	17	2	0	0	0	34^1	45	29	3	0	26	10	18.6	6.03	75	.313	.418	2	.333	0	-7	-5	-0	-0.2
Total	3	3	1	.750	28	4	2	1	0	67^2	78	38	6	0	42	30	16.0	3.99	117	.287	.382	2	.143	-1	2	5	-1	0.8

● PAUL GIEL

Giel, Paul Robert b: 2/29/32, Winona, Minn. BR/TR, 5'11", 185 lbs. Deb: 7/10/54

YEAR	TM/L	W	L	PCT	G	GS	CG	SH	SV	IP	H	R	HR	HB	BB	SO	RAT	ERA	ERA+	OAV	OOB	BH	AVG	PB	PR	PR+	PD	TPI
1954	NY-N	0	0	—	6	0	0	0	0	4^1	8	4	0	0	2	4	20.8	8.31	49	.421	.476	0	—	0	-2	-2	-0	-0.1
1955	NY-N	4	4	.500	34	2	0	0	0	82^1	70	36	8	2	50	47	13.3	3.39	119	.233	.346	1	.053	-2	6	6	-1	0.3
1958	SF-N	4	5	.444	29	9	0	0	0	92	89	56	12	2	55	55	14.3	4.70	81	.259	.365	2	.074	-2	-8	-9	1	-0.9
1959	Pit-N	0	0	—	4	0	0	0	0	7^2	17	12	0	0	6	3	27.0	14.09	27	.472	.548	0	—	0	-9	-9	0	-0.4
1960	Pit-N	2	0	1.000	16	0	0	0	0	33	35	25	3	0	15	21	13.6	5.73	65	.276	.352	0	.000	-1	-7	-7	-1	-0.5
1961	Min-A	1	0	1.000	12	0	0	0	0	19^1	24	27	6	0	17	14	19.1	9.78	43	.289	.410	1	.500	0	-12	-11	0	-0.5
	KC-A	0	0	—	1	0	0	0	0	1^2	6	7	1	0	3	1	48.6	37.80	11	.600	.692	0	—	0	-6	-6	-0	-0.3
	Yr	1	0	1.000	13	0	0	0	0	21	30	34	7	0	20	15	21.4	12.00	35	.323	.442	1	.500	0	-19	-17	0	-0.8
Total	6	11	9	.550	102	11	0	0	0	240^1	249	167	30	4	148	145	15.0	5.39	73	.271	.374	4	.073	-4	-38	-40	-0	-2.4

YEAR	TM/L	W	L	PCT	G	GS	CG	SH	SV	IP	H	R	HR	HB	BB	SO	RAT	ERA	ERA+	OAV	OOB	BH	AVG	PB	PR	PR+	PD	TPI
● **BOB GIGGIE** Giggie, Robert Thomas b: 8/13/33, Dorchester, Mass. BR/TR, 6'1", 200 lbs. Deb: 4/18/59																												
1959	Mil-N	1	0	1.000	13	0	0	0	1	20	24	10	2	0	10	15	15.3	4.05	87	.316	.395	0	.000	-0	-0	-1	1	0.0
1960	Mil-N	0	0	—	3	0	0	0	0	4^1	5	2	0	0	4	5	18.7	4.15	83	.278	.409	0	—	0	-0	-0	-0	0.0
	KC-A	1	0	1.000	10	0	0	0	0	18^2	24	12	1	0	15	8	18.8	5.79	69	.333	.448	0	.000	-0	-4	-4	0	-0.2
1962	KC-A	1	1	.500	4	2	0	0	0	14^1	17	11	5	1	3	4	13.2	6.28	67	.293	.339	0	.000	-0	-4	-3	-1	-0.5
Total	3	3	1	.750	30	2	0	0	1	57^1	70	35	8	1	32	32	16.2	5.18	74	.313	.401	0	.000	-1	-8	-9	0	-0.7
● **BILL GILBERT** Gilbert, Alfred Gideon b: 3/13/1868, Havre De Grace, Md 6', 180 lbs. Deb: 9/15/1892																												
1892	Bal-N	0	1	.000	2	1	1	0	0	14	14	15	1	0	17	5	19.9	5.79	59	.250	.425	2	.333	1	-4	-4	-1	-0.2
● **JOE GILBERT** Gilbert, Joe Dennis b: 4/20/52, Jasper, Tex. BR/TL, 6'1", 167 lbs. Deb: 4/30/72																												
1972	Mon-N	0	1	.000	22	0	0	0	0	33	41	31	3	0	18	25	16.1	8.45	42	.306	.388	0	.000	-0	-18	-17	-1	-1.0
1973	Mon-N	1	2	.333	21	0	0	0	1	29	30	18	1	0	19	17	15.2	4.97	77	.270	.377	0	.000	0	-4	-4	0	-0.4
Total	2	1	3	.250	43	0	0	0	1	62	71	49	4	0	37	42	15.7	6.82	54	.290	.383	0	.000	-0	-23	-21	-0	-1.4
● **BILL GILBRETH** Gilbreth, William Freeman b: 9/3/47, Abilene, Tex. BL/TL, 6', 180 lbs. Deb: 6/25/71																												
1971	Det-A	2	1	.667	9	5	2	0	0	30	28	17	4	2	21	14	15.3	4.80	75	.264	.395	2	.182	-0	-4	-4	0	-0.3
1972	Det-A	0	0	—	2	0	0	0	0	5	10	9	1	0	4	2	25.2	16.20	19	.476	.560	0	.000	-0	-7	-7	0	-0.4
1974	Cal-A	0	0	—	3	0	0	0	0	1^1	2	2	0	0	1	0	20.3	13.50	26	.400	.500	0	—	0	-1	-2	0	-0.1
Total	3	2	1	.667	14	5	2	0	0	36^1	40	28	5	2	26	16	16.8	6.69	53	.303	.425	2	.167	-0	-13	-12	0	-0.8
● **BOB GILKS** Gilks, Robert James b: 7/2/1864, Cincinnati, Ohio d: 8/21/44, Brunswick, Ga. BR/TR, 5'8", 178 lbs. Deb: 8/25/1887 ♦																												
1887	Cle-a	7	5	.583	13	13	12	1	0	108	146	66	1	9	42	28	12.9	3.08	141	.313	.326	29	.337	2	15	15	2	1.6
1888	Cle-a	0	2	.000	4	2	2	0	1	21	26	23	1	1	8	3	15.0	8.14	38	.292	.357	111	.229	0	-12	-12	-0	-0.9
1890	Cle-N	2	2	.500	4	3	3	0	0	31^2	34	17	0	4	9	5	13.4	4.26	84	.266	.333	116	.213	-0	-2	-2	-1	-0.3
Total	3	9	9	.500	21	18	17	1	1	160^2	206	106	2	14	59	36	13.3	3.98	101	.302	.332	323	.233	2	0	1	1	0.4
● **ED GILL** Gill, Edward James b: 8/7/1895, Somerville, Mass. d: 10/10/95, Brockton, Mass. BL/TR, 5'10", 165 lbs. Deb: 7/5/19																												
1919	Was-A	1	1	.500	16	2	0	0	0	37^1	38	25	0	2	21	7	14.7	4.82	67	.260	.361	0	.000	-1	-7	-7	-1	-0.5
● **GEORGE GILL** Gill, George Lloyd b: 2/13/09, Catchings, Miss. d: 2/21/99, Jackson, Miss. BR/TR, 6'1", 185 lbs. Deb: 5/4/37																												
1937	Det-A	11	4	.733	31	10	4	1	1	127^2	146	74	11	1	42	40	13.3	4.51	104	.285	.340	7	.140	-3	2	2	1	0.1
1938	Det-A	12	9	.571	24	23	13	1	0	164	195	82	15	2	50	30	13.6	4.12	121	.296	.348	6	.105	-4	12	15	-1	1.2
1939	Det-A	0	1	.000	3	1	0	0	0	8^2	14	8	1	0	3	1	17.7	8.31	59	.368	.415	0	.000	-0	-4	-3	0	-0.3
	StL-A	1	12	.077	27	11	5	0	0	95	139	89	10	3	34	24	16.7	7.11	68	.343	.398	4	.154	-2	-26	-22	1	-2.5
	Yr	1	13	.071	30	12	5	0	0	103^2	153	97	11	3	37	25	16.8	7.21	68	.345	.400	4	.143	-2	-30	-26	1	-2.8
Total	3	24	26	.480	85	45	22	2	1	395^1	494	253	37	6	129	95	14.3	5.05	96	.306	.360	17	.126	-9	-16	-8	2	-1.5
● **HADDIE GILL** Gill, Harold Edward b: 1/23/1899, Brockton, Mass. d: 8/1/32, Brockton, Mass. BL/TL, 5'11", 165 lbs. Deb: 8/16/23																												
1923	Cin-N	0	0	—	1	0	0	0	0	1	1	0	0	0	1	1	18.0	0.00	—	.333	.500	0	—	0	0	0	0	0.0
● **CLARAL GILLENWATER** Gillenwater, Claral Lewis b: 5/20/1900, Sims, Ind. d: 2/26/78, Bradenton, Fla. BR/TR, 6', 187 lbs. Deb: 8/20/23																												
1923	Chi-A	1	3	.250	5	3	1	1	0	21^1	28	15	2	1	6	2	14.8	5.48	72	.337	.389	0	.000	-1	-4	-4	0	-0.6
● **TOM GILLES** Gilles, Thomas Bradford b: 7/2/62, Peoria, Ill. BR/TR, 6'1", 185 lbs. Deb: 6/7/90																												
1990	Tor-A	1	0	1.000	2	0	0	0	0	1^1	2	1	0	0	0	1	13.5	6.75	59	.333	.333	0	—	0	-0	-0	0	-0.1
● **DUKE GILLESPIE** Gillespie, John Patrick "Silent John" b: 2/25/1900, Oakland, Cal. d: 2/15/54, Vallejo, Cal. BR/TR, 5'11.5", 172 lbs. Deb: 4/12/22																												
1922	Cin-N	3	3	.500	31	4	1	0	0	77^2	84	43	2	4	29	21	13.6	4.52	88	.294	.367	2	.133	-1	-4	-5	1	-0.3
● **BOB GILLESPIE** Gillespie, Robert William "Bunch" b: 10/8/18, Columbus, Ohio BR/TR, 6'4", 187 lbs. Deb: 5/11/44																												
1944	Det-A	0	1	.000	7	0	0	0	0	11	7	8	0	0	12	4	15.5	6.55	54	.194	.396	0	.000	-0	-4	-4	0	-0.3
1947	Chi-A	5	8	.385	25	17	1	0	0	118	133	71	4	1	53	36	14.3	4.73	77	.291	.366	2	.061	-3	-13	-14	3	-1.4
1948	Chi-A	0	4	.000	25	6	1	0	0	72	81	45	3	1	33	19	14.4	5.13	83	.287	.364	0	.000	-2	-7	-7	-0	-0.6
1950	Bos-A	0	0	—	1	0	0	0	0	1^1	2	3	1	0	4	0	40.5	20.25	24	.333	.600	0	—	0	-2	-2	-0	-0.1
Total	4	5	13	.278	58	23	2	0	0	202^1	223	127	8	2	102	59	14.5	5.07	76	.286	.369	2	.039	-5	-26	-27	3	-2.4
● **PAUL GILLIFORD** Gilliford, Paul Gant "Gorilla" b: 1/12/45, Bryn Mawr, Pa. BR/TL, 5'11", 210 lbs. Deb: 9/20/67																												
1967	Bal-A	0	0	—	2	0	0	0	0	3	6	4	1	0	1	2	21.0	12.00	26	.429	.467	0	—	0	-3	-3	0	-0.1
● **JACK GILLIGAN** Gilligan, John Patrick b: 10/18/1884, Chicago, Ill. d: 11/19/80, Modesto, Cal. BB/TR, 6', 190 lbs. Deb: 9/16/09																												
1909	StL-A	1	2	.333	3	3	3	0	0	23	28	19	1	2	9	4	15.3	5.48	44	.315	.390	1	.111	-1	-8	-8	-1	-1.0
1910	StL-A	0	3	.000	9	5	2	0	0	39^1	37	21	0	1	28	10	15.1	3.66	68	.253	.377	3	.200	-0	-5	-5	0	-0.4
Total	2	1	5	.167	12	8	5	0	0	62^1	65	40	1	3	37	14	15.2	4.33	57	.277	.382	4	.167	-1	-13	-13	-0	-1.4
● **GEORGE GILLPATRICK** Gillpatrick, George F. b: 2/28/1875, Holden, Mo. d: 12/15/41, Kansas City, Mo. Deb: 5/22/1898																												
1898	StL-N	0	2	.000	7	3	1	0	0	35	42	38	0	2	19	12	16.2	6.94	55	.296	.387	2	.125	-2	-13	-12	-1	-0.7
● **FRANK GILMORE** Gilmore, Frank T. "Shadow" b: 4/27/1864, Webster, Mass. d: 7/21/29, Hartford, Conn. BR, Deb: 9/11/1886																												
1886	Was-N	4	4	.500	9	9	9	1	0	75	57	35	3		22	75	9.5	2.52	130	.200	.257	0	.000	-4	7	6	-1	0.1
1887	Was-N	7	20	.259	28	27	27	1	0	234^2	339	172	7	13	92	114	13.5	3.87	105	.328	.336	13	.130	-11	5	5	-3	-0.8
1888	Was-N	1	9	.100	12	11	10	0	0	95^2	131	101	4	7	29	23	15.7	6.59	43	.323	.378	1	.024	-5	-40	-41	-2	-3.8
Total	3	12	33	.267	49	47	46	2	0	405^1	527	308	14	20	143	212	13.3	4.26	85	.306	.333	14	.082	-20	-28	-29	-6	-4.5
● **LEN GILMORE** Gilmore, Leonard Preston "Meow" b: 11/3/17, Fairview Park, Ind. BR/TR, 6'3", 175 lbs. Deb: 10/1/44																												
1944	Pit-N	0	1	.000	1	1	1	0	0	8	13	7	2	0	0	0	14.6	7.88	47	.361	.361	0	.000	-0	-4	-4	1	-0.3
● **JOHN GILROY** Gilroy, John M. b: 10/26/1869, Washington, D.C. d: 8/4/1897, Norfolk, Va. Deb: 8/30/1895																												
1895	Was-N	1	4	.200	8	4	2	0	0	41^1	63	48	3	4	24	2	19.8	6.53	73	.344	.431	7	.241	-1	-8	-8	1	-0.7
1896	Was-N	0	0	—	1	0	0	0	0	2	0	0	0	0	1	0	4.5	0.00	—	.000	.143	0	.000	-0	1	1	0	0.0
Total	2	1	4	.200	9	4	2	0	0	43^1	63	48	3	4	25	2	19.1	6.23	77	.333	.422	7	.233	-1	-7	-7	1	-0.7
● **HAL GILSON** Gilson, Harold "Lefty" b: 2/9/42, Los Angeles, Cal. BR/TL, 6'5", 195 lbs. Deb: 4/14/68																												
1968	StL-N	0	2	.000	13	0	0	0	2	21^2	27	11	1	0	11	19	15.8	4.57	63	.310	.388	0	.000	-0	-4	-4	-1	-0.6
	Hou-N	0	0	—	2	0	0	0	0	3^2	7	4	0	1	1	1	22.1	7.36	40	.412	.474	0	—	0	-2	-2	0	-0.1
	Yr	0	2	.000	15	0	0	0	2	25^1	34	15	1	1	12	20	16.7	4.97	58	.327	.402	0	.000	-0	-6	-6	-1	-0.7
● **BILLY GING** Ging, William Joseph b: 11/7/1872, Elmira, N.Y. d: 9/14/50, Elmira, N.Y. BR/TR, 5'10", 170 lbs. Deb: 9/25/1899																												
1899	Bos-N	1	0	1.000	1	1	1	0	0	8	5	1	0	0	5	2	11.3	1.13	369	.179	.303	0	.000	-0	2	2	-0	0.2
● **JOE GINGRAS** Gingras, Joseph Elzead John b: 1/10/1894, New York, N.Y. d: 9/6/47, Jersey City, N.J. BR/TR, 6'2", 188 lbs. Deb: 6/18/15																												
1915	KC-F	0	0	—	2	0	0	0	0	4	6	3	0	0	1	2	15.8	6.75	39	.353	.389	0	.000	-0	-2	-2	-0	-0.1
● **MATT GINTER** Ginter, Matthew Shane b: 12/24/77, Lexington, Ky. BR/TR, 6'2", 220 lbs. Deb: 9/1/2000																												
2000	Chi-A	1	0	1.000	7	0	0	0	0	9^1	18	14	5	0	7	6	24.1	13.50	37	.409	.490	0	—	0	-9	-9	-0	-0.7
● **ED GIOVANOLA** Giovanola, Edward Thomas b: 3/4/69, Los Gatos, Cal. BL/TR, 5'10", 170 lbs. Deb: 9/10/95 ♦																												
1999	SD-N	0	0	—	1	0	0	0	0	1^1	1	0	0	0	2	0	20.3	0.00	—	.200	.429	11	.190	0	1	1	0	0.0
● **CHARLIE GIRARD** Girard, Charles August b: 12/16/1884, Brooklyn, N.Y. d: 8/6/36, Brooklyn, N.Y. BR/TR, 5'10", 175 lbs. Deb: 9/14/10																												
1910	Phi-N	1	2	.333	7	1	0	0	1	26^2	33	26	2	2	12	11	15.9	6.41	49	.308	.388	1	.125	-0	-10	-9	-1	-1.1
● **DAVE GIUSTI** Giusti, David John b: 11/27/39, Seneca Falls, N.Y. BR/TR, 5'11", 195 lbs. Deb: 4/13/62																												
1962	Hou-N	2	3	.400	22	5	0	0	0	73^2	82	49	7	0	30	43	13.7	5.62	66	.280	.347	7	.292	3	-14	-16	1	-0.7

YEAR	TM/L	W	L	PCT	G	GS	CG	SH	SV	IP	H	R	HR	HB	BB	SO	RAT	ERA	ERA+	OAV	OOB	BH	AVG	PB	PR	PR+	PD	TPI
1964	Hou-N	0	0	—	8	0	0	0	0	25^{2}	24	10	1	0	8	16	11.2	3.16	108	.253	.311	2	.286	1	1	1	1	0.3
1965	Hou-N	8	7	.533	38	13	4	1	3	131^{1}	132	67	13	1	46	92	12.3	4.32	78	.259	.321	6	.171	2	-11	-15	1	-1.3
1966	Hou-N	15	14	.517	34	33	9	4	0	210	215	112	23	5	54	131	11.7	4.20	81	.260	.310	17	.230	5	-14	-19	-1	-2.0
1967	Hou-N	11	15	.423	37	33	8	1	1	221^{2}	231	114	20	3	58	157	11.9	4.18	79	.265	.313	13	.155	3	-20	-22	-2	-2.3
1968	Hou-N	11	14	.440	37	34	12	2	1	251	226	95	15	4	67	186	10.6	3.19	93	.239	.293	15	.183	2	-6	-7	3	-0.1
1969	StL-N	3	7	.300	22	12	2	1	0	99^{2}	96	46	7	1	37	62	12.1	3.61	99	.255	.323	5	.200	1	-0	-0	1	0.2
1970	*Pit-N	9	3	.750	66	1	0	0	26	103	98	38	7	0	39	85	12.0	3.06	128	.259	.328	3	.188	2	11	10	0	1.8
1971	*Pit-N	5	6	.455	58	0	0	0	**30**	86	79	31	5	1	31	55	11.6	2.93	116	.241	.308	1	.059	-1	5	4	-1	0.7
1972	*Pit-N	7	4	.636	54	0	0	0	22	74^{2}	59	18	3	0	20	54	9.5	1.93	172	.219	.273	0	.000	-1	13	12	1	2.6
1973	Pit-N★	9	2	.818	67	0	0	0	20	98^{2}	89	31	9	0	37	64	11.5	2.37	149	.241	.310	4	.308	1	14	13	-2	1.9
1974	*Pit-N	7	5	.583	64	2	0	0	12	105^{2}	101	43	2	0	40	53	12.0	3.32	104	.258	.327	1	.111	-0	4	2	1	0.3
1975	*Pit-N	5	4	.556	61	0	0	0	17	91^{2}	79	38	3	0	42	38	11.9	2.95	121	.237	.322	3	.300	1	7	6	0	1.0
1976	Pit-N	5	4	.556	40	0	0	0	6	58^{1}	59	31	5	0	27	24	13.3	4.32	81	.267	.347	0	.000	-0	-5	-5	0	-0.9
1977	Oak-A	3	3	.500	40	0	0	0	6	60^{1}	54	22	4	0	20	28	11.0	2.98	135	.245	.308	0	—	0	7	7	0	0.8
	Chi-N	0	2	.000	20	0	0	0	1	25^{1}	30	19	2	0	14	15	15.6	6.04	73	.297	.383	0	.000	-0	-6	-4	-0	-0.4
Total	15	100	93	.518	668	133	35	9	145	1716^{2}	1654	764	126	15	570	1103	11.7	3.60	95	.253	.315	77	.187	18	-14	-33	2	1.9
● **BRIAN GIVENS** Givens, Brian Allen b: 11/6/65, Lompoc, Cal. BR/TL, 6′6″, 220 lbs. Deb: 6/24/95																												
1995	Mil-A	5	7	.417	19	19	0	0	0	107^{1}	116	71	11	3	54	73	14.5	4.95	101	.275	.361	0	—	0	-3	0	-1	-0.1
1996	Mil-A	1	3	.250	4	4	0	0	0	14	32	22	3	0	7	10	25.1	12.86	40	.438	.488	0	—	0	-12	-11	-1	-1.7
Total	2	6	10	.375	23	23	0	0	0	121^{1}	148	93	14	3	61	83	15.7	5.86	86	.299	.379	0	—	0	-15	-11	-2	-1.8
● **DAN GLADDEN** Gladden, Clinton Daniel b: 7/7/57, San Jose, Cal. BR/TR, 5′11″, 180 lbs. Deb: 9/5/83 ◆																												
1988	Min-A	0	0	—	1	0	0	0	0	1	0	0	0	0	0	0	0.0	0.00	—	.000	.000	155	.269	0	0	0	0	0.0
1989	Min-A	0	0	—	1	0	0	0	0	1	2	1	0	0	1	0	27.0	9.00	46	.400	.500	136	.295	0	-1	-1	0	0.0
Total	2	0	0	—	2	0	0	0	0	2	2	1	0	0	1	0	13.5	4.50	91	.250	.333	1215	.270	1	-0	-0	0	0.0
● **FRED GLADDING** Gladding, Fred Earl b: 6/28/36, Flat Rock, Mich. BL/TR, 6′, 225 lbs. Deb: 7/1/61 C																												
1961	Det-A	1	0	1.000	8	0	0	0	0	16^{1}	18	7	1	2	11	11	17.1	3.31	124	.286	.408	0	.000	-0	1	1	-0	0.0
1962	Det-A	0	0	—	6	0	0	0	0	5	3	0	0	0	2	4	9.0	0.00	—	.176	.263	0	—	0	2	2	0	0.1
1963	Det-A	1	1	.500	22	0	0	0	7	27^{1}	19	6	1	0	14	24	10.9	1.98	189	.198	.300	0	.000	-0	5	5	0	0.7
1964	Det-A	7	4	.636	42	0	0	0	7	67^{1}	57	23	7	2	27	59	11.5	3.07	119	.233	.314	0	.000	-1	4	4	1	0.7
1965	Det-A	6	2	.750	46	0	0	0	5	70	63	22	6	4	29	43	12.3	2.83	123	.239	.323	0	.000	-1	5	5	-1	0.5
1966	Det-A	5	0	1.000	51	0	0	0	2	74	62	33	6	1	29	57	11.2	3.28	106	.230	.307	0	.000	-0	1	2	-1	0.0
1967	Det-A	6	4	.600	42	1	0	0	12	77	62	20	6	4	19	64	9.9	1.99	164	.227	.287	0	.000	-2	11	11	-0	1.6
1968	Hou-N	0	0	—	7	0	0	0	2	4^{1}	8	7	0	1	3	2	24.9	14.54	20	.421	.522	0	—	0	-6	-6	-0	-0.6
1969	Hou-N	4	8	.333	57	0	0	0	**29**	72^{2}	83	39	2	1	27	40	13.7	4.21	84	.289	.352	1	.100	-1	-5	-5	0	-1.2
1970	Hou-N	7	4	.636	63	0	0	0	18	71	84	39	4	3	24	46	14.1	4.06	96	.293	.354	0	.000	-1	-0	-1	1	-0.2
1971	Hou-N	4	5	.444	48	0	0	0	12	51^{1}	51	17	0	7	22	17	14.0	2.10	160	.268	.365	0	.000	-0	8	7	-1	1.4
1972	Hou-N	5	6	.455	42	0	0	0	14	48^{2}	38	16	1	2	12	18	9.6	2.77	121	.222	.281	0	.000	-1	4	3	-1	0.5
1973	Hou-N	2	0	1.000	16	0	0	0	1	16	18	8	4	0	4	9	12.4	4.50	81	.290	.333	0	—	0	-1	-2	0	-0.2
Total	13	48	34	.585	450	1	0	0	109	601	566	237	38	27	223	394	12.2	3.13	113	.252	.327	1	.016	-6	29	28	-2	3.3
● **FRED GLADE** Glade, Frederick Monroe "Lucky" b: 1/25/1876, Dubuque, Iowa d: 11/21/34, Grand Island, Neb. BR/TR, 6′, 190 lbs. Deb: 5/27/02																												
1902	Chi-N	0	1	.000	1	1	1	0	0	8	13	11	0	1	3	3	19.1	9.00	30	.361	.425	1	.333	1	-6	-6	0	-0.5
1904	StL-A	18	15	.545	35	34	30	6	1	289	248	101	2	13	58	156	9.9	2.27	109	.233	.281	19	.186	1	10	7	1	1.1
1905	StL-A	6	25	.194	32	32	28	2	0	275	257	109	3	11	58	127	10.7	2.81	90	.249	.296	9	.092	-6	-5	-9	4	-1.2
1906	StL-A	15	14	.517	35	32	28	4	1	266^{2}	215	91	4	10	59	96	9.6	2.36	109	.224	.276	13	.137	-4	10	7	-3	0.0
1907	StL-A	13	9	.591	24	22	18	2	0	202	187	81	2	9	45	71	10.7	2.67	94	.248	.298	15	.205	2	-3	-4	-4	-0.6
1908	NY-A	0	4	.000	5	5	2	0	0	32	30	18	0	4	14	11	13.5	4.22	59	.275	.378	0	.000	-1	-6	-6	-1	-0.9
Total	6	52	68	.433	132	126	107	14	2	1072^{2}	950	411	11	48	237	464	10.4	2.62	97	.240	.291	57	.150	-7	0	-11	-3	-2.1
● **JOHN GLAISER** Glaiser, John Burke "Bert" b: 7/28/1894, Yoakum, Tex. d: 3/7/59, Houston, Tex. BL/TR, 5′8″, 165 lbs. Deb: 4/20/20																												
1920	Det-A	0	0	—	9	1	0	0	1	17	23	12	1	1	8	3	16.9	6.35	59	.354	.432	0	.000	-0	-5	-5	1	-0.1
● **TOM GLASS** Glass, Thomas Joseph b: 4/29/1898, Greensboro, N.C. d: 12/15/81, Greensboro, N.C. BR/TR, 6′3″, 170 lbs. Deb: 6/12/25																												
1925	Phi-A	1	0	1.000	2	0	0	0	0	5	9	4	0	0	0	2	16.2	5.40	86	.409	.409	0	.000	-0	-1	-0	-0	-0.1
● **JACK GLASSCOCK** Glasscock, John Wesley "Pebbly Jack" b: 7/22/1859, Wheeling, W.Va. d: 2/24/47, Wheeling, W.Va. BR/TR, 5′8″, 160 lbs. Deb: 5/1/1879 M◆																												
1884	Cle-N	0	0	—	2	0	0	0	0	5	8	6	0		2	1	18.0	5.40	58	.333	.385	70	.249	0	-1	-1	1	0.0
1887	Ind-N	0	0	—	1	0	0	0	0	1	0	0	0	0	0	1	0.0	0.00	—	.000	.000	183	.349	0	0	0	0	0.0
1888	Ind-N	0	0	—	1	0	0	0	0	0^{1}	1	3	0	1	2	1	108.0	54.00	5	1.000	1.000	119	.269	0	-2	-2	0	-0.1
1889	Ind-N	0	0	—	1	0	0	0	0	0^{2}	3	2	0	0	3	0	81.0	0.00	—	.600	.750	205	.352	0	0	0	-0	0.0
Total	4	0	0	—	5	0	0	0	0	7	12	11	0	1	7	3	25.7	6.43	53	.364	.488	2082	.294	1	-2	-2	1	-0.1
● **KEITH GLAUBER** Glauber, Keith Harris b: 1/18/72, Brooklyn, N.Y. BR/TR, 6′2″, 190 lbs. Deb: 9/8/98																												
1998	Cin-N	0	0	—	3	0	0	0	0	7^{2}	6	2	0	0	1	4	8.2	2.35	182	.214	.241	0	.000	-0	2	2	-0	0.0
2000	Cin-N	0	0	—	4	0	0	0	0	7^{1}	5	3	0	1	2	4	9.8	3.68	130	.185	.267	0	.000	-0	1	1	-0	0.0
Total	2	0	0	—	7	0	0	0	0	15	11	5	0	1	3	8	9.0	3.00	151	.200	.254	0	.000	-0	2	2	-0	0.0
● **LUKE GLAVENICH** Glavenich, Luke Frank b: 1/17/1893, Jackson, Cal. d: 5/22/35, Stockton, Cal. BR/TR, 5′9.5″, 189 lbs. Deb: 4/12/13																												
1913	Cle-A	0	0	—	1	0	0	0	0	1	3	5	0	0	3	1	54.0	9.00	34	.500	.667	0	—	0	-1	-1	-0	0.0
● **TOM GLAVINE** Glavine, Thomas Michael b: 3/25/66, Concord, Mass. BL/TL, 6′1″, 190 lbs. Deb: 8/17/87																												
1987	Atl-N	2	4	.333	9	9	0	0	0	50^{1}	55	34	5	3	33	20	16.3	5.54	79	.279	.391	2	.125	-0	-8	-6	1	-0.6
1988	Atl-N	7	17	.292	34	34	1	0	0	195^{1}	201	111	12	8	63	84	12.5	4.56	81	.270	.333	11	.183	1	-24	-18	2	-1.8
1989	Atl-N	14	8	.636	29	29	6	4	0	186	172	88	20	2	40	90	10.4	3.68	99	.243	.285	10	.149	0	-4	-0	1	0.1
1990	Atl-N	10	12	.455	33	33	1	0	0	214^{1}	232	111	18	1	78	129	13.1	4.28	94	.281	.343	7	.113	0	-12	-5	1	-0.4
1991	*Atl-N★	**20**	11	.645	34	34	**9**	1	0	246^{2}	201	83	17	2	69	192	9.9	2.55	**152**	.222	.279	17	.230	4	31	**35**	3	**5.2**
1992	*Atl-N★	**20**	8	.714	33	33	7	**5**	0	225	197	81	6	2	70	129	10.8	2.76	133	.235	.295	19	.247	4	19	22	-0	3.2
1993	*Atl-N☆	**22**	6	.786	36	36	4	2	0	239^{1}	236	91	16	2	90	120	12.3	3.20	126	.259	.327	14	.173	1	23	22	0	2.5
1994	Atl-N	13	9	.591	25	25	2	0	0	165^{1}	173	76	10	1	70	140	13.3	3.97	107	.268	.341	10	.179	1	4	5	2	1.0
1995	*Atl-N	16	7	.696	29	29	3	1	0	198^{2}	182	76	9	5	66	127	11.5	3.08	139	.246	.312	14	.222	3	24	26	3	3.4
1996	*Atl-N★	15	10	.600	36	36	1	0	0	235^{1}	222	91	14	0	85	181	11.7	2.98	148	.249	.314	22	.289	6	32	36	4	4.6
1997	*Atl-N☆	14	7	.667	33	33	5	2	0	240	197	86	20	4	79	152	10.5	2.96	142	.226	.294	14	.222	4	33	33	0	3.1
1998	*Atl-N★	**20**	6	.769	33	33	4	3	0	229^{1}	202	67	13	2	74	157	10.9	2.47	168	.238	.300	17	.239	3	45	44	3	5.5
1999	*Atl-N	14	11	.560	35	35	2	0	0	234	259	115	18	4	83	138	13.3	4.12	109	.287	.349	9	.138	-0	12	10	5	1.4
2000	*Atl-N★	**21**	9	.700	35	35	4	2	0	241	222	101	24	4	65	152	10.9	3.40	133	.244	.298	10	.147	1	33	31	2	3.7
Total	14	208	125	.625	434	434	49	20	0	2900^{2}	2751	1211	202	40	965	1811	11.7	3.39	122	.251	.314	176	.196	28	209	232	27	30.9
● **RALPH GLAZE** Glaze, Daniel Ralph b: 3/13/1882, Denver, Col. d: 10/31/68, Atascadero, Cal. BR/TR, 5′9″, 165 lbs. Deb: 6/1/06																												
1906	Bos-A	4	6	.400	19	10	7	0	0	123	110	58	4	5	32	56	10.8	3.59	77	.242	.299	10	.182	0	-12	-11	0	-0.8
1907	Bos-A	9	13	.409	32	21	11	1	0	182^{1}	150	75	4	4	48	68	10.0	2.32	111	.227	.283	11	.180	0	5	5	-4	0.2
1908	Bos-A	2	2	.500	10	3	2	0	0	34^{2}	43	24	1	0	5	13	12.5	3.38	73	.253	.274	1	.077	-1	-4	-3	-1	-0.6
Total	3	15	21	.417	61	34	20	1	0	340	303	157	9	9	85	137	10.5	2.89	91	.236	.288	22	.171	-1	-11	-10	-4	-1.2
● **WHITEY GLAZNER** Glazner, Charles Franklin b: 9/17/1893, Sycamore, Ala. d: 6/6/89, Orlando, Fla. BR/TR, 5′9″, 165 lbs. Deb: 9/26/20																												
1920	Pit-N	0	0	—	2	0	0	0	0	8^{2}	9	3	0	0	2	1	11.4	3.12	103	.300	.344	0	.000	-0	0	0	-0	-0.1
1921	Pit-N	14	5	.737	36	25	15	0	1	234	214	88	5	12	58	88	10.9	2.77	139	**.250**	.306	10	.132	-3	26	27	-4	1.3
1922	Pit-N	11	12	.478	34	26	10	1	1	193	238	118	9	2	52	77	13.6	4.38	93	.309	.354	16	.246	3	-6	-7	0	-0.4
1923	Pit-N	2	1	.667	7	4	1	1	1	30	29	18	5	0	11	8	12.0	3.30	122	.250	.315	4	.333	2	2	2	0	0.4
	Phi-N	7	14	.333	28	23	12	2	1	161^{1}	195	104	11	6	63	51	14.7	4.69	98	.304	.371	9	.170	-1	-12	-1	-0	-0.2

YEAR TM/L	W	L	PCT	G	GS	CG	SH	SV	IP	H	R	HR	HB	BB	SO	RAT	ERA	ERA+	OAV	OOB	BH	AVG	PB	PR	PR+	PD	TPI
Yr	9	15	.375	35	27	13	3	2	191^1	224	122	16	6	74	59	14.3	4.47	101	.296	.363	13	.200	1	-10	1	0	0.2
1924 Phi-N	7	16	.304	35	24	8	2	0	156^2	210	108	14	4	63	41	15.9	5.92	75	.339	.403	8	.157	-4	-36	-22	1	-3.0
Total 5	41	48	.461	142	102	46	6	4	783^2	895	439	44	24	249	266	13.4	4.21	99	.295	.353	47	.181	-3	-25	-3	-3	-2.0

● JOE GLEASON Gleason, Joseph Paul b: 7/9/1895, Phelps, N.Y. d: 9/8/90, Phelps, N.Y. BR/TR, 5'10.5", 175 lbs. Deb: 9/11/20

YEAR TM/L	W	L	PCT	G	GS	CG	SH	SV	IP	H	R	HR	HB	BB	SO	RAT	ERA	ERA+	OAV	OOB	BH	AVG	PB	PR	PR+	PD	TPI
1920 Was-A	0	0	—	3	0	0	0	0	8	14	13	2	1	6	2	23.6	13.50	28	.326	.420	0	.000	1	-9	-9	0	-0.3
1922 Was-A	2	2	.500	8	5	3	0	0	40^2	53	26	3	1	18	12	15.9	4.65	83	.319	.389	2	.143	-0	-3	-4	-0	-0.4
Total 2	2	2	.500	11	5	3	0	0	48^2	67	39	5	2	24	14	17.2	6.10	63	.321	.396	2	.125	0	-11	-13	0	-0.7

● BILL GLEASON Gleason, William b: 1868, Cleveland, Ohio d: 12/2/1893, Cleveland, Ohio Deb: 4/24/1890

YEAR TM/L	W	L	PCT	G	GS	CG	SH	SV	IP	H	R	HR	HB	BB	SO	RAT	ERA	ERA+	OAV	OOB	BH	AVG	PB	PR	PR+	PD	TPI
1890 Cle-P	0	1	.000	1	1	0	0	0	4	14	16	1	0	6	0	45.0	27.00	15	.538	.625	0	.000	-0	-10	-11	-0	-1.1

● KID GLEASON Gleason, William J. b: 10/26/1866, Camden, N.J. d: 1/2/33, Philadelphia, Pa. BB/TR, 5'7", 158 lbs. Deb: 4/20/1888 FMC♦

YEAR TM/L	W	L	PCT	G	GS	CG	SH	SV	IP	H	R	HR	HB	BB	SO	RAT	ERA	ERA+	OAV	OOB	BH	AVG	PB	PR	PR+	PD	TPI
1888 Phi-N	7	16	.304	24	23	23	0	0	199^2	199	112	11	12	53	89	11.9	2.84	105	.252	.309	17	.205	0	0	3	-3	0.0
1889 Phi-N	9	15	.375	29	21	15	0	1	205	242	177	8	9	97	64	15.3	5.58	78	.285	.364	25	.253	2	-36	-26	1	-2.1
1890 Phi-N	38	17	.691	60	55	54	6	**2**	506	479	253	8	15	167	222	11.8	2.63	139	.242	.306	47	.210	-6	53	56	-0	4.5
1891 Phi-N	24	22	.522	53	44	40	1	1	418	431	237	10	13	165	100	13.1	3.51	97	.256	.328	53	.248	6	-8	-5	-3	-0.2
1892 StL-N	20	24	.455	47	45	43	2	0	400	389	244	11	10	151	133	12.4	3.33	96	.245	.314	50	.215	8	-2	-6	5	0.7
1893 StL-N	21	22	.488	48	45	37	1	1	380^1	436	276	18	10	187	86	15.0	4.61	103	.279	.360	51	.256	4	2	5	1	0.8
1894 StL-N	2	6	.250	8	8	6	0	0	58	75	50	2	3	21	9	15.4	6.05	90	.310	.372	7	.250	-0	-5	-4	1	-0.3
*Bal-N	15	5	.750	21	20	19	0	0	172	224	111	3	3	44	35	14.2	4.45	123	.312	.354	30	.349	4	17	19	-2	1.8
Yr	17	11	.607	29	28	25	0	0	230	299	161	5	6	65	44	14.5	4.85	112	.311	.359	37	.325	4	12	15	-0	1.5
1895 *Bal-N	2	4	.333	9	5	3	0	1	50^1	77	51	4	3	21	6	18.1	6.97	68	.345	.409	130	.309	2	-12	-12	-0	-1.0
Total 8	138	131	.513	299	266	240	10	6	2389^1	2552	1511	75	78	906	744	13.3	3.79	103	.265	.333	1946	.261	20	10	28	-0	4.2

● JERRY DON GLEATON Gleaton, Jerry Don b: 9/14/57, Brownwood, Tex. BL/TL, 6'3", 210 lbs. Deb: 7/11/79

YEAR TM/L	W	L	PCT	G	GS	CG	SH	SV	IP	H	R	HR	HB	BB	SO	RAT	ERA	ERA+	OAV	OOB	BH	AVG	PB	PR	PR+	PD	TPI
1979 Tex-A	0	1	.000	5	2	0	0	0	9^2	15	7	0	1	2	2	16.8	6.52	64	.375	.419	0	—	0	-2	-3	0	-0.2
1980 Tex-A	0	0	—	5	0	0	0	0	7	5	2	0	0	4	2	11.6	2.57	152	.208	.321	0	—	0	1	1	0	0.1
1981 Sea-A	4	7	.364	20	13	1	0	0	85^1	88	50	10	2	38	31	13.5	4.75	81	.273	.354	0	—	0	-10	-8	-1	-1.0
1982 Sea-A	0	0	—	3	0	0	0	0	4^2	7	7	3	1	2	1	19.3	13.50	31	.333	.417	0	—	0	-5	-5	-0	-0.2
1984 Chi-A	1	2	.333	11	0	0	0	2	18^1	20	12	2	1	6	4	13.3	3.44	121	.286	.351	0	—	0	1	1	-1	0.2
1985 Chi-A	1	0	1.000	31	0	0	0	1	29^2	37	19	3	0	13	22	15.2	5.76	75	.316	.385	0	—	0	-5	-5	-0	-0.2
1987 KC-A	4	4	.500	48	0	0	0	5	50^2	38	28	4	0	28	44	11.7	4.26	107	.216	.324	0	—	0	1	2	1	0.4
1988 KC-A	0	4	.000	42	0	0	0	3	38	33	17	2	3	17	29	12.6	3.55	112	.232	.327	0	—	0	2	2	-0	0.2
1989 KC-A	0	0	—	15	0	0	0	0	14^1	20	10	0	0	6	9	16.3	5.65	68	.345	.406	0	—	0	-3	-3	-0	-0.2
1990 Det-A	1	3	.250	57	0	0	0	13	82^2	62	27	5	3	25	56	9.8	2.94	135	.213	.282	0	—	0	9	9	-0	0.6
1991 Det-A	3	2	.600	47	0	0	0	2	75^1	74	37	7	0	39	47	13.5	4.06	102	.269	.360	0	—	0	0	1	0	0.1
1992 Pit-N	1	0	1.000	23	0	0	0	0	31^2	34	16	4	0	19	18	15.1	4.26	81	.283	.381	0	.000	0	-3	-3	-0	-0.1
Total 12	15	23	.395	307	16	1	0	26	447^1	433	232	40	11	199	265	12.9	4.25	95	.261	.345	0	.000	0	-14	-10	-0	-0.3

● MARTIN GLENDON Glendon, Martin J. b: 2/8/1877, Milwaukee, Wis. d: 11/6/50, Norwood Park, Ill. 5'8", 165 lbs. Deb: 4/18/02

YEAR TM/L	W	L	PCT	G	GS	CG	SH	SV	IP	H	R	HR	HB	BB	SO	RAT	ERA	ERA+	OAV	OOB	BH	AVG	PB	PR	PR+	PD	TPI
1902 Cin-N	0	1	.000	1	1	0	0	0	3	5	5	0	0	4	0	27.0	12.00	25	.357	.500	0	.000	-0	-3	-3	-0	-0.5
1903 Cle-A	1	2	.333	3	3	3	0	0	27^2	20	9	0	0	7	9	8.8	0.98	292	.202	.255	0	.000	-1	6	6	1	0.7
Total 2	1	3	.250	4	4	3	0	0	30^2	25	14	0	0	11	9	10.6	2.05	140	.221	.290	0	.000	-1	3	3	1	0.2

● BOB GLENN Glenn, Burdette b: 6/16/1894, W.Sunbury, Pa. d: 6/3/77, Richmond, Cal. BR/TR, Deb: 7/27/20

YEAR TM/L	W	L	PCT	G	GS	CG	SH	SV	IP	H	R	HR	HB	BB	SO	RAT	ERA	ERA+	OAV	OOB	BH	AVG	PB	PR	PR+	PD	TPI
1920 StL-N	0	0	—	2	0	0	0	0	2	2	0	0	0	0	0	9.0	0.00	—	.222	.222	0	—	0	1	1	0	0.0

● SAL GLIATTO Gliatto, Salvador Michael b: 5/7/02, Chicago, Ill. d: 11/2/95, Tyler, Tex. BB/TR, 5'8.5", 150 lbs. Deb: 4/19/30

YEAR TM/L	W	L	PCT	G	GS	CG	SH	SV	IP	H	R	HR	HB	BB	SO	RAT	ERA	ERA+	OAV	OOB	BH	AVG	PB	PR	PR+	PD	TPI
1930 Cle-A	0	0	—	8	0	0	0	2	15	21	15	1	2	9	7	19.2	6.60	73	.328	.427	0	.000	-0	-3	-3	-0	-0.2

● GEORGE GLINATSIS Glinatsis, George b: 6/29/69, Youngstown, Ohio BR/TR, 6'4", 195 lbs. Deb: 7/18/94

YEAR TM/L	W	L	PCT	G	GS	CG	SH	SV	IP	H	R	HR	HB	BB	SO	RAT	ERA	ERA+	OAV	OOB	BH	AVG	PB	PR	PR+	PD	TPI
1994 Sea-A	0	1	.000	2	2	0	0	0	5^1	9	8	2	0	6	1	25.3	13.50	36	.429	.556	0	—	0	-5	-5	-0	-0.7

● GARY GLOVER Glover, John Gary b: 12/3/76, Cleveland, Ohio BR/TR, 6'5", 200 lbs. Deb: 9/30/99

YEAR TM/L	W	L	PCT	G	GS	CG	SH	SV	IP	H	R	HR	HB	BB	SO	RAT	ERA	ERA+	OAV	OOB	BH	AVG	PB	PR	PR+	PD	TPI
1999 Tor-A	0	0	—	1	0	0	0	0	1	0	0	0	0	1	0	9.0	0.00	—	.000	.333	0	—	0	1	1	0	0.0

● ED GLYNN Glynn, Edward Paul b: 6/3/53, Flushing, N.Y. BR/TL, 6'2", 180 lbs. Deb: 9/19/75

YEAR TM/L	W	L	PCT	G	GS	CG	SH	SV	IP	H	R	HR	HB	BB	SO	RAT	ERA	ERA+	OAV	OOB	BH	AVG	PB	PR	PR+	PD	TPI
1975 Det-A	0	2	.000	3	1	0	0	0	14^2	11	8	1	0	8	8	11.7	4.30	94	.220	.328	0	—	0	-1	-0	0	0.0
1976 Det-A	1	3	.250	5	4	1	0	0	23^2	22	18	3	0	20	17	16.0	6.08	61	.265	.408	0	—	0	-7	-6	-1	-0.9
1977 Det-A	2	1	.667	8	3	0	0	0	27^1	36	17	3	0	12	13	15.8	5.27	82	.316	.381	0	—	0	-4	-3	-0	-0.3
1978 Det-A	0	0	—	10	0	0	0	0	14^2	11	5	3	0	4	9	9.2	3.07	126	.208	.263	0	—	0	1	1	1	0.1
1979 NY-N	1	4	.200	46	0	0	0	7	60	57	22	3	2	40	32	14.9	3.00	122	.259	.378	0	.000	-0	5	4	-1	0.3
1980 NY-N	3	3	.500	38	0	0	0	1	52^1	49	26	5	0	23	32	12.4	4.13	86	.246	.324	0	.000	-1	-3	-3	1	-0.4
1981 Cle-A	0	0	—	4	0	0	0	0	7^2	5	1	0	0	4	4	10.6	1.17	309	.192	.300	0	—	0	2	2	-0	0.1
1982 Cle-A	5	2	.714	47	0	0	0	4	49^2	43	27	6	0	30	54	13.2	4.17	98	.232	.340	0	—	0	-0	-0	-0	-0.1
1983 Cle-A	0	2	.000	11	0	0	0	0	12^1	22	11	2	0	6	13	20.4	5.84	73	.373	.431	0	—	0	-2	-2	-1	-0.3
1985 Mon-N	0	0	—	3	0	0	0	0	2^1	5	5	0	0	4	2	34.7	19.29	18	.455	.600	0	—	0	-4	-4	-0	-0.2
Total 10	12	17	.414	175	8	1	0	12	264^2	261	140	26	2	151	184	14.1	4.25	90	.261	.359	0	.000	-1	-13	-12	-2	-1.7

● RYAN GLYNN Glynn, Ryan David b: 11/1/74, Portsmouth, Va. BR/TR, 6'3", 195 lbs. Deb: 5/16/99

YEAR TM/L	W	L	PCT	G	GS	CG	SH	SV	IP	H	R	HR	HB	BB	SO	RAT	ERA	ERA+	OAV	OOB	BH	AVG	PB	PR	PR+	PD	TPI
1999 Tex-A	2	4	.333	13	10	0	0	0	54^2	71	46	10	1	35	39	17.6	7.24	70	.316	.410	0	.000	-0	-14	-13	-1	-1.2
2000 Tex-A	5	7	.417	16	16	0	0	0	88^2	107	65	15	3	41	33	15.3	5.58	91	.293	.369	0	.000	-0	-6	-5	-0	-0.5
Total 2	7	11	.389	29	26	0	0	0	143^1	178	111	25	4	76	72	16.2	6.22	82	.302	.385	0	.000	-0	-21	-17	-0	-1.7

● JOT GOAR Goar, Joshua Mercer b: 1/31/1870, New Lisbon, Ind. d: 4/4/47, New Castle, Ind. BR/TR, 5'9", 160 lbs. Deb: 4/18/1896

YEAR TM/L	W	L	PCT	G	GS	CG	SH	SV	IP	H	R	HR	HB	BB	SO	RAT	ERA	ERA+	OAV	OOB	BH	AVG	PB	PR	PR+	PD	TPI
1896 Pit-N	0	1	.000	3	0	0	0	0	13^1	36	33	1	1	8	3	30.4	16.88	25	.486	.542	1	.167	-1	-19	-19	-1	-1.0
1898 Cin-N	0	0	—	1	0	0	0	0	2	4	3	0	0	1	0	22.5	9.00	43	.400	.455	0	—	0	-1	-1	-0	0.0
Total 2	0	1	.000	4	0	0	0	0	15^1	40	36	1	1	9	3	29.3	15.85	26	.476	.532	1	.167	-1	-20	-20	-0	-1.0

● GEORGE GOETZ Goetz, George Burt b: Greencastle, Pa. 6'2", 180 lbs. Deb: 6/17/1889

YEAR TM/L	W	L	PCT	G	GS	CG	SH	SV	IP	H	R	HR	HB	BB	SO	RAT	ERA	ERA+	OAV	OOB	BH	AVG	PB	PR	PR+	PD	TPI
1889 Bal-a	1	0	1.000	1	1	0	0	0	9	12	6	0	0	0	2	12.0	4.00	99	.308	.308	0	.000	-1	-0	-0	0	0.0

● JOHN GOETZ Goetz, John Hardy b: 10/24/37, Goetzville, Mich. BR/TR, 6', 185 lbs. Deb: 4/16/60

YEAR TM/L	W	L	PCT	G	GS	CG	SH	SV	IP	H	R	HR	HB	BB	SO	RAT	ERA	ERA+	OAV	OOB	BH	AVG	PB	PR	PR+	PD	TPI
1960 Chi-N	0	0	—	4	0	0	0	0	6^1	10	9	2	0	4	6	19.9	12.79	30	.370	.452	0	.000	-0	-6	-6	0	-0.3

● BILL GOGOLEWSKI Gogolewski, William Joseph b: 10/26/47, Oshkosh, Wis. BL/TR, 6'4", 190 lbs. Deb: 9/3/70

YEAR TM/L	W	L	PCT	G	GS	CG	SH	SV	IP	H	R	HR	HB	BB	SO	RAT	ERA	ERA+	OAV	OOB	BH	AVG	PB	PR	PR+	PD	TPI
1970 Was-A	2	2	.500	8	5	0	0	0	33^2	33	18	2	1	25	19	15.8	4.81	74	.260	.386	0	.000	-0	-4	-5	1	-0.5
1971 Was-A	6	5	.545	27	17	4	1	0	124^1	112	39	5	2	39	70	11.1	2.75	120	.241	.302	5	.156	0	10	8	-0	0.7
1972 Tex-A	4	11	.267	36	21	2	1	2	150^2	136	74	9	6	58	95	11.9	4.24	71	.239	.316	5	.125	-1	-20	-21	-0	-2.2
1973 Tex-A	3	6	.333	49	1	0	0	6	123^2	139	67	10	1	48	77	13.7	4.22	88	.286	.351	0	—	0	-5	-7	2	-0.3
1974 Cle-A	0	0	—	5	0	0	0	0	13^2	15	7	1	1	2	3	11.9	4.61	79	.283	.321	0	—	0	-1	-2	1	0.1
1975 Chi-A	0	0	—	19	0	0	0	2	55	61	35	5	1	28	37	14.7	5.24	74	.292	.378	0	—	0	-9	-8	1	-0.3
Total 6	15	24	.385	144	44	6	2	10	501	496	240	32	12	200	301	12.7	4.02	85	.260	.334	10	.127	-1	-30	-35	5	-2.5

● GREG GOHR Gohr, Gregory James b: 10/29/67, Santa Clara, Cal. BR/TR, 6'3", 205 lbs. Deb: 4/7/93

YEAR TM/L	W	L	PCT	G	GS	CG	SH	SV	IP	H	R	HR	HB	BB	SO	RAT	ERA	ERA+	OAV	OOB	BH	AVG	PB	PR	PR+	PD	TPI
1993 Det-A	0	0	—	16	0	0	0	0	22^2	26	15	1	2	14	23	16.7	5.96	72	.289	.396	0	—	0	-4	-4	-0	-0.2
1994 Det-A	2	2	.500	8	6	0	0	0	34	36	19	3	0	21	21	15.1	4.50	108	.263	.361	0	—	0	1	1	-1	0.1
1995 Det-A	1	0	1.000	10	0	0	0	0	10^1	9	1	0	0	3	12	10.5	0.87	547	.243	.300	0	—	0	4	4	-0	0.4
1996 Det-A	4	8	.333	17	16	0	0	0	91^2	129	76	24	3	34	60	16.3	7.17	71	.328	.386	0	—	0	-22	-21	-1	-2.2
Cal-A	1	1	.500	15	0	0	0	1	24	34	20	7	0	10	15	16.5	7.50	67	.337	.396	0	—	0	-7	-7	0	-0.5
Yr	5	9	.357	32	16	0	0	1	115^2	163	96	31	3	44	75	16.3	7.24	70	.330	.388	0	—	0	-29	-28	-1	-2.7
Total 4	8	11	.421	66	22	0	0	1	182^2	234	131	35	5	82	131	15.8	6.21	79	.309	.380	0	—	0	-27	-26	-2	-2.4

● **JIM GOLDEN** Golden, James Edward b: 3/20/36, Eldon, Mo. BL/TR, 6′, 175 lbs. Deb: 9/30/60

YEAR	TM/L	W	L	PCT	G	GS	CG	SH	SV	IP	H	R	HR	HB	BB	SO	RAT	ERA	ERA+	OAV	OOB	BH	AVG	PB	PR	PR+	PD	TPI
1960	LA-N	1	0	1.000	1	1	0	0	0	7	6	5	1	0	4	4	12.9	6.43	62	.240	.345	1	.333	0	-2	-2	-0	-0.2
1961	LA-N	1	1	.500	28	0	0	0	0	42	52	30	7	0	20	18	15.4	5.79	75	.306	.379	0	.000	-0	-8	-6	-0	-0.4
1962	Hou-N	7	11	.389	37	18	5	2	1	152^{2}	163	84	13	0	50	88	12.6	4.07	92	.270	.326	12	.222	4	-2	-6	1	-0.2
1963	Hou-N	0	1	.000	3	1	0	0	0	6^{1}	12	4	0	0	2	5	19.9	5.68	55	.429	.467	0	—	0	-2	-2	0	-0.3
Total	4	9	13	.409	69	20	5	2	1	208	233	123	21	0	76	115	13.4	4.54	85	.282	.343	13	.217	4	-14	-16	0	-1.1

● **MIKE GOLDEN** Golden, Michael Henry b: 9/11/1851, Shirley, Mass. d: 1/11/29, Rockford, Ill. BR/TR, 5′8″, 168 lbs. Deb: 5/5/1875 ♦

YEAR	TM/L	W	L	PCT	G	GS	CG	SH	SV	IP	H	R	HR	HB	BB	SO	RAT	ERA	ERA+	OAV	OOB	BH	AVG	PB	PR	PR+	PD	TPI
1875	Wes-n	1	12	.077	13	13	13	0	0	113	111	88	0		12	20	9.8	1.83	133	.225	.243	6	.130	-4	5	7		0.2
	Chi-n	6	7	.462	14	14	12	1	0	119	129	95	0		8	14	10.4	1.89	120	.247	.258	40	.258	1	4	5		0.4
	Yr	7	19	.269	27	27	25	1	0	232	240	183	0		20	34	10.1	1.86	126	.236	.251	46	.229	-3	9	12		0.6
1878	Mil-N	3	13	.188	22	18	15	0	0	161	217	171	1		33	52	14.0	4.14	63	.295	.325	44	.206	-2	-33	-24	0	-2.0

● **ROY GOLDEN** Golden, Roy Kramer b: 7/12/1888, Madisonville, O. d: 10/4/61, Norwood, Ohio BR/TR, 6′1″, 195 lbs. Deb: 9/7/10

YEAR	TM/L	W	L	PCT	G	GS	CG	SH	SV	IP	H	R	HR	HB	BB	SO	RAT	ERA	ERA+	OAV	OOB	BH	AVG	PB	PR	PR+	PD	TPI
1910	StL-N	2	3	.400	7	6	3	0	0	42^{2}	44	28	3	2	33	31	16.7	4.43	67	.286	.418	4	.267	1	-7	-7	1	-0.6
1911	StL-N	4	9	.308	30	25	6	0	0	148^{2}	127	90	6	5	129	81	15.8	5.02	67	.240	.394	5	.114	-1	-27	-27	-0	-2.2
Total	2	6	12	.333	37	31	9	0	0	191^{1}	171	118	9	7	162	112	16.0	4.89	67	.250	.399	9	.153	-1	-33	-34	1	-2.8

● **FRED GOLDSMITH** Goldsmith, Fredrick Ernest b: 5/15/1852, New Haven, Conn. d: 3/28/39, Berkley, Mich. BR/TR, 6′1″, 195 lbs. Deb: 10/23/1875 U♦

YEAR	TM/L	W	L	PCT	G	GS	CG	SH	SV	IP	H	R	HR	HB	BB	SO	RAT	ERA	ERA+	OAV	OOB	BH	AVG	PB	PR	PR+	PD	TPI
1879	Tro-N	2	4	.333	8	7	7	0	0	63	61	38	0		1	31	8.9	1.57	159	.237	.240	9	.237	0	6	6	-0	0.6
1880	Chi-N	21	3	**.875**	26	24	22	4	1	210^{1}	189	80	2		18	90	8.9	1.75	138	.231	.247	37	.261	2	14	15	2	1.9
1881	Chi-N	24	13	.649	39	39	37	5	0	330	328	166	4		44	76	10.1	2.59	106	.247	.271	38	.241	3	7	5	5	1.1
1882	Chi-N	28	17	.622	45	45	45	4	0	405	377	192	7		38	109	9.2	2.42	119	.236	.254	42	.230	-1	22	20	-2	1.4
1883	Chi-N	25	19	.568	46	45	40	2	0	383^{1}	456	256	14		39	82	11.6	3.15	105	.277	.294	52	.221	-1	-0	6	1	0.5
1884	Chi-N	9	11	.450	21	21	20	1	0	188	245	140	11		29	34	13.1	4.26	74	.298	.322	11	.136	-2	-27	-22	-3	-2.3
	Bal-a	3	1	.750	4	4	3	0	0	30	29	12	0	1	2	11	9.6	2.70	128	.238	.256	2	.143	-0	2	2	1	0.3
Total	6	112	68	.622	189	185	174	16	1	1609^{2}	1685	884	38	1	171	433	10.4	2.73	107	.256	.275	191	.224	-1	24	32	4	3.5

● **HAL GOLDSMITH** Goldsmith, Harold Eugene b: 8/18/1898, Peconic, N.Y. d: 10/20/85, Riverhead, N.Y. BR/TR, 6′, 174 lbs. Deb: 6/23/26

YEAR	TM/L	W	L	PCT	G	GS	CG	SH	SV	IP	H	R	HR	HB	BB	SO	RAT	ERA	ERA+	OAV	OOB	BH	AVG	PB	PR	PR+	PD	TPI
1926	Bos-N	5	7	.417	19	15	5	0	0	101	135	62	2	1	28	16	14.6	4.37	81	.333	.377	8	.211	0	-6	-10	1	-0.9
1927	Bos-N	1	3	.250	22	5	1	0	1	71^{2}	83	34	4	0	26	13	13.7	3.52	106	.289	.348	5	.238	0	3	2	0	0.1
1928	Bos-N	0	0	—	4	0	0	0	0	8^{1}	14	5	2	0	1	1	16.2	3.24	121	.359	.375	0	.000	-0	1	1	0	0.0
1929	StL-N	0	0	—	2	0	0	0	0	4	3	3	1	0	1	0	9.0	6.75	69	.214	.267	0	.000	-0	-1	-1	-0	-0.1
Total	4	6	10	.375	47	20	6	0	1	185	235	104	9	1	56	30	14.2	4.04	90	.315	.364	13	.210	0	-3	-8	1	-0.9

● **IZZY GOLDSTEIN** Goldstein, Isidore b: 6/6/08, Odessa, Russia d: 9/24/93, Delray Beach, Fla. BB/TR, 6′, 160 lbs. Deb: 4/24/32

YEAR	TM/L	W	L	PCT	G	GS	CG	SH	SV	IP	H	R	HR	HB	BB	SO	RAT	ERA	ERA+	OAV	OOB	BH	AVG	PB	PR	PR+	PD	TPI
1932	Det-A	3	2	.600	16	6	2	0	0	56^{1}	63	42	2	3	41	14	17.1	4.47	105	.276	.393	5	.294	1	0	1	0	0.2

● **DAVE GOLTZ** Goltz, David Allan b: 6/23/49, Pelican Rapids, Minn. BR/TR, 6′4″, 215 lbs. Deb: 7/18/72

YEAR	TM/L	W	L	PCT	G	GS	CG	SH	SV	IP	H	R	HR	HB	BB	SO	RAT	ERA	ERA+	OAV	OOB	BH	AVG	PB	PR	PR+	PD	TPI
1972	Min-A	3	3	.500	15	11	2	0	1	91	75	30	5	0	26	38	10.0	2.67	121	.224	.280	3	.103	-1	4	5	-0	0.3
1973	Min-A	6	4	.600	32	10	1	0	1	106^{1}	138	68	11	2	32	65	14.6	5.25	76	.318	.368	0	—	0	-17	-15	1	-1.2
1974	Min-A	10	10	.500	28	24	5	1	1	174^{1}	192	81	14	7	45	89	12.6	3.25	115	.282	.333	0	—	0	7	9	1	1.1
1975	Min-A	14	14	.500	32	32	15	1	0	243	235	112	18	6	72	128	11.6	3.67	105	.255	.313	0	—	0	3	4	1	0.6
1976	Min-A	14	14	.500	36	35	13	4	0	249^{1}	239	113	14	5	91	133	12.1	3.36	107	.254	.323	0	—	0	5	6	0	0.7
1977	Min-A	**20**	11	.645	39	39	19	2	0	303	284	129	23	2	91	186	11.2	3.36	119	.247	.304	0	—	0	24	22	-1	2.0
1978	Min-A	15	10	.600	29	29	13	2	0	220^{1}	209	72	12	1	67	116	11.3	2.49	154	.253	.309	0	—	0	31	32	0	3.7
1979	Min-A	14	13	.519	36	35	12	1	0	250^{2}	282	124	22	1	69	132	12.6	4.16	106	.288	.336	0	—	0	2	6	-1	0.5
1980	LA-N	7	11	.389	35	27	2	2	1	171^{1}	198	91	12	0	59	91	13.5	4.31	81	.299	.356	6	.128	0	-13	-16	-0	-1.6
1981	*LA-N	2	7	.222	26	8	0	0	1	77	83	35	4	0	25	48	12.6	4.09	81	.288	.345	1	.059	-1	-5	-7	1	-0.8
1982	LA-N	0	1	.000	2	1	0	0	0	3^{2}	6	4	0	0	0	3	14.7	4.91	71	.353	.353	0	.000	-0	-1	-1	0	-0.1
	*Cal-A	8	5	.615	28	7	1	0	3	86	82	43	4	1	32	49	12.0	4.08	100	.252	.320	0	—	0	0	-0	-2	-0.2
1983	Cal-A	0	6	.000	15	6	0	0	0	63^{2}	81	48	10	1	37	27	16.8	6.22	65	.315	.403	0	—	0	-15	-16	-0	-1.3
Total	12	113	109	.509	353	264	83	13	8	2039^{2}	2104	950	149	26	646	1105	12.2	3.69	104	.269	.327	10	.106	-1	26	33	0	3.7

● **WAYNE GOMES** Gomes, Wayne Maurice b: 1/15/73, Hampton, Va. BR/TR, 6′, 215 lbs. Deb: 6/13/97

YEAR	TM/L	W	L	PCT	G	GS	CG	SH	SV	IP	H	R	HR	HB	BB	SO	RAT	ERA	ERA+	OAV	OOB	BH	AVG	PB	PR	PR+	PD	TPI
1997	Phi-N	5	1	.833	37	0	0	0	0	42^{2}	45	26	4	1	24	24	14.8	5.27	81	.274	.370	0	.000	0	-5	-5	-1	-0.7
1998	Phi-N	9	6	.600	71	0	0	0	1	93^{1}	94	48	9	3	35	86	12.7	4.24	102	.258	.328	0	.000	-0	-0	1	-1	0.1
1999	Phi-N	5	5	.500	73	0	0	0	19	74	70	38	5	2	56	58	15.6	4.26	111	.255	.384	0	.000	-0	3	4	-1	0.5
2000	Phi-N	4	6	.400	65	0	0	0	7	73^{2}	72	41	6	3	35	49	13.4	4.40	107	.262	.351	0	—	0	2	3	-1	0.2
Total	4	23	18	.561	246	0	0	0	27	283^{2}	281	153	24	9	150	217	14.0	4.44	102	.261	.356	0	.000	-0	-1	3	-4	0.1

● **LUIS GOMEZ** Gomez, Luis (Sanchez) b: 8/19/51, Guadalajara, Mex. BR/TR, 5′9″, 150 lbs. Deb: 4/28/74 ♦

YEAR	TM/L	W	L	PCT	G	GS	CG	SH	SV	IP	H	R	HR	HB	BB	SO	RAT	ERA	ERA+	OAV	OOB	BH	AVG	PB	PR	PR+	PD	TPI
1981	Atl-N	0	0	—	1	0	0	0	0	1	3	3	0	0	2	0	45.0	27.00	13	.500	.625	7	.200	0	-3	-3	-0	-0.1

● **PAT GOMEZ** Gomez, Patrick Alexander b: 3/17/68, Roseville, Cal. BL/TL, 5′11″, 185 lbs. Deb: 4/6/93

YEAR	TM/L	W	L	PCT	G	GS	CG	SH	SV	IP	H	R	HR	HB	BB	SO	RAT	ERA	ERA+	OAV	OOB	BH	AVG	PB	PR	PR+	PD	TPI
1993	SD-N	1	2	.333	27	1	0	0	0	31^{2}	35	19	2	0	19	26	15.3	5.12	81	.292	.388	0	.000	-1	-4	-3	-1	-0.4
1994	SF-N	0	1	.000	26	0	0	0	0	33^{1}	23	14	2	0	20	14	11.6	3.78	106	.211	.333	0	.000	-0	2	1	-1	0.0
1995	SF-N	0	0	—	18	0	0	0	0	14	16	8	2	0	12	15	18.0	5.14	80	.276	.400	0	.000	-0	-1	-2	-0	-0.1
Total	3	1	3	.250	71	1	0	0	0	79	74	41	6	0	51	55	14.2	4.56	90	.258	.370	0	.000	-1	-4	-4	-1	-0.5

● **RUBEN GOMEZ** Gomez, Ruben (Colon) b: 7/13/27, Arroyo, P.R. BR/TR, 6′, 175 lbs. Deb: 4/17/53

YEAR	TM/L	W	L	PCT	G	GS	CG	SH	SV	IP	H	R	HR	HB	BB	SO	RAT	ERA	ERA+	OAV	OOB	BH	AVG	PB	PR	PR+	PD	TPI
1953	NY-N	13	11	.542	29	26	13	3	0	204	166	89	17	4	101	113	12.0	3.40	126	.218	.313	15	.208	-0	20	20	2	2.3
1954	*NY-N	17	9	.654	37	32	10	4	0	221^{2}	202	85	20	7	109	106	12.9	2.88	140	.244	.337	14	.173	0	29	29	2	3.3
1955	NY-N	9	10	.474	33	31	9	3	1	185^{1}	207	103	20	7	63	79	13.5	4.56	88	.285	.348	18	.300	4	-11	-11	3	-0.4
1956	NY-N	7	17	.292	40	31	4	2	0	196^{1}	191	108	19	9	77	76	12.7	4.58	83	.259	.337	11	.183	-0	-18	-17	2	-1.7
1957	NY-N	15	13	.536	38	36	16	1	0	238^{1}	233	110	28	5	71	92	11.7	3.78	104	.254	.311	16	.184	1	3	4	2	0.8
1958	SF-N	10	12	.455	42	30	8	1	1	207^{2}	204	107	21	8	77	112	12.5	4.38	87	.261	.334	14	.200	1	-10	-13	2	-1.0
1959	Phi-N	3	8	.273	20	12	2	1	1	72^{1}	90	55	12	0	24	37	14.2	6.10	67	.300	.352	3	.176	0	-17	-15	2	-1.9
1960	Phi-N	0	3	.000	22	1	0	0	1	52^{1}	68	37	7	1	9	24	13.4	5.33	73	.321	.351	1	.083	-1	-9	-8	-1	-0.6
1962	Cle-A	1	2	.333	15	4	0	0	1	45^{1}	50	23	5	2	25	21	15.3	4.37	89	.292	.389	3	.231	0	-2	-3	1	-0.1
	Min-A	1	1	.500	6	2	1	0	0	19^{1}	17	11	3	0	11	8	13.0	4.66	88	.254	.359	0	.000	-0	-1	-1	0	-0.1
	Yr	2	3	.400	21	6	1	0	1	64^{2}	67	34	8	2	36	29	14.6	4.45	88	.282	.380	3	.167	-0	-3	-4	1	-0.2
1967	Phi-N	0	0	—	7	0	0	0	0	11^{1}	8	6	2	0	7	9	11.9	3.97	86	.211	.333	0	—	0	-1	-1	1	0.0
Total	10	76	86	.469	289	205	63	15	5	1454	1436	734	154	43	574	677	12.7	4.09	97	.259	.334	95	.199	6	-17	-18	14	0.6

● **LEFTY GOMEZ** Gomez, Vernon Louis "Goofy" b: 11/26/08, Rodeo, Cal. d: 2/17/89, Greenbrae, Cal. BL/TL, 6′2″, 173 lbs. Deb: 4/29/30 H

YEAR	TM/L	W	L	PCT	G	GS	CG	SH	SV	IP	H	R	HR	HB	BB	SO	RAT	ERA	ERA+	OAV	OOB	BH	AVG	PB	PR	PR+	PD	TPI
1930	NY-A	2	5	.286	15	6	2	0	1	60	66	41	12	1	28	22	14.3	5.55	78	.280	.358	3	.150	-2	-6	-9	1	-0.9
1931	NY-A	21	9	.700	40	26	17	1	3	243	206	88	7	4	85	150	10.9	2.67	149	.226	.295	11	.133	-3	46	39	-1	3.9
1932	*NY-A	24	7	.774	37	31	21	1	1	265^{1}	266	140	23	2	105	176	12.7	4.21	97	.259	.329	18	.173	-1	8	-4	-3	-0.9
1933	NY-A★	16	10	.615	35	30	14	4	2	234^{2}	218	108	16	0	106	**163**	12.4	3.18	122	.240	.319	9	.112	-3	29	20	-4	1.3
1934	NY-A★	**26**	5	**.839**	38	33	**25**	**6**	1	**281^{2}**	223	86	12	0	96	**158**	**10.2**	**2.33**	174	**.215**	**.282**	13	.131	-3	**68**	**60**	-2	5.5
1935	NY-A★	12	15	.444	34	30	15	2	1	246	223	104	18	2	86	138	11.4	3.18	127	.242	.309	10	.120	-6	35	26	1	1.9
1936	*NY-A☆	13	7	.650	31	30	10	0	0	188^{2}	184	104	6	1	122	105	14.6	4.39	106	.254	.362	10	.145	-3	14	6	-1	0.2
1937	*NY-A★	**21**	11	.656	34	34	25	**6**	0	278^{1}	233	88	10	1	93	**194**	10.6	**2.33**	191	**.223**	.287	21	.200	-1	**71**	**68**	-3	**6.7**
1938	*NY-A★	18	12	.600	32	32	20	**4**	0	239	239	110	7	1	99	129	12.8	3.35	135	.260	.332	13	.151	-2	38	33	2	3.5
1939	*NY-A☆	12	8	.600	26	26	14	2	0	198	173	80	11	3	84	102	11.8	3.41	128	.235	.316	11	.151	-2	27	22	-1	1.7
1940	NY-A	3	3	.500	9	5	0	0	0	27^{1}	37	20	2	1	18	14	18.4	6.59	61	.325	.421	0	.000	-1	-7	-8	-1	-1.6
1941	NY-A	15	5	**.750**	23	23	8	2	0	156^{1}	151	76	10	1	103	76	14.7	3.74	105	.250	.360	9	.153	-1	7	3	-4	-0.1
1942	NY-A	6	4	.600	13	13	2	0	0	80	67	42	4	2	65	41	15.1	4.27	80	.237	.383	5	.152	-1	-5	-8	-2	-1.1
1943	Was-A	0	1	.000	1	1	0	0	0	4^{2}	4	4	0	0	5	0	17.4	5.79	55	.250	.429	0	.000	-0	-1	-1	1	-0.2
Total	14	189	102	.649	368	320	173	28	9	2503	2290	1091	138	19	1095	1468	12.2	3.34	125	.242	.321	133	.147	-30	322	247	-15	19.9

YEAR	TM/L	W	L	PCT	G	GS	CG	SH	SV	IP	H	R	HR	HB	BB	SO	RAT	ERA	ERA+	OAV	OOB	BH	AVG	PB	PR	PR+	PD	TPI
● **JOE GONZALES**	Gonzales, Joe Madrid "Smokey" b: 3/19/15, San Francisco, Cal d: 11/16/96, Torrance, Cal. BR/TR, 5'9", 175 lbs. Deb: 8/28/37																											
1937	Bos-A	1	2	.333	8	2	2	0	0	31	37	16	1	0	11	11	13.9	4.35	109	.291	.348	0	.000	-2	1	1	0	0.0
● **RENE GONZALES**	Gonzales, Rene Adrian b: 9/3/60, Austin, Tex. BR/TR, 6'3", 201 lbs. Deb: 7/27/84 ♦																											
1993	Cal-A	0	0	—	1	0	0	0	0	1	0	0	0	0	0	0	0.0	0.00	—	.000	.000	84	.251	0	0	0	0	0.0
● **VINCE GONZALES**	Gonzales, Wenceslao (O'Reilly) b: 9/28/25, Quivican, Cuba d: 3/11/81, Ciudad Del Carmen, Campeche, Mexico BL/TL, 6'1", 165 lbs. Deb: 4/13/55																											
1955	Was-A	0	0	—	1	0	0	0	0	2	6	6	0	0	3	1	40.5	27.00	14	.500	.600	0	—	0	-5	-5	-0	-0.2
● **GABE GONZALEZ**	Gonzalez, Gabriel b: 5/24/72, Long Beach, Cal. BB/TL, 6'1", 160 lbs. Deb: 4/1/98																											
1998	Fla-N	0	0	—	3	0	0	0	0	1	1	1	0	1	1	0	27.0	9.00	45	.333	.600	0	—	0	-1	-1	0	0.0
● **JEREMI GONZALEZ**	Gonzalez, Geremis Segundo (Acosta) b: 1/8/75, Maracaibo, Venezuela BR/TR, 6'2", 200 lbs. Deb: 5/27/97																											
1997	Chi-N	11	9	.550	23	23	1	1	0	144	126	73	16	2	69	93	12.3	4.25	101	.236	.326	4	.100	-1	-1	1	-2	-0.2
1998	Chi-N	7	7	.500	20	20	1	1	0	110	124	72	13	3	41	70	13.7	5.32	83	.281	.346	6	.188	0	-13	-11	-1	-1.3
Total	2	18	16	.529	43	43	2	2	0	254	250	145	29	5	110	163	12.9	4.71	92	.256	.335	10	.139	-1	-14	-10	-2	-1.5
● **GERMAN GONZALEZ**	Gonzalez, German Jose (Caraballo) b: 3/7/62, Rio Caribe, Venez. BR/TR, 6', 170 lbs. Deb: 8/5/88																											
1988	Min-A	0	0	—	16	0	0	0	1	21^1	20	8	4	1	8	19	12.2	3.38	121	.244	.319	0	—	0	1	2	0	0.1
1989	Min-A	3	2	.600	22	0	0	0	0	29	32	17	2	4	11	25	14.6	4.66	89	.274	.356	0	—	0	-2	-2	-0	-0.2
Total	2	3	2	.600	38	0	0	0	1	50^1	52	25	6	5	19	44	13.6	4.11	100	.261	.341	0	—	0	-1	0	0	-0.1
● **JULIO GONZALEZ**	Gonzalez, Julio Enrique (Herrera) b: 12/20/20, Banes, Cuba d: 2/15/91, Banes, Cuba BR/TR, 5'11", 150 lbs. Deb: 8/9/49																											
1949	Was-A	0	0	—	13	0	0	0	0	34^1	33	20	3	1	27	5	16.0	4.72	90	.256	.389	1	.200	0	-2	-2	-0	0.0
● **LARIEL GONZALEZ**	Gonzalez, Lariel Alfonso b: 5/25/76, San Cristobal, D.R. BR/TR, 6'4", 228 lbs. Deb: 9/22/98																											
1998	Col-N	0	0	—	1	0	0	0	0	1	0	0	0	0	0	0	0.0	0.00	—	.000	.000	0	—	0	0	0	-0	0.0
● **RALPH GOOD**	Good, Ralph Nelson "Holy" b: 4/25/1886, Monticello, Me. d: 11/24/65, Waterville, Maine BR/TR, 6', 165 lbs. Deb: 7/1/10																											
1910	Bos-N	0	0	—	2	0	0	0	0	9	6	4	0	2	2	4	10.0	2.00	166	.188	.278	0	.000	-0	1	1	0	0.1
● **WILBUR GOOD**	Good, Wilbur David "Lefty" b: 9/28/1885, Punxsutawney, Pa. d: 12/30/63, Brooksville, Fla. BL/TL, 5'6", 165 lbs. Deb: 8/18/05 ♦																											
1905	NY-A	0	2	.000	5	2	0	0	0	19	18	17	1	0	14	13	15.2	4.74	62	.250	.372	3	.375	1	-4	-3	0	-0.3
● **HERB GOODALL**	Goodall, Herbert Frank b: 3/10/1870, Mansfield, Pa. d: 1/20/38, Mansfield, Pa. BR/TR, 5'9", 180 lbs. Deb: 4/29/1890																											
1890	Lou-a	8	5	.615	18	13	8	1	**4**	109	94	73	2	10	51	46	12.8	3.39	114	.225	.324	19	.422	6	6	6	1	1.2
● **JOHN GOODELL**	Goodell, John Henry William "Lefty" b: 4/5/07, Muskogee, Okla. d: 9/21/93, Mesquite, Tex. BR/TL, 5'10", 165 lbs. Deb: 4/19/28																											
1928	Chi-A	0	0	—	2	0	0	0	0	3	6	6	0	1	2	0	27.0	18.00	23	.500	.600	0	—	0	-5	-5	0	-0.2
● **DWIGHT GOODEN**	Gooden, Dwight Eugene "Doc" b: 11/16/64, Tampa, Fla. BR/TR, 6'3", 210 lbs. Deb: 4/7/84																											
1984	NY-N★	17	9	.654	31	31	7	3	0	218	161	72	7	2	73	**276**	**9.7**	2.60	136	**.202**	**.270**	14	.200	1	24	23	1	2.9
1985	NY-N☆	**24**	4	.857	35	35	**16**	8	0	**276^2**	198	51	13	2	69	**268**	8.8	**1.53**	**227**	.201	.254	21	.226	6	**64**	**62**	2	**7.6**
1986	*NY-N★	17	6	.739	33	33	12	2	0	250	197	92	17	4	80	200	10.1	2.84	125	.215	.280	7	.086	-3	25	20	2	1.8
1987	NY-N	15	7	**.682**	25	25	7	3	0	179^2	162	68	11	2	53	148	10.9	3.21	118	.244	.301	14	.219	2	18	12	-0	1.6
1988	*NY-N★	18	9	.667	34	34	10	3	0	248^1	242	98	8	6	57	175	11.1	3.19	101	.256	.303	16	.178	3	7	1	5	0.9
1989	NY-N	9	4	.692	19	17	0	0	1	118^1	93	42	9	2	47	101	10.8	2.89	113	.211	.290	8	.200	2	8	5	0	0.8
1990	NY-N	19	7	.731	34	34	2	1	0	232^2	229	106	10	7	70	223	11.8	3.83	98	.258	.317	14	.187	4	-1	-2	2	0.3
1991	NY-N	13	7	.650	27	27	3	1	0	190	185	80	12	3	56	150	11.6	3.60	101	.257	.313	15	.238	4	2	1	1	0.6
1992	NY-N	10	13	.435	31	31	3	0	0	206	197	93	11	3	70	145	11.8	3.67	95	.255	.319	19	.264	7	-4	-4	1	0.4
1993	NY-N	12	15	.444	29	29	7	2	0	208^2	188	89	16	9	61	149	11.1	3.45	116	.242	.304	14	.200	4	14	13	-0	2.0
1994	NY-N	3	4	.429	7	7	0	0	0	41^1	46	32	9	1	15	40	13.5	6.31	66	.282	.346	2	.167	-0	-10	-10	1	-1.3
1996	NY-A	11	7	.611	29	29	1	1	0	170^2	169	101	19	9	88	126	14.0	5.01	99	.259	.355	0	—	0	-0	-1	1	-0.1
1997	*NY-A	9	5	.643	20	19	0	0	0	106^1	116	61	14	7	53	66	14.9	4.91	91	.283	.374	0	.000	-0	-4	-6	1	-0.6
1998	*Cle-A	8	6	.571	23	23	0	0	0	134	135	59	13	9	51	83	13.1	3.76	127	.262	.339	0	.000	-0	13	15	-0	1.3
1999	Cle-A	3	4	.429	26	22	0	0	0	115	127	90	18	9	67	88	15.9	6.26	81	.282	.385	1	.500	2	-18	-15	0	-0.6
2000	Hou-N	0	0	—	1	1	0	0	0	4	6	4	1	0	3	1	20.3	9.00	54	.353	.450	0	.000	-0	-2	-2	0	-0.1
	TB-A	2	3	.400	8	8	0	0	0	36^2	47	32	14	3	20	23	17.2	6.63	75	.315	.407	0	—	0	-7	-7	-1	-0.8
	*NY-A	4	2	.667	18	5	0	0	2	64^1	66	28	8	0	21	31	12.2	3.36	143	.266	.323	0	.000	-0	11	11	1	1.0
	Yr	6	5	.545	26	13	0	0	2	101	113	60	22	3	41	54	14.0	4.54	107	.285	.356	0	.000	-0	4	4	1	0.2
Total	16	194	112	.634	430	410	68	24	3	2800^2	2564	1198	210	78	954	2293	11.6	3.51	110	.244	.311	145	.196	30	140	112	16	17.7
● **ART GOODWIN**	Goodwin, Arthur Ingram b: 2/27/1877, Whiteley Twnshp, Pa. d: 6/19/43, Franklin Township, Pa. TR, 5'8", 195 lbs. Deb: 10/7/05																											
1905	NY-A	0	0	—	1	0	0	0	0	0^1	2	4	0	0	2	0	108.0	81.00	4	.667	.800	0	—	0	-3	-3	0	-0.1
● **CLYDE GOODWIN**	Goodwin, Clyde Samuel b: 11/12/1886, Athens, Ohio d: 10/12/63, Dayton, Ohio BR/TR, 5'11", 145 lbs. Deb: 9/18/06																											
1906	Was-A	0	2	.000	4	3	1	0	0	22^1	20	16	0	1	13	9	13.7	4.43	59	.244	.354	1	.200	-0	-4	-5	-1	-0.4
● **JIM GOODWIN**	Goodwin, James Patrick b: 8/15/26, St.Louis, Mo. BL/TL, 6'1", 170 lbs. Deb: 4/24/48																											
1948	Chi-A	0	0	—	8	1	0	0	1	10^1	9	11	0	1	12	3	19.2	8.71	49	.237	.431	1	.500	0	-5	-5	0	-0.2
● **MARV GOODWIN**	Goodwin, Marvin Mardo b: 1/16/1891, Gordonsville, Va. d: 10/21/25, Houston, Tex. BR/TR, 5'11", 168 lbs. Deb: 9/7/16																											
1916	Was-A	0	0	—	3	0	0	0	0	5^2	5	4	0	0	3	1	12.7	3.18	88	.217	.308	0	.000	-0	-0	-0	-0	-0.1
1917	StL-N	6	4	.600	14	12	6	3	0	85^1	70	33	1	0	19	38	9.4	2.21	122	.222	.266	4	.174	-0	5	5	2	0.8
1919	StL-N	11	9	.550	33	17	7	0	0	179	163	66	3	8	33	48	10.3	2.51	111	.245	.289	12	.200	1	8	6	-1	0.8
1920	StL-N	3	8	.273	32	12	3	0	1	116^1	153	79	1	5	28	23	14.4	4.95	60	.314	.357	7	.200	-0	-23	-27	-3	-2.6
1921	StL-N	1	2	.333	14	4	1	0	1	36^1	47	21	1	1	9	7	14.1	3.72	99	.315	.358	0	.000	-1	0	-0	0	0.0
1922	StL-N	0	0	—	2	0	0	0	0	4	3	1	0	0	3	0	13.5	2.25	172	.250	.400	0	—	0	1	1	0	0.1
1925	Cin-N	0	2	.000	4	3	2	0	0	20^2	26	14	2	1	5	4	13.9	4.79	86	.317	.364	1	.250	0	-1	-2	1	0.0
Total	7	21	25	.457	102	48	19	3	2	447^1	467	218	8	15	100	121	11.7	3.30	90	.269	.315	24	.186	0	-11	-17	0	-1.0
● **RAY GORDINIER**	Gordinier, Raymond Cornelius "Gordy" b: 4/11/1892, Rochester, N.Y. d: 11/15/60, Rochester, N.Y. BB/TR, 5'8.5", 170 lbs. Deb: 9/17/21																											
1921	Bro-N	1	0	1.000	3	3	0	0	0	12	10	8	0	0	8	4	13.5	5.25	74	.227	.346	1	.250	0	-2	-2	0	-0.1
1922	Bro-N	0	0	—	5	0	0	0	0	11^1	13	11	3	0	8	5	16.7	8.74	47	.289	.396	0	.000	-0	-6	-6	-0	-0.3
Total	2	1	0	1.000	8	3	0	0	0	23^1	23	19	3	0	16	9	15.0	6.94	57	.258	.371	1	.167	-0	-8	-8	0	-0.4
● **DON GORDON**	Gordon, Donald Thomas b: 10/10/59, New York, N.Y. BR/TR, 6'1", 175 lbs. Deb: 4/10/86																											
1986	Tor-A	0	1	.000	14	0	0	0	1	21^2	28	20	1	1	8	13	15.4	7.06	60	.311	.374	0	—	0	-7	-7	-1	-0.4
1987	Tor-A	0	0	—	5	0	0	0	0	11	8	5	2	0	3	3	9.0	4.09	110	.200	.256	0	—	0	0	1	-0	0.0
	Cle-A	0	3	.000	21	0	0	0	1	39^2	49	31	3	4	12	20	14.7	4.08	111	.295	.357	0	—	0	2	2	1	0.2
	Yr	0	3	.000	26	0	0	0	1	50^2	57	36	5	4	15	23	13.5	4.09	111	.277	.338	0	—	0	2	2	1	0.2
1988	Cle-A	3	4	.429	38	0	0	0	1	59^1	65	33	5	3	19	20	13.2	4.40	94	.284	.347	0	—	0	-3	-2	1	-0.1
Total	3	3	8	.273	78	0	0	0	3	131^2	150	89	11	8	42	56	13.7	4.72	91	.286	.348	0	—	0	-8	-6	1	-0.3
● **TOM GORDON**	Gordon, Thomas b: 11/18/67, Sebring, Fla. BR/TR, 5'9", 180 lbs. Deb: 9/8/88																											
1988	KC-A	0	2	.000	5	2	0	0	0	15^2	16	9	1	0	7	18	13.2	5.17	77	.267	.343	0	—	0	-2	-2	0	-0.2
1989	KC-A	17	9	.654	49	16	1	1	1	163	122	67	10	1	86	153	11.5	3.64	106	.210	.312	0	—	0	4	4	3	0.8
1990	KC-A	12	11	.522	32	32	6	1	0	195^1	192	99	17	3	99	175	13.5	3.73	103	.257	.347	0	—	0	4	2	1	0.4
1991	KC-A	9	14	.391	45	14	1	0	1	158	129	76	16	4	87	167	12.5	3.87	107	.221	.325	0	—	0	4	4	0	0.6
1992	KC-A	6	10	.375	40	11	0	0	0	117^2	116	67	9	4	55	98	13.4	4.59	89	.258	.344	0	—	0	-8	-7	1	-0.8
1993	KC-A	12	6	.667	48	14	2	0	1	155^2	125	65	11	1	77	143	11.7	3.58	128	.223	.318	0	—	0	13	16	1	1.8
1994	KC-A	11	7	.611	24	24	0	0	0	155^1	136	79	15	3	87	126	13.1	4.35	115	.237	.340	0	—	0	8	11	2	1.2

YEAR	TM/L	W	L	PCT	G	GS	CG	SH	SV	IP	H	R	HR	HB	BB	SO	RAT	ERA	ERA+	OAV	OOB	BH	AVG	PB	PR	PR+	PD	TPI
1995	KC-A	12	12	.500	31	31	2	0	0	189	204	110	12	4	89	119	14.1	4.43	108	.279	.360	0	—	0	6	7	1	0.9
1996	Bos-A	12	9	.571	34	34	4	1	0	215^2	249	143	28	4	105	171	14.9	5.59	91	.284	.363	0	—	0	-14	-12	1	-0.9
1997	Bos-A	6	10	.375	42	25	2	1	11	182^2	155	85	10	3	78	159	11.6	3.74	124	.226	.308	0	—	0	17	18	0	1.6
1998	*Bos-A★	7	4	.636	73	0	0	0	**46**	79^1	55	24	2	0	25	78	9.1	2.72	173	.191	.256	0	—	0	17	17	-1	3.2
1999	*Bos-A	0	2	.000	21	0	0	0	11	17^2	17	11	2	1	12	24	15.3	5.60	89	.246	.366	0	—	0	-1	-1	-0	-0.2
Total	12	104	96	.520	444	203	18	4	71	1645	1516	835	133	28	807	1431	12.9	4.15	108	.244	.334	0	—	0	47	59	8	8.4
● RICK GORECKI Gorecki, Richard John b: 8/27/73, Evergreen Park, Ill. BR/TR, 6'3", 167 lbs. Deb: 9/10/97																												
1997	LA-N	1	0	1.000	4	1	0	0	0	6	9	10	3	0	6	6	22.5	15.00	26	.346	.469	0	—	0	-7	-8	-0	-1.1
1998	TB-A	1	2	.333	3	3	0	0	0	16^2	15	9	1	0	10	7	13.5	4.86	99	.259	.368	0	—	0	-0	-0	-0	0.0
Total	2	2	2	.500	7	4	0	0	0	22^2	24	19	4	0	16	13	15.9	7.54	60	.286	.400	0	—	0	-8	-8	-0	-1.1
● CHARLIE GORIN Gorin, Charles Perry b: 2/6/28, Waco, Tex. BL/TL, 5'10", 165 lbs. Deb: 5/29/54																												
1954	Mil-N	0	1	.000	5	0	0	0	0	9^2	5	3	0	0	6	12	10.2	1.86	200	.152	.282	0	.000	-0	2	2	-0	0.1
1955	Mil-N	0	0	—	2	0	0	0	0	0^1	1	2	0	0	3	0	108.0	54.00	7	.500	.800	0	—	0	-2	-2	0	-0.1
Total	2	0	1	.000	7	0	0	0	0	10	6	5	0	0	9	12	13.5	3.60	103	.171	.341	0	.000	-0	0	0	-0	0.0
● JACK GORMAN Gorman, John F. "Stooping Jack" b: 1859, St.Louis, Mo. d: 9/9/1889, St.Louis, Mo. Deb: 7/1/1883 ♦																												
1884	Pit-a	1	2	.333	3	3	3	0	0	25	22	20	0	1	5	10	10.1	4.68	71	.212	.255	4	.148	-0	-4	-4	0	-0.4
● TOM GORMAN Gorman, Thomas Aloysius b: 1/4/25, New York, N.Y. d: 12/26/92, Valley Stream, N.Y. BR/TR, 6'1", 190 lbs. Deb: 7/16/52																												
1952	*NY-A	6	2	.750	12	6	1	1	1	60^2	63	34	8	2	22	31	12.9	4.60	72	.272	.340	2	.087	-1	-6	-10	-0	-1.3
1953	*NY-A	4	5	.444	40	1	0	0	6	77	65	32	5	6	32	38	12.0	3.39	109	.226	.317	2	.133	-1	5	3	-0	0.3
1954	NY-A	0	0	—	23	0	0	0	2	36^2	30	14	1	1	14	31	11.0	2.21	156	.222	.300	0	.000	-1	6	5	0	0.3
1955	KC-A	7	6	.538	57	0	0	0	18	109	98	48	11	4	36	46	11.4	3.55	118	.246	.314	2	.083	-1	5	7	-1	0.8
1956	KC-A	9	10	.474	52	13	1	0	3	171^1	168	83	23	2	68	56	12.5	3.83	113	.258	.330	2	.051	-4	6	9	-0	0.6
1957	KC-A	5	9	.357	38	12	3	1	3	124^2	125	59	18	1	33	66	11.5	3.83	103	.261	.310	4	.121	-2	2	2	-0	0.0
1958	KC-A	4	4	.500	50	1	0	0	8	89^2	86	41	8	3	20	44	10.9	3.51	111	.258	.306	2	.118	-1	3	4	-1	0.2
1959	KC-A	1	0	1.000	17	0	0	0	1	20^1	24	21	3	1	14	9	17.3	7.08	57	.293	.402	0	—	0	-7	-7	-1	-0.5
Total	8	36	36	.500	289	33	5	2	42	689^1	659	332	77	20	239	321	12.0	3.77	105	.254	.321	14	.090	-10	11	14	-4	0.4
● TOM GORMAN Gorman, Thomas David "Big Tom" b: 3/16/16, New York, N.Y. d: 8/11/86, Closter, N.J. BR/TL, 6'2", 200 lbs. Deb: 9/14/39 U																												
1939	NY-N	0	0	—	4	0	0	0	0	5	7	4	0	0	1	2	14.4	7.20	55	.350	.381	0	.000	-0	-2	-2	0	-0.1
● TOM GORMAN Gorman, Thomas Patrick b: 12/16/57, Portland, Ore. BL/TL, 6'4", 200 lbs. Deb: 9/2/81																												
1981	Mon-N	0	0	—	9	0	0	0	0	15	12	7	0	1	6	13	11.4	4.20	83	.222	.311	0	—	0	-1	-1	0	0.0
1982	Mon-N	1	0	1.000	5	0	0	0	0	7	8	4	0	0	4	6	15.4	5.14	71	.286	.375	0	—	0	-1	-1	0	-0.1
	NY-N	0	1	.000	3	1	0	0	0	9^1	8	1	0	0	0	7	7.7	0.96	377	.235	.235	0	.000	-0	3	3	0	0.3
	Yr	1	1	.500	8	1	0	0	0	16^1	16	5	0	0	4	13	11.0	2.76	132	.258	.303	0	.000	-0	2	2	0	0.2
1983	NY-N	1	4	.200	25	4	0	0	0	49^1	45	29	3	0	15	30	10.9	4.93	74	.245	.302	1	.250	0	-7	-7	0	-0.7
1984	NY-N	6	0	1.000	36	0	0	0	0	57^2	51	20	6	1	13	40	10.1	2.97	119	.238	.285	0	.000	-0	4	4	0	0.3
1985	NY-N	4	4	.500	34	2	0	0	0	52^2	56	32	8	0	18	32	12.6	5.13	68	.277	.336	0	.000	-1	-9	-10	1	-1.4
1986	Phi-N	0	1	.000	8	0	0	0	0	11^2	21	10	0	0	5	8	20.1	7.71	50	.382	.433	0	.000	-0	-5	-5	0	-0.4
1987	SD-N	0	0	—	6	0	0	0	0	11	11	5	1	0	5	8	13.1	4.09	97	.262	.340	0	—	0	-0	-0	0	0.0
Total	7	12	10	.545	126	7	0	0	0	213^2	212	108	18	2	66	144	11.8	4.34	83	.261	.318	1	.071	-1	-17	-18	2	-2.0
● JOE GORMLEY Gormley, Joseph b: 12/20/1866, Summit Hill, Pa. d: 7/2/50, Summit Hill, Pa. BL/TL, Deb: 6/16/1891																												
1891	Phi-N	0	1	.000	1	1	1	0	0	8	10	8	0	0	5	2	16.9	5.63	61	.294	.385	0	.000	-1	-2	-2	0	-0.2
● HANK GORNICKI Gornicki, Henry Frank b: 1/14/11, Niagara Falls, N.Y d: 2/16/96, Riviera Beach, Fla BR/TR, 6'1", 145 lbs. Deb: 4/17/41																												
1941	StL-N	1	0	1.000	4	1	1	1	0	11^1	6	4	0	1	9	6	12.7	3.18	118	.158	.333	1	.250	0	1	1	-0	0.0
	Chi-N	0	0	—	1	0	0	0	0	2	3	1	0	0	0	2	13.5	4.50	78	.375	.375	0	—	0	-0	-0	0	0.0
	Yr	1	0	1.000	5	1	1	1	0	13^1	9	5	0	1	9	8	12.8	3.38	110	.196	.339	1	.250	0	0	1	0	0.0
1942	Pit-N	5	6	.455	25	14	7	2	2	112	89	45	2	1	40	48	10.4	2.57	132	.215	.286	4	.114	-1	9	10	-1	0.8
1943	Pit-N	9	13	.409	42	18	4	1	4	147	165	86	10	2	47	63	13.1	3.98	87	.286	.342	7	.175	-1	-10	-8	-1	-1.4
1946	Pit-N	0	0	—	7	0	0	0	0	12^2	12	10	0	0	11	4	16.3	3.55	99	.255	.397	0	.000	-0	-0	-0	-1	-0.1
Total	4	15	19	.441	79	33	12	4	6	285	275	146	12	4	107	123	12.2	3.38	102	.254	.323	12	.146	-2	-0	2	-2	-0.7
● JOHNNY GORSICA Gorsica, John Joseph Perry (b: John Joseph Perry Gorczyca) b: 3/29/15, Bayonne, N.J. d: 12/16/98, Charlottesville, Va. BR/TR, 6'2", 180 lbs. Deb: 4/22/40																												
1940	*Det-A	7	7	.500	29	20	5	2	0	160	170	85	10	4	57	68	13.0	4.33	110	.272	.337	12	.194	0	1	7	5	1.1
1941	Det-A	9	11	.450	33	21	8	1	2	171	193	98	14	2	55	59	13.2	4.47	102	.281	.336	17	.298	4	-6	1	4	0.9
1942	Det-A	3	2	.600	28	0	0	0	4	53	63	31	2	3	26	19	15.6	4.75	83	.310	.397	1	.100	-0	-6	-4	4	-0.1
1943	Det-A	4	5	.444	35	4	1	0	5	96^1	88	43	3	2	40	45	12.1	3.36	105	.247	.327	4	.174	0	-1	2	3	0.5
1944	Det-A	6	14	.300	34	19	8	1	4	162	192	88	5	4	32	47	12.7	4.11	87	.296	.333	7	.135	-1	-12	-9	3	-0.9
1946	Det-A	0	0	—	14	0	0	0	1	23^2	28	13	5	0	11	14	14.8	4.56	80	.301	.375	2	.667	1	-3	-2	-0	-0.1
1947	Det-A	2	0	1.000	31	0	0	0	1	57^2	44	27	5	2	26	20	11.2	3.75	101	.208	.300	2	.200	0	0	0	1	0.2
Total	7	31	39	.443	204	64	22	4	17	723^2	778	385	44	17	247	272	13.0	4.18	98	.276	.338	45	.207	4	-28	-6	20	1.6
● RICH GOSSAGE Gossage, Richard Michael "Goose" b: 7/5/51, Colorado Springs, Colo. BR/TR, 6'3", 217 lbs. Deb: 4/16/72																												
1972	Chi-A	7	1	.875	36	1	0	0	2	80	72	44	2	4	44	57	13.5	4.27	73	.247	.353	0	.000	-2	-11	-10	-1	-1.3
1973	Chi-A	0	4	.000	20	4	1	0	0	49^2	57	44	9	3	37	33	17.6	7.43	53	.311	.435	0	—	0	-20	-18	-0	-1.3
1974	Chi-A	4	6	.400	39	3	0	0	1	89^1	92	45	4	2	47	64	14.2	4.13	90	.272	.364	0	—	0	-5	-4	0	-0.4
1975	Chi-A★	9	8	.529	62	0	0	0	**26**	141^2	99	32	3	5	70	130	11.1	1.84	211	.201	.306	0	—	0	**31**	**31**	1	5.1
1976	Chi-A☆	9	17	.346	31	29	15	0	1	224	214	104	16	9	90	135	12.6	3.94	91	.254	.333	0	—	0	-10	-9	-1	-1.1
1977	Pit-N★	11	9	.550	72	0	0	0	26	133	78	27	9	2	49	151	8.7	1.62	246	.170	.253	5	.217	1	**34**	**34**	-1	**6.3**
1978	*NY-A★	10	11	.476	63	0	0	0	**27**	134^1	87	41	9	2	59	122	9.9	2.01	181	.187	.281	0	—	0	**26**	**25**	-1	4.9
1979	NY-A	5	3	.625	36	0	0	0	18	58^1	48	18	5	0	19	41	10.3	2.62	156	.227	.291	0	—	0	10	10	-1	1.8
1980	*NY-A★	6	2	.750	64	0	0	0	**33**	99	74	29	5	1	37	103	10.2	2.27	173	.211	.288	0	—	0	19	19	-1	2.7
1981	*NY-A†	3	2	.600	32	0	0	0	20	46^2	22	6	2	1	14	48	7.1	0.77	464	.141	.216	0	—	0	15	15	0	3.2
1982	NY-A☆	4	5	.444	56	0	0	0	30	93	63	23	5	0	28	102	8.8	2.23	179	.196	.261	0	—	0	19	19	-1	2.9
1983	NY-A	13	5	.722	57	0	0	0	22	87^1	82	27	5	1	25	90	11.1	2.27	172	.248	.303	0	—	0	18	17	-2	3.2
1984	*SD-N★	10	6	.625	62	0	0	0	25	102^1	75	34	6	1	36	84	9.9	2.90	123	.204	.277	4	.182	0	8	8	-1	1.4
1985	SD-N★	5	3	.625	50	0	0	0	26	79	64	21	1	1	17	52	9.3	1.82	194	.226	.272	0	.000	-1	16	15	-1	2.4
1986	SD-N	5	7	.417	45	0	0	0	21	64^2	69	36	8	2	20	63	12.7	4.45	82	.273	.331	0	.000	-1	-5	-6	-1	-1.3
1987	SD-N	5	4	.556	40	0	0	0	11	52	47	18	4	0	19	44	11.4	3.12	127	.244	.311	0	.000	-0	6	5	-1	0.9
1988	Chi-N	4	4	.500	46	0	0	0	13	43^2	50	23	3	3	15	30	14.0	4.33	83	.291	.358	0	.000	-0	-4	-3	-0	-0.7
1989	SF-N	2	1	.667	31	0	0	0	4	43^2	32	16	2	0	27	24	12.2	2.68	126	.212	.331	0	.000	-0	4	4	-1	0.2
	NY-A	1	0	1.000	11	0	0	0	1	14^1	14	6	0	3	3	6	11.3	3.77	103	.275	.327	0	—	0	0	0	0	0.0
1991	Tex-A	4	2	.667	44	0	0	0	1	40^1	33	16	4	3	16	28	11.6	3.57	113	.228	.317	0	—	0	2	2	-1	0.2
1992	Oak-A	0	2	.000	30	0	0	0	0	38	32	13	5	2	19	26	12.6	2.84	132	.230	.331	0	—	0	5	4	-0	0.2
1993	Oak-A	4	5	.444	39	0	0	0	1	47^2	49	24	6	1	26	40	14.3	4.53	90	.266	.360	0	—	0	-1	-2	-1	-0.5
1994	Sea-A	3	0	1.000	36	0	0	0	1	47^1	44	23	6	3	15	29	11.8	4.18	117	.251	.321	0	—	0	3	4	-1	0.1
Total	22	124	107	.537	1002	37	16	0	310	1809^1	1497	670	119	47	732	1502	11.3	3.01	126	.228	.310	9	.106	-3	160	156	-14	28.9
● JIM GOTT Gott, James William b: 8/3/59, Hollywood, Cal. BR/TR, 6'4", 220 lbs. Deb: 4/9/82																												
1982	Tor-A	5	10	.333	30	23	1	1	0	136	134	76	15	3	66	82	13.4	4.43	101	.255	.341	0	—	0	-5	1	-0	0.1
1983	Tor-A	9	14	.391	34	30	6	1	0	176^2	195	103	15	5	68	121	13.7	4.74	91	.280	.349	0	—	0	-13	-8	-1	-1.0
1984	Tor-A	7	6	.538	35	12	1	1	2	109^2	93	54	7	3	49	73	11.9	4.02	102	.233	.322	0	—	0	-0	1	-1	0.0
1985	SF-N	7	10	.412	26	26	2	0	0	148^1	144	73	10	1	51	78	11.9	3.88	89	.254	.317	10	.196	4	-5	-8	1	-0.3
1986	SF-N	0	0	—	9	2	0	0	1	13	16	12	0	0	13	9	20.1	7.62	46	.314	.453	0	.000	-0	-6	-6	-0	-0.3
1987	SF-N	1	0	1.000	30	3	0	0	1	56	53	32	4	2	32	63	14.0	4.50	86	.244	.347	1	.100	1	-3	-4	0	-0.2

YEAR	TM/L	W	L	PCT	G	GS	CG	SH	SV	IP	H	R	HR	HB	BB	SO	RAT	ERA	ERA+	OAV	OOB	BH	AVG	PB	PR	PR+	PD	TPI
	Pit-N	0	2	.000	25	0	0	0	13	31	28	11	0	0	8	27	10.5	1.45	283	.233	.281	0	.000	-0	9	9	-0	1.2
	Yr	1	2	.333	55	3	0	0	13	87	81	43	4	2	40	90	12.7	3.41	116	.240	.325	1	.091	0	6	5	-0	1.0
1988	Pit-N	6	6	.500	67	0	0	0	34	77^{1}	68	30	9	2	22	76	10.7	3.49	98	.243	.303	0	.000	-0	-0	-1	-0	-0.2
1989	Pit-N	0	0	—	1	0	0	0	0	0^{2}	1	0	0	0	1	1	27.0	0.00	—	.333	.500	0	—	0	0	0	0	0.0
1990	LA-N	3	5	.375	50	0	0	0	3	62	59	27	5	0	34	44	13.5	2.90	126	.257	.352	0	.000	-0	6	5	-0	0.7
1991	LA-N	4	3	.571	55	0	0	0	2	76	63	28	5	1	32	73	11.4	2.96	121	.223	.305	1	.500	0	6	5	1	0.6
1992	LA-N	3	3	.500	68	0	0	0	6	88	72	27	4	1	41	75	11.7	2.45	141	.225	.315	1	.500	0	10	10	1	1.0
1993	LA-N	4	8	.333	62	0	0	0	25	77^{2}	71	23	6	1	17	67	10.3	2.32	165	.248	.293	0	.000	-0	15	14	0	2.7
1994	LA-N	5	3	.625	37	0	0	0	2	36^{1}	46	24	3	3	20	29	17.1	5.94	66	.322	.416	0	—	0	-7	-9	0	-1.7
1995	Pit-N	2	4	.333	25	0	0	0	3	31^{1}	38	26	2	1	12	19	14.6	6.03	71	.288	.352	0	.000	-0	-6	-6	0	-1.0
Total	14	56	74	.431	554	96	10	3	91	1120	1081	546	85	23	466	837	12.6	3.87	101	.254	.331	13	.178	5	2	3	0	1.6
● **TED GOULAIT** Goulait, Theodore Lee b: 8/12/1889, St.Clair, Mich. d: 7/15/36, St.Clair, Mich. BR/TR, 5'9.5", 172 lbs. Deb: 9/28/12																												
1912	NY-N	0	0	—	1	1	1	0	0	7	11	6	0	0	4	6	19.3	6.43	53	.367	.441	1	.500	0	-2	-2	0	-0.1
● **AL GOULD** Gould, Albert Frank "Pudgy" b: 1/20/1893, Muscatine, Iowa d: 8/8/82, San Jose, Cal. BR/TR, 5'6.5", 160 lbs. Deb: 7/11/16																												
1916	Cle-A	5	6	.455	30	9	6	1	1	106^{2}	101	37	0	3	40	41	12.2	2.53	119	.256	.329	3	.103	-2	4	5	-1	0.3
1917	Cle-A	4	4	.500	27	7	1	0	0	94	95	44	1	3	52	24	14.4	3.64	78	.281	.382	5	.208	1	-10	-8	2	-0.4
Total	2	9	10	.474	57	16	7	1	1	200^{2}	196	81	1	6	92	65	13.2	3.05	96	.267	.354	8	.151	-1	-7	-3	1	-0.1
● **CHARLIE GOULD** Gould, Charles Harvey b: 8/21/1847, Cincinnati, Ohio d: 4/10/17, Flushing, N.Y. BR/TR, 6', 172 lbs. Deb: 5/5/1871 M♦																												
1876	Cin-N	0	0	—	2	0	0	0	0	4^{1}	10	9	0	22	0	0	20.8	0.00	—	.400	.400	65	.246	0	1	1	-0	0.0
● **LARRY GOWELL** Gowell, Lawrence Clyde b: 5/2/48, Lewiston, Me. BR/TR, 6'2", 182 lbs. Deb: 9/21/72																												
1972	NY-A	0	1	.000	2	1	0	0	0	7	3	1	0	0	2	7	6.4	1.29	230	.143	.217	1	1.000	1	1	1	0	0.3
● **MAURO GOZZO** Gozzo, Mauro Paul b: 3/7/66, New Britain, Conn. BR/TR, 6'3", 212 lbs. Deb: 8/8/89																												
1989	Tor-A	4	1	.800	9	3	0	0	0	31^{2}	35	19	1	1	9	10	12.8	4.83	78	.289	.344	0	—	0	-3	-4	-0	-0.6
1990	Cle-A	0	0	—	2	0	0	0	0	3	2	0	0	0	2	2	12.0	0.00	—	.182	.308	0	—	0	1	1	-0	0.1
1991	Cle-A	0	0	—	2	2	0	0	0	4^{2}	9	10	0	0	7	3	30.9	19.29	22	.450	.593	0	—	0	-8	-8	-0	-0.4
1992	Min-A	0	0	—	2	0	0	0	0	1^{2}	7	5	2	0	0	1	37.8	27.00	15	.583	.583	0	—	0	-4	-4	-0	-0.2
1993	NY-N	0	1	.000	10	0	0	0	1	14	11	5	1	0	5	6	10.3	2.57	156	.212	.281	0	—	0	2	2	-1	0.1
1994	NY-N	3	5	.375	23	8	0	0	0	69	86	48	5	1	28	33	15.0	4.83	87	.304	.369	4	.250	1	-5	-5	-0	-0.4
Total	6	7	7	.500	48	13	0	0	1	124	150	87	9	2	51	55	14.7	5.30	76	.301	.368	4	.250	1	-17	-17	-2	-1.4
● **AL GRABOWSKI** Grabowski, Alfons Francis b: 9/6/01, Syracuse, N.Y. d: 10/29/66, Memphis, N.Y. BL/TL, 5'11.5", 175 lbs. Deb: 9/11/29 F																												
1929	StL-N	3	2	.600	6	6	4	2	0	50	44	18	0	0	8	22	9.4	2.52	185	.227	.257	4	.250	2	12	12	-0	1.2
1930	StL-N	6	4	.600	33	8	1	0	1	107	120	66	7	3	49	43	14.5	4.79	105	.290	.369	12	.364	3	2	3	-0	0.4
Total	2	9	6	.600	39	14	5	2	1	157	164	84	7	3	57	65	12.8	4.07	120	.270	.335	16	.327	4	14	14	-0	1.6
● **REGGIE GRABOWSKI** Grabowski, Reginald John b: 7/16/07, Syracuse, N.Y. d: 4/2/55, Syracuse, N.Y. BR/TR, 6'0.5", 185 lbs. Deb: 4/15/32 F																												
1932	Phi-N	2	2	.500	14	2	0	0	0	34^{1}	38	18	2	2	22	15	16.3	3.67	120	.273	.380	0	.000	-1	1	2	-1	0.1
1933	Phi-N	1	3	.250	10	5	4	1	0	48	38	13	4	1	10	9	9.2	2.44	157	.220	.266	2	.125	-1	5	6	-1	0.3
1934	Phi-N	1	3	.250	27	5	0	0	0	65^{1}	114	72	13	3	23	13	19.3	9.23	51	.384	.433	1	.056	-2	-38	-28	-1	-1.8
Total	3	4	8	.333	51	12	4	1	0	147^{2}	190	103	19	6	55	37	15.3	5.73	76	.312	.375	3	.075	-3	-32	-20	-3	-1.4
● **MIKE GRACE** Grace, Michael James b: 6/20/70, Joliet, Ill. BR/TR, 6'4", 210 lbs. Deb: 9/1/95																												
1995	Phi-N	1	1	.500	2	2	0	0	0	11^{1}	10	4	0	0	4	7	11.1	3.18	133	.238	.304	0	.000	-0	1	1	0	0.2
1996	Phi-N	7	2	.778	12	12	1	1	0	80	72	33	9	1	16	49	10.0	3.49	124	.238	.279	4	.138	-0	7	7	1	0.9
1997	Phi-N	3	2	.600	6	6	1	1	0	39	32	16	3	1	10	26	9.9	3.46	123	.230	.287	1	.083	-1	3	3	-1	0.3
1998	Phi-N	4	7	.364	21	15	0	0	0	90^{1}	116	61	10	8	30	46	15.3	5.48	79	.312	.376	2	.087	-1	-12	-11	-1	-1.4
1999	Phi-N	1	4	.200	27	5	0	0	0	55	80	48	5	6	30	28	19.0	7.69	61	.346	.434	0	.000	-1	-19	-18	-0	-1.4
Total	5	16	16	.500	68	40	2	2	0	275^{2}	310	162	27	16	90	156	13.6	4.96	88	.285	.349	7	.096	-2	-21	-17	-1	-1.4
● **JOHN GRAFF** Graff, John J. b: 11/1866, Washington, D.C. d: 4/2/32, Washington, D.C. Deb: 7/19/1893																												
1893	Was-N	0	1	.000	2	1	1	0	0	12	21	21	2	1	13	4	26.3	11.25	41	.368	.493	1	.200	-0	-9	-9	-0	-0.5
● **PEACHES GRAHAM** Graham, George Frederick b: 3/23/1877, Aledo, Ill. d: 7/25/39, Long Beach, Cal. BR/TR, 5'9", 180 lbs. Deb: 9/14/02 F♦																												
1903	Chi-N	0	1	.000	1	1	0	0	0	5	9	6	0	1	3	4	23.4	5.40	58	.429	.520	0	.000	-0	-1	-1	0	-0.2
● **SKINNY GRAHAM** Graham, Kyle b: 8/14/1899, Oak Grove, Ala. d: 12/1/73, Oak Grove, Ala. BR/TR, 6'2", 172 lbs. Deb: 9/3/24																												
1924	Bos-N	0	4	.000	5	4	1	0	0	33	33	14	0	0	11	15	12.0	3.82	100	.287	.349	0	.000	-1	0	0	-0	-0.1
1925	Bos-N	7	12	.368	34	23	5	0	1	157	177	90	6	3	62	32	13.9	4.41	91	.296	.365	6	.136	-2	-3	-8	-2	-1.2
1926	Bos-N	3	3	.500	15	4	1	0	0	36^{1}	54	32	3	2	19	7	18.6	7.93	45	.370	.449	2	.167	-1	-17	-19	0	-2.6
1929	Det-A	1	3	.250	13	6	2	0	1	51^{2}	70	41	2	3	33	7	18.5	5.57	77	.340	.438	2	.105	-1	-8	-7	-1	-0.7
Total	4	11	22	.333	67	37	9	0	2	278	334	177	11	8	125	61	15.1	5.02	79	.314	.390	10	.122	-5	-27	-34	-3	-4.6
● **OSCAR GRAHAM** Graham, Oscar M. b: 7/20/1878, Plattsmouth, Neb. d: 10/15/31, Moline, Ill. BL/TL, 6'0.5", Deb: 4/16/07																												
1907	Was-A	4	9	.308	20	14	6	0	0	104	116	66	3	10	29	44	13.4	3.98	61	.284	.347	11	.229	3	-17	-19	0	-1.8
● **BILL GRAHAM** Graham, William Albert b: 1/21/37, Flemingsburg, Ky. BR/TR, 6'3", 217 lbs. Deb: 10/2/66																												
1966	Det-A	0	0	—	1	0	0	0	0	2	2	0	0	0	0	2	9.0	0.00	—	.250	.250	0	—	0	1	1	-0	0.0
1967	NY-N	1	2	.333	5	3	1	0	0	27^{1}	20	10	3	0	11	14	10.2	2.63	129	.200	.279	1	.125	-0	2	2	-1	0.1
Total	2	1	2	.333	6	3	1	0	0	29^{1}	22	10	3	0	11	16	10.1	2.45	138	.204	.277	1	.125	-0	3	3	-1	0.1
● **BILL GRAHAME** Grahame, William James b: 7/22/1884, Owosso, Mich. d: 2/15/36, Holt, Mich. TL, 6', Deb: 4/18/08																												
1908	StL-A	6	7	.462	21	13	7	0	0	117^{1}	104	46	0	12	32	47	11.4	2.30	104	.240	.310	5	.119	-3	1	1	-0	-0.2
1909	StL-A	8	14	.364	34	21	13	3	1	187^{1}	171	78	3	5	60	82	11.3	3.12	77	.256	.322	10	.159	-0	-13	-15	1	-1.7
1910	StL-A	0	8	.000	9	6	1	0	0	43	46	31	2	4	13	12	13.2	3.56	70	.297	.366	2	.154	-0	-5	-5	-2	-1.1
Total	3	14	29	.326	64	40	21	3	1	347^{2}	321	155	5	21	105	141	11.6	2.90	83	.256	.323	17	.144	-3	-17	-19	-1	-3.0
● **JOE GRAHE** Grahe, Joseph Milton b: 8/14/67, W.Palm Beach, Fla. BR/TR, 6', 200 lbs. Deb: 8/4/90																												
1990	Cal-A	3	4	.429	8	8	0	0	0	43^{1}	51	30	3	3	23	25	16.0	4.98	77	.293	.385	0	—	0	-5	-6	1	-0.7
1991	Cal-A	3	7	.300	18	10	1	0	0	73	84	43	2	3	33	40	14.8	4.81	85	.288	.366	0	—	0	-6	-6	0	-0.7
1992	Cal-A	5	6	.455	46	7	0	0	21	94^{2}	85	37	5	6	39	39	12.4	3.52	113	.246	.332	0	—	0	5	5	0	0.8
1993	Cal-A	4	1	.800	45	0	0	0	11	56^{2}	54	22	5	2	25	31	12.9	2.86	158	.251	.335	0	—	0	9	10	1	1.2
1994	Cal-A	2	5	.286	40	0	0	0	13	43^{1}	68	33	5	6	18	26	19.1	6.65	74	.362	.434	0	—	0	-9	-8	1	-1.5
1995	Col-N	4	3	.571	17	9	0	0	0	56^{2}	69	42	6	3	27	27	15.7	5.08	106	.301	.382	5	.417	1	-6	2	1	0.3
1999	Phi-N	1	4	.200	13	5	0	0	0	32^{2}	40	16	1	3	17	16	16.5	3.86	122	.308	.400	1	.143	0	3	3	0	0.4
Total	7	22	30	.423	187	39	1	0	45	400^{1}	451	223	27	26	182	204	14.8	4.41	100	.287	.370	6	.316	1	-9	1	4	-0.2
● **TOMMY GRAMLY** Gramly, Bert Thomas b: 4/19/45, Dallas, Tex. BR/TR, 6'3", 175 lbs. Deb: 4/18/68																												
1968	Cle-A	0	1	.000	3	0	0	0	0	3^{1}	3	1	0	0	2	1	13.5	2.70	110	.250	.357	0	—	0	0	0	-0	0.0
● **HANK GRAMPP** Grampp, Henry Erchardt b: 9/28/03, New York, N.Y. d: 3/24/86, New York, N.Y. BR/TR, 6'1", 185 lbs. Deb: 6/2/27																												
1927	Chi-N	0	0	—	2	0	0	0	0	3	4	3	0	0	1	3	15.0	9.00	43	.333	.385	0	—	0	-2	-2	0	-0.1
1929	Chi-N	0	1	.000	1	1	0	0	0	2	4	6	0	1	3	0	36.0	27.00	17	.500	.667	0	—	0	-5	-5	-0	-0.7
Total	2	0	1	.000	3	1	0	0	0	5	8	9	0	1	4	3	23.4	16.20	26	.400	.520	0	—	0	-7	-7	0	-0.8
● **JACK GRANEY** Graney, John Gladstone b: 6/10/1886, St.Thomas, Ont., Can. d: 4/20/78, Louisiana, Mo. BL/TL, 5'9", 180 lbs. Deb: 4/30/08 ♦																												
1908	Cle-A	0	0	—	2	0	0	0	0	3^{1}	6	2	0	0	1	0	18.9	5.40	44	.400	.438	0	—	0	-1	-1	-0	-0.1

YEAR	TM/L	W	L	PCT	G	GS	CG	SH	SV	IP	H	R	HR	HB	BB	SO	RAT	ERA	ERA+	OAV	OOB	BH	AVG	PB	PR	PR+	PD	TPI
● **JEFF GRANGER**	Granger, Jeffrey Adam b: 12/16/71, San Pedro, Cal. BR/TL, 6'4", 200 lbs. Deb: 9/16/93																											
1993	KC-A	0	0	—	1	0	0	0	0	1	3	3	0	0	2	1	45.0	27.00	17	.500	.625	0	—	0	-3	-2	0	-0.1
1994	KC-A	0	1	.000	2	2	0	0	0	9^1	13	8	2	0	6	3	18.3	6.75	74	.325	.413	0	—	0	-2	-2	0	-0.1
1996	KC-A	0	0	—	15	0	0	0	0	16^1	21	13	3	2	10	11	18.2	6.61	76	.313	.418	0	—	0	-3	-3	0	-0.1
1997	Pit-N	0	0	—	9	0	0	0	0	5	10	10	3	0	8	4	32.4	18.00	24	.417	.563	0	—	0	-8	-7	-0	-0.4
Total	4	0	1	.000	27	2	0	0	0	31^2	47	34	8	2	26	19	21.3	9.09	54	.343	.455	0	—	0	-15	-15	-0	-0.7
● **WAYNE GRANGER**	Granger, Wayne Allan b: 3/15/44, Springfield, Mass. BR/TR, 6'2", 165 lbs. Deb: 6/5/68																											
1968	*StL-N	4	2	.667	34	0	0	0	4	44	40	14	2	2	12	27	11.0	2.25	129	.238	.297	1	.200	0	4	3	2	0.7
1969	Cin-N	9	6	.600	**90**	0	0	0	27	144^2	143	64	10	7	40	68	11.8	2.80	135	.262	.320	2	.095	-0	13	15	1	2.3
1970	*Cin-N	6	5	.545	67	0	0	0	**35**	84^2	79	33	5	1	27	38	11.4	2.66	152	.252	.313	1	.100	-1	13	13	2	2.8
1971	Cin-N	7	6	.538	**70**	0	0	0	11	100	94	39	8	1	28	51	11.1	3.33	101	.251	.304	1	.143	1	2	0	3	0.5
1972	Min-A	4	6	.400	63	0	0	0	19	89^2	83	42	7	2	28	45	11.3	3.01	107	.243	.304	2	.200	0	1	2	-0	0.3
1973	StL-N	2	4	.333	33	0	0	0	5	46^2	50	29	3	2	21	14	14.1	4.24	86	.284	.367	0	.000	-0	-3	-3	-0	-0.5
	NY-A	0	1	.000	7	0	0	0	0	15^1	19	7	1	1	3	10	13.5	1.76	208	.279	.319	0	—	0	4	3	-1	0.2
1974	Chi-A	0	0	—	5	0	0	0	0	7^2	16	8	1	0	3	4	22.3	8.22	45	.432	.475	0	—	0	-4	-4	0	-0.2
1975	Hou-N	2	5	.286	55	0	0	0	5	74	76	39	7	4	23	30	12.5	3.65	93	.264	.327	0	.000	-1	-0	-2	1	-0.2
1976	Mon-N	1	0	1.000	27	0	0	0	2	32	32	15	3	2	16	16	14.1	3.66	102	.264	.360	0	.000	-0	-1	0	-0	0.0
Total	9	35	35	.500	451	0	0	0	108	638^2	632	290	47	22	201	303	12.0	3.14	113	.260	.322	7	.103	-1	28	29	8	5.9
● **GEORGE GRANT**	Grant, George Addison b: 1/6/03, E.Tallassee, Ala. d: 3/25/86, Montgomery, Ala. BR/TR, 5'11.5", 175 lbs. Deb: 9/17/23																											
1923	StL-A	0	0	—	4	0	0	0	0	8^2	15	7	0	0	3	2	18.7	5.19	80	.395	.439	0	.000	-0	-1	-1	0	0.0
1924	StL-A	1	2	.333	22	2	0	0	0	51^1	69	43	4	1	25	11	16.7	6.31	72	.325	.399	0	.000	-2	-12	-10	-1	-0.7
1925	StL-A	0	2	.000	12	0	0	0	0	16^1	26	15	2	0	8	7	18.7	6.06	77	.400	.466	1	.250	-0	-3	-2	0	-0.2
1927	Cle-A	4	6	.400	25	3	2	0	1	74^2	85	46	1	0	40	19	15.1	4.46	94	.300	.387	2	.095	-2	-3	-2	0	-0.4
1928	Cle-A	10	8	.556	28	18	6	1	0	155^1	196	102	7	2	76	39	15.9	5.04	82	.319	.395	11	.183	-2	-17	-15	2	-1.4
1929	Cle-A	0	2	.000	12	0	0	0	0	24	41	29	2	0	23	5	24.0	10.50	42	.414	.525	0	.000	-0	-17	-15	0	-1.1
1931	Pit-N	0	0	—	11	0	0	0	0	17	28	16	0	1	7	6	19.1	7.41	52	.364	.424	0	.000	-0	-7	-7	0	-0.3
Total	7	15	20	.429	114	23	8	1	1	347^1	460	258	16	4	182	89	16.7	5.65	75	.331	.410	14	.135	-8	-59	-53	3	-4.1
● **JIM GRANT**	Grant, James Ronald b: 8/4/1894, Coalville, Iowa d: 11/30/85, Des Moines, Iowa BR/TL, 5'11", 180 lbs. Deb: 4/21/23																											
1923	Phi-N	0	0	—	2	0	0	0	0	4	10	8	0	1	4	0	33.8	13.50	34	.588	.682	0	.000	-0	-4	-3	0	-0.2
● **MUDCAT GRANT**	Grant, James Timothy "Jim" b: 8/13/35, Lacoochee, Fla. BR/TR, 6'1", 186 lbs. Deb: 4/17/58																											
1958	Cle-A	10	11	.476	44	28	11	1	4	204	173	93	20	1	104	111	12.3	3.84	95	.228	.321	5	.076	-4	-2	-4	-2	-1.0
1959	Cle-A	10	7	.588	38	19	6	1	3	165^1	140	80	23	2	81	85	12.1	4.14	89	.232	.325	11	.200	1	-5	-9	-0	-0.8
1960	Cle-A	9	8	.529	33	19	5	0	0	159^2	147	88	26	2	78	75	12.8	4.40	85	.243	.332	16	.281	4	-9	-12	-1	-0.9
1961	Cle-A	15	9	.625	35	35	11	3	0	244^2	207	118	32	3	109	146	11.7	3.86	102	.227	.312	15	.170	1	4	2	1	0.3
1962	Cle-A	7	10	.412	26	23	6	1	0	149^2	128	75	24	0	81	90	12.6	4.27	91	.233	.331	8	.151	-0	-5	-7	-0	-0.7
1963	Cle-A☆	13	14	.481	38	32	10	2	1	229^1	213	107	30	4	87	157	11.9	3.69	98	.243	.314	13	.188	3	-2	-2	-3	-0.2
1964	Cle-A	3	4	.429	13	9	1	0	0	62	82	41	11	1	25	43	15.7	5.95	60	.324	.387	6	.273	4	-16	-16	0	-1.2
	Min-A	11	9	.550	26	23	10	1	1	166	162	73	21	0	36	75	10.7	2.82	127	.248	.288	10	.167	0	15	14	0	1.7
	Yr	14	13	.519	39	32	11	1	1	228	244	114	32	1	61	118	12.1	3.67	98	.270	.316	16	.195	4	-1	-2	1	0.5
1965	*Min-A★	**21**	7	**.750**	41	39	14	**6**	0	270^1	252	107	34	0	61	142	10.4	3.30	108	.247	.289	15	.155	2	5	8	1	1.1
1966	Min-A	13	13	.500	35	35	10	3	0	249	248	104	23	6	49	110	11.0	3.25	111	.260	.300	15	.192	2	5	9	2	1.4
1967	Min-A	5	6	.455	27	14	2	0	0	95^1	121	56	10	1	17	50	13.1	4.72	73	.315	.346	5	.179	0	-16	-12	-2	-1.6
1968	LA-N	6	4	.600	37	4	1	0	3	94^2	77	29	1	6	19	35	9.7	2.09	132	.226	.279	4	.129	0	9	8	1	1.0
1969	Mon-N	1	6	.143	11	10	1	0	0	50^2	64	33	7	1	14	20	14.0	4.80	77	.299	.345	2	.125	-1	-7	-6	0	-0.8
	StL-N	7	5	.583	30	3	1	0	7	63^1	62	31	9	2	22	35	12.2	4.12	87	.252	.319	5	.294	2	-4	-4	-1	-0.7
	Yr	8	11	.421	41	13	2	0	7	114	126	64	16	3	36	55	13.0	4.42	82	.274	.331	7	.212	1	-10	-10	-1	-1.5
1970	Oak-A	6	2	.750	72	0	0	0	24	123^1	104	26	8	3	30	54	10.0	1.82	194	.235	.288	2	.222	2	**26**	**25**	1	2.8
	Pit-N	2	1	.667	8	0	0	0	0	12	8	3	2	0	2	4	7.5	2.25	174	.190	.227	0	.000	-0	2	2	0	0.5
1971	Pit-N	5	3	.625	42	0	0	0	7	75	79	32	8	1	28	22	13.0	3.60	94	.274	.341	2	.250	1	-1	-2	1	-0.1
	*Oak-A	1	0	1.000	15	0	0	0	3	27^1	25	9	3	0	6	13	10.2	1.98	169	.243	.284	1	.333	0	5	4	-0	0.3
Total	14	145	119	.549	571	293	89	18	53	2441^2	2292	1105	292	33	849	1267	11.7	3.63	100	.248	.313	135	.178	16	6	-3	-3	1.1
● **MARK GRANT**	Grant, Mark Andrew b: 10/24/63, Aurora, Ill. BR/TR, 6'2", 205 lbs. Deb: 4/27/84																											
1984	SF-N	1	4	.200	11	10	0	0	1	53^2	56	40	6	1	19	32	12.7	6.37	55	.272	.336	0	.000	-2	-17	-17	-0	-1.6
1986	SF-N	0	1	.000	4	1	0	0	0	10	6	4	0	0	5	5	9.9	3.60	98	.176	.282	0	.000	-0	0	-0	-0	0.0
1987	SF-N	1	2	.333	16	8	0	0	1	61	66	29	6	1	21	32	13.0	3.54	109	.282	.344	1	.083	-0	4	2	-1	0.0
	SD-N	6	7	.462	17	17	2	1	0	102^1	104	59	16	0	52	58	13.7	4.66	85	.263	.348	3	.094	-1	-7	-8	-1	-1.0
	Yr	7	9	.438	33	25	2	1	1	163^1	170	88	22	1	73	90	13.4	4.24	92	.270	.347	4	.091	-1	-3	-6	-1	-1.0
1988	SD-N	2	8	.200	33	11	0	0	0	97^2	97	41	14	2	36	61	12.4	3.69	92	.268	.338	0	.000	-1	-3	-3	0	-0.4
1989	SD-N	8	2	.800	50	0	0	0	2	116^1	105	45	11	3	32	69	10.8	3.33	105	.248	.305	1	.050	-0	2	2	-0	0.1
1990	SD-N	1	1	.500	26	0	0	0	0	39	47	23	5	0	19	29	15.2	4.85	79	.305	.382	1	.500	0	-5	-4	1	-0.1
	Atl-N	1	2	.333	33	1	0	0	3	52^1	61	30	4	1	18	40	13.8	4.64	87	.293	.352	1	.250	1	-5	-3	-0	-0.2
	Yr	2	3	.400	59	1	0	0	3	91^1	108	53	9	1	37	69	14.4	4.73	84	.298	.365	2	.333	1	-9	-8	0	-0.3
1992	Sea-A	2	4	.333	23	10	0	0	0	81	100	39	6	2	22	42	13.8	3.89	102	.311	.358	0	—	0	1	1	-1	0.0
1993	Hou-N	0	0	—	6	0	0	0	0	11	11	4	0	0	5	6	13.1	0.82	474	.275	.356	0	—	0	4	4	1	0.3
	Col-N	0	1	.000	14	0	0	0	1	14^1	23	20	4	0	6	8	18.2	12.56	38	.377	.433	0	—	0	-14	-11	0	-0.8
	Yr	0	1	.000	20	0	0	0	1	25^1	34	24	4	0	11	14	16.0	7.46	59	.337	.402	0	—	0	-10	-8	1	-0.5
Total	8	22	32	.407	233	58	2	1	8	638^2	676	334	72	10	235	382	13.0	4.31	87	.277	.343	7	.067	-3	-38	-40	-2	-3.7
● **RICK GRAPENTHIN**	Grapenthin, Richard Ray b: 4/16/58, Linn Grove, Iowa BR/TR, 6'2", 205 lbs. Deb: 5/3/83																											
1983	Mon-N	0	1	.000	1	0	0	0	0	4	4	4	2	0	1	3	11.3	9.00	40	.267	.313	0	.000	-0	-2	-2	0	-0.4
1984	Mon-N	1	2	.333	13	1	0	0	2	23	19	9	3	0	7	9	10.2	3.52	97	.235	.295	1	.200	0	0	-0	0	0.0
1985	Mon-N	0	0	—	5	0	0	0	0	7	13	11	0	1	8	4	28.3	14.14	24	.394	.524	1	1.000	1	-8	-9	-0	-0.4
Total	3	1	3	.250	19	1	0	0	2	34	36	24	5	1	16	16	14.0	6.35	54	.279	.363	2	.286	0	-10	-12	0	-0.8
● **LOU GRASMICK**	Grasmick, Louis Junior b: 9/11/24, Baltimore, Md. BR/TR, 6', 195 lbs. Deb: 4/22/48																											
1948	Phi-N	0	0	—	2	0	0	0	0	5	3	4	1	0	8	2	19.8	7.20	55	.176	.440	1	1.000	0	-2	-2	0	0.0
● **DON GRATE**	Grate, Donald "Buckeye" b: 8/27/23, Greenfield, Ohio BR/TR, 6'2.5", 180 lbs. Deb: 7/6/45																											
1945	Phi-N	0	1	.000	4	2	0	0	0	8^1	18	16	0	0	12	6	32.4	17.28	22	.439	.566	0	.000	-0	-12	-12	-0	-1.2
1946	Phi-N	1	0	1.000	3	0	0	0	0	8	4	1	0	0	2	2	6.8	1.13	305	.160	.222	0	.000	0	2	2	-0	0.2
Total	2	1	1	.500	7	2	0	0	0	16^1	22	17	0	0	14	8	19.8	9.37	39	.333	.450	0	.000	-0	-10	-10	-1	-1.0
● **MARK GRATER**	Grater, Mark Anthony b: 1/19/64, Rochester, Pa. BR/TR, 5'10", 205 lbs. Deb: 6/12/91																											
1991	StL-N	0	0	—	3	0	0	0	0	3	5	0	0	0	2	0	21.0	0.00	—	.385	.467	0	—	0	1	1	-0	0.1
1993	Det-A	0	0	—	6	0	0	0	0	5	6	3	0	0	4	4	18.0	5.40	80	.286	.400	0	—	0	-1	-1	-0	0.0
Total	2	0	0	—	9	0	0	0	0	8	11	3	0	0	6	4	19.1	3.38	121	.324	.425	0	—	0	1	1	-0	0.1
● **BEIKER GRATEROL**	Graterol, Beiker b: 11/9/74, Lara, Venez. BR/TR, 6'2", 165 lbs. Deb: 4/9/99																											
1999	Det-A	0	1	.000	1	1	0	0	0	4	4	7	3	0	4	2	18.0	15.75	31	.250	.400	0	—	0	-5	-5	0	-0.6
● **DANNY GRAVES**	Graves, Daniel Peter b: 8/7/73, Saigon, South Vietnam BR/TR, 5'11", 200 lbs. Deb: 7/13/96																											
1996	Cle-A	2	0	1.000	15	0	0	0	0	29^2	29	18	2	0	10	22	11.8	4.55	108	.246	.305	0	—	0	1	1	-0	0.0
1997	Cle-A	0	0	—	5	0	0	0	0	11^1	15	8	2	0	9	4	19.1	4.76	99	.326	.436	0	—	0	-0	-0	-0	0.0
	Cin-N	0	0	—	10	0	0	0	0	14^2	26	14	0	0	11	7	22.7	6.14	70	.413	.500	0	.000	-0	-3	-3	0	-0.1
1998	Cin-N	2	1	.667	62	0	0	0	8	81^1	76	31	6	2	28	44	11.7	3.32	129	.251	.318	0	.000	-0	8	9	1	0.4
1999	Cin-N	8	7	.533	75	0	0	0	27	111	90	42	10	2	49	69	11.4	3.08	151	.227	.315	0	.000	-1	18	19	1	3.1

YEAR	TM/L	W	L	PCT	G	GS	CG	SH	SV	IP	H	R	HR	HB	BB	SO	RAT	ERA	ERA+	OAV	OOB	BH	AVG	PB	PR	PR+	PD	TPI
2000	Cin-N★	10	5	.667	66	0	0	0	30	91^1	81	31	8	3	42	53	12.4	2.56	186	.243	.333	1	.500	2	21	22	2	4.7
Total	5	22	13	.629	233	0	0	0	65	339^1	317	144	28	7	149	199	12.5	3.32	139	.252	.334	1	.083	0	46	48	4	8.1
● **FRANK GRAVES** Graves, Frank M. b: 11/2/1860, Cincinnati, Ohio 6', 163 lbs. Deb: 5/10/1886 ♦																												
1886	StL-N	0	0	—	1	0	0	0	0	7	10	10	0		1	2	14.1	9.00	36	.323	.344	21	.152	-0	-4	-5	-0	-0.2
● **CHARLIE GRAY** Gray, Charles A. b: 1867, Indianapolis, Ind. d: 6/1/1900, Indianapolis, Ind. Deb: 4/23/1890																												
1890	Pit-N	1	4	.200	5	4	3	0	0	31	48	35	0	1	24	10	21.2	7.55	44	.343	.442	3	.200	-0	-14	-16	-1	-1.8
● **DAVE GRAY** Gray, David Alexander b: 1/7/43, Ogden, Utah BR/TR, 6'1", 190 lbs. Deb: 6/14/64																												
1964	Bos-A	0	0	—	9	1	0	0	0	13	18	20	3	0	20	17	26.3	9.00	43	.321	.500	1	1.000	0	-8	-7	0	-0.3
● **CHUMMY GRAY** Gray, George Edward b: 7/17/1873, Rockland, Me. d: 8/14/13, Rockland, Maine TR, 5'11.5", 163 lbs. Deb: 9/14/1899																												
1899	Pit-N	3	3	.500	9	7	6	0	0	70^2	85	35	1	4	24	9	14.4	3.44	111	.297	.360	1	.038	-3	3	3	2	0.1
● **JEFF GRAY** Gray, Jeffrey Edward b: 4/10/63, Richmond, Va. BR/TR, 6'1", 175 lbs. Deb: 6/21/88																												
1988	Cin-N	0	0	—	5	0	0	0	0	9^1	12	4	0	0	4	5	15.4	3.86	93	.333	.400	0	.000	-0	-0	-0	0	0.0
1990	*Bos-A	2	4	.333	41	0	0	0	9	50^2	53	27	3	1	15	50	12.3	4.44	92	.268	.322	0	—	0	-3	-2	-0	-0.3
1991	Bos-A	2	3	.400	50	0	0	0	1	61^2	39	17	7	1	10	41	7.3	2.34	184	.181	.220	0	—	0	12	13	1	1.0
Total	3	4	7	.364	96	0	0	0	10	121^2	104	48	10	2	29	96	10.0	3.33	125	.231	.281	0	.000	-0	9	11	1	0.7
● **JOHNNY GRAY** Gray, John Leonard b: 12/11/26, W.Palm Beach, Fla. BR/TR, 6'4", 226 lbs. Deb: 7/18/54																												
1954	Phi-A	3	12	.200	18	16	5	0	0	105	111	83	10	0	91	51	17.3	6.51	60	.273	.406	1	.029	-4	-33	-29	0	-3.7
1955	KC-A	0	3	.000	8	5	0	0	0	26^2	28	23	2	1	24	11	17.9	6.41	65	.277	.421	1	.125	-0	-7	-6	-1	-0.7
1957	Cle-A	1	3	.250	7	3	1	1	0	20	21	17	1	0	13	3	15.3	5.85	64	.288	.395	0	.000	-1	-5	-5	-0	-0.9
1958	Phi-N	0	0	—	15	0	0	0	0	17^1	12	9	3	0	14	10	13.5	4.15	95	.222	.382	0	.000	-0	-0	-0	-0	0.0
Total	4	4	18	.182	48	24	6	1	0	169	172	132	16	1	142	75	16.8	6.18	64	.271	.405	2	.043	-5	-45	-41	-1	-5.3
● **DOLLY GRAY** Gray, Samuel David "Sam" b: 10/15/1897, Van Alstyne, Tex. d: 4/16/53, McKinney, Tex. BR/TR, 5'11", 175 lbs. Deb: 4/19/24																												
1924	Phi-A	8	7	.533	34	19	8	2	2	151^2	169	95	5	6	89	54	15.7	3.98	108	.284	.383	10	.175	-2	4	5	-1	0.1
1925	Phi-A	16	8	.667	32	28	14	4	3	203^2	199	90	11	3	63	80	11.7	3.27	142	.260	.319	12	.179	-2	25	30	-3	2.6
1926	Phi-A	11	12	.478	38	18	5	0	0	150^2	164	81	9	4	50	82	13.0	3.64	114	.279	.340	11	.216	1	6	8	-2	1.1
1927	Phi-A	9	6	.600	37	13	3	1	3	133^1	153	79	4	4	51	49	14.0	4.59	93	.295	.362	8	.190	-1	-7	-5	0	-0.6
1928	StL-A	20	12	.625	35	31	21	2	3	262^2	256	119	11	1	86	102	11.8	3.19	132	.260	.320	19	.188	-2	25	29	3	3.4
1929	StL-A	18	15	.545	43	37	23	**4**	1	**305**	336	142	18	1	96	109	12.8	3.72	119	.285	.340	19	.184	-2	18	23	-1	1.9
1930	StL-A	4	15	.211	27	24	7	0	0	167^2	215	133	17	4	52	51	14.5	6.28	78	.316	.368	11	.204	-2	-30	-25	-1	-2.4
1931	StL-A	11	24	.314	43	37	13	0	2	258	323	187	20	4	54	88	13.3	5.09	91	.297	.332	14	.177	-1	-20	-12	-1	-1.6
1932	StL-A	7	12	.368	52	18	7	3	4	206^2	250	126	9	1	53	79	13.2	4.53	107	.294	.336	13	.210	-0	-1	7	-1	0.5
1933	StL-A	7	4	.636	38	6	0	0	4	112	131	55	7	1	45	36	14.2	4.10	114	.301	.368	7	.219	1	2	6	-1	0.7
Total	10	111	115	.491	379	231	101	16	22	1951^1	2196	1107	111	29	639	730	13.2	4.18	108	.286	.343	124	.191	-10	23	65	-7	5.7
● **TED GRAY** Gray, Ted Glenn b: 12/31/24, Detroit, Mich. BB/TL (BR 1946), 5'11", 175 lbs. Deb: 5/15/46																												
1946	Det-A	0	2	.000	3	2	0	0	1	11^2	17	12	4	0	5	5	17.0	8.49	43	.340	.400	0	.000	-0	-6	-6	-0	-0.9
1948	Det-A	6	2	.750	26	11	3	1	0	85^1	73	43	2	3	72	60	15.6	4.22	104	.236	.385	7	.241	1	1	1	-0	0.1
1949	Det-A	10	10	.500	34	27	8	3	1	195	163	83	11	5	103	96	12.5	3.51	119	.227	.328	8	.127	-3	15	14	1	1.1
1950	Det-A★	10	7	.588	27	21	7	0	1	149^1	139	85	22	2	72	102	12.8	4.40	107	.248	.335	7	.140	-2	3	5	-2	0.1
1951	Det-A	7	14	.333	34	28	9	1	1	197^1	194	103	17	6	95	131	13.5	4.06	103	.256	.343	9	.143	-3	1	3	-1	-0.2
1952	Det-A	12	17	.414	35	32	13	2	0	224	212	118	21	3	101	138	12.7	4.14	92	.249	.331	13	.171	-2	-12	-8	1	-1.0
1953	Det-A	10	15	.400	30	28	8	0	0	176	166	102	25	7	76	115	12.7	4.60	88	.252	.336	14	.230	2	-12	-10	-1	-1.2
1954	Det-A	3	5	.375	19	10	2	0	0	72	70	48	8	2	56	29	16.0	5.38	69	.268	.401	1	.045	-2	-13	-14	-1	-1.7
1955	Chi-A	0	0	—	2	1	0	0	0	3	9	6	0	0	2	1	33.0	18.00	22	.500	.550	0	—	0	-5	-5	0	-0.2
	Cle-A	0	0	—	2	0	0	0	0	2	5	4	1	0	2	1	31.5	18.00	22	.455	.538	0	—	0	-3	-3	0	-0.1
	NY-A	0	0	—	1	1	0	0	0	3	3	1	0	0	0	1	9.0	3.00	125	.300	.300	0	.000	-0	0	0	-0	0.0
	Bal-A	1	2	.333	9	1	0	0	0	15^1	21	19	3	0	11	8	18.8	8.22	46	.344	.444	0	.000	-0	-7	-8	1	-1.2
	Yr	1	2	.333	14	3	0	0	0	23^1	38	30	4	0	15	11	20.4	9.64	40	.380	.461	0	.000	-0	-15	-16	1	-1.5
Total	9	59	74	.444	222	162	50	7	4	1134	1072	624	114	28	595	687	13.5	4.37	94	.251	.346	59	.159	-10	-38	-30	-4	-5.2
● **DOLLY GRAY** Gray, William Denton b: 12/3/1878, Houghton, Mich. d: 4/4/56, Yuba City, Cal. BL/TL, 6'2", 160 lbs. Deb: 4/13/09																												
1909	Was-A	5	19	.208	36	26	19	0	0	218	210	123	1	9	77	87	12.2	3.59	68	.258	.329	13	.146	-1	-27	-29	-1	-3.3
1910	Was-A	8	19	.296	34	29	21	3	0	229	216	106	3	10	65	84	11.4	2.63	95	.249	.309	21	.247	4	-3	-4	2	0.2
1911	Was-A	2	13	.133	28	15	6	0	0	121	160	90	4	3	40	42	15.1	5.06	65	.331	.385	10	.227	1	-23	-24	1	-2.4
Total	3	15	51	.227	98	70	46	3	0	568	586	319	8	22	182	213	12.5	3.52	75	.271	.333	44	.202	3	-53	-56	2	-5.5
● **ELI GRBA** Grba, Eli b: 8/9/34, Chicago, Ill. BR/TR, 6'2", 207 lbs. Deb: 7/10/59																												
1959	NY-A	2	5	.286	19	6	0	0	0	50^1	52	44	6	0	39	23	16.3	6.44	57	.269	.392	3	.214	1	-14	-17	-0	-1.9
1960	*NY-A	6	4	.600	24	9	1	0	1	80^2	65	45	9	2	46	32	12.6	3.68	97	.226	.337	5	.238	2	2	-1	-1	0.0
1961	LA-A	11	13	.458	40	30	8	0	2	211^2	197	119	26	7	114	105	13.5	4.25	106	.242	.340	15	.234	4	-5	5	-1	0.9
1962	LA-A	8	9	.471	40	29	1	0	1	176^1	185	101	19	2	75	90	13.4	4.54	85	.267	.340	12	.207	3	-11	-14	1	-0.9
1963	LA-A	1	2	.333	12	1	0	0	0	17^1	14	9	2	1	10	5	13.0	4.67	73	.222	.338	0	.000	-0	-2	-3	0	-0.4
Total	5	28	33	.459	135	75	10	0	4	536^1	513	318	62	12	284	255	13.6	4.48	90	.250	.345	35	.219	10	-31	-26	-1	-2.3
● **JOHN GREASON** Greason, John R. TL, Deb: 8/27/1873																												
1873	Was-n	1	6	.143	7	7	7	0	0	63	112	90	3		7	3	17.0	5.43	62	.357	.371	4	.143	-2	-15	-14		-1.1
● **BILL GREASON** Greason, William Henry "Booster" b: 9/3/24, Atlanta, Ga. BR/TR, 5'10", 170 lbs. Deb: 5/31/54																												
1954	StL-N	0	1	.000	3	2	0	0	0	4	8	8	4	0	4	2	27.0	13.50	30	.421	.522	0	.000	-0	-4	-4	0	-0.7
● **CHRIS GREEN** Green, Christopher De Wayne b: 9/5/60, Los Angeles, Cal. BL/TL, 6'2", 214 lbs. Deb: 4/17/84																												
1984	Pit-N	0	0	—	4	0	0	0	0	3	5	2	0	0	1	3	18.0	6.00	60	.417	.462	0	—	0	-1	-1	0	0.0
● **JASON GREEN** Green, David Jason b: 6/5/75, Port Hope, Ontario, Can. BR/TR, 6'1", 205 lbs. Deb: 7/23/2000																												
2000	Hou-N	1	1	.500	14	0	0	0	0	17^2	15	16	3	1	20	19	18.3	6.62	74	.234	.424	0	.000	-0	-4	-3	-0	-0.3
● **ED GREEN** Green, Edward M. b: 1850, Philadelphia, Pa. Deb: 4/22/1890																												
1890	Phi-a	7	15	.318	25	22	20	1	1	191	267	184	4	6	94	56	17.3	5.80	67	.321	.393	15	.119	-4	-41	-41	3	-3.6
● **FRED GREEN** Green, Fred Allen b: 9/14/33, Titusville, N.J. d: 12/22/96, Titusville, N.J. BR/TL, 6'4", 190 lbs. Deb: 4/15/59 F																												
1959	Pit-N	1	2	.333	17	1	0	0	1	37^1	37	16	2	0	15	20	12.5	3.13	123	.259	.329	0	.000	-1	3	3	0	0.2
1960	*Pit-N	8	4	.667	45	0	0	0	3	70	61	26	4	1	33	49	12.2	3.21	117	.243	.333	3	.375	3	4	4	-1	1.0
1961	Pit-N	0	0	—	13	0	0	0	0	20^2	27	16	2	0	9	4	15.7	4.79	83	.321	.387	0	.000	-0	-2	-2	1	-0.1
1962	Was-A	0	1	.000	5	0	0	0	0	7	7	6	3	0	6	2	16.7	6.43	63	.250	.382	0	—	0	-2	-2	0	-0.2
1964	Pit-N	0	0	—	8	0	0	0	0	7^1	10	1	1	0	0	2	12.3	1.23	286	.323	.323	0	—	0	2	2	-0	0.1
Total	5	9	7	.563	88	1	0	0	4	142^1	142	65	12	1	63	77	13.0	3.48	110	.264	.343	3	.176	2	6	5	0	1.0
● **DALLAS GREEN** Green, George Dallas b: 8/4/34, Newport, Del. BL/TR, 6'5", 210 lbs. Deb: 6/18/60 M																												
1960	Phi-N	3	6	.333	23	10	5	1	0	108^2	100	54	10	2	44	51	12.1	4.06	96	.248	.325	7	.206	0	-4	-2	-1	-0.1
1961	Phi-N	2	4	.333	42	10	1	1	1	128	160	77	8	2	47	51	14.7	4.85	84	.315	.375	5	.152	0	-12	-11	0	-0.5
1962	Phi-N	6	6	.500	37	10	2	0	1	129^1	145	58	10	5	43	58	13.4	3.83	101	.289	.352	2	.063	-1	2	1	2	0.2
1963	Phi-N	7	5	.583	40	14	4	0	2	120	134	53	10	2	38	68	13.1	3.23	100	.286	.342	3	.086	-1	1	0	1	0.0
1964	Phi-N	2	1	.667	25	0	0	0	0	42	63	31	4	2	14	21	16.9	5.79	60	.362	.416	0	.000	-0	-10	-11	-1	-0.8
1965	Was-A	0	0	—	6	2	0	0	0	14^1	14	6	0	0	3	6	10.7	3.14	111	.241	.279	0	.000	-0	1	1	0	0.0
1966	NY-N	0	0	—	4	0	0	0	0	5	6	3	2	0	2	1	14.4	5.40	67	.333	.400	0	—	0	-1	-1	0	0.0

YEAR	TM/L	W	L	PCT	G	GS	CG	SH	SV	IP	H	R	HR	HB	BB	SO	RAT	ERA	ERA+	OAV	OOB	BH	AVG	PB	PR	PR+	PD	TPI
1967	Phi-N	0	0	—	8	0	0	0	0	15	25	16	2	1	6	12	19.2	9.00	38	.362	.421	0	.000	-0	-9	-9	1	-0.4
Total	8	20	22	.476	185	46	12	2	4	562^1	647	298	46	14	197	268	13.7	4.26	88	.294	.356	17	.120	-3	-33	-33	3	-1.6
● **HARVEY GREEN**	Green, Harvey George "Buck" b: 2/9/15, Kenosha, Wis. d: 7/24/70, Franklin, La. BB/TR, 6'2.5", 185 lbs. Deb: 9/12/35																											
1935	Bro-N	0	0	—	2	0	0	0	0	1	2	1	0	1	3	0	54.0	9.00	44	.400	.667	0	—	0	-1	-1	-0	0.0
● **TYLER GREEN**	Green, Tyler Scott b: 2/18/70, Springfield, Ohio BR/TR, 6'5", 185 lbs. Deb: 4/9/93																											
1993	Phi-N	0	0	—	3	2	0	0	0	7^1	16	9	1	0	5	7	25.8	7.36	54	.444	.512	0	.000	-0	-3	-3	-0	-0.2
1995	Phi-N★	8	9	.471	26	25	4	2	0	140^2	157	86	15	4	66	85	14.5	5.31	80	.290	.371	8	.182	2	-18	-17	-1	-1.6
1997	Phi-N	4	4	.500	14	14	0	0	0	76^2	72	50	8	1	45	58	13.9	4.93	86	.247	.350	8	.308	3	-6	-6	-1	-0.3
1998	Phi-N	6	12	.333	27	27	0	0	0	159^1	142	97	23	9	85	113	13.3	5.03	86	.239	.343	6	.146	-0	-14	-12	-2	-1.3
Total	4	18	25	.419	70	68	4	2	0	384	387	242	47	14	201	263	14.1	5.16	83	.265	.359	22	.195	4	-40	-37	-3	-3.4
● **TOMMY GREENE**	Greene, Ira Thomas b: 4/6/67, Lumberton, N.C. BR/TR, 6'5", 227 lbs. Deb: 9/10/89																											
1989	Atl-N	1	2	.333	4	4	1	1	0	26^1	22	12	5	0	6	17	9.6	4.10	89	.234	.280	1	.100	-1	-2	-1	-0	-0.2
1990	Atl-N	1	0	1.000	5	2	0	0	0	12^1	14	11	3	1	9	4	17.5	8.03	50	.286	.407	0	.000	-0	-6	-5	-0	-0.4
	Phi-N	2	3	.400	10	7	0	0	0	39	36	20	5	0	17	17	12.2	4.15	92	.247	.325	2	.182	0	-2	-1	-0	-0.2
	Yr	3	3	.500	15	9	0	0	0	51^1	50	31	8	1	26	21	13.5	5.08	76	.256	.347	2	.167	0	-7	-7	-1	-0.6
1991	Phi-N	13	7	.650	36	27	3	2	0	207^2	177	85	19	3	66	154	10.7	3.38	109	.230	.294	19	.268	7	7	7	-3	1.1
1992	Phi-N	3	3	.500	13	12	0	0	0	64^1	75	39	5	0	34	39	15.2	5.32	66	.291	.373	3	.125	-1	-13	-13	-1	-1.3
1993	*Phi-N	16	4	.800	31	30	7	2	0	200	175	84	12	3	62	167	10.8	3.42	116	.233	.294	16	.222	6	14	12	-1	1.6
1994	Phi-N	2	0	1.000	7	7	0	0	0	35^2	37	20	5	0	22	28	14.9	4.54	95	.272	.373	5	.385	2	-1	-1	-0	0.1
1995	Phi-N	0	5	.000	11	6	0	0	0	33^2	45	32	6	3	20	24	18.2	8.29	51	.319	.415	0	.000	-0	-15	-15	-0	-1.9
1997	Hou-N	0	1	.000	2	2	0	0	0	9	10	7	2	0	5	11	15.0	7.00	57	.286	.375	1	.333	1	-3	-3	-0	-0.3
Total	8	38	25	.603	119	97	11	5	0	628	591	310	62	10	241	461	12.1	4.14	93	.249	.320	47	.221	14	-20	-21	-6	-1.5
● **JUNE GREENE**	Greene, Julius Foust b: 6/25/1899, Ramseur, N.C. d: 3/19/74, Glendora, Cal. BL/TR, 6'2.5", 185 lbs. Deb: 4/20/28 ♦																											
1928	Phi-N	0	0	—	1	0	0	0	0	2	5	2	0	0	0	0	22.5	9.00	47	.556	.556	3	.500	2	-1	-1	0	0.2
1929	Phi-N	0	0	—	5	0	0	0	0	13^2	33	32	2	3	9	4	29.6	19.76	26	.465	.542	4	.211	0	-23	-20	0	-0.8
Total	2	0	0	—	6	0	0	0	0	15^2	38	34	2	3	9	4	28.7	18.38	28	.475	.543	7	.280	2	-24	-21	1	-0.6
● **NELSON GREENE**	Greene, Nelson George "Lefty" b: 9/20/1900, Philadelphia, Pa. d: 4/6/83, Lebanon, Pa. BL/TL, 6', 185 lbs. Deb: 4/28/24																											
1924	Bro-N	0	1	.000	4	1	0	0	0	9	14	6	0	0	2	3	16.0	4.00	94	.350	.381	0	.000	-0	-0	-0	0	0.0
1925	Bro-N	2	0	1.000	11	0	0	0	1	22	45	28	4	0	7	4	21.3	10.64	39	.417	.452	2	.286	0	-16	-16	0	-1.3
Total	2	2	1	.667	15	1	0	0	1	31	59	34	5	0	9	7	19.7	8.71	47	.399	.433	2	.250	-0	-16	-16	1	-1.3
● **RICK GREENE**	Greene, Richard Douglas b: 1/2/71, Fort Knox, Ky. BR/TR, 6'5", 200 lbs. Deb: 6/19/99																											
1999	Cin-N	0	0	—	1	0	0	0	0	5^2	7	4	2	0	1	3	12.7	4.76	98	.292	.320	0	.000	-0	-0	-0	-0	0.0
● **KENT GREENFIELD**	Greenfield, Kent b: 7/1/02, Guthrie, Ky. d: 3/14/78, Guthrie, Ky. BR/TR, 6'1", 180 lbs. Deb: 9/28/24																											
1924	NY-N	0	1	.000	1	1	0	0	0	3	9	8	1	0	1	1	30.0	15.00	24	.500	.526	0	—	0	-4	-4	-0	-0.6
1925	NY-N	12	8	.600	29	20	12	0	0	171^2	195	86	4	2	64	66	13.7	3.88	104	.288	.352	5	.081	-6	7	3	1	-0.2
1926	NY-N	13	12	.520	39	28	8	1	1	222^2	206	111	17	5	82	74	11.8	3.96	95	.251	.322	6	.092	-5	-3	-5	-2	-1.2
1927	NY-N	2	2	.500	12	1	0	0	0	20	39	25	3	2	13	4	24.3	9.45	41	.411	.491	0	.000	-0	-12	-13	0	-2.1
	Bos-N	11	14	.440	27	26	11	1	0	190	203	92	3	5	59	59	12.6	3.84	97	.282	.341	11	.172	-2	2	-3	-0	-0.5
	Yr	13	16	.448	39	27	11	1	0	210	242	117	6	7	72	63	13.8	4.37	85	.297	.359	11	.167	-2	-11	-16	-0	-2.6
1928	Bos-N	3	11	.214	32	20	5	0	0	143^2	173	100	6	5	60	30	14.9	5.32	73	.307	.378	2	.053	-4	-21	-23	1	-2.2
1929	Bos-N	0	0	—	6	2	0	0	0	15^2	33	19	1	2	15	7	28.7	10.91	43	.465	.568	0	.000	-1	-11	-11	1	-0.5
	Bro-N	0	0	—	6	0	0	0	0	8^2	13	8	1	0	3	1	16.6	8.31	56	.382	.432	0	.000	-0	-3	-4	-0	-0.2
	Yr	0	0	—	12	2	0	0	0	24^1	46	27	2	2	18	8	24.4	9.99	47	.438	.528	0	.000	-1	-14	-15	1	-0.7
Total	6	41	48	.461	152	98	36	2	1	775^1	871	449	36	21	297	242	13.8	4.54	85	.290	.358	24	.101	-18	-46	-60	-0	-7.5
● **JOHN GREENING**	Greening, John A. (b: John A. Greenig) b: Philadelphia, Pa. Deb: 5/9/1888																											
1888	Was-N	0	1	.000	1	1	1	0	0	9	17	13	2	0	4	2	21.0	11.00	25	.405	.457	0	.000	-0	-8	-8	-0	-0.6
● **BOB GREENWOOD**	Greenwood, Robert Chandler "Greenie" b: 3/13/28, Cananea, Mexico d: 9/1/94, Hayward, Cal. BR/TR, 6'5", 200 lbs. Deb: 4/21/54																											
1954	Phi-N	1	2	.333	11	4	0	0	0	36^2	28	16	2	0	18	9	11.3	3.19	127	.209	.303	0	.000	-1	4	3	0	0.2
1955	Phi-N	0	0	—	1	0	0	0	0	2^1	7	4	1	0	0	0	27.0	15.43	26	.500	.500	0	.000	-0	-3	-3	-0	-0.2
Total	2	1	2	.333	12	4	0	0	0	39	35	20	3	0	18	9	12.2	3.92	103	.236	.319	0	.000	-1	1	0	0	0.0
● **KENNY GREER**	Greer, Kenneth William b: 5/12/67, Boston, Mass. BR/TR, 6'2", 210 lbs. Deb: 9/29/93																											
1993	NY-N	1	0	1.000	1	0	0	0	0	1	0	0	0	0	0	2	0.0	0.00	—	.000	.000	0	—	0	0	0	0	0.1
1995	SF-N	0	2	.000	8	0	0	0	0	12	15	12	3	1	5	7	15.8	5.25	78	.288	.362	0	.000	-0	-1	-2	0	-0.2
Total	2	1	2	.333	9	0	0	0	0	13	15	12	3	1	5	9	14.5	4.85	84	.273	.344	0	.000	-0	-1	-1	0	-0.1
● **DAVE GREGG**	Gregg, David Charles "Highpockets" b: 3/14/1891, Chehalis, Wash. d: 11/12/65, Clarkston, Wash. BR/TR, 6'1", 185 lbs. Deb: 6/15/13 F																											
1913	Cle-A	0	0	—	1	0	0	0	0	1	2	2	0	1	0	0	27.0	18.00	17	.400	.500	0	—	0	-2	-2	0	-0.1
● **HAL GREGG**	Gregg, Harold Dana "Skeets" b: 7/11/21, Anaheim, Cal. d: 5/13/91, Bishop, Cal. BR/TR, 6'3.5", 195 lbs. Deb: 8/18/43																											
1943	Bro-N	0	3	.000	5	4	0	0	0	18^2	21	21	2	0	21	7	20.3	9.64	35	.304	.467	0	.000	0	-13	-13	-0	-1.7
1944	Bro-N	9	16	.360	39	31	6	0	2	197^2	201	142	12	9	137	92	15.8	5.46	65	.258	.376	14	.206	-0	-41	-43	0	-4.8
1945	Bro-N†	18	13	.581	42	34	13	2	2	254^1	221	116	5	8	120	139	12.3	3.47	108	.232	.323	20	.220	3	9	8	-0	1.2
1946	Bro-N	6	4	.600	26	16	4	1	2	117^1	103	46	3	1	44	54	11.4	2.99	113	.236	.308	4	.125	-1	5	5	-2	0.1
1947	*Bro-N	4	5	.444	37	16	2	1	1	104^1	115	79	6	4	55	59	15.0	5.87	70	.272	.361	9	.265	2	-21	-20	0	-1.3
1948	Pit-N	2	4	.333	22	8	1	0	1	74^1	72	40	3	3	34	25	13.2	4.60	88	.255	.342	6	.273	2	-5	-4	-0	-0.2
1949	Pit-N	1	1	.500	8	1	0	0	0	18^2	20	10	1	1	8	9	14.0	3.38	125	.303	.387	0	.000	-0	1	2	-0	0.1
1950	Pit-N	0	1	.000	5	1	0	0	0	5^1	10	10	2	1	7	3	30.4	13.50	32	.400	.545	0	.000	-0	-6	-5	0	-0.8
1952	NY-N	0	1	.000	16	4	1	0	1	36^1	42	22	7	2	17	13	15.1	4.71	79	.286	.367	1	.125	-0	-4	-4	-1	-0.3
Total	9	40	48	.455	200	115	27	4	9	827	805	486	41	29	443	401	13.9	4.54	82	.253	.350	54	.205	4	-73	-74	-3	-7.7
● **VEAN GREGG**	Gregg, Sylveanus Augustus b: 4/13/1885, Chehalis, Wash. d: 7/29/64, Aberdeen, Wash. BR/TL, 6'1", 185 lbs. Deb: 4/12/11 F																											
1911	Cle-A	23	7	.767	34	26	22	5	0	244^2	172	67	2	10	86	125	**9.9**	**1.80**	**189**	**.205**	.286	14	.165	-4	42	43	0	4.6
1912	Cle-A	20	13	.606	37	34	26	1	2	271^1	242	99	4	10	90	184	11.3	2.59	132	.246	.316	17	.175	-3	22	24	-2	2.3
1913	Cle-A	20	13	.606	44	34	23	3	3	285^2	258	103	2	13	124	166	12.4	2.24	136	.246	.334	13	.131	-4	22	25	-4	1.9
1914	Cle-A	9	3	.750	17	12	6	1	0	96^2	88	46	0	3	48	56	12.9	3.07	94	.251	.347	6	.176	1	-4	-2	-0	-0.2
	Bos-A	3	4	.429	12	9	4	0	0	68^1	71	39	0	0	37	24	14.2	3.95	68	.283	.375	4	.211	0	-9	-10	-1	-1.0
	Yr	12	7	.632	29	21	10	1	0	165	159	85	0	3	85	80	13.5	3.44	82	.265	.358	10	.189	1	-13	-11	-2	-1.2
1915	Bos-A	4	2	.667	18	9	3	1	3	75	71	37	2	5	32	43	13.0	3.36	83	.260	.348	7	.350	2	-4	-5	0	-0.2
1916	Bos-A	2	5	.286	21	7	3	0	0	77^2	71	30	0	3	30	41	12.1	3.01	92	.259	.339	2	.111	-1	-2	-2	-0	-0.3
1918	Phi-A	9	14	.391	30	25	17	3	2	199^1	180	85	4	5	67	63	11.4	3.12	94	.251	.320	12	.169	-3	-7	-4	-1	-0.9
1925	Was-A	2	2	.500	26	5	1	0	2	74^1	87	41	3	2	38	18	15.4	4.12	103	.318	.404	3	.214	0	2	1	-1	0.0
Total	8	92	63	.594	239	161	105	14	12	1393	1240	547	17	51	552	720	11.9	2.70	117	.248	.328	78	.171	-12	63	71	-9	6.2
● **FRANK GREGORY**	Gregory, Frank Ernst b: 7/25/1888, Spring Valley Township, Wis. d: 11/5/55, Beloit, Wis. BR/TR, 5'11", 185 lbs. Deb: 9/5/12																											
1912	Cin-N	2	0	1.000	4	2	1	0	0	15^2	19	12	0	1	7	4	15.5	4.60	73	.297	.375	1	.200	0	-2	-2	-1	-0.3
● **LEE GREGORY**	Gregory, Grover Leroy b: 6/2/38, Bakersfield, Cal. BL/TL, 6'1", 180 lbs. Deb: 4/17/64																											
1964	Chi-N	0	0	—	11	0	0	0	0	18	23	8	3	0	5	8	14.0	3.50	106	.333	.378	1	.077	0	0	0	0	0.0
● **HOWIE GREGORY**	Gregory, Howard Watterson b: 11/18/1886, Hannibal, Mo. d: 5/30/70, Tulsa, Okla. BL/TR, 6', 175 lbs. Deb: 4/16/11																											
1911	StL-A	0	1	.000	3	1	0	0	0	7	11	5	0	0	4	1	19.3	5.14	66	.393	.469	0	.000	-0	-1	-1	-0	-0.2

YEAR	TM/L	W	L	PCT	G	GS	CG	SH	SV	IP	H	R	HR	HB	BB	SO	RAT	ERA	ERA+	OAV	OOB	BH	AVG	PB	PR	PR+	PD	TPI
● PAUL GREGORY	Gregory, Paul Edwin "Pop" b: 6/9/08, Tomnolen, Miss. d: 9/16/99, Southaven, Miss. BR/TR, 6'2", 180 lbs. Deb: 4/20/32																											
1932	Chi-A	5	3	.625	33	9	3	0	0	117^2	125	75	8	2	51	39	13.6	4.51	96	.273	.348	3	.079	-3	-0	-3	3	-0.1
1933	Chi-A	4	11	.267	23	17	5	0	0	103^2	124	75	10	1	47	18	14.9	4.95	86	.296	.368	5	.143	-1	-8	-8	1	-1.0
Total	2	9	14	.391	56	26	8	0	0	221^1	249	150	18	3	98	57	14.2	4.72	91	.284	.358	8	.110	-4	-8	-11	4	-1.1
● BILL GREIF	Greif, William Briley b: 4/25/50, Ft.Stockton, Tex. BR/TR, 6'5", 205 lbs. Deb: 7/19/71																											
1971	Hou-N	1	1	.500	7	3	0	0	0	16	18	10	1	2	8	14	15.8	5.06	67	.290	.389	1	.333	0	-3	-3	0	-0.3
1972	SD-N	5	16	.238	34	22	2	1	2	125^1	143	86	18	8	47	91	14.2	5.60	59	.287	.357	1	.030	-3	-30	-34	-2	-5.5
1973	SD-N	10	17	.370	36	31	9	3	1	199^1	181	88	20	5	62	120	11.2	3.21	109	.246	.309	6	.098	-2	10	6	-1	0.5
1974	SD-N	9	19	.321	43	35	7	1	1	226	244	126	17	14	95	137	14.1	4.66	77	.279	.359	4	.071	-2	-26	-28	0	-3.3
1975	SD-N	4	6	.400	59	1	0	0	9	72	74	44	7	5	38	43	14.6	3.88	90	.269	.368	0	.000	-0	-2	-3	-2	-0.7
1976	SD-N	1	3	.250	5	5	0	0	0	22^1	27	20	2	0	11	5	15.3	8.06	41	.297	.373	0	.000	-1	-11	-13	0	-1.8
	StL-N	1	5	.167	47	0	0	0	6	54^2	60	28	5	2	26	32	14.5	4.12	86	.290	.374	0	.000	0	-4	-3	-1	-0.5
	Yr	2	8	.200	52	5	0	0	6	77	87	48	7	2	37	37	14.7	5.26	66	.292	.374	0	.000	-1	-15	-16	-0	-2.3
Total	6	31	67	.316	231	97	18	5	19	715^2	747	402	70	36	287	442	13.5	4.41	79	.272	.349	12	.072	-7	-65	-78	-5	-11.6
● SETH GREISINGER	Greisinger, Seth Adam b: 7/29/75, Kansas City, Kan. BR/TR, 6'4", 190 lbs. Deb: 6/3/98																											
1998	Det-A	6	9	.400	21	21	0	0	0	130	142	79	17	4	48	66	13.4	5.12	92	.282	.350	1	.250	0	-7	-6	-2	-0.7
● BILL GREVELL	Grevell, William J. b: 3/5/1898, Williamstown, N.J. d: 6/21/23, Philadelphia, Pa. BR/TR, 5'11", 170 lbs. Deb: 5/14/19																											
1919	Phi-A	0	0	—	5	2	0	0	0	12	15	20	0	1	18	3	25.5	14.25	24	.306	.500	0	.000	-1	-15	-14	1	-0.7
● LEE GRIFFETH	Griffeth, Leon Clifford b: 5/20/25, Carmel, N.Y. BB/TL, 5'11.5", 180 lbs. Deb: 6/25/46																											
1946	Phi-A	0	0	—	10	0	0	0	0	15^1	13	7	1	2	6	4	12.3	2.93	121	.232	.328	0	.000	0	1	1	-0	0.1
● HANK GRIFFIN	Griffin, James Linton "Pepper" b: 7/11/1886, Whitehouse, Tex. d: 2/11/50, Terrell, Tex. BR/TR, 6', 165 lbs. Deb: 5/5/11																											
1911	Chi-N	0	0	—	1	1	0	0	0	1	1	2	1	0	3	1	36.0	18.00	18	.250	.571	0	—	0	-2	-2	0	-0.1
	Bos-N	0	6	.000	15	6	1	0	0	82^2	96	70	3	6	34	30	14.8	5.23	73	.305	.383	7	.233	-0	-17	-11	0	-0.7
	Yr	0	6	.000	16	7	1	0	0	83^2	97	72	4	6	37	31	15.1	5.38	71	.304	.387	7	.233	-0	-18	-13	0	-0.8
1912	Bos-N	0	0	—	3	0	0	0	0	1^2	3	5	0	1	3	0	37.8	27.00	13	.750	.875	0	—	0	-4	-4	-0	-0.2
Total	2	0	6	.000	19	7	1	0	0	85^1	100	77	4	7	40	31	15.5	5.80	66	.310	.397	7	.233	-0	-23	-17	0	-1.0
● MARTY GRIFFIN	Griffin, Martin John b: 9/2/01, San Francisco, Cal d: 11/19/51, Los Angeles, Cal. BR/TR, 6'2", 200 lbs. Deb: 7/25/28																											
1928	Bos-A	0	3	.000	11	3	0	0	0	37^2	42	21	0	0	17	9	14.1	5.02	82	.300	.376	4	.308	1	-4	-4	-0	-0.2
● MIKE GRIFFIN	Griffin, Michael Leroy b: 6/26/57, Colusa, Cal. BR/TR, 6'5", 197 lbs. Deb: 9/17/79																											
1979	NY-A	0	0	—	3	0	0	0	1	4^1	5	2	0	0	2	5	14.5	4.15	98	.313	.389	0	—	0	0	-0	-0	0.0
1980	NY-A	2	4	.333	13	9	0	0	0	54	64	36	6	1	23	25	14.7	4.83	81	.287	.356	0	—	0	-5	-6	-0	-0.5
1981	NY-A	0	0	—	2	0	0	0	0	4^1	5	1	0	0	0	4	10.4	2.08	172	.278	.278	0	—	0	1	1	0	0.1
	Chi-N	2	5	.286	16	9	0	0	1	52	64	27	4	0	9	20	12.6	4.50	82	.302	.330	2	.154	-0	-6	-4	0	-0.6
1982	SD-N	0	1	.000	7	0	0	0	0	10^1	9	4	0	0	3	4	10.5	3.48	99	.237	.293	0	.000	-0	0	-0	-0	0.0
1987	Bal-A	3	5	.375	23	6	1	0	1	74^1	78	39	9	3	33	42	13.8	4.36	101	.269	.350	0	—	0	1	0	-1	0.0
1989	Cin-N	0	0	—	3	0	0	0	0	4^1	10	6	0	0	3	1	27.0	12.46	29	.500	.565	1	1.000	0	-4	-4	-0	-0.2
Total	6	7	15	.318	67	24	1	0	3	203^2	235	115	19	4	73	101	13.8	4.60	87	.288	.349	3	.200	-0	-13	-13	-1	-1.2
● PAT GRIFFIN	Griffin, Patrick Richard b: 5/6/1893, Niles, Ohio d: 6/7/27, Youngstown, Ohio BR/TR, 6'2", 180 lbs. Deb: 7/23/14																											
1914	Cin-N	0	0	—	1	0	0	0	0	1	3	3	0	0	2	0	45.0	9.00	33	.750	.833	0	—	0	-1	-1	0	0.0
● TOM GRIFFIN	Griffin, Thomas James b: 2/22/48, Los Angeles, Cal. BR/TR, 6'3", 210 lbs. Deb: 4/10/69																											
1969	Hou-N	11	10	.524	31	31	6	3	0	188^1	156	80	19	7	93	200	12.2	3.54	100	.220	.317	9	.145	2	1	0	-2	0.1
1970	Hou-N	3	13	.188	23	20	2	1	0	111^1	118	72	9	3	72	72	15.6	5.74	68	.275	.383	2	.061	-2	-21	-24	-1	-3.2
1971	Hou-N	0	6	.000	10	6	0	0	0	37^2	44	22	4	2	20	29	15.8	4.78	71	.288	.377	1	.111	-0	-5	-6	1	-0.8
1972	Hou-N	5	4	.556	39	5	1	1	3	94^1	92	39	7	3	38	83	12.7	3.24	104	.258	.334	7	.280	3	2	1	-1	0.4
1973	Hou-N	4	6	.400	25	12	4	0	0	99^2	83	51	10	2	46	69	11.8	4.15	88	.229	.320	3	.107	0	-5	-6	0	-0.5
1974	Hou-N	14	10	.583	34	34	8	3	0	211	202	97	14	5	89	110	12.6	3.54	98	.250	.328	20	.294	8	2	-2	1	0.8
1975	Hou-N	3	8	.273	17	13	3	1	0	79^1	89	52	11	2	46	56	15.5	5.33	63	.288	.384	3	.136	-0	-15	-19	1	-2.2
1976	Hou-N	5	3	.625	20	2	0	0	0	41^2	44	29	4	1	37	33	17.7	6.05	53	.278	.418	0	.000	-0	-12	-14	0	-2.5
	SD-N	4	3	.571	11	11	2	0	0	70^1	56	27	0	1	42	36	12.7	2.94	111	.222	.336	2	.077	-2	4	3	-0	0.1
	Yr	9	6	.600	31	13	2	0	0	112	100	56	4	2	79	69	14.5	4.10	79	.244	.369	2	.065	-2	-7	-11	-0	-2.4
1977	SD-N	6	9	.400	38	20	0	0	0	151^1	144	88	17	5	88	79	14.1	4.46	79	.254	.359	6	.133	1	-9	-17	-2	-1.5
1978	Cal-A	3	4	.429	24	4	0	0	0	56	63	39	8	1	31	35	15.3	4.02	90	.279	.368	0	—	0	-1	-3	1	-0.2
1979	SF-N	5	6	.455	59	3	0	0	2	94^1	83	46	9	4	46	82	12.7	3.91	90	.237	.333	1	.071	-1	-2	-5	2	-0.5
1980	SF-N	5	1	.833	42	4	0	0	0	107^2	80	35	8	8	49	79	11.5	2.76	128	.212	.315	2	.111	0	10	10	0	0.6
1981	SF-N	8	8	.500	22	22	3	1	0	129^1	121	62	8	7	57	83	12.9	3.76	91	.249	.336	8	.195	2	-4	-5	2	-0.2
1982	Pit-N	1	3	.250	6	4	0	0	0	22^1	32	23	5	1	15	8	19.3	8.87	42	.330	.425	2	.222	0	-13	-12	0	-1.7
Total	14	77	94	.450	401	191	29	10	5	1494^2	1407	762	133	52	769	1054	13.4	4.07	86	.249	.345	66	.163	12	-68	-96	1	-11.3
● CLARK GRIFFITH	Griffith, Clark Calvin "The Old Fox" b: 11/20/1869, Clear Creek, Mo. d: 10/27/55, Washington, D.C. BR/TR, 5'6.5", 156 lbs. Deb: 4/11/1891 MH◆																											
1891	StL-a	11	8	.579	27	17	12	0	0	186^1	195	122	8	15	58	68	12.9	3.33	126	.260	.326	12	.156	-3	8	16	0	1.0
	Bos-a	3	1	.750	7	4	3	0	0	40	47	33	3	5	15	20	15.1	5.62	62	.283	.360	4	.174	2	-8	-10	-1	-0.7
	Yr	14	9	.609	34	21	15	0	0	226^1	242	155	11	20	73	88	13.3	3.74	109	.264	.332	16	.160	-1	-1	8	-1	0.3
1893	Chi-N	1	2	.333	4	2	2	0	0	19^2	24	14	1	1	5	9	13.7	5.03	92	.293	.341	2	.182	-1	-1	-1	1	-0.1
1894	Chi-N	21	14	.600	36	30	28	0	0	261^1	328	193	12	14	85	71	14.7	4.92	114	.304	.362	33	.232	-0	12	19	1	1.8
1895	Chi-N	26	14	.650	42	41	39	0	0	353	434	228	11	22	91	79	13.9	3.93	130	.298	.348	46	.319	5	33	43	1	4.2
1896	Chi-N	23	11	.676	36	35	35	0	0	317^2	370	189	3	12	70	81	12.8	3.54	128	.289	.331	36	.267	3	29	34	1	3.2
1897	Chi-N	21	18	.538	41	38	**38**	1	1	343^2	410	231	3	17	86	102	13.4	3.72	120	.293	.342	38	.235	3	23	27	3	2.9
1898	Chi-N	24	10	.706	38	38	36	4	0	325^2	305	105	1	20	64	97	10.8	**1.88**	**191**	.246	.294	20	.164	-2	63	62	1	5.8
1899	Chi-N	22	14	.611	38	38	35	0	0	319^2	329	163	5	14	65	73	11.5	2.79	134	.266	.310	31	.258	6	38	35	6	4.6
1900	Chi-N	14	13	.519	30	30	27	**4**	0	248	245	126	6	16	51	61	11.3	3.05	118	.258	.306	24	.253	5	18	16	-1	1.6
1901	Chi-A	24	7	**.774**	35	30	26	**5**	1	266^2	275	114	4	4	50	67	11.1	2.67	131	.263	.299	27	.303	14	30	25	0	3.8
1902	Chi-A	15	9	.625	28	24	20	3	0	213	247	117	11	16	47	51	13.1	4.18	81	.290	.339	20	.217	2	-14	-20	-1	-1.8
1903	NY-A	14	11	.560	25	24	22	2	0	213	201	92	3	6	33	69	10.1	2.70	116	.249	.283	11	.159	2	6	9	-3	0.9
1904	NY-A	7	5	.583	16	11	8	1	0	100^1	91	40	3	4	16	36	10.0	2.87	94	.243	.281	6	.143	-1	-3	-2	-1	-0.4
1905	NY-A	9	6	.600	25	7	4	2	1	101^2	82	30	1	1	15	46	8.7	1.68	174	.223	.255	7	.219	1	11	13	-2	1.9
1906	NY-A	2	2	.500	17	2	1	0	2	59^2	58	30	0	4	15	16	11.6	3.02	98	.258	.316	2	.111	-1	-2	-0	1	0.0
1907	NY-A	0	0	—	4	0	0	0	0	8^1	15	16	0	0	6	5	22.7	8.64	32	.395	.477	0	.000	-0	-6	-5	0	-0.3
1909	Cin-N	0	1	.000	1	1	1	0	0	6	11	8	0	0	2	3	19.5	6.00	43	.379	.419	0	.000	-0	-2	-2	1	-0.3
1912	Was-A	0	0	—	1	0	0	0	0	0	1	1	0	0	—	—	∞	—	1.000	1.000	101	.000	-0	-1	-1	0	-0.1	
1913	Was-A	0	0	—	1	0	0	0	0	1	1	0	0	0	0	0	9.0	0.00	—	.250	.250	1	1.000	1	0	0	-0	0.0
1914	Was-A	0	0	—	1	0	0	0	1	1	1	0	0	0	0	1	9.0	0.00	—	.250	.250	1	1.000	1	0	0	-0	0.1
Total	20	237	146	.619	453	372	337	22	6	3385^2	3670	1852	76	171	774	955	12.3	3.31	121	.274	.322	321	.233	35	233	259	7	28.3
● FRANK GRIFFITH	Griffith, Frank Wesley b: 11/18/1872, Gilman, Ill. d: 12/8/08, Waterman, Ill. BL/TL, Deb: 8/13/1892																											
1892	Chi-N	0	1	.000	1	1	0	0	0	4	3	5	1	0	6	3	20.3	11.25	30	.200	.429	0	.000	-0	-4	-3	-0	-0.5
1894	Cle-N	1	2	.333	7	6	3	0	0	42^1	64	62	5	9	37	15	23.4	9.99	55	.344	.474	8	.333	2	-22	-21	-0	-0.9
Total	2	1	3	.250	8	7	3	0	0	46^1	67	67	6	9	43	18	23.1	10.10	52	.333	.470	8	.320	2	-25	-24	-0	-1.4
● HAL GRIGGS	Griggs, Harold Lloyd b: 8/24/28, Shannon, Ga. BR/TR, 6', 170 lbs. Deb: 4/18/56																											
1956	Was-A	1	6	.143	34	12	1	0	1	98^2	120	82	14	1	76	48	18.0	6.02	72	.307	.421	0	.000	-1	-20	-18	1	-1.1
1957	Was-A	0	1	.000	2	2	0	0	0	13^2	11	5	1	0	7	12	11.9	3.29	118	.229	.327	1	.250	0	1	1	0	0.1
1958	Was-A	3	11	.214	32	21	3	0	0	137	138	91	20	2	74	69	14.1	5.52	69	.262	.355	5	.122	-2	-27	-26	-0	-2.5

YEAR	TM/L	W	L	PCT	G	GS	CG	SH	SV	IP	H	R	HR	HB	BB	SO	RAT	ERA	ERA+	OAV	OOB	BH	AVG	PB	PR	PR+	PD	TPI
1959	Was-A	2	8	.200	37	10	2	1	2	97^2	103	63	8	1	52	43	14.4	5.25	75	.270	.359	1	.056	-2	-15	-14	-0	-1.6
Total	4	6	26	.188	105	45	6	1	3	347	372	241	43	4	209	172	15.2	5.50	73	.276	.375	7	.089	-5	-61	-57	1	-5.1

● GUIDO GRILLI Grilli, Guido John b: 1/9/39, Memphis, Tenn. BL/TL, 6', 188 lbs. Deb: 4/12/66

YEAR	TM/L	W	L	PCT	G	GS	CG	SH	SV	IP	H	R	HR	HB	BB	SO	RAT	ERA	ERA+	OAV	OOB	BH	AVG	PB	PR	PR+	PD	TPI
1966	Bos-A	0	1	.000	6	0	0	0	0	4^2	5	6	1	0	9	4	27.0	7.71	49	.278	.519	1	.500	0	-2	-2	0	-0.3
	KC-A	0	1	.000	16	0	0	0	1	15^2	19	15	0	3	11	8	19.0	6.89	49	.302	.429	0	—	0	-6	-6	-1	-0.5
	Yr	0	2	.000	22	0	0	0	1	20^1	24	21	1	3	20	12	20.8	7.08	49	.296	.452	1	.500	0	-8	-8	-1	-0.8

● JASON GRILLI Grilli, Jason Michael b: 11/11/76, Royal Oak, Mich. BR/TR, 6'4", 185 lbs. Deb: 5/11/2000 F

YEAR	TM/L	W	L	PCT	G	GS	CG	SH	SV	IP	H	R	HR	HB	BB	SO	RAT	ERA	ERA+	OAV	OOB	BH	AVG	PB	PR	PR+	PD	TPI
2000	Fla-N	1	0	1.000	1	1	0	0	0	6^2	11	4	0	2	2	3	20.3	5.40	82	.379	.455	1	.500	0	-1	-1	-0	-0.1

● STEVE GRILLI Grilli, Stephen Joseph b: 5/2/49, Brooklyn, N.Y. BR/TR, Deb: N/A.

YEAR	TM/L	W	L	PCT	G	GS	CG	SH	SV	IP	H	R	HR	HB	BB	SO	RAT	ERA	ERA+	OAV	OOB	BH	AVG	PB	PR	PR+	PD	TPI
1975	Det-A	0	0	—	3	0	0	0	0	6^2	3	2	0	0	6	5	12.2	1.35	298	.136	.321	0	—	0	2	2	0	0.1
1976	Det-A	3	1	.750	36	0	0	0	3	66	63	43	5	5	41	36	14.9	4.64	80	.258	.376	0	—	0	-8	-6	2	-0.2
1977	Det-A	1	2	.333	30	2	0	0	0	72^2	71	42	8	3	49	49	15.2	4.83	89	.265	.384	0	—	0	-6	-4	-1	-0.3
1979	Tor-A	0	0	—	1	0	0	0	0	2^1	1	0	0	0	0	1	3.9	0.00	—	.143	.143	0	—	0	1	1	-0	0.0
Total	4	4	3	.571	70	2	0	0	3	147^2	138	87	13	8	96	91	14.7	4.51	89	.255	.375	0	—	0	-11	-8	1	-0.4

● JOHN GRIM Grim, John Helm b: 8/9/1867, Lebanon, Ky. d: 7/28/61, Indianapolis, Ind BR/TR, 6'2", 175 lbs. Deb: 9/29/1888 ♦

YEAR	TM/L	W	L	PCT	G	GS	CG	SH	SV	IP	H	R	HR	HB	BB	SO	RAT	ERA	ERA+	OAV	OOB	BH	AVG	PB	PR	PR+	PD	TPI
1890	Roc-a	0	0	—	1	0	0	0	0	3^1	3	3	0	0	4	3	18.9	0.00	—	.231	.412	51	.266	0	1	1	-0	0.1

● BOB GRIM Grim, Robert Anton b: 3/8/30, New York, N.Y. d: 10/23/96, Shawnee, Kan. BR/TR, 6'1", 185 lbs. Deb: 4/18/54

YEAR	TM/L	W	L	PCT	G	GS	CG	SH	SV	IP	H	R	HR	HB	BB	SO	RAT	ERA	ERA+	OAV	OOB	BH	AVG	PB	PR	PR+	PD	TPI
1954	NY-A	20	6	.769	37	20	8	1	0	199	175	78	9	3	85	108	11.9	3.26	106	.244	.327	10	.143	-1	10	4	-1	0.3
1955	*NY-A	7	5	.583	26	11	1	1	4	92^1	81	49	9	3	42	63	12.3	4.19	89	.238	.326	3	.120	-1	-2	-5	0	-0.7
1956	NY-A	6	1	.857	26	6	1	0	5	74^2	64	27	3	2	31	48	11.7	2.77	139	.235	.318	1	.063	-0	11	10	-1	0.9
1957	*NY-A★	12	8	.600	46	0	0	0	**19**	72	60	22	5	0	36	52	12.0	2.63	137	.239	.334	1	.111	1	9	8	0	1.8
1958	NY-A	0	1	.000	11	0	0	0	0	16^1	12	10	3	1	10	11	12.7	5.51	64	.211	.338	0	.000	-0	-3	-4	-0	-0.2
	KC-A	7	6	.538	26	14	5	1	0	113^2	118	54	7	3	41	54	12.8	3.56	110	.269	.336	6	.188	-0	3	4	-1	0.3
	Yr	7	7	.500	37	14	5	1	0	130	130	64	10	4	51	65	12.8	3.81	101	.263	.336	6	.182	-1	-1	1	-1	0.1
1959	KC-A	6	10	.375	40	9	3	1	4	125^1	124	69	10	3	57	65	13.2	4.09	98	.260	.343	3	.094	-1	-3	-1	-2	-0.4
1960	Cle-A	0	1	.000	3	0	0	0	0	2^1	6	3	0	0	1	2	27.0	11.57	32	.500	.538	0	—	0	-2	-2	0	-0.4
	Cin-N	2	2	.500	26	0	0	0	2	30^1	32	18	3	0	10	22	12.5	4.45	86	.274	.331	0	.000	-0	-2	-2	-0	-0.3
	StL-N	1	0	1.000	15	0	0	0	0	20^2	22	7	1	0	9	15	13.5	3.05	134	.272	.344	0	.000	-0	2	2	0	0.1
	Yr	3	2	.600	41	0	0	0	2	51	54	25	4	0	19	37	12.9	3.88	101	.273	.336	0	.000	-0	-1	0	-0	-0.2
1962	KC-A	0	1	.000	12	0	0	0	3	13	14	9	0	0	8	3	15.2	6.23	68	.292	.393	0	.000	-0	-3	-3	1	-0.3
Total	8	61	41	.598	268	60	18	4	37	759^2	708	346	50	15	330	443	12.5	3.61	104	.252	.334	24	.127	-4	19	11	-4	1.1

● BURLEIGH GRIMES Grimes, Burleigh Arland "Ol' Stubblebeard"
b: 8/18/1893, Emerald, Wis. d: 12/6/85, Clear Lake, Wis. BR/TR, 5'10", 175 lbs. Deb: 9/10/16 MCH

YEAR	TM/L	W	L	PCT	G	GS	CG	SH	SV	IP	H	R	HR	HB	BB	SO	RAT	ERA	ERA+	OAV	OOB	BH	AVG	PB	PR	PR+	PD	TPI
1916	Pit-N	2	3	.400	6	5	4	0	0	45^2	40	19	1	0	10	20	9.9	2.36	114	.241	.284	3	.176	-0	1	2	1	0.2
1917	Pit-N	3	16	.158	37	17	8	1	0	194	186	101	5	6	70	72	12.2	3.53	80	.260	.331	16	.232	2	-18	-14	1	-1.1
1918	Bro-N	19	9	.679	**40**	30	19	7	1	269^2	210	94	3	4	76	113	9.7	2.14	130	.216	.276	18	.200	0	19	19	4	2.6
1919	Bro-N	10	11	.476	25	21	13	1	0	181^1	179	97	2	7	60	82	12.2	3.47	86	.256	.321	17	.246	1	-11	-10	1	-0.9
1920	*Bro-N	23	11	**.676**	40	33	25	5	2	303^2	271	101	5	4	67	131	10.1	2.22	144	.238	.282	34	.306	10	31	32	3	5.3
1921	Bro-N	**22**	13	.629	37	35	**30**	2	0	302^1	313	120	6	5	76	**136**	11.7	2.83	138	.274	.322	27	.237	2	32	**35**	4	**4.4**
1922	Bro-N	17	14	.548	36	34	18	1	1	259	324	159	17	7	84	99	14.4	4.76	85	.308	.363	22	.237	4	-19	-20	4	-1.2
1923	Bro-N	21	18	.538	39	38	**33**	2	0	**327**	356	165	9	11	100	119	12.9	3.58	108	.280	.338	30	.238	3	15	11	5	2.0
1924	Bro-N	22	13	.629	38	36	**30**	1	1	**310^2**	351	161	15	6	91	135	13.0	3.82	98	.287	.339	37	.298	6	1	-3	5	0.9
1925	Bro-N	12	19	.387	33	31	19	0	0	246^2	305	164	15	7	102	73	15.1	5.04	83	.309	.377	24	.250	5	-21	-24	8	-1.2
1926	Bro-N	12	13	.480	30	29	18	1	0	225^1	238	114	4	5	88	64	13.2	3.71	103	.276	.346	18	.222	1	3	3	3	0.6
1927	NY-N	19	8	.704	39	34	15	2	2	259^2	274	116	12	4	87	102	12.7	3.54	109	.276	.337	18	.188	-0	11	9	5	1.3
1928	Pit-N	**25**	14	.641	**48**	37	**28**	**4**	3	**330^2**	311	146	11	9	77	97	10.8	2.99	136	.248	.297	42	.321	11	37	39	6	6.0
1929	Pit-N	17	7	.708	33	29	18	2	2	232^2	245	108	11	4	70	62	12.3	3.13	**152**	.269	.324	26	.286	6	**41**	**42**	3	**4.7**
1930	Bos-N	3	5	.375	11	9	1	0	0	49	72	53	4	3	22	15	17.8	7.35	67	.353	.424	3	.188	-0	-13	-13	0	-1.6
	*StL-N	13	6	.684	22	19	10	1	0	152^1	174	66	5	4	43	58	13.1	3.01	166	.293	.345	15	.263	2	33	34	1	4.0
	Yr	16	11	.593	33	28	11	1	0	201^1	246	119	9	7	65	73	14.2	4.07	123	.308	.366	18	.247	2	20	21	2	2.4
1931	*StL-N	17	9	.654	29	28	17	3	0	212^1	240	97	11	10	59	67	13.1	3.65	108	.286	.340	14	.184	-2	5	7	3	0.8
1932	*Chi-N	6	11	.353	30	18	5	1	1	141^1	174	89	8	1	50	36	14.3	4.78	79	.297	.354	11	.250	1	-14	-16	1	-1.5
1933	Chi-N	3	6	.333	17	7	3	1	3	69^2	71	29	2	1	29	12	13.0	3.49	94	.277	.353	3	.150	-1	-1	-2	1	-0.2
	StL-N	0	1	.000	4	3	0	0	1	13^2	15	13	1	1	8	4	15.8	5.27	66	.263	.364	1	.200	0	-3	-3	-1	-0.3
	Yr	3	7	.300	21	10	3	1	4	83^1	86	42	3	2	37	16	13.5	3.78	87	.275	.355	4	.160	-0	-4	-4	-0	-0.5
1934	StL-N	2	1	.667	4	0	0	0	0	7^2	5	3	1	0	2	1	8.2	3.52	120	.179	.233	0	—	0	0	1	0	0.1
	Pit-N	1	2	.333	8	4	0	0	0	27^1	36	24	0	1	10	9	15.5	7.24	57	.310	.370	1	.143	-0	-10	-9	1	-0.8
	Yr	3	3	.500	12	4	0	0	0	35	41	27	1	1	12	10	13.9	6.43	64	.285	.344	1	.143	-0	-9	-9	1	-0.7
	NY-A	1	2	.333	10	0	0	0	1	18	22	11	0	1	14	5	18.5	5.50	74	.319	.440	0	.000	-0	-2	-3	1	-0.4
Total	19	270	212	.560	616	497	314	35	18	4179^2	4412	2050	148	101	1295	1512	12.5	3.53	107	.273	.331	380	.248	52	118	121	58	23.7

● JOHN GRIMES Grimes, John Thomas b: 4/17/1869, Woodstock, Md. d: 1/17/64, San Francisco, Cal BR/TR, 5'11", 160 lbs. Deb: 7/28/1897

YEAR	TM/L	W	L	PCT	G	GS	CG	SH	SV	IP	H	R	HR	HB	BB	SO	RAT	ERA	ERA+	OAV	OOB	BH	AVG	PB	PR	PR+	PD	TPI
1897	StL-N	0	2	.000	3	1	1	0	0	19^2	24	23	0	6	8	4	17.4	5.95	74	.300	.404	2	.286	1	-4	-3	1	-0.1

● JASON GRIMSLEY Grimsley, Jason Alan b: 8/7/67, Cleveland, Tex. BR/TR, 6'3", 180 lbs. Deb: 9/8/89

YEAR	TM/L	W	L	PCT	G	GS	CG	SH	SV	IP	H	R	HR	HB	BB	SO	RAT	ERA	ERA+	OAV	OOB	BH	AVG	PB	PR	PR+	PD	TPI
1989	Phi-N	1	3	.250	4	4	0	0	0	18^1	19	13	2	0	19	7	18.7	5.89	60	.268	.422	0	.000	-1	-5	-5	0	-0.9
1990	Phi-N	3	2	.600	11	11	0	0	0	57^1	47	21	1	2	43	41	14.4	3.30	116	.227	.365	3	.188	0	3	3	1	0.4
1991	Phi-N	1	7	.125	12	12	0	0	0	61	54	34	4	3	41	42	14.5	4.87	75	.242	.367	1	.059	-1	-8	-8	1	-0.9
1993	Cle-A	3	4	.429	10	6	0	0	0	42^1	52	26	3	1	20	27	15.5	5.31	82	.302	.378	0	—	0	-5	-5	-0	-0.7
1994	Cle-A	5	2	.714	14	13	1	0	0	82^2	91	47	7	6	34	59	14.3	4.57	103	.283	.362	0	—	0	2	1	-0	0.1
1995	Cle-A	0	0	—	15	2	0	0	1	34	37	24	4	2	32	25	18.8	6.09	77	.289	.438	0	—	0	-5	-5	1	-0.2
1996	Cal-A	5	7	.417	35	20	2	1	0	130^1	150	110	14	13	74	82	16.4	6.84	73	.286	.388	0	—	0	-27	-26	2	-1.8
1999	*NY-A	7	2	.778	55	0	0	0	1	75	66	39	7	4	40	49	13.2	3.60	132	.231	.333	0	—	0	11	10	1	1.1
2000	*NY-A	3	2	.600	63	4	0	0	1	96^1	100	58	10	5	42	53	13.7	5.04	95	.268	.350	0	.000	1	-1	-3	1	0.0
Total	9	28	29	.491	219	72	3	1	3	597^1	616	372	52	36	345	385	15.0	5.11	89	.267	.371	4	.103	-0	-35	-38	6	-2.9

● ROSS GRIMSLEY Grimsley, Ross Albert I b: 6/4/22, Americus, Kan. d: 2/6/94, Memphis, Tenn. BL/TL, 6', 175 lbs. Deb: 9/3/51 F

YEAR	TM/L	W	L	PCT	G	GS	CG	SH	SV	IP	H	R	HR	HB	BB	SO	RAT	ERA	ERA+	OAV	OOB	BH	AVG	PB	PR	PR+	PD	TPI
1951	Chi-A	0	0	—	7	0	0	0	0	14	12	8	1	0	10	8	14.1	3.86	105	.235	.361	0	.000	-0	0	0	-1	-0.1

● ROSS GRIMSLEY Grimsley, Ross Albert Ii b: 1/7/50, Topeka, Kan. BL/TL, 6'3", 200 lbs. Deb: 5/16/71 F

YEAR	TM/L	W	L	PCT	G	GS	CG	SH	SV	IP	H	R	HR	HB	BB	SO	RAT	ERA	ERA+	OAV	OOB	BH	AVG	PB	PR	PR+	PD	TPI
1971	Cin-N	10	7	.588	26	26	6	3	0	161^1	151	67	15	2	43	67	10.9	3.57	94	.250	.302	6	.118	-1	-2	-4	-1	-0.6
1972	*Cin-N	14	8	.636	30	28	4	1	1	197^2	194	73	18	0	50	79	11.1	3.05	105	.260	.307	8	.121	-2	9	4	-0	0.2
1973	*Cin-N	13	10	.565	38	36	8	1	1	242^1	245	96	24	0	68	90	11.6	3.23	106	.266	.317	5	.061	-6	12	5	-2	-0.4
1974	*Bal-A	18	13	.581	40	39	17	4	1	295^2	267	111	26	3	76	158	10.5	3.07	112	.244	.295	0	—	0	18	13	0	1.3
1975	Bal-A	10	13	.435	35	32	8	1	0	197	210	95	29	1	47	89	11.8	4.07	87	.276	.319	0	—	0	-6	-13	0	-1.3
1976	Bal-A	8	7	.533	28	19	2	0	0	136^2	143	66	8	1	35	41	11.8	3.95	83	.270	.317	0	—	0	-7	-11	-1	-1.2
1977	Bal-A	14	10	.583	34	34	11	2	0	218^1	230	105	24	1	74	53	12.6	3.96	96	.277	.337	0	—	0	3	-4	2	-0.2
1978	Mon-N☆	20	11	.645	36	36	19	3	0	263	237	103	17	2	67	84	10.5	3.05	116	.243	.293	13	.144	-1	16	14	1	1.6
1979	Mon-N	10	9	.526	32	27	2	0	0	151^1	199	102	18	3	41	42	14.5	5.35	69	.322	.367	11	.200	1	-27	-29	-0	-3.1
1980	Mon-N	2	4	.333	11	7	0	0	0	41^1	61	31	5	1	12	11	16.1	6.31	57	.351	.396	2	.222	0	-12	-13	0	-1.6
	Cle-A	4	5	.444	14	11	2	0	0	74^2	103	63	11	1	24	18	15.4	6.75	60	.331	.381	0	—	0	-22	-22	-1	-2.2
1982	Bal-A	1	2	.333	21	0	0	0	0	60	65	35	7	0	22	18	13.1	5.25	77	.283	.345	0	—	0	-8	-8	0	-0.4
Total	11	124	99	.556	345	295	79	15	3	2039^1	2105	947	202	15	559	750	11.8	3.81	92	.270	.320	45	.127	-10	-27	-69	-1	-7.9

● DAN GRINER Griner, Donald Dexter "Rusty" b: 3/7/1888, Centerville, Tenn. d: 6/3/50, Bishopville, S.C. BL/TR, 6'1.5", 200 lbs. Deb: 8/17/12

YEAR	TM/L	W	L	PCT	G	GS	CG	SH	SV	IP	H	R	HR	HB	BB	SO	RAT	ERA	ERA+	OAV	OOB	BH	AVG	PB	PR	PR+	PD	TPI
1912	StL-N	3	4	.429	12	7	2	0	0	54	59	35	3	3	15	20	12.8	3.17	108	.278	.335	1	.077	-0	1	2	-1	0.0

YEAR	TM/L	W	L	PCT	G	GS	CG	SH	SV	IP	H	R	HR	HB	BB	SO	RAT	ERA	ERA+	OAV	OOB	BH	AVG	PB	PR	PR+	PD	TPI
1913	StL-N	10	22	.313	34	34	18	1	0	225	279	150	12	10	66	79	14.2	5.08	64	.312	.366	21	.259	5	-47	-46	2	-4.9
1914	StL-N	9	13	.409	37	17	11	2	2	179	163	66	3	3	57	74	11.2	2.51	111	.254	.318	14	.255	4	5	6	-1	1.0
1915	StL-N	5	11	.313	37	17	9	3	3	150^1	137	59	4	8	46	46	11.4	2.81	99	.259	.328	14	.269	4	-1	-0	-2	0.2
1916	StL-N	0	0	—	4	0	0	0	1	11	15	5	0	1	3	3	15.5	4.09	65	.341	.396	1	.250	0	-2	-2	0	-0.1
1918	Bro-N	1	5	.167	11	6	3	1	0	54^1	47	16	0	7	15	22	11.4	2.15	129	.267	.348	1	.071	-1	4	4	0	0.4
Total	6	28	55	.337	135	81	43	7	6	673^2	700	331	22	32	202	244	12.5	3.49	86	.280	.342	52	.237	12	-39	-37	-2	-3.4

● LEE GRISSOM Grissom, Lee Theo b: 10/23/07, Sherman, Tex. d: 10/4/98, Corning, Cal. BB/TL (BR 1934, 37), 6'3", 200 lbs. Deb: 9/2/34 F

YEAR	TM/L	W	L	PCT	G	GS	CG	SH	SV	IP	H	R	HR	HB	BB	SO	RAT	ERA	ERA+	OAV	OOB	BH	AVG	PB	PR	PR+	PD	TPI
1934	Cin-N	0	1	.000	4	1	0	0	0	7	13	12	0	0	7	4	25.7	15.43	26	.382	.488	0	.000	-0	-9	-9	-0	-1.0
1935	Cin-N	1	1	.500	3	3	1	0	0	21	31	10	0	0	4	13	15.0	3.86	103	.333	.361	0	.000	-1	0	0	0	0.0
1936	Cin-N	1	1	.500	6	4	0	0	0	24^1	33	18	1	0	9	13	15.5	6.29	61	.320	.375	0	.000	-1	-6	-7	0	-0.6
1937	Cin-N★	12	17	.414	50	30	14	**5**	6	223^2	193	89	7	4	93	149	11.7	3.26	114	.232	.313	7	.109	-3	16	12	-2	1.0
1938	Cin-N	2	3	.400	14	7	0	0	0	51	60	38	4	2	22	16	14.8	5.29	69	.300	.375	3	.188	-0	-9	-10	-0	-0.9
1939	*Cin-N	9	7	.563	33	21	3	0	0	153^2	145	77	14	1	56	53	11.8	4.10	93	.249	.316	4	.085	-2	-3	-5	-2	-0.8
1940	NY-A	0	0	—	5	0	0	0	0	4^2	4	0	0	0	2	1	11.6	0.00	—	.250	.333	0	—	0	2	2	0	0.1
	Bro-N	2	5	.286	14	10	3	1	0	73^2	59	30	3	0	34	56	11.4	2.81	142	.215	.302	5	.217	0	9	9	-1	0.8
1941	Bro-N	0	0	—	4	1	0	0	1	11^1	10	3	2	0	8	5	14.3	2.38	154	.238	.360	1	.500	0	2	2	-0	0.1
	Phi-N	2	13	.133	29	18	2	0	0	131^1	120	69	4	2	70	74	13.2	3.97	93	.242	.338	6	.167	-1	-5	-4	-1	-0.5
	Yr	2	13	.133	33	19	2	0	1	142^2	130	72	6	2	78	79	13.2	3.85	96	.242	.340	7	.184	-0	-3	-2	-1	-0.4
Total	8	29	48	.377	162	95	23	6	7	701^2	668	346	35	9	305	384	12.6	3.89	97	.250	.329	26	.127	-8	-3	-8	-6	-1.8

● MARV GRISSOM Grissom, Marvin Edward b: 3/31/18, Los Molinos, Cal. BR/TR, 6'3", 195 lbs. Deb: 9/10/46 FC

YEAR	TM/L	W	L	PCT	G	GS	CG	SH	SV	IP	H	R	HR	HB	BB	SO	RAT	ERA	ERA+	OAV	OOB	BH	AVG	PB	PR	PR+	PD	TPI
1946	NY-N	0	2	.000	4	3	0	0	0	18^2	17	11	1	1	13	9	14.9	4.34	79	.254	.383	1	.200	-0	-2	-2	1	-0.1
1949	Det-A	2	4	.333	27	2	0	0	0	39^1	56	32	6	1	34	17	20.8	6.41	65	.335	.450	2	.222	1	-10	-10	0	-1.2
1952	Chi-A	12	10	.545	28	24	7	1	0	166	156	79	6	3	79	97	12.9	3.74	98	.250	.337	8	.151	-1	-1	-2	-2	-0.5
1953	Bos-A	2	6	.250	13	11	1	1	0	59^1	61	34	5	1	30	31	14.0	4.70	89	.266	.354	0	.000	-3	-5	-3	-1	-0.7
	NY-N	4	2	.667	21	7	3	0	0	84^1	83	40	6	1	31	46	12.3	3.95	109	.255	.321	2	.074	-2	3	3	1	0.1
1954	*NY-N★	10	7	.588	56	3	1	1	19	122^1	100	37	13	7	50	64	11.6	2.35	171	.226	.314	5	.156	-1	23	23	-0	3.7
1955	NY-N	5	4	.556	55	0	0	0	8	89^1	76	35	6	6	41	49	12.4	2.92	138	.237	.334	2	.154	-1	11	11	0	1.2
1956	NY-N	1	1	.500	43	2	0	0	7	80^2	71	15	3	1	16	49	9.8	1.56	242	.241	.282	1	.091	-0	**20**	**20**	-1	0.9
1957	NY-N	4	4	.500	55	0	0	0	14	82^2	74	36	6	2	23	51	10.8	2.61	151	.243	.301	2	.167	0	12	12	1	1.7
1958	SF-N	7	5	.583	51	0	0	0	10	65^1	71	34	11	5	26	46	14.1	3.99	95	.287	.367	0	.000	-1	-0	-1	0	-0.3
1959	StL-N	0	0	—	3	0	0	0	0	2	6	5	2	0	0	0	27.0	22.50	19	.500	.500	0	—	0	-4	-4	0	-0.2
Total	10	47	45	.511	356	52	12	3	58	810	771	358	65	28	343	459	12.7	3.41	115	.254	.335	23	.122	-7	47	47	-0	4.6

● CONNIE GROB Grob, Conrad George b: 11/9/32, Cross Plains, Wis. d: 9/28/97, Madison, Wis. BL/TR, 6'0.5", 180 lbs. Deb: 4/22/56

YEAR	TM/L	W	L	PCT	G	GS	CG	SH	SV	IP	H	R	HR	HB	BB	SO	RAT	ERA	ERA+	OAV	OOB	BH	AVG	PB	PR	PR+	PD	TPI
1956	Was-A	4	5	.444	37	1	0	0	1	79^1	121	79	14	1	26	27	16.8	7.83	55	.353	.400	6	.333	1	-32	-30	1	-2.7

● JOHNNY GRODZICKI Grodzicki, John "Grod" b: 2/26/17, Nanticoke, Pa. d: 5/2/98, Daytona Beach, Fla. BR/TR, 6'1.5", 200 lbs. Deb: 4/18/41 C

YEAR	TM/L	W	L	PCT	G	GS	CG	SH	SV	IP	H	R	HR	HB	BB	SO	RAT	ERA	ERA+	OAV	OOB	BH	AVG	PB	PR	PR+	PD	TPI
1941	StL-N	2	1	.667	5	1	0	0	0	13^1	6	7	0	0	11	10	11.5	1.35	279	.130	.298	0	.000	0	3	3	-0	0.8
1946	StL-N	0	0	—	3	0	0	0	0	4	4	5	1	0	4	2	18.0	9.00	38	.250	.400	0	—	0	-2	-2	0	-0.1
1947	StL-N	0	1	.000	16	0	0	0	0	23^1	21	17	5	0	19	8	15.4	5.40	77	.253	.392	0	.000	-0	-3	-3	0	-0.1
Total	3	2	2	.500	24	1	0	0	0	40^2	31	29	6	0	34	20	14.4	4.43	89	.214	.363	0	.000	0	-3	-2	0	0.6

● STEVE GROMEK Gromek, Stephen Joseph b: 1/15/20, Hamtramck, Mich. BB/TR, 6'2", 180 lbs. Deb: 8/18/41

YEAR	TM/L	W	L	PCT	G	GS	CG	SH	SV	IP	H	R	HR	HB	BB	SO	RAT	ERA	ERA+	OAV	OOB	BH	AVG	PB	PR	PR+	PD	TPI
1941	Cle-A	1	1	.500	9	2	1	0	2	23^1	25	12	0	0	11	19	13.9	4.24	93	.266	.343	1	.167	-0	-0	-1	-1	-0.2
1942	Cle-A	2	0	1.000	14	0	0	0	0	44^1	46	24	2	0	23	14	14.0	3.65	94	.267	.354	5	.333	3	0	-1	-1	0.2
1943	Cle-A	0	0	—	3	0	0	0	0	4	6	4	0	0	0	4	13.5	9.00	35	.353	.353	2	1.000	1	-3	-3	-0	-0.1
1944	Cle-A	10	9	.526	35	21	12	2	1	203^2	160	74	5	3	70	115	10.3	2.56	129	**.219**	.290	19	.260	5	20	17	-3	1.8
1945	Cle-A†	19	9	.679	33	30	21	3	1	251	229	80	6	4	66	101	10.7	2.55	128	.243	.295	21	.231	3	23	20	-3	2.3
1946	Cle-A	5	15	.250	29	21	5	2	4	153^2	159	79	20	3	47	75	12.2	4.33	76	.264	.321	11	.196	0	-14	-19	-1	-2.3
1947	Cle-A	3	5	.375	29	7	0	0	4	84^1	77	43	8	1	36	39	12.2	3.74	93	.240	.318	7	.318	2	-0	-3	-0	-0.1
1948	*Cle-A	9	3	.750	38	9	4	1	2	130	109	52	10	6	51	50	11.5	2.84	143	.226	.307	6	.146	-1	21	19	-1	1.3
1949	Cle-A	4	6	.400	27	12	3	0	0	92	86	41	8	2	40	22	12.5	3.33	120	.250	.332	4	.167	-0	9	7	0	0.7
1950	Cle-A	10	7	.588	31	13	4	1	0	113^1	94	50	10	3	36	43	10.6	3.65	119	.226	.292	6	.158	-2	12	9	-0	0.9
1951	Cle-A	7	4	.636	27	8	4	0	1	107^1	98	41	6	4	29	40	11.0	2.77	137	.238	.295	8	.296	3	16	13	1	1.6
1952	Cle-A	7	7	.500	29	13	3	1	1	122^2	109	55	14	2	28	65	10.2	3.67	91	.232	.278	3	.100	-0	0	-5	-3	-0.8
1953	Cle-A	1	1	.500	5	1	0	0	0	11	11	4	0	1	3	8	12.3	3.27	115	.268	.333	0	.000	-0	1	1	-0	0.0
	Det-A	6	8	.429	19	17	6	1	1	125^2	138	70	17	8	36	59	13.0	4.51	90	.276	.335	3	.073	-4	-7	-6	-1	-1.1
	Yr	7	9	.438	24	18	6	1	1	136^2	149	74	17	9	39	67	13.0	4.41	92	.275	.334	3	.070	-4	-6	-6	-1	-1.1
1954	Det-A	18	16	.529	36	32	17	4	1	252^2	236	85	26	12	57	102	10.9	2.74	135	.246	.297	15	.190	2	28	27	-3	3.4
1955	Det-A	13	10	.565	28	25	8	2	0	181	183	89	26	9	37	73	11.4	3.98	97	.261	.307	9	.167	4	-0	-3	-2	-0.1
1956	Det-A	8	6	.571	40	13	4	0	4	141	142	74	25	9	47	64	12.6	4.28	96	.263	.332	4	.148	2	-2	-3	-2	-0.3
1957	Det-A	0	1	.000	15	1	0	0	1	23^2	32	16	3	1	13	11	17.5	6.08	63	.333	.418	0	.000	-0	-6	-6	-1	-0.4
Total	17	123	108	.532	447	225	92	17	23	2064^2	1940	893	186	68	630	904	11.5	3.41	108	.247	.309	124	.197	15	96	65	-21	6.8

● BOB GROOM Groom, Robert b: 9/12/1884, Belleville, Ill. d: 2/19/48, Belleville, Ill. BR/TR, 6'2", 175 lbs. Deb: 4/13/09

YEAR	TM/L	W	L	PCT	G	GS	CG	SH	SV	IP	H	R	HR	HB	BB	SO	RAT	ERA	ERA+	OAV	OOB	BH	AVG	PB	PR	PR+	PD	TPI
1909	Was-A	7	26	.212	44	31	17	1	0	260^2	218	114	2	13	105	131	11.6	2.87	85	.229	.314	8	.091	-6	-11	-13	4	-1.9
1910	Was-A	12	17	.414	34	30	22	3	0	257^2	244	117	8	9	77	98	11.5	2.76	90	.260	.322	11	.120	-6	-7	-8	-2	-1.6
1911	Was-A	13	17	.433	37	32	20	2	2	254^2	280	148	9	8	67	135	12.5	3.82	86	.282	.332	11	.134	-4	-13	-15	1	-1.9
1912	Was-A	24	13	.649	43	40	28	2	1	316	287	133	3	5	94	179	11.0	2.62	127	.246	.305	12	.117	-7	24	25	-2	1.9
1913	Was-A	16	16	.500	37	36	17	4	0	264^1	258	118	8	5	81	156	11.7	3.23	91	.254	.312	15	.163	1	-9	-8	1	-0.8
1914	StL-F	13	20	.394	42	34	23	1	1	280^2	281	141	9	4	75	167	11.5	3.24	94	.262	.312	15	.160	-4	-11	-6	-0	-1.0
1915	StL-F	11	11	.500	37	26	11	4	2	209	200	93	6	2	73	111	11.8	3.27	88	.261	.327	10	.152	-3	-13	-9	0	-1.2
1916	StL-A	13	9	.591	41	26	8	1	4	217^1	174	82	1	3	98	92	11.4	2.57	107	.226	.315	7	.111	-2	6	4	2	0.4
1917	StL-A	8	19	.296	38	28	11	4	3	232^2	193	80	3	5	95	82	11.3	2.94	88	.233	.315	8	.111	-4	-7	-9	-1	-1.6
1918	Cle-A	2	2	.500	14	5	0	0	0	43^1	70	42	0	1	18	8	18.5	7.06	43	.380	.438	1	.083	-1	-21	-18	0	-1.7
Total	10	119	150	.442	367	288	157	22	13	2336^1	2205	1068	49	55	783	1159	11.7	3.10	93	.254	.319	98	.128	-35	-61	-58	2	-9.4

● BUDDY GROOM Groom, Wedsel Gary b: 7/10/65, Dallas, Tex. BL/TL, 6'2", 200 lbs. Deb: 6/20/92

YEAR	TM/L	W	L	PCT	G	GS	CG	SH	SV	IP	H	R	HR	HB	BB	SO	RAT	ERA	ERA+	OAV	OOB	BH	AVG	PB	PR	PR+	PD	TPI
1992	Det-A	0	5	.000	12	7	0	0	1	38^2	48	28	4	0	22	15	16.3	5.82	68	.320	.407	0	—	0	-8	-8	-0	-0.9
1993	Det-A	0	2	.000	19	3	0	0	0	36^2	48	25	4	2	13	15	15.5	6.14	70	.322	.384	0	—	0	-7	-8	0	-0.4
1994	Det-A	0	1	.000	40	0	0	0	1	32	31	14	4	2	13	27	12.9	3.94	123	.256	.338	0	—	0	3	3	-1	0.1
1995	Det-A	1	3	.250	23	4	0	0	1	40^2	55	35	6	2	26	23	18.4	7.52	63	.322	.417	0	—	0	-13	-12	-1	-1.1
	Fla-N	1	2	.333	14	0	0	0	0	15	26	12	2	0	6	12	19.2	7.20	59	.400	.451	0	—	0	-5	-5	0	-0.8
1996	Oak-A	5	0	1.000	72	1	0	0	2	77^1	85	37	8	3	34	57	14.2	3.84	128	.281	.360	0	—	0	10	9	-1	0.4
1997	Oak-A	2	2	.500	78	0	0	0	3	64^2	75	38	9	0	24	45	13.8	5.15	88	.292	.352	0	—	0	-4	-4	0	-0.2
1998	Oak-A	3	1	.750	75	0	0	0	0	57^1	62	30	4	1	20	36	13.0	4.24	108	.274	.336	0	—	0	3	2	-1	0.1
1999	Oak-A	3	2	.600	**76**	0	0	0	0	46	48	29	1	1	18	32	13.1	5.09	91	.274	.345	0	—	0	-1	-2	1	-0.1
2000	Bal-A	6	3	.667	70	0	0	0	4	59^1	63	37	5	0	21	44	12.7	4.85	99	.275	.336	0	—	0	0	-0	0	0.0
Total	9	21	21	.500	479	15	0	0	12	467^2	541	285	47	11	197	306	14.4	5.10	90	.293	.365	0	—	0	-22	-26	-1	-2.9

● DON GROSS Gross, Donald John b: 6/30/31, Weidman, Mich. BL/TL, 5'11", 186 lbs. Deb: 7/21/55

YEAR	TM/L	W	L	PCT	G	GS	CG	SH	SV	IP	H	R	HR	HB	BB	SO	RAT	ERA	ERA+	OAV	OOB	BH	AVG	PB	PR	PR+	PD	TPI
1955	Cin-N	4	5	.444	17	11	2	1	0	67^1	79	33	11	1	16	33	12.8	4.14	102	.298	.340	3	.158	-1	-1	1	0	0.0
1956	Cin-N	3	0	1.000	19	7	2	0	0	69^1	69	25	4	1	20	47	11.7	1.95	204	.257	.310	2	.105	-1	14	15	1	0.8
1957	Cin-N	7	9	.438	43	16	5	0	1	148^1	152	75	21	3	33	73	11.4	4.31	95	.264	.307	5	.109	-2	-7	-3	-0	-0.6
1958	Pit-N	5	7	.417	40	3	0	0	7	74^2	67	37	5	1	38	59	12.8	3.98	97	.241	.334	1	.056	-1	-0	-1	1	-0.2
1959	Pit-N	1	1	.500	21	0	0	0	2	33	28	16	3	1	10	15	10.6	3.55	109	.228	.291	0	.000	-0	1	1	1	0.2
1960	Pit-N	0	0	—	5	0	0	0	0	5^1	5	2	1	0	0	3	8.4	3.38	111	.238	.238	0	—	0	0	0	-0	0.0
Total	6	20	22	.476	145	37	9	1	10	398	400	188	45	7	117	230	11.8	3.73	108	.261	.316	11	.106	-5	8	13	2	0.2

● GREG GROSS

Gross, Gregory Eugene b: 8/1/52, York, Pa. BL/TL, 5′11″, 175 lbs. Deb: 9/5/73 ♦

YEAR	TM/L	W	L	PCT	G	GS	CG	SH	SV	IP	H	R	HR	HB	BB	SO	RAT	ERA	ERA+	OAV	OOB	BH	AVG	PB	PR	PR+	PD	TPI
1986	Phi-N	0	0	—	1	0	0	0	0	0^2	1	0	0	0	1	2	27.0	0.00	—	.333	.500	25	.248	0	0	0	0	0.0
1989	Hou-N	0	0	—	1	0	0	0	0	1	3	2	0	0	1	1	36.0	18.00	19	.500	.571	15	.200	0	-2	-2	0	-0.1
Total	2	0	0	—	2	0	0	0	0	1^2	4	2	0	0	2	3	32.4	10.80	33	.444	.545	1073	.287	0	-1	-1	0	-0.1

● KEVIN GROSS

Gross, Kevin Frank b: 6/8/61, Downey, Cal. BR/TR, 6′5″, 215 lbs. Deb: 6/25/83

YEAR	TM/L	W	L	PCT	G	GS	CG	SH	SV	IP	H	R	HR	HB	BB	SO	RAT	ERA	ERA+	OAV	OOB	BH	AVG	PB	PR	PR+	PD	TPI
1983	Phi-N	4	6	.400	17	17	1	1	0	96	100	46	13	3	35	66	12.9	3.56	100	.265	.333	3	.091	-1	1	0	0	0.0
1984	Phi-N	8	5	.615	44	14	1	0	1	129	140	66	8	5	44	84	13.2	4.12	88	.277	.341	2	.067	-2	-7	-7	1	-0.7
1985	Phi-N	15	13	.536	38	31	6	2	0	205^2	194	86	11	7	81	151	12.3	3.41	108	.251	.328	9	.138	0	4	6	1	1.0
1986	Phi-N	12	12	.500	37	36	7	2	0	241^2	240	115	28	8	94	154	12.7	4.02	96	.259	.333	15	.188	3	-8	-4	-1	-0.2
1987	Phi-N	9	16	.360	34	33	3	1	0	200^2	205	107	26	10	87	110	13.5	4.35	98	.267	.350	12	.190	2	-6	-2	-2	-0.3
1988	Phi-N★	12	14	.462	33	33	5	1	0	231^2	209	101	18	11	89	162	12.0	3.69	97	.239	.317	13	.173	1	-6	-3	-0	-0.2
1989	Mon-N	11	12	.478	31	31	4	3	0	201^1	188	105	20	6	88	158	12.6	4.38	81	.247	.330	9	.141	1	-20	-19	-0	-1.9
1990	Mon-N	9	12	.429	31	26	2	1	0	163^1	171	86	9	4	65	111	13.2	4.57	80	.272	.344	10	.200	4	-14	-17	-2	-1.9
1991	LA-N	10	11	.476	46	10	0	0	3	115^2	123	55	10	2	50	95	13.6	3.58	100	.275	.351	7	.280	2	1	0	-0	0.3
1992	LA-N	8	13	.381	34	30	4	3	0	204^2	182	82	11	3	77	158	11.5	3.17	109	.241	.313	6	.095	-1	8	7	-1	0.4
1993	LA-N	13	13	.500	33	32	3	0	0	202^1	224	110	15	5	74	150	13.5	4.14	92	.281	.346	13	.203	5	-2	-8	2	-0.2
1994	LA-N	9	7	.563	25	23	1	0	1	157^1	162	64	11	2	43	124	11.8	3.60	109	.263	.314	7	.149	1	11	6	2	0.9
1995	Tex-A	9	15	.375	31	30	4	0	0	183^2	200	124	27	8	89	106	14.6	5.54	87	.279	.365	0	—	0	-17	-14	-1	-1.6
1996	Tex-A	11	8	.579	28	19	1	0	0	129^1	151	78	19	4	50	78	14.3	5.22	100	.293	.360	0	—	0	-3	0	0	0.1
1997	Ana-A	2	1	.667	12	3	0	0	0	25^1	30	20	4	1	20	20	18.1	6.75	68	.313	.436	0	.000	-0	-6	-6	0	-0.6
Total	15	142	158	.473	474	368	42	14	5	2487^2	2519	1245	230	79	986	1727	13.0	4.11	95	.264	.338	106	.161	14	-64	-61	0	-4.9

● KIP GROSS

Gross, Kip Lee b: 8/24/64, Scottsbluff, Neb. BR/TR, 6′2″, 195 lbs. Deb: 4/21/90

YEAR	TM/L	W	L	PCT	G	GS	CG	SH	SV	IP	H	R	HR	HB	BB	SO	RAT	ERA	ERA+	OAV	OOB	BH	AVG	PB	PR	PR+	PD	TPI
1990	Cin-N	0	0	—	5	0	0	0	0	6^1	6	3	0	0	2	3	11.4	4.26	93	.273	.333	0	—	0	-0	-0	-0	0.0
1991	Cin-N	6	4	.600	29	9	1	0	0	85^2	93	43	8	0	40	40	14.0	3.47	110	.279	.357	2	.091	-1	2	3	0	0.2
1992	LA-N	1	1	.500	16	1	0	0	0	23^2	32	14	1	0	10	14	16.0	4.18	82	.323	.385	2	1.000	1	-2	-2	1	0.0
1993	LA-N	0	0	—	10	0	0	0	0	15	13	1	0	0	4	12	10.2	0.60	637	.236	.288	0	—	0	6	6	-0	0.3
1999	Bos-A	0	2	.000	11	1	0	0	0	12^2	15	11	3	3	8	9	18.5	7.82	64	.294	.419	0	—	0	-4	-4	-0	-0.5
2000	Hou-N	0	1	.000	2	1	0	0	0	4^1	9	8	2	0	2	3	22.8	10.38	47	.429	.478	0	.000	-0	-3	-3	-0	-0.5
Total	6	7	8	.467	73	12	1	0	0	147^2	168	80	14	3	66	81	14.4	3.90	100	.289	.365	4	.160	-0	-1	-0	0	-0.5

● WAYNE GROSS

Gross, Wayne Dale b: 1/14/52, Riverside, Cal. BL/TR, 6′2″, 210 lbs. Deb: 8/21/76 ♦

YEAR	TM/L	W	L	PCT	G	GS	CG	SH	SV	IP	H	R	HR	HB	BB	SO	RAT	ERA	ERA+	OAV	OOB	BH	AVG	PB	PR	PR+	PD	TPI
1983	Oak-A	0	0	—	1	0	0	0	0	2^1	2	0	0	1	1	0	15.4	0.00	—	.222	.364	79	.233	0	1	1	-0	0.1

● HARLEY GROSSMAN

Grossman, Harley Joseph b: 5/5/30, Evansville, Ind. BR/TR, 6′, 170 lbs. Deb: 4/22/52

YEAR	TM/L	W	L	PCT	G	GS	CG	SH	SV	IP	H	R	HR	HB	BB	SO	RAT	ERA	ERA+	OAV	OOB	BH	AVG	PB	PR	PR+	PD	TPI
1952	Was-A	0	0	—	1	0	0	0	0	0^1	2	2	1	0	0	0	54.0	54.00	7	.667	.667	0	—	0	-2	-2	0	-0.1

● ERNIE GROTH

Groth, Ernest John "Dango" b: 12/24/1884, Cedarburg, Wis. d: 5/23/50, Milwaukee, Wis. BR/TR, 5′11″, 175 lbs. Deb: 9/6/04

YEAR	TM/L	W	L	PCT	G	GS	CG	SH	SV	IP	H	R	HR	HB	BB	SO	RAT	ERA	ERA+	OAV	OOB	BH	AVG	PB	PR	PR+	PD	TPI
1904	Chi-N	0	2	.000	3	2	2	0	1	16	22	13	1	1	6	9	16.3	5.63	47	.310	.372	0	.000	-1	-5	-5	-0	-0.7

● ERNEST GROTH

Groth, Ernest William b: 5/3/22, Beaver Falls, Pa. BR/TR, 5′9″, 185 lbs. Deb: 9/11/47

YEAR	TM/L	W	L	PCT	G	GS	CG	SH	SV	IP	H	R	HR	HB	BB	SO	RAT	ERA	ERA+	OAV	OOB	BH	AVG	PB	PR	PR+	PD	TPI
1947	Cle-A	0	0	—	2	0	0	0	0	1^1	0	0	0	0	1	1	6.8	0.00	—	.000	.250	0	—	0	1	1	0	0.0
1948	Cle-A	0	0	—	1	0	0	0	0	1	1	1	0	0	2	0	27.0	9.00	45	.250	.500	0	—	0	-1	-1	-0	0.0
1949	Chi-A	0	1	.000	3	0	0	0	0	5	2	3	2	1	3	1	10.8	5.40	77	.125	.300	0	—	0	-1	-1	-0	-0.1
Total	3	0	1	.000	6	0	0	0	0	7^1	3	4	2	1	6	2	12.3	4.91	82	.130	.333	0	—	0	-1	-1	-0	-0.1

● MATT GROTT

Grott, Matthew Allen b: 12/5/67, LaPorte, Ind. BL/TL, 6′1″, 210 lbs. Deb: 5/4/95

YEAR	TM/L	W	L	PCT	G	GS	CG	SH	SV	IP	H	R	HR	HB	BB	SO	RAT	ERA	ERA+	OAV	OOB	BH	AVG	PB	PR	PR+	PD	TPI
1995	Cin-N	0	0	—	2	0	0	0	0	1^2	6	4	1	0	0	2	32.4	21.60	19	.545	.545	0	—	0	-3	-3	0	-0.1

● ORVAL GROVE

Grove, Orval Leroy b: 8/29/19, Mineral, Kan. d: 4/20/92, Carmichael, Cal. BR/TR, 6′3″, 196 lbs. Deb: 5/28/40

YEAR	TM/L	W	L	PCT	G	GS	CG	SH	SV	IP	H	R	HR	HB	BB	SO	RAT	ERA	ERA+	OAV	OOB	BH	AVG	PB	PR	PR+	PD	TPI
1940	Chi-A	0	0	—	3	0	0	0	0	6	4	2	0	0	4	1	12.0	3.00	147	.182	.308	0	.000	-0	1	1	-0	0.0
1941	Chi-A	0	0	—	2	0	0	0	0	7	9	8	2	0	5	5	18.0	10.29	40	.321	.424	0	.000	-0	-5	-5	0	-0.2
1942	Chi-A	4	6	.400	12	8	4	0	0	66^1	77	47	1	1	33	21	15.1	5.16	70	.283	.363	5	.227	1	-11	-12	1	-1.3
1943	Chi-A	15	9	.625	32	25	18	3	2	216^1	192	84	9	4	72	76	11.1	2.75	122	.239	.304	12	.182	2	13	14	1	1.9
1944	Chi-A☆	14	15	.483	34	33	11	2	0	234^2	237	112	11	8	71	105	12.1	3.72	92	.263	.322	8	.104	-3	-8	-8	4	-0.8
1945	Chi-A	14	12	.538	33	30	16	4	1	217	233	100	12	5	68	54	12.7	3.44	96	.273	.330	7	.099	-4	-2	-3	2	-0.6
1946	Chi-A	8	13	.381	33	26	10	1	0	205^1	213	96	10	3	78	60	12.9	3.02	113	.272	.340	7	.108	-2	11	9	2	0.8
1947	Chi-A	6	8	.429	25	19	6	1	0	135^2	158	78	10	4	70	33	15.4	4.44	82	.296	.382	7	.146	-0	-11	-12	-1	-1.2
1948	Chi-A	2	10	.167	32	11	1	0	1	87^2	110	64	6	3	42	18	15.9	6.16	69	.315	.393	2	.095	-2	-18	-19	2	-2.2
1949	Chi-A	0	0	—	1	0	0	0	0	0^2	4	4	1	1	1	1	81.0	54.00	8	.667	.750	0	—	0	-4	-4	0	-0.2
Total	10	63	73	.463	207	152	66	11	4	1176^2	1237	595	62	29	444	374	13.1	3.78	93	.272	.340	48	.129	-9	-33	-37	10	-3.8

● LEFTY GROVE

Grove, Robert Moses b: 3/6/1900, Lonaconing, Md. d: 5/22/75, Norwalk, Ohio BL/TL, 6′3″, 190 lbs. Deb: 4/14/25 H

YEAR	TM/L	W	L	PCT	G	GS	CG	SH	SV	IP	H	R	HR	HB	BB	SO	RAT	ERA	ERA+	OAV	OOB	BH	AVG	PB	PR	PR+	PD	TPI
1925	Phi-A	10	12	.455	45	18	5	0	1	197	207	120	11	5	131	**116**	15.7	4.75	98	.278	.390	8	.123	-6	-8	-2	2	-0.6
1926	Phi-A	13	13	.500	45	33	20	1	6	258	227	97	6	6	101	**194**	11.7	**2.51**	**166**	.244	.322	8	.099	-5	**43**	**46**	-1	3.9
1927	Phi-A	20	13	.606	51	28	14	1	9	262^1	251	116	6	2	79	**174**	11.4	3.19	134	.252	.309	10	.125	-3	28	30	-1	3.2
1928	Phi-A	**24**	8	.750	39	31	24	4	4	261^2	228	93	10	1	64	**183**	10.1	2.58	156	.229	.277	15	.170	1	**43**	**42**	-3	**4.7**
1929	*Phi-A	20	6	**.769**	42	37	19	2	4	275^1	278	104	8	3	81	**170**	11.8	**2.81**	**151**	.262	.316	22	.216	1	**44**	**44**	-3	3.5
1930	*Phi-A	**28**	5	**.848**	**50**	32	22	2	**9**	291	273	101	8	5	60	**209**	**10.5**	**2.54**	**184**	**.247**	**.288**	22	.200	0	**68**	**69**	0	**7.2**
1931	*Phi-A	**31**	4	**.886**	41	30	**27**	**4**	5	288^2	249	84	10	1	62	**175**	**9.7**	**2.06**	**218**	.229	**.271**	23	.200	-2	**74**	**76**	-2	**8.4**
1932	Phi-A	25	10	.714	44	30	**27**	**4**	7	291^2	269	101	13	1	79	188	**10.8**	**2.84**	**159**	.241	**.292**	18	.168	0	**53**	**54**	-2	**5.8**
1933	Phi-A★	**24**	8	**.750**	45	28	**21**	2	6	275^1	280	113	12	4	83	114	12.0	3.20	134	.261	.316	9	.086	-7	33	33	0	2.9
1934	Bos-A	8	8	.500	22	12	5	0	0	109^1	149	84	5	1	32	43	15.0	6.50	74	.320	.365	6	.162	-0	-24	-19	-1	-2.3
1935	Bos-A☆	20	12	.625	35	30	23	2	1	273	269	105	6	3	65	121	**11.1**	**2.70**	**176**	.257	.302	7	.079	-5	**53**	**58**	2	6.0
1936	Bos-A★	17	12	.586	35	30	22	**6**	2	253^1	237	90	14	4	65	130	**10.9**	**2.81**	**189**	.246	**.297**	11	.138	-3	**63**	**67**	0	**6.6**
1937	Bos-A☆	17	9	.654	32	32	21	3	0	262	269	101	9	1	83	153	12.1	3.02	157	.261	.317	13	.143	-3	46	49	-1	3.9
1938	Bos-A★	14	4	.778	24	21	12	1	1	163^2	169	65	8	1	52	99	12.2	**3.08**	**160**	.263	.319	8	.148	-1	31	33	-0	3.0
1939	Bos-A☆	15	4	**.789**	23	23	17	2	0	191	180	63	8	1	58	81	11.3	**2.54**	**186**	.249	.305	9	.134	-1	44	45	-3	3.6
1940	Bos-A	7	6	.538	22	21	9	1	0	153^1	159	73	20	1	50	62	12.3	3.99	113	.269	.328	8	.151	-1	7	8	0	0.5
1941	Bos-A	7	7	.500	21	21	10	0	0	134	155	84	8	2	42	54	13.4	4.37	95	.287	.340	5	.111	-1	-3	-3	-2	-0.6
Total	17	300	141	.680	616	457	298	35	55	3940^2	3849	1594	162	42	1187	2266	11.6	3.06	148	.255	.311	202	.148	-37	595	628	-15	59.7

● CHARLIE GROVER

Grover, Charles Byrd "Bugs" b: 6/20/1890, Gallipolis, Ohio d: 5/24/71, Emmett Township, Mich. BL/TR, 6′1.5″, 185 lbs. Deb: 9/9/13

YEAR	TM/L	W	L	PCT	G	GS	CG	SH	SV	IP	H	R	HR	HB	BB	SO	RAT	ERA	ERA+	OAV	OOB	BH	AVG	PB	PR	PR+	PD	TPI
1913	Det-A	0	0	—	2	1	0	0	0	10^2	9	4	0	0	7	2	13.5	3.38	86	.265	.390	0	.000	-0	-1	-1	0	0.0

● TOM GRUBBS

Grubbs, Thomas Dillard "Judge" b: 2/22/1894, Mt.Sterling, Ky. d: 1/28/86, Lexington, Ky. BR/TR, 6′2″, 165 lbs. Deb: 10/3/20

YEAR	TM/L	W	L	PCT	G	GS	CG	SH	SV	IP	H	R	HR	HB	BB	SO	RAT	ERA	ERA+	OAV	OOB	BH	AVG	PB	PR	PR+	PD	TPI
1920	NY-N	0	1	.000	1	1	0	0	0	5	9	4	0	0	0	0	16.2	7.20	42	.409	.409	0	.000	-0	-2	-2	-0	-0.4

● HENRY GRUBER

Gruber, Henry John b: 12/14/1863, Hamden, Conn. d: 9/26/32, New Haven, Conn. BR/TR, 5′9″, 155 lbs. Deb: 7/28/1887

YEAR	TM/L	W	L	PCT	G	GS	CG	SH	SV	IP	H	R	HR	HB	BB	SO	RAT	ERA	ERA+	OAV	OOB	BH	AVG	PB	PR	PR+	PD	TPI
1887	Det-N	4	3	.571	7	7	7	0	0	62^1	84	29	3	0	21	12	12.1	2.74	148	.322	.322	10	.333	1	9	9	-1	0.7
1888	Det-N	11	14	.440	27	25	25	3	0	240	196	121	8	4	41	71	9.0	2.29	121	.213	.249	13	.141	-1	15	13	1	1.1
1889	Cle-N	7	16	.304	25	23	23	0	1	205	198	125	6	8	94	74	13.2	3.64	111	.246	.331	7	.101	-1	8	9	-0	0.7
1890	Cle-P	22	23	.489	48	44	39	1	0	383^1	464	352	15	15	204	110	16.0	4.27	93	.286	.371	36	.221	6	-2	-14	1	-0.6
1891	Cle-N	17	22	.436	44	40	35	1	0	348^2	407	258	10	7	119	79	13.8	4.13	84	.281	.338	23	.163	1	-30	-25	2	-2.0
Total	5	61	78	.439	151	139	129	5	1	1239^1	1349	885	42	34	479	346	13.4	3.67	99	.267	.332	89	.180	5	1	-7	3	-0.1

● KEN GRUNDT

Grundt, Kenneth Allan b: 8/26/69, Melrose Park, Ill. BL/TL, 6′4″, 195 lbs. Deb: 8/8/96

YEAR	TM/L	W	L	PCT	G	GS	CG	SH	SV	IP	H	R	HR	HB	BB	SO	RAT	ERA	ERA+	OAV	OOB	BH	AVG	PB	PR	PR+	PD	TPI
1996	Bos-A	0	0	—	1	0	0	0	0	0^1	1	1	0	0	0	0	27.0	27.00	19	.500	.500	0	—	0	-1	-1	0	0.0
1997	Bos-A	0	0	—	2	0	0	0	0	3	5	3	0	0	0	0	15.0	9.00	52	.357	.357	0	—	0	-1	-1	0	-0.1
Total	2	0	0	—	3	0	0	0	0	3^1	6	4	0	0	0	0	16.2	10.80	43	.375	.375	0	—	0	-2	-2	0	-0.1

YEAR	TM/L	W	L	PCT	G	GS	CG	SH	SV	IP	H	R	HR	HB	BB	SO	RAT	ERA	ERA+	OAV	OOB	BH	AVG	PB	PR	PR+	PD	TPI
● AL GRUNWALD	Grunwald, Alfred Henry "Stretch" b: 2/13/30, Los Angeles, Cal. BL/TL, 6'4", 210 lbs. Deb: 4/18/55																											
1955	Pit-N	0	0	—	3	0	0	0	0	7^2	7	4	1	0	7	2	16.4	4.70	88	.241	.389	2	.500	1	-1	-0	-0	0.0
1959	KC-A	0	1	.000	6	1	0	0	1	11^1	18	14	1	0	11	9	23.0	7.94	50	.360	.475	0	.000	-1	-5	-5	0	-0.5
Total	2	0	1	.000	9	1	0	0	1	19	25	18	2	0	18	11	20.4	6.63	61	.316	.443	2	.250	0	-6	-5	-0	-0.5
● MIKE GRZANICH	Grzanich, Michael Edward b: 8/24/72, Canton, Ill. BR/TR, 6'1", 180 lbs. Deb: 5/14/98																											
1998	Hou-N	0	0	—	1	0	0	0	0	1	1	2	0	0	2	1	27.0	18.00	23	.333	.600	0	—	0	-2	-2	0	-0.1
● JOE GRZENDA	Grzenda, Joseph Charles b: 6/8/37, Scranton, Pa. BR/TL, 6'2", 180 lbs. Deb: 4/26/61																											
1961	Det-A	1	0	1.000	4	0	0	0	0	5^2	9	5	2	0	2	0	17.5	7.94	52	.375	.423	1	1.000	0	-2	-2	0	-0.3
1964	KC-A	0	2	.000	20	0	0	0	0	25	34	15	2	1	13	17	17.3	5.40	71	.324	.403	0	.000	-0	-5	-4	1	-0.2
1966	KC-A	0	2	.000	21	0	0	0	0	22	28	8	1	0	12	14	16.4	3.27	104	.337	.421	0	.000	-0	0	0	1	0.1
1967	NY-N	0	0	—	11	0	0	0	0	16^2	14	4	0	1	8	9	12.4	2.16	157	.237	.338	0	.000	-0	2	2	-1	0.1
1969	*Min-A	4	1	.800	38	0	0	0	3	48^2	52	23	4	1	17	24	12.9	3.88	94	.281	.345	0	.000	0	-1	-1	1	0.0
1970	Was-A	3	6	.333	49	3	0	0	6	84^2	86	52	8	3	34	38	13.1	5.00	71	.267	.343	0	.000	-1	-12	-14	0	-1.7
1971	Was-A	5	2	.714	46	0	0	0	5	70^1	54	19	2	1	17	56	9.2	1.92	173	.217	.270	1	.143	-0	12	11	-0	1.3
1972	StL-N	1	0	1.000	30	0	0	0	0	35	46	24	1	3	17	15	17.0	5.66	60	.326	.410	0	.000	-0	-9	-9	0	-0.5
Total	8	14	13	.519	219	3	0	0	14	308	323	150	20	10	120	173	13.2	4.00	88	.277	.349	2	.067	-2	-15	-17	3	-1.2
● CECILIO GUANTE	Guante, Cecilio (Magallane) b: 2/1/60, Villa Mella, D.R. BR/TR, 6'3", 205 lbs. Deb: 5/1/82																											
1982	Pit-N	0	0	—	10	0	0	0	0	27	28	16	1	2	5	26	11.7	3.33	111	.264	.310	0	.000	-1	1	1	-0	0.0
1983	Pit-N	2	6	.250	49	0	0	0	9	100^1	90	45	5	2	46	82	12.4	3.32	112	.241	.327	2	.091	-1	4	4	-1	0.2
1984	Pit-N	2	3	.400	27	0	0	0	2	41^1	32	12	3	2	16	30	10.9	2.61	138	.224	.311	0	.000	-0	5	5	-1	0.5
1985	Pit-N	4	6	.400	63	0	0	0	5	109	84	34	5	5	40	92	10.7	2.72	132	.214	.295	1	.059	-1	11	10	-1	0.8
1986	Pit-N	5	2	.714	52	0	0	0	4	78	65	32	11	3	29	63	11.2	3.35	115	.225	.302	0	.000	-0	3	4	-2	0.2
1987	NY-A	3	2	.600	23	0	0	0	1	44	42	30	8	1	20	46	12.9	5.73	77	.247	.330	0	—	0	-6	-7	-1	-0.7
1988	NY-A	5	6	.455	56	0	0	0	11	75	59	25	10	5	22	61	10.3	2.88	137	.213	.283	0	—	0	9	9	-2	1.3
	Tex-A	0	0	—	7	0	0	0	1	4^2	8	1	1	0	4	4	23.1	1.93	212	.400	.500	0	—	0	1	1	-0	0.0
	Yr	5	6	.455	63	0	0	0	12	79^2	67	26	11	5	26	65	11.1	2.82	140	.226	.299	0	—	0	10	10	-2	1.3
1989	Tex-A	6	6	.500	50	0	0	0	2	69	66	35	7	4	36	69	13.8	3.91	102	.249	.348	0	—	0	-0	0	-1	0.0
1990	Cle-A	2	3	.400	26	1	0	0	0	46^2	38	26	10	3	18	30	11.4	5.01	78	.220	.304	0	—	0	-6	-6	0	-0.5
Total	9	29	34	.460	363	1	0	0	35	595	512	256	61	27	236	503	11.7	3.48	110	.232	.313	3	.061	-3	21	23	-8	1.8
● EDDIE GUARDADO	Guardado, Edward Adrian b: 10/2/70, Stockton, Cal. BR/TL, 6', 193 lbs. Deb: 6/13/93																											
1993	Min-A	3	8	.273	19	16	0	0	0	94^2	123	68	13	1	36	46	15.2	6.18	71	.319	.379	0	—	0	-19	-19	-1	-1.9
1994	Min-A	0	2	.000	4	4	0	0	0	17	26	16	3	0	4	8	15.9	8.47	58	.351	.385	0	—	0	-7	-7	-1	-0.7
1995	Min-A	4	9	.308	51	5	0	0	2	91^1	99	54	13	0	45	71	14.2	5.12	93	.280	.361	0	—	0	-4	-3	-1	-0.5
1996	Min-A	6	5	.545	**83**	0	0	0	4	73^2	61	45	12	3	33	74	11.9	5.25	97	.228	.320	0	—	0	-2	-1	-0	-0.2
1997	Min-A	0	4	.000	69	0	0	0	1	46	45	23	7	2	17	54	12.5	3.91	119	.251	.323	0	—	0	3	4	0	0.3
1998	Min-A	3	1	.750	79	0	0	0	0	65^2	66	34	10	0	28	53	12.9	4.52	106	.265	.339	0	—	0	1	2	-1	0.0
1999	Min-A	2	5	.286	63	0	0	0	2	48	37	24	6	2	25	50	12.0	4.50	113	.222	.330	0	—	0	2	3	1	0.4
2000	Min-A	7	4	.636	70	0	0	0	9	61^2	55	27	14	1	25	52	11.8	3.94	133	.238	.315	0	—	0	7	8	-1	1.4
Total	8	25	38	.397	438	25	0	0	18	498	512	291	78	9	213	408	13.3	5.06	95	.269	.345	0	—	0	-19	-12	-4	-1.2
● MARK GUBICZA	Gubicza, Mark Steven b: 8/14/62, Philadelphia, Pa. BR/TR, 6'5", 220 lbs. Deb: 4/6/84																											
1984	KC-A	10	14	.417	29	29	4	2	0	189	172	90	13	5	75	111	12.0	4.05	100	.243	.320	0	—	0	-1	-0	2	0.2
1985	*KC-A	14	10	.583	29	28	0	0	0	177^1	160	88	14	5	77	99	12.3	4.06	102	.238	.321	0	—	0	2	2	2	0.4
1986	KC-A	12	6	.667	35	24	3	2	0	180^2	155	77	8	5	84	118	12.2	3.64	117	.233	.324	0	—	0	11	12	3	1.4
1987	KC-A	13	18	.419	35	35	10	2	0	241^2	231	114	18	6	120	166	13.3	3.98	115	.259	.350	0	—	0	13	15	4	2.1
1988	KC-A★	20	8	.714	35	35	8	4	0	269^2	237	94	11	6	83	183	10.9	2.70	148	.234	.296	0	—	0	38	39	3	4.3
1989	KC-A★	15	11	.577	36	36	8	2	0	255	252	100	10	5	63	173	11.3	3.04	127	.259	.307	0	—	0	24	23	2	2.5
1990	KC-A	4	7	.364	16	16	2	0	0	94	101	48	5	4	38	71	13.7	4.50	85	.283	.358	0	—	0	-6	-7	0	-0.7
1991	KC-A	9	12	.429	26	26	0	0	0	133	168	90	10	6	42	89	14.6	5.68	73	.308	.364	0	—	0	-23	-23	2	-2.8
1992	KC-A	7	6	.538	18	18	2	1	0	111^1	110	47	8	1	36	81	11.9	3.72	109	.259	.318	0	—	0	3	4	0	0.5
1993	KC-A	5	8	.385	49	6	0	0	2	104^1	128	61	2	2	43	80	14.9	4.66	99	.307	.374	0	—	0	-4	-1	-1	-0.2
1994	KC-A	7	9	.438	22	22	0	0	0	130	158	74	11	0	26	59	12.7	4.50	111	.301	.334	0	—	0	4	7	1	0.8
1995	KC-A	12	14	.462	33	33	3	2	0	213^1	222	97	21	6	62	81	12.2	3.75	128	.272	.328	0	—	0	23	24	2	2.8
1996	KC-A	4	12	.250	19	19	2	1	0	119^1	132	70	22	7	34	55	13.0	5.13	98	.284	.343	0	—	0	-2	-2	0	-0.1
1997	Ana-A	0	1	.000	2	2	0	0	0	4^2	13	13	2	0	3	5	30.9	25.07	18	.481	.533	0	—	0	-11	-11	0	-1.4
Total	14	132	136	.493	384	329	42	16	2	2223^1	2239	1063	155	58	786	1371	12.5	3.96	109	.264	.330	0	—	0	72	84	21	9.8
● MARV GUDAT	Gudat, Marvin John b: 8/27/05, Goliad, Tex. d: 3/1/54, Los Angeles, Cal. BL/TL, 5'11", 162 lbs. Deb: 5/21/29 ♦																											
1929	Cin-N	1	1	.500	7	2	2	0	0	26^2	29	12	0	0	4	0	11.1	3.38	135	.282	.308	2	.200	-0	4	4	-1	0.1
1932	*Chi-N	0	0	—	1	0	0	0	0	1	1	0	0	0	0	2	9.0	0.00	—	.250	.250	24	.255	0	0	0	0	0.0
Total	2	1	1	.500	8	2	2	0	0	27^2	30	12	0	0	4	2	11.1	3.25	139	.280	.306	26	.250	-0	4	4	-1	0.1
● WHITEY GUESE	Guese, Theodore b: 1/24/1872, New Bremen, Ohio d: 4/8/51, Wapakoneta, Ohio BR/TR, 6'0.5", 200 lbs. Deb: 7/13/01																											
1901	Cin-N	1	4	.200	6	5	4	0	0	44^1	62	48	5	3	14	11	16.0	6.09	53	.328	.383	3	.200	1	-14	-15	-2	-1.3
● LEE GUETTERMAN	Guetterman, Arthur Lee b: 11/22/58, Chattanooga, Tenn. BL/TL, 6'8", 227 lbs. Deb: 9/12/84																											
1984	Sea-A	0	0	—	3	0	0	0	0	4^1	9	2	0	0	2	2	22.8	4.15	96	.450	.500	0	—	0	-0	-0	0	0.0
1986	Sea-A	0	4	.000	41	4	1	0	0	76	108	67	7	4	30	38	16.8	7.34	58	.347	.412	0	—	0	-27	-26	0	-1.2
1987	Sea-A	11	4	.733	25	17	2	1	0	113^1	117	60	13	2	35	42	12.2	3.81	124	.267	.324	0	—	0	8	11	1	1.4
1988	NY-A	1	2	.333	20	2	0	0	0	40^2	49	21	2	1	14	15	14.2	4.65	85	.306	.366	0	—	0	-3	-3	-0	-0.2
1989	NY-A	5	5	.500	70	0	0	0	13	103	98	31	6	0	26	51	10.8	2.45	158	.258	.305	0	—	0	17	16	2	2.0
1990	NY-A	11	7	.611	64	0	0	0	2	93	80	37	6	0	26	48	10.3	3.39	118	.236	.290	0	—	0	5	6	1	1.2
1991	NY-A	3	4	.429	64	0	0	0	6	88	91	42	6	3	25	35	12.2	3.68	113	.268	.323	0	—	0	4	4	0	0.4
1992	NY-A	1	1	.500	15	0	0	0	0	22^2	35	24	5	0	13	5	19.1	9.53	41	.354	.429	0	—	0	-14	-14	0	-1.1
	NY-N	3	4	.429	43	0	0	0	2	43^1	57	28	5	1	14	15	15.0	5.82	60	.324	.377	0	.000	-0	-11	-11	-1	-1.9
1993	StL-N	3	3	.500	40	0	0	0	1	46	41	18	1	2	16	19	11.5	2.93	135	.240	.312	1	.500	1	6	5	-1	0.6
1995	Sea-A	0	0	—	23	0	0	0	1	17	21	13	1	3	11	11	18.5	6.88	69	.300	.417	0	—	0	-4	-4	1	-0.1
1996	Sea-A	0	2	.000	17	0	0	0	0	11	11	8	0	0	10	6	17.2	4.09	121	.275	.420	0	—	0	1	1	0	0.2
Total	11	38	36	.514	425	23	3	1	25	658^1	717	351	52	16	222	287	13.1	4.33	96	.282	.343	1	.250	0	-18	-14	4	1.3
● RON GUIDRY	Guidry, Ronald Ames b: 8/28/50, Lafayette, La. BL/TL, 5'11", 162 lbs. Deb: 7/27/75																											
1975	NY-A	0	1	.000	10	1	0	0	0	15^2	15	6	0	1	9	15	14.4	3.45	107	.259	.368	0	—	0	1	0	-1	0.0
1976	*NY-A	0	0	—	7	0	0	0	0	16	20	12	1	0	4	12	13.5	5.63	61	.294	.333	0	—	0	-4	-4	0	-0.2
1977	*NY-A	16	7	.696	31	25	9	5	1	210^2	174	72	12	0	65	176	10.2	2.82	140	.224	.284	0	—	0	29	27	-1	2.8
1978	*NY-A★	**25**	3	**.893**	35	35	16	**9**	0	273^2	187	61	13	1	72	248	**8.6**	**1.74**	**208**	**.193**	**.250**	0	—	0	**62**	**60**	2	**6.5**
1979	NY-A★	18	8	.692	33	30	15	2	2	236^1	203	83	20	0	71	201	10.4	**2.78**	147	.236	.294	0	—	0	38	36	-0	3.7
1980	*NY-A	17	10	.630	37	29	5	3	1	219^2	215	97	19	1	80	166	12.1	3.56	110	.260	.326	0	—	0	12	9	2	1.2
1981	*NY-A	11	5	.688	23	21	0	0	0	127	100	41	12	1	26	104	**9.0**	2.76	129	.214	**.257**	0	—	0	13	12	1	1.5
1982	NY-A☆	14	8	.636	34	33	6	1	0	222	216	104	22	1	69	162	11.6	3.81	105	.254	.311	0	—	0	7	5	-2	0.2
1983	NY-A†	21	9	.700	31	31	**21**	3	0	250^1	232	99	26	2	60	156	10.6	3.42	114	.244	.291	0	—	0	18	14	-0	1.5
1984	NY-A	10	11	.476	29	28	5	1	0	195^2	223	102	24	2	44	127	12.4	4.51	84	.287	.327	0	—	0	-11	-16	-0	-1.6
1985	NY-A	**22**	6	**.786**	34	33	11	2	0	259	243	104	28	0	42	143	9.9	3.27	123	.248	.279	0	—	0	25	22	-1	2.1
1986	NY-A	9	12	.429	30	30	5	0	0	192^1	202	94	28	1	38	140	11.3	3.98	103	.265	.301	0	—	0	4	3	-1	0.1
1987	NY-A	5	8	.385	22	17	2	0	0	117^2	111	50	14	1	38	96	11.5	3.67	120	.248	.308	0	—	0	10	10	-0	0.9
1988	NY-A	2	3	.400	12	10	0	0	0	56	57	28	7	2	15	32	11.9	4.18	94	.259	.312	0	—	0	-1	-1	-1	-0.2
Total	14	170	91	.651	368	323	95	26	4	2392	2198	953	226	13	633	1778	10.7	3.29	119	.244	.294	0	—	0	204	175	-3	18.5

YEAR TM/L	W	L	PCT	G	GS	CG	SH	SV	IP	H	R	HR	HB	BB	SO	RAT	ERA	ERA+	OAV	OOB	BH	AVG	PB	PR	PR+	PD	TPI
● **SKIP GUINN**	Guinn, Drannon Eugene b: 10/25/44, St.Charles, Mo. BR/TL, 5'10", 180 lbs. Deb: 5/7/68																										
1968 Atl-N	0	0	—	3	0	0	0	0	5	3	2	0	0	3	4	10.8	3.60	83	.167	.286	0	—	0	-0	-0	-0	0.0
1969 Hou-N	1	2	.333	28	0	0	0	0	27	34	22	3	1	21	33	18.7	6.67	53	.304	.418	0	.000	-0	-9	-10	-0	-1.0
1971 Hou-N	0	0	—	4	0	0	0	1	4^2	1	0	0	0	3	3	7.7	0.00	—	.067	.222	0	—	0	2	2	-0	0.1
Total 3	1	2	.333	35	0	0	0	1	36^2	38	24	3	1	27	40	16.2	5.40	64	.262	.382	0	.000	-0	-8	-8	-0	-0.9
● **LEFTY GUISE**	Guise, Witt Orison b: 9/18/09, Driggs, Ark. d: 8/13/68, Little Rock, Ark. BL/TL, 6'2", 172 lbs. Deb: 9/13/40																										
1940 Cin-N	0	0	—	2	0	0	0	0	7^2	8	2	0	1	5	1	16.4	1.17	323	.296	.424	1	.333	0	2	2	0	0.2
● **DON GULLETT**	Gullett, Donald Edward b: 1/6/51, Lynn, Ky. BR/TL, 6', 190 lbs. Deb: 4/10/70 C																										
1970 *Cin-N	5	2	.714	44	2	0	0	6	77^2	54	23	4	0	44	76	11.4	2.43	166	.196	.306	4	.211	1	14	14	-1	1.4
1971 Cin-N	16	6	**.727**	35	31	4	3	0	217^2	196	73	14	2	64	107	10.8	2.65	127	.242	.299	9	.120	-2	20	18	-2	1.2
1972 *Cin-N	9	10	.474	31	16	2	0	2	134^2	127	61	15	1	43	96	11.4	3.94	82	.250	.309	8	.211	2	-7	-12	-2	-1.6
1973 *Cin-N	18	8	.692	45	30	7	4	2	228^1	198	95	24	3	69	153	10.6	3.51	97	.232	.292	12	.188	3	4	-3	-0	0.0
1974 Cin-N	17	11	.607	36	35	10	3	0	243	201	93	22	2	88	183	10.8	3.04	115	.222	.292	19	.237	4	16	13	-0	1.8
1975 *Cin-N	15	4	**.789**	22	22	8	3	0	159^2	127	49	11	2	56	98	10.4	2.42	149	.218	.289	14	.226	3	21	21	-1	2.7
1976 *Cin-N	11	3	.786	23	20	4	0	1	126	119	48	8	0	48	64	11.9	3.00	117	.253	.322	8	.182	-0	7	7	-0	0.8
1977 *NY-A	14	4	.778	22	22	7	1	0	158^1	137	67	14	1	69	116	11.8	3.58	110	.232	.314	0	—	0	9	7	-2	0.6
1978 NY-A	4	2	.667	8	8	2	0	0	44^2	46	19	3	1	20	28	13.5	3.63	100	.269	.349	0	—	0	1	0	0	0.0
Total 9	109	50	.686	266	186	44	14	11	1390	1205	528	115	12	501	921	11.1	3.11	113	.233	.302	74	.194	10	85	67	-8	6.9
● **BILL GULLICKSON**	Gullickson, William Lee b: 2/20/59, Marshall, Minn. BR/TR, 6'3", 215 lbs. Deb: 9/26/79																										
1979 Mon-N	0	0	—	1	0	0	0	0	1	2	0	0	0	0	0	18.0	0.00	—	.500	.500	0	—	0	0	0	0	0.0
1980 Mon-N	10	5	.667	24	19	5	2	0	141	127	53	6	2	50	120	11.4	3.00	119	.238	.305	7	.175	0	10	9	0	1.0
1981 *Mon-N	7	9	.438	22	22	3	2	0	157^1	142	54	3	4	34	115	10.3	2.80	125	.239	.284	7	.152	0	12	12	-1	1.1
1982 Mon-N	12	14	.462	34	34	6	0	0	236^2	231	101	25	4	61	155	11.3	3.57	102	.254	.304	10	.122	-2	1	2	-4	-0.4
1983 Mon-N	17	12	.586	34	34	10	1	0	242^1	230	108	19	4	59	120	10.9	3.75	96	.251	.299	11	.134	1	-3	-4	-1	-0.5
1984 Mon-N	12	9	.571	32	32	3	0	0	226^2	230	100	27	1	37	100	10.6	3.61	95	.265	.295	8	.110	-2	-0	-5	-4	-1.0
1985 Mon-N	14	12	.538	29	29	4	1	0	181^1	187	78	8	1	47	68	11.7	3.52	96	.271	.318	12	.188	2	2	-3	-1	-0.3
1986 Cin-N	15	12	.556	37	37	6	2	0	244^2	245	103	24	2	60	121	11.3	3.38	115	.264	.310	6	.076	-4	9	13	-2	0.7
1987 Cin-N	10	11	.476	27	27	3	1	0	165	172	99	33	2	39	89	11.6	4.85	88	.267	.310	11	.208	2	-14	-11	-2	-1.2
NY-A	4	2	.667	8	8	1	0	0	48	46	29	7	1	11	28	10.9	4.88	90	.253	.299	0	—	0	-2	-3	-1	-0.3
1990 Hou-N	10	14	.417	32	32	2	1	0	193^1	221	100	21	2	61	73	13.2	3.82	97	.287	.341	9	.158	2	-0	-2	-3	-0.4
1991 Det-A	**20**	9	.690	35	35	4	0	0	226^1	256	109	22	4	44	91	12.1	3.90	107	.288	.324	0	—	0	5	6	-3	0.5
1992 Det-A	14	13	.519	34	34	4	1	0	221^2	228	109	35	0	50	64	11.3	4.34	91	.267	.308	0	—	0	-10	-9	-0	-1.1
1993 Det-A	13	9	.591	28	28	2	0	0	159^1	186	106	28	3	44	70	13.2	5.37	80	.291	.340	0	—	0	-18	-19	0	-2.2
1994 Det-A	4	5	.444	21	19	1	0	0	115^1	156	79	24	4	25	65	14.4	5.93	82	.322	.361	0	—	0	-14	-14	1	-0.8
Total 14	162	136	.544	398	390	54	11	0	2560	2659	1228	282	34	622	1279	11.7	3.93	98	.268	.314	81	.141	-1	-24	-27	-20	-4.9
● **AD GUMBERT**	Gumbert, Addison Courtney b: 10/10/1868, Pittsburgh, Pa. d: 4/23/25, Pittsburgh, Pa. BR/TR, 5'10", 200 lbs. Deb: 9/15/1888 F																										
1888 Chi-N	3	3	.500	6	6	5	0	0	48^2	44	24	0	5	10	16	10.9	3.14	96	.234	.291	8	.333	2	-2	-1	-1	0.0
1889 Chi-N	16	13	.552	31	28	25	2	0	246^1	258	148	16	14	76	91	12.7	3.62	115	.261	.323	44	.288	11	11	14	-1	2.1
1890 Bos-P	23	12	.657	39	33	27	1	0	277^1	338	189	18	11	86	81	14.1	3.96	111	.288	.342	35	.241	5	8	13	2	1.7
1891 Chi-N	17	11	.607	32	31	24	1	0	256^1	282	149	5	10	90	73	13.4	3.58	93	.269	.332	32	.305	12	-7	-7	1	0.6
1892 Chi-N	22	19	.537	46	45	39	0	0	382^2	399	220	11	14	107	118	12.2	3.41	97	.258	.312	42	.236	4	-5	-4	1	0.5
1893 Pit-N	11	7	.611	22	20	16	2	0	162^2	207	119	5	5	78	40	16.0	5.15	88	.301	.376	21	.221	1	-9	-11	-2	-0.9
1894 Pit-N	15	14	.517	38	32	26	0	0	271^1	376	245	13	6	85	67	15.5	6.04	87	.325	.374	34	.298	6	-21	-24	1	-1.3
1895 Bro-N	11	16	.407	33	26	20	0	1	234	288	183	11	12	69	45	14.2	5.08	87	.298	.352	35	.361	11	-8	-19	-1	-0.8
1896 Bro-N	0	4	.000	5	4	2	0	0	31	34	18	2	0	11	3	13.1	3.77	109	.276	.336	2	.182	-0	2	1	1	0.2
Phi-N	5	3	.625	11	10	7	1	0	77^1	99	55	0	4	23	14	14.7	4.54	95	.308	.362	9	.265	1	-1	-2	-1	-0.1
Yr	5	7	.417	16	14	9	1	0	108^1	133	73	2	4	34	17	14.2	4.32	99	.300	.355	11	.244	1	1	-1	0	0.1
Total 9	123	102	.547	263	235	191	7	1	1987^2	2325	1350	81	81	635	548	13.8	4.27	96	.284	.341	262	.274	53	-31	-33	1	1.6
● **HARRY GUMBERT**	Gumbert, Harry Edward "Gunboat" b: 11/5/09, Elizabeth, Pa. d: 1/4/95, Wimberley, Tex. BR/TR, 6'2", 185 lbs. Deb: 9/12/35																										
1935 NY-N	1	2	.333	6	3	1	0	0	23^2	35	27	1	0	10	11	17.1	6.08	63	.330	.388	0	.000	-1	-5	-6	-0	-0.8
1936 *NY-N	11	3	.786	39	15	3	0	0	140^2	157	77	7	2	54	52	13.6	3.90	100	.281	.346	11	.250	2	2	-0	3	0.5
1937 *NY-N	10	11	.476	34	24	10	1	1	200^1	194	92	11	4	62	65	11.7	3.68	106	.257	.317	13	.181	-1	5	5	8	1.1
1938 NY-N	15	13	.536	38	33	14	1	0	235^2	238	114	13	7	84	84	12.6	4.01	94	.261	.328	13	.155	-3	-6	-6	8	-0.2
1939 NY-N	18	11	.621	36	34	14	2	0	243^2	257	132	21	1	81	81	12.5	4.32	91	.271	.329	18	.200	-0	-11	-11	6	-0.5
1940 NY-N	12	14	.462	35	30	14	2	2	237	230	110	17	3	81	77	11.9	3.76	103	.252	.316	17	.195	2	2	3	4	0.9
1941 NY-N	1	1	.500	5	5	1	0	0	32^1	34	20	3	0	18	9	14.5	4.45	83	.266	.356	2	.167	-0	-3	-3	1	-0.1
StL-N	11	5	.688	33	17	8	3	1	144^1	139	52	7	1	30	53	10.6	2.74	137	.251	.291	17	.321	6	14	16	4	2.7
Yr	12	6	.667	38	22	9	3	1	176^2	173	72	10	1	48	62	11.3	3.06	123	.254	.304	19	.292	5	11	13	4	2.6
1942 *StL-N	9	5	.643	38	19	5	0	5	163	156	67	3	1	59	52	11.9	3.26	105	.250	.315	6	.111	-2	1	3	5	0.5
1943 StL-N	10	5	.667	21	19	7	2	0	133	115	46	4	0	32	40	9.9	2.84	118	.237	.284	7	.156	-2	8	8	2	0.8
1944 StL-N	4	2	.667	10	7	3	0	1	61^1	60	23	1	0	19	16	11.6	2.49	141	.258	.313	4	.190	-0	8	7	1	0.8
Cin-N	10	8	.556	24	19	11	2	2	155^1	157	61	7	2	40	40	11.5	3.30	106	.262	.310	5	.096	-2	5	3	2	0.4
Yr	14	10	.583	34	26	14	2	3	216^2	217	84	8	2	59	56	11.5	3.07	114	.261	.311	9	.123	-2	13	11	3	1.2
1946 Cin-N	6	8	.429	36	10	5	0	4	119	112	48	8	1	42	44	11.7	3.25	103	.248	.314	8	.250	1	2	1	1	0.4
1947 Cin-N	10	10	.500	46	0	0	0	10	90^1	88	42	3	0	47	43	13.5	3.89	106	.260	.351	6	.273	1	2	2	0	0.6
1948 Cin-N	10	8	.556	**61**	0	0	0	**17**	106^1	123	50	5	0	34	25	13.3	3.47	113	.291	.344	1	.040	-1	6	5	4	1.3
1949 Cin-N	4	3	.571	29	0	0	0	2	40^2	58	28	5	1	8	12	14.8	5.53	76	.341	.374	0	.000	-1	-7	-6	1	-0.9
Pit-N	1	4	.200	16	0	0	0	3	27^2	30	20	5	0	18	5	15.6	5.86	72	.270	.372	1	.250	0	-6	-5	1	-0.8
Yr	5	7	.417	45	0	0	0	5	68^1	88	48	10	1	26	17	15.1	5.66	74	.313	.373	1	.167	-0	-12	-11	2	-1.7
1950 Pit-N	0	0	—	1	0	0	0	0	1^2	3	3	0	0	2	0	27.0	5.40	81	.333	.455	1	1.000	0	-0	-0	0	0.1
Total 15	143	113	.559	508	235	96	13	48	2156	2186	1012	121	23	721	709	12.2	3.68	102	.263	.323	130	.184	-2	18	17	50	6.8
● **BILLY GUMBERT**	Gumbert, William Skeen b: 8/8/1865, Pittsburgh, Pa. d: 4/13/46, Pittsburgh, Pa. BR/TR, 6'1.5", 200 lbs. Deb: 6/19/1890 F																										
1890 Pit-N	4	6	.400	10	10	8	0	0	79^1	96	71	0	8	31	18	15.3	5.22	63	.290	.365	9	.243	-3	-15	-18	1	-1.5
1892 Pit-N	3	2	.600	6	3	2	0	0	39^2	30	15	0	1	23	3	12.3	1.36	242	.201	.312	2	.111	-1	8	9	-1	0.8
1893 Lou-N	0	0	—	1	1	0	0	0	0^2	2	6	0	0	5	0	94.5	27.00	16	.500	.778	1	1.000	1	-2	-2	-0	0.0
Total 3	7	8	.467	17	14	10	0	0	119^2	128	92	0	9	59	21	14.7	4.06	81	.264	.355	12	.214	3	-8	-11	-1	-0.7
● **DAVE GUMPERT**	Gumpert, David Lawrence b: 5/5/58, South Haven, Mich. BR/TR, 6'1", 190 lbs. Deb: 7/25/82																										
1982 Det-A	0	0	—	5	1	0	0	1	1^2	7	6	1	0	2	0	40.5	27.00	15	.700	.750	0	—	0	-5	-5	-0	-0.5
1983 Det-A	0	2	.000	26	0	0	0	2	44^1	43	16	1	0	7	14	10.2	2.64	149	.257	.287	0	—	0	7	7	-1	0.2
1985 Chi-N	1	0	1.000	9	0	0	0	0	10^1	12	7	0	0	7	4	16.5	3.48	115	.279	.380	0	.000	-0	0	1	-0	0.0
1986 Chi-N	2	0	1.000	38	0	0	0	2	59^2	60	32	4	1	28	45	13.4	4.37	93	.267	.350	0	.000	-1	-4	-2	-1	-0.3
1987 KC-A	0	0	—	8	0	0	0	0	19^1	27	16	3	0	6	13	15.4	6.05	76	.333	.379	0	—	0	-3	-3	0	-0.1
Total 5	3	2	.600	86	1	0	0	5	135^2	149	77	9	1	50	76	13.3	4.31	95	.283	.347	0	.000	-1	-6	-3	-2	-0.7
● **RANDY GUMPERT**	Gumpert, Randall Pennington b: 1/23/18, Monocacy, Pa. BR/TR, 6'3", 205 lbs. Deb: 6/13/36																										
1936 Phi-A	1	2	.333	22	3	2	0	2	62^1	74	42	2	0	32	9	15.3	4.76	107	.295	.375	6	.273	0	2	**2**	-1	0.1
1937 Phi-A	0	0	—	10	1	0	0	0	12	16	17	1	1	15	5	24.0	12.00	39	.333	.500	1	.333	0	-10	-10	0	-0.4
1938 Phi-A	0	2	.000	4	2	0	0	0	12^1	24	18	1	0	10	1	24.8	10.95	44	.393	.479	1	.250	0	-8	-8	1	-0.9
1946 NY-A	11	3	.786	33	12	4	0	1	132^2	113	44	8	0	32	63	9.8	2.31	150	.229	.276	6	.128	-2	18	17	-1	1.5
1947 NY-A	4	1	.800	24	6	2	0	0	56^1	71	36	4	0	28	25	15.8	5.43	65	.311	.387	1	.071	-1	-11	-12	0	-1.1
1948 NY-A	1	0	1.000	15	0	0	0	0	25	27	10	0	1	6	12	12.2	2.88	142	.267	.315	0	—	0	4	4	0	0.2
Chi-A	2	6	.250	16	11	6	1	0	97^1	103	43	6	2	13	31	10.9	3.79	112	.275	.303	4	.138	-2	5	5	-1	0.1
Yr	3	6	.333	31	11	6	1	0	122^1	130	53	6	3	19	43	11.2	3.60	117	.273	.305	4	.138	-2	9	9	-1	0.3
1949 Chi-A	13	16	.448	34	32	18	3	1	234	223	111	22	1	83	78	11.8	3.81	110	.253	.318	16	.190	-1	10	10	1	1.0

YEAR	TM/L	W	L	PCT	G	GS	CG	SH	SV	IP	H	R	HR	HB	BB	SO	RAT	ERA	ERA+	OAV	OOB	BH	AVG	PB	PR	PR+	PD	TPI
1950	Chi-A	5	12	.294	40	17	6	1	0	155^1	165	87	15	4	58	48	13.2	4.75	94	.275	.343	3	.071	-4	-3	-5	-0	-0.8
1951	Chi-A☆	9	8	.529	33	16	7	1	2	141^2	156	74	20	1	34	45	12.1	4.32	93	.272	.314	15	.333	3	-3	-5	-3	-0.5
1952	Bos-A	1	0	1.000	10	1	0	0	1	19^2	15	11	1	1	5	6	9.6	4.12	96	.205	.266	0	.000	-1	-1	-0	-0	-0.1
	Was-A	4	9	.308	20	12	2	0	0	104	112	55	12	5	30	29	12.7	4.24	84	.273	.330	7	.206	0	-7	-8	-1	-1.0
	Yr	5	9	.357	30	13	2	0	1	123^2	127	66	13	6	35	35	12.2	4.22	86	.262	.320	7	.179	-0	-8	-8	-1	-1.1
Total	10	51	59	.464	261	113	47	6	7	1052^2	1099	548	92	16	346	352	12.5	4.17	98	.268	.328	60	.182	-8	-4	-11	-5	-1.9

● ERIC GUNDERSON Gunderson, Eric Andrew b: 3/29/66, Portland, Ore. BR/TL, 6′, 195 lbs. Deb: 4/11/90

YEAR	TM/L	W	L	PCT	G	GS	CG	SH	SV	IP	H	R	HR	HB	BB	SO	RAT	ERA	ERA+	OAV	OOB	BH	AVG	PB	PR	PR+	PD	TPI
1990	SF-N	1	2	.333	7	4	0	0	0	19^2	24	14	2	0	11	14	16.0	5.49	66	.293	.376	0	.000	-1	-4	-4	0	-0.6
1991	SF-N	0	0	—	2	0	0	0	1	3^1	6	4	0	0	1	2	18.9	5.40	66	.353	.389	0	—	0	-1	-1	0	0.0
1992	Sea-A	2	1	.667	9	0	0	0	0	9^1	12	12	1	1	5	2	17.4	8.68	46	.324	.419	0	—	0	-5	-5	0	-0.9
1994	NY-N	0	0	—	14	0	0	0	0	9	5	0	0	0	4	4	9.0	0.00	—	.185	.290	0	—	0	4	4	-0	0.2
1995	NY-N	1	1	.500	30	0	0	0	0	24^1	25	10	2	1	8	19	12.6	3.70	110	.269	.333	0	—	0	1	1	1	0.2
	Bos-A	2	1	.667	19	0	0	0	0	12^1	13	7	0	2	9	9	17.5	5.11	95	.295	.436	0	—	0	-1	-0	0	0.0
1996	Bos-A	0	1	.000	28	0	0	0	0	17^1	21	17	5	2	8	7	16.1	8.31	61	.300	.387	0	—	0	-6	-6	-1	-0.3
1997	Tex-A	2	1	.667	60	0	0	0	1	49^2	45	19	5	2	15	31	11.2	3.26	147	.241	.304	0	—	0	7	8	-1	0.4
1998	Tex-A	0	3	.000	68	1	0	0	0	67^2	88	43	13	1	19	41	14.4	5.19	93	.315	.361	0	—	0	-4	-3	0	-0.1
1999	Tex-A	0	0	—	11	0	0	0	0	10	20	8	1	0	2	6	19.8	7.20	71	.417	.440	0	—	0	-3	-2	-0	-0.1
2000	Tor-A	0	1	.000	6	0	0	0	0	6^1	15	6	0	1	2	2	25.6	7.11	70	.455	.500	0	—	0	-2	-1	0	-0.2
Total	10	8	11	.421	254	5	0	0	2	229	274	140	29	10	84	137	14.5	4.95	93	.299	.364	0	.000	-0	-12	-9	-0	-1.4

● RED GUNKEL Gunkel, Woodward William b: 4/15/1894, Sheffield, Ill. d: 4/19/54, Chicago, Ill. BB/TR, 5′8″, 158 lbs. Deb: 6/18/16

YEAR	TM/L	W	L	PCT	G	GS	CG	SH	SV	IP	H	R	HR	HB	BB	SO	RAT	ERA	ERA+	OAV	OOB	BH	AVG	PB	PR	PR+	PD	TPI
1916	Cle-A	0	0	—	1	0	0	0	0	1	0	2	0	1	1	1	18.0	0.00	—	.000	.500	0	—	0	0	0	-0	0.0

● LARRY GURA Gura, Lawrence Cyril b: 11/26/47, Joliet, Ill. BB/TL, 6′1″, 185 lbs. Deb: 4/30/70

YEAR	TM/L	W	L	PCT	G	GS	CG	SH	SV	IP	H	R	HR	HB	BB	SO	RAT	ERA	ERA+	OAV	OOB	BH	AVG	PB	PR	PR+	PD	TPI
1970	Chi-N	1	3	.250	20	3	1	0	1	38	35	18	6	1	23	21	14.0	3.79	119	.254	.364	0	.000	-1	1	3	0	0.2
1971	Chi-N	0	0	—	6	0	0	0	1	3	6	3	0	0	1	2	21.0	6.00	66	.400	.438	0	.000	-0	-1	-1	-0	-0.1
1972	Chi-N	0	0	—	7	0	0	0	0	12^1	11	5	3	0	3	13	10.2	3.65	104	.250	.298	0	.000	-0	-0	0	0	0.0
1973	Chi-N	2	4	.333	21	7	0	0	0	64^2	79	39	10	1	11	43	12.7	4.87	81	.296	.326	3	.200	0	-9	-6	1	-0.4
1974	NY-A	5	1	.833	8	8	4	2	0	56	54	17	2	0	12	17	10.6	2.41	146	.248	.287	0	—	0	8	7	-0	0.7
1975	NY-A	7	8	.467	26	20	5	0	0	151^1	173	65	13	3	41	65	12.9	3.51	105	.295	.344	0	—	0	5	3	-0	0.3
1976	*KC-A	4	0	1.000	20	2	1	1	1	62^2	47	20	4	1	20	22	9.8	2.30	153	.213	.281	0	—	0	9	8	1	0.6
1977	*KC-A	8	5	.615	52	6	1	1	10	106^1	108	43	8	1	28	46	11.6	3.13	129	.265	.314	0	—	0	11	11	0	1.4
1978	*KC-A	16	4	.800	35	26	8	2	0	221^2	183	73	13	4	60	81	10.0	2.72	141	.229	.286	0	—	0	26	27	2	2.6
1979	KC-A	13	12	.520	39	33	7	1	0	233^2	226	137	29	7	73	85	11.8	4.47	96	.253	.315	0	—	0	-6	-5	1	-0.4
1980	*KC-A☆	18	10	.643	36	36	16	4	0	283^1	272	107	20	5	76	113	11.2	2.95	137	.255	.307	0	—	0	34	35	1	3.3
1981	*KC-A	11	8	.579	23	23	12	2	0	172^1	139	61	11	4	35	61	9.3	2.72	133	.223	.269	0	—	0	18	17	0	1.9
1982	KC-A	18	12	.600	37	37	8	3	0	248	251	124	31	6	64	98	11.6	4.03	102	.261	.311	0	—	0	2	2	2	0.4
1983	KC-A	11	18	.379	34	31	5	0	0	200^1	220	119	23	8	76	57	13.7	4.90	84	.284	.354	0	—	0	-18	-18	3	-2.0
1984	KC-A	12	9	.571	31	25	3	0	0	168^2	175	102	26	4	67	68	13.1	5.18	78	.269	.341	0	—	0	-22	-21	1	-2.2
1985	KC-A	0	0	—	3	0	0	0	1	4^1	7	6	1	0	4	2	22.8	12.46	33	.368	.478	0	—	0	-4	-4	0	-0.2
	Chi-N	0	3	.000	5	4	0	0	0	20^1	34	19	4	1	6	7	18.1	8.41	48	.370	.414	0	.000	-0	-11	-9	0	-1.1
Total	16	126	97	.565	403	261	71	16	14	2047	2020	958	204	46	600	801	11.7	3.76	106	.260	.317	3	.091	-2	42	48	11	5.0

● CHARLIE GUTH Guth, Charles J. b: 1856, Chicago, Ill. d: 7/5/1883, Cambridge, Mass. Deb: 9/30/1880

YEAR	TM/L	W	L	PCT	G	GS	CG	SH	SV	IP	H	R	HR	HB	BB	SO	RAT	ERA	ERA+	OAV	OOB	BH	AVG	PB	PR	PR+	PD	TPI
1880	Chi-N	1	0	1.000	1	1	1	0	0	9	12	8	0		1	7	13.0	5.00	48	.293	.310	1	.250	0	-3	-3	-0	-0.2

● MARK GUTHRIE Guthrie, Mark Andrew b: 9/22/65, Buffalo, N.Y. BR/TL, 6′4″, 206 lbs. Deb: 7/25/89

YEAR	TM/L	W	L	PCT	G	GS	CG	SH	SV	IP	H	R	HR	HB	BB	SO	RAT	ERA	ERA+	OAV	OOB	BH	AVG	PB	PR	PR+	PD	TPI
1989	Min-A	2	4	.333	13	8	0	0	0	57^1	66	32	7	1	21	38	13.8	4.55	91	.292	.355	0	—	0	-4	-2	-0	-0.2
1990	Min-A	7	9	.438	24	21	3	1	0	144^2	154	65	8	1	39	101	12.1	3.79	110	.276	.325	0	—	0	2	6	1	0.6
1991	*Min-A	7	5	.583	41	12	0	0	2	98	116	52	11	1	41	72	14.5	4.32	99	.303	.372	0	—	0	-2	-0	-1	-0.1
1992	Min-A	2	3	.400	54	0	0	0	5	75	59	27	7	0	23	76	9.8	2.88	141	.215	.276	0	—	0	9	10	-0	0.7
1993	Min-A	2	1	.667	22	0	0	0	0	21	20	11	2	0	16	15	15.4	4.71	93	.267	.396	0	—	0	-1	-1	0	-0.1
1994	Min-A	4	2	.667	50	2	0	0	1	51^1	65	43	8	2	18	38	14.9	6.14	79	.316	.376	0	—	0	-8	-7	0	-0.7
1995	Min-A	5	3	.625	36	0	0	0	0	42^1	47	22	5	1	16	48	13.6	4.46	107	.290	.358	0	—	0	1	1	-1	0.1
	*LA-N	0	2	.000	24	0	0	0	0	19^2	19	11	1	1	9	19	13.3	3.66	104	.241	.326	0	.000	-0	1	0	0	0.0
1996	*LA-N	2	3	.400	66	0	0	0	1	73	65	21	3	1	22	56	10.8	2.22	174	.240	.299	0	.000	-0	16	15	-0	0.8
1997	LA-N	1	4	.200	62	0	0	0	1	69^1	71	44	12	0	30	42	13.1	5.32	72	.271	.346	1	.250	0	-9	-12	0	-0.8
1998	LA-N	2	1	.667	53	0	0	0	0	54	56	26	3	2	24	45	13.7	3.50	113	.267	.347	0	.000	-0	4	3	0	0.2
1999	Bos-A	1	1	.500	46	0	0	0	2	46^1	50	32	9	2	20	36	14.0	5.83	85	.275	.353	0	—	0	-5	-4	-0	-0.2
	Chi-N	0	2	.000	11	0	0	0	0	12^1	7	6	1	0	4	9	8.0	3.65	124	.171	.244	0	—	0	1	1	-0	0.1
2000	Chi-N	2	3	.400	19	0	0	0	0	18^2	17	11	1	1	10	17	13.5	4.82	95	.258	.364	0	.000	-0	-0	-1	-0	-0.1
	TB-A	1	1	.500	34	0	0	0	0	32	33	18	4	0	18	26	14.3	4.50	110	.262	.354	0	—	0	2	2	0	0.1
	Tor-A	0	2	.000	23	0	0	0	0	20^2	20	12	3	1	9	20	13.1	4.79	104	.263	.349	0	—	0	0	0	-0	0.0
	Yr	1	3	.250	57	0	0	0	0	52^2	53	30	7	1	27	46	13.8	4.61	108	.262	.352	0	—	0	2	2	0	0.1
Total	12	38	46	.452	578	43	3	1	12	835^2	865	433	85	14	320	658	12.9	4.18	103	.271	.340	1	.091	-1	8	10	-2	0.4

● JOHNNY GUZMAN Guzman, Dionini Ramon (Estrella) b: 1/21/71, Hatillo Palma, D.R. BR/TL, 5′10″, 155 lbs. Deb: 6/8/91

YEAR	TM/L	W	L	PCT	G	GS	CG	SH	SV	IP	H	R	HR	HB	BB	SO	RAT	ERA	ERA+	OAV	OOB	BH	AVG	PB	PR	PR+	PD	TPI
1991	Oak-A	1	0	1.000	5	0	0	0	0	5	11	5	0	0	2	3	23.4	9.00	43	.500	.542	0	—	0	-3	-3	0	-0.5
1992	Oak-A	0	0	—	2	0	0	0	0	3	8	4	0	1	0	0	27.0	12.00	31	.471	.500	0	—	0	-3	-3	-0	-0.2
Total	2	1	0	1.000	7	0	0	0	0	8	19	9	0	1	2	3	24.8	10.13	38	.487	.524	0	—	0	-5	-6	0	-0.7

● DOMINGO GUZMAN Guzman, Domingo Serrano b: 4/5/75, San Cristobal, D.R. BR/TR, 6′, 210 lbs. Deb: 9/9/99

YEAR	TM/L	W	L	PCT	G	GS	CG	SH	SV	IP	H	R	HR	HB	BB	SO	RAT	ERA	ERA+	OAV	OOB	BH	AVG	PB	PR	PR+	PD	TPI
1999	SD-N	0	1	.000	7	0	0	0	0	5	13	12	1	0	3	4	28.8	21.60	19	.464	.516	0	—	0	-9	-11	0	-1.6
2000	SD-N	0	0	—	1	0	0	0	0	1	1	1	0	2	1	0	36.0	9.00	49	.333	.667	0	—	0	-0	-1	0	0.0
Total	2	0	1	.000	8	0	0	0	0	6	14	13	1	2	4	4	30.0	19.50	22	.452	.541	0	—	0	-10	-11	0	-1.6

● GERALDO GUZMAN Guzman, Geraldo Moreno b: 11/28/72, Tenares, D.R. BR/TR, 6′2″, 180 lbs. Deb: 7/6/2000

YEAR	TM/L	W	L	PCT	G	GS	CG	SH	SV	IP	H	R	HR	HB	BB	SO	RAT	ERA	ERA+	OAV	OOB	BH	AVG	PB	PR	PR+	PD	TPI
2000	Ari-N	5	4	.556	13	10	0	0	0	60^1	66	36	8	2	22	52	13.4	5.37	86	.286	.353	0	.000	-2	-5	-5	-1	-0.9

● JOSE GUZMAN Guzman, Jose Alberto (Mirabal) b: 4/9/63, Santa Isabel, P.R. BR/TR, 6′2″, 195 lbs. Deb: 9/10/85

YEAR	TM/L	W	L	PCT	G	GS	CG	SH	SV	IP	H	R	HR	HB	BB	SO	RAT	ERA	ERA+	OAV	OOB	BH	AVG	PB	PR	PR+	PD	TPI
1985	Tex-A	3	2	.600	5	5	0	0	0	32^2	27	13	3	0	14	24	11.3	2.76	154	.214	.293	0	—	0	5	5	0	0.8
1986	Tex-A	9	15	.375	29	29	2	0	0	172^1	199	101	23	6	60	87	13.8	4.54	95	.293	.355	0	—	0	-7	-4	0	-0.5
1987	Tex-A	14	14	.500	37	30	6	0	0	208^1	196	115	30	3	82	143	12.1	4.67	96	.251	.324	0	—	0	-4	-4	1	-0.3
1988	Tex-A	11	13	.458	30	30	6	2	0	206^2	180	99	20	5	82	157	11.6	3.70	110	.231	.308	0	—	0	6	9	-0	0.9
1991	Tex-A	13	7	.650	25	25	5	1	0	169^2	152	67	10	4	84	125	12.7	3.08	131	.239	.331	0	—	0	19	18	2	2.3
1992	Tex-A	16	11	.593	33	33	5	0	0	224	229	103	17	4	73	179	12.3	3.66	104	.268	.329	0	—	0	7	4	-0	0.4
1993	Chi-N	12	10	.545	30	30	2	1	0	191	188	98	25	3	74	163	12.5	4.34	92	.258	.329	7	.111	-3	-6	-7	0	-0.9
1994	Chi-N	2	2	.500	4	4	0	0	0	19^2	22	20	1	1	13	11	16.5	9.15	45	.289	.400	0	.000	-1	-11	-11	-0	-1.7
Total	8	80	74	.519	193	186	26	4	0	1224^1	1193	616	129	26	482	889	12.5	4.05	102	.256	.329	7	.099	-3	10	9	3	1.0

● JUAN GUZMAN Guzman, Juan Andres (Correa) b: 10/28/66, Santo Domingo, D.R. BR/TR, 5′11″, 195 lbs. Deb: 6/7/91

YEAR	TM/L	W	L	PCT	G	GS	CG	SH	SV	IP	H	R	HR	HB	BB	SO	RAT	ERA	ERA+	OAV	OOB	BH	AVG	PB	PR	PR+	PD	TPI
1991	*Tor-A	10	3	.769	23	23	1	0	0	138^2	98	53	6	4	66	123	10.9	2.99	141	.197	.296	0	—	0	17	18	-2	1.4
1992	*Tor-A★	16	5	.762	28	28	1	0	0	180^2	135	56	6	1	72	165	10.4	2.64	155	.207	.287	0	—	0	26	28	-2	3.0
1993	*Tor-A	14	3	.824	33	33	2	1	0	221	211	107	17	3	110	194	13.2	3.99	109	.252	.341	0	—	0	8	8	-2	0.3
1994	Tor-A	12	11	.522	25	25	2	0	0	147^1	165	102	20	3	76	124	14.9	5.68	85	.282	.367	0	—	0	-14	-14	-2	-1.9
1995	Tor-A	4	14	.222	24	24	3	0	0	135^1	151	101	13	3	73	94	15.1	6.32	75	.281	.370	0	—	0	-24	-24	-2	-2.7
1996	Tor-A	11	8	.579	27	27	4	1	0	187^2	158	68	20	7	53	165	**10.5**	**2.93**	**171**	**.228**	**.290**	0	—	0	43	43	-1	3.8
1997	Tor-A	3	6	.333	13	13	0	0	0	60	48	42	14	2	31	52	12.2	4.95	93	.213	.314	0	—	0	-3	-2	-1	-0.4
1998	Tor-A	6	12	.333	22	22	2	0	0	145	133	83	19	6	65	113	12.7	4.41	106	.239	.325	0	.000	-0	4	4	-1	0.3
	Bal-A	4	4	.500	11	11	0	0	0	66	60	34	4	2	33	55	13.0	4.23	108	.241	.335	0	—	0	3	2	-1	0.2
	Yr	10	16	.385	33	33	2	0	0	211	193	117	23	8	98	168	12.8	4.35	107	.240	.328	0	.000	-0	7	7	-2	0.5

YEAR	TM/L	W	L	PCT	G	GS	CG	SH	SV	IP	H	R	HR	HB	BB	SO	RAT	ERA	ERA+	OAV	OOB	BH	AVG	PB	PR	PR+	PD	TPI
1999	Bal-A	5	9	.357	21	21	1	1	0	122^2	124	63	18	3	65	95	14.1	4.18	112	.264	.358	1	.167	-0	9	7	-0	0.7
	Cin-N	6	3	.667	12	12	1	0	0	77^1	70	33	10	1	21	60	10.7	3.03	154	.238	.291	3	.115	-1	13	14	-0	1.3
2000	TB-A	0	1	.000	1	1	0	0	0	1^2	7	8	2	0	2	3	48.6	43.20	11	.636	.692	0	—	0	-7	-7	0	-0.8
Total	10	91	79	.535	240	240	17	3	0	1483^1	1360	750	149	35	667	1243	12.5	4.08	112	.243	.327	4	.118	-1	77	80	-13	5.2

● SANTIAGO GUZMAN

Guzman, Santiago Donovan (b: Santiago Donovan (Guzman)) b: 7/25/49, San Pedro De Macoris, D.R. BR/TR, 6'2", 180 lbs. Deb: 9/30/69

YEAR	TM/L	W	L	PCT	G	GS	CG	SH	SV	IP	H	R	HR	HB	BB	SO	RAT	ERA	ERA+	OAV	OOB	BH	AVG	PB	PR	PR+	PD	TPI
1969	StL-N	0	1	.000	1	1	0	0	0	7^1	9	4	2	0	3	7	14.7	4.91	73	.321	.387	1	.333	0	-1	-1	-0	-0.1
1970	StL-N	1	1	.500	8	3	1	0	0	13^2	14	12	1	0	13	9	17.8	7.24	57	.275	.422	1	.200	-0	-5	-5	-0	-0.6
1971	StL-N	0	0	—	2	1	0	0	0	10	6	1	0	0	2	13	7.2	0.00	—	.162	.205	0	.000	-0	4	4	-0	0.2
1972	StL-N	0	0	—	1	0	0	0	0	1	1	1	1	0	0	0	9.0	9.00	38	.250	.250	0	—	0	-1	-1	0	0.0
Total	4	1	2	.333	12	5	1	0	0	32	30	18	4	0	18	29	13.5	4.50	85	.250	.348	2	.222	0	-3	-2	-1	-0.5

● BRUNO HAAS

Haas, Bruno Philip "Boon" b: 5/5/1891, Worcester, Mass. d: 6/5/52, Sarasota, Fla. BB/TL, 5'10", 180 lbs. Deb: 6/23/15 ♦

YEAR	TM/L	W	L	PCT	G	GS	CG	SH	SV	IP	H	R	HR	HB	BB	SO	RAT	ERA	ERA+	OAV	OOB	BH	AVG	PB	PR	PR+	PD	TPI
1915	Phi-A	0	1	.000	6	2	1	0	0	14^1	23	27	0	0	28	7	32.0	11.93	25	.404	.600	1	.056	-1	-14	-14	0	-0.9

● MOOSE HAAS

Haas, Bryan Edmund b: 4/22/56, Baltimore, Md. BR/TR, 6', 180 lbs. Deb: 9/8/76

YEAR	TM/L	W	L	PCT	G	GS	CG	SH	SV	IP	H	R	HR	HB	BB	SO	RAT	ERA	ERA+	OAV	OOB	BH	AVG	PB	PR	PR+	PD	TPI
1976	Mil-A	0	1	.000	5	2	0	0	0	16	12	8	0	0	12	9	13.5	3.94	89	.207	.343	0	—	0	-1	-1	1	0.0
1977	Mil-A	10	12	.455	32	32	6	0	0	197^2	195	104	21	2	84	113	12.8	4.33	94	.261	.338	0	—	0	-6	-5	-2	-0.8
1978	Mil-A	2	3	.400	7	6	2	0	0	30^2	33	22	6	0	8	32	12.0	6.16	61	.273	.318	0	—	0	-8	-8	-0	-1.2
1979	Mil-A	11	11	.500	29	28	8	1	0	184^2	198	112	26	0	59	95	12.5	4.78	88	.275	.330	0	—	0	-11	-12	-1	-1.3
1980	Mil-A	16	15	.516	33	33	14	3	0	252^1	246	96	25	1	56	146	10.8	3.10	125	.258	.300	0	—	0	26	23	-0	2.6
1981	*Mil-A	11	7	.611	24	22	5	0	0	137^1	146	69	10	1	40	64	12.3	4.46	77	.275	.327	0	—	0	-12	-17	-1	-2.0
1982	*Mil-A	11	8	.579	32	27	3	0	1	193^1	232	101	15	3	39	104	12.8	4.47	85	.302	.339	0	—	0	-8	-16	-2	-1.5
1983	Mil-A	13	3	.813	25	25	7	3	0	179	170	66	12	1	42	75	10.7	3.27	115	.251	.296	0	—	0	16	10	-1	0.8
1984	Mil-A	9	11	.450	31	30	4	0	0	189^1	205	91	15	0	43	84	11.8	3.99	97	.279	.318	0	—	0	0	-3	3	0.0
1985	Mil-A	8	8	.500	27	26	6	1	0	161^2	165	85	21	1	25	78	10.6	3.84	108	.260	.289	0	—	0	6	6	-1	0.4
1986	Oak-A	7	2	.778	12	12	1	0	0	72^1	58	23	4	1	19	40	9.7	2.74	142	.218	.273	0	—	0	12	10	-1	1.1
1987	Oak-A	2	2	.500	9	9	0	0	0	40^2	57	29	7	0	9	13	14.6	5.75	72	.335	.369	0	—	0	-6	-8	-0	-0.7
Total	12	100	83	.546	266	252	56	8	2	1655	1717	806	162	10	436	853	11.8	4.01	97	.269	.317	0	—	0	8	-22	-5	-2.6

● DAVE HAAS

Haas, Robert David b: 10/19/65, Independence, Mo. BR/TR, 6'1", 200 lbs. Deb: 9/8/91

YEAR	TM/L	W	L	PCT	G	GS	CG	SH	SV	IP	H	R	HR	HB	BB	SO	RAT	ERA	ERA+	OAV	OOB	BH	AVG	PB	PR	PR+	PD	TPI
1991	Det-A	1	0	1.000	11	0	0	0	0	10^2	8	8	1	1	12	6	17.7	6.75	62	.242	.457	0	—	0	-3	-3	-0	-0.3
1992	Det-A	5	3	.625	12	11	1	1	0	61^2	68	30	8	1	16	29	12.4	3.94	100	.276	.323	0	—	0	0	0	-0	0.0
1993	Det-A	1	2	.333	20	0	0	0	0	28	45	20	9	0	8	17	17.0	6.11	70	.375	.414	0	—	0	-6	-6	-0	-0.5
Total	3	7	5	.583	43	11	1	1	0	100^1	121	58	18	2	36	52	14.3	4.84	84	.303	.364	0	—	0	-9	-9	-0	-0.8

● BOB HABENICHT

Habenicht, Robert Julius "Hobby" b: 2/13/26, St.Louis, Mo. d: 12/24/80, Richmond, Va. BR/TR, 6'2", 185 lbs. Deb: 4/17/51

YEAR	TM/L	W	L	PCT	G	GS	CG	SH	SV	IP	H	R	HR	HB	BB	SO	RAT	ERA	ERA+	OAV	OOB	BH	AVG	PB	PR	PR+	PD	TPI
1951	StL-N	0	0	—	3	0	0	0	0	5	5	4	0	0	9	1	25.2	7.20	55	.278	.519	0	.000	0	-2	-2	-0	-0.1
1953	StL-A	0	0	—	1	0	0	0	0	1^2	1	1	0	1	1	1	16.2	5.40	78	.167	.375	0	—	0	-0	-0	-0	0.0
Total	2	0	0	—	4	0	0	0	0	6^2	6	5	0	1	10	2	23.0	6.75	60	.250	.486	0	.000	0	-2	-2	0	-0.1

● JOHN HABYAN

Habyan, John Gabriel b: 1/29/64, Bay Shore, N.Y. BR/TR, 6'2", 195 lbs. Deb: 9/29/85

YEAR	TM/L	W	L	PCT	G	GS	CG	SH	SV	IP	H	R	HR	HB	BB	SO	RAT	ERA	ERA+	OAV	OOB	BH	AVG	PB	PR	PR+	PD	TPI
1985	Bal-A	1	0	1.000	2	0	0	0	0	2^2	3	1	0	0	0	2	10.1	0.00	—	.250	.250	0	—	0	1	1	0	0.3
1986	Bal-A	1	3	.250	6	5	0	0	0	26^1	24	17	3	0	18	14	14.4	4.44	93	.250	.368	0	—	0	-1	-1	-0	-0.1
1987	Bal-A	6	7	.462	27	13	0	0	1	116^1	110	67	20	2	40	64	11.8	4.80	92	.248	.313	0	—	0	-4	-5	1	-0.4
1988	Bal-A	1	0	1.000	7	0	0	0	0	14^2	22	10	2	0	4	4	16.0	4.30	91	.355	.394	0	—	0	-1	-1	0	0.0
1990	NY-A	0	0	—	6	0	0	0	0	8^2	10	2	0	1	2	4	13.5	2.08	192	.294	.351	0	—	0	2	2	-0	0.1
1991	NY-A	4	2	.667	66	0	0	0	2	90	73	28	2	2	20	70	9.5	2.30	180	.225	.275	0	—	0	18	18	0	1.2
1992	NY-A	5	6	.455	56	0	0	0	7	72^2	84	32	6	2	21	44	13.3	3.84	102	.295	.347	0	—	0	1	1	1	0.2
1993	NY-A	2	1	.667	36	0	0	0	1	42^1	45	20	5	0	16	29	13.0	4.04	103	.276	.341	0	—	0	1	1	-0	0.0
	KC-A	0	0	—	12	0	0	0	0	14	14	7	1	0	4	10	11.6	4.50	102	.259	.310	0	—	0	-0	0	-0	0.0
	Yr	2	1	.667	48	0	0	0	1	56^1	59	27	6	0	20	39	12.6	4.15	103	.272	.333	0	—	0	1	1	0	0.0
1994	StL-N	1	0	1.000	52	0	0	0	1	47^1	50	17	2	0	20	46	13.3	3.23	129	.275	.347	0	—	0	5	5	1	0.3
1995	StL-N	3	2	.600	31	0	0	0	0	40^2	32	18	0	1	15	35	10.6	2.88	146	.222	.300	0	.000	-0	6	6	1	0.7
	Cal-A	1	2	.333	28	0	0	0	0	32^2	36	16	2	1	12	25	13.5	4.13	114	.279	.345	0	—	0	2	2	-1	0.1
1996	Col-N	1	1	.500	19	0	0	0	0	24	34	19	4	1	14	25	18.4	7.13	73	.347	.434	0	.000	-0	-8	-4	-0	-0.3
Total	11	26	24	.520	348	18	0	0	12	532^1	537	254	47	10	186	372	12.4	3.85	111	.265	.330	0	.000	-0	23	24	2	2.1

● WARREN HACKER

Hacker, Warren Louis b: 11/21/24, Marissa, Ill. BR/TR, 6'1", 185 lbs. Deb: 9/24/48

YEAR	TM/L	W	L	PCT	G	GS	CG	SH	SV	IP	H	R	HR	HB	BB	SO	RAT	ERA	ERA+	OAV	OOB	BH	AVG	PB	PR	PR+	PD	TPI
1948	Chi-N	0	1	.000	3	1	0	0	0	3	7	7	0	0	3	0	30.0	21.00	19	.438	.526	0	—	0	-6	-6	0	-1.0
1949	Chi-N	5	8	.385	30	12	3	0	0	125^2	141	68	7	4	53	40	14.2	4.23	95	.283	.356	7	.184	-1	-3	-3	1	-0.3
1950	Chi-N	0	1	.000	5	3	1	0	1	15^1	20	11	3	0	8	5	16.4	5.28	80	.313	.389	0	.000	-1	-2	-2	1	-0.1
1951	Chi-N	0	0	—	2	0	0	0	0	1^1	3	2	0	1	0	2	27.0	13.50	30	.500	.571	0	—	0	-1	-1	0	-0.1
1952	Chi-N	15	9	.625	33	20	12	5	1	185	144	56	17	1	31	84	**8.6**	2.58	149	**.212**	**.247**	7	.121	-2	24	25	-4	2.6
1953	Chi-N	12	19	.387	39	32	9	0	2	221^2	225	123	35	3	54	106	11.4	4.38	101	.254	.299	17	.218	0	-2	2	-3	0.0
1954	Chi-N	6	13	.316	39	18	4	1	2	158^2	157	89	28	4	37	80	11.2	4.25	99	.257	.304	13	.236	1	-3	-1	-1	-0.1
1955	Chi-N	11	15	.423	35	30	13	0	0	213	202	112	38	2	43	80	10.4	4.27	96	.245	.285	18	.250	2	-5	-4	-4	-0.6
1956	Chi-N	3	13	.188	34	24	4	0	0	168	190	103	28	1	44	65	12.6	4.66	81	.285	.330	8	.148	-2	-17	-17	-3	-1.9
1957	Cin-N	3	2	.600	15	6	0	0	0	43^1	50	26	5	3	13	18	13.7	5.19	79	.294	.355	1	.125	-0	-6	-5	-0	-0.5
	Phi-N	4	4	.500	20	10	1	0	0	74	72	40	10	1	18	33	11.1	4.50	85	.257	.304	6	.261	1	-5	-6	-1	-0.5
	Yr	7	6	.538	35	16	1	0	0	117^1	122	66	15	4	31	51	12.0	4.76	82	.271	.324	7	.226	1	-11	-11	-1	-1.0
1958	Phi-N	0	1	.000	9	1	0	0	0	17	24	17	2	0	8	4	16.9	7.41	53	.329	.395	0	.000	-0	-7	-7	-0	-0.4
1961	Chi-A	3	3	.500	42	0	0	0	8	57^1	62	26	8	1	8	40	11.1	3.77	104	.272	.300	1	.111	-1	2	1	-1	0.0
Total	12	62	89	.411	306	157	47	6	17	1283^1	1297	680	181	21	320	557	11.5	4.21	96	.259	.307	78	.195	-2	-32	-22	-15	-2.9

● JIM HACKETT

Hackett, James Joseph "Sunny Jim" b: 10/1/1877, Jacksonville, Ill. d: 3/28/61, Douglas, Mich. BR/TR, 6'2", 185 lbs. Deb: 9/14/02 ♦

YEAR	TM/L	W	L	PCT	G	GS	CG	SH	SV	IP	H	R	HR	HB	BB	SO	RAT	ERA	ERA+	OAV	OOB	BH	AVG	PB	PR	PR+	PD	TPI
1902	StL-N	0	3	.000	4	3	3	0	0	30^1	46	26	0	1	16	7	18.7	6.23	44	.348	.423	6	.286	1	-12	-12	-0	-0.9
1903	StL-N	1	3	.250	7	6	5	0	1	48^1	47	28	0	3	18	21	12.7	3.72	88	.249	.324	80	.228	1	-2	-2	0	-0.1
Total	2	1	6	.143	11	9	8	0	1	78^2	93	54	0	4	34	28	15.0	4.69	65	.290	.365	86	.231	2	-14	-14	-0	-1.0

● LUTHER HACKMAN

Hackman, Luther Gean b: 10/10/74, Columbus, Miss. BR/TR, 6'4", 195 lbs. Deb: 9/1/99

YEAR	TM/L	W	L	PCT	G	GS	CG	SH	SV	IP	H	R	HR	HB	BB	SO	RAT	ERA	ERA+	OAV	OOB	BH	AVG	PB	PR	PR+	PD	TPI
1999	Col-N	1	2	.333	5	3	0	0	0	16	26	19	5	0	12	10	21.4	10.69	54	.371	.463	1	.200	-0	-11	-7	1	-1.0
2000	StL-N	0	0	—	1	0	0	0	0	2^2	4	3	0	1	4	0	30.4	10.13	46	.400	.600	0	—	0	-2	-2	0	-0.1
Total	2	1	2	.333	6	3	0	0	0	18^2	30	22	5	1	16	10	22.7	10.61	53	.375	.485	1	.200	-0	-13	-8	1	-1.1

● HARVEY HADDIX

Haddix, Harvey "The Kitten" b: 9/18/25, Medway, Ohio d: 1/8/94, Springfield, Ohio BL/TL, 5'9.5", 170 lbs. Deb: 8/20/52 C

YEAR	TM/L	W	L	PCT	G	GS	CG	SH	SV	IP	H	R	HR	HB	BB	SO	RAT	ERA	ERA+	OAV	OOB	BH	AVG	PB	PR	PR+	PD	TPI
1952	StL-N	2	2	.500	7	6	3	0	0	42	31	18	4	2	10	31	9.2	2.79	133	.201	.259	3	.214	0	4	4	-1	0.4
1953	StL-N☆	20	9	.690	36	33	19	**6**	1	253	220	97	24	4	69	163	10.4	3.06	139	.232	.287	28	.289	10	35	34	1	4.7
1954	StL-N†	18	13	.581	43	35	13	3	4	259^2	247	114	26	3	77	184	11.3	3.57	115	.249	.305	18	.194	3	14	15	-0	2.0
1955	StL-N★	12	16	.429	37	30	9	2	1	208	216	111	27	5	62	150	12.2	4.46	91	.268	.325	12	.164	0	-10	-9	1	-0.9
1956	StL-N	1	0	1.000	4	4	1	1	0	23^2	28	15	3	0	10	16	14.5	5.32	71	.298	.365	2	.222	1	-4	-4	-0	-0.1
	Phi-N	12	8	.600	31	26	11	2	2	206^2	196	98	23	6	55	154	11.2	3.48	107	.247	.301	22	.237	4	7	6	-1	0.9
	Yr	13	8	.619	35	30	12	3	2	230^1	224	113	26	6	65	170	11.5	3.67	102	.253	.308	24	.235	5	3	1	-1	0.8
1957	Phi-N	10	13	.435	27	25	8	1	0	170^2	176	84	18	1	39	136	11.4	4.06	94	.264	.306	21	.309	7	-3	-5	-2	-0.1
1958	Cin-N	8	7	.533	29	26	8	1	0	184	191	79	28	7	43	110	11.8	3.52	118	.268	.315	11	.180	3	9	12	-1	1.1
1959	Pit-N	12	12	.500	31	29	14	2	0	224^1	189	88	26	2	49	149	**9.6**	3.13	124	.228	**.273**	12	.145	-0	20	19	-0	1.8
1960	*Pit-N	11	10	.524	29	28	4	0	1	172^1	189	87	13	1	38	101	11.9	3.97	94	.277	.316	17	.254	4	-4	-4	3	0.3
1961	Pit-N	10	6	.625	29	22	5	2	0	156	159	72	15	2	41	99	11.7	4.10	97	.266	.316	8	.143	0	-1	-2	0	-0.1
1962	Pit-N	9	6	.600	28	20	4	0	0	141^1	146	74	17	2	42	101	12.1	4.20	94	.264	.319	13	.250	4	-4	-4	-1	0.0
1963	Pit-N	3	4	.429	49	1	0	0	1	70	67	27	7	4	20	70	11.7	3.34	99	.256	.318	2	.182	1	-0	-0	0	0.0
1964	Bal-A	5	5	.500	49	0	0	0	10	89^2	68	26	4	2	23	90	9.3	2.31	155	.211	.268	0	.000	-2	13	13	1	1.5

YEAR	TM/L	W	L	PCT	G	GS	CG	SH	SV	IP	H	R	HR	HB	BB	SO	RAT	ERA	ERA+	OAV	OOB	BH	AVG	PB	PR	PR+	PD	TPI
1965	Bal-A	3	2	.600	24	0	0	0	1	33^{2}	31	22	5	2	23	21	15.0	3.48	100	.248	.373	0	.000	-0	-0	-0	-0	0.0
Total	14	136	113	.546	453	285	99	20	21	2235	2154	1012	240	43	601	1575	11.3	3.63	108	.252	.305	169	.212	35	75	74	1	11.5

● GEORGE HADDOCK

Haddock, George Silas "Gentleman George" b: 12/25/1866, Portsmouth, N.H. d: 4/18/26, Boston, Mass. BR/TR, 5'11", 155 lbs. Deb: 9/27/1888

YEAR	TM/L	W	L	PCT	G	GS	CG	SH	SV	IP	H	R	HR	HB	BB	SO	RAT	ERA	ERA+	OAV	OOB	BH	AVG	PB	PR	PR+	PD	TPI
1888	Was-N	0	2	.000	2	2	2	0	0	16	9	8	0	1	2	3	6.8	2.25	125	.148	.188	1	.200	0	1	1	1	0.2
1889	Was-N	11	19	.367	33	31	30	0	0	276^{1}	299	203	10	9	123	106	14.0	4.20	94	.268	.345	25	.223	7	-6	-8	0	0.0
1890	Buf-P	9	26	.257	35	34	31	0	0	290^{2}	366	307	15	14	149	123	16.4	5.76	71	.295	.377	36	.247	7	-49	-55	4	-3.6
1891	Bos-a	34	11	.756	51	47	37	**5**	1	379^{2}	330	172	8	14	137	169	11.4	2.49	140	.226	.299	45	.243	9	**52**	45	6	5.5
1892	Bro-N	29	13	.690	46	44	39	3	1	381^{1}	340	190	11	14	163	153	12.2	3.14	101	.229	.311	28	.177	-1	6	1	2	0.2
1893	Bro-N	8	9	.471	23	20	12	0	0	151	193	145	10	7	89	37	17.2	5.60	79	.302	.393	24	.282	4	-16	-21	-3	-1.6
1894	Phi-N	4	3	.571	10	7	5	0	0	56	63	46	0	1	34	7	15.8	5.79	88	.281	.378	5	.172	-1	-3	-4	1	-0.4
	Was-N	0	4	.000	4	4	4	0	0	29	50	40	2	1	17	1	21.1	8.69	61	.373	.447	3	.188	-1	-11	-11	-0	-1.0
	Yr	4	7	.364	14	11	9	0	0	85	113	86	2	2	51	8	17.6	6.78	76	.316	.404	8	.178	-1	-14	-16	1	-1.4
Total	7	95	87	.522	204	189	160	8	2	1580	1650	1111	56	61	714	599	13.8	4.07	93	.259	.340	167	.227	25	-25	-55	11	-0.7

● BUMP HADLEY

Hadley, Irving Darius b: 7/5/04, Lynn, Mass. d: 2/15/63, Lynn, Mass. BR/TR, 5'11", 190 lbs. Deb: 4/20/26

YEAR	TM/L	W	L	PCT	G	GS	CG	SH	SV	IP	H	R	HR	HB	BB	SO	RAT	ERA	ERA+	OAV	OOB	BH	AVG	PB	PR	PR+	PD	TPI
1926	Was-A	0	0	—	1	0	0	0	0	3	6	5	0	0	2	0	24.0	12.00	32	.429	.500	0	—	0	-3	-3	-0	-0.1
1927	Was-A	14	6	.700	30	27	13	0	0	198^{2}	177	72	2	9	86	60	12.3	2.85	142	.244	.332	19	.271	2	28	27	0	2.6
1928	Was-A	12	13	.480	33	31	16	3	0	231^{2}	236	105	4	8	100	80	13.4	3.54	113	.268	.348	17	.210	1	13	12	-0	1.3
1929	Was-A	6	16	.273	37	27	7	1	0	195^{1}	196	139	10	5	85	98	13.2	5.62	75	.263	.342	6	.097	-4	-30	-30	1	-3.1
1930	Was-A	15	11	.577	42	34	15	1	2	260^{1}	242	123	6	6	105	162	12.2	3.73	123	.247	.323	21	.226	1	27	25	-1	2.2
1931	Was-A	11	10	.524	**55**	11	2	1	8	179^{2}	145	81	4	1	92	124	11.9	3.06	140	**.218**	.314	9	.167	-1	26	25	2	2.8
1932	Chi-A	1	1	.500	3	2	1	0	1	18^{2}	17	8	2	0	8	13	12.1	3.86	112	.262	.342	1	.167	-0	1	1	0	0.1
	StL-A	13	20	.394	40	33	12	1	1	229^{2}	244	160	21	8	163	132	16.3	5.53	88	.274	.391	22	.282	4	-27	-16	-3	-1.8
	Yr	14	21	.400	43	35	13	1	2	248^{1}	261	168	23	8	171	145	15.9	5.40	89	.273	.388	23	.274	4	-25	-15	-3	-1.7
1933	StL-A	15	20	.429	45	36	19	2	3	**316^{2}**	309	152	17	3	141	149	12.9	3.92	119	.256	.335	17	.156	-4	13	24	-3	1.7
1934	StL-A	10	16	.385	39	32	7	2	1	213	212	120	14	6	127	79	14.6	4.35	115	.257	.361	13	.203	-1	3	14	-0	1.3
1935	Was-A	10	15	.400	35	32	13	0	0	230^{1}	268	143	18	4	102	77	14.6	4.92	88	.292	.366	15	.195	1	-12	-16	1	-1.2
1936	*NY-A	14	4	.778	31	17	8	1	1	173^{2}	194	97	12	1	89	74	14.7	4.35	107	.283	.366	16	.235	2	13	6	1	0.8
1937	*NY-A	11	8	.579	29	25	6	0	0	178^{1}	199	122	16	3	83	70	14.4	5.30	84	.281	.358	11	.169	1	-13	-18	1	-1.4
1938	NY-A	9	8	.529	29	17	8	1	1	167^{1}	165	79	13	3	66	61	12.6	3.60	126	.254	.325	5	.093	-1	22	18	3	1.7
1939	*NY-A	12	6	.667	26	18	7	1	2	154	132	62	10	3	85	65	12.9	2.98	146	.237	.342	11	.177	-1	28	25	2	2.8
1940	NY-A	3	5	.375	25	2	0	0	2	80	88	62	4	1	52	39	15.9	5.74	70	.276	.379	3	.111	-1	-12	-16	0	-1.5
1941	NY-N	1	0	1.000	3	2	0	0	0	13	19	10	1	0	9	4	19.4	6.23	59	.345	.438	0	.000	-0	-4	-4	-0	-0.3
	Phi-A	4	6	.400	25	9	1	0	3	102^{1}	131	69	13	2	47	31	15.8	5.01	84	.310	.381	4	.129	-1	-10	-9	-1	-0.9
Total	16	161	165	.494	528	355	135	14	25	2945^{2}	2980	1609	167	63	1442	1318	13.7	4.24	105	.263	.350	190	.189	-1	65	68	2	7.0

● MICKEY HAEFNER

Haefner, Milton Arnold b: 10/9/12, Lenzburg, Ill. d: 1/3/95, New Athens, Ill. BL/TL, 5'8", 160 lbs. Deb: 4/22/43

YEAR	TM/L	W	L	PCT	G	GS	CG	SH	SV	IP	H	R	HR	HB	BB	SO	RAT	ERA	ERA+	OAV	OOB	BH	AVG	PB	PR	PR+	PD	TPI
1943	Was-A	11	5	.688	36	13	8	1	6	165^{1}	126	56	4	4	60	65	10.3	2.29	140	.208	.283	6	.133	0	19	17	-0	1.8
1944	Was-A	12	15	.444	31	28	18	3	1	228	221	94	7	4	71	86	11.7	3.04	107	.251	.310	11	.157	-1	10	6	1	0.7
1945	Was-A	16	14	.533	37	28	19	1	3	238^{1}	226	103	10	7	69	83	11.4	3.47	89	.247	.305	20	.244	4	-3	-11	1	-0.8
1946	Was-A	14	11	.560	33	27	17	2	1	227^{2}	220	86	10	5	80	85	12.1	2.85	118	.251	.317	15	.203	4	17	13	-1	1.8
1947	Was-A	10	14	.417	31	28	14	4	1	193	195	86	8	4	85	77	13.2	3.64	102	.264	.343	8	.136	-1	1	2	-1	0.0
1948	Was-A	5	13	.278	28	20	4	0	0	147^{2}	151	86	7	6	61	45	13.3	4.02	108	.265	.342	7	.163	-1	4	5	2	0.6
1949	Was-A	5	5	.500	19	12	4	1	0	91^{2}	85	51	7	2	53	23	13.7	4.42	96	.249	.353	5	.200	1	-2	-2	1	0.0
	Chi-A	4	6	.400	14	12	4	1	1	80^{1}	84	40	9	5	41	17	14.6	4.37	95	.275	.370	6	.261	2	-2	-2	0	0.0
	Yr	9	11	.450	33	24	8	2	1	172	169	91	16	7	94	40	14.1	4.40	96	.261	.361	11	.229	2	-4	-3	1	0.0
1950	Chi-A	1	6	.143	24	9	2	0	0	70^{2}	83	49	11	2	45	17	16.6	5.73	78	.299	.400	4	.200	0	-9	-10	-1	-0.8
	Bos-N	0	2	.000	8	2	1	0	0	24	23	15	3	0	12	10	13.1	5.63	68	.247	.333	2	.286	1	-4	-5	-0	-0.3
Total	8	78	91	.462	261	179	91	13	13	1466^{2}	1414	666	76	39	577	508	12.5	3.50	102	.252	.326	84	.188	8	31	13	1	3.0

● BUD HAFEY

Hafey, Daniel Albert b: 8/6/12, Berkeley, Cal. d: 7/27/86, Sacramento, Cal. BR/TR, 6', 185 lbs. Deb: 4/21/35 F♦

YEAR	TM/L	W	L	PCT	G	GS	CG	SH	SV	IP	H	R	HR	HB	BB	SO	RAT	ERA	ERA+	OAV	OOB	BH	AVG	PB	PR	PR+	PD	TPI
1939	Phi-N	0	0	—	2	0	0	0	0	1^{1}	7	5	0	0	1	1	54.0	33.75	12	.700	.727	9	.176	-0	-4	-4	0	-0.2

● LEO HAFFORD

Hafford, Leo Edgar b: 9/17/1883, Somerville, Mass. d: 10/2/11, Willimantic, Conn. TR, 6', 170 lbs. Deb: 4/15/06

YEAR	TM/L	W	L	PCT	G	GS	CG	SH	SV	IP	H	R	HR	HB	BB	SO	RAT	ERA	ERA+	OAV	OOB	BH	AVG	PB	PR	PR+	PD	TPI
1906	Cin-N	1	1	.500	3	1	1	0	0	19	13	9	0	1	11	5	11.8	0.95	291	.191	.313	2	.222	-0	4	4	-1	0.3

● FRANK HAFNER

Hafner, Francis R. b: 8/14/1867, Hannibal, Mo. d: 3/2/57, Hannibal, Mo. TR, Deb: 5/5/1888

YEAR	TM/L	W	L	PCT	G	GS	CG	SH	SV	IP	H	R	HR	HB	BB	SO	RAT	ERA	ERA+	OAV	OOB	BH	AVG	PB	PR	PR+	PD	TPI
1888	KC-a	0	2	.000	2	2	2	0	0	18	24	23	2	1	16	5	20.5	7.00	49	.308	.432	0	.000	-1	-8	-6	-0	-0.6

● ART HAGAN

Hagan, Arthur Charles b: 3/17/1863, Providence, R.I. d: 3/25/36, Providence, R.I. TR, Deb: 6/30/1883

YEAR	TM/L	W	L	PCT	G	GS	CG	SH	SV	IP	H	R	HR	HB	BB	SO	RAT	ERA	ERA+	OAV	OOB	BH	AVG	PB	PR	PR+	PD	TPI
1883	Phi-N	1	14	.067	17	16	15	0	0	137	207	151	2		33	39	15.8	5.45	57	.342	.376	6	.102	-5	-35	-37	-1	-3.4
	Buf-N	0	2	.000	2	2	1	0	0	15	17	12	0		6	7	13.8	3.60	88	.270	.333	0	.000	-1	-1	-1	0	-0.2
	Yr	1	16	.059	19	18	16	0	0	152	224	163	2		39	46	15.6	5.27	59	.335	.371	6	.091	-7	-36	-37	-1	-3.6
1884	Buf-N	1	2	.333	3	3	3	0	0	26	53	38	1		4	4	19.7	5.88	54	.384	.401	4	.308	0	-8	-7	-1	-0.7
Total	2	2	18	.100	22	21	19	0	0	178	277	201	3		43	50	16.2	5.36	58	.343	.376	10	.127	-6	-44	-45	-2	-4.3

● CASEY HAGEMAN

Hageman, Kurt Moritz b: 5/12/1887, Mt.Oliver, Pa. d: 4/1/64, New Bedford, Pa. BR/TR, 5'10.5", 186 lbs. Deb: 9/18/11

YEAR	TM/L	W	L	PCT	G	GS	CG	SH	SV	IP	H	R	HR	HB	BB	SO	RAT	ERA	ERA+	OAV	OOB	BH	AVG	PB	PR	PR+	PD	TPI
1911	Bos-A	0	2	.000	2	2	1	0	0	17	16	8	2	1	5	8	11.6	2.12	155	.262	.328	0	.000	-0	2	2	-1	0.1
1912	Bos-A	0	0	—	2	1	0	0	0	1^{1}	5	5	0	0	3	1	54.0	27.00	13	.500	.615	0	—	0	-4	-3	-0	-0.1
1914	StL-N	2	4	.333	12	7	2	0	0	55^{1}	43	24	0	5	20	21	11.1	2.44	115	.215	.302	2	.125	-1	2	2	1	0.3
	Chi-N	1	1	.500	16	1	0	0	1	46^{2}	44	26	0	3	12	17	11.4	3.47	80	.254	.314	7	.467	3	-4	-4	-1	0.0
	Yr	3	5	.375	28	8	2	0	1	102	87	50	0	8	32	38	11.2	2.91	96	.233	.308	9	.290	2	-1	-1	-0	0.3
Total	3	3	7	.300	32	11	4	0	1	120^{1}	108	63	2	9	40	47	11.7	3.07	93	.243	.318	9	.257	2	-3	-3	-1	0.3

● KEVIN HAGEN

Hagen, Kevin Eugene b: 3/8/60, Renton, Wash. BR/TR, 6'2", 185 lbs. Deb: 6/4/83

YEAR	TM/L	W	L	PCT	G	GS	CG	SH	SV	IP	H	R	HR	HB	BB	SO	RAT	ERA	ERA+	OAV	OOB	BH	AVG	PB	PR	PR+	PD	TPI
1983	StL-N	2	2	.500	9	4	0	0	0	22^{1}	34	15	0	0	7	7	16.5	4.84	75	.362	.406	0	.000	-1	-3	-3	0	-0.5
1984	StL-N	1	0	1.000	4	0	0	0	0	7^{1}	9	2	0	0	1	2	12.3	2.45	142	.300	.323	0	—	0	1	1	-0	0.1
Total	2	3	2	.600	13	4	0	0	0	29^{2}	43	17	0	0	8	9	15.5	4.25	85	.347	.386	0	.000	-1	-2	-2	-0	-0.4

● RIP HAGERMAN

Hagerman, Zerah Zequiel b: 6/20/1888, Lyndon, Kan. d: 1/30/30, Albuquerque, N.Mex BR/TR, 6'2", 200 lbs. Deb: 4/16/09

YEAR	TM/L	W	L	PCT	G	GS	CG	SH	SV	IP	H	R	HR	HB	BB	SO	RAT	ERA	ERA+	OAV	OOB	BH	AVG	PB	PR	PR+	PD	TPI
1909	Chi-N	4	4	.500	13	7	4	1	0	79	64	29	0	2	28	32	10.7	1.82	139	.225	.298	3	.130	-0	7	6	-0	0.6
1914	Cle-A	9	15	.375	37	26	12	3	0	198	189	98	3	5	118	112	14.2	3.09	93	.265	.374	1	.016	-5	-8	-4	-3	-1.4
1915	Cle-A	6	14	.300	29	22	7	0	0	151	156	85	4	6	77	69	14.2	3.52	87	.277	.370	4	.105	-2	-10	-8	-3	-1.5
1916	Cle-A	0	0	—	2	0	0	0	0	3^{2}	5	6	1	2	2	1	22.1	12.27	25	.333	.474	0	.000	-0	-4	-4	-0	-0.2
Total	4	19	33	.365	81	55	23	4	0	431^{2}	414	218	8	15	225	214	13.6	3.09	93	.263	.360	8	.065	-9	-14	-10	-6	-2.5

● NOODLES HAHN

Hahn, Frank George b: 4/29/1879, Nashville, Tenn. d: 2/6/60, Candler, N.C. BL/TL, 5'9", 160 lbs. Deb: 4/18/1899

YEAR	TM/L	W	L	PCT	G	GS	CG	SH	SV	IP	H	R	HR	HB	BB	SO	RAT	ERA	ERA+	OAV	OOB	BH	AVG	PB	PR	PR+	PD	TPI
1899	Cin-N	23	8	.742	38	34	32	4	0	309	280	128	3	10	68	**145**	10.4	2.68	146	.242	.289	16	.147	-4	40	42	-4	2.7
1900	Cin-N	16	20	.444	39	37	29	**4**	0	311^{1}	306	145	4	7	89	**132**	11.6	3.27	112	.256	.312	24	.209	0	15	14	-0	1.4
1901	Cin-N	22	19	.537	42	42	**41**	2	0	**375^{1}**	370	159	12	9	69	**239**	10.7	2.71	118	.256	.294	24	.170	-1	26	21	-0	2.0
1902	Cin-N	23	12	.657	36	36	35	6	0	321	282	97	2	6	58	142	9.7	1.77	170	.236	.275	22	.185	0	36	41	-2	4.3
1903	Cin-N	22	12	.647	34	34	34	5	0	296	297	125	3	8	47	127	10.7	2.52	141	.262	.297	18	.161	-2	25	31	-1	2.9
1904	Cin-N	16	18	.471	35	34	33	2	0	297^{2}	258	101	3	7	35	98	9.1	2.06	143	.234	.262	17	.172	1	23	27	-0	3.1
1905	Cin-N	5	3	.625	13	8	5	1	0	77	85	44	0	2	9	17	11.2	2.81	118	.272	.297	4	.167	-1	2	4	-2	0.0
1906	NY-A	3	2	.600	6	6	3	1	0	42	38	22	0	3	6	17	10.1	3.86	77	.245	.287	4	.333	1	-5	-4	-1	-0.4
Total	8	130	94	.580	243	231	212	25	0	2029^{1}	1916	821	27	52	381	917	10.4	2.55	133	.249	.289	129	.176	-5	161	180	-11	16.0

● FRED HAHN

Hahn, Frederick Aloys b: 2/16/29, Nyack, N.Y. d: 8/16/84, Valhalla, N.Y. BR/TL, 6'3", 174 lbs. Deb: 4/19/52

YEAR	TM/L	W	L	PCT	G	GS	CG	SH	SV	IP	H	R	HR	HB	BB	SO	RAT	ERA	ERA+	OAV	OOB	BH	AVG	PB	PR	PR+	PD	TPI
1952	StL-N	0	0	—	1	0	0	0	0	2	2	2	0	0	1	0	13.5	0.00	—	.250	.333	0	—	0	1	1	0	0.1

● HAL HAID

Haid, Harold Augustine b: 12/21/1897, Barberton, Ohio d: 8/13/52, Los Angeles, Cal. BR/TR, 5'10.5", 150 lbs. Deb: 9/5/19

YEAR	TM/L	W	L	PCT	G	GS	CG	SH	SV	IP	H	R	HR	HB	BB	SO	RAT	ERA	ERA+	OAV	OOB	BH	AVG	PB	PR	PR+	PD	TPI
1919	StL-A	0	0	—	1	0	0	0	0	2	5	5	0	0	3	1	36.0	18.00	18	.556	.667	0	—	0	-3	-3	0	-0.2
1928	StL-N	2	2	.500	27	0	0	0	**5**	47	39	24	1	1	11	21	9.8	2.30	174	.218	.267	3	.375	1	9	9	0	1.0
1929	StL-N	9	9	.500	38	14	8	0	4	154^2	171	90	8	5	66	41	14.1	4.07	115	.284	.360	4	.082	-4	11	10	-1	0.6
1930	StL-N	3	2	.600	20	0	0	0	2	33	38	17	1	3	14	13	15.0	4.09	123	.297	.379	0	.000	-0	3	3	1	0.5
1931	Bos-N	0	2	.000	27	0	0	0	1	56	59	36	3	3	16	20	12.5	4.50	84	.263	.321	1	.125	-1	-4	-5	2	-0.1
1933	Chi-A	0	0	—	6	0	0	0	0	14^2	18	15	2	2	13	7	20.3	7.98	53	.310	.452	1	.250	0	-6	-6	0	-0.3
Total	6	14	15	.483	119	14	8	0	12	307^1	330	187	15	14	123	103	13.7	4.16	106	.275	.349	9	.125	-3	10	9	2	1.5

● JESSE HAINES

Haines, Jesse Joseph "Pop" b: 7/22/1893, Clayton, Ohio d: 8/5/78, Dayton, Ohio BR/TR, 6', 190 lbs. Deb: 7/20/18 CH

YEAR	TM/L	W	L	PCT	G	GS	CG	SH	SV	IP	H	R	HR	HB	BB	SO	RAT	ERA	ERA+	OAV	OOB	BH	AVG	PB	PR	PR+	PD	TPI
1918	Cin-N	0	0	—	1	0	0	0	0	5	5	1	0	0	1	2	10.8	1.80	148	.294	.333	1	1.000	0	1	0	0	0.1
1920	StL-N	13	20	.394	**47**	37	19	4	2	301^2	303	136	9	9	80	120	11.7	2.98	100	.270	.324	19	.176	-1	5	0	-5	-0.7
1921	StL-N	18	12	.600	37	29	13	**3**	0	244^1	261	112	15	8	56	84	12.0	3.50	105	.286	.333	17	.181	-3	8	5	2	0.4
1922	StL-N	11	9	.550	29	26	11	2	0	183	207	103	10	4	45	62	12.6	3.84	101	.284	.329	12	.167	-2	5	1	1	0.0
1923	StL-N	20	13	.606	37	36	23	1	0	266	283	125	7	5	75	73	12.3	3.11	125	.275	.328	20	.202	-2	26	24	0	2.4
1924	StL-N	8	19	.296	35	31	16	1	0	222^2	275	129	14	5	66	69	14.0	4.41	86	.309	.360	14	.189	-2	-13	-16	-1	-2.0
1925	StL-N	13	14	.481	29	25	15	0	0	207	234	116	11	1	52	63	12.5	4.57	95	.290	.334	13	.176	-2	-7	-6	-1	-0.9
1926	*StL-N	13	4	.765	33	20	14	3	1	183	186	76	10	2	48	46	11.6	3.25	120	.265	.314	13	.213	-1	12	13	-3	0.7
1927	StL-N	24	10	.706	38	36	**25**	**6**	1	300^2	273	114	11	5	77	89	10.6	2.72	145	.245	.297	23	.202	-1	40	41	1	4.3
1928	*StL-N	20	8	.714	33	28	20	1	0	240^1	238	98	14	6	72	77	11.8	3.18	126	.266	.324	16	.184	-1	22	22	-3	1.9
1929	StL-N	13	10	.565	28	25	12	0	0	179^2	230	123	21	2	73	59	15.3	5.71	82	.313	.376	11	.159	-3	-20	-21	-4	-2.7
1930	*StL-N	13	8	.619	29	24	14	0	1	182	215	107	15	1	54	68	13.4	4.30	117	.298	.348	16	.246	1	14	14	-3	1.2
1931	StL-N	12	3	.800	19	17	8	2	0	122^1	134	48	2	0	28	27	11.9	3.02	131	.278	.318	6	.133	-2	12	12	-1	1.0
1932	StL-N	3	5	.375	20	10	4	1	0	85^1	116	51	4	1	16	27	14.0	4.75	83	.326	.357	5	.185	0	-8	-8	-1	-0.7
1933	StL-N	9	6	.600	32	10	5	0	1	115^1	113	46	3	1	37	37	11.8	2.50	139	.252	.311	2	.067	-2	11	12	-2	1.1
1934	*StL-N	4	4	.500	37	6	0	0	1	90	86	42	6	4	19	17	10.9	3.50	121	.262	.311	3	.158	-1	**6**	**7**	2	0.7
1935	StL-N	6	5	.545	30	11	3	0	2	115^1	110	49	4	1	28	24	10.8	3.59	114	.252	.299	9	.273	1	6	6	-2	0.5
1936	StL-N	7	5	.583	25	9	4	0	1	99^1	110	44	4	1	21	19	12.0	3.90	101	.284	.323	5	.167	-1	1	1	-0	0.0
1937	StL-N	3	3	.500	16	6	2	0	0	65^2	81	36	5	1	23	18	14.4	4.52	88	.303	.361	4	.182	-0	-4	-4	-1	-0.5
Total	19	210	158	.571	555	386	208	24	10	3208^2	3460	1556	165	57	871	981	12.3	3.64	108	.280	.330	209	.186	-22	114	105	-21	6.8

● JIM HAISLIP

Haislip, James Clifton "Slim" b: 8/4/1891, Farmersville, Tex. d: 1/22/70, Dallas, Tex. BR/TR, 6'1", 186 lbs. Deb: 8/27/13

YEAR	TM/L	W	L	PCT	G	GS	CG	SH	SV	IP	H	R	HR	HB	BB	SO	RAT	ERA	ERA+	OAV	OOB	BH	AVG	PB	PR	PR+	PD	TPI
1913	Phi-N	0	0	—	1	0	0	0	0	3	4	4	0	0	3	0	21.0	6.00	56	.400	.538	0	.000	-0	-1	-1	-0	-0.1

● JOHN HALAMA

Halama, John Thadeuz b: 2/22/72, Brooklyn, N.Y. BL/TL, 6'5", 200 lbs. Deb: 4/2/98

YEAR	TM/L	W	L	PCT	G	GS	CG	SH	SV	IP	H	R	HR	HB	BB	SO	RAT	ERA	ERA+	OAV	OOB	BH	AVG	PB	PR	PR+	PD	TPI
1998	Hou-N	1	1	.500	6	6	0	0	0	32^1	37	21	0	2	13	21	14.5	5.85	69	.296	.371	0	.000	-0	-6	-7	0	-0.4
1999	Sea-A	11	10	.524	38	24	1	1	0	179	193	88	20	7	56	105	12.9	4.22	112	.281	.342	1	.200	1	13	11	2	1.3
2000	*Sea-A	14	9	.609	30	30	1	1	0	166^2	206	108	19	2	56	87	14.3	5.08	94	.308	.364	1	.500	0	-3	-5	0	-0.5
Total	3	26	20	.565	74	60	2	2	0	378	436	217	39	11	125	213	13.6	4.74	99	.295	.354	2	.118	1	4	-2	2	0.4

● ED HALBRITER

Halbriter, Edward L. b: 2/2/1860, Auburn, N.Y. d: 8/9/36, Los Angeles, Cal. Deb: 5/23/1882

YEAR	TM/L	W	L	PCT	G	GS	CG	SH	SV	IP	H	R	HR	HB	BB	SO	RAT	ERA	ERA+	OAV	OOB	BH	AVG	PB	PR	PR+	PD	TPI
1882	Phi-a	0	1	.000	1	1	1	0	0	8	17	12	1		4	4	23.6	7.88	38	.405	.457	0	.000	-1	-5	-4	-0	-0.4

● DAD HALE

Hale, Ray Luther b: 2/18/1880, Allegan, Mich. d: 2/1/46, Allegan, Mich. BR/TR, 5'10", 180 lbs. Deb: 4/21/02

YEAR	TM/L	W	L	PCT	G	GS	CG	SH	SV	IP	H	R	HR	HB	BB	SO	RAT	ERA	ERA+	OAV	OOB	BH	AVG	PB	PR	PR+	PD	TPI
1902	Bos-N	1	3	.250	8	5	3	0	0	40	57	38	1	1	16	11	16.6	6.07	47	.333	.394	0	.000	-1	-15	-14	-0	-1.4
	Bal-A	0	1	.000	3	2	1	0	0	14	21	14	0	1	6	6	18.0	4.50	84	.344	.412	0	.000	-1	-1	-1	-1	-0.2
Total	1	1	4	.200	11	7	4	0	0	54	78	52	1	2	22	17	17.0	5.67	54	.336	.398	0	.000	-2	-16	-15	-1	-1.6

● ED HALICKI

Halicki, Edward Louis b: 10/4/50, Newark, N.J. BR/TR, 6'7", 220 lbs. Deb: 7/8/74

YEAR	TM/L	W	L	PCT	G	GS	CG	SH	SV	IP	H	R	HR	HB	BB	SO	RAT	ERA	ERA+	OAV	OOB	BH	AVG	PB	PR	PR+	PD	TPI
1974	SF-N	1	8	.111	16	11	2	0	0	74^1	84	49	6	2	31	40	14.2	4.24	90	.275	.345	6	.240	1	-5	-3	-1	-0.3
1975	SF-N	9	13	.409	24	23	7	2	0	159^2	143	76	6	3	59	153	11.6	3.49	109	.240	.312	6	.113	-2	2	5	-1	0.5
1976	SF-N	12	14	.462	32	31	8	4	0	186^1	171	86	10	2	61	130	11.3	3.62	100	.246	.309	9	.170	1	-2	0	-0	0.1
1977	SF-N	16	12	.571	37	37	7	2	0	257^2	241	105	27	7	70	168	11.1	3.32	118	.244	.298	15	.176	3	17	17	-3	1.7
1978	SF-N	9	10	.474	29	28	9	4	1	199	166	74	11	7	45	105	9.9	2.85	121	.221	**.271**	9	.136	-2	16	14	-2	0.9
1979	SF-N	5	8	.385	33	19	3	1	0	125^2	134	82	12	3	47	81	13.2	4.58	76	.266	.333	7	.206	1	-12	-16	0	-1.4
1980	SF-N	0	0	—	11	2	0	0	0	25	29	15	5	0	10	14	14.0	5.40	66	.293	.358	1	.167	-0	-5	-5	0	-0.3
	Cal-A	3	1	.750	10	6	0	0	0	35^1	39	22	5	0	11	16	12.7	4.84	81	.279	.331	0	—	0	-3	-4	-1	-0.4
Total	7	55	66	.455	192	157	36	13	1	1063	1007	509	82	24	334	707	11.6	3.62	102	.247	.308	53	.165	3	8	9	-7	0.8

● DREW HALL

Hall, Andrew Clark b: 3/27/63, Louisville, Ky. BL/TL, 6'4", 205 lbs. Deb: 9/14/86

YEAR	TM/L	W	L	PCT	G	GS	CG	SH	SV	IP	H	R	HR	HB	BB	SO	RAT	ERA	ERA+	OAV	OOB	BH	AVG	PB	PR	PR+	PD	TPI
1986	Chi-N	1	2	.333	5	4	1	0	1	23^2	24	12	3	0	10	21	12.9	4.56	89	.267	.340	1	.143	0	-2	-1	-0	-0.2
1987	Chi-N	1	1	.500	21	0	0	0	1	32^2	40	31	4	0	14	20	14.9	6.89	62	.308	.375	0	.000	-0	-10	-9	-0	-0.6
1988	Chi-N	1	1	.500	19	0	0	0	1	22^1	26	20	4	1	9	22	14.5	7.66	47	.295	.367	0	.000	-0	-10	-10	0	-0.9
1989	Tex-A	2	1	.667	38	0	0	0	0	58^1	42	24	3	3	33	45	12.0	3.70	107	.207	.326	0	—	0	1	2	0	0.1
1990	Mon-N	4	7	.364	42	0	0	0	3	58^1	52	35	6	0	29	40	12.5	5.09	72	.242	.332	0	.000	-0	-8	-10	1	-1.7
Total	5	9	12	.429	125	4	1	0	5	195^1	184	122	20	4	95	148	13.0	5.21	75	.253	.343	1	.063	-1	-30	-28	-0	-3.3

● CHARLEY HALL

Hall, Charles Louis "Sea Lion" (b: Carlos Clolo)
b: 7/27/1885, Ventura, Cal. d: 12/6/43, Ventura, Cal. BL/TR, 6'1", 187 lbs. Deb: 7/12/06

YEAR	TM/L	W	L	PCT	G	GS	CG	SH	SV	IP	H	R	HR	HB	BB	SO	RAT	ERA	ERA+	OAV	OOB	BH	AVG	PB	PR	PR+	PD	TPI
1906	Cin-N	4	8	.333	14	9	9	1	1	95	86	56	1	8	50	49	13.6	3.32	83	.258	.368	6	.128	-1	-7	-6	0	-0.8
1907	Cin-N	4	2	.667	11	8	5	0	0	68	51	22	0	4	43	25	13.0	2.51	103	.226	.359	7	.269	1	-0	1	-1	0.1
1909	Bos-A	6	4	.600	11	7	3	0	0	59^2	59	24	0	3	17	27	11.9	2.56	98	.271	.332	3	.158	-1	-1	-0	-0	-0.2
1910	Bos-A	12	9	.571	35	16	13	0	2	188^2	142	68	6	9	73	95	10.7	1.91	134	.207	.292	17	.207	3	13	13	0	2.0
1911	Bos-A	8	7	.533	32	10	6	0	**4**	146^1	149	79	3	5	72	83	13.9	3.75	87	.279	.370	9	.141	-1	-7	-8	-2	-1.0
1912	*Bos-A	15	8	.652	34	20	9	2	2	191	178	85	3	4	70	83	11.9	3.02	113	.257	.329	20	.267	5	6	8	1	1.5
1913	Bos-A	5	4	.556	35	4	2	0	2	105	97	67	1	5	46	48	12.7	3.43	86	.235	.319	9	.214	1	-6	-6	-1	-0.5
1916	StL-N	0	4	.000	10	5	2	0	1	42^2	45	27	1	0	14	15	12.4	5.48	48	.280	.337	2	.143	-1	-14	-13	0	-1.3
1918	Det-A	0	1	.000	6	1	0	0	0	13^1	14	10	1	0	6	2	13.5	6.75	39	.269	.345	0	.000	-0	-6	-6	-1	-0.5
Total	9	54	47	.535	188	80	49	3	12	909^2	821	438	16	38	391	427	12.4	3.09	95	.248	.334	73	.197	7	-21	-16	-2	-0.7

● BERT HALL

Hall, Herbert Ernest b: 10/15/1888, Portland, Ore. d: 7/18/48, Seattle, Wash. BR/TR, 5'10", 178 lbs. Deb: 8/21/11

YEAR	TM/L	W	L	PCT	G	GS	CG	SH	SV	IP	H	R	HR	HB	BB	SO	RAT	ERA	ERA+	OAV	OOB	BH	AVG	PB	PR	PR+	PD	TPI
1911	Phi-N	0	1	.000	7	1	0	0	0	18	19	11	0	1	13	8	16.5	4.00	86	.297	.423	1	.333	0	-1	-1	-1	-0.1

● HERB HALL

Hall, Herbert Silas "Iron Duke" b: 6/5/1893, Steeleville, Ill. d: 7/1/70, Fresno, Cal. BB/TR, 6'4", 220 lbs. Deb: 4/28/18

YEAR	TM/L	W	L	PCT	G	GS	CG	SH	SV	IP	H	R	HR	HB	BB	SO	RAT	ERA	ERA+	OAV	OOB	BH	AVG	PB	PR	PR+	PD	TPI
1918	Det-A	0	0	—	3	0	0	0	0	6	12	11	0	2	7	1	31.5	15.00	18	.500	.636	0	.000	-0	-8	-9	0	-0.4

● JOHN HALL

Hall, John Sylvester b: 1/9/24, Muskogee, Okla. d: 1/17/95, Midwest City, Okla. BR/TR, 6'2.5", 170 lbs. Deb: 4/21/48

YEAR	TM/L	W	L	PCT	G	GS	CG	SH	SV	IP	H	R	HR	HB	BB	SO	RAT	ERA	ERA+	OAV	OOB	BH	AVG	PB	PR	PR+	PD	TPI
1948	Bro-N	0	0	—	3	0	0	0	0	4^1	4	3	1	0	2	2	12.5	6.23	64	.267	.353	0	—	0	-1	-1	0	0.0

● MARC HALL

Hall, Marcus b: 8/12/1887, Joplin, Mo. d: 2/24/15, Joplin, Mo. BR/TR, 6'1.5", 190 lbs. Deb: 8/20/10

YEAR	TM/L	W	L	PCT	G	GS	CG	SH	SV	IP	H	R	HR	HB	BB	SO	RAT	ERA	ERA+	OAV	OOB	BH	AVG	PB	PR	PR+	PD	TPI
1910	StL-A	1	7	.125	8	7	5	0	0	46^1	50	33	0	3	31	25	16.3	4.27	58	.289	.406	1	.067	-2	-9	-9	1	-1.5
1913	Det-A	10	12	.455	30	21	8	1	0	165	154	79	1	2	79	69	12.8	3.27	89	.255	.344	4	.089	-3	-6	-7	0	-1.1
1914	Det-A	4	6	.400	25	8	1	0	0	90^1	88	38	1	0	27	18	11.5	2.69	104	.267	.322	1	.043	-2	1	1	0	-0.1
Total	3	15	25	.375	63	36	14	1	0	301^2	292	150	2	5	137	112	12.9	3.25	87	.264	.348	6	.072	-7	-15	-14	1	-2.7

● DARREN HALL

Hall, Michael Darren b: 7/14/64, Marysville, Ohio BR/TR, 6'3", 205 lbs. Deb: 4/30/94

YEAR	TM/L	W	L	PCT	G	GS	CG	SH	SV	IP	H	R	HR	HB	BB	SO	RAT	ERA	ERA+	OAV	OOB	BH	AVG	PB	PR	PR+	PD	TPI
1994	Tor-A	2	3	.400	30	0	0	0	17	31^2	26	12	3	1	14	28	11.7	3.41	141	.226	.315	0	—	0	5	5	1	1.0
1995	Tor-A	0	2	.000	17	0	0	0	3	16^1	21	9	2	0	9	11	16.5	4.41	107	.309	.390	0	—	0	1	1	-0	0.1
1996	LA-N	0	2	.000	9	0	0	0	0	12	13	9	2	0	5	12	13.5	6.00	64	.271	.340	0	—	0	-2	-3	-0	-0.5
1997	LA-N	3	2	.600	63	0	0	0	2	54^2	58	15	3	0	26	39	13.8	2.30	167	.283	.364	0	—	0	12	10	1	1.1
1998	LA-N	0	3	.000	11	0	0	0	0	11^1	17	14	2	1	5	8	18.3	10.32	38	.347	.418	0	—	0	-8	-9	-0	-1.6
Total	5	5	12	.294	130	0	0	0	22	126	135	59	12	2	59	98	14.0	3.93	107	.278	.359	0	—	0	7	4	1	0.0

YEAR	TM/L	W	L	PCT	G	GS	CG	SH	SV	IP	H	R	HR	HB	BB	SO	RAT	ERA	ERA+	OAV	OOB	BH	AVG	PB	PR	PR+	PD	TPI
● DICK HALL Hall, Richard Wallace b: 9/27/30, St.Louis, Mo. BR/TR, 6'6", 200 lbs. Deb: 4/15/52 ♦																												
1955	Pit-N	6	6	.500	15	13	4	0	1	94^1	92	43	8	2	28	46	11.6	3.91	105	.253	.310	7	.175	1	1	2	-2	0.2
1956	Pit-N	0	7	.000	19	9	1	0	1	62^1	64	36	8	0	21	27	12.3	4.76	79	.270	.329	10	.345	2	-7	-7	-1	-0.5
1957	Pit-N	0	0	—	8	0	0	0	0	10	17	12	4	1	5	7	20.7	10.80	35	.362	.434	0	.000	-0	-8	-8	-0	-0.4
1959	Pit-N	0	0	—	2	1	0	0	0	8^2	12	5	1	0	1	3	13.5	3.12	124	.333	.351	0	.000	-0	1	1	-0	0.0
1960	KC-A	8	13	.381	29	28	9	1	0	182^1	183	96	28	3	38	79	11.1	4.05	98	.261	.301	6	.107	-2	-4	-1	-1	-0.4
1961	Bal-A	7	5	.583	29	13	4	2	4	122^1	102	47	10	0	30	92	9.7	3.09	124	.227	.275	5	.139	-0	13	11	1	1.1
1962	Bal-A	6	6	.500	43	6	1	0	6	118^1	102	31	9	0	19	71	9.2	2.28	162	.230	.262	4	.167	1	22	20	-0	2.2
1963	Bal-A	5	5	.500	47	3	0	0	12	111^2	91	39	12	4	16	74	8.9	2.98	116	.224	.260	13	.464	6	8	6	1	1.4
1964	Bal-A	9	1	.900	45	0	0	0	7	87^2	58	19	8	0	16	52	7.6	1.85	193	.188	.228	2	.125	-0	17	17	-0	2.1
1965	Bal-A	11	8	.579	48	0	0	0	12	93^2	84	34	8	0	11	79	9.1	3.07	113	.243	.266	5	.333	3	4	4	-1	1.0
1966	Bal-A	6	2	.750	32	0	0	0	7	66	59	30	8	3	8	44	9.5	3.95	84	.233	.265	2	.167	0	-4	-5	-0	-0.6
1967	Phi-N	10	8	.556	48	1	1	0	8	86	83	28	5	2	12	49	10.2	2.20	155	.255	.286	1	.071	-1	11	11	1	2.6
1968	Phi-N	4	1	.800	32	0	0	0	0	46	53	26	6	1	5	31	11.5	4.89	61	.296	.319	1	.333	0	-10	-10	-0	-1.1
1969	*Bal-A	5	2	.714	39	0	0	0	6	65^2	49	14	3	1	9	31	8.1	1.92	186	.213	.246	2	.286	1	12	12	-1	1.5
1970	*Bal-A	10	5	.667	32	0	0	0	3	61^1	51	25	8	0	6	30	8.4	3.08	118	.229	.249	1	.083	-1	4	4	-1	0.6
1971	*Bal-A	6	6	.500	27	0	0	0	1	43^1	52	27	4	1	11	26	13.3	4.98	67	.302	.348	2	.400	1	-7	-8	-1	-1.7
Total	16	93	75	.554	495	74	20	3	68	1259^2	1152	512	130	18	236	741	10.0	3.32	110	.244	.283	150	.210	10	55	49	-7	8.0
● BOB HALL Hall, Robert Lewis b: 12/22/23, Swissvale, Pa. d: 3/12/83, St.Petersburg, Fla BR/TR, 6'2", 195 lbs. Deb: 4/23/49																												
1949	Bos-N	6	4	.600	31	6	2	0	0	74^1	77	40	7	1	41	43	14.4	4.36	87	.272	.366	8	.364	3	-3	-5	-2	-0.6
1950	Bos-N	0	2	.000	21	4	0	0	0	50^1	58	43	8	2	33	22	16.6	6.97	55	.293	.399	1	.083	-1	-16	-19	-0	-1.0
1953	Pit-N	3	12	.200	37	17	6	1	1	152	172	99	17	1	72	68	14.5	5.39	83	.286	.364	6	.158	0	-19	-15	-1	-1.3
Total	3	9	18	.333	89	27	8	1	1	276^2	307	182	32	4	146	133	14.9	5.40	77	.284	.371	15	.208	2	-37	-38	-3	-2.9
● TOM HALL Hall, Tom Edward b: 11/23/47, Thomasville, N.C. BL/TL, 6', 155 lbs. Deb: 6/9/68																												
1968	Min-A	2	1	.667	8	4	0	0	0	29^2	27	15	1	1	12	18	12.1	2.43	127	.239	.317	0	.000	-1	2	2	-0	0.1
1969	*Min-A	8	7	.533	31	18	5	2	0	140^2	129	63	12	0	50	92	11.5	3.33	110	.243	.308	8	.186	1	5	5	-2	0.4
1970	*Min-A	11	6	.647	52	11	1	0	4	155^1	94	46	11	2	66	184	9.4	2.55	146	.173	.265	8	.182	-0	20	20	-2	1.9
1971	Min-A	4	7	.364	48	11	0	0	9	129^2	104	54	13	0	58	137	11.2	3.33	107	.216	.300	9	.265	2	2	3	1	0.6
1972	*Cin-N	10	1	.909	47	7	1	1	8	124^1	77	43	13	2	56	134	9.8	2.61	123	.173	.269	3	.100	-1	12	9	-2	0.7
1973	*Cin-N	8	5	.615	54	7	0	0	8	103^2	74	43	13	0	48	96	10.6	3.47	98	.202	.295	1	.045	-2	2	-1	-2	-0.5
1974	Cin-N	3	1	.750	40	1	0	0	1	64	54	32	9	0	30	48	11.8	4.08	86	.232	.319	0	.000	-1	-3	-4	-0	-0.4
1975	Cin-N	0	0	—	2	0	0	0	0	2	2	0	0	0	2	3	18.0	0.00	—	.250	.400	0	—	0	1	1	0	0.0
	NY-N	4	3	.571	34	4	0	0	1	60^2	58	39	10	3	31	48	13.6	4.75	73	.254	.351	2	.400	1	-8	-9	-0	-1.0
	Yr	4	3	.571	36	4	0	0	1	62^2	60	39	10	3	33	51	13.8	4.60	75	.254	.353	2	.400	1	-7	-8	-0	-1.0
1976	NY-N	1	1	.500	5	0	0	0	0	4^2	5	3	0	0	5	2	19.3	5.79	57	.250	.400	0	—	0	-1	-1	0	-0.3
	*KC-A	1	1	.500	31	0	0	0	1	30^1	28	19	4	0	18	25	13.6	4.45	79	.246	.348	0	—	0	-3	-3	1	-0.2
1977	KC-A	0	0	—	6	0	0	0	0	7^2	4	3	2	0	6	10	11.7	3.52	115	.154	.313	0	—	0	0	0	0	0.0
Total	10	52	33	.612	358	63	7	3	32	852^2	656	360	88	8	382	797	11.0	3.27	107	.211	.299	31	.161	-1	29	23	-8	1.3
● BILL HALL Hall, William Bernard "Beanie" b: 2/22/1894, Charleston, W.Va. d: 8/15/47, Newport, Ky. BR/TR, 6'2", 250 lbs. Deb: 7/4/13																												
1913	Bro-N	0	0	—	3	0	0	0	0	4^2	4	3	0	1	5	3	19.3	5.79	57	.267	.476	0	.000	-0	-1	-1	-0	-0.1
● JOHN HALLA Halla, John Arthur b: 5/13/1884, St.Louis, Mo. d: 9/30/47, ElSegundo, Cal. BL/TL, 5'11", 175 lbs. Deb: 8/18/05																												
1905	Cle-A	0	0	—	3	0	0	0	0	12^2	12	6	0	1	0	4	9.2	2.84	92	.250	.265	1	.200	-0	-0	-0	-0	0.0
● ROY HALLADAY Halladay, Harry Leroy b: 5/14/77, Denver, Colo. BR/TR, 6'6", 205 lbs. Deb: 9/20/98																												
1998	Tor-A	1	0	1.000	2	2	1	0	0	14	9	4	2	0	2	13	7.1	1.93	242	.176	.208	0	—	0	4	4	0	0.3
1999	Tor-A	8	7	.533	36	18	1	1	1	149^1	156	76	19	4	79	82	14.4	3.92	126	.270	.362	0	.000	-0	16	17	-1	1.4
2000	Tor-A	4	7	.364	19	13	0	0	0	67^2	107	87	14	2	42	44	20.1	10.64	47	.357	.439	0	—	0	-43	-42	-0	-5.0
Total	3	13	14	.481	57	33	2	1	1	231	272	167	35	6	123	139	15.6	5.77	86	.293	.379	0	.000	-0	-23	-21	-1	-3.3
● BILL HALLAHAN Hallahan, William Anthony "Wild Bill" b: 8/4/02, Binghamton, N.Y. d: 7/8/81, Binghamton, N.Y. BR/TL, 5'10.5", 170 lbs. Deb: 4/16/25																												
1925	StL-N	1	0	1.000	6	0	0	0	0	15^1	14	6	0	0	11	8	14.7	3.52	123	.259	.385	1	.333	0	1	1	0	0.1
1926	*StL-N	1	4	.200	19	3	0	0	0	56^2	45	27	1	1	32	28	12.4	3.65	107	.260	.379	4	.250	0	**1**	**2**	-1	0.1
1929	StL-N	4	4	.500	20	12	5	0	0	93^2	94	51	6	0	60	52	14.8	4.42	106	.269	.376	4	.154	-1	3	3	1	0.2
1930	*StL-N	15	9	.625	35	32	13	2	2	237^1	233	135	15	0	126	**177**	13.6	4.66	108	.260	.351	10	.123	-6	8	9	-0	0.2
1931	*StL-N	**19**	9	.679	37	30	16	3	4	248^2	242	102	10	1	112	**159**	12.8	3.29	120	.259	.339	8	.099	-4	16	17	-2	1.2
1932	StL-N	12	7	.632	25	22	13	1	1	176^1	169	79	10	0	69	108	12.1	3.11	126	.253	.323	12	.214	2	15	16	-1	1.7
1933	StL-N★	16	13	.552	36	32	16	2	0	244^1	245	114	6	0	98	93	12.6	3.50	99	.260	.330	12	.150	-0	-4	-1	-3	-0.4
1934	*StL-N	8	12	.400	32	26	10	2	0	162^2	195	93	2	0	66	70	14.4	4.26	99	.294	.358	10	.182	-1	-4	-1	-0	-0.2
1935	StL-N	15	8	.652	40	23	8	2	1	181^1	196	91	7	1	57	73	12.6	3.42	120	.275	.329	8	.143	-2	12	13	-1	1.3
1936	StL-N	2	2	.500	9	6	1	0	0	37	58	28	4	0	17	16	18.2	6.32	62	.360	.421	5	.556	3	-9	-10	0	-0.7
	Cin-N	5	9	.357	23	19	5	2	0	135	150	78	3	1	57	32	13.9	4.33	88	.287	.359	9	.191	1	-5	-8	1	-0.6
	Yr	7	11	.389	32	25	6	2	0	172	208	106	7	1	74	48	14.8	4.76	81	.305	.373	14	.250	3	-14	-18	1	-1.3
1937	Cin-N	3	9	.250	21	9	2	0	0	63	90	52	3	2	29	18	17.3	6.14	61	.345	.414	2	.095	-1	-16	-18	0	-2.9
1938	Phi-N	1	8	.111	21	10	1	0	0	89	107	59	4	2	45	22	15.6	5.46	71	.295	.376	5	.192	-0	-17	-15	-0	-1.3
Total	12	102	94	.520	324	224	90	14	8	1740^1	1838	915	71	8	779	856	13.6	4.03	102	.274	.351	90	.162	-9	2	12	-6	-1.3
● JACK HALLETT Hallett, Jack Price b: 11/13/14, Toledo, Ohio d: 6/11/82, Toledo, Ohio BR/TR, 6'4", 215 lbs. Deb: 9/13/40																												
1940	Chi-A	1	1	.500	2	2	1	0	0	14	15	10	1	1	6	9	14.1	6.43	69	.273	.355	2	.400	0	-3	-3	0	-0.3
1941	Chi-A	5	5	.500	22	6	3	0	0	74^2	96	57	7	3	38	25	16.5	6.03	68	.306	.386	4	.154	0	-16	-16	-0	-1.8
1942	Pit-N	0	1	.000	3	3	2	0	0	22^1	23	12	0	0	8	16	12.5	4.84	70	.274	.337	3	.375	2	-4	-4	0	0.0
1943	Pit-N	1	2	.333	9	4	2	1	0	47^2	36	11	0	1	11	11	9.1	1.70	205	.212	.264	4	.286	2	9	9	-1	0.7
1946	Pit-N	5	7	.417	35	9	3	1	0	115	107	48	0	0	39	64	11.4	3.29	107	.267	.332	6	.231	0	2	3	0	0.3
1948	NY-N	0	0	—	2	0	0	0	0	4	3	3	0	0	4	3	15.8	4.50	87	.214	.389	0	.000	-0	-0	-0	-0	0.0
Total	6	12	16	.429	73	24	11	2	0	277^2	280	141	8	5	106	128	12.7	4.05	92	.270	.340	19	.237	4	-12	-10	-1	-1.1
● BILL HALLMAN Hallman, William Wilson b: 3/31/1867, Pittsburgh, Pa. d: 9/11/20, Philadelphia, Pa. BR/TR, 5'8", 160 lbs. Deb: 4/23/1888 M♦																												
1896	Phi-N	0	0	—	1	0	0	0	0	2	4	4	0	0	2	0	27.0	18.00	24	.400	.500	150	.320	0	-3	-3	-0	-0.1
● CHARLIE HALLSTROM Hallstrom, Charles E. "Swedish Wonder" b: 1/22/1864, Jonkoping, Sweden d: 5/6/49, Chicago, Ill. Deb: 9/23/1885																												
1885	Pro-N	0	1	.000	1	1	1	0	0	9	18	16	3		6	0	24.0	11.00	24	.409	.480	0	.000	-1	-8	-9	-0	-0.7
● SHANE HALTER Halter, Shane David b: 11/8/69, LaPlata, Md. BR/TR, 5'10", 160 lbs. Deb: 4/6/97 ♦																												
1998	KC-A	0	0	—	1	0	0	0	0	1	1	0	0	0	0	0	9.0	0.00	—	.333	.333	45	.221	0	1	1	0	0.0
2000	Det-A	0	0	—	1	0	0	0	0	0	0	0	0	1	—	—	—	—	—	1.000	97	.261	0	0	0	0	0.0	
Total	2	0	0	—	2	0	0	0	0	1	1	0	0	0	1	0	18.0	0.00	—	.333	.500	141	.250	0	1	1	0	0.0
● DOC HAMANN Hamann, Elmer Joseph b: 12/21/1900, New Ulm, Minn. d: 1/11/73, Milwaukee, Wis. BR/TR, 6'1", 180 lbs. Deb: 9/21/22																												
1922	Cle-A	0	0	—	1	0	0	0	0	0	3	0	1	3	—	—	∞	—	1.000	1.000	99	—	0	-6	-6	0	-0.5	
● ROGER HAMBRIGHT Hambright, Roger Dee b: 3/26/49, Sunnyside, Wash. BR/TR, 5'10", 180 lbs. Deb: 7/19/71																												
1971	NY-A	3	1	.750	18	0	0	0	2	26^2	22	13	5	0	10	14	10.8	4.39	74	.224	.296	1	.500	0	-3	-4	0	-0.5
● JOHN HAMILL Hamill, John Alexander Charles b: 12/18/1860, New York, N.Y. d: 12/6/11, Bristol, R.I. BR/TR, 5'8", 158 lbs. Deb: 5/1/1884																												
1884	Was-a	2	17	.105	19	19	18	1	0	156^2	197	158	8	5	43	50	14.1	4.48	68	.287	.333	7	.099	-3	-21	-27	-1	-2.8
● DAVE HAMILTON Hamilton, David Edward b: 12/13/47, Seattle, Wash. BL/TL, 6', 190 lbs. Deb: 5/29/72																												
1972	*Oak-A	6	6	.500	25	14	1	0	0	101^1	94	34	7	1	31	55	11.2	2.93	97	.249	.307	4	.154	2	2	-1	-0	0.1
1973	Oak-A	6	4	.600	16	11	1	0	0	69^2	74	37	8	1	24	34	12.8	4.39	81	.274	.336	0	—	0	-4	-7	-1	-1.0

YEAR	TM/L	W	L	PCT	G	GS	CG	SH	SV	IP	H	R	HR	HB	BB	SO	RAT	ERA	ERA+	OAV	OOB	BH	AVG	PB	PR	PR+	PD	TPI
1974	Oak-A	7	4	.636	29	18	1	1	0	117	104	45	10	5	48	69	12.1	3.15	105	.241	.324	0	—	0	6	2	-0	0.2
1975	Oak-A	1	2	.333	11	4	0	0	0	35^2	42	19	4	0	18	20	15.1	4.04	90	.290	.368	0	—	0	-1	-2	-0	-0.1
	Chi-A	6	5	.545	30	1	0	0	6	69^2	63	23	4	0	29	51	11.9	2.84	137	.246	.323	0	—	0	7	8	0	1.3
	Yr	7	7	.500	41	5	0	0	6	105^1	105	42	8	0	47	71	13.0	3.25	117	.262	.339	0	—	0	6	6	0	1.2
1976	Chi-A	6	6	.500	45	1	0	0	10	90^1	81	38	4	4	45	62	13.0	3.59	99	.243	.340	0	—	0	-1	-0	-1	-0.1
1977	Chi-A	4	5	.444	55	0	0	0	9	67^1	71	33	6	0	33	45	13.9	3.61	114	.270	.351	0	—	0	3	4	0	0.6
1978	StL-N	0	0	—	13	0	0	0	0	14	16	13	5	0	6	8	14.1	6.43	55	.296	.367	0	.000	-0	-4	-5	0	-0.2
	Pit-N	0	2	.000	16	0	0	0	1	26^1	23	16	2	0	12	15	12.0	3.42	108	.221	.302	0	.000	-1	0	1	-0	0.0
	Yr	0	2	.000	29	0	0	0	1	40^1	39	29	7	0	18	23	12.7	4.46	82	.247	.324	0	.000	-1	-4	-4	-0	-0.2
1979	Oak-A	3	4	.429	40	7	1	0	5	82^2	80	42	5	1	43	52	13.5	3.70	110	.261	.353	0	—	0	5	3	1	0.3
1980	Oak-A	0	3	.000	21	1	0	0	0	30	44	39	6	3	28	23	22.5	11.40	33	.344	.472	0	—	0	-25	-27	-0	-2.3
Total	9	39	41	.488	301	57	4	1	31	704	692	339	61	15	317	434	13.1	3.85	93	.259	.341	4	.121	1	-11	-22	-2	-1.2
● **EARL HAMILTON**	Hamilton, Earl Andrew b: 7/19/1891, Gibson City, Ill. d: 11/17/68, Anaheim, Cal. BL/TL, 5'8", 160 lbs. Deb: 4/14/11																											
1911	StL-A	5	12	.294	32	17	10	1	0	177	191	103	4	4	69	55	13.4	3.97	85	.284	.354	6	.107	-1	-12	-12	1	-1.0
1912	StL-A	11	14	.440	41	26	17	1	2	249^2	228	117	2	9	86	139	11.6	3.24	102	.248	.319	13	.178	-0	2	2	-2	0.1
1913	StL-A	13	12	.520	31	24	19	3	1	217^1	197	95	3	9	83	101	12.0	2.57	114	.241	.318	10	.135	-2	9	9	-1	0.7
1914	StL-A	16	18	.471	44	35	20	5	2	302^1	265	111	5	10	100	111	11.2	2.50	108	.239	.307	15	.176	4	8	7	-4	0.8
1915	StL-A	9	17	.346	35	28	13	1	0	204	203	98	4	12	69	63	12.5	2.87	100	.274	.346	7	.113	-2	2	-0	-2	-0.5
1916	StL-A	0	0	—	1	0	0	0	0	4	4	5	0	0	4	0	18.0	9.00	31	.250	.400	0	—	0	-3	-3	-0	-0.2
	Det-A	1	2	.333	5	5	3	0	0	37^1	34	14	0	4	22	7	14.5	2.65	108	.254	.375	1	.077	-1	1	1	1	0.1
	StL-A	5	7	.417	22	12	3	0	0	91^1	97	44	2	2	26	25	12.3	3.05	90	.284	.339	0	.000	-1	-2	-3	-1	-0.7
	Yr	6	9	.400	28	17	6	0	0	132^2	135	63	2	6	52	32	13.1	3.12	89	.275	.352	1	.027	-2	-4	-5	-1	-0.8
1917	StL-A	0	9	.000	27	8	2	0	1	83	86	46	1	2	41	19	14.0	3.14	83	.274	.361	7	.368	3	-4	-5	-1	-0.3
1918	Pit-N	6	0	1.000	6	6	6	1	0	54	47	7	0	0	13	20	10.0	0.83	344	.242	.290	6	.286	1	12	12	-0	1.6
1919	Pit-N	8	11	.421	28	19	9	1	1	160^1	167	73	3	5	49	39	12.4	3.31	91	.280	.340	7	.135	-2	-7	-5	2	-0.7
1920	Pit-N	10	13	.435	39	23	12	0	3	230^1	223	99	2	2	69	74	11.5	3.24	99	.258	.314	10	.149	-3	-3	-1	-0	-0.4
1921	Pit-N	13	15	.464	35	30	12	2	0	225	237	103	5	8	58	59	12.1	3.36	114	.272	.323	12	.160	-0	11	12	4	1.6
1922	Pit-N	11	7	.611	33	14	9	1	2	160	183	84	6	1	40	34	12.6	3.99	102	.296	.339	9	.155	-2	2	1	-1	-0.1
1923	Pit-N	7	9	.438	28	15	5	0	1	141	148	67	6	1	42	42	12.2	3.77	106	.271	.324	9	.173	-2	4	4	2	0.4
1924	Phi-N	0	1	.000	3	0	0	0	0	6	9	9	0	1	2	2	18.0	10.50	42	.391	.462	0	.000	-0	-4	-3	0	-0.5
Total	14	115	147	.439	410	262	140	16	13	2342^2	2319	1075	43	70	773	790	12.1	3.16	102	.264	.329	112	.153	-9	13	15	-4	0.9
● **JACK HAMILTON**	Hamilton, Jack Edwin b: 12/25/38, Burlington, Iowa BR/TR, 6', 200 lbs. Deb: 4/13/62																											
1962	Phi-N	9	12	.429	41	26	4	1	2	182	185	115	18	5	107	101	14.7	5.09	76	.268	.370	3	.056	-4	-23	-25	2	-2.7
1963	Phi-N	2	1	.667	19	1	0	0	1	30	22	19	3	0	17	23	11.7	5.40	60	.200	.307	0	.000	-0	-7	-7	1	-0.7
1964	Det-A	0	1	.000	5	1	0	0	0	15	24	17	2	1	8	5	19.8	8.40	44	.364	.440	0	.000	-0	-8	-8	1	-0.5
1965	Det-A	1	1	.500	4	1	0	0	0	4^1	6	7	1	0	4	3	20.8	14.54	24	.316	.435	0	—	0	-5	-5	0	-1.0
1966	NY-N	6	13	.316	57	13	3	1	13	148^2	138	89	13	5	88	93	14.0	3.93	92	.248	.356	5	.132	-1	-5	-5	1	-0.7
1967	NY-N	2	0	1.000	17	1	0	0	1	31^1	24	15	2	1	16	22	11.8	3.73	91	.205	.306	1	.200	1	-1	-1	-0	0.0
	Cal-A	9	6	.600	26	20	0	0	0	119^1	104	47	6	1	63	74	12.7	3.24	97	.239	.337	6	.158	-0	-0	-1	-0	-0.2
1968	Cal-A	3	1	.750	21	2	1	0	2	38	34	15	0	0	15	18	11.6	3.32	88	.246	.320	1	.143	-0	-1	-2	-0	-0.2
1969	Cle-A	0	2	.000	20	0	0	0	1	30^2	37	17	2	0	23	13	17.6	4.40	86	.316	.429	0	.000	-0	-3	-2	-0	-0.2
	Chi-A	0	3	.000	8	0	0	0	0	12^1	23	16	1	0	7	5	21.9	11.68	33	.411	.476	0	—	0	-11	-10	-0	-1.8
	Yr	0	5	.000	28	0	0	0	1	43	60	33	3	0	30	18	18.8	6.49	59	.347	.443	0	.000	-0	-14	-12	-0	-2.0
Total	8	32	40	.444	218	65	8	2	20	611^2	597	357	48	13	348	357	14.1	4.53	78	.259	.359	16	.107	-6	-66	-68	4	-8.0
● **JEFF HAMILTON**	Hamilton, Jeffrey Robert b: 3/19/64, Flint, Mich. BR/TR, 6'3", 207 lbs. Deb: 6/28/86 ◆																											
1989	LA-N	0	1	.000	1	0	0	0	0	1^2	2	1	0	0	1	2	16.2	5.40	63	.286	.375	134	.245	0	-0	-0	0	-0.1
● **JOEY HAMILTON**	Hamilton, Johns Joseph b: 9/9/70, Statesboro, Ga. BR/TR, 6'4", 220 lbs. Deb: 5/24/94																											
1994	SD-N	9	6	.600	16	16	1	1	0	108^2	98	40	7	6	29	61	11.0	2.98	138	.241	.302	0	.000	-4	15	14	0	1.4
1995	SD-N	6	9	.400	31	30	2	2	0	204^1	189	89	17	11	56	123	11.3	3.08	131	.246	.307	7	.108	-2	25	22	-1	1.2
1996	*SD-N	15	9	.625	34	33	3	1	0	211^2	206	100	19	9	83	184	12.7	4.17	95	.256	.332	11	.162	1	1	-5	0	-0.3
1997	SD-N	12	7	.632	31	29	1	0	0	192^2	199	100	22	12	69	124	13.1	4.25	91	.271	.344	7	.130	1	-1	-9	-2	-0.8
1998	*SD-N	13	13	.500	34	34	0	0	0	217^1	220	113	15	8	106	147	13.8	4.27	92	.267	.356	10	.141	0	-1	-9	-0	-0.9
1999	Tor-A	7	8	.467	22	18	0	0	0	98	118	73	13	3	39	56	14.7	6.52	76	.298	.365	0	.000	-0	-18	-17	-1	-2.2
2000	Tor-A	2	1	.667	6	6	0	0	0	33	28	13	3	2	12	15	11.5	3.55	141	.233	.313	0	—	0	5	5	-0	0.4
Total	7	64	53	.547	174	166	7	4	0	1065^2	1058	528	96	51	394	710	12.7	4.07	100	.261	.334	35	.117	-3	27	2	-4	-1.2
● **STEVE HAMILTON**	Hamilton, Steve Absher b: 11/30/35, Columbia, Ky. d: 12/2/97, Morehead, Ky. BL/TL, 6'7", 195 lbs. Deb: 4/23/61 C																											
1961	Cle-A	0	0	—	2	0	0	0	0	3	2	1	0	0	3	4	15.0	3.00	131	.200	.385	1	1.000	0	0	0	0	0.1
1962	Was-A	3	8	.273	41	10	1	0	2	107^1	103	51	10	3	39	83	12.2	3.77	107	.248	.317	2	.077	-1	2	3	1	0.3
1963	Was-A	0	1	.000	3	0	0	0	0	2	5	3	0	0	2	1	31.5	13.50	27	.556	.636	0	—	0	-2	-2	0	-0.4
	*NY-A	5	1	.833	34	0	0	0	5	62^1	49	19	3	1	24	63	10.7	2.60	135	.220	.298	4	.286	1	7	7	1	1.0
	Yr	5	2	.714	37	0	0	0	5	64^1	54	22	3	1	26	64	11.3	2.94	120	.233	.313	4	.286	1	5	4	1	0.6
1964	*NY-A	7	2	.778	30	3	1	0	3	60^1	55	24	6	0	15	49	10.4	3.28	110	.246	.293	4	.200	1	2	2	0	0.4
1965	NY-A	3	1	.750	46	1	0	0	5	58^1	47	12	2	0	16	51	9.7	1.39	245	.214	.267	1	.167	0	13	13	-2	1.0
1966	NY-A	8	3	.727	44	3	1	1	3	90	69	32	8	3	22	57	9.4	3.00	111	.218	.276	1	.053	-2	4	3	-1	0.2
1967	NY-A	2	4	.333	44	0	0	0	4	62	57	25	7	1	23	55	11.8	3.48	90	.250	.321	1	.111	-0	-2	-3	0	-0.3
1968	NY-A	2	2	.500	40	0	0	0	11	50^2	37	13	0	1	13	42	9.1	2.13	136	.211	.270	0	.000	0	5	4	0	0.7
1969	NY-A	3	4	.429	38	0	0	0	2	57	39	22	7	0	21	39	9.5	3.32	105	.194	.270	0	.000	-1	2	1	-1	0.0
1970	NY-A	4	3	.571	35	0	0	0	3	45^1	36	16	3	1	16	33	10.5	2.78	127	.222	.296	0	.000	-1	5	4	0	0.6
	Chi-A	0	0	—	3	0	0	0	0	3	4	2	0	0	1	3	15.0	6.00	65	.333	.385	0	—	0	-1	-1	0	0.0
	Yr	4	3	.571	38	0	0	0	3	48^1	40	18	3	1	17	36	10.8	2.98	119	.230	.302	0	.000	-1	4	3	1	0.6
1971	*SF-N	2	2	.500	39	0	0	0	4	44^2	29	15	4	1	11	38	8.3	3.02	113	.186	.244	0	.000	-0	2	2	-0	0.1
1972	Chi-N	1	0	1.000	22	0	0	0	0	17	24	9	1	1	8	13	17.5	4.76	80	.333	.407	0	.000	-0	-2	-2	-0	-0.1
Total	12	40	31	.563	421	17	3	1	42	663	556	244	51	12	214	531	10.6	3.05	114	.229	.295	14	.125	-2	36	33	-1	3.6
● **LUKE HAMLIN**	Hamlin, Luke Daniel "Hot Potato" b: 7/3/04, Ferris Center, Mich. d: 2/18/78, Clare, Mich. BL/TR, 6'2", 168 lbs. Deb: 9/18/33																											
1933	Det-A	1	0	1.000	3	3	0	0	0	16^2	20	11	3	0	10	10	16.2	4.86	89	.294	.385	2	.400	1	-1	-1	-1	0.0
1934	Det-A	2	3	.400	20	5	1	0	1	75^1	87	48	11	0	44	30	15.7	5.38	82	.289	.380	6	.231	-0	-7	-8	-0	-0.5
1937	Bro-N	11	13	.458	39	25	11	1	1	185^2	183	96	4	0	48	93	11.2	3.59	113	.252	.298	11	.186	-1	7	9	-3	0.7
1938	Bro-N	12	15	.444	44	30	10	3	6	237^1	243	111	14	2	65	97	11.8	3.68	106	.263	.313	11	.141	-3	3	6	-4	0.0
1939	Bro-N	20	13	.606	40	36	19	2	0	269^2	255	115	27	0	54	88	10.3	3.64	111	.248	.285	13	.126	-5	8	11	-5	0.3
1940	Bro-N	9	8	.529	33	25	9	2	0	182^1	183	77	17	2	34	91	10.8	3.06	131	.256	.292	5	.086	-4	16	18	-4	0.7
1941	Bro-N	8	8	.500	30	20	5	1	1	136	139	75	14	2	41	58	12.0	4.24	87	.261	.316	6	.146	-1	-9	-9	-2	-1.2
1942	Pit-N	4	4	.500	23	14	6	1	0	112	128	58	3	1	19	38	11.9	3.94	86	.281	.312	9	.243	1	-8	-7	-2	-0.6
1944	Phi-A	6	12	.333	29	23	9	2	0	190	204	94	13	3	38	58	11.6	3.74	93	.271	.309	13	.232	3	-7	-5	-5	-0.7
Total	9	73	76	.490	261	181	70	12	9	1405	1442	685	106	10	353	563	11.6	3.77	103	.262	.308	76	.164	-8	2	15	-25	-1.3
● **PETE HAMM**	Hamm, Peter Whitfield b: 9/20/47, Buffalo, N.Y. BR/TR, 6'5", 210 lbs. Deb: 7/29/70																											
1970	Min-A	0	2	.000	10	0	0	0	0	16^1	17	10	3	0	7	3	13.2	5.51	68	.262	.333	0	.000	-0	-3	-3	-1	-0.4
1971	Min-A	2	4	.333	13	8	1	0	0	44	55	33	7	1	18	16	15.1	6.75	53	.309	.376	3	.273	1	-16	-15	0	-1.8
Total	2	2	6	.250	23	8	1	0	0	60^1	72	43	10	1	25	19	14.6	6.41	56	.296	.364	3	.250	1	-19	-18	-0	-2.2
● **ATLEE HAMMAKER**	Hammaker, Charlton Atlee b: 1/24/58, Carmel, Cal. BB/TL, 6'3", 200 lbs. Deb: 8/13/81																											
1981	KC-A	1	3	.250	10	6	0	0	0	39	44	24	2	0	12	11	12.9	5.54	65	.286	.337	0	—	0	-8	-8	-1	-0.8
1982	SF-N	12	8	.600	29	27	4	1	0	175	189	86	16	2	28	102	11.3	4.11	88	.278	.309	4	.068	-4	-10	-10	1	-1.3
1983	SF-N★	10	9	.526	23	23	8	3	0	172^1	147	57	9	3	32	127	**9.5**	**2.25**	**158**	.228	**.267**	6	.102	-1	27	25	1	2.8
1984	SF-N	2	0	1.000	6	6	0	0	0	33	32	10	2	0	9	24	11.2	2.18	161	.256	.306	2	.182	1	5	5	0	0.4

YEAR	TM/L	W	L	PCT	G	GS	CG	SH	SV	IP	H	R	HR	HB	BB	SO	RAT	ERA	ERA+	OAV	OOB	BH	AVG	PB	PR	PR+	PD	TPI
1985	SF-N	5	12	.294	29	29	1	1	0	170^2	161	81	17	0	47	100	11.0	3.74	92	.247	.298	4	.085	-3	-3	-6	1	-0.7
1987	*SF-N	10	10	.500	31	27	2	0	0	168^1	159	73	22	3	57	107	11.7	3.58	107	.248	.313	7	.123	-1	9	5	-1	0.4
1988	SF-N	9	9	.500	43	17	3	1	5	144^2	136	68	11	3	41	65	11.2	3.73	88	.248	.304	4	.121	-0	-4	-8	2	-0.8
1989	*SF-N	6	6	.500	28	9	0	0	0	76^2	78	34	5	1	23	30	12.0	3.76	90	.271	.327	7	.368	2	-2	-3	-1	-0.3
1990	SF-N	4	5	.444	25	6	0	0	0	67^1	69	33	7	0	21	28	12.0	4.28	85	.273	.328	1	.059	-1	-4	-5	-1	-0.7
	SD-N	0	4	.000	9	1	0	0	0	19^1	16	11	1	0	6	16	10.2	4.66	82	.213	.272	1	.500	0	-2	-2	-0	-0.3
	Yr	4	9	.308	34	7	0	0	0	86^2	85	44	8	0	27	44	11.6	4.36	85	.259	.315	2	.105	-0	-5	-7	-1	-1.0
1991	SD-N	0	1	.000	1	1	0	0	0	4^2	8	7	0	0	3	1	21.2	5.79	66	.364	.440	0	.000	-0	-1	-1	0	-0.2
1994	Chi-A	0	0	—	2	0	0	0	0	1^1	1	0	0	0	0	1	6.8	0.00	—	.200	.200	0	—	0	1	1	0	0.0
1995	Chi-A	0	0	—	13	0	0	0	0	6^1	11	9	2	1	8	3	28.4	12.79	35	.393	.541	0	—	0	-6	-6	0	-0.3
Total	12	59	67	.468	249	152	18	6	5	1078^2	1051	493	94	13	287	615	11.3	3.66	97	.255	.306	36	.118	-7	2	-13	1	-1.8
● **CHRIS HAMMOND**	Hammond, Christopher Andrew b: 1/21/66, Atlanta, Ga. BL/TL, 6′1″, 195 lbs. Deb: 7/16/90 F																											
1990	Cin-N	0	2	.000	3	3	0	0	0	11^1	13	9	2	0	12	4	19.9	6.35	62	.302	.455	0	.000	-0	-3	-3	0	-0.5
1991	Cin-N	7	7	.500	20	18	0	0	0	99^2	92	51	4	2	48	50	12.8	4.06	94	.250	.340	12	.353	5	-4	-3	0	0.2
1992	Cin-N	7	10	.412	28	26	0	0	0	147^1	149	75	13	3	55	79	12.6	4.21	86	.266	.334	6	.136	2	-12	-10	-0	-0.9
1993	Fla-N	11	12	.478	32	32	1	0	0	191	207	106	18	1	66	108	12.9	4.66	93	.277	.337	12	.190	4	-13	-7	0	-0.3
1994	Fla-N	4	4	.500	13	13	1	1	0	73^1	79	30	5	1	23	40	12.6	3.07	143	.281	.338	3	.136	0	9	10	-2	0.9
1995	Fla-N	9	6	.600	25	24	3	2	0	161	157	73	17	9	47	126	11.9	3.80	111	.256	.318	13	.271	6	7	7	-0	1.2
1996	Fla-N	5	8	.385	38	9	0	0	0	81	104	65	14	4	27	50	15.0	6.56	62	.315	.374	1	.067	-1	-21	-23	0	-3.2
1997	Bos-A	3	4	.429	29	8	0	0	1	65^1	81	45	5	2	27	48	15.2	5.92	78	.310	.379	0	—	0	-10	-9	0	-0.8
1998	Fla-N	0	2	.000	3	3	0	0	0	13^2	20	11	3	1	8	8	19.1	6.59	62	.357	.446	1	.200	0	-4	-4	-1	-0.5
Total	9	46	55	.455	191	136	5	3	1	843^2	902	465	81	23	313	513	13.2	4.54	91	.277	.344	48	.205	16	-50	-39	-2	-3.9
● **GRANNY HAMNER**	Hamner, Granville Wilbur b: 4/26/27, Richmond, Va. d: 9/12/93, Philadelphia, Pa. BR/TR, 5′10″, 163 lbs. Deb: 9/14/44 F♦																											
1956	Phi-N	0	1	.000	3	1	0	0	0	8^1	10	4	0	0	2	4	13.0	4.32	86	.294	.333	90	.224	1	-1	-1	-0	-0.1
1957	Phi-N	0	0	—	1	0	0	0	0	1	1	0	0	0	0	1	9.0	0.00	—	.250	.250	114	.227	0	0	0	0	0.0
1962	KC-A	0	1	.000	3	0	0	0	0	4	10	6	0	0	6	0	36.0	9.00	47	.476	.593	0	—	0	-2	-2	0	-0.4
Total	3	0	2	.000	7	1	0	0	0	13^1	21	10	0	0	8	5	19.6	5.40	72	.356	.433	1529	.262	1	-2	-2	-0	-0.5
● **RALPH HAMNER**	Hamner, Ralph Conant "Bruz" b: 9/12/16, Gibsland, La. BR/TR, 6′3″, 165 lbs. Deb: 4/28/46																											
1946	Chi-A	2	7	.222	25	7	1	0	1	71^1	80	47	2	5	39	29	15.6	4.42	77	.276	.371	3	.167	0	-7	-8	-1	-1.0
1947	Chi-N	1	2	.333	3	3	2	0	0	25	24	10	0	0	16	14	14.4	2.52	157	.267	.377	1	.125	-0	4	4	-1	0.4
1948	Chi-N	5	9	.357	27	17	5	0	0	111^1	110	63	12	5	69	53	14.9	4.69	83	.259	.369	6	.182	1	-9	-10	2	-0.9
1949	Chi-N	0	2	.000	6	1	0	0	0	12^1	22	13	1	1	8	3	22.6	8.76	46	.407	.492	0	.000	-0	-6	-6	1	-0.8
Total	4	8	20	.286	61	28	8	0	1	220	236	133	15	11	132	99	15.5	4.58	82	.275	.378	10	.164	0	-18	-21	1	-2.3
● **MIKE HAMPTON**	Hampton, Michael William b: 9/9/72, Brooksville, Fla. BR/TL, 5′10″, 180 lbs. Deb: 4/17/93																											
1993	Sea-A	1	3	.250	13	3	0	0	1	17	28	20	3	0	17	8	23.8	9.53	46	.368	.484	0	—	0	-10	-9	-0	-1.7
1994	Hou-N	2	1	.667	44	0	0	0	0	41^1	46	19	4	2	16	24	13.9	3.70	107	.282	.354	0	.000	-0	2	1	2	0.2
1995	Hou-N	9	8	.529	24	24	0	0	0	150^2	141	73	13	4	49	115	11.6	3.35	116	.247	.310	7	.146	1	14	10	0	1.1
1996	Hou-N	10	10	.500	27	27	2	1	0	160^1	175	79	12	3	49	101	12.7	3.59	108	.280	.335	10	.238	4	11	5	2	1.2
1997	*Hou-N	15	10	.600	34	34	7	2	0	223	217	105	16	2	77	139	11.9	3.83	104	.257	.321	10	.137	1	9	4	5	1.0
1998	*Hou-N	11	7	.611	32	32	1	1	0	211^2	227	92	18	5	81	137	13.3	3.36	121	.278	.347	16	.262	7	21	17	3	2.4
1999	*Hou-N★	**22**	4	**.846**	34	34	3	2	0	239	206	86	12	5	101	177	11.7	2.90	152	.241	.325	23	.311	11	44	42	2	**5.5**
2000	*NY-N	15	10	.600	33	33	3	1	0	217^2	194	89	10	8	99	151	12.4	3.14	141	.241	.330	20	.274	6	36	32	3	4.2
Total	8	85	53	.616	241	187	16	7	1	1260^2	1234	563	88	29	489	852	12.5	3.44	120	.259	.332	86	.231	28	128	102	17	13.9
● **LEE HANCOCK**	Hancock, Leland David b: 6/27/67, N.Hollywood, Cal. BL/TL, 6′4″, 215 lbs. Deb: 9/3/95																											
1995	Pit-N	0	0	—	11	0	0	0	0	14	10	3	0	0	2	6	7.7	1.93	223	.192	.222	0	—	0	4	4	-0	0.2
1996	Pit-N	0	0	—	13	0	0	0	0	18^1	21	18	5	2	10	13	16.2	6.38	68	.276	.375	0	—	0	-4	-4	1	-0.1
Total	2	0	0	—	24	0	0	0	0	32^1	31	21	5	2	12	19	12.5	4.45	97	.242	.317	0	—	0	-1	-0	1	0.1
● **GARRY HANCOCK**	Hancock, Ronald Garry b: 1/23/54, Tampa, Fla. BL/TL, 6′, 175 lbs. Deb: 7/16/78 ♦																											
1984	Oak-A	0	0	—	1	0	0	0	0	1^1	0	0	0	0	0	0	0.0	0.00	—	.000	.000	13	.217	0	1	1	0	0.0
● **RYAN HANCOCK**	Hancock, Ryan Lee b: 11/11/71, Santa Clara, Cal. BR/TR, 6′2″, 220 lbs. Deb: 6/8/96																											
1996	Cal-A	4	1	.800	11	4	0	0	0	27^2	34	23	2	2	17	19	17.2	7.48	67	.306	.408	1	1.000	0	-8	-8	0	-1.0
● **RICH HAND**	Hand, Richard Allen b: 7/10/48, Bellevue, Wash. BR/TR, 6′1″, 195 lbs. Deb: 4/9/70																											
1970	Cle-A	6	13	.316	35	25	3	1	3	159^2	132	71	27	4	69	110	11.6	3.83	103	.228	.314	6	.146	-1	-2	2	0	0.1
1971	Cle-A	2	6	.250	15	12	0	0	0	60^2	74	43	6	4	38	26	17.2	5.79	66	.311	.414	2	.125	-0	-16	-12	-1	-1.6
1972	Tex-A	10	14	.417	30	28	2	1	0	170^2	139	66	12	3	103	109	12.9	3.32	91	.226	.340	8	.154	1	-5	-6	-0	-0.7
1973	Tex-A	2	3	.400	8	7	1	0	0	41^2	49	29	2	2	19	14	15.1	5.40	69	.290	.368	0	—	0	-7	-8	-1	-0.9
	Cal-A	4	3	.571	16	6	0	0	0	54^2	58	29	5	1	21	19	13.2	3.62	98	.274	.342	0	—	0	1	-0	1	0.0
	Yr	6	6	.500	24	13	1	0	0	96^1	107	58	7	3	40	33	14.0	4.39	83	.281	.354	0	—	0	-6	-9	0	-0.9
Total	4	24	39	.381	104	78	6	2	3	487^1	452	238	52	14	250	278	13.2	4.01	88	.249	.345	16	.147	-0	-29	-25	-1	-3.1
● **JIM HANDIBOE**	Handiboe, James Edward "Nick" b: 7/17/1866, Columbus, Ohio d: 11/8/42, Columbus, Ohio BR/TR, 5′11″, 160 lbs. Deb: 5/28/1886																											
1886	Pit-a	7	7	.500	14	14	12	1	0	114	82	65	1	12	33	83	10.0	3.32	102	.195	.273	5	.114	-2	2	1	-0	-0.2
● **VERN HANDRAHAN**	Handrahan, James Vernon b: 11/27/38, Charlottetown, P.E.I., Canada BL/TR, 6′2″, 185 lbs. Deb: 4/14/64																											
1964	KC-A	0	1	.000	18	1	0	0	0	35^2	33	24	9	2	25	18	15.1	6.06	63	.252	.380	2	.222	0	-10	-8	0	-0.4
1966	KC-A	0	1	.000	16	1	0	0	1	25^1	20	12	5	1	15	18	12.8	4.26	80	.227	.346	0	.000	-0	-2	-2	0	-0.1
Total	2	0	2	.000	34	2	0	0	1	61	53	36	14	3	40	36	14.2	5.31	69	.242	.366	2	.167	-0	-12	-11	0	-0.5
● **BILL HANDS**	Hands, William Alfred b: 5/6/40, Hackensack, N.J. BR/TR, 6′2″, 185 lbs. Deb: 6/3/65																											
1965	SF-N	0	2	.000	4	2	0	0	0	6	13	11	0	0	6	5	28.5	16.50	22	.433	.528	0	.000	-0	-9	-8	0	-1.4
1966	Chi-N	8	13	.381	41	26	0	0	2	159	168	91	17	5	59	93	13.1	4.58	80	.272	.340	2	.041	-3	-17	-16	1	-2.1
1967	Chi-N	7	8	.467	49	11	3	1	6	150	134	46	9	2	48	84	11.0	2.46	144	.239	.301	4	.105	-1	15	17	-0	1.8
1968	Chi-N	16	10	.615	38	34	11	4	0	258^2	221	91	26	6	36	148	9.2	2.89	109	.231	.264	5	.061	-5	3	7	-0	0.2
1969	Chi-N	20	14	.588	41	41	18	3	0	300	268	102	21	6	73	181	10.4	2.49	162	.237	.287	9	.092	-5	37	46	1	4.8
1970	Chi-N	18	15	.545	39	38	12	2	1	265	278	121	20	4	76	170	12.2	3.70	122	.269	.322	10	.133	1	10	21	1	2.7
1971	Chi-N	12	18	.400	36	35	14	1	0	242^1	248	112	27	2	50	128	11.1	3.42	115	.260	.298	6	.083	-3	1	12	-0	1.1
1972	Chi-N	11	8	.579	32	28	6	3	0	189	168	73	12	2	47	96	10.3	3.00	127	.237	.286	1	.018	-4	10	15	-2	0.9
1973	Min-A	7	10	.412	39	15	3	1	2	142	138	69	14	2	41	78	11.5	3.49	114	.252	.307	0	—	0	5	7	-1	0.8
1974	Min-A	4	5	.444	35	10	0	0	3	115^1	130	57	9	4	25	74	12.4	4.45	84	.284	.327	0	—	0	-11	-9	-1	-0.8
	Tex-A	2	0	1.000	2	2	1	1	0	14	11	3	0	0	3	4	9.0	1.93	185	.208	.250	0	—	0	3	3	0	0.4
	Yr	6	5	.545	37	12	1	1	3	129^1	141	60	9	4	28	78	12.0	4.18	89	.276	.319	0	—	0	-8	-6	-1	-0.4
1975	Tex-A	6	7	.462	18	18	4	1	0	109^2	118	58	12	3	28	67	12.2	4.02	94	.271	.319	0	—	0	-3	-3	0	-0.3
Total	11	111	110	.502	374	260	72	17	14	1951	1895	834	167	36	492	1128	11.2	3.35	114	.253	.302	37	.078	-20	45	97	-0	8.1
● **CHRIS HANEY**	Haney, Christopher Deane b: 11/16/68, Baltimore, Md. BL/TL, 6′3″, 195 lbs. Deb: 6/21/91 F																											
1991	Mon-N	3	7	.300	16	16	0	0	0	84^2	94	49	6	1	43	51	14.7	4.04	90	.280	.363	2	.074	-2	-3	-4	1	-0.5
1992	Mon-N	2	3	.400	9	6	1	1	0	38	40	25	6	4	10	27	12.8	5.45	64	.270	.333	2	.222	0	-8	-8	-0	-1.0
	KC-A	2	3	.400	7	7	1	1	0	42	35	18	5	0	16	27	10.9	3.86	105	.226	.298	0	—	0	0	1	-1	0.0
1993	KC-A	9	9	.500	23	23	1	1	0	124	141	87	13	3	53	65	14.3	6.02	76	.286	.359	0	—	0	-23	-19	0	-2.2
1994	KC-A	2	2	.500	6	6	0	0	0	28^1	36	25	2	1	11	18	15.2	7.31	69	.333	.400	0	—	0	-8	-7	1	-0.7
1995	KC-A	3	4	.429	16	13	1	0	0	81^1	78	35	7	2	33	31	12.5	3.65	131	.262	.339	0	—	0	10	10	0	0.8
1996	KC-A	10	14	.417	35	35	4	1	0	228	267	136	29	6	51	115	12.8	4.70	107	.291	.332	0	—	0	8	8	-2	0.5
1997	KC-A	1	2	.333	8	3	0	0	0	24^2	29	16	1	2	5	16	13.1	4.38	108	.290	.336	0	—	0	1	1	0	0.1
1998	KC-A	6	6	.500	33	12	0	0	0	97^1	125	78	18	5	36	51	15.3	7.03	69	.316	.380	0	—	0	-26	-23	1	-2.2

YEAR	TM/L	W	L	PCT	G	GS	CG	SH	SV	IP	H	R	HR	HB	BB	SO	RAT	ERA	ERA+	OAV	OOB	BH	AVG	PB	PR	PR+	PD	TPI
	Chi-N	0	0	—	5	0	0	0	0	5	3	4	2	0	1	4	7.2	7.20	61	.167	.211	0	—	0	-2	-1	0	-0.1
1999	Cle-A	0	2	.000	13	4	0	0	0	40^1	43	22	3	3	16	22	13.8	4.69	108	.270	.348	0	—	0	1	2	-0	0.0
2000	Cle-A	0	0	—	1	0	0	0	0	1	1	1	0	0	1	0	18.0	9.00	56	.333	.500	0	—	0	-0	-0	0	0.0
Total	10	38	52	.422	172	125	8	4	0	794^2	892	496	92	27	276	427	13.5	5.11	90	.285	.348	4	.111	-1	-51	-43	0	-5.3

● DON HANKINS Hankins, Donald Wayne b: 2/9/02, Pendleton, Ind. d: 5/16/63, Winston-Salem, N.C BR/TR, 6'3", 183 lbs. Deb: 4/23/27

YEAR	TM/L	W	L	PCT	G	GS	CG	SH	SV	IP	H	R	HR	HB	BB	SO	RAT	ERA	ERA+	OAV	OOB	BH	AVG	PB	PR	PR+	PD	TPI
1927	Det-A	2	1	.667	20	1	0	0	2	42^2	67	39	1	0	13	10	16.9	6.33	67	.383	.426	1	.143	-1	-10	-10	0	-0.7

● FRANK HANKINSON Hankinson, Frank Edward b: 4/29/1856, New York, N.Y. d: 4/5/11, Palisades Park, N.J BR/TR, 5'11", 168 lbs. Deb: 5/1/1878 ◆

YEAR	TM/L	W	L	PCT	G	GS	CG	SH	SV	IP	H	R	HR	HB	BB	SO	RAT	ERA	ERA+	OAV	OOB	BH	AVG	PB	PR	PR+	PD	TPI
1878	Chi-N	0	1	.000	1	1	1	0	0	9	11	9	0		0	4	11.0	6.00	40	.282	.282	64	.267	0	-4	-3	-0	-0.3
1879	Chi-N	15	10	.600	26	25	25	2	0	230^2	248	134	0		27	69	10.7	2.50	103	.255	.275	31	.181	-4	-0	2	4	0.2
1880	Cle-N	1	1	.500	4	2	2	0	1	25	20	10	0		3	8	8.3	1.08	218	.215	.240	55	.209	-0	4	4	1	0.4
1885	NY-a	0	0	—	1	0	0	0	0	2	2	1	1	0	1	0	13.5	4.50	66	.500	.600	81	.224	0	-0	-0	-0	0.0
Total	4	16	12	.571	32	28	28	2	1	266^2	281	154	1	0	31	81	10.5	2.50	102	.253	.274	785	.237	-4	-0	1	5	0.3

● JIM HANLEY Hanley, James Patrick b: 10/13/1885, Providence, R.I. d: 5/1/61, Elmhurst, N.Y. BR/TL, 5'11", 165 lbs. Deb: 7/3/13

YEAR	TM/L	W	L	PCT	G	GS	CG	SH	SV	IP	H	R	HR	HB	BB	SO	RAT	ERA	ERA+	OAV	OOB	BH	AVG	PB	PR	PR+	PD	TPI
1913	NY-A	0	0	—	1	0	0	0	0	4	5	3	0	0	4	2	20.3	6.75	44	.313	.450	0	.000	-0	-2	-2	0	-0.1

● PRESTON HANNA Hanna, Preston Lee b: 9/10/54, Pensacola, Fla. BR/TR, 6'1", 195 lbs. Deb: 9/13/75

YEAR	TM/L	W	L	PCT	G	GS	CG	SH	SV	IP	H	R	HR	HB	BB	SO	RAT	ERA	ERA+	OAV	OOB	BH	AVG	PB	PR	PR+	PD	TPI
1975	Atl-N	0	0	—	4	0	0	0	0	5^2	7	1	0	2	5	2	22.2	1.59	238	.304	.467	0	—	0	1	1	-0	0.0
1976	Atl-N	0	0	—	5	0	0	0	0	8	11	5	0	0	4	3	16.9	4.50	84	.333	.405	0	.000	-0	-1	-1	-0	-0.1
1977	Atl-N	2	6	.250	17	9	1	0	1	60	69	40	6	2	34	37	15.8	4.95	90	.285	.378	1	.071	-0	-7	-3	1	-0.3
1978	Atl-N	7	13	.350	29	28	0	0	0	140^1	132	89	10	3	93	90	14.6	5.13	79	.251	.367	9	.184	1	-24	-15	-0	-1.9
1979	Atl-N	1	1	.500	6	4	0	0	0	24^1	27	11	1	0	15	15	15.5	2.96	137	.284	.382	0	.000	-0	2	3	1	0.3
1980	Atl-N	2	0	1.000	32	2	0	0	0	79^1	63	28	3	3	44	35	12.5	3.18	118	.224	.335	2	.143	0	4	5	-1	0.2
1981	Atl-N	2	1	.667	20	1	0	0	0	35^1	45	27	2	0	23	22	17.3	6.37	56	.341	.439	1	.250	0	-11	-11	2	-0.6
1982	Atl-N	3	0	1.000	20	1	0	0	0	36	36	15	3	0	28	17	16.0	3.75	100	.277	.405	2	.400	1	-1	-0	-1	0.0
	Oak-A	0	4	.000	23	2	1	0	0	48^1	54	34	3	1	33	32	16.4	5.59	70	.287	.396	0	—	0	-8	-9	-0	-0.7
Total	8	17	25	.405	156	47	2	0	1	437^1	444	250	28	11	279	253	15.1	4.61	86	.269	.378	15	.161	1	-45	-29	1	-3.1

● GERRY HANNAHS Hannahs, Gerald Ellis b: 3/6/53, Binghamton, N.Y. BL/TL, 6'3", 210 lbs. Deb: 9/8/76

YEAR	TM/L	W	L	PCT	G	GS	CG	SH	SV	IP	H	R	HR	HB	BB	SO	RAT	ERA	ERA+	OAV	OOB	BH	AVG	PB	PR	PR+	PD	TPI
1976	Mon-N	2	0	1.000	3	3	0	0	0	16	20	14	2	0	12	10	18.0	6.75	55	.323	.432	3	.375	1	-6	-5	-0	-0.5
1977	Mon-N	1	5	.167	8	7	0	0	0	37	43	27	7	0	17	21	14.6	4.86	78	.291	.364	0	.000	-0	-4	-4	-0	-0.7
1978	LA-N	0	0	—	1	0	0	0	0	2	3	2	0	0	0	5	13.5	9.00	39	.333	.333	0	—	0	-1	-1	0	-0.1
1979	LA-N	0	2	.000	4	2	0	0	1	16	10	8	2	0	13	6	12.9	3.38	108	.175	.329	1	.250	0	1	0	0	0.1
Total	4	3	7	.300	16	12	0	0	1	71	76	51	11	0	42	42	15.0	5.07	74	.275	.371	4	.211	1	-10	-10	-1	-1.2

● JIM HANNAN Hannan, James John b: 1/7/40, Jersey City, N.J. BR/TR, 6'3", 205 lbs. Deb: 4/17/62

YEAR	TM/L	W	L	PCT	G	GS	CG	SH	SV	IP	H	R	HR	HB	BB	SO	RAT	ERA	ERA+	OAV	OOB	BH	AVG	PB	PR	PR+	PD	TPI
1962	Was-A	2	4	.333	42	3	0	0	4	68	56	27	6	0	49	39	13.9	3.31	122	.230	.360	1	.091	-1	5	5	0	0.4
1963	Was-A	2	2	.500	13	2	0	0	0	27^2	23	18	2	0	17	14	13.0	4.88	76	.228	.339	0	.000	-0	-4	-4	0	-0.5
1964	Was-A	4	7	.364	49	7	0	0	3	106	108	60	13	0	45	67	13.0	4.16	89	.266	.339	3	.150	-1	-6	-5	-1	-0.7
1965	Was-A	1	1	.500	4	1	1	1	0	14^2	18	8	0	1	6	5	15.3	4.91	71	.340	.417	0	.000	-0	-2	-2	-1	-0.4
1966	Was-A	3	9	.250	30	18	2	0	0	114	125	58	9	3	59	68	14.8	4.26	81	.288	.377	2	.067	-2	-10	-10	-0	-1.2
1967	Was-A	1	1	.500	8	2	0	0	0	21^2	28	14	3	1	7	14	15.0	5.40	59	.315	.371	0	.000	-0	-5	-6	0	-0.5
1968	Was-A	10	6	.625	25	22	4	1	0	140^1	147	53	4	4	50	75	12.9	3.01	97	.272	.338	3	.064	-2	-1	-2	-0	-0.5
1969	Was-A	7	6	.538	35	28	1	1	0	158^1	138	73	17	2	91	72	13.1	3.64	95	.238	.343	6	.115	-2	-0	-3	-1	-0.5
1970	Was-A	9	11	.450	42	17	1	1	0	128	119	65	17	1	54	61	12.2	4.01	89	.250	.328	4	.129	-0	-4	-7	1	-0.9
1971	Det-A	1	0	1.000	7	0	0	0	0	11	7	4	1	1	7	6	12.3	3.27	110	.189	.333	0	.000	-0	0	0	1	0.1
	Mil-A	1	1	.500	21	1	0	0	0	32^1	38	23	7	1	21	17	16.7	5.01	69	.295	.397	0	.000	-0	-6	-6	-0	-0.4
	Yr	2	1	.667	28	1	0	0	0	43^1	45	27	8	2	28	23	15.6	4.57	77	.271	.383	0	.000	-1	-5	-5	0	-0.3
Total	10	41	48	.461	276	101	9	4	7	822	807	403	79	14	406	438	13.4	3.88	89	.261	.350	19	.091	-9	-33	-38	-1	-5.1

● LOY HANNING Hanning, Loy Vernon b: 10/18/17, Bunker, Mo. d: 6/24/86, Anaconda, Mo. BR/TR, 6'2", 175 lbs. Deb: 9/20/39

YEAR	TM/L	W	L	PCT	G	GS	CG	SH	SV	IP	H	R	HR	HB	BB	SO	RAT	ERA	ERA+	OAV	OOB	BH	AVG	PB	PR	PR+	PD	TPI
1939	StL-A	0	1	.000	4	1	0	0	0	10	6	5	1	0	4	8	9.0	3.60	135	.158	.238	0	.000	-0	1	1	0	0.1
1942	StL-A	1	1	.500	11	0	0	0	0	17^1	26	15	2	1	12	9	20.3	7.79	48	.356	.453	1	.250	0	-8	-8	1	-0.7
Total	2	1	2	.333	15	1	0	0	0	27^1	32	20	3	1	16	17	16.1	6.26	66	.288	.383	1	.200	-0	-7	-6	1	-0.6

● GREG HANSELL Hansell, Gregory Michael b: 3/12/71, Bellflower, Cal. BR/TR, 6'5", 215 lbs. Deb: 4/28/95

YEAR	TM/L	W	L	PCT	G	GS	CG	SH	SV	IP	H	R	HR	HB	BB	SO	RAT	ERA	ERA+	OAV	OOB	BH	AVG	PB	PR	PR+	PD	TPI
1995	LA-N	0	1	.000	20	0	0	0	0	19^1	29	17	5	2	6	13	17.2	7.45	51	.349	.407	0	—	0	-7	-9	-0	-0.4
1996	Min-A	3	0	1.000	50	0	0	0	3	74^1	83	48	14	2	31	46	14.0	5.69	90	.285	.358	0	—	0	-6	-5	-1	-0.3
1997	Mil-A	0	0	—	3	0	0	0	0	4^2	5	5	1	1	1	5	13.5	9.64	48	.263	.333	0	—	0	-3	-3	-0	-0.1
1999	Pit-N	1	3	.250	33	0	0	0	0	39^1	42	20	5	3	11	34	12.8	3.89	118	.280	.341	0	.000	-0	3	3	0	0.2
Total	4	4	4	.500	106	0	0	0	3	137^2	159	90	25	8	49	98	14.1	5.56	85	.293	.360	0	.000	-0	-12	-12	-1	-0.6

● ANDY HANSEN Hansen, Andrew Viggo "Swede" b: 11/12/24, Lake Worth, Fla. BR/TR, 6'3", 190 lbs. Deb: 6/30/44

YEAR	TM/L	W	L	PCT	G	GS	CG	SH	SV	IP	H	R	HR	HB	BB	SO	RAT	ERA	ERA+	OAV	OOB	BH	AVG	PB	PR	PR+	PD	TPI
1944	NY-N	3	3	.500	23	4	0	0	1	52^2	63	39	3	3	32	15	16.7	6.49	56	.301	.402	2	.167	0	-17	-16	1	-1.6
1945	NY-N	4	3	.571	23	13	4	0	3	92^2	98	52	7	2	28	37	12.4	4.66	84	.273	.329	0	.000	-3	-9	-8	2	-0.7
1947	NY-N	1	5	.167	27	9	1	0	0	82^1	78	45	8	0	38	18	12.7	4.37	93	.248	.330	4	.190	-0	-3	-3	1	-0.1
1948	NY-N	5	3	.625	36	9	3	0	1	100	96	40	4	0	36	27	11.9	2.97	133	.255	.320	1	.050	-0	11	11	-1	0.7
1949	NY-N	2	6	.250	33	2	0	0	1	66^1	58	35	7	0	28	26	11.7	4.61	86	.234	.312	0	.000	-1	-4	-5	0	-0.5
1950	NY-N	0	1	.000	31	1	0	0	3	57	64	37	8	1	26	19	14.4	5.53	74	.279	.355	0	.000	-1	-9	-9	-0	-0.6
1951	Phi-N	3	1	.750	24	0	0	0	0	39	34	14	4	1	7	11	9.7	2.54	152	.228	.268	1	.333	1	6	6	1	0.7
1952	Phi-N	5	6	.455	43	0	0	0	4	77^1	76	36	6	3	27	18	12.3	3.26	112	.259	.328	2	.182	1	4	3	1	0.7
1953	Phi-N	0	2	.000	30	1	0	0	3	51^1	60	30	6	1	24	17	14.9	4.03	104	.296	.373	2	.286	0	1	1	1	0.1
Total	9	23	30	.434	270	39	8	0	16	618^2	627	328	53	11	246	188	12.9	4.22	93	.263	.335	12	.102	-3	-19	-20	5	-1.3

● SNIPE HANSEN Hansen, Roy Emil Frederick b: 2/21/07, Chicago, Ill. d: 9/11/78, Chicago, Ill. BB/TL (BL 1930), 6'3", 195 lbs. Deb: 7/5/30

YEAR	TM/L	W	L	PCT	G	GS	CG	SH	SV	IP	H	R	HR	HB	BB	SO	RAT	ERA	ERA+	OAV	OOB	BH	AVG	PB	PR	PR+	PD	TPI
1930	Phi-N	0	7	.000	22	9	1	0	0	84^1	123	76	8	2	38	25	17.4	6.72	81	.364	.431	3	.111	-2	-16	-11	-1	-0.9
1932	Phi-N	10	10	.500	39	23	5	0	2	191	215	103	13	6	51	56	12.8	3.72	118	.278	.328	8	.127	-4	3	13	-2	0.7
1933	Phi-N	6	14	.300	32	22	8	0	1	168^1	199	103	12	4	30	47	12.5	4.44	86	.294	.328	9	.155	-3	-21	-10	-1	-1.5
1934	Phi-N	6	12	.333	50	16	5	2	3	151	194	112	15	3	61	40	15.4	5.42	87	.307	.371	10	.233	-0	-23	-10	1	-1.0
1935	Phi-N	0	1	.000	2	1	0	0	0	4^1	8	7	0	0	5	0	27.0	12.46	36	.421	.542	0	.000	-0	-4	-3	0	-0.6
	StL-A	0	1	.000	10	0	0	0	0	26^2	44	28	2	1	9	8	18.2	8.78	55	.364	.412	1	.143	-1	-13	-11	-1	-0.6
Total	5	22	45	.328	155	71	19	2	6	625^2	783	429	50	16	194	176	14.3	5.01	90	.306	.358	31	.155	-10	-73	-31	-3	-3.9

● ROY HANSEN Hansen, Roy Inglof "Ing" b: 3/6/1898, Beloit, Wis. d: 2/9/77, Beloit, Wis. BR/TR, 6', 165 lbs. Deb: 5/28/18

YEAR	TM/L	W	L	PCT	G	GS	CG	SH	SV	IP	H	R	HR	HB	BB	SO	RAT	ERA	ERA+	OAV	OOB	BH	AVG	PB	PR	PR+	PD	TPI
1918	Was-A	1	0	1.000	5	0	0	0	0	9	10	4	0	1	3	2	14.0	3.00	91	.278	.350	0	—	0	-0	-0	0	0.0

● FRANK HANSFORD Hansford, Frank Cicero b: 12/26/1874, DuQuoin, Ill. d: 12/14/52, Fort Scott, Kan. TL, 6', 180 lbs. Deb: 6/9/1898

YEAR	TM/L	W	L	PCT	G	GS	CG	SH	SV	IP	H	R	HR	HB	BB	SO	RAT	ERA	ERA+	OAV	OOB	BH	AVG	PB	PR	PR+	PD	TPI
1898	Bro-N	0	0	—	1	0	0	0	0	7	10	4	0	0	5	0	19.3	3.86	93	.333	.429	0	.000	-1	-0	-0	-0	-0.1

● DON HANSKI Hanski, Donald Thomas (b: Donald Thomas Hanyzewski) b: 2/27/16, LaPorte, Ind. d: 9/2/57, Worth, Ill. BL/TL, 5'11", 180 lbs. Deb: 5/6/43 ◆

YEAR	TM/L	W	L	PCT	G	GS	CG	SH	SV	IP	H	R	HR	HB	BB	SO	RAT	ERA	ERA+	OAV	OOB	BH	AVG	PB	PR	PR+	PD	TPI
1943	Chi-A	0	0	—	1	0	0	0	0	1	1	0	0	0	1	0	18.0	0.00	—	.333	.500	5	.238	0	0	0	-0	0.0
1944	Chi-A	0	0	—	2	0	0	0	0	3	5	4	0	0	2	0	21.0	12.00	29	.357	.438	0	.000	-0	-3	-3	-0	-0.2
Total	2	0	0	—	3	0	0	0	0	4	6	4	0	0	3	0	20.3	9.00	38	.353	.450	5	.227	-0	-2	-2	-0	-0.2

● OLLIE HANSON Hanson, Earl Sylvester b: 1/19/1896, Holbrook, Mass. d: 8/19/51, Clifton, N.J. BR/TR, 5'11", 178 lbs. Deb: 4/27/21

YEAR	TM/L	W	L	PCT	G	GS	CG	SH	SV	IP	H	R	HR	HB	BB	SO	RAT	ERA	ERA+	OAV	OOB	BH	AVG	PB	PR	PR+	PD	TPI
1921	Chi-N	0	2	.000	2	2	1	0	0	9	9	7	0	1	6	2	16.0	7.00	55	.265	.390	0	.000	-0	-3	-3	0	-0.6

● ERIK HANSON Hanson, Erik Brian b: 5/18/65, Kinnelon, N.J. BR/TR, 6'6", 210 lbs. Deb: 9/5/88

YEAR	TM/L	W	L	PCT	G	GS	CG	SH	SV	IP	H	R	HR	HB	BB	SO	RAT	ERA	ERA+	OAV	OOB	BH	AVG	PB	PR	PR+	PD	TPI
1988	Sea-A	2	3	.400	6	6	0	0	0	41^2	35	17	4	1	12	36	10.4	3.24	129	.230	.291	0	—	0	3	4	-0	0.4
1989	Sea-A	9	5	.643	17	17	1	0	0	113^1	103	44	7	5	32	75	11.1	3.18	127	.243	.304	0	—	0	9	10	0	1.3
1990	Sea-A	18	9	.667	33	33	5	1	0	236	205	88	15	2	68	211	10.5	3.24	122	.232	.289	0	—	0	18	19	-0	2.0

YEAR	TM/L	W	L	PCT	G	GS	CG	SH	SV	IP	H	R	HR	HB	BB	SO	RAT	ERA	ERA+	OAV	OOB	BH	AVG	PB	PR	PR+	PD	TPI
1991	Sea-A	8	8	.500	27	27	2	1	0	174^2	182	82	16	2	56	143	12.4	3.81	108	.269	.327	0	—	0	6	6	-1	0.4
1992	Sea-A	8	17	.320	31	30	6	1	0	186^2	209	110	14	7	57	112	13.2	4.82	83	.287	.345	0	—	0	-18	-17	0	-2.0
1993	Sea-A	11	12	.478	31	30	7	0	0	215	215	91	17	5	60	163	11.7	3.47	127	.263	.317	0	—	0	21	22	1	2.2
1994	Cin-N	5	5	.500	22	21	0	0	0	122^2	137	60	10	3	23	101	12.0	4.11	101	.283	.320	6	.154	-1	1	0	0	0.0
1995	*Bos-A☆	15	5	.750	29	29	1	1	0	186^2	187	94	17	1	59	139	11.9	4.24	115	.258	.314	0	—	0	10	13	-0	1.1
1996	Tor-A	13	17	.433	35	35	4	1	0	214^2	243	143	26	2	102	156	14.5	5.41	93	.289	.367	0	—	0	-10	-10	-3	-1.3
1997	Tor-A	0	0	—	3	2	0	0	0	15	15	13	3	0	6	18	12.6	7.80	59	.254	.323	0	—	0	-5	-5	-0	-0.3
1998	Tor-A	0	3	.000	11	8	0	0	0	49	73	34	10	1	29	21	18.9	6.24	75	.348	.429	0	—	0	-9	-9	1	-0.4
Total	11	89	84	.514	245	238	26	5	0	1555^1	1604	776	139	29	504	1175	12.4	4.15	105	.267	.327	6	.154	-1	26	35	-3	3.4

● ED HANYZEWSKI Hanyzewski, Edward Michael b: 9/18/20, Union Mills, Ind. d: 10/8/91, Fargo, N.D. BR/TR, 6'1", 200 lbs. Deb: 5/12/42

YEAR	TM/L	W	L	PCT	G	GS	CG	SH	SV	IP	H	R	HR	HB	BB	SO	RAT	ERA	ERA+	OAV	OOB	BH	AVG	PB	PR	PR+	PD	TPI
1942	Chi-N	1	1	.500	6	1	0	0	0	19	17	9	2	0	8	6	11.8	3.79	84	.254	.333	1	.200	-0	-1	-1	0	-0.1
1943	Chi-N	8	7	.533	33	16	3	0	0	130	120	54	2	2	45	55	11.6	2.56	130	.243	.309	2	.049	-4	12	11	2	1.0
1944	Chi-N	2	5	.286	14	7	3	0	0	58^1	61	33	6	1	20	19	12.7	4.47	79	.261	.322	1	.059	-1	-6	-6	3	-0.5
1945	Chi-N	0	0	—	2	1	0	0	0	4^2	7	4	1	0	1	0	15.4	5.79	63	.350	.381	0	.000	0	-1	-1	0	0.0
1946	Chi-N	1	0	1.000	3	0	0	0	0	6	8	3	0	1	5	1	21.0	4.50	74	.348	.483	0	.000	-0	-1	-1	0	-0.1
Total	5	12	13	.480	58	25	6	0	0	218	213	103	11	4	79	81	12.2	3.30	102	.254	.321	4	.062	-5	4	2	5	0.3

● MEL HARDER Harder, Melvin Leroy "Chief" b: 10/15/09, Beemer, Neb. BR/TR, 6'1", 195 lbs. Deb: 4/24/28 MC

YEAR	TM/L	W	L	PCT	G	GS	CG	SH	SV	IP	H	R	HR	HB	BB	SO	RAT	ERA	ERA+	OAV	OOB	BH	AVG	PB	PR	PR+	PD	TPI
1928	Cle-A	0	2	.000	23	1	0	0	1	49	64	42	4	0	32	15	17.6	6.61	63	.335	.430	0	.000	-1	-14	-13	-1	-0.8
1929	Cle-A	1	0	1.000	11	0	0	0	0	17^2	24	15	2	3	5	4	16.3	5.60	79	.333	.400	0	.000	-0	-3	-2	-0	-0.2
1930	Cle-A	11	10	.524	36	19	7	0	2	175^1	205	108	9	4	68	45	14.2	4.21	115	.295	.361	9	.143	-4	9	12	-1	0.7
1931	Cle-A	13	14	.481	40	24	9	0	1	194	229	119	8	6	72	63	14.2	4.36	106	.289	.352	19	.253	1	0	5	0	0.8
1932	Cle-A	15	13	.536	39	32	17	1	0	254^2	277	125	9	3	68	90	12.3	3.75	127	.272	.319	17	.181	-0	21	27	3	2.8
1933	Cle-A	15	17	.469	43	31	14	2	4	253	254	113	10	3	67	81	11.5	2.95	**151**	.259	.309	16	.190	-1	**37**	**40**	8	**5.5**
1934	Cle-A★	20	12	.625	44	29	17	**6**	4	255^1	246	97	6	7	81	91	11.8	2.61	**174**	.254	.316	14	.161	-1	54	54	2	**6.4**
1935	Cle-A★	22	11	.667	42	35	17	4	2	287^1	313	120	6	0	53	95	11.5	3.29	137	.275	.307	21	.206	-1	37	38	5	4.3
1936	Cle-A★	15	15	.500	36	30	13	0	1	224^2	294	155	13	6	71	84	14.9	5.17	97	.313	.365	11	.138	-4	-3	-3	0	-0.7
1937	Cle-A★	15	12	.556	38	30	13	0	2	233^2	269	127	9	4	86	95	13.8	4.28	108	.288	.350	15	.174	-1	9	9	2	0.9
1938	Cle-A	17	10	.630	38	29	15	2	4	240	257	115	16	5	62	102	12.2	3.83	121	.271	.319	10	.114	-5	26	22	2	1.9
1939	Cle-A	15	9	.625	29	26	12	1	1	208	213	89	15	3	64	67	12.1	3.50	126	.269	.326	10	.139	-2	26	22	-2	1.9
1940	Cle-A	12	11	.522	31	25	5	0	0	186^1	200	96	16	5	59	76	12.8	4.06	104	.278	.337	11	.177	-1	7	3	1	0.4
1941	Cle-A	5	4	.556	15	10	1	0	1	68^2	76	43	8	2	37	21	15.1	5.24	75	.279	.370	2	.080	-2	-8	-10	1	-1.3
1942	Cle-A	13	14	.481	29	29	13	4	0	198^2	179	83	8	3	82	74	12.0	3.44	100	.240	.317	8	.119	-3	5	0	1	-0.1
1943	Cle-A	8	7	.533	19	18	6	1	0	135^1	126	57	7	1	61	40	12.5	3.06	102	.254	.337	10	.213	2	4	1	-0	0.2
1944	Cle-A	12	10	.545	30	27	12	2	0	196^1	211	95	5	3	69	64	13.0	3.71	89	.278	.341	16	.216	1	-6	-9	-1	-1.0
1945	Cle-A	3	7	.300	11	11	2	0	0	76	93	37	3	0	23	16	13.7	3.67	88	.303	.352	2	.080	-2	-3	-4	1	-0.6
1946	Cle-A	5	4	.556	13	12	4	1	0	92^1	85	37	4	0	31	21	11.3	3.41	97	.249	.311	3	.086	-2	1	-1	-2	-0.5
1947	Cle-A	6	4	.600	15	15	4	1	0	80	91	41	3	1	27	17	13.4	4.50	77	.289	.347	5	.179	0	-7	-10	-1	-1.2
Total	20	223	186	.545	582	433	181	25	23	3426^1	3706	1714	161	59	1118	1161	12.8	3.80	113	.276	.334	199	.165	-27	190	183	18	19.4

● JIM HARDIN Hardin, James Warren b: 8/6/43, Morris Chapel, Tenn. d: 3/9/91, Key West, Fla. BR/TR, 6', 175 lbs. Deb: 6/23/67

YEAR	TM/L	W	L	PCT	G	GS	CG	SH	SV	IP	H	R	HR	HB	BB	SO	RAT	ERA	ERA+	OAV	OOB	BH	AVG	PB	PR	PR+	PD	TPI
1967	Bal-A	8	3	.727	19	14	5	2	0	111	85	30	5	3	27	64	9.3	2.27	139	.211	.266	5	.135	-0	12	11	-1	1.0
1968	Bal-A	18	13	.581	35	35	16	2	0	244	188	79	20	10	70	160	9.9	2.51	117	.212	.277	7	.085	-3	13	12	-0	1.1
1969	Bal-A	6	7	.462	30	20	3	1	1	137^2	128	62	18	6	43	64	11.6	3.60	99	.248	.313	7	.156	2	0	-0	-1	0.0
1970	Bal-A	6	5	.545	36	19	3	2	1	145^1	150	60	13	1	26	78	11.0	3.53	103	.267	.301	3	.067	-1	3	2	-2	-0.2
1971	Bal-A	0	0	—	6	0	0	0	0	5^2	12	5	0	0	3	3	23.8	4.76	70	.480	.536	0	—	0	-1	-1	0	0.0
	NY-A	0	2	.000	12	3	0	0	0	28^1	35	19	3	1	9	14	14.3	5.08	64	.313	.369	0	.000	-0	-5	-6	-0	-0.5
	Yr	0	2	.000	18	3	0	0	0	34	47	24	3	1	12	17	15.9	5.03	65	.343	.400	0	.000	-0	-6	-7	-0	-0.5
1972	Atl-N	5	2	.714	26	9	1	0	2	79^2	93	47	11	2	24	25	13.4	4.41	86	.287	.340	2	.095	1	-8	-5	-1	-0.4
Total	6	43	32	.573	164	100	28	7	4	751^2	691	302	70	23	202	408	11.0	3.18	104	.244	.300	24	.103	-3	14	12	-5	1.0

● CHARLIE HARDING Harding, Charles Harold "Slim" b: 1/3/1891, Nashville, Tenn. d: 10/30/71, Bold Spring, Tenn BR/TR, 6'2.5", 172 lbs. Deb: 9/18/13

YEAR	TM/L	W	L	PCT	G	GS	CG	SH	SV	IP	H	R	HR	HB	BB	SO	RAT	ERA	ERA+	OAV	OOB	BH	AVG	PB	PR	PR+	PD	TPI
1913	Det-A	0	0	—	1	0	0	0	0	2	3	1	0	0	1	0	18.0	4.50	65	.375	.444	0		0	-0	-0	0	0.0

● ALEX HARDY Hardy, David Alexander "Dooney" b: 1877, Toronto, Ont., Canada d: 4/22/40, Toronto, Ont., Can. TL, Deb: 9/4/02

YEAR	TM/L	W	L	PCT	G	GS	CG	SH	SV	IP	H	R	HR	HB	BB	SO	RAT	ERA	ERA+	OAV	OOB	BH	AVG	PB	PR	PR+	PD	TPI
1902	Chi-N	2	2	.500	4	4	4	1	0	35	29	19	0	0	12	12	10.5	3.60	75	.227	.293	3	.214	0	-3	-4	-1	-0.4
1903	Chi-N	1	1	.500	3	3	1	0	0	12^2	21	10	0	1	7	4	20.6	6.39	49	.375	.453	1	.167	0	-4	-5	0	-0.5
Total	2	3	3	.500	7	7	5	1	0	47^2	50	29	0	1	19	16	13.2	4.34	65	.272	.343	4	.200	1	-8	-8	-0	-0.9

● RED HARDY Hardy, Francis Joseph b: 1/6/23, Marmarth, N.Dak. BR/TR, 5'11", 175 lbs. Deb: 6/20/51

YEAR	TM/L	W	L	PCT	G	GS	CG	SH	SV	IP	H	R	HR	HB	BB	SO	RAT	ERA	ERA+	OAV	OOB	BH	AVG	PB	PR	PR+	PD	TPI
1951	NY-N	0	0	—	2	0	0	0	0	1^1	4	1	0	1	1	0	40.5	6.75	58	.571	.667	0	—	0	-0	-0	0	0.0

● HARRY HARDY Hardy, Harry b: 11/5/1875, Steubenville, Ohio d: 9/4/43, Steubenville, Ohio BL/TL, 5'6", 155 lbs. Deb: 9/26/05

YEAR	TM/L	W	L	PCT	G	GS	CG	SH	SV	IP	H	R	HR	HB	BB	SO	RAT	ERA	ERA+	OAV	OOB	BH	AVG	PB	PR	PR+	PD	TPI
1905	Was-A	1	1	.500	3	2	2	0	0	24	20	9	0	0	6	10	9.8	1.88	141	.227	.277	1	.111	-1	2	2	-1	-0.1
1906	Was-A	0	3	.000	5	3	2	0	0	20	35	27	0	0	12	4	21.1	9.00	29	.385	.456	0	.000	-1	-14	-14	1	-1.7
Total	2	1	4	.200	8	5	4	0	0	44	55	36	0	0	18	14	14.9	5.11	52	.307	.371	1	.067	-2	-12	-12	-0	-1.8

● LARRY HARDY Hardy, Howard Lawrence b: 1/10/48, Goose Creek, Tex. BR/TR, 5'10", 180 lbs. Deb: 4/28/74

YEAR	TM/L	W	L	PCT	G	GS	CG	SH	SV	IP	H	R	HR	HB	BB	SO	RAT	ERA	ERA+	OAV	OOB	BH	AVG	PB	PR	PR+	PD	TPI
1974	SD-N	9	4	.692	76	1	0	0	2	101^2	129	58	9	0	44	57	15.3	4.69	76	.317	.384	0	.000	-1	-12	-13	1	-1.5
1975	SD-N	0	0	—	3	0	0	0	0	2^2	8	6	3	0	2	3	33.8	13.50	26	.500	.556	0	—	0	-3	-3	-0	-0.2
1976	Hou-N	0	0	—	15	0	0	0	3	21^2	34	19	2	0	10	10	18.3	7.06	45	.362	.423	0	.000	-0	-9	-10	0	-0.5
Total	3	9	4	.692	94	1	0	0	5	126	171	83	14	0	56	70	16.2	5.29	66	.331	.396	0	.000	-1	-23	-26	1	-2.2

● JACK HARDY Hardy, John Graydon b: 10/8/59, St.Petersburg, Fla. BR/TR, 6'2", 175 lbs. Deb: 5/23/89

YEAR	TM/L	W	L	PCT	G	GS	CG	SH	SV	IP	H	R	HR	HB	BB	SO	RAT	ERA	ERA+	OAV	OOB	BH	AVG	PB	PR	PR+	PD	TPI
1989	Chi-A	0	0	—	5	0	0	0	0	12^1	14	9	1	1	5	4	14.6	6.57	58	.286	.364	0	—	0	-4	-4	1	-0.1

● STEVE HARGAN Hargan, Steven Lowell b: 9/8/42, Ft.Wayne, Ind. BR/TR, 6'3", 180 lbs. Deb: 8/3/65

YEAR	TM/L	W	L	PCT	G	GS	CG	SH	SV	IP	H	R	HR	HB	BB	SO	RAT	ERA	ERA+	OAV	OOB	BH	AVG	PB	PR	PR+	PD	TPI
1965	Cle-A	4	3	.571	17	8	1	0	2	60^1	55	26	2	1	28	37	12.5	3.43	101	.246	.332	1	.053	-1	0	0	0	-0.1
1966	Cle-A	13	10	.565	38	21	7	3	0	192	173	60	9	1	45	132	10.3	2.48	138	.241	.286	7	.121	-2	20	20	0	2.3
1967	Cle-A☆	14	13	.519	30	29	15	**6**	0	223	180	79	9	3	72	141	10.3	2.62	125	.224	.290	11	.164	1	15	16	1	2.3
1968	Cle-A	8	15	.348	32	27	4	2	0	158^1	139	81	11	5	81	78	12.8	4.15	71	.241	.340	9	.176	1	-21	-21	-2	-3.1
1969	Cle-A	5	14	.263	32	23	1	1	0	143^2	145	95	14	3	81	76	14.3	5.70	66	.265	.363	7	.159	-1	-33	-30	2	-3.4
1970	Cle-A	11	3	.786	23	19	8	1	0	142^2	101	47	14	3	53	72	9.9	2.90	137	.201	.281	5	.111	-2	13	16	1	1.4
1971	Cle-A	1	13	.071	37	16	1	0	1	113^1	138	83	18	6	56	52	15.9	6.19	62	.304	.388	2	.063	-3	-34	-27	-2	-3.5
1972	Cle-A	0	3	.000	12	1	0	0	0	20	23	16	1	0	15	10	17.1	5.85	55	.291	.404	0	.000	-0	-6	-6	0	-0.8
1974	Tex-A	12	9	.571	37	27	8	2	0	186^2	202	103	15	5	48	98	12.3	3.95	90	.275	.324	0	—	0	-7	-8	2	-0.7
1975	Tex-A	9	10	.474	33	26	8	1	0	189^1	203	96	17	6	62	93	12.9	3.80	99	.275	.336	0	—	0	-0	-1	2	0.1
1976	Tex-A	8	8	.500	35	8	2	1	1	124^1	127	63	8	3	38	63	12.2	3.62	99	.261	.318	0	—	0	-1	-0	-0	-0.1
1977	Tor-A	1	3	.250	6	5	1	0	0	29^1	36	17	2	0	14	11	15.3	5.22	81	.308	.382	0	—	0	-4	-3	0	-0.3
	Tex-A	1	0	1.000	6	0	0	0	0	12^1	22	13	2	0	5	10	19.7	8.76	47	.393	.443	0	—	0	-6	-6	-0	-0.5
	Yr	2	3	.400	12	5	1	0	0	41^2	58	30	4	0	19	21	16.6	6.26	67	.335	.401	0	—	0	-10	-9	0	-0.8
	Atl-N	0	3	.000	16	5	0	0	0	36^2	49	31	3	0	16	18	16.0	6.87	65	.325	.389	0	.000	-1	-12	-9	1	-0.6
Total	12	87	107	.448	354	215	56	17	4	1632	1593	810	125	36	614	891	12.4	3.92	91	.257	.328	42	.129	-7	-76	-62	6	-7.0

● ALAN HARGESHEIMER Hargesheimer, Alan Robert b: 11/21/54, Chicago, Ill. BR/TR, 6'3", 195 lbs. Deb: 7/14/80

YEAR	TM/L	W	L	PCT	G	GS	CG	SH	SV	IP	H	R	HR	HB	BB	SO	RAT	ERA	ERA+	OAV	OOB	BH	AVG	PB	PR	PR+	PD	TPI
1980	SF-N	4	6	.400	15	13	0	0	0	75	82	38	3	0	32	40	13.7	4.32	82	.285	.356	4	.182	1	-6	-7	-1	-0.8
1981	SF-N	1	2	.333	6	3	0	0	0	18^2	20	9	1	1	9	6	14.5	4.34	79	.299	.390	1	.200	0	-2	-2	0	-0.2
1983	Chi-N	0	0	—	5	0	0	0	0	4	6	4	0	0	2	5	18.0	9.00	42	.375	.444	0	—	0	-2	-2	-0	-0.1
1986	KC-A	0	1	.000	5	1	0	0	0	13	18	9	1	1	7	4	18.0	6.23	68	.340	.426	0	—	0	-3	-3	-0	-0.2
Total	4	5	9	.357	31	17	0	0	0	110^2	126	60	5	2	50	55	14.5	4.72	77	.297	.374	5	.185	1	-13	-14	-1	-1.3

YEAR	TM/L	W	L	PCT	G	GS	CG	SH	SV	IP	H	R	HR	HB	BB	SO	RAT	ERA	ERA+	OAV	OOB	BH	AVG	PB	PR	PR+	PD	TPI
● TIM HARIKKALA	Harikkala, Timothy Allan b: 7/15/71, W.Palm Beach, Fla. BR/TR, 6'2", 185 lbs. Deb: 5/27/95																											
1995	Sea-A	0	0	—	1	0	0	0	0	3^1	7	6	1	0	1	1	21.6	16.20	29	.412	.444	0	—	0	-4	-4	-0	-0.2
1996	Sea-A	0	1	.000	1	1	0	0	0	4^1	4	6	1	1	2	1	14.5	12.46	40	.250	.368	0	—	0	-4	-4	-0	-0.5
1999	Bos-A	1	1	.500	7	0	0	0	0	13	15	9	0	1	6	7	15.2	6.23	80	.306	.393	0	—	0	-2	-2	0	-0.2
Total	3	1	2	.333	9	1	0	0	0	20^2	26	21	2	2	9	9	16.1	9.15	54	.317	.398	0	—	0	-10	-10	0	-0.9
● MIKE HARKEY	Harkey, Michael Anthony b: 10/25/66, San Diego, Cal. BR/TR, 6'5", 220 lbs. Deb: 9/5/88																											
1988	Chi-N	0	3	.000	5	5	0	0	0	34^2	33	14	0	2	15	18	13.0	2.60	139	.248	.333	1	.091	-1	3	4	-1	0.2
1990	Chi-N	12	6	.667	27	27	2	1	0	173^2	153	71	14	7	59	94	11.3	3.26	125	.234	.305	14	.250	3	10	15	-1	1.7
1991	Chi-N	0	2	.000	4	4	0	0	0	18^2	21	11	3	0	6	15	13.0	5.30	73	.273	.325	2	.400	1	-3	-3	0	-0.2
1992	Chi-N	4	0	1.000	7	7	0	0	0	38	34	13	4	1	15	21	11.8	1.89	190	.243	.321	4	.267	1	7	7	-0	0.9
1993	Chi-N	10	10	.500	28	28	1	0	0	157^1	187	100	17	3	43	67	13.3	5.26	76	.305	.353	5	.093	-2	-21	-22	-1	-2.8
1994	Col-N	1	6	.143	24	13	0	0	0	91^2	125	61	10	1	35	39	15.8	5.79	86	.336	.395	4	.182	-1	-16	-7	1	-0.4
1995	Oak-A	4	6	.400	14	12	0	0	0	66	75	46	12	3	31	28	14.9	6.27	71	.292	.375	0	—	0	-11	-14	1	-1.6
	Cal-A	4	3	.571	12	8	1	0	0	61^1	80	32	12	1	16	28	14.2	4.55	103	.311	.354	0	—	0	1	1	-2	0.0
	Yr	8	9	.471	26	20	1	0	0	127^1	155	78	24	4	47	56	14.6	5.44	84	.302	.365	0	—	0	-10	-13	-1	-1.6
1997	LA-N	1	0	1.000	10	0	0	0	0	14^2	12	8	3	0	5	6	10.4	4.30	90	.211	.274	0	.000	-0	-0	-1	-0	-0.1
Total	8	36	36	.500	131	104	4	1	0	656	720	356	75	18	225	316	13.2	4.49	94	.281	.344	30	.183	1	-31	-18	-4	-2.3
● JOHN HARKINS	Harkins, John Joseph "Pa" b: 4/12/1859, New Brunswick, N.J d: 11/20/40, New Brunswick, N.J BR/TR, 6'1", 205 lbs. Deb: 5/2/1884																											
1884	Cle-N	12	32	.273	46	45	42	3	0	391	399	300	7		108	192	11.7	3.68	86	.249	.297	47	.205	-4	-30	-22	-1	-2.3
1885	Bro-a	14	20	.412	34	34	33	1	0	293	303	224	7	7	56	141	11.2	3.75	88	.250	.287	42	.264	5	-16	-14	4	-0.5
1886	Bro-a	15	16	.484	34	33	33	0	0	292^1	286	203	6	5	114	118	12.5	3.60	97	.244	.313	32	.225	3	-5	-4	2	0.2
1887	Bro-a	10	14	.417	24	24	22	0	0	199	339	184	6	5	77	36	15.6	6.02	72	.366	.369	30	.286	-0	-38	-38	-1	-3.2
1888	Bal-a	0	1	.000	1	1	1	0	0	8	12	12	0	0	3	2	16.9	6.75	44	.333	.385	0	.000	-0	-3	-3	0	-0.3
Total	5	51	83	.381	139	137	131	4	0	1183^1	1339	923	26	17	358	489	12.5	4.09	85	.271	.312	151	.237	4	-93	-79	5	-6.1
● SPEC HARKNESS	Harkness, Frederick Harvey b: 12/13/1887, Los Angeles, Cal. d: 5/16/52, Compton, Cal. BR/TR, 5'11", 180 lbs. Deb: 6/13/10																											
1910	Cle-A	10	7	.588	26	16	6	1	1	136^1	132	61	2	3	55	60	12.5	3.04	85	.268	.345	7	.140	-1	-8	-7	-1	-1.1
1911	Cle-A	2	2	.500	12	6	3	0	0	53^1	62	36	1	0	21	25	14.0	4.22	81	.310	.376	6	.316	1	-5	-5	-2	-0.4
Total	2	12	9	.571	38	22	9	1	1	189^2	194	97	3	3	76	85	13.0	3.37	84	.280	.354	13	.188	-0	-13	-11	-3	-1.5
● DICK HARLEY	Harley, Henry Risk b: 8/18/1874, Springfield, Ohio d: 5/16/61, Springfield, Ohio BR/TR, Deb: 4/15/05																											
1905	Bos-N	2	5	.286	9	4	4	1	0	65^2	72	45	5	1	19	19	12.6	4.66	67	.286	.338	1	.045	-2	-12	-11	2	-1.1
● LARRY HARLOW	Harlow, Larry Duane b: 11/13/51, Colorado Springs, Colo. BL/TL, 6'2", 185 lbs. Deb: 9/20/75 ♦																											
1978	Bal-A	0	0	—	1	0	0	0	0	0^2	2	5	1	0	4	1	81.0	67.50	5	.500	.750	112	.243	0	-5	-5	0	-0.2
● BILL HARMAN	Harman, William Bell b: 1/2/19, Bridgewater, Va. BR/TR, 6'4", 200 lbs. Deb: 6/17/41 ♦																											
1941	Phi-N	0	0	—	5	0	0	0	0	13	15	8	0	0	8	3	15.9	4.85	76	.319	.418	1	.071	-0	-2	-2	-0	-0.2
● BOB HARMON	Harmon, Robert Green "Hickory Bob" b: 10/15/1887, Liberal, Mo. d: 11/27/61, Monroe, La. BB/TR, 6', 187 lbs. Deb: 6/23/09																											
1909	StL-N	6	11	.353	21	17	10	0	0	159	155	85	6	4	65	48	12.7	3.68	69	.265	.342	13	.255	4	-19	-21	-0	-1.7
1910	StL-N	13	15	.464	43	33	15	0	2	236	227	128	1	7	133	87	14.0	4.46	67	.258	.360	14	.184	2	-37	-40	2	-3.9
1911	StL-N	23	16	.590	51	41	28	2	4	348	290	155	10	7	181	144	12.4	3.13	108	.235	.336	17	.153	0	11	10	1	1.2
1912	StL-N	18	18	.500	43	34	15	3	0	268	284	156	4	3	116	73	13.5	3.93	87	.281	.357	23	.232	1	-15	-15	4	-1.3
1913	StL-N	8	21	.276	42	27	16	1	2	273^1	291	135	6	6	99	66	13.0	3.92	83	.286	.353	24	.261	5	-22	-21	2	-1.3
1914	Pit-N	13	17	.433	37	30	19	2	3	245	226	84	3	7	55	61	10.6	2.53	105	.252	.300	12	.140	-1	7	3	-1	0.1
1915	Pit-N	16	17	.485	37	32	25	5	1	269^2	242	106	6	3	62	86	10.2	2.50	109	.247	.294	14	.147	1	7	7	3	1.3
1916	Pit-N	8	11	.421	31	17	10	2	0	172^2	175	78	4	1	39	62	11.2	2.81	95	.267	.309	6	.109	-3	-4	-2	3	-0.2
1918	Pit-N	2	7	.222	16	9	5	0	0	82^1	76	30	3	0	12	7	9.6	2.62	109	.254	.283	4	.148	-1	1	2	0	0.2
Total	9	107	133	.446	321	240	143	15	12	2054	1966	957	43	38	762	634	12.1	3.33	90	.260	.331	127	.184	7	-71	-76	14	-5.6
● PETE HARNISCH	Harnisch, Peter Thomas b: 9/23/66, Commack, N.Y. BB/TR, 6', 207 lbs. Deb: 9/13/88																											
1988	Bal-A	0	2	.000	2	2	0	0	0	13	13	8	1	0	9	10	15.2	5.54	71	.260	.373	0	—	0	-2	-2	0	-0.3
1989	Bal-A	5	9	.357	18	17	2	0	0	103^1	97	55	10	5	64	70	14.5	4.62	82	.249	.362	0	—	0	-8	-10	-1	-1.2
1990	Bal-A	11	11	.500	31	31	3	0	0	188^2	189	96	17	1	86	122	13.2	4.34	88	.261	.341	0	—	0	-9	-12	-2	-1.4
1991	Hou-N★	12	9	.571	33	33	4	2	0	216^2	169	71	14	5	83	172	10.7	2.70	130	**.212**	.291	6	.097	-1	24	20	-3	1.5
1992	Hou-N	9	10	.474	34	34	0	0	0	206^2	182	92	18	5	64	164	10.9	3.70	91	.233	.296	11	.164	2	-4	-8	-3	-0.8
1993	Hou-N	16	9	.640	33	33	5	**4**	0	217^2	171	84	20	6	79	185	10.6	2.98	130	**.214**	.290	7	.104	-1	26	23	-4	1.9
1994	Hou-N	8	5	.615	17	17	1	0	0	95	100	59	13	3	39	62	13.5	5.40	73	.269	.343	6	.171	1	-12	-16	-1	-1.8
1995	NY-N	2	8	.200	18	18	0	0	0	110	111	55	13	3	24	82	11.3	3.68	110	.261	.305	3	.091	-2	6	5	-1	0.1
1996	NY-N	8	12	.400	31	31	2	1	0	194^2	195	103	30	7	61	114	12.2	4.21	95	.260	.322	5	.091	-2	0	-4	-3	-0.9
1997	NY-N	0	1	.000	6	5	0	0	0	25^2	35	24	5	1	11	12	16.5	8.06	50	.327	.395	0	.000	-1	-11	-12	0	-0.6
	Mil-A	1	1	.500	4	3	0	0	0	14	13	9	1	0	12	10	16.1	5.14	90	.245	.385	0	—	0	-1	-1	-0	-0.1
1998	Cin-N	14	7	.667	32	32	2	1	0	209	176	79	24	6	64	157	10.6	3.14	136	.228	.293	7	.106	-3	25	26	-1	2.0
1999	Cin-N	16	10	.615	33	33	2	2	0	198^1	190	86	25	5	57	120	11.4	3.68	127	.252	.308	10	.152	1	20	21	-3	2.2
2000	Cin-N	8	6	.571	22	22	3	1	0	131	133	76	23	1	46	71	12.4	4.74	101	.261	.323	8	.186	1	-1	0	-1	0.1
Total	13	110	100	.524	314	311	24	11	0	1923^2	1774	897	214	48	699	1351	11.8	3.84	104	.244	.314	63	.125	-6	51	31	-21	0.7
● JACK HARPER	Harper, Charles William b: 4/2/1878, Galloway, Pa. d: 9/30/50, Jamestown, N.Y. BR/TR, 6', 178 lbs. Deb: 9/18/1899																											
1899	Cle-N	1	4	.200	5	5	5	0	0	37	44	33	3	3	12	14	14.4	3.89	95	.295	.360	2	.182	1	-0	-1	-0	0.0
1900	StL-N	0	1	.000	1	1	0	0	0	3	4	7	0	0	2	0	18.0	12.00	30	.308	.400	0	.000	-0	-3	-3	0	-0.4
1901	StL-N	23	13	.639	39	37	28	1	0	308^2	294	158	7	16	99	128	11.9	3.62	88	.249	.316	20	.172	1	-10	-16	1	-1.4
1902	StL-A	15	11	.577	29	26	20	2	0	222^1	224	131	8	8	81	74	12.7	4.13	85	.262	.332	17	.205	-0	-14	-15	1	-1.4
1903	Cin-N	8	9	.471	17	15	13	0	0	135	143	87	2	10	70	45	14.9	4.33	82	.271	.367	14	.250	2	-16	-11	1	-0.8
1904	Cin-N	23	9	.719	35	35	31	6	0	293^2	262	113	2	9	85	125	10.9	2.30	128	.234	.293	18	.159	-2	14	19	-5	1.2
1905	Cin-N	9	13	.409	26	23	15	1	1	179^1	189	116	2	8	69	70	13.3	3.86	86	.271	.344	10	.167	1	-17	-10	-0	-1.1
1906	Cin-N	1	4	.200	5	5	3	0	0	36^2	38	23	1	2	20	10	14.7	4.17	66	.286	.387	3	.273	1	-6	-6	-1	-0.7
	Chi-N	0	0	—	1	1	0	0	0	1	0	0	0	0	0	0	0.0	0.00	—	.000	.000	0	—	0	0	0	0	0.0
	Yr	1	4	.200	6	6	3	0	0	37^2	38	23	1	2	20	10	14.3	4.06	68	.279	.380	3	.273	1	-6	-5	-1	-0.7
Total	8	80	64	.556	158	148	115	10	1	1216^2	1198	668	25	56	438	466	12.5	3.55	92	.256	.327	84	.186	3	-51	-38	-3	-4.6
● GEORGE HARPER	Harper, George B. b: 8/17/1866, Milwaukee, Wis. d: 12/11/31, Stockton, Cal. BR/TR, 5'10", 165 lbs. Deb: 7/11/1894																											
1894	Phi-N	6	6	.500	12	9	7	0	0	86^1	128	84	3	2	49	24	18.7	5.32	96	.340	.418	6	.150	-4	0	-2	-1	-0.5
1896	Bro-N	4	8	.333	16	11	7	0	0	86	106	72	4	3	39	22	15.5	5.55	74	.300	.375	6	.162	0	-11	-14	1	-1.4
Total	2	10	14	.417	28	20	14	0	0	172^1	234	156	7	5	88	46	17.1	5.43	85	.321	.397	12	.156	-4	-11	-16	0	-1.9
● HARRY HARPER	Harper, Harry Clayton b: 4/24/1895, Hackensack, N.J. d: 4/23/63, New York, N.Y. BL/TL, 6'2", 165 lbs. Deb: 6/27/13																											
1913	Was-A	0	0	—	4	0	0	0	0	12^2	10	11	1	1	5	9	11.4	3.55	83	.204	.291	1	.250	0	-1	-1	0	0.0
1914	Was-A	2	1	.667	23	3	1	0	2	57	45	29	1	5	35	50	13.4	3.47	81	.211	.336	3	.250	0	-5	-4	-1	-0.3
1915	Was-A	4	4	.500	19	10	5	2	2	86^1	66	26	1	1	40	54	11.2	1.77	168	.222	.317	0	.000	-4	11	11	-2	0.5
1916	Was-A	14	10	.583	36	34	13	2	0	249^2	209	82	4	8	101	149	11.5	2.45	114	.235	.319	18	.207	1	10	10	-4	0.5
1917	Was-A	11	12	.478	31	31	10	4	0	179^1	145	85	1	5	106	99	12.8	3.01	87	.230	.345	7	.117	-3	-7	-8	-3	-1.6
1918	Was-A	11	10	.524	35	32	14	3	1	244	182	77	1	8	104	78	10.8	2.18	125	.212	.303	11	.134	-4	16	15	-5	0.3
1919	Was-A	6	21	.222	35	31	8	0	0	208	220	119	3	8	97	87	14.1	3.72	86	.284	.370	11	.169	-2	-11	-12	-1	-1.8
1920	Bos-A	5	14	.263	27	22	11	1	0	162^2	163	73	9	2	66	71	12.8	3.04	120	.275	.349	6	.120	-3	14	11	-3	0.6
1921	*NY-A	4	3	.571	8	7	4	0	0	52^2	52	23	3	2	25	22	13.5	3.76	113	.263	.351	2	.125	-1	3	3	-2	0.0
1923	Bro-N	0	1	.000	1	1	0	0	0	3^2	8	6	2	0	3	4	27.0	14.73	26	.421	.500	0	.000	-0	-4	-5	-0	-0.6
Total	10	57	76	.429	219	171	66	12	5	1256	1100	531	26	40	582	623	12.3	2.87	105	.243	.335	59	.147	-16	26	21	-21	-2.4

YEAR	TM/L	W	L	PCT	G	GS	CG	SH	SV	IP	H	R	HR	HB	BB	SO	RAT	ERA	ERA+	OAV	OOB	BH	AVG	PB	PR	PR+	PD	TPI
● **JACK HARPER**	Harper, John Wesley b: 8/5/1893, Hendricks, W.Va. d: 6/18/27, Halstead, Kan. BR/TR, 5'11", 180 lbs. Deb: 4/17/15																											
1915	Phi-A	0	0	—	3	0	0	0	0	8^{2}	5	4	0	0	1	3	6.2	3.12	94	.161	.188	0	.000	-0	-0	-0	0	0.0
● **TRAVIS HARPER**	Harper, Travis Boyd b: 5/21/76, Harrisonburg, Va. BR/TR, 6'4", 190 lbs. Deb: 8/4/2000																											
2000	TB-A	1	2	.333	6	5	1	1	0	32	30	17	5	1	15	14	12.9	4.78	104	.244	.331	0	—	0	1	1	-0	0.0
● **BILL HARPER**	Harper, William Homer "Blue Sleeve" b: 6/14/1889, Bertrand, Mo. d: 6/17/51, Somerville, Tenn. BB/TR, 6'1", 180 lbs. Deb: 6/10/11																											
1911	StL-A	0	0	—	2	0	0	0	0	8	9	9	0	1	4	6	15.8	6.75	50	.300	.400	0	.000	-0	-3	-3	0	-0.2
● **SLIM HARRELL**	Harrell, Oscar Martin b: 7/31/1890, Grandview, Tex. d: 4/30/71, Hillsboro, Tex. BR/TR, 6'3", 180 lbs. Deb: 6/21/12																											
1912	Phi-A	0	0	—	1	0	0	0	0	3	4	0	0	0	0	1	12.0	0.00	—	.364	.364	0	.000	-0	1	1	-0	0.0
● **RAY HARRELL**	Harrell, Raymond James "Cowboy" b: 2/16/12, Petrolia, Tex. d: 1/28/84, Alexandria, La. BR/TR, 6'1", 185 lbs. Deb: 4/16/35																											
1935	StL-N	1	1	.500	11	1	0	0	0	29^{2}	39	26	4	0	11	13	15.2	6.67	61	.320	.376	0	.000	-1	-9	-8	-0	-0.5
1937	StL-N	3	7	.300	35	15	1	1	1	96^{2}	99	73	7	2	59	41	14.9	5.87	68	.263	.366	1	.045	-2	-21	-20	-1	-2.1
1938	StL-N	2	3	.400	32	3	1	0	2	63	78	37	6	3	29	32	15.7	4.86	81	.308	.386	0	.000	-1	-7	-6	0	-0.6
1939	Chi-N	0	2	.000	4	2	0	0	0	17^{1}	29	16	2	0	6	5	18.2	8.31	47	.387	.432	0	.000	-1	-8	-8	0	-0.8
	Phi-N	3	7	.300	22	10	4	0	0	94^{2}	101	77	6	4	56	35	15.3	5.42	74	.270	.371	3	.115	-1	-16	-15	-3	-1.7
	Yr	3	9	.250	26	12	4	0	0	112	130	93	8	4	62	40	15.8	5.87	68	.290	.381	3	.097	-2	-24	-23	-3	-2.5
1940	Pit-N	0	0	—	3	0	0	0	0	3^{1}	5	5	0	0	2	3	18.9	8.10	47	.333	.412	0	—	0	-2	-2	-0	-0.1
1945	NY-N	0	0	—	12	0	0	0	0	25^{1}	34	22	1	1	14	7	17.4	4.97	79	.343	.430	1	.200	1	-3	-3	0	-0.1
Total	6	9	20	.310	119	31	6	1	3	330	385	256	26	10	177	136	15.6	5.70	70	.293	.381	5	.069	-5	-66	-61	-3	-5.9
● **BILL HARRELSON**	Harrelson, William Charles b: 11/17/45, Tahlequah, Okla. BB/TR, 6'5", 215 lbs. Deb: 7/31/68																											
1968	Cal-A	1	6	.143	10	5	1	0	0	33^{2}	28	23	4	1	26	22	14.7	5.08	57	.226	.364	1	.100	-0	-8	-8	-0	-1.7
● **DENNY HARRIGER**	Harriger, Dennis Scott b: 7/21/69, Kittanning, Pa. BR/TR, 5'11", 185 lbs. Deb: 6/16/98																											
1998	Det-A	0	3	.000	4	2	0	0	0	12	17	12	1	0	8	3	18.8	6.75	70	.327	.417	0	—	0	-3	-3	-0	-0.5
● **ANDY HARRINGTON**	Harrington, Andrew Francis b: 11/13/1888, Wakefield, Mass. d: 11/12/38, Malden, Mass. BR/TR, 6', 193 lbs. Deb: 9/8/13																											
1913	Cin-N	0	0	—	1	0	0	0	0	4	6	5	0	0	1	1	15.8	9.00	36	.353	.389	1	.500	0	-3	-3	-0	-0.1
● **BILL HARRINGTON**	Harrington, William Womble b: 10/3/27, Sanford, N.C. BR/TR, 5'11", 160 lbs. Deb: 4/16/53																											
1953	Phi-A	0	0	—	1	0	0	0	0	2	5	3	0	0	0	0	22.5	13.50	32	.500	.500	0	—	0	-2	-2	-0	-0.1
1955	KC-A	3	3	.500	34	1	0	0	2	76^{2}	69	41	6	2	41	26	13.1	4.11	102	.246	.347	2	.118	-1	-1	1	-1	-0.1
1956	KC-A	2	2	.500	23	1	0	0	1	37^{2}	40	27	3	0	26	14	15.8	6.45	67	.274	.384	0	.000	-1	-10	-9	-0	-0.9
Total	3	5	5	.500	58	2	0	0	3	116^{1}	114	71	9	2	67	40	14.2	5.03	84	.261	.362	2	.083	-1	-13	-10	-1	-1.1
● **BEN HARRIS**	Harris, Ben Franklin b: 12/17/1889, Donelson, Tenn. d: 4/29/27, St.Louis, Mo. BR/TR, 6', 220 lbs. Deb: 4/19/14																											
1914	KC-F	7	7	.500	31	14	5	0	1	154	179	89	7	6	41	40	13.2	4.09	68	.303	.354	9	.200	1	-21	-23	1	-1.8
1915	KC-F	0	0	—	1	0	0	0	0	2	1	0	0	0	0	0	4.5	0.00	—	.143	.143	0	—	0	1	1	0	0.1
Total	2	7	7	.500	32	14	5	0	1	156	180	89	7	6	41	40	13.1	4.04	69	.301	.352	9	.200	1	-20	-23	1	-1.7
● **LUM HARRIS**	Harris, Chalmer Luman b: 1/17/15, New Castle, Ala. d: 11/11/96, Pell City, Ala. BR/TR, 6'1", 180 lbs. Deb: 4/19/41 MC																											
1941	Phi-A	4	4	.500	33	10	5	0	2	131^{2}	134	77	16	2	51	49	12.8	4.78	88	.260	.329	11	.275	2	-9	-9	-1	-0.4
1942	Phi-A	11	15	.423	26	20	10	1	0	166	146	80	14	1	70	60	11.8	3.74	101	.234	.313	10	.161	-2	-2	1	-1	-0.1
1943	Phi-A	7	21	.250	32	27	15	1	1	216^{1}	241	122	17	3	63	55	12.8	4.20	81	.279	.330	12	.171	-1	-22	-19	-0	-2.4
1944	Phi-A	10	9	.526	23	22	12	2	0	174^{1}	193	70	8	0	26	33	11.3	3.30	105	.281	.308	10	.169	-1	2	3	-1	0.2
1946	Phi-A	3	14	.176	34	12	4	0	0	125^{1}	153	78	11	0	48	33	14.4	5.24	68	.308	.369	8	.222	1	-24	-23	3	-2.4
1947	Was-A	0	0	—	3	0	0	0	0	6^{1}	7	2	0	0	7	2	19.9	2.84	131	.318	.483	0	.000	-0	1	1	1	0.1
Total	6	35	63	.357	151	91	46	4	3	820	874	429	66	6	265	232	12.6	4.16	88	.273	.329	51	.190	-0	-54	-46	1	-5.0
● **BUBBA HARRIS**	Harris, Charles b: 2/15/26, Sulligent, Ala. BR/TR, 6'4", 204 lbs. Deb: 4/29/48																											
1948	Phi-A	5	2	.714	45	0	0	0	5	93^{2}	89	51	2	1	35	32	12.0	4.13	104	.249	.317	3	.125	-1	2	2	-0	0.0
1949	Phi-A	1	1	.500	37	0	0	0	3	84^{1}	92	57	12	1	42	18	14.4	5.44	75	.286	.370	3	.125	-2	-12	-13	2	-0.6
1951	Phi-A	0	0	—	3	0	0	0	0	4	4	4	0	1	5	2	22.5	9.00	48	.250	.455	0	—	0	-2	-2	0	-0.1
	Cle-A	0	0	—	2	0	0	0	0	4	5	2	0	0	4	1	20.3	4.50	84	.333	.474	0	—	0	-0	-0	0	0.0
	Yr	0	0	—	5	0	0	0	0	8	9	6	0	1	9	3	21.4	6.75	60	.290	.463	0	—	0	-2	-2	0	-0.1
Total	3	6	3	.667	87	0	0	0	8	186	190	114	14	3	86	53	13.5	4.84	87	.267	.349	6	.125	-3	-12	-13	2	-0.7
● **GREG HARRIS**	Harris, Greg Allen b: 11/2/55, Lynwood, Cal. BB/TR, 6', 175 lbs. Deb: 5/20/81																											
1981	NY-N	3	5	.375	16	14	0	0	1	68^{2}	65	36	8	2	28	54	12.5	4.46	78	.245	.322	4	.182	0	-7	-7	-1	-0.9
1982	Cin-N	2	6	.250	34	10	1	0	1	91^{1}	96	56	12	2	37	67	13.3	4.83	77	.274	.346	3	.167	-0	-12	-11	0	-0.9
1983	Cin-N	0	0	—	1	0	0	0	0	1	2	3	0	1	3	1	54.0	27.00	14	.500	.750	0	.000	-0	-3	-2	0	-0.1
1984	Mon-N	0	1	.000	15	0	0	0	2	17^{2}	10	4	0	2	7	15	9.7	2.04	168	.172	.284	0	.000	-0	3	3	0	0.2
	*SD-N	2	1	.667	19	1	0	0	1	36^{2}	28	14	3	2	18	30	11.8	2.70	132	.209	.312	3	.375	1	4	4	-0	0.4
	Yr	2	2	.500	34	1	0	0	3	54^{1}	38	18	3	4	25	45	11.1	2.48	142	.198	.303	3	.333	1	7	6	-0	0.6
1985	Tex-A	5	4	.556	58	0	0	0	11	113	74	35	7	5	43	111	9.7	2.47	171	.186	.274	0	—	0	21	22	1	2.1
1986	Tex-A	10	8	.556	73	0	0	0	20	111^{1}	103	40	12	1	42	95	11.8	2.83	152	.251	.322	0	—	0	17	18	1	3.3
1987	Tex-A	5	10	.333	42	19	0	0	0	140^{2}	157	92	18	4	56	106	13.9	4.86	92	.281	.351	0	—	0	-6	-6	0	-0.5
1988	Phi-N	4	6	.400	66	1	0	0	1	107	80	34	7	4	52	71	11.4	2.36	151	.209	.311	3	.333	1	13	14	-0	1.4
1989	Phi-N	2	2	.500	44	0	0	0	1	75^{1}	64	34	7	2	43	51	13.0	3.58	99	.234	.342	1	.167	1	-1	-0	1	0.1
	Bos-A	2	2	.500	15	0	0	0	0	28	21	12	1	0	15	25	11.6	2.57	160	.208	.310	0	—	0	4	5	0	0.6
1990	*Bos-A	13	9	.591	34	30	1	0	0	184^{1}	186	90	13	6	77	117	13.1	4.00	102	.265	.342	0	—	0	-2	2	3	0.5
1991	Bos-A	11	12	.478	53	21	1	0	2	173	157	79	13	5	69	127	12.0	3.85	112	.243	.321	0	—	0	5	8	2	1.2
1992	Bos-A	4	9	.308	70	2	1	0	4	107^{2}	82	38	6	4	60	73	12.2	2.51	168	.215	.327	0	—	0	17	19	0	2.3
1993	Bos-A	6	7	.462	**80**	0	0	0	8	112^{1}	95	55	7	10	60	103	13.2	3.77	123	.232	.344	0	—	0	7	10	-0	1.1
1994	Bos-A	3	4	.429	35	0	0	0	2	45^{2}	60	44	8	1	23	44	16.6	8.28	61	.321	.398	0	—	0	-18	-16	0	-2.0
	NY-A	0	1	.000	3	0	0	0	0	5	4	5	1	2	3	4	16.2	5.40	85	.222	.391	0	—	0	-0	-0	-0	-0.1
	Yr	3	5	.375	38	0	0	0	2	50^{2}	64	49	9	3	26	48	16.5	7.99	62	.312	.397	0	—	0	-18	-16	0	-2.1
1995	Mon-N	2	3	.400	45	0	0	0	0	48^{1}	45	18	6	1	16	47	11.5	2.61	165	.245	.308	1	.333	1	8	9	-0	0.8
Total	15	74	90	.451	703	98	4	0	54	1467	1329	689	129	54	652	1141	12.5	3.69	112	.243	.330	15	.221	3	51	70	7	9.5
● **GREG HARRIS**	Harris, Gregory Wade b: 12/1/63, Greensboro, N.C. BR/TR, 6'2", 187 lbs. Deb: 9/14/88																											
1988	SD-N	2	0	1.000	3	1	1	0	0	18	13	3	0	0	3	15	8.0	1.50	227	.200	.235	0	.000	-1	4	4	-0	0.4
1989	SD-N	8	9	.471	56	8	0	0	6	135	106	43	8	2	52	106	10.7	2.60	135	.215	.293	1	.053	-1	14	14	1	1.8
1990	SD-N	8	8	.500	73	0	0	0	9	117^{1}	92	35	6	4	49	97	11.1	2.30	166	.220	.307	1	.083	-0	20	20	0	2.9
1991	SD-N	9	5	.643	20	20	3	2	0	133	116	42	16	1	27	95	9.7	2.23	170	.233	.274	3	.083	-1	21	22	-1	2.1
1992	SD-N	4	8	.333	20	20	1	0	0	118	113	62	13	2	35	66	11.4	4.12	87	.252	.309	4	.129	1	-8	-7	0	-0.5
1993	SD-N	10	9	.526	22	22	4	0	0	152	151	65	18	3	39	83	11.4	3.67	113	.257	.307	9	.170	1	6	8	1	1.1
	Col-N	1	8	.111	13	13	0	0	0	73^{1}	88	62	15	4	30	40	15.0	6.50	73	.299	.372	1	.050	-2	-20	-12	0	-1.3
	Yr	11	17	.393	35	35	4	0	0	225^{1}	239	127	33	7	69	123	12.6	4.59	95	.271	.329	10	.137	-0	-14	-6	1	-0.2
1994	Col-N	3	12	.200	29	19	1	0	1	130	154	99	22	5	52	82	14.6	6.65	75	.300	.370	7	.175	-0	-35	-20	1	-2.0
1995	Min-A	0	5	.000	7	6	0	0	0	32^{2}	50	35	5	0	16	21	18.2	8.82	54	.355	.420	0	—	0	-15	-14	0	-1.6
Total	8	45	64	.413	243	109	10	2	16	909^{1}	883	446	103	21	303	605	11.9	3.98	102	.255	.319	26	.119	-3	-13	7	3	2.9
● **HERB HARRIS**	Harris, Herbert Benjamin "Hub" or "Lefty" b: 4/24/13, Chicago, Ill. d: 1/18/91, Crystal Lake, Ill. BL/TL, 6'1", 175 lbs. Deb: 7/21/36																											
1936	Phi-N	0	0	—	4	0	0	0	0	7	14	8	0	1	5	0	25.7	10.29	44	.438	.526	0	.000	-0	-5	-4	0	-0.2
● **PEP HARRIS**	Harris, Hernando Petrocelli b: 9/23/72, Lancaster, S.C. BR/TR, 6'2", 185 lbs. Deb: 8/14/96																											
1996	Cal-A	2	0	1.000	11	3	0	0	0	32^{1}	31	16	4	3	17	20	14.2	3.90	129	.254	.359	0	—	0	4	4	0	0.2
1997	Ana-A	5	4	.556	61	0	0	0	0	79^{2}	82	33	7	2	38	56	13.8	3.62	127	.274	.360	0	—	0	8	9	1	0.9

YEAR	TM/L	W	L	PCT	G	GS	CG	SH	SV	IP	H	R	HR	HB	BB	SO	RAT	ERA	ERA+	OAV	OOB	BH	AVG	PB	PR	PR+	PD	TPI
1998	Ana-A	3	1	.750	49	0	0	0	0	60	55	32	7	0	23	34	11.7	4.35	108	.239	.308	0	—	0	2	2	1	0.2
Total	3	10	5	.667	121	3	0	0	0	172	168	81	18	5	78	110	13.1	3.92	120	.258	.342	0	—	0	14	15	2	1.3
● JOE HARRIS Harris, Joseph White b: 2/1/1882, Melrose, Mass. d: 4/12/66, Melrose, Mass. BR/TR, 6'1", 198 lbs. Deb: 9/22/05																												
1905	Bos-A	1	2	.333	3	3	3	0	0	23	16	6	0	0	8	14	9.4	2.35	115	.198	.270	1	.111	-1	1	1	-0	0.0
1906	Bos-A	2	21	.087	30	24	20	1	2	235	211	130	5	7	67	99	10.9	3.52	78	.243	.303	13	.160	-2	-22	-20	6	-1.5
1907	Bos-A	0	7	.000	12	5	3	0	0	59	57	28	0	1	13	24	10.8	3.05	84	.256	.300	4	.190	-0	-3	-3	0	-0.4
Total	3	3	30	.091	45	32	26	1	2	317	284	164	5	8	88	137	10.8	3.35	81	.242	.300	18	.162	-3	-24	-22	6	-1.9
● LENNY HARRIS Harris, Leonard Anthony b: 10/28/64, Miami, Fla. BL/TR, 5'10", 205 lbs. Deb: 9/7/88 ♦																												
1998	Cin-N	0	0	—	1	0	0	0	0	1	0	0	0	0	0	1	0.0	0.00	—	.000	.000	36	.295	0	0	0	0	0.0
● MICKEY HARRIS Harris, Maurice Charles b: 1/30/17, New York, N.Y. d: 4/15/71, Farmington, Mich. BL/TL, 6', 195 lbs. Deb: 4/23/40																												
1940	Bos-A	4	2	.667	13	9	3	0	0	68^1	83	40	8	2	26	36	14.6	5.00	90	.292	.356	6	.273	2	-5	-4	0	0.0
1941	Bos-A	8	14	.364	35	22	11	1	1	194	189	86	6	2	86	111	12.9	3.25	128	.250	.328	6	.109	2	19	20	-1	2.1
1946	*Bos-A☆	17	9	.654	34	30	15	0	0	222^2	236	105	18	3	76	131	12.7	3.64	101	.268	.329	18	.231	4	-3	1	-1	0.3
1947	Bos-A	5	4	.556	15	6	1	0	0	51^2	42	20	3	0	23	35	11.3	2.44	159	.225	.310	5	.417	3	7	8	0	1.7
1948	Bos-A	7	10	.412	20	17	6	1	0	113^2	120	73	10	1	59	42	14.3	5.30	83	.273	.360	2	.063	-1	-13	-11	-2	-1.7
1949	Bos-A	2	3	.400	7	6	2	0	0	37^2	53	26	3	1	20	14	17.7	5.02	87	.323	.400	1	.083	-1	-3	-3	0	-0.4
	Was-A	2	12	.143	23	19	4	0	0	129	151	82	8	0	55	54	14.4	5.16	82	.292	.360	8	.205	1	-14	-13	-2	-1.2
	Yr	4	15	.211	30	25	6	0	0	166^2	204	108	11	1	75	68	15.1	5.13	83	.299	.369	9	.176	1	-17	-15	-2	-1.6
1950	Was-A	5	9	.357	**53**	0	0	0	**15**	98	93	56	9	1	46	41	12.9	4.78	94	.247	.330	4	.235	1	-2	-3	-1	-0.5
1951	Was-A	6	8	.429	41	0	0	0	4	87^1	87	45	6	1	43	47	13.5	3.81	107	.260	.347	3	.188	0	3	3	-1	0.4
1952	Was-A	0	0	—	1	0	0	0	0	1	1	1	1	0	0	0	9.0	9.00	40	.250	.250	0	—	0	-1	-1	-0	0.0
	Cle-A	3	0	1.000	29	0	0	0	1	46^2	42	26	6	1	21	23	12.3	4.63	72	.249	.335	1	.200	-0	-5	-7	0	-0.5
	Yr	3	0	1.000	30	0	0	0	1	47^2	43	27	7	1	21	23	12.3	4.72	71	.249	.333	1	.200	-0	-6	-8	-0	-0.5
Total	9	59	71	.454	271	109	42	2	21	1050	1097	560	78	12	455	534	13.4	4.18	98	.267	.342	54	.188	11	-16	-9	-7	0.2
● REGGIE HARRIS Harris, Reginald Allen b: 8/12/68, Waynesboro, Va. BR/TR, 6'1", 180 lbs. Deb: 7/4/90																												
1990	Oak-A	1	0	1.000	16	1	0	0	0	41^1	25	16	5	2	21	31	10.5	3.48	107	.176	.291	0	—	0	2	1	-0	0.0
1991	Oak-A	0	0	—	2	0	0	0	0	3	5	4	0	0	3	2	24.0	12.00	32	.455	.571	0	—	0	-3	-3	-0	-0.1
1996	Bos-A	0	0	—	4	0	0	0	0	4^1	7	6	2	1	5	4	27.0	12.46	41	.389	.542	0	—	0	-4	-3	-0	-0.2
1997	Phi-N	1	3	.250	50	0	0	0	0	54^1	55	33	1	5	43	45	17.1	5.30	80	.263	.401	0	—	0	-7	-6	-1	-0.5
1998	Hou-N	0	0	—	6	0	0	0	0	6	6	4	1	0	2	2	12.0	6.00	68	.261	.320	0	—	0	-1	-1	-0	-0.1
1999	Mil-N	0	0	—	8	0	0	0	0	12	8	4	1	2	7	11	12.8	3.00	151	.186	.327	0	.000	-0	2	2	-0	0.1
Total	6	2	3	.400	86	1	0	0	0	121	106	67	10	10	81	95	14.7	4.91	84	.238	.367	0	.000	-0	-10	-11	-2	-0.8
● BOB HARRIS Harris, Robert Arthur b: 5/1/17, Gillette, Wyo. d: 8/8/89, North Platte, Neb. BR/TR, 6', 185 lbs. Deb: 9/19/38																												
1938	Det-A	1	0	1.000	3	1	1	0	0	10	14	9	0	0	4	7	16.2	7.20	69	.318	.375	1	.333	0	-3	-2	0	-0.1
1939	Det-A	1	1	.500	5	1	0	0	0	18	18	8	4	0	8	9	13.0	4.00	122	.269	.347	2	.400	0	1	2	0	0.2
	StL-A	3	12	.200	28	16	6	0	0	126	162	88	5	0	71	48	16.6	5.71	85	.321	.405	7	.189	-0	-15	-11	3	-0.9
	Yr	4	13	.235	33	17	6	0	0	144	180	96	9	0	79	57	16.2	5.50	89	.315	.398	9	.214	-0	-14	-10	3	-0.7
1940	StL-A	11	15	.423	35	28	8	1	1	193^2	225	120	24	3	85	49	14.5	4.93	93	.290	.362	15	.250	3	-12	-7	-0	-0.5
1941	StL-A	12	14	.462	34	29	9	2	1	186^2	237	117	18	2	85	57	15.6	5.21	83	.312	.383	7	.115	-3	-22	-18	-2	-2.5
1942	StL-A	1	5	.167	6	6	0	0	0	33^2	37	24	2	0	17	9	14.4	5.61	66	.268	.348	0	.000	-1	-7	-7	-1	-1.2
	Phi-A	1	5	.167	16	8	2	1	0	78	77	31	5	0	24	26	11.7	2.88	131	.253	.308	7	.269	1	7	7	2	0.9
	Yr	2	10	.167	22	14	2	1	0	111^2	114	55	7	0	41	35	12.5	3.71	101	.258	.321	7	.194	0	-1	1	2	-0.3
Total	5	30	52	.366	127	89	26	4	2	646	770	397	58	5	294	205	14.9	4.96	89	.297	.370	39	.193	1	-51	-37	3	-4.1
● GENE HARRIS Harris, Tyrone Eugene b: 12/5/64, Sebring, Fla. BR/TR, 5'11", 190 lbs. Deb: 4/5/89																												
1989	Mon-N	1	1	.500	11	0	0	0	0	20	16	11	1	0	10	11	11.7	4.95	71	.242	.342	0	.000	-0	-3	-3	2	-0.2
	Sea-A	1	4	.200	10	6	0	0	1	33^1	47	27	3	1	15	14	17.0	6.48	62	.353	.423	0	—	0	-10	-9	-1	-1.2
1990	Sea-A	1	2	.333	25	0	0	0	0	38	31	25	5	1	30	43	14.7	4.74	84	.217	.356	0	—	0	-3	-3	-0	-0.2
1991	Sea-A	0	0	—	8	0	0	0	1	13^1	15	8	1	0	10	6	16.9	4.05	102	.273	.385	0	—	0	0	0	-0	0.0
1992	Sea-A	0	0	—	8	0	0	0	0	9	8	7	3	0	6	6	14.0	7.00	57	.235	.350	0	—	0	-3	-3	-0	-0.2
	SD-N	0	2	.000	14	1	0	0	0	21^1	15	8	0	1	9	19	10.5	2.95	121	.195	.287	1	.333	0	1	1	0	0.2
1993	SD-N	6	6	.500	59	0	0	0	23	59^1	57	27	3	1	37	39	14.4	3.03	136	.254	.363	0	.000	-0	7	7	1	1.5
1994	SD-N	1	1	.500	13	0	0	0	0	12^1	21	11	2	0	8	9	21.2	8.03	51	.389	.468	0	.000	-0	-5	-6	-0	-0.8
	Det-A	0	0	—	11	0	0	0	1	11^1	13	10	1	1	4	10	14.3	7.15	68	.271	.340	0	—	0	-3	-3	0	-0.1
1995	Phi-N	2	2	.500	21	0	0	0	0	19	19	9	2	0	8	9	12.8	4.26	99	.260	.333	0	—	0	-0	-0	1	0.0
	Bal-A	0	0	—	3	0	0	0	0	4	4	2	0	0	1	4	11.3	4.50	106	.267	.313	0	—	0	0	0	0	0.0
Total	7	12	18	.400	183	7	0	0	26	241	246	145	21	5	138	170	14.5	4.71	86	.267	.365	1	.167	-0	-19	-17	1	-1.0
● BUDDY HARRIS Harris, Walter Francis b: 12/5/48, Philadelphia, Pa. BR/TR, 6'7", 245 lbs. Deb: 9/10/70																												
1970	Hou-N	0	0	—	2	0	0	0	0	6^1	6	4	3	0	0	2	8.5	5.68	68	.240	.240	0	.000	-0	-1	-1	-0	-0.1
1971	Hou-N	1	1	.500	20	0	0	0	0	30^2	33	22	3	0	16	21	14.4	6.46	52	.275	.360	0	.000	-0	-10	-11	-1	-0.8
Total	2	1	1	.500	22	0	0	0	0	37	39	26	6	0	16	23	13.4	6.32	55	.269	.342	0	.000	-0	-11	-12	-1	-0.9
● BILL HARRIS Harris, William Milton b: 6/23/1900, Wylie, Tex. d: 8/21/65, Indian Trail, N.C. BR/TR, 6'1", 180 lbs. Deb: 4/22/23																												
1923	Cin-N	3	2	.600	22	3	1	0	0	69^2	79	42	3	3	18	18	12.9	5.17	75	.292	.342	6	.353	1	-9	-10	0	-0.5
1924	Cin-N	0	0	—	3	0	0	0	0	7	10	7	0	0	2	5	15.4	9.00	42	.323	.364	1	1.000	0	-4	-4	0	-0.1
1931	Pit-N	2	2	.500	4	4	3	1	0	31	21	6	0	0	9	10	8.7	0.87	442	.194	.256	1	.091	-1	10	10	0	1.3
1932	Pit-N	10	9	.526	37	17	4	0	2	168	178	84	6	6	38	63	11.9	3.64	105	.271	.317	10	.182	-1	4	3	-2	0.1
1933	Pit-N	4	4	.500	31	0	0	0	5	58^2	68	28	1	1	14	19	12.7	3.22	103	.289	.332	0	.000	-1	1	1	-1	-0.1
1934	Pit-N	0	0	—	11	1	0	0	0	19	28	15	2	1	7	8	17.1	6.63	62	.350	.409	1	.500	0	-5	-5	0	-0.2
1938	Bos-A	5	5	.500	13	11	5	1	1	80^1	83	39	5	1	21	26	11.8	4.03	122	.268	.316	6	.214	-0	7	8	-0	0.8
Total	7	24	22	.522	121	36	13	2	8	433^2	467	221	17	12	109	149	12.2	3.92	101	.276	.324	25	.203	-1	4	2	-2	1.3
● BILL HARRIS Harris, William Thomas b: 12/3/31, Duguayville, N.B., Canada BL/TR, 5'8", 187 lbs. Deb: 9/27/57																												
1957	Bro-N	0	1	.000	1	1	0	0	0	7	9	3	1	0	1	3	12.9	3.86	108	.321	.345	1	.500	0	0	0	0	0.1
1959	LA-N	0	0	—	1	0	0	0	0	1^2	0	0	0	0	3	0	16.2	0.00	—	.000	.375	0	—	0	1	1	0	0.0
Total	2	0	1	.000	2	1	0	0	0	8^2	9	3	1	0	4	3	13.5	3.12	134	.273	.351	1	.500	0	1	1	0	0.1
● BOB HARRISON Harrison, Robert Lee b: 9/22/30, St.Louis, Mo. BL/TR, 5'11", 178 lbs. Deb: 9/23/55																												
1955	Bal-A	0	0	—	1	0	0	0	0	2	3	2	0	0	4	0	31.5	9.00	42	.500	.700	0	—	0	-1	-1	-0	-0.1
1956	Bal-A	0	0	—	1	1	0	0	0	1^2	3	3	0	0	5	0	43.2	16.20	24	.375	.615	0	—	0	-2	-2	-0	-0.1
Total	2	0	0	—	2	1	0	0	0	3^2	6	5	0	0	9	0	36.8	12.27	31	.429	.652	0	—	0	-3	-4	-0	-0.2
● RORIC HARRISON Harrison, Roric Edward b: 9/20/46, Los Angeles, Cal. BR/TR, 6'3", 195 lbs. Deb: 4/18/72																												
1972	Bal-A	3	4	.429	39	2	0	0	4	94	68	24	2	4	34	62	10.1	2.30	134	.209	.292	2	.118	1	8	8	-1	0.7
1973	Atl-N	11	8	.579	38	22	3	0	5	177^1	161	90	15	3	98	130	13.3	4.16	95	.242	.342	3	.056	-2	-10	-4	-1	-0.7
1974	Atl-N	6	11	.353	20	20	3	0	0	126	148	70	12	3	49	46	14.3	4.71	80	.294	.360	7	.184	2	-15	-12	-2	-1.5
1975	Atl-N	3	4	.429	15	7	2	0	1	54^2	58	33	7	0	19	22	12.7	4.77	79	.266	.325	3	.200	1	-7	-6	0	-0.6
	Cle-A	7	7	.500	19	19	4	0	0	126	137	71	9	4	46	52	13.4	4.79	79	.275	.341	0	—	0	-14	-14	-1	-1.5
1978	Min-A	0	1	.000	9	0	0	0	0	12	18	10	0	0	11	7	21.8	7.50	51	.346	.460	0	—	0	-5	-5	-0	-0.4
Total	5	30	35	.462	140	70	12	0	10	590	590	298	45	14	257	319	13.1	4.24	88	.261	.340	15	.121	2	-43	-33	-5	-4.0
● TOM HARRISON Harrison, Thomas James b: 1/18/45, Trail, B.C., Canada BR/TR, 6'3", 200 lbs. Deb: 5/7/65 ♦																												
1965	KC-A	0	0	—	1	0	0	0	0	1	2	1	0	0	1	0	27.0	9.00	39	.667	.750	0	—	0	-1	-1	-0	0.0
● SLIM HARRISS Harriss, William Jennings Bryan b: 12/11/1896, Brownwood, Tex. d: 9/19/63, Temple, Tex. BR/TR, 6'6", 180 lbs. Deb: 4/19/20																												
1920	Phi-A	9	14	.391	31	25	11	1	0	192	226	111	5	5	57	60	13.5	4.08	99	.305	.359	7	.106	-7	-6	-1	3	-0.5

YEAR	TM/L	W	L	PCT	G	GS	CG	SH	SV	IP	H	R	HR	HB	BB	SO	RAT	ERA	ERA+	OAV	OOB	BH	AVG	PB	PR	PR+	PD	TPI
1921	Phi-A	11	16	.407	39	28	14	0	2	227^2	258	136	16	9	73	92	13.4	4.27	104	.290	.350	12	.148	-7	0	5	-1	-0.3
1922	Phi-A	9	20	.310	47	32	13	0	3	229^2	262	148	19	3	94	102	14.1	5.02	85	.290	.359	13	.176	-4	-25	-18	1	-2.4
1923	Phi-A	10	16	.385	46	28	9	0	6	209^1	221	114	9	2	95	89	13.7	4.00	103	.280	.359	4	.066	-8	-0	2	5	0.0
1924	Phi-A	6	10	.375	36	12	4	1	2	123	138	78	5	3	62	45	14.9	4.68	92	.291	.377	7	.167	-3	-6	-5	4	-0.5
1925	Phi-A	19	12	.613	46	33	15	2	1	252^2	263	118	8	6	95	95	13.0	3.49	133	.268	.336	18	.205	-3	25	31	4	3.4
1926	Phi-A	3	5	.375	12	10	2	0	0	57	66	34	0	0	22	13	13.9	4.11	102	.289	.352	1	.059	-2	-1	0	0	-0.1
	Bos-A	6	10	.375	21	18	6	1	0	113	135	66	0	2	33	34	13.5	4.46	91	.311	.362	7	.206	-0	-6	-5	1	-0.5
	Yr	9	15	.375	33	28	8	1	0	170	201	100	0	2	55	47	13.7	4.34	95	.304	.359	8	.157	-2	-6	-4	1	-0.6
1927	Bos-A	14	21	.400	44	27	11	1	1	217^2	253	127	8	9	66	77	13.6	4.18	101	.298	.355	8	.121	-5	-11	-5	1	-0.2
1928	Bos-A	8	11	.421	27	15	4	1	1	128^1	141	74	5	2	33	37	12.3	4.63	89	.287	.335	5	.139	-3	-8	-7	-2	-1.3
Total	9	95	135	.413	349	228	89	7	16	1750^1	1963	1006	75	41	630	644	13.5	4.25	100	.290	.354	82	.145	-40	-27	3	15	-2.4

● **EARL HARRIST** Harrist, Earl "Irish" b: 8/20/19, Dubach, La. d: 9/1/98, Simsboro, La. BR/TR, 6', 178 lbs. Deb: 8/18/45

YEAR	TM/L	W	L	PCT	G	GS	CG	SH	SV	IP	H	R	HR	HB	BB	SO	RAT	ERA	ERA+	OAV	OOB	BH	AVG	PB	PR	PR+	PD	TPI
1945	Cin-N	2	4	.333	14	5	1	0	0	62^1	60	30	2	1	27	15	12.7	3.61	104	.249	.327	0	.000	-2	1	1	-1	-0.2
1947	Chi-A	3	8	.273	33	4	0	0	5	93^2	85	48	3	3	49	55	13.2	3.56	103	.248	.347	5	.208	-0	2	1	1	0.2
1948	Chi-A	1	3	.250	11	1	0	0	0	23	23	17	4	3	13	14	15.3	5.87	73	.267	.382	0	.000	-1	-4	-4	0	-0.7
	Was-A	3	3	.500	23	4	0	0	0	60^2	70	35	1	3	37	21	16.3	4.60	94	.293	.394	3	.167	-1	-2	-2	-1	-0.3
	Yr	4	6	.400	34	5	0	0	0	83^2	93	52	5	6	50	35	16.0	4.95	87	.286	.391	3	.136	-2	-6	-6	-1	-1.0
1952	StL-A	2	8	.200	36	9	1	0	5	116^2	119	61	7	10	47	49	13.6	4.01	98	.269	.352	3	.097	-2	-4	-1	1	-0.3
1953	Chi-A	1	0	1.000	7	0	0	0	0	8^1	9	7	1	0	5	1	15.1	7.56	53	.290	.389	0	.000	-0	-3	-3	-0	-0.4
	Det-A	0	2	.000	8	1	0	0	0	18^2	25	19	2	0	15	7	19.3	8.68	47	.333	.444	0	.000	-0	-10	-9	1	-0.8
	Yr	1	2	.333	15	1	0	0	0	27	34	26	3	0	20	8	18.0	8.33	49	.321	.429	0	.000	-0	-13	-13	1	-1.2
Total	5	12	28	.300	132	24	2	0	10	383^1	391	217	20	20	193	162	14.2	4.34	90	.268	.361	11	.115	-7	-21	-17	0	-2.5

● **JACK HARSHMAN** Harshman, John Elvin b: 7/12/27, San Diego, Cal. BL/TL, 6'2", 185 lbs. Deb: 9/16/48 ♦

YEAR	TM/L	W	L	PCT	G	GS	CG	SH	SV	IP	H	R	HR	HB	BB	SO	RAT	ERA	ERA+	OAV	OOB	BH	AVG	PB	PR	PR+	PD	TPI
1952	NY-N	0	2	.000	2	2	0	0	0	6^1	12	10	2	0	6	6	25.6	14.21	26	.429	.529	0	.000	-0	-7	-7	0	-1.1
1954	Chi-A	14	8	.636	35	21	9	4	1	177	157	61	7	5	96	134	13.1	2.95	127	.238	.339	8	.143	3	15	15	-1	2.1
1955	Chi-A	11	7	.611	32	23	9	0	0	179^1	144	74	16	4	97	116	12.3	3.36	117	.224	.330	11	.183	4	12	12	-0	1.4
1956	Chi-A	15	11	.577	34	30	15	4	0	226^2	183	85	14	3	102	143	11.4	3.10	132	.221	.308	12	.169	6	27	26	-2	3.1
1957	Chi-A	8	8	.500	30	26	6	0	1	151^1	142	78	16	5	82	83	13.6	4.10	91	.250	.349	10	.222	5	-5	-6	-3	-0.4
1958	Bal-A	12	15	.444	34	29	17	3	4	236^1	204	89	20	3	75	161	10.7	2.89	124	.231	.294	16	.195	8	23	19	1	3.5
1959	Bal-A	0	6	.000	14	8	0	0	0	47^1	58	39	6	2	28	24	16.7	6.85	55	.319	.415	2	.200	1	-16	-16	1	-1.5
	Bos-A	2	3	.400	8	2	0	0	0	24^2	29	19	2	0	10	14	14.2	6.57	62	.284	.348	1	.143	0	-7	-7	-1	-1.1
	Cle-A	5	1	.833	13	6	5	1	1	66	46	21	6	0	13	35	8.0	2.59	142	.179	.219	7	.206	2	9	8	-0	0.9
	Yr	7	10	.412	35	16	5	1	1	138	133	79	14	2	51	73	12.1	4.76	79	.246	.313	10	.196	3	-14	-15	1	-1.7
1960	Cle-A	2	4	.333	15	8	0	0	0	54^1	50	32	7	0	30	25	13.3	3.98	94	.243	.339	3	.176	-0	-1	-1	-1	-0.2
Total	8	69	65	.515	217	155	61	12	7	1169^1	1025	508	96	22	539	741	12.2	3.50	109	.235	.323	76	.179	29	50	41	-5	6.7

● **OSCAR HARSTAD** Harstad, Oscar Theander b: 5/24/1892, Parkland, Wash. d: 11/14/85, Corvallis, Ore. BR/TR, 6', 174 lbs. Deb: 4/23/15

YEAR	TM/L	W	L	PCT	G	GS	CG	SH	SV	IP	H	R	HR	HB	BB	SO	RAT	ERA	ERA+	OAV	OOB	BH	AVG	PB	PR	PR+	PD	TPI
1915	Cle-A	3	5	.375	32	7	4	0	1	82	81	45	1	1	35	35	12.8	3.40	90	.270	.348	2	.125	-1	-4	-3	2	-0.2

● **BILLY HART** Hart, Robert Lee b: 5/16/1866, Palmyra, Mo. d: 5/14/44, Hannibal, Mo. 5'8", Deb: 7/13/1890

YEAR	TM/L	W	L	PCT	G	GS	CG	SH	SV	IP	H	R	HR	HB	BB	SO	RAT	ERA	ERA+	OAV	OOB	BH	AVG	PB	PR	PR+	PD	TPI
1890	StL-a	12	8	.600	26	24	20	0	0	201^1	188	111	6	16	66	95	12.1	3.67	118	.240	.312	15	.192	-1	5	13	-3	0.7

● **BILL HART** Hart, William Franklin b: 7/19/1865, Louisville, Ky. d: 9/19/36, Cincinnati, Ohio TR, 5'10", 163 lbs. Deb: 7/26/1886 U

YEAR	TM/L	W	L	PCT	G	GS	CG	SH	SV	IP	H	R	HR	HB	BB	SO	RAT	ERA	ERA+	OAV	OOB	BH	AVG	PB	PR	PR+	PD	TPI
1886	Phi-a	9	13	.409	22	22	22	2	0	186	183	144	7	7	66	78	12.4	3.19	110	.234	.299	10	.137	-5	5	6	1	0.3
1887	Phi-a	1	2	.333	3	3	3	0	0	26	45	22	1	1	17	4	15.9	4.50	95	.375	.380	1	.077	-2	-1	-1	0	-0.2
1892	Bro-N	9	12	.429	28	23	16	2	1	195	188	109	3	7	96	65	13.4	3.28	97	.243	.332	24	.192	3	0	-3	3	0.3
1895	Pit-N	14	17	.452	36	29	24	0	1	261^2	293	186	4	15	135	85	15.2	4.75	95	.279	.369	25	.236	-2	1	-7	6	-0.3
1896	StL-N	12	29	.293	42	41	37	0	0	336	411	271	11	15	141	65	15.2	5.12	85	.299	.370	30	.186	-5	-28	-29	6	-2.5
1897	StL-N	9	27	.250	39	38	31	0	0	294^2	395	292	10	16	148	67	17.1	6.26	70	.318	.398	39	.250	-1	-64	-60	3	-5.1
1898	Pit-N	5	9	.357	16	15	13	1	1	125	141	81	4	7	44	19	13.8	4.82	74	.282	.348	12	.240	0	-17	-18	0	-1.6
1901	Cle-A	7	11	.389	20	19	16	0	0	157^2	180	109	3	10	57	48	14.1	3.77	94	.283	.352	14	.219	-2	-2	-4	2	-0.3
Total	8	66	120	.355	206	190	162	5	3	1582	1836	1214	43	78	704	431	14.8	4.65	86	.283	.359	155	.207	-14	-105	-115	22	-9.4

● **CHUCK HARTENSTEIN** Hartenstein, Charles Oscar "Twiggy" b: 5/26/42, Seguin, Tex. BR/TR, 5'11", 165 lbs. Deb: 9/11/65 C♦

YEAR	TM/L	W	L	PCT	G	GS	CG	SH	SV	IP	H	R	HR	HB	BB	SO	RAT	ERA	ERA+	OAV	OOB	BH	AVG	PB	PR	PR+	PD	TPI
1966	Chi-N	0	0	—	5	0	0	0	0	9^1	8	2	0	1	3	4	11.6	1.93	191	.222	.300	0	—	0	2	2	0	0.1
1967	Chi-N	9	5	.643	45	0	0	0	10	73	74	27	4	1	17	20	11.3	3.08	115	.278	.324	1	.063	-1	2	4	-0	0.7
1968	Chi-N	2	4	.333	28	0	0	0	1	35^2	41	19	3	1	11	17	13.4	4.54	70	.291	.346	0	.000	-0	-6	-5	-0	-1.0
1969	Pit-N	5	4	.556	56	0	0	0	10	95^2	84	42	9	4	27	44	10.8	3.95	88	.241	.303	1	.071	-1	-4	-5	1	-0.5
1970	Pit-N	1	1	.500	17	0	0	0	1	23^2	25	15	3	0	8	14	12.5	4.56	86	.278	.337	0	.000	-0	-1	-2	1	-0.1
	StL-N	0	0	—	6	0	0	0	0	13^1	24	13	1	0	5	9	19.6	8.78	47	.375	.420	0	.000	0	-7	-7	0	-0.3
	Yr	1	1	.500	23	0	0	0	1	37	49	28	4	0	13	23	15.1	6.08	66	.318	.371	0	.000	0	-8	-9	1	-0.4
	Bos-A	0	3	.000	17	0	0	0	1	19	21	17	6	1	12	12	16.1	8.05	49	.288	.395	0	.000	0	-9	-8	-1	-1.3
1977	Tor-A	0	2	.000	13	0	0	0	0	27^1	40	22	8	1	6	15	15.5	6.59	64	.348	.385	0	—	0	-8	-7	-0	-0.5
Total	6	17	19	.472	187	0	0	0	23	297	317	157	34	9	89	135	12.6	4.52	80	.280	.337	2	.054	-2	-31	-29	2	-2.9

● **FRANK HARTER** Harter, Franklin Pierce "Chief" b: 9/19/1886, Keyesport, Ill. d: 4/14/59, Breese, Ill. BR/TR, 5'11", 165 lbs. Deb: 8/31/12

YEAR	TM/L	W	L	PCT	G	GS	CG	SH	SV	IP	H	R	HR	HB	BB	SO	RAT	ERA	ERA+	OAV	OOB	BH	AVG	PB	PR	PR+	PD	TPI
1912	Cin-N	1	2	.333	6	3	1	0	0	29^1	25	16	1	0	11	12	11.0	3.07	110	.234	.305	1	.091	-1	1	1	-1	-0.1
1913	Cin-N	1	1	.500	17	2	0	0	0	46^2	47	23	3	0	19	10	12.7	3.86	84	.272	.344	2	.143	-1	-3	-3	-1	-0.3
1914	Ind-F	1	2	.333	6	1	1	0	0	24^2	33	12	0	0	7	8	14.6	4.01	78	.330	.374	0	.000	-1	-3	-2	-0	-0.4
Total	3	3	5	.375	29	6	2	0	0	100^2	105	51	4	0	37	30	12.7	3.67	89	.276	.341	3	.091	-3	-5	-4	-2	-0.8

● **DEAN HARTGRAVES** Hartgraves, Dean Charles b: 8/12/66, Bakersfield, Cal. BR/TL, 6', 185 lbs. Deb: 5/3/95

YEAR	TM/L	W	L	PCT	G	GS	CG	SH	SV	IP	H	R	HR	HB	BB	SO	RAT	ERA	ERA+	OAV	OOB	BH	AVG	PB	PR	PR+	PD	TPI
1995	Hou-N	2	0	1.000	40	0	0	0	0	36^1	30	14	2	0	16	24	11.4	3.22	120	.227	.311	0	.000	-0	4	3	0	0.1
1996	Hou-N	0	0	—	19	0	0	0	0	19	18	11	1	1	16	16	16.6	5.21	74	.257	.402	0	—	0	-2	-3	0	-0.2
	Atl-N	1	0	1.000	20	0	0	0	0	18^2	16	10	3	1	7	14	11.6	4.34	102	.232	.312	0	.000	-0	-0	0	0	0.0
	Yr	1	0	1.000	39	0	0	0	0	37^2	34	21	4	2	23	30	14.1	4.78	87	.245	.360	0	.000	-0	-2	-3	0	-0.2
1998	SF-N	0	0	—	5	0	0	0	0	5^2	10	7	1	0	4	4	22.2	9.53	42	.385	.467	0	—	0	-3	-4	-0	-0.2
Total	3	3	0	1.000	84	0	0	0	0	79^2	74	42	7	2	43	58	13.4	4.41	91	.249	.348	0	.000	-0	-2	-4	-0	-0.3

● **MIKE HARTLEY** Hartley, Michael Edward b: 8/31/61, Hawthorne, Cal. BR/TR, 6'1", 197 lbs. Deb: 9/10/89

YEAR	TM/L	W	L	PCT	G	GS	CG	SH	SV	IP	H	R	HR	HB	BB	SO	RAT	ERA	ERA+	OAV	OOB	BH	AVG	PB	PR	PR+	PD	TPI
1989	LA-N	0	1	.000	5	0	0	0	0	6	2	1	0	0	0	4	3.0	1.50	228	.100	.100	0	.000	-0	1	1	0	0.2
1990	LA-N	6	3	.667	32	6	1	1	1	79^1	58	32	7	2	30	76	10.2	2.95	124	.200	.280	1	.077	-1	7	7	-0	0.6
1991	LA-N	2	0	1.000	40	0	0	0	1	57	53	29	7	3	37	44	14.7	4.42	81	.245	.363	0	.000	-0	-5	-5	-0	-0.3
	Phi-N	2	1	.667	18	0	0	0	1	26^1	21	11	4	3	10	19	11.6	3.76	98	.219	.312	0	.000	-0	-0	-0	-1	-0.1
	Yr	4	1	.800	58	0	0	0	2	83^1	74	40	11	6	47	63	13.7	4.21	86	.237	.348	0	.000	-0	-5	-6	-1	-0.4
1992	Phi-N	7	6	.538	46	0	0	0	0	55	54	23	5	2	23	53	12.9	3.44	102	.255	.333	0	.000	-0	0	0	-0	0.0
1993	Min-A	1	2	.333	53	0	0	0	1	81	86	38	4	7	36	57	14.3	4.00	109	.281	.370	0	—	0	3	3	-2	0.0
1995	Bos-A	0	0	—	5	0	0	0	0	7	8	7	1	2	2	2	15.4	9.00	54	.308	.400	0	—	0	-3	-3	-0	-0.1
	Bal-A	1	0	1.000	3	0	0	0	0	7	5	1	0	1	0	4	7.7	1.29	370	.217	.250	0	—	0	3	3	0	0.4
	Yr	1	0	1.000	8	0	0	0	0	14	13	8	1	2	3	6	11.6	5.14	94	.265	.333	0	—	0	-1	-0	0	0.3
Total	6	19	13	.594	202	6	1	1	4	318^2	287	142	28	19	139	259	12.6	3.70	104	.241	.330	1	.043	-2	7	5	-3	0.7

● **CHARLIE HARTMAN** Hartman, Charles Otto b: 8/10/1888, Los Angeles, Cal. d: 10/22/60, Los Angeles, Cal. Deb: 6/24/08

YEAR	TM/L	W	L	PCT	G	GS	CG	SH	SV	IP	H	R	HR	HB	BB	SO	RAT	ERA	ERA+	OAV	OOB	BH	AVG	PB	PR	PR+	PD	TPI
1908	Bos-A	0	0	—	1	0	0	0	0	2	1	1	0	0	2	1	13.5	4.50	55	.143	.333	0	—	0	-0	-0	0	0.0

● **BOB HARTMAN** Hartman, Robert Louis b: 8/28/37, Kenosha, Wis. BR/TL, 5'11", 185 lbs. Deb: 4/26/59

YEAR	TM/L	W	L	PCT	G	GS	CG	SH	SV	IP	H	R	HR	HB	BB	SO	RAT	ERA	ERA+	OAV	OOB	BH	AVG	PB	PR	PR+	PD	TPI
1959	Mil-N	0	0	—	3	0	0	0	0	1^2	6	5	0	0	2	1	43.2	27.00	13	.545	.615	0	—	0	-4	-5	-0	-0.2
1962	Cle-A	0	1	.000	8	2	0	0	0	17^1	14	10	1	0	8	11	11.4	3.12	124	.209	.293	0	.000	-1	2	1	-0	0.0
Total	2	0	1	.000	11	2	0	0	0	19	20	15	1	0	10	12	14.2	5.21	74	.256	.341	0	.000	-1	-3	-3	-0	-0.2

YEAR	TM/L	W	L	PCT	G	GS	CG	SH	SV	IP	H	R	HR	HB	BB	SO	RAT	ERA	ERA+	OAV	OOB	BH	AVG	PB	PR	PR+	PD	TPI
● RAY HARTRANFT	Hartranft, Raymond Joseph b: 9/19/1890, Quakertown, Pa. d: 2/10/55, Spring City, Pa. BL/TL, 6'1", 195 lbs. Deb: 6/16/13																											
1913	Phi-N	0	0	—	1	0	0	0	0	1	3	1	0	0	1	1	36.0	9.00	37	.500	.571	0	—	0	-1	-1	0	0.0
● JEFF HARTSOCK	Hartsock, Jeffrey Roger b: 11/19/66, Fairfield, Ohio BR/TR, 6', 190 lbs. Deb: 9/12/92																											
1992	Chi-N	0	0	—	4	0	0	0	0	9^1	15	7	2	0	4	6	18.3	6.75	53	.375	.432	0	.000	-0	-3	-3	0	-0.2
● CLINT HARTUNG	Hartung, Clinton Clarence "Floppy" or "The Hondo Hurricane" b: 8/10/22, Hondo, Tex. BR/TR, 6'4", 215 lbs. Deb: 4/15/47 ◆																											
1947	NY-N	9	7	.563	23	20	8	1	0	138	140	76	15	2	69	54	13.8	4.57	89	.263	.350	29	.309	9	-8	-8	-1	0.1
1948	NY-N	8	8	.500	36	19	6	2	1	153^1	146	89	15	5	72	42	13.1	4.75	83	.258	.347	10	.179	2	-14	-14	-0	-1.2
1949	NY-N	9	11	.450	33	25	8	0	0	154^2	156	98	16	4	86	48	14.3	5.00	80	.260	.357	12	.190	4	-17	-18	2	-1.5
1950	NY-N	3	3	.500	20	8	1	0	0	65^1	87	56	10	2	44	23	18.3	6.61	62	.326	.425	13	.302	4	-18	-18	2	-0.8
Total	4	29	29	.500	112	72	23	3	1	511^1	529	319	56	13	271	167	14.3	5.02	80	.269	.361	90	.238	19	-56	-58	3	-3.4
● PAUL HARTZELL	Hartzell, Paul Franklin b: 11/2/53, Bloomsburg, Pa. BR/TR, 6'5", 200 lbs. Deb: 4/10/76																											
1976	Cal-A	7	4	.636	37	15	7	2	2	166	166	64	6	10	43	51	11.9	2.77	120	.266	.323	0	—	0	14	11	1	0.8
1977	Cal-A	8	12	.400	41	23	6	0	4	189^1	200	92	14	4	38	79	11.5	3.57	110	.274	.313	0	—	0	11	8	1	0.9
1978	Cal-A	6	10	.375	54	12	5	0	6	157	168	67	8	5	41	55	12.3	3.44	105	.278	.329	0	—	0	6	3	1	0.5
1979	Min-A	6	10	.375	28	26	4	0	0	163	193	102	18	4	44	44	13.3	5.36	82	.301	.350	0	—	0	-20	-17	1	-1.3
1980	Bal-A	0	2	.000	6	0	0	0	0	17^2	22	14	3	0	9	5	15.8	6.62	60	.310	.387	0	—	0	-5	-5	-1	-0.6
1984	Mil-A	0	1	.000	4	1	0	0	0	10^1	17	11	0	0	6	3	20.0	7.84	49	.370	.442	0	—	0	-4	-5	0	-0.4
Total	6	27	39	.409	170	77	22	2	12	703^1	766	350	49	23	181	237	12.4	3.90	98	.282	.332	0	—	0	1	-7	3	-0.1
● BRYAN HARVEY	Harvey, Bryan Stanley b: 6/2/63, Soddy-Daisy, Tenn. BR/TR, 6'2", 212 lbs. Deb: 5/16/87																											
1987	Cal-A	0	0	—	3	0	0	0	0	5	6	0	0	0	2	3	14.4	0.00	—	.300	.364	0	—	0	2	2	-0	0.1
1988	Cal-A	7	5	.583	50	0	0	0	17	76	59	22	4	1	20	67	9.5	2.13	181	.214	.269	0	—	0	16	15	-2	2.7
1989	Cal-A	3	3	.500	51	0	0	0	25	55	36	21	6	0	41	78	12.6	3.44	111	.183	.324	0	—	0	3	2	0	0.4
1990	Cal-A	4	4	.500	54	0	0	0	25	64^1	45	24	4	0	35	82	11.2	3.22	119	.201	.309	0	—	0	5	4	-0	0.8
1991	Cal-A☆	2	4	.333	67	0	0	0	**46**	78^2	51	20	6	1	17	101	7.9	1.60	257	.178	.227	0	—	0	22	22	-0	3.7
1992	Cal-A	0	4	.000	25	0	0	0	13	28^2	22	12	4	0	11	34	10.4	2.83	141	.208	.282	0	—	0	4	4	-1	0.7
1993	Fla-N★	1	5	.167	59	0	0	0	45	69	45	14	4	0	13	73	7.6	1.70	255	.186	.227	0	—	0	18	19	-1	3.6
1994	Fla-N	0	0	—	12	0	0	0	6	10^1	12	6	1	0	4	10	13.9	5.23	84	.279	.340	0	—	0	-1	-1	0	-0.1
1995	Fla-N	0	0	—	1	0	0	0	0	0	2	1	0	1	—	—	∞	—	1.000	1.000	101	—	0	-3	-3	0	-0.3	
Total	9	17	25	.405	322	0	0	0	177	387	278	122	30	2	144	448	9.9	2.49	161	.199	.275	0	—	0	65	65	-3	11.6
● ZAZA HARVEY	Harvey, Ervin King b: 1/5/1879, Saratoga, Cal. d: 6/3/54, Santa Monica, Cal. BL/TL, 6', 190 lbs. Deb: 5/3/00 ◆																											
1900	Chi-N	0	0	—	1	0	0	0	0	4	3	0	0	0	1	0	9.0	0.00	—	.214	.267	0	.000	-1	2	2	-0	0.0
1901	Chi-A	3	7	.300	16	9	5	0	1	92	91	59	2	5	34	27	12.7	3.62	96	.255	.328	10	.250	2	0	-1	2	0.2
Total	2	3	7	.300	17	9	5	0	1	96	94	59	2	5	35	27	12.6	3.47	101	.253	.326	86	.332	2	2	0	2	0.2
● CHAD HARVILLE	Harville, Chad Ashley b: 9/16/76, Selmer, Tenn. BR/TR, 5'9", 180 lbs. Deb: 6/23/99																											
1999	Oak-A	0	2	.000	15	0	0	0	0	14^1	18	11	2	0	10	15	17.6	6.91	67	.310	.412	0	—	0	-3	-4	-0	-0.5
● SHIGETOSHI HASEGAWA	Hasegawa, Shigetoshi b: 8/1/68, Kobe, Japan BR/TR, 5'11", 160 lbs. Deb: 4/5/97																											
1997	Ana-A	3	7	.300	50	7	0	0	0	116^2	118	60	14	3	46	83	12.9	3.93	116	.269	.343	0	—	0	8	8	2	0.8
1998	Ana-A	8	3	.727	61	0	0	0	5	97^1	86	37	14	2	32	73	11.1	3.14	149	.241	.307	0	—	0	16	17	1	1.8
1999	Ana-A	4	6	.400	64	1	0	0	2	77	80	45	14	2	34	44	13.6	4.91	99	.276	.356	0	—	0	-0	-0	1	0.0
2000	Ana-A	10	5	.625	66	0	0	0	9	95^2	100	42	11	2	38	59	13.2	3.48	139	.270	.341	0	.000	-0	14	15	-0	2.3
Total	4	25	22	.532	241	8	0	0	16	386^2	384	185	53	9	150	259	12.6	3.84	124	.264	.336	0	.000	-0	39	39	3	4.9
● HERB HASH	Hash, Herbert Howard b: 2/13/11, Woolwine, Va. BR/TR, 6'1", 180 lbs. Deb: 4/19/40																											
1940	Bos-A	7	7	.500	34	12	3	1	3	120	123	68	11	5	84	36	15.9	4.95	91	.266	.385	7	.175	-0	-8	-6	1	-0.5
1941	Bos-A	1	0	1.000	4	0	0	0	1	8^1	7	5	1	0	7	3	15.1	5.40	77	.226	.368	0	.000	-0	-1	-1	0	-0.2
Total	2	8	7	.533	38	12	3	1	4	128^1	130	73	12	5	91	39	15.8	4.98	90	.264	.384	7	.167	-1	-9	-7	1	-0.7
● ANDY HASSLER	Hassler, Andrew Earl b: 10/18/51, Texas City, Tex. BL/TL, 6'5", 220 lbs. Deb: 5/30/71																											
1971	Cal-A	0	3	.000	6	4	0	0	0	18^2	25	10	0	1	15	13	19.8	3.86	84	.333	.451	0	.000	-1	-1	-1	0	-0.2
1973	Cal-A	0	4	.000	7	4	1	0	0	31^2	33	23	0	3	19	19	15.6	3.69	96	.262	.372	0	—	0	0	-1	-0	-0.1
1974	Cal-A	7	11	.389	23	22	10	2	1	162	132	64	10	9	79	76	12.2	2.61	132	.225	.326	0	—	0	18	16	0	1.8
1975	Cal-A	3	12	.200	30	18	6	1	0	133^1	158	94	12	6	53	82	14.6	5.94	60	.303	.373	0	—	0	-32	-38	1	-3.6
1976	Cal-A	0	6	.000	14	4	0	0	0	47^1	50	31	3	0	17	16	12.7	5.13	65	.284	.347	0	—	0	-8	-10	-0	-1.2
	*KC-A	5	6	.455	19	14	4	1	0	99^2	89	37	2	0	39	45	11.6	2.89	121	.242	.314	0	—	0	7	7	1	0.8
	Yr	5	12	.294	33	18	4	1	0	147	139	68	5	0	56	61	11.9	3.61	95	.256	.325	0	—	0	-1	-3	1	-0.4
1977	*KC-A	9	6	.600	29	27	3	1	0	156^1	166	88	7	5	75	83	14.2	4.20	96	.270	.354	0	—	0	-2	-3	0	-0.2
1978	KC-A	1	4	.200	11	9	1	0	0	58^1	76	36	1	2	24	26	15.7	4.32	89	.317	.383	0	—	0	-4	-3	-1	-0.3
	Bos-A	2	1	.667	13	2	0	0	1	30	38	13	0	0	13	23	15.3	3.00	138	.302	.367	0	—	0	3	3	-0	0.3
	Yr	3	5	.375	24	11	1	0	1	88^1	114	49	1	2	37	49	15.6	3.87	102	.311	.378	0	—	0	-1	1	-1	0.0
1979	Bos-A	1	2	.333	8	0	0	0	0	15^1	23	17	0	1	7	7	18.2	8.80	50	.365	.437	0	—	0	-8	-7	-0	-1.2
	NY-N	4	5	.444	29	8	1	0	4	80^1	74	35	5	0	42	53	13.0	3.70	99	.252	.345	0	.000	-2	0	-0	1	-0.2
1980	Pit-N	0	0	—	6	0	0	0	0	11^2	9	6	2	0	4	4	10.0	3.86	95	.243	.317	0	.000	-0	-0	-0	1	0.0
	Cal-A	5	1	.833	41	0	0	0	10	83	67	25	8	1	37	75	11.4	2.49	158	.214	.299	0	—	0	14	14	-1	1.2
1981	Cal-A	4	3	.571	42	0	0	0	5	75^2	72	29	8	0	33	44	12.5	3.21	114	.262	.341	0	—	0	4	4	1	0.4
1982	*Cal-A	2	1	.667	54	0	0	0	4	71^1	58	24	5	4	40	38	12.9	2.78	146	.232	.347	0	—	0	10	10	2	0.7
1983	Cal-A	0	5	.000	42	0	0	0	4	36^1	42	22	2	0	17	20	14.6	5.45	74	.302	.378	0	—	0	-6	-6	1	-0.8
1984	StL-N	1	0	1.000	3	0	0	0	0	2^1	4	3	2	0	2	1	23.1	11.57	30	.364	.462	0	—	0	-2	-2	0	-0.4
1985	StL-N	0	1	.000	10	0	0	0	0	10	9	5	0	0	4	5	11.7	1.80	197	.225	.295	0	—	0	2	2	-0	0.2
Total	14	44	71	.383	387	112	26	5	29	1123^1	1125	562	67	32	520	630	13.4	3.83	97	.264	.349	0	.000	-3	-4	-14	4	-2.8
● CHARLIE HASTINGS	Hastings, Charles Morton b: 11/11/1870, Ironton, Ohio d: 8/3/34, Parkersburg, W.Va. 5'11", 179 lbs. Deb: 5/3/1893																											
1893	Cle-N	4	5	.444	15	9	6	0	1	92	128	81	5	5	33	14	16.2	4.70	104	.320	.379	7	.179	0	-0	2	-2	0.0
1896	Pit-N	5	10	.333	17	13	9	0	1	104	126	86	1	7	44	19	15.3	5.88	71	.296	.372	8	.216	-0	-18	-20	1	-2.1
1897	Pit-N	5	4	.556	16	10	9	0	0	118	138	84	3	7	47	42	14.6	4.58	91	.289	.362	10	.233	3	-4	-6	-1	-0.1
1898	Pit-N	4	10	.286	19	13	12	0	0	137^1	142	76	2	10	52	40	13.4	3.41	104	.265	.341	10	.233	2	3	2	1	0.5
Total	4	18	29	.383	67	45	36	0	2	451^1	534	327	11	29	176	115	14.7	4.55	91	.291	.362	35	.216	5	-18	-21	-1	-1.7
● BOB HASTY	Hasty, Robert Keller b: 5/3/1896, Canton, Ga. d: 5/28/72, Dallas, Ga. BR/TR, 6'3", 210 lbs. Deb: 9/11/19																											
1919	Phi-A	0	2	.000	2	2	1	0	0	12	15	10	1	0	4	5	14.3	5.25	65	.306	.358	1	.333	0	-3	-2	-1	-0.4
1920	Phi-A	1	3	.250	19	4	1	0	0	71^2	91	53	5	0	28	12	14.9	5.02	80	.323	.384	6	.250	0	-10	-7	2	-0.2
1921	Phi-A	5	16	.238	35	22	9	0	0	179^1	238	120	8	2	40	46	14.1	4.87	92	.331	.368	20	.294	2	-12	-8	0	-0.5
1922	Phi-A	9	14	.391	28	26	14	1	0	192^1	225	110	20	3	41	33	12.6	4.26	100	.298	.336	15	.200	-2	-5	-0	-2	-0.4
1923	Phi-A	13	15	.464	44	36	10	1	1	243^1	274	146	11	9	72	56	13.1	4.44	93	.291	.347	17	.193	-3	-12	-9	-1	-1.2
1924	Phi-A	1	3	.250	18	4	0	0	0	52^2	57	36	4	1	30	15	15.0	5.64	76	.282	.378	1	.077	-1	-8	-8	2	-0.5
Total	6	29	53	.354	146	94	35	2	1	751^1	900	475	49	15	215	167	13.5	4.65	91	.305	.355	60	.221	-3	-49	-34	-0	-3.2
● MICKEY HATCHER	Hatcher, Michael Vaughn b: 3/15/55, Cleveland, Ohio BR/TR, 6'2", 200 lbs. Deb: 8/3/79 C◆																											
1989	LA-N	0	0	—	1	0	0	0	0	1	0	1	0	1	3	0	36.0	9.00	38	.000	.667	66	.295	0	-1	-1	0	0.0
● GIL HATFIELD	Hatfield, Gilbert "Colonel" b: 1/27/1855, Hoboken, N.J. d: 5/26/21, Hoboken, N.J. TR, 5'9.5", 168 lbs. Deb: 9/24/1885 F◆																											
1889	NY-N	2	4	.333	6	5	5	0	0	52	53	43	2	1	25	28	13.7	3.98	99	.256	.339	23	.184	-0	0	-0	0	0.0
1890	NY-P	1	1	.500	3	0	0	0	1	7^2	8	8	1	1	4	3	15.3	3.52	129	.258	.361	80	.279	0	1	1	-0	0.1
1891	Was-a	0	0	—	4	0	0	0	0	18	29	28	1	0	14	3	21.5	11.00	34	.349	.443	128	.256	1	-15	-14	-0	-0.6
Total	3	3	5	.375	13	5	5	0	1	77^2	90	79	4	2	43	34	15.6	5.56	71	.280	.369	295	.248	1	-14	-14	-0	-0.5

● JOHN HATFIELD
Hatfield, John Van Buskirk b: 7/20/1847, New Jersey d: 2/20/09, Long Island City, N.Y. 5'10", 165 lbs. Deb: 5/18/1871 FM◆

YEAR	TM/L	W	L	PCT	G	GS	CG	SH	SV	IP	H	R	HR	HB	BB	SO	RAT	ERA	ERA+	OAV	OOB	BH	AVG	PB	PR	PR+	PD	TPI
1874	Mut-n	0	1	.000	3	0	0	0	0	8	11	6	0		0	0	12.4	2.25	100	.314	.314	66	.226	-0	-0	-0		0.1

● HILLY HATHAWAY
Hathaway, Hillary Houston b: 9/12/69, Jacksonville, Fla. BL/TL, 6'4", 195 lbs. Deb: 9/8/92

YEAR	TM/L	W	L	PCT	G	GS	CG	SH	SV	IP	H	R	HR	HB	BB	SO	RAT	ERA	ERA+	OAV	OOB	BH	AVG	PB	PR	PR+	PD	TPI
1992	Cal-A	0	0	—	2	1	0	0	0	5^2	8	5	1	0	3	1	17.5	7.94	50	.333	.407	0	—	0	-3	-2	-0	-0.1
1993	Cal-A	4	3	.571	11	11	0	0	0	57^1	71	35	6	5	26	11	16.0	5.02	90	.326	.410	0	—	0	-4	-3	1	-0.3
Total	2	4	3	.571	13	12	0	0	0	63	79	40	7	5	29	12	16.1	5.29	85	.326	.409	0	—	0	-7	-5	0	-0.4

● RAY HATHAWAY
Hathaway, Ray Wilson b: 10/13/16, Greenville, Ohio BR/TR, 6', 165 lbs. Deb: 4/20/45

YEAR	TM/L	W	L	PCT	G	GS	CG	SH	SV	IP	H	R	HR	HB	BB	SO	RAT	ERA	ERA+	OAV	OOB	BH	AVG	PB	PR	PR+	PD	TPI
1945	Bro-N	0	1	.000	4	1	0	0	0	9	11	7	1	0	6	3	17.0	4.00	94	.297	.395	0	.000	-0	-0	-0	0	0.0

● JOE HATTEN
Hatten, Joseph Hilarian b: 11/17/16, Bancroft, Iowa d: 12/16/88, Redding, Cal. BR/TL, 6', 176 lbs. Deb: 4/21/46

YEAR	TM/L	W	L	PCT	G	GS	CG	SH	SV	IP	H	R	HR	HB	BB	SO	RAT	ERA	ERA+	OAV	OOB	BH	AVG	PB	PR	PR+	PD	TPI
1946	Bro-N	14	11	.560	42	30	13	1	2	222	207	79	10	7	110	85	13.1	2.84	119	.253	.347	6	.076	-6	14	14	-2	0.7
1947	*Bro-N	17	8	.680	42	32	11	3	0	225^1	211	95	9	5	105	76	12.8	3.63	114	.252	.339	17	.205	0	11	12	3	1.5
1948	Bro-N	13	10	.565	42	30	11	1	0	208^2	228	93	9	3	94	73	14.0	3.58	112	.283	.360	13	.206	1	9	10	4	1.5
1949	*Bro-N	12	8	.600	37	29	11	2	2	187^1	194	102	15	2	69	58	12.7	4.18	98	.271	.337	12	.179	-1	-3	-2	0	-0.3
1950	Bro-N	2	2	.500	23	8	2	1	0	68^2	82	45	10	0	31	29	14.8	4.59	89	.294	.365	2	.111	-1	-3	-4	-1	-0.4
1951	Bro-N	1	0	1.000	11	6	0	0	0	49^1	55	25	3	0	21	22	13.9	4.56	86	.281	.350	2	.133	-1	-3	-4	1	-0.2
	Chi-N	2	6	.250	23	6	1	0	0	75^1	82	48	8	1	37	23	14.3	5.14	80	.281	.364	4	.235	0	-10	-8	-0	-0.8
	Yr	3	6	.333	34	12	1	0	0	124^2	137	73	11	1	58	45	14.1	4.91	82	.281	.358	6	.188	-1	-13	-12	1	-1.0
1952	Chi-N	4	4	.500	13	8	2	0	0	50^1	65	35	6	1	25	15	16.3	6.08	63	.314	.391	1	.067	-1	-13	-12	1	-1.7
Total	7	65	49	.570	233	149	51	8	4	1087	1124	522	70	19	492	381	13.5	3.87	101	.271	.351	57	.160	-8	1	5	6	0.3

● CLYDE HATTER
Hatter, Clyde Melno b: 8/7/08, Poplar Hills, Ky. d: 10/16/37, Yosemite, Ky. BR/TL, 5'11", 170 lbs. Deb: 4/23/35

YEAR	TM/L	W	L	PCT	G	GS	CG	SH	SV	IP	H	R	HR	HB	BB	SO	RAT	ERA	ERA+	OAV	OOB	BH	AVG	PB	PR	PR+	PD	TPI
1935	Det-A	0	0	—	8	2	0	0	0	33^1	44	33	2	1	30	15	20.3	7.56	55	.319	.444	3	.300	0	-12	-13	-1	-0.7
1937	Det-A	1	0	1.000	3	0	0	0	0	9^1	17	12	0	1	11	4	28.0	11.57	40	.415	.547	0	.000	-0	-7	-7	-0	-0.6
Total	2	1	0	1.000	11	2	0	0	0	42^2	61	45	2	2	41	19	21.9	8.44	51	.341	.468	3	.231	0	-19	-21	-1	-1.3

● CHRIS HAUGHEY
Haughey, Christopher Francis "Bud" b: 10/3/25, Astoria, N.Y. BR/TR, 6'1", 180 lbs. Deb: 10/3/43

YEAR	TM/L	W	L	PCT	G	GS	CG	SH	SV	IP	H	R	HR	HB	BB	SO	RAT	ERA	ERA+	OAV	OOB	BH	AVG	PB	PR	PR+	PD	TPI
1943	Bro-N	0	1	.000	1	0	0	0	0	7	5	6	0	0	10	0	19.3	3.86	87	.238	.484	0	.000	-0	-0	-0	-0	-0.1

● GARY HAUGHT
Haught, Gary Allen b: 9/29/70, Tacoma, Wash. BB/TR, 6'1", 190 lbs. Deb: 7/16/97

YEAR	TM/L	W	L	PCT	G	GS	CG	SH	SV	IP	H	R	HR	HB	BB	SO	RAT	ERA	ERA+	OAV	OOB	BH	AVG	PB	PR	PR+	PD	TPI
1997	Oak-A	0	0	—	6	0	0	0	0	11^1	12	9	3	2	6	11	15.9	7.15	63	.279	.392	0	—	0	-3	-3	0	-0.2

● PHIL HAUGSTAD
Haugstad, Philip Donald b: 2/23/24, Black River Falls, Wis. d: 10/21/98, Black River Falls, Wis. BR/TR, 6'2", 165 lbs. Deb: 9/1/47

YEAR	TM/L	W	L	PCT	G	GS	CG	SH	SV	IP	H	R	HR	HB	BB	SO	RAT	ERA	ERA+	OAV	OOB	BH	AVG	PB	PR	PR+	PD	TPI
1947	Bro-N	1	0	1.000	6	1	0	0	0	12^2	14	4	1	0	4	4	12.8	2.84	145	.298	.353	0	.000	-0	2	2	-0	0.1
1948	Bro-N	0	0	—	1	0	0	0	0	1	1	0	0	0	0	0	9.0	0.00	—	.333	.333	0	—	0	0	0	0	0.1
1951	Bro-N	0	1	.000	21	1	0	0	0	30^2	28	25	4	3	24	22	16.1	6.46	61	.233	.374	0	.000	0	-9	-9	0	-0.4
1952	Cin-N	0	0	—	9	0	0	0	0	12	8	9	1	1	13	2	16.5	6.75	56	.190	.393	0	.000	-0	-4	-4	0	-0.2
Total	4	1	1	.500	37	2	0	0	0	56^1	51	38	6	4	41	28	15.3	5.59	70	.241	.374	0	.000	-0	-10	-10	1	-0.4

● TOM HAUSMAN
Hausman, Thomas Matthew b: 3/31/53, Mobridge, S.D. BR/TR, 6'5", 200 lbs. Deb: 4/26/75

YEAR	TM/L	W	L	PCT	G	GS	CG	SH	SV	IP	H	R	HR	HB	BB	SO	RAT	ERA	ERA+	OAV	OOB	BH	AVG	PB	PR	PR+	PD	TPI
1975	Mil-A	3	6	.333	29	9	1	0	0	112	110	57	7	6	47	46	13.1	4.10	94	.258	.340	0	—	0	-4	-3	1	-0.2
1976	Mil-A	0	0	—	3	0	0	0	0	3^1	3	2	0	0	3	1	16.2	5.40	65	.250	.400	0	—	0	-1	-1	0	0.0
1978	NY-N	3	3	.500	10	10	0	0	0	51^2	58	28	6	1	9	16	11.8	4.70	74	.287	.321	3	.176	1	-6	-7	0	-0.7
1979	NY-N	2	6	.250	19	10	1	0	2	78^2	65	25	6	4	19	33	10.1	2.75	133	.226	.284	3	.115	-1	9	8	0	0.7
1980	NY-N	6	5	.545	55	4	0	0	1	122	125	63	12	3	26	53	11.4	3.98	89	.266	.309	1	.063	-1	-5	-6	1	-0.5
1981	NY-N	0	1	.000	20	0	0	0	0	33	28	8	2	0	7	13	9.5	2.18	160	.235	.278	0	.000	0	5	5	0	0.3
1982	NY-N	1	2	.333	21	0	0	0	0	36^2	44	26	4	2	6	16	12.8	4.42	82	.295	.331	0	.000	-0	-3	-3	-1	-0.3
	Atl-N	0	0	—	3	0	0	0	0	3^2	6	2	0	0	4	2	24.5	4.91	76	.500	.625	0	—	0	-1	-0	0	0.0
	Yr	1	2	.333	24	0	0	0	0	40^1	50	28	4	2	10	18	13.8	4.46	82	.311	.358	0	.000	-0	-4	-4	-0	-0.3
Total	7	15	23	.395	160	33	2	0	3	441	439	211	37	16	121	180	11.8	3.80	96	.262	.317	7	.111	-2	-6	-8	2	-0.7

● CLEM HAUSMANN
Hausmann, Clemens Raymond b: 8/17/19, Houston, Tex. d: 8/29/72, Baytown, Tex. BR/TR, 5'9", 165 lbs. Deb: 4/28/44

YEAR	TM/L	W	L	PCT	G	GS	CG	SH	SV	IP	H	R	HR	HB	BB	SO	RAT	ERA	ERA+	OAV	OOB	BH	AVG	PB	PR	PR+	PD	TPI
1944	Bos-A	4	7	.364	32	12	3	0	2	137	139	55	6	3	69	43	13.9	3.42	99	.266	.355	3	.079	-3	0	-0	-0	-0.3
1945	Bos-A	5	7	.417	31	13	4	2	2	125	131	77	5	2	60	30	13.9	5.04	68	.270	.352	4	.103	-3	-23	-22	2	-2.2
1949	Phi-A	0	0	—	1	0	0	0	0	1	0	1	0	0	2	0	18.0	9.00	46	.000	.500	0	—	0	-1	-1	0	0.0
Total	3	9	14	.391	64	25	7	2	4	263	270	133	11	5	131	73	13.9	4.21	81	.267	.354	7	.091	-5	-24	-23	2	-2.5

● BRAD HAVENS
Havens, Bradley David b: 11/17/59, Highland Park, Mich BL/TL, 6'1", 196 lbs. Deb: 6/5/81

YEAR	TM/L	W	L	PCT	G	GS	CG	SH	SV	IP	H	R	HR	HB	BB	SO	RAT	ERA	ERA+	OAV	OOB	BH	AVG	PB	PR	PR+	PD	TPI
1981	Min-A	3	6	.333	14	12	1	1	0	78	76	33	6	1	24	43	11.7	3.58	110	.257	.315	0	—	0	1	3	-1	0.3
1982	Min-A	10	14	.417	33	32	4	1	0	208^2	201	112	32	0	80	129	12.1	4.31	99	.250	.318	0	—	0	-5	-1	-3	-0.4
1983	Min-A	5	8	.385	16	14	1	0	0	80^1	110	75	11	0	38	40	16.6	8.18	52	.333	.402	0	—	0	-37	-33	-2	-4.4
1985	Bal-A	0	1	.000	8	1	0	0	0	14^1	20	14	4	0	10	19	18.8	8.79	46	.333	.429	0	—	0	-7	-8	-0	-0.5
1986	Bal-A	3	3	.500	46	0	0	0	1	71	64	37	7	0	29	57	11.8	4.56	91	.248	.324	0	—	0	-3	-3	1	-0.2
1987	LA-N	0	0	—	31	1	0	0	1	35^1	30	18	2	1	23	23	13.8	4.33	92	.227	.346	0	.000	-0	-1	-1	-1	-0.1
1988	LA-N	0	0	—	9	0	0	0	0	9^2	15	5	1	0	4	8	17.7	4.66	72	.357	.413	0	.000	-0	-1	-1	1	0.0
	Cle-A	2	3	.400	28	0	0	0	1	57^1	62	22	7	0	17	30	12.4	3.14	131	.273	.324	0	—	0	5	6	-0	0.5
1989	Cle-A	0	0	—	7	0	0	0	0	13^1	18	6	3	0	7	6	16.9	4.05	98	.353	.431	0	—	0	-0	-0	1	0.1
	Det-A	1	2	.333	13	1	0	0	0	22^2	28	14	3	3	14	15	17.9	5.56	69	.308	.417	0	—	0	-4	-4	0	-0.5
	Yr	1	2	.333	20	1	0	0	0	36	46	20	6	3	21	21	17.5	5.00	78	.324	.422	0	—	0	-4	-5	1	-0.4
Total	8	24	37	.393	205	61	6	2	3	590^2	624	336	76	5	246	370	13.3	4.81	86	.272	.344	0	.000	-0	-53	-44	-4	-5.2

● RYAN HAWBLITZEL
Hawblitzel, Ryan Wade b: 4/30/71, West Palm Beach, Fla. BR/TR, 6'2", 170 lbs. Deb: 6/9/96

YEAR	TM/L	W	L	PCT	G	GS	CG	SH	SV	IP	H	R	HR	HB	BB	SO	RAT	ERA	ERA+	OAV	OOB	BH	AVG	PB	PR	PR+	PD	TPI
1996	Col-N	0	1	.000	8	0	0	0	0	15	18	12	2	0	6	7	14.4	6.00	87	.290	.353	0	.000	-0	-3	-1	0	-0.1

● ED HAWK
Hawk, Edward b: 5/11/1890, Neosho, Mo. d: 3/26/36, Neosho, Mo. BL/TR, 5'11", 175 lbs. Deb: 9/7/11

YEAR	TM/L	W	L	PCT	G	GS	CG	SH	SV	IP	H	R	HR	HB	BB	SO	RAT	ERA	ERA+	OAV	OOB	BH	AVG	PB	PR	PR+	PD	TPI
1911	StL-A	0	4	.000	5	4	4	0	0	37^2	38	18	1	4	8	14	11.9	3.35	101	.253	.309	2	.154	-1	-0	0	0	-0.1

● BILL HAWKE
Hawke, William Victor "Dick" b: 4/28/1870, Elsmere, Del. d: 12/11/02, Wilmington, Del. BR/TR, 5'8.5", 169 lbs. Deb: 7/28/1892

YEAR	TM/L	W	L	PCT	G	GS	CG	SH	SV	IP	H	R	HR	HB	BB	SO	RAT	ERA	ERA+	OAV	OOB	BH	AVG	PB	PR	PR+	PD	TPI
1892	StL-N	5	5	.500	14	11	10	1	0	97^1	108	59	2	8	45	55	14.9	3.70	86	.270	.355	4	.089	-4	-4	-6	0	-0.9
1893	StL-N	0	1	.000	1	1	0	0	0	5^1	9	9	0	0	3	1	20.3	5.06	93	.360	.429	1	.333	0	-0	-0	-0	0.0
	Bal-N	11	16	.407	29	29	22	1	0	225	248	175	8	9	108	69	14.6	4.76	100	.271	.354	16	.172	-4	-2	-0	0	-0.4
	Yr	11	17	.393	30	30	22	1	0	230^1	257	184	8	9	111	70	14.7	4.77	100	.274	.356	17	.177	-4	-3	-1	0	-0.4
1894	*Bal-N	16	9	.640	32	25	17	0	3	206	264	174	9	12	78	68	15.5	5.81	94	.308	.374	28	.304	2	-11	-8	1	-0.5
Total	3	32	31	.508	76	66	49	2	3	533^2	629	417	19	29	234	193	15.0	4.98	95	.286	.363	49	.210	-7	-18	-15	1	-1.8

● LA TROY HAWKINS
Hawkins, La Troy b: 12/21/72, Gary, Ind. BR/TR, 6'5", 195 lbs. Deb: 4/29/95

YEAR	TM/L	W	L	PCT	G	GS	CG	SH	SV	IP	H	R	HR	HB	BB	SO	RAT	ERA	ERA+	OAV	OOB	BH	AVG	PB	PR	PR+	PD	TPI
1995	Min-A	2	3	.400	6	6	1	0	0	27	39	29	3	1	12	9	17.3	8.67	55	.339	.406	0	—	0	-12	-12	0	-1.6
1996	Min-A	1	1	.500	7	6	0	0	0	26^1	42	24	8	0	9	24	17.4	8.20	62	.372	.418	0	—	0	-9	-9	0	-0.5
1997	Min-A	6	12	.333	20	20	0	0	0	103^1	134	71	19	4	47	58	16.1	5.84	80	.317	.390	0	.000	-0	-15	-13	0	-1.9
1998	Min-A	7	14	.333	33	33	0	0	0	190^1	227	126	27	5	61	105	13.9	5.25	91	.299	.355	0	.000	-0	-13	-10	1	-0.8
1999	Min-A	10	14	.417	33	33	1	0	0	174^1	238	136	29	1	60	103	15.4	6.66	77	.323	.375	0	.000	-0	-35	-29	-1	-3.3
2000	Min-A	2	5	.286	66	0	0	0	14	87^2	85	34	7	1	32	59	12.1	3.39	155	.256	.323	0	.000	-0	15	17	1	1.7
Total	6	28	49	.364	165	98	2	0	14	609	765	420	93	12	221	358	14.7	5.76	86	.309	.368	0	.000	-1	-68	-55	1	-6.4

● ANDY HAWKINS
Hawkins, Melton Andrew b: 1/21/60, Waco, Tex. BR/TR, 6'3", 223 lbs. Deb: 7/17/82

YEAR	TM/L	W	L	PCT	G	GS	CG	SH	SV	IP	H	R	HR	HB	BB	SO	RAT	ERA	ERA+	OAV	OOB	BH	AVG	PB	PR	PR+	PD	TPI
1982	SD-N	2	5	.286	15	10	1	0	0	63^2	66	33	4	2	27	25	13.4	4.10	84	.274	.352	0	.000	-2	-3	-5	-1	-0.8
1983	SD-N	5	7	.417	21	19	4	1	0	119^2	106	50	8	5	48	59	12.0	2.93	119	.244	.326	2	.065	-1	9	8	1	0.7
1984	*SD-N	8	9	.471	36	22	2	1	0	146	143	90	13	2	72	77	13.4	4.68	76	.254	.341	8	.195	1	-18	-18	-1	-2.0
1985	SD-N	18	8	.692	33	33	5	2	0	228^2	229	88	18	4	65	69	11.7	3.15	113	.267	.321	6	.078	-4	11	10	-1	0.6
1986	SD-N	10	8	.556	37	35	3	1	0	209^1	218	111	24	5	75	117	12.8	4.30	85	.268	.334	10	.149	-1	-13	-15	-2	-1.4

YEAR	TM/L	W	L	PCT	G	GS	CG	SH	SV	IP	H	R	HR	HB	BB	SO	RAT	ERA	ERA+	OAV	OOB	BH	AVG	PB	PR	PR+	PD	TPI
1987	SD-N	3	10	.231	24	20	0	0	0	117^2	131	71	16	2	49	51	13.9	5.05	78	.287	.358	5	.156	-0	-13	-15	0	-1.4
1988	SD-N	14	11	.560	33	33	4	2	0	217^2	196	88	16	6	76	91	11.5	3.35	102	.244	.314	7	.113	-2	3	1	-3	-0.3
1989	NY-A	15	15	.500	34	34	5	2	0	208^1	238	127	23	6	76	98	13.8	4.80	81	.290	.355	0	—	0	-21	-21	-3	-3.0
1990	NY-A	5	12	.294	28	26	2	1	0	157^2	156	101	20	2	82	74	13.7	5.37	74	.260	.351	0	—	0	-25	-24	-2	-2.5
1991	NY-A	0	2	.000	4	3	0	0	0	12^2	23	15	5	0	6	5	20.6	9.95	42	.383	.439	0	—	0	-8	-8	1	-0.9
	Oak-A	4	4	.500	15	14	1	0	0	77	68	41	5	5	36	40	12.7	4.79	80	.237	.332	0	—	0	-6	-9	0	-0.8
	Yr	4	6	.400	19	17	1	0	0	89^2	91	56	10	5	42	45	13.9	5.52	70	.262	.350	0	—	0	-14	-17	1	-1.7
Total	10	84	91	.480	280	249	27	10	0	1558^1	1574	815	152	39	612	706	12.9	4.22	87	.265	.338	38	.117	-8	-84	-97	-11	-11.8

● WYNN HAWKINS

Hawkins, Wynn Firth "Hawk" b: 2/20/36, E.Palestine, Ohio BR/TR, 6'3", 195 lbs. Deb: 4/22/60

YEAR	TM/L	W	L	PCT	G	GS	CG	SH	SV	IP	H	R	HR	HB	BB	SO	RAT	ERA	ERA+	OAV	OOB	BH	AVG	PB	PR	PR+	PD	TPI
1960	Cle-A	4	4	.500	15	9	1	0	0	66	68	32	10	1	39	39	14.7	4.23	88	.269	.369	2	.100	-1	-3	-4	1	-0.4
1961	Cle-A	7	9	.438	30	21	3	1	1	133	139	72	16	2	59	51	13.5	4.06	97	.270	.347	4	.108	-2	-1	-2	-1	-0.5
1962	Cle-A	1	0	1.000	3	0	0	0	0	3^2	9	5	1	0	1	0	24.5	7.36	53	.429	.455	0	—	0	-1	-1	-0	-0.3
Total	3	12	13	.480	48	30	4	1	1	202^2	216	109	27	3	99	90	14.1	4.17	93	.274	.357	6	.105	-2	-5	-7	-1	-1.2

● PINK HAWLEY

Hawley, Emerson P. b: 12/5/1872, Beaver Dam, Wis. d: 9/19/38, Beaver Dam, Wis. BL/TR, 5'10", 185 lbs. Deb: 8/13/1892

YEAR	TM/L	W	L	PCT	G	GS	CG	SH	SV	IP	H	R	HR	HB	BB	SO	RAT	ERA	ERA+	OAV	OOB	BH	AVG	PB	PR	PR+	PD	TPI
1892	StL-N	6	14	.300	20	20	18	0	0	166^1	160	116	4	11	63	63	12.7	3.19	100	.243	.319	12	.169	-2	2	0	-2	-0.4
1893	StL-N	5	17	.227	31	24	21	0	1	227	249	184	6	20	103	73	14.7	4.60	103	.270	.356	26	.286	7	2	3	-3	0.6
1894	StL-N	19	27	.413	53	41	36	0	0	392^2	481	306	14	21	149	120	14.9	4.90	110	.298	.365	43	.264	2	18	22	2	2.1
1895	Pit-N	31	22	.585	**56**	50	44	**4**	1	**444**^{1}	449	242	7	33	122	142	12.2	3.18	142	.258	.319	57	.308	14	**79**	70	2	**7.8**
1896	Pit-N	22	21	.512	49	43	37	2	0	378	382	197	2	28	157	137	13.5	3.57	118	.260	.343	39	.239	2	33	28	3	2.9
1897	Pit-N	18	18	.500	40	39	33	0	0	311^1	362	221	7	26	94	88	13.9	4.80	87	.288	.350	30	.231	-2	-17	-22	0	-2.1
1898	Cin-N	27	11	.711	43	37	32	3	0	331	357	163	5	22	91	69	12.8	3.37	114	.273	.331	24	.185	-4	9	16	-5	0.7
1899	Cin-N	14	17	.452	34	29	25	0	1	250^1	289	161	7	20	65	46	13.4	4.24	92	.289	.344	22	.218	-1	-11	-9	-2	-1.2
1900	NY-N	18	18	.500	41	38	**34**	2	0	329^1	377	204	7	20	89	80	13.3	3.53	103	.287	.341	25	.203	-2	6	3	4	0.5
1901	Mil-A	7	14	.333	26	23	17	0	0	182^1	228	133	3	9	41	50	13.7	4.59	78	.302	.346	19	.260	2	-19	-21	1	-1.5
Total	10	167	179	.483	393	344	297	11	3	3012^2	3334	1927	62	210	974	868	13.5	3.96	107	.277	.342	297	.241	15	103	90	-0	9.4

● SCOTT HAWLEY

Hawley, Marvin Hiram b: Painesville, Ohio d: 4/28/04, Alliance, Ohio Deb: 9/22/1894

YEAR	TM/L	W	L	PCT	G	GS	CG	SH	SV	IP	H	R	HR	HB	BB	SO	RAT	ERA	ERA+	OAV	OOB	BH	AVG	PB	PR	PR+	PD	TPI
1894	Bos-N	0	1	.000	1	1	1	0	0	7	10	6	0	2	7	1	24.4	7.71	74	.333	.487	0	.000	-1	-2	-1	0	-0.2

● HAL HAYDEL

Haydel, John Harold b: 7/9/44, Houma, La. BR/TR, 6', 190 lbs. Deb: 9/7/70

YEAR	TM/L	W	L	PCT	G	GS	CG	SH	SV	IP	H	R	HR	HB	BB	SO	RAT	ERA	ERA+	OAV	OOB	BH	AVG	PB	PR	PR+	PD	TPI
1970	Min-A	2	0	1.000	4	0	0	0	0	9	7	3	2	0	4	4	11.0	3.00	124	.226	.314	2	.667	2	1	1	-0	0.4
1971	Min-A	4	2	.667	31	0	0	0	1	40	33	19	3	2	20	29	12.4	4.27	83	.243	.348	1	.333	0	-4	-3	0	-0.4
Total	2	6	2	.750	35	0	0	0	1	49	40	22	5	2	24	33	12.1	4.04	89	.240	.342	3	.500	2	-3	-2	-0	0.0

● LEFTY HAYDEN

Hayden, Eugene Franklin b: 4/14/35, San Francisco, Cal BL/TL, 6'2", 175 lbs. Deb: 6/26/58

YEAR	TM/L	W	L	PCT	G	GS	CG	SH	SV	IP	H	R	HR	HB	BB	SO	RAT	ERA	ERA+	OAV	OOB	BH	AVG	PB	PR	PR+	PD	TPI
1958	Cin-N	0	0	—	3	0	0	0	0	3^2	5	2	0	0	1	3	14.7	4.91	84	.313	.353	0	—	0	-0	-0	-0	0.0

● BEN HAYES

Hayes, Ben Joseph b: 8/4/57, Niagara Falls, N.Y. BR/TR, 6'1", 180 lbs. Deb: 6/25/82

YEAR	TM/L	W	L	PCT	G	GS	CG	SH	SV	IP	H	R	HR	HB	BB	SO	RAT	ERA	ERA+	OAV	OOB	BH	AVG	PB	PR	PR+	PD	TPI
1982	Cin-N	2	0	1.000	26	0	0	0	2	45^2	37	12	3	0	22	38	11.6	1.97	188	.219	.309	0	.000	-0	8	9	-1	0.3
1983	Cin-N	4	6	.400	60	0	0	0	7	69^1	82	53	8	1	37	44	15.6	6.49	59	.301	.387	0	.000	-1	-22	-20	0	-3.0
Total	2	6	6	.500	86	0	0	0	9	115	119	65	11	1	59	82	14.0	4.70	80	.270	.357	0	.000	-1	-14	-11	-1	-2.7

● JIM HAYES

Hayes, James Millard "Whitey" b: 2/25/12, Montevallo, Ala. d: 11/27/93, Decatur, Ga. BL/TR, 6'1", 168 lbs. Deb: 7/13/35

YEAR	TM/L	W	L	PCT	G	GS	CG	SH	SV	IP	H	R	HR	HB	BB	SO	RAT	ERA	ERA+	OAV	OOB	BH	AVG	PB	PR	PR+	PD	TPI
1935	Was-A	2	4	.333	7	4	1	0	0	28	38	28	0	0	23	9	19.6	8.36	52	.322	.433	2	.250	-0	-12	-13	-1	-2.1

● FRED HAYNER

Hayner, Fred Ames b: 11/3/1871, Janesville, Wis. d: 1/14/29, Lake Forest, Ill. 6', 160 lbs. Deb: 8/19/1890

YEAR	TM/L	W	L	PCT	G	GS	CG	SH	SV	IP	H	R	HR	HB	BB	SO	RAT	ERA	ERA+	OAV	OOB	BH	AVG	PB	PR	PR+	PD	TPI
1890	Pit-N	0	0	—	1	0	0	0	0	4	7	9	2	0	5	1	27.0	13.50	24	.368	.500	0	.000	-0	-4	-5	0	-0.2

● HEATH HAYNES

Haynes, Heath Burnett b: 11/30/68, Wheeling, W.Va. BR/TR, 6', 175 lbs. Deb: 6/1/94

YEAR	TM/L	W	L	PCT	G	GS	CG	SH	SV	IP	H	R	HR	HB	BB	SO	RAT	ERA	ERA+	OAV	OOB	BH	AVG	PB	PR	PR+	PD	TPI
1994	Mon-N	0	0	—	4	0	0	0	0	3^2	3	1	0	0	3	1	14.7	0.00	—	.231	.375	0	—	0	2	2	-0	0.1

● JIMMY HAYNES

Haynes, Jimmy Wayne b: 9/5/72, LaGrange, Ga. BR/TR, 6'4", 185 lbs. Deb: 9/13/95

YEAR	TM/L	W	L	PCT	G	GS	CG	SH	SV	IP	H	R	HR	HB	BB	SO	RAT	ERA	ERA+	OAV	OOB	BH	AVG	PB	PR	PR+	PD	TPI
1995	Bal-A	2	1	.667	4	3	0	0	0	24	11	6	2	0	12	22	8.6	2.25	211	.136	.247	0	—	0	7	7	-0	0.8
1996	Bal-A	3	6	.333	26	11	0	0	1	89	122	84	14	2	58	65	18.4	8.29	59	.333	.427	0	—	0	-33	-34	0	-2.7
1997	Oak-A	3	6	.333	13	13	0	0	0	73^1	74	38	7	2	40	65	14.2	4.42	103	.262	.358	0	.000	-0	1	1	1	0.1
1998	Oak-A	11	9	.550	33	33	1	1	0	194^1	229	124	25	5	88	134	14.9	5.09	90	.298	.374	0	.000	0	-9	-11	-2	-1.1
1999	Oak-A	7	12	.368	30	25	0	0	0	142	158	112	21	2	80	93	15.2	6.34	73	.282	.373	0	.000	-0	-23	-28	-1	-3.1
2000	Mil-N	12	13	.480	33	33	0	0	0	199^1	228	128	21	7	100	88	15.1	5.33	86	.295	.380	8	.125	-1	-15	-17	1	-1.8
Total	6	38	47	.447	139	118	1	1	1	722	822	492	90	18	378	467	15.2	5.63	82	.290	.377	8	.110	-2	-73	-82	-1	-7.8

● JOE HAYNES

Haynes, Joseph Walton b: 9/21/17, Lincolnton, Ga. d: 1/6/67, Hopkins, Minn. BR/TR, 6'2.5", 190 lbs. Deb: 4/24/39 C

YEAR	TM/L	W	L	PCT	G	GS	CG	SH	SV	IP	H	R	HR	HB	BB	SO	RAT	ERA	ERA+	OAV	OOB	BH	AVG	PB	PR	PR+	PD	TPI
1939	Was-A	8	12	.400	27	20	10	1	0	173	186	118	10	1	78	64	13.8	5.36	81	.276	.352	14	.209	0	-14	-21	-1	-2.0
1940	Was-A	3	6	.333	22	7	1	0	0	63^1	85	50	4	1	34	23	17.1	6.54	64	.327	.407	2	.105	-2	-15	-18	-1	-2.2
1941	Chi-A	0	0	—	8	0	0	0	0	28	30	13	0	0	11	18	13.2	3.86	106	.280	.347	3	.273	0	1	1	-0	0.0
1942	Chi-A	8	5	.615	**40**	1	1	0	6	103	88	37	6	3	47	35	12.1	2.62	137	.234	.324	5	.179	0	12	11	0	1.5
1943	Chi-A	7	2	.778	35	2	1	0	3	109^1	114	51	2	2	32	37	12.2	2.96	113	.263	.316	9	.265	2	4	5	-1	0.5
1944	Chi-A	5	6	.455	33	12	8	0	2	154^1	148	55	5	0	43	44	11.1	2.57	134	.254	.306	10	.200	1	15	15	0	1.3
1945	Chi-A	5	5	.500	14	13	8	1	1	104	92	44	5	1	29	34	10.6	3.55	94	.237	.291	7	.175	-2	-2	-3	1	-0.4
1946	Chi-A	7	9	.438	32	23	9	0	2	177^1	203	80	14	4	60	60	13.6	3.76	91	.289	.349	14	.246	3	-5	-7	1	-0.2
1947	Chi-A	14	6	.700	29	22	7	2	0	182	174	65	5	2	61	50	11.7	**2.42**	**151**	.250	.312	17	.262	2	26	25	0	3.0
1948	Chi-A☆	9	10	.474	27	22	6	0	0	149^2	167	79	13	2	52	40	13.3	3.97	107	.284	.344	8	.160	-1	5	5	-2	0.2
1949	Was-A	2	9	.182	37	10	0	0	2	96^1	106	77	6	3	55	19	15.3	6.26	68	.283	.380	6	.240	1	-22	-21	1	-2.0
1950	Was-A	7	5	.583	27	10	1	1	0	101^2	124	73	14	5	46	15	15.5	5.84	77	.305	.382	7	.200	1	-14	-16	1	-1.3
1951	Was-A	1	4	.200	26	3	1	0	2	73	85	46	9	1	37	18	15.2	4.56	90	.290	.372	7	.333	2	-4	-4	-1	-0.1
1952	Was-A	0	3	.000	22	2	0	0	3	66	70	35	2	1	35	18	14.5	4.50	79	.275	.364	2	.105	-1	-6	-7	-1	-0.5
Total	14	76	82	.481	379	147	53	5	21	1581	1672	823	95	26	620	475	13.2	4.01	96	.272	.342	111	.213	7	-20	-32	-2	-2.2

● RAY HAYWARD

Hayward, Raymond Alton b: 4/27/61, Enid, Okla. BL/TL, 6'1", 190 lbs. Deb: 9/20/86

YEAR	TM/L	W	L	PCT	G	GS	CG	SH	SV	IP	H	R	HR	HB	BB	SO	RAT	ERA	ERA+	OAV	OOB	BH	AVG	PB	PR	PR+	PD	TPI
1986	SD-N	0	2	.000	3	3	0	0	0	10	16	12	1	0	4	6	18.0	9.00	41	.340	.392	0	.000	-0	-6	-6	-0	-1.0
1987	SD-N	0	0	—	4	0	0	0	0	6	12	11	3	0	3	2	22.5	16.50	24	.444	.500	0	.000	-0	-8	-9	1	-0.4
1988	Tex-A	4	6	.400	12	12	1	1	0	62^2	63	44	6	0	35	37	14.1	5.46	75	.276	.373	0	—	0	-10	-9	1	-1.2
Total	3	4	8	.333	19	15	1	1	0	78^2	91	67	10	0	42	45	15.2	6.75	60	.301	.387	0	.000	-1	-24	-23	1	-2.6

● BILL HAYWOOD

Haywood, William Kiernan b: 4/21/37, Colon, Panama BR/TR, 6'3", 205 lbs. Deb: 7/28/68

YEAR	TM/L	W	L	PCT	G	GS	CG	SH	SV	IP	H	R	HR	HB	BB	SO	RAT	ERA	ERA+	OAV	OOB	BH	AVG	PB	PR	PR+	PD	TPI
1968	Was-A	0	0	—	14	0	0	0	0	23	27	16	1	2	12	10	16.0	4.70	62	.314	.410	0	—	0	-4	-5	-0	-0.3

● ED HEAD

Head, Edward Marvin b: 1/25/18, Selma, La. d: 1/31/80, Bastrop, La. BR/TR, 6'1", 175 lbs. Deb: 7/27/40

YEAR	TM/L	W	L	PCT	G	GS	CG	SH	SV	IP	H	R	HR	HB	BB	SO	RAT	ERA	ERA+	OAV	OOB	BH	AVG	PB	PR	PR+	PD	TPI
1940	Bro-N	1	2	.333	13	5	2	0	0	39^1	40	21	0	0	18	13	13.3	4.12	97	.260	.337	2	.182	-0	-1	-1	-1	-0.2
1942	Bro-N	10	6	.625	36	15	5	1	4	136^2	118	60	11	3	47	78	11.1	3.56	92	.231	.300	13	.333	4	-4	-5	0	-0.1
1943	Bro-N	9	10	.474	47	18	7	3	6	169^2	166	75	8	0	66	83	12.3	3.66	92	.250	.318	7	.152	-2	-5	-6	1	-0.7
1944	Bro-N	4	3	.571	9	8	5	1	0	63^1	54	21	2	0	19	17	10.4	2.70	132	.232	.290	5	.263	1	6	6	-1	0.6
1946	Bro-N	3	2	.600	13	7	3	1	1	56	56	24	3	0	24	17	12.9	3.21	105	.267	.342	5	.313	2	1	1	-1	0.2
Total	5	27	23	.540	118	53	22	6	11	465	434	201	24	3	174	208	11.8	3.48	98	.245	.314	32	.244	5	-2	-4	-1	-0.2

● RALPH HEAD

Head, Ralph b: 8/30/1893, Tallapoosa, Ga. d: 10/8/62, Muscadine, Ala. BR/TR, 5'10", 175 lbs. Deb: 4/18/23

YEAR	TM/L	W	L	PCT	G	GS	CG	SH	SV	IP	H	R	HR	HB	BB	SO	RAT	ERA	ERA+	OAV	OOB	BH	AVG	PB	PR	PR+	PD	TPI
1923	Phi-N	2	9	.182	35	13	5	0	0	132^1	185	111	13	1	57	24	16.5	6.66	69	.341	.404	3	.071	-5	-39	-26	-1	-2.3

● TOM HEALEY

Healey, Thomas F. b: 1853, Cranston, R.I. d: 2/6/1891, Lewiston, Maine TR, Deb: 6/13/1878

YEAR	TM/L	W	L	PCT	G	GS	CG	SH	SV	IP	H	R	HR	HB	BB	SO	RAT	ERA	ERA+	OAV	OOB	BH	AVG	PB	PR	PR+	PD	TPI
1878	Pro-N	0	3	.000	3	3	3	0	0	24	27	17	1		7	2	12.8	3.00	74	.278	.327	2	.222	0	-2	-2	-0	-0.2
	Ind-N	6	4	.600	11	10	9	0	1	89	98	50	1		13	18	11.2	2.22	91	.270	.295	8	.178	-1	1	-2	-0	-0.3
	Yr	6	7	.462	14	13	12	0	**1**	113	125	67	2		20	20	11.5	2.39	87	.272	.302	10	.185	-1	-1	-4	-0	-0.5

● JOHN HEALY Healy, John J. "Egyptian" or "Long John" b: 10/27/1866, Cairo, Ill. d: 3/16/1899, St.Louis, Mo. BR/TR, 6'2", 158 lbs. Deb: 9/11/1885

YEAR	TM/L	W	L	PCT	G	GS	CG	SH	SV	IP	H	R	HR	HB	BB	SO	RAT	ERA	ERA+	OAV	OOB	BH	AVG	PB	PR	PR+	PD	TPI
1885	StL-N	1	7	.125	8	8	8	0	0	66	54	37	0		20	32	10.1	3.00	92	.210	.267	1	.042	-3	-1	-2	1	-0.4
1886	StL-N	17	23	.425	43	41	39	3	0	353^2	315	213	5		118	213	11.0	2.88	112	.230	.291	14	.097	-12	17	14	-2	0.1
1887	Ind-N	12	29	.293	41	41	40	3	0	341	523	292	24	15	108	75	14.2	5.17	80	.344	.350	28	.197	-4	-42	-38	-4	-3.9
1888	Ind-N	12	24	.333	37	37	36	1	0	321^1	347	199	13	15	87	124	12.6	3.89	76	.267	.320	30	.229	4	-37	-32	1	-2.7
1889	Was-N	1	11	.083	13	12	10	0	0	101	139	111	2	5	38	49	16.2	6.24	63	.317	.378	10	.222	1	-25	-26	2	-2.0
	Chi-N	1	4	.200	5	5	5	0	0	46	48	35	4	4	18	22	13.7	4.50	92	.261	.340	2	.100	-2	-2	-2	-0	-0.3
	Yr	2	15	.118	18	17	15	0	0	147	187	146	6	9	56	71	15.4	5.69	70	.301	.367	12	.185	-1	-27	-28	1	-2.3
1890	Tol-a	22	21	.512	46	46	44	2	0	389	326	201	5	24	127	225	11.0	2.89	137	.221	.293	34	.218	7	42	45	2	4.6
1891	Bal-a	8	10	.444	23	22	19	0	0	170^1	179	124	6	5	57	54	12.7	3.75	99	.261	.322	9	.141	-2	-1	-0	-5	-0.7
1892	Bal-N	3	6	.333	9	8	5	0	0	68^1	82	51	4	2	21	24	13.8	4.74	72	.286	.339	6	.222	0	-11	-10	-0	-1.0
	Lou-N	1	1	.500	2	2	2	0	0	18^1	15	7	0	0	5	4	9.8	1.96	156	.214	.267	2	.286	1	3	2	-1	0.3
	Yr	4	7	.364	11	10	7	0	0	86^2	97	58	4	2	26	28	13.0	4.15	81	.272	.325	8	.235	1	-8	-8	-1	-0.7
Total	8	78	136	.364	227	222	208	9	0	1875	2028	1270	63	70	599	822	12.4	3.84	94	.267	.318	136	.179	-9	-57	-50	-10	-6.0

● CHARLIE HEARD Heard, Charles b: 1/30/1872, Philadelphia, Pa. d: 2/20/45, Philadelphia, Pa. BR/TR, 6'2", 190 lbs. Deb: 7/14/1890 ◆

YEAR	TM/L	W	L	PCT	G	GS	CG	SH	SV	IP	H	R	HR	HB	BB	SO	RAT	ERA	ERA+	OAV	OOB	BH	AVG	PB	PR	PR+	PD	TPI
1890	Pit-N	0	6	.000	6	6	5	0	0	44	75	65	5	2	32	13	22.3	8.39	39	.366	.456	8	.186	-1	-24	-27	-1	-2.5

● JAY HEARD Heard, Jehosie b: 1/17/20, Atlanta, Ga. d: 11/18/99, Birmingham, Ala. BL/TL, 5'7", 155 lbs. Deb: 4/24/54

YEAR	TM/L	W	L	PCT	G	GS	CG	SH	SV	IP	H	R	HR	HB	BB	SO	RAT	ERA	ERA+	OAV	OOB	BH	AVG	PB	PR	PR+	PD	TPI
1954	Bal-A	0	0	—	2	0	0	0	0	3^1	6	5	1	0	3	2	24.3	13.50	27	.375	.474	0	—	0	-4	-4	0	-0.2

● BUNNY HEARN Hearn, Bunn b: 5/21/1891, Chapel Hill, N.C. d: 10/10/59, Wilson, N.C. BL/TL, 5'11", 190 lbs. Deb: 9/17/10

YEAR	TM/L	W	L	PCT	G	GS	CG	SH	SV	IP	H	R	HR	HB	BB	SO	RAT	ERA	ERA+	OAV	OOB	BH	AVG	PB	PR	PR+	PD	TPI
1910	StL-N	1	3	.250	5	5	4	0	0	39	49	22	2	1	16	14	15.2	5.08	59	.322	.391	2	.133	-0	-9	-9	-1	-0.9
1911	StL-N	0	0	—	2	0	0	0	0	2^2	7	4	1	0	0	1	23.6	13.50	25	.538	.538	0	.000	-0	-3	-3	-0	-0.2
1913	NY-N	1	1	.500	2	2	1	0	0	13	13	6	0	0	7	8	13.8	2.77	113	.277	.370	2	.400	1	1	1	-0	0.1
1915	Pit-F	6	11	.353	29	17	8	1	0	175^2	187	74	6	2	37	49	11.6	3.38	80	.285	.326	10	.189	-0	-13	-13	-1	-1.3
1918	Bos-N	5	6	.455	17	12	9	1	0	126^1	119	43	2	0	29	30	10.5	2.49	108	.256	.300	8	.178	-1	4	3	1	0.2
1920	Bos-N	0	3	.000	11	4	2	0	0	43	54	34	3	1	11	9	13.8	5.65	54	.329	.375	2	.143	-1	-12	-13	0	-0.9
Total	6	13	24	.351	66	40	24	2	0	399^2	429	183	14	4	100	111	12.0	3.56	78	.287	.333	24	.180	-2	-32	-35	-1	-3.0

● BUNNY HEARN Hearn, Elmer Lafayette b: 1/13/04, Brooklyn, N.Y. d: 3/31/74, Venice, Fla. BL/TL, 5'8", 160 lbs. Deb: 4/13/26

YEAR	TM/L	W	L	PCT	G	GS	CG	SH	SV	IP	H	R	HR	HB	BB	SO	RAT	ERA	ERA+	OAV	OOB	BH	AVG	PB	PR	PR+	PD	TPI
1926	Bos-N	4	9	.308	34	12	3	0	2	117^1	121	63	2	0	56	40	13.6	4.22	84	.276	.358	3	.100	-2	-5	-9	-2	-1.0
1927	Bos-N	0	2	.000	8	0	0	0	0	12^2	16	9	0	0	9	5	17.8	4.26	87	.327	.431	2	.400	1	-0	-1	0	0.0
1928	Bos-N	1	0	1.000	7	0	0	0	0	10	6	8	0	1	8	8	13.5	6.30	62	.167	.333	0	.000	-0	-3	-3	-0	-0.3
1929	Bos-N	2	0	1.000	10	1	0	0	0	18^1	18	10	2	0	9	12	13.3	4.42	106	.277	.365	0	.000	0	1	1	1	0.1
Total	4	7	11	.389	59	13	3	0	2	158^1	161	90	4	1	82	65	13.9	4.38	85	.273	.363	5	.132	-2	-8	-13	-2	-1.2

● JIM HEARN Hearn, James Tolbert b: 4/11/21, Atlanta, Ga. d: 6/10/98, Boca Grande, Fla. BR/TR, 6'3", 205 lbs. Deb: 4/17/47

YEAR	TM/L	W	L	PCT	G	GS	CG	SH	SV	IP	H	R	HR	HB	BB	SO	RAT	ERA	ERA+	OAV	OOB	BH	AVG	PB	PR	PR+	PD	TPI
1947	StL-N	12	7	.632	37	21	4	1	1	162	151	67	9	1	63	57	11.9	3.22	128	.248	.319	8	.145	-1	15	16	-1	1.5
1948	StL-N	8	6	.571	34	13	3	0	1	89^2	92	44	9	2	35	27	12.9	4.22	97	.271	.342	5	.200	-0	-3	-1	-2	-0.4
1949	StL-N	1	3	.250	17	4	0	0	0	42	48	27	3	2	23	18	15.6	5.14	81	.294	.388	1	.100	-0	-5	-4	0	-0.4
1950	StL-N	0	1	.000	6	0	0	0	0	9	12	11	1	0	6	4	18.0	10.00	43	.333	.429	1	1.000	0	-6	-6	-0	-0.5
	NY-N	11	3	.786	16	16	11	5	0	125	72	33	8	0	38	54	7.9	1.94	211	.169	.237	6	.136	-0	31	30	0	3.3
	Yr	11	4	.733	22	16	11	**5**	0	134	84	44	9	0	44	58	8.6	**2.49**	165	.182	.253	7	.156	0	25	24	0	2.8
1951	*NY-N	17	9	.654	34	34	11	0	0	211^1	204	102	21	2	82	66	12.3	3.62	108	.251	.321	12	.162	-0	8	7	5	1.3
1952	NY-N☆	14	7	.667	37	34	11	1	1	223^2	208	113	16	5	97	89	12.5	3.78	98	.245	.326	14	.182	4	-1	-2	4	0.6
1953	NY-N	9	12	.429	36	32	6	0	0	196^2	206	111	22	3	84	77	13.4	4.53	95	.266	.341	9	.136	0	-5	-5	2	-0.3
1954	NY-N	8	8	.500	29	18	3	2	1	130	137	71	10	2	66	45	14.2	4.15	97	.272	.359	5	.111	-1	-1	-2	1	-0.1
1955	NY-N	14	16	.467	39	33	11	1	0	226^2	225	107	27	3	66	86	11.7	3.73	108	.260	.314	12	.156	1	8	7	2	1.2
1956	NY-N	5	11	.313	30	19	2	0	1	129^1	124	74	17	3	44	66	11.9	3.97	95	.254	.319	4	.098	-3	-3	-3	-0	-0.6
1957	Phi-N	5	1	.833	36	4	1	0	3	74	79	35	7	2	18	46	12.0	3.65	104	.274	.321	0	.000	-2	2	1	0	0.0
1958	Phi-N	5	3	.625	39	1	0	0	0	73^1	88	45	6	0	27	33	14.1	4.17	95	.292	.351	0	.000	-1	-2	-2	-1	-0.4
1959	Phi-N	0	2	.000	6	0	0	0	0	11	15	7	2	0	6	1	17.2	5.73	72	.333	.412	0	.000	0	-2	-2	0	-0.3
Total	13	109	89	.551	396	229	63	10	8	1703^2	1661	847	158	25	655	669	12.4	3.81	105	.255	.326	77	.141	-3	35	35	11	4.9

● SPENCER HEATH Heath, Spencer Paul b: 11/5/1894, Chicago, Ill. d: 1/25/30, Chicago, Ill. BB/TR, 6', 170 lbs. Deb: 5/4/20

YEAR	TM/L	W	L	PCT	G	GS	CG	SH	SV	IP	H	R	HR	HB	BB	SO	RAT	ERA	ERA+	OAV	OOB	BH	AVG	PB	PR	PR+	PD	TPI
1920	Chi-A	0	0	—	4	0	0	0	0	7	19	12	1	0	2	0	27.0	15.43	24	.475	.500	0	.000	-1	-9	-9	-0	-0.5

● JEFF HEATHCOCK Heathcock, Ronald Jeffrey b: 11/18/59, Covina, Cal. BR/TR, 6'4", 205 lbs. Deb: 9/3/83

YEAR	TM/L	W	L	PCT	G	GS	CG	SH	SV	IP	H	R	HR	HB	BB	SO	RAT	ERA	ERA+	OAV	OOB	BH	AVG	PB	PR	PR+	PD	TPI
1983	Hou-N	2	1	.667	6	3	0	0	1	28	19	14	1	1	4	12	7.7	3.21	106	.181	.218	0	.000	-1	1	1	0	0.0
1985	Hou-N	3	1	.750	14	7	1	0	1	56^1	50	25	9	1	13	25	10.2	3.36	103	.239	.287	1	.063	0	2	1	0	0.1
1987	Hou-N	4	2	.667	19	2	0	0	1	42^2	44	15	4	1	9	15	11.4	3.16	124	.277	.320	0	.000	-1	4	4	-0	0.4
1988	Hou-N	0	5	.000	17	1	0	0	0	31	33	25	2	1	16	12	14.5	5.81	57	.275	.365	0	.000	-0	-8	-9	0	-1.3
Total	4	9	9	.500	56	13	1	0	3	158	146	79	16	4	42	64	10.9	3.76	95	.246	.300	1	.029	-2	-1	-4	0	-0.8

● MIKE HEATHCOTT Heathcott, Michael Joseph b: 5/16/69, Chicago, Ill. BR/TR, 6'3", 180 lbs. Deb: 8/28/98

YEAR	TM/L	W	L	PCT	G	GS	CG	SH	SV	IP	H	R	HR	HB	BB	SO	RAT	ERA	ERA+	OAV	OOB	BH	AVG	PB	PR	PR+	PD	TPI
1998	Chi-A	0	0	—	1	0	0	0	0	3	2	1	0	0	1	3	9.0	3.00	152	.182	.250	0	—	0	1	1	-0	0.0

● NEAL HEATON Heaton, Neal b: 3/3/60, Holtsville, N.Y. BL/TL, 6'1", 205 lbs. Deb: 9/3/82

YEAR	TM/L	W	L	PCT	G	GS	CG	SH	SV	IP	H	R	HR	HB	BB	SO	RAT	ERA	ERA+	OAV	OOB	BH	AVG	PB	PR	PR+	PD	TPI
1982	Cle-A	0	2	.000	8	4	0	0	0	31	32	21	1	0	16	14	13.9	5.23	78	.260	.345	0	—	0	-4	-4	-0	-0.3
1983	Cle-A	11	7	.611	39	16	4	3	7	149^1	157	79	11	1	44	75	12.2	4.16	102	.269	.321	0	—	0	-1	1	-2	0.0
1984	Cle-A	12	15	.444	38	34	4	1	0	198^2	231	128	21	1	75	75	13.9	5.21	79	.293	.354	0	—	0	-27	-24	-3	-3.1
1985	Cle-A	9	17	.346	36	33	5	1	0	207^2	244	119	19	7	80	82	14.3	4.90	84	.298	.365	0	—	0	-17	-18	-3	-2.1
1986	Cle-A	3	6	.333	12	12	2	0	0	74^1	73	42	8	1	34	24	13.1	4.24	98	.254	.335	0	—	0	-0	-1	-0	-0.1
	Min-A	4	9	.308	21	17	3	0	1	124^1	128	60	18	1	47	66	12.7	3.98	108	.273	.340	0	—	0	3	4	-1	0.4
	Yr	7	15	.318	33	29	5	0	1	198^2	201	102	26	2	81	90	12.9	4.08	104	.266	.338	0	—	0	2	4	-1	0.3
1987	Mon-N	13	10	.565	32	32	3	1	0	193^1	207	103	25	3	37	105	11.5	4.52	93	.273	.310	14	.209	2	-9	-6	-1	-0.6
1988	Mon-N	3	10	.231	32	11	0	0	2	97^1	98	54	14	3	43	43	13.3	4.99	72	.271	.354	3	.143	-0	-17	-14	-0	-1.9
1989	Pit-N	6	7	.462	42	18	1	0	0	147^1	127	55	12	6	55	67	11.5	3.05	110	.233	.311	9	.214	1	7	5	1	0.6
1990	Pit-N☆	12	9	.571	30	24	0	0	0	146	143	66	17	2	38	68	11.3	3.45	105	.263	.314	2	.047	-2	6	3	-0	0.2
1991	Pit-N	3	3	.500	42	1	0	0	0	68^2	72	37	6	4	21	34	12.7	4.33	83	.275	.338	4	.286	2	-5	-6	-1	-0.4
1992	KC-A	3	1	.750	31	0	0	0	0	41	43	21	5	1	22	29	14.5	4.17	97	.274	.367	0	—	0	-1	-0	-0	-0.1
	Mil-A	0	0	—	1	0	0	0	0	1	0	0	0	0	1	2	9.0	0.00	—	.000	.250	0	—	0	0	0	0	0.0
	Yr	3	1	.750	32	0	0	0	0	42	43	21	5	1	23	31	14.4	4.07	100	.269	.364	0	—	0	-1	-0	-0	-0.1
1993	NY-A	1	0	1.000	18	0	0	0	0	27	34	19	6	3	11	15	16.0	6.00	69	.301	.378	0	—	0	-5	-6	-0	-0.2
Total	12	80	96	.455	382	202	22	6	10	1507	1589	804	163	32	524	699	12.8	4.37	91	.273	.337	32	.171	2	-70	-66	-11	-7.6

● DAVE HEAVERLO Heaverlo, David Wallace b: 8/25/50, Ellensburg, Wash. BR/TR, 6'1", 210 lbs. Deb: 4/14/75

YEAR	TM/L	W	L	PCT	G	GS	CG	SH	SV	IP	H	R	HR	HB	BB	SO	RAT	ERA	ERA+	OAV	OOB	BH	AVG	PB	PR	PR+	PD	TPI
1975	SF-N	3	1	.750	42	0	0	0	1	64	62	18	2	1	31	35	13.2	2.39	159	.262	.349	2	.500	1	9	10	1	0.7
1976	SF-N	4	4	.500	61	0	0	0	1	75	85	45	2	2	15	40	12.2	4.44	82	.289	.328	1	.333	0	-8	-6	1	-0.6
1977	SF-N	5	1	.833	56	0	0	0	1	98^2	92	36	10	3	21	58	10.6	2.55	153	.251	.297	0	.000	-0	15	15	2	1.0
1978	Oak-A	3	6	.333	69	0	0	0	10	130	141	56	11	3	41	71	12.8	3.25	112	.281	.339	0	—	0	8	6	3	0.8
1979	Oak-A	4	11	.267	62	0	0	0	9	85^2	97	42	7	4	42	40	15.0	4.20	97	.294	.380	0	.000	-0	0	-1	0	-0.2
1980	Sea-A	6	3	.667	60	0	0	0	4	78^2	75	37	9	5	35	42	13.2	3.89	106	.253	.342	0	—	0	1	2	-2	0.1
1981	Oak-A	1	0	1.000	6	0	0	0	0	5^2	7	1	0	0	3	2	15.9	1.59	219	.292	.370	0	—	0	1	1	-0	0.2
Total	7	26	26	.500	356	0	0	0	26	537^2	559	235	41	18	188	288	12.8	3.41	113	.273	.339	3	.231	0	26	26	4	2.0

● WALLY HEBERT Hebert, Wallace Andrew "Preacher" b: 8/21/07, Lake Charles, La. d: 12/8/99, Westlake, La. BL/TL, 6'1", 195 lbs. Deb: 5/1/31

YEAR	TM/L	W	L	PCT	G	GS	CG	SH	SV	IP	H	R	HR	HB	BB	SO	RAT	ERA	ERA+	OAV	OOB	BH	AVG	PB	PR	PR+	PD	TPI
1931	StL-A	6	7	.462	23	13	5	0	0	103	128	70	11	3	43	26	15.2	5.07	91	.306	.375	9	.209	-1	-8	-5	-2	-0.8
1932	StL-A	1	12	.077	35	15	2	0	1	108^1	145	99	6	2	45	29	16.0	6.48	75	.322	.386	12	.353	2	-24	-18	0	-1.6
1933	StL-A	4	6	.400	33	10	3	0	0	88^1	114	58	4	1	35	19	15.3	5.30	88	.308	.369	9	.391	3	-10	-6	-1	-0.3

YEAR TM/L	W	L	PCT	G	GS	CG	SH	SV	IP	H	R	HR	HB	BB	SO	RAT	ERA	ERA+	OAV	OOB	BH	AVG	PB	PR	PR+	PD	TPI
1943 Pit-N	10	11	.476	34	23	12	1	0	184	197	75	3	2	45	41	11.9	2.98	117	.272	.316	13	.220	1	8	10	1	1.3
Total 4	21	36	.368	125	61	22	1	1	483^2	584	302	24	8	168	115	14.1	4.63	91	.298	.355	43	.270	5	-34	-20	-1	-1.4
● GUY HECKER	Hecker, Guy Jackson b: 4/3/1856, Youngsville, Pa. d: 12/3/38, Wooster, Ohio BR/TR, 6', 190 lbs. Deb: 5/2/1882 MU♦																										
1882 Lou-a	6	6	.500	13	11	10	0	0	104	75	49	0		5	33	**6.9**	1.30	191	**.188**	**.199**	94	.276	4	16	15	3	2.2
1883 Lou-a	28	23	.549	53	52	51	3	0	469	526	298	4		75	164	11.5	3.34	90	.266	.292	90	.271	12	-2	-20	4	-0.3
1884 Lou-a	**52**	20	.722	**75**	73	**72**	6	0	**670^2**	526	230	4	16	56	**385**	**8.0**	**1.80**	**172**	.204	**.226**	94	.297	28	108	101	7	**13.1**
1885 Lou-a	30	23	.566	53	53	51	2	0	480	454	252	6	18	54	209	9.9	2.18	148	.237	.265	81	.273	9	57	56	5	**6.7**
1886 Lou-a	26	23	.531	49	48	45	2	0	420^2	390	273	6	10	118	133	11.1	2.87	127	.231	.285	117	.341	18	27	34	1	5.1
1887 Lou-a	18	12	.600	34	32	32	2	1	285^1	375	214	9	10	50	58	12.1	4.16	105	.301	.307	149	.372	11	4	7	5	1.8
1888 Lou-a	8	17	.320	26	25	25	0	0	223^1	251	154	5	10	43	63	12.3	3.39	91	.274	.313	48	.227	2	-8	-8	1	-0.4
1889 Lou-a	5	13	.278	19	16	15	0	0	151^1	215	145	7	5	47	33	15.9	5.59	69	.324	.373	93	.284	4	-29	-29	1	-2.2
1890 Pit-N	2	9	.182	14	12	11	0	0	119^2	160	111	9	3	44	32	15.6	5.11	64	.311	.369	77	.226	2	-21	-26	1	-1.7
Total 9	175	146	.545	336	322	312	15	1	2924	2972	1726	50	72	492	1110	10.7	2.93	113	.250	.281	843	.290	90	153	130	25	24.3
● HARRY HEDGPETH	Hedgpeth, Harry Malcolm b: 9/4/1888, Fayetteville, N.C. d: 7/30/66, Richmond, Va. BL/TL, 6'1.5", 194 lbs. Deb: 10/3/13																										
1913 Was-A	0	0	—	1	0	0	0	1	1	1	0	0	0	0	0	9.0	0.00	—	.250	.250	0	—	0	0	0	0	0.1
● MIKE HEDLUND	Hedlund, Michael David "Red" b: 8/11/46, Dallas, Tex. BR/TR, 6'1", 190 lbs. Deb: 5/8/65																										
1965 Cle-A	0	0	—	6	0	0	0	0	5^1	6	4	0	0	5	4	18.6	5.06	69	.286	.423	0	.000	-0	-1	-1	-0	-0.1
1968 Cle-A	0	0	—	3	0	0	0	0	1^2	6	2	0	1	2	0	48.6	10.80	27	.545	.643	0	—	0	-1	-1	0	-0.1
1969 KC-A	3	6	.333	34	16	1	0	2	125	123	53	8	1	40	74	11.8	3.24	114	.259	.318	5	.152	-1	5	6	1	0.6
1970 KC-A	2	3	.400	9	0	0	0	0	15	18	13	6	0	7	5	15.0	7.20	52	.300	.373	0	.000	-0	-6	-6	-0	-1.2
1971 KC-A	15	8	.652	32	30	7	1	0	205^2	168	68	15	1	72	76	10.5	2.71	127	.227	.296	6	.088	-4	17	17	3	1.8
1972 KC-A	5	7	.417	29	16	1	0	0	113	119	67	10	4	41	52	13.1	4.78	64	.275	.343	6	.188	-0	-21	-22	1	-2.2
Total 6	25	24	.510	113	62	9	1	2	465^2	440	207	39	7	167	211	11.9	3.56	96	.253	.321	17	.123	-5	-7	-7	5	-1.2
● DANNY HEEP	Heep, Daniel William b: 7/3/57, San Antonio, Tex. BL/TL, 5'11", 185 lbs. Deb: 8/31/79 ♦																										
1988 *LA-N	0	0	—	1	0	0	0	0	2	2	2	1	0	0	0	9.0	9.00	37	.222	.222	36	.242	0	-1	-1	-0	-0.1
1990 *Bos-A	0	0	—	1	0	0	0	0	1	4	1	0	0	0	0	36.0	9.00	45	.667	.667	12	.174	0	-1	-1	0	0.0
Total 2	0	0	—	2	0	0	0	0	3	6	3	1	0	0	0	18.0	9.00	40	.400	.400	503	.257	0	-2	-2	-0	-0.1
● BOB HEFFNER	Heffner, Robert Frederic b: 9/13/38, Allentown, Pa. BR/TR, 6'4", 205 lbs. Deb: 6/19/63																										
1963 Bos-A	4	9	.308	20	19	3	1	0	124^2	131	61	15	2	36	77	12.2	4.26	89	.267	.319	5	.116	-1	-9	-6	-0	-0.7
1964 Bos-A	7	9	.438	55	10	1	1	6	158^2	152	81	20	3	44	112	11.3	4.08	94	.251	.305	7	.159	0	-8	-4	-1	-0.4
1965 Bos-A	0	2	.000	27	1	0	0	0	49	59	42	9	1	18	42	14.3	7.16	52	.304	.366	0	.000	-1	-20	-17	-1	-1.0
1966 Cle-A	0	1	.000	5	1	0	0	0	13	12	6	1	0	3	7	10.4	3.46	99	.240	.283	0	.000	-0	0	-0	-1	0.0
1968 Cal-A	0	0	—	7	0	0	0	0	8	6	2	0	0	6	3	13.5	2.25	129	.240	.387	0	—	0	1	1	-0	0.1
Total 5	11	21	.344	114	31	4	2	6	353^1	360	192	45	6	107	241	12.0	4.51	84	.264	.320	12	.128	-1	-36	-27	-2	-2.0
● BRONSON HEFLIN	Heflin, Bronson Wayne b: 8/29/71, Clarksville, Tenn. BR/TR, 6'3", 195 lbs. Deb: 8/1/96																										
1996 Phi-N	0	0	—	3	0	0	0	0	6^2	11	7	1	0	3	4	18.9	6.75	64	.367	.424	0	—	0	-2	-2	-0	-0.1
● RANDY HEFLIN	Heflin, Randolph Rutherford b: 9/11/18, Fredericksburg, Va. d: 8/17/99, Fredericksburg, Va. BL/TR, 6', 185 lbs. Deb: 6/9/45																										
1945 Bos-A	4	10	.286	20	14	6	2	0	102	102	52	3	4	61	39	14.7	4.06	84	.272	.380	3	.086	-3	-8	-7	1	-1.1
1946 Bos-A	0	1	.000	5	1	0	0	0	14^2	16	5	0	1	12	6	17.8	2.45	149	.296	.433	2	.667	1	2	2	1	0.3
Total 2	4	11	.267	25	15	6	2	0	116^2	118	57	3	5	73	45	15.1	3.86	89	.275	.387	5	.132	-2	-6	-5	2	-0.8
● JAKE HEHL	Hehl, Herman Jacob b: 12/8/1899, Brooklyn, N.Y. d: 7/4/61, Brooklyn, N.Y. BR/TR, 5'11", 180 lbs. Deb: 6/20/18																										
1918 Bro-N	0	0	—	1	0	0	0	0	1	0	0	0	1	0	0	9.0	0.00	—	.000	.250	0	—	0	0	0	0	0.0
● EMMET HEIDRICK	Heidrick, R. Emmet "Snags" b: 7/9/1876, Queenstown, Pa. d: 1/20/16, Clarion, Pa. BL/TR, 6', 185 lbs. Deb: 9/14/1898 ♦																										
1902 StL-A	0	0	—	1	0	0	0	0	1	0	0	0	0	0	0	0.0	0.00	—	.000	.000	129	.289	0	0	0	-0	0.0
● FRANK HEIFER	Heifer, Franklin "Heck" b: 1/18/1854, Reading, Pa. d: 8/29/1893, Reading, Pa. 5'10.5", 175 lbs. Deb: 6/4/1875 ♦																										
1875 Bos-n	0	0	—	2	0	0	0	1	2^1	6	4	0		0	0	23.1	15.43	14	.462	.462	14	.280	1	-3	-4		-0.3
● FRED HEIMACH	Heimach, Frederick Amos "Lefty" b: 1/27/01, Camden, N.J. d: 6/1/73, Ft.Myers, Fla. BL/TL, 6', 175 lbs. Deb: 10/1/20																										
1920 Phi-A	0	1	.000	1	1	0	0	0	5	13	9	0	0	1	0	25.2	14.40	28	.542	.560	0	.000	-0	-6	-5	1	-0.6
1921 Phi-A	1	0	1.000	1	1	1	0	0	9	7	0	0	0	1	1	8.0	0.00	—	.226	.250	1	.250	-0	4	4	1	0.6
1922 Phi-A	7	11	.389	37	19	7	0	1	171^2	220	117	18	3	63	47	15.0	5.03	85	.316	.375	15	.250	2	-19	-14	1	-1.0
1923 Phi-A	6	12	.333	40	19	10	0	0	208^1	238	120	14	6	69	63	13.5	4.32	95	.292	.352	30	.254	2	-8	-5	0	-0.1
1924 Phi-A	14	12	.538	40	26	10	0	0	198	243	122	2	4	60	60	14.0	4.73	91	.306	.357	29	.322	6	-11	-10	2	-0.3
1925 Phi-A	0	1	.000	10	0	0	0	0	20^1	24	10	2	1	9	6	15.0	3.98	117	.312	.391	1	.167	-0	1	1	0	0.1
1926 Phi-A	1	0	1.000	13	1	0	0	0	31^2	28	14	1	0	5	8	9.4	2.84	147	.239	.270	1	.100	-1	4	5	2	0.3
Bos-A	2	9	.182	20	13	6	0	0	102	119	72	5	0	42	17	14.2	5.65	72	.303	.370	13	.295	2	-18	-18	3	-1.1
Yr	3	9	.250	33	14	6	0	0	133^2	147	86	6	0	47	25	13.1	4.98	82	.288	.348	14	.259	2	-14	-13	5	-0.8
1928 NY-A	2	3	.400	13	9	5	0	0	68	66	30	3	1	16	25	11.0	3.31	114	.250	.295	5	.167	-1	6	4	0	0.1
1929 NY-A	11	6	.647	35	10	3	3	4	134^2	141	72	4	3	29	26	11.6	4.01	96	.272	.314	9	.184	1	4	-2	2	-0.1
1930 Bro-N	0	2	.000	9	0	0	0	0	7^1	14	5	0	0	3	1	20.9	4.91	100	.424	.472	1	.250	-0	0	0	0	0.0
1931 Bro-N	9	7	.563	31	10	7	1	1	135^1	145	66	6	1	23	43	11.2	3.46	110	.274	.306	12	.197	1	6	5	4	1.0
1932 Bro-N	9	4	.692	36	15	7	0	0	167^2	203	85	7	6	28	30	12.7	3.97	96	.299	.333	9	.164	1	-2	-3	1	0.0
1933 Bro-N	0	1	.000	10	3	0	0	0	29^2	49	33	2	2	11	7	18.8	10.01	32	.374	.431	2	.200	-0	-22	-23	-0	-1.2
Total 13	62	69	.473	296	127	56	5	7	1288^2	1510	755	64	27	360	334	13.2	4.46	90	.296	.346	128	.236	12	-61	-61	16	-2.3
● GORMAN HEIMUELLER	Heimueller, Gorman John b: 9/24/55, Los Angeles, Cal. BL/TL, 6'4", 195 lbs. Deb: 7/12/83																										
1983 Oak-A	3	5	.375	16	14	2	1	0	83^2	93	43	8	1	29	31	13.2	4.41	88	.286	.346	0	—	0	-3	-5	2	-0.2
1984 Oak-A	0	1	.000	6	0	0	0	0	14^2	21	14	2	0	7	3	17.2	6.14	61	.344	.412	0	—	0	-3	-4	0	-0.2
Total 2	3	6	.333	22	14	2	1	0	98^1	114	57	10	1	36	34	13.8	4.67	83	.295	.357	0	—	0	-7	-9	3	-0.4
● DON HEINKEL	Heinkel, Donald Elliott b: 10/20/59, Racine, Wis. BL/TR, 6', 185 lbs. Deb: 4/7/88																										
1988 Det-A	0	0	—	21	0	0	0	1	36^1	30	17	4	1	12	30	10.7	3.96	96	.219	.287	0	—	0	0	-1	-0	0.0
1989 StL-N	1	1	.500	7	5	0	0	0	26^1	40	19	2	0	7	16	16.1	5.81	63	.348	.385	0	.000	-0	-7	-6	0	-0.4
Total 2	1	1	.500	28	5	0	0	1	62^2	70	36	6	1	19	46	12.9	4.74	79	.278	.331	0	.000	-0	-7	-7	0	-0.4
● KEN HEINTZELMAN	Heintzelman, Kenneth Alphonse b: 10/14/15, Peruque, Mo. d: 8/14/2000, St.Peters, Mo. BR/TL, 5'11.5", 185 lbs. Deb: 10/3/37 F																										
1937 Pit-N	1	0	1.000	1	1	1	0	0	9	6	3	0	1	3	4	10.0	2.00	193	.207	.303	0	.000	-1	2	2	-1	0.1
1938 Pit-N	0	0	—	1	0	0	0	0	2	1	2	0	0	3	1	18.0	9.00	42	.167	.444	0	—	0	-1	-1	0	0.0
1939 Pit-N	1	1	.500	17	2	1	1	0	35^2	35	23	2	0	18	18	13.4	5.05	76	.250	.335	2	.222	0	-4	-5	-0	-0.2
1940 Pit-N	8	8	.500	39	16	5	2	3	165	193	86	7	4	65	71	14.3	4.47	85	.292	.359	9	.167	-1	-11	-12	3	-1.0
1941 Pit-N	11	11	.500	35	24	13	2	0	196	206	91	8	1	83	81	13.3	3.44	105	.272	.345	8	.127	-2	4	4	1	0.3
1942 Pit-N	8	11	.421	27	18	5	3	0	130	143	69	9	0	63	39	14.3	4.57	74	.281	.361	3	.086	-2	-18	-17	-2	-2.6
1946 Pit-N	8	12	.400	32	24	6	2	1	157^2	165	84	7	0	86	57	14.3	3.77	94	.271	.362	6	.136	-1	-6	-4	2	-0.4
1947 Pit-N	0	0	—	2	1	0	0	0	4	9	11	2	0	2	2	33.8	20.25	21	.409	.536	0	—	0	-7	-7	-0	-0.3
Phi-N	7	10	.412	24	19	8	0	1	136	144	72	12	2	46	55	12.7	4.04	99	.277	.338	5	.116	-2	0	-0	-3	-0.5
Yr	7	10	.412	26	20	8	0	1	140	153	83	14	2	52	57	13.3	4.50	89	.282	.347	5	.116	-2	-7	-8	-3	-0.8
1948 Phi-N	6	11	.353	27	16	5	2	2	130	117	66	10	1	57	43	11.3	4.29	92	.241	.307	5	.135	-1	-5	-5	-1	-0.8
1949 Phi-N	17	10	.630	33	32	15	**5**	0	250	239	96	19	1	93	65	12.0	3.02	130	.255	.323	13	.157	-1	28	26	-3	2.3
1950 *Phi-N	3	9	.250	23	17	4	1	0	125^1	122	66	10	0	54	39	12.6	4.09	99	.250	.325	2	.053	-3	1	-1	-2	-0.6
1951 Phi-N	6	12	.333	35	12	3	0	2	118^1	119	61	13	4	53	55	13.4	4.18	92	.267	.350	3	.107	-1	-3	-5	-1	-0.9
1952 Phi-N	1	3	.250	23	1	0	0	1	42^2	41	16	1	0	12	20	11.2	3.16	115	.266	.319	0	.000	-0	3	2	-1	0.1
Total 13	77	98	.440	319	183	66	18	10	1501^2	1540	746	100	14	630	564	13.1	3.93	96	.267	.341	56	.127	-16	-18	-23	-7	-4.5

YEAR	TM/L	W	L	PCT	G	GS	CG	SH	SV	IP	H	R	HR	HB	BB	SO	RAT	ERA	ERA+	OAV	OOB	BH	AVG	PB	PR	PR+	PD	TPI
● **CLARENCE HEISE**	Heise, Clarence Edward "Lefty" b: 8/7/07, Topeka, Kan. d: 5/30/99, Winter Park, Fla. BL/TL, 5'10", 172 lbs. Deb: 4/22/34																											
1934	StL-N	0	0	—	1	0	0	0	0	2	3	3	1	0	0	1	13.5	4.50	94	.300	.300	0	—	0	-0	-0	-0	0.0
● **JIM HEISE**	Heise, James Edward b: 10/2/32, Scottdale, Pa. BR/TR, 6'1", 185 lbs. Deb: 6/29/57																											
1957	Was-A	0	3	.000	8	2	0	0	0	19	25	19	2	0	16	8	19.4	8.05	48	.329	.446	0	.000	-0	-9	-9	-0	-1.2
● **ROY HEISER**	Heiser, Le Roy Barton b: 6/22/42, Baltimore, Md. BR/TR, 6'4", 190 lbs. Deb: 9/2/61																											
1961	Was-A	0	0	—	3	0	0	0	0	5^{2}	6	5	1	1	9	1	25.4	6.35	63	.261	.485	0	.000	-0	-1	-1	-0	-0.1
● **RICK HEISERMAN**	Heiserman, Richard Michael b: 2/22/73, Atlantic, Iowa BR/TR, 6'7", 225 lbs. Deb: 5/23/99																											
1999	StL-N	0	0	—	3	0	0	0	0	4^{1}	8	4	2	0	4	4	24.9	8.31	55	.400	.500	0	.000	-0	-2	-2	0	-0.1
● **CRESE HEISMANN**	Heismann, Christian Ernest b: 4/16/1880, Cincinnati, Ohio d: 11/19/51, Cincinnati, Ohio BL/TL, 6', 150 lbs. Deb: 9/25/01																											
1901	Cin-N	0	1	.000	3	2	1	0	0	13^{2}	18	9	1	3	6	6	17.8	5.93	54	.316	.409	2	.400	1	-4	-4	-1	-0.2
1902	Cin-N	2	1	.667	5	3	2	0	0	33	33	18	1	5	10	15	13.1	2.45	122	.260	.338	3	.214	0	1	2	0	0.2
	Bal-A	0	3	.000	3	3	2	0	0	16	20	17	1	2	12	2	19.1	8.44	45	.308	.430	1	.143	-1	-9	-8	-0	-1.1
Total	2	2	5	.286	11	8	5	0	0	62^{2}	71	44	3	10	28	23	15.7	4.74	69	.285	.380	6	.231	1	-11	-10	-1	-1.1
● **HARRY HEITMANN**	Heitmann, Henry Anton b: 10/6/1896, Albany, N.Y. d: 12/15/58, Brooklyn, N.Y. BR/TR, 6', 175 lbs. Deb: 7/27/18																											
1918	Bro-N	0	1	.000	1	1	0	0	0	0^{1}	4	4	0	0	0	0	108.0	108.00	3	1.000	1.000	0	—	0	-4	-4	0	-0.6
● **MEL HELD**	Held, Melvin Nicholas "Country" b: 4/12/29, Edon, Ohio BR/TR, 6'1", 178 lbs. Deb: 4/27/56																											
1956	Bal-A	0	0	—	4	0	0	0	0	7	7	4	1	0	3	4	12.9	5.14	76	.318	.400	0	—	0	-1	-1	0	0.0
● **RICK HELLING**	Helling, Ricky Allen b: 12/15/70, Devils Lake, N.D. BR/TR, 6'3", 215 lbs. Deb: 4/10/94																											
1994	Tex-A	3	2	.600	9	9	1	1	0	52	62	34	14	0	18	25	13.8	5.88	82	.295	.351	0	—	0	-6	-6	-1	-0.6
1995	Tex-A	0	2	.000	3	3	0	0	0	12^{1}	17	11	2	2	8	5	19.7	6.57	74	.340	.450	0	—	0	-3	-2	-0	-0.3
1996	Tex-A	1	2	.333	6	2	0	0	0	20^{1}	23	17	7	0	9	16	14.2	7.52	70	.280	.352	0	—	0	-6	-5	-0	-0.6
	Fla-N	2	1	.667	5	4	0	0	0	27^{2}	14	6	2	0	7	26	6.8	1.95	209	.143	.200	1	.111	-0	7	7	-1	0.6
1997	Fla-N	2	6	.250	31	8	0	0	0	76	61	38	12	4	48	53	13.4	4.38	92	.232	.359	1	.091	-1	-1	-3	-1	-0.5
	Tex-A	3	3	.500	10	8	0	0	0	55	47	29	5	2	21	46	11.5	4.58	105	.235	.314	0	.000	-0	-0	1	-1	0.0
1998	*Tex-A	**20**	7	.741	33	33	4	2	0	216^{1}	209	109	27	1	78	164	12.0	4.41	109	.253	.318	1	.200	0	6	10	-4	0.7
1999	*Tex-A	13	11	.542	35	35	3	0	0	219^{1}	228	127	41	6	85	131	13.1	4.84	105	.272	.344	0	.000	-0	1	6	-2	0.3
2000	Tex-A	16	13	.552	35	35	0	0	0	217	212	122	29	9	99	146	13.3	4.48	114	.252	.337	0	.000	-1	11	14	-2	1.4
Total	7	60	47	.561	167	137	8	3	0	896	873	493	139	24	373	612	12.8	4.65	105	.256	.334	3	.086	-2	8	21	-13	1.0
● **HORACE HELMBOLD**	Helmbold, Horace b: Philadelphia, Pa. Deb: 10/11/1890																											
1890	Phi-a	0	1	.000	1	1	1	0	0	7	17	15	0	0	6	3	29.6	14.14	27	.447	.523	0	.000	-1	-8	-8	0	-0.7
● **RUSS HEMAN**	Heman, Russell Frederick b: 2/10/33, Olive, Cal. BR/TR, 6'4", 200 lbs. Deb: 4/20/61																											
1961	Cle-A	0	0	—	6	0	0	0	1	10	8	4	0	1	8	4	15.3	3.60	109	.216	.370	0	.000	-0	0	0	0	0.0
	LA-A	0	0	—	6	0	0	0	0	10	4	3	1	1	2	2	6.3	1.80	251	.125	.200	0	.000	-0	2	3	0	0.1
	Yr	0	0	—	12	0	0	0	1	20	12	7	1	2	10	6	10.8	2.70	156	.174	.296	0	.000	-0	3	3	0	0.1
● **GEORGE HEMMING**	Hemming, George Earl "Old Wax Figger" b: 12/15/1868, Carrollton, Ohio d: 6/3/30, Springfield, Mass. BR/TR, 5'11", 170 lbs. Deb: 4/21/1890																											
1890	Cle-P	0	1	.000	3	1	1	0	0	21	25	23	1	2	19	3	19.7	6.86	58	.284	.422	2	.182	-1	-6	-7	1	-0.3
	Bro-P	8	4	.667	19	11	11	0	3	123	117	86	3	3	59	32	13.1	3.80	117	.240	.325	9	.158	-4	6	8	0	0.3
	Yr	8	5	.615	22	12	12	0	**3**	144	142	109	4	5	78	35	14.1	4.25	103	.247	.341	11	.162	-5	-0	2	1	0.0
1891	Bro-N	8	15	.348	27	22	19	1	1	199^{2}	231	173	11	11	84	83	14.7	4.96	67	.279	.353	13	.159	-1	-36	-37	1	-3.3
1892	Cin-N	0	1	.000	1	0	0	0	0	6	10	6	1	0	2	0	18.0	7.50	44	.357	.400	1	.333	0	-3	-3	0	-0.3
	Lou-N	2	2	.500	4	4	4	0	0	35	36	25	1	0	17	12	13.6	4.63	66	.255	.335	1	.077	-1	-5	-7	0	-0.6
	Yr	2	3	.400	5	4	4	0	0	41	46	31	2	0	19	12	14.3	5.05	61	.272	.346	2	.125	-1	-8	-9	0	-0.9
1893	Lou-N	18	17	.514	41	32	32	1	1	332	369	245	7	15	175	79	15.2	5.10	86	.273	.363	32	.203	-2	-16	-27	2	-2.1
1894	Lou-N	13	19	.406	35	32	32	1	1	294^{1}	358	213	7	9	133	66	15.3	4.37	117	.297	.371	33	.252	1	31	25	-1	2.0
	*Bal-N	4	0	1.000	6	6	4	0	0	45^{1}	48	22	0	2	26	4	15.1	3.57	153	.268	.367	6	.286	1	9	9	-0	0.7
	Yr	17	19	.472	41	38	36	1	1	339^{2}	406	235	7	11	159	70	15.3	4.27	121	.293	.370	39	.257	3	40	34	-1	2.7
1895	Bal-N	20	13	.606	34	31	26	1	0	262^{1}	288	155	10	6	96	43	13.4	4.05	117	.275	.339	33	.282	3	21	21	-3	1.9
1896	Bal-N	15	6	.714	25	21	20	3	0	202	233	113	9	3	54	33	12.9	4.19	102	.287	.333	25	.258	4	4	2	-3	0.2
1897	Lou-N	3	4	.429	9	8	7	0	0	67	80	59	5	1	25	7	14.2	5.10	83	.294	.356	5	.179	-1	-6	-6	1	-0.5
Total	8	91	82	.526	204	168	156	7	6	1587^{2}	1795	1120	55	52	690	362	14.4	4.53	98	.279	.353	160	.223	-0	-1	-19	-2	-2.0
● **BERNIE HENDERSON**	Henderson, Bernard "Barnyard" b: 4/12/1899, Douglassville, Tex d: 6/6/66, Linden, Tex. BR/TR, 5'9", 175 lbs. Deb: 9/5/21																											
1921	Cle-A	0	1	.000	2	1	0	0	0	3	5	5	0	0	0	1	15.0	9.00	47	.333	.333	0	.000	0	-2	-2	-0	-0.3
● **ED HENDERSON**	Henderson, Edward J. (b: Eugene J. Ball) b: 12/25/1884, Newark, N.J. d: 1/15/64, New York, N.Y. BL/TL, 5'9", 168 lbs. Deb: 5/15/14																											
1914	Pit-F	0	1	.000	6	1	1	0	0	16	14	8	2	0	8	4	12.4	3.94	73	.241	.333	0	.000	-0	-2	-2	-1	-0.2
	Ind-F	1	0	1.000	2	1	1	0	0	10	8	7	0	3	4	1	13.5	4.50	69	.229	.357	0	.000	-1	-2	-1	-0	-0.2
	Yr	1	1	.500	8	2	2	0	0	26	22	15	2	3	12	5	12.8	4.15	71	.237	.343	0	.000	-1	-4	-3	-1	-0.4
● **HARDIE HENDERSON**	Henderson, James Harding b: 10/31/1862, Philadelphia, Pa. d: 2/6/03, Philadelphia, Pa. BR/TR, 200 lbs. Deb: 5/2/1883 U																											
1883	Phi-N	0	1	.000	1	1	1	0	0	9	26	24	0		2	2	28.0	19.00	16	.481	.500	2	.250	0	-16	-16	-0	-0.9
	Bal-a	10	32	.238	45	42	38	0	0	358^{1}	383	315	4		87	145	11.8	4.02	87	.256	.297	31	.162	-6	-28	-20	-2	-2.5
1884	Bal-a	27	23	.540	52	52	50	4	0	439^{1}	382	235	9	16	116	346	10.5	2.62	132	.216	.271	46	.227	2	31	39	1	4.1
1885	Bal-a	25	35	.417	61	61	59	0	0	539^{1}	539	311	7	19	117	263	11.3	3.19	102	.253	.298	51	.223	3	4	4	-0	0.7
1886	Bal-a	3	15	.167	19	19	19	0	0	171^{1}	188	147	0	9	66	88	13.8	4.62	74	.252	.320	16	.235	2	-22	-23	2	-1.5
	Bro-a	10	4	.714	14	14	14	0	0	124	112	82	2	0	51	49	11.8	2.90	120	.232	.306	9	.180	-1	8	8	0	0.6
	Yr	13	19	.406	33	33	33	0	0	295^{1}	300	229	2	9	117	137	13.0	3.90	88	.244	.314	25	.212	1	-15	-15	2	-0.9
1887	Bro-a	5	8	.385	13	12	12	0	0	111^{2}	190	85	3	5	63	28	15.7	3.95	109	.369	.375	11	.234	-3	4	4	1	0.2
1888	Pit-N	1	3	.250	5	5	4	0	0	35^{1}	43	31	0	2	20	9	16.6	5.35	50	.289	.380	5	.278	1	-10	-11	0	-1.0
Total	6	81	121	.401	210	206	197	4	0	1788^{1}	1863	1230	25	51	522	930	11.9	3.50	98	.254	.302	171	.210	-2	-30	-12	2	-0.3
● **JOE HENDERSON**	Henderson, Joseph Lee b: 7/4/46, Lake Cormorant, Miss. BL/TR, 6'2", 195 lbs. Deb: 6/7/74																											
1974	Chi-A	1	0	1.000	5	3	0	0	0	15	21	15	2	0	11	12	19.2	8.40	44	.328	.427	0	.000	-0	-8	-8	0	-0.5
1976	Cin-N	2	0	1.000	4	0	0	0	0	11	9	1	0	0	8	7	13.9	0.00	—	.225	.354	0	—	0	4	4	0	0.9
1977	Cin-N	0	2	.000	7	0	0	0	0	9	17	13	2	0	6	8	23.0	12.00	33	.386	.460	0	.000	-0	-8	-8	-0	-1.5
Total	3	3	2	.600	16	3	0	0	0	35	47	29	4	0	25	27	18.5	6.69	56	.318	.416	0	.000	-0	-12	-11	-0	-1.1
● **ROD HENDERSON**	Henderson, Rodney Wood b: 3/11/71, Greensburg, Ky. BR/TR, 6'4", 195 lbs. Deb: 4/19/94																											
1994	Mon-N	0	1	.000	3	2	0	0	0	6^{2}	9	9	1	0	7	3	21.6	9.45	45	.333	.471	0	.000	-0	-4	-4	0	-0.5
1998	Mil-N	0	0	—	2	0	0	0	0	3^{2}	5	4	2	1	0	1	14.7	9.82	43	.313	.353	0	—	0	-2	-2	-0	-0.1
Total	2	0	1	.000	5	2	0	0	0	10^{1}	14	13	3	1	7	4	19.2	9.58	44	.326	.431	0	.000	-0	-6	-6	0	-0.6
● **BILL HENDERSON**	Henderson, William Maxwell b: 11/4/01, Pensacola, Fla. d: 10/6/66, Pensacola, Fla. BR/TR, 6', 190 lbs. Deb: 6/20/30																											
1930	NY-A	0	0	—	3	0	0	0	0	8	7	6	1	0	4	2	12.4	4.50	96	.250	.344	1	.500	0	0	-0	0	0.0
● **BOB HENDLEY**	Hendley, Charles Robert b: 4/30/39, Macon, Ga. BR/TL, 6'2", 190 lbs. Deb: 6/23/61																											
1961	Mil-N	5	7	.417	19	13	3	0	0	97	96	46	8	0	39	44	12.5	3.90	96	.262	.333	1	.032	-3	1	-2	1	-0.4
1962	Mil-N	11	13	.458	35	29	7	2	1	200	188	90	17	0	59	112	11.1	3.60	105	.247	.301	7	.119	1	8	5	1	0.6
1963	Mil-N	9	9	.500	41	24	7	3	3	169^{1}	153	80	16	1	64	105	11.6	3.93	82	.244	.315	5	.106	-1	-12	-14	1	-1.4
1964	SF-N	10	11	.476	30	29	4	1	0	163^{1}	161	71	18	2	59	104	12.2	3.64	98	.258	.325	5	.106	-1	-2	-1	-2	-0.5
1965	SF-N	0	0	—	8	2	0	0	0	15	27	22	6	1	13	8	24.6	12.60	29	.397	.500	0	.000	-0	-15	-15	0	-0.7
	Chi-N	4	4	.500	18	10	2	0	0	62	59	39	9	1	25	38	12.3	4.35	85	.244	.317	0	.000	-1	-6	-4	1	-0.6

YEAR	TM/L	W	L	PCT	G	GS	CG	SH	SV	IP	H	R	HR	HB	BB	SO	RAT	ERA	ERA+	OAV	OOB	BH	AVG	PB	PR	PR+	PD	TPI
	Yr	4	4	.500	26	12	2	0	0	77	86	61	15	2	38	46	14.7	5.96	62	.277	.360	0	.000	-2	-21	-19	1	-1.3
1966	Chi-N	4	5	.444	43	6	0	0	7	89^2	98	46	10	0	39	65	13.8	3.91	94	.285	.358	3	.167	1	-3	-2	1	-0.1
1967	Chi-N	2	0	1.000	7	0	0	0	1	12^1	17	10	4	0	3	10	14.6	6.57	54	.315	.351	0	.000	-1	-4	-4	-0	-0.8
	NY-N	3	3	.500	15	13	2	0	0	70^2	65	35	11	1	28	36	12.0	3.44	99	.241	.314	2	.111	-0	-1	-0	-2	-0.2
	Yr	5	3	.625	22	13	2	0	1	83	82	45	15	1	31	46	12.4	3.90	87	.253	.320	2	.083	-1	-5	-4	-2	-1.0
Total	7	48	52	.480	216	126	25	6	12	879^1	864	439	99	6	329	522	12.3	3.97	90	.257	.325	23	.095	-6	-34	-39	0	-4.1

● ED HENDRICKS
Hendricks, Edward "Big Ed" b: 6/20/1885, Zeeland, Mich. d: 11/28/30, Jackson, Mich. BL/TL, 6'3", 200 lbs. Deb: 9/15/10

YEAR	TM/L	W	L	PCT	G	GS	CG	SH	SV	IP	H	R	HR	HB	BB	SO	RAT	ERA	ERA+	OAV	OOB	BH	AVG	PB	PR	PR+	PD	TPI
1910	NY-N	0	1	.000	4	1	1	0	1	12	12	7	0	0	4	2	12.0	3.75	79	.261	.320	0	.000	-1	-1	-1	-1	-0.2

● ELLIE HENDRICKS
Hendricks, Elrod Jerome b: 12/22/40, Charlotte Amalie, V.I. BL/TR, 6'1", 175 lbs. Deb: 4/13/68 C◆

YEAR	TM/L	W	L	PCT	G	GS	CG	SH	SV	IP	H	R	HR	HB	BB	SO	RAT	ERA	ERA+	OAV	OOB	BH	AVG	PB	PR	PR+	PD	TPI
1978	Bal-A	0	0	—	1	0	0	0	0	2^1	1	0	0	0	1	0	7.7	0.00	—	.125	.222	6	.333	0	1	1	-0	0.1

● DON HENDRICKSON
Hendrickson, Donald William b: 7/14/13, Kewanna, Ind. d: 1/19/77, Norfolk, Va. BR/TR, 6'2", 204 lbs. Deb: 7/4/45

YEAR	TM/L	W	L	PCT	G	GS	CG	SH	SV	IP	H	R	HR	HB	BB	SO	RAT	ERA	ERA+	OAV	OOB	BH	AVG	PB	PR	PR+	PD	TPI
1945	Bos-N	4	8	.333	37	2	1	0	5	73^1	74	46	8	1	39	14	14.0	4.91	78	.261	.353	3	.167	-0	-9	-9	-1	-1.5
1946	Bos-N	0	1	.000	2	0	0	0	0	2	4	2	0	0	2	2	27.0	4.50	76	.364	.462	0	.000	-0	-0	-0	-0	-0.1
Total	2	4	9	.308	39	2	1	0	5	75^1	78	48	8	1	41	16	14.3	4.90	78	.265	.357	3	.158	-0	-9	-9	-1	-1.6

● CLAUDE HENDRIX
Hendrix, Claude Raymond b: 4/13/1889, Olathe, Kan. d: 3/22/44, Allentown, Pa. BR/TR, 6', 195 lbs. Deb: 6/7/11

YEAR	TM/L	W	L	PCT	G	GS	CG	SH	SV	IP	H	R	HR	HB	BB	SO	RAT	ERA	ERA+	OAV	OOB	BH	AVG	PB	PR	PR+	PD	TPI
1911	Pit-N	4	6	.400	22	12	6	1	1	118^2	85	52	1	1	53	57	10.5	2.73	126	.204	.295	4	.098	-1	9	9	4	1.0
1912	Pit-N	24	9	**.727**	39	32	25	4	1	288^2	256	110	6	9	105	176	11.5	2.59	126	.246	.320	39	.322	16	26	23	5	4.4
1913	Pit-N	14	15	.483	42	25	17	2	3	241	216	95	3	5	89	138	11.6	2.84	106	.248	.321	27	.273	10	10	5	2	1.8
1914	Chi-F	**29**	10	.744	**49**	37	**34**	6	5	362	262	91	6	5	77	189	**8.6**	1.69	157	**.203**	**.251**	30	.231	4	**48**	**42**	6	**5.8**
1915	Chi-F	16	15	.516	40	31	26	5	4	285	256	120	7	2	84	107	10.8	3.00	84	.241	.298	30	.265	11	-9	-17	-4	-1.1
1916	Chi-N	8	16	.333	36	24	15	3	2	218	193	81	4	6	67	117	11.0	2.68	108	.242	.306	16	.200	2	-2	5	2	1.1
1917	Chi-N	10	12	.455	40	21	13	1	1	215	202	94	3	4	72	81	11.6	2.60	112	.257	.322	22	.256	3	3	7	-2	0.9
1918	*Chi-N	20	7	**.741**	32	27	21	3	0	233	229	87	2	5	54	86	11.1	2.78	100	.259	.305	24	.264	8	-0	0	1	1.1
1919	Chi-N	10	14	.417	33	25	15	2	0	206^1	208	79	3	9	42	69	11.3	2.62	110	.266	.311	15	.192	-0	7	6	1	0.8
1920	Chi-N	9	12	.429	27	23	12	0	0	203^2	216	101	6	3	54	72	12.1	3.58	90	.273	.322	15	.181	-2	-10	-8	-1	-1.0
Total	10	144	116	.554	360	257	184	27	17	2371^1	2123	910	41	49	697	1092	10.9	2.65	110	.243	.303	222	.241	50	82	72	14	14.8

● LAFAYETTE HENION
Henion, Lafayette Marion b: 6/7/1899, Eureka, Cal. d: 7/22/55, San Luis Obispo, Cal. BR/TR, 5'11", 154 lbs. Deb: 9/10/19

YEAR	TM/L	W	L	PCT	G	GS	CG	SH	SV	IP	H	R	HR	HB	BB	SO	RAT	ERA	ERA+	OAV	OOB	BH	AVG	PB	PR	PR+	PD	TPI
1919	Bro-N	0	0	—	1	0	0	0	0	3	2	2	0	0	2	2	12.0	6.00	50	.200	.333	0	.000	-0	-1	-1	-0	-0.1

● TOM HENKE
Henke, Thomas Anthony b: 12/21/57, Kansas City, Mo. BR/TR, 6'5", 215 lbs. Deb: 9/10/82

YEAR	TM/L	W	L	PCT	G	GS	CG	SH	SV	IP	H	R	HR	HB	BB	SO	RAT	ERA	ERA+	OAV	OOB	BH	AVG	PB	PR	PR+	PD	TPI
1982	Tex-A	1	0	1.000	8	0	0	0	0	15^2	14	2	0	1	8	9	13.2	1.15	338	.246	.348	0	—	0	5	5	0	0.3
1983	Tex-A	1	0	1.000	8	0	0	0	1	16	16	6	1	0	4	17	11.3	3.38	119	.262	.308	0	—	0	1	1	0	0.1
1984	Tex-A	1	1	.500	25	0	0	0	2	28^1	36	21	0	1	20	25	18.1	6.35	65	.313	.419	0	—	0	-7	-7	-0	-0.5
1985	*Tor-A	3	3	.500	28	0	0	0	13	40	29	12	4	0	8	42	8.3	2.02	208	.206	.248	0	—	0	9	10	-0	1.9
1986	Tor-A	9	5	.643	63	0	0	0	27	91^1	63	39	6	1	32	118	9.5	3.35	126	.191	.265	0	—	0	8	9	-2	1.6
1987	Tor-A★	0	6	.000	72	0	0	0	**34**	94	62	27	10	0	25	128	8.3	2.49	181	.188	.245	0	—	0	**21**	**21**	1	2.9
1988	Tor-A	4	4	.500	52	0	0	0	25	68	60	23	6	2	24	66	11.4	2.91	135	.237	.308	0	—	0	8	8	0	1.4
1989	*Tor-A	8	3	.727	64	0	0	0	20	89	66	20	5	2	25	116	9.4	1.92	197	.205	.266	0	—	0	19	19	0	3.0
1990	Tor-A	2	4	.333	61	0	0	0	32	74^2	58	18	8	1	19	75	9.4	2.17	182	.213	.267	0	—	0	15	15	-1	2.1
1991	*Tor-A	0	2	.000	49	0	0	0	32	50^1	33	13	4	0	11	53	7.9	2.32	181	.184	.232	0	—	0	10	10	-1	1.4
1992	*Tor-A	3	2	.600	57	0	0	0	34	55^2	40	19	5	0	22	46	10.0	2.26	181	.197	.276	0	—	0	10	11	-1	2.0
1993	Tex-A	5	5	.500	66	0	0	0	40	74^1	55	25	7	1	27	79	10.0	2.91	143	.205	.280	0	—	0	12	11	1	2.2
1994	Tex-A	3	6	.333	37	0	0	0	15	38	33	16	6	0	12	39	10.7	3.79	127	.232	.292	0	—	0	4	4	-0	0.8
1995	StL-N★	1	1	.500	52	0	0	0	36	54^1	42	11	2	0	18	48	9.9	1.82	230	.209	.274	0	.000	-0	14	14	-0	2.1
Total	14	41	42	.494	642	0	0	0	311	789^2	607	252	64	9	255	861	9.9	2.67	156	.211	.278	0	.000	-0	130	130	-3	21.3

● WELDON HENLEY
Henley, Weldon b: 10/25/1880, Jasper, Ga. d: 11/16/60, Palatka, Fla. BR/TR, 6', 175 lbs. Deb: 4/23/03

YEAR	TM/L	W	L	PCT	G	GS	CG	SH	SV	IP	H	R	HR	HB	BB	SO	RAT	ERA	ERA+	OAV	OOB	BH	AVG	PB	PR	PR+	PD	TPI
1903	Phi-A	12	10	.545	29	21	13	1	0	186^1	186	108	3	12	67	86	12.8	3.91	78	.259	.333	9	.132	-3	-20	-17	-1	-2.2
1904	Phi-A	15	17	.469	36	34	31	5	0	295^2	245	126	3	19	76	130	10.3	2.53	106	.226	.289	24	.222	2	2	5	4	1.1
1905	Phi-A	4	11	.267	25	19	13	1	0	183^2	155	74	4	9	67	82	11.3	2.60	102	.231	.309	11	.169	-1	1	1	4	0.4
1907	Bro-N	1	5	.167	7	7	5	0	0	56	54	31	2	1	21	11	12.2	3.05	77	.273	.345	4	.200	1	-4	-5	2	-0.3
Total	4	32	43	.427	97	81	62	7	0	721^2	640	339	12	41	231	309	11.4	2.94	93	.240	.310	48	.184	-2	-20	-16	9	-1.0

● MIKE HENNEMAN
Henneman, Michael Alan b: 12/11/61, St.Charles, Mo. BR/TR, 6'4", 195 lbs. Deb: 5/11/87

YEAR	TM/L	W	L	PCT	G	GS	CG	SH	SV	IP	H	R	HR	HB	BB	SO	RAT	ERA	ERA+	OAV	OOB	BH	AVG	PB	PR	PR+	PD	TPI
1987	*Det-A	11	3	.786	55	0	0	0	7	96^2	86	36	8	3	30	75	11.1	2.98	142	.238	.301	0	.000	-0	16	14	0	2.0
1988	Det-A	9	6	.600	65	0	0	0	22	91^1	72	23	7	2	24	58	9.7	1.87	204	.218	.275	0	—	0	**21**	**21**	-1	4.0
1989	Det-A☆	11	4	.733	60	0	0	0	8	90	84	46	4	5	51	69	14.0	3.70	103	.251	.358	0	—	0	2	1	0	0.2
1990	Det-A	8	6	.571	69	0	0	0	22	94^1	90	36	4	3	33	50	12.0	3.05	130	.253	.321	0	—	0	9	9	1	1.7
1991	Det-A	10	2	.833	60	0	0	0	21	84^1	81	29	2	0	34	61	12.3	2.88	144	.258	.330	0	—	0	11	12	-0	2.0
1992	Det-A	2	6	.250	60	0	0	0	24	77^1	75	36	6	0	20	58	11.1	3.96	100	.256	.304	0	—	0	-0	0	1	0.1
1993	Det-A	5	3	.625	63	0	0	0	24	71^2	69	28	4	2	32	58	12.9	2.64	163	.251	.333	0	—	0	14	13	-1	2.0
1994	Det-A	1	3	.250	30	0	0	0	8	34^2	43	27	5	2	17	27	16.1	5.19	93	.297	.378	0	—	0	-1	-1	0	-0.1
1995	Det-A	0	1	.000	29	0	0	0	18	29^1	24	5	0	0	9	24	10.1	1.53	310	.222	.282	0	—	0	10	10	-1	1.4
	Hou-N	0	1	.000	21	0	0	0	8	21	21	7	1	2	4	19	11.6	3.00	129	.266	.318	0	—	0	3	2	-0	0.2
1996	*Tex-A	0	7	.000	49	0	0	0	31	42	41	28	6	0	17	34	12.4	5.79	91	.258	.330	0	—	0	-4	-2	-0	-0.4
Total	10	57	42	.576	561	0	0	0	193	732^2	686	301	47	19	271	533	12.0	3.21	130	.249	.320	0	.000	-0	81	79	-1	13.1

● GEORGE HENNESSEY
Hennessey, George "Three Star" b: 10/28/07, Slatington, Pa. d: 1/15/88, Princeton, N.J. BR/TR, 5'10", 168 lbs. Deb: 9/2/37

YEAR	TM/L	W	L	PCT	G	GS	CG	SH	SV	IP	H	R	HR	HB	BB	SO	RAT	ERA	ERA+	OAV	OOB	BH	AVG	PB	PR	PR+	PD	TPI
1937	StL-A	0	1	.000	5	0	0	0	0	7	15	8	2	0	6	4	27.0	10.29	47	.500	.583	0	—	0	-4	-4	0	-0.4
1942	Phi-N	1	1	.500	5	1	0	0	0	17	11	5	1	0	10	2	11.1	2.65	125	.180	.296	0	.000	-1	1	1	-0	0.0
1945	Chi-N	0	0	—	2	0	0	0	0	3^2	7	3	0	0	1	2	19.6	7.36	50	.438	.471	0	—	0	-1	-2	0	-0.1
Total	3	1	2	.333	12	1	0	0	0	27^2	33	16	3	0	17	8	16.3	5.20	72	.308	.403	0	.000	-1	-5	-5	-0	-0.5

● PHIL HENNIGAN
Hennigan, Phillip Winston b: 4/10/46, Jasper, Tex. BR/TR, 5'11.5", 185 lbs. Deb: 9/2/69

YEAR	TM/L	W	L	PCT	G	GS	CG	SH	SV	IP	H	R	HR	HB	BB	SO	RAT	ERA	ERA+	OAV	OOB	BH	AVG	PB	PR	PR+	PD	TPI
1969	Cle-A	2	1	.667	9	0	0	0	0	16^1	14	6	0	1	4	10	10.5	3.31	114	.241	.302	0	.000	-0	1	1	-1	0.1
1970	Cle-A	6	3	.667	42	1	0	0	3	71^2	69	34	7	4	44	43	14.7	4.02	99	.263	.377	1	.143	1	-2	-0	1	0.1
1971	Cle-A	4	3	.571	57	0	0	0	14	82	80	45	13	3	51	69	14.7	4.94	78	.261	.371	0	.000	-0	-13	-9	-1	-1.2
1972	Cle-A	5	3	.625	38	1	0	0	6	67^1	54	20	8	2	18	44	9.9	2.67	121	.226	.286	1	.083	-0	3	4	-1	0.4
1973	NY-N	0	4	.000	30	0	0	0	3	43^1	50	30	6	1	16	22	13.9	6.23	58	.289	.353	1	.333	0	-12	-13	-1	-1.3
Total	5	17	14	.548	176	2	0	0	26	280^2	267	135	34	11	133	188	13.2	4.26	86	.257	.347	3	.100	1	-25	-17	-2	-1.9

● PETE HENNING
Henning, Ernest Herman b: 12/28/1887, Crown Point, Ind. d: 11/4/39, Dyer, Ind. BR/TR, 5'11", 185 lbs. Deb: 4/17/14

YEAR	TM/L	W	L	PCT	G	GS	CG	SH	SV	IP	H	R	HR	HB	BB	SO	RAT	ERA	ERA+	OAV	OOB	BH	AVG	PB	PR	PR+	PD	TPI
1914	KC-F	5	10	.333	28	14	7	0	2	138	153	88	5	7	58	45	14.2	4.83	58	.291	.369	8	.182	0	-30	-33	0	-3.2
1915	KC-F	9	15	.375	40	20	15	1	2	207	181	88	5	3	76	73	11.3	3.17	83	.235	.307	14	.206	-1	-10	-13	4	-1.2
Total	2	14	25	.359	68	34	22	1	4	345	334	176	10	10	134	118	12.5	3.83	70	.258	.332	22	.196	-1	-40	-46	4	-4.4

● RICK HENNINGER
Henninger, Richard Lee b: 1/11/48, Hastings, Neb. BR/TR, 6'6", 225 lbs. Deb: 9/3/73

YEAR	TM/L	W	L	PCT	G	GS	CG	SH	SV	IP	H	R	HR	HB	BB	SO	RAT	ERA	ERA+	OAV	OOB	BH	AVG	PB	PR	PR+	PD	TPI
1973	Tex-A	1	0	1.000	6	2	0	0	0	23	23	8	1	0	11	6	13.3	2.74	136	.261	.343	0	—	0	3	3	-1	0.1

● RANDY HENNIS
Hennis, Randall Philip b: 12/16/65, Clearlake, Cal. BR/TR, 6'6", 220 lbs. Deb: 9/17/90

YEAR	TM/L	W	L	PCT	G	GS	CG	SH	SV	IP	H	R	HR	HB	BB	SO	RAT	ERA	ERA+	OAV	OOB	BH	AVG	PB	PR	PR+	PD	TPI
1990	Hou-N	0	0	—	3	1	0	0	0	9^2	1	0	0	1	3	4	4.7	0.00	—	.033	.147	0	.000	-0	4	4	-0	0.2

● OSCAR HENRIQUEZ
Henriquez, Oscar Eduardo b: 1/28/74, LaGuaira, Venez. BR/TR, 6'6", 220 lbs. Deb: 9/7/97

YEAR	TM/L	W	L	PCT	G	GS	CG	SH	SV	IP	H	R	HR	HB	BB	SO	RAT	ERA	ERA+	OAV	OOB	BH	AVG	PB	PR	PR+	PD	TPI
1997	Hou-N	0	1	.000	4	0	0	0	0	4	2	2	0	1	3	3	13.5	4.50	89	.167	.375	0	—	0	-0	-0	0	0.0
1998	Fla-N	0	0	—	15	0	0	0	0	20	26	22	4	1	12	19	17.5	8.55	47	.306	.398	0	.000	-0	-10	-10	-1	-0.6
Total	2	0	1	.000	19	0	0	0	0	24	28	24	4	2	15	22	16.9	7.88	51	.289	.395	0	.000	-0	-10	-11	-1	-0.6

● DWAYNE HENRY
Henry, Dwayne Allen b: 2/16/62, Elkton, Md. BR/TR, 6'3", 205 lbs. Deb: 9/7/84

YEAR	TM/L	W	L	PCT	G	GS	CG	SH	SV	IP	H	R	HR	HB	BB	SO	RAT	ERA	ERA+	OAV	OOB	BH	AVG	PB	PR	PR+	PD	TPI
1984	Tex-A	0	1	.000	3	0	0	0	0	4^1	5	4	0	0	7	2	24.9	8.31	50	.294	.500	0	—	0	-2	-2	-0	-0.4
1985	Tex-A	2	2	.500	16	0	0	0	3	21	16	7	0	0	7	20	9.9	2.57	165	.211	.277	0	—	0	4	4	-0	0.8
1986	Tex-A	1	0	1.000	19	0	0	0	0	19^1	14	11	1	1	22	17	17.2	4.66	93	.209	.411	0	—	0	-1	-1	0	0.0
1987	Tex-A	0	0	—	5	0	0	0	0	10	12	10	2	0	9	7	18.9	9.00	50	.293	.420	0	—	0	-5	-5	0	-0.2
1988	Tex-A	0	1	.000	11	0	0	0	1	10^1	15	10	1	3	9	10	23.5	8.71	47	.326	.466	0	—	0	-5	-5	-0	-0.5
1989	Atl-N	0	2	.000	12	0	0	0	1	12^2	12	6	2	0	5	16	12.1	4.26	86	.250	.321	0	—	0	-1	-1	-0	-0.2
1990	Atl-N	2	2	.500	34	0	0	0	0	38^1	41	26	3	0	25	34	15.5	5.63	72	.273	.377	0	—	0	-8	-6	-1	-0.7
1991	Hou-N	3	2	.600	52	0	0	0	2	67^2	51	25	7	2	39	51	12.2	3.19	110	.219	.336	0	.000	-0	4	3	-1	0.1
1992	Cin-N	3	3	.500	60	0	0	0	0	83^2	59	31	4	1	44	72	11.2	3.33	108	.199	.304	1	.250	0	2	2	0	0.2
1993	Cin-N	0	1	.000	3	0	0	0	0	4^2	6	8	0	0	4	2	19.3	3.86	105	.273	.385	0	.000	0	0	0	-0	0.0
	Sea-A	2	1	.667	31	1	0	0	2	54	56	40	6	2	35	35	15.5	6.67	66	.273	.384	0	—	0	-14	-13	-2	-0.9
1995	Det-A	1	0	1.000	10	0	0	0	5	8^2	11	6	0	0	10	9	21.8	6.23	76	.306	.457	0	—	0	-1	-1	-0	-0.3
Total	11	14	15	.483	256	1	0	0	14	334^2	298	184	26	9	216	275	14.1	4.65	85	.241	.357	1	.167	-0	-29	-26	-3	-2.1

● EARL HENRY
Henry, Earl Clifford "Hook" b: 6/10/17, Roseville, Ohio BL/TL, 5'11", 172 lbs. Deb: 9/23/44

YEAR	TM/L	W	L	PCT	G	GS	CG	SH	SV	IP	H	R	HR	HB	BB	SO	RAT	ERA	ERA+	OAV	OOB	BH	AVG	PB	PR	PR+	PD	TPI
1944	Cle-A	1	1	.500	2	2	1	0	0	17^2	18	9	0	0	3	5	10.7	4.58	72	.269	.300	0	.000	-0	-2	-3	0	-0.3
1945	Cle-A	0	3	.000	15	1	0	0	0	21^2	20	13	0	1	20	10	17.0	5.40	60	.253	.410	2	.500	1	-5	-5	-1	-0.6
Total	2	1	4	.200	17	3	1	0	0	39^1	38	22	0	1	23	15	14.2	5.03	65	.260	.365	2	.222	0	-7	-8	1	-0.9

● BUTCH HENRY
Henry, Floyd Bluford b: 10/7/68, ElPaso, Tex. BL/TL, 6'1", 205 lbs. Deb: 4/9/92

YEAR	TM/L	W	L	PCT	G	GS	CG	SH	SV	IP	H	R	HR	HB	BB	SO	RAT	ERA	ERA+	OAV	OOB	BH	AVG	PB	PR	PR+	PD	TPI
1992	Hou-N	6	9	.400	28	28	2	1	0	165^2	185	81	16	1	41	96	12.3	4.02	84	.285	.329	8	.148	1	-9	-13	1	-0.9
1993	Col-N	2	8	.200	20	15	1	0	0	84^2	117	66	14	1	24	39	15.1	6.59	72	.331	.375	2	.091	-1	-24	-14	-0	-1.6
	Mon-N	1	1	.500	10	1	0	0	0	18^1	18	10	1	0	4	8	10.8	3.93	106	.250	.289	0	.000	-0	0	0	-1	0.0
	Yr	3	9	.250	30	16	1	0	0	103	135	76	15	1	28	47	14.3	6.12	76	.317	.360	2	.083	-2	-24	-14	-1	-1.6
1994	Mon-N	8	3	.727	24	15	0	0	1	107^1	97	30	10	2	20	70	10.0	2.43	174	.241	.280	9	.290	3	21	21	-0	2.4
1995	Mon-N	7	9	.438	21	21	1	1	0	126^2	133	47	11	2	28	60	11.6	2.84	151	.275	.317	2	.048	-4	19	20	2	2.1
1997	Bos-A	7	3	.700	36	5	0	0	6	84^1	89	36	6	0	19	51	11.5	3.52	132	.277	.318	0	—	0	10	10	1	1.3
1998	Bos-A	0	0	—	2	2	0	0	0	9	8	4	2	1	3	6	12.0	4.00	118	.235	.316	0	—	0	1	1	0	0.1
1999	Sea-A	2	0	1.000	7	4	0	0	0	25	30	15	1	2	10	15	15.1	5.04	94	.303	.378	0	—	0	-0	-1	-0	-0.1
Total	7	33	33	.500	148	91	4	2	7	621	677	289	61	9	149	345	12.1	3.83	109	.280	.324	21	.139	-2	17	23	3	3.3

● DUTCH HENRY
Henry, Frank John b: 5/12/02, Cleveland, Ohio d: 8/23/68, Cleveland, Ohio BL/TL, 6'1", 175 lbs. Deb: 9/16/21

YEAR	TM/L	W	L	PCT	G	GS	CG	SH	SV	IP	H	R	HR	HB	BB	SO	RAT	ERA	ERA+	OAV	OOB	BH	AVG	PB	PR	PR+	PD	TPI
1921	StL-A	0	0	—	1	0	0	0	0	2	2	1	0	0	0	1	9.0	4.50	100	.250	.250	1	1.000	0	-0	-0	0	0.0
1922	StL-A	0	0	—	4	0	0	0	0	5	7	3	0	0	5	3	21.6	5.40	77	.280	.400	0	—	0	-1	-1	0	0.0
1923	Bro-N	4	6	.400	17	9	5	2	0	94^1	105	55	9	2	28	28	12.9	3.91	99	.281	.334	8	.229	1	1	-0	-0	0.0
1924	Bro-N	1	2	.333	16	4	0	0	0	46	69	33	0	0	15	11	16.4	5.67	66	.352	.398	5	.250	1	-9	-10	0	-0.5
1927	NY-N	11	6	.647	45	15	7	1	4	163^2	184	93	6	0	31	40	11.8	4.23	91	.278	.311	13	.236	1	-6	-7	-2	-0.7
1928	NY-N	3	6	.333	17	8	4	0	1	64	82	36	4	1	25	23	15.2	3.80	103	.325	.388	3	.158	-1	1	1	1	0.1
1929	NY-N	5	6	.455	27	9	4	0	1	101^1	129	52	10	1	31	27	14.3	3.82	120	.316	.366	7	.250	2	10	9	-1	0.9
	Chi-A	1	0	1.000	2	1	1	0	0	15	20	12	1	0	7	2	16.2	6.00	71	.308	.375	1	.143	0	-3	-3	-1	-0.2
1930	Chi-A	2	17	.105	35	16	4	0	0	155	211	116	12	4	48	35	15.3	4.88	95	.331	.381	12	.235	1	-4	-4	3	-0.1
Total	8	27	43	.386	164	62	25	3	6	646^1	809	401	42	8	190	170	14.0	4.39	95	.308	.356	50	.231	6	-10	-16	0	-0.5

● JIM HENRY
Henry, James Francis b: 6/26/10, Danville, Pa. d: 8/15/76, Memphis, Tenn. BR/TR, 6'2", 175 lbs. Deb: 4/23/36

YEAR	TM/L	W	L	PCT	G	GS	CG	SH	SV	IP	H	R	HR	HB	BB	SO	RAT	ERA	ERA+	OAV	OOB	BH	AVG	PB	PR	PR+	PD	TPI
1936	Bos-A	5	1	.833	21	8	2	0	0	76^1	75	43	10	2	40	36	13.8	4.60	116	.255	.348	3	.115	-1	4	6	0	0.3
1937	Bos-A	1	0	1.000	3	2	1	0	0	15^1	15	9	2	0	11	8	15.3	5.28	90	.263	.382	0	.000	-0	-1	-1	-0	-0.1
1939	Phi-N	0	1	.000	9	1	0	0	1	23	24	13	3	1	8	7	12.9	5.09	79	.276	.344	0	.000	-1	-3	-3	-1	-0.3
Total	3	6	2	.750	33	11	3	0	1	114^2	114	65	15	3	59	51	13.8	4.79	104	.260	.352	3	.083	-2	-0	2	-1	-0.1

● JOHN HENRY
Henry, John Michael b: 9/2/1863, Springfield, Mass. d: 6/11/39, Hartford, Conn. TL, Deb: 8/13/1884 ◆

YEAR	TM/L	W	L	PCT	G	GS	CG	SH	SV	IP	H	R	HR	HB	BB	SO	RAT	ERA	ERA+	OAV	OOB	BH	AVG	PB	PR	PR+	PD	TPI
1884	Cle-N	1	4	.200	5	5	5	1	0	42	46	39	2		26	23	15.4	3.64	87	.257	.351	4	.154	-1	-3	-2	1	-0.3
1885	Bal-a	2	7	.222	9	9	9	0	0	71	71	55	0	2	13	31	10.9	4.31	76	.247	.284	9	.265	1	-8	-8	2	-0.5
1886	Was-N	1	3	.250	4	4	4	0	0	27^2	35	27	1		15	19	16.3	4.23	78	.285	.362	5	.357	1	-3	-3	-0	-0.3
Total	3	4	14	.222	18	18	18	1	0	140^2	152	121	3	2	54	73	13.3	4.09	79	.258	.322	53	.243	1	-14	-13	2	-1.1

● DOUG HENRY
Henry, Richard Douglas b: 12/10/63, Sacramento, Cal. BR/TR, 6'4", 205 lbs. Deb: 7/15/91

YEAR	TM/L	W	L	PCT	G	GS	CG	SH	SV	IP	H	R	HR	HB	BB	SO	RAT	ERA	ERA+	OAV	OOB	BH	AVG	PB	PR	PR+	PD	TPI
1991	Mil-A	2	1	.667	32	0	0	0	15	36	16	4	1	0	14	28	7.5	1.00	398	.133	.224	0	—	0	12	12	-1	1.8
1992	Mil-A	1	4	.200	68	0	0	0	29	65	64	34	6	0	24	52	12.2	4.02	96	.256	.321	0	—	0	-0	-1	0	-0.2
1993	Mil-A	4	4	.500	54	0	0	0	17	55	67	37	7	3	25	38	15.5	5.56	77	.300	.378	0	—	0	-8	-8	0	-1.4
1994	Mil-A	2	3	.400	25	0	0	0	0	31^1	32	17	7	1	23	20	16.1	4.60	110	.271	.394	0	.000	-0	1	1	-0	0.2
1995	NY-N	3	6	.333	51	0	0	0	4	67	48	23	7	1	25	62	9.9	2.96	137	.198	.276	1	1.000	0	9	8	0	1.2
1996	NY-N	2	8	.200	58	0	0	0	9	75	82	48	7	1	36	58	14.3	4.68	86	.273	.353	0	.000	-1	-4	-6	-1	-0.9
1997	*SF-N	4	5	.444	75	0	0	0	3	70^2	70	45	5	1	41	69	14.3	4.71	87	.261	.361	0	.000	-0	-4	-5	-1	-0.7
1998	*Hou-N	8	2	.800	59	0	0	0	2	71	55	25	9	0	35	59	11.4	3.04	133	.216	.310	0	.000	-0	9	8	-1	0.9
1999	*Hou-N	2	3	.400	35	0	0	0	2	40^2	45	24	8	3	24	36	15.9	4.65	95	.281	.385	0	.000	-0	-0	-1	0	-0.1
2000	Hou-N	1	3	.250	45	0	0	0	1	53	39	26	10	3	28	46	11.9	4.42	111	.204	.315	0	.000	-0	1	3	0	0.2
	*SF-N	3	1	.750	27	0	0	0	0	25^1	18	10	2	1	21	16	14.2	2.49	170	.214	.377	0	—	0	6	5	-0	0.7
	Yr	4	4	.500	72	0	0	0	1	78^1	57	36	12	4	49	62	12.6	3.79	123	.207	.335	0	.000	-0	7	8	-0	0.9
Total	10	32	40	.444	529	0	0	0	82	590	536	293	69	14	296	484	12.9	3.95	106	.242	.336	1	.059	-1	23	17	-4	1.7

● BILL HENRY
Henry, William Francis b: 2/15/42, Long Beach, Cal. BL/TL, 6'3", 195 lbs. Deb: 9/13/66

YEAR	TM/L	W	L	PCT	G	GS	CG	SH	SV	IP	H	R	HR	HB	BB	SO	RAT	ERA	ERA+	OAV	OOB	BH	AVG	PB	PR	PR+	PD	TPI
1966	NY-A	0	0	—	2	0	0	0	0	3	0	0	0	0	2	3	6.0	0.00	—	.000	.200	0	—	0	1	1	0	0.1

● BILL HENRY
Henry, William Rodman b: 10/15/27, Alice, Tex. BL/TL, 6'2", 180 lbs. Deb: 4/17/52

YEAR	TM/L	W	L	PCT	G	GS	CG	SH	SV	IP	H	R	HR	HB	BB	SO	RAT	ERA	ERA+	OAV	OOB	BH	AVG	PB	PR	PR+	PD	TPI
1952	Bos-A	5	4	.556	13	10	5	0	0	76^2	75	40	7	2	36	23	13.3	3.87	102	.254	.339	8	.258	2	-2	1	-1	0.1
1953	Bos-A	5	5	.500	21	12	4	1	1	85^2	86	39	4	4	33	56	12.9	3.26	129	.260	.334	6	.188	-0	7	9	-1	0.9
1954	Bos-A	3	7	.300	24	13	3	1	0	95^2	104	56	9	1	49	38	14.5	4.52	91	.270	.354	4	.118	-1	-8	-4	-1	-0.6
1955	Bos-A	2	4	.333	17	7	0	0	0	59^2	56	28	7	0	21	23	11.6	3.32	129	.247	.310	2	.105	-1	4	6	0	0.5
1958	Chi-N	5	4	.556	44	0	0	0	6	81^1	63	27	8	1	17	58	9.0	2.88	136	.214	.259	4	.235	1	10	9	-1	1.2
1959	Chi-N	9	8	.529	**65**	0	0	0	12	134^1	111	42	19	1	26	115	9.2	2.68	147	.227	.267	6	.194	0	19	**19**	-1	2.5
1960	Cin-N★	1	5	.167	51	0	0	0	17	67^2	62	25	8	4	20	58	11.4	3.19	120	.247	.313	0	.000	-1	4	5	1	0.6
1961	*Cin-N	2	1	.667	47	0	0	0	16	53^1	50	18	8	0	15	53	11.0	2.19	185	.244	.295	0	.000	-1	11	11	0	1.2
1962	Cin-N	4	2	.667	40	0	0	0	11	37^1	40	21	5	1	20	35	14.7	4.58	88	.280	.372	1	.333	0	-3	-2	-1	-0.5
1963	Cin-N	1	3	.250	47	0	0	0	14	52	55	30	4	1	11	45	11.6	4.15	81	.279	.321	1	.167	-0	-5	-5	0	-0.6
1964	Cin-N	2	2	.500	37	0	0	0	6	52	31	9	2	3	12	28	8.0	0.87	418	.170	.234	3	.500	1	15	16	-0	1.7
1965	Cin-N	2	0	1.000	3	0	0	0	0	5	3	0	0	0	1	5	7.2	0.00	—	.176	.222	0	—	0	2	2	-0	0.4
	SF-N	2	2	.500	35	0	0	0	4	42	40	18	2	1	8	35	10.5	3.64	99	.248	.288	1	.200	0	-0	-0	-0	-0.1
	Yr	4	2	.667	38	0	0	0	4	47	43	18	2	1	9	40	10.1	3.26	111	.242	.282	1	.200	0	1	2	-1	0.3
1966	SF-N	1	1	.500	35	0	0	0	1	22	15	6	3	1	10	15	10.6	2.45	149	.190	.289	0	.000	-0	3	3	-0	0.2
1967	SF-N	2	0	1.000	28	1	0	0	2	21^2	16	5	1	2	9	23	11.2	2.08	158	.198	.293	0	.000	-0	3	3	0	0.3
1968	SF-N	0	2	.000	7	1	0	0	0	5	4	3	0	1	3	0	14.4	5.40	55	.250	.400	0	—	0	-1	-1	0	-0.3
	Pit-N	0	0	—	10	0	0	0	0	16^2	29	18	2	2	3	9	18.4	8.10	36	.382	.420	0	.000	-0	-9	-10	-1	-0.6
	Yr	0	2	.000	17	1	0	0	0	21^2	33	21	2	3	6	9	17.4	7.48	39	.359	.416	0	.000	-0	-11	-11	-1	-0.9
1969	Hou-N	0	0	—	3	0	0	0	0	5	2	1	0	0	2	2	7.2	0.00	—	.111	.200	0	—	0	2	2	-0	0.1
Total	16	46	50	.479	527	44	12	2	90	913	842	386	89	25	296	621	11.5	3.26	119	.244	.308	36	.177	-0	51	62	-6	7.0

● ROY HENSHAW
Henshaw, Roy Knikelbine b: 7/29/11, Chicago, Ill. d: 6/8/93, LaGrange, Ill. BR/TL, 5'8", 155 lbs. Deb: 4/15/33

YEAR	TM/L	W	L	PCT	G	GS	CG	SH	SV	IP	H	R	HR	HB	BB	SO	RAT	ERA	ERA+	OAV	OOB	BH	AVG	PB	PR	PR+	PD	TPI
1933	Chi-N	2	1	.667	21	0	0	0	0	38^2	32	22	0	2	20	16	12.6	4.19	78	.230	.335	2	.200	-0	-4	-4	-1	-0.4
1935	*Chi-N	13	5	.722	31	18	7	3	1	142^2	135	60	6	4	68	53	13.1	3.28	120	.249	.337	13	.255	2	12	11	-3	1.0
1936	Chi-N	6	5	.545	39	14	6	2	1	129^1	152	67	8	5	56	69	14.8	3.97	100	.296	.370	6	.136	-2	1	0	-2	-0.4

YEAR	TM/L	W	L	PCT	G	GS	CG	SH	SV	IP	H	R	HR	HB	BB	SO	RAT	ERA	ERA+	OAV	OOB	BH	AVG	PB	PR	PR+	PD	TPI
1937	Bro-N	5	12	.294	42	16	5	0	2	156^1	176	110	14	4	69	98	14.3	5.07	80	.278	.352	8	.167	-2	-20	-17	0	-1.9
1938	StL-N	5	11	.313	27	15	4	0	0	130	132	63	7	1	48	34	12.5	4.02	99	.266	.332	9	.220	-0	-3	-1	-1	-0.2
1942	Det-A	2	4	.333	23	2	0	0	1	61^2	63	32	3	1	27	24	13.3	4.09	97	.269	.347	1	.083	-1	-3	-1	-1	-0.2
1943	Det-A	0	2	.000	26	3	0	0	2	71^1	75	35	2	3	33	33	14.0	3.79	93	.276	.360	2	.111	-1	-4	-2	0	-0.2
1944	Det-A	0	0	—	7	1	0	0	0	12^1	17	12	0	0	6	10	16.8	8.76	41	.315	.383	0	.000	-1	-7	-7	0	-0.4
Total	8	33	40	.452	216	69	22	5	7	742^1	782	401	40	20	327	337	13.7	4.16	94	.271	.349	41	.179	-5	-29	-21	-8	-2.7
● **PHIL HENSIEK** Hensiek, Philip Frank "Sid" b: 10/13/01, St.Louis, Mo. d: 2/21/72, St.Louis, Mo. BR/TR, 6', 160 lbs. Deb: 8/15/35																												
1935	Was-A	0	3	.000	6	1	0	0	1	13	21	15	2	0	9	6	20.8	9.69	45	.356	.441	2	.667	1	-8	-8	-0	-1.3
● **CHUCK HENSLEY** Hensley, Charles Floyd b: 3/11/59, Tulare, Cal. BL/TL, 6'3", 190 lbs. Deb: 5/10/86																												
1986	SF-N	0	0	—	11	0	0	0	1	7^1	5	2	2	0	2	6	8.6	2.45	144	.179	.233	0	—	0	1	1	0	0.0
● **PAT HENTGEN** Hentgen, Patrick George b: 11/13/68, Detroit, Mich. BR/TR, 6'2", 200 lbs. Deb: 9/3/91																												
1991	Tor-A	0	0	—	3	1	0	0	0	7^1	5	2	1	2	3	3	12.3	2.45	172	.208	.345	0	—	0	1	1	0	0.1
1992	Tor-A	5	2	.714	28	2	0	0	0	50^1	49	30	7	0	32	39	14.5	5.36	76	.254	.360	0	—	0	-8	-7	-1	-0.9
1993	*Tor-A☆	19	9	.679	34	32	3	0	0	216^1	215	103	27	7	74	122	12.3	3.87	112	.258	.323	0	—	0	11	11	-2	1.1
1994	Tor-A★	13	8	.619	24	24	6	3	0	174^2	158	74	21	3	59	147	11.3	3.40	142	.240	.306	0	—	0	27	28	0	3.0
1995	Tor-A	10	14	.417	30	30	2	0	0	200^2	236	129	24	5	90	135	14.8	5.11	92	.290	.364	0	—	0	-9	-9	-2	-1.1
1996	Tor-A	20	10	.667	35	35	**10**	**3**	0	**265^2**	238	105	20	5	94	177	11.4	3.22	156	.241	.310	0	—	0	**53**	**53**	-1	5.2
1997	Tor-A★	15	10	.600	35	35	**9**	**3**	0	**264**	253	116	31	7	71	160	11.3	3.68	125	.254	.308	0	.000	-1	26	27	-0	2.2
1998	Tor-A	12	11	.522	29	29	0	0	0	177^2	208	109	28	5	69	94	14.3	5.17	90	.293	.360	0	.000	-1	-10	-10	-1	-1.2
1999	Tor-A	11	12	.478	34	34	1	0	0	199	225	115	32	3	65	118	13.3	4.79	103	.286	.343	1	.167	-0	2	3	-1	0.3
2000	*StL-N	15	12	.556	33	33	1	1	0	194^1	202	107	24	3	89	118	13.6	4.72	98	.276	.356	8	.133	-1	-2	-2	-1	-0.4
Total	10	120	88	.577	285	255	32	10	0	1750	1789	890	215	40	646	1113	12.7	4.21	112	.266	.334	9	.115	-2	92	95	-7	8.3
● **BILL HEPLER** Hepler, William Lewis b: 9/25/45, Covington, Va. BL/TL, 6', 160 lbs. Deb: 4/23/66																												
1966	NY-N	3	3	.500	37	3	0	0	0	69	71	30	3	3	51	25	16.3	3.52	103	.274	.399	3	.214	0	1	1	-1	0.0
● **RON HERBEL** Herbel, Ronald Samuel b: 1/16/38, Denver, Colo. d: 1/20/2000, Tacoma, Wash. BR/TR, 6'1", 195 lbs. Deb: 9/10/63																												
1963	SF-N	0	0	—	2	0	0	0	0	1^1	1	1	0	0	1	1	13.5	6.75	47	.200	.333	0	—	0	-1	-1	0	0.0
1964	SF-N	9	9	.500	40	22	7	2	1	161	162	65	7	3	61	98	12.6	3.07	116	.259	.328	0	.000	-4	8	9	2	0.7
1965	SF-N	12	9	.571	47	21	1	0	1	170^2	172	80	16	3	47	106	11.7	3.85	94	.261	.313	1	.020	-4	-6	-5	2	-0.8
1966	SF-N	4	5	.444	32	18	0	0	1	129^2	149	70	15	2	39	55	13.2	4.16	88	.291	.344	1	.026	-4	-8	-7	-1	-0.9
1967	SF-N	4	5	.444	42	11	1	1	1	125^2	125	54	10	2	35	52	11.6	3.08	107	.268	.322	3	.107	0	4	3	4	0.6
1968	SF-N	0	0	—	28	2	0	0	0	42^2	55	26	5	1	15	18	15.0	3.38	87	.309	.366	0	.000	-0	-2	-2	1	-0.1
1969	SF-N	4	1	.800	39	4	2	0	1	87^1	92	43	7	1	23	34	12.0	4.02	87	.275	.323	0	.000	-2	-4	-5	0	-0.4
1970	SD-N	7	5	.583	64	1	0	0	9	111	114	69	14	4	39	53	12.7	4.95	80	.266	.333	0	.000	-1	-11	-12	-0	-1.5
	NY-N	2	2	.500	12	0	0	0	1	13	14	3	1	0	2	8	11.1	1.38	291	.275	.302	0	—	0	4	4	-0	0.8
	Yr	9	7	.563	**76**	1	0	0	10	124	128	72	15	4	41	61	12.6	4.57	87	.267	.330	0	.000	-1	-7	-8	-1	-0.7
1971	Atl-N	0	1	.000	25	0	0	0	1	51^2	61	31	6	4	23	22	15.3	5.23	71	.300	.383	1	.091	-1	-10	-8	0	-0.5
Total	9	42	37	.532	331	79	11	3	16	894	945	442	81	20	285	447	12.6	3.83	94	.273	.332	6	.029	-15	-25	-24	7	-2.1
● **ERNIE HERBERT** Herbert, Ernie Albert "Tex" b: 1/30/1887, Hale, Mo. d: 1/13/68, Dallas, Tex. BR/TR, 5'10", 165 lbs. Deb: 7/27/13																												
1913	Cin-N	0	0	—	6	0	0	0	0	17^1	12	12	0	1	5	5	9.3	2.08	156	.179	.247	1	.250	0	2	2	-1	0.0
1914	StL-F	1	0	1.000	18	1	0	0	1	50^1	56	33	2	4	27	24	15.6	3.58	85	.293	.392	7	.538	2	-4	-3	-2	-0.1
1915	StL-F	1	0	1.000	11	1	1	0	0	48	48	21	1	3	18	23	12.9	3.38	85	.253	.327	5	.278	1	-3	-3	-1	-0.1
Total	3	2	0	1.000	35	2	1	0	1	115^2	116	66	3	8	50	52	13.5	3.27	92	.259	.344	13	.371	3	-5	-3	-4	-0.2
● **FRED HERBERT** Herbert, Frederick (b: Herbert Frederick Kemman) b: 3/4/1887, LaGrange, Ill. d: 5/29/63, Tice, Fla. BR/TR, 6', 185 lbs. Deb: 9/25/15																												
1915	NY-N	1	1	.500	2	2	1	0	0	17	12	5	0	0	4	6	8.5	1.06	242	.197	.246	1	.167	-0	3	3	0	0.4
● **RAY HERBERT** Herbert, Raymond Ernest b: 12/15/29, Detroit, Mich. BR/TR, 5'11", 185 lbs. Deb: 8/27/50																												
1950	Det-A	1	2	.333	8	3	1	0	1	22^1	20	11	1	0	12	5	12.9	3.63	129	.244	.340	2	.286	0	2	3	1	0.4
1951	Det-A	4	0	1.000	5	0	0	0	0	12^2	8	2	0	0	9	9	12.1	1.42	294	.190	.333	0	.000	-0	4	4	-0	0.7
1953	Det-A	4	6	.400	43	3	0	0	6	87^2	109	58	5	0	46	37	15.9	5.24	78	.308	.387	3	.158	-0	-12	-11	3	-1.0
1954	Det-A	3	6	.333	42	4	0	0	0	84^1	114	64	6	2	50	44	17.7	5.87	63	.334	.422	3	.176	2	-20	-21	2	-1.6
1955	KC-A	1	8	.111	23	11	2	0	0	87^2	99	65	10	1	40	30	14.4	6.26	67	.292	.368	4	.190	0	-22	-19	2	-1.5
1958	KC-A	8	8	.500	42	16	5	0	3	175	161	76	20	4	55	108	11.3	3.50	112	.248	.311	10	.192	1	5	8	2	1.1
1959	KC-A	11	11	.500	37	26	10	2	1	183^2	196	108	24	1	62	99	12.7	4.85	83	.275	.334	12	.211	2	-20	-17	-1	-1.7
1960	KC-A	14	15	.483	37	33	14	0	1	252^2	256	106	17	7	72	122	11.9	3.28	121	.267	.323	13	.171	1	17	19	3	2.5
1961	KC-A	3	6	.333	13	12	1	0	0	83^2	103	56	10	2	30	34	14.5	5.38	78	.303	.363	3	.107	-1	-13	-11	0	-1.1
	Chi-A	9	6	.600	21	20	4	0	0	137^2	142	69	15	0	36	50	11.6	4.05	97	.265	.311	12	.226	4	-0	-2	1	0.3
	Yr	12	12	.500	34	32	5	0	0	221^1	245	125	25	2	66	84	12.7	4.55	88	.280	.332	15	.185	3	-13	-13	1	-0.8
1962	Chi-A★	20	9	**.690**	35	35	12	2	0	236^2	228	90	13	1	74	115	11.5	3.27	119	.255	.312	16	.195	5	18	17	3	2.8
1963	Chi-A	13	10	.565	33	33	14	**7**	0	224^2	230	86	12	2	35	105	10.7	3.24	108	.265	.295	14	.222	6	10	7	2	1.6
1964	Chi-A	6	7	.462	20	19	1	1	0	111^2	117	50	14	2	17	40	11.0	3.47	100	.275	.306	5	.139	-1	2	-0	-1	-0.2
1965	Phi-N	5	8	.385	25	19	4	1	1	130^2	162	60	13	1	19	51	12.5	3.86	90	.309	.334	11	.268	3	-5	-6	0	-0.2
1966	Phi-N	2	5	.286	23	2	0	0	2	50^1	55	26	7	1	14	15	12.5	4.29	84	.293	.345	1	.077	-1	-4	-4	-0	-0.6
Total	14	104	107	.493	407	236	68	13	15	1881^1	2000	927	167	24	571	864	12.4	4.01	96	.276	.331	109	.192	20	-38	-35	18	1.5
● **FELIX HEREDIA** Heredia, Felix (Perez) b: 6/18/76, Barahona, D.R. BL/TL, 6', 160 lbs. Deb: 8/9/96																												
1996	Fla-N	1	1	.500	21	0	0	0	0	16^2	21	8	1	0	10	10	16.7	4.32	94	.313	.403	0	—	0	-0	-0	-1	-0.1
1997	*Fla-N	5	3	.625	56	0	0	0	0	56^2	53	30	3	5	30	54	14.0	4.29	94	.241	.345	1	.500	0	-1	-2	-2	-0.3
1998	Fla-N	0	3	.000	41	2	0	0	2	41	38	30	1	1	32	38	15.6	5.49	74	.241	.372	0	.000	-0	-6	-7	-0	-0.6
	*Chi-N	3	0	1.000	30	0	0	0	0	17^2	19	9	1	0	6	16	12.7	4.08	108	.279	.338	0	—	0	0	1	-1	0.0
	Yr	3	3	.500	71	2	0	0	2	58^2	57	39	2	1	38	54	14.7	5.06	82	.252	.362	0	.000	-0	-5	-6	-1	-0.6
1999	Chi-N	3	1	.750	69	0	0	0	1	52	56	35	7	1	25	50	14.2	4.85	93	.272	.353	2	.500	1	-2	-2	-1	-0.1
2000	Chi-N	7	3	.700	74	0	0	0	2	58^2	46	31	6	2	33	52	12.4	4.76	96	.220	.332	0	.000	-0	-1	-1	-1	-0.3
Total	5	19	11	.633	291	2	0	0	5	242^2	233	143	19	9	136	220	14.0	4.71	91	.251	.352	3	.273	1	-8	-11	-5	-1.4
● **GIL HEREDIA** Heredia, Gilbert b: 10/26/65, Nogales, Ariz. BR/TR, 6'1", 190 lbs. Deb: 9/1/91																												
1991	SF-N	0	2	.000	7	4	0	0	0	33	27	14	4	0	7	13	9.3	3.82	94	.233	.276	3	.429	1	-0	-1	-1	0.0
1992	SF-N	2	3	.400	13	4	0	0	0	30	32	20	3	1	16	15	14.7	5.40	61	.278	.371	1	.167	0	-6	-7	-1	-1.2
	Mon-N	0	0	—	7	1	0	0	0	14^2	12	3	1	0	4	7	9.8	1.84	189	.250	.308	0	.000	-0	3	3	0	0.1
	Yr	2	3	.400	20	5	0	0	0	44^2	44	23	4	1	20	22	13.1	4.23	79	.270	.353	1	.111	-0	-4	-4	-1	-1.1
1993	Mon-N	4	2	.667	20	9	1	0	2	57^1	66	28	4	2	14	40	12.9	3.92	106	.293	.340	2	.154	-0	1	2	1	0.2
1994	Mon-N	6	3	.667	39	3	0	0	0	75^1	85	34	7	2	13	62	11.9	3.46	122	.281	.314	5	.313	1	6	6	0	0.8
1995	Mon-N	5	6	.455	40	18	0	0	1	119	137	60	7	5	21	74	12.3	4.31	100	.291	.329	6	.182	-0	-2	-0	1	0.1
1996	Tex-A	2	5	.286	44	0	0	0	1	73^1	91	50	12	1	14	43	13.0	5.89	89	.301	.334	0	—	0	-7	-5	-0	-0.4
1998	Oak-A	3	3	.500	8	6	0	0	0	42^2	43	14	4	3	3	27	10.3	2.74	167	.256	.282	0	—	0	9	9	0	1.2
1999	Oak-A	13	8	.619	33	33	1	0	0	200^1	228	119	22	8	34	117	12.1	4.81	97	.283	.318	0	.000	-0	1	-4	0	-0.3
2000	*Oak-A	15	11	.577	32	32	2	0	0	198^2	214	106	24	4	66	101	12.9	4.12	116	.274	.334	1	.500	0	18	15	0	1.7
Total	9	50	43	.538	243	110	4	0	4	844^1	935	448	88	26	192	499	12.3	4.32	104	.280	.325	18	.209	2	22	17	1	2.2
● **UBALDO HEREDIA** Heredia, Ubaldo Jose (Martinez) b: 5/4/56, Ciudad Bolivar, Ven. BR/TR, 6'2", 180 lbs. Deb: 5/12/87																												
1987	Mon-N	0	1	.000	2	2	0	0	0	10	10	6	2	1	3	6	12.6	5.40	78	.263	.333	0	.000	-0	-1	-1	0	-0.1
● **WILSON HEREDIA** Heredia, Wilson b: 3/30/72, LaRomana, D.R. BR/TR, 6', 175 lbs. Deb: 4/27/95																												
1995	Tex-A	0	1	.000	6	0	0	0	0	12	9	5	2	0	15	6	18.0	3.75	129	.225	.436	0	—	0	1	1	-0	0.1
1997	Tex-A	1	0	1.000	10	0	0	0	0	19^2	14	9	2	0	16	8	13.7	3.20	150	.197	.345	0	—	0	3	3	0	0.2
Total	2	1	1	.500	16	0	0	0	0	31^2	23	14	4	0	31	14	15.3	3.41	141	.207	.380	0	—	0	4	5	-0	0.3

YEAR TM/L	W	L	PCT	G	GS	CG	SH	SV	IP	H	R	HR	HB	BB	SO	RAT	ERA	ERA+	OAV	OOB	BH	AVG	PB	PR	PR+	PD	TPI
● **MATT HERGES**	Herges, Matthew Tyler b: 4/1/70, Champaign, Ill. BL/TR, 6', 200 lbs. Deb: 8/3/99																										
1999 LA-N	0	2	.000	17	0	0	0	0	24^1	24	13	5	1	8	18	12.2	4.07	105	.255	.320	0	.000	-0	1	1	-0	0.0
2000 LA-N	11	3	.786	59	4	0	0	1	110^2	100	43	7	6	40	75	11.9	3.17	138	.249	.326	1	.077	-1	18	16	1	1.7
Total 2	11	5	.688	76	4	0	0	1	135	124	56	12	7	48	93	11.9	3.33	131	.250	.325	1	.071	-1	19	16	1	1.7
● **ART HERMAN**	Herman, Arthur b: 5/11/1871, Louisville, Ky. d: 9/20/55, Los Angeles, Cal. Deb: 6/29/1896																										
1896 Lou-N	4	6	.400	14	12	9	0	0	94^1	122	73	4	2	36	13	15.3	5.63	77	.310	.371	5	.139	-4	-13	-14	-1	-1.5
1897 Lou-N	0	1	.000	3	2	1	0	0	18	23	14	1	0	5	4	14.0	4.00	106	.307	.350	2	.333	1	1	1	0	0.2
Total 2	4	7	.364	17	14	10	0	0	112^1	145	87	5	2	41	17	15.1	5.37	80	.310	.368	7	.167	-2	-13	-13	-1	-1.3
● **DUSTIN HERMANSON**	Hermanson, Dustin Michael b: 12/21/72, Springfield, Ohio BR/TR, 6'3", 195 lbs. Deb: 5/8/95																										
1995 SD-N	3	1	.750	26	0	0	0	0	31^2	35	26	8	1	22	19	16.5	6.82	59	.280	.392	0	—	0	-9	-10	0	-1.1
1996 SD-N	1	0	1.000	8	0	0	0	0	13^2	18	15	3	0	4	11	14.5	8.56	46	.340	.386	0	—	0	-7	-7	0	-0.4
1997 Mon-N	8	8	.500	32	28	1	1	0	158^1	134	68	15	1	66	136	11.4	3.69	114	.234	.314	5	.104	-0	9	9	-0	0.8
1998 Mon-N	14	11	.560	32	30	1	0	0	187	163	80	21	3	56	154	10.7	3.13	134	.234	.294	6	.115	2	23	23	1	3.1
1999 Mon-N	9	14	.391	34	34	0	0	0	216^1	225	110	20	7	69	145	12.5	4.20	107	.271	.333	3	.047	-5	9	7	-1	0.1
2000 Mon-N	12	14	.462	38	30	2	1	4	198	226	128	26	4	75	94	13.9	4.77	99	.290	.356	8	.145	-1	-3	-1	-1	-0.3
Total 6	47	48	.495	170	122	4	2	4	805	801	427	93	16	292	559	12.4	4.17	105	.262	.330	22	.100	-3	22	20	-1	2.2
● **JESUS HERNAIZ**	Hernaiz, Jesus Rafael (Rodriguez) b: 1/8/45, Santurce, P.R. BR/TR, 6'2", 175 lbs. Deb: 6/14/74																										
1974 Phi-N	2	3	.400	27	0	0	0	1	41	53	31	6	0	25	16	17.0	5.88	64	.323	.413	0	.000	-0	-10	-9	-0	-1.1
● **LIVAN HERNANDEZ**	Hernandez, Eisler Livan b: 2/20/75, Villa Clara, Cuba BR/TR, 6'2", 220 lbs. Deb: 9/24/96 F																										
1996 Fla-N	0	0	—	1	0	0	0	0	3	3	0	0	0	2	2	15.0	0.00	—	.273	.385	1	1.000	0	1	1	-0	0.1
1997 *Fla-N	9	3	.750	17	17	0	0	0	96^1	81	39	5	3	38	72	11.4	3.18	127	.229	.310	5	.172	1	11	10	1	1.3
1998 Fla-N	10	12	.455	33	33	9	0	0	234^1	265	133	37	6	104	162	14.4	4.72	86	.289	.365	16	.195	2	-13	-18	1	-1.2
1999 Fla-N	5	9	.357	20	20	2	0	0	136	161	78	17	2	55	97	14.4	4.76	92	.294	.360	13	.289	5	-3	-6	1	0.1
SF-N	3	3	.500	10	10	0	0	0	63^2	66	32	6	0	21	47	12.3	4.38	96	.267	.325	4	.222	1	1	-1	1	0.1
Yr	8	12	.400	30	30	2	0	0	199^2	227	110	23	2	76	144	13.7	4.64	93	.286	.349	17	.270	7	-2	-8	2	0.2
2000 *SF-N	17	11	.607	33	33	5	2	0	240	254	114	22	4	73	165	12.4	3.75	113	.273	.328	21	.236	6	24	14	3	2.3
Total 5	44	38	.537	114	113	16	2	0	773^1	830	396	87	15	293	545	13.2	4.19	100	.276	.343	60	.227	15	22	-1	7	2.7
● **FERNANDO HERNANDEZ**	Hernandez, Fernando b: 6/16/71, Santiago, D.R. BR/TR, 6'2", 185 lbs. Deb: 4/3/97																										
1997 Det-A	0	0	—	2	0	0	0	0	1^1	5	6	0	1	3	2	60.8	40.50	11	.556	.692	0	—	0	-5	-5	0	-0.2
● **XAVIER HERNANDEZ**	Hernandez, Francis Xavier b: 8/16/65, Port Arthur, Tex. BL/TR, 6'2", 185 lbs. Deb: 6/4/89																										
1989 Tor-A	1	0	1.000	7	0	0	0	0	22^2	25	15	2	1	8	7	13.5	4.76	79	.278	.343	0	—	0	-2	-3	-1	-0.2
1990 Hou-N	2	1	.667	34	1	0	0	0	62^1	60	34	8	4	24	24	12.7	4.62	80	.256	.336	1	.333	0	-6	-6	-1	-0.4
1991 Hou-N	2	7	.222	32	6	0	0	3	63	66	34	6	0	32	55	14.0	4.71	74	.263	.346	0	.000	-0	-7	-9	0	-1.2
1992 Hou-N	9	1	.900	77	0	0	0	7	111	81	31	5	3	42	96	10.2	2.11	160	.200	.281	0	.000	-1	17	16	-2	1.4
1993 Hou-N	4	5	.444	72	0	0	0	9	96^2	75	37	6	1	28	101	9.7	2.61	149	.212	.272	0	.000	-1	15	14	-1	1.3
1994 NY-A	4	4	.500	31	0	0	0	6	40	48	27	7	2	21	37	16.0	5.85	78	.300	.388	0	—	0	-5	-6	1	-1.0
1995 *Cin-N	7	2	.778	59	0	0	0	3	90	95	47	8	4	31	84	13.0	4.60	90	.273	.339	0	.000	-1	-4	-5	-0	-0.6
1996 Cin-N	0	0	—	3	0	0	0	0	3	8	6	2	0	2	3	27.0	13.50	31	.471	.526	0	—	0	-3	-3	-0	-0.2
Hou-N	5	5	.500	58	0	0	0	6	74^2	69	39	11	2	26	78	11.7	4.22	92	.245	.313	0	.000	-0	0	-3	-0	-0.5
Yr	5	5	.500	61	0	0	0	6	78	77	45	13	2	28	81	12.3	4.62	84	.258	.325	0	.000	-0	-3	-7	-0	-0.7
1997 Tex-A	0	4	.000	44	0	0	0	0	49^1	51	27	7	2	22	36	13.7	4.56	105	.262	.342	0	—	0	0	1	0	0.1
1998 Tex-A	6	6	.500	46	0	0	0	1	58	43	27	5	1	30	41	11.5	3.57	135	.207	.310	0	—	0	7	8	-1	1.3
Total 10	40	35	.533	463	7	0	0	35	671	621	324	67	20	266	562	12.2	3.90	101	.244	.321	1	.027	-3	13	4	-4	-0.0
● **EVELIO HERNANDEZ**	Hernandez, Gregorio Evelio (Lopez) b: 12/24/31, Guanabacoa, Havana, Cuba BR/TR, 6'1", 195 lbs. Deb: 9/12/56																										
1956 Was-A	1	1	.500	4	4	1	0	0	22^2	24	12	2	0	8	9	12.7	4.76	91	.276	.337	2	.182	-0	-2	-1	-0	-0.1
1957 Was-A	0	0	—	14	2	0	0	0	36	38	18	2	0	20	15	14.5	4.25	92	.268	.358	0	.000	-1	-2	-1	-1	-0.2
Total 2	1	1	.500	18	6	1	0	0	58^2	62	30	4	0	28	24	13.8	4.45	91	.271	.350	2	.118	-1	-3	-2	-1	-0.3
● **WILLIE HERNANDEZ**	Hernandez, Guillermo (Villanueva) b: 11/14/54, Aguada, P.R. BL/TL, 6'3", 180 lbs. Deb: 4/9/77																										
1977 Chi-N	8	7	.533	67	1	0	0	4	110	94	42	11	1	28	78	10.1	3.03	145	.234	.285	1	.063	-1	11	15	3	2.1
1978 Chi-N	8	2	.800	54	0	0	0	3	59^2	57	26	6	1	35	38	14.0	3.77	107	.263	.368	0	.000	-0	-1	2	1	0.3
1979 Chi-N	4	4	.500	51	2	0	0	0	79	85	50	8	4	39	53	14.6	5.01	82	.281	.370	2	.250	0	-11	-7	-0	-0.6
1980 Chi-N	1	9	.100	53	7	0	0	0	108^1	115	58	8	2	45	75	13.5	4.40	89	.276	.349	4	.211	0	-10	-5	2	-0.3
1981 Chi-N	0	0	—	12	0	0	0	2	13^2	14	7	0	0	8	13	14.5	3.95	94	.280	.379	0	—	0	-1	-0	0	0.0
1982 Chi-N	4	6	.400	75	0	0	0	10	75	74	26	3	1	24	54	11.9	3.00	125	.268	.329	0	.000	-0	5	6	2	1.2
1983 Chi-N	1	0	1.000	11	0	0	0	1	19^2	16	8	0	0	6	18	10.1	3.20	119	.222	.282	1	.500	0	1	1	0	0.1
*Phi-N	8	4	.667	63	0	0	0	7	95^2	93	39	9	1	26	75	11.3	3.29	109	.254	.305	5	.385	2	4	3	-0	0.6
Yr	9	4	.692	74	1	0	0	8	115^1	109	47	9	1	32	93	11.1	3.28	110	.249	.301	6	.400	2	5	4	0	0.7
1984 *Det-A★	9	3	.750	**80**	0	0	0	32	140^1	96	30	6	4	36	112	8.7	1.92	204	.194	.254	0	—	0	**32**	**32**	-1	3.9
1985 Det-A★	8	10	.444	74	0	0	0	31	106^2	82	38	13	1	14	76	8.2	2.70	151	.210	.239	0	.000	-0	17	17	-2	3.2
1986 Det-A☆	8	7	.533	64	0	0	0	24	88^2	87	35	13	5	21	77	11.5	3.55	116	.251	.304	0	—	0	6	6	1	1.2
1987 *Det-A	3	4	.429	45	0	0	0	8	49	53	27	8	0	20	30	13.4	3.67	115	.276	.344	0	—	0	4	3	-1	0.4
1988 Det-A	6	5	.545	63	0	0	0	10	67^2	50	24	8	4	31	59	11.3	3.06	125	.208	.309	0	—	0	7	6	1	1.2
1989 Det-A	2	2	.500	32	0	0	0	15	31^1	36	21	4	1	16	30	15.2	5.74	67	.293	.379	0	—	0	-6	-7	0	-1.3
Total 13	70	63	.526	744	11	0	0	147	1044^2	952	431	97	25	349	788	11.4	3.38	118	.245	.311	13	.206	1	58	69	6	12.0
● **JEREMY HERNANDEZ**	Hernandez, Jeremy Stuart b: 7/6/66, Burbank, Cal. BR/TR, 6'6", 195 lbs. Deb: 9/2/91																										
1991 SD-N	0	0	—	9	0	0	0	2	14^1	8	1	0	0	5	9	8.2	0.00	—	.157	.232	0	.000	-0	6	6	0	0.3
1992 SD-N	1	4	.200	26	0	0	0	0	36^2	39	17	4	1	11	25	12.5	4.17	86	.291	.349	0	.000	-0	-3	-2	0	-0.3
1993 SD-N	0	2	.000	21	0	0	0	0	34^1	41	19	2	0	7	26	12.6	4.72	88	.301	.336	0	.000	-0	-3	-2	0	-0.1
Cle-A	6	5	.545	49	0	0	0	8	77^1	75	33	12	0	27	44	11.9	3.14	138	.261	.325	0	—	0	10	10	-0	1.5
1994 Fla-N	3	3	.500	21	0	0	0	9	23^1	16	9	0	2	14	13	12.3	2.70	162	.205	.340	0	.000	-0	4	4	-0	0.8
1995 Fla-N	0	0	—	7	0	0	0	0	7	12	9	2	1	3	5	20.6	11.57	36	.400	.471	0	.000	-0	-6	-6	-0	-0.3
Total 5	10	14	.417	133	0	0	0	20	193	191	88	20	4	67	122	12.2	3.64	113	.267	.333	0	.000	-1	9	10	-0	1.9
● **MANNY HERNANDEZ**	Hernandez, Manuel Antonio (Montas) b: 5/7/61, LaRomana, D.R. BR/TR, 6', 150 lbs. Deb: 6/5/86																										
1986 Hou-N	2	3	.400	9	4	0	0	0	27^2	33	15	2	0	12	9	14.6	3.90	92	.306	.375	0	.000	-1	-1	-1	-0	-0.2
1987 Hou-N	0	4	.000	6	3	0	0	0	21^2	25	15	1	1	5	12	12.9	5.40	73	.301	.348	0	.000	-1	-3	-4	0	-0.6
1989 NY-N	0	0	—	1	0	0	0	0	1	0	0	0	0	0	1	0.0	0.00	—	.000	.000	0	—	0	0	0	0	0.0
Total 3	2	7	.222	16	7	0	0	0	50^1	58	30	3	1	17	22	13.6	4.47	84	.299	.358	0	.000	-1	-3	-4	0	-0.8
● **ORLANDO HERNANDEZ**	Hernandez, Orlando P. "El Duque" b: 10/11/65, Villa Clara, Cuba BR/TR, 6'2", 210 lbs. Deb: 6/3/98 F																										
1998 *NY-A	12	4	.750	21	21	3	1	0	141	113	53	11	6	52	131	10.9	3.13	140	.222	.302	0	.000	-1	24	21	1	2.2
1999 *NY-A★	17	9	.654	33	33	2	1	0	214^1	187	108	24	8	87	157	11.8	4.12	115	.233	.315	1	.333	0	18	15	0	1.6
2000 *NY-A	12	13	.480	29	29	3	0	0	195^2	186	104	34	6	51	141	11.2	4.51	106	.247	.300	0	.000	-1	9	6	1	0.7
Total 3	41	26	.612	83	83	8	2	0	551	486	265	69	20	190	429	11.4	4.00	117	.236	.306	1	.053	-1	51	42	2	4.5
● **RAMON HERNANDEZ**	Hernandez, Ramon (Gonzalez) b: 8/31/40, Carolina, P.R. BB/TL, 5'9", 170 lbs. Deb: 4/11/67																										
1967 Atl-N	0	2	.000	46	0	0	0	5	51^2	60	27	5	2	14	28	13.2	4.18	79	.296	.347	0	.000	-0	-5	-5	1	-0.3
1968 Chi-N	0	0	—	8	0	0	0	0	9	14	11	1	1	0	3	15.0	9.00	35	.350	.366	0	—	0	-6	-6	0	-0.3
1971 Pit-N	0	1	.000	10	0	0	0	4	12^1	5	1	0	0	2	7	5.1	0.73	464	.122	.163	1	.500	0	4	4	0	0.7
1972 *Pit-N	5	0	1.000	53	0	0	0	14	70	50	14	3	3	22	47	9.6	1.67	199	.194	.265	2	.167	0	14	13	0	1.6
1973 Pit-N	4	5	.444	59	0	0	0	11	89^2	71	27	5	4	25	64	10.0	2.41	146	.218	.282	1	.125	0	13	12	1	1.5
1974 *Pit-N	5	2	.714	58	0	0	0	2	68^2	68	21	3	2	18	33	11.5	2.75	126	.258	.310	1	.250	1	7	6	-1	0.6
1975 *Pit-N	7	2	.778	46	0	0	0	5	64	62	21	0	0	28	43	12.7	2.95	120	.252	.328	0	.000	-0	5	4	1	0.7

YEAR	TM/L	W	L	PCT	G	GS	CG	SH	SV	IP	H	R	HR	HB	BB	SO	RAT	ERA	ERA+	OAV	OOB	BH	AVG	PB	PR	PR+	PD	TPI
1976	Pit-N	2	2	.500	37	0	0	0	3	43	42	17	3	1	16	17	12.3	3.56	98	.262	.333	0	.000	-0	-0	-0	-1	-0.1
	Chi-N	0	0	—	2	0	0	0	0	1^2	2	0	0	0	0	1	10.8	0.00	—	.333	.333	0	—	0	1	1	0	0.0
	Yr	2	2	.500	39	0	0	0	3	44^2	44	17	3	1	16	18	12.3	3.43	102	.265	.333	0	.000	-0	0	0	-0	-0.1
1977	Chi-N	0	0	—	6	0	0	0	1	7^2	11	9	1	0	3	4	16.4	8.22	53	.306	.359	0	.000	-0	-4	-3	0	-0.1
	Bos-A	0	1	.000	12	0	0	0	1	12^2	14	10	2	1	7	8	15.6	5.68	79	.280	.379	0	—	0	-2	-1	-0	-0.1
Total	9	23	15	.605	337	0	0	0	46	430^1	399	158	23	14	135	255	11.5	3.03	115	.245	.308	5	.125	1	26	22	1	4.2

● ROBERTO HERNANDEZ Hernandez, Roberto Manuel (Rodriguez) b: 11/11/64, Santurce, P.R. BR/TR, 6'4", 235 lbs. Deb: 9/2/91

YEAR	TM/L	W	L	PCT	G	GS	CG	SH	SV	IP	H	R	HR	HB	BB	SO	RAT	ERA	ERA+	OAV	OOB	BH	AVG	PB	PR	PR+	PD	TPI
1991	Chi-A	1	0	1.000	9	3	0	0	0	15	18	15	1	0	7	6	15.0	7.80	51	.290	.362	0	—	0	-6	-7	-0	-0.4
1992	Chi-A	7	3	.700	43	0	0	0	12	71	45	15	4	4	20	68	8.7	1.65	235	.180	.252	0	—	0	18	18	-0	2.9
1993	*Chi-A	3	4	.429	70	0	0	0	38	78^2	66	21	6	0	20	71	9.8	2.29	183	.228	.277	0	—	0	18	17	0	2.8
1994	Chi-A	4	4	.500	45	0	0	0	14	47^2	44	29	5	1	19	50	12.1	4.91	95	.238	.312	0	—	0	-1	-1	-1	-0.3
1995	Chi-A	3	7	.300	60	0	0	0	32	59^2	63	30	9	3	28	84	14.2	3.92	114	.266	.351	0	—	0	5	4	-0	0.7
1996	Chi-A★	6	5	.545	72	0	0	0	38	84^2	65	21	2	0	38	85	10.9	1.91	248	.208	.293	0	—	0	29	28	-1	**5.2**
1997	Chi-A	5	1	.833	46	0	0	0	27	48	38	15	5	1	24	47	11.8	2.44	180	.216	.313	0	—	0	11	11	0	2.2
	*SF-N	5	2	.714	28	0	0	0	4	32^2	29	9	2	0	14	35	11.8	2.48	165	.238	.316	1	.500	0	6	6	-0	1.2
1998	TB-A	2	6	.250	67	0	0	0	26	71^1	55	33	5	5	41	55	12.7	4.04	119	.212	.330	0	—	0	5	6	-0	0.9
1999	TB-A	2	3	.400	72	0	0	0	43	73^1	68	27	1	4	33	69	12.9	3.07	162	.244	.332	0	—	0	15	15	0	2.4
2000	TB-A	4	7	.364	68	0	0	0	32	73^1	76	33	9	3	23	61	12.5	3.19	155	.272	.334	0	—	0	14	14	1	2.7
Total	10	42	42	.500	580	3	0	0	266	655^1	567	248	49	21	267	631	11.7	3.04	149	.231	.312	1	.500	0	115	111	-2	20.3

● RUDY HERNANDEZ Hernandez, Rudolph Albert (Fuentes) b: 12/10/31, Santiago, D.R. BR/TR, 6'3", 185 lbs. Deb: 7/3/60

YEAR	TM/L	W	L	PCT	G	GS	CG	SH	SV	IP	H	R	HR	HB	BB	SO	RAT	ERA	ERA+	OAV	OOB	BH	AVG	PB	PR	PR+	PD	TPI
1960	Was-A	4	1	.800	21	0	0	0	0	34^2	34	24	2	1	21	22	14.5	4.41	88	.262	.368	1	.167	-0	-2	-2	-0	-0.3
1961	Was-A	0	1	.000	7	0	0	0	0	9	8	5	0	0	3	4	11.0	3.00	134	.250	.314	0	—	0	1	1	0	0.1
Total	2	4	2	.667	28	0	0	0	0	43^2	42	29	2	1	24	26	13.8	4.12	95	.259	.358	1	.167	-0	-1	-1	-0	-0.2

● WALT HERRELL Herrell, Walter William "Reds" b: 2/19/1889, Rockville, Md. d: 1/23/49, Front Royal, Va. Deb: 6/10/11

YEAR	TM/L	W	L	PCT	G	GS	CG	SH	SV	IP	H	R	HR	HB	BB	SO	RAT	ERA	ERA+	OAV	OOB	BH	AVG	PB	PR	PR+	PD	TPI
1911	Was-A	0	0	—	1	0	0	0	0	2	5	4	0	0	2	0	31.5	18.00	18	.556	.636	0	.000	-0	-3	-3	0	-0.2

● BOBBY HERRERA Herrera, Procopio Rodriguez "Tito" (b: Procopio Rodriguez (Herrera)) b: 7/26/26, Nuevo Laredo, Mex BR/TR, 6', 184 lbs. Deb: 4/19/51

YEAR	TM/L	W	L	PCT	G	GS	CG	SH	SV	IP	H	R	HR	HB	BB	SO	RAT	ERA	ERA+	OAV	OOB	BH	AVG	PB	PR	PR+	PD	TPI
1951	StL-A	0	0	—	3	0	0	0	0	2^1	6	7	2	1	4	1	42.4	27.00	16	.462	.611	0	—	0	-6	-5	-0	-0.3

● TROY HERRIAGE Herriage, William Troy "Dutch" b: 12/20/30, Tipton, Okla. BR/TR, 6'1", 170 lbs. Deb: 4/25/56

YEAR	TM/L	W	L	PCT	G	GS	CG	SH	SV	IP	H	R	HR	HB	BB	SO	RAT	ERA	ERA+	OAV	OOB	BH	AVG	PB	PR	PR+	PD	TPI
1956	KC-A	1	13	.071	31	16	1	0	0	103	135	83	16	6	64	59	17.9	6.64	65	.321	.418	3	.120	-1	-28	-25	-2	-3.2

● TOM HERRIN Herrin, Thomas Edward b: 9/12/29, Shreveport, La. d: 11/20/99, Homer, La. BR/TR, 6'3", 190 lbs. Deb: 4/13/54

YEAR	TM/L	W	L	PCT	G	GS	CG	SH	SV	IP	H	R	HR	HB	BB	SO	RAT	ERA	ERA+	OAV	OOB	BH	AVG	PB	PR	PR+	PD	TPI
1954	Bos-A	1	2	.333	14	1	0	0	0	28^1	34	23	2	0	22	8	17.8	7.31	56	.315	.431	1	.125	-0	-11	-9	1	-0.8

● ART HERRING Herring, Arthur L "Red" or "Sandy" b: 3/10/06, Altus, Okla. d: 12/2/95, Marion, Ind. BR/TR, 5'7", 168 lbs. Deb: 9/12/29

YEAR	TM/L	W	L	PCT	G	GS	CG	SH	SV	IP	H	R	HR	HB	BB	SO	RAT	ERA	ERA+	OAV	OOB	BH	AVG	PB	PR	PR+	PD	TPI
1929	Det-A	2	1	.667	4	4	2	0	0	32	38	17	0	1	19	15	16.3	4.78	90	.302	.397	3	.214	1	-2	-2	0	0.0
1930	Det-A	3	3	.500	23	6	1	0	0	77^2	97	54	2	3	36	16	15.8	5.33	90	.315	.392	3	.130	-2	-6	-4	-0	-0.5
1931	Det-A	7	13	.350	35	16	9	0	1	165	186	95	8	8	67	64	14.2	4.31	106	.281	.355	11	.200	-1	1	5	2	0.6
1932	Det-A	1	2	.333	12	0	0	0	2	22^1	25	18	2	1	15	12	16.5	5.24	90	.284	.394	0	.000	-0	-2	-1	0	-0.2
1933	Det-A	1	2	.333	24	3	1	0	0	61	61	34	6	1	20	20	12.1	3.84	112	.264	.325	1	.077	-1	3	3	-1	0.0
1934	Bro-N	2	4	.333	14	4	2	0	0	49^1	63	36	2	0	29	15	16.8	6.20	63	.307	.393	2	.143	1	-12	-13	-0	-1.3
1939	Chi-A	0	0	—	7	0	0	0	0	14^1	13	9	2	1	5	8	11.9	5.65	84	.250	.328	0	.000	-0	-2	-1	0	-0.1
1944	Bro-N	3	4	.429	12	6	3	1	1	55^1	59	28	3	1	17	19	12.5	3.42	104	.277	.333	3	.200	0	1	1	0	0.2
1945	Bro-N	7	4	.636	22	15	7	2	2	124	103	60	11	3	43	34	10.8	3.48	108	.222	.292	4	.095	-2	4	4	1	0.2
1946	Bro-N	7	2	.778	35	2	0	0	5	86	91	39	2	1	29	34	12.7	3.35	101	.277	.338	4	.182	0	1	0	2	0.2
1947	Pit-N	1	3	.250	11	0	0	0	2	10^2	18	11	3	0	4	6	18.6	8.44	50	.360	.407	0	.000	-0	-5	-5	-0	-0.9
Total	11	34	38	.472	199	56	25	3	13	697^2	754	401	41	20	284	243	13.6	4.32	96	.276	.349	31	.149	-4	-18	-14	4	-1.8

● HERB HERRING Herring, Herbert Lee b: 7/22/1891, Danville, Ark. d: 4/22/64, Tucson, Ariz. BR/TR, 5'11", 178 lbs. Deb: 9/4/12

YEAR	TM/L	W	L	PCT	G	GS	CG	SH	SV	IP	H	R	HR	HB	BB	SO	RAT	ERA	ERA+	OAV	OOB	BH	AVG	PB	PR	PR+	PD	TPI
1912	Was-A	0	0	—	1	0	0	0	0	1	1	0	0	0	1	0	18.0	0.00	—	.250	.400	0	—	0	0	0	-0	0.0

● LEFTY HERRING Herring, Silas Clarke b: 3/4/1880, Philadelphia, Pa. d: 2/11/65, Massapequa, N.Y. BL/TL, 5'11", 160 lbs. Deb: 5/16/1899 ♦

YEAR	TM/L	W	L	PCT	G	GS	CG	SH	SV	IP	H	R	HR	HB	BB	SO	RAT	ERA	ERA+	OAV	OOB	BH	AVG	PB	PR	PR+	PD	TPI
1899	Was-N	0	0	—	2	0	0	0	0	2	0	0	0	0	2	0	9.0	0.00	—	.000	.250	1	1.000	1	1	1	0	0.1

● BILL HERRING Herring, William Francis "Smoke" b: 10/31/1893, New York, N.Y. d: 9/10/62, Honesdale, Pa. BR/TR, 6'3", 185 lbs. Deb: 6/26/15

YEAR	TM/L	W	L	PCT	G	GS	CG	SH	SV	IP	H	R	HR	HB	BB	SO	RAT	ERA	ERA+	OAV	OOB	BH	AVG	PB	PR	PR+	PD	TPI
1915	Bro-F	0	0	—	3	0	0	0	0	3	5	6	1	1	2	3	24.0	15.00	18	.385	.500	0	—	0	-4	-4	-0	-0.2

● LEROY HERRMANN Herrmann, Leroy George b: 2/27/06, Steward, Ill. d: 7/3/72, Livermore, Cal. BR/TR, 5'10", 185 lbs. Deb: 7/30/32

YEAR	TM/L	W	L	PCT	G	GS	CG	SH	SV	IP	H	R	HR	HB	BB	SO	RAT	ERA	ERA+	OAV	OOB	BH	AVG	PB	PR	PR+	PD	TPI
1932	Chi-N	2	1	.667	7	0	0	0	0	12^2	18	9	0	0	9	5	19.2	6.39	59	.346	.443	1	.500	0	-4	-4	-0	-0.7
1933	Chi-N	0	1	.000	9	1	0	0	1	21	26	19	3	4	8	4	16.3	5.57	59	.299	.384	1	.167	-0	-5	-5	-1	-0.4
1935	Cin-N	3	5	.375	29	8	2	0	0	108	124	53	9	8	31	30	13.6	3.58	111	.297	.357	8	.267	1	5	5	-0	0.4
Total	3	5	7	.417	45	9	2	0	1	141^2	168	81	12	12	48	39	14.5	4.13	93	.302	.370	10	.263	1	-4	-4	-1	-0.7

● MARTY HERRMANN Herrmann, Martin John "Lefty" b: 1/10/1893, Oldenburg, Ind. d: 9/11/56, Cincinnati, Ohio BL/TL, 5'10", 150 lbs. Deb: 7/10/18 F

YEAR	TM/L	W	L	PCT	G	GS	CG	SH	SV	IP	H	R	HR	HB	BB	SO	RAT	ERA	ERA+	OAV	OOB	BH	AVG	PB	PR	PR+	PD	TPI
1918	Bro-N	0	0	—	1	0	0	0	0	1	0	0	0	0	1	0	9.0	0.00	—	.000	.250	0	—	0	0	0	-0	0.0

● FRANK HERSHEY Hershey, Frank b: 12/13/1877, Gorham, N.Y. d: 12/15/49, Canandaigua, N.Y. TR, 5'10", 175 lbs. Deb: 4/20/05

YEAR	TM/L	W	L	PCT	G	GS	CG	SH	SV	IP	H	R	HR	HB	BB	SO	RAT	ERA	ERA+	OAV	OOB	BH	AVG	PB	PR	PR+	PD	TPI
1905	Bos-N	0	1	.000	1	1	1	0	0	4	5	4	0	0	2	1	15.8	6.75	46	.313	.389	0	.000	-0	-2	-2	-0	-0.3

● OREL HERSHISER Hershiser, Orel Leonard Quinton b: 9/16/58, Buffalo, N.Y. BR/TR, 6'3", 192 lbs. Deb: 9/1/83

YEAR	TM/L	W	L	PCT	G	GS	CG	SH	SV	IP	H	R	HR	HB	BB	SO	RAT	ERA	ERA+	OAV	OOB	BH	AVG	PB	PR	PR+	PD	TPI
1983	LA-N	0	0	—	8	0	0	0	1	8	7	6	1	0	6	5	14.6	3.38	107	.233	.361	0	—	0	0	0	0	0.0
1984	LA-N	11	8	.579	45	20	8	**4**	2	189^2	160	65	9	4	50	150	10.2	2.66	133	.225	.279	10	.200	2	20	19	1	2.1
1985	*LA-N	19	3	**.864**	36	34	9	5	0	239^2	179	72	8	6	68	157	9.5	2.03	172	.206	.268	15	.197	3	42	40	2	4.3
1986	LA-N	14	14	.500	35	35	8	1	0	231^1	213	112	13	5	86	153	11.8	3.85	90	.243	.314	17	.239	4	-3	-11	1	-0.7
1987	LA-N★	16	16	.500	37	35	10	1	1	**264^2**	247	105	17	9	74	190	11.2	3.06	130	.247	.305	19	.211	4	30	28	1	**3.8**
1988	*LA-N★	**23**	8	.742	35	34	**15**	**8**	1	**267**	208	73	18	4	73	178	9.6	2.26	148	.213	.271	11	.129	-0	**35**	**33**	6	**4.7**
1989	LA-N☆	15	15	.500	35	33	8	4	0	**256^2**	226	75	9	3	77	178	10.7	2.31	148	.240	.299	14	.182	3	**34**	**32**	4	**4.7**
1990	LA-N	1	1	.500	4	4	0	0	0	25^1	26	12	1	1	4	16	11.0	4.26	86	.260	.295	0	.000	-1	-1	-2	-0	-0.2
1991	LA-N	7	2	.778	21	21	0	0	0	112	112	43	3	5	32	73	12.0	3.46	104	.259	.317	8	.258	3	3	2	1	0.6
1992	LA-N	10	15	.400	33	33	1	0	0	210^2	209	101	15	8	69	130	12.2	3.67	94	.257	.322	15	.221	4	-4	-5	3	0.2
1993	LA-N	12	14	.462	33	33	5	1	0	215^2	201	106	17	7	72	141	11.7	3.59	106	.246	.312	26	.356	10	11	6	3	1.9
1994	LA-N	6	6	.500	21	21	1	0	0	135^1	146	67	15	2	42	72	12.6	3.79	104	.279	.335	9	.205	2	6	2	2	0.6
1995	*Cle-A	16	6	.727	26	26	1	1	0	167^1	151	76	21	5	51	111	11.1	3.87	121	.244	.306	0	—	0	16	15	2	2.0
1996	*Cle-A	15	9	.625	33	33	1	0	0	206	238	115	21	12	58	125	13.5	4.24	115	.287	.343	0	—	0	17	15	4	1.9
1997	*Cle-A	14	6	.700	32	32	1	0	0	195^1	199	105	26	11	69	107	12.9	4.47	105	.272	.344	0	.000	-0	2	5	1	0.5
1998	SF-N	11	10	.524	34	34	0	0	0	202	200	105	22	13	85	126	13.3	4.41	90	.259	.343	10	.152	1	-4	-11	2	-0.7
1999	*NY-N	13	12	.520	32	32	0	0	0	179	175	92	14	11	77	89	13.2	4.58	96	.260	.345	9	.145	-1	-0	-4	2	-0.3
2000	LA-N	1	5	.167	10	6	0	0	0	24^2	42	36	5	11	14	13	24.4	13.14	33	.389	.504	0	.000	-1	-23	-25	0	-3.9
Total	18	204	150	.576	510	466	68	25	5	3130^1	2939	1366	235	117	1007	2014	11.7	3.48	111	.248	.314	163	.201	33	181	141	36	21.5

● JOE HESKETH Hesketh, Joseph Thomas b: 2/15/59, Lackawanna, N.Y. BR/TL, 6'2", 170 lbs. Deb: 8/7/84

YEAR	TM/L	W	L	PCT	G	GS	CG	SH	SV	IP	H	R	HR	HB	BB	SO	RAT	ERA	ERA+	OAV	OOB	BH	AVG	PB	PR	PR+	PD	TPI
1984	Mon-N	2	2	.500	11	5	1	1	1	45	38	12	2	0	15	32	10.6	1.80	190	.233	.298	1	.100	0	9	9	-0	0.8
1985	Mon-N	10	5	.667	25	25	2	1	0	155^1	125	52	10	0	45	113	9.8	2.49	136	.222	.280	4	.091	-1	19	17	-1	1.4
1986	Mon-N	6	5	.545	15	15	0	0	0	82^2	92	46	11	2	31	67	13.6	5.01	74	.283	.349	0	.000	-2	-12	-12	-1	-1.7
1987	Mon-N	0	0	—	18	0	0	0	1	28^2	23	12	2	2	15	31	12.6	3.14	134	.211	.317	0	.000	-0	3	3	-1	0.1
1988	Mon-N	4	3	.571	60	0	0	0	9	72^2	63	30	1	0	35	64	12.1	2.85	126	.242	.332	0	.000	0	5	6	1	0.9
1989	Mon-N	6	4	.600	43	0	0	0	3	48^1	54	34	5	0	26	44	14.9	5.77	61	.292	.379	1	.500	0	-12	-12	-1	-2.3
1990	Mon-N	1	0	1.000	2	0	0	0	0	3	2	0	0	0	2	3	12.0	0.00	—	.200	.333	0	—	0	1	1	0	0.3
	Atl-N	0	2	.000	31	0	0	0	5	31	30	23	5	1	12	21	12.5	5.81	70	.248	.321	0	.000	-0	-7	-6	-0	-0.5

YEAR	TM/L	W	L	PCT	G	GS	CG	SH	SV	IP	H	R	HR	HB	BB	SO	RAT	ERA	ERA+	OAV	OOB	BH	AVG	PB	PR	PR+	PD	TPI
	Yr	1	2	.333	33	0	0	0	5	34	32	23	5	1	14	24	12.4	5.29	76	.244	.322	0	.000	-0	-6	-5	-0	-0.2
	Bos-A	0	4	.000	12	2	0	0	0	25^2	37	12	2	0	11	26	16.8	3.51	117	.333	.393	0	—	0	1	2	-0	0.2
1991	Bos-A	12	4	.750	39	17	0	0	0	153^1	142	59	19	0	53	104	11.4	3.29	131	.250	.314	0	—	0	14	17	0	1.6
1992	Bos-A	8	9	.471	30	25	1	0	1	148^2	162	84	15	2	58	104	13.4	4.36	97	.276	.343	0	—	0	-7	-2	0	-0.2
1993	Bos-A	3	4	.429	28	5	0	0	1	53^1	62	35	4	0	29	34	15.4	5.06	91	.294	.379	0	—	0	-4	-2	-0	-0.3
1994	Bos-A	8	5	.615	25	20	0	0	0	114	117	70	9	2	46	83	13.0	4.26	118	.267	.340	0	—	0	7	9	-2	0.8
Total	11	60	47	.561	339	114	4	2	21	961^2	947	469	85	9	378	726	12.5	3.78	107	.259	.330	6	.070	-2	17	27	-2	1.1

● OTTO HESS Hess, Otto C. b: 10/10/1878, Bern, Switzerland d: 2/25/26, Tucson, Ariz. BL/TL, 6'1", 170 lbs. Deb: 8/3/02 ♦

YEAR	TM/L	W	L	PCT	G	GS	CG	SH	SV	IP	H	R	HR	HB	BB	SO	RAT	ERA	ERA+	OAV	OOB	BH	AVG	PB	PR	PR+	PD	TPI
1902	Cle-A	2	4	.333	7	4	4	0	0	43^2	67	42	0	1	23	13	18.8	5.98	58	.351	.423	1	.071	-1	-12	-13	1	-1.4
1904	Cle-A	8	7	.533	21	16	15	4	0	151^1	134	60	2	5	31	64	10.1	1.67	152	.238	.284	12	.120	-3	16	15	-0	1.1
1905	Cle-A	10	15	.400	26	25	22	4	0	213^2	179	97	1	9	72	109	11.0	3.16	83	.229	.302	44	.254	5	-12	-13	0	-0.9
1906	Cle-A	20	17	.541	43	36	33	7	**3**	333^2	274	104	4	24	85	167	10.3	1.83	143	.227	.291	31	.201	1	32	30	-2	3.4
1907	Cle-A	6	6	.500	17	14	7	0	1	93^1	84	37	1	12	37	36	12.8	2.89	87	.243	.337	4	.133	0	-4	-4	-1	-0.6
1908	Cle-A	0	0	—	4	0	0	0	0	7	11	6	0	0	1	2	15.4	5.14	46	.407	.429	0	.000	-1	-2	-2	0	-0.1
1912	Bos-N	12	17	.414	33	31	21	0	0	254	270	142	3	15	90	80	13.3	3.76	95	.283	.354	23	.245	3	-10	-5	-3	-0.5
1913	Bos-N	7	17	.292	29	27	19	2	0	218^1	231	123	13	7	70	80	12.7	3.83	86	.279	.340	26	.313	8	-15	-13	1	-0.4
1914	Bos-N	5	6	.455	14	11	7	1	1	89	89	39	2	5	33	24	12.8	3.03	91	.271	.347	11	.234	1	-2	-3	2	0.0
1915	Bos-N	0	1	.000	4	1	1	0	0	14	16	13	0	2	6	5	15.4	3.86	67	.286	.375	2	.400	1	-2	-2	-0	-0.1
Total	10	70	90	.438	198	165	129	18	5	1418	1355	663	26	80	448	580	12.0	2.98	98	.257	.324	154	.216	14	-11	-12	-2	0.5

● GEORGE HESSELBACHER Hesselbacher, George Edward b: 1/18/1895, Philadelphia, Pa. d: 2/18/80, Rydal, Pa. BR/TR, 6'2", 175 lbs. Deb: 6/29/16

YEAR	TM/L	W	L	PCT	G	GS	CG	SH	SV	IP	H	R	HR	HB	BB	SO	RAT	ERA	ERA+	OAV	OOB	BH	AVG	PB	PR	PR+	PD	TPI
1916	Phi-A	0	4	.000	6	4	2	0	0	26	37	33	3	0	22	6	20.4	7.27	39	.349	.461	1	.125	-0	-13	-13	1	-1.6

● LARRY HESTERFER Hesterfer, Lawrence b: 6/9/1878, Newark, N.J. d: 9/22/43, Cedar Grove, N.J. BR/TL, 5'8", 145 lbs. Deb: 9/5/01

YEAR	TM/L	W	L	PCT	G	GS	CG	SH	SV	IP	H	R	HR	HB	BB	SO	RAT	ERA	ERA+	OAV	OOB	BH	AVG	PB	PR	PR+	PD	TPI
1901	NY-N	0	1	.000	1	1	1	0	0	6	15	15	0	0	3	2	27.0	7.50	44	.469	.514	0	.000	0	-3	-3	-0	-0.4

● JOHNNY HETKI Hetki, John Edward b: 5/12/22, Leavenworth, Kan. BR/TR, 6'1", 205 lbs. Deb: 9/14/45

YEAR	TM/L	W	L	PCT	G	GS	CG	SH	SV	IP	H	R	HR	HB	BB	SO	RAT	ERA	ERA+	OAV	OOB	BH	AVG	PB	PR	PR+	PD	TPI
1945	Cin-N	1	2	.333	5	2	2	0	0	32^2	28	13	1	0	11	9	10.7	3.58	105	.235	.300	1	.091	-1	1	1	1	0.0
1946	Cin-N	6	6	.500	32	11	4	0	1	126^1	121	44	3	1	31	41	10.9	2.99	112	.253	.300	11	.333	3	6	5	-1	0.7
1947	Cin-N	3	4	.429	37	5	2	0	0	96	110	72	7	1	48	33	14.9	5.81	71	.287	.368	6	.222	1	-19	-18	0	-1.1
1948	Cin-N	0	1	.000	3	0	0	0	0	6^2	8	7	0	0	3	3	14.9	9.45	41	.286	.355	0	.000	0	-4	-4	-0	-0.5
1950	Cin-N	1	2	.333	22	1	0	0	0	53	53	33	9	3	27	21	14.1	5.09	83	.265	.361	2	.222	0	-6	-5	-0	-0.3
1952	StL-A	0	1	.000	3	1	0	0	0	9^1	15	7	2	0	2	4	16.4	3.86	101	.357	.386	0	.000	0	-0	0	0	0.0
1953	Pit-N	3	6	.333	54	2	0	0	3	118^1	120	60	9	1	33	37	11.7	3.95	113	.266	.318	5	.208	1	4	7	0	0.6
1954	Pit-N	4	4	.500	58	1	0	0	9	83	102	53	11	0	30	27	14.3	4.99	84	.297	.353	2	.222	-0	-8	-7	-1	-0.9
Total	8	18	26	.409	214	23	8	0	13	525^1	557	289	42	6	185	175	12.8	4.39	91	.272	.335	27	.235	5	-26	-22	-2	-1.5

● ERIC HETZEL Hetzel, Eric Paul b: 9/25/63, Crowley, La. BR/TR, 6'3", 175 lbs. Deb: 7/1/89

YEAR	TM/L	W	L	PCT	G	GS	CG	SH	SV	IP	H	R	HR	HB	BB	SO	RAT	ERA	ERA+	OAV	OOB	BH	AVG	PB	PR	PR+	PD	TPI
1989	Bos-A	2	3	.400	12	11	0	0	0	50^1	61	39	7	2	28	33	16.3	6.26	66	.296	.386	0	—	0	-13	-11	-1	-1.1
1990	Bos-A	1	4	.200	9	8	0	0	0	35	39	28	3	1	21	20	15.7	5.91	69	.281	.379	0	—	0	-8	-7	-0	-0.9
Total	2	3	7	.300	21	19	0	0	0	85^1	100	67	10	3	49	53	16.0	6.12	67	.290	.383	0	—	0	-21	-18	-2	-2.0

● ED HEUSSER Heusser, Edward Burlton "The Wild Elk Of The Wasatch"
b: 5/7/09, Salt Lake County, Utah d: 3/1/56, Aurora, Col. BB/TR (BR 1935-36, 38), 6'0.5", 187 lbs. Deb: 4/25/35

YEAR	TM/L	W	L	PCT	G	GS	CG	SH	SV	IP	H	R	HR	HB	BB	SO	RAT	ERA	ERA+	OAV	OOB	BH	AVG	PB	PR	PR+	PD	TPI
1935	StL-N	5	5	.500	33	11	2	0	2	123^1	125	50	5	2	27	39	11.2	2.92	140	.263	.305	4	.118	-1	15	16	-1	1.0
1936	StL-N	7	3	.700	42	3	0	0	3	104^1	130	73	6	4	38	26	14.8	5.43	73	.310	.373	7	.269	3	-16	-18	-0	-1.3
1938	Phi-N	0	0	—	1	0	0	0	0	1	2	3	1	0	1	0	27.0	27.00	14	.400	.500	0	—	0	-3	-3	-0	-0.1
1940	Phi-A	6	13	.316	41	6	2	0	5	110	144	84	11	2	42	39	15.4	4.99	89	.308	.368	5	.167	1	-7	-7	1	-0.9
1943	Cin-N	4	3	.571	26	10	2	1	0	91	97	40	4	0	23	28	11.9	3.46	96	.275	.319	5	.185	-1	-1	-1	-1	-0.3
1944	Cin-N	13	11	.542	30	23	17	4	2	192^2	165	59	9	1	42	42	9.7	**2.38**	**146**	.231	.275	15	.217	1	26	25	-1	3.0
1945	Cin-N	11	16	.407	31	30	18	4	1	223	248	105	10	3	60	56	12.6	3.71	101	.280	.328	19	.247	4	2	1	0	0.6
1946	Cin-N	7	14	.333	29	21	9	1	2	167^2	167	68	11	1	39	47	11.1	3.22	104	.260	.304	11	.208	2	4	2	-2	0.2
1948	Phi-N	3	2	.600	33	0	0	0	3	74	89	46	9	0	28	22	14.2	4.99	79	.299	.359	3	.158	-1	-8	-9	0	-0.6
Total	9	56	67	.455	266	104	50	10	18	1087	1167	528	66	13	300	299	12.3	3.69	101	.274	.324	69	.206	8	11	6	-5	1.6

● JOE HEVING Heving, Joseph William b: 9/2/1900, Covington, Ky. d: 4/11/70, Covington, Ky. BR/TR, 6'1", 185 lbs. Deb: 4/29/30 F

YEAR	TM/L	W	L	PCT	G	GS	CG	SH	SV	IP	H	R	HR	HB	BB	SO	RAT	ERA	ERA+	OAV	OOB	BH	AVG	PB	PR	PR+	PD	TPI
1930	NY-N	7	5	.583	41	2	0	0	6	89^2	109	57	7	1	27	37	13.8	5.22	91	.309	.360	5	.227	-0	-2	-5	4	-0.3
1931	NY-N	1	6	.143	22	0	0	0	3	42^1	48	27	4	2	11	26	13.0	4.89	76	.277	.328	1	.125	-0	-5	-6	1	-0.9
1933	Chi-A	7	5	.583	40	6	3	1	6	118	113	50	6	2	27	47	10.8	2.67	159	.249	.295	8	.211	0	21	21	0	2.2
1934	Chi-A	1	7	.125	33	2	0	0	4	88	133	85	12	3	48	40	18.8	7.26	65	.343	.419	5	.185	1	-27	-24	1	-1.8
1937	Cle-A	8	4	.667	40	0	0	0	5	72^2	92	53	6	2	30	35	15.4	4.83	95	.311	.378	5	.263	0	-2	-2	1	-0.1
1938	Cle-A	1	1	.500	3	0	0	0	0	6	10	8	0	0	5	0	22.5	9.00	52	.370	.469	0	.000	-0	-3	-3	-0	-0.5
	Bos-A	8	1	.889	16	11	7	1	2	82	94	35	5	1	22	34	12.8	3.73	132	.283	.330	4	.133	-1	10	11	2	1.1
	Yr	9	2	.818	19	11	7	1	2	88	104	43	5	1	27	34	13.5	4.09	120	.290	.341	4	.129	-2	7	8	2	0.6
1939	Bos-A	11	3	.786	46	5	1	0	7	107	124	65	8	2	34	43	13.5	3.70	128	.295	.350	6	.188	-1	**11**	**12**	0	1.4
1940	Bos-A	12	7	.632	39	7	4	0	3	119	129	63	7	3	42	55	13.2	4.01	112	.272	.335	8	.200	0	5	6	0	0.9
1941	Cle-A	5	2	.714	27	3	2	1	5	70^2	63	21	2	1	31	18	12.1	2.29	172	.240	.323	0	.000	-1	15	14	2	1.5
1942	Cle-A	5	3	.625	27	2	0	0	3	46^1	52	28	4	2	25	13	15.3	4.86	71	.278	.369	0	.000	-1	-6	-8	0	-1.4
1943	Cle-A	1	1	.500	30	1	0	0	9	72	58	23	1	2	34	34	11.8	2.75	113	.230	.326	1	.071	-0	4	3	2	0.3
1944	Cle-A	8	3	.727	**63**	1	0	0	10	119^2	106	42	2	2	41	46	11.2	1.96	169	.239	.307	4	.182	-1	**20**	19	1	2.0
1945	Bos-N	1	0	1.000	3	0	0	0	0	5^1	5	2	0	1	3	1	15.2	3.38	114	.294	.429	0	.000	-0	0	0	1	0.1
Total	13	76	48	.613	430	40	17	3	63	1038^2	1136	559	64	24	380	429	13.3	3.90	108	.279	.344	47	.170	-4	40	36	14	4.5

● JAKE HEWITT Hewitt, Charles Jacob b: 6/6/1870, Maidsville, W.Va. d: 5/18/59, Morgantown, W.Va. BL/TL, 5'7", 150 lbs. Deb: 8/6/1895

YEAR	TM/L	W	L	PCT	G	GS	CG	SH	SV	IP	H	R	HR	HB	BB	SO	RAT	ERA	ERA+	OAV	OOB	BH	AVG	PB	PR	PR+	PD	TPI
1895	Pit-N	1	0	1.000	4	2	1	0	2	13	13	6	0	1	2	4	11.1	4.15	109	.255	.296	1	.167	-1	1	1	-0	0.0

● GREG HEYDEMAN Heydeman, Gregory George b: 1/2/52, Carmel, Cal. BR/TR, 6', 180 lbs. Deb: 9/2/73

YEAR	TM/L	W	L	PCT	G	GS	CG	SH	SV	IP	H	R	HR	HB	BB	SO	RAT	ERA	ERA+	OAV	OOB	BH	AVG	PB	PR	PR+	PD	TPI
1973	LA-N	0	0	—	1	0	0	0	0	2	2	1	0	1	1	1	18.0	4.50	77	.222	.364	0	—	0	-0	-0	-0	0.0

● GREG HIBBARD Hibbard, James Gregory b: 9/13/64, New Orleans, La. BL/TL, 6', 190 lbs. Deb: 5/31/89

YEAR	TM/L	W	L	PCT	G	GS	CG	SH	SV	IP	H	R	HR	HB	BB	SO	RAT	ERA	ERA+	OAV	OOB	BH	AVG	PB	PR	PR+	PD	TPI
1989	Chi-A	6	7	.462	23	23	2	0	0	137^1	142	58	5	2	41	55	12.1	3.21	119	.268	.323	0	—	0	10	9	1	1.0
1990	Chi-A	14	9	.609	33	33	3	1	0	211	202	80	11	6	55	92	11.2	3.16	121	.255	.308	0	—	0	18	16	-1	1.6
1991	Chi-A	11	11	.500	32	29	5	0	0	194	196	107	23	2	57	71	11.8	4.31	92	.266	.320	0	—	0	-5	-7	-1	-0.8
1992	Chi-A	10	7	.588	31	28	0	0	1	176	187	92	17	7	57	69	12.8	4.40	88	.277	.340	0	—	0	-9	-11	2	-0.7
1993	Chi-N	15	11	.577	31	31	1	0	0	191	209	96	19	3	47	82	12.2	3.96	101	.286	.332	6	.092	-3	2	1	-1	-0.3
1994	Sea-A	1	5	.167	15	14	0	0	0	80^2	115	78	11	2	31	39	16.5	6.69	73	.328	.385	0	—	0	-17	-16	1	-0.9
Total	6	57	50	.533	165	158	11	1	1	990	1051	511	86	22	288	408	12.4	4.05	98	.275	.330	6	.092	-3	-0	-8	1	-0.1

● JOHN HIBBARD Hibbard, John Denison b: 12/2/1864, Chicago, Ill. d: 11/17/37, Hollywood, Cal. TL, Deb: 7/31/1884

YEAR	TM/L	W	L	PCT	G	GS	CG	SH	SV	IP	H	R	HR	HB	BB	SO	RAT	ERA	ERA+	OAV	OOB	BH	AVG	PB	PR	PR+	PD	TPI
1884	Chi-N	1	1	.500	2	2	2	1	0	17	18	10	1		9	4	14.3	2.65	118	.300	.391	0	.000	-1	1	1	-0	0.0

● BRYAN HICKERSON Hickerson, Bryan David b: 10/13/63, Bemidji, Minn. BL/TL, 6'2", 203 lbs. Deb: 7/25/91

YEAR	TM/L	W	L	PCT	G	GS	CG	SH	SV	IP	H	R	HR	HB	BB	SO	RAT	ERA	ERA+	OAV	OOB	BH	AVG	PB	PR	PR+	PD	TPI
1991	SF-N	2	2	.500	17	6	0	0	0	50	53	20	3	0	17	43	12.6	3.60	100	.275	.333	0	.000	-1	0	-0	-1	-0.3
1992	SF-N	5	3	.625	61	1	0	0	0	87^1	74	31	7	1	21	68	9.9	3.09	107	.236	.286	0	.000	-0	4	2	-2	0.0
1993	SF-N	7	5	.583	47	15	0	0	0	120^1	137	58	14	1	39	69	13.2	4.26	92	.291	.347	4	.143	-0	-3	-5	-2	-0.6
1994	SF-N	4	8	.333	28	14	0	0	1	98^1	118	60	20	1	38	59	14.4	5.40	74	.301	.364	5	.185	1	-13	-16	-2	-1.7
1995	Chi-N	2	3	.400	38	0	0	0	1	31^2	36	28	3	0	15	28	14.5	6.82	60	.283	.359	1	.500	1	-9	-10	-0	-1.3
	Col-N	1	0	1.000	18	0	0	0	0	16^2	33	24	5	1	13	12	25.4	11.88	45	.407	.495	1	1.000	1	-14	-9	-1	-0.5
	Yr	3	3	.500	56	0	0	0	1	48^1	69	52	8	1	28	40	18.2	8.57	53	.332	.414	2	.667	1	-24	-20	-1	-1.8
Total	5	21	21	.500	209	36	0	0	2	404^1	451	221	52	4	143	279	13.3	4.72	81	.286	.347	11	.149	1	-35	-41	-7	-4.4

YEAR	TM/L	W	L	PCT	G	GS	CG	SH	SV	IP	H	R	HR	HB	BB	SO	RAT	ERA	ERA+	OAV	OOB	BH	AVG	PB	PR	PR+	PD	TPI
● JIM HICKEY	Hickey, James Robert "Sid" b: 10/22/20, N.Abington, Mass. d: 9/20/97, Manchester, Conn. BR/TR, 6'1", 204 lbs. Deb: 4/25/42																											
1942	Bos-N	0	1	.000	1	1	0	0	0	1^1	4	4	1	0	2	0	40.5	20.25	16	.500	.600	0	.000	-0	-3	-2	-0	-0.4
1944	Bos-N	0	0	—	8	0	0	0	0	9^1	15	9	0	1	5	3	20.3	4.82	79	.366	.447	0	.000	-0	-1	-1	0	0.0
Total	2	0	1	.000	9	1	0	0	0	10^2	19	13	1	1	7	3	22.8	6.75	56	.388	.474	0	.000	-0	-4	-3	0	-0.4
● JACK HICKEY	Hickey, John William b: 11/3/1881, Minneapolis, Minn. d: 12/28/41, Seattle, Wash. BR/TL, 5'10", 170 lbs. Deb: 4/16/04																											
1904	Cle-A	0	1	.000	2	2	1	0	0	12^1	14	13	0	0	11	5	18.2	7.30	35	.286	.417	0	.000	-1	-6	-7	0	-0.5
● KEVIN HICKEY	Hickey, Kevin John b: 2/25/57, Chicago, Ill. BL/TL, 6'1", 200 lbs. Deb: 4/14/81																											
1981	Chi-A	0	2	.000	41	0	0	0	3	44^1	38	22	3	1	18	17	11.6	3.65	98	.232	.311	0	—	0	0	-0	1	0.1
1982	Chi-A	4	4	.500	60	0	0	0	6	78	73	32	4	2	30	38	12.1	3.00	135	.256	.331	0	—	0	9	9	2	1.2
1983	Chi-A	1	2	.333	23	0	0	0	5	20^2	23	14	5	0	11	8	14.8	5.23	80	.264	.347	0	—	0	-3	-2	-0	-0.4
1989	Bal-A	2	3	.400	51	0	0	0	2	49^1	38	16	3	1	23	28	11.3	2.92	130	.220	.315	0	—	0	5	5	-0	0.5
1990	Bal-A	1	3	.250	37	0	0	0	1	26^1	26	16	3	0	13	17	13.3	5.13	74	.265	.351	0	—	0	-4	-4	0	-0.6
1991	Bal-A	1	0	1.000	19	0	0	0	0	14	15	14	3	0	6	10	13.5	9.00	44	.278	.350	0	—	0	-8	-8	-0	-0.5
Total	6	9	14	.391	231	0	0	0	17	232^2	213	114	21	4	101	118	12.3	3.91	99	.247	.329	0	—	0	1	-1	2	0.3
● CHARLIE HICKMAN	Hickman, Charles Taylor "Cheerful Charlie" or "Piano Legs" b: 3/4/1876, Taylortown, Dunkard Township, Pa. d: 4/19/34, Morgantown, W.Va. BR/TR, 5'11.5", 215 lbs. Deb: 9/8/1897 ◆																											
1897	*Bos-N	0	0	—	2	0	0	0	1	7^2	10	5	0	0	5	0	17.6	5.87	76	.313	.405	2	.667	2	-1	-1	0	0.1
1898	Bos-N	1	2	.333	6	3	3	1	2	33	22	8	0	0	13	9	9.5	2.18	169	.188	.269	15	.259	0	5	5	-1	0.4
1899	Bos-N	6	0	1.000	11	9	5	2	1	66^1	52	38	3	8	40	14	13.6	4.48	93	.216	.346	25	.397	6	-5	-2	-1	0.2
1901	NY-N	3	5	.375	9	9	6	0	0	65	76	42	1	3	26	11	14.5	4.57	72	.290	.361	113	.278	2	-9	-9	1	-0.7
1902	Cle-A	0	1	.000	1	1	1	0	0	8	11	8	0	1	5	1	19.1	7.88	44	.324	.425	161	.378	1	-4	-4	-0	-0.3
1907	Was-A	0	0	—	1	0	0	0	0	5	4	4	0	0	5	2	16.2	3.60	67	.222	.391	55	.278	0	-1	-1	1	0.0
Total	6	10	8	.556	30	22	15	3	4	185	175	105	4	12	94	37	13.7	4.28	86	.249	.347	1176	.295	11	-14	-12	-1	-0.3
● ERNIE HICKMAN	Hickman, Ernest P. b: 1856, E.St.Louis, Ill. d: 11/19/1891, E.St.Louis, Ill Deb: 6/7/1884																											
1884	KC-U	4	13	.235	17	17	15	0	0	137^1	172	146	5		36	68	13.6	4.52	49	.287	.328	12	.167	-7	-32	-38	-1	-3.9
● JIM HICKMAN	Hickman, James Lucius b: 5/10/37, Henning, Tenn. BR/TR, 6'4", 205 lbs. Deb: 4/14/62 ◆																											
1967	LA-N	0	0	—	1	0	0	0	0	2	2	1	1	0	0	0	9.0	4.50	69	.286	.286	16	.163	0	-0	-0	-0	0.0
● JESSE HICKMAN	Hickman, Jesse Owens b: 2/18/39, Lecompte, La. BR/TR, 6'2", 186 lbs. Deb: 6/5/65																											
1965	KC-A	0	1	.000	12	0	0	0	0	15^1	9	10	3	0	8	16	10.0	5.87	59	.184	.298	0	—	0	-4	-4	-0	-0.3
1966	KC-A	0	0	—	1	0	0	0	0	1	0	0	0	0	1	0	9.0	0.00	—	.000	.333	0	—	0	0	0	-0	0.0
Total	2	0	1	.000	13	0	0	0	0	16^1	9	10	3	0	9	16	9.9	5.51	63	.176	.300	0	—	0	-4	-4	-0	-0.3
● KIRBY HIGBE	Higbe, Walter Kirby b: 4/8/15, Columbia, S.C. d: 5/6/85, Columbia, S.C. BR/TR, 5'11", 190 lbs. Deb: 10/3/37																											
1937	Chi-N	1	0	1.000	1	0	0	0	0	5	4	3	1	0	1	2	9.0	5.40	74	.182	.217	0	.000	-0	-1	-1	-0	-0.2
1938	Chi-N	0	0	—	2	2	0	0	0	10	10	6	1	0	6	4	14.4	5.40	71	.263	.364	0	.000	-0	-2	-2	1	-0.1
1939	Chi-N	2	1	.667	9	2	0	0	0	22^2	12	9	0	0	22	16	13.5	3.18	124	.158	.347	2	.286	1	2	2	-0	0.3
	Phi-N	10	14	.417	34	26	14	1	2	187^1	208	113	10	10	101	79	15.3	4.85	83	.283	.378	11	.167	-2	-19	-17	-4	-2.5
	Yr	12	15	.444	43	28	14	1	2	210	220	122	10	10	123	95	15.1	4.67	86	.272	.374	13	.178	-2	-18	-15	-4	-2.2
1940	Phi-N☆	14	19	.424	41	36	20	1	1	283	242	126	12	3	121	**137**	11.6	3.72	105	.232	.313	17	.165	-2	4	6	-1	0.4
1941	*Bro-N	**22**	9	.710	**48**	39	19	2	3	298	244	123	17	6	132	121	11.5	3.14	117	.220	.306	21	.188	1	16	17	-5	1.3
1942	Bro-N	16	11	.593	38	32	13	2	0	221^2	180	89	17	2	106	115	11.7	3.25	100	.223	.315	8	.104	-4	2	0	-1	-0.6
1943	Bro-N	13	10	.565	35	27	8	1	0	185	189	81	4	5	95	108	14.1	3.70	91	.264	.354	9	.138	-2	-6	-7	-1	-1.1
1946	Bro-N★	17	8	.680	42	29	11	3	1	210^2	178	82	6	1	107	134	12.2	3.03	111	.229	.323	10	.130	-4	9	8	0	0.6
1947	Bro-N	2	0	1.000	4	3	0	0	0	15^2	18	9	0	1	12	10	17.8	5.17	80	.295	.419	1	.200	0	-2	-2	0	-0.2
	Pit-N	11	17	.393	46	30	10	1	5	225	204	108	22	3	110	99	12.7	3.72	113	.240	.329	10	.139	-1	8	12	-4	0.9
	Yr	13	17	.433	50	33	10	1	5	240^2	222	117	22	4	122	109	13.0	3.81	111	.243	.335	11	.143	-1	10	10	-4	0.7
1948	Pit-N	8	7	.533	56	8	3	0	10	158	140	75	11	3	83	86	12.9	3.36	121	.240	.337	10	.208	1	10	12	-1	1.2
1949	Pit-N	0	2	.000	7	1	0	0	0	15^1	25	24	2	0	12	5	21.7	13.50	31	.379	.474	0	.000	-0	-16	-15	0	-1.6
	NY-N	2	0	1.000	37	2	0	0	2	80^1	72	42	12	1	41	38	12.8	3.47	115	.242	.335	1	.067	-0	5	5	1	0.1
	Yr	2	2	.500	44	3	0	0	2	95^2	97	66	14	1	53	43	14.2	5.08	79	.266	.361	1	.056	-1	-11	-11	-1	-1.5
1950	NY-N	0	3	.000	18	1	0	0	0	34^2	37	19	2	0	30	17	17.4	4.93	83	.285	.419	1	.250	0	-3	-3	1	-0.1
Total	12	118	101	.539	418	238	98	11	24	1952^1	1763	909	117	35	979	971	12.8	3.69	102	.241	.333	101	.153	-14	7	14	-16	-1.6
● IRV HIGGINBOTHAM	Higginbotham, Irving Clinton b: 4/26/1882, Homer, Neb. d: 6/12/59, Seattle, Wash. BR/TR, 6'1", 196 lbs. Deb: 8/11/06																											
1906	StL-N	1	4	.200	7	6	4	0	0	47^1	50	23	1	1	11	14	11.8	3.23	81	.266	.310	4	.222	0	-3	-3	1	-0.2
1908	StL-N	3	8	.273	19	11	7	1	0	107	113	51	0	3	33	38	12.5	3.20	74	.270	.328	5	.132	-1	-10	-10	-1	-1.3
1909	StL-N	1	0	1.000	3	1	1	0	0	11^1	5	3	0	0	2	2	5.6	1.59	159	.143	.189	0	.000	-0	1	1	-1	0.0
	Chi-N	5	2	.714	19	6	4	0	1	78	64	32	0	3	20	32	10.0	2.19	116	.213	.269	6	.231	1	4	3	-1	0.2
	Yr	6	2	.750	22	7	5	0	1	89^1	69	35	0	3	22	34	9.5	2.12	120	.205	.260	6	.207	0	5	4	-2	0.2
Total	3	10	14	.417	48	24	16	1	1	243^2	232	109	1	7	66	86	11.3	2.81	88	.246	.300	15	.176	-1	-8	-9	-2	-1.3
● DENNIS HIGGINS	Higgins, Dennis Dean b: 8/4/39, Jefferson City, Mo. BR/TR, 6'4", 190 lbs. Deb: 4/12/66																											
1966	Chi-A	1	0	1.000	42	1	0	0	5	93	66	27	9	5	33	86	10.1	2.52	126	.202	.286	3	.176	0	9	7	1	0.5
1967	Chi-A	1	2	.333	9	0	0	0	0	12^1	13	9	0	3	10	8	19.0	5.84	53	.271	.426	0	.000	-0	-4	-4	0	-0.8
1968	Was-A	4	4	.500	59	0	0	0	13	99^2	81	40	9	3	46	66	11.7	3.25	90	.226	.319	2	.133	-0	-3	-4	-1	-0.6
1969	Was-A	10	9	.526	55	0	0	0	16	85^1	79	42	7	3	56	71	14.6	3.48	100	.252	.371	1	.091	-1	1	-0	-1	-0.2
1970	Cle-A	4	6	.400	58	0	0	0	11	90^1	82	43	8	2	54	82	13.7	3.99	99	.248	.358	3	.250	1	-3	-0	1	0.1
1971	StL-N	1	0	1.000	3	0	0	0	0	7	6	3	0	0	2	6	10.3	3.86	93	.240	.296	0	.000	-0	-0	-0	0	0.0
1972	StL-N	1	2	.333	15	1	0	0	1	22^2	19	14	0	0	22	20	16.3	3.97	86	.226	.387	0	.000	-0	-1	-1	-0	-0.2
Total	7	22	23	.489	241	2	0	0	46	410^1	346	178	33	16	223	339	12.8	3.42	98	.233	.340	9	.155	0	0	-3	-1	-1.2
● EDDIE HIGGINS	Higgins, Thomas Edward "Doc" or "Irish" b: 3/18/1888, Nevada, Ill. d: 2/14/59, Elgin, Ill. BR/TR, 6'0.5", 174 lbs. Deb: 5/14/09																											
1909	StL-N	3	3	.500	16	5	5	0	0	66	68	36	4	1	17	15	11.7	4.50	56	.273	.322	4	.190	-0	-14	-15	0	-1.3
1910	StL-N	0	1	.000	2	0	0	0	0	10^1	15	8	0	0	7	1	19.2	4.35	68	.349	.440	2	.400	1	-2	-2	1	0.0
Total	2	3	4	.429	18	5	5	0	0	76^1	83	44	4	1	24	16	12.7	4.48	58	.284	.341	6	.231	1	-15	-16	1	-1.3
● ED HIGH	High, Edward T. "Lefty" b: 12/26/1876, Baltimore, Md. d: 2/10/26, Baltimore, Md. TL, Deb: 7/4/01																											
1901	Det-A	1	0	1.000	4	1	1	0	0	18	21	9	0	1	6	4	14.0	3.50	110	.288	.350	0	.000	-1	0	1	-0	0.0
● TEDDY HIGUERA	Higuera, Teodoro Valenzuela (Valenzuela) b: 11/9/58, Los Mochis, Mexico BB/TL, 5'10", 178 lbs. Deb: 4/23/85																											
1985	Mil-A	15	8	.652	32	30	7	2	0	212^1	186	105	22	3	63	127	10.7	3.90	107	.235	.293	0	—	0	6	6	-3	0.3
1986	Mil-A★	20	11	.645	34	34	15	4	0	248^1	226	84	26	3	74	207	11.0	2.79	155	.241	.299	0	—	0	38	41	-1	4.8
1987	Mil-A	18	10	.643	35	35	14	3	0	261^2	236	120	24	2	87	240	11.2	3.85	119	.241	.304	0	—	0	18	21	-2	1.7
1988	Mil-A	16	9	.640	31	31	8	1	0	227^1	168	66	15	6	59	192	**9.2**	2.45	162	.207	**.265**	0	—	0	**38**	39	1	4.3
1989	Mil-A	9	6	.600	22	22	2	1	0	135^1	125	56	9	4	48	91	11.8	3.46	111	.248	.318	0	—	0	7	6	-2	0.4
1990	Mil-A	11	10	.524	27	27	4	1	0	170	167	80	16	3	50	129	11.6	3.76	103	.256	.312	0	—	0	3	2	-1	0.2
1991	Mil-A	3	2	.600	7	6	0	0	0	36^1	37	18	2	1	10	33	11.9	4.46	89	.262	.316	0	—	0	-1	-2	-0	-0.2
1993	Mil-A	1	3	.250	8	8	0	0	0	30	43	24	4	1	16	27	18.0	7.20	59	.333	.411	0	—	0	-10	-10	-1	-1.1
1994	Mil-A	1	5	.167	17	12	0	0	0	58^2	74	55	13	2	36	35	17.2	7.06	71	.311	.406	0	—	0	-15	-13	0	-1.0
Total	9	94	64	.595	213	205	50	12	0	1380	1262	608	131	25	443	1081	11.3	3.61	117	.243	.306	0	—	0	85	91	-9	9.4
● WHITEY HILCHER	Hilcher, Walter Frank b: 2/28/09, Chicago, Ill. d: 11/21/62, Minneapolis, Minn. BR/TR, 6', 174 lbs. Deb: 9/17/31																											
1931	Cin-N	0	1	.000	2	1	0	0	0	12	16	5	0	1	4	5	15.8	3.00	125	.320	.382	0	.000	-1	1	1	-0	0.0
1932	Cin-N	0	3	.000	11	2	0	0	0	18^2	24	19	3	0	10	16	16.4	7.71	50	.316	.395	1	.333	0	-8	-8	0	-1.0
1935	Cin-N	2	0	1.000	4	2	1	1	0	19^1	19	6	0	0	5	9	11.2	2.79	142	.264	.312	1	.167	-0	3	3	1	0.3

YEAR TM/L	W	L	PCT	G	GS	CG	SH	SV	IP	H	R	HR	HB	BB	SO	RAT	ERA	ERA+	OAV	OOB	BH	AVG	PB	PR	PR+	PD	TPI
1936 Cin-N	1	2	.333	14	1	0	0	0	35	44	31	3	1	14	10	15.2	6.17	62	.299	.364	0	.000	-1	-8	-10	-1	-0.9
Total 4	3	6	.333	31	6	1	1	0	85	103	61	6	2	33	28	14.6	5.29	73	.299	.363	2	.095	-2	-13	-14	-0	-1.6
● ORAL HILDEBRAND Hildebrand, Oral Clyde b: 4/7/07, Indianapolis, Ind. d: 9/8/77, Southport, Ind. BR/TR, 6'3", 175 lbs. Deb: 9/8/31																											
1931 Cle-A	2	1	.667	5	2	2	0	0	26^2	25	16	0	3	13	6	13.8	4.39	105	.243	.345	2	.182	-1	-0	1	-0	0.0
1932 Cle-A	8	6	.571	27	15	7	0	0	129^1	124	69	7	0	62	49	12.9	3.69	129	.249	.333	7	.146	-3	11	14	-2	0.8
1933 Cle-A☆	16	11	.593	36	31	15	**6**	0	220^1	205	110	8	1	88	90	12.0	3.76	118	.245	.318	16	.190	-1	13	16	-0	1.6
1934 Cle-A	11	9	.550	33	28	10	1	1	198	225	112	14	3	99	72	14.9	4.50	101	.282	.364	13	.171	-1	-0	1	1	0.0
1935 Cle-A	9	8	.529	34	20	8	0	5	171^1	171	85	12	3	63	49	12.4	3.94	114	.263	.331	9	.164	-2	10	11	-0	0.8
1936 Cle-A	10	11	.476	36	21	9	0	4	174^2	197	107	10	4	83	65	14.6	4.90	103	.283	.362	12	.190	0	3	3	-1	0.2
1937 StL-A	8	17	.320	30	27	12	1	1	201^1	228	127	18	3	87	75	14.2	5.14	94	.284	.356	14	.200	-1	-12	-7	-1	-0.8
1938 StL-A	8	10	.444	23	23	10	0	0	163	194	104	18	3	73	66	14.9	5.69	87	.297	.370	15	.254	1	-16	-13	-3	-1.2
1939 *NY-A	10	4	.714	21	15	7	1	2	126^2	102	44	11	1	41	50	10.2	3.06	143	.219	.284	8	.182	-1	22	19	-1	1.7
1940 NY-A	1	1	.500	13	0	0	0	0	19^1	19	7	1	1	14	5	15.8	1.86	217	.268	.395	0	.000	-0	5	5	-0	0.4
Total 10	83	78	.516	258	182	80	9	13	1430^2	1490	781	99	22	623	527	13.4	4.35	107	.267	.343	96	.187	-9	36	49	-8	3.5
● TOM HILGENDORF Hilgendorf, Thomas Eugene b: 3/10/42, Clinton, Iowa BB/TL, 6'1", 190 lbs. Deb: 8/15/69																											
1969 StL-N	0	0	—	6	0	0	0	2	6^1	3	1	0	0	2	2	7.1	1.42	252	.150	.227	1	1.000	1	2	2	-0	0.2
1970 StL-N	0	4	.000	23	0	0	0	3	20^2	22	11	0	0	13	13	15.2	3.92	105	.272	.372	0	.000	-0	0	0	0	0.1
1972 Cle-A	3	1	.750	19	5	1	0	0	47	51	16	4	2	21	25	14.2	2.68	120	.283	.365	1	.077	-1	2	3	0	0.2
1973 Cle-A	5	3	.625	48	1	1	0	6	94^2	87	38	9	3	36	58	12.0	3.14	125	.242	.316	0	—	0	7	8	1	0.9
1974 Cle-A	4	3	.571	35	0	0	0	3	48^1	58	26	6	1	17	23	14.2	4.84	75	.302	.362	0	—	0	-7	-7	0	-1.0
1975 Phi-N	7	3	.700	53	0	0	0	0	96^2	81	32	6	1	38	52	11.2	2.14	175	.230	.307	3	.250	1	16	17	1	1.8
Total 6	19	14	.576	184	6	2	0	14	313^2	302	124	25	7	127	173	12.5	3.04	122	.255	.331	5	.185	1	21	23	2	2.2
● ERIK HILJUS Hiljus, Erik Kristian b: 12/25/72, Panorama City, Cal. BR/TR, 6'5", 230 lbs. Deb: 9/10/99																											
1999 Det-A	0	0	—	6	0	0	0	0	8^2	7	5	2	0	5	1	12.5	5.19	94	.241	.353	0	—	0	-0	-0	-0	0.0
2000 Det-A	0	0	—	3	0	0	0	0	3^2	5	3	1	0	1	2	14.7	7.36	65	.333	.375	0	—	0	-1	-1	-0	-0.1
Total 2	0	0	—	9	0	0	0	0	12^1	12	8	3	0	6	3	13.1	5.84	83	.273	.360	0	—	0	-1	-1	-0	-0.1
● CARMEN HILL Hill, Carmen Proctor "Specs" or "Bunker" b: 10/1/1895, Royalton, Minn. d: 1/1/90, Indianapolis, Ind. BR/TR, 6'1", 180 lbs. Deb: 8/24/15																											
1915 Pit-N	2	1	.667	8	3	2	1	0	47	42	8	0	2	13	24	10.9	1.15	238	.255	.317	2	.154	0	8	8	1	0.7
1916 Pit-N	0	0	—	2	0	0	0	0	6^1	11	10	0	1	5	5	24.2	8.53	31	.611	.708	0	—	0	-4	-4	-0	-0.2
1918 Pit-N	2	3	.400	6	4	3	0	0	43^2	24	11	0	0	17	15	8.5	1.24	232	.160	.246	2	.167	0	7	8	0	1.0
1919 Pit-N	0	0	—	4	0	0	0	0	5	12	6	0	0	1	1	23.4	9.00	33	.480	.500	0	—	0	-3	-3	0	-0.2
1922 NY-N	2	1	.667	8	4	0	0	0	28^1	33	15	0	0	5	6	12.1	4.76	84	.295	.325	2	.182	-0	-2	-2	1	-0.2
1926 Pit-N	3	3	.500	6	6	4	1	0	39^2	42	17	2	2	9	8	12.0	3.40	116	.288	.338	3	.176	-1	2	2	1	0.4
1927 *Pit-N	22	11	.667	43	31	22	2	3	277^2	260	125	12	4	80	95	11.2	3.24	127	.249	.305	22	.212	2	21	26	1	3.0
1928 Pit-N	16	10	.615	36	31	16	1	2	237	229	110	16	4	81	73	11.9	3.53	115	.259	.324	20	.233	2	12	14	3	1.3
1929 Pit-N	2	3	.400	27	3	0	0	3	79	94	45	4	0	35	28	14.7	3.99	120	.297	.366	1	.036	-3	6	7	0	0.1
StL-N	0	0	—	3	1	0	0	0	8^2	10	10	2	1	8	1	19.7	8.31	56	.303	.452	0	.000	-0	-3	-4	0	-0.2
Yr	2	3	.400	30	4	0	0	3	87^2	104	55	6	1	43	29	15.2	4.41	108	.297	.376	1	.032	-4	**3**	**3**	0	-0.1
1930 StL-N	0	1	.000	4	2	0	0	0	14^2	12	12	2	0	13	8	15.3	7.36	68	.240	.397	1	.333	0	-4	-4	-0	-0.2
Total 10	49	33	.598	147	85	47	5	8	787	769	369	38	14	267	264	12.0	3.44	116	.261	.326	53	.191	-0	40	48	1	5.5
● RED HILL Hill, Clifford Joseph b: 1/20/1893, Marshall, Tex. d: 8/11/38, ElPaso, Tex. BB/TL, Deb: 4/21/17																											
1917 Phi-A	0	0	—	1	0	0	0	0	2^2	5	4	0	0	1	0	20.3	6.75	41	.385	.429	0	—	0	-1	-1	0	0.0
● DAVE HILL Hill, David Burnham b: 11/11/37, New Orleans, La. BR/TR, 6'2", 170 lbs. Deb: 8/22/57																											
1957 KC-A	0	0	—	2	0	0	0	0	2^1	6	7	3	0	3	1	34.7	27.00	15	.462	.563	0	—	0	-6	-6	-0	-0.3
● DONNIE HILL Hill, Donald Earl b: 11/12/60, Pomona, Cal. BB/TR, 5'10", 160 lbs. Deb: 7/25/83 ♦																											
1990 Cal-A	0	0	—	1	0	0	0	0	1	0	0	0	0	1	1	9.0	0.00	—	.000	.250	93	.264	0	0	0	0	0.0
● GARRY HILL Hill, Garry Alton b: 11/3/46, Rutherfordton, N.C. BR/TR, 6'2", 195 lbs. Deb: 6/12/69																											
1969 Atl-N	0	1	.000	1	1	0	0	0	2^1	6	4	1	0	1	2	27.0	15.43	23	.462	.500	0	—	0	-3	-3	0	-0.5
● HERBERT HILL Hill, Herbert Lee b: 8/19/1891, Hutchins, Tex. d: 9/2/70, Farmers Branch, Tex. BR/TR, 5'11.5", 175 lbs. Deb: 7/17/15																											
1915 Cle-A	0	0	—	1	0	0	0	0	2	1	0	0	0	2	0	13.5	0.00	—	.250	.500	0	—	0	1	1	-0	0.0
● KEN HILL Hill, Kenneth Wade b: 12/14/65, Lynn, Mass. BR/TR, 6'2", 175 lbs. Deb: 9/3/88																											
1988 StL-N	0	1	.000	4	1	0	0	0	14	16	9	0	0	6	6	14.1	5.14	68	.286	.355	0	.000	-0	-3	-3	0	-0.2
1989 StL-N	7	15	.318	33	33	2	1	0	196^2	186	92	9	5	99	112	13.3	3.80	96	.252	.344	9	.153	-0	-6	-3	0	-0.4
1990 StL-N	5	6	.455	17	14	1	0	0	78^2	79	49	7	1	33	58	12.9	5.49	70	.264	.339	4	.211	1	-15	-15	0	-1.7
1991 StL-N	11	10	.524	30	30	0	0	0	181^1	147	76	15	6	67	121	10.9	3.57	104	.224	.302	5	.100	-1	2	3	0	0.2
1992 Mon-N	16	9	.640	33	33	3	3	0	218	187	76	13	3	75	150	10.9	2.68	129	.230	.298	11	.177	5	20	19	1	3.0
1993 Mon-N	9	7	.563	28	28	2	0	0	183^2	163	84	7	6	74	90	11.9	3.23	129	.238	.318	6	.115	-1	17	19	3	1.8
1994 Mon-N★	**16**	5	.762	23	23	2	1	0	154^2	145	61	12	6	44	85	11.3	3.32	127	.248	.307	7	.146	-0	15	16	1	2.2
1995 StL-N	6	7	.462	18	18	0	0	0	110^1	125	71	16	0	45	50	13.9	5.06	83	.286	.353	6	.194	1	-11	-11	1	-0.9
*Cle-A	4	1	.800	12	11	1	0	0	74^2	77	36	5	1	32	48	13.3	3.98	118	.268	.344	0	—	0	6	6	2	0.5
1996 *Tex-A	16	10	.615	35	35	7	**3**	0	250^2	250	110	19	6	95	170	12.6	3.63	145	.263	.334	0	—	0	38	43	2	4.0
1997 Tex-A	5	8	.385	19	19	0	0	0	111	129	69	11	2	56	68	15.2	5.19	92	.298	.381	0	—	0	-8	-5	3	-0.2
Ana-A	4	4	.500	12	12	1	0	0	79	65	34	8	1	39	38	12.0	3.65	126	.223	.316	1	.500	1	8	8	0	0.8
Yr	9	12	.429	31	31	1	0	0	190	194	103	19	3	95	106	13.8	4.55	103	.268	.355	1	.500	1	1	3	3	0.6
1998 Ana-A	9	6	.600	19	19	0	0	0	103	123	60	6	3	47	57	15.1	4.98	94	.311	.388	0	.000	-0	-4	-3	2	-0.2
1999 Ana-A	4	11	.267	26	22	0	0	0	128^1	129	72	14	4	76	76	14.7	4.77	102	.270	.375	0	.000	-0	1	1	2	0.3
2000 Ana-A	5	7	.417	16	16	0	0	0	78^2	102	59	16	2	53	50	18.0	6.52	76	.323	.423	1	.333	0	-14	-13	1	-1.5
Chi-A	0	1	.000	2	1	0	0	0	3	5	8	0	0	6	0	33.0	24.00	21	.455	.647	0	—	0	-6	-6	0	-0.9
Yr	5	8	.385	18	17	0	0	0	81^2	107	67	16	2	59	50	18.5	7.16	69	.327	.433	1	.333	0	-20	-20	1	-2.4
Total 13	117	108	.520	327	315	19	8	0	1965^2	1928	966	158	46	847	1179	12.9	4.03	107	.259	.339	50	.150	4	42	56	20	6.8
● MILT HILL Hill, Milton Giles b: 8/22/65, Atlanta, Ga. BR/TR, 6', 180 lbs. Deb: 8/1/91																											
1991 Cin-N	1	1	.500	22	0	0	0	0	33^1	36	14	1	0	8	20	11.9	3.78	101	.295	.338	0	.000	-0	-0	0	-0	-0.1
1992 Cin-N	0	0	—	14	0	0	0	1	20	15	9	1	1	5	10	9.4	3.15	114	.211	.273	0	—	0	1	1	-0	0.0
1993 Cin-N	3	0	1.000	19	0	0	0	0	28^2	34	18	5	0	9	23	13.5	5.65	71	.301	.352	0	.000	-0	-5	-5	-1	-0.6
1994 Atl-N	0	0	—	10	0	0	0	0	11^1	18	10	3	0	6	10	19.1	7.94	53	.367	.436	0	—	0	-5	-5	-0	-0.2
Sea-A	1	0	1.000	13	0	0	0	0	23^2	30	19	4	0	11	16	15.6	6.46	76	.306	.376	0	—	0	-4	-4	-0	-0.2
Total 4	5	1	.833	78	0	0	0	1	117	133	70	14	1	39	79	13.3	5.08	81	.294	.351	0	.000	-0	-14	-13	-2	-1.1
● BILL HILL Hill, William Cicero "Still Bill" b: 8/2/1874, Chattanooga, Tenn. d: 1/28/38, Cincinnati, Ohio BL/TL, 6'1", 201 lbs. Deb: 4/18/1896 F																											
1896 Lou-N	9	28	.243	43	39	32	0	2	319^2	353	229	14	18	155	104	14.8	4.31	101	.278	.364	24	.207	-5	2	1	4	0.0
1897 Lou-N	7	17	.292	27	26	20	1	0	199	209	127	6	17	69	55	13.3	3.62	118	.268	.341	7	.095	-8	15	14	2	0.8
1898 Cin-N	13	14	.481	33	32	26	2	0	262	261	146	3	17	119	75	13.6	3.98	96	.258	.346	13	.133	-7	-11	-4	1	-0.9
1899 Cle-N	3	6	.333	11	10	7	0	0	72^1	96	67	0	4	39	26	17.3	6.97	53	.318	.403	4	.129	-2	-25	-28	0	-2.7
Bal-N	3	4	.429	8	7	6	0	0	61	64	35	1	3	18	17	12.5	3.25	122	.270	.329	7	.292	1	4	5	1	0.6
Bro-N	1	0	1.000	2	1	1	0	1	11	11	3	0	0	6	3	13.9	0.82	478	.262	.354	3	.600	2	4	4	-0	0.6
Yr	7	10	.412	21	18	14	0	1	144^1	171	105	1	7	63	46	15.0	4.93	77	.294	.370	14	.233	0	-17	-18	1	-1.5
Total 4	36	69	.343	124	115	92	3	3	925	994	607	24	59	406	280	14.2	4.16	99	.273	.355	58	.167	-20	-11	-6	7	-1.6
● HOMER HILLEBRAND Hillebrand, Homer Hiller Henry b: 10/10/1879, Freeport, Ill. d: 1/20/74, Elsinore, Cal. BR/TL, 5'8", 165 lbs. Deb: 4/24/05 ♦																											
1905 Pit-N	5	2	.714	10	6	4	0	1	60^2	43	20	0	2	19	37	9.5	2.82	107	.198	.269	26	.236	1	1	1	-1	0.2
1906 Pit-N	3	2	.600	7	5	4	1	0	53	42	19	1	1	21	32	10.9	2.21	121	.220	.300	5	.238	1	3	3	1	0.5

YEAR	TM/L	W	L	PCT	G	GS	CG	SH	SV	IP	H	R	HR	HB	BB	SO	RAT	ERA	ERA+	OAV	OOB	BH	AVG	PB	PR	PR+	PD	TPI
1908	Pit-N	0	0	—	1	0	0	0	0	1	1	0	0	0	0	1	9.0	0.00	—	.333	.333	0	—	0	0	0	-0	0.0
Total	3	8	4	.667	18	11	8	1	1	114^{2}	86	39	1	3	40	70	10.1	2.51	113	.209	.284	31	.237	2	4	4	1	0.7

● **SHAWN HILLEGAS** Hillegas, Shawn Patrick b: 8/21/64, Dos Palos, Cal. BR/TR, 6'2", 208 lbs. Deb: 8/9/87

YEAR	TM/L	W	L	PCT	G	GS	CG	SH	SV	IP	H	R	HR	HB	BB	SO	RAT	ERA	ERA+	OAV	OOB	BH	AVG	PB	PR	PR+	PD	TPI
1987	LA-N	4	3	.571	12	10	0	0	0	58	52	27	5	0	31	51	12.9	3.57	111	.241	.336	0	.000	-1	3	3	-1	0.1
1988	LA-N	3	4	.429	11	10	0	0	0	56^{2}	54	26	5	3	17	30	11.8	4.13	81	.250	.314	2	.133	0	-4	-5	-1	-0.7
	Chi-A	3	2	.600	6	6	0	0	0	40	30	16	4	1	18	26	11.0	3.15	126	.207	.299	0	—	0	4	4	-0	0.4
1989	Chi-A	7	11	.389	50	13	0	0	3	119^{2}	132	67	12	3	51	76	14.0	4.74	80	.279	.353	0	—	0	-11	-13	-1	-1.9
1990	Chi-A	0	0	—	7	0	0	0	0	11^{1}	4	1	0	0	5	5	7.1	0.79	483	.111	.220	0	—	0	4	4	0	0.2
1991	Cle-A	3	4	.429	51	3	0	0	7	83	67	42	7	2	46	66	12.5	4.34	96	.223	.330	0	—	0	-2	-2	-0	-0.2
1992	NY-A	1	8	.111	21	9	1	1	0	78^{1}	96	52	12	0	33	46	14.8	5.51	71	.306	.372	0	—	0	-14	-14	-1	-1.5
	Oak-A	0	0	—	5	0	0	0	0	7^{2}	8	5	1	0	4	3	14.1	2.35	160	.276	.364	0	—	0	1	1	-0	0.0
	Yr	1	8	.111	26	9	1	1	0	86	104	57	13	0	37	49	14.8	5.23	75	.303	.371	0	—	0	-12	-13	-1	-1.5
1993	Oak-A	3	6	.333	18	11	0	0	0	60^{2}	78	48	8	4	33	29	17.1	6.97	59	.317	.406	0	—	0	-18	-21	-1	-2.6
Total	7	24	38	.387	181	62	1	1	10	515^{1}	521	284	54	13	238	332	13.5	4.61	84	.264	.347	2	.069	-1	-37	-42	-6	-6.2

● **FRANK HILLER** Hiller, Frank Walter "Dutch" b: 7/13/20, Newark, N.J. d: 1/8/87, West Chester, Pa. BR/TR, 6', 200 lbs. Deb: 5/25/46

YEAR	TM/L	W	L	PCT	G	GS	CG	SH	SV	IP	H	R	HR	HB	BB	SO	RAT	ERA	ERA+	OAV	OOB	BH	AVG	PB	PR	PR+	PD	TPI
1946	NY-A	0	2	.000	3	1	0	0	0	11^{1}	13	7	2	0	6	4	15.1	4.76	72	.295	.380	1	.250	0	-2	-2	-0	-0.3
1948	NY-A	5	2	.714	22	5	1	0	0	62^{1}	59	29	8	1	30	25	13.0	4.04	101	.244	.330	6	.375	2	2	0	0	0.2
1949	NY-A	0	2	.000	4	0	0	0	1	7^{2}	9	5	0	0	7	3	18.8	5.87	69	.290	.421	1	.500	0	-1	-2	-0	-0.3
1950	Chi-N	12	5	.706	38	17	9	2	1	153	153	68	16	4	32	55	11.1	3.53	119	.258	.300	5	.114	-3	10	11	1	0.9
1951	Chi-N	6	12	.333	24	21	6	2	1	141^{1}	147	83	17	9	31	50	11.9	4.84	85	.268	.317	6	.125	-2	-14	-11	1	-1.4
1952	Cin-N	5	8	.385	28	15	6	1	1	124^{1}	129	67	7	6	37	50	12.5	4.63	81	.271	.331	5	.167	1	-12	-12	0	-1.0
1953	NY-N	2	1	.667	19	1	0	0	0	33^{2}	43	29	6	4	15	10	16.6	6.15	70	.303	.385	2	.500	1	-7	-7	1	-0.4
Total	7	30	32	.484	138	60	22	5	4	533^{2}	553	288	56	24	158	197	12.4	4.42	92	.266	.325	26	.176	-1	-24	-22	3	-2.3

● **JOHN HILLER** Hiller, John Frederick b: 4/8/43, Toronto, Ont., Canada BR/TL, 6', 195 lbs. Deb: 9/6/65

YEAR	TM/L	W	L	PCT	G	GS	CG	SH	SV	IP	H	R	HR	HB	BB	SO	RAT	ERA	ERA+	OAV	OOB	BH	AVG	PB	PR	PR+	PD	TPI
1965	Det-A	0	0	—	5	0	0	0	1	6	5	0	0	0	1	4	9.0	0.00	—	.227	.261	0	—	0	2	2	-0	0.1
1966	Det-A	0	0	—	1	0	0	0	0	2	2	2	0	0	2	1	18.0	9.00	39	.286	.444	0	—	0	-1	-1	-0	-0.1
1967	Det-A	4	3	.571	23	6	2	2	3	65	57	20	4	0	9	49	9.1	2.63	124	.233	.260	2	.133	-0	4	5	-0	0.5
1968	*Det-A	9	6	.600	39	12	4	1	2	128	92	37	9	0	51	78	10.1	2.39	126	.200	.280	3	.081	-2	8	9	-0	0.8
1969	Det-A	4	4	.500	40	8	1	1	4	99^{1}	97	50	13	1	44	74	12.9	3.99	94	.257	.336	6	.286	2	-4	-3	-1	-0.2
1970	Det-A	6	6	.500	47	5	1	1	3	104	82	39	12	2	46	89	11.3	3.03	123	.219	.307	0	.000	-2	8	8	-1	0.6
1972	*Det-A	1	2	.333	24	3	1	0	3	44^{1}	39	13	4	3	13	26	11.2	2.03	156	.232	.299	0	.000	-0	5	5	1	0.5
1973	Det-A	10	5	.667	**65**	0	0	0	**38**	125^{1}	89	21	7	0	39	124	9.2	1.44	285	.198	.262	0	—	0	**33**	**35**	0	**6.6**
1974	Det-A☆	17	14	.548	59	0	0	0	13	150	127	51	10	3	62	134	11.5	2.64	144	.231	.312	0	—	0	16	19	-2	3.8
1975	Det-A	2	3	.400	36	0	0	0	14	70^{2}	52	20	6	0	36	87	11.2	2.17	186	.205	.303	0	—	0	13	14	-0	1.6
1976	Det-A	12	8	.600	56	1	1	1	13	121	93	37	7	2	67	117	12.0	2.38	156	.219	.329	0	.000	-0	15	**17**	-1	3.1
1977	Det-A	8	14	.364	45	8	3	0	7	124	120	59	15	1	61	115	13.2	3.56	121	.258	.345	0	—	0	7	10	-1	1.6
1978	Det-A	9	4	.692	51	0	0	0	15	92^{1}	64	27	6	0	35	74	9.6	2.34	166	.202	.281	0	—	0	15	15	-1	2.6
1979	Det-A	4	7	.364	43	0	0	0	9	79^{1}	83	47	14	0	55	46	15.7	5.22	83	.274	.385	0	—	0	-9	-8	-0	-1.1
1980	Det-A	1	0	1.000	11	0	0	0	0	30^{2}	38	15	3	0	14	18	15.3	4.40	94	.309	.380	0	—	0	-1	-1	-0	-0.1
Total	15	87	76	.534	545	43	13	6	125	1242	1040	438	110	12	535	1036	11.5	2.83	134	.229	.312	11	.109	-3	113	127	-8	20.3

● **DAVE HILLMAN** Hillman, Darius Dutton b: 9/14/27, Dungannon, Va. BR/TR, 5'11", 168 lbs. Deb: 4/30/55

YEAR	TM/L	W	L	PCT	G	GS	CG	SH	SV	IP	H	R	HR	HB	BB	SO	RAT	ERA	ERA+	OAV	OOB	BH	AVG	PB	PR	PR+	PD	TPI
1955	Chi-N	0	0	—	25	3	0	0	0	57^{2}	63	36	10	1	25	23	13.9	5.31	77	.283	.357	1	.100	0	-8	-8	0	-0.4
1956	Chi-N	0	2	.000	2	2	0	0	0	12^{1}	11	7	0	0	5	6	11.7	2.19	172	.216	.286	0	.000	-1	2	2	0	0.3
1957	Chi-N	6	11	.353	32	14	1	0	1	103^{1}	115	52	13	0	37	53	13.2	4.35	89	.280	.340	0	.000	-2	-5	-6	-0	-1.1
1958	Chi-N	4	8	.333	31	16	3	0	1	125^{2}	132	57	12	0	31	65	11.7	3.15	124	.265	.308	6	.146	-1	11	11	-0	0.8
1959	Chi-N	8	11	.421	39	24	4	1	0	191	178	84	17	1	43	88	10.5	3.53	112	.248	.292	9	.150	1	9	9	1	1.0
1960	Bos-A	0	3	.000	16	3	0	0	0	36^{2}	41	27	6	0	12	14	13.0	5.65	72	.281	.335	0	.000	-0	-7	-6	0	-0.5
1961	Bos-A	3	2	.600	28	1	0	0	0	78	70	26	8	0	23	39	10.7	2.77	151	.242	.298	0	.000	-2	11	12	0	0.5
1962	Cin-N	0	0	—	2	0	0	0	0	3^{2}	8	4	0	0	1	0	22.1	9.82	41	.421	.450	0	—	0	-2	-2	-0	-0.1
	NY-N	0	0	—	13	1	0	0	1	15^{2}	21	12	5	1	8	8	17.2	6.32	66	.333	.417	0	.000	-0	-4	-4	0	-0.2
	Yr	0	0	—	15	1	0	0	1	19^{1}	29	16	5	1	9	8	18.2	6.98	59	.354	.424	0	.000	-0	-7	-6	-0	-0.3
Total	8	21	37	.362	188	64	8	1	3	624	639	305	71	3	185	296	11.9	3.87	103	.264	.317	16	.098	-5	6	8	1	0.3

● **ERIC HILLMAN** Hillman, John Eric b: 4/27/66, Gary, Ind. BL/TL, 6'10", 225 lbs. Deb: 5/18/92

YEAR	TM/L	W	L	PCT	G	GS	CG	SH	SV	IP	H	R	HR	HB	BB	SO	RAT	ERA	ERA+	OAV	OOB	BH	AVG	PB	PR	PR+	PD	TPI
1992	NY-N	2	2	.500	11	8	0	0	0	52^{1}	67	31	9	2	10	16	13.6	5.33	65	.318	.354	1	.077	-1	-11	-11	-1	-0.9
1993	NY-N	2	9	.182	27	22	3	1	0	145	173	83	12	4	24	60	12.5	3.97	101	.299	.331	7	.159	-0	1	1	-1	0.0
1994	NY-N	0	3	.000	11	6	0	0	0	34^{2}	45	30	9	2	11	20	15.1	7.79	54	.321	.379	0	.000	-1	-14	-14	-0	-1.1
Total	3	4	14	.222	49	36	3	1	0	232	285	144	30	8	45	96	13.1	4.85	81	.306	.344	8	.123	-2	-23	-24	-1	-2.0

● **CHARLIE HILSEY** Hilsey, Charles T. b: 3/23/1864, Philadelphia, Pa. d: 10/31/18, Philadelphia, Pa. 5'7", 180 lbs. Deb: 9/27/1883 ♦

YEAR	TM/L	W	L	PCT	G	GS	CG	SH	SV	IP	H	R	HR	HB	BB	SO	RAT	ERA	ERA+	OAV	OOB	BH	AVG	PB	PR	PR+	PD	TPI
1883	Phi-N	0	3	.000	3	3	3	0	0	26	36	26	1		4	8	13.8	5.54	56	.305	.328	1	.100	-1	-7	-7	-0	-0.7
1884	Phi-a	2	1	.667	3	3	3	0	0	27	29	19	0	0	5	10	11.3	4.67	73	.257	.288	5	.208	0	-4	-4	1	-0.3
Total	2	2	4	.333	6	6	6	0	0	53	65	45	1	0	9	18	12.6	5.09	64	.281	.308	6	.176	-1	-11	-11	0	-1.0

● **HOWARD HILTON** Hilton, Howard James b: 1/3/64, Oxnard, Cal. BR/TR, 6'3", 230 lbs. Deb: 4/9/90

YEAR	TM/L	W	L	PCT	G	GS	CG	SH	SV	IP	H	R	HR	HB	BB	SO	RAT	ERA	ERA+	OAV	OOB	BH	AVG	PB	PR	PR+	PD	TPI
1990	StL-N	0	0	—	2	0	0	0	0	3	2	0	0	0	3	2	15.0	0.00	—	.182	.357	0	—	0	1	1	-0	0.1

● **BRETT HINCHLIFFE** Hinchliffe, Brett b: 7/21/74, Detroit, Mich. BR/TR, 6'5", 190 lbs. Deb: 4/5/99

YEAR	TM/L	W	L	PCT	G	GS	CG	SH	SV	IP	H	R	HR	HB	BB	SO	RAT	ERA	ERA+	OAV	OOB	BH	AVG	PB	PR	PR+	PD	TPI
1999	Sea-A	0	4	.000	11	4	0	0	0	30^{2}	41	31	10	4	21	14	19.4	8.80	54	.323	.434	0	—	0	-13	-14	-0	-1.5
2000	Ana-A	0	0	—	2	0	0	0	0	1^{2}	1	1	0	0	1	0	10.8	5.40	92	.167	.286	0	—	0	-0	-0	-0	0.0
Total	2	0	4	.000	13	4	0	0	0	32^{1}	42	32	10	4	22	14	18.9	8.63	55	.316	.428	0	—	0	-13	-14	-0	-1.5

● **SAM HINDS** Hinds, Samuel Russell b: 7/11/53, Frederick, Md. BR/TR, 6'6", 215 lbs. Deb: 5/21/77

YEAR	TM/L	W	L	PCT	G	GS	CG	SH	SV	IP	H	R	HR	HB	BB	SO	RAT	ERA	ERA+	OAV	OOB	BH	AVG	PB	PR	PR+	PD	TPI
1977	Mil-A	0	3	.000	29	1	0	0	2	72^{1}	72	42	5	2	40	46	14.2	4.73	86	.266	.364	0	—	0	-5	-5	-0	-0.3

● **PAUL HINES** Hines, Paul A. b: 3/1/1852, Washington, D.C. d: 7/10/35, Hyattsville, Md. BR/TR, 5'9.5", 173 lbs. Deb: 4/20/1872 ♦

YEAR	TM/L	W	L	PCT	G	GS	CG	SH	SV	IP	H	R	HR	HB	BB	SO	RAT	ERA	ERA+	OAV	OOB	BH	AVG	PB	PR	PR+	PD	TPI
1884	*Pro-N	0	0	—	1	0	0	0	0	1	3	1	0		0	0	27.0	0.00	—	.500	.500	148	.302	0	0	0	-0	0.0

● **PAUL HINRICHS** Hinrichs, Paul Edwin "Herky" b: 8/31/25, Marengo, Iowa BR/TR, 6', 180 lbs. Deb: 5/16/51

YEAR	TM/L	W	L	PCT	G	GS	CG	SH	SV	IP	H	R	HR	HB	BB	SO	RAT	ERA	ERA+	OAV	OOB	BH	AVG	PB	PR	PR+	PD	TPI
1951	Bos-A	0	0	—	4	0	0	0	0	3^{1}	7	8	1	0	4	1	29.7	21.60	21	.412	.524	0	—	0	-6	-6	0	-0.3

● **DUTCH HINRICHS** Hinrichs, William Louis b: 4/27/1889, Orange, Cal. d: 8/18/72, Kingsburg, Cal. BR/TR, 6'3", 195 lbs. Deb: 6/25/10

YEAR	TM/L	W	L	PCT	G	GS	CG	SH	SV	IP	H	R	HR	HB	BB	SO	RAT	ERA	ERA+	OAV	OOB	BH	AVG	PB	PR	PR+	PD	TPI
1910	Was-A	0	1	.000	3	0	0	0	1	7	10	7	0	0	3	5	16.7	2.57	97	.357	.419	0	.000	-1	-0	-0	-0	-0.1

● **JERRY HINSLEY** Hinsley, Jerry Dean b: 4/9/44, Hugo, Okla. BR/TR, 5'11", 165 lbs. Deb: 4/18/64

YEAR	TM/L	W	L	PCT	G	GS	CG	SH	SV	IP	H	R	HR	HB	BB	SO	RAT	ERA	ERA+	OAV	OOB	BH	AVG	PB	PR	PR+	PD	TPI
1964	NY-N	0	2	.000	9	2	0	0	0	15^{1}	21	17	0	0	7	11	16.4	8.22	44	.313	.378	0	.000	-0	-8	-8	-1	-1.0
1967	NY-N	0	0	—	2	0	0	0	0	5	6	2	0	0	4	3	18.0	3.60	94	.316	.435	0	—	0	-0	-0	0	0.0
Total	2	0	2	.000	11	2	0	0	0	20^{1}	27	19	0	0	11	14	16.8	7.08	50	.314	.392	0	.000	-0	-8	-8	-1	-1.0

● **RICH HINTON** Hinton, Richard Michael b: 5/22/47, Tucson, Ariz. BL/TL, 6'2", 185 lbs. Deb: 7/17/71

YEAR	TM/L	W	L	PCT	G	GS	CG	SH	SV	IP	H	R	HR	HB	BB	SO	RAT	ERA	ERA+	OAV	OOB	BH	AVG	PB	PR	PR+	PD	TPI
1971	Chi-A	3	4	.429	18	2	0	0	0	24^{1}	27	12	1	1	6	15	12.6	4.44	81	.310	.362	0	.000	-0	-3	-2	1	-0.4
1972	NY-A	1	0	1.000	7	3	0	0	0	16^{2}	20	11	2	0	8	13	15.1	4.86	61	.299	.373	0	.000	-0	-3	-4	-0	-0.3
	Tex-A	0	1	.000	5	0	0	0	0	11^{1}	7	10	1	0	10	4	13.5	2.38	127	.171	.333	1	.500	1	1	1	0	0.2
	Yr	1	1	.500	12	3	0	0	0	28	27	21	3	0	18	17	14.5	3.86	77	.250	.357	1	.200	1	-2	-3	-0	-0.1
1975	Chi-A	1	0	1.000	15	0	0	0	0	37^{1}	41	22	2	0	15	30	13.5	4.82	81	.270	.335	0	—	0	-4	-4	1	-0.1
1976	Cin-N	1	2	.333	12	1	0	0	0	17^{2}	30	15	4	0	11	8	20.9	7.64	46	.380	.456	0	.000	-0	-8	-8	-0	-1.3
1978	Chi-A	2	6	.250	29	4	2	0	1	80^{2}	78	38	5	2	28	48	12.0	4.02	95	.261	.328	0	—	0	-2	-2	-1	-0.3
1979	Chi-A	1	2	.333	16	2	0	0	2	41^{2}	57	30	4	2	8	27	14.5	6.05	71	.331	.368	0	—	0	-8	-8	1	-0.5

YEAR TM/L	W	L	PCT	G	GS	CG	SH	SV	IP	H	R	HR	HB	BB	SO	RAT	ERA	ERA+	OAV	OOB	BH	AVG	PB	PR	PR+	PD	TPI
Sea-A	0	2	.000	14	1	0	0	0	20	23	14	4	2	5	7	13.5	5.40	81	.284	.341	0	—	0	-3	-2	-0	-0.2
Yr	1	4	.200	30	3	0	0	2	61^2	80	44	8	4	13	34	14.2	5.84	74	.316	.359	0	—	0	-11	-10	0	-0.7
Total 6	9	17	.346	116	13	2	0	3	249^2	283	152	23	7	91	152	13.7	4.87	78	.289	.354	1	.143	0	-31	-29	0	-2.9

● HERB HIPPAUF Hippauf, Herbert August b: 5/9/39, New York, N.Y. d: 7/17/95, Santa Clara, Cal. BR/TL, 6', 180 lbs. Deb: 4/27/66

YEAR TM/L	W	L	PCT	G	GS	CG	SH	SV	IP	H	R	HR	HB	BB	SO	RAT	ERA	ERA+	OAV	OOB	BH	AVG	PB	PR	PR+	PD	TPI
1966 Atl-N	0	1	.000	3	0	0	0	0	2^2	6	5	0	0	1	1	23.6	13.50	27	.462	.500	0	—	0	-3	-3	-0	-0.6

● HARLEY HISNER Hisner, Harley Parnell b: 11/6/26, Maples, Ind. BR/TR, 6'1", 185 lbs. Deb: 9/30/51

YEAR TM/L	W	L	PCT	G	GS	CG	SH	SV	IP	H	R	HR	HB	BB	SO	RAT	ERA	ERA+	OAV	OOB	BH	AVG	PB	PR	PR+	PD	TPI
1951 Bos-A	0	1	.000	1	1	0	0	0	6	7	3	0	0	4	3	16.5	4.50	99	.292	.393	1	.500	0	-0	-0	0	0.0

● STERLING HITCHCOCK Hitchcock, Sterling Alex b: 4/29/71, Fayetteville, N.C. BL/TL, 6'1", 192 lbs. Deb: 9/11/92

YEAR TM/L	W	L	PCT	G	GS	CG	SH	SV	IP	H	R	HR	HB	BB	SO	RAT	ERA	ERA+	OAV	OOB	BH	AVG	PB	PR	PR+	PD	TPI
1992 NY-A	0	2	.000	3	3	0	0	0	13	23	12	2	1	6	6	20.8	8.31	47	.377	.441	0	—	0	-6	-6	0	-0.8
1993 NY-A	1	2	.333	6	6	0	0	0	31	32	18	4	1	14	26	13.6	4.65	90	.271	.353	0	—	0	-1	-2	-0	-0.2
1994 NY-A	4	1	.800	23	5	1	0	2	49^1	48	24	3	0	29	37	14.0	4.20	109	.265	.367	0	—	0	3	2	-0	0.2
1995 *NY-A	11	10	.524	27	27	4	1	0	168^1	155	91	22	5	68	121	12.2	4.70	98	.245	.323	0	—	0	0	-2	-3	-0.4
1996 Sea-A	13	9	.591	35	35	0	0	0	196^2	245	131	27	7	73	132	14.9	5.35	93	.309	.372	0	—	0	-8	-9	-1	-0.9
1997 SD-N	10	11	.476	32	28	1	0	0	161	172	102	24	4	55	106	12.9	5.20	75	.276	.339	5	.100	-1	-18	-26	-1	-3.1
1998 *SD-N	9	7	.563	39	27	2	1	1	176^1	169	83	29	9	48	158	11.5	3.93	100	.251	.309	7	.140	-1	6	-0	-2	-0.3
1999 SD-N	12	14	.462	33	33	1	0	0	205^2	202	99	29	5	76	194	12.4	4.11	102	.254	.323	5	.082	-3	10	2	-1	-0.1
2000 SD-N	1	6	.143	11	11	0	0	0	65^2	69	38	12	5	26	61	13.7	4.93	89	.267	.346	0	.000	-3	-2	-4	-0	-0.6
Total 9	61	62	.496	209	175	9	2	3	1067	1115	598	152	37	395	841	13.0	4.69	92	.270	.339	17	.093	-7	-15	-45	-8	-6.2

● BRUCE HITT Hitt, Bruce Smith b: 3/14/1897, Comanche, Tex. d: 11/10/73, Portland, Ore. BR/TR, 6'1", 190 lbs. Deb: 9/23/17

YEAR TM/L	W	L	PCT	G	GS	CG	SH	SV	IP	H	R	HR	HB	BB	SO	RAT	ERA	ERA+	OAV	OOB	BH	AVG	PB	PR	PR+	PD	TPI
1917 StL-N	0	0	—	2	0	0	0	0	4	7	6	1	0	1	1	18.0	9.00	30	.368	.400	0	.000	-0	-3	-3	0	-0.2

● ROY HITT Hitt, Roy Wesley "Rhino" b: 6/22/1887, Carleton, Neb. d: 2/8/56, Pomona, Cal. BL/TL, 5'10", 200 lbs. Deb: 4/27/07

YEAR TM/L	W	L	PCT	G	GS	CG	SH	SV	IP	H	R	HR	HB	BB	SO	RAT	ERA	ERA+	OAV	OOB	BH	AVG	PB	PR	PR+	PD	TPI
1907 Cin-N	6	10	.375	21	18	14	2	0	153^1	143	76	2	12	56	63	12.4	3.40	76	.258	.339	10	.179	-0	-16	-13	-1	-1.5

● LLOYD HITTLE Hittle, Lloyd Eldon "Red" b: 2/21/24, Lodi, Cal. BR/TL, 5'10.5", 164 lbs. Deb: 6/12/49

YEAR TM/L	W	L	PCT	G	GS	CG	SH	SV	IP	H	R	HR	HB	BB	SO	RAT	ERA	ERA+	OAV	OOB	BH	AVG	PB	PR	PR+	PD	TPI
1949 Was-A	5	7	.417	36	9	3	2	0	109	123	62	2	0	57	32	14.9	4.21	101	.285	.369	4	.143	-2	-0	1	-1	-0.2
1950 Was-A	2	4	.333	11	4	1	0	0	43^1	60	27	1	0	17	9	16.0	4.98	90	.326	.383	1	.077	-1	-2	-2	1	-0.3
Total 2	7	11	.389	47	13	4	2	0	152^1	183	89	3	0	74	41	15.2	4.43	98	.298	.373	5	.122	-3	-2	-2	0	-0.5

● MYRIL HOAG Hoag, Myril Oliver b: 3/9/08, Davis, Cal. d: 7/28/71, High Springs, Fla BR/TR, 5'11", 180 lbs. Deb: 4/15/31 ♦

YEAR TM/L	W	L	PCT	G	GS	CG	SH	SV	IP	H	R	HR	HB	BB	SO	RAT	ERA	ERA+	OAV	OOB	BH	AVG	PB	PR	PR+	PD	TPI
1939 StL-A★	0	0	—	1	0	0	0	0	1	0	0	0	0	0	0	0.0	0.00	—	.000	.000	142	.295	0	1	1	0	0.0
1945 Cle-A	0	0	—	2	0	0	0	0	3	3	0	0	0	1	0	12.0	0.00	—	.300	.364	27	.211	0	1	1	0	0.1
Total 2	0	0	—	3	0	0	0	0	4	3	0	0	0	1	0	9.0	0.00	—	.214	.267	854	.271	1	2	2	0	0.1

● ED HOBAUGH Hobaugh, Edward Russell b: 6/27/34, Kittanning, Pa. BR/TR, 6', 176 lbs. Deb: 4/19/61

YEAR TM/L	W	L	PCT	G	GS	CG	SH	SV	IP	H	R	HR	HB	BB	SO	RAT	ERA	ERA+	OAV	OOB	BH	AVG	PB	PR	PR+	PD	TPI
1961 Was-A	7	9	.438	26	18	3	0	0	126^1	142	68	12	1	64	67	14.7	4.42	91	.281	.363	4	.098	-2	-6	-6	0	-0.8
1962 Was-A	2	1	.667	26	2	0	0	1	69^1	66	36	9	0	25	37	11.8	3.76	107	.258	.324	2	.167	0	2	2	-1	0.1
1963 Was-A	0	0	—	9	1	0	0	0	16	20	13	3	2	6	11	15.8	6.19	60	.308	.384	1	.500	2	-5	-4	0	0.0
Total 3	9	10	.474	61	21	3	0	1	211^2	228	117	24	3	95	115	13.9	4.34	92	.276	.352	7	.127	-1	-8	-8	-0	-0.7

● GLEN HOBBIE Hobbie, Glen Frederick b: 4/24/36, Witt, Ill. BR/TR, 6'2", 195 lbs. Deb: 9/20/57

YEAR TM/L	W	L	PCT	G	GS	CG	SH	SV	IP	H	R	HR	HB	BB	SO	RAT	ERA	ERA+	OAV	OOB	BH	AVG	PB	PR	PR+	PD	TPI
1957 Chi-N	0	0	—	2	0	0	0	0	4^1	6	5	0	0	5	3	22.8	10.38	37	.333	.478	0	.000	-0	-3	-3	0	-0.2
1958 Chi-N	10	6	.625	55	16	2	1	2	168^1	163	80	13	7	93	91	14.1	3.74	105	.252	.353	7	.146	-2	4	3	4	0.5
1959 Chi-N	16	13	.552	46	33	10	3	0	234	204	105	15	6	106	138	12.2	3.69	107	.236	.324	9	.114	-3	7	7	1	0.5
1960 Chi-N	16	20	.444	46	36	16	4	1	258^2	253	130	27	9	101	134	12.6	3.97	95	.256	.330	13	.151	1	-6	-5	4	-0.2
1961 Chi-N	7	13	.350	36	29	7	2	2	198^2	207	113	26	6	54	103	12.1	4.26	98	.268	.321	11	.167	2	-5	-2	3	0.4
1962 Chi-N	5	14	.263	42	23	5	0	0	162	198	112	18	3	62	87	14.6	5.22	79	.304	.367	6	.122	-1	-23	-18	1	-2.0
1963 Chi-N	7	10	.412	36	24	4	1	0	165^1	172	80	17	6	49	94	12.4	3.92	90	.270	.328	4	.080	-2	-12	-7	-1	-1.1
1964 Chi-N	0	3	.000	8	4	0	0	0	27^1	39	29	4	1	10	14	16.5	7.90	47	.325	.382	0	.000	-1	-13	-12	0	-1.1
StL-N	1	2	.333	13	5	1	0	1	44^1	41	23	4	1	15	18	11.6	4.26	89	.241	.306	2	.154	1	-4	-2	1	0.0
Yr	1	5	.167	21	9	1	0	1	71^2	80	52	8	2	25	32	13.4	5.65	67	.276	.338	2	.111	1	-17	-14	1	-1.1
Total 8	62	81	.434	284	170	45	11	6	1263	1283	677	124	39	495	682	12.9	4.20	93	.264	.337	52	.131	-5	-55	-41	13	-3.2

● JOHN HOBBS Hobbs, John Douglas b: 11/11/56, Philadelphia, Pa. BR/TL, 6'3", 190 lbs. Deb: 8/31/81

YEAR TM/L	W	L	PCT	G	GS	CG	SH	SV	IP	H	R	HR	HB	BB	SO	RAT	ERA	ERA+	OAV	OOB	BH	AVG	PB	PR	PR+	PD	TPI
1981 Min-A	0	0	—	4	0	0	0	0	5^2	5	2	0	2	6	1	20.6	3.18	124	.238	.448	0	—	0	0	0	-0	0.0

● HARRY HOCH Hoch, Harry Keller b: 1/9/1887, Woodside, Del. d: 10/26/81, Lewes, Del. BR/TR, 5'10.5", 165 lbs. Deb: 4/16/08

YEAR TM/L	W	L	PCT	G	GS	CG	SH	SV	IP	H	R	HR	HB	BB	SO	RAT	ERA	ERA+	OAV	OOB	BH	AVG	PB	PR	PR+	PD	TPI
1908 Phi-N	2	1	.667	3	3	2	0	0	26	20	10	0	2	13	4	12.1	2.77	88	.211	.318	1	.200	1	-1	-1	0	0.0
1914 StL-A	0	2	.000	15	2	1	0	0	54	55	31	1	2	27	13	14.0	3.00	90	.284	.377	1	.056	-2	-2	-2	2	-0.1
1915 StL-A	0	4	.000	12	3	1	0	0	40	52	49	2	3	26	9	18.2	7.20	40	.311	.413	2	.200	0	-19	-20	-0	-1.8
Total 3	2	7	.222	30	8	4	0	0	120	127	90	3	7	66	26	15.0	4.35	62	.279	.378	4	.121	-1	-22	-22	2	-1.9

● CHUCK HOCKENBERY Hockenbery, Charles Marion b: 12/15/50, LaCrosse, Wis. BB/TR, 6'1", 195 lbs. Deb: 7/4/75

YEAR TM/L	W	L	PCT	G	GS	CG	SH	SV	IP	H	R	HR	HB	BB	SO	RAT	ERA	ERA+	OAV	OOB	BH	AVG	PB	PR	PR+	PD	TPI
1975 Cal-A	0	5	.000	16	4	0	0	1	41	48	27	3	3	19	15	15.4	5.27	68	.296	.380	0	—	0	-7	-8	-0	-1.0

● GEORGE HOCKETTE Hockette, George Edward "Lefty" b: 4/7/08, Perth, Miss. d: 1/20/74, Plantation, Fla. BL/TL, 6', 174 lbs. Deb: 9/17/34

YEAR TM/L	W	L	PCT	G	GS	CG	SH	SV	IP	H	R	HR	HB	BB	SO	RAT	ERA	ERA+	OAV	OOB	BH	AVG	PB	PR	PR+	PD	TPI
1934 Bos-A	2	1	.667	3	3	3	2	0	27^1	22	5	3	0	6	14	9.2	1.65	292	.218	.262	3	.273	0	9	9	-0	1.0
1935 Bos-A	2	3	.400	23	4	0	0	0	61	83	43	6	1	12	11	14.2	5.16	92	.329	.362	2	.143	-1	-5	-3	3	0.0
Total 2	4	4	.500	26	7	3	2	0	88^1	105	48	9	1	18	25	12.6	4.08	117	.297	.333	5	.200	-0	4	6	3	1.0

● SHOVEL HODGE Hodge, Clarence Clemet b: 7/6/1893, Mount Andrew, Ala. d: 12/31/67, Ft.Walton Beach, Fla. BL/TR, 6'4", 190 lbs. Deb: 9/6/20

YEAR TM/L	W	L	PCT	G	GS	CG	SH	SV	IP	H	R	HR	HB	BB	SO	RAT	ERA	ERA+	OAV	OOB	BH	AVG	PB	PR	PR+	PD	TPI
1920 Chi-A	1	1	.500	4	2	1	0	0	19^2	15	14	0	0	12	5	12.4	2.29	165	.224	.342	0	.000	-1	3	3	-1	0.1
1921 Chi-A	6	8	.429	36	10	5	0	2	142^2	191	118	7	5	54	25	15.8	6.56	65	.335	.397	17	.327	3	-36	-37	3	-2.5
1922 Chi-A	7	6	.538	35	8	2	0	1	139	154	73	3	2	65	37	14.3	4.14	98	.300	.381	12	.207	-1	-2	-1	1	-0.1
Total 3	14	15	.483	75	20	8	0	3	301^1	360	205	10	7	131	67	14.9	5.17	80	.313	.387	29	.250	1	-34	-35	4	-2.5

● ED HODGE Hodge, Ed Oliver b: 4/19/58, Bellflower, Cal. BL/TL, 6'2", 192 lbs. Deb: 5/1/84

YEAR TM/L	W	L	PCT	G	GS	CG	SH	SV	IP	H	R	HR	HB	BB	SO	RAT	ERA	ERA+	OAV	OOB	BH	AVG	PB	PR	PR+	PD	TPI
1984 Min-A	4	3	.571	25	15	0	0	0	100	116	59	13	1	29	59	13.1	4.77	88	.291	.340	0	—	0	-9	-6	-2	-0.6

● KEVIN HODGES Hodges, Kevin Jon b: 6/24/73, Houston, Tex. BR/TR, 6'4", 200 lbs. Deb: 4/24/2000

YEAR TM/L	W	L	PCT	G	GS	CG	SH	SV	IP	H	R	HR	HB	BB	SO	RAT	ERA	ERA+	OAV	OOB	BH	AVG	PB	PR	PR+	PD	TPI
2000 Sea-A	0	0	—	13	0	0	0	0	17^1	18	10	4	2	12	7	16.6	5.19	92	.310	.444	0	—	0	-1	-1	-0	-0.1

● ELI HODKEY Hodkey, Aloysius Joseph b: 11/3/17, Lorain, Ohio BL/TL, 6'4", 185 lbs. Deb: 9/12/46

YEAR TM/L	W	L	PCT	G	GS	CG	SH	SV	IP	H	R	HR	HB	BB	SO	RAT	ERA	ERA+	OAV	OOB	BH	AVG	PB	PR	PR+	PD	TPI
1946 Phi-N	0	1	.000	2	1	0	0	0	4^1	9	6	0	0	5	0	29.1	12.46	28	.391	.500	0	.000	-0	-4	-4	-0	-0.8

● CHARLIE HODNETT Hodnett, Charles b: 1861, Iowa d: 4/25/1890, St.Louis, Mo. Deb: 5/3/1883

YEAR TM/L	W	L	PCT	G	GS	CG	SH	SV	IP	H	R	HR	HB	BB	SO	RAT	ERA	ERA+	OAV	OOB	BH	AVG	PB	PR	PR+	PD	TPI
1883 StL-a	2	2	.500	4	4	3	0	0	32	28	10	1		7	6	9.8	1.41	248	.220	.261	2	.182	-0	7	7	-0	0.7
1884 StL-U	12	2	.857	14	14	12	1	0	121	121	56	0		16	41	10.2	2.01	119	.243	.267	12	.207	-1	6	5	-2	0.1
Total 2	14	4	.778	18	18	15	1	0	153	149	66	1		23	47	10.1	1.88	139	.239	.266	14	.203	-1	13	12	-2	0.8

● GEORGE HODSON Hodson, George S. b: 6/1870, Pennsylvania TR, Deb: 8/9/1894

YEAR TM/L	W	L	PCT	G	GS	CG	SH	SV	IP	H	R	HR	HB	BB	SO	RAT	ERA	ERA+	OAV	OOB	BH	AVG	PB	PR	PR+	PD	TPI
1894 Bos-N	4	4	.500	12	11	8	0	0	74	103	66	4	5	35	12	17.4	5.84	97	.326	.402	3	.100	-4	-4	-1	-1	-0.5
1895 Phi-N	1	2	.333	4	2	1	0	0	17	27	23	4	0	9	6	19.1	9.53	50	.355	.424	0	.000	-1	-9	-9	-1	-1.1
Total 2	5	6	.455	16	13	9	0	0	91	130	89	8	5	44	18	17.7	6.53	84	.332	.406	3	.086	-5	-13	-10	-2	-1.6

● BILLY HOEFT Hoeft, William Frederick b: 5/17/32, Oshkosh, Wis. BL/TL, 6'3", 205 lbs. Deb: 4/18/52

YEAR TM/L	W	L	PCT	G	GS	CG	SH	SV	IP	H	R	HR	HB	BB	SO	RAT	ERA	ERA+	OAV	OOB	BH	AVG	PB	PR	PR+	PD	TPI
1952 Det-A	2	7	.222	34	10	1	0	4	125	123	66	14	5	63	67	13.8	4.32	88	.260	.353	6	.150	-1	-9	-7	1	-0.5
1953 Det-A	9	14	.391	29	27	9	0	2	197^2	223	113	24	4	58	90	13.0	4.83	84	.283	.335	11	.172	0	-18	-16	-2	-1.8
1954 Det-A	7	15	.318	34	25	10	4	1	175	180	93	22	4	59	114	12.5	4.58	81	.266	.328	10	.192	4	-17	-17	-2	-1.8
1955 Det-A☆	16	7	.696	32	29	17	**7**	0	220	187	75	17	6	75	133	11.0	2.99	129	.229	.298	17	.207	3	24	22	-3	2.1

YEAR	TM/L	W	L	PCT	G	GS	CG	SH	SV	IP	H	R	HR	HB	BB	SO	RAT	ERA	ERA+	OAV	OOB	BH	AVG	PB	PR	PR+	PD	TPI
1956	Det-A	20	14	.588	38	34	18	4	0	248	276	127	22	5	104	172	14.0	4.06	101	.287	.360	20	.250	6	3	1	-3	0.5
1957	Det-A	9	11	.450	34	28	10	1	1	207	188	85	15	5	69	111	11.4	3.48	111	.244	.310	10	.149	2	7	9	-2	0.8
1958	Det-A	10	9	.526	36	21	6	0	3	143	148	70	15	1	49	94	12.5	4.15	97	.268	.328	12	.273	3	-6	-2	-2	-0.1
1959	Det-A	1	1	.500	2	2	0	0	0	9	6	5	0	1	4	2	11.0	5.00	81	.188	.297	1	.333	0	-1	-1	0	-0.2
	Bos-A	0	3	.000	5	3	0	0	0	17^2	22	12	1	1	8	8	15.8	5.60	72	.319	.397	0	.000	-0	-3	-3	0	-0.4
	Bal-A	1	1	.500	16	3	0	0	0	41	50	29	6	0	19	30	15.1	5.71	66	.307	.379	3	.250	1	-8	-9	-0	-0.4
	Yr	2	5	.286	23	8	0	0	0	67^2	78	46	7	2	31	40	14.8	5.59	70	.295	.374	4	.222	0	-13	-13	0	-1.0
1960	Bal-A	2	1	.667	19	0	0	0	0	18^2	18	10	2	0	14	14	15.4	4.34	88	.240	.360	0	.000	-0	-1	-1	0	-0.1
1961	Bal-A	7	4	.636	35	12	3	1	3	138	106	37	7	1	55	100	10.6	2.02	190	.216	.296	7	.179	1	**31**	29	1	2.5
1962	Bal-A	4	8	.333	57	4	0	0	7	113^2	103	62	7	1	43	73	11.6	4.59	81	.243	.315	3	.158	3	-8	-12	0	-1.0
1963	SF-N	2	0	1.000	23	0	0	0	4	24^1	26	12	5	0	10	8	13.3	4.44	72	.271	.340	1	1.000	1	-3	-3	-0	-0.4
1964	Mil-N	4	0	1.000	42	0	0	0	4	73^1	76	35	9	1	18	47	11.7	3.80	93	.271	.318	2	.222	1	-2	-2	0	0.0
1965	Chi-N	2	2	.500	29	2	1	0	1	51^1	41	21	3	0	20	44	10.7	2.81	131	.215	.289	3	.273	1	4	5	-1	0.4
1966	Chi-N	1	2	.333	36	0	0	0	3	41	43	28	4	1	14	30	12.7	4.61	80	.264	.326	1	.250	0	-5	-4	1	-0.3
	SF-N	0	2	.000	4	0	0	0	0	3^2	4	3	0	0	3	3	17.2	7.36	50	.250	.368	0	—	0	-2	-1	-0	-0.3
	Yr	1	4	.200	40	0	0	0	3	44^2	47	31	4	1	17	33	13.1	4.84	76	.263	.330	1	.250	0	-6	-6	0	-0.6
Total	15	97	101	.490	505	200	75	17	33	1847^1	1820	883	173	36	685	1140	12.4	3.94	98	.259	.327	107	.202	24	-15	-15	-11	-1.0

● ART HOELSKOETTER

Hoelskoetter, Arthur "Holley" or "Hoss" (a.k.a. Arthur H. Hostetter) b: 9/30/1882, St.Louis, Mo. d: 8/3/54, St.Louis, Mo. BR/TR, 6'2", Deb: 9/10/05 ♦

YEAR	TM/L	W	L	PCT	G	GS	CG	SH	SV	IP	H	R	HR	HB	BB	SO	RAT	ERA	ERA+	OAV	OOB	BH	AVG	PB	PR	PR+	PD	TPI
1905	StL-N	0	1	.000	1	1	1	0	0	6	6	6	1	0	5	4	16.5	1.50	199	.273	.407	20	.241	0	1	1	0	0.2
1906	StL-N	1	4	.200	12	3	2	0	0	58^1	53	37	1	1	34	20	13.6	4.63	57	.240	.344	71	.224	1	-13	-13	-1	-1.1
1907	StL-N	0	0	—	2	0	0	0	0	11	9	16	0	2	10	8	17.2	5.73	44	.209	.382	98	.247	0	-4	-4	-1	-0.2
Total	3	1	5	.167	15	4	3	0	0	75^1	68	59	2	3	49	32	14.3	4.54	58	.238	.355	225	.236	1	-16	-16	-1	-1.1

● JOE HOERNER

Hoerner, Joseph Walter b: 11/12/36, Dubuque, Iowa d: 10/4/96, Hermann, Mo. BR/TL, 6'1", 200 lbs. Deb: 9/27/63

YEAR	TM/L	W	L	PCT	G	GS	CG	SH	SV	IP	H	R	HR	HB	BB	SO	RAT	ERA	ERA+	OAV	OOB	BH	AVG	PB	PR	PR+	PD	TPI
1963	Hou-N	0	0	—	1	0	0	0	0	3	2	0	0	0	0	2	6.0	0.00	—	.182	.182	0	.000	-0	1	1	0	0.1
1964	Hou-N	0	0	—	7	0	0	0	0	11	13	11	3	0	6	4	15.5	4.91	70	.310	.396	0	.000	-0	-2	-2	0	-0.1
1966	StL-N	5	1	.833	57	0	0	0	13	76	57	16	5	4	21	63	9.7	1.54	233	.212	.279	1	.125	1	17	17	-1	2.0
1967	*StL-N	4	4	.500	57	0	0	0	15	66	52	25	5	1	20	50	10.0	2.59	127	.225	.290	2	.182	0	6	5	-0	0.9
1968	*StL-N	8	2	.800	47	0	0	0	17	48^2	34	9	2	0	12	42	8.5	1.48	196	.192	.243	0	.000	-1	8	8	0	1.7
1969	StL-N	2	3	.400	45	0	0	0	15	53^1	44	18	5	1	9	35	9.1	2.87	125	.230	.269	0	.000	-1	4	4	0	0.6
1970	Phi-N☆	9	5	.643	44	0	0	0	9	57^2	53	20	5	1	20	39	11.5	2.65	151	.247	.314	2	.200	1	9	9	-2	1.7
1971	Phi-N	4	5	.444	49	0	0	0	9	73	57	19	6	1	21	57	9.7	1.97	179	.215	.275	1	.100	-1	12	12	-0	1.8
1972	Phi-N	0	2	.000	15	0	0	0	3	21^2	21	6	2	1	5	12	11.2	2.08	173	.259	.310	0	.000	-0	3	4	-1	0.4
	Atl-N	1	3	.250	25	0	0	0	2	23^1	34	18	4	1	8	19	16.6	6.56	58	.351	.406	0	.000	-0	-8	-7	-0	-1.3
	Yr	1	5	.167	40	0	0	0	5	45	55	24	6	2	13	31	14.0	4.40	84	.309	.363	0	.000	-1	-5	-3	-1	-0.9
1973	Atl-N	2	2	.500	20	0	0	0	2	12^2	17	9	1	0	4	10	14.9	6.39	62	.333	.382	0	—	0	-4	-3	-0	-0.7
	KC-A	2	0	1.000	22	0	0	0	4	19^1	28	11	0	0	13	15	19.1	5.12	80	.329	.418	0	—	0	-3	-2	-0	-0.3
1974	KC-A	2	3	.400	30	0	0	0	2	35^1	32	15	3	4	12	24	12.2	3.82	100	.244	.327	0	—	0	-1	0	-1	-0.1
1975	Phi-N	0	0	—	25	0	0	0	0	21	25	6	3	1	8	20	14.6	2.57	146	.298	.366	0	.000	-0	2	3	-1	0.0
1976	Tex-A	0	4	.000	41	0	0	0	8	35	41	22	3	0	19	15	15.4	5.14	70	.315	.403	0	—	0	-6	-6	1	-1.0
1977	Cin-N	0	0	—	8	0	0	0	0	5^2	9	8	3	3	3	5	23.8	12.71	31	.375	.500	0	—	0	-6	-5	-0	-0.3
Total	14	39	34	.534	493	0	0	0	99	562^2	519	213	50	18	181	412	11.5	2.99	120	.249	.314	6	.102	-1	35	36	-7	5.4

● LEFTY HOERST

Hoerst, Frank Joseph b: 8/11/17, Philadelphia, Pa. d: 2/18/2000, Maple Shade, N.J. BL/TL, 6'3", 192 lbs. Deb: 4/26/40

YEAR	TM/L	W	L	PCT	G	GS	CG	SH	SV	IP	H	R	HR	HB	BB	SO	RAT	ERA	ERA+	OAV	OOB	BH	AVG	PB	PR	PR+	PD	TPI
1940	Phi-N	1	0	1.000	6	0	0	0	0	12	12	7	1	0	8	3	15.0	5.25	74	.250	.357	0	.000	-0	-2	-2	1	-0.1
1941	Phi-N	3	10	.231	37	11	1	0	0	105^2	111	70	7	1	50	33	13.8	5.20	71	.275	.357	4	.182	0	-18	-17	2	-1.7
1942	Phi-N	4	16	.200	33	22	5	0	1	150^2	162	99	11	1	78	52	14.4	5.20	64	.271	.357	7	.152	-0	-32	-32	2	-3.7
1946	Phi-N	1	6	.143	18	7	2	0	0	68^1	77	42	4	1	36	17	15.0	4.61	74	.288	.375	1	.059	-1	-9	-9	1	-1.1
1947	Phi-N	1	1	.500	4	1	0	0	0	11^1	19	12	1	0	3	0	17.5	7.94	50	.358	.393	2	.500	1	-5	-5	0	-0.6
Total	5	10	33	.233	98	41	8	0	1	348	381	230	24	3	175	105	14.5	5.17	68	.279	.362	14	.154	-1	-66	-64	4	-7.2

● CHET HOFF

Hoff, Chester Cornelius "Red" b: 5/8/1891, Ossining, N.Y. d: 9/17/98, Daytona Beach, Fla. BL/TL, 5'9", 162 lbs. Deb: 9/6/11

YEAR	TM/L	W	L	PCT	G	GS	CG	SH	SV	IP	H	R	HR	HB	BB	SO	RAT	ERA	ERA+	OAV	OOB	BH	AVG	PB	PR	PR+	PD	TPI
1911	NY-A	0	1	.000	5	1	0	0	0	20^2	21	8	0	0	7	10	12.2	2.18	165	.262	.322	2	.286	0	3	3	1	0.2
1912	NY-A	0	1	.000	5	1	0	0	0	15^2	20	14	0	0	6	14	14.9	6.89	52	.303	.361	1	.200	0	-6	-5	-0	-0.3
1913	NY-A	0	0	—	2	0	0	0	0	3	0	0	0	0	1	2	3.0	0.00	—	.000	.111	0	.000	-0	1	1	-0	0.0
1915	StL-A	2	2	.500	11	3	2	0	0	43^2	26	16	0	1	24	23	10.5	1.24	232	.169	.285	3	.176	-1	8	8	1	0.7
Total	4	2	4	.333	23	5	2	0	0	83	67	38	0	1	38	49	11.5	2.49	127	.218	.305	6	.200	-1	6	6	1	0.6

● BILL HOFFER

Hoffer, William Leopold "Chick" or "Wizard" b: 11/8/1870, Cedar Rapids, Iowa d: 7/21/59, Cedar Rapids, Iowa BR/TR, 5'9", 155 lbs. Deb: 4/26/1895

YEAR	TM/L	W	L	PCT	G	GS	CG	SH	SV	IP	H	R	HR	HB	BB	SO	RAT	ERA	ERA+	OAV	OOB	BH	AVG	PB	PR	PR+	PD	TPI
1895	*Bal-N	31	6	**.838**	41	38	32	**4**	0	314	296	146	9	19	124	80	12.6	3.21	148	.245	.325	27	.214	-3	55	54	-2	4.3
1896	*Bal-N	25	7	**.781**	35	35	32	3	0	309	317	151	1	12	95	93	12.3	3.38	127	.263	.323	38	.304	11	34	32	2	3.6
1897	*Bal-N	22	11	.667	38	33	29	1	0	303^1	350	188	5	17	104	62	14.0	4.30	97	.287	.351	33	.237	2	0	-5	0	-0.3
1898	Bal-N	0	4	.000	4	4	4	0	0	34^1	62	44	0	1	16	5	20.7	7.34	49	.387	.446	5	.208	0	-14	-14	-0	-1.2
	Pit-N	3	0	1.000	4	3	3	0	0	31	26	7	0	0	15	11	11.9	1.74	204	.226	.315	1	.091	-1	6	6	-0	0.5
	Yr	3	4	.429	8	7	7	0	0	65^1	88	51	0	1	31	16	16.5	4.68	76	.320	.391	6	.171	-0	-8	-8	-0	-0.7
1899	Pit-N	8	10	.444	23	19	15	2	0	163^2	169	98	5	10	64	44	13.4	3.63	105	.267	.343	18	.198	-1	4	3	0	0.2
1901	Cle-A	3	8	.273	16	10	10	0	**3**	99	113	78	2	1	35	19	13.5	4.55	78	.283	.343	6	.136	-1	-10	-11	0	-1.1
Total	6	92	46	.667	161	142	125	10	3	1254^1	1333	712	22	60	453	314	13.2	3.75	112	.270	.339	128	.229	6	75	66	-0	6.0

● DANNY HOFFMAN

Hoffman, Daniel John b: 3/2/1880, Canton, Conn. d: 3/14/22, Manchester, Conn. BL/TL, 5'9", 175 lbs. Deb: 4/20/03 ♦

YEAR	TM/L	W	L	PCT	G	GS	CG	SH	SV	IP	H	R	HR	HB	BB	SO	RAT	ERA	ERA+	OAV	OOB	BH	AVG	PB	PR	PR+	PD	TPI
1903	Phi-A	0	0	—	1	0	0	0	0	3	2	1	0	0	2	0	12.0	3.00	102	.182	.308	61	.246	0	-0	0	-0	0.0

● FRANK HOFFMAN

Hoffman, Frank J. "The Texas Wonder" b: Houston, Tex. TR, Deb: 8/13/1888

YEAR	TM/L	W	L	PCT	G	GS	CG	SH	SV	IP	H	R	HR	HB	BB	SO	RAT	ERA	ERA+	OAV	OOB	BH	AVG	PB	PR	PR+	PD	TPI
1888	KC-a	3	9	.250	12	12	12	0	0	104	102	71	3	6	42	38	13.0	2.77	124	.248	.326	6	.154	-1	3	7	0	0.6

● GUY HOFFMAN

Hoffman, Guy Alan b: 7/9/56, Ottawa, Ill. BL/TL, 5'9", 185 lbs. Deb: 7/4/79

YEAR	TM/L	W	L	PCT	G	GS	CG	SH	SV	IP	H	R	HR	HB	BB	SO	RAT	ERA	ERA+	OAV	OOB	BH	AVG	PB	PR	PR+	PD	TPI
1979	Chi-A	0	5	.000	24	0	0	0	2	30^1	30	18	0	1	23	18	16.0	5.34	80	.261	.388	0	—	0	-4	-4	0	-0.5
1980	Chi-A	1	0	1.000	23	1	0	0	1	37^2	38	12	1	0	17	24	13.1	2.63	154	.268	.346	0	—	0	6	6	-1	0.2
1983	Chi-A	1	0	1.000	11	0	0	0	0	6	14	5	1	0	2	2	24.0	7.50	56	.483	.516	0	—	0	-2	-2	-0	-0.3
1986	Chi-N	6	2	.750	32	8	1	0	0	84	92	37	6	2	29	47	13.2	3.86	105	.288	.351	1	.067	-1	-1	2	-1	-0.1
1987	Cin-N	9	10	.474	36	22	0	0	0	158^2	160	83	20	4	49	87	12.1	4.37	97	.265	.325	5	.111	-2	-5	-2	-2	-0.5
1988	Tex-A	0	0	—	11	0	0	0	0	22^1	22	14	5	1	8	9	12.5	5.24	78	.247	.316	0	—	0	-3	-3	-0	-0.1
Total	6	17	17	.500	137	31	1	0	3	339	356	169	33	8	128	187	13.1	4.25	98	.274	.343	6	.100	-2	-9	-3	-4	-1.3

● TREVOR HOFFMAN

Hoffman, Trevor William b: 10/13/67, Bellflower, Cal. BR/TR, 6', 205 lbs. Deb: 4/6/93 F

YEAR	TM/L	W	L	PCT	G	GS	CG	SH	SV	IP	H	R	HR	HB	BB	SO	RAT	ERA	ERA+	OAV	OOB	BH	AVG	PB	PR	PR+	PD	TPI
1993	Fla-N	2	2	.500	28	0	0	0	2	35^2	24	13	5	0	19	26	10.9	3.28	132	.185	.289	0	.000	-0	3	4	0	0.4
	SD-N	2	4	.333	39	0	0	0	3	54^1	56	30	5	1	20	53	12.8	4.31	96	.264	.330	1	.200	0	-2	-1	-0	-0.1
	Yr	4	6	.400	67	0	0	0	5	90	80	43	10	1	39	79	12.0	3.90	108	.234	.314	1	.143	-0	1	3	0	0.3
1994	SD-N	4	4	.500	47	0	0	0	20	56	39	16	4	0	20	68	9.5	2.57	160	.193	.266	0	.000	-0	10	10	0	1.9
1995	SD-N	7	4	.636	55	0	0	0	31	53^1	48	25	10	0	14	52	10.5	3.88	104	.235	.284	1	.500	1	2	1	-1	0.2
1996	*SD-N	9	5	.643	70	0	0	0	42	88	50	23	6	2	31	111	8.5	2.25	177	.161	.241	0	.000	-1	19	18	-0	3.5
1997	SD-N	6	4	.600	70	0	0	0	37	81^1	59	25	9	0	24	111	9.2	2.66	146	.200	.260	1	.333	0	14	12	-1	2.3
1998	*SD-N★	4	2	.667	66	0	0	0	**53**	73	41	12	2	1	21	86	7.8	1.48	265	.165	.232	0	.000	-0	22	21	-1	4.2
1999	SD-N★	2	3	.400	64	0	0	0	40	67^1	48	23	5	0	15	73	8.4	2.14	196	.197	.243	1	.333	1	18	17	-1	2.8
2000	SD-N★	4	7	.364	70	0	0	0	43	72^1	61	29	7	0	11	85	9.0	2.99	146	.224	.254	0	—	0	13	12	-0	2.2
Total	8	40	35	.533	509	0	0	0	271	581^1	426	196	53	4	175	665	9.4	2.72	150	.201	.263	4	.138	-0	101	92	-4	17.4

● BILL HOFFMAN

Hoffman, William Joseph b: 3/3/18, Philadelphia, Pa. BL/TL, 5'9", 170 lbs. Deb: 8/13/39

YEAR	TM/L	W	L	PCT	G	GS	CG	SH	SV	IP	H	R	HR	HB	BB	SO	RAT	ERA	ERA+	OAV	OOB	BH	AVG	PB	PR	PR+	PD	TPI
1939	Phi-N	0	0	—	3	0	0	0	0	6	8	9	2	3	7	1	27.0	13.50	30	.333	.529	0	.000	-0	-6	-6	-0	-0.3

YEAR	TM/L	W	L	PCT	G	GS	CG	SH	SV	IP	H	R	HR	HB	BB	SO	RAT	ERA	ERA+	OAV	OOB	BH	AVG	PB	PR	PR+	PD	TPI
● **JOHN HOFFORD**	Hofford, John William b: 5/25/1863, Philadelphia, Pa. d: 12/16/15, Philadelphia, Pa. Deb: 9/26/1885																											
1885	Pit-a	0	3	.000	3	3	3	0	0	25	28	16	1	0	9	21	13.3	3.60	89	.275	.333	1	.125	-1	-1	-1	0	-0.1
1886	Pit-a	3	6	.333	9	9	9	0	0	81	88	66	1	2	40	25	14.4	4.33	78	.261	.343	10	.294	3	-8	-9	1	-0.4
Total	2	3	9	.250	12	12	12	0	0	106	116	82	2	2	49	46	14.2	4.16	80	.264	.341	11	.262	2	-9	-10	1	-0.5
● **GEORGE HOGAN**	Hogan, George A. b: 9/25/1885, Marion, Ohio d: 2/22/22, Bartlesville, Okla BR/TR, 6', 160 lbs. Deb: 4/18/14 F																											
1914	KC-F	0	1	.000	4	1	0	0	0	13	12	9	1	1	7	7	13.8	4.15	67	.255	.364	0	.000	-1	-2	-2	0	-0.2
● **EDDIE HOGAN**	Hogan, Robert Edward b: 4/1860, St.Louis, Mo. BR, 5'7", 153 lbs. Deb: 7/5/1882 ♦																											
1882	StL-a	0	1	.000	1	1	1	0	0	8	10	7	0		0	4	11.3	1.13	249	.286	.286	1	.333	0	1	1	-1	0.1
● **BRAD HOGG**	Hogg, Carter Bradley b: 3/26/1888, Buena Vista, Ga. d: 4/2/35, Buena Vista, Ga. BR/TR, 6', 185 lbs. Deb: 9/1/11																											
1911	Bos-N	0	3	.000	8	3	2	0	1	25^{2}	33	20	0	1	14	8	16.8	6.66	57	.337	.425	4	.444	1	-9	-7	0	-0.6
1912	Bos-N	1	1	.500	10	1	0	0	1	31	37	32	2	2	16	12	16.0	6.97	51	.308	.399	1	.091	-1	-12	-11	-0	-0.8
1915	Chi-N	1	0	1.000	2	2	1	1	0	13	12	3	1	1	6	0	13.2	2.08	134	.245	.339	0	.000	-0	1	1	0	0.1
1918	Phi-N	13	13	.500	29	25	17	3	1	228	201	83	3	6	61	81	10.6	2.53	119	.245	.302	18	.228	3	6	11	2	1.9
1919	Phi-N	5	12	.294	22	19	13	0	0	150^{1}	163	85	7	5	55	48	13.4	4.43	73	.292	.360	17	.283	3	-25	-18	-2	-1.9
Total	5	20	29	.408	71	50	33	4	3	448	446	223	13	15	152	149	12.3	3.70	85	.271	.338	40	.247	5	-40	-25	0	-1.3
● **BILL HOGG**	Hogg, William Johnston "Buffalo Bill" b: 9/11/1881, Port Huron, Mich. d: 12/8/09, New Orleans, La. BR/TR, 6', 200 lbs. Deb: 4/25/05																											
1905	NY-A	9	13	.409	39	22	9	3	1	205	178	104	1	13	101	125	12.8	3.20	92	.236	.336	4	.060	-6	-13	-6	-5	-1.7
1906	NY-A	14	13	.519	28	25	15	3	0	206	171	77	5	12	72	107	11.1	2.93	101	.229	.307	9	.125	-5	-5	1	-5	-0.9
1907	NY-A	10	8	.556	25	21	13	0	0	166^{2}	173	84	3	6	83	64	14.1	3.08	91	.270	.359	11	.183	-0	-10	-5	-2	-0.8
1908	NY-A	4	16	.200	24	21	6	0	0	152^{1}	155	89	4	4	63	72	13.1	3.01	82	.262	.337	4	.093	-3	-10	-9	-2	-1.7
Total	4	37	50	.425	116	89	43	6	1	730	677	354	13	35	319	368	12.7	3.06	92	.248	.334	28	.116	-14	-38	-18	-13	-5.1
● **CHIEF HOGSETT**	Hogsett, Elon Chester b: 11/2/03, Brownell, Kan. BL/TL, 6', 190 lbs. Deb: 9/18/29																											
1929	Det-A	1	2	.333	4	4	2	1	0	28^{2}	34	10	0	1	9	9	13.8	2.83	152	.312	.370	2	.200	-0	5	5	0	0.4
1930	Det-A	9	8	.529	33	17	4	0	1	146	174	102	9	9	63	54	15.2	5.42	88	.300	.377	17	.293	3	-13	-10	2	-0.5
1931	Det-A	3	9	.250	22	12	5	0	2	112^{1}	150	80	8	5	33	47	15.1	5.93	77	.324	.375	11	.234	0	-19	-16	0	-1.4
1932	Det-A	11	9	.550	47	15	7	0	7	178	201	97	8	5	66	56	13.8	3.54	133	.286	.351	14	.246	3	19	22	2	2.8
1933	Det-A	6	10	.375	45	2	0	0	9	116	137	78	7	4	56	39	15.3	4.50	96	.296	.377	8	.211	-0	-3	-2	1	-0.3
1934	*Det-A	3	2	.600	26	0	0	0	3	50^{1}	61	34	4	1	19	23	14.5	4.29	102	.303	.367	3	.231	-0	1	1	1	0.1
1935	*Det-A	6	6	.500	40	0	0	0	5	96^{2}	109	45	1	5	49	39	15.2	3.54	118	.288	.377	6	.261	2	10	7	3	1.3
1936	Det-A	0	1	.000	3	0	0	0	0	4	8	7	1	0	1	1	20.3	9.00	55	.400	.429	0	—	0	-2	-2	0	-0.2
	StL-A	13	15	.464	39	29	10	0	1	215^{1}	278	153	15	15	90	67	16.0	5.52	97	.310	.383	10	.143	-2	-11	-3	1	-0.4
	Yr	13	16	.448	42	29	10	0	1	219^{1}	286	160	16	15	91	68	16.1	5.58	96	.312	.384	10	.143	-2	-13	-5	1	-0.6
1937	StL-A	6	19	.240	37	26	8	1	2	177^{1}	245	144	19	5	75	68	16.5	6.29	77	.328	.393	13	.210	0	-33	-28	-1	-3.2
1938	Was-A	5	6	.455	31	9	1	0	3	91	107	73	12	8	36	33	14.9	6.03	75	.292	.368	7	.304	3	-13	-16	0	-1.4
1944	Det-A	0	0	—	3	0	0	0	0	6^{1}	7	6	1	2	4	5	18.5	0.00	—	.250	.382	0	.000	-0	2	2	-0	0.1
Total	11	63	87	.420	330	114	37	2	33	1222	1511	829	85	60	501	441	15.3	5.02	94	.305	.376	91	.226	8	-57	-41	9	-2.7
● **CAL HOGUE**	Hogue, Calvin Grey b: 10/24/27, Dayton, Ohio BR/TR, 6', 185 lbs. Deb: 7/15/52																											
1952	Pit-N	1	8	.111	19	12	3	0	0	83^{2}	79	56	7	4	68	34	16.2	4.84	82	.258	.399	6	.250	1	-10	-7	-2	-0.7
1953	Pit-N	1	1	.500	3	2	2	0	0	19	19	13	4	1	16	10	17.1	5.21	86	.250	.387	0	.000	-1	-2	-1	0	-0.2
1954	Pit-N	0	1	.000	3	2	0	0	0	11	11	6	1	0	12	7	18.8	4.91	85	.282	.451	0	.000	-0	-1	-1	0	-0.1
Total	3	2	10	.167	25	16	5	0	0	113^{2}	109	75	12	5	96	51	16.6	4.91	83	.259	.402	6	.188	0	-13	-10	-1	-1.0
● **BOBBY HOGUE**	Hogue, Robert Clinton b: 4/5/21, Miami, Fla. d: 12/22/87, Miami, Fla. BR/TR, 5'10", 195 lbs. Deb: 4/24/48																											
1948	Bos-N	8	2	.800	40	1	0	0	2	86^{1}	88	34	4	2	19	43	11.4	3.23	119	.265	.309	2	.095	-1	7	6	-1	0.5
1949	Bos-N	2	2	.500	33	0	0	0	3	72	78	30	4	2	25	23	13.1	3.13	121	.280	.343	6	.286	1	7	6	2	0.6
1950	Bos-N	3	5	.375	36	1	0	0	7	62^{2}	69	35	8	4	31	15	14.9	5.03	77	.280	.370	3	.231	1	-6	-9	1	-1.1
1951	Bos-N	0	0	—	3	0	0	0	0	5	4	3	1	0	3	0	12.6	5.40	68	.235	.350	1	.500	0	-1	-1	-0	0.0
	StL-A	1	1	.500	18	0	0	0	1	29^{2}	31	17	1	0	23	11	16.4	5.16	85	.279	.403	2	.667	1	-3	-2	1	0.0
	*NY-A	1	0	1.000	7	0	0	0	0	7^{1}	4	0	0	0	3	2	8.6	0.00	—	.174	.269	0	—	0	3	3	0	0.4
	Yr	2	1	.667	25	0	0	0	1	37	35	17	1	0	26	13	14.8	4.14	104	.261	.381	2	.667	1	-0	1	1	0.4
1952	NY-A	3	5	.375	27	0	0	0	4	47^{1}	52	30	6	1	25	12	14.8	5.32	62	.294	.384	3	.273	0	-9	-12	-1	-2.1
	StL-A	0	1	.000	8	1	0	0	0	16^{1}	10	5	1	0	13	2	12.7	2.76	142	.179	.333	0	.000	-0	2	2	0	0.1
	Yr	3	6	.333	35	1	0	0	4	63^{2}	62	35	7	1	38	14	14.3	4.66	74	.266	.371	3	.231	0	-7	-9	-1	-2.0
Total	5	18	16	.529	172	3	0	0	17	326^{2}	336	154	25	9	142	108	13.4	3.97	96	.271	.350	17	.233	3	0	-6	1	-1.6
● **WALLY HOLBOROW**	Holborow, Walter Albert b: 11/30/13, New York, N.Y. d: 7/14/86, Ft.Lauderdale, Fla. BR/TR, 5'11", 187 lbs. Deb: 9/27/44																											
1944	Was-A	0	0	—	1	0	0	0	0	3	0	0	0	0	2	1	6.0	0.00	—	.000	.182	0	—	0	1	1	0	0.1
1945	Was-A	1	1	.500	15	1	1	1	0	31^{1}	20	9	0	0	16	14	10.3	2.30	135	.189	.295	0	.000	-0	4	3	-1	0.1
1948	Phi-A	1	2	.333	5	1	1	0	0	17^{1}	32	12	1	0	7	3	20.3	5.71	75	.421	.470	2	.500	1	-3	-3	1	-0.2
Total	3	2	3	.400	21	2	2	1	0	51^{2}	52	21	1	0	25	18	13.4	3.31	106	.272	.356	2	.333	1	2	1	-0	0.0
● **KEN HOLCOMBE**	Holcombe, Kenneth Edward b: 8/23/18, Burnsville, N.C. BR/TR, 5'11.5", 169 lbs. Deb: 4/27/45																											
1945	NY-A	3	3	.500	23	2	0	0	0	55^{1}	43	19	2	0	27	20	11.4	1.79	194	.226	.323	2	.133	-1	10	10	-0	0.9
1948	Cin-N	0	0	—	2	0	0	0	0	2^{1}	3	2	0	0	0	2	11.6	7.71	51	.300	.300	0	—	0	-1	-1	-0	-0.1
1950	Chi-A	3	10	.231	24	15	5	0	1	96	122	68	10	0	45	37	15.7	4.59	98	.307	.378	5	.156	-2	-0	-1	-0	-0.3
1951	Chi-A	11	12	.478	28	23	12	2	0	159^{1}	142	69	9	1	68	39	11.9	3.78	107	.241	.321	11	.250	1	6	5	2	0.9
1952	Chi-A	0	5	.000	7	7	1	0	0	35	38	24	3	2	18	12	14.9	6.17	59	.286	.379	0	.000	-1	-10	-10	-1	-1.3
	StL-A	0	2	.000	12	1	0	0	0	21	20	10	1	0	9	7	12.4	3.86	101	.263	.341	1	.333	0	-0	0	0	0.1
	Yr	0	7	.000	19	8	1	0	0	56	58	34	4	2	27	19	14.0	5.30	71	.278	.366	1	.077	-1	-10	-9	1	-1.2
1953	Bos-A	1	0	1.000	3	0	0	0	1	6	9	4	0	0	3	1	18.0	6.00	70	.333	.400	0	.000	-0	-1	-1	0	-0.2
Total	6	18	32	.360	99	48	18	2	2	375	377	196	25	3	170	118	13.2	3.98	101	.265	.345	19	.179	-3	3	2	3	-0.0
● **DAVID HOLDRIDGE**	Holdridge, David Allen b: 2/5/69, Wayne, Mich. BR/TR, 6'3", 190 lbs. Deb: 8/8/98																											
1998	Sea-A	0	0	—	7	0	0	0	0	6^{2}	6	3	0	0	4	6	13.5	4.05	115	.231	.333	0	—	0	0	0	-0	0.0
● **FRED HOLDSWORTH**	Holdsworth, Fredrick William b: 5/29/52, Detroit, Mich. BR/TR, 6'1", 190 lbs. Deb: 7/27/72																											
1972	Det-A	0	1	.000	2	2	0	0	0	7	13	10	0	0	2	5	19.3	12.86	25	.419	.455	1	.333	0	-8	-7	-0	-0.8
1973	Det-A	0	1	.000	5	2	0	0	0	14^{2}	13	11	3	0	6	9	11.7	6.75	61	.236	.311	0	—	0	-5	-4	-0	-0.3
1974	Det-A	0	3	.000	8	5	0	0	0	35^{2}	40	20	4	1	14	16	13.9	4.29	89	.286	.355	0	—	0	-3	-2	-1	-0.3
1976	Bal-A	4	1	.800	16	0	0	0	2	39^{2}	24	9	0	0	13	24	8.4	2.04	160	.179	.252	0	—	0	7	6	-0	0.8
1977	Bal-A	0	1	.000	12	0	0	0	0	14^{1}	17	11	0	1	16	4	21.3	6.28	61	.333	.500	0	—	0	-4	-4	-0	-0.3
	Mon-N	3	3	.500	14	6	0	0	0	42^{1}	35	17	6	0	18	21	11.3	3.19	120	.230	.312	0	.000	-1	3	3	0	0.3
1978	Mon-N	0	0	—	6	0	0	0	0	8^{2}	16	10	3	0	8	3	24.9	7.27	49	.381	.480	0	—	0	-4	-4	-0	-0.2
1980	Mil-A	0	0	—	9	0	0	0	0	19^{2}	24	12	2	0	9	12	15.1	4.58	85	.286	.355	0	—	0	-1	-2	0	0.0
Total	7	7	10	.412	72	15	0	0	2	182	182	100	18	2	86	94	13.4	4.40	84	.264	.347	1	.077	-1	-13	-15	-2	-0.8
● **WALTER HOLKE**	Holke, Walter Henry "Union Man" b: 12/25/1892, St.Louis, Mo. d: 10/12/54, St.Louis, Mo. BB/TL, 6'1.5", 185 lbs. Deb: 10/6/14 C♦																											
1923	Phi-N	0	0	—	1	0	0	0	0	0^{1}	1	0	0	0	0	0	27.0	0.00	—	.500	.500	175	.311	0	0	0	0	0.0
● **AL HOLLAND**	Holland, Alfred Willis b: 8/16/52, Roanoke, Va. BR/TL, 5'11", 207 lbs. Deb: 9/5/77																											
1977	Pit-N	0	0	—	2	0	0	0	0	2^{1}	4	2	0	0	0	1	15.4	7.71	52	.400	.400	0	—	0	-1	-1	0	0.0
1979	SF-N	0	0	—	3	0	0	0	0	7	3	0	0	0	5	7	10.3	0.00	—	.125	.276	0	—	0	3	3	-0	0.1
1980	SF-N	5	3	.625	54	0	0	0	7	82^{1}	71	21	2	1	34	65	11.6	1.75	203	.233	.312	1	.200	1	17	17	0	2.1
1981	SF-N	7	5	.583	47	3	0	0	7	100^{2}	87	31	4	2	44	78	11.9	2.41	142	.233	.317	1	.063	-1	12	12	-1	1.3
1982	SF-N	7	3	.700	58	7	0	0	5	129^{2}	115	56	12	1	40	97	10.8	3.33	108	.231	.289	2	.059	-3	4	4	0	0.0
1983	*Phi-N	8	4	.667	68	0	0	0	25	91^{2}	63	26	8	0	30	100	9.1	2.26	158	.188	.255	0	.000	-1	14	14	-2	2.2

YEAR	TM/L	W	L	PCT	G	GS	CG	SH	SV	IP	H	R	HR	HB	BB	SO	RAT	ERA	ERA+	OAV	OOB	BH	AVG	PB	PR	PR+	PD	TPI
1984	Phi-N☆	5	10	.333	68	0	0	0	29	98^1	82	38	14	1	30	61	10.3	3.39	107	.225	.286	0	.000	-1	2	3	-2	0.3
1985	Phi-N	0	1	.000	3	0	0	0	1	4	5	2	0	0	4	1	20.3	4.50	82	.333	.474	0	—	0	-0	-0	0	0.0
	Pit-N	1	3	.250	38	0	0	0	4	58^2	48	22	5	0	17	47	10.0	3.38	106	.227	.285	2	.400	2	1	1	-1	0.2
	Yr	1	4	.200	41	0	0	0	5	62^2	53	24	5	0	21	48	10.6	3.45	104	.235	.300	2	.400	2	1	1	-1	0.2
	Cal-A	0	1	.000	15	0	0	0	0	24^1	17	4	4	0	10	14	10.0	1.48	278	.193	.276	0	—	0	7	7	-0	0.3
1986	NY-A	1	0	1.000	25	1	0	0	0	40^2	44	29	5	0	9	37	11.7	5.09	80	.268	.306	0	—	0	-4	-5	-1	-0.3
1987	NY-A	0	0	—	3	0	0	0	0	6^1	9	10	1	0	9	5	25.6	14.21	31	.321	.486	0	—	0	-7	-7	0	-0.3
Total	10	34	30	.531	384	11	0	0	78	646	548	241	55	5	232	513	10.9	2.98	122	.227	.296	6	.083	-2	49	47	-6	5.9
● **MUL HOLLAND**	Holland, Howard Arthur b: 1/6/03, Franklin, Va. d: 2/16/69, Winchester, Va. BR/TR, 6′4″, 185 lbs. Deb: 5/25/26																											
1926	Cin-N	0	0	—	3	0	0	0	0	6^2	3	1	0	0	5	0	10.8	1.35	273	.136	.296	1	.500	0	2	2	1	0.2
1927	NY-N	1	0	1.000	2	0	0	0	0	2	0	0	0	0	3	0	13.5	0.00	—	.000	.333	0	—	0	1	1	-0	0.2
1929	StL-N	0	1	.000	8	0	0	0	0	14^1	13	15	3	1	7	5	13.2	9.42	50	.232	.328	1	.250	0	-7	-8	-0	-0.4
Total	3	1	1	.500	13	0	0	0	0	23	16	16	3	1	15	5	12.5	6.26	69	.190	.320	2	.333	1	-5	-5	0	0.0
● **BILL HOLLAND**	Holland, William David "Dutch" b: 6/4/15, Varina, N.C. d: 4/5/97, Goldsboro, N.C. BL/TL, 6′1″, 190 lbs. Deb: 9/17/39																											
1939	Was-A	0	1	.000	3	0	0	0	0	4	6	5	1	0	5	2	24.8	11.25	39	.400	.550	0	—	0	-3	-3	0	-0.5
● **ED HOLLEY**	Holley, Edward Edgar b: 7/23/1899, Benton, Ky. d: 10/26/86, Paducah, Ky. BR/TR, 6′1.5″, 195 lbs. Deb: 5/24/28																											
1928	Chi-N	0	0	—	13	1	0	0	0	31	31	15	1	2	16	10	14.2	3.77	102	.265	.363	0	.000	-0	1	0	-1	-0.1
1932	Phi-N	11	14	.440	34	30	16	2	0	228	247	114	15	6	55	87	12.2	3.95	112	.273	.319	12	.132	-6	-2	10	-2	0.3
1933	Phi-N	13	15	.464	30	28	12	3	0	206^2	219	93	18	13	62	56	12.8	3.53	108	.273	.335	12	.162	-2	-4	6	-3	0.3
1934	Phi-N	1	8	.111	15	13	2	0	0	72^2	85	62	10	4	31	14	14.9	7.18	66	.294	.370	5	.208	-1	-25	-17	-1	-1.9
	Pit-N	0	3	.000	5	4	0	0	0	9^1	20	16	1	2	6	2	27.0	15.43	27	.426	.509	2	1.000	2	-12	-12	0	-1.7
	Yr	1	11	.083	20	17	2	0	0	82	105	78	11	6	37	16	16.2	8.12	57	.313	.391	7	.269	1	-37	-28	-1	-3.6
Total	4	25	40	.385	97	76	30	5	0	547^2	602	300	45	27	170	169	13.1	4.40	95	.279	.339	31	.158	-8	-42	-11	-6	-3.1
● **BUG HOLLIDAY**	Holliday, James Wear b: 2/8/1867, St.Louis, Mo. d: 2/15/10, Cincinnati, Ohio BR/TR, 5′11″, 151 lbs. Deb: 4/17/1889 U♦																											
1892	Cin-N	0	0	—	1	0	0	0	0	4	13	5	0	0	1	0	31.5	11.25	29	.520	.538	177	.294	0	-4	-4	0	-0.1
1896	Cin-N	0	0	—	1	0	0	0	0	1	4	3	0	1	2	0	63.0	0.00	—	.571	.700	27	.321	0	0	0	-0	0.0
Total	2	0	0	—	2	0	0	0	0	5	17	8	0	1	3	0	37.8	9.00	39	.531	.583	1141	.312	1	-3	-3	-0	-0.1
● **CARL HOLLING**	Holling, Carl b: 7/9/1896, Dana, Cal. d: 7/18/62, Santa Rosa, Cal. BR/TR, 6′1″, 172 lbs. Deb: 4/19/21																											
1921	Det-A	3	7	.300	35	11	4	0	4	136	162	95	8	4	58	38	14.8	4.30	99	.305	.378	13	.271	1	-0	-0	2	0.2
1922	Det-A	1	1	.500	5	1	0	0	0	9^1	21	16	1	2	5	2	27.0	15.43	25	.525	.596	0	.000	-0	-12	-12	0	-1.9
Total	2	4	8	.333	40	12	4	0	4	145^1	183	111	9	6	63	40	15.6	5.02	85	.320	.394	13	.260	1	-12	-13	2	-1.7
● **AL HOLLINGSWORTH**	Hollingsworth, Albert Wayne "Boots" b: 2/25/08, St.Louis, Mo. d: 4/28/96, Austin, Tex. BL/TL, 6′, 174 lbs. Deb: 4/16/35 C																											
1935	Cin-N	6	13	.316	38	22	8	0	0	173^1	165	90	5	1	76	89	12.6	3.89	102	.243	.321	8	.148	-2	2	2	1	0.0
1936	Cin-N	9	10	.474	29	25	9	0	0	184	204	97	4	5	66	76	13.5	4.16	92	.281	.345	23	.315	7	-3	-7	-2	-0.1
1937	Cin-N	9	15	.375	43	24	11	1	5	202^1	224	108	8	2	73	74	13.3	3.91	95	.278	.339	19	.250	3	0	-4	1	-0.1
1938	Cin-N	2	2	.500	9	4	1	0	0	34	43	28	2	0	12	13	14.6	7.15	51	.307	.362	3	.250	1	-13	-14	0	-1.3
	Phi-N	5	16	.238	24	21	11	1	0	174^1	177	89	4	0	77	80	13.1	3.82	102	.264	.340	15	.224	-0	-1	1	-2	-0.1
	Yr	7	18	.280	33	25	12	1	0	208^1	220	117	6	0	89	93	13.3	4.36	88	.272	.344	18	.228	1	-13	-12	-2	-1.4
1939	Phi-N	1	9	.100	15	10	3	0	0	60	78	48	2	0	27	24	15.8	5.85	69	.317	.385	2	.100	-1	-13	-12	-0	-1.8
	Bro-N	1	2	.333	8	5	1	0	0	27^1	33	17	1	1	11	11	14.8	5.27	76	.311	.381	1	.125	-1	-4	-4	1	-0.3
	Yr	2	11	.154	23	15	4	0	0	87^1	111	65	3	1	38	35	15.5	5.67	71	.315	.384	3	.107	-2	-17	-16	1	-2.1
1940	Was-A	1	0	1.000	3	2	0	0	0	18	18	12	0	0	11	7	14.5	5.50	76	.261	.363	1	.167	0	-2	-3	1	0.0
1942	StL-A	10	6	.625	33	18	7	1	4	161	173	70	4	2	52	60	12.7	2.96	125	.272	.329	10	.179	0	12	13	0	1.3
1943	StL-A	6	13	.316	35	20	9	1	3	154	169	81	7	2	51	63	13.0	4.21	79	.281	.339	7	.140	-1	-16	-15	-1	-2.0
1944	*StL-A	5	7	.417	26	10	3	2	1	92^2	108	51	3	1	37	22	14.2	4.47	81	.291	.357	2	.071	-2	-11	-9	-1	-1.3
1945	StL-A	12	9	.571	26	22	15	1	1	173^1	164	60	4	0	68	64	12.0	2.70	130	.251	.322	12	.197	1	13	15	2	2.1
1946	StL-A	0	0	—	5	0	0	0	0	11	23	8	1	0	4	3	22.1	6.55	57	.411	.450	0	.000	-0	-4	-3	-1	-0.2
	Chi-A	3	2	.600	21	2	0	0	1	55	63	29	2	0	22	22	13.9	4.58	74	.288	.353	0	.000	-1	-7	-7	-0	-0.8
	Yr	3	2	.600	26	2	0	0	1	66	86	37	3	0	26	25	15.3	4.91	71	.313	.372	0	.000	-1	-10	-11	-1	-1.0
Total	11	70	104	.402	315	185	78	7	15	1520^1	1642	788	47	14	587	608	13.3	3.99	93	.275	.341	103	.196	3	-44	-44	-2	-4.6
● **BONNIE HOLLINGSWORTH**	Hollingsworth, John Burnette b: 12/26/1895, Jacksboro, Tenn. d: 1/4/90, Knoxville, Tenn. BR/TR, 5′10″, 170 lbs. Deb: 5/30/22																											
1922	Pit-N	0	0	—	9	0	0	0	0	13^2	17	14	0	1	8	7	17.1	7.90	52	.315	.413	0	—	0	-6	-6	-0	-0.3
1923	Was-A	3	7	.300	17	8	1	0	0	72^2	72	43	3	3	50	26	15.5	4.09	92	.272	.393	2	.091	-1	-1	-3	-1	-0.5
1924	Bro-N	1	0	1.000	3	1	1	0	0	8^2	8	6	0	0	10	7	18.7	6.23	60	.267	.450	0	.000	-1	-2	-2	0	-0.3
1928	Bos-N	0	2	.000	7	2	0	0	0	22^1	30	19	2	0	13	10	17.3	5.24	75	.341	.426	1	.167	-0	-3	-3	0	-0.2
Total	4	4	9	.308	36	11	2	0	0	117^1	127	82	5	4	81	50	16.3	4.91	78	.291	.406	3	.097	-2	-12	-15	-1	-1.3
● **JESSIE HOLLINS**	Hollins, Jessie Edward b: 1/27/70, Conroe, Tex. BR/TR, 6′3″, 190 lbs. Deb: 9/19/92																											
1992	Chi-N	0	0	—	4	0	0	0	0	4^2	8	7	1	0	5	0	25.1	13.50	27	.400	.520	0	—	0	-5	-5	-0	-0.3
● **JOHN HOLLISON**	Hollison, John Henry "Swede" b: 5/3/1870, Chicago, Ill. d: 8/19/69, Chicago, Ill. BR/TL, 5′8″, 162 lbs. Deb: 8/13/1892																											
1892	Chi-N	0	0	—	1	0	0	0	0	4	1	1	1	0	0	2	2.3	2.25	148	.077	.077	0	.000	-0	0	0	0	0.0
● **BOBO HOLLOMAN**	Holloman, Alva Lee b: 3/7/25, Thomaston, Ga. d: 5/1/87, Athens, Ga. BR/TR, 6′2″, 207 lbs. Deb: 4/18/53																											
1953	StL-A	3	7	.300	22	10	1	1	0	65^1	69	41	2	1	50	25	16.5	5.23	80	.275	.397	2	.105	-2	-9	-7	-0	-1.1
● **JIM HOLLOWAY**	Holloway, James Madison b: 9/22/08, Plaquemine, La. d: 4/15/97, Baton Rouge, La. BR/TR, 6′1″, 165 lbs. Deb: 5/17/29																											
1929	Phi-N	0	0	—	3	0	0	0	0	4^2	10	7	2	0	5	1	28.9	13.50	38	.455	.556	1	1.000	0	-5	-4	-0	-0.1
● **KEN HOLLOWAY**	Holloway, Kenneth Eugene (b: Kenneth Eugene Hollaway) b: 8/8/1897, Barwick, Ga. d: 9/25/68, Thomasville, Ga. BR/TR, 6′, 185 lbs. Deb: 8/27/22																											
1922	Det-A	0	0	—	1	0	0	0	0	1	1	1	0	0	0	1	9.0	0.00	—	.250	.250	0	—	0	0	0	0	0.0
1923	Det-A	11	10	.524	42	24	7	1	1	194	232	117	12	10	75	55	14.7	4.45	87	.302	.372	8	.123	-5	-10	-13	1	-1.6
1924	Det-A	14	6	.700	49	13	5	0	3	181^1	209	105	6	6	61	46	13.7	4.07	101	.299	.361	11	.190	-1	3	1	2	0.2
1925	Det-A	13	4	.765	38	14	6	0	2	157^2	170	90	8	2	67	29	13.6	4.62	93	.282	.356	11	.229	-0	-4	-6	-2	-0.7
1926	Det-A	4	6	.400	36	12	3	0	2	139	192	94	2	8	42	43	15.7	5.12	79	.343	.397	11	.239	0	-17	-16	0	-1.0
1927	Det-A	11	12	.478	36	23	11	1	6	183^1	210	103	10	4	61	36	13.5	4.07	103	.299	.359	8	.129	-5	1	3	2	0.0
1928	Det-A	4	8	.333	30	11	5	0	2	120^1	137	67	2	5	32	32	13.0	4.34	95	.291	.343	4	.121	-2	-4	-3	1	-0.4
1929	Cle-A	6	5	.545	25	11	6	2	0	119	118	52	2	2	37	32	11.9	3.03	147	.264	.323	7	.171	-2	16	18	-2	1.1
1930	Cle-A	1	1	.500	12	2	0	0	2	30	49	32	5	0	14	8	18.9	8.40	57	.374	.434	0	.000	-2	-13	-11	1	-0.9
	NY-A	0	0	—	16	0	0	0	0	34^1	52	23	3	0	8	11	15.7	5.24	82	.374	.408	3	.231	-0	-2	-4	-0	-0.2
	Yr	1	1	.500	28	2	0	0	2	64^1	101	55	8	0	22	19	17.2	6.72	68	.374	.421	3	.120	-3	-15	-16	1	-1.1
Total	9	64	52	.552	285	110	43	4	18	1160	1370	684	50	37	397	293	14.0	4.40	95	.303	.364	63	.167	-18	-29	-30	4	-3.5
● **JEFF HOLLY**	Holly, Jeffrey Owen b: 3/1/53, San Pedro, Cal. BL/TL, 6′5″, 210 lbs. Deb: 5/1/77																											
1977	Min-A	2	3	.400	18	5	0	0	0	48^1	57	37	8	1	12	32	13.0	6.89	58	.300	.345	0	—	0	-15	-16	-1	-1.5
1978	Min-A	1	1	.500	15	1	0	0	0	35^1	28	15	1	0	18	12	11.7	3.57	108	.222	.319	0	—	0	1	1	0	0.1
1979	Min-A	0	0	—	6	0	0	0	0	6^1	10	7	0	0	3	5	18.5	7.11	62	.385	.448	0	—	0	-2	-2	0	-0.1
Total	3	3	4	.429	39	6	0	0	0	90	95	59	9	1	33	49	12.9	5.60	71	.278	.343	0	—	0	-16	-16	-0	-1.5
● **BRAD HOLMAN**	Holman, Bradley Thomas b: 2/9/68, Kansas City, Mo. BR/TR, 6′5″, 200 lbs. Deb: 7/4/93 F																											
1993	Sea-A	1	3	.250	19	0	0	0	3	36^1	27	17	1	5	16	17	11.9	3.72	119	.208	.318	0	—	0	3	3	-1	0.3
● **BRIAN HOLMAN**	Holman, Brian Scott b: 1/25/65, Denver, Colo. BR/TR, 6′4″, 185 lbs. Deb: 6/25/88 F																											
1988	Mon-N	4	8	.333	18	16	1	1	0	100^1	101	39	3	0	34	58	12.1	3.23	112	.264	.324	3	.107	-1	2	4	-1	0.2

YEAR	TM/L	W	L	PCT	G	GS	CG	SH	SV	IP	H	R	HR	HB	BB	SO	RAT	ERA	ERA+	OAV	OOB	BH	AVG	PB	PR	PR+	PD	TPI
1989	Mon-N	1	2	.333	10	3	0	0	0	31^2	34	18	2	1	15	23	14.2	4.83	73	.270	.352	1	.125	-0	-5	-5	-0	-0.5
	Sea-A	8	10	.444	23	22	6	2	0	159^2	160	68	9	6	62	82	12.9	3.44	117	.261	.335	0	—	0	8	10	1	1.2
1990	Sea-A	11	11	.500	28	28	3	0	0	189^2	188	92	17	6	66	121	12.3	4.03	98	.260	.327	0	.000	-0	-2	-1	-1	-0.3
1991	Sea-A	13	14	.481	30	30	5	3	0	195^1	199	86	16	10	77	108	13.2	3.69	112	.268	.345	0	—	0	9	9	2	1.4
Total	4	37	45	.451	109	99	15	6	0	676^2	682	303	47	23	254	392	12.8	3.71	107	.263	.335	4	.108	-1	12	18	-0	2.0
● SCOTT HOLMAN	Holman, Randy Scott b: 9/18/58, Santa Paula, Cal. BR/TR, 6'1", 190 lbs. Deb: 9/20/80																											
1980	NY-N	0	0	—	4	0	0	0	0	7	6	2	0	0	1	3	9.0	1.29	277	.250	.280	0	—	0	2	2	-0	0.1
1982	NY-N	2	1	.667	4	4	1	0	0	26^2	23	10	2	0	7	11	10.1	2.36	154	.232	.283	2	.222	0	4	4	1	0.5
1983	NY-N	1	7	.125	35	10	0	0	0	101	90	48	7	1	52	44	12.7	3.74	97	.242	.336	5	.217	0	-1	-1	2	0.2
Total	3	3	8	.273	43	14	1	0	0	134^2	119	60	9	1	60	58	12.0	3.34	109	.240	.324	7	.219	1	4	4	2	0.8
● SHAWN HOLMAN	Holman, Shawn Leroy b: 11/10/64, Sewickley, Pa. BR/TR, 6'2", 185 lbs. Deb: 9/5/89																											
1989	Det-A	0	0	—	5	0	0	0	0	10	8	2	0	0	11	9	17.1	1.80	212	.211	.388	0	—	0	2	2	-0	0.1
● DARREN HOLMES	Holmes, Darren Lee b: 4/25/66, Asheville, N.C. BR/TR, 6', 199 lbs. Deb: 9/1/90																											
1990	LA-N	0	1	.000	14	0	0	0	0	17^1	15	10	1	0	11	19	13.5	5.19	71	.238	.351	0	—	0	-3	-3	-0	-0.2
1991	Mil-A	1	4	.200	40	0	0	0	3	76^1	90	43	6	1	27	59	13.9	4.72	84	.295	.354	0	—	0	-5	-6	1	-0.3
1992	Mil-A	4	4	.500	41	0	0	0	6	42^1	35	12	1	2	11	31	10.2	2.55	151	.224	.284	0	—	0	7	6	0	1.3
1993	Col-N	3	3	.500	62	0	0	0	25	66^2	56	31	6	2	20	60	10.5	4.05	118	.222	.285	0	—	0	-0	5	-0	0.6
1994	Col-N	0	3	.000	29	0	0	0	3	28^1	35	25	5	1	24	33	19.1	6.35	78	.313	.438	0	.000	-0	-7	-4	-0	-0.4
1995	*Col-N	6	1	.857	68	0	0	0	14	66^2	59	26	3	1	28	61	11.9	3.24	166	.237	.317	0	.000	-0	7	12	1	1.7
1996	Col-N	5	4	.556	62	0	0	0	1	77	78	41	8	1	28	73	12.5	3.97	131	.259	.324	0	.000	-0	2	9	-1	0.9
1997	Col-N	9	2	.818	42	6	0	0	3	89^1	113	58	12	0	36	70	15.0	5.34	97	.314	.376	3	.158	-0	-11	-1	1	-0.1
1998	NY-A	0	3	.000	34	0	0	0	2	51^1	53	19	4	2	14	31	12.1	3.33	132	.270	.325	0	—	0	8	6	-0	0.3
1999	*Ari-N	4	3	.571	44	0	0	0	0	48^2	50	21	3	1	25	35	14.1	3.70	124	.262	.350	0	.000	-0	5	5	0	0.6
2000	Ari-N	0	0	—	4	0	0	0	1	2^1	5	3	0	0	1	2	23.1	11.57	40	.455	.500	0	—	0	-2	-2	0	-0.1
	StL-N	0	1	.000	5	0	0	0	0	8^1	12	9	2	1	3	5	17.3	9.72	48	.364	.432	0	.000	-0	-5	-5	-0	-0.5
	Bal-A	0	0	—	5	0	0	0	0	4^2	13	13	3	0	5	6	34.7	25.07	19	.481	.563	0	—	0	-10	-11	-0	-0.5
	Ari-N	0	0	—	4	0	0	0	0	4	7	3	1	1	0	3	18.0	6.75	68	.389	.421	0	—	0	-1	-1	0	0.0
	Yr	0	1	.000	13	0	0	0	1	14^2	24	15	3	2	4	10	18.4	9.20	50	.387	.441	0	.000	-0	-8	-8	-0	-0.6
Total	11	32	29	.525	454	6	0	0	58	583^1	621	314	55	13	233	488	13.4	4.47	106	.273	.344	3	.115	-1	-16	15	1	3.3
● CHICK HOLMES	Holmes, Elwood Marter b: 3/22/1896, Beverly, N.J. d: 4/15/54, Camden, N.J. TR, Deb: 6/27/18																											
1918	Phi-A	0	0	—	2	0	0	0	0	2	4	5	0	1	1	0	27.0	13.50	22	.400	.500	0	—	0	-2	-2	-0	-0.1
● JIM HOLMES	Holmes, James Scott b: 8/2/1882, Lawrenceburg, Ky. d: 3/10/60, Jacksonville, Fla. Deb: 9/8/06																											
1906	Phi-A	0	1	.000	3	1	0	0	0	9	10	11	0	1	8	1	19.0	4.00	68	.286	.432	3	.600	1	-1	-1	0	0.0
1908	Bro-N	1	4	.200	13	1	1	0	0	40	37	19	0	3	20	10	13.5	3.37	69	.270	.375	1	.077	-1	-4	-5	-2	-0.9
Total	2	1	5	.167	16	2	1	0	0	49	47	30	0	4	28	11	14.5	3.49	69	.273	.387	4	.222	0	-6	-6	-2	-0.9
● DUCKY HOLMES	Holmes, James William b: 1/28/1869, Des Moines, Iowa d: 8/6/32, Truro, Iowa BL/TR, 5'6", 170 lbs. Deb: 8/8/1895 ♦																											
1895	Lou-N	1	0	1.000	2	1	1	0	0	14	16	11	1	1	4	0	13.5	5.79	80	.281	.339	60	.373	1	-2	-2	0	0.0
1896	Lou-N	0	1	.000	2	1	0	0	0	12	26	23	0	0	8	3	25.5	7.50	58	.433	.500	38	.270	0	-4	-4	0	-0.2
Total	2	1	1	.500	4	2	1	0	0	26	42	34	1	1	12	3	19.0	6.58	68	.359	.423	1014	.281	1	-6	-6	0	-0.2
● HERM HOLSHOUSER	Holshouser, Herman Alexander b: 1/20/07, Rockwell, N.C. d: 7/26/94, Concord, N.C. BR/TR, 6', 170 lbs. Deb: 4/15/30																											
1930	StL-A	0	1	.000	25	1	0	0	1	62^1	103	63	8	3	28	37	19.3	7.80	63	.376	.439	2	.125	-1	-22	-19	-0	-0.9
● CHRIS HOLT	Holt, Christopher Michael b: 9/18/71, Dallas, Tex. BR/TR, 6'4", 205 lbs. Deb: 9/1/96																											
1996	Hou-N	0	1	.000	4	0	0	0	0	4^2	5	3	0	0	3	0	15.4	5.79	67	.263	.364	0	.000	-0	-1	-1	0	-0.2
1997	Hou-N	8	12	.400	33	32	0	0	0	209^2	211	98	17	8	61	95	12.0	3.52	114	.263	.321	6	.090	-3	16	12	0	0.7
1999	*Hou-N	5	13	.278	32	26	0	0	1	164	193	92	12	8	57	115	14.2	4.66	95	.303	.367	3	.067	-2	-2	-5	-1	-0.7
2000	Hou-N	8	16	.333	34	32	3	1	0	207	247	131	22	8	75	136	14.3	5.35	91	.303	.368	6	.100	-2	-16	-10	-0	-1.2
Total	4	21	42	.333	103	90	3	1	1	585^1	656	324	51	24	196	346	13.5	4.51	98	.289	.351	15	.087	-8	-3	-5	-1	-1.4
● VERN HOLTGRAVE	Holtgrave, Lavern George "Woody" b: 10/18/42, Aviston, Ill. BR/TR, 6'1", 183 lbs. Deb: 9/26/65																											
1965	Det-A	0	0	—	1	0	0	0	0	3	4	2	0	0	2	2	18.0	6.00	58	.308	.400	0	—	0	-1	-1	-0	-0.1
● BRIAN HOLTON	Holton, Brian John b: 11/29/59, McKeesport, Pa. BR/TR, 6', 193 lbs. Deb: 9/9/85																											
1985	LA-N	1	1	.500	3	0	0	0	0	4	9	7	0	0	1	1	22.5	9.00	39	.450	.476	0	—	0	-2	-3	0	-0.5
1986	LA-N	2	3	.400	12	3	0	0	0	24^1	28	13	1	1	6	24	12.9	4.44	78	.292	.340	0	.000	-1	-2	-3	0	-0.6
1987	LA-N	3	2	.600	53	1	0	0	2	83^1	87	39	11	0	32	58	12.9	3.89	102	.269	.335	1	.200	0	2	1	1	0.1
1988	*LA-N	7	3	.700	45	0	0	0	1	84^2	69	19	1	1	26	49	10.2	1.70	196	.228	.292	0	.000	-1	16	16	-0	1.8
1989	Bal-A	5	7	.417	39	12	0	0	0	116^1	140	63	11	1	39	51	13.9	4.02	94	.300	.355	0	—	0	-2	-3	-0	-0.3
1990	Bal-A	2	3	.400	33	0	0	0	0	58	68	31	7	0	21	27	13.8	4.50	85	.292	.350	0	—	0	-4	-5	1	-0.3
Total	6	20	19	.513	185	16	0	0	3	370^2	401	172	31	3	125	210	12.8	3.62	102	.278	.337	1	.050	-1	9	4	1	0.2
● MIKE HOLTZ	Holtz, Michael James b: 10/10/72, Arlington, Va. BL/TL, 5'9", 172 lbs. Deb: 7/11/96																											
1996	Cal-A	3	3	.500	30	0	0	0	0	29^1	21	11	1	3	19	31	13.2	2.45	204	.204	.344	0	—	0	8	8	0	1.5
1997	Ana-A	3	4	.429	66	0	0	0	2	43^1	38	21	7	2	15	40	11.4	3.32	138	.228	.299	0	.000	-0	6	6	1	0.9
1998	Ana-A	2	2	.500	53	0	0	0	1	30^1	38	16	0	1	15	29	16.0	4.75	99	.322	.403	0	—	0	-0	-0	-1	-0.1
1999	Ana-A	2	3	.400	28	0	0	0	0	22^1	26	20	3	2	15	17	17.3	8.06	60	.295	.410	0	—	0	-8	-8	1	-1.4
2000	Ana-A	3	4	.500	61	0	0	0	0	41	37	26	4	2	18	40	12.5	5.05	98	.248	.337	0	—	0	-1	-0	1	0.0
Total	5	13	15	.464	238	0	0	0	3	166^1	160	94	15	10	82	157	13.6	4.49	107	.256	.351	0	.000	-0	6	6	2	0.9
● KEN HOLTZMAN	Holtzman, Kenneth Dale b: 11/3/45, St.Louis, Mo. BR/TL, 6'2", 175 lbs. Deb: 9/4/65																											
1965	Chi-N	0	0	—	3	0	0	0	0	4	2	4	1	0	3	3	11.3	2.25	164	.143	.294	0	—	0	1	1	0	0.0
1966	Chi-N	11	16	.407	34	33	9	0	0	220^2	194	104	27	4	68	171	10.8	3.79	97	.235	.296	9	.123	-3	-5	-3	-2	-0.8
1967	Chi-N	9	0	1.000	12	12	3	0	0	92^2	76	31	11	2	44	62	11.8	2.53	140	.222	.314	7	.200	1	9	10	0	1.1
1968	Chi-N	11	14	.440	34	32	6	3	1	215	201	89	17	6	76	151	11.8	3.35	94	.248	.317	10	.125	-2	-9	-4	1	-0.6
1969	Chi-N	17	13	.567	39	39	12	6	0	261^1	248	117	18	5	93	176	11.9	3.58	112	.247	.314	15	.150	-1	0	12	-1	1.0
1970	Chi-N	17	11	.607	39	38	15	1	0	287^2	271	125	30	3	94	202	11.5	3.38	133	.248	.309	21	.200	1	22	32	0	3.1
1971	Chi-N	9	15	.375	30	29	9	3	0	195	213	108	18	2	64	143	12.9	4.48	88	.276	.333	9	.130	-1	-22	-10	-1	-1.4
1972	*Oak-A☆	19	11	.633	39	37	16	4	0	265^1	232	83	23	4	52	134	9.8	2.51	114	.236	.278	16	.178	2	17	11	0	1.5
1973	*Oak-A★	21	13	.618	40	40	16	4	0	297^1	275	109	22	4	66	157	10.4	2.97	120	.243	.287	0	—	0	28	21	-1	2.2
1974	*Oak-A	19	17	.528	39	38	9	3	0	255^1	273	111	14	3	51	117	11.5	3.07	108	.272	.309	0	—	0	16	8	0	1.1
1975	*Oak-A	18	14	.563	39	38	13	2	0	266^1	217	111	16	7	108	122	11.2	3.14	116	.222	.303	0	.000	-0	19	15	3	2.0
1976	Bal-A	5	4	.556	13	13	6	1	0	97^2	100	34	4	1	35	25	12.5	2.86	115	.271	.336	0	—	0	7	5	1	0.6
	NY-A	9	7	.563	21	21	10	2	0	149	165	74	14	0	35	41	12.1	4.17	82	.283	.323	0	—	0	-11	-13	-1	-1.3
	Yr	14	11	.560	34	34	16	3	0	246^2	265	108	18	1	70	66	12.3	3.65	92	.278	.328	0	—	0	-3	-8	1	-0.7
1977	NY-A	2	3	.400	18	11	0	0	0	71^2	105	55	7	1	24	14	16.3	5.78	68	.362	.413	0	—	0	-14	-15	2	-0.7
1978	NY-A	1	0	1.000	5	3	0	0	0	17^2	21	8	2	0	9	3	15.3	4.08	89	.313	.395	0	—	0	-1	-1	1	0.0
	Chi-N	0	3	.000	23	6	0	0	2	53	61	40	10	1	35	36	16.5	6.11	66	.286	.390	2	.200	0	-15	-11	-0	-0.7
1979	Chi-N	6	9	.400	23	20	3	2	0	117^2	133	70	15	6	53	44	14.7	4.59	90	.287	.368	10	.233	2	-11	-5	-2	-0.6
Total	15	174	150	.537	451	410	127	31	3	2867^1	2787	1273	249	49	910	1601	11.8	3.49	105	.255	.315	99	.163	-1	32	50	1	6.5
● MARK HOLZEMER	Holzemer, Mark Harold b: 8/20/69, Littleton, Colo. BL/TL, 6', 165 lbs. Deb: 8/21/93																											
1993	Cal-A	0	3	.000	5	4	0	0	0	23^1	34	24	2	3	13	10	19.3	8.87	51	.340	.431	0	—	0	-12	-11	0	-1.1
1995	Cal-A	0	1	.000	12	0	0	0	0	8^1	11	6	1	1	7	5	20.5	5.40	87	.306	.432	0	—	0	-1	-1	-1	-0.1
1996	Cal-A	1	0	1.000	25	0	0	0	0	24^2	35	28	7	3	8	20	16.8	8.76	57	.327	.390	0	—	0	-10	-10	1	-0.4
1997	Sea-A	0	0	—	14	0	0	0	1	9	9	6	0	0	8	7	17.0	6.00	75	.250	.386	0	—	0	-1	-2	1	0.0

YEAR TM/L	W	L	PCT	G	GS	CG	SH	SV	IP	H	R	HR	HB	BB	SO	RAT	ERA	ERA+	OAV	OOB	BH	AVG	PB	PR	PR+	PD	TPI
1998 Oak-A	1	0	1.000	13	0	0	0	0	9^2	13	6	1	1	3	3	15.8	5.59	82	.333	.395	0	—	0	-1	-1	-0	-0.1
2000 Phi-N	0	1	.000	25	0	0	0	0	25^2	36	23	4	1	8	19	15.8	7.71	61	.336	.388	0	.000	-0	-9	-8	-0	-0.4
Total 6	2	5	.286	94	4	0	0	1	100^2	138	93	15	9	47	64	17.3	7.69	61	.325	.403	0	.000	-0	-34	-33	0	-2.1

● RICK HONEYCUTT Honeycutt, Frederick Wayne b: 6/29/54, Chattanooga, Tenn. BL/TL, 5'11", 190 lbs. Deb: 8/24/77

YEAR TM/L	W	L	PCT	G	GS	CG	SH	SV	IP	H	R	HR	HB	BB	SO	RAT	ERA	ERA+	OAV	OOB	BH	AVG	PB	PR	PR+	PD	TPI
1977 Sea-A	0	1	.000	10	3	0	0	0	29	26	16	7	3	11	17	12.4	4.34	95	.239	.325	0	—	0	-1	-1	-1	-0.1
1978 Sea-A	5	11	.313	26	24	4	1	0	134^1	150	81	12	3	49	50	13.5	4.89	78	.285	.349	0	—	0	-17	-16	1	-1.5
1979 Sea-A	11	12	.478	33	28	8	1	0	194	201	103	22	6	67	83	12.7	4.04	108	.268	.333	0	—	0	4	7	-1	0.6
1980 Sea-A☆	10	17	.370	30	30	9	1	0	203^1	221	99	22	3	60	79	12.6	3.94	105	.280	.333	0	—	0	2	4	-0	0.5
1981 Tex-A	11	6	.647	20	20	8	2	0	127^2	120	49	12	0	17	40	9.7	3.31	105	.246	.272	0	—	0	5	2	1	0.4
1982 Tex-A	5	17	.227	30	26	4	1	0	164	201	103	20	3	54	64	14.2	5.27	74	.305	.360	0	—	0	-22	-27	1	-2.9
1983 Tex-A★	14	8	.636	25	25	5	2	0	174^2	168	59	9	6	37	56	10.9	**2.42**	**166**	.262	.308	0	—	0	**32**	31	3	**4.2**
*LA-N	2	3	.400	9	7	1	0	0	39	46	26	6	2	13	18	14.1	5.77	62	.297	.359	1	.083	-1	-9	-9	2	-1.0
1984 LA-N	10	9	.526	29	28	6	2	0	183^2	180	72	11	2	51	75	11.4	2.84	124	.258	.310	8	.143	-0	15	14	2	1.7
1985 *LA-N	8	12	.400	31	25	1	0	1	142	141	71	9	1	49	67	12.1	3.42	102	.261	.323	5	.132	0	3	1	3	0.4
1986 LA-N	11	9	.550	32	28	0	0	0	171	164	71	9	3	45	100	11.2	3.32	104	.249	.300	3	.070	0	8	3	2	0.5
1987 LA-N	2	12	.143	27	20	1	1	0	115^2	133	74	10	2	45	92	14.0	4.59	87	.278	.343	7	.233	2	-6	-8	-0	-0.7
Oak-A	1	4	.200	7	4	0	0	0	23^2	25	17	3	2	9	10	13.7	5.32	78	.275	.353	0	—	0	-2	-3	-0	-0.6
1988 *Oak-A	3	2	.600	55	0	0	0	7	79^2	74	36	6	3	25	47	11.5	3.50	108	.253	.318	0	—	0	4	3	1	0.3
1989 *Oak-A	2	2	.500	64	0	0	0	12	76^2	56	26	5	1	26	52	9.7	2.35	157	.207	.279	0	—	0	13	12	1	1.0
1990 *Oak-A	2	2	.500	63	0	0	0	7	63^1	46	23	2	1	22	38	9.8	2.70	138	.204	.278	0	.000	-0	9	8	1	0.6
1991 Oak-A	2	4	.333	43	0	0	0	0	37^2	37	16	3	2	20	26	14.1	3.58	107	.261	.360	0	—	0	2	1	0	0.2
1992 *Oak-A	1	4	.200	54	0	0	0	3	39	41	19	2	3	10	32	12.5	3.69	102	.272	.329	0	—	0	1	0	-1	0.0
1993 Oak-A	1	4	.200	52	0	0	0	1	41^2	30	18	2	1	20	21	11.0	2.81	146	.211	.313	0	—	0	7	6	-0	0.7
1994 Tex-A	1	2	.333	42	0	0	0	1	25	37	21	4	2	9	18	17.3	7.20	67	.349	.410	0	—	0	-7	-7	1	-0.6
1995 Oak-A	5	1	.833	49	0	0	0	2	44^2	37	13	5	1	9	21	9.5	2.42	185	.231	.276	0	—	0	11	11	-0	1.3
NY-A	0	0	—	3	0	0	0	0	1	2	3	1	0	1	0	27.0	27.00	17	.400	.500	0	—	0	-2	-3	0	-0.1
Yr	5	1	.833	52	0	0	0	2	45^2	39	16	6	1	10	21	9.9	2.96	151	.236	.284	0	—	0	9	8	-0	1.2
1996 *StL-N	2	1	.667	61	0	0	0	4	47^1	42	15	3	0	7	30	9.3	2.85	147	.240	.269	0	.000	1	7	7	1	0.6
1997 StL-N	0	0	—	2	0	0	0	0	2	5	3	0	0	1	2	27.0	13.50	31	.500	.545	0	—	0	-2	-2	-0	-0.1
Total 21	109	143	.433	797	268	47	11	38	2160	2183	1034	185	50	657	1038	12.0	3.72	104	.264	.322	24	.132	2	56	35	15	5.4

● DON HOOD Hood, Donald Harris b: 10/16/49, Florence, S.C. BL/TL, 6'2", 180 lbs. Deb: 7/16/73

YEAR TM/L	W	L	PCT	G	GS	CG	SH	SV	IP	H	R	HR	HB	BB	SO	RAT	ERA	ERA+	OAV	OOB	BH	AVG	PB	PR	PR+	PD	TPI
1973 *Bal-A	3	2	.600	8	4	1	1	1	32^1	31	17	1	1	6	18	10.6	3.90	96	.256	.297	0	—	0	-0	-1	-1	-0.1
1974 Bal-A	1	1	.500	20	2	0	0	1	57^1	47	26	1	0	20	26	10.5	3.45	100	.223	.290	0	—	0	1	0	-0	0.0
1975 Cle-A	6	10	.375	29	19	2	0	0	135^1	136	76	16	0	57	51	12.8	4.39	86	.268	.342	0	—	0	-9	-9	-2	-1.1
1976 Cle-A	3	5	.375	33	6	0	0	1	77^2	89	46	5	4	41	32	15.5	4.87	72	.296	.387	0	—	0	-12	-12	0	-1.2
1977 Cle-A	2	1	.667	41	5	1	0	0	105	87	42	3	4	49	62	12.0	3.00	132	.224	.317	0	—	0	13	11	-2	0.4
1978 Cle-A	5	6	.455	36	19	1	0	0	154^2	166	82	13	1	77	73	14.2	4.48	84	.278	.361	0	—	0	-12	-13	0	-0.8
1979 Cle-A	1	0	1.000	13	0	0	0	1	22	13	9	1	1	14	7	11.5	3.68	116	.169	.304	0	—	0	1	1	0	0.1
NY-A	3	1	.750	27	6	0	0	1	67^1	62	24	3	2	30	22	12.6	3.07	133	.252	.338	0	—	0	9	8	0	0.5
Yr	4	1	.800	40	6	0	0	2	89^1	75	33	4	3	44	29	12.3	3.22	128	.232	.330	0	—	0	10	9	1	0.6
1980 StL-N	4	6	.400	33	8	1	0	0	82^1	90	39	2	2	34	35	13.8	3.39	109	.288	.362	4	.200	-0	2	3	1	0.4
1982 KC-A	4	0	1.000	30	3	0	0	1	66^2	71	31	7	2	22	31	12.8	3.51	117	.276	.338	0	—	0	4	4	0	0.3
1983 KC-A	2	3	.400	27	0	0	0	0	47^2	48	20	5	2	14	17	12.1	2.27	180	.273	.333	0	—	0	10	10	1	1.1
Total 10	34	35	.493	297	72	6	1	6	848^1	840	412	57	19	364	374	13.0	3.79	101	.263	.342	4	.200	-0	6	3	-0	-0.4

● WALLY HOOD Hood, Wallace James Jr. b: 9/24/25, Los Angeles, Cal. BR/TR, 6'1", 190 lbs. Deb: 9/23/49 F

YEAR TM/L	W	L	PCT	G	GS	CG	SH	SV	IP	H	R	HR	HB	BB	SO	RAT	ERA	ERA+	OAV	OOB	BH	AVG	PB	PR	PR+	PD	TPI
1949 NY-A	0	0	—	2	0	0	0	0	2^1	0	0	0	0	1	2	3.9	0.00	—	.000	.143	0	—	0	1	1	-0	0.0

● CHRIS HOOK Hook, Christopher Wayne b: 8/4/68, San Diego, Cal. BR/TR, 6'5", 230 lbs. Deb: 4/30/95

YEAR TM/L	W	L	PCT	G	GS	CG	SH	SV	IP	H	R	HR	HB	BB	SO	RAT	ERA	ERA+	OAV	OOB	BH	AVG	PB	PR	PR+	PD	TPI
1995 SF-N	5	1	.833	45	0	0	0	0	52^1	55	33	7	3	29	40	15.0	5.50	74	.274	.373	0	.000	-0	-8	-8	-0	-0.9
1996 SF-N	0	1	.000	10	0	0	0	0	13^1	16	13	3	2	14	4	21.6	7.43	55	.308	.471	1	.500	0	-5	-5	0	-0.3
Total 2	5	2	.714	55	0	0	0	0	65^2	71	46	10	5	43	44	16.3	5.89	69	.281	.395	1	.200	0	-12	-13	0	-1.2

● JAY HOOK Hook, James Wesley b: 11/18/36, Waukegan, Ill. BL/TR, 6'2", 182 lbs. Deb: 9/3/57

YEAR TM/L	W	L	PCT	G	GS	CG	SH	SV	IP	H	R	HR	HB	BB	SO	RAT	ERA	ERA+	OAV	OOB	BH	AVG	PB	PR	PR+	PD	TPI
1957 Cin-N	0	1	.000	3	2	0	0	0	10	6	7	0	0	8	6	12.6	4.50	91	.176	.333	0	.000	-0	-1	-0	0	-0.1
1958 Cin-N	0	1	.000	1	1	0	0	0	3	3	4	2	0	2	5	15.0	12.00	35	.250	.357	0	.000	-0	-3	-2	-0	-0.4
1959 Cin-N	5	5	.500	17	15	4	0	0	79	79	46	10	3	39	37	13.8	5.13	79	.266	.357	3	.125	-1	-10	-10	-0	-1.2
1960 Cin-N	11	18	.379	36	33	10	2	0	222	222	119	31	5	73	103	12.2	4.50	85	.263	.325	6	.083	-3	-18	-16	1	-2.3
1961 Cin-N	1	3	.250	22	5	0	0	0	62^2	83	55	14	5	22	36	15.8	7.76	52	.322	.386	2	.133	-1	-26	-25	-1	-1.6
1962 NY-N	8	19	.296	37	34	13	0	0	213^2	230	137	31	8	71	113	13.0	4.84	86	.273	.335	14	.203	2	-21	-15	-0	-1.4
1963 NY-N	4	14	.222	41	20	3	0	1	152^2	168	104	21	9	53	89	13.6	5.48	64	.281	.348	9	.237	2	-37	-32	-1	-3.4
1964 NY-N	0	1	.000	3	2	0	0	0	9^2	17	10	2	0	7	5	22.3	9.31	38	.395	.480	0	.000	-0	-6	-6	0	-0.5
Total 8	29	62	.319	160	112	30	2	1	752^2	808	482	111	30	275	394	13.3	5.23	75	.276	.344	34	.151	-2	-123	-106	-4	-10.9

● BUCK HOOKER Hooker, William Edward b: 8/28/1880, Richmond, Va. d: 7/2/29, Richmond, Va. TR, 5'6", Deb: 9/5/02

YEAR TM/L	W	L	PCT	G	GS	CG	SH	SV	IP	H	R	HR	HB	BB	SO	RAT	ERA	ERA+	OAV	OOB	BH	AVG	PB	PR	PR+	PD	TPI
1902 Cin-N	0	1	.000	1	1	1	0	0	8	11	5	0	0	0	0	12.4	4.50	67	.324	.324	0	.000	-0	-2	-1	-0	-0.2
1903 Cin-N	0	0	—	1	0	0	0	0	2^1	2	0	0	0	2	0	15.4	0.00	—	.250	.400	0	.000	-0	1	1	-0	0.0
Total 2	0	1	.000	2	1	1	0	0	10^1	13	5	1	0	2	0	13.1	3.48	90	.310	.341	0	.000	-1	-1	-0	-1	-0.2

● HARRY HOOPER Hooper, Harry Bartholomew b: 8/24/1887, Bell Station, Cal. d: 12/18/74, Santa Cruz, Cal. BL/TR, 5'10", 168 lbs. Deb: 4/16/09 H♦

YEAR TM/L	W	L	PCT	G	GS	CG	SH	SV	IP	H	R	HR	HB	BB	SO	RAT	ERA	ERA+	OAV	OOB	BH	AVG	PB	PR	PR+	PD	TPI
1913 Bos-A	0	0	—	1	0	0	0	0	2	2	0	0	0	1	0	13.5	0.00	—	.333	.429	169	.288	0	1	1	-0	0.0

● BOB HOOPER Hooper, Robert Nelson b: 5/30/22, Leamington, Ont., Canada d: 3/17/80, New Brunswick, N.J BR/TR, 5'11", 195 lbs. Deb: 4/19/50

YEAR TM/L	W	L	PCT	G	GS	CG	SH	SV	IP	H	R	HR	HB	BB	SO	RAT	ERA	ERA+	OAV	OOB	BH	AVG	PB	PR	PR+	PD	TPI
1950 Phi-A	15	10	.600	45	20	3	0	5	170^1	181	108	15	1	91	58	14.4	5.02	91	.272	.361	7	.125	-2	-8	-9	3	-1.0
1951 Phi-A	12	10	.545	38	23	9	0	5	189	192	98	13	3	61	64	12.2	4.38	98	.267	.327	15	.208	-1	-5	-2	1	-0.2
1952 Phi-A	8	15	.348	43	14	4	0	6	144^1	158	100	13	4	68	40	14.3	5.18	76	.279	.361	8	.195	1	-24	-18	3	-2.4
1953 Cle-A	5	4	.556	43	0	0	0	7	69^1	50	37	4	2	38	16	11.7	4.02	93	.206	.318	1	.083	-1	-0	-2	1	-0.3
1954 Cle-A	0	0	—	17	0	0	0	2	34^2	39	22	3	1	16	12	14.5	4.93	74	.289	.368	0	.000	-1	-5	-5	0	-0.3
1955 Cin-N	0	2	.000	8	0	0	0	0	13	20	12	2	0	6	6	18.0	7.62	56	.357	.419	0	.000	-0	-5	-5	0	-0.6
Total 6	40	41	.494	194	57	16	0	25	620^2	640	377	50	11	280	196	13.5	4.80	87	.268	.348	31	.166	-4	-48	-41	8	-4.9

● LEON HOOTEN Hooten, Michael Leon b: 4/4/48, Downey, Cal. BR/TR, 5'11", 180 lbs. Deb: 4/13/74

YEAR TM/L	W	L	PCT	G	GS	CG	SH	SV	IP	H	R	HR	HB	BB	SO	RAT	ERA	ERA+	OAV	OOB	BH	AVG	PB	PR	PR+	PD	TPI
1974 Oak-A	0	0	—	6	0	0	0	0	8^1	6	3	1	1	4	1	11.9	3.24	103	.207	.324	0	—	0	0	0	0	0.0

● BURT HOOTON Hooton, Burt Carlton b: 2/7/50, Greenville, Tex. BR/TR, 6'1", 210 lbs. Deb: 6/17/71 C

YEAR TM/L	W	L	PCT	G	GS	CG	SH	SV	IP	H	R	HR	HB	BB	SO	RAT	ERA	ERA+	OAV	OOB	BH	AVG	PB	PR	PR+	PD	TPI
1971 Chi-N	2	0	1.000	3	3	2	1	0	21^1	8	5	2	0	10	22	7.6	2.11	187	.111	.220	0	.000	-1	3	4	-0	0.3
1972 Chi-N	11	14	.440	33	31	9	3	0	218^1	201	78	13	1	81	132	11.7	2.80	136	.246	.315	9	.125	-1	16	22	1	2.6
1973 Chi-N	14	17	.452	42	34	9	2	0	239^2	248	107	12	4	73	134	12.2	3.68	107	.270	.327	9	.129	-0	-0	7	-1	0.7
1974 Chi-N	7	11	.389	48	21	3	1	1	176^1	214	112	16	3	51	94	13.7	4.80	80	.299	.348	3	.060	-4	-23	-18	3	-1.8
1975 Chi-N	0	2	.000	3	3	0	0	0	11	18	12	2	0	4	5	18.0	8.18	47	.383	.431	0	.000	-0	-6	-5	1	-0.7
LA-N	18	7	.720	31	30	12	4	0	223^2	172	76	16	0	64	148	9.5	2.82	121	.210	.267	9	.129	1	20	16	-2	1.6
Yr	18	9	.667	34	33	12	4	0	234^2	190	88	18	0	68	153	9.9	3.07	112	.219	.276	9	.123	0	15	10	-1	0.9
1976 LA-N	11	15	.423	33	33	8	4	0	226^2	203	93	16	1	60	116	10.5	3.26	104	.241	.292	6	.097	-2	6	3	-2	0.0
1977 *LA-N	12	7	.632	32	31	6	2	1	223^1	184	74	14	3	60	153	10.0	2.62	146	.225	.281	11	.164	-0	32	31	0	2.5
1978 *LA-N	19	10	.655	32	32	10	3	0	236	196	74	17	0	61	104	9.8	2.71	130	.226	.277	10	.149	1	23	22	-1	2.6
1979 LA-N	11	10	.524	29	29	12	1	0	212	191	85	11	2	63	129	10.9	2.97	123	.244	.302	11	.147	-1	18	16	-0	1.4
1980 LA-N	14	8	.636	34	33	4	2	1	206^2	194	90	22	0	64	118	11.2	3.66	96	.249	.306	4	.063	-3	-1	-4	-0	-0.7
1981 *LA-N★	11	6	.647	23	23	5	4	0	142^1	124	42	3	2	33	74	10.1	2.28	146	.237	.285	8	.190	2	19	17	-1	2.3
1982 LA-N	4	7	.364	21	21	2	2	0	120^2	130	57	5	2	33	51	12.3	4.03	86	.275	.325	3	.086	-1	-6	-8	0	-0.7
1983 LA-N	9	8	.529	33	27	2	0	0	160	156	86	21	2	59	87	12.2	4.22	85	.254	.321	8	.160	1	-10	-11	-0	-1.0

YEAR	TM/L	W	L	PCT	G	GS	CG	SH	SV	IP	H	R	HR	HB	BB	SO	RAT	ERA	ERA+	OAV	OOB	BH	AVG	PB	PR	PR+	PD	TPI
1984	LA-N	3	6	.333	54	6	0	0	4	110	109	43	5	0	43	62	12.4	3.44	103	.263	.333	1	.071	-1	2	1	-0	0.0
1985	Tex-A	5	8	.385	29	20	2	0	0	124	149	78	18	0	40	62	13.7	5.23	81	.297	.349	0	—	0	-15	-13	-1	-1.3
Total	15	151	136	.526	480	377	86	29	7	2652	2497	1112	193	20	799	1491	11.3	3.38	108	.250	.306	92	.123	-9	79	79	-4	7.8
● JOHN HOOVER	Hoover, John Nicklaus b: 11/22/62, Fresno, Cal. BR/TR, 6′2″, 190 lbs. Deb: 5/23/90																											
1990	Tex-A	0	0	—	2	0	0	0	0	4^2	8	6	0	0	3	0	21.2	11.57	34	.364	.440	0	—	0	-4	-4	-0	-0.2
● DICK HOOVER	Hoover, Richard Lloyd b: 12/11/25, Columbus, Ohio d: 4/12/81, Lake Placid, Fla. BL/TL, 6′, 170 lbs. Deb: 4/16/52																											
1952	Bos-N	0	0	—	2	0	0	0	0	4^2	8	4	1	0	3	0	21.2	7.71	47	.348	.423	0	—	0	-2	-2	-0	-0.1
● JOHN HOPE	Hope, John Alan b: 12/21/70, Ft.Lauderdale, Fla. BR/TR, 6′3″, 195 lbs. Deb: 8/29/93																											
1993	Pit-N	0	2	.000	7	7	0	0	0	38	47	19	2	2	8	8	13.5	4.03	101	.313	.356	1	.077	-1	0	0	0	0.0
1994	Pit-N	0	0	—	9	0	0	0	0	14	18	12	1	2	4	6	15.4	5.79	75	.310	.375	1	.333	0	-2	-2	0	-0.1
1995	Pit-N	0	0	—	3	0	0	0	0	2^1	8	8	0	3	4	2	57.9	30.86	14	.615	.750	0	—	0	-7	-7	-0	-0.3
1996	Pit-N	1	3	.250	5	4	0	0	0	19^1	17	18	5	2	11	13	14.0	6.98	63	.243	.361	1	.200	-0	-6	-5	0	-0.9
Total	4	1	5	.167	24	11	0	0	0	73^2	90	57	8	9	27	29	15.4	5.99	70	.309	.385	3	.143	-1	-15	-14	1	-1.3
● SAM HOPE	Hope, Samuel b: 12/4/1878, Brooklyn, N.Y. d: 6/30/46, Greenport, N.Y. BR/TR, 5′10″, Deb: 8/5/07																											
1907	Phi-A	0	0	—	1	0	0	0	0	0^1	3	1	0	0	0	0	81.0	0.00	—	.750	.750	0	—	0	0	0	0	0.0
● PAUL HOPKINS	Hopkins, Paul Henry b: 9/25/04, Chester, Conn. BR/TR, 6′, 175 lbs. Deb: 9/29/27																											
1927	Was-A	1	0	1.000	2	1	0	0	0	9	13	6	1	0	4	5	17.0	5.00	81	.361	.425	2	.667	1	-1	-1	0	0.0
1929	Was-A	0	1	.000	7	0	0	0	0	16^1	15	5	1	0	9	5	13.2	2.20	192	.250	.348	0	.000	-1	4	4	-0	0.1
	StL-A	0	0	—	2	0	0	0	0	2	0	0	0	0	2	1	9.0	0.00	—	.000	.286	0	—	0	1	1	-0	0.0
	Yr	0	1	.000	9	0	0	0	0	18^1	15	5	1	0	11	6	12.8	1.96	217	.231	.342	0	.000	-1	5	5	-0	0.1
Total	2	1	1	.500	11	1	0	0	0	27^1	28	11	2	0	15	11	14.2	2.96	142	.277	.371	2	.333	1	4	4	-0	0.1
● LEFTY HOPPER	Hopper, Clarence F. b: 5/27/1875, Jersey City, N.J. d: 9/27/59, San Diego, Cal. TL, Deb: 10/10/1898																											
1898	Bro-N	0	2	.000	2	2	2	0	0	11	14	11	0	0	5	5	15.5	4.91	73	.304	.373	0	.000	-1	-2	-2	0	-0.3
● JIM HOPPER	Hopper, James McDaniel b: 9/1/19, Charlotte, N.C. d: 1/23/82, Charlotte, N.C. BR/TR, 6′1″, 175 lbs. Deb: 4/21/46																											
1946	Pit-N	0	1	.000	2	1	0	0	0	4	6	5	1	0	3	1	20.3	11.25	31	.316	.409	0	—	0	-3	-3	0	-0.6
● BILL HOPPER	Hopper, William Booth "Bird Dog" b: 10/26/1890, Jackson, Tenn. d: 1/14/65, Allen Park, Mich. BR/TR, 6′, 175 lbs. Deb: 9/11/13																											
1913	StL-N	0	3	.000	3	3	2	0	0	24	20	14	2	3	8	3	11.6	3.75	86	.230	.316	3	.375	1	-1	-1	-0	0.0
1914	StL-N	0	0	—	3	0	0	0	0	5	6	3	0	0	5	1	19.8	3.60	78	.286	.423	0	—	0	-0	-0	0	0.0
1915	Was-A	0	1	.000	13	0	0	0	1	31^1	39	23	0	1	16	8	16.1	4.60	65	.348	.434	1	.200	0	-6	-6	1	-0.2
Total	3	0	4	.000	19	3	2	0	1	60^1	65	40	2	4	29	12	14.6	4.18	73	.295	.387	4	.308	1	-8	-7	1	-0.2
● JOHN HORAN	Horan, Patrick J. b: 1863, Ireland 5′10.5″, 160 lbs. Deb: 5/17/1884																											
1884	CP-U	3	6	.333	13	10	9	0	0	98	94	73	0		24	55	10.8	3.49	70	.236	.279	6	.088	-8	-11	-11	-1	-1.4
● JOE HORLEN	Horlen, Joel Edward b: 8/14/37, San Antonio, Tex. BR/TR, 6′, 175 lbs. Deb: 9/4/61																											
1961	Chi-A	1	3	.250	5	4	0	0	0	17^2	25	15	2	0	13	11	19.4	6.62	59	.338	.437	0	.000	-1	-5	-5	0	-1.0
1962	Chi-A	7	6	.538	20	19	5	1	0	108^2	108	62	10	2	43	63	12.7	4.89	80	.262	.335	2	.053	-3	-11	-12	2	-1.3
1963	Chi-A	11	7	.611	33	21	3	0	0	124	122	50	10	2	55	61	13.0	3.27	107	.261	.341	9	.225	1	5	3	1	0.7
1964	Chi-A	13	9	.591	32	28	9	2	0	210^2	142	54	11	4	55	138	**8.6**	1.88	184	**.190**	**.250**	11	.159	-1	41	39	3	4.4
1965	Chi-A	13	13	.500	34	34	7	4	0	219	203	88	16	3	39	125	10.1	2.88	111	.245	.281	9	.132	0	14	8	-0	1.0
1966	Chi-A	10	13	.435	37	29	4	2	1	211	185	64	14	6	53	124	10.4	2.43	130	.233	.286	4	.067	-4	24	19	6	2.4
1967	Chi-A☆	19	7	**.731**	35	35	13	**6**	0	258	188	66	13	4	58	103	**8.7**	**2.06**	**151**	.203	**.253**	14	.169	1	**34**	**31**	3	3.7
1968	Chi-A	12	14	.462	35	35	4	1	0	223^2	197	75	16	14	70	102	11.3	2.37	127	.238	.308	7	.104	-1	15	16	2	2.1
1969	Chi-A	13	16	.448	36	35	7	2	0	235^2	237	105	20	5	77	121	12.2	3.78	102	.261	.323	14	.182	-1	-4	2	-1	0.0
1970	Chi-A	6	16	.273	28	26	4	0	0	172^1	198	99	18	4	41	77	12.7	4.86	80	.287	.331	6	.115	-2	-22	-17	4	-1.8
1971	Chi-A	8	9	.471	34	18	3	0	2	137^1	150	72	12	5	30	82	12.1	4.26	84	.284	.329	4	.100	-2	-12	-10	1	-1.3
1972	*Oak-A	3	4	.429	32	6	0	0	1	84	74	33	3	4	20	58	10.5	3.00	95	.236	.291	3	.176	-0	1	-1	1	-0.1
Total	12	116	117	.498	361	290	59	18	4	2002	1829	783	145	53	554	1065	11.0	3.11	110	.243	.300	83	.134	-12	79	67	22	8.8
● TRADER HORNE	Horne, Berlyn Dale "Sonny" b: 4/12/1899, Bachman, Ohio d: 2/3/83, Franklin, Ohio BB/TR, 5′9″, 155 lbs. Deb: 4/24/29																											
1929	Chi-N	1	1	.500	11	1	0	0	0	23	24	20	3	0	21	6	17.6	5.09	91	.273	.413	2	.400	0	-1	-1	0	0.0
● JACK HORNER	Horner, William Frank b: 9/21/1863, Baltimore, Md. d: 7/14/10, New Orleans, La. BR, Deb: 5/7/1894																											
1894	Bal-N	0	1	.000	2	1	1	0	1	11	15	12	0	1	7	2	18.8	9.00	61	.319	.418	1	.167	-0	-4	-4	0	-0.3
● JOE HORNUNG	Hornung, Michael Joseph "Ubbo Ubbo" b: 6/12/1857, Carthage, N.Y. d: 10/30/31, Howard Beach, N.Y. BR/TR, 5′8.5″, 164 lbs. Deb: 5/1/1879 U♦																											
1880	Buf-N	0	0	—	1	0	0	0	0	3	2	2	0		1	0	9.0	6.00	41	.167	.231	91	.266	0	-1	-1	0	0.0
● HANSON HORSEY	Horsey, Hanson b: 11/26/1889, Galena, Md. d: 12/1/49, Millington, Md. BR/TR, 5′11″, 165 lbs. Deb: 4/27/12																											
1912	Cin-N	0	0	—	1	0	0	0	0	4	14	10	0	0	3	0	38.3	22.50	15	.609	.654	0	.000	-0	-8	-9	-0	-0.4
● VINCE HORSMAN	Horsman, Vincent Stanley Joseph b: 3/9/67, Halifax, N.S., Can. BR/TL, 6′2″, 180 lbs. Deb: 9/5/91																											
1991	Tor-A	0	0	—	4	0	0	0	0	4	2	0	0	0	3	2	11.3	0.00	—	.167	.333	0	—	0	2	2	-0	0.1
1992	Oak-A	2	1	.667	58	0	0	0	1	43^1	39	13	3	0	21	18	12.5	2.49	150	.252	.341	0	—	0	7	6	-0	0.4
1993	Oak-A	2	0	1.000	40	0	0	0	0	25	25	15	2	3	15	17	15.5	5.40	76	.255	.371	0	—	0	-3	-4	-0	-0.3
1994	Oak-A	0	1	.000	33	0	0	0	0	29^1	29	17	2	1	11	20	12.6	4.91	90	.266	.339	0	—	0	-0	-2	1	0.0
1995	Min-A	0	0	—	6	0	0	0	0	9	12	8	2	0	4	4	16.0	7.00	68	.333	.400	0	—	0	-2	-2	-0	-0.1
Total	5	4	2	.667	141	0	0	0	1	110^2	107	53	9	4	54	61	13.4	4.07	101	.261	.353	0	—	0	3	1	-1	0.1
● OSCAR HORSTMANN	Horstmann, Oscar Theodore b: 6/2/1891, Alma, Mo. d: 5/11/77, Salina, Kan. BR/TR, 5′11″, 165 lbs. Deb: 4/18/17																											
1917	StL-N	9	4	.692	35	11	4	1	1	138^2	111	67	5	4	54	50	11.0	3.44	78	.225	.307	9	.196	1	-11	-12	-0	-1.1
1918	StL-N	0	2	.000	9	2	0	0	0	23	29	18	0	0	14	6	16.8	5.48	49	.349	.443	0	.000	-0	-7	-7	1	-0.5
1919	StL-N	0	1	.000	6	2	0	0	0	15	14	6	0	0	12	5	15.6	3.00	93	.264	.400	1	.500	0	-0	-0	0	0.0
Total	3	9	7	.563	50	15	4	1	1	176^2	154	91	5	4	80	61	12.1	3.67	74	.245	.334	10	.192	1	-18	-19	1	-1.6
● ELMER HORTON	Horton, Elmer E. "Herky Jerky" b: 9/4/1869, Hamilton, Ohio d: 8/12/20, Vienna, N.Y. Deb: 9/24/1896																											
1896	Pit-N	0	2	.000	2	2	2	0	0	15	22	18	0	1	9	3	19.2	9.60	44	.338	.427	0	.000	-1	-9	-9	-1	-0.9
1898	Bro-N	0	1	.000	1	1	1	0	0	9	16	13	0	0	6	0	22.0	10.00	36	.381	.458	1	.250	-0	-6	-6	-0	-0.5
Total	2	0	3	.000	3	3	3	0	0	24	38	31	0	1	15	3	20.3	9.75	41	.355	.439	1	.091	-1	-15	-16	-1	-1.4
● RICKY HORTON	Horton, Ricky Neal b: 7/30/59, Poughkeepsie, N.Y. BL/TL, 6′2″, 195 lbs. Deb: 4/7/84																											
1984	StL-N	9	4	.692	37	18	1	1	1	125^2	140	53	14	1	39	76	12.9	3.44	101	.285	.339	2	.065	-2	2	1	3	0.2
1985	*StL-N	3	2	.600	49	3	0	0	1	89^2	84	30	5	3	34	59	12.1	2.91	122	.251	.326	1	.063	-0	7	6	2	0.5
1986	StL-N	4	3	.571	42	9	1	0	3	100^1	77	25	7	1	26	49	9.3	2.24	163	.218	.273	1	.056	0	17	16	2	1.3
1987	*StL-N	8	3	.727	67	6	0	0	7	125	127	58	15	0	42	55	12.2	3.82	109	.263	.323	5	.172	0	4	5	2	0.7
1988	Chi-A	6	10	.375	52	9	1	0	2	109^1	120	64	6	5	36	28	13.3	4.86	82	.291	.355	0	—	0	-11	-11	1	-1.3
	*LA-N	1	1	.500	12	0	0	0	0	9	11	7	2	0	2	8	13.0	5.00	67	.306	.342	0	—	0	-2	-2	1	-0.3
1989	LA-N	0	0	—	23	0	0	0	0	26^2	35	15	1	1	11	12	15.9	5.06	68	.343	.412	0	.000	-0	-5	-5	-0	-0.3
	StL-N	0	3	.000	11	8	0	0	0	45^2	50	24	2	3	10	14	12.4	4.73	77	.282	.332	3	.273	1	-6	-5	0	-0.2
	Yr	0	3	.000	34	8	0	0	0	72^1	85	39	3	4	21	26	13.7	4.85	73	.305	.362	3	.250	1	-11	-10	0	-0.5
1990	StL-N	1	1	.500	32	0	0	0	1	42	52	25	3	1	22	18	16.1	4.93	78	.315	.399	0	.000	-0	-5	-5	2	-0.1
Total	7	32	27	.542	325	53	3	1	15	673^1	696	301	55	15	222	319	12.5	3.76	100	.273	.334	12	.109	-1	1	-1	12	0.5
● DAVE HOSKINS	Hoskins, David Taylor b: 8/3/25, Greenwood, Miss. d: 4/2/70, Flint, Mich. BL/TR, 6′1″, 180 lbs. Deb: 4/18/53																											
1953	Cle-A	9	3	.750	26	7	3	0	1	112^2	102	57	9	4	38	55	11.5	3.99	94	.243	.312	15	.259	4	0	-3	0	0.1

YEAR	TM/L	W	L	PCT	G	GS	CG	SH	SV	IP	H	R	HR	HB	BB	SO	RAT	ERA	ERA+	OAV	OOB	BH	AVG	PB	PR	PR+	PD	TPI
1954	Cle-A	0	1	.000	14	1	0	0	0	26^2	29	10	3	0	10	9	13.2	3.04	121	.284	.348	0	.000	-1	2	2	-0	0.0
Total	2	9	4	.692	40	8	3	0	1	139^1	131	67	12	4	48	64	11.8	3.81	98	.251	.319	15	.227	3	2	-1	0	0.1

● GENE HOST Host, Eugene Earl "Twinkles" or "Slick" b: 1/1/33, Leeper, Pa. d: 8/20/98, Nashville, Tenn. BB/TL, 5'11", 190 lbs. Deb: 9/16/56

YEAR	TM/L	W	L	PCT	G	GS	CG	SH	SV	IP	H	R	HR	HB	BB	SO	RAT	ERA	ERA+	OAV	OOB	BH	AVG	PB	PR	PR+	PD	TPI
1956	Det-A	0	0	—	1	1	0	0	0	4^2	9	4	2	0	2	5	21.2	7.71	53	.409	.458	0	.000	-0	-2	-2	-0	-0.1
1957	KC-A	0	2	.000	11	2	0	0	0	23^2	29	19	5	0	14	9	16.4	7.23	55	.315	.406	0	.000	-1	-9	-8	0	-0.7
Total	2	0	2	.000	12	3	0	0	0	28^1	38	23	7	0	16	14	17.2	7.31	55	.333	.415	0	.000	-1	-11	-10	0	-0.8

● BYRON HOUCK Houck, Byron Simon "Duke" b: 8/28/1891, Prosper, Minn. d: 6/17/69, Santa Cruz, Cal. BR/TR, 6', 175 lbs. Deb: 5/15/12

YEAR	TM/L	W	L	PCT	G	GS	CG	SH	SV	IP	H	R	HR	HB	BB	SO	RAT	ERA	ERA+	OAV	OOB	BH	AVG	PB	PR	PR+	PD	TPI
1912	Phi-A	8	8	.500	30	17	10	0	1	180^2	148	79	1	12	74	75	11.7	2.94	105	.234	.326	4	.065	-7	8	3	-1	-0.4
1913	Phi-A	14	6	.700	41	19	4	1	0	176	147	93	3	6	122	71	14.1	4.14	67	.214	.337	5	.083	-4	-24	-29	-1	-3.5
1914	Phi-A	0	0	—	3	3	0	0	0	11	14	9	0	0	6	4	16.4	3.27	80	.318	.400	1	.333	0	-1	-1	-0	0.0
	Bro-F	2	6	.250	17	9	3	0	0	92	95	48	4	2	43	45	13.7	3.13	92	.272	.355	7	.233	2	-2	-3	-3	-0.3
1918	StL-A	2	4	.333	27	2	0	0	2	71^2	58	24	0	0	29	29	10.9	2.39	115	.225	.303	3	.150	-1	**3**	**3**	-1	0.1
Total	4	26	24	.520	118	50	17	1	3	531^1	462	253	8	20	274	224	12.8	3.30	87	.234	.334	20	.114	-9	-16	-26	-6	-4.1

● CHARLIE HOUGH Hough, Charles Oliver b: 1/5/48, Honolulu, Hawaii BR/TR, 6'2", 190 lbs. Deb: 8/12/70 C

YEAR	TM/L	W	L	PCT	G	GS	CG	SH	SV	IP	H	R	HR	HB	BB	SO	RAT	ERA	ERA+	OAV	OOB	BH	AVG	PB	PR	PR+	PD	TPI
1970	LA-N	0	0	—	8	0	0	0	2	17	18	11	7	0	11	8	15.4	5.29	72	.265	.367	1	.333	0	-2	-3	0	-0.1
1971	LA-N	0	0	—	4	0	0	0	0	4^1	3	3	1	0	3	4	12.5	4.15	78	.200	.333	0	—	0	-0	-0	0	0.0
1972	LA-N	0	0	—	2	0	0	0	0	2^2	2	1	0	1	2	4	16.9	3.38	99	.200	.385	0	—	0	0	-0	0	0.0
1973	LA-N	4	2	.667	37	0	0	0	5	71^2	52	24	3	6	45	70	12.9	2.76	125	.207	.341	3	.214	0	7	6	0	0.6
1974	*LA-N	9	4	.692	49	0	0	0	1	96	65	45	12	4	40	63	10.2	3.75	91	.196	.291	0	.000	-1	-1	-4	-0	-0.6
1975	LA-N	3	7	.300	38	0	0	0	4	61	43	25	3	8	34	34	12.5	2.95	116	.195	.323	2	.333	1	5	3	-1	0.6
1976	LA-N	12	8	.600	77	0	0	0	18	142^2	102	43	6	8	77	81	11.8	2.21	153	.200	.314	6	.286	2	**21**	**19**	-1	**3.4**
1977	*LA-N	6	12	.333	70	1	0	0	22	127^1	98	53	10	7	70	105	12.4	3.32	115	.213	.326	4	.182	1	8	7	-1	1.3
1978	*LA-N	5	5	.500	55	0	0	0	7	93^1	69	38	6	5	48	66	11.8	3.28	107	.205	.313	4	.333	1	3	2	-0	0.4
1979	LA-N	7	5	.583	42	14	0	0	0	151^1	152	88	16	8	66	76	13.4	4.76	77	.264	.348	6	.158	-0	-17	-19	0	-1.4
1980	LA-N	1	3	.250	19	1	0	0	1	32^1	37	21	4	2	21	25	16.7	5.57	63	.291	.400	1	.500	0	-7	-8	-1	-0.9
	Tex-A	2	2	.500	16	2	2	1	0	61^1	54	30	2	3	37	47	13.8	3.96	98	.240	.355	0	—	0	1	-0	-0	-0.1
1981	Tex-A	4	1	.800	21	5	2	0	1	82	61	30	4	3	31	69	10.4	2.96	117	.207	.290	0	—	0	6	5	-1	0.2
1982	Tex-A	16	13	.552	34	34	12	2	0	228	217	111	21	7	72	128	11.7	3.95	98	.251	.314	0	—	0	3	-2	1	-0.1
1983	Tex-A	15	13	.536	34	33	11	3	0	252	219	96	22	3	95	152	11.3	3.18	126	.238	.311	0	—	0	25	24	4	2.9
1984	Tex-A	16	14	.533	36	36	**17**	1	0	266	260	127	26	9	94	164	12.3	3.76	111	.255	.324	0	—	0	7	11	3	1.5
1985	Tex-A	14	16	.467	34	34	14	1	0	250^1	198	102	23	7	83	141	10.4	3.31	128	.215	.285	0	—	0	23	25	1	2.9
1986	Tex-A★	17	10	.630	33	33	7	2	0	230^1	188	115	32	9	89	146	11.2	3.79	114	.221	.302	0	—	0	10	13	1	1.5
1987	Tex-A	18	13	.581	40	40	13	0	0	**285^1**	238	159	36	19	124	223	12.0	3.79	119	.223	.314	0	—	0	22	22	3	2.5
1988	Tex-A	15	16	.484	34	34	10	0	0	252	202	111	20	12	126	174	12.1	3.32	123	.221	.324	0	—	0	18	21	4	2.8
1989	Tex-A	10	13	.435	30	30	5	1	0	182	168	97	28	6	95	94	13.3	4.35	91	.245	.342	0	—	0	-9	-8	-2	-1.0
1990	Tex-A	12	12	.500	32	32	5	0	0	218^2	190	108	24	11	119	114	13.2	4.07	96	.235	.342	0	—	0	-4	-4	-0	-0.4
1991	Chi-A	9	10	.474	31	29	4	1	0	199^1	167	98	21	11	94	107	12.3	4.02	99	.229	.326	0	—	0	2	-1	0	0.0
1992	Chi-A	7	12	.368	27	27	4	0	0	176^1	160	88	19	7	66	76	11.9	3.93	98	.239	.314	0	—	0	0	-1	-1	-0.2
1993	Fla-N	9	16	.360	34	34	0	0	0	204^1	202	109	20	8	71	126	12.4	4.27	101	.259	.328	2	.032	-5	-5	1	2	-0.2
1994	Fla-N	5	9	.357	21	21	1	0	0	113^2	118	74	17	10	52	65	14.3	5.15	85	.274	.366	4	.121	-1	-12	-9	0	-1.1
Total	25	216	216	.500	858	440	107	13	61	3801^1	3283	1807	383	174	1665	2362	12.1	3.75	106	.233	.322	33	.146	-2	104	102	13	14.5

● CRAIG HOUSE House, Craig Michael b: 7/8/77, Naha A.F.B., Okinawa, Japan BR/TR, 6'2", 210 lbs. Deb: 8/6/2000

YEAR	TM/L	W	L	PCT	G	GS	CG	SH	SV	IP	H	R	HR	HB	BB	SO	RAT	ERA	ERA+	OAV	OOB	BH	AVG	PB	PR	PR+	PD	TPI
2000	Col-N	1	1	.500	16	0	0	0	0	13^2	13	11	3	2	17	8	21.1	7.24	82	.265	.471	0	—	0	-4	-2	0	-0.2

● PAT HOUSE House, Patrick Lory b: 9/1/40, Boise, Idaho BL/TL, 6'3", 185 lbs. Deb: 9/6/67

YEAR	TM/L	W	L	PCT	G	GS	CG	SH	SV	IP	H	R	HR	HB	BB	SO	RAT	ERA	ERA+	OAV	OOB	BH	AVG	PB	PR	PR+	PD	TPI
1967	Hou-N	1	0	1.000	6	0	0	0	1	4	3	2	0	1	0	2	9.0	4.50	74	.214	.267	0	—	0	-1	-1	0	-0.1
1968	Hou-N	1	1	.500	18	0	0	0	0	16^1	21	15	0	2	6	6	16.0	7.71	38	.323	.397	0	—	0	-9	-9	-0	-1.1
Total	2	2	1	.667	24	0	0	0	1	20^1	24	17	0	3	6	8	14.6	7.08	43	.304	.375	0	—	0	-9	-9	0	-1.2

● TOM HOUSE House, Thomas Ross b: 4/29/47, Seattle, Wash. BL/TL, 5'11", 190 lbs. Deb: 6/23/71 C

YEAR	TM/L	W	L	PCT	G	GS	CG	SH	SV	IP	H	R	HR	HB	BB	SO	RAT	ERA	ERA+	OAV	OOB	BH	AVG	PB	PR	PR+	PD	TPI
1971	Atl-N	1	0	1.000	11	1	0	0	0	20^2	20	8	2	1	3	11	10.5	3.05	122	.263	.300	2	.400	1	1	1	0	0.1
1972	Atl-N	0	0	—	8	0	0	0	2	9^1	7	3	1	1	6	7	13.5	2.89	131	.226	.368	0	.000	-0	1	1	0	0.0
1973	Atl-N	4	2	.667	52	0	0	0	4	67^1	58	37	13	2	31	42	12.2	4.68	84	.243	.335	2	.200	0	-8	-5	-0	-0.5
1974	Atl-N	6	2	.750	56	0	0	0	11	102^2	74	26	5	3	27	64	9.1	1.93	197	.203	.264	4	.400	1	19	20	1	2.3
1975	Atl-N	7	7	.500	58	0	0	0	11	79^1	79	39	2	2	36	36	13.3	3.18	119	.262	.344	1	.111	-0	4	5	1	1.1
1976	Bos-A	1	3	.250	36	0	0	0	4	43^2	39	22	4	2	19	27	12.4	4.33	90	.241	.328	0	—	0	-4	-2	1	-0.1
1977	Bos-A	1	0	1.000	8	0	0	0	0	7^2	15	11	0	0	6	6	24.7	12.91	35	.405	.488	0	—	0	-8	-6	-0	-0.7
	Sea-A	4	5	.444	26	11	1	0	1	89^1	94	42	12	4	19	39	11.8	3.93	105	.268	.313	0	—	0	1	2	-1	0.1
	Yr	5	5	.500	34	11	1	0	1	97	109	53	12	4	25	45	12.8	4.64	90	.281	.331	0	—	0	-6	-5	-1	-0.6
1978	Sea-A	5	4	.556	34	9	3	0	0	116	130	70	10	5	35	29	13.2	4.66	82	.289	.347	0	—	0	-11	-11	-0	-0.8
Total	8	29	23	.558	289	21	4	0	33	536	516	258	49	20	182	261	12.1	3.79	103	.256	.324	9	.257	1	-4	6	1	1.5

● FRED HOUSE House, Willard Edwin b: 10/3/1890, Cabool, Mo. d: 11/16/23, Kansas City, Mo. BR/TR, 6'3", 190 lbs. Deb: 4/22/13

YEAR	TM/L	W	L	PCT	G	GS	CG	SH	SV	IP	H	R	HR	HB	BB	SO	RAT	ERA	ERA+	OAV	OOB	BH	AVG	PB	PR	PR+	PD	TPI
1913	Det-A	1	2	.333	19	2	0	0	0	53^2	64	40	1	2	17	16	13.9	5.20	56	.325	.384	0	.000	-1	-14	-14	1	-0.7

● CHARLIE HOUSEHOLDER Householder, Charles F. b: 1856, Harrisburg, Pa. BR/TR, 5'7", 150 lbs. Deb: 4/20/1884 ♦

YEAR	TM/L	W	L	PCT	G	GS	CG	SH	SV	IP	H	R	HR	HB	BB	SO	RAT	ERA	ERA+	OAV	OOB	BH	AVG	PB	PR	PR+	PD	TPI
1884	CP-U	0	0	—	2	0	0	0	0	3	4	3	0		0	3	12.0	3.00	81	.308	.308	74	.239	-0	-0	-0	-0	0.0

● FRANK HOUSEMAN Houseman, Frank b: Netherlands Deb: 9/2/1886

YEAR	TM/L	W	L	PCT	G	GS	CG	SH	SV	IP	H	R	HR	HB	BB	SO	RAT	ERA	ERA+	OAV	OOB	BH	AVG	PB	PR	PR+	PD	TPI
1886	Bal-a	0	1	.000	1	1	1	0	0	8	6	3	0	1	1	5	9.0	3.38	101	.182	.229	1	.250	-0	0	0	0	0.0

● JOE HOUSER Houser, Joseph William b: 7/3/1891, Steubenville, Ohio d: 1/3/53, Orlando, Fla. BL/TL, 5'9.5", 160 lbs. Deb: 4/24/14

YEAR	TM/L	W	L	PCT	G	GS	CG	SH	SV	IP	H	R	HR	HB	BB	SO	RAT	ERA	ERA+	OAV	OOB	BH	AVG	PB	PR	PR+	PD	TPI
1914	Buf-F	0	1	.000	7	2	0	0	0	23	21	16	1	0	20	6	16.0	5.48	54	.250	.394	1	.143	-0	-7	-6	1	-0.3

● ART HOUTTEMAN Houtteman, Arthur Joseph b: 8/7/27, Detroit, Mich. BR/TR, 6'2", 188 lbs. Deb: 4/29/45

YEAR	TM/L	W	L	PCT	G	GS	CG	SH	SV	IP	H	R	HR	HB	BB	SO	RAT	ERA	ERA+	OAV	OOB	BH	AVG	PB	PR	PR+	PD	TPI
1945	Det-A	0	2	.000	13	0	0	0	0	25^1	27	17	1	1	11	9	13.9	5.33	66	.270	.348	0	.000	-1	-6	-5	1	-0.4
1946	Det-A	0	1	.000	1	1	0	0	0	8	15	8	1	0	0	2	16.9	9.00	41	.385	.385	1	.500	0	-5	-5	-0	-0.4
1947	Det-A	7	2	.778	23	9	7	2	0	110^2	106	51	6	1	36	58	11.6	3.42	110	.247	.306	12	.300	2	4	4	-0	0.5
1948	Det-A	2	16	.111	43	20	4	0	10	164^1	186	101	11	2	52	74	13.1	4.66	94	.287	.342	11	.196	-2	-7	-5	4	-0.4
1949	Det-A	15	10	.600	34	25	13	2	0	203^2	227	101	19	5	59	85	12.9	3.71	112	.282	.335	19	.244	1	11	10	5	1.7
1950	Det-A★	19	12	.613	41	34	21	**4**	4	274^2	257	112	29	8	99	88	11.9	3.54	132	.251	.322	14	.151	-3	32	34	3	3.5
1952	Det-A	8	20	.286	35	28	10	2	1	221	218	116	19	5	65	109	11.7	4.36	87	.253	.309	7	.101	-4	-17	-13	1	-1.9
1953	Det-A	2	6	.250	16	9	3	1	1	68^2	87	50	11	4	29	28	15.7	5.90	69	.309	.381	3	.158	0	-15	-14	-0	-1.4
	Cle-A	7	7	.500	22	13	6	1	3	109	113	56	4	5	25	40	11.8	3.80	99	.269	.318	5	.147	-1	2	-1	0	-0.2
	Yr	9	13	.409	38	22	9	2	4	177^2	200	106	15	9	54	68	13.3	4.61	84	.285	.344	8	.151	-1	-12	-15	-0	-1.6
1954	*Cle-A	15	7	.682	32	25	11	1	0	188	198	80	14	3	59	68	12.4	3.35	110	.273	.330	18	.277	5	8	7	2	1.4
1955	Cle-A	10	6	.625	35	12	3	1	0	124^1	126	63	15	2	44	53	12.5	3.98	100	.265	.330	6	.158	-1	-0	0	2	0.2
1956	Cle-A	2	2	.500	22	4	0	0	1	46^2	60	39	5	4	31	19	18.3	6.56	64	.317	.424	2	.167	-1	-12	-12	0	-1.0
1957	Cle-A	0	0	—	3	0	0	0	0	4	6	3	1	0	3	3	20.3	6.75	55	.353	.450	0	—	0	-1	-1	-0	-0.1
	Bal-A	0	0	—	5	1	0	0	0	6^2	20	13	0	0	3	3	31.1	17.55	20	.513	.548	1	.500	0	-10	-11	0	-0.5
	Yr	0	0	—	8	1	0	0	0	10^2	26	16	1	0	6	6	27.0	13.50	27	.464	.516	1	.500	0	-12	-12	0	-0.6
Total	12	87	91	.489	325	181	78	14	20	1555	1646	810	136	40	516	639	12.7	4.14	99	.272	.333	99	.193	-4	-16	-11	17	1.0

● ED HOVLIK Hovlik, Edward Charles b: 8/20/1891, Cleveland, Ohio d: 3/19/55, Painesville, Ohio BR/TR, 6', 180 lbs. Deb: 7/14/18 F

YEAR	TM/L	W	L	PCT	G	GS	CG	SH	SV	IP	H	R	HR	HB	BB	SO	RAT	ERA	ERA+	OAV	OOB	BH	AVG	PB	PR	PR+	PD	TPI
1918	Was-A	2	1	.667	8	2	1	0	0	28	25	10	0	0	10	10	11.3	1.29	212	.272	.343	1	.125	-1	5	5	-1	0.4
1919	Was-A	0	0	—	3	0	0	0	0	5^2	12	10	0	0	9	3	33.4	12.71	25	.480	.618	0	.000	-0	-6	-6	0	-0.3
Total	2	2	1	.667	11	2	1	0	0	33^2	37	20	0	0	19	13	15.0	3.21	88	.316	.412	1	.100	-1	-1	-2	-0	0.1

YEAR	TM/L	W	L	PCT	G	GS	CG	SH	SV	IP	H	R	HR	HB	BB	SO	RAT	ERA	ERA+	OAV	OOB	BH	AVG	PB	PR	PR+	PD	TPI
● **JOE HOVLIK**	Hovlik, Joseph b: 8/16/1884, Czechoslovakia d: 11/3/51, Oxford Junction, Ia BR/TR, 5′10.5″, 194 lbs. Deb: 7/10/09 F																											
1909	Was-A	0	0	—	3	0	0	0	0	6	13	10	0	1	3	1	25.5	4.50	54	.419	.486	0	.000	0	-1	-1	0	0.0
1910	Was-A	0	0	—	1	0	0	0	0	1^{2}	6	5	0	1	0	0	37.8	16.20	15	.500	.538	0	—	0	-3	-3	-0	-0.1
1911	Chi-A	2	0	1.000	12	3	1	1	0	47	47	21	1	0	20	24	12.8	3.06	105	.257	.330	1	.077	-0	1	1	1	0.1
Total	3	2	0	1.000	16	3	1	1	0	54^{2}	66	36	1	2	23	25	15.0	3.62	86	.292	.363	1	.067	-0	-2	-3	1	0.0
● **BRUCE HOWARD**	Howard, Bruce Ernest b: 3/23/43, Salisbury, Md. BB/TR, 6′2″, 180 lbs. Deb: 9/4/63 F																											
1963	Chi-A	2	1	.667	7	0	0	0	1	17	12	7	0	0	14	9	13.8	2.65	132	.207	.361	1	.250	0	2	2	-0	0.3
1964	Chi-A	2	1	.667	3	3	1	1	0	22^{1}	10	2	0	1	8	17	7.7	0.81	429	.139	.235	0	.000	-1	7	7	-0	0.9
1965	Chi-A	9	8	.529	30	22	1	1	0	148	123	61	13	1	72	120	11.9	3.47	92	.224	.316	6	.146	2	-0	-5	-1	-0.4
1966	Chi-A	9	5	.643	27	21	4	2	0	149	110	48	14	1	44	85	9.4	2.30	138	.202	.263	3	.070	-1	19	16	0	1.4
1967	Chi-A	3	10	.231	30	17	1	0	0	112^{2}	102	55	9	3	52	76	12.5	3.43	90	.240	.327	5	.179	1	-3	-4	1	-0.3
1968	Bal-A	0	2	.000	10	5	0	0	0	31	30	16	2	2	26	19	16.8	3.77	78	.268	.414	2	.286	2	-3	-3	0	0.0
	Was-A	1	4	.200	13	7	0	0	0	48^{2}	62	30	7	0	23	23	15.7	5.36	54	.330	.403	0	.000	-2	-13	-14	1	-1.4
	Yr	1	6	.143	23	12	0	0	0	79^{2}	92	46	9	2	49	42	16.2	4.74	62	.307	.407	2	.087	0	-16	-16	1	-1.4
Total	6	26	31	.456	120	75	7	4	1	528^{2}	449	219	45	8	239	349	11.8	3.18	99	.231	.317	17	.116	2	9	-2	1	0.5
● **CHRIS HOWARD**	Howard, Christian b: 11/18/65, Lynn, Mass. BR/TL, 6′, 185 lbs. Deb: 9/21/93																											
1993	Chi-A	1	0	1.000	3	0	0	0	0	2^{1}	2	0	0	0	3	1	19.3	0.00	—	.286	.500	0	—	0	1	1	-0	0.2
1994	Bos-A	1	0	1.000	37	0	0	0	1	39^{2}	35	17	5	0	12	22	10.7	3.63	139	.233	.290	0	—	0	5	6	-0	0.2
1995	Tex-A	0	0	—	4	0	0	0	0	4	3	0	0	0	1	2	9.0	0.00	—	.231	.286	0	—	0	2	2	-0	0.1
Total	3	2	0	1.000	44	0	0	0	1	46	40	17	5	0	16	25	11.0	3.13	159	.235	.301	0	—	0	8	9	-1	0.5
● **DAVID HOWARD**	Howard, David Wayne b: 2/26/67, Sarasota, Fla. BB/TR, 6′, 175 lbs. Deb: 4/14/91 F◆																											
1994	KC-A	0	0	—	1	0	0	0	0	2	2	1	0	0	5	0	31.5	4.50	111	.286	.583	19	.229	0	0	0	-0	0.0
● **EARL HOWARD**	Howard, Earl Nycum b: 6/25/1893, Everett, Pa. d: 4/4/37, Everett, Pa. BR/TR, 6′1″, 160 lbs. Deb: 4/18/18																											
1918	StL-N	0	0	—	1	0	0	0	0	2	0	0	0	0	2	0	9.0	0.00	—	.000	.286	0	—	0	1	1	1	0.1
● **FRED HOWARD**	Howard, Fred Irving b: 9/2/56, Portland, Maine BR/TR, 6′3″, 190 lbs. Deb: 5/26/79																											
1979	Chi-A	1	5	.167	28	6	0	0	0	68	73	34	5	1	32	36	14.0	3.57	119	.283	.364	0	—	0	5	5	-1	0.3
● **DEL HOWARD**	Howard, George Elmer b: 12/24/1877, Kenney, Ill. d: 12/24/56, Seattle, Wash. BL/TR, 6′, 180 lbs. Deb: 4/15/05 F◆																											
1905	Pit-N	0	0	—	1	0	0	0	0	6	4	7	1	1	1	0	9.0	0.00	—	.200	.273	127	.292	0	2	2	0	0.2
● **LEE HOWARD**	Howard, Lee Vincent b: 11/11/23, Staten Island, N.Y BL/TL, 6′2″, 175 lbs. Deb: 9/22/46																											
1946	Pit-N	0	1	.000	3	2	1	0	0	13^{1}	14	3	0	0	9	6	15.5	2.03	174	.286	.397	0	.000	-1	2	2	-0	0.1
1947	Pit-N	0	0	—	2	0	0	0	0	2^{2}	4	1	1	0	0	2	13.5	3.38	125	.333	.333	0	—	0	0	0	-0	0.0
Total	2	0	1	.000	5	2	1	0	0	16	18	4	1	0	9	8	15.2	2.25	162	.295	.386	0	.000	-1	2	2	-0	0.1
● **CAL HOWE**	Howe, Calvin Earl b: 11/27/24, Rock Falls, Ill. BL/TL, 6′3″, 205 lbs. Deb: 9/26/52																											
1952	Chi-N	0	0	—	1	0	0	0	0	2	0	0	0	0	1	2	4.5	0.00	—	.000	.143	0	—	0	1	1	-0	0.0
● **LES HOWE**	Howe, Lester Curtis "Lucky" b: 8/24/1895, Brooklyn, N.Y. d: 7/16/76, Woodmere, N.Y. BR/TR, 5′11.5″, 170 lbs. Deb: 8/18/23																											
1923	Bos-A	1	0	1.000	12	2	0	0	0	30	23	10	0	1	7	7	9.3	2.40	171	.211	.265	0	.000	-1	5	6	0	0.2
1924	Bos-A	1	0	1.000	4	0	0	0	0	7^{1}	11	6	1	1	2	3	17.2	7.36	59	.423	.483	1	.500	0	-3	-2	0	-0.2
Total	2	2	0	1.000	16	2	0	0	0	37^{1}	34	16	1	2	9	10	10.8	3.38	123	.252	.308	1	.125	-1	3	3	0	0.0
● **STEVE HOWE**	Howe, Steven Roy b: 3/10/58, Pontiac, Mich. BL/TL, 6′1″, 180 lbs. Deb: 4/11/80																											
1980	LA-N	7	9	.438	59	0	0	0	17	84^{2}	83	33	1	2	22	39	11.4	2.66	132	.256	.307	1	.091	-1	9	8	1	1.8
1981	*LA-N	5	3	.625	41	0	0	0	8	54	51	17	2	0	18	32	11.5	2.50	133	.254	.315	0	.000	0	6	5	-1	0.8
1982	LA-N★	7	5	.583	66	0	0	0	13	99^{1}	87	27	3	0	17	49	9.4	2.08	167	.240	.274	0	.000	-1	17	16	-0	2.1
1983	LA-N	4	7	.364	46	0	0	0	18	68^{2}	55	15	2	1	12	52	8.9	1.44	250	.217	.256	1	.125	0	17	17	1	3.6
1985	LA-N	1	1	.500	19	0	0	0	3	22	30	17	2	1	5	11	14.7	4.91	71	.319	.360	0	—	0	-3	-4	0	-0.4
	Min-A	2	3	.400	13	0	0	0	0	19	28	16	1	0	7	10	16.6	6.16	72	.333	.385	0	—	0	-4	-3	-0	-0.7
1987	Tex-A	3	3	.500	24	0	0	0	1	31^{1}	33	15	2	3	8	19	12.6	4.31	104	.280	.341	0	—	0	1	1	0	0.1
1991	NY-A	3	1	.750	37	0	0	0	3	48^{1}	39	12	1	3	7	34	9.1	1.68	247	.222	.263	0	—	0	13	13	0	1.1
1992	NY-A	3	0	1.000	20	0	0	0	6	22	9	7	1	0	3	12	4.9	2.45	160	.122	.156	0	—	0	4	4	1	0.7
1993	NY-A	3	5	.375	51	0	0	0	4	50^{2}	58	31	7	3	10	19	12.6	4.97	84	.297	.341	0	—	0	-4	-5	1	-0.6
1994	NY-A	3	0	1.000	40	0	0	0	15	40	28	8	2	0	7	18	7.9	1.80	254	.194	.232	0	—	0	13	13	-0	1.7
1995	*NY-A	6	3	.667	56	0	0	0	2	49	66	29	7	4	17	28	16.0	4.96	93	.324	.387	0	—	0	-1	-2	1	-0.2
1996	NY-A	0	1	.000	25	0	0	0	1	17	19	12	1	1	6	5	13.8	6.35	78	.284	.351	0	—	0	-3	-3	0	-0.1
Total	12	47	41	.534	497	0	0	0	91	606	586	239	32	18	139	328	11.0	3.03	129	.255	.303	2	.074	-1	64	60	3	9.9
● **HARRY HOWELL**	Howell, Henry Harry b: 11/14/1876, New Jersey d: 5/22/56, Spokane, Wash. BR/TR, 5′9″, Deb: 10/10/1898 U◆																											
1898	Bro-N	2	0	1.000	2	2	2	0	0	18	15	11	0	1	11	2	13.5	5.00	72	.224	.342	2	.250	0	-3	-3	0	-0.2
1899	Bal-N	13	8	.619	28	25	21	0	1	209^{1}	248	126	1	10	69	58	14.1	3.91	101	.294	.355	12	.146	-3	-1	1	1	-0.2
1900	*Bro-N	6	5	.545	21	10	7	2	0	110^{1}	131	69	4	3	36	26	13.9	3.75	102	.294	.351	12	.286	4	-1	1	1	0.5
1901	Bal-A	14	21	.400	37	34	32	1	0	294^{2}	333	188	5	7	79	93	12.8	3.67	106	.281	.330	41	.218	1	0	6	-1	0.6
1902	Bal-A	9	15	.375	26	23	19	1	0	199	243	136	5	7	48	33	13.5	4.12	92	.301	.346	93	.268	5	-12	-7	4	0.2
1903	NY-A	9	6	.600	25	15	13	0	0	155^{2}	140	79	4	6	44	62	11.0	3.53	89	.240	.300	23	.217	2	-10	-7	3	-0.1
1904	StL-A	13	21	.382	34	33	32	2	0	299^{2}	254	99	1	13	60	122	9.8	2.19	113	.230	.278	25	.221	5	14	10	9	3.0
1905	StL-A	15	22	.405	38	37	**35**	4	0	323	252	109	2	12	101	198	10.2	1.98	129	.217	.286	26	.193	3	24	21	18	**5.0**
1906	StL-A	15	14	.517	35	33	30	6	1	276^{2}	233	98	1	10	61	140	9.9	2.11	122	.231	.282	13	.126	-3	18	15	8	2.1
1907	StL-A	16	15	.516	42	35	26	2	3	316^{1}	258	112	3	8	88	118	10.1	1.93	130	.225	.285	27	.237	6	21	21	8	3.8
1908	StL-A	18	18	.500	41	32	27	2	1	324^{1}	279	103	1	17	70	117	10.2	1.89	127	.240	.293	22	.183	1	18	18	0	2.3
1909	StL-A	1	1	.500	10	3	0	0	0	37^{1}	42	21	0	3	8	16	12.8	3.13	77	.294	.344	6	.176	0	-3	-3	-0	-0.2
1910	StL-A	0	0	—	1	0	0	0	0	3^{1}	7	7	0	0	2	1	24.3	10.80	23	.467	.529	0	.000	-0	-3	-3	0	-0.2
Total	13	131	146	.473	340	282	244	20	6	2567^{2}	2435	1158	27	97	677	986	11.2	2.74	108	.252	.307	302	.217	21	63	64	51	16.6
● **JAY HOWELL**	Howell, Jay Canfield b: 11/26/55, Miami, Fla. BR/TR, 6′3″, 205 lbs. Deb: 8/10/80																											
1980	Cin-N	0	0	—	5	0	0	0	0	3^{1}	8	5	0	1	0	1	24.3	13.50	27	.471	.500	0	—	0	-4	-4	-0	-0.2
1981	Chi-N	2	0	1.000	10	2	0	0	0	22^{1}	23	13	3	2	10	10	14.1	4.84	76	.277	.368	0	.000	0	-3	-3	1	-0.1
1982	NY-A	2	3	.400	6	6	0	0	0	28	42	25	1	0	13	21	17.7	7.71	52	.341	.404	0	—	0	-11	-12	-0	-1.7
1983	NY-A	1	5	.167	19	12	2	0	0	82	89	53	7	3	35	61	13.9	5.38	73	.275	.351	0	—	0	-12	-14	0	-0.9
1984	NY-A	9	4	.692	61	1	0	0	7	103^{2}	86	33	5	0	34	109	10.4	2.69	141	.223	.286	0	—	0	15	13	2	1.9
1985	Oak-A☆	9	8	.529	63	0	0	0	29	98	98	32	5	1	31	68	11.9	2.85	136	.261	.319	0	—	0	14	12	0	2.4
1986	Oak-A	3	6	.333	38	0	0	0	16	53^{1}	53	23	3	1	23	42	13.0	3.38	115	.262	.341	0	—	0	5	3	-0	0.6
1987	Oak-A★	3	4	.429	36	0	0	0	16	44^{1}	48	30	6	1	21	35	14.2	5.89	70	.277	.359	0	—	0	-7	-9	-0	-1.8
1988	*LA-N	5	3	.625	50	0	0	0	21	65	44	16	1	1	21	70	9.1	2.08	161	.188	.258	0	.000	-0	10	9	-0	1.7
1989	LA-N★	5	3	.625	56	0	0	0	28	79^{2}	60	15	3	0	22	55	9.3	1.58	216	.211	.268	0	.000	-0	17	17	-0	2.8
1990	LA-N	5	5	.500	45	0	0	0	16	66	59	17	5	6	20	59	11.6	2.18	168	.242	.315	0	.000	-0	12	11	-0	2.1
1991	LA-N	6	5	.545	44	0	0	0	16	51	39	19	3	1	11	40	9.0	3.18	113	.213	.262	0	—	0	3	2	0	0.5
1992	LA-N	1	3	.250	41	0	0	0	4	46^{2}	41	9	2	1	18	36	11.6	1.54	224	.230	.305	0	—	0	10	10	0	1.1
1993	Atl-N	3	3	.500	54	0	0	0	0	58^{1}	48	16	3	0	16	37	9.9	2.31	174	.229	.283	0	—	0	11	11	-0	1.0
1994	Tex-A	4	1	.800	40	0	0	0	2	43	44	29	10	1	16	22	12.8	5.44	89	.262	.330	0	—	0	-3	-3	0	-0.3
Total	15	58	53	.523	568	21	2	0	155	844^{2}	782	335	57	19	291	666	11.6	3.34	114	.246	.313	0	.000	-1	57	45	2	9.1
● **KEN HOWELL**	Howell, Kenneth b: 11/28/60, Detroit, Mich. BR/TR, 6′3″, 228 lbs. Deb: 6/25/84																											
1984	LA-N	5	5	.500	32	1	0	0	6	51^{1}	51	21	1	1	9	54	10.7	3.33	106	.267	.303	0	.000	-1	1	1	0	0.2
1985	*LA-N	4	7	.364	56	0	0	0	12	86	66	41	8	0	35	85	10.6	3.77	92	.208	.287	0	.000	-0	-2	-3	0	-0.4
1986	LA-N	6	12	.333	62	0	0	0	12	97^{2}	86	48	7	3	63	104	14.0	3.87	89	.239	.357	0	.000	-1	-2	-5	-1	-1.1

YEAR	TM/L	W	L	PCT	G	GS	CG	SH	SV	IP	H	R	HR	HB	BB	SO	RAT	ERA	ERA+	OAV	OOB	BH	AVG	PB	PR	PR+	PD	TPI
1987	LA-N	3	4	.429	40	2	0	0	1	55	54	32	7	0	29	60	13.6	4.91	81	.265	.356	1	.250	0	-5	-6	-0	-0.7
1988	LA-N	0	1	.000	4	1	0	0	0	12^{2}	16	10	0	0	4	12	14.2	6.39	52	.320	.370	0	.000	-0	-4	-4	-0	-0.4
1989	Phi-N	12	12	.500	33	32	1	1	0	204	155	84	11	2	86	164	10.7	3.44	103	.215	.300	6	.092	-2	1	2	-1	-0.1
1990	Phi-N	8	7	.533	18	18	2	0	0	106^{2}	106	60	12	3	49	70	13.3	4.64	82	.260	.343	2	.067	-1	-10	-10	-1	-1.4
Total	7	38	48	.442	245	54	3	1	31	613^{1}	534	296	46	9	275	549	12.0	3.95	91	.237	.323	9	.079	-5	-19	-23	-3	-3.9

● DIXIE HOWELL

Howell, Millard b: 1/7/20, Bowman, Ky. d: 3/18/60, Hollywood, Fla. BL/TR, 6′2″, 210 lbs. Deb: 9/14/40

YEAR	TM/L	W	L	PCT	G	GS	CG	SH	SV	IP	H	R	HR	HB	BB	SO	RAT	ERA	ERA+	OAV	OOB	BH	AVG	PB	PR	PR+	PD	TPI
1940	Cle-A	0	0	—	3	0	0	0	0	5	2	1	0	0	4	2	10.8	1.80	234	.143	.333	0	—	0	1	1	0	0.1
1949	Cin-N	0	1	.000	5	1	0	0	0	13^{1}	21	12	3	0	8	7	19.6	8.10	52	.362	.439	1	.111	-0	-6	-6	0	-0.4
1955	Chi-A	8	3	.727	35	0	0	0	9	73^{2}	70	27	1	0	25	25	11.6	2.93	135	.250	.311	8	.381	2	8	8	1	1.7
1956	Chi-A	5	6	.455	34	1	0	0	4	64^{1}	79	39	3	2	36	28	16.4	4.62	89	.309	.398	4	.235	2	-3	-4	0	-0.4
1957	Chi-A	6	5	.545	37	0	0	0	6	68^{1}	64	25	6	0	30	37	12.4	3.29	113	.255	.335	5	.185	4	4	3	1	1.0
1958	Chi-A	0	0	—	1	0	0	0	0	1^{2}	0	0	0	0	0	0	0.0	0.00	—	.000	.000	0	—	0	1	1	0	0.0
Total	6	19	15	.559	115	2	0	0	19	226^{1}	236	104	13	2	103	99	13.6	3.78	104	.273	.352	18	.243	8	5	4	2	2.0

● ROLAND HOWELL

Howell, Roland Boatner "Billiken" b: 1/3/1892, Napoleonville, La. d: 3/31/73, Baton Rouge, La. BR/TR, 6′4″, 210 lbs. Deb: 6/14/12

YEAR	TM/L	W	L	PCT	G	GS	CG	SH	SV	IP	H	R	HR	HB	BB	SO	RAT	ERA	ERA+	OAV	OOB	BH	AVG	PB	PR	PR+	PD	TPI
1912	StL-N	0	0	—	3	0	0	0	0	1^{2}	5	5	0	0	5	0	54.0	27.00	13	.556	.714	0	—	0	-4	-4	-0	-0.2

● BOBBY HOWRY

Howry, Bobby Dean b: 8/4/73, Phoenix, Ariz. BL/TR, 6′5″, 215 lbs. Deb: 6/21/98

YEAR	TM/L	W	L	PCT	G	GS	CG	SH	SV	IP	H	R	HR	HB	BB	SO	RAT	ERA	ERA+	OAV	OOB	BH	AVG	PB	PR	PR+	PD	TPI
1998	Chi-A	0	3	.000	44	0	0	0	9	54^{1}	37	20	7	2	19	51	9.6	3.15	145	.194	.274	0	—	0	9	9	-0	0.6
1999	Chi-A	5	3	.625	69	0	0	0	28	67^{2}	58	34	8	3	38	80	13.2	3.59	136	.229	.337	0	—	0	10	10	-1	1.5
2000	*Chi-A	2	4	.333	65	0	0	0	7	71	54	26	6	4	29	60	11.0	3.17	157	.216	.307	0	—	0	14	14	-0	1.2
Total	3	7	10	.412	178	0	0	0	44	193	149	80	21	9	86	191	11.4	3.31	146	.215	.309	0	—	0	33	32	-1	3.3

● PETER HOY

Hoy, Peter Alexander b: 6/29/66, Brockville, Ont., Canada BL/TR, 6′7″, 220 lbs. Deb: 4/11/92

YEAR	TM/L	W	L	PCT	G	GS	CG	SH	SV	IP	H	R	HR	HB	BB	SO	RAT	ERA	ERA+	OAV	OOB	BH	AVG	PB	PR	PR+	PD	TPI
1992	Bos-A	0	0	—	5	0	0	0	0	3^{2}	8	3	0	0	2	2	24.5	7.36	57	.471	.526	0	—	0	-1	-1	0	0.0

● TEX HOYLE

Hoyle, Roland Edison b: 7/17/21, Carbondale, Pa. d: 7/4/94, Carbondale, Pa. BR/TR, 6′4″, 170 lbs. Deb: 4/18/52

YEAR	TM/L	W	L	PCT	G	GS	CG	SH	SV	IP	H	R	HR	HB	BB	SO	RAT	ERA	ERA+	OAV	OOB	BH	AVG	PB	PR	PR+	PD	TPI
1952	Phi-A	0	0	—	3	0	0	0	0	2^{1}	9	7	2	0	1	1	38.6	27.00	15	.563	.588	0	—	0	-6	-6	0	-0.3

● LA MARR HOYT

Hoyt, Dewey La Marr b: 1/1/55, Columbia, S.C. BR/TR, 6′1″, 222 lbs. Deb: 9/14/79

YEAR	TM/L	W	L	PCT	G	GS	CG	SH	SV	IP	H	R	HR	HB	BB	SO	RAT	ERA	ERA+	OAV	OOB	BH	AVG	PB	PR	PR+	PD	TPI
1979	Chi-A	0	0	—	2	0	0	0	0	3	2	0	0	0	0	0	6.0	0.00	—	.200	.200	0	—	0	1	1	-0	0.1
1980	Chi-A	9	3	.750	24	13	3	1	0	112^{1}	123	66	8	2	41	55	13.3	4.57	88	.281	.345	0	—	0	-7	-7	-2	-0.8
1981	Chi-A	9	3	.750	43	1	0	0	10	90^{2}	80	40	10	3	28	60	11.0	3.57	100	.240	.305	0	—	0	1	0	-1	-0.1
1982	Chi-A	**19**	15	.559	39	32	14	2	0	239^{2}	248	104	17	2	48	124	11.2	3.53	115	.266	.303	0	—	0	15	14	-1	1.7
1983	*Chi-A	**24**	10	.706	36	36	11	1	0	260^{2}	236	115	27	1	31	148	**9.3**	3.66	115	.238	**.262**	0	—	0	12	15	5	2.4
1984	Chi-A	13	18	.419	34	34	11	1	0	235^{2}	244	127	31	5	43	126	11.2	4.47	93	.266	.302	0	—	0	-12	-8	1	-0.8
1985	SD-N★	16	8	.667	31	31	8	3	0	210^{1}	210	85	20	2	20	83	9.9	3.47	102	.261	.281	4	.063	-4	3	2	1	-0.1
1986	SD-N	8	11	.421	35	25	1	0	0	159	170	100	27	3	68	85	13.6	5.15	71	.276	.351	6	.130	-1	-25	-27	-2	-3.1
Total	8	98	68	.590	244	172	48	8	10	1311^{1}	1313	637	140	18	279	681	11.0	3.99	99	.260	.302	10	.091	-5	-12	-8	1	-0.7

● WAITE HOYT

Hoyt, Waite Charles "Schoolboy" b: 9/9/1899, Brooklyn, N.Y. d: 8/25/84, Cincinnati, Ohio BR/TR, 6′, 180 lbs. Deb: 7/24/18 H

YEAR	TM/L	W	L	PCT	G	GS	CG	SH	SV	IP	H	R	HR	HB	BB	SO	RAT	ERA	ERA+	OAV	OOB	BH	AVG	PB	PR	PR+	PD	TPI
1918	NY-N	0	0	—	1	0	0	0	0	1	0	0	0	0	0	2	0.0	0.00	—	.000	.000	0	.000	-0	0	0	0	0.0
1919	Bos-A	4	6	.400	13	11	6	1	0	105^{1}	99	42	1	0	22	28	10.3	3.25	93	.262	.303	5	.132	-3	-0	-3	1	-0.4
1920	Bos-A	6	6	.500	22	11	6	2	1	121^{1}	123	72	2	1	47	45	12.7	4.38	83	.270	.339	5	.116	-3	-8	-10	1	-1.1
1921	*NY-A	19	13	.594	43	32	21	1	3	282^{1}	301	121	3	5	81	102	12.3	3.09	137	.276	.329	22	.222	-2	37	36	-1	3.4
1922	*NY-A	19	12	.613	37	31	17	3	0	265	271	114	13	9	76	95	12.1	3.43	117	.269	.326	20	.217	1	18	17	-2	1.7
1923	*NY-A	17	9	.654	37	28	19	1	1	238^{2}	227	97	9	4	66	60	11.2	3.02	131	.253	.307	16	.190	-2	26	25	-1	2.1
1924	NY-A	18	13	.581	46	32	14	2	4	247	295	117	8	3	76	71	13.6	3.79	110	.300	.352	10	.133	-5	12	10	-0	0.6
1925	NY-A	11	14	.440	46	30	17	1	6	243	283	124	14	1	78	86	13.4	4.00	107	.292	.346	24	.304	6	11	7	3	1.4
1926	*NY-A	16	12	.571	40	28	12	1	4	217^{2}	224	112	4	2	62	79	11.9	3.85	100	.264	.316	16	.211	-0	4	0	-3	-0.3
1927	*NY-A	**22**	7	**.759**	36	32	23	3	1	256^{1}	242	90	10	4	54	86	10.5	2.63	146	.251	.294	22	.222	0	43	37	-0	3.8
1928	*NY-A	23	7	.767	42	31	19	3	**8**	273	279	118	16	1	60	67	11.2	3.36	112	.272	.313	28	.257	2	21	13	-1	1.3
1929	NY-A	10	9	.526	30	25	12	0	1	201^{2}	219	115	9	3	69	57	13.0	4.24	91	.279	.339	17	.224	1	0	-9	-2	-0.8
1930	NY-A	2	2	.500	8	7	2	0	0	47^{2}	64	27	7	0	9	10	13.8	4.53	95	.317	.346	1	.063	-2	-1	-1	-0	-0.3
	Det-A	9	8	.529	26	20	8	1	4	135^{2}	176	89	7	2	47	25	14.9	4.78	100	.313	.368	9	.196	-2	-2	0	-3	-0.5
	Yr	11	10	.524	34	27	10	1	4	183^{1}	240	116	14	2	56	35	14.6	4.71	99	.314	.363	10	.161	-4	-1	-1	-3	-0.8
1931	Det-A	3	8	.273	16	12	5	0	0	92	124	70	2	2	32	10	15.5	5.87	78	.319	.374	4	.133	-2	-15	-13	-0	-1.4
	*Phi-A	10	5	.667	16	14	9	2	0	111	130	60	9	0	37	30	13.5	4.22	107	.298	.353	13	.302	3	2	3	1	0.7
	Yr	13	13	.500	32	26	14	2	0	203	254	130	11	2	69	40	14.4	4.97	91	.308	.363	17	.233	0	-13	-9	0	-0.7
1932	Bro-N	1	3	.250	8	4	0	0	1	26^{2}	38	27	3	0	12	7	16.9	7.76	49	.342	.407	0	.000	-1	-12	-12	1	-1.5
	NY-N	5	7	.417	18	12	3	0	0	97^{1}	103	43	6	5	25	29	12.3	3.42	109	.275	.328	3	.097	-2	5	3	1	0.2
	Yr	6	10	.375	26	16	3	0	1	124	141	70	9	5	37	36	13.3	4.35	86	.290	.347	3	.081	-3	-7	-9	2	-1.3
1933	Pit-N	5	7	.417	36	8	4	1	4	117	118	45	3	1	19	44	10.6	2.92	114	.262	.293	5	.156	-1	5	5	1	0.5
1934	Pit-N	15	6	.714	48	17	8	3	5	190^{2}	184	75	6	2	43	105	10.8	2.93	141	.252	.296	10	.179	-1	24	25	-1	2.5
1935	Pit-N	7	11	.389	39	11	5	0	6	164	187	72	8	1	27	63	11.8	3.40	121	.285	.315	14	.259	2	11	13	-0	1.5
1936	Pit-N	7	5	.583	22	9	6	0	1	116^{2}	115	44	5	3	20	37	10.6	2.70	150	.255	.291	6	.154	-1	17	17	1	1.6
1937	Pit-N	1	2	.333	11	0	0	0	2	28	31	14	3	0	6	21	11.9	4.50	86	.270	.306	1	.083	-1	-2	-2	-1	-0.4
	Bro-N	7	7	.500	27	19	10	1	0	167	180	83	5	0	30	44	11.3	3.23	125	.270	.301	4	.083	-2	13	14	-1	0.8
	Yr	8	9	.471	38	19	10	1	2	195	211	97	8	0	36	65	11.4	3.42	117	.270	.302	5	.083	-3	11	13	-2	0.4
1938	Bro-N	0	3	.000	6	1	0	0	0	16^{1}	24	9	1	0	5	3	16.0	4.96	79	.333	.377	0	.000	-0	-2	-2	-0	-0.3
Total	21	237	182	.566	674	425	226	26	52	3762^{1}	4037	1780	154	49	1003	1206	12.2	3.59	112	.276	.325	255	.198	-17	210	177	-7	15.1

● AL HRABOSKY

Hrabosky, Alan Thomas b: 7/21/49, Oakland, Cal. BR/TL, 5′11″, 185 lbs. Deb: 6/16/70

YEAR	TM/L	W	L	PCT	G	GS	CG	SH	SV	IP	H	R	HR	HB	BB	SO	RAT	ERA	ERA+	OAV	OOB	BH	AVG	PB	PR	PR+	PD	TPI
1970	StL-N	2	1	.667	16	1	0	0	0	19	22	10	2	0	7	12	13.7	4.74	87	.286	.345	0	.000	-0	-1	-1	-1	-0.3
1971	StL-N	0	0	—	1	0	0	0	0	2	2	0	0	0	0	2	9.0	0.00	—	.250	.250	0	—	0	1	1	-0	0.0
1972	StL-N	1	0	1.000	5	0	0	0	0	7	2	0	0	0	3	9	6.4	0.00	—	.087	.192	0	.000	-0	3	3	-0	0.4
1973	StL-N	2	4	.333	44	0	0	0	5	56	45	15	2	2	21	57	10.9	2.09	175	.220	.298	0	.000	-0	10	10	-1	1.1
1974	StL-N	8	1	.889	65	0	0	0	9	88^{1}	71	34	3	1	38	82	11.2	2.95	121	.221	.306	4	.308	1	7	6	-1	0.8
1975	StL-N	13	3	.813	65	0	0	0	**22**	97^{1}	72	27	3	1	33	82	9.8	1.66	226	.205	.275	3	.200	1	**21**	**22**	-2	4.6
1976	StL-N	8	6	.571	68	0	0	0	13	95^{1}	89	42	5	4	39	73	12.5	3.30	107	.252	.333	0	.000	0	2	2	-0	0.4
1977	StL-N	6	5	.545	65	0	0	0	10	86^{1}	82	44	12	3	41	68	13.1	4.38	88	.256	.346	0	.000	-1	-4	-5	-1	-0.9
1978	*KC-A	8	7	.533	58	0	0	0	20	75	52	24	6	1	35	60	10.6	2.88	133	.200	.297	0	—	0	7	8	-0	1.6
1979	KC-A	9	4	.692	58	0	0	0	11	65	67	31	3	1	41	39	15.1	3.74	114	.272	.378	0	—	0	4	4	-2	0.6
1980	Atl-N	4	2	.667	45	0	0	0	3	59^{2}	50	27	8	0	31	31	12.2	3.62	104	.223	.318	0	.000	-0	-0	1	-2	-0.1
1981	Atl-N	1	1	.500	24	0	0	0	1	33^{2}	24	5	1	0	9	13	8.8	1.07	335	.207	.264	0	.000	-0	9	9	-1	0.5
1982	Atl-N	2	1	.667	31	0	0	0	3	37^{1}	41	25	5	0	17	20	14.0	5.54	67	.285	.360	1	.333	0	-8	-7	-1	-0.7
Total	13	64	35	.646	545	1	0	0	97	722	619	284	50	13	315	548	11.8	3.10	121	.234	.318	8	.143	0	49	52	-11	8.0

● CARL HUBBELL

Hubbell, Carl Owen "King Carl" or "The Mealticket"
b: 6/22/03, Carthage, Mo. d: 11/21/88, Scottsdale, Ariz. BR/TL (BB 1928-29, 31-32), 6′, 170 lbs. Deb: 7/26/28 H

YEAR	TM/L	W	L	PCT	G	GS	CG	SH	SV	IP	H	R	HR	HB	BB	SO	RAT	ERA	ERA+	OAV	OOB	BH	AVG	PB	PR	PR+	PD	TPI
1928	NY-N	10	6	.625	20	14	8	1	1	124	117	49	7	3	21	37	10.2	2.83	138	.248	.284	5	.106	-3	16	15	2	1.8
1929	NY-N	18	11	.621	39	35	19	1	1	268	273	128	17	6	67	106	11.6	3.69	124	.265	.313	12	.129	-6	30	27	5	2.4
1930	NY-N	17	12	.586	37	32	17	3	2	241^{2}	263	120	11	11	58	117	12.4	3.87	122	.278	.327	13	.151	-5	29	24	-1	1.8
1931	NY-N	14	12	.538	36	30	21	4	3	248	211	88	14	4	67	155	**10.2**	2.65	139	**.227**	**.282**	20	.241	4	34	30	-2	3.3
1932	NY-N	18	11	.621	40	32	22	0	2	284	260	96	20	4	40	137	**9.6**	2.50	148	.238	**.268**	26	.241	4	43	40	6	**5.0**
1933	*NY-N★	**23**	12	.657	45	33	22	**10**	5	**308^{2}**	256	69	6	3	47	156	**8.9**	**1.66**	**193**	.227	**.260**	20	.183	1	**58**	**55**	7	**7.8**
1934	NY-N★	21	12	.636	49	35	**25**	5	**8**	313	286	100	17	2	37	118	**9.3**	**2.30**	**168**	.239	**.263**	23	.197	-1	**61**	**57**	4	6.3
1935	NY-N☆	23	12	.657	42	35	24	1	0	302^{2}	314	125	27	3	49	150	10.9	3.27	118	.263	.294	26	.239	4	25	20	4	3.0
1936	*NY-N★	**26**	6	**.813**	42	34	25	3	3	304	265	81	7	5	57	123	**9.7**	**2.31**	**169**	.236	**.276**	25	.227	1	**58**	**55**	1	**5.7**
1937	*NY-N★	**22**	8	**.733**	39	32	18	4	4	261^{2}	261	108	18	3	55	**159**	11.0	3.20	122	.257	.298	21	.216	1	21	20	-1	2.1

YEAR	TM/L	W	L	PCT	G	GS	CG	SH	SV	IP	H	R	HR	HB	BB	SO	RAT	ERA	ERA+	OAV	OOB	BH	AVG	PB	PR	PR+	PD	TPI
1938	NY-N☆	13	10	.565	24	22	13	1	1	179	171	70	16	2	33	104	**10.4**	3.07	123	.249	**.285**	9	.155	-2	14	14	-1	1.4
1939	NY-N	11	9	.550	29	18	10	0	2	154	150	60	11	2	24	62	**10.3**	2.75	143	.249	**.280**	8	.151	-1	20	20	1	2.5
1940	NY-N★	11	12	.478	31	28	11	2	0	214^{1}	220	102	22	2	59	86	11.8	3.65	106	.259	.309	15	.185	-0	5	5	1	0.6
1941	NY-N☆	11	9	.550	26	22	11	1	1	164	169	73	10	2	53	75	12.3	3.57	104	.266	.325	8	.140	-2	1	2	-3	-0.2
1942	NY-N☆	11	8	.579	24	20	11	0	0	157^{1}	158	75	17	1	34	61	11.0	3.95	85	.259	.299	11	.183	-0	-11	-10	-1	-1.2
1943	NY-N	4	4	.500	12	11	3	0	0	66	87	36	7	0	24	31	15.1	4.91	70	.322	.378	4	.200	-0	-11	-11	-1	-1.2
Total	16	253	154	.622	535	433	260	36	33	3590^{1}	3461	1380	227	53	725	1677	10.6	2.98	130	.251	.291	246	.191	-5	394	364	22	41.1
● **BILL HUBBELL**	Hubbell, Wilbert William b: 6/17/1897, San Francisco, Cal. d: 8/3/80, Lakewood, Colo. BR/TR, 6'1.5", 195 lbs. Deb: 9/24/19																											
1919	NY-N	1	1	.500	2	2	2	0	0	18^{1}	19	4	0	2	2	3	11.3	1.96	143	.260	.299	1	.125	-1	2	2	-0	0.1
1920	NY-N	0	1	.000	14	0	0	0	2	30	26	12	2	1	15	8	12.6	2.10	143	.239	.336	1	.200	-0	3	3	1	0.3
	Phi-N	9	9	.500	24	18	9	1	2	150	176	77	3	4	42	26	13.3	3.84	89	.301	.352	7	.132	-3	-12	-6	-2	-1.3
	Yr	9	10	.474	38	18	9	1	4	180	202	89	5	5	57	34	13.2	3.55	94	.291	.349	8	.138	-3	-8	-4	-1	-1.0
1921	Phi-N	9	16	.360	36	30	15	1	2	220^{1}	269	146	18	3	38	43	12.7	4.33	98	.306	.337	12	.160	-2	-13	-2	-1	-0.4
1922	Phi-N	7	15	.318	35	26	11	1	1	189	257	136	14	4	41	33	14.4	5.00	93	.317	.353	12	.171	-2	-19	-6	0	-0.7
1923	Phi-N	1	6	.143	22	5	1	0	0	55	102	70	13	2	17	8	19.8	8.35	55	.394	.435	4	.235	0	-27	-20	0	-2.1
1924	Phi-N	10	9	.526	36	22	9	2	2	179	233	103	9	2	45	30	14.1	4.83	92	.324	.365	13	.220	-1	-19	-6	0	-0.6
1925	Phi-N	0	0	—	2	0	0	0	0	2^{2}	5	4	0	0	1	0	20.3	0.00	—	.385	.429	0	.000	-0	1	1	1	0.1
	Bro-N	3	6	.333	33	5	3	0	1	86^{2}	120	59	8	2	24	16	15.2	5.30	79	.337	.382	3	.150	0	-10	-11	1	-0.9
	Yr	3	6	.333	35	5	3	0	1	89^{1}	125	63	8	2	25	16	15.3	5.14	82	.339	.384	3	.143	0	-9	-10	2	-0.8
Total	7	40	63	.388	204	108	50	5	10	931	1207	611	67	20	225	167	14.0	4.68	89	.317	.359	53	.172	-8	-93	-47	0	-5.5
● **EARL HUCKLEBERRY**	Huckleberry, Earl Eugene b: 5/23/10, Konawa, Okla. d: 2/25/99, Seminole, Okla. BR/TR, 5'11", 165 lbs. Deb: 9/13/35																											
1935	Phi-A	1	0	1.000	1	1	0	0	0	6^{2}	8	7	1	0	4	2	16.2	9.45	48	.296	.387	0	.000	-0	-4	-4	-0	-0.4
● **JOHN HUDEK**	Hudek, John Raymond b: 8/8/66, Tampa, Fla. BB/TR, 6'1", 200 lbs. Deb: 4/23/94																											
1994	Hou-N★	0	2	.000	42	0	0	0	16	39^{1}	24	14	5	1	18	39	9.8	2.97	133	.174	.274	0	—	0	5	5	-0	0.5
1995	Hou-N	2	2	.500	19	0	0	0	7	20	19	12	3	0	5	29	10.8	5.40	72	.247	.293	1	1.000	1	-3	-4	1	-0.6
1996	Hou-N	2	0	1.000	15	0	0	0	2	16	12	5	2	0	5	14	9.6	2.81	138	.207	.270	0	—	0	3	2	1	0.3
1997	Hou-N	1	3	.250	40	0	0	0	4	40^{2}	38	27	8	3	33	36	16.4	5.98	67	.252	.396	0	—	0	-8	-9	0	-1.0
1998	NY-N	1	4	.200	28	0	0	0	0	27	23	13	2	2	19	28	14.7	4.00	103	.237	.373	0	—	0	1	0	0	0.1
	Cin-N	4	2	.667	30	0	0	0	0	37	27	14	6	2	28	40	13.9	2.43	176	.206	.354	0	.000	-0	7	8	-1	1.0
	Yr	5	6	.455	58	0	0	0	0	64	50	27	8	4	47	68	14.2	3.09	136	.219	.362	0	.000	-0	8	8	-0	1.1
1999	Cin-N	0	1	.000	2	0	0	0	0	1	4	3	1	0	3	0	63.0	27.00	17	.667	.778	0	—	0	-2	-2	0	-0.4
	Atl-N	0	1	.000	15	0	0	0	0	16^{2}	21	14	1	1	11	18	17.8	6.48	69	.296	.398	0	.000	-0	-4	-4	0	-0.2
	Yr	0	2	.000	17	0	0	0	0	17^{2}	25	17	2	1	14	18	20.4	7.64	59	.325	.435	0	.000	-0	-6	-6	0	-0.6
	Tor-A	0	0	—	3	0	0	0	0	3^{2}	8	5	1	0	1	2	22.1	12.27	40	.471	.500	0	—	0	-3	-3	-0	-0.1
Total	6	10	15	.400	194	0	0	0	29	201^{1}	176	107	29	9	123	206	13.8	4.43	93	.236	.351	1	.200	0	-4	-8	1	-0.4
● **WILLIS HUDLIN**	Hudlin, George Willis "Ace" b: 5/23/06, Wagoner, Okla. BR/TR, 6', 190 lbs. Deb: 8/15/26 C																											
1926	Cle-A	1	3	.250	8	2	1	0	0	32^{1}	25	13	1	2	13	6	11.1	2.78	146	.227	.320	1	.125	0	4	5	2	0.7
1927	Cle-A	18	12	.600	43	30	18	1	0	264^{2}	291	132	3	11	83	65	13.1	4.01	105	.283	.343	24	.250	2	4	5	3	1.1
1928	Cle-A	14	14	.500	42	26	10	0	7	220^{1}	231	114	7	7	90	62	13.4	4.04	103	.279	.355	14	.194	-0	0	2	2	0.5
1929	Cle-A	17	15	.531	40	33	22	2	1	280^{1}	299	122	7	1	73	60	12.0	3.34	133	.272	.318	19	.196	-3	28	33	7	3.7
1930	Cle-A	13	16	.448	37	33	13	1	1	216^{2}	255	133	12	1	76	60	13.8	4.57	106	.293	.351	16	.219	-1	2	6	5	1.0
1931	Cle-A	15	14	.517	44	34	15	1	4	254^{1}	313	155	14	1	88	83	14.2	4.60	100	.301	.356	20	.200	1	-6	1	4	0.5
1932	Cle-A	12	8	.600	33	21	12	0	2	181^{2}	204	108	10	1	59	65	13.1	4.71	101	.278	.332	13	.203	1	-5	1	1	0.2
1933	Cle-A	5	13	.278	34	17	6	0	1	147^{1}	161	85	7	3	61	44	13.7	3.97	112	.275	.346	6	.146	-1	5	7	4	1.1
1934	Cle-A	15	10	.600	36	26	15	1	4	195	210	109	8	5	65	58	12.9	4.75	96	.277	.338	14	.206	3	-6	-4	5	0.2
1935	Cle-A	15	11	.577	36	29	14	3	5	231^{2}	252	107	8	3	61	45	12.3	3.69	122	.277	.324	24	.279	6	20	21	0	2.7
1936	Cle-A	1	5	.167	27	7	1	0	0	64	112	74	1	2	31	20	20.4	9.00	56	.397	.460	2	.111	-1	-28	-28	1	-2.0
1937	Cle-A	12	11	.522	35	23	10	2	2	175^{2}	213	106	8	2	43	31	13.2	4.10	112	.295	.337	10	.169	-1	10	10	3	1.3
1938	Cle-A	8	8	.500	29	15	8	0	1	127	158	80	13	2	45	27	14.5	4.89	95	.303	.361	5	.116	-2	-1	-4	1	-0.5
1939	Cle-A	9	10	.474	27	20	7	0	3	143	175	85	6	1	42	28	13.7	4.91	90	.303	.352	9	.188	1	-5	-8	5	-0.4
1940	Cle-A	2	1	.667	4	4	2	0	0	23^{2}	31	13	3	0	2	8	12.5	4.94	85	.316	.330	1	.125	-0	-1	-2	-0	-0.2
	Was-A	1	2	.333	8	6	1	0	0	37^{1}	50	33	9	2	5	9	13.7	6.51	64	.314	.343	1	.100	-1	-9	-10	0	-0.7
	StL-A	0	1	.000	6	1	0	0	0	11^{1}	19	16	0	0	8	4	21.4	11.12	41	.358	.443	1	.500	0	-8	-8	0	-0.5
	Yr	3	4	.429	18	11	3	0	0	72^{1}	100	62	12	2	15	21	14.6	6.72	63	.323	.358	3	.150	-1	-19	-20	0	-1.4
	NY-N	0	1	.000	1	1	0	0	0	5	9	6	1	0	1	1	18.0	10.80	36	.409	.435	0	.000	-0	-4	-4	0	-0.5
1944	StL-A	0	1	.000	1	0	0	0	0	2	3	2	0	0	0	1	13.5	4.50	80	.300	.300	0	—	0	-0	-0	-0	0.0
Total	16	158	156	.503	491	328	155	11	31	2613^{1}	3011	1493	118	44	846	677	13.4	4.41	102	.289	.345	180	.201	4	-0	25	42	8.2
● **CHARLIE HUDSON**	Hudson, Charles b: 8/18/49, Ada, Okla. BL/TL, 6'3", 185 lbs. Deb: 5/21/72																											
1972	StL-N	1	0	1.000	12	0	0	0	0	12^{1}	10	8	0	1	7	4	13.1	5.11	67	.233	.353	0	—	0	-2	-2	0	-0.2
1973	Tex-A	4	2	.667	25	4	1	1	1	62^{1}	59	35	3	0	31	34	13.0	4.62	81	.254	.342	0	—	0	-6	-6	0	-0.6
1975	Cal-A	0	1	.000	3	1	0	0	0	5^{2}	7	6	0	0	4	0	17.5	9.53	37	.304	.407	0	—	0	-4	-4	0	-0.6
Total	3	5	3	.625	40	5	1	1	1	80^{1}	76	49	3	1	42	38	13.3	5.04	73	.255	.349	0	—	0	-11	-13	0	-1.4
● **CHARLES HUDSON**	Hudson, Charles Lynn b: 3/16/59, Ennis, Tex. BB/TR, 6'3", 185 lbs. Deb: 5/31/83																											
1983	*Phi-N	8	8	.500	26	26	3	0	0	169^{1}	158	73	13	0	53	101	11.2	3.35	107	.248	.305	5	.093	-2	5	4	-1	0.1
1984	Phi-N	9	11	.450	30	30	1	1	0	173^{2}	181	101	12	2	52	94	12.2	4.04	90	.265	.319	5	.089	-2	-9	-8	-2	-1.3
1985	Phi-N	8	13	.381	38	26	3	0	0	193	188	92	23	1	74	122	12.3	3.78	98	.252	.320	8	.140	-1	-4	-2	-2	-0.5
1986	Phi-N	7	10	.412	33	23	0	0	0	144	165	87	20	0	58	82	13.9	4.94	78	.291	.357	2	.047	-3	-19	-17	-0	-2.1
1987	NY-A	11	7	.611	35	16	6	2	0	154^{2}	137	63	19	3	57	100	11.5	3.61	122	.239	.311	0	—	0	15	14	-2	1.3
1988	NY-A	6	6	.500	28	12	1	0	2	106^{1}	93	53	9	4	36	58	11.3	4.49	88	.235	.306	0	—	0	-6	-6	-0	-0.7
1989	Det-A	1	5	.167	18	7	0	0	0	66^{2}	75	49	14	2	31	23	14.6	6.35	60	.288	.369	0	—	0	-18	-19	-1	-1.6
Total	7	50	60	.455	208	140	14	3	2	1007^{2}	997	518	110	12	361	580	12.2	4.14	93	.258	.324	20	.095	-8	-36	-34	-8	-4.8
● **HAL HUDSON**	Hudson, Hal Campbell "Bud" or "Lefty" b: 5/4/27, Grosse Pointe, Mich. BL/TL, 5'10", 175 lbs. Deb: 4/20/52																											
1952	StL-A	0	0	—	3	0	0	0	0	5^{2}	9	8	0	0	6	0	23.8	12.71	31	.360	.484	0	.000	-0	-6	-5	-0	-0.3
	Chi-A	0	0	—	2	0	0	0	0	4	7	2	0	0	1	4	18.0	2.25	162	.389	.421	0	—	0	1	1	-0	0.0
	Yr	0	0	—	5	0	0	0	0	9^{2}	16	10	0	0	7	4	21.4	8.38	45	.372	.460	0	.000	-0	-5	-5	-0	-0.3
1953	Chi-A	0	0	—	1	0	0	0	0	0^{2}	0	0	0	0	0	0	0.0	0.00	—	.000	.000	0	—	0	0	0	0	0.0
Total	2	0	0	—	6	0	0	0	0	10^{1}	16	10	0	0	7	4	20.0	7.84	49	.364	.451	0	.000	-0	-5	-4	-0	-0.3
● **JESSE HUDSON**	Hudson, Jesse James b: 7/22/48, Mansfield, La. BL/TL, 6'2", 165 lbs. Deb: 9/19/69																											
1969	NY-N	0	0	—	1	0	0	0	0	2	2	1	0	0	2	3	18.0	4.50	81	.250	.400	0	—	0	-0	-0	0	0.0
● **JOE HUDSON**	Hudson, Joseph Paul b: 9/29/70, Philadelphia, Pa. BR/TR, 6'1", 175 lbs. Deb: 6/10/95																											
1995	*Bos-A	0	1	.000	39	0	0	0	1	46	53	21	2	2	23	29	15.3	4.11	119	.301	.388	0	—	0	3	4	-0	0.2
1996	Bos-A	3	5	.375	36	0	0	0	1	45	57	35	4	0	32	19	17.8	5.40	94	.318	.422	0	—	0	-2	-2	0	-0.2
1997	Bos-A	3	1	.750	26	0	0	0	0	35^{2}	39	16	1	4	14	14	14.4	3.53	131	.289	.373	0	—	0	4	4	1	0.5
1998	Mil-N	0	0	—	1	0	0	0	0	0^{1}	2	6	0	0	4	0	162.0	162.00	3	1.000	1.000	0	—	0	-6	-6	0	-0.2
Total	4	6	7	.462	102	0	0	0	2	127	151	78	7	6	73	62	16.3	4.82	101	.307	.403	0	—	0	-1	1	0	0.3
● **NAT HUDSON**	Hudson, Nathaniel P. b: 1/12/1859, Chicago, Ill. d: 3/14/28, Chicago, Ill. BR/TR, Deb: 4/18/1886																											
1886	*StL-a	16	10	.615	29	27	25	0	**1**	234^{1}	224	122	3	2	62	100	11.1	3.03	113	.243	.293	35	.233	1	11	11	-1	0.9
1887	StL-a	4	4	.500	9	9	7	0	0	67	111	57	2	4	20	15	15.4	4.97	91	.349	.357	16	.308	0	-5	-3	-2	-0.4
1888	StL-a	25	10	**.714**	39	37	36	5	0	333	283	155	8	15	59	130	9.6	2.54	128	.222	.264	50	.255	5	19	25	-1	2.5
1889	StL-a	3	2	.600	9	5	4	0	0	60	71	47	2	4	15	13	13.5	4.20	101	.285	.336	13	.250	0	-2	0	-1	0.0
Total	4	48	26	.649	86	78	72	5	1	694^{1}	689	381	15	25	156	258	11.0	3.08	114	.249	.291	114	.253	6	23	33	-4	3.0

YEAR	TM/L	W	L	PCT	G	GS	CG	SH	SV	IP	H	R	HR	HB	BB	SO	RAT	ERA	ERA+	OAV	OOB	BH	AVG	PB	PR	PR+	PD	TPI
● **REX HUDSON**	Hudson, Rex Haughton b: 8/11/53, Tulsa, Okla. BB/TR, 5'11", 165 lbs. Deb: 7/27/74																											
1974	LA-N	0	0	—	1	0	0	0	0	2	6	5	2	0	0	0	27.0	22.50	15	.500	.500	0	—	0	-4	-5	-0	-0.2
● **SID HUDSON**	Hudson, Sidney Charles b: 1/3/15, Coalfield, Tenn. BR/TR, 6'4", 180 lbs. Deb: 4/18/40 C																											
1940	Was-A	17	16	.515	38	31	19	3	1	252	272	149	20	3	81	96	12.7	4.57	91	.274	.330	22	.237	2	-5	-12	1	-1.0
1941	Was-A★	13	14	.481	33	33	17	3	0	249^2	242	124	12	1	97	108	12.3	3.46	117	.253	.322	16	.186	-0	19	17	2	1.8
1942	Was-A☆	10	17	.370	35	31	19	1	2	239^1	266	140	9	5	70	72	12.8	4.36	84	.276	.328	19	.213	1	-19	-19	3	-1.5
1946	Was-A	8	11	.421	31	15	6	1	1	142^1	160	75	9	4	37	35	12.7	3.60	93	.280	.328	12	.279	3	-2	-4	2	0.0
1947	Was-A	6	9	.400	20	17	5	1	0	106	113	66	8	1	58	37	14.6	5.60	66	.272	.363	12	.308	2	-22	-22	1	-2.4
1948	Was-A	4	16	.200	39	29	4	0	1	182	217	128	11	6	107	53	16.3	5.88	74	.299	.394	14	.237	2	-32	-31	3	-2.4
1949	Was-A	8	17	.320	40	27	11	2	1	209	234	117	11	5	91	54	14.2	4.22	101	.283	.357	16	.239	2	-1	1	4	0.6
1950	Was-A	14	14	.500	30	30	17	0	0	237^2	261	129	17	6	98	75	13.8	4.09	110	.284	.356	20	.215	-1	13	11	3	1.3
1951	Was-A	5	12	.294	23	19	8	0	0	138^2	168	90	8	4	52	43	14.5	5.13	80	.302	.365	12	.273	2	-15	-16	3	-1.3
1952	Was-A	3	4	.429	7	7	6	0	0	62^2	59	22	4	0	29	24	12.6	2.73	130	.257	.340	4	.167	-0	7	6	2	0.9
	Bos-A	7	9	.438	21	18	7	0	0	134^1	145	64	9	7	36	50	12.6	3.62	109	.276	.330	8	.174	-1	1	4	4	0.8
	Yr	10	13	.435	28	25	13	0	0	197	204	86	13	7	65	74	12.6	3.34	114	.270	.333	12	.171	-1	7	10	6	1.7
1953	Bos-A	6	9	.400	30	17	4	0	2	156	164	65	13	4	49	60	12.5	3.52	120	.269	.327	7	.140	-2	8	11	1	0.8
1954	Bos-A	3	4	.429	33	5	0	0	5	71^1	83	43	5	2	30	27	14.5	4.42	93	.296	.369	2	.154	-1	-5	-2	0	-0.3
Total	12	104	152	.406	380	279	123	11	13	2181	2384	1212	136	48	835	734	13.5	4.28	95	.278	.345	164	.220	9	-54	-55	28	-2.7
● **TIM HUDSON**	Hudson, Timothy Adam b: 7/14/75, Columbus, Ga. BR/TR, 6', 160 lbs. Deb: 6/8/99																											
1999	Oak-A	11	2	.846	21	21	1	0	0	136^1	121	56	8	4	62	132	12.3	3.23	144	.237	.324	1	.250	1	25	22	2	2.1
2000	*Oak-A★	**20**	6	**.769**	32	32	2	2	0	202^1	169	100	24	7	82	169	11.5	4.14	115	.227	.309	0	.000	-0	18	15	-1	1.5
Total	2	31	8	.795	53	53	3	2	0	338^2	290	156	32	11	144	301	11.8	3.77	125	.231	.315	1	.143	0	42	37	1	3.6
● **AL HUENKE**	Huenke, Albert Alfred b: 6/26/1891, New Bremen, Ohio d: 9/20/74, St.Marys, Ohio BR/TR, 6', 175 lbs. Deb: 10/6/14																											
1914	NY-N	0	0	—	1	0	0	0	0	2	2	1	0	0	0	2	9.0	4.50	59	.250	.250	0	.000	-0	-0	-0	-0	0.0
● **PHIL HUFFMAN**	Huffman, Phillip Lee b: 6/20/58, Freeport, Tex. BR/TR, 6'2", 180 lbs. Deb: 4/10/79																											
1979	Tor-A	6	18	.250	31	31	2	1	0	173	220	130	25	0	68	56	15.0	5.77	75	.304	.364	0	—	0	-30	-26	0	-3.0
1985	Bal-A	0	0	—	2	1	0	0	0	4^2	7	8	1	0	5	2	23.1	15.43	26	.350	.480	0	—	0	-6	-6	0	-0.3
Total	2	6	18	.250	33	32	2	1	0	177^2	227	138	26	0	73	58	15.2	6.03	72	.305	.367	0	—	0	-36	-32	0	-3.3
● **ED HUGHES**	Hughes, Edward J. b: 10/5/1880, Chicago, Ill. d: 10/11/27, McHenry, Ill. BR/TR, 6'1", 180 lbs. Deb: 8/29/02 F♦																											
1905	Bos-A	3	2	.600	6	4	2	0	0	33^1	38	27	0	1	9	8	13.0	4.59	59	.288	.338	3	.214	-0	-7	-7	-2	-1.1
1906	Bos-A	0	0	—	2	0	0	0	0	10	15	7	0	0	3	3	16.2	5.40	51	.349	.391	1	.000	-0	-3	-3	-0	-0.2
Total	2	3	2	.600	8	4	2	0	0	43^1	53	34	0	1	12	11	13.7	4.78	57	.303	.351	4	.190	-1	-10	-10	-2	-1.3
● **JAY HUGHES**	Hughes, James Jay b: 1/22/1874, Sacramento, Cal. d: 6/2/24, Sacramento, Cal. BR/TR, 185 lbs. Deb: 4/18/1898 F																											
1898	Bal-N	23	12	.657	38	35	31	5	0	300^2	268	152	4	18	100	81	11.6	3.20	112	.237	.309	37	.226	4	14	13	2	1.9
1899	Bro-N	**28**	6	**.824**	35	35	30	3	0	291^2	250	121	6	14	119	99	11.8	2.68	146	.231	.316	27	.252	5	38	39	2	4.6
1901	Bro-N	17	12	.586	31	29	24	0	0	250^2	265	125	3	12	102	96	13.6	3.27	103	.269	.345	16	.176	-1	2	2	1	0.2
1902	Bro-N	15	10	.600	30	29	26	0	0	245	223	114	3	9	51	92	10.4	2.87	97	.243	.289	19	.209	4	-2	-3	1	0.3
Total	4	83	40	.675	134	128	111	8	0	1088	1006	512	16	53	372	368	11.8	3.00	114	.245	.315	99	.219	13	51	52	7	7.0
● **JIM HUGHES**	Hughes, James Michael b: 7/2/51, Los Angeles, Cal. BR/TR, 6'3", 190 lbs. Deb: 9/14/74																											
1974	Min-A	0	2	.000	2	2	1	0	0	10^1	8	8	2	0	4	8	10.5	5.23	71	.216	.293	0	—	0	-2	-2	0	-0.3
1975	Min-A	16	14	.533	37	34	12	2	0	249^2	241	119	17	13	127	130	13.7	3.82	100	.255	.351	0	—	0	-1	0	1	0.1
1976	Min-A	9	14	.391	37	26	3	0	0	177	190	113	17	8	73	87	13.8	4.98	72	.281	.358	0	—	0	-29	-27	-1	-3.3
1977	Min-A	0	0	—	2	0	0	0	0	4^1	4	1	0	0	1	1	10.4	2.08	192	.250	.294	0	—	0	1	1	-0	0.0
Total	4	25	30	.455	78	62	16	2	0	441^1	443	241	36	21	205	226	13.6	4.30	87	.265	.352	0	—	0	-31	-28	-1	-3.5
● **JIM HUGHES**	Hughes, James Robert b: 3/21/23, Chicago, Ill. BR/TR, 6'1", 200 lbs. Deb: 9/13/52																											
1952	Bro-N	2	1	.667	6	0	0	0	0	18^2	16	4	0	0	11	8	13.0	1.45	252	.235	.342	0	.000	-0	5	5	-1	0.6
1953	*Bro-N	4	3	.571	48	0	0	0	9	85^2	80	33	6	1	41	49	12.8	3.47	123	.245	.332	4	.286	1	8	8	-1	0.7
1954	Bro-N	8	4	.667	**60**	0	0	0	**24**	86^2	76	36	7	0	44	58	12.5	3.22	127	.239	.331	3	.188	-0	8	8	-1	1.4
1955	Bro-N	0	2	.000	24	0	0	0	6	42^2	41	22	10	0	19	20	12.7	4.22	96	.256	.335	0	.000	-2	-1	-1	0	-0.2
1956	Bro-N	0	0	—	5	0	0	0	0	12	10	7	3	0	4	8	10.5	5.25	76	.233	.298	0	.000	-0	-2	-2	-0	-0.1
	Chi-N	1	3	.250	25	1	0	0	0	45^1	43	35	4	4	30	20	15.3	5.16	73	.259	.385	2	.286	1	-7	-7	-1	-0.5
	Yr	1	3	.250	30	1	0	0	0	57^1	53	42	7	4	34	28	14.3	5.18	74	.254	.368	2	.222	0	-9	-9	-1	-0.6
1957	Chi-A	0	0	—	4	0	0	0	0	5	12	6	0	0	3	2	27.0	10.80	35	.462	.517	0	—	0	-4	-4	0	-0.2
Total	6	15	13	.536	172	1	0	0	39	296	278	143	30	5	152	165	13.2	3.83	106	.251	.344	9	.170	-1	7	7	-3	1.7
● **MICKEY HUGHES**	Hughes, Michael J. b: 10/25/1866, New York, N.Y. d: 4/10/31, Jersey City, N.J. TR, 5'6", 165 lbs. Deb: 4/22/1888 F																											
1888	Bro-a	25	13	.658	40	40	40	2	0	363	281	163	5	6	98	159	9.5	2.13	140	.206	.262	19	.137	-7	38	35	-1	2.4
1889	*Bro-a	9	8	.529	20	17	13	0	0	153	172	120	6	7	86	54	15.6	4.35	86	.275	.369	12	.176	-3	-9	-11	-0	-1.2
1890	Bro-N	4	4	.500	9	8	6	0	0	66^1	77	47	1	4	30	22	15.1	5.16	67	.282	.362	1	.038	-4	-12	-13	0	-1.5
	Phi-a	1	3	.250	6	5	4	0	0	41^1	64	56	0	5	21	15	19.6	5.44	71	.344	.425	2	.125	-1	-7	-7	-1	-0.6
Total	3	39	28	.582	75	70	63	2	0	623^2	594	386	12	22	235	250	12.3	3.22	102	.243	.315	34	.137	-14	10	4	-1	-0.9
● **DICK HUGHES**	Hughes, Richard Henry b: 2/13/38, Stephens, Ark. BR/TR, 6'3", 195 lbs. Deb: 9/11/66																											
1966	StL-N	2	1	.667	6	2	1	1	1	21	12	4	0	2	7	20	9.0	1.71	209	.162	.253	2	.400	1	4	4	0	0.8
1967	*StL-N	16	6	**.727**	37	27	12	3	3	222^1	164	72	22	5	48	161	**8.8**	2.67	123	**.203**	**.252**	10	.128	-1	17	16	-2	1.2
1968	*StL-N	2	2	.500	25	5	0	0	4	64	45	25	7	0	21	49	9.3	3.52	82	.202	.270	0	.000	-1	-4	-5	1	-0.4
Total	3	20	9	.690	68	34	13	4	8	307^1	221	101	29	7	76	230	8.9	2.78	116	.200	.256	12	.122	-2	18	16	-1	1.6
● **TOM HUGHES**	Hughes, Thomas Edward b: 9/13/34, Ancon, C.Z. BL/TR, 6'2", 180 lbs. Deb: 9/13/59																											
1959	StL-N	0	2	.000	2	2	0	0	0	4	9	9	2	0	2	2	24.8	15.75	27	.409	.458	0	.000	-0	-5	-5	-0	-0.8
● **TOM HUGHES**	Hughes, Thomas James "Long Tom" b: 11/29/1878, Chicago, Ill. d: 2/8/56, Chicago, Ill. BR/TR, 6'1", 175 lbs. Deb: 9/7/00 F																											
1900	Chi-N	1	1	.500	3	3	3	0	0	21	31	14	0	1	7	12	16.7	5.14	70	.341	.394	0	.000	-0	-3	-4	0	-0.3
1901	Chi-N	10	23	.303	37	35	32	1	0	308^1	309	166	4	17	115	225	12.9	3.24	100	.259	.333	14	.119	-8	3	-0	-2	-1.0
1902	Bal-A	7	5	.583	13	13	12	1	0	108^1	120	57	2	2	32	45	12.8	3.90	97	.281	.334	6	.140	-2	-4	-2	1	-0.3
	Bos-A	3	3	.500	9	8	4	0	0	49^1	51	31	0	1	24	15	13.9	3.28	109	.267	.352	11	.367	2	2	2	-0	0.4
	Yr	10	8	.556	22	21	16	1	0	157^2	171	88	2	3	56	60	13.1	3.71	100	.277	.340	17	.233	0	-2	0	1	0.1
1903	*Bos-A	20	7	.741	33	31	25	5	0	244^2	232	95	5	9	60	112	11.1	2.57	118	.249	.301	26	.280	7	11	12	-4	1.5
1904	NY-A	7	11	.389	19	18	12	1	0	136^1	141	72	3	5	48	75	12.8	3.70	73	.268	.334	13	.241	1	-17	-14	-3	-1.9
	Was-A	3	12	.200	16	14	14	0	0	124^1	133	67	4	6	34	48	12.5	3.47	77	.274	.330	13	.228	3	-12	-11	-1	-1.0
	Yr	10	23	.303	35	32	26	1	0	260^2	274	139	7	11	82	123	12.7	3.59	75	.271	.332	26	.234	4	-29	-25	-3	-2.9
1905	Was-A	17	20	.459	39	35	26	6	0	291^1	239	113	3	10	79	149	10.1	2.35	113	.225	.285	22	.212	4	10	10	-4	1.3
1906	Was-A	7	17	.292	30	24	18	1	0	204	230	118	5	3	81	90	13.9	3.62	73	.287	.355	14	.212	3	-21	-23	-4	-2.6
1907	Was-A	7	14	.333	34	23	18	2	**4**	211	206	104	1	12	47	102	11.3	3.11	78	.258	.309	19	.237	3	-13	-17	-1	-1.4
1908	Was-A	18	15	.545	43	31	24	3	4	276^1	224	91	3	6	77	165	10.0	2.21	103	.227	.287	17	.195	2	6	2	1	0.7
1909	Was-A	4	7	.364	22	13	7	2	1	120^1	113	56	1	5	33	77	11.3	2.69	90	.246	.303	3	.083	-2	-3	-4	-0	-0.6
1911	Was-A	11	17	.393	34	27	17	2	0	223	251	128	7	4	77	86	13.4	3.47	95	.288	.348	15	.185	-1	-3	-5	-2	-0.9
1912	Was-A	13	10	.565	31	26	11	1	0	196	201	99	8	6	78	108	13.1	2.94	113	.270	.344	13	.194	1	8	9	0	1.0
1913	Was-A	4	12	.250	36	12	4	0	6	129^2	129	81	6	15	61	59	14.2	4.30	69	.253	.350	4	.111	-1	-20	-19	1	-2.4
Total	13	132	174	.431	399	313	227	25	15	2644	2610	1292	52	102	853	1368	12.1	3.09	93	.259	.323	190	.198	12	-57	-64	-18	-7.5
● **TOM HUGHES**	Hughes, Thomas L. "Salida Tom" b: 1/28/1884, Coal Creek, Colo. d: 11/1/61, Los Angeles, Cal. BR/TR, 6'2", 175 lbs. Deb: 9/18/06																											
1906	NY-A	1	0	1.000	3	1	1	0	0	15	11	8	2	0	1	5	7.2	4.20	71	.208	.222	1	.200	0	-3	-2	-1	-0.2
1907	NY-A	2	0	1.000	4	3	2	0	0	27	16	10	0	2	11	10	9.7	2.67	105	.174	.276	1	.143	-0	-0	0	-1	-0.1

YEAR	TM/L	W	L	PCT	G	GS	CG	SH	SV	IP	H	R	HR	HB	BB	SO	RAT	ERA	ERA+	OAV	OOB	BH	AVG	PB	PR	PR+	PD	TPI
1909	NY-A	7	8	.467	24	15	9	2	2	118^2	109	42	3	4	37	69	11.4	2.65	95	.249	.313	5	.128	0	-2	-2	-1	-0.2
1910	NY-A	7	9	.438	23	15	11	0	1	151^2	153	77	2	3	37	64	11.5	3.50	76	.271	.320	9	.164	-1	-17	-13	1	-1.4
1914	Bos-N	2	0	1.000	2	2	1	0	0	17	14	7	0	0	4	11	9.5	2.65	104	.226	.273	0	.000	-1	0	0	1	0.0
1915	Bos-N	16	14	.533	**50**	25	17	4	**9**	280^1	208	88	4	11	58	171	8.9	2.12	122	.213	.265	9	.100	-3	20	16	-2	1.2
1916	Bos-N	16	3	**.842**	40	13	7	1	5	161	121	46	2	8	51	97	10.1	2.35	106	.215	.290	10	.192	2	5	3	-1	0.4
1917	Bos-N	5	3	.625	11	8	6	2	0	74	54	21	1	3	30	40	10.6	1.95	131	.216	.307	0	.000	-3	6	5	-0	0.2
1918	Bos-N	0	2	.000	3	3	1	0	0	18^1	17	10	0	0	6	9	11.3	3.44	78	.250	.311	2	.333	1	-1	-2	0	0.0
Total	9	56	39	.589	160	85	55	9	17	863	703	309	14	31	235	476	10.1	2.56	102	.229	.291	37	.130	-4	8	4	-4	-0.1
● **TOMMY HUGHES**	Hughes, Thomas Owen b: 10/7/19, Wilkes-Barre, Pa. d: 11/28/90, Wilkes-Barre, Pa. BR/TR, 6'1", 190 lbs. Deb: 4/19/41																											
1941	Phi-N	9	14	.391	34	24	5	2	0	170	187	106	12	4	82	59	14.5	4.45	83	.280	.362	11	.200	0	-15	-14	1	-1.5
1942	Phi-N	12	18	.400	40	31	19	0	1	253	224	105	8	0	99	77	11.5	3.06	108	.238	.310	8	.100	-5	7	7	3	0.6
1946	Phi-N	6	9	.400	29	13	3	2	1	111	123	64	5	1	44	34	13.6	4.38	78	.281	.349	3	.097	-1	-12	-12	-1	-1.7
1947	Phi-N	4	11	.267	29	15	4	1	1	127	121	52	5	0	59	44	12.8	3.47	115	.265	.350	2	.050	-4	8	8	0	0.5
1948	Cin-N	0	4	.000	12	4	0	0	0	27	43	28	3	0	24	7	22.3	9.00	43	.364	.472	1	.143	-0	-15	-15	-0	-1.9
Total	5	31	56	.356	144	87	31	5	3	688	698	355	33	5	308	221	13.2	3.92	91	.266	.344	25	.117	-10	-27	-26	2	-4.0
● **VERN HUGHES**	Hughes, Vernon Alexander "Lefty" b: 4/15/1893, Etna, Pa. d: 9/26/61, Sewickley, Pa. BL/TL, 5'10", 155 lbs. Deb: 7/6/14																											
1914	Bal-F	0	0	—	3	0	0	0	0	5^2	5	4	0	0	3	0	12.7	3.18	95	.250	.348	0	.000	-0	-0	-0	-0	0.0
● **BILL HUGHES**	Hughes, William Nesbert b: 11/18/1896, Philadelphia, Pa. d: 2/25/63, Birmingham, Ala. BR/TR, 5'10.5", 155 lbs. Deb: 9/15/21																											
1921	Pit-N	0	0	—	1	0	0	0	0	2	3	1	0	1	1	2	22.5	4.50	85	.375	.500	0	—	0	-0	-0	0	0.0
● **BILL HUGHES**	Hughes, William R. b: 11/25/1866, Blandinsville, Ill. d: 8/25/43, Santa Ana, Cal. BL/TL, Deb: 9/28/1884 ◆																											
1885	Phi-a	0	2	.000	2	2	2	0	0	16^2	18	17	0	2	10	4	16.2	4.86	71	.269	.380	3	.188	0	-3	-2	-0	-0.2
● **JIM HUGHEY**	Hughey, James Ulysses "Coldwater Jim" b: 3/8/1869, Wakeshma, Mich. d: 3/29/45, Coldwater, Mich. TR, 6', Deb: 9/29/1891																											
1891	Mil-a	1	0	1.000	2	1	1	0	0	15	18	6	0	0	3	9	12.6	3.00	146	.286	.318	1	.143	-1	1	2	0	0.1
1893	Chi-N	0	1	.000	2	2	1	0	0	9	14	16	0	1	3	4	18.0	11.00	42	.341	.400	0	.000	0	-6	-6	0	-0.4
1896	Pit-N	6	8	.429	25	14	11	0	0	155	171	108	3	7	67	48	14.2	4.99	84	.278	.355	14	.215	-1	-11	-14	-3	-1.3
1897	Pit-N	6	10	.375	25	17	13	0	1	149^1	193	115	3	7	45	38	14.8	5.06	82	.310	.364	8	.127	-5	-13	-15	-2	-1.8
1898	StL-N	7	24	.226	35	33	31	0	0	283^2	325	169	2	11	71	74	12.9	3.93	96	.285	.333	11	.113	-5	-10	-4	-1	-1.0
1899	Cle-N	4	30	.118	36	34	32	0	0	283	403	244	9	22	88	54	16.3	5.41	68	.334	.389	18	.162	-5	-49	-57	-4	-5.9
1900	StL-N	5	7	.417	20	12	11	0	0	112^2	147	90	4	6	40	23	15.4	5.19	70	.314	.375	7	.171	0	-19	-20	-2	-1.8
Total	7	29	80	.266	145	113	100	0	1	1007^2	1271	748	21	54	317	250	14.7	4.87	80	.306	.363	59	.153	-17	-106	-111	-11	-12.1
● **TEX HUGHSON**	Hughson, Cecil Carlton b: 2/9/16, Buda, Tex. d: 8/6/93, Austin, Tex. BR/TR, 6'3", 198 lbs. Deb: 4/16/41																											
1941	Bos-A	5	3	.625	12	8	4	0	0	61	70	30	3	1	13	22	12.4	4.13	101	.289	.328	1	.059	-1	0	0	0	-0.1
1942	Bos-A☆	**22**	6	.786	38	30	**22**	4	4	**281**	258	92	10	1	75	**113**	10.7	2.59	144	.245	.296	18	.176	1	33	**35**	1	3.7
1943	Bos-A★	12	15	.444	35	32	**20**	4	2	266	242	87	23	2	73	114	10.7	2.64	126	.247	.300	9	.105	-4	19	20	1	1.7
1944	Bos-A★	18	5	**.783**	28	23	19	2	5	203^1	172	57	4	2	41	112	**9.5**	2.26	151	.225	**.267**	10	.152	-1	26	26	-0	3.0
1946	*Bos-A	20	11	.645	39	35	21	6	3	278	252	89	15	2	51	172	9.9	2.75	133	.238	.274	12	.132	-2	23	27	-2	2.6
1947	Bos-A	12	11	.522	29	26	13	3	0	189^1	173	86	17	2	71	119	11.7	3.33	117	.244	.314	2	.033	-6	8	11	-0	0.7
1948	Bos-A	3	1	.750	15	0	0	0	0	19^1	21	14	0	0	7	6	13.0	5.12	86	.276	.337	0	.000	-0	-2	-2	-1	-0.4
1949	Bos-A	4	2	.667	29	2	0	0	3	77^2	82	49	5	1	41	35	14.4	5.33	82	.268	.356	1	.045	-3	-10	-8	-2	-1.0
Total	8	96	54	.640	225	156	99	19	17	1375^2	1270	504	77	11	372	693	10.8	2.94	125	.245	.297	53	.119	-15	99	109	-3	10.2
● **RICK HUISMAN**	Huisman, Richard Allen b: 5/17/69, Oak Park, Ill. BR/TR, 6'3", 200 lbs. Deb: 9/4/95																											
1995	KC-A	0	0	—	7	0	0	0	0	9^2	14	8	2	0	1	12	14.0	7.45	64	.333	.349	0	—	0	-3	-3	-0	-0.1
1996	KC-A	2	1	.667	22	0	0	0	1	29^1	25	15	4	0	18	23	13.2	4.60	109	.231	.341	0	—	0	1	1	0	0.1
Total	2	2	1	.667	29	0	0	0	1	39	39	23	6	0	19	35	13.4	5.31	93	.260	.343	0	—	0	-2	-2	0	0.0
● **MARK HUISMANN**	Huismann, Mark Lawrence b: 5/11/58, Littleton, Colo. BR/TR, 6'3", 195 lbs. Deb: 8/16/83																											
1983	KC-A	2	1	.667	13	0	0	0	0	30^2	29	20	1	0	17	20	13.5	5.58	73	.250	.346	0	—	0	-5	-5	-1	-0.5
1984	*KC-A	3	3	.500	38	0	0	0	3	75	84	38	7	1	21	54	12.7	4.20	96	.286	.335	0	—	0	-2	-1	0	-0.1
1985	KC-A	1	0	1.000	9	0	0	0	0	18^2	14	4	1	0	3	9	8.2	1.93	216	.219	.254	0	—	0	5	5	0	0.2
1986	KC-A	0	1	.000	10	0	0	0	1	17^1	18	8	1	0	6	13	12.5	4.15	103	.269	.329	0	—	0	0	0	0	0.0
	Sea-A	3	3	.500	36	1	0	0	4	80	80	39	18	1	19	59	11.2	3.71	115	.256	.301	0	—	0	4	5	0	0.4
	Yr	3	4	.429	46	1	0	0	5	97^1	98	47	19	1	25	72	11.5	3.79	112	.259	.306	0	—	0	4	5	0	0.4
1987	Sea-A	0	0	—	6	0	0	0	0	14^2	10	10	1	2	4	15	9.8	4.91	96	.196	.281	0	—	0	-1	-0	0	0.0
	Cle-A	2	3	.400	20	0	0	0	2	35^1	38	22	6	0	8	23	11.7	5.09	89	.271	.311	0	—	0	-2	-2	-0	-0.3
	Yr	2	3	.400	26	0	0	0	2	50	48	32	7	2	12	38	11.2	5.04	91	.251	.302	0	—	0	-3	-2	0	-0.3
1988	Det-A	1	0	1.000	5	0	0	0	0	5^1	6	3	0	0	2	6	13.5	5.06	76	.286	.348	0	—	0	-1	-1	0	-0.1
1989	Bal-A	0	0	—	8	0	0	0	1	11^1	13	8	0	0	0	13	10.3	6.35	60	.277	.277	0	—	0	-3	-3	1	-0.1
1990	Pit-N	1	0	1.000	2	0	0	0	0	3	6	5	2	1	1	2	24.0	9.00	40	.462	.533	0	—	0	-2	-2	-0	-0.4
1991	Pit-N	0	0	—	5	0	0	0	0	5	7	6	0	0	2	5	16.2	7.20	50	.304	.360	0	—	0	-2	-2	0	-0.1
Total	9	13	11	.542	152	1	0	0	11	296^1	305	163	37	5	83	219	11.9	4.40	95	.266	.318	0	—	0	-8	-7	1	-1.0
● **HARRY HULIHAN**	Hulihan, Harry Joseph b: 4/18/1899, Rutland, Vt. d: 9/11/80, Rutland, Vt. BR/TL, 5'11", 170 lbs. Deb: 8/16/22																											
1922	Bos-N	2	3	.400	7	6	2	0	0	40	40	23	0	4	26	16	15.7	3.15	127	.274	.398	2	.154	-0	4	4	-1	0.3
● **HANK HULVEY**	Hulvey, James Hensel b: 7/18/1897, Mount Sidney, Va. d: 4/9/82, Mount Sidney, Va. BB/TR, 6', 180 lbs. Deb: 9/5/23																											
1923	Phi-A	0	1	.000	1	1	0	0	0	7	10	6	1	0	2	2	15.4	7.71	53	.357	.400	1	.500	0	-3	-3	0	-0.3
● **TOM HUME**	Hume, Thomas Hubert b: 3/29/53, Cincinnati, Ohio BR/TR, 6'1", 185 lbs. Deb: 5/25/77 C																											
1977	Cin-N	3	3	.500	14	5	0	0	0	43	54	36	5	0	17	22	14.9	7.12	55	.305	.366	2	.200	1	-15	-15	-0	-1.7
1978	Cin-N	8	11	.421	42	23	3	0	1	174	198	89	12	4	50	90	13.0	4.14	86	.289	.341	3	.067	-3	-11	-11	0	-1.4
1979	*Cin-N	10	9	.526	57	12	2	0	17	163	162	54	12	0	33	80	10.8	2.76	**136**	.262	.300	8	.174	0	18	18	0	2.4
1980	Cin-N	9	10	.474	78	0	0	0	25	137	121	44	6	3	38	68	10.6	2.56	140	.240	.297	3	.188	1	16	16	3	3.0
1981	Cin-N	9	4	.692	51	0	0	0	13	67^2	63	27	7	1	31	27	12.6	3.46	103	.259	.345	0	.000	-0	0	1	-0	0.1
1982	Cin-N★	2	6	.250	46	0	0	0	17	63^2	57	24	2	1	21	22	11.2	3.11	119	.245	.310	0	.000	-1	4	4	-1	0.6
1983	Cin-N	3	5	.375	48	0	0	0	9	66	66	40	8	3	41	34	15.0	4.77	80	.264	.374	0	.000	-1	-8	-7	1	-0.9
1984	Cin-N	4	13	.235	54	8	0	0	3	113^1	142	83	14	1	41	59	14.6	5.64	67	.309	.367	3	.136	-0	-26	-22	1	-3.1
1985	Cin-N	3	5	.375	56	0	0	0	3	80	65	33	7	3	35	50	11.6	3.26	116	.224	.314	0	.000	-1	3	4	-0	0.4
1986	Phi-N	4	1	.800	48	1	0	0	4	94^1	89	37	5	3	34	51	12.0	2.77	140	.252	.323	0	.000	-1	10	11	1	0.6
1987	Phi-N	1	4	.200	38	6	0	0	0	70^2	75	48	10	4	41	29	15.3	5.60	76	.277	.380	3	.200	0	-12	-10	0	-0.6
	Cin-N	1	0	1.000	11	0	0	0	0	13^1	14	6	0	1	2	4	11.5	4.05	105	.292	.333	0	—	0	0	0	-0	0.0
	Yr	2	4	.333	49	6	0	0	0	84	89	54	10	5	43	33	14.7	5.36	79	.279	.373	3	.200	0	-12	-10	0	-0.6
Total	11	57	71	.445	543	55	5	0	92	1086	1106	521	88	24	384	536	12.5	3.85	97	.268	.334	22	.120	-5	-21	-13	5	-0.6
● **BILL HUMPHREY**	Humphrey, Byron William b: 6/17/11, Vienna, Mo. d: 2/13/92, Springfield, Mo. BR/TR, 6', 180 lbs. Deb: 4/24/38																											
1938	Bos-A	0	0	—	2	0	0	0	0	2	5	2	0	0	1	0	27.0	9.00	55	.500	.545	0	—	0	-1	-1	-0	0.0
● **BOB HUMPHREYS**	Humphreys, Robert William b: 8/18/35, Covington, Va. BR/TR, 5'11", 170 lbs. Deb: 9/8/62																											
1962	Det-A	0	1	.000	4	0	0	0	1	5	8	4	3	0	2	3	18.0	7.20	57	.381	.435	0	—	0	-2	-2	0	-0.3
1963	StL-N	0	1	.000	9	0	0	0	0	10^2	11	8	4	1	7	8	16.0	5.06	70	.282	.404	0	—	0	-2	-2	0	-0.2
1964	*StL-N	2	0	1.000	28	0	0	0	2	42^2	32	14	3	1	15	36	10.1	2.53	150	.213	.289	1	.250	1	5	6	-0	0.4
1965	Chi-N	2	0	1.000	41	0	0	0	0	65^2	59	25	6	2	27	38	12.1	3.15	117	.244	.325	0	.000	-0	3	4	-1	0.1
1966	Was-A	7	3	.700	58	1	0	0	3	111^2	91	38	6	4	28	88	9.9	2.82	123	.229	.287	2	.167	1	8	8	-0	0.8
1967	Was-A	6	2	.750	48	2	0	0	4	105^2	93	54	13	2	41	54	11.6	4.17	76	.238	.314	2	.133	1	-11	-12	-1	-1.1
1968	Was-A	5	7	.417	56	0	0	0	2	92^2	78	40	13	0	30	56	10.5	3.69	79	.233	.296	2	.400	1	-7	-8	1	-1.0
1969	Was-A	3	3	.500	47	0	0	0	5	79^2	69	37	3	1	38	43	12.2	3.05	114	.233	.322	1	.077	-1	5	4	0	0.3

YEAR	TM/L	W	L	PCT	G	GS	CG	SH	SV	IP	H	R	HR	HB	BB	SO	RAT	ERA	ERA+	OAV	OOB	BH	AVG	PB	PR	PR+	PD	TPI
1970	Was-A	0	0	—	5	0	0	0	0	6^2	4	2	1	0	9	6	17.6	1.35	263	.200	.448	0	—	0	2	2	0	0.1
	Mil-A	2	4	.333	23	1	0	0	3	45^2	37	18	3	2	22	32	12.0	3.15	120	.222	.319	0	.000	-1	3	3	-0	0.4
	Yr	2	4	.333	28	1	0	0	3	52^1	41	20	4	2	31	38	12.7	2.92	129	.219	.336	0	.000	-1	5	5	0	0.5
Total	9	27	21	.563	319	4	0	0	20	566	482	240	55	13	219	364	11.4	3.36	101	.234	.312	8	.131	1	3	3	-2	-0.5

● BERT HUMPHRIES

Humphries, Albert b: 9/26/1880, California, Pa. d: 9/21/45, Orlando, Fla. BR/TR, 5'11.5", 182 lbs. Deb: 4/16/10

YEAR	TM/L	W	L	PCT	G	GS	CG	SH	SV	IP	H	R	HR	HB	BB	SO	RAT	ERA	ERA+	OAV	OOB	BH	AVG	PB	PR	PR+	PD	TPI
1910	Phi-N	0	0	—	5	0	0	0	2	9^2	13	8	0	1	3	3	15.8	4.66	67	.317	.378	0	.000	0	-2	-2	0	-0.1
1911	Phi-N	3	1	.750	11	5	2	0	1	41	56	25	1	6	10	13	15.8	4.17	83	.339	.398	5	.333	3	-4	-3	-1	-0.1
	Cin-N	4	3	.571	14	7	3	0	0	65	62	25	3	6	18	16	11.9	2.35	141	.266	.335	1	.063	-1	8	7	0	0.7
	Yr	7	4	.636	25	12	5	0	1	106	118	50	4	12	28	29	13.4	3.06	110	.296	.361	6	.194	2	4	4	-0	0.6
1912	Cin-N	9	11	.450	30	15	9	1	2	158^2	162	77	6	8	36	58	11.7	3.23	104	.270	.319	7	.137	-2	3	2	-1	-0.1
1913	Chi-N	16	4	**.800**	28	20	13	2	1	181	169	70	10	2	24	61	9.7	2.69	118	.250	.277	12	.194	1	10	10	-2	0.9
1914	Chi-N	10	11	.476	34	21	8	2	0	171	162	80	5	2	37	62	10.6	2.68	104	.250	.293	13	.236	2	2	2	2	0.6
1915	Chi-N	8	13	.381	31	22	10	4	3	171^2	183	69	6	5	23	45	11.1	2.31	120	.280	.309	8	.174	0	8	9	-2	0.9
Total	6	50	43	.538	153	90	45	9	9	798	807	354	31	30	151	258	11.1	2.79	110	.267	.309	46	.186	3	26	25	-3	2.8

● JOHNNY HUMPHRIES

Humphries, John William b: 6/23/15, Clifton Forge, Va d: 6/24/65, New Orleans, La. BR/TR, 6'1", 185 lbs. Deb: 5/8/38

YEAR	TM/L	W	L	PCT	G	GS	CG	SH	SV	IP	H	R	HR	HB	BB	SO	RAT	ERA	ERA+	OAV	OOB	BH	AVG	PB	PR	PR+	PD	TPI
1938	Cle-A	9	8	.529	**45**	6	1	0	6	103^1	105	69	6	1	63	56	14.7	5.23	89	.264	.367	3	.103	-1	-5	-7	-1	-1.2
1939	Cle-A	2	4	.333	15	1	0	0	2	28^1	30	30	0	1	32	12	20.0	8.26	53	.294	.467	0	.000	-1	-11	-13	-0	-2.3
1940	Cle-A	0	2	.000	19	1	1	0	1	33^2	35	35	5	2	29	17	17.6	8.29	51	.269	.410	0	.000	-1	-15	-16	-1	-1.0
1941	Chi-A	4	2	.667	14	6	4	4	1	73^1	63	18	2	1	22	25	10.6	1.84	223	.230	.290	2	.087	-1	19	19	-1	1.2
1942	Chi-A	12	12	.500	28	28	17	2	0	228^1	227	85	9	7	59	71	11.5	2.68	134	.257	.309	18	.225	5	25	24	-2	2.8
1943	Chi-A	11	11	.500	28	27	8	2	0	188^1	198	86	7	6	54	51	12.3	3.30	101	.268	.322	20	.290	5	-0	1	-2	0.6
1944	Chi-A	8	10	.444	30	20	8	0	1	169	170	75	9	4	57	42	12.3	3.67	93	.267	.331	10	.189	0	-5	-5	-3	-0.8
1945	Chi-A	6	14	.300	22	21	10	1	1	153	172	83	11	3	48	33	13.1	4.24	78	.282	.337	8	.148	-3	-15	-16	-4	-2.5
1946	Phi-N	0	0	—	10	1	0	0	0	24^2	24	17	1	1	9	10	12.4	4.01	85	.258	.330	2	.250	0	-2	-2	-1	-0.2
Total	9	52	63	.452	211	111	49	9	12	1002	1024	498	50	26	373	317	12.8	3.78	97	.265	.334	63	.191	4	-9	-13	-14	-3.4

● BEN HUNT

Hunt, Benjamin Franklin "High Pockets" b: 11/10/1888, Eufaula, Okla. d: 9/27/27, Greybull, Wyo. BL/TL, 6'5", 190 lbs. Deb: 8/24/10

YEAR	TM/L	W	L	PCT	G	GS	CG	SH	SV	IP	H	R	HR	HB	BB	SO	RAT	ERA	ERA+	OAV	OOB	BH	AVG	PB	PR	PR+	PD	TPI
1910	Bos-A	2	3	.400	7	7	3	0	0	46^2	45	22	4	0	20	19	12.5	4.05	63	.266	.344	1	.056	-2	-8	-8	-1	-1.0
1913	StL-N	0	1	.000	2	1	0	0	0	8	6	5	0	1	9	6	18.0	3.38	96	.240	.457	0	.000	-0	-0	-0	1	0.0
Total	2	2	4	.333	9	8	3	0	0	54^2	51	27	4	1	29	25	13.3	3.95	67	.263	.362	1	.050	-2	-8	-8	-0	-1.0

● KEN HUNT

Hunt, Kenneth Raymond b: 12/14/38, Ogden, Utah BR/TR, 6'4", 200 lbs. Deb: 4/16/61

YEAR	TM/L	W	L	PCT	G	GS	CG	SH	SV	IP	H	R	HR	HB	BB	SO	RAT	ERA	ERA+	OAV	OOB	BH	AVG	PB	PR	PR+	PD	TPI
1961	*Cin-N	9	10	.474	29	22	4	0	0	136^1	130	70	13	6	66	75	13.3	3.96	103	.257	.349	7	.179	0	1	2	-1	0.1

● GEORGE HUNTER

Hunter, George Henry b: 7/8/1887, Buffalo, N.Y. d: 1/11/68, Harrisburg, Pa. BB/TL, 5'8.5", 165 lbs. Deb: 5/4/09 F♦

YEAR	TM/L	W	L	PCT	G	GS	CG	SH	SV	IP	H	R	HR	HB	BB	SO	RAT	ERA	ERA+	OAV	OOB	BH	AVG	PB	PR	PR+	PD	TPI
1909	Bro-N	4	10	.286	16	13	10	0	0	113^1	104	48	2	3	38	43	11.5	2.46	105	.254	.322	28	.228	2	2	2	0	0.5

● CATFISH HUNTER

Hunter, James Augustus "Jim" b: 4/8/46, Hertford, N.C. d: 8/30/99, Hertford, N.C. BR/TR, 6', 195 lbs. Deb: 5/13/65 H

YEAR	TM/L	W	L	PCT	G	GS	CG	SH	SV	IP	H	R	HR	HB	BB	SO	RAT	ERA	ERA+	OAV	OOB	BH	AVG	PB	PR	PR+	PD	TPI
1965	KC-A	8	8	.500	32	20	3	2	0	133	124	68	21	2	46	82	11.6	4.26	82	.246	.311	6	.150	-1	-12	-11	-2	-1.5
1966	KC-A☆	9	11	.450	30	25	4	0	0	176^2	158	87	17	2	64	103	11.4	4.02	84	.239	.308	9	.153	1	-12	-12	-3	-1.6
1967	KC-A★	13	17	.433	35	35	13	5	0	259^2	209	91	16	2	84	196	10.2	2.81	113	.219	.284	18	.196	4	12	11	-5	1.2
1968	Oak-A	13	13	.500	36	34	11	2	1	234	210	99	29	4	69	172	10.9	3.35	84	.238	.296	19	.232	5	-10	-15	-3	-1.4
1969	Oak-A	12	15	.444	38	35	10	3	0	247	210	99	34	5	85	150	10.9	3.35	103	.234	.304	19	.224	4	8	3	-1	0.6
1970	Oak-A★	18	14	.563	40	40	9	1	0	262^1	253	124	32	9	74	178	11.5	3.81	93	.250	.307	18	.200	4	-3	-8	-2	-0.7
1971	*Oak-A	21	11	.656	37	37	16	4	0	273^2	225	103	27	4	80	181	10.2	2.96	113	.223	.282	36	.350	13	15	12	-4	2.4
1972	*Oak-A☆	21	7	**.750**	38	37	16	5	0	295^1	200	74	21	3	70	191	8.3	2.04	140	.189	.242	23	.219	3	34	29	-3	2.9
1973	*Oak-A★	21	5	**.808**	36	36	11	3	0	256^1	222	105	39	1	69	124	10.3	3.34	106	.232	.284	1	1.000	1	14	7	-4	0.3
1974	*Oak-A★	**25**	12	.676	41	41	23	6	0	318^1	268	97	25	4	46	143	**9.0**	**2.49**	134	.229	**.260**	0	—	0	**40**	32	-4	3.3
1975	NY-A★	**23**	14	.622	39	39	**30**	7	0	**328**	248	107	25	5	83	177	**9.2**	2.58	143	**.208**	**.263**	0	—	0	44	42	-4	4.1
1976	*NY-A★	17	15	.531	36	36	21	2	0	298^2	268	126	28	3	68	173	10.2	3.53	97	.241	.286	0	.000	-0	-0	-4	-2	-0.6
1977	*NY-A	9	9	.500	22	22	8	1	0	143^1	137	83	29	3	47	52	11.7	4.71	84	.250	.313	0	—	0	-10	-12	-3	-1.6
1978	*NY-A	12	6	.667	21	20	5	1	0	118	98	49	16	1	35	56	10.2	3.58	101	.226	.286	0	—	0	3	1	-1	0.0
1979	NY-A	2	9	.182	19	19	1	0	0	105	128	68	15	1	34	34	14.0	5.31	77	.312	.366	0	—	0	-13	-15	-1	-1.4
Total	15	224	166	.574	500	476	181	42	1	3449^1	2958	1380	374	49	954	2012	10.3	3.26	104	.231	.287	149	.226	33	111	56	-40	6.0

● JIM HUNTER

Hunter, James Mac Gregor b: 6/22/64, Jersey City, N.J. BR/TR, 6'3", 205 lbs. Deb: 5/17/91

YEAR	TM/L	W	L	PCT	G	GS	CG	SH	SV	IP	H	R	HR	HB	BB	SO	RAT	ERA	ERA+	OAV	OOB	BH	AVG	PB	PR	PR+	PD	TPI
1991	Mil-A	0	5	.000	8	6	0	0	0	31	45	26	3	4	17	14	19.2	7.26	55	.349	.440	0	—	0	-11	-12	1	-1.5

● RICH HUNTER

Hunter, Richard Thomas b: 9/25/74, Pasadena, Cal. BR/TR, 6'1", 185 lbs. Deb: 4/6/96

YEAR	TM/L	W	L	PCT	G	GS	CG	SH	SV	IP	H	R	HR	HB	BB	SO	RAT	ERA	ERA+	OAV	OOB	BH	AVG	PB	PR	PR+	PD	TPI
1996	Phi-N	3	7	.300	14	14	0	0	0	69^1	84	54	10	5	33	32	15.8	6.49	67	.303	.387	3	.167	0	-17	-16	0	-1.9

● LEM HUNTER

Hunter, Robert Lemuel b: 1/16/1863, Warren, Ohio d: 11/9/56, W.Lafayette, Ohio Deb: 9/1/1883 ♦

YEAR	TM/L	W	L	PCT	G	GS	CG	SH	SV	IP	H	R	HR	HB	BB	SO	RAT	ERA	ERA+	OAV	OOB	BH	AVG	PB	PR	PR+	PD	TPI
1883	Cle-N	0	0	—	1	0	0	0	0	6^1	10	7	0		2	4	17.1	1.42	222	.370	.414	1	.250	-0	1	1	0	0.0

● WILLARD HUNTER

Hunter, Willard Mitchell b: 3/8/34, Newark, N.J. BR/TL, 6'2", 180 lbs. Deb: 4/16/62

YEAR	TM/L	W	L	PCT	G	GS	CG	SH	SV	IP	H	R	HR	HB	BB	SO	RAT	ERA	ERA+	OAV	OOB	BH	AVG	PB	PR	PR+	PD	TPI
1962	LA-N	0	0	—	1	0	0	0	0	2	6	10	1	0	4	1	45.0	40.50	9	.545	.667	0	—	0	-8	-9	0	-0.4
	NY-N	1	6	.143	27	6	1	0	0	63	67	41	9	1	34	40	14.6	5.57	75	.270	.360	3	.231	0	-11	-9	-1	-1.0
	Yr	1	6	.143	28	6	1	0	0	65	73	51	10	1	38	41	15.5	6.65	63	.282	.376	3	.231	0	-20	-17	-1	-1.4
1964	NY-N	3	3	.500	41	0	0	0	5	49	54	25	4	2	9	22	11.9	4.41	81	.284	.323	1	1.000	0	-5	-4	-0	-0.6
Total	2	4	9	.308	69	6	1	0	5	114	127	76	14	3	47	63	14.0	5.68	69	.283	.355	4	.286	1	-24	-22	-1	-2.0

● WALT HUNTZINGER

Huntzinger, Walter Henry "Shakes" b: 2/6/1899, Pottsville, Pa. d: 8/11/81, Upper Darby, Pa. BR/TR, 6', 150 lbs. Deb: 9/29/23

YEAR	TM/L	W	L	PCT	G	GS	CG	SH	SV	IP	H	R	HR	HB	BB	SO	RAT	ERA	ERA+	OAV	OOB	BH	AVG	PB	PR	PR+	PD	TPI
1923	NY-N	0	1	.000	2	1	0	0	0	8	9	7	0	0	1	2	11.3	7.88	49	.290	.313	0	.000	-0	-3	-4	-0	-0.4
1924	NY-N	1	1	.500	12	2	0	0	1	32^1	41	19	3	0	9	6	13.9	4.45	82	.318	.362	4	.500	1	-2	-3	-0	-0.1
1925	NY-N	5	1	.833	26	1	0	0	0	64^1	68	30	3	0	17	19	11.9	3.50	115	.281	.328	1	.091	-1	**6**	**4**	-1	0.2
1926	StL-N	0	4	.000	9	4	2	0	0	34	35	19	4	0	14	9	13.0	4.24	92	.267	.338	0	.000	-1	-2	-1	1	-0.2
	Chi-N	1	1	.500	11	0	0	0	2	28^2	26	8	0	3	8	4	11.6	0.94	408	.260	.333	1	.143	-1	9	9	0	0.7
	Yr	1	5	.167	20	4	2	0	2	62^2	61	27	4	3	22	13	12.4	2.73	142	.264	.336	1	.067	-2	8	8	1	0.5
Total	4	7	8	.467	60	8	2	0	3	167^1	179	83	10	3	49	40	12.4	3.60	108	.283	.337	6	.167	-1	8	6	-1	0.2

● TOM HURD

Hurd, Thomas Carr "Whitey" b: 5/27/24, Danville, Va. d: 9/5/82, Waterloo, Iowa BR/TR, 5'9", 155 lbs. Deb: 7/30/54

YEAR	TM/L	W	L	PCT	G	GS	CG	SH	SV	IP	H	R	HR	HB	BB	SO	RAT	ERA	ERA+	OAV	OOB	BH	AVG	PB	PR	PR+	PD	TPI
1954	Bos-A	2	0	1.000	16	0	0	0	1	29^2	21	11	2	0	12	14	10.0	3.03	135	.198	.280	1	.333	0	2	3	0	0.3
1955	Bos-A	8	6	.571	43	0	0	0	5	80^2	72	32	7	1	38	48	12.4	3.01	142	.242	.330	1	.071	-1	8	11	-0	1.7
1956	Bos-A	3	4	.429	40	0	0	0	5	76	84	52	5	3	47	34	15.9	5.33	87	.289	.393	6	.500	2	-10	-5	-1	-0.4
Total	3	13	10	.565	99	0	0	0	11	186^1	177	95	14	4	97	96	13.4	3.96	111	.255	.350	8	.276	1	1	8	-1	1.6

● BRUCE HURST

Hurst, Bruce Vee b: 3/24/58, St.George, Utah BL/TL, 6'3", 215 lbs. Deb: 4/12/80

YEAR	TM/L	W	L	PCT	G	GS	CG	SH	SV	IP	H	R	HR	HB	BB	SO	RAT	ERA	ERA+	OAV	OOB	BH	AVG	PB	PR	PR+	PD	TPI
1980	Bos-A	2	2	.500	12	7	0	0	0	30^2	39	33	4	2	16	16	16.7	9.10	46	.307	.393	0	—	0	-17	-16	-0	-1.7
1981	Bos-A	2	0	1.000	5	5	0	0	0	23	23	11	1	1	12	11	14.1	4.30	90	.258	.353	0	—	0	-2	-1	-1	-0.1
1982	Bos-A	3	7	.300	28	19	0	0	0	117	161	87	16	3	40	53	15.7	5.77	75	.333	.388	0	—	0	-22	-18	1	-1.3
1983	Bos-A	12	12	.500	33	32	6	2	0	211^1	241	102	22	3	62	115	13.0	4.09	107	.290	.342	0	—	0	-0	6	1	0.7
1984	Bos-A	12	12	.500	33	33	9	2	0	218	232	106	25	6	88	136	13.5	3.92	106	.271	.343	0	—	0	2	6	0	0.6
1985	Bos-A	11	13	.458	35	31	6	1	0	229^1	243	123	31	3	70	189	12.4	4.51	95	.273	.328	0	—	0	-9	-6	0	-0.5
1986	*Bos-A	13	8	.619	25	25	11	4	0	174^1	169	63	18	3	50	167	11.5	2.99	139	.256	.311	0	—	0	23	23	-1	2.5
1987	Bos-A☆	15	13	.536	33	33	15	3	0	238^2	239	124	35	1	76	190	11.9	4.41	103	.262	.320	0	—	0	2	4	0	0.4
1988	*Bos-A	18	6	.750	33	32	7	1	0	216^2	222	98	21	2	65	166	12.0	3.66	113	.264	.318	0	—	0	8	11	0	1.2
1989	SD-N	15	11	.577	33	33	**10**	2	0	244^2	214	84	16	0	66	179	10.3	2.69	130	.237	.289	5	.071	-2	22	22	1	2.3
1990	SD-N	11	9	.550	33	33	9	**4**	0	223^2	188	85	21	1	63	162	10.1	3.14	122	.228	.284	6	.090	-2	16	17	0	1.2
1991	SD-N	15	8	.652	31	31	4	0	0	221^2	201	89	17	3	59	141	10.7	3.29	116	.241	.293	9	.134	-0	10	12	-1	1.1
1992	SD-N	14	9	.609	32	32	6	4	0	217^1	223	96	22	0	51	131	11.3	3.85	93	.267	.309	11	.159	1	-8	-6	-1	-0.6

YEAR	TM/L	W	L	PCT	G	GS	CG	SH	SV	IP	H	R	HR	HB	BB	SO	RAT	ERA	ERA+	OAV	OOB	BH	AVG	PB	PR	PR+	PD	TPI
1993	SD-N	0	1	.000	2	2	0	0	0	4^{1}	9	7	0	0	3	3	24.9	12.46	33	.409	.480	0	—	0	-4	-4	0	-0.6
	Col-N	0	1	.000	3	3	0	0	0	8^{2}	6	5	1	0	3	6	9.3	5.19	92	.194	.265	0	.000	-0	-1	-0	0	0.0
	Yr	0	2	.000	5	5	0	0	0	13	15	12	1	0	6	9	14.5	7.62	60	.283	.356	0	.000	-0	-5	-4	0	-0.6
1994	Tex-A	2	1	.667	8	8	0	0	0	38	53	30	8	0	16	24	16.3	7.11	68	.342	.404	0	—	0	-10	-10	-1	-0.7
Total	15	145	113	.562	379	359	83	23	0	2417^{1}	2463	1143	258	28	740	1689	12.0	3.92	104	.265	.321	31	.113	-3	9	38	2	4.5

● JAMES HURST
Hurst, James Lavon b: 6/1/67, Plantation, Fla. BL/TL, 6', 160 lbs. Deb: 4/4/94

YEAR	TM/L	W	L	PCT	G	GS	CG	SH	SV	IP	H	R	HR	HB	BB	SO	RAT	ERA	ERA+	OAV	OOB	BH	AVG	PB	PR	PR+	PD	TPI
1994	Tex-A	0	0	—	8	0	0	0	0	10^{2}	17	12	1	0	8	5	21.1	10.13	48	.362	.455	0	—	0	-6	-6	0	-0.3

● JONATHAN HURST
Hurst, Jonathan b: 10/20/66, New York, N.Y. BR/TR, 6'3", 175 lbs. Deb: 6/9/92

YEAR	TM/L	W	L	PCT	G	GS	CG	SH	SV	IP	H	R	HR	HB	BB	SO	RAT	ERA	ERA+	OAV	OOB	BH	AVG	PB	PR	PR+	PD	TPI
1992	Mon-N	1	1	.500	3	3	0	0	0	16^{1}	18	10	1	1	7	4	14.3	5.51	63	.281	.361	0	.000	-0	-4	-4	-0	-0.5
1994	NY-N	0	1	.000	7	0	0	0	0	10	15	14	5	0	5	6	18.0	12.60	33	.341	.408	0	—	0	-9	-9	-0	-0.8
Total	2	1	2	.333	10	3	0	0	0	26^{1}	33	24	6	1	12	10	15.7	8.20	46	.306	.380	0	.000	-0	-13	-13	-0	-1.3

● BILL HURST
Hurst, William Hansel b: 4/28/70, Miami Beach, Fla. BR/TR, 6'7", 220 lbs. Deb: 9/18/96

YEAR	TM/L	W	L	PCT	G	GS	CG	SH	SV	IP	H	R	HR	HB	BB	SO	RAT	ERA	ERA+	OAV	OOB	BH	AVG	PB	PR	PR+	PD	TPI
1996	Fla-N	0	0	—	2	0	0	0	0	2	3	0	0	0	1	1	18.0	0.00	—	.333	.400	0	—	0	1	1	-0	0.0

● EDWIN HURTADO
Hurtado, Edwin Amilgar b: 2/1/70, Barquisimeto, Venez. BR/TR, 6'3", 215 lbs. Deb: 5/22/95

YEAR	TM/L	W	L	PCT	G	GS	CG	SH	SV	IP	H	R	HR	HB	BB	SO	RAT	ERA	ERA+	OAV	OOB	BH	AVG	PB	PR	PR+	PD	TPI
1995	Tor-A	5	2	.714	14	10	1	0	0	77^{2}	81	50	11	5	40	33	14.6	5.45	87	.275	.371	0	—	0	-6	-6	-1	-0.5
1996	Sea-A	2	5	.286	16	4	0	0	2	47^{2}	61	42	10	0	30	36	17.2	7.74	64	.324	.417	0	—	0	-15	-15	1	-1.8
1997	Sea-A	1	2	.333	13	1	0	0	0	19	25	19	5	2	15	10	19.9	9.00	50	.329	.452	0	—	0	-9	-10	1	-1.2
Total	3	8	9	.471	43	15	1	0	2	144^{1}	167	111	26	7	85	79	16.2	6.67	71	.299	.398	0	—	0	-30	-31	1	-3.5

● BILL HUSTED
Husted, William J. b: 10/11/1866, Gloucester, N.J. d: 5/17/41, Gloucester, N.J. Deb: 4/29/1890

YEAR	TM/L	W	L	PCT	G	GS	CG	SH	SV	IP	H	R	HR	HB	BB	SO	RAT	ERA	ERA+	OAV	OOB	BH	AVG	PB	PR	PR+	PD	TPI
1890	Phi-P	5	10	.333	18	17	12	0	0	129	148	105	2	5	67	33	15.3	4.88	88	.276	.361	6	.107	-6	-9	-9	-2	-1.3

● BERT HUSTING
Husting, Berthold Juneau "Pete" b: 3/6/1878, Fond Du Lac, Wis. d: 9/3/48, Milwaukee, Wis. BR/TR, 5'10.5", 185 lbs. Deb: 8/16/00

YEAR	TM/L	W	L	PCT	G	GS	CG	SH	SV	IP	H	R	HR	HB	BB	SO	RAT	ERA	ERA+	OAV	OOB	BH	AVG	PB	PR	PR+	PD	TPI
1900	Pit-N	0	0	—	2	0	0	0	0	8	10	5	2	1	5	7	18.0	5.63	65	.303	.410	0	.000	-1	-2	-2	1	-0.1
1901	Mil-A	9	15	.375	34	26	19	0	1	217^{1}	234	151	5	13	95	67	14.2	4.27	84	.272	.353	19	.202	-1	-14	-16	5	-1.1
1902	Bos-A	0	1	.000	1	1	1	0	0	8	15	15	0	0	8	4	25.9	9.00	40	.395	.500	1	.250	1	-5	-5	0	-0.4
	Phi-A	14	5	.737	32	27	17	1	0	204	240	126	7	9	91	44	15.0	3.79	97	.293	.370	13	.159	-3	-5	-3	2	-0.3
	Yr	14	6	.700	33	28	18	1	0	212	255	141	7	9	99	48	15.4	3.99	92	.298	.377	14	.163	-3	-10	-7	3	-0.7
Total	3	23	21	.523	69	54	37	1	1	437^{1}	499	297	14	23	199	122	14.8	4.16	87	.285	.366	33	.180	-4	-26	-25	8	-1.9

● JOHNNY HUTCHINGS
Hutchings, John Richard Joseph b: 4/14/16, Chicago, Ill. d: 4/27/63, Indianapolis, Ind. BB/TR, 6'2", 250 lbs. Deb: 4/26/40

YEAR	TM/L	W	L	PCT	G	GS	CG	SH	SV	IP	H	R	HR	HB	BB	SO	RAT	ERA	ERA+	OAV	OOB	BH	AVG	PB	PR	PR+	PD	TPI
1940	*Cin-N	2	1	.667	19	4	0	0	0	54	53	21	3	1	18	18	12.0	3.50	108	.260	.323	2	.154	0	2	2	-1	0.0
1941	Cin-N	0	0	—	8	0	0	0	0	11	12	6	0	0	4	5	13.1	4.09	88	.279	.340	0	—	0	-1	-1	0	0.0
	Bos-N	1	6	.143	36	7	1	1	2	95^{2}	110	59	6	4	22	36	12.8	4.14	86	.287	.333	4	.148	0	-5	-6	0	-0.4
	Yr	1	6	.143	44	7	1	1	2	106^{2}	122	65	6	4	26	41	12.8	4.13	86	.286	.333	4	.148	0	-6	-7	0	-0.4
1942	Bos-N	1	0	1.000	20	3	0	0	0	65^{2}	66	33	2	2	34	27	14.0	4.39	76	.260	.352	1	.050	-2	-8	-8	-1	-0.7
1944	Bos-N	1	4	.200	14	7	1	0	1	56^{2}	55	30	3	1	26	26	13.0	3.97	96	.252	.335	1	.067	-1	-2	-1	-1	-0.2
1945	Bos-N	7	6	.538	57	12	3	2	3	185	173	87	21	4	75	99	12.3	3.75	102	.244	.320	13	.241	2	1	2	0	0.3
1946	Bos-N	0	1	.000	1	1	0	0	0	3	5	3	1	0	1	1	18.0	9.00	38	.357	.400	0	.000	-0	-2	-2	-0	-0.3
Total	6	12	18	.400	155	34	5	3	6	471	474	239	36	12	180	212	12.7	3.96	93	.260	.330	21	.162	-1	-15	-14	-2	-1.3

● FRED HUTCHINSON
Hutchinson, Frederick Charles b: 8/12/19, Seattle, Wash. d: 11/12/64, Bradenton, Fla. BL/TR, 6'2", 200 lbs. Deb: 5/2/39 M◆

YEAR	TM/L	W	L	PCT	G	GS	CG	SH	SV	IP	H	R	HR	HB	BB	SO	RAT	ERA	ERA+	OAV	OOB	BH	AVG	PB	PR	PR+	PD	TPI
1939	Det-A	3	6	.333	13	12	3	0	0	84^{2}	95	56	9	0	51	22	15.5	5.21	94	.287	.382	13	.382	3	-6	-3	-0	0.0
1940	*Det-A	3	7	.300	17	10	1	0	0	76	85	52	6	2	26	32	13.4	5.68	84	.281	.342	8	.267	0	-11	-7	0	-0.7
1946	Det-A	14	11	.560	28	26	16	3	2	207	184	78	14	0	66	138	10.9	3.09	118	.236	.295	28	.315	8	10	13	3	2.7
1947	Det-A	18	10	.643	33	25	18	3	2	219^{2}	211	84	14	2	61	113	11.2	3.03	124	.251	.304	32	.302	11	16	18	2	3.7
1948	Det-A	13	11	.542	33	28	15	0	0	221	223	119	32	1	48	92	**11.1**	4.32	101	.258	**.297**	23	.205	4	-1	1	3	0.9
1949	Det-A	15	7	.682	33	21	9	4	1	188^{2}	167	70	18	1	52	54	**10.5**	2.96	141	.237	**.290**	18	.247	4	26	25	2	3.4
1950	Det-A	17	8	.680	39	26	10	1	0	231^{2}	269	119	18	5	48	71	12.5	3.96	118	.290	.329	31	.326	10	16	18	2	2.9
1951	Det-A★	10	10	.500	31	20	9	2	2	188^{1}	204	84	12	2	27	53	11.1	3.68	113	.275	.302	16	.188	-2	9	10	2	1.0
1952	Det-A	2	1	.667	12	1	0	0	0	37^{1}	40	16	4	1	9	12	12.1	3.38	113	.276	.323	1	.056	-1	1	2	2	0.2
1953	Det-A	0	0	—	3	0	0	0	0	9^{2}	9	3	0	0	0	4	8.4	2.79	146	.243	.243	1	.167	0	1	1	-0	0.1
Total	10	95	71	.572	242	169	81	13	7	1464	1487	681	127	14	388	591	11.6	3.73	113	.262	.311	171	.263	39	62	77	15	14.2

● IRA HUTCHINSON
Hutchinson, Ira Kendall b: 8/31/10, Chicago, Ill. d: 8/21/73, Chicago, Ill. BR/TR, 5'10.5", 180 lbs. Deb: 9/24/33

YEAR	TM/L	W	L	PCT	G	GS	CG	SH	SV	IP	H	R	HR	HB	BB	SO	RAT	ERA	ERA+	OAV	OOB	BH	AVG	PB	PR	PR+	PD	TPI
1933	Chi-A	0	0	—	1	1	0	0	0	4	7	6	1	0	3	2	22.5	13.50	31	.368	.455	1	.500	0	-4	-4	-0	-0.2
1937	Bos-N	4	6	.400	31	8	1	0	0	91^{2}	99	44	4	1	35	29	13.3	3.73	96	.286	.353	3	.115	-1	2	-2	1	-0.2
1938	Bos-N	9	8	.529	36	12	4	1	4	151	150	58	3	4	61	38	12.8	2.74	125	.258	.332	9	.173	-1	18	13	1	1.4
1939	Bro-N	5	2	.714	41	1	0	0	1	105^{2}	103	54	9	1	51	46	13.2	4.34	93	.265	.352	1	.037	-3	-5	-4	1	-0.4
1940	StL-N	4	2	.667	20	2	1	0	1	63^{1}	68	27	3	0	19	19	12.4	3.13	128	.271	.322	4	.222	0	5	6	0	0.6
1941	StL-N	1	5	.167	29	0	0	0	5	46^{2}	32	23	3	2	19	19	10.2	3.86	98	.196	.288	2	.250	0	-1	-0	0	0.0
1944	Bos-N	9	7	.563	40	8	1	1	1	119^{2}	136	59	8	3	53	22	14.4	4.21	91	.296	.373	4	.138	-1	-8	-5	1	-0.6
1945	Bos-N	2	3	.400	11	0	0	0	1	28^{2}	33	18	2	1	8	4	13.2	5.02	76	.277	.328	0	.000	-1	-4	-4	1	-0.7
Total	8	34	33	.507	209	32	7	2	13	610^{2}	628	289	33	12	249	179	13.1	3.76	100	.270	.344	24	.140	-7	2	-1	5	-0.1

● BILL HUTCHISON
Hutchison, William Forrest "Wild Bill"
b: 12/17/1859, New Haven, Conn. d: 3/19/26, Kansas City, Mo. BR/TR, 5'9", 175 lbs. Deb: 6/10/1884

YEAR	TM/L	W	L	PCT	G	GS	CG	SH	SV	IP	H	R	HR	HB	BB	SO	RAT	ERA	ERA+	OAV	OOB	BH	AVG	PB	PR	PR+	PD	TPI
1884	KC-U	1	1	.500	2	2	2	0	0	17	14	11	0		1	5	7.9	2.65	84	.209	.221	2	.250	-0	-0	-1	2	0.0
1889	Chi-N	16	17	.485	37	36	33	3	0	318	306	206	11	8	117	136	12.2	3.54	118	.245	.314	21	.158	-5	17	21	5	1.7
1890	Chi-N	**42**	25	.627	**71**	**66**	**65**	5	**2**	**603**	505	315	20	13	199	289	10.7	2.70	135	.220	.286	53	.203	-4	58	63	5	5.8
1891	Chi-N	**44**	19	.698	**66**	58	**56**	4	1	**561**	508	283	26	7	178	261	11.1	2.81	119	.232	.292	45	.185	-1	34	33	-2	2.7
1892	Chi-N	**36**	36	.500	**75**	70	**67**	5	1	**622**	571	316	11	13	190	**314**	11.2	2.76	120	.234	.293	57	.217	3	36	38	4	4.5
1893	Chi-N	16	24	.400	44	40	38	2	0	348^{1}	420	266	9	13	156	80	15.2	4.75	97	.289	.364	41	.253	1	-3	-5	-3	-0.5
1894	Chi-N	14	16	.467	37	34	28	0	0	279^{1}	374	257	9	18	140	60	17.1	6.03	93	.317	.398	42	.309	6	-22	-12	-1	-0.5
1895	Chi-N	13	21	.382	38	35	30	2	0	291	371	218	13	13	129	85	15.9	4.73	107	.306	.378	25	.198	-7	2	11	-0	0.3
1897	StL-N	1	4	.200	6	5	2	0	0	40	55	41	5	2	22	5	17.8	6.07	72	.324	.407	5	.278	1	-8	-7	-1	-0.7
Total	9	183	163	.529	376	346	321	21	4	3079^{2}	3124	1913	104	87	1132	1235	12.7	3.59	111	.255	.323	291	.216	-6	113	137	8	13.3

● HERB HUTSON
Hutson, George Herbert b: 7/17/49, Savannah, Ga. BR/TR, 6'2", 205 lbs. Deb: 4/10/74

YEAR	TM/L	W	L	PCT	G	GS	CG	SH	SV	IP	H	R	HR	HB	BB	SO	RAT	ERA	ERA+	OAV	OOB	BH	AVG	PB	PR	PR+	PD	TPI
1974	Chi-N	0	2	.000	20	2	0	0	0	28^{2}	24	15	3	1	15	22	12.6	3.45	111	.233	.336	0	.000	-0	1	1	-1	0.0

● MARK HUTTON
Hutton, Mark Steven b: 2/6/70, South Adelaide, Australia BR/TR, 6'6", 240 lbs. Deb: 7/23/93

YEAR	TM/L	W	L	PCT	G	GS	CG	SH	SV	IP	H	R	HR	HB	BB	SO	RAT	ERA	ERA+	OAV	OOB	BH	AVG	PB	PR	PR+	PD	TPI
1993	NY-A	1	1	.500	7	4	0	0	0	22	24	17	2	1	17	12	17.2	5.73	73	.293	.420	0	—	0	-3	-4	-0	-0.3
1994	NY-A	0	0	—	2	0	0	0	0	3^{2}	4	3	0	0	0	1	9.8	4.91	93	.250	.250	0	—	0	-0	-0	-0	0.0
1996	NY-A	0	2	.000	12	2	0	0	0	30^{1}	32	19	3	1	18	25	15.1	5.04	98	.269	.370	0	—	0	-0	-0	-1	-0.1
	Fla-N	5	1	.833	13	9	0	0	0	56^{1}	47	23	6	3	18	31	10.9	3.67	111	.222	.292	6	.316	2	3	3	-1	0.4
1997	Fla-N	3	1	.750	32	0	0	0	0	47^{2}	50	24	7	2	19	29	13.4	3.78	107	.286	.362	0	—	0	2	1	1	0.2
	Col-N	0	1	.000	8	1	0	0	0	12^{2}	22	10	3	4	7	10	23.4	7.11	73	.407	.508	0	.000	-0	-4	-2	-0	-0.2
	Yr	3	2	.600	40	1	0	0	0	60^{1}	72	34	10	6	26	39	15.5	4.48	95	.314	.398	0	.000	-0	-2	-1	1	0.0
1998	Cin-N	0	1	.000	10	2	0	0	0	17	24	14	2	1	17	3	22.2	7.41	58	.348	.483	1	1.000	0	-6	-6	1	-0.2
Total	5	9	7	.563	84	18	0	0	0	189^{2}	203	110	23	12	96	111	14.8	4.75	91	.279	.372	7	.304	3	-8	-9	-1	-0.2

● TOM HUTTON
Hutton, Thomas George b: 4/20/46, Los Angeles, Cal. BL/TL, 5'11", 180 lbs. Deb: 9/16/66 ◆

YEAR	TM/L	W	L	PCT	G	GS	CG	SH	SV	IP	H	R	HR	HB	BB	SO	RAT	ERA	ERA+	OAV	OOB	BH	AVG	PB	PR	PR+	PD	TPI
1980	Mon-N	0	0	—	1	0	0	0	0	1	3	3	1	0	1	1	36.0	27.00	13	.500	.571	12	.218	0	-3	-3	0	-0.1

● DICK HYDE
Hyde, Richard Elde b: 8/3/28, Hindsboro, Ill. BR/TR, 5'11", 170 lbs. Deb: 4/23/55

YEAR	TM/L	W	L	PCT	G	GS	CG	SH	SV	IP	H	R	HR	HB	BB	SO	RAT	ERA	ERA+	OAV	OOB	BH	AVG	PB	PR	PR+	PD	TPI
1955	Was-A	0	0	—	3	0	0	0	0	2	2	1	0	0	1	1	13.5	4.50	85	.286	.375	0	—	0	-0	-0	-0	0.0
1957	Was-A	4	3	.571	52	2	0	0	1	109^{1}	104	54	4	7	56	46	13.7	4.12	95	.261	.361	3	.167	-0	-4	-3	1	-0.1
1958	Was-A	10	3	.769	53	0	0	0	18	103	82	26	1	2	35	49	10.4	1.75	218	.220	.291	0	.000	-2	**23**	**23**	2	3.8

YEAR	TM/L	W	L	PCT	G	GS	CG	SH	SV	IP	H	R	HR	HB	BB	SO	RAT	ERA	ERA+	OAV	OOB	BH	AVG	PB	PR	PR+	PD	TPI
1959	Was-A	2	5	.286	37	0	0	0	4	54^{1}	56	34	5	2	27	29	14.1	4.97	79	.269	.359	0	.000	-1	-7	-6	2	-0.7
1960	Was-A	0	1	.000	9	0	0	0	0	8^{2}	11	4	2	1	5	4	17.7	4.15	94	.355	.459	0	—	0	-0	-0	-0	0.0
1961	Bal-A	1	2	.333	15	0	0	0	0	21	18	14	1	1	13	15	13.7	5.57	69	.228	.344	1	1.000	0	-4	-4	1	-0.3
Total	6	17	14	.548	169	2	0	0	23	298^{1}	273	133	13	13	137	144	12.8	3.56	109	.249	.339	4	.093	-2	8	10	6	2.7
● JIM HYNDMAN	Hyndman, James Harvey b: 7/9/1866, Hamilton, Ontario, Canada d: 1/16/34, Alamosa, Colo. Deb: 7/23/1886 ♦																											
1886	Phi-a	0	1	.000	1	1	0	0	0	2	5	10	1	1	5	1	49.5	27.00	13	.455	.647	0	.000	-1	-5	-5	0	-0.7
● PAT HYNES	Hynes, Patrick J. b: 3/12/1884, St.Louis, Mo. d: 3/12/07, St.Louis, Mo. TL, Deb: 9/27/03 ♦																											
1903	StL-N	0	1	.000	1	1	1	0	0	9	10	6	0	0	6	1	16.0	4.00	82	.294	.400	0	.000	-0	-1	-1	-1	-0.2
1904	StL-A	1	0	1.000	5	2	1	0	0	26	35	21	1	0	7	6	14.5	6.23	40	.321	.362	60	.236	0	-10	-11	-1	-0.7
Total	2	1	1	.500	6	3	2	0	0	35	45	27	1	0	13	7	14.9	5.66	47	.315	.372	60	.233	0	-11	-12	-2	-0.9
● HAM IBURG	Iburg, Herman Edward b: 10/29/1877, San Francisco, Cal d: 2/11/45, San Francisco, Cal BR/TR, 5'11", 165 lbs. Deb: 4/17/02																											
1902	Phi-N	11	18	.379	30	29	20	1	0	236	286	141	1	11	62	106	13.7	3.89	72	.299	.349	12	.138	-5	-29	-28	0	-3.5
● GARY IGNASIAK	Ignasiak, Gary Raymond b: 9/1/49, Anchorville, Mich. BR/TL, 5'11", 185 lbs. Deb: 9/20/73 F																											
1973	Det-A	0	0	—	3	0	0	0	0	4^{2}	5	2	0	0	3	4	15.4	3.86	106	.278	.381	0	—	0	-0	0	0	0.0
● MIKE IGNASIAK	Ignasiak, Michael James b: 3/12/66, Mt.Clemens, Mich. BB/TR, 5'11", 175 lbs. Deb: 8/22/91 F																											
1991	Mil-A	2	1	.667	4	1	0	0	0	12^{2}	7	8	2	0	8	10	10.7	5.68	70	.163	.294	0	—	0	-2	-2	-0	-0.5
1993	Mil-A	1	1	.500	27	0	0	0	0	37	32	17	2	2	21	28	13.4	3.65	117	.241	.353	0	—	0	3	3	-1	0.1
1994	Mil-A	3	1	.750	23	5	0	0	0	47^{2}	51	25	5	1	13	24	12.3	4.53	111	.276	.327	0	—	0	1	3	-1	0.1
1995	Mil-A	4	1	.800	25	0	0	0	0	39^{2}	51	27	5	2	23	26	17.2	5.90	85	.325	.418	0	—	0	-5	-4	-1	-0.4
Total	4	10	4	.714	79	6	0	0	0	137	141	77	14	5	65	88	13.9	4.80	98	.272	.359	0	—	0	-3	-1	-2	-0.7
● BLAISE ILSLEY	Ilsley, Blaise Francis b: 4/9/64, Alpena, Mich. BL/TL, 6'1", 195 lbs. Deb: 4/4/94																											
1994	Chi-N	0	0	—	10	0	0	0	0	15	25	13	2	0	9	9	20.4	7.80	53	.385	.459	0	.000	-0	-6	-6	0	-0.3
● DOC IMLAY	Imlay, Harry Miller b: 1/12/1889, Allentown, N.J. d: 10/7/48, Bordentown, N.J. BR/TR, 5'11", 168 lbs. Deb: 7/7/13																											
1913	Phi-N	0	0	—	9	0	0	0	0	13^{2}	19	13	1	0	7	7	17.1	7.24	46	.358	.433	0	.000	-0	-6	-6	0	-0.3
● BOB INGERSOLL	Ingersoll, Robert Randolph b: 1/8/1883, Rapid City, S.D. d: 1/13/27, Minneapolis, Minn. BR/TR, 5'11.5", 175 lbs. Deb: 4/23/14																											
1914	Cin-N	0	0	—	4	0	0	0	0	6	5	2	0	1	5	2	16.5	3.00	98	.250	.423	1	1.000	0	-0	-0	-0	0.0
● BERT INKS	Inks, Albert John b: 1/27/1871, Ligonier, Ind. d: 10/3/41, Ligonier, Ind. BL/TL, 6'3", 175 lbs. Deb: 9/2/1891																											
1891	Bro-N	3	10	.231	13	13	11	1	0	96^{1}	99	70	2	6	43	47	13.8	4.02	82	.256	.339	10	.286	2	-7	-8	-0	-0.7
1892	Bro-N	4	2	.667	9	8	4	1	0	58	48	34	0	4	33	25	13.2	3.88	82	.216	.328	10	.400	3	-4	-5	0	-0.1
	Was-N	1	2	.333	3	3	3	0	0	21	29	27	0	2	10	11	17.6	5.14	63	.315	.394	3	.300	1	-4	-4	-0	-0.5
	Yr	5	4	.556	12	11	7	1	0	79	77	61	0	6	43	36	14.4	4.22	76	.245	.347	13	.371	4	-8	-9	-0	-0.6
1894	Bal-N	9	4	.692	22	14	10	0	1	133	181	108	4	11	54	30	16.6	5.55	98	.321	.391	18	.316	2	-3	-1	-1	-0.1
	Lou-N	2	6	.250	8	8	8	0	0	59^{2}	87	70	2	1	34	8	18.4	6.49	79	.336	.415	12	.444	3	-8	-10	0	-0.6
	Yr	11	10	.524	30	22	18	0	1	192^{2}	268	178	6	12	88	38	17.2	5.84	92	.326	.399	30	.357	5	-11	-10	-1	-0.7
1895	Lou-N	7	20	.259	28	27	21	0	0	205^{1}	294	197	3	15	78	42	17.0	6.40	72	.331	.394	21	.250	-0	-37	-42	1	-3.7
1896	Phi-N	0	1	.000	3	1	0	0	0	10^{1}	21	13	1	1	5	2	23.5	7.84	55	.412	.474	1	.200	-0	-4	-4	-1	-0.4
	Cin-N	1	1	.500	3	3	2	0	0	20	21	13	0	1	9	2	13.9	4.50	103	.269	.352	0	.000	-1	-0	0	-1	-0.1
	Yr	1	2	.333	6	4	2	0	0	30^{1}	42	26	1	2	14	4	17.2	5.64	80	.326	.400	1	.083	-1	-4	-4	-1	-0.5
Total	5	27	46	.370	89	77	59	2	1	603^{2}	780	532	12	41	266	167	16.2	5.52	81	.307	.382	75	.300	9	-68	-73	-2	-6.2
● JEFF INNIS	Innis, Jeffrey David b: 7/5/62, Decatur, Ill. BR/TR, 6', 170 lbs. Deb: 5/16/87																											
1987	NY-N	0	1	.000	17	1	0	0	0	25^{2}	29	9	5	1	4	28	11.9	3.16	120	.279	.312	0	.000	-0	3	2	-0	0.1
1988	NY-N	1	1	.500	12	0	0	0	0	19	19	6	0	0	2	14	9.9	1.89	170	.250	.269	0	—	0	3	3	-1	0.2
1989	NY-N	0	1	.000	29	0	0	0	0	39^{2}	38	16	2	1	8	16	10.7	3.18	103	.255	.297	0	.000	-0	1	0	1	0.1
1990	NY-N	1	3	.250	18	0	0	0	1	26^{1}	19	9	4	1	10	12	10.3	2.39	157	.209	.294	0	—	0	4	4	0	0.6
1991	NY-N	0	2	.000	69	0	0	0	0	84^{2}	66	30	2	0	23	47	9.5	2.66	137	.219	.274	0	.000	-0	10	9	3	0.8
1992	NY-N	6	9	.400	76	0	0	0	1	88	85	32	4	6	36	39	13.0	2.86	121	.266	.351	0	.000	-0	6	6	2	1.2
1993	NY-N	2	3	.400	67	0	0	0	3	76^{2}	81	39	5	6	38	36	14.7	4.11	98	.278	.373	0	—	0	-1	-1	1	0.0
Total	7	10	20	.333	288	1	0	0	5	360	337	141	22	15	121	192	11.8	3.05	119	.253	.322	0	.000	-1	27	24	6	3.0
● DANE IORG	Iorg, Dane Charles b: 5/11/50, Eureka, Cal. BL/TR, 6', 180 lbs. Deb: 4/9/77 F♦																											
1986	SD-N	0	0	—	2	0	0	0	0	3	5	4	2	0	1	2	18.0	12.00	31	.357	.400	24	.226	0	-3	-3	-0	-0.1
● HOOKS IOTT	Iott, Clarence Eugene b: 12/3/19, Mountain Grove, Mo. d: 8/17/80, St.Petersburg, Fla BB/TL, 6'2", 200 lbs. Deb: 9/6/41																											
1941	StL-A	0	0	—	2	0	0	0	0	2	2	2	0	0	1	1	13.5	9.00	48	.250	.333	0	—	0	-1	-1	0	0.0
1947	StL-A	0	1	.000	4	0	0	0	0	8^{1}	15	16	4	0	14	6	31.3	16.20	24	.375	.537	0	.000	-0	-12	-11	0	-1.1
	NY-N	3	8	.273	20	9	2	1	0	71^{1}	67	50	3	1	52	46	15.1	5.93	69	.251	.375	3	.143	1	-15	-15	-0	-1.8
Total	2	3	9	.250	26	9	2	1	0	81^{2}	84	68	7	1	67	53	16.8	7.05	58	.267	.397	3	.130	1	-27	-27	0	-2.9
● HIDEKI IRABU	Irabu, Hideki b: 5/5/69, Hyogo, Japan BR/TR, 6'4", 240 lbs. Deb: 7/10/97																											
1997	NY-A	5	4	.556	13	9	0	0	0	53^{1}	69	47	15	1	20	56	15.2	7.09	63	.311	.370	0	.000	-0	-15	-16	-0	-2.2
1998	NY-A	13	9	.591	29	28	2	1	0	173	148	79	27	9	76	126	12.1	4.06	108	.233	.324	1	.250	0	11	7	-2	0.6
1999	*NY-A	11	7	.611	32	27	2	1	0	169^{1}	180	98	26	6	46	133	12.3	4.84	98	.267	.319	0	.000	-0	1	-2	-2	-0.4
2000	Mon-N	2	5	.286	11	11	0	0	0	54^{2}	77	45	9	1	14	42	15.1	7.24	65	.339	.380	2	.125	-1	-16	-15	-0	-1.6
Total	4	31	25	.554	85	75	4	2	0	450^{1}	474	269	77	17	156	357	12.9	5.10	90	.269	.335	3	.120	-1	-19	-27	-5	-3.6
● DARYL IRVINE	Irvine, Daryl Keith b: 11/15/64, Harrisonburg, Va. BR/TR, 6'3", 195 lbs. Deb: 4/28/90																											
1990	Bos-A	1	1	.500	11	0	0	0	0	17^{1}	15	10	0	0	10	9	13.0	4.67	87	.246	.352	0	—	0	-1	-1	0	-0.1
1991	Bos-A	0	0	—	9	0	0	0	0	18	25	13	2	2	9	8	18.0	6.00	72	.321	.404	0	—	0	-4	-3	0	-0.1
1992	Bos-A	3	4	.429	21	0	0	0	0	28	31	20	1	2	14	10	15.1	6.11	69	.287	.379	0	—	0	-7	-5	0	-1.1
Total	3	4	5	.444	41	0	0	0	0	63^{1}	71	43	3	4	33	27	15.3	5.68	74	.287	.380	0	—	0	-12	-10	1	-1.3
● ARTHUR IRWIN	Irwin, Arthur Albert "Doc" or "Sandy" b: 2/14/1858, Toronto, Ont., Can. d: 7/16/21, AtSea Atlantic Ocean N.Y. To Boston BL/TR, 5'8.5", 158 lbs. Deb: 5/1/1880 FMU♦																											
1884	*Pro-N	0	0	—	1	0	0	0	0	3	5	2	0		1	0	18.0	3.00	95	.357	.400	97	.240	0	-0	-0	0	0.0
1889	Was-N	0	0	—	1	0	0	0	0	1	1	1	0	0	0	0	9.0	0.00	—	.250	.250	73	.233	0	0	0	-0	0.0
Total	2	0	0	—	2	0	0	0	0	4	6	3	0	0	1	0	15.8	2.25	139	.333	.368	982	.251	0	0	0	-0	0.0
● BILL IRWIN	Irwin, William Franklin "Phil" b: 9/16/1859, Neville, Ohio d: 8/7/33, Ft.Thomas, Ky. BR/TR, 6', 195 lbs. Deb: 8/30/1886																											
1886	Cin-a	0	2	.000	2	2	2	0	0	17	18	19	2	0	8	6	13.8	5.82	60	.247	.321	0	.000	-0	-4	-4	0	-0.4
● FRANK ISBELL	Isbell, William Frank "Bald Eagle" b: 8/21/1875, Delevan, N.Y. d: 7/15/41, Wichita, Kan. BL/TR, 5'11", 190 lbs. Deb: 5/1/1898 ♦																											
1898	Chi-N	4	7	.364	13	9	7	0	0	81	86	54	0	7	42	16	15.0	3.56	101	.270	.368	37	.233	-0	0	0	-0	0.0
1901	Chi-A	0	0	—	1	0	0	0	0	1	2	1	0	0	0	0	18.0	9.00	39	.400	.400	143	.257	0	-1	-1	0	0.0
1902	Chi-A	0	0	—	1	1	0	0	0	1	3	2	0	0	1	1	36.0	9.00	38	.500	.571	130	.252	0	-1	-1	1	0.0
1906	*Chi-A	0	0	—	1	0	0	0	0	2	1	0	0	0	0	2	4.5	0.00	—	.143	.143	153	.279	0	1	1	-0	0.0
1907	Chi-A	0	0	—	1	0	0	0	1	0^{1}	0	0	0	0	0	0	0.0	0.00	—	.000	.000	118	.243	0	0	0	0	0.1
Total	5	4	7	.364	17	10	7	0	1	85^{1}	92	57	0	7	43	19	15.0	3.59	99	.273	.367	1056	.250	1	-0	-0	1	0.1
● JASON ISRINGHAUSEN	Isringhausen, Jason Derik b: 9/7/72, Brighton, Ill. BR/TR, 6'3", 195 lbs. Deb: 7/17/95																											
1995	NY-N	9	2	.818	14	14	1	0	0	93	88	29	6	2	31	55	11.7	2.81	144	.254	.319	4	.148	1	14	13	-1	1.5
1996	NY-N	6	14	.300	27	27	2	1	0	171^{2}	190	103	13	8	73	114	14.2	4.77	84	.284	.361	13	.255	6	-10	-15	0	-0.9
1997	NY-N	2	2	.500	6	6	0	0	0	29^{2}	40	27	3	1	22	25	19.1	7.58	53	.336	.444	1	.143	-0	-11	-12	-1	-1.3
1999	NY-N	1	3	.250	13	5	0	0	1	39^{1}	43	29	7	2	22	31	15.3	6.41	68	.279	.376	1	.083	-0	-8	-9	0	-0.8

YEAR	TM/L	W	L	PCT	G	GS	CG	SH	SV	IP	H	R	HR	HB	BB	SO	RAT	ERA	ERA+	OAV	OOB	BH	AVG	PB	PR	PR+	PD	TPI
	Oak-A	0	1	.000	20	0	0	0	8	25^1	21	6	2	1	12	20	12.1	2.13	218	.223	.318	0	—	0	8	7	0	0.7
2000	*Oak-A★	6	4	.600	66	0	0	0	33	69	67	34	6	3	32	57	13.3	3.78	126	.252	.339	0	—	0	9	8	0	1.5
Total	5	24	26	.480	146	52	3	1	42	428	449	228	37	17	192	302	13.8	4.37	96	.272	.354	19	.196	6	1	-8	-0	0.7
● AL JACKSON	Jackson, Alvin Neill b: 12/26/35, Waco, Tex. BL/TL, 5'10", 169 lbs. Deb: 6/1/59 C																											
1959	Pit-N	0	0	—	8	3	0	0	0	18	30	14	1	0	8	13	19.0	6.50	60	.405	.463	1	.200	0	-5	-5	-0	-0.3
1961	Pit-N	1	0	1.000	3	2	1	0	0	23^2	20	10	2	0	4	15	9.1	3.42	117	.233	.267	0	.000	-1	2	2	1	0.1
1962	NY-N	8	20	.286	36	33	12	4	0	231^1	244	132	16	5	78	118	12.7	4.40	95	.273	.335	5	.068	-5	-12	-5	4	-0.6
1963	NY-N	13	17	.433	37	34	11	0	1	227	237	128	25	12	84	142	13.2	3.96	88	.267	.338	16	.203	2	-17	-11	2	-1.1
1964	NY-N	11	16	.407	40	31	11	3	1	213^1	229	115	18	4	60	112	12.4	4.26	84	.272	.323	11	.153	2	-17	-16	0	-1.6
1965	NY-N	8	20	.286	37	31	7	3	1	205^1	217	111	17	8	61	120	12.5	4.34	81	.271	.329	7	.117	-1	-18	-19	2	-2.2
1966	StL-N	13	15	.464	36	30	11	3	0	232^2	222	82	18	3	45	90	10.4	2.51	143	.250	.288	13	.176	2	28	28	4	4.2
1967	StL-N	9	4	.692	38	11	1	1	1	107	117	61	7	1	29	43	12.4	3.95	83	.279	.327	8	.258	2	-7	-8	2	-0.5
1968	NY-N	3	7	.300	25	9	0	0	3	92^2	88	42	5	2	17	59	10.4	3.69	82	.249	.287	7	.250	1	-7	-7	1	-0.6
1969	NY-N	0	0	—	9	0	0	0	0	11	18	13	1	1	4	10	18.8	10.64	34	.353	.411	0	.000	-0	-9	-8	0	-0.4
	Cin-N	1	0	1.000	33	0	0	0	3	27^1	27	17	5	3	17	16	15.5	5.27	71	.260	.379	1	.250	0	-5	-4	-0	-0.3
	Yr	1	0	1.000	42	0	0	0	3	38^1	45	30	6	4	21	26	16.4	6.81	55	.290	.389	1	.200	0	-14	-13	-0	-0.7
Total	10	67	99	.404	302	184	54	14	10	1389^1	1449	725	115	39	407	738	12.3	3.98	91	.268	.324	69	.159	3	-67	-55	16	-3.3
● CHARLIE JACKSON	Jackson, Charles Bernard b: 8/4/1876, Versailles, Ohio d: 11/23/57, Scottsbluff, Neb. TR, Deb: 8/11/05																											
1905	Det-A	0	2	.000	2	2	1	0	0	11	14	12	1	0	7	3	17.2	5.73	48	.311	.404	1	.250	0	-4	-4	-0	-0.6
● DANNY JACKSON	Jackson, Danny Lynn b: 1/5/62, San Antonio, Tex. BR/TL, 6', 205 lbs. Deb: 9/11/83																											
1983	KC-A	1	1	.500	4	3	0	0	0	19	26	12	1	0	6	9	15.2	5.21	78	.325	.372	0	—	0	-2	-2	0	-0.2
1984	KC-A	2	6	.250	15	11	1	0	0	76	84	41	4	5	35	40	14.7	4.26	95	.285	.370	0	—	0	-2	-2	-0	-0.2
1985	*KC-A	14	12	.538	32	32	4	3	0	208	209	94	7	6	76	114	12.6	3.42	122	.261	.329	0	—	0	17	17	-1	1.9
1986	KC-A	11	12	.478	32	27	4	1	1	185^2	177	83	13	4	79	115	12.6	3.20	133	.256	.335	0	—	0	20	22	-1	2.4
1987	KC-A	9	18	.333	36	34	11	2	0	224	219	115	11	7	109	152	13.5	4.02	114	.258	.347	0	—	0	11	13	-2	1.3
1988	Cin-N☆	**23**	8	.742	35	35	**15**	6	0	260^2	206	86	13	2	71	161	9.6	2.73	132	.218	.275	13	.144	-0	21	24	2	3.1
1989	Cin-N	6	11	.353	20	20	1	0	0	115^2	122	78	10	1	57	70	14.0	5.60	64	.271	.354	8	.222	1	-27	-25	-1	-3.2
1990	*Cin-N	6	6	.500	22	21	0	0	0	117^1	119	54	11	2	40	76	12.3	3.61	110	.266	.329	2	.054	-2	3	4	-1	0.1
1991	Chi-N	1	5	.167	17	14	0	0	0	70^2	89	59	8	1	48	31	17.6	6.75	58	.309	.409	2	.087	-1	-24	-21	-1	-1.8
1992	Chi-N	4	9	.308	19	19	0	0	0	113	117	59	5	3	48	51	13.4	4.22	85	.270	.346	3	.083	-2	-9	-7	-1	-1.2
	*Pit-N	4	4	.500	15	15	0	0	0	88^1	94	40	1	1	29	46	12.6	3.36	103	.276	.334	2	.083	-1	1	1	0	0.0
	Yr	8	13	.381	34	34	0	0	0	201^1	211	99	6	4	77	97	13.1	3.84	92	.272	.341	5	.083	-3	-7	-7	-1	-1.2
1993	*Phi-N	12	11	.522	32	32	2	1	0	210^1	214	105	12	4	80	120	12.8	3.77	105	.263	.332	5	.077	-2	7	5	-2	0.1
1994	Phi-N★	14	6	.700	25	25	4	1	0	179^1	183	71	13	2	46	129	11.6	3.26	132	.266	.314	9	.158	1	19	20	1	2.3
1995	StL-N	2	12	.143	19	19	2	1	0	100^2	120	82	10	6	48	52	15.6	5.90	71	.303	.387	5	.161	0	-19	-19	-1	-2.3
1996	*StL-N	1	1	.500	13	4	0	0	0	36^1	33	18	3	1	16	27	12.4	4.46	94	.243	.327	3	.333	1	-1	-1	0	0.1
1997	StL-N	1	2	.333	4	4	0	0	0	18^2	26	17	3	2	8	13	17.4	7.71	54	.347	.424	1	.143	-0	-7	-7	0	-0.9
	SD-N	1	7	.125	13	9	0	0	0	49	72	47	8	3	20	19	17.4	7.53	52	.353	.419	1	.077	-0	-18	-22	-1	-2.9
	Yr	2	9	.182	17	13	0	0	0	67^2	98	64	11	5	28	32	17.4	7.58	52	.351	.420	2	.100	-1	-25	-29	-1	-3.8
Total	15	112	131	.461	353	324	44	15	1	2072^2	2110	1061	133	50	816	1225	12.9	4.01	100	.266	.338	54	.126	-6	-11	2	-7	-1.4
● DARRELL JACKSON	Jackson, Darrell Preston b: 4/3/56, Los Angeles, Cal. BB/TL, 5'10", 150 lbs. Deb: 6/16/78																											
1978	Min-A	4	6	.400	19	15	1	1	0	92^1	89	53	9	2	48	54	13.5	4.48	86	.256	.350	0	—	0	-7	-7	-1	-0.7
1979	Min-A	4	4	.500	24	8	1	0	0	69^1	89	36	5	1	26	43	15.1	4.28	103	.319	.379	0	—	0	-0	1	1	0.1
1980	Min-A	9	9	.500	32	25	1	0	1	172	161	81	15	2	69	90	12.1	3.87	113	.250	.325	0	—	0	3	9	-0	0.8
1981	Min-A	3	3	.500	14	5	0	0	0	32^2	35	16	1	1	19	26	15.2	4.41	90	.282	.382	0	—	0	-3	-2	-1	-0.3
1982	Min-A	0	5	.000	13	7	0	0	0	44^2	51	33	6	1	24	16	15.3	6.25	68	.297	.386	0	—	0	-11	-10	-0	-1.0
Total	5	20	27	.426	102	60	3	1	1	411	425	219	36	7	186	229	13.5	4.38	96	.272	.352	0	—	0	-18	-8	-2	-1.1
● DARRIN JACKSON	Jackson, Darrin Jay b: 8/22/62, Los Angeles, Cal. BR/TR, 6', 185 lbs. Deb: 6/17/85 ♦																											
1991	SD-N	0	0	—	1	0	0	0	0	2	3	2	0	0	2	0	22.5	9.00	42	.375	.500	94	.262	0	-1	-1	-0	-0.1
● GRANT JACKSON	Jackson, Grant Dwight "Buck" b: 9/28/42, Fostoria, Ohio BB/TL, 6', 190 lbs. Deb: 9/3/65 C																											
1965	Phi-N	1	1	.500	6	2	0	0	0	13^2	17	11	4	0	5	15	14.5	7.24	48	.304	.361	0	.000	-0	-6	-6	0	-0.8
1966	Phi-N	0	0	—	2	0	0	0	0	1^2	2	1	0	0	3	0	27.0	5.40	67	.333	.556	0	—	0	-0	-0	0	0.0
1967	Phi-N	2	3	.400	43	4	0	0	1	84^1	86	40	3	2	43	83	14.0	3.84	89	.267	.357	2	.133	-0	-4	-4	-2	-0.4
1968	Phi-N	1	6	.143	33	6	1	0	1	61	59	28	4	0	20	49	11.7	2.95	102	.248	.306	3	.300	1	0	0	0	0.2
1969	Phi-N☆	14	18	.438	38	35	13	4	1	253	237	114	16	5	92	180	11.9	3.34	106	.249	.318	12	.140	-0	7	6	-2	0.5
1970	Phi-N	5	15	.250	32	23	1	0	0	149^2	170	94	17	1	61	104	14.0	5.29	76	.288	.356	4	.091	-2	-21	-22	0	-2.7
1971	*Bal-A	4	3	.571	29	9	0	0	0	77^2	72	31	7	2	20	51	10.9	3.13	107	.249	.302	2	.091	0	3	2	-0	0.2
1972	Bal-A	1	1	.500	32	0	0	0	8	41	33	14	1	0	9	34	9.2	2.63	117	.217	.261	0	.000	-0	2	2	0	0.2
1973	*Bal-A	8	0	1.000	45	0	0	0	9	80^1	54	18	5	0	24	47	8.7	1.90	196	.198	.263	0	—	0	17	17	-0	2.0
1974	*Bal-A	6	4	.600	49	0	0	0	12	66^2	48	19	7	1	22	56	9.6	2.57	135	.198	.268	0	—	0	8	7	-1	1.1
1975	Bal-A	4	3	.571	41	0	0	0	7	48^1	42	18	3	1	21	39	11.9	3.35	105	.241	.327	0	—	0	2	1	-0	0.1
1976	Bal-A	1	1	.500	13	0	0	0	3	19^1	19	11	1	2	9	14	14.0	5.12	64	.268	.366	0	—	0	-3	-4	-0	-0.6
	*NY-A	6	0	1.000	21	2	1	1	1	58^2	38	11	1	1	16	25	8.4	1.69	203	.186	.249	0	—	0	12	12	-1	1.1
	Yr	7	1	.875	34	2	1	1	4	78	57	22	2	3	25	39	9.8	2.54	133	.207	.281	0	—	0	9	8	-2	0.5
1977	Pit-N	5	3	.625	49	2	0	0	4	91	81	44	11	1	39	41	12.0	3.86	103	.240	.321	6	.333	2	1	1	-1	0.2
1978	Pit-N	7	5	.583	60	0	0	0	5	77^1	89	32	5	1	32	45	14.2	3.26	114	.298	.367	3	.250	1	3	4	0	0.7
1979	*Pit-N	8	5	.615	72	0	0	0	14	82	67	32	9	2	35	39	11.4	2.96	131	.230	.317	0	.000	-1	7	8	-1	1.3
1980	Pit-N	8	4	.667	61	0	0	0	9	71	71	24	4	0	20	31	11.5	2.92	125	.275	.327	0	.000	-1	5	6	-0	0.9
1981	Pit-N	1	2	.333	35	0	0	0	4	32^1	30	10	1	0	10	17	11.1	2.51	144	.248	.305	0	.000	-0	4	4	-1	0.3
	Mon-N	1	0	1.000	10	0	0	0	0	10^2	14	9	2	0	9	4	19.4	7.59	46	.333	.451	0	—	0	-5	-5	0	-0.4
	Yr	2	2	.500	45	0	0	0	4	43	44	19	3	0	19	21	13.2	3.77	95	.270	.346	0	.000	-0	-1	-1	-1	-0.1
1982	KC-A	3	1	.750	20	0	0	0	0	38^1	42	27	7	2	21	15	15.3	5.17	79	.271	.365	0	—	0	-5	-5	-0	-0.5
	Pit-N	0	0	—	1	0	0	0	0	0^2	1	1	1	0	0	0	13.5	13.50	28	.333	.333	0	—	0	-1	-1	-0	0.0
Total	18	86	75	.534	692	83	16	5	79	1358^2	1272	589	109	21	511	889	11.9	3.46	104	.251	.322	32	.136	-2	26	23	-9	3.4
● JOHN JACKSON	Jackson, John Lewis b: 7/15/09, Wynnefield, Pa. d: 10/22/56, Somers Point, N.J. BR/TR, 6'2", 180 lbs. Deb: 6/20/33																											
1933	Phi-N	2	2	.500	10	7	1	0	0	54	74	42	3	5	35	11	19.0	6.00	64	.329	.430	3	.143	-1	-16	-11	-2	-1.1
● LARRY JACKSON	Jackson, Lawrence Curtis b: 6/2/31, Nampa, Idaho d: 8/28/90, Boise, Idaho BR/TR, 6'2", 190 lbs. Deb: 4/17/55																											
1955	StL-N	9	14	.391	37	25	4	1	2	177^1	189	93	25	9	72	88	13.7	4.31	94	.277	.353	3	.053	-6	-5	-5	0	-1.1
1956	StL-N	2	2	.500	51	1	0	0	9	85^1	75	44	5	1	45	50	12.8	4.11	92	.240	.337	1	.091	-0	-3	-3	2	0.0
1957	StL-N★	15	9	.625	41	22	6	2	1	210^1	196	84	21	4	57	96	11.0	3.47	114	.248	.302	13	.181	0	10	11	4	1.6
1958	StL-N★	13	13	.500	49	23	11	1	8	198	211	93	21	10	51	124	12.4	3.68	112	.272	.325	9	.150	-2	6	9	-2	0.8
1959	StL-N	14	13	.519	40	37	12	3	0	256	271	103	13	4	64	145	11.9	3.30	128	.270	.316	9	.112	-3	18	25	-0	2.1
1960	StL-N★	18	13	.581	43	38	14	3	0	**282**	277	123	22	3	70	171	11.2	3.48	118	.257	.304	20	.211	2	9	18	-2	1.9
1961	StL-N	14	11	.560	33	28	12	3	0	211	203	99	20	4	56	113	11.2	3.75	117	.252	.303	13	.176	0	7	14	2	1.7
1962	StL-N	16	11	.593	36	35	11	2	0	252^1	267	121	25	6	64	112	12.0	3.75	114	.269	.318	15	.169	2	6	14	1	1.6
1963	Chi-N★	14	18	.438	37	37	13	4	0	275	256	102	11	6	54	153	10.3	2.55	137	.245	.286	17	.195	2	22	27	2	3.9
1964	Chi-N	**24**	11	.686	40	38	19	3	0	297^2	265	114	17	1	58	148	9.8	3.14	118	.235	.273	20	.175	1	13	18	7	2.9
1965	Chi-N	14	21	.400	39	39	12	4	0	257^1	268	126	28	5	57	131	11.5	3.85	96	.267	.310	11	.128	1	-9	-4	3	-0.2
1966	Chi-N	0	2	.000	3	2	0	0	0	8	14	13	3	0	4	5	20.3	13.50	27	.368	.429	0	.000	-0	-9	-9	0	-1.4
	Phi-N	15	13	.536	35	33	12	5	0	247	243	93	22	5	58	107	11.1	2.99	120	.259	.306	13	.146	-0	17	17	1	2.0
	Yr	15	15	.500	38	35	12	**5**	0	255	257	106	25	5	62	112	11.4	3.32	108	.264	.311	13	.141	-1	8	8	2	0.6
1967	Phi-N	13	15	.464	40	37	11	4	0	261^2	242	111	17	6	54	139	10.4	3.10	110	.241	.284	14	.161	0	8	9	4	1.5

YEAR	TM/L	W	L	PCT	G	GS	CG	SH	SV	IP	H	R	HR	HB	BB	SO	RAT	ERA	ERA+	OAV	OOB	BH	AVG	PB	PR	PR+	PD	TPI
1968	Phi-N	13	17	.433	34	34	12	2	0	243^2	229	86	9	4	60	127	10.8	2.77	109	.248	.297	12	.141	-0	6	6	2	0.9
Total	14	194	183	.515	558	429	149	37	20	3262^2	3206	1405	259	68	824	1709	11.3	3.40	113	.256	.306	170	.156	-5	95	148	25	18.2
● **MIKE JACKSON** Jackson, Michael Ray b: 12/22/64, Houston, Tex. BR/TR, 6', 200 lbs. Deb: 8/11/86																												
1986	Phi-N	0	0	—	9	0	0	0	0	13^1	12	5	2	2	4	3	12.2	3.38	114	.250	.333	0	—	0	1	1	-0	0.0
1987	Phi-N	3	10	.231	55	7	0	0	1	109^1	88	55	16	3	56	93	12.1	4.20	101	.250	.319	2	.118	-0	-1	1	-1	-0.1
1988	Sea-A	6	5	.545	62	0	0	0	4	99^1	74	37	10	2	43	76	10.8	2.63	159	.209	.298	0	—	0	15	16	-0	1.7
1989	Sea-A	4	6	.400	65	0	0	0	7	99^1	81	43	8	6	54	94	12.8	3.17	127	.223	.333	0	—	0	8	9	-1	0.9
1990	Sea-A	5	7	.417	63	0	0	0	3	77^1	64	42	8	2	44	69	12.8	4.54	87	.229	.338	0	—	0	-5	-5	1	-0.6
1991	Sea-A	7	7	.500	72	0	0	0	14	88^2	64	35	5	6	34	74	10.6	3.25	127	.201	.290	0	—	0	8	9	-1	1.4
1992	SF-N	6	6	.500	67	0	0	0	2	82	76	35	7	4	33	80	12.4	3.73	89	.252	.333	0	.000	-0	-2	-4	-0	-0.6
1993	SF-N	6	6	.500	**81**	0	0	0	1	77^1	58	28	7	3	24	70	9.9	3.03	129	.204	.273	2	.667	2	9	8	0	1.3
1994	SF-N	3	2	.600	36	0	0	0	4	42^1	23	8	4	2	11	51	7.7	1.49	270	.164	.235	0	.000	-0	**13**	12	0	1.6
1995	*Cin-N	6	1	.857	40	0	0	0	2	49	38	13	5	1	19	41	10.7	2.39	173	.213	.293	1	.250	0	10	10	-1	1.2
1996	Sea-A	1	1	.500	73	0	0	0	6	72	61	32	11	6	24	70	11.4	3.63	137	.225	.302	0	—	0	11	11	1	0.6
1997	*Cle-A	2	5	.286	71	0	0	0	15	75	59	33	3	4	29	74	11.0	3.24	145	.215	.300	0	—	0	11	12	2	1.5
1998	*Cle-A	1	1	.500	69	0	0	0	40	64	43	11	4	4	13	55	8.4	1.55	309	.195	.252	0	—	0	**22**	**22**	1	3.0
1999	*Cle-A	3	4	.429	72	0	0	0	39	68^2	60	32	11	2	26	55	11.5	4.06	124	.232	.307	0	—	0	6	7	-1	1.4
Total	14	53	61	.465	835	7	0	0	138	1017^2	801	409	101	47	414	905	11.2	3.26	130	.217	.304	5	.185	1	105	108	3	13.3
● **MIKE JACKSON** Jackson, Michael Warren b: 3/27/46, Paterson, N.J. BL/TL, 6'3", 190 lbs. Deb: 5/10/70																												
1970	Phi-N	1	1	.500	5	0	0	0	0	6^1	6	1	0	0	4	4	14.2	1.42	281	.286	.400	1	1.000	0	2	2	0	0.4
1971	StL-N	0	0	—	1	0	0	0	0	0^2	1	0	0	0	1	0	27.0	0.00	—	.333	.500	0	.000	-0	0	0	0	0.0
1972	KC-A	1	2	.333	7	3	0	0	0	19^2	24	14	0	0	14	15	17.4	6.41	47	.320	.427	0	.000	-1	-7	-7	1	-1.0
1973	KC-A	0	0	—	9	0	0	0	0	22^1	25	17	3	1	20	13	18.5	6.85	60	.301	.442	0	—	0	-8	-6	-0	-0.3
	Cle-A	0	0	—	1	0	0	0	0	0^2	1	0	0	0	0	1	13.5	0.00	—	.333	.333	0	—	0	0	0	0	0.0
	Yr	0	0	—	10	0	0	0	0	23	26	17	3	1	20	14	18.4	6.65	62	.302	.439	0	—	0	-7	-6	-0	-0.3
Total	4	2	3	.400	23	3	0	0	0	49^2	57	32	3	1	39	33	17.6	5.80	63	.308	.431	1	.143	-0	-12	-11	1	-0.9
● **ROY LEE JACKSON** Jackson, Roy Lee b: 5/1/54, Opelika, Ala. BR/TR, 6'2", 194 lbs. Deb: 9/13/77																												
1977	NY-N	0	2	.000	4	4	0	0	0	24	25	16	2	3	15	13	16.1	6.00	62	.263	.381	0	.000	-1	-6	-6	-1	-0.6
1978	NY-N	0	0	—	4	2	0	0	0	12^2	21	13	2	2	6	6	20.6	9.24	38	.429	.509	2	.667	1	-8	-8	0	-0.3
1979	NY-N	1	0	1.000	8	0	0	0	0	16^1	11	4	1	1	5	10	9.4	2.20	165	.200	.279	1	1.000	0	3	3	0	0.2
1980	NY-N	1	7	.125	24	8	1	0	1	70^2	78	37	4	0	20	58	12.5	4.20	85	.287	.336	3	.188	1	-5	-5	-1	-0.6
1981	Tor-A	1	2	.333	39	0	0	0	7	62	65	23	5	1	25	27	13.2	2.61	151	.275	.347	0	—	0	7	9	0	0.6
1982	Tor-A	8	8	.500	48	2	0	0	6	97	77	37	7	2	31	71	10.2	3.06	147	.218	.284	0	—	0	11	14	0	2.3
1983	Tor-A	8	3	.727	49	0	0	0	7	92	92	48	6	3	41	48	13.3	4.50	96	.267	.351	0	—	0	-4	-2	0	-0.2
1984	Tor-A	7	8	.467	54	0	0	0	10	86	73	40	12	1	31	58	11.0	3.56	115	.230	.301	0	—	0	4	5	0	0.9
1985	SD-N	2	3	.400	22	2	0	0	2	40	32	13	4	1	13	28	10.3	2.70	131	.224	.293	1	.000	-1	4	4	0	0.4
1986	Min-A	0	1	.000	28	0	0	0	1	58^1	57	29	7	3	16	32	11.7	3.86	112	.256	.314	0	—	0	2	3	-1	0.1
Total	10	28	34	.452	280	18	1	0	34	559	531	260	50	17	203	351	12.1	3.77	108	.254	.325	6	.194	1	9	17	-1	2.8
● **TONY JACOBS** Jacobs, Anthony Robert b: 8/5/25, Dixmoor, Ill. d: 12/21/80, Nashville, Tenn. BB/TR, 5'9", 150 lbs. Deb: 9/19/48																												
1948	Chi-N	0	0	—	1	0	0	0	0	2	3	1	1	0	0	2	13.5	4.50	87	.333	.333	0	—	0	-0	-0	0	0.0
1955	StL-N	0	0	—	1	0	0	0	0	2	6	4	1	0	1	1	31.5	18.00	23	.500	.538	0	.000	-0	-3	-3	-0	-0.1
Total	2	0	0	—	2	0	0	0	0	4	9	5	2	0	1	3	22.5	11.25	35	.429	.455	0	.000	-0	-3	-3	-0	-0.1
● **ART JACOBS** Jacobs, Arthur Edward b: 8/28/02, Luckey, Ohio d: 6/8/67, Inglewood, Cal. BL/TL, 5'10", 170 lbs. Deb: 6/18/39																												
1939	Cin-N	0	0	—	1	0	0	0	1	1	2	1	0	0	1	0	27.0	9.00	43	.400	.500	0	—	0	-1	-1	-0	-0.1
● **BUCKY JACOBS** Jacobs, Newton Smith b: 3/21/13, Altavista, Va. d: 6/15/90, Richmond, Va. BR/TR, 5'11", 155 lbs. Deb: 6/27/37																												
1937	Was-A	1	1	.500	11	1	0	0	0	22^1	26	12	0	0	11	8	14.9	4.84	92	.295	.374	0	.000	-1	-1	-1	0	-0.1
1939	Was-A	0	0	—	2	0	0	0	0	3	1	0	0	0	0	1	3.0	0.00	—	.100	.100	0	—	0	2	2	-0	0.1
1940	Was-A	0	1	.000	9	0	0	0	0	15	16	11	1	2	9	6	16.2	6.00	69	.271	.386	0	.000	-0	-3	-3	1	-0.1
Total	3	1	2	.333	22	1	0	0	0	40^1	43	23	1	2	20	15	14.5	4.91	88	.274	.363	0	.000	-1	-2	-3	2	-0.1
● **ELMER JACOBS** Jacobs, William Elmer b: 8/10/1892, Salem, Mo. d: 2/10/58, Salem, Mo. BR/TR, 6', 165 lbs. Deb: 4/23/14																												
1914	Phi-N	1	3	.250	14	7	1	0	0	50^2	65	38	2	3	20	17	15.6	4.80	61	.342	.413	0	.000	-2	-11	-10	0	-0.9
1916	Pit-N	6	10	.375	34	17	8	0	0	153	151	70	2	4	38	46	11.4	2.94	91	.258	.308	3	.075	-2	-5	-4	-2	-0.8
1917	Pit-N	6	19	.240	38	25	10	1	2	227^1	214	87	3	5	76	58	11.7	2.81	101	.262	.329	12	.179	-1	-2	1	2	0.1
1918	Pit-N	0	1	.000	8	4	0	0	0	23^1	31	18	0	0	14	2	17.4	5.79	50	.344	.433	2	.286	0	-8	-7	1	-0.3
	Phi-N	9	5	.643	18	14	12	4	1	123	91	39	3	4	42	33	10.0	2.41	124	.210	.285	6	.158	-1	5	7	-2	0.6
	Yr	9	6	.600	26	18	12	4	1	146^1	122	57	3	4	56	35	11.2	2.95	101	.233	.312	8	.178	-1	-3	0	-1	0.3
1919	Phi-N	6	10	.375	17	15	13	0	0	128^2	150	66	5	6	44	37	14.0	3.85	84	.304	.368	8	.178	-1	-13	-8	1	-1.0
	StL-N	3	6	.333	17	8	4	1	1	85^1	81	30	2	5	25	31	11.7	2.53	110	.264	.329	8	.348	3	4	3	-0	0.7
	Yr	9	16	.360	34	23	17	1	1	214	231	96	7	11	69	68	13.1	3.32	92	.289	.353	16	.235	2	-10	-6	1	-0.3
1920	StL-N	4	8	.333	23	9	1	0	1	77^2	91	56	2	5	33	21	14.9	5.21	57	.296	.374	5	.192	-0	-18	-20	1	-2.8
1924	Chi-N	11	12	.478	38	22	13	1	1	190^1	181	93	9	2	72	50	12.1	3.74	104	.258	.329	6	.111	-4	3	3	1	0.1
1925	Chi-N	2	3	.400	18	4	1	1	1	55^2	63	37	9	1	22	19	13.9	5.17	84	.274	.340	3	.231	-0	-6	-5	0	-0.4
1927	Chi-A	2	4	.333	25	8	2	1	0	74^1	105	49	3	4	37	22	17.7	4.60	88	.354	.432	3	.150	-1	-4	-5	2	-0.3
Total	9	50	81	.382	250	133	65	9	7	1189^1	1223	583	40	39	423	336	12.8	3.55	91	.275	.343	56	.161	-8	-57	-43	5	-5.0
● **BEANY JACOBSON** Jacobson, Albert L. (b: Albin L. Jacobson) b: 6/5/1881, Port Washington, Wis. d: 1/31/33, Decatur, Ill. BL/TL, 6', 170 lbs. Deb: 4/30/04																												
1904	Was-A	5	23	.179	33	30	23	1	0	253^2	276	135	6	3	57	75	11.9	3.55	75	.278	.319	8	.091	-6	-27	-24	2	-3.0
1905	Was-A	7	8	.467	22	17	12	0	0	144^1	139	83	1	5	35	50	11.2	3.30	80	.255	.305	7	.159	1	-10	-11	-2	-1.1
1906	StL-A	9	9	.500	24	15	12	0	0	155	146	68	3	4	27	53	10.3	2.50	103	.252	.290	5	.091	-4	3	2	-0	-0.3
1907	StL-A	1	6	.143	7	7	6	0	0	57^1	55	28	1	0	26	16	12.7	2.98	84	.255	.335	4	.222	-0	-3	-3	-0	-0.4
	Bos-A	0	0	—	2	1	0	0	0	2	2	3	0	0	3	1	22.5	9.00	29	.250	.455	0	—	0	-1	-1	0	-0.1
	Yr	1	6	.143	9	8	6	0	0	59^1	57	31	1	0	29	17	13.0	3.19	79	.254	.340	4	.222	-0	-4	-4	-0	-0.5
Total	4	22	46	.324	88	70	53	1	0	612^1	618	317	11	12	148	195	11.4	3.19	82	.264	.311	24	.117	-9	-38	-39	-1	-4.9
● **LARRY JACOBUS** Jacobus, Stuart Louis b: 12/18/1893, Cincinnati, Ohio d: 8/19/65, N.College Hill, O. BB/TR, 6'2", 186 lbs. Deb: 7/15/18																												
1918	Cin-N	0	1	.000	5	0	0	0	0	17^1	25	12	0	0	1	8	13.5	5.71	47	.368	.377	0	.000	-1	-6	-6	-0	-0.4
● **JASON JACOME** Jacome, Jason James b: 11/24/70, Tulsa, Okla. BL/TL, 6'1", 155 lbs. Deb: 7/2/94																												
1994	NY-N	4	3	.571	8	8	1	1	0	54	54	17	3	0	17	30	11.8	2.67	157	.269	.326	1	.063	-1	9	9	1	1.1
1995	NY-N	0	4	.000	5	5	0	0	0	21	33	24	3	1	15	11	21.0	10.29	39	.359	.454	0	.000	-1	-14	-15	-0	-2.1
	KC-A	4	6	.400	15	14	1	0	0	84	101	52	15	1	21	39	13.2	5.36	89	.300	.343	0	—	0	-6	-5	2	-0.4
1996	KC-A	0	4	.000	49	2	0	0	1	47^2	67	27	5	2	22	32	17.2	4.72	106	.337	.408	0	—	0	1	2	2	0.3
1997	KC-A	0	0	—	7	0	0	0	0	6^2	13	7	2	1	5	3	25.7	9.45	50	.448	.543	0	—	0	-4	-3	1	-0.1
	Cle-A	2	0	1.000	21	4	0	0	0	42^2	45	26	8	0	15	24	12.7	5.27	89	.269	.330	0	—	0	-3	-3	-0	-0.1
	Yr	2	0	1.000	28	4	0	0	0	49^1	58	33	10	1	20	27	14.4	5.84	80	.296	.364	0	—	0	-7	-6	1	-0.2
1998	Cle-A	0	1	.000	1	1	0	0	0	5	10	8	2	0	3	2	23.4	14.40	33	.435	.500	0	—	0	-5	-5	-0	-0.6
Total	5	10	18	.357	106	34	2	1	1	261	323	161	38	5	98	141	14.7	5.34	87	.308	.370	1	.043	-2	-22	-21	5	-1.9
● **PAT JACQUEZ** Jacquez, Patrick Thomas b: 4/23/47, Stockton, Cal. BR/TR, 6', 200 lbs. Deb: 4/18/71																												
1971	Chi-A	0	0	—	2	0	0	0	0	2	4	1	0	0	2	1	27.0	4.50	80	.444	.545	0	.000	-0	-0	-0	0	0.0
● **THOMAS JACQUEZ** Jacquez, Thomas Patrick b: 12/29/75, Stockton, Cal. BL/TL, 6'2", 195 lbs. Deb: 9/9/2000																												
2000	Phi-N	0	0	—	9	0	0	0	1	7^1	10	9	2	0	3	6	16.0	11.05	43	.333	.394	0	—	0	-5	-5	0	-0.2

YEAR	TM/L	W	L	PCT	G	GS	CG	SH	SV	IP	H	R	HR	HB	BB	SO	RAT	ERA	ERA+	OAV	OOB	BH	AVG	PB	PR	PR+	PD	TPI
● **JAKE JAECKEL**	Jaeckel, Paul Henry b: 4/1/42, E.Los Angeles, Cal. BR/TR, 5'10", 170 lbs. Deb: 9/19/64																											
1964	Chi-N	1	0	1.000	4	0	0	0	1	8	4	0	0	0	3	2	7.9	0.00	—	.160	.250	0	.000	-0	3	3	-0	0.5
● **CHARLIE JAEGER**	Jaeger, Charles Thomas b: 4/17/1875, Ottawa, Ill. d: 9/27/42, Ottawa, Ill. BR/TR, Deb: 9/9/04																											
1904	Det-A	3	3	.500	8	6	5	0	0	49	49	29	0	6	15	13	12.9	2.57	99	.261	.335	1	.059	-2	0	-0	-1	-0.3
● **JOE JAEGER**	Jaeger, Joseph Peter "Zip" b: 3/3/1895, St.Cloud, Minn. d: 12/13/63, Hampton, Iowa BR/TR, 6'1", 190 lbs. Deb: 7/28/20																											
1920	Chi-N	0	0	—	2	0	0	0	0	3	6	6	0	0	4	0	30.0	12.00	27	.500	.625	0	.000	-0	-3	-3	0	-0.2
● **SIG JAKUCKI**	Jakucki, Sigmund "Jack" b: 8/20/09, Camden, N.J. d: 5/28/79, Galveston, Tex. BR/TR, 6'2.5", 198 lbs. Deb: 8/30/36																											
1936	StL-A	0	3	.000	7	2	0	0	0	20^2	32	22	2	1	12	9	19.6	8.71	62	.348	.429	0	.000	-1	-8	-7	0	-0.8
1944	*StL-A	13	9	.591	35	24	12	4	3	198	211	89	17	3	54	67	12.2	3.55	101	.268	.318	11	.151	-2	-3	1	1	0.1
1945	StL-A	12	10	.545	30	24	15	1	2	192^1	188	84	9	1	65	55	11.9	3.51	100	.257	.318	13	.186	0	-3	0	0	0.1
Total	3	25	22	.532	72	50	27	5	5	411	431	195	28	5	131	131	12.4	3.79	96	.268	.325	24	.161	-2	-14	-6	1	-0.6
● **LEFTY JAMERSON**	Jamerson, Charles Dewey "Charlie" b: 1/26/1900, Enfield, Ill. d: 8/4/80, Mocksville, N.C. BL/TL, 6'1", 195 lbs. Deb: 8/16/24																											
1924	Bos-A	0	0	—	1	0	0	0	0	1	1	2	0	0	3	0	36.0	18.00	24	.250	.571	0	—	0	-2	-1	-0	-0.1
● **JEFF JAMES**	James, Jeffrey Lynn "Jesse" b: 9/29/41, Indianapolis, Ind. BR/TR, 6'3", 195 lbs. Deb: 4/13/68																											
1968	Phi-N	4	4	.500	29	13	1	1	0	116	112	61	8	4	46	83	12.6	4.27	70	.256	.332	4	.121	-1	-17	-16	0	-1.2
1969	Phi-N	2	2	.500	6	5	1	0	0	31^2	36	20	5	0	14	21	14.2	5.40	66	.288	.360	2	.182	-0	-6	-7	-0	-0.8
Total	2	6	6	.500	35	18	2	1	0	147^2	148	81	13	4	60	104	12.9	4.51	69	.263	.338	6	.136	-1	-23	-23	-0	-2.0
● **JOHNNY JAMES**	James, John Phillip b: 7/23/33, Bonners Ferry, Idaho BL/TR, 5'10", 160 lbs. Deb: 9/6/58																											
1958	NY-A	0	0	—	1	0	0	0	0	3	2	0	0	0	4	1	18.0	0.00	—	.250	.500	0	.000	-0	1	1	0	0.1
1960	NY-A	5	1	.833	28	0	0	0	2	43^1	38	22	3	3	26	29	13.9	4.36	82	.248	.368	0	.000	-0	-2	-4	0	-0.5
1961	NY-A	0	0	—	1	0	0	0	0	1^1	1	0	0	0	0	2	6.8	0.00	—	.250	.250	0	—	0	1	1	0	0.0
	LA-A	0	2	.000	36	3	0	0	0	71^1	66	44	12	2	54	41	15.4	5.30	85	.246	.377	0	.000	-1	-10	-6	-0	-0.4
	Yr	0	2	.000	37	3	0	0	0	72^2	67	44	12	2	54	43	15.2	5.20	86	.246	.375	0	.000	-1	-10	-5	-0	-0.4
Total	3	5	3	.625	66	3	0	0	2	119	107	66	15	5	84	73	14.8	4.76	87	.247	.375	0	.000	-2	-11	-8	0	-0.8
● **MIKE JAMES**	James, Michael Elmo b: 8/15/67, Ft.Walton Beach, Fla. BR/TR, 6'4", 215 lbs. Deb: 4/29/95																											
1995	Cal-A	3	0	1.000	46	0	0	0	1	55^2	49	27	6	3	26	36	12.6	3.88	121	.238	.332	0	—	0	5	5	-0	0.2
1996	Cal-A	5	5	.500	69	0	0	0	1	81	62	27	7	10	42	65	12.7	2.67	188	.214	.333	0	—	0	21	21	1	2.3
1997	Ana-A	5	5	.500	58	0	0	0	7	62^2	69	32	3	5	28	57	14.6	4.31	106	.283	.368	0	—	0	2	2	0	0.3
1998	Ana-A	0	0	—	11	0	0	0	0	14	10	3	0	0	7	12	10.9	1.93	243	.208	.309	0	—	0	4	4	-0	0.2
2000	*StL-N	2	2	.500	51	0	0	0	2	51^1	40	22	7	3	24	41	11.7	3.16	147	.219	.319	0	.000	-0	8	8	-0	0.6
Total	5	15	12	.556	235	0	0	0	11	264^2	230	111	23	21	127	211	12.9	3.37	141	.237	.338	0	.000	-0	41	41	0	3.6
● **RICK JAMES**	James, Richard Lee b: 10/11/47, Sheffield, Ala. BR/TR, 6'2.5", 205 lbs. Deb: 9/20/67																											
1967	Chi-N	0	1	.000	3	1	0	0	0	4^2	9	8	1	0	2	2	21.2	13.50	26	.529	.579	0	.000	-0	-5	-5	-0	-0.9
● **BOB JAMES**	James, Robert Harvey b: 8/15/58, Glendale, Cal. BR/TR, 6'4", 230 lbs. Deb: 9/7/78																											
1978	Mon-N	0	1	.000	4	1	0	0	0	4	4	4	1	0	4	3	18.0	9.00	39	.267	.421	0	—	0	-2	-2	-0	-0.5
1979	Mon-N	0	0	—	2	0	0	0	0	2	2	3	0	0	3	1	22.5	13.50	27	.250	.455	0	—	0	-2	-2	-0	-0.1
1982	Mon-N	0	0	—	7	0	0	0	0	9	10	6	0	0	8	11	18.0	6.00	61	.294	.429	0	—	0	-2	-2	-0	-0.1
	Det-A	0	2	.000	12	1	0	0	0	19^2	22	13	4	0	8	20	13.7	5.03	81	.278	.345	0	—	0	-2	-2	-0	-0.2
1983	Det-A	0	0	—	4	0	0	0	0	4	5	5	2	0	3	4	18.0	11.25	35	.313	.421	0	—	0	-3	-3	-0	-0.2
	Mon-N	1	0	1.000	27	0	0	0	7	50	37	17	3	3	23	56	11.3	2.88	125	.210	.312	2	.286	0	4	4	1	0.4
1984	Mon-N	6	6	.500	62	0	0	0	10	96	92	47	6	4	45	91	13.2	3.66	94	.251	.339	2	.143	-0	-1	-3	-1	-0.5
1985	Chi-A	8	7	.533	69	0	0	0	32	110	90	31	5	2	23	88	9.4	2.13	203	.226	.271	0	—	0	25	**26**	-1	4.7
1986	Chi-A	5	4	.556	49	0	0	0	14	58^1	61	36	8	4	23	32	13.6	5.25	82	.268	.345	0	—	0	-7	-6	-1	-1.1
1987	Chi-A	4	6	.400	43	0	0	0	10	54	54	32	10	4	17	34	12.5	4.67	99	.256	.323	0	—	0	-1	-0	0	-0.1
Total	8	24	26	.480	279	2	0	0	73	407	377	194	39	17	157	340	12.2	3.80	105	.246	.323	4	.190	0	8	9	-2	2.3
● **LEFTY JAMES**	James, William A. b: 7/1/1889, Glen Roy, Ohio d: 5/3/33, Glen Roy, Ohio BL/TL, 5'11.5", 175 lbs. Deb: 4/13/12																											
1912	Cle-A	0	1	.000	3	1	0	0	1	6	8	9	0	2	4	2	21.0	7.50	45	.348	.483	0	.000	-0	-3	-3	-0	-0.5
1913	Cle-A	2	3	.400	11	4	3	0	0	39	42	27	0	3	9	18	12.5	3.00	101	.273	.325	3	.231	-0	-0	0	-1	-0.1
1914	Cle-A	0	3	.000	17	6	1	0	0	50^2	44	23	0	2	32	16	13.9	3.20	90	.251	.373	0	.000	-1	-3	-2	1	-0.1
Total	3	2	7	.222	31	11	4	0	1	95^2	94	59	0	7	45	36	13.7	3.39	88	.267	.361	3	.107	-1	-6	-4	0	-0.7
● **BILL JAMES**	James, William Henry "Big Bill" b: 1/20/1887, Detroit, Mich. d: 5/24/42, Venice, Cal. BB/TR, 6'4", 195 lbs. Deb: 6/12/11																											
1911	Cle-A	2	4	.333	8	6	4	0	0	51^2	58	37	1	2	32	21	16.0	4.88	70	.284	.387	1	.059	-1	-9	-8	-1	-1.0
1912	Cle-A	0	0	—	3	0	0	0	0	13^2	15	11	0	0	9	5	15.8	4.61	74	.288	.393	0	.000	-0	-2	-2	-1	-0.2
1914	StL-A	15	14	.517	44	35	20	3	1	284	269	121	4	6	109	109	12.2	2.85	95	.257	.330	10	.112	-3	-3	-5	5	-0.3
1915	StL-A	6	10	.375	34	22	8	0	1	170^1	155	89	2	7	92	58	13.4	3.59	80	.255	.359	8	.190	1	-12	-14	2	-1.0
	Det-A	7	3	.700	11	9	3	1	0	67	57	26	1	0	33	24	12.1	2.42	125	.243	.336	6	.286	2	4	4	1	1.0
	Yr	13	13	.500	45	31	11	1	1	237^1	212	115	3	7	125	82	13.0	3.26	89	.251	.352	14	.222	2	-9	-9	3	0.0
1916	Det-A	8	12	.400	30	20	8	0	1	151^2	141	76	1	11	79	61	13.7	3.68	78	.255	.360	3	.068	-3	-14	-14	-0	-2.1
1917	Det-A	13	10	.565	34	23	10	2	1	198	163	71	2	12	96	62	12.3	2.09	127	.229	.330	12	.211	2	13	12	-0	1.7
1918	Det-A	6	11	.353	19	18	8	1	0	122	127	68	3	5	68	42	14.8	3.76	71	.279	.379	5	.109	-3	-13	-16	2	-2.1
1919	Det-A	1	0	1.000	2	1	0	0	0	9^1	12	6	0	0	7	3	18.3	5.79	55	.324	.432	1	.250	0	-3	-3	0	-0.3
	Bos-A	3	5	.375	13	7	4	0	0	72^2	74	42	2	3	39	12	14.4	4.09	74	.280	.379	3	.143	-1	-7	-9	0	-0.9
	*Chi-A	3	2	.600	5	5	3	2	0	39^1	39	12	0	2	14	11	12.6	2.52	126	.281	.355	2	.143	-1	3	3	-1	0.2
	Yr	7	7	.500	20	13	7	2	0	121^1	125	60	2	5	60	26	14.1	3.71	83	.284	.376	6	.154	-2	-6	-9	-0	-1.0
Total	8	64	71	.474	203	146	68	9	4	1179^2	1110	559	16	48	578	408	13.2	3.20	88	.258	.352	51	.142	-8	-44	-50	8	-5.0
● **BILL JAMES**	James, William Lawrence "Seattle Bill" b: 3/12/1892, Iowa Hill, Cal. d: 3/10/71, Oroville, Cal. BR/TR, 6'3", 196 lbs. Deb: 4/17/13																											
1913	Bos-N	6	10	.375	24	14	10	1	0	135^2	134	75	4	7	57	73	13.1	2.79	118	.264	.347	12	.255	1	6	7	0	1.0
1914	*Bos-N	26	7	**.788**	46	37	30	4	3	332^1	261	91	7	13	118	156	10.6	1.90	145	.225	.304	33	.256	4	**33**	**32**	-1	**3.7**
1915	Bos-N	5	4	.556	13	9	4	0	0	68^1	68	28	3	2	22	23	12.1	3.03	86	.269	.332	1	.048	-2	-2	-4	1	-0.5
1919	Bos-N	0	0	—	1	0	0	0	0	5^1	6	2	0	0	2	1	13.5	3.38	85	.273	.333	0	.000	-0	-0	-0	0	0.0
Total	4	37	21	.638	84	60	44	5	3	541^2	469	196	14	22	199	253	11.5	2.28	126	.242	.319	46	.231	4	37	36	1	4.2
● **CHARLIE JAMIESON**	Jamieson, Charles Devine "Cuckoo" b: 2/7/1893, Paterson, N.J. d: 10/27/69, Paterson, N.J. BL/TL, 5'8.5", 165 lbs. Deb: 9/20/15 ♦																											
1916	Was-A	0	0	—	1	0	0	0	0	4	2	2	0	0	3	2	11.3	4.50	62	.143	.294	36	.248	0	-1	-1	0	0.0
1917	Was-A	0	0	—	1	0	0	0	0	2^1	10	10	0	0	2	1	46.3	38.57	7	.625	.667	6	.171	0	-9	-9	-0	-0.4
1918	Phi-A	2	1	.667	5	2	1	0	0	23	24	17	0	2	13	2	15.3	4.30	68	.261	.364	84	.202	0	-4	-3	-0	-0.4
1919	Cle-A	0	0	—	4	1	0	0	0	13	12	9	0	0	8	0	13.8	5.54	60	.250	.357	6	.353	0	-3	-3	-0	-0.1
1922	Cle-A	0	0	—	2	0	0	0	0	5^2	7	3	0	0	4	2	17.5	3.18	126	.318	.423	183	.323	1	1	1	-0	0.0
Total	5	2	1	.667	13	3	1	0	0	48	55	41	0	2	30	7	16.3	6.19	51	.286	.388	1990	.303	2	-17	-16	-1	-0.9
● **JERRY JANESKI**	Janeski, Gerard Joseph b: 4/18/46, Pasadena, Cal. BR/TR, 6'4", 205 lbs. Deb: 4/10/70																											
1970	Chi-A	10	17	.370	35	35	4	1	0	205^2	247	125	22	5	63	79	13.8	4.77	82	.300	.353	5	.076	-4	-24	-19	1	-2.5
1971	Was-A	1	5	.167	23	10	0	0	1	61^2	72	38	5	3	34	19	15.9	4.96	67	.304	.398	3	.214	1	-10	-12	1	-1.0
1972	Tex-A	0	1	.000	4	1	0	0	0	12^2	11	5	0	0	7	7	12.8	2.84	106	.229	.327	0	.000	-0	0	0	0	0.0
Total	3	11	23	.324	62	46	4	1	1	280	330	168	27	8	104	105	14.2	4.72	79	.298	.362	8	.098	-4	-34	-30	2	-3.5
● **LARRY JANSEN**	Jansen, Lawrence Joseph b: 7/16/20, Verboort, Ore. BR/TR, 6'2", 190 lbs. Deb: 4/17/47 C																											
1947	NY-N	21	5	**.808**	42	30	20	1	1	248	241	102	23	1	57	104	10.9	3.16	129	.262	.306	16	.186	-0	25	25	-0	2.4
1948	NY-N	18	12	.600	42	36	15	4	2	277	283	125	25	3	54	126	11.0	3.61	109	.265	.303	13	.137	-2	11	10	2	1.0
1949	NY-N	15	16	.484	37	35	17	3	0	259^2	271	130	36	2	62	113	11.6	3.85	104	.263	.306	16	.165	-0	6	4	3	0.6

YEAR	TM/L	W	L	PCT	G	GS	CG	SH	SV	IP	H	R	HR	HB	BB	SO	RAT	ERA	ERA+	OAV	OOB	BH	AVG	PB	PR	PR+	PD	TPI
1950	NY-N★	19	13	.594	40	35	21	**5**	3	275	238	106	31	1	55	161	**9.6**	3.01	136	.232	**.271**	16	.167	-0	35	34	2	3.8
1951	*NY-N☆	**23**	11	.676	39	34	18	3	0	278^2	254	102	26	3	56	145	10.1	3.04	129	.239	.279	9	.094	-5	29	28	3	2.9
1952	NY-N	11	11	.500	34	27	8	1	2	167^1	183	91	16	6	47	74	12.7	4.09	91	.281	.335	8	.178	3	-7	-7	2	-0.4
1953	NY-N	11	16	.407	36	26	6	0	1	184^2	185	96	24	2	55	88	11.8	4.14	104	.256	.311	8	.133	-1	3	3	-1	0.2
1954	NY-N	2	2	.500	13	7	0	0	0	40^2	57	32	5	1	15	15	16.2	5.98	68	.337	.395	4	.286	1	-9	-9	1	-0.6
1956	Cin-N	2	3	.400	8	7	2	0	1	34^2	39	20	5	1	9	16	12.7	5.19	77	.281	.329	0	.000	-1	-5	-4	-0	-0.7
Total	9	122	89	.578	291	237	107	17	10	1765^2	1751	804	191	20	410	842	11.1	3.58	112	.258	.302	90	.150	-6	87	83	11	9.2
● **MARTY JANZEN**	Janzen, Martin Thomas b: 5/31/73, Homestead, Fla. BR/TR, 6'3", 197 lbs. Deb: 5/12/96																											
1996	Tor-A	4	6	.400	15	11	0	0	0	73^2	95	65	16	2	38	47	16.5	7.33	68	.317	.397	0	—	0	-19	-19	-1	-2.0
1997	Tor-A	2	1	.667	12	0	0	0	0	25	23	11	4	0	13	17	13.0	3.60	128	.250	.343	0	—	0	3	3	-0	0.3
Total	2	6	7	.462	27	11	0	0	0	98^2	118	76	20	2	51	64	15.6	6.39	77	.301	.384	0	—	0	-16	-16	-1	-1.7
● **KEVIN JARVIS**	Jarvis, Kevin Thomas b: 8/1/69, Lexington, Ky. BL/TR, 6'2", 200 lbs. Deb: 4/6/94																											
1994	Cin-N	1	1	.500	6	3	0	0	0	17^2	22	14	4	0	5	10	13.8	7.13	58	.301	.346	1	.250	0	-6	-6	0	-0.6
1995	Cin-N	3	4	.429	19	11	1	1	0	79	91	56	13	3	32	33	14.4	5.70	72	.292	.363	3	.143	-0	-13	-14	0	-1.1
1996	Cin-N	8	9	.471	24	20	2	1	0	120^1	152	93	17	2	43	63	14.7	5.98	71	.305	.362	6	.167	-0	-24	-23	-1	-2.8
1997	Cin-N	0	1	.000	9	0	0	0	1	13^1	21	16	4	1	7	12	19.6	10.13	42	.344	.420	0	.000	-0	-9	-9	-0	-0.7
	Min-A	0	0	—	6	2	0	0	0	13	23	18	4	0	8	9	21.5	12.46	37	.371	.443	0	—	0	-11	-11	-0	-0.5
	Det-A	0	3	.000	17	3	0	0	0	41^2	55	28	9	0	14	27	14.9	5.40	85	.318	.369	0	—	0	-4	-4	-0	-0.3
	Yr	0	3	.000	23	5	0	0	0	54^2	78	46	13	0	22	36	16.5	7.08	65	.332	.389	0	—	0	-15	-15	-1	-0.8
1999	Oak-A	0	1	.000	4	1	0	0	0	14	28	19	6	1	6	11	22.5	11.57	40	.418	.473	0	—	0	-10	-11	0	-0.6
2000	Col-N	3	4	.429	24	19	0	-0	0	115	138	83	26	4	33	60	13.7	5.95	100	.300	.352	3	.088	-2	-17	-0	0	-0.2
Total	6	15	23	.395	109	59	3	2	1	414	530	327	83	11	148	225	15.0	6.43	73	.310	.369	13	.135	-2	-94	-73	-2	-6.8
● **RAY JARVIS**	Jarvis, Raymond Arnold b: 5/10/46, Providence, R.I. BR/TR, 6'2", 198 lbs. Deb: 4/15/69																											
1969	Bos-A	5	6	.455	29	12	2	0	1	100^1	105	59	8	3	43	36	13.5	4.75	80	.274	.352	2	.069	-2	-13	-10	1	-1.2
1970	Bos-A	0	1	.000	15	0	0	0	0	16	17	12	1	2	14	8	18.6	3.94	101	.274	.423	0	—	0	-0	0	0	0.0
Total	2	5	7	.417	44	12	2	0	1	116^1	122	71	9	5	57	44	14.2	4.64	82	.274	.363	2	.069	-2	-13	-10	1	-1.2
● **PAT JARVIS**	Jarvis, Robert Patrick b: 3/18/41, Carlyle, Ill. BR/TR, 5'10.5", 180 lbs. Deb: 8/4/66																											
1966	Atl-N	6	2	.750	10	9	3	1	0	62^1	46	16	1	1	12	41	8.5	2.31	157	.206	.250	0	.000	-2	9	9	-1	0.8
1967	Atl-N	15	10	.600	32	30	7	1	0	194	195	86	15	4	62	118	12.1	3.66	91	.260	.320	6	.085	-3	-6	-8	-2	-1.4
1968	Atl-N	16	12	.571	34	34	14	1	0	256	202	82	15	2	50	157	8.9	2.60	115	.214	.255	12	.141	0	11	11	-3	1.0
1969	*Atl-N	13	11	.542	37	33	4	1	0	217^1	204	113	25	1	73	123	11.5	4.43	81	.246	.308	8	.113	-2	-20	-20	-0	-2.3
1970	Atl-N	16	16	.500	36	34	11	1	0	254	240	110	21	0	72	173	11.1	3.61	119	.247	.299	15	.183	-0	12	18	2	2.3
1971	Atl-N	6	14	.300	35	23	3	3	1	162^1	162	81	16	3	51	68	12.0	4.10	91	.261	.320	5	.106	-2	-11	-6	1	-0.9
1972	Atl-N	11	7	.611	37	6	0	0	2	98^2	94	50	7	0	44	56	12.6	4.10	92	.260	.341	3	.125	-0	-7	-3	1	-0.5
1973	Mon-N	2	1	.667	28	0	0	0	0	39^1	37	21	6	1	16	19	12.4	3.20	119	.250	.327	0	.000	-0	2	3	-0	0.1
Total	8	85	73	.538	249	169	42	8	3	1284	1180	559	106	12	380	755	11.0	3.58	101	.243	.300	49	.121	-10	-11	4	-3	-0.9
● **HI JASPER**	Jasper, Henry W. b: 11/15/1880, St.Louis, Mo. d: 5/22/37, St.Louis, Mo. BR/TR, 5'11", 180 lbs. Deb: 4/19/14																											
1914	Chi-A	1	0	1.000	16	0	0	0	0	32^1	22	22	0	1	20	19	12.0	3.34	80	.210	.341	0	.000	-1	-2	-2	1	-0.1
1915	Chi-A	0	1	.000	3	2	1	0	0	15^2	8	8	2	0	9	15	9.8	4.60	65	.157	.283	2	.286	0	-3	-3	1	0.0
1916	StL-N	5	6	.455	21	9	2	0	1	107	97	54	0	7	42	37	12.3	3.28	81	.254	.339	7	.212	1	-8	-7	2	-0.5
1919	Cle-A	4	5	.444	12	10	5	0	0	82^2	83	41	1	0	28	25	12.1	3.59	93	.269	.330	3	.103	-2	-3	-2	1	-0.4
Total	4	10	12	.455	52	21	8	0	1	237^2	210	125	3	8	99	96	12.0	3.48	84	.248	.333	12	.162	-2	-16	-15	5	-1.0
● **LARRY JASTER**	Jaster, Larry Edward b: 1/13/44, Midland, Mich. BL/TL, 6'3.5", 205 lbs. Deb: 9/17/65																											
1965	StL-N	3	0	1.000	4	3	3	0	0	28	21	5	1	0	7	10	9.0	1.61	239	.206	.257	2	.200	0	6	6	-1	0.7
1966	StL-N	11	5	.688	26	21	6	**5**	0	151^2	124	57	17	5	45	92	10.3	3.26	110	.227	.291	8	.178	1	6	5	-1	0.6
1967	*StL-N	9	7	.563	34	23	2	1	3	152^1	141	57	12	2	44	87	11.0	3.01	109	.244	.300	5	.100	-1	6	5	-2	0.1
1968	*StL-N	9	13	.409	31	21	3	1	0	154^1	153	63	13	6	38	70	11.5	3.50	83	.262	.313	6	.140	0	-9	-11	-2	-1.7
1969	Mon-N	1	6	.143	24	11	1	0	0	77	95	60	17	2	28	39	14.6	5.49	67	.302	.362	8	.421	3	-16	-15	-2	-1.1
1970	Atl-N	1	1	.500	14	0	0	0	0	22^1	33	18	5	0	8	9	16.5	6.85	63	.359	.410	0	.000	-0	-7	-6	1	-0.4
1972	Atl-N	1	1	.500	5	1	0	0	0	12^1	12	7	4	0	8	6	14.6	5.11	74	.267	.377	0	.000	-0	-2	-2	-0	-0.3
Total	7	35	33	.515	138	80	15	7	3	598	579	267	69	15	178	313	11.6	3.64	93	.256	.314	29	.170	3	-16	-17	-7	-2.1
● **AL JAVERY**	Javery, Alva William "Beartracks" b: 6/5/18, Worcester, Mass. d: 8/16/77, Putnam, Conn. BR/TR, 6'3", 183 lbs. Deb: 4/23/40																											
1940	Bos-N	2	4	.333	29	4	1	0	1	83^1	99	62	2	2	36	42	14.8	5.51	68	.293	.364	2	.087	-1	-15	-17	-2	-1.4
1941	Bos-N	10	11	.476	34	23	9	1	1	160^2	181	88	5	6	65	54	14.1	4.31	83	.283	.355	6	.103	-4	-12	-14	1	-1.9
1942	Bos-N	12	16	.429	42	37	19	5	0	261	251	106	8	3	78	85	11.4	3.03	110	.251	.307	9	.105	-5	8	9	2	0.6
1943	Bos-N★	17	16	.515	41	35	19	5	0	**303**	288	130	13	4	99	134	11.6	3.21	106	.248	.309	17	.163	-3	6	7	2	0.7
1944	Bos-N☆	10	19	.345	40	33	11	3	3	254	248	119	12	2	118	137	13.0	3.54	108	.262	.345	12	.152	-3	2	7	-2	0.3
1945	Bos-N	2	7	.222	17	14	2	1	0	77^1	92	59	4	0	51	18	16.6	6.28	61	.295	.394	6	.207	-0	-21	-21	1	-2.0
1946	Bos-N	0	1	.000	2	1	0	0	0	3^1	5	5	0	0	5	0	27.0	13.50	25	.417	.588	0	.000	-0	-4	-4	-0	-0.7
Total	7	53	74	.417	205	147	61	15	5	1142^2	1164	569	44	17	452	470	12.9	3.80	94	.264	.335	52	.137	-15	-37	-31	2	-4.4
● **JOEY JAY**	Jay, Joseph Richard b: 8/15/35, Middletown, Conn. BB/TR, 6'4", 228 lbs. Deb: 7/21/53																											
1953	Mil-N	1	0	1.000	3	1	1	1	0	10	6	0	0	0	5	4	9.9	0.00	—	.188	.297	0	.000	-0	5	5	-0	0.4
1954	Mil-N	1	0	1.000	15	1	0	0	0	18	21	13	2	1	16	13	19.0	6.50	57	.304	.442	0	—	0	-5	-6	-0	-0.3
1955	Mil-N	0	0	—	12	1	0	0	0	19	23	11	2	0	13	3	17.1	4.74	79	.324	.429	2	.667	1	-1	-2	-1	-0.1
1957	Mil-N	0	0	—	1	0	0	0	1	0^2	0	0	0	0	0	0	0.0	0.00	—	.000	.000	0	—	0	0	0	0	0.1
1958	Mil-N	7	5	.583	18	12	6	3	0	96^2	60	25	8	1	43	74	9.7	2.14	164	.177	.272	3	.094	-1	19	17	0	1.9
1959	Mil-N	6	11	.353	34	19	4	1	0	136^1	130	71	11	5	64	88	13.1	4.09	87	.248	.336	3	.086	-1	-2	-9	2	-1.0
1960	Mil-N	9	8	.529	32	11	3	0	1	133^1	128	60	10	6	59	90	13.0	3.24	106	.254	.339	7	.156	0	8	3	-0	0.3
1961	*Cin-N☆	**21**	10	.677	34	34	14	**4**	0	247^1	217	102	25	5	92	157	11.4	3.53	115	.236	.309	8	.090	-5	14	15	-1	1.0
1962	Cin-N	21	14	.600	39	37	16	4	0	273	269	121	26	4	100	155	12.3	3.76	107	.260	.327	15	.167	3	6	8	-2	1.0
1963	Cin-N	7	18	.280	30	22	4	1	1	170	172	91	19	3	73	116	13.1	4.29	78	.266	.343	8	.160	0	-19	-18	-0	-2.4
1964	Cin-N	11	11	.500	34	23	10	0	2	183	167	75	17	3	36	134	10.1	3.39	107	.245	.285	3	.057	-3	3	4	-2	0.0
1965	Cin-N	9	8	.529	37	24	4	1	1	155^2	150	83	21	4	63	102	12.5	4.22	89	.252	.328	2	.041	-3	-12	-8	-0	-1.1
1966	Cin-N	6	2	.750	12	10	1	1	0	73^2	78	33	8	3	23	44	12.7	3.91	100	.275	.335	3	.115	-1	-2	-0	-1	-0.2
	Atl-N	0	4	.000	9	8	0	0	1	29^2	39	29	4	1	20	19	18.2	7.89	46	.315	.414	1	.125	-0	-14	-14	-0	-1.7
	Yr	6	6	.500	21	18	1	1	1	103^1	117	62	12	4	43	63	14.3	5.05	76	.287	.360	4	.118	-1	-17	-13	-1	-1.9
Total	13	99	91	.521	310	203	63	16	7	1546^1	1460	714	153	36	607	999	12.2	3.77	99	.251	.325	55	.114	-10	-1	-6	-6	-2.1
● **DOMINGO JEAN**	Jean, Domingo (Luisa) b: 1/9/69, San Pedro De Macoris, D.R. BR/TR, 6'2", 175 lbs. Deb: 8/8/93																											
1993	NY-A	1	1	.500	10	6	0	0	0	40^1	37	20	7	0	19	20	12.5	4.46	93	.237	.320	0	—	0	-1	-1	-0	-0.1
● **TEX JEANES**	Jeanes, Ernest Lee b: 12/19/1900, Maypearl, Tex. d: 4/5/73, Longview, Tex. BR/TR, 6', 176 lbs. Deb: 4/20/21 ♦																											
1922	Cle-A	0	0	—	1	0	0	0	0	0	0	0	0	1	—	—	—	—	—	1.000	99	.000	0	0	0	0	0.0	
1927	NY-N	0	0	—	1	0	0	0	0	1	2	1	0	0	2	0	36.0	9.00	43	.400	.571	6	.300	0	-1	-1	-0	0.0
Total	2	0	0	—	2	0	0	0	0	1	2	1	0	0	3	0	45.0	9.00	43	.400	.625	20	.274	0	-1	-1	-0	0.0
● **GEORGE JEFFCOAT**	Jeffcoat, George Edward b: 12/24/13, New Brookland, S.C d: 10/13/78, Leesville, S.C. BR/TR, 5'11.5", 175 lbs. Deb: 4/20/36 F																											
1936	Bro-N	5	6	.455	40	5	3	0	3	95^2	84	58	7	8	63	46	14.6	4.52	92	.239	.366	3	.130	-1	-5	-4	-1	-0.6
1937	Bro-N	1	3	.250	21	3	1	1	0	54^1	58	33	4	1	27	29	14.2	5.13	79	.274	.358	0	.000	-2	-7	-6	-0	-0.6
1939	Bro-N	0	0	—	1	0	0	0	0	2	2	0	0	0	0	1	9.0	0.00	—	.286	.286	0	—	0	1	1	-0	0.0
1943	Bos-N	1	2	.333	8	1	0	0	0	17^2	15	10	1	0	10	10	12.7	3.06	112	.217	.316	2	.500	1	1	1	0	0.2
Total	4	7	11	.389	70	9	4	1	3	169^2	159	101	12	9	100	86	14.2	4.51	89	.248	.358	5	.128	-2	-11	-9	-1	-1.0

● HAL JEFFCOAT Jeffcoat, Harold Bentley b: 9/6/24, W.Columbia, S.C. BR/TR, 5'10.5", 185 lbs. Deb: 4/20/48 F◆

YEAR	TM/L	W	L	PCT	G	GS	CG	SH	SV	IP	H	R	HR	HB	BB	SO	RAT	ERA	ERA+	OAV	OOB	BH	AVG	PB	PR	PR+	PD	TPI
1954	Chi-N	5	6	.455	43	3	1	0	7	104	110	63	12	4	58	35	14.9	5.19	81	.276	.373	8	.258	2	-13	-11	1	-0.8
1955	Chi-N	8	6	.571	50	1	0	0	6	100^{2}	107	46	5	4	53	32	14.7	2.95	139	.276	.369	4	.174	1	12	13	1	1.9
1956	Cin-N	8	2	.800	38	16	2	0	2	171	189	79	12	5	55	55	13.1	3.84	104	.281	.340	8	.148	-1	-1	2	3	0.4
1957	Cin-N	12	13	.480	37	31	10	1	0	207	236	117	29	7	46	63	12.6	4.52	91	.294	.338	14	.203	6	-15	-9	-1	-0.5
1958	Cin-N	6	8	.429	49	0	0	0	9	75	76	34	8	2	26	35	12.5	3.72	111	.268	.333	5	.556	2	2	3	2	1.1
1959	Cin-N	0	1	.000	17	0	0	0	1	21^{2}	21	8	3	0	10	12	12.9	3.32	122	.253	.333	1	1.000	1	2	2	0	0.2
	StL-N	0	1	.000	11	0	0	0	0	17^{2}	33	18	4	0	9	7	21.4	9.17	46	.402	.462	0	.000	-0	-10	-9	0	-0.5
	Yr	0	2	.000	28	0	0	0	1	39^{1}	54	26	7	0	19	19	16.7	5.95	70	.327	.397	1	.250	0	-9	-8	0	-0.3
Total	6	39	37	.513	245	51	13	1	25	697	772	365	73	22	257	239	13.6	4.22	97	.285	.352	487	.248	10	-24	-9	5	1.8

● MIKE JEFFCOAT Jeffcoat, James Michael b: 8/3/59, Pine Bluff, Ark. BL/TL, 6'2", 187 lbs. Deb: 8/21/83

YEAR	TM/L	W	L	PCT	G	GS	CG	SH	SV	IP	H	R	HR	HB	BB	SO	RAT	ERA	ERA+	OAV	OOB	BH	AVG	PB	PR	PR+	PD	TPI
1983	Cle-A	1	3	.250	11	2	0	0	0	32^{2}	32	13	1	1	13	9	12.7	3.31	129	.256	.331	0	—	0	3	3	-0	0.3
1984	Cle-A	5	2	.714	63	1	0	0	1	75^{1}	82	28	7	1	24	41	12.8	2.99	137	.281	.338	0	—	0	8	9	1	0.8
1985	Cle-A	0	0	—	9	0	0	0	0	9^{2}	8	5	1	0	6	4	13.0	2.79	148	.235	.350	0	—	0	1	1	1	0.1
	SF-N	0	2	.000	19	1	0	0	0	22	27	13	4	2	6	10	14.3	5.32	65	.307	.365	0	.000	0	-4	-5	1	-0.3
1987	Tex-A	0	1	.000	2	2	0	0	0	7	11	10	4	0	4	1	19.3	12.86	35	.355	.429	0	—	0	-7	-6	-0	-0.7
1988	Tex-A	0	2	.000	5	2	0	0	0	10	19	13	1	2	5	5	23.4	11.70	35	.432	.510	0	—	0	-9	-8	0	-1.3
1989	Tex-A	9	6	.600	22	22	2	2	0	130^{2}	139	65	7	4	33	64	12.1	3.58	111	.270	.319	0	—	0	4	6	0	0.6
1990	Tex-A	5	6	.455	44	12	1	0	5	110^{2}	122	57	12	2	28	58	12.4	4.47	88	.283	.330	0	—	0	-7	-7	-1	-0.8
1991	Tex-A	5	3	.625	70	0	0	0	1	79^{2}	104	46	8	4	25	43	15.0	4.63	87	.320	.376	1	1.000	1	-5	-5	0	-0.4
1992	Tex-A	0	1	.000	6	3	0	0	0	19^{2}	28	17	2	0	5	6	15.1	7.32	52	.350	.388	0	—	0	-7	-8	0	-0.4
1994	Fla-N	0	0	—	4	0	0	0	0	2^{2}	4	3	2	0	0	1	13.5	10.13	43	.364	.364	0	—	0	-2	-2	-0	-0.1
Total	10	25	26	.490	255	45	3	2	7	500	576	270	49	16	149	242	13.3	4.37	91	.292	.346	1	.500	1	-23	-21	0	-2.2

● JESSE JEFFERSON Jefferson, Jesse Harrison b: 3/3/49, Midlothian, Va. BR/TR, 6'3", 195 lbs. Deb: 6/23/73

YEAR	TM/L	W	L	PCT	G	GS	CG	SH	SV	IP	H	R	HR	HB	BB	SO	RAT	ERA	ERA+	OAV	OOB	BH	AVG	PB	PR	PR+	PD	TPI
1973	Bal-A	6	5	.545	18	15	3	0	0	100^{2}	104	53	15	0	46	52	13.4	4.11	91	.267	.345	0	—	0	-3	-4	1	-0.3
1974	Bal-A	1	0	1.000	20	2	0	0	0	57^{1}	55	30	2	0	38	31	14.6	4.40	79	.261	.373	0	—	0	-5	-6	0	-0.3
1975	Bal-A	0	2	.000	4	0	0	0	0	7^{2}	5	3	0	0	8	4	15.3	2.35	150	.227	.433	0	—	0	1	1	0	0.3
	Chi-A	5	9	.357	22	21	1	0	0	107^{2}	100	69	11	2	94	67	16.4	5.10	76	.249	.394	0	—	0	-16	-14	0	-1.6
	Yr	5	11	.313	26	21	1	0	0	115^{1}	105	72	11	2	102	71	16.3	4.92	79	.248	.397	0	—	0	-14	-13	1	-1.3
1976	Chi-A	2	5	.286	19	9	0	0	0	62^{1}	86	62	4	2	42	30	18.8	8.52	42	.339	.436	0	—	0	-35	-34	1	-3.2
1977	Tor-A	9	17	.346	33	33	8	0	0	217	224	123	23	1	83	114	12.8	4.31	98	.269	.336	0	—	0	-6	-2	0	-0.2
1978	Tor-A	7	16	.304	31	30	9	2	0	211^{2}	214	109	28	3	86	97	12.9	4.38	90	.267	.340	0	—	0	-14	-10	0	-1.0
1979	Tor-A	2	10	.167	34	10	2	0	1	116	150	75	19	2	45	43	15.3	5.51	79	.328	.390	0	—	0	-16	-14	1	-1.2
1980	Tor-A	4	13	.235	29	18	2	2	0	121^{2}	130	78	12	2	52	53	13.6	5.47	79	.281	.357	0	—	0	-19	-15	1	-1.7
	Pit-N	1	0	1.000	1	1	0	0	0	6^{2}	3	1	0	0	2	4	6.8	1.35	270	.143	.217	0	.000	-0	2	2	0	0.3
1981	Cal-A	2	4	.333	26	5	0	0	0	77	80	39	4	2	24	27	12.4	3.62	101	.269	.328	0	—	0	0	0	-1	-0.1
Total	9	39	81	.325	237	144	25	4	1	1085^{2}	1151	642	118	14	520	522	14.0	4.81	83	.277	.360	0	.000	-0	-111	-98	3	-9.0

● FERGIE JENKINS Jenkins, Ferguson Arthur b: 12/13/43, Chatham, Ont., Can. BR/TR, 6'5", 210 lbs. Deb: 9/10/65 H

YEAR	TM/L	W	L	PCT	G	GS	CG	SH	SV	IP	H	R	HR	HB	BB	SO	RAT	ERA	ERA+	OAV	OOB	BH	AVG	PB	PR	PR+	PD	TPI
1965	Phi-N	2	1	.667	7	0	0	0	1	12^{1}	7	3	2	0	2	10	6.6	2.19	158	.159	.196	0	.000	-0	2	2	-0	0.3
1966	Phi-N	0	0	—	1	0	0	0	0	2^{1}	3	2	0	0	1	2	15.4	3.86	93	.273	.333	0	—	0	-0	-0	-0	0.0
	Chi-N	6	8	.429	60	12	2	1	5	182	147	75	24	3	51	148	9.9	3.31	111	.219	.277	7	.137	1	6	7	-2	0.4
	Yr	6	8	.429	61	12	2	1	5	184^{1}	150	77	24	3	52	150	10.0	3.32	111	.220	.278	7	.137	1	6	7	-2	0.4
1967	Chi-N★	20	13	.606	38	38	**20**	3	0	289^{1}	230	101	30	4	83	236	9.9	2.80	127	.217	.277	14	.151	1	19	23	2	3.0
1968	Chi-N	20	15	.571	40	40	20	3	0	308	255	96	26	3	65	260	9.4	2.63	120	.222	.266	16	.160	2	12	17	-1	2.2
1969	Chi-N	21	15	.583	43	42	23	7	1	311^{1}	284	122	27	8	71	**273**	10.5	3.21	126	.242	.290	15	.139	-1	13	25	0	2.8
1970	Chi-N	22	16	.579	40	39	**24**	3	0	313	265	128	30	7	60	274	**9.5**	3.39	133	.224	**.265**	14	.124	-3	23	35	-1	3.6
1971	Chi-N★	**24**	13	.649	39	39	**30**	3	0	**325**	304	114	29	5	37	263	9.6	2.77	142	.246	.271	28	.243	10	25	37	2	5.8
1972	Chi-N☆	20	12	.625	36	36	23	5	0	289^{1}	253	111	32	7	62	184	10.0	3.20	119	.234	.280	20	.183	1	8	18	3	2.5
1973	Chi-N	14	16	.467	38	38	7	2	0	271	267	133	35	4	57	170	10.9	3.89	102	.259	.301	10	.119	-1	-7	2	3	0.4
1974	Tex-A	**25**	12	.676	41	41	**29**	6	0	328^{1}	286	117	27	8	45	225	9.3	2.82	126	.232	.264	1	.500	0	29	28	-0	3.1
1975	Tex-A	17	18	.486	37	37	22	4	0	270	261	130	37	9	56	157	10.9	3.93	96	.251	.295	0	—	0	-4	-5	1	-0.5
1976	Bos-A	12	11	.522	30	29	12	2	0	209	201	85	20	5	43	142	10.7	3.27	120	.253	.296	0	—	0	6	13	-1	1.4
1977	Bos-A	10	10	.500	28	28	11	1	0	193	190	91	30	0	36	105	10.5	3.68	122	.257	.291	0	—	0	8	16	1	1.6
1978	Tex-A	18	8	.692	34	30	16	4	0	249	228	92	21	3	41	157	9.8	3.04	124	.245	.279	0	—	0	20	20	2	2.2
1979	Tex-A	16	14	.533	37	37	10	3	0	259	252	127	40	3	81	164	11.7	4.07	102	.256	.314	0	—	0	5	3	4	0.7
1980	Tex-A	12	12	.500	29	29	12	0	0	198	190	90	22	4	52	129	11.2	3.77	103	.250	.301	0	—	0	6	3	1	0.4
1981	Tex-A	5	8	.385	19	16	1	0	0	106	122	55	14	0	40	63	13.8	4.50	77	.290	.351	0	—	0	-10	-13	2	-1.2
1982	Chi-N	14	15	.483	34	34	4	1	0	217^{1}	221	92	19	5	68	134	12.2	3.15	119	.264	.323	10	.149	-1	11	14	-0	1.6
1983	Chi-N	6	9	.400	33	29	1	1	0	167^{1}	176	89	19	6	46	96	12.3	4.30	88	.275	.329	13	.245	3	-12	-9	-1	-0.5
Total	19	284	226	.557	664	594	267	49	7	4500^{2}	4142	1853	484	84	997	3192	10.4	3.34	115	.243	.289	148	.165	13	161	245	14	29.8

● JACK JENKINS Jenkins, Warren Washington b: 12/22/42, Covington, Va. BR/TR, 6'2", 195 lbs. Deb: 9/13/62

YEAR	TM/L	W	L	PCT	G	GS	CG	SH	SV	IP	H	R	HR	HB	BB	SO	RAT	ERA	ERA+	OAV	OOB	BH	AVG	PB	PR	PR+	PD	TPI
1962	Was-A	0	1	.000	3	1	1	0	0	13^{1}	12	6	4	0	7	10	12.8	4.05	100	.245	.339	0	.000	-0	-0	-0	-0	-0.1
1963	Was-A	0	2	.000	4	2	0	0	0	12^{1}	16	8	2	0	12	5	20.4	5.84	64	.340	.475	1	.333	0	-3	-3	0	-0.4
1969	LA-N	0	0	—	1	0	0	0	0	1	0	0	0	0	0	1	0.0	0.00	—	.000	.000	0	—	0	0	0	0	0.0
Total	3	0	3	.000	8	3	1	0	0	26^{2}	28	14	6	0	19	16	15.9	4.73	82	.283	.398	1	.143	-0	-3	-3	0	-0.5

● WILLIE JENSEN Jensen, William Christian b: 11/17/1889, Philadelphia, Pa. d: 3/27/17, Philadelphia, Pa. BL/TR, 5'11.5", 170 lbs. Deb: 9/10/12

YEAR	TM/L	W	L	PCT	G	GS	CG	SH	SV	IP	H	R	HR	HB	BB	SO	RAT	ERA	ERA+	OAV	OOB	BH	AVG	PB	PR	PR+	PD	TPI
1912	Det-A	1	2	.333	5	4	1	0	0	33	43	23	1	2	18	8	17.2	4.91	66	.339	.429	0	.000	-2	-6	-6	-0	-0.7
1914	Phi-A	0	1	.000	1	1	1	0	0	9	7	4	1	0	2	1	9.0	2.00	131	.226	.273	0	.000	0	1	1	0	0.1
Total	2	1	3	.250	6	5	2	0	0	42	50	27	2	2	20	9	15.4	4.29	73	.316	.400	0	.000	-2	-5	-6	-0	-0.6

● MIKE JERZEMBECK Jerzembeck, Michael Joseph b: 5/18/72, Queens, N.Y. BR/TR, 6'1", 185 lbs. Deb: 8/8/98

YEAR	TM/L	W	L	PCT	G	GS	CG	SH	SV	IP	H	R	HR	HB	BB	SO	RAT	ERA	ERA+	OAV	OOB	BH	AVG	PB	PR	PR+	PD	TPI
1998	NY-A	0	1	.000	3	2	0	0	0	6^{1}	9	9	2	0	4	1	18.5	12.79	34	.346	.433	0	—	0	-6	-6	-0	-0.7

● VIRGIL JESTER Jester, Virgil Milton b: 7/23/27, Denver, Colo. BR/TR, 5'11", 188 lbs. Deb: 6/18/52

YEAR	TM/L	W	L	PCT	G	GS	CG	SH	SV	IP	H	R	HR	HB	BB	SO	RAT	ERA	ERA+	OAV	OOB	BH	AVG	PB	PR	PR+	PD	TPI
1952	Bos-N	3	5	.375	19	8	4	1	0	73	80	31	5	1	23	25	12.8	3.33	108	.283	.339	4	.211	1	3	2	-1	0.3
1953	Mil-N	0	0	—	2	0	0	0	0	2	4	5	1	0	4	0	36.0	22.50	17	.400	.571	0	—	0	-4	-5	0	-0.2
Total	2	3	5	.375	21	8	4	1	0	75	84	36	6	1	27	25	13.4	3.84	94	.287	.349	4	.211	1	-1	-2	-1	0.1

● GERMAN JIMENEZ Jimenez, German (Camarena) b: 12/5/62, Santiago, Mex. BL/TL, 5'11", 200 lbs. Deb: 6/28/88

YEAR	TM/L	W	L	PCT	G	GS	CG	SH	SV	IP	H	R	HR	HB	BB	SO	RAT	ERA	ERA+	OAV	OOB	BH	AVG	PB	PR	PR+	PD	TPI
1988	Atl-N	1	6	.143	15	9	0	0	0	55^{2}	65	39	4	1	12	26	12.6	5.01	73	.294	.333	1	.059	-1	-10	-8	-1	-1.1

● JOSE JIMENEZ Jimenez, Jose b: 7/7/73, San Pedro De Macoris, D.R. BR/TR, 6'3", 170 lbs. Deb: 9/9/98

YEAR	TM/L	W	L	PCT	G	GS	CG	SH	SV	IP	H	R	HR	HB	BB	SO	RAT	ERA	ERA+	OAV	OOB	BH	AVG	PB	PR	PR+	PD	TPI
1998	StL-N	3	0	1.000	4	3	0	0	0	21^{1}	22	8	0	0	8	12	12.7	2.95	142	.262	.326	0	.000	-1	3	3	0	0.3
1999	StL-N	5	14	.263	29	28	2	2	0	163	173	114	16	11	71	113	14.1	5.85	78	.275	.359	5	.094	-3	-23	-23	2	-2.3
2000	Col-N	5	2	.714	72	0	0	0	24	70^{2}	63	27	4	3	28	44	12.0	3.18	186	.239	.319	2	.500	0	11	17	-0	2.5
Total	3	13	16	.448	105	31	2	2	24	255	258	149	20	14	107	169	13.4	4.87	101	.264	.345	7	.111	-3	-9	1	1	0.5

● JUAN JIMENEZ Jimenez, Juan Antonio (Martes) b: 3/8/49, LaTorre, La Vega, D.R. BR/TR, 6'1", 165 lbs. Deb: 9/9/74

YEAR	TM/L	W	L	PCT	G	GS	CG	SH	SV	IP	H	R	HR	HB	BB	SO	RAT	ERA	ERA+	OAV	OOB	BH	AVG	PB	PR	PR+	PD	TPI
1974	Pit-N	0	0	—	4	0	0	0	0	4	6	4	0	0	2	2	18.0	6.75	51	.353	.421	0	—	0	-1	-2	-0	-0.1

● MIGUEL JIMENEZ Jimenez, Miguel Anthony b: 8/19/69, New York, N.Y. BR/TR, 6'2", 205 lbs. Deb: 9/12/93

YEAR	TM/L	W	L	PCT	G	GS	CG	SH	SV	IP	H	R	HR	HB	BB	SO	RAT	ERA	ERA+	OAV	OOB	BH	AVG	PB	PR	PR+	PD	TPI
1993	Oak-A	1	0	1.000	5	4	0	0	0	27	27	12	5	1	16	13	14.7	4.00	102	.262	.367	0	—	0	1	0	-1	-0.1
1994	Oak-A	1	4	.200	8	7	0	0	0	34	38	33	9	1	32	22	18.8	7.41	60	.275	.415	0	—	0	-10	-12	0	-1.3
Total	2	2	4	.333	13	11	0	0	0	61	65	45	14	2	48	35	17.0	5.90	73	.270	.395	0	—	0	-9	-12	-1	-1.4

● TOMMY JOHN John, Thomas Edward b: 5/22/43, Terre Haute, Ind. BR/TL, 6'3", 185 lbs. Deb: 9/6/63

YEAR	TM/L	W	L	PCT	G	GS	CG	SH	SV	IP	H	R	HR	HB	BB	SO	RAT	ERA	ERA+	OAV	OOB	BH	AVG	PB	PR	PR+	PD	TPI
1963	Cle-A	0	2	.000	6	3	0	0	0	20^{1}	23	10	1	0	6	9	12.8	2.21	164	.284	.333	0	.000	-1	3	3	-0	0.2

YEAR	TM/L	W	L	PCT	G	GS	CG	SH	SV	IP	H	R	HR	HB	BB	SO	RAT	ERA	ERA+	OAV	OOB	BH	AVG	PB	PR	PR+	PD	TPI
1964	Cle-A	2	9	.182	25	14	2	1	0	94^1	97	53	10	0	35	65	12.6	3.91	92	.262	.326	5	.208	0	-3	-3	1	-0.3
1965	Chi-A	14	7	.667	39	27	6	1	3	183^2	162	67	12	2	58	126	10.9	3.09	103	.237	.298	10	.169	2	8	2	3	0.8
1966	Chi-A	14	11	.560	34	33	10	**5**	0	223	195	76	13	7	57	138	10.5	2.62	121	.235	.290	10	.145	2	20	15	1	2.0
1967	Chi-A	10	13	.435	31	29	9	**6**	0	178^1	143	62	12	5	47	110	9.8	2.47	126	.219	.277	8	.157	-0	15	13	6	2.4
1968	Chi-A★	10	5	.667	25	25	5	1	0	177^1	135	45	10	12	49	117	9.9	1.98	153	.212	.280	12	.194	2	20	20	6	2.8
1969	Chi-A	9	11	.450	33	33	6	2	0	232^1	230	91	16	1	90	128	12.4	3.25	119	.261	.330	9	.114	-2	10	15	7	1.8
1970	Chi-A	12	17	.414	37	37	10	3	0	269^1	253	117	19	9	101	138	12.1	3.27	119	.251	.324	17	.202	1	13	18	4	2.4
1971	Chi-A	13	16	.448	38	35	10	3	0	229^1	244	115	17	5	58	131	12.0	3.61	100	.274	.321	10	.145	-1	-4	-0	-1	-0.3
1972	LA-N	11	5	.688	29	29	4	1	0	186^2	172	68	14	3	40	117	10.4	2.89	115	.244	.287	10	.159	-1	12	10	4	1.1
1973	LA-N	16	7	**.696**	36	31	4	2	0	218	202	88	16	4	50	116	10.6	3.10	111	.246	.293	15	.203	2	14	9	7	1.9
1974	LA-N	13	3	.813	22	22	5	3	0	153	133	51	4	1	42	78	10.4	2.59	132	.235	.289	6	.118	-1	18	15	2	1.6
1976	LA-N	10	10	.500	31	31	6	2	0	207	207	76	7	0	61	91	11.7	3.09	110	.261	.314	7	.109	-2	10	7	-1	0.4
1977	*LA-N	20	7	.741	31	31	11	3	0	220^1	225	82	12	3	50	123	11.4	2.78	138	.267	.311	14	.177	1	28	26	2	3.5
1978	*LA-N☆	17	10	.630	33	30	7	0	1	213	230	95	11	5	53	124	12.2	3.30	107	.271	.318	8	.121	-1	7	5	2	0.7
1979	NY-A☆	21	9	.700	37	36	17	3	0	276^1	268	109	9	4	65	111	11.0	2.96	138	.260	.306	0	—	0	**39**	36	2	3.8
1980	*NY-A★	22	9	.710	36	36	16	**6**	0	265^1	270	115	13	6	56	78	11.3	3.43	115	.268	.311	0	—	0	18	15	1	1.7
1981	*NY-A	9	8	.529	20	20	7	0	0	140^1	135	50	10	3	39	50	11.4	2.63	136	.256	.311	0	—	0	16	15	1	2.0
1982	NY-A	10	10	.500	30	26	9	2	0	186^2	190	84	11	3	34	54	10.9	3.66	109	.266	.302	0	—	0	9	7	2	0.8
	*Cal-A	4	2	.667	7	7	1	0	0	35	49	18	4	0	5	14	13.9	3.86	105	.336	.358	0	—	0	1	1	1	0.2
	Yr	14	12	.538	37	33	10	2	0	221^2	239	102	15	3	39	68	11.4	3.69	108	.278	.311	0	—	0	10	8	2	1.0
1983	Cal-A	11	13	.458	34	34	9	0	0	234^2	287	126	20	2	49	65	13.0	4.33	93	.304	.340	0	—	0	-7	-8	1	-0.6
1984	Cal-A	7	13	.350	32	29	4	1	0	181^1	223	97	15	4	56	47	14.0	4.52	88	.306	.359	0	—	0	-10	-11	0	-1.0
1985	Cal-A	2	4	.333	12	6	0	0	0	38^1	51	22	3	1	15	17	15.7	4.70	88	.329	.392	0	—	0	-2	-3	1	-0.2
	Oak-A	2	6	.250	11	11	0	0	0	48	66	37	6	1	13	8	15.0	6.19	62	.332	.376	0	—	0	-11	-13	1	-1.7
	Yr	4	10	.286	23	17	0	0	0	86^1	117	59	9	2	28	25	15.3	5.53	72	.331	.383	0	—	0	-13	-16	2	-1.9
1986	NY-A	5	3	.625	13	10	1	0	0	70^2	73	27	8	2	15	28	11.5	2.93	140	.275	.319	0	—	0	10	9	1	1.1
1987	NY-A	13	6	.684	33	33	3	1	0	187^2	212	95	12	6	47	63	12.7	4.03	109	.288	.336	0	—	0	9	8	-1	0.6
1988	NY-A	9	8	.529	35	32	0	0	0	176^1	221	96	11	6	46	81	13.9	4.49	88	.308	.355	0	—	0	-10	-11	2	-0.7
1989	NY-A	2	7	.222	10	10	0	0	0	63^2	87	45	6	3	22	18	15.8	5.80	67	.336	.394	0	—	0	-13	-14	2	-1.4
Total	26	288	231	.555	760	700	162	46	4	4710^1	4783	2017	302	98	1259	2245	11.7	3.34	110	.265	.316	141	.157	1	217	186	55	25.6

● AUGIE JOHNS Johns, Augustus Francis "Lefty" b: 9/10/1899, St.Louis, Mo. d: 9/12/75, San Antonio, Tex. BL/TL, 5'8.5", 170 lbs. Deb: 4/16/26

YEAR	TM/L	W	L	PCT	G	GS	CG	SH	SV	IP	H	R	HR	HB	BB	SO	RAT	ERA	ERA+	OAV	OOB	BH	AVG	PB	PR	PR+	PD	TPI
1926	Det-A	6	4	.600	35	14	3	1	1	112^2	117	77	6	5	69	40	15.3	5.35	76	.271	.377	4	.143	-1	-17	-16	-2	-1.6
1927	Det-A	0	0	—	1	0	0	0	0	1	1	1	0	0	1	1	18.0	9.00	47	.333	.500	0	—	0	-1	-1	0	0.0
Total	2	6	4	.600	36	14	3	1	1	113^2	118	78	6	5	70	41	15.3	5.38	75	.271	.378	4	.143	-1	-17	-17	-2	-1.6

● DOUG JOHNS Johns, Douglas Alan b: 12/19/67, South Bend, Ind. BR/TL, 6'2", 185 lbs. Deb: 7/8/95

YEAR	TM/L	W	L	PCT	G	GS	CG	SH	SV	IP	H	R	HR	HB	BB	SO	RAT	ERA	ERA+	OAV	OOB	BH	AVG	PB	PR	PR+	PD	TPI
1995	Oak-A	5	3	.625	11	9	1	1	0	54^2	44	32	5	5	26	25	12.3	4.61	97	.226	.332	0	—	0	1	-1	1	0.0
1996	Oak-A	6	12	.333	40	23	1	0	1	158	187	112	21	6	69	71	14.9	5.98	82	.297	.372	0	—	0	-17	-19	2	-1.5
1998	Bal-A	3	3	.500	31	10	0	0	1	86^2	108	46	9	4	32	34	15.0	4.57	100	.321	.387	2	1.000	1	1	-0	2	0.3
1999	Bal-A	6	4	.600	32	5	0	0	0	86^2	81	45	9	8	25	50	11.8	4.47	105	.248	.317	0	.000	-0	4	2	0	0.2
Total	4	20	22	.476	114	47	2	1	2	386	420	235	44	23	152	180	13.9	5.13	92	.282	.358	2	.667	1	-12	-18	6	-1.0

● OLLIE JOHNS Johns, Oliver Tracy b: 8/21/1879, Trenton, Ohio d: 6/17/61, Hamilton, Ohio BL/TL, Deb: 9/24/05

YEAR	TM/L	W	L	PCT	G	GS	CG	SH	SV	IP	H	R	HR	HB	BB	SO	RAT	ERA	ERA+	OAV	OOB	BH	AVG	PB	PR	PR+	PD	TPI
1905	Cin-N	1	0	1.000	4	1	1	0	1	18	31	22	1	0	4	8	17.5	3.50	94	.369	.398	1	.200	-0	-1	-0	-0	0.0

● ABE JOHNSON Johnson, Abraham b: Chicago, Ill. Deb: 7/16/1893

YEAR	TM/L	W	L	PCT	G	GS	CG	SH	SV	IP	H	R	HR	HB	BB	SO	RAT	ERA	ERA+	OAV	OOB	BH	AVG	PB	PR	PR+	PD	TPI
1893	Chi-N	0	0	—	1	0	0	0	1	1	2	4	0	1	2	0	45.0	36.00	13	.400	.625	0	—	0	-3	-4	-0	-0.5

● RANKIN JOHNSON Johnson, Adam Rankin Jr. b: 3/1/17, Hayden, Ariz. BR/TR, 6'3", 177 lbs. Deb: 4/17/41 F

YEAR	TM/L	W	L	PCT	G	GS	CG	SH	SV	IP	H	R	HR	HB	BB	SO	RAT	ERA	ERA+	OAV	OOB	BH	AVG	PB	PR	PR+	PD	TPI
1941	Phi-A	1	0	1.000	7	0	0	0	0	10	14	10	0	0	3	0	15.3	3.60	116	.326	.370	0	.000	-0	1	1	0	0.1

● RANKIN JOHNSON Johnson, Adam Rankin Sr. "Tex" b: 2/4/1888, Burnet, Tex. d: 7/2/72, Williamsport, Pa. BR/TR, 6'1.5", 185 lbs. Deb: 4/20/14 F

YEAR	TM/L	W	L	PCT	G	GS	CG	SH	SV	IP	H	R	HR	HB	BB	SO	RAT	ERA	ERA+	OAV	OOB	BH	AVG	PB	PR	PR+	PD	TPI
1914	Bos-A	3	9	.250	16	13	4	2	0	99^1	92	41	2	3	34	24	11.7	3.08	87	.265	.336	4	.133	-1	-4	-4	-2	-0.8
	Chi-F	9	5	.643	16	14	12	2	0	120	88	29	5	4	29	60	9.1	**1.58**	169	.209	.267	4	.108	-3	17	16	-1	1.3
1915	Chi-F	2	4	.333	11	6	3	0	1	57	58	34	2	1	23	19	12.9	4.42	57	.270	.343	1	.045	-3	-11	-13	-2	-1.7
	Bal-F	7	11	.389	23	19	12	2	1	150^2	143	68	3	1	58	62	12.1	3.35	86	.255	.326	8	.157	-2	-10	-8	-3	-1.3
	Yr	9	15	.375	34	25	15	2	2	207^2	201	102	5	2	81	81	12.3	3.64	76	.259	.331	9	.123	-5	-21	-20	-5	-3.0
1918	StL-N	1	1	.500	6	1	0	0	0	23	20	10	0	0	7	4	10.6	2.74	99	.263	.325	1	.250	0	0	-0	1	0.1
Total	3	22	30	.423	72	53	31	6	2	450	401	182	12	9	151	169	11.2	2.92	93	.248	.315	18	.125	-9	-7	-10	-7	-2.4

● ART JOHNSON Johnson, Arthur Gilbert b: 2/15/1897, Warren, Pa. d: 6/7/82, Sarasota, Fla. BB/TL, 6'1", 167 lbs. Deb: 9/18/27

YEAR	TM/L	W	L	PCT	G	GS	CG	SH	SV	IP	H	R	HR	HB	BB	SO	RAT	ERA	ERA+	OAV	OOB	BH	AVG	PB	PR	PR+	PD	TPI
1927	NY-N	0	0	—	1	0	0	0	0	3	1	1	0	0	1	0	6.0	0.00	—	.125	.222	0	—	0	1	1	-0	0.1

● ART JOHNSON Johnson, Arthur Henry "Lefty" b: 7/16/16, Winchester, Mass. BL/TL, 6'2", 185 lbs. Deb: 9/22/40

YEAR	TM/L	W	L	PCT	G	GS	CG	SH	SV	IP	H	R	HR	HB	BB	SO	RAT	ERA	ERA+	OAV	OOB	BH	AVG	PB	PR	PR+	PD	TPI
1940	Bos-N	0	1	.000	2	1	0	0	0	6	10	7	0	1	3	1	21.0	10.50	35	.345	.424	0	.000	-0	-4	-5	0	-0.6
1941	Bos-N	7	15	.318	43	18	6	0	1	183^1	189	92	7	5	71	70	13.0	3.53	101	.270	.342	8	.145	-2	2	1	0	-0.1
1942	Bos-N	0	0	—	4	0	0	0	0	6^1	4	1	0	1	5	0	14.2	1.42	235	.190	.370	0	.000	-0	1	1	-0	0.0
Total	3	7	16	.304	49	19	6	0	1	195^2	203	100	7	7	79	71	13.3	3.68	97	.271	.346	8	.140	-2	-1	-3	1	-0.7

● BEN JOHNSON Johnson, Benjamin Franklin b: 5/16/31, Greenwood, S.C. BR/TR, 6'2", 190 lbs. Deb: 9/6/59

YEAR	TM/L	W	L	PCT	G	GS	CG	SH	SV	IP	H	R	HR	HB	BB	SO	RAT	ERA	ERA+	OAV	OOB	BH	AVG	PB	PR	PR+	PD	TPI
1959	Chi-N	0	0	—	4	2	0	0	0	16^2	17	5	1	0	4	6	11.3	2.16	183	.262	.304	0	.000	-0	3	3	-0	0.1
1960	Chi-N	2	1	.667	17	0	0	0	1	29^1	39	21	3	1	11	9	15.6	4.91	77	.355	.418	0	.000	-0	-4	-4	1	-0.3
Total	2	2	1	.667	21	2	0	0	1	46	56	26	4	1	15	15	14.1	3.91	98	.320	.377	0	.000	-1	-0	-0	0	-0.2

● CHET JOHNSON Johnson, Chester Lillis "Chesty Chet" b: 8/1/17, Redmond, Wash. d: 4/10/83, Seattle, Wash. BL/TL, 6', 175 lbs. Deb: 9/12/46 F

YEAR	TM/L	W	L	PCT	G	GS	CG	SH	SV	IP	H	R	HR	HB	BB	SO	RAT	ERA	ERA+	OAV	OOB	BH	AVG	PB	PR	PR+	PD	TPI
1946	StL-A	0	0	—	5	3	0	0	0	18	20	12	0	0	13	8	16.5	5.00	75	.286	.398	0	.000	-1	-3	-2	-1	-0.3

● BART JOHNSON Johnson, Clair Barth b: 1/3/50, Torrance, Cal. BR/TR, 6'5", 215 lbs. Deb: 9/8/69

YEAR	TM/L	W	L	PCT	G	GS	CG	SH	SV	IP	H	R	HR	HB	BB	SO	RAT	ERA	ERA+	OAV	OOB	BH	AVG	PB	PR	PR+	PD	TPI
1969	Chi-A	1	3	.250	4	3	0	0	0	22^1	22	11	2	0	6	18	11.3	3.22	120	.259	.308	1	.167	0	1	1	-0	0.3
1970	Chi-A	4	7	.364	18	15	2	1	0	89^2	92	53	11	2	46	71	14.1	4.82	81	.268	.358	8	.276	2	-11	-9	-0	-0.8
1971	Chi-A	12	10	.545	53	16	4	0	14	178	148	67	9	6	111	153	13.4	2.93	123	.227	.345	11	.193	0	11	13	-1	1.7
1972	Chi-A	0	3	.000	9	0	0	0	1	13^2	18	20	2	1	13	9	21.1	9.22	34	.327	.464	0	.000	-0	-9	-9	0	-1.8
1973	Chi-A	3	3	.500	22	9	0	0	0	80^2	76	39	6	2	40	56	13.2	4.13	96	.252	.343	0	—	0	-3	-1	-0	-0.1
1974	Chi-A	10	4	.714	18	18	8	2	0	121^2	105	42	6	1	32	76	10.2	2.74	136	.229	.281	0	—	0	12	13	-2	1.2
1976	Chi-A	9	16	.360	32	32	8	3	0	211^1	231	115	19	1	62	91	12.5	4.73	75	.282	.334	0	—	0	-28	-27	0	-2.8
1977	Chi-A	4	5	.444	29	4	0	0	2	92	114	48	5	2	38	46	15.1	4.01	102	.302	.369	0	—	0	1	1	-0	0.1
Total	8	43	51	.457	185	97	22	6	17	809^1	806	395	60	15	348	520	13.0	3.94	95	.261	.339	20	.215	3	-27	-17	-4	-2.2

● CONNIE JOHNSON Johnson, Clifford b: 12/27/22, Stone Mountain, Ga BR/TR, 6'4", 200 lbs. Deb: 4/17/53

YEAR	TM/L	W	L	PCT	G	GS	CG	SH	SV	IP	H	R	HR	HB	BB	SO	RAT	ERA	ERA+	OAV	OOB	BH	AVG	PB	PR	PR+	PD	TPI
1953	Chi-A	4	4	.500	14	10	2	1	0	60^2	55	27	4	2	38	44	14.1	3.56	113	.238	.351	1	.050	-2	3	3	-1	0.1
1955	Chi-A	7	4	.636	17	16	5	2	0	99	95	40	5	1	52	72	13.5	3.45	114	.251	.343	5	.152	-1	6	5	-1	0.3
1956	Chi-A	0	1	.000	5	2	0	0	0	12^1	11	5	1	0	7	6	13.1	3.65	112	.234	.333	0	.000	-0	1	1	0	0.0
	Bal-A	9	10	.474	26	25	9	2	0	183^2	165	79	12	1	62	130	11.2	3.43	114	.239	.303	15	.259	3	15	11	-3	1.1
	Yr	9	11	.450	31	27	9	2	0	196	176	84	13	1	69	136	11.3	3.44	114	.239	.305	15	.246	3	16	11	-3	1.1
1957	Bal-A	14	11	.560	35	30	14	3	0	242	212	93	17	3	66	177	10.5	3.20	112	.235	.289	12	.135	-4	16	11	-4	0.3
1958	Bal-A	6	9	.400	26	17	4	0	1	118^1	116	58	13	0	32	68	11.3	3.88	93	.260	.310	7	.206	1	-1	-4	-2	-0.5
Total	5	40	39	.506	123	100	34	8	1	716	654	302	52	7	257	497	11.5	3.44	109	.243	.310	40	.169	-3	38	27	-10	1.3

● DANE JOHNSON Johnson, Dane Edward b: 2/10/63, Coral Gables, Fla. BR/TR, 6'5", 205 lbs. Deb: 5/30/94

YEAR	TM/L	W	L	PCT	G	GS	CG	SH	SV	IP	H	R	HR	HB	BB	SO	RAT	ERA	ERA+	OAV	OOB	BH	AVG	PB	PR	PR+	PD	TPI
1994	Chi-A	2	1	.667	15	0	0	0	0	12^1	16	9	2	0	11	7	19.7	6.57	71	.327	.450	0	—	0	-2	-3	-0	-0.5
1996	Tor-A	0	0	—	10	0	0	0	0	9	5	3	0	0	5	7	10.0	3.00	167	.161	.278	0	—	0	2	2	0	0.1

YEAR	TM/L	W	L	PCT	G	GS	CG	SH	SV	IP	H	R	HR	HB	BB	SO	RAT	ERA	ERA+	OAV	OOB	BH	AVG	PB	PR	PR+	PD	TPI
1997	Oak-A	4	1	.800	38	0	0	0	2	45^2	49	28	4	2	31	43	16.2	4.53	100	.272	.385	0	—	0	0	-0	-1	-0.1
Total	3	6	2	.750	63	0	0	0	2	67	70	40	6	2	47	57	16.0	4.70	98	.269	.385	0	—	0	-0	-1	-1	-0.5

● DAVE JOHNSON Johnson, David Charles b: 10/4/48, Abilene, Tex. BR/TR, 6'1", 183 lbs. Deb: 7/2/74

YEAR	TM/L	W	L	PCT	G	GS	CG	SH	SV	IP	H	R	HR	HB	BB	SO	RAT	ERA	ERA+	OAV	OOB	BH	AVG	PB	PR	PR+	PD	TPI
1974	Bal-A	2	2	.500	11	0	0	0	2	15^1	17	5	1	0	5	6	12.9	2.93	118	.274	.328	0	—	0	1	1	-0	0.2
1975	Bal-A	0	1	.000	6	0	0	0	0	8^2	8	4	0	0	7	4	15.6	4.15	85	.250	.385	0	—	0	-0	-1	0	-0.1
1977	Min-A	2	5	.286	30	6	0	0	0	72^2	86	42	7	5	23	33	14.1	4.58	87	.299	.361	0	—	0	-4	-5	0	-0.4
1978	Min-A	0	2	.000	6	1	0	0	0	12	15	11	1	0	9	7	18.0	7.50	51	.313	.421	0	—	0	-5	-5	0	-0.7
Total	4	4	10	.286	53	7	0	0	2	108^2	126	62	9	5	44	50	14.5	4.64	83	.293	.365	0	—	0	-8	-10	-0	-1.0

● DAVE JOHNSON Johnson, David Wayne b: 10/24/59, Baltimore, Md. BR/TR, 5'11", 183 lbs. Deb: 5/29/87

YEAR	TM/L	W	L	PCT	G	GS	CG	SH	SV	IP	H	R	HR	HB	BB	SO	RAT	ERA	ERA+	OAV	OOB	BH	AVG	PB	PR	PR+	PD	TPI
1987	Pit-N	0	0	—	5	0	0	0	0	6^1	13	7	1	0	2	4	21.3	9.95	41	.448	.484	0	—	0	-4	-4	0	-0.2
1989	Bal-A	4	7	.364	14	14	4	0	0	89^1	90	44	11	4	28	26	12.3	4.23	90	.265	.328	0	—	0	-3	-4	-2	-0.7
1990	Bal-A	13	9	.591	30	29	3	0	0	180	196	83	30	3	43	68	12.1	4.10	93	.280	.324	0	—	0	-4	-6	-3	-1.0
1991	Bal-A	4	8	.333	22	14	0	0	0	84	127	68	18	4	24	38	16.6	7.07	56	.349	.395	0	—	0	-28	-30	-1	-3.6
1993	Det-A	1	1	.500	6	0	0	0	0	8^1	13	13	3	2	5	7	21.6	12.96	33	.342	.444	0	—	0	-8	-8	-0	-1.4
Total	5	22	25	.468	77	57	7	0	0	368	439	215	63	13	102	143	13.5	5.11	75	.298	.349	0	—	0	-47	-53	-6	-6.9

● DON JOHNSON Johnson, Donald Roy b: 11/12/26, Portland, Ore. BR/TR, 6'3", 200 lbs. Deb: 4/20/47

YEAR	TM/L	W	L	PCT	G	GS	CG	SH	SV	IP	H	R	HR	HB	BB	SO	RAT	ERA	ERA+	OAV	OOB	BH	AVG	PB	PR	PR+	PD	TPI
1947	NY-A	4	3	.571	15	8	2	0	0	54^1	57	26	2	1	23	16	13.4	3.64	97	.270	.345	0	.000	-2	0	-1	-1	-0.3
1950	NY-A	1	0	1.000	8	0	0	0	0	18	35	21	2	0	12	9	23.5	10.00	43	.398	.470	0	.000	-0	-11	-12	-0	-0.6
	StL-A	5	6	.455	25	12	4	1	1	96	126	72	14	1	55	31	17.1	6.09	81	.325	.410	2	.069	-3	-16	-11	-1	-1.4
	Yr	6	6	.500	33	12	4	1	1	114	161	93	16	1	67	40	18.1	6.71	72	.338	.421	2	.063	-4	-27	-22	-1	-2.0
1951	StL-A	0	1	.000	6	3	0	0	0	15	27	26	4	1	18	8	27.6	12.60	35	.391	.523	1	.333	0	-14	-13	0	-0.7
	Was-A	7	11	.389	21	20	8	1	0	143^2	138	67	9	2	58	52	12.4	3.95	104	.255	.329	4	.085	-5	3	2	-0	-0.3
	Yr	7	12	.368	27	23	8	1	0	158^2	165	93	13	3	76	60	13.8	4.76	87	.270	.354	5	.100	-5	-11	-11	-0	-1.0
1952	Was-A	0	5	.000	29	6	0	0	2	69	80	41	4	4	33	37	15.3	4.43	80	.287	.370	1	.077	-1	-6	-7	-0	-0.7
1954	Chi-A	8	7	.533	46	16	3	3	7	144	129	53	14	0	43	68	10.8	3.13	119	.243	.300	1	.029	-3	10	10	0	0.7
1955	Bal-A	2	4	.333	31	5	0	0	1	68	89	46	4	0	35	27	16.4	5.82	65	.333	.411	0	.000	-1	-14	-16	0	-1.4
1958	SF-N	0	1	.000	17	0	0	0	1	23	31	19	2	2	8	14	16.0	6.26	61	.323	.387	0	.000	-0	-6	-6	-0	-0.4
Total	7	27	38	.415	198	70	17	5	12	631	712	371	55	11	285	262	14.4	4.78	84	.288	.364	9	.058	-16	-54	-55	-2	-5.1

● EARL JOHNSON Johnson, Earl Douglas "Lefty" b: 4/2/19, Redmond, Wash. d: 12/3/94, Seattle, Wash. BL/TL, 6'3", 190 lbs. Deb: 7/20/40 F

YEAR	TM/L	W	L	PCT	G	GS	CG	SH	SV	IP	H	R	HR	HB	BB	SO	RAT	ERA	ERA+	OAV	OOB	BH	AVG	PB	PR	PR+	PD	TPI
1940	Bos-A	6	2	.750	17	10	2	0	0	70^1	69	33	0	2	39	26	14.1	4.09	110	.260	.359	2	.074	-3	2	3	1	0.1
1941	Bos-A	4	5	.444	17	12	4	0	0	93^2	90	57	4	3	51	46	13.8	4.52	92	.247	.344	10	.294	2	-4	-4	2	0.1
1946	*Bos-A	5	4	.556	29	5	0	0	3	80	78	39	5	2	39	40	13.4	3.71	99	.250	.337	5	.227	2	-2	-0	-0	0.1
1947	Bos-A	12	11	.522	45	17	6	3	8	142^1	129	63	7	2	62	65	12.2	2.97	131	.246	.328	12	.273	1	12	14	2	2.7
1948	Bos-A	10	4	.714	35	3	1	0	5	91^1	98	49	7	0	42	45	13.8	4.53	97	.276	.353	3	.097	-3	-2	-1	2	-0.3
1949	Bos-A	3	6	.333	19	3	0	0	0	49^1	65	45	1	4	29	20	17.9	7.48	58	.327	.422	0	.000	-1	-18	-16	-1	-2.6
1950	Bos-A	0	0	—	11	0	0	0	0	13^2	18	11	0	1	8	6	17.8	7.24	68	.333	.429	0	.000	-0	-4	-3	1	-0.1
1951	Det-A	0	0	—	6	0	0	0	1	5^2	9	5	0	0	2	2	17.5	6.35	66	.375	.423	0	—	0	-1	-1	0	-0.1
Total	8	40	32	.556	179	50	13	3	17	546^1	556	302	24	14	272	250	13.9	4.30	96	.265	.353	32	.187	-2	-18	-9	7	-0.1

● WALT JOHNSON Johnson, Ellis Walter b: 12/8/1892, Minneapolis, Minn. d: 1/4/65, Minneapolis, Minn. BR/TR, 6'0.5", 180 lbs. Deb: 7/6/12

YEAR	TM/L	W	L	PCT	G	GS	CG	SH	SV	IP	H	R	HR	HB	BB	SO	RAT	ERA	ERA+	OAV	OOB	BH	AVG	PB	PR	PR+	PD	TPI
1912	Chi-A	0	0	—	3	0	0	0	0	11^2	11	6	0	1	7	7	14.7	3.86	83	.262	.380	0	.000	-0	-1	-1	-0	-0.1
1915	Chi-A	0	0	—	1	0	0	0	0	2	3	2	0	0	0	3	13.5	9.00	33	.333	.333	0	—	0	-1	-1	-0	-0.1
1917	Phi-A	0	2	.000	4	2	0	0	0	13^2	15	12	0	0	5	8	13.2	7.24	38	.294	.357	0	.000	0	-7	-7	0	-0.8
Total	3	0	2	.000	8	2	0	0	0	27^1	29	20	0	1	12	18	13.8	5.93	50	.284	.365	0	.000	0	-9	-9	-0	-1.0

● ERNIE JOHNSON Johnson, Ernest Thorwald b: 6/16/24, Brattleboro, Vt. BR/TR, 6'4", 195 lbs. Deb: 4/28/50

YEAR	TM/L	W	L	PCT	G	GS	CG	SH	SV	IP	H	R	HR	HB	BB	SO	RAT	ERA	ERA+	OAV	OOB	BH	AVG	PB	PR	PR+	PD	TPI
1950	Bos-N	2	0	1.000	16	1	0	0	0	20^2	37	21	1	0	13	15	21.8	6.97	55	.394	.467	1	.500	0	-6	-8	1	-0.5
1952	Bos-N	6	3	.667	29	10	2	1	1	92	100	53	8	2	31	45	13.0	4.11	88	.270	.329	2	.091	-0	-4	-5	1	-0.4
1953	Mil-N	4	3	.571	36	1	0	0	0	81	79	34	4	3	22	36	11.6	2.67	147	.263	.320	1	.071	-1	15	12	0	0.8
1954	Mil-N	5	2	.714	40	4	1	0	2	99^1	77	34	11	1	34	68	10.1	2.81	133	.219	.290	3	.231	0	14	11	1	0.9
1955	Mil-N	5	7	.417	40	2	0	0	4	92	81	38	5	2	55	43	13.5	3.42	110	.240	.349	2	.100	-1	6	4	-0	0.3
1956	Mil-N	4	3	.571	36	0	0	0	6	51	54	21	9	1	21	26	13.4	3.71	93	.270	.342	1	.250	0	0	-2	0	-0.2
1957	*Mil-N	7	3	.700	30	0	0	0	4	65	67	29	9	1	26	44	13.0	3.88	90	.265	.336	6	.353	3	0	-3	1	-0.1
1958	Mil-N	3	1	.750	15	0	0	0	1	23^1	35	21	4	1	10	13	17.7	8.10	43	.357	.422	0	.000	0	-11	-13	0	-2.0
1959	Bal-A	4	1	.800	31	1	0	0	1	50^1	57	32	6	3	19	29	14.1	4.11	92	.286	.357	2	.333	0	-1	-2	0	-0.1
Total	9	40	23	.635	273	19	3	1	19	574^2	587	283	57	14	231	319	13.0	3.77	98	.266	.340	18	.180	2	13	-6	5	-1.3

● FRED JOHNSON Johnson, Frederick Edward "Deacon" or "Cactus" b: 3/10/1894, Tolar, Tex. d: 6/14/73, Kerrville, Tex. BR/TR, 6', 185 lbs. Deb: 9/27/22

YEAR	TM/L	W	L	PCT	G	GS	CG	SH	SV	IP	H	R	HR	HB	BB	SO	RAT	ERA	ERA+	OAV	OOB	BH	AVG	PB	PR	PR+	PD	TPI
1922	NY-N	0	2	.000	2	2	1	0	0	18	20	8	3	0	1	8	10.5	4.00	100	.294	.304	0	.000	-1	0	0	-0	-0.1
1923	NY-N	2	0	1.000	3	2	1	0	0	17	11	8	2	0	7	5	9.5	4.24	90	.177	.261	0	.000	-1	-0	-1	1	-0.1
1938	StL-A	3	7	.300	17	6	3	0	3	69	91	50	7	1	27	24	15.5	5.61	89	.316	.377	6	.240	-0	-6	-5	-2	-0.7
1939	StL-A	0	1	.000	5	2	1	0	0	14	23	12	0	0	9	2	20.6	6.43	76	.383	.464	0	.000	-1	-3	-2	1	-0.1
Total	4	5	10	.333	27	12	6	0	3	118	145	78	12	1	44	39	14.5	5.26	88	.303	.363	6	.154	-2	-9	-8	0	-1.0

● CHIEF JOHNSON Johnson, George Howard "Murphy" or "Big Murph" b: 3/30/1886, Winnebago, Neb. d: 6/12/22, Des Moines, Iowa BR/TR, 5'11.5", 190 lbs. Deb: 4/16/13

YEAR	TM/L	W	L	PCT	G	GS	CG	SH	SV	IP	H	R	HR	HB	BB	SO	RAT	ERA	ERA+	OAV	OOB	BH	AVG	PB	PR	PR+	PD	TPI
1913	Cin-N	14	16	.467	44	31	13	3	0	269	251	137	8	7	86	107	11.5	3.01	108	.256	.320	10	.114	-3	6	7	0	0.5
1914	Cin-N	0	0	—	1	1	0	0	0	4	6	4	0	0	2	1	18.0	6.75	43	.333	.400	0	—	0	-2	-2	-0	-0.1
	KC-F	9	10	.474	20	19	12	2	0	134	157	76	2	4	33	78	13.0	3.16	88	.298	.345	6	.122	-2	-4	-6	-3	-1.2
1915	KC-F	17	17	.500	46	34	19	4	2	281^1	253	121	5	8	71	118	10.6	2.75	96	.242	.295	11	.126	-4	-1	-4	2	-0.6
Total	3	40	43	.482	111	85	44	9	2	688^1	667	338	15	19	192	304	11.5	2.95	98	.259	.315	27	.121	-9	-1	-4	-1	-1.4

● HANK JOHNSON Johnson, Henry Ward b: 5/21/06, Bradenton, Fla. d: 8/20/82, Bradenton, Fla. BR/TR (BB 1933), 5'11.5", 175 lbs. Deb: 4/17/25

YEAR	TM/L	W	L	PCT	G	GS	CG	SH	SV	IP	H	R	HR	HB	BB	SO	RAT	ERA	ERA+	OAV	OOB	BH	AVG	PB	PR	PR+	PD	TPI
1925	NY-A	1	3	.250	24	4	2	1	0	67	88	58	3	8	37	25	17.9	6.85	62	.319	.414	1	.059	-1	-18	-20	1	-1.0
1926	NY-A	0	0	—	1	0	0	0	1	1	2	2	0	0	2	0	36.0	18.00	21	.400	.571	0	—	0	-2	-2	-0	-0.3
1928	NY-A	14	9	.609	31	22	10	1	0	199	188	107	16	12	104	110	13.7	4.30	88	.250	.351	19	.241	2	-6	-13	0	-1.1
1929	NY-A	3	3	.500	12	8	2	0	0	42^2	37	28	5	0	39	24	16.0	5.06	76	.237	.390	1	.071	-1	-4	-6	-1	-0.9
1930	NY-A	14	11	.560	44	15	7	1	2	175^1	177	112	12	2	104	115	14.5	4.67	92	.265	.366	17	.266	5	-0	-8	2	-0.3
1931	NY-A	13	8	.619	40	23	8	0	4	196^1	176	114	13	1	102	106	12.8	4.72	84	.234	.326	15	.195	2	-7	-18	-3	-1.8
1932	NY-A	2	2	.500	5	4	2	0	0	31^1	34	18	7	0	15	27	14.1	4.88	83	.266	.343	3	.231	0	-1	-3	0	-0.3
1933	Bos-A	8	6	.571	25	21	7	0	1	155^1	156	84	13	3	74	65	13.5	4.06	108	.263	.348	12	.231	3	4	5	-2	0.6
1934	Bos-A	6	8	.429	31	14	7	1	1	124^1	162	95	12	5	53	66	15.9	5.36	90	.316	.385	10	.233	1	-12	-7	-1	-0.7
1935	Bos-A	2	1	.667	13	2	0	0	1	31	41	21	3	0	14	14	16.0	5.52	86	.331	.399	0	.000	-1	-4	-2	-1	-0.4
1936	Phi-A	0	2	.000	3	3	0	0	0	11^2	16	16	4	1	10	6	20.8	7.71	66	.296	.415	1	.250	-0	-3	-3	-0	-0.4
1939	Cin-N	0	3	.000	20	0	0	0	1	31^1	30	10	1	0	13	10	12.4	2.01	191	.268	.344	2	.400	1	7	6	-1	0.6
Total	12	63	56	.529	249	116	45	4	11	1066^1	1107	665	89	32	567	568	14.4	4.75	88	.268	.361	81	.215	9	-47	-69	-6	-6.0

● JIM JOHNSON Johnson, James Brian b: 11/3/45, Muskegon, Mich. d: 12/6/87, North Muskegon, Mich. BL/TL, 5'11", 175 lbs. Deb: 4/13/70

YEAR	TM/L	W	L	PCT	G	GS	CG	SH	SV	IP	H	R	HR	HB	BB	SO	RAT	ERA	ERA+	OAV	OOB	BH	AVG	PB	PR	PR+	PD	TPI
1970	SF-N	1	0	1.000	3	0	0	0	0	6^2	8	6	0	0	5	2	17.6	8.10	49	.320	.433	0	.000	0	-3	-3	0	-0.4

● JASON JOHNSON Johnson, Jason Michael b: 10/27/73, Santa Barbara, Cal. BR/TR, 6'6", 220 lbs. Deb: 8/27/97

YEAR	TM/L	W	L	PCT	G	GS	CG	SH	SV	IP	H	R	HR	HB	BB	SO	RAT	ERA	ERA+	OAV	OOB	BH	AVG	PB	PR	PR+	PD	TPI
1997	Pit-N	0	0	—	3	0	0	0	0	6	10	4	2	0	1	3	16.5	6.00	72	.400	.423	0	.000	-0	-1	-1	-0	-0.1
1998	TB-A	2	5	.286	13	13	0	0	0	60	74	38	9	3	27	36	15.6	5.70	84	.306	.382	0	.000	-0	-7	-6	-1	-0.7
1999	Bal-A	8	7	.533	22	21	0	0	0	115^1	120	74	16	3	55	71	13.9	5.46	86	.266	.350	0	.000	-0	-8	-10	-1	-1.2
2000	Bal-A	1	10	.091	25	13	0	0	0	107^2	119	95	21	4	61	79	15.4	7.02	68	.278	.373	0	.000	-0	-25	-28	-2	-2.4
Total	4	11	22	.333	63	47	0	0	0	289	323	211	48	10	144	189	14.9	6.10	78	.282	.367	0	.000	-1	-41	-44	-5	-4.4

● **JERRY JOHNSON** Johnson, Jerry Michael b: 12/3/43, Miami, Fla. BR/TR, 6'3", 200 lbs. Deb: 7/17/68

YEAR	TM/L	W	L	PCT	G	GS	CG	SH	SV	IP	H	R	HR	HB	BB	SO	RAT	ERA	ERA+	OAV	OOB	BH	AVG	PB	PR	PR+	PD	TPI
1968	Phi-N	4	4	.500	16	11	2	0	0	80^2	82	33	5	2	29	40	12.6	3.24	93	.264	.330	2	.080	-0	-2	-2	1	-0.2
1969	Phi-N	6	13	.316	33	21	4	2	1	147^1	151	76	18	3	57	82	12.9	4.28	83	.268	.338	9	.209	2	-11	-12	-1	-1.4
1970	StL-N	2	0	1.000	7	0	0	0	1	11^1	6	4	1	0	3	5	7.1	3.18	130	.146	.205	0	.000	0	1	1	-0	0.2
	SF-N	3	4	.429	33	1	0	0	3	65^1	67	39	5	1	38	44	14.6	4.27	93	.266	.364	1	.067	-1	-2	-2	-0	-0.4
	Yr	5	4	.556	40	1	0	0	4	76^2	73	43	6	1	41	49	13.5	4.11	97	.249	.343	1	.063	-1	-0	-1	-1	-0.2
1971	*SF-N	12	9	.571	67	0	0	0	18	109	93	42	9	1	48	85	11.7	2.97	114	.230	.313	2	.154	-0	6	5	-0	1.1
1972	SF-N	8	6	.571	48	0	0	0	8	73^1	73	40	4	0	40	57	13.9	4.42	79	.261	.353	0	.000	-1	-8	-8	0	-1.6
1973	Cle-A	5	6	.455	39	1	0	0	5	59^2	70	48	7	0	39	45	16.4	6.18	63	.299	.399	0	—	0	-16	-15	0	-2.6
1974	Hou-N	2	1	.667	34	0	0	0	0	45	47	26	2	0	24	32	14.2	4.80	72	.276	.366	0	.000	-0	-6	-7	0	-0.4
1975	SD-N	3	1	.750	21	4	0	0	0	54	60	37	3	0	31	18	15.2	5.17	67	.282	.373	1	.083	-0	-9	-11	-1	-0.8
1976	SD-N	1	3	.250	24	1	0	0	0	39	39	27	0	0	26	27	15.0	5.31	62	.260	.369	0	.000	-0	-8	-9	-0	-1.0
1977	Tor-A	2	4	.333	43	0	0	0	5	86	91	50	9	0	54	54	15.2	4.60	91	.279	.382	0	—	0	-5	-4	-0	-0.3
Total	10	48	51	.485	365	39	6	2	41	770^2	779	422	63	7	389	489	13.7	4.31	83	.265	.352	15	.123	-2	-59	-62	-1	-7.4

● **JOHNNY JOHNSON** Johnson, John Clifford "Swede" b: 9/29/14, Belmore, Ohio d: 6/26/91, Iron Mountain, Mich. BL/TL, 6', 182 lbs. Deb: 4/19/44

YEAR	TM/L	W	L	PCT	G	GS	CG	SH	SV	IP	H	R	HR	HB	BB	SO	RAT	ERA	ERA+	OAV	OOB	BH	AVG	PB	PR	PR+	PD	TPI
1944	NY-A	0	2	.000	22	1	0	0	3	26^2	25	14	0	1	24	11	16.9	4.05	86	.243	.391	3	.500	1	-2	-2	-1	-0.1
1945	Chi-A	3	0	1.000	29	0	0	0	4	69^2	85	39	2	1	35	38	15.6	4.26	78	.306	.385	4	.286	2	-7	-7	-1	-0.3
Total	2	3	2	.600	51	1	0	0	7	96^1	110	53	2	2	59	49	16.0	4.20	80	.289	.387	7	.350	3	-9	-9	-2	-0.4

● **YOUNGY JOHNSON** Johnson, John Godfred b: 7/22/1877, San Francisco, Cal. d: 8/28/36, Berkeley, Cal. TR, Deb: 4/29/1897

YEAR	TM/L	W	L	PCT	G	GS	CG	SH	SV	IP	H	R	HR	HB	BB	SO	RAT	ERA	ERA+	OAV	OOB	BH	AVG	PB	PR	PR+	PD	TPI
1897	Phi-N	1	2	.333	5	2	1	0	0	29	39	24	0	2	12	7	16.4	4.66	90	.320	.390	1	.077	-2	-1	-2	-0	-0.3
1899	NY-N	0	0	—	1	0	0	0	0	2	0	0	0	0	2	1	9.0	0.00	—	.000	.250	0	.000	-0	1	1	0	0.0
Total	2	1	2	.333	6	2	1	0	0	31	39	24	0	2	14	8	16.0	4.35	96	.305	.382	1	.071	-2	-0	-1	-0	-0.3

● **JOHN HENRY JOHNSON** Johnson, John Henry b: 8/21/56, Houston, Tex. BL/TL, 6'2", 190 lbs. Deb: 4/10/78

YEAR	TM/L	W	L	PCT	G	GS	CG	SH	SV	IP	H	R	HR	HB	BB	SO	RAT	ERA	ERA+	OAV	OOB	BH	AVG	PB	PR	PR+	PD	TPI
1978	Oak-A	11	10	.524	33	30	7	2	0	186	164	81	18	0	82	91	11.9	3.39	108	.238	.319	0	—	0	8	6	-3	0.3
1979	Oak-A	2	8	.200	14	13	1	0	0	84^2	89	45	13	1	36	50	13.4	4.36	93	.269	.342	0	—	0	-1	-3	-1	-0.4
	Tex-A	2	6	.250	17	12	1	0	0	82^1	79	50	12	1	36	46	12.7	4.92	85	.255	.334	0	—	0	-6	-7	-1	-0.6
	Yr	4	14	.222	31	25	2	0	0	167	168	95	25	2	72	96	13.0	4.63	89	.262	.338	0	—	0	-8	-10	-1	-1.0
1980	Tex-A	2	2	.500	33	0	0	0	4	38^2	27	12	2	1	15	44	10.0	2.33	168	.199	.283	0	—	0	7	7	0	0.8
1981	Tex-A	3	1	.750	24	0	0	0	2	23^2	19	7	2	1	6	8	9.9	2.66	130	.232	.292	0	—	0	3	2	1	0.5
1983	Bos-A	3	2	.600	34	1	0	0	1	53^1	58	28	3	1	20	51	13.3	3.71	118	.283	.350	0	—	0	2	4	-0	0.3
1984	Bos-A	1	2	.333	30	3	0	0	1	63^2	64	26	7	0	27	57	12.9	3.53	118	.260	.333	0	—	0	3	4	-0	0.2
1986	Mil-A	2	1	.667	19	0	0	0	1	44	43	15	2	0	10	42	10.8	2.66	163	.251	.293	0	—	0	7	8	-1	0.5
1987	Mil-A	0	1	.000	10	2	0	0	0	26^1	42	30	1	0	18	18	20.5	9.57	48	.365	.451	0	—	0	-15	-14	0	-0.6
Total	8	26	33	.441	214	61	9	2	9	602^2	585	294	60	5	250	407	12.5	3.90	102	.256	.331	0	—	0	9	6	-5	1.0

● **JOHN JOHNSON** Johnson, John Louis (b: John Louis Mercer) b: 11/18/1869, Pekin, Ill. d: 1/28/41, Kansas City, Mo. TL, 5'10", 165 lbs. Deb: 9/11/1894

YEAR	TM/L	W	L	PCT	G	GS	CG	SH	SV	IP	H	R	HR	HB	BB	SO	RAT	ERA	ERA+	OAV	OOB	BH	AVG	PB	PR	PR+	PD	TPI
1894	Phi-N	1	1	.500	4	3	2	0	0	32^2	44	30	3	1	15	10	16.5	6.06	84	.319	.390	3	.188	-1	-3	-4	0	-0.2

● **JONATHAN JOHNSON** Johnson, Jonathan Kent b: 7/16/74, LaGrange, Ga. BR/TR, 6', 180 lbs. Deb: 9/27/98

YEAR	TM/L	W	L	PCT	G	GS	CG	SH	SV	IP	H	R	HR	HB	BB	SO	RAT	ERA	ERA+	OAV	OOB	BH	AVG	PB	PR	PR+	PD	TPI
1998	Tex-A	0	0	—	1	1	0	0	0	4^1	5	4	0	0	5	3	20.8	8.31	58	.313	.476	0	—	0	-2	-2	0	-0.1
1999	Tex-A	0	0	—	1	0	0	0	0	3	9	5	0	1	2	3	36.0	15.00	34	.529	.600	0	—	0	-3	-3	-0	-0.1
2000	Tex-A	1	1	.500	15	0	0	0	0	29	34	23	3	6	19	23	18.3	6.21	82	.291	.415	0	—	0	-4	-3	1	-0.1
Total	3	1	1	.500	17	1	0	0	0	36^1	48	32	3	7	26	29	20.1	7.18	71	.320	.443	0	—	0	-9	-8	1	-0.3

● **JOE JOHNSON** Johnson, Joseph Richard b: 10/30/61, Brookline, Mass. BR/TR, 6'2", 195 lbs. Deb: 7/25/85

YEAR	TM/L	W	L	PCT	G	GS	CG	SH	SV	IP	H	R	HR	HB	BB	SO	RAT	ERA	ERA+	OAV	OOB	BH	AVG	PB	PR	PR+	PD	TPI
1985	Atl-N	4	4	.500	15	14	1	0	0	85^2	95	44	9	3	24	34	12.8	4.10	94	.285	.339	1	.043	-1	-5	-2	-2	-0.4
1986	Atl-N	6	7	.462	17	15	2	0	0	87	101	58	8	2	35	49	14.3	4.97	80	.289	.358	3	.115	-1	-12	-9	2	-1.1
	Tor-A	7	2	.778	16	15	0	0	0	88	94	39	3	3	22	39	12.2	3.89	109	.281	.331	0	—	0	3	3	-1	0.2
1987	Tor-A	3	5	.375	14	14	0	0	0	66^2	77	44	10	2	18	27	13.1	5.13	88	.289	.339	0	—	0	-5	-5	-0	-0.5
Total	3	20	18	.526	62	58	3	0	0	327^1	367	185	30	10	99	149	13.1	4.48	92	.286	.342	4	.082	-2	-19	-12	-2	-1.8

● **KEN JOHNSON** Johnson, Kenneth Travis b: 6/16/33, W.Palm Beach, Fla. BR/TR, 6'4", 210 lbs. Deb: 9/13/58

YEAR	TM/L	W	L	PCT	G	GS	CG	SH	SV	IP	H	R	HR	HB	BB	SO	RAT	ERA	ERA+	OAV	OOB	BH	AVG	PB	PR	PR+	PD	TPI
1958	KC-A	0	0	—	2	0	0	0	0	2^1	6	7	1	0	3	1	34.7	27.00	14	.429	.529	0	—	0	-6	-6	0	-0.3
1959	KC-A	1	1	.500	2	2	0	0	0	11	11	6	2	0	5	8	13.1	4.09	98	.268	.348	0	.000	-0	-0	-0	0	0.0
1960	KC-A	5	10	.333	42	6	2	0	3	120^1	120	68	16	7	45	83	12.9	4.26	93	.263	.338	5	.167	-1	-5	-4	2	-0.3
1961	KC-A	0	4	.000	6	1	0	0	0	9^1	11	11	2	0	7	4	17.4	10.61	39	.297	.409	0	.000	-0	-7	-6	1	-1.1
	*Cin-N	6	2	.750	15	11	3	1	1	83	71	33	11	2	22	42	10.3	3.25	125	.229	.284	6	.240	1	7	7	1	0.9
1962	Hou-N	7	16	.304	33	31	5	1	0	197	195	100	18	7	46	178	11.3	3.84	97	.257	.305	4	.077	-3	2	-2	1	-0.4
1963	Hou-N	11	17	.393	37	32	6	1	1	224	204	86	12	8	50	148	10.5	2.65	119	.242	.291	5	.068	-4	16	13	2	1.5
1964	Hou-N	11	16	.407	35	35	7	1	0	218	209	100	15	7	44	117	10.7	3.63	94	.250	.293	6	.079	-2	-2	-5	1	-0.7
1965	Hou-N	3	2	.600	8	8	1	0	0	51^2	52	25	4	4	11	28	11.7	4.18	80	.267	.319	2	.111	-0	-4	-5	1	-0.4
	Mil-N	13	8	.619	29	26	8	1	2	179^2	165	75	15	3	37	123	10.3	3.21	110	.240	.282	7	.115	-2	7	6	-3	0.2
	Yr	16	10	.615	37	34	9	1	2	231^1	217	100	19	7	48	151	10.6	3.42	102	.246	.290	9	.114	-2	3	2	-2	-0.2
1966	Atl-N	14	8	.636	32	31	11	2	0	215^2	213	89	24	0	46	105	10.8	3.30	110	.262	.301	10	.143	0	7	8	0	0.8
1967	Atl-N	13	9	.591	29	29	6	0	0	210^1	191	78	19	7	38	85	10.1	2.74	121	.244	.285	9	.127	-0	15	14	-2	1.3
1968	Atl-N	5	8	.385	31	16	1	0	0	135	145	58	10	9	25	57	11.9	3.47	86	.279	.324	7	.175	-0	-7	-7	-1	-0.8
1969	Atl-N	0	1	.000	9	2	0	0	1	29	32	17	4	0	9	20	12.7	4.97	73	.283	.336	0	.000	-0	-4	-4	0	-0.3
	NY-A	1	2	.333	12	0	0	0	0	26	19	11	1	0	11	21	10.4	3.46	101	.202	.286	0	.000	-0	0	0	1	0.1
	Chi-N	1	2	.333	9	1	0	0	1	19	17	8	2	0	13	18	14.2	2.84	142	.230	.345	0	.000	-0	2	2	-0	0.3
1970	Mon-N	0	0	—	3	0	0	0	0	6	9	6	1	2	1	4	18.0	7.50	55	.321	.387	0	—	0	-2	-2	0	-0.1
Total	13	91	106	.462	334	231	50	7	9	1737^1	1670	778	157	56	413	1042	11.1	3.46	101	.253	.302	61	.114	-12	18	8	5	0.7

● **KEN JOHNSON** Johnson, Kenneth Wandersee "Hook" b: 1/14/23, Topeka, Kan. BL/TL, 6'1", 185 lbs. Deb: 9/18/47

YEAR	TM/L	W	L	PCT	G	GS	CG	SH	SV	IP	H	R	HR	HB	BB	SO	RAT	ERA	ERA+	OAV	OOB	BH	AVG	PB	PR	PR+	PD	TPI
1947	StL-N	1	0	1.000	2	1	1	0	0	10	2	1	0	1	5	8	7.2	0.00	—	.063	.211	2	.500	1	5	5	0	0.5
1948	StL-N	2	4	.333	13	4	0	0	0	45^1	43	27	1	1	30	20	14.7	4.76	86	.262	.379	6	.300	2	-4	-3	-0	-0.3
1949	StL-N	0	1	.000	14	2	0	0	0	33^2	29	28	1	3	35	18	17.9	6.42	65	.250	.435	2	.250	0	-9	-8	1	-0.2
1950	StL-N	0	0	—	2	0	0	0	0	2	1	1	0	0	3	1	18.0	0.00	—	.167	.444	0	—	0	1	1	0	0.1
	*Phi-N	4	1	.800	14	8	3	1	0	60^2	61	32	3	1	43	32	15.6	4.01	101	.260	.376	3	.158	-0	1	0	0	0.0
	Yr	4	1	.800	16	8	3	1	0	62^2	62	33	3	1	46	33	15.7	3.88	105	.257	.378	3	.158	-0	2	1	0	0.1
1951	Phi-N	5	8	.385	20	18	4	3	0	106^1	103	56	8	3	68	58	14.7	4.57	84	.259	.371	5	.143	-1	-7	-9	-0	-1.1
1952	Det-A	0	0	—	9	1	0	0	0	11^1	12	11	1	0	11	10	18.3	6.35	60	.273	.418	1	.333	0	-3	-3	0	-0.1
Total	6	12	14	.462	74	34	8	4	0	269^1	251	156	14	9	195	147	15.2	4.58	87	.252	.379	19	.213	1	-17	-18	1	-1.1

● **LLOYD JOHNSON** Johnson, Lloyd William "Eppa" b: 12/24/10, Santa Rosa, Cal. d: 10/8/80, Stockton, Cal. BL/TL, 6'4", 204 lbs. Deb: 4/21/34

YEAR	TM/L	W	L	PCT	G	GS	CG	SH	SV	IP	H	R	HR	HB	BB	SO	RAT	ERA	ERA+	OAV	OOB	BH	AVG	PB	PR	PR+	PD	TPI
1934	Pit-N	0	0	—	1	0	0	0	0	1	1	0	0	0	0	0	9.0	0.00	—	.333	.333	0	—	0	0	0	-0	0.0

● **MARK JOHNSON** Johnson, Mark J. b: 5/2/75, Dayton, Ohio BR/TR, 6'3", 226 lbs. Deb: 4/7/2000

YEAR	TM/L	W	L	PCT	G	GS	CG	SH	SV	IP	H	R	HR	HB	BB	SO	RAT	ERA	ERA+	OAV	OOB	BH	AVG	PB	PR	PR+	PD	TPI
2000	Det-A	0	1	.000	9	3	0	0	0	24	25	23	3	1	16	11	15.8	7.50	64	.266	.378	0	—	0	-7	-7	0	-0.3

● **MIKE JOHNSON** Johnson, Michael Keith b: 10/3/75, Edmonton, Alberta, Canada BL/TR, 6'2", 175 lbs. Deb: 4/6/97

YEAR	TM/L	W	L	PCT	G	GS	CG	SH	SV	IP	H	R	HR	HB	BB	SO	RAT	ERA	ERA+	OAV	OOB	BH	AVG	PB	PR	PR+	PD	TPI
1997	Bal-A	0	1	.000	14	5	0	0	2	39^2	52	36	12	1	16	29	15.7	7.94	56	.317	.381	0	—	0	-15	-16	-0	-0.8
	Mon-N	2	5	.286	11	11	0	0	0	50	54	34	8	0	21	28	13.5	5.94	71	.277	.347	1	.077	-1	-10	-10	0	-1.2
1998	Mon-N	0	2	.000	2	2	0	0	0	7^1	16	12	4	1	2	4	23.3	14.73	29	.432	.475	1	.333	0	-9	-9	-0	-1.2
1999	Mon-N	0	0	—	3	1	0	0	0	8^1	12	8	2	0	7	6	20.5	8.64	52	.324	.432	1	.250	0	-4	-4	0	-0.2
2000	Mon-N	5	6	.455	41	13	0	0	0	101^1	107	73	18	9	53	70	15.0	6.39	74	.269	.367	4	.182	0	-20	-19	-1	-1.7
Total	4	7	14	.333	71	32	0	0	2	206^2	241	163	44	11	99	137	15.3	6.97	65	.290	.373	7	.167	-0	-57	-57	-1	-5.1

● **MIKE JOHNSON** Johnson, Michael Norton b: 3/2/51, Slayton, Minn. BR/TR, 6'1", 185 lbs. Deb: 7/25/74

YEAR	TM/L	W	L	PCT	G	GS	CG	SH	SV	IP	H	R	HR	HB	BB	SO	RAT	ERA	ERA+	OAV	OOB	BH	AVG	PB	PR	PR+	PD	TPI
1974	SD-N	0	2	.000	18	0	0	0	0	21^1	29	13	1	1	15	15	19.0	4.64	77	.326	.429	0	—	0	-2	-3	-0	-0.2

● RANDY JOHNSON

Johnson, Randall David b: 9/10/63, Walnut Creek, Cal. BR/TL, 6'10", 225 lbs. Deb: 9/15/88

YEAR	TM/L	W	L	PCT	G	GS	CG	SH	SV	IP	H	R	HR	HB	BB	SO	RAT	ERA	ERA+	OAV	OOB	BH	AVG	PB	PR	PR+	PD	TPI
1988	Mon-N	3	0	1.000	4	4	1	0	0	26	23	8	3	0	7	25	10.4	2.42	149	.225	.275	1	.111	-0	3	3	-1	0.2
1989	Mon-N	0	4	.000	7	6	0	0	0	29^2	29	25	2	0	26	26	16.7	6.67	53	.264	.404	1	.143	-0	-10	-10	-0	-1.2
	Sea-A	7	9	.438	22	22	2	0	0	131	118	75	11	3	70	104	13.1	4.40	92	.244	.344	0	—	0	-7	-5	0	-0.5
1990	Sea-A☆	14	11	.560	33	33	5	2	0	219^2	174	103	26	5	120	194	12.3	3.65	109	.216	.321	0	—	0	7	8	-1	0.7
1991	Sea-A	13	10	.565	33	33	2	1	0	201^1	151	96	15	12	152	228	14.1	3.98	104	.213	.361	0	—	0	3	3	-1	0.3
1992	Sea-A	12	14	.462	31	31	6	2	0	210^1	154	104	13	18	144	**241**	13.5	3.77	106	**.206**	.347	0	—	0	4	5	-1	0.5
1993	Sea-A★	19	8	.704	35	34	10	3	1	255^1	185	97	22	16	99	**308**	10.6	3.24	136	**.203**	.292	0	—	0	31	33	1	3.2
1994	Sea-A★	13	6	.684	23	23	**9**	**4**	0	172	132	65	14	6	72	**204**	11.0	3.19	153	.216	.304	0	—	0	31	32	2	3.4
1995	*Sea-A★	18	2	**.900**	30	30	6	3	0	214^1	159	65	12	6	65	**294**	**9.7**	**2.48**	**191**	**.201**	**.267**	0	—	0	**53**	**54**	1	**4.6**
1996	Sea-A	5	0	1.000	14	8	0	0	1	61^1	48	27	8	2	25	85	11.0	3.67	135	.211	.294	0	—	0	9	9	0	0.7
1997	*Sea-A★	20	4	**.833**	30	29	5	2	0	213	147	60	20	10	77	291	9.9	2.28	197	**.194**	.277	0	—	0	54	53	-1	5.6
1998	Sea-A	9	10	.474	23	23	6	2	0	160	146	90	19	11	60	213	12.2	4.33	107	.240	.320	1	.143	-0	6	5	1	0.6
	*Hou-N	10	1	.909	11	11	4	4	0	84^1	57	12	4	3	26	116	9.2	1.28	317	.191	.262	2	.063	-2	28	27	-1	3.4
1999	*Ari-N★	17	9	.654	35	35	**12**	2	0	**271^2**	207	86	30	9	70	**364**	9.5	**2.48**	**184**	.208	.267	12	.124	-3	**63**	**63**	-1	5.2
2000	Ari-N★	19	7	**.731**	35	35	**8**	**3**	0	248^2	202	89	23	6	76	**347**	10.3	2.64	**175**	.224	.289	13	.157	-0	**55**	**55**	-1	5.1
Total	13	179	95	.653	366	357	76	28	2	2498^2	1932	1002	222	107	1089	3040	11.3	3.19	138	.213	.305	30	.128	-6	329	333	-2	31.8

● BOB JOHNSON

Johnson, Robert Dale b: 4/25/43, Aurora, Ill. BL/TR, 6'4", 220 lbs. Deb: 9/19/69

YEAR	TM/L	W	L	PCT	G	GS	CG	SH	SV	IP	H	R	HR	HB	BB	SO	RAT	ERA	ERA+	OAV	OOB	BH	AVG	PB	PR	PR+	PD	TPI
1969	NY-N	0	0	—	2	0	0	0	1	1^2	1	0	0	0	1	1	10.8	0.00	—	.167	.286	0	—	0	1	1	-0	0.1
1970	KC-A	8	13	.381	40	26	10	1	4	214	178	82	18	11	82	206	11.4	3.07	122	.228	.310	6	.105	-1	15	16	-1	1.3
1971	*Pit-N	9	10	.474	31	27	7	1	0	174^2	170	73	19	7	55	101	12.0	3.45	98	.259	.323	3	.063	-1	0	-1	-1	-0.4
1972	*Pit-N	4	4	.500	31	11	1	0	3	115^2	98	40	14	4	46	79	11.5	2.96	112	.231	.312	5	.143	-0	6	5	-2	0.1
1973	Pit-N	4	2	.667	50	2	0	0	4	92	98	41	12	5	34	68	13.4	3.62	97	.276	.348	0	.000	-1	1	-1	-2	-0.4
1974	Cle-A	3	4	.429	14	10	0	0	0	72	75	42	12	3	37	36	14.4	4.38	83	.273	.365	0	—	0	-6	-6	-0	-0.6
1977	Atl-N	0	1	.000	15	0	0	0	0	22^1	24	18	7	2	14	16	16.1	7.25	61	.270	.381	1	.333	0	-8	-6	-1	-0.3
Total	7	28	34	.452	183	76	18	2	12	692^1	644	296	82	32	269	507	12.3	3.48	102	.249	.327	15	.096	-4	9	6	-7	-0.2

● ROY JOHNSON

Johnson, Roy "Hardrock" b: 10/1/1895, Madill, Okla. d: 1/10/86, Scottsdale, Ariz. BR/TR, 6', 185 lbs. Deb: 8/7/18 MC

YEAR	TM/L	W	L	PCT	G	GS	CG	SH	SV	IP	H	R	HR	HB	BB	SO	RAT	ERA	ERA+	OAV	OOB	BH	AVG	PB	PR	PR+	PD	TPI
1918	Phi-A	1	5	.167	10	8	3	0	0	50	47	32	0	2	34	12	14.9	3.42	86	.254	.376	1	.067	-2	-4	-3	-0	-0.5

● JING JOHNSON

Johnson, Russell Conwell b: 10/9/1894, Parker Ford, Pa. d: 12/6/50, Pottstown, Pa. BR/TR, 5'9", 172 lbs. Deb: 6/27/16

YEAR	TM/L	W	L	PCT	G	GS	CG	SH	SV	IP	H	R	HR	HB	BB	SO	RAT	ERA	ERA+	OAV	OOB	BH	AVG	PB	PR	PR+	PD	TPI
1916	Phi-A	2	9	.182	12	12	8	0	0	84^1	90	46	3	0	39	25	13.8	3.74	76	.288	.368	2	.074	-1	-8	-8	3	-0.8
1917	Phi-A	9	12	.429	34	23	13	0	0	191	184	76	3	5	56	55	11.5	2.78	99	.260	.319	12	.203	2	-2	-1	2	0.4
1919	Phi-A	9	15	.375	34	25	12	0	0	202	222	106	8	3	62	67	12.8	3.61	95	.291	.346	14	.194	0	-9	-4	5	0.1
1927	Phi-A	4	2	.667	17	3	2	0	0	51^2	42	20	2	4	16	16	10.8	3.48	122	.235	.312	2	.167	-0	4	4	1	0.5
1928	Phi-A	0	0	—	3	0	0	0	0	10^2	13	8	1	0	5	3	15.2	5.06	79	.310	.383	2	.500	1	-1	-1	0	0.0
Total	5	24	38	.387	100	63	35	0	0	539^2	551	256	17	12	178	166	12.4	3.35	95	.275	.338	32	.184	2	-17	-9	10	0.2

● SI JOHNSON

Johnson, Silas Kenneth b: 10/5/06, Danway, Ill. d: 5/12/94, Sheridan, Ill. BR/TR, 5'11.5", 185 lbs. Deb: 5/2/28

YEAR	TM/L	W	L	PCT	G	GS	CG	SH	SV	IP	H	R	HR	HB	BB	SO	RAT	ERA	ERA+	OAV	OOB	BH	AVG	PB	PR	PR+	PD	TPI
1928	Cin-N	0	0	—	3	0	0	0	0	10^1	9	5	0	0	5	1	12.2	4.35	91	.250	.341	1	.250	0	-0	-0	-0	0.0
1929	Cin-N	0	0	—	1	0	0	0	0	2	2	1	0	0	1	0	13.5	4.50	101	.250	.333	0	—	0	0	0	-0	0.0
1930	Cin-N	3	1	.750	35	3	0	0	0	78^1	86	54	5	4	31	47	13.9	4.94	98	.286	.360	4	.235	-0	0	-1	-0	-0.1
1931	Cin-N	11	19	.367	42	33	14	0	0	262^1	273	131	5	6	74	95	12.1	3.77	99	.269	.323	13	.149	-3	3	-1	-5	-0.9
1932	Cin-N	13	15	.464	42	27	14	2	2	245	246	109	8	2	57	94	11.2	3.27	118	.259	.302	10	.125	-4	17	16	-0	1.3
1933	Cin-N	7	18	.280	34	28	14	4	1	211^1	212	101	7	3	54	51	11.5	3.49	97	.263	.312	3	.042	-7	-4	-2	-1	-1.1
1934	Cin-N	7	22	.241	46	31	9	0	3	215^2	264	150	15	7	84	89	14.8	5.22	78	.297	.362	10	.139	-3	-28	-27	-3	-3.7
1935	Cin-N	5	11	.313	30	20	4	1	0	130	155	106	14	3	59	40	15.0	6.23	64	.293	.367	1	.024	-4	-32	-33	-1	-3.8
1936	Cin-N	0	0	—	2	0	0	0	0	4	7	6	1	0	0	2	15.8	13.50	28	.368	.368	0	—	0	-4	-5	-0	-0.2
	StL-N	5	3	.625	12	9	3	1	0	61^2	82	30	4	1	11	21	13.7	4.38	90	.314	.344	4	.190	-0	-2	-3	-1	-0.5
	Yr	5	3	.625	14	9	3	1	0	65^2	89	36	5	1	11	23	13.8	4.93	80	.318	.346	4	.190	-0	-7	-7	-1	-0.7
1937	StL-N	12	12	.500	38	21	12	1	1	192^1	222	92	14	1	43	64	12.4	3.32	120	.292	.330	9	.138	-3	13	14	-2	1.1
1938	StL-N	0	3	.000	6	3	0	0	0	15^2	27	17	0	0	6	4	19.0	7.47	53	.380	.429	0	.000	-0	-6	-6	0	-0.9
1940	Phi-N	5	14	.263	37	14	5	0	1	138^1	145	81	13	2	42	58	12.3	4.88	80	.268	.323	6	.140	-2	-16	-15	-2	-2.2
1941	Phi-N	5	12	.294	39	21	6	1	2	163^1	207	91	8	1	54	80	14.4	4.52	82	.309	.362	7	.149	-2	-16	-15	-1	-1.7
1942	Phi-N	8	19	.296	39	26	10	1	0	195^1	198	96	6	1	72	78	12.5	3.69	90	.266	.332	6	.103	-4	-8	-8	-3	-1.7
1943	Phi-N	8	3	.727	21	14	9	1	2	113	110	48	4	0	25	46	10.8	3.27	103	.252	.292	6	.182	0	1	1	-0	0.1
1946	Phi-N	0	0	—	1	0	0	0	0	3	7	4	1	0	0	2	21.0	3.00	114	.538	.538	1	1.000	0	0	0	-0	0.0
	Bos-N	6	5	.545	28	12	5	1	1	127	134	47	8	4	35	41	12.3	2.76	124	.272	.325	5	.135	-2	9	9	-1	0.5
	Yr	6	5	.545	29	12	5	1	1	130	141	51	9	4	35	43	12.5	2.77	124	.279	.330	6	.158	-1	9	9	-1	0.5
1947	Bos-N	6	8	.429	36	10	3	0	2	112^2	124	57	7	1	34	27	12.7	4.23	92	.275	.327	1	.033	-3	-2	-4	3	-0.5
Total	17	101	165	.380	492	272	108	13	15	2281^1	2510	1226	120	36	687	840	12.8	4.09	92	.279	.333	87	.123	-37	-76	-79	-17	-14.3

● SYL JOHNSON

Johnson, Sylvester W (Born Sylvester Johnson)
b: 12/31/1900, Portland, Ore. d: 2/20/85, Portland, Ore. BR/TR, 5'11", 180 lbs. Deb: 4/24/22 C

YEAR	TM/L	W	L	PCT	G	GS	CG	SH	SV	IP	H	R	HR	HB	BB	SO	RAT	ERA	ERA+	OAV	OOB	BH	AVG	PB	PR	PR+	PD	TPI
1922	Det-A	7	3	.700	29	8	3	0	0	97	99	52	7	4	30	29	12.3	3.71	105	.273	.336	8	.222	-0	4	2	-2	0.0
1923	Det-A	12	7	.632	37	18	7	0	0	176^1	181	82	12	3	47	93	11.8	3.98	97	.274	.325	10	.161	-1	0	-2	-5	-0.8
1924	Det-A	5	4	.556	29	9	2	0	3	104	117	63	8	5	42	55	14.2	4.93	83	.287	.360	7	.206	-0	-8	-10	-1	-0.9
1925	Det-A	0	2	.000	6	0	0	0	0	13	11	7	1	0	10	5	14.5	3.46	124	.250	.389	0	.000	-1	1	1	0	0.1
1926	StL-N	0	3	.000	19	6	1	0	1	49	54	27	3	2	15	10	13.0	4.22	92	.297	.357	0	.000	-2	-2	-2	-1	-0.3
1927	StL-N	0	0	—	2	0	0	0	0	3	3	2	1	0	0	2	9.0	6.00	66	.250	.250	0	—	0	-1	-1	0	0.0
1928	*StL-N	8	4	.667	34	6	2	0	3	120	117	53	6	4	33	66	11.6	3.90	103	.259	.315	6	.158	-0	1	1	-1	0.0
1929	StL-N	13	7	.650	42	19	12	3	3	182^1	186	88	11	7	56	80	12.3	3.60	129	.265	.325	7	.117	-2	23	22	-4	1.4
1930	*StL-N	12	10	.545	32	24	9	2	2	187^2	215	105	13	4	38	92	12.3	4.65	108	.293	.332	15	.214	-0	7	8	-3	0.4
1931	*StL-N	11	9	.550	32	24	12	2	2	186	186	73	9	2	29	82	10.5	3.00	131	.255	.286	14	.233	2	18	19	-3	1.8
1932	StL-N	5	14	.263	32	22	7	0	2	164^2	199	103	14	4	35	70	13.0	4.92	80	.299	.338	10	.196	-1	-19	-18	-1	-2.0
1933	StL-N	3	3	.500	35	1	0	0	3	84	89	45	7	3	16	28	11.6	4.29	81	.271	.311	5	.238	0	-9	-7	-2	-0.7
1934	Cin-N	0	0	—	2	0	0	0	0	6^2	9	6	2	0	0	0	12.2	2.70	151	.310	.310	1	.500	1	1	1	-0	0.1
	Phi-N	5	9	.357	42	10	4	3	3	133^2	122	58	14	1	24	54	9.9	3.50	135	.242	.277	8	.195	-1	8	16	-4	1.1
	Yr	5	9	.357	44	10	4	3	3	140^1	131	64	16	1	24	54	10.0	3.46	136	.245	.279	9	.209	1	9	17	-4	1.2
1935	Phi-N	10	8	.556	37	18	8	1	6	174^2	182	79	15	3	31	89	11.1	3.56	128	.265	.299	14	.241	1	9	17	-3	1.5
1936	Phi-N	5	7	.417	39	8	1	0	7	111	129	60	10	3	29	48	13.1	4.30	106	.288	.335	9	.250	-0	-3	3	-2	0.1
1937	Phi-N	4	10	.286	32	15	4	0	3	138	155	81	19	2	22	46	11.7	5.02	86	.288	.318	7	.146	-3	-17	-10	-1	-1.2
1938	Phi-N	2	7	.222	22	6	2	0	0	83	87	43	4	0	11	21	10.6	4.23	92	.267	.291	1	.034	-3	-4	-3	-2	-0.8
1939	Phi-N	8	8	.500	22	13	6	0	2	111	112	50	10	1	15	37	10.4	3.81	105	.264	.291	5	.152	-1	1	2	-1	0.1
1940	Phi-N	2	2	.500	17	2	2	0	2	40^2	37	22	6	0	5	13	9.3	4.20	93	.236	.259	0	.000	-1	-2	-1	-0	-0.3
Total	19	112	117	.489	542	209	82	11	43	2165^2	2290	1099	172	48	488	920	11.7	4.06	104	.273	.316	127	.181	-10	8	41	-36	-0.4

● TOM JOHNSON

Johnson, Thomas Raymond b: 4/2/51, St.Paul, Minn. BR/TR, 6'1", 185 lbs. Deb: 9/10/74

YEAR	TM/L	W	L	PCT	G	GS	CG	SH	SV	IP	H	R	HR	HB	BB	SO	RAT	ERA	ERA+	OAV	OOB	BH	AVG	PB	PR	PR+	PD	TPI
1974	Min-A	2	0	1.000	4	0	0	0	1	7	4	1	0	0	0	4	5.1	0.00	—	.167	.167	0	—	0	3	3	-0	0.6
1975	Min-A	1	2	.333	18	0	0	0	3	38^2	40	23	4	2	21	17	14.7	4.19	92	.263	.360	0	—	0	-2	-2	-0	-0.1
1976	Min-A	3	1	.750	18	1	0	0	0	48^1	44	14	2	0	8	37	9.7	2.61	137	.243	.275	0	—	0	5	5	0	0.4
1977	Min-A	16	7	.696	71	0	0	0	15	146^2	152	57	11	5	47	87	12.5	3.13	128	.272	.334	0	—	0	15	14	1	2.5
1978	Min-A	1	4	.200	18	0	0	0	3	32^2	42	22	2	2	17	21	16.8	5.51	70	.318	.404	0	—	0	-6	-6	0	-0.9
Total	5	23	14	.622	129	1	0	0	22	273^1	282	117	19	9	93	166	12.6	3.39	114	.269	.334	0	—	0	15	15	1	2.5

● VIC JOHNSON

Johnson, Victor Oscar b: 8/3/20, Eau Claire, Wis. BR/TL, 6', 160 lbs. Deb: 5/3/44

YEAR	TM/L	W	L	PCT	G	GS	CG	SH	SV	IP	H	R	HR	HB	BB	SO	RAT	ERA	ERA+	OAV	OOB	BH	AVG	PB	PR	PR+	PD	TPI
1944	Bos-A	0	3	.000	7	5	0	0	0	27^1	42	22	0	0	15	7	18.8	6.26	54	.362	.435	0	.000	-1	-9	-9	1	-0.9
1945	Bos-A	6	4	.600	26	9	4	1	2	85^1	90	41	4	2	46	21	14.6	4.01	85	.276	.369	5	.167	-1	-6	-6	1	-0.7
1946	Cle-A	0	1	.000	9	1	0	0	0	13^2	20	14	1	0	8	3	18.4	9.22	36	.357	.438	0	.000	-0	-9	-10	1	-0.6
Total	3	6	8	.429	42	15	4	1	2	126^1	152	77	5	2	69	31	15.9	5.06	67	.305	.392	5	.119	-3	-23	-23	2	-2.2

YEAR	TM/L	W	L	PCT	G	GS	CG	SH	SV	IP	H	R	HR	HB	BB	SO	RAT	ERA	ERA+	OAV	OOB	BH	AVG	PB	PR	PR+	PD	TPI
● WALTER JOHNSON	Johnson, Walter Perry "Barney" or "The Big Train" b: 11/6/1887, Humboldt, Kan. d: 12/10/46, Washington, D.C. BR/TR, 6'1", 200 lbs. Deb: 8/2/07 MH ♦																											
1907	Was-A	5	9	.357	14	12	11	2	0	110^1	100	35	1	2	20	71	10.0	1.88	129	.244	.282	4	.111	-2	8	7	-2	0.5
1908	Was-A	14	14	.500	36	30	23	6	1	256^1	194	75	0	11	53	160	9.1	1.65	139	.211	.262	13	.165	3	21	19	-4	2.1
1909	Was-A	13	25	.342	40	36	27	4	1	296^1	247	112	1	15	84	164	10.5	2.22	110	.221	.284	13	.129	-3	9	7	-2	0.4
1910	Was-A	25	17	.595	**45**	42	**38**	8	1	**370**	262	92	1	13	76	**313**	8.5	1.36	183	.205	.257	24	.175	1	48	47	-1	5.8
1911	Was-A	25	13	.658	40	37	**36**	**6**	1	322^1	292	119	8	8	70	207	10.3	1.90	173	.238	.283	30	.234	3	**52**	**51**	4	6.5
1912	Was-A	33	12	.733	50	37	34	7	2	369	259	89	2	16	76	**303**	**8.6**	**1.39**	**240**	**.196**	**.248**	38	.264	9	**79**	**79**	1	**11.1**
1913	Was-A	**36**	7	**.837**	48	36	**29**	**11**	2	**346**	232	56	9	9	38	**243**	**7.3**	**1.14**	**258**	**.187**	**.217**	35	.261	10	**69**	**69**	0	**10.8**
1914	Was-A	**28**	18	.609	**51**	40	**33**	**9**	1	**371^2**	287	88	3	11	74	**225**	9.0	1.72	164	.217	.265	30	.221	8	42	44	2	**7.1**
1915	Was-A	**27**	13	.675	47	39	**35**	**7**	4	**336^2**	258	83	1	19	56	**203**	**8.9**	1.55	**192**	.214	**.260**	34	.231	6	**52**	**52**	2	**7.7**
1916	Was-A	**25**	20	.556	48	38	**36**	3	1	**369^2**	290	105	0	9	82	**228**	9.3	1.90	147	.220	.270	32	.225	8	38	37	-5	5.2
1917	Was-A	23	16	.590	47	34	30	8	3	326	248	105	3	14	68	**188**	9.1	2.21	119	.211	.263	33	.254	10	16	15	-1	3.0
1918	Was-A	**23**	13	.639	39	29	29	**8**	3	326	241	71	2	8	70	**162**	**8.8**	**1.27**	**215**	.210	**.260**	40	.267	6	**55**	**54**	-3	**7.8**
1919	Was-A	20	14	.588	39	29	27	**7**	2	290^1	235	73	0	7	51	**147**	9.1	**1.49**	**216**	**.219**	**.259**	24	.192	2	**56**	**56**	0	**7.2**
1920	Was-A	8	10	.444	21	15	12	4	3	143^2	135	68	5	5	27	78	10.5	3.13	119	.245	.286	17	.266	4	11	10	-1	1.4
1921	Was-A	17	14	.548	35	32	25	1	1	264	265	122	7	2	92	**143**	12.2	3.51	117	.263	.326	30	.270	4	23	18	-3	2.0
1922	Was-A	15	16	.484	41	31	23	4	4	280	283	115	8	7	99	105	12.5	2.99	129	.267	.334	22	.204	-1	33	29	1	2.9
1923	Was-A	17	12	.586	42	34	18	3	4	261	263	112	9	20	73	**130**	12.3	3.48	108	.269	.333	18	.194	1	15	9	-2	0.8
1924	*Was-A	**23**	7	**.767**	38	38	20	**6**	0	277^2	233	97	10	10	77	**158**	**10.4**	**2.72**	148	**.224**	**.284**	32	.283	7	**47**	42	-1	**4.7**
1925	*Was-A	20	7	.741	30	29	16	3	0	229	217	95	7	7	78	108	11.9	3.07	138	**.250**	.317	42	.433	17	34	31	-4	**4.5**
1926	Was-A	15	16	.484	33	33	22	2	0	260^2	259	120	13	5	73	125	11.6	3.63	107	.263	.317	20	.194	1	11	7	-5	0.4
1927	Was-A	5	6	.455	18	15	7	1	0	107^2	113	70	7	7	26	48	12.2	5.10	80	.278	.332	16	.348	6	-11	-13	0	-0.5
Total	21	417	279	.599	802	666	531	110	34	5914^1	4913	1902	97	205	1363	3509	9.9	2.17	147	.227	.279	547	.235	99	706	680	-23	91.4
● BILL JOHNSON	Johnson, William Charles b: 10/6/60, Wilmington, Del. BR/TR, 6'5", 205 lbs. Deb: 9/6/83																											
1983	Chi-N	1	0	1.000	10	0	0	0	0	12^1	17	6	0	0	3	4	14.6	4.38	87	.347	.385	0	—	0	-1	-1	0	0.0
1984	Chi-N	0	0	—	4	0	0	0	0	5^1	4	1	0	0	1	3	8.4	1.69	232	.235	.278	0	—	0	1	1	0	0.1
Total	2	1	0	1.000	14	0	0	0	0	17^2	21	7	0	0	4	7	12.7	3.57	108	.318	.357	0	—	0	0	0	1	0.1
● JEFF JOHNSON	Johnson, William Jeffrey b: 8/4/66, Durham, N.C. BR/TL, 6'3", 200 lbs. Deb: 6/5/91																											
1991	NY-A	6	11	.353	23	23	0	0	0	127	156	89	15	6	33	62	13.8	5.95	70	.305	.354	0	—	0	-26	-25	1	-2.8
1992	NY-A	2	3	.400	13	8	0	0	0	52^2	71	44	4	2	23	14	16.4	6.66	59	.329	.398	0	—	0	-16	-16	-0	-1.3
1993	NY-A	0	2	.000	2	2	0	0	0	2^2	12	10	1	0	2	0	47.3	30.38	14	.600	.636	0	—	0	-8	-8	-0	-1.2
Total	3	8	16	.333	38	33	0	0	0	182^1	239	143	20	8	58	76	15.1	6.52	63	.320	.375	0	—	0	-50	-49	1	-5.3
● JOEL JOHNSTON	Johnston, Joel Raymond b: 3/8/67, West Chester, Pa. BR/TR, 6'4", 220 lbs. Deb: 9/5/91																											
1991	KC-A	1	0	1.000	13	0	0	0	0	22^1	9	1	0	0	9	21	7.3	0.40	1024	.120	.214	0	—	0	9	9	-0	0.5
1992	KC-A	0	0	—	5	0	0	0	0	2^2	3	4	2	0	2	0	16.9	13.50	30	.273	.385	0	—	0	-3	-3	-0	-0.1
1993	Pit-N	2	4	.333	33	0	0	0	2	53^1	38	20	7	0	19	31	9.6	3.38	120	.203	.277	2	.333	1	4	4	-1	0.5
1994	Pit-N	0	0	—	4	0	0	0	0	3^1	14	12	0	2	4	5	54.0	29.70	15	.583	.667	0	—	0	-9	-9	-0	-0.4
1995	Bos-A	0	1	.000	4	0	0	0	0	4	2	5	1	1	3	4	13.5	11.25	43	.143	.333	0	—	0	-3	-3	-0	-0.5
Total	5	3	5	.375	59	0	0	0	2	85^2	66	42	10	3	37	61	11.1	4.31	96	.212	.302	2	.333	1	-2	-2	-1	-0.0
● JOHN JOHNSTONE	Johnstone, John William b: 11/25/68, Liverpool, N.Y. BR/TR, 6'3", 195 lbs. Deb: 9/3/93																											
1993	Fla-N	0	2	.000	7	0	0	0	0	10^2	16	8	1	0	7	5	19.4	5.91	73	.340	.426	0	—	0	-2	-2	-0	-0.3
1994	Fla-N	1	2	.333	17	0	0	0	0	21^1	23	20	4	1	16	23	16.9	5.91	74	.264	.385	0	—	0	-4	-4	0	-0.4
1995	Fla-N	0	0	—	4	0	0	0	0	4^2	7	2	1	0	2	3	17.4	3.86	109	.333	.391	0	—	0	0	0	-0	0.0
1996	Hou-N	1	0	1.000	9	0	0	0	0	13	17	8	2	0	5	5	15.2	5.54	70	.321	.379	0	—	0	-2	-3	-0	-0.2
1997	SF-N	0	0	—	10	0	0	0	0	16^2	12	4	0	4	6	14	11.9	2.16	189	.218	.338	0	.000	-0	4	4	0	0.2
	Oak-A	0	0	—	5	0	0	0	0	6^1	7	2	0	0	7	4	19.9	2.84	159	.292	.452	0	—	0	1	1	-0	0.0
	SF-N	0	0	—	3	0	0	0	0	2	3	3	1	0	1	1	18.0	13.50	30	.333	.400	0	—	0	-2	-2	-0	-0.1
1998	SF-N	6	5	.545	70	0	0	0	0	88	72	32	10	1	38	86	11.4	3.07	129	.224	.307	0	.000	-0	11	9	-1	0.9
1999	SF-N	4	6	.400	62	0	0	0	3	65^2	48	24	8	1	20	56	9.5	2.60	161	.203	.267	0	—	0	14	13	0	1.8
2000	SF-N	3	4	.429	47	0	0	0	0	50	64	35	11	2	13	37	14.2	6.30	67	.322	.369	0	.000	-0	-9	-13	0	-1.5
Total	8	15	19	.441	234	0	0	0	3	278^1	269	138	38	9	115	234	12.7	4.01	103	.255	.334	0	.000	-1	12	4	-1	0.4
● ROY JOINER	Joiner, Roy Merrill "Pop" b: 10/30/06, Red Bluff, Cal. d: 12/26/89, Red Bluff, Cal. BL/TL, 6', 170 lbs. Deb: 4/30/34																											
1934	Chi-N	0	1	.000	20	2	0	0	0	34	61	33	3	0	8	9	18.3	8.21	47	.391	.421	2	.200	-0	-16	-17	-0	-0.9
1935	Chi-N	0	0	—	2	0	0	0	0	3^1	6	4	0	0	2	0	21.6	5.40	73	.429	.500	0	.000	-0	-1	-1	0	0.0
1940	NY-N	3	2	.600	30	2	0	0	1	53	66	26	8	5	17	25	14.9	3.40	114	.308	.373	3	.273	1	3	3	0	0.3
Total	3	3	3	.500	52	4	0	0	1	90^1	133	63	11	5	27	34	16.4	5.28	74	.346	.397	5	.227	0	-13	-14	0	-0.6
● DAVE JOLLY	Jolly, David "Gabby" b: 10/14/24, Stony Point, N.C. d: 5/27/63, Durham, N.C. BR/TR, 6', 165 lbs. Deb: 5/9/53																											
1953	Mil-N	0	1	.000	24	0	0	0	0	38^1	34	16	4	1	27	23	14.6	3.52	111	.239	.365	1	.500	1	3	2	0	0.2
1954	Mil-N	11	6	.647	47	1	0	0	10	111^1	87	36	6	2	64	62	12.4	2.43	154	.215	.326	9	.290	3	20	18	0	3.2
1955	Mil-N	2	3	.400	36	0	0	0	1	58^1	58	42	6	1	51	23	17.0	5.71	66	.258	.397	1	.167	0	-11	-14	1	-1.0
1956	Mil-N	2	3	.400	29	0	0	0	7	45^2	39	21	7	0	35	20	14.6	3.74	92	.228	.359	0	.000	-0	0	-2	-1	-0.3
1957	Mil-N	1	1	.500	23	0	0	0	1	37^2	37	22	4	3	21	27	14.6	5.02	70	.264	.372	3	.600	1	-5	-7	0	-0.2
Total	5	16	14	.533	159	1	0	0	19	291^1	255	137	27	7	198	155	14.2	3.77	98	.236	.357	14	.292	5	8	-3	0	1.9
● COWBOY JONES	Jones, Albert Edward "Bronco" b: 8/23/1874, Golden, Colo. d: 2/9/58, Inglewood, Cal. BL/TL, 5'11", 160 lbs. Deb: 6/24/1898																											
1898	Cle-N	4	4	.500	9	9	7	0	0	72	76	44	0	4	29	26	13.6	3.00	121	.269	.345	2	.071	-3	5	5	-2	0.0
1899	StL-N	6	5	.545	12	12	9	0	0	85^1	111	51	1	6	22	28	14.7	3.59	111	.314	.364	5	.172	0	3	4	2	0.6
1900	StL-N	13	19	.406	39	36	29	3	0	292^2	334	185	10	19	82	68	13.4	3.57	102	.286	.343	21	.179	-3	4	2	5	0.4
1901	StL-N	2	6	.250	10	9	7	0	0	76^1	97	51	4	3	22	25	14.4	4.48	71	.307	.358	4	.148	0	-10	-12	2	-0.8
Total	4	25	34	.424	70	66	52	3	0	526^1	618	331	15	32	155	147	13.8	3.63	100	.292	.349	32	.159	-5	2	-0	6	0.2
● ALEX JONES	Jones, Alexander b: 12/25/1869, Pittsburgh, Pa. d: 4/4/41, Woodville, Pa. BL/TL, 5'6", 135 lbs. Deb: 9/25/1889																											
1889	Pit-N	1	0	1.000	1	1	1	0	0	9	7	5	0	0	1	10	8.0	3.00	125	.206	.229	1	.200	0	1	1	0	0.1
1892	Lou-N	5	11	.313	18	16	13	1	0	146^2	130	90	3	9	56	44	12.0	3.31	93	.228	.307	8	.145	-1	-0	-4	2	-0.3
	Was-N	0	3	.000	4	4	3	0	0	27	33	23	0	2	14	7	16.3	4.00	81	.289	.377	3	.273	0	-2	-2	-1	-0.2
	Yr	5	14	.263	22	20	16	1	0	173^2	163	113	3	11	70	51	12.6	3.42	91	.238	.319	11	.167	-1	-3	-7	1	-0.5
1894	Phi-N	1	0	1.000	1	1	1	0	0	9	10	4	0	0	0	2	10.0	2.00	255	.278	.278	1	.250	-0	3	3	0	0.3
1903	Det-A	0	1	.000	2	2	0	0	0	8^2	19	15	0	0	6	2	26.0	12.46	23	.432	.500	0	.000	-1	-9	-9	-0	-0.8
Total	4	7	15	.318	26	24	18	1	0	200^1	199	137	3	11	77	65	12.9	3.73	86	.249	.324	13	.165	-1	-7	-12	1	-0.9
● AL JONES	Jones, Alfornia b: 2/10/59, Charleston, Miss. BR/TR, 6'4", 210 lbs. Deb: 8/6/83																											
1983	Chi-A	0	0	—	2	0	0	0	0	2^1	3	1	0	0	2	2	19.3	3.86	109	.375	.500	0	—	0	0	0	-0	0.0
1984	Chi-A	1	1	.500	20	0	0	0	5	20^1	23	10	3	1	11	15	15.5	4.43	94	.299	.393	0	—	0	-1	-1	0	-0.1
1985	Chi-A	1	0	1.000	5	0	0	0	0	6	3	2	0	0	3	2	9.0	1.50	288	.167	.286	0	—	0	2	2	0	0.3
Total	3	2	1	.667	27	0	0	0	5	28^2	29	13	3	1	16	19	14.4	3.77	112	.282	.383	0	—	0	1	1	0	0.2
● ART JONES	Jones, Arthur Lennox b: 2/7/06, Kershaw, S.C. d: 11/25/80, Columbia, S.C. BR/TR, 6', 165 lbs. Deb: 4/23/32																											
1932	Bro-N	0	0	—	1	0	0	0	0	1	2	2	0	0	1	0	27.0	18.00	21	.667	.750	0	—	0	-2	-2	0	-0.1
● BARRY JONES	Jones, Barry Louis b: 2/15/63, Centerville, Ind. BR/TR, 6'4", 225 lbs. Deb: 7/18/86																											
1986	Pit-N	3	4	.429	26	0	0	0	3	37^1	29	16	3	0	21	29	12.1	2.89	133	.215	.321	1	.200	0	3	4	1	0.8
1987	Pit-N	2	4	.333	32	0	0	0	1	43^1	55	34	6	0	23	28	16.2	5.61	73	.314	.394	0	.000	-0	-7	-7	0	-0.9
1988	Pit-N	1	1	.500	42	0	0	0	2	56^1	57	21	3	1	21	31	12.6	3.04	112	.271	.341	0	.000	-0	3	2	0	0.1
	Chi-A	2	2	.500	17	0	0	0	1	26	15	7	3	0	17	17	11.1	2.42	164	.170	.305	0	—	0	4	4	0	0.7
1989	Chi-A	3	2	.600	22	0	0	0	1	30^1	22	12	2	1	8	17	9.2	2.37	161	.208	.270	0	—	0	5	5	1	0.9

YEAR	TM/L	W	L	PCT	G	GS	CG	SH	SV	IP	H	R	HR	HB	BB	SO	RAT	ERA	ERA+	OAV	OOB	BH	AVG	PB	PR	PR+	PD	TPI
1990	Chi-A	11	4	.733	65	0	0	0	1	74	62	20	2	1	33	45	11.7	2.31	166	.235	.322	0	—	0	13	13	2	2.7
1991	Mon-N	4	9	.308	**77**	0	0	0	13	88^2	76	35	8	1	33	46	11.2	3.35	108	.246	.321	0	.000	-0	3	3	1	0.5
1992	Phi-N	5	6	.455	44	0	0	0	0	54^1	65	30	3	2	24	19	15.1	4.64	75	.305	.381	0	.000	-0	-7	-7	1	-1.3
	NY-N	2	0	1.000	17	0	0	0	1	15^1	20	16	0	0	11	11	18.2	9.39	37	.317	.419	0	—	0	-10	-10	0	-1.3
	Yr	7	6	.538	61	0	0	0	1	69^2	85	46	3	2	35	30	15.8	5.68	61	.308	.390	0	.000	-0	-17	-17	1	-2.6
1993	Chi-A	0	1	.000	6	0	0	0	0	7^1	14	8	2	0	3	7	20.9	8.59	49	.412	.459	0	—	0	-3	-4	-0	-0.4
Total	8	33	33	.500	348	0	0	0	23	433	415	199	32	6	194	250	12.8	3.66	102	.260	.342	1	.063	-1	5	3	5	1.8
● **CALVIN JONES**	Jones, Calvin Douglas b: 9/26/63, Compton, Cal. BR/TR, 6'3", 185 lbs. Deb: 6/14/91																											
1991	Sea-A	2	2	.500	27	0	0	0	2	46^1	33	14	0	1	29	42	12.2	2.53	163	.209	.335	0	—	0	8	8	0	0.8
1992	Sea-A	3	5	.375	38	1	0	0	0	61^2	50	39	8	2	47	49	14.4	5.69	70	.226	.367	0	—	0	-12	-12	-0	-1.4
Total	2	5	7	.417	65	1	0	0	2	108	83	53	8	3	76	91	13.5	4.33	93	.219	.354	0	—	0	-4	-3	0	-0.6
● **DEACON JONES**	Jones, Carroll Elmer b: 12/20/1892, Arcadia, Kan. d: 12/28/52, Pittsburg, Kan. BR/TR, 6'1", 174 lbs. Deb: 9/23/16																											
1916	Det-A	0	0	—	1	0	0	0	0	7	7	3	0	0	5	2	15.4	2.57	111	.269	.387	0	.000	-0	0	0	-0	0.0
1917	Det-A	4	4	.500	24	6	2	0	0	77	69	34	0	6	26	28	11.8	2.92	91	.256	.334	0	.000	-1	-2	-2	1	-0.2
1918	Det-A	3	2	.600	21	4	1	0	0	67	60	35	0	1	38	15	13.3	3.09	86	.244	.347	5	.185	-1	-2	-3	1	-0.2
Total	3	7	6	.538	46	10	3	0	0	151	136	72	0	7	69	45	12.6	2.98	89	.251	.343	5	.114	-2	-4	-5	2	-0.4
● **BUMPUS JONES**	Jones, Charles Leander b: 1/1/1870, Cedarville, Ohio d: 6/25/38, Xenia, Ohio BR/TR, Deb: 10/15/1892																											
1892	Cin-N	1	0	1.000	1	1	1	0	0	9	0	1	0	0	4	3	4.0	0.00	—	.000	.129	0	.000	-0	3	3	-1	0.3
1893	Cin-N	1	3	.250	6	5	2	0	0	28^2	37	37	1	5	23	6	20.4	10.05	48	.303	.433	4	.250	1	-17	-16	-1	-1.5
	NY-N	0	1	.000	1	1	0	0	0	4	5	5	0	1	10	1	36.0	11.25	41	.294	.571	0	—	0	-3	-3	1	-0.4
	Yr	1	4	.200	7	6	2	0	0	32^2	42	42	1	6	33	7	22.3	10.19	47	.302	.455	4	.250	1	-20	-19	-0	-1.9
Total	2	2	4	.333	8	7	3	0	0	41^2	42	43	1	6	37	10	18.4	7.99	56	.253	.407	4	.222	1	-17	-16	-1	-1.6
● **CHARLEY JONES**	Jones, Charles Wesley "Baby" (b: Benjamin Wesley Rippay) b: 4/30/1850, Alamance Co., N.C. BR/TR, 5'11.5", 202 lbs. Deb: 5/4/1875 U♦																											
1887	NY-a	0	0	—	2	0	0	0	0	3	6	2	0	0	4	0	18.0	3.00	142	.545	.545	75	.290	0	0	0	-0	0.0
● **DALE JONES**	Jones, Dale Eldon "Nubs" b: 12/17/18, Marquette, Neb. d: 11/8/80, Orlando, Fla. BR/TR, 6'1", 172 lbs. Deb: 9/7/41																											
1941	Phi-N	0	1	.000	2	1	0	0	0	8^1	13	11	0	0	6	2	20.5	7.56	49	.342	.432	1	.333	0	-4	-4	-1	-0.3
● **JACK JONES**	Jones, Daniel Albion "Jumping Jack" b: 10/23/1860, Litchfield, Conn. d: 10/19/36, Wallingford, Conn. TR, Deb: 7/9/1883																											
1883	Det-N	6	5	.545	12	12	9	1	0	92^2	103	63	0		19	33	11.8	3.50	89	.259	.293	8	.190	-2	-4	-4	-2	-0.6
	Phi-a	5	2	.714	7	7	7	0	0	65	58	38	1		6	28	8.9	2.63	135	.223	.241	6	.240	-0	5	6	-0	0.5
Total	1	11	7	.611	19	19	16	1	0	157^2	161	101	1		25	61	10.6	3.14	105	.245	.273	14	.209	-2	1	2	-2	-0.1
● **DICK JONES**	Jones, Decatur Poindexter b: 5/22/02, Meadville, Miss. d: 8/2/94, Burlingame, Cal. BL/TR, 6', 184 lbs. Deb: 9/11/26																											
1926	Was-A	2	1	.667	4	3	1	0	0	21	20	10	0	0	11	3	13.3	4.29	90	.263	.356	2	.200	-0	-1	-1	0	-0.1
1927	Was-A	0	0	—	2	0	0	0	0	3^1	8	11	0	0	5	1	35.1	21.60	19	.444	.565	0	—	0	-6	-7	-0	-0.3
Total	2	2	1	.667	6	3	1	0	0	24^1	28	21	0	0	16	4	16.3	6.66	58	.298	.400	2	.200	-0	-7	-8	-0	-0.4
● **DOUG JONES**	Jones, Douglas Reid b: 6/24/57, Lebanon, Ind. BR/TR, 6'2", 195 lbs. Deb: 4/9/82																											
1982	Mil-A	0	0	—	4	0	0	0	0	2^2	5	3	1	0	1	1	20.3	10.13	37	.385	.429	0	—	0	-2	-2	0	-0.1
1986	Cle-A	1	0	1.000	11	0	0	0	1	18	18	5	0	1	6	12	12.5	2.50	166	.257	.325	0	—	0	3	3	0	0.2
1987	Cle-A	6	5	.545	49	0	0	0	8	91^1	101	45	4	6	24	87	12.9	3.15	144	.281	.336	0	—	0	13	14	1	1.8
1988	Cle-A★	3	4	.429	51	0	0	0	37	83^1	69	26	1	2	16	72	9.4	2.27	182	.218	.260	0	—	0	16	17	0	2.7
1989	Cle-A★	7	10	.412	59	0	0	0	32	80^2	76	25	4	1	13	65	10.0	2.34	169	.251	.284	0	—	0	14	14	1	3.1
1990	Cle-A☆	5	5	.500	66	0	0	0	43	84^1	66	26	5	2	22	55	9.6	2.56	153	.218	.275	0	—	0	13	13	-1	2.4
1991	Cle-A	4	8	.333	36	4	0	0	7	63^1	87	42	7	0	17	48	14.8	5.54	75	.320	.360	0	—	0	-10	-10	1	-1.7
1992	Hou-N★	11	8	.579	80	0	0	0	36	111^2	96	29	5	5	17	93	9.5	1.85	182	.235	.274	0	.000	-0	21	20	-1	4.2
1993	Hou-N	4	10	.286	71	0	0	0	26	85^1	102	46	7	5	21	66	13.5	4.54	85	.298	.348	0	—	0	-5	-7	-0	-1.3
1994	Phi-N★	2	4	.333	47	0	0	0	27	54	55	14	2	0	6	38	10.2	2.17	198	.255	.275	1	1.000	0	12	**13**	0	2.4
1995	Bal-A	0	4	.000	52	0	0	0	22	46^2	55	30	6	2	16	42	14.1	5.01	95	.286	.348	0	—	0	-2	-1	0	-0.2
1996	Chi-N	2	2	.500	28	0	0	0	2	32^1	41	20	4	1	7	26	13.6	5.01	87	.306	.345	0	—	0	-3	-2	-0	-0.3
	Mil-A	5	0	1.000	24	0	0	0	1	31^2	31	13	3	2	13	34	13.1	3.41	152	.254	.336	0	—	0	6	6	0	0.8
1997	Mil-A	6	6	.500	75	0	0	0	36	80^1	62	20	4	3	9	82	8.3	2.02	229	.215	.246	0	—	0	23	23	-0	4.5
1998	Mil-N	3	4	.429	46	0	0	0	12	54	65	32	15	4	11	43	13.3	5.17	83	.298	.343	0	.000	-0	-6	-5	0	-0.8
	*Cle-A	1	2	.333	23	0	0	0	1	31^1	34	12	2	0	6	28	11.5	3.45	138	.279	.313	0	—	0	4	5	1	0.4
1999	Oak-A	5	5	.500	70	0	0	0	10	104	106	43	10	3	24	63	11.5	3.55	131	.267	.314	0	—	0	15	13	-1	1.2
2000	*Oak-A	4	2	.667	54	0	0	0	2	73^1	86	34	6	2	18	54	13.0	3.93	121	.292	.337	0	—	0	8	7	0	0.5
Total	16	69	79	.466	846	4	0	0	303	1128^1	1155	465	86	39	247	909	11.5	3.30	129	.264	.309	1	.143	0	122	120	0	19.8
● **EARL JONES**	Jones, Earl Leslie "Lefty" b: 6/11/19, Fresno, Cal. d: 1/24/89, Fresno, Cal. BL/TL, 5'10.5", 190 lbs. Deb: 7/6/45																											
1945	StL-A	0	0	—	10	0	0	0	1	28^1	18	10	0	0	18	13	11.4	2.54	139	.184	.310	2	.200	1	3	3	-1	0.2
● **ELIJAH JONES**	Jones, Elijah Albert "Bumpus" b: 1/27/1882, Oxford, Mich. d: 4/29/43, Pontiac, Mich. BR/TR, 5'11.5", Deb: 4/13/07																											
1907	Det-A	0	1	.000	4	1	1	0	1	16	23	15	0	1	4	9	15.8	5.06	51	.338	.384	0	.000	-1	-4	-4	-0	-0.4
1909	Det-A	1	1	.500	2	2	0	0	0	10	10	3	0	0	0	2	9.0	2.70	93	.278	.278	1	.250	0	-0	-0	-0	-0.1
Total	2	1	2	.333	6	3	1	0	1	26	33	18	0	1	4	11	13.2	4.15	62	.317	.349	1	.125	-0	-5	-4	-1	-0.5
● **GARY JONES**	Jones, Gareth Howell b: 6/12/45, Huntington Park, Cal. BL/TL, 6', 191 lbs. Deb: 9/25/70 F																											
1970	NY-A	0	0	—	2	0	0	0	0	2	3	0	0	0	1	2	18.0	0.00	—	.375	.444	0	—	0	1	1	-0	0.0
1971	NY-A	0	0	—	12	0	0	0	0	14	19	14	1	0	7	10	16.7	9.00	36	.317	.388	0	.000	-0	-9	-10	-0	-0.5
Total	2	0	0	—	14	0	0	0	0	16	22	14	1	0	8	12	16.9	7.88	42	.324	.395	0	.000	-0	-8	-9	-0	-0.5
● **GORDON JONES**	Jones, Gordon Bassett b: 4/2/30, Portland, Ore. d: 4/25/94, Lodi, Cal. BR/TR, 6', 190 lbs. Deb: 8/6/54 C																											
1954	StL-N	4	4	.500	11	10	4	2	0	81	78	25	3	1	19	48	10.9	2.00	206	.248	.293	3	.125	-1	19	19	-0	1.7
1955	StL-N	1	4	.200	15	9	0	0	0	57	66	38	10	1	28	46	15.0	5.84	70	.286	.365	1	.071	-1	-11	-11	-1	-1.0
1956	StL-N	0	2	.000	5	1	0	0	0	11^1	14	9	2	0	5	6	15.1	5.56	68	.311	.380	0	.000	-0	-2	-2	0	-0.4
1957	NY-N	0	1	.000	10	0	0	0	0	11^2	16	9	1	1	3	5	15.4	6.17	64	.320	.370	1	.500	0	-3	-3	-1	-0.2
1958	SF-N	3	1	.750	11	1	0	0	1	30^1	33	11	2	1	5	8	11.6	2.37	161	.284	.320	0	.000	-1	5	5	1	0.6
1959	SF-N	3	2	.600	31	0	0	0	2	43^2	45	23	6	1	19	29	13.4	4.33	88	.280	.359	0	.000	-0	-2	-3	-0	-0.4
1960	Bal-A	1	1	.500	29	0	0	0	2	55	59	28	9	1	13	30	11.9	4.42	86	.281	.326	2	.400	1	-3	-4	0	-0.1
1961	Bal-A	0	0	—	3	0	0	0	1	5	5	3	3	0	0	4	9.0	5.40	71	.250	.250	0	—	0	-1	-1	-0	-0.1
1962	KC-A	3	2	.600	21	0	0	0	6	32^2	31	23	10	0	14	28	12.4	6.34	67	.252	.328	0	.000	-1	-9	-7	-0	-1.3
1964	Hou-N	0	1	.000	34	0	0	0	0	50	58	24	3	0	14	28	13.0	4.14	83	.290	.336	1	.250	0	-3	-4	-0	-0.2
1965	Hou-N	0	0	—	1	0	0	0	0	1	0	0	0	0	0	0	0.0	0.00	—	.000	.000	0	—	0	0	0	-0	0.0
Total	11	15	18	.455	171	21	4	2	12	378^2	405	193	49	6	120	232	12.6	4.16	94	.275	.332	8	.119	-3	-10	-11	-2	-1.4
● **HENRY JONES**	Jones, Henry "Baldy" b: Pittsburgh, Pa. Deb: 4/22/1890																											
1890	Pit-N	2	1	.667	5	4	2	0	0	31	35	25	1	0	14	13	14.2	3.48	95	.276	.348	2	.222	-0	0	-1	-1	-0.1
● **JIMMY JONES**	Jones, James Condia b: 4/20/64, Dallas, Tex. BR/TR, 6'2", 190 lbs. Deb: 9/21/86																											
1986	SD-N	2	0	1.000	3	3	1	1	0	18	10	6	1	0	3	15	6.5	2.50	147	.164	.203	1	.167	-0	2	2	-0	0.2
1987	SD-N	9	7	.563	30	22	2	1	0	145^2	154	85	14	5	54	51	13.2	4.14	96	.270	.339	8	.163	1	-1	-3	1	0.0
1988	SD-N	9	14	.391	29	29	3	0	0	179	192	98	14	3	44	82	12.0	4.12	82	.277	.323	9	.164	2	-13	-15	1	-1.4
1989	NY-A	2	1	.667	11	6	0	0	0	48	56	29	7	2	16	25	13.9	5.25	74	.293	.354	0	—	0	-7	-7	1	-0.3
1990	NY-A	1	2	.333	17	7	0	0	0	50	72	42	8	1	23	25	17.3	6.30	63	.344	.412	0	—	0	-13	-13	-1	-0.7
1991	Hou-N	6	8	.429	26	22	1	1	0	135^1	143	73	9	3	51	88	13.1	4.39	80	.270	.337	7	.184	2	-11	-14	1	-1.0
1992	Hou-N	10	6	.625	25	23	0	0	0	139^1	135	64	13	5	39	69	11.6	4.07	83	.258	.315	6	.167	2	-9	-11	-1	-1.1

YEAR TM/L	W	L	PCT	G	GS	CG	SH	SV	IP	H	R	HR	HB	BB	SO	RAT	ERA	ERA+	OAV	OOB	BH	AVG	PB	PR	PR+	PD	TPI
1993 Mon-N	4	1	.800	12	6	0	0	0	39^2	47	34	6	0	9	21	12.7	6.35	66	.285	.322	1	.111	0	-10	-9	-0	-1.0
Total 8	43	39	.524	153	118	7	3	0	755	809	431	72	19	239	376	12.7	4.46	82	.275	.333	32	.166	7	-62	-71	3	-5.3
● JIM JONES Jones, James Tilford "Sheriff" b: 12/25/1876, London, Ky. d: 5/6/53, London, Ky. BR/TR, 5'10", 162 lbs. Deb: 6/29/1897 ◆																											
1897 Lou-N	0	0	—	1	0	0	0	0	6^2	19	22	1	2	5	0	35.1	18.90	23	.500	.578	1	.250	1	-11	-11	-0	-0.4
1901 NY-N	0	1	.000	1	1	1	0	0	5	6	6	0	0	2	3	14.4	10.80	31	.300	.364	19	.209	0	-4	-4	-0	-0.5
Total 2	0	1	.000	2	1	1	0	0	11^2	25	28	1	2	7	3	26.2	15.43	25	.431	.507	79	.230	1	-15	-15	-0	-0.9
● JEFF JONES Jones, Jeffrey Allen b: 7/29/56, Detroit, Mich. BR/TR, 6'3", 210 lbs. Deb: 4/10/80																											
1980 Oak-A	1	3	.250	35	0	0	0	5	44^1	32	21	2	1	26	34	12.0	2.84	133	.204	.321	0	—	0	6	5	1	0.6
1981 *Oak-A	4	1	.800	33	0	0	0	3	61	51	27	7	3	40	43	13.9	3.39	103	.233	.359	0	—	0	2	1	-1	0.0
1982 Oak-A	3	1	.750	18	2	0	0	0	37	44	29	6	1	26	18	17.3	5.11	77	.306	.415	0	—	0	-4	-5	-0	-0.5
1983 Oak-A	1	1	.500	13	1	0	0	0	29^2	43	19	7	2	8	14	16.1	5.76	67	.339	.387	0	—	0	-6	-7	-0	-0.4
1984 Oak-A	0	3	.000	13	0	0	0	0	33	31	14	4	0	12	19	11.7	3.55	106	.258	.326	0	—	0	2	1	-0	0.1
Total 5	9	9	.500	112	3	0	0	8	205	201	110	26	7	112	128	14.0	3.95	94	.262	.361	0	—	0	-0	-5	-0	-0.2
● BROADWAY JONES Jones, Jesse Frank b: 11/15/1898, Millsboro, Del. d: 9/7/77, Lewes, Del. BR/TR, 5'9", 154 lbs. Deb: 7/4/23																											
1923 Phi-N	0	0	—	3	0	0	0	0	8	5	8	0	0	7	1	13.5	9.00	51	.185	.353	1	.500	0	-4	-3	-0	-0.2
● JOHNNY JONES Jones, John Paul "Admiral" b: 8/25/1892, Arcadia, La. d: 6/5/80, Ruston, La. BR/TR, 6'1", 151 lbs. Deb: 4/24/19																											
1919 NY-N	0	0	—	2	0	0	0	1	6^2	9	4	0	1	3	3	17.6	5.40	52	.310	.394	0	.000	-0	-2	-2	0	-0.1
1920 Bos-N	1	0	1.000	3	1	0	0	0	9^2	16	7	1	0	5	6	19.6	6.52	47	.372	.438	1	.250	1	-4	-4	0	-0.3
Total 2	1	0	1.000	5	1	0	0	1	16^1	25	11	1	1	8	9	18.7	6.06	49	.347	.420	1	.143	0	-5	-6	0	-0.4
● STACY JONES Jones, Joseph Stacy b: 5/26/67, Gadsden, Ala. BR/TR, 6'6", 225 lbs. Deb: 7/30/91																											
1991 Bal-A	0	0	—	4	1	0	0	0	11	11	6	1	0	5	10	13.1	4.09	97	.256	.333	0	—	0	0	-0	0	0.0
1996 Chi-A	0	0	—	2	0	0	0	0	2	0	0	0	0	1	1	4.5	0.00	—	.000	.143	0	—	0	1	1	-0	0.0
Total 2	0	0	—	6	1	0	0	0	13	11	6	1	0	6	11	11.8	3.46	118	.224	.309	0	—	0	1	1	0	0.0
● KEN JONES Jones, Kenneth Frederick "Broadway" b: 4/13/03, Dover, N.J. d: 5/15/91, Hartford, Conn. BR/TR, 6'3", 193 lbs. Deb: 5/19/24																											
1924 Det-A	0	0	—	1	0	0	0	0	2	1	0	0	0	1	0	9.0	0.00	—	.143	.250	0	—	0	1	1	-0	0.0
1930 Bos-N	0	1	.000	8	1	0	0	0	19^2	28	16	1	0	4	4	14.6	5.95	83	.359	.390	1	.200	-0	-2	-2	0	-0.1
Total 2	0	1	.000	9	1	0	0	0	21^2	29	16	1	0	5	4	14.1	5.40	90	.341	.378	1	.200	-0	-1	-1	0	-0.1
● MARCUS JONES Jones, Marcus Ray b: 3/29/75, Bellflower, Cal. BR/TR, 6'5", 235 lbs. Deb: 7/17/2000																											
2000 Oak-A	0	0	—	1	1	0	0	0	2^1	5	4	1	0	3	1	30.9	15.43	31	.417	.533	0	.000	-0	-3	-3	-0	-0.1
● MIKE JONES Jones, Michael b: 7/6/1865, Hamilton, Ont., Canada d: 3/24/1894, Hamilton, Ont., Canada BL/TL, 5'11.5", 168 lbs. Deb: 8/12/1890																											
1890 Lou-a	2	0	1.000	3	3	2	0	0	22	21	12	2	0	9	6	12.3	3.27	118	.244	.316	4	.444	2	1	1	-0	0.2
● MIKE JONES Jones, Michael Carl b: 7/30/59, Penfield, N.Y. BL/TL, 6'6", 215 lbs. Deb: 9/6/80																											
1980 KC-A	0	1	.000	3	1	0	0	0	4^2	6	7	0	0	5	2	21.2	11.57	35	.333	.478	0	—	0	-4	-4	-0	-0.7
1981 *KC-A	6	3	.667	12	11	0	0	0	75^2	74	30	7	2	28	29	12.4	3.21	112	.256	.326	0	—	0	4	3	0	0.4
1984 *KC-A	2	3	.400	23	12	0	0	0	81	86	48	10	1	36	43	13.7	4.89	83	.270	.346	0	—	0	-8	-8	-1	-0.5
1985 KC-A	3	3	.500	33	1	0	0	0	64	62	40	6	0	39	32	14.2	4.78	87	.257	.361	0	—	0	-4	-4	-0	-0.4
Total 4	11	10	.524	71	25	0	0	0	225^1	228	125	23	3	108	106	13.5	4.43	89	.263	.347	0	—	0	-13	-13	-1	-1.2
● ODELL JONES Jones, Odell b: 1/13/53, Tulare, Cal. BR/TR, 6'3", 175 lbs. Deb: 9/11/75																											
1975 Pit-N	0	0	—	2	0	0	0	0	3	1	0	0	0	0	2	3.0	0.00	—	.100	.100	0	—	0	1	1	-0	0.1
1977 Pit-N	3	7	.300	34	15	1	0	0	108	118	63	14	3	31	66	12.7	5.08	78	.278	.332	4	.143	-1	-14	-13	-1	-1.4
1978 Pit-N	2	0	1.000	3	1	0	0	0	9	7	3	0	0	4	10	11.0	2.00	185	.206	.289	0	.000	-0	2	2	-0	0.4
1979 Sea-A	3	11	.214	25	19	3	0	0	118^2	151	90	16	3	58	72	16.1	6.07	72	.317	.395	0	—	0	-24	-22	-2	-2.3
1981 Pit-N	4	5	.444	13	8	0	0	0	54^1	51	23	3	0	23	30	12.3	3.31	109	.250	.326	2	.200	-0	1	2	0	0.3
1983 Tex-A	3	6	.333	42	0	0	0	10	67	56	28	4	2	22	50	10.7	3.09	130	.223	.291	0	—	0	7	7	-1	1.0
1984 Tex-A	2	4	.333	33	0	0	0	2	59^1	62	28	7	2	23	28	13.2	3.64	114	.281	.354	0	—	0	3	3	1	0.4
1986 Bal-A	2	2	.500	21	0	0	0	0	49^1	58	22	4	0	23	32	14.8	3.83	108	.305	.380	0	—	0	2	2	-0	0.1
1988 Mil-A	5	0	1.000	28	2	0	0	1	80^2	75	47	8	1	29	48	11.7	4.35	92	.251	.319	0	—	0	-3	-3	-1	-0.3
Total 9	24	35	.407	201	45	4	0	13	549^1	579	304	56	11	213	338	13.2	4.42	92	.275	.344	6	.154	-1	-26	-22	-5	-1.7
● OSCAR JONES Jones, Oscar Winfield "Flip Flap" b: 1/21/1879, London Grove, Pa. d: 10/8/46, Perkasie, Pa. BR/TR, 5'7", 163 lbs. Deb: 4/20/03																											
1903 Bro-N	19	14	.576	38	36	31	4	0	324^1	320	159	4	19	77	95	11.5	2.94	109	.260	.313	32	.256	3	12	9	-3	0.8
1904 Bro-N	17	25	.405	46	41	38	0	0	377	387	175	7	17	92	96	11.8	2.75	100	.270	.321	24	.175	-1	-0	0	-7	-0.8
1905 Bro-N	8	15	.348	29	20	14	0	1	174	197	121	6	9	56	66	13.6	4.66	62	.285	.347	13	.200	-0	-32	-35	-4	-4.4
Total 3	44	54	.449	113	97	83	4	1	875^1	904	455	17	45	225	257	12.1	3.20	92	.269	.324	69	.211	2	-20	-25	-14	-4.4
● PERCY JONES Jones, Percy Lee b: 10/28/1899, Harwood, Tex. d: 3/18/79, Dallas, Tex. BR/TL, 5'11.5", 175 lbs. Deb: 8/6/20																											
1920 Chi-N	0	0	—	4	0	0	0	0	7	15	10	1	1	3	0	24.4	11.57	28	.455	.514	0	.000	-0	-7	-6	-0	-0.4
1921 Chi-N	3	5	.375	32	3	1	0	0	98^2	116	57	2	4	39	46	14.5	4.56	84	.295	.365	6	.222	-0	-9	-8	-2	-0.8
1922 Chi-N	8	9	.471	44	24	7	2	1	162	197	104	10	5	68	45	15.0	4.78	88	.314	.385	4	.085	-4	-12	-10	0	-1.3
1925 Chi-N	6	6	.500	28	13	6	1	0	124	123	74	12	5	71	60	14.4	4.65	93	.263	.366	6	.154	-3	-5	-4	2	-0.4
1926 Chi-N	12	7	.632	30	20	10	2	2	160^1	151	64	3	5	90	80	13.8	3.09	125	.256	.359	13	.260	3	13	13	-1	1.6
1927 Chi-N	7	8	.467	30	11	5	1	0	112^2	123	67	3	6	72	37	16.1	4.07	95	.285	.394	14	.350	3	-2	-3	2	0.1
1928 Chi-N	10	6	.625	39	19	9	1	3	154	167	80	4	7	56	41	13.4	4.03	95	.288	.358	11	.196	-0	-1	-3	-0	-0.4
1929 Bos-N	7	15	.318	35	22	11	1	1	188^1	219	112	15	4	84	69	14.7	4.64	101	.298	.373	9	.148	-3	2	1	1	-0.1
1930 Pit-N	0	1	.000	9	2	0	0	0	19	26	20	3	3	11	3	18.9	6.63	75	.329	.430	0	.000	-0	-4	-3	-1	-0.2
Total 9	53	57	.482	251	114	49	8	6	1026	1137	588	53	40	494	381	14.7	4.34	95	.289	.374	63	.194	-5	-24	-24	1	-1.9
● RANDY JONES Jones, Randall Leo b: 1/12/50, Fullerton, Cal. BR/TL, 6', 178 lbs. Deb: 6/16/73																											
1973 SD-N	7	6	.538	20	19	6	1	0	139^2	129	58	13	1	37	77	10.8	3.16	110	.241	.291	8	.167	0	8	5	0	0.5
1974 SD-N	8	22	.267	40	34	4	1	2	208^1	217	118	16	5	78	124	13.0	4.45	80	.270	.339	10	.154	-1	-19	-21	2	-2.6
1975 SD-N★	20	12	.625	37	36	18	6	0	285	242	94	17	0	56	103	**9.4**	**2.24**	**155**	.232	.271	11	.133	-1	44	41	5	**5.2**
1976 SD-N★	**22**	14	.611	40	40	**25**	5	0	**315^1**	274	109	15	4	50	93	**9.4**	2.74	120	.234	**.267**	6	.058	-6	27	20	8	2.5
1977 SD-N	6	12	.333	27	25	1	0	0	147^1	173	85	12	0	36	44	12.8	4.58	77	.291	.332	5	.116	-1	-11	-19	4	-1.7
1978 SD-N	13	14	.481	37	36	7	2	0	253	263	104	6	0	64	71	11.6	2.88	116	.272	.317	15	.183	1	20	14	2	1.7
1979 SD-N	11	12	.478	39	39	6	0	0	263	257	120	17	3	64	112	11.1	3.63	97	.259	.306	15	.174	0	3	-3	4	0.2
1980 SD-N	5	13	.278	24	24	4	3	0	154^1	165	71	14	0	29	53	11.3	3.91	88	.276	.310	3	.067	-3	-5	-8	3	-0.9
1981 NY-N	1	8	.111	13	12	0	0	0	59^1	65	48	8	1	38	14	15.8	4.85	72	.274	.377	2	.118	-1	-9	-9	2	-1.2
1982 NY-N	7	10	.412	28	20	2	1	0	107^2	130	68	11	4	51	44	15.5	4.60	79	.304	.384	4	.148	0	-12	-11	3	-1.3
Total 10	100	123	.448	305	285	73	19	2	1933	1915	875	129	18	503	735	11.3	3.42	101	.260	.309	79	.132	-12	46	8	32	2.4
● BOBBY JONES Jones, Robert Joseph b: 2/10/70, Fresno, Cal. BR/TR, 6'4", 225 lbs. Deb: 8/14/93																											
1993 NY-N	2	4	.333	9	9	0	0	0	61^2	61	35	6	2	22	35	12.4	3.65	110	.262	.331	1	.050	-2	3	3	-0	0.1
1994 NY-N	12	7	.632	24	24	1	1	0	160	157	75	10	4	56	80	12.2	3.15	133	.257	.324	5	.109	-2	19	18	2	2.1
1995 NY-N	10	10	.500	30	30	3	1	0	195^2	209	107	20	7	53	127	12.4	4.19	97	.274	.327	9	.161	-1	-0	-3	-0	-0.4
1996 NY-N	12	8	.600	31	31	3	1	0	195^2	219	102	26	3	46	116	12.3	4.42	91	.288	.331	7	.117	-1	-4	-9	0	-0.8
1997 NY-N★	15	9	.625	30	30	2	1	0	193^1	177	88	24	2	63	125	11.3	3.63	111	.242	.304	8	.129	-0	12	9	2	1.2
1998 NY-N	9	9	.500	30	30	0	0	0	195^1	192	94	23	8	53	115	11.7	4.05	102	.262	.319	9	.188	1	4	2	1	0.4
1999 NY-N	3	3	.500	12	9	0	0	0	59^1	69	37	3	2	11	31	12.4	5.61	78	.295	.332	5	.313	2	-7	-8	-0	-0.5
2000 *NY-N	11	6	.647	27	27	1	0	0	154^2	171	90	25	5	49	85	13.1	5.06	87	.281	.339	2	.045	-3	-7	-12	-2	-1.5
Total 8	74	56	.569	193	190	10	4	0	1215^2	1255	628	137	33	353	714	12.1	4.13	100	.269	.325	46	.131	-5	20	1	2	0.6
● BOBBY JONES Jones, Robert Mitchell b: 4/11/72, Orange, N.J. BR/TL, 6', 185 lbs. Deb: 5/18/97																											
1997 Col-N	1	1	.500	4	4	0	0	0	19^1	30	18	2	0	12	5	19.6	8.38	62	.380	.462	1	.200	0	-9	-6	-0	-0.5

YEAR	TM/L	W	L	PCT	G	GS	CG	SH	SV	IP	H	R	HR	HB	BB	SO	RAT	ERA	ERA+	OAV	OOB	BH	AVG	PB	PR	PR+	PD	TPI
1998	Col-N	7	8	.467	35	20	1	0	0	141^{1}	153	87	12	6	66	109	14.3	5.22	99	.282	.366	8	.178	-1	-15	-1	-1	-0.2
1999	Col-N	6	10	.375	30	20	0	0	0	112^{1}	132	91	24	6	77	74	17.2	6.33	92	.292	.402	4	.148	-1	-22	-5	-2	-0.8
2000	NY-N	0	1	.000	11	1	0	0	0	21^{2}	18	11	2	3	14	20	14.5	4.15	106	.222	.357	1	.500	1	1	1	0	0.1
Total	4	14	20	.412	80	45	1	0	0	294^{2}	333	207	40	15	169	208	15.8	5.77	93	.288	.386	14	.177	-1	-45	-11	-2	-1.4
● **SAM JONES** Jones, Samuel "Toothpick Sam" b: 12/14/25, Stewartsville, Ohio d: 11/5/71, Morgantown, W.Va. BR/TR, 6'4", 200 lbs. Deb: 9/22/51																												
1951	Cle-A	0	1	.000	2	1	0	0	0	8^{2}	4	2	0	0	5	4	9.3	2.08	182	.143	.273	0	.000	-0	2	2	-0	0.1
1952	Cle-A	2	3	.400	14	4	0	0	1	36	38	30	6	4	37	28	19.8	7.25	46	.270	.434	1	.100	-1	-14	-17	-1	-2.2
1955	Chi-N★	14	20	.412	36	34	12	4	0	241^{2}	175	118	22	14	185	**198**	13.9	4.10	100	**.206**	.357	14	.182	-2	-2	-0	-0	-0.2
1956	Chi-N	9	14	.391	33	28	8	2	0	188^{2}	155	93	21	8	115	**176**	13.3	3.91	96	.221	.338	10	.175	0	-3	-3	-1	-0.4
1957	StL-N	12	9	.571	28	27	10	2	0	182^{2}	164	77	17	6	71	154	11.9	3.60	110	.239	.316	10	.159	-1	6	7	0	0.7
1958	StL-N	14	13	.519	35	35	14	2	0	250	204	95	23	6	107	**225**	11.4	2.88	143	.223	.309	9	.100	-6	30	**33**	-0	2.8
1959	SF-N★	**21**	15	.583	50	35	16	**4**	4	270^{2}	232	99	18	8	109	209	11.6	**2.83**	135	**.228**	.307	11	.129	-2	**34**	31	-2	**3.6**
1960	SF-N	18	14	.563	39	35	13	3	0	234	200	112	18	4	91	190	11.3	3.19	109	.230	.306	16	.200	1	15	8	-2	1.0
1961	SF-N	8	8	.500	37	17	2	0	1	128^{1}	134	72	12	8	57	105	14.0	4.49	85	.264	.348	5	.139	-1	-7	-10	-2	-1.4
1962	Det-A	2	4	.333	30	6	1	0	1	81^{1}	77	39	13	2	35	73	12.6	3.65	111	.254	.335	2	.095	-1	3	4	-0	0.2
1963	StL-N	2	0	1.000	11	0	0	0	2	11	15	12	0	0	5	8	16.4	9.00	39	.319	.385	0	.000	0	-7	-6	-0	-1.2
1964	Bal-A	0	0	—	7	0	0	0	0	10^{1}	5	3	1	0	5	6	8.7	2.61	137	.152	.263	0	—	0	1	1	-0	0.1
Total	12	102	101	.502	322	222	76	17	9	1643^{1}	1403	752	151	60	822	1376	12.5	3.59	108	.230	.328	78	.149	-11	58	51	-8	3.1
● **SAM JONES** Jones, Samuel Pond "Sad Sam" b: 7/26/1892, Woodsfield, Ohio d: 7/6/66, Barnesville, Ohio BR/TR, 6', 170 lbs. Deb: 6/13/14																												
1914	Cle-A	0	0	—	1	0	0	0	0	3^{1}	2	1	0	0	2	0	10.8	2.70	107	.200	.333	1	.500	0	0	0	0	0.0
1915	Cle-A	4	9	.308	48	9	2	0	4	145^{2}	131	78	0	1	63	42	12.0	3.65	84	.252	.334	5	.156	-0	-11	-9	0	-0.8
1916	Bos-A	0	1	.000	12	0	0	0	1	27	25	14	0	0	10	7	11.7	3.67	76	.272	.343	2	.333	0	-3	-3	-0	-0.1
1917	Bos-A	0	1	.000	9	1	0	0	1	16^{1}	15	9	1	0	6	5	11.6	4.41	59	.259	.328	0	.000	-1	-3	-3	1	-0.3
1918	*Bos-A	16	5	**.762**	24	21	16	5	0	184	151	66	1	8	70	44	11.2	2.25	119	.230	.312	10	.175	2	11	9	-1	1.1
1919	Bos-A	12	20	.375	35	31	21	5	1	245	258	120	4	7	95	67	13.2	3.75	81	.278	.350	11	.136	-0	-14	-21	3	-2.3
1920	Bos-A	13	16	.448	37	33	21	3	0	274	302	143	9	4	79	86	12.6	3.94	93	.288	.340	20	.217	1	-4	-9	-1	-0.9
1921	Bos-A	23	16	.590	40	38	25	**5**	1	298^{2}	318	122	1	6	78	98	12.1	3.22	131	.279	.329	24	.240	5	35	34	-3	4.1
1922	*NY-A	13	13	.500	45	28	20	0	**8**	260	270	132	16	3	76	81	12.1	3.67	109	.275	.329	23	.264	8	11	10	-1	1.6
1923	*NY-A	21	8	.724	39	27	18	3	4	243	239	114	11	6	69	68	11.6	3.63	109	.257	.312	19	.224	2	10	8	1	1.2
1924	NY-A	9	6	.600	36	21	8	3	3	178^{2}	187	85	6	1	76	53	13.3	3.63	115	.276	.350	9	.176	-0	12	11	-1	0.7
1925	NY-A	15	21	.417	43	31	14	1	2	246^{2}	267	147	14	3	104	92	13.6	4.63	92	.281	.354	13	.162	-3	-7	-10	0	-1.5
1926	*NY-A	9	8	.529	39	23	6	1	5	161	186	104	6	4	80	69	15.1	4.98	77	.298	.381	10	.204	1	-17	-21	-1	-2.1
1927	StL-A	8	14	.364	30	26	11	0	0	189^{2}	211	121	13	3	102	72	15.0	4.32	101	.282	.371	6	.109	-2	-4	1	-2	-0.3
1928	Was-A	17	7	.708	30	27	19	4	0	224^{2}	209	89	5	3	78	63	11.6	2.84	141	.252	.319	20	.253	6	30	29	1	3.6
1929	Was-A	9	9	.500	24	24	8	1	0	153^{2}	156	80	5	3	49	36	12.2	3.92	108	.264	.324	8	.157	0	5	5	-1	0.4
1930	Was-A	15	7	.682	25	25	14	1	0	183^{1}	195	95	4	3	61	60	12.7	4.07	113	.277	.337	9	.148	-1	12	11	-1	0.8
1931	Was-A	9	10	.474	25	24	8	1	1	148	185	88	10	4	47	58	14.4	4.32	99	.304	.358	15	.313	4	1	-0	-0	0.3
1932	Chi-A	10	15	.400	30	28	10	0	0	200^{1}	217	123	9	3	75	64	13.3	4.22	102	.270	.335	11	.193	2	6	2	3	0.7
1933	Chi-A	10	12	.455	27	25	11	2	0	176^{2}	181	80	13	4	65	60	12.7	3.36	126	.265	.333	9	.155	-0	18	17	-1	1.8
1934	Chi-A	8	12	.400	27	26	11	1	0	183^{1}	217	120	16	2	60	60	13.7	5.11	93	.289	.343	12	.200	2	-12	-7	-2	-0.7
1935	Chi-A	8	7	.533	21	19	7	0	0	140	162	77	8	1	51	38	13.8	4.05	114	.284	.343	8	.167	0	6	9	0	0.8
Total	22	229	217	.513	647	487	250	36	31	3883	4084	2008	152	69	1396	1223	12.9	3.84	104	.274	.339	245	.197	25	81	62	-8	8.1
● **SHELDON JONES** Jones, Sheldon Leslie "Available" b: 2/2/22, Tecumseh, Neb. d: 4/18/91, Greenville, N.C. BR/TR, 6', 180 lbs. Deb: 9/9/46																												
1946	NY-N	1	2	.333	6	4	1	0	0	28	21	10	4	1	17	24	12.5	3.21	107	.208	.328	2	.250	0	1	1	-0	0.1
1947	NY-N	2	2	.500	15	6	0	0	0	55^{2}	51	27	2	3	29	24	13.4	3.88	105	.250	.352	2	.125	-1	1	1	-1	-0.1
1948	NY-N	16	8	.667	55	21	8	1	5	201^{1}	204	89	16	6	90	82	13.4	3.35	117	.263	.344	13	.203	1	14	13	0	1.6
1949	NY-N	15	12	.556	42	27	11	1	0	207^{1}	198	93	19	10	88	79	12.8	3.34	119	.248	.331	8	.121	-3	16	15	-0	1.4
1950	NY-N	13	16	.448	40	28	11	2	2	199	188	114	26	7	90	97	12.9	4.61	89	.249	.335	6	.105	-2	-10	-12	-2	-1.9
1951	*NY-N	6	11	.353	41	12	2	0	4	120^{1}	119	77	12	4	52	58	13.1	4.26	92	.260	.340	3	.097	-1	-4	-5	0	-0.7
1952	Bos-N	1	4	.200	39	1	0	0	1	70	81	45	7	1	31	40	14.5	4.76	76	.286	.359	1	.125	-0	-8	-9	0	-0.7
1953	Chi-N	0	2	.000	22	2	0	0	0	38^{1}	47	24	3	5	16	9	16.0	5.40	82	.299	.382	0	.000	-1	-5	-4	0	-0.3
Total	8	54	57	.486	260	101	33	4	12	920	909	479	89	37	413	413	13.3	3.96	100	.258	.342	35	.136	-7	4	1	-3	-0.6
● **SHERMAN JONES** Jones, Sherman Jarvis "Roadblock" b: 2/10/35, Winton, N.C. BL/TR, 6'4", 205 lbs. Deb: 8/2/60																												
1960	SF-N	1	1	.500	16	0	0	0	1	32	37	17	3	1	11	10	13.8	3.09	112	.291	.353	2	.286	0	2	1	-1	0.1
1961	*Cin-N	1	1	.500	24	2	0	0	2	55	51	32	6	2	27	32	13.1	4.42	92	.256	.351	2	.182	0	-2	-2	-0	-0.1
1962	NY-N	0	4	.000	8	3	0	0	0	23^{1}	31	22	3	2	8	11	15.8	7.71	54	.326	.390	3	.429	1	-10	-9	0	-1.1
Total	3	2	6	.250	48	5	0	0	3	110^{1}	119	71	12	5	46	53	13.9	4.73	83	.283	.360	7	.280	1	-10	-10	-1	-1.1
● **STEVE JONES** Jones, Steven Howell b: 4/22/41, Huntington Park, Cal. BL/TL, 5'10", 175 lbs. Deb: 8/15/67 F																												
1967	Chi-A	2	2	.500	11	3	0	0	0	25^{2}	21	13	1	0	12	17	11.6	4.21	74	.223	.311	1	.250	0	-3	-3	-0	-0.5
1968	Was-A	1	2	.333	7	0	0	0	0	10^{2}	8	8	3	0	7	11	12.7	5.91	49	.205	.326	0	.000	-0	-3	-4	-0	-0.8
1969	KC-A	2	3	.400	20	4	0	0	0	44^{2}	45	25	3	3	24	31	14.5	4.23	87	.260	.360	1	.125	0	-3	-3	0	-0.2
Total	3	5	7	.417	38	7	0	0	0	81	74	46	7	3	43	59	13.3	4.44	76	.242	.341	2	.154	1	-9	-9	-1	-1.5
● **RICK JONES** Jones, Thomas Fredrick b: 4/16/55, Jacksonville, Fla. BL/TL, 6'5", 190 lbs. Deb: 4/18/76																												
1976	Bos-A	5	3	.625	24	14	1	0	0	104^{1}	133	48	6	1	26	45	13.8	3.36	116	.311	.352	0	—	0	2	6	-0	0.4
1977	Sea-A	1	4	.200	10	10	0	0	0	42^{1}	47	25	10	0	37	16	17.9	5.10	81	.283	.414	0	—	0	-5	-5	0	-0.5
1978	Sea-A	0	2	.000	3	2	0	0	0	12^{1}	17	8	1	0	7	11	17.5	5.84	65	.315	.393	0	—	0	-3	-3	-0	-0.4
Total	3	6	9	.400	37	26	1	0	0	159	197	81	17	1	70	72	15.2	4.02	99	.304	.373	0	—	0	-6	-1	-0	-0.5
● **TIM JONES** Jones, Timmothy Byron b: 1/24/54, Sacramento, Cal. BB/TR, 6'5", 220 lbs. Deb: 9/4/77																												
1977	Pit-N	1	0	1.000	3	1	0	0	0	10	4	0	0	0	3	5	6.3	0.00	—	.118	.189	0	.000	-0	4	4	-0	0.4
● **TODD JONES** Jones, Todd Barton Givin b: 4/24/68, Marietta, Ga. BL/TR, 6'3", 200 lbs. Deb: 7/7/93																												
1993	Hou-N	1	2	.333	27	0	0	0	2	37^{1}	28	14	4	1	15	25	10.6	3.13	124	.214	.299	0	—	0	4	3	-0	0.2
1994	Hou-N	5	2	.714	48	0	0	0	5	72^{2}	52	23	3	1	26	63	9.8	2.72	145	.202	.278	2	.400	1	12	11	-1	1.0
1995	Hou-N	6	5	.545	68	0	0	0	15	99^{2}	89	38	8	6	52	96	13.3	3.07	126	.237	.339	1	.200	0	12	10	-1	1.2
1996	Hou-N	6	3	.667	51	0	0	0	17	57^{1}	61	30	5	5	32	44	15.4	4.40	88	.274	.377	0	.000	-0	-1	-4	-0	-0.7
1997	Det-A	5	4	.556	68	0	0	0	31	70	60	29	3	1	35	70	12.3	3.09	149	.231	.324	0	—	0	12	12	-1	2.1
1998	Det-A	1	4	.200	65	0	0	0	28	63^{1}	58	38	7	2	36	57	13.6	4.97	95	.249	.354	0	—	0	-2	-2	0	-0.2
1999	Det-A	4	4	.500	65	0	0	0	30	66^{1}	64	30	7	1	35	64	13.6	3.80	128	.259	.353	0	—	0	8	8	-1	1.3
2000	Det-A★	2	4	.333	67	0	0	0	**42**	64	67	28	6	1	25	67	13.1	3.52	136	.276	.346	0	—	0	10	9	-1	1.6
Total	8	30	28	.517	459	0	0	0	170	530^{2}	479	230	43	18	256	486	12.8	3.54	122	.243	.336	3	.273	1	54	47	-5	6.5
● **TIM JONES** Jones, William Timothy b: 12/1/62, Sumter, S.C. BL/TR, 5'10", 175 lbs. Deb: 7/26/88 ♦																												
1990	StL-N	0	0	—	1	0	0	0	0	1^{1}	1	2	0	0	2	0	20.3	6.75	57	.167	.375	28	.219	0	-0	-0	0	0.0
● **CLAUDE JONNARD** Jonnard, Claude Alfred b: 11/23/1897, Nashville, Tenn. d: 8/27/59, Nashville, Tenn. BR/TR, 6'1", 165 lbs. Deb: 10/1/21 F																												
1921	NY-N	0	0	—	1	0	0	0	1	4	4	0	0	0	0	7	9.0	0.00	—	.267	.267	0	.000	-0	2	2	-0	0.1
1922	NY-N	6	1	.857	33	0	0	0	**5**	96	96	45	7	3	28	44	11.9	3.84	104	.272	.331	1	.042	-3	3	2	-2	-0.3
1923	*NY-N	4	3	.571	**45**	1	1	0	**5**	96	105	45	6	0	35	45	13.1	3.28	116	.279	.340	1	.038	-3	8	6	-1	0.1
1924	*NY-N	3	5	.375	34	3	1	0	5	89^{2}	80	33	2	2	24	40	10.6	2.41	152	.229	.282	1	.045	-3	**15**	**13**	-0	0.9
1926	StL-A	0	2	.000	12	3	0	0	1	36	46	29	1	0	24	13	17.5	6.00	71	.313	.409	0	.000	-1	-8	-6	1	-0.3
1929	Chi-N	0	1	.000	12	2	0	0	0	27^{2}	41	27	4	1	11	11	17.2	7.48	62	.320	.379	2	.200	1	-9	-9	0	-0.3
Total	6	13	12	.520	137	9	2	0	17	349^{1}	372	179	20	6	122	160	12.9	3.79	104	.272	.334	5	.056	-9	10	6	-1	0.2
● **CHARLIE JORDAN** Jordan, Charles T. "Kid" b: 10/4/1871, Baltimore, Md. d: 6/1/28, Hazleton, Pa. Deb: 7/31/1896																												
1896	Phi-N	0	0	—	2	0	0	0	0	4^{2}	9	4	0	0	2	3	21.2	7.71	56	.409	.458	1	.500	0	-2	-2	0	-0.1

YEAR	TM/L	W	L	PCT	G	GS	CG	SH	SV	IP	H	R	HR	HB	BB	SO	RAT	ERA	ERA+	OAV	OOB	BH	AVG	PB	PR	PR+	PD	TPI
● **HARRY JORDAN**	Jordan, Harry J. b: 2/14/1873, Pittsburgh, Pa. d: 3/1/20, Pittsburgh, Pa. Deb: 9/25/1894																											
1894	Pit-N	1	0	1.000	1	1	1	0	0	9	10	7	0	1	2	1	13.0	4.00	131	.278	.333	0	.000	-0	1	1	-0	0.1
1895	Pit-N	0	2	.000	2	2	2	0	0	17	24	15	0	1	6	4	16.4	4.24	107	.329	.387	2	.286	-0	1	1	-0	0.0
Total	2	1	2	.333	3	3	3	0	0	26	34	22	0	2	8	5	15.2	4.15	115	.312	.370	2	.200	-0	2	2	-1	0.1
● **MILT JORDAN**	Jordan, Milton Mignot b: 5/24/27, Mineral Springs, Pa. d: 5/13/93, Ithaca, N.Y. BR/TR, 6'2.5", 207 lbs. Deb: 4/16/53																											
1953	Det-A	0	1	.000	8	1	0	0	0	17	26	13	3	0	5	4	16.4	5.82	70	.366	.408	1	.500	0	-3	-3	0	-0.1
● **NILES JORDAN**	Jordan, Niles Chapman b: 12/1/25, Lyman, Wash. BL/TL, 5'11", 180 lbs. Deb: 8/26/51																											
1951	Phi-N	2	3	.400	5	5	2	1	0	36^{2}	35	15	4	0	8	11	10.6	3.19	121	.250	.291	1	.077	-1	3	3	-1	0.2
1952	Cin-N	0	1	.000	3	1	0	0	0	6^{1}	14	7	1	0	3	2	24.2	9.95	38	.452	.500	0	.000	-0	-4	-4	0	-0.6
Total	2	2	4	.333	8	6	2	1	0	43	49	22	5	0	11	13	12.6	4.19	92	.287	.330	1	.071	-1	-1	-2	-1	-0.4
● **RIP JORDAN**	Jordan, Raymond Willis "Lanky" b: 9/28/1889, Portland, Me. d: 6/5/60, Meriden, Conn. BL/TR, 6', 172 lbs. Deb: 6/25/12																											
1912	Chi-A	0	0	—	4	0	0	0	0	12^{1}	13	8	2	1	3	1	12.4	5.11	63	.289	.347	0	.000	-1	-2	-3	-0	-0.2
1919	Was-A	0	0	—	1	1	0	0	0	4	6	5	1	0	2	2	18.0	11.25	29	.353	.421	0	.000	-0	-4	-4	-0	-0.2
Total	2	0	0	—	5	1	0	0	0	16^{1}	19	13	3	1	5	3	13.8	6.61	48	.306	.368	0	.000	-1	-6	-6	-1	-0.4
● **RICARDO JORDAN**	Jordan, Ricardo b: 6/27/70, Boynton Beach, Fla BL/TL, 5'11", 165 lbs. Deb: 6/23/95																											
1995	Tor-A	1	0	1.000	15	0	0	0	1	15	18	11	3	2	13	10	19.8	6.60	71	.305	.446	0	—	0	-3	-3	0	-0.2
1996	Phi-N	2	2	.500	26	0	0	0	0	25	18	6	0	0	12	17	10.8	1.80	240	.202	.297	0	.000	-0	7	7	-0	0.9
1997	NY-N	1	2	.333	22	0	0	0	0	27	31	17	1	2	15	19	16.0	5.33	76	.304	.403	0	.000	-0	-3	-4	0	-0.4
1998	Cin-N	1	0	1.000	6	0	0	0	0	3^{1}	4	9	2	0	7	1	29.7	24.30	18	.308	.550	0	—	0	-7	-7	0	-1.3
Total	4	5	4	.556	69	0	0	0	1	70^{1}	71	43	6	4	47	47	15.6	5.25	82	.270	.389	0	.000	-0	-7	-8	-0	-1.0
● **ORVILLE JORGENS**	Jorgens, Orville Edward b: 6/4/08, Rockford, Ill. d: 1/11/92, Colorado Springs, Colo. BR/TR, 6'1", 180 lbs. Deb: 4/19/35 F																											
1935	Phi-N	10	15	.400	**53**	24	6	0	2	188^{1}	216	129	12	8	96	57	15.3	4.83	94	.283	.370	6	.097	-5	-17	-5	3	-0.8
1936	Phi-N	8	8	.500	39	21	4	0	0	167^{1}	196	110	16	7	69	58	14.6	4.79	95	.290	.361	12	.200	-1	-14	-4	1	-0.4
1937	Phi-N	3	4	.429	52	9	1	0	3	140^{2}	159	83	12	5	68	34	14.8	4.41	98	.298	.383	5	.143	-1	-8	-1	2	0.0
Total	3	21	27	.438	144	54	11	0	5	496^{1}	571	322	40	20	233	149	14.9	4.70	95	.290	.370	23	.146	-7	-39	-11	5	-1.2
● **ADDIE JOSS**	Joss, Adrian b: 4/12/1880, Woodland, Wis. d: 4/14/11, Toledo, Ohio BR/TR, 6'3", 185 lbs. Deb: 4/26/02 H																											
1902	Cle-A	17	13	.567	32	29	28	**5**	0	269^{1}	225	120	2	13	75	106	10.5	2.77	124	.228	.291	12	.117	-5	24	21	6	2.1
1903	Cle-A	18	13	.581	32	31	31	3	0	283^{2}	232	105	3	9	37	120	**8.8**	2.19	130	.223	**.256**	22	.193	0	24	22	4	2.8
1904	Cle-A	14	10	.583	25	24	20	5	0	192^{1}	160	51	0	7	30	83	9.2	**1.59**	159	.227	.266	10	.132	-4	22	21	0	2.3
1905	Cle-A	20	12	.625	33	32	31	3	0	286	246	90	4	11	46	132	9.5	2.01	131	.234	.273	13	.134	-0	20	20	5	2.8
1906	Cle-A	21	9	.700	34	31	28	9	1	282	220	81	3	3	43	106	8.5	1.72	152	.218	.252	21	.210	2	30	29	2	3.7
1907	Cle-A	**27**	11	.711	42	38	34	6	2	338^{2}	279	100	3	7	54	127	9.0	1.83	137	.227	.263	13	.114	-5	27	26	9	3.4
1908	Cle-A	24	11	.686	42	35	29	9	2	325	232	77	2	2	30	130	**7.3**	**1.16**	**205**	**.197**	**.218**	15	.155	2	44	44	2	6.0
1909	Cle-A	14	13	.519	33	28	24	4	0	242^{2}	198	71	0	4	31	67	8.6	1.71	150	.226	.255	8	.100	-3	21	22	0	2.3
1910	Cle-A	5	5	.500	13	12	9	1	0	107^{1}	96	35	2	2	18	49	9.7	2.26	114	.245	.282	4	.111	-1	3	4	2	0.4
Total	9	160	97	.623	286	260	234	45	5	2327	1888	730	19	58	364	920	8.9	1.89	142	.223	.260	118	.144	-14	216	209	30	25.8
● **MIKE JOYCE**	Joyce, Michael Lewis b: 2/12/41, Detroit, Mich. BR/TR, 6'2", 193 lbs. Deb: 7/2/62																											
1962	Chi-A	2	1	.667	25	1	0	0	2	43^{1}	40	17	2	0	14	9	11.2	3.32	118	.247	.307	3	.429	1	3	3	0	0.3
1963	Chi-A	0	0	—	6	0	0	0	0	10^{2}	13	10	1	0	8	7	17.7	8.44	42	.289	.396	0	—	0	-6	-6	-0	-0.3
Total	2	2	1	.667	31	1	0	0	2	54	53	27	3	0	22	16	12.5	4.33	88	.256	.328	3	.429	1	-3	-3	0	0.0
● **DICK JOYCE**	Joyce, Richard Edward b: 11/18/43, Portland, Me. BL/TL, 6'5", 225 lbs. Deb: 9/3/65																											
1965	KC-A	0	1	.000	5	3	0	0	0	13	12	7	0	0	4	7	11.1	2.77	126	.240	.296	0	.000	-0	1	1	-0	0.0
● **BOB JOYCE**	Joyce, Robert Emmett b: 1/14/15, Stockton, Cal. d: 12/10/81, San Francisco, Cal BR/TR, 6'1", 180 lbs. Deb: 5/4/39																											
1939	Phi-A	3	5	.375	30	6	1	0	0	107^{2}	156	91	13	1	37	25	16.2	6.69	70	.337	.387	3	.086	-3	-25	-23	1	-1.6
1946	NY-N	3	4	.429	14	7	2	0	0	60^{2}	79	43	3	0	20	24	14.7	5.34	64	.315	.365	3	.158	0	-13	-13	1	-1.2
Total	2	6	9	.400	44	13	3	0	0	168^{1}	235	134	16	1	57	49	15.7	6.20	69	.329	.380	6	.111	-3	-38	-36	2	-2.8
● **MIKE JUDD**	Judd, Michael Galen b: 6/30/75, San Diego, Cal. BR/TR, 6'2", 200 lbs. Deb: 9/28/97																											
1997	LA-N	0	0	—	1	0	0	0	0	2^{2}	4	0	0	0	0	4	13.5	0.00	—	.364	.364	0	.000	-0	1	1	-0	0.0
1998	LA-N	0	0	—	7	0	0	0	0	11^{1}	19	19	4	1	9	14	23.0	15.09	26	.373	.475	0	.000	-0	-14	-15	1	-0.7
1999	LA-N	3	1	.750	7	4	0	0	0	28	30	17	4	1	12	22	13.8	5.46	78	.280	.358	0	.000	-0	-3	-4	0	-0.5
2000	LA-N	0	1	.000	1	1	0	0	0	4	4	7	2	1	3	5	18.0	15.75	28	.250	.400	1	1.000	1	-5	-5	-0	-0.7
Total	4	3	2	.600	16	5	0	0	0	46	57	43	10	3	24	45	16.4	8.41	50	.308	.396	1	.125	0	-20	-23	0	-1.9
● **RALPH JUDD**	Judd, Ralph Wesley b: 12/7/01, Perrysburg, Ohio d: 5/6/57, Lapeer, Mich. BL/TR, 5'10", 170 lbs. Deb: 10/2/27																											
1927	Was-A	0	0	—	1	0	0	0	1	4	8	3	0	0	2	2	22.5	6.75	60	.400	.455	0	.000	-0	-1	-1	-0	-0.1
1929	NY-N	3	0	1.000	18	0	0	0	0	50^{2}	49	19	4	0	11	21	10.7	2.66	172	.261	.302	0	.000	-2	12	11	0	0.4
1930	NY-N	0	0	—	2	0	0	0	0	7^{2}	13	8	0	0	3	0	18.8	5.87	81	.394	.444	0	.000	-1	-1	-1	-0	-0.1
Total	3	3	0	1.000	21	0	0	0	1	62^{1}	70	30	4	0	16	23	12.4	3.32	138	.290	.335	0	.000	-3	10	9	0	0.2
● **OSCAR JUDD**	Judd, Thomas William Oscar "Ossie" b: 2/14/08, London, Ont., Can. d: 12/27/95, Ingersoll, Ont., Can. BL/TL, 6'0.5", 180 lbs. Deb: 4/16/41																											
1941	Bos-A	0	0	—	7	0	0	0	1	12^{1}	15	12	1	0	10	5	18.2	8.76	48	.300	.417	2	.500	2	-6	-6	0	-0.1
1942	Bos-A	8	10	.444	31	19	11	0	2	150^{1}	135	72	3	2	90	70	13.6	3.89	96	.239	.346	18	.269	6	-4	-3	-0	0.3
1943	Bos-A☆	11	6	.647	23	20	8	1	0	155^{1}	131	58	2	3	69	53	11.8	2.90	114	.230	.317	14	.259	4	7	7	2	1.4
1944	Bos-A	1	1	.500	9	6	1	0	0	30	30	16	1	0	15	9	13.5	3.60	94	.261	.346	2	.182	1	-1	-1	-0	0.0
1945	Bos-A	0	1	.000	2	1	0	0	0	6^{1}	10	8	1	0	3	5	18.5	8.53	40	.333	.394	1	.500	0	-4	-4	0	-0.4
	Phi-N	5	4	.556	23	9	3	1	2	82^{2}	80	47	3	1	40	36	13.2	3.81	101	.254	.340	8	.267	3	-0	0	1	0.4
1946	Phi-N	11	12	.478	30	24	12	1	2	173^{1}	169	86	6	1	90	65	13.5	3.53	97	.260	.350	25	.316	8	-2	-2	4	1.1
1947	Phi-N	4	15	.211	32	19	8	1	0	146^{2}	155	86	6	3	69	54	13.9	4.60	87	.279	.361	12	.188	2	-9	-10	1	-0.7
1948	Phi-N	0	2	.000	4	1	0	0	0	14^{1}	19	14	1	0	11	7	18.8	6.91	57	.317	.423	1	.167	0	-5	-5	-0	-0.5
Total	8	40	51	.440	161	99	43	4	7	771^{1}	744	399	24	10	397	304	13.4	3.90	93	.256	.347	83	.262	26	-23	-22	8	1.5
● **JEFF JUDEN**	Juden, Jeffrey Daniel b: 1/19/71, Salem, Mass. BR/TR, 6'8", 265 lbs. Deb: 9/15/91																											
1991	Hou-N	0	2	.000	4	3	0	0	0	18	19	14	3	0	7	11	13.0	6.00	59	.275	.342	0	.000	-1	-5	-5	-1	-0.6
1993	Hou-N	0	1	.000	2	0	0	0	0	5	4	3	1	0	4	7	14.4	5.40	72	.222	.364	0	—	0	-1	-1	-0	-0.2
1994	Phi-N	1	4	.200	6	5	0	0	0	27^{2}	29	25	4	1	12	22	13.7	6.18	69	.276	.356	1	.111	-0	-6	-6	-0	-0.9
1995	Phi-N	2	4	.333	13	10	1	0	0	62^{2}	53	31	6	5	31	47	12.8	4.02	105	.235	.340	1	.056	-1	1	1	-0	0.0
1996	SF-N	4	0	1.000	36	0	0	0	0	41^{2}	39	23	7	1	20	35	13.0	4.10	100	.250	.339	0	.000	-0	-1	-0	-0	-0.1
	Mon-N	1	0	1.000	22	0	0	0	0	32^{2}	22	12	1	4	14	26	11.0	2.20	196	.188	.296	0	—	0	7	8	-1	0.3
	Yr	5	0	1.000	58	0	0	0	0	74^{1}	61	35	8	5	34	61	12.1	3.27	128	.223	.321	0	.000	-0	8	8	-1	0.2
1997	Mon-N	11	5	.688	22	22	3	0	0	130	125	64	17	9	57	107	13.2	4.22	99	.255	.344	6	.140	0	-0	-0	-2	-0.2
	*Cle-A	0	1	.000	8	5	0	0	0	31^{1}	32	21	6	1	15	29	13.8	5.46	86	.264	.350	0	—	0	-3	-3	-0	-0.2
1998	Mil-N	7	11	.389	24	24	2	0	0	138^{1}	149	91	20	10	66	109	14.6	5.53	77	.277	.367	5	.122	-1	-20	-19	-1	-2.3
	Ana-A	1	3	.250	8	6	0	0	0	40	33	32	7	2	18	39	11.9	6.75	70	.217	.308	0	—	0	-9	-9	-0	-0.8
1999	NY-A	0	1	.000	2	1	0	0	0	5^{2}	5	9	1	1	3	9	14.3	1.59	298	.200	.310	0	—	0	2	2	0	0.3
Total	8	27	32	.458	147	76	6	0	0	533	510	325	73	34	247	441	13.4	4.81	89	.253	.344	13	.109	-3	-33	-32	-5	-4.7
● **HOWIE JUDSON**	Judson, Howard Kolls b: 2/16/26, Hebron, Ill. BR/TR, 6'1", 195 lbs. Deb: 4/22/48																											
1948	Chi-A	4	5	.444	40	5	1	0	8	107^{1}	102	60	7	3	56	38	13.5	4.78	89	.255	.351	3	.103	-2	-6	-6	0	-0.7
1949	Chi-A	1	14	.067	26	12	3	0	1	108	114	65	13	1	70	36	15.4	4.58	91	.274	.380	2	.065	-3	-5	-5	0	-0.9
1950	Chi-A	2	3	.400	46	3	1	0	0	112	105	53	10	2	63	34	13.7	3.94	114	.252	.353	2	.100	-1	**8**	**7**	-2	0.1
1951	Chi-A	5	6	.455	27	14	3	0	1	121^{2}	124	67	9	2	55	43	13.4	3.77	107	.264	.343	4	.121	-2	5	4	0	0.1
1952	Chi-A	0	1	.000	21	0	0	0	1	34	30	17	4	0	22	15	13.8	4.24	86	.244	.359	0	.000	-0	-2	-2	-0	-0.2

YEAR	TM/L	W	L	PCT	G	GS	CG	SH	SV	IP	H	R	HR	HB	BB	SO	RAT	ERA	ERA+	OAV	OOB	BH	AVG	PB	PR	PR+	PD	TPI
1953	Cin-N	0	1	.000	10	6	0	0	0	38^2	58	28	8	0	11	11	16.1	5.59	78	.341	.381	1	.111	1	-6	-5	0	-0.2
1954	Cin-N	5	7	.417	37	8	0	0	3	93^1	86	47	9	3	42	27	12.6	3.95	106	.251	.338	2	.083	-2	1	2	-2	0.0
Total	7	17	37	.315	207	48	8	0	14	615	619	337	60	11	319	204	13.9	4.29	98	.265	.356	14	.093	-9	-4	-6	-3	-1.8
● **KEN JUNGELS**	Jungels, Kenneth Peter "Curly" b: 6/23/16, Aurora, Ill. d: 9/9/75, West Bend, Wis. BR/TR, 6'1", 180 lbs. Deb: 9/15/37																											
1937	Cle-A	0	0	—	2	0	0	0	0	3	3	1	0	0	1	0	12.0	0.00	—	.273	.333	0	—	0	2	2	0	0.1
1938	Cle-A	1	0	1.000	9	0	0	0	0	15^1	21	16	1	2	18	7	24.1	8.80	53	.339	.500	0	.000	-1	-7	-7	-0	-0.5
1940	Cle-A	0	0	—	2	0	0	0	0	3^1	3	1	0	0	1	1	10.8	2.70	156	.273	.333	0	.000	-0	1	1	0	0.0
1941	Cle-A	0	0	—	6	0	0	0	0	13^2	17	12	4	1	8	6	17.1	7.24	54	.293	.388	0	.000	-0	-5	-5	-0	-0.3
1942	Pit-N	0	0	—	6	0	0	0	0	13^2	12	11	0	0	4	7	10.5	6.59	51	.235	.291	1	.500	0	-5	-5	0	-0.2
Total	5	1	0	1.000	25	0	0	0	0	49	56	41	5	3	32	21	16.7	6.80	60	.290	.399	1	.100	-1	-14	-15	-0	-0.9
● **MIKE JUREWICZ**	Jurewicz, Michael Allen b: 9/20/45, Buffalo, N.Y. BB/TL, 6'3", 205 lbs. Deb: 9/7/65																											
1965	NY-A	0	0	—	2	0	0	0	0	2^1	5	2	0	0	1	2	23.1	7.71	44	.417	.462	0	—	0	-1	-1	-0	-0.1
● **AL JURISICH**	Jurisich, Alvin Joseph b: 8/25/21, New Orleans, La. d: 11/3/81, New Orleans, La. BR/TR, 6'2", 193 lbs. Deb: 4/26/44																											
1944	*StL-N	7	9	.438	30	14	5	2	1	130	102	53	7	5	65	53	11.9	3.39	104	.221	.323	8	.178	-1	3	2	-1	0.0
1945	StL-N	3	3	.500	27	6	1	0	0	71^2	61	45	7	1	41	42	12.9	5.15	73	.232	.338	2	.087	-2	-11	-11	-1	-1.1
1946	Phi-N	4	3	.571	13	10	2	1	1	68^1	71	30	9	1	31	34	13.6	3.69	93	.263	.341	3	.130	-0	-2	-2	-1	-0.4
1947	Phi-N	1	7	.125	34	12	5	0	3	118^1	110	69	15	1	52	48	12.4	4.94	81	.258	.340	1	.032	-3	-12	-12	-2	-1.2
Total	4	15	22	.405	104	42	13	3	5	388^1	344	197	38	8	189	177	12.5	4.24	87	.242	.334	14	.115	-6	-21	-24	-5	-2.7
● **WALT JUSTIS**	Justis, Walter Newton "Smoke" b: 8/17/1883, Moores Hill, Ind. d: 10/4/41, Greendale, Ind. BR/TR, 5'11.5", 195 lbs. Deb: 8/1/05																											
1905	Det-A	0	0	—	2	0	0	0	0	3^1	4	3	0	1	6	0	29.7	8.10	34	.308	.550	0	—	0	-2	-2	-0	-0.1
● **HEROLD JUUL**	Juul, Earl Herold b: 5/21/1893, Chicago, Ill. d: 1/4/42, Chicago, Ill. BR/TR, 5'9.5", 150 lbs. Deb: 4/24/14																											
1914	Bro-F	0	3	.000	9	3	0	0	0	29	26	24	0	1	31	16	18.0	6.21	46	.248	.423	2	.222	-0	-11	-11	-0	-1.0
● **HERB JUUL**	Juul, Herbert Victor b: 2/2/1886, Chicago, Ill. d: 11/14/28, Chicago, Ill. BL/TL, 5'11", 150 lbs. Deb: 7/11/11 ♦																											
1911	Cin-N	0	0	—	1	0	0	0	0	4	3	2	0	0	4	2	15.8	4.50	74	.231	.412	0	.000	-0	-0	-1	-0	-0.1
● **JIM KAAT**	Kaat, James Lee b: 11/7/38, Zeeland, Mich. BL/TL, 6'4", 217 lbs. Deb: 8/2/59 C♦																											
1959	Was-A	0	2	.000	3	2	0	0	0	5	7	9	1	2	4	2	23.4	12.60	31	.350	.500	0	.000	-0	-5	-5	0	-0.8
1960	Was-A	1	5	.167	13	9	0	0	0	50	48	39	8	5	31	25	15.1	5.58	70	.255	.375	2	.143	-1	-9	-9	0	-1.0
1961	Min-A	9	17	.346	36	29	8	1	0	200^2	188	105	12	11	82	122	12.6	3.90	109	.248	.331	15	.238	3	3	7	3	1.5
1962	Min-A☆	18	14	.563	39	35	16	**5**	1	269	243	106	23	18	75	173	11.2	3.14	130	.243	.307	18	.180	3	25	27	6	4.1
1963	Min-A	10	10	.500	31	27	7	1	1	178^1	195	96	24	9	38	105	12.2	4.19	87	.274	.319	8	.131	-0	-11	-11	4	-0.7
1964	Min-A	17	11	.607	36	34	13	0	1	243	231	100	23	9	60	171	11.1	3.22	111	.251	.304	14	.169	5	11	10	3	1.9
1965	*Min-A	18	11	.621	45	42	7	2	2	264^1	267	121	25	5	63	154	11.4	2.83	126	.258	.304	23	.247	6	19	21	3	3.4
1966	Min-A★	**25**	13	.658	41	41	**19**	3	0	**304^2**	271	114	29	3	55	205	9.7	2.75	131	.235	.271	23	.195	4	23	27	0	3.9
1967	Min-A	16	13	.552	42	38	13	2	0	263^1	269	110	21	9	42	211	10.9	3.04	114	.260	.295	17	.172	3	6	11	1	1.7
1968	Min-A	14	12	.538	30	29	9	2	0	208	192	78	16	3	40	130	10.2	2.94	105	.243	.282	12	.156	0	1	3	-0	0.4
1969	Min-A	14	13	.519	40	32	10	0	1	242^1	252	114	23	9	75	139	12.5	3.49	105	.265	.325	18	.207	6	4	4	-3	0.8
1970	*Min-A	14	10	.583	45	34	4	1	0	230^1	244	110	26	3	58	120	11.9	3.56	105	.273	.319	15	.197	3	4	4	2	1.0
1971	Min-A	13	14	.481	39	38	15	4	0	260^1	275	104	16	6	47	137	11.3	3.32	107	.268	.304	15	.161	-0	4	7	-0	0.7
1972	Min-A	10	2	.833	15	15	5	0	0	113^1	94	36	6	0	20	64	9.1	2.06	156	.227	.263	13	.289	5	13	14	-0	2.2
1973	Min-A	11	12	.478	29	28	7	2	0	181^2	206	101	26	4	39	93	12.3	4.41	90	.282	.322	0	—	0	-12	-9	-1	-1.1
	Chi-A	4	1	.800	7	7	3	1	0	42^2	44	23	4	0	4	16	10.1	4.22	94	.260	.277	0	—	0	-2	-1	-1	-0.2
	Yr	15	13	.536	36	35	10	3	0	224^1	250	124	30	4	43	109	11.9	4.37	91	.278	.314	0	—	0	-14	-10	-2	-1.3
1974	Chi-A	21	13	.618	42	39	15	3	0	277^1	263	106	18	6	63	142	10.8	2.92	128	.250	.296	0	.000	-0	22	24	-2	2.7
1975	Chi-A★	20	14	.588	43	41	12	1	0	303^2	321	121	20	9	77	142	12.1	3.11	125	.274	.324	0	—	0	23	25	-2	2.5
1976	*Phi-N	12	14	.462	38	35	7	1	0	227^2	241	95	21	0	32	83	10.8	3.48	102	.274	.300	14	.177	2	1	2	-3	0.1
1977	Phi-N	6	11	.353	35	27	2	0	0	160^1	211	100	20	2	40	55	14.2	5.39	74	.320	.361	10	.189	1	-26	-24	-2	-2.4
1978	Phi-N	8	5	.615	26	24	2	1	0	140^1	150	67	9	5	32	48	12.0	4.10	87	.280	.326	7	.146	-1	-8	-8	-2	-1.0
1979	Phi-N	1	0	1.000	3	1	0	0	0	8^1	9	4	1	0	5	2	15.1	4.32	89	.281	.378	0	.000	0	-1	-0	-0	0.0
	NY-A	2	3	.400	40	1	0	0	2	58^1	64	29	4	2	14	23	12.3	3.86	106	.287	.335	0	—	0	2	2	-1	0.1
1980	NY-A	0	1	.000	4	0	0	0	0	5	8	5	0	0	4	1	21.6	7.20	55	.381	.480	0	—	0	-2	-2	1	-0.3
	StL-N	8	7	.533	49	14	6	1	4	129^2	140	61	6	0	33	36	12.0	3.82	97	.281	.325	5	.143	1	-3	-2	-2	-0.3
1981	StL-N	6	6	.500	41	1	0	0	4	53	60	25	2	0	17	8	13.1	3.40	105	.299	.353	3	.375	1	1	1	1	0.4
1982	*StL-N	5	3	.625	62	2	0	0	2	75	79	40	6	2	23	35	12.5	4.08	89	.276	.334	0	.000	-1	-4	-4	1	-0.5
1983	StL-N	0	0	—	24	0	0	0	0	34^2	48	19	5	0	10	19	15.1	3.89	93	.327	.369	0	.000	-0	-1	-1	0	-0.1
Total	25	283	237	.544	898	625	180	31	18	4530^1	4620	2038	395	122	1083	2461	11.6	3.45	107	.264	.311	232	.185	41	76	118	6	19.0
● **GEORGE KAHLER**	Kahler, George Runnells "Krum" b: 9/6/1889, Athens, Ohio d: 2/7/24, Battle Creek, Va. BR/TR, 6', 183 lbs. Deb: 8/13/10																											
1910	Cle-A	6	4	.600	12	12	8	2	0	95^1	80	35	0	4	46	38	12.3	1.60	161	.237	.335	5	.143	-2	10	10	-1	0.8
1911	Cle-A	9	8	.529	30	17	10	0	1	154^1	153	78	1	13	66	97	13.5	3.27	104	.270	.360	9	.167	-2	1	2	-1	-0.1
1912	Cle-A	12	19	.387	41	32	17	3	1	246^1	263	135	1	11	121	104	14.4	3.69	92	.291	.382	9	.112	-5	-10	-8	-4	-1.7
1913	Cle-A	5	11	.313	24	15	5	0	0	117^2	118	56	1	4	32	43	11.8	3.14	97	.266	.322	2	.061	-3	-3	-1	-3	-0.8
1914	Cle-A	0	1	.000	2	1	1	0	0	14	17	10	0	0	7	3	15.4	3.86	75	.309	.387	0	.000	-0	-2	-1	-0	-0.2
Total	5	32	43	.427	109	77	41	5	2	627^2	631	314	3	32	272	285	13.4	3.17	101	.274	.358	25	.121	-13	-4	2	-9	-2.0
● **DON KAINER**	Kainer, Donald Wayne b: 9/3/55, Houston, Tex. BR/TR, 6'3", 205 lbs. Deb: 9/6/80																											
1980	Tex-A	0	0	—	4	3	0	0	0	19^2	22	7	0	3	9	10	15.6	1.83	213	.289	.386	0	—	0	5	5	1	0.4
● **DON KAISER**	Kaiser, Clyde Donald "Tiger" b: 2/3/35, Byng, Okla. BR/TR, 6'5", 195 lbs. Deb: 7/20/55																											
1955	Chi-N	0	0	—	11	0	0	0	0	18^1	20	11	2	1	5	11	12.8	5.40	76	.274	.329	0	.000	-0	-3	-3	-0	-0.2
1956	Chi-N	4	9	.308	27	22	5	1	0	150^1	144	69	15	1	52	74	11.8	3.59	105	.247	.310	2	.043	-5	3	3	-0	-0.3
1957	Chi-N	2	6	.250	20	13	1	0	0	72	91	48	4	0	28	23	14.9	5.00	77	.316	.377	2	.105	-1	-9	-9	2	-0.8
Total	3	6	15	.286	58	35	6	1	0	240^2	255	128	21	2	85	108	12.8	4.15	92	.270	.332	4	.059	-6	-9	-9	1	-1.3
● **JEFF KAISER**	Kaiser, Jeffrey Patrick b: 7/24/60, Wyandotte, Mich. BR/TL, 6'3", 195 lbs. Deb: 4/11/85																											
1985	Oak-A	0	0	—	15	0	0	0	0	16^2	25	32	6	1	20	10	24.8	14.58	26	.342	.489	0	—	0	-19	-21	1	-1.0
1987	Cle-A	0	0	—	2	0	0	0	0	3^1	4	6	1	1	3	2	21.6	16.20	28	.286	.444	0	—	0	-4	-4	0	-0.2
1988	Cle-A	0	0	—	3	0	0	0	0	2^2	2	0	0	0	1	0	10.1	0.00	—	.286	.375	0	—	0	1	1	0	0.1
1989	Cle-A	0	1	.000	6	0	0	0	0	3^2	5	5	1	0	5	4	24.5	7.36	54	.313	.476	0	—	0	-1	-1	-0	-0.3
1990	Cle-A	0	0	—	5	0	0	0	0	12^2	16	5	2	0	7	9	16.3	3.55	111	.308	.390	0	—	0	1	1	0	0.0
1991	Det-A	0	1	.000	10	0	0	0	2	5	6	5	1	0	5	4	19.8	9.00	46	.286	.423	0	—	0	-3	-3	0	-0.5
1993	Cin-N	0	0	—	3	0	0	0	0	3^1	4	1	0	0	2	4	16.2	2.70	149	.286	.375	0	—	0	0	0	-0	0.0
	NY-N	0	0	—	6	0	0	0	0	4^2	6	6	1	0	3	5	17.4	11.57	35	.353	.450	0	—	0	-4	-4	0	-0.2
	Yr	0	0	—	9	0	0	0	0	8	10	7	1	0	5	9	16.9	7.88	51	.323	.417	0	—	0	-3	-3	0	-0.2
Total	7	0	2	.000	50	0	0	0	2	52	68	60	12	2	46	38	20.1	9.17	44	.318	.443	0	—	0	-30	-30	1	-2.1
● **BOB KAISER**	Kaiser, Robert Thomas b: 4/29/50, Cincinnati, Ohio BB/TL, 5'10", 175 lbs. Deb: 9/3/71																											
1971	Cle-A	0	0	—	5	0	0	0	0	6	8	3	2	2	3	4	19.5	4.50	85	.333	.448	0	—	0	-1	-0	0	0.0
● **GEORGE KAISERLING**	Kaiserling, George b: 5/12/1893, Steubenville, Ohio d: 3/2/18, Steubenville, Ohio BR/TR, 6', 175 lbs. Deb: 4/20/14																											
1914	Ind-F	17	10	.630	37	33	20	1	0	275^1	288	119	8	17	72	75	12.3	3.11	100	.274	.330	11	.112	-7	-7	0	-3	-1.0
1915	New-F	15	15	.500	41	29	16	5	2	261^1	246	90	1	9	73	75	11.3	2.24	114	.257	.316	12	.152	-3	14	10	-1	0.7
Total	2	32	25	.561	78	62	36	6	2	536^2	534	209	9	26	145	150	11.8	2.68	106	.266	.323	23	.130	-10	8	9	-5	-0.3
● **BILL KALFASS**	Kalfass, William Philip "Lefty" b: 3/3/16, New York, N.Y. d: 9/8/68, Brooklyn, N.Y. BR/TL, 6'3.5", 190 lbs. Deb: 9/15/37																											
1937	Phi-A	1	0	1.000	3	1	1	0	0	12	10	4	0	0	10	9	15.0	3.00	157	.233	.377	0	.000	-1	2	2	-0	0.1

YEAR	TM/L	W	L	PCT	G	GS	CG	SH	SV	IP	H	R	HR	HB	BB	SO	RAT	ERA	ERA+	OAV	OOB	BH	AVG	PB	PR	PR+	PD	TPI
● **RUDY KALLIO**	Kallio, Rudolph b: 12/14/1892, Portland, Ore. d: 4/6/79, Newport, Ore. BR/TR, 5'10", 160 lbs. Deb: 4/25/18																											
1918	Det-A	8	13	.381	30	22	10	2	0	181^1	178	91	0	1	76	70	12.7	3.62	73	.261	.336	9	.161	-1	-17	-20	-0	-2.4
1919	Det-A	0	0	—	12	1	0	0	1	22^1	28	15	0	1	8	3	14.9	5.64	57	.326	.389	0	.000	-1	-6	-6	-0	-0.4
1925	Bos-A	1	4	.200	7	4	0	0	0	18^2	28	18	0	1	9	2	18.3	7.71	59	.364	.437	2	.333	0	-7	-6	-0	-1.1
Total	3	9	17	.346	49	27	10	2	1	222^1	234	124	0	3	93	75	13.4	4.17	69	.277	.351	11	.167	-1	-30	-33	-1	-3.9
● **SCOTT KAMIENIECKI**	Kamieniecki, Scott Andrew b: 4/19/64, Mt.Clemens, Mich. BR/TR, 6', 195 lbs. Deb: 6/18/91																											
1991	NY-A	4	4	.500	9	9	0	0	0	55^1	54	24	8	3	22	34	12.8	3.90	106	.256	.335	0	—	0	1	1	1	0.2
1992	NY-A	6	14	.300	28	28	4	0	0	188	193	100	13	5	74	88	13.0	4.36	90	.269	.342	0	—	0	-9	-9	-1	-0.9
1993	NY-A	10	7	.588	30	20	2	0	1	154^1	163	73	17	3	59	72	13.1	4.08	102	.277	.346	0	—	0	4	1	1	0.2
1994	NY-A	8	6	.571	22	16	1	0	0	117^1	115	53	13	3	59	71	13.6	3.76	122	.261	.353	0	—	0	14	11	0	1.2
1995	*NY-A	7	6	.538	17	16	1	0	0	89^2	83	43	8	3	49	43	13.6	4.01	115	.246	.346	0	—	0	7	6	-1	0.7
1996	NY-A	1	2	.333	7	5	0	0	0	22^2	36	30	6	2	19	15	22.6	11.12	44	.364	.475	0	—	0	-15	-16	0	-1.5
1997	*Bal-A	10	6	.625	30	30	0	0	0	179^1	179	83	20	4	67	109	12.5	4.01	110	.261	.330	0	.000	-0	11	8	2	0.8
1998	Bal-A	2	6	.250	12	11	0	0	0	54^2	67	41	7	4	26	25	16.0	6.75	68	.313	.398	0	—	0	-13	-14	1	-1.5
1999	Bal-A	2	4	.333	43	3	0	0	2	56^1	52	32	4	4	29	39	13.6	4.95	95	.250	.353	0	—	0	-2	-2	2	0.0
2000	Cle-A	1	3	.250	26	0	0	0	0	33^1	42	22	6	1	20	29	17.0	5.67	88	.311	.404	0	—	0	-3	-2	0	-0.2
	Atl-N	2	1	.667	26	0	0	0	2	24^2	22	18	3	0	22	17	16.1	5.47	83	.239	.386	0	—	0	-2	-3	1	-0.2
Total	10	53	59	.473	250	138	8	0	5	975^2	1006	519	105	32	446	542	13.7	4.52	97	.270	.353	0	.000	-0	-5	-17	7	-1.2
● **BOB KAMMEYER**	Kammeyer, Robert Lynn b: 12/2/50, Kansas City, Kan. BR/TR, 6'4", 210 lbs. Deb: 7/3/78																											
1978	NY-A	0	0	—	7	0	0	0	0	21^2	24	15	1	2	6	11	13.3	5.82	62	.276	.337	0	—	0	-5	-5	1	-0.2
1979	NY-A	0	0	—	1	0	0	0	0	0	7	2	1	0	—	—	∞	—	1.000	1.000	97	—	0	-8	-8	0	-0.6	
Total	2	0	0	—	8	0	0	0	0	21^2	31	23	3	3	6	11	16.6	9.14	40	.330	.388	0	—	0	-13	-14	1	-0.8
● **IKE KAMP**	Kamp, Alphonse Francis b: 9/5/1900, Roxbury, Mass. d: 2/25/55, Boston, Mass. BB/TL, 6', 170 lbs. Deb: 9/16/24																											
1924	Bos-N	0	1	.000	1	1	0	0	0	7	9	5	0	0	5	4	18.0	5.14	74	.360	.467	0	.000	-0	-1	-1	0	-0.1
1925	Bos-N	2	4	.333	24	4	1	0	0	58^1	68	38	0	0	35	20	15.9	5.09	79	.301	.395	2	.167	-0	-5	-7	0	-0.6
Total	2	2	5	.286	25	5	1	0	0	65^1	77	43	0	0	40	24	16.1	5.10	78	.307	.402	2	.154	-0	-6	-9	1	-0.7
● **HARRY KANE**	Kane, Harry "Klondike" (b: Harry Cohen) b: 7/27/1883, Hamburg, Ark. d: 9/15/32, Portland, Ore. BL/TL, Deb: 8/8/02																											
1902	StL-A	0	1	.000	4	1	1	0	0	23	34	21	2	0	16	7	19.6	5.48	64	.343	.435	1	.111	-1	-5	-5	-0	-0.3
1903	Det-A	0	2	.000	3	3	2	0	0	18	26	22	0	1	8	10	17.5	8.50	34	.338	.407	1	.143	-0	-11	-11	-1	-1.0
1905	Phi-N	1	1	.500	2	2	2	1	0	17	12	6	0	0	8	12	10.6	1.59	184	.203	.299	1	.167	-0	3	3	-0	0.2
1906	Phi-N	1	3	.250	6	3	2	0	0	28	28	16	0	3	18	14	15.8	3.86	68	.255	.374	0	.000	-1	-4	-4	0	-0.6
Total	4	2	7	.222	15	9	7	1	0	86	100	65	2	4	50	43	16.1	4.81	62	.290	.386	3	.100	-2	-17	-18	-1	-1.7
● **ERV KANTLEHNER**	Kantlehner, Erving Leslie "Peanuts" b: 7/31/1892, San Jose, Cal. d: 2/3/90, Santa Barbara, Cal. BL/TL, 6', 190 lbs. Deb: 4/17/14																											
1914	Pit-N	3	2	.600	21	5	3	2	0	67	51	33	0	3	39	26	12.5	3.09	86	.218	.337	1	.067	-0	-2	-3	-0	-0.3
1915	Pit-N	5	12	.294	29	18	10	1	3	163	135	60	1	4	58	64	10.9	2.26	121	.230	.304	15	.288	3	9	9	1	1.4
1916	Pit-N	5	15	.250	34	21	7	2	2	165	151	72	1	4	57	49	11.6	3.16	85	.249	.317	8	.174	-0	-10	-9	1	-0.9
	Phi-N	0	0	—	3	0	0	0	0	4	7	4	0	0	3	2	22.5	9.00	29	.500	.588	0	—	0	-3	-3	0	-0.1
	Yr	5	15	.250	37	21	7	2	2	169	158	76	1	4	60	51	11.8	3.30	81	.254	.324	8	.174	-0	-13	-11	1	-1.0
Total	3	13	29	.310	87	44	20	5	5	399	344	169	2	11	157	141	11.5	2.84	95	.239	.318	24	.212	2	-6	-6	2	0.1
● **MATT KARCHNER**	Karchner, Matthew Dean b: 6/28/67, Berwick, Pa. BR/TR, 6'4", 245 lbs. Deb: 7/18/95																											
1995	Chi-A	4	2	.667	31	0	0	0	0	32	33	8	2	1	12	24	12.9	1.69	264	.275	.346	0	—	0	11	10	0	1.7
1996	Chi-A	7	4	.636	50	0	0	0	1	59^1	61	42	10	2	41	46	15.8	5.76	82	.266	.382	0	—	0	-5	-7	-1	-1.2
1997	Chi-A	3	1	.750	52	0	0	0	15	52^2	50	18	4	0	26	30	13.0	2.91	151	.258	.345	0	—	0	10	9	-0	1.0
1998	Chi-A	2	4	.333	32	0	0	0	11	36^2	33	21	2	5	19	30	14.0	5.15	88	.243	.356	0	—	0	-2	-3	0	-0.4
	*Chi-N	3	1	.750	29	0	0	0	0	28	30	18	6	2	14	22	14.8	5.14	86	.263	.354	0	—	0	-3	-2	0	-0.3
1999	Chi-N	1	0	1.000	16	0	0	0	0	18	16	5	3	2	9	9	13.5	2.50	181	.235	.342	0	—	0	4	4	-0	0.2
2000	Chi-N	1	1	.500	13	0	0	0	0	14^2	19	11	3	0	11	5	18.4	6.14	74	.311	.417	0	—	0	-2	-3	0	-0.2
Total	6	21	13	.618	223	0	0	0	27	241^1	242	123	30	12	132	166	14.4	4.21	108	.262	.362	0	—	0	12	9	-1	0.8
● **PAUL KARDOW**	Kardow, Paul Otto "Tex" b: 9/19/15, Humble, Tex. d: 4/27/68, San Antonio, Tex. BR/TR, 6'6", 210 lbs. Deb: 7/1/36																											
1936	Cle-A	0	0	—	2	0	0	0	0	2	1	1	0	0	2	0	13.5	4.50	112	.167	.375	0	—	0	0	0	-0	0.0
● **ED KARGER**	Karger, Edwin "Loose" b: 5/6/1883, San Angelo, Tex. d: 9/9/57, Delta, Colo. BL/TL, 5'11", 185 lbs. Deb: 4/15/06																											
1906	Pit-N	2	3	.400	6	2	0	0	0	28	21	11	0	2	9	8	10.3	1.93	139	.204	.281	1	.091	-1	2	2	1	0.5
	StL-N	5	16	.238	25	20	17	0	1	191^2	193	85	0	7	43	73	11.4	2.72	97	.271	.319	17	.233	4	-2	-2	3	0.6
	Yr	7	19	.269	31	22	17	0	1	219^2	214	96	0	9	52	81	11.3	2.62	100	.263	.314	18	.214	3	0	0	4	1.1
1907	StL-N	15	19	.441	39	32	29	6	1	314	257	102	2	10	65	137	9.5	2.04	123	.223	.270	20	.179	1	15	16	4	2.5
1908	StL-N	4	9	.308	22	15	9	1	0	141^1	148	77	1	2	50	34	12.7	3.06	77	.260	.322	13	.241	3	-11	-11	-1	-0.8
1909	Cin-N	1	3	.250	9	5	1	0	0	34^1	26	22	0	2	30	8	15.2	4.46	58	.217	.382	3	.273	2	-7	-7	-0	-0.6
	Bos-A	5	2	.714	12	6	3	0	0	68	71	29	0	3	22	17	12.7	3.18	79	.273	.337	3	.125	-0	-5	-5	-0	-0.6
1910	Bos-A	11	7	.611	27	25	16	1	1	183^1	162	75	5	5	53	81	10.8	3.19	80	.230	.289	20	.294	6	-14	-13	-2	-0.8
1911	Bos-A	5	8	.385	25	18	6	1	0	131	134	70	4	4	42	57	12.4	3.37	97	.272	.334	11	.234	3	-0	-1	-0	0.2
Total	6	48	67	.417	165	123	81	9	3	1091^2	1012	471	12	35	314	415	11.2	2.79	94	.246	.305	88	.220	18	-22	-20	5	1.0
● **ANDY KARL**	Karl, Anton Andrew b: 4/8/14, Mt.Vernon, N.Y. d: 4/8/89, LaJolla, Cal. BR/TR, 6'1.5", 175 lbs. Deb: 4/24/43																											
1943	Bos-A	1	1	.500	11	0	0	0	1	26	31	11	0	0	13	6	15.2	3.46	96	.310	.389	2	.286	0	-0	-0	1	0.1
	Phi-N	1	2	.333	9	2	0	0	0	26^2	44	22	0	0	11	4	18.6	7.09	48	.383	.437	2	.250	1	-11	-11	0	-1.0
1944	Phi-N	3	2	.600	38	0	0	0	2	89	76	32	1	1	21	26	9.9	2.33	155	.237	.287	3	.200	1	**13**	**13**	1	0.9
1945	Phi-N	8	8	.500	**67**	2	1	0	**15**	180^2	175	80	7	3	50	51	11.4	2.99	128	.253	.306	7	.143	-2	**16**	**17**	1	1.6
1946	Phi-N	3	7	.300	39	0	0	0	5	65^1	84	37	6	1	22	15	14.7	4.96	69	.321	.375	1	.100	-0	-11	-11	1	-1.7
1947	Bos-N	2	3	.400	27	0	0	0	3	35	41	18	2	0	13	5	13.9	3.86	101	.318	.380	1	.167	-0	1	0	2	0.2
Total	5	18	23	.439	191	4	1	0	26	422^2	451	200	16	5	130	107	12.5	3.51	104	.279	.334	16	.168	-0	7	7	6	0.1
● **SCOTT KARL**	Karl, Randall Scott b: 8/9/71, Fontana, Cal. BL/TL, 6'2", 195 lbs. Deb: 5/4/95																											
1995	Mil-A	6	7	.462	25	18	1	0	0	124	141	65	10	3	50	59	14.1	4.14	121	.288	.358	0	—	0	8	11	0	1.0
1996	Mil-A	13	9	.591	32	32	3	1	0	207^1	220	124	29	11	72	121	13.2	4.86	107	.271	.338	0	—	0	3	7	-1	0.6
1997	Mil-A	10	13	.435	32	32	1	0	0	193^1	212	103	23	4	67	119	13.2	4.47	103	.279	.340	0	.000	-0	2	3	-0	0.3
1998	Mil-N	10	11	.476	33	33	0	0	0	192^1	219	104	21	4	66	102	13.5	4.40	97	.290	.350	4	.071	-2	-3	-3	2	-0.3
1999	Mil-N	11	11	.500	33	33	0	0	0	197^2	246	121	21	8	69	74	14.7	4.78	95	.312	.373	11	.183	3	-0	-5	2	0.0
2000	Col-N	2	3	.400	17	9	0	0	0	65^2	95	56	14	3	33	29	18.0	7.68	77	.343	.419	4	.286	0	-22	-10	1	-0.6
	Ana-A	2	2	.500	6	4	0	0	0	21^2	31	21	2	0	12	9	17.9	6.65	75	.337	.413	0	—	0	-4	-4	-1	-0.6
Total	6	54	56	.491	178	161	5	1	0	1002	1164	594	120	33	369	513	14.1	4.81	100	.293	.358	19	.142	1	-21	-3	4	0.4
● **BILL KARNS**	Karns, William Arthur b: 12/28/1875, Richmond, Iowa d: 11/15/41, Seattle, Wash. BL/TL, Deb: 8/1/01																											
1901	Bal-A	1	0	1.000	3	1	1	0	0	17	30	18	0	0	9	5	20.6	6.35	61	.380	.443	1	.143	-1	-5	-4	-0	-0.3
● **RYAN KARP**	Karp, Ryan Jason b: 4/5/70, Los Angeles, Cal. BL/TL, 6'4", 220 lbs. Deb: 6/23/95																											
1995	Phi-N	0	0	—	1	0	0	0	0	2	1	1	0	0	3	2	18.0	4.50	94	.143	.400	0	—	0	-0	-0	-0	0.0
1997	Phi-N	1	1	.500	15	1	0	0	0	15	12	12	2	2	9	18	13.8	5.40	79	.218	.348	0	—	0	-2	-2	-0	-0.2
Total	2	1	1	.500	16	1	0	0	0	17	13	13	2	2	12	20	14.3	5.29	80	.210	.355	0	—	0	-2	-2	-0	-0.2
● **HERB KARPEL**	Karpel, Herbert "Lefty" b: 12/27/17, Brooklyn, N.Y. d: 1/24/95, San Diego, Cal. BL/TL, 5'9.5", 180 lbs. Deb: 4/19/46																											
1946	NY-A	0	0	—	2	0	0	0	0	1^2	4	2	0	0	0	0	21.6	10.80	32	.500	.500	0	—	0	-1	-1	-0	-0.1
● **BENN KARR**	Karr, Benjamin Joyce "Baldy" b: 11/28/1893, Mt.Pleasant, Miss. d: 12/8/68, Memphis, Tenn. BL/TR, 6', 175 lbs. Deb: 4/20/20																											
1920	Bos-A	3	8	.273	26	2	0	0	1	91^2	109	55	3	1	24	21	13.2	4.81	76	.304	.349	21	.280	6	-10	-12	-1	-0.9

YEAR	TM/L	W	L	PCT	G	GS	CG	SH	SV	IP	H	R	HR	HB	BB	SO	RAT	ERA	ERA+	OAV	OOB	BH	AVG	PB	PR	PR+	PD	TPI
1921	Bos-A	8	7	.533	26	7	5	0	0	117^{2}	123	53	8	1	38	37	12.4	3.67	115	.283	.342	16	.258	1	8	7	-0	0.9
1922	Bos-A	5	12	.294	41	13	7	0	1	183^{1}	212	115	10	5	45	41	12.9	4.47	92	.302	.348	21	.214	-1	-9	-7	-1	-0.7
1925	Cle-A	11	12	.478	32	24	12	1	0	197^{2}	248	127	8	6	80	41	15.2	4.78	92	.317	.385	24	.261	4	-8	-8	2	-0.2
1926	Cle-A	5	6	.455	30	7	4	0	1	113^{1}	137	72	9	6	41	23	14.6	5.00	81	.291	.355	10	.222	2	-12	-12	1	-0.7
1927	Cle-A	3	3	.500	22	5	1	0	2	76^{2}	92	49	5	1	32	17	14.7	5.05	83	.315	.385	4	.200	1	-8	-7	2	-0.3
Total	6	35	48	.422	177	58	29	1	5	780^{1}	921	471	43	20	260	180	13.9	4.60	90	.303	.362	96	.245	12	-40	-39	2	-1.9
● **STEVE KARSAY** Karsay, Stefan Andrew b: 3/24/72, Flushing, N.Y. BR/TR, 6'3", 210 lbs. Deb: 8/17/93																												
1993	Oak-A	3	3	.500	8	8	0	0	0	49	49	23	4	2	16	33	12.3	4.04	101	.258	.322	0	—	0	2	0	-1	0.0
1994	Oak-A	1	1	.500	4	4	1	0	0	28	26	8	1	1	8	15	11.3	2.57	172	.252	.313	0	—	0	7	6	0	0.4
1997	Oak-A	3	12	.200	24	24	0	0	0	132^{2}	166	92	20	9	47	92	15.1	5.77	79	.304	.369	0	—	0	-18	-18	-1	-1.8
1998	Cle-A	0	2	.000	11	1	0	0	0	24^{1}	31	16	3	2	6	13	14.4	5.92	81	.310	.361	0	—	0	-3	-3	-0	-0.2
1999	*Cle-A	10	2	.833	50	3	0	0	1	78^{2}	71	29	6	2	30	68	11.8	2.97	170	.247	.323	0	—	0	17	17	0	2.3
2000	Cle-A	5	9	.357	72	0	0	0	20	76^{2}	79	33	5	3	25	66	12.6	3.76	133	.266	.329	0	.000	-0	10	10	1	2.0
Total	6	22	29	.431	169	40	1	0	21	389^{1}	422	201	39	19	132	287	13.2	4.37	107	.277	.342	0	.000	-0	14	13	-1	2.7
● **TAKASHI KASHIWADA** Kashiwada, Takashi b: 5/14/71, Tokyo, Japan BL/TL, 5'11", 165 lbs. Deb: 5/1/97																												
1997	NY-N	3	1	.750	35	0	0	0	0	31^{1}	35	15	4	3	18	19	16.1	4.31	94	.289	.394	0	.000	-0	-0	-1	0	-0.1
● **JACK KATOLL** Katoll, John "Big Jack" b: 6/24/1872, Germany d: 6/18/55, Hartland, Ill. BR/TR, 5'11", 195 lbs. Deb: 9/9/1898																												
1898	Chi-N	0	1	.000	2	1	1	0	0	11	8	4	0	0	1	3	7.4	0.82	438	.200	.220	0	.000	-1	3	3	-0	0.2
1899	Chi-N	1	1	.500	2	2	2	0	0	18	17	15	0	1	4	1	11.0	6.00	62	.250	.301	0	.000	-1	-4	-5	0	-0.4
1901	Chi-A	11	10	.524	27	25	19	0	0	208	231	126	3	11	53	59	12.8	2.81	124	.278	.330	10	.125	-4	20	16	2	1.2
1902	Chi-A	0	0	—	1	0	0	0	0	1	1	0	0	0	0	2	9.0	0.00	—	.250	.250	0	.000	-0	0	0	0	0.0
	Bal-A	5	10	.333	15	13	13	0	0	123	175	106	5	2	32	25	15.3	4.02	94	.334	.375	10	.175	-0	-6	-3	4	0.0
	Yr	5	10	.333	16	13	13	0	0	124	176	106	5	2	32	27	15.2	3.99	94	.333	.374	10	.172	-0	-6	-3	4	0.0
Total	4	17	22	.436	47	41	35	0	0	361	432	251	8	14	90	90	13.4	3.32	109	.294	.341	20	.134	-6	13	12	6	1.0
● **BOB KATZ** Katz, Robert Clyde b: 1/30/11, Lancaster, Pa. d: 12/14/62, St.Joseph, Mich. BR/TR, 5'11.5", 190 lbs. Deb: 5/12/44																												
1944	Cin-N	0	1	.000	6	2	0	0	0	18^{1}	17	9	0	0	7	4	11.8	3.93	89	.254	.324	0	.000	-1	-1	-1	1	0.0
● **CURT KAUFMAN** Kaufman, Curt Gerrard b: 7/19/57, Omaha, Neb. BR/TR, 6'2", 175 lbs. Deb: 9/10/82																												
1982	NY-A	1	0	1.000	7	0	0	0	0	8^{2}	9	5	2	0	6	1	15.6	5.19	77	.265	.375	0	—	0	-1	-1	-0	-0.1
1983	NY-A	0	0	—	4	0	0	0	0	8^{2}	10	3	0	0	4	8	14.5	3.12	125	.303	.378	0	—	0	1	1	-0	0.0
1984	Cal-A	2	3	.400	29	1	0	0	1	69	68	37	13	0	20	41	11.5	4.57	87	.254	.306	0	—	0	-4	-5	0	-0.3
Total	3	3	3	.500	40	1	0	0	1	86^{1}	87	45	15	0	30	50	12.2	4.48	89	.260	.321	0	—	0	-4	-5	0	-0.4
● **TONY KAUFMANN** Kaufmann, Anthony Charles b: 12/16/1900, Chicago, Ill. d: 6/4/82, Elgin, Ill. BR/TR, 5'11", 165 lbs. Deb: 9/23/21 C♦																												
1921	Chi-N	1	0	1.000	2	1	1	0	1	13	12	6	0	0	3	6	10.4	4.15	92	.240	.283	2	.400	1	-1	-0	-1	0.0
1922	Chi-N	7	13	.350	37	14	4	1	3	153	161	81	15	5	57	45	13.1	4.06	103	.273	.343	9	.200	1	1	2	-1	0.3
1923	Chi-N	14	10	.583	33	24	18	2	3	206^{1}	209	97	14	11	67	72	12.5	3.10	129	.264	.330	16	.216	3	21	21	-1	2.4
1924	Chi-N	16	11	.593	34	26	16	3	0	208^{1}	218	104	21	4	66	79	12.4	4.02	97	.272	.330	24	.316	6	-3	-3	-1	0.1
1925	Chi-N	13	13	.500	31	23	14	2	2	196	221	107	9	7	77	49	14.0	4.50	96	.292	.363	15	.192	1	-5	-4	-0	-0.3
1926	Chi-N	9	7	.563	26	22	14	1	2	169^{2}	169	71	6	6	44	52	11.6	3.02	127	.262	.316	15	.250	2	15	15	-2	1.4
1927	Chi-N	3	3	.500	9	6	3	0	0	53^{1}	75	44	8	4	19	21	16.5	6.41	60	.338	.400	5	.313	3	-15	-15	2	-1.0
	Phi-N	0	3	.000	5	5	1	0	0	18^{2}	37	25	2	0	8	4	21.7	10.61	39	.425	.474	1	.143	0	-14	-13	-0	-1.5
	StL-N	0	0	—	1	0	0	0	0	0^{1}	4	3	0	0	1	0	135.0	81.00	5	1.000	1.000	0	—	0	-3	-3	0	-0.1
	Yr	3	6	.333	15	11	4	0	0	72^{1}	116	72	10	4	28	25	18.4	7.84	50	.371	.429	6	.261	3	-32	-31	1	-2.6
1928	StL-N	0	0	—	4	1	0	0	0	4^{2}	8	5	1	1	4	2	25.1	9.64	41	.444	.565	0	—	0	-3	-3	-0	-0.1
1930	StL-N	0	1	.000	2	1	0	0	0	10^{1}	15	9	2	0	4	2	16.5	7.84	64	.357	.413	1	.333	0	-3	-3	-0	-0.2
1931	StL-N	1	1	.500	15	1	0	0	1	49	65	34	3	1	17	13	15.2	6.06	65	.319	.374	2	.111	-1	-12	-11	0	-0.7
1935	StL-N	0	0	—	3	0	0	0	0	3^{2}	4	1	0	0	1	0	12.3	2.45	167	.286	.333	0	—	0	1	1	0	0.0
Total	11	64	62	.508	202	124	71	9	12	1086^{1}	1198	587	81	39	368	345	13.3	4.18	97	.284	.347	91	.220	17	-22	-17	-5	0.3
● **GREG KEAGLE** Keagle, Gregory Charles b: 6/28/71, Corning, N.Y. BR/TR, 6'1", 185 lbs. Deb: 4/1/96																												
1996	Det-A	3	6	.333	26	6	0	0	0	87^{2}	104	76	13	9	68	70	18.6	7.39	68	.298	.425	0	—	0	-23	-22	-0	-1.9
1997	Det-A	3	5	.375	11	10	0	0	0	45^{1}	58	33	9	5	18	33	16.1	6.55	70	.309	.384	0	.000	-0	-10	-10	-0	-1.4
1998	Det-A	0	5	.000	9	7	0	0	0	38^{2}	46	26	5	4	20	25	16.3	5.59	85	.295	.389	0	—	0	-4	-4	0	-0.4
Total	3	6	16	.273	46	23	0	0	0	171^{2}	208	135	27	18	106	128	17.4	6.76	72	.300	.406	0	.000	-0	-37	-36	-1	-3.7
● **STEVE KEALEY** Kealey, Steven William b: 5/13/47, Torrance, Cal. BR/TR, 6', 185 lbs. Deb: 9/9/68																												
1968	Cal-A	0	1	.000	6	0	0	0	0	10	10	3	0	0	5	4	13.5	2.70	108	.256	.341	0	—	0	0	0	-1	0.0
1969	Cal-A	2	0	1.000	15	3	1	1	0	36^{2}	48	18	4	1	13	17	15.2	3.93	89	.322	.380	0	.000	-1	-1	-2	-1	-0.3
1970	Cal-A	1	0	1.000	17	0	0	0	1	21^{2}	19	11	2	0	6	14	10.4	4.15	87	.260	.316	1	.250	0	-1	-1	-1	-0.1
1971	Chi-A	2	2	.500	54	1	0	0	6	77^{1}	69	40	10	0	26	50	11.1	3.84	94	.239	.302	2	.200	1	-3	-2	-0	-0.1
1972	Chi-A	3	2	.600	40	0	0	0	4	57^{1}	50	21	4	0	12	37	9.7	3.30	95	.234	.274	0	.000	-0	-1	-1	-1	-0.2
1973	Chi-A	0	0	—	7	0	0	0	0	11^{1}	23	22	2	0	7	4	23.8	15.09	26	.418	.484	0	—	0	-14	-14	-0	-0.7
Total	6	8	5	.615	139	4	1	1	11	214^{1}	219	115	22	1	69	126	12.1	4.28	80	.267	.325	3	.115	-0	-21	-20	-3	-1.4
● **ED KEAS** Keas, Edward James b: 2/2/1863, Dubuque, Iowa d: 1/12/40, Dubuque, Iowa Deb: 8/25/1888																												
1888	Cle-a	3	3	.500	6	6	6	0	0	51	53	28	1	1	12	18	11.6	2.29	135	.259	.303	2	.087	-2	4	4	1	0.3
● **RAY KEATING** Keating, Raymond Herbert b: 7/21/1891, Bridgeport, Conn. d: 12/28/63, Sacramento, Cal. BR/TR, 5'11", 185 lbs. Deb: 9/12/12																												
1912	NY-A	0	3	.000	6	5	3	0	0	35^{2}	36	27	0	1	18	21	13.9	5.80	62	.265	.355	6	.375	1	-10	-8	0	-0.4
1913	NY-A	6	12	.333	28	21	9	2	0	151^{1}	147	77	3	2	51	83	11.9	3.21	93	.253	.316	3	.070	-3	-5	-4	-2	-0.9
1914	NY-A	8	11	.421	34	25	14	0	0	210	198	94	1	5	67	109	11.6	2.96	93	.253	.316	12	.169	-0	-5	-5	2	-0.2
1915	NY-A	3	6	.333	11	10	8	1	0	79^{1}	66	41	3	3	45	37	12.9	3.63	81	.228	.337	4	.154	-1	-6	-6	1	-0.6
1916	NY-A	5	6	.455	14	11	6	0	0	91	91	42	4	2	37	35	12.9	3.07	94	.272	.349	7	.241	1	-2	-2	2	0.1
1918	NY-A	2	2	.500	15	6	1	0	0	48^{1}	39	27	0	2	30	16	13.2	3.91	72	.238	.362	3	.188	-0	-6	-6	0	-0.5
1919	Bos-N	7	11	.389	22	14	9	1	0	136	129	61	2	2	45	48	11.6	2.98	96	.261	.325	7	.152	-1	-1	-2	2	-0.2
Total	7	31	51	.378	130	92	50	4	0	751^{2}	706	369	13	17	293	349	12.2	3.29	88	.254	.329	42	.170	-2	-35	-32	5	-2.7
● **BOB KEATING** Keating, Robert M. b: 9/22/1862, Springfield, Mass d: 1/19/22, Springfield, Mass. BL/TL, 6'4", 190 lbs. Deb: 8/27/1887																												
1887	Bal-a	0	1	.000	1	1	1	0	0	9	22	16	0	0	6	0	22.0	11.00	37	.449	.449	1	.250	-0	-7	-7	0	-0.5
● **CACTUS KECK** Keck, Frank Joseph b: 1/13/1899, St.Louis, Mo. d: 2/6/81, Kirkwood, Mo. BR/TR, 5'11", 170 lbs. Deb: 5/26/22																												
1922	Cin-N	7	6	.538	27	15	5	1	1	131	138	71	4	5	29	27	11.8	3.37	119	.276	.322	7	.159	-1	11	9	-3	0.3
1923	Cin-N	3	6	.333	35	6	1	0	2	87	84	49	5	3	32	16	12.3	3.72	104	.254	.325	1	.059	-1	3	1	1	0.1
Total	2	10	12	.455	62	21	6	1	3	218	222	120	9	8	61	43	12.0	3.51	112	.267	.323	8	.131	-2	13	11	-3	0.4
● **DAVE KEEFE** Keefe, David Edwin b: 1/9/1897, Williston, Vt. d: 2/4/78, Kansas City, Mo. BL/TR, 5'9", 165 lbs. Deb: 4/21/17 C																												
1917	Phi-A	1	0	1.000	3	0	0	0	0	5	5	4	0	0	4	1	16.2	1.80	153	.278	.409	0	.000	-0	0	1	0	0.1
1919	Phi-A	0	1	.000	1	1	1	0	0	9	8	4	0	0	3	5	11.0	4.00	86	.242	.306	0	.000	-0	-1	-1	0	-0.1
1920	Phi-A	6	7	.462	31	13	7	1	0	130^{1}	129	60	2	6	30	41	11.4	2.97	136	.262	.313	10	.250	-0	12	14	1	1.4
1921	Phi-A	2	9	.182	44	12	4	0	1	173	214	126	19	5	64	68	14.7	4.68	95	.311	.374	10	.175	-3	-8	-4	-2	-0.7
1922	Cle-A	0	0	—	18	1	0	0	0	36^{1}	47	30	2	0	12	11	14.6	6.19	65	.333	.386	2	.333	1	-9	-9	-0	-0.4
Total	5	9	17	.346	97	27	12	1	1	353^{2}	403	224	23	11	113	126	13.4	4.15	101	.294	.352	22	.206	-3	-5	2	-1	0.3
● **GEORGE KEEFE** Keefe, George W. b: 1/7/1867, Washington, D.C. d: 8/24/35, Washington, D.C. BL/TL, 5'9", 168 lbs. Deb: 7/30/1886																												
1886	Was-N	0	3	.000	4	4	4	0	0	31^{1}	28	22	0		15	5	12.4	5.17	64	.233	.319	0	.000	-2	-6	-7	-1	-0.7
1887	Was-N	0	1	.000	1	1	1	0	0	8	20	20	1	2	4	0	24.8	9.00	45	.417	.440	0	.000	-1	-4	-4	-0	-0.4
1888	Was-N	6	7	.462	13	13	13	1	0	114	87	55	2	4	43	52	10.6	2.84	99	.206	.286	9	.214	1	0	-0	1	0.2

YEAR	TM/L	W	L	PCT	G	GS	CG	SH	SV	IP	H	R	HR	HB	BB	SO	RAT	ERA	ERA+	OAV	OOB	BH	AVG	PB	PR	PR+	PD	TPI
1889	Was-N	8	18	.308	30	27	24	0	0	230	266	182	6	4	143	90	16.2	5.13	77	.281	.378	16	.163	-2	-28	-31	-2	-2.9
1890	Buf-P	6	16	.273	25	22	22	0	0	196	280	229	11	5	138	55	19.4	6.52	63	.321	.417	16	.203	1	-50	-55	-1	-4.1
1891	Was-a	0	3	.000	5	4	4	0	1	37	44	42	0	1	17	11	15.1	2.68	140	.286	.360	2	.143	-0	4	4	1	0.3
Total	6	20	48	.294	78	71	68	1	1	616^1	725	550	20	16	360	213	16.0	5.05	74	.283	.374	43	.172	-3	-85	-92	-4	-7.6
● JOHN KEEFE Keefe, John Thomas b: 5/5/1867, Fitchburg, Mass. d: 8/9/37, Fitchburg, Mass. TL, Deb: 4/28/1890																												
1890	Syr-a	17	24	.415	43	41	36	2	0	352^1	355	234	9	25	148	120	13.5	4.32	82	.254	.336	30	.191	-5	-17	-34	0	-3.3
● BOBBY KEEFE Keefe, Robert Francis b: 6/16/1882, Folsom, Cal. d: 12/7/64, Sacramento, Cal. BR/TR, 5'11", 155 lbs. Deb: 4/15/07																												
1907	NY-A	3	5	.375	19	3	0	0	3	57^2	60	18	1	1	20	20	12.6	2.50	112	.270	.333	1	.053	-2	0	2	0	0.1
1911	Cin-N	12	13	.480	39	26	15	0	3	234^1	196	88	7	3	76	105	10.6	2.69	123	.229	.294	6	.086	-2	19	17	-5	0.9
1912	Cin-N	1	3	.250	17	6	0	0	2	68^2	78	52	0	4	33	29	15.1	5.24	64	.289	.375	3	.167	-1	-14	-15	0	-0.9
Total	3	16	21	.432	75	35	15	0	8	360^2	334	158	8	8	129	154	11.8	3.14	103	.248	.317	10	.093	-5	5	4	-5	0.1
● TIM KEEFE Keefe, Timothy John "Smiling Tim" or "Sir Timothy" b: 1/1/1857, Cambridge, Mass. d: 4/23/33, Cambridge, Mass. BR/TR, 5'10.5", 185 lbs. Deb: 8/6/1880 UH																												
1880	Tro-N	6	6	.500	12	12	12	0	0	105	68	27	0		16	39	**7.2**	**0.86**	**294**	**.178**	**.212**	10	.233	-0	18	18	1	2.1
1881	Tro-N	18	27	.400	45	45	45	4	0	403	434	243	4		83	103	11.5	3.24	91	.270	.305	35	.230	4	-21	-12	-0	-0.8
1882	Tro-N	17	26	.395	43	42	41	1	0	376	367	221	4		78	111	10.7	2.49	114	.243	.280	43	.228	5	17	15	5	2.3
1883	NY-a	41	27	.603	**68**	68	**68**	5	0	**619**	488	244	6		108	**359**	**8.7**	2.41	138	**.203**	**.237**	57	.220	4	61	63	6	6.5
1884	*NY-a	37	17	.685	58	58	56	4	0	483	380	196	5	15	71	334	8.7	2.25	138	**.204**	.239	50	.238	12	53	48	0	5.7
1885	NY-N	32	13	.711	46	46	45	7	0	400	300	154	6		102	227	9.0	**1.58**	**170**	.203	.255	27	.163	-1	55	51	0	5.0
1886	NY-N	**42**	20	.677	**64**	64	**62**	2	0	**535**	479	250	9		102	297	9.8	2.56	126	.231	.267	35	.171	1	45	40	1	3.8
1887	NY-N	35	19	.648	56	56	54	2	0	476^2	536	260	11	11	108	189	**10.3**	3.12	121	**.272**	**.276**	62	.294	8	51	37	3	4.1
1888	*NY-N	**35**	12	**.745**	51	51	48	**8**	0	434^1	317	140	5	12	90	**335**	**8.7**	**1.74**	**157**	**.196**	.243	23	.127	-6	**54**	**50**	1	4.4
1889	*NY-N	28	13	.683	47	45	39	3	1	364	319	212	9	18	151	225	12.1	3.31	119	**.228**	.312	23	.154	-4	28	26	2	2.2
1890	NY-P	17	11	.607	30	30	23	1	0	229	225	137	6	8	89	89	12.7	3.38	134	.246	.318	10	.109	-5	22	28	1	2.2
1891	NY-N	2	5	.286	8	7	4	0	0	55	70	57	1	4	27	30	16.5	5.24	61	.299	.381	2	.095	-1	-12	-13	0	-1.3
	Phi-N	3	6	.333	11	10	9	0	1	78^1	82	55	2	4	30	34	13.3	3.91	87	.259	.331	5	.172	0	-5	-4	0	-0.4
	Yr	5	11	.313	19	17	13	0	1	133^1	152	112	3	8	57	64	14.6	4.45	75	.276	.353	7	.140	-1	-16	-17	1	-1.7
1892	Phi-N	19	16	.543	39	38	31	2	0	313^1	279	142	4	13	98	136	11.2	2.36	138	.229	.293	10	.085	-7	32	31	-1	2.2
1893	Phi-N	10	7	.588	22	22	17	0	0	178	202	131	3	13	80	56	14.9	4.40	104	.277	.359	18	.228	0	5	4	-2	0.1
Total	14	342	225	.603	600	594	554	39	2	5049^2	4546	2469	75	98	1233	2564	10.3	2.62	126	.231	.275	410	.195	11	405	382	18	38.1
● ED KEEGAN Keegan, Edward Charles b: 7/8/39, Camden, N.J. BR/TR, 6'3", 165 lbs. Deb: 8/24/59																												
1959	Phi-N	0	3	.000	3	3	0	0	0	9	19	18	2	1	13	3	33.0	18.00	23	.432	.569	0	.000	-0	-14	-13	-0	-1.9
1961	KC-A	0	0	—	6	0	0	0	1	6	6	5	0	0	5	3	16.5	4.50	93	.261	.393	0	—	0	-0	-0	-0	0.0
1962	Phi-N	0	0	—	4	0	0	0	0	8	6	2	1	1	5	5	13.5	2.25	172	.214	.353	0	—	0	2	1	-0	0.0
Total	3	0	3	.000	13	3	0	0	1	23	31	25	3	2	23	11	21.9	9.00	45	.326	.467	0	.000	-0	-13	-12	-1	-1.9
● BOB KEEGAN Keegan, Robert Charles "Smiley" b: 8/4/20, Rochester, N.Y. BR/TR, 6'2.5", 207 lbs. Deb: 5/24/53																												
1953	Chi-A	7	5	.583	22	11	4	2	1	98^2	80	34	4	2	33	32	10.5	2.74	147	.223	.293	9	.321	2	14	14	1	1.9
1954	Chi-A★	16	9	.640	31	27	14	2	2	209^2	211	84	16	1	82	61	12.6	3.09	121	.266	.336	9	.120	-2	15	15	-1	1.4
1955	Chi-A	2	5	.286	18	11	1	0	0	58^2	83	39	4	1	28	29	17.2	5.83	68	.336	.406	6	.333	2	-12	-12	0	-1.1
1956	Chi-A	5	7	.417	20	16	4	0	0	105^1	119	56	15	2	35	32	13.3	3.93	104	.286	.344	4	.125	-1	3	2	-0	0.1
1957	Chi-A	10	8	.556	30	20	6	2	2	142^2	131	62	22	2	37	36	10.7	3.53	106	.243	.294	4	.103	-1	4	3	-1	0.1
1958	Chi-A	0	2	.000	14	2	0	0	0	29^2	44	25	9	0	18	8	18.8	6.07	60	.358	.440	0	.000	-1	-8	-8	1	-0.5
Total	6	40	36	.526	135	87	29	6	5	644^2	668	300	70	8	233	198	12.7	3.66	105	.270	.335	32	.163	-2	16	14	-1	1.9
● BURT KEELEY Keeley, Burton Elwood "Speed" b: 11/2/1879, Wilmington, Ill. d: 5/3/52, Ely, Minn. BR/TR, 5'9", 170 lbs. Deb: 4/18/08																												
1908	Was-A	6	11	.353	28	15	12	1	1	169	173	87	3	4	48	68	12.0	2.98	77	.259	.313	5	.102	-3	-11	-14	2	-1.5
1909	Was-A	0	0	—	2	0	0	0	0	7	12	13	0	1	1	0	18.0	11.57	21	.364	.400	1	.500	0	-7	-7	1	-0.2
Total	2	6	11	.353	30	15	12	1	1	176	185	100	3	5	49	68	12.2	3.32	69	.264	.317	6	.118	-3	-18	-21	2	-1.7
● VIC KEEN Keen, Howard Victor b: 3/16/1899, Bel Air, Md. d: 12/10/76, Salisbury, Md. BR/TR, 5'9", 165 lbs. Deb: 8/13/18																												
1918	Phi-A	0	1	.000	1	1	0	0	0	8	9	3	1	0	1	1	11.3	3.38	87	.300	.323	0	.000	-0	-1	-0	-1	-0.1
1921	Chi-N	0	3	.000	5	4	1	0	0	25	29	17	0	1	9	9	14.0	4.68	82	.319	.386	0	.000	-0	-2	-2	0	-0.3
1922	Chi-N	1	2	.333	7	2	2	0	1	34^2	36	20	4	1	10	11	12.2	3.89	108	.275	.331	4	.333	1	1	1	-0	0.1
1923	Chi-N	12	8	.600	35	17	10	0	1	177	169	70	8	5	57	46	11.7	3.00	133	.255	.319	8	.151	-3	20	20	-2	1.6
1924	Chi-N	15	14	.517	40	28	15	0	3	234^2	242	112	17	4	80	75	12.5	3.80	103	.272	.335	12	.156	-4	2	3	-3	-0.4
1925	Chi-N	2	6	.250	30	8	1	0	1	83^1	125	61	8	0	41	19	17.9	6.26	69	.359	.427	6	.240	0	-18	-18	1	-1.3
1926	*StL-N	10	9	.526	26	21	12	1	0	152	179	89	15	1	42	29	13.1	4.56	86	.295	.342	3	.057	-6	-12	-11	-2	-1.9
1927	StL-N	2	1	.667	21	0	0	0	0	33^2	39	21	3	2	8	12	13.1	4.81	82	.293	.343	1	.250	0	-3	-3	0	-0.2
Total	8	42	44	.488	165	81	41	1	6	748^1	828	393	56	14	248	202	13.1	4.11	97	.287	.346	34	.148	-12	-15	-11	-6	-2.5
● KID KEENAN Keenan, Harry Leon b: 1875, Louisville, Ky. d: 6/11/03, Covington, Ky. TR, Deb: 8/11/1891																												
1891	Cin-a	0	1	.000	1	1	1	0	0	8	6	9	0	1	4	5	12.4	0.00	—	.200	.314	2	.500	0	3	3	-0	0.4
● JIM KEENAN Keenan, James William b: 2/10/1858, New Haven, Conn. d: 9/21/26, Cincinnati, Ohio BR/TR, 5'10", 186 lbs. Deb: 5/17/1875 ♦																												
1884	Ind-a	0	0	—	1	0	0	0	0	3	2	1	0	0	0	0	6.0	3.00	110	.182	.182	73	.293	0	0	0	-0	0.0
1885	Cin-a	0	0	—	1	0	0	0	0	8	7	2	0	0	1	0	9.0	1.13	290	.233	.258	35	.265	0	2	2	0	0.1
1886	Cin-a	0	1	.000	2	0	0	0	0	8	8	5	0	0	3	2	12.4	3.38	104	.258	.324	40	.270	0	0	0	-0	0.0
Total	3	0	1	.000	4	0	0	0	0	19	17	8	0	0	4	2	9.9	2.37	142	.236	.276	463	.246	1	2	2	-0	0.1
● JIMMIE KEENAN Keenan, James William "Sparkplug" b: 5/25/1898, Avon, N.Y. d: 6/5/80, Seminole, Fla. BL/TL, 5'7", 155 lbs. Deb: 9/9/20																												
1920	Phi-N	0	0	—	1	0	0	0	0	3	3	1	0	0	1	2	12.0	3.00	114	.333	.400	0	.000	-0	0	0	0	0.0
1921	Phi-N	1	2	.333	15	2	0	0	0	32^1	48	31	3	1	15	7	17.8	6.68	63	.364	.432	0	.000	-1	-10	-8	-1	-0.8
Total	2	1	2	.333	16	2	0	0	0	35^1	51	32	3	1	16	9	17.3	6.37	65	.362	.430	0	.000	-2	-10	-8	-1	-0.8
● JEFF KEENER Keener, Jeffrey Bruce b: 1/14/59, Pana, Ill. BL/TR, 6', 170 lbs. Deb: 6/8/82																												
1982	StL-N	1	1	.500	19	0	0	0	0	22^1	19	8	1	0	19	25	15.3	1.61	225	.235	.380	0	—	0	5	5	0	0.4
1983	StL-N	0	0	—	4	0	0	0	0	4^1	6	4	0	1	1	4	16.6	8.31	44	.333	.400	0	—	0	-2	-2	0	-0.1
Total	2	1	1	.500	23	0	0	0	0	26^2	25	12	1	1	20	29	15.5	2.70	134	.253	.383	0	—	0	3	3	0	0.3
● JOE KEENER Keener, Joseph Donald b: 4/21/53, San Pedro, Cal. BR/TR, 6'4", 200 lbs. Deb: 9/18/76																												
1976	Mon-N	0	1	.000	2	2	0	0	0	4^1	7	7	0	1	8	1	33.2	10.38	36	.389	.593	0	.000	-0	-3	-3	0	-0.6
● HARRY KEENER Keener, Joshua Harry "Beans" b: 9/1869, Easton, Pa. d: 3/5/12, Easton, Pa. TR, Deb: 6/27/1896																												
1896	Phi-N	3	11	.214	16	13	11	0	0	113^1	144	102	5	9	39	28	15.2	5.88	73	.307	.371	16	.314	2	-19	-20	0	-1.6
● RICKEY KEETON Keeton, Rickey b: 3/18/57, Cincinnati, Ohio BR/TR, 6'2", 190 lbs. Deb: 5/27/80																												
1980	Mil-A	2	2	.500	5	5	0	0	0	28^1	35	15	4	0	9	8	14.0	4.76	81	.307	.358	0	—	0	-2	-3	0	-0.4
1981	Mil-A	1	0	1.000	17	0	0	0	0	35^1	47	21	4	0	11	9	14.8	5.09	67	.329	.377	0	—	0	-6	-7	0	-0.3
Total	2	3	2	.600	22	5	0	0	0	63^2	82	36	8	0	20	17	14.4	4.95	73	.319	.368	0	—	0	-8	-10	0	-0.7
● FRANK KEFFER Keffer, Frank b: Harrisburg, Pa. Deb: 4/19/1890																												
1890	Syr-a	1	1	.500	2	1	1	0	0	16	15	13	0	0	9	4	13.5	5.63	63	.242	.338	1	.143	-1	-3	-4	0	-0.4
● CHET KEHN Kehn, Chester Lawrence b: 10/30/21, San Diego, Cal. d: 4/5/84, San Diego, Cal. BR/TR, 5'11", 168 lbs. Deb: 4/30/42																												
1942	Bro-N	0	0	—	3	1	0	0	0	7^2	8	6	2	0	4	3	14.1	7.04	46	.267	.353	2	1.000	1	-3	-3	0	0.0
● KATSY KEIFER Keifer, Sherman Carl b: 9/3/1891, California, Pa. d: 2/19/27, Outwood, Ky. BB/TL, Deb: 10/8/14																												
1914	Ind-F	1	0	1.000	1	1	1	0	0	9	6	2	0	0	2	2	8.0	2.00	156	.194	.242	1	.333	0	1	1	0	0.1

YEAR	TM/L	W	L	PCT	G	GS	CG	SH	SV	IP	H	R	HR	HB	BB	SO	RAT	ERA	ERA+	OAV	OOB	BH	AVG	PB	PR	PR+	PD	TPI
● RANDY KEISLER Keisler, Randy Dean b: 2/24/76, Richards, Tex. BL/TL, 6'3", 190 lbs. Deb: 9/10/2000																												
2000	NY-A	1	0	1.000	4	1	0	0	0	10^{2}	16	14	1	0	8	6	20.3	11.81	41	.364	.462	0	—	0	-8	-9	-0	-0.6
● MIKE KEKICH Kekich, Michael Dennis b: 4/2/45, San Diego, Cal. BR/TL, 6'1", 200 lbs. Deb: 6/9/65																												
1965	LA-N	0	1	.000	5	1	0	0	0	10^{1}	10	12	2	0	13	9	20.0	9.58	34	.263	.451	0	.000	-0	-7	-8	-0	-0.7
1968	LA-N	2	10	.167	25	20	1	1	0	115	116	54	9	1	46	84	12.8	3.91	71	.267	.339	3	.081	-2	-12	-16	-1	-1.9
1969	NY-A	4	6	.400	28	13	1	0	1	105	91	58	11	2	49	66	12.2	4.54	77	.236	.325	3	.111	-1	-11	-13	-1	-1.4
1970	NY-A	6	3	.667	26	14	1	0	0	98^{2}	103	59	12	1	55	63	14.5	4.83	73	.267	.360	3	.094	-1	-12	-15	-1	-1.5
1971	NY-A	10	9	.526	37	24	3	0	0	170^{1}	167	89	13	4	82	93	13.4	4.07	80	.257	.344	8	.154	-0	-11	-17	1	-1.6
1972	NY-A	10	13	.435	29	28	2	0	0	175^{1}	172	77	13	4	76	78	12.9	3.70	80	.263	.344	8	.136	-1	-12	-15	-1	-2.1
1973	NY-A	1	1	.500	5	4	0	0	0	14^{2}	20	15	1	2	14	4	22.1	9.20	40	.351	.493	0	—	0	-9	-9	-0	-1.1
	Cle-A	1	4	.200	16	6	0	0	0	50	73	47	6	0	35	26	19.4	7.02	56	.349	.443	0	—	0	-18	-17	-1	-1.6
	Yr	2	5	.286	21	10	0	0	0	64^{2}	93	62	7	2	49	30	20.0	7.52	51	.350	.454	0	—	0	-27	-26	-2	-2.7
1975	Tex-A	0	0	—	23	0	0	0	2	31^{1}	33	16	2	0	21	19	15.5	3.73	101	.282	.391	0	—	0	0	0	1	0.1
1977	Sea-A	5	4	.556	41	2	0	0	3	90	90	58	11	3	51	55	14.4	5.60	74	.265	.365	0	—	0	-15	-15	-0	-1.4
Total	9	39	51	.433	235	112	8	1	6	860^{2}	875	485	80	17	442	497	13.9	4.59	73	.268	.358	25	.120	-5	-107	-125	-4	-13.2
● GEORGE KELB Kelb, George Francis "Pugger" or "Lefty" b: 7/17/1870, Toledo, Ohio d: 10/20/36, Toledo, Ohio BL/TL, Deb: 4/17/1898																												
1898	Cle-N	0	1	.000	3	1	1	0	0	16^{1}	23	17	0	4	1	8	15.4	4.41	82	.329	.373	1	.200	-0	-1	-1	0	-0.1
● HAL KELLEHER Kelleher, Harold Joseph b: 6/24/13, Philadelphia, Pa. d: 8/27/89, Cape May Court House, N.J. BR/TR, 6', 165 lbs. Deb: 9/17/35																												
1935	Phi-N	2	0	1.000	3	3	2	1	0	25	26	7	0	1	12	12	14.0	1.80	252	.260	.345	3	.375	1	6	7	0	0.6
1936	Phi-N	0	5	.000	14	4	1	0	0	44	60	38	2	3	29	13	18.8	5.32	85	.331	.432	2	.167	-0	-6	-3	0	-0.4
1937	Phi-N	2	4	.333	27	2	1	0	0	58^{1}	72	51	3	7	31	20	17.0	6.63	65	.308	.404	3	.176	-0	-18	-13	-0	-1.2
1938	Phi-N	0	0	—	6	0	0	0	0	7^{1}	16	15	0	0	9	4	30.7	18.41	21	.432	.543	1	.500	0	-12	-12	0	-0.5
Total	4	4	9	.308	50	9	4	1	0	134^{2}	174	111	5	11	81	49	17.8	5.95	74	.315	.413	9	.231	0	-30	-21	0	-1.5
● RON KELLER Keller, Ronald Lee b: 6/3/43, Indianapolis, Ind. BR/TR, 6'2", 200 lbs. Deb: 7/9/66																												
1966	Min-A	0	0	—	2	0	0	0	0	5^{1}	7	4	1	0	1	1	13.5	5.06	71	.318	.348	0	.000	-0	-1	-1	0	-0.1
1968	Min-A	0	1	.000	7	1	0	0	0	16	18	6	2	1	4	11	12.9	2.81	110	.305	.359	0	.000	-0	0	0	0	0.0
Total	2	0	1	.000	9	1	0	0	0	21^{1}	25	10	3	1	5	12	13.1	3.38	95	.309	.356	0	.000	-0	-1	-0	0	-0.1
● AL KELLETT Kellett, Alfred Henry b: 10/30/01, Red Bank, N.J. d: 7/14/60, New York, N.Y. BR/TR, 6'3", 200 lbs. Deb: 7/1/23																												
1923	Phi-A	0	1	.000	5	0	0	0	0	10	11	9	0	0	8	1	17.1	6.30	65	.282	.404	1	.333	0	-3	-2	1	-0.1
1924	Bos-A	0	0	—	1	0	0	0	0	0	0	0	0	2	—	—	∞	—	—	1.000	103	—	0	-2	-2	0	-0.2	
Total	2	0	1	.000	6	0	0	0	0	10	11	11	0	0	10	1	18.9	8.10	51	.282	.429	1	.333	0	-5	-4	1	-0.3
● HARRY KELLEY Kelley, Harry Leroy b: 2/13/06, Parkin, Ark. d: 3/23/58, Parkin, Ark. BR/TR, 5'9.5", 170 lbs. Deb: 4/16/25																												
1925	Was-A	1	1	.500	6	1	0	0	0	16	30	23	0	0	12	7	23.6	9.00	47	.405	.488	0	.000	-1	-8	-9	1	-0.9
1926	Was-A	0	0	—	7	1	0	0	0	10	17	10	0	1	8	6	23.4	8.10	48	.405	.510	0	.000	-0	-5	-5	-0	-0.3
1936	Phi-A	15	12	.556	35	27	20	1	3	235^{1}	250	112	21	2	75	82	12.5	3.86	132	.275	.332	18	.198	-1	31	32	-2	2.9
1937	Phi-A	13	21	.382	41	29	14	0	0	205	267	154	16	3	79	68	15.3	5.36	88	.306	.365	16	.225	1	-17	-14	-1	-1.9
1938	Phi-A	0	2	.000	4	3	0	0	0	8	17	16	0	0	10	3	30.4	16.88	29	.436	.551	0	.000	-0	-11	-11	-0	-1.6
	Was-A	9	8	.529	38	14	7	2	1	148^{1}	162	90	12	1	46	44	12.7	4.49	100	.276	.330	12	.250	1	5	0	0	0.2
	Yr	9	10	.474	42	17	7	2	1	156^{1}	179	106	12	1	56	47	13.6	5.12	88	.286	.346	12	.240	1	-6	-11	0	-1.4
1939	Was-A	4	3	.571	15	3	2	0	1	53^{2}	69	32	2	3	14	20	14.4	4.70	93	.314	.363	4	.267	1	-0	-2	-0	-0.2
Total	6	42	47	.472	146	78	43	3	5	676^{1}	812	437	51	10	244	230	14.2	4.86	98	.296	.356	50	.216	0	-5	-8	-2	-1.8
● DICK KELLEY Kelley, Richard Anthony b: 1/8/40, Boston, Mass d: 12/12/91, Northridge, Cal. BR/TL, 6', 175 lbs. Deb: 4/15/64																												
1964	Mil-N	0	0	—	2	0	0	0	0	2	2	4	0	0	3	2	22.5	18.00	20	.250	.455	0	—	0	-3	-3	-0	-0.2
1965	Mil-N	1	1	.500	21	4	0	0	0	45	37	15	5	0	20	31	11.4	3.00	117	.226	.310	0	.000	-1	3	3	-0	0.1
1966	Atl-N	7	5	.583	20	13	2	2	0	81	75	36	6	3	21	50	11.0	3.22	113	.247	.302	1	.036	-3	3	4	-2	0.1
1967	Atl-N	2	9	.182	39	9	1	1	2	98	88	48	8	1	42	75	12.0	3.77	88	.247	.328	4	.250	1	-4	-5	1	-0.3
1968	Atl-N	2	4	.333	31	11	1	1	1	98	86	36	4	1	45	73	12.1	2.76	109	.238	.324	1	.043	-1	3	3	1	0.2
1969	SD-N	4	8	.333	27	23	1	1	0	136	113	60	11	5	61	96	11.8	3.57	99	.230	.321	5	.106	-2	0	1	-2	-0.1
1971	SD-N	2	3	.400	48	1	0	0	2	59^{2}	52	26	5	4	23	42	11.9	3.47	95	.232	.315	1	.333	0	0	-1	0	-0.1
Total	7	18	30	.375	188	61	5	5	5	519^{2}	453	225	39	14	215	369	11.8	3.39	100	.237	.319	12	.096	-5	2	-1	2	-0.4
● TOM KELLEY Kelley, Thomas Henry b: 1/5/44, Manchester, Conn. BR/TR, 6', 191 lbs. Deb: 5/5/64																												
1964	Cle-A	0	0	—	6	0	0	0	0	9^{2}	9	9	1	1	9	7	17.7	5.59	64	.237	.396	0	—	0	-2	-2	-0	-0.1
1965	Cle-A	2	1	.667	4	4	1	0	0	30	19	8	3	0	13	31	9.6	2.40	145	.186	.278	2	.222	0	4	4	-0	0.4
1966	Cle-A	4	8	.333	31	7	1	0	0	95^{1}	97	55	14	0	42	64	13.1	4.34	79	.264	.340	4	.143	-1	-10	-10	-1	-1.4
1967	Cle-A	0	0	—	1	0	0	0	0	1	0	0	0	0	2	0	18.0	0.00	—	.000	.500	0	—	0	0	0	0	0.1
1971	Atl-N	9	5	.643	28	20	5	0	0	143	140	56	8	1	69	68	13.2	2.96	126	.262	.347	2	.047	-4	8	11	-1	0.6
1972	Atl-N	5	7	.417	27	14	2	1	0	116^{1}	122	65	12	0	65	59	14.5	4.56	83	.272	.364	3	.088	-2	-14	-9	-3	-1.3
1973	Atl-N	0	1	.000	7	0	0	0	0	12^{2}	13	5	0	0	7	5	14.2	2.84	139	.289	.385	0	.000	-0	1	1	0	0.1
Total	7	20	22	.476	104	45	9	1	0	408	400	198	38	2	207	234	13.4	3.75	98	.260	.349	11	.095	-6	-13	-4	-5	-1.6
● ALEX KELLNER Kellner, Alexander Raymond b: 8/26/24, Tucson, Ariz. d: 5/3/96, Tucson, Ariz. BR/TL, 6', 200 lbs. Deb: 4/29/48 F																												
1948	Phi-A	0	0	—	13	1	0	0	0	23	21	20	0	2	16	14	15.3	7.83	55	.239	.368	0	.000	-1	-9	-9	-0	-0.5
1949	Phi-A☆	20	12	.625	38	27	19	0	1	245	243	120	18	2	129	94	13.7	3.75	110	.261	.352	20	.217	1	12	10	-0	1.3
1950	Phi-A	8	20	.286	36	29	15	0	2	225^{1}	253	157	28	2	112	85	14.7	5.47	83	.282	.363	16	.200	-1	-22	-23	-2	-2.7
1951	Phi-A	11	14	.440	33	29	11	1	0	209^{2}	218	118	20	4	93	94	13.5	4.46	96	.272	.350	18	.228	-1	-8	-4	-1	-0.6
1952	Phi-A	12	14	.462	34	33	14	1	2	231^{1}	223	124	21	4	86	105	12.2	4.36	91	.252	.321	17	.207	0	-18	-10	-2	-1.1
1953	Phi-A	11	12	.478	25	25	14	2	0	201^{2}	210	98	8	4	51	81	11.8	3.93	109	.269	.317	15	.217	-1	2	8	-2	0.7
1954	Phi-A	6	17	.261	27	27	8	1	0	173^{2}	204	118	16	6	88	69	15.4	5.39	72	.301	.387	10	.182	-0	-32	-27	0	-3.1
1955	KC-A	11	8	.579	30	24	6	3	0	162^{2}	164	81	18	5	60	75	12.7	4.20	99	.265	.335	12	.214	2	-4	-1	-0	0.2
1956	KC-A	7	4	.636	20	17	5	0	0	91^{2}	103	49	15	2	33	44	13.5	4.32	100	.289	.353	6	.200	-0	-2	0	0	0.0
1957	KC-A	6	5	.545	28	21	3	0	0	132^{2}	141	65	18	2	41	72	12.5	4.27	93	.278	.335	11	.234	4	-7	-4	0	0.1
1958	KC-A	0	2	.000	7	6	0	0	0	33^{2}	40	24	5	0	8	22	12.8	5.88	66	.315	.356	1	.091	-0	-8	-7	0	-0.4
	Cin-N	7	3	.700	18	7	4	0	0	82	74	24	8	3	20	42	10.6	2.30	180	.243	.296	10	.357	3	15	16	-2	2.0
1959	StL-N	2	1	.667	12	4	0	0	0	37	31	17	9	1	10	19	10.2	3.16	134	.220	.276	2	.222	0	3	4	-0	0.3
Total	12	101	112	.474	321	250	99	9	5	1849^{1}	1925	1015	184	37	747	816	13.2	4.41	95	.270	.343	138	.215	7	-78	-46	-8	-3.8
● WALT KELLNER Kellner, Walter Joseph b: 4/26/29, Tucson, Ariz. BR/TR, 6', 200 lbs. Deb: 9/6/52 F																												
1952	Phi-A	0	0	—	1	0	0	0	0	4	4	3	0	0	3	2	15.8	6.75	59	.250	.368	0	.000	-0	-1	-1	-0	-0.1
1953	Phi-A	0	0	—	2	0	0	0	0	3	1	2	0	1	4	4	18.0	6.00	71	.111	.429	0	—	0	-1	-1	0	0.0
Total	2	0	0	—	3	0	0	0	0	7	5	5	0	1	7	6	16.7	6.43	64	.200	.394	0	.000	-0	-2	-2	0	-0.1
● AL KELLOGG Kellogg, Albert C. b: 9/9/1886, Providence, R.I. d: 7/21/53, Portland, Ore. TL, 6'3", 208 lbs. Deb: 9/25/08																												
1908	Phi-A	0	2	.000	3	3	2	0	0	17	20	19	1	1	9	8	15.9	5.82	44	.294	.385	1	.125	-0	-6	-6	0	-0.6
● WIN KELLUM Kellum, Winford Ansley b: 4/11/1876, Waterford, Ont., Canada d: 8/10/51, Big Rapids, Mich. BB/TL, 5'10", 190 lbs. Deb: 4/26/01																												
1901	Bos-A	2	3	.400	6	6	5	0	0	48	61	42	3	3	7	8	13.3	6.38	55	.305	.338	3	.167	-1	-14	-16	1	-1.2
1904	Cin-N	15	10	.600	31	24	22	1	2	224^{2}	206	98	1	10	46	70	10.5	2.60	113	.244	.291	13	.159	2	3	8	1	1.1
1905	StL-N	3	3	.500	11	7	5	1	0	74	70	30	1	1	10	19	9.9	2.92	102	.255	.283	5	.200	1	1	0	1	0.2
Total	3	20	16	.556	48	37	32	2	2	346^{2}	337	170	5	14	63	97	10.7	3.19	95	.255	.297	21	.168	2	-10	-6	3	0.1
● BRYAN KELLY Kelly, Bryan Keith b: 2/24/59, Silver Spring, Md. BR/TR, 6'2", 195 lbs. Deb: 9/2/86																												
1986	Det-A	1	2	.333	6	4	0	0	0	20	21	11	4	0	10	18	13.9	4.50	92	.269	.352	0	—	0	-1	-1	0	-0.1
1987	Det-A	0	1	.000	5	0	0	0	0	10^{2}	12	6	2	0	7	10	16.0	5.06	84	.286	.388	0	—	0	-1	-1	-0	-0.1
Total	2	1	3	.250	11	4	0	0	0	30^{2}	33	17	6	0	17	28	14.7	4.70	89	.275	.365	0	—	0	-1	-2	0	-0.2

YEAR	TM/L	W	L	PCT	G	GS	CG	SH	SV	IP	H	R	HR	HB	BB	SO	RAT	ERA	ERA+	OAV	OOB	BH	AVG	PB	PR	PR+	PD	TPI
● **ED KELLY**	Kelly, Edward Leo b: 12/10/1888, Pawtucket, R.I. d: 11/4/28, Red Lodge, Mont. BR/TR, 5'11.5", 173 lbs. Deb: 4/14/14																											
1914	Bos-A	0	0	—	3	0	0	0	0	2^1	1	1	0	0	1	4	7.7	0.00	—	.100	.182	0	.000	-0	1	1	0	0.0
● **GEORGE KELLY**	Kelly, George Lange "Highpockets" b: 9/10/1895, San Francisco, Cal. d: 10/13/84, Burlingame, Cal. BR/TR, 6'4", 190 lbs. Deb: 8/18/15 FCH♦																											
1917	NY-N	1	0	1.000	1	0	0	0	0	5	4	0	0	0	1	2	9.0	0.00	—	.211	.250	0	.000	-0	2	2	-0	0.3
● **HERB KELLY**	Kelly, Herbert Barrett "Moke" b: 6/4/1892, Mobile, Ala. d: 5/18/73, Torrance, Cal. BL/TL, 5'9", 160 lbs. Deb: 9/25/14																											
1914	Pit-N	0	2	.000	5	2	2	0	0	25^2	24	11	1	0	7	6	10.9	2.45	108	.253	.304	2	.222	0	1	1	-0	0.0
1915	Pit-N	1	1	.500	5	1	0	0	0	11	10	9	0	1	4	6	12.3	4.09	67	.250	.333	1	.500	1	-2	-2	1	-0.1
Total	2	1	3	.250	10	3	2	0	0	36^2	34	20	1	1	11	12	11.3	2.95	91	.252	.313	3	.273	1	-1	-1	1	-0.1
● **MIKE KELLY**	Kelly, Michael J. b: 11/9/02, St.Louis, Mo. BR/TR, 6'1", 178 lbs. Deb: 9/3/26																											
1926	Phi-N	0	0	—	4	0	0	0	0	6^2	9	7	0	1	4	2	18.9	9.45	44	.346	.452	0	.000	-0	-4	-4	-0	-0.3
● **KING KELLY**	Kelly, Michael Joseph b: 12/31/1857, Troy, N.Y. d: 11/8/1894, Boston, Mass. BR/TR, 5'10", 170 lbs. Deb: 5/1/1878 MH♦																											
1880	Chi-N	0	0	—	1	0	0	0	0	3	3	2	0		1	1	12.0	0.00	—	.250	.308	100	.291	0	1	1	-0	0.0
1883	Chi-N	0	0	—	1	0	0	0	0	1	1	0	0		0	0	9.0	0.00	—	.333	.333	109	.255	0	0	0	0	0.0
1884	Chi-N	0	1	.000	2	0	0	0	0	5^1	12	11	2		2	1	23.6	8.44	37	.400	.438	160	.354	1	-3	-3	-0	-0.4
1887	Bos-N	1	0	1.000	3	0	0	0	0	13	31	16	1	0	14	0	21.5	3.46	117	.437	.437	211	.391	1	1	1	-0	0.1
1890	Bos-P	1	0	1.000	1	0	0	0	0	2	1	1	0	0	2	2	13.5	4.50	98	.143	.333	111	.326	0	-0	-0	-0	0.0
1891	Cin-a	0	1	.000	3	0	0	0	0	15^1	21	15	2	1	7	0	17.0	5.28	78	.313	.387	84	.297	1	-3	-2	0	0.0
1892	*Bos-N	0	0	—	1	0	0	0	0	6	8	4	0	3	4	0	22.5	1.50	234	.308	.455	53	.189	0	1	1	-0	0.0
Total	7	2	2	.500	12	0	0	0	0	45^2	77	49	5	4	30	4	19.1	4.14	92	.356	.411	1868	.314	4	-3	-2	-0	-0.3
● **REN KELLY**	Kelly, Reynolds Joseph b: 11/18/1899, San Francisco, Cal d: 8/24/63, Millbrae, Cal. BR/TR, 6', 183 lbs. Deb: 9/18/23 F																											
1923	Phi-A	0	0	—	1	0	0	0	0	7	7	3	0	0	4	1	14.1	2.57	160	.259	.355	0	.000	-0	1	1	-0	0.0
● **BOB KELLY**	Kelly, Robert Edward b: 10/4/27, Cleveland, Ohio BR/TR, 6', 180 lbs. Deb: 5/4/51																											
1951	Chi-N	7	4	.636	35	11	4	0	0	123^2	130	70	8	1	55	48	13.5	4.66	88	.275	.352	5	.161	-1	-10	-7	-0	-0.7
1952	Chi-N	4	9	.308	31	15	3	2	0	125^1	114	62	7	3	46	50	11.7	3.59	107	.236	.306	8	.216	0	2	4	1	0.4
1953	Chi-N	0	1	.000	14	0	0	0	0	17	27	19	2	1	9	6	19.6	9.53	47	.375	.451	0	.000	-0	-10	-9	0	-0.4
	Cin-N	1	2	.333	28	5	0	0	2	66^1	71	36	7	0	26	29	13.2	4.34	100	.276	.343	2	.118	-1	-0	0	0	-0.1
	Yr	1	3	.250	42	5	0	0	2	83^1	98	55	9	1	35	35	14.5	5.40	81	.298	.367	2	.111	-1	-10	-9	1	-0.5
1958	Cin-N	0	0	—	2	1	0	0	0	2	3	1	0	0	3	1	27.0	4.50	92	.500	.667	0	—	0	-0	-0	0	0.0
	Cle-A	0	2	.000	13	3	0	0	0	27^2	29	18	4	1	13	12	14.0	5.20	70	.282	.368	1	.250	0	-4	-5	0	-0.3
Total	4	12	18	.400	123	35	7	2	2	362	374	206	28	6	152	146	13.2	4.50	90	.268	.343	16	.178	-1	-22	-18	1	-1.1
● **BILL KELSO**	Kelso, William Eugene b: 2/19/40, Kansas City, Mo. BR/TR, 6'4", 215 lbs. Deb: 7/31/64																											
1964	LA-A	2	0	1.000	10	1	1	1	0	23^2	19	6	3	1	9	21	11.0	2.28	144	.218	.299	0	.000	-0	4	3	0	0.2
1966	Cal-A	1	1	.500	5	0	0	0	0	11^1	11	3	1	1	6	11	14.3	2.38	141	.244	.346	0	.000	-0	1	1	-0	0.2
1967	Cal-A	5	3	.625	69	1	0	0	11	112	85	41	6	4	63	91	12.2	2.97	106	.219	.333	2	.105	-1	3	2	1	0.2
1968	Cin-N	4	1	.800	35	0	0	0	1	54	56	26	6	3	15	39	12.3	4.00	79	.277	.336	0	.000	-1	-6	-5	-1	-0.6
Total	4	12	5	.706	119	2	1	1	12	201	171	76	16	9	93	162	12.2	3.13	102	.237	.331	2	.059	-2	2	1	-0	0.0
● **RUSS KEMMERER**	Kemmerer, Russell Paul "Rusty" or "Dutch" b: 11/1/31, Pittsburgh, Pa. BR/TR, 6'3", 200 lbs. Deb: 6/27/54																											
1954	Bos-A	5	3	.625	19	9	2	1	0	75^1	71	35	4	2	41	37	13.6	3.82	108	.257	.357	3	.143	-0	-1	2	0	0.2
1955	Bos-A	1	1	.500	7	2	0	0	0	17^1	18	14	3	0	15	13	17.1	7.27	59	.269	.402	0	.000	-0	-6	-5	-0	-0.6
1957	Bos-A	0	0	—	1	0	0	0	0	4	5	2	0	0	2	1	15.8	4.50	89	.333	.412	0	.000	-0	-0	-0	-0	0.0
	Was-A	7	11	.389	39	26	6	0	0	172^1	214	110	20	2	71	81	15.0	4.96	79	.309	.375	3	.067	-1	-22	-20	-3	-2.2
	Yr	7	11	.389	40	26	6	0	0	176^1	219	112	20	2	73	82	15.0	4.95	79	.310	.376	3	.065	-1	-23	-20	-3	-2.2
1958	Was-A	6	15	.286	40	30	6	0	0	224^1	234	122	25	4	74	111	12.5	4.61	83	.270	.330	11	.159	-2	-21	-20	-1	-1.9
1959	Was-A	8	17	.320	37	28	8	0	0	206	221	116	20	4	71	89	12.9	4.50	87	.276	.338	8	.133	-1	-15	-13	0	-1.5
1960	Was-A	0	2	.000	3	3	0	0	0	17^1	18	15	2	1	10	10	15.1	7.79	50	.269	.372	0	.000	0	-8	-7	1	-0.6
	Chi-A	6	3	.667	36	7	2	1	2	120^2	111	45	5	1	45	76	11.7	2.98	127	.248	.318	0	.000	-3	12	11	0	0.5
	Yr	6	5	.545	39	10	2	1	2	138	129	60	7	2	55	86	12.1	3.59	106	.250	.325	0	.000	-3	4	3	1	-0.1
1961	Chi-A	3	3	.500	47	2	0	0	2	96^2	102	53	10	0	26	35	11.9	4.38	89	.278	.326	3	.200	1	-4	-5	1	-0.1
1962	Chi-A	2	1	.667	20	0	0	0	0	28	30	14	3	0	11	17	13.2	3.86	101	.270	.336	1	.500	1	0	0	1	0.2
	Hou-N	5	3	.625	36	2	0	0	3	68	72	34	10	3	15	23	11.9	4.10	91	.272	.318	3	.333	1	-1	-3	0	-0.2
1963	Hou-N	0	0	—	17	0	0	0	1	36^2	48	28	1	0	8	12	13.7	5.65	56	.320	.354	2	.286	0	-10	-11	1	-0.5
Total	9	43	59	.422	302	109	24	2	8	1066^2	1144	588	103	17	389	505	13.1	4.46	86	.277	.342	34	.128	-5	-76	-71	1	-6.7
● **DUTCH KEMNER**	Kemner, Herman John b: 3/4/1899, Quincy, Ill. d: 1/16/88, Quincy, Ill. BR/TR, 5'10.5", 175 lbs. Deb: 4/19/29																											
1929	Cin-N	0	0	—	9	0	0	0	1	15^1	19	13	0	0	8	10	15.8	7.63	60	.328	.409	1	.250	0	-5	-5	0	-0.2
● **ED KENNA**	Kenna, Edward Benninghaus "The Pitching Poet" b: 10/17/1877, Charleston, W.Va. d: 3/22/12, Grant, Fla. TR, 6', 180 lbs. Deb: 5/5/02																											
1902	Phi-A	1	1	.500	2	1	1	0	0	17	19	15	1	1	11	5	16.4	5.29	69	.284	.392	1	.125	-0	-3	-3	0	-0.3
● **VERN KENNEDY**	Kennedy, Lloyd Vernon b: 3/20/07, Kansas City, Mo. d: 1/28/93, Mendon, Mo. BL/TR, 6', 175 lbs. Deb: 9/18/34																											
1934	Chi-A	0	2	.000	3	3	1	0	0	19^1	21	8	1	0	9	7	14.0	3.72	127	.300	.380	2	.286	0	2	2	1	0.2
1935	Chi-A	11	11	.500	31	25	16	2	1	211^2	211	110	17	4	95	65	13.2	3.91	118	.262	.343	18	.247	1	13	16	2	1.8
1936	Chi-A☆	21	9	.700	35	34	20	1	0	274^1	282	167	13	3	147	99	14.2	4.63	112	.268	.360	32	.283	5	13	17	1	2.0
1937	Chi-A	14	13	.519	32	30	15	1	0	221	238	150	16	3	124	114	14.9	5.09	90	.273	.366	20	.230	2	-12	-12	0	-1.0
1938	Det-A☆	12	9	.571	33	26	11	0	2	190^1	215	123	13	1	113	53	15.6	5.06	99	.287	.381	23	.291	3	-6	-1	2	0.3
1939	Det-A	0	3	.000	4	4	1	0	0	21	25	15	4	1	9	9	15.0	6.43	76	.301	.376	2	.286	0	-4	-3	1	-0.3
	StL-A	9	17	.346	33	27	12	1	0	191^2	229	130	18	1	115	55	16.2	5.73	85	.297	.389	10	.149	-2	-24	-17	-1	-2.2
	Yr	9	20	.310	37	31	13	1	0	212^2	254	145	22	2	124	64	16.1	5.80	84	.297	.388	12	.162	-2	-28	-21	0	-2.5
1940	StL-A	12	17	.414	34	32	18	0	0	222^1	263	149	18	3	122	70	15.7	5.59	82	.298	.385	25	.298	6	-30	-24	2	-1.7
1941	StL-A	2	4	.333	6	6	2	0	0	45	44	27	5	0	27	6	14.2	4.40	98	.259	.360	6	.400	2	-1	-0	0	0.2
	Was-A	1	7	.125	17	7	2	0	0	66^1	77	49	5	2	39	22	16.0	5.70	71	.297	.393	3	.143	-1	-11	-13	0	-1.3
	Yr	3	11	.214	23	13	4	0	0	111^1	121	76	10	2	66	28	15.3	5.17	80	.282	.380	9	.250	2	-13	-13	0	-1.1
1942	Cle-A	4	8	.333	28	12	4	0	1	108	99	57	1	1	50	37	12.5	4.08	84	.244	.328	6	.200	1	-5	-8	0	-0.7
1943	Cle-A	10	7	.588	28	17	8	1	0	146^2	130	47	4	2	59	63	11.7	2.45	127	.242	.319	12	.231	1	14	11	1	1.6
1944	Cle-A	2	5	.286	12	10	2	0	0	59	66	36	0	0	37	17	15.7	5.03	66	.289	.389	2	.087	-2	-11	-12	1	-1.4
	Phi-N	1	5	.167	12	7	3	0	0	55^1	60	31	3	0	20	23	13.0	4.23	85	.269	.329	6	.286	1	-4	-4	0	-0.3
1945	Phi-N	0	3	.000	12	3	0	0	0	36	43	29	2	0	14	13	14.3	5.50	70	.297	.358	2	.182	0	-7	-7	1	-0.4
	Cin-N	5	12	.294	24	20	11	1	1	157^2	170	74	10	3	69	38	13.8	4.00	94	.280	.356	12	.226	2	-3	-4	1	-0.1
	Yr	5	15	.250	36	23	11	1	1	193^2	213	103	12	3	83	51	13.9	4.28	88	.283	.356	14	.219	2	-10	-11	2	-0.5
Total	12	104	132	.441	344	263	126	7	5	2025^2	2173	1202	130	24	1049	691	14.4	4.67	94	.277	.363	181	.244	19	-77	-62	13	-3.3
● **MONTE KENNEDY**	Kennedy, Monty Calvin b: 5/11/22, Amelia, Va. d: 3/1/97, Midlothian, Va. BR/TL, 6'2", 185 lbs. Deb: 4/18/46																											
1946	NY-N	9	10	.474	38	27	10	1	1	186^2	153	80	14	4	116	71	13.2	3.42	101	.224	.340	15	.234	2	-0	0	-0	0.2
1947	NY-N	9	12	.429	34	24	9	0	0	148^1	158	90	8	4	88	60	15.2	4.85	84	.272	.372	8	.167	-1	-13	-13	-0	-1.6
1948	NY-N	3	9	.250	25	16	7	1	0	114^1	118	64	10	3	57	63	14.0	4.01	98	.264	.351	4	.129	-1	-1	-1	-1	-0.3
1949	NY-N	12	14	.462	38	32	14	4	1	223^1	208	105	13	3	100	95	12.5	3.43	116	.242	.323	12	.145	-1	15	14	-2	1.1
1950	NY-N	5	4	.556	36	17	5	0	2	114^1	120	65	14	3	53	41	13.9	4.72	87	.269	.351	2	.056	-3	-7	-8	-0	-0.9
1951	*NY-N	1	2	.333	29	5	1	0	0	68	68	25	0	0	31	22	13.1	2.25	174	.270	.350	3	.200	0	13	13	-0	0.6
1952	NY-N	3	4	.429	31	6	2	1	0	83^1	73	37	6	2	31	48	11.4	3.02	122	.230	.303	2	.091	-1	7	6	1	0.4
1953	NY-N	0	0	—	18	0	0	0	0	22^2	30	18	2	1	19	11	19.9	7.15	60	.337	.459	0	.000	-0	-7	-7	0	-0.3
Total	8	42	55	.433	249	127	48	7	4	961	928	484	67	20	495	411	13.5	3.84	101	.253	.344	46	.153	-5	6	4	-4	-0.8
● **TED KENNEDY**	Kennedy, Theodore A. b: 2/1865, Henry, Ill. d: 10/31/07, St.Louis, Mo. BL/TR, Deb: 6/12/1885																											
1885	Chi-N	7	2	.778	9	9	8	0	0	78^2	91	54	5		28	36	13.6	3.43	88	.288	.346	3	.083	-4	-5	-3	-0	-0.7

YEAR TM/L	W	L	PCT	G	GS	CG	SH	SV	IP	H	R	HR	HB	BB	SO	RAT	ERA	ERA+	OAV	OOB	BH	AVG	PB	PR	PR+	PD	TPI
1886 Phi-a	5	15	.250	20	19	19	0	0	172^{2}	196	143	4	8	65	68	14.0	4.53	77	.271	.338	3	.044	-9	-21	-20	1	-2.4
Lou-a	0	4	.000	4	4	4	0	0	32	53	43	1	1	16	14	19.7	5.34	68	.351	.417	1	.077	-1	-7	-6	-1	-0.7
Yr	5	19	.208	24	23	23	0	0	204^{2}	249	186	5	9	81	82	14.9	4.66	76	.285	.352	4	.049	-10	-28	-25	0	-3.1
Total 2	12	21	.364	33	32	31	0	0	283^{1}	340	240	10	9	109	118	14.5	4.32	78	.286	.350	7	.060	-14	-33	-28	-0	-3.8

● BILL KENNEDY Kennedy, William Aulton "Lefty" b: 3/14/21, Carnesville, Ga. d: 4/9/83, Seattle, Wash. BL/TL, 6'2", 195 lbs. Deb: 4/26/48

YEAR TM/L	W	L	PCT	G	GS	CG	SH	SV	IP	H	R	HR	HB	BB	SO	RAT	ERA	ERA+	OAV	OOB	BH	AVG	PB	PR	PR+	PD	TPI
1948 Cle-A	1	0	1.000	6	3	0	0	0	11^{1}	16	14	0	0	13	12	23.0	11.12	37	.333	.475	2	.667	1	-9	-9	0	-0.6
StL-A	7	8	.467	26	20	3	0	0	132	132	82	10	5	104	77	16.4	4.70	97	.259	.389	11	.250	1	-6	-2	-1	-0.2
Yr	8	8	.500	32	23	3	0	0	143^{1}	148	96	10	5	117	89	17.0	5.21	87	.265	.397	13	.277	2	-15	-11	-1	-0.8
1949 StL-A	4	11	.267	48	16	2	0	1	153^{2}	172	97	12	3	73	69	14.5	4.69	97	.285	.365	6	.150	-2	-8	-2	-2	-0.5
1950 StL-A	0	0	—	1	0	0	0	0	2	1	1	0	0	2	1	13.5	0.00	—	.143	.333	0	—	0	1	1	-0	0.0
1951 StL-A	1	5	.167	19	5	1	0	0	56	76	37	4	1	37	29	18.3	5.79	76	.332	.427	2	.125	-2	-10	-8	1	-0.8
1952 Chi-A	2	2	.500	**47**	1	0	0	5	70^{2}	54	27	4	1	38	46	11.8	2.80	130	.213	.318	3	.231	0	7	7	-1	0.4
1953 Bos-A	0	0	—	16	0	0	0	2	24^{1}	24	13	2	1	17	14	15.5	3.70	114	.255	.375	1	.500	0	1	1	-0	0.1
1956 Cin-N	0	0	—	1	0	0	0	0	2	6	4	1	0	0	0	27.0	18.00	22	.667	.667	0	—	0	-3	-3	-0	-0.1
1957 Cin-N	0	2	.000	8	0	0	0	3	12^{2}	16	9	1	1	5	8	15.6	6.39	64	.314	.386	0	.000	0	-4	-3	0	-0.6
Total 8	15	28	.349	172	45	6	0	11	464^{2}	497	284	34	12	289	256	15.5	4.73	92	.275	.379	25	.208	-1	-31	-19	-2	-2.3

● BILL KENNEDY Kennedy, William Gorman b: 12/22/18, Alexandria, Va. d: 8/20/95, Alexandria, Va. BL/TL, 6'1", 175 lbs. Deb: 5/1/42

YEAR TM/L	W	L	PCT	G	GS	CG	SH	SV	IP	H	R	HR	HB	BB	SO	RAT	ERA	ERA+	OAV	OOB	BH	AVG	PB	PR	PR+	PD	TPI
1942 Was-A	0	1	.000	8	2	1	0	2	18	21	18	1	0	10	4	15.5	8.00	46	.296	.383	0	.000	-1	-9	-9	1	-0.6
1946 Was-A	1	2	.333	21	2	0	0	3	39	40	29	1	0	29	18	15.9	6.00	56	.270	.390	1	.125	-0	-11	-12	-0	-1.1
1947 Was-A	0	0	—	2	0	0	0	0	6^{2}	10	8	1	0	5	1	20.3	8.10	46	.370	.469	0	.000	-0	-3	-3	0	-0.2
Total 3	1	3	.250	31	4	1	0	5	63^{2}	71	55	3	0	44	23	16.3	6.79	51	.289	.397	1	.071	-1	-23	-24	0	-1.9

● BRICKYARD KENNEDY Kennedy, William Park b: 10/7/1867, Bellaire, Ohio d: 9/23/15, Bellaire, Ohio BR/TR, 5'11", 160 lbs. Deb: 4/26/1892

YEAR TM/L	W	L	PCT	G	GS	CG	SH	SV	IP	H	R	HR	HB	BB	SO	RAT	ERA	ERA+	OAV	OOB	BH	AVG	PB	PR	PR+	PD	TPI
1892 Bro-N	13	8	.619	26	21	18	0	1	191	189	115	3	4	95	108	13.6	3.86	82	.248	.334	14	.165	-1	-12	-15	-0	-1.5
1893 Bro-N	25	20	.556	46	44	40	2	1	382^{2}	376	238	15	7	168	107	13.0	3.72	119	.249	.327	39	.248	2	40	32	5	3.4
1894 Bro-N	24	20	.545	48	41	34	0	2	360^{2}	445	291	15	11	149	107	15.1	4.92	101	.300	.368	49	.304	4	17	1	3	0.6
1895 Bro-N	19	12	.613	40	34	27	2	1	288^{2}	341	199	14	7	95	41	13.8	5.05	87	.289	.346	40	.305	4	-9	-23	-0	-1.5
1896 Bro-N	17	20	.459	42	38	28	1	1	305^{2}	334	211	12	12	130	76	14.0	4.42	93	.276	.352	23	.189	-7	-2	-10	3	-1.3
1897 Bro-N	18	20	.474	44	40	36	2	1	343^{1}	370	206	6	8	149	81	13.8	3.91	105	.273	.348	40	.272	4	15	8	2	1.2
1898 Bro-N	16	22	.421	40	39	38	0	0	339^{1}	360	183	12	5	123	73	12.9	3.37	107	.270	.334	34	.252	3	9	8	6	1.6
1899 Bro-N	22	9	.710	40	33	27	2	2	277^{1}	297	133	11	3	86	55	12.5	2.79	140	.273	.329	27	.248	4	33	34	0	3.6
1900 Bro-N	20	13	.606	42	35	26	2	0	292	316	160	5	8	111	75	13.4	3.91	98	.276	.344	37	.301	7	-7	-2	1	0.5
1901 Bro-N	3	5	.375	14	8	6	0	0	85^{1}	80	40	1	1	24	28	11.1	3.06	110	.246	.300	6	.167	-1	3	3	-0	0.0
1902 NY-N	1	4	.200	6	6	4	1	0	38^{2}	44	25	0	0	16	9	14.0	3.96	71	.286	.353	4	.267	1	-5	-5	-1	-0.5
1903 *Pit-N	9	6	.600	18	15	10	1	0	125^{1}	130	62	0	2	57	39	13.6	3.45	94	.277	.357	21	.362	8	-2	-3	-1	0.3
Total 12	187	159	.540	406	354	294	13	9	3030	3282	1863	94	68	1203	799	13.5	3.96	103	.273	.343	334	.261	27	79	36	16	6.4

● ART KENNEY Kenney, Arthur Joseph b: 4/29/16, Milford, Mass. BL/TL, 6', 175 lbs. Deb: 7/1/38

YEAR TM/L	W	L	PCT	G	GS	CG	SH	SV	IP	H	R	HR	HB	BB	SO	RAT	ERA	ERA+	OAV	OOB	BH	AVG	PB	PR	PR+	PD	TPI
1938 Bos-N	0	0	—	2	0	0	0	0	2^{1}	3	4	0	0	8	2	42.4	15.43	22	.300	.611	0	—	0	-3	-3	0	-0.2

● ED KENT Kent, Edward C. b: 1859, New York BR/TR, 5'6.5", 152 lbs. Deb: 8/14/1884

YEAR TM/L	W	L	PCT	G	GS	CG	SH	SV	IP	H	R	HR	HB	BB	SO	RAT	ERA	ERA+	OAV	OOB	BH	AVG	PB	PR	PR+	PD	TPI
1884 Tol-a	0	1	.000	1	1	1	0	0	9	14	11	0	1	3	4	18.0	6.00	57	.298	.353	0	.000	-1	-3	-2	0	-0.2

● MAURY KENT Kent, Maurice Allen b: 9/17/1885, Marshalltown, Ia. d: 4/19/66, Iowa City, Iowa BR/TR, 6', 168 lbs. Deb: 4/15/12

YEAR TM/L	W	L	PCT	G	GS	CG	SH	SV	IP	H	R	HR	HB	BB	SO	RAT	ERA	ERA+	OAV	OOB	BH	AVG	PB	PR	PR+	PD	TPI
1912 Bro-N	5	5	.500	20	9	2	1	0	93	107	74	3	1	46	24	14.9	4.84	69	.296	.377	8	.229	1	-15	-16	1	-1.3
1913 Bro-N	0	0	—	3	0	0	0	0	7^{1}	5	2	0	0	3	1	9.8	2.45	134	.192	.276	0	.000	-0	1	1	-0	0.0
Total 2	5	5	.500	23	9	2	1	0	100^{1}	112	76	3	1	49	25	14.5	4.66	72	.289	.371	8	.211	1	-14	-15	1	-1.3

● MATT KEOUGH Keough, Matthew Lon b: 7/3/55, Pomona, Cal. BR/TR, 6'3", 190 lbs. Deb: 9/3/77 F

YEAR TM/L	W	L	PCT	G	GS	CG	SH	SV	IP	H	R	HR	HB	BB	SO	RAT	ERA	ERA+	OAV	OOB	BH	AVG	PB	PR	PR+	PD	TPI
1977 Oak-A	1	3	.250	7	6	0	0	0	42^{2}	39	25	4	1	22	23	13.1	4.85	83	.247	.343	0	—	0	-4	-4	-1	-0.4
1978 Oak-A★	8	15	.348	32	32	6	0	0	197^{1}	178	90	9	4	85	108	12.2	3.24	113	.241	.323	0	—	0	12	9	2	1.2
1979 Oak-A	2	17	.105	30	28	7	1	0	176^{2}	220	115	18	7	78	95	15.5	5.04	80	.315	.389	0	—	0	-16	-20	2	-1.7
1980 Oak-A	16	13	.552	34	32	20	2	0	250	218	94	24	5	94	121	11.4	2.92	130	.236	.310	0	—	0	31	26	-1	2.7
1981 *Oak-A	10	6	.625	19	19	10	2	0	140^{1}	125	56	11	0	45	60	10.9	3.40	102	.239	.299	0	—	0	4	1	-2	-0.1
1982 Oak-A	11	18	.379	34	34	10	2	0	209^{1}	233	144	38	5	101	75	14.6	5.72	68	.284	.366	0	—	0	-38	-44	-3	-5.3
1983 Oak-A	2	3	.400	14	4	0	0	0	44	50	29	7	0	31	28	16.6	5.52	70	.284	.391	0	—	0	-7	-9	-1	-0.9
NY-A	3	4	.429	12	12	0	0	0	55^{2}	59	42	12	2	20	26	13.1	5.17	75	.266	.332	0	—	0	-7	-8	-0	-0.9
Yr	5	7	.417	26	16	0	0	0	99^{2}	109	71	19	2	51	54	14.6	5.33	73	.274	.359	0	—	0	-14	-17	-1	-1.8
1985 StL-N	0	1	.000	4	1	0	0	0	10	10	5	0	1	4	10	13.5	4.50	79	.278	.366	0	.000	-0	-1	-1	0	-0.1
1986 Chi-N	2	2	.500	19	2	0	0	0	29	36	17	4	1	12	19	15.2	4.97	82	.316	.386	2	.400	1	-4	-3	-0	-0.3
Hou-N	3	2	.600	10	5	0	0	0	35	22	14	5	1	18	25	10.5	3.09	117	.180	.291	4	.364	1	2	2	-1	0.4
Yr	5	4	.556	29	7	0	0	0	64	58	31	9	2	30	44	12.7	3.94	97	.246	.336	6	.375	2	-2	-1	-1	0.1
Total 9	58	84	.408	215	175	53	7	0	1190	1190	631	132	27	510	590	13.1	4.17	91	.262	.341	6	.333	2	-27	-51	-5	-5.4

● KURT KEPSHIRE Kepshire, Kurt David b: 7/3/59, Bridgeport, Conn. BL/TR, 6'1", 180 lbs. Deb: 7/4/84

YEAR TM/L	W	L	PCT	G	GS	CG	SH	SV	IP	H	R	HR	HB	BB	SO	RAT	ERA	ERA+	OAV	OOB	BH	AVG	PB	PR	PR+	PD	TPI
1984 StL-N	6	5	.545	17	16	2	2	0	109	100	47	7	0	44	71	11.9	3.30	105	.249	.323	2	.056	-2	4	2	-2	-0.2
1985 StL-N	10	9	.526	32	29	0	0	0	153^{1}	155	89	16	0	71	67	13.3	4.75	75	.264	.343	6	.118	-1	-20	-21	-2	-2.6
1986 StL-N	0	1	.000	2	1	0	0	0	8	8	4	2	0	4	6	13.5	4.50	81	.258	.343	0	.000	-0	-1	-1	0	-0.1
Total 3	16	15	.516	51	46	2	2	0	270^{1}	263	140	25	0	119	144	12.7	4.16	85	.258	.335	8	.091	-3	-17	-20	-3	-2.9

● CHARLIE KERFELD Kerfeld, Charles Patrick b: 9/28/63, Knob Noster, Mo. BR/TR, 6'6", 225 lbs. Deb: 7/27/85

YEAR TM/L	W	L	PCT	G	GS	CG	SH	SV	IP	H	R	HR	HB	BB	SO	RAT	ERA	ERA+	OAV	OOB	BH	AVG	PB	PR	PR+	PD	TPI
1985 Hou-N	4	2	.667	11	6	0	0	0	44^{1}	44	22	2	0	25	30	14.0	4.06	85	.268	.365	0	.000	-1	-2	-3	-1	-0.6
1986 *Hou-N	11	2	.846	61	0	0	0	7	93^{2}	71	32	5	2	42	77	11.0	2.59	139	.213	.305	1	.111	-0	12	11	-1	1.5
1987 Hou-N	0	2	.000	21	0	0	0	0	29^{2}	34	22	3	1	21	17	17.0	6.67	59	.309	.424	0	.000	-0	-9	-9	-0	-0.6
1990 Hou-N	0	2	.000	5	0	0	0	0	3^{1}	9	6	0	0	6	4	40.5	16.20	23	.529	.652	0	—	0	-5	-5	-0	-0.9
Atl-N	3	1	.750	25	0	0	0	2	30^{2}	31	22	2	0	23	27	15.8	5.58	72	.270	.391	0	—	0	-6	-5	-1	-0.7
Yr	3	3	.500	30	0	0	0	2	34	40	28	2	0	29	31	18.3	6.62	61	.303	.429	0	—	0	-11	-9	-1	-1.6
Total 4	18	9	.667	123	6	0	0	9	201^{2}	189	104	12	3	117	155	13.8	4.20	88	.256	.360	1	.038	-2	-10	-12	-2	-1.3

● GUS KERIAZAKOS Keriazakos, Constantine Nicholas b: 7/28/31, W.Orange, N.J. d: 5/4/96, Hilton Head, S.C. BR/TR, 6'3", 187 lbs. Deb: 10/1/50

YEAR TM/L	W	L	PCT	G	GS	CG	SH	SV	IP	H	R	HR	HB	BB	SO	RAT	ERA	ERA+	OAV	OOB	BH	AVG	PB	PR	PR+	PD	TPI
1950 Chi-A	0	1	.000	1	1	0	0	0	2^{1}	7	5	0	0	5	1	46.3	19.29	23	.500	.632	1	1.000	0	-4	-4	-0	-0.5
1954 Was-A	2	3	.400	22	3	2	0	0	59^{2}	59	29	4	0	30	33	13.4	3.77	94	.262	.349	1	.067	-1	-0	-1	-0	-0.2
1955 KC-A	0	1	.000	5	1	0	0	0	11^{2}	15	16	4	0	7	8	17.0	12.34	34	.333	.423	0	.000	-0	-11	-10	-0	-0.8
Total 3	2	5	.286	28	5	2	0	0	73^{2}	81	50	8	0	42	42	15.0	5.62	65	.285	.377	2	.105	-1	-15	-16	-0	-1.5

● BILL KERKSIECK Kerksieck, Wayman William b: 12/6/13, Ulm, Ark. d: 3/11/70, Stuttgart, Ark. BR/TR, 6'1", 183 lbs. Deb: 6/21/39

YEAR TM/L	W	L	PCT	G	GS	CG	SH	SV	IP	H	R	HR	HB	BB	SO	RAT	ERA	ERA+	OAV	OOB	BH	AVG	PB	PR	PR+	PD	TPI
1939 Phi-N	0	2	.000	23	2	1	0	0	62^{2}	81	52	13	0	32	13	16.2	7.18	56	.328	.405	1	.083	-0	-23	-22	-1	-1.1

● JIM KERN Kern, James Lester b: 3/15/49, Gladwin, Mich. BR/TR, 6'5", 205 lbs. Deb: 9/6/74

YEAR TM/L	W	L	PCT	G	GS	CG	SH	SV	IP	H	R	HR	HB	BB	SO	RAT	ERA	ERA+	OAV	OOB	BH	AVG	PB	PR	PR+	PD	TPI
1974 Cle-A	0	1	.000	4	3	1	0	0	15^{1}	16	9	1	0	14	11	17.6	4.70	77	.262	.400	0	—	0	-2	-2	-0	-0.1
1975 Cle-A	1	2	.333	13	7	0	0	0	71^{2}	60	31	5	5	45	55	13.8	3.77	101	.233	.357	0	—	0	0	0	0	0.0
1976 Cle-A	10	7	.588	50	2	0	0	15	117^{2}	91	38	2	5	50	111	11.2	2.37	147	.222	.314	0	—	0	15	15	-0	2.6
1977 Cle-A★	8	10	.444	60	0	0	0	18	92	85	39	3	6	47	91	13.5	3.42	116	.260	.363	0	—	0	7	6	0	1.1
1978 Cle-A★	10	10	.500	58	0	0	0	13	99^{1}	77	36	4	3	58	95	12.5	3.08	122	.224	.342	0	.000	-0	8	7	1	1.6
1979 Tex-A★	13	5	.722	71	0	0	0	29	143	99	35	5	2	62	136	10.3	1.57	265	.199	.290	0	—	0	**42**	**42**	-1	**6.8**
1980 Tex-A	3	11	.214	38	1	0	0	2	63^{1}	65	38	4	2	45	40	15.9	4.83	81	.279	.400	0	—	0	-6	-7	0	-1.3
1981 Tex-A	1	2	.333	23	0	0	0	6	30	21	10	0	1	22	20	13.2	2.70	129	.204	.349	0	—	0	3	3	-0	0.4
1982 Cin-N	3	5	.375	50	0	0	0	2	76	61	27	3	2	48	43	13.1	2.84	130	.222	.342	0	.000	-0	6	7	1	0.7
Chi-A	2	1	.667	13	1	0	0	3	28	20	16	3	0	12	23	10.3	5.14	79	.204	.291	0	—	0	-3	-3	0	-0.4
1983 Chi-A	0	0	—	1	0	0	0	0	0^{2}	1	1	0	0	0	0	13.5	0.00	—	.333	.333	0	—	0	0	0	0	0.0

YEAR	TM/L	W	L	PCT	G	GS	CG	SH	SV	IP	H	R	HR	HB	BB	SO	RAT	ERA	ERA+	OAV	OOB	BH	AVG	PB	PR	PR+	PD	TPI
1984	Phi-N	0	1	.000	8	0	0	0	0	13^1	20	16	3	0	10	8	20.3	10.13	36	.339	.435	0	.000	-0	-10	-9	-0	-0.7
	Mil-A	1	0	1.000	6	0	0	0	0	4^2	6	0	0	0	3	4	17.4	0.00	—	.300	.391	0	—	0	2	2	-0	0.4
1985	Mil-A	0	1	.000	5	0	0	0	0	11	14	8	1	0	5	3	15.5	6.55	64	.318	.388	0	—	0	-3	-3	1	-0.2
1986	Cle-A	1	1	.500	16	0	0	0	0	27^1	34	28	1	3	23	11	19.8	7.90	53	.298	.429	0	—	0	-11	-11	0	-0.7
Total	13	53	57	.482	416	14	1	0	88	793^1	670	332	35	29	444	651	13.0	3.32	116	.235	.344	0	.000	-1	49	46	1	10.2
● DICKIE KERR Kerr, Richard Henry b: 7/3/1893, St.Louis, Mo. d: 5/4/63, Houston, Tex. BL/TL, 5′7″, 155 lbs. Deb: 4/25/19																												
1919	*Chi-A	13	7	.650	39	17	10	1	0	212^1	208	78	2	2	64	79	11.6	2.88	110	.259	.316	17	.250	5	8	7	1	1.2
1920	Chi-A	21	9	.700	45	27	19	3	**5**	253^2	266	116	7	4	72	72	12.1	3.37	112	.278	.331	14	.156	-4	12	11	3	1.1
1921	Chi-A	19	17	.528	44	37	25	3	1	308^2	357	182	12	11	96	80	13.5	4.72	90	.295	.352	25	.238	5	-15	-17	-0	-1.2
1925	Chi-A	0	1	.000	12	2	0	0	0	36^2	45	23	3	1	18	4	15.7	5.15	81	.304	.383	4	.333	1	-3	-4	0	-0.1
Total	4	53	34	.609	140	83	54	7	6	811^1	876	399	24	18	250	235	12.7	3.84	99	.281	.338	60	.218	7	2	-2	4	1.0
● JOE KERRIGAN Kerrigan, Joseph Thomas b: 11/30/54, Philadelphia, Pa. BR/TR, 6′5″, 205 lbs. Deb: 7/9/76 C																												
1976	Mon-N	2	6	.250	38	0	0	0	1	56^2	63	27	3	2	23	22	14.0	3.81	98	.289	.362	0	.000	-0	-2	-1	1	0.0
1977	Mon-N	3	5	.375	66	0	0	0	11	89^1	80	37	4	3	33	43	11.7	3.22	118	.241	.315	0	.000	-1	7	6	1	0.6
1978	Bal-A	3	1	.750	26	2	0	0	3	71^2	75	44	10	2	36	41	14.2	4.77	74	.273	.361	0	—	0	-8	-11	2	-0.5
1980	Bal-A	0	0	—	1	0	0	0	0	2^1	3	1	0	0	0	1	11.6	3.86	103	.273	.273	0	—	0	0	0	0	0.0
Total	4	8	12	.400	131	2	0	0	15	220	221	109	17	7	92	107	13.1	3.89	95	.264	.342	0	.000	-1	-3	-5	3	0.1
● RICK KESTER Kester, Richard Lee b: 7/7/46, Iola, Kan. BR/TR, 6′, 190 lbs. Deb: 8/18/68																												
1968	Atl-N	0	0	—	5	0	0	0	0	6^1	8	4	0	0	3	9	15.6	5.68	53	.308	.379	0	—	0	-2	-2	-0	-0.1
1969	Atl-N	0	0	—	1	0	0	0	0	2	5	3	1	0	0	2	22.5	13.50	27	.455	.455	0	—	0	-2	-2	-0	-0.1
1970	Atl-N	0	0	—	15	0	0	0	0	32^1	36	24	3	0	19	20	15.3	5.57	77	.283	.377	0	.000	-1	-5	-4	-1	-0.4
Total	3	0	0	—	21	0	0	0	0	40^2	49	31	4	0	22	31	15.7	5.98	68	.299	.382	0	.000	-1	-10	-8	-1	-0.6
● GUS KETCHUM Ketchum, Augustus Franklin b: 3/21/1897, Royse City, Tex. d: 9/6/80, Oklahoma City, Okla. BR/TR, 5′9.5″, 170 lbs. Deb: 8/7/22																												
1922	Phi-A	0	1	.000	6	0	0	0	0	16	19	12	2	1	8	4	15.8	5.63	76	.302	.389	0	.000	-1	-3	-2	-1	-0.2
● HENRY KEUPPER Keupper, Henry J. b: 6/24/1887, Staunton, Ill. d: 8/14/60, Marion, Ill. BL/TL, 6′1″, 185 lbs. Deb: 4/19/14																												
1914	StL-F	8	20	.286	42	25	12	1	0	213	256	132	3	4	49	70	13.1	4.27	71	.291	.332	17	.250	1	-33	-28	2	-2.9
● JIMMY KEY Key, James Edward b: 4/22/61, Huntsville, Ala. BR/TL, 6′1″, 190 lbs. Deb: 4/6/84																												
1984	Tor-A	4	5	.444	63	0	0	0	10	62	70	37	8	1	32	44	15.0	4.65	88	.286	.371	0	—	0	-4	-4	1	-0.5
1985	*Tor-A★	14	6	.700	35	32	3	0	0	212^2	188	77	22	2	50	85	10.2	3.00	140	.237	.284	0	—	0	27	28	4	2.9
1986	Tor-A	14	11	.560	36	35	4	2	0	232	222	98	24	3	74	141	11.6	3.57	118	.256	.317	0	—	0	16	17	3	1.9
1987	Tor-A	17	8	.680	36	36	8	1	0	261	210	93	24	2	66	161	**9.6**	**2.76**	**163**	**.221**	**.273**	0	—	0	**50**	**50**	2	**4.6**
1988	Tor-A	12	5	.706	21	21	2	2	0	131^1	127	55	13	5	30	65	11.1	3.29	120	.250	.298	0	—	0	10	10	-0	1.2
1989	*Tor-A	13	14	.481	33	33	5	1	0	216	226	99	18	3	27	118	10.7	3.88	98	.270	.295	0	—	0	0	-2	2	-0.1
1990	Tor-A	13	7	.650	27	27	0	0	0	154^2	169	79	20	1	22	88	11.2	4.25	93	.281	.307	0	—	0	-6	-5	0	-0.6
1991	*Tor-A★	16	12	.571	33	33	2	2	0	209^1	207	84	12	3	44	125	10.9	3.05	138	.254	.295	0	—	0	24	26	3	3.6
1992	*Tor-A	13	13	.500	33	33	4	2	0	216^2	205	88	24	4	59	117	11.1	3.53	116	.248	.301	0	—	0	10	13	0	1.5
1993	NY-A★	18	6	**.750**	34	34	4	2	0	236^2	219	84	26	1	43	173	10.0	3.00	139	.246	.282	0	—	0	35	32	0	3.0
1994	NY-A★	**17**	4	.810	25	25	1	0	0	168	177	68	10	3	52	97	12.4	3.27	140	.273	.330	0	—	0	29	26	3	3.2
1995	NY-A	1	2	.333	5	5	0	0	0	30^1	40	20	3	0	6	14	13.6	5.64	82	.323	.354	0	—	0	-3	-4	0	-0.3
1996	*NY-A	12	11	.522	30	30	0	0	0	169^1	171	93	21	2	58	116	12.3	4.68	106	.266	.329	0	—	0	6	5	1	0.7
1997	*Bal-A†	16	10	.615	34	34	1	1	0	212^1	210	90	24	5	82	141	12.6	3.43	128	.261	.333	0	.000	-0	27	24	2	2.8
1998	Bal-A	6	3	.667	25	11	0	0	0	79^1	77	39	5	3	23	53	11.7	4.20	109	.258	.317	0	—	0	4	3	0	0.3
Total	15	186	117	.614	470	389	34	13	10	2591^2	2518	1104	254	38	668	1538	11.2	3.51	122	.255	.305	0	.000	-0	225	220	21	24.2
● BRIAN KEYSER Keyser, Brian Lee b: 10/31/66, Castro Valley, Cal. BR/TR, 6′1″, 180 lbs. Deb: 6/2/95																												
1995	Chi-A	5	6	.455	23	10	0	0	0	92^1	114	53	10	2	27	48	13.9	4.97	90	.306	.356	0	—	0	-3	-6	1	-0.5
1996	Chi-A	1	2	.333	28	0	0	0	1	59^2	78	35	3	0	28	19	16.0	4.98	95	.328	.398	0	—	0	0	-2	2	0.1
Total	2	6	8	.429	51	10	0	0	1	152	192	88	13	2	55	67	14.7	4.97	92	.314	.373	0	—	0	-2	-7	3	-0.4
● MASAO KIDA Kida, Masao b: 9/12/68, Tokyo, Japan BR/TR, 6′2″, 209 lbs. Deb: 4/5/99																												
1999	Det-A	1	0	1.000	49	0	0	0	1	64^2	73	48	6	4	30	50	14.9	6.26	78	.289	.373	0	—	0	-10	-10	-0	-0.5
2000	Det-A	0	0	—	2	0	0	0	0	2^2	5	3	1	0	0	0	16.9	10.13	47	.385	.385	0	—	0	-2	-2	0	0.0
Total	2	1	0	1.000	51	0	0	0	1	67^1	78	51	7	4	30	50	15.0	6.42	76	.293	.373	0	—	0	-12	-12	-0	-0.5
● DANA KIECKER Kiecker, Dana Ervin b: 2/25/61, Sleepy Eye, Minn. BR/TR, 6′3″, 180 lbs. Deb: 4/12/90																												
1990	*Bos-A	8	9	.471	32	25	0	0	0	152	145	74	7	9	54	93	12.3	3.97	103	.253	.328	0	—	0	-1	2	2	0.4
1991	Bos-A	2	3	.400	18	5	0	0	0	40^1	56	34	6	2	23	21	18.1	7.36	58	.344	.431	0	—	0	-15	-13	1	-1.3
Total	2	10	12	.455	50	30	0	0	0	192^1	201	108	13	11	77	114	13.5	4.68	88	.273	.351	0	—	0	-15	-11	3	-0.9
● JOE KIEFER Kiefer, Joseph William "Harlem Joe" or "Smoke" b: 7/19/1899, W.Leyden, N.Y. d: 7/5/75, Utica, N.Y. BR/TR, 5′11″, 190 lbs. Deb: 10/1/20																												
1920	Chi-A	0	1	.000	2	1	0	0	0	4^2	7	8	0	1	5	1	25.1	15.43	24	.333	.481	0	.000	-0	-6	-6	-0	-0.9
1925	Bos-A	0	2	.000	2	2	0	0	0	15	20	12	0	1	9	4	18.0	6.00	76	.351	.448	0	.000	-1	-3	-2	1	-0.3
1926	Bos-A	0	2	.000	11	1	0	0	0	30	29	19	2	2	16	4	14.1	4.80	85	.266	.370	1	.143	-0	-3	-2	0	-0.1
Total	3	0	5	.000	15	4	0	0	0	49^2	56	39	2	4	30	9	16.3	6.16	68	.299	.407	1	.077	-1	-11	-11	1	-1.3
● MARK KIEFER Kiefer, Mark Andrew b: 11/13/68, Orange, Cal. BR/TR, 6′4″, 175 lbs. Deb: 9/20/93 F																												
1993	Mil-A	0	0	—	6	0	0	0	1	9^1	3	0	0	1	5	7	8.7	0.00	—	.097	.243	0	—	0	4	4	0	0.2
1994	Mil-A	1	0	1.000	7	0	0	0	0	10^2	15	12	4	0	8	8	19.4	8.44	60	.357	.460	0	—	0	-4	-4	-0	-0.3
1995	Mil-A	4	1	.800	24	0	0	0	0	49^2	37	20	6	0	27	41	11.6	3.44	145	.203	.306	0	—	0	7	8	-1	0.6
1996	Mil-A	0	0	—	7	0	0	0	0	10	15	9	1	0	5	5	18.0	8.10	64	.366	.435	0	—	0	-3	-3	-0	-0.2
Total	4	5	1	.833	44	0	0	0	1	79^2	70	41	11	1	45	61	13.1	4.29	115	.236	.339	0	—	0	4	5	-2	0.3
● JOHN KIELY Kiely, John Francis b: 10/4/64, Boston, Mass. BR/TR, 6′3″, 210 lbs. Deb: 7/26/91																												
1991	Det-A	0	1	.000	7	0	0	0	0	6^2	13	11	0	1	9	1	31.1	14.85	28	.448	.590	0	—	0	-8	-8	-0	-1.0
1992	Det-A	4	2	.667	39	0	0	0	0	55	44	14	2	0	28	18	11.8	2.13	186	.224	.321	0	—	0	11	11	2	1.4
1993	Det-A	0	2	.000	8	0	0	0	0	11^2	13	11	2	1	13	5	20.8	7.71	56	.295	.466	0	—	0	-4	-4	1	-0.6
Total	3	4	5	.444	54	0	0	0	0	73^1	70	36	4	2	50	24	15.0	4.17	97	.260	.380	0	—	0	-1	-1	3	-0.2
● LEO KIELY Kiely, Leo Patrick "Kiki" b: 11/30/29, Hoboken, N.J. d: 1/18/84, Montclair, N.J. BL/TL, 6′2″, 180 lbs. Deb: 6/27/51																												
1951	Bos-A	7	7	.500	17	16	4	0	0	113^1	106	48	9	2	39	46	11.7	3.34	134	.251	.317	5	.143	-1	10	13	1	1.5
1954	Bos-A	5	8	.385	28	19	4	1	0	131	153	74	12	1	58	59	14.6	3.50	117	.295	.367	9	.180	0	3	8	-1	0.7
1955	Bos-A	3	3	.500	33	4	0	0	6	90	91	31	5	0	37	36	12.8	2.80	153	.269	.341	5	.192	-0	12	14	1	1.2
1956	Bos-A	2	2	.500	23	0	0	0	3	31^1	47	25	1	2	14	9	18.1	5.17	89	.362	.432	1	.167	-0	-4	-2	0	-0.3
1958	Bos-A	5	2	.714	47	0	0	0	12	81	77	31	3	2	18	26	10.8	3.00	134	.254	.300	0	.000	-2	7	9	1	0.9
1959	Bos-A	3	3	.500	41	0	0	0	7	55^2	67	26	8	1	18	30	13.9	4.20	97	.299	.354	0	.000	-1	-2	-1	1	-0.1
1960	KC-A	1	2	.333	20	0	0	0	1	20^2	21	4	1	1	5	6	11.8	1.74	229	.266	.318	0	.000	0	5	5	1	0.9
Total	7	26	27	.491	209	39	8	1	29	523	562	239	39	9	189	212	13.1	3.37	125	.279	.343	20	.144	-4	31	46	5	4.8
● DARRYL KILE Kile, Darryl Andrew b: 12/2/68, Garden Grove, Cal. BR/TR, 6′5″, 185 lbs. Deb: 4/8/91																												
1991	Hou-N	7	11	.389	37	22	0	0	0	153^2	144	81	16	6	84	100	13.7	3.69	95	.246	.347	0	.000	-3	-0	-3	-2	-0.8
1992	Hou-N	5	10	.333	22	22	2	0	0	125^1	124	61	8	4	63	90	13.7	3.95	85	.261	.352	5	.156	1	-6	-8	-2	-1.1
1993	Hou-N☆	15	8	.652	32	26	4	2	0	171^2	152	73	12	15	69	141	12.4	3.51	110	.239	.327	5	.094	-1	10	7	-2	0.6
1994	Hou-N	9	6	.600	24	24	0	0	0	147^2	153	84	13	9	82	105	14.9	4.57	87	.275	.377	7	.149	1	-6	-11	-1	-0.9
1995	Hou-N	4	12	.250	25	21	0	0	0	127	114	81	5	12	73	113	14.1	4.96	78	.240	.355	4	.111	0	-11	-17	2	-1.6
1996	Hou-N	12	11	.522	35	33	4	0	0	219	233	113	16	16	97	219	14.2	4.19	92	.276	.362	10	.137	1	1	-8	1	-0.7
1997	*Hou-N☆	19	7	.731	34	34	6	4	0	255^2	208	87	19	10	94	205	11.0	2.57	156	.225	.303	11	.124	0	46	43	2	4.4

YEAR	TM/L	W	L	PCT	G	GS	CG	SH	SV	IP	H	R	HR	HB	BB	SO	RAT	ERA	ERA+	OAV	OOB	BH	AVG	PB	PR	PR+	PD	TPI
1998	Col-N	13	17	.433	36	35	4	1	0	230^1	257	141	28	7	96	158	14.1	5.20	100	.287	.361	18	.254	2	-25	-1	0	0.2
1999	Col-N	8	13	.381	32	32	1	0	0	190^2	225	150	33	6	109	116	16.0	6.61	88	.298	.391	7	.135	-2	-43	-13	-1	-1.5
2000	*StL-N★	20	9	.690	34	34	5	1	0	232^1	215	109	33	13	58	192	11.1	3.91	118	.247	.304	9	.123	0	19	19	0	2.1
Total	10	112	104	.519	311	283	26	8	0	1853^1	1825	980	183	98	825	1439	13.3	4.27	100	.260	.346	76	.135	-1	-15	1	-2	0.7
● JOHN KILEY	Kiley, John Frederick b: 7/1/1859, Dedham, Mass. d: 12/18/40, Norwood, Mass. BL/TL, 5'7", 147 lbs. Deb: 5/1/1884 ♦																											
1891	Bos-N	0	1	.000	1	1	1	0	0	8	13	9	3	0	5	1	20.3	6.75	54	.351	.429	0	.000	0	-3	-3	0	-0.2
● PAUL KILGUS	Kilgus, Paul Nelson b: 2/2/62, Bowling Green, Ky. BL/TL, 6'1", 185 lbs. Deb: 6/7/87																											
1987	Tex-A	2	7	.222	25	12	0	0	0	89^1	95	45	14	2	31	42	12.9	4.13	109	.271	.334	0	—	0	3	4	-1	0.2
1988	Tex-A	12	15	.444	32	32	5	3	0	203^1	190	105	18	10	71	88	12.0	4.16	98	.243	.314	0	—	0	-4	-2	1	-0.1
1989	*Chi-N	6	10	.375	35	23	0	0	2	145^2	164	90	9	5	49	61	13.5	4.39	86	.283	.344	3	.073	-3	-14	-9	0	-1.2
1990	Tor-A	0	0	—	11	0	0	0	0	16^1	19	11	2	1	7	7	14.9	6.06	65	.306	.386	0	—	0	-4	-4	0	-0.2
1991	Bal-A	0	2	.000	38	0	0	0	1	62	60	38	8	3	24	32	12.6	5.08	78	.256	.333	0	—	0	-7	-8	2	-0.2
1993	StL-N	1	0	1.000	22	1	0	0	1	28^2	18	2	1	1	8	21	8.5	0.63	632	.180	.248	1	.200	0	11	11	0	0.6
Total	6	21	34	.382	163	68	5	3	4	545^1	546	291	52	22	190	251	12.5	4.19	97	.259	.327	4	.087	-2	-15	-8	2	-0.9
● MIKE KILKENNY	Kilkenny, Michael David b: 4/11/45, Bradford, Ont., Can. BR/TL, 6'3.5", 175 lbs. Deb: 4/11/69																											
1969	Det-A	8	6	.571	39	15	6	4	2	128^1	99	54	13	4	63	97	11.6	3.37	111	.211	.310	2	.054	-2	4	5	-0	0.3
1970	Det-A	7	6	.538	36	21	3	0	0	129	141	77	10	2	70	105	14.9	5.16	72	.279	.369	3	.077	-3	-21	-21	0	-2.1
1971	Det-A	4	5	.444	30	11	2	0	1	86^1	83	52	8	2	44	47	13.4	5.00	72	.247	.338	2	.083	-2	-15	-13	-0	-1.5
1972	Det-A	0	0	—	1	0	0	0	0	1	1	1	1	0	0	0	9.0	9.00	35	.250	.250	0	—	0	-1	-1	0	0.0
	Oak-A	0	0	—	1	0	0	0	0	1	0	0	0	0	0	0	0.0	0.00	—	.000	.000	0	—	0	0	0	-0	0.0
	SD-N	0	0	—	5	0	0	0	0	4^1	7	4	1	0	3	5	20.8	8.31	40	.350	.435	0	—	0	-2	-3	0	-0.1
	Cle-A	4	1	.800	22	7	1	0	1	58	51	23	5	0	39	44	14.0	3.41	95	.237	.354	1	.071	-1	-2	-1	1	-0.1
	Yr	4	1	.800	24	7	1	0	1	60	52	24	6	0	39	44	18.5	3.45	94	.234	.349	1	.071	-1	-2	-1	1	-0.1
1973	Cle-A	0	0	—	5	0	0	0	0	2	5	5	1	1	5	3	49.5	22.50	17	.455	.647	0	—	0	-4	-4	0	-0.2
Total	5	23	18	.561	139	54	12	4	4	410	387	216	39	9	224	301	13.6	4.43	82	.248	.345	8	.070	-8	-41	-36	1	-3.7
● EVANS KILLEEN	Killeen, Evans Henry b: 2/27/36, Brooklyn, N.Y. BR/TR, 6', 190 lbs. Deb: 9/7/59																											
1959	KC-A	0	0	—	4	0	0	0	0	5^2	4	3	0	0	4	1	12.7	4.76	84	.211	.348	0	—	0	-1	-0	-0	-0.1
● HENRY KILLEEN	Killeen, Henry b: 5/1872, Troy, N.Y. 5'9", 150 lbs. Deb: 9/11/1891																											
1891	Cle-N	0	1	.000	1	1	1	0	0	8^2	11	8	1	0	8	3	19.7	6.23	56	.297	.422	0	.000	-0	-3	-3	0	-0.2
● FRANK KILLEN	Killen, Frank Bissell "Lefty" b: 11/30/1870, Pittsburgh, Pa. d: 12/3/39, Pittsburgh, Pa. BL/TL, 6'1", 200 lbs. Deb: 8/27/1891																											
1891	Mil-a	7	4	.636	11	11	11	2	0	96^2	73	42	1	3	51	38	11.8	1.68	262	.202	.306	8	.229	1	22	25	-0	2.5
1892	Was-N	29	26	.527	60	52	46	2	0	459^2	448	286	15	20	182	147	12.7	3.31	98	.245	.321	37	.199	10	-1	-3	3	1.0
1893	Pit-N	**36**	14	.720	55	48	38	2	0	415	401	235	12	15	140	99	12.1	3.64	125	.246	.312	47	.275	14	47	43	1	5.3
1894	Pit-N	14	11	.560	28	28	20	1	0	204	261	148	3	5	86	62	15.5	4.50	117	.308	.375	21	.262	0	19	17	1	1.5
1895	Pit-N	5	5	.500	13	11	6	0	0	95	113	77	2	1	57	25	16.2	5.49	82	.291	.383	13	.342	4	-8	-11	1	-0.4
1896	Pit-N	**30**	18	.625	**52**	50	**44**	**5**	0	**432^1**	476	244	7	14	119	134	12.7	3.41	123	.277	.329	40	.231	9	46	39	2	4.4
1897	Pit-N	17	23	.425	42	41	**38**	1	0	337^1	417	246	4	8	76	99	13.4	4.46	94	.301	.341	32	.248	5	-6	-11	-1	-0.7
1898	Pit-N	10	11	.476	23	23	17	0	0	177^2	201	106	3	11	41	48	12.8	3.75	95	.283	.332	17	.262	2	-3	-4	-0	-0.2
	Was-N	6	9	.400	17	16	15	0	0	128^1	149	80	4	2	29	43	12.6	3.58	102	.288	.328	15	.273	3	0	1	-0	0.5
	Yr	16	20	.444	40	39	32	0	0	306	350	186	7	13	70	91	12.7	3.68	98	.285	.330	32	.267	5	-2	-3	-1	0.3
1899	Was-N	0	2	.000	2	2	1	0	0	12	18	11	0	1	4	3	17.3	6.00	65	.346	.404	1	.200	-0	-3	-3	-1	-0.4
	Bos-N	7	5	.583	12	12	11	0	0	99^1	108	65	3	3	26	23	12.4	4.26	98	.276	.326	7	.171	-2	-4	-1	-0	-0.3
	Yr	7	7	.500	14	14	12	0	0	111^1	126	76	3	4	30	26	12.9	4.45	93	.284	.335	8	.174	-3	-7	-4	-1	-0.7
1900	Chi-N	3	3	.500	6	6	6	0	0	54	65	31	1	2	11	4	13.0	4.67	77	.297	.336	3	.150	-1	-6	-7	-0	-0.6
Total	10	164	131	.556	321	300	253	13	0	2511^1	2730	1571	55	85	822	725	13.0	3.78	109	.272	.332	241	.241	44	104	92	5	12.6
● ED KILLIAN	Killian, Edwin Henry "Twilight Ed" b: 11/12/1876, Racine, Wis. d: 7/18/28, Detroit, Mich. BL/TL, 5'11", 170 lbs. Deb: 8/25/03																											
1903	Cle-A	3	4	.429	9	8	7	3	0	61^2	61	24	1	4	13	18	11.4	2.48	115	.257	.307	5	.179	-1	3	3	-0	0.2
1904	Det-A	15	20	.429	40	34	32	4	0	331^2	293	118	0	17	93	124	10.9	2.44	104	.238	.301	18	.143	-3	6	4	-5	-0.5
1905	Det-A	23	14	.622	39	37	33	**8**	0	313^1	263	108	0	13	102	110	10.9	2.27	120	.230	.300	32	.271	6	13	16	-4	2.2
1906	Det-A	10	6	.625	21	16	14	0	2	149^2	165	71	0	5	54	47	13.5	3.43	81	.283	.348	9	.170	-1	-12	-11	-2	-1.4
1907	*Det-A	25	13	.658	42	34	29	3	0	314	286	103	2	11	91	96	11.1	1.78	147	.245	.306	39	.320	10	27	28	-2	4.5
1908	*Det-A	12	9	.571	27	23	15	0	1	180^2	170	78	3	8	53	47	11.5	2.99	81	.252	.314	10	.137	-3	-12	-11	3	-1.4
1909	Det-A	11	9	.550	25	19	14	3	1	173^1	150	45	1	6	49	54	10.6	1.71	147	.236	.297	10	.161	-1	15	15	-1	1.6
1910	Det-A	4	3	.571	11	9	5	1	0	74	75	38	2	6	27	20	13.1	3.04	87	.268	.345	4	.148	-1	-4	-3	-1	-0.5
Total	8	103	78	.569	214	180	149	22	4	1598^1	1463	585	9	70	482	516	11.3	2.38	110	.246	.310	127	.209	6	35	41	-12	4.7
● JACK KILLILAY	Killilay, John William b: 5/24/1887, Leavenworth, Kan. d: 10/21/68, Tulsa, Okla. BR/TR, 5'11", 165 lbs. Deb: 5/13/11																											
1911	Bos-A	4	2	.667	14	7	1	0	0	61	65	26	0	10	36	28	16.4	3.54	93	.302	.425	1	.042	-2	-1	-2	0	-0.4
● MATT KILROY	Kilroy, Matthew Aloysius "Matches" b: 6/21/1866, Philadelphia, Pa. d: 3/2/40, Philadelphia, Pa. BL/TL, 5'9", 175 lbs. Deb: 4/17/1886 F																											
1886	Bal-a	29	34	.460	**68**	68	**66**	5	0	583	476	350	10	19	182	**513**	10.5	3.37	102	.210	.274	38	.174	-5	5	4	6	0.4
1887	Bal-a	**46**	19	.708	**69**	69	**66**	**6**	0	**589^1**	742	326	9	20	157	217	11.6	3.07	134	.300	.306	90	.333	9	**80**	**71**	10	**7.6**
1888	Bal-a	17	21	.447	40	40	35	2	0	321	347	224	5	23	79	135	12.6	4.04	74	.266	.319	26	.179	-0	-35	-39	-1	-3.8
1889	Bal-a	29	25	.537	59	56	**55**	5	0	480^2	476	283	8	27	142	217	12.1	2.85	139	.250	.312	57	.274	10	54	57	8	**6.8**
1890	Bos-P	9	15	.375	30	27	18	0	1	217^2	268	161	14	15	87	48	15.3	4.26	103	.290	.361	20	.215	-0	-1	3	1	0.3
1891	Cin-a	1	4	.200	7	6	4	0	0	45^1	51	42	1	8	19	6	15.5	2.98	138	.274	.366	3	.150	-1	4	5	0	0.4
1892	Was-N	1	1	.500	4	3	2	0	0	26^1	20	11	0	2	15	1	12.6	2.39	136	.202	.319	2	.200	-0	3	3	2	0.3
1893	Lou-N	3	2	.600	5	5	5	1	0	35	57	41	2	4	23	4	21.6	9.00	49	.354	.447	7	.438	3	-17	-19	1	-1.5
1894	Lou-N	0	5	.000	8	7	3	0	0	37	46	34	2	2	20	11	16.5	3.89	131	.301	.389	2	.118	-2	6	5	1	0.5
1898	Chi-N	6	7	.462	13	11	10	0	0	100^1	119	67	2	11	30	18	14.4	4.31	83	.292	.357	22	.229	2	-8	-8	1	-0.6
Total	10	141	133	.515	303	292	264	19	1	2435^2	2602	1539	53	131	754	1170	12.3	3.47	109	.263	.314	267	.244	15	92	84	28	10.4
● MIKE KILROY	Kilroy, Michael Joseph b: 11/4/1872, Philadelphia, Pa. d: 10/2/60, Philadelphia, Pa. BR/TR, 5'11", 180 lbs. Deb: 9/1/1888 F																											
1888	Bal-a	0	1	.000	1	1	1	0	0	9	12	9	1	0	5	1	17.0	8.00	37	.308	.386	0	.000	-1	-5	-5	-0	-0.4
1891	Phi-N	0	2	.000	3	1	0	0	0	10	15	14	1	2	4	3	18.9	9.90	34	.333	.412	2	.400	1	-7	-7	-0	-0.9
Total	2	0	3	.000	4	2	1	0	0	19	27	23	2	2	9	4	18.0	9.00	36	.321	.400	2	.222	0	-12	-12	-0	-1.3
● BYUNG-HYUN KIM	Kim, Byung-Hyun b: 1/21/79, Kwangju, South Korea BR/TR, 5'11", 176 lbs. Deb: 5/29/99																											
1999	Ari-N	1	2	.333	25	0	0	0	1	27^1	20	15	2	5	20	31	14.8	4.61	99	.211	.375	0	.000	-0	-0	-0	1	0.1
2000	Ari-N	6	6	.500	61	1	0	0	14	70^2	52	39	9	9	46	111	13.6	4.46	104	.200	.340	0	.000	-0	1	1	0	0.2
Total	2	7	8	.467	86	1	0	0	15	98	72	54	11	14	66	142	14.0	4.50	102	.203	.349	0	.000	-0	1	1	1	0.3
● NEWT KIMBALL	Kimball, Newell W. b: 3/27/15, Logan, Utah BR/TR, 6'2.5", 190 lbs. Deb: 5/7/37																											
1937	Chi-N	0	0	—	2	0	0	0	0	5	12	8	1	0	1	0	23.4	10.80	37	.444	.464	0	.000	-0	-4	-4	0	-0.2
1938	Chi-N	0	0	—	1	0	0	0	0	1	3	1	0	0	0	1	27.0	9.00	43	.500	.500	0	—	0	-1	-1	0	0.0
1940	Bro-N	3	1	.750	21	0	0	0	1	33^2	29	15	2	0	15	21	11.8	3.21	125	.238	.321	0	.000	-1	2	3	-0	0.2
	StL-N	1	0	1.000	2	1	1	0	0	14	11	5	1	0	6	6	10.9	2.57	155	.208	.288	2	.333	1	2	2	-0	0.2
	Yr	4	1	.800	23	1	1	0	1	47^2	40	20	3	0	21	27	11.5	3.02	132	.229	.311	2	.182	0	4	5	-1	0.4
1941	Bro-N	3	1	.750	15	5	1	0	1	52	43	22	0	0	29	17	12.5	3.63	101	.225	.327	3	.214	0	-0	0	-0	0.0
1942	Bro-N	2	0	1.000	14	1	0	0	0	29^1	27	13	0	1	19	8	14.4	3.68	89	.265	.385	1	.200	-0	-1	-1	-2	-0.2
1943	Bro-N	1	1	.500	5	0	0	0	1	11	9	2	0	0	5	2	11.5	1.64	205	.214	.298	0	.000	-0	2	2	-0	0.4
	Phi-N	1	6	.143	34	6	2	0	2	89^2	85	47	4	1	42	33	12.8	4.12	82	.253	.338	3	.188	1	-7	-7	-2	-0.7
	Yr	2	7	.222	39	6	2	0	3	100^2	94	49	4	1	47	35	12.7	3.84	88	.249	.333	3	.158	1	-5	-5	-2	-0.3
Total	6	11	9	.550	94	13	4	0	5	235^2	219	113	8	2	117	88	12.9	3.78	94	.249	.339	9	.180	1	-6	-6	-4	-0.3

YEAR	TM/L	W	L	PCT	G	GS	CG	SH	SV	IP	H	R	HR	HB	BB	SO	RAT	ERA	ERA+	OAV	OOB	BH	AVG	PB	PR	PR+	PD	TPI
● **SAM KIMBER**	Kimber, Samuel Jackson b: 10/29/1852, Philadelphia, Pa. d: 11/7/25, Philadelphia, Pa. BR/TR, 5′10.5″, 165 lbs. Deb: 5/1/1884																											
1884	Bro-a	18	20	.474	41	41	41	4	0	361^1	364	240	6	15	72	122	11.2	3.81	87	.247	.289	21	.148	-5	-23	-19	-1	-2.2
1885	Pro-N	0	1	.000	1	1	1	0	0	8	15	13	1		5	4	22.5	11.25	24	.405	.476	0	.000	-0	-7	-8	0	-0.6
Total	2	18	21	.462	42	42	42	4	0	369^1	379	253	7	15	77	126	11.5	3.97	83	.251	.294	21	.145	-6	-30	-27	-1	-2.8
● **HARRY KIMBERLIN**	Kimberlin, Harry Lydle "Murphy" or "Mule Trader" b: 3/13/09, Sullivan, Mo. d: 12/31/99, Poplar Bluff, Mo. BR/TR, 6′3″, 175 lbs. Deb: 7/11/36																											
1936	StL-A	0	0	—	13	0	0	0	0	20	24	13	3	0	16	4	18.0	5.40	100	.296	.412	0	.000	-0	-1	-0	-0	-0.1
1937	StL-A	0	2	.000	3	2	1	0	0	15^1	16	13	2	0	9	5	14.7	2.35	206	.254	.347	1	.200	0	4	4	-0	0.5
1938	StL-A	0	0	—	1	1	1	0	0	8	8	3	1	0	3	1	12.4	3.38	147	.286	.355	0	.000	-0	1	1	-0	0.0
1939	StL-A	1	2	.333	17	3	0	0	0	41	59	35	6	2	19	11	17.6	5.49	89	.326	.396	3	.333	0	-4	-3	0	-0.1
Total	4	1	4	.200	34	6	2	0	0	84^1	107	64	12	2	47	21	16.6	4.70	106	.303	.388	4	.250	0	0	3	-1	0.3
● **HAL KIME**	Kime, Harold Lee "Lefty" b: 3/15/1899, W.Salem, Ohio d: 5/16/39, Columbus, Ohio BL/TL, 5′9″, 160 lbs. Deb: 6/19/20																											
1920	StL-N	0	0	—	4	0	0	0	0	7	9	4	0	1	2	1	15.4	2.57	116	.333	.400	0	.000	-0	0	0	0	0.0
● **CHAD KIMSEY**	Kimsey, Clyde Elias b: 8/6/06, Copperhill, Tenn. d: 12/3/42, Pryor, Okla. BL/TR, 6′2″, 200 lbs. Deb: 4/21/29																											
1929	StL-A	3	6	.333	24	3	1	0	1	64^1	83	42	2	0	19	13	14.3	5.04	88	.340	.388	8	.267	3	-6	-4	3	0.0
1930	StL-A	6	10	.375	42	4	1	0	1	113^1	139	87	8	2	45	32	14.8	6.35	77	.312	.377	24	.343	7	-21	-18	1	-1.3
1931	StL-A	4	6	.400	42	1	0	0	7	94^1	121	60	1	2	27	27	14.3	4.39	106	.312	.360	10	.270	5	-0	**2**	2	1.0
1932	StL-A	4	2	.667	33	0	0	0	3	78^1	85	45	3	0	33	13	13.6	4.02	121	.281	.352	6	.333	1	4	7	1	0.7
	Chi-A	1	1	.500	7	0	0	0	2	11	8	4	0	1	5	6	11.5	2.45	176	.211	.318	0	.000	-0	2	2	1	0.5
	Yr	5	3	.625	40	0	0	0	5	89^1	93	49	3	1	38	19	13.3	3.83	125	.274	.348	6	.300	1	6	**9**	2	1.2
1933	Chi-A	4	1	.800	28	2	0	0	0	96	124	67	7	4	36	19	15.4	5.53	77	.318	.381	5	.152	-2	-13	-14	1	-0.7
1936	Det-A	2	3	.400	22	0	0	0	3	52	58	36	2	1	29	11	15.2	4.85	102	.284	.376	5	.313	2	1	1	2	0.4
Total	6	24	29	.453	198	10	2	0	17	509^1	618	341	23	10	194	121	14.5	5.07	92	.307	.371	58	.282	16	-33	-23	11	0.6
● **ELLIS KINDER**	Kinder, Ellis Raymond "Old Folks" b: 7/26/14, Atkins, Ark. d: 10/16/68, Jackson, Tenn. BR/TR, 6′, 195 lbs. Deb: 4/30/46																											
1946	StL-A	3	3	.500	33	7	1	0	1	86^2	78	35	8	0	36	59	11.8	3.32	112	.241	.318	1	.053	-1	2	4	-1	0.0
1947	StL-A	8	15	.348	34	26	10	2	1	194^1	201	105	11	0	82	110	13.1	4.49	86	.264	.336	8	.129	-4	-17	-13	-3	-2.0
1948	Bos-A	10	7	.588	28	22	10	1	0	178	183	84	10	2	63	53	12.5	3.74	117	.266	.330	6	.097	-4	11	13	-3	0.4
1949	Bos-A	23	6	**.793**	43	30	19	**6**	4	252	251	103	21	2	99	138	12.6	3.36	130	.260	.330	12	.130	-4	24	27	-4	2.0
1950	Bos-A	14	12	.538	48	23	11	1	9	207	212	105	23	1	78	95	12.7	4.26	115	.263	.328	13	.183	-1	7	14	-2	1.3
1951	Bos-A	11	2	.846	**63**	2	1	0	**14**	127	108	42	8	0	46	84	10.9	2.55	175	.230	.298	4	.118	-3	**22**	**25**	-2	2.5
1952	Bos-A	5	6	.455	23	10	4	0	4	97^2	85	33	11	1	28	50	10.5	2.58	153	.234	.290	0	.000	-4	12	14	-0	1.2
1953	Bos-A	10	6	.625	**69**	0	0	0	**27**	107	84	30	8	2	38	39	10.4	1.85	227	.215	.288	11	.379	3	**26**	**27**	0	**5.6**
1954	Bos-A	8	8	.500	48	2	0	0	15	107	106	47	7	0	36	67	11.9	3.62	114	.260	.321	5	.185	0	1	5	-2	0.8
1955	Bos-A	5	5	.500	43	0	0	0	18	66^2	57	22	4	1	15	31	9.9	2.84	151	.229	.275	3	.250	0	8	10	-1	1.9
1956	StL-N	2	0	1.000	22	0	0	0	6	25^2	23	11	3	0	9	4	11.2	3.51	108	.245	.311	0	.000	-0	1	1	-1	0.0
	Chi-A	3	1	.750	29	0	0	0	3	29^2	33	10	2	0	8	19	12.4	2.73	150	.277	.323	0	.000	-0	5	5	-1	0.6
1957	Chi-A	0	0	—	1	0	0	0	0	1	0	0	0	0	1	0	9.0	0.00	—	.000	.250	0	—	0	0	0	-0	0.0
Total	12	102	71	.590	484	122	56	10	102	1479^2	1421	627	116	9	539	749	12.0	3.43	125	.252	.318	63	.142	-19	101	131	-17	14.3
● **SILVER KING**	King, Charles Frederick (b: Charles Frederick Koenig) b: 1/11/1868, St.Louis, Mo. d: 5/21/38, St.Louis, Mo. BR/TR, 6′, 170 lbs. Deb: 9/28/1886																											
1886	KC-N	1	3	.250	5	5	5	0	0	39	43	35	1		9	23	12.0	4.85	78	.243	.280	1	.045	-2	-7	-4	1	-0.4
1887	*StL-a	32	12	.727	46	44	43	2	1	390	510	231	4	17	109	128	12.2	3.78	120	.309	.316	70	.285	-4	22	31	-3	1.8
1888	*StL-a	**45**	20	.692	**66**	64	**64**	**6**	0	**584^2**	435	203	6	30	76	258	**8.3**	**1.63**	**200**	.200	**.237**	43	.208	9	**93**	**99**	-1	**10.6**
1889	StL-a	35	16	.686	56	53	47	2	1	458	462	257	15	21	125	188	11.9	3.14	134	.254	.309	43	.228	1	36	50	-3	4.1
1890	Chi-P	30	22	.577	56	56	48	**4**	0	461	420	233	5	15	163	185	11.7	**2.69**	**161**	**.232**	.301	31	.168	-6	**79**	**82**	6	**6.9**
1891	Pit-N	14	29	.326	48	44	40	3	1	384^1	382	243	7	18	144	160	12.7	3.11	105	.250	.321	25	.169	-1	10	7	-2	0.4
1892	NY-N	22	24	.478	51	47	45	1	0	410^1	392	250	15	21	171	170	12.8	3.29	98	.242	.322	34	.209	6	-0	-3	-1	0.1
1893	NY-N	3	4	.429	7	7	4	0	0	49	69	58	4	2	26	13	17.8	8.63	54	.322	.401	3	.176	1	-22	-22	-0	-2.0
	Cin-N	5	6	.455	17	15	8	1	1	105	119	69	2	7	56	30	15.6	4.89	98	.277	.369	6	.162	-0	-3	-1	-0	-0.1
	Yr	8	10	.444	24	22	12	1	1	154	188	127	6	9	82	43	16.3	6.08	78	.292	.380	9	.167	1	-24	-22	-0	-2.1
1896	Was-N	10	7	.588	22	16	12	0	1	145^1	179	106	3	4	43	35	14.0	4.09	108	.300	.351	16	.276	3	4	5	-3	0.5
1897	Was-N	6	9	.400	23	19	12	0	1	154	196	118	7	11	45	32	14.7	4.79	91	.307	.363	11	.193	0	-8	-8	1	-0.5
Total	10	203	152	.572	397	370	328	19	6	3180^2	3207	1803	69	146	967	1222	11.9	3.18	122	.253	.308	283	.213	7	205	243	-6	21.4
● **CLYDE KING**	King, Clyde Edward b: 5/23/24, Goldsboro, N.C. BB/TR, 6′1″, 175 lbs. Deb: 6/21/44 MC																											
1944	Bro-N	2	1	.667	14	3	1	0	0	43^2	42	18	1	1	12	14	11.3	3.09	115	.256	.311	2	.200	-0	3	2	-1	0.0
1945	Bro-N	5	5	.500	42	2	0	0	3	112^1	131	64	8	0	48	29	14.3	4.09	92	.295	.364	4	.125	-2	-4	-4	1	-0.5
1947	Bro-N	6	5	.545	29	9	2	0	0	87^2	85	34	11	0	29	31	11.7	2.77	149	.252	.311	3	.115	-1	13	13	-1	1.3
1948	Bro-N	0	1	.000	9	0	0	0	0	12^1	14	11	3	1	6	5	15.3	8.03	50	.286	.375	0	.000	-0	-6	-5	0	-0.4
1951	Bro-N	14	7	.667	48	3	1	0	6	121^1	118	64	15	3	50	33	12.7	4.15	94	.263	.341	4	.138	0	-3	-3	0	-0.5
1952	Bro-N	2	0	1.000	23	0	0	0	0	42^2	56	25	5	1	12	17	14.6	5.06	72	.318	.365	0	.000	-1	-6	-7	1	-0.3
1953	Cin-N	3	6	.333	35	4	0	0	2	76	78	47	15	2	32	21	13.3	5.21	84	.271	.348	0	.000	-1	-8	-7	-0	-0.8
Total	7	32	25	.561	200	21	4	0	11	496	524	263	58	8	189	150	13.1	4.14	95	.275	.343	13	.114	-4	-11	-11	-0	-1.2
● **CURTIS KING**	King, Curtis Albert b: 10/25/70, Norristown, Pa. BR/TR, 6′5″, 205 lbs. Deb: 8/1/97																											
1997	StL-N	4	2	.667	30	0	0	0	0	29^1	38	14	0	1	11	13	15.3	2.76	150	.325	.388	0	.000	-0	5	5	0	0.8
1998	StL-N	2	0	1.000	36	0	0	0	2	51	50	20	5	3	20	28	12.9	3.53	119	.262	.341	0	.000	-1	4	4	1	0.2
1999	StL-N	0	0	—	2	0	0	0	0	1	3	2	0	0	0	1	27.0	18.00	25	.500	.500	0	—	0	-1	-1	0	-0.1
Total	3	6	2	.750	68	0	0	0	2	81^1	91	36	5	4	31	42	13.9	3.43	122	.290	.361	0	.000	-1	7	7	1	0.9
● **ERIC KING**	King, Eric Steven b: 4/10/64, Oxnard, Cal. BR/TR, 6′2″, 215 lbs. Deb: 5/15/86																											
1986	Det-A	11	4	.733	33	16	3	1	3	138^1	108	54	11	8	63	79	11.6	3.51	118	.216	.313	0	—	0	10	10	0	1.0
1987	*Det-A	6	9	.400	55	4	0	0	9	116	111	67	15	4	60	89	13.6	4.89	87	.251	.345	0	—	0	-5	-9	2	-0.9
1988	Det-A	4	1	.800	23	5	0	0	3	68^2	60	28	5	5	34	45	13.0	3.41	112	.233	.334	0	—	0	4	3	-1	0.2
1989	Chi-A	9	10	.474	25	25	1	1	0	159^1	144	69	13	4	64	72	12.0	3.39	113	.244	.322	0	—	0	9	8	-0	0.8
1990	Chi-A	12	4	.750	25	25	2	2	0	151	135	59	10	6	40	70	10.8	3.28	117	.237	.294	0	—	0	11	9	-1	0.8
1991	Cle-A	6	11	.353	25	24	2	1	0	150^2	166	83	7	3	44	59	12.7	4.60	90	.279	.332	0	—	0	-8	-7	-2	-0.9
1992	Det-A	4	6	.400	17	14	0	0	1	79^1	90	47	12	1	28	45	13.5	5.22	76	.285	.345	0	—	0	-11	-11	-1	-1.3
Total	7	52	45	.536	203	113	8	5	16	863^1	814	407	73	31	333	459	12.3	3.97	101	.249	.324	0	—	0	9	3	-3	-0.3
● **KEVIN KING**	King, Kevin Ray b: 2/11/69, Atwater, Cal. BL/TL, 6′4″, 170 lbs. Deb: 9/2/93																											
1993	Sea-A	0	1	.000	13	0	0	0	0	11^2	9	8	3	1	4	8	10.8	6.17	72	.231	.318	0	—	0	-2	-2	-0	-0.2
1994	Sea-A	0	2	.000	19	0	0	0	0	15^1	21	13	0	1	17	6	22.9	7.04	69	.333	.481	0	—	0	-4	-4	0	-0.4
1995	Sea-A	0	0	—	2	0	0	0	0	3^2	7	5	0	1	1	3	22.1	12.27	39	.412	.474	0	—	0	-3	-3	-0	-0.2
Total	3	0	3	.000	34	0	0	0	0	30^2	37	26	3	3	22	17	18.2	7.34	64	.311	.431	0	—	0	-9	-9	-0	-0.8
● **NELLIE KING**	King, Nelson Joseph b: 3/15/28, Shenandoah, Pa. BR/TR, 6′6″, 185 lbs. Deb: 4/15/54																											
1954	Pit-N	0	0	—	4	0	0	0	0	7	10	5	0	0	1	3	14.1	5.14	81	.400	.423	0	—	0	-1	-1	0	0.0
1955	Pit-N	1	3	.250	17	4	0	0	0	54^1	60	24	2	2	14	21	12.6	2.98	138	.286	.336	0	.000	-2	6	7	-0	0.2
1956	Pit-N	4	1	.800	38	0	0	0	5	60	54	24	8	1	19	25	11.1	3.15	120	.241	.303	0	.000	-1	4	4	-1	0.2
1957	Pit-N	2	1	.667	36	0	0	0	1	52	69	27	7	2	16	23	15.1	4.50	84	.337	.390	0	.000	-1	-4	-4	-0	-0.3
Total	4	7	5	.583	95	4	0	0	6	173^1	193	80	17	5	50	72	12.9	3.58	109	.291	.345	0	.000	-3	6	6	-1	0.1
● **RAY KING**	King, Raymond Keith b: 1/15/74, Chicago, Ill. BL/TL, 6′1″, 225 lbs. Deb: 5/21/99																											
1999	Chi-N	0	0	—	10	0	0	0	0	10^2	11	8	2	1	10	5	18.6	5.91	76	.289	.449	0	.000	-0	-2	-2	-0	-0.1
2000	Mil-N	3	2	.600	36	0	0	0	0	28^2	18	7	1	0	10	19	8.8	1.26	363	.180	.255	0	—	0	11	11	0	1.7
Total	2	3	2	.600	46	0	0	0	0	39^1	29	15	3	1	20	24	11.4	2.52	181	.210	.314	0	.000	-0	9	9	0	1.6

YEAR TM/L	W	L	PCT	G	GS	CG	SH	SV	IP	H	R	HR	HB	BB	SO	RAT	ERA	ERA+	OAV	OOB	BH	AVG	PB	PR	PR+	PD	TPI
● BRIAN KINGMAN Kingman, Brian Paul b: 7/27/54, Los Angeles, Cal. BR/TR, 6'2", 200 lbs. Deb: 6/28/79																											
1979 Oak-A	8	7	.533	18	17	5	1	0	112^2	113	59	10	3	33	58	11.9	4.31	94	.258	.314	0	—	0	-1	-3	-2	-0.6
1980 Oak-A	8	20	.286	32	30	10	1	0	211^1	209	105	21	4	82	116	12.6	3.83	99	.256	.326	0	—	0	5	-1	-2	-0.4
1981 *Oak-A	3	6	.333	18	15	3	1	0	100^1	112	48	10	4	32	52	13.3	3.95	88	.286	.347	0	—	0	-3	-5	-2	-0.6
1982 Oak-A	4	12	.250	23	20	3	0	1	122^2	131	64	11	7	57	46	14.3	4.48	87	.279	.365	0	—	0	-5	-8	-3	-1.2
1983 SF-N	0	0	—	3	0	0	0	0	4^2	10	6	0	0	1	1	21.2	7.71	46	.417	.440	0	—	0	-2	-2	-0	-0.1
Total 5	23	45	.338	94	82	21	3	1	551^2	575	282	52	18	205	273	13.0	4.13	92	.269	.338	0	—	0	-7	-21	-9	-2.9
● DAVE KINGMAN Kingman, David Arthur b: 12/21/48, Pendleton, Ore. BR/TR, 6'6", 210 lbs. Deb: 7/30/71 ◆																											
1973 SF-N	0	0	—	2	0	0	0	0	4	3	4	0	0	6	4	20.3	9.00	43	.200	.429	62	.203	1	-2	-2	-0	-0.1
● DENNIS KINNEY Kinney, Dennis Paul b: 2/26/52, Toledo, Ohio BL/TL, 6'1", 190 lbs. Deb: 4/9/78																											
1978 Cle-A	0	2	.000	18	0	0	0	5	38^2	37	21	3	1	14	19	12.1	4.42	85	.259	.329	0	—	0	-3	-3	-0	-0.2
SD-N	0	1	.000	7	0	0	0	0	7	6	5	3	0	4	2	12.9	6.43	52	.222	.323	0	.000	-0	-2	-3	-0	-0.4
1979 SD-N	0	0	—	13	0	0	0	0	18	17	8	2	1	8	11	13.0	3.50	101	.250	.338	0	.000	-0	0	0	-0	0.0
1980 SD-N	4	6	.400	50	0	0	0	1	82^2	79	45	3	1	37	40	12.7	4.25	81	.252	.333	1	.083	-0	-6	-8	-0	-1.0
1981 Det-A	0	0	—	6	0	0	0	0	3^2	5	4	0	0	4	3	22.1	9.82	38	.313	.450	0	—	0	-3	-2	-0	-0.1
1982 Oak-A	0	0	—	3	0	0	0	0	4^1	9	4	1	0	4	0	27.0	8.31	47	.474	.565	0	—	0	-2	-2	-0	-0.1
Total 5	4	9	.308	97	0	0	0	6	154^1	153	87	12	3	71	75	13.2	4.55	78	.261	.344	1	.071	-1	-15	-18	-1	-1.8
● MATT KINNEY Kinney, Matthew John b: 12/16/76, Bangor, Me. BR/TR, 6'5", 220 lbs. Deb: 8/18/2000																											
2000 Min-A	2	2	.500	8	8	0	0	0	42^1	41	26	7	0	25	24	14.0	5.10	103	.261	.363	0	—	0	-1	1	-0	0.0
● WALT KINNEY Kinney, Walter William b: 9/9/1893, Denison, Tex. d: 7/1/71, Escondido, Cal. BL/TL, 6'2", 186 lbs. Deb: 7/26/18																											
1918 Bos-A	0	0	—	5	0	0	0	0	15	5	3	0	2	8	4	9.0	1.80	149	.106	.263	0	.000	-1	2	2	-0	0.0
1919 Phi-A	9	15	.375	43	21	13	0	2	202^2	199	110	7	8	91	97	13.2	3.64	94	.262	.347	25	.284	5	-9	-5	3	0.6
1920 Phi-A	2	4	.333	10	8	5	1	0	61	59	38	3	1	28	19	13.0	3.10	130	.261	.345	9	.346	2	5	6	0	0.7
1923 Phi-A	0	1	.000	5	1	0	0	0	12	11	13	0	0	9	9	15.0	7.50	55	.229	.351	1	.167	1	-5	-4	-0	-0.3
Total 4	11	20	.355	63	30	18	1	2	290^2	274	164	10	11	136	129	13.0	3.59	99	.254	.343	35	.280	7	-8	-2	2	1.0
● MIKE KINNUNEN Kinnunen, Michael John b: 4/1/58, Seattle, Wash. BL/TL, 6'1", 185 lbs. Deb: 6/12/80																											
1980 Min-A	0	0	—	21	0	0	0	0	24^2	29	18	1	1	9	8	14.2	5.11	86	.290	.355	0	—	0	-3	-2	0	-0.1
1986 Bal-A	0	0	—	9	0	0	0	0	7	8	6	1	0	5	1	16.7	6.43	64	.308	.419	0	—	0	-2	-2	0	-0.1
1987 Bal-A	0	0	—	18	0	0	0	0	20	27	14	3	0	16	14	19.3	4.95	89	.338	.448	0	—	0	-1	-1	-0	-0.1
Total 3	0	0	—	48	0	0	0	0	51^2	64	38	5	1	30	23	16.5	5.23	84	.311	.401	0	—	0	-6	-5	0	-0.3
● ED KINSELLA Kinsella, Edward William "Rube" b: 1/15/1882, Lexington, Ill. d: 1/17/76, Bloomington, Ill. BR/TR, 6'1.5", 175 lbs. Deb: 9/16/05																											
1905 Pit-N	0	1	.000	3	2	2	0	0	17	19	6	0	1	3	11	12.2	2.65	113	.292	.333	0	.000	-0	1	1	-1	-0.1
1910 StL-A	1	3	.250	10	5	2	0	0	50	62	30	0	2	16	10	14.4	3.78	65	.321	.379	3	.250	2	-7	-7	1	-0.3
Total 2	1	4	.200	13	7	4	0	0	67	81	36	0	3	19	21	13.8	3.49	75	.314	.368	3	.200	2	-6	-7	0	-0.4
● MATT KINZER Kinzer, Matthew Roy b: 6/17/63, Indianapolis, Ind. BR/TR, 6'2", 210 lbs. Deb: 5/18/89																											
1989 StL-N	0	2	.000	8	1	0	0	0	13^1	25	20	3	0	4	8	19.6	12.83	28	.403	.439	0	.000	-0	-14	-13	-0	-1.7
1990 Det-A	0	0	—	1	0	0	0	0	1^2	3	3	0	0	3	1	32.4	16.20	24	.375	.545	0	—	0	-2	-2	-0	-0.1
Total 2	0	2	.000	9	1	0	0	0	15	28	23	3	0	7	9	21.0	13.20	28	.400	.455	0	.000	-0	-16	-15	-1	-1.8
● HARRY KINZY Kinzy, Henry Hershel "Slim" b: 7/19/10, Hallsville, Tex. BR/TR, 6'4", 185 lbs. Deb: 6/8/34																											
1934 Chi-A	0	1	.000	13	2	1	0	0	34^1	38	23	1	4	31	12	19.1	4.98	95	.290	.440	3	.300	1	-2	-1	-0	0.0
● FRED KIPP Kipp, Fred Leo b: 10/1/31, Piqua, Kan. BL/TL, 6'4", 200 lbs. Deb: 9/10/57																											
1957 Bro-N	0	0	—	1	0	0	0	0	4	6	4	2	0	0	3	13.5	9.00	46	.333	.333	0	.000	-0	-2	-2	0	-0.1
1958 LA-N	6	6	.500	40	9	0	0	0	102^1	107	60	16	1	45	58	13.5	5.01	82	.273	.349	9	.250	1	-12	-10	1	-0.9
1959 LA-N	0	0	—	2	0	0	0	0	2^2	2	0	0	0	3	1	16.9	0.00	—	.222	.417	0	—	0	1	1	0	0.1
1960 NY-A	0	1	.000	4	0	0	0	0	4^1	4	3	0	0	0	2	8.3	6.23	57	.250	.250	0	—	0	-1	-1	0	-0.3
Total 4	6	7	.462	47	9	0	0	0	113^1	119	67	18	1	48	64	13.3	5.08	80	.274	.347	9	.243	1	-14	-12	1	-1.2
● BOB KIPPER Kipper, Robert Wayne b: 7/8/64, Aurora, Ill. BR/TL, 6'2", 200 lbs. Deb: 4/12/85																											
1985 Cal-A	0	1	.000	2	1	0	0	0	3^1	7	8	1	0	3	0	27.0	21.60	19	.467	.556	0	—	0	-6	-7	0	-1.0
Pit-N	1	2	.333	5	4	0	0	0	24^2	21	16	4	0	7	13	10.2	5.11	70	.221	.275	2	.250	0	-4	-4	0	-0.4
1986 Pit-N	6	8	.429	20	19	0	0	0	114	123	60	17	2	34	81	12.6	4.03	95	.271	.324	1	.030	-3	-4	-2	-1	-0.6
1987 Pit-N	5	9	.357	24	20	1	1	0	110^2	117	74	25	2	52	83	13.9	5.94	69	.271	.352	8	.242	2	-23	-22	-0	-2.3
1988 Pit-N	2	6	.250	50	0	0	0	0	65	54	33	7	2	26	39	11.4	3.74	91	.234	.317	0	.000	-0	-2	-2	1	-0.2
1989 Pit-N	3	4	.429	52	0	0	0	4	83	55	29	5	0	33	58	9.5	2.93	115	.188	.270	1	.111	-0	5	4	-1	0.3
1990 Pit-N	5	2	.714	41	1	0	0	3	62^2	44	24	7	3	26	35	10.5	3.02	120	.195	.286	1	.143	-0	5	4	-0	0.5
1991 *Pit-N	2	2	.500	52	0	0	0	4	60	66	34	7	0	22	38	13.2	4.65	77	.276	.337	0	.000	-0	-6	-7	-1	-0.7
1992 Min-A	3	3	.500	25	0	0	0	0	38^2	40	23	8	3	14	22	13.3	4.42	92	.268	.343	0	—	0	-2	-2	0	-0.2
Total 8	27	37	.422	271	45	1	1	11	562	527	301	81	12	217	369	12.1	4.34	86	.247	.320	13	.137	-1	-37	-39	-2	-4.6
● THORNTON KIPPER Kipper, Thornton John b: 9/27/28, Bagley, Wis. BR/TR, 6'3", 190 lbs. Deb: 6/7/53																											
1953 Phi-N	3	3	.500	20	3	0	0	0	45^2	59	26	8	0	12	15	14.0	4.73	89	.319	.360	1	.091	-1	-2	-3	-0	-0.4
1954 Phi-N	0	0	—	11	0	0	0	1	13^2	22	13	0	1	12	5	23.0	7.90	51	.379	.493	0	.000	-0	-6	-6	0	-0.3
1955 Phi-N	0	1	.000	24	0	0	0	0	39^2	47	23	4	1	22	15	15.9	4.99	80	.301	.391	1	.333	0	-4	-5	-1	-0.3
Total 3	3	4	.429	55	3	0	0	1	99	128	62	12	2	46	35	16.0	5.27	78	.321	.394	2	.125	-1	-12	-13	-1	-1.0
● CLAY KIRBY Kirby, Clayton Laws b: 6/25/48, Washington, D.C. d: 10/11/91, Arlington, Va. BR/TR, 6'3", 185 lbs. Deb: 4/11/69																											
1969 SD-N	7	20	.259	35	35	2	0	0	215^2	204	108	18	6	100	113	12.9	3.80	93	.252	.339	4	.061	-2	-5	-6	-2	-1.1
1970 SD-N	10	16	.385	36	34	6	1	0	214^2	198	118	29	9	120	154	13.7	4.53	88	.248	.352	11	.149	-0	-11	-13	-2	-1.6
1971 SD-N	15	13	.536	38	36	13	2	0	267^1	213	99	20	3	103	231	10.7	2.83	117	.216	.292	8	.093	-3	19	15	-0	1.2
1972 SD-N	12	14	.462	34	34	9	2	0	238^2	197	87	21	2	116	175	11.9	3.13	105	.226	.318	5	.068	-4	9	4	-1	-0.1
1973 SD-N	8	18	.308	34	31	4	2	0	191^2	214	122	30	1	66	129	13.2	4.79	73	.282	.341	5	.093	-3	-24	-29	-2	-3.9
1974 Cin-N	12	9	.571	36	35	7	1	0	230^2	210	97	15	2	91	160	11.8	3.28	107	.242	.316	7	.095	-3	9	6	-2	-0.1
1975 Cin-N	10	6	.625	26	19	1	0	0	110^2	113	63	13	5	54	48	14.0	4.72	76	.263	.352	6	.188	1	-13	-14	-2	-1.9
1976 Mon-N	1	8	.111	22	15	0	0	0	78^2	81	61	10	2	63	51	16.7	5.72	65	.273	.403	1	.056	-1	-19	-16	-1	-1.9
Total 8	75	104	.419	261	239	42	8	0	1548	1430	755	156	30	713	1061	12.6	3.84	92	.246	.331	47	.098	-15	-36	-56	-13	-9.4
● JOHN KIRBY Kirby, John F. b: 1/13/1865, St.Louis, Mo. d: 10/6/31, St.Louis, Mo. TR, 5'8", 172 lbs. Deb: 8/1/1884																											
1884 KC-U	0	1	.000	2	2	1	0	0	11	13	10	0		2	1	12.3	4.09	55	.277	.306	1	.143	-1	-2	-2	1	-0.2
1885 StL-N	5	8	.385	14	14	14	0	0	129^1	118	66	0		44	46	11.3	3.55	77	.241	.303	3	.060	-6	-10	-12	-2	-1.6
1886 StL-N	11	26	.297	41	41	38	1	0	325	329	222	9		134	129	12.8	3.30	98	.252	.322	15	.110	-9	1	-3	-1	-1.2
1887 Ind-N	1	6	.143	8	8	5	0	0	62	113	64	3	2	43	7	16.7	6.10	68	.377	.381	4	.138	-2	-14	-13	-1	-1.3
Cle-a	0	5	.000	5	5	5	0	0	41	90	53	1	2	28	6	20.2	9.00	48	.354	.432	3	.167	-1	-21	-21	-0	-1.7
1888 KC-a	1	4	.200	5	5	5	0	0	43	48	36	0	1	7	11	11.7	4.19	82	.273	.304	1	.063	-2	-5	-3	-0	-0.5
Total 5	18	50	.265	75	75	68	1	0	611^1	711	451	13	5	258	200	13.3	4.09	80	.281	.332	27	.105	-21	-53	-55	-3	-6.5
● LA RUE KIRBY Kirby, La Rue b: 12/30/1889, Eureka, Mich. d: 6/10/61, Lansing, Mich. BB/TR, 6', 185 lbs. Deb: 8/7/12 ◆																											
1912 NY-N	1	0	1.000	3	1	1	0	0	11	13	7	1	1	6	2	16.4	5.73	59	.295	.392	1	.200	0	-3	-3	0	-0.2
1915 StL-F	0	0	—	1	0	0	0	0	7	7	5	1	0	2	7	11.6	5.14	56	.269	.321	38	.213	0	-2	-2	-0	-0.1
Total 2	1	0	1.000	4	1	1	0	0	18	20	12	2	1	8	9	14.5	5.50	58	.286	.367	87	.230	0	-5	-5	-0	-0.3
● MIKE KIRCHER Kircher, Michael Andrew (b: Wolfgang Andrew Kerscher) b: 9/30/1897, Rochester, N.Y. d: 6/26/72, Rochester, N.Y. BB/TR, 6', 180 lbs. Deb: 8/8/19																											
1919 Phi-A	0	0	—	2	0	0	0	0	8	15	8	0	0	3	2	20.3	7.88	44	.429	.474	0	.000	-0	-4	-4	-1	-0.3

YEAR TM/L	W	L	PCT	G	GS	CG	SH	SV	IP	H	R	HR	HB	BB	SO	RAT	ERA	ERA+	OAV	OOB	BH	AVG	PB	PR	PR+	PD	TPI
1920 StL-N	2	1	.667	9	3	1	0	0	36^2	50	23	0	2	5	5	14.0	5.40	55	.333	.363	3	.273	0	-9	-10	-1	-0.9
1921 StL-N	0	1	.000	3	0	0	0	0	3^1	4	3	0	1	1	2	16.2	8.10	45	.364	.462	0	—	0	-2	-2	0	-0.3
Total 3	2	2	.500	14	3	1	0	0	48	69	34	0	3	9	9	15.2	6.00	52	.352	.389	3	.214	-0	-15	-16	-2	-1.5

● BILL KIRK Kirk, William Partlemore b: 7/19/35, Coatesville, Pa. BL/TL, 6', 165 lbs. Deb: 9/23/61

YEAR TM/L	W	L	PCT	G	GS	CG	SH	SV	IP	H	R	HR	HB	BB	SO	RAT	ERA	ERA+	OAV	OOB	BH	AVG	PB	PR	PR+	PD	TPI
1961 KC-A	0	0	—	1	1	0	0	0	3	6	4	2	0	1	3	21.0	12.00	35	.375	.412	0	—	0	-3	-3	-0	-0.1

● DON KIRKWOOD Kirkwood, Donald Paul b: 9/24/49, Pontiac, Mich. BR/TR, 6'3", 188 lbs. Deb: 9/13/74

YEAR TM/L	W	L	PCT	G	GS	CG	SH	SV	IP	H	R	HR	HB	BB	SO	RAT	ERA	ERA+	OAV	OOB	BH	AVG	PB	PR	PR+	PD	TPI
1974 Cal-A	0	0	—	3	0	0	0	0	7^1	12	8	0	0	6	4	22.1	8.59	40	.375	.474	0	—	0	-4	-4	-0	-0.2
1975 Cal-A	6	5	.545	44	2	0	0	7	84	85	38	6	0	28	49	12.1	3.11	115	.270	.329	0	—	0	6	4	-0	0.6
1976 Cal-A	6	12	.333	28	26	4	0	0	157^2	167	91	12	1	57	78	12.8	4.62	72	.278	.341	0	—	0	-19	-24	1	-2.4
1977 Cal-A	1	0	1.000	13	0	0	0	1	17^2	20	12	3	0	9	10	14.8	5.09	77	.290	.372	0	—	0	-2	-2	1	0.0
Chi-A	1	1	.500	16	0	0	0	0	40	49	27	3	1	10	24	13.5	5.17	79	.310	.355	0	—	0	-5	-5	0	-0.2
Yr	2	1	.667	29	0	0	0	1	57^2	69	39	6	1	19	34	13.9	5.15	79	.304	.360	0	—	0	-7	-7	1	-0.2
1978 Tor-A	4	5	.444	16	9	3	0	0	68	76	36	6	0	25	29	13.4	4.24	93	.289	.351	0	—	0	-3	-2	0	-0.2
Total 5	18	23	.439	120	37	7	0	8	374^2	409	212	30	2	135	194	13.1	4.37	82	.284	.347	0	—	0	-27	-33	2	-2.4

● HARRY KIRSCH Kirsch, Harry Louis "Casey" b: 10/17/1887, Pittsburgh, Pa. d: 12/25/25, Overbrook, Pa. BR/TR, 5'11", 170 lbs. Deb: 4/16/10

YEAR TM/L	W	L	PCT	G	GS	CG	SH	SV	IP	H	R	HR	HB	BB	SO	RAT	ERA	ERA+	OAV	OOB	BH	AVG	PB	PR	PR+	PD	TPI
1910 Cle-A	0	0	—	2	0	0	0	0	3	5	2	0	0	1	5	18.0	6.00	43	.385	.429	0	—	0	-1	-1	-0	-0.1

● GARLAND KISER Kiser, Garland Routhard b: 7/8/68, Charlotte, N.C. BL/TL, 6'3", 190 lbs. Deb: 9/9/91

YEAR TM/L	W	L	PCT	G	GS	CG	SH	SV	IP	H	R	HR	HB	BB	SO	RAT	ERA	ERA+	OAV	OOB	BH	AVG	PB	PR	PR+	PD	TPI
1991 Cle-A	0	0	—	7	0	0	0	0	4^2	7	5	0	1	4	3	23.1	9.64	43	.368	.500	0	—	0	-3	-3	-0	-0.2

● RUBE KISINGER Kisinger, Charles Samuel b: 12/13/1876, Adrian, Mich. d: 7/14/41, Huron, Ohio BR/TR, 6', 190 lbs. Deb: 9/10/02

YEAR TM/L	W	L	PCT	G	GS	CG	SH	SV	IP	H	R	HR	HB	BB	SO	RAT	ERA	ERA+	OAV	OOB	BH	AVG	PB	PR	PR+	PD	TPI
1902 Det-A	2	3	.400	5	5	5	0	0	43^1	48	20	0	3	14	7	13.5	3.12	117	.281	.346	3	.158	-1	2	3	-0	0.1
1903 Det-A	7	9	.438	16	14	13	2	0	118^2	118	58	0	2	27	33	11.1	2.96	98	.259	.303	6	.128	-3	0	-1	1	-0.3
Total 2	9	12	.429	21	19	18	2	0	162	166	78	0	5	41	40	11.8	3.00	103	.265	.315	9	.136	-4	2	2	1	-0.2

● BRUCE KISON Kison, Bruce Eugene b: 2/18/50, Pasco, Wash. BR/TR, 6'4", 178 lbs. Deb: 7/4/71 C

YEAR TM/L	W	L	PCT	G	GS	CG	SH	SV	IP	H	R	HR	HB	BB	SO	RAT	ERA	ERA+	OAV	OOB	BH	AVG	PB	PR	PR+	PD	TPI
1971 *Pit-N	6	5	.545	18	13	2	1	0	95^1	93	40	6	6	36	60	12.7	3.40	100	.259	.337	2	.065	-1	1	-0	1	0.0
1972 *Pit-N	9	7	.563	32	18	6	1	3	152	123	61	11	9	69	102	11.9	3.26	102	.220	.316	10	.189	2	3	1	-1	0.2
1973 Pit-N	3	0	1.000	7	7	0	0	0	43^2	36	17	4	1	24	26	12.6	3.09	114	.232	.339	1	.083	0	3	2	0	0.2
1974 *Pit-N	9	8	.529	40	16	1	0	2	129	123	64	8	11	57	71	13.3	3.49	99	.247	.338	4	.108	-0	2	-0	1	0.0
1975 *Pit-N	12	11	.522	33	29	6	0	0	192	160	89	10	4	92	89	12.0	3.23	110	.227	.320	7	.119	-2	9	7	2	0.8
1976 Pit-N	14	9	.609	31	29	6	1	1	193	180	83	10	3	52	98	11.0	3.08	113	.247	.299	12	.203	4	9	9	1	1.5
1977 Pit-N	9	10	.474	33	32	3	1	0	193	209	113	25	6	55	122	12.6	4.90	81	.278	.333	18	.261	5	-21	-19	1	-1.2
1978 Pit-N	6	6	.500	28	11	0	0	0	96	81	40	3	5	39	62	11.7	3.19	116	.229	.314	4	.138	1	4	5	1	0.8
1979 *Pit-N	13	7	.650	33	25	3	1	0	172^1	157	70	13	4	45	105	10.8	3.19	122	.246	.300	8	.145	0	11	13	1	1.6
1980 Cal-A	3	6	.333	13	13	2	1	0	73^1	73	46	5	3	32	28	13.3	4.91	80	.264	.346	0	—	0	-7	-8	-1	-0.9
1981 Cal-A	1	1	.500	11	4	0	0	0	44	40	18	8	0	14	19	11.0	3.48	105	.241	.300	0	—	0	1	1	1	0.1
1982 *Cal-A	10	5	.667	33	16	3	1	1	142	120	54	15	5	44	86	10.7	3.17	128	.226	.292	0	—	0	14	14	2	1.6
1983 Cal-A	11	5	.688	26	17	4	1	2	126^2	128	59	13	4	43	83	12.4	4.05	99	.264	.330	0	—	0	0	-0	1	0.1
1984 Cal-A	4	5	.444	20	7	0	0	2	65^1	72	42	10	6	28	66	14.6	5.37	74	.280	.364	0	—	0	-10	-10	1	-1.3
1985 Bos-A	5	3	.625	22	9	0	0	1	92	98	43	9	1	32	56	12.8	4.11	104	.274	.335	0	—	0	2	2	1	0.3
Total 15	115	88	.567	380	246	36	8	12	1809^2	1693	839	150	68	662	1073	12.1	3.66	102	.248	.321	66	.163	8	20	16	11	3.8

● BILL KISSINGER Kissinger, William Francis "Shang" b: 8/15/1871, Dayton, Ky. d: 4/20/29, Cincinnati, Ohio BR/TR, 185 lbs. Deb: 5/30/1895 ◆

YEAR TM/L	W	L	PCT	G	GS	CG	SH	SV	IP	H	R	HR	HB	BB	SO	RAT	ERA	ERA+	OAV	OOB	BH	AVG	PB	PR	PR+	PD	TPI
1895 Bal-N	1	0	1.000	2	2	1	0	0	11^1	18	11	0	0	2	3	15.9	3.97	120	.353	.377	1	.200	-0	1	1	-0	0.0
StL-N	4	12	.250	24	14	9	0	0	140^2	222	145	8	8	51	31	18.0	6.72	72	.352	.408	24	.247	-2	-30	-29	0	-2.4
Yr	5	12	.294	26	16	10	0	0	152	240	156	8	8	53	34	17.8	6.51	74	.352	.406	25	.245	-2	-29	-28	0	-2.4
1896 StL-N	2	9	.182	20	12	11	0	1	136	209	136	5	8	55	22	18.0	6.49	67	.349	.411	22	.301	1	-32	-32	2	-1.7
1897 StL-N	0	4	.000	7	4	2	0	0	31^1	51	50	2	8	15	5	21.3	11.49	38	.362	.451	13	.333	2	-25	-24	0	-1.9
Total 3	7	25	.219	53	32	23	0	1	319^1	500	342	15	24	123	61	18.2	6.99	66	.352	.413	60	.280	1	-86	-85	2	-6.0

● FRANK KITSON Kitson, Frank R. b: 9/11/1869, Hopkins, Mich. d: 4/14/30, Allegan, Mich. BL/TR, 5'11", 165 lbs. Deb: 5/19/1898

YEAR TM/L	W	L	PCT	G	GS	CG	SH	SV	IP	H	R	HR	HB	BB	SO	RAT	ERA	ERA+	OAV	OOB	BH	AVG	PB	PR	PR+	PD	TPI
1898 Bal-N	8	5	.615	17	13	13	1	0	119^1	123	71	0	8	35	32	12.5	3.24	110	.265	.327	27	.314	4	5	5	0	0.8
1899 Bal-N	22	16	.579	40	37	34	2	0	326^2	327	144	6	12	65	75	11.1	2.78	142	.260	.303	27	.201	-2	39	42	-2	3.7
1900 *Bro-N	15	13	.536	40	30	21	2	**4**	253^1	283	152	12	9	56	55	12.4	4.19	92	.282	.326	32	.294	5	-14	-10	-5	-0.9
1901 Bro-N	19	11	.633	38	32	26	5	2	280^2	312	135	9	10	67	127	12.5	2.98	112	.279	.326	35	.263	5	11	11	-3	1.4
1902 Bro-N	19	13	.594	32	31	29	3	0	268^2	256	105	4	7	52	109	10.6	2.85	97	.251	.292	32	.276	8	-2	-2	2	0.7
1903 Det-A	15	16	.484	31	28	28	2	0	257^2	277	112	8	5	38	102	11.2	2.58	113	.274	.303	21	.181	-1	11	10	-2	0.7
1904 Det-A	9	13	.409	26	24	19	0	0	199^2	211	100	7	7	38	69	11.5	3.07	83	.272	.312	15	.208	1	-10	-12	-0	-1.2
1905 Det-A	12	14	.462	33	27	21	3	1	225^2	230	120	3	11	57	78	11.9	3.47	79	.266	.319	16	.184	-1	-20	-18	-2	-2.3
1906 Was-A	6	14	.300	30	21	15	1	0	197	196	97	2	6	57	59	11.8	3.65	72	.262	.320	22	.244	8	-21	-23	-0	-1.3
1907 Was-A	0	3	.000	5	3	2	0	0	32	41	20	1	2	9	11	14.6	3.94	61	.313	.366	1	.100	-0	-5	-6	-1	-0.7
NY-A	4	0	1.000	12	4	3	0	0	61	75	31	0	4	17	14	14.2	3.10	90	.305	.360	7	.280	1	-4	-2	-1	-0.2
Yr	4	3	.571	17	7	5	0	0	93	116	51	1	6	26	25	14.3	3.39	79	.308	.362	8	.229	0	-9	-7	-2	-0.9
Total 10	129	118	.522	304	250	211	19	7	2221^2	2331	1087	52	81	491	731	11.8	3.18	99	.270	.315	235	.240	27	-11	-5	-15	0.7

● MALACHI KITTRIDGE Kittridge, Malachi Jeddidah "Jeddidah" b: 10/12/1869, Clinton, Mass. d: 6/23/28, Gary, Ind. BR/TR, 5'7", 170 lbs. Deb: 4/19/1890 M◆

YEAR TM/L	W	L	PCT	G	GS	CG	SH	SV	IP	H	R	HR	HB	BB	SO	RAT	ERA	ERA+	OAV	OOB	BH	AVG	PB	PR	PR+	PD	TPI
1896 Chi-N	0	0	—	1	0	0	0	0	1^2	2	2	0	0	1	0	16.2	5.40	84	.286	.375	48	.223	-0	-0	-0	-0	0.0

● HUGO KLAERNER Klaerner, Hugo Emil "Dutch" b: 10/15/08, Fredericksburg, Tex. d: 2/3/82, Fredericksburg, Tex. BR/TR, 5'11", 190 lbs. Deb: 9/10/34

YEAR TM/L	W	L	PCT	G	GS	CG	SH	SV	IP	H	R	HR	HB	BB	SO	RAT	ERA	ERA+	OAV	OOB	BH	AVG	PB	PR	PR+	PD	TPI
1934 Chi-A	0	2	.000	3	3	1	0	0	17^1	24	21	4	0	16	9	20.8	10.90	43	.329	.449	2	.333	1	-12	-11	1	-0.8

● FRED KLAGES Klages, Frederick Albert Anthony b: 10/31/43, Ambridge, Pa. BR/TR, 6'2", 185 lbs. Deb: 9/11/66

YEAR TM/L	W	L	PCT	G	GS	CG	SH	SV	IP	H	R	HR	HB	BB	SO	RAT	ERA	ERA+	OAV	OOB	BH	AVG	PB	PR	PR+	PD	TPI
1966 Chi-A	1	0	1.000	3	3	0	0	0	15^2	9	4	0	0	7	6	9.2	1.72	184	.167	.262	3	.500	1	3	3	0	0.3
1967 Chi-A	4	4	.500	11	9	0	0	0	44^2	43	19	6	1	16	17	12.1	3.83	81	.256	.324	3	.000	-1	-3	-4	-1	-0.9
Total 2	5	4	.556	14	12	0	0	0	60^1	52	23	6	1	23	23	11.3	3.28	95	.234	.309	3	.167	-0	0	-1	-1	-0.6

● AL KLAWITTER Klawitter, Albert "Dutch" b: 4/12/1888, Wilkes-Barre, Pa. d: 5/2/50, Milwaukee, Wis. BR/TR, 5'11.5", 187 lbs. Deb: 9/20/09

YEAR TM/L	W	L	PCT	G	GS	CG	SH	SV	IP	H	R	HR	HB	BB	SO	RAT	ERA	ERA+	OAV	OOB	BH	AVG	PB	PR	PR+	PD	TPI
1909 NY-N	1	1	.500	6	3	2	0	1	27	24	11	1	0	13	6	12.3	2.00	128	.247	.336	3	.333	1	2	2	1	0.4
1910 NY-N	0	0	—	1	0	0	0	0	1	2	1	0	0	2	0	36.0	9.00	33	.400	.571	0	—	0	-1	-1	-0	-0.1
1913 Det-A	1	2	.333	8	3	1	0	0	32	39	25	0	0	15	10	15.2	5.91	49	.305	.378	0	.000	-2	-11	-11	0	-1.0
Total 3	2	3	.400	15	6	3	0	1	60	65	37	1	0	30	16	14.3	4.20	66	.283	.365	3	.150	-0	-9	-10	1	-0.7

● TOM KLAWITTER Klawitter, Thomas Carl b: 6/24/58, LaCrosse, Wis. BR/TL, 6'2", 190 lbs. Deb: 4/14/85

YEAR TM/L	W	L	PCT	G	GS	CG	SH	SV	IP	H	R	HR	HB	BB	SO	RAT	ERA	ERA+	OAV	OOB	BH	AVG	PB	PR	PR+	PD	TPI
1985 Min-A	0	0	—	7	2	0	0	0	9^1	7	7	2	0	13	5	19.3	6.75	65	.226	.455	0	—	0	-3	-2	0	-0.1

● HAL KLEINE Kleine, Harold John b: 6/8/23, St.Louis, Mo. d: 12/10/57, St.Louis, Mo. BL/TL, 6'2", 193 lbs. Deb: 4/26/44

YEAR TM/L	W	L	PCT	G	GS	CG	SH	SV	IP	H	R	HR	HB	BB	SO	RAT	ERA	ERA+	OAV	OOB	BH	AVG	PB	PR	PR+	PD	TPI
1944 Cle-A	1	2	.333	11	6	1	0	0	40^2	38	29	0	0	36	13	16.4	5.75	57	.248	.392	2	.143	-1	-11	-12	-1	-0.9
1945 Cle-A	0	0	—	3	0	0	0	0	7	8	4	0	0	7	5	19.3	3.86	84	.286	.429	1	.333	1	-0	-0	-0	0.0
Total 2	1	2	.333	14	6	1	0	0	47^2	46	33	0	0	43	18	16.8	5.48	60	.254	.397	3	.176	-0	-11	-12	-1	-0.9

● TED KLEINHANS Kleinhans, Theodore Otto (b: Traugott Otto Kleinhans) b: 4/8/1899, Deer Park, Wis. d: 7/24/85, Redington Beach, Fla. BR/TL, 6', 170 lbs. Deb: 4/20/34

YEAR TM/L	W	L	PCT	G	GS	CG	SH	SV	IP	H	R	HR	HB	BB	SO	RAT	ERA	ERA+	OAV	OOB	BH	AVG	PB	PR	PR+	PD	TPI
1934 Phi-N	0	0	—	5	0	0	0	0	6	11	8	1	0	3	2	21.0	9.00	52	.379	.438	0	.000	-0	-3	-2	0	-0.1
Cin-N	2	6	.250	24	9	0	0	0	80	107	63	2	1	38	23	16.4	5.74	71	.321	.392	3	.130	-1	-15	-15	1	-1.2
Yr	2	6	.250	29	9	0	0	0	86	118	71	3	1	41	25	16.7	5.97	69	.326	.396	3	.125	-1	-18	-17	2	-1.3
1936 NY-A	1	1	.500	19	0	0	0	1	29^1	36	25	0	0	23	10	18.1	5.83	80	.300	.413	1	.167	-0	-3	-4	-0	-0.3
1937 Cin-N	1	2	.333	7	3	1	0	0	27^1	29	13	1	1	12	13	13.8	2.30	162	.271	.350	2	.250	0	5	5	1	0.4

YEAR	TM/L	W	L	PCT	G	GS	CG	SH	SV	IP	H	R	HR	HB	BB	SO	RAT	ERA	ERA+	OAV	OOB	BH	AVG	PB	PR	PR+	PD	TPI
1938	Cin-N	0	0	—	1	0	0	0	0	1	2	1	0	0	0	0	18.0	9.00	41	.400	.400	0	—	0	-1	-1	-0	0.0
Total	4	4	9	.308	56	12	1	0	1	143^2	185	110	4	2	76	48	16.5	5.26	79	.311	.391	6	.158	-1	-16	-18	1	-1.2
● NUB KLEINKE	Kleinke, Norbert George b: 5/19/11, Fond Du Lac, Wis. d: 3/16/50, Off Marin Coast, Cal. BR/TR, 6'1", 170 lbs. Deb: 4/25/35																											
1935	StL-N	0	0	—	4	2	0	0	0	12^2	19	8	1	0	3	5	15.6	4.97	82	.358	.393	0	.000	-0	-1	-1	-0	-0.1
1937	StL-N	1	1	.500	5	2	1	0	0	20^2	25	14	0	0	7	9	13.9	4.79	83	.321	.376	0	.000	-1	-2	-2	0	-0.2
Total	2	1	1	.500	9	4	1	0	0	33^1	44	22	1	0	10	14	14.6	4.86	83	.336	.383	0	.000	-2	-3	-3	0	-0.3
● ED KLEPFER	Klepfer, Edward Lloyd "Big Ed" b: 3/17/1888, Summerville, Pa. d: 8/9/50, Tulsa, Okla. BR/TR, 6', 185 lbs. Deb: 7/4/11																											
1911	NY-A	0	0	—	2	0	0	0	0	4	5	3	0	0	2	4	15.8	6.75	53	.250	.318	0	.000	-0	-2	-1	0	-0.1
1913	NY-A	0	1	.000	8	1	0	0	0	24^2	38	22	2	2	12	10	19.0	7.66	39	.373	.448	1	.167	0	-13	-13	0	-0.6
1915	Chi-A	1	0	1.000	3	2	1	0	0	12^2	11	4	0	0	5	3	11.4	2.84	105	.234	.308	0	.000	-0	0	0	-0	0.0
	Cle-A	1	6	.143	8	7	2	0	0	43	47	25	0	0	11	13	12.1	2.09	146	.283	.328	2	.167	-0	4	4	1	0.7
	Yr	2	6	.250	11	9	3	0	0	55^2	58	29	0	0	16	16	12.0	2.26	134	.272	.323	2	.133	-0	4	5	0	0.7
1916	Cle-A	6	6	.500	31	13	4	1	2	143	136	52	0	4	46	62	11.7	2.52	119	.262	.327	1	.025	-4	5	7	-0	0.2
1917	Cle-A	14	4	.778	41	27	9	0	1	213	208	84	0	0	55	66	11.1	2.37	120	.264	.312	2	.032	-6	7	10	-2	0.0
1919	Cle-A	0	0	—	5	0	0	0	0	7^1	12	14	1	0	6	7	22.1	7.36	45	.375	.474	0	.000	-0	-3	-3	0	-0.2
Total	6	22	17	.564	98	50	16	1	3	447^2	457	204	3	6	137	165	12.1	2.81	104	.273	.330	6	.048	-11	-2	6	-1	-0.0
● ED KLIEMAN	Klieman, Edward Frederick "Specs" or "Babe" b: 3/21/18, Norwood, Ohio d: 11/15/79, Homosassa, Fla. BR/TR, 6'1", 190 lbs. Deb: 9/24/43																											
1943	Cle-A	0	1	.000	1	1	1	0	0	9	8	1	0	0	5	2	13.0	1.00	311	.286	.394	0	.000	-0	2	2	-0	0.2
1944	Cle-A	11	13	.458	47	19	5	1	5	178^1	185	73	4	7	70	44	13.2	3.38	98	.274	.348	6	.105	-3	1	-2	1	-0.5
1945	Cle-A	5	8	.385	38	12	4	1	4	126^1	123	60	3	4	49	33	12.5	3.85	84	.261	.336	8	.200	1	-7	-9	3	-0.5
1946	Cle-A	0	0	—	9	0	0	0	0	15	18	13	0	0	10	2	16.8	6.60	50	.290	.389	0	.000	-0	-5	-6	-1	-0.4
1947	Cle-A	5	4	.556	**58**	0	0	0	**17**	92	78	32	5	2	39	21	11.6	3.03	115	.231	.315	2	.105	-1	7	5	2	0.8
1948	*Cle-A	3	2	.600	44	0	0	0	4	79^2	62	26	3	2	46	18	12.4	2.60	156	.229	.345	2	.143	-0	**15**	**14**	1	1.0
1949	Was-A	0	0	—	2	0	0	0	0	3	8	6	0	0	3	1	33.0	18.00	24	.500	.579	1	1.000	-0	-5	-5	-0	-0.2
	Chi-A	2	0	1.000	18	0	0	0	3	33	33	15	2	0	15	9	13.1	3.00	139	.273	.353	2	.250	0	4	4	0	0.4
	Yr	2	0	1.000	20	0	0	0	3	36	41	21	2	0	18	10	14.8	4.25	98	.299	.381	3	.333	1	-0	-0	1	0.2
1950	Phi-A	0	0	—	5	0	0	0	0	5^2	10	6	0	2	2	0	22.2	9.53	48	.357	.438	0	.000	-0	-3	-3	-0	-0.2
Total	8	26	28	.481	222	32	10	2	33	542	525	232	17	17	239	130	13.0	3.49	100	.261	.345	21	.146	-3	10	1	6	0.6
● RON KLIMKOWSKI	Klimkowski, Ronald Bernard b: 3/1/44, Jersey City, N.J. BR/TR, 6'2", 190 lbs. Deb: 9/15/69																											
1969	NY-A	0	0	—	3	1	0	0	0	14	6	1	0	0	5	3	7.1	0.64	542	.130	.216	0	.000	-0	5	5	-0	0.2
1970	NY-A	6	7	.462	45	3	1	1	1	98^1	80	36	7	3	33	40	10.6	2.65	132	.223	.294	1	.053	-2	12	10	0	1.1
1971	Oak-A	2	2	.500	26	0	0	0	2	45^1	37	19	3	1	23	25	12.1	3.38	99	.220	.318	2	.400	1	0	-0	1	0.2
1972	NY-A	0	3	.000	16	2	0	0	1	31^1	32	15	3	1	15	11	13.8	4.02	74	.271	.358	0	.000	-1	-3	-4	0	-0.5
Total	4	8	12	.400	90	6	1	1	4	189	155	71	13	5	76	79	11.2	2.90	116	.224	.306	3	.091	-2	13	10	1	1.0
● BOBBY KLINE	Kline, John Robert b: 1/27/29, St.Petersburg, Fla BR/TR, 6', 179 lbs. Deb: 4/11/55 ◆																											
1955	Was-A	0	0	—	1	0	0	0	0	1	4	3	1	0	1	0	45.0	27.00	14	.667	.714	31	.221	0	-3	-3	0	-0.1
● BOB KLINE	Kline, Robert George "Junior" b: 12/9/09, Enterprise, Ohio d: 3/16/87, Westerville, Ohio BR/TR, 6'3", 200 lbs. Deb: 9/17/30																											
1930	Bos-A	0	0	—	1	0	0	0	0	1	1	0	0	0	0	0	9.0	0.00	—	.333	.333	0	—	0	1	1	0	0.0
1931	Bos-A	5	5	.500	28	10	3	0	0	98	110	54	3	3	35	25	13.6	4.41	98	.298	.364	9	.333	2	-0	-1	2	0.3
1932	Bos-A	11	13	.458	47	19	4	1	2	172	203	117	10	1	76	31	14.7	5.28	85	.294	.365	7	.130	-3	-15	-15	3	-1.8
1933	Bos-A	7	8	.467	46	8	1	0	4	127	127	70	5	6	67	16	14.2	4.54	97	.265	.362	6	.176	-1	-4	-2	3	0.0
1934	Phi-A	6	2	.750	20	0	0	0	1	39^2	50	34	6	0	13	14	14.3	6.35	69	.314	.366	3	.333	1	-8	-9	1	-1.3
	Was-A	1	0	1.000	6	0	0	0	0	4	10	8	0	1	4	1	33.8	15.75	27	.500	.600	0	—	0	-5	-5	0	-0.9
	Yr	7	2	.778	26	0	0	0	1	43^2	60	42	6	1	17	15	16.1	7.21	61	.335	.396	3	.333	1	-13	-14	2	-2.2
Total	5	30	28	.517	148	37	8	1	7	441^2	501	283	24	11	195	87	14.4	5.05	87	.291	.367	25	.202	-1	-32	-32	9	-3.7
● RON KLINE	Kline, Ronald Lee b: 3/9/32, Callery, Pa. BR/TR, 6'3", 205 lbs. Deb: 4/21/52																											
1952	Pit-N	0	7	.000	27	11	0	0	0	78^2	74	55	3	6	66	27	16.7	5.49	73	.253	.401	0	.000	-2	-15	-12	-1	-1.3
1955	Pit-N	6	13	.316	36	19	2	1	2	136^2	161	78	13	5	53	48	14.4	4.15	99	.298	.366	5	.132	-2	-2	-1	2	0.0
1956	Pit-N	14	18	.438	44	39	9	2	2	264	263	110	26	5	81	125	11.9	3.38	112	.263	.321	10	.127	-3	12	12	-0	1.1
1957	Pit-N	9	16	.360	40	31	11	2	0	205	214	107	27	1	61	88	12.1	4.04	94	.268	.321	4	.061	-6	-4	-6	-1	-1.3
1958	Pit-N	13	16	.448	32	32	11	2	0	237^1	220	96	25	0	92	109	11.8	3.53	110	.252	.323	2	.027	-6	11	9	1	0.5
1959	Pit-N	11	13	.458	33	29	7	0	0	186	186	95	23	2	70	91	12.5	4.26	91	.263	.331	8	.136	-2	-6	-8	-1	-1.2
1960	StL-N	4	9	.308	34	17	1	0	1	117^2	133	86	21	0	43	54	13.5	6.04	68	.284	.344	5	.143	-2	-30	-23	1	-2.4
1961	LA-A	3	6	.333	26	12	0	0	0	104^2	119	62	16	1	44	70	14.1	4.90	92	.288	.358	3	.097	-2	-10	-4	1	-0.4
	Det-A	5	3	.625	10	8	3	1	0	56^1	53	25	3	0	17	27	11.2	2.72	151	.245	.300	3	.167	0	8	8	-1	1.1
	Yr	8	9	.471	36	20	3	1	1	161	172	87	19	1	61	97	13.1	4.14	106	.273	.339	6	.122	-2	-2	4	0	0.7
1962	Det-A	3	6	.333	36	4	0	0	2	77^1	88	40	9	2	28	47	13.7	4.31	94	.284	.347	2	.125	-1	-3	-2	1	-0.2
1963	Was-A	3	8	.273	62	1	0	0	17	93^2	85	36	3	3	30	49	11.3	2.79	133	.249	.316	1	.091	-0	9	9	-1	1.4
1964	Was-A	10	7	.588	61	0	0	0	14	81^1	81	29	4	2	21	40	11.5	2.32	159	.262	.313	1	.167	0	12	12	-0	2.6
1965	Was-A	7	6	.538	74	0	0	0	**29**	99^1	106	36	7	2	32	52	12.7	2.63	132	.275	.333	0	.000	-1	9	9	-1	1.6
1966	Was-A	6	4	.600	63	0	0	0	23	90^1	79	32	12	0	17	46	9.6	2.39	145	.237	.274	1	.167	-0	10	11	-2	1.6
1967	Min-A	7	1	.875	54	0	0	0	5	71^2	71	33	10	1	15	36	10.9	3.77	92	.261	.302	0	.000	-1	-4	-2	-1	-0.4
1968	Pit-N	12	5	.706	56	0	0	0	7	112^2	94	26	3	2	31	48	10.1	1.68	174	.234	.293	0	.000	-1	**16**	**16**	-1	2.5
1969	Pit-N	1	3	.250	20	0	0	0	3	31^1	37	23	3	1	5	15	12.5	5.81	60	.296	.328	0	.000	-1	-8	-8	-0	-1.2
	SF-N	0	2	.000	7	0	0	0	0	11	16	6	1	0	6	7	18.0	4.09	86	.364	.440	0	—	0	-1	-1	-0	-0.1
	Yr	1	5	.167	27	0	0	0	3	42	53	29	4	1	11	22	13.9	5.36	65	.314	.359	0	.000	-1	-8	-9	-0	-1.3
	Bos-A	0	1	.000	16	0	0	0	1	17	24	11	4	0	17	7	21.7	4.76	80	.329	.456	0	—	0	-2	-2	0	-0.1
1970	Atl-N	0	0	—	5	0	0	0	1	6^1	9	5	4	0	2	3	15.6	7.11	60	.321	.367	0	—	0	-2	-2	-0	-0.1
Total	17	114	144	.442	736	203	44	8	108	2078	2113	991	217	33	731	989	12.5	3.75	101	.266	.331	45	.092	-28	1	12	-5	3.7
● STEVE KLINE	Kline, Steven Jack b: 10/6/47, Wenatchee, Wash. BR/TR, 6'3", 205 lbs. Deb: 7/10/70																											
1970	NY-A	6	6	.500	16	15	5	0	0	100^1	99	42	8	0	24	49	11.0	3.41	103	.254	.298	5	.179	2	3	1	1	0.4
1971	NY-A	12	13	.480	31	30	15	1	0	222^1	206	87	21	0	37	81	9.8	2.96	109	.244	.276	9	.136	-0	13	7	3	1.1
1972	NY-A	16	9	.640	32	32	11	4	0	236^1	210	79	11	10	44	58	10.1	2.40	123	.237	.281	7	.092	-3	18	15	2	1.6
1973	NY-A	4	7	.364	14	13	2	1	0	74	76	39	5	1	31	19	13.1	4.01	91	.270	.344	0	—	0	-2	-3	-0	-0.4
1974	NY-A	2	2	.500	4	4	0	0	0	26	26	12	3	1	5	6	11.1	3.46	102	.263	.305	0	—	0	0	0	-0	0.0
	Cle-A	3	8	.273	16	11	1	0	0	71	70	44	9	4	31	17	13.3	5.07	71	.266	.352	0	—	0	-11	-11	1	-1.5
	Yr	5	10	.333	20	15	1	0	0	97	96	56	12	5	36	23	12.7	4.64	78	.265	.340	0	—	0	-11	-11	1	-1.5
1977	Atl-N	0	0	—	16	0	0	0	1	20^1	21	15	4	0	12	10	14.6	6.64	67	.259	.355	0	—	0	-6	-4	0	-0.3
Total	6	43	45	.489	129	105	34	6	1	750^1	708	318	61	16	184	240	10.9	3.26	101	.249	.298	21	.124	-1	15	4	5	0.9
● STEVE KLINE	Kline, Steven James b: 8/22/72, Sunbury, Pa. BB/TL, 6'2", 200 lbs. Deb: 4/2/97																											
1997	Cle-A	3	1	.750	20	1	0	0	0	26^1	42	19	6	1	13	17	19.1	5.81	81	.365	.434	0	—	0	-4	-3	-1	-0.5
	Mon-N	1	3	.250	26	0	0	0	0	26^1	31	18	4	1	10	20	14.4	6.15	68	.304	.372	0	.000	-0	-6	-6	0	-0.8
1998	Mon-N	3	6	.333	78	0	0	0	1	71^2	62	25	4	3	41	76	13.3	2.76	152	.228	.335	0	.000	-0	12	12	0	1.3
1999	Mon-N	7	4	.636	**82**	0	0	0	0	69^2	56	32	8	3	33	69	11.9	3.75	120	.218	.314	0	.000	-0	6	6	2	1.0
2000	Mon-N	1	5	.167	**83**	0	0	0	14	82^1	88	36	8	3	27	64	12.9	3.50	135	.278	.341	0	.000	-0	10	11	-0	1.0
Total	4	15	19	.441	289	1	0	0	15	276^1	279	130	30	11	124	246	13.5	3.84	116	.263	.346	0	.000	-1	19	19	1	2.0
● BILL KLING	Kling, William b: 1/14/1867, Kansas City, Mo. d: 8/26/34, Kansas City, Mo. BL/TR, 6', 190 lbs. Deb: 8/13/1891 F																											
1891	Phi-N	4	2	.667	12	7	4	0	0	75	91	61	2	2	32	26	15.0	4.32	79	.289	.358	6	.194	1	-8	-7	-1	-0.5
1892	Bal-N	0	2	.000	2	2	0	0	0	11	17	16	1	2	7	7	21.3	11.45	30	.340	.441	1	.250	1	-10	-9	-0	-1.0
1895	Lou-N	0	0	—	1	0	0	0	0	1	0	0	0	0	1	0	9.0	0.00	—	.000	.250	0	.000	-0	1	1	0	0.0
Total	3	4	4	.500	15	9	4	0	0	87	108	77	3	4	40	33	15.7	5.17	66	.293	.369	7	.194	1	-18	-17	-1	-1.5

● SCOTT KLINGENBECK

Klingenbeck, Scott Edward b: 2/3/71, Cincinnati, Ohio BR/TR, 6′2″, 205 lbs. Deb: 6/2/94

YEAR	TM/L	W	L	PCT	G	GS	CG	SH	SV	IP	H	R	HR	HB	BB	SO	RAT	ERA	ERA+	OAV	OOB	BH	AVG	PB	PR	PR+	PD	TPI
1994	Bal-A	1	0	1.000	1	1	0	0	0	7	6	4	1	1	4	5	14.1	3.86	130	.240	.367	0	—	0	1	1	-0	0.1
1995	Bal-A	2	2	.500	6	5	0	0	0	31^1	32	17	6	0	18	15	14.4	4.88	97	.269	.365	0	—	0	-1	-0	1	0.0
	Min-A	0	2	.000	18	4	0	0	0	48^1	69	48	16	4	24	27	18.1	8.57	56	.338	.418	0	—	0	-21	-20	-1	-1.0
	Yr	2	4	.333	24	9	0	0	0	79^2	101	65	22	4	42	42	16.6	7.12	67	.313	.398	0	—	0	-21	-21	-0	-1.0
1996	Min-A	1	1	.500	10	3	0	0	0	28^2	42	28	5	1	10	15	16.6	7.85	65	.339	.393	0	—	0	-9	-8	0	-0.5
1998	Cin-N	1	3	.250	4	4	0	0	0	22^2	26	17	6	1	7	13	13.5	5.96	72	.286	.343	0	.000	-1	-4	-4	0	-0.6
Total	4	5	8	.385	39	17	0	0	0	138	175	114	34	7	63	75	16.0	6.91	69	.311	.387	0	.000	-1	-34	-32	0	-2.0

● BOB KLINGER

Klinger, Robert Harold b: 6/4/08, Allenton, Mo. d: 8/19/77, Villa Ridge, Mo. BR/TR, 6′, 180 lbs. Deb: 4/19/38

YEAR	TM/L	W	L	PCT	G	GS	CG	SH	SV	IP	H	R	HR	HB	BB	SO	RAT	ERA	ERA+	OAV	OOB	BH	AVG	PB	PR	PR+	PD	TPI
1938	Pit-N	12	5	.706	28	21	10	1	1	159^1	152	63	7	6	42	58	11.3	2.99	127	.253	.308	10	.167	-2	14	14	0	1.3
1939	Pit-N	14	17	.452	37	33	10	2	0	225	251	120	11	3	81	64	13.4	4.36	88	.284	.346	17	.202	0	-11	-13	3	-1.3
1940	Pit-N	8	13	.381	39	22	3	0	3	142	196	102	5	5	53	48	16.1	5.39	71	.329	.388	6	.143	-2	-24	-25	1	-3.4
1941	Pit-N	9	4	.692	35	9	3	0	4	116^2	127	58	5	1	30	36	12.2	3.93	92	.276	.322	8	.250	2	-4	-4	0	-0.3
1942	Pit-N	8	11	.421	37	19	8	1	1	152^2	151	69	6	3	45	58	11.7	3.24	104	.252	.307	8	.200	1	1	2	1	0.5
1943	Pit-N	11	8	.579	33	25	14	3	0	195	185	77	6	0	58	65	11.2	2.72	128	.252	.307	16	.246	3	14	16	0	1.8
1946	*Bos-A	3	2	.600	28	1	0	0	**9**	57	49	16	1	1	25	16	11.8	2.37	155	.238	.323	5	.313	1	7	8	-0	1.0
1947	Bos-A	1	1	.500	28	0	0	0	5	42	42	20	5	1	24	12	14.4	3.86	101	.253	.351	1	.111	-1	-1	0	-0	-0.1
Total	8	66	61	.520	265	130	48	7	23	1089^2	1153	525	46	20	358	357	12.6	3.68	100	.271	.331	71	.204	3	-3	-0	5	-0.5

● JOE KLINK

Klink, Joseph Charles b: 2/3/62, Johnstown, Pa. BL/TL, 5′11″, 175 lbs. Deb: 4/9/87

YEAR	TM/L	W	L	PCT	G	GS	CG	SH	SV	IP	H	R	HR	HB	BB	SO	RAT	ERA	ERA+	OAV	OOB	BH	AVG	PB	PR	PR+	PD	TPI
1987	Min-A	0	1	.000	12	0	0	0	0	23	37	18	4	0	11	17	18.8	6.65	70	.359	.421	0	—	0	-6	-5	-0	-0.3
1990	*Oak-A	0	0	—	40	0	0	0	1	39^2	34	9	1	0	18	19	11.8	2.04	182	.233	.317	0	—	0	8	8	-1	0.3
1991	Oak-A	10	3	.769	62	0	0	0	2	62	60	30	4	5	21	34	12.5	4.35	88	.259	.333	0	—	0	-2	-4	0	-0.7
1993	Fla-N	0	2	.000	59	0	0	0	0	37^2	37	22	0	0	24	22	14.6	5.02	86	.266	.374	0	.000	-0	-4	-3	-1	-0.2
1996	Sea-A	0	0	—	3	0	0	0	0	2^1	3	1	1	0	1	2	15.4	3.86	128	.300	.364	0	—	0	0	0	-0	0.0
Total	5	10	6	.625	176	0	0	0	3	164^2	171	80	10	5	75	94	13.7	4.26	95	.271	.354	0	.000	-0	-3	-4	-2	-0.9

● JOHNNY KLIPPSTEIN

Klippstein, John Calvin b: 10/17/27, Washington, D.C. BR/TR, 6′1″, 185 lbs. Deb: 5/3/50

YEAR	TM/L	W	L	PCT	G	GS	CG	SH	SV	IP	H	R	HR	HB	BB	SO	RAT	ERA	ERA+	OAV	OOB	BH	AVG	PB	PR	PR+	PD	TPI
1950	Chi-N	2	9	.182	33	11	3	0	1	104^2	112	69	9	4	64	51	15.5	5.25	80	.279	.383	11	.333	4	-13	-12	-1	-0.8
1951	Chi-N	6	6	.500	35	11	1	1	2	123^2	125	71	10	6	53	56	13.4	4.29	95	.263	.344	4	.108	-2	-5	-3	0	-0.4
1952	Chi-N	9	14	.391	41	25	7	2	3	202^2	208	110	17	6	89	110	13.5	4.44	87	.265	.344	11	.175	1	-16	-13	1	-1.1
1953	Chi-N	10	11	.476	48	19	5	0	6	167^2	169	115	15	8	107	113	15.2	4.83	92	.258	.369	9	.155	-1	-10	-7	-2	-1.0
1954	Chi-N	4	11	.267	36	21	4	0	1	148	155	104	13	4	96	69	15.5	5.29	79	.272	.381	6	.133	-2	-20	-17	1	-1.6
1955	Cin-N	9	10	.474	39	14	3	2	0	138	120	66	13	4	60	68	12.0	3.39	125	.233	.318	2	.065	-2	10	12	-0	1.3
1956	Cin-N	12	11	.522	37	29	11	0	1	211	219	103	26	10	82	86	13.3	4.09	97	.275	.350	7	.099	-4	-8	-3	1	-0.6
1957	Cin-N	8	11	.421	46	18	3	1	3	146	146	84	17	3	68	99	13.4	5.05	81	.261	.344	3	.073	-3	-19	-14	-1	-2.2
1958	Cin-N	3	2	.600	12	4	0	0	1	33	37	20	5	1	14	22	14.2	4.91	84	.285	.359	1	.125	-0	-4	-3	-1	-0.5
	LA-N	3	5	.375	45	0	0	0	9	90	81	40	12	2	44	73	12.7	3.80	108	.248	.341	1	.050	-2	2	3	-0	0.1
	Yr	6	7	.462	57	4	0	0	10	123	118	60	17	3	58	95	13.1	4.10	100	.259	.346	2	.071	-2	-2	0	-1	-0.4
1959	*LA-N	4	0	1.000	28	0	0	0	2	45^2	48	31	8	2	33	30	16.4	5.91	72	.276	.397	1	.143	-0	-10	-8	-0	-0.8
1960	Cle-A	5	5	.500	49	0	0	0	**14**	74^1	53	30	8	1	35	46	10.8	2.91	129	.205	.303	2	.143	-0	8	7	0	1.2
1961	Was-A	2	2	.500	42	1	0	0	0	71^2	83	59	13	4	43	41	16.3	6.78	59	.297	.399	1	.143	-0	-22	-22	1	-1.1
1962	Cin-N	7	6	.538	40	7	0	0	4	108^2	113	66	13	4	64	67	15.0	4.47	90	.278	.381	3	.125	0	-6	-5	0	-0.5
1963	Phi-N	5	6	.455	49	1	0	0	8	112	80	28	3	3	46	86	10.4	1.93	168	.204	.293	1	.038	-2	17	17	-1	1.6
1964	Phi-N	2	1	.667	11	0	0	0	1	22^1	22	10	6	2	8	13	12.9	4.03	86	.250	.327	0	.000	-0	-1	-1	1	-0.2
	Min-A	0	4	.000	33	0	0	0	2	45^2	44	12	4	1	20	39	12.8	1.97	181	.260	.342	0	.000	0	8	8	1	0.9
1965	*Min-A	9	3	.750	56	0	0	0	5	76^1	59	22	8	3	31	59	11.0	2.24	159	.217	.304	0	.000	-1	10	11	-1	1.7
1966	Min-A	1	1	.500	26	0	0	0	3	39^2	35	15	2	2	20	26	12.9	3.40	106	.238	.337	0	.000	-0	0	1	-0	0.0
1967	Det-A	0	0	—	5	0	0	0	0	6^2	6	4	1	0	1	4	9.5	5.40	60	.250	.280	0	—	0	-2	-2	-0	-0.1
Total	18	101	118	.461	711	161	37	6	66	1967^2	1915	1059	203	70	978	1158	13.6	4.24	94	.258	.350	63	.125	-14	-80	-53	-0	-4.1

● FRED KLOBEDANZ

Klobedanz, Frederick Augustus "Duke"
b: 6/13/1871, Waterbury, Conn. d: 4/12/40, Waterbury, Conn. BL/TL, 5′11″, 190 lbs. Deb: 8/20/1896

YEAR	TM/L	W	L	PCT	G	GS	CG	SH	SV	IP	H	R	HR	HB	BB	SO	RAT	ERA	ERA+	OAV	OOB	BH	AVG	PB	PR	PR+	PD	TPI
1896	Bos-N	6	4	.600	10	9	9	0	0	80^2	69	41	5	7	31	26	11.9	3.01	151	.229	.316	13	.317	2	12	13	-1	1.5
1897	*Bos-N	26	7	**.788**	38	37	30	2	0	309^1	344	198	13	23	125	92	14.3	4.60	97	.279	.357	48	.324	9	-10	-4	-4	0.1
1898	Bos-N	19	10	.655	35	33	25	0	0	270^2	281	168	13	12	99	51	13.0	3.89	95	.266	.336	27	.213	0	-8	-6	-1	-0.6
1899	Bos-N	1	4	.200	5	5	4	0	0	33^1	39	22	2	2	9	8	13.5	4.86	86	.291	.345	2	.182	1	-4	-2	1	-0.2
1902	Bos-N	1	0	1.000	1	1	1	0	0	8	9	1	0	1	2	4	13.5	1.13	251	.281	.343	1	.500	1	1	1	-0	0.3
Total	5	53	25	.679	89	85	69	2	0	702	742	430	33	45	266	181	13.5	4.12	101	.269	.343	91	.277	13	-9	2	-6	1.1

● STAN KLOPP

Klopp, Stanley Harold "Betz" b: 12/22/10, Womelsdorf, Pa. d: 3/11/80, Robesonia, Pa. BR/TR, 6′1.5″, 180 lbs. Deb: 4/30/44

YEAR	TM/L	W	L	PCT	G	GS	CG	SH	SV	IP	H	R	HR	HB	BB	SO	RAT	ERA	ERA+	OAV	OOB	BH	AVG	PB	PR	PR+	PD	TPI
1944	Bos-N	1	2	.333	24	0	0	0	0	46^1	47	36	1	0	33	17	15.5	4.27	89	.272	.388	2	.286	0	-3	-2	-1	-0.2

● BRENT KNACKERT

Knackert, Brent Bradley b: 8/1/69, Los Angeles, Cal. BR/TR, 6′3″, 185 lbs. Deb: 4/10/90

YEAR	TM/L	W	L	PCT	G	GS	CG	SH	SV	IP	H	R	HR	HB	BB	SO	RAT	ERA	ERA+	OAV	OOB	BH	AVG	PB	PR	PR+	PD	TPI
1990	Sea-A	1	1	.500	24	2	0	0	0	37^1	50	28	5	2	21	28	17.6	6.51	61	.313	.399	0	—	0	-11	-10	-0	-0.5
1996	Bos-A	0	1	.000	8	0	0	0	0	10	16	12	1	0	7	5	20.7	9.00	56	.356	.442	0	—	0	-4	-4	1	-0.3
Total	2	1	2	.333	32	2	0	0	0	47^1	66	40	6	2	28	33	18.3	7.04	60	.322	.409	0	—	0	-15	-15	0	-0.8

● CHRIS KNAPP

Knapp, Robert Christian b: 9/16/53, Cherry Point, N.C. BR/TR, 6′5″, 195 lbs. Deb: 9/4/75

YEAR	TM/L	W	L	PCT	G	GS	CG	SH	SV	IP	H	R	HR	HB	BB	SO	RAT	ERA	ERA+	OAV	OOB	BH	AVG	PB	PR	PR+	PD	TPI
1975	Chi-A	0	0	—	2	0	0	0	0	2	2	1	0	0	4	3	27.0	4.50	86	.250	.500	0	—	0	-0	-0	0	0.0
1976	Chi-A	3	1	.750	11	6	1	0	0	52^1	54	31	5	1	32	41	15.0	4.82	74	.273	.377	0	—	0	-8	-7	-0	-0.6
1977	Chi-A	12	7	.632	27	26	4	0	0	146^1	166	90	16	7	61	103	14.4	4.80	85	.283	.357	0	—	0	-12	-11	-1	-1.3
1978	Cal-A	14	8	.636	30	29	6	0	0	188^1	178	94	25	2	67	126	11.8	4.21	86	.250	.317	0	—	0	-9	-13	-2	-1.6
1979	*Cal-A	5	5	.500	20	18	3	0	0	98	109	73	8	2	35	36	13.4	5.51	74	.275	.337	0	—	0	-14	-16	-0	-1.4
1980	Cal-A	2	11	.154	32	20	1	0	1	117^1	133	83	18	8	51	46	14.7	6.14	64	.289	.369	0	—	0	-27	-29	-1	-3.0
Total	6	36	32	.529	122	99	15	0	1	604^1	642	372	72	20	250	355	13.6	4.99	78	.272	.347	0	—	0	-70	-77	-5	-7.9

● FRANK KNAUSS

Knauss, Frank H. b: 1868, Cleveland, Ohio BL/TL, 5′10″, 170 lbs. Deb: 6/25/1890

YEAR	TM/L	W	L	PCT	G	GS	CG	SH	SV	IP	H	R	HR	HB	BB	SO	RAT	ERA	ERA+	OAV	OOB	BH	AVG	PB	PR	PR+	PD	TPI
1890	Col-a	17	12	.586	37	34	28	3	2	275^2	206	131	3	21	106	148	10.9	2.81	128	**.202**	.290	24	.226	5	33	26	-1	2.6
1891	Cle-N	0	3	.000	3	3	1	0	0	15	23	29	2	4	8	6	21.0	7.20	48	.338	.438	1	.167	-0	-6	-6	0	-0.9
1892	Cin-N	0	0	—	1	0	0	0	0	8	13	9	0	0	5	2	20.3	3.38	97	.351	.429	1	.333	0	-0	-0	0	0.0
1894	Cle-N	0	1	.000	2	2	1	0	0	11	7	9	0	3	14	2	19.6	5.73	95	.179	.429	0	.000	-1	-0	-0	1	0.0
1895	NY-N	0	0	—	1	1	0	0	0	3^2	9	7	0	0	2	1	27.0	17.18	27	.450	.500	0	.000	-0	-5	-5	-0	-0.2
Total	5	17	16	.515	44	40	30	3	2	313^1	258	185	5	28	135	159	12.1	3.30	111	.218	.312	26	.217	4	20	13	-0	1.5

● RUDY KNEISCH

Kneisch, Rudolph Frank b: 4/10/1899, Baltimore, Md. d: 4/6/65, Baltimore, Md. BR/TL, 5′10.5″, 175 lbs. Deb: 9/21/26

YEAR	TM/L	W	L	PCT	G	GS	CG	SH	SV	IP	H	R	HR	HB	BB	SO	RAT	ERA	ERA+	OAV	OOB	BH	AVG	PB	PR	PR+	PD	TPI
1926	Det-A	0	1	.000	2	2	1	0	0	17	18	7	2	2	6	4	13.8	2.65	153	.273	.351	0	.000	-1	3	3	0	0.1

● PHIL KNELL

Knell, Philip Louis b: 3/12/1865, San Francisco, Cal d: 6/5/44, Santa Monica, Cal. BR/TL, 5′7.5″, 154 lbs. Deb: 7/6/1888

YEAR	TM/L	W	L	PCT	G	GS	CG	SH	SV	IP	H	R	HR	HB	BB	SO	RAT	ERA	ERA+	OAV	OOB	BH	AVG	PB	PR	PR+	PD	TPI
1888	Pit-N	1	2	.333	3	3	3	0	0	26^1	20	19	1	5	18	15	14.7	3.76	71	.217	.374	1	.091	-1	-3	-3	-0	-0.4
1890	Phi-P	22	11	.667	35	31	30	2	0	286^2	287	199	10	28	166	99	15.1	3.83	112	.249	.358	29	.220	-1	13	14	0	1.1
1891	Col-a	28	27	.509	58	52	47	**5**	0	462	363	228	4	54	226	228	12.5	2.92	118	**.209**	.319	34	.158	-9	41	29	5	2.4
1892	Was-N	9	13	.409	22	21	17	1	0	170	156	114	4	11	76	74	12.9	3.65	89	.234	.323	8	.118	-5	-7	-8	-0	-1.2
	Phi-N	5	5	.500	11	9	7	0	0	80	87	47	0	11	35	43	15.0	4.05	80	.266	.357	3	.088	-3	-7	-7	-2	-1.1
	Yr	14	18	.438	33	30	24	1	0	250	243	161	4	22	111	117	13.5	3.78	86	.245	.334	11	.108	-7	-14	-15	-2	-2.3
1894	Pit-N	0	0	—	1	0	0	0	0	7	11	9	0	1	6	0	23.1	11.57	45	.355	.474	0	.000	-1	-5	-5	1	-0.2
	Lou-N	7	21	.250	32	28	25	0	0	247	330	237	9	14	104	67	16.3	5.32	96	.317	.387	31	.274	0	0	-6	-2	-0.6
	Yr	7	21	.250	33	28	25	0	0	254	341	246	9	15	110	67	16.5	5.49	93	.318	.389	31	.267	-0	-5	-11	-2	-0.8
1895	Lou-N	0	6	.000	10	6	3	0	0	56^2	75	66	3	6	21	19	16.2	6.51	71	.314	.383	6	.231	0	-11	-12	1	-0.8
	Cle-N	7	5	.583	20	13	9	0	0	116^2	149	100	7	6	53	30	16.0	5.40	92	.306	.381	11	.200	-3	-8	-5	0	-0.6

YEAR	TM/L	W	L	PCT	G	GS	CG	SH	SV	IP	H	R	HR	HB	BB	SO	RAT	ERA	ERA+	OAV	OOB	BH	AVG	PB	PR	PR+	PD	TPI
	Yr	7	11	.389	30	19	12	0	0	173^1	224	166	10	12	74	49	16.1	5.76	84	.309	.382	17	.210	-3	-19	-17	1	-1.4
Total	6	79	90	.467	192	163	141	8	0	1452^1	1478	1019	38	136	705	575	14.4	4.05	99	.256	.351	123	.187	-21	14	-6	2	-1.4

● CHARLIE KNEPPER Knepper, Charles b: 2/18/1871, Anderson, Ind. d: 2/6/46, Muncie, Ind. BR/TR, 6'4", 190 lbs. Deb: 5/26/1899

YEAR	TM/L	W	L	PCT	G	GS	CG	SH	SV	IP	H	R	HR	HB	BB	SO	RAT	ERA	ERA+	OAV	OOB	BH	AVG	PB	PR	PR+	PD	TPI
1899	Cle-N	4	22	.154	27	26	26	0	0	219^2	307	190	11	15	77	43	16.3	5.78	64	.329	.390	12	.135	-5	-47	-53	-1	-5.1

● BOB KNEPPER Knepper, Robert Wesley b: 5/25/54, Akron, Ohio BL/TL, 6'2", 200 lbs. Deb: 9/10/76

YEAR	TM/L	W	L	PCT	G	GS	CG	SH	SV	IP	H	R	HR	HB	BB	SO	RAT	ERA	ERA+	OAV	OOB	BH	AVG	PB	PR	PR+	PD	TPI
1976	SF-N	1	2	.333	4	4	0	0	0	25^1	26	9	0	0	7	11	11.9	3.24	112	.277	.327	1	.111	-0	1	1	0	0.1
1977	SF-N	11	9	.550	27	27	6	2	0	166	151	73	14	3	72	100	12.3	3.36	116	.242	.323	10	.182	1	10	10	-1	1.2
1978	SF-N	17	11	.607	36	35	16	**6**	0	260	218	85	10	4	85	147	10.6	2.63	131	.229	.295	5	.063	-3	**27**	25	-2	2.0
1979	SF-N	9	12	.429	34	34	6	2	0	207^1	241	117	30	3	77	123	13.9	4.64	75	.289	.352	12	.182	3	-21	-28	-1	-2.4
1980	SF-N	9	16	.360	35	33	8	1	0	215^1	242	114	15	8	61	103	13.0	4.10	87	.281	.335	10	.152	-0	-12	-13	2	-1.3
1981	*Hou-N★	9	5	.643	22	22	6	5	0	156^2	128	41	5	4	38	75	9.8	2.18	151	.226	.280	7	.149	1	23	21	-1	1.9
1982	Hou-N	5	15	.250	33	29	4	0	1	180	193	100	14	3	60	108	12.8	4.45	75	.278	.338	3	.058	-2	-17	-24	1	-2.6
1983	Hou-N	6	13	.316	35	29	4	3	0	203	202	93	12	4	71	125	12.3	3.19	107	.261	.326	12	.182	3	10	5	1	0.9
1984	Hou-N	15	10	.600	35	34	11	3	0	233^2	223	93	26	1	55	140	10.7	3.20	104	.251	.296	13	.171	4	10	4	-1	0.7
1985	Hou-N	15	13	.536	37	37	4	0	0	241	253	119	21	3	54	131	11.6	3.55	98	.271	.313	11	.141	0	1	-2	-3	-0.5
1986	*Hou-N	17	12	.586	40	38	8	**5**	0	258	232	100	19	4	62	143	10.4	3.14	115	.242	.290	9	.099	-3	17	14	2	1.4
1987	Hou-N	8	17	.320	33	31	1	0	0	177^2	226	118	26	4	54	76	14.4	5.27	74	.313	.364	5	.098	-1	-23	-28	2	-3.3
1988	Hou-N★	14	5	.737	27	27	3	2	0	175	156	70	13	2	67	103	11.6	3.14	106	.243	.316	6	.125	-1	6	4	2	0.6
1989	Hou-N	4	10	.286	22	20	0	0	0	113	135	78	12	2	60	45	15.7	5.89	58	.303	.388	7	.226	5	-30	-32	1	-3.0
	SF-N	3	2	.600	13	6	1	1	0	52	55	20	4	1	15	19	12.3	3.46	98	.270	.323	1	.083	1	0	-0	-1	-0.1
	Yr	7	12	.368	35	26	1	1	0	165	190	98	16	3	75	64	14.6	5.13	66	.292	.368	8	.186	6	-30	-33	0	-3.1
1990	SF-N	3	3	.500	12	7	0	0	0	44^1	56	28	7	1	19	24	15.4	5.68	64	.311	.380	3	.231	1	-9	-10	0	-1.1
Total	15	146	155	.485	445	413	78	30	1	2708	2737	1258	228	47	857	1473	12.1	3.68	95	.264	.323	115	.137	7	-6	-55	1	-5.5

● LOU KNERR Knerr, Wallace Luther b: 8/21/21, Strasburg, Pa. d: 3/23/80, Denver, Pa. BR/TR, 6'1", 210 lbs. Deb: 4/17/45

YEAR	TM/L	W	L	PCT	G	GS	CG	SH	SV	IP	H	R	HR	HB	BB	SO	RAT	ERA	ERA+	OAV	OOB	BH	AVG	PB	PR	PR+	PD	TPI
1945	Phi-A	5	11	.313	27	17	5	0	0	130	142	77	6	1	74	41	15.0	4.22	81	.283	.376	9	.191	-1	-12	-11	0	-1.4
1946	Phi-A	3	16	.158	30	22	6	0	0	148^1	171	95	13	1	67	58	14.5	5.40	66	.288	.361	9	.180	0	-31	-30	-0	-3.4
1947	Was-A	0	0	—	6	0	0	0	0	9	17	13	1	0	8	5	25.0	11.00	34	.405	.500	1	1.000	0	-7	-7	0	-0.3
Total	3	8	27	.229	63	39	11	0	0	287^1	330	185	20	2	149	104	15.1	5.04	69	.290	.373	19	.194	-1	-51	-48	0	-5.1

● ELMER KNETZER Knetzer, Elmer Ellsworth "Baron" b: 7/22/1885, Carrick, Pa. d: 10/3/75, Pittsburgh, Pa. BR/TR, 5'10", 180 lbs. Deb: 9/11/09

YEAR	TM/L	W	L	PCT	G	GS	CG	SH	SV	IP	H	R	HR	HB	BB	SO	RAT	ERA	ERA+	OAV	OOB	BH	AVG	PB	PR	PR+	PD	TPI
1909	Bro-N	1	3	.250	5	4	3	0	0	35^2	33	22	2	0	22	7	13.9	3.03	86	.252	.359	0	.000	-2	-2	-2	1	-0.3
1910	Bro-N	7	5	.583	20	15	10	3	0	132^2	122	63	1	1	60	56	12.4	3.19	95	.255	.339	2	.053	-3	-2	-2	-2	-0.6
1911	Bro-N	11	12	.478	35	20	11	3	0	204	202	101	1	1	93	66	13.1	3.49	96	.277	.359	6	.097	-4	-2	-4	-1	-0.8
1912	Bro-N	7	9	.438	33	16	4	1	0	140^1	135	86	6	4	70	61	13.4	4.55	74	.254	.345	5	.135	-1	-18	-19	-0	-2.0
1914	Pit-F	20	12	.625	37	30	20	3	1	272	257	123	9	2	88	146	11.5	2.88	100	.254	.315	9	.099	-9	0	-0	2	-0.8
1915	Pit-F	18	14	.563	41	33	22	3	3	279	256	105	5	1	89	120	11.2	2.58	105	.251	.311	12	.132	-7	5	4	-0	-0.3
1916	Bos-N	0	2	.000	2	0	0	0	0	5	11	9	0	0	2	2	23.4	7.20	35	.524	.565	0	—	0	-3	-3	1	-0.5
	Cin-N	5	12	.294	36	16	12	0	1	171^1	161	76	6	3	48	70	11.1	2.89	90	.252	.307	8	.154	-1	-5	-6	3	-0.4
	Yr	5	14	.263	38	16	12	0	1	176^1	172	85	6	3	50	72	11.5	3.01	86	.261	.316	8	.154	-1	-8	-8	3	-0.9
1917	Cin-N	0	0	—	11	0	0	0	1	27^1	29	18	0	2	12	7	14.2	2.96	88	.282	.368	0	.000	-0	-1	-1	0	-0.1
Total	8	69	69	.500	220	134	82	13	6	1267^1	1206	603	30	14	484	535	12.1	3.15	93	.258	.330	42	.109	-26	-27	-32	2	-5.8

● LON KNIGHT Knight, Alonzo P. b: 6/16/1853, Philadelphia, Pa. d: 4/23/32, Philadelphia, Pa. BR/TR, 5'11.5", 165 lbs. Deb: 9/4/1875 MU♦

YEAR	TM/L	W	L	PCT	G	GS	CG	SH	SV	IP	H	R	HR	HB	BB	SO	RAT	ERA	ERA+	OAV	OOB	BH	AVG	PB	PR	PR+	PD	TPI
1875	Ath-n	6	5	.545	13	13	12	0	0	107	114	73	0		12	15	10.6	2.27	105	.259	.278	6	.128	-3	-1	1		-0.1
1876	Phi-N	10	22	.313	34	32	27	0	0	282	383	288	0		34	12	13.3	2.62	93	.289	.315	60	.248	-1	-10	-6	-1	-0.6
1884	Phi-a	0	1	.000	2	1	1	0	0	14	24	19	0	1	4	2	18.6	9.00	38	.348	.392	131	.271	0	-9	-8	0	-0.4
1885	Phi-a	0	0	—	1	0	0	0	0	5	4	1	0	0	2	1	10.8	1.80	191	.103	.146	25	.210	-0	1	1	0	0.1
	Pro-N	0	0	—	1	0	0	0	0	4	4	4	1		4	1	18.0	6.75	40	.235	.381	13	.160	-0	-2	-2	-0	-0.1
Total	3	10	23	.303	38	33	28	0	0	305	415	312	1	1	44	16	13.6	2.95	84	.286	.315	549	.245	-1	-20	-15	-1	-1.0

● JACK KNIGHT Knight, Elma Russell b: 1/12/1895, Pittsboro, Miss. d: 7/30/76, San Antonio, Tex. BL/TR, 6', 175 lbs. Deb: 9/20/22

YEAR	TM/L	W	L	PCT	G	GS	CG	SH	SV	IP	H	R	HR	HB	BB	SO	RAT	ERA	ERA+	OAV	OOB	BH	AVG	PB	PR	PR+	PD	TPI
1922	StL-N	0	0	—	1	1	0	0	0	4	9	4	0	0	3	1	27.0	9.00	43	.474	.545	1	.500	0	-2	-2	0	-0.1
1925	Phi-N	7	6	.538	33	11	4	0	3	105^1	161	100	14	1	36	19	16.9	6.84	70	.354	.402	9	.205	-1	-30	-22	-1	-2.4
1926	Phi-N	3	12	.200	35	15	5	0	2	142^2	206	122	14	0	48	29	16.0	6.62	63	.347	.396	12	.214	0	-44	-36	5	-2.8
1927	Bos-N	0	0	—	3	0	0	0	0	3	6	5	0	0	2	0	24.0	15.00	25	.429	.500	0	—	0	-4	-4	1	-0.1
Total	4	10	18	.357	72	27	9	0	5	255	382	231	28	1	89	49	16.7	6.85	64	.353	.403	22	.216	0	-80	-64	4	-5.4

● GEORGE KNIGHT Knight, George Henry b: 11/24/1855, Lakeville, Conn. d: 10/4/12, Lakeville, Conn. Deb: 9/28/1875

YEAR	TM/L	W	L	PCT	G	GS	CG	SH	SV	IP	H	R	HR	HB	BB	SO	RAT	ERA	ERA+	OAV	OOB	BH	AVG	PB	PR	PR+	PD	TPI
1875	NH-n	1	0	1.000	1	1	1	0	0	9	12	6	0		0	0	12.0	3.00	69	.293	.293	0	.000	-1	-1	-1		-0.1

● JOE KNIGHT Knight, Joseph William "Quiet Joe" b: 9/28/1859, Port Stanley, Ont., Canada d: 10/16/38, Lynhurst, Ont., Canada BL/TL, 5'11", 185 lbs. Deb: 5/16/1884 ♦

YEAR	TM/L	W	L	PCT	G	GS	CG	SH	SV	IP	H	R	HR	HB	BB	SO	RAT	ERA	ERA+	OAV	OOB	BH	AVG	PB	PR	PR+	PD	TPI
1884	Phi-N	2	4	.333	6	6	6	0	0	51	66	53	2		21	8	15.4	5.47	55	.293	.354	6	.250	1	-14	-14	-0	-1.2

● HUB KNOLLS Knolls, Oscar Edward b: 12/18/1883, Valparaiso, Ind. d: 7/1/46, Chicago, Ill. TR, 6'2", 190 lbs. Deb: 5/1/06

YEAR	TM/L	W	L	PCT	G	GS	CG	SH	SV	IP	H	R	HR	HB	BB	SO	RAT	ERA	ERA+	OAV	OOB	BH	AVG	PB	PR	PR+	PD	TPI
1906	Bro-N	0	0	—	2	0	0	0	0	6^2	13	5	0	0	2	3	20.3	4.05	62	.382	.417	1	1.000	1	-1	-1	-1	0.0

● JACK KNOTT Knott, John Henry b: 3/2/07, Dallas, Tex. d: 10/13/81, Brownwood, Tex. BR/TR, 6'2.5", 200 lbs. Deb: 4/13/33

YEAR	TM/L	W	L	PCT	G	GS	CG	SH	SV	IP	H	R	HR	HB	BB	SO	RAT	ERA	ERA+	OAV	OOB	BH	AVG	PB	PR	PR+	PD	TPI
1933	StL-A	1	8	.111	20	9	0	0	0	82^2	88	51	11	2	33	19	13.4	5.01	93	.269	.340	7	.304	1	-7	-3	-1	-0.3
1934	StL-A	10	3	.769	45	10	2	0	4	138	149	86	17	1	67	56	14.2	4.96	101	.278	.359	4	.133	-1	-7	1	1	0.0
1935	StL-A	11	8	.579	48	19	7	2	**7**	187^2	219	119	8	1	78	45	14.3	4.60	104	.287	.353	7	.115	-5	-3	4	1	0.0
1936	StL-A	9	17	.346	47	23	9	0	6	192^2	272	174	15	4	93	60	17.2	7.29	74	.330	.401	4	.070	-5	-48	-38	-1	-4.7
1937	StL-A	8	18	.308	38	22	8	0	2	191^1	220	117	25	5	91	74	14.9	4.89	99	.291	.370	8	.140	-4	-6	-1	-2	-0.7
1938	StL-A	1	2	.333	7	4	0	0	0	30	35	19	3	0	15	8	15.0	4.80	104	.285	.362	1	.100	-1	-0	1	-0	-0.1
	Chi-A	5	10	.333	20	18	9	0	0	131	135	70	8	0	54	35	13.0	4.05	121	.271	.342	5	.125	-2	11	12	1	1.0
	Yr	6	12	.333	27	22	9	0	0	161	170	89	11	0	69	43	13.4	4.19	117	.273	.346	6	.120	-3	11	12	1	0.9
1939	Chi-A	11	6	.647	25	23	8	0	0	149^2	157	71	13	1	41	56	12.0	4.15	114	.269	.318	8	.151	-3	8	9	-1	0.5
1940	Chi-A	11	9	.550	25	23	4	2	0	158	166	88	12	2	52	44	12.5	4.56	97	.265	.324	5	.088	-4	-3	-2	-1	-0.7
1941	Phi-A	13	11	.542	27	26	11	0	0	194^1	212	108	20	2	81	54	13.7	4.40	95	.279	.350	5	.077	-3	-5	-5	-3	-1.0
1942	Phi-A	2	10	.167	20	14	4	0	0	95^1	127	84	7	1	36	31	15.5	5.57	68	.310	.367	4	.138	-1	-20	-18	1	-2.0
1946	Phi-A	0	1	.000	3	1	0	0	0	6^1	7	4	1	1	1	2	12.8	5.68	62	.280	.333	0	—	0	-2	-1	-0	-0.2
Total	11	82	103	.443	325	192	62	4	19	1557	1787	991	140	20	642	484	14.2	4.97	95	.287	.355	58	.120	-29	-83	-44	-5	-8.2

● ED KNOUFF Knouff, Edward "Fred" b: 6/1868, Philadelphia, Pa. d: 9/14/1900, Philadelphia, Pa. BR/TR, 210 lbs. Deb: 7/1/1885 ♦

YEAR	TM/L	W	L	PCT	G	GS	CG	SH	SV	IP	H	R	HR	HB	BB	SO	RAT	ERA	ERA+	OAV	OOB	BH	AVG	PB	PR	PR+	PD	TPI
1885	Phi-a	7	6	.538	14	13	12	0	0	106	103	76	0	9	44	43	13.2	3.65	94	.228	.309	9	.188	-2	-5	-2	1	-0.3
1886	Bal-a	0	1	.000	1	1	1	0	0	9	2	5	0	3	5	8	10.0	2.00	171	.067	.263	0	.000	-0	1	1	1	0.2
1887	Bal-a	2	6	.250	9	9	6	0	0	63	120	79	0	13	41	27	19.0	7.57	54	.388	.413	10	.313	0	-23	-25	0	-2.1
	StL-a	4	2	.667	6	6	6	1	0	50	76	34	0	3	36	18	14.2	4.50	101	.298	.364	11	.193	-1	-1	0	-0	-0.1
	Yr	6	8	.429	15	15	12	1	0	113	196	113	0	16	77	45	16.9	6.21	69	.439	.393	21	.236	-1	-24	-24	0	-2.2
1888	StL-a	5	4	.556	9	9	9	0	0	81	66	45	0	8	37	25	12.3	2.67	122	.214	.314	3	.097	-2	4	5	-2	0.1
	Cle-a	0	1	.000	2	2	1	0	0	9	8	2	0	1	3	2	12.0	1.00	309	.229	.308	1	.167	0	2	2	1	0.3
	Yr	5	5	.500	11	11	10	0	0	90	74	47	0	9	40	27	12.3	2.50	130	.216	.314	4	.108	-2	6	7	-1	0.4
1889	Phi-a	2	0	1.000	3	3	2	0	0	25	37	17	2	1	9	5	16.9	3.96	96	.333	.388	3	.250	0	-0	-0	-1	0.0
Total	5	20	20	.500	44	43	37	1	0	343	412	258	2	38	175	128	14.4	4.17	89	.282	.344	37	.196	-4	-22	-17	0	-1.9

● DAROLD KNOWLES Knowles, Darold Duane b: 12/9/41, Brunswick, Mo. BL/TL, 6', 190 lbs. Deb: 4/18/65 C

YEAR	TM/L	W	L	PCT	G	GS	CG	SH	SV	IP	H	R	HR	HB	BB	SO	RAT	ERA	ERA+	OAV	OOB	BH	AVG	PB	PR	PR+	PD	TPI
1965	Bal-A	0	1	.000	5	1	0	0	0	14^2	14	15	2	3	10	12	16.6	9.20	38	.250	.391	0	.000	-0	-9	-9	0	-0.6
1966	Phi-N	6	5	.545	69	0	0	0	13	100^1	98	38	4	7	46	88	13.5	3.05	118	.260	.351	4	.250	0	6	6	2	1.1
1967	Was-A	6	8	.429	61	1	0	0	14	113^1	91	37	5	4	52	85	11.7	2.70	117	.228	.322	1	.063	-1	7	6	2	1.0

YEAR	TM/L	W	L	PCT	G	GS	CG	SH	SV	IP	H	R	HR	HB	BB	SO	RAT	ERA	ERA+	OAV	OOB	BH	AVG	PB	PR	PR+	PD	TPI
1968	Was-A	1	1	.500	32	0	0	0	4	41^1	38	11	0	1	12	37	11.1	2.18	134	.241	.298	1	.250	1	4	3	0	0.4
1969	Was-A★	9	2	.818	53	0	0	0	13	84^1	73	25	8	4	31	59	11.5	2.24	155	.236	.314	1	.077	0	13	12	0	2.0
1970	Was-A	2	14	.125	71	0	0	0	27	119^1	100	36	4	4	58	71	12.2	2.04	175	.231	.328	1	.050	-1	22	21	2	**3.7**
1971	Was-A	2	2	.500	12	0	0	0	2	15^1	17	6	2	0	6	16	13.5	3.52	94	.266	.329	0	.000	-0	-0	-0	-0	-0.1
	*Oak-A	5	2	.714	43	0	0	0	7	52^2	40	22	3	3	16	40	10.1	3.59	93	.221	.295	1	.125	-0	-1	-2	1	-0.2
	Yr	7	4	.636	55	0	0	0	9	68	57	28	5	3	22	56	10.9	3.57	93	.233	.304	1	.100	-1	-1	-2	1	-0.3
1972	Oak-A	5	1	.833	54	0	0	0	11	65^2	49	12	1	0	37	36	11.8	1.37	208	.212	.321	3	.250	1	12	12	3	2.0
1973	*Oak-A	6	8	.429	52	5	1	1	9	99	87	44	7	3	49	46	12.6	3.09	115	.246	.343	0	—	0	8	5	2	1.0
1974	Oak-A	3	3	.500	45	1	0	0	3	53^1	61	29	6	2	35	18	16.5	4.22	79	.296	.403	0	—	0	-4	-6	1	-0.6
1975	Chi-N	6	9	.400	58	0	0	0	15	88^1	107	61	3	3	36	63	14.9	5.81	66	.298	.367	1	.067	-1	-21	-18	3	-3.3
1976	Chi-N	5	7	.417	58	0	0	0	9	71^2	61	30	6	2	22	39	10.7	2.89	134	.242	.308	1	.143	1	5	7	2	1.7
1977	Tex-A	5	2	.714	42	0	0	0	4	50^1	50	22	3	2	23	14	13.4	3.22	127	.272	.359	0	—	0	5	5	1	0.8
1978	Mon-N	3	3	.500	60	0	0	0	6	72	63	20	5	0	30	34	11.6	2.38	149	.250	.330	1	.167	-0	10	9	2	1.1
1979	StL-N	2	5	.286	48	0	0	0	6	48^2	54	27	5	0	17	22	13.1	4.07	93	.277	.335	0	.000	-0	-2	-2	-1	-0.3
1980	StL-N	0	1	.000	2	0	0	0	0	1^2	3	2	1	0	0	1	16.2	10.80	34	.375	.375	0	—	0	-1	-1	-0	-0.3
Total	16	66	74	.471	765	8	1	1	143	1092	1006	437	65	38	480	681	12.6	3.12	112	.250	.336	15	.120	-2	54	47	20	9.4
● **TOM KNOWLSON**	Knowlson, Thomas Herbert “Doc” b: 4/23/1895, Pittsburgh, Pa. d: 4/11/43, Miami Shores, Fla. BB/TR, 5′11″, 178 lbs. Deb: 7/3/15																											
1915	Phi-A	4	6	.400	18	9	8	0	0	100^2	99	53	1	6	60	24	14.8	3.49	84	.273	.386	3	.083	-3	-6	-6	-0	-0.9
● **BILL KNOWLTON**	Knowlton, William Young b: 8/18/1892, Philadelphia, Pa. d: 2/25/44, Philadelphia, Pa. BR/TR, Deb: 9/3/20																											
1920	Phi-A	0	1	.000	1	1	0	0	0	5^2	9	9	0	3	3	5	23.8	4.76	84	.346	.469	0	.000	-0	-1	-0	0	-0.1
● **KURT KNUDSEN**	Knudsen, Kurt David b: 2/20/67, Arlington Heights, Ill. BR/TR, 6′3″, 200 lbs. Deb: 5/16/92																											
1992	Det-A	2	3	.400	48	1	0	0	5	70^2	70	39	9	1	41	51	14.3	4.58	86	.264	.365	0	—	0	-5	-5	0	-0.4
1993	Det-A	3	2	.600	30	0	0	0	2	37^2	41	22	9	4	16	29	14.6	4.78	90	.281	.367	0	—	0	-2	-2	-0	-0.3
1994	Det-A	1	0	1.000	4	0	0	0	0	5^1	7	8	2	0	11	1	30.4	13.50	36	.304	.529	0	—	0	-5	-5	-0	-0.7
Total	3	6	5	.545	82	1	0	0	7	113^2	118	69	20	5	68	81	15.1	5.07	81	.272	.377	0	—	0	-12	-12	-0	-1.4
● **MARK KNUDSON**	Knudson, Mark Richard b: 10/28/60, Denver, Colo. BR/TR, 6′5″, 215 lbs. Deb: 7/8/85																											
1985	Hou-N	0	2	.000	2	2	0	0	0	11	21	11	0	0	3	4	19.6	9.00	39	.429	.462	0	.000	0	-7	-7	-0	-0.9
1986	Hou-N	1	5	.167	9	7	0	0	0	42^2	48	23	5	1	15	20	13.5	4.22	85	.279	.340	0	.000	-1	-2	-3	-1	-0.5
	Mil-A	0	1	.000	4	1	0	0	0	17^2	22	15	7	0	5	9	13.8	7.64	57	.286	.329	0	—	0	-7	-6	-0	-0.3
1987	Mil-A	4	4	.500	15	8	1	0	0	62	88	46	7	0	14	26	14.8	5.37	85	.331	.364	0	—	0	-6	-5	-1	-0.7
1988	Mil-A	0	0	—	5	0	0	0	0	16	17	3	1	0	2	7	10.7	1.13	354	.279	.302	0	—	0	5	5	0	0.3
1989	Mil-A	8	5	.615	40	7	1	0	0	123^2	110	50	15	3	29	47	10.3	3.35	115	.237	.286	0	—	0	7	7	-1	0.5
1990	Mil-A	10	9	.526	30	27	4	2	0	168^1	187	84	14	3	40	56	12.3	4.12	94	.282	.325	0	—	0	-4	-4	-2	-0.6
1991	Mil-A	1	3	.250	12	7	0	0	0	35	54	33	8	1	15	23	18.0	7.97	50	.355	.417	0	—	0	-15	-16	-0	-1.5
1993	Col-N	0	0	—	4	0	0	0	0	5^2	16	14	4	0	5	3	33.4	22.24	21	.471	.538	0	.000	-0	-11	-9	-0	-0.5
Total	8	24	29	.453	121	59	6	2	0	482	563	279	61	8	128	195	13.1	4.72	84	.290	.337	0	.000	-1	-40	-41	-5	-4.2
● **KEVIN KOBEL**	Kobel, Kevin Richard b: 10/2/53, Buffalo, N.Y. BR/TL, 6′1″, 195 lbs. Deb: 9/8/73																											
1973	Mil-A	0	1	.000	2	1	0	0	0	8^1	9	8	2	0	8	4	18.4	8.64	44	.273	.415	0	—	0	-4	-5	-0	-0.5
1974	Mil-A	6	14	.300	34	24	3	2	0	169^1	166	84	16	2	54	74	11.8	3.99	91	.258	.317	0	—	0	-7	-7	1	-0.7
1976	Mil-A	0	1	.000	3	0	0	0	0	4	6	5	3	1	3	1	22.5	11.25	31	.375	.500	0	—	0	-3	-3	0	-0.6
1978	NY-N	5	6	.455	32	11	1	0	0	108^1	95	42	9	2	30	51	10.6	2.91	120	.239	.295	4	.160	0	8	7	-1	0.7
1979	NY-N	6	8	.429	30	27	1	1	0	161^2	169	74	14	3	46	67	12.1	3.51	104	.274	.328	9	.196	0	4	3	0	0.3
1980	NY-N	1	4	.200	14	1	0	0	0	24^1	36	21	5	0	11	8	17.4	7.03	51	.353	.416	0	.000	-0	-9	-10	-0	-1.8
Total	6	18	34	.346	115	64	5	3	0	476	481	234	49	8	152	205	12.1	3.88	93	.266	.326	13	.178	0	-12	-15	0	-2.6
● **ALAN KOCH**	Koch, Alan Goodman b: 3/25/38, Decatur, Ala. BR/TR, 6′4″, 195 lbs. Deb: 7/26/63																											
1963	Det-A	1	1	.500	7	1	0	0	0	10	21	12	3	1	9	5	27.9	10.80	35	.467	.564	2	.667	1	-8	-8	0	-1.2
1964	Det-A	0	0	—	3	0	0	0	0	4	6	3	1	0	3	1	20.3	6.75	54	.375	.474	0	—	0	-1	-1	-0	-0.1
	Was-A	3	10	.231	32	14	1	0	0	114	110	64	18	3	43	67	12.3	4.89	76	.253	.325	8	.250	2	-16	-15	-2	-1.6
	Yr	3	10	.231	35	14	1	0	0	118	116	67	19	3	46	68	12.6	4.96	75	.258	.331	8	.250	2	-17	-16	-2	-1.7
Total	2	4	11	.267	42	15	1	0	0	128	137	79	22	4	55	73	13.8	5.41	68	.277	.354	10	.286	3	-25	-24	-2	-2.9
● **BILLY KOCH**	Koch, William Christopher b: 12/14/74, Rockville Centre, N.Y. BR/TR, 6′3″, 218 lbs. Deb: 5/5/99																											
1999	Tor-A	0	5	.000	56	0	0	0	31	63^2	55	26	5	3	30	57	12.4	3.39	146	.235	.330	0	.000	-0	10	11	1	1.7
2000	Tor-A	9	3	.750	68	0	0	0	33	78^2	78	28	6	2	18	60	11.2	2.63	190	.258	.304	0	.000	-0	20	20	0	3.8
Total	2	9	8	.529	124	0	0	0	64	142^1	133	54	11	5	48	117	11.8	2.97	167	.248	.316	0	.000	-0	30	31	1	5.5
● **DICK KOECHER**	Koecher, Richard Finlay “Highpockets” b: 3/30/26, Philadelphia, Pa. BL/TL, 6′5″, 196 lbs. Deb: 9/29/46																											
1946	Phi-N	0	1	.000	1	1	0	0	0	2^2	7	3	0	0	1	2	27.0	10.13	34	.467	.500	0	.000	-0	-2	-2	-0	-0.4
1947	Phi-N	0	2	.000	3	2	1	0	0	17	20	12	1	1	10	4	16.4	4.76	84	.299	.397	0	.000	-1	-1	-1	0	-0.2
1948	Phi-N	0	1	.000	3	0	0	0	0	6	4	2	0	0	3	2	10.5	3.00	132	.235	.350	0	—	0	1	1	-0	0.1
Total	3	0	4	.000	7	3	1	0	0	25^2	31	17	1	1	14	8	16.1	4.91	80	.313	.404	0	.000	-1	-3	-3	0	-0.5
● **MARK KOENIG**	Koenig, Mark Anthony b: 7/19/04, San Francisco, Cal. d: 4/22/93, Willows, Cal. BB/TR, 6′, 180 lbs. Deb: 9/8/25 ♦																											
1930	Det-A	0	1	.000	2	1	0	0	0	9	11	10	0	1	8	6	20.0	10.00	48	.314	.455	64	.240	0	-5	-5	-0	-0.4
1931	Det-A	0	0	—	3	0	0	0	0	7	7	5	0	0	11	3	23.1	6.43	71	.280	.500	92	.253	0	-2	-1	0	0.0
Total	2	0	1	.000	5	1	0	0	0	16	18	15	0	1	19	9	21.4	8.44	56	.300	.475	1190	.279	0	-7	-6	-0	-0.4
● **WILL KOENIGSMARK**	Koenigsmark, William Thomas b: 2/27/1896, Waterloo, Ill. d: 7/1/72, Waterloo, Ill. BR/TR, 6′4″, 180 lbs. Deb: 9/10/19																											
1919	StL-N	0	0	—	1	0	0	0	0	0	2	0	0	1	—	—	∞	—	1.000	1.000	96	—	0	-2	-2	0	-0.2	
● **ELMER KOESTNER**	Koestner, Elmer Joseph “Bob” b: 11/30/1885, Piper City, Ill. d: 10/27/59, Fairbury, Ill. BR/TR, 6′1.5″, 175 lbs. Deb: 4/23/10																											
1910	Cle-A	5	10	.333	27	13	8	1	2	145	145	76	0	6	63	44	13.3	3.04	85	.282	.367	15	.313	2	-8	-7	-2	-0.6
1914	Chi-N	0	0	—	4	0	0	0	0	6^1	6	5	0	0	4	6	14.2	2.84	98	.261	.370	0	.000	-0	-0	-0	-0	0.0
	Cin-N	0	0	—	5	1	0	0	0	18^1	18	15	0	0	9	6	13.3	4.42	66	.265	.351	2	.400	1	-3	-3	0	-0.1
	Yr	0	0	—	9	1	0	0	0	24^2	24	20	0	0	13	12	13.5	4.01	72	.264	.356	2	.333	1	-3	-3	0	-0.1
Total	2	5	10	.333	36	14	8	1	2	169^2	169	96	0	6	76	56	13.3	3.18	83	.279	.365	17	.315	3	-12	-10	-2	-0.7
● **JOE KOHLMAN**	Kohlman, Joseph James “Blackie” b: 1/28/13, Philadelphia, Pa. d: 3/16/74, Philadelphia, Pa. BR/TR, 6′, 160 lbs. Deb: 9/26/37																											
1937	Was-A	1	0	1.000	2	2	1	0	0	13	15	7	0	0	3	3	12.5	4.15	107	.283	.321	1	.200	-0	1	0	-0	0.0
1938	Was-A	0	0	—	7	0	0	0	0	14^1	12	10	1	0	11	5	14.4	6.28	72	.240	.377	0	.000	-0	-2	-3	0	-0.1
Total	2	1	0	1.000	9	2	1	0	0	27^1	27	17	1	0	14	8	13.5	5.27	85	.262	.350	1	.125	-1	-2	-3	-0	-0.1
● **RYAN KOHLMEIER**	Kohlmeier, Ryan Lyle b: 6/25/77, Salina, Kan. BR/TR, 6′2″, 195 lbs. Deb: 7/29/2000																											
2000	Bal-A	0	1	.000	25	0	0	0	13	26^1	30	9	1	0	15	17	15.4	2.39	200	.291	.381	0	—	0	7	7	-0	0.8
● **BRANDON KOLB**	Kolb, Brandon Charles b: 11/20/73, Oakland, Cal. BR/TR, 6′1″, 190 lbs. Deb: 5/12/2000																											
2000	SD-N	0	1	.000	11	0	0	0	0	14	16	8	0	0	11	12	17.4	4.50	97	.296	.415	0	.000	-0	0	-0	-0	-0.1
● **DANNY KOLB**	Kolb, Daniel Lee b: 3/29/75, Sterling, Ill. BR/TR, 6′4″, 185 lbs. Deb: 6/4/99																											
1999	Tex-A	2	1	.667	16	0	0	0	0	31	33	18	2	1	15	15	14.2	4.65	109	.268	.353	0	—	0	1	1	0	0.2
2000	Tex-A	0	0	—	1	0	0	0	0	0^2	5	5	0	0	2	0	94.5	67.50	8	.833	.875	0	—	0	-5	-4	0	-0.2
Total	2	2	1	.667	17	0	0	0	0	31^2	38	23	2	1	17	15	15.9	5.97	85	.295	.381	0	—	0	-4	-3	0	0.0
● **EDDIE KOLB**	Kolb, Edward William b: 7/20/1880, Cincinnati, Ohio BR/TR, Deb: 10/15/1899																											
1899	Cle-N	0	1	.000	1	1	1	0	0	8	18	19	0	1	5	1	27.0	10.13	36	.439	.511	1	.250	-0	-6	-6	-1	-0.5

YEAR	TM/L	W	L	PCT	G	GS	CG	SH	SV	IP	H	R	HR	HB	BB	SO	RAT	ERA	ERA+	OAV	OOB	BH	AVG	PB	PR	PR+	PD	TPI
● RAY KOLP	Kolp, Raymond Carl "Jockey" b: 10/1/1894, New Berlin, Ohio d: 7/29/67, New Orleans, La. BR/TR, 5'10.5", 187 lbs. Deb: 4/16/21																											
1921	StL-A	8	7	.533	37	18	5	1	0	166^2	208	111	12	0	51	43	14.0	4.97	90	.314	.363	7	.127	-5	-13	-9	1	-1.1
1922	StL-A	14	4	.778	32	18	9	1	0	169^2	199	89	10	5	36	54	12.7	3.93	106	.292	.332	17	.298	5	2	4	-4	0.4
1923	StL-A	5	12	.294	34	17	11	1	1	171^1	178	91	11	6	54	44	12.5	3.89	107	.273	.335	6	.111	-4	2	5	-2	-0.1
1924	StL-A	5	7	.417	25	12	5	1	0	96^2	131	65	4	4	25	29	14.9	5.68	79	.329	.375	6	.200	-0	-16	-12	-1	-1.3
1927	Cin-N	3	3	.500	24	5	2	1	3	82^1	86	38	5	1	29	28	12.7	3.06	124	.278	.342	6	.200	-0	8	7	0	0.5
1928	Cin-N	13	10	.565	44	23	12	1	3	209	219	87	9	4	55	61	12.0	3.19	124	.280	.330	15	.214	3	19	18	1	2.2
1929	Cin-N	8	10	.444	30	16	4	1	0	145^1	151	75	8	1	39	27	11.8	4.03	113	.278	.328	8	.163	-2	11	9	1	0.9
1930	Cin-N	7	12	.368	37	19	5	2	3	168^1	180	86	10	0	34	40	11.4	4.22	114	.278	.314	12	.245	1	14	12	-1	1.1
1931	Cin-N	4	9	.308	30	10	2	0	1	107	144	66	8	4	39	24	15.7	4.96	75	.332	.392	4	.125	-1	-13	-15	-1	-1.9
1932	Cin-N	6	10	.375	32	18	7	2	1	159^2	176	80	13	3	27	42	11.6	3.89	99	.280	.313	9	.184	-1	-0	-1	-2	-0.4
1933	Cin-N	6	9	.400	30	14	4	0	3	150^1	168	73	7	1	23	28	11.5	3.53	96	.290	.318	7	.156	-1	-3	-2	1	-0.2
1934	Cin-N	0	2	.000	28	2	0	0	3	61^2	78	36	1	2	12	19	13.4	4.52	90	.312	.348	1	.083	-1	-3	-3	2	-0.1
Total	12	79	95	.454	383	172	66	11	18	1688	1918	897	98	31	424	439	12.7	4.08	102	.292	.338	98	.184	-7	8	13	-6	0.0
● HAL KOLSTAD	Kolstad, Harold Everette b: 6/1/35, Rice Lake, Wis. BR/TR, 5'9", 190 lbs. Deb: 4/22/62																											
1962	Bos-A	0	2	.000	27	2	0	0	2	61^1	65	44	11	2	35	36	15.0	5.43	76	.269	.366	1	.056	-2	-10	-9	0	-0.6
1963	Bos-A	0	2	.000	7	0	0	0	0	11	16	16	4	2	6	6	19.6	13.09	29	.340	.436	0	.000	-0	-12	-11	-0	-1.7
Total	2	0	4	.000	34	2	0	0	2	72^1	81	60	15	4	41	42	15.7	6.59	62	.280	.377	1	.053	-2	-22	-19	0	-2.3
● ED KONETCHY	Konetchy, Edward Joseph "Big Ed" b: 9/3/1885, LaCrosse, Wis. d: 5/27/47, Ft.Worth, Tex. BR/TR, 6'2.5", 195 lbs. Deb: 6/29/07 ♦																											
1910	StL-N	0	0	—	1	0	0	0	0	4	4	2	0	0	1	0	11.3	4.50	66	.267	.313	157	.302	0	-1	-1	-0	0.0
1913	StL-N	1	0	1.000	1	0	0	0	0	4^2	1	0	0	0	4	3	9.6	0.00	—	.071	.278	139	.276	0	2	2	-0	0.4
1918	Bos-N	0	1	.000	1	1	1	0	0	8	14	8	1	0	2	3	18.0	6.75	40	.378	.410	103	.236	0	-4	-4	-0	-0.4
Total	3	1	1	.500	3	1	1	0	0	16^2	19	10	1	0	7	6	14.0	4.32	67	.288	.356	2150	.281	1	-3	-3	-1	0.0
● DOUG KONIECZNY	Konieczny, Douglas James b: 9/27/51, Detroit, Mich. BR/TR, 6'4", 220 lbs. Deb: 9/11/73																											
1973	Hou-N	0	1	.000	2	2	0	0	0	13	12	8	0	0	4	6	11.1	5.54	66	.279	.340	0	.000	-0	-3	-3	-0	-0.2
1974	Hou-N	0	3	.000	6	3	0	0	0	16	18	15	0	2	12	8	18.0	7.88	44	.290	.421	0	.000	-1	-8	-8	-0	-1.3
1975	Hou-N	6	13	.316	32	29	4	1	0	171	184	93	15	1	87	89	14.3	4.47	76	.280	.365	8	.160	1	-16	-22	-2	-2.3
1977	Hou-N	1	1	.500	4	4	0	0	0	21	26	15	1	1	8	7	15.0	6.00	60	.302	.368	1	.143	-0	-5	-6	0	-0.5
Total	4	7	18	.280	44	38	4	1	0	221	240	131	16	4	111	110	14.5	4.93	69	.283	.368	9	.138	-0	-31	-40	-2	-4.3
● ALEX KONIKOWSKI	Konikowski, Alexander James "Whitey" b: 6/8/28, Throop, Pa. d: 9/28/97, Seymour, Conn. BR/TR, 6'1", 187 lbs. Deb: 6/16/48																											
1948	NY-N	2	3	.400	22	1	0	0	1	33^1	46	34	7	0	17	9	17.0	7.56	52	.346	.420	0	.000	0	-13	-13	1	-1.7
1951	*NY-N	0	0	—	3	0	0	0	0	4	2	0	0	0	0	5	4.5	0.00	—	.154	.154	0	—	0	2	2	0	0.1
1954	NY-N	0	0	—	10	0	0	0	0	12	10	10	1	0	12	6	16.5	7.50	54	.244	.415	0	.000	-0	-5	-5	-0	-0.3
Total	3	2	3	.400	35	1	0	0	1	49^1	58	44	8	0	29	20	15.9	6.93	57	.310	.403	0	.000	0	-16	-16	0	-1.9
● JIM KONSTANTY	Konstanty, Casimir James b: 3/2/17, Strykersville, N.Y. d: 6/11/76, Oneonta, N.Y. BR/TR, 6'1.5", 202 lbs. Deb: 6/18/44																											
1944	Cin-N	6	4	.600	20	12	5	1	0	112^2	113	46	11	1	33	19	11.7	2.80	125	.266	.320	10	.294	2	10	9	1	1.1
1946	Bos-N	0	1	.000	10	1	0	0	0	15^1	17	9	2	0	7	9	14.1	5.28	65	.283	.358	0	.000	0	-3	-3	1	-0.1
1948	Phi-N	1	0	1.000	6	0	0	0	2	9^2	7	1	0	0	2	7	8.4	0.93	424	.233	.281	0	.000	-0	3	3	-0	0.4
1949	Phi-N	9	5	.643	53	0	0	0	7	97	98	38	9	1	29	43	11.9	3.25	121	.280	.337	3	.176	-0	9	8	1	1.2
1950	*Phi-N★	16	7	.696	**74**	0	0	0	**22**	152	108	51	11	0	50	56	9.4	2.66	152	.205	.274	4	.108	-2	**25**	**24**	-1	3.7
1951	Phi-N	4	11	.267	58	1	0	0	9	115^2	127	58	9	0	31	27	12.3	4.05	95	.282	.328	3	.158	-0	-1	-3	1	-0.2
1952	Phi-N	5	3	.625	42	2	2	1	6	80	87	44	9	0	21	16	12.1	3.94	93	.274	.319	1	.071	-0	-2	-3	-0	-0.3
1953	Phi-N	14	10	.583	48	19	7	0	5	170^2	198	90	18	3	42	45	12.8	4.43	95	.290	.334	11	.220	-0	-3	-4	0	-0.5
1954	Phi-N	2	3	.400	33	1	0	0	3	50^1	62	27	7	0	12	11	13.2	3.75	108	.316	.356	0	.000	-2	2	2	0	0.0
	NY-A	1	1	.500	9	0	0	0	2	18^1	11	2	0	0	6	3	8.3	0.98	350	.183	.258	0	.000	-0	6	5	0	0.7
1955	NY-A	7	2	.778	45	0	0	0	11	73^2	68	28	5	0	24	19	11.2	2.32	161	.247	.308	1	.125	-0	13	12	-0	1.8
1956	NY-A	0	0	—	8	0	0	0	2	11	15	6	3	0	6	6	17.2	4.91	79	.319	.396	0	.000	-0	-1	-1	-0	-0.1
	StL-N	1	1	.500	27	0	0	0	5	39^1	46	20	4	0	6	7	11.9	4.58	83	.301	.327	0	—	0	-4	-3	-1	-0.3
Total	11	66	48	.579	433	36	14	2	74	945^2	957	420	88	5	269	268	11.7	3.46	112	.268	.320	33	.163	-5	54	45	2	7.4
● DENNIS KONUSZEWSKI	Konuszewski, Dennis John b: 2/4/71, Bridgeport, Mich. BR/TR, 6'3", 210 lbs. Deb: 8/4/95																											
1995	Pit-N	0	0	—	1	0	0	0	0	0^1	3	2	0	0	1	0	108.0	54.00	8	1.000	1.000	0	—	0	-2	-2	0	-0.1
● ERNIE KOOB	Koob, Ernest Gerald b: 9/11/1892, Keeler, Mich. d: 11/12/41, Lemay, Mo. BL/TL, 5'10", 160 lbs. Deb: 6/23/15																											
1915	StL-A	4	5	.444	28	13	6	0	1	133^2	119	50	2	10	50	37	12.1	2.36	122	.254	.339	5	.135	-1	9	8	-2	0.2
1916	StL-A	11	8	.579	33	20	10	2	2	166^2	153	54	1	6	56	26	11.6	2.54	108	.252	.321	0	.000	-1	5	4	-4	0.0
1917	StL-A	6	14	.300	39	18	3	1	1	133^2	139	81	1	6	57	47	13.6	3.91	67	.280	.361	4	.114	-1	-18	-20	1	-2.9
1919	StL-A	2	4	.333	25	4	0	0	0	66	77	37	3	2	23	11	13.9	4.64	72	.296	.358	0	.000	-2	-10	-9	0	-1.0
Total	4	23	31	.426	125	55	19	3	4	500	488	222	7	24	186	121	12.6	3.13	90	.266	.342	9	.070	-5	-15	-18	-4	-3.7
● CAL KOONCE	Koonce, Calvin Lee b: 11/18/40, Fayetteville, N.C. d: 10/28/93, Winston-Salem, N.C. BR/TR, 6'1", 185 lbs. Deb: 4/14/62																											
1962	Chi-N	10	10	.500	35	30	3	1	0	190^2	200	93	17	7	86	84	13.8	3.97	105	.271	.353	6	.094	-4	-0	4	-1	-0.1
1963	Chi-N	2	6	.250	21	13	0	0	0	72^2	75	43	9	2	32	44	13.5	4.58	77	.273	.353	2	.105	-0	-10	-8	1	-0.8
1964	Chi-N	3	0	1.000	6	2	0	0	0	31	30	8	1	0	7	17	10.7	2.03	183	.254	.296	0	.000	-1	5	6	2	0.6
1965	Chi-N	7	9	.438	38	23	3	1	0	173	181	83	17	6	52	88	12.4	3.69	100	.271	.329	5	.102	-0	-3	-0	-0	0.0
1966	Chi-N	5	5	.500	45	5	0	0	2	108^2	113	57	13	1	35	65	12.3	3.81	97	.268	.325	3	.130	0	-2	-2	1	0.0
1967	Chi-N	2	2	.500	34	0	0	0	2	51	52	27	2	1	21	28	13.1	4.59	77	.268	.343	0	.000	-1	-7	-6	1	-0.5
	NY-N	3	3	.500	11	6	2	1	0	45	45	16	2	0	7	24	10.4	2.80	121	.259	.287	2	.154	-0	3	3	1	0.5
	Yr	5	5	.500	45	6	2	1	2	96	97	43	4	1	28	52	11.8	3.75	93	.264	.317	2	.100	-1	-4	-3	2	0.0
1968	NY-N	6	4	.600	55	2	0	0	11	97	80	27	4	1	32	50	10.5	2.41	125	.235	.303	0	.000	-1	6	6	-1	0.7
1969	NY-N	6	3	.667	40	0	0	0	7	83	85	53	8	3	42	48	14.1	4.99	73	.269	.360	4	.235	0	-13	-12	1	-1.3
1970	NY-N	0	2	.000	13	0	0	0	0	22	25	9	2	1	14	10	16.4	3.27	123	.301	.408	0	.000	-0	2	2	0	0.2
	Bos-A	3	4	.429	23	8	1	0	2	76^1	64	32	7	3	29	37	11.3	3.54	112	.231	.311	2	.095	-0	2	3	2	0.5
1971	Bos-A	0	1	.000	13	1	0	0	0	21	22	16	3	0	11	9	14.1	5.57	66	.278	.367	0	.000	0	-5	-4	1	-0.1
Total	10	47	49	.490	334	90	9	3	24	971^1	972	464	85	25	368	504	12.6	3.78	98	.264	.335	24	.100	-6	-23	-8	9	-0.3
● JERRY KOOSMAN	Koosman, Jerome Martin b: 12/23/42, Appleton, Minn. BR/TL, 6'2", 208 lbs. Deb: 4/14/67																											
1967	NY-N	0	2	.000	9	3	0	0	0	22^1	22	17	3	0	19	11	16.5	6.04	56	.259	.394	0	.000	0	-7	-7	0	-0.5
1968	NY-N★	19	12	.613	35	34	17	7	0	263^2	221	72	16	8	69	178	10.2	2.08	145	.228	.285	7	.077	-3	26	27	-1	3.0
1969	*NY-N★	17	9	.654	32	32	16	6	0	241	187	66	14	4	68	180	9.7	2.28	161	.216	.277	4	.048	-7	35	36	-1	3.1
1970	NY-N	12	7	.632	30	29	5	1	0	212	189	87	22	2	71	118	11.1	3.14	128	.237	.300	6	.086	-2	21	21	-3	1.2
1971	NY-N	6	11	.353	26	24	4	0	0	165^2	160	66	12	1	51	96	11.5	3.04	112	.256	.313	8	.160	0	8	7	-1	0.6
1972	NY-N	11	12	.478	34	24	4	1	1	163	155	81	14	6	52	147	11.8	4.14	81	.250	.314	4	.085	-3	-12	-14	0	-2.2
1973	*NY-N	14	15	.483	35	35	12	3	0	263	234	93	18	4	76	156	10.7	2.84	128	.242	.300	8	.103	-3	24	23	-1	2.0
1974	NY-N	15	11	.577	35	35	13	0	0	265	258	113	16	7	85	188	11.9	3.36	106	.257	.320	16	.186	2	8	6	-0	0.8
1975	NY-N	14	13	.519	36	34	11	4	2	239^2	234	106	19	4	98	173	12.6	3.42	101	.261	.337	14	.179	1	6	1	-1	0.3
1976	NY-N	21	10	.677	34	32	17	3	0	247^1	205	81	19	1	66	200	9.9	2.69	123	.226	.279	17	.215	3	22	18	0	2.6
1977	NY-N	8	20	.286	32	32	6	1	0	226^2	195	102	17	4	81	192	11.1	3.49	107	.232	.302	8	.111	-3	11	7	-2	0.3
1978	NY-N	3	15	.167	38	32	3	0	2	235^1	221	110	17	8	84	160	12.0	3.75	93	.255	.327	6	.086	-3	-4	-7	2	-0.7
1979	Min-A	20	13	.606	37	36	10	2	0	263^2	268	108	19	3	83	157	12.1	3.38	130	.268	.326	0	—	0	25	29	2	3.5
1980	Min-A	16	13	.552	38	34	8	0	2	243^1	252	119	24	5	69	149	12.1	4.03	108	.272	.326	0	—	0	0	8	1	1.0
1981	Min-A	3	9	.250	19	13	2	1	5	94^1	98	49	8	0	34	55	12.6	4.20	94	.272	.335	0	—	0	-6	-2	0	-0.3
	Chi-A	1	4	.200	8	3	1	0	0	27	27	10	2	0	7	21	11.3	3.33	107	.260	.306	0	—	0	1	1	-0	0.1
	Yr	4	13	.235	27	16	3	1	5	121^1	125	59	10	0	41	76	12.3	4.01	97	.269	.329	0	—	0	-5	-2	-0	-0.2
1982	Chi-A	11	7	.611	42	19	3	1	3	173^1	194	81	9	2	38	88	12.1	3.84	105	.287	.327	0	—	0	5	4	0	0.4
1983	*Chi-A	11	7	.611	37	24	2	1	2	169^2	176	96	19	6	53	90	12.5	4.77	88	.266	.326	0	—	0	-13	-10	0	-1.0

YEAR	TM/L	W	L	PCT	G	GS	CG	SH	SV	IP	H	R	HR	HB	BB	SO	RAT	ERA	ERA+	OAV	OOB	BH	AVG	PB	PR	PR+	PD	TPI
1984	Phi-N	14	15	.483	36	34	3	1	0	224	232	95	8	3	60	137	11.9	3.25	112	.267	.317	8	.108	-3	8	9	-1	0.8
1985	Phi-N	6	4	.600	19	18	3	1	0	99^1	107	56	14	3	34	60	13.0	4.62	80	.276	.340	3	.088	-2	-11	-10	-0	-1.1
Total	19	222	209	.515	612	527	140	33	17	3839^1	3635	1608	290	71	1198	2556	11.5	3.36	110	.252	.313	109	.119	-22	148	146	-6	13.9
● HOWIE KOPLITZ	Koplitz, Howard Dean b: 5/4/38, Oshkosh, Wis. BR/TR, 5'11", 195 lbs. Deb: 9/8/61																											
1961	Det-A	2	0	1.000	4	1	1	0	0	12	16	6	0	0	8	9	18.0	2.25	182	.327	.421	0	.000	-1	2	2	-0	0.3
1962	Det-A	3	0	1.000	10	6	1	0	0	37^2	54	24	5	0	10	10	15.3	5.26	77	.342	.381	3	.231	1	-5	-5	0	-0.3
1964	Was-A	0	0	—	6	1	0	0	0	17	20	9	3	0	13	9	17.5	4.76	78	.290	.402	0	.000	-0	-2	-2	0	-0.1
1965	Was-A	4	7	.364	33	11	0	0	1	106^2	97	51	11	3	48	59	12.5	4.05	86	.249	.336	3	.100	-1	-7	-7	1	-0.7
1966	Was-A	0	0	—	1	0	0	0	0	2	0	0	0	0	1	0	4.5	0.00	—	.000	.200	0	—	0	1	1	0	0.1
Total	5	9	7	.563	54	19	2	0	1	175^1	187	90	19	3	80	87	13.9	4.21	87	.280	.359	6	.118	-1	-11	-10	1	-0.7
● GEORGE KORINCE	Korince, George Eugene "Moose" b: 1/10/46, Ottawa, Ont., Canada BR/TR, 6'3", 210 lbs. Deb: 9/10/66																											
1966	Det-A	0	0	—	2	0	0	0	0	3	1	0	0	1	3	2	15.0	0.00	—	.091	.333	0	—	0	1	1	-0	0.1
1967	Det-A	1	0	1.000	9	0	0	0	0	14	10	8	1	0	11	11	13.5	5.14	63	.204	.350	0	.000	-0	-3	-3	0	-0.2
Total	2	1	0	1.000	11	0	0	0	0	17	11	8	1	1	14	13	13.8	4.24	78	.183	.347	0	.000	-0	-2	-2	-0	-0.1
● JIM KORWAN	Korwan, James "Long Jim" b: 3/4/1874, Brooklyn, N.Y. d: 7/24/1899, Brooklyn, N.Y. BR/TR, 6'1", 181 lbs. Deb: 4/24/1894																											
1894	Bro-N	0	0	—	1	0	0	0	0	5	9	14	1	0	5	2	25.2	14.40	34	.391	.500	0	.000	-0	-5	-6	0	-0.2
1897	Chi-N	1	2	.333	5	4	3	0	0	34	47	36	1	1	28	12	20.1	5.82	77	.324	.437	0	.000	-2	-6	-5	2	-0.4
Total	2	1	2	.333	6	4	3	0	0	39	56	50	2	1	33	14	20.8	6.92	65	.333	.446	0	.000	-2	-11	-10	2	-0.6
● BILL KOSKI	Koski, William John "T-Bone" b: 2/6/32, Madera, Cal. BR/TR, 6'4", 185 lbs. Deb: 4/28/51																											
1951	Pit-N	0	1	.000	13	1	0	0	0	27	26	23	2	0	28	6	18.0	6.67	63	.257	.419	0	.000	-1	-8	-7	-1	-0.5
● DAVE KOSLO	Koslo, George Bernard (b: George Bernard Koslowski) b: 3/31/20, Menasha, Wis. d: 12/1/75, Menasha, Wis. BL/TL, 5'11", 180 lbs. Deb: 9/12/41																											
1941	NY-N	1	2	.333	4	3	2	0	0	23^2	17	6	0	0	10	12	10.3	1.90	194	.202	.287	1	.111	-1	5	5	-1	0.5
1942	NY-N	3	6	.333	19	11	3	1	0	78	79	49	7	1	32	42	12.9	5.08	66	.261	.333	3	.120	-0	-15	-15	-1	-1.7
1946	NY-N	14	19	.424	40	35	17	3	1	265^1	251	119	15	5	101	121	12.1	3.63	95	.249	.320	11	.125	-3	-6	-5	2	-0.8
1947	NY-N	15	10	.600	39	31	10	3	0	217^1	223	118	23	3	82	86	12.8	4.39	93	.259	.326	10	.128	-1	-8	-8	-1	-1.0
1948	NY-N	8	10	.444	35	18	5	3	3	149	168	69	7	1	62	58	14.0	3.87	102	.290	.359	5	.114	-1	2	1	-1	-0.1
1949	NY-N	11	14	.440	38	23	15	0	4	212	193	72	13	0	43	64	**10.0**	**2.50**	**159**	.239	**.278**	10	.145	1	**36**	**35**	0	**4.2**
1950	NY-N	13	15	.464	40	22	7	1	3	186^2	190	89	18	5	68	56	12.7	3.91	105	.268	.337	8	.123	-1	5	4	-0	0.4
1951	*NY-N	10	9	.526	39	16	5	2	3	149^2	153	68	18	2	45	54	12.0	3.31	118	.258	.313	5	.100	-1	11	10	2	1.3
1952	NY-N	10	7	.588	41	17	8	2	5	166^1	154	66	10	2	47	67	11.0	3.19	116	.242	.296	2	.037	-4	10	9	1	0.7
1953	NY-N	6	12	.333	37	12	2	0	2	111^2	135	70	8	1	36	36	13.9	4.76	90	.296	.349	1	.033	-3	-6	-6	1	-1.1
1954	Bal-A	0	1	.000	3	1	0	0	0	14^1	20	7	1	0	3	3	14.4	3.14	114	.333	.365	0	.000	-0	1	1	-0	0.0
	Mil-N	1	1	.500	12	0	0	0	1	17^1	13	6	0	0	9	7	11.4	3.12	120	.228	.333	0	.000	-0	2	1	-1	0.1
1955	Mil-N	0	1	.000	1	0	0	0	0	0	1	1	0	0	—	—	∞	—	1.000	1.000	93	—	0	-1	-1	0	-0.1	
Total	12	92	107	.462	348	189	74	15	22	1591^1	1597	740	121	20	538	606	12.2	3.68	105	.260	.321	56	.109	-15	34	32	2	2.4
● JOE KOSTAL	Kostal, Joseph William "Cudgey" b: 3/17/1876, Chicago, Ill. d: 10/17/33, Guelph, Ont., Can. BR/TR, 5'6", 130 lbs. Deb: 7/14/1896																											
1896	Lou-N	0	0	—	2	0	0	0	0	2	4	4	0	0	0	0	18.0	0.00	—	.400	.400	0	—	0	1	1	-0	0.0
● SANDY KOUFAX	Koufax, Sanford (b: Sanford Braun) b: 12/30/35, Brooklyn, N.Y. BR/TL, 6'2", 210 lbs. Deb: 6/24/55 H																											
1955	Bro-N	2	2	.500	12	5	2	2	0	41^2	33	15	2	1	28	30	13.4	3.02	134	.216	.341	0	.000	-2	5	5	-0	0.2
1956	Bro-N	2	4	.333	16	10	0	0	0	58^2	66	37	10	0	29	30	14.6	4.91	81	.286	.365	2	.118	-0	-7	-6	-1	-0.7
1957	Bro-N	5	4	.556	34	13	2	0	0	104^1	83	49	14	2	51	122	11.7	3.88	107	.216	.311	0	.000	-3	-0	3	-2	-0.3
1958	LA-N	11	11	.500	40	26	5	0	1	158^2	132	89	19	1	105	131	13.5	4.48	91	**.220**	.337	6	.122	-2	-9	-7	-0	-1.1
1959	*LA-N	8	6	.571	35	23	6	1	2	153^1	136	74	23	0	92	173	13.4	4.05	104	.235	.340	6	.111	-1	-2	3	-1	0.0
1960	LA-N	8	13	.381	37	26	7	2	1	175	133	83	20	1	100	197	12.0	3.91	102	**.207**	.315	7	.123	-2	-3	1	-1	-0.2
1961	LA-N★	18	13	.581	42	35	15	2	1	255^2	212	117	27	3	96	**269**	10.9	3.52	123	**.222**	.295	5	.065	-5	15	22	-3	1.6
1962	LA-N☆	14	7	.667	28	26	11	2	1	184^1	134	61	13	2	57	216	**9.4**	**2.54**	143	**.197**	**.261**	6	.087	-3	29	24	-2	2.1
1963	*LA-N☆	**25**	5	.833	40	40	20	**11**	0	311	214	68	18	3	58	**306**	**8.0**	**1.88**	161	**.189**	**.230**	7	.064	-4	**49**	**43**	-4	3.4
1964	LA-N☆	19	5	**.792**	29	28	15	**7**	1	223	154	49	13	0	53	223	**8.4**	**1.74**	**187**	**.191**	**.241**	7	.095	-2	45	41	-4	4.0
1965	*LA-N★	**26**	8	**.765**	43	41	**27**	8	2	**335^2**	216	90	26	5	71	**382**	**7.8**	**2.04**	160	**.179**	**.228**	20	.177	5	**56**	**50**	-2	5.5
1966	*LA-N★	**27**	9	.750	41	41	**27**	**5**	0	**323**	241	74	19	0	77	**317**	8.9	**1.73**	**191**	.205	.253	9	.076	-5	**67**	**62**	-4	**6.0**
Total	12	165	87	.655	397	314	137	40	9	2324^1	1754	806	204	18	817	2396	10.0	2.76	131	.205	.276	75	.097	-25	243	226	-25	20.5
● JOE KOUKALIK	Koukalik, Joseph b: 3/3/1880, Chicago, Ill. d: 12/27/45, Chicago, Ill. 5'8", 160 lbs. Deb: 9/1/04																											
1904	Bro-N	0	1	.000	1	1	1	0	0	8	10	3	0	0	4	1	15.8	1.13	244	.333	.412	0	.000	-0	1	1	-0	0.1
● LOU KOUPAL	Koupal, Louis Laddie b: 12/19/1898, Tabor, S.D. d: 12/8/61, San Gabriel, Cal. BR/TR, 5'11", 175 lbs. Deb: 4/17/25																											
1925	Pit-N	0	0	—	6	0	0	0	0	9	14	10	1	0	7	0	21.0	9.00	50	.378	.477	0	.000	-0	-5	-4	0	-0.2
1926	Pit-N	0	2	.000	6	2	1	0	0	19^2	22	9	0	1	8	7	14.2	3.20	123	.289	.365	1	.250	0	1	2	-0	0.2
1928	Bro-N	1	0	1.000	17	1	1	0	1	37^1	43	22	0	1	15	10	14.2	2.41	165	.303	.373	1	.111	-1	7	7	1	0.4
1929	Bro-N	0	1	.000	18	3	0	0	4	40^1	49	36	3	0	25	17	16.5	5.36	86	.308	.402	1	.071	-2	-3	-3	-1	-0.3
	Phi-N	5	5	.500	15	11	3	0	2	86^2	106	56	5	2	29	18	14.2	4.78	109	.305	.362	4	.125	-2	-1	4	-1	0.1
	Yr	5	6	.455	33	14	3	0	6	127	155	92	8	2	54	35	15.0	4.96	101	.306	.375	5	.109	-4	-3	1	-1	-0.2
1930	Phi-N	0	4	.000	13	4	1	0	0	36^2	52	35	4	1	17	11	17.2	8.59	64	.344	.414	1	.083	-1	-15	-12	-1	-1.2
1937	StL-A	4	9	.308	26	13	6	0	0	105^2	150	87	10	0	55	24	17.5	6.56	74	.339	.412	3	.094	-3	-23	-19	-0	-2.2
Total	6	10	21	.323	101	34	12	0	7	335^1	436	255	23	5	156	87	16.0	5.58	86	.322	.394	11	.106	-9	-38	-28	-2	-3.2
● FABIAN KOWALIK	Kowalik, Fabian Lorenz b: 4/22/08, Falls City, Tex. d: 8/14/54, Karnes City, Tex. BR/TR (BB 1932, 35), 5'11", 185 lbs. Deb: 9/4/32																											
1932	Chi-A	0	1	.000	2	1	0	0	0	10^1	16	11	2	1	4	2	18.3	6.97	62	.340	.404	5	.385	1	-3	-3	-0	-0.2
1935	*Chi-N	2	2	.500	20	2	1	0	1	55	60	31	2	0	19	20	12.9	4.42	89	.280	.339	3	.200	-0	-2	-3	1	-0.2
1936	Chi-N	0	2	.000	6	0	0	0	1	16	24	12	1	0	7	1	17.4	6.75	59	.358	.419	0	.000	-1	-5	-5	0	-0.6
	Phi-N	1	5	.167	22	8	2	0	0	77	100	57	5	2	31	19	15.5	5.38	84	.308	.372	13	.228	-0	-12	-6	-2	-0.6
	Bos-N	0	1	.000	1	1	1	0	0	9	18	8	0	0	2	0	20.0	8.00	48	.419	.444	2	.400	1	-4	-4	0	-0.3
	Yr	1	8	.111	29	9	3	0	1	102	142	77	6	2	40	20	16.2	5.82	75	.326	.386	15	.224	-0	-20	-15	-1	-1.5
Total	3	3	11	.214	51	12	4	0	2	167^1	218	119	10	3	63	42	15.3	5.43	78	.313	.373	23	.242	-0	-26	-21	-1	-1.9
● JOE KRAEMER	Kraemer, Joseph Wayne b: 9/10/64, Olympia, Wash. BL/TL, 6'2", 185 lbs. Deb: 8/22/89																											
1989	Chi-N	0	1	.000	1	1	0	0	0	3^2	7	6	0	0	2	5	22.1	4.91	77	.368	.429	0	.000	-0	-1	-0	-0	-0.1
1990	Chi-N	0	0	—	18	0	0	0	0	25	31	25	2	2	14	16	16.9	7.20	57	.310	.405	0	—	0	-9	-8	0	-0.4
Total	2	0	1	.000	19	1	0	0	0	28^2	38	31	2	2	16	21	17.6	6.91	59	.319	.409	0	.000	-0	-10	-8	0	-0.5
● JOE KRAKAUSKAS	Krakauskas, Joseph Victor Lawrence b: 3/28/15, Montreal, Que., Can d: 7/8/60, Hamilton, Ont., Can BL/TL, 6'1", 203 lbs. Deb: 9/9/37																											
1937	Was-A	4	1	.800	5	4	3	0	0	40	33	14	0	0	22	18	12.4	2.70	164	.226	.327	2	.125	-0	9	8	-1	0.8
1938	Was-A	7	5	.583	29	10	5	1	0	121^1	99	61	4	3	88	104	14.1	3.12	145	.220	.352	6	.182	1	23	20	-1	1.7
1939	Was-A	11	17	.393	39	29	12	0	1	217^1	230	125	13	1	114	110	14.3	4.60	95	.276	.364	16	.208	3	1	-6	-2	-0.6
1940	Was-A	1	6	.143	32	10	2	0	2	109	137	90	7	0	73	68	17.3	6.44	65	.309	.406	8	.250	1	-25	-29	1	-1.4
1941	Cle-A	1	2	.333	12	5	0	0	0	41^2	39	25	3	0	29	25	14.7	4.10	96	.245	.362	1	.077	-1	0	-1	1	-0.1
1942	Cle-A	0	0	—	3	0	0	0	0	7	7	3	1	0	4	2	14.1	3.86	89	.259	.355	0	.000	-0	-0	-0	1	0.0
1946	Cle-A	2	5	.286	29	5	0	0	1	47^1	60	31	2	0	25	20	16.2	5.51	60	.314	.394	0	.000	-1	-11	-12	1	-1.8
Total	7	26	36	.419	149	63	22	1	4	583^2	605	349	30	4	355	347	14.9	4.53	93	.269	.369	33	.180	2	-4	-21	-1	-1.4
● JACK KRALICK	Kralick, John Francis b: 6/1/35, Youngstown, Ohio BL/TL, 6'2", 180 lbs. Deb: 4/15/59																											
1959	Was-A	0	0	—	6	0	0	0	0	12^1	13	9	5	0	6	7	13.9	6.57	60	.289	.373	0	.000	-0	-4	-4	1	-0.1
1960	Was-A	8	6	.571	35	18	7	2	1	151	139	54	12	4	45	71	11.2	3.04	128	.245	.305	5	.122	-1	14	14	-1	1.1
1961	Min-A	13	11	.542	33	33	11	2	0	242	257	101	21	3	64	137	12.0	3.61	118	.274	.323	13	.151	-2	11	16	2	1.4
1962	Min-A	12	11	.522	39	37	7	1	0	242^2	239	121	31	3	61	139	11.2	3.86	106	.258	.305	18	.202	3	3	6	1	0.9

YEAR	TM/L	W	L	PCT	G	GS	CG	SH	SV	IP	H	R	HR	HB	BB	SO	RAT	ERA	ERA+	OAV	OOB	BH	AVG	PB	PR	PR+	PD	TPI
1963	Min-A	1	4	.200	5	5	1	1	0	25^{2}	28	16	2	1	8	13	13.0	3.86	94	.280	.339	1	.167	1	-1	-1	0	0.0
	Cle-A	13	9	.591	28	27	10	3	0	197^{1}	187	70	19	0	41	116	10.4	2.92	124	.249	.288	11	.183	1	16	15	-1	1.7
	Yr	14	13	.519	33	32	11	4	0	223	215	86	21	1	49	129	10.7	3.03	120	.253	.294	12	.182	2	15	15	-1	1.7
1964	Cle-A☆	12	7	.632	30	29	8	3	0	190^{2}	196	79	17	9	51	119	12.1	3.21	112	.267	.322	10	.156	-1	9	8	0	0.7
1965	Cle-A	5	11	.313	30	16	1	0	0	86	106	58	9	2	21	34	13.5	4.92	71	.298	.340	3	.143	-1	-14	-14	-1	-2.5
1966	Cle-A	3	4	.429	27	4	0	0	0	68^{1}	69	30	9	1	20	31	11.9	3.82	90	.268	.324	1	.077	-1	-3	-3	1	-0.3
1967	Cle-A	0	2	.000	2	0	0	0	0	2	4	3	0	0	1	1	22.5	9.00	36	.444	.500	0	—	0	-1	-1	1	-0.2
Total	9	67	65	.508	235	169	45	12	1	1218	1238	541	125	23	318	668	11.7	3.56	108	.264	.314	62	.162	0	30	38	3	2.7
● **STEVE KRALY**	Kraly, Steve Charles "Lefty" b: 4/18/29, Whiting, Ind. BL/TL, 5'10", 152 lbs. Deb: 8/9/53																											
1953	NY-A	0	2	.000	5	3	0	0	1	25	19	10	2	2	16	8	13.3	3.24	114	.209	.339	0	.000	-1	2	1	0	0.0
● **JACK KRAMER**	Kramer, John Henry b: 1/5/18, New Orleans, La. d: 5/18/95, Metairie, La. BR/TR, 6'2", 190 lbs. Deb: 4/25/39																											
1939	StL-A	9	16	.360	40	31	10	2	0	211^{2}	269	150	18	3	127	68	17.0	5.83	84	.318	.409	9	.136	-1	-28	-21	-1	-2.2
1940	StL-A	3	7	.300	16	9	1	0	0	64^{2}	86	48	4	0	26	12	15.6	6.26	73	.327	.388	1	.050	-1	-14	-12	0	-1.5
1941	StL-A	4	3	.571	29	3	0	0	2	59^{1}	69	48	5	0	40	20	16.5	5.16	83	.289	.391	0	.000	1	-7	-5	0	-0.5
1943	StL-A	0	0	—	3	0	0	0	0	9	11	8	0	1	8	4	20.0	8.00	42	.297	.435	1	.500	1	-5	-5	-0	-0.2
1944	*StL-A	17	13	.567	33	31	18	1	0	257	233	94	3	1	75	124	10.8	2.49	145	.241	.297	14	.165	1	27	30	3	4.1
1945	StL-A†	10	15	.400	29	25	15	3	2	193	190	85	13	0	73	99	12.3	3.36	105	.254	.320	9	.148	-0	0	3	1	0.5
1946	StL-A★	13	11	.542	31	28	13	3	0	194^{2}	190	84	6	0	68	69	11.9	3.19	117	.257	.319	8	.136	-1	7	11	-0	1.1
1947	StL-A☆	11	16	.407	33	28	9	1	1	199^{1}	206	123	16	2	89	77	13.4	4.97	78	.270	.348	7	.113	-2	-28	-23	1	-2.9
1948	Bos-A	18	5	**.783**	29	29	14	2	0	205	233	104	12	0	64	72	13.0	4.35	101	.284	.336	11	.151	-1	-1	1	-3	-0.2
1949	Bos-A	6	8	.429	21	18	7	2	1	111^{2}	126	70	8	1	49	24	14.2	5.16	85	.286	.358	9	.257	3	-12	-10	-1	-0.8
1950	NY-N	3	6	.333	35	9	1	0	1	86^{2}	91	46	6	2	39	27	13.7	3.53	116	.268	.346	2	.100	1	6	6	0	0.6
1951	NY-N	0	0	—	4	1	0	0	0	4^{2}	11	8	0	0	3	2	27.0	15.43	25	.524	.583	0	—	0	-6	-6	0	-0.3
	NY-A	1	3	.250	19	3	0	0	0	40^{2}	46	27	1	0	21	15	14.8	4.65	82	.280	.362	1	.100	-0	-2	-4	-1	-0.5
Total	12	95	103	.480	322	215	88	14	7	1637^{1}	1761	895	92	10	682	613	13.5	4.24	96	.276	.347	72	.144	0	-63	-33	0	-2.8
● **RANDY KRAMER**	Kramer, Randall John b: 9/20/60, Palo Alto, Cal. BR/TR, 6'2", 170 lbs. Deb: 9/11/88																											
1988	Pit-N	1	2	.333	5	1	0	0	0	10	12	6	1	1	1	7	12.6	5.40	63	.316	.350	0	.000	-0	-2	-2	-0	-0.5
1989	Pit-N	5	9	.357	35	15	1	1	2	111^{1}	90	53	10	7	61	52	12.8	3.96	85	.224	.337	5	.152	-0	-6	-8	-1	-1.1
1990	Pit-N	0	1	.000	12	2	0	0	0	25^{2}	27	15	3	2	9	15	13.3	4.91	74	.273	.345	0	.000	-1	-3	-4	1	-0.2
	Chi-N	0	2	.000	10	2	0	0	0	20^{1}	20	10	3	1	12	12	14.6	3.98	102	.253	.359	0	.000	-0	-0	0	-0	0.0
	Yr	0	3	.000	22	4	0	0	0	46	47	25	6	3	21	27	13.9	4.50	85	.264	.351	0	.000	-1	-4	-3	0	-0.2
1992	Sea-A	0	1	.000	4	4	0	0	0	16^{1}	30	14	2	1	7	6	20.9	7.71	52	.400	.458	0	—	0	-7	-7	-0	-0.4
Total	4	6	15	.286	66	24	1	1	2	183^{2}	179	98	19	12	90	92	13.8	4.51	78	.259	.354	5	.122	-1	-18	-20	-2	-2.2
● **TOM KRAMER**	Kramer, Thomas Joseph b: 1/9/68, Cincinnati, Ohio BB/TR, 6', 185 lbs. Deb: 9/12/91																											
1991	Cle-A	0	0	—	4	0	0	0	0	4^{2}	10	9	1	0	6	4	30.9	17.36	24	.476	.593	0	—	0	-7	-7	-0	-0.3
1993	Cle-A	7	3	.700	39	16	1	0	0	121	126	60	19	2	59	71	13.9	4.02	108	.269	.353	0	—	0	4	4	-1	0.2
Total	2	7	3	.700	43	16	1	0	0	125^{2}	136	69	20	2	65	75	14.5	4.51	96	.278	.364	0	—	0	-3	-2	-1	-0.1
● **GENE KRAPP**	Krapp, Eugene Hamlet "Rubber Arm" b: 5/12/1887, Rochester, N.Y. d: 4/13/23, Detroit, Mich. BR/TR, 5'5", 165 lbs. Deb: 4/14/11																											
1911	Cle-A	13	9	.591	35	26	14	1	1	222	188	115	1	13	138	132	13.7	3.41	100	.232	.353	17	.230	4	-1	0	4	0.8
1912	Cle-A	2	5	.286	9	7	4	0	0	58^{2}	57	39	0	4	42	22	15.8	4.60	74	.273	.404	7	.318	1	-8	-8	2	-0.4
1914	Buf-F	16	14	.533	36	29	18	1	0	252^{2}	198	83	4	12	115	106	11.6	2.49	119	.210	.304	11	.143	-2	11	13	5	1.8
1915	Buf-F	9	19	.321	38	30	14	1	0	231	188	106	6	4	123	93	12.3	3.51	80	.230	.333	9	.129	-3	-20	-18	7	-1.6
Total	4	40	47	.460	118	92	50	3	1	764^{1}	631	343	11	33	418	353	12.7	3.23	95	.227	.335	44	.181	-1	-19	-12	19	0.6
● **JACK KRAUS**	Kraus, John William "Tex" or "Texas Jack" b: 4/26/18, San Antonio, Tex. d: 1/2/76, San Antonio, Tex. BR/TL, 6'4", 190 lbs. Deb: 4/25/43																											
1943	Phi-N	9	15	.375	34	25	10	1	2	199^{2}	197	83	7	0	78	48	12.4	3.16	107	.259	.328	4	.067	-5	5	5	1	0.2
1945	Phi-N	4	9	.308	19	13	0	0	0	81^{2}	96	55	3	4	40	28	15.4	5.40	71	.293	.376	3	.120	-1	-15	-14	0	-2.0
1946	NY-N	2	1	.667	17	1	0	0	0	25	25	17	4	1	15	7	14.8	6.12	56	.260	.366	0	.000	-0	-8	-7	1	-0.8
Total	3	15	25	.375	70	39	10	1	2	306^{1}	318	155	14	5	133	83	13.4	4.00	88	.268	.345	7	.080	-6	-17	-17	2	-2.6
● **HARRY KRAUSE**	Krause, Harry William "Hal" b: 7/12/1887, San Francisco, Cal. d: 10/23/40, San Francisco, Cal BB/TL, 5'10", 165 lbs. Deb: 4/20/08																											
1908	Phi-A	1	1	.500	4	2	2	0	0	21	20	11	0	3	4	10	11.6	2.57	100	.247	.307	0	.000	-1	-0	-0	-1	-0.2
1909	Phi-A	18	8	.692	32	21	16	7	0	213	151	49	2	13	49	139	9.0	**1.39**	**173**	.204	.266	12	.156	-1	26	25	-3	2.7
1910	Phi-A	6	6	.500	16	11	9	2	0	112^{1}	99	46	4	8	42	60	11.9	2.88	82	.254	.339	8	.211	1	-5	-7	-2	-0.9
1911	Phi-A	11	8	.579	27	19	12	1	2	169	155	65	2	9	47	85	11.2	3.04	104	.251	.313	15	.254	2	6	2	-3	0.1
1912	Phi-A	0	2	.000	4	2	0	0	0	5^{1}	10	8	0	1	2	3	21.9	13.50	23	.435	.500	1	.250	0	-6	-7	0	-1.1
	Cle-A	0	1	.000	2	2	0	0	0	4^{2}	11	6	0	0	2	1	25.1	11.57	29	.500	.542	0	—	0	-4	-4	-0	-0.7
	Yr	0	3	.000	6	4	0	0	0	10	21	14	0	1	4	4	23.4	12.60	26	.467	.520	1	.250	0	-10	-11	-0	-1.8
Total	5	36	26	.581	85	57	39	10	2	525^{1}	446	185	8	34	146	298	10.7	2.50	107	.238	.305	36	.195	1	16	10	-9	-0.1
● **LEW KRAUSSE**	Krausse, Lewis Bernard Jr. b: 4/25/43, Media, Pa. BR/TR, 5'11", 186 lbs. Deb: 6/16/61 F																											
1961	KC-A	2	5	.286	12	8	2	1	0	55^{2}	49	33	3	1	46	32	15.5	4.85	86	.243	.386	2	.118	-1	-5	-4	-1	-0.6
1964	KC-A	0	2	.000	5	4	0	0	0	14^{2}	22	14	1	2	9	9	20.3	7.36	52	.349	.446	0	.000	0	-6	-5	-0	-0.7
1965	KC-A	2	4	.333	7	5	0	0	0	25	29	14	1	0	8	22	13.3	5.04	69	.284	.336	0	.000	-1	-4	-4	-1	-1.0
1966	KC-A	14	9	.609	36	22	4	1	3	177^{2}	144	69	8	6	63	87	10.8	2.99	114	.222	.297	8	.154	0	9	8	-3	0.8
1967	KC-A	7	17	.292	48	19	0	0	6	160	140	85	17	4	67	96	11.9	4.27	75	.236	.317	6	.146	1	-19	-20	-0	-2.9
1968	Oak-A	10	11	.476	36	25	2	0	4	185	147	68	16	3	62	105	10.3	3.11	91	.217	.286	9	.161	3	-3	-6	-2	-0.6
1969	Oak-A	7	7	.500	43	16	4	2	7	140	134	75	23	5	48	85	12.0	4.44	78	.256	.325	8	.167	4	-13	-16	-1	-1.4
1970	Mil-A	13	18	.419	37	35	8	1	0	216	235	130	33	4	67	130	12.8	4.75	80	.275	.330	9	.138	1	-25	-23	-0	-2.9
1971	Mil-A	8	12	.400	43	22	1	0	0	180^{1}	164	67	23	5	62	92	11.5	2.94	118	.239	.307	1	.023	-3	10	11	-1	0.7
1972	Bos-A	1	3	.250	24	7	0	0	1	60^{2}	74	48	9	3	28	35	15.6	6.38	51	.308	.387	2	.125	-0	-22	-20	1	-1.4
1973	StL-N	0	0	—	1	0	0	0	0	2	2	0	0	0	1	1	13.5	0.00	—	.250	.333	0	—	0	1	1	0	0.1
1974	Atl-N	4	3	.571	29	4	0	0	0	66^{2}	65	32	3	2	32	27	13.4	4.18	91	.258	.346	2	.333	2	-4	-3	-1	-0.1
Total	12	68	91	.428	321	167	21	5	21	1283^{2}	1205	635	137	35	493	721	12.2	4.00	85	.248	.322	47	.133	6	-81	-84	-9	-10.0
● **LEW KRAUSSE**	Krausse, Lewis Bernard Sr. b: 6/8/12, Media, Pa. d: 9/6/88, Sarasota, Fla. BR/TR, 6'0.5", 167 lbs. Deb: 6/11/31 F																											
1931	Phi-A	1	0	1.000	3	1	1	0	0	11	6	6	2	0	6	1	9.8	4.09	110	.150	.261	0	.000	0	0	0	0	0.1
1932	Phi-A	4	1	.800	20	3	2	1	0	57	64	31	3	0	24	16	13.9	4.58	99	.281	.349	2	.133	-0	-1	-0	1	0.0
Total	2	5	1	.833	23	4	3	1	0	68	70	37	5	0	30	17	13.2	4.50	100	.261	.336	2	.118	0	-0	0	1	0.1
● **KEN KRAVEC**	Kravec, Kenneth Peter b: 7/29/51, Cleveland, Ohio BL/TL, 6'2", 185 lbs. Deb: 9/4/75																											
1975	Chi-A	0	1	.000	2	1	0	0	0	4^{1}	1	3	0	0	8	1	18.7	6.23	62	.071	.409	0	—	0	-1	-1	1	-0.2
1976	Chi-A	1	5	.167	9	8	1	0	0	49^{2}	49	28	3	1	32	38	14.9	4.89	73	.257	.366	0	—	0	-8	-7	-0	-0.8
1977	Chi-A	11	8	.579	26	25	6	1	0	166^{2}	161	87	12	6	57	125	12.1	4.10	100	.250	.317	0	—	0	-1	-0	0	0.0
1978	Chi-A	11	16	.407	30	30	7	2	0	203	188	104	22	10	95	154	13.0	4.08	94	.245	.336	0	—	0	-7	-6	-1	-0.8
1979	Chi-A	15	13	.536	36	35	10	3	1	250	208	115	20	14	111	132	12.0	3.74	114	.233	.327	0	—	0	14	14	-1	1.3
1980	Chi-A	3	6	.333	20	15	0	0	0	81^{2}	100	71	13	5	44	37	16.4	6.94	58	.298	.387	0	—	0	-26	-26	0	-2.4
1981	Chi-N	1	6	.143	24	12	0	0	0	78^{1}	80	48	5	4	39	50	14.1	5.06	73	.268	.361	0	.000	-1	-14	-11	1	-1.0
1982	Chi-N	1	1	.500	13	2	0	0	0	25	27	20	3	0	18	20	16.2	6.12	61	.267	.378	0	.000	-0	-7	-6	-0	-0.5
Total	8	43	56	.434	160	128	24	6	1	858^{2}	814	476	78	40	404	557	13.2	4.47	90	.251	.341	0	.000	-1	-49	-44	-0	-4.4
● **RAY KRAWCZYK**	Krawczyk, Raymond Allen b: 10/9/59, Pittsburgh, Pa. BR/TR, 6'1", 186 lbs. Deb: 6/29/84																											
1984	Pit-N	0	0	—	4	0	0	0	0	5^{1}	7	2	0	0	4	3	18.6	3.38	107	.350	.458	0	—	0	0	0	-0	0.0
1985	Pit-N	0	2	.000	8	0	0	0	0	8^{1}	20	13	1	1	6	9	29.2	14.04	26	.455	.529	0	—	0	-10	-10	0	-1.8
1986	Pit-N	0	1	.000	12	0	0	0	0	12^{1}	17	13	3	0	10	7	19.7	7.30	53	.321	.429	0	—	0	-5	-5	-0	-0.4
1988	Cal-A	0	1	.000	14	1	0	0	1	24^{1}	29	13	2	2	8	17	14.4	4.81	80	.299	.364	0	—	0	-2	-3	1	-0.1

YEAR	TM/L	W	L	PCT	G	GS	CG	SH	SV	IP	H	R	HR	HB	BB	SO	RAT	ERA	ERA+	OAV	OOB	BH	AVG	PB	PR	PR+	PD	TPI
1989	Mil-A	0	0	—	1	0	0	0	0	2	4	3	0	0	1	6	22.5	13.50	28	.400	.455	0	—	0	-2	-2	0	-0.1
Total	5	0	4	.000	39	1	0	0	1	52^{1}	77	44	6	3	29	42	18.7	7.05	54	.344	.426	0	—	0	-19	-19	0	-2.4
● **FRANK KREEGER**	Kreeger, Frank d: 7/14/1899, Shelby Co., Ill. Deb: 7/28/1884 ♦																											
1884	KC-U	0	1	.000	1	1	0	0	0	7	9	8	0		5	3	18.0	0.00	—	.290	.389	0	.000	-1	2	2	0	0.2
● **RAY KREMER**	Kremer, Remy Peter "Wiz" b: 3/23/1893, Oakland, Cal. d: 2/8/65, Pinole, Cal. BR/TR, 6'1", 190 lbs. Deb: 4/18/24																											
1924	Pit-N	18	10	.643	**41**	30	17	**4**	1	259^{1}	262	102	7	4	51	64	11.0	3.19	120	.265	.304	13	.151	-4	19	19	-2	1.3
1925	*Pit-N	17	8	.680	40	27	14	0	2	214^{2}	232	106	19	9	47	62	12.1	3.69	121	.278	.323	14	.197	1	14	18	-3	1.6
1926	Pit-N	**20**	6	**.769**	37	26	18	3	5	231^{1}	221	79	9	4	51	74	10.7	**2.61**	**151**	.252	.296	21	.253	2	**31**	**33**	-3	**3.6**
1927	*Pit-N	19	8	.704	35	28	18	3	2	226	205	73	9	0	53	63	10.3	**2.47**	**166**	.244	.289	14	.169	-1	36	39	-3	4.0
1928	Pit-N	15	13	.536	34	31	17	1	0	219	253	124	15	4	68	61	13.4	4.64	87	.297	.352	14	.179	0	-16	-14	-4	-1.9
1929	Pit-N	18	10	.643	34	27	14	0	0	221^{2}	226	114	21	1	60	66	11.7	4.26	112	.271	.320	11	.128	-2	11	12	-3	0.8
1930	Pit-N	**20**	12	.625	39	38	18	1	0	**276**	366	181	29	1	63	58	14.0	5.02	99	.322	.359	16	.157	-4	-2	-1	-4	-0.9
1931	Pit-N	11	15	.423	30	30	15	1	0	230	246	110	6	5	65	58	12.4	3.33	116	.271	.323	17	.227	4	14	13	-6	1.2
1932	Pit-N	4	3	.571	11	10	3	1	0	56^{2}	61	35	5	1	16	6	12.4	4.29	89	.270	.321	2	.105	-1	-3	-3	-2	-0.6
1933	Pit-N	1	0	1.000	7	0	0	0	0	20	36	26	2	0	9	4	20.2	10.35	32	.387	.441	0	.000	-1	-16	-16	1	-0.8
Total	10	143	85	.627	308	247	134	14	10	1954^{2}	2108	950	122	29	483	516	12.1	3.76	113	.278	.323	122	.178	-7	90	103	-27	8.3
● **JIM KREMMEL**	Kremmel, James Louis b: 2/28/48, Belleville, Ill. BL/TL, 6', 175 lbs. Deb: 7/4/73																											
1973	Tex-A	0	2	.000	4	2	0	0	0	9	15	10	1	2	6	6	23.0	9.00	41	.366	.469	0	—	0	-5	-5	-0	-1.0
1974	Chi-N	0	2	.000	23	2	0	0	0	31	37	21	3	1	18	22	16.3	5.23	73	.303	.397	0	.000	-0	-5	-5	-0	-0.3
Total	2	0	4	.000	27	4	0	0	0	40	52	31	4	3	24	28	17.8	6.07	63	.319	.416	0	.000	-0	-11	-10	-0	-1.3
● **RED KRESS**	Kress, Ralph b: 1/2/07, Columbia, Cal. d: 11/29/62, Los Angeles, Cal. BR/TR, 5'11.5", 165 lbs. Deb: 9/24/27 C♦																											
1935	Was-A	0	0	—	3	0	0	0	0	5^{2}	8	9	0	0	5	5	20.6	12.71	34	.333	.448	75	.298	1	-5	-5	0	-0.2
1946	NY-N	0	0	—	1	0	0	0	0	3^{2}	5	5	1	1	1	1	17.2	12.27	28	.333	.412	0	.000	0	-4	-4	1	-0.1
Total	2	0	0	—	4	0	0	0	0	9^{1}	13	14	1	1	6	6	19.3	12.54	32	.333	.435	1454	.286	1	-9	-9	1	-0.3
● **LOU KRETLOW**	Kretlow, Louis Henry "Lena" b: 6/27/21, Apache, Okla. BR/TR, 6'2", 185 lbs. Deb: 9/26/46																											
1946	Det-A	1	0	1.000	1	1	1	0	0	9	7	3	2	0	2	4	9.0	3.00	122	.206	.250	2	.500	1	1	1	-0	0.2
1948	Det-A	2	1	.667	5	2	1	0	0	23^{1}	21	14	1	0	11	9	12.3	4.63	94	.233	.317	4	.500	1	-1	-1	0	0.0
1949	Det-A	3	2	.600	25	10	1	0	0	76	85	58	5	1	69	40	18.4	6.16	68	.290	.427	0	.000	-4	-17	-17	2	-1.1
1950	StL-A	0	2	.000	9	2	0	0	0	14^{1}	25	19	2	2	18	10	28.3	11.93	41	.403	.549	0	.000	-0	-12	-10	-0	-1.2
	Chi-A	0	0	—	11	1	0	0	0	21^{1}	17	13	1	0	27	14	18.6	3.80	118	.221	.423	0	.000	-1	2	2	-1	0.0
	Yr	0	2	.000	20	3	0	0	0	35^{2}	42	32	3	2	45	24	22.5	7.07	66	.302	.478	0	.000	-1	-10	-9	-1	-1.2
1951	Chi-A	6	9	.400	26	18	7	1	0	137	129	77	7	3	74	89	13.5	4.20	96	.250	.347	4	.083	-5	-1	-3	-0	-0.8
1952	Chi-A	4	4	.500	19	11	4	2	1	79	52	31	5	1	56	63	12.4	2.96	123	.186	.323	1	.050	-1	6	6	-1	0.4
1953	Chi-A	0	0	—	9	3	0	0	0	20^{2}	12	11	2	1	30	15	18.7	3.48	116	.171	.426	0	.000	-0	1	1	1	0.1
	StL-A	1	5	.167	22	11	0	0	0	81	93	56	5	0	52	37	16.1	5.11	82	.286	.385	5	.200	-1	-10	-8	-2	-0.7
	Yr	1	5	.167	31	14	0	0	0	101^{2}	105	67	7	1	82	52	16.6	4.78	87	.266	.393	5	.172	-1	-9	-7	-1	-0.6
1954	Bal-A	6	11	.353	32	20	5	0	0	166^{2}	169	83	12	1	82	82	13.6	4.37	82	.269	.354	8	.157	-0	-12	-15	0	-1.4
1955	Bal-A	0	4	.000	15	5	0	0	0	38^{1}	50	39	3	1	27	26	18.3	8.22	46	.316	.419	1	.091	-1	-18	-19	1	-1.7
1956	KC-A	4	9	.308	25	20	3	0	0	118^{2}	121	75	17	0	74	61	14.8	5.31	82	.262	.364	2	.061	-3	-15	-12	-1	-1.5
Total	10	27	47	.365	199	104	22	3	1	785^{1}	781	479	62	10	522	450	15.0	4.87	82	.261	.372	27	.114	-13	-76	-77	-1	-7.7
● **RICK KREUGER**	Kreuger, Richard Allen b: 11/3/48, Grand Rapids, Mich. BR/TL, 6'2", 185 lbs. Deb: 9/6/75																											
1975	Bos-A	0	0	—	2	0	0	0	0	4	3	2	0	0	1	1	9.0	4.50	91	.200	.250	0	—	0	-0	-0	0	0.0
1976	Bos-A	2	1	.667	8	4	1	0	0	31	31	14	3	0	16	12	13.6	4.06	96	.272	.362	0	—	0	-2	-0	1	0.0
1977	Bos-A	0	1	.000	1	0	0	0	0	0	2	0	0	0	—	—	∞	—	1.000	1.000	111	—	0	-2	-2	0	-0.2	
1978	Cle-A	0	0	—	6	0	0	0	0	9^{1}	6	4	1	0	3	7	8.7	3.86	97	.194	.265	0	—	0	-0	-0	0	0.0
Total	4	2	2	.500	17	4	1	0	0	44^{1}	42	22	4	0	20	20	12.6	4.47	87	.259	.341	0	—	0	-4	-3	1	-0.2
● **FRANK KREUTZER**	Kreutzer, Franklin James b: 2/7/39, Buffalo, N.Y. BR/TL, 6'1", 190 lbs. Deb: 9/20/62																											
1962	Chi-A	0	0	—	1	0	0	0	0	1^{1}	0	0	0	0	1	1	6.8	0.00	—	.000	.200	0	—	0	1	1	0	0.0
1963	Chi-A	1	0	1.000	1	1	0	0	0	5	3	1	1	0	1	0	7.2	1.80	195	.188	.235	0	.000	-0	1	1	0	0.2
1964	Chi-A	3	1	.750	17	2	0	0	1	40^{1}	37	15	1	0	18	32	12.3	3.35	103	.239	.318	1	.125	-0	1	1	1	0.1
	Was-A	2	6	.250	13	9	0	0	0	45^{1}	48	26	6	1	23	27	14.3	4.76	78	.267	.353	0	.000	-1	-6	-5	0	-1.0
	Yr	5	7	.417	30	11	0	0	1	85^{2}	85	41	7	1	41	59	13.3	4.10	87	.254	.337	1	.053	-1	-5	-5	1	-0.9
1965	Was-A	2	6	.250	33	14	2	1	0	85^{1}	73	48	7	2	54	65	13.6	4.32	80	.232	.348	1	.045	-1	-8	-8	-2	-1.0
1966	Was-A	0	5	.000	9	6	0	0	0	31^{1}	30	24	9	1	10	24	11.8	6.03	57	.236	.297	2	.250	0	-9	-9	0	-1.2
1969	Was-A	0	0	—	4	0	0	0	0	2	3	1	0	0	2	2	22.5	4.50	77	.333	.455	0	—	0	-0	-0	0	0.0
Total	6	8	18	.308	78	32	2	1	1	210^{2}	194	115	24	4	109	151	13.1	4.40	80	.241	.334	4	.078	-2	-20	-21	-1	-2.9
● **KURT KRIEGER**	Krieger, Kurt Ferdinand "Dutch" b: 9/16/26, Traisen, Austria d: 8/16/70, St.Louis, Mo. BR/TR, 6'3", 212 lbs. Deb: 4/21/49																											
1949	StL-N	0	0	—	1	0	0	0	0	1	0	0	0	0	1	0	9.0	0.00	—	.000	.250	0	—	0	0	0	-0	0.0
1951	StL-N	0	0	—	2	0	0	0	0	4	6	7	1	0	5	3	24.8	15.75	25	.353	.500	0	—	0	-5	-5	0	-0.2
Total	2	0	0	—	3	0	0	0	0	5	6	7	1	0	6	3	21.6	12.60	32	.300	.462	0	—	0	-5	-5	0	-0.2
● **HOWIE KRIST**	Krist, Howard Wilbur "Spud" b: 2/28/16, W.Henrietta, N.Y. d: 4/23/89, Buffalo, N.Y. BL/TR, 6'1", 175 lbs. Deb: 9/12/37																											
1937	StL-N	3	1	.750	6	4	1	0	0	27^{2}	34	13	0	0	10	6	14.3	4.23	94	.304	.361	0	.000	-1	-1	-1	-1	-0.3
1938	StL-N	0	0	—	2	0	0	0	0	1^{1}	1	0	0	0	0	1	6.8	0.00	—	.250	.250	0	—	0	1	1	0	0.0
1941	StL-N	10	0	1.000	37	8	2	0	2	114	107	57	10	1	35	36	11.3	4.03	93	.246	.304	9	.237	1	-5	-3	-1	-0.3
1942	StL-N	13	3	.813	34	8	3	0	1	118^{1}	103	34	2	2	43	47	11.3	2.51	136	.233	.304	6	.143	-1	11	12	-2	1.2
1943	*StL-N	11	5	.688	34	17	9	2	3	164^{1}	141	57	5	4	62	57	11.3	2.90	116	.233	.309	10	.167	-2	9	8	-5	0.1
1946	StL-N	0	2	.000	15	0	0	0	0	18^{2}	22	15	3	1	8	3	14.9	6.75	51	.306	.383	0	—	0	-7	-7	0	-0.7
Total	6	37	11	.771	128	37	15	2	6	444^{1}	408	176	20	8	158	150	11.6	3.32	106	.244	.313	25	.168	-3	7	10	-9	0.0
● **RICK KRIVDA**	Krivda, Rick Michael b: 1/19/70, McKeesport, Pa. BR/TL, 6'1", 180 lbs. Deb: 7/7/95																											
1995	Bal-A	2	7	.222	13	13	1	0	0	75^{1}	76	40	9	4	25	53	12.5	4.54	105	.266	.333	0	—	0	1	2	-1	0.1
1996	Bal-A	3	5	.375	22	11	0	0	0	81^{2}	89	48	14	1	39	54	14.2	4.96	99	.283	.363	0	—	0	0	-0	-1	-0.1
1997	Bal-A	4	2	.667	10	10	0	0	0	50	67	36	7	0	18	29	15.3	6.30	70	.328	.383	0	—	0	-10	-11	0	-1.1
1998	Cle-A	2	0	1.000	11	1	0	0	0	25	24	10	2	0	16	10	14.4	3.24	147	.250	.357	0	—	0	4	4	-0	0.3
	Cin-N	0	2	.000	16	1	0	0	0	26^{1}	41	34	7	3	19	19	21.5	11.28	38	.366	.470	0	.000	-0	-21	-20	-0	-1.4
Total	4	11	16	.407	72	36	1	0	0	258^{1}	297	168	39	8	117	165	14.7	5.57	84	.293	.371	0	.000	-0	-24	-25	-2	-2.2
● **GUS KROCK**	Krock, August H. b: 5/9/1866, Milwaukee, Wis. d: 3/22/05, Pasadena, Cal. BR/TR, 6', 196 lbs. Deb: 4/24/1888																											
1888	Chi-N	25	14	.641	39	39	39	4	0	339^{2}	295	143	20	9	45	161	9.2	2.44	124	.227	.258	22	.164	-3	16	21	-3	1.5
1889	Chi-N	3	3	.500	7	7	5	0	0	60^{2}	86	43	10	2	14	16	15.1	4.90	85	.323	.362	4	.167	-1	-6	-5	0	-0.5
	Ind-N	2	2	.500	4	4	3	0	0	32	48	38	2	0	14	10	17.4	7.31	57	.336	.395	5	.357	1	-12	-11	-1	-0.9
	Was-N	2	4	.333	6	6	6	0	0	48	65	50	1	1	22	17	16.5	5.25	75	.314	.383	2	.087	-2	-7	-7	-0	-0.8
	Yr	7	9	.438	17	17	14	0	0	140^{2}	199	131	13	3	50	43	16.1	5.57	73	.323	.377	11	.180	-2	-24	-23	-1	-2.2
1890	Buf-P	0	3	.000	4	3	3	0	0	25	43	37	1	0	15	5	20.9	6.12	67	.364	.436	1	.083	-1	-5	-6	0	-0.5
Total	3	32	26	.552	60	59	56	4	0	505^{1}	537	311	34	12	110	209	11.7	3.49	97	.264	.306	34	.164	-7	-14	-5	-4	-1.2
● **RUBE KROH**	Kroh, Floyd Myron b: 8/25/1886, Friendship, N.Y. d: 3/17/44, New Orleans, La. BL/TL, 6'2", 186 lbs. Deb: 9/30/06																											
1906	Bos-A	1	0	1.000	1	1	1	1	0	9	2	0	0	0	4	5	6.0	0.00	—	.074	.194	0	.000	-0	3	3	0	0.3
1907	Bos-A	1	4	.200	7	5	1	0	0	34^{1}	33	13	0	2	8	8	11.3	2.62	98	.256	.309	3	.273	0	-0	-0	-0	0.0
1908	Chi-N	0	0	—	2	1	0	0	0	12	9	3	0	0	4	11	9.8	1.50	157	.200	.265	0	.000	-0	1	1	0	0.1
1909	Chi-N	9	4	.692	17	13	10	2	0	120^{1}	97	26	2	1	30	51	9.6	1.65	154	.224	.276	6	.150	-0	13	12	1	1.5
1910	Chi-N	3	1	.750	6	4	1	0	0	34^{1}	33	19	1	2	15	16	13.1	4.46	65	.254	.340	3	.250	0	-5	-6	1	-0.6

YEAR	TM/L	W	L	PCT	G	GS	CG	SH	SV	IP	H	R	HR	HB	BB	SO	RAT	ERA	ERA+	OAV	OOB	BH	AVG	PB	PR	PR+	PD	TPI
1912	Bos-N	0	0	—	3	1	0	0	0	6^1	8	4	0	0	6	1	19.9	5.68	63	.364	.500	1	.500	0	-2	-1	1	0.0
Total	6	14	9	.609	36	25	13	3	0	216^1	182	65	3	5	67	92	10.6	2.29	115	.232	.296	13	.181	-0	9	8	3	1.3

● **GARY KROLL** Kroll, Gary Melvin b: 7/8/41, Culver City, Cal. BR/TR, 6'6", 220 lbs. Deb: 7/26/64

YEAR	TM/L	W	L	PCT	G	GS	CG	SH	SV	IP	H	R	HR	HB	BB	SO	RAT	ERA	ERA+	OAV	OOB	BH	AVG	PB	PR	PR+	PD	TPI
1964	Phi-N	0	0	—	2	0	0	0	0	3	3	1	0	0	2	2	15.0	3.00	116	.250	.357	0	—	0	0	0	-0	0.0
	NY-N	0	1	.000	8	2	0	0	0	21^2	19	11	1	1	15	24	14.5	4.15	86	.241	.368	1	.333	0	-1	-1	1	0.0
	Yr	0	1	.000	10	2	0	0	0	24^2	22	12	1	1	17	26	14.6	4.01	89	.242	.367	1	.333	0	-1	-1	1	0.0
1965	NY-N	6	6	.500	32	11	1	0	1	87	83	48	12	6	41	62	13.4	4.45	79	.249	.342	3	.115	-1	-9	-9	-0	-1.2
1966	Hou-N	0	0	—	10	0	0	0	0	23^2	26	10	2	0	11	22	14.1	3.80	90	.280	.356	0	.000	-0	-1	-1	0	-0.1
1969	Cle-A	0	0	—	19	0	0	0	0	24	16	14	3	0	22	28	14.3	4.13	91	.188	.355	0	—	0	-1	-1	-0	-0.1
Total	4	6	7	.462	71	13	1	0	1	159^1	147	84	18	7	91	138	13.8	4.24	84	.244	.350	4	.125	-1	-12	-12	1	-1.4

● **MARC KROON** Kroon, Marc Jason b: 4/2/73, Bronx, N.Y. BB/TR, 6'2", 195 lbs. Deb: 7/7/95

YEAR	TM/L	W	L	PCT	G	GS	CG	SH	SV	IP	H	R	HR	HB	BB	SO	RAT	ERA	ERA+	OAV	OOB	BH	AVG	PB	PR	PR+	PD	TPI
1995	SD-N	0	1	.000	2	0	0	0	0	1^2	1	2	0	0	2	2	16.2	10.80	37	.200	.429	0	—	0	-1	-1	-0	-0.2
1997	SD-N	0	1	.000	12	0	0	0	0	11^1	14	9	2	1	5	12	15.9	6.35	61	.280	.357	0	—	0	-3	-3	-0	-0.3
1998	SD-N	0	0	—	2	0	0	0	0	2^1	0	0	0	0	1	2	3.9	0.00	—	.000	.125	0	—	0	1	1	-0	0.0
	Cin-N	0	0	—	4	0	0	0	0	5^1	7	8	0	1	8	4	27.0	13.50	32	.333	.533	0	—	0	-5	-5	0	-0.2
	Yr	0	0	—	6	0	0	0	0	7^2	7	8	0	1	9	6	20.0	9.39	44	.250	.447	0	—	0	-4	-5	0	-0.2
Total	3	0	2	.000	20	0	0	0	0	20^2	22	19	2	2	16	20	17.4	7.84	51	.265	.396	0	—	0	-8	-9	-0	-0.7

● **BILL KRUEGER** Krueger, William Culp b: 4/24/58, Waukegan, Ill. BL/TL, 6'5", 210 lbs. Deb: 4/10/83

YEAR	TM/L	W	L	PCT	G	GS	CG	SH	SV	IP	H	R	HR	HB	BB	SO	RAT	ERA	ERA+	OAV	OOB	BH	AVG	PB	PR	PR+	PD	TPI
1983	Oak-A	7	6	.538	17	16	2	0	0	109^2	104	54	7	2	53	58	13.0	3.61	107	.252	.340	0	—	0	6	3	-2	0.1
1984	Oak-A	10	10	.500	26	24	1	0	0	142	156	95	9	2	85	61	15.4	4.75	79	.285	.383	0	—	0	-12	-17	-2	-2.2
1985	Oak-A	9	10	.474	32	23	2	0	0	151^1	165	95	13	2	69	56	14.0	4.52	85	.276	.353	0	—	0	-6	-12	-1	-1.4
1986	Oak-A	1	2	.333	11	3	0	0	1	34^1	40	25	4	0	13	10	13.9	6.03	64	.301	.363	0	—	0	-7	-9	1	-0.7
1987	Oak-A	0	3	.000	9	0	0	0	0	5^2	9	7	0	0	8	2	27.0	9.53	43	.360	.515	0	—	0	-3	-4	-0	-0.7
	LA-N	0	0	—	2	0	0	0	0	2^1	3	2	0	0	1	2	15.4	0.00	—	.250	.308	0	—	0	1	1	-0	0.0
1988	LA-N	0	0	—	1	1	0	0	0	2^1	4	3	0	1	2	1	27.0	11.57	29	.364	.500	0	—	0	-2	-2	0	-0.1
1989	Mil-A	3	2	.600	34	5	0	0	3	93^2	96	43	9	0	33	72	12.4	3.84	100	.264	.325	0	—	0	0	0	-0	0.0
1990	Mil-A	6	8	.429	30	17	0	0	0	129	137	70	10	3	54	64	13.5	3.98	98	.276	.351	0	—	0	-1	-1	-1	-0.2
1991	Sea-A	11	8	.579	35	25	1	0	0	175	194	82	15	4	60	91	13.3	3.60	115	.289	.351	0	—	0	10	10	1	1.1
1992	Min-A	10	6	.625	27	27	2	2	0	161^1	166	82	18	3	46	86	12.0	4.30	95	.263	.317	0	—	0	-6	-4	-3	-0.7
	Mon-N	0	2	.000	9	2	0	0	0	17^1	23	13	0	1	7	13	16.1	6.75	51	.315	.383	0	.000	-0	-6	-6	-0	-0.7
1993	Det-A	6	4	.600	32	7	0	0	0	82	90	43	6	4	30	60	13.6	3.40	126	.285	.354	0	—	0	8	8	-0	0.9
1994	Det-A	0	2	.000	16	2	0	0	0	19^2	26	24	3	1	17	17	20.1	9.61	50	.321	.444	0	—	0	-10	-10	0	-0.8
	SD-N	3	2	.600	8	7	1	0	0	41	42	24	5	1	7	30	11.0	4.83	85	.259	.294	6	.500	3	-3	-3	0	-0.1
1995	SD-N	0	0	—	6	0	0	0	0	7^2	13	6	1	0	4	6	20.0	7.04	57	.371	.436	0	—	0	-2	-3	-0	-0.1
	Sea-A	2	1	.667	6	5	0	0	0	20	37	17	4	0	4	10	18.4	5.85	81	.407	.432	0	—	0	-3	-2	-0	-0.3
Total	13	68	66	.507	301	164	9	2	4	1194^1	1305	685	104	24	493	639	13.7	4.35	92	.280	.352	6	.400	2	-37	-50	-8	-5.9

● **ABE KRUGER** Kruger, Abraham b: 2/14/1885, Morris Run, Pa. d: 7/4/62, Elmira, N.Y. BR/TR, 6'2", 190 lbs. Deb: 10/6/08

YEAR	TM/L	W	L	PCT	G	GS	CG	SH	SV	IP	H	R	HR	HB	BB	SO	RAT	ERA	ERA+	OAV	OOB	BH	AVG	PB	PR	PR+	PD	TPI
1908	Bro-N	0	1	.000	2	1	0	0	0	6^1	5	5	0	3	3	2	15.6	4.26	55	.238	.407	0	.000	-0	-1	-1	1	-0.2

● **MIKE KRUKOW** Krukow, Michael Edward b: 1/21/52, Long Beach, Cal. BR/TR, 6'5", 205 lbs. Deb: 9/6/76

YEAR	TM/L	W	L	PCT	G	GS	CG	SH	SV	IP	H	R	HR	HB	BB	SO	RAT	ERA	ERA+	OAV	OOB	BH	AVG	PB	PR	PR+	PD	TPI
1976	Chi-N	0	0	—	2	0	0	0	0	4^1	6	4	0	0	2	1	16.6	8.31	47	.333	.400	0	.000	-0	-2	-2	-0	-0.1
1977	Chi-N	8	14	.364	34	33	1	1	0	172	195	96	16	3	61	106	13.6	4.40	100	.281	.341	11	.200	-0	-9	-0	1	0.0
1978	Chi-N	9	3	.750	27	20	3	1	0	138^1	125	62	11	5	53	81	11.9	3.90	103	.243	.320	11	.244	3	-5	2	-0	0.4
1979	Chi-N	9	9	.500	28	28	0	0	0	164^2	172	84	13	3	81	119	14.0	4.21	98	.275	.361	16	.314	5	-9	-1	-2	0.2
1980	Chi-N	10	15	.400	34	34	3	0	0	205	200	117	13	8	80	130	12.6	4.39	89	.258	.334	16	.246	2	-18	-10	-3	-1.1
1981	Chi-N	9	9	.500	25	25	2	1	0	144^1	146	68	11	2	55	101	12.7	3.68	101	.264	.333	9	.180	-0	-3	0	0	0.1
1982	Phi-N	13	11	.542	33	33	7	2	0	208	211	87	8	3	82	138	12.8	3.12	118	.268	.339	13	.181	-0	11	13	2	1.5
1983	SF-N	11	11	.500	31	31	2	1	0	184^1	189	95	17	3	76	136	13.1	3.95	90	.261	.333	16	.254	5	-7	-9	-2	-0.6
1984	SF-N	11	12	.478	35	33	3	1	1	199^1	234	117	22	5	78	141	14.3	4.56	77	.290	.356	10	.139	-1	-21	-24	-2	-2.8
1985	SF-N	8	11	.421	28	28	6	1	0	194^2	176	80	19	3	49	150	10.5	3.38	102	.238	.288	12	.218	5	5	2	-0	0.6
1986	SF-N★	20	9	.690	34	34	10	2	0	245	204	90	24	4	55	178	9.7	3.05	116	.223	.271	12	.146	0	18	14	-1	1.5
1987	*SF-N	5	6	.455	30	28	3	0	0	163	182	98	24	2	46	104	12.7	4.80	80	.288	.338	9	.167	1	-13	-18	1	-0.9
1988	SF-N	7	4	.636	20	20	1	0	0	124^2	111	51	13	5	31	75	10.6	3.54	92	.236	.291	3	.073	-0	-1	-4	-0	-0.4
1989	SF-N	4	3	.571	8	8	0	0	0	43	37	20	5	1	18	18	11.7	3.98	85	.236	.318	1	.063	-1	-2	-3	0	-0.6
Total	14	124	117	.515	369	355	41	10	1	2190^2	2188	1069	196	47	767	1478	12.3	3.90	96	.260	.325	139	.193	17	-55	-39	-5	-2.2

● **AL KRUMM** Krumm, Albert b: 1/13/1865, Pittsburgh, Pa. d: 6/15/37, San Diego, Cal. TR, Deb: 5/17/1889

YEAR	TM/L	W	L	PCT	G	GS	CG	SH	SV	IP	H	R	HR	HB	BB	SO	RAT	ERA	ERA+	OAV	OOB	BH	AVG	PB	PR	PR+	PD	TPI
1889	Pit-N	0	1	.000	1	1	1	0	0	9	8	11	0	0	10	4	18.0	10.00	37	.229	.400	0	.000	-1	-6	-7	-0	-0.5

● **JEFF KUBENKA** Kubenka, Jeffrey Scot b: 8/24/74, Weimar, Tex. BR/TL, 6'2", 191 lbs. Deb: 9/6/98

YEAR	TM/L	W	L	PCT	G	GS	CG	SH	SV	IP	H	R	HR	HB	BB	SO	RAT	ERA	ERA+	OAV	OOB	BH	AVG	PB	PR	PR+	PD	TPI
1998	LA-N	1	0	1.000	6	0	0	0	0	9^1	4	1	0	0	8	10	11.6	0.96	411	.138	.324	0	—	0	3	3	0	0.4
1999	LA-N	0	1	.000	6	0	0	0	0	7^2	13	12	1	0	4	2	20.0	11.74	37	.371	.436	1	1.000	1	-6	-7	0	-0.6
Total	2	1	1	.500	12	0	0	0	0	17	17	13	1	0	12	12	15.4	5.82	71	.266	.382	1	1.000	1	-3	-3	1	-0.2

● **TIM KUBINSKI** Kubinski, Timothy Mark b: 1/20/72, Pullman, Wash. BL/TL, 6'4", 205 lbs. Deb: 7/16/97

YEAR	TM/L	W	L	PCT	G	GS	CG	SH	SV	IP	H	R	HR	HB	BB	SO	RAT	ERA	ERA+	OAV	OOB	BH	AVG	PB	PR	PR+	PD	TPI
1997	Oak-A	0	0	—	11	0	0	0	0	12^2	12	9	2	1	6	10	13.5	5.68	80	.255	.352	0	—	0	-2	-2	0	-0.1
1999	Oak-A	0	0	—	14	0	0	0	0	12^1	14	8	3	1	5	7	14.6	5.84	80	.280	.357	0	—	0	-1	-2	0	0.0
Total	2	0	0	—	25	0	0	0	0	25	26	17	5	2	11	17	14.0	5.76	80	.268	.355	0	—	0	-3	-3	1	-0.1

● **JOHNNY KUCAB** Kucab, John Albert b: 12/17/19, Olyphant, Pa. d: 5/26/77, Youngstown, Ohio BR/TR, 6'2", 185 lbs. Deb: 9/14/50

YEAR	TM/L	W	L	PCT	G	GS	CG	SH	SV	IP	H	R	HR	HB	BB	SO	RAT	ERA	ERA+	OAV	OOB	BH	AVG	PB	PR	PR+	PD	TPI
1950	Phi-A	1	1	.500	4	2	2	0	0	26	29	10	4	0	8	8	12.8	3.46	131	.282	.333	1	.111	-0	3	3	-1	0.1
1951	Phi-A	4	3	.571	30	1	0	0	4	74^2	76	37	9	1	23	23	12.1	4.22	101	.265	.322	0	.000	-2	-1	0	-2	-0.3
1952	Phi-A	0	1	.000	25	0	0	0	2	51^1	64	37	5	1	20	17	14.9	5.26	75	.312	.376	2	.200	-0	-9	-7	-0	-0.4
Total	3	5	5	.500	59	3	2	0	6	152	169	84	18	2	51	48	13.1	4.44	95	.284	.343	3	.086	-2	-7	-3	-2	-0.6

● **JACK KUCEK** Kucek, John Andrew Charles b: 6/8/53, Warren, Ohio BR/TR, 6'2", 200 lbs. Deb: 8/8/74

YEAR	TM/L	W	L	PCT	G	GS	CG	SH	SV	IP	H	R	HR	HB	BB	SO	RAT	ERA	ERA+	OAV	OOB	BH	AVG	PB	PR	PR+	PD	TPI
1974	Chi-A	1	4	.200	9	7	0	0	0	37^2	48	25	3	1	21	25	16.7	5.26	71	.320	.407	0	—	0	-7	-6	1	-0.7
1975	Chi-A	0	0	—	2	0	0	0	0	3^2	9	6	0	0	4	2	31.9	4.91	79	.500	.591	0	—	0	-0	-0	-0	0.0
1976	Chi-A	0	0	—	2	0	0	0	0	4^2	9	5	2	0	4	2	25.1	9.64	37	.429	.520	0	—	0	-3	-3	-0	-0.2
1977	Chi-A	0	1	.000	8	3	0	0	0	34^2	35	20	4	2	10	25	12.2	3.63	113	.267	.329	0	—	0	2	2	1	0.2
1978	Chi-A	2	3	.400	10	5	3	0	0	52	42	23	5	0	27	30	11.9	3.29	116	.220	.317	0	—	0	3	3	-0	0.2
1979	Chi-A	0	0	—	1	0	0	0	0	0^2	0	4	0	0	3	0	40.5	0.00	—	.000	.500	0	—	0	0	0	0	0.0
	Phi-N	1	0	1.000	4	0	0	0	0	4^1	6	4	2	0	1	2	14.5	8.31	46	.333	.368	0	—	0	-2	-2	-0	-0.4
1980	Tor-A	3	8	.273	23	12	0	0	1	68	83	56	9	1	41	35	16.5	6.75	64	.300	.392	0	—	0	-20	-17	-1	-2.5
Total	7	7	16	.304	59	27	3	0	2	205^2	232	139	25	4	111	121	15.2	5.12	78	.287	.376	0	—	0	-28	-25	0	-3.4

● **JOHNNY KUCKS** Kucks, John Charles b: 7/27/33, Hoboken, N.J. BR/TR, 6'3", 184 lbs. Deb: 4/17/55

YEAR	TM/L	W	L	PCT	G	GS	CG	SH	SV	IP	H	R	HR	HB	BB	SO	RAT	ERA	ERA+	OAV	OOB	BH	AVG	PB	PR	PR+	PD	TPI
1955	*NY-A	8	7	.533	29	13	3	1	0	126^2	122	54	8	2	44	49	11.9	3.41	110	.252	.317	2	.050	-4	8	5	-0	0.1
1956	*NY-A☆	18	9	.667	34	31	12	3	0	224^1	223	113	19	10	72	67	12.2	3.85	100	.261	.326	11	.143	-2	8	0	-0	-0.1
1957	*NY-A	8	10	.444	37	23	4	1	2	179^1	169	82	13	8	59	78	11.8	3.56	101	.251	.319	6	.109	-2	4	1	3	0.2
1958	*NY-A	8	8	.500	34	15	4	1	4	126	132	67	14	6	39	46	12.6	3.93	90	.269	.331	5	.125	-1	-2	-6	1	-0.7
1959	NY-A	0	1	.000	9	1	0	0	0	16^2	21	16	5	0	9	9	16.2	8.64	42	.323	.405	0	.000	-0	-9	-10	0	-0.5
	KC-A	8	11	.421	33	23	6	1	1	151^1	163	76	10	12	42	51	12.9	3.87	104	.278	.339	4	.085	-3	-0	2	1	0.1
	Yr	8	12	.400	42	24	6	1	1	168	184	92	15	12	51	60	13.2	4.34	91	.282	.345	4	.082	-3	-9	-7	2	-0.4
1960	KC-A	4	10	.286	31	17	1	0	0	114	140	85	22	1	43	38	14.5	6.00	66	.306	.367	4	.133	-1	-27	-25	-0	-2.8
Total	6	54	56	.491	207	123	30	7	7	938^1	970	493	91	39	308	338	12.6	4.10	92	.269	.333	32	.110	-12	-18	-33	5	-3.7

YEAR	TM/L	W	L	PCT	G	GS	CG	SH	SV	IP	H	R	HR	HB	BB	SO	RAT	ERA	ERA+	OAV	OOB	BH	AVG	PB	PR	PR+	PD	TPI
● **BERT KUCZYNSKI** Kuczynski, Bernard Carl b: 1/8/20, Philadelphia, Pa. d: 1/19/97, Allentown, Pa. BR/TR, 6′, 195 lbs. Deb: 6/2/43																												
1943	Phi-A	0	1	.000	6	1	0	0	0	24^2	36	15	2	2	9	8	17.1	4.01	85	.336	.398	0	.000	-0	-2	-2	-0	-0.1
● **FRED KUHAULUA** Kuhaulua, Fred Mahele b: 2/23/53, Honolulu, Hawaii BL/TL, 5′11″, 175 lbs. Deb: 8/2/77																												
1977	Cal-A	0	0	—	3	1	0	0	0	6^1	15	11	1	0	7	3	31.3	15.63	25	.455	.550	0	—	0	-8	-9	0	-0.4
1981	SD-N	1	0	1.000	5	4	0	0	0	29^1	28	10	1	0	9	16	11.4	2.45	133	.257	.314	1	.111	-0	3	3	-1	0.0
Total	2	1	0	1.000	8	5	0	0	0	35^2	43	21	2	0	16	19	14.9	4.79	70	.303	.373	1	.111	-0	-5	-6	-1	-0.4
● **BUB KUHN** Kuhn, Bernard Daniel b: 10/12/1899, Vicksburg, Mich. d: 11/20/56, Detroit, Mich. BL/TR, 6′1.5″, 182 lbs. Deb: 9/1/24																												
1924	Cle-A	0	1	.000	1	0	0	0	0	1	4	3	1	0	0	0	36.0	27.00	16	.667	.667	0	—	0	-3	-3	0	-0.4
● **JOHN KULL** Kull, John A. (b: John A Kolonauski) b: 6/24/1882, Shenandoah, Pa. d: 3/30/36, Schuylkill Haven, Pa. BL/TL, 6′2″, 190 lbs. Deb: 10/2/09																												
1909	Phi-A	1	0	1.000	1	0	0	0	0	3	3	1	0	1	5	4	27.0	3.00	80	.250	.500	1	1.000	0	-0	-0	0	0.0
● **MIKE KUME** Kume, John Michael b: 5/19/26, Premier, W.Va. BR/TR, 6′1″, 195 lbs. Deb: 8/26/55																												
1955	KC-A	0	2	.000	6	4	0	0	0	23^2	35	23	1	3	15	7	20.2	7.99	52	.354	.453	1	.125	-0	-11	-10	-0	-0.7
● **JEFF KUNKEL** Kunkel, Jeffrey William b: 3/25/62, W.Palm Beach, Fla. BR/TR, 6′2″, 180 lbs. Deb: 7/23/84 F♦																												
1988	Tex-A	0	0	—	1	0	0	0	0	1	0	0	0	0	0	1	0.0	0.00	—	.000	.000	35	.227	0	0	0	0	0.0
1989	Tex-A	0	0	—	1	0	0	0	0	1^2	4	4	1	0	3	0	37.8	21.60	18	.444	.583	79	.270	0	-3	-3	0	-0.1
Total	2	0	0	—	2	0	0	0	0	2^2	4	4	1	0	3	1	23.6	13.50	30	.333	.467	192	.221	1	-3	-3	0	-0.1
● **BILL KUNKEL** Kunkel, William Gustave James b: 7/7/36, Hoboken, N.J. d: 5/4/85, Red Bank, N.J. BR/TR, 6′1″, 187 lbs. Deb: 4/15/61 FU																												
1961	KC-A	3	4	.429	58	2	0	0	4	88^2	103	58	11	0	32	46	13.7	5.18	81	.289	.348	1	.125	-0	-11	-9	0	-0.8
1962	KC-A	0	0	—	9	0	0	0	0	7^2	8	7	3	0	4	6	14.1	3.52	120	.258	.343	0	—	0	0	1	-0	0.0
1963	NY-A	3	2	.600	22	0	0	0	0	46^1	42	15	3	0	13	31	10.7	2.72	129	.239	.291	2	.333	1	5	4	-1	0.4
Total	3	6	6	.500	89	2	0	0	4	142^2	153	80	17	0	49	83	12.7	4.29	92	.272	.330	3	.214	1	-6	-5	-1	-0.4
● **EARL KUNZ** Kunz, Earl Dewey "Pinches" b: 12/25/1899, Sacramento, Cal. d: 4/14/63, Sacramento, Cal. BR/TR, 5′10″, 170 lbs. Deb: 4/19/23																												
1923	Pit-N	1	2	.333	21	2	1	0	1	45^2	48	33	2	0	24	12	14.2	5.52	73	.293	.383	1	.083	-1	-8	-8	-1	-0.7
● **RYAN KUROSAKI** Kurosaki, Ryan Yoshitomo b: 7/3/52, Honolulu, Hawaii BR/TR, 5′10″, 160 lbs. Deb: 5/20/75																												
1975	StL-N	0	0	—	7	0	0	0	0	13	15	11	3	0	7	6	15.2	7.62	49	.283	.367	0	.000	-0	-6	-5	-0	-0.3
● **HAL KURTZ** Kurtz, Harold James "Bud" b: 8/20/43, Washington, D.C. BR/TR, 6′3″, 205 lbs. Deb: 4/18/68																												
1968	Cle-A	1	0	1.000	28	0	0	0	1	38	37	24	2	5	15	16	13.5	5.21	57	.255	.345	0	.000	-0	-9	-10	-1	-0.6
● **ED KUSEL** Kusel, Edward D. b: 2/15/1886, Cleveland, Ohio d: 10/20/48, Cleveland, Ohio TR, 6′, 165 lbs. Deb: 9/18/09																												
1909	StL-A	0	3	.000	3	3	3	0	0	24	43	28	1	0	1	2	16.5	7.13	34	.384	.389	3	.300	1	-12	-13	-1	-1.3
● **EMIL KUSH** Kush, Emil Benedict b: 11/4/16, Chicago, Ill. d: 11/26/69, River Grove, Ill. BR/TR, 5′11″, 185 lbs. Deb: 9/21/41																												
1941	Chi-N	0	0	—	2	0	0	0	0	4	2	1	0	0	0	2	4.5	2.25	156	.143	.143	0	.000	-0	1	1	-0	0.0
1942	Chi-N	0	0	—	1	0	0	0	0	2	1	0	0	0	1	1	9.0	0.00	—	.167	.286	0	.000	-0	1	1	0	0.1
1946	Chi-N	9	2	.818	40	6	1	1	2	129^2	120	47	4	3	43	50	11.5	3.05	109	.253	.319	8	.211	0	5	4	2	0.6
1947	Chi-N	8	3	.727	47	1	1	0	5	91	80	38	8	3	53	44	13.5	3.36	117	.247	.358	5	.250	1	7	6	1	1.0
1948	Chi-N	1	4	.200	34	1	0	0	3	72	70	39	5	2	37	31	13.6	4.38	89	.253	.345	2	.154	0	-3	-4	1	-0.2
1949	Chi-N	3	3	.500	26	0	0	0	2	47^2	51	21	7	2	24	22	14.5	3.78	107	.283	.374	3	.333	1	1	1	1	0.4
Total	6	21	12	.636	150	8	2	1	12	346^1	324	146	24	10	158	150	12.8	3.48	106	.254	.341	18	.220	2	12	9	5	1.9
● **CRAIG KUSICK** Kusick, Craig Robert b: 9/30/48, Milwaukee, Wis. BR/TR, 6′3″, 232 lbs. Deb: 9/8/73 ♦																												
1979	Tor-A	0	0	—	1	0	0	0	0	3^2	3	2	1	0	0	0	7.4	4.91	89	.214	.214	11	.204	0	-0	-0	-0	0.0
● **MARTY KUTYNA** Kutyna, Marion John b: 11/14/32, Philadelphia, Pa. BR/TR, 6′, 190 lbs. Deb: 9/19/59																												
1959	KC-A	0	0	—	4	0	0	0	1	7^1	7	0	0	0	1	1	9.8	0.00	—	.250	.276	0	—	0	3	3	0	0.2
1960	KC-A	3	2	.600	51	0	0	0	4	61^2	64	33	7	0	32	20	14.0	3.94	101	.274	.361	1	.200	-0	-0	0	0	0.0
1961	Was-A	6	8	.429	50	6	0	0	3	143	147	79	12	2	48	64	12.4	3.97	101	.271	.332	7	.206	-0	1	1	3	0.4
1962	Was-A	5	6	.455	54	0	0	0	0	78	83	42	9	0	27	25	12.7	4.04	100	.275	.334	1	.125	-0	-1	-0	1	0.1
Total	4	14	16	.467	159	6	0	0	8	290	301	154	28	2	108	110	12.8	3.88	103	.272	.338	9	.191	-0	3	4	4	0.7
● **JERRY KUTZLER** Kutzler, Jerry Scott b: 3/25/65, Waukegan, Ill. BL/TR, 6′1″, 175 lbs. Deb: 4/28/90																												
1990	Chi-A	2	1	.667	7	7	0	0	0	31^1	38	23	2	0	14	21	14.9	6.03	64	.304	.374	0	—	0	-7	-8	-0	-0.7
● **BOB KUZAVA** Kuzava, Robert Leroy "Sarge" b: 5/28/23, Wyandotte, Mich. BB/TL, 6′2″, 204 lbs. Deb: 9/21/46																												
1946	Cle-A	1	0	1.000	2	2	0	0	0	12	9	7	0	1	11	4	15.8	3.00	110	.191	.356	1	.200	-0	1	0	0	0.1
1947	Cle-A	1	1	.500	4	4	1	1	0	21^2	22	10	1	1	9	9	13.3	4.15	84	.265	.344	1	.111	-1	-1	-2	1	-0.1
1949	Chi-A	10	6	.625	29	18	9	1	0	156^2	139	76	6	1	91	83	13.3	4.02	104	.240	.344	2	.036	-6	3	3	-2	-0.6
1950	Chi-A	1	3	.250	10	7	1	0	0	44^1	43	28	5	0	27	21	14.2	5.68	79	.257	.361	1	.083	-0	-5	-6	0	-0.5
	Was-A	8	7	.533	22	22	8	1	0	155	156	80	8	1	75	84	13.5	3.95	114	.263	.346	5	.100	-2	11	10	-1	0.6
	Yr	9	10	.474	32	29	9	1	0	199^1	199	108	13	1	102	105	13.6	4.33	104	.261	.350	6	.097	-2	5	4	-1	0.1
1951	Was-A	3	3	.500	8	8	3	0	0	52^1	57	34	5	2	28	22	15.0	5.50	74	.284	.377	3	.176	-0	-8	-8	0	-0.8
	*NY-A	8	4	.667	23	8	4	1	5	82^1	76	27	5	1	27	50	11.4	2.40	159	.241	.303	3	.136	0	16	14	-1	2.0
	Yr	11	7	.611	31	16	7	1	5	134^2	133	61	10	3	55	72	12.8	3.61	109	.258	.333	6	.154	0	8	5	-1	1.2
1952	*NY-A	8	8	.500	28	12	6	1	3	133	115	53	7	1	63	67	12.1	3.45	96	.240	.329	4	.093	-1	3	-2	-2	-0.6
1953	*NY-A	6	5	.545	33	6	2	2	4	92^1	92	35	9	0	34	48	12.3	3.31	111	.264	.330	1	.048	-1	7	4	-2	0.2
1954	NY-A	1	3	.250	20	3	0	0	1	39^2	46	30	3	0	18	22	14.5	5.45	63	.297	.370	0	.000	-0	-8	-10	-1	-1.1
	Bal-A	1	3	.250	4	4	0	0	0	23^2	30	11	0	0	11	15	15.6	4.18	86	.323	.394	0	.000	-1	-1	-2	-1	-0.4
	Yr	2	6	.250	24	7	0	0	1	63^1	76	41	3	0	29	37	14.9	4.97	70	.306	.379	0	.000	-1	-9	-11	-1	-1.5
1955	Bal-A	0	1	.000	6	1	0	0	0	12^1	10	7	0	0	4	5	10.2	3.65	105	.222	.286	0	.000	-0	0	0	-1	0.0
	Phi-N	1	0	1.000	17	4	0	0	0	32^1	47	26	5	0	12	13	16.4	7.24	55	.333	.386	1	.143	-0	-11	-12	0	-0.6
1957	Pit-N	0	0	—	4	0	0	0	0	2	3	2	0	0	3	1	27.0	9.00	42	.333	.500	0	—	0	-1	-1	-0	-0.1
	StL-N	0	0	—	3	0	0	0	0	2^1	4	1	0	0	2	2	23.1	3.86	103	.364	.462	0	—	0	0	0	0	0.0
	Yr	0	0	—	7	0	0	0	0	4^1	7	3	0	0	5	3	24.9	6.23	62	.350	.480	0	—	0	-1	-1	0	-0.1
Total	10	49	44	.527	213	99	34	7	13	862	849	427	54	8	415	446	13.3	4.05	97	.260	.345	22	.086	-14	5	-13	-8	-1.9
● **CLEM LABINE** Labine, Clement Walter b: 8/6/26, Lincoln, R.I. BR/TR, 6′, 180 lbs. Deb: 4/18/50																												
1950	Bro-N	0	0	—	1	0	0	0	0	2	2	1	0	0	1	0	13.5	4.50	91	.286	.375	0	—	0	-0	-0	-0	0.0
1951	Bro-N	5	1	.833	14	6	5	2	0	65^1	52	17	4	0	20	39	9.9	2.20	178	.223	.285	3	.143	-1	13	13	-1	0.9
1952	Bro-N	8	4	.667	25	9	0	0	0	77	76	44	3	1	47	43	14.5	5.14	71	.259	.364	1	.045	-2	-12	-13	-1	-1.9
1953	*Bro-N	11	6	.647	37	7	0	0	7	110^1	92	39	9	0	30	44	10.0	2.77	154	.225	.278	2	.071	-1	19	18	0	2.7
1954	Bro-N	7	6	.538	47	2	0	0	5	108^1	101	60	7	1	56	43	13.1	4.15	98	.247	.339	1	.033	-2	-1	-1	1	-0.2
1955	*Bro-N	13	5	.722	**60**	8	1	0	11	144^1	121	61	12	0	55	67	11.0	3.24	125	.229	.301	3	.097	1	13	13	3	2.0
1956	*Bro-N☆	10	6	.625	62	3	1	0	**19**	115^2	111	48	11	3	39	75	11.9	3.35	119	.253	.318	2	.087	-1	5	8	1	1.2
1957	Bro-N★	5	7	.417	58	0	0	0	**17**	104^2	104	50	8	1	27	67	11.4	3.44	121	.259	.307	2	.100	-1	5	8	2	1.2
1958	LA-N	6	6	.500	52	2	0	0	14	104	112	55	8	1	33	43	12.6	4.15	99	.283	.340	1	.056	-1	-2	-1	0	-0.2
1959	*LA-N	5	10	.333	56	0	0	0	9	84^2	91	39	11	1	25	37	12.4	3.93	108	.282	.335	0	.000	-2	0	3	1	0.4
1960	LA-N	0	1	.000	13	0	0	0	1	17	26	12	1	0	8	15	18.0	5.82	68	.356	.420	1	.500	1	-4	-3	-0	-0.2
	Det-A	0	3	.000	14	0	0	0	2	19^1	19	12	2	0	12	6	14.4	5.12	77	.257	.360	0	.000	-0	-3	-2	0	-0.4
	*Pit-N	3	0	1.000	15	0	0	0	3	30^1	29	5	0	1	11	21	12.2	1.48	253	.254	.325	0	.000	-0	8	8	0	0.9
1961	Pit-N	4	1	.800	56	1	0	0	8	92^2	102	43	4	2	31	49	13.1	3.69	108	.284	.344	1	.100	-0	4	3	-1	0.1
1962	NY-N	0	0	—	3	0	0	0	0	4	5	6	1	0	1	2	13.5	11.25	37	.278	.316	0	—	0	-3	-3	0	-0.1
Total	13	77	56	.579	513	38	7	2	96	1079^2	1043	492	81	11	396	551	12.1	3.63	112	.256	.323	17	.075	-11	41	49	8	6.4

● BOB LACEY Lacey, Robert Joseph b: 8/25/53, Fredericksburg, Va. BR/TL, 6'5", 210 lbs. Deb: 5/13/77

YEAR	TM/L	W	L	PCT	G	GS	CG	SH	SV	IP	H	R	HR	HB	BB	SO	RAT	ERA	ERA+	OAV	OOB	BH	AVG	PB	PR	PR+	PD	TPI
1977	Oak-A	6	8	.429	64	0	0	0	7	121^{2}	100	46	13	0	43	69	10.6	3.03	133	.234	.304	0	—	0	14	14	3	1.9
1978	Oak-A	8	9	.471	**74**	0	0	0	5	119^{2}	126	52	10	1	35	60	12.2	3.01	121	.270	.323	0	—	0	10	9	2	1.5
1979	Oak-A	1	5	.167	42	0	0	0	4	47^{2}	66	34	7	1	24	33	17.2	5.85	69	.327	.401	0	—	0	-9	-10	0	-1.2
1980	Oak-A	3	2	.600	47	1	1	1	6	79^{2}	68	29	7	1	21	45	10.2	2.94	129	.234	.288	0	—	0	10	8	-0	0.6
1981	Cle-A	0	0	—	14	0	0	0	0	21^{1}	36	20	5	0	3	11	16.5	7.59	48	.371	.390	0	—	0	-9	-9	-0	-0.5
	Tex-A	0	0	—	1	0	0	0	0	1	1	1	1	0	0	0	9.0	9.00	39	.250	.250	0	—	0	-1	-1	0	0.0
	Yr	0	0	—	15	0	0	0	0	22^{1}	37	21	6	0	3	11	16.1	7.66	47	.366	.385	0	—	0	-10	-10	0	-0.5
1983	Cal-A	1	2	.333	8	0	0	0	0	8^{2}	12	5	1	0	0	7	12.5	5.19	78	.343	.343	0	—	0	-1	-1	-0	-0.2
1984	SF-N	1	3	.250	34	1	0	0	0	51	55	26	5	0	13	26	12.0	3.88	91	.276	.321	2	.333	1	-2	-2	0	-0.1
Total	7	20	29	.408	284	2	1	1	22	450^{2}	464	213	49	3	139	251	12.1	3.67	104	.269	.325	2	.333	1	13	7	5	2.0

● MARCEL LACHEMANN Lachemann, Marcel Ernest b: 6/13/41, Los Angeles, Cal. BR/TR, 6', 185 lbs. Deb: 6/4/69 FMC

YEAR	TM/L	W	L	PCT	G	GS	CG	SH	SV	IP	H	R	HR	HB	BB	SO	RAT	ERA	ERA+	OAV	OOB	BH	AVG	PB	PR	PR+	PD	TPI
1969	Oak-A	4	1	.800	28	0	0	0	2	43^{1}	43	24	1	2	19	16	13.3	3.95	87	.261	.344	0	.000	-0	-2	-3	1	-0.3
1970	Oak-A	3	3	.500	41	0	0	0	3	58^{1}	58	20	6	2	18	39	12.0	2.78	128	.266	.328	0	.000	-1	6	5	1	0.6
1971	Oak-A	0	0	—	1	0	0	0	0	0^{1}	2	2	0	0	1	0	81.0	54.00	6	1.000	1.000	0	—	0	-2	-2	0	-0.1
Total	3	7	4	.636	70	0	0	0	5	102	103	46	7	4	38	55	12.8	3.44	102	.268	.340	0	.000	-1	3	1	2	0.2

● AL LACHOWICZ Lachowicz, Allen Robert b: 9/6/60, Pittsburgh, Pa. BR/TR, 6'3", 198 lbs. Deb: 9/13/83

YEAR	TM/L	W	L	PCT	G	GS	CG	SH	SV	IP	H	R	HR	HB	BB	SO	RAT	ERA	ERA+	OAV	OOB	BH	AVG	PB	PR	PR+	PD	TPI
1983	Tex-A	0	1	.000	2	1	0	0	0	8	9	2	0	0	2	8	12.4	2.25	179	.281	.324	0	—	0	2	2	0	0.2

● LACKEY Lackey b: Columbus, Ohio Deb: 10/2/1890

YEAR	TM/L	W	L	PCT	G	GS	CG	SH	SV	IP	H	R	HR	HB	BB	SO	RAT	ERA	ERA+	OAV	OOB	BH	AVG	PB	PR	PR+	PD	TPI
1890	Phi-a	0	0	—	1	0	0	0	0	2	1	4	0	0	3	1	18.0	9.00	43	.143	.400	0	.000	-0	-1	-1	-0	-0.1

● FRANK LaCORTE LaCorte, Frank Joseph b: 10/13/51, San Jose, Cal. BR/TR, 6'1", 180 lbs. Deb: 9/8/75

YEAR	TM/L	W	L	PCT	G	GS	CG	SH	SV	IP	H	R	HR	HB	BB	SO	RAT	ERA	ERA+	OAV	OOB	BH	AVG	PB	PR	PR+	PD	TPI
1975	Atl-N	0	3	.000	3	2	0	0	0	13^{2}	13	10	1	0	6	10	12.5	5.27	72	.245	.322	0	.000	-1	-2	-2	0	-0.5
1976	Atl-N	3	12	.200	19	17	1	0	0	105^{1}	97	58	6	6	53	79	13.3	4.70	81	.249	.348	3	.091	-2	-14	-10	-0	-1.5
1977	Atl-N	1	8	.111	14	7	0	0	0	37	67	51	10	2	29	28	23.8	11.68	38	.394	.488	2	.200	-0	-32	-26	0	-4.4
1978	Atl-N	0	1	.000	2	2	0	0	0	14^{2}	9	6	0	0	4	7	8.0	3.68	110	.180	.241	0	.000	-0	-0	1	-0	-0.1
1979	Atl-N	0	0	—	6	0	0	0	0	8^{1}	9	7	2	0	5	6	15.1	7.56	54	.273	.368	0	.000	-0	-4	-3	-0	-0.2
	Hou-N	1	2	.333	12	3	0	0	0	27	21	16	3	0	10	24	10.3	5.00	70	.208	.279	0	.000	-0	-4	-5	-1	-0.6
	Yr	1	2	.333	18	3	0	0	0	35^{1}	30	23	5	0	15	30	11.5	5.60	65	.224	.302	0	.000	-0	-7	-8	-1	-0.8
1980	*Hou-N	8	5	.615	55	0	0	0	11	83	61	29	4	0	43	66	11.3	2.82	117	.210	.311	1	.167	0	7	5	-2	0.7
1981	*Hou-N	4	2	.667	37	0	0	0	5	42	41	18	1	0	21	40	13.3	3.64	90	.258	.344	1	.333	0	-1	-2	-0	-0.3
1982	Hou-N	1	5	.167	55	0	0	0	7	76^{1}	71	44	5	0	46	51	13.8	4.48	74	.247	.350	0	.000	-1	-7	-11	-2	-1.2
1983	Hou-N	4	4	.500	37	0	0	0	3	53^{1}	35	32	8	2	28	48	11.0	5.06	67	.190	.304	1	.200	0	-8	-10	-0	-1.5
1984	Cal-A	1	2	.333	13	1	0	0	0	29^{1}	33	26	9	0	13	13	14.1	7.06	56	.282	.354	0	—	0	-10	-10	-0	-0.9
Total	10	23	44	.343	253	32	1	0	26	490	457	297	49	10	258	372	13.3	5.01	72	.249	.345	8	.104	-4	-75	-77	-7	-10.5

● MIKE LaCOSS LaCoss, Michael James (b: Michael James Marks) b: 5/30/56, Glendale, Cal. BR/TR, 6'4", 190 lbs. Deb: 7/18/78

YEAR	TM/L	W	L	PCT	G	GS	CG	SH	SV	IP	H	R	HR	HB	BB	SO	RAT	ERA	ERA+	OAV	OOB	BH	AVG	PB	PR	PR+	PD	TPI
1978	Cin-N	4	8	.333	16	15	2	1	0	96	104	56	5	1	46	31	14.2	4.50	79	.288	.370	2	.067	-2	-10	-10	-1	-1.4
1979	*Cin-N★	14	8	.636	35	32	6	1	0	205^{2}	202	92	13	2	79	73	12.4	3.50	107	.263	.333	9	.129	-1	5	5	1	0.5
1980	Cin-N	10	12	.455	34	29	4	2	0	169^{1}	207	101	9	1	68	59	14.7	4.62	78	.303	.367	5	.091	-3	-19	-20	1	-2.5
1981	Cin-N	4	7	.364	20	13	1	1	1	78	102	55	7	1	30	22	15.3	6.12	58	.325	.386	0	.000	-2	-23	-22	0	-3.0
1982	Hou-N	6	6	.500	41	8	0	0	0	115	107	41	3	4	54	51	12.9	2.90	115	.252	.342	6	.250	2	9	6	-1	0.7
1983	Hou-N	5	7	.417	38	17	2	0	1	138	142	81	10	2	56	53	13.0	4.43	77	.273	.346	3	.086	-2	-12	-17	1	-1.5
1984	Hou-N	7	5	.583	39	18	2	1	3	132	132	64	3	0	55	86	12.8	4.02	83	.261	.334	4	.129	-1	-6	-11	0	-1.0
1985	KC-A	1	1	.500	21	0	0	0	1	40^{2}	49	25	2	0	29	26	17.3	5.09	82	.304	.411	0	—	0	-4	-4	0	-0.2
1986	SF-N	10	13	.435	37	31	4	1	0	204^{1}	179	99	14	6	70	86	11.2	3.57	99	.240	.310	14	.230	6	4	-1	1	0.6
1987	*SF-N	13	10	.565	39	26	2	1	0	171	184	78	16	2	63	79	13.1	3.68	104	.283	.348	3	.060	-2	8	3	4	0.5
1988	SF-N	7	7	.500	19	19	1	1	0	114^{1}	99	55	5	1	47	70	11.6	3.62	90	.234	.312	8	.242	3	-2	-5	3	0.1
1989	*SF-N	10	10	.500	45	18	1	0	6	150^{1}	143	62	3	7	65	78	12.9	3.17	106	.255	.340	3	.073	-1	5	4	-1	0.4
1990	SF-N	6	4	.600	13	12	1	0	0	77^{2}	75	37	5	0	39	39	13.2	3.94	93	.259	.347	1	.043	-1	-1	-3	-1	-0.5
1991	SF-N	1	5	.167	18	5	0	0	0	47^{1}	61	39	4	2	24	30	16.5	7.23	50	.314	.395	2	.222	1	-19	-20	-0	-2.2
Total	14	98	103	.488	415	243	26	9	12	1739^{2}	1786	885	99	29	725	783	13.1	4.02	88	.270	.345	60	.125	-4	-65	-95	8	-9.5

● KERRY LACY Lacy, Kerry Ardeen b: 8/7/72, Chattanooga, Tenn. BR/TR, 6'2", 195 lbs. Deb: 8/16/96

YEAR	TM/L	W	L	PCT	G	GS	CG	SH	SV	IP	H	R	HR	HB	BB	SO	RAT	ERA	ERA+	OAV	OOB	BH	AVG	PB	PR	PR+	PD	TPI
1996	Bos-A	2	0	1.000	11	0	0	0	0	10^{2}	15	5	2	1	8	9	20.3	3.38	150	.333	.444	0	—	0	2	2	0	0.3
1997	Bos-A	1	1	.500	33	0	0	0	3	45^{2}	60	34	7	0	22	18	16.2	6.11	76	.314	.385	0	—	0	-8	-7	-1	-0.4
Total	2	3	1	.750	44	0	0	0	3	56^{1}	75	39	9	1	30	27	16.9	5.59	84	.318	.397	0	—	0	-6	-5	-1	-0.1

● PETE LADD Ladd, Peter Linwood b: 7/17/56, Portland, Maine BR/TR, 6'3", 240 lbs. Deb: 8/17/79

YEAR	TM/L	W	L	PCT	G	GS	CG	SH	SV	IP	H	R	HR	HB	BB	SO	RAT	ERA	ERA+	OAV	OOB	BH	AVG	PB	PR	PR+	PD	TPI
1979	Hou-N	1	1	.500	10	0	0	0	0	12^{1}	8	5	1	2	8	6	13.1	2.92	121	.178	.327	0	.000	-0	1	1	0	0.2
1982	*Mil-A	1	3	.250	16	0	0	0	3	18	16	8	5	0	6	12	11.0	4.00	95	.239	.301	0	—	0	0	-0	-1	-0.1
1983	Mil-A	3	4	.429	44	0	0	0	25	49^{1}	30	17	3	1	16	41	8.6	2.55	147	.172	.246	0	—	0	8	7	-0	1.4
1984	Mil-A	4	9	.308	54	1	0	0	3	91	94	58	16	1	38	75	13.2	5.24	74	.266	.339	0	—	0	-13	-15	-2	-2.1
1985	Mil-A	0	0	—	29	0	0	0	2	45^{2}	58	26	5	2	10	22	13.8	4.53	92	.315	.357	0	—	0	-2	-2	-0	-0.1
1986	Sea-A	8	6	.571	52	0	0	0	6	70^{2}	69	33	10	3	18	53	11.5	3.82	111	.258	.313	0	—	0	3	3	-1	0.5
Total	6	17	23	.425	205	1	0	0	39	287	275	147	40	9	96	209	11.9	4.14	96	.252	.318	0	.000	-0	-2	-6	-4	-0.2

● DOYLE LADE Lade, Doyle Marion "Porky" b: 2/17/21, Fairbury, Neb. d: 5/18/2000, Lincoln, Neb. BR/TR (BB 1946-47), 5'10", 183 lbs. Deb: 9/18/46

YEAR	TM/L	W	L	PCT	G	GS	CG	SH	SV	IP	H	R	HR	HB	BB	SO	RAT	ERA	ERA+	OAV	OOB	BH	AVG	PB	PR	PR+	PD	TPI
1946	Chi-N	0	2	.000	3	2	0	0	0	15^{1}	15	8	0	1	3	8	11.2	4.11	81	.238	.284	1	.200	-0	-1	-1	0	-0.2
1947	Chi-N	11	10	.524	34	25	7	1	0	187^{1}	202	105	15	1	79	62	13.5	3.94	100	.276	.347	13	.217	2	2	0	2	0.5
1948	Chi-N	5	6	.455	19	12	6	0	0	87^{1}	99	44	4	1	31	29	13.5	4.02	97	.283	.343	5	.156	-1	-1	-1	1	-0.1
1949	Chi-N	4	5	.444	36	13	5	1	1	129^{2}	141	73	14	2	58	43	14.0	5.00	81	.274	.350	7	.219	2	-14	-14	0	-0.7
1950	Chi-N	5	6	.455	34	12	2	0	2	117^{2}	126	68	14	2	50	36	13.6	4.74	89	.275	.349	10	.286	3	-8	-7	3	0.0
Total	5	25	29	.463	126	64	20	2	3	537^{1}	583	298	47	7	221	178	13.6	4.39	91	.275	.346	36	.220	6	-21	-23	7	-0.5

● STEVE LADEW Ladew, Stephen b: St.Louis, Mo. Deb: 9/27/1889 ♦

YEAR	TM/L	W	L	PCT	G	GS	CG	SH	SV	IP	H	R	HR	HB	BB	SO	RAT	ERA	ERA+	OAV	OOB	BH	AVG	PB	PR	PR+	PD	TPI
1889	KC-a	0	0	—	1	0	0	0	0	2	1	4	0	0	3	0	18.0	4.50	93	.143	.400	0	.000	-0	-0	-0	0	0.0

● FLIP LAFFERTY Lafferty, Frank Bernard b: 5/4/1854, Scranton, Pa. d: 2/8/10, Wilmington, Del. TR, Deb: 9/15/1876 ♦

YEAR	TM/L	W	L	PCT	G	GS	CG	SH	SV	IP	H	R	HR	HB	BB	SO	RAT	ERA	ERA+	OAV	OOB	BH	AVG	PB	PR	PR+	PD	TPI
1876	Phi-N	0	1	.000	1	1	1	0	0	9	5	3	0		0	0	5.0	0.00	—	.152	.152	0	.000	-1	2	2	0	0.2

● ED LAFITTE Lafitte, Edward Francis "Doc" b: 4/7/1886, New Orleans, La. d: 4/12/71, Jenkintown, Pa. BR/TR, 6'2", 188 lbs. Deb: 4/16/09

YEAR	TM/L	W	L	PCT	G	GS	CG	SH	SV	IP	H	R	HR	HB	BB	SO	RAT	ERA	ERA+	OAV	OOB	BH	AVG	PB	PR	PR+	PD	TPI
1909	Det-A	0	1	.000	3	1	1	0	1	14	22	14	2	1	2	11	16.1	3.86	65	.344	.373	1	.250	0	-2	-2	0	-0.2
1911	Det-A	11	8	.579	29	20	15	0	1	172^{1}	205	113	2	5	52	63	13.7	3.92	88	.302	.356	11	.157	-2	-11	-8	-2	-1.2
1912	Det-A	0	0	—	1	0	0	0	0	1^{2}	2	4	0	0	2	0	21.6	16.20	20	.333	.500	0	—	0	-2	-2	0	-0.1
1914	Bro-F	18	15	.545	42	33	23	0	2	290^{2}	260	110	7	16	127	137	12.5	2.63	109	.248	.338	26	.257	3	8	8	3	1.5
1915	Bro-F	6	9	.400	17	15	7	0	1	117^{2}	126	66	6	1	57	34	14.1	3.90	70	.288	.371	14	.264	2	-15	-16	-2	-1.9
	Buf-F	2	2	.500	14	5	1	1	1	50^{1}	53	25	1	2	22	17	13.8	3.40	82	.286	.368	2	.118	-1	-4	-3	0	-0.4
	Yr	8	11	.421	31	20	8	1	2	168	179	91	7	3	79	51	14.0	3.75	73	.287	.370	16	.229	1	-19	-19	-2	-2.3
Total	5	37	35	.514	106	74	47	1	6	646^{2}	668	332	18	25	262	262	13.3	3.33	90	.276	.353	54	.220	1	-26	-24	-0	-2.3

● ED LAGGER Lagger, Edwin Joseph b: 7/14/12, Joliet, Ill. d: 11/10/81, Joliet, Ill. BR/TR, 6'3", 200 lbs. Deb: 6/15/34

YEAR	TM/L	W	L	PCT	G	GS	CG	SH	SV	IP	H	R	HR	HB	BB	SO	RAT	ERA	ERA+	OAV	OOB	BH	AVG	PB	PR	PR+	PD	TPI
1934	Phi-A	0	0	—	8	0	0	0	0	18	27	23	1	1	14	2	21.0	11.00	40	.342	.447	0	.000	-1	-13	-14	1	-0.6

● LERRIN LaGROW LaGrow, Lerrin Harris b: 7/8/48, Phoenix, Ariz. BR/TR, 6'5", 220 lbs. Deb: 7/28/70

YEAR	TM/L	W	L	PCT	G	GS	CG	SH	SV	IP	H	R	HR	HB	BB	SO	RAT	ERA	ERA+	OAV	OOB	BH	AVG	PB	PR	PR+	PD	TPI
1970	Det-A	0	1	.000	10	0	0	0	0	12^{1}	16	11	2	0	6	7	16.1	7.30	51	.308	.379	0	.000	-0	-5	-5	-0	-0.4
1972	*Det-A	0	1	.000	16	0	0	0	2	27^{1}	22	4	0	0	6	9	9.2	1.32	240	.222	.267	0	—	0	5	5	-0	0.3
1973	Det-A	1	5	.167	21	3	0	0	3	54	54	26	8	1	23	33	13.0	4.33	94	.263	.341	0	—	0	-3	-1	1	-0.1
1974	Det-A	8	19	.296	37	34	11	0	0	216^{1}	245	132	21	3	80	85	13.6	4.66	82	.287	.350	0	—	0	-25	-19	3	-2.0

YEAR	TM/L	W	L	PCT	G	GS	CG	SH	SV	IP	H	R	HR	HB	BB	SO	RAT	ERA	ERA+	OAV	OOB	BH	AVG	PB	PR	PR+	PD	TPI
1975	Det-A	7	14	.333	32	26	7	2	0	164^1	183	105	15	2	66	75	13.7	4.38	92	.280	.348	0	—	0	-11	-6	-2	-0.9
1976	StL-N	0	1	.000	8	2	1	0	0	24^1	21	4	0	1	7	10	10.7	1.48	239	.241	.305	0	.000	-1	5	6	0	0.2
1977	Chi-A	7	3	.700	66	0	0	0	25	98^2	81	32	10	1	35	63	10.7	2.46	166	.230	.302	0	—	0	18	18	1	2.7
1978	Chi-A	6	5	.545	52	0	0	0	16	88	85	47	9	3	38	41	12.9	4.40	87	.260	.342	0	—	0	-6	-6	2	-0.7
1979	Chi-A	0	3	.000	11	2	0	0	1	17^2	27	21	2	1	16	9	22.4	9.17	46	.346	.463	0	—	0	-10	-10	-0	-1.5
	LA-N	5	1	.833	31	0	0	0	4	37	38	16	2	0	18	22	13.6	3.41	107	.270	.352	1	.333	0	1	1	-0	0.2
1980	Phi-N	0	2	.000	25	0	0	0	3	39	42	22	5	0	17	21	13.6	4.15	91	.276	.349	1	.250	0	-2	-1	-0	-0.1
Total	10	34	55	.382	309	67	19	2	54	779	814	420	74	12	312	375	13.1	4.11	94	.271	.342	2	.154	-0	-32	-19	2	-2.3
● JEFF LAHTI	Lahti, Jeffrey Allen b: 10/8/56, Oregon City, Ore. BR/TR, 6′, 180 lbs. Deb: 6/27/82																											
1982	*StL-N	5	4	.556	33	1	0	0	0	56^2	53	27	3	2	21	22	12.1	3.81	95	.245	.318	1	.077	-1	-1	-1	2	-0.1
1983	StL-N	3	3	.500	53	0	0	0	0	74	64	31	2	1	29	26	11.4	3.16	115	.240	.316	0	.000	-1	4	4	1	0.3
1984	StL-N	4	2	.667	63	0	0	0	1	84^2	69	36	6	2	34	45	11.2	3.72	93	.225	.306	1	.167	-0	-1	-2	0	-0.1
1985	*StL-N	5	2	.714	52	0	0	0	19	68^1	63	15	3	0	26	41	11.7	1.84	192	.251	.321	0	.000	-1	13	13	-0	1.9
1986	StL-N	0	0	—	4	0	0	0	0	2^1	3	0	0	0	1	3	15.4	0.00	—	.333	.400	0	—	0	1	1	-0	0.0
Total	5	17	11	.607	205	1	0	0	20	286	252	109	14	5	111	137	11.6	3.12	114	.240	.316	2	.053	-3	16	14	2	2.0
● EDDIE LAKE	Lake, Edward Erving "Sparky" b: 3/18/16, Antioch, Cal. d: 6/7/95, Castro Valley, Cal. BR/TR, 5′7″, 160 lbs. Deb: 9/26/39 ♦																											
1944	Bos-A	0	0	—	6	0	0	0	0	19^1	20	13	2	3	11	7	15.8	4.19	81	.278	.395	26	.206	1	-2	-2	0	0.0
● JOE LAKE	Lake, Joseph Henry b: 1/6/1881, Brooklyn, N.Y. d: 6/30/50, Brooklyn, N.Y. BR/TR, 6′, 185 lbs. Deb: 4/21/08																											
1908	NY-A	9	22	.290	38	27	19	2	0	269^1	252	157	6	6	77	118	11.2	3.17	78	.242	.298	21	.188	0	-23	-20	-4	-2.7
1909	NY-A	14	11	.560	31	26	17	3	1	215^1	180	81	2	5	59	117	10.2	1.88	135	.225	.283	14	.173	1	14	15	5	2.6
1910	StL-A	11	17	.393	35	29	24	1	2	261^1	243	116	2	1	77	141	11.1	2.20	112	.248	.304	21	.231	2	9	8	1	1.2
1911	StL-A	10	15	.400	30	25	14	2	0	215^1	245	115	3	4	40	69	12.1	3.30	102	.282	.316	21	.262	2	1	2	6	1.0
1912	StL-A	1	7	.125	11	6	4	0	0	57	70	41	0	1	16	28	13.7	4.42	75	.314	.363	3	.150	-1	-7	-7	2	-0.8
	Det-A	9	11	.450	26	14	11	0	1	162^2	190	94	3	3	39	86	12.8	3.10	105	.296	.340	9	.145	-3	4	3	0	0.1
	Yr	10	18	.357	37	20	15	0	1	219^2	260	135	3	4	55	114	13.1	3.44	95	.301	.346	12	.146	-5	-3	-4	2	-0.7
1913	Det-A	8	7	.533	28	12	6	0	1	137	149	67	3	0	24	35	11.4	3.28	89	.278	.309	12	.267	4	-5	-6	3	0.2
Total	6	62	90	.408	199	139	95	8	5	1318	1329	671	19	20	332	594	11.5	2.85	99	.261	.309	101	.206	4	-7	-5	12	1.6
● AL LAKEMAN	Lakeman, Albert Wesley "Moose" b: 12/31/18, Cincinnati, Ohio d: 5/25/76, Spartanburg, S.C. BR/TR, 6′2″, 195 lbs. Deb: 4/19/42 C♦																											
1948	Phi-N	0	0	—	1	0	0	0	0	0^2	1	1	1	0	0	0	13.5	13.50	29	.333	.333	11	.162	0	-1	-1	-0	0.0
● JACK LAMABE	Lamabe, John Alexander b: 10/3/36, Farmingdale, N.Y. BR/TR, 6′1″, 198 lbs. Deb: 4/17/62																											
1962	Pit-N	3	1	.750	46	0	0	0	2	78	70	35	4	0	40	56	12.7	2.88	136	.238	.329	0	.000	-1	9	9	1	0.5
1963	Bos-A	7	4	.636	65	2	0	0	6	151^1	139	63	8	4	46	93	11.2	3.15	120	.247	.308	3	.094	-1	8	10	1	0.8
1964	Bos-A	9	13	.409	39	25	3	0	1	177^1	235	123	25	2	57	109	14.9	5.89	65	.318	.369	6	.115	-1	-45	-38	-0	-4.3
1965	Bos-A	0	3	.000	14	0	0	0	0	25^1	34	24	5	3	14	17	18.1	8.17	46	.340	.436	0	.000	-0	-13	-12	0	-1.3
	Hou-N	0	2	.000	3	2	0	0	0	12^2	17	9	3	0	3	6	14.2	4.26	79	.315	.351	1	.250	0	-1	-1	-0	-0.2
1966	Chi-A	7	9	.438	34	17	3	2	0	121^1	116	55	9	1	35	67	11.3	3.93	81	.251	.305	2	.057	-2	-7	-11	-0	-1.6
1967	Chi-A	1	0	1.000	3	0	0	0	0	5	7	2	0	0	1	3	14.4	1.80	172	.318	.348	0	—	0	1	1	0	0.2
	NY-N	0	3	.000	16	2	0	0	1	31^2	24	15	4	0	8	23	9.1	3.98	85	.200	.250	0	.000	-0	-2	-2	-0	-0.2
	*StL-N	3	4	.429	23	1	1	1	4	47^2	43	16	2	0	10	30	10.0	2.83	116	.244	.285	2	.200	0	3	2	-0	0.4
	Yr	3	7	.300	39	3	1	1	5	79^1	67	31	6	0	18	53	9.6	3.29	101	.226	.271	2	.133	-0	1	0	-0	0.2
1968	Chi-N	3	2	.600	42	0	0	0	1	61^1	68	33	7	1	24	30	13.6	4.26	74	.289	.358	1	.200	0	-9	-7	-1	-0.6
Total	7	33	41	.446	285	49	7	3	15	711^2	753	375	67	11	238	434	12.7	4.24	85	.272	.333	15	.096	-6	-55	-50	0	-6.3
● AL LaMACCHIA	LaMacchia, Alfred Anthony b: 7/22/21, St.Louis, Mo. BR/TR, 5′10.5″, 190 lbs. Deb: 9/27/43																											
1943	StL-A	0	1	.000	1	1	0	0	0	4	9	6	0	0	2	2	24.8	11.25	30	.450	.500	0	.000	-0	-4	-3	-0	-0.6
1945	StL-A	2	0	1.000	5	0	0	0	0	9	6	2	0	0	3	2	9.0	2.00	176	.207	.281	0	.000	-0	1	1	0	0.3
1946	StL-A	0	0	—	8	0	0	0	0	15	17	10	2	0	7	3	14.4	6.00	62	.279	.353	0	.000	-0	-4	-4	-0	-0.2
	Was-A	0	1	.000	2	0	0	0	0	2^2	6	5	1	0	2	0	27.0	16.88	20	.462	.533	0	—	0	-4	-4	-0	-0.7
	Yr	0	1	.000	10	0	0	0	0	17^2	23	15	3	0	9	3	16.3	7.64	48	.311	.386	0	.000	-0	-8	-7	-0	-0.9
Total	3	2	2	.500	16	1	0	0	0	30^2	38	23	3	0	14	7	15.3	6.46	55	.309	.380	0	.000	-1	-10	-9	-1	-1.2
● FRANK LaMANNA	LaManna, Frank "Hank" b: 8/22/19, Waterton, Pa. d: 9/1/80, Syracuse, N.Y. BR/TR, 6′2.5″, 195 lbs. Deb: 4/16/40																											
1940	Bos-N	1	0	1.000	5	1	1	0	0	13^1	13	8	1	0	8	3	14.2	4.73	79	.271	.375	1	.200	0	-1	-2	0	-0.1
1941	Bos-N	5	4	.556	35	4	0	0	1	72^2	77	52	5	1	56	23	16.6	5.33	67	.285	.410	9	.281	1	-14	-14	1	-1.4
1942	Bos-N	0	1	.000	5	0	0	0	0	6^2	5	4	1	0	3	2	10.8	5.40	62	.208	.296	0	.000	-0	-2	-2	-0	-0.3
Total	3	6	5	.545	45	5	1	0	1	92^2	95	64	7	1	67	28	15.8	5.24	68	.278	.398	10	.256	1	-17	-18	1	-1.8
● FRANK LAMANSKE	Lamanske, Frank James "Lefty" b: 9/30/06, Oglesby, Ill. d: 8/4/71, Olney, Ill. BL/TL, 5′11″, 170 lbs. Deb: 4/27/35																											
1935	Bro-N	0	0	—	2	0	0	0	0	3^2	5	3	0	0	1	1	14.7	7.36	54	.313	.353	0	.000	-0	-1	-1	0	-0.1
● WAYNE LaMASTER	LaMaster, Noble Wayne b: 2/13/07, Speed, Ind. d: 8/4/89, New Albany, Ind. BL/TL, 5′8″, 170 lbs. Deb: 4/19/37																											
1937	Phi-N	15	19	.441	50	30	10	1	4	220^1	255	139	24	2	82	135	13.8	5.31	82	.290	.352	15	.190	-2	-34	-22	-4	-3.6
1938	Phi-N	4	7	.364	18	12	1	1	0	63^2	80	58	8	3	31	35	16.1	7.77	50	.301	.380	9	.409	4	-28	-27	1	-3.3
	Bro-N	0	1	.000	3	0	0	0	0	11^1	17	6	0	0	3	3	15.9	4.76	82	.340	.377	1	.167	-0	-1	-1	-0	-0.1
	Yr	4	8	.333	21	12	1	1	0	75	97	64	8	3	34	38	16.1	7.32	53	.307	.380	10	.357	4	-29	-28	1	-3.4
Total	2	19	27	.413	71	42	11	2	4	295^1	352	203	32	5	116	173	14.4	5.82	72	.295	.360	25	.234	1	-64	-48	-4	-7.0
● JOHN LAMB	Lamb, John Andrew b: 7/20/46, Sharon, Conn. BR/TR, 6′3″, 180 lbs. Deb: 8/12/70																											
1970	Pit-N	0	1	.000	23	0	0	0	3	32^1	23	10	2	2	13	24	10.6	2.78	140	.209	.304	0	.000	-0	5	4	-1	0.1
1971	Pit-N	0	0	—	2	0	0	0	0	4^1	3	0	0	0	1	1	8.3	0.00	—	.188	.235	0	.000	-0	2	2	0	0.1
1973	Pit-N	0	1	.000	22	0	0	0	2	29^2	37	24	3	0	10	11	14.3	6.07	58	.308	.362	0	.000	-0	-8	-9	0	-0.5
Total	3	0	2	.000	47	0	0	0	5	66^1	63	34	5	2	24	36	12.1	4.07	91	.256	.327	0	.000	-1	-2	-3	-1	-0.3
● RAY LAMB	Lamb, Raymond Richard b: 12/28/44, Glendale, Cal. BR/TR, 6′1″, 175 lbs. Deb: 8/1/69																											
1969	LA-N	0	1	.000	10	0	0	0	1	15	12	3	2	0	7	11	11.4	1.80	185	.235	.328	0	.000	-0	3	3	0	0.2
1970	LA-N	6	1	.857	35	0	0	0	0	57	59	27	4	4	27	32	14.2	3.79	101	.277	.369	0	.000	-0	2	0	-1	-0.1
1971	Cle-A	6	12	.333	43	21	3	1	1	158^1	147	67	11	1	69	91	12.3	3.35	114	.247	.326	4	.093	-2	2	8	-2	0.4
1972	Cle-A	5	6	.455	34	9	0	0	0	107^2	101	42	5	1	29	64	11.0	3.09	104	.248	.299	0	.000	-1	-0	2	-1	-0.1
1973	Cle-A	3	3	.500	32	1	0	0	2	86	98	44	7	2	42	60	14.9	4.60	85	.291	.373	0	—	0	-7	-6	-0	-0.5
Total	5	20	23	.465	154	31	3	1	4	424	417	183	29	8	174	258	12.7	3.54	104	.260	.335	4	.058	-4	-1	7	-4	-0.1
● CLAYTON LAMBERT	Lambert, Clayton Patrick b: 3/26/17, Summit, Ill. d: 4/3/81, Ogden, Utah BR/TR, 6′2″, 185 lbs. Deb: 4/22/46																											
1946	Cin-N	2	2	.500	23	4	2	0	1	52^2	48	27	3	1	20	20	11.8	4.27	78	.251	.325	2	.154	-1	-5	-6	-1	-0.6
1947	Cin-N	0	0	—	3	0	0	0	0	5^2	12	10	3	0	6	1	28.6	15.88	26	.444	.545	0	.000	-0	-7	-7	0	-0.3
Total	2	2	2	.500	26	4	2	0	1	58^1	60	37	6	1	26	21	13.4	5.40	63	.275	.355	2	.143	-1	-12	-13	-1	-0.9
● GENE LAMBERT	Lambert, Eugene Marion b: 4/26/21, Crenshaw, Miss. d: 2/10/2000, Germantown, Tenn. BR/TR, 5′11″, 175 lbs. Deb: 9/14/41																											
1941	Phi-N	0	1	.000	2	1	0	0	0	9	11	2	0	0	2	3	13.0	2.00	185	.297	.333	0	.000	-0	2	2	-0	0.1
1942	Phi-N	0	0	—	1	0	0	0	0	1	3	1	0	0	0	1	27.0	9.00	37	.500	.500	0	—	0	-1	-1	0	0.0
Total	2	0	1	.000	3	1	0	0	0	10	14	3	0	0	2	4	14.4	2.70	136	.326	.356	0	.000	-0	1	1	0	0.1
● OTIS LAMBETH	Lambeth, Otis Samuel b: 5/13/1890, Berlin, Kan. d: 6/5/76, Moran, Kan. BR/TR, 6′, 175 lbs. Deb: 7/16/16																											
1916	Cle-A	4	4	.500	15	9	3	0	1	74	69	33	1	3	38	28	13.4	2.92	103	.256	.354	3	.111	-1	-1	1	-2	-0.3
1917	Cle-A	7	6	.538	26	10	2	0	2	97^1	97	48	2	11	30	27	12.8	3.14	90	.274	.349	6	.188	-0	-5	-3	-1	-0.6
1918	Cle-A	0	0	—	2	0	0	0	0	7	10	5	0	0	6	3	20.6	6.43	47	.370	.485	1	1.000	0	-3	-2	0	-0.1
Total	3	11	10	.524	43	19	5	0	3	178^1	176	86	3	14	74	58	13.3	3.18	92	.270	.357	10	.167	-1	-9	-5	-3	-1.0

YEAR TM/L	W	L	PCT	G	GS	CG	SH	SV	IP	H	R	HR	HB	BB	SO	RAT	ERA	ERA+	OAV	OOB	BH	AVG	PB	PR	PR+	PD	TPI
● FRED LAMLINE	Lamline, Frederick Arthur "Dutch" (b: Frederick Arthur Lamlein) b: 8/14/1887, Port Huron, Mich. d: 9/20/70, Port Huron, Mich. BR/TR, 5'11", 171 lbs. Deb: 9/18/12																										
1912 Chi-A	0	0	—	1	0	0	0	0	2	7	7	0	0	2	1	40.5	31.50	10	.583	.643	0	—	0	-6	-7	0	-0.3
1915 StL-N	0	0	—	4	0	0	0	0	19	21	4	0	2	3	11	12.3	1.42	196	.300	.347	1	.125	-0	3	3	0	0.1
Total 2	0	0	—	5	0	0	0	0	21	28	11	0	2	5	12	15.0	4.29	66	.341	.393	1	.125	-0	-3	-3	0	-0.2
● DENNIS LAMP	Lamp, Dennis Patrick b: 9/23/52, Los Angeles, Cal. BR/TR, 6'3", 210 lbs. Deb: 8/21/77																										
1977 Chi-N	0	2	.000	11	3	0	0	0	30	43	21	3	2	8	12	15.9	6.30	70	.344	.393	3	.375	1	-8	-6	0	-0.2
1978 Chi-N	7	15	.318	37	36	6	3	0	223^2	221	96	16	4	56	73	11.3	3.30	122	.258	.307	15	.205	0	7	16	3	1.9
1979 Chi-N	11	10	.524	38	32	6	1	0	200^1	223	96	14	5	46	86	12.3	3.50	118	.287	.331	9	.155	-1	5	13	4	1.5
1980 Chi-N	10	14	.417	41	37	2	1	0	202^2	259	123	16	1	82	83	15.2	5.20	76	.317	.380	6	.098	-3	-36	-26	2	-2.9
1981 Chi-A	7	6	.538	27	10	3	0	0	127	103	41	4	1	43	71	10.4	2.41	149	.222	.289	0	—	0	18	17	1	1.8
1982 Chi-A	11	8	.579	44	27	3	2	5	189^2	206	96	9	6	59	78	12.9	3.99	101	.279	.337	0	—	0	2	1	2	0.3
1983 *Chi-A	7	7	.500	49	5	1	0	15	116^1	123	52	6	4	29	44	12.1	3.71	113	.275	.325	0	—	0	5	6	0	0.8
1984 Tor-A	8	8	.500	56	4	0	0	9	85	97	53	9	1	38	45	14.4	4.55	90	.285	.359	0	—	0	-5	-4	1	-0.7
1985 *Tor-A	11	0	1.000	53	1	0	0	2	105^2	96	42	7	0	27	68	10.5	3.32	127	.247	.296	0	—	0	10	10	2	1.2
1986 Tor-A	2	6	.250	40	2	0	0	2	73	93	50	5	0	23	30	14.3	5.05	84	.309	.358	0	—	0	-7	-7	0	-0.7
1987 Oak-A	1	3	.250	36	5	0	0	0	56^2	76	38	5	1	22	36	15.7	5.08	81	.326	.387	0	—	0	-4	-6	-0	-0.4
1988 Bos-A	7	6	.538	46	0	0	0	0	82^2	92	39	3	2	19	49	12.3	3.48	118	.284	.328	0	—	0	5	6	1	1.0
1989 Bos-A	4	2	.667	42	0	0	0	2	112^1	96	37	4	0	27	61	9.9	2.32	177	.235	.283	0	—	0	20	21	2	1.3
1990 *Bos-A	3	5	.375	47	1	0	0	0	105^2	114	61	10	3	30	49	12.5	4.68	87	.279	.333	0	—	0	-9	-7	0	-0.4
1991 Bos-A	6	3	.667	51	0	0	0	0	92	100	54	8	3	31	57	13.1	4.70	92	.275	.337	0	—	0	-6	-4	-0	-0.4
1992 Pit-N	1	1	.500	21	0	0	0	0	28	33	16	3	2	9	15	14.1	5.14	67	.292	.355	0	.000	-0	-5	-5	0	-0.4
Total 16	96	96	.500	639	163	21	7	35	1830^2	1975	915	122	35	549	857	12.6	3.93	104	.278	.333	33	.164	-3	-9	27	18	3.7
● HENRY LAMPE	Lampe, Henry Joseph b: 9/19/1872, Boston, Mass. d: 9/16/36, Dorchester, Mass. BR/TL, 5'11.5", 175 lbs. Deb: 5/14/1894																										
1894 Bos-N	0	1	.000	2	1	0	0	0	5^1	17	19	5	0	7	1	40.5	11.81	48	.531	.615	0	.000	-0	-4	-3	0	-0.4
1895 Phi-N	0	2	.000	7	3	2	0	0	44	68	54	3	1	33	18	20.9	7.57	63	.347	.443	2	.125	-1	-14	-14	-0	-0.6
Total 2	0	3	.000	9	4	2	0	0	49^1	85	73	8	1	40	19	23.0	8.03	61	.373	.468	2	.111	-1	-17	-17	0	-1.0
● DICK LANAHAN	Lanahan, Richard Anthony b: 9/27/11, Washington, D.C. d: 3/12/75, Rochester, Minn. BL/TL, 6', 186 lbs. Deb: 9/15/35																										
1935 Was-A	0	3	.000	3	3	0	0	0	20^2	27	13	2	2	17	10	20.0	5.66	76	.314	.438	1	.167	-0	-3	-3	-0	-0.4
1937 Was-A	0	1	.000	6	2	0	0	0	11^1	16	16	2	1	13	2	23.8	12.71	35	.320	.469	0	.000	-0	-10	-11	0	-0.7
1940 Pit-N	6	8	.429	40	8	4	0	2	108	121	63	8	1	42	45	13.7	4.25	90	.279	.345	4	.118	-2	-5	-5	-0	-0.8
1941 Pit-N	0	1	.000	7	0	0	0	0	12	13	9	1	2	3	5	13.5	5.25	69	.283	.353	0	.000	-0	-2	-2	-0	-0.2
Total 4	6	13	.316	56	13	4	0	2	152	177	101	13	6	75	62	15.3	5.15	76	.288	.371	5	.119	-2	-20	-21	0	-2.1
● LES LANCASTER	Lancaster, Lester Wayne b: 4/21/62, Dallas, Tex. BR/TR, 6'2", 200 lbs. Deb: 4/7/87																										
1987 Chi-N	8	3	.727	27	18	0	0	0	132^1	138	76	14	1	51	78	12.9	4.90	87	.268	.335	4	.082	-2	-12	-9	-1	-0.9
1988 Chi-N	4	6	.400	44	3	1	0	5	85^2	89	42	4	1	34	36	13.0	3.78	95	.273	.343	1	.050	-1	-3	-2	1	-0.3
1989 *Chi-N	4	2	.667	42	0	0	0	8	72^2	60	12	2	0	15	56	9.3	1.36	276	.226	.267	2	.182	0	17	18	-1	1.8
1990 Chi-N	9	5	.643	55	6	1	1	6	109	121	57	11	1	40	65	13.4	4.62	88	.283	.346	1	.050	-1	-10	-6	1	-0.7
1991 Chi-N	9	7	.563	64	11	1	0	3	156	150	68	13	4	49	102	11.7	3.52	110	.256	.317	5	.179	0	3	6	-1	0.5
1992 Det-A	3	4	.429	41	1	0	0	0	86^2	101	66	11	3	51	35	16.1	6.33	63	.294	.389	0	—	0	-23	-23	-1	-1.7
1993 StL-N	4	1	.800	50	0	0	0	0	61^1	56	24	5	1	21	36	11.4	2.93	135	.242	.308	0	.000	-0	8	7	-1	0.5
Total 7	41	28	.594	323	39	3	1	22	703^2	715	345	60	11	261	408	12.6	4.05	98	.265	.333	13	.098	-4	-20	-7	-2	-0.8
● GARY LANCE	Lance, Gary Dean b: 9/21/48, Greenville, S.C. BB/TR, 6'3", 195 lbs. Deb: 9/28/77																										
1977 KC-A	0	1	.000	1	0	0	0	0	2	2	1	0	0	2	0	18.0	4.50	90	.286	.444	0	—	0	-0	-0	-0	0.0
● DOC LANDIS	Landis, Samuel H. b: 8/16/1854, Philadelphia, Pa. BR, 5'11", 172 lbs. Deb: 5/2/1882																										
1882 Phi-a	1	1	.500	2	2	2	0	0	17	16	12	1		1	13	9.0	3.18	94	.232	.243	2	.167	-0	-1	-0	-0	-0.1
Bal-a	11	28	.282	42	40	35	0	0	343	416	257	7		46	62	12.1	3.38	81	.281	.302	29	.166	-6	-27	-24	-2	-2.8
Yr	12	29	.293	44	42	37	0	0	360	432	269	8		47	75	12.0	3.38	82	.278	.300	31	.166	-7	-28	-24	-3	-2.9
● BILL LANDIS	Landis, William Henry b: 10/8/42, Hanford, Cal. BL/TL, 6'2", 178 lbs. Deb: 9/28/63																										
1963 KC-A	0	0	—	1	0	0	0	0	1^2	0	0	0	0	1	3	5.4	0.00	—	.000	.167	0	—	0	1	1	-0	0.0
1967 Bos-A	1	0	1.000	18	1	0	0	0	25^2	24	16	6	0	11	23	12.3	5.26	66	.253	.330	0	.000	-0	-6	-5	-1	-0.4
1968 Bos-A	3	3	.500	38	1	0	0	3	60	48	22	4	2	30	59	12.0	3.15	100	.223	.324	0	.000	-1	-1	0	-1	-0.2
1969 Bos-A	5	5	.500	45	5	0	0	1	82^1	82	53	7	3	49	50	14.6	5.25	73	.269	.375	0	.000	-0	-15	-13	0	-1.4
Total 4	9	8	.529	102	7	0	0	4	169^2	154	91	17	5	91	135	13.3	4.46	79	.248	.349	0	.000	-1	-21	-16	-2	-2.0
● LARRY LANDRETH	Landreth, Larry Robert b: 3/11/55, Stratford, Ont., Can BR/TR, 6'1", 175 lbs. Deb: 9/16/76																										
1976 Mon-N	1	2	.333	3	3	0	0	0	11	13	8	1	0	10	7	18.8	4.09	91	.310	.442	0	.000	-0	-1	-0	-0	-0.1
1977 Mon-N	0	2	.000	4	1	0	0	0	9^1	16	11	0	0	8	5	23.1	9.64	40	.381	.480	0	.000	-0	-6	-6	-0	-1.1
Total 2	1	4	.200	7	4	0	0	0	20^1	29	19	1	0	18	12	20.8	6.64	57	.345	.461	0	.000	-1	-7	-6	-1	-1.2
● JOE LANDRUM	Landrum, Joseph Butler b: 12/13/28, Columbia, S.C. BR/TR, 5'11", 180 lbs. Deb: 7/13/50 F																										
1950 Bro-N	0	0	—	7	0	0	0	1	6^2	12	8	2	1	1	5	18.9	8.10	51	.414	.452	0	—	0	-3	-3	0	-0.1
1952 Bro-N	1	3	.250	9	5	2	0	0	38	46	24	3	1	10	17	13.5	5.21	70	.301	.348	1	.125	-0	-6	-7	-0	-0.7
Total 2	1	3	.250	16	5	2	0	1	44^2	58	32	5	2	11	22	14.3	5.64	66	.319	.364	1	.125	-0	-9	-10	0	-0.8
● BILL LANDRUM	Landrum, Thomas William b: 8/17/57, Columbia, S.C. BR/TR, 6'2", 200 lbs. Deb: 8/31/86 F																										
1986 Cin-N	0	0	—	10	0	0	0	0	13^1	23	11	0	0	4	14	18.2	6.75	57	.390	.429	0	.000	-0	-4	-4	-0	-0.3
1987 Cin-N	3	2	.600	44	2	0	0	2	65	68	35	3	0	34	42	14.1	4.71	90	.292	.382	1	.200	0	-4	-3	1	-0.2
1988 Chi-N	1	0	1.000	7	0	0	0	0	12^1	19	8	1	0	3	6	16.1	5.84	62	.365	.400	0	.000	-0	-3	-3	-0	-0.3
1989 Pit-N	2	3	.400	56	0	0	0	26	81	60	18	2	0	28	51	9.8	1.67	202	.205	.275	0	.000	-0	17	16	-0	1.9
1990 *Pit-N	7	3	.700	54	0	0	0	13	71^2	69	22	4	0	21	39	11.3	2.13	170	.262	.317	1	.111	0	13	12	-0	2.1
1991 *Pit-N	4	4	.500	61	0	0	0	17	76^1	76	32	4	0	19	45	11.2	3.18	112	.252	.297	0	.000	-0	4	3	-1	0.4
1992 Mon-N	1	1	.500	18	0	0	0	0	20	27	16	3	2	9	7	17.1	7.20	48	.325	.404	0	—	0	-8	-8	-0	-0.8
1993 Cin-N	0	2	.000	18	0	0	0	0	21^2	18	9	1	0	6	14	10.0	3.74	108	.231	.286	0	—	0	1	1	1	0.1
Total 8	18	15	.545	268	2	0	0	58	361^1	360	151	18	2	124	218	12.1	3.39	109	.265	.327	2	.080	-1	14	12	-0	2.9
● JERRY LANE	Lane, Gerald Hal b: 2/7/26, Ashland, N.Y. d: 7/24/88, Chattanooga, Tenn BR/TR, 6'0.5", 205 lbs. Deb: 7/7/53																										
1953 Was-A	1	4	.200	20	2	0	0	0	56^2	64	33	3	1	16	26	12.9	4.92	79	.288	.339	1	.111	0	-6	-7	-0	-0.5
1954 Cin-N	1	0	1.000	3	0	0	0	0	10^2	9	2	0	0	3	2	10.1	1.69	248	.237	.293	0	.000	-0	3	3	-1	0.2
1955 Cin-N	0	2	.000	8	0	0	0	1	11	11	6	2	0	6	5	13.9	4.91	86	.289	.386	0	—	0	-1	-1	-0	-0.1
Total 3	2	6	.250	31	2	0	0	1	78^1	84	41	5	1	25	33	12.6	4.48	89	.282	.340	1	.077	0	-4	-4	-1	-0.4
● SAM LANFORD	Lanford, Lewis Grover b: 1/8/1886, Woodruff, S.C. d: 9/14/70, Woodruff, S.C. BR/TR, 5'7", 155 lbs. Deb: 8/19/07																										
1907 Was-A	0	1	.000	2	1	0	0	0	7	10	10	0	3	5	2	23.1	5.14	47	.333	.474	1	.333	0	-2	-2	-0	-0.3
● WALT LANFRANCONI	Lanfranconi, Walter Oswald b: 11/9/16, Barre, Vt. d: 8/18/86, Barre, Vt. BR/TR, 5'7.5", 155 lbs. Deb: 9/12/41																										
1941 Chi-N	0	1	.000	2	1	0	0	0	6	7	3	0	0	2	1	13.5	3.00	117	.280	.333	0	.000	-0	0	0	-0	0.0
1947 Bos-N	4	4	.500	36	4	1	0	1	64	65	23	2	0	27	18	12.9	2.95	132	.272	.346	0	.000	-1	**8**	**7**	1	0.8
Total 2	4	5	.444	38	5	1	0	1	70	72	26	2	0	29	19	13.0	2.96	131	.273	.345	0	.000	-1	8	7	1	0.8
● MARTY LANG	Lang, Martin John b: 9/27/05, Hooper, Neb. d: 1/13/68, Lakewood, Colo. BR/TL, 5'11", 160 lbs. Deb: 7/4/30																										
1930 Pit-N	0	0	—	2	0	0	0	0	1^2	9	10	2	0	3	2	64.8	54.00	9	.692	.750	0	—	0	-9	-9	-0	-0.4
● CHIP LANG	Lang, Robert David b: 8/21/52, Pittsburgh, Pa. BR/TR, 6'4", 205 lbs. Deb: 9/8/75																										
1975 Mon-N	0	0	—	1	1	0	0	0	1^2	2	2	0	0	3	2	27.0	10.80	36	.333	.556	0	—	0	-1	-1	-0	-0.1

YEAR	TM/L	W	L	PCT	G	GS	CG	SH	SV	IP	H	R	HR	HB	BB	SO	RAT	ERA	ERA+	OAV	OOB	BH	AVG	PB	PR	PR+	PD	TPI
1976	Mon-N	1	3	.250	29	2	0	0	0	62^1	56	32	3	3	34	30	13.4	4.19	89	.242	.347	1	.167	-0	-5	-3	0	-0.2
Total	2	1	3	.250	30	3	0	0	0	64	58	34	3	3	37	32	13.8	4.36	86	.245	.354	1	.167	-0	-6	-4	0	-0.3
● **ERV LANGE**	Lange, Erwin Henry b: 8/12/1887, Forest Park, Ill. d: 4/24/71, Maywood, Ill. BR/TR, 5'10", 170 lbs. Deb: 4/19/14																											
1914	Chi-F	12	11	.522	36	22	10	2	2	190	162	69	3	3	55	87	10.4	2.23	119	.224	.282	9	.176	2	14	10	-3	1.0
● **FRANK LANGE**	Lange, Frank Herman "Seagan" b: 10/28/1883, Columbis, Wis. d: 12/26/45, Madison, Wis. BR/TR, 5'11", 180 lbs. Deb: 5/16/10																											
1910	Chi-A	9	4	.692	23	15	6	1	0	130^2	93	48	2	9	54	98	10.7	1.65	145	.204	.301	13	.255	3	13	11	-2	1.3
1911	Chi-A	8	8	.500	29	22	8	1	0	161^2	151	77	3	3	77	104	12.9	3.23	100	.251	.339	22	.289	8	2	-0	-1	0.7
1912	Chi-A	10	10	.500	31	20	11	2	3	165^1	165	85	4	4	68	96	12.9	3.27	98	.270	.347	14	.215	2	1	-1	-1	0.0
1913	Chi-A	1	3	.250	12	3	0	0	0	40^2	46	24	0	1	20	20	14.8	4.87	60	.295	.379	3	.167	1	-9	-9	0	-0.6
Total	4	28	25	.528	95	60	25	4	3	498^1	455	234	9	17	219	318	12.5	2.96	100	.249	.335	52	.248	14	7	1	-2	1.4
● **DICK LANGE**	Lange, Richard Otto b: 9/1/48, Harbor Beach, Mich. BR/TR, 5'10", 185 lbs. Deb: 9/9/72																											
1972	Cal-A	0	0	—	2	1	0	0	0	7^2	7	4	0	0	2	8	10.6	4.70	62	.233	.281	0	.000	-0	-1	-2	0	-0.1
1973	Cal-A	2	1	.667	17	4	1	0	0	52^2	61	30	9	1	21	27	14.2	4.44	80	.292	.359	0	—	0	-4	-6	-1	-0.3
1974	Cal-A	3	8	.273	21	18	1	0	0	113^2	111	63	10	4	47	57	12.8	3.80	91	.248	.325	0	—	0	-2	-5	-1	-0.6
1975	Cal-A	4	6	.400	30	8	1	0	1	102	119	70	12	1	53	45	15.3	5.21	68	.292	.374	0	—	0	-16	-20	-0	-1.8
Total	4	9	15	.375	70	31	3	0	1	276	298	167	31	6	123	137	13.9	4.47	78	.272	.349	0	.000	-0	-23	-32	-1	-2.8
● **RICK LANGFORD**	Langford, James Rick b: 3/20/52, Farmville, Va. BR/TR, 6', 180 lbs. Deb: 6/13/76																											
1976	Pit-N	0	1	.000	12	1	0	0	0	23	27	17	2	0	14	17	16.0	6.26	56	.307	.402	1	.200	0	-7	-7	0	-0.3
1977	Oak-A	8	19	.296	37	31	6	1	0	208^1	223	107	18	2	73	141	12.9	4.02	100	.273	.334	0	—	0	1	0	1	0.2
1978	Oak-A	7	13	.350	37	24	4	2	0	175^2	169	77	15	3	56	92	11.7	3.43	106	.253	.314	0	—	0	7	4	1	0.6
1979	Oak-A	12	16	.429	34	29	14	1	0	218^2	233	114	22	4	57	101	12.1	4.28	95	.273	.322	0	—	0	-1	-6	2	-0.4
1980	Oak-A	19	12	.613	35	33	**28**	2	0	**290**	276	119	29	1	64	102	10.6	3.26	116	.255	.297	0	—	0	25	18	1	1.8
1981	*Oak-A	12	10	.545	24	24	**18**	2	0	195^1	190	81	14	3	58	84	11.6	2.99	116	.255	.311	0	—	0	15	11	-2	1.0
1982	Oak-A	11	16	.407	32	31	15	2	0	237^1	265	121	33	2	49	79	12.0	4.21	93	.281	.318	0	.000	-0	-3	-8	1	-0.8
1983	Oak-A	0	4	.000	7	7	0	0	0	20	43	28	4	2	10	2	24.7	12.15	32	.448	.509	0	—	0	-18	-19	-0	-2.8
1984	Oak-A	0	0	—	3	2	0	0	0	8^2	15	8	2	0	2	2	17.7	8.31	45	.366	.395	0	—	0	-4	-5	-0	-0.3
1985	Oak-A	3	5	.375	23	3	0	0	0	59	60	24	8	0	15	21	11.4	3.51	110	.261	.306	0	—	0	4	2	-0	0.3
1986	Oak-A	1	10	.091	16	11	0	0	0	55	69	49	13	1	18	30	14.4	7.36	53	.300	.353	0	—	0	-19	-23	-1	-3.7
Total	11	73	106	.408	260	196	85	10	0	1491	1570	745	160	18	416	671	12.1	4.01	95	.271	.322	1	.167	0	-1	-31	3	-4.4
● **MARK LANGSTON**	Langston, Mark Edward b: 8/20/60, San Diego, Cal. BR/TL, 6'2", 190 lbs. Deb: 4/7/84																											
1984	Sea-A	17	10	.630	35	33	5	2	0	225	188	99	16	8	118	**204**	12.6	3.40	118	.230	.332	0	—	0	15	15	1	1.8
1985	Sea-A	7	14	.333	24	24	2	0	0	126^2	122	85	22	2	91	72	15.3	5.47	77	.255	.376	0	—	0	-19	-17	2	-2.3
1986	Sea-A	12	14	.462	37	36	9	0	0	239^1	234	142	30	4	123	**245**	13.6	4.85	88	.255	.346	0	—	0	-18	-16	-1	-1.5
1987	Sea-A★	19	13	.594	35	35	14	3	0	272	242	132	30	5	114	**262**	11.9	3.84	123	.238	.318	0	—	0	19	26	1	2.8
1988	Sea-A	15	11	.577	35	35	9	3	0	261^1	222	108	32	3	110	235	11.5	3.34	125	.233	.314	0	—	0	18	23	3	2.5
1989	Sea-A	4	5	.444	10	10	2	1	0	73^1	60	30	3	4	19	60	10.2	3.56	113	.221	.282	0	—	0	3	4	-0	0.4
	Mon-N	12	9	.571	24	24	6	4	0	176^2	138	57	13	0	93	175	11.8	2.39	148	.218	.318	11	.172	0	22	22	-0	2.7
1990	Cal-A	10	17	.370	33	33	5	1	0	223	215	120	13	5	104	195	13.1	4.40	87	.259	.345	0	—	0	-12	-14	2	-1.3
1991	Cal-A☆	19	8	.704	34	34	7	0	0	246^1	190	89	30	2	96	183	10.5	3.00	137	.215	.293	0	—	0	30	30	3	3.2
1992	Cal-A★	13	14	.481	32	32	9	2	0	229	206	103	14	6	74	174	11.2	3.66	109	.242	.307	0	.000	-0	7	8	2	1.1
1993	Cal-A★	16	11	.593	35	35	7	0	0	256^1	220	100	22	1	85	196	10.7	3.20	142	.234	.298	0	—	0	32	36	3	3.8
1994	Cal-A	7	8	.467	18	18	2	1	0	119^1	121	67	19	0	54	109	13.2	4.68	105	.268	.346	0	—	0	2	3	2	0.5
1995	Cal-A	15	7	.682	31	31	2	1	0	200^1	212	109	21	3	64	142	12.5	4.63	102	.272	.330	0	—	0	2	2	2	0.4
1996	Cal-A	6	5	.545	18	18	2	0	0	123^1	116	68	18	2	45	83	11.9	4.82	104	.247	.316	0	—	0	2	3	2	0.4
1997	Ana-A	2	4	.333	9	9	0	0	0	47^2	61	34	8	0	29	30	17.0	5.85	78	.316	.405	0	—	0	-7	-7	1	-0.6
1998	*SD-N	4	6	.400	22	16	0	0	0	81^1	107	55	11	1	41	56	16.5	5.86	67	.325	.402	2	.083	-0	-15	-19	1	-2.0
1999	Cle-A	1	2	.333	25	5	0	0	0	61^2	69	40	9	0	29	43	14.3	5.25	96	.287	.364	1	.500	0	-3	0	0	0.0
Total	16	179	158	.531	457	428	81	18	0	2962^2	2723	1438	311	46	1289	2464	12.3	3.97	108	.246	.327	14	.152	-0	81	101	21	11.9
● **MAX LANIER**	Lanier, Hubert Max b: 8/18/15, Denton, N.C. BR/TL, 5'10", 187 lbs. Deb: 4/20/38 F																											
1938	StL-N	0	3	.000	18	3	1	0	0	45	57	30	1	2	28	14	17.4	4.20	94	.317	.414	1	.100	-0	-2	-1	-0	-0.1
1939	StL-N	2	1	.667	7	6	2	0	0	37^2	29	11	0	1	13	14	10.3	2.39	172	.220	.295	4	.286	1	6	7	-0	0.5
1940	StL-N	9	6	.600	35	11	4	2	3	105	113	50	1	1	38	49	13.0	3.34	119	.276	.339	6	.200	-0	6	7	1	1.1
1941	StL-N	10	8	.556	35	18	8	2	3	153	126	59	4	1	59	93	10.9	2.82	133	.225	.300	10	.192	-1	14	15	2	1.9
1942	*StL-N	13	8	.619	34	20	8	2	2	161	137	55	4	2	60	93	11.1	2.96	116	.234	.308	12	.255	2	6	8	1	1.4
1943	*StL-N☆	15	7	.682	32	25	14	2	3	213^1	195	62	3	2	75	123	11.5	1.90	**177**	.246	.312	12	.164	-2	**35**	**35**	0	3.6
1944	*StL-N†	17	12	.586	33	30	16	5	0	224^1	192	82	5	3	71	141	10.7	2.65	133	.234	.297	14	.182	-0	24	22	-0	2.7
1945	StL-N	2	2	.500	4	4	3	0	0	26	22	10	0	0	8	16	10.4	1.73	216	.222	.280	2	.182	-0	6	6	0	0.9
1946	StL-N	6	0	1.000	6	6	6	2	0	56	45	13	1	1	19	36	10.4	1.93	179	.228	.300	5	.200	-0	9	9	-0	1.0
1949	StL-N	5	4	.556	15	15	4	1	0	92	92	42	5	0	35	37	12.4	3.82	109	.261	.328	2	.074	-2	2	3	-1	0.1
1950	StL-N	11	9	.550	27	27	10	2	0	181^1	173	70	13	1	68	89	12.0	3.13	137	.249	.317	11	.162	-1	20	23	0	2.2
1951	StL-N	11	9	.550	31	23	9	2	1	160	149	60	14	1	50	59	11.2	3.26	122	.248	.306	8	.151	-2	12	12	0	1.3
1952	NY-N	7	12	.368	37	16	6	1	5	137	124	64	11	3	65	47	12.6	3.94	94	.244	.333	11	.268	3	-3	-4	3	0.0
1953	NY-N	0	0	—	3	0	0	0	0	5^1	8	4	1	0	3	2	18.6	6.75	64	.381	.458	0	.000	-0	-1	-1	0	-0.1
	StL-A	0	1	.000	10	1	0	0	0	22^1	28	18	2	0	19	8	18.9	7.25	58	.322	.443	1	.167	-0	-8	-7	-0	-0.4
Total	14	108	82	.568	327	204	91	21	17	1619^1	1490	630	65	18	611	821	11.8	3.01	125	.247	.318	99	.185	-3	127	134	5	16.1
● **FRANK LANKFORD**	Lankford, Frank Greenfield b: 3/26/71, Atlanta, Ga. BR/TR, 6'2", 190 lbs. Deb: 3/31/98																											
1998	LA-N	0	2	.000	12	0	0	0	1	19^2	23	13	2	2	7	7	14.6	5.95	67	.287	.360	0	.000	-0	-4	-5	1	-0.3
● **JOHNNY LANNING**	Lanning, John Young "Tobacco Chewin' Johnny" b: 9/6/10, Asheville, N.C. d: 11/8/89, Asheville, N.C. BR/TR, 6'1", 185 lbs. Deb: 4/17/36 F																											
1936	Bos-N	7	11	.389	28	20	3	1	0	153	154	75	9	0	55	33	12.3	3.65	105	.263	.326	7	.135	-2	6	3	-2	0.0
1937	Bos-N	5	7	.417	32	11	4	1	2	116^2	107	59	10	1	40	37	11.4	3.93	91	.236	.300	4	.121	-1	-0	-5	-0	-0.6
1938	Bos-N	8	7	.533	32	18	4	1	0	138	146	74	5	1	52	39	13.0	3.72	92	.267	.332	9	.188	-1	1	-5	-1	-0.6
1939	Bos-N	5	6	.455	37	6	3	0	4	129	120	53	6	2	53	45	12.2	3.42	108	.252	.329	6	.143	-1	7	4	0	0.3
1940	Pit-N	8	4	.667	38	7	2	0	2	115^2	119	59	8	0	39	42	12.3	4.05	94	.268	.327	7	.200	1	-3	-3	0	-0.2
1941	Pit-N	11	11	.500	34	23	9	0	1	175^2	175	72	6	0	47	41	11.4	3.13	116	.256	.304	6	.107	-2	10	10	1	1.1
1942	Pit-N	6	8	.429	34	8	2	1	1	119^1	125	52	7	1	26	31	11.5	3.32	102	.274	.314	4	.138	-0	-0	1	-0	0.0
1943	Pit-N	4	1	.800	12	2	0	0	2	27	23	10	0	0	9	11	10.7	2.33	149	.223	.286	1	.167	-0	3	3	-1	0.6
1945	Pit-N	0	0	—	1	0	0	0	0	2	8	8	1	0	0	0	36.0	36.00	11	.571	.571	0	—	0	-7	-7	0	-0.3
1946	Pit-N	4	5	.444	27	9	3	0	1	91	97	36	3	1	31	16	12.8	3.07	115	.269	.329	3	.143	-0	3	4	1	0.5
1947	Bos-N	0	0	—	3	0	0	0	0	3^2	4	5	0	0	6	0	24.5	9.82	40	.400	.625	0	—	0	-2	-3	0	-0.1
Total	11	58	60	.492	278	104	30	4	13	1071	1078	503	55	6	358	295	12.1	3.58	101	.261	.321	47	.146	-7	19	5	-1	0.7
● **RED LANNING**	Lanning, Lester Alfred b: 5/13/1895, Harvard, Ill. d: 6/13/62, Bristol, Conn. BL/TL, 5'9", 165 lbs. Deb: 6/20/16 ♦																											
1916	Phi-A	0	3	.000	6	3	1	0	0	24^1	38	27	1	2	17	9	21.1	8.14	35	.362	.460	6	.182	1	-14	-14	0	-1.4
● **TOM LANNING**	Lanning, Thomas Newton b: 4/22/07, Asheville, N.C. d: 11/4/67, Marietta, Ga. BL/TL, 6'1", 165 lbs. Deb: 9/14/38 F																											
1938	Phi-N	0	1	.000	3	1	0	0	0	7	9	7	0	0	2	2	14.1	6.43	60	.300	.344	1	1.000	0	-2	-2	-0	-0.2
● **GENE LANSING**	Lansing, Eugene Hewitt "Jigger" b: 1/11/1898, Albany, N.Y. d: 1/18/45, Rensselaer, N.Y. BR/TR, 6'1", 185 lbs. Deb: 4/27/22																											
1922	Bos-N	0	1	.000	15	1	0	0	0	40^2	46	28	1	0	22	14	15.0	5.98	67	.301	.389	0	.000	-1	-8	-9	-0	-0.6
● **PAUL LaPALME**	LaPalme, Paul Edmore "Lefty" b: 12/14/23, Springfield, Mass. BL/TL, 5'10", 184 lbs. Deb: 5/28/51																											
1951	Pit-N	1	5	.167	22	8	1	1	0	54^1	79	48	6	1	31	24	18.4	6.29	67	.333	.413	1	.100	-0	-14	-12	-1	-1.2
1952	Pit-N	1	2	.333	31	2	0	0	0	59^2	56	33	6	1	37	25	14.2	3.92	102	.253	.363	1	.100	-0	-1	0	1	0.0

YEAR	TM/L	W	L	PCT	G	GS	CG	SH	SV	IP	H	R	HR	HB	BB	SO	RAT	ERA	ERA+	OAV	OOB	BH	AVG	PB	PR	PR+	PD	TPI
1953	Pit-N	8	16	.333	35	24	7	1	2	176^1	191	107	20	0	64	86	13.0	4.59	97	.272	.333	5	.085	-5	-6	-2	-2	-0.9
1954	Pit-N	4	10	.286	33	15	2	0	0	120^2	147	79	15	0	54	57	15.0	5.52	76	.302	.372	5	.143	-0	-19	-17	-0	-1.8
1955	StL-N	4	3	.571	56	0	0	0	3	91^2	76	36	10	1	34	39	10.9	2.75	148	.228	.301	4	.211	0	13	13	1	1.1
1956	StL-N	0	0	—	1	0	0	0	0	0^2	4	6	0	0	2	0	81.0	81.00	5	.667	.750	0	—	0	-6	-6	-0	-0.3
	Cin-N	2	4	.333	11	2	0	0	0	27	26	14	7	0	4	4	10.0	4.67	85	.257	.286	2	.500	1	-3	-2	-0	-0.3
	Yr	2	4	.333	12	2	0	0	0	27^2	30	20	7	0	6	4	11.7	6.51	61	.280	.319	2	.500	1	-8	-7	-0	-0.6
	Chi-A	3	1	.750	29	0	0	0	2	45^2	31	14	2	0	27	23	11.4	2.36	173	.195	.312	0	.000	-1	9	9	1	0.8
1957	Chi-A	1	4	.200	35	0	0	0	7	40^1	35	16	5	1	19	19	12.3	3.35	112	.235	.325	2	.500	1	2	2	1	0.5
Total	7	24	45	.348	253	51	10	2	14	616^1	645	353	71	4	272	277	13.4	4.42	95	.269	.345	20	.136	-4	-25	-15	-0	-2.1
● ANDY LAPIHUSKA	Lapihuska, Andrew "Apples" b: 11/1/22, Delmont, N.J. d: 2/17/96, Millville, R.I. BL/TR, 5'10.5", 175 lbs. Deb: 9/12/42																											
1942	Phi-N	0	2	.000	3	2	0	0	0	20^2	17	13	0	2	13	8	13.9	5.23	63	.221	.348	2	.286	0	-4	-4	0	-0.3
1943	Phi-N	0	0	—	1	0	0	0	0	2^1	5	6	1	0	3	0	30.9	23.14	15	.417	.533	0	.000	-0	-5	-5	-0	-0.3
Total	2	0	2	.000	4	2	0	0	0	23	22	19	1	2	16	8	15.7	7.04	47	.247	.374	2	.222	0	-10	-10	0	-0.6
● DAVE LaPOINT	LaPoint, David Jeffrey b: 7/29/59, Glens Falls, N.Y. BL/TL, 6'3", 215 lbs. Deb: 9/10/80																											
1980	Mil-A	1	0	1.000	5	3	0	0	1	15	17	14	2	0	13	5	18.0	6.00	65	.293	.423	0	—	0	-3	-4	-1	-0.3
1981	StL-N	1	0	1.000	3	2	0	0	0	10^2	12	5	1	1	3	4	12.7	4.22	84	.293	.341	0	.000	-1	-1	-1	0	-0.1
1982	*StL-N	9	3	.750	42	21	0	0	0	152^2	170	63	8	3	52	81	13.3	3.42	106	.290	.350	2	.053	-3	3	4	-3	-0.4
1983	StL-N	12	9	.571	37	29	1	0	0	191^1	191	92	12	4	84	113	13.1	3.95	92	.267	.347	9	.153	1	-7	-7	-1	-0.7
1984	StL-N	12	10	.545	33	33	2	1	0	193	205	94	9	1	77	130	13.2	3.96	88	.278	.347	4	.068	-3	-8	-11	-2	-1.6
1985	SF-N	7	17	.292	31	31	2	1	0	206^2	215	99	18	0	74	122	12.6	3.57	96	.269	.331	10	.167	2	1	-3	-2	-0.3
1986	Det-A	3	6	.333	16	8	0	0	0	67^2	85	49	11	0	32	36	15.6	5.72	72	.307	.379	0	—	0	-12	-12	-1	-1.4
	SD-N	1	4	.200	24	4	0	0	0	61^1	67	37	8	1	24	41	13.5	4.26	86	.276	.343	0	.000	-1	-4	-4	-0	-0.4
1987	StL-N	1	1	.500	6	2	0	0	0	16	26	12	4	0	5	8	17.4	6.75	62	.351	.392	0	.000	-0	-5	-5	0	-0.5
	Chi-A	6	3	.667	14	12	2	1	0	82^2	69	29	7	1	31	43	11.0	2.94	156	.224	.297	0	—	0	14	15	2	1.6
1988	Chi-A	10	11	.476	25	25	1	1	0	161^1	151	69	10	2	47	79	11.2	3.40	117	.245	.300	0	—	0	10	10	-2	1.0
	Pit-N	4	2	.667	8	8	1	0	0	52	54	18	4	0	10	19	11.1	2.77	123	.271	.306	1	.063	-1	4	4	0	0.3
1989	NY-A	6	9	.400	20	20	0	0	0	113^2	146	73	12	2	45	51	15.3	5.62	69	.310	.373	0	—	0	-22	-22	-2	-2.7
1990	NY-A	7	10	.412	28	27	2	0	0	157^2	180	84	11	1	57	67	13.6	4.11	97	.292	.353	0	—	0	-3	-2	-0	-0.2
1991	Phi-N	0	1	.000	2	2	0	0	0	5	10	10	0	1	6	3	30.6	16.20	23	.435	.567	0	.000	-0	-7	-7	0	-1.0
Total	12	80	86	.482	294	227	11	4	1	1486^2	1598	748	117	17	559	802	13.2	4.02	93	.277	.343	26	.104	-6	-39	-45	-12	-6.7
● YOVANNY LARA	Lara, Yovanny B. b: 9/20/75, San Cristobal, D.R. BR/TR, 6'4", 180 lbs. Deb: 6/28/2000																											
2000	Mon-N	0	0	—	6	0	0	0	0	5^2	5	4	0	0	8	3	20.6	6.35	74	.250	.464	0	—	0	-1	-1	-0	-0.1
● ANDY LARKIN	Larkin, Andrew Dane b: 6/27/74, Chelan, Wash. BR/TR, 6'4", 180 lbs. Deb: 9/29/96																											
1996	Fla-N	0	0	—	1	1	0	0	0	5	3	1	0	1	4	2	14.4	1.80	226	.176	.364	0	.000	-0	1	1	-0	0.0
1998	Fla-N	3	8	.273	17	14	0	0	0	74^2	101	87	12	4	55	43	19.3	9.64	42	.329	.437	4	.138	-1	-45	-48	-0	-5.4
2000	Cin-N	0	0	—	3	0	0	0	0	6^2	6	4	1	0	5	7	14.9	5.40	88	.240	.367	0	.000	-0	-1	-0	-0	0.0
	KC-A	0	3	.000	18	0	0	0	1	19^1	29	20	5	0	11	17	18.6	8.84	57	.349	.426	0	—	0	-8	-8	-0	-1.1
Total	3	3	11	.214	39	15	0	0	1	105^2	139	112	18	5	75	69	18.7	8.86	48	.322	.428	4	.125	-1	-52	-55	-0	-6.5
● TERRY LARKIN	Larkin, Frank S. d: 9/16/1894, Brooklyn, N.Y. BR/TR, Deb: 5/20/1876 ♦																											
1876	NY-N	0	1	.000	1	1	1	0	0	9	9	7	0		0	0	9.0	3.00	71	.231	.231	0	.000	-1	-1	-1	-0	-0.2
1877	Har-N	29	25	.537	56	56	55	4	0	501	510	285	2		53	96	10.1	2.14	114	**.245**	.264	52	.228	6	37	19	-1	2.0
1878	Chi-N	29	26	.527	56	56	56	1	0	506	511	288	4		31	163	9.6	2.24	108	.246	.257	65	.288	13	4	10	-4	1.7
1879	Chi-N	31	23	.574	58	58	57	4	0	513^1	514	277	5		30	142	9.5	2.44	105	.240	**.250**	50	.219	1	3	7	-7	0.1
1880	Tro-N	0	5	.000	5	5	3	0	0	38	83	65	1		10	5	22.0	8.76	29	.421	.449	3	.150	-0	-27	-25	0	-2.2
Total	5	89	80	.527	176	176	172	9	0	1567^1	1627	922	12		124	406	10.1	2.43	102	.249	.263	198	.234	19	17	10	-12	1.4
● PAT LARKIN	Larkin, Patrick Clibborn b: 6/14/60, Arcadia, Cal. BL/TL, 6', 180 lbs. Deb: 7/16/83																											
1983	SF-N	0	0	—	5	0	0	0	0	10^1	13	6	1	2	3	6	15.7	4.35	81	.317	.391	0	.000	-0	-1	-1	-0	-0.1
● STEVE LARKIN	Larkin, Stephen Patrick b: 12/9/10, Cincinnati, Ohio d: 5/2/69, Norristown, Pa. BR/TR, 6'1", 195 lbs. Deb: 5/6/34																											
1934	Det-A	0	0	—	2	1	0	0	0	6	8	7	0	0	5	8	19.5	1.50	293	.296	.406	1	.333	1	2	2	0	0.2
● DAVE LaROCHE	LaRoche, David Eugene b: 5/14/48, Colorado Springs, Colo. BL/TL, 6'2", 200 lbs. Deb: 5/11/70 C																											
1970	Cal-A	4	1	.800	38	0	0	0	4	49^2	41	20	6	4	21	44	12.0	3.44	105	.224	.317	2	.250	1	2	1	0	0.3
1971	Cal-A	5	1	.833	56	0	0	0	9	72	55	21	3	1	27	63	10.4	2.50	130	.212	.289	1	.091	-0	8	6	-1	0.6
1972	Min-A	5	7	.417	62	0	0	0	10	95^1	72	33	9	6	39	79	11.0	2.83	114	.209	.300	1	.091	0	3	4	0	0.6
1973	Chi-N	4	1	.800	45	0	0	0	4	54^1	55	37	7	1	29	34	14.1	5.80	68	.274	.368	2	.500	1	-13	-10	1	-0.8
1974	Chi-N	5	6	.455	49	4	0	0	5	92	103	54	9	3	47	49	15.0	4.79	80	.286	.373	9	.333	3	-12	-9	-0	-0.9
1975	Cle-A	5	3	.625	61	0	0	0	17	82^1	61	26	5	2	57	94	13.1	2.19	173	.210	.344	0	—	0	15	15	1	2.2
1976	Cle-A☆	1	4	.200	61	0	0	0	21	96^1	57	25	2	1	49	104	10.0	2.24	156	.175	.285	0	—	0	14	14	-1	1.3
1977	Cle-A	2	2	.500	13	0	0	0	4	18^2	15	13	3	0	7	18	10.6	5.30	75	.234	.310	0	—	0	-3	-3	-0	-0.6
	Cal-A★	6	5	.545	46	0	0	0	13	81^1	64	31	8	2	37	61	11.4	3.10	127	.218	.310	0	—	0	9	8	-0	1.2
	Yr	8	7	.533	59	0	0	0	17	100	79	44	11	2	44	79	11.3	3.51	112	.221	.310	0	—	0	6	5	-0	0.6
1978	Cal-A	10	9	.526	59	0	0	0	25	95^2	73	35	7	2	48	70	11.6	2.82	128	.215	.316	0	—	0	10	9	-0	1.8
1979	*Cal-A	7	11	.389	53	1	0	0	10	85^2	107	54	13	2	32	59	14.8	5.57	73	.314	.376	0	—	0	-13	-15	1	-2.7
1980	Cal-A	3	5	.375	52	9	1	0	4	128	122	62	14	3	39	89	11.5	4.08	97	.256	.317	0	—	0	-0	-2	-1	-0.2
1981	*NY-A	4	1	.800	26	1	0	0	0	47	38	16	3	1	16	24	10.5	2.49	144	.229	.301	0	—	0	6	6	-1	0.5
1982	NY-A	4	2	.667	25	0	0	0	0	50	54	19	4	1	11	31	11.9	3.42	117	.273	.314	0	—	0	4	3	-0	0.3
1983	NY-A	0	0	—	1	0	0	0	0	1	2	2	1	0	0	0	18.0	18.00	22	.400	.400	0	—	0	-2	-2	0	-0.1
Total	14	65	58	.528	647	15	1	0	126	1049^1	919	448	94	29	459	819	12.1	3.53	106	.239	.325	15	.246	4	27	23	-1	3.5
● JOHN LaROSE	LaRose, Henry John b: 10/25/51, Pawtucket, R.I. BL/TL, 6'1", 185 lbs. Deb: 9/20/78																											
1978	Bos-A	0	0	—	1	0	0	0	0	2	3	5	1	0	3	0	27.0	22.50	18	.375	.545	0	—	0	-4	-4	0	-0.2
● DON LARSEN	Larsen, Don James b: 8/7/29, Michigan City, Ind. BR/TR, 6'4", 227 lbs. Deb: 4/18/53																											
1953	StL-A	7	12	.368	38	22	7	2	2	192^2	201	99	11	4	64	96	12.6	4.16	101	.267	.328	23	.284	5	-3	1	-1	0.8
1954	Bal-A	3	21	.125	29	28	12	1	0	201^2	213	106	18	1	89	80	13.5	4.37	82	.274	.349	22	.250	8	-15	-18	0	-1.1
1955	*NY-A	9	2	.818	19	13	5	1	2	97	81	38	8	2	51	44	12.4	3.06	122	.229	.329	6	.146	2	10	8	-1	1.0
1956	*NY-A	11	5	.688	38	20	6	1	1	179^2	133	72	19	7	96	107	11.8	3.26	119	.204	.313	19	.241	6	18	13	-1	1.6
1957	*NY-A	10	4	.714	27	20	4	1	0	139^2	113	68	12	0	87	81	12.9	3.74	96	.220	.333	14	.250	5	1	-2	-0	0.2
1958	*NY-A	9	6	.600	19	19	5	3	0	114^1	100	43	4	4	52	55	12.3	3.07	115	.233	.322	15	.306	9	9	6	-1	1.5
1959	NY-A	6	7	.462	25	18	3	1	0	124^2	122	65	14	2	76	69	14.4	4.33	84	.260	.365	12	.255	4	-7	-10	-0	-0.6
1960	KC-A	1	10	.091	22	15	0	0	0	83^2	97	55	11	0	42	43	15.0	5.38	74	.293	.373	6	.207	0	-14	-13	-1	-1.6
1961	KC-A	1	0	1.000	8	1	0	0	0	15	21	9	2	1	11	13	19.8	4.20	100	.344	.452	6	.300	1	-0	-0	0	0.2
	Chi-A	7	2	.778	25	3	0	0	2	74^1	64	36	5	1	29	53	11.4	4.12	95	.231	.306	8	.320	3	-1	-2	0	0.1
	Yr	8	2	.800	33	4	0	0	2	89^1	85	45	7	2	40	66	12.8	4.13	96	.251	.334	14	.311	4	-1	-2	0	0.3
1962	*SF-N	5	4	.556	49	0	0	0	11	86^1	83	44	9	2	47	58	13.8	4.38	87	.256	.354	5	.200	1	-4	-6	0	-0.6
1963	SF-N	7	7	.500	46	0	0	0	3	62	46	23	8	0	30	44	11.0	3.05	105	.203	.296	2	.182	0	2	1	0	0.3
1964	SF-N	0	1	.000	6	0	0	0	0	10^1	10	5	0	0	6	6	13.9	4.35	82	.256	.356	0	.000	-0	-1	-1	-0	-0.1
	Hou-N	4	8	.333	30	10	2	1	1	103^1	92	36	4	1	20	58	9.8	2.26	151	.233	.272	3	.097	0	15	14	0	1.7
	Yr	4	9	.308	36	10	2	1	1	113^2	102	41	4	1	26	64	10.2	2.45	140	.235	.280	3	.094	0	14	13	0	1.6
1965	Hou-N	0	0	—	1	1	0	0	0	5^1	8	3	0	0	3	1	18.6	5.06	66	.348	.423	0	.000	-0	-1	-1	0	0.0
	Bal-A	1	2	.333	27	1	0	0	1	54	53	22	4	1	20	40	12.3	2.67	130	.255	.323	3	.273	1	5	5	1	0.5
1967	Chi-N	0	0	—	3	0	0	0	0	4	5	4	1	0	2	1	15.8	9.00	39	.333	.412	0	—	0	-3	-2	0	-0.1
Total	14	81	91	.471	412	171	44	11	23	1548	1442	728	130	26	725	849	12.8	3.78	99	.247	.332	144	.242	46	10	-9	-1	3.8

YEAR	TM/L	W	L	PCT	G	GS	CG	SH	SV	IP	H	R	HR	HB	BB	SO	RAT	ERA	ERA+	OAV	OOB	BH	AVG	PB	PR	PR+	PD	TPI
● DAN LARSON	Larson, Daniel James b: 7/4/54, Los Angeles, Cal. BR/TR, 6′, 180 lbs. Deb: 7/18/76																											
1976	Hou-N	5	8	.385	13	13	5	0	0	92^1	81	40	3	1	28	42	10.7	3.02	106	.236	.296	9	.290	4	5	2	0	0.7
1977	Hou-N	1	7	.125	32	10	1	0	1	97^2	108	72	13	2	45	44	14.3	5.81	62	.280	.358	6	.214	1	-21	-27	0	-1.9
1978	Phi-N	0	0	—	1	0	0	0	0	1	1	1	1	0	1	2	18.0	9.00	40	.250	.400	0	—	0	-1	-1	0	0.0
1979	Phi-N	1	1	.500	3	3	0	0	0	19	17	9	1	1	9	9	12.8	4.26	90	.250	.346	0	.000	-1	-1	-1	0	-0.1
1980	Phi-N	0	5	.000	12	7	0	0	0	45^2	46	24	4	0	24	17	13.8	3.15	120	.271	.361	2	.154	0	2	3	-1	0.3
1981	Phi-N	3	0	1.000	5	4	1	0	0	28	27	13	4	0	15	15	13.5	4.18	87	.260	.353	1	.111	0	-2	-2	-0	-0.2
1982	Chi-N	0	4	.000	12	6	0	0	0	39^2	51	30	4	2	18	22	16.1	5.67	66	.327	.403	3	.273	0	-9	-8	1	-0.6
Total	7	10	25	.286	78	43	7	0	1	323^1	331	189	30	6	140	151	13.3	4.40	81	.269	.346	21	.216	4	-26	-32	1	-1.8
● AL LARY	Lary, Alfred Allen b: 9/26/28, Northport, Ala. BR/TR, 6′3″, 185 lbs. Deb: 9/6/54 F♦																											
1954	Chi-N	0	0	—	1	1	0	0	0	6	3	2	0	0	7	4	15.0	3.00	140	.150	.370	1	.500	0	1	1	0	0.1
1962	Chi-N	0	1	.000	15	3	0	0	0	34	42	27	5	0	15	18	15.1	7.15	58	.311	.380	1	.167	0	-12	-11	-0	-0.5
Total	2	0	1	.000	16	4	0	0	0	40	45	29	5	0	22	22	15.1	6.52	64	.290	.379	2	.250	1	-11	-10	-0	-0.4
● FRANK LARY	Lary, Frank Strong "Mule" or "The Yankee Killer" b: 4/10/30, Northport, Ala. BR/TR, 5′11″, 180 lbs. Deb: 9/14/54 F																											
1954	Det-A	0	0	—	3	0	0	0	0	3^2	4	1	0	0	3	5	17.2	2.45	150	.286	.412	0	—	0	1	1	-0	0.0
1955	Det-A	14	15	.483	36	31	16	2	1	235	232	100	10	6	89	98	12.5	3.10	124	.262	.334	16	.195	1	22	20	1	2.6
1956	Det-A	**21**	13	.618	41	38	20	3	1	**294**	289	116	20	12	116	165	12.8	3.15	131	.257	.333	19	.184	0	33	32	-0	3.4
1957	Det-A	11	16	.407	40	35	12	2	3	237^2	250	111	23	12	72	107	12.6	3.98	97	.276	.337	9	.123	-3	-5	-3	0	-0.6
1958	Det-A	16	15	.516	39	34	**19**	3	1	**260^1**	249	91	20	12	68	131	11.4	2.90	139	.251	.307	15	.170	-1	25	31	-0	3.4
1959	Det-A	17	10	.630	32	32	11	3	0	223	225	109	23	11	46	137	11.4	3.55	114	.261	.307	10	.125	-2	8	12	-0	1.1
1960	Det-A★	15	15	.500	38	36	**15**	2	1	**274^1**	262	125	25	19	62	149	11.3	3.51	113	.249	.302	17	.183	4	11	13	-2	1.6
1961	Det-A★	23	9	.719	36	36	**22**	4	0	275^1	252	117	24	6	66	146	10.6	3.24	127	.243	.293	25	.231	4	24	26	4	3.6
1962	Det-A	2	6	.250	17	14	2	1	0	80	98	59	17	4	21	41	13.8	5.74	71	.297	.346	4	.167	1	-16	-14	-1	-1.3
1963	Det-A	4	9	.308	16	14	6	0	0	107^1	90	40	15	5	26	46	10.1	3.27	114	.226	.281	8	.229	1	4	5	1	0.9
1964	Det-A	0	2	.000	6	4	0	0	0	18	24	15	3	3	10	6	18.5	7.00	52	.316	.416	0	.000	-1	-7	-7	-1	-0.8
	NY-N	2	3	.400	13	8	3	1	1	57^1	62	33	7	4	14	27	12.6	4.55	79	.279	.333	2	.118	1	-6	-6	-0	-0.5
	Mil-N	1	0	1.000	5	2	0	0	0	12^1	15	7	4	0	0	4	10.9	4.38	80	.306	.306	0	.000	-0	-1	-1	1	0.0
	Yr	3	3	.500	18	10	3	1	1	69^2	77	40	11	4	14	31	12.3	4.52	79	.284	.329	2	.100	0	-8	-7	0	-0.5
1965	NY-N	1	3	.250	14	7	0	0	1	57^1	48	24	2	1	16	23	10.2	2.98	118	.233	.291	4	.211	0	4	3	0	0.3
	Chi-A	1	0	1.000	14	1	0	0	2	26^2	23	12	4	2	7	14	10.8	4.05	79	.230	.294	1	.500	0	-2	-3	0	-0.1
Total	12	128	116	.525	350	292	126	21	11	2162^1	2123	960	197	97	616	1099	11.8	3.49	113	.257	.316	130	.177	5	95	110	3	13.6
● FRED LASHER	Lasher, Frederick Walter b: 8/19/41, Poughkeepsie, N.Y. BR/TR, 6′4″, 210 lbs. Deb: 4/12/63																											
1963	Min-A	0	0	—	11	0	0	0	0	11^1	12	10	1	0	11	10	18.3	4.76	76	.286	.434	0	.000	-0	-1	-1	0	0.0
1967	Det-A	2	1	.667	17	0	0	0	9	30	25	14	1	1	11	28	11.1	3.90	84	.221	.296	1	.111	-0	-2	-2	-0	-0.4
1968	*Det-A	5	1	.833	34	0	0	0	5	48^2	37	19	5	0	22	32	10.9	3.33	90	.215	.304	1	.111	-0	-2	-2	1	-0.2
1969	Det-A	2	1	.667	32	0	0	0	0	44	34	16	5	2	22	26	11.9	3.07	122	.224	.330	0	.000	-0	3	3	0	0.2
1970	Det-A	1	3	.250	12	0	0	0	3	9	10	6	0	1	12	8	23.0	5.00	75	.278	.469	0	.000	-0	-1	-1	0	-0.3
	Cle-A	1	7	.125	43	1	0	0	5	57^2	57	34	6	3	30	44	14.0	4.06	98	.264	.361	0	.000	-1	-2	-1	-1	-0.3
	Yr	2	10	.167	55	1	0	0	8	66^2	67	40	6	4	42	52	15.3	4.18	94	.266	.379	0	.000	-1	-3	-2	-1	-0.6
1971	Cal-A	0	0	—	2	0	0	0	0	1^1	4	4	0	0	2	0	40.5	27.00	12	.667	.750	0	—	0	-3	-4	-0	-0.2
Total	6	11	13	.458	151	1	0	0	22	202	179	103	18	7	110	148	13.2	3.88	91	.243	.347	2	.063	-2	-10	-7	0	-1.2
● BILL LASKEY	Laskey, William Alan b: 12/20/57, Toledo, Ohio BR/TR, 6′5″, 190 lbs. Deb: 4/23/82																											
1982	SF-N	13	12	.520	32	31	7	1	0	189^1	186	74	14	2	43	88	11.0	3.14	115	.261	.304	8	.129	-2	10	10	0	1.1
1983	SF-N	13	10	.565	25	25	1	0	0	148^1	151	75	18	3	45	81	12.1	4.19	85	.266	.323	5	.106	0	-9	-11	-1	-1.6
1984	SF-N	9	14	.391	35	34	2	0	0	207^2	222	112	20	6	50	71	12.0	4.33	81	.273	.320	4	.063	-3	-17	-19	-3	-2.5
1985	SF-N	5	11	.313	19	19	0	0	0	114	110	55	10	0	39	42	11.8	3.55	97	.255	.317	4	.133	1	1	-1	0	-0.1
	Mon-N	0	5	.000	11	7	0	0	0	34^1	55	36	9	2	14	18	18.6	9.44	36	.362	.423	1	.143	-0	-22	-24	1	-2.9
	Yr	5	16	.238	30	26	0	0	0	148^1	165	91	19	2	53	60	13.3	4.91	70	.283	.345	5	.135	0	-22	-26	1	-3.0
1986	SF-N	1	1	.500	20	0	0	0	1	27^1	28	14	5	0	13	8	13.5	4.28	82	.275	.357	0	.000	-0	-2	-2	0	-0.2
1988	Cle-A	1	0	1.000	17	0	0	0	1	24^1	32	16	0	0	6	17	14.1	5.18	80	.320	.358	0	—	0	-3	-3	0	-0.1
Total	6	42	53	.442	159	116	10	1	2	745^1	784	382	76	13	210	325	12.2	4.14	86	.272	.325	22	.105	-4	-43	-50	-2	-6.3
● BILL LASLEY	Lasley, Willard Almond b: 7/13/02, Gallipolis, Ohio d: 8/21/90, Seattle, Wash. BB/TR, 6′, 175 lbs. Deb: 9/19/24																											
1924	StL-A	0	0	—	2	0	0	0	0	4	7	3	0	0	2	0	20.3	6.75	67	.412	.474	0	.000	-0	-1	-1	-0	-0.1
● TOM LASORDA	Lasorda, Thomas Charles b: 9/22/27, Norristown, Pa. BL/TL, 5′10″, 175 lbs. Deb: 8/5/54 MCH																											
1954	Bro-N	0	0	—	4	0	0	0	0	9	8	5	2	0	5	5	13.0	5.00	82	.242	.342	0	.000	-0	-1	-1	-0	-0.1
1955	Bro-N	0	0	—	4	1	0	0	0	4	5	6	1	1	6	4	27.0	13.50	30	.313	.522	0	—	0	-4	-4	-0	-0.2
1956	KC-A	0	4	.000	18	5	0	0	1	45^1	40	38	6	3	45	28	17.5	6.15	70	.240	.409	1	.077	-1	-10	-9	0	-0.8
Total	3	0	4	.000	26	6	0	0	1	58^1	53	49	9	4	56	37	17.4	6.48	66	.245	.409	1	.071	-2	-15	-14	0	-1.1
● BILL LATHAM	Latham, William Carol b: 8/29/60, Birmingham, Ala. BL/TL, 6′2″, 190 lbs. Deb: 4/15/85																											
1985	NY-N	1	3	.250	7	3	0	0	0	22^2	21	10	1	0	7	10	11.1	3.97	87	.250	.308	1	.333	1	-1	-1	1	-0.1
1986	Min-A	0	1	.000	7	2	0	0	0	16	24	14	1	1	6	8	17.4	7.31	59	.358	.419	0	—	0	-6	-5	-1	-0.3
Total	2	1	4	.200	14	5	0	0	0	38^2	45	24	2	1	13	18	13.7	5.35	71	.298	.358	1	.333	1	-6	-7	0	-0.4
● BILL LATHROP	Lathrop, William George b: 8/12/1891, Hanover, Wis. d: 11/20/58, Janesville, Wis. BR/TR, 6′2.5″, 184 lbs. Deb: 7/29/13																											
1913	Chi-A	0	1	.000	6	0	0	0	0	17	16	11	0	1	12	9	15.4	4.24	69	.262	.392	0	.000	-1	-2	-2	0	-0.2
1914	Chi-A	1	2	.333	19	1	0	0	0	47^2	41	20	0	2	19	7	11.7	2.64	102	.241	.325	0	.000	-1	1	0	1	-0.1
Total	2	1	3	.250	25	1	0	0	0	64^2	57	31	0	3	31	16	12.7	3.06	90	.247	.343	0	.000	-2	-2	-2	1	-0.3
● BARRY LATMAN	Latman, Arnold Barry b: 5/21/36, Los Angeles, Cal. BR/TR, 6′3″, 210 lbs. Deb: 9/10/57																											
1957	Chi-A	1	2	.333	7	2	0	0	1	12^1	12	11	2	1	13	9	19.0	8.03	47	.267	.441	0	.000	-0	-6	-6	0	-1.1
1958	Chi-A	3	0	1.000	13	3	1	1	0	47^2	27	7	1	1	17	28	8.5	0.76	481	.162	.243	1	.083	-0	16	16	-1	0.8
1959	Chi-A	8	5	.615	37	21	5	2	0	156	138	71	15	4	72	97	12.3	3.75	100	.235	.323	6	.128	-1	2	0	-3	-0.4
1960	Cle-A	7	7	.500	31	20	4	0	0	147^1	146	78	19	6	72	94	13.7	4.03	93	.258	.348	9	.220	1	-3	-5	-1	-0.4
1961	Cle-A☆	13	5	.722	45	18	4	2	5	176^2	163	84	23	5	54	108	11.3	4.02	98	.244	.306	4	.073	-3	-0	-2	-3	-0.8
1962	Cle-A	8	13	.381	45	21	7	1	5	179^1	179	96	23	5	72	117	12.8	4.17	93	.261	.336	10	.189	2	-4	-6	-1	-0.5
1963	Cle-A	7	12	.368	38	21	4	2	2	149^1	146	90	23	6	52	133	12.3	4.94	73	.257	.325	8	.182	2	-22	-22	3	-2.1
1964	LA-A	6	10	.375	40	18	2	1	2	138	128	72	15	7	52	81	12.2	3.85	85	.244	.321	5	.125	-1	-3	-10	-1	-1.2
1965	Cal-A	1	1	.500	18	0	0	0	0	31^2	30	12	3	0	16	18	13.1	2.84	120	.254	.343	0	.000	-0	2	2	-1	0.0
1966	Hou-N	2	7	.222	31	9	1	1	1	103	88	42	5	7	35	74	11.4	2.71	126	.233	.310	4	.154	0	10	9	-0	0.7
1967	Hou-N	3	6	.333	39	1	0	0	0	77^2	73	42	13	6	34	70	13.1	4.52	73	.252	.342	1	.091	-1	-10	-11	0	-1.2
Total	11	59	68	.465	344	134	28	10	16	1219	1130	605	142	48	489	829	12.3	3.91	94	.246	.325	48	.145	-1	-17	-35	-8	-6.2
● BILL LATTIMORE	Lattimore, William Hershel "Slothful Bill" b: 5/25/1884, Roxton, Tex. d: 10/30/19, Colorado Springs, Colo. BL/TL, 5′9″, 165 lbs. Deb: 4/17/08																											
1908	Cle-A	1	2	.333	4	4	1	1	0	24	24	16	0	0	7	5	11.6	4.50	53	.247	.298	4	.444	1	-6	-6	-1	-0.6
● CHUCK LAUER	Lauer, John Charles b: 1865, Pittsburgh, Pa. TR, Deb: 7/17/1884 ♦																											
1884	Pit-a	0	2	.000	3	3	2	0	0	19	23	25	0	3	9	8	16.6	7.58	44	.277	.368	5	.114	-1	-9	-9	-1	-0.8
● GEORGE LAUZERIQUE	Lauzerique, George Albert b: 7/22/47, Havana, Cuba BR/TR, 6′1″, 180 lbs. Deb: 9/17/67																											
1967	KC-A	0	2	.000	3	2	0	0	0	16	11	4	2	1	6	10	10.1	2.25	142	.193	.281	0	.000	-0	2	2	0	0.2
1968	Oak-A	0	0	—	1	0	0	0	0	1	0	0	0	0	1	0	9.0	0.00	—	.000	.333	0	—	0	0	0	0	0.0
1969	Oak-A	3	4	.429	19	8	1	0	0	61^1	58	32	14	2	27	39	12.8	4.70	73	.250	.333	2	.100	-1	-7	-9	1	-1.0
1970	Mil-A	1	2	.333	11	4	1	0	0	35	41	27	7	1	14	24	14.4	6.94	55	.295	.364	2	.200	1	-13	-12	-0	-0.9
Total	4	4	8	.333	34	14	2	0	0	113^1	110	63	23	4	48	73	12.9	5.00	70	.256	.336	4	.121	-0	-18	-19	1	-1.7

YEAR	TM/L	W	L	PCT	G	GS	CG	SH	SV	IP	H	R	HR	HB	BB	SO	RAT	ERA	ERA+	OAV	OOB	BH	AVG	PB	PR	PR+	PD	TPI

● GARY LAVELLE Lavelle, Gary Robert b: 1/3/49, Scranton, Pa. BB/TL, 6'1", 200 lbs. Deb: 9/10/74

YEAR	TM/L	W	L	PCT	G	GS	CG	SH	SV	IP	H	R	HR	HB	BB	SO	RAT	ERA	ERA+	OAV	OOB	BH	AVG	PB	PR	PR+	PD	TPI
1974	SF-N	0	3	.000	10	0	0	0	0	16^2	14	7	1	0	10	12	13.0	2.16	176	.222	.329	0	.000	-0	3	3	-0	0.4
1975	SF-N	6	3	.667	65	0	0	0	8	82^1	80	30	3	3	48	51	14.3	2.95	129	.260	.365	1	.111	-0	6	7	0	0.9
1976	SF-N	10	6	.625	65	0	0	0	12	110^1	102	37	6	2	52	71	12.7	2.69	135	.246	.333	1	.077	-1	10	11	-2	1.6
1977	SF-N★	7	7	.500	73	0	0	0	20	118^1	106	35	4	0	37	93	10.9	2.05	191	.239	.298	0	.000	-2	24	24	1	3.5
1978	SF-N	13	10	.565	67	0	0	0	14	97^2	96	41	3	2	44	63	13.1	3.32	104	.263	.345	1	.067	-1	3	2	0	0.3
1979	SF-N	7	9	.438	70	0	0	0	20	96^2	86	31	5	2	42	80	12.1	2.51	139	.247	.332	1	.250	0	13	11	0	2.3
1980	SF-N	6	8	.429	62	0	0	0	9	100	106	43	4	0	36	66	12.8	3.42	104	.275	.336	0	.000	-1	2	1	0	0.1
1981	SF-N	2	6	.250	34	3	0	0	4	65^2	58	33	3	2	23	45	11.4	3.84	89	.244	.316	3	.273	1	-3	-3	1	-0.2
1982	SF-N	10	7	.588	68	0	0	0	8	104^2	97	35	6	1	29	76	10.9	2.67	135	.247	.300	2	.154	0	11	11	2	2.1
1983	SF-N☆	7	4	.636	56	0	0	0	20	87	73	33	4	0	19	68	9.5	2.59	137	.229	.272	0	.000	-2	10	9	2	1.6
1984	SF-N	5	4	.556	77	0	0	0	12	101	92	34	5	1	42	71	12.0	2.76	127	.246	.324	0	.000	-0	9	9	-1	0.8
1985	*Tor-A	5	7	.417	69	0	0	0	8	72^2	54	30	5	0	36	50	11.1	3.10	136	.214	.313	0	—	0	8	9	-0	1.5
1987	Tor-A	2	3	.400	23	0	0	0	1	27^2	36	20	2	0	19	17	17.9	5.53	82	.313	.410	0	—	0	-3	-3	0	-0.5
	Oak-A	0	0	—	6	0	0	0	0	4^1	4	4	0	0	3	6	14.5	8.31	50	.267	.389	0	—	0	-2	-2	-0	-0.1
	Yr	2	3	.400	29	0	0	0	1	32	40	24	2	0	22	23	17.4	5.91	75	.308	.408	0	—	0	-5	-5	0	-0.6
Total	13	80	77	.510	745	3	0	0	136	1085	1004	413	51	13	440	769	12.1	2.93	125	.249	.325	9	.081	-6	93	90	4	14.3

● JIMMY LAVENDER Lavender, James Sanford b: 3/25/1884, Barnesville, Ga. d: 1/12/60, Cartersville, Ga. BR/TR, 5'11", 165 lbs. Deb: 4/23/12

YEAR	TM/L	W	L	PCT	G	GS	CG	SH	SV	IP	H	R	HR	HB	BB	SO	RAT	ERA	ERA+	OAV	OOB	BH	AVG	PB	PR	PR+	PD	TPI
1912	Chi-N	16	13	.552	42	31	15	3	3	251^2	240	116	8	10	89	109	12.1	3.04	109	.257	.328	13	.149	-3	10	8	1	0.6
1913	Chi-N	10	14	.417	40	20	10	0	2	204	206	111	6	13	98	91	14.0	3.66	87	.267	.359	8	.118	-4	-10	-11	-2	-1.8
1914	Chi-N	11	11	.500	37	28	11	2	0	214^1	191	106	11	11	87	87	12.1	3.07	91	.247	.331	11	.175	2	-7	-7	3	-0.1
1915	Chi-N	10	16	.385	41	24	13	1	4	220	178	77	5	10	67	117	10.4	2.58	108	.228	.298	9	.134	-2	4	5	3	0.7
1916	Chi-N	10	14	.417	36	25	9	4	2	188	163	76	3	9	62	91	11.2	2.82	103	.240	.312	8	.151	-2	-4	2	-1	-0.1
1917	Phi-N	6	8	.429	28	14	7	0	1	129^1	119	61	5	3	44	52	11.6	3.55	79	.250	.317	5	.139	-1	-12	-10	-2	-1.4
Total	6	63	76	.453	224	142	65	10	12	1207^1	1097	547	38	56	447	547	11.9	3.09	97	.249	.325	54	.144	-9	-19	-12	2	-2.1

● RON LAW Law, Ronald David b: 3/14/46, Hamilton, Ont., Can. BR/TR, 6'2", 165 lbs. Deb: 6/29/69

YEAR	TM/L	W	L	PCT	G	GS	CG	SH	SV	IP	H	R	HR	HB	BB	SO	RAT	ERA	ERA+	OAV	OOB	BH	AVG	PB	PR	PR+	PD	TPI
1969	Cle-A	3	4	.429	35	1	0	0	1	52^1	68	34	2	2	34	29	17.9	4.99	76	.325	.424	1	.143	-0	-8	-7	0	-0.9

● VANCE LAW Law, Vance Aaron b: 10/1/56, Boise, Idaho BR/TR, 6'2", 190 lbs. Deb: 6/1/80 F♦

YEAR	TM/L	W	L	PCT	G	GS	CG	SH	SV	IP	H	R	HR	HB	BB	SO	RAT	ERA	ERA+	OAV	OOB	BH	AVG	PB	PR	PR+	PD	TPI
1986	Mon-N	0	0	—	3	0	0	0	0	4	3	2	0	0	2	0	11.3	2.25	164	.214	.313	81	.225	1	1	1	0	0.1
1987	Mon-N	0	0	—	3	0	0	0	0	3^1	5	2	0	0	0	2	13.5	5.40	78	.333	.333	119	.273	1	-0	-0	0	0.0
1991	Oak-A	0	0	—	1	0	0	0	0	0^2	1	0	0	0	1	0	27.0	0.00	—	.333	.500	28	.209	0	0	0	0	0.0
Total	3	0	0	—	7	0	0	0	0	8	9	4	0	0	3	2	13.5	3.38	116	.281	.343	972	.256	2	0	0	0	0.1

● VERN LAW Law, Vernon Sanders "Deacon" b: 3/12/30, Meridian, Idaho BR/TR, 6'2", 195 lbs. Deb: 6/11/50 FC

YEAR	TM/L	W	L	PCT	G	GS	CG	SH	SV	IP	H	R	HR	HB	BB	SO	RAT	ERA	ERA+	OAV	OOB	BH	AVG	PB	PR	PR+	PD	TPI
1950	Pit-N	7	9	.438	27	17	5	1	0	128	137	83	11	4	49	57	13.4	4.92	89	.272	.341	3	.073	-2	-11	-7	-2	-1.2
1951	Pit-N	6	9	.400	28	14	2	1	2	114	109	66	9	6	51	41	13.1	4.50	94	.253	.341	11	.344	5	-7	-3	-1	0.0
1954	Pit-N	9	13	.409	39	18	7	0	3	161^2	201	109	20	3	56	57	14.5	5.51	76	.311	.368	12	.231	3	-26	-23	-1	-2.4
1955	Pit-N	10	10	.500	43	24	8	1	1	200^2	221	98	19	1	61	82	12.7	3.81	108	.280	.333	16	.254	3	5	7	0	1.0
1956	Pit-N	8	16	.333	39	32	6	0	2	195^2	218	110	24	6	49	60	12.6	4.32	87	.281	.329	10	.175	1	-12	-12	-1	-1.3
1957	Pit-N	10	8	.556	31	25	9	3	1	172^2	172	72	18	2	32	55	10.7	2.87	132	.256	.291	12	.190	1	19	18	-2	1.8
1958	Pit-N	14	12	.538	35	29	6	1	3	202^1	235	103	16	1	39	56	12.2	3.96	98	.297	.331	12	.194	6	-0	-2	-0	0.3
1959	Pit-N	18	9	.667	34	33	20	2	1	266	245	91	25	2	53	110	10.2	2.98	130	.243	.282	16	.167	1	29	27	1	2.8
1960	*Pit-N★	20	9	.690	35	35	**18**	3	0	271^2	266	104	25	4	40	120	10.3	3.08	122	.257	.287	17	.181	3	21	20	1	2.6
1961	Pit-N	3	4	.429	11	10	1	0	0	59^1	72	33	10	1	18	20	13.8	4.70	85	.305	.357	5	.263	1	-4	-5	1	-0.3
1962	Pit-N	10	7	.588	23	20	7	2	0	139^1	156	67	21	1	27	78	11.9	3.94	100	.276	.310	14	.311	5	0	-0	1	0.6
1963	Pit-N	4	5	.444	18	12	1	1	0	76^2	91	45	11	0	13	31	12.2	4.93	67	.296	.325	5	.217	1	-14	-14	1	-1.3
1964	Pit-N	12	13	.480	35	29	7	5	0	192	203	85	18	1	32	93	11.1	3.61	97	.270	.300	19	.311	8	-2	-2	1	0.6
1965	Pit-N	17	9	.654	29	28	13	4	0	217^1	182	66	17	3	35	101	9.1	2.15	163	.229	.264	20	.244	4	33	33	1	4.7
1966	Pit-N	12	8	.600	31	28	8	4	0	177^2	203	85	19	4	24	88	11.7	4.05	88	.292	.320	16	.242	5	-9	-10	2	-0.4
1967	Pit-N	2	6	.250	25	10	1	0	0	97	122	57	5	1	18	43	13.1	4.18	81	.308	.340	3	.111	-0	-9	-9	-0	-0.7
Total	16	162	147	.524	483	364	119	28	13	2672	2833	1274	268	40	597	1092	11.7	3.77	101	.272	.314	191	.216	45	14	15	2	6.8

● BROOKS LAWRENCE Lawrence, Brooks Ulysses "Bull" b: 1/30/25, Springfield, Ohio d: 4/27/2000, Springfield, Ohio BR/TR, 6', 205 lbs. Deb: 6/24/54

YEAR	TM/L	W	L	PCT	G	GS	CG	SH	SV	IP	H	R	HR	HB	BB	SO	RAT	ERA	ERA+	OAV	OOB	BH	AVG	PB	PR	PR+	PD	TPI
1954	StL-N	15	6	.714	35	18	8	0	1	158^2	141	71	17	8	72	72	12.5	3.74	110	.243	.335	10	.189	0	6	6	0	0.8
1955	StL-N	3	8	.273	46	10	2	1	1	96	102	73	11	7	58	52	15.7	6.56	62	.278	.387	2	.095	-2	-27	-27	1	-2.8
1956	Cin-N☆	19	10	.655	49	30	11	1	0	218^2	210	109	26	2	71	96	11.6	3.99	100	.256	.317	11	.157	-1	-5	-0	3	0.2
1957	Cin-N	16	13	.552	49	32	12	1	4	250^1	234	111	26	8	76	121	11.4	3.52	117	.247	.309	14	.171	-0	10	15	-0	1.7
1958	Cin-N	8	13	.381	46	23	6	2	5	181	194	89	12	4	55	74	12.6	4.13	100	.275	.331	6	.113	-2	-4	0	-0	-0.2
1959	Cin-N	7	12	.368	43	14	3	0	10	128^1	144	74	17	4	45	64	13.5	4.77	85	.281	.344	6	.150	-1	-12	-10	-0	-1.6
1960	Cin-N	1	0	1.000	7	0	0	0	1	7^2	9	12	1	0	8	2	20.0	10.57	36	.310	.459	0	—	0	-6	-6	0	-0.8
Total	7	69	62	.527	275	127	42	5	22	1040^2	1034	539	110	33	385	481	12.6	4.25	96	.261	.332	49	.154	-5	-38	-19	4	-2.7

● BOB LAWRENCE Lawrence, Robert Andrew "Larry" b: 12/14/1899, Brooklyn, N.Y. d: 11/6/83, Jamaica, N.Y. BR/TR, 5'11", 180 lbs. Deb: 7/19/24

YEAR	TM/L	W	L	PCT	G	GS	CG	SH	SV	IP	H	R	HR	HB	BB	SO	RAT	ERA	ERA+	OAV	OOB	BH	AVG	PB	PR	PR+	PD	TPI
1924	Chi-A	0	0	—	1	0	0	0	0	1	1	1	0	0	1	1	18.0	9.00	46	.250	.400	0	—	0	-1	-1	0	0.0

● SEAN LAWRENCE Lawrence, Sean Christopher b: 9/2/70, Oak Park, Ill. BL/TL, 6'4", 215 lbs. Deb: 8/25/98

YEAR	TM/L	W	L	PCT	G	GS	CG	SH	SV	IP	H	R	HR	HB	BB	SO	RAT	ERA	ERA+	OAV	OOB	BH	AVG	PB	PR	PR+	PD	TPI
1998	Pit-N	2	1	.667	7	3	0	0	0	19^2	25	16	4	0	10	12	16.0	7.32	59	.313	.389	0	.000	-1	-7	-7	-0	-0.9

● ROXIE LAWSON Lawson, Alfred Voyle b: 4/13/06, Donnellson, Iowa d: 4/9/77, Stockport, Iowa BR/TR, 6', 170 lbs. Deb: 8/3/30

YEAR	TM/L	W	L	PCT	G	GS	CG	SH	SV	IP	H	R	HR	HB	BB	SO	RAT	ERA	ERA+	OAV	OOB	BH	AVG	PB	PR	PR+	PD	TPI
1930	Cle-A	1	2	.333	7	4	2	0	0	33^2	46	27	1	0	23	10	18.4	6.15	79	.324	.418	1	.091	-1	-6	-5	-0	-0.4
1931	Cle-A	0	2	.000	17	3	0	0	0	55^2	72	50	5	0	36	20	17.5	7.60	61	.304	.396	2	.143	-0	-20	-17	-1	-0.9
1933	Det-A	0	1	.000	4	2	0	0	0	16	17	16	2	0	17	6	19.1	7.31	59	.270	.425	0	.000	-1	-5	-5	0	-0.3
1935	Det-A	3	1	.750	7	4	4	2	2	40	34	11	3	0	24	16	13.0	1.57	265	.233	.341	4	.308	1	13	12	1	1.3
1936	Det-A	8	6	.571	41	8	3	0	3	128	139	87	13	4	71	34	15.0	5.48	90	.281	.376	10	.222	1	-6	-8	1	-0.6
1937	Det-A	18	7	.720	37	29	15	0	1	217^1	236	141	17	1	115	68	14.6	5.26	89	.271	.357	21	.259	3	-15	-14	-1	-1.2
1938	Det-A	8	9	.471	27	16	5	0	1	127	154	85	13	0	82	39	16.7	5.46	92	.299	.395	2	.044	-5	-9	-6	1	-1.1
1939	Det-A	1	1	.500	2	1	0	0	0	11^1	7	7	1	0	7	4	11.1	4.76	103	.167	.286	0	.000	-1	-0	0	0	0.0
	StL-A	3	7	.300	36	14	5	0	0	150^2	181	93	10	2	83	43	15.9	5.32	92	.307	.394	8	.186	-1	-12	-7	-1	-0.5
	Yr	4	8	.333	38	15	5	0	0	162	188	100	11	2	90	47	15.6	5.28	92	.297	.387	8	.170	-2	-12	-7	-0	-0.5
1940	StL-A	5	3	.625	30	2	0	0	4	72	77	45	5	0	54	18	16.4	5.13	89	.278	.396	1	.045	-3	-6	-4	-0	-0.7
Total	9	47	39	.547	208	83	34	2	11	851^2	963	562	70	7	512	258	15.7	5.37	89	.285	.380	49	.173	-6	-67	-56	-2	-4.4

● AL LAWSON Lawson, Alfred William b: 3/24/1869, London, England d: 11/29/54, San Antonio, Tex. BR/TR, 5'11", 161 lbs. Deb: 5/13/1890

YEAR	TM/L	W	L	PCT	G	GS	CG	SH	SV	IP	H	R	HR	HB	BB	SO	RAT	ERA	ERA+	OAV	OOB	BH	AVG	PB	PR	PR+	PD	TPI
1890	Bos-N	0	1	.000	1	1	1	0	0	9	12	7	0	0	4	1	16.0	4.00	94	.308	.372	0	.000	-0	-0	-0	0	0.0
	Pit-N	0	2	.000	2	2	1	0	0	10	15	20	0	0	10	2	22.5	9.00	37	.333	.455	0	.000	-1	-6	-7	0	-0.9
	Yr	0	3	.000	3	3	2	0	0	19	27	27	0	0	14	3	19.4	6.63	53	.321	.418	0	.000	-1	-6	-7	0	-0.9

● BOB LAWSON Lawson, Robert Baker b: 8/23/1876, Brookneal, Va. d: 10/28/52, Durham, N.C. BR/TR, 5'10", 170 lbs. Deb: 5/7/01

YEAR	TM/L	W	L	PCT	G	GS	CG	SH	SV	IP	H	R	HR	HB	BB	SO	RAT	ERA	ERA+	OAV	OOB	BH	AVG	PB	PR	PR+	PD	TPI
1901	Bos-N	2	2	.500	6	4	4	0	0	46	45	28	0	3	28	12	14.9	3.33	109	.254	.365	4	.148	-0	-0	1	1	0.1
1902	Bal-A	0	2	.000	3	2	1	0	0	13	21	11	0	2	3	5	18.0	4.85	78	.362	.413	1	.167	-0	-2	-1	1	-0.2
Total	2	2	4	.333	9	6	5	0	0	59	66	39	0	5	31	17	15.6	3.66	100	.281	.376	5	.152	-1	-2	-0	1	-0.1

● STEVE LAWSON Lawson, Steven George b: 12/28/50, Oakland, Cal. BR/TL, 6'1", 175 lbs. Deb: 8/3/72

YEAR	TM/L	W	L	PCT	G	GS	CG	SH	SV	IP	H	R	HR	HB	BB	SO	RAT	ERA	ERA+	OAV	OOB	BH	AVG	PB	PR	PR+	PD	TPI
1972	Tex-A	0	0	—	13	0	0	0	1	16	13	6	1	0	10	13	12.9	2.81	107	.213	.324	1	1.000	0	0	0	-0	0.1

● BRETT LAXTON Laxton, Brett William b: 10/5/73, Stratford, N.J. BL/TR, 6'2", 205 lbs. Deb: 6/21/99

YEAR	TM/L	W	L	PCT	G	GS	CG	SH	SV	IP	H	R	HR	HB	BB	SO	RAT	ERA	ERA+	OAV	OOB	BH	AVG	PB	PR	PR+	PD	TPI
1999	Oak-A	0	1	.000	3	2	0	0	0	9^2	12	12	1	2	7	9	19.6	7.45	62	.316	.447	0	—	0	-3	-3	-0	-0.3
2000	KC-A	0	1	.000	6	1	0	0	0	16^2	23	15	0	2	10	14	18.9	8.10	62	.348	.449	0	—	0	-6	-6	-1	-0.3
Total	2	0	2	.000	9	3	0	0	0	26^1	35	27	1	4	17	23	19.1	7.86	62	.337	.448	0	—	0	-9	-9	-1	-0.6

YEAR	TM/L	W	L	PCT	G	GS	CG	SH	SV	IP	H	R	HR	HB	BB	SO	RAT	ERA	ERA+	OAV	OOB	BH	AVG	PB	PR	PR+	PD	TPI
● **BILL LAXTON**	Laxton, William Harry b: 1/5/48, Camden, N.J. BL/TL, 6'1", 190 lbs. Deb: 9/15/70																											
1970	Phi-N	0	0	—	2	0	0	0	0	2	2	3	2	1	2	2	22.5	13.50	30	.250	.455	0	—	0	-2	-2	-0	-0.1
1971	SD-N	0	2	.000	18	0	0	0	0	27^2	32	25	4	1	26	23	19.2	6.83	48	.305	.447	0	—	0	-10	-11	0	-0.8
1974	SD-N	0	1	.000	30	1	0	0	0	44^2	37	22	5	3	38	40	15.7	4.03	89	.226	.380	1	.200	0	-2	-2	-0	-0.1
1976	Det-A	0	5	.000	26	3	0	0	2	94^2	77	49	13	6	51	74	12.7	4.09	91	.221	.331	0	—	0	-6	-4	-2	-0.4
1977	Sea-A	3	2	.600	43	0	0	0	3	72^2	62	44	10	4	39	49	13.0	4.95	83	.233	.340	0	—	0	-7	-7	-1	-0.6
	Cle-A	0	0	—	2	0	0	0	0	1^2	2	1	0	0	2	1	21.6	5.40	73	.286	.444	0	—	0	-0	-0	0	0.0
	Yr	3	2	.600	45	0	0	0	3	74^1	64	45	10	4	41	50	13.2	4.96	83	.234	.343	0	—	0	-7	-7	-1	-0.6
Total	5	3	10	.231	121	4	0	0	5	243^1	212	144	34	15	158	189	14.2	4.73	80	.236	.359	1	.200	0	-28	-26	-3	-2.0
● **TIM LAYANA**	Layana, Timothy Joseph b: 3/2/64, Inglewood, Cal. d: 6/26/99, Bakersfield, Cal. BR/TR, 6'2", 195 lbs. Deb: 4/9/90																											
1990	Cin-N	5	3	.625	55	0	0	0	2	80	71	33	7	2	44	53	13.2	3.49	113	.244	.347	0	.000	-1	3	4	0	0.4
1991	Cin-N	0	2	.000	22	0	0	0	0	20^2	23	18	1	0	11	14	14.8	6.97	55	.277	.362	0	.000	-0	-8	-7	0	-0.6
1993	SF-N	0	0	—	1	0	0	0	0	2	7	5	1	0	1	1	36.0	22.50	17	.538	.571	0	—	0	-4	-4	0	-0.2
Total	3	5	5	.500	78	0	0	0	2	102^2	101	56	9	2	56	68	13.9	4.56	86	.261	.357	0	.000	-1	-9	-7	1	-0.4
● **DANNY LAZAR**	Lazar, John Daniel b: 11/14/43, East Chicago, Ind. BL/TL, 6'1", 190 lbs. Deb: 6/21/68																											
1968	Chi-A	0	1	.000	8	1	0	0	0	13^1	14	6	1	0	4	11	12.2	4.05	75	.269	.321	0	.000	0	-2	-1	0	-0.1
1969	Chi-A	0	0	—	9	3	0	0	0	20^2	21	15	5	1	11	9	14.4	6.53	59	.280	.379	0	.000	-0	-7	-6	-0	-0.4
Total	2	0	1	.000	17	4	0	0	0	34	35	21	6	1	15	20	13.5	5.56	63	.276	.357	0	.000	-0	-8	-7	-0	-0.5
● **JACK LAZORKO**	Lazorko, Jack Thomas b: 3/30/56, Hoboken, N.J. BR/TR, 5'11", 200 lbs. Deb: 6/4/84																											
1984	Mil-A	0	1	.000	15	1	0	0	1	39^2	37	19	7	1	22	24	13.6	4.31	89	.245	.345	0	—	0	-1	-2	0	-0.1
1985	Sea-A	0	0	—	15	0	0	0	1	20^1	23	10	1	3	8	7	15.0	3.54	119	.291	.378	0	—	0	1	1	1	0.1
1986	Det-A	0	0	—	3	0	0	0	0	6^2	8	3	0	0	4	3	16.2	4.05	102	.296	.387	0	—	0	0	0	0	0.0
1987	Cal-A	5	6	.455	26	11	2	0	0	117^2	108	68	20	2	44	55	11.8	4.59	94	.248	.320	0	—	0	-2	-4	2	-0.2
1988	Cal-A	0	1	.000	10	3	0	0	0	37^2	37	15	5	1	16	19	12.9	3.35	116	.255	.333	0	—	0	3	2	0	0.1
Total	5	5	8	.385	69	15	2	0	2	222	213	115	33	7	94	108	12.7	4.22	98	.254	.334	0	—	0	1	-2	3	-0.1
● **CHARLIE LEA**	Lea, Charles William b: 12/25/56, Orleans, France BR/TR, 6'4", 197 lbs. Deb: 6/12/80																											
1980	Mon-N	7	5	.583	21	19	0	0	0	104	103	51	5	2	55	56	13.8	3.72	96	.262	.356	3	.081	-2	-1	-2	-1	-0.5
1981	Mon-N	5	4	.556	16	11	2	2	0	64^1	63	34	4	1	26	31	12.6	4.62	76	.268	.344	2	.133	-0	-8	-8	-0	-1.1
1982	Mon-N	12	10	.545	27	27	4	2	0	177^2	145	70	16	0	56	115	10.2	3.24	113	.222	.283	8	.123	-1	7	8	-1	0.7
1983	Mon-N	16	11	.593	33	33	8	4	0	222	195	87	15	1	84	137	11.4	3.12	115	.238	.309	8	.114	-2	13	12	-1	1.1
1984	Mon-N★	15	10	.600	30	30	8	0	0	224^1	198	82	19	3	68	123	10.8	2.89	119	.239	.299	8	.111	-3	18	14	0	1.3
1987	Mon-N	0	1	.000	1	1	0	0	0	1	4	4	1	0	2	1	54.0	36.00	12	.571	.667	0	—	0	-4	-3	0	-0.5
1988	Min-A	7	7	.500	24	23	0	0	0	130	156	79	19	5	50	72	14.6	4.85	84	.301	.368	0	—	0	-13	-11	-1	-1.1
Total	7	62	48	.564	152	144	22	8	0	923^1	864	407	79	12	341	535	11.9	3.54	102	.250	.320	29	.112	-7	12	9	-4	-0.1
● **RICK LEACH**	Leach, Richard Max b: 5/4/57, Ann Arbor, Mich. BL/TL, 6', 195 lbs. Deb: 4/30/81 ♦																											
1984	Tor-A	0	0	—	1	0	0	0	0	1	2	3	1	0	2	0	36.0	27.00	15	.400	.571	23	.261	0	-3	-2	0	-0.1
● **TERRY LEACH**	Leach, Terry Hester b: 3/13/54, Selma, Ala. BR/TR, 6', 215 lbs. Deb: 8/12/81																											
1981	NY-N	1	1	.500	21	1	0	0	0	35^1	26	11	2	0	12	16	9.7	2.55	137	.205	.273	0	.000	1	4	4	1	0.3
1982	NY-N	2	1	.667	21	1	1	1	3	45^1	46	22	2	0	18	30	12.7	4.17	87	.271	.340	1	.125	-0	-3	-3	-0	-0.2
1985	NY-N	3	4	.429	22	4	1	1	1	55^2	48	19	3	1	14	30	10.2	2.91	119	.235	.288	2	.167	1	4	4	1	0.6
1986	NY-N	0	0	—	6	0	0	0	0	6^2	6	3	0	0	3	4	12.2	2.70	131	.222	.300	0	—	0	1	1	0	0.0
1987	NY-N	11	1	.917	44	12	1	1	0	131^1	132	54	14	1	29	61	11.1	3.22	117	.262	.304	2	.061	-2	13	9	1	0.7
1988	*NY-N	7	2	.778	52	0	0	0	3	92	95	32	5	3	24	51	11.9	2.54	127	.268	.320	2	.143	0	9	7	2	1.0
1989	NY-N	0	0	—	10	0	0	0	0	21^1	19	11	1	1	4	2	10.1	4.22	78	.244	.289	0	.000	-0	-2	-2	1	-0.1
	KC-A	5	6	.455	30	3	0	0	0	73^2	78	46	4	1	36	34	14.0	4.15	93	.278	.362	0	—	0	-2	-2	1	-0.2
1990	Min-A	2	5	.286	55	0	0	0	2	81^2	84	31	2	1	21	46	11.7	3.20	130	.268	.316	0	—	0	7	8	1	0.7
1991	*Min-A	1	2	.333	50	0	0	0	0	67^1	82	28	3	0	14	32	12.8	3.61	118	.299	.333	0	—	0	4	5	1	0.4
1992	Chi-A	6	5	.545	51	0	0	0	0	73^2	57	17	2	4	20	22	9.9	1.95	198	.215	.280	0	—	0	16	16	1	2.3
1993	Chi-A	0	0	—	14	0	0	0	1	16	15	5	0	1	2	3	10.1	2.81	149	.250	.286	0	—	0	3	3	-1	0.1
Total	11	38	27	.585	376	21	3	3	10	700	688	279	38	13	197	331	11.5	3.15	119	.259	.313	7	.097	-1	53	48	8	5.6
● **LUIS LEAL**	Leal, Luis Enrique (Alvarado) b: 3/21/57, Barquisimeto, Ven. BR/TR, 6'3", 205 lbs. Deb: 5/25/80																											
1980	Tor-A	3	4	.429	13	10	1	0	0	59^2	72	35	6	1	31	26	15.7	4.53	95	.314	.398	0	—	0	-3	-1	-1	-0.2
1981	Tor-A	7	13	.350	29	19	3	0	1	129^2	127	63	8	5	44	71	12.2	3.68	107	.254	.321	0	—	0	-0	4	-1	0.5
1982	Tor-A	12	15	.444	38	38	10	0	0	249^2	250	113	24	3	79	111	12.0	3.93	114	.262	.320	0	—	0	4	14	-1	1.3
1983	Tor-A	13	12	.520	35	35	7	1	0	217^1	216	113	23	6	65	116	11.9	4.31	100	.257	.315	0	—	0	-6	0	-1	0.0
1984	Tor-A	13	8	.619	35	35	6	2	0	222^1	221	106	27	4	77	134	12.2	3.89	106	.258	.323	0	—	0	3	5	0	0.5
1985	Tor-A	3	6	.333	15	14	0	0	0	67^1	82	46	13	3	24	33	14.6	5.75	73	.303	.366	0	—	0	-12	-11	0	-1.3
Total	6	51	58	.468	165	151	27	3	1	946	968	476	101	22	320	491	12.5	4.14	103	.265	.328	0	—	0	-14	11	-2	0.8
● **KING LEAR**	Lear, Charles Bernard b: 1/23/1891, Greencastle, Pa. d: 10/31/76, Waynesboro, Pa. BR/TR, 6', 175 lbs. Deb: 5/2/14																											
1914	Cin-N	1	2	.333	17	4	3	1	1	55^2	55	23	3	2	19	20	12.3	3.07	95	.271	.339	3	.188	1	-2	-1	-0	0.0
1915	Cin-N	6	10	.375	40	15	9	0	0	167^2	169	73	7	6	45	46	11.8	3.01	95	.270	.324	8	.170	-1	-5	-3	-4	-0.8
Total	2	7	12	.368	57	19	12	1	1	223^1	224	96	10	8	64	66	11.9	3.02	95	.270	.328	11	.175	-0	-6	-3	-4	-0.8
● **FRANK LEARY**	Leary, Francis Patrick b: 2/26/1881, Wayland, Mass. d: 10/4/07, Natick, Mass. TR, Deb: 4/30/07																											
1907	Cin-N	0	1	.000	2	1	0	0	0	8	7	2	0	0	6	4	14.6	1.13	231	.269	.406	0	.000	-0	1	1	0	0.2
● **JACK LEARY**	Leary, John J. b: 1858, New Haven, Conn. TL, 5'11", 186 lbs. Deb: 8/21/1880 ♦																											
1880	Bos-N	0	1	.000	1	1	0	0	0	3	8	5	0		0	1	24.0	15.00	15	.727	.727	0	.000	-0	-4	-4	0	-0.6
1881	Det-N	0	2	.000	2	2	1	0	0	13	13	6	0		2	2	10.4	4.15	70	.255	.283	3	.273	1	-2	-2	-0	-0.2
1882	Pit-a	1	0	1.000	3	2	1	0	0	18^2	28	22	0		3	5	14.9	6.27	42	.326	.348	75	.292	1	-7	-8	0	-0.3
	Bal-a	2	1	.667	3	3	3	0	0	26	29	22	1		8	2	12.8	1.38	199	.264	.314	4	.222	0	4	4	-0	0.4
	Yr	3	1	.750	6	5	4	0	0	44^2	57	44	1		11	7	13.7	3.43	79	.291	.329	79	.287	1	-4	-4	0	0.1
1884	Alt-U	0	3	.000	3	3	2	0	0	24	31	30	0		2	7	12.4	5.25	51	.292	.306	3	.091	-2	-7	-6	-0	-0.7
	CP-U	0	2	.000	2	1	1	0	0	10	14	14	0		5	6	17.1	5.40	45	.311	.380	7	.175	-1	-3	-3	-0	-0.5
	Yr	0	5	.000	5	4	3	0	0	34	45	44	0		7	13	13.8	5.29	49	.298	.329	10	.137	-3	-11	-10	-0	-1.2
Total	4	3	9	.250	14	12	8	0	0	94^2	123	99	1		20	23	13.6	4.56	59	.301	.333	125	.232	-2	-21	-19	-0	-1.9
● **TIM LEARY**	Leary, Timothy James b: 12/23/58, Santa Monica, Cal. BR/TR, 6'3", 205 lbs. Deb: 4/12/81																											
1981	NY-N	0	0	—	1	1	0	0	0	2	0	0	0	0	1	3	4.5	0.00	—	.000	.143	0	.000	-0	1	1	0	0.0
1983	NY-N	1	1	.500	2	2	1	0	0	10^2	15	10	0	0	4	9	16.0	3.38	108	.319	.373	1	.333	0	0	0	0	0.1
1984	NY-N	3	3	.500	20	7	0	0	0	53^2	61	28	2	2	18	29	13.6	4.02	88	.285	.346	3	.300	2	-3	-3	-1	-0.2
1985	Mil-A	1	4	.200	5	5	0	0	0	33^1	40	18	5	1	8	29	13.2	4.05	103	.296	.340	0	—	0	0	0	1	0.1
1986	Mil-A	12	12	.500	33	30	3	2	0	188^1	216	97	20	7	53	110	13.2	4.21	103	.289	.342	0	—	0	-0	3	1	0.4
1987	LA-N	3	11	.214	39	12	0	0	1	107^2	121	62	15	2	36	61	13.3	4.76	83	.285	.344	7	.304	2	-8	-10	1	-0.9
1988	*LA-N	17	11	.607	35	34	9	6	0	228^2	201	87	13	6	56	180	10.4	2.91	115	.234	.285	18	.269	6	14	11	2	2.1
1989	LA-N	6	7	.462	19	17	2	0	0	117^1	107	45	9	2	37	59	11.2	3.38	101	.247	.309	2	.061	-2	2	1	1	-0.1
	Cin-N	2	7	.222	14	14	0	0	0	89^2	98	39	8	3	31	64	13.2	3.71	97	.278	.342	5	.192	2	-2	-1	0	0.1
	Yr	8	14	.364	33	31	2	0	0	207	205	84	17	5	68	123	12.1	3.52	99	.261	.324	7	.119	-1	-0	-0	1	0.0
1990	NY-A	9	19	.321	31	31	6	1	0	208	202	105	18	7	78	138	12.4	4.11	97	.257	.330	0	—	0	-4	-3	2	-0.2
1991	NY-A	4	10	.286	28	18	1	0	0	120^2	150	89	20	4	57	83	15.7	6.49	64	.312	.389	0	—	0	-32	-31	-0	-3.1
1992	NY-A	5	6	.455	18	15	2	0	0	97	84	62	9	4	57	34	13.5	5.57	70	.245	.359	0	—	0	-17	-18	-1	-1.8
	Sea-A	3	4	.429	8	8	1	0	0	44	47	27	3	5	30	12	16.8	4.91	81	.280	.404	0	—	0	-5	-5	1	-0.6
	Yr	8	10	.444	26	23	3	0	0	141	131	89	12	9	87	46	14.5	5.36	74	.256	.374	0	—	0	-22	-22	-0	-2.4

YEAR	TM/L	W	L	PCT	G	GS	CG	SH	SV	IP	H	R	HR	HB	BB	SO	RAT	ERA	ERA+	OAV	OOB	BH	AVG	PB	PR	PR+	PD	TPI
1993	Sea-A	11	9	.550	33	27	0	0	0	169^1	202	104	21	8	58	68	14.2	5.05	87	.300	.362	0	—	0	-13	-12	1	-1.1
1994	Tex-A	1	1	.500	6	3	0	0	0	21	26	19	4	1	11	9	16.3	8.14	59	.306	.392	0	—	0	-8	-8	0	-0.6
Total	13	78	105	.426	292	224	25	9	1	1491^1	1570	792	147	52	535	888	13.0	4.36	90	.273	.340	36	.221	9	-76	-75	7	-5.8

● GEORGE LeCLAIR
LeClair, George Lewis "Frenchy" b: 10/18/1886, Milton, Vt. d: 10/10/18, Farnham, Que., Can. BR/TR, 5'9", 170 lbs. Deb: 6/5/14

YEAR	TM/L	W	L	PCT	G	GS	CG	SH	SV	IP	H	R	HR	HB	BB	SO	RAT	ERA	ERA+	OAV	OOB	BH	AVG	PB	PR	PR+	PD	TPI
1914	Pit-F	5	2	.714	22	7	5	1	0	103^1	99	52	0	1	25	49	10.9	4.01	72	.262	.309	5	.147	-2	-13	-13	0	-1.0
1915	Pit-F	1	2	.333	14	3	1	0	1	45^2	43	20	1	0	13	10	11.0	3.35	81	.253	.306	2	.154	-1	-3	-3	1	-0.3
	Buf-F	0	0	—	1	0	0	0	0	3	4	2	0	0	1	2	15.0	6.00	47	.333	.385	0	—	0	-1	-1	-0	-0.1
	Bal-F	1	8	.111	18	9	6	1	1	84	76	43	2	0	22	30	10.5	2.46	116	.246	.296	2	.083	-2	2	4	0	0.2
	Yr	2	10	.167	33	12	7	1	2	132^2	123	65	3	0	36	42	10.8	2.85	99	.251	.302	4	.108	-3	-2	-1	1	-0.2
Total	2	7	12	.368	55	19	12	2	2	236	222	117	3	1	61	91	10.8	3.36	85	.255	.305	9	.127	-5	-15	-13	1	-1.2

● RAZOR LEDBETTER
Ledbetter, Ralph Overton b: 12/8/1894, Rutherford College, N.C. d: 2/1/69, W.Palm Beach, Fla. BR/TR, 6'3", 190 lbs. Deb: 4/16/15

YEAR	TM/L	W	L	PCT	G	GS	CG	SH	SV	IP	H	R	HR	HB	BB	SO	RAT	ERA	ERA+	OAV	OOB	BH	AVG	PB	PR	PR+	PD	TPI
1915	Det-A	0	0	—	1	0	0	0	0	1	1	0	0	0	0	0	9.0	0.00	—	.333	.333	0	—	0	0	0	0	0.0

● COREY LEE
Lee, Corey Wayne b: 12/26/74, Raleigh, N.C. BB/TL, 6'2", 180 lbs. Deb: 8/24/99

YEAR	TM/L	W	L	PCT	G	GS	CG	SH	SV	IP	H	R	HR	HB	BB	SO	RAT	ERA	ERA+	OAV	OOB	BH	AVG	PB	PR	PR+	PD	TPI
1999	Tex-A	0	1	.000	1	0	0	0	0	1	2	3	1	0	1	0	27.0	27.00	19	.400	.500	0	—	0	-2	-2	0	-0.4

● DAVID LEE
Lee, David Emmer b: 3/12/73, Pittsburgh, Pa. BR/TR, 6'1", 200 lbs. Deb: 5/22/99

YEAR	TM/L	W	L	PCT	G	GS	CG	SH	SV	IP	H	R	HR	HB	BB	SO	RAT	ERA	ERA+	OAV	OOB	BH	AVG	PB	PR	PR+	PD	TPI
1999	Col-N	3	2	.600	36	0	0	0	0	49	43	21	4	4	29	38	14.0	3.67	158	.247	.367	1	.200	-0	5	9	0	0.8
2000	Col-N	0	0	—	7	0	0	0	1	5^2	10	9	3	1	6	6	27.0	11.12	53	.357	.486	0	—	0	-4	-3	-0	-0.1
Total	2	3	2	.600	43	0	0	0	1	54^2	53	30	7	5	35	44	15.3	4.45	131	.262	.384	1	.200	-0	1	7	-0	0.7

● DON LEE
Lee, Donald Edward b: 2/26/34, Globe, Ariz. BR/TR, 6'4", 210 lbs. Deb: 4/23/57 F

YEAR	TM/L	W	L	PCT	G	GS	CG	SH	SV	IP	H	R	HR	HB	BB	SO	RAT	ERA	ERA+	OAV	OOB	BH	AVG	PB	PR	PR+	PD	TPI
1957	Det-A	1	3	.250	11	6	0	0	0	38^2	48	22	6	1	18	19	15.6	4.66	83	.308	.383	2	.167	-0	-4	-3	-0	-0.4
1958	Det-A	0	0	—	1	0	0	0	0	2	1	2	1	1	1	0	13.5	9.00	45	.143	.333	0	—	0	-1	-1	-0	-0.1
1960	Was-A	8	7	.533	44	20	1	0	3	165	160	72	16	3	64	88	12.4	3.44	113	.258	.330	5	.116	-0	8	8	1	0.8
1961	Min-A	3	6	.333	37	10	4	0	3	115	93	49	12	4	35	65	10.3	3.52	120	.221	.288	2	.067	-3	6	9	2	0.6
1962	Min-A	3	3	.500	9	9	1	0	0	52	51	27	8	7	24	28	14.2	4.50	91	.256	.357	4	.211	0	-3	-2	0	-0.2
	LA-A	8	8	.500	27	22	4	2	2	153^1	153	64	12	3	39	74	11.4	3.11	124	.256	.305	9	.184	-0	15	13	-2	1.1
	Yr	11	11	.500	36	31	5	2	2	205^1	204	91	20	10	63	102	12.1	3.46	113	.256	.319	13	.191	0	12	10	-2	0.9
1963	LA-A	8	11	.421	40	22	3	2	1	154	148	74	12	9	51	89	12.2	3.68	93	.251	.320	7	.156	-1	-1	-5	-1	-0.7
1964	LA-A	5	4	.556	33	8	0	0	2	89^1	99	39	6	1	25	73	12.6	2.72	121	.279	.328	6	.261	2	9	6	-1	0.8
1965	Cal-A	0	1	.000	10	0	0	0	0	14	21	11	4	1	5	12	17.4	6.43	53	.350	.409	1	.333	1	-5	-5	-0	-0.3
	Hou-N	0	0	—	7	0	0	0	0	8	8	3	0	1	3	3	13.5	3.38	99	.267	.353	0	.000	-0	-0	-0	0	0.0
1966	Hou-N	2	0	1.000	9	0	0	0	0	18	17	5	1	0	4	9	10.5	2.50	137	.250	.292	1	1.000	1	2	2	-1	0.3
	Chi-N	2	1	.667	16	0	0	0	0	19	28	19	3	0	12	7	18.9	7.11	52	.346	.430	0	—	0	-7	-7	-0	-1.0
	Yr	4	1	.800	25	0	0	0	0	37	45	24	4	0	16	16	14.8	4.86	73	.302	.370	1	1.000	1	-5	-5	1	-0.7
Total	9	40	44	.476	244	97	13	4	11	828^1	827	387	81	31	281	467	12.4	3.61	104	.260	.326	37	.164	-1	20	14	1	0.9

● MARK LEE
Lee, Mark Linden b: 6/14/53, Inglewood, Cal. BR/TR, 6'4", 225 lbs. Deb: 4/23/78

YEAR	TM/L	W	L	PCT	G	GS	CG	SH	SV	IP	H	R	HR	HB	BB	SO	RAT	ERA	ERA+	OAV	OOB	BH	AVG	PB	PR	PR+	PD	TPI
1978	SD-N	5	1	.833	56	0	0	0	2	85	74	34	2	2	36	31	11.9	3.28	101	.240	.324	0	.000	-1	3	0	2	0.1
1979	SD-N	2	4	.333	46	1	0	0	5	65	88	34	3	2	25	25	15.9	4.29	82	.332	.394	2	.333	1	-4	-6	1	-0.5
1980	Pit-N	0	1	.000	4	0	0	0	0	5^2	5	3	0	0	3	2	12.7	4.76	77	.227	.320	0	—	0	-1	-1	0	0.0
1981	Pit-N	0	2	.000	12	0	0	0	2	19^2	17	6	1	0	5	5	10.1	2.75	131	.233	.282	1	.500	0	2	2	1	0.4
Total	4	7	8	.467	118	1	0	0	9	175^1	184	77	6	4	69	63	13.2	3.64	95	.275	.347	3	.231	1	-0	-4	4	0.0

● MARK LEE
Lee, Mark Owen b: 7/20/64, Williston, N.Dak. BL/TL, 6'3", 198 lbs. Deb: 9/8/88

YEAR	TM/L	W	L	PCT	G	GS	CG	SH	SV	IP	H	R	HR	HB	BB	SO	RAT	ERA	ERA+	OAV	OOB	BH	AVG	PB	PR	PR+	PD	TPI
1988	KC-A	0	0	—	4	0	0	0	0	5	6	2	0	0	1	0	12.6	3.60	111	.300	.333	0	—	0	0	0	0	0.0
1990	Mil-A	1	0	1.000	11	0	0	0	0	21^1	20	5	1	0	4	14	10.1	2.11	184	.256	.293	0	—	0	4	4	-0	0.2
1991	Mil-A	2	5	.286	62	0	0	0	1	67^2	72	33	10	1	31	43	13.8	3.86	103	.283	.364	0	—	0	2	1	1	0.1
1995	Bal-A	2	0	1.000	39	0	0	0	1	33^1	31	18	5	1	18	27	13.5	4.86	98	.246	.345	0	—	0	-1	-0	-1	-0.1
Total	4	5	5	.500	116	0	0	0	2	127^1	129	58	16	2	54	84	13.1	3.82	109	.270	.346	0	—	0	6	5	-1	0.2

● MIKE LEE
Lee, Michael Randall b: 5/19/41, Bell, Cal. BL/TL, 6'5", 220 lbs. Deb: 5/6/60

YEAR	TM/L	W	L	PCT	G	GS	CG	SH	SV	IP	H	R	HR	HB	BB	SO	RAT	ERA	ERA+	OAV	OOB	BH	AVG	PB	PR	PR+	PD	TPI
1960	Cle-A	0	0	—	7	0	0	0	0	9	6	2	1	1	11	6	18.0	2.00	187	.207	.439	0	—	0	2	2	-0	0.1
1963	LA-A	1	1	.500	6	4	0	0	0	26	30	11	3	1	14	11	15.6	3.81	90	.300	.391	0	.000	-1	-1	-1	1	-0.1
Total	2	1	1	.500	13	4	0	0	0	35	36	13	4	2	25	17	16.2	3.34	105	.279	.404	0	.000	-1	1	1	1	0.0

● BOB LEE
Lee, Robert Dean "Moose" or "Horse" b: 11/26/37, Ottumwa, Iowa BR/TR, 6'3", 230 lbs. Deb: 4/15/64

YEAR	TM/L	W	L	PCT	G	GS	CG	SH	SV	IP	H	R	HR	HB	BB	SO	RAT	ERA	ERA+	OAV	OOB	BH	AVG	PB	PR	PR+	PD	TPI
1964	LA-A	6	5	.545	64	5	0	0	19	137	87	31	6	1	58	111	9.6	1.51	217	.182	.272	0	.000	-2	**32**	**30**	-2	2.8
1965	Cal-A☆	9	7	.563	69	0	0	0	23	131^1	95	35	11	1	42	89	9.5	1.92	177	.205	.272	3	.143	1	22	22	-1	3.4
1966	Cal-A	5	4	.556	61	0	0	0	16	101^2	90	39	8	1	31	46	10.8	2.74	122	.237	.297	0	.000	-0	8	7	-1	0.8
1967	LA-N	0	0	—	4	0	0	0	0	6^2	6	8	2	1	3	2	13.5	5.40	57	.222	.323	0	—	0	-2	-2	-0	-0.1
	Cin-N	3	3	.500	27	1	0	0	2	50^2	51	26	0	0	25	33	13.5	4.44	84	.262	.345	3	.375	1	-6	-4	-1	-0.4
	Yr	3	3	.500	31	1	0	0	2	57^1	57	34	2	1	28	35	13.5	4.55	81	.257	.343	3	.375	1	-8	-5	-1	-0.5
1968	Cin-N	2	4	.333	44	1	0	0	3	65^1	73	38	4	1	37	34	15.3	5.10	62	.302	.396	1	.200	0	-15	-13	-1	-1.5
Total	5	25	23	.521	269	7	0	0	63	492^2	402	177	31	5	196	315	11.0	2.70	125	.225	.304	7	.104	-1	40	37	-6	5.0

● ROY LEE
Lee, Roy Edwin b: 9/28/17, Elmira, N.Y. d: 11/11/85, St.Louis, Mo. BL/TL, 5'11.5", 175 lbs. Deb: 9/23/45

YEAR	TM/L	W	L	PCT	G	GS	CG	SH	SV	IP	H	R	HR	HB	BB	SO	RAT	ERA	ERA+	OAV	OOB	BH	AVG	PB	PR	PR+	PD	TPI
1945	NY-N	0	2	.000	3	1	0	0	0	7	8	9	3	0	3	0	14.1	11.57	34	.267	.333	0	.000	-0	-6	-6	-0	-1.0

● SANG-HOON LEE
Lee, Sang-Hoon b: 3/11/71, Seoul, South Korea BL/TL, 6'1", 190 lbs. Deb: 6/29/2000

YEAR	TM/L	W	L	PCT	G	GS	CG	SH	SV	IP	H	R	HR	HB	BB	SO	RAT	ERA	ERA+	OAV	OOB	BH	AVG	PB	PR	PR+	PD	TPI
2000	Bos-A	0	0	—	9	0	0	0	0	11^2	11	4	2	1	5	6	13.1	3.09	165	.262	.354	0	—	0	2	3	0	0.1

● TOM LEE
Lee, Thomas Frank b: 6/8/1862, Philadelphia, Pa. d: 3/4/1886, Milwaukee, Wis. Deb: 6/14/1884

YEAR	TM/L	W	L	PCT	G	GS	CG	SH	SV	IP	H	R	HR	HB	BB	SO	RAT	ERA	ERA+	OAV	OOB	BH	AVG	PB	PR	PR+	PD	TPI
1884	Chi-N	1	4	.200	5	5	5	0	0	45^1	55	43	12		15	14	13.9	3.77	83	.272	.323	3	.125	-2	-4	-3	-0	-0.4
	Bal-U	5	8	.385	15	14	12	0	0	122	121	88	1		29	81	11.1	3.39	79	.242	.283	23	.280	-2	-13	-9	0	-0.8
Total	1	6	12	.333	20	19	17	0	0	167^1	176	131	13		44	95	11.8	3.50	80	.250	.295	26	.245	-4	-17	-12	0	-1.2

● THORNTON LEE
Lee, Thornton Starr "Lefty" b: 9/13/06, Sonoma, Cal. d: 6/9/97, Tucson, Ariz. BL/TL, 6'3", 205 lbs. Deb: 9/19/33 F

YEAR	TM/L	W	L	PCT	G	GS	CG	SH	SV	IP	H	R	HR	HB	BB	SO	RAT	ERA	ERA+	OAV	OOB	BH	AVG	PB	PR	PR+	PD	TPI
1933	Cle-A	1	1	.500	3	2	2	0	0	17^1	13	9	1	0	11	7	12.5	4.15	107	.203	.320	3	.375	1	0	1	-0	0.2
1934	Cle-A	1	1	.500	24	6	0	0	0	85^2	105	57	8	3	44	41	16.0	5.04	90	.308	.392	2	.095	-1	-5	-5	0	-0.3
1935	Cle-A	7	10	.412	32	20	8	1	1	180^2	179	90	6	4	71	81	12.7	4.04	112	.259	.331	12	.197	-1	8	9	2	0.8
1936	Cle-A	3	5	.375	43	8	2	0	3	127	138	86	2	2	67	49	14.7	4.89	103	.271	.358	5	.122	-2	**2**	2	2	0.1
1937	Chi-A	12	10	.545	30	25	13	2	0	204^2	209	91	17	1	60	80	11.9	3.52	131	.260	.312	15	.211	1	25	25	1	2.3
1938	Chi-A	13	12	.520	33	30	18	1	1	245^1	252	123	12	3	94	77	12.8	3.49	140	.263	.331	25	.258	6	36	**38**	-2	3.7
1939	Chi-A	15	11	.577	33	29	15	2	3	235	260	121	14	3	70	81	12.8	4.21	112	.285	.338	15	.165	-3	11	13	0	1.0
1940	Chi-A	12	13	.480	28	27	24	1	0	228	223	100	13	2	56	87	11.1	3.47	127	.254	.300	23	.274	4	23	24	-3	2.4
1941	Chi-A★	22	11	.667	35	34	**30**	3	1	300^1	258	98	18	4	92	130	**10.6**	**2.37**	**173**	.232	**.293**	29	.254	5	**59**	**58**	-2	**6.7**
1942	Chi-A	2	6	.250	11	8	6	1	0	76	82	38	4	2	31	25	13.6	3.32	109	.278	.351	6	.200	0	3	2	-2	0.1
1943	Chi-A	5	9	.357	19	19	7	1	0	127	129	66	8	4	50	35	13.0	4.18	80	.266	.340	3	.071	-4	-12	-12	-3	-1.9
1944	Chi-A	3	9	.250	15	14	6	0	0	113^1	105	51	3	1	25	39	10.4	3.02	114	.246	.290	4	.095	-3	5	5	2	0.4
1945	Chi-A†	15	12	.556	29	28	19	1	0	228^1	208	81	6	10	76	108	11.6	2.44	136	.245	.314	14	.179	-1	23	23	-1	2.4
1946	Chi-A	2	4	.333	7	7	2	0	0	43^1	39	24	1	1	23	23	13.1	3.53	97	.244	.342	4	.267	1	-0	-1	-0	-0.1
1947	Chi-A	3	7	.300	21	11	2	1	1	86^2	86	50	5	2	56	57	15.0	4.47	82	.261	.372	6	.207	0	-7	-8	0	-0.8
1948	NY-N	1	3	.250	11	4	1	0	1	32^2	41	20	3	1	12	17	14.9	4.41	89	.304	.365	1	.091	-1	-2	-2	0	-0.3
Total	16	117	124	.485	374	272	155	14	10	2331^1	2327	1105	121	43	838	937	12.4	3.56	119	.260	.326	167	.200	1	169	172	-7	16.7

● BILL LEE
Lee, William Crutcher "Big Bill" b: 10/21/09, Plaquemine, La. d: 6/15/77, Plaquemine, La. BR/TR, 6'3", 195 lbs. Deb: 4/29/34

YEAR	TM/L	W	L	PCT	G	GS	CG	SH	SV	IP	H	R	HR	HB	BB	SO	RAT	ERA	ERA+	OAV	OOB	BH	AVG	PB	PR	PR+	PD	TPI
1934	Chi-N	13	14	.481	35	29	16	4	1	214^1	218	91	9	2	74	104	12.3	3.40	114	.263	.325	10	.132	-2	16	12	2	1.2
1935	*Chi-N	20	6	**.769**	39	32	18	3	1	252	241	106	11	5	84	100	11.8	2.96	133	.251	.314	24	.235	2	30	28	-0	2.8

YEAR	TM/L	W	L	PCT	G	GS	CG	SH	SV	IP	H	R	HR	HB	BB	SO	RAT	ERA	ERA+	OAV	OOB	BH	AVG	PB	PR	PR+	PD	TPI
1936	Chi-N	18	11	.621	43	33	20	**4**	1	258^2	238	106	14	3	93	102	11.6	3.31	121	.246	.314	12	.138	-3	21	20	1	1.8
1937	Chi-N	14	15	.483	42	34	17	2	3	272^1	289	122	14	0	73	108	12.0	3.54	113	.273	.320	15	.172	-1	11	13	3	1.5
1938	*Chi-N★	**22**	9	**.710**	44	37	19	**9**	2	291	281	95	18	2	74	121	11.0	**2.66**	**144**	.252	.299	20	.198	1	**37**	**37**	1	**4.0**
1939	Chi-N★	19	15	.559	37	36	20	1	0	282^1	295	125	18	1	85	105	12.1	3.44	114	.272	.325	13	.126	-4	15	15	5	1.7
1940	Chi-N	9	17	.346	37	30	9	1	0	211^1	246	129	12	2	70	70	13.5	5.03	75	.294	.350	10	.132	-2	-28	-31	-1	-3.5
1941	Chi-N	8	14	.364	28	22	12	0	1	167^1	179	87	6	2	43	62	12.0	3.76	93	.270	.316	11	.186	1	-2	-5	1	-0.4
1942	Chi-N	13	13	.500	32	30	18	1	0	219^2	221	99	4	1	67	75	11.8	3.85	83	.258	.312	11	.159	1	-13	-16	1	-1.6
1943	Chi-N	3	7	.300	13	12	4	0	0	78^1	83	37	4	0	27	18	12.6	3.56	94	.273	.332	7	.269	1	-2	-2	-1	-0.2
	Phi-N	1	5	.167	13	7	2	0	3	60^2	70	35	4	1	21	17	13.6	4.60	73	.298	.358	1	.059	-2	-8	-8	-1	-1.1
	Yr	4	12	.250	26	19	6	0	3	139	153	72	8	1	48	35	13.1	4.01	84	.284	.344	8	.186	-0	-10	-10	-2	-1.3
1944	Phi-N	10	11	.476	31	28	11	3	1	208^1	199	88	9	3	57	50	11.2	3.15	115	.248	.300	14	.194	-0	11	11	2	1.2
1945	Phi-N	3	6	.333	13	13	2	0	0	77^1	107	52	0	0	30	13	15.9	4.66	82	.318	.374	4	.167	-1	-7	-7	0	-0.7
	Bos-N	6	3	.667	16	13	6	1	0	106^1	112	43	6	0	36	12	12.5	2.79	137	.279	.338	4	.129	-1	12	12	1	1.0
	Yr	9	9	.500	29	26	8	1	0	183^2	219	95	6	0	66	25	14.0	3.58	107	.297	.354	8	.145	-1	5	5	1	0.3
1946	Bos-N	10	9	.526	25	21	8	0	0	140	148	73	7	1	45	32	12.5	4.18	82	.273	.330	8	.170	-1	-12	-12	1	-1.4
1947	Chi-N	0	2	.000	14	2	0	0	0	24	26	16	2	1	14	9	15.4	4.50	88	.268	.366	1	.333	0	-1	-2	0	-0.1
Total	14	169	157	.518	462	379	182	29	13	2864	2953	1304	138	24	893	998	12.2	3.54	106	.266	.322	165	.168	-10	78	67	14	6.2

● BILL LEE

Lee, William Francis "Spaceman" b: 12/28/46, Burbank, Cal. BL/TL, 6'3", 210 lbs. Deb: 6/25/69

YEAR	TM/L	W	L	PCT	G	GS	CG	SH	SV	IP	H	R	HR	HB	BB	SO	RAT	ERA	ERA+	OAV	OOB	BH	AVG	PB	PR	PR+	PD	TPI
1969	Bos-A	1	3	.250	20	1	0	0	0	52	56	27	9	2	28	45	14.9	4.50	85	.281	.376	0	.000	-1	-5	-4	-0	-0.4
1970	Bos-A	2	2	.500	11	5	0	0	1	37	48	20	3	0	14	19	15.1	4.62	86	.320	.378	0	.000	-1	-4	-3	1	-0.3
1971	Bos-A	9	2	.818	47	3	0	0	2	102	102	35	7	1	46	74	13.1	2.74	135	.256	.335	5	.217	0	8	10	0	1.2
1972	Bos-A	7	4	.636	47	0	0	0	5	84^1	75	31	5	1	32	43	11.5	3.20	101	.248	.322	3	.188	1	-1	0	3	0.5
1973	Bos-A☆	17	11	.607	38	33	18	1	1	284^2	275	100	20	5	76	120	11.3	2.75	146	.257	.309	0	—	0	34	38	1	3.8
1974	Bos-A	17	15	.531	38	37	16	1	0	282^1	320	123	25	4	67	95	12.5	3.51	110	.290	.333	0	—	0	4	10	4	1.5
1975	*Bos-A	17	9	.654	41	34	17	4	0	260	274	123	20	3	69	78	12.0	3.95	104	.273	.322	0	—	0	-5	4	2	0.5
1976	Bos-A	5	7	.417	24	14	1	0	3	96	124	68	13	3	28	29	14.5	5.63	70	.307	.356	0	—	0	-22	-16	1	-1.9
1977	Bos-A	9	5	.643	27	16	4	0	1	128	155	67	14	0	29	31	12.9	4.43	102	.306	.344	0	—	0	-5	1	2	0.3
1978	Bos-A	10	10	.500	28	24	8	1	0	177	198	89	20	2	59	44	13.2	3.46	119	.285	.343	0	—	0	6	12	0	1.3
1979	Mon-N	16	10	.615	33	33	6	3	0	222	230	91	20	1	46	59	11.2	3.04	121	.265	.303	16	.216	2	17	16	1	2.1
1980	Mon-N	4	6	.400	24	18	2	0	0	118	156	71	13	3	22	34	13.8	4.96	72	.319	.352	9	.220	1	-18	-18	-0	-1.4
1981	*Mon-N	5	6	.455	31	7	0	0	6	88^2	90	33	6	2	14	34	10.8	2.94	119	.265	.298	8	.364	3	5	5	3	1.4
1982	Mon-N	0	0	—	7	0	0	0	0	12^1	19	7	1	0	1	8	14.6	4.38	83	.352	.364	0	—	0	-1	-1	0	0.0
Total	14	119	90	.569	416	225	72	10	19	1944^1	2122	885	176	27	531	713	12.4	3.62	107	.280	.329	41	.208	5	14	54	16	8.6

● WATTY LEE

Lee, Wyatt Arnold b: 8/12/1879, Lynch Station, Va. d: 3/6/36, Washington, D.C. BL/TL, 5'10.5", 171 lbs. Deb: 4/30/01 ♦

YEAR	TM/L	W	L	PCT	G	GS	CG	SH	SV	IP	H	R	HR	HB	BB	SO	RAT	ERA	ERA+	OAV	OOB	BH	AVG	PB	PR	PR+	PD	TPI
1901	Was-A	16	16	.500	36	33	25	2	0	262	328	184	14	11	45	63	13.2	4.40	83	.303	.337	33	.256	4	-21	-21	2	-1.5
1902	Was-A	5	6	.455	13	10	10	0	0	98	118	66	5	8	20	24	13.4	5.05	73	.298	.344	100	.256	3	-16	-14	1	-1.0
1903	Was-A	8	12	.400	22	20	15	2	0	166^2	169	86	5	7	40	70	11.7	3.08	102	.262	.313	48	.208	1	-2	1	3	0.6
1904	Pit-N	1	2	.333	5	3	1	0	0	22^2	34	25	0	3	9	5	18.3	8.74	31	.337	.407	4	.333	1	-15	-15	0	-1.5
Total	4	30	36	.455	76	66	51	4	0	549^1	649	361	24	29	114	162	13.0	4.29	81	.292	.334	185	.242	10	-55	-48	5	-3.4

● SAM LEEVER

Leever, Samuel "Deacon" or "The Goshen Schoolmaster"
b: 12/23/1871, Goshen, Ohio d: 5/19/53, Goshen, Ohio BR/TR, 5'10.5", 175 lbs. Deb: 5/26/1898

YEAR	TM/L	W	L	PCT	G	GS	CG	SH	SV	IP	H	R	HR	HB	BB	SO	RAT	ERA	ERA+	OAV	OOB	BH	AVG	PB	PR	PR+	PD	TPI
1898	Pit-N	1	0	1.000	5	3	2	0	0	33	26	10	0	1	5	15	8.7	2.45	145	.215	.252	3	.250	0	4	4	-0	0.2
1899	Pit-N	21	23	.477	**51**	39	35	4	**3**	**379**	353	191	7	11	122	121	11.5	3.18	120	.247	.311	33	.226	3	28	27	2	3.0
1900	*Pit-N	15	13	.536	30	29	25	3	0	232^2	236	101	2	8	48	84	11.3	2.71	134	.263	.306	18	.205	0	26	24	-1	2.4
1901	Pit-N	14	5	.737	21	20	18	2	0	176	182	82	2	7	39	82	11.7	2.86	114	.265	.311	13	.183	-0	9	8	2	0.9
1902	Pit-N	15	7	.682	28	26	23	4	2	222	203	73	2	8	31	86	9.8	2.39	115	.243	.277	16	.178	-0	10	9	-4	0.4
1903	*Pit-N	25	7	**.781**	36	34	30	**7**	1	284^1	255	98	2	5	60	90	10.1	**2.06**	**157**	.238	.282	19	.165	-4	38	38	-0	3.4
1904	Pit-N	18	11	.621	34	32	26	1	0	253^1	224	85	2	5	54	63	10.1	2.17	127	.237	.282	26	.263	7	16	16	-1	2.4
1905	Pit-N	20	5	**.800**	33	29	20	3	1	229^2	199	94	3	12	54	81	10.4	2.70	111	.231	.286	9	.102	-4	8	8	0	0.4
1906	Pit-N	22	7	.759	36	31	25	6	0	260^1	232	84	3	7	48	76	9.9	2.32	115	.243	.284	20	.211	2	9	10	-5	0.7
1907	Pit-N	14	9	.609	31	24	17	5	0	216^2	182	70	3	8	46	65	9.8	1.66	147	.229	.278	11	.151	-1	20	19	-5	1.4
1908	Pit-N	15	7	.682	38	20	14	4	2	192^2	179	60	1	6	41	28	10.6	2.10	110	.249	.295	9	.148	0	6	4	-4	0.1
1909	Pit-N	8	1	.889	19	4	2	0	2	70	74	30	0	4	14	23	11.8	2.83	96	.276	.322	4	.167	0	-2	-1	0	-0.1
1910	Pit-N	6	5	.545	26	8	4	0	2	111	104	45	2	6	25	33	10.9	2.76	112	.259	.313	2	.065	-3	3	4	1	0.2
Total	13	194	100	.660	388	299	241	39	13	2660^2	2449	1023	29	88	587	847	10.6	2.47	123	.245	.293	183	.184	1	175	170	-15	15.4

● BILL LEFEBVRE

Lefebvre, Wilfred Henry "Lefty" b: 11/11/15, Natick, R.I. BL/TL, 5'11.5", 180 lbs. Deb: 6/10/38 ♦

YEAR	TM/L	W	L	PCT	G	GS	CG	SH	SV	IP	H	R	HR	HB	BB	SO	RAT	ERA	ERA+	OAV	OOB	BH	AVG	PB	PR	PR+	PD	TPI
1938	Bos-A	0	0	—	1	0	0	0	0	4	8	6	2	1	0	0	20.3	13.50	37	.400	.429	1	1.000	1	-4	-4	-0	-0.1
1939	Bos-A	1	1	.500	5	3	0	0	0	26^1	35	17	2	0	14	8	16.7	5.81	81	.333	.412	3	.300	1	-3	-3	-1	-0.2
1943	Was-A	2	0	1.000	6	3	1	0	0	32^1	33	18	3	0	16	10	13.6	4.45	72	.268	.353	4	.286	2	-4	-5	-0	-0.1
1944	Was-A	2	4	.333	24	4	2	0	3	69^2	86	48	3	1	21	18	14.0	4.52	72	.305	.355	16	.258	3	-8	-10	-0	-0.4
Total	4	5	5	.500	36	10	3	0	3	132^1	162	89	10	2	51	36	14.6	5.03	71	.306	.369	24	.276	7	-20	-22	-1	-0.8

● CRAIG LEFFERTS

Lefferts, Craig Lindsay b: 9/29/57, Munich, W.Germany BL/TL, 6'1", 210 lbs. Deb: 4/7/83

YEAR	TM/L	W	L	PCT	G	GS	CG	SH	SV	IP	H	R	HR	HB	BB	SO	RAT	ERA	ERA+	OAV	OOB	BH	AVG	PB	PR	PR+	PD	TPI
1983	Chi-N	3	4	.429	56	5	0	0	1	89	80	35	13	2	29	60	11.2	3.13	121	.243	.308	2	.111	-1	5	6	0	0.4
1984	*SD-N	3	4	.429	62	0	0	0	10	105^2	88	29	4	1	24	56	9.6	2.13	168	.229	.276	5	.294	1	17	17	-1	1.4
1985	SD-N	7	6	.538	60	0	0	0	2	83^1	75	34	7	0	30	48	11.3	3.35	106	.244	.312	1	.250	0	2	2	-0	0.3
1986	SD-N	9	8	.529	**83**	0	0	0	4	107^2	98	41	7	1	44	72	12.0	3.09	118	.253	.331	1	.125	1	8	7	2	1.3
1987	SD-N	2	2	.500	33	0	0	0	2	51^1	56	29	9	2	15	39	12.8	4.38	90	.272	.327	1	.333	0	-2	-2	-1	-0.2
	*SF-N	3	3	.500	44	0	0	0	4	47^1	36	18	4	0	18	18	10.3	3.23	119	.216	.292	1	.250	1	4	3	-1	0.4
	Yr	5	5	.500	77	0	0	0	6	98^2	92	47	13	2	33	57	11.6	3.83	102	.247	.311	2	.286	1	3	1	-1	0.2
1988	SF-N	3	8	.273	64	0	0	0	11	92^1	74	33	7	1	23	58	9.6	2.92	112	.225	.278	0	.000	-1	5	4	-1	0.3
1989	*SF-N	2	4	.333	70	0	0	0	20	107	93	38	11	1	22	71	9.8	2.69	126	.233	.275	0	.000	-1	10	8	-1	0.6
1990	SD-N	7	5	.583	56	0	0	0	23	78^2	68	26	10	1	22	60	10.4	2.52	152	.228	.283	1	.250	0	11	11	0	2.3
1991	SD-N	1	6	.143	54	0	0	0	23	69	74	35	5	1	14	48	11.6	3.91	97	.285	.324	0	.000	-1	-2	-1	0	-0.1
1992	SD-N	13	9	.591	27	27	0	0	0	163^1	180	76	16	0	35	81	11.8	3.69	97	.285	.322	4	.077	-3	-3	-2	-1	-0.6
	Bal-A	1	3	.250	5	5	1	0	0	33	34	19	3	0	6	23	10.9	4.09	99	.268	.301	0	—	0	-1	-0	-1	-0.1
1993	Tex-A	3	9	.250	52	8	0	0	0	83^1	102	57	17	1	28	58	14.1	6.05	69	.304	.360	0	—	0	-16	-18	0	-2.2
1994	Cal-A	1	1	.500	30	0	0	0	1	34^2	50	20	7	0	12	27	16.1	4.67	105	.350	.400	0	—	0	1	1	-1	0.0
Total	12	58	72	.446	696	45	1	0	101	1145^2	1108	490	120	11	322	719	11.3	3.43	108	.257	.311	16	.121	-3	40	37	-4	3.8

● PHIL LEFTWICH

Leftwich, Philip Dale b: 5/19/69, Lynchburg, Va. BR/TR, 6'5", 205 lbs. Deb: 7/29/93

YEAR	TM/L	W	L	PCT	G	GS	CG	SH	SV	IP	H	R	HR	HB	BB	SO	RAT	ERA	ERA+	OAV	OOB	BH	AVG	PB	PR	PR+	PD	TPI
1993	Cal-A	4	6	.400	12	12	1	0	0	80^2	81	35	5	3	27	31	12.4	3.79	119	.262	.327	0	—	0	5	6	-0	0.7
1994	Cal-A	5	10	.333	20	20	1	0	0	114	127	75	16	3	42	67	13.6	5.68	86	.283	.349	0	—	0	-11	-10	-0	-1.1
1996	Cal-A	0	1	.000	2	2	0	0	0	7^1	12	9	1	0	3	4	18.4	7.36	68	.375	.429	0	—	0	-2	-2	0	-0.2
Total	3	9	17	.346	34	34	2	0	0	202	220	119	22	6	72	102	13.3	4.99	95	.279	.344	0	—	0	-8	-5	-0	-0.6

● REGIS LEHENY

Leheny, Regis Francis b: 1/5/08, Pittsburgh, Pa. d: 11/2/76, Pittsburgh, Pa. BL/TL, 6'0.5", 180 lbs. Deb: 5/21/32

YEAR	TM/L	W	L	PCT	G	GS	CG	SH	SV	IP	H	R	HR	HB	BB	SO	RAT	ERA	ERA+	OAV	OOB	BH	AVG	PB	PR	PR+	PD	TPI
1932	Bos-A	0	0	—	2	0	0	0	0	2^2	5	5	0	0	3	1	27.0	16.88	27	.417	.533	0	.000	-0	-4	-4	0	-0.2

● JIM LEHEW

Lehew, James Anthony b: 8/19/37, Baltimore, Md. BR/TR, 6', 185 lbs. Deb: 9/13/61

YEAR	TM/L	W	L	PCT	G	GS	CG	SH	SV	IP	H	R	HR	HB	BB	SO	RAT	ERA	ERA+	OAV	OOB	BH	AVG	PB	PR	PR+	PD	TPI
1961	Bal-A	0	0	—	2	0	0	0	0	2	1	0	0	0	0	0	4.5	0.00	—	.167	.167	0	—	0	1	1	0	0.1
1962	Bal-A	0	0	—	6	0	0	0	0	9^2	10	3	0	0	3	2	12.1	1.86	199	.303	.361	0	.000	-0	2	2	0	0.1
Total	2	0	0	—	8	0	0	0	0	11^2	11	3	0	0	3	2	10.8	1.54	241	.282	.333	0	.000	-0	3	3	0	0.2

● KEN LEHMAN

Lehman, Kenneth Karl b: 6/10/28, Seattle, Wash. BL/TL, 6', 186 lbs. Deb: 9/5/52

YEAR	TM/L	W	L	PCT	G	GS	CG	SH	SV	IP	H	R	HR	HB	BB	SO	RAT	ERA	ERA+	OAV	OOB	BH	AVG	PB	PR	PR+	PD	TPI
1952	*Bro-N	1	2	.333	4	3	0	0	0	15^1	19	11	1	0	6	7	14.7	5.28	69	.297	.357	0	.000	0	-3	-3	0	-0.5
1956	Bro-N	2	3	.400	25	4	0	0	0	49^1	65	35	11	0	23	29	16.1	5.66	70	.325	.395	3	.300	1	-10	-9	1	-0.7

YEAR	TM/L	W	L	PCT	G	GS	CG	SH	SV	IP	H	R	HR	HB	BB	SO	RAT	ERA	ERA+	OAV	OOB	BH	AVG	PB	PR	PR+	PD	TPI
1957	Bro-N	0	0	—	3	0	0	0	0	7	7	0	0	0	1	3	10.3	0.00	—	.259	.286	1	.500	0	3	3	0	0.2
	Bal-A	8	3	.727	30	3	1	0	6	68	57	21	1	0	22	32	10.5	2.78	129	.232	.295	4	.200	1	8	6	-1	1.2
1958	Bal-A	2	1	.667	31	1	1	0	0	62	64	26	5	2	18	36	12.2	3.48	103	.276	.333	1	.071	-1	2	1	0	-0.1
1961	Phi-N	1	1	.500	41	2	0	0	1	63^1	61	32	6	1	25	27	12.4	4.26	96	.260	.333	0	.000	-1	-2	-1	1	0.0
Total	5	14	10	.583	134	13	2	0	7	265	273	125	24	3	95	134	12.6	3.91	97	.272	.337	9	.161	1	-2	-3	2	0.1
● NORM LEHR	Lehr, Norman Carl Michael "King" b: 5/28/01, Rochester, N.Y. d: 7/17/68, Livonia, N.Y. BR/TR, 6', 168 lbs. Deb: 5/20/26																											
1926	Cle-A	0	0	—	4	0	0	0	0	14^2	11	5	0	0	4	4	9.2	3.07	132	.216	.273	0	.000	-1	2	2	1	0.1
● HANK LEIBER	Leiber, Henry Edward b: 1/17/11, Phoenix, Ariz. d: 11/8/93, Tucson, Ariz. BR/TR, 6'1.5", 205 lbs. Deb: 4/16/33 ♦																											
1942	NY-N	0	1	.000	1	1	1	0	0	9	9	9	0	1	5	5	15.0	6.00	56	.290	.405	32	.218	0	-3	-3	0	-0.2
● CHARLIE LEIBRANDT	Leibrandt, Charles Louis b: 10/4/56, Chicago, Ill. BR/TL, 6'3", 200 lbs. Deb: 9/17/79																											
1979	*Cin-N	0	0	—	3	0	0	0	0	4^1	2	2	0	0	2	1	8.3	0.00	—	.154	.267	0	—	0	2	2	0	0.1
1980	Cin-N	10	9	.526	36	27	5	2	0	173^2	200	84	15	2	54	62	13.3	4.25	84	.292	.346	11	.196	1	-12	-13	1	-1.1
1981	Cin-N	1	1	.500	7	4	1	1	0	30	28	12	0	0	15	9	12.9	3.60	99	.262	.352	0	.000	-0	-0	-0	0	0.0
1982	Cin-N	5	7	.417	36	11	0	0	2	107^2	130	68	4	2	48	34	15.0	5.10	73	.308	.381	2	.080	-1	-18	-16	-0	-1.9
1984	*KC-A	11	7	.611	23	23	0	0	0	143^2	158	65	11	3	38	53	12.5	3.63	111	.277	.326	0	—	0	6	6	-2	0.6
1985	*KC-A	17	9	.654	33	33	8	3	0	237^2	223	86	17	2	68	108	11.1	2.69	155	.248	.302	0	—	0	39	39	4	4.5
1986	KC-A	14	11	.560	35	34	8	1	0	231^1	238	112	18	4	63	108	11.9	4.09	104	.268	.319	0	—	0	3	4	2	0.6
1987	KC-A	16	11	.593	35	35	8	3	0	240^1	235	104	23	1	74	151	11.6	3.41	134	.253	.308	0	—	0	28	30	4	3.5
1988	KC-A	13	12	.520	35	35	7	2	0	243	244	98	20	4	62	125	11.5	3.19	125	.264	.313	0	—	0	21	22	2	2.4
1989	KC-A	5	11	.313	33	27	3	1	0	161	196	98	13	2	54	73	14.1	5.14	75	.304	.360	0	—	0	-22	-23	-0	-2.1
1990	Atl-N	9	11	.450	24	24	5	2	0	162^1	164	72	9	4	35	76	11.3	3.16	128	.261	.304	9	.180	1	12	15	1	2.0
1991	*Atl-N	15	13	.536	36	36	1	1	0	229^2	212	105	18	4	56	128	10.7	3.49	112	.245	.294	3	.043	-4	5	10	4	1.1
1992	*Atl-N	15	7	.682	32	31	5	2	0	193	191	78	9	5	42	104	11.1	3.36	109	.258	.302	7	.121	-1	3	6	3	0.9
1993	Tex-A	9	10	.474	26	26	1	0	0	150^1	169	84	15	4	45	89	13.1	4.55	91	.284	.339	0	—	0	-4	-7	5	-0.2
Total	14	140	119	.541	394	346	52	18	2	2308	2390	1068	172	37	656	1121	12.0	3.71	108	.268	.321	32	.120	-5	62	78	25	10.4
● LEFTY LEIFIELD	Leifield, Albert Peter b: 9/5/1883, Trenton, Ill. d: 10/10/70, Alexandria, Va. BL/TL, 6'1", 165 lbs. Deb: 9/3/05 C																											
1905	Pit-N	5	2	.714	8	7	6	1	0	56	52	24	0	4	14	10	11.3	2.89	104	.248	.307	7	.350	3	1	1	1	0.5
1906	Pit-N	18	13	.581	37	31	24	8	1	255^2	214	90	3	14	68	111	10.4	1.87	143	.231	.294	11	.125	-3	22	23	1	2.6
1907	Pit-N	20	16	.556	40	33	24	6	1	286	270	107	1	12	100	112	12.0	2.33	105	.256	.328	15	.147	0	5	3	4	0.8
1908	Pit-N	15	14	.517	34	26	18	5	2	218^2	168	69	1	12	86	87	10.9	2.10	110	.212	.299	17	.227	3	6	5	-0	1.0
1909	*Pit-N	19	8	.704	32	26	13	3	0	201^2	172	76	4	6	54	43	10.4	2.37	115	.229	.286	14	.192	2	5	8	-2	1.0
1910	Pit-N	15	13	.536	40	30	13	3	2	218^1	197	84	6	10	67	64	11.3	2.64	117	.253	.320	11	.183	0	10	11	3	1.7
1911	Pit-N	16	16	.500	42	37	26	2	1	318	301	114	7	16	82	111	11.3	2.63	131	.260	.318	24	.235	6	27	28	-1	3.2
1912	Pit-N	1	2	.333	6	1	1	0	0	23^2	29	15	0	2	10	8	15.6	4.18	78	.302	.380	1	.143	0	-2	-3	1	-0.2
	Chi-N	7	2	.778	13	9	4	1	0	70^2	68	26	0	3	21	23	11.7	2.42	137	.258	.319	3	.115	-1	8	7	1	0.9
	Yr	8	4	.667	19	10	5	1	0	94^1	97	41	0	5	31	31	12.7	2.86	116	.269	.336	4	.121	-1	6	5	2	0.7
1913	Chi-N	0	1	.000	6	1	0	0	0	21^1	28	14	0	0	5	4	13.9	5.48	58	.329	.367	0	.000	-1	-5	-6	1	-0.3
1918	StL-A	2	6	.250	15	6	3	1	0	67	61	23	1	2	19	22	11.0	2.55	107	.252	.312	1	.053	-2	2	1	1	0.1
1919	StL-A	6	4	.600	19	9	6	2	0	92	96	40	4	4	25	18	12.2	2.93	113	.270	.325	3	.100	-2	3	4	1	0.2
1920	StL-A	0	0	—	4	0	0	0	0	9	17	12	0	0	3	3	20.0	7.00	56	.405	.444	0	.000	-0	-3	-3	-0	-0.2
Total	12	124	97	.561	296	216	138	32	7	1838	1673	694	27	85	554	616	11.3	2.47	116	.248	.313	107	.175	6	77	80	10	11.3
● DAVE LEIPER	Leiper, David Paul b: 6/18/62, Whittier, Cal. BL/TL, 6'1", 160 lbs. Deb: 9/2/84																											
1984	Oak-A	1	0	1.000	8	0	0	0	0	7	12	7	2	0	5	3	21.9	9.00	42	.353	.436	0	—	0	-4	-4	0	-0.5
1986	Oak-A	2	2	.500	33	0	0	0	1	31^2	28	17	3	2	18	15	13.6	4.83	80	.252	.366	0	—	0	-2	-4	0	-0.4
1987	Oak-A	2	1	.667	45	0	0	0	1	52^1	49	28	6	1	18	33	11.7	3.78	109	.246	.312	0	—	0	4	2	1	0.2
	SD-N	1	0	1.000	12	0	0	0	1	16	16	8	2	0	5	10	11.8	4.50	88	.267	.323	0	—	0	-1	-1	-0	-0.1
1988	SD-N	3	0	1.000	35	0	0	0	1	54	45	19	1	0	14	33	9.8	2.17	157	.231	.282	1	.500	0	8	8	0	0.5
1989	SD-N	0	1	.000	22	0	0	0	0	28^2	40	19	2	2	20	7	19.5	5.02	70	.333	.437	0	.000	-0	-5	-5	1	-0.2
1994	Oak-A	0	0	—	26	0	0	0	1	18^2	13	4	0	1	6	14	9.6	1.93	230	.206	.286	0	—	0	6	6	-0	0.2
1995	Oak-A	1	1	.500	24	0	0	0	0	22^2	23	10	3	1	13	10	14.7	3.57	125	.258	.359	0	—	0	3	2	-0	0.1
	Mon-N	0	2	.000	26	0	0	0	2	22	16	8	2	0	6	12	9.0	2.86	150	.200	.256	0	.000	-0	3	3	0	0.4
1996	Phi-N	2	0	1.000	26	0	0	0	0	21	31	16	4	0	7	10	16.3	6.43	67	.348	.396	0	—	0	-5	-5	0	-0.4
	Mon-N	0	1	.000	7	0	0	0	0	4	9	5	0	0	2	3	24.8	11.25	38	.474	.524	0	—	0	-3	-3	0	-0.6
	Yr	2	1	.667	33	0	0	0	0	25	40	21	4	0	9	13	17.6	7.20	60	.370	.419	0	—	0	-8	-8	0	-1.0
Total	8	12	8	.600	264	0	0	0	7	278	282	141	25	7	114	150	13.0	3.98	100	.266	.342	1	.250	0	4	-1	2	-0.8
● JACK LEIPER	Leiper, John Henry Thomas b: 12/23/1867, Chester, Pa. d: 8/23/60, West Goshen, Pa. BL/TL, 5'11", Deb: 9/4/1891																											
1891	Col-a	2	2	.500	6	5	4	0	0	45	41	43	3	4	39	19	16.8	5.40	64	.234	.385	3	.143	-2	-8	-10	-1	-0.8
● JOHN LEISTER	Leister, John William b: 1/3/61, San Antonio, Tex. BR/TR, 6'2", 200 lbs. Deb: 5/28/87																											
1987	Bos-A	0	2	.000	8	6	0	0	0	30^1	49	31	9	0	12	16	18.1	9.20	50	.368	.421	0	—	0	-16	-15	-1	-0.9
1990	Bos-A	0	0	—	2	1	0	0	0	5^2	7	5	0	0	4	3	17.5	4.76	86	.304	.407	0	—	0	-1	-0	-0	0.0
Total	2	0	2	.000	10	7	0	0	0	36	56	36	9	0	16	19	18.0	8.50	53	.359	.419	0	—	0	-16	-16	-1	-0.9
● AL LEITER	Leiter, Alois Terry b: 10/23/65, Toms River, N.J. BL/TL, 6'3", 215 lbs. Deb: 9/15/87 F																											
1987	NY-A	2	2	.500	4	4	0	0	0	22^2	24	16	2	0	15	28	15.5	6.35	69	.273	.379	0	—	0	-5	-5	-0	-0.7
1988	NY-A	4	4	.500	14	14	0	0	0	57^1	49	27	7	5	33	60	13.7	3.92	101	.231	.348	0	—	0	0	0	1	0.1
1989	NY-A	1	2	.333	4	4	0	0	0	26^2	23	20	1	2	21	22	15.5	6.08	64	.235	.380	0	—	0	-6	-7	-0	-0.6
	Tor-A	0	0	—	1	1	0	0	0	6^2	9	3	1	0	2	4	14.9	4.05	93	.310	.355	0	—	0	-0	-0	-0	0.0
	Yr	1	2	.333	5	5	0	0	0	33^1	32	23	2	2	23	26	15.4	5.67	68	.252	.375	0	—	0	-7	-7	-1	-0.6
1990	Tor-A	0	0	—	4	0	0	0	0	6^1	1	0	0	0	2	5	4.3	0.00	—	.050	.136	0	—	0	3	3	0	0.2
1991	Tor-A	0	0	—	3	0	0	0	0	1^2	3	5	0	0	5	1	43.2	27.00	16	.429	.667	0	—	0	-4	-4	0	-0.2
1992	Tor-A	0	0	—	1	0	0	0	0	1	1	1	0	0	2	0	27.0	9.00	45	.200	.429	0	—	0	-1	-1	0	0.0
1993	*Tor-A	9	6	.600	34	12	1	1	2	105	93	52	8	4	56	66	13.1	4.11	105	.240	.342	0	—	0	3	3	-1	0.3
1994	Tor-A	6	7	.462	20	20	1	0	0	111^2	125	68	6	2	65	100	15.5	5.08	95	.285	.380	0	—	0	-3	-3	-0	-0.3
1995	Tor-A	11	11	.500	28	28	2	1	0	183	162	80	15	6	108	153	13.6	3.64	130	.238	.347	0	—	0	22	22	-2	2.1
1996	Fla-N★	16	12	.571	33	33	2	1	0	215^1	153	74	14	11	119	200	11.8	2.93	139	**.202**	.319	7	.100	-2	31	29	-1	3.0
1997	*Fla-N	11	9	.550	27	27	0	0	0	151^1	133	78	13	12	91	132	14.0	4.34	93	.241	.360	5	.104	-1	-2	-5	-2	-0.9
1998	NY-N	17	6	.739	28	28	4	2	0	193	151	55	8	11	71	174	10.9	2.47	167	.216	.298	6	.105	0	38	37	-2	4.0
1999	*NY-N	13	12	.520	32	32	1	1	0	213	209	107	19	9	93	162	13.1	4.23	104	.262	.346	6	.105	-2	8	4	-3	-0.1
2000	*NY-N★	16	8	.667	31	31	2	1	0	208	176	84	19	11	76	200	11.4	3.20	138	.228	.307	3	.052	-4	33	29	1	2.8
Total	14	106	79	.573	264	234	13	7	2	1502^2	1312	670	113	73	759	1307	12.8	3.73	116	.237	.336	27	.093	-8	116	100	-10	9.7
● MARK LEITER	Leiter, Mark Edward b: 4/13/63, Joliet, Ill. BR/TR, 6'3", 210 lbs. Deb: 7/24/90 F																											
1990	NY-A	1	1	.500	8	3	0	0	0	26^1	33	20	5	2	9	21	15.0	6.84	58	.314	.379	0	—	0	-9	-8	1	-0.5
1991	Det-A	9	7	.563	38	15	1	0	1	134^2	125	66	16	6	50	103	12.1	4.21	99	.245	.319	0	—	0	-2	-1	-1	-0.1
1992	Det-A	8	5	.615	35	14	1	0	0	112	116	57	9	3	43	75	13.0	4.18	95	.277	.348	0	—	0	-3	-3	0	-0.3
1993	Det-A	6	6	.500	27	13	1	0	0	106^2	111	61	17	3	44	70	13.3	4.73	91	.267	.341	0	—	0	-5	-5	-1	-0.6
1994	Cal-A	4	7	.364	40	7	0	0	2	95^1	99	56	13	9	35	71	13.5	4.72	104	.265	.343	0	—	0	1	2	1	0.2
1995	SF-N	10	12	.455	30	29	7	1	0	195^2	185	91	19	17	55	129	11.8	3.82	107	.254	.321	6	.098	-2	8	6	-3	0.1
1996	SF-N	4	10	.286	23	22	1	0	0	135^1	151	93	25	9	50	118	14.0	5.19	79	.283	.355	6	.143	-0	-14	-17	-2	-1.7
	Mon-N	4	2	.667	12	12	1	0	0	69^2	68	35	12	7	19	46	12.1	4.39	98	.254	.320	2	.080	-1	-1	-1	1	-0.1
	Yr	8	12	.400	35	34	2	0	0	205	219	128	37	16	69	164	13.3	4.92	85	.273	.343	8	.119	-2	-16	-17	-1	-1.8
1997	Phi-N	10	17	.370	31	31	3	0	0	182^2	216	132	25	9	64	148	14.2	5.67	75	.292	.355	6	.118	-1	-30	-28	1	-3.5
1998	Phi-N	7	5	.583	69	0	0	0	23	88^2	67	36	8	8	47	84	12.4	3.55	122	.216	.334	0	.000	-0	7	8	0	1.2

YEAR	TM/L	W	L	PCT	G	GS	CG	SH	SV	IP	H	R	HR	HB	BB	SO	RAT	ERA	ERA+	OAV	OOB	BH	AVG	PB	PR	PR+	PD	TPI
1999	Sea-A	0	0	—	2	0	0	0	0	1^1	2	1	0	0	0	1	13.5	6.75	70	.333	.333	0	—	0	-0	-0	0	0.0
Total	10	63	72	.467	315	146	15	1	26	1148^1	1173	648	149	73	416	866	13.0	4.60	92	.266	.339	20	.110	-5	-48	-48	-2	-5.3
● BILL LEITH Leith, William "Shady Bill" b: 5/31/1873, Matteawan, N.Y. d: 7/16/40, Beacon, N.Y. TL, Deb: 9/25/1899																												
1899	Was-N	0	0	—	1	0	0	0	0	2	4	5	0	1	2	1	31.5	18.00	22	.400	.538	0	.000	-0	-3	-3	-0	-0.2
● DOC LEITNER Leitner, George Aloysius b: 9/14/1865, Piermont, N.Y. d: 5/18/37, New York, N.Y. BR/TR, 5'11.5", 185 lbs. Deb: 8/10/1887																												
1887	Ind-N	2	6	.250	8	8	8	0	0	65	110	66	6	0	41	27	15.2	5.68	73	.358	.358	4	.148	-3	-12	-11	-2	-1.3
● DUMMY LEITNER Leitner, George Michael b: 6/19/1872, Parkton, Md. d: 2/20/60, Baltimore, Md. BL/TR, 5'7", 120 lbs. Deb: 6/29/01																												
1901	Phi-A	0	0	—	1	0	0	0	0	2	1	0	0	0	1	1	9.0	0.00	—	.143	.250	0	.000	-0	1	1	-0	0.0
	NY-N	0	2	.000	2	2	2	0	0	18	27	9	0	1	4	3	16.0	4.50	73	.342	.381	1	.143	-0	-2	-2	-0	-0.3
1902	Cle-A	0	0	—	1	1	0	0	0	8	11	4	0	0	1	0	13.5	4.50	77	.324	.343	1	.250	0	-1	-1	0	0.0
	Chi-A	0	0	—	1	0	0	0	0	4	9	7	0	2	2	0	29.3	13.50	25	.450	.542	0	.000	-0	-4	-5	0	-0.2
	Yr	0	0	—	2	1	0	0	0	12	20	11	0	2	3	0	18.8	7.50	46	.370	.424	1	.143	-0	-5	-6	1	-0.2
Total	2	0	2	.000	5	3	2	0	0	32	48	20	0	3	8	4	16.6	5.34	63	.343	.391	2	.133	-1	-7	-7	0	-0.5
● BILL LELIVELT Lelivelt, William John b: 10/21/1884, Chicago, Ill. d: 2/14/68, Chicago, Ill. BR/TR, 5'10", 168 lbs. Deb: 7/19/09 F																												
1909	Det-A	0	1	.000	4	2	1	0	1	20	27	12	0	0	2	4	13.0	4.50	56	.325	.341	2	.333	1	-4	-4	0	-0.2
1910	Det-A	0	1	.000	1	1	1	0	0	9	6	4	0	0	3	2	9.0	1.00	263	.207	.281	1	.500	1	2	2	0	0.3
Total	2	0	2	.000	5	3	2	0	1	29	33	16	0	0	5	6	11.8	3.41	75	.295	.325	3	.375	2	-3	-3	0	0.1
● DAVE LEMANCZYK Lemanczyk, David Lawrence b: 8/17/50, Syracuse, N.Y. BR/TR, 6'4", 235 lbs. Deb: 4/15/73																												
1973	Det-A	0	0	—	1	0	0	0	0	2^1	4	3	0	0	0	0	15.4	11.57	35	.364	.364	0	—	0	-2	-2	-0	-0.1
1974	Det-A	2	1	.667	22	3	0	0	0	78^2	79	43	12	2	44	52	14.3	4.00	95	.261	.358	0	—	0	-3	-2	1	0.0
1975	Det-A	2	7	.222	26	6	4	0	0	109	120	62	8	3	46	67	14.0	4.46	90	.281	.355	0	—	0	-8	-5	0	-0.4
1976	Det-A	4	6	.400	20	10	1	0	0	81^1	86	47	7	0	34	51	13.3	5.09	73	.271	.342	0	—	0	-14	-12	1	-1.3
1977	Tor-A	13	16	.448	34	34	11	0	0	252	278	143	20	4	87	105	13.2	4.25	99	.282	.343	0	—	0	-5	-1	0	-0.1
1978	Tor-A	4	14	.222	29	20	3	0	0	136^2	170	97	16	3	65	62	15.7	6.26	63	.313	.389	0	—	0	-38	-34	-1	-3.9
1979	Tor-A☆	8	10	.444	22	20	11	3	0	143	137	65	12	6	45	63	11.8	3.71	117	.258	.324	0	—	0	8	10	0	1.1
1980	Tor-A	2	5	.286	10	8	0	0	0	43^1	57	29	4	0	15	10	15.0	5.40	80	.322	.375	0	—	0	-7	-5	1	-0.6
	Cal-A	2	4	.333	21	2	0	0	0	66^2	81	40	8	2	27	19	14.9	4.32	91	.301	.369	0	—	0	-2	-3	-2	-0.4
	Yr	4	9	.308	31	10	0	0	0	110	138	69	12	2	42	29	14.9	4.75	86	.309	.371	0	—	0	-9	-8	-1	-1.0
Total	8	37	63	.370	185	103	30	3	0	913	1012	529	87	20	363	429	13.8	4.62	88	.284	.354	0	—	0	-71	-53	0	-5.7
● DENNY LEMASTER Lemaster, Denver Clayton b: 2/25/39, Corona, Cal. BR/TL, 6'1", 185 lbs. Deb: 7/15/62																												
1962	Mil-N	3	4	.429	17	12	4	1	0	86^2	75	36	11	3	32	69	11.4	3.01	126	.233	.308	4	.121	-1	9	8	-2	0.3
1963	Mil-N	11	14	.440	46	31	10	1	1	237	199	87	30	1	85	190	10.8	3.04	106	.227	.296	14	.189	3	7	5	-3	0.5
1964	Mil-N	17	11	.607	39	35	9	3	1	221	216	112	27	4	75	185	12.0	4.15	85	.252	.315	9	.134	0	-15	-16	0	-1.8
1965	Mil-N	7	13	.350	32	23	4	1	0	146^1	140	75	12	3	58	111	12.4	4.43	80	.251	.325	4	.089	-1	-14	-15	-0	-2.0
1966	Atl-N	11	8	.579	27	27	10	3	0	171	170	78	25	1	41	139	11.2	3.74	97	.258	.303	7	.119	-1	-2	-2	-2	-0.5
1967	Atl-N†	9	9	.500	31	31	8	2	0	215^1	184	86	20	3	72	148	10.8	3.34	99	.229	.295	7	.104	-2	1	-1	-1	-0.3
1968	Hou-N	10	15	.400	33	32	7	2	0	224	231	79	11	4	72	146	12.3	2.81	105	.262	.321	2	.031	-3	4	4	-3	-0.3
1969	Hou-N	13	17	.433	38	37	11	1	1	244^2	232	97	20	1	72	173	11.2	3.16	112	.246	.300	15	.170	3	12	10	-1	1.5
1970	Hou-N	7	12	.368	39	21	3	0	3	162	169	88	22	2	65	103	13.1	4.56	85	.268	.338	8	.178	2	-9	-13	-2	-1.3
1971	Hou-N	0	2	.000	42	0	0	0	2	60	59	23	4	1	22	28	12.3	3.45	98	.262	.331	1	.167	-0	0	-1	-0	-0.1
1972	Mon-N	2	0	1.000	13	0	0	0	0	19^2	28	17	2	1	6	13	16.0	7.78	46	.329	.380	1	.333	1	-9	-9	-1	-0.8
Total	11	90	105	.462	357	249	66	14	8	1787^2	1703	778	184	24	600	1305	11.7	3.58	96	.249	.312	72	.130	1	-18	-28	-13	-4.8
● DICK LeMAY LeMay, Richard Paul b: 8/28/38, Cincinnati, Ohio BL/TL, 6'3", 190 lbs. Deb: 6/13/61																												
1961	SF-N	3	6	.333	27	5	1	0	3	83^1	65	35	11	4	36	54	11.3	3.56	107	.217	.309	2	.077	-2	4	2	-0	0.1
1962	SF-N	0	1	.000	9	0	0	0	1	9^1	9	8	2	0	9	5	17.4	7.71	49	.265	.419	0	—	0	-4	-4	0	-0.5
1963	Chi-N	0	1	.000	9	1	0	0	0	15^1	26	9	1	0	4	10	17.6	5.28	66	.394	.429	0	.000	-0	-3	-3	-0	-0.2
Total	3	3	8	.273	45	6	1	0	4	108	100	52	14	4	49	69	12.8	4.17	91	.250	.338	2	.071	-1	-3	-5	-0	-0.6
● BOB LEMON Lemon, Robert Granville b: 9/22/20, San Bernardino, Cal. d: 1/11/2000, Long Beach, Cal. BL/TR, 6', 185 lbs. Deb: 9/9/41 MCH♦																												
1946	Cle-A	4	5	.444	32	5	1	0	1	94	77	40	1	0	68	39	13.9	2.49	133	.229	.359	16	.180	2	11	9	4	1.4
1947	Cle-A	11	5	.688	37	15	6	1	3	167^1	150	68	7	4	97	65	13.5	3.44	101	.242	.348	18	.321	9	5	1	4	1.6
1948	*Cle-A☆	20	14	.588	43	37	**20**	**10**	2	**293^2**	231	104	12	3	129	147	11.1	2.82	144	.216	.302	34	.286	14	**48**	43	8	**7.0**
1949	Cle-A☆	22	10	.688	37	33	22	2	1	279^2	211	101	19	6	137	138	11.4	2.99	133	.211	.309	29	.269	16	37	33	6	**5.8**
1950	Cle-A☆	**23**	11	.676	44	37	**22**	3	3	**288**	281	144	28	2	146	**170**	13.4	3.84	113	.257	.345	37	.272	17	23	16	5	3.8
1951	Cle-A★	17	14	.548	42	34	17	1	2	263^1	244	119	18	2	124	132	12.6	3.52	108	.244	.328	21	.206	5	18	9	4	1.8
1952	Cle-A★	22	11	.667	42	36	**28**	5	4	**309^2**	236	104	15	6	105	131	10.1	2.50	134	**.208**	.279	28	.226	7	40	32	7	4.9
1953	Cle-A☆	21	15	.583	41	36	23	5	1	**286^2**	283	119	16	11	110	98	12.7	3.36	112	.262	.336	26	.232	8	20	13	8	3.3
1954	*Cle-A★	**23**	7	.767	36	33	**21**	2	0	258^1	228	95	12	4	92	110	11.3	2.72	135	.237	.307	21	.214	6	29	28	4	**4.2**
1955	Cle-A	**18**	10	.643	35	31	5	0	2	211^1	218	103	17	5	74	100	12.6	3.88	103	.266	.330	19	.244	6	2	3	2	1.1
1956	Cle-A	20	14	.588	39	35	**21**	2	3	255^1	230	103	23	6	89	94	11.5	3.03	139	.239	.307	18	.194	5	32	33	4	**5.2**
1957	Cle-A	6	11	.353	21	17	2	0	0	117^1	129	70	9	7	64	45	15.3	4.60	81	.287	.385	3	.065	-3	-11	-12	3	-1.5
1958	Cle-A	0	1	.000	11	1	0	0	0	25^1	41	15	3	1	16	8	20.6	5.33	68	.376	.460	3	.231	0	-4	-5	1	-0.2
Total	13	207	128	.618	460	350	188	31	22	2850	2559	1185	180	57	1251	1277	12.2	3.23	119	.241	.324	274	.232	90	251	202	60	38.4
● DAVE LEMONDS Lemonds, David Lee b: 7/5/48, Charlotte, N.C. BL/TL, 6'1.5", 180 lbs. Deb: 6/30/69																												
1969	Chi-N	0	1	.000	2	1	0	0	0	4^2	5	2	0	0	5	0	19.3	3.86	104	.313	.476	0	.000	-0	-0	0	0	0.0
1972	Chi-A	4	7	.364	31	18	0	0	0	94^2	87	39	6	1	38	69	12.0	2.95	106	.247	.322	3	.120	-1	1	2	-0	0.1
Total	2	4	8	.333	33	19	0	0	0	99^1	92	41	6	1	43	69	12.3	2.99	106	.250	.330	3	.115	-1	1	2	-0	0.1
● MARK LEMONGELLO Lemongello, Mark b: 7/21/55, Jersey City, N.J. BR/TR, 6'1", 180 lbs. Deb: 9/14/76																												
1976	Hou-N	3	1	.750	4	4	1	0	0	29	26	12	2	0	7	9	10.2	2.79	115	.236	.282	0	.000	-1	2	1	1	0.2
1977	Hou-N	9	14	.391	34	30	5	0	0	214^2	237	88	20	3	52	83	12.2	3.48	103	.281	.325	6	.087	-4	10	2	-1	-0.2
1978	Hou-N	9	14	.391	33	30	9	1	1	210^1	204	100	20	9	66	77	11.9	3.94	84	.259	.323	11	.172	1	-8	-16	-0	-1.5
1979	Tor-A	1	9	.100	18	10	2	0	0	83	97	64	14	3	34	40	14.5	6.29	69	.299	.371	0	—	0	-19	-17	1	-1.7
Total	4	22	38	.367	89	74	17	1	1	537	564	264	56	15	159	209	12.4	4.06	88	.273	.329	17	.121	-3	-15	-31	1	-3.2
● ED LENNON Lennon, Edward Francis b: 8/17/1897, Philadelphia, Pa. d: 9/13/47, Philadelphia, Pa. BR/TR, 5'11", 170 lbs. Deb: 6/30/28																												
1928	Phi-N	0	0	—	5	0	0	0	0	12^1	19	14	0	0	10	6	21.2	8.76	49	.373	.475	0	.000	-1	-7	-6	-0	-0.4
● DANILO LEON Leon, Danilo Enrique (Lineco) b: 4/3/67, LaConcepcion, Venez. BR/TR, 6'1", 170 lbs. Deb: 6/6/92																												
1992	Tex-A	1	1	.500	15	0	0	0	0	18^1	18	14	5	3	10	15	15.2	5.89	65	.254	.369	0	—	0	-4	-4	0	-0.4
● IZZY LEON Leon, Isidoro (Becerra) b: 1/4/11, Cruces, Las Villas, Cuba BR/TR, 5'10", 160 lbs. Deb: 6/21/45																												
1945	Phi-N	0	4	.000	14	4	0	0	0	38^2	49	25	3	0	19	11	15.8	5.35	72	.312	.386	1	.111	-0	-7	-6	0	-0.6
● MAX LEON Leon, Maximino (Molino) b: 2/4/50, Pozo Hondo, Aculo, Mexico BR/TR, 6', 170 lbs. Deb: 7/18/73																												
1973	Atl-N	2	2	.500	12	1	1	0	0	27	30	18	6	3	9	18	14.0	5.33	74	.278	.350	2	.286	0	-5	-4	-0	-0.5
1974	Atl-N	4	7	.364	34	2	1	1	3	75	68	22	5	1	14	38	10.0	2.64	144	.242	.280	2	.133	-1	8	9	1	1.4
1975	Atl-N	2	1	.667	50	1	0	0	6	85	90	52	5	7	33	53	13.8	4.13	92	.274	.352	3	.333	1	-5	-3	1	0.0
1976	Atl-N	2	4	.333	30	0	0	0	3	36	32	15	2	2	15	16	12.3	2.75	138	.234	.318	0	.000	-0	3	4	-1	0.6
1977	Atl-N	4	4	.500	31	9	0	0	1	81^2	89	42	9	9	25	44	13.6	3.97	112	.280	.349	6	.316	1	-0	4	0	0.5
1978	Atl-N	0	0	—	5	0	0	0	0	5^2	6	4	1	1	4	1	17.5	6.35	64	.273	.407	0	—	0	-2	-1	-0	-0.1
Total	6	14	18	.438	162	13	2	1	13	310^1	315	153	28	23	100	170	12.7	3.71	107	.264	.332	13	.250	1	-1	9	1	1.9
● DENNIS LEONARD Leonard, Dennis Patrick b: 5/8/51, Brooklyn, N.Y. BR/TR, 6'1", 190 lbs. Deb: 9/4/74																												
1974	KC-A	0	4	.000	5	4	0	0	0	22	28	15	0	3	12	8	17.6	5.32	72	.329	.430	0	—	0	-4	-3	1	-0.5

YEAR	TM/L	W	L	PCT	G	GS	CG	SH	SV	IP	H	R	HR	HB	BB	SO	RAT	ERA	ERA+	OAV	OOB	BH	AVG	PB	PR	PR+	PD	TPI
1975	KC-A	15	7	.682	32	30	8	0	0	212^1	212	98	18	9	90	146	13.2	3.77	102	.263	.344	0	—	0	0	2	0	0.2
1976	*KC-A	17	10	.630	35	34	16	2	0	259	247	113	16	11	70	150	11.4	3.51	100	.255	.313	0	—	0	0	-0	-4	-0.4
1977	*KC-A	**20**	12	.625	38	37	21	5	1	292^2	246	117	18	8	79	244	10.2	3.04	133	.227	.285	0	—	0	33	33	-2	3.2
1978	*KC-A	21	17	.553	40	40	20	4	0	294^2	283	125	27	9	78	183	11.3	3.33	115	.254	.308	0	—	0	15	16	0	2.1
1979	KC-A	14	12	.538	32	32	12	**5**	0	236	226	117	33	2	56	126	10.8	4.08	105	.253	.299	0	—	0	4	5	0	0.5
1980	*KC-A	20	11	.645	38	38	9	3	0	280^1	271	127	30	1	80	155	11.3	3.79	107	.253	.306	0	—	0	8	8	-0	0.8
1981	*KC-A	13	11	.542	26	26	9	2	0	**201^2**	202	79	15	3	41	107	11.0	2.99	121	.258	.298	0	—	0	15	14	0	1.7
1982	KC-A	10	6	.625	21	21	2	0	0	130^2	145	82	20	2	46	58	13.3	5.10	80	.279	.340	0	—	0	-15	-15	1	-1.5
1983	KC-A	6	3	.667	10	10	1	0	0	63	69	29	3	0	19	31	12.6	3.71	110	.277	.328	0	—	0	3	3	0	0.4
1985	KC-A	0	0	—	2	0	0	0	0	2	1	0	0	0	0	1	4.5	0.00	—	.143	.143	0	—	0	1	1	-0	0.0
1986	KC-A	8	13	.381	33	30	5	2	0	192^2	207	106	22	4	51	114	12.2	4.44	96	.275	.324	0	—	0	-5	-4	0	-0.3
Total	12	144	106	.576	312	302	103	23	1	2187	2137	1008	202	52	622	1323	11.6	3.70	107	.257	.312	0	—	0	55	60	-3	6.2

● ELMER LEONARD

Leonard, Elmer Ellsworth "Tiny" b: 11/12/1888, Napa, Cal. d: 5/27/81, Napa, Cal. BR/TR, 6'3.5", 210 lbs. Deb: 6/22/11

YEAR	TM/L	W	L	PCT	G	GS	CG	SH	SV	IP	H	R	HR	HB	BB	SO	RAT	ERA	ERA+	OAV	OOB	BH	AVG	PB	PR	PR+	PD	TPI
1911	Phi-A	2	2	.500	5	1	1	0	0	19	26	11	0	2	10	10	18.0	2.84	111	.329	.418	2	.286	1	1	1	-1	0.1

● DUTCH LEONARD

Leonard, Emil John b: 3/25/09, Auburn, Ill. d: 4/17/83, Springfield, Ill. BR/TR, 6', 175 lbs. Deb: 8/31/33 C

YEAR	TM/L	W	L	PCT	G	GS	CG	SH	SV	IP	H	R	HR	HB	BB	SO	RAT	ERA	ERA+	OAV	OOB	BH	AVG	PB	PR	PR+	PD	TPI
1933	Bro-N	2	3	.400	10	3	2	0	0	40	42	17	0	0	10	6	11.7	2.93	110	.261	.304	0	.000	-1	2	1	0	0.0
1934	Bro-N	14	11	.560	44	21	11	2	5	183^2	210	90	12	4	33	58	12.1	3.28	119	.286	.320	12	.179	-1	16	13	1	1.8
1935	Bro-N	2	9	.182	43	11	4	0	**8**	137^2	152	67	11	1	29	41	11.9	3.92	101	.280	.318	1	.026	-4	1	1	-1	-0.5
1936	Bro-N	0	0	—	16	0	0	0	1	32	34	18	2	0	5	8	11.0	3.66	113	.262	.289	2	.400	0	1	2	1	0.2
1938	Was-A	12	15	.444	33	31	15	3	0	223^1	221	109	11	7	53	68	**11.3**	3.43	132	.256	**.305**	19	.232	3	34	29	0	3.3
1939	Was-A	20	8	.714	34	34	21	2	0	269^1	273	124	16	5	59	88	11.3	3.54	123	.262	.305	21	.221	0	32	26	2	2.5
1940	Was-A☆	14	19	.424	35	35	23	2	0	289	328	136	19	2	78	124	12.7	3.49	120	.286	.332	16	.158	-5	29	23	5	2.3
1941	Was-A	18	13	.581	34	33	19	4	0	256	271	117	6	3	54	91	11.5	3.45	117	.270	.309	9	.102	-5	20	17	-1	1.3
1942	Was-A	2	2	.500	6	5	1	1	0	35	28	16	1	0	5	15	8.5	4.11	89	.214	.243	1	.100	-0	-2	-2	-0	-0.2
1943	Was-A★	11	13	.458	31	30	15	2	1	219^2	218	96	9	4	46	51	11.0	3.28	98	.257	.298	7	.104	-4	0	-2	2	-0.5
1944	Was-A☆	14	14	.500	32	31	17	3	0	229^1	222	97	8	3	37	62	10.3	3.06	106	.252	.284	18	.228	2	9	5	1	0.9
1945	Was-A†	17	7	.708	31	29	12	4	1	216	208	72	5	2	35	96	10.2	2.13	146	.248	.279	18	.231	1	30	25	0	3.0
1946	Was-A	10	10	.500	26	23	7	2	0	161^2	182	85	9	4	36	62	12.4	3.56	94	.281	.323	9	.170	-1	-1	-4	3	-0.2
1947	Phi-N	17	12	.586	32	29	19	3	0	235	224	86	14	2	57	103	10.8	2.68	149	.258	.306	14	.175	-1	36	35	3	4.4
1948	Phi-N	12	17	.414	34	31	16	1	0	225^2	226	85	9	4	54	92	11.3	2.51	157	.265	.312	12	.145	-3	36	36	4	4.6
1949	Chi-N	7	16	.304	33	28	10	1	0	180	198	94	4	7	43	83	12.4	4.15	97	.272	.319	12	.203	0	-2	-2	1	-0.1
1950	Chi-N	5	1	.833	35	1	0	0	6	74	70	41	7	2	27	28	12.0	3.77	111	.248	.318	1	.063	-2	3	3	0	0.2
1951	Chi-N☆	10	6	.625	41	1	0	0	3	81^2	69	30	3	2	28	30	10.9	2.64	155	.234	.305	0	.000	-3	12	13	2	2.3
1952	Chi-N	2	2	.500	45	0	0	0	11	66^2	56	18	3	3	24	37	11.2	2.16	178	.235	.313	2	.200	-0	12	12	2	1.4
1953	Chi-N	2	3	.400	45	0	0	0	8	62^2	72	34	9	1	24	27	13.9	4.60	97	.289	.354	3	.300	1	-2	-1	0	0.0
Total	20	191	181	.513	640	376	192	30	44	3218^1	3304	1432	158	56	737	1170	11.5	3.25	119	.265	.309	177	.168	-21	267	231	24	26.7

● DUTCH LEONARD

Leonard, Hubert Benjamin b: 4/16/1892, Birmingham, Ohio d: 7/11/52, Fresno, Cal. BL/TL, 5'10.5", 185 lbs. Deb: 4/12/13

YEAR	TM/L	W	L	PCT	G	GS	CG	SH	SV	IP	H	R	HR	HB	BB	SO	RAT	ERA	ERA+	OAV	OOB	BH	AVG	PB	PR	PR+	PD	TPI
1913	Bos-A	14	17	.452	42	28	14	3	1	259^1	245	108	0	4	94	144	11.9	2.39	123	.253	.321	15	.181	1	16	16	-3	1.6
1914	Bos-A	19	5	.792	36	25	17	7	3	224^2	139	34	3	8	60	176	**8.3**	**0.96**	**280**	**.180**	**.246**	10	.147	-1	**44**	**44**	-3	4.7
1915	*Bos-A	15	7	.682	32	21	10	2	0	183^1	130	57	3	14	67	116	10.4	2.36	118	**.208**	.299	14	.264	5	12	9	-4	1.1
1916	*Bos-A	18	12	.600	48	34	17	6	6	274	244	87	6	8	66	144	10.4	2.36	117	.247	.300	17	.200	2	14	13	-6	1.0
1917	Bos-A	16	17	.485	37	36	26	4	1	294^1	257	88	4	5	72	144	10.2	2.17	119	.236	.286	9	.087	-6	16	14	-5	0.3
1918	Bos-A	8	6	.571	16	16	12	3	0	125^2	119	51	0	2	53	47	12.5	2.72	99	.254	.332	8	.186	0	1	-1	-2	-0.2
1919	Det-A	14	13	.519	29	28	18	4	0	217^1	212	89	7	7	65	102	11.8	2.77	115	.254	.313	11	.155	-3	11	10	-4	0.5
1920	Det-A	10	17	.370	28	27	10	3	0	191^1	192	107	8	8	63	76	12.4	4.33	86	.271	.338	12	.211	2	-11	-13	-1	-1.6
1921	Det-A	11	13	.458	36	32	16	1	1	245	273	125	15	10	63	120	12.7	3.75	114	.286	.336	14	.171	-4	15	14	-3	0.6
1924	Det-A	3	2	.600	9	7	3	0	1	51^1	68	32	1	1	18	26	15.3	4.56	90	.327	.383	4	.211	-0	-2	-3	-0	-0.3
1925	Det-A	11	4	.733	18	18	9	0	0	125^2	143	73	7	1	43	65	13.4	4.51	95	.289	.347	10	.200	-1	-2	-3	-2	-0.6
Total	11	139	113	.552	331	272	152	33	13	2192	2022	851	54	68	664	1160	11.3	2.76	115	.249	.311	124	.173	-5	114	100	-33	7.1

● DAVE LEONHARD

Leonhard, David Paul b: 1/22/41, Arlington, Va. BR/TR, 5'11", 165 lbs. Deb: 9/21/67

YEAR	TM/L	W	L	PCT	G	GS	CG	SH	SV	IP	H	R	HR	HB	BB	SO	RAT	ERA	ERA+	OAV	OOB	BH	AVG	PB	PR	PR+	PD	TPI
1967	Bal-A	0	0	—	3	2	0	0	1	14^1	11	5	1	1	6	9	11.3	3.14	100	.200	.290	0	.000	-1	0	0	0	0.0
1968	Bal-A	7	7	.500	28	18	5	2	1	126^1	95	46	10	2	57	61	11.0	3.13	93	.216	.309	4	.129	-1	-2	-3	1	-0.3
1969	*Bal-A	7	4	.636	37	3	1	1	1	94	78	28	8	0	38	37	11.1	2.49	143	.228	.305	2	.095	-0	12	11	-1	1.2
1970	Bal-A	0	0	—	23	0	0	0	1	28^1	32	18	5	0	18	14	15.9	5.08	72	.294	.394	0	.000	0	-4	-5	1	-0.1
1971	*Bal-A	2	3	.400	12	6	1	1	1	54	51	18	5	1	19	18	11.8	2.83	118	.252	.320	5	.278	1	4	3	1	0.5
1972	Bal-A	0	0	—	14	0	0	0	0	20	20	10	3	0	12	7	14.4	4.50	69	.260	.360	1	1.000	1	-3	-3	0	-0.1
Total	6	16	14	.533	117	29	7	4	5	337	287	125	32	4	150	146	11.8	3.15	103	.234	.320	12	.156	1	6	4	3	1.2

● RUDY LEOPOLD

Leopold, Rudolph Matas b: 7/27/05, Grand Cane, La. d: 9/3/65, Baton Rouge, La. BL/TL, 6', 160 lbs. Deb: 7/4/28

YEAR	TM/L	W	L	PCT	G	GS	CG	SH	SV	IP	H	R	HR	HB	BB	SO	RAT	ERA	ERA+	OAV	OOB	BH	AVG	PB	PR	PR+	PD	TPI
1928	Chi-A	0	0	—	2	0	0	0	0	2^1	3	3	0	0	0	0	11.6	3.86	105	.273	.273	0	.000	-0	0	0	-0	0.0

● RANDY LERCH

Lerch, Randy Louis b: 10/9/54, Sacramento, Cal. BL/TL, 6'5", 190 lbs. Deb: 9/14/75

YEAR	TM/L	W	L	PCT	G	GS	CG	SH	SV	IP	H	R	HR	HB	BB	SO	RAT	ERA	ERA+	OAV	OOB	BH	AVG	PB	PR	PR+	PD	TPI
1975	Phi-N	0	0	—	3	0	0	0	0	7	6	5	1	0	1	8	9.0	6.43	58	.231	.259	0	—	0	-2	-2	-0	-0.1
1976	Phi-N	0	0	—	1	0	0	0	1	3	3	1	0	0	0	0	9.0	3.00	118	.250	.250	1	1.000	1	0	0	-0	0.1
1977	Phi-N	10	6	.625	32	28	3	0	0	168^2	207	102	20	1	75	81	15.1	5.07	79	.312	.383	9	.167	-0	-22	-19	2	-1.5
1978	*Phi-N	11	8	.579	33	28	5	0	0	184	183	89	15	1	70	96	12.4	3.96	90	.263	.332	15	.250	7	-8	-8	1	0.0
1979	Phi-N	10	13	.435	37	35	6	1	0	214	228	98	20	3	60	92	12.2	3.74	102	.281	.333	11	.153	1	-0	2	2	0.5
1980	Phi-N	4	14	.222	30	22	2	0	0	150	178	98	15	0	55	57	14.0	5.16	74	.302	.362	12	.267	3	-26	-22	1	-2.0
1981	*Mil-A	7	9	.438	23	18	1	0	0	110^2	134	63	8	0	43	53	14.4	4.31	80	.303	.365	0	—	0	-8	-12	0	-1.5
1982	Mil-A	8	7	.533	21	20	1	1	0	108^2	123	68	12	3	51	33	14.7	4.97	76	.286	.366	0	—	0	-11	-15	-1	-1.9
	Mon-N	2	0	1.000	6	4	0	0	0	23^2	26	11	0	0	8	4	12.9	3.42	107	.289	.347	2	.250	0	0	1	-0	0.1
1983	Mon-N	1	3	.250	19	5	0	0	0	38^2	45	29	6	1	18	24	14.9	6.75	53	.292	.370	2	.222	1	-13	-14	-0	-1.2
	SF-N	1	0	1.000	7	0	0	0	0	10^2	9	4	1	0	8	6	14.3	3.38	105	.231	.362	0	—	0	0	0	0	0.0
	Yr	2	3	.400	26	5	0	0	0	49^1	54	33	7	1	26	30	14.8	6.02	60	.280	.368	2	.222	1	-13	-14	-0	-1.2
1984	SF-N	5	3	.625	37	4	0	0	2	72^1	80	36	3	1	36	48	14.6	4.23	83	.287	.370	2	.133	1	-5	-6	1	-0.5
1986	Phi-N	1	1	.500	4	0	0	0	0	8	10	8	0	0	7	5	19.1	7.88	49	.286	.405	1	.333	1	-4	-3	-0	-0.6
Total	11	60	64	.484	253	164	18	2	3	1099^1	1232	612	101	10	432	507	13.7	4.53	82	.289	.356	55	.206	15	-97	-97	4	-8.6

● JOHN LEROY

Leroy, John Michael b: 4/19/75, Bellevue, Wash. BR/TR, 6'3", 175 lbs. Deb: 9/26/97

YEAR	TM/L	W	L	PCT	G	GS	CG	SH	SV	IP	H	R	HR	HB	BB	SO	RAT	ERA	ERA+	OAV	OOB	BH	AVG	PB	PR	PR+	PD	TPI
1997	Atl-N	1	0	1.000	1	0	0	0	0	2	1	0	0	0	3	3	18.0	0.00	—	.143	.400	0	—	0	1	1	-0	0.2

● LOUIS LeROY

LeRoy, Louis Paul "Chief" b: 2/18/1879, Omro, Wis. d: 10/10/44, Shawano, Wis. BR/TR, 5'10", 180 lbs. Deb: 9/22/05

YEAR	TM/L	W	L	PCT	G	GS	CG	SH	SV	IP	H	R	HR	HB	BB	SO	RAT	ERA	ERA+	OAV	OOB	BH	AVG	PB	PR	PR+	PD	TPI
1905	NY-A	1	1	.500	3	3	2	0	0	24	26	14	2	1	1	8	10.5	3.75	78	.277	.292	1	.125	-0	-3	-2	-0	-0.2
1906	NY-A	2	0	1.000	11	2	1	0	1	44^2	33	19	0	2	12	28	9.5	2.22	134	.209	.273	2	.143	-1	2	3	1	0.2
1910	Bos-A	0	0	—	1	0	0	0	0	4	7	9	1	0	2	3	20.3	11.25	23	.389	.450	0	.000	-0	-4	-4	0	-0.2
Total	3	3	1	.750	15	5	3	0	1	72^2	66	42	3	3	15	39	10.4	3.22	91	.244	.292	3	.130	-1	-4	-2	1	-0.2

● BARRY LERSCH

Lersch, Barry Lee b: 9/7/44, Denver, Colo. BB/TR, 6', 180 lbs. Deb: 4/8/69

YEAR	TM/L	W	L	PCT	G	GS	CG	SH	SV	IP	H	R	HR	HB	BB	SO	RAT	ERA	ERA+	OAV	OOB	BH	AVG	PB	PR	PR+	PD	TPI
1969	Phi-N	0	3	.000	10	0	0	0	2	17^2	20	14	6	1	10	13	15.8	7.13	50	.286	.383	0	.000	-0	-7	-7	1	-1.2
1970	Phi-N	6	3	.667	42	11	3	0	3	138	119	52	17	1	47	92	10.9	3.26	123	.232	.297	2	.065	-2	12	11	-1	0.5
1971	Phi-N	5	14	.263	38	30	3	0	0	214^1	203	97	28	3	50	113	10.7	3.78	93	.252	.298	10	.169	2	-7	-6	-1	-0.4
1972	Phi-N	4	6	.400	36	8	3	1	0	100^2	86	37	8	3	33	48	10.9	3.04	118	.231	.299	0	.000	-2	5	6	-0	0.3
1973	Phi-N	3	6	.333	42	4	0	0	1	98^1	105	49	10	2	27	51	12.3	4.39	87	.279	.330	3	.176	0	-8	-6	-0	-0.6
1974	StL-N	0	0	—	1	0	0	0	0	1^1	3	6	1	0	5	0	54.0	40.50	9	.429	.667	0	—	0	-5	-6	0	-0.3
Total	6	18	32	.360	169	53	9	1	6	570^1	536	255	70	10	172	317	11.3	3.82	97	.250	.308	15	.113	-3	-11	-7	-1	-1.7

● DON LESHNOCK

Leshnock, Donald Lee b: 11/25/46, Youngstown, Ohio BR/TL, 6'3", 195 lbs. Deb: 6/7/72

YEAR	TM/L	W	L	PCT	G	GS	CG	SH	SV	IP	H	R	HR	HB	BB	SO	RAT	ERA	ERA+	OAV	OOB	BH	AVG	PB	PR	PR+	PD	TPI
1972	Det-A	0	0	—	1	0	0	0	0	1	2	0	0	0	0	2	18.0	0.00	—	.400	.400	0	—	0	0	0	0	0.0

YEAR TM/L	W	L	PCT	G	GS	CG	SH	SV	IP	H	R	HR	HB	BB	SO	RAT	ERA	ERA+	OAV	OOB	BH	AVG	PB	PR	PR+	PD	TPI
● CURTIS LESKANIC	Leskanic, Curtis John b: 4/2/68, Homestead, Pa. BR/TR, 6', 180 lbs. Deb: 6/27/93																										
1993 Col-N	1	5	.167	18	8	0	0	0	57	59	40	7	2	27	30	13.9	5.37	89	.266	.351	2	.154	0	-8	-3	-0	-0.3
1994 Col-N	1	1	.500	8	3	0	0	0	22^1	27	14	2	0	10	17	14.9	5.64	88	.314	.385	1	.167	0	-4	-1	-0	-0.1
1995 *Col-N	6	3	.667	**76**	0	0	0	10	98	83	38	7	0	33	107	10.7	3.40	159	.226	.289	1	.143	-0	9	17	2	1.8
1996 Col-N	7	5	.583	70	0	0	0	6	73^2	82	51	12	2	38	76	14.9	6.23	84	.285	.372	1	.333	0	-16	-7	-1	-1.1
1997 Col-N	4	0	1.000	55	0	0	0	2	58^1	59	36	8	0	24	53	12.8	5.55	93	.271	.343	0	.000	-0	-9	-2	-0	-0.2
1998 Col-N	6	4	.600	66	0	0	0	2	75^2	75	37	9	1	40	55	13.8	4.40	118	.258	.349	0	.000	-0	-1	5	-0	0.6
1999 Col-N	6	2	.750	63	0	0	0	0	85	87	54	7	5	49	77	14.9	5.08	114	.272	.377	2	.500	1	-5	5	1	0.6
2000 Mil-N	9	3	.750	73	0	0	0	12	77^1	58	23	7	3	51	75	13.0	2.56	178	.212	.341	0	.000	-0	18	17	1	2.9
Total 8	40	23	.635	429	11	0	0	32	547^1	530	293	59	13	272	490	13.4	4.59	113	.256	.347	7	.184	1	-17	31	2	4.2
● BRAD LESLEY	Lesley, Bradley Jay b: 9/11/58, Turlock, Cal. BR/TR, 6'6", 230 lbs. Deb: 7/31/82																										
1982 Cin-N	0	2	.000	28	0	0	0	4	38^1	27	13	1	0	13	29	9.4	2.58	144	.197	.267	0	.000	-0	4	5	-0	0.3
1983 Cin-N	0	0	—	5	0	0	0	0	8^1	9	2	1	0	0	5	9.7	2.16	177	.290	.290	0	—	0	1	1	-0	0.1
1984 Cin-N	0	1	.000	16	0	0	0	2	19^1	17	11	3	0	14	7	14.4	5.12	74	.246	.373	1	.500	0	-3	-3	0	-0.1
1985 Mil-A	1	0	1.000	5	0	0	0	0	6^1	8	7	2	0	2	5	14.2	9.95	42	.296	.345	0	—	0	-4	-4	-0	-0.5
Total 4	1	3	.250	54	0	0	0	6	72^1	61	33	7	0	29	46	11.2	3.86	98	.231	.307	1	.333	0	-2	-1	-0	-0.2
● WALT LEVERENZ	Leverenz, Walter Fred "Tiny" b: 7/21/1887, Chicago, Ill. d: 3/19/73, Atascadero, Cal. BL/TL, 5'10", 175 lbs. Deb: 4/18/13																										
1913 StL-A	6	17	.261	30	27	13	2	1	202^2	159	80	3	12	89	87	11.5	2.58	114	.222	.318	12	.176	-1	8	8	-1	0.6
1914 StL-A	1	12	.077	27	16	5	0	0	111^1	107	67	5	4	63	41	14.1	3.80	71	.264	.368	6	.182	-0	-13	-14	-1	-1.7
1915 StL-A	1	2	.333	5	1	0	0	0	9	11	9	0	1	8	3	20.0	8.00	36	.333	.476	0	.000	-0	-5	-5	0	-1.0
Total 3	8	31	.205	62	44	18	2	1	323	277	156	8	17	160	131	12.7	3.15	91	.240	.341	18	.176	-1	-10	-11	-3	-2.1
● DIXIE LEVERETT	Leverett, Gorham Vance b: 3/29/1894, Georgetown, Tex. d: 2/20/57, Beaverton, Ore. BR/TR, 5'11", 190 lbs. Deb: 5/6/22																										
1922 Chi-A	13	10	.565	33	27	16	4	2	223^2	224	95	11	3	79	60	12.3	3.34	122	.264	.329	21	.253	3	18	18	-1	1.9
1923 Chi-A	10	13	.435	38	24	9	0	3	192^2	212	108	6	6	64	64	13.2	4.06	97	.280	.341	16	.267	4	-2	-2	-1	0.1
1924 Chi-A	2	3	.400	21	11	4	0	0	99	123	72	2	3	41	29	15.2	5.82	71	.314	.383	6	.188	-1	-17	-19	0	-0.9
1926 Chi-A	1	1	.500	6	3	1	0	0	24	31	18	1	0	7	12	14.3	6.00	64	.316	.362	1	.143	-0	-5	-6	0	-0.4
1929 Bos-N	3	7	.300	24	12	3	0	1	97^2	135	81	5	5	30	28	15.7	6.36	74	.339	.393	6	.188	-0	-18	-18	-0	-1.6
Total 5	29	34	.460	122	77	33	4	6	637	725	374	25	17	221	193	13.6	4.51	92	.291	.353	50	.234	6	-25	-27	-1	-0.9
● HOD LEVERETTE	Leverette, Horace Wilbur "Levy" b: 2/4/1889, Shreveport, La. d: 4/10/58, St.Petersburg, Fla BR/TR, 6', 180 lbs. Deb: 4/22/20																										
1920 StL-A	0	2	.000	3	2	0	0	0	10^1	9	6	1	0	12	0	18.3	5.23	75	.250	.438	0	.000	-1	-2	-1	1	-0.2
● AL LEVINE	Levine, Alan Brian b: 5/22/68, Park Ridge, Ill. BL/TR, 6'3", 180 lbs. Deb: 6/22/96																										
1996 Chi-A	0	1	.000	16	0	0	0	0	18^1	22	14	1	1	7	12	14.7	5.40	88	.289	.357	0	—	0	-1	-1	1	0.0
1997 Chi-A	2	2	.500	25	0	0	0	0	27^1	35	22	4	2	16	22	17.5	6.91	63	.313	.408	0	—	0	-7	-8	0	-0.9
1998 Tex-A	0	1	.000	30	0	0	0	0	58	68	30	6	0	16	19	13.0	4.50	107	.294	.340	0	—	0	1	2	-0	0.1
1999 Ana-A	1	1	.500	50	1	0	0	0	85	76	40	13	3	29	37	11.4	3.39	143	.247	.318	0	—	0	14	14	0	0.7
2000 Ana-A	3	4	.429	51	5	0	0	2	95^1	98	44	10	2	49	42	14.1	3.87	128	.266	.355	0	—	0	11	12	-0	0.7
Total 5	6	9	.400	172	6	0	0	2	284	299	150	34	8	117	132	13.4	4.25	114	.273	.347	0	—	0	18	19	1	0.6
● ALLEN LEVRAULT	Levrault, Allen Harry b: 8/15/77, Fall River, Mass. BR/TR, 6'3", 240 lbs. Deb: 6/13/2000																										
2000 Mil-N	0	1	.000	5	1	0	0	0	12	10	7	0	0	7	9	12.8	4.50	101	.238	.347	0	.000	-0	0	0	-0	-0.1
● DUTCH LEVSEN	Levsen, Emil Henry b: 4/29/1898, Wyoming, Iowa d: 3/12/72, St.Louis Park, Minn. BR/TR, 6', 180 lbs. Deb: 9/28/23																										
1923 Cle-A	0	0	—	3	0	0	0	0	4^1	4	0	0	0	0	1	8.3	0.00	—	.267	.267	0	.000	-0	2	2	1	0.2
1924 Cle-A	1	1	.500	4	1	1	0	0	16^1	22	8	0	0	4	3	14.3	4.41	97	.333	.371	0	.000	-1	-0	-0	0	-0.1
1925 Cle-A	1	2	.333	4	3	2	0	0	24^1	30	16	1	1	16	9	17.4	5.55	80	.313	.416	2	.250	0	-3	-3	-1	-0.3
1926 Cle-A	16	13	.552	33	31	18	2	0	237^1	235	110	11	8	85	53	12.4	3.41	119	.261	.330	17	.205	-0	16	17	-1	1.7
1927 Cle-A	3	7	.300	25	13	2	1	0	80^1	96	54	1	2	37	15	15.1	5.49	77	.303	.379	5	.200	-1	-12	-11	1	-1.2
1928 Cle-A	0	3	.000	11	3	0	0	0	41^1	39	30	4	2	31	7	15.7	5.44	76	.258	.391	0	.000	-2	-6	-6	-0	-0.6
Total 6	21	26	.447	80	51	23	3	0	404	426	218	17	13	173	88	13.6	4.17	99	.276	.354	24	.178	-4	-4	-2	1	-0.3
● DENNIS LEWALLYN	Lewallyn, Dennis Dale b: 8/11/53, Pensacola, Fla. BR/TR, 6'4", 200 lbs. Deb: 9/21/75																										
1975 LA-N	0	0	—	2	0	0	0	0	3	1	0	0	0	0	0	3.0	0.00	—	.100	.100	0	—	0	1	1	0	0.1
1976 LA-N	1	1	.500	4	2	0	0	0	16^2	12	5	1	0	6	4	9.7	2.16	157	.207	.281	0	.000	-1	2	2	0	0.3
1977 LA-N	3	1	.750	5	1	0	0	1	17	22	8	4	0	4	8	13.8	4.24	90	.306	.342	0	.000	-1	-1	-1	-0	-0.3
1978 LA-N	0	0	—	1	0	0	0	0	2	2	0	0	0	0	0	9.0	0.00	—	.250	.250	0	—	0	1	1	-0	0.0
1979 LA-N	0	1	.000	7	0	0	0	0	12^1	19	8	0	1	5	1	18.2	5.11	71	.358	.424	1	.500	0	-2	-2	0	-0.1
1980 Tex-A	0	0	—	4	0	0	0	0	5^2	7	5	0	0	4	1	17.5	7.94	49	.304	.407	0	—	0	-2	-3	0	-0.1
1981 Cle-A	0	0	—	7	0	0	0	0	13^1	16	8	1	0	2	11	12.2	5.40	67	.296	.321	0	—	0	-3	-3	-0	-0.2
1982 Cle-A	0	1	.000	4	0	0	0	0	10^1	13	8	3	0	1	3	12.2	6.97	59	.310	.326	0	—	0	-3	-3	-0	-0.3
Total 8	4	4	.500	34	3	0	0	1	80^1	92	42	6	1	22	28	12.9	4.48	82	.287	.335	1	.077	-1	-6	-7	0	-0.6
● DAN LEWANDOWSKI	Lewandowski, Daniel William b: 1/6/28, Buffalo, N.Y. d: 7/19/96, Hamilton, Ont., Can. BR/TR, 6', 180 lbs. Deb: 9/22/51																										
1951 StL-N	0	1	.000	2	0	0	0	0	1	3	1	0	0	1	1	36.0	9.00	44	.500	.571	0	—	0	-1	-1	0	-0.1
● LEWIS	Lewis b: Brooklyn, N.Y. Deb: 7/12/1890 ♦																										
1890 Buf-P	0	1	.000	1	1	0	0	0	3	13	20	3	0	7	1	60.0	60.00	7	.591	.690	1	.200	-0	-19	-19	1	-1.6
● TED LEWIS	Lewis, Edward Morgan "Parson" b: 12/25/1872, Machynlleth, Wales d: 5/24/36, Durham, N.H. BR/TR, 5'10.5", 158 lbs. Deb: 7/6/1896																										
1896 Bos-N	1	4	.200	6	5	4	0	0	41^2	37	32	2	0	27	12	13.8	3.24	140	.236	.348	2	.111	-2	5	6	1	0.4
1897 *Bos-N	21	12	.636	38	34	30	2	1	290	316	177	11	10	125	65	14.0	3.85	116	.275	.351	28	.248	-2	15	19	-5	1.1
1898 Bos-N	26	8	**.765**	41	33	29	1	2	313^1	267	131	9	9	109	72	11.1	2.90	127	.229	.300	37	.282	4	25	27	-1	2.8
1899 Bos-N	17	11	.607	29	25	23	2	0	234^2	245	119	10	8	73	60	12.5	3.49	119	.269	.328	25	.260	0	9	16	-4	1.2
1900 Bos-N	13	12	.520	30	22	19	1	0	209	215	122	11	4	86	66	13.1	4.13	100	.265	.339	10	.137	-4	-10	-0	-3	-0.6
1901 Bos-A	16	17	.485	39	34	31	1	1	316^1	299	172	14	8	91	103	11.3	3.53	100	.247	.304	21	.174	-2	5	0	-2	-0.4
Total 6	94	64	.595	183	153	136	7	4	1405	1379	753	57	39	511	378	12.4	3.53	113	.255	.324	123	.223	-5	49	68	-13	4.5
● DUFFY LEWIS	Lewis, George Edward b: 4/18/1888, San Francisco, Cal d: 6/17/79, Salem, N.H. BL/TL, 5'10.5", 165 lbs. Deb: 4/16/10 C♦																										
1913 Bos-A	0	0	—	1	0	0	0	0	1	3	2	0	0	0	1	27.0	18.00	16	.500	.500	164	.298	0	-2	-2	-0	-0.1
● JIM LEWIS	Lewis, James Martin b: 10/12/55, Miami, Fla. BR/TR, 6'3", 190 lbs. Deb: 9/12/79																										
1979 Sea-A	0	0	—	2	0	0	0	0	2^1	10	7	1	0	1	0	42.4	15.43	28	.625	.647	0	—	0	-3	-3	-0	-0.1
1982 NY-A	0	0	—	1	0	0	0	0	0^2	3	7	0	0	3	0	81.0	54.00	7	.500	.667	0	—	0	-4	-4	0	-0.2
1983 Min-A	0	0	—	6	0	0	0	0	18	24	13	5	1	7	8	16.0	6.50	66	.324	.390	0	—	0	-5	-4	0	-0.2
1985 Sea-A	0	1	.000	2	1	0	0	0	4^2	8	4	1	2	1	1	21.2	7.71	55	.421	.500	0	—	0	-2	-2	-0	-0.3
Total 4	0	1	.000	11	1	0	0	0	25^2	45	31	7	3	12	9	21.0	8.77	49	.391	.462	0	—	0	-13	-12	-0	-0.8
● JIM LEWIS	Lewis, James Steven b: 7/20/64, Jackson, Mich. BR/TR, 6'2", 200 lbs. Deb: 8/9/91																										
1991 SD-N	0	0	—	12	0	0	0	0	13	14	7	2	0	11	10	17.3	4.15	92	.275	.403	0	.000	-0	-1	-0	1	0.0
● RICHIE LEWIS	Lewis, Richie Todd b: 1/25/66, Muncie, Ind. BR/TR, 5'10", 175 lbs. Deb: 7/31/92																										
1992 Bal-A	1	1	.500	2	2	0	0	0	6^2	13	8	1	0	7	4	27.0	10.80	37	.406	.513	0	—	0	-5	-5	0	-0.8
1993 Fla-N	6	3	.667	57	0	0	0	0	77^1	68	37	7	1	43	65	13.0	3.26	133	.239	.340	1	.500	0	7	9	1	1.0
1994 Fla-N	1	4	.200	45	0	0	0	0	54	62	44	7	1	38	45	16.8	5.67	77	.284	.393	0	.000	-0	-9	-7	-0	-0.7
1995 Fla-N	0	1	.000	21	1	0	0	0	36	30	15	9	1	15	32	11.5	3.75	112	.224	.307	0	.000	-0	2	2	-0	0.1
1996 Det-A	4	6	.400	72	0	0	0	2	90^1	78	45	9	4	65	78	14.6	4.18	121	.238	.370	0	.000	-0	8	9	-1	0.7
1997 Oak-A	2	0	1.000	14	0	0	0	0	18^2	24	21	7	1	15	12	19.3	9.64	47	.316	.435	0	—	0	-11	-11	0	-0.9
Cin-N	0	0	—	4	0	0	0	0	5^2	4	5	3	0	3	4	11.1	6.35	67	.200	.304	1	1.000	0	-1	-1	-0	0.0

YEAR	TM/L	W	L	PCT	G	GS	CG	SH	SV	IP	H	R	HR	HB	BB	SO	RAT	ERA	ERA+	OAV	OOB	BH	AVG	PB	PR	PR+	PD	TPI
1998	Bal-A	0	0	—	2	1	0	0	0	4^2	8	8	2	0	5	4	25.1	15.43	30	.421	.542	0	—	0	-6	-6	-0	-0.3
Total	7	14	15	.483	217	4	0	0	2	293^1	287	183	45	8	191	244	14.9	4.88	94	.258	.371	2	.200	1	-15	-10	-1	-0.9
● **SCOTT LEWIS**	Lewis, Scott Allen b: 12/5/65, Grants Pass, Ore. BR/TR, 6'3", 178 lbs. Deb: 9/25/90																											
1990	Cal-A	1	1	.500	2	2	1	0	0	16^1	10	4	2	0	2	9	6.6	2.20	174	.172	.200	0	—	0	3	3	-0	0.3
1991	Cal-A	3	5	.375	16	11	0	0	0	60^1	81	43	9	2	21	37	15.5	6.27	66	.316	.373	0	—	0	-15	-14	-0	-1.6
1992	Cal-A	4	0	1.000	21	2	0	0	0	38^1	36	18	3	2	14	18	12.2	3.99	100	.255	.331	0	—	0	-0	0	1	0.1
1993	Cal-A	1	2	.333	15	4	0	0	0	32	37	16	3	2	12	10	14.3	4.22	107	.311	.383	0	—	0	0	1	-1	0.0
1994	Cal-A	0	1	.000	20	0	0	0	0	31	46	23	5	2	10	10	16.8	6.10	80	.359	.414	0	—	0	-4	-4	0	-0.2
Total	5	9	9	.500	74	19	1	0	0	178	210	104	22	8	59	84	14.0	5.01	85	.299	.360	0	—	0	-16	-14	-0	-1.4
● **BERT LEWIS**	Lewis, William Burton b: 10/3/1895, Tonawanda, N.Y. d: 3/24/50, Tonawanda, N.Y. BR/TR, 6'2", 176 lbs. Deb: 4/19/24																											
1924	Phi-N	0	0	—	12	0	0	0	0	18	23	12	1	1	7	3	15.5	6.00	74	.315	.383	0	.000	-1	-4	-3	0	-0.2
● **TERRY LEY**	Ley, Terrence Richard b: 2/21/47, Portland, Ore. BL/TL, 6', 190 lbs. Deb: 8/20/71																											
1971	NY-A	0	0	—	6	0	0	0	0	9	9	9	1	2	9	7	20.0	5.00	65	.257	.435	0	—	0	-2	-2	0	-0.1
● **AL LIBKE**	Libke, Albert Walter b: 9/12/18, Tacoma, Wash. BL/TR, 6'4", 215 lbs. Deb: 4/19/45 ◆																											
1945	Cin-N	0	0	—	4	0	0	0	0	4^1	3	0	0	0	3	2	12.5	0.00	—	.200	.333	127	.283	1	2	2	0	0.1
1946	Cin-N	0	0	—	1	1	0	0	0	5	4	2	0	0	3	2	12.6	3.60	93	.235	.350	109	.253	0	-0	-0	-0	0.0
Total	2	0	0	—	5	1	0	0	0	9^1	7	2	0	0	6	4	12.5	1.93	183	.219	.342	236	.268	2	2	2	0	0.1
● **DON LIDDLE**	Liddle, Donald Eugene b: 5/25/25, Mt.Carmel, Ill. d: 6/5/2000, Mt.Carmel, Ill. BL/TL, 5'10", 165 lbs. Deb: 4/17/53																											
1953	Mil-N	7	6	.538	31	15	4	0	2	128^2	119	54	6	2	55	63	12.3	3.08	127	.248	.328	3	.088	-2	17	13	-1	1.0
1954	*NY-N	9	4	.692	28	19	4	3	0	126^2	100	48	5	3	55	44	11.2	3.06	132	.223	.312	7	.189	2	14	14	-1	1.4
1955	NY-N	10	4	.714	33	13	4	0	1	106^1	97	54	18	4	61	56	13.7	4.23	95	.246	.353	5	.185	1	-2	-2	-1	-0.2
1956	NY-N	1	2	.333	11	5	1	0	1	41^1	45	22	5	1	14	21	13.1	3.92	97	.278	.339	2	.167	-0	-1	-1	0	0.0
	StL-N	1	2	.333	14	2	0	0	0	24^2	36	25	8	0	18	14	19.7	8.39	45	.353	.450	0	.000	-0	-13	-13	-0	-1.4
	Yr	2	4	.333	25	7	1	0	1	66	81	47	13	1	32	35	15.5	5.59	68	.307	.384	2	.143	-0	-13	-13	0	-1.4
Total	4	28	18	.609	117	54	13	3	4	427^2	397	203	42	10	203	198	12.8	3.75	106	.250	.339	17	.152	1	16	11	-2	0.8
● **CORY LIDLE**	Lidle, Cory Fulton b: 3/22/72, Hollywood, Cal. BR/TR, 5'11", 175 lbs. Deb: 5/8/97																											
1997	NY-N	7	2	.778	54	2	0	0	2	81^2	86	38	7	3	20	54	12.0	3.53	114	.274	.323	0	.000	-0	6	5	-1	0.4
1999	TB-A	1	0	1.000	5	1	0	0	0	5	8	4	0	0	2	4	18.0	7.20	69	.364	.417	0	—	0	-1	-1	0	-0.2
2000	TB-A	4	6	.400	31	11	0	0	0	96^2	114	61	13	3	29	62	13.6	5.03	99	.294	.348	0	.000	-0	-1	-1	1	0.0
Total	3	12	8	.600	90	14	0	0	2	183^1	208	103	20	6	51	120	13.0	4.42	103	.287	.339	0	.000	-0	4	3	1	0.2
● **DUTCH LIEBER**	Lieber, Charles Edwin b: 2/1/10, Alameda, Cal. d: 12/31/61, Sawtelle, Cal. BR/TR, 6'0.5", 180 lbs. Deb: 4/18/35																											
1935	Phi-A	1	1	.500	18	1	0	0	2	46^2	45	18	1	1	19	14	12.5	3.09	147	.263	.340	2	.143	-1	7	7	0	0.3
1936	Phi-A	0	1	.000	3	0	0	0	0	11^2	17	11	0	0	6	1	17.7	7.71	66	.362	.434	0	.000	-0	-3	-3	1	-0.2
Total	2	1	2	.333	21	1	0	0	2	58^1	62	29	1	1	25	15	13.6	4.01	116	.284	.361	2	.118	-2	4	4	1	0.1
● **JON LIEBER**	Lieber, Jonathan Ray b: 4/2/70, Council Bluffs, Iowa BL/TR, 6'3", 220 lbs. Deb: 5/15/94																											
1994	Pit-N	6	7	.462	17	17	1	0	0	108^2	116	62	12	1	25	71	11.8	3.73	116	.271	.313	4	.103	-2	6	7	-1	0.5
1995	Pit-N	4	7	.364	21	12	0	0	0	72^2	103	56	7	4	14	45	15.0	6.32	68	.346	.383	1	.048	-2	-17	-16	1	-2.1
1996	Pit-N	9	5	.643	51	15	0	0	1	142	156	70	19	3	28	94	11.9	3.99	109	.279	.316	7	.194	2	4	6	2	0.8
1997	Pit-N	11	14	.440	33	32	1	0	0	188^1	193	102	23	1	51	160	11.7	4.49	96	.263	.312	7	.121	-0	-6	-4	0	-0.5
1998	Pit-N	8	14	.364	29	28	2	0	1	171	182	93	23	3	40	138	11.8	4.11	105	.269	.313	8	.167	0	2	4	-1	0.4
1999	Chi-N	10	11	.476	31	31	3	1	0	203^1	226	107	28	1	46	186	12.1	4.07	111	.279	.319	7	.121	-1	11	10	-1	0.8
2000	Chi-N	12	11	.522	35	35	6	1	0	**251**	248	130	36	10	54	192	11.2	4.41	104	.256	.303	18	.220	3	6	4	1	0.8
Total	7	60	69	.465	217	170	13	2	2	1137	1224	620	148	23	258	886	11.9	4.32	102	.274	.317	52	.152	1	6	11	1	0.7
● **GLENN LIEBHARDT**	Liebhardt, Glenn Ignatius "Sandy" b: 7/31/10, Cleveland, Ohio d: 3/14/92, Winston-Salem, N.C. BR/TR, 5'10.5", 170 lbs. Deb: 4/22/30 F																											
1930	Phi-A	0	1	.000	5	0	0	0	0	9	14	12	2	0	8	2	22.0	11.00	42	.359	.468	0	.000	-0	-6	-6	-0	-0.6
1936	StL-A	0	0	—	24	0	0	0	0	55^1	98	58	4	2	27	20	20.7	8.78	61	.375	.438	0	.000	-2	-23	-20	-2	-1.1
1938	StL-A	0	0	—	2	0	0	0	0	3	4	2	1	0	0	1	12.0	6.00	83	.308	.308	0	—	0	-0	-0	0	0.0
Total	3	0	1	.000	31	0	0	0	0	67^1	116	72	7	2	35	23	20.5	8.96	59	.371	.437	0	.000	-2	-30	-26	-2	-1.7
● **GLENN LIEBHARDT**	Liebhardt, Glenn John b: 3/10/1883, Milton, Ind. d: 7/13/56, Cleveland, Ohio BR/TR, 5'10", 175 lbs. Deb: 10/2/06 F																											
1906	Cle-A	2	0	1.000	2	2	2	0	0	18	13	4	0	0	1	9	7.0	1.50	175	.206	.219	0	.000	-1	2	2	0	0.2
1907	Cle-A	18	14	.563	38	34	27	4	1	280^1	254	100	1	10	85	110	11.2	2.05	122	.244	.307	14	.161	-1	15	14	1	1.6
1908	Cle-A	15	16	.484	38	26	19	3	0	262	222	93	2	3	81	146	10.5	2.20	109	.235	.297	14	.175	0	6	6	1	0.7
1909	Cle-A	1	5	.167	12	4	1	0	1	52^1	54	28	0	1	16	15	12.2	2.92	87	.314	.376	0	.000	-2	-3	-2	-2	-0.6
Total	4	36	35	.507	90	66	49	7	2	612^2	543	225	3	14	183	280	10.9	2.17	113	.244	.306	28	.147	-4	21	20	0	1.9
● **KERRY LIGTENBERG**	Ligtenberg, Kerry Dale b: 5/11/71, Rapid City, S.Dak. BR/TR, 6'2", 185 lbs. Deb: 8/12/97																											
1997	*Atl-N	1	0	1.000	15	0	0	0	1	15	12	5	4	0	4	19	9.6	3.00	140	.211	.262	0	—	0	2	2	-0	0.1
1998	*Atl-N	3	2	.600	75	0	0	0	30	73	51	24	6	0	24	79	9.2	2.71	153	.193	.260	0	—	0	12	12	-2	1.4
2000	*Atl-N	2	3	.400	59	0	0	0	12	52^1	43	21	7	0	24	51	11.5	3.61	125	.226	.313	0	—	0	6	5	-1	0.6
Total	3	6	5	.545	149	0	0	0	43	140^1	106	50	17	0	52	149	10.1	3.08	140	.207	.281	0	—	0	20	19	-3	2.1
● **GENE LILLARD**	Lillard, Robert Eugene b: 11/12/13, Santa Barbara, Cal d: 4/12/91, Goleta, Cal. BR/TR, 5'10.5", 178 lbs. Deb: 5/8/36 F◆																											
1939	Chi-N	3	5	.375	20	7	2	0	0	55	68	48	2	3	36	31	17.5	6.55	60	.309	.413	1	.100	1	-16	-16	0	-1.9
1940	StL-N	0	1	.000	2	1	0	0	0	4^2	8	7	1	1	4	2	25.1	13.50	30	.364	.481	0	—	0	-5	-5	0	-0.8
Total	2	3	6	.333	22	8	2	0	0	59^2	76	55	3	4	40	33	18.1	7.09	56	.314	.420	8	.182	1	-21	-21	0	-2.7
● **JIM LILLIE**	Lillie, James J. "Grasshopper" (b: James J. Lilly) b: 7/27/1861, New Haven, Conn. d: 11/9/1890, Kansas City, Mo. Deb: 5/17/1883 ◆																											
1883	Buf-N	0	1	.000	3	0	0	0	0	12	16	12	0		2	4	13.5	3.00	106	.302	.327	47	.234	0	0	0	0	0.0
1884	Buf-N	0	1	.000	2	1	0	0	0	13	22	24	0		5	4	18.7	6.23	51	.324	.370	105	.223	-0	-5	-4	0	-0.2
1886	KC-N	0	0	—	1	0	0	0	0	6	8	5	0		1	0	13.5	4.50	84	.348	.375	73	.175	-0	-1	-0	0	0.0
Total	3	0	2	.000	6	1	0	0	0	31	46	41	0		8	8	15.7	4.65	71	.319	.355	332	.219	-0	-5	-4	1	-0.2
● **DEREK LILLIQUIST**	Lilliquist, Derek Jansen b: 2/20/66, Winter Park, Fla. BL/TL, 6', 214 lbs. Deb: 4/13/89																											
1989	Atl-N	8	10	.444	32	30	0	0	0	165^2	202	87	16	2	34	79	12.9	3.97	92	.301	.337	12	.190	0	-9	-5	-1	-0.7
1990	Atl-N	2	8	.200	12	11	0	0	0	61^2	75	45	10	1	19	34	13.9	6.28	64	.301	.353	8	.348	4	-17	-14	-1	-1.7
	SD-N	3	3	.500	16	7	1	1	0	60^1	61	29	6	2	23	29	12.8	4.33	88	.266	.339	3	.150	-0	-4	-3	-2	-0.5
	Yr	5	11	.313	28	18	1	1	0	122	136	74	16	3	42	63	13.4	5.31	74	.285	.346	11	.256	4	-21	-18	-3	-2.2
1991	SD-N	0	2	.000	6	2	0	0	0	14^1	25	14	3	0	4	7	18.2	8.79	43	.379	.414	0	.000	-0	-8	-8	0	-0.9
1992	Cle-A	5	3	.625	71	0	0	0	6	61^2	39	13	5	2	18	47	8.6	1.75	223	.186	.257	0	—	0	15	15	0	2.1
1993	Cle-A	4	4	.500	56	2	0	0	10	64	64	20	5	1	19	40	11.8	2.25	193	.263	.319	0	—	0	15	15	-0	2.0
1994	Cle-A	1	3	.250	36	0	0	0	1	29^1	34	17	6	1	8	15	13.2	4.91	96	.304	.355	0	—	0	-0	-1	-1	-0.1
1995	Bos-A	2	1	.667	28	0	0	0	0	23	27	17	7	0	9	9	14.1	6.26	78	.303	.367	0	—	0	-4	-3	-0	-0.4
1996	Cin-N	0	0	—	5	0	0	0	0	3^2	5	3	1	0	0	1	12.3	7.36	58	.357	.357	0	—	0	-1	-1	0	0.0
Total	8	25	34	.424	262	52	1	1	17	483^2	532	245	59	9	134	261	12.6	4.13	97	.283	.333	23	.213	4	-13	-8	-4	-0.2
● **TED LILLY**	Lilly, Theodore Roosevelt b: 1/4/76, Lamita, Cal. BL/TL, 6'1", 180 lbs. Deb: 5/14/99																											
1999	Mon-N	0	1	.000	9	3	0	0	0	23^2	30	20	7	3	9	28	16.0	7.61	59	.309	.385	1	.200	0	-8	-8	0	-0.4
2000	NY-A	0	0	—	7	0	0	0	0	8	8	6	1	0	5	11	14.6	5.63	85	.235	.333	0	—	0	-1	-1	0	0.0
Total	2	0	1	.000	16	3	0	0	0	31^2	38	26	8	3	14	39	15.6	7.11	64	.290	.372	1	.200	0	-9	-9	0	-0.4
● **JOSE LIMA**	Lima, Jose Desiderio Rodriguez (b: Jose Desiderio Rodriguez (Lima)) b: 9/30/72, Santiago, D.R. BR/TR, 6'2", 170 lbs. Deb: 4/20/94																											
1994	Det-A	0	1	.000	3	1	0	0	0	6^2	11	10	2	0	3	7	18.9	13.50	36	.355	.412	0	—	0	-6	-6	-0	-0.7

YEAR	TM/L	W	L	PCT	G	GS	CG	SH	SV	IP	H	R	HR	HB	BB	SO	RAT	ERA	ERA+	OAV	OOB	BH	AVG	PB	PR	PR+	PD	TPI
1995	Det-A	3	9	.250	15	15	0	0	0	73^2	85	52	10	4	18	37	13.1	6.11	78	.288	.338	0	—	0	-11	-11	-2	-1.6
1996	Det-A	5	6	.455	39	4	0	0	3	72^2	87	48	13	5	22	59	14.1	5.70	89	.296	.355	0	—	0	-6	-5	2	-0.5
1997	*Hou-N	1	6	.143	52	1	0	0	2	75	79	45	9	5	16	63	12.0	5.28	76	.271	.321	0	.000	-0	-9	-11	-1	-1.1
1998	Hou-N	16	8	.667	33	33	3	1	0	233^1	229	100	34	7	32	169	10.3	3.70	109	.256	.287	11	.139	-1	14	10	1	0.8
1999	*Hou-N★	21	10	.677	35	35	3	0	0	246^1	256	108	30	2	44	187	11.0	3.58	123	.265	.298	6	.080	-4	27	24	-2	2.0
2000	Hou-N	7	16	.304	33	33	0	0	0	196^1	251	152	48	2	68	124	14.7	6.65	74	.313	.369	10	.167	-1	-44	-36	-1	-3.5
Total	7	53	56	.486	210	122	6	1	5	904	998	515	146	25	203	646	12.2	4.87	92	.279	.323	27	.124	-6	-35	-41	-3	-4.6
● EZRA LINCOLN	Lincoln, Ezra Perry b: 11/17/1868, Raynham, Mass. d: 5/7/51, Taunton, Mass. BL/TL, 5′11″, 160 lbs. Deb: 5/2/1890																											
1890	Cle-N	3	11	.214	15	15	13	0	0	118	157	102	1	1	53	22	16.1	4.42	81	.310	.376	8	.157	-3	-11	-11	0	-1.2
	Syr-a	0	3	.000	3	3	2	0	0	20	33	27	1	1	4	6	17.1	10.35	34	.359	.392	0	.000	-1	-14	-17	-0	-1.6
Total	1	3	14	.176	18	18	15	0	0	138	190	129	2	2	57	28	16.2	5.28	68	.317	.378	8	.136	-4	-26	-26	0	-2.8
● MIKE LINCOLN	Lincoln, Michael George b: 4/10/75, Carmichael, Cal. BR/TR, 6′2″, 211 lbs. Deb: 4/7/99																											
1999	Min-A	3	10	.231	18	15	0	0	0	76^1	102	59	11	1	26	27	15.2	6.84	75	.321	.374	0	.000	-0	-17	-14	0	-1.9
2000	Min-A	0	3	.000	8	4	0	0	0	20^2	36	25	10	2	13	15	22.2	10.89	48	.383	.468	0	—	0	-14	-12	-0	-1.3
Total	2	3	13	.188	26	19	0	0	0	97	138	84	21	3	39	42	16.7	7.70	67	.335	.396	0	.000	-0	-30	-26	0	-3.2
● VIVE LINDAMAN	Lindaman, Vivan Alexander b: 10/28/1877, Charles City, Iowa d: 2/13/27, Charles City, Iowa BR/TR, 6′1″, 200 lbs. Deb: 4/14/06																											
1906	Bos-N	12	23	.343	39	36	32	2	0	307^1	303	132	4	11	90	115	11.8	2.43	111	.264	.324	14	.132	-2	7	9	-2	0.7
1907	Bos-N	11	15	.423	34	28	24	2	1	260	252	130	10	15	108	90	13.0	3.63	70	.265	.349	11	.122	-2	-34	-30	-2	-3.4
1908	Bos-N	12	16	.429	43	30	21	2	1	270^2	246	112	7	10	70	68	10.8	2.36	102	.249	.306	15	.176	0	0	1	-3	-0.2
1909	Bos-N	1	6	.143	15	6	6	1	0	66	75	44	1	1	28	13	14.2	4.64	61	.299	.371	6	.273	1	-15	-12	-1	-1.3
Total	4	36	60	.375	131	100	83	7	2	904	876	418	22	37	296	286	12.0	2.92	88	.263	.329	46	.152	-3	-41	-33	-8	-4.2
● PAUL LINDBLAD	Lindblad, Paul Aaron b: 8/9/41, Chanute, Kan. BL/TL, 6′1″, 195 lbs. Deb: 9/15/65																											
1965	KC-A	0	1	.000	4	0	0	0	0	7^1	12	9	3	1	0	12	16.0	11.05	32	.353	.371	0	.000	-0	-6	-6	0	-0.7
1966	KC-A	5	10	.333	38	14	0	0	1	121	138	63	14	3	37	69	13.2	4.17	82	.292	.348	5	.147	0	-10	-10	0	-1.2
1967	KC-A	5	8	.385	46	10	1	1	6	115^2	106	59	15	6	35	83	11.4	3.58	89	.241	.306	7	.206	2	-4	-5	-0	-0.5
1968	Oak-A	4	3	.571	47	1	0	0	2	56^1	51	19	6	0	14	42	10.4	2.40	118	.237	.284	3	.375	1	4	3	0	0.6
1969	Oak-A	9	6	.600	60	0	0	0	9	78^1	72	37	8	2	33	64	12.3	4.14	83	.240	.319	4	.333	1	-4	-6	-0	-1.2
1970	Oak-A	8	2	.800	62	0	0	0	3	63^1	52	23	7	0	28	42	11.4	2.70	131	.222	.305	0	.000	-1	7	6	-0	0.9
1971	Oak-A	1	0	1.000	8	0	0	0	0	16	18	7	1	1	2	4	11.8	3.94	85	.295	.328	1	.333	0	-1	-1	0	0.0
	Was-A	6	4	.600	43	0	0	0	8	83^2	58	25	6	2	29	50	9.6	2.58	128	.196	.272	3	.158	0	8	7	1	1.1
	Yr	7	4	.636	51	0	0	0	8	99^2	76	32	7	3	31	54	9.9	2.80	118	.213	.281	4	.182	1	7	6	1	1.1
1972	Tex-A	5	8	.385	**66**	0	0	0	9	99^2	95	31	7	0	29	51	11.2	2.62	115	.257	.311	3	.200	0	5	5	-1	0.7
1973	*Oak-A	1	5	.167	36	3	0	0	2	78	89	38	8	3	28	33	13.8	3.69	96	.292	.357	0	—	0	1	-1	-1	-0.2
1974	Oak-A	4	4	.500	45	2	0	0	6	100^2	85	30	4	2	30	46	10.5	2.06	162	.231	.292	0	—	0	18	15	0	1.4
1975	*Oak-A	9	1	.900	68	0	0	0	7	122^1	105	44	6	0	43	58	10.9	2.72	134	.237	.305	0	.000	-0	15	13	1	1.3
1976	Oak-A	6	5	.545	65	0	0	0	5	114^2	111	50	5	3	24	37	10.8	3.06	110	.253	.296	0	—	0	6	4	1	0.5
1977	Tex-A	4	5	.444	42	1	0	0	4	98^2	103	50	16	1	29	46	12.1	4.20	98	.270	.324	0	—	0	-1	-1	0	-0.1
1978	Tex-A	1	1	.500	18	0	0	0	2	39^2	41	16	2	2	15	25	13.2	3.63	104	.279	.354	0	—	0	1	1	0	0.0
	*NY-A	0	0	—	7	1	0	0	0	18^1	21	9	4	0	8	9	14.2	4.42	82	.284	.354	0	—	0	-1	-2	0	0.0
	Yr	1	1	.500	25	1	0	0	2	58	62	25	6	2	23	34	13.5	3.88	96	.281	.354	0	—	0	-1	-1	0	0.0
Total	14	68	63	.519	655	32	1	1	64	1213^2	1157	510	112	26	384	671	11.6	3.29	104	.253	.314	26	.195	4	35	19	2	2.6
● LYMAN LINDE	Linde, Lyman Gilbert b: 9/30/20, Rolling Prairie, Wis. d: 10/24/95, Beaver Dam, Wis. BR/TR, 5′11″, 185 lbs. Deb: 9/11/47																											
1947	Cle-A	0	0	—	1	0	0	0	0	0^2	3	2	0	0	1	0	54.0	27.00	13	.600	.667	0	—	0	-2	-2	0	-0.1
1948	Cle-A	0	0	—	3	0	0	0	0	10	9	6	1	0	4	0	11.7	5.40	75	.243	.317	0	.000	-0	-1	-2	-0	-0.1
Total	2	0	0	—	4	0	0	0	0	10^2	12	8	1	0	5	0	14.3	6.75	60	.286	.362	0	.000	-0	-3	-3	-0	-0.2
● JOHNNY LINDELL	Lindell, John Harlan b: 8/30/16, Greeley, Colo. d: 8/27/85, Newport Beach, Cal. BR/TR, 6′4.5″, 217 lbs. Deb: 4/18/41 ◆																											
1942	NY-A	2	1	.667	23	2	0	0	1	52^2	52	25	3	1	22	28	12.8	3.76	92	.254	.329	6	.250	1	-1	-2	-0	0.0
1953	Pit-N	5	16	.238	27	23	13	1	0	175^2	173	106	17	6	116	102	15.1	4.71	95	.262	.377	26	.286	6	-8	-4	3	1.2
	Phi-N	1	1	.500	5	3	2	0	0	23^1	22	16	0	0	23	16	17.4	4.24	99	.259	.417	7	.389	2	0	-0	-0	0.2
	Yr	6	17	.261	32	26	15	1	0	199	195	122	17	6	139	118	15.4	4.66	95	.261	.382	33	.303	8	-8	-5	2	1.4
Total	2	8	18	.308	55	28	15	1	1	251^2	247	147	20	7	161	146	14.8	4.47	95	.260	.371	762	.273	9	-9	-7	2	1.4
● ERNIE LINDEMANN	Lindemann, Ernest b: 6/10/1883, New York, N.Y. d: 12/27/51, Brooklyn, N.Y. BR/TR, Deb: 6/28/07																											
1907	Bos-N	0	0	—	1	1	0	0	0	6^1	6	5	0	0	4	3	14.2	5.68	45	.286	.400	1	.500	0	-2	-2	0	-0.1
● CARL LINDQUIST	Lindquist, Carl Emil b: 5/9/19, Morris Run, Pa. BR/TR, 6′2″, 185 lbs. Deb: 9/27/43																											
1943	Bos-N	0	2	.000	2	2	0	0	0	13	17	10	3	0	4	1	14.5	6.23	55	.315	.362	0	.000	-1	-4	-4	0	-0.5
1944	Bos-N	0	0	—	5	0	0	0	0	8^2	8	5	1	0	2	4	10.4	3.12	123	.222	.263	0	.000	-0	0	1	-0	0.0
Total	2	0	2	.000	7	2	0	0	0	21^2	25	15	4	0	6	5	12.9	4.98	72	.278	.323	0	.000	-1	-4	-3	-0	-0.5
● JIM LINDSEY	Lindsey, James Kendrick b: 1/24/1898, Greensburg, La. d: 10/25/63, Jackson, La. BR/TR, 6′1″, 175 lbs. Deb: 5/1/22																											
1922	Cle-A	4	5	.444	29	5	0	0	1	83^2	105	60	4	3	24	29	14.2	6.02	67	.324	.376	4	.167	-1	-18	-19	-1	-1.9
1924	Cle-A	0	0	—	3	0	0	0	0	3	8	7	0	0	3	0	33.0	21.00	20	.500	.579	0	.000	-1	-6	-6	0	-0.3
1929	StL-N	1	1	.500	2	2	1	0	0	16^1	20	11	1	1	2	8	12.7	5.51	85	.290	.319	1	.200	-0	-1	-2	-0	-0.2
1930	*StL-N	7	5	.583	39	6	3	0	5	105^2	131	59	6	4	46	50	15.4	4.43	113	.312	.385	8	.286	1	6	7	-3	0.5
1931	*StL-N	6	4	.600	35	2	1	1	7	74^2	77	32	2	0	45	32	14.7	2.77	142	.270	.370	1	.111	-0	**9**	**9**	-0	1.3
1932	StL-N	3	3	.500	33	5	0	0	3	89^1	96	53	6	2	38	31	13.7	4.94	80	.279	.354	3	.143	-1	-10	-10	-1	-0.9
1933	StL-N	0	0	—	1	0	0	0	0	2	2	1	0	0	1	1	13.5	4.50	77	.286	.375	0	—	0	-0	-0	-0	0.0
1934	Cin-N	0	0	—	4	0	0	0	0	4	4	3	0	1	2	2	15.8	4.50	91	.286	.412	0	—	0	-0	-0	0	0.0
	StL-N	0	1	.000	11	0	0	0	1	14	21	13	2	0	3	7	15.4	6.43	66	.328	.358	0	.000	-0	-4	-3	-0	-0.3
	Yr	0	1	.000	15	0	0	0	1	18	25	16	2	1	5	9	15.5	6.00	70	.321	.369	0	.000	-0	-4	-4	-0	-0.3
1937	Bro-N	0	1	.000	20	0	0	0	2	38^1	43	22	4	1	12	15	13.1	3.52	115	.295	.352	1	.167	-0	2	2	-1	0.0
Total	9	21	20	.512	177	20	5	1	19	431	507	261	25	12	176	175	14.5	4.70	91	.300	.370	18	.186	-3	-23	-21	-6	-1.8
● AXEL LINDSTROM	Lindstrom, Axel Olaf b: 8/26/1895, Gustavsberg, Sweden d: 6/24/40, Asheville, N.C. BR/TR, 5′10″, 180 lbs. Deb: 10/3/16																											
1916	Phi-A	0	0	—	1	0	0	0	1	4	2	2	0	1	0	1	6.8	4.50	63	.182	.250	1	.500	0	-1	-1	-0	0.0
● SCOTT LINEBRINK	Linebrink, Scott Cameron b: 8/4/76, Austin, Tex. BR/TR, 6′3″, 185 lbs. Deb: 4/15/2000																											
2000	SF-N	0	0	—	3	0	0	0	0	2^1	7	3	1	0	2	0	34.7	11.57	37	.500	.563	0	—	0	-2	-2	0	-0.1
	Hou-N	0	0	—	8	0	0	0	0	9^2	11	5	3	3	6	6	18.6	4.66	105	.289	.426	1	1.000	0	-0	0	-0	0.0
	Yr	0	0	—	11	0	0	0	0	12	18	8	4	3	8	6	21.8	6.00	79	.346	.460	1	1.000	0	-2	-2	-0	-0.1
● DICK LINES	Lines, Richard George b: 8/17/38, Montreal, Que., Can. BR/TL, 6′1″, 175 lbs. Deb: 4/16/66																											
1966	Was-A	5	2	.714	53	0	0	0	2	83	63	23	4	1	24	49	9.5	2.28	152	.213	.274	0	.000	-1	11	11	2	1.0
1967	Was-A	2	5	.286	54	0	0	0	4	85^2	83	43	6	0	24	54	11.2	3.36	94	.245	.295	1	.111	1	-1	-2	0	-0.1
Total	2	7	7	.500	107	0	0	0	6	168^2	146	66	10	1	48	103	10.4	2.83	117	.230	.285	1	.053	-1	9	9	2	0.9
● FRED LINK	Link, Edward Theodore "Laddie" b: 3/11/1886, Columbus, Ohio d: 5/22/39, Houston, Tex. BL/TL, 6′, 170 lbs. Deb: 4/15/10																											
1910	Cle-A	5	6	.455	22	13	6	1	1	127^2	121	53	0	7	50	55	12.5	3.17	82	.259	.340	7	.167	-1	-9	-8	-1	-1.0
	StL-A	0	1	.000	3	3	0	0	0	17	24	10	0	1	13	5	20.1	4.24	58	.375	.487	1	.167	-0	-3	-3	-0	-0.2
	Yr	5	7	.417	25	16	6	1	1	144^2	145	63	0	8	63	60	13.4	3.30	78	.273	.359	8	.167	-1	-12	-11	-2	-1.2
● ED LINKE	Linke, Edward Karl "Babe" b: 11/9/11, Chicago, Ill. d: 6/21/88, Chicago, Ill. BR/TR, 5′11″, 180 lbs. Deb: 4/27/33																											
1933	Was-A	1	0	1.000	3	2	0	0	0	16	15	10	0	0	11	6	14.6	5.06	83	.250	.366	1	.167	0	-1	-2	-0	-0.1
1934	Was-A	2	2	.500	7	4	2	0	0	34^2	38	20	1	0	9	9	12.2	4.15	104	.277	.322	2	.182	0	1	1	0	0.1
1935	Was-A	11	7	.611	40	22	10	1	3	178	211	111	6	1	80	51	14.8	5.01	86	.296	.367	20	.294	6	-11	-14	-1	-0.8

YEAR	TM/L	W	L	PCT	G	GS	CG	SH	SV	IP	H	R	HR	HB	BB	SO	RAT	ERA	ERA+	OAV	OOB	BH	AVG	PB	PR	PR+	PD	TPI
1936	Was-A	1	5	.167	13	6	1	0	0	52	73	46	4	0	14	11	15.1	7.10	67	.330	.370	6	.400	5	-12	-14	1	-0.7
1937	Was-A	6	1	.857	36	7	0	0	3	128^2	158	89	11	4	59	61	15.5	5.60	79	.304	.379	10	.217	1	-14	-17	-0	-0.8
1938	StL-A	1	7	.125	21	2	0	0	0	39^2	60	37	6	0	33	18	21.1	7.94	63	.357	.463	2	.200	0	-14	-13	1	-1.9
Total	6	22	22	.500	120	43	13	1	6	449	555	313	28	5	206	156	15.4	5.61	79	.305	.377	41	.263	12	-51	-60	0	-4.2
● **ROYCE LINT**	Lint, Royce James b: 1/1/21, Birmingham, Ala. BL/TL, 6'1", 165 lbs. Deb: 4/13/54																											
1954	StL-N	2	3	.400	30	4	1	1	0	70^1	75	46	9	0	30	36	13.4	4.86	85	.273	.344	1	.100	1	-6	-6	1	-0.2
● **DOUG LINTON**	Linton, Douglas Warren b: 2/9/65, Santa Ana, Cal. BR/TR, 6'1", 190 lbs. Deb: 8/3/92																											
1992	Tor-A	1	3	.250	8	3	0	0	0	24	31	23	5	0	17	16	18.0	8.63	47	.323	.425	0	—	0	-12	-12	-0	-1.6
1993	Tor-A	0	1	.000	4	1	0	0	0	11	11	8	0	1	9	4	17.2	6.55	66	.256	.396	0	—	0	-3	-3	-0	-0.2
	Cal-A	2	0	1.000	19	0	0	0	0	25^2	35	22	8	0	14	19	17.2	7.71	59	.324	.402	0	—	0	-10	-9	-0	-0.6
	Yr	2	1	.667	23	1	0	0	0	36^2	46	30	8	1	23	23	17.2	7.36	61	.305	.400	0	—	0	-12	-11	-0	-0.8
1994	NY-N	6	2	.750	32	3	0	0	0	50^1	74	27	4	0	20	29	16.8	4.47	94	.341	.397	0	.000	-1	-1	-2	-1	-0.4
1995	KC-A	0	1	.000	7	2	0	0	0	22^1	22	21	4	2	10	13	13.7	7.25	66	.256	.347	0	—	0	-6	-6	0	-0.3
1996	KC-A	7	9	.438	21	18	0	0	0	104	111	65	13	8	26	87	12.5	5.02	100	.271	.327	0	—	0	-0	-0	-1	-0.1
1999	Bal-A	1	4	.200	14	8	0	0	0	59	69	41	14	2	25	31	14.6	5.95	79	.296	.369	0	—	0	-7	-9	0	-0.6
Total	6	17	20	.459	105	35	0	0	0	296^1	353	207	48	13	121	199	14.8	5.86	79	.296	.367	0	.000	-1	-40	-40	-1	-3.8
● **FRANK LINZY**	Linzy, Frank Alfred b: 9/15/40, Ft.Gibson, Okla BR/TR, 6'1", 190 lbs. Deb: 8/14/63																											
1963	SF-N	0	0	—	8	1	0	0	0	16^2	22	9	0	1	10	14	17.8	4.86	66	.324	.418	0	.000	-0	-3	-3	0	-0.2
1965	SF-N	9	3	.750	57	0	0	0	21	81^2	76	19	2	3	23	35	11.2	1.43	251	.250	.309	4	.222	1	**19**	**19**	5	4.8
1966	SF-N	7	11	.389	51	0	0	0	16	100^1	107	40	4	2	34	57	12.8	2.96	124	.273	.334	3	.150	0	7	8	1	1.7
1967	SF-N	7	7	.500	57	0	0	0	17	95^2	67	21	4	0	34	38	9.5	1.51	218	.203	.277	0	.000	-2	20	19	3	4.0
1968	SF-N	9	8	.529	57	0	0	0	12	94^2	76	30	1	1	27	36	9.9	2.09	141	.218	.277	0	.000	-1	9	9	4	2.3
1969	SF-N	14	9	.609	58	0	0	0	11	116^1	129	57	5	3	38	62	13.2	3.64	96	.283	.342	8	.267	3	-1	-2	3	0.3
1970	SF-N	2	1	.667	20	0	0	0	1	25^2	33	20	2	1	11	16	15.8	7.01	57	.327	.398	0	.000	-0	-8	-9	0	-1.0
	StL-N	3	5	.375	47	0	0	0	2	61^1	66	26	3	0	23	19	13.1	3.67	112	.282	.346	0	.000	-1	3	3	1	0.4
	Yr	5	6	.455	67	0	0	0	3	87	99	46	5	1	34	35	13.9	4.66	88	.296	.362	0	.000	-1	-6	-6	1	-0.6
1971	StL-N	4	3	.571	50	0	0	0	6	59^1	49	18	2	0	27	24	11.5	2.12	170	.226	.311	2	.500	1	9	9	1	1.5
1972	Mil-A	2	2	.500	47	0	0	0	12	77^1	70	30	4	2	27	24	11.5	3.03	101	.248	.318	1	.111	-0	0	0	1	0.1
1973	Mil-A	2	6	.250	42	1	0	0	13	63	68	34	7	1	21	21	12.9	3.57	105	.282	.342	0	—	0	2	1	0	0.2
1974	Phi-N	3	2	.600	22	0	0	0	0	24^2	27	11	1	0	7	12	12.4	3.28	115	.284	.333	0	—	0	1	1	1	0.3
Total	11	62	57	.521	516	2	0	0	111	816^2	790	315	35	14	282	358	12.0	2.85	122	.257	.323	18	.149	0	58	58	20	14.4
● **ANGELO LiPETRI**	LiPetri, Michael Angelo b: 7/6/30, Brooklyn, N.Y. BR/TR, 6'1.5", 180 lbs. Deb: 4/25/56																											
1956	Phi-N	0	0	—	6	0	0	0	0	11	7	5	2	1	3	8	9.0	3.27	114	.175	.250	0	.000	-0	1	1	0	0.0
1958	Phi-N	0	0	—	4	0	0	0	0	4	6	5	1	1	0	1	15.8	11.25	35	.353	.389	0	—	0	-3	-3	0	-0.1
Total	2	0	0	—	10	0	0	0	0	15	13	10	3	2	3	9	10.8	5.40	70	.228	.290	0	.000	-0	-3	-3	0	-0.1
● **TOM LIPP**	Lipp, Thomas Charles (b: Thomas Charles Lieb) b: 6/4/1870, Baltimore, Md. d: 5/30/32, Baltimore, Md. 5'11.5", 170 lbs. Deb: 9/18/1897																											
1897	Phi-N	0	1	.000	1	1	0	0	0	3	8	5	0	0	2	1	30.0	15.00	28	.471	.526	1	1.000	0	-4	-4	-0	-0.5
● **NIG LIPSCOMB**	Lipscomb, Gerard b: 2/24/11, Rutherfordton, N.C d: 2/27/78, Huntersville, N.C. BR/TR, 6', 175 lbs. Deb: 4/23/37 ♦																											
1937	StL-A	0	0	—	3	0	0	0	0	9^2	13	9	3	0	5	1	16.8	6.52	74	.333	.409	31	.323	1	-2	-2	-0	-0.1
● **FELIPE LIRA**	Lira, Antonio Felipe b: 4/26/72, Santa Teresa, Venez. BR/TR, 6', 170 lbs. Deb: 4/27/95																											
1995	Det-A	9	13	.409	37	22	0	0	1	146^1	151	74	17	8	56	89	13.2	4.31	111	.271	.346	0	—	0	7	7	-1	0.9
1996	Det-A	6	14	.300	32	32	3	2	0	194^2	204	123	30	10	66	113	12.9	5.22	97	.269	.336	0	—	0	-5	-4	2	-0.1
1997	Det-A	5	7	.417	20	15	1	1	0	92	101	61	15	2	45	64	14.5	5.77	80	.277	.360	0	—	0	-12	-12	2	-1.1
	Sea-A	0	4	.000	8	3	0	0	0	18^2	31	21	3	4	10	9	21.7	9.16	49	.365	.455	0	—	0	-10	-10	-0	-1.6
	Yr	5	11	.313	28	18	1	1	0	110^2	132	82	18	6	55	73	15.7	6.34	72	.294	.378	0	—	0	-22	-22	2	-2.7
1998	Sea-A	1	0	1.000	7	0	0	0	0	15^2	22	10	5	0	5	16	15.5	4.60	101	.319	.365	0	—	0	0	0	0	0.0
1999	Det-A	0	0	—	2	0	0	0	0	3^1	7	5	2	0	2	3	24.3	10.80	45	.389	.450	0	—	0	-2	-2	0	-0.1
2000	Mon-N	5	8	.385	53	7	0	0	0	101^2	129	71	11	4	36	51	15.0	5.40	87	.310	.371	4	.211	2	-9	-8	1	-0.6
Total	6	26	46	.361	159	79	4	3	1	572^1	645	365	83	28	220	345	14.0	5.25	92	.284	.355	4	.211	2	-31	-27	4	-2.6
● **HOD LISENBEE**	Lisenbee, Horace Milton b: 9/23/1898, Clarksville, Tenn d: 11/14/87, Clarksville, Tenn. BR/TR, 5'11", 170 lbs. Deb: 4/23/27																											
1927	Was-A	18	9	.667	39	34	17	**4**	0	242	221	114	6	3	78	105	11.2	3.57	114	.245	.307	11	.133	-5	15	14	-2	0.6
1928	Was-A	2	6	.250	16	9	3	0	0	77	102	58	4	5	32	13	16.2	6.08	66	.326	.397	4	.174	-0	-17	-18	-1	-1.6
1929	Bos-A	0	0	—	5	0	0	0	0	8^2	10	5	1	0	4	2	14.5	5.19	82	.294	.368	0	.000	-0	-1	-1	0	-0.1
1930	Bos-A	10	17	.370	37	31	15	0	0	237^1	254	130	20	5	86	47	13.1	4.40	105	.280	.346	20	.267	1	7	6	-4	0.3
1931	Bos-A	5	12	.294	41	17	6	0	0	164^2	190	108	13	3	49	42	13.2	5.19	83	.281	.332	12	.226	0	-15	-17	-2	-1.5
1932	Bos-A	0	4	.000	19	6	3	0	0	73^1	87	55	9	1	25	13	13.9	5.65	80	.296	.353	1	.048	-2	-10	-9	-1	-0.7
1936	Phi-A	1	7	.125	19	7	4	0	0	85^2	115	69	9	0	24	17	14.6	6.20	82	.322	.365	3	.120	-1	-11	-10	-1	-0.9
1945	Cin-N	1	3	.250	31	3	0	0	1	80^1	97	56	12	2	16	14	12.9	5.49	68	.294	.330	0	.000	-3	-15	-16	-1	-1.1
Total	8	37	58	.389	207	107	48	4	1	969	1076	595	74	19	314	253	13.1	4.81	90	.282	.340	51	.169	-10	-47	-52	-11	-5.0
● **AD LISKA**	Liska, Adolph James b: 7/10/06, Dwight, Neb. d: 11/30/98, Portland, Ore. BR/TR, 5'11.5", 160 lbs. Deb: 4/17/29																											
1929	Was-A	3	9	.250	24	10	4	0	0	94^1	87	53	1	3	42	33	12.6	4.77	89	.249	.335	5	.172	-1	-6	-6	3	-0.4
1930	Was-A	9	7	.563	32	16	7	1	1	150^2	140	69	6	5	71	40	12.9	3.29	140	.250	.340	5	.096	-4	23	22	6	2.2
1931	Was-A	0	1	.000	2	1	0	0	0	4	9	3	0	0	1	2	22.5	6.75	64	.450	.476	0	.000	-0	-1	-1	0	-0.2
1932	Phi-N	2	0	1.000	8	0	0	0	1	26^2	22	5	0	1	10	6	11.1	1.69	261	.239	.320	0	.000	-1	6	7	1	0.6
1933	Phi-N	3	1	.750	45	1	0	0	1	75^2	96	46	5	0	26	23	14.5	4.52	84	.310	.363	1	.071	-1	-10	-5	4	0.0
Total	5	17	18	.486	111	28	11	1	3	351^1	354	176	12	9	150	104	13.1	3.87	112	.266	.344	11	.107	-7	13	18	14	2.2
● **MARK LITTELL**	Littell, Mark Alan b: 1/17/53, Cape Girardeau, Mo. BL/TR, 6'3", 210 lbs. Deb: 6/14/73																											
1973	KC-A	1	3	.250	8	7	1	0	0	38	44	25	5	0	23	16	15.9	5.68	72	.288	.381	0	—	0	-8	-6	-0	-0.6
1975	KC-A	1	2	.333	7	3	1	0	0	24^1	19	11	1	0	15	19	12.6	3.70	104	.229	.347	0	—	0	0	0	1	0.1
1976	*KC-A	8	4	.667	60	1	0	0	16	104	68	26	1	0	60	92	11.1	2.08	169	.188	.304	0	.000	-0	**17**	17	-1	2.4
1977	*KC-A	8	4	.667	48	5	0	0	12	104^2	73	49	6	1	55	106	11.1	3.61	112	.198	.304	0	.000	-0	5	5	-1	0.5
1978	StL-N	4	8	.333	72	2	0	0	11	106^1	80	38	8	4	59	130	12.1	2.79	126	.213	.326	0	.000	-0	9	9	-1	1.0
1979	StL-N	9	4	.692	63	0	0	0	13	82^1	60	22	2	0	39	67	10.8	2.19	172	.203	.296	0	.000	-1	14	14	-1	2.5
1980	StL-N	0	2	.000	14	0	0	0	2	10^2	14	11	2	0	7	7	17.7	9.28	40	.318	.412	0	.000	-0	-7	-6	-0	-1.3
1981	StL-N	1	3	.250	28	1	0	0	2	41	36	21	2	0	31	22	14.7	4.39	81	.237	.366	2	.250	0	-4	-4	-1	-0.4
1982	StL-N	0	1	.000	16	0	0	0	0	20^2	22	14	1	0	15	7	16.1	5.23	69	.272	.385	0	.000	-0	-4	-4	-1	-0.3
Total	9	32	31	.508	316	19	2	0	56	532	416	217	28	5	304	466	12.3	3.32	112	.217	.326	2	.059	-2	23	24	-4	3.9
● **JEFF LITTLE**	Little, Donald Jeffrey b: 12/25/54, Fremont, Ohio BR/TL, 6'6", 220 lbs. Deb: 9/6/80																											
1980	StL-N	1	1	.500	7	2	0	0	0	18^2	18	9	0	0	9	17	13.0	3.86	96	.250	.333	1	.167	-0	-1	-0	-0	-0.1
1982	Min-A	2	0	1.000	33	0	0	0	0	36^1	33	20	6	0	27	26	14.9	4.21	101	.244	.370	0	—	0	-1	0	-1	0.0
Total	2	3	1	.750	40	2	0	0	0	55	51	29	6	0	36	43	14.2	4.09	99	.246	.358	1	.167	-0	-1	-0	-1	-0.1
● **JOHN LITTLEFIELD**	Littlefield, John Andrew b: 1/5/54, Covina, Cal. BR/TR, 6'2", 200 lbs. Deb: 6/8/80																											
1980	StL-N	5	5	.500	52	0	0	0	9	66	71	31	2	1	20	22	12.5	3.14	118	.282	.337	0	.000	-1	3	4	0	0.6
1981	SD-N	2	3	.400	42	0	0	0	2	64	53	28	5	1	28	21	11.5	3.66	89	.235	.322	0	.000	-0	-1	-3	-0	-0.3
Total	2	7	8	.467	94	0	0	0	11	130	124	59	7	2	48	43	12.0	3.39	103	.259	.330	0	.000	-1	2	1	-0	0.3
● **DICK LITTLEFIELD**	Littlefield, Richard Bernard b: 3/18/26, Detroit, Mich. d: 11/20/97, Detroit, Mich. BL/TL, 6', 180 lbs. Deb: 7/7/50																											
1950	Bos-A	2	2	.500	15	2	0	0	1	23^1	27	25	7	1	24	13	20.1	9.26	53	.297	.448	0	.000	-1	-12	-11	1	-1.5
1951	Chi-A	1	1	.500	4	2	0	0	0	9^2	9	12	1	0	17	7	24.2	8.38	48	.243	.481	0	.000	0	-5	-5	-0	-0.8
1952	Det-A	0	3	.000	28	1	0	0	1	47^2	46	24	4	0	25	32	13.4	4.34	88	.257	.348	1	.143	-0	-4	-3	-1	-0.3

YEAR	TM/L	W	L	PCT	G	GS	CG	SH	SV	IP	H	R	HR	HB	BB	SO	RAT	ERA	ERA+	OAV	OOB	BH	AVG	PB	PR	PR+	PD	TPI
	StL-A	2	3	.400	7	5	3	0	0	46^1	35	18	4	0	17	34	10.1	2.72	144	.205	.277	1	.063	-2	5	6	-1	0.3
	Yr	2	6	.250	35	6	3	0	1	94	81	42	8	0	42	66	11.8	3.54	109	.231	.314	2	.087	-2	1	3	-2	0.0
1953	StL-A	7	12	.368	36	22	2	0	0	152^1	153	93	17	4	84	104	14.2	5.08	83	.264	.361	8	.190	-1	-18	-14	-1	-1.7
1954	Bal-A	0	0	—	3	0	0	0	0	6	8	7	0	1	6	5	22.5	10.50	34	.333	.484	0	.000	-0	-5	-5	-0	-0.3
	Pit-N	10	11	.476	23	21	7	1	0	155	140	78	10	2	85	92	13.2	3.60	116	.239	.337	8	.163	0	8	10	-3	1.0
1955	Pit-N	5	12	.294	35	17	4	1	0	130	148	91	15	2	68	70	15.1	5.12	80	.290	.375	6	.176	0	-16	-14	-2	-1.8
1956	Pit-N	0	0	—	6	2	0	0	0	12^2	14	8	2	0	6	10	14.2	4.26	88	.286	.364	0	.000	-0	-1	-1	-0	-0.1
	StL-N	0	2	.000	3	2	0	0	0	9^2	9	9	2	0	4	5	12.1	7.45	51	.237	.310	0	.000	-0	-4	-4	-0	-0.7
	NY-N	4	4	.500	31	7	0	0	2	97	78	45	16	0	39	65	10.9	4.08	93	.231	.310	2	.083	-2	-3	-3	0	-0.4
	Yr	4	6	.400	40	11	0	0	2	119^1	101	62	20	0	49	80	11.3	4.37	86	.238	.316	2	.071	-2	-8	-8	-1	-1.2
1957	Chi-N	2	3	.400	48	2	0	0	4	65^2	76	46	12	1	37	51	15.6	5.35	72	.295	.385	2	.182	0	-11	-11	-1	-1.0
1958	Mil-N	0	1	.000	4	0	0	0	1	6^1	7	5	2	1	1	7	12.8	4.26	83	.280	.333	0	—	0	-0	-1	-0	-0.1
Total	9	33	54	.379	243	83	16	2	9	761^2	750	461	92	12	413	495	13.9	4.71	86	.260	.355	28	.145	-5	-65	-54	-9	-7.4
● CARLISLE LITTLEJOHN Littlejohn, Charles Carlisle b: 10/6/01, Irene, Tex. d: 10/27/77, Kansas City, Mo. BR/TR, 5'10", 175 lbs. Deb: 5/11/27																												
1927	StL-N	3	1	.750	14	2	1	0	0	42	47	21	4	0	14	16	13.1	4.50	88	.292	.349	5	.417	2	-3	-3	-1	-0.2
1928	StL-N	2	1	.667	12	2	1	0	0	32	36	16	2	0	14	6	14.1	3.66	109	.286	.357	0	.000	-2	1	1	-0	-0.1
Total	2	5	2	.714	26	4	2	0	0	74	83	37	6	0	28	22	13.5	4.14	96	.289	.352	5	.217	-0	-2	-1	-1	-0.3
● GREG LITTON Litton, Jon Gregory b: 7/13/64, New Orleans, La. BR/TR, 6', 190 lbs. Deb: 5/2/89 ♦																												
1991	SF-N	0	0	—	1	0	0	0	0	1	1	1	0	0	3	0	36.0	9.00	40	.250	.571	23	.181	0	-1	-1	0	0.0
● BUDDY LIVELY Lively, Everett Adrian "Red" b: 2/14/25, Birmingham, Ala. BR/TR, 6'0.5", 200 lbs. Deb: 4/17/47 F																												
1947	Cin-N	4	7	.364	38	17	3	1	0	123	126	75	16	0	63	52	13.8	4.68	88	.265	.351	6	.188	2	-9	-8	-0	-0.5
1948	Cin-N	0	0	—	10	0	0	0	0	22^2	13	7	0	1	11	12	9.9	2.38	164	.165	.275	0	.000	-0	4	4	-1	0.1
1949	Cin-N	4	6	.400	31	10	3	1	1	103^1	91	47	11	0	53	30	12.5	3.92	107	.245	.339	4	.154	0	1	3	-1	0.2
Total	3	8	13	.381	79	27	6	2	1	249	230	129	27	1	127	94	12.9	4.16	99	.248	.339	10	.167	1	-3	-1	-2	-0.2
● JACK LIVELY Lively, Henry Everett b: 5/29/1885, Joppa, Ala. d: 12/5/67, Arab, Ala. BR/TR, 5'9", 185 lbs. Deb: 4/16/11 F																												
1911	Det-A	7	5	.583	18	14	10	0	0	113^2	143	73	1	7	34	45	14.6	4.59	75	.313	.369	11	.256	3	-16	-14	-1	-1.1
● WES LIVENGOOD Livengood, Wesley Amos b: 7/18/10, Salisbury, N.C. d: 9/2/96, Winston-Salem, N.C. BR/TR, 6'2", 172 lbs. Deb: 5/30/39																												
1939	Cin-N	0	0	—	5	0	0	0	0	5^2	9	6	3	0	3	4	19.1	9.53	40	.360	.429	0	—	0	-4	-4	0	-0.2
● JAKE LIVINGSTONE Livingstone, Jacob M. b: 1/1/1880, St.Petersburg, Russia d: 3/22/49, Wassaic, N.Y. Deb: 9/6/01																												
1901	NY-N	0	0	—	2	0	0	0	0	12	26	13	0	3	7	6	27.0	9.00	37	.433	.514	1	.167	0	-8	-8	-0	-0.4
● CLEM LLEWELLYN Llewellyn, Clement Manly "Lew" b: 8/1/1895, Dobson, N.C. d: 11/26/69, Concord, N.C. BL/TR, 6'2", 195 lbs. Deb: 6/18/22																												
1922	NY-A	0	0	—	1	0	0	0	0	1	1	0	0	0	0	0	9.0	0.00	—	.250	.250	0	—	0	0	0	-0	0.0
● GRAEME LLOYD Lloyd, Graeme John b: 4/9/67, Victoria, Australia BL/TL, 6'7", 234 lbs. Deb: 4/11/93																												
1993	Mil-A	3	4	.429	55	0	0	0	0	63^2	64	24	5	3	13	31	11.3	2.83	151	.256	.301	0	—	0	11	10	1	1.1
1994	Mil-A	2	3	.400	43	0	0	0	3	47	49	28	4	3	15	31	12.8	5.17	97	.269	.335	0	—	0	-2	-1	-0	-0.1
1995	Mil-A	0	5	.000	33	0	0	0	4	32	28	16	4	0	8	13	10.1	4.50	111	.246	.295	0	—	0	1	2	0	0.3
1996	Mil-A	2	4	.333	52	0	0	0	0	51	49	19	3	1	17	24	11.8	2.82	184	.254	.318	0	—	0	12	13	-0	1.2
	*NY-A	0	2	.000	13	0	0	0	0	5^2	12	11	1	0	5	6	27.0	17.47	28	.429	.515	0	—	0	-8	-8	-0	-1.4
	Yr	2	6	.250	65	0	0	0	0	56^2	61	30	4	1	22	30	13.3	4.29	121	.276	.344	0	—	0	4	5	-0	-0.2
1997	*NY-A	1	1	.500	46	0	0	0	1	49	55	24	6	1	20	26	14.0	3.31	135	.293	.364	0	—	0	7	6	0	0.3
1998	*NY-A	3	0	1.000	50	0	0	0	0	37^2	26	10	3	2	6	20	8.1	1.67	262	.191	.236	0	—	0	12	12	-0	0.8
1999	Tor-A	5	3	.625	74	0	0	0	3	72	68	36	11	4	23	47	11.9	3.63	136	.250	.318	0	—	0	10	10	-1	0.9
Total	7	16	22	.421	366	0	0	0	11	358	351	168	37	14	107	198	11.9	3.62	131	.258	.318	0	—	0	43	44	-1	3.1
● ESTEBAN LOAIZA Loaiza, Esteban Antonio Veyna b: 12/31/71, Tijuana, Mexico BR/TR, 6'4", 190 lbs. Deb: 4/29/95																												
1995	Pit-N	8	9	.471	32	31	1	0	0	172^2	205	115	21	5	55	85	13.8	5.16	83	.300	.357	10	.192	1	-19	-16	1	-1.2
1996	Pit-N	2	3	.400	10	10	1	1	0	52^2	65	32	11	2	19	32	14.7	4.96	88	.308	.371	2	.118	-1	-4	-3	1	-0.3
1997	Pit-N	11	11	.500	33	32	1	0	0	196^1	214	99	17	12	56	122	12.9	4.13	104	.279	.338	10	.167	-0	2	4	-1	0.3
1998	Pit-N	6	5	.545	21	14	0	0	0	91^2	96	50	13	3	30	53	12.7	4.52	95	.275	.338	7	.241	1	-3	-2	2	0.0
	Tex-A	3	6	.333	14	14	1	0	0	79^1	103	57	15	2	22	55	14.4	5.90	82	.316	.363	0	—	0	-11	-9	-0	-0.9
1999	*Tex-A	9	5	.643	30	15	0	0	0	120^1	128	65	10	0	40	77	12.6	4.56	111	.275	.332	0	—	0	4	7	0	0.7
2000	Tex-A	5	6	.455	20	17	0	0	1	107^1	133	67	21	3	31	75	14.0	5.37	95	.302	.352	0	.000	-0	-5	-3	1	-0.2
	Tor-A	5	7	.417	14	14	1	1	0	92	95	45	8	10	26	62	12.8	3.62	138	.270	.338	0	—	0	13	14	-0	1.5
	Yr	10	13	.435	34	31	1	1	1	199^1	228	112	29	13	57	137	13.5	4.56	111	.288	.346	0	.000	-0	8	11	1	1.3
Total	6	49	52	.485	174	147	5	2	1	912^1	1039	530	116	37	279	561	13.4	4.72	98	.289	.347	29	.180	1	-23	-10	3	-0.1
● HARRY LOCHHEAD Lochhead, Robert Henry b: 3/29/1876, Stockton, Cal. d: 8/22/09, Stockton, Cal. BR/TR, 5'11", 172 lbs. Deb: 4/16/1899 ♦																												
1899	Cle-N	0	0	—	1	0	0	0	0	3^2	4	2	0	0	2	0	14.7	0.00	—	.286	.375	129	.238	0	2	2	-0	0.1
● CHUCK LOCKE Locke, Charles Edward b: 5/5/32, Malden, Mo. BR/TR, 5'11", 185 lbs. Deb: 9/16/55																												
1955	Bal-A	0	0	—	2	0	0	0	0	3	0	0	0	0	1	1	3.0	0.00	—	.000	.100	0	—	0	1	1	0	0.1
● BOBBY LOCKE Locke, Lawrence Donald b: 3/3/34, Rowes Run, Pa. BR/TR, 5'11", 185 lbs. Deb: 6/18/59																												
1959	Cle-A	3	2	.600	24	7	0	0	2	77^2	66	33	6	3	41	40	12.7	3.13	118	.233	.336	8	.333	3	6	5	0	0.7
1960	Cle-A	3	5	.375	32	11	2	2	2	123	121	51	10	2	37	53	11.7	3.37	111	.255	.311	9	.237	3	7	5	2	0.9
1961	Cle-A	4	4	.500	37	4	0	0	2	95^1	112	50	12	2	40	37	14.5	4.53	87	.300	.371	4	.211	0	-5	-6	1	-0.4
1962	StL-N	0	0	—	1	0	0	0	0	2	1	0	0	0	2	1	13.5	0.00	—	.143	.333	0	—	0	1	1	0	0.1
	Phi-N	1	0	1.000	5	0	0	0	0	15^2	16	12	4	0	10	9	14.9	5.74	67	.262	.366	2	.286	0	-3	-3	1	-0.1
	Yr	1	0	1.000	6	0	0	0	0	17^2	17	12	4	0	12	10	14.8	5.09	77	.250	.363	2	.286	0	-2	-2	1	0.0
1963	Phi-N	0	0	—	9	0	0	0	0	10^2	10	7	0	0	5	7	12.7	5.91	55	.244	.326	0	.000	-0	-3	-3	-0	-0.2
1964	Phi-N	0	0	—	8	0	0	0	0	19^1	21	6	2	0	6	11	12.6	2.79	124	.276	.329	0	.000	-0	2	1	0	0.1
1965	Cin-N	0	1	.000	11	0	0	0	0	17^1	20	15	2	0	8	8	14.5	5.71	66	.299	.373	0	.000	0	-4	-4	1	-0.1
1967	Cal-A	3	0	1.000	9	1	0	0	2	19^1	14	6	1	1	3	7	8.4	2.33	135	.203	.247	2	.667	1	2	2	0	0.5
1968	Cal-A	2	3	.400	29	0	0	0	2	36^1	51	29	3	1	13	21	16.1	6.44	45	.331	.387	0	.000	-0	-14	-15	-1	-2.3
Total	9	16	15	.516	165	23	2	2	10	416^2	432	209	40	9	165	194	13.1	4.02	91	.269	.340	25	.255	8	-12	-17	4	-0.8
● RON LOCKE Locke, Ronald Thomas b: 4/4/42, Wakefield, R.I. BR/TL, 5'11", 168 lbs. Deb: 4/23/64																												
1964	NY-N	1	2	.333	25	3	0	0	0	41^1	46	23	3	1	22	17	15.0	3.48	103	.289	.379	0	.000	-0	0	0	-0	0.0
● BOB LOCKER Locker, Robert Awtry b: 3/15/38, George, Iowa BB/TR, 6'3", 200 lbs. Deb: 4/14/65																												
1965	Chi-A	5	2	.714	51	0	0	0	2	91^1	71	36	6	2	30	69	10.1	3.15	101	.216	.285	0	.000	-2	3	0	3	0.2
1966	Chi-A	9	8	.529	56	0	0	0	12	95	73	32	2	5	23	70	9.6	2.46	129	.206	.264	4	.250	1	10	8	3	2.1
1967	Chi-A	7	5	.583	**77**	0	0	0	20	124^2	102	34	5	10	23	80	9.7	2.09	148	.222	.274	0	.000	-1	16	15	5	2.4
1968	Chi-A	5	4	.556	70	0	0	0	10	90^1	78	27	4	1	27	62	10.6	2.29	132	.234	.293	0	.000	-1	7	7	2	1.2
1969	Chi-A	2	3	.400	17	0	0	0	4	22	26	18	6	0	6	15	13.1	6.55	59	.292	.337	0	.000	-0	-7	-6	0	-1.2
	Sea-A	3	3	.500	51	0	0	0	6	78^1	69	29	3	3	26	46	11.3	2.18	167	.234	.302	1	.083	-0	13	13	2	1.3
	Yr	5	6	.455	68	0	0	0	10	100^1	95	47	9	3	32	61	11.7	3.14	117	.247	.310	1	.077	-1	5	6	2	0.1
1970	Mil-A	0	1	.000	28	0	0	0	3	31^2	37	18	1	5	10	19	14.8	3.41	111	.306	.382	0	.000	-0	1	1	-0	0.0
	Oak-A	3	3	.500	38	0	0	0	4	56^1	49	21	1	1	19	33	11.0	2.88	123	.232	.299	1	.167	-0	5	4	1	0.6
	Yr	3	4	.429	66	0	0	0	7	88	86	39	2	6	29	52	12.4	3.07	118	.259	.330	1	.143	-0	6	6	0	0.6
1971	*Oak-A	7	2	.778	47	0	0	0	6	72^1	68	28	2	1	19	46	10.9	2.86	117	.249	.300	0	.000	-0	5	4	1	0.7
1972	*Oak-A	6	1	.857	56	0	0	0	10	78	69	25	1	2	16	47	10.0	2.65	108	.235	.280	0	.000	0	4	2	-1	0.2
1973	Chi-N	10	6	.625	63	0	0	0	18	106^1	96	40	6	4	42	76	12.0	2.54	156	.244	.323	1	.067	-1	13	15	2	2.9

YEAR	TM/L	W	L	PCT	G	GS	CG	SH	SV	IP	H	R	HR	HB	BB	SO	RAT	ERA	ERA+	OAV	OOB	BH	AVG	PB	PR	PR+	PD	TPI
1975	Chi-N	0	1	.000	22	0	0	0	0	32^2	38	21	3	2	16	14	15.4	4.96	78	.306	.394	0	—	0	-5	-4	1	-0.1
Total	10	57	39	.594	576	0	0	0	95	879	776	329	40	36	257	577	10.9	2.75	122	.237	.300	7	.074	-4	65	60	18	10.3
● SKIP LOCKWOOD	Lockwood, Claude Edward b: 8/17/46, Boston, Mass. BR/TR, 6', 190 lbs. Deb: 4/23/65 ♦																											
1969	Sea-A	0	1	.000	6	3	0	0	0	23	24	9	3	0	6	10	11.7	3.52	103	.279	.326	0	.000	-1	0	0	0	0.0
1970	Mil-A	5	12	.294	27	26	3	1	0	173^2	173	91	22	6	79	93	13.4	4.30	88	.266	.351	12	.226	2	-11	-10	-1	-0.8
1971	Mil-A	10	15	.400	33	32	5	1	0	208	191	93	13	5	91	115	12.4	3.33	104	.246	.329	5	.081	-1	3	3	-3	-0.1
1972	Mil-A	8	15	.348	29	27	5	3	0	170	148	75	11	4	71	106	11.8	3.60	84	.232	.313	7	.132	-1	-10	-11	-3	-1.8
1973	Mil-A	5	12	.294	37	15	3	0	0	154^2	164	75	10	6	59	87	13.3	3.90	97	.280	.352	0	—	0	-1	-2	0	-0.2
1974	Cal-A	2	5	.286	37	2	0	0	1	81^1	81	42	8	5	32	39	13.1	4.32	80	.264	.343	0	—	0	-6	-8	-0	-0.7
1975	NY-N	1	3	.250	24	0	0	0	2	48^1	28	9	3	1	25	61	10.1	1.49	232	.174	.289	1	.167	-0	12	11	-1	0.9
1976	NY-N	10	7	.588	56	0	0	0	19	94^1	62	31	6	2	34	108	9.3	2.67	124	.186	.266	6	.333	3	9	7	-0	1.7
1977	NY-N	4	8	.333	63	0	0	0	20	104	87	40	5	4	31	84	10.6	3.38	111	.227	.291	3	.200	-0	6	4	-2	0.4
1978	NY-N	7	13	.350	57	0	0	0	15	90^2	78	36	10	0	31	73	10.8	3.57	98	.236	.302	2	.182	1	0	-1	-2	-0.2
1979	NY-N	2	5	.286	27	0	0	0	9	42^1	33	7	3	0	14	42	10.0	1.49	245	.224	.292	0	.000	-0	11	10	-1	2.1
1980	Bos-A	3	1	.750	24	1	0	0	2	45^2	61	31	4	0	17	11	15.4	5.32	79	.321	.377	0	—	0	-6	-5	-1	-0.6
Total	12	57	97	.370	420	106	16	5	68	1236	1130	539	98	33	490	829	12.0	3.55	100	.246	.323	40	.154	3	5	-2	-13	0.7
● MILO LOCKWOOD	Lockwood, Milo Hathaway b: 4/7/1858, Solon, Ohio d: 10/9/1897, Economy, Pa. 5'10", 160 lbs. Deb: 4/17/1884 ♦																											
1884	Was-U	1	9	.100	11	10	6	0	0	67^2	99	95	4		15	48	15.2	7.45	32	.319	.351	14	.209	-2	-38	-39	1	-3.8
● BILLY LOES	Loes, William b: 12/13/29, Long Island City, N.Y. BR/TR, 6'1", 170 lbs. Deb: 5/18/50																											
1950	Bro-N	0	0	—	10	0	0	0	0	12^2	16	11	5	0	5	2	14.9	7.82	52	.314	.375	0	.000	0	-5	-5	-0	-0.3
1952	*Bro-N	13	8	.619	39	21	8	4	1	187^1	154	62	12	3	71	115	11.0	2.69	135	.224	.299	5	.093	-3	22	20	-0	1.9
1953	*Bro-N	14	8	.636	32	25	9	1	0	162^2	165	92	21	3	53	75	12.2	4.54	94	.261	.322	7	.125	-2	-5	-5	3	-0.6
1954	Bro-N	13	5	.722	28	21	6	0	0	147^2	154	73	14	1	60	97	13.1	4.14	99	.269	.339	6	.118	-2	-1	-1	-1	-0.4
1955	*Bro-N	10	4	.714	22	19	6	0	0	128	116	59	16	2	46	85	11.5	3.59	113	.240	.308	4	.091	-3	6	7	-0	0.4
1956	Bro-N	0	1	.000	1	1	0	0	0	1^1	5	6	1	0	1	2	40.5	40.50	10	.556	.600	0	—	0	-5	-5	0	-0.7
	Bal-A	2	7	.222	21	6	1	0	3	56^2	65	33	4	2	23	22	14.3	4.76	82	.291	.363	3	.176	-1	-4	-6	1	-0.8
1957	Bal-A★	12	7	.632	31	18	8	3	4	155^1	142	59	8	4	37	86	10.6	3.24	111	.245	.295	4	.080	-3	9	6	2	0.6
1958	Bal-A	3	9	.250	32	10	1	0	5	114	106	51	10	8	44	44	12.5	3.63	99	.252	.334	2	.067	-2	2	-0	0	-0.3
1959	Bal-A	4	7	.364	37	0	0	0	14	64^1	58	31	5	3	25	34	12.0	4.06	93	.239	.317	1	.125	-0	-1	-2	1	-0.3
1960	SF-N	3	2	.600	37	0	0	0	5	45^2	40	26	9	4	17	28	12.0	4.93	71	.247	.333	1	.250	0	-6	-8	1	-0.9
1961	SF-N	6	5	.545	26	18	3	1	0	114^2	114	62	13	5	39	55	12.4	4.24	90	.258	.325	5	.156	-0	-3	-6	0	-0.5
Total	11	80	63	.559	316	139	42	9	32	1190^1	1135	565	118	35	421	645	12.0	3.89	99	.252	.321	38	.110	-17	9	-5	6	-1.9
● CARLTON LOEWER	Loewer, Carlton Ernest b: 9/24/73, Lafayette, La. BR/TR, 6'6", 220 lbs. Deb: 6/14/98																											
1998	Phi-N	7	8	.467	21	21	1	0	0	122^2	154	86	18	3	39	58	14.4	6.09	71	.312	.366	3	.086	-1	-25	-23	-1	-2.6
1999	Phi-N	2	6	.250	20	13	2	1	0	89^2	100	54	9	0	26	48	12.6	5.12	92	.287	.337	5	.227	1	-6	-4	-1	-0.3
Total	2	9	14	.391	41	34	3	1	0	212^1	254	140	27	3	65	106	13.6	5.68	79	.302	.354	8	.140	-1	-31	-27	-2	-2.9
● FRANK LOFTUS	Loftus, Francis Patrick b: 3/10/1898, Scranton, Pa. d: 10/27/80, Belchertown, Mass. BR/TR, 5'9", 190 lbs. Deb: 9/26/26																											
1926	Was-A	0	0	—	1	0	0	0	0	1	3	2	0	0	2	0	45.0	9.00	43	.600	.714	0	—	0	-1	-1	-0	0.0
● BOB LOGAN	Logan, Robert Dean "Lefty" b: 2/10/10, Thompson, Neb. d: 5/20/78, Indianapolis, Ind. BR/TL, 5'10", 170 lbs. Deb: 4/18/35																											
1935	Bro-N	0	1	.000	2	0	0	0	0	2^2	2	1	0	0	1	1	10.1	3.38	118	.182	.250	0	—	0	0	0	0	0.1
1937	Det-A	0	0	—	1	0	0	0	0	0^2	1	0	0	0	1	1	27.0	0.00	—	.333	.500	0	—	0	0	0	0	0.0
	Chi-N	0	0	—	4	0	0	0	1	6^1	6	1	0	0	4	2	14.2	1.42	280	.261	.370	0	.000	-0	2	2	-0	0.1
1938	Chi-N	0	2	.000	14	0	0	0	2	22^2	18	9	0	1	17	10	14.3	2.78	138	.222	.364	0	.000	-0	3	3	-0	0.2
1941	Cin-N	0	1	.000	2	0	0	0	0	3^1	5	5	0	0	5	0	27.0	8.10	44	.333	.500	0	—	0	-2	-2	0	-0.3
1945	Bos-N	7	11	.389	34	25	5	1	1	187	213	84	9	1	53	53	12.9	3.18	121	.283	.331	13	.213	1	13	14	0	1.4
Total	5	7	15	.318	57	25	5	1	4	222^2	245	100	9	2	81	67	13.3	3.15	122	.277	.339	13	.200	1	16	17	0	1.5
● BILL LOHRMAN	Lohrman, William Le Roy b: 5/22/13, Brooklyn, N.Y. d: 9/13/99, Poughkeepsie, N.Y BR/TR, 6'1", 185 lbs. Deb: 6/19/34																											
1934	Phi-N	0	1	.000	4	0	0	0	1	6	5	5	0	0	1	2	9.0	4.50	105	.217	.250	1	.500	0	-0	0	0	0.1
1937	NY-N	1	0	1.000	2	1	1	0	1	10	5	1	0	0	2	3	6.3	0.90	432	.152	.200	0	.000	-0	3	3	0	0.4
1938	NY-N	9	6	.600	31	14	3	0	0	152	152	72	9	2	33	52	11.1	3.32	114	.253	.294	4	.082	-4	8	8	2	0.5
1939	NY-N	12	13	.480	38	24	9	1	1	185^2	200	91	15	3	45	70	12.0	4.07	96	.282	.327	14	.233	4	-3	-3	-0	0.0
1940	NY-N	10	15	.400	31	27	11	4	1	195	200	98	19	3	43	73	11.4	3.78	103	.264	.306	8	.123	-2	1	2	2	0.2
1941	NY-N	9	10	.474	33	20	6	2	3	159	184	87	7	0	40	61	12.7	4.02	92	.286	.327	11	.229	4	-7	-6	0	-0.2
1942	StL-N	1	1	.500	5	0	0	0	0	12^2	11	3	0	0	2	6	9.2	1.42	241	.244	.277	2	.667	1	3	3	0	0.5
	NY-N	13	4	.765	26	19	12	2	0	158	143	52	11	2	33	41	10.1	2.56	131	.240	.282	7	.121	-3	13	14	-1	1.1
	Yr	14	5	.737	31	19	12	2	0	170^2	154	55	11	2	35	47	10.1	2.48	136	.240	.281	9	.148	-2	16	17	-1	1.6
1943	NY-N	5	6	.455	17	12	3	0	1	80^1	110	51	7	2	25	16	15.3	5.15	67	.324	.374	1	.037	-3	-16	-15	-1	-2.2
	Bro-N	0	2	.000	6	2	2	0	0	27^2	29	14	2	1	10	5	13.0	3.58	94	.274	.342	1	.143	0	-1	-1	-0	0.0
	Yr	5	8	.385	23	14	5	0	1	108	139	65	9	3	35	21	14.8	4.75	72	.312	.366	2	.059	-3	-16	-16	-1	-2.2
1944	Bro-N	0	0	—	3	0	0	0	0	2^2	4	0	0	0	4	1	27.0	0.00	—	.500	.667	0	—	0	1	1	-0	0.0
	Cin-N	0	1	.000	2	1	0	0	0	1^2	5	5	0	0	2	0	37.8	27.00	13	.500	.583	0	—	0	-4	-5	-0	-0.8
	Yr	0	1	.000	5	1	0	0	0	4^1	9	5	0	0	6	1	31.2	10.38	34	.500	.625	0	—	0	-3	-3	-0	-0.8
Total	9	60	59	.504	198	120	47	9	8	990^2	1048	479	70	13	240	330	11.8	3.69	101	.271	.315	49	.153	-3	-1	2	3	-0.4
● RICH LOISELLE	Loiselle, Richard Frank b: 1/12/72, Neenah, Wis. BR/TR, 6'5", 225 lbs. Deb: 9/7/96																											
1996	Pit-N	1	0	1.000	5	3	0	0	0	20^2	22	8	3	0	8	9	13.1	3.05	143	.268	.333	2	.250	1	3	3	0	0.2
1997	Pit-N	1	5	.167	72	0	0	0	29	72^2	76	29	7	1	24	66	12.5	3.10	139	.269	.328	0	.000	-0	9	9	-1	1.3
1998	Pit-N	2	7	.222	54	0	0	0	19	55	56	26	2	2	36	48	15.4	3.44	125	.262	.373	0	—	0	5	5	0	1.1
1999	Pit-N	3	2	.600	13	0	0	0	0	15^1	16	9	2	2	9	14	15.8	5.28	87	.281	.397	0	—	0	-1	-1	1	-0.2
2000	Pit-N	2	3	.400	40	0	0	0	0	42^1	43	27	5	3	30	32	16.2	5.10	90	.262	.386	0	—	0	-2	-2	-0	-0.3
Total	5	9	17	.346	184	3	0	0	48	206	213	99	19	8	107	169	14.3	3.76	117	.266	.358	2	.222	0	13	14	0	2.1
● MICKEY LOLICH	Lolich, Michael Stephen b: 9/12/40, Portland, Ore. BB/TL, 6', 210 lbs. Deb: 5/12/63																											
1963	Det-A	5	9	.357	33	18	4	0	0	144^1	145	64	13	5	56	103	12.8	3.55	105	.265	.338	2	.056	-1	1	3	-1	0.1
1964	Det-A	18	9	.667	44	33	12	6	2	232	196	88	26	5	64	192	10.3	3.26	112	.225	.282	7	.109	1	9	10	-2	1.0
1965	Det-A	15	9	.625	43	37	7	3	3	243^2	216	103	23	12	72	226	11.1	3.44	101	.236	.301	5	.058	-6	1	1	-2	-0.7
1966	Det-A	14	14	.500	40	33	5	1	3	203^2	204	119	24	6	83	173	12.9	4.77	73	.257	.331	9	.141	1	-30	-29	-3	-3.9
1967	Det-A	14	13	.519	31	30	11	**6**	0	204	165	71	14	7	56	174	10.1	3.04	107	.221	.282	12	.197	3	4	5	-2	0.7
1968	*Det-A	17	9	.654	39	32	8	4	1	220	178	84	23	11	65	197	10.4	3.19	94	.219	.286	8	.114	0	-5	-4	-2	-0.8
1969	Det-A☆	19	11	.633	37	36	15	1	1	280^2	214	111	22	14	122	271	11.2	3.14	119	.210	.304	8	.088	-3	15	18	-0	1.6
1970	Det-A	14	19	.424	40	39	13	3	0	272^2	272	125	27	5	109	230	12.7	3.80	98	.260	.333	11	.134	1	-2	-2	1	0.0
1971	Det-A★	**25**	14	.641	45	45	**29**	4	0	**376**	336	133	36	7	92	**308**	10.4	2.92	123	.237	.287	15	.130	1	23	27	-4	2.5
1972	*Det-A★	22	14	.611	41	41	23	4	0	327^1	282	100	29	11	74	250	10.1	2.50	126	.234	.284	6	.067	-0	21	23	-4	2.2
1973	Det-A	16	15	.516	42	42	17	3	0	308^2	315	143	35	5	79	214	11.6	3.82	107	.266	.315	0	—	0	0	9	-1	0.7
1974	Det-A	16	21	.432	41	41	27	3	0	308	310	155	38	3	78	202	11.4	4.15	92	.268	.316	0	—	0	-18	-11	-4	-1.6
1975	Det-A	12	18	.400	32	32	19	1	0	240^2	260	119	19	0	64	139	12.1	3.78	107	.279	.325	0	—	0	0	6	-2	0.6
1976	NY-N	8	13	.381	31	30	5	2	0	192^2	184	83	14	0	52	120	11.0	3.22	102	.252	.302	7	.130	0	6	2	-1	0.1
1978	SD-N	2	1	.667	20	2	0	0	1	34^2	30	6	0	1	11	13	10.9	1.56	214	.240	.307	0	.000	-0	8	7	-0	0.6
1979	SD-N	0	2	.000	27	5	0	0	0	49^1	59	33	4	0	22	20	14.8	4.74	75	.304	.375	0	.000	-0	-5	-7	0	-0.4
Total	16	217	191	.532	586	496	195	41	11	3638^1	3366	1537	347	92	1099	2832	11.3	3.44	104	.246	.306	90	.110	-4	27	58	-25	2.7
● TIM LOLLAR	Lollar, William Timothy b: 3/17/56, Poplar Bluff, Mo. BL/TL, 6'3", 200 lbs. Deb: 6/28/80																											
1980	NY-A	1	0	1.000	14	1	0	0	2	32^1	33	14	3	0	20	13	14.8	3.34	118	.280	.384	0	—	0	3	2	0	0.1
1981	SD-N	2	8	.200	24	11	0	0	1	76^2	87	56	4	3	51	38	16.6	6.10	53	.293	.402	3	.167	1	-22	-26	2	-2.8
1982	SD-N	16	9	.640	34	34	4	2	0	232^2	192	82	20	4	87	150	10.9	3.13	110	.224	.298	21	.247	9	12	8	0	1.8

YEAR	TM/L	W	L	PCT	G	GS	CG	SH	SV	IP	H	R	HR	HB	BB	SO	RAT	ERA	ERA+	OAV	OOB	BH	AVG	PB	PR	PR+	PD	TPI
1983	SD-N	7	12	.368	30	30	1	0	0	175^2	170	98	22	4	85	135	13.3	4.61	76	.258	.347	14	.241	6	-19	-23	-2	-1.8
1984	*SD-N	11	13	.458	31	31	3	2	0	195^2	168	89	18	1	105	131	12.6	3.91	91	.234	.333	15	.221	7	-7	-7	-2	-0.4
1985	Chi-A	3	5	.375	18	13	0	0	0	83	83	48	10	1	58	61	15.4	4.66	93	.266	.383	0	—	0	-5	-3	-0	-0.3
	Bos-A	5	5	.500	16	10	1	0	1	67	57	37	9	1	40	44	13.2	4.57	94	.230	.339	0	.000	-0	-3	-2	-1	-0.4
	Yr	8	10	.444	34	23	1	0	1	150	140	85	19	2	98	105	14.4	4.62	93	.250	.364	0	.000	-0	-8	-5	-1	-0.7
1986	Bos-A	2	0	1.000	32	1	0	0	0	43	51	35	7	3	34	28	18.4	6.91	60	.304	.429	1	1.000	0	-13	-13	1	-0.5
Total	7	47	52	.475	199	131	9	4	4	906	841	459	93	17	480	600	13.3	4.27	85	.249	.345	54	.234	23	-54	-64	-3	-4.3
● VIC LOMBARDI	Lombardi, Victor Alvin b: 9/20/22, Reedley, Cal. d: 12/7/97, Fresno, Cal. BL/TL, 5'7", 158 lbs. Deb: 4/18/45																											
1945	Bro-N	10	11	.476	38	24	9	0	4	203^2	195	106	11	5	86	64	12.6	3.31	113	.252	.331	13	.183	-1	11	10	-1	0.9
1946	Bro-N	13	10	.565	41	25	13	2	3	193	170	76	10	2	84	60	11.9	2.89	117	.235	.316	14	.230	2	11	11	0	1.4
1947	*Bro-N	12	11	.522	33	20	7	3	3	174^2	156	73	12	2	65	72	11.5	2.99	138	.241	.312	16	.242	2	21	22	1	3.0
1948	Pit-N	10	9	.526	38	17	9	0	4	163	156	72	9	2	67	54	12.4	3.70	110	.255	.330	10	.208	1	5	7	1	0.9
1949	Pit-N	5	5	.500	34	12	4	0	1	134	149	74	14	3	68	64	14.8	4.57	92	.286	.372	17	.347	5	-8	-5	1	0.3
1950	Pit-N	0	5	.000	39	2	0	0	1	76^1	93	61	14	2	48	26	16.9	6.60	66	.310	.409	4	.250	1	-21	-18	0	-0.9
Total	6	50	51	.495	223	100	42	5	16	944^2	919	462	70	16	418	340	12.9	3.68	106	.257	.337	74	.238	10	19	24	3	5.6
● LOU LOMBARDO	Lombardo, Louis b: 11/18/28, Carlstadt, N.J. BL/TL, 6'2", 210 lbs. Deb: 9/22/48																											
1948	NY-N	0	0	—	2	0	0	0	0	5^1	5	4	1	1	5	0	18.6	6.75	58	.250	.423	0	.000	-0	-2	-2	0	-0.1
● KEVIN LOMON	Lomon, Kevin Dale b: 11/20/71, Fort Smith, Ark. BR/TR, 6'1", 195 lbs. Deb: 4/27/95																											
1995	NY-N	0	1	.000	6	0	0	0	0	9^1	17	8	0	0	5	6	21.2	6.75	60	.405	.468	0	—	0	-3	-3	-0	-0.3
1996	Atl-N	0	0	—	6	0	0	0	0	7^1	7	4	0	1	3	1	13.5	4.91	90	.259	.355	0	—	0	-1	-0	1	0.0
Total	2	0	1	.000	12	0	0	0	0	16^2	24	12	0	1	8	7	17.8	5.94	71	.348	.423	0	—	0	-3	-3	0	-0.3
● JIM LONBORG	Lonborg, James Reynold b: 4/16/42, Santa Maria, Cal. BR/TR, 6'5", 210 lbs. Deb: 4/23/65																											
1965	Bos-A	9	17	.346	32	31	7	1	0	185^1	193	112	20	3	65	113	12.7	4.47	83	.262	.324	8	.136	0	-21	-14	-2	-2.0
1966	Bos-A	10	10	.500	45	23	3	1	2	181^2	173	86	18	7	55	131	11.6	3.86	98	.249	.310	5	.093	-2	-9	-1	-1	-0.4
1967	*Bos-A☆	**22**	9	.710	39	39	15	2	0	273^1	228	102	23	19	83	**246**	10.9	3.16	110	.225	.296	14	.141	-1	2	9	-2	0.6
1968	Bos-A	6	10	.375	23	17	4	1	0	113^1	89	57	11	11	59	73	12.6	4.29	74	.216	.330	11	.282	3	-16	-13	-2	-1.7
1969	Bos-A	7	11	.389	29	23	4	0	0	143^2	148	78	15	7	65	100	13.8	4.51	84	.270	.355	4	.098	-1	-14	-11	-0	-1.3
1970	Bos-A	4	1	.800	9	4	0	0	0	34	33	12	3	0	9	21	11.1	3.18	125	.260	.309	4	.444	2	2	3	0	0.7
1971	Bos-A	10	7	.588	27	26	5	1	0	167^2	167	86	15	14	67	100	13.3	4.13	90	.259	.342	9	.170	0	-12	-8	1	-0.6
1972	Mil-A	14	12	.538	33	30	11	2	1	223	197	75	17	11	76	143	11.5	2.83	108	.238	.311	10	.145	-1	6	5	-2	0.4
1973	Phi-N	13	16	.448	38	30	6	0	0	199^1	218	124	25	9	80	106	13.9	4.88	78	.279	.353	8	.136	0	-27	-23	-1	-3.1
1974	Phi-N	17	13	.567	39	39	16	3	0	283	280	113	22	6	70	121	11.3	3.21	118	.261	.310	9	.096	-4	13	17	-4	0.9
1975	Phi-N	8	6	.571	27	26	6	2	0	159^1	161	84	12	5	45	72	11.9	4.12	91	.257	.312	1	.023	-3	-9	-7	0	-0.8
1976	*Phi-N	18	10	.643	33	32	8	1	1	222	210	85	18	5	50	118	10.7	3.08	115	.249	.294	11	.164	1	11	11	-3	1.2
1977	*Phi-N	11	4	.733	25	25	4	1	0	157^2	157	77	15	5	50	76	12.1	4.11	97	.261	.323	5	.104	-2	-3	-2	-1	-0.5
1978	Phi-N	8	10	.444	22	22	1	0	0	113^2	132	69	16	2	45	48	14.2	5.23	68	.293	.359	6	.176	1	-21	-21	-0	-2.9
1979	Phi-N	0	1	.000	4	1	0	0	0	7^1	14	10	3	1	4	7	23.3	11.05	35	.389	.463	0	.000	-0	-6	-6	-0	-0.7
Total	15	157	137	.534	425	368	90	15	4	2464^1	2400	1170	233	105	823	1475	12.2	3.86	94	.255	.322	105	.136	-5	-104	-58	-18	-10.2
● JOEY LONG	Long, Joey J. b: 7/15/70, Sidney, O. BR/TL, 6'2", 220 lbs. Deb: 4/25/97																											
1997	SD-N	0	0	—	10	0	0	0	0	11	17	11	1	1	8	8	21.3	8.18	47	.340	.441	0	—	0	-5	-6	0	-0.3
● LEP LONG	Long, Lester b: 7/12/1888, Summit, N.J. d: 10/21/58, Birmingham, Ala. BR/TR, 5'10", 153 lbs. Deb: 6/29/11																											
1911	Phi-A	0	0	—	4	0	0	0	0	8	15	6	0	0	5	4	22.5	4.50	70	.405	.476	0	.000	-0	-1	-1	0	-0.1
● RED LONG	Long, Nelson b: 9/28/1876, Burlington, Ont., Canada d: 8/11/29, Hamilton, Ont., Can BR/TR, 6'1", 190 lbs. Deb: 9/11/02																											
1902	Bos-N	0	0	—	1	1	1	0	0	8	4	2	0	1	3	5	9.0	1.13	251	.148	.258	0	.000	-0	1	1	-0	0.0
● BOB LONG	Long, Robert Earl b: 11/11/54, Jasper, Tenn. BR/TR, 6'3", 178 lbs. Deb: 9/2/81																											
1981	Pit-N	1	2	.333	5	3	0	0	0	19^2	23	14	2	0	10	8	15.1	5.95	60	.299	.379	0	.000	-0	-5	-5	-1	-0.7
1985	Sea-A	0	0	—	28	0	0	0	0	38^1	30	17	7	2	17	29	11.5	3.76	112	.210	.302	0	—	0	2	2	-0	0.1
Total	2	1	2	.333	33	3	0	0	0	58	53	31	9	2	27	37	12.7	4.50	89	.241	.329	0	.000	-0	-4	-3	-1	-0.6
● TOM LONG	Long, Thomas Francis "Little Hawk" b: 4/22/1898, Memphis, Tenn. d: 9/16/73, Louisville, Ky. BL/TL, 5'9", 154 lbs. Deb: 4/26/24																											
1924	Bro-N	0	0	—	1	0	0	0	0	2	2	2	0	0	2	0	18.0	9.00	42	.333	.500	0	—	0	-1	-1	-0	-0.1
● BILL LONG	Long, William Douglas b: 2/29/60, Cincinnati, Ohio BR/TR, 6', 185 lbs. Deb: 7/21/85																											
1985	Chi-A	0	1	.000	4	3	0	0	0	14	25	17	4	0	5	13	19.3	10.29	42	.391	.435	0	—	0	-10	-9	0	-0.5
1987	Chi-A	8	8	.500	29	23	5	2	1	169	179	85	20	3	28	72	11.2	4.37	105	.272	.304	0	—	0	2	4	0	0.3
1988	Chi-A	8	11	.421	47	18	3	0	2	174	187	89	21	4	43	77	12.1	4.03	99	.280	.327	0	—	0	-1	-1	-0	-0.1
1989	Chi-A	5	5	.500	30	8	0	0	1	98^2	101	49	8	4	37	51	13.0	3.92	97	.265	.336	0	—	0	-0	-1	0	-0.1
1990	Chi-A	0	1	.000	4	0	0	0	0	5^2	6	5	2	0	2	2	12.7	6.35	60	.261	.320	0	—	0	-2	-2	0	-0.2
	Chi-N	6	1	.857	42	0	0	0	5	55^2	66	29	8	1	21	32	14.2	4.37	94	.301	.365	0	.000	-0	-4	-2	0	-0.2
1991	Mon-N	0	0	—	3	0	0	0	0	1^2	4	2	0	0	4	0	43.2	10.80	34	.500	.667	0	—	0	-1	-1	-0	-0.1
Total	6	27	27	.500	159	52	8	2	9	518^2	568	276	63	12	140	247	12.5	4.37	95	.281	.331	0	.000	-0	-15	-12	1	-0.9
● BRIAN LOONEY	Looney, Brian James b: 9/26/69, New Haven, Conn. BL/TL, 5'10", 180 lbs. Deb: 9/26/93																											
1993	Mon-N	0	0	—	3	1	0	0	0	6	8	2	0	0	2	7	15.0	3.00	139	.308	.357	0	.000	-0	1	1	0	0.0
1994	Mon-N	0	0	—	1	0	0	0	0	2	4	5	1	1	0	2	22.5	22.50	19	.400	.455	0	—	0	-4	-4	-0	-0.2
1995	Bos-A	0	1	.000	3	1	0	0	0	4^2	12	9	1	0	4	2	30.9	17.36	28	.545	.615	0	—	0	-7	-6	0	-1.0
Total	3	0	1	.000	7	2	0	0	0	12^2	24	16	2	1	6	11	22.0	11.37	39	.414	.477	0	.000	-0	-10	-9	-0	-1.2
● BRADEN LOOPER	Looper, Braden La Vern b: 10/28/74, Weatherford, Okla. BR/TR, 6'4", 210 lbs. Deb: 3/31/98																											
1998	StL-N	0	1	.000	4	0	0	0	0	3^1	5	4	1	0	1	4	16.2	5.40	78	.357	.400	0	—	0	-0	-0	-0	-0.1
1999	Fla-N	3	3	.500	72	0	0	0	0	83	96	43	7	1	31	50	13.9	3.80	115	.293	.356	0	—	0	7	5	-1	0.3
2000	Fla-N	5	1	.833	73	0	0	0	2	67^1	71	41	3	5	36	29	15.0	4.41	100	.268	.366	0	.000	-0	2	0	0	0.0
Total	3	8	5	.615	149	0	0	0	2	153^2	172	88	11	6	68	83	14.4	4.10	107	.283	.361	0	.000	-0	8	5	-1	0.2
● PETE LOOS	Loos, Ivan b: 3/23/1878, Philadelphia, Pa. d: 2/23/56, Darby, Pa. TR, Deb: 5/2/01																											
1901	Phi-A	0	1	.000	1	1	0	0	0	1	2	5	0	0	4	0	54.0	27.00	14	.400	.667	0	—	0	-3	-3	0	-0.4
● ED LOPAT	Lopat, Edmund Walter (b: Edmund Walter Lopatynski) b: 6/21/18, New York, N.Y. d: 6/15/92, Darien, Conn. BL/TL, 5'10", 185 lbs. Deb: 4/30/44 MC																											
1944	Chi-A	11	10	.524	27	25	13	1	0	210	217	96	12	2	59	75	11.9	3.26	105	.265	.316	25	.309	6	4	4	1	1.2
1945	Chi-A	10	13	.435	26	24	17	1	1	199^1	226	101	8	6	56	74	13.0	4.11	81	.285	.336	24	.293	5	-16	-18	-1	-1.5
1946	Chi-A	13	13	.500	29	29	20	2	0	231	216	80	18	1	48	89	10.3	2.73	125	.248	.288	22	.253	6	20	18	1	2.9
1947	Chi-A	16	13	.552	31	31	22	3	0	252^2	241	88	17	2	73	109	11.3	2.81	130	.253	.307	19	.198	0	25	24	-1	2.6
1948	NY-A	17	11	.607	33	31	13	3	0	226^2	246	106	16	2	66	83	12.5	3.65	112	.284	.336	14	.173	-1	16	11	2	1.2
1949	*NY-A	15	10	.600	31	30	14	4	1	215^1	222	93	19	5	69	70	12.4	3.26	124	.269	.330	20	.263	7	22	20	0	2.8
1950	*NY-A	18	8	.692	35	32	15	3	1	236^1	244	110	19	4	65	72	11.9	3.47	124	.266	.317	19	.232	8	29	23	1	3.1
1951	*NY-A★	21	9	.700	31	31	20	4	0	234^2	209	86	12	3	71	93	**10.9**	2.91	131	.239	**.298**	15	.179	1	31	26	2	3.3
1952	*NY-A	10	5	.667	20	19	10	2	0	149^1	127	47	11	4	53	56	11.1	2.53	131	.234	.307	9	.173	1	19	15	0	1.5
1953	*NY-A	16	4	**.800**	25	24	9	3	0	178^1	169	58	13	4	32	50	10.3	**2.42**	**152**	.250	.288	12	.190	1	31	27	1	3.2
1954	NY-A	12	4	.750	26	23	7	0	0	170	189	74	14	6	33	54	12.1	3.55	97	.288	.328	1	.018	-5	3	-2	-1	-0.8
1955	NY-A	4	8	.333	16	12	3	1	0	86^2	101	45	12	1	16	24	12.3	3.74	100	.294	.328	4	.138	-1	2	0	-1	-0.2
	Bal-A	3	4	.429	10	7	1	0	0	49	57	24	8	3	9	10	12.7	4.22	90	.294	.335	3	.176	0	-1	-2	1	-0.2
	Yr	7	12	.368	26	19	4	1	0	135^2	158	69	20	4	25	34	12.4	3.91	96	.294	.330	7	.152	-1	1	-2	-0	-0.4
Total	12	166	112	.597	340	318	164	27	3	2439^1	2464	1008	179	43	650	859	11.6	3.21	116	.264	.315	187	.211	29	186	145	4	19.1

YEAR TM/L	W	L	PCT	G	GS	CG	SH	SV	IP	H	R	HR	HB	BB	SO	RAT	ERA	ERA+	OAV	OOB	BH	AVG	PB	PR	PR+	PD	TPI
● **ART LOPATKA** Lopatka, Arthur Joseph b: 5/28/19, Chicago, Ill. BB/TL, 5'10", 170 lbs. Deb: 9/12/45																											
1945 StL-N	1	0	1.000	4	1	1	0	0	11^2	7	4	0	1	3	5	8.5	1.54	243	.159	.229	1	.250	0	3	3	-0	0.2
1946 Phi-N	0	1	.000	4	1	0	0	0	5^1	13	11	1	0	4	4	28.7	16.88	20	.448	.515	0	—	0	-8	-8	0	-1.2
Total 2	1	1	.500	8	2	1	0	0	17	20	15	1	1	7	9	14.8	6.35	57	.274	.346	1	.250	0	-5	-5	-0	-1.0
● **ALBIE LOPEZ** Lopez, Albert Anthony b: 8/18/71, Mesa, Ariz. BR/TR, 6'2", 205 lbs. Deb: 7/6/93																											
1993 Cle-A	3	1	.750	9	9	0	0	0	49^2	49	34	7	1	32	25	14.9	5.98	73	.262	.373	0	—	0	-9	-9	-0	-0.6
1994 Cle-A	1	2	.333	4	4	1	1	0	17	20	11	3	1	6	18	14.3	4.24	112	.290	.355	0	—	0	1	1	-0	0.1
1995 Cle-A	0	0	—	6	2	0	0	0	23	17	8	4	1	7	22	9.8	3.13	150	.205	.275	0	—	0	4	4	-0	0.2
1996 Cle-A	5	4	.556	13	10	0	0	0	62	80	47	14	2	22	45	15.1	6.39	77	.311	.370	0	—	0	-10	-11	-0	-1.2
1997 Cle-A	3	7	.300	37	6	0	0	0	76^2	101	61	11	4	40	63	17.0	6.93	68	.321	.404	0	.000	-0	-20	-19	1	-1.9
1998 TB-A	7	4	.636	54	0	0	0	1	79^2	73	31	7	3	32	62	12.2	2.60	185	.249	.329	0	.000	-0	18	19	1	2.4
1999 TB-A	3	2	.600	51	0	0	0	1	64	66	40	8	1	24	37	12.8	4.64	107	.263	.330	0	—	0	2	2	-0	0.1
2000 TB-A	11	13	.458	45	24	4	1	2	185^1	199	95	24	1	70	96	13.1	4.13	120	.277	.342	0	.000	-1	16	17	-1	1.7
Total 8	33	33	.500	219	55	5	2	4	557^1	605	327	78	14	233	368	13.8	4.73	102	.278	.352	0	.000	-1	3	6	-1	0.8
● **AURELIO LOPEZ** Lopez, Aurelio Alejandro (Rios) b: 9/21/48, Tecamachalco, Mexico d: 9/22/92, Matehuala, Mex. BR/TR, 6', 220 lbs. Deb: 9/1/74																											
1974 KC-A	0	0	—	8	1	0	0	0	16	21	12	0	0	10	5	17.4	5.63	68	.344	.437	0	—	0	-4	-3	0	-0.2
1978 StL-N	4	2	.667	25	4	0	0	0	65	52	35	4	1	32	46	11.8	4.29	82	.218	.313	3	.214	0	-5	-6	-1	-0.6
1979 Det-A	10	5	.667	61	0	0	0	21	127	95	37	12	3	51	106	10.6	2.41	180	.210	.294	0	—	0	26	27	-0	3.8
1980 Det-A	13	6	.684	67	1	0	0	21	124	125	56	15	3	45	97	12.6	3.77	109	.263	.330	0	—	0	4	5	-1	0.7
1981 Det-A	5	2	.714	29	3	0	0	3	81^2	70	34	8	2	31	53	11.4	3.64	104	.233	.309	0	—	0	0	1	-0	0.1
1982 Det-A	3	1	.750	19	0	0	0	3	41	41	27	8	0	19	26	13.2	5.27	77	.268	.349	0	—	0	-5	-5	0	-0.6
1983 Det-A☆	9	8	.529	57	0	0	0	18	115^1	87	36	12	1	49	90	10.7	2.81	140	.210	.295	0	—	0	16	15	-1	2.4
1984 *Det-A	10	1	.909	71	0	0	0	14	137^2	109	51	16	2	52	94	10.7	2.94	133	.221	.298	0	—	0	16	15	-2	1.3
1985 Det-A	3	7	.300	51	0	0	0	5	86^1	82	50	15	1	41	53	12.9	4.80	85	.250	.335	0	—	0	-6	-7	-0	-0.8
1986 *Hou-N	3	3	.500	45	0	0	0	7	78	64	32	6	0	25	44	10.3	3.46	104	.221	.283	0	.000	-1	2	1	-2	-0.2
1987 Hou-N	2	1	.667	26	0	0	0	1	38	39	22	6	2	12	21	12.6	4.50	87	.273	.338	0	.000	-0	-2	-3	-0	-0.2
Total 11	62	36	.633	459	9	0	0	93	910	785	392	102	15	367	635	11.5	3.56	111	.234	.313	3	.125	-1	42	40	-8	5.7
● **RAMON LOPEZ** Lopez, Jose Ramon (Hevia) b: 5/26/33, Las Villas, Cuba d: 9/4/82, Miami, Fla. BR/TR, 6', 175 lbs. Deb: 8/21/66																											
1966 Cal-A	0	1	.000	4	1	0	0	0	7	4	5	1	0	4	2	10.3	5.14	65	.154	.267	0	—	0	-1	-1	-0	-0.2
● **MARCELINO LOPEZ** Lopez, Marcelino Pons b: 9/23/43, Havana, Cuba BR/TL, 6'3", 210 lbs. Deb: 4/14/63																											
1963 Phi-N	1	0	1.000	4	2	0	0	0	6	8	5	0	0	7	2	22.5	6.00	54	.333	.484	0	.000	-0	-2	-2	0	-0.3
1965 Cal-A	14	13	.519	35	32	8	1	1	215^1	185	79	12	4	82	122	11.3	2.93	116	.230	.305	14	.203	3	13	12	4	2.3
1966 Cal-A	7	14	.333	37	32	6	2	1	199	188	95	20	9	68	132	12.0	3.93	85	.251	.321	11	.190	2	-11	-13	2	-1.0
1967 Cal-A	0	2	.000	4	3	0	0	0	9	11	10	1	0	9	6	20.0	9.00	35	.324	.465	1	.500	0	-6	-6	-0	-1.1
Bal-A	1	0	1.000	4	4	0	0	0	17^2	15	5	1	0	10	15	12.7	2.55	124	.227	.329	0	.000	-0	1	1	-1	0.0
Yr	1	2	.333	8	7	0	0	0	26^2	26	15	2	0	19	21	15.2	4.73	67	.260	.378	1	.143	0	-4	-5	-1	-1.1
1969 *Bal-A	5	3	.625	27	4	0	0	0	69^1	65	34	3	2	34	57	13.1	4.41	81	.252	.344	3	.214	1	-6	-7	-1	-0.7
1970 *Bal-A	1	1	.500	25	3	0	0	0	60^2	47	19	2	0	37	49	12.5	2.08	176	.217	.331	1	.077	0	11	11	-1	0.5
1971 Mil-A	2	7	.222	31	11	0	0	0	67^2	64	48	5	0	60	42	16.5	4.66	75	.251	.394	1	.059	-1	-9	-9	1	-1.2
1972 Cle-A	0	0	—	4	2	0	0	0	8^1	8	5	0	0	10	1	19.4	5.40	60	.276	.462	0	.000	-0	-2	-2	-0	-0.1
Total 8	31	40	.437	171	93	14	3	2	653	591	300	44	15	317	426	12.7	3.62	94	.243	.334	31	.171	4	-11	-15	4	-1.6
● **RODRIGO LOPEZ** Lopez, Rodrigo (Munoz) b: 12/14/75, Tlalnepantla, Mex. BR/TR, 6'1", 180 lbs. Deb: 4/29/2000																											
2000 SD-N	0	3	.000	6	6	0	0	0	24^2	40	24	5	0	13	17	19.3	8.76	50	.377	.445	1	.111	-0	-11	-13	0	-1.2
● **BRIS LORD** Lord, Bristol Robotham "The Human Eyeball" b: 9/21/1883, Upland, Pa. d: 11/13/64, Prince Frederick, Md. BR/TR, 5'9", 185 lbs. Deb: 4/21/05 ♦																											
1907 Phi-A	0	0	—	1	0	0	0	0	1	3	2	0	0	0	0	27.0	9.00	29	.500	.500	31	.182	0	-1	-1	-0	0.0
● **LEFTY LORENZEN** Lorenzen, Adolph Andreas b: 1/12/1893, Davenport, Iowa d: 3/5/63, Davenport, Iowa BL/TL, 5'10", 164 lbs. Deb: 9/12/13																											
1913 Det-A	0	0	—	1	0	0	0	0	2	4	4	0	0	3	0	31.5	18.00	16	.667	.778	1	.500	0	-3	-3	1	-0.1
● **ANDREW LORRAINE** Lorraine, Andrew Jason b: 8/11/72, Los Angeles, Cal. BL/TL, 6'3", 195 lbs. Deb: 7/17/94																											
1994 Cal-A	0	2	.000	4	3	0	0	0	18^2	30	23	7	0	11	10	19.8	10.61	46	.366	.441	0	—	0	-12	-12	0	-0.9
1995 Chi-A	0	0	—	5	0	0	0	0	8	3	3	0	1	2	5	6.8	3.38	132	.111	.200	0	—	0	1	1	-0	0.0
1997 Oak-A	3	1	.750	12	6	0	0	0	29^2	45	22	2	1	15	18	18.5	6.37	71	.354	.427	0	—	0	-6	-6	-0	-0.7
1998 Sea-A	0	0	—	4	0	0	0	0	3^2	3	1	0	0	4	0	17.2	2.45	189	.250	.438	0	—	0	1	1	-0	0.0
1999 Chi-N	2	5	.286	11	11	2	1	0	61^2	71	42	9	0	22	40	13.6	5.55	81	.293	.352	2	.133	0	-7	-7	-0	-0.7
2000 Chi-N	1	2	.333	8	5	0	0	0	32	36	25	5	0	18	25	15.2	6.47	71	.286	.375	1	.125	-0	-7	-7	-1	-0.6
Cle-A	0	0	—	10	0	0	0	0	9^1	8	4	1	0	5	5	12.5	3.86	130	.222	.317	0	—	0	1	1	0	0.1
Total 6	6	10	.375	54	25	2	1	0	163	196	120	24	2	77	103	15.2	6.18	74	.301	.376	3	.130	0	-28	-29	-1	-2.8
● **JOE LOTZ** Lotz, Joseph Peter "Smokey" b: 1/2/1891, Remsen, Iowa d: 1/1/71, Castro Valley, Cal. BR/TR, 5'8.5", 175 lbs. Deb: 7/15/16																											
1916 StL-N	0	3	.000	12	3	1	0	0	40	31	20	1	1	17	18	11.0	4.27	62	.225	.314	4	.333	1	-7	-7	-1	-0.5
● **ART LOUDELL** Loudell, Arthur (b: Arthur Laudel) b: 4/10/1882, Latham, Mo. d: 2/19/61, Kansas City, Mo. BR/TR, 5'11", 173 lbs. Deb: 8/13/10																											
1910 Det-A	1	1	.500	5	2	1	0	0	21^1	23	13	0	0	14	12	15.6	3.38	78	.284	.389	1	.143	-0	-2	-2	-1	-0.2
● **LARRY LOUGHLIN** Loughlin, Larry John b: 8/16/41, Tacoma, Wash. d: 1/26/99, Denver, Colo. BL/TL, 6'1", 190 lbs. Deb: 5/27/67																											
1967 Phi-N	0	0	—	3	0	0	0	0	5^1	9	9	1	0	4	5	21.9	15.19	22	.375	.464	1	1.000	1	-7	-7	-0	-0.3
● **DON LOUN** Loun, Donald Nelson b: 11/9/40, Frederick, Md. BR/TL, 6'2", 185 lbs. Deb: 9/23/64																											
1964 Was-A	1	1	.500	2	2	1	1	0	13	13	4	0	0	3	3	11.1	2.08	178	.250	.291	0	.000	-0	2	2	0	0.4
● **SLIM LOVE** Love, Edward Haughton b: 8/1/1890, Love, Miss. d: 11/30/42, Memphis, Tenn. BL/TL, 6'7", 195 lbs. Deb: 9/8/13																											
1913 Was-A	1	0	1.000	5	1	0	0	1	16^2	14	5	0	0	6	5	10.8	1.62	182	.226	.294	1	.200	0	2	2	-1	0.1
1916 NY-A	2	0	1.000	20	1	0	0	0	47^2	46	29	2	0	23	21	13.0	4.91	59	.274	.361	0	.000	-2	-11	-10	-0	-0.8
1917 NY-A	6	5	.545	33	9	2	0	1	130^1	115	50	0	1	57	82	11.9	2.35	114	.251	.335	6	.167	-1	5	5	-2	0.1
1918 NY-A	13	12	.520	38	29	13	1	1	228^2	207	92	3	10	116	95	13.1	3.07	92	.253	.353	17	.230	2	-7	-6	-5	-0.9
1919 Det-A	6	4	.600	22	8	4	0	1	89^2	92	40	3	6	40	46	13.9	3.01	106	.275	.363	6	.222	0	2	2	-2	0.0
1920 Det-A	0	0	—	1	0	0	0	0	4^1	6	4	0	0	4	2	20.8	8.31	45	.375	.500	0	—	0	-2	-2	0	-0.1
Total 6	28	21	.571	119	48	19	1	4	517^1	480	220	8	17	246	251	12.9	3.04	94	.259	.351	30	.192	-0	-11	-10	-9	-1.6
● **VANCE LOVELACE** Lovelace, Vance Odell b: 8/9/63, Tampa, Fla. BL/TL, 6'5", 205 lbs. Deb: 9/10/88																											
1988 Cal-A	0	0	—	3	0	0	0	0	1^1	2	2	1	0	3	0	33.8	13.50	29	.400	.625	0	—	0	-1	-1	0	-0.1
1989 Cal-A	0	0	—	1	0	0	0	0	1	0	0	0	0	1	1	9.0	0.00	—	.000	.250	0	—	0	0	0	0	0.0
1990 Sea-A	0	0	—	5	0	0	0	0	2^1	3	1	0	1	6	1	38.6	3.86	103	.300	.588	0	—	0	0	0	-0	0.0
Total 3	0	0	—	9	0	0	0	0	4^2	5	3	1	1	10	2	30.9	5.79	68	.278	.552	0	—	0	-1	-1	-0	-0.1
● **LYNN LOVENGUTH** Lovenguth, Lynn Richard b: 11/29/22, Camden, N.Y. BL/TR, 5'10.5", 170 lbs. Deb: 4/18/55																											
1955 Phi-N	0	1	.000	14	0	0	0	0	18	17	9	1	2	10	14	14.5	4.50	88	.258	.372	0	.000	-0	-1	-1	-0	-0.1
1957 StL-N	0	1	.000	2	1	0	0	0	9	6	3	0	0	6	6	12.0	2.00	198	.182	.308	0	.000	-0	2	2	-0	0.1
Total 2	0	2	.000	16	1	0	0	0	27	23	12	1	2	16	20	13.7	3.67	108	.232	.350	0	.000	-1	1	1	-1	0.0
● **JOHN LOVETT** Lovett, John b: 5/6/1877, Monday, Ohio d: 12/5/37, Murray City, Ohio Deb: 5/22/03																											
1903 StL-N	0	0	—	3	1	0	0	0	5	6	5	0	1	5	3	21.6	5.40	60	.300	.462	1	.333	0	-1	-1	-0	0.0
● **LEN LOVETT** Lovett, Leonard Walker b: 7/17/1852, Lancaster Co., Pa d: 11/18/22, Newark, Del. BR/TR, Deb: 8/4/1873 ♦																											
1873 Res-n	0	1	.000	1	1	1	0	0	9	22	16	0		1	1	23.0	7.00	48	.400	.411	2	.400	0	-4	-4		-0.2

● TOM LOVETT Lovett, Thomas Joseph b: 12/7/1863, Providence, R.I. d: 3/19/28, Providence, R.I. BR, 5'8", 162 lbs. Deb: 6/4/1885

YEAR	TM/L	W	L	PCT	G	GS	CG	SH	SV	IP	H	R	HR	HB	BB	SO	RAT	ERA	ERA+	OAV	OOB	BH	AVG	PB	PR	PR+	PD	TPI
1885	Phi-a	7	8	.467	16	16	15	1	0	138^2	130	96	3	5	38	56	11.2	3.70	93	.236	.291	13	.224	-0	-7	-4	-1	-0.4
1889	*Bro-a	17	10	.630	29	28	23	1	0	229	234	132	3	8	65	92	12.1	4.32	86	.256	.311	19	.190	-1	-12	-16	-0	-1.5
1890	*Bro-N	30	11	**.732**	44	41	39	4	0	372	327	195	14	17	141	124	11.7	2.78	124	.229	.306	33	.201	-1	33	28	-0	2.4
1891	Bro-N	23	19	.548	44	43	39	3	0	365^2	361	229	14	20	129	129	12.6	3.69	90	.248	.318	25	.163	-5	-14	-16	-2	-2.1
1893	Bro-N	3	5	.375	14	8	6	0	1	96	134	92	2	6	35	15	16.4	6.56	67	.321	.381	9	.180	-2	-20	-24	-1	-1.7
1894	Bos-N	8	6	.571	15	13	10	0	0	104	155	96	12	3	36	23	16.8	5.97	95	.341	.394	7	.143	-5	-7	-3	-1	-0.7
Total	6	88	59	.599	162	149	132	9	1	1305^1	1341	840	48	59	444	439	12.7	3.94	94	.257	.322	106	.185	-13	-28	-35	-5	-4.0

● PETE LOVRICH Lovrich, Peter b: 10/16/42, Blue Island, Ill. BR/TR, 6'4", 200 lbs. Deb: 4/26/63

YEAR	TM/L	W	L	PCT	G	GS	CG	SH	SV	IP	H	R	HR	HB	BB	SO	RAT	ERA	ERA+	OAV	OOB	BH	AVG	PB	PR	PR+	PD	TPI
1963	KC-A	1	1	.500	20	1	0	0	0	20^2	25	23	5	1	10	16	15.7	7.84	50	.291	.371	0	—	0	-10	-8	-1	-0.8

● GROVER LOWDERMILK Lowdermilk, Grover Cleveland "Slim" b: 1/15/1885, Sandborn, Ind. d: 3/31/68, Odin, Ill. BR/TR, 6'4", 190 lbs. Deb: 7/3/09 F

YEAR	TM/L	W	L	PCT	G	GS	CG	SH	SV	IP	H	R	HR	HB	BB	SO	RAT	ERA	ERA+	OAV	OOB	BH	AVG	PB	PR	PR+	PD	TPI
1909	StL-N	0	2	.000	7	3	1	0	0	29	28	24	0	3	30	14	18.9	6.21	41	.292	.473	1	.100	-1	-12	-12	-0	-0.9
1911	StL-N	0	1	.000	11	2	1	1	0	33^1	37	30	1	2	33	15	19.4	7.29	46	.301	.456	1	.111	-1	-14	-15	0	-0.7
1912	Chi-N	0	1	.000	2	1	1	0	0	13	17	18	1	0	14	8	21.5	9.69	34	.304	.443	0	.000	-1	-9	-9	-0	-0.6
1915	StL-A	9	17	.346	38	29	14	1	0	222^1	183	110	1	16	133	130	13.4	3.12	92	.234	.357	9	.125	-3	-4	-6	0	-1.0
	Det-A	4	1	.800	7	5	0	0	0	28	17	16	0	1	24	18	13.5	4.18	73	.185	.359	1	.125	-0	-4	-3	0	-0.6
	Yr	13	18	.419	45	34	14	1	0	250^1	200	126	1	17	157	148	13.4	3.24	89	.229	.357	10	.125	-3	-8	-10	0	-1.6
1916	Det-A	0	0	—	1	0	0	0	0	0^1	0	0	0	0	3	0	81.0	0.00	—	.000	.750	0	—	0	0	0	0	0.0
	Cle-A	1	5	.167	10	9	2	0	0	51^1	52	33	0	3	45	28	17.5	3.16	95	.277	.424	3	.167	-0	-2	-1	0	-0.1
	Yr	1	5	.167	11	9	2	0	0	51^2	52	33	0	3	48	28	17.9	3.14	96	.275	.429	3	.167	-0	-2	-1	0	-0.1
1917	StL-A	2	1	.667	3	2	2	1	0	19	16	5	0	0	4	9	9.5	1.42	183	.225	.267	0	.000	-1	3	3	0	0.3
1918	StL-A	2	6	.250	13	11	4	0	0	80	74	44	1	3	38	25	12.9	3.15	87	.255	.347	7	.250	1	-3	-4	2	0.1
1919	StL-A	0	0	—	7	0	0	0	0	12	6	2	0	5	4	6	11.3	0.75	442	.176	.349	0	.000	-0	3	3	-0	0.2
	*Chi-A	5	5	.500	20	11	5	0	0	96^2	95	44	0	4	43	43	13.2	2.79	114	.268	.353	3	.088	-3	5	4	1	0.2
	Yr	5	5	.500	27	11	5	0	0	108^2	101	46	0	9	47	49	13.0	2.57	125	.260	.353	3	.086	-4	8	8	1	0.4
1920	Chi-A	0	0	—	3	0	0	0	0	5^1	9	4	0	0	5	0	23.6	6.75	56	.409	.519	0	—	0	-2	-2	1	0.0
Total	9	23	39	.371	122	73	30	3	0	590^1	534	330	4	37	376	296	14.4	3.58	82	.253	.375	25	.131	-8	-40	-42	5	-3.1

● LOU LOWDERMILK Lowdermilk, Louis Bailey b: 2/23/1887, Sandborn, Ind. d: 12/27/75, Centralia, Ill. BR/TL, 6'1", 180 lbs. Deb: 4/20/11 F

YEAR	TM/L	W	L	PCT	G	GS	CG	SH	SV	IP	H	R	HR	HB	BB	SO	RAT	ERA	ERA+	OAV	OOB	BH	AVG	PB	PR	PR+	PD	TPI
1911	StL-N	3	4	.429	16	3	3	0	0	65	72	39	0	5	29	20	14.7	3.46	98	.304	.391	2	.111	-1	-0	-1	-2	-0.3
1912	StL-N	1	1	.500	4	1	1	0	1	15	14	8	0	0	9	2	13.8	3.00	114	.246	.348	1	.250	0	1	1	0	0.1
Total	2	4	5	.444	20	4	4	0	1	80	86	47	0	5	38	22	14.5	3.37	100	.293	.383	3	.136	-1	0	0	-2	-0.2

● DEREK LOWE Lowe, Derek Christopher b: 6/1/73, Dearborn, Mich. BR/TR, 6'6", 170 lbs. Deb: 4/26/97

YEAR	TM/L	W	L	PCT	G	GS	CG	SH	SV	IP	H	R	HR	HB	BB	SO	RAT	ERA	ERA+	OAV	OOB	BH	AVG	PB	PR	PR+	PD	TPI
1997	Sea-A	2	4	.333	12	9	0	0	0	53	59	43	11	2	20	39	13.8	6.96	65	.282	.351	0	.000	-0	-14	-15	-0	-1.4
	Bos-A	0	2	.000	8	0	0	0	0	16	15	6	0	2	3	13	11.3	3.38	137	.268	.328	0	.000	-0	2	2	0	0.3
	Yr	2	6	.250	20	9	0	0	0	69	74	49	11	4	23	52	13.2	6.13	74	.279	.346	0	.000	-0	-12	-12	0	-1.1
1998	*Bos-A	3	9	.250	63	10	0	0	4	123	126	65	5	4	42	77	12.6	4.02	117	.267	.332	0	.000	-0	9	9	2	1.0
1999	*Bos-A	6	3	.667	74	0	0	0	15	109^1	84	35	7	4	25	80	9.3	2.63	189	.208	.261	0	—	0	27	28	0	2.6
2000	Bos-A★	4	4	.500	74	0	0	0	**42**	91^1	90	27	6	2	22	79	11.2	2.56	199	.257	.305	0	.000	-0	**24**	**25**	1	3.9
Total	4	15	22	.405	231	19	0	0	61	392^2	374	176	29	14	112	288	11.5	3.67	132	.251	.309	0	.000	-0	48	50	3	6.4

● GEORGE LOWE Lowe, George Wesley "Doc" b: 4/25/1895, Ridgefield Park, N.J. d: 9/2/81, Somers Point, N.J. BR/TR, 6'2", 180 lbs. Deb: 7/28/20

YEAR	TM/L	W	L	PCT	G	GS	CG	SH	SV	IP	H	R	HR	HB	BB	SO	RAT	ERA	ERA+	OAV	OOB	BH	AVG	PB	PR	PR+	PD	TPI
1920	Cin-N	0	0	—	1	0	0	0	0	2	1	0	0	0	1	0	9.0	0.00	—	.167	.286	0	—	0	1	1	-0	0.0

● SEAN LOWE Lowe, Jonathan Sean b: 3/29/71, Dallas, Tex. BR/TR, 6'2", 205 lbs. Deb: 8/29/97

YEAR	TM/L	W	L	PCT	G	GS	CG	SH	SV	IP	H	R	HR	HB	BB	SO	RAT	ERA	ERA+	OAV	OOB	BH	AVG	PB	PR	PR+	PD	TPI
1997	StL-N	0	2	.000	6	4	0	0	0	17^1	27	21	2	1	10	8	19.7	9.35	44	.360	.442	1	.333	0	-10	-10	-0	-0.9
1998	StL-N	0	3	.000	4	1	0	0	0	5^1	11	9	1	0	5	2	27.0	15.19	28	.440	.533	0	.000	-0	-6	-7	-0	-1.1
1999	Chi-A	4	1	.800	64	0	0	0	0	95^2	90	39	10	4	46	62	13.2	3.67	133	.262	.355	0	—	0	13	13	0	0.6
2000	Chi-A	4	1	.800	50	5	0	0	0	70^2	78	47	10	6	39	53	15.7	5.48	91	.284	.384	0	—	0	-4	-4	-0	-0.3
Total	4	8	7	.533	124	10	0	0	0	189	206	116	23	11	100	125	15.1	5.19	93	.287	.382	1	.200	0	-8	-8	-0	-1.7

● BOBBY LOWE Lowe, Robert Lincoln "Link" b: 7/10/1868, Pittsburgh, Pa. d: 12/8/51, Detroit, Mich. BR/TR, 5'10", 150 lbs. Deb: 4/19/1890 M◆

YEAR	TM/L	W	L	PCT	G	GS	CG	SH	SV	IP	H	R	HR	HB	BB	SO	RAT	ERA	ERA+	OAV	OOB	BH	AVG	PB	PR	PR+	PD	TPI
1891	Bos-N	0	0	—	1	0	0	0	0	1	3	1	0	0	1	0	36.0	9.00	41	.500	.571	129	.260	0	-1	-1	-0	0.0

● TURK LOWN Lown, Omar Joseph b: 5/30/24, Brooklyn, N.Y. BR/TR, 6'1", 185 lbs. Deb: 4/24/51

YEAR	TM/L	W	L	PCT	G	GS	CG	SH	SV	IP	H	R	HR	HB	BB	SO	RAT	ERA	ERA+	OAV	OOB	BH	AVG	PB	PR	PR+	PD	TPI
1951	Chi-N	4	9	.308	31	18	3	1	0	127	125	80	14	1	90	39	15.3	5.46	75	.260	.378	8	.205	1	-21	-19	0	-1.5
1952	Chi-N	4	11	.267	33	19	5	0	0	156^2	154	87	13	3	93	73	14.4	4.37	88	.257	.359	7	.140	-0	-11	-9	1	-0.7
1953	Chi-N	8	7	.533	49	12	2	0	3	148^1	166	93	20	2	84	76	15.3	5.16	86	.282	.373	6	.125	-2	-14	-11	2	-1.0
1954	Chi-N	0	2	.000	15	0	0	0	0	22	23	18	1	0	15	16	15.5	6.14	68	.261	.369	0	—	0	-5	-5	1	-0.3
1956	Chi-N	9	8	.529	61	0	0	0	13	110^2	95	49	10	1	78	74	14.2	3.58	105	.240	.366	5	.217	2	2	2	-1	0.6
1957	Chi-N	5	7	.417	**67**	0	0	0	12	93	74	45	10	0	51	51	12.1	3.77	103	.221	.324	2	.200	0	1	1	2	0.3
1958	Chi-N	0	0	—	4	0	0	0	0	4	2	2	0	0	3	4	11.3	4.50	87	.154	.313	0	—	0	-0	-0	-0	0.0
	Cin-N	0	2	.000	11	0	0	0	0	11^2	12	8	2	0	12	9	18.5	5.40	77	.273	.429	0	.000	-0	-2	-2	-0	-0.3
	Yr	0	2	.000	15	0	0	0	0	15^2	14	10	2	0	15	13	16.7	5.17	79	.246	.403	0	.000	-0	-2	-2	-0	-0.3
	Chi-A	3	3	.500	27	0	0	0	8	40^2	49	22	1	0	28	40	17.0	3.98	91	.308	.412	3	.333	1	-1	-2	0	-0.2
1959	*Chi-A	9	2	.818	60	0	0	0	**15**	93^1	73	32	12	2	42	63	11.3	2.89	130	.215	.305	3	.250	1	10	9	1	1.5
1960	Chi-A	2	3	.400	45	0	0	0	5	67^1	60	31	6	0	34	39	12.6	3.88	98	.239	.330	1	.200	1	-0	-1	0	0.0
1961	Chi-A	7	5	.583	59	0	0	0	11	101	87	37	13	0	35	50	10.9	2.76	142	.238	.304	0	.000	-2	14	13	-1	1.5
1962	Chi-A	4	2	.667	42	0	0	0	6	56^1	58	21	3	1	25	40	13.4	3.04	129	.269	.347	0	.000	-0	6	6	1	0.8
Total	11	55	61	.474	504	49	10	1	73	1032	978	525	105	10	590	574	13.8	4.12	96	.252	.352	35	.164	1	-21	-18	7	0.7

● SAM LOWRY Lowry, Samuel Joseph b: 3/25/20, Philadelphia, Pa. d: 12/1/92, Philadelphia, Pa. BR/TR, 5'11", 170 lbs. Deb: 9/19/42

YEAR	TM/L	W	L	PCT	G	GS	CG	SH	SV	IP	H	R	HR	HB	BB	SO	RAT	ERA	ERA+	OAV	OOB	BH	AVG	PB	PR	PR+	PD	TPI
1942	Phi-A	0	0	—	1	0	0	0	0	3	3	2	0	0	1	0	12.0	6.00	63	.250	.308	0	.000	-0	-1	-1	-0	-0.1
1943	Phi-A	0	0	—	5	0	0	0	0	18	18	10	1	0	9	3	13.5	5.00	68	.269	.355	1	.167	-0	-3	-3	0	-0.2
Total	2	0	0	—	6	0	0	0	0	21	21	12	1	0	10	3	13.3	5.14	67	.266	.348	1	.143	-0	-4	-4	0	-0.3

● MIKE LOYND Loynd, Michael Wallace b: 3/26/64, St.Louis, Mo. BR/TR, 6'4", 210 lbs. Deb: 7/24/86

YEAR	TM/L	W	L	PCT	G	GS	CG	SH	SV	IP	H	R	HR	HB	BB	SO	RAT	ERA	ERA+	OAV	OOB	BH	AVG	PB	PR	PR+	PD	TPI
1986	Tex-A	2	2	.500	9	8	0	0	1	42	49	30	4	2	19	33	15.0	5.36	80	.290	.368	0	—	0	-5	-5	0	-0.4
1987	Tex-A	1	5	.167	26	8	0	0	1	69^1	82	53	14	1	38	48	15.7	6.10	74	.287	.372	0	—	0	-13	-12	-1	-1.0
Total	2	3	7	.300	35	16	0	0	2	111^1	131	83	18	3	57	81	15.4	5.82	76	.288	.371	0	—	0	-18	-17	-1	-1.4

● PAT LUBY Luby, John Perkins b: 6/1869, Charleston, S.C. d: 4/24/1899, Charleston, S.C. TR, 6', 185 lbs. Deb: 6/16/1890

YEAR	TM/L	W	L	PCT	G	GS	CG	SH	SV	IP	H	R	HR	HB	BB	SO	RAT	ERA	ERA+	OAV	OOB	BH	AVG	PB	PR	PR+	PD	TPI
1890	Chi-N	20	9	.690	34	31	26	0	1	267^2	226	129	6	15	95	85	11.3	3.19	115	.222	.298	31	.267	8	11	13	-2	1.7
1891	Chi-N	8	11	.421	30	24	18	0	1	206	221	148	11	19	94	52	14.6	4.76	70	.264	.352	24	.245	7	-32	-33	-0	-1.8
1892	Chi-N	11	16	.407	31	27	24	1	0	252^1	248	157	10	10	103	66	12.9	3.07	108	.247	.323	31	.190	1	6	7	1	0.8
1895	Lou-N	1	5	.167	11	6	5	0	0	71^1	115	90	5	7	19	12	17.8	6.81	68	.357	.405	15	.283	3	-16	-18	1	-0.8
Total	4	40	41	.494	106	88	73	1	2	797^1	810	524	32	51	311	215	13.2	3.88	92	.254	.331	101	.235	18	-31	-28	-1	-0.1

● RED LUCAS Lucas, Charles Frederick "The Nashville Narcissus"
b: 4/28/02, Columbia, Tenn. d: 7/9/86, Nashville, Tenn. BL/TR, 5'9.5", 170 lbs. Deb: 4/19/23 ◆

YEAR	TM/L	W	L	PCT	G	GS	CG	SH	SV	IP	H	R	HR	HB	BB	SO	RAT	ERA	ERA+	OAV	OOB	BH	AVG	PB	PR	PR+	PD	TPI
1923	NY-N	0	0	—	3	0	0	0	1	5^1	9	5	0	0	4	3	21.9	0.00	—	.346	.433	0	.000	-0	2	2	1	0.1
1924	Bos-N	1	4	.200	27	4	1	0	0	83^2	112	60	5	6	18	30	14.6	5.16	74	.332	.377	11	.333	2	-12	-13	1	-0.4
1926	Cin-N	8	5	.615	39	11	7	1	2	154	161	68	6	2	30	34	11.3	3.68	100	.277	.314	23	.303	6	2	0	-1	0.9
1927	Cin-N	18	11	.621	37	23	19	4	2	239^2	231	96	6	0	39	51	10.1	3.38	112	.256	.287	47	.313	7	14	11	-1	2.4
1928	Cin-N	13	9	.591	27	19	13	**4**	1	167^1	164	73	9	0	42	35	11.1	3.39	117	.258	.304	23	.315	6	11	11	-0	1.9
1929	Cin-N	19	12	.613	32	32	**28**	2	0	270	267	119	14	1	58	72	**10.9**	3.60	127	**.257**	**.297**	41	.293	11	33	30	0	4.1
1930	Cin-N	14	16	.467	33	28	18	1	1	210^2	270	135	15	1	44	53	13.5	5.38	90	.315	.349	38	.336	15	-10	-13	-3	-0.4
1931	Cin-N	14	13	.519	29	29	**24**	3	0	238	261	110	10	0	39	56	11.3	3.59	104	.280	.309	43	.281	11	7	4	1	1.7
1932	Cin-N	13	17	.433	31	31	**28**	0	0	269^1	261	110	10	1	35	63	9.9	2.94	131	.249	.274	43	.287	13	28	28	-0	4.5

YEAR TM/L	W	L	PCT	G	GS	CG	SH	SV	IP	H	R	HR	HB	BB	SO	RAT	ERA	ERA+	OAV	OOB	BH	AVG	PB	PR	PR+	PD	TPI
1933 Cin-N	10	16	.385	29	29	21	3	0	219^{2}	248	106	13	2	18	40	11.0	3.40	100	.289	.305	35	.287	12	-2	-0	0	1.4
1934 Pit-N	10	9	.526	29	22	12	1	0	172^{2}	198	89	14	2	40	44	12.5	4.38	94	.283	.324	23	.219	3	-6	-5	-3	-0.5
1935 Pit-N	8	6	.571	20	19	8	2	0	125^{2}	136	60	10	2	23	29	11.5	3.44	119	.272	.307	21	.318	8	8	9	-1	1.6
1936 Pit-N	15	4	.789	27	22	12	0	0	175^{2}	178	70	7	3	26	53	10.6	3.18	128	.257	.287	26	.241	4	16	17	-1	2.0
1937 Pit-N	8	10	.444	20	20	9	1	0	126^{1}	150	69	12	1	23	20	12.4	4.27	90	.290	.322	22	.268	5	-5	-6	-2	-0.4
1938 Pit-N	6	3	.667	13	13	4	0	0	84	90	33	5	1	16	19	11.5	3.54	107	.283	.319	5	.109	-2	2	2	-1	-0.1
Total 15	157	135	.538	396	302	204	22	7	2542	2736	1203	136	22	455	602	11.4	3.72	107	.275	.308	404	.281	98	92	78	-9	18.8

● GARY LUCAS

Lucas, Gary Paul b: 11/8/54, Riverside, Cal. BL/TL, 6'5", 200 lbs. Deb: 4/16/80

YEAR TM/L	W	L	PCT	G	GS	CG	SH	SV	IP	H	R	HR	HB	BB	SO	RAT	ERA	ERA+	OAV	OOB	BH	AVG	PB	PR	PR+	PD	TPI
1980 SD-N	5	8	.385	46	18	0	0	3	150	138	59	8	1	43	85	10.9	3.24	106	.250	.306	6	.171	-0	6	3	1	0.3
1981 SD-N	7	7	.500	**57**	0	0	0	13	90	78	26	1	3	36	53	11.7	2.00	163	.247	.330	1	.100	-1	**15**	13	0	2.5
1982 SD-N	1	10	.091	65	0	0	0	16	97^{1}	89	42	5	1	29	64	11.0	3.24	106	.245	.303	0	.000	-1	4	2	1	0.3
1983 SD-N	5	8	.385	62	0	0	0	17	91	85	38	9	0	34	60	11.8	2.87	122	.245	.312	0	.000	-1	8	7	-1	0.9
1984 Mon-N	0	3	.000	55	0	0	0	8	53	54	20	4	0	20	42	12.6	2.72	126	.267	.333	0	.000	-0	5	4	2	0.5
1985 Mon-N	6	2	.750	49	0	0	0	1	67^{2}	63	29	6	0	24	31	11.6	3.19	106	.251	.316	0	.000	-1	3	2	-0	0.1
1986 *Cal-A	4	1	.800	27	0	0	0	2	45^{2}	45	19	1	0	6	31	10.1	3.15	131	.253	.277	0	—	0	5	5	1	0.6
1987 Cal-A	1	5	.167	48	0	0	0	3	74^{1}	66	41	7	2	35	44	12.5	3.63	119	.241	.331	0	—	0	7	6	1	0.6
Total 8	29	44	.397	409	18	0	0	63	669	618	274	41	7	227	410	11.5	3.01	118	.249	.314	7	.087	-4	53	42	4	5.8

● RAY LUCAS

Lucas, Ray Wesley "Luke" b: 10/2/08, Springfield, Ohio d: 10/9/69, Harrison, Mich. BR/TR, 6'2", 175 lbs. Deb: 9/28/29

YEAR TM/L	W	L	PCT	G	GS	CG	SH	SV	IP	H	R	HR	HB	BB	SO	RAT	ERA	ERA+	OAV	OOB	BH	AVG	PB	PR	PR+	PD	TPI
1929 NY-N	0	0	—	3	0	0	0	1	8	3	0	0	0	3	1	6.8	0.00	—	.111	.200	1	.500	0	4	4	0	0.3
1930 NY-N	0	0	—	6	0	0	0	0	10^{1}	9	8	2	1	10	1	17.4	6.97	68	.265	.444	0	.000	-0	-2	-3	1	-0.1
1931 NY-N	0	0	—	1	0	0	0	0	2	1	1	1	0	1	0	9.0	4.50	82	.143	.250	0	—	0	-0	-0	-0	0.0
1933 Bro-N	0	0	—	2	0	0	0	0	5	6	4	0	1	4	0	19.8	7.20	45	.316	.458	0	—	0	-2	-2	0	-0.1
1934 Bro-N	1	1	.500	10	2	0	0	0	30^{2}	39	24	2	3	14	3	16.4	6.75	58	.328	.412	2	.333	1	-9	-10	1	-0.4
Total 5	1	1	.500	22	2	0	0	1	56	58	37	5	5	32	5	15.3	5.79	71	.282	.391	3	.333	1	-10	-11	2	-0.3

● JOE LUCEY

Lucey, Joseph Earl "Scootch" b: 3/27/1897, Holyoke, Mass. d: 7/30/80, Holyoke, Mass. BR/TR, 6', 168 lbs. Deb: 7/6/20 ♦

YEAR TM/L	W	L	PCT	G	GS	CG	SH	SV	IP	H	R	HR	HB	BB	SO	RAT	ERA	ERA+	OAV	OOB	BH	AVG	PB	PR	PR+	PD	TPI
1925 Bos-A	0	1	.000	7	2	0	0	0	11	18	20	0	0	14	2	26.2	9.00	50	.360	.500	2	.133	-1	-6	-5	1	-0.4

● CON LUCID

Lucid, Cornelius Cecil b: 2/24/1874, Dublin, Ireland d: 6/25/31, Houston, Tex. 5'7", 170 lbs. Deb: 5/1/1893

YEAR TM/L	W	L	PCT	G	GS	CG	SH	SV	IP	H	R	HR	HB	BB	SO	RAT	ERA	ERA+	OAV	OOB	BH	AVG	PB	PR	PR+	PD	TPI
1893 Lou-N	0	1	.000	2	1	0	0	0	6	10	14	0	1	10	0	31.5	15.00	29	.357	.538	1	.333	0	-7	-7	-0	-0.8
1894 Bro-N	5	3	.625	10	9	7	0	0	71^{1}	87	68	6	9	44	15	17.7	6.56	75	.298	.406	7	.212	-2	-10	-14	-2	-1.3
1895 Bro-N	10	7	.588	21	19	12	2	0	137	164	113	4	7	72	24	16.0	5.52	80	.292	.380	13	.245	2	-11	-19	-1	-1.5
Phi-N	6	3	.667	10	10	7	1	0	69^{2}	80	56	3	9	35	19	16.0	5.94	81	.284	.380	10	.345	4	-9	-9	-2	-0.7
Yr	16	10	.615	31	29	19	3	0	206^{2}	244	169	7	16	107	43	16.0	5.66	80	.289	.380	23	.280	6	-20	-28	-2	-2.2
1896 Phi-N	1	4	.200	5	5	5	0	0	42	75	43	2	2	17	3	20.1	8.36	52	.383	.437	2	.125	-2	-19	-19	-1	-1.7
1897 StL-N	1	5	.167	6	6	5	0	0	49	66	46	0	0	26	4	16.9	3.67	120	.319	.395	3	.176	-0	3	4	1	0.4
Total 5	23	23	.500	54	50	36	3	0	375	482	340	15	28	204	65	17.1	6.02	76	.308	.397	36	.238	2	-52	-63	-5	-5.6

● LOU LUCIER

Lucier, Louis Joseph b: 3/23/18, Northbridge, Mass. BR/TR, 5'8", 160 lbs. Deb: 4/23/43

YEAR TM/L	W	L	PCT	G	GS	CG	SH	SV	IP	H	R	HR	HB	BB	SO	RAT	ERA	ERA+	OAV	OOB	BH	AVG	PB	PR	PR+	PD	TPI
1943 Bos-A	3	4	.429	16	9	3	0	0	74	94	35	1	2	33	23	15.7	3.89	85	.322	.394	4	.200	-0	-5	-5	3	-0.1
1944 Bos-A	0	0	—	3	0	0	0	0	5^{1}	7	3	0	0	7	2	23.6	5.06	67	.292	.452	0	.000	-0	-1	-1	-0	-0.1
Phi-N	0	0	—	1	0	0	0	0	2	3	3	0	0	2	1	22.5	13.50	27	.333	.455	0	—	0	-2	-2	-0	-0.1
1945 Phi-N	0	1	.000	13	0	0	0	1	20^{1}	14	9	1	0	5	5	8.4	2.21	173	.194	.247	1	.250	0	4	4	1	0.3
Total 3	3	5	.375	33	9	3	0	1	101^{2}	118	50	2	2	47	31	14.8	3.81	90	.297	.374	5	.200	-0	-4	-4	4	0.0

● WILLIE LUDOLPH

Ludolph, William Francis "Wee Willie" b: 1/21/1900, San Francisco, Cal d: 4/8/52, Oakland, Cal. BR/TR, 6'1.5", 170 lbs. Deb: 5/28/24

YEAR TM/L	W	L	PCT	G	GS	CG	SH	SV	IP	H	R	HR	HB	BB	SO	RAT	ERA	ERA+	OAV	OOB	BH	AVG	PB	PR	PR+	PD	TPI
1924 Det-A	0	0	—	3	0	0	0	0	5^{2}	5	3	0	1	2	1	12.7	4.76	86	.250	.348	0	.000	-0	-0	-0	0	0.0

● ERIC LUDWICK

Ludwick, Eric David b: 12/14/71, Whiteman Afb, Mo. BR/TR, 6'5", 210 lbs. Deb: 9/1/96

YEAR TM/L	W	L	PCT	G	GS	CG	SH	SV	IP	H	R	HR	HB	BB	SO	RAT	ERA	ERA+	OAV	OOB	BH	AVG	PB	PR	PR+	PD	TPI
1996 StL-N	0	1	.000	6	1	0	0	0	10	11	11	4	1	3	12	13.5	9.00	47	.275	.341	0	.000	-0	-5	-5	-0	-0.5
1997 StL-N	0	1	.000	5	0	0	0	0	6^{2}	12	7	1	0	6	7	24.3	9.45	44	.400	.500	0	—	0	-4	-4	-0	-0.5
Oak-A	1	4	.200	6	5	0	0	0	24	32	24	7	1	16	14	18.4	8.25	55	.330	.430	0	.000	-0	-10	-10	0	-1.6
1998 Fla-N	1	4	.200	13	6	0	0	0	32^{2}	46	31	7	0	17	27	17.4	7.44	55	.333	.406	0	.000	-1	-12	-13	-0	-1.7
1999 Tor-A	0	0	—	1	0	0	0	0	1	3	3	0	0	2	0	45.0	27.00	18	.500	.625	0	—	0	-2	-2	0	-0.1
Total 4	2	10	.167	31	12	0	0	0	74^{1}	104	76	19	2	44	60	18.2	8.35	51	.334	.420	0	.000	-1	-33	-35	-0	-4.4

● STEVE LUEBBER

Luebber, Stephen Lee b: 7/9/49, Clinton, Mo. BR/TR, 6'3", 195 lbs. Deb: 6/27/71

YEAR TM/L	W	L	PCT	G	GS	CG	SH	SV	IP	H	R	HR	HB	BB	SO	RAT	ERA	ERA+	OAV	OOB	BH	AVG	PB	PR	PR+	PD	TPI
1971 Min-A	2	5	.286	18	12	0	0	1	68	73	42	7	4	37	35	15.1	5.03	71	.278	.375	1	.053	-2	-12	-11	0	-1.2
1972 Min-A	0	0	—	2	0	0	0	0	2^{1}	3	0	0	0	2	1	19.3	0.00	—	.333	.455	0	—	0	1	1	0	0.1
1976 Min-A	4	5	.444	38	12	2	1	2	119^{1}	109	57	9	1	62	45	13.0	4.00	90	.248	.342	0	—	0	-6	-5	-1	-0.5
1979 Tor-A	0	0	—	1	0	0	0	0	0	2	0	0	1	—	—	∞	—	1.000	1.000	103	—	0	-1	-1	0	-0.1	
1981 Bal-A	0	0	—	7	0	0	0	0	16^{2}	26	14	3	1	4	12	16.7	7.56	48	.366	.408	0	—	0	-7	-7	0	-0.3
Total 5	6	10	.375	66	24	2	1	3	206^{1}	213	114	19	6	106	93	14.2	4.62	77	.271	.362	1	.053	-2	-26	-24	-1	-2.0

● LARRY LUEBBERS

Luebbers, Larry Christopher b: 10/11/69, Cincinnati, Ohio BR/TR, 6'6", 190 lbs. Deb: 7/3/93

YEAR TM/L	W	L	PCT	G	GS	CG	SH	SV	IP	H	R	HR	HB	BB	SO	RAT	ERA	ERA+	OAV	OOB	BH	AVG	PB	PR	PR+	PD	TPI
1993 Cin-N	2	5	.286	14	14	0	0	0	77^{1}	74	49	7	1	38	38	13.2	4.54	89	.261	.350	6	.250	1	-4	-4	-1	-0.3
1999 StL-N	3	3	.500	8	8	1	0	0	45^{2}	46	27	8	3	16	16	12.8	5.12	89	.261	.333	2	.125	-0	-3	-3	0	-0.3
2000 Cin-N	0	2	.000	14	1	0	0	1	20^{1}	27	15	1	0	12	9	17.3	6.20	77	.333	.419	0	—	0	-4	-3	1	-0.2
Total 3	5	10	.333	36	23	1	0	1	143^{1}	147	91	16	4	66	63	13.6	4.96	87	.272	.355	8	.200	1	-11	-10	-0	-0.8

● DICK LUEBKE

Luebke, Richard Raymond b: 4/8/35, Chicago, Ill. d: 12/4/74, San Diego, Cal. BR/TL, 6'4", 200 lbs. Deb: 8/11/62

YEAR TM/L	W	L	PCT	G	GS	CG	SH	SV	IP	H	R	HR	HB	BB	SO	RAT	ERA	ERA+	OAV	OOB	BH	AVG	PB	PR	PR+	PD	TPI
1962 Bal-A	0	1	.000	10	0	0	0	0	13^{1}	12	4	0	0	6	7	12.2	2.70	137	.250	.333	0	—	0	2	2	-0	0.1

● RICK LUECKEN

Luecken, Richard Fred b: 11/15/60, McAllen, Tex. BR/TR, 6'6", 210 lbs. Deb: 6/6/89

YEAR TM/L	W	L	PCT	G	GS	CG	SH	SV	IP	H	R	HR	HB	BB	SO	RAT	ERA	ERA+	OAV	OOB	BH	AVG	PB	PR	PR+	PD	TPI
1989 KC-A	2	1	.667	19	0	0	0	1	23^{2}	23	9	3	0	13	16	13.7	3.42	113	.258	.353	0	—	0	1	1	-0	0.1
1990 Atl-N	1	4	.200	36	0	0	0	1	53	73	36	5	3	30	35	18.0	5.77	70	.336	.424	1	.333	1	-12	-10	0	-0.8
Tor-A	0	0	—	1	0	0	0	0	1	2	1	1	0	1	0	27.0	9.00	44	.500	.600	0	—	0	-1	-1	0	0.0
Total 2	3	5	.375	56	0	0	0	2	77^{2}	98	46	9	3	44	51	16.8	5.10	78	.316	.406	1	.333	1	-11	-9	-0	-0.7

● HENRY LUFF

Luff, Henry T. b: 9/14/1856, Philadelphia, Pa. d: 10/11/16, Philadelphia, Pa. 5'11", 175 lbs. Deb: 4/21/1875 ♦

YEAR TM/L	W	L	PCT	G	GS	CG	SH	SV	IP	H	R	HR	HB	BB	SO	RAT	ERA	ERA+	OAV	OOB	BH	AVG	PB	PR	PR+	PD	TPI
1875 NH-n	1	6	.143	10	7	5	0	0	68^{2}	98	91	2		3	5	13.2	3.28	63	.295	.301	45	.271	3	-8	-10		-0.6

● URBANO LUGO

Lugo, Rafael Urbano (Colina) b: 8/12/62, Punto Fijo, Venez. BR/TR, 6', 190 lbs. Deb: 4/28/85

YEAR TM/L	W	L	PCT	G	GS	CG	SH	SV	IP	H	R	HR	HB	BB	SO	RAT	ERA	ERA+	OAV	OOB	BH	AVG	PB	PR	PR+	PD	TPI
1985 Cal-A	3	4	.429	20	10	1	0	0	83	86	36	10	4	29	42	12.9	3.69	112	.274	.343	0	—	0	4	4	0	0.3
1986 Cal-A	1	1	.500	6	3	0	0	0	21^{1}	21	9	4	0	6	9	11.4	3.80	108	.266	.318	0	—	0	1	1	-0	0.0
1987 Cal-A	0	2	.000	7	5	0	0	0	28	42	34	8	0	18	24	19.3	9.32	46	.339	.423	0	—	1	-15	-16	-0	-0.9
1988 Cal-A	0	0	—	1	0	0	0	0	2	2	2	1	0	1	1	13.5	9.00	43	.250	.333	0	—	0	-1	-1	-0	-0.1
1989 Mon-N	0	0	—	3	0	0	0	0	4	4	3	1	0	0	3	9.0	6.75	52	.250	.250	0	—	0	-1	-1	-0	-0.1
1990 Det-A	2	0	1.000	13	1	0	0	0	24^{1}	30	19	9	3	13	12	17.0	7.03	56	.313	.411	0	—	0	-8	-8	1	-0.5
Total 6	6	7	.462	50	19	1	0	0	162^{2}	185	103	33	7	67	91	14.3	5.31	77	.290	.364	0	—	0	-21	-22	0	-1.3

● WILD BILL LUHRSEN

Luhrsen, William Ferdinand b: 4/14/1884, Buckley, Ill. d: 8/15/73, Little Rock, Ark. BR/TR, 5'9", 165 lbs. Deb: 8/23/13

YEAR TM/L	W	L	PCT	G	GS	CG	SH	SV	IP	H	R	HR	HB	BB	SO	RAT	ERA	ERA+	OAV	OOB	BH	AVG	PB	PR	PR+	PD	TPI
1913 Pit-N	3	1	.750	5	3	2	0	0	29	25	10	3	2	16	11	13.3	2.48	122	.248	.361	0	.000	-1	2	2	1	0.2

● AL LUKENS

Lukens, Albert P. b: 11/1868, Pennsylvania 5'9", 168 lbs. Deb: 6/23/1894

YEAR TM/L	W	L	PCT	G	GS	CG	SH	SV	IP	H	R	HR	HB	BB	SO	RAT	ERA	ERA+	OAV	OOB	BH	AVG	PB	PR	PR+	PD	TPI
1894 Phi-N	0	1	.000	3	2	1	0	0	15	26	22	0	3	10	0	23.4	10.20	50	.377	.476	0	.000	-2	-8	-9	-0	-0.5

● RALPH LUMENTI

Lumenti, Raphael Anthony b: 12/21/36, Milford, Mass. BL/TL, 6'3", 185 lbs. Deb: 9/7/57

YEAR TM/L	W	L	PCT	G	GS	CG	SH	SV	IP	H	R	HR	HB	BB	SO	RAT	ERA	ERA+	OAV	OOB	BH	AVG	PB	PR	PR+	PD	TPI
1957 Was-A	0	1	.000	3	2	0	0	0	9^{1}	9	7	1	1	5	8	14.5	6.75	58	.250	.357	0	.000	-0	-3	-3	0	-0.3
1958 Was-A	1	2	.333	8	4	0	0	0	21	21	20	2	1	36	20	24.9	8.57	44	.266	.500	2	.250	0	-11	-11	0	-1.3

YEAR	TM/L	W	L	PCT	G	GS	CG	SH	SV	IP	H	R	HR	HB	BB	SO	RAT	ERA	ERA+	OAV	OOB	BH	AVG	PB	PR	PR+	PD	TPI
1959	Was-A	0	0	—	2	0	0	0	0	3	2	0	0	0	1	2	9.0	0.00	—	.200	.273	0	—	0	1	1	-0	0.1
Total	3	1	3	.250	13	6	0	0	0	33^1	32	27	3	2	42	30	20.5	7.29	53	.256	.450	2	.200	-0	-13	-13	0	-1.5
● **MEMO LUNA** Luna, Guillermo Romero b: 6/25/30, Tacubaya, Mexico BL/TL, 6', 168 lbs. Deb: 4/20/54																												
1954	StL-N	0	1	.000	1	1	0	0	0	0^2	2	2	0	0	2	0	54.0	27.00	15	.667	.800	0	—	0	-2	-2	-0	-0.3
● **JACK LUNDBOM** Lundbom, John Frederick b: 3/10/1877, Manistee, Mich. d: 10/31/49, Manistee, Mich. BR/TR, 6'0.5", 187 lbs. Deb: 5/9/02																												
1902	Cle-A	1	1	.500	8	3	1	0	0	34	48	35	1	1	16	7	17.2	6.62	52	.333	.404	4	.267	1	-11	-12	-0	-0.6
● **CARL LUNDGREN** Lundgren, Carl Leonard b: 2/16/1880, Marengo, Ill. d: 8/21/34, Marengo, Ill. BR/TR, 5'11", 175 lbs. Deb: 6/19/02																												
1902	Chi-N	9	9	.500	18	18	17	1	0	160	158	59	2	6	45	68	11.8	1.97	137	.258	.315	7	.106	-4	14	13	-3	0.7
1903	Chi-N	11	9	.550	27	20	16	0	**3**	193	191	103	1	6	60	67	12.0	2.94	107	.262	.323	7	.115	-1	7	4	-2	0.0
1904	Chi-N	17	9	.654	31	27	25	2	1	242	203	97	2	4	77	106	10.6	2.60	102	.226	.290	20	.222	4	4	2	-1	0.4
1905	Chi-N	13	5	.722	23	19	16	3	0	169^1	132	58	3	9	53	69	10.3	2.23	134	.220	.293	11	.180	1	15	14	1	1.6
1906	Chi-N	17	6	.739	27	24	21	5	2	207^2	160	63	3	8	89	103	11.1	2.21	119	.221	.313	12	.179	2	10	10	-1	1.2
1907	Chi-N	18	7	.720	28	25	21	7	0	207	130	42	0	2	92	84	9.7	1.17	212	**.185**	.282	7	.106	-3	**30**	30	-0	3.6
1908	Chi-N	6	9	.400	23	15	9	1	0	138^2	149	72	5	0	56	38	13.3	4.22	56	.284	.353	7	.149	-1	-29	-29	-2	-3.3
1909	Chi-N	0	1	.000	2	1	0	0	0	4^1	6	2	0	0	4	0	20.8	4.15	61	.353	.476	1	.500	0	-1	-1	-0	-0.2
Total	8	91	55	.623	179	149	125	19	6	1322	1129	496	16	35	476	535	11.2	2.42	113	.235	.308	72	.157	-2	50	45	-8	4.0
● **DEL LUNDGREN** Lundgren, Ebin Delmar b: 9/21/1899, Lindsborg, Kan. d: 10/19/84, Lindsborg, Kan. BR/TR, 5'8", 160 lbs. Deb: 4/27/24																												
1924	Pit-N	0	1	.000	8	1	0	0	0	16^2	25	13	0	1	3	4	15.7	6.48	59	.403	.439	0	.000	-1	-5	-5	0	-0.3
1926	Bos-A	0	2	.000	18	2	0	0	0	31	35	28	2	3	28	11	19.2	7.55	54	.307	.455	0	.000	-0	-12	-12	0	-0.7
1927	Bos-A	5	12	.294	30	17	5	2	0	136^1	160	100	7	4	87	39	16.6	6.27	67	.302	.405	7	.159	-2	-32	-30	-2	-3.4
Total	3	5	15	.250	56	20	5	2	0	184	220	141	9	8	118	54	16.9	6.51	64	.312	.416	7	.137	-3	-49	-47	-2	-4.4
● **DAVID LUNDQUIST** Lundquist, David Bruce b: 6/4/73, Beverly, Mass. BR/TR, 6'2", 200 lbs. Deb: 4/6/99																												
1999	Chi-A	1	1	.500	17	0	0	0	0	22	28	21	3	1	12	18	16.8	8.59	57	.315	.402	0	—	0	-9	-9	-0	-0.7
● **DOLF LUQUE** Luque, Adolfo Domingo De Guzman "The Pride Of Havana" b: 8/4/1890, Havana, Cuba d: 7/3/57, Havana, Cuba BR/TR, 5'7", 160 lbs. Deb: 5/20/14 C																												
1914	Bos-N	0	1	.000	2	1	1	0	0	8^2	5	5	0	0	4	1	9.3	4.15	66	.167	.265	0	.000	-0	-1	-1	-1	-0.2
1915	Bos-N	0	0	—	2	1	0	0	0	5	6	3	0	0	4	3	18.0	3.60	72	.286	.400	0	.000	-0	-0	-1	0	0.0
1918	Cin-N	6	3	.667	12	10	9	1	0	83	84	44	1	1	32	26	12.7	3.80	70	.277	.348	9	.321	5	-10	-11	-0	-0.7
1919	*Cin-N	10	3	.769	30	9	6	2	3	106	89	35	2	2	36	40	10.8	2.63	105	.237	.308	4	.125	-0	3	2	1	0.3
1920	Cin-N	13	9	.591	37	23	10	1	1	207^2	168	65	5	4	60	72	10.1	2.51	121	**.225**	.286	17	.266	4	14	12	-2	1.6
1921	Cin-N	17	19	.472	41	36	25	**3**	3	304	318	132	13	1	64	102	11.3	3.38	106	.273	.312	30	.270	6	14	7	1	1.4
1922	Cin-N	13	23	.361	39	33	18	0	0	261	266	123	7	1	72	79	11.7	3.31	121	.268	.318	18	.209	2	23	20	0	2.6
1923	Cin-N	**27**	8	**.771**	41	37	28	**6**	2	322	279	90	2	5	88	151	10.4	**1.93**	**200**	**.235**	.291	21	.202	2	**74**	**72**	1	**7.7**
1924	Cin-N	10	15	.400	31	28	13	2	0	219^1	229	99	5	2	53	86	11.7	3.16	119	.271	.316	13	.178	-1	17	15	1	1.6
1925	Cin-N	16	18	.471	36	36	22	**4**	0	291	263	109	7	2	78	140	**10.6**	**2.63**	**156**	**.239**	**.291**	26	.255	5	**53**	**50**	4	**6.3**
1926	Cin-N	13	16	.448	34	31	16	1	0	233^2	231	123	7	2	77	83	11.9	3.43	108	.260	.321	27	.346	8	10	7	2	1.8
1927	Cin-N	13	12	.520	29	27	17	2	0	230^2	225	103	10	0	56	76	11.0	3.20	118	.260	.305	18	.217	2	18	16	4	2.1
1928	Cin-N	11	10	.524	33	29	11	1	1	234^1	254	112	12	2	84	72	13.1	3.57	111	.284	.347	8	.119	-1	11	10	-2	0.5
1929	Cin-N	5	16	.238	32	22	8	1	0	176	213	103	7	2	56	43	13.9	4.50	101	.310	.364	15	.278	4	4	1	0	0.5
1930	Bro-N	14	8	.636	31	24	16	2	2	199	221	107	18	0	58	62	12.6	4.30	114	.287	.337	18	.240	1	15	14	1	1.5
1931	Bro-N	7	6	.538	19	15	5	0	0	102^2	122	59	6	1	27	25	13.1	4.56	84	.297	.342	4	.133	0	-8	-9	-1	-1.0
1932	NY-N	6	7	.462	38	5	1	0	5	110	128	53	4	0	32	32	13.1	4.01	93	.290	.338	1	.040	-2	-2	-4	1	-0.5
1933	*NY-N	8	2	.800	35	0	0	0	4	80^1	75	27	4	0	19	23	10.5	2.69	119	.251	.296	5	.263	1	6	5	0	0.7
1934	NY-N	4	3	.571	26	0	0	0	7	42^1	54	20	3	1	17	12	15.3	3.83	101	.316	.381	2	.286	1	1	0	1	0.2
1935	NY-N	1	0	1.000	2	0	0	0	0	3^2	1	0	0	0	1	2	4.9	0.00	—	.077	.143	1	1.000	0	2	2	-0	0.4
Total	20	194	179	.520	550	367	206	26	28	3220^1	3231	1412	113	26	918	1130	11.7	3.24	117	.265	.318	237	.227	37	245	207	13	26.8
● **JOHNNY LUSH** Lush, John Charles b: 10/8/1885, Williamsport, Pa. d: 11/18/46, Beverly Hills, Cal BL/TL, 5'9.5", 165 lbs. Deb: 4/22/04 ♦																												
1904	Phi-N	0	6	.000	7	6	3	0	0	42^2	52	40	0	7	27	27	18.1	3.59	75	.301	.415	102	.276	2	-4	-4	1	-0.3
1905	Phi-N	2	0	1.000	2	2	1	0	0	17	12	4	0	1	8	8	11.1	1.59	184	.194	.296	5	.313	1	3	3	0	0.4
1906	Phi-N	18	15	.545	37	35	24	5	0	281	254	128	2	16	119	151	12.5	2.37	110	.236	.321	56	.264	7	8	8	3	2.1
1907	Phi-N	3	5	.375	8	8	5	2	0	57^1	48	22	0	3	21	20	11.3	2.98	81	.227	.306	8	.200	1	-3	-4	1	-0.4
	StL-N	7	10	.412	20	19	15	3	0	144	132	63	2	8	42	71	11.4	2.50	100	.246	.311	23	.280	5	-0	0	-0	0.8
	Yr	10	15	.400	28	27	20	5	0	201^1	180	85	2	11	63	91	11.4	2.64	94	.241	.309	31	.254	6	-4	-3	0	0.4
1908	StL-N	11	18	.379	38	32	23	3	1	250^2	221	102	6	11	57	93	10.4	2.12	111	.231	.283	15	.169	1	7	7	0	1.0
1909	StL-N	11	18	.379	34	28	21	2	0	221^1	215	96	1	10	69	66	12.0	3.13	81	.260	.324	22	.239	4	-13	-15	-1	-1.4
1910	StL-N	14	13	.519	36	25	13	1	1	225^1	235	116	6	7	70	54	12.5	3.20	93	.276	.336	21	.226	4	-4	-6	-2	-0.4
Total	7	66	85	.437	182	155	105	16	2	1239^1	1169	571	17	63	413	490	11.9	2.68	97	.249	.318	252	.254	24	-7	-11	1	1.8
● **SPARKY LYLE** Lyle, Albert Walter b: 7/22/44, DuBois, Pa. BL/TL, 6'1", 192 lbs. Deb: 7/4/67																												
1967	Bos-A	1	2	.333	27	0	0	0	5	43^1	33	13	3	2	14	42	10.2	2.28	153	.213	.287	2	.250	1	5	5	-0	0.5
1968	Bos-A	6	1	.857	49	0	0	0	11	65^2	67	25	6	0	14	52	11.1	2.74	115	.261	.299	1	.125	-0	2	3	-1	0.3
1969	Bos-A	8	3	.727	71	0	0	0	17	102^2	91	33	8	1	48	93	12.3	2.54	150	.240	.327	2	.118	-1	12	14	1	2.0
1970	Bos-A	1	7	.125	63	0	0	0	20	67^1	62	37	5	1	34	51	13.0	3.88	102	.244	.336	0	.000	-1	-1	1	-1	-0.1
1971	Bos-A	6	4	.600	50	0	0	0	16	52^1	41	16	5	0	23	37	11.0	2.75	134	.228	.315	3	1.000	1	4	5	0	1.3
1972	NY-A	9	5	.643	59	0	0	0	**35**	107^2	84	25	3	0	29	75	9.4	1.92	154	.216	.271	4	.190	1	**14**	**13**	-1	2.8
1973	NY-A★	5	9	.357	51	0	0	0	27	82^1	66	30	4	0	18	63	9.2	2.51	146	.216	.259	0	—	0	12	11	0	2.3
1974	NY-A	9	3	.750	66	0	0	0	15	114	93	30	6	1	43	89	10.8	1.66	213	.226	.300	0	.000	-0	**25**	**24**	-1	3.1
1975	NY-A	5	7	.417	49	0	0	0	6	89^1	94	34	1	2	36	65	13.3	3.12	118	.275	.347	0	—	0	7	6	0	0.8
1976	*NY-A☆	7	8	.467	64	0	0	0	**23**	103^2	82	33	5	0	42	61	10.8	2.26	152	.225	.305	0	—	0	15	14	-1	2.6
1977	*NY-A★	13	5	.722	**72**	0	0	0	26	137	131	41	7	2	33	68	10.9	2.17	182	.257	.305	0	—	0	**29**	**28**	-1	**4.6**
1978	*NY-A	9	3	.750	59	0	0	0	9	111^2	116	46	6	4	33	33	12.3	3.47	105	.278	.337	0	—	0	4	2	0	0.3
1979	Tex-A	5	8	.385	67	0	0	0	13	95	78	37	9	0	28	48	10.0	3.13	133	.226	.284	0	—	0	12	11	-1	1.6
1980	Tex-A	3	2	.600	49	0	0	0	8	80^2	97	47	9	0	28	43	13.9	4.69	83	.306	.362	0	—	0	-6	-7	-0	-0.6
	Phi-N	0	0	—	10	0	0	0	2	14	11	5	0	0	6	6	10.9	1.93	197	.220	.304	0	—	0	3	3	-1	0.1
1981	*Phi-N	9	6	.600	48	0	0	0	2	75	85	40	4	1	33	29	14.3	4.44	82	.301	.377	2	.400	1	-8	-7	1	-1.1
1982	Phi-N	3	3	.500	34	0	0	0	2	36^2	50	23	3	0	12	12	15.2	5.15	71	.327	.376	1	.500	1	-6	-6	1	-0.8
	Chi-A	0	0	—	11	0	0	0	1	12	11	4	0	0	7	6	13.5	3.00	135	.262	.367	0	—	0	1	1	-0	0.1
Total	16	99	76	.566	899	0	0	0	238	1390^1	1292	519	84	14	481	873	11.6	2.88	127	.251	.316	15	.192	2	122	121	-4	19.8
● **JIM LYLE** Lyle, James Charles b: 7/24/1900, Lake, Miss. d: 10/10/77, Williamsport, Pa. BR/TR, 6'1", 180 lbs. Deb: 10/2/25																												
1925	Was-A	0	0	—	1	0	0	0	0	3	5	2	0	0	1	3	18.0	6.00	70	.333	.375	0	—	0	-1	-1	-0	0.0
● **ADRIAN LYNCH** Lynch, Adrian Ryan b: 2/9/1897, Laurens, Iowa d: 3/16/34, Davenport, Iowa BB/TR, 6'1.5", 185 lbs. Deb: 8/4/20																												
1920	StL-A	2	0	1.000	5	3	1	0	0	22^1	23	15	1	1	17	8	16.5	5.24	75	.277	.406	2	.222	0	-4	-3	-1	-0.3
● **ED LYNCH** Lynch, Edward Francis b: 2/25/56, Brooklyn, N.Y. BR/TR, 6'6", 230 lbs. Deb: 8/31/80																												
1980	NY-N	1	1	.500	5	4	0	0	0	19^1	24	12	0	1	5	9	14.0	5.12	69	.304	.353	2	.333	0	-3	-3	0	-0.3
1981	NY-N	4	5	.444	17	13	0	0	0	80^1	79	32	6	1	21	27	11.3	2.91	120	.254	.303	3	.143	1	5	5	-1	0.6
1982	NY-N	4	8	.333	43	12	0	0	2	139^1	145	57	6	1	40	51	12.0	3.55	102	.273	.325	0	.000	-3	1	1	-1	-0.4
1983	NY-N	10	10	.500	30	27	1	0	0	174^2	208	94	17	3	41	44	13.0	4.28	85	.302	.344	8	.154	-1	-12	-12	-1	-1.5
1984	NY-N	9	8	.529	40	13	0	0	2	124	169	77	14	4	24	62	14.3	4.50	79	.324	.359	6	.222	1	-12	-13	-1	-1.8
1985	NY-N	10	8	.556	31	29	6	1	0	191	188	76	19	1	27	65	10.2	3.44	101	.256	.283	4	.077	-2	3	1	-4	-0.6
1986	NY-N	0	0	—	1	0	0	0	0	1^2	2	0	0	0	0	1	10.8	0.00	—	.286	.286	0	—	0	1	1	-0	0.0
	Chi-N	7	5	.583	23	13	1	1	0	99^2	105	48	10	1	23	57	11.6	3.79	107	.279	.322	1	.033	-2	-1	3	-1	0.0
	Yr	7	5	.583	24	13	1	1	0	101^1	107	48	10	1	23	58	11.6	3.73	108	.279	.321	1	.033	-2	-0	3	-1	0.0

YEAR	TM/L	W	L	PCT	G	GS	CG	SH	SV	IP	H	R	HR	HB	BB	SO	RAT	ERA	ERA+	OAV	OOB	BH	AVG	PB	PR	PR+	PD	TPI
1987	Chi-N	2	9	.182	58	8	0	0	4	110^{1}	130	74	17	2	48	80	14.7	5.38	80	.295	.367	3	.188	-0	-16	-13	1	-1.2
Total	8	47	54	.465	248	119	8	2	8	940^{1}	1050	470	89	14	229	396	12.4	4.00	92	.284	.329	27	.114	-6	-35	-32	-8	-5.2

● JACK LYNCH

Lynch, John H. b: 2/5/1857, New York, N.Y d: 4/20/23, Bronx, N.Y. BR/TR, 5'8", 185 lbs. Deb: 5/2/1881

YEAR	TM/L	W	L	PCT	G	GS	CG	SH	SV	IP	H	R	HR	HB	BB	SO	RAT	ERA	ERA+	OAV	OOB	BH	AVG	PB	PR	PR+	PD	TPI
1881	Buf-N	10	9	.526	20	19	17	0	0	165^{2}	203	112	2		29	32	12.6	3.59	77	.297	.325	13	.167	-3	-15	-15	1	-1.5
1883	NY-a	13	15	.464	29	29	29	1	0	255	263	161	6		25	119	10.2	4.09	82	.250	.267	20	.187	-3	-22	-21	-1	-2.1
1884	NY-a	37	15	.712	55	53	53	5	0	496	420	225	10	10	42	292	8.6	2.67	117	.215	.236	30	.152	7	32	26	-5	1.1
1885	NY-a	23	21	.523	44	43	43	1	0	379	410	243	17	3	42	177	10.8	3.61	82	.263	.283	30	.196	2	-15	-30	-5	-3.0
1886	NY-a	20	30	.400	51	50	50	1	0	432^{2}	485	307	10	12	116	193	12.8	3.95	86	.271	.320	27	.160	-6	-24	-26	-3	-3.1
1887	NY-a	7	14	.333	21	21	21	0	0	187	281	158	8	4	36	45	13.7	5.10	83	.335	.338	21	.233	-4	-17	-18	2	-1.5
1890	Bro-a	0	1	.000	1	1	1	0	0	9	22	18	1	0	5	1	27.0	12.00	32	.449	.500	3	.750	2	-8	-8	1	-0.4
Total	7	110	105	.512	221	216	214	8	0	1924^{1}	2084	1224	54	29	295	859	11.1	3.69	89	.263	.289	144	.180	-18	-69	-93	-10	-10.5

● MIKE LYNCH

Lynch, Michael Joseph b: 6/28/1880, Holyoke, Mass. d: 4/2/27, Garrison, N.Y. BR/TR, 6'2", 170 lbs. Deb: 6/21/04

YEAR	TM/L	W	L	PCT	G	GS	CG	SH	SV	IP	H	R	HR	HB	BB	SO	RAT	ERA	ERA+	OAV	OOB	BH	AVG	PB	PR	PR+	PD	TPI
1904	Pit-N	15	11	.577	27	24	24	1	0	222^{2}	200	90	1	15	91	95	12.4	2.71	101	.243	.330	20	.230	4	1	1	-2	0.2
1905	Pit-N	17	8	.680	33	22	13	0	2	206^{1}	191	102	3	5	107	106	13.2	3.79	79	.254	.351	11	.136	-1	-18	-18	0	-2.2
1906	Pit-N	6	5	.545	18	12	7	0	0	119	101	48	2	8	31	48	10.6	2.42	110	.232	.295	8	.205	-0	3	3	-1	0.2
1907	Pit-N	2	2	.500	7	4	2	0	0	36	37	21	0	1	22	9	15.0	2.25	108	.282	.390	3	.250	1	1	1	1	0.3
	NY-N	3	6	.333	12	10	7	0	1	72	68	35	3	0	30	34	12.3	3.38	73	.249	.323	8	.296	2	-7	-7	0	-0.6
	Yr	5	8	.385	19	14	9	0	1	108	105	56	3	1	52	43	13.2	3.00	82	.260	.346	11	.282	3	-6	-6	2	-0.3
Total	4	43	32	.573	97	72	53	1	3	656	597	296	9	29	281	292	12.4	3.05	91	.248	.333	50	.203	5	-21	-20	-1	-2.1

● TOM LYNCH

Lynch, Thomas S. b: 1863, Peru, Ill. d: 5/13/03, Peru, Ill. BL, 5'11", 175 lbs. Deb: 8/5/1884

YEAR	TM/L	W	L	PCT	G	GS	CG	SH	SV	IP	H	R	HR	HB	BB	SO	RAT	ERA	ERA+	OAV	OOB	BH	AVG	PB	PR	PR+	PD	TPI
1884	Chi-N	0	0	—	1	1	0	0	0	7	7	4	1		3	2	12.9	2.57	122	.241	.313	0	.000	-1	0	0	0	0.0

● RED LYNN

Lynn, Japhet Monroe b: 12/27/13, Kenney, Tex. d: 10/27/77, Bellville, Tex. BR/TR, 6', 162 lbs. Deb: 4/25/39

YEAR	TM/L	W	L	PCT	G	GS	CG	SH	SV	IP	H	R	HR	HB	BB	SO	RAT	ERA	ERA+	OAV	OOB	BH	AVG	PB	PR	PR+	PD	TPI
1939	Det-A	0	1	.000	4	0	0	0	0	8^{1}	11	8	2	1	3	3	16.2	8.64	57	.324	.395	0	.000	-0	-4	-3	0	-0.3
	NY-N	1	0	1.000	26	0	0	0	1	49^{2}	44	21	3	2	21	22	12.1	3.08	127	.240	.325	0	.000	-1	5	5	-1	0.0
1940	NY-N	4	3	.571	33	0	0	0	3	42^{1}	40	21	3	1	24	25	13.8	3.83	101	.247	.348	0	.000	-1	0	0	-1	-0.1
1944	Chi-N	5	4	.556	22	7	4	1	1	84^{1}	80	41	4	1	37	35	12.6	4.06	87	.251	.331	6	.207	0	-4	-5	1	-0.3
Total	3	10	8	.556	85	7	4	1	5	184^{2}	175	91	12	5	85	85	12.9	3.95	96	.251	.336	6	.146	-1	-3	-4	-1	-0.7

● AL LYONS

Lyons, Albert Harold b: 7/18/18, St.Joseph, Mo. d: 12/20/65, Inglewood, Cal. BR/TR, 6'2", 195 lbs. Deb: 4/19/44

YEAR	TM/L	W	L	PCT	G	GS	CG	SH	SV	IP	H	R	HR	HB	BB	SO	RAT	ERA	ERA+	OAV	OOB	BH	AVG	PB	PR	PR+	PD	TPI
1944	NY-A	0	0	—	11	0	0	0	0	39^{2}	43	22	2	2	24	14	15.7	4.54	77	.291	.397	9	.346	2	-5	-5	-1	-0.1
1946	NY-A	0	1	.000	2	1	0	0	0	8^{1}	11	5	0	1	6	4	19.4	5.40	64	.314	.429	0	.000	-1	-2	-2	0	-0.2
1947	NY-A	1	0	1.000	6	0	0	0	0	11	18	11	2	0	9	7	22.1	9.00	39	.367	.466	4	.667	2	-6	-7	0	-0.4
	Pit-N	1	2	.333	13	0	0	0	0	28^{1}	36	24	4	1	12	16	15.6	7.31	58	.300	.368	2	.200	1	-10	-9	1	-0.6
1948	Bos-N	1	0	1.000	7	0	0	0	0	12^{2}	17	11	1	0	8	5	17.8	7.82	49	.309	.397	2	.167	0	-5	-6	1	-0.3
Total	4	3	3	.500	39	1	0	0	0	100	125	73	9	4	59	46	16.9	6.30	59	.307	.400	17	.293	5	-29	-28	2	-1.6

● CURT LYONS

Lyons, Curt Russell b: 10/17/74, Greencastle, Ind. BR/TR, 6'5", 230 lbs. Deb: 9/19/96

YEAR	TM/L	W	L	PCT	G	GS	CG	SH	SV	IP	H	R	HR	HB	BB	SO	RAT	ERA	ERA+	OAV	OOB	BH	AVG	PB	PR	PR+	PD	TPI
1996	Cin-N	2	0	1.000	3	3	0	0	0	16	17	8	1	1	7	14	14.1	4.50	94	.274	.357	0	.000	-1	-0	-0	-0	-0.1

● GEORGE LYONS

Lyons, George Tony "Smooth" b: 1/25/1891, Bible Grove, Ill. d: 8/12/81, Nevada, Mo. BR/TR, 5'11", 180 lbs. Deb: 9/6/20

YEAR	TM/L	W	L	PCT	G	GS	CG	SH	SV	IP	H	R	HR	HB	BB	SO	RAT	ERA	ERA+	OAV	OOB	BH	AVG	PB	PR	PR+	PD	TPI
1920	StL-N	2	1	.667	7	2	1	0	0	23^{1}	21	8	2	1	9	5	12.0	3.09	97	.262	.344	1	.143	-0	0	-0	1	0.0
1924	StL-A	3	2	.600	26	6	2	0	0	77^{2}	97	52	2	5	45	25	17.0	5.21	87	.323	.420	5	.250	-0	-8	-6	1	-0.2
Total	2	5	3	.625	33	8	3	0	0	101	118	60	4	6	54	30	15.9	4.72	88	.311	.405	6	.222	-0	-8	-6	2	-0.2

● HARRY LYONS

Lyons, Harry Pratt b: 3/25/1866, Chester, Pa. d: 6/29/12, Mauricetown, N.J. BR/TR, 5'10.5", 157 lbs. Deb: 8/29/1887 ◆

YEAR	TM/L	W	L	PCT	G	GS	CG	SH	SV	IP	H	R	HR	HB	BB	SO	RAT	ERA	ERA+	OAV	OOB	BH	AVG	PB	PR	PR+	PD	TPI
1890	Roc-a	0	0	—	1	0	0	0	0	3^{2}	8	7	0	0	1	2	22.1	12.27	29	.421	.450	152	.260	0	-3	-4	0	-0.1

● HERSH LYONS

Lyons, Herschel Englebert b: 7/23/15, Fresno, Cal. BR/TR, 5'11", 195 lbs. Deb: 4/17/41

YEAR	TM/L	W	L	PCT	G	GS	CG	SH	SV	IP	H	R	HR	HB	BB	SO	RAT	ERA	ERA+	OAV	OOB	BH	AVG	PB	PR	PR+	PD	TPI
1941	StL-N	0	0	—	1	0	0	0	0	1^{1}	1	0	0	0	3	1	27.0	0.00	—	.200	.500	0	—	0	1	1	0	0.1

● STEVE LYONS

Lyons, Stephen John b: 6/3/60, Tacoma, Wash. BL/TR, 6'3", 195 lbs. Deb: 4/15/85 ◆

YEAR	TM/L	W	L	PCT	G	GS	CG	SH	SV	IP	H	R	HR	HB	BB	SO	RAT	ERA	ERA+	OAV	OOB	BH	AVG	PB	PR	PR+	PD	TPI
1990	Chi-A	0	0	—	1	0	0	0	0	2	2	1	0	0	4	1	27.0	4.50	85	.250	.500	28	.192	0	-0	-0	0	0.0
1991	Bos-A	0	0	—	1	0	0	0	0	1	2	0	0	0	0	1	18.0	0.00	—	.400	.400	51	.241	0	0	0	0	0.0
Total	2	0	0	—	2	0	0	0	0	3	4	1	0	0	4	2	24.0	3.00	133	.308	.471	545	.252	0	0	0	0	0.0

● TED LYONS

Lyons, Theodore Amar b: 12/28/1900, Lake Charles, La. d: 7/25/86, Sulphur, La. BB/TR, 5'11", 200 lbs. Deb: 7/2/23 MCH◆

YEAR	TM/L	W	L	PCT	G	GS	CG	SH	SV	IP	H	R	HR	HB	BB	SO	RAT	ERA	ERA+	OAV	OOB	BH	AVG	PB	PR	PR+	PD	TPI
1923	Chi-A	2	1	.667	9	1	0	0	0	22^{2}	30	21	2	1	15	6	18.3	6.35	62	.323	.422	1	.200	0	-6	-6	1	-0.6
1924	Chi-A	12	11	.522	41	22	12	0	3	216^{1}	279	143	10	2	72	52	14.7	4.87	85	.322	.375	17	.221	0	-15	-18	-3	-1.9
1925	Chi-A	**21**	11	.656	43	32	19	**5**	3	262^{2}	274	111	7	2	83	45	12.3	3.26	128	.278	.335	18	.186	-3	33	28	2	2.9
1926	Chi-A	18	16	.529	39	31	24	3	2	283^{2}	268	108	6	1	106	51	11.9	3.01	128	.252	.320	22	.212	-0	32	28	4	3.4
1927	Chi-A	**22**	14	.611	39	34	**30**	2	2	**307^{2}**	291	125	7	0	67	71	10.5	2.84	143	.251	.292	28	.255	5	**45**	**42**	0	**5.2**
1928	Chi-A	15	14	.517	39	27	21	0	6	240	276	133	11	2	68	60	13.0	3.98	102	.295	.344	23	.253	1	2	2	2	0.5
1929	Chi-A	14	20	.412	37	31	21	1	2	259^{1}	276	136	11	2	76	57	12.3	4.10	105	.278	.331	20	.220	1	4	5	3	1.0
1930	Chi-A	22	15	.595	42	36	**29**	1	1	**297^{2}**	331	160	12	2	57	69	11.8	3.78	122	.285	.319	38	.311	8	29	28	3	4.1
1931	Chi-A	4	6	.400	22	12	7	0	0	101	117	50	6	0	33	16	13.4	4.01	106	.296	.350	5	.152	-1	4	3	-1	0.1
1932	Chi-A	10	15	.400	33	26	19	1	2	230^{2}	243	104	10	3	71	58	12.4	3.28	132	.272	.327	19	.260	5	31	28	-1	3.1
1933	Chi-A	10	21	.323	36	27	14	2	1	228	260	142	10	0	74	74	13.2	4.38	97	.280	.333	26	.286	6	-3	-4	0	0.2
1934	Chi-A	11	13	.458	30	24	21	0	1	205^{1}	249	138	15	2	66	53	13.9	4.87	97	.293	.345	26	.206	1	-8	-3	2	0.0
1935	Chi-A	15	8	.652	23	22	19	3	0	190^{2}	194	79	15	3	56	54	11.9	3.02	153	.262	.317	18	.220	-0	30	33	-1	3.5
1936	Chi-A	10	13	.435	26	24	15	1	0	182	227	115	21	3	45	48	13.6	5.14	101	.305	.347	11	.157	-3	-2	1	1	0.0
1937	Chi-A	12	7	.632	22	22	11	0	0	169^{1}	182	86	21	1	45	45	12.1	4.15	111	.278	.326	12	.211	1	9	9	0	1.0
1938	Chi-A	9	11	.450	23	23	17	1	0	194^{2}	238	93	13	0	52	54	13.4	3.70	132	.299	.342	14	.194	-1	24	25	2	2.3
1939	Chi-A☆	14	6	.700	21	21	16	0	0	172^{2}	162	71	7	1	26	65	**9.9**	2.76	171	.247	**.276**	18	.295	4	36	37	-1	4.2
1940	Chi-A	12	8	.600	22	22	17	**4**	0	186^{1}	188	85	17	0	37	72	10.9	3.24	137	.252	.287	18	.240	2	24	24	-2	2.3
1941	Chi-A	12	10	.545	22	22	19	2	0	187^{1}	199	87	9	4	37	63	11.5	3.70	111	.269	.308	20	.270	4	9	8	1	1.3
1942	Chi-A	14	6	.700	20	20	20	1	0	180^{1}	167	52	11	2	26	50	9.7	**2.10**	**172**	.245	.275	16	.239	4	31	31	1	**4.0**
1946	Chi-A	1	4	.200	5	5	5	0	0	42^{2}	38	17	2	0	9	10	9.9	2.32	147	.235	.275	3	.000	-1	6	5	0	0.5
Total	21	260	230	.531	594	484	356	27	23	4161	4489	2056	223	31	1121	1073	12.2	3.67	118	.276	.324	364	.233	32	313	304	12	37.1

● TOBY LYONS

Lyons, Thomas A. b: 3/27/1869, Cambridge, Mass. d: 8/27/20, Boston, Mass. Deb: 4/18/1890

YEAR	TM/L	W	L	PCT	G	GS	CG	SH	SV	IP	H	R	HR	HB	BB	SO	RAT	ERA	ERA+	OAV	OOB	BH	AVG	PB	PR	PR+	PD	TPI
1890	Syr-a	0	2	.000	3	3	2	0	0	22^{1}	40	36	1	1	21	6	25.0	10.48	34	.377	.484	4	.333	1	-16	-19	0	-1.0

● RICK LYSANDER

Lysander, Richard Eugene b: 2/21/53, Huntington Park, Cal. BR/TR, 6'2", 190 lbs. Deb: 4/12/80

YEAR	TM/L	W	L	PCT	G	GS	CG	SH	SV	IP	H	R	HR	HB	BB	SO	RAT	ERA	ERA+	OAV	OOB	BH	AVG	PB	PR	PR+	PD	TPI
1980	Oak-A	0	0	—	5	0	0	0	0	13^{2}	24	13	3	0	4	5	18.4	7.90	48	.381	.418	0	—	0	-6	-7	0	-0.3
1983	Min-A	5	12	.294	61	4	1	1	3	125	132	63	8	2	43	58	12.7	3.38	126	.275	.337	0	—	0	10	12	1	1.6
1984	Min-A	4	3	.571	36	0	0	0	5	56^{2}	62	23	2	0	27	22	14.1	3.49	121	.283	.362	0	—	0	3	4	0	0.6
1985	Min-A	0	2	.000	35	1	0	0	3	61	72	43	3	0	22	26	13.9	6.05	73	.305	.364	0	—	0	-13	-10	-1	-0.6
Total	4	9	17	.346	137	5	1	1	11	256^{1}	290	142	16	2	96	111	13.6	4.28	99	.291	.354	0	—	0	-6	-1	0	1.3

● BILL LYSTON

Lyston, William Edward b: 1863, Near Baltimore, Md. d: 8/4/44, Baltimore, Md. TR, Deb: 8/29/1891

YEAR	TM/L	W	L	PCT	G	GS	CG	SH	SV	IP	H	R	HR	HB	BB	SO	RAT	ERA	ERA+	OAV	OOB	BH	AVG	PB	PR	PR+	PD	TPI
1891	Col-a	0	1	.000	1	1	1	0	0	6	10	8	0	1	6	1	25.5	10.50	33	.357	.486	0	.000	-0	-5	-5	-0	-0.5
1894	Cle-N	0	0	—	1	1	0	0	0	3^{2}	5	6	1	0	4	0	22.1	9.82	56	.313	.450	0	.000	-0	-2	-2	-0	-0.1
Total	2	0	1	.000	2	2	1	0	0	9^{2}	15	14	1	1	10	1	24.2	10.24	41	.341	.473	0	.000	-0	-6	-7	-0	-0.6

● DUKE MAAS

Maas, Duane Fredrick b: 1/31/29, Utica, Mich. d: 12/7/76, Mt.Clemens, Mich. BR/TR, 5'10", 170 lbs. Deb: 4/21/55

YEAR	TM/L	W	L	PCT	G	GS	CG	SH	SV	IP	H	R	HR	HB	BB	SO	RAT	ERA	ERA+	OAV	OOB	BH	AVG	PB	PR	PR+	PD	TPI
1955	Det-A	5	6	.455	18	16	5	2	0	86^{2}	91	52	7	2	50	42	14.8	4.88	79	.271	.369	5	.167	0	-9	-10	0	-1.1
1956	Det-A	0	7	.000	26	7	0	0	0	63^{1}	81	51	9	6	32	34	16.9	6.54	63	.313	.401	3	.188	0	-17	-17	-0	-1.7
1957	Det-A	10	14	.417	45	26	8	2	6	219^{1}	210	92	23	4	65	116	11.4	3.28	118	.252	.309	6	.085	-4	12	14	0	1.1
1958	KC-A	4	5	.444	10	7	3	1	1	55^{1}	49	25	3	1	13	19	10.2	3.90	100	.241	.290	3	.176	0	-1	0	0	0.1

YEAR TM/L	W	L	PCT	G	GS	CG	SH	SV	IP	H	R	HR	HB	BB	SO	RAT	ERA	ERA+	OAV	OOB	BH	AVG	PB	PR	PR+	PD	TPI
*NY-A	7	3	.700	22	13	2	1	0	101^1	93	51	9	2	36	50	11.6	3.82	92	.242	.310	3	.088	-2	-1	-3	-1	-0.6
Yr	11	8	.579	32	20	5	2	1	156^2	142	76	12	3	49	69	11.1	3.85	95	.242	.304	6	.118	-1	-1	-3	-1	-0.5
1959 NY-A	14	8	.636	38	21	3	1	4	138	149	82	14	2	53	67	13.3	4.43	82	.278	.345	5	.125	-1	-9	-13	1	-2.0
1960 *NY-A	5	1	.833	35	1	0	0	4	70^1	70	44	6	1	35	28	13.6	4.09	87	.265	.353	0	.000	-1	-2	-4	1	-0.4
1961 NY-A	0	0	—	1	0	0	0	0	0^1	2	2	0	0	0	0	54.0	54.00	7	1.000	1.000	0	—	0	-2	-2	0	-0.1
Total 7	45	44	.506	195	91	21	7	15	734^2	745	399	71	18	284	356	12.8	4.19	90	.264	.336	25	.117	-7	-27	-35	0	-4.7
● **BOB MABE** Mabe, Robert Lee b: 10/8/29, Danville, Va. BR/TR, 5'11", 165 lbs. Deb: 4/18/58																											
1958 StL-N	3	9	.250	31	13	4	0	0	111^2	113	66	11	4	41	74	12.7	4.51	91	.260	.330	1	.042	-2	-7	-5	0	-0.6
1959 Cin-N	4	2	.667	18	1	0	0	3	29^2	29	28	6	0	19	8	14.6	5.46	74	.254	.361	0	.000	-1	-5	-5	0	-1.0
1960 Bal-A	0	0	—	2	0	0	0	0	0^2	4	6	0	0	1	0	67.5	27.00	14	.571	.625	0	—	0	-2	-2	-0	-0.1
Total 3	7	11	.389	51	14	4	0	3	142	146	100	17	4	61	82	13.4	4.82	85	.263	.340	1	.032	-3	-14	-11	-0	-1.7
● **JOHN MABRY** Mabry, John Steven b: 10/17/70, Wilmington, Del. BL/TR, 6'4", 195 lbs. Deb: 4/23/94 ♦																											
2000 Sea-A	0	0	—	1	0	0	0	0	0^2	3	2	0	0	1	0	54.0	27.00	18	.600	.667	25	.243	0	-2	-2	0	-0.1
● **MAC MacARTHUR** MacArthur, Malcolm b: 1/19/1862, Glasgow, Scotland d: 10/18/32, Detroit, Mich. TR, 5'9.5", 164 lbs. Deb: 5/2/1884																											
1884 Ind-a	1	5	.167	6	6	6	0	0	52	57	49	1	2	21	19	13.8	5.02	66	.263	.333	2	.095	-2	-10	-10	0	-1.0
● **FRANK MacCORMACK** MacCormack, Frank Louis b: 9/21/54, Jersey City, N.J. BR/TR, 6'4", 210 lbs. Deb: 6/14/76																											
1976 Det-A	0	5	.000	9	8	0	0	0	32^2	35	24	1	1	34	14	19.3	5.79	64	.294	.455	0	.000	-0	-8	-7	-0	-1.0
1977 Sea-A	0	0	—	3	3	0	0	0	7	4	3	0	3	12	4	24.4	3.86	107	.174	.500	0	—	0	0	0	0	0.0
Total 2	0	5	.000	12	11	0	0	0	39^2	39	27	1	4	46	18	20.2	5.45	70	.275	.464	0	.000	-0	-8	-7	-0	-1.0
● **ROB MacDONALD** MacDonald, Robert Joseph b: 4/27/65, East Orange, N.J. BL/TR, 6'3", 208 lbs. Deb: 8/14/90																											
1990 Tor-A	0	0	—	4	0	0	0	0	2^1	0	0	0	0	2	0	7.7	0.00	—	.000	.250	0	—	0	1	1	-0	0.0
1991 *Tor-A	3	3	.500	45	0	0	0	0	53^2	51	19	5	0	25	24	12.7	2.85	148	.252	.335	0	—	0	7	8	-1	0.7
1992 Tor-A	1	0	1.000	27	0	0	0	0	47^1	50	24	4	1	16	26	12.7	4.37	94	.270	.332	0	—	0	-2	-1	-1	-0.2
1993 Det-A	3	3	.500	68	0	0	0	3	65^2	67	42	8	1	33	39	13.8	5.35	80	.268	.356	0	—	0	-7	-8	1	-0.6
1995 NY-A	1	1	.500	33	0	0	0	0	46^1	50	25	7	1	22	41	14.2	4.86	95	.282	.365	0	—	0	-1	-1	-0	-0.1
1996 NY-N	0	2	.000	20	0	0	0	0	19	16	10	2	0	9	12	11.8	4.26	94	.235	.325	0	—	0	-0	-1	-0	-0.1
Total 6	8	9	.471	197	0	0	0	3	234^1	234	120	26	3	107	142	13.2	4.34	99	.264	.345	0	—	0	-2	-2	-2	-0.3
● **BILL MACDONALD** Macdonald, William Paul b: 3/28/29, Alameda, Cal. d: 5/4/91, Shasta Lake, Cal. BR/TR, 5'10", 170 lbs. Deb: 5/6/50																											
1950 Pit-N	8	10	.444	32	20	6	2	1	153	138	88	17	1	88	60	13.4	4.29	102	.243	.346	6	.122	-2	-3	1	-3	-0.3
1953 Pit-N	0	1	.000	4	1	0	0	0	7^1	12	10	0	1	8	4	25.8	12.27	36	.400	.538	0	—	0	-7	-6	-0	-0.7
Total 2	8	11	.421	36	21	6	2	1	160^1	150	98	17	2	96	64	13.9	4.66	94	.251	.356	6	.122	-2	-9	-5	-3	-1.0
● **JIMMY MACE** Mace, Harry L. b: Washington, D.C. 5'11", 185 lbs. Deb: 5/5/1891																											
1891 Was-a	0	1	.000	3	1	1	0	0	16	18	14	0	1	8	3	15.2	7.31	51	.273	.360	0	.000	-1	-6	-6	-0	-0.4
● **DANNY MacFAYDEN** MacFayden, Daniel Knowles "Deacon Danny" b: 6/10/05, N.Truro, Mass. d: 8/26/72, Brunswick, Me. BR/TR, 5'11", 170 lbs. Deb: 8/25/26																											
1926 Bos-A	0	1	.000	3	1	1	0	0	13	10	7	0	0	7	1	11.8	4.85	84	.217	.321	1	.333	0	-1	-1	1	0.0
1927 Bos-A	5	8	.385	34	16	6	1	2	160^1	176	88	9	6	59	42	13.5	4.27	99	.294	.363	13	.283	4	-2	-1	-2	0.2
1928 Bos-A	9	15	.375	33	28	9	0	0	195	215	123	12	7	78	61	13.8	4.75	87	.289	.361	9	.143	-1	-15	-14	-1	-1.6
1929 Bos-A	10	18	.357	32	27	14	4	0	221	225	108	8	5	81	61	12.7	3.62	118	.271	.340	13	.176	-3	15	16	2	1.7
1930 Bos-A	11	14	.440	36	33	18	1	2	269^1	293	141	9	6	93	76	13.1	4.21	109	.281	.343	13	.141	-4	13	12	2	0.7
1931 Bos-A	16	12	.571	35	32	17	2	0	230^2	263	121	4	7	79	74	13.6	4.02	107	.281	.341	10	.123	-5	9	7	2	0.5
1932 Bos-A	1	10	.091	12	11	6	0	0	77^2	91	55	3	1	33	29	14.5	5.10	88	.289	.358	3	.120	-2	-5	-5	0	-0.7
NY-A	7	5	.583	17	15	9	0	1	121^1	137	69	11	2	37	33	13.1	3.93	104	.281	.334	5	.102	-3	7	2	-2	-0.2
Yr	8	15	.348	29	26	15	0	1	199	228	124	14	3	70	62	13.6	4.39	97	.284	.344	8	.108	-4	2	-3	-1	-0.9
1933 NY-A	3	2	.600	25	6	2	0	0	90^1	120	62	8	2	37	28	15.8	5.88	66	.319	.383	1	.029	-4	-16	-22	-0	-1.4
1934 NY-A	4	3	.571	22	11	4	0	0	96	110	57	5	2	31	41	13.4	4.50	90	.288	.345	4	.103	-2	-0	-5	-1	-0.6
1935 Cin-N	1	2	.333	7	4	1	0	0	36	39	22	1	0	13	13	13.0	4.75	84	.281	.342	1	.091	-1	-3	-3	1	-0.2
Bos-N	5	13	.278	28	20	7	1	0	151^2	200	96	8	5	34	46	14.2	5.10	74	.314	.354	8	.157	-1	-18	-24	2	-2.3
Yr	6	15	.286	35	24	8	1	0	187^2	239	118	9	5	47	59	14.0	5.04	76	.308	.352	9	.145	-2	-21	-27	3	-2.5
1936 Bos-N	17	13	.567	37	31	21	2	0	266^2	268	97	5	5	66	86	11.4	2.87	134	.259	.307	8	.096	-5	34	30	3	2.9
1937 Bos-N	14	14	.500	32	32	16	2	0	246	250	96	5	2	60	70	11.4	2.93	123	.268	.313	13	.157	-2	27	20	1	2.0
1938 Bos-N	14	9	.609	29	29	19	5	0	219^2	208	82	6	5	64	58	11.3	2.95	116	.247	.304	9	.117	-4	20	13	-1	0.7
1939 Bos-N	8	14	.364	33	28	8	0	2	191^2	221	100	11	4	59	46	13.3	3.90	95	.291	.345	12	.179	-1	0	-5	1	-0.4
1940 Pit-N	5	4	.556	35	8	0	0	2	91^1	112	47	5	4	27	24	14.1	3.55	107	.302	.356	5	.179	-0	3	3	1	0.3
1941 Was-A	0	1	.000	5	0	0	0	0	7	12	9	1	0	5	3	21.9	10.29	39	.375	.459	0	—	0	-5	-5	0	-0.5
1943 Bos-N	2	1	.667	10	1	0	0	0	21^1	31	14	1	1	9	5	17.3	5.91	58	.344	.410	1	.250	0	-6	-6	-0	-0.8
Total 17	132	159	.454	465	333	158	18	9	2706	2981	1394	112	64	872	797	13.0	3.96	101	.281	.340	129	.142	-34	58	12	10	0.3
● **JULIO MACHADO** Machado, Julio Segundo (Rondon) b: 12/1/65, Zulia, Venezuela BR/TR, 5'9", 165 lbs. Deb: 9/7/89																											
1989 NY-N	0	1	.000	10	0	0	0	0	11	9	4	0	0	3	14	9.8	3.27	100	.214	.267	0	—	0	0	-0	-0	0.0
1990 NY-N	4	1	.800	27	0	0	0	0	34^1	32	13	4	2	17	27	13.4	3.15	119	.248	.345	0	—	0	2	2	-0	0.3
Mil-A	0	0	—	10	0	0	0	3	13	9	1	0	0	8	12	11.8	0.69	561	.191	.309	0	—	0	5	5	-0	0.2
1991 Mil-A	3	3	.500	54	0	0	0	3	88^2	65	36	12	3	55	98	12.5	3.45	115	.211	.336	0	—	0	6	5	-1	0.3
Total 3	7	5	.583	101	0	0	0	6	147	115	54	16	5	83	151	12.4	3.12	124	.219	.331	0	—	0	14	12	-1	0.8
● **CHUCK MACHEMEHL** Machemehl, Charles Walter b: 4/20/47, Brenham, Tex. BR/TR, 6'4", 200 lbs. Deb: 4/6/71																											
1971 Cle-A	0	2	.000	14	0	0	0	3	18^1	16	16	2	0	15	9	15.2	6.38	60	.246	.387	1	.500	0	-6	-5	0	-0.6
● **DENNY MACK** Mack, Dennis Joseph (b: Dennis Joseph McGee) b: 1851, Easton, Pa. d: 4/10/1888, Wilkes-Barre, Pa. BR/TR, 5'7", 164 lbs. Deb: 5/6/1871 MU♦																											
1871 Rok-n	0	1	.000	3	1	1	0	0	13	20	30	0		3	1	15.9	3.46	118	.299	.329	30	.246	-0	1	1		0.1
● **FRANK MACK** Mack, Frank George "Stubby" b: 2/2/1900, Oklahoma City, Okla. d: 7/2/71, Clearwater, Fla. BR/TR, 6'1.5", 180 lbs. Deb: 8/16/22																											
1922 Chi-A	2	2	.500	8	4	1	1	0	34^1	36	16	2	0	16	11	13.6	3.67	111	.281	.361	3	.250	1	1	2	-1	0.1
1923 Chi-A	0	1	.000	11	0	0	0	0	23^1	23	13	0	0	11	6	13.1	4.24	93	.284	.370	0	.000	-1	-1	-1	0	-0.1
1925 Chi-A	0	0	—	8	0	0	0	0	13^1	24	14	1	0	13	6	25.0	9.45	44	.444	.552	1	.333	0	-7	-8	-0	-0.4
Total 3	2	3	.400	27	4	1	1	0	71	83	43	3	0	40	23	15.6	4.94	82	.316	.406	4	.190	0	-7	-7	-1	-0.4
● **TONY MACK** Mack, Tony Lynn b: 4/30/61, Lexington, Ky. BR/TR, 5'10", 177 lbs. Deb: 7/27/85																											
1985 Cal-A	0	1	.000	1	1	0	0	0	2^1	8	4	0	0	0	0	30.9	15.43	27	.571	.571	0	—	0	-3	-3	-0	-0.5
● **BILL MACK** Mack, William Francis b: 2/12/1885, Elmira, N.Y. d: 9/30/71, Elmira, N.Y. BL/TL, 6'1", 155 lbs. Deb: 7/14/08																											
1908 Chi-N	0	0	—	2	0	0	0	0	6	5	3	1	1	1	2	10.5	3.00	78	.263	.333	2	.667	1	-0	-0	-0	0.1
● **KEN MacKENZIE** MacKenzie, Kenneth Purvis b: 3/10/34, Gore Bay, Ont., Can. BR/TL, 6', 185 lbs. Deb: 5/2/60																											
1960 Mil-N	0	1	.000	9	0	0	0	0	8^1	9	7	2	0	3	9	13.0	6.48	53	.281	.343	0	.000	-0	-3	-3	-0	-0.4
1961 Mil-N	0	1	.000	5	0	0	0	0	7	8	5	1	1	2	5	14.1	5.14	73	.296	.367	0	.000	-0	-1	-1	0	-0.1
1962 NY-N	5	4	.556	42	1	0	0	1	80	87	47	10	3	34	51	13.9	4.95	84	.280	.356	1	.083	-1	-9	-6	1	-0.7
1963 NY-N	3	1	.750	34	0	0	0	3	58	63	35	11	2	12	41	11.9	4.97	70	.267	.308	0	.000	-1	-11	-9	-1	-0.9
StL-N	0	0	—	8	0	0	0	0	9	9	6	1	0	3	7	12.0	4.00	89	.250	.308	0	—	0	-1	-0	-0	-0.1
Yr	3	1	.750	42	0	0	0	3	67	72	41	12	2	15	48	12.0	4.84	72	.265	.308	0	.000	-1	-12	-9	-1	-1.0
1964 SF-N	0	0	—	10	0	0	0	1	9	9	7	1	0	3	3	12.0	5.00	71	.265	.324	0	—	0	-1	-1	0	0.0
1965 Hou-N	0	3	.000	21	0	0	0	0	37	46	22	7	0	6	26	12.6	3.89	86	.299	.325	3	.273	1	-1	-2	-0	-0.1
Total 6	8	10	.444	129	1	0	0	5	208^1	231	129	33	6	63	142	13.0	4.80	78	.278	.334	4	.111	-2	-27	-24	-1	-2.3
● **JOHN MACKINSON** Mackinson, John Joseph b: 10/29/23, Orange, N.J. d: 10/17/89, Reseda, Cal. BR/TR, 5'10.5", 160 lbs. Deb: 4/16/53																											
1953 Phi-A	0	0	—	1	0	0	0	0	1^1	1	0	0	0	2	0	20.3	0.00	—	.200	.429	0	—	0	1	1	0	0.0

YEAR	TM/L	W	L	PCT	G	GS	CG	SH	SV	IP	H	R	HR	HB	BB	SO	RAT	ERA	ERA+	OAV	OOB	BH	AVG	PB	PR	PR+	PD	TPI
1955	StL-N	0	1	.000	8	1	0	0	0	20^2	24	18	3	1	10	8	15.2	7.84	52	.296	.380	0	.000	-0	-9	-9	-0	-0.4
Total	2	0	1	.000	9	1	0	0	0	22	25	18	3	1	12	8	15.5	7.36	55	.291	.384	0	.000	-0	-8	-8	-0	-0.4

● BILLY MacLEOD

MacLeod, William Daniel b: 5/13/42, Gloucester, Mass. BL/TL, 6'2", 190 lbs. Deb: 9/13/62

YEAR	TM/L	W	L	PCT	G	GS	CG	SH	SV	IP	H	R	HR	HB	BB	SO	RAT	ERA	ERA+	OAV	OOB	BH	AVG	PB	PR	PR+	PD	TPI
1962	Bos-A	0	1	.000	2	0	0	0	0	1^2	4	1	0	0	1	2	27.0	5.40	76	.444	.500	0	—	0	-0	-0	-0	-0.1

● MAX MACON

Macon, Max Cullen b: 10/14/15, Pensacola, Fla. d: 8/5/89, Jupiter, Fla. BL/TL, 6'3", 175 lbs. Deb: 4/21/38 ♦

YEAR	TM/L	W	L	PCT	G	GS	CG	SH	SV	IP	H	R	HR	HB	BB	SO	RAT	ERA	ERA+	OAV	OOB	BH	AVG	PB	PR	PR+	PD	TPI
1938	StL-N	4	11	.267	38	12	5	1	2	129^1	133	83	9	4	61	39	13.8	4.11	96	.268	.352	11	.306	2	-5	-2	1	0.0
1940	Bro-N	1	0	1.000	2	0	0	0	0	2	5	5	2	0	0	1	22.5	22.50	18	.455	.455	1	1.000	0	-4	-4	-0	-0.6
1942	Bro-N	5	3	.625	14	8	4	1	1	84	67	22	3	2	33	27	10.9	1.93	169	.220	.300	12	.279	4	13	13	-0	1.6
1943	Bro-N	7	5	.583	25	9	0	0	0	77	91	54	4	4	32	21	14.8	5.96	56	.291	.364	9	.164	-1	-22	-22	1	-3.2
1944	Bos-N	0	0	—	1	0	0	0	0	3	10	7	2	0	1	1	33.0	21.00	18	.556	.579	100	.273	0	-6	-5	0	-0.2
1947	Bos-N	0	0	—	1	0	0	0	0	2	1	0	0	0	1	1	9.0	0.00	—	.167	.286	0	.000	-0	1	1	0	0.0
Total	6	17	19	.472	81	29	9	2	3	297^1	307	171	20	10	128	90	13.5	4.24	85	.267	.345	133	.265	5	-23	-21	1	-2.4

● HARRY MacPHERSON

MacPherson, Harry William b: 7/10/26, N.Andover, Mass. BR/TR, 5'10", 150 lbs. Deb: 8/14/44

YEAR	TM/L	W	L	PCT	G	GS	CG	SH	SV	IP	H	R	HR	HB	BB	SO	RAT	ERA	ERA+	OAV	OOB	BH	AVG	PB	PR	PR+	PD	TPI
1944	Bos-N	0	0	—	1	0	0	0	0	1	0	0	0	0	1	1	9.0	0.00	—	.000	.250	0	—	0	0	0	0	0.0

● JIMMY MACULLAR

Macullar, James F. "Little Mac" b: 1/16/1855, Boston, Mass. d: 4/8/24, Baltimore, Md. BR/TL, 5'6", 155 lbs. Deb: 5/5/1879 MU♦

YEAR	TM/L	W	L	PCT	G	GS	CG	SH	SV	IP	H	R	HR	HB	BB	SO	RAT	ERA	ERA+	OAV	OOB	BH	AVG	PB	PR	PR+	PD	TPI
1885	Bal-a	0	0	—	1	0	0	0	0	1	0	0	0	0	0	0	0.0	0.00	—	.000	.000	61	.191	0	0	0	-0	0.0
1886	Bal-a	0	0	—	1	0	0	0	0	2	4	3	0	0	0	1	18.0	9.00	38	.400	.400	55	.205	0	-1	-1	-0	-0.1
Total	2	0	0	—	2	0	0	0	0	3	4	3	0	0	0	1	12.0	6.00	56	.308	.308	319	.207	0	-1	-1	-0	-0.1

● KEITH MacWHORTER

MacWhorter, Keith b: 12/30/55, Worcester, Mass. BR/TR, 6'4", 190 lbs. Deb: 5/10/80

YEAR	TM/L	W	L	PCT	G	GS	CG	SH	SV	IP	H	R	HR	HB	BB	SO	RAT	ERA	ERA+	OAV	OOB	BH	AVG	PB	PR	PR+	PD	TPI
1980	Bos-A	0	3	.000	14	2	0	0	0	42^1	46	27	3	2	18	21	14.0	5.53	76	.280	.359	0	—	0	-7	-6	0	-0.3

● LEN MADDEN

Madden, Leonard Joseph "Lefty" b: 7/2/1890, Toledo, Ohio d: 9/9/49, Toledo, Ohio BL/TL, 6'2", 165 lbs. Deb: 8/31/12

YEAR	TM/L	W	L	PCT	G	GS	CG	SH	SV	IP	H	R	HR	HB	BB	SO	RAT	ERA	ERA+	OAV	OOB	BH	AVG	PB	PR	PR+	PD	TPI
1912	Chi-N	0	1	.000	6	2	0	0	0	12^1	16	10	1	1	9	5	19.0	2.92	114	.302	.413	1	.250	0	1	1	-0	0.0

● MIKE MADDEN

Madden, Michael Anthony b: 1/13/58, Denver, Colo. BL/TL, 6'1", 190 lbs. Deb: 4/5/83

YEAR	TM/L	W	L	PCT	G	GS	CG	SH	SV	IP	H	R	HR	HB	BB	SO	RAT	ERA	ERA+	OAV	OOB	BH	AVG	PB	PR	PR+	PD	TPI
1983	Hou-N	9	5	.643	28	13	0	0	0	94^2	76	37	4	1	45	44	11.6	3.14	109	.231	.325	1	.045	-1	5	3	0	0.3
1984	Hou-N	2	3	.400	17	7	0	0	0	40^2	46	27	1	0	35	29	17.9	5.53	60	.297	.426	2	.333	1	-9	-11	-1	-1.2
1985	Hou-N	0	0	—	13	0	0	0	0	19	29	15	1	0	11	16	18.9	4.26	81	.363	.440	0	—	0	-1	-2	-0	-0.1
1986	Hou-N	1	2	.333	13	6	0	0	0	39^2	47	20	3	0	22	30	15.7	4.08	88	.297	.383	0	.000	-1	-2	-2	-0	-0.2
Total	4	12	10	.545	71	26	0	0	0	194	198	99	9	1	113	119	14.5	3.94	87	.274	.373	3	.081	-1	-6	-12	-1	-1.2

● KID MADDEN

Madden, Michael Joseph b: 10/22/1866, Portland, Me. d: 3/16/1896, Portland, Maine BL/TL, 5'7.5", 130 lbs. Deb: 5/6/1887

YEAR	TM/L	W	L	PCT	G	GS	CG	SH	SV	IP	H	R	HR	HB	BB	SO	RAT	ERA	ERA+	OAV	OOB	BH	AVG	PB	PR	PR+	PD	TPI
1887	Bos-N	21	14	.600	37	37	36	3	0	321	439	203	20	20	122	81	12.9	3.79	107	.317	.327	44	.306	4	10	10	-2	0.9
1888	Bos-N	7	11	.389	20	18	17	1	0	165	142	76	6	15	24	53	9.9	2.95	97	.228	.273	11	.164	-2	-2	-2	-1	-0.3
1889	Bos-N	10	10	.500	22	19	18	1	1	178	194	131	7	16	71	64	14.2	4.40	95	.269	.348	25	.291	2	-8	-4	0	-0.2
1890	Bos-P	3	2	.600	10	7	5	1	1	62	85	55	2	8	25	24	17.1	4.79	92	.313	.387	7	.184	-1	-4	-3	1	-0.2
1891	Bos-a	0	1	.000	1	1	1	0	0	8	10	12	2	3	6	6	21.4	6.75	52	.294	.442	2	.667	1	-3	-3	0	-0.2
	Bal-a	13	12	.520	32	27	20	1	1	224	239	168	4	24	88	56	14.1	4.10	91	.264	.345	29	.271	5	-10	-9	4	-0.1
	Yr	13	13	.500	33	28	21	1	1	232	249	180	6	27	94	62	14.4	4.19	89	.265	.349	31	.282	6	-12	-12	4	-0.3
Total	5	54	50	.519	122	109	97	7	3	958	1109	645	41	86	336	284	13.2	3.92	97	.282	.332	118	.265	10	-15	-12	4	-0.1

● MORRIS MADDEN

Madden, Morris De Wayne b: 8/31/60, Laurens, S.C. BL/TL, 6' ", 155 lbs. Deb: 6/11/87

YEAR	TM/L	W	L	PCT	G	GS	CG	SH	SV	IP	H	R	HR	HB	BB	SO	RAT	ERA	ERA+	OAV	OOB	BH	AVG	PB	PR	PR+	PD	TPI
1987	Det-A	0	0	—	2	0	0	0	0	1^2	4	3	0	0	3	0	37.8	16.20	26	.444	.583	0	—	0	-2	-2	-0	-0.1
1988	Pit-N	0	0	—	5	0	0	0	0	5^2	5	0	0	0	7	3	19.1	0.00	—	.294	.500	0	—	0	2	2	0	0.1
1989	Pit-N	2	2	.500	9	3	0	0	0	14	17	14	0	0	13	6	19.3	7.07	48	.327	.462	0	.000	-0	-6	-6	-1	-1.3
Total	3	2	2	.500	16	3	0	0	0	21^1	26	17	0	0	23	9	20.7	5.91	58	.333	.485	0	.000	-0	-6	-6	-1	-1.3

● NICK MADDOX

Maddox, Nicholas b: 11/9/1886, Govans, Md. d: 11/27/54, Pittsburgh, Pa. BL/TR, 6', 175 lbs. Deb: 9/13/07

YEAR	TM/L	W	L	PCT	G	GS	CG	SH	SV	IP	H	R	HR	HB	BB	SO	RAT	ERA	ERA+	OAV	OOB	BH	AVG	PB	PR	PR+	PD	TPI
1907	Pit-N	5	1	.833	6	6	6	1	0	54	32	8	0	4	13	38	8.2	0.83	292	.178	.249	5	.250	2	10	10	-0	1.5
1908	Pit-N	23	8	.742	36	32	22	4	1	260^2	209	89	5	11	90	70	10.7	2.28	101	.223	.298	25	.266	8	2	1	-1	0.9
1909	*Pit-N	13	8	.619	31	27	17	4	0	203^1	173	72	2	15	39	56	10.0	2.21	123	.232	.283	15	.224	4	9	11	-1	1.4
1910	Pit-N	2	3	.400	20	7	2	0	0	87^1	73	40	0	5	28	29	10.9	3.40	91	.246	.321	6	.214	1	-4	-3	-0	-0.1
Total	4	43	20	.683	93	72	47	9	1	605^1	487	209	7	35	170	193	10.3	2.29	112	.225	.292	51	.244	15	17	18	-2	3.7

● GREG MADDUX

Maddux, Gregory Alan b: 4/14/66, San Angelo, Tex. BR/TR, 6', 170 lbs. Deb: 9/3/86 F

YEAR	TM/L	W	L	PCT	G	GS	CG	SH	SV	IP	H	R	HR	HB	BB	SO	RAT	ERA	ERA+	OAV	OOB	BH	AVG	PB	PR	PR+	PD	TPI
1986	Chi-N	2	4	.333	6	5	1	0	0	31	44	20	3	1	11	20	16.3	5.52	73	.336	.392	4	.333	1	-6	-5	0	-0.7
1987	Chi-N	6	14	.300	30	27	1	1	0	155^2	181	111	17	4	74	101	15.0	5.61	76	.294	.374	5	.119	-2	-26	-22	6	-2.0
1988	Chi-N☆	18	8	.692	34	34	9	3	0	249	230	97	13	9	81	140	11.6	3.18	114	.244	.309	19	.198	2	8	11	2	1.7
1989	*Chi-N	19	12	.613	35	35	7	1	0	238^1	222	90	13	6	82	135	11.7	2.95	128	.249	.317	17	.210	2	15	20	3	3.2
1990	Chi-N	15	15	.500	35	35	8	2	0	237	242	116	11	4	71	144	12.0	3.46	118	.265	.321	12	.145	-2	9	15	8	2.5
1991	Chi-N	15	11	.577	37	37	7	2	0	**263**	232	113	18	6	66	198	10.4	3.35	116	.237	.289	18	.205	3	10	15	5	2.3
1992	Chi-N★	**20**	11	.645	35	35	9	4	0	**268**	201	68	7	14	70	199	9.6	2.18	**165**	.210	.273	15	.170	2	**40**	**41**	6	**6.1**
1993	*Atl-N	20	10	.667	36	36	**8**	1	0	**267**	228	85	14	6	52	197	**9.6**	**2.36**	**170**	.232	**.274**	15	.165	-1	**50**	**50**	7	**6.1**
1994	Atl-N★	**16**	6	.727	25	25	**10**	**3**	0	**202**	150	44	4	6	31	156	**8.3**	**1.56**	**272**	**.207**	**.245**	14	.222	2	**60**	**60**	3	**7.3**
1995	*Atl-N★	**19**	2	**.905**	28	28	**10**	**3**	0	**209^2**	147	39	8	4	23	181	**7.5**	**1.63**	**262**	.197	**.225**	11	.153	-0	**59**	**60**	6	**6.7**
1996	*Atl-N☆	15	11	.577	35	35	5	1	0	245	225	85	11	3	28	172	9.4	2.72	162	.241	.265	10	.147	-1	41	44	10	5.4
1997	*Atl-N★	19	4	**.826**	33	33	5	2	0	232^2	200	58	9	6	20	177	8.7	2.20	191	.236	.258	7	.104	-1	52	52	3	5.2
1998	*Atl-N★	18	9	.667	34	34	9	**5**	0	251	201	75	13	7	45	204	**9.1**	**2.22**	**187**	.220	**.262**	18	.240	4	**56**	**55**	7	**7.1**
1999	*Atl-N	19	9	.679	33	33	4	0	0	219^1	258	103	16	4	37	136	12.3	3.57	126	.294	.325	11	.172	3	24	23	7	3.6
2000	*Atl-N†	19	9	.679	35	35	6	**3**	0	249^1	225	91	19	10	42	190	10.0	3.00	151	.238	.277	15	.188	2	45	43	8	**5.5**
Total	15	240	135	.640	471	467	99	31	0	3318	2986	1195	176	90	733	2350	10.3	2.83	145	.241	.288	191	.179	13	436	460	82	60.0

● MIKE MADDUX

Maddux, Michael Ausley b: 8/27/61, Dayton, Ohio BL/TR, 6'2", 190 lbs. Deb: 6/3/86 F

YEAR	TM/L	W	L	PCT	G	GS	CG	SH	SV	IP	H	R	HR	HB	BB	SO	RAT	ERA	ERA+	OAV	OOB	BH	AVG	PB	PR	PR+	PD	TPI
1986	Phi-N	3	7	.300	16	16	0	0	0	78	88	56	6	3	34	44	14.4	5.42	71	.286	.362	1	.045	-1	-15	-13	-1	-1.7
1987	Phi-N	2	0	1.000	7	2	0	0	0	17	17	5	0	0	5	15	11.6	2.65	160	.254	.306	0	.000	-0	3	3	-0	0.2
1988	Phi-N	4	3	.571	25	11	0	0	0	88^2	91	41	6	5	34	59	13.2	3.76	95	.275	.351	3	.130	-0	-3	-2	1	0.0
1989	Phi-N	1	3	.250	16	4	2	1	1	43^2	52	29	3	2	14	26	14.0	5.15	69	.304	.364	0	.000	-1	-8	-8	2	-0.6
1990	LA-N	0	1	.000	11	2	0	0	0	20^2	24	15	3	1	4	11	12.6	6.53	56	.293	.333	0	.000	-0	-6	-7	-0	-0.4
1991	SD-N	7	2	.778	64	1	0	0	5	98^2	78	30	4	1	27	57	9.7	2.46	154	.221	.278	1	.077	-0	13	14	1	1.4
1992	SD-N	2	2	.500	50	1	0	0	5	79^2	71	25	2	0	24	60	10.7	2.37	151	.236	.292	1	.111	-0	10	11	2	0.8
1993	NY-N	3	8	.273	58	0	0	0	5	75	67	34	3	4	27	57	11.8	3.60	112	.243	.319	0	.000	-0	4	4	1	0.6
1994	NY-N	2	1	.667	27	0	0	0	2	44	45	25	7	0	13	32	11.9	5.11	82	.263	.315	0	.000	-0	-4	-5	-0	-0.4
1995	Pit-N	1	0	1.000	8	0	0	0	0	9	14	9	0	0	3	4	17.0	9.00	48	.359	.405	0	—	0	-5	-5	0	-0.2
	*Bos-A	4	1	.800	36	4	0	0	1	89^2	86	40	5	2	15	65	10.3	3.61	135	.247	.282	0	—	0	11	12	0	0.6
1996	Bos-A	3	2	.600	23	7	0	0	0	64^1	76	37	12	5	27	32	15.1	4.48	113	.295	.372	0	—	0	4	4	0	0.4
1997	Sea-A	1	0	1.000	6	0	0	0	0	10^2	20	12	1	1	8	7	24.5	10.13	44	.400	.492	0	—	0	-7	-7	-0	-0.5
1998	Mon-N	3	4	.429	51	0	0	0	0	55^2	50	24	3	1	15	33	10.7	3.72	113	.243	.297	0	.000	-0	3	3	0	0.4
1999	Mon-N	0	0	—	4	0	0	0	0	5	9	5	1	1	3	4	23.4	9.00	50	.409	.500	0	—	0	-2	-3	-0	-0.1
	LA-N	1	1	.500	49	0	0	0	0	54^2	54	21	5	4	19	41	12.7	3.29	130	.261	.335	0	—	0	8	6	-0	0.3
	Yr	1	1	.500	53	0	0	0	0	59^2	63	26	6	5	22	45	13.6	3.77	114	.275	.352	0	—	0	5	4	-0	0.2
2000	Hou-N	2	2	.500	21	0	0	0	0	27^1	31	20	6	2	12	17	14.8	6.26	78	.282	.363	0	.000	-0	-5	-4	0	-0.5
Total	15	39	37	.513	472	48	2	1	20	861^2	873	428	67	32	284	564	12.4	4.05	101	.265	.329	6	.065	-4	0	6	8	0.3

● TONY MADIGAN

Madigan, William J. "Tice" b: 7/1868, Washington, D.C. d: 12/4/54, Washington, D.C. TR, 5'5.5", 126 lbs. Deb: 7/10/1886

YEAR	TM/L	W	L	PCT	G	GS	CG	SH	SV	IP	H	R	HR	HB	BB	SO	RAT	ERA	ERA+	OAV	OOB	BH	AVG	PB	PR	PR+	PD	TPI
1886	Was-N	1	13	.071	14	13	13	0	0	114^2	154	110	3		44	29	15.5	4.87	68	.310	.366	4	.083	-4	-20	-20	0	-2.2

YEAR	TM/L	W	L	PCT	G	GS	CG	SH	SV	IP	H	R	HR	HB	BB	SO	RAT	ERA	ERA+	OAV	OOB	BH	AVG	PB	PR	PR+	PD	TPI
● **DAVE MADISON**	Madison, David Pledger b: 2/1/21, Brooksville, Miss. d: 12/8/85, Macon, Miss. BR/TR, 6'3", 190 lbs. Deb: 9/26/50																											
1950	NY-A	0	0	—	1	0	0	0	0	3	3	2	1	0	1	1	12.0	6.00	72	.273	.333	0	—	0	-0	-1	-0	0.0
1952	StL-A	4	2	.667	31	4	0	0	0	78	78	46	7	4	48	35	15.0	4.38	89	.264	.374	2	.118	-1	-6	-4	0	-0.4
	Det-A	1	1	.500	10	1	0	0	0	15	16	14	1	1	10	7	16.2	7.80	49	.291	.409	0	.000	0	-7	-6	-0	-0.8
	Yr	5	3	.625	41	5	0	0	0	93	94	60	8	5	58	42	15.2	4.94	79	.268	.379	2	.105	-1	-13	-10	-0	-1.2
1953	Det-A	3	4	.429	32	1	0	0	0	62	76	55	7	3	44	27	17.9	6.82	60	.303	.413	1	.091	-1	-19	-19	0	-1.9
Total	3	8	7	.533	74	6	0	0	0	158	173	117	16	8	103	70	16.2	5.70	70	.282	.392	3	.100	-2	-33	-29	0	-3.1
● **ALEX MADRID**	Madrid, Alexander b: 4/18/63, Springerville, Ariz BR/TR, 6'3", 200 lbs. Deb: 7/20/87																											
1987	Mil-A	0	0	—	3	0	0	0	0	5^1	11	9	1	0	1	1	20.3	15.19	30	.440	.462	0	—	0	-6	-6	-0	-0.3
1988	Phi-N	1	1	.500	5	2	1	0	0	16^1	15	5	0	0	6	2	11.6	2.76	129	.246	.313	0	.000	-0	1	1	-0	0.1
1989	Phi-N	1	2	.333	6	3	0	0	0	24^2	32	16	3	1	14	13	17.1	5.47	65	.314	.402	0	.000	-0	-5	-5	-1	-0.7
Total	3	2	3	.400	14	5	1	0	0	46^1	58	30	4	1	21	16	15.5	5.63	65	.309	.381	0	.000	-1	-10	-10	-1	-0.9
● **CALVIN MADURO**	Maduro, Calvin Gregory b: 9/5/74, Santa Cruz, Aruba BR/TR, 6', 175 lbs. Deb: 9/8/96																											
1996	Phi-N	0	1	.000	4	2	0	0	0	15^1	13	6	1	2	3	11	10.6	3.52	123	.232	.295	0	.000	-0	1	1	-0	0.0
1997	Phi-N	3	7	.300	15	13	0	0	0	71	83	59	12	3	41	31	16.1	7.23	59	.294	.390	1	.050	-2	-24	-23	-1	-2.8
2000	Bal-A	0	0	—	15	2	0	0	0	23^1	29	25	8	2	16	18	18.1	9.64	50	.315	.427	0	—	0	-12	-13	-0	-0.6
Total	3	3	8	.273	34	17	0	0	0	109^2	125	90	21	7	60	60	15.8	7.22	61	.291	.386	1	.042	-2	-35	-35	-1	-3.4
● **HECTOR MAESTRI**	Maestri, Hector Anibal (Garcia) b: 4/19/35, Havana, Cuba BR/TR, 5'10", 158 lbs. Deb: 9/24/60																											
1960	Was-A	0	0	—	1	0	0	0	0	2	1	0	0	0	1	1	9.0	0.00	—	.167	.286	0	—	0	1	1	-0	0.0
1961	Was-A	0	1	.000	1	1	0	0	0	6	6	3	1	0	2	2	12.0	1.50	268	.250	.308	0	.000	-0	2	2	-0	0.3
Total	2	0	1	.000	2	1	0	0	0	8	7	3	1	0	3	3	11.3	1.13	354	.233	.303	0	.000	-0	3	3	-0	0.3
● **BILL MAGEE**	Magee, William J. b: 7/6/1875, Canada BR/TR, 5'10", 154 lbs. Deb: 5/18/1897																											
1897	Lou-N	4	12	.250	23	17	13	1	0	156^1	187	137	6	10	101	44	17.2	5.41	79	.294	.399	13	.210	-2	-19	-20	1	-1.6
1898	Lou-N	16	15	.516	38	33	29	3	0	295^1	294	163	8	19	129	55	13.5	4.05	88	.258	.343	14	.126	-9	-15	-16	-2	-2.3
1899	Lou-N	3	7	.300	12	10	6	1	0	71	91	58	1	9	28	13	16.2	5.20	74	.311	.388	3	.111	-2	-11	-11	1	-1.2
	Phi-N	3	5	.375	9	9	7	0	0	70	82	50	0	7	32	4	15.6	5.66	65	.292	.378	5	.161	-2	-14	-16	-1	-1.6
	Was-N	1	4	.200	8	7	4	0	0	42	54	45	3	7	28	11	19.1	8.57	46	.312	.428	5	.333	1	-22	-21	1	-1.7
	Yr	7	16	.304	29	26	17	1	0	183	227	153	4	23	88	28	16.6	6.15	62	.304	.394	13	.178	-2	-47	-48	1	-4.5
1901	StL-N	0	0	—	1	1	0	0	0	8	8	4	0	0	4	3	13.5	4.50	71	.258	.343	2	.500	1	-1	-1	-0	0.0
	NY-N	0	4	.000	6	5	4	0	0	42^1	56	36	4	4	11	14	15.1	5.95	56	.316	.370	2	.143	-1	-12	-13	0	-1.0
	Yr	0	4	.000	7	6	4	0	0	50^1	64	40	4	4	15	17	14.8	5.72	57	.308	.366	4	.222	1	-13	-14	-0	-1.0
1902	NY-N	0	0	—	2	1	0	0	0	5	5	2	0	0	1	2	10.8	3.60	78	.263	.300	0	.000	-0	-0	-0	-0	0.0
	Phi-N	2	4	.333	8	7	6	0	0	53^2	61	28	1	3	18	15	13.8	3.69	76	.285	.349	4	.211	-0	-5	-5	-0	-0.6
	Yr	2	4	.333	10	8	6	0	0	58^2	66	30	1	3	19	17	13.5	3.68	77	.283	.345	4	.200	-1	-6	-6	-0	-0.6
Total	5	29	51	.363	107	90	69	5	0	743^2	838	523	23	59	352	161	15.1	4.94	75	.283	.370	48	.169	-13	-100	-103	-0	-10.0
● **SAL MAGLIE**	Maglie, Salvatore Anthony "The Barber" b: 4/26/17, Niagara Falls, N.Y d: 12/28/92, Niagara Falls, N.Y BR/TR, 6'2", 180 lbs. Deb: 8/9/45 C																											
1945	NY-N	5	4	.556	13	10	7	3	0	84^1	72	22	2	2	22	32	10.2	2.35	167	.231	.286	5	.167	-1	14	14	0	1.4
1950	NY-N	18	4	**.818**	47	16	12	**5**	1	206	169	71	14	10	86	96	11.6	2.71	**151**	.226	.314	8	.121	-1	33	32	3	3.3
1951	*NY-N★	**23**	6	.793	42	37	22	3	4	298	254	110	27	6	86	146	10.4	2.93	**134**	**.230**	.289	17	.152	-3	**34**	**33**	1	3.0
1952	NY-N☆	18	8	.692	35	31	12	5	1	216	199	80	16	6	75	112	11.7	2.92	127	.244	.312	5	.072	-3	20	19	1	1.9
1953	NY-N	8	9	.471	27	24	9	3	0	145^1	158	79	19	1	47	80	12.8	4.15	103	.278	.334	13	.271	2	2	2	-2	0.3
1954	*NY-N	14	6	.700	34	32	9	1	2	218^1	222	83	21	3	70	117	12.2	3.26	124	.262	.320	8	.127	-2	20	19	0	1.4
1955	NY-N	9	5	.643	23	21	6	0	0	129^2	142	67	18	3	48	71	13.4	3.75	107	.278	.344	5	.125	-2	4	4	-2	0.0
	Cle-A	0	2	.000	10	2	0	0	2	25^2	26	14	0	1	7	11	11.9	3.86	103	.252	.306	0	.000	-0	0	0	-1	-0.1
1956	Cle-A	0	0	—	2	0	0	0	0	5	6	2	1	0	2	2	14.4	3.60	117	.300	.364	0	—	0	0	0	-0	0.0
	*Bro-N	13	5	.722	28	26	9	3	0	191	154	65	21	5	52	108	9.9	2.87	**138**	.222	.281	9	.129	-3	19	22	-2	1.4
1957	Bro-N	6	6	.500	19	17	4	1	1	101^1	94	42	12	4	26	50	11.0	2.93	142	.245	.300	1	.034	-3	11	13	-1	1.1
	NY-A	2	0	1.000	6	3	1	1	3	26	22	6	1	1	7	9	10.4	1.73	207	.227	.286	2	.250	0	6	6	-0	0.6
1958	NY-A	1	1	.500	7	3	0	0	0	23^1	27	12	3	0	9	7	13.9	4.63	76	.300	.364	1	.143	1	-2	-3	0	-0.1
	StL-N	2	6	.250	10	10	2	0	0	53	46	31	14	2	25	21	12.4	4.75	87	.232	.324	2	.125	-1	-5	-4	-1	-0.6
Total	10	119	62	.657	303	232	93	25	14	1723	1591	684	169	44	562	862	11.5	3.15	127	.245	.309	76	.135	-16	156	159	-2	13.6
● **MIKE MAGNANTE**	Magnante, Michael Anthony b: 6/17/65, Glendale, Cal. BL/TL, 6'1", 190 lbs. Deb: 4/22/91																											
1991	KC-A	0	1	.000	38	0	0	0	0	55	55	19	3	0	23	42	12.8	2.45	168	.262	.335	0	—	0	10	10	-0	0.5
1992	KC-A	4	9	.308	44	12	0	0	0	89^1	115	53	5	2	35	31	15.3	4.94	82	.325	.389	0	—	0	-10	-8	2	-0.9
1993	KC-A	1	2	.333	7	6	0	0	0	35^1	37	16	3	1	11	16	12.5	4.08	113	.282	.343	0	—	0	1	2	0	0.2
1994	KC-A	2	3	.400	36	1	0	0	0	47	55	27	5	0	16	21	13.6	4.60	109	.289	.345	0	—	0	1	2	0	0.2
1995	KC-A	1	1	.500	28	0	0	0	0	44^2	45	23	6	2	16	28	12.7	4.23	113	.268	.339	0	—	0	2	3	1	0.2
1996	KC-A	2	2	.500	38	0	0	0	0	54	58	38	5	4	24	32	14.3	5.67	88	.282	.368	0	—	0	-4	-4	2	-0.1
1997	*Hou-N	3	1	.750	40	0	0	0	1	47^2	39	16	2	0	11	43	9.4	2.27	177	.223	.269	0	.000	-0	10	10	-0	0.7
1998	Hou-N	4	7	.364	48	0	0	0	2	51^2	56	28	2	4	26	39	15.0	4.88	83	.276	.369	2	1.000	1	-4	-5	2	-0.6
1999	Ana-A	5	2	.714	53	0	0	0	0	69^1	68	30	2	3	29	44	13.0	3.38	144	.262	.342	0	—	0	12	11	1	1.1
2000	*Oak-A	1	1	.500	55	0	0	0	0	39^2	50	22	3	2	19	17	16.1	4.31	111	.309	.388	0	.000	-0	3	2	2	0.2
Total	10	23	29	.442	387	19	0	0	3	533^2	578	272	36	18	210	313	13.6	4.11	109	.281	.352	2	.333	1	22	22	10	1.5
● **JIM MAGNUSON**	Magnuson, James Robert b: 8/18/46, Marinette, Wis. d: 5/30/91, Green Bay, Wis. BR/TL, 6'2", 190 lbs. Deb: 6/28/70																											
1970	Chi-A	1	5	.167	13	6	0	0	0	44^2	45	28	7	1	16	20	12.5	4.84	81	.263	.330	0	.000	-1	-6	-4	-0	-0.7
1971	Chi-A	1	1	.500	15	4	0	0	0	30	30	18	0	2	16	11	14.4	4.50	80	.265	.366	0	.000	-0	-3	-3	-0	-0.2
1973	NY-A	0	1	.000	8	0	0	0	0	27^1	38	17	2	0	9	9	15.5	4.28	86	.342	.392	0	—	0	-1	-2	0	-0.1
Total	3	2	7	.222	36	10	0	0	0	102	113	63	9	3	41	40	13.9	4.59	82	.286	.358	0	.000	-2	-10	-9	0	-1.0
● **JOE MAGRANE**	Magrane, Joseph David b: 7/2/64, Des Moines, Iowa BR/TL, 6'6", 230 lbs. Deb: 4/25/87																											
1987	*StL-N	9	7	.563	27	26	4	2	0	170^1	157	75	9	10	60	101	12.0	3.54	117	.245	.320	7	.135	1	10	12	-0	1.1
1988	StL-N	5	9	.357	24	24	4	3	0	165^1	133	57	6	2	51	100	10.1	**2.18**	**160**	.217	.280	8	.167	1	23	24	2	2.5
1989	StL-N	18	9	.667	34	33	9	3	0	234^2	219	81	5	6	72	127	11.4	2.91	125	.251	.313	11	.138	1	15	18	-1	2.0
1990	StL-N	10	17	.370	31	31	3	2	0	203^1	204	86	10	8	59	100	12.0	3.59	107	.264	.322	7	.127	-0	5	5	1	0.8
1992	StL-N	1	2	.333	5	5	0	0	0	31^1	34	15	2	2	15	20	14.6	4.02	84	.279	.367	2	.200	1	-2	-2	-0	-0.1
1993	StL-N	8	10	.444	22	20	0	0	0	116	127	68	15	5	37	38	13.1	4.97	80	.286	.348	4	.114	-1	-12	-13	0	-1.8
	Cal-A	3	2	.600	8	8	0	0	0	48	48	27	4	0	21	24	12.9	3.94	115	.265	.342	0	—	0	2	3	2	0.5
1994	Cal-A	2	6	.250	20	11	1	0	0	74	89	63	18	6	51	33	17.8	7.30	67	.300	.412	0	—	0	-20	-19	-0	-1.7
1996	Chi-A	1	5	.167	19	8	0	0	0	53^2	70	45	10	3	25	21	16.4	6.88	69	.318	.395	0	—	0	-11	-13	-0	-1.2
Total	8	57	67	.460	190	166	21	10	0	1096^2	1081	517	79	42	391	564	12.4	3.81	103	.260	.330	39	.139	3	11	16	3	2.1
● **PETE MAGRINI**	Magrini, Peter Alexander b: 6/8/42, San Francisco, Cal. BR/TR, 6', 195 lbs. Deb: 4/13/66																											
1966	Bos-A	0	1	.000	3	1	0	0	0	7^1	8	9	0	1	8	3	20.9	9.82	39	.308	.486	0	.000	-0	-5	-4	-0	-0.6
● **ART MAHAFFEY**	Mahaffey, Arthur b: 6/4/38, Cincinnati, Ohio BR/TR, 6'2", 200 lbs. Deb: 7/30/60																											
1960	Phi-N	7	3	.700	14	12	5	1	0	93^1	78	29	9	1	34	56	10.9	2.31	168	.229	.301	3	.100	-2	15	16	-1	1.4
1961	Phi-N★	11	19	.367	36	32	12	3	0	219^1	205	110	27	7	70	158	11.6	4.10	99	.249	.314	8	.127	-2	-2	-1	-2	-0.4
1962	Phi-N★	19	14	.576	41	39	20	2	0	274	253	131	36	12	81	177	11.4	3.94	98	.246	.309	13	.141	1	0	-2	-4	-0.6
1963	Phi-N	7	10	.412	26	22	6	1	0	149	143	73	18	5	48	97	11.8	3.99	81	.255	.319	10	.200	2	-12	-13	-1	-1.2
1964	Phi-N	12	9	.571	34	29	2	2	0	157^1	161	84	17	6	82	80	14.2	4.52	77	.269	.362	6	.120	0	-17	-19	-2	-2.5
1965	Phi-N	2	5	.286	22	9	1	0	0	71	82	53	11	7	32	52	15.3	6.21	56	.294	.381	2	.095	-1	-21	-22	-1	-2.2
1966	StL-N	1	4	.200	12	5	0	0	1	35	37	27	7	1	21	19	15.2	6.43	56	.276	.378	0	.000	-1	-11	-11	-1	-1.6
Total	7	59	64	.480	185	148	46	9	1	999	959	507	125	39	368	639	12.3	4.17	89	.255	.328	42	.134	-2	-47	-51	-11	-7.1

● ROY MAHAFFEY Mahaffey, Lee Roy "Popeye" b: 2/9/03, Belton, S.C. d: 7/23/69, Anderson, S.C. BR/TR, 6', 180 lbs. Deb: 8/31/26

YEAR	TM/L	W	L	PCT	G	GS	CG	SH	SV	IP	H	R	HR	HB	BB	SO	RAT	ERA	ERA+	OAV	OOB	BH	AVG	PB	PR	PR+	PD	TPI
1926	Pit-N	0	0	—	4	0	0	0	0	4^{2}	5	4	0	1	1	3	13.5	0.00	—	.294	.368	0	.000	-0	2	2	-0	0.0
1927	Pit-N	1	0	1.000	2	1	0	0	0	9^{1}	9	8	0	3	9	4	20.3	7.71	53	.300	.500	2	.400	0	-4	-4	-0	-0.3
1930	Phi-A	9	5	.643	33	17	6	0	0	152^{2}	186	108	16	4	53	38	14.3	5.01	93	.298	.357	7	.119	-5	-6	-6	-1	-1.0
1931	*Phi-A	15	4	.789	30	20	8	0	2	162^{1}	161	87	9	3	82	59	13.6	4.21	107	.258	.347	12	.190	1	3	5	-3	0.3
1932	Phi-A	13	13	.500	37	28	13	0	0	222^{2}	245	136	27	5	96	106	14.0	5.09	89	.274	.348	15	.172	-1	-15	-14	-2	-1.6
1933	Phi-A	13	10	.565	33	23	9	0	0	179^{1}	198	114	5	4	74	66	13.9	5.17	83	.275	.346	14	.215	-0	-18	-18	-2	-2.0
1934	Phi-A	6	7	.462	37	14	3	0	2	129	142	88	10	1	55	37	13.8	5.37	82	.276	.347	13	.271	2	-13	-15	-2	-1.2
1935	Phi-A	8	4	.667	27	17	5	0	0	136	153	66	11	5	42	39	13.2	3.90	116	.283	.341	9	.176	-2	8	9	-1	0.4
1936	StL-A	2	6	.250	21	9	1	0	1	60	82	62	6	1	40	13	18.5	8.10	66	.315	.409	1	.063	-1	-20	-17	-2	-2.0
Total	9	67	49	.578	224	129	45	0	5	1056	1181	673	84	27	452	365	14.1	5.01	90	.280	.353	73	.184	-7	-63	-56	-13	-7.4

● LOU MAHAFFEY Mahaffey, Louis Wood b: 1/3/1874, Kentucky d: 10/26/49, Torrance, Cal. BR, 5'9", 170 lbs. Deb: 4/26/1898

YEAR	TM/L	W	L	PCT	G	GS	CG	SH	SV	IP	H	R	HR	HB	BB	SO	RAT	ERA	ERA+	OAV	OOB	BH	AVG	PB	PR	PR+	PD	TPI
1898	Lou-N	0	1	.000	1	1	1	0	0	9	10	9	0	0	5	1	15.0	3.00	119	.278	.366	0	.000	-0	1	1	-0	0.0

● ART MAHAN Mahan, Arthur Leo b: 6/8/13, Somerville, Mass. BL/TL, 5'11", 178 lbs. Deb: 4/30/40 ♦

YEAR	TM/L	W	L	PCT	G	GS	CG	SH	SV	IP	H	R	HR	HB	BB	SO	RAT	ERA	ERA+	OAV	OOB	BH	AVG	PB	PR	PR+	PD	TPI
1940	Phi-N	0	0	—	1	0	0	0	0	1	1	0	0	0	0	0	9.0	0.00	—	.333	.333	133	.244	0	0	0	-0	0.0

● RON MAHAY Mahay, Ronald Matthew b: 6/28/71, Crestwood, Ill. BL/TL, 6'2", 185 lbs. Deb: 5/21/95 ♦

YEAR	TM/L	W	L	PCT	G	GS	CG	SH	SV	IP	H	R	HR	HB	BB	SO	RAT	ERA	ERA+	OAV	OOB	BH	AVG	PB	PR	PR+	PD	TPI
1997	Bos-A	3	0	1.000	28	0	0	0	0	25	19	7	3	0	11	22	10.8	2.52	184	.204	.288	0	—	0	6	6	-0	0.6
1998	Bos-A	1	1	.500	29	0	0	0	1	26	26	16	2	2	15	14	14.9	3.46	136	.263	.371	0	—	0	3	4	-1	0.2
1999	Oak-A	2	0	1.000	6	1	0	0	1	19^{1}	8	4	2	0	3	15	5.1	1.86	250	.123	.162	0	—	0	6	6	-0	0.6
2000	Oak-A	0	1	.000	5	2	0	0	0	16	26	18	4	0	9	5	19.7	9.00	53	.366	.438	0	—	0	-7	-8	-0	-0.4
	Fla-N	1	0	1.000	18	0	0	0	0	25^{1}	31	17	6	0	16	27	16.7	6.04	73	.310	.405	2	.500	1	-4	-5	0	-0.1
Total	4	7	2	.778	86	3	0	0	2	111^{2}	110	62	17	2	54	83	13.4	4.35	106	.257	.343	6	.250	1	4	4	-1	0.9

● MICKEY MAHLER Mahler, Michael James b: 7/30/52, Montgomery, Ala. BB/TL, 6'3", 189 lbs. Deb: 9/13/77 F

YEAR	TM/L	W	L	PCT	G	GS	CG	SH	SV	IP	H	R	HR	HB	BB	SO	RAT	ERA	ERA+	OAV	OOB	BH	AVG	PB	PR	PR+	PD	TPI
1977	Atl-N	1	2	.333	5	5	0	0	0	23	31	19	4	1	9	14	16.0	6.26	71	.326	.390	3	.500	2	-6	-4	-0	-0.3
1978	Atl-N	4	11	.267	34	21	1	0	0	134^{2}	130	82	16	7	66	92	13.6	4.68	87	.255	.349	4	.098	-2	-16	-8	-1	-1.2
1979	Atl-N	5	11	.313	26	18	1	0	0	100	123	72	11	3	47	71	15.6	5.85	69	.304	.381	3	.111	-1	-23	-18	-0	-2.7
1980	Pit-N	0	0	—	2	0	0	0	0	1	4	7	1	0	3	1	63.0	63.00	6	.571	.700	0	—	0	-7	-7	0	-0.3
1981	Cal-A	0	0	—	6	0	0	0	0	6^{1}	1	0	0	0	2	5	4.3	0.00	—	.056	.150	0	—	0	3	3	0	0.1
1982	Cal-A	2	0	1.000	6	0	0	0	0	8	9	1	0	0	6	5	16.9	1.13	361	.300	.417	0	—	0	3	3	-0	0.5
1985	Mon-N	1	4	.200	9	7	1	1	1	48^{1}	40	22	3	1	24	32	12.1	3.54	96	.229	.325	3	.188	1	0	-1	-1	-0.1
	Det-A	1	2	.333	3	2	0	0	0	20^{2}	19	8	2	0	4	14	10.0	1.74	234	.241	.277	0	—	0	6	5	-0	0.8
1986	Tex-A	0	2	.000	29	5	0	0	3	63	71	31	3	3	29	28	14.7	4.14	104	.295	.377	0	—	0	0	1	-0	0.0
	Tor-A	0	0	—	2	0	0	0	0	1	1	0	0	1	0	0	18.0	0.00	—	.200	.333	0	—	0	0	0	0	0.0
	Yr	0	2	.000	31	5	0	0	3	64	72	31	3	4	29	28	14.8	4.08	106	.293	.376	0	—	0	1	2	0	0.0
Total	8	14	32	.304	122	58	3	1	4	406	429	242	40	16	190	262	14.1	4.68	86	.274	.359	13	.144	-1	-41	-27	-3	-3.2

● RICK MAHLER Mahler, Richard Keith b: 8/5/53, Austin, Tex. BR/TR, 6'1", 202 lbs. Deb: 4/20/79 F

YEAR	TM/L	W	L	PCT	G	GS	CG	SH	SV	IP	H	R	HR	HB	BB	SO	RAT	ERA	ERA+	OAV	OOB	BH	AVG	PB	PR	PR+	PD	TPI
1979	Atl-N	0	0	—	15	0	0	0	0	22	28	16	4	0	11	12	16.0	6.14	66	.311	.386	1	.500	0	-6	-5	-0	-0.2
1980	Atl-N	0	0	—	2	0	0	0	0	3^{2}	2	1	0	0	0	1	4.9	2.45	153	.154	.154	0	—	0	0	1	0	0.0
1981	Atl-N	8	6	.571	34	14	1	0	2	112^{1}	109	41	5	1	43	54	12.3	2.80	128	.258	.328	4	.148	-1	9	9	1	1.2
1982	*Atl-N	9	10	.474	39	33	5	2	0	205^{1}	213	105	18	1	62	105	12.1	4.21	89	.272	.327	11	.190	2	-14	-10	2	-0.6
1983	Atl-N	0	0	—	10	0	0	0	0	14^{1}	16	8	0	0	9	7	15.7	5.02	77	.296	.397	0	.000	-0	-2	-2	-0	-0.1
1984	Atl-N	13	10	.565	38	29	9	1	0	222	209	86	13	3	62	106	11.1	3.12	124	.251	.305	21	.296	5	12	17	2	2.5
1985	Atl-N	17	15	.531	39	39	6	1	0	266^{2}	272	116	24	2	79	107	11.9	3.48	111	.268	.322	14	.156	-1	4	10	1	1.2
1986	Atl-N	14	18	.438	39	39	7	1	0	237^{2}	283	139	25	3	95	137	14.4	4.88	82	.301	.367	16	.193	2	-31	-22	2	-2.4
1987	Atl-N	8	13	.381	39	28	3	1	0	197	212	118	24	2	85	95	13.7	4.98	87	.283	.357	16	.193	2	-31	-22	2	-2.4
1988	Atl-N	9	16	.360	39	34	5	0	0	249	279	125	17	8	42	131	11.9	3.69	100	.282	.317	9	.125	-2	-6	-0	1	-0.1
1989	Cin-N	9	13	.409	40	31	5	2	0	220^{2}	242	113	15	10	51	102	12.4	3.83	94	.282	.329	11	.177	2	-8	-5	-0	-0.4
1990	*Cin-N	7	6	.538	35	16	2	1	4	134^{2}	134	67	16	3	39	68	11.8	4.28	92	.261	.317	4	.114	-1	-7	-5	-0	-0.6
1991	Mon-N	1	3	.250	10	6	0	0	0	37^{1}	37	17	2	0	15	17	12.5	3.62	100	.268	.340	1	.111	-0	0	0	1	0.0
	Atl-N	1	1	.500	13	2	0	0	0	28^{2}	33	20	2	2	13	10	15.1	5.65	69	.282	.364	1	.200	0	-6	-5	0	-0.3
	Yr	2	4	.333	23	8	0	0	0	66	70	37	4	2	28	27	13.6	4.50	83	.275	.351	2	.143	-0	-6	-6	1	-0.3
Total	13	96	111	.464	392	271	43	9	6	1951^{1}	2069	972	165	35	606	952	12.5	3.99	96	.275	.332	104	.179	7	-75	-30	10	-0.7

● PAT MAHOMES Mahomes, Patrick Lavon b: 8/9/70, Bryan, Tex. BR/TR, 6'4", 210 lbs. Deb: 4/12/92

YEAR	TM/L	W	L	PCT	G	GS	CG	SH	SV	IP	H	R	HR	HB	BB	SO	RAT	ERA	ERA+	OAV	OOB	BH	AVG	PB	PR	PR+	PD	TPI
1992	Min-A	3	4	.429	14	13	0	0	0	69^{2}	73	41	5	0	37	44	14.2	5.04	81	.279	.368	0	—	0	-8	-7	-1	-0.7
1993	Min-A	1	5	.167	12	5	0	0	0	37^{1}	47	34	8	1	16	23	15.4	7.71	57	.309	.379	0	—	0	-14	-14	0	-1.8
1994	Min-A	9	5	.643	21	21	0	0	0	120	121	68	22	1	62	53	13.8	4.72	103	.269	.359	0	—	0	1	2	-1	0.1
1995	Min-A	4	10	.286	47	7	0	0	3	94^{2}	100	74	22	2	47	67	14.2	6.37	75	.271	.356	0	—	0	-17	-17	0	-2.1
1996	Min-A	1	4	.200	20	5	0	0	0	45	63	38	10	0	27	30	18.0	7.20	71	.330	.413	0	—	0	-11	-10	0	-0.9
	Bos-A	2	0	1.000	11	0	0	0	2	12^{1}	9	8	3	0	6	6	10.9	5.84	87	.209	.306	0	—	0	-1	-1	-0	-0.2
	Yr	3	4	.429	31	5	0	0	2	57^{1}	72	46	13	0	33	36	16.5	6.91	74	.308	.393	0	—	0	-12	-11	0	-1.1
1997	Bos-A	1	0	1.000	10	0	0	0	0	10	15	10	2	2	10	5	24.3	8.10	57	.366	.509	0	—	0	-4	-4	-0	-0.4
1999	*NY-N	8	0	1.000	39	0	0	0	0	63^{2}	44	26	7	2	37	51	11.7	3.68	119	.197	.317	5	.313	2	6	5	-1	0.7
2000	NY-N	5	3	.625	53	5	0	0	0	94	96	63	15	2	66	76	15.7	5.46	81	.263	.379	4	.235	1	-9	-11	1	-0.6
Total	8	34	31	.523	227	56	0	0	5	546^{2}	568	362	94	10	308	355	14.6	5.55	83	.271	.367	9	.273	3	-57	-57	-1	-5.9

● AL MAHON Mahon, Alfred Gwinn "Lefty" b: 9/23/09, Albion, Neb. d: 12/26/77, New Haven, Conn. BL/TL, 5'11", 160 lbs. Deb: 4/22/30

YEAR	TM/L	W	L	PCT	G	GS	CG	SH	SV	IP	H	R	HR	HB	BB	SO	RAT	ERA	ERA+	OAV	OOB	BH	AVG	PB	PR	PR+	PD	TPI
1930	Phi-A	0	0	—	3	0	0	0	0	4^{1}	11	11	0	0	7	0	37.4	22.85	20	.579	.692	0	.000	0	-9	-9	0	-0.3

● CHRIS MAHONEY Mahoney, Christopher John b: 6/11/1885, Milton, Mass. d: 7/15/54, Visalia, Cal. BR/TR, 5'9", 160 lbs. Deb: 7/12/10

YEAR	TM/L	W	L	PCT	G	GS	CG	SH	SV	IP	H	R	HR	HB	BB	SO	RAT	ERA	ERA+	OAV	OOB	BH	AVG	PB	PR	PR+	PD	TPI
1910	Bos-A	0	1	.000	2	1	0	0	1	11	16	11	1	0	5	6	17.2	3.27	78	.327	.389	1	.143	-0	-1	-1	1	-0.1

● MIKE MAHONEY Mahoney, George W. "Big Mike" b: 12/5/1873, Boston, Mass. d: 1/3/40, Boston, Mass. BR, 6'4", 220 lbs. Deb: 5/18/1897 ♦

YEAR	TM/L	W	L	PCT	G	GS	CG	SH	SV	IP	H	R	HR	HB	BB	SO	RAT	ERA	ERA+	OAV	OOB	BH	AVG	PB	PR	PR+	PD	TPI
1897	Bos-N	0	0	—	1	0	0	0	0	1	3	2	0	0	1	1	36.0	18.00	25	.500	.571	1	.500	0	-2	-1	0	0.0

● BOB MAHONEY Mahoney, Robert Paul b: 6/20/28, LeRoy, Minn. BR/TR, 6'1", 185 lbs. Deb: 5/3/51

YEAR	TM/L	W	L	PCT	G	GS	CG	SH	SV	IP	H	R	HR	HB	BB	SO	RAT	ERA	ERA+	OAV	OOB	BH	AVG	PB	PR	PR+	PD	TPI
1951	Chi-A	0	0	—	3	0	0	0	0	6^{2}	5	4	1	0	5	3	13.5	5.40	75	.208	.345	0	—	0	-1	-1	-0	-0.1
	StL-A	2	5	.286	30	4	0	0	0	81	86	47	7	0	41	30	14.1	4.44	99	.274	.358	4	.222	-0	-3	-0	-1	-0.1
	Yr	2	5	.286	33	4	0	0	0	87^{2}	91	51	8	0	46	33	14.1	4.52	97	.269	.357	4	.222	-0	-4	-1	-1	-0.2
1952	StL-A	0	0	—	3	0	0	0	0	3	8	6	0	0	4	1	36.0	18.00	22	.500	.600	0	—	0	-5	-4	-0	-0.2
Total	2	2	5	.286	36	4	0	0	0	90^{2}	99	57	8	0	50	34	14.8	4.96	88	.280	.369	4	.222	-0	-9	-6	-1	-0.4

● DUSTER MAILS Mails, John Walter "Walter" or "The Great"
b: 10/1/1894, San Quentin, Cal. d: 7/5/74, San Francisco, Cal BL/TL, 6', 195 lbs. Deb: 9/28/15

YEAR	TM/L	W	L	PCT	G	GS	CG	SH	SV	IP	H	R	HR	HB	BB	SO	RAT	ERA	ERA+	OAV	OOB	BH	AVG	PB	PR	PR+	PD	TPI
1915	Bro-N	0	1	.000	2	0	0	0	0	5	6	5	2	0	5	3	19.8	3.60	77	.333	.478	0	.000	-0	-0	-0	0	-0.1
1916	Bro-N	0	1	.000	11	0	0	0	0	17^{1}	15	9	1	0	9	13	12.5	3.63	74	.242	.338	1	.250	0	-2	-2	-0	-0.1
1920	*Cle-A	7	0	1.000	9	8	6	2	0	63^{1}	54	18	1	0	18	25	10.2	1.85	206	.230	.285	4	.200	0	14	14	-1	1.3
1921	Cle-A	14	8	.636	34	24	10	2	2	194^{1}	210	103	4	2	89	87	13.9	3.94	108	.283	.361	6	.094	-4	8	7	-3	0.0
1922	Cle-A	4	7	.364	26	13	4	1	0	104	122	69	8	4	40	54	14.4	5.28	76	.291	.359	5	.161	-0	-14	-15	0	-1.3
1925	StL-N	7	7	.500	21	16	9	0	0	131	145	78	11	7	58	49	14.4	4.60	94	.279	.360	6	.133	-2	-5	-4	-1	-0.7
1926	StL-N	0	1	.000	1	0	0	0	0	1	2	1	0	0	1	1	27.0	0.00	—	.400	.500	0	—	0	0	0	0	0.1
Total	7	32	25	.561	104	61	29	5	2	516	554	283	27	13	220	232	13.7	4.10	100	.277	.352	22	.133	-7	0	0	-5	-0.8

● WOODY MAIN Main, Forrest Harry b: 2/12/22, Delano, Cal. d: 6/27/92, Whittier, Cal. BR/TR, 6'3.5", 195 lbs. Deb: 4/21/48

YEAR	TM/L	W	L	PCT	G	GS	CG	SH	SV	IP	H	R	HR	HB	BB	SO	RAT	ERA	ERA+	OAV	OOB	BH	AVG	PB	PR	PR+	PD	TPI
1948	Pit-N	1	1	.500	17	0	0	0	0	27	35	27	4	0	19	12	18.0	8.33	49	.324	.425	0	.000	-0	-13	-12	0	-0.8
1950	Pit-N	1	0	1.000	12	0	0	0	1	20^{1}	21	12	2	1	11	12	14.6	4.87	90	.256	.351	2	.400	0	-2	-1	0	0.0
1952	Pit-N	2	12	.143	48	11	2	0	2	153^{1}	149	78	14	0	52	79	11.8	4.46	90	.253	.314	2	.054	-3	-12	-7	-3	-1.3

YEAR	TM/L	W	L	PCT	G	GS	CG	SH	SV	IP	H	R	HR	HB	BB	SO	RAT	ERA	ERA+	OAV	OOB	BH	AVG	PB	PR	PR+	PD	TPI
1953	Pit-N	0	0	—	2	0	0	0	0	4	5	5	1	0	2	4	15.8	11.25	40	.294	.368	0	—	0	-3	-3	-0	-0.1
Total	4	4	13	.235	79	11	2	0	3	204^2	210	122	21	1	84	107	13.0	5.14	79	.264	.335	4	.091	-3	-30	-23	-3	-2.2
● **ALEX MAIN**	Main, Miles Grant b: 5/13/1884, Montrose, Mich. d: 12/29/65, Royal Oak, Mich. BL/TR, 6'5", 195 lbs. Deb: 4/18/14																											
1914	Det-A	6	6	.500	32	12	5	1	3	138^1	131	51	2	3	59	55	12.6	2.67	105	.259	.340	4	.100	-2	1	2	4	0.4
1915	KC-F	13	14	.481	35	28	18	2	3	230	181	88	4	5	75	91	10.2	2.54	103	.222	.291	15	.197	-0	5	2	3	0.6
1918	Phi-N	2	2	.500	8	4	1	1	0	35	30	20	1	5	16	14	13.1	4.63	65	.240	.349	1	.091	-1	-7	-6	0	-0.7
Total	3	21	22	.488	75	44	24	4	6	403^1	342	159	7	13	150	160	11.3	2.77	98	.236	.313	20	.157	-3	-1	-2	7	0.3
● **JIM MAINS**	Mains, James Royal b: 6/12/22, Bridgton, Maine d: 3/17/69, Bridgton, Maine BR/TR, 6'2", 190 lbs. Deb: 8/22/43																											
1943	Phi-A	0	1	.000	1	1	1	0	0	8	9	5	0	0	3	4	13.5	5.63	60	.281	.343	0	.000	0	-2	-2	-0	-0.2
● **WILLARD MAINS**	Mains, Willard Eben "Grasshopper" b: 7/7/1868, N.Windham, Maine d: 5/23/23, Bridgton, Maine TR, 6'2", 190 lbs. Deb: 8/3/1888																											
1888	Chi-N	1	1	.500	2	2	1	0	0	11	8	10	0	1	6	5	12.3	4.91	62	.211	.333	1	.143	-0	-3	-2	-0	-0.3
1891	Cin-a	12	12	.500	30	23	19	0	0	204	196	127	3	12	107	76	13.9	2.69	153	.244	.342	22	.244	1	23	29	3	3.2
	Mil-a	0	2	.000	2	2	1	0	0	10	14	19	1	0	10	2	21.6	10.80	41	.318	.444	3	.600	1	-8	-6	0	-0.7
	Yr	12	14	.462	32	25	20	0	0	214	210	146	4	12	117	78	14.3	3.07	134	.248	.347	25	.263	2	15	23	3	2.5
1896	Bos-N	3	2	.600	8	5	3	0	1	42^2	43	35	1	2	31	13	16.0	5.48	83	.261	.384	6	.273	-0	-5	-4	-0	-0.4
Total	3	16	17	.485	42	32	24	0	1	267^2	261	191	5	15	154	96	14.5	3.53	117	.249	.353	32	.258	2	7	17	3	1.8
● **OSWALDO MAIRENA**	Mairena, Oswaldo Antonio b: 7/30/75, Chinandega, Nicaragua BL/TL, 5'11", 165 lbs. Deb: 9/5/2000																											
2000	Chi-N	0	0	—	2	0	0	0	0	2	7	4	1	0	2	0	40.5	18.00	25	.583	.643	0	—	0	-3	-3	-0	-0.1
● **FRANK MAKOSKY**	Makosky, Frank b: 1/20/10, Boonton, N.J. d: 1/10/87, Stroudsburg, Pa. BR/TR, 6'1", 185 lbs. Deb: 4/30/37																											
1937	NY-A	5	2	.714	26	1	1	0	3	58	64	42	6	0	24	27	13.7	4.97	90	.277	.345	5	.313	1	-2	-3	2	-0.1
● **TOM MAKOWSKI**	Makowski, Thomas Anthony b: 12/22/50, Buffalo, N.Y. BR/TL, 5'11", 185 lbs. Deb: 5/1/75																											
1975	Det-A	0	0	—	3	0	0	0	0	9^1	10	11	2	0	9	3	18.3	4.82	84	.278	.422	0	—	0	-1	-1	0	0.0
● **JOHN MALARKEY**	Malarkey, John S. "Liz" b: 5/4/1872, Springfield, Ohio d: 10/29/49, Cincinnati, Ohio TR, 5'11", 155 lbs. Deb: 9/21/1894																											
1894	Was-N	2	1	.667	3	3	3	0	0	26	42	22	1	0	5	3	16.3	4.15	127	.359	.385	1	.071	-2	3	3	-1	0.0
1895	Was-N	0	8	.000	22	8	5	0	2	100^2	135	113	3	8	60	32	18.1	5.99	80	.316	.410	5	.135	-4	-14	-13	-1	-1.2
1896	Was-N	0	1	.000	1	1	0	0	0	7	9	7	1	0	3	0	15.4	1.29	343	.310	.375	1	.500	1	2	2	0	0.4
1899	Chi-N	0	1	.000	1	1	1	0	0	9	19	13	0	1	5	7	25.0	13.00	29	.422	.490	1	.200	0	-9	-10	0	-0.6
1902	Bos-N	8	10	.444	21	19	17	1	1	170^1	158	82	0	0	58	39	11.4	2.59	109	.246	.309	13	.210	2	4	4	2	0.9
1903	Bos-N	11	16	.407	32	27	25	2	0	253	266	150	5	11	96	98	13.3	3.09	104	.272	.344	14	.161	1	5	3	2	0.6
Total	6	21	37	.362	80	59	51	3	3	566	629	387	10	20	227	179	13.9	3.64	96	.281	.353	35	.169	-2	-8	-9	2	0.1
● **BILL MALARKEY**	Malarkey, William John b: 11/26/1878, Port Byron, Ill. d: 12/12/56, Phoenix, Ariz. BR/TR, 5'10", 185 lbs. Deb: 4/16/08																											
1908	NY-N	0	2	.000	15	0	0	0	2	35	31	16	1	1	10	12	10.8	2.57	94	.242	.302	0	.000	-1	-1	-1	-0	-0.2
● **CARLOS MALDONADO**	Maldonado, Carlos Cesar (Delgado) b: 10/18/66, Chepo, Panama BB/TR, 6'2", 210 lbs. Deb: 9/16/90																											
1990	KC-A	0	0	—	4	0	0	0	0	6	9	6	0	0	4	9	19.5	9.00	43	.346	.433	0	—	0	-3	-4	-0	-0.2
1991	KC-A	0	0	—	5	0	0	0	0	7^2	11	9	0	0	9	1	23.5	8.22	50	.333	.476	0	—	0	-4	-3	-0	-0.2
1993	Mil-A	2	2	.500	29	0	0	0	1	37^1	40	20	2	0	17	18	13.7	4.58	93	.282	.358	0	—	0	-1	-1	-0	-0.1
Total	3	2	2	.500	38	0	0	0	1	51	60	35	2	0	30	28	15.9	5.65	74	.299	.390	0	—	0	-8	-8	-1	-0.5
● **CY MALIS**	Malis, Cyrus Sol b: 2/26/07, Philadelphia, Pa. d: 1/12/71, N.Hollywood, Cal. BR/TR, 5'11", 175 lbs. Deb: 8/17/34																											
1934	Phi-N	0	0	—	1	0	0	0	0	3^2	4	2	0	0	2	1	14.7	4.91	96	.267	.353	0	—	0	-0	-0	-0	0.0
● **MAL MALLETTE**	Mallette, Malcolm Francis b: 1/30/22, Syracuse, N.Y. BL/TL, 6'2", 200 lbs. Deb: 9/25/50																											
1950	Bro-N	0	0	—	2	0	0	0	0	1^1	2	0	0	0	1	2	20.3	0.00	—	.333	.429	0	—	0	1	1	0	0.0
● **ROB MALLICOAT**	Mallicoat, Robbin Dale b: 11/16/64, St.Helens, Ore. BL/TL, 6'3", 180 lbs. Deb: 9/11/87																											
1987	Hou-N	0	0	—	4	1	0	0	0	6^2	8	5	0	0	6	4	18.9	6.75	58	.320	.452	0	—	0	-2	-2	0	-0.1
1991	Hou-N	0	2	.000	24	0	0	0	1	23^1	22	10	2	2	13	18	14.3	3.86	91	.259	.370	0	.000	-0	-0	-1	-1	-0.2
1992	Hou-N	0	0	—	23	0	0	0	0	23^2	26	19	2	5	19	20	19.0	7.23	47	.283	.431	0	.000	-0	-10	-11	-0	-0.6
Total	3	0	2	.000	51	1	0	0	1	53^2	56	34	4	7	38	42	16.9	5.70	61	.277	.409	0	.000	-0	-12	-14	-1	-0.9
● **ALEX MALLOY**	Malloy, Archibald Alexander "Lick" b: 10/31/1886, Laurinburg, N.C. d: 3/1/61, Ferris, Tex. BR/TR, 6'2", 180 lbs. Deb: 9/10/10																											
1910	StL-A	0	6	.000	7	6	4	0	0	52^2	47	26	0	2	17	27	11.3	2.56	97	.261	.332	1	.063	-1	-0	-1	0	-0.2
● **HERM MALLOY**	Malloy, Herman "Tug" b: 6/1/1885, Massillon, Ohio d: 5/9/42, Louisville, Ohio BR/TR, 6', Deb: 10/6/07																											
1907	Det-A	0	1	.000	1	1	1	0	0	8	13	10	1	0	5	6	20.3	5.63	46	.371	.450	1	.250	0	-3	-3	-0	-0.3
1908	Det-A	0	2	.000	3	2	2	0	0	17	20	11	1	2	4	8	13.8	3.71	65	.278	.333	3	.333	1	-2	-2	1	-0.1
Total	2	0	3	.000	4	3	3	0	0	25	33	21	2	2	9	14	15.8	4.32	57	.308	.373	4	.308	1	-5	-5	1	-0.4
● **BOB MALLOY**	Malloy, Robert Paul b: 5/28/18, Canonsburg, Pa. BR/TR, 5'11", 185 lbs. Deb: 5/4/43																											
1943	Cin-N	0	0	—	6	0	0	0	0	10	14	8	1	0	8	4	19.8	6.30	53	.778	.846	2	.667	1	-3	-3	-0	-0.1
1944	Cin-N	1	1	.500	9	0	0	0	0	23^1	22	10	0	0	11	4	12.7	3.09	113	.265	.351	0	.000	-1	1	1	0	0.0
1946	Cin-N	2	5	.286	27	3	1	0	2	72	71	29	2	2	26	24	12.4	2.75	122	.265	.334	5	.278	1	5	5	1	0.5
1947	Cin-N	0	0	—	1	0	0	0	0	1	3	2	1	0	0	1	27.0	18.00	23	.600	.600	0	—	0	-2	-2	0	-0.1
1949	StL-A	1	1	.500	5	0	0	0	0	9^2	6	3	0	0	7	2	12.1	2.79	162	.200	.351	0	.000	-0	2	2	0	0.3
Total	5	4	7	.364	48	3	1	0	2	116	116	52	4	2	52	35	13.2	3.26	106	.287	.371	7	.226	1	3	3	-1	0.6
● **BOB MALLOY**	Malloy, Robert William b: 11/24/64, Arlington, Va. BR/TR, 6'5", 200 lbs. Deb: 5/26/87																											
1987	Tex-A	0	0	—	2	2	0	0	0	11	13	11	6	0	3	8	13.1	6.55	69	.271	.314	0	—	0	-3	-3	-0	-0.1
1990	Mon-N	0	0	—	1	0	0	0	0	2	1	0	0	0	1	1	9.0	0.00	—	.143	.250	0	—	0	1	1	-0	0.0
Total	2	0	0	—	3	2	0	0	0	13	14	11	6	0	4	9	12.5	5.54	79	.255	.305	0	—	0	-2	-2	-0	-0.1
● **CHUCK MALONE**	Malone, Charles Ray b: 7/8/65, Harrisburg, Ark. BR/TR, 6'7", 250 lbs. Deb: 9/6/90																											
1990	Phi-N	1	0	1.000	7	0	0	0	0	7^1	3	4	1	0	11	7	17.2	3.68	104	.130	.412	0	—	0	0	0	-0	0.0
● **MARTIN MALONE**	Malone, Martin Deb: 6/20/1872																											
1872	Eck-n	0	3	.000	3	3	3	0	0	27	85	86	1		0	0	28.3	10.33	33	.445	.445	5	.313	1	-20	-22		-1.3
● **PAT MALONE**	Malone, Perce Leigh b: 9/25/02, Altoona, Pa. d: 5/13/43, Altoona, Pa. BL/TR (BB 1935-37), 6', 200 lbs. Deb: 4/12/28																											
1928	Chi-N	18	13	.581	42	25	16	2	2	250^2	218	99	15	6	99	155	11.6	2.84	136	.236	.314	18	.189	1	32	29	0	3.4
1929	*Chi-N	**22**	10	.688	40	30	19	**5**	2	267	283	120	12	6	102	**166**	13.2	3.57	129	.276	.345	22	.210	2	34	32	-3	3.1
1930	Chi-N	**20**	9	.690	45	35	**22**	1	4	271^2	290	145	14	6	96	142	13.0	3.94	124	.271	.334	26	.248	5	31	29	-2	2.8
1931	Chi-N	16	9	.640	36	30	12	2	0	228^1	229	115	9	4	88	112	12.7	3.90	99	.258	.328	17	.215	2	-1	-1	0	0.0
1932	*Chi-N	15	17	.469	37	32	17	2	0	237	222	111	13	6	78	120	11.6	3.38	111	.244	.308	14	.179	0	13	10	-3	1.0
1933	Chi-N	10	14	.417	31	26	13	2	0	186^1	186	91	10	5	59	72	12.1	3.91	84	.258	.318	10	.159	-2	-12	-14	-1	-1.9
1934	Chi-N	14	7	.667	34	21	8	1	0	191	200	85	14	3	55	111	12.2	3.53	110	.270	.322	11	.172	-2	11	8	-1	0.4
1935	NY-A	3	5	.375	29	2	0	0	3	56^1	53	45	7	1	33	25	13.9	5.43	75	.252	.357	0	.000	-3	-6	-10	-0	-1.5
1936	*NY-A	12	4	.750	35	9	5	0	**9**	134^2	144	60	4	4	60	72	13.9	3.81	122	.273	.352	10	.196	-1	18	14	-2	1.3
1937	NY-A	4	4	.500	28	9	3	0	6	92	109	65	5	4	35	49	14.5	5.48	81	.291	.357	1	.030	-5	-9	-11	-2	-1.5
Total	10	134	92	.593	357	219	115	15	26	1915	1934	936	103	45	705	1024	12.6	3.74	111	.262	.330	129	.188	-2	112	87	-14	7.1
● **CHARLIE MALONEY**	Maloney, Charles Michael b: 5/22/1886, Cambridge, Mass. d: 1/17/67, Arlington, Mass. BR/TR, 5'8", 155 lbs. Deb: 8/10/08																											
1908	Bos-N	0	0	—	1	0	0	0	0	2	3	1	0	0	1	0	18.0	4.50	54	.429	.500	0	—	0	-0	-0	0	0.0
● **JIM MALONEY**	Maloney, James William b: 6/2/40, Fresno, Cal. BL/TR, 6'2", 207 lbs. Deb: 7/27/60																											
1960	Cin-N	2	6	.250	11	10	2	1	0	63^2	61	35	5	2	37	48	14.1	4.66	82	.255	.360	2	.111	-0	-6	-6	-0	-0.7

YEAR	TM/L	W	L	PCT	G	GS	CG	SH	SV	IP	H	R	HR	HB	BB	SO	RAT	ERA	ERA+	OAV	OOB	BH	AVG	PB	PR	PR+	PD	TPI
1961	*Cin-N	6	7	.462	27	11	1	0	2	94^2	86	54	16	1	59	57	13.9	4.37	93	.242	.352	11	.379	4	-4	-3	-1	-0.1
1962	Cin-N	9	7	.563	22	17	3	0	1	115^1	90	52	11	2	66	105	12.3	3.51	115	.214	.323	8	.186	0	6	6	-1	0.7
1963	Cin-N	23	7	.767	33	33	13	6	0	250^1	183	84	17	6	88	265	10.0	2.77	121	.202	.276	15	.169	1	14	16	-2	1.8
1964	Cin-N	15	10	.600	31	31	11	2	0	216	175	72	16	1	83	214	10.8	2.71	133	.222	.297	11	.151	1	20	21	-2	2.4
1965	Cin-N★	20	9	.690	33	33	14	5	0	255^1	189	77	13	5	110	244	10.7	2.54	148	.206	.295	20	.225	7	28	32	-1	4.4
1966	Cin-N	16	8	.667	32	32	10	**5**	0	224^2	174	75	18	10	90	216	11.0	2.80	139	.214	.300	18	.222	3	20	25	-0	3.0
1967	Cin-N	15	11	.577	30	29	6	3	0	196^1	181	76	8	3	72	153	11.7	3.25	115	.247	.317	11	.159	-0	3	10	-1	1.2
1968	Cin-N	16	10	.615	33	32	8	5	0	207	183	100	17	2	80	181	11.5	3.61	88	.239	.313	18	.243	6	-14	-10	-2	-0.8
1969	Cin-N	12	5	.706	30	27	6	3	0	178^2	135	64	11	1	86	102	11.2	2.77	136	.208	.302	11	.200	6	16	19	-1	2.3
1970	Cin-N	0	1	.000	7	3	0	0	1	16^2	26	22	3	2	15	7	23.2	11.34	36	.366	.489	0	.000	-0	-13	-14	0	-0.8
1971	Cal-A	0	3	.000	13	4	0	0	0	30^1	35	18	3	1	24	13	17.8	5.04	64	.294	.417	1	.200	0	-5	-6	-0	-0.6
Total	12	134	84	.615	302	262	74	30	4	1849	1518	729	138	36	810	1605	11.5	3.19	115	.224	.310	126	.201	26	64	94	-10	12.8
● **SEAN MALONEY**	Maloney, Sean Patrick b: 5/25/71, South Kingstown, R.I. BR/TR, 6'7", 210 lbs. Deb: 4/28/97																											
1997	Mil-A	0	0	—	3	0	0	0	0	7	7	4	1	2	2	5	14.1	5.14	90	.304	.407	0	—	0	-0	-0	-0	0.0
1998	LA-N	0	1	.000	11	0	0	0	0	12^2	13	7	2	2	5	11	14.2	4.97	80	.265	.357	0	.000	-0	-1	-2	0	-0.1
Total	2	0	1	.000	14	0	0	0	0	19^2	20	11	3	4	7	16	14.2	5.03	83	.278	.373	0	.000	-0	-1	-2	0	-0.1
● **PAUL MALOY**	Maloy, Paul Augustus "Biff" b: 6/4/1892, Bascom, Ohio d: 3/18/76, Sandusky, Ohio BR/TR, 5'11", 185 lbs. Deb: 7/11/13																											
1913	Bos-A	0	0	—	2	0	0	0	0	2	2	2	0	2	1	0	22.5	9.00	33	.286	.500	0	—	0	-1	-1	-0	-0.1
● **GORDON MALTZBERGER**	Maltzberger, Gordon Ralph "Maltzy" b: 9/4/12, Utopia, Tex. d: 12/11/74, Rialto, Cal. BR/TR, 6', 170 lbs. Deb: 4/27/43 C																											
1943	Chi-A	7	4	.636	37	0	0	0	**14**	98^2	86	29	8	2	24	48	10.2	2.46	136	.236	.287	3	.120	0	9	9	0	1.4
1944	Chi-A	10	5	.667	46	0	0	0	**12**	91^1	81	31	2	1	19	49	10.0	2.96	116	.235	.277	3	.136	-1	5	5	-1	0.8
1946	Chi-A	2	0	1.000	19	0	0	0	2	39^2	30	7	3	1	6	17	8.4	1.59	215	.205	.242	0	.000	-0	8	8	-1	0.4
1947	Chi-A	1	4	.200	33	0	0	0	5	63^2	61	26	4	1	25	22	12.3	3.39	108	.257	.331	1	.143	1	2	2	1	0.3
Total	4	20	13	.606	135	0	0	0	33	293^1	258	93	17	5	74	136	10.3	2.70	128	.236	.288	7	.117	0	25	24	0	2.9
● **AL MAMAUX**	Mamaux, Albert Leon b: 5/30/1894, Pittsburgh, Pa. d: 1/2/63, Santa Monica, Cal. BR/TR, 6'0.5", 168 lbs. Deb: 9/23/13																											
1913	Pit-N	0	0	—	1	0	0	0	0	3	2	1	0	0	2	2	12.0	3.00	101	.167	.286	0	.000	-0	0	0	0	0.0
1914	Pit-N	5	2	.714	13	6	4	2	0	63	41	19	1	2	24	30	9.6	1.71	155	.186	.272	5	.250	1	8	7	1	1.0
1915	Pit-N	21	8	.724	38	30	17	8	0	251^2	182	70	3	9	96	152	10.3	2.04	134	.208	.293	15	.163	-2	20	20	-3	1.6
1916	Pit-N	21	15	.583	45	37	26	1	2	310	264	123	3	9	136	163	11.9	2.53	106	.239	.327	21	.191	1	3	5	0	0.8
1917	Pit-N	2	11	.154	16	13	5	0	0	85^2	92	59	1	3	50	22	15.2	5.25	54	.278	.378	7	.226	0	-24	-22	-1	-3.1
1918	Bro-N	0	1	.000	2	1	0	0	0	8	14	6	0	0	2	2	18.0	6.75	41	.438	.471	0	.000	-0	-4	-3	1	-0.4
1919	Bro-N	10	12	.455	30	22	16	2	0	199^1	174	89	2	4	66	80	11.0	2.66	112	.245	.312	11	.175	0	6	7	-1	0.7
1920	*Bro-N	12	8	.600	41	17	9	2	4	190^2	172	70	2	4	63	101	11.3	2.69	119	.255	.322	10	.167	-0	9	11	-1	1.0
1921	Bro-N	3	3	.500	12	1	0	0	1	43	36	17	1	1	13	21	10.5	3.14	124	.240	.305	2	.182	-0	3	3	1	0.5
1922	Bro-N	1	4	.200	37	7	1	0	3	87^2	97	46	7	2	33	35	13.6	3.70	110	.290	.358	4	.235	3	4	4	0	0.5
1923	Bro-N	0	2	.000	5	1	0	0	0	13	20	13	0	0	6	5	18.0	8.31	47	.385	.448	1	.500	0	-6	-7	-0	-0.8
1924	NY-A	1	1	.500	14	2	0	0	0	38	44	28	2	1	20	12	15.4	5.68	73	.308	.396	1	.077	-1	-6	-7	-1	-0.5
Total	12	76	67	.531	254	137	78	15	10	1293	1138	541	22	35	511	625	11.7	2.90	104	.245	.325	77	.182	2	13	17	-3	1.3
● **HAL MANDERS**	Manders, Harold Carl b: 6/14/17, Waukee, Iowa BR/TR, 6', 187 lbs. Deb: 8/12/41																											
1941	Det-A	1	0	1.000	8	0	0	0	0	15^1	13	5	0	1	8	7	12.9	2.35	194	.236	.344	0	.000	-1	3	3	-0	0.1
1942	Det-A	2	0	1.000	18	0	0	0	0	33	39	19	4	1	15	14	15.0	4.09	97	.307	.385	1	.250	0	-2	-0	0	0.0
1946	Det-A	0	0	—	2	0	0	0	0	6	8	7	1	1	2	3	16.5	10.50	35	.364	.440	1	.500	-0	-5	-4	-0	-0.2
	Chi-N	0	1	.000	2	1	0	0	0	6	11	6	1	1	3	4	22.5	9.00	37	.423	.500	0	.000	-0	-4	-4	-0	-0.6
Total	3	3	1	.750	30	1	0	0	0	60^1	71	37	6	4	28	28	15.4	4.77	84	.309	.393	2	.167	-0	-7	-5	-1	-0.7
● **LEO MANGUM**	Mangum, Leo Allan "Blackie" b: 5/24/1896, Durham, N.C. d: 7/9/74, Lima, Ohio BR/TR, 6'1", 187 lbs. Deb: 7/11/24																											
1924	Chi-A	1	4	.200	13	7	1	0	0	47	69	43	3	1	25	12	18.2	7.09	58	.359	.436	1	.071	-1	-15	-16	0	-1.4
1925	Chi-A	1	0	1.000	7	0	0	0	0	15	25	15	0	0	6	6	18.6	7.80	53	.373	.425	2	.500	1	-6	-6	-0	-0.3
1928	NY-N	0	0	—	1	1	0	0	0	3	6	5	0	0	5	1	33.0	15.00	26	.500	.647	1	1.000	0	-4	-4	1	-0.1
1932	Bos-N	0	0	—	7	0	0	0	0	10^1	17	8	1	0	0	3	14.8	5.23	72	.333	.333	0	.000	-0	-2	-2	1	0.0
1933	Bos-N	4	3	.571	25	5	2	1	0	84	93	33	2	0	11	28	11.1	3.32	92	.280	.303	2	.091	-2	0	-3	2	-0.2
1934	Bos-N	5	3	.625	29	3	1	0	1	94^1	127	67	9	0	23	28	14.3	5.72	67	.315	.352	9	.281	2	-17	-21	1	-1.3
1935	Bos-N	0	0	—	3	0	0	0	0	4^2	6	3	0	0	2	0	15.4	3.86	98	.300	.364	0	—	0	0	-0	-0	0.0
Total	7	11	10	.524	85	16	4	1	1	258^1	343	174	15	1	72	78	14.5	5.37	68	.318	.362	15	.200	0	-43	-53	4	-3.3
● **JIM MANN**	Mann, James Joseph b: 11/17/74, Brockton, Mass. BR/TR, 6'3", 225 lbs. Deb: 5/29/2000																											
2000	NY-N	0	0	—	2	0	0	0	0	2^2	6	3	1	0	1	0	23.6	10.13	44	.429	.467	0	—	0	-2	-2	-0	-0.1
● **ERNIE MANNING**	Manning, Ernest Devon "Ed" b: 10/9/1890, Florala, Ala. d: 4/28/73, Pensacola, Fla. BL/TR, 6', 175 lbs. Deb: 5/3/14																											
1914	StL-A	0	0	—	4	0	0	0	0	10	11	6	0	0	3	3	12.6	3.60	75	.297	.350	0	.000	-0	-1	-1	0	-0.1
● **JIM MANNING**	Manning, James Benjamin b: 7/21/43, L'Anse, Mich. BR/TR, 6'1", 185 lbs. Deb: 4/15/62																											
1962	Min-A	0	0	—	5	1	0	0	0	7	14	10	0	1	1	3	20.6	5.14	79	.389	.421	0	.000	-0	-1	-1	0	0.0
● **JACK MANNING**	Manning, John E. b: 12/20/1853, Braintree, Mass. d: 8/15/29, Boston, Mass. BR/TR, 5'8.5", 158 lbs. Deb: 4/23/1873 M♦																											
1874	Bal-n	4	16	.200	22	20	17	0	0	176^2	222	168	2		12	12	11.9	2.09	107	.266	.277	61	.351	7	2	3		0.8
1875	Bos-n	16	2	.889	27	18	8	1	6	144	152	86	1		14	34	10.4	2.38	90	.247	.263	94	.270	4	-2	-4		-0.3
1876	Bos-N	18	5	.783	34	20	13	0	**5**	197^1	213	139	1		32	24	11.2	2.14	105	.243	.279	76	.258	3	4	3	0	0.4
1877	Cin-N	0	4	.000	10	4	2	0	1	44	83	65	1		7	6	18.4	6.95	38	.379	.398	80	.317	4	-20	-22	0	-1.4
1878	Bos-N	1	0	1.000	3	1	1	0	0	11^1	24	19	1		5	2	23.0	14.29	17	.393	.439	63	.254	0	-15	-15	0	-0.9
Total	2 n	20	18	.526	49	38	25	1	6	320^2	374	254	3		26	46	11.2	2.22	99	.258	.271	199	.290	11	-0	-1		0.5
Total	3	19	9	.679	47	25	16	0	6	252^2	320	223	3		44	32	13.0	3.53	66	.276	.311	725	.256	7	-32	-34	1	-1.9
● **RUBE MANNING**	Manning, Walter S. b: 4/29/1883, Chambersburg, Pa. d: 4/23/30, Williamsport, Pa. BR/TR, 6', 180 lbs. Deb: 9/25/07																											
1907	NY-A	0	1	.000	1	1	1	0	0	9	8	3	0	1	3	3	12.0	3.00	93	.242	.324	0	.000	-0	-0	-0	-0	-0.1
1908	NY-A	13	16	.448	41	26	19	2	1	245	228	114	4	18	86	113	12.2	2.94	84	.256	.334	17	.187	0	-15	-12	-1	-1.6
1909	NY-A	7	11	.389	26	21	11	2	1	173	167	76	2	9	48	71	11.7	3.17	80	.265	.326	11	.183	-0	-13	-12	-1	-1.3
1910	NY-A	2	4	.333	16	9	4	0	0	75	80	43	4	4	25	25	13.1	3.72	71	.283	.349	5	.192	0	-10	-8	-1	-0.7
Total	4	22	32	.407	84	57	35	4	2	502	483	236	10	32	162	212	12.1	3.14	81	.263	.333	33	.183	-0	-39	-33	-3	-3.7
● **RAMON MANON**	Manon, Ramon (Reyes) b: 1/20/68, Santo Domingo, D.R. BR/TR, 6', 150 lbs. Deb: 4/19/90																											
1990	Tex-A	0	0	—	1	0	0	0	0	2	3	3	0	0	3	0	27.0	13.50	29	.333	.500	0	—	0	-2	-2	0	-0.1
● **TOM MANSELL**	Mansell, Thomas E. "Brick" b: 1/1/1855, Auburn, N.Y. d: 10/6/34, Auburn, N.Y. BL/TR, 5'8", 160 lbs. Deb: 5/1/1879 F♦																											
1883	Det-N	0	0	—	1	0	0	0	0	6^2	21	18	2		5	3	35.1	18.90	16	.553	.605	29	.221	0	-12	-12	-0	-0.4
● **LOU MANSKE**	Manske, Louis Hugo b: 7/4/1884, Milwaukee, Wis. d: 4/27/63, Milwaukee, Wis. BL/TL, 6', Deb: 8/31/06																											
1906	Pit-N	0	0	—	2	1	0	0	0	8	12	6	0	0	5	6	19.1	5.63	48	.387	.472	0	.000	-1	-3	-3	-0	-0.2
● **MATT MANTEI**	Mantei, Matthew Bruce b: 7/7/73, Tampa, Fla. BR/TR, 6'1", 180 lbs. Deb: 6/18/95																											
1995	Fla-N	0	1	.000	12	0	0	0	0	13^1	12	8	1	0	13	15	16.9	4.73	89	.245	.403	0	—	0	-1	-1	0	0.0
1996	Fla-N	1	0	1.000	14	0	0	0	0	18^1	13	13	2	1	21	25	17.2	6.38	64	.197	.398	0	.000	-0	-4	-5	1	-0.2
1998	Fla-N	3	4	.429	42	0	0	0	9	54^2	38	19	1	7	23	63	11.2	2.96	137	.203	.313	1	.333	0	8	7	-0	1.0
1999	Fla-N	1	2	.333	35	0	0	0	10	36^1	24	11	4	2	25	50	12.6	2.72	160	.186	.327	0	.000	-0	7	7	-0	0.8
	*Ari-N	0	1	.000	30	0	0	0	22	29	20	10	1	3	19	49	13.0	2.79	164	.192	.333	0	—	0	6	6	0	1.0
	Yr	1	3	.250	65	0	0	0	32	65^1	44	21	5	5	44	99	12.8	2.76	162	.189	.330	0	.000	-0	13	13	0	1.8
2000	Ari-N	1	1	.500	47	0	0	0	17	45^1	31	24	4	2	35	53	13.5	4.57	101	.193	.343	0	—	0	0	0	-0	0.0
Total	5	6	9	.400	180	0	0	0	58	197	138	85	13	15	136	255	13.2	3.70	117	.198	.341	1	.200	0	16	14	1	2.6

● BARRY MANUEL Manuel, Barry Paul b: 8/12/65, Mamou, La. BR/TR, 5'11", 180 lbs. Deb: 9/6/91

YEAR	TM/L	W	L	PCT	G	GS	CG	SH	SV	IP	H	R	HR	HB	BB	SO	RAT	ERA	ERA+	OAV	OOB	BH	AVG	PB	PR	PR+	PD	TPI
1991	Tex-A	1	0	1.000	8	0	0	0	0	16	7	2	0	0	6	5	7.3	1.13	359	.143	.236	0	—	0	5	5	1	0.4
1992	Tex-A	1	0	1.000	3	0	0	0	0	5^2	6	3	2	1	1	9	12.7	4.76	80	.261	.320	0	—	0	-1	-1	-0	-0.1
1996	Mon-N	4	1	.800	53	0	0	0	0	86	70	34	10	7	26	62	10.8	3.24	133	.219	.293	0	.000	-0	9	10	-1	0.4
1997	NY-N	0	1	.000	19	0	0	0	0	25^2	35	18	6	1	13	21	17.2	5.26	77	.324	.402	0	.000	-0	-3	-4	-1	-0.3
1998	Ari-N	1	0	1.000	13	0	0	0	0	15^2	17	14	5	1	14	12	18.4	7.47	56	.266	.405	0	—	0	-6	-6	-0	-0.4
Total	5	7	2	.778	96	0	0	0	0	149	135	71	23	10	60	109	12.4	3.87	109	.240	.324	0	.000	-1	6	6	-1	0.0

● MOXIE MANUEL Manuel, Mark Garfield b: 10/16/1881, Metropolis, Ill. d: 4/26/24, Memphis, Tenn. BR/TR, 5'11", 170 lbs. Deb: 9/25/05

YEAR	TM/L	W	L	PCT	G	GS	CG	SH	SV	IP	H	R	HR	HB	BB	SO	RAT	ERA	ERA+	OAV	OOB	BH	AVG	PB	PR	PR+	PD	TPI
1905	Was-A	0	0	—	3	1	1	0	0	10	9	9	0	1	3	3	11.7	5.40	49	.243	.317	1	.250	0	-3	-3	0	-0.1
1908	Chi-A	3	4	.429	18	6	3	0	1	60^1	52	25	0	2	25	25	11.8	3.28	71	.243	.328	1	.063	-1	-6	-7	0	-0.9
Total	2	3	4	.429	21	7	4	0	1	70^1	61	34	0	3	28	28	11.8	3.58	66	.243	.326	2	.100	-1	-9	-10	0	-1.0

● DICK MANVILLE Manville, Richard Wesley b: 12/25/26, Des Moines, Iowa BR/TR, 6'4", 192 lbs. Deb: 4/30/50

YEAR	TM/L	W	L	PCT	G	GS	CG	SH	SV	IP	H	R	HR	HB	BB	SO	RAT	ERA	ERA+	OAV	OOB	BH	AVG	PB	PR	PR+	PD	TPI
1950	Bos-N	0	0	—	1	0	0	0	0	2	0	0	0	0	3	2	13.5	0.00	—	.000	.300	0	—	0	1	1	-0	0.0
1952	Chi-N	0	0	—	11	0	0	0	0	17	25	17	2	0	12	6	19.6	7.94	48	.362	.457	1	.500	0	-8	-7	0	-0.3
Total	2	0	0	—	12	0	0	0	0	19	25	17	2	0	15	8	18.9	7.11	54	.329	.440	1	.500	0	-7	-7	0	-0.3

● JOSIAS MANZANILLO Manzanillo, Josias (Adams) b: 10/16/67, San Pedro De Macoris, D.R. BR/TR, 6', 190 lbs. Deb: 10/5/91 F

YEAR	TM/L	W	L	PCT	G	GS	CG	SH	SV	IP	H	R	HR	HB	BB	SO	RAT	ERA	ERA+	OAV	OOB	BH	AVG	PB	PR	PR+	PD	TPI
1991	Bos-A	0	0	—	1	0	0	0	0	1	2	2	0	0	3	1	45.0	18.00	24	.400	.625	0	—	0	-2	-1	0	-0.1
1993	Mil-A	1	1	.500	10	1	0	0	1	17	22	20	1	2	10	10	18.0	9.53	45	.314	.415	0	—	0	-10	-10	1	-1.0
	NY-N	0	0	—	6	0	0	0	0	12	8	7	1	0	9	11	12.8	3.00	134	.186	.327	0	.000	-0	1	1	-0	0.0
1994	NY-N	3	2	.600	37	0	0	0	2	47^1	34	15	4	3	13	48	9.5	2.66	157	.200	.269	0	.000	-0	8	8	-0	0.8
1995	NY-N	1	2	.333	12	0	0	0	0	16	18	15	3	0	6	14	13.5	7.88	51	.273	.333	0	—	0	-7	-7	-0	-1.1
	NY-A	0	0	—	11	0	0	0	0	17^1	19	4	1	2	9	11	15.6	2.08	222	.279	.380	0	—	0	5	5	0	0.3
1997	Sea-A	0	1	.000	16	0	0	0	0	18^1	19	13	3	0	17	18	17.7	5.40	83	.275	.419	0	.000	-0	-2	-2	-0	-0.1
1999	NY-N	0	0	—	12	0	0	0	0	18^2	19	12	5	2	4	25	12.1	5.79	76	.264	.321	1	1.000	0	-3	-3	0	-0.1
2000	Pit-N	2	2	.500	43	0	0	0	0	58^2	50	23	6	0	32	39	12.6	3.38	136	.240	.342	0	.000	-0	8	8	-1	0.4
Total	7	7	8	.467	148	1	0	0	3	206^1	191	111	24	9	103	177	13.2	4.41	99	.248	.343	1	.100	-1	1	-1	-1	-0.9

● RAVELO MANZANILLO Manzanillo, Ravelo (Adams) b: 10/17/63, San Pedro De Macoris, D.R. BL/TL, 6', 210 lbs. Deb: 9/25/88 F

YEAR	TM/L	W	L	PCT	G	GS	CG	SH	SV	IP	H	R	HR	HB	BB	SO	RAT	ERA	ERA+	OAV	OOB	BH	AVG	PB	PR	PR+	PD	TPI
1988	Chi-A	0	1	.000	2	2	0	0	0	9^1	7	6	1	1	12	10	19.3	5.79	69	.212	.435	0	—	0	-2	-2	0	-0.2
1994	Pit-N	4	2	.667	46	0	0	0	1	50	45	30	4	3	42	39	16.2	4.14	104	.245	.393	2	.667	1	0	1	0	0.2
1995	Pit-N	0	0	—	5	0	0	0	0	3^2	3	3	0	1	2	1	14.7	4.91	88	.231	.375	0	.000	-0	-0	-0	0	0.0
Total	3	4	3	.571	53	2	0	0	1	63	55	39	5	5	56	50	16.6	4.43	96	.239	.399	2	.500	1	-2	-1	0	0.0

● ROLLA MAPEL Mapel, Rolla Hamilton "Lefty" b: 3/9/1890, Lees Summit, Mo. d: 4/6/66, San Diego, Cal. BL/TL, 5'11.5", 165 lbs. Deb: 8/31/19

YEAR	TM/L	W	L	PCT	G	GS	CG	SH	SV	IP	H	R	HR	HB	BB	SO	RAT	ERA	ERA+	OAV	OOB	BH	AVG	PB	PR	PR+	PD	TPI
1919	StL-A	0	3	.000	4	3	2	0	0	20	17	12	0	3	17	2	16.6	4.50	74	.262	.435	1	.167	-0	-3	-3	1	-0.3

● PAUL MARAK Marak, Paul Patrick b: 8/2/65, Lakenheath, England BR/TR, 6'2", 175 lbs. Deb: 9/1/90

YEAR	TM/L	W	L	PCT	G	GS	CG	SH	SV	IP	H	R	HR	HB	BB	SO	RAT	ERA	ERA+	OAV	OOB	BH	AVG	PB	PR	PR+	PD	TPI
1990	Atl-N	1	2	.333	7	7	1	1	0	39	39	16	2	3	19	15	14.1	3.69	109	.267	.363	1	.091	-0	0	1	1	0.2

● GEORGES MARANDA Maranda, Georges Henri b: 1/15/32, Levis, Que., Can. d: 7/14/2000, Levis, Que., Can. BR/TR, 6'2", 195 lbs. Deb: 4/26/60

YEAR	TM/L	W	L	PCT	G	GS	CG	SH	SV	IP	H	R	HR	HB	BB	SO	RAT	ERA	ERA+	OAV	OOB	BH	AVG	PB	PR	PR+	PD	TPI
1960	SF-N	1	4	.200	17	4	0	0	0	50^2	50	32	6	0	30	28	14.2	4.62	75	.254	.352	2	.167	-0	-5	-7	2	-0.5
1962	Min-A	1	3	.250	32	4	0	0	0	72^2	69	43	10	4	35	36	13.4	4.46	92	.252	.345	4	.250	1	-4	-3	1	0.0
Total	2	2	7	.222	49	8	0	0	0	123^1	119	75	16	4	65	64	13.7	4.52	85	.253	.348	6	.214	1	-9	-10	2	-0.5

● FIRPO MARBERRY Marberry, Fredrick b: 11/30/1898, Streetman, Tex. d: 6/30/76, Mexia, Tex. BR/TR, 6'1", 190 lbs. Deb: 8/11/23 U

YEAR	TM/L	W	L	PCT	G	GS	CG	SH	SV	IP	H	R	HR	HB	BB	SO	RAT	ERA	ERA+	OAV	OOB	BH	AVG	PB	PR	PR+	PD	TPI
1923	Was-A	4	0	1.000	11	4	2	0	0	44^2	42	16	1	3	17	18	12.5	2.82	133	.258	.339	2	.143	-1	6	5	-0	0.3
1924	*Was-A	11	12	.478	**50**	14	6	0	**15**	195^1	190	88	3	9	70	68	12.4	3.09	131	.262	.335	8	.136	-4	25	22	-1	2.1
1925	*Was-A	9	5	.643	**55**	0	0	0	**15**	93^1	84	50	4	4	45	53	12.8	3.47	122	.246	.341	5	.263	1	**10**	**8**	1	1.5
1926	Was-A	12	7	.632	**64**	5	3	0	**22**	138	120	55	4	3	66	43	12.3	3.00	129	.243	.336	6	.176	-1	16	14	-1	2.0
1927	Was-A	10	7	.588	56	10	2	0	9	155^1	177	92	4	3	68	74	14.4	4.64	88	.296	.371	5	.122	-3	-9	-10	-1	-1.5
1928	Was-A	13	13	.500	**48**	11	7	1	3	161^1	160	79	4	3	42	76	11.4	3.85	104	.268	.319	5	.109	-4	3	3	-1	-0.1
1929	Was-A	19	12	.613	**49**	26	16	0	**11**	250^1	233	100	6	6	69	121	**11.1**	3.06	139	.252	**.308**	19	.235	2	33	33	-2	**3.8**
1930	Was-A	15	5	.750	33	22	9	2	1	185	190	92	15	0	53	56	11.8	4.09	113	.270	.321	24	.329	5	12	11	-1	1.3
1931	Was-A	16	4	.800	45	25	11	1	7	219	211	92	13	3	63	88	11.4	3.45	124	.252	.307	19	.232	1	23	21	-2	1.7
1932	Was-A	8	4	.667	**54**	15	8	1	**13**	197^2	202	98	13	2	72	66	12.6	4.01	108	.268	.333	11	.167	-2	10	7	1	0.4
1933	Det-A	16	11	.593	37	32	15	1	2	238^1	232	98	13	1	61	84	**11.1**	3.29	131	.254	**.302**	11	.122	-5	26	27	-3	1.9
1934	*Det-A	15	5	.750	38	19	6	1	3	155^2	174	92	12	0	48	64	12.8	4.57	96	.276	.327	12	.218	2	-1	-3	-2	-0.3
1935	Det-A	0	1	.000	5	2	1	0	0	19	22	11	2	0	9	7	14.7	4.26	98	.289	.365	1	.200	0	0	-0	-0	0.0
1936	NY-N	0	0	—	1	0	0	0	0	0^1	1	1	0	0	0	0	27.0	0.00	—	.500	.500	0	.000	-0	0	0	-0	0.0
	Was-A	0	2	.000	5	1	0	0	0	14	11	7	2	1	3	4	9.6	3.86	124	.208	.263	0	.000	-0	2	2	-0	0.1
Total	14	148	88	.627	551	186	86	7	101	2067^1	2049	971	96	38	686	822	12.1	3.63	116	.262	.325	128	.192	-8	156	138	-12	13.2

● WALT MARBET Marbet, Walter William b: 9/13/1890, Plymouth Co., Ia. d: 9/24/56, Hohenwald, Tenn. BR/TR, 6'1", 175 lbs. Deb: 6/17/13

YEAR	TM/L	W	L	PCT	G	GS	CG	SH	SV	IP	H	R	HR	HB	BB	SO	RAT	ERA	ERA+	OAV	OOB	BH	AVG	PB	PR	PR+	PD	TPI
1913	StL-N	0	1	.000	3	1	0	0	0	3^1	9	7	0	0	4	1	35.1	16.20	20	.500	.591	0	—	0	-5	-5	-0	-0.9

● PHIL MARCHILDON Marchildon, Philip Joseph "Babe"
b: 10/25/13, Penetanguishene, Ont., Canada d: 1/10/97, Toronto, Ont., Can. BR/TR, 5'11", 175 lbs. Deb: 9/22/40

YEAR	TM/L	W	L	PCT	G	GS	CG	SH	SV	IP	H	R	HR	HB	BB	SO	RAT	ERA	ERA+	OAV	OOB	BH	AVG	PB	PR	PR+	PD	TPI
1940	Phi-A	0	2	.000	2	2	1	0	0	10	12	9	1	0	8	4	18.0	7.20	62	.286	.400	0	.000	-0	-3	-3	0	-0.5
1941	Phi-A	10	15	.400	30	27	14	1	0	204^1	188	94	15	3	118	74	13.6	3.57	117	.245	.348	11	.167	1	13	14	-3	1.3
1942	Phi-A	17	14	.548	38	31	18	1	1	244	215	126	14	4	140	110	13.2	4.20	90	.235	.339	20	.238	3	-15	-11	-3	-1.3
1945	Phi-A	0	1	.000	3	2	0	0	0	9	5	5	0	0	11	2	16.0	4.00	86	.179	.410	1	.500	1	-1	-1	0	0.0
1946	Phi-A	13	16	.448	36	29	16	1	1	226^2	197	104	14	4	114	95	12.5	3.49	101	.237	.332	5	.067	-6	0	1	-2	-0.6
1947	Phi-A	19	9	.679	35	35	21	2	0	276^2	228	110	15	7	141	128	12.2	3.22	118	.224	.323	15	.153	-2	15	18	-3	1.2
1948	Phi-A	9	15	.375	33	30	12	1	0	226^1	214	133	19	4	131	66	13.9	4.53	95	.251	.353	5	.069	-5	-6	-6	-1	-1.2
1949	Phi-A	0	3	.000	7	6	0	0	0	16	24	23	3	1	19	2	24.8	11.81	35	.358	.506	1	.167	-0	-14	-14	-0	-2.0
1950	Bos-A	0	0	—	1	0	0	0	0	1^1	1	1	0	0	2	0	20.3	6.75	73	.200	.429	0	—	0	-0	-0	-0	0.0
Total	9	68	75	.476	185	162	82	6	2	1214^1	1084	605	81	23	684	481	13.3	3.93	100	.240	.342	58	.143	-10	-10	-1	-11	-3.1

● JOHNNY MARCUM Marcum, John Alfred "Footsie" b: 9/9/09, Campbellsburg, Ky. d: 9/10/84, Louisville, Ky. BL/TR, 5'11", 197 lbs. Deb: 9/7/33 ♦

YEAR	TM/L	W	L	PCT	G	GS	CG	SH	SV	IP	H	R	HR	HB	BB	SO	RAT	ERA	ERA+	OAV	OOB	BH	AVG	PB	PR	PR+	PD	TPI
1933	Phi-A	3	2	.600	5	5	4	2	0	37	28	12	0	0	20	14	11.7	1.95	220	.200	.300	2	.167	0	10	10	0	1.3
1934	Phi-A	14	11	.560	37	31	17	2	0	232	257	131	13	4	88	92	13.5	4.50	97	.280	.346	30	.268	6	-0	-3	-0	0.2
1935	Phi-A	17	12	.586	39	27	19	2	3	242^2	256	125	9	2	83	99	12.6	4.08	111	.268	.328	37	.311	9	10	12	-3	1.9
1936	Bos-A	8	13	.381	31	23	9	1	1	174	194	100	14	0	52	57	12.7	4.81	110	.281	.332	18	.205	1	4	9	0	1.0
1937	Bos-A	13	11	.542	37	23	9	1	3	183^2	230	104	17	2	47	59	13.7	4.85	98	.306	.348	23	.267	5	-5	-2	1	0.3
1938	Bos-A	5	6	.455	15	11	7	0	0	92^1	113	49	11	0	25	25	13.5	4.09	120	.298	.342	5	.135	-1	7	8	-1	0.7
1939	StL-A	2	5	.286	12	6	2	0	0	47^2	66	43	12	1	10	14	14.5	7.74	63	.332	.367	10	.455	3	-17	-14	-0	-1.4
	Chi-A	3	3	.500	19	6	2	0	0	90	125	66	15	0	19	32	14.4	6.00	79	.326	.357	16	.281	2	-14	-12	-1	-0.5
	Yr.	5	8	.385	31	12	4	0	0	137^2	191	109	27	1	29	46	14.4	6.60	72	.328	.361	26	.329	6	-30	-27	-1	-1.9
Total	7	65	63	.508	195	132	69	8	7	1099^1	1269	630	91	9	344	392	13.3	4.66	101	.287	.340	141	.265	25	-4	7	-4	3.5

● LEO MARENTETTE Marentette, Leo John b: 2/18/41, Detroit, Mich. BR/TR, 6'2", 200 lbs. Deb: 9/26/65

YEAR	TM/L	W	L	PCT	G	GS	CG	SH	SV	IP	H	R	HR	HB	BB	SO	RAT	ERA	ERA+	OAV	OOB	BH	AVG	PB	PR	PR+	PD	TPI
1965	Det-A	0	0	—	2	0	0	0	0	3	1	0	0	0	1	3	6.0	0.00	—	.111	.200	0	—	0	1	1	0	0.1
1969	Mon-N	0	0	—	3	0	0	0	0	5^1	9	4	1	0	1	4	16.9	6.75	55	.391	.417	0	.000	-0	-2	-2	0	-0.1
Total	2	0	0	—	5	0	0	0	0	8^1	10	4	1	0	2	7	13.0	4.32	83	.313	.353	0	.000	-0	-1	-1	0	0.0

● JOE MARGONERI Margoneri, Joseph Emanuel b: 1/13/30, Somerset, Pa. BL/TL, 6', 185 lbs. Deb: 4/25/56

YEAR	TM/L	W	L	PCT	G	GS	CG	SH	SV	IP	H	R	HR	HB	BB	SO	RAT	ERA	ERA+	OAV	OOB	BH	AVG	PB	PR	PR+	PD	TPI
1956	NY-N	6	6	.500	23	13	2	0	0	91^2	88	45	12	0	49	49	13.5	3.93	96	.254	.346	3	.103	-1	-2	-1	-0	-0.3
1957	NY-N	1	1	.500	13	2	1	0	0	34^1	44	23	1	1	21	18	17.3	5.24	75	.314	.407	0	.000	-1	-5	-5	-0	-0.4
Total	2	7	7	.500	36	15	3	0	0	126	132	68	13	1	70	67	14.5	4.29	89	.271	.364	3	.081	-2	-7	-6	-1	-0.7

YEAR	TM/L	W	L	PCT	G	GS	CG	SH	SV	IP	H	R	HR	HB	BB	SO	RAT	ERA	ERA+	OAV	OOB	BH	AVG	PB	PR	PR+	PD	TPI
● JUAN MARICHAL	Marichal, Juan Antonio (Sanchez) "Manito" b: 10/20/37, Laguna Verde, D.R. BR/TR, 6′, 185 lbs. Deb: 7/19/60 H																											
1960	SF-N	6	2	.750	11	11	6	1	0	81^1	59	29	5	0	28	58	9.6	2.66	131	.200	.269	4	.129	0	10	8	0	0.7
1961	SF-N	13	10	.565	29	27	9	3	0	185	183	88	24	2	48	124	11.3	3.89	98	.257	.306	7	.119	-2	3	-2	-1	-0.5
1962	*SF-N★	18	11	.621	37	36	18	3	1	262^2	233	112	34	3	90	153	11.2	3.36	113	.234	.300	21	.236	4	17	13	-1	1.7
1963	SF-N☆	**25**	8	.758	41	40	18	5	0	**321**^{1}	259	102	27	2	61	248	9.0	2.41	133	.216	.256	20	.179	3	31	29	-3	3.0
1964	SF-N★	21	8	.724	33	33	**22**	4	0	269	241	89	18	1	52	206	9.8	2.48	144	.236	.273	14	.144	-1	32	32	1	3.4
1965	SF-N★	22	13	.629	39	37	24	**10**	1	295^1	224	78	27	4	46	240	8.3	2.13	**169**	.205	.240	17	.173	1	46	47	-0	**5.9**
1966	SF-N★	25	6	**.806**	37	36	25	4	0	307^1	228	88	32	5	36	222	**7.9**	2.23	165	**.202**	**.230**	28	.250	6	47	48	0	5.7
1967	SF-N★	14	10	.583	26	26	18	2	0	202^1	195	79	20	1	42	166	10.6	2.76	119	.249	.288	14	.177	3	14	12	-2	1.6
1968	SF-N★	**26**	9	.743	38	38	**30**	5	0	**326**	295	106	21	6	46	218	9.6	2.43	121	.238	.269	20	.163	1	20	19	3	2.7
1969	SF-N☆	21	11	.656	37	36	27	**8**	0	299^2	244	90	15	6	54	205	**9.1**	**2.10**	**167**	.222	.263	15	.138	-1	**50**	48	4	5.6
1970	SF-N	12	10	.545	34	33	14	1	0	242^2	269	128	28	1	48	123	11.8	4.12	97	.277	.312	5	.059	-6	-2	-4	2	-0.7
1971	*SF-N★	18	11	.621	37	37	18	4	0	279	244	113	27	3	56	159	9.8	2.94	116	.233	.274	14	.133	0	17	15	3	1.8
1972	SF-N	6	16	.273	25	24	6	0	0	165	176	82	15	3	46	72	12.3	3.71	94	.277	.329	10	.196	1	-5	-4	0	-0.4
1973	SF-N	11	15	.423	34	32	9	2	0	207^1	231	104	22	1	37	87	11.7	3.82	100	.277	.309	13	.188	1	-3	0	4	0.5
1974	Bos-A	5	1	.833	11	9	0	0	0	57^1	61	32	3	2	14	21	12.1	4.87	79	.270	.318	0	—	0	-8	-6	-0	-0.6
1975	LA-N	0	1	.000	2	2	0	0	0	6	11	9	2	0	5	1	24.0	13.50	25	.407	.500	0	.000	-0	-7	-7	0	-0.9
Total	16	243	142	.631	471	457	244	52	2	3507^1	3153	1329	320	40	709	2303	10.0	2.89	122	.237	.278	202	.165	10	262	251	9	29.5
● DAN MARION	Marion, Donald G. "Rube" b: 7/31/1890, Cleveland, Ohio d: 1/18/33, Milwaukee, Wis. BR/TR, 6′1″, 187 lbs. Deb: 4/23/14																											
1914	Bro-F	3	2	.600	17	9	4	0	0	89^1	97	52	1	6	38	41	14.2	3.93	73	.281	.362	7	.194	-2	-10	-11	-1	-0.8
1915	Bro-F	12	9	.571	35	25	15	2	0	208^1	193	92	1	3	64	46	11.2	3.20	85	.248	.308	13	.176	-2	-11	-11	-1	-1.3
Total	2	15	11	.577	52	34	19	2	0	297^2	290	144	2	9	102	87	12.1	3.42	81	.258	.325	20	.182	-3	-21	-22	-2	-2.1
● DUKE MARKELL	Markell, Harry Duquesne (b: Harry Duquesne Makowsky) b: 8/17/23, Paris, France d: 6/14/84, Ft.Lauderdale, Fla. BR/TR, 6′1.5″, 209 lbs. Deb: 9/6/51																											
1951	StL-A	1	1	.500	5	2	1	0	0	21^1	25	16	3	0	20	10	19.0	6.33	69	.298	.433	1	.167	-0	-5	-4	-1	-0.4
● CLIFF MARKLE	Markle, Clifford Monroe b: 5/3/1894, Dravosburg, Pa. d: 5/24/74, Temple City, Cal. BR/TR, 5′9″, 163 lbs. Deb: 9/18/15																											
1915	NY-A	2	0	1.000	3	2	2	0	0	23	15	3	1	0	6	12	8.2	0.39	750	.185	.241	0	.000	0	7	7	-1	0.5
1916	NY-A	4	3	.571	11	7	3	1	0	45^2	41	26	0	4	31	14	15.0	4.53	64	.256	.390	0	.000	-1	-9	-8	-0	-1.4
1921	Cin-N	2	6	.250	10	6	5	0	0	67	75	36	0	0	20	23	12.8	3.76	95	.291	.342	3	.125	-2	0	-1	-1	-0.4
1922	Cin-N	4	5	.444	25	3	2	1	0	75^2	75	41	3	0	33	34	12.8	3.81	105	.268	.345	3	.150	-0	2	2	-0	0.1
1924	NY-A	0	3	.000	7	3	0	0	0	23^1	29	26	5	0	20	7	18.9	8.87	47	.333	.458	0	.000	-1	-12	-12	-1	-1.4
Total	5	12	17	.414	56	21	12	2	0	234^2	235	132	9	4	110	90	13.4	4.10	87	.271	.356	6	.087	-5	-12	-14	-3	-2.6
● DICK MARLOWE	Marlowe, Richard Burton b: 6/27/29, Hickory, N.C. d: 12/30/68, Toledo, Ohio BR/TR, 6′2″, 170 lbs. Deb: 9/19/51																											
1951	Det-A	0	1	.000	2	1	0	0	0	1^2	5	6	0	0	2	1	37.8	32.40	13	.500	.583	0	—	0	-5	-5	-0	-0.8
1952	Det-A	0	2	.000	4	1	0	0	0	11	21	10	1	0	3	3	19.6	7.36	52	.420	.453	0	.000	-0	-5	-4	-0	-0.7
1953	Det-A	6	7	.462	42	11	2	0	0	119^2	152	74	13	2	42	52	14.7	5.26	77	.319	.377	7	.219	-0	-17	-16	1	-1.6
1954	Det-A	5	4	.556	38	2	0	0	2	84	76	45	11	0	40	39	12.4	4.18	88	.244	.330	3	.167	0	-4	-5	1	-0.5
1955	Det-A	1	0	1.000	4	1	1	0	1	15	12	4	1	0	4	9	9.6	1.80	213	.218	.271	0	.000	-0	4	4	-0	0.2
1956	Det-A	1	1	.500	7	1	0	0	0	11	12	8	1	0	9	4	17.2	5.73	72	.279	.404	0	.000	-0	-2	-2	0	-0.3
	Chi-A	0	0	—	1	0	0	0	0	1	2	1	1	0	1	0	27.0	9.00	46	.500	.600	0	—	0	-1	-1	-0	0.0
	Yr	1	1	.500	8	1	0	0	0	12	14	9	2	0	10	4	18.0	6.00	69	.298	.421	0	.000	-0	-2	-3	-0	-0.3
Total	6	13	15	.464	98	17	3	0	3	243^1	280	148	28	2	101	108	14.2	4.99	78	.295	.364	10	.175	-1	-30	-29	-2	-3.7
● LOU MARONE	Marone, Louis Stephen b: 12/3/45, San Diego, Cal. BR/TL, 5′11″, 185 lbs. Deb: 5/30/69																											
1969	Pit-N	1	1	.500	29	0	0	0	0	35^1	24	10	2	2	13	25	9.9	2.55	137	.195	.283	0	—	0	4	4	-1	0.2
1970	Pit-N	0	0	—	1	0	0	0	0	2^1	2	1	1	0	0	0	7.7	3.86	101	.222	.222	0	—	0	0	0	-0	0.0
Total	2	1	1	.500	30	0	0	0	0	37^2	26	11	3	2	13	25	9.8	2.63	134	.197	.279	0	—	0	4	4	-1	0.2
● RUBE MARQUARD	Marquard, Richard William b: 10/9/1886, Cleveland, Ohio d: 6/1/80, Baltimore, Md. BB/TL, 6′3″, 180 lbs. Deb: 9/25/08 H																											
1908	NY-N	0	1	.000	1	1	0	0	0	5	6	5	0	1	2	2	16.2	3.60	67	.316	.409	0	.000	-0	-1	-1	-0	-0.1
1909	NY-N	5	13	.278	29	21	8	0	1	173	155	81	2	9	73	109	12.3	2.60	98	.248	.335	8	.148	-1	-0	-1	-0	-0.3
1910	NY-N	4	4	.500	13	8	2	0	0	70^2	65	35	2	4	40	52	13.9	4.46	67	.254	.363	3	.111	-2	-11	-12	-0	-1.4
1911	*NY-N	24	7	**.774**	45	33	22	5	3	277^2	221	98	9	4	106	**237**	10.7	2.50	135	.219	.296	17	.163	-1	28	27	-4	2.3
1912	*NY-N	**26**	11	.703	43	38	22	1	1	294^2	286	112	9	3	80	175	11.3	2.57	132	.255	.306	21	.219	2	28	27	-3	2.9
1913	*NY-N	23	10	.697	42	33	20	4	3	288	248	100	10	3	49	151	9.4	2.50	125	.237	.273	23	.219	2	23	20	-6	1.8
1914	NY-N	12	22	.353	39	33	15	4	2	268	261	117	9	2	47	92	10.4	3.06	87	.262	.297	15	.179	-1	-8	-13	1	-1.6
1915	NY-N	9	8	.529	27	21	10	2	2	169	178	85	8	1	33	79	11.3	3.73	69	.272	.308	6	.109	-3	-18	-24	-0	-2.6
	Bro-N	2	2	.500	6	3	0	0	1	24^2	29	17	0	0	5	13	12.4	6.20	45	.276	.309	1	.125	-0	-9	-9	-0	-1.4
	Yr	11	10	.524	33	24	10	2	3	193^2	207	102	8	1	38	92	11.4	4.04	64	.273	.308	7	.111	-3	-28	-33	-0	-4.0
1916	*Bro-N	13	6	.684	36	21	15	2	5	205	169	54	2	0	38	107	9.1	1.58	170	.229	.267	9	.143	-1	24	24	-4	2.0
1917	Bro-N	19	12	.613	37	29	14	2	0	232^2	200	84	5	0	60	117	10.1	2.55	110	.232	.282	15	.200	0	4	6	-4	0.4
1918	Bro-N	9	18	.333	34	29	19	4	0	239	231	97	7	1	59	89	11.0	2.64	106	.260	.307	13	.171	-2	3	4	-2	0.0
1919	Bro-N	3	3	.500	8	7	3	0	0	59	54	17	1	0	10	29	9.8	2.29	130	.244	.277	6	.261	1	4	4	-1	0.4
1920	*Bro-N	10	7	.588	28	26	10	1	0	189^2	181	83	5	1	35	89	10.3	3.23	99	.251	.287	10	.169	-1	-2	-0	-4	-0.6
1921	Cin-N	17	14	.548	39	36	18	2	0	265^2	291	123	8	7	50	88	11.8	3.39	106	.285	.323	19	.200	-1	12	6	-3	0.2
1922	Bos-N	11	15	.423	39	25	7	0	1	198	255	131	12	0	66	57	14.6	5.09	79	.322	.374	14	.222	-1	-22	-25	1	-2.6
1923	Bos-N	11	14	.440	38	29	11	3	0	239	265	127	10	2	65	78	12.5	3.73	107	.288	.337	12	.140	-6	7	7	0	0.0
1924	Bos-N	1	2	.333	6	6	1	0	0	36	33	17	3	1	13	10	11.8	3.00	127	.254	.326	3	.273	0	3	3	-0	0.3
1925	Bos-N	2	8	.200	26	8	0	0	0	72	105	60	5	0	27	19	16.5	5.75	70	.341	.394	3	.136	-1	-12	-15	-2	-2.0
Total	18	201	177	.532	536	407	197	30	19	3306^2	3233	1443	107	39	858	1593	11.2	3.08	103	.260	.310	198	.179	-17	53	36	-31	-2.3
● ISIDRO MARQUEZ	Marquez, Isidro (Espinoza) b: 5/15/65, Navojoa, Mexico BR/TR, 6′3″, 190 lbs. Deb: 4/26/95																											
1995	Chi-A	0	1	.000	7	0	0	0	0	6^2	9	5	3	0	2	8	14.9	6.75	66	.321	.367	0	—	0	-2	-2	-0	-0.2
● JIM MARQUIS	Marquis, James Milburn b: 11/18/1900, Yoakum, Tex. d: 8/5/92, Jackson, Cal. BR/TR, 5′11″, 174 lbs. Deb: 8/8/25																											
1925	NY-A	0	0	—	2	0	0	0	0	7^1	12	8	1	0	6	0	22.1	9.82	43	.414	.514	0	.000	-0	-4	-5	0	-0.2
● JASON MARQUIS	Marquis, Jason Scott b: 8/21/78, Manhasset, N.Y. BL/TR, 6′1″, 185 lbs. Deb: 6/6/2000																											
2000	Atl-N	1	0	1.000	15	0	0	0	0	23^1	23	16	4	1	12	17	13.9	5.01	90	.261	.356	0	.000	-0	-1	-1	0	-0.1
● CONNIE MARRERO	Marrero, Conrado Eugenio (Ramos) b: 5/1/11, Las Villas, Cuba BR/TR, 5′5″, 158 lbs. Deb: 4/21/50																											
1950	Was-A	6	10	.375	27	19	8	1	1	152	159	84	17	4	55	63	12.9	4.50	100	.269	.335	6	.122	-1	1	-0	-3	-0.4
1951	Was-A☆	11	9	.550	25	25	16	2	0	187	198	87	8	3	71	66	13.1	3.90	105	.268	.335	10	.164	-2	5	4	-2	0.1
1952	Was-A	11	8	.579	22	22	16	2	0	184^1	175	68	9	4	53	77	11.3	2.88	123	.249	.305	5	.079	-5	16	14	-3	0.6
1953	Was-A	8	7	.533	22	20	10	2	2	145^2	130	56	14	5	48	65	11.3	3.03	129	.241	.309	6	.125	-2	16	14	-1	1.1
1954	Was-A	3	6	.333	22	8	1	0	0	66^1	74	37	12	0	22	26	13.0	4.75	75	.287	.343	0	.000	-1	-8	-9	-1	-1.3
Total	5	39	40	.494	118	94	51	7	3	735^1	736	332	60	16	249	297	12.3	3.67	108	.260	.323	27	.114	-11	30	23	-10	0.1
● BUCK MARROW	Marrow, Charles Kennon b: 8/29/09, Tarboro, N.C. d: 11/21/82, Newport News, Va. BR/TR, 6′4″, 200 lbs. Deb: 7/3/32																											
1932	Det-A	2	5	.286	18	7	2	0	1	63^2	70	40	6	6	29	31	14.8	4.81	98	.278	.366	3	.158	-0	-2	-1	1	0.0
1937	Bro-N	1	2	.333	6	3	1	0	0	16^1	19	13	2	0	9	2	15.4	6.61	61	.284	.368	0	.000	-1	-5	-5	0	-0.8
1938	Bro-N	0	1	.000	15	0	0	0	0	19^2	23	10	1	3	11	6	16.9	4.58	85	.291	.398	0	.000	-0	-2	-1	0	-0.1
Total	3	3	8	.273	39	10	3	0	1	99^2	112	63	9	9	49	39	15.4	5.06	88	.281	.373	3	.120	-1	-9	-7	1	-0.9
● ED MARS	Mars, Edward M. b: 12/4/1866, Chicago, Ill. d: 12/9/41, Chicago, Ill. 5′9″, 166 lbs. Deb: 8/12/1890																											
1890	Syr-a	9	5	.643	16	14	14	0	0	121^1	132	80	2	5	49	59	13.8	4.67	76	.269	.341	14	.275	4	-11	-17	1	-1.1

YEAR	TM/L	W	L	PCT	G	GS	CG	SH	SV	IP	H	R	HR	HB	BB	SO	RAT	ERA	ERA+	OAV	OOB	BH	AVG	PB	PR	PR+	PD	TPI
● **CUDDLES MARSHALL** Marshall, Clarence Westly b: 4/28/25, Bellingham, Wash. BR/TR, 6'3", 200 lbs. Deb: 4/24/46																												
1946	NY-A	3	4	.429	23	11	1	0	0	81	96	49	4	0	56	32	16.9	5.33	65	.308	.413	4	.143	-1	-16	-17	1	-1.3
1948	NY-A	0	0	—	1	0	0	0	0	1	0	0	0	0	3	0	27.0	0.00	—	.000	.500	0	—	0	0	0	-0	0.0
1949	NY-A	3	0	1.000	21	2	0	0	3	49^1	48	31	3	2	48	13	17.9	5.11	79	.259	.417	1	.111	-0	-5	-6	1	-0.4
1950	StL-A	1	3	.250	28	2	0	0	1	53^2	72	52	1	1	51	24	20.8	7.88	63	.321	.449	4	.333	0	-20	-16	-1	-1.1
Total	4	7	7	.500	73	15	1	0	4	185	216	132	8	3	158	69	18.3	5.98	67	.298	.426	9	.184	-1	-41	-40	0	-2.8
● **MIKE MARSHALL** Marshall, Michael Grant b: 1/15/43, Adrian, Mich. BR/TR, 5'10", 180 lbs. Deb: 5/31/67																												
1967	Det-A	1	3	.250	37	0	0	0	10	59	51	15	6	2	20	41	11.1	1.98	165	.233	.303	2	.222	0	8	8	1	1.0
1969	Sea-A	3	10	.231	20	14	3	1	0	87^2	99	54	8	2	35	47	14.0	5.13	71	.281	.350	7	.259	3	-15	-15	3	-1.4
1970	Hou-N	0	1	.000	4	0	0	0	0	5^1	8	5	0	1	4	5	21.9	8.44	46	.400	.520	0	—	0	-3	-3	1	-0.4
	Mon-N	3	7	.300	24	5	0	0	3	64^2	56	34	4	0	29	38	11.8	3.48	118	.225	.306	1	.091	0	4	5	2	0.9
	Yr	3	8	.273	28	5	0	0	3	70	64	39	4	1	33	43	12.6	3.86	106	.238	.323	1	.091	0	2	2	2	0.5
1971	Mon-N	5	8	.385	66	0	0	0	23	111^1	100	56	9	4	50	85	12.4	4.28	82	.247	.336	3	.188	0	-10	-9	3	-1.1
1972	Mon-N	14	8	.636	**65**	0	0	0	18	116	82	26	3	2	47	95	10.2	1.78	199	.202	.289	3	.136	0	**22**	**22**	0	5.0
1973	Mon-N	14	11	.560	**92**	0	0	0	**31**	179	163	62	10	4	75	124	12.2	2.66	143	.252	.333	8	.242	1	20	**22**	3	4.2
1974	*LA-N★	15	12	.556	**106**	0	0	0	**21**	208^1	191	66	9	1	56	143	10.7	2.42	141	.247	.299	8	.235	1	**28**	**24**	1	3.7
1975	LA-N☆	9	14	.391	57	0	0	0	13	109^1	98	46	8	4	39	64	11.6	3.29	104	.242	.315	1	.067	-1	4	2	2	0.4
1976	LA-N	4	3	.571	30	0	0	0	8	62^2	64	33	2	1	25	39	12.9	4.45	76	.270	.342	0	.000	0	-7	-8	2	-0.8
	Atl-N	2	1	.667	24	0	0	0	6	36^2	35	15	4	1	14	17	12.3	3.19	119	.259	.333	1	.167	0	1	2	0	0.3
	Yr	6	4	.600	54	0	0	0	14	99^1	99	48	6	2	39	56	12.7	3.99	89	.266	.339	1	.091	1	-5	-5	2	-0.5
1977	Atl-N	1	0	1.000	4	0	0	0	0	6	12	6	1	0	2	6	21.0	9.00	50	.400	.438	1	1.000	0	-3	-3	-0	-0.4
	Tex-A	2	2	.500	12	4	0	0	1	35^2	42	19	0	2	13	18	14.4	4.04	101	.304	.373	0	—	0	0	0	0	0.0
1978	Min-A	10	12	.455	54	0	0	0	21	99	80	31	3	1	37	56	10.7	2.45	156	.225	.300	0	—	0	15	15	1	3.3
1979	Min-A	10	15	.400	**90**	1	0	0	**32**	142^2	132	47	8	4	48	81	11.6	2.65	166	.254	.322	0	—	0	25	27	3	5.6
1980	Min-A	1	3	.250	18	0	0	0	1	32^1	42	23	2	2	12	13	15.6	6.12	71	.323	.389	0	—	0	-7	-6	1	-0.6
1981	NY-N	3	2	.600	20	0	0	0	0	31	26	10	2	0	8	8	9.9	2.61	133	.224	.274	0	—	0	3	3	-0	0.5
Total	14	97	112	.464	723	24	3	1	188	1386^2	1281	548	79	31	514	880	11.9	3.14	118	.249	.321	35	.196	6	85	88	20	20.2
● **RUBE MARSHALL** Marshall, Roy De Verne "Cy" b: 1/19/1890, Salineville, Ohio d: 6/11/80, Dover, Ohio BR/TR, 5'11", 170 lbs. Deb: 9/28/12																												
1912	Phi-N	0	1	.000	2	1	0	0	0	3	12	11	0	0	1	2	39.0	21.00	17	.632	.650	0	—	0	-6	-5	0	-0.8
1913	Phi-N	0	1	.000	14	1	0	0	1	45^1	54	29	2	1	22	18	15.3	4.57	73	.297	.376	1	.091	-1	-7	-6	0	-0.4
1914	Phi-N	6	7	.462	27	17	7	0	1	134^1	144	77	2	5	50	49	13.3	3.75	78	.279	.349	6	.140	-2	-14	-11	1	-1.2
1915	Buf-F	2	1	.667	21	4	2	0	0	59^1	62	34	1	2	33	21	14.7	3.94	71	.281	.379	5	.294	1	-8	-7	-1	-0.4
Total	4	8	10	.444	64	23	9	0	2	242	272	151	5	8	106	90	14.4	4.17	72	.290	.367	12	.169	-2	-35	-30	-0	-2.8
● **DAMASO MARTE** Marte, Damaso (Sabinon) b: 2/14/75, Santo Domingo, D.R. BL/TL, 6', 170 lbs. Deb: 6/30/99																												
1999	Sea-A	0	1	.000	5	0	0	0	0	8^2	16	9	3	0	6	3	22.8	9.35	51	.390	.468	0	—	0	-4	-5	-0	-0.4
● **PHONNEY MARTIN** Martin, Alphonse Case b: 8/4/1845, New York, N.Y. d: 5/24/33, Hollis, N.Y. 5'7", 148 lbs. Deb: 4/26/1872 M♦																												
1872	Tro-n	1	2	.333	8	3	0	0	0	37^1	70	59	0		2	1	17.4	4.82	75	.350	.356	36	.308	1	-5	-5		-0.2
	Eck-n	2	7	.222	10	9	9	0	0	85	144	106	1		4	2	15.7	4.24	80	.321	.327	12	.154	-3	-6	-9		-0.7
	Yr	3	9	.250	18	12	9	0	0	122^1	214	165	1		6	3	16.2	4.41	78	.330	.336	48	.246	-2	-11	-14		-0.9
1873	Mut-n	0	1	.000	6	1	1	0	0	34	50	37	0		7	1	15.1	3.44	92	.294	.322	31	.221	-0	-1	-1		-0.2
Total	2 n	3	10	.231	24	13	10	0	0	156^1	264	202	1		13	4	15.9	4.20	75	.322	.333	79	.236	-3	-17	-19		-1.1
● **BARNEY MARTIN** Martin, Barnes Robertson b: 3/3/23, Columbia, S.C. d: 10/30/97, Columbia, S.C. BR/TR, 5'11", 170 lbs. Deb: 4/22/53 F																												
1953	Cin-N	0	0	—	1	0	0	0	0	2	3	2	0	0	1	1	18.0	9.00	48	.333	.400	0	—	0	-1	-1	-0	-0.1
● **RENIE MARTIN** Martin, Donald Renie b: 8/30/55, Dover, Del. BR/TR, 6'4", 190 lbs. Deb: 5/9/79																												
1979	KC-A	0	3	.000	25	0	0	0	5	34^2	32	20	1	1	14	25	12.2	5.19	82	.248	.326	0	—	0	-4	-3	1	-0.3
1980	*KC-A	10	10	.500	32	20	2	0	2	137^1	133	84	18	1	70	68	13.4	4.39	92	.255	.345	0	—	0	-5	-5	-0	-0.7
1981	*KC-A	4	5	.444	29	0	0	0	4	61^2	55	25	2	0	29	25	12.3	2.77	130	.244	.331	0	—	0	6	6	1	1.0
1982	SF-N	7	10	.412	29	25	1	0	0	141^1	148	91	14	0	64	63	13.5	4.65	77	.274	.350	13	.265	3	-16	-16	1	-1.4
1983	SF-N	2	4	.333	37	6	0	0	1	94^1	95	50	11	3	51	43	14.2	4.20	84	.268	.365	9	.346	4	-6	-7	1	0.2
1984	SF-N	1	1	.500	12	0	0	0	0	23^1	29	13	2	0	16	8	17.4	3.86	91	.305	.405	3	.500	1	-1	-1	1	0.1
	Phi-N	0	2	.000	9	0	0	0	0	15^2	17	12	2	0	12	5	16.7	4.60	79	.274	.392	0	.000	-0	-2	-2	1	-0.1
	Yr	1	3	.250	21	0	0	0	0	39	46	25	4	0	28	13	17.1	4.15	86	.293	.400	3	.375	1	-2	-3	2	0.0
Total	6	24	35	.407	173	51	3	0	12	508^1	509	295	50	5	256	237	13.6	4.27	88	.264	.352	25	.301	8	-28	-29	5	-1.2
● **SPEED MARTIN** Martin, Elwood Good b: 9/15/1893, Wawawai, Wash. d: 6/14/83, Lemon Grove, Cal. BR/TR, 6', 165 lbs. Deb: 7/5/17																												
1917	StL-A	0	2	.000	9	2	0	0	0	15^2	20	13	0	0	5	5	14.4	5.74	45	.339	.391	0	.000	-0	-5	-6	1	-0.6
1918	Chi-N	5	2	.714	9	5	4	1	1	53^2	47	19	0	1	14	16	10.4	1.84	151	.246	.301	3	.188	-0	5	6	1	0.8
1919	Chi-N	8	8	.500	35	14	7	2	2	163^2	158	58	2	4	52	54	11.8	2.47	117	.259	.321	8	.182	-1	8	8	2	0.8
1920	Chi-N	4	15	.211	35	13	6	0	2	136	165	96	2	1	50	44	14.3	4.83	66	.305	.365	7	.159	-0	-26	-24	1	-3.1
1921	Chi-N	11	15	.423	37	28	13	1	1	217^1	245	115	12	2	68	86	13.0	4.35	88	.298	.353	17	.233	1	-14	-13	2	-1.0
1922	Chi-N	1	0	1.000	1	1	0	0	0	6	10	5	0	0	2	2	18.0	7.50	56	.385	.429	0	.000	0	-2	-2	-0	-0.3
Total	6	29	42	.408	126	63	30	4	6	592^1	645	306	16	8	191	207	12.8	3.78	87	.287	.344	35	.194	-0	-33	-32	7	-3.4
● **FRED MARTIN** Martin, Fred Turner b: 6/27/15, Williams, Okla. d: 6/11/79, Chicago, Ill. BR/TR, 6'1", 185 lbs. Deb: 4/21/46 C																												
1946	StL-N	2	1	.667	6	3	2	0	0	28^2	29	13	0	0	8	19	11.6	4.08	85	.254	.303	3	.273	0	-2	-2	0	-0.1
1949	StL-N	6	0	1.000	21	5	3	0	0	70	65	24	3	0	20	30	10.9	2.44	170	.243	.295	6	.300	1	12	13	0	1.1
1950	StL-N	4	2	.667	30	2	0	0	0	63^1	87	43	4	1	30	19	16.8	5.12	84	.331	.401	4	.267	1	-7	-6	1	-0.3
Total	3	12	3	.800	57	10	5	0	0	162	181	80	7	1	58	68	13.3	3.78	108	.281	.341	13	.283	2	3	5	1	0.7
● **DOC MARTIN** Martin, Harold Winthrop b: 9/23/1887, Roxbury, Mass. d: 4/14/35, Milton, Mass. BR/TR, 5'11", 165 lbs. Deb: 10/7/08																												
1908	Phi-A	0	1	.000	1	1	0	0	0	2	2	4	0	1	3	2	27.0	13.50	19	.286	.545	0	.000	-0	-2	-2	-0	-0.4
1911	Phi-A	1	1	.500	11	3	1	0	0	38	40	26	1	5	17	21	14.7	4.50	70	.272	.367	3	.214	0	-5	-6	0	-0.2
1912	Phi-A	0	0	—	2	0	0	0	0	4^1	5	5	0	1	5	4	22.8	10.38	30	.333	.524	0	.000	-1	-3	-4	0	-0.2
Total	3	1	2	.333	14	4	1	0	0	44^1	47	35	1	7	25	27	16.0	5.48	57	.278	.393	3	.167	-0	-11	-12	1	-0.8
● **PEPPER MARTIN** Martin, Johnny Leonard Roosevelt "The Wild Horse Of The Osage" b: 2/29/04, Temple, Okla. d: 3/5/65, McAlester, Okla. BR/TR, 5'8", 170 lbs. Deb: 4/16/28 C♦																												
1934	*StL-N★	0	0	—	1	0	0	0	0	2	1	1	0	0	0	0	4.5	4.50	94	.167	.167	131	.289	0	-0	-0	0	0.0
1936	StL-N	0	0	—	1	0	0	0	0	2	1	0	0	0	2	0	13.5	0.00	—	.200	.429	177	.309	1	1	1	-0	0.0
Total	2	0	0	—	2	0	0	0	0	4	2	1	0	0	2	0	9.0	2.25	181	.182	.308	1227	.298	1	1	1	0	0.0
● **JOHN MARTIN** Martin, John Robert b: 4/11/56, Wyandotte, Mich. BB/TL, 6', 190 lbs. Deb: 8/27/80																												
1980	StL-N	2	3	.400	9	5	1	0	0	42	39	20	1	0	9	23	10.3	4.29	86	.247	.287	3	.273	1	-3	-3	-1	-0.3
1981	StL-N	8	5	.615	17	15	4	0	0	102^2	85	43	10	2	26	36	9.9	3.42	104	.228	.283	7	.212	2	1	2	0	0.4
1982	StL-N	4	5	.444	24	7	0	0	0	66	56	33	6	0	30	21	11.7	4.23	86	.230	.314	1	.091	-0	-5	-4	-1	-0.7
1983	StL-N	3	1	.750	26	5	0	0	0	66^1	60	31	6	2	26	29	11.9	3.53	103	.242	.319	4	.222	1	1	1	1	0.2
	Det-A	0	0		15	0	0	0	1	13^1	15	11	2	0	4	11	12.8	7.43	53	.294	.345	0	—	0	-5	-5	0	-0.3
Total	4	17	14	.548	91	32	5	0	1	290^1	255	138	25	4	95	120	11.0	3.94	92	.238	.302	15	.205	3	-11	-10	-1	-0.7
● **MORRIE MARTIN** Martin, Morris Webster "Lefty" b: 9/3/22, Dixon, Mo. BL/TL, 6', 180 lbs. Deb: 4/25/49																												
1949	Bro-N	1	3	.250	10	4	0	0	0	30^2	39	25	5	2	15	15	16.4	7.04	58	.320	.403	2	.200	-0	-10	-10	0	-1.1
1951	Phi-A	11	4	.733	35	13	3	1	0	138	139	70	13	5	63	35	13.5	3.78	113	.259	.343	11	.220	-1	5	7	2	0.8
1952	Phi-A	0	2	.000	5	5	0	0	0	25^1	32	19	1	2	15	13	17.4	6.39	62	.302	.398	1	.111	-1	-8	-6	-0	-0.5
1953	Phi-A	10	12	.455	58	11	2	0	7	156^1	158	85	12	8	59	64	13.0	4.43	97	.262	.336	4	.095	-4	-8	-2	-0	-0.7
1954	Phi-A	2	4	.333	13	6	2	0	0	52^2	57	32	9	2	19	24	13.3	5.47	71	.278	.345	4	.235	0	-10	-9	-0	-0.9
	Chi-A	5	4	.556	35	2	1	0	5	70	52	18	5	1	24	31	9.9	2.06	182	.210	.282	2	.133	-0	13	13	-1	1.7

YEAR	TM/L	W	L	PCT	G	GS	CG	SH	SV	IP	H	R	HR	HB	BB	SO	RAT	ERA	ERA+	OAV	OOB	BH	AVG	PB	PR	PR+	PD	TPI
	Yr	7	8	.467	48	8	3	0	5	122^2	109	50	14	3	43	55	11.4	3.52	108	.241	.311	6	.188	-0	3	4	-1	0.8
1955	Chi-A	2	3	.400	37	0	0	0	2	52	50	27	4	2	20	22	12.5	3.63	109	.259	.335	3	.300	0	2	2	1	0.3
1956	Chi-A	1	0	1.000	10	0	0	0	0	18^1	21	10	1	0	7	9	13.7	4.91	84	.292	.354	1	.200	0	-2	-2	0	-0.1
	Bal-A	1	1	.500	9	0	0	0	0	5	10	6	1	1	2	3	23.4	10.80	36	.400	.464	0	—	0	-4	-4	-0	-0.8
	Yr	2	1	.667	19	0	0	0	0	23^1	31	16	2	1	9	12	15.8	6.17	66	.320	.383	1	.200	0	-5	-6	0	-0.9
1957	StL-N	0	0	—	4	1	0	0	0	10^2	5	3	0	1	4	7	8.4	2.53	157	.143	.250	0	.000	-0	2	2	0	0.1
1958	StL-N	3	1	.750	17	0	0	0	0	24^2	19	13	3	2	12	16	12.0	4.74	87	.211	.317	0	.000	-1	-2	-2	-0	-0.3
	Cle-A	2	0	1.000	14	0	0	0	1	18^2	20	7	0	0	8	5	13.5	2.41	151	.294	.368	0	—	0	3	3	-0	0.3
1959	Chi-N	0	0	—	3	0	0	0	0	2^1	5	5	2	1	1	1	27.0	19.29	20	.455	.538	0	—	0	-4	-4	0	-0.2
Total	10	38	34	.528	250	42	8	1	15	604^2	607	320	56	27	249	245	13.1	4.29	95	.262	.341	28	.170	-6	-23	-13	1	-1.4
● PAT MARTIN	Martin, Patrick Francis b: 4/13/1892, Brooklyn, N.Y. d: 2/4/49, Brooklyn, N.Y. BL/TL, 5'11.5", 170 lbs. Deb: 9/20/19																											
1919	Phi-A	0	2	.000	2	2	1	0	0	11	11	8	0	0	8	6	15.5	4.09	84	.256	.373	0	.000	-0	-1	-1	-0	-0.2
1920	Phi-A	1	4	.200	8	5	2	0	0	32^1	48	36	2	4	25	14	21.4	6.12	66	.364	.478	4	.400	1	-8	-7	-1	-0.9
Total	2	1	6	.143	10	7	3	0	0	43^1	59	44	2	4	33	20	19.9	5.61	69	.337	.453	4	.308	1	-9	-8	-1	-1.1
● PAUL MARTIN	Martin, Paul Charles b: 3/10/32, Brownstown, Pa. BR/TR, 6'6", 235 lbs. Deb: 7/2/55																											
1955	Pit-N	0	1	.000	7	1	0	0	0	7	13	12	0	1	17	3	39.9	14.14	29	.464	.674	0	—	0	-8	-8	-0	-0.9
● RAY MARTIN	Martin, Raymond Joseph b: 3/13/25, Norwood, Mass. BR/TR, 6'2", 177 lbs. Deb: 8/15/43																											
1943	Bos-N	0	0	—	2	0	0	0	0	3^1	3	3	0	0	1	1	10.8	8.10	42	.231	.286	0	.000	-0	-2	-2	0	-0.1
1947	Bos-N	1	0	1.000	1	1	1	0	0	9	7	1	0	0	4	2	11.0	1.00	389	.212	.297	0	.000	-0	3	3	0	0.4
1948	Bos-N	0	0	—	2	0	0	0	0	2^1	0	0	0	0	1	0	3.9	0.00	—	.000	.125	0	—	0	1	1	-0	0.0
Total	3	1	0	1.000	5	1	1	0	0	14^2	10	4	0	0	6	3	9.8	2.45	154	.189	.271	0	.000	-0	2	2	1	0.3
● TOM MARTIN	Martin, Thomas Edgar b: 5/21/70, Charleston, S.C. BL/TL, 6'1", 185 lbs. Deb: 4/2/97																											
1997	*Hou-N	5	3	.625	55	0	0	0	2	56	52	13	2	1	23	36	12.2	2.09	191	.254	.332	0	.000	-0	13	13	-0	1.6
1998	Cle-A	1	1	.500	14	0	0	0	0	14^2	29	21	3	0	12	9	25.2	12.89	37	.408	.494	0	—	0	-13	-13	0	-1.4
1999	Cle-A	0	1	.000	6	0	0	0	0	9^1	13	9	2	0	3	8	15.4	8.68	58	.325	.372	0	—	0	-4	-4	-0	-0.3
2000	Cle-A	1	0	1.000	31	0	0	0	0	33^1	32	16	3	1	15	21	13.0	4.05	123	.254	.338	0	—	0	3	3	0	0.2
Total	4	7	5	.583	106	0	0	0	2	113^1	126	59	10	2	53	74	14.4	4.61	97	.285	.364	0	.000	-0	-1	-2	-1	0.1
● JOE MARTINA	Martina, Joseph John "Oyster Joe" b: 7/8/1889, New Orleans, La. d: 3/22/62, New Orleans, La. BR/TR, 6', 183 lbs. Deb: 4/19/24																											
1924	*Was-A	6	8	.429	24	14	8	0	0	125^1	129	69	7	6	56	57	13.7	4.67	86	.271	.355	14	.326	3	-6	-9	-2	-0.8
● ALFREDO MARTINEZ	Martinez, Alfredo b: 3/15/57, Los Angeles, Cal. BR/TR, 6'3", 185 lbs. Deb: 4/20/80																											
1980	Cal-A	7	9	.438	30	23	4	1	0	149^1	150	81	14	1	59	57	12.7	4.52	87	.259	.328	0	—	0	-8	-10	-2	-1.1
1981	Cal-A	0	0	—	2	0	0	0	0	6	5	2	1	0	3	4	12.0	3.00	122	.227	.320	0	—	0	0	0	0	0.0
Total	2	7	9	.438	32	23	4	1	0	155^1	155	83	15	1	62	61	12.6	4.46	88	.257	.328	0	—	0	-7	-9	-2	-1.1
● DAVE MARTINEZ	Martinez, David b: 9/26/64, New York, N.Y. BL/TL, 5'10", 175 lbs. Deb: 6/15/86 ♦																											
1990	Mon-N	0	0	—	1	0	0	0	0	0^1	2	2	0	0	2	0	108.0	54.00	7	.667	.800	109	.279	0	-2	-2	0	-0.1
1995	Chi-A	0	0	—	1	0	0	0	0	1	0	0	0	0	2	0	18.0	0.00	—	.000	.400	93	.307	0	1	1	0	0.0
Total	2	0	0	—	2	0	0	0	0	1^1	2	2	0	0	4	0	40.5	13.50	32	.333	.600	1531	.275	1	-1	-1	0	-0.1
● TIPPY MARTINEZ	Martinez, Felix Anthony b: 5/31/50, LaJunta, Colo. BL/TL, 5'10", 180 lbs. Deb: 8/9/74																											
1974	NY-A	0	0	—	10	0	0	0	0	12^2	14	7	0	1	9	10	17.1	4.26	83	.286	.407	0	—	0	-1	-1	-0	-0.1
1975	NY-A	1	2	.333	23	2	0	0	8	37	27	15	2	1	32	20	14.6	2.68	138	.208	.368	0	—	0	5	4	-1	0.5
1976	NY-A	2	0	1.000	11	0	0	0	2	28	18	6	1	0	14	14	10.3	1.93	177	.191	.296	0	—	0	5	5	1	0.5
	Bal-A	3	1	.750	28	0	0	0	8	41^2	32	13	0	1	28	31	13.2	2.59	126	.222	.353	0	—	0	4	3	1	0.6
	Yr	5	1	.833	39	0	0	0	10	69^2	50	19	1	1	42	45	12.0	2.33	143	.210	.331	0	—	0	9	8	2	1.1
1977	Bal-A	5	1	.833	41	0	0	0	9	50	47	17	2	0	27	29	13.3	2.70	141	.266	.363	0	—	0	8	7	1	1.1
1978	Bal-A	3	3	.500	42	0	0	0	5	69	77	41	4	1	40	57	15.4	4.83	73	.281	.375	0	—	0	-8	-11	1	-0.9
1979	*Bal-A	10	3	.769	39	0	0	0	3	78	59	29	0	1	31	61	10.5	2.88	139	.210	.291	0	—	0	12	10	1	1.7
1980	Bal-A	4	4	.500	53	0	0	0	10	80^2	69	30	5	1	34	68	11.6	3.01	132	.240	.322	0	—	0	9	9	2	1.2
1981	Bal-A	3	3	.500	37	0	0	0	11	59	48	21	4	0	32	50	12.2	2.90	125	.231	.333	0	—	0	5	5	1	0.8
1982	Bal-A	8	8	.500	76	0	0	0	16	95	81	39	6	1	37	78	11.3	3.41	119	.240	.317	0	—	0	7	7	-0	1.3
1983	*Bal-A☆	9	3	.750	65	0	0	0	21	103^1	76	30	10	0	37	81	9.8	2.35	169	.211	.284	0	—	0	20	19	2	3.1
1984	Bal-A	4	9	.308	55	0	0	0	17	89^2	88	42	9	0	51	72	14.0	3.91	99	.260	.356	0	—	0	1	-0	0	-0.1
1985	Bal-A	3	3	.500	49	0	0	0	4	70	70	48	8	0	37	47	13.8	5.40	75	.261	.351	0	—	0	-10	-11	1	-0.9
1986	Bal-A	0	2	.000	14	0	0	0	1	16	18	10	1	0	12	11	16.9	5.63	74	.295	.411	0	—	0	-3	-3	0	-0.3
1988	Min-A	0	0	—	3	0	0	0	0	4	8	9	1	1	4	3	29.3	18.00	23	.471	.591	0	—	0	-6	-6	-0	-0.3
Total	14	55	42	.567	546	2	0	0	115	834	732	357	53	8	425	632	12.6	3.45	111	.242	.337	0	—	0	48	37	9	8.2
● JAVIER MARTINEZ	Martinez, Javier Antonio b: 2/5/77, Bayamon, P.R. BR/TR, 6'2", 210 lbs. Deb: 4/2/98																											
1998	Pit-N	0	1	.000	37	0	0	0	0	41	39	32	5	4	34	42	16.9	4.83	89	.248	.395	0	.000	-0	-3	-2	-1	-0.2
● BUCK MARTINEZ	Martinez, John Albert b: 11/7/48, Redding, Cal. BR/TR, 5'10", 190 lbs. Deb: 6/18/69 ♦																											
1979	Mil-A	0	0	—	1	0	0	0	0	1	1	1	0	0	1	0	18.0	9.00	46	.250	.400	53	.270	0	-1	-1	0	0.0
● DENNIS MARTINEZ	Martinez, Jose Dennis (Emilia) "El Presidente" b: 5/14/55, Granada, Nicaragua BR/TR, 6'1", 185 lbs. Deb: 9/14/76																											
1976	Bal-A	1	2	.333	4	2	1	0	0	27^2	23	8	1	0	8	18	10.1	2.60	126	.237	.295	0	—	0	3	2	0	0.3
1977	Bal-A	14	7	.667	42	13	5	0	4	166^2	157	86	10	8	64	107	12.4	4.10	93	.253	.330	0	—	0	-1	-6	0	-0.7
1978	Bal-A	16	11	.593	40	38	15	2	0	276^1	257	121	20	3	93	142	11.5	3.52	100	.250	.314	0	—	0	8	-0	4	0.4
1979	*Bal-A	15	16	.484	40	39	**18**	3	0	**292^1**	279	129	28	1	78	132	11.0	3.66	110	.253	.303	0	—	0	18	12	3	1.5
1980	Bal-A	6	4	.600	25	12	2	0	1	99^2	103	44	12	2	44	42	13.5	3.97	100	.272	.351	0	—	0	1	-0	0	0.0
1981	Bal-A	**14**	5	.737	25	24	9	2	0	179	173	84	10	2	62	88	11.9	3.32	109	.254	.318	0	—	0	7	6	4	1.1
1982	Bal-A	16	12	.571	40	39	10	2	0	252	262	123	30	7	87	111	12.7	4.21	96	.267	.331	0	—	0	-4	-5	0	-0.5
1983	Bal-A	7	16	.304	32	25	4	0	0	153	209	108	21	2	45	71	15.1	5.53	72	.330	.376	0	—	0	-25	-27	5	-3.0
1984	Bal-A	6	9	.400	34	20	2	0	0	141^2	145	81	26	5	37	77	11.9	5.02	77	.263	.315	0	—	0	-16	-18	1	-1.6
1985	Bal-A	13	11	.542	33	31	3	1	0	180	203	110	29	9	63	68	13.8	5.15	78	.288	.353	0	—	0	-20	-23	0	-2.6
1986	Bal-A	0	0	—	4	0	0	0	0	6^2	11	5	0	0	2	2	17.6	6.75	61	.367	.406	0	—	0	-2	-2	0	-0.1
	Mon-N	3	6	.333	19	15	1	1	0	98	103	52	11	3	28	63	12.3	4.59	81	.274	.329	3	.100	-0	-9	-10	1	-0.8
1987	Mon-N	11	4	.733	22	22	2	1	0	144^2	133	59	9	6	40	84	11.1	3.30	128	.244	.302	3	.065	-2	13	14	0	1.2
1988	Mon-N	15	13	.536	34	34	9	2	0	235^1	215	94	21	6	55	120	10.6	2.72	133	.239	.287	15	.192	2	19	22	0	2.9
1989	Mon-N	16	7	.696	34	33	5	2	0	232	227	88	21	7	49	142	11.0	3.18	111	.257	.301	9	.125	-1	8	9	3	1.1
1990	Mon-N★	10	11	.476	32	32	7	2	0	226	191	80	16	6	49	156	9.8	2.95	124	.228	.275	7	.103	-2	21	18	1	1.6
1991	Mon-N★	14	11	.560	31	31	**9**	**5**	0	222	187	70	9	4	62	123	10.3	**2.39**	151	.226	.283	11	.153	1	**32**	31	4	4.0
1992	Mon-N★	16	11	.593	32	32	6	0	0	226^1	172	75	12	9	60	147	9.6	2.47	141	.211	.273	14	.189	1	26	26	3	3.5
1993	Mon-N	15	9	.625	35	34	2	0	1	224^2	211	110	27	11	64	138	11.5	3.85	109	.246	.307	11	.159	-0	5	8	3	1.1
1994	Cle-A	11	6	.647	24	24	7	3	0	176^2	166	75	14	7	44	92	11.1	3.52	134	.247	.301	0	—	0	25	24	2	2.2
1995	*Cle-A★	12	5	.706	28	28	3	2	0	187	174	71	17	12	46	99	11.2	3.08	153	.247	.304	0	—	0	34	34	4	3.1
1996	Cle-A	9	6	.600	20	20	1	1	0	112	122	63	12	2	37	48	12.9	4.50	109	.278	.337	0	—	0	6	5	2	0.8
1997	Sea-A	1	5	.167	9	9	0	0	0	49	65	46	8	7	29	17	18.6	7.71	58	.327	.430	0	—	0	-17	-18	-0	-1.7
1998	*Atl-N	4	6	.400	53	5	1	1	2	91	109	53	8	3	19	62	13.0	4.45	93	.295	.335	1	.091	-0	-2	-3	1	-0.2
Total	23	245	193	.559	692	562	122	30	8	3999^2	3897	1835	372	122	1165	2149	11.7	3.70	106	.256	.314	74	.142	-3	132	104	43	13.6
● JOSE MARTINEZ	Martinez, Jose Miguel (Martinez) b: 4/1/71, Guayubin, D.R. BR/TR, 6'2", 180 lbs. Deb: 5/10/94																											
1994	SD-N	0	2	.000	4	1	0	0	0	12	18	9	2	0	5	7	17.3	6.75	61	.375	.434	0	.000	-0	-3	-4	0	-0.5
● MARTY MARTINEZ	Martinez, Orlando (Oliva) b: 8/23/41, Havana, Cuba BB/TR, 6'1", 175 lbs. Deb: 5/2/62 MC♦																											
1969	Hou-N	0	0	—	1	0	0	0	0	0^2	1	1	1	0	0	0	13.5	13.50	26	.333	.333	61	.308	0	-1	-1	-0	0.0

YEAR	TM/L	W	L	PCT	G	GS	CG	SH	SV	IP	H	R	HR	HB	BB	SO	RAT	ERA	ERA+	OAV	OOB	BH	AVG	PB	PR	PR+	PD	TPI
● **PEDRO MARTINEZ**	Martinez, Pedro (Aquino) b: 11/29/68, Villa Mella, D.R. BL/TL, 6'2", 185 lbs. Deb: 6/29/93																											
1993	SD-N	3	1	.750	32	0	0	0	0	37	23	11	4	1	13	32	9.0	2.43	170	.172	.250	0	.000	-0	7	7	-0	0.6
1994	SD-N	3	2	.600	48	1	0	0	3	68^1	52	31	4	1	49	52	13.4	2.90	142	.210	.342	0	.000	-1	10	9	1	0.8
1995	Hou-N	0	0	—	25	0	0	0	0	20^2	29	18	3	2	16	17	20.5	7.40	52	.330	.443	0	—	0	-7	-9	0	-0.4
1996	NY-N	0	0	—	5	0	0	0	0	7	8	7	1	0	7	6	19.3	6.43	62	.296	.441	0	—	0	-2	-2	0	-0.1
	Cin-N	0	0	—	4	0	0	0	0	3	5	2	1	0	1	3	18.0	6.00	71	.357	.400	0	—	0	-1	-1	-0	0.0
	Yr	0	0	—	9	0	0	0	0	10	13	9	2	0	8	9	18.9	6.30	65	.317	.429	0	—	0	-2	-3	-0	-0.1
1997	Cin-N	1	1	.500	8	0	0	0	0	6^2	8	9	1	1	7	4	21.6	9.45	45	.286	.444	0	—	0	-4	-4	-0	-0.7
Total	5	7	4	.636	122	1	0	0	3	142^2	125	78	14	5	93	114	14.1	3.97	103	.232	.350	0	.000	-1	3	2	1	0.2
● **PEDRO MARTINEZ**	Martinez, Pedro Jaime (b: Pedro Jaime (Martinez)) b: 10/25/71, Manoguayabo, D.R. BR/TR, 5'11", 170 lbs. Deb: 9/24/92 F																											
1992	LA-N	0	1	.000	2	1	0	0	0	8	6	2	0	0	1	8	7.9	2.25	153	.200	.226	0	.000	-0	1	1	-0	0.1
1993	LA-N	10	5	.667	65	2	0	0	2	107	76	34	5	4	57	119	11.5	2.61	147	.201	.312	0	.000	-0	17	15	-2	1.8
1994	Mon-N	11	5	.688	24	23	1	1	1	144^2	115	58	11	11	45	142	10.6	3.42	124	.220	.295	4	.091	-1	13	13	-1	1.1
1995	Mon-N	14	10	.583	30	30	2	2	0	194^2	158	79	21	11	66	174	10.9	3.51	122	.227	.304	7	.111	-3	15	17	-0	1.5
1996	Mon-N★	13	10	.565	33	33	4	1	0	216^2	189	100	19	3	70	222	10.9	3.70	117	.232	.296	6	.094	-2	13	15	-2	1.0
1997	Mon-N★	17	8	.680	31	31	**13**	4	0	241^1	158	65	16	9	67	305	**8.7**	**1.90**	**221**	**.184**	**.250**	8	.116	-1	**62**	**62**	1	**6.3**
1998	*Bos-A☆	19	7	.731	33	33	3	2	0	233^2	188	82	26	8	67	251	10.1	2.89	163	.217	.280	0	.000	-1	46	47	-2	4.5
1999	*Bos-A★	**23**	4	**.852**	31	29	5	1	0	213^1	160	56	9	9	37	**313**	**8.7**	**2.07**	**241**	**.205**	**.249**	0	.000	-0	**66**	**68**	-0	**8.1**
2000	Bos-A†	18	6	.750	29	29	7	**4**	0	217	128	44	17	14	32	**284**	**7.2**	**1.74**	**292**	**.167**	**.214**	0	—	0	**77**	**78**	2	**8.5**
Total	9	125	56	.691	278	211	35	15	3	1576^1	1178	520	124	69	442	1818	9.6	2.68	168	.206	.271	25	.098	-8	309	315	-5	32.9
● **RAMON MARTINEZ**	Martinez, Ramon Jaime (b: Ramon Jaime (Martinez)) b: 3/22/68, Santo Domingo, D.R. BR/TR, 6'4", 173 lbs. Deb: 8/13/88 F																											
1988	LA-N	1	3	.250	9	6	0	0	0	35^2	27	17	0	0	22	23	12.4	3.79	88	.216	.333	0	.000	-1	-1	-2	-0	-0.3
1989	LA-N	6	4	.600	15	15	2	2	0	98^2	79	39	11	5	41	89	11.4	3.19	107	.219	.308	6	.162	0	3	3	1	0.4
1990	LA-N★	20	6	.769	33	33	**12**	3	0	234^1	191	89	22	4	67	223	10.1	2.92	126	.220	.279	10	.125	-2	23	20	0	2.0
1991	LA-N	17	13	.567	33	33	6	4	0	220^1	190	89	18	7	69	150	10.9	3.27	110	.229	.294	9	.117	-1	10	8	-1	0.8
1992	LA-N	8	11	.421	25	25	1	1	0	150^2	141	82	11	5	69	101	12.8	4.00	86	.245	.331	6	.120	-1	-8	-9	-1	-1.4
1993	LA-N	10	12	.455	32	32	4	3	0	211^2	202	88	15	4	104	127	13.2	3.44	111	.255	.344	9	.129	-2	14	9	2	0.9
1994	LA-N	12	7	.632	24	24	4	**3**	0	170	160	83	18	6	56	119	11.8	3.97	99	.249	.315	18	.273	5	5	-1	-1	0.3
1995	*LA-N	17	7	.708	30	30	4	2	0	206^1	176	95	19	5	81	138	11.4	3.66	104	.231	.309	11	.172	1	12	3	-0	0.5
1996	*LA-N	15	6	.714	28	27	2	2	0	168^2	153	76	12	8	86	133	13.2	3.42	113	.245	.344	7	.119	-2	15	9	1	0.9
1997	LA-N	10	5	.667	22	22	1	0	0	133^2	123	64	14	6	68	120	13.3	3.64	106	.243	.339	8	.190	1	8	4	1	0.5
1998	LA-N	7	3	.700	15	15	1	0	0	101^2	76	41	8	3	41	91	10.6	2.83	140	.206	.291	6	.176	1	16	14	1	1.5
1999	*Bos-A	2	1	.667	4	4	0	0	0	20^2	14	8	2	2	8	15	10.5	3.05	163	.192	.289	0	—	0	4	4	-0	0.6
2000	Bos-A	10	8	.556	27	27	0	0	0	127^2	143	94	16	9	67	89	15.4	6.13	83	.283	.377	1	.200	0	-17	-14	-1	-1.7
Total	13	135	86	.611	297	293	37	20	0	1880	1675	865	166	64	779	1418	12.1	3.62	106	.238	.320	91	.154	0	84	46	1	5.0
● **ROGELIO MARTINEZ**	Martinez, Rogelio (Ulloa) "Limonar" b: 11/5/18, Cidra, Cuba BR/TR, 6', 180 lbs. Deb: 7/13/50																											
1950	Was-A	0	1	.000	2	1	0	0	0	1^1	4	4	0	0	2	0	40.5	27.00	17	.500	.600	0	—	0	-3	-3	-0	-0.6
● **SILVIO MARTINEZ**	Martinez, Silvio Ramon (Cabrera) b: 8/19/55, Santiago, D.R. BR/TR, 5'10", 170 lbs. Deb: 4/9/77																											
1977	Chi-A	0	1	.000	10	0	0	0	1	21	28	14	4	0	12	10	17.1	5.57	74	.337	.421	0	—	0	-3	-3	0	-0.2
1978	StL-N	9	8	.529	22	22	5	2	0	138^1	114	65	11	2	71	45	12.2	3.64	97	.228	.326	8	.170	0	-1	-2	-1	-0.3
1979	StL-N	15	8	.652	32	29	7	2	0	206^2	204	92	14	0	67	102	11.8	3.27	115	.259	.317	8	.129	-2	11	11	-3	0.7
1980	StL-N	5	10	.333	25	20	2	0	0	119^2	127	75	8	2	48	39	13.3	4.81	77	.273	.343	3	.086	-2	-16	-14	-2	-2.0
1981	StL-N	2	5	.286	18	16	0	0	0	97	95	48	4	1	39	34	12.5	3.99	89	.260	.333	7	.200	1	-5	-5	-1	-0.3
Total	5	31	32	.492	107	87	14	4	1	582^2	568	294	41	5	237	230	12.5	3.88	95	.258	.331	26	.145	-3	-15	-13	-7	-2.1
● **WILLIE MARTINEZ**	Martinez, William Jose b: 1/4/78, Barquisimeto, Venez. BR/TR, 6'2", 180 lbs. Deb: 6/14/2000																											
2000	Cle-A	0	0	—	1	0	0	0	0	3	1	1	0	0	1	1	6.0	3.00	167	.111	.200	0	—	0	1	1	0	0.1
● **WEDO MARTINI**	Martini, Guido Joe "Southern" b: 7/1/13, Birmingham, Ala. d: 10/28/70, Philadelphia, Pa. BR/TR, 5'10", 165 lbs. Deb: 7/28/35																											
1935	Phi-A	0	2	.000	3	2	0	0	0	6^1	8	13	0	0	11	1	27.0	17.05	27	.333	.543	0	.000	-0	-9	-9	1	-1.3
● **JOE MARTY**	Marty, Joseph Anton b: 9/1/13, Sacramento, Cal. d: 10/4/84, Sacramento, Cal. BR/TR, 6', 182 lbs. Deb: 4/22/37 ♦																											
1939	Phi-N	0	0	—	1	0	0	0	0	4	2	2	0	0	3	1	11.3	4.50	89	.154	.313	76	.254	0	-0	-0	-0	0.0
● **RANDY MARTZ**	Martz, Randy Carl b: 5/28/56, Harrisburg, Pa. BL/TR, 6'4", 210 lbs. Deb: 9/6/80																											
1980	Chi-N	1	2	.333	6	6	0	0	0	30^1	28	14	1	0	11	5	11.6	2.08	189	.241	.307	1	.111	-1	5	6	1	0.6
1981	Chi-N	5	7	.417	33	14	1	0	6	107^2	103	49	6	1	49	32	12.8	3.68	101	.256	.338	6	.214	1	-2	0	0	0.1
1982	Chi-N	11	10	.524	28	24	1	0	1	147^2	157	80	17	3	36	40	11.9	4.21	89	.272	.318	6	.143	1	-10	-7	1	-0.8
1983	Chi-A	0	0	—	1	1	0	0	0	5	4	2	0	0	4	1	14.4	3.60	117	.211	.348	0	—	0	0	0	-0	0.0
Total	4	17	19	.472	68	45	2	0	7	290^2	292	145	24	4	100	78	12.3	3.78	99	.262	.325	13	.165	1	-7	-1	1	-0.1
● **ONAN MASAOKA**	Masaoka, Onan Kainoa Satoshi b: 10/27/77, Hilo, Hawaii BR/TL, 6', 186 lbs. Deb: 4/5/99																											
1999	LA-N	2	4	.333	54	0	0	0	1	66^2	55	33	8	2	47	61	14.0	4.32	99	.222	.350	0	.000	-0	2	-0	-1	-0.2
2000	LA-N	1	1	.500	29	0	0	0	0	27	23	12	2	1	15	27	13.0	4.00	110	.230	.336	0	—	0	2	1	-0	0.1
Total	2	3	5	.375	83	0	0	0	1	93^2	78	45	10	3	62	88	13.7	4.23	102	.224	.346	0	.000	-0	4	1	-2	-0.1
● **DEL MASON**	Mason, Adelbert William b: 10/29/1883, Newfane, N.Y. d: 12/31/62, Winter Park, Fla. BR/TR, 6', 160 lbs. Deb: 4/23/04																											
1904	Was-A	0	3	.000	5	3	2	0	0	33	45	30	1	2	13	16	16.4	6.00	44	.326	.392	0	.000	-2	-12	-12	-1	-1.2
1906	Cin-N	0	1	.000	2	1	1	0	0	12	10	6	1	1	6	4	12.8	4.50	61	.250	.362	0	.000	-1	-2	-2	-0	-0.3
1907	Cin-N	5	12	.294	25	17	13	1	0	146	144	68	2	6	55	45	12.6	3.14	83	.277	.353	8	.182	-0	-11	-8	1	-0.9
Total	3	5	16	.238	32	21	16	1	0	191	199	104	4	9	74	65	13.3	3.72	70	.286	.362	8	.125	-3	-26	-22	0	-2.4
● **CHARLIE MASON**	Mason, Charles E. b: 6/25/1853, New Orleans, La. d: 10/21/36, Philadelphia, Pa. BR/TR, 175 lbs. Deb: 4/26/1875 M♦																											
1875	Was-n	0	0	—	1	0	0	0	0	2	3	2	0	1	0	18.0		4.50	53	.300	.364	3	.091	-0	-1	-0		0.0
● **ERNIE MASON**	Mason, Ernest b: New Orleans, La. d: 7/30/04, Covington, La. Deb: 7/17/1894																											
1894	StL-N	0	3	.000	4	2	2	0	0	22^2	34	29	1	0	10	3	17.5	7.15	76	.343	.404	3	.250	-0	-5	-4	-1	-0.4
● **HANK MASON**	Mason, Henry b: 6/19/31, Marshall, Mo. BR/TR, 6', 185 lbs. Deb: 9/12/58																											
1958	Phi-N	0	0	—	1	0	0	0	0	5	7	7	0	1	2	3	18.0	10.80	37	.368	.455	0	.000	-0	-4	-4	-0	-0.2
1960	Phi-N	0	0	—	3	0	0	0	0	5^2	9	6	1	0	5	3	22.2	9.53	41	.375	.483	0	.000	-0	-4	-3	-0	-0.2
Total	2	0	0	—	4	0	0	0	0	10^2	16	13	1	1	7	6	20.3	10.13	39	.372	.471	0	.000	-0	-7	-7	-0	-0.4
● **MIKE MASON**	Mason, Michael Paul b: 11/21/58, Faribault, Minn. BL/TL, 6'2", 205 lbs. Deb: 9/13/82																											
1982	Tex-A	1	2	.333	4	4	0	0	0	23	21	13	3	0	9	8	11.7	5.09	76	.244	.316	0	—	0	-3	-3	0	-0.3
1983	Tex-A	0	2	.000	5	0	0	0	0	10^2	10	7	0	1	6	9	14.3	5.91	68	.244	.354	0	—	0	-2	-2	0	-0.4
1984	Tex-A	9	13	.409	36	24	4	0	0	184^1	159	78	18	2	51	113	10.4	3.61	115	.233	.288	0	—	0	8	11	-1	1.1
1985	Tex-A	8	15	.348	38	30	1	1	0	179	212	113	22	3	73	92	14.5	4.83	88	.299	.366	0	—	0	-13	-12	-0	-1.3
1986	Tex-A	7	3	.700	27	22	2	1	0	135	135	71	11	0	56	85	12.7	4.33	99	.257	.329	0	—	0	-2	-0	0	0.0
1987	Tex-A	0	2	.000	8	6	0	0	0	29	37	20	6	4	22	21	19.6	5.59	80	.322	.447	0	—	0	-4	-4	0	-0.2
	Chi-N	4	1	.800	17	4	0	0	0	38	43	25	4	1	23	28	15.9	5.68	75	.303	.404	2	.222	0	-7	-6	-0	-0.6
1988	Min-A	0	1	.000	5	0	0	0	0	6^2	8	8	1	0	9	7	23.0	10.80	38	.286	.459	0	—	0	-5	-5	-0	-0.6
Total	7	29	39	.426	140	90	7	2	0	605^2	625	335	65	11	249	363	13.2	4.53	93	.268	.342	2	.222	0	-28	-20	-1	-2.3
● **ROGER MASON**	Mason, Roger Le Roy b: 9/18/58, Bellaire, Mich. BR/TR, 6'6", 220 lbs. Deb: 9/4/84																											
1984	Det-A	1	1	.500	5	2	0	0	1	22	23	11	1	0	10	15	13.5	4.50	87	.271	.347	0	—	0	-1	-1	0	-0.1
1985	SF-N	1	3	.250	5	5	1	1	0	29^2	28	13	1	0	11	26	11.8	2.12	162	.243	.310	1	.091	-0	5	5	-0	0.6
1986	SF-N	3	4	.429	11	11	1	0	0	60	56	35	5	3	30	43	13.4	4.80	74	.250	.346	1	.048	-2	-7	-9	-1	-1.2

YEAR	TM/L	W	L	PCT	G	GS	CG	SH	SV	IP	H	R	HR	HB	BB	SO	RAT	ERA	ERA+	OAV	OOB	BH	AVG	PB	PR	PR+	PD	TPI
1987	SF-N	1	1	.500	5	5	0	0	0	26	30	15	4	0	10	18	13.8	4.50	86	.303	.367	1	.125	0	-1	-2	0	-0.1
1989	Hou-N	0	0	—	2	0	0	0	0	1^1	2	3	0	0	2	3	27.0	20.25	17	.333	.500	0	—	0	-2	-3	0	-0.1
1991	*Pit-N	3	2	.600	24	0	0	0	3	29^2	21	11	2	1	6	21	8.5	3.03	118	.200	.250	0	—	0	2	2	0	0.4
1992	*Pit-N	5	7	.417	65	0	0	0	8	88	80	41	11	4	33	56	12.0	4.09	84	.246	.323	0	.000	-1	-6	-6	-1	-1.2
1993	SD-N	0	7	.000	34	0	0	0	0	50	43	20	1	2	18	39	11.3	3.24	128	.242	.318	0	.000	-0	4	5	-0	0.6
	*Phi-N	5	5	.500	34	0	0	0	0	49^2	47	28	9	0	16	32	11.4	4.89	81	.246	.304	1	.333	0	-5	-5	-1	-1.0
	Yr	5	12	.294	68	0	0	0	0	99^2	90	48	10	2	34	71	11.4	4.06	100	.244	.311	1	.167	-0	-0	-0	-2	-0.4
1994	Phi-N	1	1	.500	6	0	0	0	0	8^2	11	6	2	0	5	7	16.6	5.19	83	.306	.390	0	—	0	-1	-1	-0	-0.2
	NY-N	2	4	.333	41	0	0	0	1	51^1	44	23	6	2	20	26	11.6	3.51	119	.232	.311	0	—	0	4	4	-1	0.3
	Yr	3	5	.375	47	0	0	0	1	60	55	29	8	2	25	33	12.3	3.75	112	.243	.324	0	—	0	3	3	-1	0.1
Total	9	22	35	.386	232	23	2	1	13	416^1	385	206	42	12	161	286	12.1	4.02	94	.248	.323	4	.071	-2	-8	-12	-5	-2.0

● WALT MASTERS

Masters, Walter Thomas b: 3/28/07, Pen Argyl, Pa. d: 7/10/92, Ottawa, Ont., Can. BR/TR, 5'10.5", 180 lbs. Deb: 7/9/31

YEAR	TM/L	W	L	PCT	G	GS	CG	SH	SV	IP	H	R	HR	HB	BB	SO	RAT	ERA	ERA+	OAV	OOB	BH	AVG	PB	PR	PR+	PD	TPI
1931	Was-A	0	0	—	3	0	0	0	1	9	7	2	0	0	4	1	11.0	2.00	215	.226	.314	0	.000	-0	2	2	1	0.1
1937	Phi-N	0	0	—	1	0	0	0	0	1	5	4	0	0	1	0	54.0	36.00	12	.714	.750	0	—	0	-4	-3	-0	-0.2
1939	Phi-A	0	0	—	4	0	0	0	0	11	15	9	0	0	8	2	18.8	6.55	72	.306	.404	0	.000	-0	-2	-2	0	-0.1
Total	3	0	0	—	8	0	0	0	1	21	27	15	0	0	13	3	17.1	6.00	75	.310	.400	0	.000	-1	-4	-3	1	-0.2

● PAUL MASTERSON

Masterson, Paul Nicholas "Lefty" (b: Paul Nicholas Nastasowski)
b: 10/16/15, Chicago, Ill. d: 11/27/97, Chicago, Ill. BL/TL, 5'11", 165 lbs. Deb: 9/15/40

YEAR	TM/L	W	L	PCT	G	GS	CG	SH	SV	IP	H	R	HR	HB	BB	SO	RAT	ERA	ERA+	OAV	OOB	BH	AVG	PB	PR	PR+	PD	TPI
1940	Phi-N	0	0	—	2	0	0	0	0	5	5	4	0	0	2	3	12.6	7.20	54	.263	.333	0	.000	-0	-2	-2	0	-0.1
1941	Phi-N	1	0	1.000	2	1	1	0	0	11^1	11	6	0	0	6	8	13.5	4.76	78	.250	.340	0	.000	-1	-1	-1	0	-0.2
1942	Phi-N	0	0	—	4	0	0	0	0	8^1	10	6	1	0	5	3	16.2	6.48	51	.303	.395	0	—	0	-3	-3	0	-0.2
Total	3	1	0	1.000	8	1	1	0	0	24^2	26	16	1	0	13	14	14.2	5.84	62	.271	.358	0	.000	-1	-6	-6	0	-0.5

● WALT MASTERSON

Masterson, Walter Edward b: 6/22/20, Philadelphia, Pa. BR/TR, 6'2", 189 lbs. Deb: 5/8/39

YEAR	TM/L	W	L	PCT	G	GS	CG	SH	SV	IP	H	R	HR	HB	BB	SO	RAT	ERA	ERA+	OAV	OOB	BH	AVG	PB	PR	PR+	PD	TPI
1939	Was-A	2	2	.500	24	5	1	0	0	58^1	66	44	2	2	48	12	17.9	5.55	78	.293	.422	2	.154	-0	-6	-8	-1	-0.6
1940	Was-A	3	13	.188	31	19	3	0	2	130^1	128	92	6	3	88	68	15.1	4.90	85	.257	.371	7	.184	0	-8	-11	-1	-1.3
1941	Was-A	4	3	.571	34	6	1	0	3	78^1	101	56	3	1	53	40	17.8	5.97	68	.321	.420	2	.105	-1	-16	-17	1	-1.5
1942	Was-A	5	9	.357	25	15	8	4	2	142^2	138	75	6	2	54	63	12.2	3.34	109	.251	.321	7	.156	-0	5	5	-2	0.2
1945	Was-A	1	2	.333	4	2	1	1	0	25	21	8	1	0	10	14	11.2	1.08	287	.228	.304	1	.111	-1	6	6	0	0.7
1946	Was-A	5	6	.455	29	9	2	0	1	91^1	105	70	8	3	67	61	17.2	6.01	56	.295	.411	2	.080	-1	-25	-28	0	-3.2
1947	Was-A★	12	16	.429	35	31	14	4	1	253	215	98	11	2	97	135	11.2	3.13	119	.234	.309	11	.133	-3	16	17	3	1.8
1948	Was-A★	8	15	.348	33	27	9	2	2	188	171	88	12	4	122	72	14.2	3.83	113	.247	.363	11	.193	-0	10	11	-2	1.0
1949	Was-A	3	2	.600	10	7	3	0	0	53	42	22	4	3	21	17	11.2	3.23	132	.216	.303	1	.056	-1	6	6	1	0.4
	Bos-A	3	4	.429	18	5	1	0	4	55	58	30	2	0	35	19	15.2	4.25	102	.283	.387	2	.118	-0	-0	1	-1	-0.1
	Yr	6	6	.500	28	12	4	0	4	108	100	52	6	3	56	36	13.3	3.75	115	.251	.347	3	.086	-2	5	7	-0	0.3
1950	Bos-A	8	6	.571	33	15	6	0	1	129^1	145	91	15	1	82	60	15.9	5.64	87	.287	.387	6	.136	-3	-15	-10	1	-1.0
1951	Bos-A	3	0	1.000	30	1	0	0	2	59^1	53	24	1	0	32	39	12.9	3.34	134	.228	.322	2	.182	-1	5	7	0	0.3
1952	Bos-A	1	1	.500	5	1	0	0	0	9^1	18	12	1	0	11	3	28.0	11.57	34	.400	.518	0	.000	0	-8	-7	0	-1.3
	Was-A	9	8	.529	24	21	11	0	2	160^2	153	71	11	3	72	89	12.8	3.70	96	.253	.336	6	.120	-1	-0	-3	1	-0.3
	Yr	10	9	.526	29	22	11	0	2	170	171	83	12	3	83	92	13.6	4.13	87	.263	.350	6	.115	-1	-9	-11	1	-1.6
1953	Was-A	10	12	.455	29	20	10	4	0	166^1	145	79	16	3	62	95	11.4	3.63	107	.232	.304	7	.137	-1	7	5	0	0.6
1956	Det-A	1	1	.500	35	0	0	0	0	49^2	54	28	2	1	32	28	15.8	4.17	99	.289	.395	1	.250	0	-0	-0	-0	-0.1
Total	14	78	100	.438	399	184	70	15	20	1649^2	1613	888	101	28	886	815	13.8	4.15	96	.258	.353	68	.140	-14	-24	-27	0	-4.4

● LEN MATARAZZO

Matarazzo, Leonard b: 9/12/28, New Castle, Pa. BR/TR, 6'4", 195 lbs. Deb: 9/6/52

YEAR	TM/L	W	L	PCT	G	GS	CG	SH	SV	IP	H	R	HR	HB	BB	SO	RAT	ERA	ERA+	OAV	OOB	BH	AVG	PB	PR	PR+	PD	TPI
1952	Phi-A	0	0	—	1	0	0	0	0	1	1	0	0	0	1	0	18.0	0.00	—	.250	.400	0	—	0	0	0	-0	0.0

● GREG MATHEWS

Mathews, Gregory Inman b: 5/17/62, Harbor City, Cal. BR/TL, 6'2", 180 lbs. Deb: 6/3/86

YEAR	TM/L	W	L	PCT	G	GS	CG	SH	SV	IP	H	R	HR	HB	BB	SO	RAT	ERA	ERA+	OAV	OOB	BH	AVG	PB	PR	PR+	PD	TPI
1986	StL-N	11	8	.579	23	22	1	0	0	145^1	139	61	15	2	44	67	11.5	3.65	100	.259	.317	2	.047	-3	1	-0	-2	-0.5
1987	*StL-N	11	11	.500	32	32	2	1	0	197^2	184	87	17	0	71	108	11.6	3.73	111	.249	.314	13	.191	1	8	9	-1	0.9
1988	StL-N	4	6	.400	13	13	1	0	0	68	61	34	4	2	33	31	12.7	4.24	82	.247	.340	4	.174	0	-6	-6	0	-0.7
1990	StL-N	0	5	.000	11	10	0	0	0	50^2	53	34	2	2	30	18	15.1	5.33	72	.277	.381	3	.214	1	-9	-8	1	-0.5
1992	Phi-N	2	3	.400	14	7	0	0	0	52^1	54	31	7	1	24	27	13.6	5.16	68	.270	.351	0	.000	-1	-10	-10	-1	-1.0
Total	5	28	33	.459	93	84	4	1	0	514	491	247	45	7	202	251	12.3	4.08	94	.256	.330	22	.136	-1	-15	-15	-3	-1.8

● BOBBY MATHEWS

Mathews, Robert T. b: 11/21/1851, Baltimore, Md. d: 4/17/1898, Baltimore, Md. BR/TR, 5'5.5", 140 lbs. Deb: 5/4/1871 U♦

YEAR	TM/L	W	L	PCT	G	GS	CG	SH	SV	IP	H	R	HR	HB	BB	SO	RAT	ERA	ERA+	OAV	OOB	BH	AVG	PB	PR	PR+	PD	TPI
1871	Kek-n	6	11	.353	19	19	19	**1**	0	169	261	243	5		21	17	15.0	5.17	88	.305	.322	24	.270	-3	-18	-10		-0.7
1872	Bal-n	25	18	.581	49	47	39	0	0	406	480	356	3		52	**55**	11.8	3.19	115	.257	.277	50	.224	-8	20	21		0.8
1873	Mut-n	29	23	.558	52	52	47	2	0	443	489	348	5		62	**75**	11.2	2.56	123	.251	.274	43	.193	-2	34	30		1.9
1874	Mut-n	42	22	.656	65	65	62	**4**	0	578	652	371	3		41	**101**	10.8	1.90	118	.261	.273	72	.242	-2	19	22		1.4
1875	Mut-n	29	38	.433	70	70	**69**	3	0	**625^2**	711	421	4		20	75	10.5	2.49	94	.260	.265	48	.182	-10	-18	-10		-2.2
1876	NY-N	21	34	.382	56	56	55	2	0	516	693	395	8		24	37	12.5	2.86	75	.298	.308	40	.181	-10	-32	-45	-3	-4.5
1877	Cin-N	3	12	.200	15	15	13	0	0	129^1	208	132	0		17	9	15.7	4.04	66	.339	.357	10	.169	-3	-18	-21	-1	-2.2
1879	Pro-N	12	6	.667	27	25	15	1	**1**	189	194	85	4		26	90	10.5	2.29	103	.258	.282	35	.202	-0	4	2	0	0.1
1881	Pro-N	4	8	.333	14	14	10	1	0	102^1	121	81	2		21	28	12.5	3.17	84	.268	.300	11	.193	-2	-4	-6	-1	-0.8
	Bos-N	1	0	1.000	5	1	1	0	2	23	22	11	0		11	5	12.9	2.35	113	.239	.320	12	.169	-1	1	1	-0	0.0
	Yr	5	8	.385	19	15	11	1	**2**	125^1	143	92	2		32	33	12.6	3.02	88	.263	.304	23	.180	-3	-3	-5	-2	-0.8
1882	Bos-N	19	15	.559	34	32	31	0	0	285	278	151	5		22	153	9.5	2.87	100	.232	.246	38	.225	-2	1	-0	-4	-0.6
1883	Phi-a	30	13	.698	44	44	41	1	0	381	396	224	11		31	203	10.1	2.46	144	.251	.265	31	.186	-7	36	43	-1	3.2
1884	Phi-a	30	18	.625	49	49	48	3	0	430^2	401	238	10	12	49	286	9.7	3.32	102	.232	.258	34	.185	-5	-4	3	-2	-0.4
1885	Phi-a	30	17	.638	48	48	46	2	0	422^1	394	229	3	20	57	286	10.0	2.43	142	.233	.267	30	.168	-7	38	45	0	3.5
1886	Phi-a	13	9	.591	24	24	22	0	0	197^2	226	148	3	13	53	93	13.3	3.96	88	.267	.320	21	.239	-0	-11	-10	0	-0.9
1887	Phi-a	3	4	.429	7	7	7	0	0	58	100	64	4	3	25	9	16.0	6.67	64	.361	.368	9	.310	-0	-15	-15	0	-1.3
Total	5 n	131	112	.539	255	253	236	10	0	2221^2	2593	1739	20	0	196	323	11.3	2.68	108	.261	.276	237	.216	-25	37	51		1.2
Total	10	166	136	.550	323	315	289	10	3	2734^1	3033	1758	50	48	336	1199	11.2	3.00	100	.263	.285	271	.194	-38	-3	-0	-11	-3.9

● TERRY MATHEWS

Mathews, Terry Alan b: 10/5/64, Alexandria, La. BL/TR, 6'2", 225 lbs. Deb: 6/21/91

YEAR	TM/L	W	L	PCT	G	GS	CG	SH	SV	IP	H	R	HR	HB	BB	SO	RAT	ERA	ERA+	OAV	OOB	BH	AVG	PB	PR	PR+	PD	TPI
1991	Tex-A	4	0	1.000	34	2	0	0	1	57^1	54	24	5	1	18	51	11.5	3.61	112	.251	.312	0	—	0	3	3	0	0.2
1992	Tex-A	2	4	.333	40	0	0	0	0	42^1	48	29	4	1	31	26	17.0	5.95	64	.294	.410	0	—	0	-9	-11	0	-1.3
1994	Fla-N	2	1	.667	24	2	0	0	0	43	45	16	4	1	9	21	11.5	3.35	131	.268	.309	3	.500	1	4	5	0	0.4
1995	Fla-N	4	4	.500	57	0	0	0	3	82^2	70	32	9	1	27	72	10.7	3.38	125	.235	.301	6	.462	3	7	8	-0	0.9
1996	Fla-N	2	4	.333	57	0	0	0	4	55	59	33	7	1	27	49	14.2	4.91	83	.273	.357	0	.000	-0	-4	-5	0	-0.6
	*Bal-A	2	2	.500	14	0	0	0	0	18^2	20	7	3	0	7	13	13.0	3.38	146	.282	.346	0	—	0	3	3	-0	0.6
1997	*Bal-A	4	4	.500	57	0	0	0	1	63^1	63	35	8	0	36	39	14.1	4.41	100	.267	.364	0	—	0	1	0	0	0.0
1998	Bal-A	0	1	.000	17	0	0	0	0	20^1	26	15	6	0	8	10	15.0	6.20	74	.342	.405	0	—	0	-3	-4	1	-0.1
1999	KC-A	2	1	.667	24	1	0	0	1	39	44	21	4	2	17	19	14.5	4.38	114	.289	.368	0	.000	-0	2	3	-0	0.2
Total	8	22	21	.512	324	5	0	0	10	421^2	429	212	50	7	180	300	13.1	4.25	101	.269	.346	9	.375	3	4	2	1	0.3

● T. J. MATHEWS

Mathews, Timothy Jay b: 1/9/70, Belleville, Ill. BR/TR, 6'2", 200 lbs. Deb: 7/28/95 F

YEAR	TM/L	W	L	PCT	G	GS	CG	SH	SV	IP	H	R	HR	HB	BB	SO	RAT	ERA	ERA+	OAV	OOB	BH	AVG	PB	PR	PR+	PD	TPI
1995	StL-N	1	1	.500	23	0	0	0	2	29^2	21	7	1	0	11	28	9.7	1.52	276	.200	.276	0	.000	-0	9	9	1	0.7
1996	*StL-N	2	6	.250	67	0	0	0	6	83^2	62	32	8	2	32	80	10.3	3.01	139	.203	.282	0	.000	-0	11	11	-2	0.9
1997	StL-N	4	4	.500	40	0	0	0	0	46	41	14	4	1	18	46	11.7	2.15	193	.238	.314	0	.000	-0	10	10	-0	1.6
	Oak-A	6	2	.750	24	0	0	0	3	28^2	34	18	5	1	12	24	14.8	4.40	103	.293	.364	0	—	0	1	0	-0	0.1
1998	Oak-A	7	4	.636	66	0	0	0	1	72^2	71	44	6	4	29	53	12.9	4.58	100	.258	.338	0	—	0	1	-0	-1	-0.1
1999	Oak-A	9	5	.643	50	0	0	0	3	59	46	28	9	2	20	42	10.4	3.81	122	.215	.288	0	—	0	7	6	0	1.1
2000	Oak-A	2	3	.400	50	0	0	0	0	59^2	73	40	10	2	25	42	15.1	6.03	79	.303	.373	0	—	0	-7	-9	1	-0.5
Total	6	31	25	.554	320	0	0	0	15	379^1	348	183	43	12	147	315	12.0	3.80	117	.244	.319	0	.000	-0	31	28	-1	3.8

YEAR	TM/L	W	L	PCT	G	GS	CG	SH	SV	IP	H	R	HR	HB	BB	SO	RAT	ERA	ERA+	OAV	OOB	BH	AVG	PB	PR	PR+	PD	TPI
● CHRISTY MATHEWSON	Mathewson, Christopher "Matty" or "Big Six" b: 8/12/1880, Factoryville, Pa. d: 10/7/25, Saranac Lake, N.Y. BR/TR, 6'1.5", 195 lbs. Deb: 7/17/00 FMCH																											
1900	NY-N	0	3	.000	6	1	1	0	0	33^2	37	32	1	4	20	15	16.3	5.08	71	.278	.389	2	.182	0	-5	-6	0	-0.3
1901	NY-N	20	17	.541	40	38	36	5	0	336	288	131	3	13	97	221	10.7	2.41	137	.230	.292	28	.215	-1	34	34	8	4.2
1902	NY-N	14	17	.452	35	33	30	**8**	0	284^2	246	118	3	10	77	164	10.5	2.12	133	.233	.292	26	.200	1	21	22	4	2.9
1903	NY-N	30	13	.698	45	42	37	3	2	366^1	321	136	4	10	100	**267**	10.6	2.26	148	.231	.287	28	.226	3	**41**	43	2	**5.1**
1904	NY-N	33	12	.733	48	46	33	4	1	367^2	306	120	7	4	78	**212**	9.5	2.03	134	.226	.270	30	.226	6	29	29	6	4.7
1905	*NY-N	**31**	9	.775	43	37	32	**8**	3	338^2	252	85	4	1	64	**206**	**8.4**	**1.28**	**230**	.205	**.245**	30	.236	10	**65**	**64**	6	**9.9**
1906	NY-N	22	12	.647	38	35	22	6	1	266^2	262	100	3	3	77	128	11.5	2.97	88	.259	.313	24	.264	7	-10	-11	4	-0.2
1907	NY-N	**24**	12	.667	41	36	31	**8**	2	315	250	88	5	2	53	**178**	**8.7**	2.00	124	.212	**.247**	20	.187	3	17	17	1	2.4
1908	NY-N	**37**	11	.771	**56**	44	**34**	**11**	**5**	**390^2**	285	86	5	3	42	**259**	**7.6**	**1.43**	**169**	.200	**.225**	20	.155	1	**41**	**42**	10	**7.2**
1909	NY-N	25	6	**.806**	37	33	26	8	2	275^1	192	57	2	0	36	149	**7.5**	**1.14**	**223**	.200	**.228**	25	.263	7	44	44	6	**7.1**
1910	NY-N	**27**	9	.750	38	35	**27**	2	0	318^1	292	100	5	3	60	184	10.0	1.89	157	.248	.286	25	.234	7	**40**	**39**	7	**6.1**
1911	*NY-N	26	13	.667	45	37	29	5	3	307	303	102	5	1	38	141	10.0	**1.99**	**169**	.259	.283	22	.196	0	**48**	**47**	7	**6.7**
1912	*NY-N	23	12	.657	43	34	27	0	5	310	311	107	5	2	34	134	10.1	2.12	159	.260	**.281**	29	.264	5	**44**	**44**	0	5.3
1913	*NY-N	25	11	.694	40	35	25	4	2	306	291	94	8	0	21	93	**9.2**	**2.06**	**152**	.252	**.266**	19	.184	-0	**39**	**37**	4	**4.8**
1914	NY-N	24	13	.649	41	35	29	5	2	312	314	133	16	2	23	80	9.8	3.00	88	.263	.278	23	.219	6	-7	-13	2	-0.7
1915	NY-N	8	14	.364	27	24	11	1	0	186	199	97	9	1	20	57	10.6	3.58	72	.277	.298	8	.157	3	-17	-23	1	-2.2
1916	NY-N	3	4	.429	12	6	4	1	2	65^2	59	27	3	0	7	16	9.0	2.33	104	.243	.264	0	.000	-1	2	1	2	0.2
	Cin-N	1	0	1.000	1	1	1	0	0	9	15	8	1	0	1	3	16.0	8.00	32	.366	.381	3	.600	1	-5	-5	0	-0.3
	Yr	4	4	.500	13	7	5	1	2	74^2	74	35	4	0	8	19	9.9	3.01	81	.261	.281	3	.136	1	-3	-5	2	-0.1
Total	17	373	188	.665	636	552	435	79	30	4788^2	4223	1621	89	59	848	2507	9.6	2.13	136	.236	.273	362	.215	59	421	408	68	62.9
● HENRY MATHEWSON	Mathewson, Henry b: 12/24/1886, Factoryville, Pa. d: 7/1/17, Factoryville, Pa. BR/TR, 6'3", 175 lbs. Deb: 9/28/06 F																											
1906	NY-N	0	1	.000	2	1	1	0	1	10	7	7	0	1	14	2	19.8	5.40	48	.194	.431	0	.000	-0	-3	-3	0	-0.3
1907	NY-N	0	0	—	1	0	0	0	1	1	1	0	0	0	0	0	9.0	0.00	—	.250	.250	0	—	0	0	0	-0	0.1
Total	2	0	1	.000	3	1	1	0	2	11	8	7	0	1	14	2	18.8	4.91	53	.200	.418	0	.000	-0	-3	-3	0	-0.2
● CARL MATHIAS	Mathias, Carl Lynwood "Stubby" b: 6/13/36, Bechtelsville, Pa. BB/TL, 5'11", 195 lbs. Deb: 7/31/60																											
1960	Cle-A	0	1	.000	7	0	0	0	0	15^1	14	7	2	0	8	13	12.9	3.52	106	.233	.324	0	.000	-0	1	0	0	0.0
1961	Was-A	0	1	.000	4	3	0	0	0	13^2	22	19	3	1	4	7	17.8	11.20	36	.361	.409	1	.200	-0	-11	-11	-0	-0.7
Total	2	0	2	.000	11	3	0	0	0	29	36	26	5	1	12	20	15.2	7.14	54	.298	.366	1	.167	-0	-10	-11	0	-0.7
● RON MATHIS	Mathis, Ronald Vance b: 9/25/58, Kansas City, Mo. BR/TR, 6', 175 lbs. Deb: 4/13/85																											
1985	Hou-N	3	5	.375	23	8	0	0	1	70	83	54	7	1	27	34	14.3	6.04	57	.293	.357	1	.071	-1	-19	-21	-0	-2.3
1987	Hou-N	0	1	.000	8	0	0	0	0	12	10	8	2	0	11	8	15.8	5.25	75	.233	.389	0	.000	-0	-2	-2	0	-0.1
Total	2	3	6	.333	31	8	0	0	1	82	93	62	9	1	38	42	14.5	5.93	60	.285	.362	1	.063	-1	-21	-23	-0	-2.4
● JON MATLACK	Matlack, Jonathan Trumpbour b: 1/19/50, West Chester, Pa. BL/TL, 6'3", 205 lbs. Deb: 7/11/71 C																											
1971	NY-N	0	3	.000	7	6	0	0	0	37	31	18	2	0	15	24	11.2	4.14	83	.228	.305	3	.273	1	-3	-3	-1	-0.2
1972	NY-N	15	10	.600	34	32	8	4	0	244	215	79	14	2	71	169	10.6	2.32	145	.234	.291	10	.128	1	31	29	-1	3.0
1973	*NY-N	14	16	.467	34	34	14	3	0	242	210	93	16	2	99	205	11.6	3.20	113	.236	.314	9	.138	2	13	12	1	1.7
1974	NY-N★	13	15	.464	34	34	14	**7**	0	265^1	221	82	8	5	76	195	10.2	2.41	148	.226	.285	8	.101	-4	36	35	-0	3.2
1975	NY-N★	16	12	.571	33	32	8	3	0	228^2	224	105	15	1	58	154	11.1	3.38	102	.254	.300	7	.100	0	6	2	-2	0.1
1976	NY-N☆	17	10	.630	35	35	16	**6**	0	262	236	94	18	3	57	153	10.2	2.95	112	.242	.286	17	.193	4	16	11	-1	1.4
1977	NY-N	7	15	.318	26	26	5	3	0	169	175	86	19	2	43	123	11.7	4.21	89	.273	.321	3	.060	-2	-5	-9	0	-1.2
1978	Tex-A	15	13	.536	35	33	18	2	1	270	252	93	14	4	51	157	10.2	2.27	166	.245	.284	0	—	0	45	45	0	4.8
1979	Tex-A	5	4	.556	13	13	2	0	0	85	98	43	9	1	15	35	12.1	4.13	101	.293	.325	0	—	0	1	0	0	0.1
1980	Tex-A	10	10	.500	35	34	8	1	1	234^2	265	111	17	0	48	142	12.0	3.68	106	.287	.323	0	—	0	9	6	-3	0.2
1981	Tex-A	4	7	.364	17	16	1	1	0	104^1	101	59	8	1	41	43	12.3	4.14	84	.258	.330	0	—	0	-6	-8	-0	-0.8
1982	Tex-A	7	7	.500	33	14	1	0	1	147^2	158	64	14	2	37	78	12.0	3.53	110	.275	.321	0	—	0	9	6	0	0.6
1983	Tex-A	2	4	.333	25	9	2	0	0	73^1	90	43	7	3	27	38	14.7	4.66	86	.307	.372	0	—	0	-5	-5	1	-0.3
Total	13	125	126	.498	361	318	97	30	3	2363	2276	970	161	26	638	1516	11.2	3.18	114	.254	.305	57	.129	2	148	121	-5	12.6
● AL MATTERN	Mattern, Alonzo Albert b: 6/16/1883, W.Rush, N.Y. d: 11/6/58, West Rush, N.Y. BL/TL, 5'10", 165 lbs. Deb: 9/16/08																											
1908	Bos-N	1	2	.333	5	3	1	1	0	30^1	30	10	0	0	6	8	10.7	2.08	116	.265	.303	1	.125	-0	1	1	-0	0.0
1909	Bos-N	15	21	.417	47	32	24	2	3	316^1	322	142	4	3	108	98	12.3	2.85	99	.268	.330	17	.168	-1	-9	-1	3	0.1
1910	Bos-N	16	19	.457	**51**	37	17	**6**	1	305	288	145	5	6	121	94	12.2	2.98	112	.257	.332	16	.163	-4	2	11	1	0.8
1911	Bos-N	4	15	.211	33	21	11	0	0	186^1	228	129	13	1	63	51	14.1	4.97	77	.320	.376	11	.175	-2	-33	-21	2	-1.9
1912	Bos-N	0	1	.000	2	1	0	0	0	6^1	10	9	0	0	1	3	15.6	7.11	50	.313	.333	0	.000	-0	-3	-2	0	-0.3
Total	5	36	58	.383	138	94	53	9	4	844^1	878	435	22	10	299	254	12.7	3.37	95	.276	.340	45	.165	-8	-41	-14	5	-1.3
● C. V. MATTESON	Matteson, Clifford Virgil b: 11/1861, Ohio d: 12/18/31, Seville, Ohio Deb: 6/13/1884 ♦																											
1884	StL-U	1	0	1.000	1	1	1	0	0	6	9	11	1		3	3	18.0	9.00	27	.321	.387	0	.000	-1	-4	-4	-0	-0.5
● EDDIE MATTESON	Matteson, Henry Edson "Matty" b: 9/7/1884, Guys Mills, Pa. d: 9/1/43, Westfield, N.Y. BR/TR, 5'10.5", 160 lbs. Deb: 5/30/14																											
1914	Phi-N	3	2	.600	15	3	2	0	0	58	58	29	1	1	23	28	12.7	3.10	95	.278	.352	4	.182	-0	-2	-1	-2	-0.3
1918	Was-A	5	3	.625	14	6	2	0	0	67^2	57	20	2	1	15	17	9.7	1.73	158	.238	.286	2	.105	-2	8	8	-1	0.6
Total	2	8	5	.615	29	9	4	0	0	125^2	115	49	3	2	38	45	11.1	2.36	120	.257	.318	6	.146	-2	6	6	-3	0.3
● JOE MATTHEWS	Matthews, John Joseph "Lefty" b: 9/29/1898, Baltimore, Md. d: 2/8/68, Hagerstown, Md. BB/TL, 6', 170 lbs. Deb: 9/18/22																											
1922	Bos-N	0	1	.000	3	1	0	0	0	10	5	6	1	1	6	0	10.8	3.60	111	.143	.286	0	.000	-0	1	0	-0	0.0
● MIKE MATTHEWS	Matthews, Michael Scott b: 10/24/73, Fredericksburg, Va. BL/TL, 6'2", 175 lbs. Deb: 5/31/2000																											
2000	StL-N	0	0	—	14	0	0	0	0	9^1	15	12	2	1	10	8	25.1	11.57	40	.349	.481	0	—	0	-7	-7	-0	-0.3
● WILLIAM MATTHEWS	Matthews, William Calvin b: 1/12/1878, Mahanoy City, Pa. d: 1/23/46, Mt.Carbon, Pa. TR, Deb: 8/28/09																											
1909	Bos-A	0	0	—	5	1	0	0	0	16^2	16	8	1	0	10	6	14.0	3.24	77	.271	.377	0	.000	-1	-1	-1	-0	-0.2
● DALE MATTHEWSON	Matthewson, Dale Wesley b: 5/15/23, Catasauqua, Pa. d: 2/20/84, Blairsville, Ga. BR/TR, 5'11.5", 145 lbs. Deb: 7/3/43																											
1943	Phi-N	0	3	.000	11	1	0	0	0	26	26	14	1	0	8	8	11.8	4.85	70	.271	.327	0	.000	-0	-4	-4	-0	-0.5
1944	Phi-N	0	0	—	17	0	0	0	0	32	27	14	1	0	16	8	12.1	3.94	92	.237	.331	1	.333	-0	-1	-1	-0	-0.1
Total	2	0	3	.000	28	1	0	0	0	58	53	28	2	0	24	16	11.9	4.34	81	.252	.329	1	.200	-0	-5	-5	-0	-0.6
● MIKE MATTIMORE	Mattimore, Michael Joseph b: 1859, Renovo, Pa. d: 4/28/31, Butte, Mont. BL/TL, 5'8.5", 160 lbs. Deb: 5/3/1887 ♦																											
1887	NY-N	3	3	.500	7	7	6	1	0	57^1	75	39	2	4	28	12	12.4	2.35	160	.307	.319	8	.250	-0	11	10	-1	0.7
1888	Phi-a	15	10	.600	26	24	24	4	0	221	221	146	6	13	65	80	12.2	3.38	88	.251	.312	38	.268	7	-8	-10	4	0.0
1889	Phi-a	2	1	.667	5	1	0	0	1	31	43	27	0	1	13	6	16.5	5.81	65	.319	.383	17	.233	1	-7	-7	-0	-0.5
	KC-a	0	0	—	1	0	0	0	0	3	3	3	1	0	2	1	15.0	3.00	139	.250	.357	12	.160	-0	0	0	-0	0.0
	Yr	2	1	.667	6	1	0	0	1	34	46	30	1	1	15	7	16.4	5.56	69	.313	.380	29	.196	1	-6	-7	-0	-0.5
1890	Bro-a	6	13	.316	19	19	19	0	0	178^1	201	149	3	13	76	33	14.6	4.54	86	.276	.355	17	.132	-3	-13	-13	-0	-1.3
Total	4	26	27	.491	58	51	50	5	1	490^2	543	364	12	31	184	132	13.4	3.83	90	.271	.334	92	.204	5	-17	-20	2	-1.1
● EARL MATTINGLY	Mattingly, Laurence Earl b: 11/4/04, Newport, Md. d: 9/8/93, Brookeville, Md. BR/TR, 5'10.5", 164 lbs. Deb: 4/15/31																											
1931	Bro-N	0	1	.000	8	0	0	0	0	14^1	15	4	0	2	10	6	17.0	2.51	152	.268	.397	0	.000	-0	2	2	1	0.1
● RICK MATULA	Matula, Richard Carlton b: 11/22/53, Wharton, Tex. BR/TR, 6', 190 lbs. Deb: 4/8/79																											
1979	Atl-N	8	10	.444	28	28	1	0	0	171^1	193	90	14	3	64	67	13.7	4.15	98	.286	.350	5	.094	-3	-8	-2	1	-0.4
1980	Atl-N	11	13	.458	33	30	3	1	0	176^2	195	100	17	0	60	62	13.0	4.58	82	.286	.343	6	.105	-3	-19	-16	1	-2.1
1981	Atl-N	0	0	—	5	0	0	0	0	7	8	5	1	0	2	0	12.9	6.43	56	.286	.333	0	.000	-0	-2	-2	0	-0.1
Total	3	19	23	.452	66	58	4	1	0	355	396	195	32	3	126	129	13.3	4.41	88	.286	.347	11	.099	-6	-29	-19	2	-2.6

YEAR	TM/L	W	L	PCT	G	GS	CG	SH	SV	IP	H	R	HR	HB	BB	SO	RAT	ERA	ERA+	OAV	OOB	BH	AVG	PB	PR	PR+	PD	TPI
● **HARRY MATUZAK**	Matuzak, Harry George "Matty" b: 1/27/10, Omer, Mich. d: 11/16/78, Fairhope, Ala. BR/TR, 5′11.5″, 185 lbs. Deb: 4/19/34																											
1934	Phi-A	0	3	.000	11	0	0	0	0	24	28	16	2	1	10	9	14.6	4.88	90	.292	.364	1	.167	0	-1	-1	0	-0.1
1936	Phi-A	0	1	.000	6	1	0	0	0	15	21	14	0	0	4	8	15.0	7.20	71	.318	.357	0	.000	-0	-4	-3	-0	-0.2
Total	2	0	4	.000	17	1	0	0	0	39	49	30	2	1	14	17	14.8	5.77	81	.302	.362	1	.111	-0	-5	-5	0	-0.3
● **HAL MAUCK**	Mauck, Alfred Maris b: 3/6/1869, Princeton, Ind. d: 4/27/21, Princeton, Ind. BR/TR, 5′11″, 185 lbs. Deb: 4/29/1893																											
1893	Chi-N	8	10	.444	23	18	12	1	0	143	168	112	2	9	60	23	14.9	4.41	105	.284	.359	9	.148	-5	4	4	-1	-0.2
● **AL MAUL**	Maul, Albert Joseph "Smiling Al" b: 10/9/1865, Philadelphia, Pa. d: 5/3/58, Philadelphia, Pa. BR/TR, 6′, 175 lbs. Deb: 6/20/1884 ♦																											
1884	Phi-U	0	1	.000	1	1	1	0	0	8	10	7	0		1	7	12.4	4.50	52	.286	.306	0	.000	-1	-2	-2	-0	-0.3
1887	Phi-N	4	2	.667	7	5	4	0	0	50^1	87	50	2	2	15	18	15.9	5.54	76	.369	.374	32	.451	3	-8	-7	0	-0.4
1888	Pit-N	0	2	.000	3	1	1	0	0	17	26	20	0	0	5	12	16.4	6.35	42	.342	.383	54	.208	1	-7	-7	0	-0.7
1889	Pit-N	1	4	.200	6	4	4	0	0	42	64	53	3	1	28	11	19.9	9.86	38	.340	.429	71	.276	2	-27	-31	1	-2.1
1890	Pit-P	16	12	.571	30	28	26	2	0	246^2	258	189	13	12	104	81	13.6	3.79	103	.257	.335	42	.259	7	12	3	5	1.2
1891	Pit-N	1	2	.333	8	3	3	0	1	39	44	22	0	3	16	13	14.5	2.31	142	.273	.350	28	.188	1	5	4	-0	0.3
1893	Was-N	12	21	.364	37	33	29	1	0	297	355	254	17	18	144	72	15.7	5.30	87	.288	.370	34	.254	10	-21	-22	0	-1.0
1894	Was-N	11	15	.423	28	26	21	0	0	201^2	272	200	12	10	73	34	15.8	5.98	88	.319	.379	30	.242	3	-15	-16	2	-1.1
1895	Was-N	10	5	.667	16	16	14	0	0	135^2	136	67	5	3	37	34	11.7	**2.45**	**195**	.257	.309	18	.250	1	35	35	1	3.3
1896	Was-N	5	2	.714	8	8	7	0	0	62	75	50	0	4	20	18	14.4	3.63	121	.296	.357	8	.286	2	5	5	-1	0.5
1897	Was-N	0	1	.000	1	1	0	0	0	2	4	2	0	0	1	0	22.5	9.00	48	.400	.455	0	.000	-0	-1	-1	0	-0.2
	Bal-N	0	0	—	2	2	0	0	0	7^2	9	8	0	4	8	2	24.7	7.04	59	.290	.488	1	.333	0	-2	-3	-0	-0.1
	Yr	0	1	.000	3	3	0	0	0	9^2	13	10	0	4	9	2	24.2	7.45	56	.317	.481	1	.250	-0	-3	-4	-0	-0.3
1898	Bal-N	20	7	.741	28	28	26	1	0	239^2	207	74	3	4	49	31	9.8	2.10	170	.231	.274	19	.204	4	40	40	-5	3.9
1899	Bro-N	2	0	1.000	4	4	2	0	0	26	35	19	1	2	6	2	14.9	4.50	87	.321	.368	3	.273	0	-2	-2	0	-0.1
1900	Phi-N	2	3	.400	5	4	3	0	0	38	53	31	2	2	3	6	13.7	6.16	59	.329	.349	3	.200	0	-10	-11	0	-1.1
1901	NY-N	0	3	.000	3	3	2	0	0	19	39	27	1	2	8	5	23.2	11.37	29	.419	.476	3	.375	1	-17	-17	0	-1.7
Total	15	84	80	.512	187	167	143	4	1	1431^2	1674	1073	59	67	518	346	14.1	4.43	96	.285	.349	346	.249	32	-15	-30	4	0.4
● **ERNIE MAUN**	Maun, Ernest Gerald b: 2/3/01, Clearwater, Kan. d: 1/1/87, Corpus Christi, Tex. BR/TR, 6′, 165 lbs. Deb: 5/16/24																											
1924	NY-N	2	1	.667	22	0	0	0	1	35	46	24	2	1	10	5	14.7	5.91	62	.326	.375	2	.667	1	-8	-9	-1	-0.7
1926	Phi-N	1	4	.200	14	5	0	0	0	37^2	57	36	4	1	18	9	18.2	6.45	64	.339	.406	3	.250	-0	-11	-9	-0	-1.0
Total	2	3	5	.375	36	5	0	0	1	72^2	103	60	6	2	28	14	16.5	6.19	63	.333	.392	5	.333	1	-19	-18	-1	-1.7
● **DICK MAUNEY**	Mauney, Richard b: 1/26/20, Concord, N.C. d: 2/6/70, Albemarle, N.C. BR/TR, 5′11.5″, 164 lbs. Deb: 6/13/45																											
1945	Phi-N	6	10	.375	20	16	6	2	1	122^2	127	54	7	2	27	35	11.4	3.08	124	.268	.310	6	.146	-0	10	10	1	1.3
1946	Phi-N	6	4	.600	24	7	3	1	2	90	98	36	4	3	18	31	11.9	2.70	127	.279	.320	4	.167	-1	7	7	0	0.8
1947	Phi-N	0	0	—	9	1	0	0	1	16^1	15	8	1	1	7	6	12.7	3.86	104	.288	.383	0	.000	-0	0	0	1	0.1
Total	3	12	14	.462	53	24	9	3	4	229	240	98	12	6	52	72	11.7	2.99	123	.274	.319	10	.149	-1	17	18	2	2.2
● **HARRY MAUPIN**	Maupin, Harry Carr b: 7/11/1872, Wellsville, Mo. d: 8/25/52, Parsons, Kan. 5′7″, 150 lbs. Deb: 10/5/1898																											
1898	StL-N	0	2	.000	2	2	2	0	0	18	22	11	0	3	3	3	14.0	5.50	69	.297	.350	3	.429	1	-4	-3	-1	-0.3
1899	Cle-N	0	3	.000	5	3	2	0	0	25	55	36	0	1	7	3	22.7	12.60	29	.437	.470	0	.000	-2	-24	-26	-1	-2.2
Total	2	0	5	.000	7	5	4	0	0	43	77	47	0	4	10	6	19.0	9.63	39	.385	.425	3	.176	-1	-28	-28	-2	-2.5
● **DAVID MAURER**	Maurer, David Charles b: 2/23/75, Minneapolis, Minn. BR/TL, 6′2″, 205 lbs. Deb: 7/22/2000																											
2000	SD-N	1	0	1.000	14	0	0	0	0	14^2	15	8	2	2	5	13	13.5	3.68	119	.263	.344	0	—	0	2	1	-0	0.0
● **RALPH MAURIELLO**	Mauriello, Ralph "Tami" b: 8/25/34, Brooklyn, N.Y. BR/TR, 6′3″, 195 lbs. Deb: 9/13/58																											
1958	LA-N	1	1	.500	3	2	0	0	0	11^2	10	6	1	0	8	11	13.9	4.63	89	.238	.360	0	.000	-1	-1	-1	-0	-0.2
● **TIM MAUSER**	Mauser, Timothy Edward b: 10/4/66, Fort Worth, Tex. BR/TR, 6′, 185 lbs. Deb: 7/7/91																											
1991	Phi-N	0	0	—	3	0	0	0	0	10^2	18	10	3	0	3	6	17.7	7.59	48	.367	.404	0	.000	-0	-5	-5	-0	-0.3
1993	Phi-N	0	0	—	8	0	0	0	0	16^1	15	9	1	1	7	14	12.7	4.96	80	.238	.324	0	.000	-0	-2	-2	1	0.0
	SD-N	0	1	.000	28	0	0	0	0	37^2	36	19	5	0	17	32	12.7	3.58	116	.248	.327	0	.000	-0	2	2	1	0.2
	Yr	0	1	.000	36	0	0	0	0	54	51	28	6	1	24	46	12.7	4.00	102	.245	.326	0	.000	-0	0	1	1	0.2
1994	SD-N	2	4	.333	35	0	0	0	2	49	50	21	3	1	19	32	12.9	3.49	118	.269	.340	1	.250	0	4	3	-0	0.4
1995	SD-N	0	1	.000	5	0	0	0	0	5^2	4	6	0	0	9	9	20.6	9.53	42	.190	.433	0	.000	-0	-3	-4	-0	-0.6
Total	4	2	6	.250	79	0	0	0	2	119^1	123	65	12	2	55	93	13.6	4.37	93	.265	.345	1	.071	-0	-4	-4	1	-0.3
● **BRIAN MAXCY**	Maxcy, David Brian b: 5/4/71, Amory, Miss. BR/TR, 6′1″, 170 lbs. Deb: 5/27/95																											
1995	Det-A	4	5	.444	41	0	0	0	0	52^1	61	48	6	2	31	20	16.2	6.88	69	.293	.390	0	—	0	-13	-12	1	-1.6
1996	Det-A	0	0	—	2	0	0	0	0	3^1	8	5	2	0	2	1	27.0	13.50	37	.471	.526	0	—	0	-3	-3	0	-0.1
Total	2	4	5	.444	43	0	0	0	0	55^2	69	53	8	2	33	21	16.8	7.28	66	.307	.400	0	—	0	-16	-15	2	-1.7
● **LARRY MAXIE**	Maxie, Larry Hans b: 10/10/40, Upland, Cal. BR/TR, 6′4″, 220 lbs. Deb: 8/30/69																											
1969	Atl-N	0	0	—	2	0	0	0	0	3	1	1	0	1	1	1	9.0	3.00	120	.111	.273	0	—	0	0	0	0	0.0
● **BERT MAXWELL**	Maxwell, James Albert b: 10/17/1886, Texarkana, Ark. d: 12/10/61, Brady, Tex. BB/TR, 6′, 180 lbs. Deb: 9/12/06																											
1906	Pit-N	0	1	.000	1	1	0	0	0	8	8	6	0	0	2	1	11.3	5.63	48	.286	.333	0	.000	-0	-3	-3	0	-0.3
1908	Phi-A	0	0	—	4	0	0	0	0	13	23	21	0	2	9	7	23.5	11.08	23	.348	.442	0	.000	-1	-13	-11	-0	-0.7
1911	NY-N	1	2	.333	4	3	3	0	0	31	37	15	0	2	7	8	13.4	2.90	116	.311	.359	1	.111	-0	2	2	1	0.2
1914	Bro-F	3	4	.429	12	8	6	1	1	71^1	76	31	0	1	24	19	12.7	3.28	88	.276	.337	2	.087	-2	-3	-3	1	-0.5
Total	4	4	7	.364	21	12	9	1	1	123^1	144	73	0	5	42	35	13.9	4.16	71	.295	.357	3	.075	-3	-17	-16	1	-1.3
● **DARRELL MAY**	May, Darrell Kevin b: 6/13/72, San Bernardino, Cal. BL/TL, 6′2″, 170 lbs. Deb: 9/10/95																											
1995	Atl-N	0	0	—	2	0	0	0	0	4	10	5	0	0	0	1	22.5	11.25	38	.500	.500	0	—	0	-3	-3	0	-0.1
1996	Pit-N	0	1	.000	5	2	0	0	0	8^2	15	10	5	1	4	5	20.8	9.35	47	.357	.426	1	.333	0	-5	-5	0	-0.4
	Cal-A	0	0	—	5	0	0	0	0	2^2	3	3	1	0	2	1	16.9	10.13	49	.333	.455	0	—	0	-2	-2	-0	-0.1
1997	Ana-A	2	1	.667	29	2	0	0	0	51^2	56	31	6	0	25	42	14.1	5.23	88	.277	.357	0	.000	-0	-4	-4	-0	-0.2
Total	3	2	2	.500	41	4	0	0	0	67	84	49	12	1	31	49	15.6	6.31	72	.308	.380	1	.200	0	-13	-13	-0	-0.8
● **JAKIE MAY**	May, Frank Spruiell b: 11/25/1895, Youngsville, N.C. d: 6/3/70, Wendell, N.C. BR/TL, 5′8″, 178 lbs. Deb: 6/26/17																											
1917	StL-N	0	0	—	15	1	0	0	0	29^1	29	13	0	3	11	18	13.2	3.38	80	.302	.391	0	.000	-1	-2	-2	2	0.0
1918	StL-N	5	6	.455	29	15	6	0	0	152^2	149	83	2	13	69	61	13.6	3.83	71	.264	.358	3	.067	-1	-18	-19	-2	-1.7
1919	StL-N	3	12	.200	28	19	8	1	0	125^2	99	64	1	14	87	58	14.3	3.22	87	.230	.377	6	.162	-1	-4	-6	-1	-1.0
1920	StL-N	1	4	.200	16	5	3	0	0	70^2	65	38	0	7	37	33	13.9	3.06	98	.251	.360	5	.227	1	1	-1	-2	-0.1
1921	StL-N	1	3	.250	5	5	1	0	0	21	29	14	0	0	12	5	17.6	4.71	78	.333	.414	2	.333	1	-2	-3	-1	-0.4
1924	Cin-N	3	3	.500	38	3	2	0	**6**	99	104	39	2	6	29	59	12.6	3.00	126	.276	.337	3	.111	-2	10	9	-0	0.4
1925	Cin-N	8	9	.471	36	12	7	1	2	137^1	146	74	3	7	45	74	13.0	3.87	106	.272	.337	8	.186	0	6	4	0	0.5
1926	Cin-N	13	9	.591	45	15	9	1	3	167^2	175	66	4	7	44	103	12.1	3.22	115	.276	.329	7	.146	-1	11	9	-1	0.9
1927	Cin-N	15	12	.556	44	28	17	2	1	235^2	242	110	4	14	70	121	12.4	3.51	108	.274	.337	14	.184	0	11	7	1	0.8
1928	Cin-N	3	5	.375	21	11	1	1	1	79^1	99	44	1	1	35	39	15.3	4.42	89	.315	.386	8	.296	1	-4	-4	-1	-0.4
1929	Cin-N	10	14	.417	41	24	10	0	3	199	219	111	7	5	75	92	13.5	4.61	99	.285	.352	13	.203	-1	2	-1	-0	-0.2
1930	Cin-N	3	11	.214	26	18	5	1	0	112^1	147	83	6	6	41	44	15.5	5.77	84	.320	.383	5	.128	-1	-10	-12	0	-1.2
1931	Chi-N	5	5	.500	31	4	1	0	2	79	81	35	2	3	43	38	14.5	3.87	100	.275	.372	5	.227	1	-0	-0	0	0.1
1932	*Chi-N	2	2	.500	35	0	0	0	1	53^2	61	34	3	2	19	20	13.8	4.36	86	.281	.345	1	.125	-0	-3	-4	-0	-0.3
Total	14	72	95	.431	410	160	70	7	19	1562^1	1645	808	35	88	617	765	13.5	3.88	97	.278	.355	80	.171	-4	-3	-23	-6	-2.6
● **RUDY MAY**	May, Rudolph b: 7/18/44, Coffeyville, Kan. BL/TL, 6′3″, 207 lbs. Deb: 4/18/65																											
1965	Cal-A	4	9	.308	30	19	2	1	0	124	111	59	7	4	78	76	14.0	3.92	87	.245	.361	6	.200	3	-6	-7	-2	-0.6
1969	Cal-A	10	13	.435	43	25	4	0	2	180^1	142	81	20	3	66	133	10.5	3.44	101	.220	.296	4	.082	-2	4	1	-1	-0.1
1970	Cal-A	7	13	.350	38	34	2	2	0	208^2	190	102	20	3	81	164	11.8	4.01	90	.245	.319	6	.087	-2	-7	-9	0	-1.1

YEAR	TM/L	W	L	PCT	G	GS	CG	SH	SV	IP	H	R	HR	HB	BB	SO	RAT	ERA	ERA+	OAV	OOB	BH	AVG	PB	PR	PR+	PD	TPI
1971	Cal-A	11	12	.478	32	31	7	2	0	208^1	160	74	12	2	87	156	10.8	3.02	107	.213	.297	10	.147	0	10	5	-1	0.5
1972	Cal-A	12	11	.522	35	30	10	3	1	205^1	162	79	15	0	82	169	10.7	2.94	99	.215	.293	7	.113	-1	3	-0	-2	-0.4
1973	Cal-A	7	17	.292	34	28	10	4	0	185	177	101	20	3	80	134	12.6	4.38	81	.254	.333	0	—	0	-11	-18	2	-1.9
1974	Cal-A	0	1	.000	18	3	0	0	2	27	29	24	2	1	10	12	13.3	7.00	49	.274	.342	0	—	0	-10	-11	1	-0.4
	NY-A	8	4	.667	17	15	8	2	0	114^1	75	36	5	4	48	90	10.0	2.28	155	.188	.282	0	—	0	17	16	-2	1.5
	Yr	8	5	.615	35	18	8	2	2	141^1	104	60	7	5	58	102	10.6	3.18	110	.206	.295	0	—	0	7	5	-0	1.1
1975	NY-A	14	12	.538	32	31	13	1	0	212	179	87	9	2	99	145	11.9	3.06	121	.231	.320	0	—	0	17	15	-1	1.6
1976	NY-A	4	3	.571	11	11	2	1	0	68	49	32	5	1	28	38	10.3	3.57	96	.206	.292	0	—	0	-0	-1	0	-0.1
	Bal-A	11	7	.611	24	21	5	1	0	152^1	156	73	11	0	42	71	11.7	3.78	87	.267	.316	0	—	0	-4	-9	-1	-1.1
	Yr	15	10	.600	35	32	7	2	0	220^1	205	105	16	1	70	109	11.3	3.72	89	.249	.309	0	—	0	-5	-10	-1	-1.2
1977	Bal-A	18	14	.563	37	37	11	4	0	251^2	243	114	25	5	78	105	11.7	3.61	105	.255	.315	0	—	0	13	6	-3	0.4
1978	Mon-N	8	10	.444	27	23	4	1	0	144	141	73	15	6	42	87	11.8	3.88	91	.255	.315	6	.143	0	-5	-6	-2	-0.8
1979	Mon-N	10	3	.769	33	7	2	1	0	93^2	88	30	4	4	31	67	11.8	2.31	159	.255	.324	3	.143	-0	15	14	1	2.0
1980	*NY-A	15	5	.750	41	17	3	1	3	175^1	144	56	14	0	39	133	**9.4**	**2.46**	**160**	.224	**.268**	0	—	0	31	29	0	3.3
1981	*NY-A	6	11	.353	27	22	4	0	1	147^2	137	71	10	2	41	79	11.0	4.14	86	.246	.300	0	—	0	-8	-10	1	-0.9
1982	NY-A	6	6	.500	41	6	0	0	3	106	109	43	4	1	14	85	10.5	2.89	138	.267	.292	0	—	0	14	13	1	1.5
1983	NY-A	1	5	.167	15	0	0	0	0	18^1	22	15	1	1	12	16	17.2	6.87	57	.293	.398	0	—	0	-6	-6	0	-1.2
Total	16	152	156	.494	535	360	87	24	12	2622	2314	1150	199	42	958	1760	11.4	3.46	102	.238	.310	42	.123	-2	66	24	-7	2.2

● SCOTT MAY

May, Scott Francis b: 11/11/61, West Bend, Wis. BR/TR, 6'1", 185 lbs. Deb: 9/2/88

YEAR	TM/L	W	L	PCT	G	GS	CG	SH	SV	IP	H	R	HR	HB	BB	SO	RAT	ERA	ERA+	OAV	OOB	BH	AVG	PB	PR	PR+	PD	TPI
1988	Tex-A	0	0	—	3	1	0	0	0	7^1	8	7	3	0	4	4	14.7	8.59	48	.296	.387	0	—	0	-4	-4	0	-0.2
1991	Chi-N	0	0	—	2	0	0	0	0	2	6	4	0	0	1	1	31.5	18.00	22	.545	.583	0	—	0	-3	-3	-0	-0.2
Total	2	0	0	—	5	1	0	0	0	9^1	14	11	3	0	5	5	18.3	10.61	38	.368	.442	0	—	0	-7	-7	-0	-0.4

● BUCKSHOT MAY

May, William Herbert b: 12/13/1899, Bakersfield, Cal. d: 3/15/84, Bakersfield, Cal. BR/TR, 6'2", 169 lbs. Deb: 5/9/24

YEAR	TM/L	W	L	PCT	G	GS	CG	SH	SV	IP	H	R	HR	HB	BB	SO	RAT	ERA	ERA+	OAV	OOB	BH	AVG	PB	PR	PR+	PD	TPI
1924	Pit-N	0	0	—	1	0	0	0	0	1	2	0	0	0	0	1	18.0	0.00	—	.500	.500	0	—	0	0	0	0	0.0

● ED MAYER

Mayer, Edwin David b: 11/30/31, San Francisco, Cal BL/TL, 6'2", 185 lbs. Deb: 9/15/57

YEAR	TM/L	W	L	PCT	G	GS	CG	SH	SV	IP	H	R	HR	HB	BB	SO	RAT	ERA	ERA+	OAV	OOB	BH	AVG	PB	PR	PR+	PD	TPI
1957	Chi-N	0	0	—	3	1	0	0	0	7^2	8	5	2	1	2	3	12.9	5.87	66	.258	.324	1	.500	0	-2	-2	0	0.0
1958	Chi-N	2	2	.500	19	0	0	0	1	23^2	15	12	0	3	16	14	12.9	3.80	103	.190	.347	1	.200	-0	0	0	-0	0.0
Total	2	2	2	.500	22	1	0	0	1	31^1	23	17	2	4	18	17	12.9	4.31	91	.209	.341	2	.286	0	-1	-1	0	0.0

● ERSKINE MAYER

Mayer, Erskine John (b: James Erskine) b: 1/16/1889, Atlanta, Ga. d: 3/10/57, Los Angeles, Cal. BR/TR, 6', 168 lbs. Deb: 9/4/12 F

YEAR	TM/L	W	L	PCT	G	GS	CG	SH	SV	IP	H	R	HR	HB	BB	SO	RAT	ERA	ERA+	OAV	OOB	BH	AVG	PB	PR	PR+	PD	TPI
1912	Phi-N	0	1	.000	7	1	0	0	0	21^1	27	15	1	1	7	5	14.8	6.33	57	.318	.376	0	.000	-0	-7	-6	0	-0.3
1913	Phi-N	9	9	.500	39	19	7	2	1	170^2	172	77	6	9	46	51	12.0	3.11	107	.272	.330	6	.120	-2	2	4	0	0.2
1914	Phi-N	21	19	.525	48	38	24	4	2	321	308	135	8	13	91	116	11.6	2.58	114	.256	.315	21	.194	2	8	12	4	2.2
1915	*Phi-N	21	15	.583	43	33	20	2	2	274^2	240	94	9	14	59	114	10.3	2.36	116	.243	.295	21	.239	5	12	12	1	2.2
1916	Phi-N	7	7	.500	28	16	7	2	0	140	148	58	7	4	33	62	11.9	3.15	84	.281	.328	5	.132	-1	-8	-8	3	-0.5
1917	Phi-N	11	6	.647	28	18	11	1	0	160	160	62	6	4	33	64	11.1	2.76	102	.268	.310	10	.196	-0	-1	1	-0	0.0
1918	Phi-N	7	4	.636	13	13	7	0	0	104	108	46	2	4	26	16	11.9	3.12	96	.276	.328	8	.216	1	-4	-1	-0	-0.1
	Pit-N	9	3	.750	15	14	11	1	0	123^1	122	40	1	4	27	25	11.2	2.26	127	.268	.314	7	.167	2	7	8	-2	0.8
	Yr	16	7	.696	28	27	18	1	0	227^1	230	86	3	8	53	41	11.5	2.65	110	.272	.320	15	.190	2	3	7	-2	0.7
1919	Pit-N	5	3	.625	18	10	6	0	1	88^1	100	50	2	2	12	20	11.6	4.48	67	.267	.294	6	.207	0	-15	-14	-1	-1.4
	*Chi-A	1	3	.250	6	2	0	0	0	23^2	30	23	1	0	11	9	15.6	8.37	38	.316	.387	0	.000	-1	-14	-14	-0	-1.9
Total	8	91	70	.565	245	164	93	12	6	1427	1415	600	43	55	345	482	11.4	2.96	99	.264	.316	84	.185	5	-21	-5	4	1.2

● SAM MAYER

Mayer, Samuel Frankel (b: Samuel Frankel Erskine) b: 2/28/1893, Atlanta, Ga. d: 7/1/62, Atlanta, Ga. BR/TL, 5'10", 164 lbs. Deb: 9/14/15 F♦

YEAR	TM/L	W	L	PCT	G	GS	CG	SH	SV	IP	H	R	HR	HB	BB	SO	RAT	ERA	ERA+	OAV	OOB	BH	AVG	PB	PR	PR+	PD	TPI
1915	Was-A	0	0	—	1	0	0	0	0	0	0	0	0	2	—	—	—	—	—	1.000	101	.241	0	0	0	0	0.0	

● BRENT MAYNE

Mayne, Brent Danem b: 4/19/68, Loma Linda, Cal. BL/TR, 6'1", 190 lbs. Deb: 9/18/90 ♦

YEAR	TM/L	W	L	PCT	G	GS	CG	SH	SV	IP	H	R	HR	HB	BB	SO	RAT	ERA	ERA+	OAV	OOB	BH	AVG	PB	PR	PR+	PD	TPI
2000	Col-N	1	0	1.000	1	0	0	0	0	1	1	0	0	0	1	0	18.0	0.00	—	.250	.400	101	.301	0	1	1	0	0.1

● AL MAYS

Mays, Albert C. b: 5/17/1865, Canal Dover, Ohio d: 5/7/05, Parkersburg, W.Va. BR, Deb: 5/10/1885

YEAR	TM/L	W	L	PCT	G	GS	CG	SH	SV	IP	H	R	HR	HB	BB	SO	RAT	ERA	ERA+	OAV	OOB	BH	AVG	PB	PR	PR+	PD	TPI
1885	Lou-a	6	11	.353	17	17	17	0	0	150	129	102	3	8	43	61	10.8	2.76	117	.219	.282	13	.213	0	8	8	-0	0.7
1886	NY-a	11	27	.289	41	40	39	1	0	350	330	231	7	14	140	163	12.4	3.39	101	.240	.317	16	.119	-9	2	1	-1	-0.8
1887	NY-a	17	34	.333	52	52	50	0	0	441^1	687	359	11	20	136	124	14.4	4.73	90	.347	.353	55	.238	-1	-21	-24	6	-1.5
1888	Bro-a	9	9	.500	18	18	17	1	0	160^2	150	81	1	11	32	67	10.8	2.80	107	.238	.287	5	.079	-4	5	3	2	0.1
1889	Col-a	10	7	.588	21	19	13	1	0	140	167	119	4	4	56	52	14.6	4.82	75	.287	.354	7	.130	-1	-15	-20	1	-1.8
1890	Col-a	0	1	.000	1	1	1	0	0	9	14	13	0	1	8	2	23.0	8.00	45	.341	.460	0	.000	-0	-4	-5	-1	-0.4
Total	6	53	89	.373	150	147	137	3	0	1251	1477	905	26	58	415	469	13.1	3.91	94	.284	.328	96	.176	-16	-26	-36	7	-3.7

● CARL MAYS

Mays, Carl William "Sub" b: 11/12/1891, Liberty, Ky. d: 4/4/71, ElCajon, Cal. BL/TR, 5'11.5", 195 lbs. Deb: 4/15/15

YEAR	TM/L	W	L	PCT	G	GS	CG	SH	SV	IP	H	R	HR	HB	BB	SO	RAT	ERA	ERA+	OAV	OOB	BH	AVG	PB	PR	PR+	PD	TPI
1915	Bos-A	6	5	.545	38	6	2	0	**7**	131^2	119	54	0	5	21	65	9.9	2.60	107	.244	.282	9	.237	2	5	3	2	0.6
1916	*Bos-A	18	13	.581	44	24	14	2	3	245	208	79	3	9	74	76	10.7	2.39	116	.234	.299	18	.234	7	12	11	9	3.3
1917	Bos-A	22	9	.710	35	33	27	2	0	289	230	81	1	14	74	91	9.9	1.74	148	.221	.282	27	.252	6	30	28	8	4.9
1918	*Bos-A	21	13	.618	35	33	**30**	**8**	0	293^1	230	94	2	11	81	114	9.9	2.21	121	.221	.284	30	.288	10	19	16	9	4.2
1919	Bos-A	5	11	.313	21	16	14	2	2	146	131	57	3	5	40	53	10.8	2.47	123	.247	.306	8	.151	-2	12	10	3	1.2
	NY-A	9	3	.750	13	13	12	1	0	120	96	34	2	5	37	54	10.4	1.65	193	.216	.283	14	.311	3	21	21	1	2.7
	Yr	14	14	.500	34	29	26	3	2	266	227	91	5	10	77	107	10.6	2.10	148	.233	.295	22	.224	1	33	31	4	3.9
1920	NY-A	26	11	.703	45	37	26	**6**	2	312	310	127	13	7	84	92	11.6	3.06	125	.263	.316	26	.239	2	26	26	6	3.6
1921	*NY-A	**27**	9	**.750**	**49**	38	30	1	**7**	**336**^{2}	332	145	11	9	76	70	11.1	3.05	139	.257	.303	49	.343	12	46	45	3	5.8
1922	*NY-A	13	14	.481	34	29	21	1	2	240	257	111	12	7	50	41	11.8	3.60	111	.285	.327	23	.250	1	12	11	6	1.8
1923	NY-A	5	2	.714	23	7	2	0	0	81^1	119	59	8	4	32	16	17.2	6.20	64	.357	.420	4	.148	1	-20	-21	3	-1.2
1924	Cin-N	20	9	.690	37	27	15	2	0	226	238	97	3	4	36	63	11.1	3.15	120	.270	.302	24	.289	7	18	16	8	3.5
1925	Cin-N	3	5	.375	12	5	3	0	2	51^2	60	22	0	2	13	10	13.1	3.31	124	.294	.342	4	.250	1	6	5	1	0.8
1926	Cin-N	19	12	.613	39	33	**24**	3	1	281	286	112	3	4	53	58	11.0	3.14	118	.269	.306	22	.224	2	21	18	10	3.1
1927	Cin-N	3	7	.300	14	9	6	0	0	82	89	39	1	1	10	17	11.0	3.51	108	.276	.300	13	.406	5	4	3	4	1.3
1928	Cin-N	4	1	.800	14	6	4	1	1	62^2	67	33	3	0	22	10	12.8	3.88	102	.275	.335	8	.296	1	1	1	0	0.2
1929	NY-N	7	2	.778	37	8	1	0	4	123	140	67	8	2	31	32	12.7	4.32	106	.287	.333	12	.353	4	5	4	2	0.8
Total	15	208	126	.623	490	324	231	29	31	3021^1	2912	1211	73	89	734	862	11.1	2.92	119	.257	.307	291	.268	64	217	194	74	36.6

● JOE MAYS

Mays, Joseph Emerson b: 12/10/75, Flint, Mich. BB/TR, 6'1", 160 lbs. Deb: 4/7/99

YEAR	TM/L	W	L	PCT	G	GS	CG	SH	SV	IP	H	R	HR	HB	BB	SO	RAT	ERA	ERA+	OAV	OOB	BH	AVG	PB	PR	PR+	PD	TPI
1999	Min-A	6	11	.353	49	20	2	1	0	171	179	92	24	2	67	115	13.1	4.37	117	.270	.338	0	.000	0	10	13	1	1.2
2000	Min-A	7	15	.318	31	28	2	1	0	160^1	193	105	20	2	67	102	14.7	5.56	95	.299	.366	2	.400	1	-11	-5	1	-0.4
Total	2	13	26	.333	80	48	4	2	0	331^1	372	197	44	4	134	217	13.9	4.94	105	.284	.352	2	.250	1	-2	8	2	0.8

● MATT MAYSEY

Maysey, Matthew Samuel b: 1/8/67, Hamilton, Ont., Canada BR/TR, 6'4", 225 lbs. Deb: 7/8/92

YEAR	TM/L	W	L	PCT	G	GS	CG	SH	SV	IP	H	R	HR	HB	BB	SO	RAT	ERA	ERA+	OAV	OOB	BH	AVG	PB	PR	PR+	PD	TPI
1992	Mon-N	0	0	—	2	0	0	0	0	2^1	4	1	1	1	0	1	19.3	3.86	90	.364	.417	0	—	0	-0	-0	-0	0.0
1993	Mil-A	1	2	.333	23	0	0	0	1	22	28	14	4	1	13	10	17.2	5.73	74	.322	.416	1	1.000	0	-3	-4	-1	-0.5
Total	2	1	2	.333	25	0	0	0	1	24^1	32	15	5	2	13	11	17.4	5.55	75	.327	.416	1	1.000	0	-3	-4	-1	-0.5

● JACK McADAMS

McAdams, George D. b: 12/17/1886, Benton, Ark. d: 5/21/37, San Francisco, Cal BR/TR, 6'1.5", 170 lbs. Deb: 7/22/11

YEAR	TM/L	W	L	PCT	G	GS	CG	SH	SV	IP	H	R	HR	HB	BB	SO	RAT	ERA	ERA+	OAV	OOB	BH	AVG	PB	PR	PR+	PD	TPI
1911	StL-N	0	0	—	6	0	0	0	0	9^2	7	5	0	2	5	4	13.0	3.72	91	.226	.368	0	.000	-0	-0	-0	0	0.0

● BILL McAFEE

McAfee, William Fort b: 9/7/07, Smithville, Ga. d: 7/8/58, Culpeper, Va. BR/TR, 6'2", 186 lbs. Deb: 5/12/30

YEAR	TM/L	W	L	PCT	G	GS	CG	SH	SV	IP	H	R	HR	HB	BB	SO	RAT	ERA	ERA+	OAV	OOB	BH	AVG	PB	PR	PR+	PD	TPI
1930	Chi-N	0	0	—	2	0	0	0	0	1	3	5	0	0	2	0	45.0	0.00	—	.375	.500	0	—	0	1	1	-0	0.0
1931	Bos-N	0	1	.000	18	1	0	0	0	29^2	39	22	2	0	10	9	14.9	6.37	59	.333	.386	0	.000	-0	-8	-9	0	-0.4
1932	Was-A	6	1	.857	8	5	2	0	0	41^1	47	22	3	0	22	10	15.0	3.92	110	.287	.371	2	.111	-2	3	2	1	0.2
1933	Was-A	3	2	.600	27	1	0	0	5	53	64	40	3	1	21	14	14.6	6.62	63	.296	.361	4	.267	2	-14	-15	0	-1.3
1934	StL-A	1	0	1.000	28	0	0	0	0	61^2	84	48	4	3	26	11	16.5	5.84	86	.332	.401	3	.188	-0	-9	-5	-1	-0.3
Total	5	10	4	.714	83	7	2	0	5	186^2	237	137	12	4	81	44	15.5	5.69	78	.313	.382	9	.173	0	-28	-26	1	-1.8

● **JIMMY McALEER** McAleer, James Robert "Loafer" b: 7/10/1864, Youngstown, Ohio d: 4/29/31, Youngstown, Ohio BR/TR, 6', 175 lbs. Deb: 4/24/1889 M◆

YEAR	TM/L	W	L	PCT	G	GS	CG	SH	SV	IP	H	R	HR	HB	BB	SO	RAT	ERA	ERA+	OAV	OOB	BH	AVG	PB	PR	PR+	PD	TPI
1901	Cle-A	0	0	—	1	0	0	0	0	0^1	2	3	0	0	3	0	135.0	0.00	—	.667	.833	1	.143	-0	0	0	0	0.0

● **JACK McALEESE** McAleese, John James b: 1877, Sharon, Pa. d: 11/15/50, New York, N.Y. BR/TR, 5'8", Deb: 8/10/01 ◆

YEAR	TM/L	W	L	PCT	G	GS	CG	SH	SV	IP	H	R	HR	HB	BB	SO	RAT	ERA	ERA+	OAV	OOB	BH	AVG	PB	PR	PR+	PD	TPI
1901	Chi-A	0	0	—	1	0	0	0	0	3	7	3	0	0	1	1	24.0	9.00	39	.438	.471	0	.000	-0	-2	-2	0	-0.1

● **SPORT McALLISTER** McAllister, Lewis William b: 7/23/1874, Austin, Miss. d: 7/17/62, Wyandotte, Mich. BB/TR, 5'11", 180 lbs. Deb: 8/7/1896 ◆

YEAR	TM/L	W	L	PCT	G	GS	CG	SH	SV	IP	H	R	HR	HB	BB	SO	RAT	ERA	ERA+	OAV	OOB	BH	AVG	PB	PR	PR+	PD	TPI
1896	Cle-N	0	0	—	1	0	0	0	0	4	9	3	0	0	2	0	24.8	6.75	67	.450	.500	6	.222	-0	-1	-1	0	0.0
1897	Cle-N	1	2	.333	4	3	3	0	0	28	29	20	3	0	9	10	12.2	4.50	100	.266	.322	30	.219	-0	-1	-0	1	0.0
1898	Cle-N	3	4	.429	9	7	6	0	0	65^1	73	43	2	3	23	9	13.6	4.55	80	.281	.346	13	.228	1	-7	-7	-1	-0.6
1899	Cle-N	0	1	.000	3	1	1	0	0	16	29	22	0	4	10	2	24.2	9.56	39	.387	.483	99	.237	0	-10	-11	-0	-0.5
Total	4	4	7	.364	17	11	10	0	0	113^1	140	88	5	7	44	21	15.2	5.32	73	.302	.371	358	.247	1	-19	-18	0	-1.1

● **ERNIE McANALLY** McAnally, Ernest Lee b: 8/15/46, Pittsburg, Tex. BR/TR, 6'1", 190 lbs. Deb: 4/11/71

YEAR	TM/L	W	L	PCT	G	GS	CG	SH	SV	IP	H	R	HR	HB	BB	SO	RAT	ERA	ERA+	OAV	OOB	BH	AVG	PB	PR	PR+	PD	TPI
1971	Mon-N	11	12	.478	31	25	8	2	0	177^2	150	85	9	8	87	98	12.4	3.90	91	.228	.326	7	.117	-2	-8	-7	0	-1.1
1972	Mon-N	6	15	.286	29	27	4	2	0	170	165	79	13	4	71	102	12.7	3.81	93	.259	.337	6	.113	-2	-7	-5	3	-0.4
1973	Mon-N	7	9	.438	27	24	4	0	0	147	158	84	13	3	54	72	13.2	4.04	95	.274	.340	9	.184	-1	-6	-3	-0	-0.5
1974	Mon-N	6	13	.316	25	21	5	2	0	128^2	126	73	10	4	56	79	13.0	4.48	86	.256	.336	5	.119	-2	-12	-8	1	-1.3
Total	4	30	49	.380	112	97	21	6	0	623^1	599	321	45	19	268	351	12.8	4.03	91	.253	.334	27	.132	-6	-33	-24	3	-3.3

● **JAMIE McANDREW** McAndrew, James Brian b: 9/2/67, Williamsport, Pa. BR/TR, 6'2", 190 lbs. Deb: 7/17/95 F

YEAR	TM/L	W	L	PCT	G	GS	CG	SH	SV	IP	H	R	HR	HB	BB	SO	RAT	ERA	ERA+	OAV	OOB	BH	AVG	PB	PR	PR+	PD	TPI
1995	Mil-A	2	3	.400	10	4	0	0	0	36^1	37	21	2	1	12	19	12.4	4.71	106	.266	.329	0	—	0	0	1	-1	0.1
1997	Mil-A	1	1	.500	5	4	0	0	0	19^1	24	19	1	2	23	8	22.8	8.38	55	.304	.471	0	—	0	-8	-8	-0	-0.7
Total	2	3	4	.429	15	8	0	0	0	55^2	61	40	3	3	35	27	16.0	5.98	81	.280	.387	0	—	0	-8	-7	-1	-0.6

● **JIM McANDREW** McAndrew, James Clement b: 1/11/44, Lost Nation, Iowa BR/TR, 6'2", 185 lbs. Deb: 7/21/68 F

YEAR	TM/L	W	L	PCT	G	GS	CG	SH	SV	IP	H	R	HR	HB	BB	SO	RAT	ERA	ERA+	OAV	OOB	BH	AVG	PB	PR	PR+	PD	TPI
1968	NY-N	4	7	.364	12	12	2	1	0	79	66	20	5	4	17	46	9.9	2.28	133	.230	.282	1	.045	-1	6	6	-1	0.7
1969	NY-N	6	7	.462	27	21	4	2	0	135	112	57	12	2	44	90	10.5	3.47	106	.225	.291	5	.135	0	2	3	-1	0.1
1970	NY-N	10	14	.417	32	27	9	3	2	184^1	166	77	18	2	38	111	10.1	3.56	113	.239	.281	8	.148	1	10	10	-2	1.1
1971	NY-N	2	5	.286	24	10	0	0	0	90^1	78	50	10	1	32	42	11.1	4.38	78	.227	.294	1	.043	-1	-9	-10	1	-0.8
1972	NY-N	11	8	.579	28	23	4	0	1	160^2	133	54	12	5	38	81	9.9	2.80	120	.225	.278	2	.047	-2	12	10	-1	0.8
1973	NY-N	3	8	.273	23	12	0	0	1	80^1	109	60	9	3	31	38	16.0	5.38	67	.330	.393	2	.133	2	-15	-16	-1	-1.9
1974	SD-N	1	4	.200	15	5	1	0	0	41^2	48	30	7	0	13	16	13.2	5.62	64	.284	.335	1	.143	0	-9	-10	-1	-1.1
Total	7	37	53	.411	161	110	20	6	4	771^1	712	348	73	17	213	424	11.0	3.65	98	.245	.300	20	.100	-3	-4	-6	-6	-1.1

● **DIXIE McARTHUR** McArthur, Oland Alexander b: 2/1/1892, Vernon, Ala. d: 5/31/86, West Point, Miss. BR/TR, 6'1", 185 lbs. Deb: 7/10/14

YEAR	TM/L	W	L	PCT	G	GS	CG	SH	SV	IP	H	R	HR	HB	BB	SO	RAT	ERA	ERA+	OAV	OOB	BH	AVG	PB	PR	PR+	PD	TPI
1914	Pit-N	0	0	—	1	0	0	0	0	1	1	1	0	0	0	1	9.0	0.00	—	.250	.250	0	—	0	0	0	0	0.0

● **WICKEY McAVOY** McAvoy, James Eugene b: 10/22/1894, Rochester, N.Y. d: 7/6/73, Rochester, N.Y. BR/TR, 5'11", 172 lbs. Deb: 9/29/13 ◆

YEAR	TM/L	W	L	PCT	G	GS	CG	SH	SV	IP	H	R	HR	HB	BB	SO	RAT	ERA	ERA+	OAV	OOB	BH	AVG	PB	PR	PR+	PD	TPI
1918	Phi-A	0	0	—	1	0	0	0	0	0^2	1	1	1	0	0	0	13.5	13.50	22	.500	.500	66	.244	0	-1	-1	0	0.0

● **TOM McAVOY** McAvoy, Thomas John b: 8/12/36, Brooklyn, N.Y. BL/TL, 6'3", 200 lbs. Deb: 9/27/59

YEAR	TM/L	W	L	PCT	G	GS	CG	SH	SV	IP	H	R	HR	HB	BB	SO	RAT	ERA	ERA+	OAV	OOB	BH	AVG	PB	PR	PR+	PD	TPI
1959	Was-A	0	0	—	1	0	0	0	0	2^2	1	0	0	0	2	0	10.1	0.00	—	.125	.300	0	.000	-0	1	1	0	0.1

● **AL McBEAN** McBean, Alvin O'Neal b: 5/15/38, Charlotte Amalie, V.I. BR/TR, 6', 180 lbs. Deb: 7/2/61

YEAR	TM/L	W	L	PCT	G	GS	CG	SH	SV	IP	H	R	HR	HB	BB	SO	RAT	ERA	ERA+	OAV	OOB	BH	AVG	PB	PR	PR+	PD	TPI
1961	Pit-N	3	2	.600	27	2	0	0	0	74^1	72	35	4	4	42	49	14.3	3.75	106	.263	.369	4	.267	1	2	2	2	0.5
1962	Pit-N	15	10	.600	33	29	6	2	0	189^2	212	93	11	7	65	119	13.5	3.70	106	.285	.348	14	.209	2	5	5	0	0.8
1963	Pit-N	13	3	.813	55	7	2	1	11	122^1	100	42	5	2	39	74	10.4	2.57	128	.222	.287	6	.194	2	10	10	2	1.8
1964	Pit-N	8	3	.727	58	0	0	0	22	89^2	76	23	4	4	17	41	9.7	1.91	184	.234	.280	1	.083	-1	**16**	**16**	4	3.3
1965	Pit-N	6	6	.500	62	1	0	0	18	114	111	33	5	3	42	54	12.3	2.29	153	.260	.331	6	.222	1	16	16	1	2.4
1966	Pit-N	4	3	.571	47	0	0	0	3	86^2	95	38	9	2	24	54	12.6	3.22	111	.280	.332	1	.100	-1	4	3	1	0.3
1967	Pit-N	7	4	.636	51	8	5	0	4	131	118	41	6	1	43	54	11.1	2.54	132	.248	.312	6	.207	2	12	12	0	1.4
1968	Pit-N	9	12	.429	36	28	9	2	0	198^1	204	88	10	5	63	100	12.3	3.58	82	.269	.330	13	.194	2	-13	-15	4	-0.9
1969	SD-N	0	1	.000	1	1	0	0	0	7	10	4	1	0	2	1	15.4	5.14	69	.345	.387	1	.500	0	-1	-1	-0	-0.1
	LA-N	2	6	.250	31	0	0	0	4	48^1	46	22	6	2	21	26	12.8	3.91	85	.258	.343	0	.000	0	-2	-3	-1	-0.7
	Yr	2	7	.222	32	1	0	0	4	55^1	56	26	7	2	23	27	13.2	4.07	82	.271	.349	1	.200	0	-3	-5	-1	-0.8
1970	LA-N	0	0	—	1	0	0	0	0	1	1	0	0	0	0	0	9.0	0.00	—	.333	.333	0	—	0	0	0	-0	0.0
	Pit-N	0	0	—	7	0	0	0	1	10	13	11	2	0	7	3	18.0	8.10	48	.317	.417	0	.000	-0	-4	-5	0	-0.2
	Yr	0	0	—	8	0	0	0	1	11	14	11	2	0	7	3	17.2	7.36	53	.318	.412	0	.000	-0	-4	-4	0	-0.2
Total	10	67	50	.573	409	76	22	5	63	1072^1	1058	430	63	30	365	575	12.2	3.13	111	.262	.327	52	.197	9	45	41	13	8.6

● **PRYOR McBEE** McBee, Pryor Edward "Lefty" b: 6/20/01, Blanco, Okla. d: 4/19/63, Roseville, Cal. BR/TL, 6'1", 190 lbs. Deb: 5/22/26

YEAR	TM/L	W	L	PCT	G	GS	CG	SH	SV	IP	H	R	HR	HB	BB	SO	RAT	ERA	ERA+	OAV	OOB	BH	AVG	PB	PR	PR+	PD	TPI
1926	Chi-A	0	0	—	1	0	0	0	0	1^1	1	2	0	0	3	1	27.0	6.75	57	.250	.571	0	—	0	-0	-0	0	0.0

● **DICK McBRIDE** McBride, James Dickson b: 1845, Philadelphia, Pa. d: 10/10/16, Philadelphia, Pa. TR, 5'9", 150 lbs. Deb: 5/20/1871 M

YEAR	TM/L	W	L	PCT	G	GS	CG	SH	SV	IP	H	R	HR	HB	BB	SO	RAT	ERA	ERA+	OAV	OOB	BH	AVG	PB	PR	PR+	PD	TPI
1871	Ath-n	18	5	**.783**	25	25	25	0	0	222	285	223	3		40	15	13.2	4.58	88	.280	.307	31	.235	-4	-9	-14		-1.1
1872	Ath-n	30	14	.682	47	47	47	1	0	419^1	508	349	3		26	44	11.5	2.85	124	.265	.275	74	.287	5	37	33		2.5
1873	Ath-n	24	19	.558	46	46	38	**3**	0	382^2	453	325	3		47	25	11.8	3.32	103	.263	.282	71	.281	3	-3	4		0.4
1874	Ath-n	33	22	.600	55	55	55	0	0	487	514	344	6		32	37	**10.1**	**1.64**	**141**	**.240**	**.251**	57	.217	-7	**30**	**34**		1.7
1875	Ath-n	44	14	.759	60	60	59	6	0	538	607	297	4		24	27	10.6	2.33	103	.267	.275	73	.270	3	-6	4		-0.2
1876	Bos-N	0	4	.000	4	4	3	0	0	33	53	35	1		5	2	15.8	2.73	83	.342	.374	3	.188	-1	-2	-2	-0	-0.3
Total	5 n	149	74	.668	233	233	224	10	0	2049	2367	1538	19		169	148	11.1	2.70	111	.261	.274	306	.260	-0	49	68		3.3

● **KEN McBRIDE** McBride, Kenneth Faye b: 8/12/35, Huntsville, Ala. BR/TR, 6', 195 lbs. Deb: 8/4/59 C

YEAR	TM/L	W	L	PCT	G	GS	CG	SH	SV	IP	H	R	HR	HB	BB	SO	RAT	ERA	ERA+	OAV	OOB	BH	AVG	PB	PR	PR+	PD	TPI
1959	Chi-A	0	1	.000	11	2	0	0	1	22^2	20	11	1	0	17	12	14.7	3.18	118	.230	.356	1	.167	-0	2	2	1	0.1
1960	Chi-A	0	1	.000	5	0	0	0	0	4^2	6	2	0	1	3	4	19.3	3.86	98	.333	.455	0	—	0	0	-0	-0	0.0
1961	LA-A☆	12	15	.444	38	36	11	1	1	241^2	229	114	28	7	102	180	12.6	3.65	124	.252	.332	7	.084	-5	10	21	4	2.0
1962	LA-A†	11	5	.688	24	23	6	4	0	149^1	136	66	9	9	70	83	13.0	3.50	110	.249	.344	9	.164	0	8	6	5	1.1
1963	LA-A★	13	12	.520	36	36	11	2	0	251	198	101	22	14	82	147	10.5	3.26	105	.218	.293	15	.172	2	10	5	3	1.0
1964	LA-A	4	13	.235	29	21	0	0	1	116^1	104	77	14	16	75	66	15.1	5.26	62	.239	.370	6	.214	3	-21	-28	3	-3.1
1965	Cal-A	0	3	.000	8	4	0	0	0	22	24	17	1	2	14	11	16.4	6.14	55	.270	.381	0	.000	-0	-7	-7	-0	-0.9
Total	7	40	50	.444	151	122	28	7	3	807^2	717	388	75	49	363	503	12.6	3.79	101	.240	.332	38	.144	-0	2	2	15	0.2

● **PETE McBRIDE** McBride, Peter William b: 7/9/1875, Adams, Mass. d: 7/3/44, N.Adams, Mass. BR/TR, 5'10", 170 lbs. Deb: 9/20/1898

YEAR	TM/L	W	L	PCT	G	GS	CG	SH	SV	IP	H	R	HR	HB	BB	SO	RAT	ERA	ERA+	OAV	OOB	BH	AVG	PB	PR	PR+	PD	TPI
1898	Cle-N	0	1	.000	1	1	1	0	0	7	9	6	0	1	4	6	18.0	6.43	56	.310	.412	2	1.000	2	-2	-2	-0	-0.1
1899	StL-N	2	4	.333	11	6	4	0	0	64	65	46	4	4	40	26	15.3	4.08	98	.263	.375	5	.185	0	-2	-1	-1	-0.1
Total	2	2	5	.286	12	7	5	0	0	71	74	52	4	5	44	32	15.6	4.31	91	.268	.378	7	.241	2	-4	-3	-1	-0.2

● **RALPH McCABE** McCabe, Ralph Herbert "Mack" b: 10/21/18, Napanee, Ont., Can. d: 5/3/74, Windsor, Ont., Can. BR/TR, 6'4", 195 lbs. Deb: 9/18/46

YEAR	TM/L	W	L	PCT	G	GS	CG	SH	SV	IP	H	R	HR	HB	BB	SO	RAT	ERA	ERA+	OAV	OOB	BH	AVG	PB	PR	PR+	PD	TPI
1946	Cle-A	0	1	.000	1	1	0	0	0	4	5	5	3	1	2	3	18.0	11.25	29	.313	.421	0	.000	-0	-3	-4	0	-0.6

● **DICK McCABE** McCabe, Richard James b: 2/21/1896, Mamaroneck, N.Y. d: 4/11/50, Buffalo, N.Y. BR/TR, 5'10.5", 159 lbs. Deb: 5/30/18

YEAR	TM/L	W	L	PCT	G	GS	CG	SH	SV	IP	H	R	HR	HB	BB	SO	RAT	ERA	ERA+	OAV	OOB	BH	AVG	PB	PR	PR+	PD	TPI
1918	Bos-A	0	1	.000	3	1	0	0	0	9^2	13	4	0	0	2	3	14.0	2.79	96	.351	.385	0	.000	-0	-0	-0	0	0.0
1922	Chi-A	1	0	1.000	3	0	0	0	0	3^1	4	2	0	0	0	1	10.8	5.40	75	.308	.308	0	—	0	-1	-0	-0	-0.1
Total	2	1	1	.500	6	1	0	0	0	13	17	6	0	0	2	4	13.2	3.46	88	.340	.365	0	.000	-0	-1	-1	-0	-0.1

● **TIM McCABE** McCabe, Timothy J. b: 10/19/1894, Ironton, Mo. d: 4/12/77, Ironton, Mo. BR/TR, 6', 190 lbs. Deb: 8/16/15

YEAR	TM/L	W	L	PCT	G	GS	CG	SH	SV	IP	H	R	HR	HB	BB	SO	RAT	ERA	ERA+	OAV	OOB	BH	AVG	PB	PR	PR+	PD	TPI
1915	StL-A	3	1	.750	7	4	4	1	0	41^2	25	11	1	1	9	17	7.6	1.30	221	.177	.232	1	.067	-1	8	7	-1	0.6
1916	StL-A	2	0	1.000	13	0	0	0	0	25^2	29	20	0	2	7	7	13.3	3.16	87	.282	.339	0	.000	-0	-1	-1	1	0.0
1917	StL-A	0	0	—	1	0	0	0	0	2^1	4	6	1	0	4	2	30.9	23.14	11	.400	.571	0	—	0	-5	-5	0	-0.3
1918	StL-A	0	0	—	1	0	0	0	0	1^1	2	2	0	0	1	0	20.3	13.50	20	.333	.429	0	—	0	-2	-2	-0	-0.1
Total	4	5	1	.833	22	4	4	1	0	71	60	39	2	3	21	26	10.6	2.92	96	.231	.296	1	.053	-1	-0	-1	1	0.2

YEAR	TM/L	W	L	PCT	G	GS	CG	SH	SV	IP	H	R	HR	HB	BB	SO	RAT	ERA	ERA+	OAV	OOB	BH	AVG	PB	PR	PR+	PD	TPI
● **HARRY McCAFFERY**	McCaffery, Harry Charles b: 11/25/1858, St.Louis, Mo. d: 4/19/28, St.Louis, Mo. BR/TR, 5'10.5", 185 lbs. Deb: 6/15/1882 U♦																											
1885	Cin-a	1	0	1.000	1	1	1	0	0	9	13	9	1	2	2	2	17.0	6.00	54	.342	.405	0	.000	-1	-3	-3	-0	-0.3
● **BILL McCAHAN**	McCahan, William Glenn b: 6/7/21, Philadelphia, Pa. d: 7/3/86, Fort Worth, Tex. BR/TR, 5'11", 200 lbs. Deb: 9/15/46																											
1946	Phi-A	1	1	.500	4	2	2	1	0	18	16	2	0	0	9	6	12.5	1.00	355	.246	.338	2	.400	1	5	5	0	0.7
1947	Phi-A	10	5	.667	29	19	10	1	0	165^1	160	73	7	0	62	47	12.1	3.32	115	.252	.318	9	.164	-1	7	9	1	0.8
1948	Phi-A	4	7	.364	17	15	5	0	0	86^2	98	58	8	0	65	20	16.9	5.71	75	.284	.398	8	.258	1	-14	-14	-1	-1.5
1949	Phi-A	1	1	.500	7	4	0	0	0	20^2	23	9	0	0	9	3	13.9	2.61	157	.291	.364	1	.200	-0	4	4	-0	0.3
Total	4	16	14	.533	57	40	17	2	0	290^2	297	142	15	0	145	76	13.7	3.84	103	.264	.348	20	.208	1	2	4	-1	0.3
● **WINDY McCALL**	McCall, John William b: 7/18/25, San Francisco, Cal. BL/TL, 6', 180 lbs. Deb: 4/25/48																											
1948	Bos-A	0	1	.000	1	1	0	0	0	1^1	6	3	1	0	1	0	47.3	20.25	22	.600	.636	0	—	0	-2	-2	0	-0.4
1949	Bos-A	0	0	—	5	0	0	0	0	9^1	13	12	2	0	10	8	22.2	11.57	38	.333	.469	2	.667	1	-8	-7	-0	-0.3
1950	Pit-N	0	0	—	2	0	0	0	0	6^2	12	7	2	0	4	5	21.6	9.45	46	.387	.457	0	.000	0	-4	-4	0	-0.2
1954	NY-N	2	5	.286	33	4	0	0	2	61	50	26	5	3	29	38	12.1	3.25	124	.219	.315	0	.000	-1	6	5	-1	0.4
1955	NY-N	6	5	.545	42	6	4	0	3	95	86	45	8	6	37	50	12.2	3.69	109	.244	.326	2	.118	-1	4	4	1	0.4
1956	NY-N	3	4	.429	46	4	0	0	7	77^1	74	36	7	1	20	41	11.1	3.61	105	.252	.302	3	.200	-0	1	1	-2	0.0
1957	NY-N	0	0	—	5	0	0	0	0	3	8	5	1	1	2	2	33.0	15.00	26	.533	.611	0	—	0	-4	-4	-0	-0.2
Total	7	11	15	.423	134	15	4	0	12	253^2	249	134	26	11	103	144	12.9	4.22	94	.257	.335	7	.146	-1	-7	-7	-3	-0.3
● **LARRY McCALL**	McCall, Larry Stephen b: 9/8/52, Asheville, N.C. BL/TR, 6'2", 195 lbs. Deb: 9/10/77																											
1977	NY-A	0	1	.000	2	0	0	0	0	6	12	7	1	0	1	0	19.5	7.50	53	.375	.394	0	—	0	-2	-2	-0	-0.4
1978	NY-A	1	1	.500	5	1	0	0	0	16	20	10	2	1	6	7	15.2	5.63	65	.323	.391	0	—	0	-3	-4	0	-0.4
1979	Tex-A	1	0	1.000	2	1	0	0	0	8^1	7	2	0	0	3	3	10.8	2.16	193	.226	.294	0	—	0	2	2	0	0.2
Total	3	2	2	.500	9	2	0	0	0	30^1	39	19	3	1	10	10	14.8	5.04	76	.312	.368	0	—	0	-4	-4	0	-0.6
● **DUTCH McCALL**	McCall, Robert Leonard b: 12/27/20, Columbia, Tenn. d: 1/7/96, Little Rock, Ark. BL/TL, 6'1", 184 lbs. Deb: 4/27/48																											
1948	Chi-N	4	13	.235	30	20	5	0	0	151^1	158	93	14	1	85	89	14.5	4.82	81	.268	.361	9	.170	1	-14	-16	1	-1.4
● **RANDY McCAMENT**	McCament, Larry Randall b: 7/29/62, Albuquerque, N.Mex. BR/TR, 6'3", 195 lbs. Deb: 6/28/89																											
1989	SF-N	1	1	.500	25	0	0	0	0	36^2	32	22	4	1	23	12	13.7	3.93	86	.241	.357	1	.333	0	-2	-2	0	0.0
1990	SF-N	0	0	—	3	0	0	0	0	6	8	2	0	0	5	5	19.5	3.00	122	.333	.448	0	.000	-0	1	0	-0	0.0
Total	2	1	1	.500	28	0	0	0	0	42^2	40	24	4	1	28	17	14.6	3.80	90	.255	.371	1	.250	0	-1	-2	0	0.0
● **GENE McCANN**	McCann, Henry Eugene "Mike" b: 6/13/1876, Baltimore, Md. d: 4/26/43, New York, N.Y. TR, 5'10", 185 lbs. Deb: 4/19/01																											
1901	Bro-N	2	3	.400	6	5	3	0	0	34	34	25	1	4	16	9	14.3	3.44	97	.260	.358	0	.000	-1	-0	-0	0	-0.1
1902	Bro-N	1	2	.333	3	3	3	0	0	30	32	18	0	0	12	9	13.2	2.40	115	.274	.341	1	.083	-1	1	1	1	0.1
Total	2	3	5	.375	9	8	6	0	0	64	66	43	1	4	28	18	13.8	2.95	104	.266	.350	1	.045	-2	1	1	1	0.0
● **ARCH McCARTHY**	McCarthy, Archibald Joseph b: Ypsilanti, Mich. TR, 6', 160 lbs. Deb: 8/14/02																											
1902	Det-A	2	7	.222	10	8	8	0	0	72	90	57	2	4	31	10	15.6	6.13	60	.306	.380	2	.071	-3	-20	-19	-2	-2.2
● **GREG McCARTHY**	McCarthy, Gregory O'Neil b: 10/30/68, Norwalk, Conn. BL/TL, 6'2", 195 lbs. Deb: 8/28/96																											
1996	Sea-A	0	0	—	10	0	0	0	0	9^2	8	2	0	4	4	7	14.9	1.86	266	.229	.372	0	—	0	3	3	0	0.2
1997	Sea-A	1	1	.500	37	0	0	0	0	29^2	26	21	4	1	16	34	13.0	5.46	82	.230	.331	0	—	0	-3	-3	0	-0.2
1998	Sea-A	1	2	.333	29	0	0	0	0	23^1	18	13	6	3	17	25	14.7	5.01	92	.214	.365	0	—	0	-1	-1	1	0.0
Total	3	2	3	.400	76	0	0	0	0	62^2	52	36	10	8	37	66	13.9	4.74	98	.224	.350	0	—	0	-0	-1	1	0.0
● **JOHNNY McCARTHY**	McCarthy, John Joseph b: 1/7/10, Chicago, Ill. d: 9/13/73, Mundelein, Ill. BL/TL, 6'1.5", 185 lbs. Deb: 9/2/34 ♦																											
1939	NY-N	0	0	—	1	0	0	0	0	5	8	4	1	0	2	0	18.0	7.20	55	.364	.417	21	.262	0	-2	-2	0	0.0
● **TOMMY McCARTHY**	McCarthy, Thomas Francis Michael b: 7/24/1863, Boston, Mass. d: 8/5/22, Boston, Mass. BR/TR, 5'7", 170 lbs. Deb: 7/10/1884 MH♦																											
1884	Bos-U	0	7	.000	7	6	5	0	0	56	73	53	2		14	18	14.0	4.82	49	.296	.333	45	.215	-2	-15	-16	1	-1.4
1886	Phi-N	0	0	—	1	0	0	0	0	1	0	0	0		1	1	9.0	0.00	—	.000	.250	5	.185	0	0	0	0	0.0
1888	*StL-a	0	1	.000	2	1	0	0	0	5^1	5	5	1	0	2	1	11.8	5.06	64	.238	.304	140	.274	0	-1	-1	-0	-0.2
1889	StL-a	0	0	—	1	0	0	0	0	5	4	4	0	0	6	1	18.0	7.20	59	.211	.400	176	.291	0	-2	-2	-0	-0.1
1891	StL-a	0	0	—	1	0	0	0	0	1	2	2	0	0	0	0	18.0	9.00	47	.400	.400	176	.309	0	-1	-0	-0	0.0
1894	Bos-N	0	0	—	1	0	0	0	0	2	1	1	0	0	3	0	18.0	4.50	126	.143	.400	188	.349	0	0	0	-0	0.0
Total	6	0	8	.000	13	7	5	0	0	70^1	85	65	3	0	26	21	14.2	4.99	54	.281	.338	1495	.292	-1	-18	-18	1	-1.7
● **TOM McCARTHY**	McCarthy, Thomas Michael b: 6/18/61, Lundstahl, W.Ger. BR/TR, 6', 180 lbs. Deb: 7/5/85																											
1985	Bos-A	0	0	—	3	0	0	0	0	5	7	6	1	0	4	2	19.8	10.80	40	.350	.458	0	—	0	-4	-4	-0	-0.2
1988	Chi-A	2	0	1.000	6	0	0	0	1	13	9	2	0	2	2	5	9.0	1.38	287	.191	.255	0	—	0	4	4	0	0.6
1989	Chi-A	1	2	.333	31	0	0	0	0	66^2	72	32	8	2	20	27	12.7	3.51	109	.280	.337	0	—	0	3	2	1	0.2
Total	3	3	2	.600	40	0	0	0	1	84^2	88	40	9	4	26	34	12.5	3.61	107	.272	.333	0	—	0	3	2	1	0.6
● **TOM McCARTHY**	McCarthy, Thomas Patrick b: 5/22/1884, Ft.Wayne, Ind. d: 3/28/33, Mishawaka, Ind. TR, 5'7", 170 lbs. Deb: 5/10/08																											
1908	Cin-N	0	1	.000	1	1	0	0	0	3^2	6	5	0	0	3	3	22.1	9.82	23	.300	.391	0	.000	-0	-3	-3	0	-0.5
	Pit-N	0	0	—	2	1	0	0	0	6	3	1	0	0	6	1	13.5	0.00	—	.176	.391	0	.000	-0	2	2	1	0.1
	Bos-N	7	3	.700	14	11	7	2	0	94	77	24	0	1	28	27	10.1	1.63	148	.235	.298	6	.171	0	8	8	0	1.0
	Yr	7	4	.636	17	13	7	2	0	103^2	86	30	0	1	37	31	10.8	1.82	132	.236	.308	6	.146	-1	6	7	1	0.6
1909	Bos-N	0	5	.000	8	7	3	0	0	46^1	47	28	3	2	28	11	15.0	3.50	81	.272	.379	2	.125	-0	-5	-3	0	-0.3
Total	2	7	9	.438	25	20	10	2	0	150	133	58	3	3	65	42	12.1	2.34	108	.248	.332	8	.140	-1	2	3	1	0.3
● **BILL McCARTHY**	McCarthy, William Thomas b: 4/11/1882, Ashland, Mass. d: 5/29/39, Boston, Mass. BR/TR, 5'11", 180 lbs. Deb: 4/21/06																											
1906	Bos-N	0	0	—	1	0	0	0	0	2	2	6	0	0	3	0	22.5	9.00	30	.182	.357	0	.000	-0	-1	-1	-0	-0.1
● **JOHN McCARTY**	McCarty, John A. b: St.Louis, Mo. TR, Deb: 4/18/1889																											
1889	KC-a	8	6	.571	15	14	13	0	0	119^2	147	108	4	6	61	36	16.1	3.91	107	.293	.376	18	.228	-2	-1	3	-0	0.1
● **KIRK McCASKILL**	McCaskill, Kirk Edward b: 4/9/61, Kapuskasing, Ont., Canada BR/TR, 6'1", 196 lbs. Deb: 5/1/85																											
1985	Cal-A	12	12	.500	30	29	6	1	0	189^2	189	105	23	4	64	102	12.2	4.70	88	.258	.321	0	—	0	-12	-12	-0	-1.4
1986	*Cal-A	17	10	.630	34	33	10	2	0	246^1	207	98	19	5	92	202	11.1	3.36	123	.229	.303	0	—	0	23	21	-0	2.1
1987	Cal-A	4	6	.400	14	13	1	1	0	74^2	84	52	14	2	34	56	14.5	5.67	76	.286	.364	0	—	0	-10	-12	1	-1.2
1988	Cal-A	8	6	.571	23	23	4	2	0	146^1	155	78	9	1	61	98	13.3	4.31	90	.274	.346	0	—	0	-5	-7	0	-0.6
1989	Cal-A	15	10	.600	32	32	6	4	0	212	202	73	16	3	59	107	11.2	2.93	130	.254	.308	0	—	0	23	21	2	2.7
1990	Cal-A	12	11	.522	29	29	2	1	0	174^1	161	77	9	2	72	78	12.1	3.25	118	.244	.320	0	—	0	13	11	2	1.6
1991	Cal-A	10	19	.345	30	30	1	0	0	177^2	193	93	19	3	66	71	13.3	4.26	97	.283	.349	0	—	0	-3	-3	1	-0.4
1992	Chi-A	12	13	.480	34	34	0	0	0	209	193	116	11	6	95	109	12.7	4.18	93	.242	.328	0	—	0	-5	-7	2	-0.6
1993	*Chi-A	4	8	.333	30	14	0	0	2	113^2	144	71	12	1	36	65	14.3	5.23	80	.313	.364	0	—	0	-11	-14	2	-1.1
1994	Chi-A	1	4	.200	40	0	0	0	3	52^2	51	22	6	0	22	37	12.5	3.42	137	.252	.326	0	—	0	8	8	0	0.7
1995	Chi-A	6	4	.600	55	1	0	0	2	81	97	50	10	5	33	50	15.0	4.89	91	.302	.376	0	—	0	-2	-4	0	-0.4
1996	Chi-A	5	5	.500	29	4	0	0	0	51^2	72	41	6	2	31	28	18.3	6.97	68	.344	.434	0	—	0	-11	-13	1	-2.0
Total	12	106	108	.495	380	242	30	11	7	1729	1748	876	154	34	665	1003	12.7	4.12	99	.264	.334	0	—	0	7	-10	9	-0.6
● **STEVE McCATTY**	McCatty, Steven Earl b: 3/20/54, Detroit, Mich. BR/TR, 6'3", 205 lbs. Deb: 9/17/77																											
1977	Oak-A	0	0	—	4	2	0	0	0	14^1	16	9	1	1	7	9	15.1	5.02	80	.276	.364	0	—	0	-2	-2	-1	-0.1
1978	Oak-A	0	0	—	9	0	0	0	0	20	26	14	1	0	9	10	15.7	4.50	81	.310	.376	0	—	0	-2	-2	-0	-0.1
1979	Oak-A	11	12	.478	31	23	8	0	0	185^2	207	106	17	10	80	87	14.4	4.22	96	.284	.363	0	—	0	0	-3	-2	-0.5
1980	Oak-A	14	14	.500	33	31	11	1	0	221^2	202	104	27	8	99	114	12.5	3.86	98	.240	.325	0	—	0	5	-2	-1	-0.4
1981	*Oak-A	**14**	7	.667	22	22	16	**4**	0	185^2	140	50	12	2	61	91	9.8	**2.33**	150	**.211**	.279	0	—	0	**28**	**25**	-1	2.8
1982	Oak-A	6	3	.667	21	20	2	0	0	128^2	124	62	16	4	70	66	13.8	3.99	98	.255	.354	0	—	0	1	-1	-1	-0.1
1983	Oak-A	6	9	.400	38	24	3	2	5	167	156	79	16	1	82	65	12.9	3.99	97	.247	.334	0	—	0	2	-2	-2	-0.4

YEAR	TM/L	W	L	PCT	G	GS	CG	SH	SV	IP	H	R	HR	HB	BB	SO	RAT	ERA	ERA+	OAV	OOB	BH	AVG	PB	PR	PR+	PD	TPI
1984	Oak-A	8	14	.364	33	30	4	0	0	179^2	206	101	24	1	71	63	13.9	4.76	79	.289	.355	0	—	0	-15	-21	-2	-2.5
1985	Oak-A	4	4	.500	30	9	1	0	0	85^2	95	56	10	4	41	36	14.7	5.57	69	.286	.371	0	—	0	-14	-17	0	-1.4
Total	9	63	63	.500	221	161	45	7	5	1188^1	1172	581	124	31	520	541	13.0	3.99	95	.258	.339	0	—	0	4	-26	-9	-2.7
● **AL McCAULEY** McCauley, Allen A. b: 3/4/1863, Indianapolis, Ind. d: 8/24/17, Wayne Twnshp., Ind BL/TL, 6', 180 lbs. Deb: 6/21/1884 ♦																												
1884	Ind-a	2	7	.222	10	9	9	0	0	76	87	74	2	0	25	34	13.3	5.09	65	.261	.313	10	.189	2	-16	-15	2	-1.1
● **JOE McCLAIN** McClain, Joseph Fred b: 5/5/33, Johnson City, Tenn. BR/TR, 6', 183 lbs. Deb: 4/14/61																												
1961	Was-A	8	18	.308	33	29	7	2	1	212	221	105	22	4	48	76	11.6	3.86	104	.270	.313	14	.206	1	4	4	-3	0.3
1962	Was-A	0	4	.000	10	4	0	0	0	24	33	25	8	2	11	6	17.3	9.38	43	.327	.404	1	.143	-0	-14	-14	0	-1.9
Total	2	8	22	.267	43	33	7	2	1	236	254	130	30	6	59	82	12.2	4.42	91	.276	.324	15	.200	1	-11	-11	-3	-1.6
● **PAUL McCLELLAN** McClellan, Paul William b: 2/3/66, San Mateo, Cal. BR/TR, 6'2", 180 lbs. Deb: 9/2/90																												
1990	SF-N	0	1	.000	4	1	0	0	0	7^2	14	10	3	1	6	2	24.7	11.74	31	.389	.488	1	.500	0	-7	-7	0	-0.7
1991	SF-N	3	6	.333	13	12	1	0	0	71	68	41	12	1	25	44	11.9	4.56	79	.252	.318	3	.143	-0	-7	-8	-1	-1.0
Total	2	3	7	.300	17	13	1	0	0	78^2	82	51	15	2	31	46	13.2	5.26	68	.268	.339	4	.174	0	-14	-15	-1	-1.7
● **JIM McCLOSKEY** McCloskey, James Ellwood "Irish" b: 5/26/10, Danville, Pa. d: 8/18/71, Jersey City, N.J. BL/TL, 5'9.5", 180 lbs. Deb: 4/21/36																												
1936	Bos-N	0	0	—	4	1	0	0	0	8	14	10	1	1	3	2	20.3	11.25	34	.378	.439	0	.000	-0	-6	-7	0	-0.3
● **JOHN McCLOSKEY** McCloskey, James John b: 8/20/1882, Wyoming, Pa. d: 6/5/19, Wilkes-Barre, Pa. Deb: 5/3/06																												
1906	Phi-N	3	2	.600	9	4	3	0	0	41	46	21	2	1	9	6	12.3	2.85	92	.280	.322	3	.200	0	-1	-1	-1	-0.2
1907	Phi-N	0	0	—	3	0	0	0	0	9	15	9	0	1	6	3	22.0	7.00	35	.417	.512	0	.000	-0	-5	-5	0	-0.3
Total	2	3	2	.600	12	4	3	0	0	50	61	30	2	2	15	9	14.0	3.60	72	.305	.359	3	.158	-0	-6	-6	-1	-0.5
● **BOB McCLURE** McClure, Robert Craig b: 4/29/52, Oakland, Cal. BR/TL, 5'11", 170 lbs. Deb: 8/13/75 C																												
1975	KC-A	1	0	1.000	12	0	0	0	1	15^1	4	0	0	0	14	15	10.6	0.00	—	.077	.273	0	—	0	6	6	-0	0.4
1976	KC-A	0	0	—	8	0	0	0	0	4	3	4	0	0	8	3	24.8	9.00	39	.214	.500	0	—	0	-2	-2	-0	-0.1
1977	Mil-A	2	1	.667	68	0	0	0	6	71^1	64	25	2	1	34	57	12.5	2.52	162	.249	.339	0	—	0	12	12	2	0.9
1978	Mil-A	2	6	.250	44	0	0	0	9	65	53	30	8	6	30	47	12.3	3.74	101	.223	.325	0	—	0	0	0	-1	0.0
1979	Mil-A	5	2	.714	36	0	0	0	5	51	53	29	6	3	24	37	14.1	3.88	108	.269	.357	0	—	0	2	2	-0	0.2
1980	Mil-A	5	8	.385	52	5	2	1	10	90^2	83	34	6	2	37	47	12.1	3.08	126	.241	.318	0	—	0	10	8	-1	1.2
1981	*Mil-A	0	0	—	4	0	0	0	0	7^2	7	3	1	0	4	6	12.9	3.52	97	.233	.324	0	—	0	0	-0	-0	0.0
1982	*Mil-A	12	7	.632	34	26	5	0	0	172^2	160	90	21	4	74	99	12.4	4.22	90	.248	.329	0	—	0	-3	-9	-1	-0.9
1983	Mil-A	9	9	.500	24	23	4	0	0	142	152	75	11	5	68	68	14.3	4.50	83	.277	.362	0	—	0	-7	-13	-1	-1.5
1984	Mil-A	4	8	.333	39	18	1	0	1	139^2	154	76	9	2	52	68	13.4	4.38	88	.282	.347	0	—	0	-6	-8	-0	-0.7
1985	Mil-A	4	1	.800	38	1	0	0	3	85^2	91	43	10	3	30	57	13.0	4.31	97	.274	.340	0	—	0	-2	-1	-0	-0.1
1986	Mil-A	2	1	.667	13	0	0	0	0	16^1	18	7	2	0	10	11	15.4	3.86	112	.286	.384	0	—	0	1	1	-0	0.1
	Mon-N	2	5	.286	52	0	0	0	6	62^2	53	22	2	1	23	42	11.1	3.02	123	.232	.306	1	.250	0	5	5	0	0.6
1987	Mon-N	6	1	.857	52	0	0	0	5	52^1	47	30	8	0	20	33	11.5	3.44	122	.241	.312	0	.000	-0	4	4	0	0.6
1988	Mon-N	1	3	.250	19	0	0	0	2	19	23	13	3	1	6	12	14.2	6.16	58	.307	.366	0	.000	-0	-6	-5	0	-1.1
	NY-N	1	0	1.000	14	0	0	0	1	11	12	5	1	1	2	7	12.3	4.09	79	.279	.326	0	—	0	-1	-1	-0	-0.1
	Yr	2	3	.400	33	0	0	0	3	30	35	18	4	2	8	19	13.5	5.40	64	.297	.352	0	.000	-0	-6	-6	-0	-1.2
1989	Cal-A	6	1	.857	48	0	0	0	3	52^1	39	14	2	1	15	36	9.5	1.55	247	.212	.275	0	—	0	14	13	-1	1.7
1990	Cal-A	2	0	1.000	11	0	0	0	0	7	7	6	0	0	3	6	12.9	6.43	60	.269	.345	0	—	0	-2	-2	0	-0.4
1991	Cal-A	0	0	—	13	0	0	0	0	9^2	13	11	3	1	5	5	17.7	9.31	44	.317	.404	0	—	0	-6	-6	0	-0.3
	StL-N	1	1	.500	32	0	0	0	0	23	24	8	1	1	8	15	12.9	3.13	119	.282	.351	1	1.000	0	1	1	-0	0.2
1992	StL-N	2	2	.500	71	0	0	0	0	54	52	21	6	2	25	24	13.2	3.17	107	.261	.350	0	—	0	2	1	-0	0.1
1993	Fla-N	1	1	.500	14	0	0	0	0	6^1	13	5	2	0	5	6	25.6	7.11	61	.419	.500	0	—	0	-2	-2	0	-0.4
Total	19	68	57	.544	698	73	12	1	52	1158^2	1125	551	104	34	497	701	12.9	3.81	101	.257	.338	2	.222	0	22	7	-4	0.4
● **HARRY McCLUSKEY** McCluskey, Harry Robert b: 3/29/1892, Clay Center, Ohio d: 6/7/62, Toledo, Ohio BL/TL, 5'11.5", 173 lbs. Deb: 7/29/15																												
1915	Cin-N	0	0	—	3	0	0	0	0	5	4	3	0	0	0	2	7.2	5.40	53	.182	.182	0	.000	-0	-1	-1	-0	-0.1
● **ALEX McCOLL** McColl, Alexander Boyd "Red" b: 3/29/1894, Eagleville, Ohio d: 2/6/91, Kingsville, Ohio BB/TR, 6'1", 178 lbs. Deb: 8/27/33																												
1933	*Was-A	1	0	1.000	4	1	1	0	0	17	13	5	0	0	7	5	10.6	2.65	158	.210	.290	2	.333	1	3	3	-0	0.2
1934	Was-A	3	4	.429	42	2	1	0	1	112	129	56	6	1	36	29	13.3	3.86	112	.291	.345	3	.097	-2	8	6	2	0.4
Total	2	4	4	.500	46	3	2	0	1	129	142	61	6	1	43	34	13.0	3.70	116	.281	.338	5	.135	-1	11	9	2	0.6
● **RALPH McCONNAUGHEY** McConnaughey, Ralph James b: 8/5/1889, Vandergrift, Pa. d: 6/4/66, Detroit, Mich. BR/TR, 5'8.5", 166 lbs. Deb: 7/8/14																												
1914	Ind-F	0	2	.000	7	2	1	0	0	26	23	15	3	1	16	7	13.8	4.85	64	.245	.360	1	.125	-0	-6	-5	-0	-0.4
● **GEORGE McCONNELL** McConnell, George Neely "Slats" b: 9/16/1877, Shelbyville, Tenn d: 5/10/64, Chattanooga, Tenn. BR/TR, 6'3", 190 lbs. Deb: 4/13/09 ♦																												
1909	NY-A	0	1	.000	2	1	0	0	0	4	3	2	0	0	3	4	13.5	2.25	112	.231	.375	9	.209	0	0	0	1	0.1
1912	NY-A	8	12	.400	23	20	19	0	0	176^2	172	96	3	4	52	91	11.6	2.75	131	.269	.328	27	.297	3	11	15	5	2.8
1913	NY-A	4	15	.211	35	20	8	0	3	180	162	90	2	7	60	72	11.4	3.20	94	.245	.314	12	.179	-1	-5	-4	5	-0.1
1914	Chi-N	0	1	.000	1	1	0	0	0	7	3	1	0	0	3	3	7.7	1.29	216	.125	.222	0	.000	-0	1	1	0	0.2
1915	Chi-F	**25**	10	**.714**	44	35	23	4	1	303	262	103	8	8	89	151	10.7	2.20	114	.232	.292	31	.248	4	18	11	3	2.2
1916	Chi-N	4	12	.250	28	21	8	1	0	171^1	137	66	8	5	35	82	9.3	2.57	113	.223	.271	9	.158	-2	1	6	2	0.5
Total	6	41	51	.446	133	98	58	5	4	842	739	358	21	24	242	403	10.7	2.60	112	.240	.300	88	.229	4	26	30	15	5.7
● **BILLY McCOOL** McCool, William John b: 7/14/44, Batesville, Ind. BR/TL, 6'2", 203 lbs. Deb: 4/24/64																												
1964	Cin-N	6	5	.545	40	3	0	0	7	89^1	66	27	3	1	29	87	9.7	2.42	150	.206	.274	0	.000	-2	11	12	-2	1.3
1965	Cin-N	9	10	.474	62	2	0	0	21	105^1	93	53	9	4	47	120	12.3	4.27	88	.237	.324	1	.037	-2	-9	-6	-0	-1.4
1966	Cin-N☆	8	8	.500	57	0	0	0	18	105^1	76	32	5	3	41	104	10.3	2.48	157	.205	.290	3	.167	-0	13	15	2	3.1
1967	Cin-N	3	7	.300	31	11	0	0	2	97^1	92	45	8	5	56	83	14.1	3.42	110	.246	.352	2	.077	-1	-1	3	-1	0.1
1968	Cin-N	3	4	.429	30	4	0	0	2	50^2	59	35	4	0	41	30	17.8	4.97	64	.294	.413	1	.125	-0	-11	-10	-1	-1.5
1969	SD-N	3	5	.375	54	0	0	0	7	58^2	59	32	2	6	42	35	16.4	4.30	82	.266	.396	0	.000	-0	-5	-5	-0	-0.8
1970	StL-N	0	3	.000	18	0	0	0	1	21^2	20	15	0	0	16	12	15.0	6.23	66	.250	.375	0	.000	-0	-5	-5	0	-0.7
Total	7	32	42	.432	292	20	0	0	58	528^1	465	239	31	19	272	471	12.9	3.59	103	.237	.336	7	.069	-6	-6	6	-1	0.1
● **JIM McCORMICK** McCormick, James b: 11/3/1856, Glasgow, Scotland d: 3/10/18, Paterson, N.J. BR/TR, 5'10.5", 215 lbs. Deb: 5/20/1878 M																												
1878	Ind-N	5	8	.385	14	14	12	1	0	117	128	47	0		15	36	11.0	1.69	120	.269	.292	8	.143	-3	8	5	2	0.4
1879	Cle-N	20	40	.333	62	60	59	3	0	546^1	582	308	4		74	197	10.8	2.42	103	.259	.282	62	.220	-1	4	5	4	0.7
1880	Cle-N	**45**	28	.616	**74**	74	**72**	7	0	**657^2**	585	274	2		75	260	9.0	1.85	127	.226	.247	71	.246	1	38	**37**	1	**4.0**
1881	Cle-N	26	30	.464	59	58	**57**	2	0	526	484	267	4		84	178	9.7	2.45	107	.235	.265	79	.256	6	19	11	-3	1.2
1882	Cle-N	**36**	30	.545	**68**	67	**65**	4	0	**595^2**	550	274	14		103	200	9.9	2.37	118	.238	.271	57	.218	-4	35	29	-2	2.1
1883	Cle-N	28	12	**.700**	43	41	36	1	1	342	316	151	1		65	145	10.0	**1.84**	**171**	.233	.268	37	.236	-1	49	50	7	5.4
1884	Cle-N	19	22	.463	42	41	39	3	0	359	357	206	17		75	182	10.8	2.86	110	.247	.285	50	.263	2	5	11	0	1.3
	Cin-U	21	3	**.875**	24	24	24	**7**	0	210	151	57	3		14	161	**7.1**	**1.54**	**166**	**.188**	**.202**	27	.245	-6	21	**23**	2	1.7
1885	Pro-N	1	3	.250	4	4	4	0	0	37	34	26	1		20	8	13.1	2.43	110	.234	.327	3	.214	0	2	1	3	0.4
	*Chi-N	20	4	.833	24	24	24	3	0	215	187	103	8		40	88	9.5	2.43	124	.224	.260	23	.223	0	9	13	3	1.5
	Yr	21	7	.750	28	28	28	3	0	252	221	129	9		60	96	10.0	2.43	122	.226	.271	26	.222	1	11	14	5	1.9
1886	*Chi-N	31	11	.738	42	42	38	2	0	347^2	341	165	18		100	172	11.4	2.82	128	.253	.304	41	.236	2	19	28	2	3.0
1887	Pit-N	13	23	.361	36	36	36	0	0	322^1	461	217	12	12	84	77	13.2	4.30	90	.328	.334	35	.254	-1	-8	-16	5	-1.0
Total	10	265	214	.553	492	485	466	33	1	4275^2	4176	2095	84	12	749	1704	10.2	2.43	117	.245	.274	493	.237	-4	202	200	23	20.7
● **JERRY McCORMICK** McCormick, John b: Philadelphia, Pa. d: 9/19/05, Philadelphia, Pa. Deb: 5/1/1883 ♦																												
1884	Phi-U	0	0	—	1	0	0	0	0	2	5	4	1	0	3	22.5		9.00	26	.455	.455	84	.285	-0	-1	-2	-0	-0.1
● **MIKE McCORMICK** McCormick, Michael Francis b: 9/29/38, Pasadena, Cal. BL/TL, 6'2", 195 lbs. Deb: 9/3/56																												
1956	NY-N	0	1	.000	3	2	0	0	0	6^2	7	7	1	0	10	4	23.0	9.45	40	.269	.472	0	.000	-0	-4	-4	-0	-0.5

YEAR	TM/L	W	L	PCT	G	GS	CG	SH	SV	IP	H	R	HR	HB	BB	SO	RAT	ERA	ERA+	OAV	OOB	BH	AVG	PB	PR	PR+	PD	TPI
1957	NY-N	3	1	.750	24	5	1	0	0	74^2	79	37	7	3	32	50	13.7	4.10	96	.280	.360	6	.273	1	-2	-1	-1	0.0
1958	SF-N	11	8	.579	42	28	8	2	1	178^1	192	103	20	3	60	82	12.9	4.59	83	.276	.336	12	.222	1	-13	-16	2	-1.2
1959	SF-N	12	16	.429	47	31	7	3	4	225^2	213	117	24	1	86	151	12.0	3.99	96	.248	.317	7	.106	-2	-1	-5	1	-0.6
1960	SF-N★	15	12	.556	40	34	15	4	3	253	228	87	15	1	65	154	10.5	**2.70**	129	.241	.291	16	.182	1	**30**	24	3	2.9
1961	SF-N★	13	16	.448	40	35	13	3	0	250	235	99	33	2	75	163	11.2	3.20	119	.249	.306	15	.188	1	23	18	-2	1.8
1962	SF-N	5	5	.500	28	15	1	0	0	98^2	112	64	18	1	45	42	14.4	5.38	71	.286	.361	3	.107	0	-16	-18	-1	-1.6
1963	Bal-A	6	8	.429	25	21	2	0	0	136	132	70	18	0	66	75	13.1	4.30	81	.256	.340	8	.174	1	-10	-13	-0	-1.2
1964	Bal-A	0	2	.000	4	2	0	0	0	17^1	21	10	1	0	8	13	15.1	5.19	69	.288	.358	1	.167	-0	-3	-3	-0	-0.3
1965	Was-A	8	8	.500	44	21	3	1	1	158	158	64	17	0	36	88	11.1	3.36	103	.260	.301	3	.073	-1	2	2	-1	0.0
1966	Was-A	11	14	.440	41	32	8	3	0	216	193	98	23	2	51	101	10.3	3.46	100	.236	.282	14	.212	3	-1	0	-1	0.3
1967	SF-N	**22**	10	.688	40	35	14	5	0	262^1	220	88	25	5	81	150	10.5	2.85	115	.226	.289	10	.119	0	15	13	-2	1.4
1968	SF-N	12	14	.462	38	28	9	2	1	198^1	196	92	17	2	49	121	11.2	3.58	82	.254	.300	6	.103	1	-13	-14	-2	-2.0
1969	SF-N	11	9	.550	32	28	9	0	0	196^2	175	81	20	1	77	76	11.6	3.34	105	.237	.310	9	.136	1	6	4	-1	0.3
1970	SF-N	3	4	.429	23	11	1	0	2	78^1	80	58	15	3	36	37	13.7	6.20	64	.262	.346	4	.160	0	-19	-20	1	-1.6
	NY-A	2	0	1.000	9	4	0	0	0	20^2	26	15	2	0	13	12	17.0	6.10	58	.295	.386	1	.200	0	-5	-6	-1	-0.6
1971	KC-A	0	0	—	4	1	0	0	0	9^2	14	10	0	0	5	2	17.7	9.31	37	.350	.422	0	.000	-0	-6	-6	1	-0.2
Total	16	134	128	.511	484	333	91	23	12	2380^1	2281	1100	256	24	795	1321	11.7	3.73	95	.251	.313	115	.156	9	-17	-48	-5	-3.1

● **HARRY McCORMICK** McCormick, Patrick Henry b: 10/25/1855, Syracuse, N.Y. d: 8/8/1889, Syracuse, N.Y. BR/TR, 5'9", 155 lbs. Deb: 5/1/1879

YEAR	TM/L	W	L	PCT	G	GS	CG	SH	SV	IP	H	R	HR	HB	BB	SO	RAT	ERA	ERA+	OAV	OOB	BH	AVG	PB	PR	PR+	PD	TPI
1879	Syr-N	18	33	.353	54	54	49	5	0	457^1	517	291	3		31	96	10.8	2.99	79	.266	.277	51	.222	-0	-25	-33	-7	-3.5
1881	Wor-N	1	8	.111	9	9	9	1	0	78^1	89	50	1		15	7	11.9	3.56	85	.275	.307	6	.133	-2	-7	-4	-1	-0.7
1882	Cin-a	14	11	.560	25	25	24	3	0	219^2	177	87	4		42	33	9.0	1.52	174	.206	.243	12	.129	-5	29	28	0	2.2
1883	Cin-a	8	6	.571	15	15	14	1	0	128^2	139	70	1		27	21	11.6	2.87	113	.258	.294	17	.309	4	6	6	1	0.8
Total	4	41	58	.414	103	103	96	10	0	884	922	498	9		115	157	10.6	2.66	98	.252	.274	86	.203	-4	3	-4	-7	-1.2

● **BILL McCORRY** McCorry, William Charles b: 7/9/1887, Saranac Lake, N.Y. d: 3/22/73, Augusta, Ga. BL/TR, 5'9", 157 lbs. Deb: 9/17/09

YEAR	TM/L	W	L	PCT	G	GS	CG	SH	SV	IP	H	R	HR	HB	BB	SO	RAT	ERA	ERA+	OAV	OOB	BH	AVG	PB	PR	PR+	PD	TPI
1909	StL-A	0	2	.000	2	2	2	0	0	15	29	21	1	0	6	10	21.0	9.00	27	.397	.443	0	.000	-0	-11	-11	-1	-1.2

● **LES McCRABB** McCrabb, Lester William "Buster" b: 11/4/14, Wakefield, Pa. BR/TR, 5'11", 175 lbs. Deb: 9/7/39 C

YEAR	TM/L	W	L	PCT	G	GS	CG	SH	SV	IP	H	R	HR	HB	BB	SO	RAT	ERA	ERA+	OAV	OOB	BH	AVG	PB	PR	PR+	PD	TPI
1939	Phi-A	1	2	.333	5	4	2	0	0	35^2	42	20	4	1	10	11	13.4	4.04	117	.290	.340	0	.000	-2	2	3	-0	0.0
1940	Phi-A	0	0	—	4	0	0	0	0	11^2	19	13	2	1	2	4	17.0	6.94	64	.365	.400	1	.250	0	-3	-3	0	-0.1
1941	Phi-A	9	13	.409	26	23	11	1	2	157^1	188	105	16	3	49	40	13.7	5.49	76	.293	.346	8	.143	-2	-24	-23	-2	-3.0
1942	Phi-A	0	0	—	1	0	0	0	0	4	14	14	2	1	2	0	38.3	31.50	12	.560	.607	0	.000	-0	-12	-12	0	-0.5
1950	Phi-A	0	0	—	2	0	0	0	0	1^1	7	4	0	0	0	2	47.3	27.00	17	.636	.636	0	—	0	-3	-3	0	-0.2
Total	5	10	15	.400	38	27	13	1	2	210	270	156	24	6	63	57	14.5	5.96	72	.309	.359	9	.122	-4	-40	-39	-1	-3.8

● **ED McCREERY** McCreery, Esley Porterfield "Big Ed" b: 12/24/1889, Cripple Creek, Colo. d: 10/19/60, Sacramento, Cal. BR/TR, 6', 190 lbs. Deb: 8/16/14

YEAR	TM/L	W	L	PCT	G	GS	CG	SH	SV	IP	H	R	HR	HB	BB	SO	RAT	ERA	ERA+	OAV	OOB	BH	AVG	PB	PR	PR+	PD	TPI
1914	Det-A	1	0	1.000	3	1	0	0	0	4	6	5	0	0	3	4	20.3	11.25	25	.316	.409	0	.000	-0	-4	-4	0	-0.7

● **TOM McCREERY** McCreery, Thomas Livingston b: 10/19/1874, Beaver, Pa. d: 7/3/41, Beaver, Pa. BB/TR, 5'11", 180 lbs. Deb: 6/8/1895 ♦

YEAR	TM/L	W	L	PCT	G	GS	CG	SH	SV	IP	H	R	HR	HB	BB	SO	RAT	ERA	ERA+	OAV	OOB	BH	AVG	PB	PR	PR+	PD	TPI
1895	Lou-N	3	1	.750	8	4	3	1	1	48^2	51	40	0	5	38	14	17.4	5.36	86	.266	.400	35	.324	1	-3	-4	1	0.0
1896	Lou-N	0	1	.000	1	1	0	0	0	1	4	10	1	0	5	0	81.0	36.00	12	.571	.750	155	.351	0	-4	-4	0	-0.5
1900	Pit-N	0	0	—	1	0	0	0	0	3	3	4	2	0	1	0	12.0	12.00	30	.250	.308	29	.220	0	-3	-3	0	-0.1
Total	3	3	2	.600	10	5	3	1	1	52^2	58	54	3	5	44	14	18.3	6.32	72	.275	.412	857	.289	2	-9	-11	1	-0.6

● **LANCE McCULLERS** McCullers, Lance Graye b: 3/8/64, Tampa, Fla. BB/TR, 6'1", 218 lbs. Deb: 8/12/85

YEAR	TM/L	W	L	PCT	G	GS	CG	SH	SV	IP	H	R	HR	HB	BB	SO	RAT	ERA	ERA+	OAV	OOB	BH	AVG	PB	PR	PR+	PD	TPI
1985	SD-N	0	2	.000	21	0	0	0	5	35	23	15	3	1	16	27	10.3	2.31	153	.195	.296	0	.000	-0	5	5	0	0.4
1986	SD-N	10	10	.500	70	7	0	0	5	136	103	46	12	4	58	92	10.9	2.78	132	.216	.306	2	.091	0	14	14	-1	1.9
1987	SD-N	8	10	.444	78	0	0	0	16	123^1	115	60	11	2	59	126	12.8	3.72	106	.244	.331	1	.071	-1	5	3	1	0.5
1988	SD-N	3	6	.333	60	0	0	0	10	97^2	70	29	8	0	55	81	11.5	2.49	137	.205	.315	2	.250	1	10	10	0	1.2
1989	NY-A	4	3	.571	52	1	0	0	3	84^2	83	46	9	3	37	82	13.1	4.57	85	.255	.337	0	—	0	-6	-7	-0	-0.6
1990	NY-A	1	0	1.000	11	0	0	0	0	15	14	8	2	0	6	11	12.0	3.60	111	.241	.313	0	—	0	1	1	0	0.0
	Det-A	1	0	1.000	9	1	0	0	0	29^2	18	11	2	0	13	20	9.4	2.73	145	.170	.261	0	—	0	4	4	0	0.1
	Yr	2	0	1.000	20	1	0	0	0	44^2	32	19	4	0	19	31	10.3	3.02	131	.195	.279	0	—	0	4	5	-1	0.1
1992	Tex-A	1	0	1.000	5	0	0	0	0	5	1	4	0	0	8	3	16.2	5.40	70	.067	.391	0	—	0	-1	-1	0	-0.1
Total	7	28	31	.475	306	9	0	0	39	526^1	427	219	47	10	252	442	11.8	3.25	115	.223	.317	5	.104	0	32	29	-1	3.4

● **CHARLIE McCULLOUGH** McCullough, Charles F. b: 1867, Dublin, Ireland TR, 6'1", 185 lbs. Deb: 4/23/1890

YEAR	TM/L	W	L	PCT	G	GS	CG	SH	SV	IP	H	R	HR	HB	BB	SO	RAT	ERA	ERA+	OAV	OOB	BH	AVG	PB	PR	PR+	PD	TPI
1890	Bro-a	4	21	.160	26	25	24	0	0	215^2	247	174	5	16	102	61	15.2	4.59	85	.279	.364	2	.023	-12	-17	-16	-2	-2.7
	Syr-a	1	2	.333	3	3	3	0	0	26	29	25	1	0	14	8	14.9	7.27	49	.274	.358	1	.111	0	-10	-12	-0	-0.9
	Yr	5	23	.179	29	28	27	0	0	241^2	276	199	6	16	116	69	15.2	4.88	79	.278	.363	3	.032	-12	-27	-27	-3	-3.6

● **PAUL McCULLOUGH** McCullough, Paul Willard b: 7/28/1898, New Castle, Pa. d: 11/7/70, New Castle, Pa. BR/TR, 5'9.5", 190 lbs. Deb: 7/2/29

YEAR	TM/L	W	L	PCT	G	GS	CG	SH	SV	IP	H	R	HR	HB	BB	SO	RAT	ERA	ERA+	OAV	OOB	BH	AVG	PB	PR	PR+	PD	TPI
1929	Was-A	0	0	—	3	0	0	0	0	7^1	7	7	1	0	2	3	11.0	8.59	49	.250	.300	0	.000	-0	-4	-4	-0	-0.2

● **PHIL McCULLOUGH** McCullough, Pinson Lamar b: 7/22/17, Stockbridge, Ga. BR/TR, 6'4", 204 lbs. Deb: 4/22/42

YEAR	TM/L	W	L	PCT	G	GS	CG	SH	SV	IP	H	R	HR	HB	BB	SO	RAT	ERA	ERA+	OAV	OOB	BH	AVG	PB	PR	PR+	PD	TPI
1942	Was-A	0	0	—	1	0	0	0	0	3	5	4	0	0	2	2	21.0	6.00	61	.333	.412	0	.000	-0	-1	-1	0	0.0

● **JEFF McCURRY** McCurry, Jeffrey Dee b: 1/21/70, Tokyo, Japan BR/TR, 6'7", 210 lbs. Deb: 5/6/95

YEAR	TM/L	W	L	PCT	G	GS	CG	SH	SV	IP	H	R	HR	HB	BB	SO	RAT	ERA	ERA+	OAV	OOB	BH	AVG	PB	PR	PR+	PD	TPI
1995	Pit-N	1	4	.200	55	0	0	0	1	61	82	38	9	5	30	27	17.3	5.02	86	.337	.421	0	.000	-0	-6	-5	0	-0.4
1996	Det-A	0	0	—	2	0	0	0	0	3^1	9	9	3	0	2	0	29.7	24.30	21	.474	.524	0	—	0	-7	-7	1	-0.2
1997	Col-N	1	4	.200	33	0	0	0	0	40^2	43	22	7	0	20	19	13.9	4.43	117	.277	.360	0	.000	-0	-1	3	-0	0.3
1998	Pit-N	1	3	.250	16	0	0	0	0	19^1	24	14	4	1	9	11	15.8	6.52	66	.324	.405	0	—	0	-5	-5	0	-0.8
1999	Hou-N	0	1	.000	5	0	0	0	0	4	11	8	1	0	2	3	29.3	15.75	28	.478	.520	0	—	0	-5	-5	-0	-0.9
Total	5	3	12	.200	111	0	0	0	1	128^1	169	91	24	6	63	60	16.7	5.89	78	.329	.408	0	.000	-0	-24	-17	0	-2.0

● **LINDY McDANIEL** McDaniel, Lyndall Dale b: 12/13/35, Hollis, Okla. BR/TR, 6'3", 195 lbs. Deb: 9/2/55 F

YEAR	TM/L	W	L	PCT	G	GS	CG	SH	SV	IP	H	R	HR	HB	BB	SO	RAT	ERA	ERA+	OAV	OOB	BH	AVG	PB	PR	PR+	PD	TPI
1955	StL-N	0	0	—	4	2	0	0	0	19	22	10	4	0	7	7	13.7	4.74	86	.293	.354	1	.200	-0	-1	-1	0	-0.1
1956	StL-N	7	6	.538	39	7	1	0	0	116^1	121	60	7	0	42	59	12.6	3.40	111	.273	.335	7	.219	2	5	5	1	0.8
1957	StL-N	15	9	.625	30	26	10	1	0	191	196	87	13	3	53	75	11.9	3.49	114	.266	.317	19	.257	4	8	10	-0	1.6
1958	StL-N	5	7	.417	26	17	2	1	0	108^2	139	76	17	2	31	47	14.2	5.80	71	.305	.352	2	.067	-3	-22	-19	1	-2.0
1959	StL-N	14	12	.538	62	7	1	0	**15**	132	144	61	11	1	41	86	12.7	3.82	111	.283	.338	1	.034	-2	2	6	2	1.2
1960	StL-N★	12	4	.750	65	2	1	0	**26**	116^1	85	28	8	1	24	105	8.5	2.09	196	.207	.253	6	.231	1	**22**	**24**	1	**4.6**
1961	StL-N	10	6	.625	55	0	0	0	9	94^1	117	57	11	2	31	65	14.3	4.87	90	.305	.361	4	.235	-0	-9	-4	1	-0.7
1962	StL-N	3	10	.231	55	2	0	0	14	107	96	53	12	1	29	79	10.6	4.12	104	.239	.292	2	.095	-1	-2	2	2	0.3
1963	Chi-N	13	7	.650	57	0	0	0	**22**	88	82	32	9	0	27	75	11.1	2.86	123	.251	.308	2	.091	-0	4	6	0	1.3
1964	Chi-N	1	7	.125	63	0	0	0	15	95	104	43	4	1	23	71	12.1	3.88	96	.276	.319	2	.125	-1	-4	-2	0	-0.2
1965	Chi-N	5	6	.455	71	0	0	0	2	128^2	115	45	12	0	47	92	11.3	2.59	142	.241	.309	0	.000	-1	14	15	2	1.4
1966	SF-N	10	5	.667	64	0	0	0	6	121^2	103	48	5	0	35	93	10.2	2.66	138	.228	.284	2	.091	-1	13	13	1	1.7
1967	SF-N	2	6	.250	41	3	0	0	3	72^2	69	34	5	2	24	48	11.8	3.72	88	.248	.313	1	.091	-1	-3	-4	2	-0.3
1968	SF-N	0	0	—	12	0	0	0	0	19^1	30	16	2	0	5	9	16.3	7.45	40	.357	.393	0	.000	-0	-10	-10	0	-0.5
	NY-A	4	1	.800	24	0	0	0	10	51^1	30	10	5	1	12	43	7.5	1.75	165	.166	.222	0	.000	-1	7	7	2	1.1
1969	NY-A	5	6	.455	51	0	0	0	5	83^2	84	37	4	0	23	60	11.5	3.55	98	.261	.310	0	.000	-1	1	-1	1	0.0
1970	NY-A	9	5	.643	62	0	0	0	29	111^2	88	29	7	0	23	81	8.9	2.01	175	.217	.259	4	.167	0	21	20	1	3.5
1971	NY-A	5	10	.333	44	0	0	0	4	69^2	82	41	12	0	24	39	13.7	5.04	64	.296	.352	1	.111	-0	-12	-15	0	-3.1
1972	NY-A	3	1	.750	37	0	0	0	0	68	54	23	4	0	25	47	10.5	2.25	131	.217	.288	2	.286	1	6	6	1	0.6
1973	NY-A	12	6	.667	47	3	1	0	10	160^1	148	54	11	1	49	93	11.1	2.86	128	.250	.309	0	.000	-0	17	15	3	2.1
1974	KC-A	1	4	.200	38	5	2	0	1	106^2	109	50	6	0	24	47	11.2	3.46	111	.265	.306	0	—	0	2	4	1	0.3
1975	KC-A	5	1	.833	40	0	0	0	1	78	81	40	3	0	24	40	12.1	4.15	93	.273	.327	0	—	0	-3	-2	-0	-0.2
Total	21	141	119	.542	987	74	18	2	172	2139^1	2099	934	172	15	623	1361	11.5	3.45	109	.258	.312	56	.148	-4	55	73	23	13.4

YEAR TM/L	W	L	PCT	G	GS	CG	SH	SV	IP	H	R	HR	HB	BB	SO	RAT	ERA	ERA+	OAV	OOB	BH	AVG	PB	PR	PR+	PD	TPI
● VON McDANIEL McDaniel, Max Von b: 4/18/39, Hollis, Okla. d: 8/20/95, Lawton, Okla. BR/TR, 6'2.5", 180 lbs. Deb: 6/13/57 F																											
1957 StL-N	7	5	.583	17	13	4	2	0	86^{2}	71	37	7	1	31	45	10.7	3.22	123	.225	.296	0	.000	-3	6	7	-1	0.4
1958 StL-N	0	0	—	2	1	0	0	0	2	5	3	0	0	5	0	45.0	13.50	31	.500	.667	0	—	0	-2	-2	-0	-0.1
Total 2	7	5	.583	19	14	4	2	0	88^{2}	76	40	7	1	36	45	11.5	3.45	115	.233	.311	0	.000	-3	4	5	-1	0.3
● JOE McDERMOTT McDermott, Joseph Deb: 5/4/1871 ♦																											
1872 Eck-n	0	7	.000	7	7	7	0	0	63	143	144	3		12	1	22.1	8.14	42	.377	.396	9	.281	2	-32	-36		-2.1
● MICKEY McDERMOTT McDermott, Maurice Joseph "Maury" b: 8/29/28, Poughkeepsie, N.Y. BL/TL, 6'2", 170 lbs. Deb: 4/24/48 C♦																											
1948 Bos-A	0	0	—	7	0	0	0	0	23^{1}	16	18	2	1	35	17	20.1	6.17	71	.208	.460	3	.375	1	-5	-5	1	-0.1
1949 Bos-A	5	4	.556	12	12	6	2	0	80	63	37	5	3	52	50	13.3	4.05	108	.220	.345	7	.212	1	1	3	-0	0.3
1950 Bos-A	7	3	.700	38	15	4	0	5	130	119	80	8	2	124	96	17.0	5.19	94	.249	.406	16	.364	6	-9	-4	1	0.4
1951 Bos-A	8	8	.500	34	19	9	1	3	172	141	72	9	5	92	127	12.5	3.35	133	.226	.330	18	.273	2	15	20	1	2.1
1952 Bos-A	10	9	.526	30	21	7	2	0	162	139	70	14	3	92	117	13.0	3.72	106	.234	.340	14	.226	3	-1	4	-0	0.6
1953 Bos-A	18	10	.643	32	30	8	4	0	206^{1}	169	82	9	2	109	92	12.2	3.01	140	.224	.323	28	.301	7	23	26	1	4.2
1954 Was-A	7	15	.318	30	26	11	1	1	196^{1}	172	95	8	3	110	95	13.1	3.44	103	.239	.342	19	.200	3	6	3	1	0.6
1955 Was-A	10	10	.500	31	20	8	1	1	156	140	75	9	9	100	78	14.4	3.75	102	.243	.364	25	.263	7	4	1	0	1.0
1956 *NY-A	2	6	.250	23	9	1	0	0	87	85	46	10	0	47	38	13.7	4.24	91	.261	.354	11	.212	3	-1	-4	-0	-0.1
1957 KC-A	1	4	.200	29	4	0	0	0	69	68	47	9	0	50	29	15.4	5.48	72	.266	.386	12	.245	3	-13	-11	1	0.0
1958 Det-A	0	0	—	2	0	0	0	0	2	6	4	0	0	2	0	36.0	9.00	45	.500	.571	1	.333	0	-1	-1	-0	0.0
1961 StL-N	1	0	1.000	19	0	0	0	4	27	29	17	3	0	15	15	14.7	3.67	120	.271	.361	1	.071	-1	1	2	-0	0.0
KC-A	0	0	—	4	0	0	0	0	5^{2}	14	12	0	0	10	3	38.1	14.29	29	.452	.585	1	.200	1	-6	-6	-0	-0.3
Total 12	69	69	.500	291	156	54	11	14	1316^{2}	1161	655	86	28	838	757	13.9	3.91	105	.240	.355	156	.252	36	14	29	4	8.7
● MIKE McDERMOTT McDermott, Michael H. b: 5/6/1864, Fall River, Mass. d: 5/7/47, Fall River, Mass. 5'10", 152 lbs. Deb: 9/2/1889																											
1889 Lou-a	1	8	.111	9	9	9	0	0	84^{1}	108	65	4	2	34	22	15.4	4.16	92	.302	.365	6	.182	-1	-3	-3	-0	-0.3
● MIKE McDERMOTT McDermott, Michael Joseph b: 9/7/1862, St.Louis, Mo. d: 6/30/43, St.Louis, Mo. TR, 5'8", 145 lbs. Deb: 4/20/1895																											
1895 Lou-N	4	19	.174	33	26	18	0	0	207^{1}	258	203	8	11	103	42	16.1	5.99	77	.300	.382	13	.159	-2	-28	-32	1	-2.6
1896 Lou-N	2	7	.222	12	10	4	1	0	65	87	77	4	6	44	12	19.0	7.34	59	.318	.423	8	.296	1	-21	-22	1	-2.0
1897 Cle-N	4	5	.444	9	7	4	0	0	62	75	44	2	3	25	12	15.0	4.50	100	.296	.367	8	.320	1	-1	-0	1	0.1
StL-N	1	2	.333	4	4	1	0	0	21^{1}	23	23	2	0	19	3	17.7	9.28	47	.274	.408	2	.222	-0	-12	-11	1	-1.0
Yr	5	7	.417	13	11	5	0	0	83^{1}	98	67	4	3	44	15	15.7	5.72	78	.291	.378	10	.294	1	-13	-11	2	-0.9
Total 3	11	33	.250	58	47	27	1	0	355^{2}	443	347	16	20	191	69	16.5	6.17	74	.301	.389	31	.217	0	-62	-65	4	-5.5
● DANNY McDEVITT McDevitt, Daniel Eugene b: 11/18/32, New York, N.Y. BL/TL, 5'10", 175 lbs. Deb: 6/17/57																											
1957 Bro-N	7	4	.636	22	17	5	2	0	119	105	55	5	6	72	90	13.8	3.25	128	.238	.353	6	.154	-0	8	11	2	1.1
1958 LA-N	2	6	.250	13	10	2	0	0	48^{1}	71	43	6	0	31	26	19.0	7.45	55	.355	.442	2	.133	-0	-19	-17	-1	-2.4
1959 LA-N	10	8	.556	39	22	6	2	4	145	149	83	16	14	51	106	13.3	3.97	106	.263	.339	5	.109	-2	-0	4	0	0.3
1960 LA-N	0	4	.000	24	7	0	0	0	53	51	26	7	6	42	30	16.8	4.25	93	.260	.406	2	.200	0	-3	-2	-0	-0.1
1961 NY-A	1	2	.333	8	2	0	0	1	13	18	11	2	1	8	8	18.7	7.62	49	.353	.450	0	.000	0	-5	-6	0	-1.1
Min-A	1	0	1.000	16	1	0	0	0	26^{2}	20	11	1	4	19	15	14.5	2.36	179	.213	.368	0	.000	-0	5	5	0	0.3
Yr	2	2	.500	24	3	0	0	1	39^{2}	38	22	3	5	27	23	15.9	4.08	100	.262	.395	0	.000	-0	-0	-0	0	-0.8
1962 KC-A	0	3	.000	33	1	0	0	2	51	47	37	5	1	41	28	15.7	5.82	73	.250	.387	2	.222	0	-11	-9	1	-0.4
Total 6	21	27	.438	155	60	13	4	7	456	461	266	42	32	264	303	14.9	4.40	94	.265	.372	17	.138	-3	-25	-12	2	-2.3
● ALLEN McDILL McDill, Allen Gabriel b: 8/23/71, Greenville, Miss. BL/TL, 6', 155 lbs. Deb: 5/15/97																											
1997 KC-A	0	0	—	3	0	0	0	0	4	3	6	1	1	8	2	27.0	13.50	35	.214	.522	0	—	0	-4	-4	0	-0.2
1998 KC-A	0	0	—	7	0	0	0	0	6	9	7	3	0	2	3	16.5	10.50	46	.333	.379	0	—	0	-4	-4	0	-0.2
2000 Det-A	0	0	—	13	0	0	0	0	10	13	9	2	1	1	7	13.5	7.20	66	.317	.349	0	—	0	-3	-3	-0	-0.1
Total 3	0	0	—	23	0	0	0	0	20	25	22	6	2	11	12	17.1	9.45	51	.305	.400	0	—	0	-10	-10	0	-0.5
● HANK McDONALD McDonald, Henry Monroe b: 1/16/11, Santa Monica, Cal. d: 10/17/82, Hemet, Cal. BR/TR, 6'3", 200 lbs. Deb: 4/16/31																											
1931 Phi-A	2	4	.333	19	10	1	1	0	70^{1}	62	43	3	1	41	23	13.3	3.71	121	.239	.346	2	.095	-1	5	6	-1	0.2
1933 Phi-A	1	1	.500	4	1	0	0	0	12^{1}	14	12	0	0	4	1	13.1	5.11	84	.264	.316	0	.000	-0	-1	-1	-0	-0.2
StL-A	0	4	.000	25	5	0	0	0	58^{1}	83	59	6	3	34	22	18.5	8.64	54	.332	.418	2	.143	-1	-28	-24	-0	-1.4
Yr	1	5	.167	29	6	0	0	0	70^{2}	97	71	6	3	38	23	17.6	8.02	57	.320	.401	2	.111	-1	-29	-25	-0	-1.6
Total 2	3	9	.250	48	16	1	1	0	141	159	114	9	4	79	46	15.4	5.87	77	.283	.375	4	.103	-2	-24	-20	-1	-1.4
● JIM McDONALD McDonald, Jimmie Le Roy "Hot Rod" b: 5/17/27, Grants Pass, Ore. BR/TR (BB 1950-51), 5'10.5", 185 lbs. Deb: 7/27/50																											
1950 Bos-A	1	0	1.000	9	0	0	0	0	19	23	9	1	1	10	5	16.1	3.79	129	.329	.420	1	.333	1	2	2	1	0.3
1951 StL-A	4	7	.364	16	11	5	0	1	84	84	48	5	2	46	28	14.1	4.07	108	.260	.356	6	.207	-0	0	3	1	0.4
1952 NY-A	3	4	.429	26	5	1	0	0	69^{1}	71	31	1	2	40	20	14.7	3.50	95	.268	.368	6	.316	3	1	-2	3	0.5
1953 *NY-A	9	7	.563	27	18	6	2	0	129^{2}	128	64	4	1	39	43	11.7	3.82	97	.260	.316	4	.098	-3	3	-2	2	-0.3
1954 NY-A	4	1	.800	16	10	3	1	0	71	54	28	3	1	45	20	12.7	3.17	108	.213	.334	4	.211	2	4	2	1	0.4
1955 Bal-A	3	5	.375	21	8	0	0	0	51^{2}	76	48	5	0	30	20	18.5	7.14	53	.345	.424	2	.182	1	-18	-20	1	-2.4
1956 Chi-A	0	2	.000	8	3	0	0	0	18^{2}	29	18	2	1	7	10	17.8	8.68	47	.377	.435	0	.000	-0	-9	-10	-0	-0.9
1957 Chi-A	0	1	.000	10	0	0	0	0	22^{1}	18	8	2	0	10	12	11.3	2.01	185	.234	.322	0	.000	0	4	4	-0	0.2
1958 Chi-A	0	0	—	3	0	0	0	0	2^{1}	6	8	1	0	4	0	38.6	19.29	19	.429	.556	0	—	0	-4	-4	0	-0.2
Total 9	24	27	.471	136	55	15	3	1	468	489	262	24	8	231	158	14.0	4.27	89	.273	.359	23	.180	4	-17	-26	8	-2.0
● JOHN McDONALD McDonald, John Joseph (b: John Joseph McDonnell) b: 1/27/1883, Throop, Pa. d: 4/9/50, Roselle, N.J. BR/TR, 6'1", 170 lbs. Deb: 9/3/07																											
1907 Was-A	0	0	—	1	0	0	0	0	6	12	11	0	0	2	3	21.0	9.00	27	.414	.452	1	.333	1	-4	-5	-0	-0.2
● BEN McDONALD McDonald, Larry Benard b: 11/24/67, Baton Rouge, La. BR/TR, 6'7", 213 lbs. Deb: 9/6/89																											
1989 Bal-A	1	0	1.000	6	0	0	0	0	7^{1}	8	7	2	0	4	3	14.7	8.59	44	.286	.375	0	—	0	-4	-4	0	-0.5
1990 Bal-A	8	5	.615	21	15	3	2	0	118^{2}	88	36	9	0	35	65	9.3	2.43	157	.205	.265	0	—	0	20	19	0	2.0
1991 Bal-A	6	8	.429	21	21	1	0	0	126^{1}	126	71	16	1	43	85	12.1	4.84	82	.261	.323	0	—	0	-10	-13	-1	-1.4
1992 Bal-A	13	13	.500	35	35	4	2	0	227	213	113	32	9	74	158	11.7	4.24	95	.247	.313	0	—	0	-7	-5	1	-0.4
1993 Bal-A	13	14	.481	34	34	7	1	0	220^{1}	185	92	17	5	86	171	11.3	3.39	132	.228	.306	0	—	0	23	26	3	3.2
1994 Bal-A	14	7	.667	24	24	5	1	0	157^{1}	151	75	14	2	54	94	11.8	4.06	123	.255	.319	0	—	0	13	16	1	1.9
1995 Bal-A	3	6	.333	14	13	1	0	0	80	67	40	10	3	38	62	12.1	4.16	114	.224	.318	0	—	0	5	5	1	0.6
1996 Mil-A	12	10	.545	35	35	2	0	0	221^{1}	228	104	25	6	67	146	12.2	3.90	133	.264	.322	0	—	0	27	31	-0	2.5
1997 Mil-A	8	7	.533	21	21	1	0	0	133	120	68	13	5	36	110	10.9	4.06	114	.237	.294	0	.000	0	8	8	0	0.8
Total 9	78	70	.527	211	198	24	6	0	1291^{1}	1186	606	138	31	437	894	11.5	3.91	115	.243	.310	0	.000	0	74	83	4	8.7
● McDOOLAN McDoolan Deb: 4/14/1873																											
1873 Mar-n	0	1	.000	1	1	1	0	0	9	18	24	0		0	0	18.0	3.00	108	.305	.305	0	.000	-1	0	0		0.0
● SANDY McDOUGAL McDougal, John Auchanbolt b: 5/21/1874, Buffalo, N.Y. d: 10/2/10, Buffalo, N.Y. BR/TR, 5'10", 155 lbs. Deb: 6/12/1895																											
1895 Bro-N	0	0	—	1	0	0	0	1	3	3	4	0	0	5	2	24.0	12.00	37	.250	.471	0	.000	-0	-2	-3	-0	-0.2
1905 StL-N	1	4	.200	5	5	5	0	0	44^{2}	50	24	0	0	12	10	12.5	3.43	87	.301	.348	2	.133	-1	-2	-2	3	0.0
Total 2	1	4	.200	6	5	5	0	1	47^{2}	53	28	0	0	17	12	13.2	3.97	78	.298	.359	2	.125	-1	-5	-5	3	-0.2
● DEWEY McDOUGAL McDougal, John H. b: 9/19/1871, Aledo, Ill. d: 4/28/36, Galesburg, Ill. TR, 170 lbs. Deb: 4/24/1895																											
1895 StL-N	3	10	.231	18	14	10	0	0	114^{2}	187	146	11	10	46	23	19.1	8.32	58	.360	.423	6	.146	-2	-45	-44	-1	-3.5
1896 StL-N	0	1	.000	3	1	0	0	0	10	13	11	2	1	4	0	16.2	8.10	54	.310	.383	0	.000	-1	-4	-4	1	-0.3
Total 2	3	11	.214	21	15	10	0	0	124^{2}	200	157	13	11	50	23	18.8	8.30	58	.357	.420	6	.136	-3	-49	-48	-0	-3.8
● JACK McDOWELL McDowell, Jack Burns b: 1/16/66, Van Nuys, Cal. BR/TR, 6'5", 180 lbs. Deb: 9/15/87																											
1987 Chi-A	3	0	1.000	4	4	0	0	0	28	16	6	1	2	6	15	7.7	1.93	238	.168	.233	0	—	0	8	8	0	0.9
1988 Chi-A	5	10	.333	26	26	1	0	0	158^{2}	147	85	12	7	68	84	12.6	3.97	100	.245	.329	0	—	0	0	0	-1	-0.1

YEAR	TM/L	W	L	PCT	G	GS	CG	SH	SV	IP	H	R	HR	HB	BB	SO	RAT	ERA	ERA+	OAV	OOB	BH	AVG	PB	PR	PR+	PD	TPI
1990	Chi-A	14	9	.609	33	33	4	0	0	205	189	93	20	7	77	165	12.0	3.82	100	.244	.317	0	—	0	2	0	-0	0.0
1991	Chi-A★	17	10	.630	35	35	**15**	3	0	253^{2}	212	97	19	4	82	191	10.6	3.41	117	.228	.293	0	—	0	20	17	0	1.7
1992	Chi-A★	20	10	.667	34	34	**13**	1	0	260^{2}	247	95	21	7	75	178	11.4	3.18	122	.251	.309	0	—	0	22	20	-1	2.1
1993	*Chi-A★	**22**	10	.688	34	34	10	**4**	0	256^{2}	261	104	20	3	69	158	11.7	3.37	125	.266	.316	0	—	0	28	24	2	3.0
1994	Chi-A	10	9	.526	25	25	6	2	0	181	186	82	12	5	42	127	11.6	3.73	125	.266	.312	0	—	0	22	19	-0	1.7
1995	*NY-A	15	10	.600	30	30	**8**	2	0	217^{2}	211	106	25	5	78	157	12.2	3.93	118	.254	.322	0	—	0	19	17	0	1.7
1996	*Cle-A	13	9	.591	30	30	5	1	0	192	214	119	22	4	67	141	13.4	5.11	96	.282	.343	0	—	0	-2	-5	1	-0.3
1997	Cle-A	3	3	.500	8	6	0	0	0	40^{2}	44	25	6	1	18	38	13.9	5.09	92	.282	.360	0	—	0	-2	-2	0	-0.2
1998	Ana-A	5	3	.625	14	14	0	0	0	76	96	45	11	1	19	45	13.7	5.09	92	.311	.353	0	—	0	-4	-3	0	-0.3
1999	Ana-A	0	4	.000	4	4	0	0	0	19	31	17	4	2	5	12	18.0	8.05	60	.369	.418	0	—	0	-7	-7	1	-1.0
Total	12	127	87	.593	277	275	62	13	0	1889	1854	874	173	48	606	1311	11.9	3.85	111	.257	.319	0	—	0	105	89	2	9.2

● ROGER McDOWELL

McDowell, Roger Alan b: 12/21/60, Cincinnati, Ohio BR/TR, 6'1", 182 lbs. Deb: 4/11/85

YEAR	TM/L	W	L	PCT	G	GS	CG	SH	SV	IP	H	R	HR	HB	BB	SO	RAT	ERA	ERA+	OAV	OOB	BH	AVG	PB	PR	PR+	PD	TPI
1985	NY-N	6	5	.545	62	2	0	0	17	127^{1}	108	43	9	1	37	70	10.3	2.83	122	.230	.287	3	.158	0	11	9	2	1.3
1986	*NY-N	14	9	.609	75	0	0	0	22	128	107	48	4	3	42	65	10.7	3.02	117	.228	.296	5	.278	1	10	8	3	2.0
1987	NY-N	7	5	.583	56	0	0	0	25	88^{2}	95	41	7	2	28	32	12.7	4.16	91	.276	.334	3	.231	1	-1	-4	1	-0.5
1988	*NY-N	5	5	.500	62	0	0	0	16	89	80	31	1	3	31	46	11.5	2.63	123	.238	.308	3	.333	2	8	6	2	1.3
1989	NY-N	1	5	.167	25	0	0	0	4	35^{1}	34	21	1	2	16	15	13.2	3.31	99	.254	.342	1	.500	0	1	-0	2	0.2
	Phi-N	3	3	.500	44	0	0	0	19	56^{2}	45	15	2	1	22	32	10.8	1.11	319	.220	.298	0	.000	-0	15	15	1	2.7
	Yr	4	8	.333	69	0	0	0	23	92	79	36	3	3	38	47	11.7	1.96	176	.233	.316	1	.333	0	16	15	3	2.9
1990	Phi-N	6	8	.429	72	0	0	0	22	86^{1}	92	41	2	2	35	39	13.4	3.86	99	.286	.359	0	.000	-0	-1	-0	1	0.1
1991	Phi-N	3	6	.333	38	0	0	0	3	59	61	28	1	2	32	28	14.5	3.20	115	.266	.361	0	.000	-0	3	3	2	0.6
	LA-N	6	3	.667	33	0	0	0	7	42^{1}	39	12	3	0	16	22	11.7	2.55	141	.257	.327	0	—	0	5	5	1	1.1
	Yr	9	9	.500	71	0	0	0	10	101^{1}	100	40	4	2	48	50	13.3	2.93	124	.262	.348	0	.000	-0	9	8	2	1.7
1992	LA-N	6	10	.375	65	0	0	0	14	83^{2}	103	46	3	1	42	50	15.7	4.09	84	.306	.384	0	.000	1	-5	-6	2	-1.0
1993	LA-N	5	3	.625	54	0	0	0	2	68	76	32	2	2	30	27	14.3	2.25	170	.288	.365	1	.500	0	14	13	3	1.8
1994	LA-N	0	3	.000	32	0	0	0	0	41^{1}	50	25	3	1	22	29	15.9	5.23	75	.303	.388	0	.000	-0	-5	-6	0	-0.4
1995	Tex-A	7	4	.636	64	0	0	0	4	85	86	39	5	6	34	49	13.3	4.02	120	.277	.359	0	—	0	7	7	2	1.1
1996	Bal-A	1	1	.500	41	0	0	0	4	59^{1}	69	32	7	2	23	20	14.3	4.25	116	.296	.364	0	—	0	5	5	2	0.4
Total	12	70	70	.500	723	2	0	0	159	1050	1045	454	50	28	410	524	12.7	3.30	114	.263	.336	16	.222	6	67	55	23	10.7

● SAM McDOWELL

McDowell, Samuel Edward Thomas "Sudden Sam" b: 9/21/42, Pittsburgh, Pa. BL/TL, 6'5", 218 lbs. Deb: 9/15/61

YEAR	TM/L	W	L	PCT	G	GS	CG	SH	SV	IP	H	R	HR	HB	BB	SO	RAT	ERA	ERA+	OAV	OOB	BH	AVG	PB	PR	PR+	PD	TPI
1961	Cle-A	0	0	—	1	1	0	0	0	6^{1}	3	0	0	0	5	5	11.4	0.00	—	.136	.296	0	.000	-0	3	3	0	0.1
1962	Cle-A	3	7	.300	25	13	0	0	1	87^{2}	81	64	9	4	70	70	15.9	6.06	64	.243	.381	4	.154	-1	-20	-22	-0	-2.3
1963	Cle-A	3	5	.375	14	12	3	1	0	65	63	37	6	0	44	63	14.8	4.85	75	.256	.369	4	.211	0	-9	-9	-0	-1.0
1964	Cle-A	11	6	.647	31	24	6	2	1	173^{1}	148	60	8	3	100	177	13.0	2.70	133	.229	.336	8	.143	0	18	17	-1	1.6
1965	Cle-A★	17	11	.607	42	35	14	3	4	273	178	80	9	6	132	**325**	10.4	**2.18**	**160**	**.185**	.287	12	.126	-3	**39**	**39**	1	4.0
1966	Cle-A†	9	8	.529	35	28	8	**5**	3	194^{1}	130	66	12	6	102	**225**	11.0	2.87	120	**.188**	.298	12	.200	1	12	12	1	1.4
1967	Cle-A	13	15	.464	37	37	10	1	0	236^{1}	201	112	21	7	123	236	12.6	3.85	85	.233	.333	15	.183	1	-16	-15	-1	-1.7
1968	Cle-A★	15	14	.517	38	37	11	3	0	269	181	78	13	10	110	**283**	10.1	1.81	164	.189	.279	13	.153	0	35	35	-1	4.1
1969	Cle-A★	18	14	.563	39	38	18	4	1	285	222	111	13	7	102	**279**	10.5	2.94	128	.213	.288	16	.174	-1	22	25	-0	2.7
1970	Cle-A★	20	12	.625	39	39	19	1	0	**305**	236	108	25	7	131	**304**	11.0	2.92	136	.213	.300	13	.124	-3	27	**33**	-2	2.8
1971	Cle-A†	13	17	.433	35	31	8	2	1	214^{2}	160	89	22	3	153	192	13.2	3.40	113	.207	.340	13	.178	-1	2	9	-2	1.0
1972	SF-N	10	8	.556	28	25	4	0	0	164^{1}	155	86	12	6	86	122	13.5	4.33	81	.253	.350	7	.119	-1	-16	-15	-0	-1.7
1973	SF-N	1	2	.333	18	3	0	0	3	40	45	23	4	0	29	35	16.6	4.50	85	.285	.396	2	.167	-0	-4	-3	0	-0.3
	NY-A	5	8	.385	16	15	2	1	0	95^{2}	73	47	4	0	64	75	12.9	3.95	93	.212	.335	0	—	0	-1	-3	0	-0.3
1974	NY-A	1	6	.143	13	7	0	0	0	48	42	27	6	0	41	33	15.6	4.69	75	.236	.379	0	—	0	-6	-6	-1	-0.9
1975	Pit-N	2	1	.667	14	1	0	0	0	34^{2}	30	11	0	0	20	29	13.0	2.86	124	.242	.347	0	.000	-1	3	3	0	0.1
Total	15	141	134	.513	425	346	103	23	14	2492^{1}	1948	999	164	59	1312	2453	12.0	3.17	112	.215	.318	119	.154	-8	88	106	-5	9.6

● CHUCK McELROY

McElroy, Charles Dwayne b: 10/1/67, Port Arthur, Tex. BL/TL, 6', 195 lbs. Deb: 9/4/89

YEAR	TM/L	W	L	PCT	G	GS	CG	SH	SV	IP	H	R	HR	HB	BB	SO	RAT	ERA	ERA+	OAV	OOB	BH	AVG	PB	PR	PR+	PD	TPI
1989	Phi-N	0	0	—	11	0	0	0	0	10^{1}	12	2	1	0	4	8	13.9	1.74	204	.286	.348	0	—	0	2	2	-0	0.1
1990	Phi-N	0	1	.000	16	0	0	0	0	14	24	13	0	0	10	16	21.9	7.71	50	.369	.453	0	—	0	-6	-6	-0	-0.4
1991	Chi-N	6	2	.750	71	0	0	0	3	101^{1}	73	33	7	0	57	92	11.5	1.95	199	.210	.322	3	.300	1	**20**	**21**	1	1.8
1992	Chi-N	4	7	.364	72	0	0	0	6	83^{2}	73	40	5	0	51	83	13.3	3.55	102	.237	.345	4	.667	3	-0	1	-1	0.3
1993	Chi-N	2	2	.500	49	0	0	0	0	47^{1}	51	30	4	1	25	31	14.6	4.56	88	.280	.370	0	.000	-1	-3	-3	-0	-0.3
1994	Cin-N	1	2	.333	52	0	0	0	5	57^{2}	52	15	3	0	15	38	10.5	2.34	177	.244	.294	1	.167	-0	12	12	-1	0.6
1995	Cin-N	3	4	.429	44	0	0	0	0	40^{1}	46	29	5	1	15	27	13.8	6.02	68	.291	.356	0	.000	-0	-8	-9	-0	-1.4
1996	Cin-N	2	0	1.000	12	0	0	0	0	12^{1}	13	10	2	0	10	13	16.8	6.57	65	.265	.390	0	.000	-0	-3	-3	-0	-0.5
	Cal-A	5	1	.833	40	0	0	0	0	36^{2}	32	12	2	2	13	32	11.5	2.95	170	.239	.315	0	—	0	8	8	1	1.3
1997	Ana-A	0	0	—	13	0	0	0	0	15^{2}	17	7	2	0	3	18	11.5	3.45	133	.270	.303	0	—	0	2	2	-0	0.1
	Chi-A	1	3	.250	48	0	0	0	1	59^{1}	56	29	3	2	19	44	11.7	3.94	111	.247	.310	0	—	0	4	3	1	0.3
	Yr	1	3	.250	61	0	0	0	1	75	73	36	5	2	22	62	11.6	3.84	115	.252	.309	0	—	0	6	5	0	0.4
1998	Col-N	6	4	.600	78	0	0	0	2	68^{1}	68	23	3	0	24	61	12.1	2.90	179	.268	.331	1	.200	-0	10	14	-1	1.8
1999	Col-N	3	1	.750	41	0	0	0	0	40^{2}	48	29	9	0	28	37	16.8	6.20	94	.296	.400	0	.000	-0	-7	-1	1	-0.1
	NY-N	0	0	—	15	0	0	0	0	13^{1}	12	5	0	1	8	7	14.2	3.38	130	.250	.368	0	—	0	2	2	-0	0.0
	Yr	3	1	.750	56	0	0	0	0	54	60	34	9	1	36	44	16.2	5.50	99	.286	.393	0	.000	-0	-6	-0	-0	-0.1
2000	Bal-A	3	0	1.000	43	2	0	0	0	63^{1}	60	36	6	2	34	50	13.6	4.69	102	.247	.344	0	—	0	2	1	-0	0.0
Total	12	36	27	.571	605	2	0	0	17	664^{1}	637	313	52	9	316	557	13.0	3.74	117	.255	.341	9	.231	2	34	45	-1	3.6

● JIM McELROY

McElroy, James D. b: 11/5/1862, Napa Co., Cal. d: 7/24/1889, Needles, Cal. 5'10", 170 lbs. Deb: 5/26/1884

YEAR	TM/L	W	L	PCT	G	GS	CG	SH	SV	IP	H	R	HR	HB	BB	SO	RAT	ERA	ERA+	OAV	OOB	BH	AVG	PB	PR	PR+	PD	TPI
1884	Phi-N	1	12	.077	13	13	13	0	0	111	115	112	1		54	45	13.7	4.86	61	.254	.333	7	.146	-3	-23	-23	-0	-2.3
	Wil-U	0	1	.000	1	1	0	0	0	5	10	6	0		0	3	18.0	10.80	25	.385	.385	0	.000	-0	-5	-4	0	-0.5
Total	1	1	13	.071	14	14	13	0	0	116	125	118	1		54	48	13.9	5.12	58	.261	.336	7	.140	-4	-28	-28	0	-2.8

● WILL McENANEY

McEnaney, William Henry b: 2/14/52, Springfield, Ohio BL/TL, 6', 180 lbs. Deb: 7/3/74

YEAR	TM/L	W	L	PCT	G	GS	CG	SH	SV	IP	H	R	HR	HB	BB	SO	RAT	ERA	ERA+	OAV	OOB	BH	AVG	PB	PR	PR+	PD	TPI
1974	Cin-N	2	1	.667	24	0	0	0	2	27	24	16	4	0	9	13	11.0	4.33	81	.250	.314	0	—	0	-2	-3	-1	-0.4
1975	*Cin-N	5	2	.714	70	0	0	0	15	91	92	29	6	2	23	48	11.6	2.47	146	.264	.314	0	.000	-2	12	12	1	1.0
1976	*Cin-N	2	6	.250	55	0	0	0	7	72^{1}	97	44	3	1	23	28	15.1	4.85	72	.323	.373	1	.167	1	-11	-11	0	-1.3
1977	Mon-N	3	5	.375	69	0	0	0	3	86^{2}	92	39	6	2	22	38	12.0	3.95	97	.271	.319	0	.000	-1	-0	-1	-0	-0.2
1978	Pit-N	0	0	—	6	0	0	0	0	8^{2}	15	11	3	1	2	6	18.7	10.38	36	.395	.439	0	—	0	-7	-6	0	-0.3
1979	StL-N	0	3	.000	45	0	0	0	2	64	60	26	3	2	16	15	11.0	2.95	128	.251	.304	0	.000	-0	6	6	2	0.4
Total	6	12	17	.414	269	0	0	0	29	349^{2}	380	165	25	8	95	148	12.4	3.76	97	.279	.330	1	.032	-2	-2	-4	-1	-0.8

● LOU McEVOY

McEvoy, Louis Anthony b: 5/30/02, Williamsburg, Kan. d: 12/17/53, Webster Groves, Mo BR/TR, 6'2.5", 203 lbs. Deb: 4/28/30

YEAR	TM/L	W	L	PCT	G	GS	CG	SH	SV	IP	H	R	HR	HB	BB	SO	RAT	ERA	ERA+	OAV	OOB	BH	AVG	PB	PR	PR+	PD	TPI
1930	NY-A	1	3	.250	28	1	0	0	3	52^{1}	64	51	4	2	29	14	16.3	6.71	64	.288	.375	2	.125	-1	-12	-15	-1	-1.3
1931	NY-A	0	0	—	6	0	0	0	1	12^{1}	19	17	1	1	12	3	23.4	12.41	32	.358	.485	0	.000	-1	-11	-13	0	-0.6
Total	2	1	3	.250	34	1	0	0	4	64^{2}	83	68	5	3	41	17	17.7	7.79	54	.302	.398	2	.100	-2	-23	-28	-1	-1.9

● BARNEY McFADDEN

McFadden, Bernard Joseph b: 2/22/1874, Eckley, Pa. d: 4/28/24, Mauch Chunk, Pa. BR/TR, 6'1", 195 lbs. Deb: 4/24/01

YEAR	TM/L	W	L	PCT	G	GS	CG	SH	SV	IP	H	R	HR	HB	BB	SO	RAT	ERA	ERA+	OAV	OOB	BH	AVG	PB	PR	PR+	PD	TPI
1901	Cin-N	3	4	.429	8	5	4	0	0	46	54	39	2	6	40	11	19.6	6.07	53	.290	.431	3	.150	-1	-14	-15	1	-1.8
1902	Phi-N	0	1	.000	1	1	1	0	0	9	14	13	0	0	7	3	21.0	8.00	35	.350	.447	0	.000	-0	-5	-5	0	-0.5
Total	2	3	5	.375	9	6	5	0	0	55	68	52	2	6	47	14	19.8	6.38	49	.301	.434	3	.130	-2	-19	-20	1	-2.3

● DAN McFARLAN

McFarlan, Anderson Daniel b: 11/1/1873, Gainesville, Tex. d: 9/23/24, Louisville, Ky. Deb: 9/2/1895 F

YEAR	TM/L	W	L	PCT	G	GS	CG	SH	SV	IP	H	R	HR	HB	BB	SO	RAT	ERA	ERA+	OAV	OOB	BH	AVG	PB	PR	PR+	PD	TPI
1895	Lou-N	0	7	.000	7	7	6	0	0	46	80	56	4	5	15	10	19.6	6.65	70	.376	.429	5	.238	-1	-10	-11	1	-1.1
1899	Bro-N	0	0	—	1	0	0	0	0	6	6	1	1	0	3	0	13.5	1.50	261	.261	.346	0	.000	-0	2	2	0	0.1
	Was-N	8	18	.308	32	28	22	1	0	211^{2}	268	166	5	11	64	41	14.6	4.76	82	.308	.363	16	.186	-0	-21	-20	-1	-2.0
	Yr	8	18	.308	33	28	22	1	0	217^{2}	274	167	6	11	67	41	14.6	4.67	84	.307	.363	16	.182	-1	-20	-18	-0	-1.9
Total	2	8	25	.242	40	35	28	1	0	263^{2}	354	223	10	16	82	51	15.4	5.02	81	.320	.375	21	.193	-1	-29	-28	1	-3.0

● CHAPPIE McFARLAND McFarland, Charles A. b: 3/13/1875, White Hall, Ill. d: 12/14/24, Houston, Tex. TR, 6'1", Deb: 9/15/02 F

YEAR	TM/L	W	L	PCT	G	GS	CG	SH	SV	IP	H	R	HR	HB	BB	SO	RAT	ERA	ERA+	OAV	OOB	BH	AVG	PB	PR	PR+	PD	TPI
1902	StL-N	0	1	.000	2	1	1	0	0	11	11	7	1	0	3	3	11.5	5.73	48	.262	.311	0	.000	-1	-4	-4	0	-0.3
1903	StL-N	9	19	.321	28	26	25	1	0	229	253	133	2	6	48	76	12.1	3.07	106	.284	.325	8	.108	-4	5	5	2	0.4
1904	StL-N	14	18	.438	32	31	28	1	0	269^{1}	266	149	7	4	56	111	10.9	3.21	84	.248	.288	13	.131	-2	-14	-15	7	-1.3
1905	StL-N	8	18	.308	31	28	22	3	1	250^{1}	281	145	3	6	65	85	12.7	3.81	78	.284	.332	14	.165	1	-22	-23	1	-2.1
1906	StL-N	2	1	.667	6	4	2	0	1	37^{1}	33	18	1	0	8	16	9.9	1.93	136	.219	.258	2	.133	-1	3	3	1	0.3
	Pit-N	1	3	.250	6	5	2	1	0	35^{1}	39	14	0	2	7	11	12.2	2.55	105	.298	.343	5	.385	1	0	0	0	0.2
	Bro-N	0	1	.000	1	1	1	0	0	9	10	8	1	0	5	5	15.0	8.00	32	.286	.375	0	.000	-0	-5	-6	-0	-0.5
	Yr	3	5	.375	13	10	5	1	1	81^{2}	82	40	2	2	20	32	11.5	2.87	92	.259	.307	7	.226	0	-2	-2	1	0.0
Total	5	34	61	.358	106	96	81	6	2	841^{1}	893	474	15	18	192	307	11.8	3.35	87	.270	.313	42	.143	-6	-37	-39	11	-3.3

● CHRIS McFARLAND McFarland, Christopher b: 8/17/1861, Fall River, Mass. d: 5/24/18, New Bedford, Mass. 5'9", 170 lbs. Deb: 4/19/1884 ◆

YEAR	TM/L	W	L	PCT	G	GS	CG	SH	SV	IP	H	R	HR	HB	BB	SO	RAT	ERA	ERA+	OAV	OOB	BH	AVG	PB	PR	PR+	PD	TPI
1884	Bal-U	0	1	.000	1	1	0	0	0	3	9	10	1		1	3	30.0	15.00	18	.500	.526	3	.214	-0	-4	-4	-0	-0.5

● MONTE McFARLAND McFarland, Lamont Amos b: 11/7/1872, White Hall, Ill. d: 11/15/13, Peoria, Ill. Deb: 9/14/1895 F

YEAR	TM/L	W	L	PCT	G	GS	CG	SH	SV	IP	H	R	HR	HB	BB	SO	RAT	ERA	ERA+	OAV	OOB	BH	AVG	PB	PR	PR+	PD	TPI
1895	Chi-N	2	0	1.000	2	2	2	0	0	14	21	11	0	0	5	5	16.7	5.14	99	.339	.388	1	.143	-1	-1	-0	0	-0.1
1896	Chi-N	0	4	.000	4	3	2	0	0	25	32	25	0	2	21	3	19.8	7.20	63	.308	.433	0	.000	-2	-8	-7	0	-0.9
Total	2	2	4	.333	6	5	4	0	0	39	53	36	0	2	26	8	18.7	6.46	73	.319	.418	1	.053	-3	-8	-7	1	-1.0

● JACK McFETRIDGE McFetridge, John Reed b: 8/25/1869, Philadelphia, Pa. d: 1/10/17, Philadelphia, Pa. 6', 175 lbs. Deb: 6/7/1890

YEAR	TM/L	W	L	PCT	G	GS	CG	SH	SV	IP	H	R	HR	HB	BB	SO	RAT	ERA	ERA+	OAV	OOB	BH	AVG	PB	PR	PR+	PD	TPI
1890	Phi-N	1	0	1.000	1	1	1	0	0	9	5	1	0	0	2	4	7.0	1.00	366	.156	.206	3	.750	1	3	3	-0	0.4
1903	Phi-N	1	11	.083	14	13	11	0	0	103	120	71	2	3	49	31	15.0	4.89	67	.299	.379	6	.176	0	-19	-19	-1	-1.8
Total	2	2	11	.154	15	14	12	0	0	112	125	72	2	3	51	35	14.4	4.58	72	.288	.367	9	.237	2	-16	-16	-1	-1.4

● ANDY McGAFFIGAN McGaffigan, Andrew Joseph b: 10/25/56, W.Palm Beach, Fla. BR/TR, 6'3", 195 lbs. Deb: 9/22/81

YEAR	TM/L	W	L	PCT	G	GS	CG	SH	SV	IP	H	R	HR	HB	BB	SO	RAT	ERA	ERA+	OAV	OOB	BH	AVG	PB	PR	PR+	PD	TPI
1981	NY-A	0	0	—	2	0	0	0	0	7	5	3	1	0	3	2	10.3	2.57	139	.200	.286	0	—	0	1	1	-0	0.0
1982	SF-N	1	0	1.000	4	0	0	0	0	8	5	1	0	1	1	4	7.9	0.00	—	.179	.233	0	.000	-0	3	3	-0	0.4
1983	SF-N	3	9	.250	43	16	0	0	2	134^{1}	131	67	17	1	39	93	11.5	4.29	83	.255	.309	2	.067	-1	-10	-11	-3	-1.4
1984	Mon-N	3	4	.429	21	3	0	0	1	46	37	14	2	0	15	39	10.2	2.54	135	.220	.284	0	.000	-1	5	5	-0	0.6
	Cin-N	0	2	.000	9	3	0	0	0	23	23	14	2	0	8	18	12.1	5.48	69	.261	.323	0	.000	-0	-5	-4	-1	-0.4
	Yr	3	6	.333	30	6	0	0	1	69	60	28	4	0	23	57	10.8	3.52	101	.234	.297	0	.000	-1	1	0	-1	0.2
1985	Cin-N	3	3	.500	15	15	2	0	0	94^{1}	88	40	4	2	30	83	11.4	3.72	102	.247	.309	1	.034	-2	-1	1	0	-0.1
1986	Mon-N	10	5	.667	48	14	1	1	2	142^{2}	114	49	9	2	55	104	10.8	2.65	140	.223	.301	2	.061	-2	17	17	-2	1.3
1987	Mon-N	5	2	.714	69	0	0	0	12	120^{1}	105	38	5	3	42	100	11.2	2.39	176	.235	.305	0	.000	-1	23	24	-0	1.5
1988	Mon-N	6	0	1.000	63	0	0	0	4	91^{1}	81	31	4	2	37	71	11.8	2.76	131	.233	.311	0	.000	-0	7	8	-1	0.5
1989	Mon-N	3	5	.375	57	0	0	0	2	75	85	40	3	3	30	40	14.2	4.68	76	.293	.365	1	1.000	0	-10	-9	-1	-1.1
1990	SF-N	0	0	—	4	0	0	0	0	4^{2}	10	9	2	0	4	4	27.0	17.36	21	.455	.538	0	—	0	-7	-7	-0	-0.4
	KC-A	4	3	.571	24	11	0	0	1	78^{2}	75	40	6	2	28	49	12.0	3.09	124	.248	.315	0	—	0	7	7	-1	0.5
1991	KC-A	0	0	—	4	0	0	0	0	8	14	5	0	0	2	3	18.0	4.50	92	.389	.421	0	—	0	-0	-0	-0	0.0
Total	11	38	33	.535	363	62	3	1	24	833^{1}	773	351	55	16	294	610	11.7	3.38	111	.247	.314	6	.048	-7	30	33	-10	1.4

● JACK McGEACHY McGeachy, John Charles b: 5/23/1864, Clinton, Mass. d: 4/5/30, Cambridge, Mass. BR/TR, 5'8", 165 lbs. Deb: 6/17/1886 ◆

YEAR	TM/L	W	L	PCT	G	GS	CG	SH	SV	IP	H	R	HR	HB	BB	SO	RAT	ERA	ERA+	OAV	OOB	BH	AVG	PB	PR	PR+	PD	TPI
1887	Ind-N	0	1	.000	1	0	0	0	0	6^{1}	17	17	2	0	4	3	24.2	11.37	36	.415	.415	114	.278	0	-5	-5	0	-0.5
1888	Ind-N	0	0	—	1	0	0	0	0	5	5	5	1	0	3	0	14.4	7.20	41	.238	.333	99	.219	0	-2	-2	-0	-0.1
1889	Ind-N	0	0	—	3	0	0	0	0	4^{2}	7	9	2	0	6	3	25.1	11.57	36	.333	.481	142	.267	0	-4	-4	-0	-0.2
Total	3	0	1	.000	5	0	0	0	0	16	29	31	5	0	13	6	21.4	10.13	37	.349	.413	609	.247	0	-11	-11	-0	-0.8

● BILL McGEE McGee, William Henry "Fiddler Bill" b: 11/16/09, Batchtown, Ill. d: 2/11/87, St.Louis, Mo. BR/TR, 6'1", 215 lbs. Deb: 9/29/35

YEAR	TM/L	W	L	PCT	G	GS	CG	SH	SV	IP	H	R	HR	HB	BB	SO	RAT	ERA	ERA+	OAV	OOB	BH	AVG	PB	PR	PR+	PD	TPI
1935	StL-N	1	0	1.000	1	1	1	0	0	9	3	1	0	0	1	2	4.0	1.00	410	.103	.133	1	.333	0	3	3	-0	0.3
1936	StL-N	1	1	.500	7	2	0	0	0	16	23	14	3	0	4	8	15.2	7.88	50	.359	.397	1	.250	0	-7	-7	0	-0.7
1937	StL-N	1	0	1.000	4	1	1	0	0	14	13	4	1	1	4	9	11.6	2.57	155	.255	.321	1	.200	-0	2	2	0	0.1
1938	StL-N	7	12	.368	47	25	10	1	5	216	216	101	4	1	78	104	12.3	3.21	123	.257	.321	14	.209	1	14	17	-0	1.5
1939	StL-N	12	5	.706	43	17	5	4	0	156	155	68	14	0	59	56	12.3	3.81	108	.261	.328	8	.145	-2	2	5	0	0.3
1940	StL-N	16	10	.615	38	31	11	3	0	218	222	108	13	2	96	78	13.2	3.80	105	.263	.340	13	.178	-1	1	4	-3	0.1
1941	StL-N	0	1	.000	4	3	0	0	0	14	17	9	1	1	13	2	19.9	5.14	73	.298	.437	0	.000	-1	-2	-2	-0	-0.2
	NY-N	2	9	.182	22	14	1	0	0	106	117	68	9	0	54	41	14.5	4.92	75	.285	.368	5	.161	-1	-15	-14	-2	-1.6
	Yr	2	10	.167	26	17	1	0	0	120	134	77	10	1	67	43	15.2	4.95	75	.286	.377	5	.143	-2	-18	-16	-2	-1.8
1942	NY-N	6	3	.667	31	8	2	1	1	104	95	50	8	1	46	40	12.3	2.94	114	.244	.326	3	.103	-2	4	5	-1	0.1
Total	8	46	41	.529	197	102	31	9	6	853	861	423	53	6	355	340	12.9	3.74	104	.263	.336	46	.170	-6	2	14	-5	-0.1

● CONNY McGEEHAN McGeehan, Cornelius Bernard b: 8/25/1882, Drifton, Pa. d: 7/4/07, Hazleton, Pa. Deb: 7/15/03 F

YEAR	TM/L	W	L	PCT	G	GS	CG	SH	SV	IP	H	R	HR	HB	BB	SO	RAT	ERA	ERA+	OAV	OOB	BH	AVG	PB	PR	PR+	PD	TPI
1903	Phi-A	1	0	1.000	3	0	0	0	0	10	9	5	0	1	1	4	9.9	4.50	68	.237	.275	0	.000	-1	-2	-2	0	-0.2

● KEVIN McGEHEE McGehee, George Kevin b: 1/18/69, Alexandria, La. BR/TR, 6', 190 lbs. Deb: 8/23/93

YEAR	TM/L	W	L	PCT	G	GS	CG	SH	SV	IP	H	R	HR	HB	BB	SO	RAT	ERA	ERA+	OAV	OOB	BH	AVG	PB	PR	PR+	PD	TPI
1993	Bal-A	0	0	—	5	0	0	0	0	16^{2}	18	11	5	2	7	7	14.6	5.94	76	.281	.370	0	—	0	-3	-3	0	-0.1

● PAT McGEHEE McGehee, Patrick Henry b: 7/2/1888, Meadville, Miss. d: 12/30/46, Paducah, Ky. BL/TR, 6'2.5", 180 lbs. Deb: 8/23/12

YEAR	TM/L	W	L	PCT	G	GS	CG	SH	SV	IP	H	R	HR	HB	BB	SO	RAT	ERA	ERA+	OAV	OOB	BH	AVG	PB	PR	PR+	PD	TPI
1912	Det-A	0	0	—	1	1	0	0	0	0	1	0	0	1	—	—	—	—	1.000	1.000	98	—	0	0	0	0	0.0	

● RANDY McGILBERRY McGilberry, Randall Kent b: 10/29/53, Mobile, Ala. BB/TR, 6'1", 195 lbs. Deb: 9/6/77

YEAR	TM/L	W	L	PCT	G	GS	CG	SH	SV	IP	H	R	HR	HB	BB	SO	RAT	ERA	ERA+	OAV	OOB	BH	AVG	PB	PR	PR+	PD	TPI
1977	KC-A	0	1	.000	3	0	0	0	0	7	7	4	1	0	1	1	10.3	5.14	79	.280	.308	0	—	0	-1	-1	0	-0.1
1978	KC-A	0	1	.000	18	0	0	0	0	25^{2}	27	16	2	0	18	12	15.8	4.21	91	.276	.388	0	—	0	-1	-1	0	0.0
Total	2	0	2	.000	21	0	0	0	0	32^{2}	34	20	3	0	19	13	14.6	4.41	88	.276	.373	0	—	0	-2	-2	0	-0.1

● BILL McGILL McGill, William John "Parson" b: 6/29/1880, Galva, Kan. d: 8/7/59, Alva, Okla. BR/TR, 6'2", Deb: 9/16/07

YEAR	TM/L	W	L	PCT	G	GS	CG	SH	SV	IP	H	R	HR	HB	BB	SO	RAT	ERA	ERA+	OAV	OOB	BH	AVG	PB	PR	PR+	PD	TPI
1907	StL-A	1	0	1.000	2	2	1	0	0	18^{1}	22	8	0	0	2	8	11.8	3.44	73	.301	.320	0	.000	-1	-2	-2	-0	-0.2

● WILLIE McGILL McGill, William Vaness "Kid" b: 11/10/1873, Atlanta, Ga. d: 8/29/44, Indianapolis, Ind. TL, 5'6.5", 170 lbs. Deb: 5/8/1890

YEAR	TM/L	W	L	PCT	G	GS	CG	SH	SV	IP	H	R	HR	HB	BB	SO	RAT	ERA	ERA+	OAV	OOB	BH	AVG	PB	PR	PR+	PD	TPI
1890	Cle-P	11	9	.550	24	20	19	0	0	183^{2}	222	146	5	12	96	82	16.2	4.12	97	.286	.373	10	.147	2	2	-3	1	0.1
1891	Cin-a	2	5	.286	8	8	6	0	0	65	69	56	1	3	37	19	15.1	4.98	82	.263	.361	2	.100	0	-9	-6	-1	-0.5
	StL-a	18	9	.667	33	29	20	1	1	233^{1}	207	140	10	12	126	146	13.3	2.70	155	.230	.332	13	.157	-0	26	34	-4	2.8
	Yr	20	14	.588	41	37	26	1	1	298^{1}	276	196	11	15	163	165	13.7	3.20	131	.237	.339	15	.146	-0	17	29	-5	2.3
1892	Cin-N	1	1	.500	3	3	1	0	0	17	18	14	0	0	5	7	12.2	5.29	62	.261	.311	2	.286	0	-4	-4	0	-0.3
1893	Chi-N	17	18	.486	39	34	26	1	0	302^{2}	311	206	6	14	181	91	15.0	4.61	101	.258	.361	29	.234	2	2	1	-5	-0.1
1894	Chi-N	7	19	.269	27	23	22	0	0	208	272	195	2	10	117	58	17.3	5.84	96	.312	.400	20	.244	0	-12	-5	-2	-0.6
1895	Phi-N	10	8	.556	20	20	13	0	0	146	177	122	2	4	81	70	16.2	5.55	86	.295	.382	14	.222	-0	-12	-12	0	-1.1
1896	Phi-N	5	4	.556	12	11	7	0	0	79^{2}	87	62	0	4	53	29	16.3	5.31	81	.275	.386	6	.207	-0	-8	-9	0	-0.8
Total	7	71	73	.493	166	148	114	2	1	1235^{1}	1363	941	26	59	696	502	15.4	4.57	100	.272	.368	96	.202	4	-15	2	-11	-0.5

● JOHN McGILLEN McGillen, John Joseph b: 8/6/17, Eddystone, Pa. d: 8/11/87, Upland, Pa. BL/TL, 6'1", 175 lbs. Deb: 4/20/44

YEAR	TM/L	W	L	PCT	G	GS	CG	SH	SV	IP	H	R	HR	HB	BB	SO	RAT	ERA	ERA+	OAV	OOB	BH	AVG	PB	PR	PR+	PD	TPI
1944	Phi-A	0	0	—	2	0	0	0	0	1	1	2	0	0	2	0	27.0	18.00	19	.333	.600	0	—	0	-2	-2	-0	-0.1

● JIM McGINLEY McGinley, James William b: 10/2/1878, Groveland, Mass. d: 9/20/61, Haverhill, Mass. BR/TR, 5'9.5", 165 lbs. Deb: 9/22/04

YEAR	TM/L	W	L	PCT	G	GS	CG	SH	SV	IP	H	R	HR	HB	BB	SO	RAT	ERA	ERA+	OAV	OOB	BH	AVG	PB	PR	PR+	PD	TPI
1904	StL-N	2	1	.667	3	3	3	0	0	27	28	8	0	3	6	6	12.3	2.00	135	.267	.325	1	.091	-1	2	2	-1	0.0
1905	StL-N	0	1	.000	1	1	0	0	0	3	5	6	1	0	2	0	21.0	15.00	20	.333	.412	1	1.000	0	-4	-4	-0	-0.6
Total	2	2	2	.500	4	4	3	0	0	30	33	14	1	3	8	6	13.2	3.30	83	.275	.336	2	.167	-0	-2	-2	-2	-0.6

● DAN McGINN McGinn, Daniel Michael b: 11/29/43, Omaha, Neb. BL/TL, 6', 190 lbs. Deb: 9/3/68

YEAR	TM/L	W	L	PCT	G	GS	CG	SH	SV	IP	H	R	HR	HB	BB	SO	RAT	ERA	ERA+	OAV	OOB	BH	AVG	PB	PR	PR+	PD	TPI
1968	Cin-N	0	1	.000	14	0	0	0	0	12	13	7	1	1	11	16	18.8	5.25	60	.271	.417	0	.000	-0	-3	-3	0	-0.2
1969	Mon-N	7	10	.412	74	1	0	0	6	132^{1}	123	67	8	5	65	112	13.1	3.94	93	.245	.337	5	.172	1	-5	-4	1	-0.3
1970	Mon-N	7	10	.412	52	19	3	2	0	130^{2}	154	88	13	7	78	83	16.5	5.44	76	.296	.395	4	.114	-2	-20	-19	2	-2.2
1971	Mon-N	1	4	.200	28	6	1	0	0	71	74	51	7	1	42	40	14.8	5.96	59	.274	.374	4	.235	0	-20	-19	1	-1.1

YEAR	TM/L	W	L	PCT	G	GS	CG	SH	SV	IP	H	R	HR	HB	BB	SO	RAT	ERA	ERA+	OAV	OOB	BH	AVG	PB	PR	PR+	PD	TPI
1972	Chi-N	0	5	.000	42	2	0	0	4	62^{2}	78	46	5	4	29	42	15.9	5.89	65	.301	.380	2	.250	1	-17	-13	-1	-1.2
Total	5	15	30	.333	210	28	4	2	10	408^{2}	442	259	34	18	225	293	15.1	5.11	74	.276	.372	15	.165	-0	-65	-57	3	-5.0
● JUMBO McGINNIS	McGinnis, George Washington b: 2/22/1864, Alton, Mo. d: 5/18/34, St.Louis, Mo. 5'10", 197 lbs. Deb: 5/2/1882																											
1882	StL-a	25	18	.581	45	45	43	3	0	388^{1}	391	241	2		53	134	10.3	2.60	108	.245	.269	44	.217	1	4	9	-5	0.4
1883	StL-a	28	16	.636	45	45	41	**6**	0	382^{2}	325	174	3		69	128	9.3	2.33	150	.215	.249	36	.200	-6	41	47	1	3.9
1884	StL-a	24	16	.600	40	40	39	5	0	354^{1}	331	196	4	12	35	141	9.6	2.84	115	.233	.258	34	.233	3	16	16	-1	1.6
1885	StL-a	6	6	.500	13	13	12	3	0	112	98	65	1	6	19	41	9.9	3.38	97	.225	.267	11	.220	0	-2	-1	-1	-0.3
1886	StL-a	5	5	.500	10	10	10	1	0	87^{2}	107	75	2	7	27	30	14.5	3.80	91	.288	.347	7	.189	-1	-3	-4	0	-0.4
	Bal-a	11	13	.458	26	25	24	0	0	209^{1}	235	141	6	14	48	70	12.8	3.48	98	.280	.329	16	.188	-1	-1	-1	-0	-0.2
	Yr	16	18	.471	36	35	34	1	0	297	342	216	8	21	75	100	13.3	3.58	96	.282	.335	23	.189	-2	-4	-5	-0	-0.6
1887	Cin-a	3	5	.375	8	8	8	0	0	69^{1}	128	66	3	8	43	18	17.7	5.45	80	.388	.402	7	.219	-0	-9	-8	-0	-0.7
Total	6	102	79	.564	187	186	177	18	0	1603^{2}	1615	958	21	47	294	562	10.7	2.95	112	.248	.281	155	.211	-5	47	59	-7	4.3
● GUS McGINNIS	McGinnis, Gus b: 8/1870, Painesville, Ohio d: 4/20/04, Barnesville, Ohio TL, 5'11", 168 lbs. Deb: 4/27/1893																											
1893	Chi-N	2	5	.286	13	5	3	0	0	67^{1}	85	67	2	3	31	13	15.9	5.35	87	.299	.374	6	.240	2	-5	-5	0	-0.2
	Phi-N	1	3	.250	5	4	4	1	0	37^{1}	39	20	0	2	17	12	14.0	4.34	105	.262	.345	3	.200	-1	1	1	0	0.1
	Yr	3	8	.273	18	9	7	1	0	104^{2}	124	87	2	5	48	25	15.2	4.99	92	.286	.364	9	.225	1	-4	-4	1	-0.1
● JOE McGINNITY	McGinnity, Joseph Jerome "Iron Man" (b: Joseph Jerome McGinty) b: 3/19/1871, Rock Island, Ill. d: 11/14/29, Brooklyn, N.Y. BR/TR, 5'11", 206 lbs. Deb: 4/18/1899 CH																											
1899	Bal-N	**28**	16	.636	48	41	38	4	2	366^{1}	358	164	3	26	93	74	11.7	2.68	148	.256	.314	28	.193	-5	48	51	1	4.8
1900	*Bro-N	**28**	8	**.778**	44	37	32	1	0	**343**	350	179	5	40	113	93	13.2	2.94	131	.264	.340	28	.193	-5	29	33	-2	2.2
1901	Bal-A	26	20	.565	**48**	43	**39**	1	1	**382**	412	219	7	21	96	75	12.5	3.56	109	.272	.324	31	.209	-4	5	12	-1	0.7
1902	Bal-A	13	10	.565	25	23	19	0	0	198^{2}	219	100	3	8	46	39	12.4	3.44	110	.280	.327	25	.287	4	3	7	-2	0.9
	NY-N	8	8	.500	19	16	16	1	0	153	122	52	1	9	32	67	9.6	2.06	136	.219	.273	8	.121	-4	12	13	1	0.9
1903	NY-N	**31**	20	.608	**55**	48	**44**	3	2	**434**	391	162	4	19	109	171	10.8	2.43	138	.236	.291	34	.206	-2	41	**43**	-4	3.9
1904	NY-N	**35**	8	**.814**	**51**	44	38	**9**	**5**	**408**	307	103	8	13	86	144	9.0	**1.61**	**169**	.206	.256	25	.176	-1	**51**	**51**	3	**5.6**
1905	*NY-N	21	15	.583	**46**	38	26	2	3	320^{1}	289	131	6	14	71	125	10.5	2.87	102	.240	.290	28	.233	6	5	2	2	1.0
1906	NY-N	**27**	12	.692	**45**	37	32	3	2	339^{2}	316	127	1	7	71	105	10.4	2.25	116	.246	.289	15	.130	-3	14	14	1	1.3
1907	NY-N	18	18	.500	**47**	34	23	3	**4**	310^{1}	320	126	6	15	58	120	11.4	3.16	78	.266	.308	18	.175	0	-24	-23	2	-2.6
1908	NY-N	11	7	.611	37	20	7	5	**5**	186	192	73	8	7	37	55	11.4	2.27	106	.267	.310	11	.180	-0	2	3	-1	0.1
Total	10	246	142	.634	465	381	314	32	24	3441^{1}	3276	1436	52	179	812	1068	11.2	2.66	120	.249	.302	251	.194	-14	186	203	-0	18.8
● KEVIN McGLINCHY	McGlinchy, Kevin Michael b: 6/28/77, Malden, Mass. BR/TR, 6'5", 220 lbs. Deb: 4/5/99																											
1999	*Atl-N	7	3	.700	64	0	0	0	0	70^{1}	66	25	6	1	30	67	12.4	2.82	160	.255	.334	0	.000	-0	14	13	-1	1.5
2000	Atl-N	0	0	—	10	0	0	0	0	8^{1}	11	4	1	0	6	9	18.4	2.16	210	.314	.415	0	—	0	2	2	0	0.1
Total	2	7	3	.700	74	0	0	0	0	78^{2}	77	29	7	1	36	76	13.0	2.75	164	.262	.344	0	.000	-0	16	16	-1	1.6
● LYNN McGLOTHEN	McGlothen, Lynn Everatt b: 3/27/50, Monroe, La. d: 8/14/84, Dubach, La. BL/TR, 6'2", 195 lbs. Deb: 6/25/72																											
1972	Bos-A	8	7	.533	22	22	4	1	0	145	135	66	9	7	59	112	12.5	3.41	94	.247	.328	10	.189	1	-6	-3	3	0.2
1973	Bos-A	1	2	.333	6	3	0	0	0	23	39	23	6	1	8	16	18.8	8.22	49	.386	.436	0	—	0	-11	-10	-0	-1.1
1974	StL-N★	16	12	.571	31	31	8	3	0	237^{1}	212	80	12	2	89	142	11.5	2.69	133	.241	.312	15	.181	-1	25	24	1	2.8
1975	StL-N	15	13	.536	35	34	9	2	0	239	231	110	21	4	97	146	12.5	3.92	96	.254	.329	7	.087	-5	-8	-4	-2	-1.2
1976	StL-N	13	15	.464	33	32	10	4	0	205	209	96	10	4	68	106	12.3	3.91	91	.268	.330	15	.211	2	-9	-8	-2	-1.0
1977	SF-N	2	9	.182	21	15	2	0	0	80	94	62	9	1	52	42	16.5	5.62	70	.299	.401	2	.105	-1	-15	-15	-2	-2.0
1978	SF-N	0	0	—	5	1	0	0	0	12^{2}	15	9	0	0	4	9	13.5	4.97	69	.313	.365	0	.000	-0	-2	-2	-0	-0.2
	Chi-N	5	3	.625	49	1	0	0	0	80	77	33	7	0	39	60	13.0	3.04	133	.257	.342	3	.231	1	5	8	-2	0.7
	Yr	5	3	.625	54	2	0	0	0	92^{2}	92	42	7	0	43	69	13.1	3.30	120	.264	.345	3	.188	0	3	6	-2	0.5
1979	Chi-N	13	14	.481	42	29	6	1	2	212	236	103	27	3	55	147	12.5	4.12	100	.283	.330	16	.225	1	-9	0	-2	-0.1
1980	Chi-N	12	14	.462	39	27	2	2	0	182^{1}	211	105	24	1	64	119	13.6	4.79	82	.293	.352	10	.196	2	-24	-16	-2	-2.2
1981	Chi-N	1	4	.200	20	6	0	0	0	54^{2}	71	32	1	1	28	26	16.5	4.77	77	.317	.395	1	.083	-1	-8	-6	1	-0.5
	Chi-A	0	0	—	11	0	0	0	0	21^{2}	14	10	0	1	7	12	9.1	4.15	86	.189	.268	0	—	0	-1	-1	-0	-0.1
1982	NY-A	0	0	—	4	0	0	0	0	5	9	6	1	0	2	2	19.8	10.80	37	.375	.423	0	—	0	-4	-4	0	-0.2
Total	11	86	93	.480	318	201	41	13	2	1497^{2}	1553	735	127	25	572	939	12.9	3.98	94	.270	.339	79	.173	-1	-66	-38	-7	-4.9
● PAT McGLOTHIN	McGlothin, Ezra Mac b: 10/20/20, Coalfield, Tenn. BL/TR, 6'3.5", 180 lbs. Deb: 4/25/49																											
1949	Bro-N	1	1	.500	7	0	0	0	0	15^{2}	13	8	2	0	5	11	10.3	4.60	89	.224	.286	0	.000	-0	-1	-1	1	-0.1
1950	Bro-N	0	0	—	1	0	0	0	0	2	5	3	0	0	1	2	27.0	13.50	30	.455	.500	0	—	0	-2	-2	-0	-0.1
Total	2	1	1	.500	8	0	0	0	0	17^{2}	18	11	2	0	6	13	12.2	5.60	73	.261	.320	0	.000	-0	-3	-3	1	-0.2
● JIM McGLOTHLIN	McGlothlin, James Milton "Red" b: 10/6/43, Los Angeles, Cal. d: 12/23/75, Union, Ky. BR/TR, 6'1", 185 lbs. Deb: 9/20/65																											
1965	Cal-A	0	3	.000	3	3	1	0	0	18	18	9	1	0	7	9	12.5	3.50	97	.261	.329	0	.000	-1	-0	-0	-0	-0.1
1966	Cal-A	3	1	.750	19	11	0	0	0	67^{2}	79	37	9	1	19	41	13.2	4.52	74	.292	.340	1	.059	-0	-8	-9	-0	-0.5
1967	Cal-A★	12	8	.600	32	29	9	**6**	0	197^{1}	163	74	13	4	56	137	10.2	2.96	106	.226	.286	8	.140	-0	6	4	1	0.5
1968	Cal-A	10	15	.400	40	32	8	0	3	208^{1}	187	87	19	8	60	135	11.0	3.54	82	.244	.305	7	.111	-1	-13	-15	2	-1.8
1969	Cal-A	8	16	.333	37	35	4	1	0	201	188	86	19	5	58	96	11.2	3.18	110	.249	.307	7	.121	-1	10	7	2	0.9
1970	*Cin-N	14	10	.583	35	34	5	3	0	210^{2}	192	91	19	3	86	97	12.0	3.59	113	.245	.322	8	.121	1	11	11	5	1.8
1971	Cin-N	8	12	.400	30	26	6	0	0	170^{2}	151	65	15	4	47	93	10.7	3.22	104	.243	.301	7	.137	1	5	3	1	0.5
1972	*Cin-N	9	8	.529	31	21	3	1	0	145	165	71	15	0	49	69	13.3	3.91	82	.287	.343	8	.174	3	-7	-12	-0	-1.1
1973	Cin-N	3	3	.500	24	9	0	0	0	63^{1}	91	52	13	0	23	18	16.2	6.68	51	.340	.392	2	.125	0	-21	-25	1	-2.0
	Chi-A	0	1	.000	5	1	0	0	0	18^{1}	13	8	2	0	13	14	12.8	3.93	101	.203	.338	0	—	0	-0	0	0	0.0
Total	9	67	77	.465	256	201	36	11	3	1300^{1}	1247	580	125	25	418	709	11.7	3.61	94	.255	.317	48	.126	2	-18	-35	11	-1.8
● STONEY McGLYNN	McGlynn, Ulysses Simpson Grant b: 5/26/1872, Lancaster, Pa. d: 8/26/41, Manitowoc, Wis. BR/TR, 5'11", 185 lbs. Deb: 9/20/06																											
1906	StL-N	2	2	.500	6	6	6	0	0	48	43	16	0	1	15	25	11.1	2.44	108	.249	.312	1	.059	-1	1	1	2	0.2
1907	StL-N	14	25	.359	45	39	**33**	3	1	**352^{1}**	329	159	6	4	112	109	11.4	2.91	86	.251	.312	25	.200	3	-17	-16	-1	-1.6
1908	StL-N	1	6	.143	16	6	4	0	1	75^{2}	76	40	0	2	17	23	11.3	3.45	68	.256	.301	2	.077	-1	-9	-9	1	-0.9
Total	3	17	33	.340	67	51	43	3	2	476	448	215	6	7	144	157	11.3	2.95	85	.252	.310	28	.167	0	-25	-24	2	-2.3
● MICKEY McGOWAN	McGowan, Tullis Earl b: 11/26/21, Dothan, Ala. BL/TL, 6'2", 200 lbs. Deb: 4/22/48																											
1948	NY-N	0	0	—	3	0	0	0	0	3^{2}	3	3	1	0	4	2	17.2	7.36	53	.231	.412	0	.000	-0	-1	-1	0	-0.1
● HOWARD McGRANER	McGraner, Howard "Muck" b: 9/11/1889, Hamley Run, Ohio d: 10/22/52, Zaleski, Ohio BL/TL, 5'7", 155 lbs. Deb: 9/12/12																											
1912	Cin-N	1	0	1.000	4	0	0	0	0	19	22	17	2	1	7	5	14.2	7.11	47	.293	.361	2	.250	1	-8	-8	1	-0.3
● TUG McGRAW	McGraw, Frank Edwin b: 8/30/44, Martinez, Cal. BR/TL, 6', 185 lbs. Deb: 4/18/65																											
1965	NY-N	2	7	.222	37	9	2	0	1	97^{2}	88	47	8	3	48	57	12.8	3.32	106	.249	.344	3	.130	-1	2	2	-1	0.1
1966	NY-N	2	9	.182	15	12	1	0	0	62^{1}	72	38	11	0	25	34	14.0	5.34	68	.294	.359	4	.235	1	-12	-12	-0	-1.8
1967	NY-N	0	3	.000	4	4	0	0	0	17^{1}	13	16	3	0	13	18	13.5	7.79	44	.206	.342	1	.250	0	-9	-8	0	-1.1
1969	*NY-N	9	3	.750	42	4	1	0	12	100^{1}	89	31	6	0	47	92	12.2	2.24	163	.243	.329	4	.167	0	**15**	**16**	1	2.4
1970	NY-N	4	6	.400	57	0	0	0	10	90^{2}	77	40	6	1	49	81	12.6	3.28	123	.231	.332	4	.308	1	8	8	1	1.2
1971	NY-N	11	4	.733	51	1	0	0	8	111	73	22	4	3	41	109	9.5	1.70	200	.189	.271	4	.222	2	**22**	**21**	-1	3.4
1972	NY-N★	8	6	.571	54	0	0	0	27	106	71	26	3	3	40	92	9.7	1.70	198	.197	.282	2	.100	-0	21	20	-0	3.9
1973	*NY-N	5	6	.455	60	2	0	0	25	118^{2}	106	53	11	3	55	81	12.4	3.87	94	.243	.331	4	.167	1	-3	-3	0	-0.3
1974	NY-N	6	11	.353	41	4	1	1	3	88^{2}	96	43	12	0	32	54	13.0	4.16	86	.279	.340	1	.071	-0	-5	-6	-1	-1.2
1975	Phi-N☆	9	6	.600	56	0	0	0	14	102^{2}	84	38	6	3	36	55	10.8	2.98	126	.226	.299	2	.154	-0	7	8	-0	1.4
1976	*Phi-N	7	6	.538	58	0	0	0	11	97^{1}	81	34	4	0	42	76	11.4	2.50	142	.226	.307	1	.143	0	11	11	-1	1.7
1977	*Phi-N	7	3	.700	45	0	0	0	9	79	62	25	6	1	24	58	9.9	2.62	153	.221	.284	4	.400	2	11	12	0	1.9
1978	*Phi-N	8	7	.533	55	1	0	0	9	89^{2}	82	39	6	0	23	63	10.5	3.21	111	.245	.293	0	.000	-0	4	4	0	0.6
1979	Phi-N	4	3	.571	65	1	0	0	16	83^{2}	83	56	9	2	29	57	12.3	5.16	74	.259	.324	1	.167	-0	-13	-12	-1	-1.6
1980	*Phi-N	5	4	.556	57	0	0	0	20	92^{1}	62	16	3	2	23	75	8.5	1.46	260	.194	.253	2	.250	0	**22**	**23**	0	3.3

YEAR	TM/L	W	L	PCT	G	GS	CG	SH	SV	IP	H	R	HR	HB	BB	SO	RAT	ERA	ERA+	OAV	OOB	BH	AVG	PB	PR	PR+	PD	TPI
1981	*Phi-N	2	4	.333	34	0	0	0	10	44	35	13	2	0	14	26	10.0	2.66	136	.219	.282	0	.000	-0	4	5	-1	0.8
1982	Phi-N	3	3	.500	34	0	0	0	5	39^2	50	19	3	1	12	25	14.3	4.31	85	.305	.356	0	.000	-0	-3	-3	0	-0.4
1983	Phi-N	2	1	.667	34	1	0	0	0	55^2	58	24	4	0	19	30	12.4	3.56	100	.271	.330	1	.333	0	0	0	0	0.0
1984	Phi-N	2	0	1.000	25	0	0	0	0	38	36	17	1	0	10	26	10.9	3.79	96	.245	.293	1	.333	0	-1	-1	0	0.0
Total	19	96	92	.511	824	39	5	1	180	1514^2	1318	597	108	22	582	1109	11.4	3.14	116	.237	.312	39	.182	5	82	85	-1	14.3

● JOHN McGRAW

McGraw, John (b: Roy Elmer Hoar) b: 12/8/1890, Intercourse, Pa. d: 4/27/67, Torrance, Cal. BR/TR, 5'9", 160 lbs. Deb: 7/29/14

YEAR	TM/L	W	L	PCT	G	GS	CG	SH	SV	IP	H	R	HR	HB	BB	SO	RAT	ERA	ERA+	OAV	OOB	BH	AVG	PB	PR	PR+	PD	TPI
1914	Bro-F	0	0	—	1	0	0	0	0	2	0	0	0	1	0	2	4.5	0.00	—	.000	.143	0	—	0	1	1	-0	0.0

● BOB McGRAW

McGraw, Robert Emmett b: 4/10/1895, LaVeta, Colo. d: 6/2/78, Boise, Idaho BR/TR, 6'2", 160 lbs. Deb: 9/25/17

YEAR	TM/L	W	L	PCT	G	GS	CG	SH	SV	IP	H	R	HR	HB	BB	SO	RAT	ERA	ERA+	OAV	OOB	BH	AVG	PB	PR	PR+	PD	TPI
1917	NY-A	0	1	.000	2	2	1	0	0	11	9	5	0	0	3	3	9.8	0.82	328	.257	.316	0	.000	-0	2	2	-0	0.1
1918	NY-A	0	1	.000	1	1	0	0	0	0	0	0	0	4	—	—	∞	—	—	1.000	102	—	0	-4	-4	0		-0.4
1919	NY-A	1	0	1.000	6	0	0	0	0	16^1	11	6	1	1	10	3	12.1	3.31	97	.216	.355	0	.000	-0	-0	-0	-0	0.0
	Bos-A	0	2	.000	10	1	0	0	0	26^2	33	23	0	3	17	6	17.9	6.75	45	.347	.461	1	.100	-1	-10	-12	-1	-0.9
	Yr	1	2	.333	16	1	0	0	0	43	44	29	1	4	27	9	15.7	5.44	57	.301	.424	1	.077	-1	-11	-12	-1	-0.9
1920	NY-A	0	0	—	15	0	0	0	0	27	24	18	1	1	20	11	15.0	4.67	82	.240	.372	0	.000	-1	-3	-3	-1	-0.3
1925	Bro-N	0	2	.000	2	2	2	0	0	19^2	14	9	0	0	13	3	12.4	3.20	130	.222	.355	1	.167	-0	2	2	-1	0.1
1926	Bro-N	9	13	.409	33	21	10	0	1	174^1	197	104	12	2	67	49	13.7	4.59	83	.292	.358	8	.145	-2	-15	-15	-1	-1.9
1927	Bro-N	0	1	.000	1	1	0	0	0	4	5	5	1	0	2	2	15.8	9.00	44	.313	.389	0	.000	-0	-2	-2	0	-0.4
	StL-N	4	5	.444	18	12	4	1	0	94	121	65	3	0	30	37	14.5	5.07	78	.323	.373	6	.182	1	-12	-12	1	-0.8
	Yr	4	6	.400	19	13	4	1	0	98	126	70	4	0	32	39	14.5	5.23	75	.322	.374	6	.176	1	-14	-14	1	-1.2
1928	Phi-N	7	8	.467	39	3	0	0	1	120	148	86	7	2	56	28	15.5	5.18	83	.317	.392	4	.111	-2	-16	-11	-1	-1.5
1929	Phi-N	5	5	.500	41	4	0	0	4	86^1	113	68	6	2	43	22	16.5	5.73	91	.324	.401	4	.200	0	-10	-5	1	-0.4
Total	9	26	38	.406	168	47	17	1	6	579^1	675	393	31	11	265	164	14.8	5.00	81	.303	.380	24	.138	-6	-67	-59	-2	-6.4

● TOM McGRAW

McGraw, Thomas Virgil b: 12/8/67, Portland, Ore. BL/TL, 6'2", 195 lbs. Deb: 5/7/97

YEAR	TM/L	W	L	PCT	G	GS	CG	SH	SV	IP	H	R	HR	HB	BB	SO	RAT	ERA	ERA+	OAV	OOB	BH	AVG	PB	PR	PR+	PD	TPI
1997	StL-N	0	0	—	2	0	0	0	0	1^2	2	0	0	0	1	0	16.2	0.00	—	.333	.429	0	—	0	1	1	0	0.0

● SCOTT McGREGOR

McGregor, Scott Houston b: 1/18/54, Inglewood, Cal. BB/TL, 6'1", 190 lbs. Deb: 9/19/76

YEAR	TM/L	W	L	PCT	G	GS	CG	SH	SV	IP	H	R	HR	HB	BB	SO	RAT	ERA	ERA+	OAV	OOB	BH	AVG	PB	PR	PR+	PD	TPI
1976	Bal-A	0	1	.000	3	2	0	0	0	14^2	17	7	0	0	5	6	13.5	3.68	89	.293	.349	0	—	0	-0	-1	0	0.0
1977	Bal-A	3	5	.375	29	5	1	0	4	114	119	57	8	7	30	55	12.3	4.42	86	.275	.333	0	—	0	-4	-8	-1	-0.7
1978	Bal-A	15	13	.536	35	32	13	4	1	233	217	98	19	1	47	94	10.2	3.32	106	.248	.287	0	—	0	12	5	0	0.6
1979	*Bal-A	13	6	.684	27	23	7	2	0	174^2	165	70	19	2	23	81	**9.8**	3.35	120	.248	**.275**	0	—	0	17	14	-1	1.2
1980	Bal-A	20	8	.714	36	36	12	4	0	252	254	101	16	2	58	119	11.2	3.32	119	.265	.308	0	—	0	20	18	-3	1.6
1981	Bal-A☆	13	5	.722	24	22	8	3	0	160	167	63	13	0	40	82	11.6	3.26	111	.273	.318	0	—	0	7	7	1	0.8
1982	Bal-A	14	12	.538	37	37	7	1	0	226^1	238	126	31	1	52	84	11.6	4.61	88	.267	.308	0	—	0	-13	-14	-1	-1.6
1983	*Bal-A	18	7	.720	36	36	12	2	0	260	271	101	24	1	45	86	11.0	3.18	125	.269	.301	0	—	0	26	23	-1	2.0
1984	Bal-A	15	12	.556	30	30	10	3	0	196^1	216	93	18	5	54	67	12.6	3.94	98	.280	.331	0	—	0	1	-1	2	0.0
1985	Bal-A	14	14	.500	35	34	8	1	0	204	226	118	34	1	65	86	12.9	4.81	84	.283	.337	0	—	0	-15	-18	-1	-2.2
1986	Bal-A	11	15	.423	34	33	4	2	0	203	216	110	35	3	57	95	12.2	4.52	92	.270	.321	0	—	0	-8	-9	-1	-1.0
1987	Bal-A	2	7	.222	26	15	1	1	0	85^1	112	69	15	3	35	39	15.8	6.64	66	.326	.393	0	—	0	-21	-21	3	-1.6
1988	Bal-A	0	3	.000	4	4	0	0	0	17^1	27	18	3	0	7	10	17.7	8.83	44	.370	.425	0	—	0	-9	-10	1	-1.2
Total	13	138	108	.561	356	309	83	23	5	2140^2	2245	1031	235	26	518	904	11.7	3.99	98	.271	.316	0	—	0	13	-17	-2	-2.1

● SLIM McGREW

McGrew, Walter Howard b: 8/5/1899, Yoakum, Tex. d: 8/21/67, Houston, Tex. BR/TR, 6'7.5", 235 lbs. Deb: 4/18/22

YEAR	TM/L	W	L	PCT	G	GS	CG	SH	SV	IP	H	R	HR	HB	BB	SO	RAT	ERA	ERA+	OAV	OOB	BH	AVG	PB	PR	PR+	PD	TPI
1922	Was-A	0	0	—	1	0	0	0	0	1^2	4	6	0	0	2	1	32.4	10.80	36	.500	.600	0	.000	-0	-1	-1	0	-0.1
1923	Was-A	0	0	—	3	0	0	0	0	5	11	9	0	0	3	1	25.2	12.60	30	.440	.500	0	.000	-0	-5	-5	0	-0.2
1924	Was-A	0	1	.000	6	2	0	0	0	23^1	25	15	1	0	12	8	14.3	5.01	80	.281	.366	0	.000	-1	-2	-3	-1	-0.3
Total	3	0	1	.000	10	2	0	0	0	30	40	30	1	0	17	10	17.1	6.60	60	.328	.410	0	.000	-2	-8	-9	0	-0.6

● McGUIRE

McGuire Deb: 6/16/1894

YEAR	TM/L	W	L	PCT	G	GS	CG	SH	SV	IP	H	R	HR	HB	BB	SO	RAT	ERA	ERA+	OAV	OOB	BH	AVG	PB	PR	PR+	PD	TPI
1894	Cin-N	0	0	—	1	0	0	0	0	6	15	9	0	0	5	1	30.0	10.50	53	.469	.541	1	.250	-0	-3	-3	0	-0.1

● DEACON McGUIRE

McGuire, James Thomas b: 11/18/1863, Youngstown, Ohio d: 10/31/36, Duck Lake, Mich. BR/TR, 6'1", 185 lbs. Deb: 6/21/1884 MC♦

YEAR	TM/L	W	L	PCT	G	GS	CG	SH	SV	IP	H	R	HR	HB	BB	SO	RAT	ERA	ERA+	OAV	OOB	BH	AVG	PB	PR	PR+	PD	TPI
1890	Roc-a	0	0	—	1	0	0	0	0	4	10	5	0	0	1	1	24.8	6.75	53	.455	.478	99	.299	0	-1	-2	0	0.0

● TOM McGUIRE

McGuire, Thomas Patrick "Elmer" b: 2/1/1892, Chicago, Ill. d: 12/7/59, Phoenix, Ariz. BR/TR, 6', 175 lbs. Deb: 4/18/14

YEAR	TM/L	W	L	PCT	G	GS	CG	SH	SV	IP	H	R	HR	HB	BB	SO	RAT	ERA	ERA+	OAV	OOB	BH	AVG	PB	PR	PR+	PD	TPI
1914	Chi-F	5	6	.455	24	12	7	0	0	131^1	143	76	7	4	57	37	14.0	3.70	72	.288	.366	19	.271	4	-12	-17	0	-0.7
1919	Chi-A	0	0	—	1	0	0	0	0	3	5	4	0	0	3	0	24.0	9.00	35	.500	.615	0	.000	-0	-2	-2	0	-0.1
Total	2	5	6	.455	25	12	7	0	0	134^1	148	80	7	4	60	37	14.2	3.82	70	.292	.371	19	.268	3	-14	-19	1	-0.8

● BILL McGUNNIGLE

McGunnigle, William Henry "Gunner" b: 1/1/1855, Boston, Mass. d: 3/9/1899, Brockton, Mass. BR/TR, 5'9", 155 lbs. Deb: 5/2/1879 M♦

YEAR	TM/L	W	L	PCT	G	GS	CG	SH	SV	IP	H	R	HR	HB	BB	SO	RAT	ERA	ERA+	OAV	OOB	BH	AVG	PB	PR	PR+	PD	TPI
1879	Buf-N	9	5	.643	14	13	13	2	0	120	113	66	0		16	62	9.7	2.63	99	**.235**	.260	30	.175	-2	-2	-0	1	-0.1
1880	Buf-N	2	3	.400	5	5	4	1	0	37	43	19	0		8	3	12.4	3.41	72	.279	.315	4	.182	-1	-4	-4	-1	-0.6
Total	2	11	8	.579	19	18	17	3	0	157	156	85	0		24	65	10.3	2.81	92	.246	.274	35	.173	-3	-6	-4	0	-0.7

● MARTY McHALE

McHale, Martin Joseph b: 10/30/1888, Stoneham, Mass. d: 5/7/79, Hempstead, N.Y. BR/TR, 5'11.5", 174 lbs. Deb: 9/28/10

YEAR	TM/L	W	L	PCT	G	GS	CG	SH	SV	IP	H	R	HR	HB	BB	SO	RAT	ERA	ERA+	OAV	OOB	BH	AVG	PB	PR	PR+	PD	TPI
1910	Bos-A	0	2	.000	2	2	1	0	0	13^2	15	8	0	1	6	14	14.5	4.61	55	.259	.338	0	.000	-1	-3	-3	-0	-0.5
1911	Bos-A	0	0	—	4	1	0	0	0	9^1	19	12	1	1	3	3	22.2	9.64	34	.475	.523	0	.000	-0	-7	-7	0	-0.3
1913	NY-A	2	4	.333	7	6	4	1	0	48^2	49	21	1	1	10	11	11.1	2.96	101	.266	.308	0	.000	-1	-0	0	-1	-0.2
1914	NY-A	6	16	.273	31	23	12	0	1	191	195	82	3	4	33	75	10.9	2.97	93	.268	.303	12	.200	2	-5	-4	-3	-0.7
1915	NY-A	3	7	.300	13	11	6	0	0	78^1	86	45	1	0	19	25	12.1	4.25	69	.277	.318	3	.143	1	-11	-11	0	-1.3
1916	Bos-A	0	1	.000	2	1	0	0	0	6	7	7	0	1	4	1	18.0	3.00	92	.280	.400	0	—	0	-0	-0	0	0.1
	Cle-A	0	0	—	5	0	0	0	0	11^1	10	7	1	0	6	2	12.7	5.56	54	.270	.372	0	.000	-0	-3	-3	-0	-0.2
	Yr	0	1	.000	7	1	0	0	0	17^1	17	14	1	1	10	3	14.5	4.67	63	.274	.384	0	.000	0	-4	-3	0	-0.1
Total	6	11	30	.268	64	44	23	1	1	358^1	381	182	7	8	81	131	11.8	3.57	80	.275	.319	15	.140	-0	-30	-29	-4	-3.1

● VANCE McILREE

McIlree, Vance Elmer b: 10/14/1897, Riverside, Iowa d: 5/6/59, Kansas City, Mo. BR/TR, 6', 160 lbs. Deb: 9/13/21

YEAR	TM/L	W	L	PCT	G	GS	CG	SH	SV	IP	H	R	HR	HB	BB	SO	RAT	ERA	ERA+	OAV	OOB	BH	AVG	PB	PR	PR+	PD	TPI
1921	Was-A	0	0	—	1	0	0	0	0	1	1	1	0	0	0	0	9.0	9.00	46	.200	.200	0	—	0	-1	-1	-0	0.0

● IRISH McILVEEN

McIlveen, Henry Cooke b: 7/27/1880, Belfast, Ireland d: 10/18/60, Lorain, Ohio BL/TL, 5'11.5", 180 lbs. Deb: 7/10/06 ♦

YEAR	TM/L	W	L	PCT	G	GS	CG	SH	SV	IP	H	R	HR	HB	BB	SO	RAT	ERA	ERA+	OAV	OOB	BH	AVG	PB	PR	PR+	PD	TPI
1906	Pit-N	0	1	.000	2	1	0	0	0	7	10	6	1	0	2	3	15.4	7.71	35	.357	.400	2	.400	1	-4	-4	0	-0.4

● STOVER McILWAIN

McIlwain, Stover William "Smokey" (b: William Stover McIlwain)
b: 9/22/39, Savannah, Ga. d: 1/15/66, Buffalo, N.Y. BR/TR, 6'4", 195 lbs. Deb: 9/25/57

YEAR	TM/L	W	L	PCT	G	GS	CG	SH	SV	IP	H	R	HR	HB	BB	SO	RAT	ERA	ERA+	OAV	OOB	BH	AVG	PB	PR	PR+	PD	TPI
1957	Chi-A	0	0	—	1	0	0	0	0	1	2	0	0	0	1	0	27.0	0.00	—	.500	.600	0	—	0	0	0	-0	0.0
1958	Chi-A	0	0	—	1	1	0	0	0	4	4	1	1	0	0	4	9.0	2.25	162	.250	.250	0	.000	-0	1	1	-0	0.0
Total	2	0	0	—	2	1	0	0	0	5	6	1	1	0	1	4	12.6	1.80	203	.300	.333	0	.000	-0	1	1	-0	0.0

● HARRY McINTIRE

McIntire, John Reid b: 1/11/1879, Dayton, Ohio d: 1/9/49, Daytona Beach, Fla. BR/TR, 5'11", 180 lbs. Deb: 4/14/05

YEAR	TM/L	W	L	PCT	G	GS	CG	SH	SV	IP	H	R	HR	HB	BB	SO	RAT	ERA	ERA+	OAV	OOB	BH	AVG	PB	PR	PR+	PD	TPI
1905	Bro-N	8	25	.242	40	35	29	1	1	308^2	340	188	6	20	101	135	13.4	3.70	78	.285	.351	34	.246	7	-24	-29	-3	-2.3
1906	Bro-N	13	21	.382	39	31	25	4	3	276	254	123	2	14	89	121	11.6	2.97	85	.247	.316	18	.175	1	-10	-14	-1	-1.7
1907	Bro-N	7	15	.318	28	22	19	3	0	199^2	178	82	6	7	79	49	11.9	2.39	98	.248	.329	15	.217	5	2	-1	-1	0.4
1908	Bro-N	11	20	.355	40	35	26	4	2	288	259	106	5	20	90	108	11.5	2.69	87	.252	.324	20	.200	2	-10	-11	-2	-1.2
1909	Bro-N	7	17	.292	32	26	20	2	1	228	200	114	5	21	91	84	12.3	3.63	71	.246	.337	13	.171	1	-26	-26	-0	-2.6
1910	*Chi-N	13	9	.591	28	19	10	2	0	176	152	70	5	10	50	65	10.8	3.07	94	.240	.305	17	.258	3	-1	-4	-1	-0.2
1911	Chi-N	11	7	.611	25	17	9	1	0	149	147	81	5	4	33	56	11.1	4.11	81	.257	.302	14	.264	4	-12	-14	-0	-1.1
1912	Chi-N	1	2	.333	4	3	2	0	0	23^2	22	11	0	0	6	8	10.6	3.80	87	.256	.304	3	.300	1	-1	-1	-0	0.0
1913	Cin-N	0	1	.000	1	0	0	0	0	1	3	3	0	0	0	0	27.0	27.00	12	.600	.600	0	—	0	-3	-3	-0	-0.4
Total	9	71	117	.378	237	188	140	17	7	1650	1555	778	34	96	539	626	11.9	3.22	83	.256	.326	134	.218	24	-85	-103	-7	-9.1

● JOE McINTOSH

McIntosh, Joseph Anthony b: 8/4/51, Billings, Mont. BB/TR, 6'2", 185 lbs. Deb: 4/5/74

YEAR	TM/L	W	L	PCT	G	GS	CG	SH	SV	IP	H	R	HR	HB	BB	SO	RAT	ERA	ERA+	OAV	OOB	BH	AVG	PB	PR	PR+	PD	TPI
1974	SD-N	0	4	.000	10	5	0	0	0	37^1	36	19	3	1	17	22	13.0	3.62	99	.250	.333	0	.000	-1	0	-0	-0	-0.2

YEAR TM/L	W	L	PCT	G	GS	CG	SH	SV	IP	H	R	HR	HB	BB	SO	RAT	ERA	ERA+	OAV	OOB	BH	AVG	PB	PR	PR+	PD	TPI
1975 SD-N	8	15	.348	37	28	4	1	0	183	195	88	14	2	60	71	12.6	3.69	94	.273	.332	9	.188	2	-1	-4	-0	-0.3
Total 2	8	19	.296	47	33	4	1	0	220^{1}	231	107	17	3	77	93	12.7	3.68	95	.270	.332	9	.155	1	-1	-5	-1	-0.5
● **FRANK McINTYRE**	McIntyre, Frank W. b: 7/12/1859, Walled Lake, Mich. d: 7/8/1887, Detroit, Mich. Deb: 5/16/1883																										
1883 Det-N	1	0	1.000	1	1	1	0	0	11	11	10	0		1	0	9.8	0.82	380	.234	.250	0	.000	-0	3	3	0	0.2
Col-a	1	1	.500	2	2	2	0	0	19	20	19	0		7	6	12.8	5.21	59	.253	.314	0	.000	-0	-4	-5	-1	-0.5
Total 1	2	1	.667	3	3	3	0	0	30	31	29	0		8	6	11.7	3.60	86	.246	.291	0	.000	-1	-1	-2	-1	-0.3
● **DOC McJAMES**	McJames, James McCutchen (b: James Mc Cutchen James) b: 8/27/1873, Williamsburg, S.C. d: 9/23/01, Charleston, S.C. TR, Deb: 9/24/1895																										
1895 Was-N	1	1	.500	2	2	2	0	0	17	17	11	0	0	16	9	17.5	1.59	302	.258	.402	1	.143	-1	6	6	0	0.5
1896 Was-N	12	20	.375	37	33	29	0	1	280^{1}	310	208	2	6	135	103	14.5	4.27	103	.278	.359	18	.162	-9	3	4	-0	-0.4
1897 Was-N	15	23	.395	44	39	33	**3**	2	323^{2}	361	212	7	21	137	**156**	14.4	3.61	120	.280	.358	21	.169	-7	25	26	0	1.8
1898 Bal-N	27	15	.643	45	42	40	2	0	374	327	148	5	12	113	178	10.9	2.36	152	.234	.296	27	.181	-4	52	51	-3	4.3
1899 Bro-N	18	15	.545	37	34	27	1	1	275^{1}	295	166	4	10	122	105	14.0	3.50	112	.274	.353	19	.170	-5	11	12	3	1.0
1901 Bro-N	5	6	.455	13	12	6	0	0	91	104	71	1	7	40	42	14.9	4.75	71	.285	.367	1	.029	-4	-14	-14	-2	-1.9
Total 6	78	80	.494	178	162	137	6	4	1361^{1}	1414	816	19	56	563	593	13.4	3.43	116	.266	.343	87	.162	-30	82	85	-1	5.3
● **ARCHIE McKAIN**	McKain, Archie Richard "Happy" b: 5/12/11, Delphos, Kan. d: 5/21/85, Salina, Kan. BB/TL (BL 1941, 43), 5'10", 175 lbs. Deb: 4/25/37																										
1937 Bos-A	8	8	.500	36	18	3	0	2	137	152	84	7	0	64	66	14.2	4.66	102	.273	.348	13	.265	3	-1	1	0	0.4
1938 Bos-A	5	4	.556	37	5	1	0	6	99^{2}	119	60	6	2	44	27	14.9	4.52	109	.297	.369	2	.065	-2	3	**4**	2	0.3
1939 Det-A	5	6	.455	32	11	4	1	4	129^{2}	120	66	6	0	54	49	12.1	3.68	133	.247	.322	9	.220	4	14	16	-2	1.5
1940 *Det-A	5	0	1.000	27	0	0	0	3	51	48	18	2	0	25	24	12.9	2.82	168	.247	.333	1	.143	0	9	10	1	1.1
1941 Det-A	2	1	.667	15	0	0	0	0	43	58	24	3	0	11	14	14.4	5.02	90	.330	.369	0	.000	-1	-4	-2	2	0.0
StL-A	0	1	.000	8	0	0	0	1	10	16	9	2	1	4	2	18.9	8.10	53	.364	.429	0	.000	-0	-4	-4	1	-0.4
Yr	2	2	.500	23	0	0	0	1	53	74	33	5	1	15	16	15.3	5.60	80	.336	.381	0	.000	-1	-9	-6	3	-0.4
1943 StL-A	1	1	.500	10	0	0	0	0	16	16	9	0	0	6	6	12.4	3.94	84	.242	.306	0	.000	-0	-1	-1	0	-0.1
Total 6	26	21	.553	165	34	8	1	16	486^{1}	529	270	26	3	208	188	13.7	4.26	112	.275	.347	25	.176	3	15	25	4	2.8
● **HAL McKAIN**	McKain, Harold Le Roy b: 7/10/06, Logan, Iowa d: 1/24/70, Sacramento, Cal. BL/TR, 5'11", 185 lbs. Deb: 9/22/27																										
1927 Cle-A	0	1	.000	2	1	0	0	0	11	18	6	0	0	4	5	18.0	4.09	103	.391	.440	0	.000	-1	0	0	0	0.0
1929 Chi-A	6	9	.400	34	10	4	1	1	158	158	84	10	10	85	33	14.4	3.65	117	.275	.378	10	.227	2	11	11	4	1.5
1930 Chi-A	6	4	.600	32	5	0	0	5	89	108	67	0	3	42	52	15.5	5.56	83	.299	.377	13	.419	7	-9	-9	1	-0.2
1931 Chi-A	6	9	.400	27	8	3	0	0	112	134	82	10	3	57	39	15.6	5.71	75	.295	.377	5	.119	-1	-16	-19	2	-1.9
1932 Chi-A	0	0	—	8	0	0	0	0	11^{1}	17	15	1	0	5	7	17.5	11.12	39	.340	.400	0	.000	-0	-8	-9	0	-0.4
Total 5	18	23	.439	103	24	7	1	6	381^{1}	435	254	21	16	193	136	15.2	4.93	88	.293	.380	28	.230	8	-23	-25	7	-1.0
● **REEVE McKAY**	McKay, Reeve Stewart "Rip" b: 11/16/1881, Morgan, Tex. d: 1/18/46, Dallas, Tex. TR, 6'1.5", 168 lbs. Deb: 10/2/15																										
1915 StL-A	0	0	—	1	0	0	0	0	1	1	1	0	0	0	0	9.0	9.00	32	.500	.500	0	—	0	-1	-1	0	0.0
● **JIM McKEE**	McKee, James Marion b: 2/1/47, Columbus, Ohio BR/TR, 6'7", 215 lbs. Deb: 9/15/72																										
1972 Pit-N	1	0	1.000	2	0	0	0	0	5	2	0	0	0	1	4	5.4	0.00	—	.125	.176	0	—	0	2	2	-0	0.4
1973 Pit-N	0	1	.000	15	1	0	0	0	27	31	21	2	1	17	13	16.3	5.67	62	.287	.389	0	.000	-0	-6	-7	-0	-0.4
Total 2	1	1	.500	17	1	0	0	0	32	33	21	2	1	18	17	14.6	4.78	73	.266	.364	0	.000	-0	-4	-5	-1	0.0
● **ROGERS McKEE**	McKee, Rogers Hornsby b: 9/16/26, Shelby, N.C. BL/TL, 6'1", 160 lbs. Deb: 8/18/43																										
1943 Phi-N	1	0	1.000	4	1	1	0	0	13^{1}	12	9	0	0	5	1	11.5	6.08	56	.226	.293	1	.200	0	-4	-4	0	-0.2
1944 Phi-N	0	0	—	1	0	0	0	0	2	2	1	1	0	1	0	13.5	4.50	80	.250	.333	0	—	0	-0	-0	0	0.0
Total 2	1	0	1.000	5	1	1	0	0	15^{1}	14	10	1	0	6	1	11.7	5.87	58	.230	.299	1	.200	0	-4	-4	0	-0.2
● **TIM McKEITHAN**	McKeithan, Emmett James b: 11/2/06, Lawndale, N.C. d: 8/20/69, Forest City, N.C. BR/TR, 6'2", 182 lbs. Deb: 7/21/32																										
1932 Phi-A	0	1	.000	4	2	0	0	0	12^{2}	18	11	0	0	5	0	16.3	7.11	64	.340	.397	0	.000	0	-4	-4	0	-0.2
1933 Phi-A	1	0	1.000	3	1	0	0	0	9	10	4	0	0	4	3	14.0	4.00	107	.278	.350	1	.333	0	0	0	0	0.1
1934 Phi-A	0	0	—	3	0	0	0	0	4	7	7	2	0	5	0	27.0	15.75	28	.389	.522	0	.000	-0	-5	-5	-0	-0.3
Total 3	1	1	.500	10	3	0	0	0	25^{2}	35	22	2	0	14	3	17.2	7.36	60	.327	.405	1	.143	0	-8	-8	0	-0.4
● **RUSS McKELVY**	McKelvy, Russell Errett b: 9/8/1854, Swissvale, Pa. d: 10/19/15, Omaha, Neb. BR/TR, Deb: 5/1/1878 ♦																										
1878 Ind-N	0	2	.000	4	1	1	0	0	25	38	23	1		3	3	14.8	2.16	94	.322	.339	57	.225	0	0	-0	1	0.1
● **KIT McKENNA**	McKenna, James William b: 2/10/1873, Lynchburg, Va. d: 3/31/41, Lynchburg, Va. TR, Deb: 7/7/1898																										
1898 Bro-N	2	6	.250	14	9	7	0	0	100^{2}	118	75	4	17	57	27	17.2	5.63	64	.290	.399	9	.225	0	-23	-23	2	-1.3
1899 Bal-N	2	3	.400	8	4	4	0	1	45	66	38	1	3	19	7	17.6	4.60	86	.340	.407	1	.059	-1	-4	-3	-0	-0.4
Total 2	4	9	.308	22	13	11	0	1	145^{2}	184	113	5	20	76	34	17.3	5.31	70	.306	.402	10	.175	-0	-26	-26	1	-1.7
● **LIMB McKENRY**	McKenry, Frank Gordon "Big Pete" b: 8/13/1888, Piney Flats, Tenn. d: 11/1/56, Fresno, Cal. BR/TR, 6'4", 205 lbs. Deb: 8/27/15																										
1915 Cin-N	5	5	.500	21	11	5	0	0	110^{1}	94	43	2	3	39	37	11.1	2.94	97	.238	.311	5	.152	0	-2	-1	1	0.1
1916 Cin-N	1	1	.500	6	1	0	0	0	14^{2}	14	8	0	2	8	2	14.7	4.30	60	.259	.375	2	.400	2	-3	-3	-0	-0.2
Total 2	6	6	.500	27	12	5	0	0	125	108	51	2	5	47	39	11.5	3.10	91	.241	.319	7	.184	2	-5	-4	1	-0.1
● **JOEL McKEON**	McKeon, Joel Jacob b: 2/25/63, Covington, Ky. BL/TL, 6', 185 lbs. Deb: 5/6/86																										
1986 Chi-A	3	1	.750	30	0	0	0	1	33	18	10	2	0	17	18	9.5	2.45	176	.165	.278	0	—	0	6	7	-1	0.7
1987 Chi-A	1	2	.333	13	0	0	0	0	21	27	22	8	0	15	14	18.0	9.43	49	.318	.420	0	—	0	-12	-11	-0	-1.3
Total 2	4	3	.571	43	0	0	0	1	54	45	32	10	0	32	32	12.8	5.17	86	.232	.341	0	—	0	-5	-4	1	-0.6
● **LARRY McKEON**	McKeon, Lawrence G. b: 3/25/1866, New York d: 7/18/15, Indianapolis, Ind 5'10", 168 lbs. Deb: 5/1/1884																										
1884 Ind-a	18	41	.305	61	60	59	2	0	512	488	350	20	18	94	308	10.5	3.50	94	.235	.275	53	.212	-3	-14	-12	8	-0.6
1885 Cin-a	20	13	.606	33	33	32	2	0	290	273	143	5	13	50	117	10.4	2.86	114	.241	.281	20	.165	-5	13	13	-0	0.7
1886 Cin-a	8	8	.500	19	19	16	0	0	156	174	118	6	3	54	46	13.3	5.08	69	.276	.336	19	.253	1	-28	-26	1	-1.9
KC-N	0	2	.000	3	3	3	0	0	21	44	32	0		8	3	22.3	10.71	35	.411	.452	0	.000	-1	-17	-14	0	-1.0
Total 3	46	64	.418	116	115	110	4	0	979	979	643	31	34	206	474	11.2	3.71	90	.248	.291	92	.202	-9	-47	-41	8	-2.8
● **TONY McKNIGHT**	McKnight, Tony Mark b: 6/29/77, Texarkana, Ark. BL/TR, 6'5", 205 lbs. Deb: 8/10/2000																										
2000 Hou-N	4	1	.800	6	6	1	0	0	35	35	19	4	2	9	23	11.8	3.86	127	.245	.299	0	.000	-2	3	4	0	0.3
● **DENNY McLAIN**	McLain, Dennis Dale b: 3/29/44, Chicago, Ill. BR/TR, 6'1", 185 lbs. Deb: 9/21/63																										
1963 Det-A	2	1	.667	3	3	2	0	0	21	20	12	2	0	16	22	15.4	4.29	87	.253	.379	1	.200	1	-2	-1	1	0.0
1964 Det-A	4	5	.444	19	16	3	0	0	100	84	48	16	1	37	70	11.0	4.05	90	.225	.297	5	.135	-1	-5	-4	-2	-0.7
1965 Det-A	16	6	.727	33	29	13	4	1	220^{1}	174	73	25	2	62	192	9.7	2.61	133	.216	.273	4	.054	-4	21	21	-0	1.7
1966 Det-A★	20	14	.588	38	38	14	4	0	264^{1}	205	120	42	3	104	192	10.6	3.92	89	.214	.294	17	.183	2	-14	-13	-1	-1.5
1967 Det-A	17	16	.515	37	37	10	3	0	235	209	110	35	3	73	161	10.9	3.79	86	.237	.297	10	.118	-3	-15	-14	-2	-2.4
1968 *Det-A★	**31**	6	**.838**	41	41	**28**	6	0	**336**	241	86	31	6	63	280	8.3	1.96	154	.200	.243	18	.162	0	38	39	1	**4.8**
1969 Det-A★	**24**	9	.727	42	41	23	**9**	0	**325**	288	105	25	4	67	181	9.9	2.80	134	.237	.279	17	.160	-1	30	33	-5	2.6
1970 Det-A	3	5	.375	14	14	1	0	0	91^{1}	100	51	19	3	28	52	12.9	4.63	80	.273	.330	2	.065	-2	-9	-9	0	-0.9
1971 Was-A	10	22	.313	33	32	9	3	0	216^{2}	233	115	31	3	72	103	12.8	4.28	77	.281	.341	6	.103	-1	-20	-24	-1	-3.4
1972 Oak-A	1	2	.333	5	5	0	0	0	22^{1}	32	17	4	0	8	8	16.1	6.04	47	.323	.374	0	.000	-0	-7	-9	0	-1.1
Atl-N	3	5	.375	15	8	2	0	1	54	60	41	12	1	18	21	13.2	6.50	58	.279	.338	2	.167	0	-18	-15	-1	-2.1
Total 10	131	91	.590	280	264	105	29	2	1886	1646	778	242	26	548	1282	10.6	3.39	101	.234	.292	82	.133	-9	-1	5	-10	-3.0
● **BARNEY McLAUGHLIN**	McLaughlin, Bernard b: 1857, Ireland d: 2/13/21, Lowell, Mass. BR/TR, Deb: 8/2/1884 F♦																										
1884 KC-U	1	3	.250	7	4	4	0	0	48^{2}	62	44	2		15	14	14.2	5.36	42	.291	.338	37	.228	-1	-16	-18	0	-1.1
● **BYRON McLAUGHLIN**	McLaughlin, Byron Scott b: 9/29/55, Van Nuys, Cal. BR/TR, 6'1", 185 lbs. Deb: 9/18/77																										
1977 Sea-A	0	0	—	1	0	0	0	0	1^{1}	5	4	1	0	0	1	33.8	27.00	15	.625	.625	0	—	0	-3	-3	0	-0.2
1978 Sea-A	4	8	.333	20	17	4	0	0	107	97	58	15	6	39	87	11.9	4.37	87	.238	.314	0	—	0	-7	-6	-2	-0.8

YEAR	TM/L	W	L	PCT	G	GS	CG	SH	SV	IP	H	R	HR	HB	BB	SO	RAT	ERA	ERA+	OAV	OOB	BH	AVG	PB	PR	PR+	PD	TPI
1979	Sea-A	7	7	.500	47	7	1	0	14	123^2	114	58	13	2	60	74	12.8	4.22	104	.251	.340	0	—	0	0	2	-2	0.1
1980	Sea-A	3	6	.333	45	4	0	0	2	90^2	124	74	15	2	50	41	17.5	6.85	60	.331	.412	0	—	0	-28	-27	-2	-2.6
1983	Cal-A	2	4	.333	16	7	0	0	0	55^2	63	32	3	2	22	45	14.1	5.17	78	.286	.357	0	—	0	-7	-7	-0	-0.7
Total	5	16	25	.390	129	35	5	0	16	378^1	403	226	47	12	171	248	13.9	5.11	80	.275	.356	0	—	0	-45	-41	-5	-4.2
● **FRANK McLAUGHLIN**	McLaughlin, Francis Edward b: 6/19/1856, Lowell, Mass. d: 4/5/17, Lowell, Mass. BR/TR, 5′9″, 160 lbs. Deb: 8/9/1882 F♦																											
1883	Pit-a	0	0	—	2	0	0	0	0	9	14	21	0		3	1	17.0	13.00	25	.333	.378	25	.219	0	-10	-10	-0	-0.4
1884	KC-U	0	0	—	2	1	0	0	0	10	15	12	0		2	3	15.3	5.40	41	.326	.354	28	.228	-0	-3	-4	-1	-0.2
Total	2	0	0	—	4	1	0	0	0	19	29	33	0		5	4	16.1	9.00	30	.330	.366	97	.228	-0	-13	-14	-1	-0.6
● **JIM McLAUGHLIN**	McLaughlin, James Thomas b: 11/18/1860, Cleveland, Ohio d: 11/16/1895, Cleveland, Ohio BL/TL, 157 lbs. Deb: 5/30/1884																											
1884	Bal-a	1	2	.333	3	2	2	0	0	22	27	22	2	0	11	8	15.5	3.68	94	.300	.376	5	.227	0	-1	-0	0	0.0
● **JOEY McLAUGHLIN**	McLaughlin, Joey Richard b: 7/11/56, Tulsa, Okla. BR/TR, 6′2″, 205 lbs. Deb: 6/11/77																											
1977	Atl-N	0	0	—	3	2	0	0	0	6	10	10	3	0	3	0	19.5	15.00	30	.385	.448	0	.000	-0	-7	-6	0	-0.3
1979	Atl-N	5	3	.625	37	0	0	0	5	69	54	23	3	1	34	40	11.6	2.48	164	.224	.322	2	.182	0	10	11	-1	1.4
1980	Tor-A	6	9	.400	55	10	0	0	4	135^2	159	79	16	4	53	70	14.3	4.51	96	.302	.370	0	—	0	-7	-3	-0	-0.3
1981	Tor-A	1	5	.167	40	0	0	0	10	60	55	24	2	0	21	38	11.4	2.85	138	.249	.314	0	—	0	5	7	-0	0.9
1982	Tor-A	8	6	.571	44	0	0	0	8	70	54	27	7	1	30	49	10.9	3.21	140	.212	.297	0	—	0	7	9	1	1.9
1983	Tor-A	7	4	.636	50	0	0	0	9	64^2	63	33	11	0	37	47	13.9	4.45	97	.259	.357	0	—	0	-3	-1	-0	-0.2
1984	Tor-A	0	0	—	6	0	0	0	0	10^2	12	6	0	0	7	3	16.0	2.53	162	.286	.388	0	—	0	2	2	0	0.1
	Tex-A	2	1	.667	15	0	0	0	0	32^2	33	17	4	0	13	21	12.7	4.41	94	.260	.329	0	—	0	-1	-1	-1	-0.1
	Yr	2	1	.667	21	0	0	0	0	43^1	45	23	4	0	20	24	13.5	3.95	105	.266	.344	0	—	0	0	1	-0	0.0
Total	7	29	28	.509	250	12	0	0	36	448^2	440	219	46	6	198	268	12.9	3.85	110	.262	.341	2	.167	-0	5	18	-0	3.4
● **JUD McLAUGHLIN**	McLaughlin, Justin Theodore b: 3/24/12, Brighton, Mass. d: 9/27/64, Cambridge, Mass. BL/TL, 5′11″, 155 lbs. Deb: 6/23/31																											
1931	Bos-A	0	0	—	9	0	0	0	0	12	23	16	1	0	8	3	23.3	12.00	36	.397	.470	0	—	0	-10	-10	0	-0.4
1932	Bos-A	0	0	—	1	0	0	0	0	3	5	5	0	0	4	0	27.0	15.00	30	.385	.529	0	.000	-0	-4	-3	0	-0.2
1933	Bos-A	0	0	—	6	0	0	0	0	8^2	14	7	1	0	5	1	19.7	6.23	70	.359	.432	0	—	0	-2	-2	-0	-0.1
Total	3	0	0	—	16	0	0	0	0	23^2	42	28	2	0	17	4	22.4	10.27	42	.382	.465	0	.000	-0	-16	-16	0	-0.7
● **BO McLAUGHLIN**	McLaughlin, Michael Duane b: 10/23/53, Oakland, Cal. BR/TR, 6′5″, 210 lbs. Deb: 7/20/76																											
1976	Hou-N	4	5	.444	17	11	4	2	1	79	71	31	6	2	17	32	10.3	2.85	112	.244	.290	0	.000	-1	6	3	0	0.3
1977	Hou-N	4	7	.364	46	6	0	0	5	84^2	81	44	6	6	34	59	12.9	4.25	84	.260	.344	0	.000	-1	-3	-7	1	-0.9
1978	Hou-N	0	1	.000	12	1	0	0	2	23^1	30	17	2	2	16	10	18.5	5.01	66	.313	.421	0	.000	-0	-4	-5	-0	-0.3
1979	Hou-N	1	2	.333	12	0	0	0	0	16^1	22	15	2	0	4	12	14.3	5.51	64	.314	.351	0	.000	-0	-3	-4	0	-0.6
	Atl-N	1	1	.500	37	1	0	0	0	49^2	63	33	2	2	16	45	14.7	4.89	83	.303	.358	0	.000	-1	-6	-4	-1	-0.4
	Yr	2	3	.400	49	1	0	0	0	66	85	48	4	2	20	57	14.6	5.05	78	.306	.357	0	.000	-1	-10	-8	-1	-1.0
1981	Oak-A	0	0	—	11	0	0	0	1	11^2	17	15	1	1	9	3	20.8	11.57	30	.333	.443	0	—	0	-10	-11	-0	-0.6
1982	Oak-A	0	4	.000	21	2	1	0	0	48^1	51	31	3	1	27	27	14.7	4.84	81	.267	.361	0	—	0	-4	-5	0	-0.3
Total	6	10	20	.333	156	21	5	2	9	313	335	186	22	14	123	188	13.6	4.49	80	.275	.348	0	.000	-3	-25	-33	0	-2.8
● **PAT McLAUGHLIN**	McLaughlin, Patrick Elmer b: 8/17/10, Taylor, Tex. d: 11/1/99, Houston, Tex. BR/TR, 6′2″, 175 lbs. Deb: 4/25/37																											
1937	Det-A	0	2	.000	10	3	0	0	0	32^2	39	23	3	0	16	8	15.2	6.34	74	.291	.367	1	.100	-1	-6	-6	-1	-0.4
1940	Phi-A	0	0	—	1	0	0	0	0	1^2	4	3	1	0	1	0	27.0	16.20	27	.444	.500	0	—	0	-2	-2	0	-0.1
1945	Det-A	0	0	—	1	0	0	0	0	1	2	2	0	0	0	0	18.0	9.00	39	.400	.400	0	—	0	-1	-1	-0	0.0
Total	3	0	2	.000	12	3	0	0	0	35^1	45	28	4	0	17	8	15.8	6.88	67	.304	.376	1	.100	-1	-9	-9	-1	-0.5
● **WARREN McLAUGHLIN**	McLaughlin, Warren A. b: 1/22/1876, N.Plainfield, N.J. d: 10/22/23, Plainfield, N.J. TL, Deb: 7/7/00																											
1900	Phi-N	0	0	—	1	0	0	0	0	6	4	4	0	0	6	1	15.0	4.50	80	.190	.370	1	.500	1	-1	-1	0	0.0
1902	Pit-N	3	0	1.000	3	3	3	0	0	26	27	13	0	1	9	13	12.8	2.77	99	.267	.333	4	.364	1	0	-0	-1	0.0
1903	Phi-N	0	3	.000	3	2	2	0	0	23	38	24	0	1	11	3	19.6	7.04	46	.376	.442	2	.200	0	-10	-10	-1	-1.0
Total	3	3	3	.500	7	5	5	0	0	55	69	41	0	2	26	17	15.9	4.75	64	.309	.386	7	.304	2	-10	-10	-2	-1.0
● **AL McLEAN**	McLean, Albert Eldon "Elrod" b: 9/20/12, Chicago, Ill. d: 9/29/90, Asheboro, N.C. BR/TR, 6′, 175 lbs. Deb: 7/16/35																											
1935	Was-A	0	0	—	4	0	0	0	0	8^2	12	8	0	0	5	3	17.7	7.27	59	.324	.405	0	.000	-0	-3	-3	-0	-0.2
● **WAYNE McLELAND**	McLeland, Wayne Gaffney "Nubbin" b: 8/29/24, Milton, Iowa BR/TR, 6′, 180 lbs. Deb: 4/20/51																											
1951	Det-A	0	1	.000	6	1	0	0	0	11	20	10	1	1	4	0	20.5	8.18	51	.400	.455	0	.000	-0	-5	-5	0	-0.4
1952	Det-A	0	0	—	4	0	0	0	0	2^2	4	3	0	0	6	0	33.8	10.13	38	.444	.667	0	—	0	-2	-2	-0	-0.1
Total	2	0	1	.000	10	1	0	0	0	13^2	24	13	1	1	10	0	23.0	8.56	48	.407	.500	0	.000	-0	-7	-7	0	-0.5
● **CAL McLISH**	McLish, Calvin Coolidge Julius Caesar Tuskahoma "Buster" b: 12/1/25, Anadarko, Okla. BB/TR, 6′1″, 200 lbs. Deb: 5/13/44 C																											
1944	Bro-N	3	10	.231	23	13	3	0	0	84	110	81	10	1	48	24	17.0	7.82	45	.321	.406	7	.219	0	-39	-40	-2	-5.2
1946	Bro-N	0	0	—	1	0	0	0	0	0	1	0	0	0	—	—	∞	—	1.000	1.000	99	—	0	-2	-2	0	-0.2	
1947	Pit-N	0	0	—	1	0	0	0	0	1	2	2	0	1	0	0	27.0	18.00	23	.400	.500	0	—	0	-2	-1	0	0.0
1948	Pit-N	0	0	—	2	1	0	0	0	5	8	5	0	0	2	1	18.0	9.00	45	.400	.455	0	.000	-0	-3	-3	0	-0.1
1949	Chi-N	1	1	.500	8	2	0	0	0	23	31	21	5	0	12	6	16.8	5.87	69	.341	.417	3	.333	2	-5	-5	1	-0.2
1951	Chi-N	4	10	.286	30	17	5	1	0	145^2	159	76	16	3	52	46	13.2	4.45	92	.283	.347	5	.119	-1	-8	-6	-0	-0.6
1956	Cle-A	2	4	.333	37	2	0	0	1	61^2	67	36	5	0	32	27	14.4	4.96	85	.282	.367	1	.111	1	-6	-5	1	-0.2
1957	Cle-A	9	7	.563	42	7	2	0	1	144^1	118	55	11	2	67	88	11.7	2.74	135	.220	.309	8	.186	3	17	16	1	2.1
1958	Cle-A	16	8	.667	39	30	13	0	1	225^2	214	92	25	1	70	97	11.4	2.99	122	.251	.309	6	.094	-1	19	17	0	1.7
1959	Cle-A★	19	8	.704	35	32	13	0	1	235^1	253	110	26	5	72	113	12.6	3.63	101	.270	.326	14	.189	1	6	1	3	0.6
1960	Cin-N	4	14	.222	37	21	2	1	0	151^1	170	85	16	7	48	56	13.4	4.16	92	.287	.348	2	.049	-3	-7	-6	1	-0.9
1961	Chi-A	10	13	.435	31	27	4	0	1	162^1	178	87	21	1	47	80	12.5	4.38	89	.280	.330	9	.167	-1	-6	-9	2	-1.0
1962	Phi-N	11	5	.688	32	24	5	1	1	154^2	184	84	15	2	45	71	13.4	4.25	91	.293	.343	4	.078	-2	-5	-7	-1	-0.8
1963	Phi-N	13	11	.542	32	32	10	2	0	209^2	184	85	14	4	56	98	10.5	3.26	99	.239	.294	14	.203	4	1	-1	2	0.5
1964	Phi-N	0	1	.000	2	1	0	0	0	5^1	6	3	0	0	1	6	11.8	3.38	103	.261	.292	0	.000	-0	0	0	0	0.0
Total	15	92	92	.500	352	209	57	5	6	1609	1685	824	164	27	552	713	12.7	4.01	93	.270	.332	73	.149	4	-39	-50	9	-4.3
● **SAM McMACKIN**	McMackin, Samuel b: 1872, Cleveland, Ohio d: 2/11/03, Columbus, Ohio BR/TL, Deb: 9/4/02																											
1902	Chi-A	0	0	—	1	0	0	0	0	3	1	1	0	0	0	2	3.0	0.00	—	.100	.100	0	.000	-0	1	1	0	0.1
	Det-A	0	1	.000	1	1	1	0	0	8^1	9	5	0	1	4	2	15.1	3.24	113	.273	.368	2	.500	1	0	0	0	0.1
	Yr	0	1	.000	2	1	1	0	0	11^1	10	6	0	1	4	4	11.9	2.38	150	.233	.313	2	.400	0	2	2	1	0.2
● **JACK McMAHAN**	McMahan, Jack Wally b: 7/22/32, Hot Springs, Ark. BR/TL, 6′, 175 lbs. Deb: 4/18/56																											
1956	Pit-N	0	0	—	11	0	0	0	0	13^1	18	9	1	0	9	9	18.2	6.08	62	.340	.435	0	.000	-0	-3	-3	0	-0.2
	KC-A	0	5	.000	23	9	0	0	0	61^2	69	40	7	2	31	13	14.9	4.82	90	.290	.376	0	.000	-2	-5	-3	-0	-0.5
Total	1	0	5	.000	34	9	0	0	0	75	87	49	8	2	40	22	15.5	5.04	84	.299	.387	0	.000	-2	-8	-7	0	-0.7
● **DON McMAHON**	McMahon, Donald John b: 1/4/30, Brooklyn, N.Y. d: 7/22/87, Los Angeles, Cal. BR/TR, 6′2″, 222 lbs. Deb: 6/30/57 C																											
1957	*Mil-N	2	3	.400	32	0	0	0	9	46^2	33	13	0	0	29	46	12.0	1.54	227	.196	.315	2	.250	1	12	11	-0	1.7
1958	*Mil-N☆	7	2	.778	38	0	0	0	8	58^2	50	25	4	2	29	37	12.4	3.68	96	.235	.332	1	.111	0	2	-1	-0	-0.2
1959	Mil-N	5	3	.625	60	0	0	0	**15**	80^2	81	26	5	1	37	55	13.3	2.57	138	.259	.339	2	.222	1	12	10	-1	1.3
1960	Mil-N	3	6	.333	48	0	0	0	10	63^2	66	48	9	2	32	50	14.1	5.94	58	.263	.351	0	.000	-1	-15	-19	0	-3.2
1961	Mil-N	6	4	.600	53	0	0	0	8	92	84	35	4	2	51	55	13.4	2.84	132	.249	.351	3	.188	0	12	10	1	1.3
1962	Mil-N	0	1	.000	2	0	0	0	0	3	3	2	1	0	0	3	9.0	6.00	63	.250	.250	0	—	0	-1	-1	-0	-0.2
	Hou-N	5	5	.500	51	0	0	0	8	76^2	53	14	4	1	33	69	10.2	1.53	245	.201	.292	1	.083	-1	21	20	-0	2.8
	Yr	5	6	.455	53	0	0	0	8	79^2	56	16	5	1	33	72	10.2	1.69	221	.203	.290	1	.083	-1	20	19	-0	2.6
1963	Hou-N	1	5	.167	49	2	0	0	5	80	83	38	10	0	26	51	12.3	4.05	78	.270	.327	1	.083	0	-7	-8	-0	-0.7
1964	Cle-A	6	4	.600	70	0	0	0	16	101	67	31	7	2	52	92	10.8	2.41	150	.189	.297	2	.143	-0	14	13	-1	1.6
1965	Cle-A	3	3	.500	58	0	0	0	11	85	79	36	8	1	37	60	12.4	3.28	106	.248	.329	2	.222	0	2	2	1	0.3

YEAR	TM/L	W	L	PCT	G	GS	CG	SH	SV	IP	H	R	HR	HB	BB	SO	RAT	ERA	ERA+	OAV	OOB	BH	AVG	PB	PR	PR+	PD	TPI
1966	Cle-A	1	1	.500	12	0	0	0	1	12^1	8	4	1	0	6	5	10.2	2.92	118	.190	.292	0	.000	-0	1	1	-0	0.1
	Bos-A	8	7	.533	49	0	0	0	9	78	65	29	7	3	38	57	12.2	2.65	143	.232	.330	1	.091	-0	7	9	-1	1.9
	Yr	9	8	.529	61	0	0	0	10	90^1	73	33	8	3	44	62	12.0	2.69	140	.227	.325	1	.077	-0	7	10	-1	2.0
1967	Bos-A	1	2	.333	11	0	0	0	2	17^2	14	8	3	0	13	10	13.8	3.57	98	.215	.346	0	.000	-0	-1	-0	0	0.0
	Chi-A	5	0	1.000	52	0	0	0	3	91^2	54	21	5	6	27	74	8.5	1.67	186	.173	.252	2	.182	0	16	15	-0	0.9
	Yr	6	2	.750	63	0	0	0	5	109^1	68	29	8	6	40	84	9.4	1.98	160	.180	.270	2	.154	-0	15	15	-0	0.9
1968	Chi-A	2	1	.667	25	0	0	0	0	46	31	10	2	3	20	32	10.6	1.96	155	.190	.290	1	.333	0	5	5	-1	0.3
	*Det-A	3	1	.750	20	0	0	0	1	35^2	22	8	2	0	10	33	8.1	2.02	149	.180	.242	0	.000	-0	4	4	-0	0.4
	Yr	5	2	.714	45	0	0	0	1	81^2	53	18	4	3	30	65	9.5	1.98	152	.186	.270	1	.143	-0	9	9	-1	0.7
1969	Det-A	3	5	.375	34	0	0	0	11	37	25	17	2	1	18	38	10.7	3.89	96	.192	.295	0	.000	-1	-1	-1	0	-0.2
	SF-N	3	1	.750	13	0	0	0	2	23^2	13	9	1	0	9	21	8.4	3.04	115	.157	.239	1	.333	0	1	1	0	0.3
1970	SF-N	9	5	.643	61	0	0	0	19	94^1	70	32	9	2	45	74	11.2	2.96	135	.202	.297	2	.143	0	11	11	-1	1.9
1971	*SF-N	10	6	.625	61	0	0	0	4	82	73	40	9	7	37	71	12.8	4.06	84	.242	.338	0	.000	-1	-5	-6	1	-1.2
1972	SF-N	3	3	.500	44	0	0	0	5	63	46	26	8	1	21	45	9.7	3.71	94	.206	.278	1	.250	0	-2	-2	-0	-0.2
1973	SF-N	4	0	1.000	22	0	0	0	6	30^1	21	5	1	0	7	20	8.3	1.48	258	.189	.237	1	1.000	0	7	8	0	1.4
1974	SF-N	0	0	—	9	0	0	0	0	11^2	13	5	2	0	2	5	11.6	3.09	124	.283	.313	0	—	0	1	1	-0	0.0
Total	18	90	68	.570	874	2	0	0	153	1310^2	1054	482	104	34	579	1003	11.4	2.96	119	.221	.310	23	.137	-1	96	85	-1	10.3
● **DOC McMAHON**	McMahon, Henry John b: 12/19/1886, Woburn, Mass. d: 12/11/29, Woburn, Mass. Deb: 10/6/08																											
1908	Bos-A	1	0	1.000	1	1	1	0	0	9	14	3	0	0	0	3	14.0	3.00	82	.350	.350	2	.400	1	-1	-1	-0	0.0
● **SADIE McMAHON**	McMahon, John Joseph b: 9/19/1867, Wilmington, Del. d: 2/20/54, Wilmington, Del BR/TR, 5'9.5", 165 lbs. Deb: 7/5/1889																											
1889	Phi-a	14	12	.538	28	27	27	2	0	242	230	160	5	14	102	117	12.9	3.53	107	.243	.325	16	.154	-6	8	7	4	0.4
1890	Phi-a	29	18	.617	48	46	44	0	1	410	414	238	5	20	133	225	12.4	3.34	116	.254	.318	40	.229	3	24	25	9	3.4
	Bal-a	7	3	.700	12	11	11	1	0	99	84	49	1	6	33	66	11.2	3.00	135	.223	.296	4	.103	-4	10	11	2	0.7
	Yr	**36**	21	.632	**60**	57	**55**	1	1	**509**	498	287	6	26	166	**291**	12.2	3.27	120	.248	.314	44	.206	-1	34	36	11	4.1
1891	Bal-a	**35**	24	.593	61	58	**53**	**5**	1	**503**	493	259	13	17	149	219	11.8	2.81	133	.248	.306	43	.205	-3	51	51	5	4.9
1892	Bal-N	19	25	.432	48	46	44	2	1	397	430	260	9	9	145	118	13.2	3.24	106	.265	.329	25	.141	-9	2	8	0	-0.1
1893	Bal-N	23	18	.561	43	40	35	0	1	346^1	378	232	6	9	156	79	14.1	4.37	109	.269	.346	36	.243	-3	12	14	-1	0.9
1894	Bal-N	25	8	.758	35	33	26	0	0	275^2	317	175	7	9	111	60	14.3	4.21	130	.285	.355	36	.286	0	34	37	3	3.4
1895	*Bal-N	10	4	.714	15	15	15	**4**	0	122^1	110	54	1	4	32	37	10.7	2.94	162	.237	.291	16	.314	1	25	25	-1	2.2
1896	Bal-N	11	9	.550	22	22	19	0	0	175^2	195	109	4	3	55	33	13.0	3.48	123	.279	.334	9	.123	-7	17	16	0	0.8
1897	Bro-N	0	6	.000	9	7	5	0	0	63	75	56	1	3	29	13	15.3	5.86	70	.293	.372	5	.200	-1	-11	-13	0	-1.0
Total	9	173	127	.577	321	305	279	14	4	2634	2726	1592	52	94	945	967	12.9	3.51	118	.260	.326	230	.204	-29	172	182	21	15.6
● **JOHN McMAKIN**	McMakin, John Weaver "Spartanburg John" b: 3/6/1878, Spartanburg, S.C. d: 9/25/56, Lyman, S.C. BR/TL, 5'11", 165 lbs. Deb: 4/19/02																											
1902	Bro-N	2	2	.500	4	4	4	0	0	32	34	18	0	2	11	6	13.2	3.09	89	.272	.341	2	.182	1	-1	-1	-0	-0.1
● **JOE McMANUS**	McManus, Joab Logan b: 9/7/1887, Palmyra, Ill. d: 12/23/55, Beckley, W.Va. BR/TR, 5'11", 180 lbs. Deb: 4/12/13																											
1913	Cin-N	0	0	—	1	0	0	0	0	2	3	4	0	0	4	1	31.5	18.00	18	.375	.583	0	—	0	-3	-3	0	-0.1
● **PAT McMANUS**	McManus, Patrick b: 1858, Ireland d: 10/6/17, Brooklyn, N.Y. Deb: 5/22/1879																											
1879	Tro-N	0	2	.000	2	2	2	0	0	21	24	21	1		1	6	10.7	3.00	83	.258	.266	1	.125	-1	-1	-1	0	-0.1
● **GREG McMICHAEL**	McMichael, Gregory Winston b: 12/1/66, Knoxville, Tenn. BR/TR, 6'3", 215 lbs. Deb: 4/12/93																											
1993	*Atl-N	2	3	.400	74	0	0	0	19	91^2	68	22	3	0	29	89	9.5	2.06	195	.206	.270	0	.000	-0	20	20	2	1.8
1994	Atl-N	4	6	.400	51	0	0	0	21	58^2	66	29	1	0	19	47	13.0	3.84	111	.280	.333	0	.000	-0	2	3	-1	0.4
1995	*Atl-N	7	2	.778	67	0	0	0	2	80^2	64	27	8	0	32	74	10.7	2.79	153	.213	.289	0	.000	-0	13	13	-1	1.2
1996	*Atl-N	5	3	.625	73	0	0	0	2	86^2	84	37	4	1	27	78	11.6	3.22	137	.253	.311	0	—	0	10	11	1	1.0
1997	NY-N	7	10	.412	73	0	0	0	7	87^2	73	34	8	2	27	81	10.5	2.98	136	.233	.298	2	.667	1	12	11	1	2.2
1998	NY-N	1	2	.333	22	0	0	0	0	22^2	23	12	1	1	14	22	15.1	3.97	104	.271	.380	0	—	0	1	0	1	0.1
	LA-N	0	1	.000	12	0	0	0	1	14^1	17	8	1	1	6	11	15.1	4.40	90	.309	.387	0	—	0	-0	-1	1	0.0
	NY-N	4	1	.800	30	0	0	0	1	31	41	19	7	2	15	22	16.8	4.06	102	.318	.397	0	.000	-0	1	0	-1	-0.1
	Yr	5	4	.556	64	0	0	0	2	68	81	39	9	4	35	55	15.9	4.10	100	.301	.390	0	.000	-0	1	-0	1	0.0
1999	NY-N	1	1	.500	19	0	0	0	0	18^2	20	10	3	0	8	18	13.5	4.82	91	.270	.341	0	—	0	-1	-1	-0	-0.1
	Oak-A	0	0	—	17	0	0	0	0	15	15	9	3	2	12	3	17.4	5.40	86	.283	.433	0	—	0	-1	-1	-0	-0.1
2000	Atl-N	0	0	—	15	0	0	0	0	16^1	12	8	3	0	4	14	8.8	4.41	103	.214	.267	0	—	0	0	0	0	0.0
Total	8	31	29	.517	453	0	0	0	53	523^1	483	215	42	9	193	459	11.8	3.25	130	.246	.316	2	.133	-0	57	56	2	6.4
● **GEORGE McMULLEN**	McMullen, George b: California Deb: 7/2/1887																											
1887	NY-a	2	1	.667	3	3	2	0	0	21	44	25	2	0	19	2	18.9	7.71	55	.393	.393	1	.083	-2	-8	-8	0	-0.8
● **JOHN McMULLIN**	McMullin, John F. "Lefty" b: 1848, Philadelphia, Pa. d: 4/11/1881, Philadelphia, Pa. BR/TL, 5'9", 160 lbs. Deb: 5/9/1871 ♦																											
1871	Tro-n	12	15	.444	29	29	28	0	0	249	430	362	4		75	12	18.3	5.53	76	.342	.379	38	.279	1	-36	-37		-2.1
1872	Mut-n	1	0	1.000	3	1	1	0	1	15	18	15	0		2	1	12.0	3.60	94	.247	.267	61	.257	0	0	-0		0.0
1873	Ath-n	1	0	1.000	1	1	1	0	0	8	10	5	0		1	2	12.4	2.25	152	.303	.324	62	.273	0	1	1		0.1
1875	Phi-n	0	0	—	4	0	0	0	0	11^1	32	23	0		1	0	26.2	7.94	29	.464	.471	57	.257	1	-7	-7		-0.3
Total	4 n	14	15	.483	37	31	30	0	1	283^1	490	405	4		79	15	18.1	5.43	42	.342	.376	308	.285	2	-101	-97		-2.3
● **CRAIG McMURTRY**	McMurtry, Joe Craig b: 11/5/59, Troy, Tex. BR/TR, 6'5", 195 lbs. Deb: 4/10/83																											
1983	Atl-N	15	9	.625	36	35	6	3	0	224^2	204	86	13	1	88	105	11.7	3.08	126	.243	.315	6	.086	-4	14	19	3	1.9
1984	Atl-N	9	17	.346	37	30	0	0	0	183^1	184	100	16	1	102	99	14.1	4.32	89	.268	.363	6	.115	-1	-15	-9	4	-0.9
1985	Atl-N	0	3	.000	17	6	0	0	1	45	56	36	6	1	27	28	16.8	6.60	58	.306	.398	1	.071	-1	-15	-13	1	-0.9
1986	Atl-N	1	6	.143	37	5	0	0	0	79^2	82	46	7	2	43	50	14.3	4.74	84	.265	.359	2	.125	-0	-9	-6	0	-0.5
1988	Tex-A	3	3	.500	32	0	0	0	3	60	37	16	5	1	24	35	9.3	2.25	182	.180	.270	0	—	0	12	12	1	1.3
1989	Tex-A	0	0	—	19	0	0	0	0	23	29	21	3	2	13	14	17.2	7.43	53	.312	.407	0	—	0	-9	-9	0	-0.4
1990	Tex-A	0	3	.000	23	3	0	0	0	41^2	43	25	4	1	30	14	16.0	4.32	91	.281	.402	0	—	0	-2	-2	1	-0.1
1995	Hou-N	0	1	.000	11	0	0	0	0	10^1	15	11	0	1	9	4	21.8	7.84	49	.357	.481	0	.000	-0	-4	-5	0	-0.4
Total	8	28	42	.400	212	79	6	3	4	667^2	650	341	54	10	336	349	13.4	4.08	96	.259	.348	15	.098	-6	-29	-12	10	-0.0
● **EDGAR McNABB**	McNabb, Edgar J. "Texas" b: 10/24/1865, Coshocton, Ohio d: 2/28/1894, Pittsburgh, Pa. BR/TR, 5'11.5", 170 lbs. Deb: 5/12/1893																											
1893	Bal-N	8	7	.533	21	14	12	0	0	142	167	109	5	8	53	18	14.5	4.12	115	.284	.352	13	.194	-2	9	10	0	0.6
● **DAVE McNALLY**	McNally, David Arthur b: 10/31/42, Billings, Mont. BR/TL, 5'11", 190 lbs. Deb: 9/26/62																											
1962	Bal-A	1	0	1.000	1	1	1	1	0	9	2	0	0	0	3	4	5.0	0.00	—	.071	.161	0	.000	-0	4	4	0	0.5
1963	Bal-A	7	8	.467	29	20	2	0	1	125^2	133	67	9	5	55	78	13.8	4.58	76	.276	.356	2	.053	-2	-13	-16	-1	-2.1
1964	Bal-A	9	11	.450	30	23	5	3	0	159^1	157	72	15	9	51	88	12.3	3.67	97	.260	.327	7	.137	0	-1	-2	0	-0.2
1965	Bal-A	11	6	.647	35	29	6	2	0	198^2	163	69	15	6	73	116	11.0	2.85	122	.222	.298	6	.092	-3	13	14	0	0.9
1966	*Bal-A	13	6	.684	34	33	5	1	0	213	212	91	22	4	64	158	11.8	3.17	105	.256	.313	15	.195	3	6	4	0	0.6
1967	Bal-A	7	7	.500	24	22	3	1	0	119	134	65	13	2	39	70	13.2	4.54	69	.295	.354	6	.158	0	-17	-19	-2	-2.3
1968	Bal-A	22	10	.688	35	35	18	5	0	273	175	67	24	10	55	202	**7.9**	1.95	150	.182	.234	11	.128	4	31	30	-3	4.0
1969	*Bal-A★	20	7	.741	41	40	11	4	0	268^2	232	103	21	5	84	166	10.8	3.22	111	.234	.297	8	.085	-2	12	11	-4	0.4
1970	*Bal-A☆	**24**	9	.727	40	40	16	1	0	296	277	114	29	7	78	185	11.0	3.22	113	.250	.304	14	.133	4	16	14	-2	1.7
1971	*Bal-A	21	5	**.808**	30	30	11	1	0	224^1	188	75	24	5	58	91	10.1	2.89	116	.229	.284	12	.162	3	14	12	-0	1.6
1972	Bal-A★	13	17	.433	36	36	12	6	0	241	220	85	15	2	68	120	10.8	2.95	105	.247	.302	12	.152	2	3	4	1	0.7
1973	*Bal-A	17	17	.500	38	38	17	4	0	266	247	100	16	5	81	87	11.3	3.21	116	.251	.312	0	—	0	18	16	1	2.1
1974	*Bal-A	16	10	.615	39	37	13	4	1	259	260	112	19	8	81	111	12.1	3.58	97	.270	.331	0	—	0	1	-4	2	-0.1
1975	Mon-N	3	6	.333	12	12	0	0	0	77^1	88	50	8	4	36	36	14.9	5.24	73	.280	.362	4	.190	2	-14	-11	-1	-1.0
Total	14	184	119	.607	424	396	120	33	2	2730	2488	1070	230	72	826	1512	11.2	3.24	106	.245	.306	97	.133	10	75	56	-8	6.8
● **TIM McNAMARA**	McNamara, Timothy Augustine b: 11/20/1898, Millville, Mass. d: 11/5/94, N.Smithfield, R.I. BR/TR, 5'11", 170 lbs. Deb: 4/27/22																											
1922	Bos-N	3	4	.429	24	5	4	2	0	70^2	55	26	2	1	26	16	10.4	2.42	165	.225	.303	2	.118	-1	**13**	**13**	-0	1.0

YEAR	TM/L	W	L	PCT	G	GS	CG	SH	SV	IP	H	R	HR	HB	BB	SO	RAT	ERA	ERA+	OAV	OOB	BH	AVG	PB	PR	PR+	PD	TPI
1923	Bos-N	3	13	.188	32	16	3	0	0	139^1	185	95	8	5	29	32	14.1	4.91	81	.320	.357	7	.179	1	-14	-14	-2	-1.5
1924	Bos-N	8	12	.400	35	21	6	2	0	179	242	119	9	3	31	35	13.9	5.18	74	.334	.364	6	.140	-1	-26	-27	1	-2.6
1925	Bos-N	0	0	—	1	0	0	0	0	0^2	6	6	0	0	2	1	108.0	81.00	5	.857	.889	0	—	0	-6	-6	0	-0.3
1926	NY-N	0	0	—	6	0	0	0	0	6	7	6	0	0	4	4	16.5	9.00	42	.304	.407	0	—	0	-3	-4	0	-0.2
Total	5	14	29	.326	98	42	13	4	0	395^2	495	252	19	9	92	88	13.6	4.78	82	.314	.355	15	.152	-1	-36	-39	-2	-3.6
● GORDON McNAUGHTON McNaughton, Gordon Joseph b: 7/31/10, Chicago, Ill. d: 8/6/42, Chicago, Ill. BR/TR, 6'1", 190 lbs. Deb: 8/13/32																												
1932	Bos-A	0	1	.000	6	2	0	0	0	21	21	15	1	3	22	6	19.7	6.43	70	.259	.434	2	.250	0	-5	-5	1	-0.1
● HARRY McNEAL McNeal, John Harley b: 8/13/1878, Iberia, Ohio d: 1/11/45, Cleveland, Ohio BL/TR, 6'2", 175 lbs. Deb: 8/5/01																												
1901	Cle-A	5	5	.500	12	10	9	0	0	85^1	120	68	4	8	30	15	16.7	4.43	80	.328	.391	6	.162	-2	-7	-9	-2	-1.1
● BRIAN McNICHOL McNichol, Brian David b: 5/20/74, Fairfax, Va. BL/TL, 6'5", 225 lbs. Deb: 9/7/99																												
1999	Chi-N	0	2	.000	4	2	0	0	0	10^2	15	8	4	1	7	12	19.4	6.75	67	.333	.434	0	.000	-0	-3	-3	-0	-0.4
● ED McNICHOL McNichol, Edwin Briggs b: 1/10/1879, Martins Ferry, O. d: 11/1/52, Salineville, O. BR/TR, 5'5", 170 lbs. Deb: 7/9/04																												
1904	Bos-N	2	12	.143	17	15	12	1	0	122	120	70	3	5	74	39	14.7	4.28	64	.262	.371	4	.093	-4	-21	-20	-2	-2.6
● FRANK McPARTLIN McPartlin, Frank b: 2/16/1872, Hoosick Falls, N.Y d: 11/13/43, New York, N.Y. TR, 6', 180 lbs. Deb: 8/22/1899																												
1899	NY-N	0	0	—	1	0	0	0	0	4	4	4	0	2	3	2	20.3	4.50	83	.267	.450	0	.000	-0	-0	-0	0	0.0
● JOHN McPHERSON McPherson, John Jacob b: 3/9/1869, Easton, Pa. d: 9/30/41, Easton, Pa. TR, Deb: 7/12/01																												
1901	Phi-A	0	1	.000	1	1	0	0	0	4	7	5	0	1	4	0	27.0	11.25	34	.368	.500	0	.000	-0	-3	-3	0	-0.5
1904	Phi-N	1	12	.077	15	12	11	1	0	128	130	82	1	6	46	32	12.8	3.66	73	.264	.334	3	.064	-4	-13	-14	0	-1.7
Total	2	1	13	.071	16	13	11	1	0	132	137	87	1	7	50	32	13.2	3.89	70	.268	.341	3	.063	-4	-16	-18	1	-2.2
● HERB McQUAID McQuaid, Herbert George b: 3/29/1899, San Francisco, Cal d: 4/4/66, Richmond, Cal. BR/TR, 6'2", 185 lbs. Deb: 6/22/23																												
1923	Cin-N	1	0	1.000	12	1	0	0	0	34^1	31	11	0	3	10	9	11.5	2.36	164	.238	.308	0	.000	-1	6	6	1	0.3
1926	NY-A	1	0	1.000	17	1	0	0	0	38^1	48	34	5	2	13	6	14.8	6.10	63	.329	.391	0	.000	-1	-9	-10	0	-0.5
Total	2	2	0	1.000	29	2	0	0	0	72^2	79	45	5	5	23	15	13.3	4.33	89	.286	.352	0	.000	-2	-3	-4	1	-0.2
● MIKE McQUEEN McQueen, Michael Robert b: 8/30/50, Oklahoma City, Okla BL/TL, 5'11", 190 lbs. Deb: 10/2/69																												
1969	Atl-N	0	0	—	1	1	0	0	0	3	2	1	0	0	3	3	15.0	3.00	120	.182	.357	0	—	0	0	0	-0	0.0
1970	Atl-N	1	5	.167	22	8	1	0	1	66	67	48	10	1	31	54	13.5	5.59	77	.266	.349	6	.300	2	-11	-9	-1	-0.6
1971	Atl-N	4	1	.800	17	3	0	0	1	56	47	24	7	2	23	38	11.6	3.54	105	.228	.312	4	.211	0	-0	1	-1	0.0
1972	Atl-N	0	5	.000	23	7	1	0	1	78^1	79	45	11	1	44	40	14.2	4.60	83	.260	.355	2	.087	-2	-10	-6	-1	-0.7
1974	Cin-N	0	0	—	10	0	0	0	0	15	17	10	4	0	11	5	16.8	5.40	65	.288	.400	1	1.000	0	-3	-3	-1	-0.2
Total	5	5	11	.313	73	19	2	0	3	218^1	212	128	32	4	112	140	13.5	4.66	84	.255	.346	13	.206	1	-24	-17	-4	-1.5
● GEORGE McQUILLAN McQuillan, George Watt b: 5/1/1885, Brooklyn, N.Y. d: 3/30/40, Columbus, Ohio BR/TR, 5'11.5", 175 lbs. Deb: 5/8/07																												
1907	Phi-N	4	0	1.000	6	5	5	3	0	41	21	3	0	1	11	28	7.2	0.66	368	.158	.228	4	.364	3	8	8	-2	1.1
1908	Phi-N	23	17	.575	48	42	32	7	2	359^2	263	88	1	6	91	114	9.0	1.53	159	.207	.263	18	.151	-1	33	35	-3	3.8
1909	Phi-N	13	16	.448	41	28	16	4	2	247^2	202	87	5	1	54	96	9.3	2.14	121	.226	.271	9	.118	-3	12	12	-2	0.8
1910	Phi-N	9	6	.600	24	17	13	3	1	152^1	109	42	2	3	50	71	9.6	**1.60**	196	.204	.276	7	.149	-1	24	25	-0	2.4
1911	Cin-N	2	6	.250	19	5	2	0	0	77	92	60	2	4	31	28	14.8	4.68	71	.308	.380	2	.091	-1	-11	-12	-1	-1.3
1913	Pit-N	8	6	.571	25	16	7	0	1	141^2	144	60	1	1	35	59	11.4	3.43	88	.273	.319	4	.103	-1	-4	-7	-1	-0.8
1914	Pit-N	13	17	.433	45	28	15	0	4	259^1	248	100	8	8	60	96	11.0	2.98	89	.261	.310	5	.068	-4	-6	-10	0	-1.6
1915	Pit-N	8	10	.444	30	20	9	0	1	149	160	64	1	2	39	56	12.1	2.84	96	.284	.332	4	.091	-3	-1	-2	0	-0.5
	Phi-N	4	3	.571	9	8	5	0	0	63^2	60	31	1	1	11	13	10.2	2.12	129	.247	.282	1	.043	-2	4	4	-1	0.2
	Yr	12	13	.480	39	28	14	0	1	212^2	220	95	2	3	50	69	11.6	2.62	104	.273	.317	5	.075	-5	3	3	-1	-0.3
1916	Phi-N	1	7	.125	21	3	1	0	2	62	58	33	2	3	15	22	11.0	2.76	96	.251	.305	1	.091	-1	-1	-1	-0	-0.2
1918	Cle-A	0	1	.000	5	1	0	0	1	23	25	10	0	0	4	7	11.3	2.35	128	.284	.315	0	.000	-0	1	2	0	0.1
Total	10	85	89	.489	273	173	105	17	14	1576^1	1382	578	23	30	401	590	10.4	2.38	114	.241	.294	55	.117	-14	62	59	-9	4.0
● HUGH McQUILLAN McQuillan, Hugh A. "Handsome Hugh" b: 9/15/1897, New York, N.Y. d: 8/26/47, New York, N.Y. BR/TR, 6', 170 lbs. Deb: 7/26/18																												
1918	Bos-N	1	0	1.000	1	1	1	0	0	9	7	3	0	0	5	1	12.0	3.00	90	.219	.324	1	.250	0	-0	-0	0	0.0
1919	Bos-N	2	3	.400	16	7	2	0	1	60	66	34	3	1	14	13	12.2	3.45	83	.288	.332	4	.222	0	-4	-4	-1	-0.4
1920	Bos-N	11	15	.423	38	26	17	1	5	225^2	230	110	3	2	70	53	12.0	3.55	86	.273	.330	19	.257	6	-10	-13	2	-0.6
1921	Bos-N	13	17	.433	45	31	13	2	5	250	284	137	9	2	90	94	13.5	4.00	91	.291	.352	18	.205	1	-6	-10	0	-0.9
1922	Bos-N	5	10	.333	28	17	7	0	0	136	154	70	3	1	56	33	14.0	4.24	94	.299	.369	7	.167	-1	-2	-4	1	-0.4
	*NY-N	6	5	.545	15	13	5	0	1	94^1	111	48	7	0	34	24	13.8	3.82	105	.301	.360	7	.189	-1	3	2	-1	0.0
	Yr	11	15	.423	43	30	12	0	1	230^1	265	118	10	1	90	57	13.9	4.06	98	.300	.365	14	.177	-2	1	-2	-0	-0.4
1923	*NY-N	15	14	.517	38	32	15	5	0	229^2	224	96	12	5	66	75	11.6	3.41	112	.259	.315	14	.171	-2	15	11	-1	0.9
1924	*NY-N	14	8	.636	27	23	14	1	3	184	179	68	8	2	43	49	11.0	2.69	136	.259	.304	14	.209	-1	24	21	-2	2.1
1925	NY-N	2	3	.400	14	11	2	0	1	70	95	49	9	1	23	23	15.3	6.04	67	.343	.395	3	.143	-1	-14	-16	1	-1.0
1926	NY-N	11	10	.524	33	22	12	1	0	167	171	72	7	1	42	47	11.5	3.72	101	.271	.318	7	.132	-3	2	1	2	0.0
1927	NY-N	5	4	.556	11	9	5	0	0	58	73	32	4	1	22	17	14.9	4.50	86	.309	.371	4	.211	1	-4	-4	0	-0.5
	Bos-N	3	5	.375	13	12	2	0	0	78	109	65	2	2	24	17	15.6	5.54	67	.332	.381	5	.227	0	-14	-17	0	-1.4
	Yr	8	9	.471	24	21	7	0	0	136	182	97	6	3	46	34	15.3	5.10	74	.323	.377	9	.220	1	-18	-21	0	-1.9
Total	10	88	94	.484	279	204	95	10	16	1561^2	1703	784	67	18	489	446	12.7	3.83	95	.284	.340	103	.195	0	-10	-33	1	-2.2
● NORM McRAE McRae, Norman b: 9/26/47, Elizabeth, N.J. BR/TR, 6'1", 195 lbs. Deb: 9/13/69																												
1969	Det-A	0	0	—	3	0	0	0	0	3	2	2	0	0	1	3	9.0	6.00	62	.200	.273	0	—	0	-1	-1	-0	0.0
1970	Det-A	0	0	—	19	0	0	0	0	31^1	26	13	1	1	25	16	14.9	2.87	130	.226	.369	0	.000	-0	3	3	1	0.2
Total	2	0	0	—	22	0	0	0	0	34^1	28	15	1	1	26	19	14.4	3.15	119	.224	.362	0	.000	-0	2	2	0	0.2
● TRICK McSORLEY McSorley, John Bernard b: 12/6/1852, St.Louis, Mo. d: 2/9/36, St.Louis, Mo. BR/TR, 5'4", 142 lbs. Deb: 5/6/1875 ◆																												
1884	Tol-a	0	0	—	1	0	0	0	0	2	5	2	0	0	0	1	22.5	4.50	76	.556	.556	17	.250	0	-0	-0	-0	0.0
● BILL McTIGUE McTigue, William Patrick "Rebel" b: 1/3/1891, Nashville, Tenn. d: 5/8/20, Nashville, Tenn. BL/TL, 6'1.5", 175 lbs. Deb: 5/2/11 ◆																												
1911	Bos-N	0	5	.000	14	8	0	0	0	37	37	32	3	2	49	23	21.4	7.05	54	.280	.481	1	.083	-1	-15	-12	-1	-1.5
1912	Bos-N	2	0	1.000	10	1	1	0	0	34^2	39	26	0	0	18	17	14.8	5.45	66	.289	.373	1	.077	-1	-8	-7	1	-0.4
1916	Det-A	0	0	—	3	0	0	0	0	5^1	5	6	0	0	5	1	16.9	5.06	57	.278	.435	0	.000	-0	-1	-1	0	0.0
Total	3	2	5	.286	27	9	1	0	0	77	81	64	3	2	72	41	18.1	6.19	59	.284	.432	2	.077	-2	-24	-20	0	-1.9
● CAL McVEY McVey, Calvin Alexander b: 8/30/1850, Montrose, Iowa d: 8/20/26, San Francisco, Cal BR/TR, 5'9", 170 lbs. Deb: 5/5/1871 M◆																												
1875	Bos-n	1	0	1.000	3	2	0	0	1	11	15	9	0		1	1	13.1	4.91	44	.294	.308	138	.355	2	-3	-4		-0.3
1876	Chi-N	5	2	.714	11	6	5	0	2	59^1	57	22	0		2	9	8.9	1.52	161	.233	.241	107	.345	3	5	6	0	0.7
1877	Chi-N	4	8	.333	17	10	6	0	**2**	92	129	87	2		11	20	13.7	4.50	66	.301	.319	98	.368	6	-17	-15	-1	-1.3
1879	Cin-N	0	2	.000	3	1	1	0	0	14	34	23	1		2	7	23.1	8.36	28	.453	.468	105	.297	1	-9	-10	0	-1.0
Total	3	9	12	.429	31	17	12	0	4	165^1	220	132	3		15	36	12.8	3.76	73	.294	.309	393	.327	10	-21	-18	-1	-1.6
● DOUG McWEENY McWeeny, Douglas Lawrence "Buzz" b: 8/17/1896, Chicago, Ill. d: 1/1/53, Melrose Park, Ill. BR/TR, 6'2", 190 lbs. Deb: 4/24/21																												
1921	Chi-A	3	6	.333	27	8	3	0	2	97^2	127	76	7	0	45	46	15.8	6.08	70	.325	.394	1	.032	-4	-20	-20	-1	-2.0
1922	Chi-A	0	1	.000	4	1	0	0	0	10^2	13	8	0	0	7	5	16.9	5.91	69	.325	.426	0	.000	0	-2	-2	-0	-0.2
1924	Chi-A	1	3	.250	13	5	2	0	0	43^1	47	25	2	2	17	18	13.7	4.57	90	.294	.369	0	.000	-0	-2	-2	3	0.1
1926	Bro-N	11	13	.458	42	24	10	1	1	216^1	213	97	6	8	84	96	12.7	3.04	126	.258	.333	7	.109	-4	19	19	-1	1.4
1927	Bro-N	4	8	.333	34	22	6	0	1	164^1	167	80	13	8	70	73	13.4	3.56	111	.266	.347	2	.043	-4	7	7	1	0.2
1928	Bro-N	14	14	.500	42	32	12	**4**	1	244	218	108	11	5	114	79	12.4	3.17	125	.235	.322	14	.173	-1	22	22	3	2.5
1929	Bro-N	4	10	.286	36	22	4	0	1	146	167	119	17	3	93	59	16.2	6.10	76	.288	.390	5	.104	-2	-22	-25	-2	-2.3
1930	Cin-N	0	2	.000	8	2	0	0	0	25^2	28	23	0	0	20	10	16.8	7.36	66	.283	.403	1	.143	-0	-7	-7	0	-0.5
Total	8	37	57	.394	206	116	37	5	6	948	980	536	56	26	450	386	13.8	4.17	98	.269	.353	30	.104	-16	-5	-7	2	-0.8

YEAR	TM/L	W	L	PCT	G	GS	CG	SH	SV	IP	H	R	HR	HB	BB	SO	RAT	ERA	ERA+	OAV	OOB	BH	AVG	PB	PR	PR+	PD	TPI
● **LARRY McWILLIAMS**	McWilliams, Larry Dean b: 2/10/54, Wichita, Kan. BL/TL, 6'5", 180 lbs. Deb: 7/17/78																											
1978	Atl-N	9	3	.750	15	15	3	1	0	99^1	84	38	11	2	35	42	11.0	2.81	144	.224	.294	2	.063	-2	9	12	1	1.4
1979	Atl-N	3	2	.600	13	13	1	0	0	66^1	69	41	4	4	22	32	12.9	5.56	73	.272	.339	5	.208	1	-13	-10	1	-0.5
1980	Atl-N	9	14	.391	30	30	4	1	0	163^2	188	97	27	7	39	77	12.9	4.95	76	.285	.332	8	.157	-0	-24	-21	-0	-2.7
1981	Atl-N	2	1	.667	6	5	2	1	0	37^2	31	13	2	0	8	23	9.3	3.11	115	.230	.273	1	.100	-0	2	2	1	0.2
1982	Atl-N	2	3	.400	27	2	0	0	0	37^2	52	30	3	2	20	24	17.7	6.21	60	.327	.409	1	.167	0	-11	-10	2	-1.0
	Pit-N	6	5	.545	19	18	2	2	1	121^2	106	49	9	4	24	94	9.9	3.11	120	.232	.276	6	.188	-0	7	8	2	0.9
	Yr	8	8	.500	46	20	2	2	1	159^1	158	79	12	6	44	118	11.7	3.84	97	.256	.312	7	.184	-0	-4	-2	4	-0.1
1983	Pit-N	15	8	.652	35	35	8	4	0	238	205	99	19	3	87	199	11.2	3.25	114	.230	.300	9	.114	-3	10	12	1	0.9
1984	Pit-N	12	11	.522	34	32	7	2	1	227^1	226	86	18	2	78	149	12.1	2.93	123	.263	.326	9	.122	-3	17	17	0	1.4
1985	Pit-N	7	9	.438	30	19	2	0	0	126^1	139	70	9	7	62	52	14.8	4.70	76	.283	.371	5	.125	-1	-15	-16	-0	-1.9
1986	Pit-N	3	11	.214	49	15	0	0	0	122^1	129	75	16	7	49	80	13.6	5.15	75	.268	.345	4	.138	0	-19	-17	-0	-1.8
1987	Atl-N	0	1	.000	9	2	0	0	0	20^1	25	15	2	2	7	13	15.0	5.75	76	.301	.370	1	.200	0	-4	-3	0	-0.1
1988	StL-N	6	9	.400	42	17	2	1	1	136	130	64	10	4	45	70	11.8	3.90	89	.253	.319	6	.162	1	-7	-6	-0	-0.6
1989	Phi-N	2	11	.154	40	16	2	1	0	120^2	123	67	3	4	49	54	13.1	4.10	87	.265	.340	3	.111	-1	-8	-7	1	-0.7
	KC-A	2	2	.500	8	5	1	0	0	32^2	31	15	2	3	8	24	11.6	4.13	93	.254	.316	0	—	0	-1	-1	-0	-0.1
1990	KC-A	0	0	—	13	0	0	0	0	8^1	10	9	2	1	9	7	21.6	9.72	40	.313	.476	0	—	0	-5	-6	0	-0.2
Total	13	78	90	.464	370	224	34	13	3	1558^1	1548	768	137	52	542	940	12.4	3.99	93	.259	.326	60	.135	-8	-65	-46	8	-4.8
● **RUSTY MEACHAM**	Meacham, Russell Loren b: 1/27/68, Stuart, Fla. BR/TR, 6'2", 175 lbs. Deb: 6/29/91																											
1991	Det-A	2	1	.667	10	4	0	0	0	27^2	35	17	4	0	11	14	15.0	5.20	80	.315	.377	0	—	0	-3	-3	0	-0.3
1992	KC-A	10	4	.714	64	0	0	0	2	101^2	88	39	5	1	21	64	9.7	2.74	148	.233	.275	0	—	0	14	14	2	2.1
1993	KC-A	2	2	.500	15	0	0	0	0	21	31	15	2	3	5	13	16.7	5.57	82	.326	.379	0	—	0	-3	-2	0	-0.3
1994	KC-A	3	3	.500	36	0	0	0	4	50^2	51	23	7	2	12	36	11.5	3.73	134	.263	.313	0	—	0	6	7	0	0.8
1995	KC-A	4	3	.571	49	0	0	0	2	59^2	72	36	6	1	19	30	13.9	4.98	96	.304	.358	0	—	0	-2	-1	0	-0.1
1996	Sea-A	1	1	.500	15	5	0	0	1	42^1	57	28	9	4	13	25	15.7	5.74	86	.328	.387	0	—	0	-3	-4	-1	-0.2
2000	Hou-N	0	0	—	5	0	0	0	0	4^2	8	6	3	0	2	3	19.3	11.57	42	.381	.435	0	—	0	-4	-3	0	-0.1
Total	7	22	14	.611	194	9	0	0	9	307^2	342	164	36	11	83	185	12.8	4.30	106	.283	.334	0	—	0	5	8	3	1.9
● **JOHNNY MEADOR**	Meador, John Davis b: 12/4/1892, Madison, N.C. d: 4/11/70, Winston-Salem, N.C BR/TR, 5'10.5", 165 lbs. Deb: 4/24/20																											
1920	Pit-N	0	2	.000	12	2	0	0	0	36^1	48	18	1	0	7	5	13.6	4.21	76	.340	.372	1	.167	-0	-4	-4	1	-0.2
● **LEE MEADOWS**	Meadows, Henry Lee "Specs" b: 7/12/1894, Oxford, N.C. d: 1/29/63, Daytona Beach, Fla BL/TR (BB 1920-21, 26, 28), 6', 190 lbs. Deb: 4/19/15																											
1915	StL-N	13	11	.542	39	26	14	1	0	244	232	112	5	5	88	104	12.0	2.99	93	.259	.329	8	.096	-4	-6	-5	-3	-1.2
1916	StL-N	12	23	.343	**51**	36	11	1	2	289	261	117	3	14	119	120	12.3	2.58	102	.247	.332	15	.158	-1	1	2	1	0.2
1917	StL-N	15	9	.625	43	37	18	4	2	265^2	253	99	5	4	90	100	11.8	3.08	87	.262	.328	9	.101	-6	-11	-12	-3	-2.0
1918	StL-N	8	14	.364	30	23	12	0	1	165^1	176	91	1	10	56	49	13.2	3.59	75	.280	.348	7	.127	-2	-15	-17	-2	-2.5
1919	StL-N	4	10	.286	22	12	3	1	0	92	100	44	3	2	30	28	12.9	3.03	92	.292	.352	3	.103	-2	-1	-3	3	-0.3
	Phi-N	8	10	.444	18	17	15	3	0	158^1	128	55	2	7	49	88	10.5	2.33	138	.229	.300	6	.118	-3	10	14	-1	1.2
	Yr	12	20	.375	40	29	18	4	0	250^1	228	99	5	9	79	116	11.4	2.59	118	.253	.320	9	.112	-5	9	13	2	0.9
1920	Phi-N	16	14	.533	35	33	19	3	0	247	249	104	5	8	90	95	12.6	2.84	120	.270	.341	14	.171	-3	8	15	0	1.5
1921	Phi-N	11	16	.407	28	27	15	2	0	194^1	226	118	10	4	62	52	13.5	4.31	98	.288	.343	13	.210	2	-11	-1	4	0.4
1922	Phi-N	12	18	.400	33	33	19	2	0	237	264	127	8	11	71	62	13.1	4.03	116	.288	.346	27	.314	3	2	15	3	2.4
1923	Phi-N	1	3	.250	8	5	0	0	1	19^2	40	32	0	0	15	10	25.2	13.27	35	.430	.509	4	.400	2	-20	-16	0	-2.5
	Pit-N	16	10	.615	31	25	17	1	0	227	250	97	3	1	44	66	11.7	3.01	133	.284	.319	22	.250	3	25	25	2	3.1
	Yr	17	13	.567	39	30	17	1	1	246^2	290	129	3	1	59	76	12.8	3.83	106	.298	.339	26	.265	5	5	6	2	0.6
1924	Pit-N	13	12	.520	36	30	15	3	0	229^1	240	99	7	4	51	61	11.6	3.26	118	.278	.322	16	.195	-1	16	15	-1	1.2
1925	*Pit-N	19	10	.655	35	31	20	1	1	255^1	272	128	11	8	67	87	12.2	3.67	122	.273	.323	17	.175	-1	17	22	1	2.1
1926	Pit-N	**20**	9	.690	36	31	15	1	0	226^2	254	125	10	4	52	54	12.3	3.97	99	.287	.329	20	.227	-1	-4	-1	3	0.1
1927	*Pit-N	19	10	.655	40	38	**25**	2	0	299^1	315	131	11	8	66	84	11.7	3.40	121	.273	.317	18	.157	-5	17	23	-1	1.4
1928	Pit-N	1	1	.500	4	2	1	0	0	10	18	11	0	0	5	3	20.7	8.10	50	.383	.442	2	.500	1	-5	-4	-0	-0.7
1929	Pit-N	0	0	—	1	0	0	0	0	0^2	2	1	0	0	1	0	40.5	13.50	35	.500	.600	0	.000	-0	-1	-1	-0	0.0
Total	15	188	180	.511	490	406	219	25	7	3160^2	3280	1491	84	90	956	1063	12.3	3.37	106	.274	.332	201	.180	-19	22	68	6	4.4
● **BRIAN MEADOWS**	Meadows, Matthew Brian b: 11/21/75, Montgomery, Ala. BR/TR, 6'4", 210 lbs. Deb: 4/4/98																											
1998	Fla-N	11	13	.458	31	31	1	0	0	174^1	222	106	20	3	46	88	14.0	5.21	78	.315	.359	7	.130	-1	-19	-23	-1	-2.8
1999	Fla-N	11	15	.423	31	31	0	0	0	178^1	214	117	31	5	57	72	13.9	5.60	78	.302	.358	7	.140	0	-21	-26	-1	-3.1
2000	SD-N	7	8	.467	22	22	0	0	0	124^2	150	80	24	8	50	53	15.0	5.34	82	.301	.374	6	.150	-1	-10	-14	-0	-1.5
	KC-A	6	2	.750	11	10	2	0	0	71^2	84	39	8	0	14	26	12.3	4.77	105	.293	.326	0	—	0	1	2	-1	0.1
Total	3	35	38	.479	95	94	3	0	0	549	670	342	83	16	167	239	14.0	5.31	82	.305	.358	20	.139	-1	-48	-61	-2	-7.3
● **RUFUS MEADOWS**	Meadows, Rufus Rivers b: 8/25/07, Chase City, Va. d: 5/10/70, Wichita, Kan. BL/TL, 5'11", 175 lbs. Deb: 4/23/26																											
1926	Cin-N	0	0	—	1	0	0	0	0	0^1	0	0	0	0	0	0	0.0	0.00	—	.000	.000	0	.000	-0	0	0	0	0.0
● **DAVE MEADS**	Meads, David Donald b: 1/7/64, Montclair, N.J. BL/TL, 6', 175 lbs. Deb: 4/13/87																											
1987	Hou-N	5	3	.625	45	0	0	0	0	48^2	60	31	8	1	16	32	14.2	5.55	71	.321	.377	1	.333	1	-8	-9	-1	-1.3
1988	Hou-N	3	1	.750	22	2	0	0	0	39^2	37	20	4	0	14	27	11.6	3.18	105	.240	.304	1	.250	1	1	1	-0	0.2
Total	2	8	4	.667	67	2	0	0	0	88^1	97	51	12	1	30	59	13.0	4.48	82	.284	.344	2	.286	1	-7	-8	-1	-1.1
● **GEORGE MEAKIM**	Meakim, George Clinton b: 7/11/1865, Brooklyn, N.Y. d: 2/17/23, Queens, N.Y. BR/TR, 5'7.5", 154 lbs. Deb: 5/2/1890																											
1890	*Lou-a	12	7	.632	28	21	16	3	1	192	173	100	4	5	63	123	11.3	2.91	132	.233	.298	11	.153	-2	21	20	-1	1.4
1891	Phi-a	1	4	.200	6	6	4	0	0	35	51	45	1	1	22	13	19.0	6.94	55	.329	.416	3	.200	0	-13	-12	2	-1.0
1892	Chi-N	0	1	.000	1	1	1	0	0	9	18	14	0	0	2	0	20.0	11.00	30	.400	.426	2	.400	0	-8	-8	-0	-0.5
	Cin-N	1	1	.500	3	3	1	0	0	13^2	19	18	1	2	9	4	19.8	8.56	38	.317	.423	0	.000	-1	-8	-8	0	-0.9
	Yr	1	2	.333	4	4	2	0	0	22^2	37	32	1	2	11	4	19.9	9.53	35	.352	.424	2	.200	-0	-16	-16	-0	-1.4
1895	Lou-N	1	0	1.000	1	1	1	0	0	7	7	2	0	0	4	2	14.1	2.57	180	.259	.355	1	.333	0	2	2	0	0.2
Total	4	15	13	.536	39	32	23	3	1	256^2	268	179	6	8	100	142	13.2	4.03	95	.260	.331	17	.170	-2	-6	-6	1	-0.8
● **GIL MECHE**	Meche, Gilbert Allen b: 9/8/78, Lafayette, La. BR/TR, 6'3", 180 lbs. Deb: 7/6/99																											
1999	Sea-A	8	4	.667	16	15	0	0	0	85^2	73	48	9	2	57	47	13.9	4.73	100	.237	.360	0	—	0	1	0	-0	0.0
2000	Sea-A	4	4	.500	15	15	1	1	0	85^2	75	37	7	1	40	60	12.2	3.78	127	.240	.328	0	—	0	11	10	-1	0.7
Total	2	12	8	.600	31	30	1	1	0	171^1	148	85	16	3	97	107	13.0	4.25	112	.238	.344	0	—	0	12	10	-1	0.7
● **JIM MECIR**	Mecir, James Jason b: 5/16/70, Bayside, N.Y. BB/TR, 6'1", 195 lbs. Deb: 9/4/95																											
1995	Sea-A	0	0	—	2	0	0	0	0	4^2	5	1	0	0	2	3	13.5	0.00	—	.263	.333	0	—	0	2	2	-0	0.1
1996	NY-A	1	1	.500	26	0	0	0	0	40^1	42	24	6	0	23	38	14.5	5.13	96	.275	.369	0	—	0	-1	-1	2	0.1
1997	NY-A	0	4	.000	25	0	0	0	0	33^2	36	23	5	2	10	25	12.8	5.88	76	.279	.340	0	—	0	-5	-5	-0	-0.6
1998	TB-A	7	2	.778	68	0	0	0	0	84	68	30	6	3	33	77	11.1	3.11	154	.225	.308	0	.000	-0	14	15	2	1.6
1999	TB-A	0	1	.000	17	0	0	0	0	20^2	15	7	0	1	14	15	13.1	2.61	191	.203	.337	0	—	0	5	5	0	0.3
2000	TB-A	7	2	.778	38	0	0	0	1	49^2	35	17	2	1	22	33	10.5	3.08	161	.201	.294	0	—	0	10	10	-1	1.6
	*Oak-A	3	1	.750	25	0	0	0	4	35^1	35	14	2	1	14	37	12.7	2.80	170	.255	.329	0	—	0	8	8	-0	0.9
	Yr	10	3	.769	63	0	0	0	5	85	70	31	4	2	36	70	11.4	2.96	165	.225	.309	0	—	0	18	18	-1	2.5
Total	6	18	11	.621	201	0	0	0	5	268^1	236	116	21	8	118	228	12.1	3.62	133	.239	.325	0	.000	-0	35	35	3	4.0
● **DOC MEDICH**	Medich, George Francis b: 12/9/48, Aliquippa, Pa. BR/TR, 6'5", 227 lbs. Deb: 9/5/72																											
1972	NY-A	0	0	—	1	1	0	0	0	0	2	0	0	2	—	—	∞	—	1.000	1.000	96	—	0	-2	-2	0	-0.2	
1973	NY-A	14	9	.609	34	32	11	3	0	235	217	84	20	3	74	145	11.3	2.95	124	.241	.300	0	—	0	23	20	-2	1.6
1974	NY-A	19	15	.559	38	38	17	4	0	279^2	275	122	24	8	91	154	12.0	3.60	98	.259	.323	0	—	0	1	-2	-1	-0.4
1975	NY-A	16	16	.500	38	37	15	2	0	272^1	271	115	25	1	72	132	11.4	3.50	105	.264	.313	0	—	0	9	6	-3	0.4
1976	Pit-N	8	11	.421	29	26	3	0	0	179	193	80	10	2	48	86	12.2	3.52	99	.281	.330	5	.096	-2	-0	-1	1	-0.1
1977	Oak-A	10	6	.625	26	25	1	0	0	147^2	155	89	19	3	49	74	12.6	4.69	86	.265	.325	0	—	0	-10	-11	-1	-1.2

YEAR	TM/L	W	L	PCT	G	GS	CG	SH	SV	IP	H	R	HR	HB	BB	SO	RAT	ERA	ERA+	OAV	OOB	BH	AVG	PB	PR	PR+	PD	TPI
	Sea-A	2	0	1.000	3	3	1	0	0	22^1	26	9	1	2	4	3	12.9	3.63	114	.286	.330	0	—	0	1	1	-1	0.0
	Yr	12	6	.667	29	28	2	0	0	170	181	98	20	5	53	77	12.7	4.55	89	.268	.326	0	—	0	-9	-10	-2	-1.2
	NY-N	0	1	.000	1	1	0	0	0	7	6	3	0	0	1	3	9.0	3.86	97	.261	.292	0	.000	-0	0	-0	-0	-0.1
1978	Tex-A	9	8	.529	28	22	6	2	2	171	166	78	10	3	52	71	11.6	3.74	101	.255	.313	0	—	0	1	0	1	0.1
1979	Tex-A	10	7	.588	29	19	4	1	0	149	156	78	9	4	49	58	12.6	4.17	100	.269	.330	0	—	0	1	-0	1	0.1
1980	Tex-A	14	11	.560	34	32	6	0	0	204^1	230	104	13	3	56	91	12.7	3.92	100	.285	.334	0	—	0	3	-0	-1	-0.2
1981	Tex-A	10	6	.625	20	20	4	**4**	0	143^1	136	51	8	2	33	65	10.7	3.08	113	.252	.297	0	—	0	9	7	1	0.8
1982	Tex-A	7	11	.389	21	21	2	0	0	122^2	146	73	8	3	61	37	15.4	5.06	77	.307	.390	0	—	0	-13	-17	0	-2.1
	*Mil-A	5	4	.556	10	10	1	0	0	63	57	37	4	1	32	36	12.9	5.00	76	.242	.335	0	—	0	-6	-9	-1	-1.2
	Yr	12	15	.444	31	31	3	0	0	185^2	203	110	12	4	93	73	14.5	5.04	76	.286	.371	0	—	0	-20	-26	-0	-3.3
Total	11	124	105	.541	312	287	71	16	2	1996^1	2036	925	151	35	624	955	12.1	3.78	99	.266	.324	5	.093	-2	15	-9	-5	-2.5

● RAFAEL MEDINA Medina, Rafael Eduardo b: 2/15/75, Panama City, Panama BR/TR, 6'3", 194 lbs. Deb: 4/2/98

YEAR	TM/L	W	L	PCT	G	GS	CG	SH	SV	IP	H	R	HR	HB	BB	SO	RAT	ERA	ERA+	OAV	OOB	BH	AVG	PB	PR	PR+	PD	TPI
1998	Fla-N	2	6	.250	12	12	0	0	0	67^1	76	50	8	3	52	49	17.5	6.01	67	.289	.412	1	.053	-2	-13	-15	-1	-1.7
1999	Fla-N	1	1	.500	20	0	0	0	0	23^1	20	15	3	1	20	16	15.8	5.79	75	.227	.376	0	—	0	-3	-4	-0	-0.3
Total	2	3	7	.300	32	12	0	0	0	90^2	96	65	11	4	72	65	17.1	5.96	69	.274	.403	1	.053	-2	-16	-19	-1	-2.0

● IRV MEDLINGER Medlinger, Irving John b: 6/18/27, Chicago, Ill. d: 9/3/75, Wheeling, Ill. BL/TL, 5'11", 185 lbs. Deb: 4/20/49

YEAR	TM/L	W	L	PCT	G	GS	CG	SH	SV	IP	H	R	HR	HB	BB	SO	RAT	ERA	ERA+	OAV	OOB	BH	AVG	PB	PR	PR+	PD	TPI
1949	StL-A	0	0	—	3	0	0	0	0	4	11	13	1	0	3	4	31.5	27.00	17	.478	.538	0	—	0	-10	-9	-0	-0.4
1951	StL-A	0	0	—	6	0	0	0	0	9^2	10	10	1	0	12	5	20.5	8.38	52	.270	.449	0	—	0	-5	-4	-0	-0.2
Total	2	0	0	—	9	0	0	0	0	13^2	21	23	2	0	15	9	23.7	13.83	32	.350	.480	0	—	0	-15	-13	-0	-0.6

● SCOTT MEDVIN Medvin, Scott Howard b: 9/16/61, North Olmsted, O. BR/TR, 6'1", 195 lbs. Deb: 5/11/88

YEAR	TM/L	W	L	PCT	G	GS	CG	SH	SV	IP	H	R	HR	HB	BB	SO	RAT	ERA	ERA+	OAV	OOB	BH	AVG	PB	PR	PR+	PD	TPI
1988	Pit-N	3	0	1.000	17	0	0	0	0	27^2	23	16	1	1	9	16	10.7	4.88	70	.230	.300	0	.000	-0	-4	-5	0	-0.5
1989	Pit-N	0	1	.000	6	0	0	0	0	6^1	6	5	0	0	5	4	15.6	5.68	59	.240	.367	0	—	0	-2	-2	0	-0.2
1990	Sea-A	0	1	.000	5	0	0	0	0	4^1	7	4	0	1	2	1	20.8	6.23	64	.368	.455	0	—	0	-1	-1	0	-0.2
Total	3	3	2	.600	28	0	0	0	0	38^1	36	25	1	2	16	21	12.7	5.17	67	.250	.333	0	.000	-0	-7	-7	1	-0.9

● PETE MEEGAN Meegan, Peter J. "Steady Pete" b: 11/13/1863, San Francisco, Cal d: 3/15/05, San Francisco, Cal Deb: 8/12/1884

YEAR	TM/L	W	L	PCT	G	GS	CG	SH	SV	IP	H	R	HR	HB	BB	SO	RAT	ERA	ERA+	OAV	OOB	BH	AVG	PB	PR	PR+	PD	TPI
1884	Ric-a	7	12	.368	22	22	22	1	0	179	177	130	7	14	29	106	11.1	4.32	77	.246	.288	12	.160	-2	-21	-20	2	-1.7
1885	Pit-a	7	8	.467	18	16	14	1	0	146	146	90	1	10	38	58	12.0	3.39	95	.247	.303	13	.194	-1	-2	-3	-1	-0.4
Total	2	14	20	.412	40	38	36	2	0	325	323	220	8	24	67	164	11.5	3.90	84	.246	.295	25	.176	-3	-24	-23	1	-2.1

● BILL MEEHAN Meehan, William Thomas b: 9/4/1889, Osceola Mills, Pa. d: 10/8/82, Douglas, Wyo. BR/TR, 5'9", 155 lbs. Deb: 9/17/15

YEAR	TM/L	W	L	PCT	G	GS	CG	SH	SV	IP	H	R	HR	HB	BB	SO	RAT	ERA	ERA+	OAV	OOB	BH	AVG	PB	PR	PR+	PD	TPI
1915	Phi-A	0	1	.000	1	1	0	0	0	4	7	5	0	0	3	4	22.5	11.25	26	.389	.476	1	1.000	0	-4	-4	0	-0.5

● ROY MEEKER Meeker, Charles Roy b: 9/15/1900, Lead Mine, Mo. d: 3/25/29, Orlando, Fla. BL/TL, 5'9", 175 lbs. Deb: 9/22/23

YEAR	TM/L	W	L	PCT	G	GS	CG	SH	SV	IP	H	R	HR	HB	BB	SO	RAT	ERA	ERA+	OAV	OOB	BH	AVG	PB	PR	PR+	PD	TPI
1923	Phi-A	3	0	1.000	5	2	2	0	0	25	24	10	0	0	13	12	13.3	3.60	114	.253	.343	1	.111	-1	1	1	-0	0.1
1924	Phi-A	5	12	.294	30	14	5	1	0	146	166	86	7	5	81	37	15.5	4.68	91	.288	.381	11	.229	-0	-7	-6	-1	-0.7
1926	Cin-N	0	2	.000	7	1	1	0	0	21	24	18	1	0	9	5	14.1	6.43	57	.324	.398	0	.000	-1	-6	-7	0	-0.6
Total	3	8	14	.364	42	17	8	1	0	192	214	114	8	5	103	54	15.1	4.73	89	.287	.377	12	.190	-2	-12	-11	-1	-1.2

● JOUETT MEEKIN Meekin, George Jouett b: 2/21/1867, New Albany, Ind. d: 12/14/44, New Albany, Ind. BR/TR, 6'1", 180 lbs. Deb: 6/13/1891

YEAR	TM/L	W	L	PCT	G	GS	CG	SH	SV	IP	H	R	HR	HB	BB	SO	RAT	ERA	ERA+	OAV	OOB	BH	AVG	PB	PR	PR+	PD	TPI
1891	Lou-a	9	16	.360	28	25	24	2	0	221^1	223	154	2	6	106	141	13.6	4.27	85	.253	.337	21	.223	4	-14	-16	-2	-1.2
1892	Lou-N	7	10	.412	19	18	17	0	0	156^1	168	108	3	6	78	67	14.5	4.03	76	.264	.350	5	.078	-5	-13	-18	0	-1.9
	Was-N	3	10	.231	14	14	13	1	0	112	112	91	2	4	48	58	13.2	3.46	94	.250	.328	6	.133	-1	-2	-3	0	-0.3
	Yr	10	20	.333	33	32	30	1	0	268^1	280	199	5	10	126	125	14.0	3.79	83	.258	.341	11	.101	-5	-15	-20	0	-2.2
1893	Was-N	10	15	.400	31	28	24	1	0	245	289	201	6	7	140	91	16.0	4.96	93	.285	.376	29	.257	3	-8	-9	1	-0.4
1894	*NY-N	33	9	**.786**	53	49	41	1	2	418^1	414	240	13	11	176	137	12.9	3.66	143	.256	.333	48	.276	6	78	75	-3	5.7
1895	NY-N	16	11	.593	29	29	24	1	0	225^2	296	170	10	9	73	76	15.1	5.30	87	.312	.366	28	.292	4	-13	-17	-1	-1.2
1896	NY-N	26	14	.650	42	41	34	0	0	334^1	378	205	8	15	127	110	14.0	3.82	110	.283	.351	43	.299	12	20	15	-3	2.1
1897	NY-N	20	11	.645	37	34	30	2	0	303^2	328	176	9	8	99	83	12.9	3.76	110	.273	.333	41	.299	6	18	14	-3	1.3
1898	NY-N	16	18	.471	38	37	34	1	0	320	329	185	9	12	108	82	12.6	3.77	92	.264	.328	27	.209	1	-6	-11	-5	-1.4
1899	NY-N	5	11	.313	18	18	16	0	0	148^1	169	103	4	8	70	30	15.0	4.37	86	.286	.369	12	.207	1	-9	-10	-3	-1.1
	Bos-N	7	6	.538	13	13	12	0	0	108	111	52	0	2	23	23	11.3	2.83	147	.266	.307	7	.171	-1	12	15	-2	1.1
	Yr	12	17	.414	31	31	28	0	0	256^1	280	155	4	10	93	53	13.4	3.72	105	.278	.344	19	.192	-1	4	6	-5	0.0
1900	Pit-N	0	2	.000	2	2	1	0	0	13	20	21	1	1	8	3	20.1	6.92	52	.351	.439	0	.000	-1	-5	-5	-1	-0.6
Total	10	152	133	.533	324	308	270	9	2	2606	2837	1706	67	89	1056	901	13.8	4.06	103	.273	.345	267	.243	29	60	32	-22	2.1

● PHIL MEELER Meeler, Charles Phillip b: 7/3/48, South Boston, Va. BR/TR, 6'5", 215 lbs. Deb: 5/10/72

YEAR	TM/L	W	L	PCT	G	GS	CG	SH	SV	IP	H	R	HR	HB	BB	SO	RAT	ERA	ERA+	OAV	OOB	BH	AVG	PB	PR	PR+	PD	TPI
1972	Det-A	0	1	.000	7	0	0	0	0	8^1	10	6	0	0	7	5	18.4	4.32	73	.303	.425	0	.000	-0	-1	-1	0	-0.1

● RUSS MEERS Meers, Russell Harlan "Babe" b: 11/28/18, Tilton, Ill. d: 11/16/94, Lancaster, Pa. BL/TL, 5'10", 170 lbs. Deb: 9/28/41

YEAR	TM/L	W	L	PCT	G	GS	CG	SH	SV	IP	H	R	HR	HB	BB	SO	RAT	ERA	ERA+	OAV	OOB	BH	AVG	PB	PR	PR+	PD	TPI
1941	Chi-N	0	1	.000	1	1	0	0	0	8	5	2	0	1	0	5	6.8	1.13	312	.172	.200	0	.000	-0	2	2	-0	0.2
1946	Chi-N	1	2	.333	7	2	0	0	0	11^1	10	6	0	0	10	2	15.9	3.18	104	.238	.385	1	1.000	0	0	0	0	0.1
1947	Chi-N	2	0	1.000	35	1	0	0	0	64^1	61	34	5	2	38	28	14.1	4.48	88	.263	.371	2	.143	-1	-3	-4	-0	-0.3
Total	3	3	3	.500	43	4	0	0	0	83^2	76	42	5	3	48	35	13.7	3.98	96	.251	.359	3	.176	-0	-0	-2	-0	0.0

● HEINIE MEINE Meine, Henry William "The Count Of Luxemburg" b: 5/1/1896, St.Louis, Mo. d: 3/18/68, St.Louis, Mo. BR/TR, 5'11", 180 lbs. Deb: 8/16/22

YEAR	TM/L	W	L	PCT	G	GS	CG	SH	SV	IP	H	R	HR	HB	BB	SO	RAT	ERA	ERA+	OAV	OOB	BH	AVG	PB	PR	PR+	PD	TPI
1922	StL-A	0	0	—	1	0	0	0	0	4	5	3	1	0	2	0	15.8	4.50	92	.313	.389	0	.000	-0	-0	-0	0	0.0
1929	Pit-N	7	6	.538	22	13	7	1	1	108	120	62	4	7	34	19	13.4	4.50	106	.291	.355	4	.103	-2	3	3	-2	0.0
1930	Pit-N	6	8	.429	20	16	4	0	1	117^1	168	89	6	5	44	18	16.6	6.14	81	.346	.406	5	.122	-3	-15	-15	3	-1.4
1931	Pit-N	**19**	13	.594	36	35	22	3	0	**284**	278	121	8	7	87	58	11.8	2.98	129	.254	.313	14	.146	-2	28	28	-0	2.6
1932	Pit-N	12	9	.571	28	25	13	1	1	172^1	193	92	6	3	45	32	12.6	3.86	99	.278	.324	10	.164	-2	0	-1	-1	-0.4
1933	Pit-N	15	8	.652	32	29	12	2	0	207^1	227	99	10	2	50	50	12.1	3.65	91	.278	.321	13	.173	-1	-7	-8	-3	-1.3
1934	Pit-N	7	6	.538	26	14	2	0	0	106^1	134	60	12	1	25	22	13.5	4.32	95	.306	.345	3	.107	-1	-3	-2	-1	-0.5
Total	7	66	50	.569	165	132	60	7	3	999^1	1125	526	47	25	287	199	12.9	3.95	101	.284	.337	49	.144	-12	5	4	-4	-1.0

● FRANK MEINKE Meinke, Frank Louis b: 10/18/1863, Chicago, Ill. d: 11/8/31, Chicago, Ill. BR, 5'10.5", 172 lbs. Deb: 5/1/1884 F♦

YEAR	TM/L	W	L	PCT	G	GS	CG	SH	SV	IP	H	R	HR	HB	BB	SO	RAT	ERA	ERA+	OAV	OOB	BH	AVG	PB	PR	PR+	PD	TPI
1884	Det-N	8	23	.258	35	31	31	1	0	289	341	217	10		63	124	12.6	3.18	91	.275	.310	56	.164	-3	-6	-9	-2	-1.1
1885	Det-N	0	1	.000	1	1	0	0	0	5	13	12	0		4	0	30.6	3.60	79	.433	.500	0	.000	-0	-0	-0	0	-0.1
Total	2	8	24	.250	36	32	31	1	0	294	354	229	10		67	124	12.9	3.18	91	.279	.315	56	.163	-3	-7	-10	-2	-1.2

● SAM MEJIAS Mejias, Samuel Elias b: 5/9/52, Santiago, D.R. BR/TR, 6', 170 lbs. Deb: 9/6/76 C♦

YEAR	TM/L	W	L	PCT	G	GS	CG	SH	SV	IP	H	R	HR	HB	BB	SO	RAT	ERA	ERA+	OAV	OOB	BH	AVG	PB	PR	PR+	PD	TPI
1978	Mon-N	0	0	—	1	0	0	0	0	1	0	0	0	1	0	0	9.0	0.00	—	.000	.250	13	.232	0	0	0	0	0.0

● JOSE MELENDEZ Melendez, Jose Luis (Garcia) b: 9/2/65, Naguabo, P.R. BR/TR, 6'2", 175 lbs. Deb: 9/11/90

YEAR	TM/L	W	L	PCT	G	GS	CG	SH	SV	IP	H	R	HR	HB	BB	SO	RAT	ERA	ERA+	OAV	OOB	BH	AVG	PB	PR	PR+	PD	TPI
1990	Sea-A	0	0	—	3	0	0	0	0	5^1	8	8	2	1	3	7	20.3	11.81	34	.333	.429	0	—	0	-5	-5	-0	-0.2
1991	SD-N	8	5	.615	31	9	0	0	3	93^2	77	35	11	1	24	60	9.8	3.27	116	.221	.273	2	.100	-0	4	5	-1	0.6
1992	SD-N	6	7	.462	56	3	0	0	0	89^1	82	32	9	3	20	82	10.6	2.92	123	.249	.298	0	.000	-0	6	6	-1	0.7
1993	Bos-A	2	1	.667	9	0	0	0	0	16	10	4	2	0	5	14	8.4	2.25	206	.179	.246	0	—	0	4	4	0	0.7
1994	Bos-A	0	1	.000	10	0	0	0	0	16^1	20	11	3	2	8	9	16.5	6.06	83	.323	.417	0	—	0	-2	-2	0	-0.1
Total	5	16	14	.533	109	12	0	0	3	220^2	197	90	27	7	60	172	10.8	3.47	111	.241	.298	2	.080	-1	7	9	-2	1.7

● STEVE MELTER Melter, Stephen Blazius b: 1/2/1886, Cherokee, Iowa d: 1/28/62, Mishawaka, Ind. BR/TR, 6'2", 180 lbs. Deb: 6/27/09

YEAR	TM/L	W	L	PCT	G	GS	CG	SH	SV	IP	H	R	HR	HB	BB	SO	RAT	ERA	ERA+	OAV	OOB	BH	AVG	PB	PR	PR+	PD	TPI
1909	StL-N	0	1	.000	23	1	0	0	3	64^1	79	49	1	2	20	24	14.1	3.50	72	.322	.378	2	.133	-0	-6	-7	1	-0.3

● CLIFF MELTON Melton, Clifford George "Mickey Mouse" or "Mountain Music"
b: 1/3/12, Brevard, N.C. d: 7/28/86, Baltimore, Md. BL/TL, 6'5.5", 203 lbs. Deb: 4/25/37

YEAR	TM/L	W	L	PCT	G	GS	CG	SH	SV	IP	H	R	HR	HB	BB	SO	RAT	ERA	ERA+	OAV	OOB	BH	AVG	PB	PR	PR+	PD	TPI
1937	*NY-N	20	9	.690	46	27	14	2	**7**	248	216	90	9	6	55	142	10.1	2.61	149	.233	.280	10	.122	-5	36	35	4	3.9
1938	NY-N	14	14	.500	36	31	10	1	0	243	266	126	19	1	61	101	12.1	3.89	97	.276	.319	14	.175	-1	-3	-3	2	-0.3
1939	NY-N	12	15	.444	41	23	9	2	5	207^1	214	94	7	4	65	95	12.3	3.56	110	.269	.327	12	.182	-1	8	8	1	1.0
1940	NY-N	10	11	.476	37	21	4	1	2	166^2	185	103	9	3	68	91	13.8	4.91	79	.285	.355	12	.222	2	-20	-19	2	-1.8

YEAR	TM/L	W	L	PCT	G	GS	CG	SH	SV	IP	H	R	HR	HB	BB	SO	RAT	ERA	ERA+	OAV	OOB	BH	AVG	PB	PR	PR+	PD	TPI
1941	NY-N	8	11	.421	42	22	9	3	1	194^1	181	83	14	2	61	100	11.3	3.01	123	.246	.305	7	.115	-3	13	15	4	1.4
1942	NY-N†	11	5	.688	23	17	12	2	1	143^2	122	51	9	2	33	61	9.8	2.63	128	.229	.276	11	.234	2	11	11	3	1.8
1943	NY-N	9	13	.409	34	28	6	2	0	186^1	184	85	7	3	69	55	12.4	3.19	108	.257	.325	8	.148	0	4	5	3	1.0
1944	NY-N	2	2	.500	13	10	1	0	0	64^1	78	40	5	1	19	15	13.7	4.06	90	.294	.344	3	.120	-2	-3	-3	1	-0.2
Total	8	86	80	.518	272	179	65	13	16	1453^2	1446	672	79	22	431	660	11.8	3.42	109	.259	.314	77	.164	-9	47	50	20	6.8
● RUBE MELTON	Melton, Reuben Franklin b: 2/27/17, Cramerton, N.C. d: 9/11/71, Greer, S.C. BR/TR, 6'5", 205 lbs. Deb: 4/17/41																											
1941	Phi-N	1	5	.167	25	5	2	0	0	83^2	81	48	7	0	47	57	13.8	4.73	78	.258	.355	2	.105	-1	-10	-9	-1	-0.9
1942	Phi-N	9	20	.310	42	29	10	1	4	209^1	180	95	7	3	114	107	12.8	3.70	89	.234	.335	8	.123	-1	-9	-9	-2	-1.5
1943	Bro-N	5	8	.385	30	17	4	2	0	119^1	106	62	3	5	79	63	14.3	3.92	86	.243	.365	4	.105	-2	-7	-8	-1	-1.2
1944	Bro-N	9	13	.409	37	23	6	1	0	187^1	178	92	1	2	96	91	13.3	3.46	103	.254	.345	7	.123	-3	3	2	0	0.0
1946	Bro-N	6	3	.667	24	12	3	2	1	99^2	72	27	3	3	52	44	11.5	1.99	170	.206	.314	3	.107	-2	16	16	-0	1.2
1947	Bro-N	0	1	.000	4	1	0	0	0	4^2	7	7	1	0	7	1	27.0	13.50	31	.350	.519	1	1.000	0	-5	-5	-0	-0.8
Total	6	30	50	.375	162	87	25	6	5	704	624	331	22	13	395	363	13.2	3.62	95	.241	.344	25	.120	-9	-12	-14	-5	-3.2
● MARIO MENDOZA	Mendoza, Mario (Aizpuru) b: 12/26/50, Chihuahua, Mex. BR/TR, 5'11", 187 lbs. Deb: 4/26/74 ♦																											
1977	Pit-N	0	0	—	1	0	0	0	0	2	3	3	1	0	2	0	22.5	13.50	30	.375	.500	16	.198	0	-2	-2	0	-0.1
● MIKE MENDOZA	Mendoza, Michael Joseph b: 11/26/55, Inglewood, Cal. BR/TR, 6'5", 215 lbs. Deb: 9/7/79 ♦																											
1979	Hou-N	0	0	—	1	0	0	0	0	1	0	0	0	0	0	0	0.0	0.00	—	.000	.000	0	—	0	0	0	0	0.0
● RAMIRO MENDOZA	Mendoza, Ramiro b: 6/15/72, Los Santos, Panama BR/TR, 6'2", 154 lbs. Deb: 5/25/96																											
1996	NY-A	4	5	.444	12	11	0	0	0	53	80	43	5	4	10	34	16.0	6.79	73	.343	.381	0	—	0	-11	-11	1	-1.4
1997	*NY-A	8	6	.571	39	15	0	0	2	133^2	157	67	15	5	28	82	12.8	4.24	105	.292	.333	0	—	0	5	3	2	0.5
1998	*NY-A	10	2	.833	41	14	1	1	1	130^1	131	50	9	9	30	56	11.7	3.25	135	.264	.318	0	—	0	20	18	1	1.6
1999	*NY-A	9	9	.500	53	6	0	0	3	123^2	141	68	13	3	27	80	12.4	4.29	110	.284	.325	0	—	0	8	6	2	1.0
2000	NY-A	7	4	.636	14	9	1	1	0	65^2	66	32	9	4	20	30	12.3	4.25	113	.260	.324	0	—	0	5	4	-0	0.5
Total	5	38	26	.594	159	55	2	2	6	506^1	575	260	51	25	115	282	12.7	4.27	108	.285	.332	0	—	0	28	19	5	2.2
● FRANK MENECHINO	Menechino, Frank b: 1/7/71, Staten Island, N.Y. BR/TR, 5'9", 175 lbs. Deb: 9/7/99 ♦																											
2000	*Oak-A	0	0	—	1	0	0	0	0	1	6	4	1	0	0	0	54.0	36.00	13	.750	.750	37	.255	0	-3	-4	0	-0.2
● JOCK MENEFEE	Menefee, John b: 1/15/1868, Rowlesburg, W.Va. d: 3/11/53, Belle Vernon, Pa. BR/TR, 6', 165 lbs. Deb: 8/17/1892 ♦																											
1892	Pit-N	0	0	—	1	0	0	0	0	4	10	6	0	0	2	0	27.0	11.25	29	.455	.500	0	.000	-0	-4	-4	0	-0.2
1893	Lou-N	8	7	.533	15	15	14	1	0	129^1	150	95	3	3	40	30	13.4	4.24	104	.281	.335	20	.274	4	6	2	2	0.7
1894	Lou-N	8	17	.320	28	24	20	1	0	211^2	258	153	3	9	50	43	13.5	4.29	119	.298	.342	13	.165	-6	24	20	2	1.4
	Pit-N	5	8	.385	13	13	13	0	0	111^2	159	95	4	2	39	33	16.1	5.40	97	.331	.383	12	.255	0	-1	-2	2	0.0
	Yr	13	25	.342	41	37	33	1	0	323^1	417	248	7	11	89	76	14.4	4.68	110	.309	.357	25	.198	-5	23	18	4	1.4
1895	Pit-N	0	1	.000	2	1	0	0	0	1^2	2	8	0	1	7	0	54.0	16.20	28	.286	.667	0	—	0	-2	-2	0	-0.3
1898	NY-N	0	1	.000	1	1	1	0	0	9^1	11	8	0	2	2	3	14.5	4.82	72	.289	.357	0	.000	-1	-1	-1	0	-0.2
1900	Chi-N	9	4	.692	16	13	11	0	0	117	140	74	1	10	35	30	14.2	3.85	94	.296	.357	5	.109	-3	-2	-3	-2	-0.7
1901	Chi-N	8	12	.400	21	20	19	0	0	182^1	201	102	4	6	34	55	11.9	3.80	85	.278	.315	39	.257	4	-10	-12	-1	-0.7
1902	Chi-N	12	10	.545	22	21	20	3	0	197^1	201	81	1	6	26	60	10.6	2.42	112	.264	.293	50	.231	3	8	6	-1	0.9
1903	Chi-N	8	10	.444	20	17	13	1	0	147	157	85	3	6	38	39	12.3	3.00	105	.275	.327	13	.203	1	4	2	3	0.6
Total	9	58	70	.453	139	125	111	6	0	1111^1	1289	707	19	45	273	293	13.0	3.81	101	.288	.335	152	.222	2	23	7	6	1.5
● TONY MENENDEZ	Menendez, Antonio Gustavo (Remon) b: 2/20/65, Havana, Cuba BR/TR, 6'2", 190 lbs. Deb: 6/22/92																											
1992	Cin-N	1	0	1.000	3	0	0	0	0	4^2	1	1	1	0	0	5	1.9	1.93	187	.067	.067	0	—	0	1	1	-0	0.2
1993	Pit-N	2	0	1.000	14	0	0	0	0	21	20	8	4	1	4	13	10.7	3.00	135	.256	.301	0	.000	-0	2	2	-0	0.2
1994	SF-N	0	1	.000	6	0	0	0	0	3^1	8	8	2	0	2	2	27.0	21.60	19	.471	.526	0	—	0	-6	-7	-0	-1.2
Total	3	3	1	.750	23	0	0	0	0	29	29	17	7	1	6	20	11.2	4.97	80	.264	.308	0	.000	-0	-3	-3	-1	-0.8
● PAUL MENHART	Menhart, Paul Gerard b: 3/25/69, St.Louis, Mo. BR/TR, 6'2", 190 lbs. Deb: 4/27/95																											
1995	Tor-A	1	4	.200	21	9	1	0	0	78^2	72	49	9	6	47	50	14.3	4.92	96	.248	.364	0	—	0	-2	-2	-0	-0.1
1996	Sea-A	2	2	.500	11	6	0	0	0	42	55	36	9	2	25	18	17.6	7.29	68	.327	.421	0	—	0	-11	-11	1	-0.8
1997	SD-N	2	3	.400	9	8	0	0	0	44	42	23	6	0	13	22	11.3	4.70	83	.256	.311	0	.000	-1	-2	-4	-0	-0.6
Total	3	5	9	.357	41	23	1	0	0	164^2	169	108	24	8	85	90	14.3	5.47	83	.272	.366	0	.000	-1	-15	-17	0	-1.5
● MIKE MEOLA	Meola, Emile Michael b: 10/19/05, New York, N.Y. d: 9/1/76, Fair Lawn, N.J. BR/TR, 5'11", 175 lbs. Deb: 4/24/33																											
1933	Bos-A	0	0	—	3	0	0	0	0	2^1	5	6	0	0	2	1	27.0	23.14	19	.417	.500	0	—	0	-5	-5	-0	-0.2
1936	StL-A	0	1	.000	9	0	0	0	0	19^1	29	20	0	1	13	6	20.0	9.31	58	.358	.453	1	.500	1	-9	-8	0	-0.3
	Bos-A	0	2	.000	6	3	1	0	1	21^1	29	17	0	1	10	8	16.9	5.48	97	.326	.400	1	.143	-0	-1	-0	1	0.0
	Yr	0	3	.000	15	3	1	0	1	40^2	58	37	0	2	23	14	18.4	7.30	73	.341	.426	2	.222	0	-10	-8	1	-0.3
Total	2	0	3	.000	18	3	1	0	1	43	63	43	0	2	25	15	18.8	8.16	65	.346	.431	2	.222	0	-15	-13	1	-0.5
● HECTOR MERCADO	Mercado, Hector Luis b: 4/29/74, Catano, P.R. BL/TL, 6'3", 205 lbs. Deb: 4/4/2000																											
2000	Cin-N	0	0	—	12	0	0	0	0	14	12	7	2	0	8	13	12.9	4.50	106	.240	.345	0	.000	-0	0	0	-0	0.0
● JOSE MERCEDES	Mercedes, Jose Miguel (Santana) b: 3/5/71, ElSeibo, D.R. BR/TR, 6'1", 180 lbs. Deb: 5/31/94																											
1994	Mil-A	2	0	1.000	19	0	0	0	0	31	22	9	4	2	16	11	11.6	2.32	217	.216	.333	0	—	0	9	9	-1	0.4
1995	Mil-A	0	1	.000	5	0	0	0	0	7^1	12	9	1	0	8	6	24.5	9.82	51	.375	.500	0	—	0	-4	-4	-0	-0.4
1996	Mil-A	0	2	.000	11	0	0	0	0	16^2	20	18	6	0	5	6	13.5	9.18	57	.294	.342	0	—	0	-8	-7	-0	-0.7
1997	Mil-A	7	10	.412	29	23	2	1	0	159	146	76	24	5	53	80	11.5	3.79	122	.248	.316	0	.000	-0	14	15	-2	1.2
1998	Mil-N	2	2	.500	7	5	0	0	0	32	42	25	5	1	9	11	14.6	6.75	63	.316	.364	1	.091	-0	-9	-9	-1	-1.0
2000	Bal-A	14	7	.667	36	20	1	0	0	145^2	150	71	15	3	64	70	13.4	4.02	119	.270	.349	0	.000	-0	15	13	-1	1.4
Total	6	25	22	.532	107	48	3	1	0	391^2	392	208	55	11	155	184	12.8	4.34	109	.265	.339	1	.071	-1	16	16	-5	0.9
● WIN MERCER	Mercer, George Barclay b: 6/20/1874, Chester, W.Va. d: 1/12/03, San Francisco, Cal BR/TR, 5'7", 140 lbs. Deb: 4/21/1894 ♦																											
1894	Was-N	17	23	.425	50	39	30	0	3	339^1	445	285	9	14	126	72	15.5	3.85	137	.313	.375	48	.291	3	56	54	2	5.1
1895	Was-N	13	23	.361	44	38	32	0	2	313^1	432	281	17	18	96	85	15.7	4.42	108	.322	.376	51	.254	0	12	13	-1	1.1
1896	Was-N	25	18	.581	46	45	38	2	0	366^1	456	266	10	20	117	94	14.6	4.13	107	.302	.360	38	.244	0	10	11	1	1.1
1897	Was-N	21	20	.512	**47**	43	35	**3**	**3**	342	403	219	5	28	104	91	14.1	3.18	136	.291	.353	44	.317	8	43	44	-1	4.9
1898	Was-N	12	18	.400	33	30	24	0	0	233^2	309	181	3	18	71	52	15.3	4.81	76	.316	.373	80	.321	8	-31	-29	-1	-2.5
1899	Was-N	7	14	.333	23	21	21	0	0	186	234	128	2	6	53	28	14.2	4.60	85	.307	.356	112	.299	5	-15	-14	3	-0.5
1900	NY-N	13	17	.433	33	29	26	1	0	242^2	303	138	5	20	58	39	14.1	3.86	94	.305	.355	73	.294	7	-4	-7	2	0.1
1901	Was-A	9	13	.409	24	22	19	1	1	179^2	217	126	8	10	50	31	13.9	4.56	80	.295	.348	42	.300	6	-18	-18	1	-1.1
1902	Det-A	15	18	.455	35	33	28	4	1	281^2	282	129	5	10	80	40	11.9	3.04	120	.261	.318	18	.180	-2	17	19	4	2.1
Total	9	132	164	.446	335	300	253	11	10	2484^2	3081	1753	64	144	755	532	14.4	3.98	107	.302	.358	506	.285	35	69	73	8	10.3
● JACK MERCER	Mercer, Harry Vernon b: 3/10/1889, Zanesville, Ohio d: 6/25/45, Dayton, Ohio Deb: 8/2/10																											
1910	Pit-N	0	0	—	1	0	0	0	0	1	0	0	0	0	2	1	18.0	0.00	—	.000	.500	0	—	0	0	0	0	0.0
● MARK MERCER	Mercer, Mark Kenneth b: 5/22/54, Fort Bragg, N.C. BL/TL, 6'5", 220 lbs. Deb: 9/1/81																											
1981	Tex-A	0	1	.000	7	0	0	0	2	7^2	7	4	1	0	7	8	16.4	4.70	74	.241	.389	0	—	0	-1	-1	0	-0.2
● KENT MERCKER	Mercker, Kent Franklin b: 2/1/68, Indianapolis, Ind. BL/TL, 6'2", 195 lbs. Deb: 9/22/89																											
1989	Atl-N	0	0	—	2	1	0	0	0	4^1	8	6	0	0	6	4	29.1	12.46	29	.400	.538	0	.000	-0	-4	-4	-0	-0.2
1990	Atl-N	4	7	.364	36	0	0	0	7	48^1	43	22	6	2	24	39	12.8	3.17	128	.236	.332	0	.000	-0	3	4	-1	0.8
1991	*Atl-N	5	3	.625	50	4	0	0	6	73^1	56	23	5	1	35	62	11.3	2.58	151	.211	.305	1	.100	-0	9	10	-1	1.1
1992	*Atl-N	3	2	.600	53	0	0	0	6	68^1	51	27	4	3	35	49	11.7	3.42	107	.207	.313	0	.000	-0	1	2	-2	-0.1
1993	*Atl-N	3	1	.750	43	6	0	0	0	66	52	24	2	2	36	59	12.3	2.86	140	.212	.318	0	.000	-1	9	9	-1	0.2
1994	Atl-N	9	4	.692	20	17	2	1	0	112^1	90	46	16	0	45	111	10.8	3.45	123	.220	.297	2	.054	-2	10	10	0	0.8
1995	*Atl-N	7	8	.467	29	26	0	0	0	143	140	73	16	3	61	102	12.8	4.15	103	.258	.336	5	.104	-2	0	2	0	0.0

YEAR	TM/L	W	L	PCT	G	GS	CG	SH	SV	IP	H	R	HR	HB	BB	SO	RAT	ERA	ERA+	OAV	OOB	BH	AVG	PB	PR	PR+	PD	TPI
1996	Bal-A	3	6	.333	14	12	0	0	0	58	73	56	12	3	35	22	17.2	7.76	64	.307	.402	0	—	0	-18	-19	-1	-2.2
	Cle-A	1	0	1.000	10	0	0	0	0	11^2	10	4	1	0	3	7	10.0	3.09	159	.244	.295	0	—	0	2	2	-0	0.2
	Yr	4	6	.400	24	12	0	0	0	69^2	83	60	13	3	38	29	16.0	6.98	71	.297	.387	0	—	0	-15	-16	-1	-2.0
1997	Cin-N	8	11	.421	28	25	0	0	0	144^2	135	65	16	2	62	75	12.4	3.92	109	.250	.329	7	.156	1	5	6	0	0.8
1998	StL-N	11	11	.500	30	29	0	0	0	161^2	199	99	11	3	53	72	14.2	5.07	83	.310	.366	8	.148	1	-15	-16	-1	-1.9
1999	StL-N	6	5	.545	25	18	0	0	0	103^2	125	73	16	2	51	64	15.5	5.12	89	.303	.383	5	.179	1	-6	-6	-1	-0.6
	*Bos-A	2	0	1.000	5	5	0	0	0	25^2	23	12	0	1	13	17	13.0	3.51	142	.235	.330	0	—	0	4	4	0	0.3
2000	Ana-A	1	3	.250	21	7	0	0	0	48^1	57	35	12	2	29	30	16.4	6.52	76	.300	.398	0	—	0	-9	-8	-0	-0.6
Total	12	63	61	.508	366	150	2	1	19	1069^1	1062	565	117	24	488	713	13.2	4.31	100	.261	.343	28	.115	-4	-9	-2	-7	-1.4

● SPIKE MERENA

Merena, John Joseph b: 11/18/09, Paterson, N.J. d: 3/9/77, Bridgeport, Conn. BL/TL, 6', 185 lbs. Deb: 9/16/34

YEAR	TM/L	W	L	PCT	G	GS	CG	SH	SV	IP	H	R	HR	HB	BB	SO	RAT	ERA	ERA+	OAV	OOB	BH	AVG	PB	PR	PR+	PD	TPI
1934	Bos-A	1	2	.333	4	3	2	1	0	24^2	20	8	2	1	16	7	13.5	2.92	165	.222	.346	1	.143	-0	4	5	-1	0.4

● RON MERIDITH

Meridith, Ronald Knox b: 11/26/56, San Pedro, Cal. BL/TL, 6', 175 lbs. Deb: 9/16/84

YEAR	TM/L	W	L	PCT	G	GS	CG	SH	SV	IP	H	R	HR	HB	BB	SO	RAT	ERA	ERA+	OAV	OOB	BH	AVG	PB	PR	PR+	PD	TPI
1984	Chi-N	0	0	—	3	0	0	0	0	5^1	6	5	1	0	2	4	13.5	3.38	116	.273	.333	0	—	0	0	0	-0	0.0
1985	Chi-N	3	2	.600	32	0	0	0	1	46^1	53	24	3	1	24	23	15.2	4.47	90	.301	.388	1	.250	0	-4	-2	0	-0.2
1986	Tex-A	1	0	1.000	5	0	0	0	0	3	2	1	0	0	1	2	9.0	3.00	144	.286	.375	0	—	0	0	0	0	0.1
1987	Tex-A	1	0	1.000	11	0	0	0	0	20^2	25	18	7	0	12	17	16.1	6.10	74	.298	.385	0	—	0	-4	-4	0	-0.1
Total	4	5	2	.714	51	0	0	0	1	75^1	86	48	11	1	39	46	15.1	4.78	87	.298	.383	1	.250	0	-8	-5	1	-0.2

● BRETT MERRIMAN

Merriman, Brett Alan b: 7/15/66, Jacksonville, Ill. BR/TR, 6'2", 180 lbs. Deb: 4/8/93

YEAR	TM/L	W	L	PCT	G	GS	CG	SH	SV	IP	H	R	HR	HB	BB	SO	RAT	ERA	ERA+	OAV	OOB	BH	AVG	PB	PR	PR+	PD	TPI
1993	Min-A	1	1	.500	19	0	0	0	0	27	36	29	3	3	23	14	20.7	9.67	45	.343	.473	0	—	0	-16	-16	0	-1.0
1994	Min-A	0	1	.000	15	0	0	0	0	17	18	13	0	4	14	10	19.1	6.35	77	.269	.424	0	—	0	-3	-3	-0	-0.2
Total	2	1	2	.333	34	0	0	0	0	44	54	42	3	7	37	24	20.0	8.39	54	.314	.454	0	—	0	-19	-18	-0	-1.2

● GEORGE MERRITT

Merritt, George Washington b: 4/14/1880, Paterson, N.J. d: 2/21/38, Memphis, Tenn. TR, 6', 160 lbs. Deb: 9/6/01 ◆

YEAR	TM/L	W	L	PCT	G	GS	CG	SH	SV	IP	H	R	HR	HB	BB	SO	RAT	ERA	ERA+	OAV	OOB	BH	AVG	PB	PR	PR+	PD	TPI
1901	Pit-N	3	0	1.000	3	3	3	0	0	24	28	18	0	2	5	5	13.1	4.88	67	.289	.337	3	.273	1	-4	-4	-0	-0.4
1903	Pit-N	0	0	—	1	0	0	0	0	4	4	3	0	0	1	2	11.3	2.25	144	.267	.313	4	.148	0	0	0	-0	0.0
Total	2	3	0	1.000	4	3	3	0	0	28	32	21	0	2	6	7	12.9	4.50	73	.286	.333	10	.213	1	-4	-4	-0	-0.4

● JIM MERRITT

Merritt, James Joseph b: 12/9/43, Altadena, Cal. BL/TL, 6'2", 180 lbs. Deb: 8/2/65

YEAR	TM/L	W	L	PCT	G	GS	CG	SH	SV	IP	H	R	HR	HB	BB	SO	RAT	ERA	ERA+	OAV	OOB	BH	AVG	PB	PR	PR+	PD	TPI
1965	*Min-A	5	4	.556	16	9	1	0	2	76^2	68	29	11	0	20	61	10.3	3.17	112	.239	.289	3	.136	0	2	3	-0	0.4
1966	Min-A	7	14	.333	31	18	5	1	3	144	112	57	17	0	33	124	9.1	3.38	107	.212	.258	4	.103	1	3	3	-0	0.4
1967	Min-A	13	7	.650	37	28	11	4	0	227^2	196	72	21	7	30	161	9.2	2.53	137	.230	.262	10	.135	0	18	22	-2	1.8
1968	Min-A	12	16	.429	38	34	11	1	1	238^1	207	102	21	7	52	181	10.0	3.25	95	.232	.279	10	.141	0	-7	-4	1	-0.4
1969	Cin-N	17	9	.654	42	36	8	1	0	251	269	127	33	5	61	144	12.0	4.37	86	.273	.318	11	.143	0	-22	-16	-3	-1.8
1970	*Cin-N★	20	12	.625	35	35	12	1	0	234	248	114	21	1	53	136	11.6	4.08	99	.270	.311	14	.169	3	-1	-1	-2	-0.1
1971	Cin-N	1	11	.083	28	11	0	0	0	107	115	55	14	3	31	38	12.5	4.37	77	.279	.334	4	.138	0	-11	-12	-2	-1.5
1972	Cin-N	1	0	1.000	4	1	0	0	0	8	13	4	1	0	2	4	16.9	4.50	71	.361	.395	0	.000	-0	-1	-1	-0	-0.2
1973	Tex-A	5	13	.278	35	19	8	1	1	160	191	79	18	1	34	65	12.7	4.05	92	.296	.332	0	—	0	-4	-6	-1	-0.7
1974	Tex-A	0	0	—	26	1	0	0	0	32^2	46	17	3	0	6	18	14.3	4.13	86	.329	.356	0	—	0	-2	-2	-1	-0.2
1975	Tex-A	0	0	—	5	0	0	0	0	3^2	3	1	0	1	0	0	9.8	0.00	—	.214	.267	0	—	0	2	2	-0	0.1
Total	11	81	86	.485	297	192	56	9	7	1483	1468	657	160	25	322	932	11.0	3.65	98	.257	.300	56	.141	3	-24	-10	-10	-2.2

● LLOYD MERRITT

Merritt, Lloyd Wesley b: 4/8/33, St.Louis, Mo. BR/TR, 6', 189 lbs. Deb: 4/22/57

YEAR	TM/L	W	L	PCT	G	GS	CG	SH	SV	IP	H	R	HR	HB	BB	SO	RAT	ERA	ERA+	OAV	OOB	BH	AVG	PB	PR	PR+	PD	TPI
1957	StL-N	1	2	.333	44	0	0	0	7	65^1	60	29	7	4	28	35	12.7	3.31	120	.251	.339	0	.000	-0	4	5	0	0.3

● SAM MERTES

Mertes, Samuel Blair "Sandow" b: 8/6/1872, San Francisco, Cal. d: 3/11/45, San Francisco, Cal BR/TR, 6', 225 lbs. Deb: 6/30/1896 ◆

YEAR	TM/L	W	L	PCT	G	GS	CG	SH	SV	IP	H	R	HR	HB	BB	SO	RAT	ERA	ERA+	OAV	OOB	BH	AVG	PB	PR	PR+	PD	TPI
1902	Chi-A	1	0	1.000	1	0	0	0	0	8	6	2	0	0	0	0	6.8	1.13	301	.207	.207	140	.282	0	2	2	-1	0.2

● JIM MERTZ

Mertz, James Verlin b: 8/10/16, Lima, Ohio BR/TR, 5'10.5", 170 lbs. Deb: 5/1/43

YEAR	TM/L	W	L	PCT	G	GS	CG	SH	SV	IP	H	R	HR	HB	BB	SO	RAT	ERA	ERA+	OAV	OOB	BH	AVG	PB	PR	PR+	PD	TPI
1943	Was-A	5	7	.417	33	10	2	0	3	116^2	109	65	7	0	58	53	12.9	4.63	69	.251	.339	7	.184	0	-17	-19	0	-1.9

● JOSE MESA

Mesa, Jose Ramon Nova (b: Jose Ramon Nova (Mesa)) b: 5/22/66, Pueblo Viejo, D.R. BR/TR, 6'3", 225 lbs. Deb: 9/10/87

YEAR	TM/L	W	L	PCT	G	GS	CG	SH	SV	IP	H	R	HR	HB	BB	SO	RAT	ERA	ERA+	OAV	OOB	BH	AVG	PB	PR	PR+	PD	TPI
1987	Bal-A	1	3	.250	6	5	0	0	0	31^1	38	23	7	0	15	17	15.2	6.03	73	.297	.371	0	—	0	-5	-6	-1	-0.7
1990	Bal-A	3	2	.600	7	7	0	0	0	46^2	37	20	2	1	27	24	12.5	3.86	99	.218	.328	0	—	0	-0	-0	-0	-0.1
1991	Bal-A	6	11	.353	23	23	2	1	0	123^2	151	86	11	3	62	64	15.7	5.97	66	.307	.388	0	—	0	-26	-29	1	-3.2
1992	Bal-A	3	8	.273	13	12	0	0	0	67^2	77	41	9	2	27	22	14.1	5.19	78	.287	.357	0	—	0	-9	-9	0	-1.2
	Cle-A	4	4	.500	15	15	1	1	0	93	92	45	5	2	43	40	13.3	4.16	94	.262	.346	0	—	0	-2	-3	-1	-0.2
	Yr	7	12	.368	28	27	1	1	0	160^2	169	86	14	4	70	62	13.6	4.59	86	.273	.351	0	—	0	-12	-11	-0	-1.4
1993	Cle-A	10	12	.455	34	33	3	0	0	208^2	232	122	21	7	62	118	13.0	4.92	88	.286	.342	0	—	0	-13	-13	-0	-1.2
1994	Cle-A	7	5	.583	51	0	0	0	2	73	71	33	3	3	26	63	12.3	3.82	124	.254	.325	0	—	0	8	7	0	1.1
1995	*Cle-A★	3	0	1.000	62	0	0	0	**46**	64	49	9	3	0	17	58	9.3	1.13	418	.216	.270	0	—	0	**26**	**26**	1	4.4
1996	*Cle-A☆	2	7	.222	69	0	0	0	39	72^1	69	32	6	3	28	64	12.4	3.73	131	.257	.333	0	—	0	10	10	-1	1.7
1997	*Cle-A	4	4	.500	66	0	0	0	16	82^1	83	28	7	3	28	69	12.5	2.40	195	.259	.324	0	—	0	20	20	-0	2.4
1998	Cle-A	3	4	.429	44	0	0	0	1	54	61	36	7	4	20	35	14.2	5.17	92	.282	.354	0	—	0	-3	-2	-1	-0.2
	SF-N	5	3	.625	32	0	0	0	0	30^2	30	14	1	0	18	28	14.1	3.52	113	.256	.356	0	—	0	2	2	-1	0.3
1999	Sea-A	3	6	.333	68	0	0	0	33	68^2	84	42	11	4	40	42	16.8	4.98	95	.305	.401	0	—	0	-1	-2	-0	-0.3
2000	*Sea-A	4	6	.400	66	0	0	0	1	80^2	89	48	11	5	41	84	15.1	5.36	89	.280	.371	0	—	0	-4	-5	0	-0.5
Total	12	58	75	.436	556	95	6	2	138	1096^2	1163	579	104	37	454	728	13.6	4.42	99	.274	.350	0	—	0	2	-3	-1	2.3

● BUD MESSENGER

Messenger, Andrew Warren b: 2/1/1898, Grand Blanc, Mich. d: 11/4/71, Lansing, Mich. BR/TR, 6', 175 lbs. Deb: 7/31/24

YEAR	TM/L	W	L	PCT	G	GS	CG	SH	SV	IP	H	R	HR	HB	BB	SO	RAT	ERA	ERA+	OAV	OOB	BH	AVG	PB	PR	PR+	PD	TPI
1924	Cle-A	2	0	1.000	5	2	1	0	0	25	28	13	4	0	14	4	15.1	4.32	99	.283	.372	1	.125	-0	-0	-0	-0	-0.1

● ANDY MESSERSMITH

Messersmith, John Alexander b: 8/6/45, Toms River, N.J. BR/TR, 6'1", 200 lbs. Deb: 7/4/68

YEAR	TM/L	W	L	PCT	G	GS	CG	SH	SV	IP	H	R	HR	HB	BB	SO	RAT	ERA	ERA+	OAV	OOB	BH	AVG	PB	PR	PR+	PD	TPI
1968	Cal-A	4	2	.667	28	5	2	1	4	81^1	44	21	3	1	35	74	8.9	2.21	132	.157	.253	2	.100	-1	7	6	0	0.6
1969	Cal-A	16	11	.593	40	33	10	2	2	250	169	81	17	5	100	211	9.9	2.52	138	**.190**	.276	12	.156	2	31	28	-1	3.2
1970	Cal-A	11	10	.524	37	26	6	1	5	194^2	144	75	21	6	78	162	10.5	3.01	120	**.205**	.290	11	.157	0	15	14	1	1.5
1971	Cal-A☆	20	13	.606	38	38	14	4	0	276^2	224	112	16	7	121	179	11.5	2.99	108	.218	.304	16	.172	4	15	8	1	1.5
1972	Cal-A	8	11	.421	25	21	10	3	2	169^2	125	56	5	2	68	142	10.3	2.81	104	.207	.290	10	.189	2	5	2	0	0.6
1973	LA-N	14	10	.583	33	33	10	3	0	249^2	196	90	24	6	77	177	10.1	2.70	127	.214	.279	15	.169	2	27	22	-0	2.2
1974	*LA-N★	**20**	6	**.769**	39	39	13	3	0	292^1	227	93	24	3	94	221	**10.0**	2.59	132	.212	**.278**	23	.240	9	34	29	0	3.5
1975	LA-N☆	19	14	.576	42	40	**19**	**7**	1	**321^2**	244	92	22	5	96	213	9.7	2.29	149	**.213**	.276	17	.157	2	**48**	**43**	-2	4.4
1976	Atl-N†	11	11	.500	29	28	12	3	1	207^1	166	83	14	2	74	135	10.5	3.04	125	.219	.290	12	.179	0	11	16	1	1.8
1977	Atl-N	5	4	.556	16	16	1	0	0	102^1	101	54	12	2	39	69	12.5	4.40	101	.256	.326	4	.118	-0	-5	1	-0	0.0
1978	NY-A	0	3	.000	6	5	0	0	0	22^1	24	21	7	1	15	16	16.1	5.64	64	.267	.377	0	—	0	-5	-5	-0	-0.6
1979	LA-N	2	4	.333	11	11	1	0	0	62^1	55	34	9	0	34	26	12.9	4.91	74	.244	.344	2	.091	-1	-8	-9	0	-0.9
Total	12	130	99	.568	344	295	98	27	15	2230^1	1719	812	174	40	831	1625	10.5	2.86	121	.212	.289	124	.170	20	174	152	-1	17.8

● TOM METCALF

Metcalf, Thomas John b: 7/16/40, Amherst, Wis. BR/TR, 6'2.5", 174 lbs. Deb: 8/4/63

YEAR	TM/L	W	L	PCT	G	GS	CG	SH	SV	IP	H	R	HR	HB	BB	SO	RAT	ERA	ERA+	OAV	OOB	BH	AVG	PB	PR	PR+	PD	TPI
1963	NY-A	1	0	1.000	8	0	0	0	0	13	12	4	1	0	3	3	10.4	2.77	127	.250	.294	0	—	0	1	1	-0	0.1

● DEWEY METIVIER

Metivier, George Dewey b: 5/6/1898, Cambridge, Mass. d: 3/2/47, Cambridge, Mass. BL/TR, 5'11", 175 lbs. Deb: 9/15/22

YEAR	TM/L	W	L	PCT	G	GS	CG	SH	SV	IP	H	R	HR	HB	BB	SO	RAT	ERA	ERA+	OAV	OOB	BH	AVG	PB	PR	PR+	PD	TPI
1922	Cle-A	2	0	1.000	2	2	2	0	0	18	18	9	1	1	3	1	11.0	4.50	89	.265	.306	1	.167	-0	-1	-1	-1	-0.1
1923	Cle-A	4	2	.667	26	5	1	0	1	73^1	111	66	1	6	38	9	19.0	6.50	61	.368	.448	3	.150	-0	-21	-21	0	-1.5
1924	Cle-A	1	5	.167	26	6	1	0	3	76^1	110	50	3	0	34	14	17.0	5.31	81	.358	.422	3	.125	-2	-9	-9	-1	-0.9
Total	3	7	7	.500	54	13	4	0	4	167^2	239	125	5	7	75	24	17.2	5.74	72	.353	.423	7	.140	-2	-31	-30	-1	-2.5

● BUTCH METZGER

Metzger, Clarence Edward b: 5/23/52, Lafayette, Ind. BR/TR, 6'1", 185 lbs. Deb: 9/8/74

YEAR	TM/L	W	L	PCT	G	GS	CG	SH	SV	IP	H	R	HR	HB	BB	SO	RAT	ERA	ERA+	OAV	OOB	BH	AVG	PB	PR	PR+	PD	TPI
1974	SF-N	1	0	1.000	10	0	0	0	0	12^2	11	5	0	0	12	5	16.3	3.55	107	.239	.397	0	—	0	0	0	-0	0.0
1975	SD-N	1	0	1.000	4	0	0	0	0	4^2	6	4	1	0	4	6	19.3	7.71	45	.316	.435	0	—	0	-2	-2	0	-0.4
1976	SD-N	11	4	.733	77	0	0	0	16	123^1	119	44	5	3	52	89	12.7	2.92	112	.258	.337	0	.000	-0	8	5	-0	0.7

YEAR	TM/L	W	L	PCT	G	GS	CG	SH	SV	IP	H	R	HR	HB	BB	SO	RAT	ERA	ERA+	OAV	OOB	BH	AVG	PB	PR	PR+	PD	TPI
1977	SD-N	0	0	—	17	1	0	0	0	22^2	27	16	5	1	12	6	15.9	5.56	64	.307	.396	0	.000	-0	-4	-6	-0	-0.4
	StL-N	4	2	.667	58	0	0	0	7	92^2	78	36	8	1	38	48	11.4	3.11	124	.228	.307	0	.000	-0	8	8	-1	0.4
	Yr	4	2	.667	75	1	0	0	7	115^1	105	52	13	2	50	54	12.3	3.59	106	.244	.326	0	.000	-1	4	3	-1	0.0
1978	NY-N	1	3	.250	25	0	0	0	0	37^1	48	28	4	1	22	21	17.1	6.51	54	.324	.415	0	—	0	-12	-13	-1	-1.3
Total	5	18	9	.667	191	1	0	0	23	293^1	289	133	23	6	140	175	13.3	3.74	94	.262	.348	0	.000	-1	-2	-7	-2	-1.0
● BRIAN MEYER	Meyer, Brian Scott b: 1/29/63, Camden, N.J. BR/TR, 6', 190 lbs. Deb: 9/3/88																											
1988	Hou-N	0	0	—	8	0	0	0	0	12^1	9	2	2	0	4	10	9.5	1.46	228	.225	.295	0	—	0	3	3	1	0.2
1989	Hou-N	0	1	.000	12	0	0	0	1	18	16	13	0	1	13	13	15.0	4.50	75	.239	.370	0	—	0	-2	-2	0	-0.1
1990	Hou-N	0	4	.000	14	0	0	0	1	20^1	16	7	3	0	6	6	9.7	2.21	168	.211	.268	0	.000	-0	4	3	1	0.8
Total	3	0	5	.000	34	0	0	0	2	50^2	41	22	5	1	23	29	11.5	2.84	123	.224	.314	0	.000	-0	4	4	1	0.9
● JACK MEYER	Meyer, John Robert b: 3/23/32, Philadelphia, Pa. d: 3/9/67, Philadelphia, Pa. BR/TR, 6'1", 175 lbs. Deb: 4/16/55																											
1955	Phi-N	6	11	.353	50	5	0	0	**16**	110^1	75	50	14	3	66	97	11.7	3.43	116	.190	.310	2	.100	0	8	7	-1	1.1
1956	Phi-N	7	11	.389	41	7	2	0	2	96	86	49	8	4	51	66	13.2	4.41	84	.242	.343	4	.200	1	-7	-7	0	-1.1
1957	Phi-N	0	2	.000	19	2	0	0	0	37^2	44	30	6	1	28	34	17.4	5.73	66	.297	.412	1	.167	0	-8	-8	0	-0.3
1958	Phi-N	3	6	.333	37	5	1	0	2	90^1	77	38	8	1	33	87	11.1	3.59	110	.232	.303	5	.278	1	4	4	-1	0.3
1959	Phi-N	5	3	.625	47	1	1	0	1	93^2	76	43	9	1	53	71	12.5	3.36	122	.222	.328	1	.071	-1	6	7	0	0.5
1960	Phi-N	3	1	.750	7	4	0	0	0	25	25	13	2	0	11	18	13.0	4.32	90	.272	.350	1	.125	-0	-2	-1	-0	-0.2
1961	Phi-N	0	0	—	1	0	0	0	0	2	2	2	1	0	2	2	18.0	9.00	45	.286	.444	0	—	0	-1	-1	-0	-0.1
Total	7	24	34	.414	202	24	4	0	21	455	385	225	48	10	244	375	12.6	3.92	100	.230	.332	14	.163	1	0	0	-1	0.2
● BOB MEYER	Meyer, Robert Bernard b: 8/4/39, Toledo, Ohio BR/TL, 6'2", 185 lbs. Deb: 4/20/64																											
1964	NY-A	0	3	.000	7	1	0	0	0	18^1	16	12	1	0	12	12	13.7	4.91	74	.235	.350	0	.000	-0	-3	-3	1	-0.4
	LA-A	1	1	.500	6	5	0	0	0	18	25	10	2	1	13	13	19.5	5.00	66	.333	.438	0	.000	-1	-3	-4	0	-0.4
	KC-A	1	4	.200	9	7	2	0	0	42	37	23	2	0	33	30	15.0	3.86	99	.248	.385	0	.000	-1	-1	-0	-1	-0.2
	Yr	2	8	.200	22	13	2	0	0	78^1	78	45	5	1	58	55	15.7	4.37	84	.267	.390	0	.000	-2	-6	-6	-0	-1.0
1969	Sea-A	0	3	.000	6	5	1	0	0	32^2	30	14	4	2	10	17	11.6	3.31	110	.252	.321	1	.091	-1	1	1	-1	-0.1
1970	Mil-A	0	1	.000	10	0	0	0	0	18^1	24	13	2	0	12	20	17.7	6.38	59	.329	.424	1	.333	0	-5	-5	0	-0.2
Total	3	2	12	.143	38	18	3	0	0	129^1	132	72	11	3	80	92	15.0	4.38	84	.273	.379	2	.057	-3	-11	-10	-1	-1.3
● RUSS MEYER	Meyer, Russell Charles "Rowdy" or "The Mad Monk" b: 10/25/23, Peru, Ill. d: 11/16/98, Oglesby, Ill. BB/TR, 6'1", 185 lbs. Deb: 9/13/46 C																											
1946	Chi-N	0	0	—	4	1	0	0	1	17	21	7	2	0	10	10	16.4	3.18	104	.309	.397	1	.200	0	0	0	0	0.1
1947	Chi-N	3	2	.600	23	2	1	0	0	45	43	17	4	1	14	22	11.6	3.40	116	.257	.319	3	.250	0	3	3	-0	0.3
1948	Chi-N	10	10	.500	29	26	8	3	0	164^2	157	75	8	1	77	89	12.8	3.66	107	.254	.338	6	.107	-3	5	5	-0	0.2
1949	Phi-N	17	8	.680	37	28	14	2	1	213	199	84	14	1	70	78	11.4	3.08	128	.250	.311	10	.143	-1	23	21	-2	2.0
1950	*Phi-N	9	11	.450	32	25	3	0	1	159^2	193	108	21	2	67	74	14.8	5.30	76	.304	.373	7	.140	-1	-21	-23	1	-2.5
1951	Phi-N	8	9	.471	28	24	7	2	0	168	172	69	13	2	55	65	12.3	3.48	111	.263	.322	5	.104	-2	9	7	-3	0.2
1952	Phi-N	13	14	.481	37	32	14	1	1	232^1	235	99	10	2	65	92	11.7	3.14	116	.260	.311	7	.089	-2	15	14	-2	1.1
1953	*Bro-N	15	5	.750	34	32	10	2	0	191^1	201	109	25	1	63	106	12.5	4.56	93	.269	.327	11	.147	-2	-6	-6	-0	-0.8
1954	Bro-N	11	6	.647	36	28	6	2	0	180^1	193	89	17	2	49	70	12.2	3.99	102	.275	.324	2	.043	-3	2	2	-2	-0.4
1955	*Bro-N	6	2	.750	18	11	2	1	0	73	86	46	8	0	31	26	14.4	5.42	75	.300	.368	1	.037	-3	-11	-11	1	-1.2
1956	Chi-N	1	6	.143	20	9	0	0	0	57	71	41	11	2	26	28	15.6	6.32	60	.313	.388	1	.083	-1	-16	-16	2	-1.6
	Cin-N	0	0	—	1	0	0	0	0	1	1	0	0	0	0	1	9.0	0.00	—	.250	.250	0	—	0	0	0	0	0.0
	Yr	1	6	.143	21	9	0	0	0	58	72	41	11	2	26	29	15.5	6.21	61	.312	.386	1	.083	-1	-16	-16	2	-1.6
1957	Bos-A	0	0	—	2	1	0	0	0	5	10	5	0	0	3	1	23.4	5.40	74	.417	.481	1	1.000	0	-1	-1	1	0.1
1959	KC-A	1	0	1.000	18	0	0	0	1	24	24	12	3	1	11	10	13.5	4.50	89	.261	.346	0	.000	-0	-2	-1	-0	-0.1
Total	13	94	73	.563	319	219	65	13	5	1531^1	1606	761	136	15	541	672	12.7	3.99	99	.271	.334	55	.114	-18	2	-8	-5	-2.6
● LEVI MEYERLE	Meyerle, Levi Samuel "Long Levi" b: 7/1845, Philadelphia, Pa. d: 11/4/21, Philadelphia, Pa. BR/TR, 6'1", 177 lbs. Deb: 5/20/1871 ♦																											
1871	Ath-n	0	0	—	1	0	0	0	0	1	1	1	0		2	0	27.0	9.00	45	.250	.500	64	.492	1	-1	-1		0.0
1876	Phi-N	0	2	.000	2	2	2	0	0	18	28	23	0		1	0	14.5	5.00	48	.333	.345	87	.336	1	-5	-5	-0	-0.4
● DAN MICELI	Miceli, Daniel b: 9/9/70, Newark, N.J. BR/TR, 6', 207 lbs. Deb: 9/9/93																											
1993	Pit-N	0	0	—	9	0	0	0	0	5^1	6	3	0	0	3	4	15.2	5.06	80	.273	.360	0	—	0	-1	-1	-0	0.0
1994	Pit-N	2	1	.667	28	0	0	0	2	27^1	28	19	5	2	11	27	13.5	5.93	73	.267	.347	0	.000	-0	-5	-5	0	-0.5
1995	Pit-N	4	4	.500	58	0	0	0	21	58	61	30	7	4	28	56	14.4	4.66	93	.270	.360	0	.000	-0	-3	-2	-1	-0.5
1996	Pit-N	2	10	.167	44	9	0	0	1	85^2	99	65	15	3	45	66	15.4	5.78	76	.291	.379	0	.000	-1	-15	-13	-2	-1.9
1997	Det-A	3	2	.600	71	0	0	0	3	82^2	77	49	13	1	38	79	12.6	5.01	92	.248	.332	0	—	0	-4	-4	-1	-0.3
1998	*SD-N	10	5	.667	67	0	0	0	2	72^2	64	28	6	1	27	70	11.4	3.22	122	.238	.310	1	1.000	1	8	6	-1	1.1
1999	SD-N	4	5	.444	66	0	0	0	2	68^2	67	39	7	2	36	59	13.8	4.46	94	.266	.362	0	.000	-0	1	-2	-1	-0.3
2000	Fla-N	6	4	.600	45	0	0	0	0	48^2	45	23	4	1	18	40	11.8	4.25	104	.242	.312	0	—	0	2	1	-1	0.1
Total	8	31	31	.500	388	9	0	0	31	449	447	256	57	14	206	401	13.4	4.71	91	.261	.346	1	.053	-2	-17	-21	-6	-2.3
● GENE MICHAEL	Michael, Eugene Richard "Stick" b: 6/2/38, Kent, Ohio BB/TR, 6'2", 183 lbs. Deb: 7/15/66 MC♦																											
1968	NY-A	0	0	—	1	0	0	0	0	3	5	5	0	1	0	3	18.0	0.00	—	.357	.400	23	.198	0	1	1	0	0.1
● JOHN MICHAELS	Michaels, John Joseph b: 7/10/07, Bridgeport, Conn. d: 11/18/96, Sebring, Fla. BL/TL, 5'10.5", 154 lbs. Deb: 4/16/32																											
1932	Bos-A	1	6	.143	28	8	2	0	0	80^2	101	59	4	3	27	16	14.6	5.13	88	.304	.362	3	.143	-1	-6	-6	1	-0.4
● JOHN MICHAELSON	Michaelson, John August "Mike" b: 8/12/1893, Tivalkoski, Finland d: 4/16/68, Woodruff, Wis. BR/TR, 5'9", 165 lbs. Deb: 8/28/21																											
1921	Chi-A	0	0	—	2	0	0	0	0	2^2	4	3	0	0	1	1	16.9	10.13	42	.400	.455	0	—	0	-2	-2	-0	-0.1
● CHRIS MICHALAK	Michalak, Christian Matthew b: 1/4/71, Joliet, Ill. BL/TL, 6'2", 195 lbs. Deb: 8/22/98																											
1998	Ari-N	0	0	—	5	0	0	0	0	5^1	9	7	1	0	4	5	21.9	11.81	36	.375	.464	0	—	0	-4	-5	-0	-0.2
● GLENN MICKENS	Mickens, Glenn Roger b: 7/26/30, Wilmar, Cal. BR/TR, 6', 175 lbs. Deb: 7/19/53																											
1953	Bro-N	0	1	.000	4	2	0	0	0	6^1	11	9	2	0	4	5	21.3	11.37	37	.393	.469	0	.000	-0	-5	-5	0	-0.6
● JIM MIDDLETON	Middleton, James Blaine "Rifle Jim" b: 5/28/1889, Argos, Ind. d: 1/12/74, Argos, Ind. BR/TR, 5'11.5", 165 lbs. Deb: 4/18/17																											
1917	NY-N	1	1	.500	13	0	0	0	1	36	35	18	1	1	8	9	11.0	2.75	93	.255	.301	0	.000	-1	-0	-1	1	-0.1
1921	Det-A	6	11	.353	38	10	2	0	**7**	121^2	149	83	5	2	44	31	14.4	5.03	85	.302	.361	5	.147	-2	-10	-10	1	-1.4
Total	2	7	12	.368	51	10	2	0	8	157^2	184	101	6	3	52	40	13.6	4.51	86	.292	.348	5	.119	-3	-10	-12	2	-1.5
● JOHN MIDDLETON	Middleton, John Wayne "Lefty" b: 4/11/1900, Mt.Calm, Tex. d: 11/3/86, Amarillo, Tex. BL/TL, 6'1", 185 lbs. Deb: 9/6/22																											
1922	Cle-A	0	1	.000	2	1	0	0	0	7^1	8	7	1	0	6	2	17.2	7.36	54	.286	.412	1	.333	0	-3	-3	0	-0.3
● DICK MIDKIFF	Midkiff, Richard b: 9/28/14, Gonzales, Tex. d: 10/30/56, Temple, Tex. BR/TR, 6'2", 185 lbs. Deb: 4/24/38																											
1938	Bos-A	1	1	.500	13	2	0	0	0	35^1	43	30	5	0	21	10	16.3	5.09	97	.305	.395	2	.200	0	-1	-1	0	0.0
● GARY MIELKE	Mielke, Gary Roger b: 1/28/63, St.James, Minn. BR/TR, 6'3", 185 lbs. Deb: 8/19/87																											
1987	Tex-A	0	0	—	3	0	0	0	0	3	3	2	2	0	1	3	12.0	6.00	75	.250	.308	0	—	0	-1	-1	-0	0.0
1989	Tex-A	1	0	1.000	43	0	0	0	1	49^2	52	18	4	2	25	26	14.3	3.26	122	.280	.371	0	—	0	3	4	-0	0.2
1990	Tex-A	0	3	.000	33	0	0	0	1	41	42	17	4	2	15	13	13.0	3.73	105	.271	.343	0	—	0	1	1	0	0.1
Total	3	1	3	.250	79	0	0	0	1	93^2	97	37	10	4	41	42	13.6	3.56	112	.275	.357	0	—	0	4	4	-0	0.3
● PETE MIKKELSEN	Mikkelsen, Peter James b: 10/25/39, Staten Island, N.Y. BR/TR, 6'2", 220 lbs. Deb: 4/17/64																											
1964	*NY-A	7	4	.636	50	0	0	0	12	86	79	35	3	4	41	63	13.0	3.56	102	.247	.340	1	.063	-1	1	1	-0	0.1
1965	NY-A	4	9	.308	41	3	0	0	1	82^1	78	40	10	3	36	69	12.8	3.28	104	.249	.332	1	.100	-0	2	1	-0	0.3
1966	Pit-N	9	8	.529	71	0	0	0	14	126	106	45	8	5	51	76	11.6	3.07	116	.234	.318	3	.150	-0	7	7	-0	1.0
1967	Pit-N	1	2	.333	32	0	0	0	2	56^1	50	29	7	3	19	30	11.5	4.31	78	.237	.309	0	.000	-0	-6	-6	-1	-0.5
	Chi-N	0	0	—	7	0	0	0	0	7	9	6	1	1	5	0	19.3	6.43	55	.333	.455	0	—	0	-2	-2	-0	-0.1
	Yr	1	2	.333	39	0	0	0	2	63^1	59	35	8	4	24	30	12.4	4.55	74	.248	.327	0	.000	-0	-8	-8	-1	-0.6

YEAR	TM/L	W	L	PCT	G	GS	CG	SH	SV	IP	H	R	HR	HB	BB	SO	RAT	ERA	ERA+	OAV	OOB	BH	AVG	PB	PR	PR+	PD	TPI
1968	Chi-N	0	0	—	3	0	0	0	0	4^2	7	4	3	0	1	5	15.4	7.71	41	.350	.381	1	1.000	0	-2	-2	0	-0.1
	StL-N	0	0	—	5	0	0	0	0	16	10	5	0	0	7	8	9.6	1.13	257	.179	.270	0	.000	-0	3	3	-1	0.1
	Yr	0	0	—	8	0	0	0	0	20^2	17	9	3	0	8	13	10.9	2.61	113	.224	.298	1	.250	0	1	1	-1	0.0
1969	LA-N	7	5	.583	48	0	0	0	4	81^1	57	34	9	4	30	51	10.1	2.77	120	.193	.277	1	.167	-0	8	5	1	0.9
1970	LA-N	4	2	.667	33	0	0	0	6	62	48	20	5	4	20	47	10.5	2.76	139	.211	.287	2	.333	1	9	8	0	1.0
1971	LA-N	8	5	.615	41	0	0	0	5	74	67	38	10	1	17	46	10.3	3.65	89	.242	.288	2	.200	0	-1	-4	1	-0.6
1972	LA-N	5	5	.500	33	0	0	0	5	57^2	65	32	3	5	23	41	14.5	4.06	82	.283	.360	0	.000	-0	-4	-5	-0	-1.0
Total	9	45	40	.529	364	3	0	0	49	653^1	576	288	59	30	250	436	11.8	3.38	102	.237	.316	11	.133	-2	13	6	2	1.1

● HANK MIKLOS Miklos, John Joseph b: 11/27/10, Chicago, Ill. d: 3/29/2000, Adrian, Mich. BL/TL, 5'11", 175 lbs. Deb: 4/23/44

YEAR	TM/L	W	L	PCT	G	GS	CG	SH	SV	IP	H	R	HR	HB	BB	SO	RAT	ERA	ERA+	OAV	OOB	BH	AVG	PB	PR	PR+	PD	TPI
1944	Chi-N	0	0	—	2	0	0	0	0	7	9	6	1	0	3	0	15.4	7.71	46	.333	.400	0	.000	-0	-3	-3	1	-0.1

● BOB MILACKI Milacki, Robert b: 7/28/64, Trenton, N.J. BR/TR, 6'4", 234 lbs. Deb: 9/18/88

YEAR	TM/L	W	L	PCT	G	GS	CG	SH	SV	IP	H	R	HR	HB	BB	SO	RAT	ERA	ERA+	OAV	OOB	BH	AVG	PB	PR	PR+	PD	TPI
1988	Bal-A	2	0	1.000	3	3	1	1	0	25	9	2	1	0	9	18	6.5	0.72	543	.110	.198	0	—	0	9	9	0	0.8
1989	Bal-A	14	12	.538	37	36	3	2	0	243	233	105	21	2	88	113	12.0	3.74	102	.254	.320	0	—	0	4	2	-0	0.1
1990	Bal-A	5	8	.385	27	24	1	1	0	135^1	143	73	18	0	61	60	13.6	4.46	85	.273	.349	0	—	0	-8	-10	1	-0.8
1991	Bal-A	10	9	.526	31	26	3	1	0	184	175	86	17	1	53	108	11.2	4.01	99	.253	.307	0	—	0	2	-1	1	0.0
1992	Bal-A	6	8	.429	23	20	0	0	1	115^2	140	78	16	2	44	51	14.5	5.84	69	.296	.358	0	—	0	-24	-23	-1	-2.5
1993	Cle-A	1	1	.500	5	2	0	0	0	16	19	8	3	0	11	7	16.9	3.38	129	.302	.405	0	—	0	2	2	0	0.2
1994	KC-A	0	5	.000	10	10	0	0	0	55^2	68	43	6	1	20	17	14.4	6.14	82	.298	.357	0	—	0	-8	-7	1	-0.4
1996	Sea-A	1	4	.200	7	4	0	0	0	21	30	20	3	0	15	13	19.3	6.86	72	.330	.425	0	—	0	-4	-4	-0	-0.8
Total	8	39	47	.453	143	125	8	5	1	795^2	817	415	85	6	301	387	12.7	4.38	91	.266	.333	0	—	0	-28	-34	2	-3.4

● MIKE MILCHIN Milchin, Michael Wayne b: 2/28/68, Knoxville, Tenn. BL/TL, 6'3", 190 lbs. Deb: 5/14/96

YEAR	TM/L	W	L	PCT	G	GS	CG	SH	SV	IP	H	R	HR	HB	BB	SO	RAT	ERA	ERA+	OAV	OOB	BH	AVG	PB	PR	PR+	PD	TPI
1996	Min-A	2	1	.667	26	0	0	0	0	21^2	31	21	6	0	12	19	17.9	8.31	62	.341	.417	0	—	0	-8	-7	0	-0.8
	Bal-A	1	0	1.000	13	0	0	0	0	11	13	7	0	0	5	10	14.7	5.73	86	.325	.400	0	—	0	-1	-1	0	0.0
	Yr	3	1	.750	39	0	0	0	0	32^2	44	28	6	0	17	29	16.8	7.44	68	.336	.412	0	—	0	-9	-9	0	-0.8

● CARL MILES Miles, Carl Thomas b: 3/22/18, Trenton, Mo. BB/TL, 5'11", 178 lbs. Deb: 6/8/40

YEAR	TM/L	W	L	PCT	G	GS	CG	SH	SV	IP	H	R	HR	HB	BB	SO	RAT	ERA	ERA+	OAV	OOB	BH	AVG	PB	PR	PR+	PD	TPI
1940	Phi-A	0	0	—	2	0	0	0	0	8	9	12	2	0	8	6	19.1	13.50	33	.281	.425	3	.750	2	-8	-8	-0	-0.2

● JIM MILES Miles, James Charlie b: 8/8/43, Grenada, Miss. BR/TR, 6'2", 210 lbs. Deb: 9/7/68

YEAR	TM/L	W	L	PCT	G	GS	CG	SH	SV	IP	H	R	HR	HB	BB	SO	RAT	ERA	ERA+	OAV	OOB	BH	AVG	PB	PR	PR+	PD	TPI
1968	Was-A	0	0	—	3	0	0	0	0	4^1	8	6	0	0	2	5	20.8	12.46	23	.421	.476	0	—	0	-5	-5	-0	-0.3
1969	Was-A	0	1	.000	10	1	0	0	0	20^1	19	15	2	4	15	15	16.8	6.20	56	.257	.409	1	.333	0	-6	-6	1	-0.2
Total	2	0	1	.000	13	1	0	0	0	24^2	27	21	2	4	17	20	17.5	7.30	46	.290	.421	1	.333	0	-10	-11	1	-0.5

● SAM MILITELLO Militello, Sam Salvatore b: 11/26/69, Tampa, Fla. BR/TR, 6'3", 200 lbs. Deb: 8/9/92

YEAR	TM/L	W	L	PCT	G	GS	CG	SH	SV	IP	H	R	HR	HB	BB	SO	RAT	ERA	ERA+	OAV	OOB	BH	AVG	PB	PR	PR+	PD	TPI
1992	NY-A	3	3	.500	9	9	0	0	0	60	43	24	6	2	32	42	11.6	3.45	114	.195	.302	0	—	0	3	3	-1	0.2
1993	NY-A	1	1	.500	3	2	0	0	0	9^1	10	8	1	2	7	5	18.3	6.75	62	.270	.413	0	—	0	-3	-3	0	-0.5
Total	2	4	4	.500	12	11	0	0	0	69^1	53	32	7	4	39	47	12.5	3.89	102	.205	.319	0	—	0	1	0	-1	-0.3

● JOHNNY MILJUS Miljus, John Kenneth "Jovo" or "Big Serb"
b: 6/30/1895, Pittsburgh, Pa. d: 2/11/76, Fort Harrison, Mont. BR/TR, 6'1", 178 lbs. Deb: 10/2/15

YEAR	TM/L	W	L	PCT	G	GS	CG	SH	SV	IP	H	R	HR	HB	BB	SO	RAT	ERA	ERA+	OAV	OOB	BH	AVG	PB	PR	PR+	PD	TPI
1915	Pit-F	0	0	—	1	0	0	0	0	1	1	0	0	0	0	0	9.0	0.00	—	.250	.250	0	—	0	0	0	0	0.0
1917	Bro-N	0	1	.000	4	1	1	0	0	15	14	3	0	3	8	9	15.0	0.60	466	.250	.373	0	.000	-1	4	4	-0	0.1
1920	Bro-N	1	0	1.000	9	0	0	0	0	23^1	24	10	2	0	4	9	10.8	3.09	104	.267	.298	2	.333	1	0	0	1	0.2
1921	Bro-N	6	3	.667	28	9	3	0	1	93^2	115	49	1	2	27	37	13.8	4.23	92	.312	.362	5	.167	-2	-5	-3	2	-0.3
1927	*Pit-N	8	3	.727	19	6	3	2	0	75^2	62	21	0	0	17	24	9.4	1.90	216	.228	.273	5	.179	-1	17	18	2	2.5
1928	Pit-N	5	7	.417	21	10	3	0	1	69^2	90	48	2	3	33	26	16.3	5.30	77	.313	.389	8	.308	1	-10	-9	-0	-1.3
	Cle-A	1	4	.200	11	4	1	0	1	50^2	46	25	1	0	20	19	11.7	2.66	156	.243	.316	3	.200	-0	8	8	-0	0.7
1929	Cle-A	8	8	.500	34	15	4	0	2	128^1	174	93	10	3	64	42	16.9	5.19	86	.331	.406	11	.256	1	-13	-10	0	-1.0
Total	7	29	26	.527	127	45	15	2	5	457^1	526	249	16	11	173	166	14.0	3.92	104	.293	.359	34	.222	0	0	7	4	0.9

● DYAR MILLER Miller, Dyar K b: 5/29/46, Batesville, Ind. BR/TR, 6'1", 195 lbs. Deb: 6/9/75 C

YEAR	TM/L	W	L	PCT	G	GS	CG	SH	SV	IP	H	R	HR	HB	BB	SO	RAT	ERA	ERA+	OAV	OOB	BH	AVG	PB	PR	PR+	PD	TPI
1975	Bal-A	6	3	.667	30	0	0	0	8	46^1	32	14	3	0	16	33	9.3	2.72	129	.199	.271	0	—	0	6	4	0	0.9
1976	Bal-A	2	4	.333	49	0	0	0	7	88^2	79	31	5	1	36	37	11.8	2.94	111	.246	.324	0	—	0	6	4	-1	0.2
1977	Bal-A	2	2	.500	12	0	0	0	1	22^1	25	14	6	0	10	9	14.1	5.64	67	.278	.350	0	—	0	-4	-5	-0	-0.8
	Cal-A	4	4	.500	41	0	0	0	4	92^1	81	35	10	0	30	49	10.8	3.02	130	.242	.304	0	—	0	11	10	-1	0.8
	Yr	6	6	.500	53	0	0	0	5	114^2	106	49	16	0	40	58	11.5	3.53	111	.249	.314	0	—	0	7	5	-1	0.0
1978	Cal-A	6	2	.750	41	0	0	0	1	84^2	85	29	3	5	41	34	13.9	2.66	136	.264	.356	0	—	0	11	9	-2	0.7
1979	Cal-A	1	0	1.000	14	1	0	0	0	35^1	44	14	2	2	13	16	15.0	3.31	123	.319	.386	0	—	0	4	3	-1	0.1
	Tor-A	0	0	—	10	0	0	0	0	15^1	27	18	3	0	5	7	18.8	10.57	41	.391	.432	0	—	0	-11	-10	-0	-0.5
	Yr	1	0	1.000	24	1	0	0	0	50^2	71	32	5	2	18	23	16.2	5.51	76	.343	.401	0	—	0	-7	-8	-1	-0.4
1980	NY-N	1	2	.333	31	0	0	0	1	42	37	9	1	0	11	28	10.3	1.93	185	.242	.293	0	.000	-0	8	8	-1	0.5
1981	NY-N	1	0	1.000	23	0	0	0	0	38^1	49	20	2	1	15	22	15.3	3.29	106	.327	.392	1	.333	0	1	1	-1	0.0
Total	7	23	17	.575	251	1	0	0	22	465^1	459	184	35	9	177	235	12.5	3.23	113	.264	.335	1	.250	0	30	23	-7	1.9

● ELMER MILLER Miller, Elmer Joseph "Lefty" b: 4/17/03, Detroit, Mich. d: 1/8/87, Corona, Cal. BL/TL, 5'11", 189 lbs. Deb: 6/21/29 ♦

YEAR	TM/L	W	L	PCT	G	GS	CG	SH	SV	IP	H	R	HR	HB	BB	SO	RAT	ERA	ERA+	OAV	OOB	BH	AVG	PB	PR	PR+	PD	TPI
1929	Phi-N	0	1	.000	8	2	0	0	0	11^1	12	18	1	3	21	5	28.6	11.12	47	.279	.537	9	.237	0	-8	-7	-0	-0.5

● FRANK MILLER Miller, Frank Lee "Bullet" b: 5/13/1886, Allegan, Mich. d: 2/19/74, Allegan, Mich. BR/TR, 6', 188 lbs. Deb: 7/12/13

YEAR	TM/L	W	L	PCT	G	GS	CG	SH	SV	IP	H	R	HR	HB	BB	SO	RAT	ERA	ERA+	OAV	OOB	BH	AVG	PB	PR	PR+	PD	TPI
1913	Chi-A	0	1	.000	1	1	0	0	0	1^2	4	5	0	0	3	2	37.8	27.00	11	.571	.700	0	—	0	-4	-4	0	-0.6
1916	Pit-N	7	10	.412	30	20	10	2	1	173	135	55	4	7	49	88	9.9	2.29	117	.226	.292	7	.137	-1	6	7	-1	0.6
1917	Pit-N	10	19	.345	38	28	14	5	1	224	216	98	1	5	60	92	11.3	3.13	91	.251	.304	9	.118	-4	-11	-7	1	-1.3
1918	Pit-N	11	8	.579	23	23	14	2	0	170^1	152	60	1	7	37	47	10.4	2.38	121	.250	.301	6	.105	-3	7	9	-0	0.6
1919	Pit-N	13	12	.520	32	26	16	3	0	201^2	170	79	6	5	34	59	9.3	3.03	99	.234	.272	7	.106	-5	-3	-0	1	-0.5
1922	Bos-N	11	13	.458	31	23	14	2	1	200	213	100	7	2	60	65	12.4	3.51	114	.279	.333	8	.118	-5	13	11	1	0.8
1923	Bos-N	0	3	.000	8	6	0	0	1	39^1	54	26	2	3	11	6	15.6	4.58	87	.335	.389	1	.143	-0	-3	-3	-1	-0.3
Total	7	52	66	.441	163	127	68	14	4	1010	944	423	21	29	254	359	10.9	3.01	104	.253	.306	38	.117	-18	-7	14	1	-0.7

● FRED MILLER Miller, Frederick Holman "Speedy" b: 6/28/1886, Fairfield, Ind. d: 5/2/53, Brookville, Ind. BL/TL, 6'2", 190 lbs. Deb: 7/8/10

YEAR	TM/L	W	L	PCT	G	GS	CG	SH	SV	IP	H	R	HR	HB	BB	SO	RAT	ERA	ERA+	OAV	OOB	BH	AVG	PB	PR	PR+	PD	TPI
1910	Bro-N	1	1	.500	6	2	0	0	0	21	25	19	1	3	13	2	17.6	4.71	64	.309	.423	2	.250	0	-4	-4	0	-0.3

● BERT MILLER Miller, Herbert A. b: 10/26/1875, Riley, Mich. d: 6/14/37, Flint, Mich. Deb: 7/15/1897

YEAR	TM/L	W	L	PCT	G	GS	CG	SH	SV	IP	H	R	HR	HB	BB	SO	RAT	ERA	ERA+	OAV	OOB	BH	AVG	PB	PR	PR+	PD	TPI
1897	Lou-N	0	1	.000	4	1	1	0	0	17	32	23	0	0	3	3	18.5	7.94	54	.395	.417	1	.167	-1	-7	-7	0	-0.3

● OX MILLER Miller, John Anthony b: 5/4/15, Gause, Tex. BR/TR, 6'1", 190 lbs. Deb: 8/7/43

YEAR	TM/L	W	L	PCT	G	GS	CG	SH	SV	IP	H	R	HR	HB	BB	SO	RAT	ERA	ERA+	OAV	OOB	BH	AVG	PB	PR	PR+	PD	TPI
1943	Was-A	0	0	—	3	0	0	0	0	6	10	7	1	0	5	1	22.5	10.50	31	.370	.469	0	.000	-0	-5	-5	1	-0.2
	StL-A	0	0	—	2	0	0	0	0	6	7	8	2	2	3	3	18.0	12.00	28	.304	.429	0	.000	-0	-6	-6	1	-0.2
	Yr	0	0	—	5	0	0	0	0	12	17	15	3	2	8	4	20.3	11.25	29	.340	.450	0	.000	-0	-11	-11	1	-0.4
1945	StL-A	2	1	.667	4	3	3	0	0	28^1	23	5	2	0	5	4	8.9	1.59	222	.219	.255	2	.182	-0	6	6	-1	0.5
1946	StL-A	1	3	.250	11	3	0	0	1	35^1	52	28	5	0	15	12	17.1	6.88	54	.338	.396	2	.286	1	-13	-12	1	-1.1
1947	Chi-N	1	2	.333	4	4	1	0	0	16	31	18	2	0	5	7	20.3	10.13	39	.397	.434	3	.429	2	-11	-11	-0	-1.4
Total	4	4	6	.400	24	10	4	0	1	91^2	123	66	12	2	33	27	15.5	6.38	57	.318	.374	7	.259	2	-29	-27	0	-2.4

● JOHN MILLER Miller, John Ernest b: 5/30/41, Baltimore, Md. BR/TR, 6'2", 210 lbs. Deb: 9/22/62

YEAR	TM/L	W	L	PCT	G	GS	CG	SH	SV	IP	H	R	HR	HB	BB	SO	RAT	ERA	ERA+	OAV	OOB	BH	AVG	PB	PR	PR+	PD	TPI
1962	Bal-A	1	1	.500	2	1	0	0	0	10	2	1	0	0	5	4	6.3	0.90	411	.065	.194	0	.000	-0	3	3	0	0.7
1963	Bal-A	1	1	.500	3	2	0	0	0	17	12	6	0	0	14	16	13.8	3.18	109	.194	.342	0	.000	-1	1	1	-0	0.0
1965	Bal-A	6	4	.600	16	16	1	0	0	93^1	75	38	4	1	58	71	12.9	3.18	109	.223	.338	3	.100	-1	3	3	0	0.3
1966	Bal-A	4	8	.333	23	16	0	0	0	100^2	92	59	15	0	58	81	13.4	4.74	70	.241	.342	4	.118	-1	-15	-16	1	-1.9
1967	Bal-A	0	0	—	2	0	0	0	0	6	7	5	1	2	3	6	18.0	7.50	42	.304	.429	0	—	0	-3	-3	0	-0.1
Total	5	12	14	.462	46	35	1	0	0	227	188	109	20	3	138	178	13.0	3.89	88	.225	.337	7	.096	-3	-10	-12	1	-1.0

● CYCLONE MILLER Miller, Joseph H. b: 9/24/1859, Springfield, Mass d: 10/13/16, New London, Conn. TL, 5'9.5", 165 lbs. Deb: 7/11/1884

YEAR	TM/L	W	L	PCT	G	GS	CG	SH	SV	IP	H	R	HR	HB	BB	SO	RAT	ERA	ERA+	OAV	OOB	BH	AVG	PB	PR	PR+	PD	TPI
1884	CP-U	1	0	1.000	1	1	1	0	0	9	4	2	0		0	13	4.0	1.00	244	.125	.125	1	.250	-0	1	1	1	0.2
	Pro-N	3	2	.600	6	5	2	0	0	34^2	36	24	0		11	12	12.2	2.08	137	.259	.313	1	.043	-3	3	3	-1	0.1
	Phi-N	0	1	.000	1	1	1	0	0	9	17	19	5		6	1	23.0	10.00	30	.386	.460	0	.000	-1	-7	-7	0	-0.5
	Yr	3	3	.500	7	6	3	0	0	43^2	53	43	5		17	13	14.4	3.71	78	.290	.350	1	.037	-4	-4	-4	-1	-0.4
1886	Phi-a	10	8	.556	19	19	19	1	0	169^2	158	109	6	4	59	99	11.7	2.97	118	.239	.305	9	.136	-1	9	10	1	0.9
Total	2	14	11	.560	27	26	23	1	0	222^1	215	154	11	4	76	125	11.9	3.04	110	.245	.308	11	.113	-5	7	7	1	0.7

● WHITEY MILLER Miller, Kenneth Albert b: 5/2/15, St.Louis, Mo. d: 4/3/91, St.Louis, Mo. BR/TR, 6'1", 195 lbs. Deb: 9/15/44

YEAR	TM/L	W	L	PCT	G	GS	CG	SH	SV	IP	H	R	HR	HB	BB	SO	RAT	ERA	ERA+	OAV	OOB	BH	AVG	PB	PR	PR+	PD	TPI
1944	NY-N	0	1	.000	4	0	0	0	0	5	1	2	0	0	4	2	9.0	0.00	—	.059	.238	0	.000	-0	2	2	0	0.4

● KURT MILLER Miller, Kurt Everett b: 8/24/72, Tucson, Ariz. BR/TR, 6'5", 205 lbs. Deb: 6/11/94

YEAR	TM/L	W	L	PCT	G	GS	CG	SH	SV	IP	H	R	HR	HB	BB	SO	RAT	ERA	ERA+	OAV	OOB	BH	AVG	PB	PR	PR+	PD	TPI
1994	Fla-N	1	3	.250	4	4	0	0	0	20	26	18	3	2	7	11	15.7	8.10	54	.317	.385	1	.167	-0	-9	-8	1	-1.2
1996	Fla-N	1	3	.250	26	5	0	0	0	46^1	57	41	5	2	33	30	17.9	6.80	60	.313	.424	3	.375	1	-13	-15	0	-1.0
1997	Fla-N	0	1	.000	7	0	0	0	0	7^1	12	8	2	1	7	7	24.5	9.82	41	.364	.488	0	—	0	-5	-5	-0	-0.6
1998	Chi-N	0	0	—	3	0	0	0	0	4	3	0	0	0	0	6	6.8	0.00	—	.200	.200	0	—	0	2	2	-0	0.1
1999	Chi-N	0	0	—	4	0	0	0	0	3	6	6	1	0	3	1	27.0	18.00	25	.462	.563	0	—	0	-4	-5	-0	-0.2
Total	5	2	7	.222	44	9	0	0	0	80^2	104	73	11	5	50	55	17.7	7.48	56	.320	.418	4	.286	1	-29	-30	0	-2.9

● LARRY MILLER Miller, Larry Don b: 6/19/37, Topeka, Kan. BL/TL, 6', 195 lbs. Deb: 6/21/64

YEAR	TM/L	W	L	PCT	G	GS	CG	SH	SV	IP	H	R	HR	HB	BB	SO	RAT	ERA	ERA+	OAV	OOB	BH	AVG	PB	PR	PR+	PD	TPI
1964	LA-N	4	8	.333	16	14	1	0	0	79^2	87	44	1	2	28	50	13.2	4.18	78	.275	.338	7	.269	2	-6	-9	-1	-1.1
1965	NY-N	1	4	.200	28	5	0	0	0	57^1	66	32	6	1	25	36	14.4	5.02	70	.289	.362	2	.182	0	-9	-10	-0	-0.8
1966	NY-N	0	2	.000	4	1	0	0	0	8^1	9	7	3	0	4	7	14.0	7.56	48	.273	.351	1	.500	0	-4	-4	-0	-0.7
Total	3	5	14	.263	48	20	1	0	0	145^1	162	83	10	3	57	93	13.7	4.71	72	.281	.349	10	.256	2	-19	-23	-1	-2.6

● RED MILLER Miller, Leo Alphonso b: 2/11/1897, Philadelphia, Pa. d: 10/20/73, Orlando, Fla. BR/TR, 5'11", 195 lbs. Deb: 4/13/23

YEAR	TM/L	W	L	PCT	G	GS	CG	SH	SV	IP	H	R	HR	HB	BB	SO	RAT	ERA	ERA+	OAV	OOB	BH	AVG	PB	PR	PR+	PD	TPI
1923	Phi-N	0	0	—	1	0	0	0	0	1^2	6	6	0	0	1	0	37.8	32.40	14	.545	.583	0	.000	-0	-5	-4	-0	-0.2

● PAUL MILLER Miller, Paul Robert b: 4/27/65, Burlington, Wis. BR/TR, 6'5", 215 lbs. Deb: 7/30/91

YEAR	TM/L	W	L	PCT	G	GS	CG	SH	SV	IP	H	R	HR	HB	BB	SO	RAT	ERA	ERA+	OAV	OOB	BH	AVG	PB	PR	PR+	PD	TPI
1991	Pit-N	0	0	—	1	1	0	0	0	5	4	3	0	0	3	2	12.6	5.40	66	.222	.333	0	.000	-0	-1	-1	-0	-0.1
1992	Pit-N	1	0	1.000	6	0	0	0	0	11^1	11	3	0	0	1	5	9.5	2.38	145	.256	.273	0	.000	-0	1	1	-0	0.1
1993	Pit-N	0	0	—	3	2	0	0	0	10	15	6	2	0	2	2	15.3	5.40	75	.349	.378	0	.000	-0	-2	-1	-0	-0.1
Total	3	1	0	1.000	10	3	0	0	0	26^1	30	12	2	0	6	9	12.3	4.10	90	.288	.327	0	.000	-1	-1	-1	-1	-0.1

● RALPH MILLER Miller, Ralph Darwin b: 3/15/1873, Cincinnati, Ohio d: 5/8/73, Cincinnati, Ohio BR/TR, 5'11", 170 lbs. Deb: 5/4/1898

YEAR	TM/L	W	L	PCT	G	GS	CG	SH	SV	IP	H	R	HR	HB	BB	SO	RAT	ERA	ERA+	OAV	OOB	BH	AVG	PB	PR	PR+	PD	TPI
1898	Bro-N	4	14	.222	23	21	16	0	0	151^2	161	119	4	13	86	43	15.4	5.34	67	.270	.374	12	.194	-1	-29	-30	3	-2.7
1899	Bal-N	1	3	.250	6	4	3	0	0	37	44	28	0	4	14	3	15.1	4.38	90	.295	.371	2	.182	1	-2	-2	-1	0.0
Total	2	5	17	.227	29	25	19	0	0	188^2	205	147	4	17	100	46	15.4	5.15	71	.275	.374	14	.192	1	-31	-31	2	-2.7

● RALPH MILLER Miller, Ralph Henry "Moose" or "Lefty" b: 1/14/1899, Vinton, Iowa d: 2/18/67, White Bear Lake, Minn. BR/TL, 6'1.5", 190 lbs. Deb: 9/16/21 F

YEAR	TM/L	W	L	PCT	G	GS	CG	SH	SV	IP	H	R	HR	HB	BB	SO	RAT	ERA	ERA+	OAV	OOB	BH	AVG	PB	PR	PR+	PD	TPI
1921	Was-A	0	0	—	1	0	0	0	0	1	0	0	0	0	0	0	0.0	0.00	—	.000	.000	0	—	0	0	0	-0	0.0

● RANDY MILLER Miller, Randall Scott b: 3/18/53, Oxnard, Cal. BR/TR, 6'1", 180 lbs. Deb: 9/7/77

YEAR	TM/L	W	L	PCT	G	GS	CG	SH	SV	IP	H	R	HR	HB	BB	SO	RAT	ERA	ERA+	OAV	OOB	BH	AVG	PB	PR	PR+	PD	TPI
1977	Bal-A	0	0	—	1	0	0	0	0	0^2	4	3	0	0	0	0	54.0	40.50	9	.800	.800	0	—	0	-3	-3	-0	-0.1
1978	Mon-N	0	1	.000	5	0	0	0	0	7	11	9	1	0	3	6	18.0	10.29	34	.393	.452	0	.000	-0	-5	-5	0	-0.7
Total	2	0	1	.000	6	0	0	0	0	7^2	15	12	1	0	3	6	21.1	12.91	28	.455	.500	0	.000	-0	-8	-8	-0	-0.8

● BOB MILLER Miller, Robert Gerald b: 7/15/35, Berwyn, Ill. BR/TL, 6'1", 185 lbs. Deb: 6/25/53

YEAR	TM/L	W	L	PCT	G	GS	CG	SH	SV	IP	H	R	HR	HB	BB	SO	RAT	ERA	ERA+	OAV	OOB	BH	AVG	PB	PR	PR+	PD	TPI
1953	Det-A	1	2	.333	13	1	0	0	0	36^1	43	25	2	1	21	9	16.1	5.94	68	.289	.380	1	.125	-1	-8	-7	0	-0.6
1954	Det-A	1	1	.500	32	1	0	0	1	69^2	62	25	1	0	26	27	11.4	2.45	150	.244	.314	2	.133	-0	10	10	-1	0.4
1955	Det-A	2	1	.667	7	3	1	0	0	25^1	26	12	4	0	12	11	13.5	2.49	154	.263	.342	2	.222	0	4	4	-0	0.4
1956	Det-A	0	2	.000	11	3	0	0	0	31^2	37	23	5	0	22	16	16.8	5.68	72	.308	.415	1	.143	0	-5	-6	-1	-0.3
1962	Cin-N	0	0	—	6	0	0	0	0	5^1	14	13	1	2	3	4	32.1	21.94	18	.538	.613	0	.000	-0	-11	-10	0	-0.5
	NY-N	2	2	.500	17	0	0	0	1	20^1	24	16	2	1	8	8	14.6	7.08	59	.312	.384	0	.000	-0	-7	-6	-0	-1.1
	Yr	2	2	.500	23	0	0	0	1	25^2	38	29	3	3	11	12	18.2	10.17	41	.369	.444	0	.000	-0	-18	-16	0	-1.6
Total	5	6	8	.429	86	8	1	0	2	188^2	206	114	15	4	92	75	14.4	4.72	83	.284	.368	6	.146	-1	-17	-17	-1	-1.7

● BOB MILLER Miller, Robert John b: 6/16/26, Detroit, Mich. BR/TR, 6'3", 190 lbs. Deb: 9/16/49

YEAR	TM/L	W	L	PCT	G	GS	CG	SH	SV	IP	H	R	HR	HB	BB	SO	RAT	ERA	ERA+	OAV	OOB	BH	AVG	PB	PR	PR+	PD	TPI
1949	Phi-N	0	0	—	3	0	0	0	0	2^2	2	0	0	0	2	0	13.5	0.00	—	.200	.333	0	—	0	1	1	0	0.1
1950	*Phi-N	11	6	.647	35	22	7	2	1	174	190	78	9	5	57	44	13.0	3.57	113	.277	.337	11	.180	-1	11	9	2	1.0
1951	Phi-N	2	1	.667	17	3	0	0	0	34^1	47	33	2	1	18	10	17.3	6.82	56	.331	.410	3	.429	1	-11	-12	-1	-0.9
1952	Phi-N	0	1	.000	3	1	0	0	0	9	13	6	2	0	1	2	14.0	6.00	61	.351	.368	0	.000	-0	-2	-2	0	-0.2
1953	Phi-N	8	9	.471	35	20	8	3	2	157^1	169	76	14	2	42	63	12.2	4.00	105	.271	.319	10	.182	-1	5	4	-1	0.2
1954	Phi-N	7	9	.438	30	16	5	0	0	150	176	84	14	3	39	42	13.1	4.56	89	.300	.347	8	.160	0	-8	-9	1	-0.7
1955	Phi-N	8	4	.667	40	0	0	0	1	89^2	80	26	6	1	28	28	10.9	2.41	165	.242	.304	5	.278	1	16	16	0	2.1
1956	Phi-N	3	6	.333	49	6	3	1	5	122^1	115	55	14	3	34	53	11.2	3.24	115	.248	.303	2	.091	-1	7	7	-0	0.4
1957	Phi-N	2	5	.286	32	1	0	0	6	60^1	61	18	4	1	17	12	11.8	2.69	142	.265	.319	2	.250	2	8	8	-1	1.1
1958	Phi-N	1	1	.500	17	0	0	0	0	22^1	36	30	7	0	9	9	18.1	11.69	34	.360	.413	0	.000	-0	-19	-19	-0	-1.5
Total	10	42	42	.500	261	69	23	6	15	822	889	406	72	16	247	263	12.6	3.96	101	.277	.332	41	.184	1	8	2	1	1.6

● BOB MILLER Miller, Robert Lane (b: Robert Lane Gemeinweiser) b: 2/18/39, St.Louis, Mo. d: 8/6/93, Rancho Bernardo, Cal. BR/TR, 6'1", 182 lbs. Deb: 6/26/57 C

YEAR	TM/L	W	L	PCT	G	GS	CG	SH	SV	IP	H	R	HR	HB	BB	SO	RAT	ERA	ERA+	OAV	OOB	BH	AVG	PB	PR	PR+	PD	TPI
1957	StL-N	0	0	—	5	0	0	0	0	9	13	9	2	0	5	7	18.0	7.00	57	.325	.400	0	—	0	-3	-3	0	-0.1
1959	StL-N	4	3	.571	11	10	3	0	0	70^2	66	31	2	1	21	43	11.2	3.31	128	.248	.306	5	.208	0	5	7	1	0.8
1960	StL-N	4	3	.571	15	7	0	0	0	52^2	53	21	2	1	17	33	12.1	3.42	120	.262	.323	2	.143	-1	2	4	0	0.4
1961	StL-N	1	3	.250	34	5	0	0	3	74^1	82	41	6	0	46	39	15.5	4.24	104	.290	.389	5	.357	2	-2	1	1	0.3
1962	NY-N	1	12	.077	33	21	1	0	0	143^2	146	98	20	6	62	91	13.4	4.89	86	.259	.339	5	.122	-1	-15	-11	2	-0.7
1963	LA-N	10	8	.556	42	23	2	0	1	187	171	71	7	3	65	125	11.5	2.89	105	.244	.311	4	.070	-3	8	3	5	0.6
1964	LA-N	7	7	.500	**74**	2	0	0	9	137^2	115	49	1	2	63	94	11.8	2.62	124	.226	.314	3	.158	1	14	10	2	1.5
1965	*LA-N	6	7	.462	61	1	0	0	9	103	82	37	9	3	26	77	9.7	2.97	110	.225	.282	0	.000	-1	7	4	-0	0.5
1966	*LA-N	4	2	.667	46	0	0	0	5	84^1	70	31	5	1	29	58	10.7	2.77	119	.230	.299	1	.077	-1	8	5	-1	0.2
1967	LA-N	2	9	.182	52	4	0	0	0	85^2	88	46	9	3	27	32	12.4	4.31	72	.273	.335	1	.125	-0	-9	-13	1	-1.5
1968	Min-A	0	3	.000	45	0	0	0	2	72^1	65	26	1	5	24	41	11.7	2.74	113	.239	.312	1	.143	-0	2	3	1	0.2
1969	*Min-A	5	5	.500	48	11	1	0	3	119^1	118	42	9	0	32	57	11.3	3.02	121	.264	.313	0	.000	-3	8	8	1	0.5
1970	Cle-A	2	2	.500	15	2	0	0	1	28	35	14	1	0	15	15	16.1	4.18	95	.310	.391	1	.200	0	-1	-1	-1	-0.1
	Chi-A	4	6	.400	15	12	0	0	0	70	88	42	11	4	33	36	16.1	5.01	78	.315	.396	4	.174	0	-10	-8	2	-0.8
	Yr	6	8	.429	30	14	0	0	1	98	123	56	12	4	48	51	16.1	4.78	82	.314	.394	5	.179	1	-12	-9	1	-0.9
	Chi-N	0	0	—	7	1	0	0	2	9	6	5	3	0	6	4	12.0	5.00	90	.194	.324	0	—	0	-1	-0	0	0.0
1971	Chi-N	0	0	—	2	0	0	0	0	7	10	4	0	0	1	2	14.1	5.14	77	.357	.379	0	.000	-0	-1	-1	0	0.0
	SD-N	7	3	.700	38	0	0	0	7	63^2	53	12	0	1	26	36	11.3	1.41	234	.227	.308	0	.000	-1	15	14	1	2.6
	*Pit-N	1	2	.333	16	0	0	0	3	28	20	8	1	0	13	13	10.6	1.29	263	.200	.292	0	.000	0	7	7	0	0.9
	Yr	8	5	.615	56	0	0	0	10	98^2	83	24	1	1	40	51	11.3	1.64	205	.230	.308	0	.000	-1	20	20	2	3.5
1972	*Pit-N	5	2	.714	36	0	0	0	3	54^1	54	19	3	1	24	18	13.1	2.65	125	.263	.343	0	.000	-0	5	4	-0	0.5
1973	SD-N	0	0	—	18	0	0	0	0	30^2	29	18	4	0	12	15	12.0	4.11	85	.244	.313	0	.000	-0	-1	-2	0	-0.2
	NY-N	0	0	—	1	0	0	0	0	1	0	0	0	0	0	1	0.0	0.00	—	.000	.000	0	—	0	0	0	0	0.0
	Yr	0	0	—	19	0	0	0	0	31^2	29	18	4	0	12	16	11.7	3.98	88	.238	.306	0	.000	-0	-1	-2	-1	-0.2
	Det-A	4	2	.667	22	0	0	0	1	42	34	16	3	0	22	23	12.0	3.43	119	.230	.329	0	—	0	2	3	0	0.4
1974	NY-N	2	2	.500	58	0	0	0	2	78	89	39	2	1	39	35	14.9	3.58	100	.296	.378	1	.111	-0	0	-0	0	0.0
Total	17	69	81	.460	694	99	7	0	51	1551^1	1487	679	101	32	608	895	12.3	3.37	105	.255	.328	33	.110	-8	39	32	18	6.0

YEAR	TM/L	W	L	PCT	G	GS	CG	SH	SV	IP	H	R	HR	HB	BB	SO	RAT	ERA	ERA+	OAV	OOB	BH	AVG	PB	PR	PR+	PD	TPI
● BOB MILLER Miller, Robert W. b: 1862, d: 5/23/31, Newark, N.J. Deb: 8/30/1890																												
1890	Roc-a	3	7	.300	13	12	11	0	1	92^1	89	58	2	3	26	20	11.5	4.29	83	.246	.302	6	.150	-1	-4	-8	0	-0.8
1891	Was-a	2	5	.286	7	7	3	0	0	42	53	51	3	6	24	13	17.8	4.29	87	.298	.399	2	.111	-2	-3	-3	1	-0.4
Total	2	5	12	.294	20	19	14	0	1	134^1	142	109	5	9	50	33	13.5	4.29	84	.263	.336	8	.138	-3	-7	-11	1	-1.2
● ROGER MILLER Miller, Roger Wesley b: 8/1/54, Connellsville, Pa. d: 4/26/93, Mill Run, Pa. BR/TR, 6'3", 200 lbs. Deb: 9/8/74																												
1974	Mil-A	0	0	—	2	0	0	0	0	2^1	3	3	1	1	0	2	15.4	11.57	31	.300	.364	0	—	0	-2	-2	-0	-0.1
● RONNIE MILLER Miller, Roland Arthur b: 8/28/18, Mason City, Iowa d: 1/6/98, Ferguson, Mo. BB/TR, 5'11", 167 lbs. Deb: 9/10/41																												
1941	Was-A	0	0	—	1	0	0	0	0	2	2	1	0	0	1	0	13.5	4.50	90	.333	.429	0	—	0	-0	-0	-0	0.0
● ROSCOE MILLER Miller, Roscoe Clyde "Roxy" or "Rubberlegs" b: 12/2/1876, Greenville, Ind. d: 4/18/13, Corydon, Ind. BR/TR, 6'2", 190 lbs. Deb: 4/25/01																												
1901	Det-A	23	13	.639	38	36	35	3	1	332	339	168	1	13	98	79	12.2	2.95	130	.261	.320	27	.208	0	26	31	4	3.3
1902	Det-A	6	12	.333	20	18	15	1	1	148^2	158	85	3	9	57	39	13.6	3.69	99	.273	.347	11	.183	-2	-2	-1	1	-0.2
	NY-N	1	8	.111	10	9	7	0	0	72^2	77	40	1	5	11	15	11.5	4.58	61	.271	.310	1	.048	-2	-15	-14	-1	-1.8
1903	NY-N	2	5	.286	15	8	6	0	**3**	85	101	53	1	1	24	30	13.3	4.13	81	.302	.351	5	.161	-1	-8	-7	-1	-0.7
1904	Pit-N	7	7	.500	19	17	11	2	0	134^1	133	67	4	4	39	35	11.8	3.35	82	.256	.313	2	.043	-4	-9	-9	-1	-1.4
Total	4	39	45	.464	102	88	74	6	5	772^2	808	413	10	32	229	198	12.5	3.45	100	.268	.326	46	.160	-8	-7	1	2	-0.8
● RUSS MILLER Miller, Russell Lewis b: 3/25/1900, Etna, Ohio d: 4/30/62, Bucyrus, Ohio BR/TR, 5'11", 165 lbs. Deb: 9/24/27 F																												
1927	Phi-N	1	1	.500	2	2	1	0	0	15^1	21	9	2	1	3	4	14.7	5.28	78	.339	.379	1	.333	0	-2	-2	-0	-0.2
1928	Phi-N	0	12	.000	33	12	1	0	1	108	137	79	14	0	34	19	14.3	5.42	79	.315	.365	4	.148	-1	-17	-13	0	-1.3
Total	2	1	13	.071	35	14	2	0	1	123^1	158	88	16	1	37	23	14.3	5.40	79	.318	.366	5	.167	-1	-19	-15	0	-1.5
● STU MILLER Miller, Stuart Leonard b: 12/26/27, Northampton, Mass. BR/TR, 5'11.5", 165 lbs. Deb: 8/12/52																												
1952	StL-N	6	3	.667	12	11	6	2	0	88	63	25	3	2	26	64	9.3	2.05	182	.197	.262	3	.120	-1	16	16	3	1.9
1953	StL-N	7	8	.467	40	18	8	2	4	137^2	161	86	19	2	47	79	13.7	5.56	77	.293	.351	8	.186	1	-19	-20	5	-1.5
1954	StL-N	2	3	.400	19	4	0	0	2	46^2	55	36	5	3	29	22	16.8	5.79	71	.307	.412	4	.308	1	-9	-9	2	-0.6
1956	StL-N	0	1	.000	3	0	0	0	1	7^1	12	6	3	0	5	5	20.9	4.91	77	.387	.472	0	.000	-0	-1	-1	0	-0.1
	Phi-N	5	8	.385	24	15	2	0	0	106^2	109	65	16	4	51	55	13.8	4.47	83	.263	.349	4	.160	2	-8	-9	0	-0.8
	Yr	5	9	.357	27	15	2	0	1	114	121	71	19	4	56	60	14.3	4.50	83	.271	.358	4	.154	2	-9	-10	0	-0.9
1957	NY-N	7	9	.438	38	13	0	0	1	124	110	53	15	3	45	60	11.5	3.63	108	.242	.315	2	.057	-3	3	4	2	0.3
1958	SF-N	6	9	.400	41	20	4	1	0	182	160	60	16	2	49	119	10.4	**2.47**	**154**	.233	**.286**	6	.120	-0	30	28	1	2.3
1959	SF-N	8	7	.533	59	9	2	0	8	167^2	164	66	15	5	57	95	12.1	2.84	134	.260	.326	2	.044	-3	**21**	19	3	1.7
1960	SF-N	7	6	.538	47	3	2	0	2	101^2	100	49	9	3	31	65	11.9	3.90	89	.256	.315	5	.200	1	-2	-5	2	-0.4
1961	SF-N★	14	5	.737	63	0	0	0	**17**	122	95	41	4	1	37	89	9.8	2.66	143	.215	.277	4	.200	2	**19**	**17**	2	3.3
1962	*SF-N	5	8	.385	59	0	0	0	19	107	107	55	8	2	42	78	12.7	4.12	92	.268	.341	2	.125	-0	-2	-4	0	-0.6
1963	Bal-A	5	8	.385	**71**	0	0	0	**27**	112^1	93	36	5	3	53	114	11.9	2.24	155	.232	.326	5	.313	2	17	16	2	3.1
1964	Bal-A	7	7	.500	66	0	0	0	23	97	77	37	7	3	34	87	10.6	3.06	117	.222	.297	1	.111	-0	6	6	1	1.1
1965	Bal-A	14	7	.667	67	0	0	0	24	119^1	87	26	5	1	32	104	9.1	1.89	184	.207	.265	1	.063	-1	21	21	1	**4.6**
1966	Bal-A	9	4	.692	51	0	0	0	18	92	65	24	5	4	22	67	8.9	2.25	148	.201	.260	2	.105	-1	12	11	-1	1.9
1967	Bal-A	3	10	.231	42	0	0	0	8	81^1	63	28	5	1	36	60	11.1	2.55	124	.220	.309	0	.000	-1	6	6	-0	0.9
1968	Atl-N	0	0	—	2	0	0	0	0	1^1	1	4	0	0	4	1	33.8	27.00	11	.500	.833	0	—	0	-4	-4	0	-0.2
Total	16	105	103	.505	704	93	24	5	154	1694	1522	697	140	39	600	1164	11.5	3.24	115	.242	.312	49	.133	-2	107	91	22	16.9
● TRAVIS MILLER Miller, Travis Eugene b: 11/2/72, Dayton, Ohio BR/TL, 6'3", 205 lbs. Deb: 8/25/96																												
1996	Min-A	1	2	.333	7	7	0	0	0	26^1	45	29	7	0	9	15	18.5	9.23	55	.388	.432	0	—	0	-12	-12	-1	-1.1
1997	Min-A	1	5	.167	13	7	0	0	0	48^1	64	49	8	1	23	26	16.4	7.63	61	.320	.393	0	—	0	-16	-16	0	-1.5
1998	Min-A	0	2	.000	14	0	0	0	0	23^1	25	10	0	0	11	23	13.9	3.86	124	.272	.350	0	—	0	2	2	-0	0.1
1999	Min-A	2	2	.500	52	0	0	0	0	49^2	55	19	3	0	16	40	12.9	2.72	187	.284	.338	0	—	0	12	13	0	0.9
2000	Min-A	2	3	.400	67	0	0	0	1	67	83	35	4	1	32	62	15.6	3.90	135	.297	.372	0	—	0	8	9	-0	0.6
Total	5	6	14	.300	153	14	0	0	1	214^2	272	142	22	2	91	166	15.3	5.11	98	.309	.375	0	—	0	-7	-2	-0	-1.0
● TREVER MILLER Miller, Trever Douglas b: 5/29/73, Louisville, Ky. BR/TL, 6'3", 175 lbs. Deb: 9/4/96																												
1996	Det-A	0	4	.000	5	4	0	0	0	16^2	28	17	3	2	9	8	21.1	9.18	55	.384	.464	0	—	0	-8	-8	0	-1.2
1998	*Hou-N	2	0	1.000	37	1	0	0	1	53^1	57	21	4	1	20	30	13.2	3.04	133	.266	.332	1	.333	1	7	6	-0	0.3
1999	*Hou-N	3	2	.600	47	0	0	0	1	49^2	58	29	6	5	29	37	16.7	5.07	87	.299	.404	0	.000	-0	-3	-4	0	-0.4
2000	Phi-N	0	0	—	14	0	0	0	0	14	19	16	3	1	9	10	18.6	8.36	57	.317	.414	0	—	0	-6	-6	0	-0.2
	LA-N	0	0	—	2	0	0	0	0	2^1	8	6	0	1	3	1	46.3	23.14	19	.571	.667	0	—	0	-5	-5	-0	-0.2
	Yr	0	0	—	16	0	0	0	0	16^1	27	22	3	2	12	11	22.6	10.47	45	.365	.466	0	—	0	-11	-10	0	-0.4
Total	4	5	6	.455	105	5	0	0	2	136	170	89	16	10	70	86	16.5	5.43	81	.306	.394	1	.167	0	-14	-16	0	-1.7
● WADE MILLER Miller, Wade T. b: 9/13/76, Reading, Pa. BR/TR, 6'2", 185 lbs. Deb: 7/7/99																												
1999	Hou-N	0	1	.000	5	1	0	0	0	10^1	17	11	4	0	5	8	19.2	9.58	46	.362	.423	0	.000	-0	-6	-6	0	-0.5
2000	Hou-N	6	6	.500	16	16	2	0	0	105	104	66	14	3	42	89	12.8	5.14	95	.257	.332	4	.100	-2	-6	-3	0	-0.4
Total	2	6	7	.462	21	17	2	0	0	115^1	121	77	18	3	47	97	13.3	5.54	87	.268	.341	4	.098	-2	-12	-9	0	-0.9
● JAKE MILLER Miller, Walter b: 2/28/1898, Wagram, Ohio d: 8/20/75, Venice, Fla. BL/TL, 6'2", 170 lbs. Deb: 9/11/24 F																												
1924	Cle-A	0	1	.000	2	2	1	0	0	12	13	6	0	0	5	4	13.5	3.00	142	.265	.333	0	.000	-1	2	2	0	0.0
1925	Cle-A	10	13	.435	32	22	13	0	2	190^1	207	85	4	7	62	51	13.1	3.31	133	.279	.340	13	.183	-3	23	23	0	2.2
1926	Cle-A	7	4	.636	18	11	5	3	1	82^2	99	34	1	2	18	24	13.0	3.27	124	.307	.348	2	.083	-2	7	7	-1	0.6
1927	Cle-A	10	8	.556	34	23	11	0	0	185^1	189	80	4	6	48	53	11.8	3.21	131	.271	.324	8	.138	-4	19	20	1	1.4
1928	Cle-A	8	9	.471	25	24	8	0	0	158	203	89	6	5	43	37	14.3	4.44	93	.332	.381	7	.135	-4	-7	-5	1	-0.8
1929	Cle-A	14	12	.538	29	29	14	2	0	206	227	98	7	7	60	58	12.8	3.58	124	.279	.334	15	.200	-3	15	19	1	1.9
1930	Cle-A	4	4	.500	24	9	1	0	0	88^1	147	89	6	4	38	31	19.3	7.13	68	.373	.433	10	.303	1	-24	-22	2	-1.3
1931	Cle-A	2	1	.667	10	5	1	1	0	41^1	45	26	2	0	19	17	13.9	4.35	106	.273	.348	1	.077	-1	0	1	1	0.0
1933	Chi-A	5	6	.455	26	14	4	2	0	105^2	130	75	3	6	47	30	15.6	5.62	75	.297	.373	7	.189	-1	-16	-16	1	-1.4
Total	9	60	58	.508	200	139	58	8	3	1069^2	1260	582	33	37	340	305	13.8	4.09	106	.298	.355	63	.171	-19	19	29	6	2.6
● WALT MILLER Miller, Walter W. b: 10/19/1884, Spiceland, Ind. d: 3/1/56, Marion, Ind. BR/TR, 5'11.5", 180 lbs. Deb: 9/20/11																												
1911	Bro-N	0	1	.000	3	2	0	0	0	11	16	14	0	1	6	0	18.8	6.55	51	.356	.442	0	.000	-1	-4	-4	-0	-0.4
● BILL MILLER Miller, William Francis "Wild Bill" b: 4/12/10, Hannibal, Mo. d: 2/26/82, Hannibal, Mo. BR/TR, 6', 180 lbs. Deb: 10/2/37																												
1937	StL-A	0	1	.000	1	1	0	0	0	4	7	6	1	1	4	1	27.0	13.50	36	.389	.522	0	.000	-0	-4	-4	0	-0.5
● BILL MILLER Miller, William Paul "Lefty" or "Hooks" b: 7/26/27, Minersville, Pa. BL/TL, 6', 175 lbs. Deb: 4/20/52																												
1952	NY-A	4	6	.400	21	13	5	2	0	88	78	43	5	2	49	45	13.2	3.48	96	.241	.345	6	.214	1	2	-2	-0	-0.1
1953	NY-A	2	1	.667	13	3	0	0	1	34	46	19	3	1	19	17	17.5	4.76	77	.324	.407	2	.200	0	-3	-4	1	-0.3
1954	NY-A	0	1	.000	2	1	0	0	0	5^2	9	4	0	0	1	6	15.9	6.35	54	.375	.400	0	.000	-0	-2	-2	-0	-0.3
1955	Bal-A	0	1	.000	5	1	0	0	0	4	3	6	0	0	10	4	29.3	13.50	28	.200	.520	1	1.000	0	-4	-4	0	-0.8
Total	4	6	9	.400	41	18	5	2	1	131^2	136	72	8	3	79	72	14.9	4.24	81	.270	.372	9	.225	1	-7	-13	0	-1.5
● JOHN MILLIGAN Milligan, John Alexander b: 1/22/04, Schuylerville, N.Y. d: 5/15/72, Fort Pierce, Fla. BR/TL, 5'10", 172 lbs. Deb: 8/11/28																												
1928	Phi-N	2	5	.286	13	7	3	0	0	68	69	39	2	1	32	22	13.5	4.37	98	.274	.358	1	.050	-2	-3	-1	1	-0.2
1929	Phi-N	0	1	.000	8	3	0	0	0	9^2	29	19	0	2	10	2	38.2	16.76	31	.527	.612	1	.333	0	-13	-11	0	-0.9
1930	Phi-N	1	2	.333	9	2	1	0	0	28^1	26	16	0	2	21	7	15.6	3.18	172	.255	.392	1	.111	-1	6	7	1	0.6
1931	Phi-N	0	0	—	3	0	0	0	0	8	11	5	0	1	4	6	18.0	3.38	126	.324	.410	0	.000	-0	0	1	-0	0.0
1934	Was-A	0	0	—	2	0	0	0	0	2^2	6	3	0	0	0	1	20.3	10.13	43	.500	.500	0	—	0	-2	-2	0	-0.1
Total	5	3	8	.273	35	12	4	0	0	116^2	141	82	2	6	67	38	16.5	5.17	90	.310	.405	3	.088	-3	-11	-6	2	-0.6

YEAR TM/L	W	L	PCT	G	GS	CG	SH	SV	IP	H	R	HR	HB	BB	SO	RAT	ERA	ERA+	OAV	OOB	BH	AVG	PB	PR	PR+	PD	TPI
● BILLY MILLIGAN Milligan, William Joseph b: 8/19/1878, Buffalo, N.Y. d: 10/14/28, Buffalo, N.Y. BR/TL, 5'7", Deb: 4/30/01																											
1901 Phi-A	0	3	.000	6	3	2	0	0	33	43	24	1	2	14	5	16.1	4.36	86	.312	.383	5	.333	2	-3	-2	-0	0.0
1904 NY-N	0	1	.000	5	1	1	0	2	25	36	22	2	1	4	6	14.8	5.40	51	.310	.339	1	.111	0	-7	-7	-0	-0.4
Total 2	0	4	.000	11	4	3	0	2	58	79	46	3	3	18	11	15.5	4.81	69	.311	.364	6	.250	2	-10	-9	-1	-0.4
● BOB MILLIKEN Milliken, Robert Fogle "Bobo" b: 8/25/26, Majorsville, W.Va. BR/TR, 6', 195 lbs. Deb: 4/22/53 C																											
1953 *Bro-N	8	4	.667	37	10	3	0	2	117^2	94	52	13	0	42	65	10.4	3.37	127	.214	.283	4	.118	-1	12	12	-2	0.8
1954 Bro-N	5	2	.714	24	3	0	0	2	62^2	58	31	12	2	18	25	11.2	4.02	102	.246	.305	3	.176	-0	0	0	-1	-0.1
Total 2	13	6	.684	61	13	3	0	4	180^1	152	83	25	2	60	90	10.7	3.59	117	.225	.290	7	.137	-2	12	12	-3	0.7
● ALAN MILLS Mills, Alan Bernard b: 10/18/66, Lakeland, Fla. BR/TR, 6'1", 192 lbs. Deb: 4/14/90																											
1990 NY-A	1	5	.167	36	0	0	0	0	41^2	48	21	4	1	33	24	17.7	4.10	97	.298	.421	0	—	0	-1	-1	1	0.0
1991 NY-A	1	1	.500	6	2	0	0	0	16^1	16	9	1	0	8	11	13.2	4.41	94	.254	.338	0	—	0	-1	-0	1	0.0
1992 Bal-A	10	4	.714	35	3	0	0	2	103^1	78	33	5	1	54	60	11.6	2.61	154	.215	.319	0	—	0	15	16	1	2.2
1993 Bal-A	5	4	.556	45	0	0	0	4	100^1	80	39	14	4	51	68	12.1	3.23	139	.225	.328	0	—	0	12	14	-0	1.1
1994 Bal-A	3	3	.500	47	0	0	0	2	45^1	43	26	7	2	24	44	13.7	5.16	97	.251	.350	0	—	0	-2	-1	-1	-0.1
1995 Bal-A	3	0	1.000	21	0	0	0	0	23	30	20	4	2	18	16	19.6	7.43	64	.309	.427	0	—	0	-7	-7	-1	-0.8
1996 *Bal-A	3	2	.600	49	0	0	0	3	54^2	40	26	10	1	35	50	12.5	4.28	115	.208	.333	0	—	0	4	4	0	0.4
1997 *Bal-A	2	3	.400	39	0	0	0	0	38^2	41	23	5	1	33	32	17.5	4.89	90	.268	.401	0	—	0	-1	-2	-0	-0.3
1998 Bal-A	3	4	.429	72	0	0	0	2	77	55	32	8	1	50	57	12.4	3.74	122	.203	.329	0	—	0	8	7	0	0.6
1999 LA-N	3	4	.429	68	0	0	0	0	72^1	70	33	10	4	43	49	14.6	3.73	115	.261	.371	0	.000	-0	7	5	-1	0.3
2000 LA-N	2	1	.667	18	0	0	0	1	25^2	31	12	3	1	16	18	16.8	4.21	104	.304	.403	0	.000	-0	1	1	-0	0.1
Bal-A	2	0	1.000	23	0	0	0	1	23^2	25	17	6	1	19	18	17.1	6.46	74	.263	.391	0	—	0	-4	-5	-0	-0.4
Total 11	38	31	.551	459	5	0	0	15	622	557	291	77	19	384	447	13.9	3.99	111	.243	.356	0	.000	-0	32	32	0	3.1
● ART MILLS Mills, Arthur Grant b: 3/2/03, Utica, N.Y. d: 7/23/75, Utica, N.Y. BR/TR, 5'10", 155 lbs. Deb: 4/16/27 FC																											
1927 Bos-N	0	1	.000	15	1	0	0	0	37^2	41	19	1	3	18	7	14.8	3.82	97	.287	.378	0	.000	-1	0	-0	1	0.0
1928 Bos-N	0	0	—	4	0	0	0	0	7^2	17	11	3	2	8	0	31.7	12.91	30	.472	.587	0	.000	-0	-8	-8	-0	-0.4
Total 2	0	1	.000	19	1	0	0	0	45^1	58	30	4	5	26	7	17.7	5.36	70	.324	.424	0	.000	-1	-7	-9	1	-0.4
● LEFTY MILLS Mills, Howard Robinson b: 5/12/10, Dedham, Mass. d: 9/23/82, Riverside, Cal. BL/TL, 6'1", 187 lbs. Deb: 6/10/34																											
1934 StL-A	0	0	—	4	0	0	0	0	8^2	10	4	0	0	11	2	21.8	4.15	120	.303	.477	1	.333	0	0	1	-0	0.0
1937 StL-A	1	1	.500	2	2	1	0	0	12^2	16	13	1	0	10	10	18.5	6.39	75	.286	.394	0	.000	-1	-2	-2	0	-0.3
1938 StL-A	10	12	.455	30	27	15	1	0	210^1	216	139	16	8	116	134	14.5	5.31	94	.262	.358	6	.091	-3	-12	-8	-2	-1.0
1939 StL-A	4	11	.267	34	14	4	0	2	144^1	147	114	16	8	113	103	16.7	6.55	74	.264	.395	11	.234	1	-31	-26	-1	-2.2
1940 StL-A	0	6	.000	26	5	1	0	0	59	64	55	7	3	52	18	18.2	7.78	59	.275	.413	2	.154	-0	-22	-20	0	-1.7
Total 5	15	30	.333	96	48	21	1	2	435	453	325	40	19	302	267	16.0	6.06	81	.266	.382	20	.149	-3	-67	-55	-3	-5.2
● DICK MILLS Mills, Richard Alan b: 1/29/45, Boston, Mass. BR/TR, 6'3", 195 lbs. Deb: 9/7/70																											
1970 Bos-A	0	0	—	2	0	0	0	0	3^2	6	4	0	1	3	3	24.5	2.45	161	.353	.476	0	—	0	1	1	0	0.0
● WILLIE MILLS Mills, William Grant "Wee Willie" b: 8/15/1877, Schenevus, N.Y. d: 7/5/14, Norwood, N.Y. BR/TR, 5'7", 150 lbs. Deb: 7/13/01 F																											
1901 NY-N	0	2	.000	2	2	2	0	0	16	21	15	2	1	4	3	14.6	8.44	39	.313	.361	1	.167	0	-9	-9	-0	-0.8
● KEVIN MILLWOOD Millwood, Kevin Austin b: 12/24/74, Gastonia, N.C. BR/TR, 6'4", 205 lbs. Deb: 7/14/97																											
1997 Atl-N	5	3	.625	12	8	0	0	0	51^1	55	26	1	2	21	42	13.7	4.03	104	.281	.356	0	.000	-1	1	1	-0	0.0
1998 Atl-N	17	8	.680	31	29	3	1	0	174^1	175	86	18	3	56	163	12.1	4.08	102	.258	.318	4	.080	-1	3	2	-1	0.0
1999 *Atl-N★	18	7	.720	33	33	2	0	0	228	168	80	24	4	59	205	**9.1**	2.68	168	**.202**	**.258**	12	.154	0	48	47	-2	4.5
2000 *Atl-N	10	13	.435	36	35	0	0	0	212^2	213	115	26	3	62	168	11.8	4.66	97	.258	.312	7	.119	-1	-0	-3	-3	-0.6
Total 4	50	31	.617	112	105	5	1	0	666^1	611	307	69	12	198	578	11.1	3.78	116	.242	.300	23	.116	-3	51	46	-6	3.9
● AL MILNAR Milnar, Albert Joseph "Happy" (b: Albert Joseph Mlinar) b: 12/26/13, Cleveland, Ohio BL/TL, 6'2", 195 lbs. Deb: 4/30/36																											
1936 Cle-A	1	2	.333	4	3	1	0	0	22	26	20	0	0	18	9	18.0	7.36	68	.286	.404	3	.300	0	-6	-6	0	-0.5
1938 Cle-A	3	1	.750	23	5	2	0	1	68^1	90	48	5	0	26	29	15.3	5.00	93	.320	.378	4	.154	-0	-2	-3	0	-0.2
1939 Cle-A	14	12	.538	37	26	12	2	3	209	212	96	11	0	99	76	13.4	3.79	116	.264	.345	20	.253	4	19	15	0	2.0
1940 Cle-A☆	18	10	.643	37	33	15	**4**	3	242^1	242	120	14	1	99	99	12.7	3.27	129	.257	.328	17	.181	-1	30	27	-5	2.2
1941 Cle-A	12	19	.387	35	30	9	1	0	229^1	236	128	9	1	116	82	13.9	4.36	90	.266	.352	14	.171	2	-5	-11	-3	-1.3
1942 Cle-A	6	8	.429	28	19	8	2	0	157	146	82	3	4	85	35	13.5	4.13	84	.251	.350	12	.171	2	-8	-13	1	-0.7
1943 Cle-A	1	3	.250	16	6	0	0	0	39	51	38	0	1	35	12	20.1	8.08	38	.329	.455	4	.211	0	-21	-23	0	-2.1
StL-A	1	2	.333	3	2	1	0	0	14^2	23	11	0	0	9	7	19.6	5.52	60	.354	.432	2	.333	1	-4	-4	0	-0.5
Yr	2	5	.286	19	8	1	0	0	53^2	74	49	0	1	44	19	20.0	7.38	43	.336	.449	6	.240	1	-24	-26	0	-2.6
1946 StL-A	1	1	.500	4	2	1	1	0	14^2	15	4	1	0	6	1	12.9	2.45	152	.278	.350	3	.750	1	2	2	-0	0.4
Phi-N	0	0	—	1	1	0	0	0	0	2	0	0	2	—	—	∞	—	1.000	1.000	101	—	0	-4	-4	0	-0.3	
Total 8	57	58	.496	188	127	49	10	7	996^1	1043	551	43	7	495	350	14.0	4.22	96	.270	.354	79	.203	9	2	-19	-6	-1.0
● GEORGE MILSTEAD Milstead, George Earl "Cowboy" b: 6/26/03, Cleburne, Tex. d: 8/9/77, Cleburne, Tex. BL/TL, 5'10", 144 lbs. Deb: 6/27/24																											
1924 Chi-N	1	1	.500	13	2	1	0	0	29^2	41	25	3	1	13	6	16.7	6.07	64	.328	.396	1	.167	0	-7	-7	0	-0.4
1925 Chi-N	1	1	.500	5	3	1	0	0	21	26	12	0	0	8	7	14.6	3.00	144	.310	.370	0	.000	-1	3	3	0	0.2
1926 Chi-N	1	5	.167	18	4	0	0	2	55^1	63	30	0	1	24	14	14.3	3.58	107	.309	.384	1	.053	-2	2	2	2	0.2
Total 3	3	7	.300	36	9	2	0	2	106	130	67	3	2	45	27	15.0	4.16	95	.315	.385	2	.063	-3	-3	-2	3	0.0
● ERIC MILTON Milton, Eric Robert b: 8/4/75, State College, Pa. BL/TL, 6'3", 200 lbs. Deb: 4/5/98																											
1998 Min-A	8	14	.364	32	32	1	0	0	172^1	195	113	25	2	70	107	13.9	5.64	85	.282	.349	4	.444	1	-19	-16	-1	-1.7
1999 Min-A	7	11	.389	34	34	5	2	0	206^1	190	111	28	3	63	163	11.2	4.49	113	.243	.302	0	.000	0	9	13	-2	0.8
2000 Min-A	13	10	.565	33	33	0	0	0	200	205	123	35	7	44	160	11.5	4.86	108	.260	.305	0	.000	-0	1	8	-2	0.6
Total 3	28	35	.444	99	99	6	2	0	578^2	590	347	88	12	177	430	12.1	4.96	102	.261	.318	4	.308	1	-9	6	-6	-0.3
● LARRY MILTON Milton, Samuel Lawrence "Tug" b: 5/4/1879, Owensboro, Ky. d: 5/16/42, Hannibal, Mo. TR, Deb: 5/7/03																											
1903 StL-N	0	0	—	1	0	0	0	0	4	3	1	0	0	1	0	9.0	2.25	145	.200	.250	1	.500	0	0	0	0	0.1
● MIKE MIMBS Mimbs, Michael Randall b: 2/13/69, Macon, Ga. BL/TL, 6'2", 180 lbs. Deb: 5/6/95																											
1995 Phi-N	9	7	.563	35	19	2	1	1	136^2	127	70	10	6	75	93	13.7	4.15	102	.250	.353	5	.143	-1	1	1	1	0.1
1996 Phi-N	3	9	.250	21	17	0	0	0	99^1	116	66	13	2	41	56	14.4	5.53	78	.294	.364	4	.121	-1	-14	-13	-1	-1.5
1997 Phi-N	0	3	.000	17	1	0	0	0	28^2	31	27	6	3	27	29	19.2	7.53	56	.272	.424	0	.000	-0	-11	-10	-1	-1.0
Total 3	12	19	.387	73	37	2	1	1	264^2	274	163	29	11	143	178	14.6	5.03	85	.270	.366	9	.129	-2	-24	-22	-1	-2.4
● COTTON MINAHAN Minahan, Edmund Joseph b: 12/10/1882, Springfield, Ohio d: 5/20/58, E.Orange, N.J. BR/TR, 6', 190 lbs. Deb: 4/21/07																											
1907 Cin-N	0	2	.000	2	2	1	0	0	14	12	8	0	1	13	4	16.7	1.29	202	.261	.433	0	.000	-1	2	2	-1	0.2
● RUDY MINARCIN Minarcin, Rudolph Anthony "Buster" b: 3/25/30, N.Vandergrift, Pa. BR/TR, 6', 195 lbs. Deb: 4/11/55																											
1955 Cin-N	5	9	.357	41	12	3	1	1	115^2	116	73	17	3	51	45	13.2	4.90	86	.261	.341	5	.179	-1	-11	-8	2	-0.8
1956 Bos-A	1	0	1.000	3	1	0	0	0	9^2	9	4	2	1	8	5	16.8	2.79	165	.250	.400	1	.500	1	1	2	0	0.2
1957 Bos-A	0	0	—	26	0	0	0	2	44^2	44	30	5	1	30	20	15.1	4.43	90	.267	.383	0	.000	0	-3	-2	-0	-0.1
Total 3	6	9	.400	70	13	3	1	3	170	169	107	24	5	89	70	13.9	4.66	90	.262	.356	6	.188	0	-13	-8	2	-0.7
● NATE MINCHEY Minchey, Nathan Derek b: 8/31/69, Austin, Tex. BR/TR, 6'8", 225 lbs. Deb: 9/12/93																											
1993 Bos-A	1	2	.333	5	5	1	0	0	33	35	16	5	0	8	18	11.7	3.55	131	.265	.307	0	—	0	3	4	-1	0.3
1994 Bos-A	2	3	.400	6	5	0	0	0	23	44	26	1	0	14	15	22.7	8.61	59	.427	.496	0	—	0	-10	-9	0	-1.4
1996 Bos-A	0	2	.000	2	2	0	0	0	6	16	11	1	0	5	4	31.5	15.00	34	.533	.600	0	—	0	-7	-7	0	-0.9
1997 Col-N	0	0	—	2	0	0	0	0	2	5	3	0	0	1	1	27.0	13.50	38	.556	.600	0	—	0	-2	-2	0	0.0
Total 4	3	7	.300	15	12	1	0	0	64	100	56	7	0	28	38	18.0	6.75	72	.365	.424	0	—	0	-16	-13	-0	-2.0

● RAY MINER Miner, Raymond Theadore "Lefty" b: 4/4/1897, Glens Falls, N.Y. d: 9/15/63, Glenridge, N.Y. BR/TL, 5'11", 160 lbs. Deb: 9/15/21

YEAR	TM/L	W	L	PCT	G	GS	CG	SH	SV	IP	H	R	HR	HB	BB	SO	RAT	ERA	ERA+	OAV	OOB	BH	AVG	PB	PR	PR+	PD	TPI
1921	Phi-A	0	0	—	1	0	0	0	0	1	2	4	0	0	3	0	45.0	36.00	12	.400	.625	0	—	0	-4	-3	-0	-0.2

● CRAIG MINETTO Minetto, Craig Stephen b: 4/25/54, Stockton, Cal. BL/TL, 6', 185 lbs. Deb: 7/4/78

YEAR	TM/L	W	L	PCT	G	GS	CG	SH	SV	IP	H	R	HR	HB	BB	SO	RAT	ERA	ERA+	OAV	OOB	BH	AVG	PB	PR	PR+	PD	TPI
1978	Oak-A	0	0	—	4	1	0	0	0	12	13	10	1	2	7	3	16.5	3.75	97	.283	.400	0	—	0	0	-0	-0	0.0
1979	Oak-A	1	5	.167	36	13	0	0	0	118^1	131	85	16	3	58	64	14.6	5.55	73	.282	.365	0	—	0	-17	-21	-2	-1.1
1980	Oak-A	0	2	.000	7	1	0	0	1	8	11	7	2	0	3	5	15.8	7.88	48	.324	.378	0	—	0	-3	-4	-0	-0.8
1981	Oak-A	0	0	—	8	0	0	0	0	6^2	7	2	0	1	4	4	16.2	2.70	129	.280	.400	0	—	0	1	1	-0	0.0
Total	4	1	7	.125	55	15	0	0	1	145	162	104	19	6	72	76	14.9	5.40	74	.284	.370	0	—	0	-20	-24	-2	-1.9

● STEVE MINGORI Mingori, Stephen Bernard b: 2/29/44, Kansas City, Mo. BL/TL, 5'10", 170 lbs. Deb: 8/5/70

YEAR	TM/L	W	L	PCT	G	GS	CG	SH	SV	IP	H	R	HR	HB	BB	SO	RAT	ERA	ERA+	OAV	OOB	BH	AVG	PB	PR	PR+	PD	TPI
1970	Cle-A	1	0	1.000	21	0	0	0	1	20^1	17	8	2	1	12	16	13.3	2.66	149	.227	.341	0	.000	-0	2	3	0	0.2
1971	Cle-A	1	2	.333	54	0	0	0	4	56^2	31	10	2	1	24	45	8.9	1.43	268	.166	.264	1	.500	0	13	14	1	1.1
1972	Cle-A	0	6	.000	41	0	0	0	10	57	67	28	4	2	36	47	16.6	3.95	82	.293	.393	1	.125	-0	-6	-4	1	-0.6
1973	Cle-A	0	0	—	5	0	0	0	0	11^2	10	8	3	0	10	4	15.4	6.17	64	.233	.377	0	—	0	-3	-3	1	-0.1
	KC-A	3	3	.500	19	1	0	0	1	56^1	59	21	6	3	23	46	13.6	3.04	136	.267	.344	0	—	0	5	6	-0	0.6
	Yr	3	3	.500	24	1	0	0	1	68	69	29	9	3	33	50	13.9	3.57	114	.261	.350	0	—	0	2	4	1	0.5
1974	KC-A	2	3	.400	36	0	0	0	2	67^1	53	31	4	2	23	43	10.4	2.81	136	.212	.284	0	—	0	6	7	2	0.8
1975	KC-A	0	3	.000	36	0	0	0	2	50^1	42	21	2	1	20	25	11.3	2.50	154	.226	.304	0	.000	-0	7	7	0	0.5
1976	*KC-A	5	5	.500	55	0	0	0	10	85^1	73	23	3	3	25	38	10.7	2.32	151	.238	.301	0	—	0	11	11	3	1.9
1977	*KC-A	2	4	.333	43	0	0	0	4	64	59	26	4	1	19	19	11.1	3.09	131	.254	.313	0	—	0	7	7	1	0.7
1978	*KC-A	1	4	.200	45	0	0	0	7	69	64	25	5	3	16	28	10.8	2.74	140	.242	.292	0	—	0	8	8	0	0.8
1979	KC-A	3	3	.500	30	1	0	0	1	46^2	69	36	10	1	17	18	16.8	5.79	74	.348	.403	0	—	0	-8	-8	-1	-1.0
Total	10	18	33	.353	385	2	0	0	42	584^2	544	237	45	18	225	329	12.1	3.03	126	.248	.323	2	.167	-0	43	50	7	4.9

● PAUL MINNER Minner, Paul Edison "Lefty" b: 7/30/23, New Wilmington, Pa. BL/TL, 6'5", 210 lbs. Deb: 9/12/46

YEAR	TM/L	W	L	PCT	G	GS	CG	SH	SV	IP	H	R	HR	HB	BB	SO	RAT	ERA	ERA+	OAV	OOB	BH	AVG	PB	PR	PR+	PD	TPI
1946	Bro-N	0	1	.000	3	0	0	0	0	4	6	4	1	0	3	3	20.3	6.75	50	.333	.429	0	—	0	-1	-2	-0	-0.3
1948	Bro-N	4	3	.571	28	2	0	0	1	62^2	61	23	5	0	26	23	12.5	2.44	164	.257	.331	4	.190	1	11	11	0	1.3
1949	*Bro-N	3	1	.750	27	1	0	0	2	47^1	49	22	7	1	18	17	12.9	3.80	108	.272	.342	3	.214	-0	1	2	0	0.2
1950	Chi-N	8	13	.381	39	24	9	1	4	190^1	217	105	18	1	72	99	13.7	4.11	102	.287	.350	14	.215	2	1	2	3	0.7
1951	Chi-N	6	17	.261	33	28	14	3	1	201^2	219	97	20	0	64	68	12.6	3.79	108	.277	.331	18	.254	5	4	7	3	1.6
1952	Chi-N	14	9	.609	28	27	12	2	0	180^2	180	84	13	1	54	61	11.7	3.74	103	.258	.312	15	.234	6	-0	2	2	1.1
1953	Chi-N	12	15	.444	31	27	9	2	1	201	227	109	15	3	40	64	12.1	4.21	106	.283	.320	15	.221	2	2	5	4	1.2
1954	Chi-N	11	11	.500	32	29	12	0	1	218	236	107	19	1	50	79	11.8	3.96	106	.280	.321	13	.171	3	3	6	1	0.9
1955	Chi-N	9	9	.500	22	22	7	1	0	157^2	173	67	15	1	47	53	12.6	3.48	117	.283	.335	13	.232	2	10	10	2	1.5
1956	Chi-N	2	5	.286	10	9	1	0	0	47	60	38	9	2	19	14	15.5	6.89	55	.324	.393	3	.250	2	-16	-16	0	-1.8
Total	10	69	84	.451	253	169	64	9	10	1310^1	1428	656	122	10	393	481	12.6	3.94	105	.279	.332	98	.219	22	12	27	15	6.4

● DON MINNICK Minnick, Donald Athey b: 4/14/31, Lynchburg, Va. BR/TR, 6'3", 195 lbs. Deb: 9/23/57

YEAR	TM/L	W	L	PCT	G	GS	CG	SH	SV	IP	H	R	HR	HB	BB	SO	RAT	ERA	ERA+	OAV	OOB	BH	AVG	PB	PR	PR+	PD	TPI
1957	Was-A	0	1	.000	2	1	0	0	0	9^1	14	8	1	0	2	7	15.4	4.82	81	.341	.372	0	.000	-0	-1	-1	-0	-0.1

● BLAS MINOR Minor, Blas b: 3/20/66, Merced, Cal. BR/TR, 6'3", 203 lbs. Deb: 7/28/92

YEAR	TM/L	W	L	PCT	G	GS	CG	SH	SV	IP	H	R	HR	HB	BB	SO	RAT	ERA	ERA+	OAV	OOB	BH	AVG	PB	PR	PR+	PD	TPI
1992	Pit-N	0	0	—	1	0	0	0	0	2	3	2	0	0	0	0	13.5	4.50	77	.333	.333	0	—	0	-0	-0	0	0.0
1993	Pit-N	8	6	.571	65	0	0	0	2	94^1	94	43	8	4	26	84	11.8	4.10	99	.263	.320	2	.200	1	-1	-0	1	0.1
1994	Pit-N	0	1	.000	17	0	0	0	1	19	27	17	4	1	9	17	17.5	8.05	54	.351	.425	0	—	0	-8	-8	-0	-0.4
1995	NY-N	4	2	.667	35	0	0	0	1	46^2	44	21	6	1	13	43	11.2	3.66	111	.253	.309	0	.000	-0	3	2	0	0.2
1996	NY-N	0	0	—	17	0	0	0	0	25^2	23	11	4	0	6	20	10.2	3.51	115	.237	.282	0	.000	-0	2	2	0	0.1
	Sea-A	0	1	.000	11	0	0	0	0	25^1	27	14	6	0	11	14	13.5	4.97	100	.276	.349	0	—	0	0	-0	-0	0.0
1997	Hou-N	1	0	1.000	11	0	0	0	1	12	13	7	1	1	5	6	14.3	4.50	89	.277	.358	0	—	0	-0	-1	0	-0.1
Total	6	13	10	.565	157	0	0	0	5	225	231	115	29	7	70	184	12.3	4.40	95	.269	.329	2	.154	0	-4	-6	1	-0.1

● JIM MINSHALL Minshall, James Edward b: 7/4/47, Covington, Ky. BR/TR, 6'6", 215 lbs. Deb: 9/14/74

YEAR	TM/L	W	L	PCT	G	GS	CG	SH	SV	IP	H	R	HR	HB	BB	SO	RAT	ERA	ERA+	OAV	OOB	BH	AVG	PB	PR	PR+	PD	TPI
1974	Pit-N	0	1	.000	5	0	0	0	0	4^1	1	1	0	0	2	3	6.2	0.00	—	.083	.214	0	—	0	2	2	-0	0.4
1975	Pit-N	0	0	—	1	0	0	0	0	1	0	0	0	0	2	2	18.0	0.00	—	.000	.400	0	—	0	0	0	0	0.0
Total	2	0	1	.000	6	0	0	0	0	5^1	1	1	0	0	4	5	8.4	0.00	—	.067	.263	0	—	0	2	2	-0	0.4

● GREG MINTON Minton, Gregory Brian b: 7/29/51, Lubbock, Tex. BB/TR, 6'2", 190 lbs. Deb: 9/7/75

YEAR	TM/L	W	L	PCT	G	GS	CG	SH	SV	IP	H	R	HR	HB	BB	SO	RAT	ERA	ERA+	OAV	OOB	BH	AVG	PB	PR	PR+	PD	TPI
1975	SF-N	1	1	.500	4	2	0	0	0	17	19	14	1	1	11	6	16.4	6.88	55	.288	.397	0	.000	-1	-6	-6	1	-0.6
1976	SF-N	0	3	.000	10	2	0	0	0	25^2	32	18	0	1	12	7	15.8	4.91	74	.317	.395	1	.200	-0	-4	-4	-0	-0.4
1977	SF-N	1	1	.500	2	2	0	0	0	14	14	8	0	0	4	5	11.6	4.50	87	.264	.316	1	.333	1	-1	-1	0	0.0
1978	SF-N	0	1	.000	11	0	0	0	0	15^2	22	14	3	1	8	6	17.8	8.04	43	.338	.419	0	.000	-0	-8	-8	0	-0.5
1979	SF-N	4	3	.571	46	0	0	0	4	79^2	59	25	0	2	27	33	9.9	1.81	194	.215	.289	0	.000	-0	17	16	2	1.7
1980	SF-N	4	6	.400	68	0	0	0	19	91^1	81	28	0	0	34	42	11.3	2.46	144	.243	.313	1	.125	-0	12	11	2	1.8
1981	SF-N	4	5	.444	55	0	0	0	21	84^1	84	28	0	0	36	29	12.8	2.88	119	.267	.342	0	.000	-1	6	5	3	1.0
1982	SF-N★	10	4	.714	78	0	0	0	30	123	108	29	5	2	42	58	11.1	1.83	197	.244	.313	3	.176	0	**24**	**24**	1	**4.0**
1983	SF-N	7	11	.389	73	0	0	0	22	106^2	117	51	6	0	47	38	13.8	3.54	100	.283	.356	6	.545	4	1	-0	-0	0.4
1984	SF-N	4	9	.308	74	1	0	0	19	124^1	130	60	6	0	57	48	13.5	3.76	93	.267	.344	1	.048	-1	-2	-4	2	-0.4
1985	SF-N	5	4	.556	68	0	0	0	4	96^2	98	42	6	0	54	37	14.2	3.54	97	.272	.367	0	.000	-1	1	-1	2	0.1
1986	SF-N	4	4	.500	48	0	0	0	5	68^2	63	35	4	1	34	34	12.8	3.93	90	.251	.343	2	.400	2	-2	-3	2	0.0
1987	SF-N	1	0	1.000	15	0	0	0	1	23^1	30	9	2	1	10	9	15.8	3.47	111	.323	.394	0	.000	-0	2	1	0	0.0
	Cal-A	5	4	.556	41	0	0	0	10	76	71	28	4	1	29	35	12.0	3.08	140	.257	.330	0	—	0	12	11	2	1.6
1988	Cal-A	4	5	.444	44	0	0	0	7	79	67	37	1	3	34	46	11.8	2.85	136	.233	.320	0	—	0	10	9	2	1.3
1989	Cal-A	4	3	.571	62	0	0	0	8	90	76	22	4	2	37	42	11.5	2.20	174	.230	.311	0	—	0	17	17	2	1.6
1990	Cal-A	1	1	.500	11	0	0	0	0	15^1	11	4	1	1	7	4	11.2	2.35	163	.212	.317	0	—	0	3	3	0	0.3
Total	16	59	65	.476	710	7	0	0	150	1130^2	1082	452	43	16	483	479	12.6	3.10	118	.257	.336	15	.146	2	81	71	19	11.9

● STEVE MINTZ Mintz, Stephen Wayne b: 11/24/68, Wilmington, N.C. BL/TR, 5'11", 190 lbs. Deb: 5/18/95

YEAR	TM/L	W	L	PCT	G	GS	CG	SH	SV	IP	H	R	HR	HB	BB	SO	RAT	ERA	ERA+	OAV	OOB	BH	AVG	PB	PR	PR+	PD	TPI
1995	SF-N	1	2	.333	14	0	0	0	0	19^1	26	16	4	2	12	7	18.6	7.45	55	.329	.430	0	.000	-0	-7	-7	-0	-1.0
1999	Ana-A	0	0	—	3	0	0	0	0	5	8	2	1	0	2	2	18.0	3.60	135	.381	.435	0	—	0	1	1	-0	0.0
Total	2	1	2	.333	17	0	0	0	0	24^1	34	18	5	2	14	9	18.5	6.66	64	.340	.431	0	.000	-0	-6	-7	-1	-1.0

● GINO MINUTELLI Minutelli, Gino Michael b: 5/23/64, Wilmington, Del. BL/TL, 6', 180 lbs. Deb: 9/18/90

YEAR	TM/L	W	L	PCT	G	GS	CG	SH	SV	IP	H	R	HR	HB	BB	SO	RAT	ERA	ERA+	OAV	OOB	BH	AVG	PB	PR	PR+	PD	TPI
1990	Cin-N	0	0	—	2	0	0	0	0	1	0	1	0	1	2	0	27.0	9.00	44	.000	.500	0	—	0	-1	-1	0	0.0
1991	Cin-N	0	2	.000	16	3	0	0	0	25^1	30	17	5	0	18	21	17.1	6.04	63	.288	.393	0	.000	-0	-7	-6	0	-0.4
1993	SF-N	0	1	.000	9	0	0	0	0	14^1	7	9	2	0	15	10	13.8	3.77	104	.152	.361	0	.000	-0	0	0	-0	-0.1
Total	3	0	3	.000	27	3	0	0	0	40^2	37	27	7	1	35	31	16.2	5.31	73	.242	.386	0	.000	-1	-7	-7	0	-0.5

● PAUL MIRABELLA Mirabella, Paul Thomas b: 3/20/54, Belleville, N.J. BL/TL, 6'2", 196 lbs. Deb: 7/28/78

YEAR	TM/L	W	L	PCT	G	GS	CG	SH	SV	IP	H	R	HR	HB	BB	SO	RAT	ERA	ERA+	OAV	OOB	BH	AVG	PB	PR	PR+	PD	TPI
1978	Tex-A	3	2	.600	10	4	0	0	1	28	30	18	2	0	17	23	15.1	5.79	65	.286	.385	0	—	0	-6	-6	-0	-1.1
1979	NY-A	0	4	.000	10	1	0	0	0	14^1	16	15	3	1	10	4	17.0	8.79	46	.276	.391	0	—	0	-7	-8	-0	-1.4
1980	Tor-A	5	12	.294	33	22	3	1	0	130^2	151	73	11	3	66	53	15.2	4.34	99	.294	.378	0	—	0	-4	-0	0	0.0
1981	Tor-A	0	0	—	8	1	0	0	0	14^2	20	16	2	1	7	9	17.2	7.36	54	.313	.389	0	—	0	-6	-5	-0	-0.3
1982	Tex-A	1	1	.500	40	0	0	0	3	50^2	46	28	4	2	22	29	12.4	4.80	81	.241	.326	0	—	0	-4	-5	-0	-0.3
1983	Bal-A	0	0	—	3	2	0	0	0	9^2	9	6	1	0	7	4	14.9	5.59	71	.243	.364	0	—	0	-2	-2	-0	-0.1
1984	Sea-A	2	5	.286	52	1	0	0	3	68	74	39	6	1	32	41	14.2	4.37	91	.282	.363	0	—	0	-3	-3	1	-0.2
1985	Sea-A	0	0	—	10	0	0	0	0	13^2	9	4	0	2	4	8	9.9	1.32	320	.188	.278	0	—	0	4	4	-0	0.2
1986	Sea-A	0	0	—	8	0	0	0	0	6^1	13	7	1	0	3	6	22.7	8.53	50	.419	.471	0	—	0	-3	-3	0	-0.1
1987	Mil-A	2	1	.667	29	0	0	0	2	29^1	30	20	0	0	16	14	14.1	4.91	93	.268	.359	0	—	0	-1	-1	1	0.0
1988	Mil-A	2	2	.500	38	0	0	0	4	60	44	12	3	0	21	33	9.8	1.65	242	.204	.274	0	—	0	16	16	1	1.2
1989	Mil-A	0	0	—	13	0	0	0	0	15^1	18	14	1	1	7	6	15.3	7.63	50	.290	.371	0	—	0	-6	-7	0	-0.3

YEAR	TM/L	W	L	PCT	G	GS	CG	SH	SV	IP	H	R	HR	HB	BB	SO	RAT	ERA	ERA+	OAV	OOB	BH	AVG	PB	PR	PR+	PD	TPI
1990	Mil-A	4	2	.667	44	2	0	0	0	59	66	32	9	2	27	28	14.5	3.97	98	.281	.360	0	—	0	-0	-1	-0	-0.1
Total	13	19	29	.396	298	33	3	1	13	499^2	526	284	43	13	239	258	14.0	4.45	92	.272	.356	0	—	0	-24	-20	0	-2.5
● ANGEL MIRANDA																												
Miranda, Angel Luis (Andujar) b: 11/9/69, Arecibo, P.R. BL/TL, 6′1″, 195 lbs. Deb: 6/5/93																												
1993	Mil-A	4	5	.444	22	17	2	0	0	120	100	53	12	2	52	88	11.6	3.30	129	.226	.310	0	—	0	14	13	-1	0.8
1994	Mil-A	2	5	.286	8	8	1	0	0	46	39	28	8	0	27	24	12.9	5.28	95	.234	.340	0	—	0	-2	-1	-1	-0.2
1995	Mil-A	4	5	.444	30	10	0	0	1	74	83	47	8	0	49	45	16.1	5.23	95	.291	.395	0	—	0	-4	-2	-0	-0.2
1996	Mil-A	7	6	.538	46	12	0	0	1	109^1	116	68	12	2	69	78	15.4	4.94	105	.277	.382	0	—	0	1	3	-1	0.2
1997	Mil-A	0	0	—	10	0	0	0	0	14	17	6	1	3	9	8	18.6	3.86	120	.309	.433	0	—	0	1	1	0	0.1
Total	5	17	21	.447	116	47	3	0	2	363^1	355	202	41	7	206	243	14.1	4.46	108	.260	.359	0	—	0	9	13	-3	0.7
● MIKE MISURACA																												
Misuraca, Michael William b: 8/21/68, Long Beach, Cal. BR/TR, 6′, 190 lbs. Deb: 7/27/97																												
1997	Mil-A	0	0	—	5	0	0	0	0	10^1	15	13	5	0	7	10	19.2	11.32	41	.333	.423	0	—	0	-8	-8	-0	-0.4
● ROY MITCHELL																												
Mitchell, Albert Roy b: 4/19/1885, Belton, Tex. d: 9/8/59, Temple, Tex. BR/TR, 5′9.5″, 170 lbs. Deb: 9/10/10																												
1910	StL-A	4	2	.667	6	6	6	0	0	52	43	24	0	2	12	23	9.9	2.60	95	.244	.300	4	.211	0	-0	-1	1	0.0
1911	StL-A	4	8	.333	28	12	8	1	0	133^1	134	79	4	6	45	40	12.5	3.85	88	.273	.341	11	.224	1	-7	-7	-0	-0.4
1912	StL-A	3	4	.429	13	7	5	0	0	62	81	36	2	4	17	22	14.8	4.65	71	.323	.375	6	.316	3	-9	-9	-1	-0.7
1913	StL-A	13	16	.448	33	27	21	4	1	245^1	265	111	6	5	47	59	11.6	3.01	97	.280	.318	13	.148	-1	-2	-2	-1	-0.5
1914	StL-A	4	5	.444	28	9	4	0	**4**	103^1	134	77	1	6	38	38	15.5	4.35	62	.320	.384	7	.206	1	-19	-19	0	-1.6
1918	Chi-A	0	1	.000	2	2	0	0	0	12	18	14	1	0	4	3	16.5	7.50	36	.346	.393	0	.000	-0	-6	-6	0	-0.5
	Cin-N	4	0	1.000	5	3	3	2	0	36^1	27	3	0	0	5	9	7.9	0.74	359	.208	.237	3	.214	0	8	8	-0	1.0
1919	Cin-N	0	1	.000	7	1	0	0	0	31	32	16	0	0	9	10	11.9	2.32	119	.276	.328	0	.000	-2	2	2	1	0.0
Total	7	32	37	.464	122	67	47	7	5	675^1	734	360	14	23	177	204	12.4	3.42	86	.284	.336	44	.187	3	-34	-35	-1	-2.7
● CHARLIE MITCHELL																												
Mitchell, Charles Ross b: 6/24/62, Dickson, Tenn. BR/TR, 6′3″, 170 lbs. Deb: 8/9/84 F																												
1984	Bos-A	0	0	—	10	0	0	0	0	16^1	14	7	1	2	6	7	12.1	2.76	151	.226	.314	0	—	0	2	2	0	0.1
1985	Bos-A	0	0	—	2	0	0	0	0	1^2	5	3	1	0	0	2	27.0	16.20	26	.500	.500	0	—	0	-2	-2	0	-0.1
Total	2	0	0	—	12	0	0	0	0	18	19	10	2	2	6	9	13.5	4.00	105	.264	.338	0	—	0	0	0	0	0.0
● CLARENCE MITCHELL																												
Mitchell, Clarence Elmer b: 2/22/1891, Franklin, Neb. d: 11/6/63, Grand Island, Neb. BL/TL, 5′11.5″, 190 lbs. Deb: 6/2/11 C♦																												
1911	Det-A	1	0	1.000	5	1	0	0	0	14^1	20	13	1	0	7	4	17.0	8.16	42	.351	.422	2	.500	1	-8	-7	-1	-0.4
1916	Cin-N	11	10	.524	29	24	17	1	0	194^2	211	87	4	10	45	52	12.3	3.14	83	.285	.334	28	.239	2	-11	-12	1	-0.8
1917	Cin-N	9	15	.375	32	20	10	2	1	159^1	166	73	4	2	34	37	11.4	3.22	81	.268	.308	25	.278	4	-9	-11	0	-1.2
1918	Bro-N	0	1	.000	1	1	0	0	0	0^1	4	4	0	0	0	0	108.0	108.00	3	1.000	1.000	6	.250	0	-4	-4	0	-0.6
1919	Bro-N	7	5	.583	23	11	9	0	0	108^2	123	49	0	0	23	43	12.1	3.06	97	.297	.334	18	.367	6	-2	-1	1	0.7
1920	*Bro-N	5	2	.714	19	7	3	1	1	78^2	85	35	1	0	23	18	12.4	3.09	104	.288	.340	25	.234	1	0	1	1	0.3
1921	Bro-N	11	9	.550	37	18	13	**3**	2	190	206	91	7	5	46	39	12.2	2.89	135	.280	.327	24	.264	3	19	21	3	2.7
1922	Bro-N	0	3	.000	5	3	0	0	0	12^2	28	24	0	1	7	1	25.6	14.21	29	.467	.529	45	.290	2	-14	-14	1	-2.1
1923	Phi-N	9	10	.474	29	19	8	1	0	139^1	170	93	8	4	46	41	14.2	4.72	98	.299	.355	21	.269	3	-11	-2	-3	-0.1
1924	Phi-N	6	13	.316	30	26	9	1	1	165	223	113	10	6	58	36	15.7	5.62	79	.321	.379	26	.255	-1	-32	-18	3	-1.6
1925	Phi-N	10	17	.370	32	26	12	1	1	199^1	245	130	23	5	51	46	13.6	5.28	90	.302	.347	18	.196	-2	-22	-10	4	-0.9
1926	Phi-N	9	14	.391	28	25	12	0	1	178^2	232	111	7	4	55	52	14.7	4.58	90	.318	.369	19	.244	1	-15	-8	4	-0.4
1927	Phi-N	6	3	.667	13	12	8	1	0	94^2	99	44	7	2	28	17	12.3	4.09	101	.271	.327	10	.238	2	-2	0	1	0.3
1928	Phi-N	0	0	—	3	0	0	0	0	5^2	13	6	0	0	2	0	23.8	9.53	45	.542	.577	1	.250	0	-3	-3	0	-0.1
	*StL-N	8	9	.471	19	18	9	1	0	150	149	59	8	3	38	31	11.4	3.30	121	.265	.315	7	.125	-3	12	12	2	1.1
	Yr	8	9	.471	22	18	9	1	0	155^2	162	65	8	3	40	31	11.9	3.53	114	.276	.326	8	.133	-3	8	8	3	1.0
1929	StL-N	8	11	.421	25	22	16	0	0	173	221	89	13	5	60	39	14.9	4.27	109	.320	.379	18	.273	4	9	8	-1	1.0
1930	StL-N	1	0	1.000	1	1	0	0	0	3	5	2	0	0	2	1	21.0	6.00	84	.357	.438	1	.500	0	-0	-0	-0	0.0
	NY-N	10	3	.769	24	16	5	0	0	129	151	68	10	1	36	40	13.1	3.98	119	.298	.346	12	.255	0	14	11	2	1.2
	Yr	11	3	.786	25	17	5	0	0	132	156	70	10	1	38	41	13.3	4.02	118	.300	.349	13	.265	1	14	11	2	1.2
1931	NY-N	13	11	.542	27	25	13	0	0	190^1	221	103	12	3	52	39	13.1	4.07	91	.285	.332	16	.219	2	-4	-8	-2	-0.9
1932	NY-N	1	3	.250	8	3	1	0	2	30^1	41	21	1	1	11	7	15.7	4.15	89	.325	.384	2	.200	0	-1	-2	-1	-0.3
Total	18	125	139	.473	390	278	145	12	9	2217	2613	1215	116	52	624	543	13.4	4.12	95	.297	.347	324	.252	26	-86	-53	17	-2.1
● CRAIG MITCHELL																												
Mitchell, Craig Seton b: 4/14/54, Santa Rosa, Cal. BR/TR, 6′3″, 180 lbs. Deb: 9/25/75																												
1975	Oak-A	0	1	.000	1	1	0	0	0	3^2	6	5	0	0	2	2	19.6	12.27	30	.375	.444	0	—	0	-3	-4	0	-0.5
1976	Oak-A	0	0	—	1	0	0	0	0	3^1	3	1	0	0	0	0	8.1	2.70	124	.231	.231	0	—	0	0	0	0	0.0
1977	Oak-A	0	1	.000	3	1	0	0	0	5^2	9	6	1	0	2	1	17.5	7.94	51	.346	.393	0	—	0	-2	-2	-0	-0.4
Total	3	0	2	.000	5	2	0	0	0	12^2	18	12	1	0	4	3	15.6	7.82	48	.327	.373	0	—	0	-6	-6	0	-0.9
● FRED MITCHELL																												
Mitchell, Frederick Francis (b: Frederick Francis Yapp) b: 6/5/1878, Cambridge, Mass. d: 10/13/70, Newton, Mass. BR/TR, 5′9.5″, 185 lbs. Deb: 4/27/01 MC♦																												
1901	Bos-A	6	6	.500	17	13	10	0	0	108^2	115	67	2	11	51	34	14.7	3.81	93	.268	.360	7	.159	-1	-2	-4	0	-0.4
1902	Bos-A	0	1	.000	1	0	0	0	0	4	8	5	1	0	5	2	29.3	11.25	32	.421	.542	0	.000	-0	-3	-3	0	-0.5
	Phi-A	5	8	.385	18	14	9	0	1	107^2	120	71	4	8	59	22	15.6	3.59	102	.282	.380	9	.188	-1	-0	1	2	0.2
	Yr	5	9	.357	19	14	9	0	1	111^2	128	76	5	8	64	24	16.1	3.87	95	.288	.388	9	.184	-1	-4	-2	3	-0.3
1903	Phi-N	11	16	.407	28	28	24	1	0	227	250	155	4	19	102	69	14.7	4.48	73	.284	.370	19	.200	-1	-31	-30	-3	-3.3
1904	Phi-N	4	7	.364	13	13	11	0	0	108^2	133	62	3	7	25	29	13.7	3.40	79	.306	.353	17	.207	1	-8	-9	3	-0.4
	Bro-N	2	5	.286	8	8	8	1	0	66	73	37	0	3	23	16	13.5	3.82	72	.291	.357	7	.292	2	-8	-8	1	-0.4
	Yr	6	12	.333	21	21	19	1	0	174^2	206	99	3	10	48	45	13.6	3.56	76	.300	.355	24	.226	4	-16	-17	4	-0.8
1905	Bro-N	3	7	.300	12	10	9	0	0	96^1	107	73	2	5	38	44	14.0	4.76	61	.285	.358	15	.190	0	-19	-21	1	-1.7
Total	5	31	50	.383	97	86	71	2	1	718^1	806	470	16	53	303	216	14.6	4.10	78	.286	.366	120	.210	1	-71	-74	5	-6.5
● JOHN MITCHELL																												
Mitchell, John Kyle b: 8/11/65, Dickson, Tenn. BR/TR, 6′2″, 195 lbs. Deb: 9/8/86 F																												
1986	NY-N	0	1	.000	4	1	0	0	0	10	10	4	1	0	4	2	12.6	3.60	98	.278	.350	0	.000	-0	0	-0	0	0.0
1987	NY-N	3	6	.333	20	19	1	0	0	111^2	124	64	6	2	36	57	13.1	4.11	92	.279	.336	4	.114	-1	-0	-4	1	-0.3
1988	NY-N	0	0	—	1	0	0	0	0	1	2	0	0	0	1	1	27.0	0.00	—	.500	.600	0	.000	-0	0	0	0	0.0
1989	NY-N	0	1	.000	2	0	0	0	0	3	3	7	0	0	4	4	21.0	6.00	54	.231	.412	0	—	0	-1	-1	-0	-0.2
1990	Bal-A	6	6	.500	24	17	0	0	0	114^1	133	63	7	3	48	43	14.5	4.64	82	.300	.372	0	—	0	-9	-11	1	-1.0
Total	5	9	14	.391	51	37	1	0	0	240	272	138	14	5	93	107	13.9	4.35	87	.289	.356	4	.105	-1	-10	-16	2	-1.5
● LARRY MITCHELL																												
Mitchell, Larry Paul b: 10/16/71, Flint, Mich. BR/TR, 6′1″, 200 lbs. Deb: 8/11/96																												
1996	Phi-N	0	0	—	7	0	0	0	0	12	14	6	1	0	5	7	14.3	4.50	96	.311	.380	0	.000	-0	-0	-0	-0	-0.1
● MONROE MITCHELL																												
Mitchell, Monroe Barr b: 9/11/01, Starkville, Miss. d: 9/4/76, Valdosta, Ga. BR/TL, 6′1.5″, 170 lbs. Deb: 7/11/23																												
1923	Was-A	2	4	.333	10	6	3	1	2	41^2	57	35	0	1	22	8	17.3	6.48	58	.350	.430	3	.250	1	-12	-13	-1	-1.7
● PAUL MITCHELL																												
Mitchell, Paul Michael b: 8/19/49, Worcester, Mass. BR/TR, 6′1″, 195 lbs. Deb: 7/1/75																												
1975	Bal-A	3	0	1.000	11	4	1	0	0	57	41	23	8	0	19	31	9.5	3.63	97	.204	.273	0	—	0	1	-1	-1	-0.1
1976	Oak-A	9	7	.563	26	26	4	1	0	142	169	74	15	1	30	67	12.7	4.25	79	.294	.331	0	—	0	-11	-15	-1	-1.6
1977	Oak-A	0	3	.000	5	3	0	0	0	13^2	21	16	3	0	7	5	18.4	10.54	38	.339	.406	0	—	0	-10	-10	0	-1.6
	Sea-A	3	3	.500	9	9	0	0	0	39^2	50	26	7	1	16	20	15.2	4.99	83	.311	.376	0	—	0	-4	-4	0	-0.5
	Yr	3	6	.333	14	12	0	0	0	53^1	71	42	10	1	23	25	16.0	6.41	64	.318	.385	0	—	0	-14	-14	1	-2.1
1978	Sea-A	8	14	.364	29	29	4	2	0	168	173	86	21	2	79	75	13.6	4.18	91	.270	.352	0	—	0	-7	-7	-1	-0.9
1979	Sea-A	1	4	.200	10	6	1	0	0	36^2	46	26	4	0	15	18	15.0	4.42	99	.309	.372	0	—	0	-1	-0	-0	0.0
	Mil-A	3	3	.500	18	8	0	0	0	75	81	50	11	3	10	32	11.3	5.76	73	.276	.307	0	—	0	-13	-13	-1	-1.0
	Yr	4	7	.364	28	14	1	0	0	111^2	127	76	15	3	25	50	12.5	5.32	80	.287	.330	0	—	0	-14	-13	-1	-1.0
1980	Mil-A	5	5	.500	17	11	1	1	1	89^1	92	40	7	1	15	29	10.9	3.53	110	.267	.300	0	—	0	5	4	0	0.4
Total	6	32	39	.451	125	96	11	4	1	621^1	673	341	76	8	191	277	12.6	4.45	85	.278	.332	0	—	0	-40	-46	-3	-5.3

YEAR TM/L	W	L	PCT	G	GS	CG	SH	SV	IP	H	R	HR	HB	BB	SO	RAT	ERA	ERA+	OAV	OOB	BH	AVG	PB	PR	PR+	PD	TPI
● **BOBBY MITCHELL** Mitchell, Robert McKasha b: 2/6/1856, Cincinnati, Ohio d: 5/1/33, Springfield, Ohio BL/TL, 5'5", 135 lbs. Deb: 9/6/1877 ♦																											
1877 Cin-N	6	5	.545	12	12	11	1	0	100	123	69	0		11	41	12.1	3.51	75	.281	.299	10	.204	-0	-8	-10	-0	-0.9
1878 Cin-N	7	2	.778	9	9	9	1	0	80	69	32	1		18	51	9.8	2.14	100	**.223**	.265	12	.245	1	2	-0	0	0.1
1879 Cle-N	7	15	.318	23	22	20	0	0	194^{2}	236	153	0		42	90	12.9	3.28	76	.283	.317	16	.147	-4	-17	-17	-4	-2.2
1882 StL-a	0	1	.000	1	1	0	0	0	7	12	13	0		2	2	18.0	7.71	36	.353	.389	0	.000	-1	-4	-4	-0	-0.4
Total 4	20	23	.465	45	44	40	2	0	381^{2}	440	267	1		73	184	12.1	3.18	77	.272	.304	38	.180	-5	-27	-31	-4	-3.4
● **WILLIE MITCHELL** Mitchell, William b: 12/1/1889, Pleasant Grove, Miss. d: 11/23/73, Sardis, Miss. BR/TL, 6', 176 lbs. Deb: 9/22/09																											
1909 Cle-A	1	2	.333	3	3	3	0	0	23	18	6	0	4	10	8	12.5	1.57	163	.225	.340	2	.286	1	2	2	0	0.4
1910 Cle-A	12	8	.600	35	18	11	1	0	183^{2}	155	77	2	15	55	102	11.0	2.60	100	.236	.310	10	.159	-3	-2	-0	-2	-0.6
1911 Cle-A	7	14	.333	30	22	9	0	0	177^{1}	190	102	1	13	60	78	13.3	3.76	91	.284	.354	7	.109	-5	-8	-7	-1	-1.3
1912 Cle-A	5	8	.385	29	15	8	0	1	163^{2}	149	88	0	7	56	94	11.7	2.80	121	.240	.309	6	.113	-4	9	11	-3	0.1
1913 Cle-A	14	8	.636	35	22	14	4	0	217	153	62	1	8	88	141	10.3	1.91	159	.199	.288	10	.143	-2	25	26	-3	2.1
1914 Cle-A	11	17	.393	39	32	16	3	1	257	228	127	3	7	124	179	12.6	3.19	91	.238	.330	7	.086	-3	-13	-8	-5	-1.8
1915 Cle-A	11	14	.440	36	30	12	1	1	236	210	103	1	2	84	149	11.3	2.82	108	.241	.309	10	.127	-5	3	6	-4	-0.3
1916 Cle-A	2	5	.286	12	6	1	0	1	43^{2}	55	35	1	0	19	24	15.3	5.15	58	.309	.376	0	.000	-1	-11	-10	-1	-1.7
Det-A	7	5	.583	23	17	7	2	0	127^{2}	119	53	1	5	48	60	12.1	3.31	86	.253	.329	9	.250	2	-7	-6	-3	-0.7
Yr	9	10	.474	35	23	8	2	1	171^{1}	174	88	2	5	67	84	12.9	3.78	77	.269	.342	9	.191	1	-18	-16	-4	-2.4
1917 Det-A	12	8	.600	30	22	12	5	0	185^{1}	172	66	2	13	46	80	11.2	2.19	121	.250	.309	7	.119	-3	10	10	-2	0.4
1918 Det-A	0	1	.000	1	1	0	0	0	4	3	4	0	0	5	2	18.0	9.00	30	.200	.400	0	.000	-0	-3	-3	0	-0.5
1919 Det-A	1	2	.333	3	2	0	0	0	13^{2}	12	8	2	1	10	4	15.1	5.27	61	.255	.397	1	.200	0	-3	-3	0	-0.6
Total 11	83	92	.474	276	190	93	16	4	1632	1464	731	14	75	605	921	11.8	2.88	103	.243	.320	69	.130	-24	3	17	-23	-4.5
● **VINEGAR BEND MIZELL** Mizell, Wilmer David b: 8/13/30, Leakesville, Miss. d: 2/21/99, Kerrville, Tex. BR/TL, 6'3.5", 205 lbs. Deb: 4/22/52																											
1952 StL-N	10	8	.556	30	30	7	2	0	190	171	89	12	1	103	146	13.0	3.65	102	.237	.333	3	.044	-5	2	1	-2	-0.6
1953 StL-N	13	11	.542	33	33	10	1	0	224^{1}	193	93	12	4	114	173	12.5	3.49	122	.227	.321	7	.084	-4	20	19	-0	1.4
1956 StL-N	14	14	.500	33	33	11	3	0	208^{2}	172	93	20	7	92	153	11.7	3.62	104	.222	.310	8	.107	-3	3	4	0	0.2
1957 StL-N	8	10	.444	33	21	7	2	0	149^{1}	136	69	18	1	51	87	11.3	3.74	106	.241	.305	4	.089	-2	2	4	1	0.3
1958 StL-N	10	14	.417	30	29	8	2	0	189^{2}	178	81	17	2	91	80	12.9	3.42	121	.252	.339	7	.115	-3	11	14	-1	1.3
1959 StL-N†	13	10	.565	31	30	8	1	0	201^{1}	196	104	21	8	89	108	13.1	4.20	101	.252	.334	14	.187	1	-6	1	-2	-0.1
1960 StL-N	1	3	.250	9	9	0	0	0	55^{1}	64	31	7	0	28	42	15.0	4.55	90	.291	.371	2	.111	-1	-5	-3	0	-0.2
*Pit-N	13	5	.722	23	23	8	3	0	155^{2}	141	59	7	3	46	71	11.0	3.12	120	.247	.306	7	.137	-1	11	11	-3	0.8
Yr	14	8	.636	32	32	8	3	0	211	205	90	14	3	74	113	12.0	3.50	110	.259	.325	9	.130	-1	6	8	-2	0.6
1961 Pit-N	7	10	.412	25	17	2	1	0	100	120	61	16	0	31	37	13.6	5.04	79	.299	.350	3	.130	-1	-11	-12	-3	-2.0
1962 Pit-N	1	1	.500	4	3	0	0	0	16^{1}	15	10	3	1	10	6	14.3	4.96	79	.254	.371	0	.000	-0	-2	-2	0	-0.2
NY-N	0	2	.000	17	2	0	0	0	38	48	35	10	1	25	15	17.5	7.34	57	.324	.425	2	.250	0	-14	-13	-1	-0.7
Yr	1	3	.250	21	5	0	0	0	54^{1}	63	45	13	2	35	21	16.6	6.63	62	.304	.410	2	.143	-0	-16	-15	-0	-0.9
Total 9	90	88	.506	268	230	61	15	0	1528^{2}	1434	725	143	28	680	918	12.6	3.85	104	.247	.329	57	.111	-19	12	25	-9	0.2
● **DAVE MLICKI** Mlicki, David John b: 6/8/68, Cleveland, Ohio BR/TR, 6'4", 190 lbs. Deb: 9/12/92																											
1992 Cle-A	0	2	.000	4	4	0	0	0	21^{2}	23	14	3	1	16	16	16.6	4.98	78	.280	.404	0	—	0	-2	-3	1	-0.2
1993 Cle-A	0	0	—	3	3	0	0	0	13^{1}	11	6	2	2	6	7	12.8	3.38	129	.220	.328	0	—	0	1	1	-0	0.1
1995 NY-N	9	7	.563	29	25	0	0	0	160^{2}	160	82	23	4	54	123	12.2	4.26	95	.256	.319	2	.051	-1	-1	-4	-1	-0.5
1996 NY-N	6	7	.462	51	2	0	0	1	90	95	46	9	6	33	83	13.4	3.30	122	.277	.351	1	.100	-0	9	8	-1	0.8
1997 NY-N	8	12	.400	32	32	1	1	0	193^{2}	194	89	21	5	76	157	12.8	4.00	101	.259	.332	9	.188	2	5	1	-2	0.1
1998 NY-N	1	4	.200	10	10	1	0	0	57	68	38	8	5	25	39	15.5	5.68	73	.297	.378	3	.188	1	-9	-10	0	-0.7
LA-N	7	3	.700	20	20	2	1	0	124^{1}	120	64	15	2	38	78	11.6	4.05	98	.253	.311	2	.059	-2	3	-1	-0	-0.3
Yr	8	7	.533	30	30	3	1	0	181^{1}	188	102	23	7	63	117	12.8	4.57	88	.267	.333	5	.100	-1	-7	-12	0	-1.0
1999 LA-N	0	1	.000	2	0	0	0	0	7^{1}	10	4	1	0	2	1	14.7	4.91	87	.323	.364	1	1.000	1	-0	-1	-0	0.0
Det-A	14	12	.538	31	31	2	0	0	191^{2}	209	108	24	12	70	119	13.7	4.60	106	.276	.347	0	.000	0	6	6	-1	0.6
2000 Det-A	6	11	.353	24	21	0	0	0	119^{1}	143	79	17	3	44	57	14.3	5.58	86	.291	.353	0	.000	-0	-9	-11	0	-1.2
Total 8	51	59	.464	206	148	6	2	1	979	1033	530	123	40	364	680	13.2	4.41	97	.270	.339	18	.117	1	1	-14	-5	-1.3
● **KEVIN MMAHAT** Mmahat, Kevin Paul b: 11/9/64, Memphis, Tenn. BL/TL, 6'5", 220 lbs. Deb: 9/9/89																											
1989 NY-A	0	2	.000	4	2	0	0	0	7^{2}	13	12	2	1	8	3	25.8	12.91	30	.406	.537	0	—	0	-8	-8	-0	-1.3
● **MIKE MODAK** Modak, Michael b: 5/18/22, Campbell, Ohio d: 12/12/95, Lakeland, Fla. BR/TR, 5'10.5", 195 lbs. Deb: 7/4/45																											
1945 Cin-N	1	2	.333	20	3	1	1	1	42^{1}	52	27	0	0	23	7	15.9	5.74	65	.308	.391	1	.100	-1	-9	-9	-1	-0.8
● **BRIAN MOEHLER** Moehler, Brian Merritt b: 12/31/71, Rockingham, N.C. BR/TR, 6'3", 195 lbs. Deb: 9/22/96																											
1996 Det-A	0	1	.000	2	2	0	0	0	10^{1}	11	10	1	0	8	2	16.5	4.35	116	.262	.380	0	—	0	1	1	-0	0.0
1997 Det-A	11	12	.478	31	31	2	1	0	175^{1}	198	97	22	5	61	97	13.6	4.67	98	.285	.347	0	.000	-0	-2	-2	0	-0.2
1998 Det-A	14	13	.519	33	33	4	3	0	221^{1}	220	103	30	2	56	123	11.3	3.90	121	.259	.307	0	.000	-0	19	20	0	2.1
1999 Det-A	10	16	.385	32	32	2	2	0	196^{1}	229	116	22	7	59	106	13.5	5.04	97	.294	.349	0	.000	-0	-4	-4	2	-0.2
2000 Det-A	12	9	.571	29	29	2	0	0	178	222	99	20	2	40	103	13.3	4.50	106	.305	.343	0	.000	-0	8	6	2	0.7
Total 5	47	51	.480	127	127	10	6	0	781^{1}	880	425	95	16	224	431	12.9	4.50	105	.285	.336	0	.000	-1	22	21	4	2.4
● **DENNIS MOELLER** Moeller, Dennis Michael b: 9/15/67, Tarzana, Cal. BR/TL, 6'2", 195 lbs. Deb: 7/28/92																											
1992 KC-A	0	3	.000	5	4	0	0	0	18	24	17	5	0	11	6	17.5	7.00	58	.333	.422	0	—	0	-6	-6	0	-0.8
1993 Pit-N	1	0	1.000	10	0	0	0	0	16^{1}	26	20	2	1	7	13	18.7	9.92	41	.356	.420	0	—	0	-11	-11	0	-0.6
Total 2	1	3	.250	15	4	0	0	0	34^{1}	50	37	7	1	18	19	18.1	8.39	48	.345	.421	0	—	0	-17	-16	1	-1.4
● **JOE MOELLER** Moeller, Joseph Douglas b: 2/15/43, Blue Island, Ill. BR/TR, 6'5", 208 lbs. Deb: 4/12/62																											
1962 LA-N	6	5	.545	19	15	1	0	1	85^{2}	87	55	10	0	58	46	15.2	5.25	69	.266	.377	7	.212	1	-12	-17	1	-1.7
1964 LA-N	7	13	.350	27	24	1	0	0	145^{1}	153	89	14	4	31	97	11.6	4.21	77	.265	.307	3	.067	-2	-11	-17	-0	-2.4
1966 *LA-N	2	4	.333	29	8	0	0	0	78^{2}	73	31	4	3	14	31	10.3	2.52	131	.244	.285	2	.167	1	10	7	1	0.8
1967 LA-N	0	0	—	6	0	0	0	0	5	9	5	1	0	3	2	21.6	9.00	34	.409	.480	0	—	0	-3	-4	0	-0.2
1968 LA-N	1	1	.500	3	3	0	0	0	16	17	10	1	1	2	11	11.3	5.06	55	.270	.303	0	.000	-1	-4	-4	0	-0.6
1969 LA-N	1	0	1.000	23	4	0	0	1	51^{1}	54	23	4	0	13	25	11.7	3.33	100	.278	.324	2	.200	0	2	-0	1	0.1
1970 LA-N	7	9	.438	31	19	2	1	4	135^{1}	131	63	16	1	43	63	11.6	3.92	98	.248	.306	6	.154	0	2	-1	-2	-0.3
1971 LA-N	2	4	.333	28	1	0	0	1	66^{1}	72	32	5	0	12	32	11.4	3.80	85	.279	.311	0	.000	-0	-2	-4	1	-0.4
Total 8	26	36	.419	166	74	4	1	7	583^{2}	596	308	55	9	176	307	12.0	4.01	86	.263	.318	20	.129	-2	-20	-40	2	-4.7
● **RON MOELLER** Moeller, Ronald Ralph "The Kid" b: 10/13/38, Cincinnati, Ohio BL/TL, 6', 180 lbs. Deb: 9/8/56																											
1956 Bal-A	0	1	.000	4	1	0	0	0	8^{2}	10	5	0	0	3	2	13.5	4.15	94	.286	.342	0	.000	-0	0	-0	-0	-0.1
1958 Bal-A	0	0	—	4	0	0	0	0	4^{1}	6	2	0	0	3	3	18.7	4.15	87	.333	.429	0	—	0	-0	-0	0	0.0
1961 LA-A	4	8	.333	33	18	1	1	0	112^{2}	122	80	15	2	83	87	16.5	5.83	77	.275	.392	6	.207	2	-23	-15	1	-1.1
1963 LA-A	0	0	—	3	0	0	0	0	2^{2}	5	2	1	0	1	2	20.3	6.75	51	.385	.429	0	—	0	-1	-1	0	0.0
Was-A	2	0	1.000	8	3	0	0	0	24^{1}	31	17	4	1	10	10	15.5	6.29	59	.316	.385	2	.222	0	-7	-7	-1	-0.6
Yr	2	0	1.000	11	3	0	0	0	27	36	19	5	1	11	12	16.0	6.33	58	.324	.390	2	.222	0	-8	-8	-1	-0.6
Total 4	6	9	.400	52	22	1	1	0	152^{2}	174	106	20	3	100	104	16.3	5.78	74	.287	.390	8	.205	2	-31	-23	0	-1.8
● **SAM MOFFETT** Moffett, Samuel R. b: 3/14/1857, Wheeling, W.Va. d: 5/5/07, Butte, Mont. BR/TR, 6', 175 lbs. Deb: 5/15/1884 F♦																											
1884 Cle-N	3	19	.136	24	22	21	0	0	197^{2}	236	165	9		58	84	13.4	3.87	81	.284	.330	47	.184	-3	-20	-15	2	-1.3
1887 Ind-N	1	5	.167	6	6	6	0	0	50	70	45	1	4	23	3	13.3	3.78	110	.323	.335	6	.143	-2	2	2	-0	-0.1
1888 Ind-N	2	5	.286	7	7	6	1	0	56	62	40	3	2	17	7	13.0	4.66	64	.278	.335	4	.114	-1	-11	-10	-2	-1.2
Total 3	6	29	.171	37	35	33	1	0	303^{2}	368	250	13	6	98	94	13.3	4.00	82	.289	.332	57	.171	-6	-29	-23	-0	-2.6
● **RANDY MOFFITT** Moffitt, Randall James b: 10/13/48, Long Beach, Cal. BR/TR, 6'3", 190 lbs. Deb: 6/11/72																											
1972 SF-N	1	5	.167	40	0	0	0	4	70^{2}	72	31	5	2	30	37	13.2	3.69	94	.266	.343	0	.000	-1	-2	-2	0	-0.2
1973 SF-N	4	4	.500	60	0	0	0	14	100^{1}	86	30	9	1	31	65	10.6	2.42	158	.225	.285	1	.059	-1	14	15	-1	1.3

YEAR	TM/L	W	L	PCT	G	GS	CG	SH	SV	IP	H	R	HR	HB	BB	SO	RAT	ERA	ERA+	OAV	OOB	BH	AVG	PB	PR	PR+	PD	TPI
1974	SF-N	5	7	.417	61	1	0	0	15	102	99	52	9	2	29	49	11.5	4.50	85	.256	.311	5	.313	2	-10	-7	1	-0.8
1975	SF-N	4	5	.444	55	0	0	0	11	74	73	35	6	3	32	39	13.1	3.89	98	.257	.339	3	.214	1	-2	-1	-0	-0.1
1976	SF-N	6	6	.500	58	0	0	0	14	103	92	36	6	1	35	50	11.2	2.27	160	.238	.303	2	.143	-0	14	15	-0	2.1
1977	SF-N	4	9	.308	64	0	0	0	11	87^2	91	41	4	3	39	68	13.7	3.59	109	.273	.355	0	.000	-0	3	3	1	0.6
1978	SF-N	8	4	.667	70	0	0	0	12	81^2	79	35	5	3	33	52	12.7	3.31	104	.258	.336	1	.143	0	3	1	-1	0.1
1979	SF-N	2	5	.286	28	0	0	0	2	35	53	33	5	2	14	16	17.7	7.71	45	.356	.418	0	.000	-0	-15	-18	-0	-3.3
1980	SF-N	1	1	.500	13	0	0	0	0	16^2	18	10	2	1	4	10	12.4	4.86	73	.281	.333	0	.000	-0	-2	-2	0	-0.3
1981	SF-N	0	0	—	10	0	0	0	0	11^1	15	10	2	0	2	11	13.5	7.94	43	.313	.340	0	—	0	-6	-6	-0	-0.4
1982	Hou-N	2	4	.333	30	0	0	0	3	41^2	36	15	3	5	13	20	11.7	3.02	110	.228	.307	0	.000	-0	3	2	-1	0.1
1983	Tor-A	6	2	.750	45	0	0	0	10	57^1	52	27	5	1	24	38	12.1	3.77	115	.243	.322	0	—	0	2	3	0	0.5
Total	12	43	52	.453	534	1	0	0	96	781^1	766	355	61	24	286	455	12.4	3.65	102	.257	.327	12	.140	-1	1	6	-3	-0.4
● HERB MOFORD Moford, Herbert b: 8/6/28, Brooksville, Ky. BR/TR, 6′1″, 175 lbs. Deb: 4/12/55																												
1955	StL-N	1	1	.500	14	1	0	0	2	24	29	23	5	1	15	8	16.9	7.88	52	.299	.398	0	.000	-0	-10	-10	1	-0.9
1958	Det-A	4	9	.308	25	11	6	0	1	109^2	83	45	10	9	42	58	11.0	3.61	112	.214	.305	1	.027	-4	2	5	1	0.3
1959	Bos-A	0	2	.000	4	2	0	0	0	8^2	10	11	3	0	6	7	16.6	11.42	36	.286	.390	0	.000	-0	-7	-7	0	-1.2
1962	NY-N	0	1	.000	7	0	0	0	0	15	21	15	3	0	1	5	13.2	7.20	58	.318	.328	1	.250	0	-5	-5	-0	-0.3
Total	4	5	13	.278	50	14	6	0	3	157^1	143	94	21	10	64	78	12.4	5.03	81	.244	.329	2	.045	-4	-21	-16	2	-2.1
● GEORGE MOGRIDGE Mogridge, George Anthony b: 2/18/1889, Rochester, N.Y. d: 3/4/62, Rochester, N.Y. BL/TL, 6′2″, 165 lbs. Deb: 8/17/11																												
1911	Chi-A	0	2	.000	4	1	0	0	0	12^2	12	10	1	0	1	5	9.2	4.97	65	.255	.271	2	.400	0	-2	-3	-0	-0.3
1912	Chi-A	3	4	.429	17	8	2	0	3	64^2	69	32	2	1	15	31	11.8	4.04	79	.264	.307	2	.125	-0	-5	-6	-1	-0.7
1915	NY-A	2	3	.400	6	5	3	1	0	41	33	11	0	3	11	11	10.3	1.76	167	.219	.285	1	.083	-1	5	5	-1	0.6
1916	NY-A	6	12	.333	30	21	10	2	0	194^2	174	71	3	7	45	66	10.4	2.31	125	.252	.305	14	.212	1	11	12	1	1.4
1917	NY-A	9	11	.450	29	25	15	1	0	196^1	185	82	5	9	39	46	10.7	2.98	90	.255	.301	11	.159	-1	-7	-6	1	-0.7
1918	NY-A	16	13	.552	**45**	19	13	1	**7**	239^1	232	78	6	8	43	62	10.6	2.18	130	.263	.304	15	.190	-0	16	17	3	2.5
1919	NY-A	10	9	.526	35	18	13	3	0	169	159	68	6	7	46	58	11.3	2.77	115	.250	.307	6	.125	-1	9	8	1	0.9
1920	NY-A	5	9	.357	26	15	7	0	1	125^1	146	83	4	3	36	35	13.3	4.31	89	.287	.338	7	.167	-1	-7	-7	1	-0.7
1921	Was-A	18	14	.563	38	36	21	4	0	288	301	119	12	7	66	101	11.7	3.00	137	.269	.313	15	.153	-5	41	37	2	3.3
1922	Was-A	18	13	.581	34	32	18	3	0	251^2	300	120	12	11	72	61	13.7	3.58	108	.304	.358	21	.244	4	13	8	-1	1.3
1923	Was-A	13	13	.500	33	30	17	3	1	211	228	90	10	3	56	62	12.2	3.11	121	.285	.334	17	.227	1	20	16	1	2.1
1924	*Was-A	16	11	.593	30	30	13	2	0	213	217	97	2	7	61	48	12.0	3.76	107	.270	.327	13	.176	-2	11	7	0	0.5
1925	Was-A	3	4	.429	10	8	3	0	0	53	58	27	2	4	18	12	13.6	4.08	104	.291	.362	2	.105	-2	2	1	-0	-0.1
	StL-A	1	1	.500	2	2	1	0	0	15^1	17	10	2	1	5	8	13.5	5.87	80	.279	.343	0	.000	-0	-3	-2	0	-0.2
	Yr	4	5	.444	12	10	4	0	0	68^1	75	37	4	5	23	20	13.6	4.48	97	.288	.358	2	.087	-2	-1	-1	0	-0.3
1926	Bos-N	6	10	.375	39	10	2	0	3	142	173	82	6	3	36	46	13.4	4.50	79	.311	.356	8	.174	-1	-11	-16	2	-1.5
1927	Bos-N	6	4	.600	20	1	0	0	5	48^2	48	23	4	2	15	26	12.0	3.70	100	.257	.319	3	.200	-0	1	0	1	0.1
Total	15	132	133	.498	398	261	138	20	20	2265^2	2352	1003	77	76	565	678	11.9	3.23	109	.273	.323	137	.182	-8	95	76	11	8.5
● GEORGE MOHART Mohart, George Benjamin b: 3/6/1892, Buffalo, N.Y. d: 10/2/70, Silver Creek, N.Y. BR/TR, 5′9″, 165 lbs. Deb: 4/15/20																												
1920	Bro-N	0	1	.000	13	1	0	0	0	35^2	33	17	0	3	7	13	10.9	1.77	181	.250	.303	1	.125	-0	5	6	1	0.4
1921	Bro-N	0	0	—	2	0	0	0	0	7	8	5	0	1	1	1	12.9	3.86	101	.296	.345	1	.500	0	-0	0	-0	0.0
Total	2	0	1	.000	15	1	0	0	0	42^2	41	22	0	4	8	14	11.2	2.11	157	.258	.310	2	.200	0	5	6	1	0.4
● MIKE MOHLER Mohler, Michael Ross b: 7/26/68, Dayton, Ohio BR/TL, 6′2″, 195 lbs. Deb: 4/7/93																												
1993	Oak-A	1	6	.143	42	9	0	0	0	64^1	57	45	10	2	44	42	14.4	5.60	73	.241	.364	0	—	0	-9	-11	0	-1.1
1994	Oak-A	0	1	.000	1	1	0	0	0	2^1	2	3	1	0	2	4	15.4	7.71	57	.167	.286	0	—	0	-1	-1	0	-0.2
1995	Oak-A	1	1	.500	28	0	0	0	1	23^2	16	8	0	0	18	15	12.9	3.04	147	.198	.343	0	—	0	4	4	-0	0.3
1996	Oak-A	6	3	.667	72	0	0	0	7	81	79	36	9	1	41	64	13.4	3.67	134	.263	.354	0	—	0	12	12	1	1.3
1997	Oak-A	1	10	.091	62	10	0	0	1	101^2	116	65	11	7	54	66	15.7	5.13	88	.301	.397	0	—	0	-6	-7	1	-0.6
1998	Oak-A	3	3	.500	57	0	0	0	0	61	70	38	6	4	26	42	14.8	5.16	89	.289	.368	0	—	0	-3	-4	-1	-0.4
1999	StL-N	1	1	.500	48	0	0	0	1	49^1	47	26	3	1	23	31	13.0	4.38	104	.254	.340	0	.000	-0	1	1	-1	-0.1
2000	StL-N	1	1	.500	22	0	0	0	0	19	26	20	1	2	15	8	20.4	9.00	51	.321	.439	1	1.000	0	-9	-9	-1	-0.8
	Cle-A	0	1	.000	2	0	0	0	0	1	1	1	1	0	0	2	9.0	9.00	56	.250	.250	0	—	0	-0	-0	0	-0.1
Total	8	14	27	.341	334	20	0	0	10	403^1	414	242	42	17	223	274	14.6	4.91	93	.271	.370	1	.250	0	-12	-16	-0	-1.7
● DALE MOHORCIC Mohorcic, Dale Robert b: 1/25/56, Cleveland, Ohio BR/TR, 6′3″, 220 lbs. Deb: 5/31/86																												
1986	Tex-A	2	4	.333	58	0	0	0	7	79	86	25	5	1	15	29	11.6	2.51	172	.279	.315	0	—	0	15	15	0	1.3
1987	Tex-A	7	6	.538	74	0	0	0	16	99^1	88	34	11	2	19	48	9.9	2.99	150	.244	.286	0	—	0	16	17	2	2.6
1988	Tex-A	2	6	.250	43	0	0	0	5	52	62	35	6	5	20	25	15.1	4.85	84	.295	.370	0	—	0	-5	-4	0	-0.6
	NY-A	2	2	.500	13	0	0	0	1	22^2	21	7	1	3	9	19	13.1	2.78	142	.239	.330	0	—	0	3	3	-1	0.5
	Yr	4	8	.333	56	0	0	0	6	74^2	83	42	7	8	29	44	14.5	4.22	96	.279	.358	0	—	0	-2	-1	-0	-0.1
1989	NY-A	2	1	.667	32	0	0	0	2	57^2	65	41	8	6	18	24	13.9	4.99	78	.286	.355	0	—	0	-7	-7	1	-0.3
1990	Mon-N	1	2	.333	34	0	0	0	2	53	56	21	6	4	18	29	13.2	3.23	113	.286	.358	1	.125	-0	3	3	0	0.2
Total	5	16	21	.432	254	0	0	0	33	363^2	378	163	37	21	99	174	12.3	3.49	119	.272	.330	1	.125	-0	25	26	3	3.7
● BILL MOISAN Moisan, William Joseph b: 7/30/25, Bradford, Mass. BL/TR, 6′1″, 170 lbs. Deb: 9/17/53																												
1953	Chi-N	0	0	—	3	0	0	0	0	5	5	3	0	1	2	1	14.4	5.40	82	.278	.381	0	—	0	-1	-1	0	0.0
● CARLTON MOLESWORTH Molesworth, Carlton b: 2/15/1876, Frederick, Md. d: 7/25/61, Frederick, Md. BL/TL, 5′6″, 200 lbs. Deb: 9/14/1895																												
1895	Was-N	0	2	.000	4	3	1	0	0	16	33	34	1	4	15	7	29.3	14.63	33	.418	.531	1	.143	-1	-18	-17	-0	-1.4
● GABE MOLINA Molina, Cruz Gabriel b: 5/3/75, Denver, Colo. BR/TR, 5′11″, 190 lbs. Deb: 5/1/99																												
1999	Bal-A	1	2	.333	20	0	0	0	0	23	22	19	4	0	16	14	14.9	6.65	71	.256	.373	0	—	0	-5	-5	-0	-0.6
2000	Bal-A	0	0	—	9	0	0	0	0	13	25	14	2	0	9	8	23.5	9.00	53	.397	.472	0	—	0	-6	-6	-0	-0.3
	Atl-N	0	0	—	2	0	0	0	0	2	3	4	1	1	1	1	22.5	9.00	50	.375	.500	0	—	0	-1	-1	-0	-0.1
Total	2	1	2	.333	31	0	0	0	0	38	50	37	7	1	26	23	18.2	7.58	62	.318	.418	0	—	0	-11	-12	-1	-1.0
● RICHIE MOLONEY Moloney, Richard Henry b: 6/7/50, Brookline, Mass. BR/TR, 6′3″, 185 lbs. Deb: 9/20/70																												
1970	Chi-A	0	0	—	1	0	0	0	0	1	2	0	0	0	0	1	18.0	0.00	—	.400	.400	0	—	0	0	0	0	0.0
● VINCE MOLYNEAUX Molyneaux, Vincent Leo b: 8/17/1888, Lewiston, N.Y. d: 5/4/50, Stamford, Conn. BR/TR, 6′, 180 lbs. Deb: 7/5/17																												
1917	StL-A	0	0	—	7	0	0	0	0	22	18	15	0	0	20	4	15.5	4.91	53	.237	.396	0	.000	-1	-5	-6	0	-0.3
1918	Bos-A	1	0	1.000	6	0	0	0	0	10^2	3	4	0	0	8	1	9.3	3.38	80	.086	.256	0	.000	-0	-1	-1	0	-0.1
Total	2	1	0	1.000	13	0	0	0	0	32^2	21	19	0	0	28	5	13.5	4.41	60	.189	.353	0	.000	-1	-6	-7	1	-0.4
● RINTY MONAHAN Monahan, Edward Francis b: 4/28/28, Brooklyn, N.Y. BR/TR, 6′1.5″, 195 lbs. Deb: 8/9/53																												
1953	Phi-A	0	0	—	4	0	0	0	0	10^2	11	5	0	0	7	2	15.2	4.22	102	.275	.383	0	.000	-0	-0	0	-0	-0.1
● BILL MONBOUQUETTE Monbouquette, William Charles b: 8/11/36, Medford, Mass. BR/TR, 5′11″, 195 lbs. Deb: 7/18/58 C																												
1958	Bos-A	3	4	.429	10	8	3	0	0	54^1	52	25	4	0	20	30	11.9	3.31	121	.251	.317	3	.176	-1	3	4	-1	0.4
1959	Bos-A	7	7	.500	34	17	4	0	0	151^2	165	86	15	3	33	87	11.9	4.15	98	.285	.327	3	.065	-4	-5	-2	-0	-0.5
1960	Bos-A★	14	11	.560	35	30	12	3	0	215	217	91	18	2	68	134	12.0	3.64	111	.263	.320	6	.092	-3	6	9	-0	0.7
1961	Bos-A	14	14	.500	32	32	12	1	0	236^1	233	106	24	0	100	161	12.7	3.39	123	.254	.327	9	.130	-1	17	20	-1	2.0
1962	Bos-A☆	15	13	.536	35	35	11	4	0	235^1	227	100	22	3	65	153	11.3	3.33	124	.251	.303	7	.096	-3	17	20	-4	1.5
1963	Bos-A☆	20	10	.667	37	36	13	1	0	266^2	258	119	31	0	42	174	10.1	3.81	99	.250	.280	10	.114	-3	-5	-1	1	-0.3
1964	Bos-A	13	14	.481	36	35	7	5	1	234	258	114	34	1	40	120	11.5	4.04	95	.277	.308	6	.083	-2	-11	-4	0	-0.7
1965	Bos-A	10	18	.357	35	35	10	2	0	228^2	239	114	32	1	40	110	11.0	3.70	101	.269	.301	4	.059	-3	-6	1	0	-0.2
1966	Det-A	7	8	.467	30	14	2	1	0	102^2	120	60	14	3	22	61	12.7	4.73	74	.293	.333	4	.154	-0	-15	-14	-1	-2.0
1967	Det-A	0	0	—	2	0	0	0	0	2	1	0	0	0	0	2	4.5	0.00	—	.143	.143	0	—	0	1	1	0	0.1
	NY-A	6	5	.545	33	10	2	1	1	133^1	122	39	6	4	17	53	9.7	2.36	132	.246	.277	5	.156	-0	13	12	-1	0.9
	Yr	6	5	.545	35	10	2	1	1	135^1	123	39	6	4	17	55	9.6	2.33	134	.245	.275	5	.156	-0	14	12	-1	1.0

YEAR	TM/L	W	L	PCT	G	GS	CG	SH	SV	IP	H	R	HR	HB	BB	SO	RAT	ERA	ERA+	OAV	OOB	BH	AVG	PB	PR	PR+	PD	TPI
1968	NY-A	5	7	.417	17	11	2	0	0	89^1	92	47	7	3	13	32	10.9	4.43	65	.264	.296	3	.115	0	-14	-16	1	-1.9
	SF-N	0	1	.000	7	0	0	0	1	12^1	11	9	4	0	2	5	9.5	3.65	81	.239	.271	0	—	0	-1	-1	0	-0.1
Total	11	114	112	.504	343	263	78	18	3	1961^2	1995	910	211	20	462	1122	11.4	3.68	104	.263	.307	60	.103	-20	-2	28	-6	-0.1
● **SID MONGE**	Monge, Isidro Pedroza b: 4/11/51, Agua Prieta, Mexico BB/TL, 6'2", 195 lbs. Deb: 9/12/75																											
1975	Cal-A	0	2	.000	4	2	2	0	0	23^2	22	12	3	1	10	17	12.5	4.18	85	.242	.324	0	—	0	-1	-2	-0	-0.2
1976	Cal-A	6	7	.462	32	13	2	0	0	117^2	108	50	10	1	49	53	12.1	3.37	99	.248	.326	0	—	0	2	-1	-1	-0.1
1977	Cal-A	0	1	.000	4	0	0	0	1	12^1	14	6	2	0	6	4	14.6	2.92	135	.304	.385	0	—	0	2	1	0	0.2
	Cle-A	1	2	.333	33	0	0	0	3	39	47	31	6	0	27	25	17.1	6.23	63	.309	.413	0	—	0	-9	-10	-1	-0.9
	Yr	1	3	.250	37	0	0	0	4	51^1	61	37	8	0	33	29	16.5	5.44	73	.308	.407	0	—	0	-8	-9	-1	-0.7
1978	Cle-A	4	3	.571	48	2	0	0	6	84^2	71	36	4	0	51	54	13.0	2.76	136	.225	.332	0	—	0	10	9	-0	0.8
1979	Cle-A☆	12	10	.545	76	0	0	0	19	131	96	37	9	1	64	108	11.1	2.40	177	.209	.307	0	—	0	27	27	-0	5.0
1980	Cle-A	3	5	.375	67	0	0	0	14	94^1	80	39	12	3	40	61	11.7	3.53	116	.227	.311	0	—	0	5	6	-2	0.5
1981	Cle-A	3	5	.375	31	0	0	0	4	58	58	31	9	0	21	41	12.3	4.34	84	.266	.331	0	—	0	-4	-5	-1	-0.7
1982	Phi-N	7	1	.875	47	0	0	0	2	72	70	35	8	2	22	43	11.8	3.75	98	.256	.316	1	.111	-0	-1	-1	1	0.0
1983	Phi-N	3	0	1.000	14	0	0	0	0	11^2	20	10	4	0	6	7	20.1	6.94	51	.377	.441	0	.000	-0	-4	-4	-0	-0.9
	SD-N	7	3	.700	47	0	0	0	7	68^2	65	24	4	1	31	32	12.7	3.15	111	.257	.340	1	.100	-0	4	3	-0	0.3
	Yr	10	3	.769	61	0	0	0	7	80^1	85	34	8	1	37	39	13.8	3.70	95	.278	.358	1	.091	-1	-1	-2	-1	-0.6
1984	SD-N	2	1	.667	13	0	0	0	0	15	17	10	3	0	17	7	20.4	4.80	74	.293	.453	0	.000	-0	-2	-2	-0	-0.4
	Det-A	1	0	1.000	19	0	0	0	0	36	40	21	5	2	12	19	13.5	4.25	92	.282	.346	0	—	0	-1	-1	-1	-0.2
Total	10	49	40	.551	435	17	4	0	56	764	708	342	79	11	356	471	12.7	3.53	107	.248	.334	2	.095	-1	26	21	-6	3.4
● **ED MONROE**	Monroe, Edward Oliver "Peck" b: 2/22/1895, Louisville, Ky. d: 4/29/69, Louisville, Ky. BR/TR, 6'5", 187 lbs. Deb: 5/29/17																											
1917	NY-A	1	0	1.000	9	1	1	0	1	28^2	35	15	1	2	6	12	13.5	3.45	78	.310	.355	2	.167	-0	-3	-2	-0	-0.2
1918	NY-A	0	0	—	1	0	0	0	0	2	1	2	0	0	2	1	13.5	4.50	63	.143	.333	0	—	0	-0	-0	0	0.0
Total	2	1	0	1.000	10	1	1	0	1	30^2	36	17	1	2	8	13	13.5	3.52	77	.300	.354	2	.167	-0	-3	-3	0	-0.2
● **LARRY MONROE**	Monroe, Lawrence James b: 6/20/56, Detroit, Mich. BR/TR, 6'4", 200 lbs. Deb: 8/23/76																											
1976	Chi-A	0	1	.000	8	2	0	0	0	21^2	23	11	0	0	13	9	15.0	4.15	86	.284	.383	0	—	0	-2	-1	-0	-0.1
● **ZACH MONROE**	Monroe, Zachary Charles b: 7/8/31, Peoria, Ill. BR/TR, 6', 198 lbs. Deb: 6/27/58																											
1958	*NY-A	4	2	.667	21	6	1	0	1	58	57	29	8	0	27	18	13.0	3.26	108	.263	.344	2	.118	-1	3	2	0	0.2
1959	NY-A	0	0	—	3	0	0	0	0	3^1	3	2	2	0	2	1	13.5	5.40	67	.231	.333	0	—	0	-1	-1	0	0.0
Total	2	4	2	.667	24	6	1	0	1	61^1	60	31	10	0	29	19	13.1	3.38	105	.261	.344	2	.118	-1	3	1	1	0.2
● **JOHN MONTAGUE**	Montague, John Evans b: 9/12/47, Newport News, Va. BR/TR, 6'2", 213 lbs. Deb: 9/9/73																											
1973	Mon-N	0	0	—	4	0	0	0	0	7^2	8	3	0	1	2	7	12.9	3.52	109	.286	.355	0	.000	-0	0	0	-0	0.0
1974	Mon-N	3	4	.429	46	1	0	0	3	82^2	73	37	5	4	38	43	12.5	3.16	122	.241	.333	1	.100	-0	4	6	-2	0.4
1975	Mon-N	0	1	.000	12	0	0	0	2	17^2	23	11	4	2	6	9	15.8	5.60	68	.324	.392	0	.000	-0	-4	-3	-0	-0.3
	Phi-N	0	0	—	3	0	0	0	0	5	8	5	1	0	4	1	21.6	9.00	42	.400	.500	0	—	0	-3	-3	0	-0.1
	Yr	0	1	.000	15	0	0	0	2	22^2	31	16	5	2	10	10	17.1	6.35	60	.341	.417	0	.000	-0	-7	-6	0	-0.4
1977	Sea-A	8	12	.400	47	15	2	0	4	182^1	193	95	20	4	75	98	13.4	4.29	96	.272	.345	0	—	0	-4	-3	1	-0.2
1978	Sea-A	1	3	.250	19	0	0	0	2	43^2	52	31	2	0	24	14	15.7	6.18	62	.308	.394	0	—	0	-12	-11	-1	-1.1
1979	Sea-A	6	4	.600	41	1	0	0	1	116^1	125	73	14	2	47	60	13.5	5.57	79	.284	.356	0	—	0	-17	-15	1	-1.1
	*Cal-A	2	0	1.000	14	0	0	0	6	17^2	16	12	3	0	9	6	12.7	5.09	80	.242	.333	0	—	0	-2	-2	-1	-0.4
	Yr	8	4	.667	55	1	0	0	7	134	141	85	17	2	56	66	13.4	5.51	79	.279	.353	0	—	0	-19	-17	-0	-1.5
1980	Cal-A	4	2	.667	37	0	0	0	3	73^2	97	47	8	1	21	22	14.5	5.13	77	.324	.371	0	—	0	-9	-10	0	-0.8
Total	7	24	26	.480	223	17	2	0	21	546^2	595	314	57	14	226	260	13.7	4.76	86	.283	.356	1	.083	-0	-46	-41	-1	-3.6
● **RAFAEL MONTALVO**	Montalvo, Rafael Edgardo (Torres) b: 3/31/64, Rio Piedras, P.R. BR/TR, 6', 185 lbs. Deb: 4/13/86																											
1986	Hou-N	0	0	—	1	0	0	0	0	1	1	1	0	0	2	0	27.0	9.00	40	.250	.500	0	—	0	-1	-1	0	0.0
● **AURELIO MONTEAGUDO**	Monteagudo, Aurelio Faustino (Cintra) b: 11/19/43, Caibarien, Cuba d: 11/10/90, Saltillo, Mexico BR/TR, 5'11", 185 lbs. Deb: 9/1/63 F																											
1963	KC-A	0	0	—	4	0	0	0	0	7	4	2	0	0	3	3	9.0	2.57	152	.182	.280	0	—	0	1	1	0	0.1
1964	KC-A	0	4	.000	11	6	0	0	0	31^1	40	32	11	1	10	14	14.6	8.90	43	.317	.372	2	.286	1	-18	-17	-0	-1.8
1965	KC-A	0	0	—	4	0	0	0	0	7	5	4	1	0	4	5	11.6	3.86	90	.185	.290	0	—	0	-0	-0	-0	0.0
1966	KC-A	0	0	—	6	0	0	0	0	12^2	12	4	0	0	7	3	13.5	2.84	120	.261	.358	0	—	0	1	1	-0	0.0
	Hou-N	0	0	—	10	0	0	0	1	15^1	14	8	1	0	11	7	14.7	4.70	73	.241	.362	0	.000	-0	-2	-2	-0	-0.1
1967	Chi-A	0	1	.000	1	1	0	0	0	1^1	4	3	1	0	2	0	40.5	20.25	15	.500	.600	0	—	0	-3	-3	-0	-0.4
1970	KC-A	1	1	.500	21	0	0	0	0	27^1	20	11	2	1	9	18	9.9	2.96	126	.200	.273	0	.000	-0	2	2	-1	0.1
1973	Cal-A	2	1	.667	15	0	0	0	3	30	23	18	2	4	16	8	12.9	4.20	85	.215	.339	0	—	0	-1	-2	0	-0.3
Total	7	3	7	.300	72	7	0	0	4	132	122	82	18	6	62	58	13.0	5.05	72	.247	.338	2	.200	1	-20	-21	-1	-2.4
● **RENE MONTEAGUDO**	Monteagudo, Rene (Miranda) b: 3/12/16, Havana, Cuba d: 9/14/73, Hialeah, Fla. BL/TL, 5'7", 165 lbs. Deb: 9/6/38 F♦																											
1938	Was-A	1	1	.500	5	3	2	0	0	22	26	15	3	0	15	13	16.8	5.73	79	.286	.387	3	.500	1	-2	-3	-1	-0.2
1940	Was-A	2	6	.250	27	8	3	0	2	100^2	128	70	7	3	52	64	16.4	6.08	69	.316	.398	6	.182	0	-19	-22	-1	-1.6
1945	Phi-N	0	0	—	14	0	0	0	0	45^2	67	42	1	2	28	16	19.1	7.49	51	.347	.435	58	.301	2	-19	-18	-1	-0.7
Total	3	3	7	.300	46	11	5	0	2	168^1	221	127	11	5	95	93	17.2	6.42	64	.321	.407	78	.289	4	-40	-44	-3	-2.5
● **JOHN MONTEFUSCO**	Montefusco, John Joseph "Count" b: 5/25/50, Long Branch, N.J. BR/TR, 6'1", 180 lbs. Deb: 9/3/74																											
1974	SF-N	3	2	.600	7	5	1	1	0	39^1	41	22	3	0	19	34	13.7	4.81	79	.256	.335	4	.286	3	-5	-4	-0	-0.3
1975	SF-N	15	9	.625	35	34	10	4	0	243^2	210	85	11	8	86	215	11.2	2.88	132	.233	.305	7	.087	-2	20	24	-1	1.9
1976	SF-N★	16	14	.533	37	36	11	**6**	0	253^1	224	90	11	4	74	172	10.7	2.84	128	.238	.296	8	.103	-2	19	21	-4	1.9
1977	SF-N	7	12	.368	26	25	4	0	0	157^1	170	82	10	3	46	110	12.5	3.49	112	.273	.326	6	.122	-1	7	7	-2	0.6
1978	SF-N	11	9	.550	36	36	3	0	0	238^2	233	110	25	4	68	177	11.5	3.81	91	.255	.310	4	.057	-3	-6	-10	-2	-1.2
1979	SF-N	3	8	.273	22	22	0	0	0	137	145	64	15	2	51	76	13.0	3.94	89	.279	.346	7	.167	2	-3	-7	0	-0.4
1980	SF-N	4	8	.333	22	17	1	0	0	113^1	120	61	15	2	39	85	12.8	4.37	81	.265	.327	1	.033	-2	-10	-11	-1	-1.4
1981	Atl-N	2	3	.400	26	9	0	0	1	77^1	75	32	9	0	27	34	11.9	3.49	103	.260	.324	1	.067	-1	0	1	0	0.0
1982	SD-N	10	11	.476	32	32	1	0	0	184^1	177	93	17	3	41	83	10.8	4.00	86	.251	.295	5	.086	-2	-8	-12	-1	-1.5
1983	SD-N	9	4	.692	31	10	1	0	4	95^1	94	38	6	1	32	52	12.0	3.30	106	.265	.327	1	.053	-1	4	2	-1	0.1
	NY-A	5	0	1.000	6	6	0	0	0	38	39	14	3	1	10	15	11.8	3.32	118	.271	.323	0	—	0	3	3	-1	0.3
1984	NY-A	5	3	.625	11	11	0	0	0	55^1	55	26	5	1	13	23	11.2	3.58	106	.253	.299	0	—	0	3	1	-1	0.1
1985	NY-A	0	0	—	3	1	0	0	0	7	12	8	3	0	2	2	18.0	10.29	39	.387	.424	0	—	0	-5	-5	0	-0.2
1986	NY-A	0	0	—	4	0	0	0	0	12^1	9	3	2	0	5	3	10.2	2.19	187	.200	.280	0	—	0	3	3	0	0.2
Total	13	90	83	.520	298	244	32	11	5	1652^1	1604	728	135	29	513	1081	11.7	3.54	103	.255	.314	44	.097	-10	22	17	-12	0.1
● **MANNY MONTEJO**	Montejo, Manuel (Bofill) b: 10/16/35, Caibarien, Cuba BR/TR, 5'11", 150 lbs. Deb: 7/25/61																											
1961	Det-A	0	0	—	12	0	0	0	0	16^1	13	7	2	2	6	15	11.6	3.86	106	.217	.309	0	—	0	0	0	-1	0.0
● **RICH MONTELEONE**	Monteleone, Richard b: 3/22/63, Tampa, Fla. BR/TR, 6'2", 234 lbs. Deb: 4/15/87																											
1987	Sea-A	0	0	—	3	0	0	0	0	7	10	5	2	1	4	2	19.3	6.43	74	.345	.441	0	—	0	-2	-1	0	0.0
1988	Cal-A	0	0	—	3	0	0	0	0	4^1	4	0	0	1	1	3	12.5	0.00	—	.222	.300	0	—	0	2	2	0	0.1
1989	Cal-A	2	2	.500	24	0	0	0	0	39^2	39	15	3	1	13	27	12.0	3.18	120	.255	.317	0	—	0	3	3	1	0.3
1990	NY-A	0	1	.000	5	0	0	0	0	7^1	8	5	0	0	2	8	12.3	6.14	65	.276	.323	0	—	0	-2	-2	0	-0.2
1991	NY-A	3	1	.750	26	0	0	0	0	47	42	27	5	0	19	34	11.7	3.64	114	.236	.310	0	—	0	2	3	1	0.3
1992	NY-A	7	3	.700	47	0	0	0	0	92^2	82	35	7	0	27	62	10.6	3.30	119	.235	.290	0	—	0	7	6	-1	0.6
1993	NY-A	7	4	.636	42	0	0	0	0	85^2	85	52	14	0	35	50	12.6	4.94	84	.262	.333	0	—	0	-6	-8	0	-0.8
1994	SF-N	4	3	.571	39	0	0	0	0	45^1	43	18	6	0	13	16	11.1	3.18	126	.253	.306	0	.000	-0	5	4	-1	0.5
1995	Cal-A	1	0	1.000	9	0	0	0	0	9	8	2	1	0	3	5	11.0	2.00	235	.267	.333	0	—	0	3	3	-0	0.2
1996	Cal-A	0	3	.000	12	0	0	0	0	15^1	23	11	5	1	2	5	15.3	5.87	85	.348	.377	0	—	0	-1	-1	-1	-0.3
Total	10	24	17	.585	210	0	0	0	0	353^1	344	170	43	4	119	212	11.9	3.87	106	.255	.318	0	.000	-0	12	9	-1	0.7

YEAR	TM/L	W	L	PCT	G	GS	CG	SH	SV	IP	H	R	HR	HB	BB	SO	RAT	ERA	ERA+	OAV	OOB	BH	AVG	PB	PR	PR+	PD	TPI
● **JEFF MONTGOMERY** Montgomery, Jeffrey Thomas b: 1/7/62, Wellston, Ohio BR/TR, 5′11″, 180 lbs. Deb: 8/1/87																												
1987	Cin-N	2	2	.500	14	1	0	0	0	19^1	25	15	2	0	9	13	15.8	6.52	65	.313	.382	0	.000	-0	-5	-5	0	-0.9
1988	KC-A	7	2	.778	45	0	0	0	1	62^2	54	25	6	2	30	47	12.4	3.45	116	.231	.323	0	—	0	4	4	0	0.5
1989	KC-A	7	3	.700	63	0	0	0	18	92	66	16	3	2	25	94	9.1	1.37	282	.198	.258	0	—	0	**26**	**26**	-1	3.5
1990	KC-A	6	5	.545	73	0	0	0	24	94^1	81	36	6	5	34	94	11.4	2.39	161	.227	.303	0	—	0	16	16	0	2.4
1991	KC-A	4	4	.500	67	0	0	0	33	90	83	32	6	2	28	77	11.3	2.90	142	.246	.307	0	—	0	12	12	-0	1.7
1992	KC-A★	1	6	.143	65	0	0	0	39	82^2	61	23	5	3	27	69	9.9	2.18	187	.205	.278	0	—	0	16	17	2	2.9
1993	KC-A★	7	5	.583	69	0	0	0	**45**	87^1	65	22	3	2	23	66	9.3	2.27	203	.206	.264	0	—	0	**20**	**21**	1	4.3
1994	KC-A	2	3	.400	42	0	0	0	27	44^2	48	21	5	1	15	50	12.9	4.03	124	.276	.337	0	—	0	4	5	-1	0.8
1995	KC-A	2	3	.400	54	0	0	0	31	65^2	60	27	7	2	25	49	11.9	3.43	140	.252	.328	0	—	0	9	10	0	1.4
1996	KC-A☆	4	6	.400	48	0	0	0	24	63^1	59	31	14	3	19	45	11.5	4.26	118	.251	.315	0	—	0	5	5	1	1.1
1997	KC-A	1	4	.200	55	0	0	0	14	59^1	53	24	9	0	18	48	10.8	3.49	135	.240	.297	0	—	0	7	8	0	0.9
1998	KC-A	2	5	.286	56	0	0	0	36	56	58	35	8	2	22	54	13.2	4.98	97	.264	.336	0	—	0	-2	-1	-0	-0.2
1999	KC-A	1	4	.200	49	0	0	0	12	51^1	72	40	7	2	21	27	16.7	6.84	73	.343	.408	0	—	0	-11	-10	1	-1.1
Total	13	46	52	.469	700	1	0	0	304	868^2	785	347	81	26	296	733	11.5	3.27	134	.241	.310	0	.000	-0	101	106	3	17.3
● **MONTY MONTGOMERY** Montgomery, Monty Bryson b: 9/1/46, Albemarle, N.C. BR/TR, 6′3″, 200 lbs. Deb: 9/14/71																												
1971	KC-A	3	0	1.000	3	2	0	0	0	21^1	16	5	0	0	3	12	8.0	2.11	163	.205	.235	0	.000	-0	3	3	0	0.4
1972	KC-A	3	3	.500	9	8	1	1	0	56^1	55	21	2	0	17	24	11.5	3.04	100	.263	.319	3	.176	1	0	0	-0	0.0
Total	2	6	3	.667	12	10	1	1	0	77^2	71	26	2	0	20	36	10.5	2.78	113	.247	.296	3	.125	0	3	3	-0	0.4
● **STEVE MONTGOMERY** Montgomery, Steven Lewis b: 12/25/70, Westminster, Cal. BR/TR, 6′4″, 210 lbs. Deb: 4/3/96																												
1996	Oak-A	1	0	1.000	8	0	0	0	0	13^2	18	14	5	0	13	8	20.4	9.22	53	.310	.437	0	—	0	-6	-7	-1	-0.4
1997	Oak-A	0	1	.000	4	0	0	0	0	6^1	10	7	2	0	8	1	25.6	9.95	46	.385	.529	0	—	0	-4	-4	-0	-0.5
1999	Phi-N	1	5	.167	53	0	0	0	3	64^2	54	25	10	0	31	55	11.8	3.34	141	.229	.318	1	1.000	0	9	10	-1	0.8
2000	SD-N	0	2	.000	7	0	0	0	0	5^2	6	6	3	0	4	3	15.9	7.94	55	.273	.385	0	—	0	-2	-2	0	-0.4
Total	4	2	8	.200	72	0	0	0	3	90^1	88	52	20	0	56	67	14.3	4.98	95	.257	.362	1	1.000	0	-3	-3	-1	-0.5
● **RAMON MONZANT** Monzant, Ramon Segundo (Espina) b: 1/4/33, Maracaibo, Venez. BR/TR, 6′, 165 lbs. Deb: 7/2/54																												
1954	NY-N	0	0	—	6	1	0	0	0	7^2	8	5	0	0	11	5	22.3	4.70	86	.276	.475	0	.000	-0	-1	-1	-0	-0.1
1955	NY-N	4	8	.333	28	12	3	0	0	94^2	98	47	11	3	43	54	13.7	3.99	101	.278	.361	3	.125	-1	0	0	-1	-0.2
1956	NY-N	1	0	1.000	4	1	1	0	0	13	8	7	4	0	7	11	10.4	4.15	91	.170	.278	0	.000	-1	-1	-1	-0	-0.1
1957	NY-N	3	2	.600	24	2	0	0	0	49^2	55	27	6	2	16	37	13.2	3.99	99	.286	.348	3	.300	1	-1	-0	-1	-0.1
1958	SF-N	8	11	.421	43	16	4	1	1	150^2	160	89	20	6	57	93	13.3	4.72	81	.273	.344	8	.163	-1	-13	-16	1	-1.8
1960	SF-N	0	0	—	1	0	0	0	0	1	1	1	1	0	0	1	9.0	9.00	39	.250	.250	0	—	0	-1	-1	0	0.0
Total	6	16	21	.432	106	32	8	1	1	316^2	330	176	42	11	134	201	13.5	4.38	89	.273	.350	14	.157	-2	-15	-17	-1	-2.3
● **ERIC MOODY** Moody, Eric Lane b: 1/6/71, Greenville, S.C. BR/TR, 6′6″, 185 lbs. Deb: 8/3/97																												
1997	Tex-A	0	1	.000	10	1	0	0	0	19	26	10	4	0	2	12	13.3	4.26	112	.329	.346	0	—	0	1	1	-0	0.0
● **LEO MOON** Moon, Leo "Lefty" b: 6/22/1899, Bellemont, N.C. d: 8/25/70, New Orleans, La. BR/TL, 5′11″, 165 lbs. Deb: 7/9/32																												
1932	Cle-A	0	0	—	1	0	0	0	0	5^2	11	8	0	0	7	1	28.6	11.12	43	.379	.500	1	.500	0	-4	-4	0	-0.1
● **JIM MOONEY** Mooney, Jim Irving b: 9/4/06, Mooresburg, Tenn. d: 4/27/79, Johnson City, Tenn BR/TL, 5′11″, 168 lbs. Deb: 8/14/31																												
1931	NY-N	7	1	.875	10	8	6	2	0	71^2	71	19	1	1	16	38	11.1	2.01	184	.262	.306	4	.160	-1	15	14	-1	1.3
1932	NY-N	6	10	.375	29	18	4	1	0	124^2	154	79	18	0	42	37	14.1	5.05	73	.299	.352	5	.122	-2	-16	-19	-2	-2.4
1933	StL-N	2	5	.286	21	8	2	0	1	77^1	87	36	1	0	26	14	13.2	3.72	93	.296	.353	1	.050	-2	-3	-2	1	-0.3
1934	*StL-N	2	4	.333	32	7	1	0	1	82^1	114	59	3	4	49	27	18.3	5.47	77	.326	.414	1	.053	-2	-13	-11	-1	-1.1
Total	4	17	20	.459	92	41	13	3	2	356	426	193	23	5	133	116	14.3	4.25	89	.298	.360	11	.105	-7	-18	-19	-3	-2.5
● **BILL MOONEYHAM** Mooneyham, William Craig b: 8/16/60, Livermore, Cal. BR/TR, 6′, 175 lbs. Deb: 4/19/86																												
1986	Oak-A	4	5	.444	45	6	0	0	2	99^2	103	53	4	3	67	75	15.6	4.52	86	.270	.384	0	—	0	-4	-8	1	-0.6
● **BALOR MOORE** Moore, Balor Lilbon b: 1/25/51, Smithville, Tex. BL/TL, 6′2″, 184 lbs. Deb: 5/21/70																												
1970	Mon-N	0	2	.000	6	2	0	0	0	9^2	14	9	0	0	8	6	20.5	7.45	55	.368	.478	1	.333	0	-4	-4	0	-0.6
1972	Mon-N	9	9	.500	22	22	6	3	0	147^2	122	61	15	5	59	161	11.3	3.47	102	.226	.307	8	.145	-0	-0	1	0	0.1
1973	Mon-N	7	16	.304	35	32	3	1	0	176^1	151	98	18	3	109	151	13.4	4.49	85	.233	.346	3	.057	-3	-16	-13	-1	-1.9
1974	Mon-N	0	2	.000	8	2	0	0	0	13^2	13	8	1	0	15	16	18.4	3.95	97	.245	.412	0	.000	-0	-0	-0	-0	-0.1
1977	Cal-A	0	2	.000	7	3	0	0	0	22^2	28	19	7	3	10	14	16.3	3.97	99	.298	.383	0	—	0	0	-0	-1	-0.1
1978	Tor-A	6	9	.400	37	18	2	0	0	144^1	165	85	16	7	54	75	14.1	4.93	80	.294	.363	0	—	0	-18	-15	1	-1.3
1979	Tor-A	5	7	.417	34	16	5	0	0	139^1	135	85	17	8	79	51	14.3	4.84	90	.262	.369	0	—	0	-10	-7	-1	-0.6
1980	Tor-A	1	1	.500	31	3	0	0	1	64^2	76	43	6	4	31	22	15.4	5.29	82	.309	.395	0	—	0	-9	-7	-0	-0.4
Total	8	28	48	.368	180	98	16	4	1	718^1	704	408	80	30	365	496	13.8	4.52	87	.261	.355	12	.106	-3	-57	-44	-1	-4.9
● **BRAD MOORE** Moore, Bradley Alan b: 6/21/64, Loveland, Colo. BR/TR, 6′1″, 185 lbs. Deb: 6/14/88																												
1988	Phi-N	0	0	—	5	0	0	0	0	5^2	4	0	0	0	4	2	12.7	0.00	—	.267	.421	0	—	0	2	2	0	0.1
1990	Phi-N	0	0	—	3	0	0	0	0	2^2	4	1	0	0	2	1	20.3	3.38	113	.400	.500	0	—	0	0	0	0	0.0
Total	2	0	0	—	8	0	0	0	0	8^1	8	1	0	0	6	3	15.1	1.08	338	.320	.452	0	—	0	2	2	0	0.1
● **CARLOS MOORE** Moore, Carlos Whitman b: 8/13/06, Clinton, Tenn. d: 7/2/58, New Orleans, La. BR/TR, 6′1.5″, 180 lbs. Deb: 5/4/30																												
1930	Was-A	0	0	—	4	0	0	0	0	11^2	9	3	0	0	4	2	10.0	2.31	199	.225	.295	0	.000	-1	3	3	-0	0.1
● **DEE MOORE** Moore, D C b: 4/6/14, Hedley, Tex. d: 7/2/97, Williston, N.Dak. BR/TR, 5′11″, 190 lbs. Deb: 9/12/36 ♦																												
1936	Cin-N	0	0	—	2	1	0	0	0	7	3	1	0	0	2	3	6.4	0.00	—	.120	.185	4	.400	1	3	3	0	0.3
● **DONNIE MOORE** Moore, Donnie Ray b: 2/13/54, Lubbock, Tex. d: 7/18/89, Anaheim, Cal. BL/TR, 6′, 185 lbs. Deb: 9/14/75																												
1975	Chi-N	0	0	—	4	1	0	0	0	8^2	12	4	1	0	4	8	16.6	4.15	93	.316	.381	0	.000	-0	-1	-0	-0	-0.1
1977	Chi-N	4	2	.667	27	1	0	0	0	48^2	51	27	1	0	18	34	12.8	4.07	108	.285	.350	3	.300	1	-1	2	1	0.4
1978	Chi-N	9	7	.563	71	1	0	0	4	102^2	117	55	7	2	31	50	13.1	4.12	98	.287	.340	4	.267	1	-6	-1	0	0.0
1979	Chi-N	1	4	.200	39	1	0	0	1	73	95	46	8	2	25	43	15.0	5.18	80	.321	.378	2	.154	0	-12	-8	1	-0.4
1980	StL-N	1	1	.500	11	0	0	0	0	21^2	25	15	1	1	5	10	12.9	6.23	59	.298	.344	3	.750	2	-6	-6	-1	-0.4
1981	Mil-A	0	0	—	3	0	0	0	0	4	4	3	0	0	4	2	18.0	6.75	51	.286	.444	0	—	0	-1	-2	0	-0.1
1982	*Atl-N	3	1	.750	16	0	0	0	1	27^2	32	13	1	2	7	17	13.3	4.23	88	.294	.347	0	.000	-0	-2	-1	0	-0.2
1983	Atl-N	2	3	.400	43	0	0	0	6	68^2	72	30	6	0	10	41	10.7	3.67	106	.279	.306	4	.500	1	-0	2	-1	0.2
1984	Atl-N	4	5	.444	47	0	0	0	16	64^1	63	27	3	1	18	47	11.5	2.94	131	.258	.312	0	.000	-0	5	6	0	1.1
1985	Cal-A★	8	8	.500	65	0	0	0	31	103	91	28	9	0	21	72	9.8	1.92	214	.237	.277	0	—	0	**25**	25	-1	5.1
1986	*Cal-A	4	5	.444	49	0	0	0	21	72^2	60	28	10	0	22	53	10.2	2.97	139	.228	.288	0	—	0	10	9	-1	1.5
1987	Cal-A	2	2	.500	14	0	0	0	5	26^2	28	12	2	0	13	17	13.8	2.70	160	.259	.339	0	—	0	5	5	-1	0.8
1988	Cal-A	5	2	.714	27	0	0	0	4	33	48	20	4	0	8	22	15.3	4.91	79	.343	.378	0	—	0	-3	-4	0	-0.8
Total	13	43	40	.518	416	4	0	0	89	654^2	698	308	53	8	186	416	12.3	3.67	110	.276	.328	16	.281	5	13	26	-1	7.1
● **EARL MOORE** Moore, Earl Alonzo "Big Ebbie" or "Crossfire" b: 7/29/1879, Pickerington, O. d: 11/28/61, Columbus, Ohio BR/TR, 6′, 195 lbs. Deb: 4/25/01																												
1901	Cle-A	16	14	.533	31	30	28	4	0	251^1	234	129	4	8	107	99	12.5	2.90	122	.244	.325	16	.162	-5	21	19	-4	1.0
1902	Cle-A	17	18	.486	36	34	29	4	1	293	304	158	8	7	101	84	12.7	2.95	117	.268	.331	24	.212	-0	20	17	-1	1.6
1903	Cle-A	20	8	.714	29	27	27	3	0	247^2	196	88	0	5	62	148	9.6	**1.74**	**164**	**.217**	.271	8	.092	-5	**34**	32	-3	2.7
1904	Cle-A	12	11	.522	26	24	22	1	0	227^2	186	83	2	10	61	139	10.2	2.25	113	.224	.285	12	.140	-2	9	7	-7	-0.3
1905	Cle-A	15	15	.500	31	30	28	3	0	269	232	111	6	18	92	131	11.4	2.64	99	.234	.311	10	.104	-4	0	-0	-2	-0.8
1906	Cle-A	1	1	.500	5	4	2	0	0	29^2	27	15	1	2	18	8	14.3	3.94	66	.245	.362	0	.000	-1	-4	-4	-1	-0.5
1907	Cle-A	1	1	.500	3	2	1	0	0	19^1	18	14	0	1	8	7	12.6	4.66	54	.250	.333	0	.000	-1	-5	-5	0	-0.5
	NY-A	2	6	.250	12	9	3	0	1	64	72	49	1	4	30	28	14.9	3.94	71	.286	.371	6	.273	1	-10	-7	-0	-0.9
	Yr	3	7	.300	15	11	4	0	1	83^1	90	63	1	5	38	35	14.4	4.10	66	.278	.362	6	.207	0	-14	-12	-0	-1.4
1908	Phi-N	2	1	.667	3	3	3	1	0	26	20	4	0	2	8	16	10.4	0.00	—	.217	.294	2	.222	0	7	7	-1	1.0

YEAR	TM/L	W	L	PCT	G	GS	CG	SH	SV	IP	H	R	HR	HB	BB	SO	RAT	ERA	ERA+	OAV	OOB	BH	AVG	PB	PR	PR+	PD	TPI
1909	Phi-N	18	12	.600	38	34	24	4	0	299^{2}	238	93	7	9	108	173	10.7	2.10	124	.210	.283	9	.094	-4	17	17	-5	0.6
1910	Phi-N	22	15	.595	46	35	18	**6**	0	283	228	98	5	10	121	**185**	11.4	2.58	121	.228	.318	20	.230	2	14	17	-4	2.0
1911	Phi-N	15	19	.441	42	36	21	5	1	308^{1}	265	123	11	12	164	174	12.9	2.63	131	.240	.345	11	.109	-6	27	28	-3	1.9
1912	Phi-N	9	14	.391	31	24	10	1	0	182^{1}	186	101	3	7	77	79	13.3	3.31	110	.275	.355	6	.107	-4	2	6	-2	0.0
1913	Phi-N	1	3	.250	12	5	0	0	1	52	50	37	3	1	40	24	15.8	5.02	66	.254	.382	0	.000	-2	-10	-9	1	-0.8
	Chi-N	1	1	.500	7	2	0	0	0	28^{1}	34	19	3	0	12	12	14.6	4.45	71	.321	.390	1	.125	-0	-4	-4	1	-0.2
	Yr	2	4	.333	19	7	0	0	1	80^{1}	84	56	6	1	52	36	15.3	4.82	68	.277	.385	1	.042	-2	-14	-13	2	-1.0
1914	Buf-F	11	15	.423	36	27	14	2	2	194^{2}	184	109	3	10	99	96	13.5	4.30	69	.263	.362	9	.161	-2	-31	-28	-2	-3.8
Total	14	163	154	.514	388	326	230	34	6	2776	2474	1231	57	106	1108	1403	12.0	2.78	110	.241	.321	134	.141	-34	87	88	-33	3.0
● **EUEL MOORE**	Moore, Euel Walton "Chief" b: 5/27/08, Reagan, Okla. d: 2/12/89, Tishomingo, Okla. BR/TR, 6'2", 185 lbs. Deb: 7/8/34																											
1934	Phi-N	5	7	.417	20	16	3	0	1	122^{1}	145	60	9	0	41	38	13.7	4.05	117	.288	.342	5	.109	-4	0	8	-1	0.2
1935	Phi-N	1	6	.143	15	8	1	0	1	40^{1}	63	40	5	2	20	15	19.0	7.81	58	.354	.425	6	.400	1	-17	-13	0	-1.8
	NY-N	1	0	1.000	6	0	0	0	0	8	9	5	0	0	4	3	14.6	5.63	69	.281	.361	0	.000	-0	-1	-2	0	-0.2
	Yr	2	6	.250	21	8	1	0	1	48^{1}	72	45	5	2	24	18	18.2	7.45	59	.343	.415	6	.353	1	-18	-15	0	-2.0
1936	Phi-N	2	3	.400	20	5	1	0	1	54^{1}	76	50	4	1	12	19	14.7	6.96	65	.311	.346	4	.222	-0	-18	-13	-1	-1.2
Total	3	9	16	.360	61	29	5	0	3	225	293	155	18	3	77	75	14.9	5.48	84	.306	.360	15	.185	-3	-36	-19	-3	-3.0
● **GENE MOORE**	Moore, Eugene Sr. "Blue Goose" b: 11/9/1885, Lancaster, Tex. d: 8/31/38, Dallas, Tex. BL/TL, 6'2", 185 lbs. Deb: 9/28/09 F																											
1909	Pit-N	0	0	—	1	0	0	0	0	2	4	4	0	0	3	2	31.5	18.00	15	.364	.500	0	.000	-0	-3	-3	-0	-0.2
1910	Pit-N	2	1	.667	4	1	0	0	0	17^{1}	19	7	1	0	7	9	13.5	3.12	99	.268	.333	0	.000	-1	-0	-0	0	-0.1
1912	Cin-N	0	1	.000	5	2	0	0	1	14^{2}	17	11	0	2	11	6	18.4	4.91	68	.304	.435	0	.000	-1	-2	-3	-0	-0.3
Total	3	2	2	.500	10	3	0	0	1	34	40	22	1	2	21	17	16.7	4.76	67	.290	.391	0	.000	-2	-6	-6	0	-0.6
● **FRANK MOORE**	Moore, Frank J. b: 9/12/1877, Dover, Ohio d: 5/20/64, Portsmouth, Ohio BR/TR, 6'4", 200 lbs. Deb: 6/14/05																											
1905	Pit-N	0	0	—	1	0	0	0	0	3	2	0	0	0	0	1	6.0	0.00	—	.200	.200	0	.000	-0	1	1	-0	0.0
● **JIM MOORE**	Moore, James Stanford b: 12/14/03, Prescott, Ark. d: 5/19/73, Seattle, Wash. BR/TR, 6', 165 lbs. Deb: 9/21/28																											
1928	Cle-A	0	1	.000	1	1	1	0	0	9	5	2	0	0	5	1	10.0	2.00	207	.161	.278	0	.000	-0	2	2	-0	0.1
1929	Cle-A	0	0	—	2	0	0	0	0	5^{2}	6	6	1	0	4	0	15.9	9.53	47	.273	.385	0	.000	-0	-3	-3	0	-0.1
1930	Chi-A	2	1	.667	9	5	2	0	1	40	42	18	0	0	12	11	12.1	3.60	128	.268	.320	3	.231	-0	5	5	-0	0.3
1931	Chi-A	0	2	.000	33	4	0	0	0	83^{2}	93	52	3	1	27	15	13.0	4.95	86	.282	.338	1	.063	-1	-5	-7	1	-0.3
1932	Chi-A	0	0	—	1	0	0	0	0	1	1	0	0	0	1	2	18.0	0.00	—	.250	.400	0	.000	-0	0	0	0	0.0
Total	5	2	4	.333	46	10	3	0	1	139^{1}	147	78	4	1	49	29	12.7	4.52	97	.270	.332	4	.114	-2	-1	-2	1	0.0
● **WHITEY MOORE**	Moore, Lloyd Albert b: 6/10/12, Tuscarawas, Ohio d: 12/10/87, Uhrichsville, O. BR/TR, 6'1", 195 lbs. Deb: 9/27/36																											
1936	Cin-N	1	0	1.000	1	0	0	0	0	5	3	3	0	0	3	4	10.8	5.40	71	.167	.286	0	.000	-0	-1	-1	-0	-0.2
1937	Cin-N	0	3	.000	13	6	0	0	0	38^{2}	32	22	1	4	39	27	17.5	4.89	76	.239	.424	0	.000	-1	-4	-5	-0	-0.5
1938	Cin-N	6	4	.600	19	11	3	1	0	90^{1}	66	41	4	3	42	38	11.1	3.49	105	.205	.302	2	.077	-2	3	2	-1	-0.2
1939	*Cin-N	13	12	.520	42	24	9	2	3	187^{2}	177	88	10	6	95	81	13.3	3.45	111	.254	.348	6	.098	-4	10	8	-1	0.5
1940	*Cin-N	8	8	.500	25	15	5	1	1	116^{2}	100	48	8	7	56	60	12.6	3.63	104	.231	.329	5	.128	-1	3	2	-3	-0.2
1941	Cin-N	2	1	.667	23	4	1	0	0	61^{2}	62	35	2	3	45	17	16.1	4.38	82	.256	.379	3	.167	-1	-5	-5	-1	-0.4
1942	Cin-N	0	0	—	1	0	0	0	0	1	0	0	0	0	1	0	9.0	0.00	—	.000	.250	0	—	0	0	0	-0	0.0
	StL-N	0	1	.000	9	0	0	0	0	12^{1}	10	6	0	1	11	1	16.1	4.38	78	.217	.379	0	.000	-0	-1	-1	-1	-0.2
	Yr	0	1	.000	10	0	0	0	0	13^{1}	10	6	0	1	12	1	15.5	4.05	84	.204	.371	0	.000	-0	-1	-1	-1	-0.2
Total	7	30	29	.508	133	60	18	4	4	513^{1}	450	243	25	24	292	228	13.4	3.75	100	.237	.346	16	.103	-10	4	-0	-7	-1.2
● **MARCUS MOORE**	Moore, Marcus Braymont b: 11/2/70, Oakland, Cal. BB/TR, 6'5", 195 lbs. Deb: 7/8/93																											
1993	Col-N	3	1	.750	27	0	0	0	0	26^{1}	30	25	4	1	20	13	17.4	6.84	70	.291	.411	0	.000	-0	-8	-5	-1	-0.8
1994	Col-N	1	1	.500	29	0	0	0	0	33^{2}	33	26	4	5	21	33	15.8	6.15	81	.252	.376	0	.000	-0	-7	-4	-0	-0.2
1996	Cin-N	3	3	.500	23	0	0	0	2	26^{1}	26	21	3	2	22	27	17.1	5.81	73	.263	.407	1	.333	1	-5	-5	-1	-0.9
Total	3	7	5	.583	79	0	0	0	2	86^{1}	89	72	11	8	63	73	16.7	6.25	75	.267	.396	1	.200	0	-20	-13	-2	-1.9
● **MIKE MOORE**	Moore, Michael Wayne b: 11/26/59, Eakly, Okla. BR/TR, 6'4", 205 lbs. Deb: 4/11/82																											
1982	Sea-A	7	14	.333	28	27	1	1	0	144^{1}	159	91	21	2	79	73	15.0	5.36	79	.285	.376	0	—	0	-21	-17	1	-2.0
1983	Sea-A	6	8	.429	22	21	3	2	0	128	130	75	10	3	60	108	13.6	4.71	91	.267	.352	0	—	0	-9	-6	2	-0.4
1984	Sea-A	7	17	.292	34	33	6	0	0	212	236	127	16	5	85	158	13.8	4.97	80	.282	.352	0	—	0	-23	-23	3	-2.0
1985	Sea-A	17	10	.630	35	34	14	2	0	247	230	100	18	4	70	155	11.1	3.46	122	.247	.302	0	—	0	19	20	2	2.3
1986	Sea-A	11	13	.458	38	37	11	1	1	266	279	141	28	12	94	146	13.0	4.30	99	.273	.341	0	—	0	-3	-1	-1	-0.2
1987	Sea-A	9	19	.321	33	33	12	0	0	231	268	145	29	0	84	115	13.7	4.71	100	.292	.351	0	.000	-0	-6	1	1	0.1
1988	Sea-A	9	15	.375	37	32	9	3	1	228^{2}	196	104	24	3	63	182	10.3	3.78	110	.232	.287	0	—	0	5	9	1	1.0
1989	*Oak-A★	19	11	.633	35	35	6	3	0	241^{2}	193	82	14	2	83	172	10.4	2.61	141	.219	.288	0	—	0	34	31	2	3.9
1990	*Oak-A	13	15	.464	33	33	3	0	0	199^{1}	204	113	14	3	84	73	13.1	4.65	80	.267	.342	0	—	0	-16	-22	1	-2.5
1991	Oak-A	17	8	.680	33	33	3	1	0	210	176	75	11	5	105	153	12.3	2.96	130	.229	.326	0	—	0	27	22	2	2.7
1992	*Oak-A	17	12	.586	36	36	2	0	0	223	229	113	20	8	103	117	13.7	4.12	91	.268	.353	0	—	0	-4	-10	-1	-1.2
1993	Det-A	13	9	.591	36	36	4	3	0	213^{2}	227	135	35	3	89	89	13.4	5.22	82	.271	.343	0	—	0	-21	-22	4	-1.6
1994	Det-A	11	10	.524	25	25	4	0	0	154^{1}	152	97	27	3	89	62	14.2	5.42	89	.263	.364	0	—	0	-11	-10	3	-0.8
1995	Det-A	5	15	.250	25	25	1	0	0	132^{2}	179	118	24	2	68	64	16.9	7.53	63	.323	.399	0	—	0	-41	-40	1	-4.6
Total	14	161	176	.478	450	440	79	16	2	2831^{2}	2858	1516	291	55	1156	1667	12.9	4.39	95	.264	.338	0	.000	-0	-70	-71	22	-5.3
● **RAY MOORE**	Moore, Raymond Leroy "Farmer" b: 6/1/26, Meadows, Md. d: 3/2/95, Clinton, Md. BR/TR, 6'1", 205 lbs. Deb: 8/1/52																											
1952	Bro-N	1	2	.333	14	2	0	0	0	28^{1}	29	17	3	2	26	11	18.1	4.76	76	.274	.425	0	.000	-0	-3	-4	-0	-0.4
1953	Bro-N	0	1	.000	1	1	1	0	0	8	6	3	1	0	4	4	11.3	3.38	126	.214	.313	0	.000	-0	1	1	-0	0.0
1955	Bal-A	10	10	.500	46	14	3	1	6	151^{2}	128	75	14	4	80	80	12.6	3.92	97	.229	.329	6	.136	-2	1	-2	-2	-0.6
1956	Bal-A	12	7	.632	32	27	9	1	0	185	161	90	12	1	99	105	12.7	4.18	94	.238	.336	19	.271	6	-1	-6	-2	-0.1
1957	Bal-A	11	13	.458	34	32	7	1	0	227^{1}	196	99	17	2	112	117	12.3	3.72	97	.236	.328	18	.214	4	2	-3	-2	-0.2
1958	Chi-A	9	7	.563	32	20	4	2	2	136^{2}	107	63	10	0	70	73	11.7	3.82	95	.220	.318	9	.205	2	-1	-3	-1	-0.2
1959	*Chi-A	3	6	.333	29	8	0	0	0	89^{2}	86	46	10	1	46	49	13.3	4.12	91	.261	.354	2	.087	-1	-3	-4	-1	-0.5
1960	Chi-A	1	1	.500	14	0	0	0	0	20^{2}	19	13	5	0	11	3	13.1	5.66	67	.253	.349	0	.000	-0	-4	-4	-0	-0.4
	Was-A	3	2	.600	37	0	0	0	13	65^{2}	49	24	5	1	27	29	10.6	2.88	135	.213	.298	1	.071	-1	7	7	-2	0.6
	Yr	4	3	.571	51	0	0	0	13	86^{1}	68	37	10	1	38	32	11.2	3.54	109	.223	.311	1	.063	-1	3	3	-2	0.2
1961	Min-A	4	4	.500	46	0	0	0	14	56^{1}	49	23	8	1	38	45	14.1	3.67	115	.233	.353	0	.000	0	2	3	-0	0.6
1962	Min-A	8	3	.727	49	0	0	0	9	64^{2}	55	35	8	2	30	58	12.1	4.73	86	.231	.322	0	.000	-1	-5	-5	-1	-1.0
1963	Min-A	1	3	.250	31	1	0	0	2	38^{2}	50	34	8	1	17	38	15.8	6.98	52	.309	.378	1	.333	0	-14	-14	0	-1.5
Total	11	63	59	.516	365	105	24	5	46	1072^{2}	935	522	101	15	560	612	12.7	4.06	93	.238	.335	56	.187	6	-18	-33	-10	-3.7
● **BARRY MOORE**	Moore, Robert Barry b: 4/3/43, Statesville, N.C. BL/TL, 6'1", 190 lbs. Deb: 5/29/65																											
1965	Was-A	0	0	—	1	0	0	0	0	1	1	1	0	0	1	0	18.0	0.00	—	.333	.500	0	—	0	0	0	-0	0.0
1966	Was-A	3	3	.500	12	11	1	0	0	62^{1}	55	26	3	1	39	28	13.7	3.75	92	.240	.353	2	.105	-1	-2	-2	0	-0.3
1967	Was-A	7	11	.389	27	26	3	1	0	143^{2}	127	67	15	3	71	74	12.6	3.76	84	.240	.333	6	.130	-0	-8	-10	1	-1.1
1968	Was-A	4	6	.400	32	18	0	0	3	117^{2}	116	55	8	2	42	56	12.2	3.37	87	.261	.327	3	.097	-1	-5	-6	1	-0.6
1969	Was-A	9	8	.529	31	25	4	0	0	134	123	70	12	2	67	51	12.9	4.30	81	.246	.338	9	.209	2	-10	-13	-2	-1.5
1970	Cle-A	3	5	.375	13	12	0	0	0	70^{1}	70	34	8	1	46	35	15.0	4.22	94	.262	.373	2	.095	-1	-4	-2	1	-0.3
	Chi-A	0	4	.000	24	7	0	0	0	70^{2}	85	56	12	8	34	34	16.2	6.37	61	.302	.393	5	.263	1	-21	-18	1	-0.8
	Yr	3	9	.250	37	19	0	0	0	141	155	90	20	9	80	69	15.6	5.30	74	.283	.383	7	.175	-0	-25	-20	1	-1.1
Total	6	26	37	.413	140	99	8	1	3	599^{2}	577	309	58	17	300	278	13.4	4.16	82	.256	.348	27	.151	-1	-50	-51	2	-4.6
● **BOBBY MOORE**	Moore, Robert Devell b: 11/8/58, Jena, La. BR/TR, 6'4", 200 lbs. Deb: 9/11/85																											
1985	SF-N	0	0	—	11	0	0	0	0	16^{2}	18	6	1	0	10	10	15.1	3.24	106	.269	.364	0	.000	-0	1	0	-1	-0.1
● **ROY MOORE**	Moore, Roy Daniel b: 10/26/1898, Austin, Tex. d: 4/5/51, Seattle, Wash. BB/TL, 6', 185 lbs. Deb: 4/15/20																											
1920	Phi-A	1	13	.071	24	14	5	0	0	132^{2}	161	89	6	3	64	45	15.5	4.68	86	.314	.393	10	.200	-1	-13	-9	2	-0.8

YEAR	TM/L	W	L	PCT	G	GS	CG	SH	SV	IP	H	R	HR	HB	BB	SO	RAT	ERA	ERA+	OAV	OOB	BH	AVG	PB	PR	PR+	PD	TPI
1921	Phi-A	10	10	.500	29	26	12	0	0	191^2	206	110	4	4	122	64	15.6	4.51	99	.280	.385	19	.257	3	-5	-1	2	0.5
1922	Phi-A	0	3	.000	15	6	0	0	0	50^2	65	43	1	3	32	29	17.8	7.64	56	.319	.418	5	.263	1	-20	-18	-0	-0.8
	Det-A	0	0	—	9	0	0	0	2	19^2	29	14	0	5	10	9	20.1	5.95	65	.367	.468	3	.429	1	-4	-5	0	-0.1
	Yr	0	3	.000	24	6	0	0	2	70^1	94	57	1	8	42	38	18.4	7.17	58	.332	.432	8	.308	2	-24	-23	-0	-0.9
1923	Det-A	0	0	—	3	0	0	0	1	12	15	4	0	0	11	7	19.5	3.00	129	.288	.413	0	.000	-0	1	1	1	0.1
Total	4	11	26	.297	80	46	17	0	3	406^2	476	260	11	15	239	154	16.2	4.98	85	.300	.397	37	.239	4	-41	-32	4	-1.1
● **TERRY MOORE**	Moore, Terry Bluford b: 5/27/12, Vernon, Ala. d: 3/29/95, Collinsville, Ill. BR/TR, 5'11", 195 lbs. Deb: 4/16/35 MC◆																											
1939	StL-N★	0	0	—	1	0	0	0	0	1	0	0	0	0	0	1	0.0	0.00	—	.000	.000	123	.295	0	0	0	0	0.0
● **TOMMY MOORE**	Moore, Tommy Joe b: 7/7/48, Lynwood, Cal. BR/TR, 5'11", 175 lbs. Deb: 9/15/72																											
1972	NY-N	0	0	—	3	1	0	0	0	12^1	12	4	1	0	1	5	9.5	2.92	115	.273	.289	1	.333	0	1	1	0	0.1
1973	NY-N	0	1	.000	3	1	0	0	0	3^1	6	5	1	0	3	1	24.3	10.80	34	.400	.500	0	—	0	-3	-3	-0	-0.5
1975	StL-N	0	0	—	10	0	0	0	0	18^2	15	10	2	0	12	6	13.0	3.86	98	.203	.314	1	.500	0	-0	-0	0	0.1
	Tex-A	0	2	.000	12	0	0	0	0	21	31	21	1	1	12	15	18.9	8.14	46	.352	.436	0	—	0	-10	-10	0	-0.8
1977	Sea-A	2	1	.667	14	1	0	0	0	33	36	22	1	3	21	13	16.4	4.91	84	.281	.395	0	—	0	-3	-3	-1	-0.3
Total	4	2	4	.333	42	3	0	0	0	88^1	100	62	6	4	49	40	15.6	5.40	71	.287	.381	2	.400	1	-16	-15	-0	-1.4
● **TREY MOORE**	Moore, Warren Neal b: 10/2/72, Houston, Tex. BL/TL, 6'1", 200 lbs. Deb: 4/5/98																											
1998	Mon-N	2	5	.286	13	11	0	0	0	61	78	37	5	1	17	35	14.2	5.02	84	.306	.352	4	.235	1	-5	-6	0	-0.4
2000	Mon-N	1	5	.167	8	8	0	0	0	35^1	55	31	7	4	21	24	20.4	6.62	71	.364	.455	1	.125	-0	-8	-7	-1	-1.0
Total	2	3	10	.231	21	19	0	0	0	96^1	133	68	12	5	38	59	16.4	5.61	78	.328	.392	5	.200	1	-13	-13	-0	-1.4
● **CY MOORE**	Moore, William Austin b: 2/7/05, Elberton, Ga. d: 3/28/72, Augusta, Ga. BR/TR, 6'1", 178 lbs. Deb: 6/7/29																											
1929	Bro-N	3	3	.500	32	3	0	0	2	68	87	45	3	0	31	17	15.6	5.56	83	.320	.389	3	.188	-0	-6	-7	-1	-0.7
1930	Bro-N	0	0	—	1	0	0	0	0	0	2	0	0	0	—	—	—	—	1.000	1.000	99	—	0	0	0	0	0.0	
1931	Bro-N	1	2	.333	23	1	1	0	0	61^2	62	31	5	4	13	35	11.5	3.79	100	.262	.311	2	.154	-1	0	0	0	-0.1
1932	Bro-N	0	3	.000	20	2	0	0	0	48^2	56	32	3	1	17	21	13.7	4.81	79	.293	.354	3	.214	0	-5	-5	0	-0.2
1933	Phi-N	8	9	.471	36	18	9	3	1	161^1	177	74	7	3	42	53	12.4	3.74	102	.279	.326	3	.063	-4	-7	1	0	-0.3
1934	Phi-N	4	9	.308	35	15	3	0	0	126^2	163	98	11	2	65	55	16.3	6.47	73	.309	.387	6	.143	-3	-34	-21	-1	-2.2
Total	6	16	26	.381	147	39	13	3	3	466^1	547	281	29	10	168	181	14.0	4.86	86	.293	.355	17	.128	-8	-52	-32	-2	-3.5
● **BILL MOORE**	Moore, William Christopher b: 9/3/02, Corning, N.Y. d: 1/24/84, Corning, N.Y. BR/TR, 6'3", 195 lbs. Deb: 4/15/25																											
1925	Det-A	0	0	—	1	0	0	0	0	0	0	0	0	3	—	—	∞	—	—	1.000	98	—	0	-2	-2	0	-0.2	
● **WILCY MOORE**	Moore, William Wilcy "Cy" b: 5/20/1897, Bonita, Tex. d: 3/29/63, Hollis, Okla. BR/TR, 6', 195 lbs. Deb: 4/14/27																											
1927	*NY-A	19	7	.731	50	12	6	1	**13**	213	185	68	3	1	59	75	**10.4**	**2.28**	**169**	**.234**	**.289**	6	.080	-7	44	40	8	5.1
1928	NY-A	4	4	.500	35	2	0	0	2	60^1	71	44	4	0	31	18	15.2	4.18	90	.286	.366	2	.143	-1	-1	-3	1	-0.3
1929	NY-A	6	4	.600	41	0	0	0	8	61	64	36	4	0	19	21	12.2	4.13	93	.268	.322	1	.067	-2	**1**	-2	2	-0.3
1931	Bos-A	11	13	.458	53	15	8	1	**10**	185^1	195	88	7	1	55	37	12.2	3.88	111	.269	.322	9	.161	-3	10	9	6	1.3
1932	Bos-A	4	10	.286	37	2	0	0	4	84^1	98	59	5	1	42	28	15.0	5.23	86	.284	.363	1	.045	-2	-7	-7	3	-1.0
	*NY-A	2	0	1.000	10	1	0	0	4	25	27	8	1	0	6	8	11.9	2.52	162	.273	.314	0	.000	-1	5	5	-0	0.4
	Yr	6	10	.375	47	3	0	0	8	109^1	125	67	6	1	48	36	14.3	4.61	95	.282	.353	1	.033	-4	-2	-3	3	-0.6
1933	NY-A	5	6	.455	35	0	0	0	8	62	92	53	1	0	20	17	16.3	5.52	70	.333	.378	2	.133	-1	-9	-12	0	-2.2
Total	6	51	44	.537	261	32	14	2	49	691	732	356	25	3	232	204	12.6	3.70	110	.269	.327	21	.102	-17	44	29	20	3.0
● **BOB MOORHEAD**	Moorhead, Charles Robert b: 1/23/38, Chambersburg, Pa. d: 12/3/86, Lemoyne, Pa. BR/TR, 6'1", 208 lbs. Deb: 4/11/62																											
1962	NY-N	0	2	.000	38	7	0	0	0	105^1	118	69	13	4	42	63	14.0	4.53	92	.289	.361	1	.045	-1	-7	-4	2	0.0
1965	NY-N	0	1	.000	9	0	0	0	0	14^1	16	7	0	0	5	5	13.2	4.40	80	.271	.328	0	—	0	-1	-1	0	-0.1
Total	2	0	3	.000	47	7	0	0	0	119^2	134	76	13	4	47	68	13.9	4.51	91	.287	.357	1	.045	-1	-8	-5	3	-0.1
● **BOB MOOSE**	Moose, Robert Ralph b: 10/9/47, Export, Pa. d: 10/9/76, Martins Ferry, Ohio BR/TR, 6', 200 lbs. Deb: 9/19/67																											
1967	Pit-N	1	0	1.000	2	2	1	0	0	14^2	14	6	1	1	4	7	11.7	3.68	91	.259	.322	2	.333	1	-1	-1	-0	0.1
1968	Pit-N	8	12	.400	38	22	3	3	3	171^1	136	61	5	3	41	126	9.5	2.73	107	.218	.269	5	.093	-2	5	4	2	0.5
1969	Pit-N	14	3	.824	44	19	6	1	4	170	149	64	9	5	62	165	11.4	2.91	120	.231	.303	4	.075	-1	13	11	1	1.1
1970	*Pit-N	11	10	.524	28	27	9	2	0	189^2	186	88	14	3	64	119	12.0	3.99	98	.262	.326	12	.182	3	1	-2	-1	0.0
1971	*Pit-N	11	7	.611	30	18	3	1	1	140	169	73	12	2	35	68	13.2	4.11	82	.301	.344	4	.103	-1	-10	-12	0	-1.5
1972	*Pit-N	13	10	.565	31	30	6	3	1	226	213	84	11	4	47	144	10.5	2.91	114	.248	.290	12	.169	3	14	11	1	1.5
1973	Pit-N	12	13	.480	33	29	6	3	0	201^1	219	86	11	4	70	111	13.1	3.53	100	.280	.342	9	.134	-0	3	-0	2	0.1
1974	Pit-N	1	5	.167	7	6	0	0	0	35^2	59	30	4	2	7	15	17.2	7.57	46	.386	.420	2	.182	0	-16	-17	2	-2.1
1975	Pit-N	2	2	.500	23	5	1	0	0	67^2	63	30	4	2	25	34	12.0	3.72	95	.246	.318	3	.167	0	-1	-1	2	0.1
1976	Pit-N	3	9	.250	53	2	0	0	10	88	100	44	4	4	32	38	13.9	3.68	95	.294	.362	3	.250	2	-2	-2	-0	-0.1
Total	10	76	71	.517	289	160	35	13	19	1304^1	1308	566	75	30	387	827	11.9	3.50	98	.262	.319	56	.141	4	8	-8	8	-0.3
● **JAKE MOOTY**	Mooty, Jake T. b: 4/13/12, Millsap, Tex. d: 4/20/70, Fort Worth, Tex. BR/TR, 5'10.5", 170 lbs. Deb: 9/9/36																											
1936	Cin-N	0	0	—	8	0	0	0	1	13^2	10	6	0	0	4	11	9.2	3.95	97	.204	.264	0	.000	-0	0	-0	-0	-0.1
1937	Cin-N	0	3	.000	14	2	0	0	1	39	54	39	2	0	22	11	17.5	8.31	45	.327	.406	0	.000	-1	-19	-21	-0	-1.6
1940	Chi-N	6	6	.500	20	12	6	0	1	114	101	45	11	1	49	42	11.9	2.92	128	.243	.325	10	.263	2	12	11	2	1.1
1941	Chi-N	8	9	.471	33	14	7	1	4	153^1	143	69	9	2	56	45	11.8	3.35	105	.251	.320	10	.200	1	5	3	1	0.5
1942	Chi-N	2	5	.286	19	10	1	0	1	84^1	89	48	11	0	44	28	14.2	4.70	68	.265	.350	6	.214	0	-13	-15	0	-1.1
1943	Chi-N	0	0	—	2	0	0	0	0	1	2	0	0	0	1	1	27.0	0.00	—	.400	.500	0	—	0	0	0	0	0.0
1944	Det-A	0	0	—	15	0	0	0	0	28^1	35	20	0	1	18	7	17.2	4.45	80	.310	.409	1	.143	-0	-3	-3	-0	-0.2
Total	7	16	23	.410	111	38	14	1	8	433^2	434	227	33	4	194	145	13.1	4.03	88	.263	.341	27	.205	1	-18	-24	-1	-1.4
● **DAVID MORAGA**	Moraga, David Michael b: 7/8/75, Torrance, Cal. BL/TL, 6', 184 lbs. Deb: 6/11/2000																											
2000	Mon-N	0	0	—	3	0	0	0	0	1^2	6	7	0	0	2	2	43.2	37.80	12	.600	.667	0	—	0	-6	-6	-0	-0.3
	Col-N	0	0	—	1	0	0	0	0	1	4	5	1	1	0	0	45.0	45.00	13	.667	.714	0	—	0	-4	-3	0	-0.1
	Yr	0	0	—	4	0	0	0	0	2^2	10	12	1	1	2	2	43.9	40.50	13	.625	.684	0	—	0	-11	-9	0	-0.4
● **HIKER MORAN**	Moran, Albert Thomas b: 1/1/12, Rochester, N.Y. d: 1/7/98, Saratoga Springs, N.Y. BR/TR, 6'4.5", 185 lbs. Deb: 9/29/38																											
1938	Bos-N	0	0	—	1	0	0	0	0	3	1	0	0	0	1	0	6.0	0.00	—	.111	.200	0	.000	-0	1	1	-0	0.0
1939	Bos-N	1	1	.500	6	2	1	0	0	20	21	10	3	0	11	4	14.4	4.50	82	.276	.368	1	.200	1	-1	-2	-0	-0.1
Total	2	1	1	.500	7	2	1	0	0	23	22	10	3	0	12	4	13.3	3.91	94	.259	.351	1	.167	0	-0	-1	-1	-0.1
● **BILL MORAN**	Moran, Carl William "Bugs" b: 9/26/50, Portsmouth, Va. BR/TR, 6'4", 210 lbs. Deb: 4/12/74																											
1974	Chi-A	1	3	.250	15	5	0	0	0	46^1	57	27	5	6	23	17	16.7	4.66	80	.302	.394	0	—	0	-5	-5	-1	-0.5
● **CHARLIE MORAN**	Moran, Charles Barthell "Uncle Charlie" b: 2/22/1878, Nashville, Tenn. d: 6/14/49, Horse Cave, Ky. BR/TR, 5'8", 180 lbs. Deb: 9/9/03 U◆																											
1903	StL-N	0	1	.000	3	2	2	0	0	24	30	29	0	1	19	7	18.8	5.25	62	.297	.413	6	.429	1	-5	-5	-1	-0.2
● **HARRY MORAN**	Moran, Harry Edwin b: 4/2/1889, Slater, W.Va. d: 11/28/62, Beckley, W.Va. BL/TL, 6'1", 165 lbs. Deb: 6/23/12																											
1912	Det-A	0	1	.000	5	2	1	0	0	14^2	19	14	1	2	12	3	20.3	4.91	66	.339	.471	1	.200	-0	-3	-3	-0	-0.2
1914	Buf-F	10	7	.588	34	16	7	2	2	154	159	87	7	11	53	73	13.0	4.27	69	.276	.348	10	.196	-0	-24	-22	-1	-2.4
1915	New-F	13	9	.591	34	23	13	2	2	205^2	193	80	2	18	66	87	12.1	2.54	101	.262	.337	11	.180	-1	4	1	1	0.2
Total	3	23	17	.575	73	41	21	4	2	374^1	371	181	10	31	131	163	12.8	3.34	82	.271	.348	22	.188	-1	-22	-25	-0	-2.4
● **SAM MORAN**	Moran, Samuel b: 9/16/1870, Rochester, N.Y. d: 8/27/1897, Rochester, N.Y. TL, 160 lbs. Deb: 8/28/1895																											
1895	Pit-N	2	4	.333	10	6	6	0	0	62^2	78	63	2	3	51	19	19.0	7.47	60	.300	.420	4	.154	-1	-19	-22	0	-1.5
● **FORREST MORE**	More, Forrest b: 9/30/1883, Hayden, Ind. d: 8/17/68, Columbus, Ind. BR/TR, 6', 180 lbs. Deb: 4/15/09																											
1909	StL-N	1	5	.167	15	2	1	0	0	50	48	33	0	3	20	17	12.8	5.04	50	.258	.340	2	.154	1	-14	-14	1	-1.5
	Bos-N	1	5	.167	10	4	3	0	0	48^2	47	47	0	4	20	10	13.1	4.44	64	.270	.359	1	.067	-1	-10	-8	0	-1.0
	Yr	2	10	.167	25	6	4	0	0	98^2	95	80	0	7	40	27	13.0	4.74	56	.264	.349	3	.107	-1	-24	-22	1	-2.5

YEAR	TM/L	W	L	PCT	G	GS	CG	SH	SV	IP	H	R	HR	HB	BB	SO	RAT	ERA	ERA+	OAV	OOB	BH	AVG	PB	PR	PR+	PD	TPI
● DAVE MOREHEAD Morehead, David Michael “Moe” b: 9/5/42, San Diego, Cal. BR/TR, 6′1″, 185 lbs. Deb: 4/13/63																												
1963	Bos-A	10	13	.435	29	29	6	1	0	174^2	137	82	20	0	99	136	12.2	3.81	99	.211	.316	6	.105	-3	-4	-1	1	-0.3
1964	Bos-A	8	15	.348	32	30	3	1	0	166^2	156	101	14	4	112	139	14.7	4.97	78	.248	.365	5	.093	-2	-25	-19	-1	-2.7
1965	Bos-A	10	18	.357	34	33	5	2	0	192^2	157	103	18	3	113	163	12.8	4.06	92	.217	.326	8	.131	0	-13	-7	-2	-1.1
1966	Bos-A	1	2	.333	12	5	0	0	0	28	31	17	7	0	7	20	12.2	5.46	70	.274	.317	3	.500	1	-6	-5	-0	-0.4
1967	*Bos-A	5	4	.556	10	9	1	1	0	47^2	48	24	0	2	22	40	13.6	4.34	80	.264	.350	1	.083	-0	-6	-4	-1	-0.9
1968	Bos-A	1	4	.200	11	9	3	1	0	55	52	17	3	2	20	28	12.1	2.45	129	.249	.320	2	.125	-0	3	4	-1	0.2
1969	KC-A	2	3	.400	21	2	0	0	0	33	28	22	7	0	28	32	15.3	5.73	64	.239	.386	0	.000	0	-8	-7	-0	-1.0
1970	KC-A	3	5	.375	28	17	1	0	1	121^2	121	64	9	1	62	69	13.6	3.62	103	.261	.349	6	.167	-0	1	2	-2	-0.1
Total	8	40	64	.385	177	134	19	6	1	819^1	730	430	78	12	463	627	13.2	4.15	90	.237	.338	31	.127	-5	-57	-37	-7	-6.3
● SETH MOREHEAD Morehead, Seth Marvin “Moe” b: 8/15/34, Houston, Tex. BL/TL, 6′0.5″, 195 lbs. Deb: 4/27/57																												
1957	Phi-N	1	1	.500	34	1	1	0	1	58^2	57	27	1	2	20	36	12.1	3.68	103	.254	.321	0	.000	-1	1	1	-1	-0.1
1958	Phi-N	1	6	.143	27	11	0	0	0	92^1	121	67	8	1	26	54	14.4	5.85	68	.319	.365	4	.182	0	-19	-19	-2	-1.4
1959	Phi-N	0	2	.000	3	3	0	0	0	10	15	11	3	1	3	8	17.1	9.90	41	.333	.388	0	.000	-0	-7	-6	0	-1.0
	Chi-N	0	1	.000	11	2	0	0	0	18^2	25	13	1	0	8	9	15.9	4.82	82	.313	.375	1	.500	1	-2	-2	-1	-0.1
	Yr	0	3	.000	14	5	0	0	0	28^2	40	24	4	1	11	17	16.3	6.59	61	.320	.380	1	.200	0	-8	-8	-1	-1.1
1960	Chi-N	2	9	.182	45	7	2	0	4	123^1	123	61	17	2	46	64	12.5	3.94	96	.258	.326	4	.138	-1	-2	-2	-0	-0.3
1961	Mil-N	1	0	1.000	12	0	0	0	0	15^1	16	11	4	1	7	13	14.1	6.46	58	.271	.358	0	—	0	-4	-5	-0	-0.3
Total	5	5	19	.208	132	24	3	0	5	318^1	357	190	34	7	110	184	13.4	4.81	80	.282	.343	9	.145	-1	-33	-34	-4	-3.2
● RAMON MOREL Morel, Ramon Rafael b: 8/15/74, Villa Gonzalez, D.R. BR/TR, 6′2″, 175 lbs. Deb: 7/6/95																												
1995	Pit-N	0	1	.000	5	0	0	0	0	6^1	6	2	0	0	2	3	11.4	2.84	152	.300	.364	0	—	0	1	1	0	0.2
1996	Pit-N	2	1	.667	29	0	0	0	0	42	57	27	4	1	19	22	16.5	5.36	82	.324	.393	0	.000	-0	-5	-4	-1	-0.4
1997	Pit-N	0	0	—	5	0	0	0	0	7^2	11	4	2	0	4	4	17.6	4.70	91	.344	.417	0	—	0	-0	-0	0	0.0
	Chi-N	0	0	—	3	0	0	0	0	3^2	3	2	1	0	3	3	14.7	4.91	88	.214	.353	0	—	0	-0	-0	-0	0.0
	Yr	0	0	—	8	0	0	0	0	11^1	14	6	3	0	7	7	16.7	4.76	90	.304	.396	0	—	0	-1	-1	0	0.0
Total	3	2	2	.500	42	0	0	0	0	59^2	77	35	7	1	28	32	16.0	4.98	87	.318	.391	0	.000	-0	-5	-4	-0	-0.2
● LEW MOREN Moren, Lewis Howard “Hicks” b: 8/4/1883, Pittsburgh, Pa. d: 11/2/66, Pittsburgh, Pa. BR/TR, 5′11″, 150 lbs. Deb: 9/21/03																												
1903	Pit-N	0	1	.000	1	1	1	0	0	6	9	7	0	1	2	2	18.0	9.00	36	.346	.414	0	.000	-0	-4	-4	-0	-0.5
1904	Pit-N	0	0	—	1	0	0	0	0	4	7	6	1	1	4	0	27.0	9.00	30	.412	.545	0	.000	-0	-3	-3	0	-0.1
1907	Phi-N	11	18	.379	37	31	21	3	1	255	202	106	3	9	101	98	11.0	2.54	95	.226	.311	6	.081	-2	-2	-3	-0	-0.7
1908	Phi-N	8	9	.471	28	16	9	4	0	154	146	68	1	2	49	72	11.5	2.92	83	.258	.320	12	.245	2	-10	-8	0	-0.8
1909	Phi-N	16	15	.516	40	31	19	2	1	257^2	226	103	6	4	93	110	11.3	2.65	98	.239	.309	10	.111	-3	-2	-2	-5	-1.1
1910	Phi-N	13	14	.481	34	26	12	1	1	205^1	207	104	6	9	82	74	13.1	3.55	88	.269	.347	11	.149	-1	-12	-9	-0	-1.3
Total	6	48	57	.457	141	105	62	10	3	882	797	394	17	26	331	356	11.8	2.95	90	.248	.323	39	.134	-5	-32	-30	-5	-4.5
● ANGEL MORENO Moreno, Angel (Veneroso) b: 6/6/55, LaMendosa Soledad, Mex. BL/TL, 5′9″, 165 lbs. Deb: 8/15/81																												
1981	Cal-A	1	3	.250	8	4	1	0	0	31^1	27	10	2	0	14	12	11.8	2.87	127	.233	.315	0	—	0	3	3	-0	0.3
1982	Cal-A	3	7	.300	13	8	2	0	1	49^1	55	31	7	1	23	22	14.4	4.74	86	.288	.367	0	—	0	-4	-4	-0	-0.7
Total	2	4	10	.286	21	12	3	0	1	80^2	82	41	9	1	37	34	13.4	4.02	97	.267	.348	0	—	0	-1	-1	-0	-0.4
● JULIO MORENO Moreno, Julio (Gonzalez) b: 1/28/22, Guines, Cuba d: 1/2/87, Miami, Fla. BR/TR, 5′8″, 165 lbs. Deb: 9/8/50																												
1950	Was-A	1	1	.500	4	3	1	0	0	21^1	22	13	1	1	12	7	14.8	4.64	97	.268	.368	1	.125	-1	-0	-0	0	-0.1
1951	Was-A	5	11	.313	31	18	5	0	2	132^2	132	82	18	1	80	37	14.4	4.88	84	.256	.357	7	.175	-1	-11	-12	0	-1.4
1952	Was-A	9	9	.500	26	22	7	0	0	147^1	154	75	10	5	52	62	12.9	3.97	90	.270	.337	6	.122	-2	-5	-7	-1	-1.1
1953	Was-A	3	1	.750	12	2	1	0	0	35^1	41	11	2	0	13	13	13.8	2.80	139	.291	.351	0	.000	-1	5	4	-0	0.3
Total	4	18	22	.450	73	45	14	0	2	336^2	349	181	31	7	157	119	13.7	4.25	91	.267	.349	14	.132	-5	-12	-15	-1	-2.3
● ORBER MORENO Moreno, Orber (Aquiles) b: 4/27/77, Caracas, Venez. BR/TR, 6′2″, 190 lbs. Deb: 5/25/99																												
1999	KC-A	0	0	—	7	0	0	0	0	8	4	5	1	0	6	7	11.3	5.63	89	.143	.294	0	—	0	-1	-1	0	0.0
● ROGER MORET Moret, Rogelio (Torres) b: 9/16/49, Guayama, P.R. BB/TL, 6′4″, 175 lbs. Deb: 9/13/70																												
1970	Bos-A	1	0	1.000	3	1	0	0	0	8^1	7	3	0	0	4	2	11.9	3.24	122	.226	.314	0	.000	-0	0	1	-0	0.0
1971	Bos-A	4	3	.571	13	7	4	1	0	71	50	24	5	2	40	47	11.7	2.92	127	.205	.322	2	.087	-1	4	6	-0	0.4
1972	Bos-A	0	0	—	3	0	0	0	0	5	5	3	0	0	6	4	19.8	3.60	90	.263	.440	0	.000	-0	-0	-0	-0	0.0
1973	Bos-A	13	2	.867	30	15	5	2	3	156^1	138	60	19	3	67	90	12.0	3.17	127	.238	.320	0	—	0	11	14	-0	1.3
1974	Bos-A	9	10	.474	31	21	10	1	2	173^1	158	79	15	2	79	111	12.4	3.74	103	.243	.327	0	—	0	-2	2	-2	0.0
1975	*Bos-A	14	3	.824	36	16	4	1	1	145	132	60	8	2	76	80	13.0	3.60	113	.248	.344	0	—	0	3	7	-1	0.7
1976	Atl-N	3	5	.375	27	12	1	0	1	77^1	84	44	7	1	27	30	13.0	5.00	76	.280	.341	3	.130	-1	-13	-10	-0	-1.1
1977	Tex-A	3	3	.500	18	8	0	0	4	72^1	59	41	6	0	38	39	12.1	3.73	110	.220	.317	0	—	0	3	3	-1	0.1
1978	Tex-A	0	1	.000	7	2	0	0	1	14^2	23	8	1	1	2	5	16.0	4.91	77	.390	.419	0	—	0	-2	-2	-0	-0.2
Total	9	47	27	.635	168	82	24	5	12	723^1	656	322	61	11	339	408	12.5	3.66	108	.245	.332	5	.100	-2	5	21	-6	1.2
● DAVE MOREY Morey, David Beale b: 2/25/1889, Malden, Mass. d: 1/4/86, Oak Bluffs, Mass. BL/TR, 6′, 185 lbs. Deb: 7/4/13																												
1913	Phi-A	0	0	—	2	0	0	0	0	4	2	2	0	1	2	1	11.3	4.50	61	.182	.357	0	.000	-0	-1	-1	0	0.0
● CY MORGAN Morgan, Cyril Arlon b: 11/11/1895, Lakeville, Mass. d: 9/11/46, Lakeville, Mass. BR/TR, 6′, 170 lbs. Deb: 6/8/21																												
1921	Bos-N	1	1	.500	17	0	0	0	1	30^1	37	24	0	1	17	8	16.3	6.53	56	.314	.404	0	.000	-1	-9	-10	1	-0.6
1922	Bos-N	0	0	—	2	0	0	0	0	1^1	8	8	0	0	2	0	67.5	27.00	15	.667	.714	0	—	0	-3	-3	-0	-0.2
Total	2	1	1	.500	19	0	0	0	1	31^2	45	32	0	1	19	8	18.5	7.39	50	.346	.433	0	.000	-1	-13	-14	1	-0.8
● CY MORGAN Morgan, Harry Richard b: 11/10/1878, Pomeroy, Ohio d: 6/28/62, Wheeling, W.Va. BR/TR, 6′, 175 lbs. Deb: 9/18/03																												
1903	StL-A	0	2	.000	2	1	1	0	0	13	12	12	0	2	6	6	13.8	4.15	70	.245	.351	1	.250	0	-2	-2	-0	-0.3
1904	StL-A	0	2	.000	8	3	2	0	0	51	51	23	3	2	10	24	11.1	3.71	67	.262	.304	1	.056	-2	-6	-7	1	-0.5
1905	StL-A	2	5	.286	13	8	5	1	0	77^1	82	59	1	9	37	44	14.9	3.61	71	.273	.370	8	.258	2	-8	-10	2	-0.5
1907	StL-A	2	5	.286	10	6	4	0	0	55	77	43	3	2	17	14	15.7	6.05	42	.333	.384	2	.100	-1	-21	-22	1	-2.4
	Bos-A	6	6	.500	16	13	9	2	0	114^1	77	35	1	3	34	50	9.0	1.97	131	.193	.262	2	.057	-4	7	8	-1	0.3
	Yr	8	11	.421	26	19	13	2	0	169^1	154	78	4	5	51	64	11.2	3.30	78	.245	.307	4	.073	-5	-14	-14	1	-2.1
1908	Bos-A	14	13	.519	30	26	17	2	1	205	166	78	7	10	90	99	11.7	2.46	100	.226	.319	8	.127	-3	-1	0	1	-0.3
1909	Bos-A	2	6	.250	12	10	5	0	1	64^2	52	19	0	6	31	30	12.4	2.37	106	.240	.350	1	.050	-2	1	1	2	0.2
	Phi-A	16	11	.593	28	26	21	5	0	228^2	152	56	3	16	71	81	9.4	1.65	146	.191	.271	8	.108	-3	21	20	-2	1.9
	Yr	18	17	.514	40	36	26	5	1	293^1	204	75	3	22	102	111	10.1	1.81	134	**.202**	.289	9	.096	-4	22	21	1	2.1
1910	Phi-A	18	12	.600	36	34	23	3	0	290^2	214	92	0	18	117	134	10.8	1.55	153	.216	.310	14	.141	-4	31	28	1	2.7
1911	Phi-A	15	7	.682	38	30	15	2	1	249^2	217	109	0	21	113	136	12.7	2.70	117	.243	.341	15	.160	-5	18	13	3	0.8
1912	Phi-A	3	8	.273	16	14	5	0	0	93^2	75	56	0	5	51	47	12.6	3.75	82	.226	.338	1	.033	-3	-4	-7	2	-0.8
1913	Cin-N	0	1	.000	1	1	0	0	0	2^1	5	4	0	1	1	2	27.0	15.43	21	.500	.583	0	.000	-0	-3	-3	0	-0.5
Total	10	78	78	.500	210	172	107	15	3	1445^1	1180	586	18	95	578	667	11.5	2.51	105	.229	.318	61	.125	-25	32	19	12	0.6
● BILL MORGAN Morgan, Henry William b: 10/1857, Washington, D.C. Deb: 5/4/1875 ♦																												
1875	RS-n	1	3	.250	7	4	4	1	0	42	40	40	0		1	7	8.8	1.29	170	.212	.216	18	.261	1	4	4		0.4
● MIKE MORGAN Morgan, Michael Thomas b: 10/8/59, Tulare, Cal. BR/TR, 6′2″, 215 lbs. Deb: 6/11/78																												
1978	Oak-A	0	3	.000	3	3	1	0	0	12^1	19	12	1	0	8	0	19.7	7.30	50	.373	.458	0	—	0	-5	-5	1	-0.9
1979	Oak-A	2	10	.167	13	13	2	0	0	77^1	102	57	7	3	50	17	18.0	5.94	68	.332	.431	0	—	0	-15	-17	1	-2.0
1982	NY-A	7	11	.389	30	23	2	0	0	150^1	167	77	15	2	67	71	14.1	4.37	91	.285	.360	0	—	0	-5	-6	1	-0.6
1983	Tor-A	0	3	.000	16	4	0	0	0	45^1	48	26	6	0	21	22	13.7	5.16	84	.273	.350	0	—	0	-5	-4	1	-0.2
1985	Sea-A	1	1	.500	2	2	0	0	0	6	11	8	2	0	5	2	24.0	12.00	35	.393	.485	0	—	0	-5	-5	0	-0.8
1986	Sea-A	11	17	.393	37	33	9	1	1	216^1	243	122	24	4	86	116	13.9	4.53	94	.286	.354	0	—	0	-8	-7	-0	-0.8
1987	Sea-A	12	17	.414	34	31	8	2	0	207	245	117	25	5	53	85	13.2	4.65	102	.296	.342	0	—	0	-4	2	1	0.4
1988	Bal-A	1	6	.143	22	10	2	0	1	71^1	70	45	6	1	23	29	11.9	5.43	72	.255	.315	0	—	0	-11	-12	0	-1.1

YEAR	TM/L	W	L	PCT	G	GS	CG	SH	SV	IP	H	R	HR	HB	BB	SO	RAT	ERA	ERA+	OAV	OOB	BH	AVG	PB	PR	PR+	PD	TPI
1989	LA-N	8	11	.421	40	19	0	0	0	152^2	130	51	6	2	33	72	9.7	2.53	135	.234	.280	3	.083	-2	16	15	4	2.2
1990	LA-N	11	15	.423	33	33	6	**4**	0	211	216	100	19	5	60	106	12.0	3.75	98	.266	.321	8	.113	-2	1	-2	3	-0.1
1991	LA-N★	14	10	.583	34	33	5	1	1	236^1	197	85	12	3	61	140	9.9	2.78	129	.226	.279	7	.092	-3	24	22	2	2.1
1992	Chi-N	16	8	.667	34	34	6	1	0	240	203	80	14	3	79	123	10.7	2.55	142	.234	.300	8	.108	-2	26	27	2	2.7
1993	Chi-N	10	15	.400	32	32	1	1	0	207^2	206	100	15	7	74	111	12.4	4.03	99	.262	.331	4	.061	-4	0	-1	0	-0.4
1994	Chi-N	2	10	.167	15	15	1	0	0	80^2	111	65	12	4	35	57	16.7	6.69	62	.338	.409	3	.125	-1	-22	-23	-1	-2.9
1995	Chi-N	2	1	.667	4	4	0	0	0	24^2	19	8	2	1	9	15	10.6	2.19	188	.216	.296	1	.143	-0	5	5	1	0.7
	StL-N	5	6	.455	17	17	1	0	0	106^2	114	48	10	5	25	46	12.2	3.88	108	.283	.333	1	.032	-2	4	4	2	0.3
	Yr	7	7	.500	21	21	1	0	0	131^1	133	56	12	6	34	61	11.9	3.56	117	.271	.326	2	.053	-2	9	9	2	1.0
1996	StL-N	4	8	.333	18	18	0	0	0	103	118	63	14	0	40	55	13.8	5.24	80	.294	.358	2	.061	-3	-12	-12	-1	-1.5
	Cin-N	2	3	.400	5	5	0	0	0	27^1	28	9	2	1	7	19	11.9	2.30	184	.267	.319	0	.000	-1	6	6	-0	0.9
	Yr	6	11	.353	23	23	0	0	0	130^1	146	72	16	1	47	74	13.4	4.63	91	.289	.350	2	.050	-3	-6	-6	-1	-0.6
1997	Cin-N	9	12	.429	31	30	1	0	0	162	165	91	13	8	49	103	12.3	4.78	89	.266	.328	4	.091	-2	-10	-9	-0	-1.2
1998	Min-A	4	2	.667	18	17	0	0	0	98	108	41	13	7	24	50	12.8	3.49	137	.286	.340	1	.500	0	13	14	1	0.9
	*Chi-N	0	1	.000	5	5	0	0	0	22^2	30	21	8	1	15	10	18.3	7.15	62	.323	.422	4	.667	2	-7	-7	1	-0.1
1999	Tex-A	13	10	.565	34	25	1	0	0	140	184	108	25	7	48	61	15.4	6.24	82	.323	.383	1	.250	0	-21	-17	1	-2.2
2000	Ari-N	5	5	.500	60	4	0	0	5	101^2	123	55	10	1	40	56	14.5	4.87	95	.311	.375	7	.438	2	-3	-3	-0	-0.1
Total	20	139	185	.429	537	410	46	10	8	2700^1	2857	1389	261	70	912	1366	12.8	4.22	97	.275	.338	54	.109	-16	-39	-36	17	-4.7

● TOM MORGAN

Morgan, Tom Stephen "Plowboy" b: 5/20/30, ElMonte, Cal. d: 1/13/87, Anaheim, Cal. BR/TR, 6'2", 195 lbs. Deb: 4/20/51 C

YEAR	TM/L	W	L	PCT	G	GS	CG	SH	SV	IP	H	R	HR	HB	BB	SO	RAT	ERA	ERA+	OAV	OOB	BH	AVG	PB	PR	PR+	PD	TPI
1951	*NY-A	9	3	.750	27	16	4	2	2	124^2	119	56	11	3	36	57	11.4	3.68	104	.253	.310	12	.273	2	6	2	2	0.5
1952	NY-A	5	4	.556	16	12	2	1	2	93^2	86	34	8	4	33	35	11.8	3.07	108	.252	.325	6	.182	1	6	3	3	0.7
1954	NY-A	11	5	.688	32	17	7	4	1	143	149	58	8	5	40	34	12.2	3.34	103	.274	.330	7	.143	0	6	2	3	0.5
1955	*NY-A	7	3	.700	40	1	0	0	10	72	72	29	3	5	24	17	12.6	3.25	115	.267	.338	4	.222	0	6	4	2	0.9
1956	*NY-A	6	7	.462	41	0	0	0	11	71^1	74	41	2	3	27	20	13.1	4.16	93	.284	.357	2	.154	-0	-0	-3	1	-0.4
1957	KC-A	9	7	.563	46	13	5	0	7	143^2	160	76	19	3	61	32	14.0	4.64	85	.299	.373	3	.091	-2	-14	-10	4	-1.1
1958	Det-A	2	5	.286	39	1	0	0	1	62^2	70	28	7	1	4	32	10.8	3.16	128	.286	.300	2	.200	-0	4	6	-0	0.6
1959	Det-A	1	4	.200	46	1	0	0	9	92^2	94	48	11	6	18	39	11.5	3.98	102	.265	.311	9	.391	4	-1	1	-0	0.4
1960	Det-A	3	2	.600	22	0	0	0	1	29	33	17	6	0	10	12	13.3	4.66	85	.295	.352	0	—	0	-3	-2	0	-0.3
	Was-A	1	3	.250	14	0	0	0	0	24	36	15	6	1	5	11	15.8	3.75	104	.343	.378	0	.000	-1	0	0	-0	0.0
	Yr	4	5	.444	36	0	0	0	1	53	69	32	12	1	15	23	14.4	4.25	92	.318	.365	0	.000	-1	-2	-2	0	-0.3
1961	LA-A	8	2	.800	59	0	0	0	10	91^2	74	31	7	5	17	39	9.4	2.36	191	.224	.272	1	.083	-1	17	20	1	2.4
1962	LA-A	5	2	.714	48	0	0	0	9	58^2	53	23	6	1	19	29	11.2	2.91	132	.247	.311	0	.000	-1	7	6	-1	0.7
1963	LA-A	0	0	—	13	0	0	0	1	16^1	20	11	1	3	6	7	16.0	5.51	62	.313	.397	0	.000	-0	-3	-4	-0	-0.2
Total	12	67	47	.588	443	61	18	7	64	1023^1	1040	467	95	40	300	364	12.1	3.61	106	.270	.329	46	.186	3	32	27	13	4.7

● GENE MORIARITY

Moriarity, Eugene John b: 1/5/1865, Holyoke, Mass. BL/TL, 5'8", 130 lbs. Deb: 6/18/1884 ♦

YEAR	TM/L	W	L	PCT	G	GS	CG	SH	SV	IP	H	R	HR	HB	BB	SO	RAT	ERA	ERA+	OAV	OOB	BH	AVG	PB	PR	PR+	PD	TPI
1884	Ind-a	0	2	.000	2	2	2	0	0	13^2	16	13	0	1	7	4	15.8	5.27	62	.267	.353	8	.216	0	-3	-3	0	-0.3
1885	Det-N	0	0	—	1	0	0	0	0	2	3	3	0	0	1	1	18.0	9.00	32	.300	.364	1	.026	-0	-1	-1	-0	-0.1
Total	2	0	2	.000	3	2	2	0	0	15^2	19	16	0	1	8	5	16.1	5.74	56	.271	.354	41	.152	-0	-4	-4	0	-0.4

● JOHN MORLAN

Morlan, John Glen b: 11/22/47, Columbus, Ohio BR/TR, 6', 178 lbs. Deb: 7/20/73

YEAR	TM/L	W	L	PCT	G	GS	CG	SH	SV	IP	H	R	HR	HB	BB	SO	RAT	ERA	ERA+	OAV	OOB	BH	AVG	PB	PR	PR+	PD	TPI
1973	Pit-N	2	2	.500	10	7	1	0	0	41	42	18	4	0	23	23	14.3	3.95	89	.276	.371	2	.182	1	-1	-2	-1	-0.2
1974	Pit-N	0	3	.000	39	0	0	0	0	65	54	37	2	3	48	38	14.5	4.29	81	.227	.363	0	.000	-1	-5	-6	-1	-0.5
Total	2	2	5	.286	49	7	1	0	0	106	96	55	6	3	71	61	14.4	4.16	84	.246	.366	2	.111	0	-6	-8	-1	-0.7

● ALVIN MORMAN

Morman, Alvin b: 1/6/69, Rockingham, N.C. BL/TL, 6'3", 210 lbs. Deb: 4/2/96

YEAR	TM/L	W	L	PCT	G	GS	CG	SH	SV	IP	H	R	HR	HB	BB	SO	RAT	ERA	ERA+	OAV	OOB	BH	AVG	PB	PR	PR+	PD	TPI
1996	Hou-N	4	1	.800	53	0	0	0	0	42	43	24	8	0	24	31	14.4	4.93	79	.261	.354	0	—	0	-3	-5	0	-0.5
1997	*Cle-A	0	0	—	34	0	0	0	2	18^1	19	13	2	1	14	13	16.7	5.89	80	.268	.395	0	.000	-0	-3	-2	-0	-0.1
1998	Cle-A	0	1	.000	31	0	0	0	0	22	25	13	1	0	11	16	14.7	5.32	90	.298	.379	0	—	0	-2	-1	0	0.0
	SF-N	0	1	.000	9	0	0	0	0	7	8	4	4	0	3	7	14.1	5.14	77	.276	.344	0	—	0	-1	-1	0	-0.1
1999	KC-A	2	4	.333	49	0	0	0	1	53^1	66	27	6	4	23	31	15.7	4.05	124	.307	.384	0	—	0	5	6	1	0.6
Total	4	6	7	.462	176	0	0	0	3	142^2	161	81	21	5	75	98	15.2	4.79	95	.285	.374	0	.000	-0	-3	-4	1	-0.1

● DAN MOROGIELLO

Morogiello, Daniel Joseph b: 3/26/55, Brooklyn, N.Y. BL/TL, 6'1", 200 lbs. Deb: 5/20/83

YEAR	TM/L	W	L	PCT	G	GS	CG	SH	SV	IP	H	R	HR	HB	BB	SO	RAT	ERA	ERA+	OAV	OOB	BH	AVG	PB	PR	PR+	PD	TPI
1983	Bal-A	0	1	.000	22	0	0	0	1	37^2	39	10	1	1	10	15	11.9	2.39	166	.265	.316	0	—	0	7	7	-1	0.3

● JIM MORONEY

Moroney, James Francis b: 12/4/1883, Boston, Mass. d: 2/26/29, Philadelphia, Pa. BL/TL, 6'1", 175 lbs. Deb: 4/24/06

YEAR	TM/L	W	L	PCT	G	GS	CG	SH	SV	IP	H	R	HR	HB	BB	SO	RAT	ERA	ERA+	OAV	OOB	BH	AVG	PB	PR	PR+	PD	TPI
1906	Bos-N	0	3	.000	3	3	3	0	0	27	28	20	1	6	12	11	15.3	5.33	50	.259	.365	1	.100	-1	-8	-8	0	-0.8
1910	Phi-N	1	2	.333	12	2	1	0	1	42	43	20	1	4	11	13	12.4	2.14	146	.295	.360	0	.000	-1	4	4	-0	0.2
1912	Chi-N	1	1	.500	10	3	1	0	1	23^2	25	13	0	4	17	5	17.5	4.56	73	.316	.460	3	.500	1	-3	-3	-0	-0.2
Total	3	2	6	.250	25	8	5	0	2	92^2	96	53	2	14	40	29	14.6	3.69	83	.288	.388	4	.154	-1	-7	-6	-1	-0.8

● BILL MORRELL

Morrell, Willard Blackmer b: 4/9/1893, Hyde Park, Mass. d: 8/5/75, Birmingham, Ala. BR/TR, 6', 172 lbs. Deb: 4/20/26

YEAR	TM/L	W	L	PCT	G	GS	CG	SH	SV	IP	H	R	HR	HB	BB	SO	RAT	ERA	ERA+	OAV	OOB	BH	AVG	PB	PR	PR+	PD	TPI
1926	Was-A	3	3	.500	26	2	1	0	1	69^2	83	48	5	2	29	16	14.7	5.30	73	.311	.383	4	.235	1	-10	-12	-1	-0.9
1930	NY-N	0	0	—	2	0	0	0	0	8	6	1	0	0	1	3	7.9	1.13	421	.214	.241	0	.000	-0	3	3	0	0.1
1931	NY-N	5	3	.625	20	7	2	0	1	66	83	34	4	0	27	16	15.0	4.36	85	.306	.369	2	.111	-0	-4	-5	-0	-0.6
Total	3	8	6	.571	48	9	3	0	2	143^2	172	83	9	2	57	35	14.5	4.64	83	.304	.370	6	.162	-0	-10	-13	-1	-1.4

● JOHN MORRILL

Morrill, John Francis "Honest John" b: 2/19/1855, Boston, Mass. d: 4/2/32, Brookline, Mass. BR/TR, 5'10.5", 155 lbs. Deb: 4/24/1876 M♦

YEAR	TM/L	W	L	PCT	G	GS	CG	SH	SV	IP	H	R	HR	HB	BB	SO	RAT	ERA	ERA+	OAV	OOB	BH	AVG	PB	PR	PR+	PD	TPI
1880	Bos-N	0	0	—	3	0	0	0	0	10^2	9	3	0		1	0	8.4	0.84	269	.273	.294	81	.237	0	2	2	0	0.1
1881	Bos-N	0	1	.000	3	0	0	0	1	5^2	9	8	0		1	0	15.9	6.35	42	.333	.357	90	.289	1	-2	-2	-0	-0.4
1882	Bos-N	0	0	—	1	0	0	0	0	2	3	0	0		0	2	13.5	0.00	—	.375	.375	101	.289	0	1	1	0	0.0
1883	Bos-N	1	0	1.000	2	1	1	0	0	13	15	11	0		4	5	13.2	2.77	112	.268	.317	129	.319	1	1	0	-0	0.1
1884	Bos-N	0	1	.000	7	1	1	0	**2**	23	34	23	0		6	13	15.7	7.43	39	.315	.351	114	.260	1	-11	-12	0	-0.6
1886	Bos-N	0	0	—	1	0	0	0	0	4	5	1	0		0	2	11.3	0.00	—	.313	.313	106	.247	0	1	1	0	0.1
1889	Was-N	0	0	—	1	0	0	0	0	0^1	0	0	0	0	0	0	0.0	0.00	—	.000	.000	27	.185	0	0	0	0	0.0
Total	7	1	2	.333	18	2	2	0	3	58^2	75	46	0	0	12	22	13.3	4.30	66	.301	.333	1312	.265	4	-9	-10	0	-0.7

● DANNY MORRIS

Morris, Danny Walker b: 6/11/46, Greenville, Ky. BR/TR, 6'1", 200 lbs. Deb: 9/10/68

YEAR	TM/L	W	L	PCT	G	GS	CG	SH	SV	IP	H	R	HR	HB	BB	SO	RAT	ERA	ERA+	OAV	OOB	BH	AVG	PB	PR	PR+	PD	TPI
1968	Min-A	0	1	.000	3	2	0	0	0	10^2	11	5	0	0	4	6	12.7	1.69	183	.262	.326	0	.000	-0	2	2	0	0.1
1969	Min-A	0	1	.000	3	1	0	0	0	5^1	5	4	1	0	4	1	15.2	5.06	72	.238	.360	0	—	0	-1	-1	0	-0.1
Total	2	0	2	.000	6	3	0	0	0	16	16	9	1	0	8	7	13.5	2.81	117	.254	.338	0	.000	-0	1	1	0	0.0

● E. MORRIS

Morris, E. b: Trenton, N.J. Deb: 9/11/1884 ♦

YEAR	TM/L	W	L	PCT	G	GS	CG	SH	SV	IP	H	R	HR	HB	BB	SO	RAT	ERA	ERA+	OAV	OOB	BH	AVG	PB	PR	PR+	PD	TPI
1884	Bal-U	0	0	—	1	0	0	0	0	1	2	2	0		2	0	36.0	9.00	30	.400	.571	0	.000	-1	-1	-1	-0	-0.1

● ED MORRIS

Morris, Edward "Cannonball" b: 9/29/1862, Brooklyn, N.Y. d: 4/12/37, Pittsburgh, Pa. BB/TL, 5'7", 165 lbs. Deb: 5/1/1884

YEAR	TM/L	W	L	PCT	G	GS	CG	SH	SV	IP	H	R	HR	HB	BB	SO	RAT	ERA	ERA+	OAV	OOB	BH	AVG	PB	PR	PR+	PD	TPI
1884	Col-a	34	13	**.723**	52	52	47	3	0	429^2	335	159	3	13	51	302	8.4	2.18	139	.204	.234	37	.186	2	51	44	2	4.5
1885	Pit-a	39	24	.619	**63**	63	**63**	**7**	0	**581**	459	245	5	14	101	**298**	**8.9**	2.35	137	**.208**	**.247**	44	.186	-5	58	56	-1	4.6
1886	Pit-a	**41**	20	.672	64	63	63	**12**	**1**	555^1	455	244	5	7	118	326	**9.4**	2.45	138	.214	**.258**	38	.167	-7	62	59	-1	4.5
1887	Pit-N	14	22	.389	38	38	37	1	0	317^2	446	225	13	8	71	91	12.9	4.31	90	.322	.326	30	.229	-4	-8	-16	-2	-1.9
1888	Pit-N	29	23	.558	**55**	55	**54**	5	0	480	470	216	7	8	74	135	10.4	2.31	116	.245	.276	19	.101	-11	29	21	1	0.9
1889	Pit-N	6	13	.316	21	21	18	0	0	170	196	107	4	6	48	40	13.2	4.86	91	.280	.332	7	.097	-5	-2	-8	-2	-1.2
1890	Pit-P	8	7	.533	18	15	15	1	0	144^1	178	116	5	3	35	25	13.5	4.86	80	.290	.332	9	.143	-4	-10	-17	-3	-1.7
Total	7	171	122	.584	311	307	297	29	1	2678	2539	1312	42	59	498	1217	10.2	2.82	116	.240	.273	184	.165	-35	179	143	-5	9.7

● JIM MORRIS

Morris, James Samuel b: 1/19/64, Brownwood, Tex. BL/TL, 6'3", 215 lbs. Deb: 9/18/99

YEAR	TM/L	W	L	PCT	G	GS	CG	SH	SV	IP	H	R	HR	HB	BB	SO	RAT	ERA	ERA+	OAV	OOB	BH	AVG	PB	PR	PR+	PD	TPI
1999	TB-A	0	0	—	5	0	0	0	0	4^2	3	3	1	1	2	3	11.6	5.79	86	.167	.286	0	—	0	-0	-0	-0	0.0
2000	TB-A	0	0	—	16	0	0	0	0	10^1	10	9	1	0	7	10	14.8	4.35	114	.250	.362	0	—	0	1	1	-0	0.0
Total	2	0	0	—	21	0	0	0	0	15	13	12	2	1	9	13	13.8	4.80	103	.224	.338	0	—	0	0	0	-1	0.0

YEAR	TM/L	W	L	PCT	G	GS	CG	SH	SV	IP	H	R	HR	HB	BB	SO	RAT	ERA	ERA+	OAV	OOB	BH	AVG	PB	PR	PR+	PD	TPI
● **JACK MORRIS**	Morris, John Scott b: 5/16/55, St.Paul, Minn. BR/TR, 6'3", 200 lbs. Deb: 7/26/77																											
1977	Det-A	1	1	.500	7	6	1	0	0	45^2	38	20	4	0	23	28	12.0	3.74	115	.235	.330	0	—	0	2	3	0	0.1
1978	Det-A	3	5	.375	28	7	0	0	0	106	107	57	8	3	49	48	13.5	4.33	90	.268	.352	0	—	0	-7	-5	-0	-0.4
1979	Det-A	17	7	.708	27	27	9	1	0	197^2	179	76	19	4	59	113	11.0	3.28	132	.244	.304	0	—	0	21	23	-1	2.5
1980	Det-A	16	15	.516	36	36	11	2	0	250	252	125	20	4	87	112	12.3	4.18	99	.262	.326	0	—	0	-4	-2	3	0.1
1981	Det-A★	**14**	7	.667	25	25	15	1	0	198	153	69	14	2	78	97	10.6	3.05	124	.218	.298	0	—	0	14	16	-0	1.6
1982	Det-A	17	16	.515	37	37	17	3	0	266^1	247	131	37	0	96	135	11.6	4.06	100	.247	.312	0	—	0	1	0	-0	0.0
1983	Det-A	20	13	.606	37	37	20	1	0	**293^2**	257	117	30	3	83	**232**	10.5	3.34	117	.233	.289	0	—	0	24	20	-1	2.0
1984	*Det-A★	19	11	.633	35	35	9	1	0	240^1	221	108	20	2	87	148	11.6	3.60	109	.241	.308	0	—	0	11	9	2	1.2
1985	Det-A★	16	11	.593	35	35	13	4	0	257	212	102	21	5	110	191	11.5	3.33	122	.225	.309	0	—	0	23	22	-1	2.0
1986	Det-A	21	8	.724	35	35	15	**6**	0	267	229	105	40	0	82	223	10.5	3.27	126	.229	.287	0	—	0	27	26	0	2.6
1987	*Det-A★	18	11	.621	34	34	13	0	0	266	227	111	39	1	93	208	10.9	3.38	125	.228	.294	0	.000	-0	32	27	-2	2.4
1988	Det-A	15	13	.536	34	34	10	2	0	235	225	115	20	4	83	168	11.9	3.94	97	.251	.318	0	—	0	1	-3	0	-0.4
1989	Det-A	6	14	.300	24	24	10	0	0	170^1	189	102	23	2	59	115	13.2	4.86	79	.283	.342	0	—	0	-18	-20	1	-2.0
1990	Det-A	15	18	.455	36	36	**11**	3	0	249^2	231	144	26	6	97	162	12.0	4.51	88	.242	.316	0	—	0	-16	-15	-1	-1.9
1991	*Min-A★	18	12	.600	35	35	10	2	0	246^2	226	107	18	5	92	163	11.8	3.43	125	.245	.317	0	—	0	18	22	-1	2.5
1992	*Tor-A	**21**	6	.778	34	34	6	1	0	240^2	222	114	18	10	80	132	11.7	4.04	101	.246	.314	0	—	0	-2	1	-1	0.1
1993	Tor-A	7	12	.368	27	27	4	1	0	152^2	189	116	18	3	65	103	15.2	6.19	70	.302	.371	0	—	0	-31	-32	-2	-3.4
1994	Cle-A	10	6	.625	23	23	1	0	0	141^1	163	96	14	4	67	100	14.9	5.60	84	.292	.371	0	—	0	-13	-14	0	-1.3
Total	18	254	186	.577	549	527	175	28	0	3824	3567	1815	389	58	1390	2478	11.8	3.90	105	.247	.316	0	.000	-0	83	79	-4	7.7
● **JOHN MORRIS**	Morris, John Wallace b: 8/23/41, Lewes, Del. BR/TL, 6'1", 198 lbs. Deb: 7/19/66																											
1966	Phi-N	1	1	.500	13	0	0	0	0	13^2	15	8	2	1	3	8	12.5	5.27	68	.278	.328	0	—	0	-3	-3	0	-0.3
1968	Bal-A	2	0	1.000	19	0	0	0	0	31^2	19	11	4	4	17	22	11.4	2.56	114	.173	.305	0	.000	-1	1	1	0	0.0
1969	Sea-A	0	0	—	6	0	0	0	0	12^2	16	10	2	0	8	8	17.1	6.39	57	.308	.400	1	1.000	1	-4	-4	1	0.0
1970	Mil-A	4	3	.571	20	9	2	0	0	73^1	70	33	4	2	22	40	11.5	3.93	97	.253	.312	3	.176	0	-2	-1	1	0.0
1971	Mil-A	2	2	.500	43	1	0	0	1	67^2	69	34	4	1	27	42	12.9	3.72	93	.270	.342	1	.200	0	-2	-2	1	0.0
1972	SF-N	0	0	—	7	0	0	0	0	6^1	9	6	2	0	2	5	15.6	4.26	82	.310	.355	0	—	0	-1	-1	0	0.0
1973	SF-N	1	0	1.000	7	0	0	0	0	6^1	12	8	0	0	3	3	21.3	8.53	45	.429	.484	0	.000	-0	-3	-3	0	-0.5
1974	SF-N	1	1	.500	17	0	0	0	1	20^2	17	7	1	0	4	9	9.1	3.05	125	.215	.253	1	1.000	0	1	2	-1	0.2
Total	8	11	7	.611	132	10	2	0	2	232^1	227	117	19	8	86	137	12.4	3.95	90	.256	.328	6	.194	1	-11	-10	3	-0.6
● **BUGS MORRIS**	Morris, Joseph Harley (a.k.a. Joseph Harley Bennett In 1918) b: 4/19/1892, Weir City, Kan. d: 11/21/57, Noel, Mo. BR/TR, 5'9.5", 163 lbs. Deb: 7/20/18																											
1918	StL-A	0	2	.000	4	2	0	0	0	10^1	12	7	1	0	7	0	16.5	3.48	79	.308	.413	1	.250	0	-1	-1	0	-0.1
1921	Chi-A	0	3	.000	3	2	1	0	0	17^2	19	14	1	0	16	2	17.8	6.11	69	.297	.438	2	.333	0	-4	-4	1	-0.4
	StL-A	0	0	—	3	1	0	0	0	5^2	11	10	1	2	6	3	30.2	14.29	31	.407	.543	1	1.000	0	-6	-6	-0	-0.3
	Yr	0	3	.000	6	3	1	0	0	23^1	30	24	2	2	22	5	20.8	8.10	53	.330	.470	3	.429	1	-10	-10	0	-0.7
Total	2	0	5	.000	10	5	1	0	0	33^2	42	31	3	2	29	5	19.5	6.68	57	.323	.453	4	.364	1	-11	-11	1	-0.8
● **MATT MORRIS**	Morris, Matthew Christian b: 8/9/74, Middletown, N.Y. BR/TR, 6'5", 210 lbs. Deb: 4/4/97																											
1997	StL-N	12	9	.571	33	33	3	0	0	217	208	88	12	7	69	149	11.8	3.19	130	.258	.322	15	.205	3	24	23	-2	2.2
1998	StL-N	7	5	.583	17	17	2	1	0	113^2	101	37	8	3	42	79	11.6	2.53	166	.243	.317	2	.069	-0	21	21	0	2.1
2000	*StL-N	3	3	.500	31	0	0	0	4	53	53	22	3	2	17	34	12.2	3.57	130	.261	.324	1	.333	0	6	6	-1	0.6
Total	3	22	17	.564	81	50	5	1	4	383^2	362	147	23	12	128	262	11.8	3.05	139	.254	.321	18	.171	3	52	51	-3	4.9
● **ED MORRIS**	Morris, Walter Edward "Big Ed" b: 12/7/1899, Foshee, Ala. d: 3/3/32, Century, Fla. BR/TR, 6'2", 185 lbs. Deb: 8/5/22																											
1922	Chi-N	0	0	—	5	0	0	0	0	12	22	17	1	0	6	5	21.0	8.25	51	.386	.444	1	.250	-0	-6	-5	-0	-0.3
1928	Bos-A	19	15	.559	47	29	20	0	5	257^2	255	118	7	5	80	104	11.9	3.53	117	.264	.323	14	.154	-4	15	16	-2	1.5
1929	Bos-A	14	14	.500	33	26	17	2	1	208^1	227	118	7	2	95	73	14.0	4.45	96	.282	.360	16	.232	2	-5	-4	-2	-0.4
1930	Bos-A	4	9	.308	18	9	3	0	0	65^1	67	42	1	0	38	28	14.5	4.13	112	.260	.355	6	.316	2	4	3	-0	0.7
1931	Bos-A	5	7	.417	37	14	3	0	0	130^2	131	80	4	5	74	46	14.5	4.75	91	.260	.361	6	.158	-2	-5	-7	0	-0.6
Total	5	42	45	.483	140	78	43	2	6	674	702	375	20	12	293	256	13.4	4.19	101	.271	.348	43	.195	-1	3	4	-4	0.9
● **BILL MORRISETTE**	Morrisette, William Lee b: 1/17/1893, Baltimore, Md. d: 3/25/66, Virginia Beach, Va BR/TR, 6', 176 lbs. Deb: 9/19/15																											
1915	Phi-A	2	0	1.000	4	1	1	0	0	20	15	6	0	0	5	11	9.0	1.35	217	.195	.244	2	.286	0	4	4	0	0.4
1916	Phi-A	0	0	—	1	0	0	0	0	4	6	3	0	0	5	2	24.8	6.75	42	.429	.579	0	.000	0	-2	-2	1	0.0
1920	Det-A	1	1	.500	8	3	1	0	0	27	25	21	0	3	19	15	15.7	4.33	86	.245	.379	0	.000	-1	-2	-2	-0	-0.3
Total	3	3	1	.750	13	4	2	0	0	51	46	30	0	3	29	28	13.8	3.35	100	.238	.347	2	.125	-1	0	-0	0	0.1
● **JIM MORRISON**	Morrison, James Forrest b: 9/23/52, Pensacola, Fla. BR/TR, 5'11", 182 lbs. Deb: 9/18/77 ◆																											
1988	Atl-N	0	0	—	3	0	0	0	0	3^2	3	0	0	0	2	1	12.3	0.00	—	.214	.313	14	.152	0	1	1	-0	0.1
● **JOHNNY MORRISON**	Morrison, John Dewey "Jughandle Johnny" b: 10/22/1895, Pellville, Ky. d: 3/20/66, Louisville, Ky. BR/TR, 5'11", 188 lbs. Deb: 9/28/20 F																											
1920	Pit-N	1	0	1.000	2	1	1	1	0	7	4	0	0	0	1	3	6.4	0.00	—	.167	.200	0	.000	-0	2	2	0	0.3
1921	Pit-N	9	7	.563	21	17	11	**3**	0	144	131	49	3	1	33	52	10.3	2.88	133	.258	.305	5	.119	-1	15	15	-0	1.4
1922	Pit-N	17	11	.607	45	33	20	**5**	1	286^1	315	130	10	6	87	104	12.8	3.43	119	.286	.341	20	.198	-2	21	21	0	1.5
1923	Pit-N	25	13	.658	42	37	27	2	2	301^2	287	136	6	5	110	114	12.0	3.49	115	.253	.321	21	.183	-3	17	17	-0	1.5
1924	Pit-N	11	16	.407	**41**	25	10	0	2	237^2	213	114	7	4	73	85	11.0	3.75	102	.245	.307	13	.169	-2	3	2	-2	-0.2
1925	*Pit-N	17	14	.548	**44**	26	10	0	**4**	211	245	113	12	7	60	60	13.3	3.88	115	.291	.343	13	.178	-2	9	13	-2	1.2
1926	Pit-N	6	8	.429	26	13	6	2	2	122^1	119	52	2	2	44	39	12.1	3.38	116	.267	.335	3	.077	-4	6	7	-2	0.2
1927	Pit-N	3	2	.600	21	2	1	0	3	53^2	63	27	2	0	21	21	14.1	4.19	98	.304	.368	2	.154	-0	-2	-0	-1	-0.2
1929	Bro-N	13	7	.650	39	10	4	0	**8**	136^2	150	87	11	3	61	57	14.1	4.48	103	.279	.355	7	.163	-2	4	2	-3	-0.2
1930	Bro-N	1	2	.333	16	0	0	0	1	34^2	47	29	4	0	16	11	16.4	5.45	90	.346	.414	0	.000	-1	-2	-2	-0	-0.2
Total	10	103	80	.563	297	164	90	13	23	1535	1574	737	57	28	506	546	12.4	3.65	113	.271	.332	84	.164	-18	74	79	-12	5.3
● **MIKE MORRISON**	Morrison, Michael b: 2/6/1867, Erie, Pa. d: 6/16/55, Erie, Pa. BR/TR, 5'8.5", 156 lbs. Deb: 4/19/1887																											
1887	Cle-a	12	25	.324	40	40	35	0	0	316^2	590	341	13	22	205	158	17.4	4.92	88	.390	.398	38	.250	-4	-22	-20	10	-1.2
1888	Cle-a	1	3	.250	4	4	4	0	0	35	40	35	3	1	19	14	15.4	5.40	57	.278	.366	4	.235	-0	-9	-9	0	-0.8
1890	Syr-a	6	9	.400	17	14	13	1	0	127	131	112	4	13	81	69	15.9	5.88	60	.258	.374	29	.242	3	-28	-36	2	-2.7
	Bal-a	1	2	.333	4	4	3	0	0	26	15	20	0	2	20	13	12.8	3.81	107	.163	.325	1	.111	-1	0	1	1	0.1
	Yr	7	11	.389	21	18	16	1	0	153	146	132	4	15	101	82	15.4	5.53	66	.244	.366	30	.233	3	-28	-35	3	-2.6
Total	3	20	39	.339	65	62	55	1	0	504^2	776	508	20	38	325	254	16.7	5.14	78	.344	.387	72	.242	-2	-59	-63	12	-4.6
● **PHIL MORRISON**	Morrison, Philip Melvin b: 10/18/1894, Rockport, Ind. d: 1/18/55, Lexington, Ky. BB/TR, 6'2", 190 lbs. Deb: 9/30/21 F																											
1921	Pit-N	0	0	—	1	0	0	0	0	0^2	1	0	0	0	0	1	13.5	0.00	—	.333	.333	0	—	0	0	0	0	0.0
● **HANK MORRISON**	Morrison, Stephen Henry b: 5/22/1866, Olneyville, R.I. d: 9/30/27, Attleboro, Mass. BR/TR, 5'10", 180 lbs. Deb: 5/28/1887																											
1887	Ind-N	3	4	.429	7	7	5	0	0	57	106	73	2	1	27	13	16.9	7.58	55	.373	.375	5	.179	-2	-22	-21	-1	-2.0
● **GUY MORRISON**	Morrison, Walter Guy b: 8/29/1895, Hinton, W.Va. d: 8/14/34, Grand Rapids, Mich BR/TR, 5'11", 185 lbs. Deb: 8/31/27																											
1927	Bos-N	1	2	.333	11	3	1	0	0	34^1	40	22	1	0	15	6	14.4	4.46	83	.296	.367	1	.125	1	-2	-3	1	-0.1
1928	Bos-N	0	0	—	1	0	0	0	0	3	4	4	1	0	3	0	21.0	12.00	33	.308	.438	0	—	0	-3	-3	0	-0.1
Total	2	1	2	.333	12	3	1	0	0	37^1	44	26	2	0	18	6	14.9	5.06	74	.297	.373	1	.125	1	-5	-6	1	-0.2
● **FRANK MORRISSEY**	Morrissey, Michael Joseph "Deacon" b: 5/5/1876, Baltimore, Md. d: 2/22/39, Baltimore, Md. TR, 5'4", 140 lbs. Deb: 7/13/01																											
1901	Bos-A	0	0	—	1	0	0	0	0	4^1	5	1	0	2	2	1	18.7	2.08	170	.278	.409	0	.000	-1	1	1	0	0.0
1902	Chi-N	1	3	.250	5	5	5	0	0	40	40	16	0	2	8	13	11.2	2.25	120	.260	.305	2	.091	-1	2	2	0	0.1
Total	2	1	3	.250	6	5	5	0	0	44^1	45	17	0	4	10	14	12.0	2.23	125	.262	.317	2	.080	-1	3	3	1	0.1

YEAR	TM/L	W	L	PCT	G	GS	CG	SH	SV	IP	H	R	HR	HB	BB	SO	RAT	ERA	ERA+	OAV	OOB	BH	AVG	PB	PR	PR+	PD	TPI
● CARL MORTON Morton, Carl Wendle b: 1/18/44, Kansas City, Mo. d: 4/12/83, Tulsa, Okla. BR/TR, 6', 200 lbs. Deb: 4/11/69																												
1969	Mon-N	0	3	.000	8	5	0	0	0	29^{1}	29	15	2	2	18	16	15.0	4.60	80	.264	.377	0	.000	-0	-3	-3	1	-0.3
1970	Mon-N	18	11	.621	43	37	10	4	0	284^{2}	281	123	27	4	125	154	13.0	3.60	114	.262	.341	15	.161	2	14	16	1	1.8
1971	Mon-N	10	18	.357	36	35	9	0	1	213^{2}	252	129	22	4	83	84	14.3	4.80	74	.295	.360	14	.182	2	-32	-30	2	-3.1
1972	Mon-N	7	13	.350	27	27	3	1	0	172	170	84	16	3	53	51	11.8	3.92	91	.258	.316	7	.135	1	-9	-7	1	-0.6
1973	Atl-N	15	10	.600	38	37	10	4	0	256^{1}	254	114	18	4	70	112	11.5	3.41	116	.259	.311	17	.181	4	7	14	0	1.7
1974	Atl-N	16	12	.571	38	38	7	1	0	274^{2}	293	110	10	2	89	113	12.6	3.15	120	.277	.334	10	.112	-4	15	19	-1	1.4
1975	Atl-N	17	16	.515	39	39	11	2	0	277^{2}	302	122	19	3	82	78	12.5	3.50	108	.278	.330	15	.160	-1	4	8	0	0.9
1976	Atl-N	4	9	.308	26	24	1	1	0	140^{1}	172	79	6	5	45	42	14.2	4.17	91	.306	.362	8	.178	-0	-10	-5	2	-0.3
Total	8	87	92	.486	255	242	51	13	1	1648^{2}	1753	776	120	27	565	650	12.8	3.73	102	.275	.336	86	.156	3	-14	14	6	1.5
● CHARLIE MORTON Morton, Charles Hazen b: 10/12/1854, Kingsville, Ohio d: 12/9/21, Massillon, Ohio BR/TR, 150 lbs. Deb: 5/2/1882 MU♦																												
1884	Tol-a	0	1	.000	3	1	1	0	0	23^{1}	18	14	0	1	5	7	9.3	3.09	111	.209	.261	18	.162	-0	0	1	-1	0.0
● GUY MORTON Morton, Guy Sr. "The Alabama Blossom" b: 6/1/1893, Vernon, Ala. d: 10/18/34, Sheffield, Ala. BR/TR, 6'1", 175 lbs. Deb: 6/20/14 F																												
1914	Cle-A	1	13	.071	25	13	5	0	1	128	116	62	1	3	55	80	12.2	3.02	95	.257	.341	1	.029	-4	-4	-2	-1	-0.8
1915	Cle-A	16	15	.516	34	27	15	6	1	240	189	75	5	2	60	134	9.4	2.14	143	.216	.268	12	.146	-4	21	23	-0	2.5
1916	Cle-A	12	6	.667	27	18	9	0	0	149^{2}	139	63	1	3	42	88	11.1	2.89	104	.246	.302	12	.211	-1	-1	2	-1	0.0
1917	Cle-A	10	10	.500	35	18	6	1	2	161	158	74	3	2	59	62	12.2	2.74	103	.266	.335	4	.085	-4	-1	2	-2	-0.5
1918	Cle-A	14	8	.636	30	28	13	1	0	214^{2}	189	87	1	3	77	123	11.3	2.64	114	.240	.310	12	.156	-1	3	8	-1	0.6
1919	Cle-A	9	9	.500	26	20	9	3	0	147^{1}	128	65	3	0	47	64	10.7	2.81	119	.233	.293	9	.161	-2	7	8	-1	0.7
1920	Cle-A	8	6	.571	29	17	6	1	1	137	140	80	2	1	57	72	13.0	4.47	85	.270	.344	10	.217	-1	-10	-10	-2	-1.3
1921	Cle-A	8	3	.727	30	7	3	2	0	107^{2}	98	45	1	2	32	45	11.0	2.76	155	.244	.303	6	.171	-2	18	18	-2	1.2
1922	Cle-A	14	9	.609	38	23	13	3	0	202^{2}	218	117	7	4	85	102	13.6	4.00	100	.277	.351	13	.191	-2	1	0	3	0.2
1923	Cle-A	6	6	.500	33	14	3	2	1	129^{1}	133	67	3	2	56	54	13.3	4.24	93	.276	.354	7	.159	-2	-4	-4	-1	-0.6
1924	Cle-A	0	1	.000	10	0	0	0	0	12^{1}	12	12	0	0	13	6	18.2	6.57	65	.250	.410	0	.000	-0	-3	-3	-0	-0.3
Total	11	98	86	.533	317	185	82	19	6	1629^{2}	1520	747	27	22	583	830	11.7	3.13	108	.251	.319	86	.157	-24	27	46	-7	1.7
● KEVIN MORTON Morton, Kevin Joseph b: 8/3/68, Norwalk, Conn. BR/TL, 6'2", 185 lbs. Deb: 7/5/91																												
1991	Bos-A	6	5	.545	16	15	1	0	0	86^{1}	93	49	9	1	40	45	14.0	4.59	94	.284	.363	0	—	0	-5	-3	1	-0.2
● SPARROW MORTON Morton, William P. TL, Deb: 7/15/1884																												
1884	Phi-N	0	2	.000	2	2	2	0	0	17	16	20	0		11	5	14.3	5.29	56	.222	.325	3	.375	1	-4	-4	-0	-0.3
● EARL MOSELEY Moseley, Earl Victor "Vic" b: 9/7/1884, Middleburg, Ohio d: 7/1/63, Alliance, Ohio BR/TR, 5'9.5", 168 lbs. Deb: 6/17/13																												
1913	Bos-A	8	5	.615	24	15	7	3	0	120^{2}	105	56	1	0	49	62	11.5	3.13	94	.245	.322	3	.081	-2	-3	-3	1	-0.4
1914	Ind-F	19	18	.514	43	38	29	4	1	316^{2}	303	149	5	4	123	205	12.2	3.47	90	.258	.330	12	.110	-8	-20	-11	-0	-2.1
1915	New-F	15	15	.500	38	32	22	5	1	268	222	87	2	2	99	142	10.8	**1.91**	134	.229	.302	13	.148	-4	**24**	21	-4	1.4
1916	Cin-N	7	10	.412	31	15	7	0	1	150^{1}	145	75	5	0	69	60	12.8	3.89	67	.257	.338	4	.087	-2	-21	-22	-2	-2.9
Total	4	49	48	.505	136	100	65	12	3	855^{2}	775	367	13	6	340	469	11.8	3.01	94	.247	.322	32	.114	-17	-20	-17	-4	-4.0
● WALTER MOSER Moser, Walter Fredrick b: 2/27/1881, Concord, N.C. d: 12/10/46, Philadelphia, Pa. BR/TR, 5'9", 170 lbs. Deb: 9/3/06																												
1906	Phi-N	0	4	.000	6	4	4	0	0	42^{2}	49	35	0	1	15	17	13.7	3.59	73	.295	.357	0	.000	-2	-5	-5	-1	-0.7
1911	Bos-A	0	1	.000	6	3	1	0	0	24^{2}	37	28	0	1	11	11	17.9	4.01	82	.366	.434	0	.000	-1	-2	-2	0	-0.2
	StL-A	0	2	.000	2	2	0	0	0	3^{1}	11	12	0	0	4	2	40.5	21.60	16	.478	.556	1	1.000	0	-7	-7	0	-1.0
	Yr	0	3	.000	8	5	1	0	0	28	48	40	0	1	15	13	20.6	6.11	54	.387	.457	1	.125	-1	-9	-9	0	-1.2
Total	2	0	7	.000	14	9	5	0	0	70^{2}	97	75	0	2	30	30	16.4	4.58	63	.334	.401	1	.045	-2	-13	-13	-1	-1.9
● JOHN MOSES Moses, John William b: 8/9/57, Los Angeles, Cal. BB/TL, 5'10", 170 lbs. Deb: 8/23/82 C♦																												
1989	Min-A	0	0	—	1	0	0	0	0	1	0	0	0	0	1	0	9.0	0.00	—	.000	.333	68	.281	0	0	0	0	0.0
1990	Min-A	0	0	—	2	0	0	0	0	2	5	3	0	0	2	0	31.5	13.50	31	.455	.538	38	.221	0	-2	-2	-0	-0.1
Total	2	0	0	—	3	0	0	0	0	3	5	3	0	0	3	0	24.0	9.00	46	.385	.500	438	.254	0	-2	-2	-0	-0.1
● PAUL MOSKAU Moskau, Paul Richard b: 12/20/53, St.Joseph, Mo. BR/TR, 6'2", 210 lbs. Deb: 6/21/77																												
1977	Cin-N	6	6	.500	20	19	2	2	0	108	116	51	10	1	40	71	13.1	4.00	98	.278	.342	7	.184	2	-1	-1	1	0.2
1978	Cin-N	6	4	.600	26	25	2	1	1	145	139	65	17	3	57	88	12.4	3.97	89	.255	.329	10	.204	4	-6	-7	-2	-0.3
1979	Cin-N	5	4	.556	21	15	1	0	0	106^{1}	107	53	9	0	51	58	13.4	3.89	96	.263	.345	3	.081	-2	-2	-2	1	-0.3
1980	Cin-N	9	7	.563	33	19	2	1	2	152^{2}	147	69	13	1	41	94	11.1	4.01	89	.257	.308	7	.159	-0	-7	-7	0	-0.8
1981	Cin-N	2	1	.667	27	1	0	0	2	54^{2}	54	31	4	1	32	32	14.3	4.94	72	.258	.360	0	.000	-0	-9	-8	1	-0.5
1982	Pit-N	1	3	.250	13	5	0	0	0	35	43	21	7	0	8	15	13.1	4.37	85	.303	.340	1	.091	-1	-3	-2	-0	-0.4
1983	Chi-N	3	2	.600	8	8	0	0	0	32	44	25	7	0	14	16	16.3	6.75	56	.331	.395	2	.182	0	-11	-10	-0	-1.3
Total	7	32	27	.542	148	92	7	4	5	633^{2}	650	315	67	6	243	374	12.8	4.22	87	.268	.336	30	.153	2	-39	-38	-0	-3.4
● JIM MOSOLF Mosolf, James Frederick b: 8/21/05, Puyallup, Wash. d: 12/28/79, Dallas, Ore. BL/TR, 5'10", 186 lbs. Deb: 9/9/29 ♦																												
1930	Pit-N	0	0	—	1	0	0	0	0	0^{1}	1	1	0	0	0	1	27.0	27.00	18	.500	.500	17	.333	0	-1	-1	0	0.0
● MAL MOSS Moss, Charles Malcolm b: 4/18/05, Sullivan, Ind. d: 2/5/83, Savannah, Ga. BR/TL, 6', 175 lbs. Deb: 4/29/30																												
1930	Chi-N	0	0	—	12	1	0	0	1	18^{2}	18	13	0	0	14	4	15.4	6.27	78	.254	.376	3	.273	0	-3	-3	0	-0.1
● RAY MOSS Moss, Raymond Earl b: 12/5/01, Chattanooga, Tenn. d: 8/9/98, Chattanooga, Tenn. BR/TR, 6'1", 185 lbs. Deb: 4/17/26																												
1926	Bro-N	0	0	—	1	0	0	0	0	1	3	1	0	0	0	0	27.0	9.00	42	.600	.600	0	.000	0	-1	-1	-0	0.0
1927	Bro-N	1	0	1.000	1	1	0	0	0	8^{1}	11	3	0	0	1	1	13.0	3.24	122	.333	.353	1	.333	1	1	1	-0	0.1
1928	Bro-N	0	3	.000	22	5	1	1	1	60^{1}	62	43	5	0	35	5	14.5	4.92	81	.279	.377	8	.320	2	-6	-6	-0	-0.1
1929	Bro-N	11	6	.647	39	20	7	2	0	182	214	115	9	7	81	59	14.9	5.04	92	.296	.373	5	.076	-5	-7	-9	-2	-1.3
1930	Bro-N	9	6	.600	36	11	5	0	1	118^{1}	127	78	13	4	55	30	14.1	5.10	96	.270	.352	6	.154	-2	-2	-2	-2	-0.6
1931	Bro-N	0	0	—	1	0	0	0	0	1	1	0	0	0	1	0	18.0	0.00	—	.333	.500	0	—	0	0	0	0	0.0
	Bos-N	1	3	.250	12	5	0	0	0	45	56	32	2	0	16	14	14.4	4.60	82	.306	.362	2	.133	-1	-4	-4	0	-0.4
	Yr	1	3	.250	13	5	0	0	0	46	57	32	2	0	17	14	14.5	4.50	84	.306	.365	2	.133	-1	-3	-4	0	-0.4
Total	6	22	18	.550	112	42	13	3	2	416	474	272	29	11	189	109	14.6	4.95	91	.289	.367	22	.148	-5	-18	-21	-4	-2.3
● DON MOSSI Mossi, Donald Louis "The Sphinx" b: 1/11/29, St.Helena, Cal. BL/TL, 6'1", 195 lbs. Deb: 4/17/54																												
1954	*Cle-A	6	1	.857	40	5	2	0	7	93	56	22	5	1	39	55	9.3	1.94	190	.176	.268	3	.158	0	**18**	**18**	-1	1.6
1955	Cle-A	4	3	.571	57	1	0	0	9	81^{2}	81	28	4	1	18	69	11.0	2.42	164	.253	.295	1	.111	0	14	14	2	1.7
1956	Cle-A	6	5	.545	48	3	0	0	11	87^{2}	79	38	6	1	33	59	11.6	3.59	117	.240	.311	3	.150	0	6	6	0	0.8
1957	Cle-A★	11	10	.524	36	22	6	1	2	159	165	82	16	2	57	97	12.7	4.13	90	.265	.329	12	.218	2	-6	-7	-1	-0.8
1958	Cle-A	7	8	.467	43	5	0	0	3	101^{2}	106	49	6	4	30	55	12.4	3.90	94	.269	.327	3	.115	-2	-1	-3	0	-0.5
1959	Det-A	17	9	.654	34	30	15	3	0	228	210	92	20	3	49	125	10.3	3.36	121	.243	.286	13	.169	0	13	17	0	1.9
1960	Det-A	9	8	.529	23	22	9	2	0	158^{1}	158	68	17	1	32	69	10.9	3.47	114	.258	.296	5	.116	-0	7	8	-1	0.8
1961	Det-A	15	7	.682	35	34	12	1	0	240^{1}	237	97	29	0	47	137	10.6	2.96	139	.258	.294	13	.165	1	28	30	0	2.7
1962	Det-A	11	13	.458	35	27	8	1	1	180^{1}	195	92	24	1	36	121	11.6	4.19	97	.270	.305	9	.164	1	-4	-2	-2	-0.3
1963	Det-A	7	7	.500	24	16	3	0	2	122^{2}	110	58	20	4	17	68	9.6	3.74	100	.236	.269	8	.205	2	-2	0	-0	0.2
1964	Chi-A	3	1	.750	34	0	0	0	7	40	37	16	9	1	7	36	10.1	2.93	118	.240	.278	1	.167	-0	3	2	-0	0.3
1965	KC-A	5	8	.385	51	0	0	0	7	55^{1}	59	30	0	0	20	41	12.8	3.74	93	.278	.341	0	.000	-1	-2	-2	-0	-0.4
Total	12	101	80	.558	460	165	55	8	50	1548	1493	672	156	19	385	932	11.0	3.43	114	.252	.299	71	.163	4	74	82	-2	8.0
● EARL MOSSOR Mossor, Earl Dalton b: 7/21/25, Forbus, Tenn. d: 12/29/88, Batavia, Ohio BL/TR, 6'1", 175 lbs. Deb: 4/30/51																												
1951	Bro-N	0	0	—	3	0	0	0	0	1^{2}	2	6	1	0	7	1	48.6	32.40	12	.333	.692	1	1.000	0	-5	-5	-0	-0.2
● DANNY MOTA Mota, Daniel (Avila) b: 10/9/75, Seybol, D.R. BR/TR, 6', 180 lbs. Deb: 9/15/2000																												
2000	Min-A	0	0	—	4	0	0	0	0	5^{1}	10	5	1	0	1	3	18.6	8.44	62	.370	.393	0	—	0	-2	-2	-0	-0.1

YEAR	TM/L	W	L	PCT	G	GS	CG	SH	SV	IP	H	R	HR	HB	BB	SO	RAT	ERA	ERA+	OAV	OOB	BH	AVG	PB	PR	PR+	PD	TPI
● **GUILLERMO MOTA**	Mota, Guillermo b: 7/25/73, San Pedro De Macoris, D.R. BR/TR, 6'6", 200 lbs. Deb: 5/2/99																											
1999	Mon-N	2	4	.333	51	0	0	0	0	55^1	54	24	5	2	25	27	13.2	2.93	153	.257	.342	1	1.000	1	10	10	1	1.1
2000	Mon-N	1	1	.500	29	0	0	0	0	30	27	21	3	2	12	24	12.3	6.00	79	.245	.331	0	.000	-0	-5	-4	-0	-0.3
Total	2	3	5	.375	80	0	0	0	0	85^1	81	45	8	4	37	51	12.9	4.01	114	.253	.338	1	.500	1	6	5	1	0.8
● **GLEN MOULDER**	Moulder, Glen Hubert b: 9/28/17, Cleveland, Okla. d: 11/27/94, Decatur, Ga. BR/TR, 6', 180 lbs. Deb: 4/28/46																											
1946	Bro-N	0	0	—	1	0	0	0	0	2	2	1	1	0	1	1	13.5	4.50	75	.286	.375	0	—	0	-0	-0	-0	0.0
1947	StL-A	4	2	.667	32	2	0	0	2	73	78	37	4	0	43	23	14.9	3.82	101	.283	.379	4	.235	-0	-1	0	1	0.1
1948	Chi-A	3	6	.333	33	9	0	0	2	85^2	108	67	8	1	54	26	17.1	6.41	66	.316	.411	6	.300	2	-20	-21	-0	-1.8
Total	3	7	8	.467	66	11	0	0	4	160^2	188	105	13	1	98	50	16.1	5.21	78	.301	.396	10	.270	1	-21	-20	1	-1.7
● **FRANK MOUNTAIN**	Mountain, Frank Henry b: 5/17/1860, Ft.Edward, N.Y. d: 11/19/39, Schenectady, N.Y. BR/TR, 5'11", 185 lbs. Deb: 7/19/1880 ♦																											
1880	Tro-N	1	1	.500	2	2	2	0	0	17	23	17	0		6	2	15.4	5.29	48	.307	.358	2	.222	-0	-6	-5	0	-0.5
1881	Det-N	3	4	.429	7	7	7	0	0	60	80	63	2		18	13	14.7	5.25	56	.292	.336	4	.160	-0	-17	-15	-1	-1.4
1882	Wor-N	0	5	.000	5	5	5	0	0	42	47	30	0		11	5	12.4	3.00	104	.255	.297	1	.063	-2	-0	1	-1	-0.2
	Phi-a	2	6	.250	8	8	8	0	0	69	72	49	1		11	15	10.8	3.91	76	.251	.279	12	.333	2	-9	-6	1	-0.3
	Wor-N	2	11	.154	13	13	11	0	0	102	138	93	4		24	24	14.3	3.97	78	.299	.334	19	.271	2	-12	-9	-1	-0.8
1883	Col-a	26	33	.441	59	59	57	4	0	503	546	345	8		123	159	12.0	3.60	86	.259	.300	60	.217	7	-16	-31	1	-2.1
1884	Col-a	23	17	.575	42	41	40	5	**1**	360^2	289	163	7	11	78	156	9.4	2.45	124	.209	.257	50	.238	9	32	25	4	3.7
1885	Pit-a	1	4	.200	5	5	5	0	0	46	56	31	1	2	24	7	16.0	4.30	75	.320	.408	2	.100	-1	-5	-6	0	-0.5
1886	Pit-a	0	2	.000	2	2	2	0	0	16	22	21	0	5	14	2	23.1	7.88	43	.319	.466	8	.145	0	-8	-8	0	-0.7
Total	7	58	83	.411	143	142	137	9	1	1215^2	1273	812	23	18	309	383	11.8	3.47	88	.254	.299	158	.220	16	-41	-56	4	-2.8
● **BILL MOUNTJOY**	Mountjoy, William Henry "Medicine Bill" b: 12/11/1858, London, Ontario, Canada d: 5/19/1894, London, Ont., Can. BL/TR, 5'6", 150 lbs. Deb: 9/29/1883																											
1883	Cin-a	0	1	.000	1	1	1	0	0	8	9	4	0		2	3	12.4	2.25	144	.265	.306	0	.000	-1	1	1	-0	0.0
1884	Cin-a	19	12	.613	33	33	32	3	0	289	274	148	5	16	43	96	10.4	2.93	114	.238	.275	18	.151	-3	10	13	-0	0.8
1885	Cin-a	10	7	.588	17	17	17	1	0	153^2	149	89	5	7	52	50	12.2	3.16	103	.247	.314	10	.167	0	1	2	-1	0.1
	Bal-a	2	4	.333	6	6	6	1	0	53	72	47	1	4	13	15	15.1	5.43	60	.316	.363	1	.056	-0	-13	-13	1	-1.0
	Yr	12	11	.522	23	23	23	2	0	206^2	221	136	6	11	65	65	12.9	3.75	87	.266	.327	11	.141	0	-11	-11	-0	-0.9
Total	3	31	24	.564	57	57	56	5	0	503^2	504	288	11	27	110	164	11.5	3.25	102	.250	.297	29	.145	-4	-0	3	-1	-0.1
● **ED MOYER**	Moyer, Charles Edward b: 8/15/1885, Andover, Ohio d: 11/18/62, Jacksonville, Fla. Deb: 7/20/10																											
1910	Was-A	0	3	.000	6	3	2	0	0	25	22	15	1	3	13	3	13.7	3.24	77	.253	.369	1	.125	-1	-2	-2	1	-0.2
● **JAMIE MOYER**	Moyer, Jamie b: 11/18/62, Sellersville, Pa. BL/TL, 6', 170 lbs. Deb: 6/16/86																											
1986	Chi-N	7	4	.636	16	16	1	1	0	87^1	107	52	10	3	42	45	15.7	5.05	80	.311	.391	2	.091	-0	-13	-9	1	-0.9
1987	Chi-N	12	15	.444	35	33	1	0	0	201	210	127	28	5	97	147	14.0	5.10	84	.271	.355	14	.230	3	-23	-18	2	-1.6
1988	Chi-N	9	15	.375	34	30	3	1	0	202	212	84	20	4	55	121	12.1	3.48	104	.272	.324	5	.083	-2	-0	3	3	0.4
1989	Tex-A	4	9	.308	15	15	1	0	0	76	84	51	10	2	33	44	14.1	4.86	82	.283	.358	0	—	0	-8	-7	1	-1.0
1990	Tex-A	2	6	.250	33	10	1	0	0	102^1	115	59	6	4	39	58	13.9	4.66	84	.290	.360	0	—	0	-8	-8	0	-0.6
1991	StL-N	0	5	.000	8	7	0	0	0	31^1	38	21	5	1	16	20	15.8	5.74	65	.319	.404	0	.000	-1	-7	-7	-0	-1.0
1993	Bal-A	12	9	.571	25	25	3	1	0	152	154	63	11	6	38	90	11.7	3.43	131	.265	.316	0	—	0	15	17	1	2.3
1994	Bal-A	5	7	.417	23	23	0	0	0	149	158	81	23	2	38	87	12.0	4.77	105	.271	.317	0	—	0	1	4	-0	0.2
1995	Bal-A	8	6	.571	27	18	0	0	0	115^2	117	70	18	3	30	65	11.7	5.21	91	.265	.316	0	—	0	-6	-6	1	-0.5
1996	Bos-A	7	1	.875	23	10	0	0	0	90	111	50	14	1	27	50	13.9	4.50	113	.300	.349	0	—	0	5	6	0	0.5
	Sea-A	6	2	.750	11	11	0	0	0	70^2	66	36	9	1	19	29	11.0	3.31	150	.243	.295	0	—	0	13	13	-1	1.2
	Yr	13	3	.813	34	21	0	0	0	160^2	177	86	23	2	46	79	12.6	3.98	126	.276	.326	0	—	0	18	19	-0	1.7
1997	*Sea-A	17	5	.773	30	30	2	0	0	188^2	187	82	21	7	43	113	11.3	3.86	117	.256	.304	1	.333	0	15	14	2	1.6
1998	Sea-A	15	9	.625	34	34	4	3	0	234^1	234	99	23	10	42	158	11.0	3.53	131	.256	.296	0	.000	-0	29	29	0	2.6
1999	Sea-A	14	8	.636	32	32	4	0	0	228	235	108	23	9	48	137	11.5	3.87	123	.267	.312	1	.500	1	25	23	4	2.4
2000	Sea-A	13	10	.565	26	26	0	0	0	154	173	103	22	3	53	98	13.4	5.49	87	.281	.341	0	.000	-0	-10	-12	2	-1.3
Total	14	131	111	.541	372	320	20	6	0	2082^1	2201	1086	243	61	620	1262	12.5	4.30	104	.272	.328	23	.144	1	28	41	17	4.3
● **RON MROZINSKI**	Mrozinski, Ronald Frank b: 9/16/30, White Haven, Pa. BR/TL, 5'11", 160 lbs. Deb: 6/20/54																											
1954	Phi-N	1	1	.500	15	4	1	0	0	48	49	26	10	0	25	26	13.9	4.50	90	.261	.347	1	.083	-1	-2	-2	-1	-0.3
1955	Phi-N	0	2	.000	22	1	0	0	1	34^1	38	26	2	4	19	18	16.0	6.55	61	.299	.407	0	.000	-1	-10	-10	-0	-0.7
Total	2	1	3	.250	37	5	1	0	1	82^1	87	52	12	4	44	44	14.8	5.36	75	.276	.372	1	.063	-2	-12	-12	-1	-1.0
● **PHIL MUDROCK**	Mudrock, Philip Ray b: 6/12/37, Louisville, Colo. BR/TR, 6'1", 190 lbs. Deb: 4/19/63																											
1963	Chi-N	0	0	—	1	0	0	0	0	1	2	1	0	0	0	0	18.0	9.00	39	.400	.400	0	—	0	-1	-1	-0	0.0
● **GORDIE MUELLER**	Mueller, Joseph Gordon b: 12/10/22, Baltimore, Md. BR/TR, 6'4", 200 lbs. Deb: 4/19/50																											
1950	Bos-A	0	0	—	8	0	0	0	0	7	11	8	1	0	13	1	30.9	10.29	48	.344	.533	0	.000	-0	-4	-4	0	-0.2
● **LES MUELLER**	Mueller, Leslie Clyde b: 3/4/19, Belleville, Ill. BR/TR, 6'3", 190 lbs. Deb: 8/15/41																											
1941	Det-A	0	0	—	4	0	0	0	0	13	9	9	1	0	10	8	13.2	4.85	94	.205	.352	0	.000	-0	-1	-0	0	0.0
1945	*Det-A	6	8	.429	26	18	6	2	1	134^2	117	63	8	2	58	42	11.8	3.68	96	.234	.316	8	.182	0	-5	-2	-2	-0.4
Total	2	6	8	.429	30	18	6	2	1	147^2	126	72	9	2	68	50	11.9	3.78	95	.231	.319	8	.170	0	-6	-3	-2	-0.4
● **WILLIE MUELLER**	Mueller, Willard Lawrence b: 8/30/56, West Bend, Wis. BR/TR, 6'4", 220 lbs. Deb: 8/12/78																											
1978	Mil-A	1	0	1.000	5	0	0	0	0	12^2	16	11	1	0	6	6	15.6	6.39	59	.291	.361	0	—	0	-4	-4	0	-0.3
1981	Mil-A	0	0	—	1	0	0	0	0	2	4	1	0	0	0	1	18.0	4.50	76	.400	.400	0	—	0	-0	-0	0	0.0
Total	2	1	0	1.000	6	0	0	0	0	14^2	20	12	1	0	6	7	16.0	6.14	61	.308	.366	0	—	0	-4	-4	0	-0.3
● **BILLY MUFFETT**	Muffett, Billy Arnold "Muff" b: 9/21/30, Hammond, Ind. BR/TR, 6'1", 198 lbs. Deb: 8/3/57 C																											
1957	StL-N	3	2	.600	23	0	0	0	8	44	35	11	1	0	13	21	9.8	2.25	176	.222	.281	0	.000	-1	8	8	-1	1.0
1958	StL-N	4	6	.400	35	6	1	0	5	84	107	52	11	5	42	41	16.5	4.93	84	.316	.399	4	.200	0	-9	-7	-1	-0.9
1959	SF-N	0	0	—	5	0	0	0	0	6^2	11	6	2	0	3	3	18.9	5.40	71	.407	.467	0	—	0	-1	-1	-0	-0.1
1960	Bos-A	6	4	.600	23	14	4	1	0	125	116	53	6	5	36	75	11.3	3.24	125	.242	.301	11	.268	2	9	11	-0	1.0
1961	Bos-A	3	11	.214	38	11	2	0	2	112^2	130	87	18	2	36	47	13.4	5.67	73	.291	.346	5	.217	2	-21	-18	-0	-1.9
1962	Bos-A	0	0	—	1	1	0	0	0	4	8	4	0	0	2	1	22.5	9.00	46	.471	.526	0	.000	-0	-2	-2	-0	-0.1
Total	6	16	23	.410	125	32	7	1	15	376^1	407	213	38	12	132	188	13.2	4.33	94	.277	.342	20	.217	3	-16	-10	-2	-1.0
● **JOE MUICH**	Muich, Ignatius Andrew b: 11/23/03, St.Louis, Mo. d: 7/2/93, St.Louis, Mo. BR/TR, 6'2", 175 lbs. Deb: 9/4/24																											
1924	Bos-N	0	0	—	3	0	0	0	0	9	19	12	1	0	5	1	24.0	11.00	35	.432	.490	0	.000	-1	-7	-7	-0	-0.4
● **JOE MUIR**	Muir, Joseph Allen b: 11/26/22, Oriole, Md. d: 6/25/80, Baltimore, Md. BL/TL, 6'1", 172 lbs. Deb: 4/21/51																											
1951	Pit-N	0	2	.000	9	1	0	0	0	16^1	11	6	2	0	7	5	9.9	2.76	153	.180	.265	0	.000	-0	2	3	1	0.4
1952	Pit-N	2	3	.400	12	5	1	0	0	35^2	42	28	3	0	18	17	15.1	6.31	63	.288	.366	1	.111	-0	-10	-9	-0	-1.1
Total	2	2	5	.286	21	6	1	0	0	52	53	34	5	0	25	22	13.5	5.19	78	.256	.336	1	.100	-0	-8	-6	1	-0.7
● **HUGH MULCAHY**	Mulcahy, Hugh Noyes "Losing Pitcher" b: 9/9/13, Brighton, Mass. BR/TR, 6'2", 190 lbs. Deb: 7/24/35 C																											
1935	Phi-N	1	5	.167	18	5	0	0	1	52^2	62	35	2	5	25	11	15.7	4.78	95	.295	.383	0	.000	-2	-4	-1	1	-0.3
1936	Phi-N	1	1	.500	3	2	2	0	0	22^2	20	8	0	2	12	2	13.5	3.18	143	.238	.347	2	.250	0	2	3	0	0.3
1937	Phi-N	8	18	.308	**56**	26	9	1	3	215^2	256	147	17	7	97	54	15.0	5.13	84	.296	.372	11	.151	-3	-29	-17	3	-1.8
1938	Phi-N	10	20	.333	46	34	15	0	1	267^1	294	162	14	6	120	90	14.1	4.61	84	.278	.354	16	.170	-2	-24	-21	1	-2.2
1939	Phi-N	9	16	.360	38	32	14	1	4	225^2	246	144	19	11	93	59	14.0	4.99	80	.282	.359	12	.158	-3	-27	-24	0	-2.6
1940	Phi-N☆	13	22	.371	36	36	21	3	0	280	283	141	12	3	91	82	12.1	3.60	108	.261	.320	19	.202	1	8	9	3	1.5
1945	Phi-N	1	3	.250	5	4	1	0	0	28^1	33	17	1	0	9	2	13.3	3.81	101	.295	.347	0	.000	-1	-0	0	1	0.0
1946	Phi-N	2	4	.333	16	5	1	0	0	62^2	69	34	3	5	33	12	15.4	4.45	77	.295	.393	3	.188	1	-7	-7	1	-0.4

YEAR TM/L	W	L	PCT	G	GS	CG	SH	SV	IP	H	R	HR	HB	BB	SO	RAT	ERA	ERA+	OAV	OOB	BH	AVG	PB	PR	PR+	PD	TPI
1947 Pit-N	0	0	—	2	1	0	0	0	6^2	8	7	1	0	7	2	20.3	4.05	104	.333	.484	1	.333	0	0	0	1	0.1
Total 9	45	89	.336	220	145	63	5	9	1161^2	1271	695	69	39	487	314	13.9	4.49	89	.280	.355	64	.165	-9	-82	-59	11	-5.4
● **MARK MULDER** Mulder, Mark Alan b: 8/5/77, South Holland, Ill. BL/TL, 6'6", 200 lbs. Deb: 4/18/2000																											
2000 Oak-A	9	10	.474	27	27	0	0	0	154	191	106	22	4	69	88	15.4	5.44	88	.308	.380	0	.000	-0	-9	-12	0	-1.2
● **TERRY MULHOLLAND** Mulholland, Terence John b: 3/9/63, Uniontown, Pa. BR/TL, 6'3", 206 lbs. Deb: 6/8/86																											
1986 SF-N	1	7	.125	15	10	0	0	0	54^2	51	33	3	1	35	27	14.3	4.94	71	.251	.364	1	.053	-1	-7	-9	-1	-1.4
1988 SF-N	2	1	.667	9	6	2	1	0	46	50	20	3	1	7	18	11.3	3.72	88	.281	.312	0	.000	-1	-1	-2	0	-0.2
1989 SF-N	0	0	—	5	1	0	0	0	11	15	5	0	0	4	6	15.5	4.09	83	.319	.373	0	.000	-0	-1	-1	0	0.0
Phi-N	4	7	.364	20	17	2	1	0	104^1	122	61	8	4	32	60	13.6	5.00	71	.292	.348	2	.059	-2	-17	-17	1	-1.8
Yr	4	7	.364	25	18	2	1	0	115^1	137	66	8	4	36	66	13.8	4.92	72	.295	.350	2	.056	-2	-18	-18	1	-1.8
1990 Phi-N	9	10	.474	33	26	6	1	0	180^2	172	78	15	2	42	75	10.8	3.34	115	.252	.297	6	.097	-2	9	10	-3	0.4
1991 Phi-N	16	13	.552	34	34	8	3	0	232	231	100	15	3	49	142	11.0	3.61	102	.260	.301	7	.087	-4	2	2	-2	-0.4
1992 Phi-N	13	11	.542	32	32	**12**	2	0	229	227	101	14	3	46	125	10.8	3.81	92	.261	.300	8	.096	-2	-8	-8	1	-0.9
1993 *Phi-N★	12	9	.571	29	28	7	2	0	191	177	80	20	3	40	116	10.4	3.25	122	.241	.283	4	.065	-4	17	16	-1	1.0
1994 NY-A	6	7	.462	24	19	2	0	0	120^2	150	94	24	3	37	72	14.2	6.49	71	.303	.355	0	—	0	-23	-27	-1	-2.4
1995 SF-N	5	13	.278	29	24	2	0	0	149	190	112	25	4	38	65	14.0	5.80	71	.313	.357	5	.102	-0	-27	-29	-1	-3.0
1996 Phi-N	8	7	.533	21	21	3	0	0	133^1	157	74	17	3	21	52	12.2	4.66	93	.293	.323	8	.178	1	-6	-5	-2	-0.6
Sea-A	5	4	.556	12	12	0	0	0	69^1	75	38	5	2	28	34	13.6	4.67	106	.286	.360	0	—	0	3	2	-1	0.2
1997 Chi-N	6	12	.333	25	25	1	0	0	157	162	79	20	9	45	74	12.4	4.07	106	.271	.331	8	.163	-0	2	4	2	0.6
SF-N	0	1	.000	15	2	0	0	0	29^2	28	21	4	2	6	25	10.9	5.16	79	.248	.298	1	.167	0	-3	-4	0	-0.1
Yr	6	13	.316	40	27	1	0	0	186^2	190	100	24	11	51	99	12.2	4.24	101	.267	.326	9	.164	0	-1	1	2	0.5
1998 *Chi-N	6	5	.545	70	6	0	0	3	112	100	49	7	4	39	72	11.5	2.89	152	.235	.306	5	.294	2	17	18	-2	1.7
1999 Chi-N	6	6	.500	26	16	0	0	0	110	137	71	16	1	32	44	13.9	5.15	88	.309	.357	3	.094	-2	-7	-8	-0	-0.9
*Atl-N	4	2	.667	16	8	0	0	1	60^1	64	24	5	0	13	39	11.5	2.98	151	.274	.312	2	.125	-0	11	10	1	1.0
Yr	10	8	.556	42	24	0	0	1	170^1	201	95	21	1	45	83	13.1	4.39	103	.297	.342	5	.104	-2	3	2	0	0.1
2000 *Atl-N	9	9	.500	54	20	1	0	1	156^2	198	96	24	4	41	78	14.0	5.11	89	.308	.354	9	.250	2	-8	-10	-2	-1.0
Total 14	112	124	.475	469	307	46	10	5	2146^2	2306	1136	225	49	555	1124	12.2	4.28	95	.275	.324	69	.114	-14	-48	-55	-9	-7.8
● **TONY MULLANE** Mullane, Anthony John "Count" or "The Apollo Of The Box" b: 1/20/1859, Cork, Ireland d: 4/25/44, Chicago, Ill. BB/TR (BL 1882, TB 1882 (part1893 (PART)), 5'10.5", 165 lbs. Deb: 8/27/1881 ◆																											
1881 Det-N	1	4	.200	5	5	5	0	0	44	55	42	2		17	7	14.7	4.91	59	.302	.362	5	.263	-0	-10	-9	0	-0.8
1882 Lou-a	30	24	.556	**55**	55	51	5	0	460^1	418	212	4		78	**170**	9.7	1.88	132	.226	.257	78	.257	11	41	33	11	5.4
1883 StL-a	35	15	**.700**	53	49	49	3	**1**	460^2	372	222	3		74	191	8.7	2.19	**159**	.207	.238	69	.225	1	57	63	1	5.9
1884 Tol-a	36	26	.581	67	65	64	**7**	0	567	481	276	5	32	89	325	9.6	2.52	135	.214	.255	97	.276	15	46	53	10	7.4
1886 Cin-a	33	27	.550	63	56	55	1	0	529^2	501	315	11	18	166	250	11.6	3.70	95	.242	.303	73	.225	2	-15	-10	2	-0.6
1887 Cin-a	31	17	.646	48	48	47	**6**	0	416^1	535	234	11	32	121	97	12.3	3.24	134	.309	.322	60	.279	2	49	50	-1	4.5
1888 Cin-a	26	16	.619	44	42	41	4	**1**	380^1	341	194	9	29	75	186	10.5	2.84	112	.231	.282	44	.251	5	9	14	-0	1.7
1889 Cin-a	11	9	.550	33	24	17	0	**5**	220	218	133	4	13	89	112	13.1	2.99	131	.251	.329	58	.296	9	21	22	-1	2.2
1890 Cin-N	12	10	.545	25	21	21	0	1	209	175	101	7	8	96	91	12.0	2.24	159	.220	.311	79	.276	7	31	31	0	3.4
1891 Cin-N	23	26	.469	51	47	42	1	0	426^1	390	250	15	18	187	124	12.6	3.23	104	.234	.318	31	.148	-5	6	7	1	0.3
1892 Cin-N	21	13	.618	37	34	30	3	1	295	222	131	12	12	127	109	11.0	2.59	126	**.201**	.290	20	.169	-1	23	22	6	2.7
1893 Cin-N	6	6	.500	15	13	11	0	0	122^1	130	84	4	9	65	24	15.0	4.41	108	.264	.360	15	.288	3	3	5	0	0.6
Bal-N	12	16	.429	34	26	23	0	1	244^2	277	177	4	7	124	71	15.0	4.45	107	.277	.360	26	.228	-3	6	8	3	0.7
Yr	18	22	.450	49	39	34	0	**2**	367	407	261	8	16	189	95	15.0	4.44	107	.273	.360	41	.247	-0	9	13	3	1.3
1894 Bal-N	6	9	.400	21	15	9	0	4	122^2	155	117	4	9	90	43	18.5	6.31	87	.305	.417	21	.396	5	-13	-11	-1	-0.7
Cle-N	1	2	.333	4	4	3	0	0	33	46	35	3	0	10	3	15.3	7.64	72	.326	.371	1	.077	-1	-8	-8	2	-0.4
Yr	7	11	.389	25	19	12	0	**4**	155^2	201	152	7	7	100	46	17.8	6.59	83	.310	.407	22	.333	4	-22	-19	1	-1.1
Total 13	284	220	.563	555	504	468	30	15	4531^1	4316	2523	98	185	1408	1803	11.5	3.05	118	.241	.298	677	.247	50	245	267	33	32.3
● **SCOTT MULLEN** Mullen, Kenneth Scott b: 1/17/75, San Benito, Tex. BR/TL, 6'2", 190 lbs. Deb: 8/31/2000																											
2000 KC-A	0	0	—	11	0	0	0	0	10^1	10	5	2	0	3	7	11.3	4.35	115	.244	.295	0	—	0	1	1	-0	0.0
● **JOE MULLIGAN** Mulligan, Joseph Ignatius "Big Joe" b: 7/31/13, Weymouth, Mass. d: 6/5/86, W.Roxbury, Mass. BR/TR, 6'4", 210 lbs. Deb: 6/28/34																											
1934 Bos-A	1	0	1.000	14	2	1	0	0	44^2	46	21	1	2	27	13	15.1	3.63	132	.279	.387	0	.000	-1	4	5	0	0.1
● **DICK MULLIGAN** Mulligan, Richard Charles b: 3/18/18, Swoyersville, Pa. d: 12/15/92, Victoria, Tex. BL/TL, 6', 167 lbs. Deb: 9/24/41																											
1941 Was-A	0	1	.000	1	1	1	0	0	9	11	5	0	0	2	2	13.0	5.00	81	.306	.342	0	.000	-0	-1	-1	0	-0.1
1946 Phi-N	2	2	.500	19	5	1	0	1	54^2	61	32	0	4	27	16	15.1	4.77	72	.289	.380	0	.000	-1	-8	-8	0	-0.7
Bos-N	1	0	1.000	4	0	0	0	0	15^1	6	4	1	0	9	4	8.8	2.35	146	.122	.259	0	.000	-1	2	2	-0	0.1
Yr	3	2	.600	23	5	1	0	1	70	67	36	1	4	36	20	13.8	4.24	81	.258	.357	0	.000	-1	-6	-6	-0	-0.6
1947 Bos-N	0	0	—	1	0	0	0	0	2	4	2	0	0	1	1	22.5	9.00	43	.400	.455	0	—	0	-1	-1	-0	-0.1
Total 3	3	3	.500	25	6	2	0	1	81	82	43	1	4	39	23	13.9	4.44	79	.268	.358	0	.000	-1	-8	-8	-0	-0.8
● **GEORGE MULLIN** Mullin, George Joseph "Wabash George" b: 7/4/1880, Toledo, Ohio d: 1/7/44, Wabash, Ind. BR/TR, 5'11", 188 lbs. Deb: 5/4/02 ◆																											
1902 Det-A	13	16	.448	35	30	25	0	0	260	282	155	4	7	95	78	13.3	3.67	99	.277	.343	39	.325	9	-3	-1	2	1.1
1903 Det-A	19	15	.559	41	36	31	6	**2**	320^2	284	128	4	8	106	170	11.2	2.25	130	.237	.303	35	.278	8	26	24	5	4.2
1904 Det-A	17	23	.425	45	44	42	7	0	382^1	345	154	1	10	131	161	11.4	2.40	106	.242	.310	45	.290	11	8	6	8	3.2
1905 Det-A	21	21	.500	44	41	**35**	1	0	**347^2**	303	149	4	8	138	168	11.6	2.51	109	.236	.314	35	.259	6	6	8	7	2.6
1906 Det-A	21	18	.538	40	40	35	2	0	330	315	139	3	15	108	123	11.9	2.78	99	.254	.322	32	.225	3	-3	-1	3	0.7
1907 *Det-A	20	20	.500	46	42	35	5	3	357^1	346	153	1	15	106	146	11.8	2.59	100	.256	.318	34	.217	3	-2	0	4	1.0
1908 *Det-A	17	13	.567	39	30	26	1	0	290^2	301	142	1	7	71	121	11.7	3.10	78	.271	.319	32	.256	8	-23	-22	3	-1.1
1909 *Det-A	**29**	8	**.784**	40	35	29	3	1	303^2	258	96	1	8	78	124	10.2	2.22	113	.234	.289	27	.214	5	9	10	1	2.0
1910 Det-A	21	12	.636	38	32	27	5	0	289	260	125	7	14	102	98	11.7	2.87	92	.254	.330	33	.256	6	-11	-7	1	0.0
1911 Det-A	18	10	.643	30	29	25	2	0	234^1	245	99	7	12	61	87	12.2	3.07	113	.276	.331	28	.286	8	7	10	-2	1.6
1912 Det-A	12	17	.414	30	29	22	2	0	226	214	112	3	9	92	88	12.5	3.54	92	.255	.335	25	.278	9	-6	-7	0	0.2
1913 Det-A	1	6	.143	7	7	4	0	0	52^1	53	28	1	2	18	16	12.6	2.75	106	.268	.335	7	.350	3	1	1	0	0.5
Was-A	3	5	.375	11	9	3	0	0	57^1	69	34	1	5	25	14	15.5	5.02	59	.283	.361	4	.190	0	-13	-13	1	-1.5
Yr	4	11	.267	18	16	7	0	0	109^2	122	62	2	7	43	30	14.1	3.94	75	.276	.350	11	.268	3	-12	-12	1	-1.0
1914 Ind-F	14	10	.583	36	20	11	1	2	203	202	100	4	10	91	74	13.4	2.70	115	.261	.346	24	.312	8	4	9	-4	1.4
1915 New-F	2	2	.500	5	4	3	0	0	32^1	41	22	0	0	16	14	15.9	5.85	44	.318	.393	1	.100	-0	-11	-13	-1	-1.4
Total 14	228	196	.538	487	428	353	35	8	3686^2	3518	1636	42	130	1238	1482	11.9	2.82	101	.255	.322	401	.262	87	-12	7	28	14.5
● **GREG MULLINS** Mullins, Gregory E. b: 12/13/71, Palatka, Fla. BL/TL, 5'10", 160 lbs. Deb: 9/18/98																											
1998 Mil-N	0	0	—	2	0	0	0	0	1	1	0	0	1	0	1	18.0	0.00	—	.250	.400	0	—	0	0	0	0	0.0
● **DOMINIC MULRENAN** Mulrenan, Dominic Joseph b: 12/18/1893, Woburn, Mass. d: 7/27/64, Melrose, Mass. BR/TR, 5'11", 170 lbs. Deb: 4/24/21																											
1921 Chi-A	2	8	.200	12	10	3	0	0	56	84	52	2	2	36	10	19.6	7.23	59	.359	.449	3	.150	-1	-18	-19	0	-2.6
● **FRANK MULRONEY** Mulroney, Francis Joseph b: 4/8/03, Mallard, Iowa d: 11/11/85, Aberdeen, Wash. BR/TR, 6', 170 lbs. Deb: 4/15/30																											
1930 Bos-A	0	1	.000	2	0	0	0	0	3	3	2	0	0	0	2	9.0	3.00	154	.273	.273	0	—	0	1	1	0	0.1
● **BOB MUNCRIEF** Muncrief, Robert Cleveland b: 1/28/16, Madill, Okla. d: 2/6/96, Duncanville, Tex. BR/TR, 6'2", 190 lbs. Deb: 9/30/37																											
1937 StL-A	0	0	—	1	1	0	0	0	2	3	2	1	0	2	0	22.5	4.50	107	.300	.417	0	—	0	0	0	-0	0.0
1939 StL-A	0	0	—	2	0	0	0	0	3	7	5	1	0	3	1	30.0	15.00	32	.500	.588	0	—	0	-3	-3	-0	-0.2
1941 StL-A	13	9	.591	36	24	12	2	1	214^1	221	95	18	5	53	67	11.7	3.65	118	.266	.314	18	.237	2	12	15	-1	1.5
1942 StL-A	6	8	.429	24	18	7	1	0	134^1	149	61	11	0	31	39	12.1	3.89	95	.280	.319	5	.111	-1	-3	-3	-0	-0.4
1943 StL-A	13	12	.520	35	27	12	3	1	205	211	80	13	2	48	80	11.5	2.81	118	.264	.307	10	.152	-2	11	12	-3	0.9
1944 *StL-A★	13	8	.619	33	27	12	3	1	219^1	216	83	11	3	50	88	11.0	3.08	117	.258	.302	18	.231	1	9	12	-1	1.2
1945 StL-A	13	4	.765	27	15	10	1	1	145^2	132	51	8	2	44	54	11.0	2.72	130	.239	.297	3	.067	-4	10	12	-1	0.9
1946 StL-A	3	12	.200	29	14	4	1	0	115^1	149	75	6	0	31	49	14.0	4.99	75	.314	.356	1	.031	-3	-19	-15	-1	-2.2

YEAR	TM/L	W	L	PCT	G	GS	CG	SH	SV	IP	H	R	HR	HB	BB	SO	RAT	ERA	ERA+	OAV	OOB	BH	AVG	PB	PR	PR+	PD	TPI
1947	StL-A	8	14	.364	31	23	7	0	0	176^1	210	108	14	2	51	74	13.4	4.90	79	.299	.348	6	.105	-3	-23	-19	0	-2.4
1948	*Cle-A	5	4	.556	21	9	1	1	0	72^1	76	37	8	0	31	24	13.3	3.98	102	.279	.353	2	.111	-1	2	1	-0	-0.1
1949	Pit-N	1	5	.167	13	4	1	0	3	35^2	44	27	8	0	13	11	14.4	6.31	67	.310	.368	1	.143	-0	-9	-8	1	-1.2
	Chi-N	5	6	.455	34	3	1	0	2	75	80	42	9	1	31	36	13.4	4.56	88	.276	.348	4	.286	1	-4	-4	-0	-0.5
	Yr	6	11	.353	47	7	2	0	5	110^2	124	69	17	1	44	47	13.7	5.12	80	.287	.354	5	.238	1	-13	-13	1	-1.7
1951	NY-A	0	0	—	2	0	0	0	0	3	5	3	0	0	4	2	27.0	9.00	43	.417	.563	0	—	0	-2	-2	0	-0.1
Total	12	80	82	.494	288	165	67	11	9	1401^1	1503	669	108	15	392	525	12.3	3.80	100	.275	.325	68	.155	-10	-20	-3	-7	-2.6

● **RED MUNGER** Munger, George David b: 10/4/18, Houston, Tex. d: 7/23/96, Houston, Tex. BR/TR, 6'2", 200 lbs. Deb: 5/1/43

YEAR	TM/L	W	L	PCT	G	GS	CG	SH	SV	IP	H	R	HR	HB	BB	SO	RAT	ERA	ERA+	OAV	OOB	BH	AVG	PB	PR	PR+	PD	TPI
1943	StL-N	9	5	.643	32	9	5	0	2	93^1	101	47	2	0	42	45	13.8	3.95	85	.281	.357	6	.214	1	-6	-6	1	-0.7
1944	StL-N†	11	3	.786	21	12	7	2	2	121	92	23	2	2	41	55	10.0	1.34	263	.212	.284	5	.114	-3	31	30	3	3.7
1946	*StL-N	2	2	.500	10	7	2	0	1	48^2	47	19	0	0	12	28	10.9	3.33	104	.255	.301	4	.250	1	0	1	2	0.3
1947	StL-N☆	16	5	.762	40	31	13	6	3	224^1	218	94	12	2	76	123	11.9	3.37	123	.255	.318	15	.185	1	17	19	3	1.9
1948	StL-N	10	11	.476	39	25	7	2	0	166	179	91	13	1	74	72	13.8	4.50	91	.272	.347	8	.160	0	-10	-7	2	-0.6
1949	StL-N★	15	8	.652	35	28	12	2	2	188^1	179	86	13	2	87	82	12.8	3.87	108	.255	.339	17	.258	4	4	6	1	1.1
1950	StL-N	7	8	.467	32	20	5	1	0	154^2	158	73	15	3	70	61	13.4	3.90	110	.262	.342	7	.137	-2	4	7	0	0.4
1951	StL-N	4	6	.400	23	11	3	0	0	94^2	106	58	13	0	46	44	14.5	5.32	74	.286	.365	5	.172	-0	-14	-14	2	-1.2
1952	StL-N	0	1	.000	1	1	0	0	0	4^1	7	6	2	1	1	1	18.7	12.46	30	.389	.450	0	.000	-0	-4	-4	0	-0.6
	Pit-N	0	3	.000	5	4	0	0	0	26^1	30	21	5	0	10	8	13.7	7.18	56	.283	.345	0	.000	-1	-10	-9	1	-0.8
	Yr	0	4	.000	6	5	0	0	0	30^2	37	27	7	1	11	9	14.4	7.92	50	.298	.360	0	.000	-1	-14	-13	1	-1.4
1956	Pit-N	3	4	.429	35	13	0	0	2	107	126	56	8	0	41	45	14.0	4.04	93	.299	.361	3	.107	-0	-3	-3	-1	-0.3
Total	10	77	56	.579	273	161	54	13	12	1228^2	1243	574	85	11	500	564	12.8	3.83	103	.264	.336	70	.174	0	8	17	13	3.2

● **VAN MUNGO** Mungo, Van Lingle b: 6/8/11, Pageland, S.C. d: 2/12/85, Pageland, S.C. BR/TR, 6'2", 185 lbs. Deb: 9/7/31 C

YEAR	TM/L	W	L	PCT	G	GS	CG	SH	SV	IP	H	R	HR	HB	BB	SO	RAT	ERA	ERA+	OAV	OOB	BH	AVG	PB	PR	PR+	PD	TPI
1931	Bro-N	3	1	.750	5	4	2	1	0	31	27	9	0	1	13	12	11.9	2.32	164	.241	.325	3	.250	1	5	5	-1	0.7
1932	Bro-N	13	11	.542	39	33	11	1	2	223^1	224	120	9	6	115	107	13.9	4.43	86	.260	.351	16	.203	0	-14	-16	2	-1.3
1933	Bro-N	16	15	.516	41	28	18	3	0	248	223	89	7	0	84	110	11.1	2.72	118	.236	.298	15	.179	-0	17	14	1	1.8
1934	Bro-N★	18	16	.529	45	38	22	3	3	**315^1**	300	137	15	3	104	184	11.6	3.37	116	.249	.310	30	.248	4	24	20	2	2.6
1935	Bro-N	16	10	.615	37	26	18	**4**	2	214^1	205	100	13	2	90	143	12.5	3.65	109	.252	.328	26	.289	5	9	8	1	1.5
1936	Bro-N☆	18	19	.486	45	37	22	2	3	311^2	275	137	8	3	118	**238**	11.4	3.35	123	**.234**	.305	22	.179	-4	23	26	2	2.7
1937	Bro-N★	9	11	.450	25	21	14	0	3	161	136	65	3	3	56	122	10.9	2.91	139	**.229**	.298	16	.250	2	18	20	3	3.0
1938	Bro-N	4	11	.267	24	18	6	2	0	133^1	133	78	11	2	72	72	14.0	3.92	100	.259	.353	9	.191	1	-2	-0	1	0.2
1939	Bro-N	4	5	.444	14	10	1	0	0	77^1	70	36	7	3	33	34	12.3	3.26	124	.239	.322	10	.345	2	6	6	-1	1.0
1940	Bro-N	1	0	1.000	7	0	0	0	1	22	24	6	1	0	10	9	13.9	2.45	163	.282	.358	0	.000	-1	3	4	-0	0.1
1941	Bro-N	0	0	—	2	0	0	0	0	2	1	1	0	0	2	0	13.5	4.50	81	.143	.333	0	—	0	-0	-0	0	0.0
1942	NY-N	1	2	.333	9	5	0	0	0	36^1	38	32	4	0	21	27	14.6	5.94	57	.273	.369	3	.214	-0	-11	-10	0	-0.8
1943	NY-N	3	7	.300	45	13	2	2	2	154^1	140	68	7	6	79	83	13.1	3.91	88	.243	.341	7	.159	-1	-9	-8	1	-0.5
1945	NY-N†	14	7	.667	26	26	7	2	0	183	161	77	4	4	71	101	11.6	3.20	122	.238	.314	17	.233	4	12	14	-0	1.9
Total	14	120	115	.511	364	259	123	20	16	2113	1957	955	89	33	868	1242	12.2	3.47	110	.245	.321	174	.221	13	83	83	11	12.9

● **MANNY MUNIZ** Muniz, Manuel (Rodriguez) b: 12/31/47, Caguas, P.R. BR/TR, 5'11", 190 lbs. Deb: 9/3/71

YEAR	TM/L	W	L	PCT	G	GS	CG	SH	SV	IP	H	R	HR	HB	BB	SO	RAT	ERA	ERA+	OAV	OOB	BH	AVG	PB	PR	PR+	PD	TPI
1971	Phi-N	0	1	.000	5	0	0	0	0	10^1	9	8	2	0	8	6	14.8	6.97	51	.225	.354	0	.000	-0	-4	-4	-0	-0.4

● **SCOTT MUNNINGHOFF** Munninghoff, Scott Andrew b: 12/5/58, Cincinnati, Ohio BR/TR, 6', 175 lbs. Deb: 4/13/80

YEAR	TM/L	W	L	PCT	G	GS	CG	SH	SV	IP	H	R	HR	HB	BB	SO	RAT	ERA	ERA+	OAV	OOB	BH	AVG	PB	PR	PR+	PD	TPI
1980	Phi-N	0	0	—	4	0	0	0	0	6	8	3	0	0	5	2	19.5	4.50	84	.320	.433	1	1.000	1	-1	-0	0	0.1

● **LES MUNNS** Munns, Leslie Ernest "Big Ed" or "Nemo" b: 12/1/08, Fort Bragg, Cal. d: 2/28/97, Cedar Rapids, Ia. BR/TR, 6'5", 212 lbs. Deb: 4/22/34

YEAR	TM/L	W	L	PCT	G	GS	CG	SH	SV	IP	H	R	HR	HB	BB	SO	RAT	ERA	ERA+	OAV	OOB	BH	AVG	PB	PR	PR+	PD	TPI
1934	Bro-N	3	7	.300	33	9	4	0	0	99^1	106	67	7	0	60	41	15.0	4.71	83	.280	.378	7	.241	2	-7	-9	2	-0.4
1935	Bro-N	1	3	.250	21	5	0	0	1	58^1	74	47	5	4	33	13	17.1	5.55	72	.319	.413	3	.188	-0	-10	-10	-2	-0.8
1936	StL-N	0	3	.000	7	1	0	0	1	24	23	18	2	0	12	4	13.1	3.00	131	.240	.324	1	.111	-1	3	3	1	0.3
Total	3	4	13	.235	61	15	4	0	2	181^2	203	132	14	4	105	58	15.5	4.76	83	.287	.382	11	.204	1	-14	-17	1	-0.9

● **OSCAR MUNOZ** Munoz, Juan Oscar b: 9/25/69, Hialeah, Fla. BR/TR, 6'3", 222 lbs. Deb: 8/6/95

YEAR	TM/L	W	L	PCT	G	GS	CG	SH	SV	IP	H	R	HR	HB	BB	SO	RAT	ERA	ERA+	OAV	OOB	BH	AVG	PB	PR	PR+	PD	TPI
1995	Min-A	2	1	.667	10	3	0	0	0	35^1	40	28	6	1	17	25	14.8	5.60	85	.276	.356	0	—	0	-3	-3	-0	-0.3

● **MIKE MUNOZ** Munoz, Michael Anthony b: 7/12/65, Baldwin Park, Cal. BL/TL, 6'2", 200 lbs. Deb: 9/6/89

YEAR	TM/L	W	L	PCT	G	GS	CG	SH	SV	IP	H	R	HR	HB	BB	SO	RAT	ERA	ERA+	OAV	OOB	BH	AVG	PB	PR	PR+	PD	TPI
1989	LA-N	0	0	—	3	0	0	0	0	2^2	5	5	1	0	2	3	23.6	16.88	20	.417	.500	0	—	0	-4	-4	0	-0.2
1990	LA-N	0	1	.000	8	0	0	0	0	5^2	6	2	0	0	3	2	14.3	3.18	115	.300	.391	0	.000	-0	0	0	-0	0.0
1991	Det-A	0	0	—	6	0	0	0	0	9^1	14	10	0	0	5	3	18.3	9.64	43	.350	.422	0	—	0	-6	-6	0	-0.2
1992	Det-A	1	2	.333	65	0	0	0	2	48	44	16	3	0	25	23	12.9	3.00	132	.246	.338	0	—	0	5	5	2	0.5
1993	Det-A	0	1	.000	8	0	0	0	0	3	4	2	1	0	6	1	30.0	6.00	72	.308	.526	0	—	0	-1	-1	0	-0.1
	Col-N	2	1	.667	21	0	0	0	0	18	21	12	1	0	9	16	15.0	4.50	106	.309	.390	0	—	0	1	0	0	0.1
1994	Col-N	4	2	.667	57	0	0	0	1	45^2	37	22	3	0	31	32	13.4	3.74	133	.223	.345	0	—	0	2	5	2	0.8
1995	*Col-N	2	4	.333	64	0	0	0	2	43^2	54	38	9	1	27	37	16.9	7.42	73	.307	.402	1	.500	1	-16	-8	1	-0.8
1996	Col-N	2	2	.500	54	0	0	0	0	44^2	55	33	4	1	16	45	14.5	6.65	79	.302	.362	0	.000	-0	-12	-6	1	-0.3
1997	Col-N	3	3	.500	64	0	0	0	2	45^2	52	25	4	0	13	26	12.8	4.53	114	.294	.342	0	.000	-0	-2	3	-0	0.3
1998	Col-N	2	2	.500	40	0	0	0	3	41^1	53	32	2	1	16	24	15.2	5.66	91	.312	.374	0	.000	-0	-7	-2	0	-0.2
1999	Tex-A	2	1	.667	56	0	0	0	1	52^2	52	24	5	1	18	27	12.1	3.93	129	.263	.327	0	—	0	6	6	0	0.4
2000	Tex-A	0	1	.000	7	0	0	0	0	4	11	6	1	0	3	1	31.5	13.50	38	.524	.583	0	—	0	-4	-4	-0	-0.6
Total	12	18	20	.474	453	0	0	0	11	364^1	408	227	34	4	174	240	14.5	5.19	95	.287	.366	1	.143	1	-38	-9	6	-0.3

● **BOBBY MUNOZ** Munoz, Roberto (Sbert) b: 3/3/68, Rio Piedras, P.R. BR/TR, 6'7", 252 lbs. Deb: 5/29/93

YEAR	TM/L	W	L	PCT	G	GS	CG	SH	SV	IP	H	R	HR	HB	BB	SO	RAT	ERA	ERA+	OAV	OOB	BH	AVG	PB	PR	PR+	PD	TPI
1993	NY-A	3	3	.500	38	0	0	0	0	45^2	48	27	1	0	26	33	14.6	5.32	78	.270	.363	0	—	0	-5	-6	-0	-0.7
1994	Phi-N	7	5	.583	21	14	1	0	1	104^1	101	40	8	1	35	59	11.8	2.67	161	.252	.314	7	.206	1	18	18	1	2.2
1995	Phi-N	0	2	.000	3	3	0	0	0	15^2	15	13	2	3	9	6	15.5	5.74	74	.268	.397	0	.000	-1	-3	-3	-0	-0.3
1996	Phi-N	0	3	.000	6	6	0	0	0	25^1	42	28	5	1	7	8	17.8	7.82	55	.375	.417	1	.143	0	-10	-10	-0	-0.9
1997	Phi-N	1	5	.167	8	7	0	0	0	33^1	47	35	4	2	15	20	17.3	8.91	48	.338	.410	3	.300	1	-17	-17	0	-2.3
1998	Bal-A	0	0	—	9	1	0	0	0	12	18	13	4	1	6	6	18.8	9.75	47	.383	.463	0	—	0	-7	-7	-0	-0.3
Total	6	11	18	.379	85	31	1	0	1	236^1	271	156	24	8	98	132	14.4	5.18	83	.290	.363	11	.196	2	-24	-24	0	-2.3

● **PETER MUNRO** Munro, Peter Daniel b: 6/14/75, Flushing, N.Y. BR/TR, 6'2", 200 lbs. Deb: 4/6/99

YEAR	TM/L	W	L	PCT	G	GS	CG	SH	SV	IP	H	R	HR	HB	BB	SO	RAT	ERA	ERA+	OAV	OOB	BH	AVG	PB	PR	PR+	PD	TPI
1999	Tor-A	0	2	.000	31	2	0	0	0	55^1	70	38	6	2	23	38	15.5	6.02	82	.318	.388	0	—	0	-7	-7	0	-0.3
2000	Tor-A	1	1	.500	9	3	0	0	0	25^2	38	22	1	3	16	16	20.0	5.96	84	.355	.452	0	.000	-0	-3	-3	0	-0.2
Total	2	1	3	.250	40	5	0	0	0	81	108	60	7	5	39	54	16.9	6.00	83	.330	.410	0	.000	-0	-10	-9	0	-0.5

● **STEVE MURA** Mura, Stephen Andrew b: 2/12/55, New Orleans, La. BR/TR, 6'2", 190 lbs. Deb: 9/5/78

YEAR	TM/L	W	L	PCT	G	GS	CG	SH	SV	IP	H	R	HR	HB	BB	SO	RAT	ERA	ERA+	OAV	OOB	BH	AVG	PB	PR	PR+	PD	TPI
1978	SD-N	0	2	.000	5	2	0	0	0	7^2	15	10	1	0	5	5	23.5	11.74	28	.441	.513	0	.000	-0	-7	-8	-0	-1.4
1979	SD-N	4	4	.500	38	5	0	0	2	73	57	30	6	1	37	59	11.7	3.08	115	.217	.316	0	.000	-1	5	4	-0	0.3
1980	SD-N	8	7	.533	37	23	3	1	2	168^2	149	74	9	3	86	109	12.7	3.68	93	.246	.343	7	.137	-0	-1	-5	0	-0.4
1981	SD-N	5	14	.263	23	22	2	0	0	138^2	156	72	10	0	50	70	13.4	4.28	76	.285	.344	6	.136	-0	-12	-17	1	-2.0
1982	StL-N	12	11	.522	35	30	7	1	0	184^1	196	89	16	0	80	84	13.5	4.05	90	.278	.352	3	.057	-4	-9	-9	1	-1.5
1983	Chi-A	0	0	—	6	0	0	0	0	12^1	13	11	1	0	6	4	13.9	4.38	96	.260	.339	0	—	0	-0	-0	-0	0.0
1985	Oak-A	1	1	.500	23	1	0	0	1	48	41	25	3	0	25	29	12.4	4.13	94	.225	.319	0	—	0	0	-2	-0	-0.1
Total	7	30	39	.435	167	83	12	2	5	632^2	627	311	46	4	289	360	13.1	4.00	88	.263	.343	16	.101	-5	-25	-36	-1	-5.1

● **MASANORI MURAKAMI** Murakami, Masanori b: 5/6/44, Otsuki, Japan BL/TL, 6', 180 lbs. Deb: 9/1/64

YEAR	TM/L	W	L	PCT	G	GS	CG	SH	SV	IP	H	R	HR	HB	BB	SO	RAT	ERA	ERA+	OAV	OOB	BH	AVG	PB	PR	PR+	PD	TPI
1964	SF-N	1	0	1.000	9	0	0	0	1	15	8	3	1	0	1	15	5.4	1.80	198	.163	.180	0	.000	-0	3	3	-1	0.1
1965	SF-N	4	1	.800	45	1	0	0	8	74^1	57	31	9	3	22	85	9.9	3.75	96	.205	.271	2	.154	-0	-2	-1	-2	-0.3
Total	2	5	1	.833	54	1	0	0	9	89^1	65	34	10	3	23	100	9.2	3.43	105	.199	.258	2	.125	-1	1	2	-2	-0.2

● **TIM MURCHISON** Murchison, Thomas Malcolm b: 10/8/1896, Liberty, N.C. d: 10/20/62, Liberty, N.C. BR/TL, 6', 185 lbs. Deb: 6/21/17

YEAR	TM/L	W	L	PCT	G	GS	CG	SH	SV	IP	H	R	HR	HB	BB	SO	RAT	ERA	ERA+	OAV	OOB	BH	AVG	PB	PR	PR+	PD	TPI
1917	StL-N	0	0	—	1	0	0	0	0	1	0	0	0	0	2	2	18.0	0.00	—	.000	.400	0	—	0	0	0	0	0.0

YEAR	TM/L	W	L	PCT	G	GS	CG	SH	SV	IP	H	R	HR	HB	BB	SO	RAT	ERA	ERA+	OAV	OOB	BH	AVG	PB	PR	PR+	PD	TPI
1920	Cle-A	0	0	—	2	0	0	0	0	5	3	1	0	0	4	0	12.6	0.00	—	.200	.368	0	.000	-0	2	2	1	0.1
Total	2	0	0	—	3	0	0	0	0	6	3	1	0	0	6	2	13.5	0.00	—	.167	.375	0	.000	-0	2	2	1	0.1
● **RED MURFF**	Murff, John Robert b: 4/1/21, Burlington, Tex. BR/TR, 6'3", 195 lbs. Deb: 4/21/56																											
1956	Mil-N	0	0	—	14	1	0	0	1	24^1	25	14	3	0	7	18	11.8	4.44	78	.272	.323	1	.200	0	-2	-3	0	-0.1
1957	Mil-N	2	2	.500	12	1	0	0	2	26	31	14	3	0	11	13	14.5	4.85	72	.301	.368	0	.000	-1	-3	-4	0	-0.7
Total	2	2	2	.500	26	2	0	0	3	50^1	56	28	6	0	18	31	13.2	4.65	75	.287	.347	1	.091	-1	-5	-7	1	-0.8
● **CON MURPHY**	Murphy, Cornelius B. "Monk" or "Razzle Dazzle" b: 10/15/1863, Worcester, Mass. d: 8/1/14, Worcester, Mass. TR, 5'9", 130 lbs. Deb: 9/11/1884																											
1884	Phi-N	0	3	.000	3	3	3	0	0	26	37	34	1		6	10	14.9	6.58	45	.319	.352	0	.000	-1	-10	-10	0	-0.9
1890	Bro-P	4	10	.286	20	14	11	0	2	139	168	134	2	6	82	29	16.6	4.79	93	.286	.379	15	.217	-1	-9	-5	-1	-0.5
Total	2	4	13	.235	23	17	14	0	2	165	205	168	3	6	88	39	16.3	5.07	83	.292	.375	15	.190	-3	-19	-15	-0	-1.4
● **DANNY MURPHY**	Murphy, Daniel Francis b: 8/23/42, Beverly, Mass. BL/TR, 5'11", 185 lbs. Deb: 6/18/60 ♦																											
1969	Chi-A	2	1	.667	17	0	0	0	4	31^1	28	8	2	2	10	16	11.5	2.01	192	.252	.325	0	.000	0	6	6	-0	0.8
1970	Chi-A	2	3	.400	51	0	0	0	5	80^2	82	55	11	4	49	42	15.1	5.69	69	.273	.382	2	.333	2	-18	-15	-1	-0.9
Total	2	4	4	.500	68	0	0	0	9	112	110	63	13	6	59	58	14.1	4.66	83	.268	.368	23	.177	2	-12	-9	-1	-0.1
● **DAN MURPHY**	Murphy, Daniel Lee b: 9/18/64, Artesia, Cal. BR/TR, 6'2", 195 lbs. Deb: 8/10/89																											
1989	SD-N	0	0	—	7	0	0	0	0	6^1	6	6	1	0	4	1	14.2	5.68	62	.231	.333	0	—	0	-2	-2	-0	-0.1
● **ED MURPHY**	Murphy, Edward J. b: 1/22/1877, Auburn, N.Y. d: 1/29/35, Weedsport, N.Y. TR, 6'1", 186 lbs. Deb: 4/23/1898																											
1898	Phi-N	1	2	.333	7	3	2	0	0	30	41	23	3	1	10	8	15.6	5.10	67	.323	.377	5	.357	1	-5	-6	1	-0.3
1901	StL-N	10	9	.526	23	21	16	0	0	165	201	105	5	1	32	42	12.8	4.20	76	.298	.331	16	.250	3	-16	-20	2	-1.4
1902	StL-N	10	6	.625	23	17	12	1	1	164	187	86	7	2	31	37	12.1	3.02	91	.286	.321	16	.262	1	-4	-5	2	-0.2
1903	StL-N	4	8	.333	15	12	9	0	0	106	108	62	2	6	38	16	12.9	3.31	99	.262	.333	13	.203	-1	-0	-1	0	-0.1
Total	4	25	25	.500	68	53	39	1	1	465	537	276	17	10	111	103	12.7	3.64	84	.288	.331	50	.246	5	-26	-30	5	-2.0
● **JOHN MURPHY**	Murphy, John Henry 5'11", 165 lbs. Deb: 4/17/1884																											
1884	Wil-U	0	6	.000	7	6	5	0	0	48	52	36	3		2	27	10.1	3.00	89	.259	.266	2	.065	-4	-3	-2	-1	-0.5
	Alt-U	5	6	.455	14	10	10	0	0	111^2	141	90	3		9	46	12.1	3.87	69	.289	.302	14	.149	-7	-18	-14	1	-1.4
	Yr	5	12	.294	21	16	15	0	0	159^2	193	126	6		11	73	11.5	3.61	74	.280	.291	16	.128	-11	-21	-15	0	-1.9
● **JOHNNY MURPHY**	Murphy, John Joseph "Grandma" "Fireman" Or "Fordham Johnny" b: 7/14/08, New York, N.Y. d: 1/14/70, New York, N.Y. BR/TR, 6'2", 190 lbs. Deb: 5/19/32																											
1932	NY-A	0	0	—	2	0	0	0	0	3^1	7	6	0	0	3	2	27.0	16.20	25	.438	.526	1	1.000	1	-4	-5	0	-0.2
1934	NY-A	14	10	.583	40	20	10	0	4	207^2	193	79	11	0	76	70	11.7	3.12	130	.250	.317	7	.099	-3	32	24	1	2.3
1935	NY-A	10	5	.667	40	8	4	0	5	117	110	67	7	0	55	28	12.7	4.08	99	.243	.325	5	.156	2	5	-0	-1	0.1
1936	*NY-A	9	3	.750	27	5	2	0	5	88	90	38	5	1	36	34	13.0	3.38	138	.262	.334	13	.361	4	16	14	1	2.1
1937	*NY-A☆	13	4	.765	39	4	0	0	10	110	121	59	7	1	50	36	14.1	4.17	107	.277	.352	8	.229	2	5	3	4	1.0
1938	*NY-A☆	8	2	.800	32	2	1	0	**11**	91^1	90	47	5	1	41	43	13.0	4.24	107	.256	.336	2	.063	-3	**6**	3	1	0.2
1939	*NY-A☆	3	6	.333	38	0	0	0	**19**	61^1	57	33	2	0	28	30	12.5	4.40	99	.252	.335	2	.182	1	1	-0	1	0.0
1940	NY-A	8	4	.667	35	1	0	0	9	63^1	58	27	5	0	15	23	10.4	3.69	109	.247	.292	1	.077	0	5	3	1	0.5
1941	*NY-A	8	3	.727	35	0	0	0	**15**	77^1	68	20	1	0	40	29	12.6	1.98	199	.237	.330	1	.056	-1	**19**	**18**	-1	2.8
1942	NY-A	4	10	.286	31	0	0	0	**11**	58	66	27	2	2	23	24	14.1	3.41	101	.293	.364	2	.154	0	2	0	0	0.1
1943	*NY-A	12	4	.750	37	0	0	0	8	68	44	22	2	0	30	31	9.8	2.51	128	.183	.273	1	.053	-2	6	5	-0	0.9
1946	NY-A	4	2	.667	27	0	0	0	7	45	40	22	4	0	19	19	11.8	3.40	102	.240	.317	0	.000	-0	1	0	1	0.1
1947	Bos-A	0	0	—	32	0	0	0	3	54^2	41	17	1	0	28	9	11.4	2.80	139	.206	.304	3	.273	1	6	6	0	0.4
Total	13	93	53	.637	415	40	17	0	107	1045	985	464	52	5	444	378	12.4	3.50	117	.249	.326	46	.154	-0	98	72	8	10.3
● **JOE MURPHY**	Murphy, Joseph Akin b: 9/7/1866, St.Louis, Mo. d: 3/28/51, Coral Gables, Fla. 5'11", 160 lbs. Deb: 4/28/1886																											
1886	Cin-a	2	3	.400	5	5	5	0	0	46	50	34	0	1	21	11	14.1	4.89	72	.256	.332	0	.000	-3	-7	-7	-1	-0.9
	StL-N	0	4	.000	4	4	3	0	0	33	45	41	3		16	11	16.6	8.18	39	.319	.389	3	.214	0	-18	-19	-0	-1.5
	StL-a	1	0	1.000	1	1	1	0	0	7	5	4	0	0	3	3	10.3	3.86	89	.179	.258	0	.000	-1	-0	-0	-0	-0.1
1887	StL-a	1	0	1.000	1	1	1	0	0	9	17	8	0	0	4	5	17.0	5.00	91	.378	.378	1	.167	-1	-1	-0	0	-0.1
Total	2	4	7	.364	11	11	10	0	0	95	117	87	3	1	44	30	15.0	5.97	59	.286	.351	4	.098	-4	-26	-26	-2	-2.6
● **ROB MURPHY**	Murphy, Robert Albert b: 5/26/60, Miami, Fla. BL/TL, 6'2", 215 lbs. Deb: 9/13/85																											
1985	Cin-N	0	0	—	2	0	0	0	0	3	2	2	1	0	2	1	12.0	6.00	63	.200	.333	0	—	0	-1	-1	-0	0.0
1986	Cin-N	6	0	1.000	34	0	0	0	1	50^1	26	4	0	0	21	36	8.4	0.72	542	.155	.249	0	.000	-0	17	17	0	2.0
1987	Cin-N	8	5	.615	87	0	0	0	3	100^2	91	37	7	0	32	99	11.0	3.04	140	.239	.299	1	.200	0	12	13	0	1.6
1988	Cin-N	0	6	.000	**76**	0	0	0	3	84^2	69	31	3	1	38	74	11.5	3.08	116	.229	.318	0	—	0	3	5	1	0.4
1989	Bos-A	5	7	.417	74	0	0	0	9	105	97	38	7	1	41	107	11.9	2.74	150	.251	.325	0	—	0	13	15	1	1.9
1990	*Bos-A	0	6	.000	68	0	0	0	7	57	85	46	10	1	32	54	18.6	6.32	65	.348	.426	0	—	0	-15	-14	0	-1.5
1991	Sea-A	0	1	.000	57	0	0	0	4	48	47	17	4	1	19	34	12.6	3.00	138	.250	.322	0	—	0	6	6	0	0.3
1992	Hou-N	3	1	.750	59	0	0	0	0	55^2	56	28	2	0	21	42	12.4	4.04	83	.260	.326	0	.000	-0	-3	-4	1	-0.2
1993	StL-N	5	7	.417	73	0	0	0	1	64^2	73	37	8	1	20	41	13.1	4.87	82	.290	.344	1	.500	0	-6	-7	-0	-1.1
1994	StL-N	4	3	.571	50	0	0	0	2	40^1	35	18	7	0	13	25	10.7	3.79	110	.230	.291	0	—	0	2	2	-0	0.3
	NY-A	0	0	—	3	0	0	0	0	1^2	3	3	2	0	0	0	16.2	16.20	28	.375	.375	0	—	0	-2	-2	0	-0.1
1995	LA-N	0	1	.000	6	0	0	0	0	5	6	7	2	0	3	2	16.2	12.60	30	.300	.391	1	1.000	1	-5	-5	0	-0.8
	Fla-N	1	1	.500	8	0	0	0	0	7^1	8	9	1	0	5	5	16.0	9.82	43	.286	.394	0	—	0	-5	-5	0	-0.8
	Yr	1	2	.333	14	0	0	0	0	12^1	14	16	3	0	8	7	16.1	10.95	37	.292	.393	1	1.000	1	-9	-10	0	-1.6
Total	11	32	38	.457	597	0	0	0	30	623^1	598	277	54	5	247	520	12.3	3.64	109	.254	.326	3	.250	1	17	22	2	2.0
● **BOB MURPHY**	Murphy, Robert J. b: 12/26/1866, Dutchess Co., N.Y. Deb: 5/27/1890																											
1890	NY-N	1	0	1.000	3	2	1	0	0	18	23	17	0	0	10	8	16.5	5.50	64	.303	.384	1	.111	-1	-4	-4	-0	-0.3
	Bro-a	3	9	.250	12	12	10	0	0	96	121	95	6	5	46	26	16.1	5.72	68	.299	.377	9	.180	0	-20	-19	2	-1.6
Total	1	4	9	.308	15	14	11	0	0	114	144	112	6	5	56	34	16.2	5.68	67	.299	.378	10	.169	-1	-24	-23	2	-1.9
● **TOM MURPHY**	Murphy, Thomas Andrew b: 12/30/45, Cleveland, Ohio BR/TR, 6'3", 185 lbs. Deb: 6/13/68																											
1968	Cal-A	5	6	.455	15	15	3	0	0	99^1	67	30	5	5	28	56	9.1	2.17	134	.191	.261	0	.000	-3	9	8	-1	0.5
1969	Cal-A	10	16	.385	36	35	4	0	0	215^2	213	110	12	21	69	100	12.6	4.21	83	.260	.333	10	.141	-0	-14	-18	1	-1.9
1970	Cal-A	16	13	.552	39	38	5	2	0	227	223	114	32	7	81	99	12.3	4.24	85	.261	.330	14	.184	3	-13	-16	-1	-1.7
1971	Cal-A	6	17	.261	37	36	7	0	0	243^1	228	108	24	9	82	89	11.8	3.77	86	.256	.325	13	.173	1	-8	-15	1	-1.1
1972	Cal-A	0	0	—	6	0	0	0	0	10	13	6	0	0	8	2	18.9	5.40	54	.342	.457	0	.000	-0	-3	-3	1	-0.1
	KC-A	4	4	.500	18	9	1	1	1	70^1	77	26	3	6	16	34	12.7	3.07	99	.287	.341	0	.000	-1	0	-0	1	-0.1
	Yr	4	4	.500	24	9	1	1	1	80^1	90	32	3	6	24	36	13.4	3.36	90	.294	.357	0	.000	-1	-3	-3	1	-0.2
1973	StL-N	3	7	.300	19	13	2	0	0	88^2	89	38	5	3	22	42	11.6	3.76	97	.269	.320	4	.174	0	-1	-1	1	0.0
1974	Mil-A	10	10	.500	70	0	0	0	20	123	97	27	6	2	51	47	11.0	1.90	190	.224	.309	1	.500	0	24	24	2	**5.0**
1975	Mil-A	1	9	.100	52	0	0	0	20	72^1	85	43	5	5	27	32	14.6	4.60	83	.295	.366	0	—	0	-7	-6	0	-1.1
1976	Mil-A	0	1	.000	15	0	0	0	1	18^1	25	18	2	2	9	7	17.7	7.36	47	.313	.396	0	—	0	-8	-8	0	-0.5
	Bos-A	4	5	.444	37	0	0	0	8	81	91	43	5	2	25	32	13.1	3.44	114	.290	.346	0	—	0	1	4	-0	0.5
	Yr	4	6	.400	52	0	0	0	9	99^1	116	61	7	4	34	39	14.0	4.17	92	.294	.356	0	—	0	-7	-3	0	0.0
1977	Bos-A	0	1	.000	16	0	0	0	0	30^2	44	25	6	0	12	13	16.4	6.75	67	.338	.394	0	—	0	-9	-7	0	-0.3
	Tor-A	2	1	.667	19	1	0	0	2	52	63	22	6	1	18	26	14.2	3.63	116	.304	.363	0	—	0	3	3	-0	0.2
	Yr	2	2	.500	35	1	0	0	2	82^2	107	47	12	1	30	39	15.0	4.79	90	.318	.375	0	—	0	-7	-4	0	-0.1
1978	Tor-A	6	9	.400	50	0	0	0	7	94	87	43	11	0	37	36	11.9	3.93	100	.256	.329	0	—	0	-2	0	2	0.2
1979	Tor-A	1	2	.333	10	0	0	0	0	18^1	23	11	1	0	8	6	15.2	5.40	81	.311	.378	0	—	0	-2	-2	1	-0.2
Total	12	68	101	.402	439	147	22	3	59	1444	1425	664	123	63	493	621	12.3	3.78	94	.263	.332	42	.145	0	-31	-37	7	-0.6
● **WALTER MURPHY**	Murphy, Walter Joseph b: 9/27/07, New York, N.Y. d: 3/23/76, Houston, Tex. BR/TR, 6'1.5", 180 lbs. Deb: 4/19/31																											
1931	Bos-A	0	0	—	2	0	0	0	0	2	4	2	0	0	1	0	22.5	9.00	48	.444	.500	0	—	0	-1	-1	-0	-0.1

YEAR	TM/L	W	L	PCT	G	GS	CG	SH	SV	IP	H	R	HR	HB	BB	SO	RAT	ERA	ERA+	OAV	OOB	BH	AVG	PB	PR	PR+	PD	TPI
● **AMBY MURRAY**	Murray, Ambrose Joseph b: 6/4/13, Fall River, Mass. d: 2/6/97, Port Salerno, Fla. BL/TL, 5'7", 150 lbs. Deb: 7/5/36																											
1936	Bos-N	0	0	—	4	1	0	0	0	11	15	5	1	0	3	2	14.7	4.09	94	.319	.360	1	.250	0	-0	-0	0	0.0
● **DALE MURRAY**	Murray, Dale Albert b: 2/2/50, Cuero, Tex. BR/TR, 6'4", 205 lbs. Deb: 7/7/74																											
1974	Mon-N	1	1	.500	32	0	0	0	10	69^2	46	12	1	0	23	31	8.9	1.03	373	.187	.257	0	.000	-1	20	21	0	1.2
1975	Mon-N	15	8	.652	63	0	0	0	9	111^1	134	59	0	3	39	43	14.2	3.96	97	.305	.365	3	.214	1	-4	-1	3	0.0
1976	Mon-N	4	9	.308	**81**	0	0	0	13	113^1	117	47	1	0	37	35	12.2	3.26	114	.277	.336	0	.000	-1	3	6	4	1.1
1977	Cin-N	7	2	.778	61	1	0	0	4	102	125	60	13	2	46	42	15.3	4.94	80	.314	.388	2	.167	-0	-12	-11	0	-1.0
1978	Cin-N	1	1	.500	15	0	0	0	2	32^2	34	20	1	1	17	25	14.3	4.13	86	.272	.364	0	.000	-0	-2	-2	1	-0.1
	NY-N	8	5	.615	53	0	0	0	5	86^1	85	39	4	2	36	37	12.8	3.65	96	.266	.345	0	.000	-0	-1	-2	2	-0.1
	Yr	9	6	.600	68	0	0	0	7	119	119	59	5	3	53	62	13.2	3.78	93	.268	.350	0	.000	-1	-3	-4	2	-0.2
1979	NY-N	4	8	.333	58	0	0	0	4	97	105	58	6	0	52	37	14.6	4.82	76	.287	.376	0	.000	-0	-12	-13	1	-1.5
	Mon-N	1	2	.333	9	0	0	0	1	13^1	14	4	1	0	3	4	11.5	2.70	136	.292	.333	0	.000	-0	2	1	-1	0.2
	Yr	5	10	.333	67	0	0	0	5	110^1	119	62	7	0	55	41	14.2	4.57	80	.287	.371	0	.000	-1	-10	-12	0	-1.3
1980	Mon-N	0	1	.000	16	0	0	0	0	29^1	39	23	3	0	12	16	15.6	6.14	58	.315	.375	0	.000	-0	-8	-8	-1	-0.5
1981	Tor-A	1	0	1.000	11	0	0	0	0	15^1	12	2	0	0	5	12	10.0	1.17	336	.211	.274	0	—	0	4	4	1	0.4
1982	Tor-A	8	7	.533	56	0	0	0	11	111	115	48	3	3	32	60	12.2	3.16	142	.268	.323	0	—	0	11	15	3	2.5
1983	NY-A	2	4	.333	40	0	0	0	1	94^1	113	56	5	1	22	45	13.0	4.48	87	.297	.337	0	—	0	-4	-6	0	-0.4
1984	NY-A	1	2	.333	19	0	0	0	0	23^2	30	15	2	2	5	13	14.1	4.94	77	.306	.352	0	—	0	-2	-3	-0	-0.4
1985	NY-A	0	0	—	3	0	0	0	0	2	4	3	0	0	0	0	18.0	13.50	30	.400	.400	0	—	0	-2	-2	-0	-0.1
	Tex-A	0	0	—	1	0	0	0	0	1	3	2	0	0	0	0	27.0	18.00	24	.750	.750	0	—	0	-2	-1	0	-0.1
	Yr	0	0	—	4	0	0	0	0	3	7	5	0	0	0	0	21.0	15.00	27	.500	.500	0	—	0	-4	-4	0	-0.2
Total	12	53	50	.515	518	1	0	0	60	902^1	976	448	40	14	329	400	13.2	3.85	100	.282	.346	5	.077	-3	-8	0	13	1.2
● **DAN MURRAY**	Murray, Daniel Saffle b: 11/21/73, Los Alamitos, Cal. BR/TR, 6'1", 193 lbs. Deb: 8/9/99																											
1999	NY-N	0	0	—	1	0	0	0	0	2	4	3	0	0	2	1	27.0	13.50	32	.444	.545	0	—	0	-2	-2	0	-0.1
	KC-A	0	0	—	4	0	0	0	0	8^1	9	8	4	1	4	8	15.1	6.48	77	.265	.359	0	—	0	-1	-1	0	-0.1
2000	KC-A	0	0	—	10	0	0	0	0	19^1	20	10	7	1	10	16	14.4	4.66	108	.278	.373	0	—	0	1	1	1	0.1
Total	2	0	0	—	15	0	0	0	0	29^2	33	21	11	2	16	25	15.5	5.76	86	.287	.383	0	—	0	-3	-3	1	-0.1
● **GEORGE MURRAY**	Murray, George King "Smiler" b: 9/23/1898, Charlotte, N.C. d: 10/18/55, Memphis, Tenn. BR/TR, 6'2", 200 lbs. Deb: 5/8/22																											
1922	NY-A	3	2	.600	22	2	0	0	0	56^2	53	27	0	1	26	14	12.7	3.97	101	.255	.340	5	.278	2	**0**	**0**	-0	0.2
1923	Bos-A	7	11	.389	39	18	5	0	0	177^2	190	111	9	7	87	40	14.4	4.91	84	.291	.380	9	.164	-3	-18	-15	-2	-1.8
1924	Bos-A	2	9	.182	28	7	0	0	0	80^1	97	68	6	7	32	27	15.2	6.72	65	.307	.383	4	.182	-1	-22	-20	0	-2.3
1926	Was-A	6	3	.667	12	12	5	0	0	81^1	89	56	1	6	37	28	14.6	5.64	69	.287	.374	5	.139	-2	-15	-17	-1	-1.7
1927	Was-A	1	1	.500	7	3	0	0	0	18	18	18	1	2	15	5	17.5	7.00	58	.265	.412	1	.167	-0	-6	-6	-1	-0.6
1933	Chi-A	0	0	—	2	0	0	0	0	2^1	3	2	0	0	2	0	19.3	7.71	55	.375	.500	0	—	0	-1	-1	0	0.0
Total	6	19	26	.422	110	42	10	0	0	416^1	450	282	17	23	199	114	14.5	5.38	76	.288	.376	24	.175	-4	-61	-59	-3	-6.2
● **HEATH MURRAY**	Murray, Heath Robertson b: 4/19/73, Troy, O. BL/TL, 6'4", 205 lbs. Deb: 5/24/97																											
1997	SD-N	1	2	.333	17	3	0	0	0	33^1	50	25	3	4	21	16	20.3	6.75	58	.376	.475	0	.000	-1	-9	-12	-1	-1.0
1999	SD-N	0	4	.000	22	8	0	0	0	50	60	33	7	1	26	25	15.7	5.76	73	.297	.380	2	.154	0	-7	-9	-0	-0.6
Total	2	1	6	.143	39	11	0	0	0	83^1	110	58	10	5	47	41	17.5	6.16	66	.328	.419	2	.105	-1	-16	-21	-1	-1.6
● **JIM MURRAY**	Murray, James Francis "Big Jim" b: 12/31/1900, Scranton, Pa. d: 7/15/73, Queens, N.Y. BB/TL, 6'2", 210 lbs. Deb: 7/3/22																											
1922	Bro-N	0	0	—	4	0	0	0	1	6	8	3	0	0	3	3	16.5	4.50	90	.320	.393	1	.500	0	-0	-0	-0	0.0
● **JOE MURRAY**	Murray, Joseph Ambrose b: 11/11/20, Wilkes-Barre, Pa. BL/TL, 6', 165 lbs. Deb: 8/17/50																											
1950	Phi-A	0	3	.000	8	2	0	0	0	30	34	20	1	0	21	8	16.5	5.70	80	.283	.390	0	.000	-2	-4	-4	1	-0.4
● **MATT MURRAY**	Murray, Matthew Michael b: 9/26/70, Boston, Mass. BL/TR, 6'6", 240 lbs. Deb: 8/12/95																											
1995	Atl-N	0	2	.000	4	1	0	0	0	10^2	10	8	3	1	5	3	13.5	6.75	63	.256	.356	1	.500	0	-3	-3	0	-0.4
	Bos-A	0	1	.000	2	1	0	0	0	3^1	11	10	1	0	3	1	37.8	18.90	26	.524	.583	0	—	0	-5	-5	0	-0.8
Total	1	0	3	.000	6	2	0	0	0	14	21	18	4	1	8	4	19.3	9.64	46	.350	.435	1	.500	0	-8	-8	1	-1.2
● **PAT MURRAY**	Murray, Patrick Joseph b: 7/18/1897, Scottsville, N.Y. d: 11/5/83, Rochester, N.Y. BR/TL, 6', 175 lbs. Deb: 7/1/19																											
1919	Phi-N	0	2	.000	8	2	1	0	0	34^1	50	28	0	4	12	11	17.3	6.29	51	.347	.412	0	.000	-1	-13	-11	-0	-0.8
● **DENNIS MUSGRAVES**	Musgraves, Dennis Eugene b: 12/25/43, Indianapolis, Ind. BR/TR, 6'4", 188 lbs. Deb: 7/9/65																											
1965	NY-N	0	0	—	5	1	0	0	0	16	11	2	0	2	7	11	11.3	0.56	627	.200	.313	0	.000	-0	5	5	-0	0.3
● **STAN MUSIAL**	Musial, Stanley Frank "Stan The Man" b: 11/21/20, Donora, Pa. BL/TL, 6', 175 lbs. Deb: 9/17/41 H♦																											
1952	StL-N★	0	0	—	1	0	0	0	0	0	0	0	0	0	—	—	—	—	.000	.000	100	.336	1	0	0	0		0.0
● **JEFF MUSSELMAN**	Musselman, Jeffrey Joseph b: 6/21/63, Doylestown, Pa. BL/TL, 6', 180 lbs. Deb: 9/2/86																											
1986	Tor-A	0	0	—	6	0	0	0	0	5^1	8	7	1	0	5	4	21.9	10.13	42	.333	.448	0	—	0	-4	-3	0	-0.2
1987	Tor-A	12	5	.706	68	1	0	0	3	89	75	43	7	3	54	54	13.3	4.15	109	.237	.354	0	—	0	3	4	1	0.7
1988	Tor-A	8	5	.615	15	15	0	0	0	85	80	34	4	3	30	39	12.0	3.18	124	.252	.322	0	—	0	8	7	-1	0.9
1989	Tor-A	0	1	.000	5	3	0	0	0	11	19	15	2	0	9	3	22.9	10.64	36	.404	.500	0	—	0	-8	-9	-0	-0.7
	NY-N	3	2	.600	20	0	0	0	0	26^1	27	11	1	0	14	11	14.0	3.08	106	.267	.357	0	—	0	1	1	2	0.3
1990	NY-N	0	2	.000	28	0	0	0	0	32	40	22	3	1	11	14	14.6	5.63	67	.310	.369	0	.000	-0	-6	-7	0	-0.4
Total	5	23	15	.605	142	19	0	0	3	248^2	249	132	18	7	123	125	13.7	4.31	94	.266	.356	0	.000	0	-6	-7	2	0.6
● **RON MUSSELMAN**	Musselman, Ralph Ronald b: 11/11/54, Wilmington, N.C. BR/TR, 6'2", 185 lbs. Deb: 8/18/82																											
1982	Sea-A	1	0	1.000	12	0	0	0	0	15^2	18	7	2	1	6	9	14.4	3.45	123	.300	.373	0	—	0	1	1	0	0.1
1984	Tor-A	0	2	.000	11	0	0	0	1	21^1	18	7	2	0	10	9	11.8	2.11	195	.225	.311	0	—	0	4	5	-0	0.4
1985	Tor-A	3	0	1.000	25	4	0	0	0	52^1	59	28	2	0	24	29	14.3	4.47	94	.284	.358	0	—	0	-2	-1	-1	-0.2
Total	3	4	2	.667	48	4	0	0	1	89^1	95	42	6	1	40	47	13.7	3.73	112	.273	.350	0	—	0	4	5	-1	0.3
● **PAUL MUSSER**	Musser, Paul b: 6/24/1889, Millheim, Pa. d: 7/7/73, State College, Pa. BR/TR, 6', 175 lbs. Deb: 6/6/12																											
1912	Was-A	0	0	—	7	2	0	0	2	20^2	16	7	0	2	16	10	14.8	2.61	128	.225	.382	0	.000	-1	2	2	0	0.0
1919	Bos-A	0	2	.000	5	4	1	0	0	19^2	26	16	0	0	8	14	15.6	4.12	73	.342	.405	0	.000	-1	-2	-3	-0	-0.4
Total	2	0	2	.000	12	6	1	0	2	40^1	42	23	0	2	24	24	15.2	3.35	95	.286	.393	0	.000	-2	-0	-1	0	-0.4
● **BARNEY MUSSILL**	Mussill, Bernard James b: 10/1/19, Bower Hill, Pa. BR/TL, 6'1", 200 lbs. Deb: 4/20/44																											
1944	Phi-N	0	1	.000	16	0	0	0	0	19^1	20	16	1	0	13	5	15.4	6.05	60	.267	.375	0	.000	-0	-5	-5	-0	-0.3
● **MIKE MUSSINA**	Mussina, Michael Cole b: 12/8/68, Williamsport, Pa. BR/TR, 6'2", 185 lbs. Deb: 8/4/91																											
1991	Bal-A	4	5	.444	12	12	2	0	0	87^2	77	31	7	1	21	52	10.2	2.87	138	.239	.288	0	—	0	12	11	-0	1.0
1992	Bal-A★	18	5	**.783**	32	32	8	4	0	241	212	70	16	2	48	130	**9.8**	2.54	159	.239	**.279**	0	—	0	38	39	-0	3.6
1993	Bal-A☆	14	6	.700	25	25	3	2	0	167^2	163	84	20	3	44	117	11.3	4.46	101	.256	.307	0	—	0	-2	1	-0	0.0
1994	Bal-A★	16	5	.762	24	24	3	0	0	176^1	163	63	19	1	42	99	10.5	3.06	164	.248	.294	0	—	0	34	37	1	4.1
1995	Bal-A	**19**	9	.679	32	32	7	**4**	0	221^2	187	86	24	1	50	158	9.7	3.29	145	.226	.271	0	—	0	35	36	-1	4.0
1996	*Bal-A	19	11	.633	36	36	4	1	0	243^1	264	137	31	3	69	204	12.4	4.81	102	.275	.326	0	—	0	5	3	1	0.4
1997	*Bal-A☆	15	8	.652	33	33	4	1	0	224^2	197	87	27	3	54	218	10.2	3.20	138	.234	.282	1	.250	0	34	31	0	2.9
1998	Bal-A	13	10	.565	29	29	4	2	0	206^1	189	85	22	4	41	175	10.2	3.49	131	.242	.283	0	.000	-0	27	25	3	2.7
1999	Bal-A★	18	7	.720	31	31	4	0	0	203^1	207	88	16	1	52	172	11.5	3.50	134	.268	.315	3	.273	1	31	28	5	3.6
2000	Bal-A	11	15	.423	34	34	6	1	0	**237^2**	236	105	28	3	46	210	10.8	3.79	126	.255	.293	0	.000	-1	30	27	0	2.5
Total	10	147	81	.645	288	288	45	15	0	2009^2	1895	836	210	22	467	1535	10.7	3.53	130	.249	.294	4	.174	0	244	239	9	24.8
● **ALEX MUSTAIKIS**	Mustaikis, Alexander Dominick b: 3/26/09, Chelsea, Mass. d: 1/17/70, Scranton, Pa. BR/TR, 6'3", 180 lbs. Deb: 7/7/40																											
1940	Bos-A	0	1	.000	6	1	0	0	0	15	15	18	1	0	15	6	18.0	9.00	50	.254	.405	2	.333	1	-8	-7	1	-0.3

YEAR	TM/L	W	L	PCT	G	GS	CG	SH	SV	IP	H	R	HR	HB	BB	SO	RAT	ERA	ERA+	OAV	OOB	BH	AVG	PB	PR	PR+	PD	TPI
● JEFF MUTIS Mutis, Jeffrey Thomas b: 12/20/66, Allentown, Pa. BL/TL, 6'2", 185 lbs. Deb: 6/15/91																												
1991	Cle-A	0	3	.000	3	3	0	0	0	12^1	23	16	1	0	7	6	21.9	11.68	36	.397	.462	0	—	0	-10	-10	-0	-1.5
1992	Cle-A	0	2	.000	3	2	0	0	0	11^1	24	14	4	0	6	8	23.8	9.53	41	.429	.484	0	—	0	-7	-7	0	-1.0
1993	Cle-A	3	6	.333	17	13	1	1	0	81	93	56	14	7	33	29	14.8	5.78	75	.289	.367	0	—	0	-13	-13	1	-1.1
1994	Fla-N	1	0	1.000	35	0	0	0	0	38^1	51	25	6	1	15	30	15.7	5.40	81	.331	.394	0	.000	-0	-5	-4	0	-0.2
Total	4	4	11	.267	58	18	1	1	0	143	191	111	25	8	61	73	16.4	6.48	66	.324	.395	0	.000	-0	-35	-34	1	-3.8
● ELMER MYERS Myers, Elmer Glenn b: 3/2/1894, York Springs, Pa. d: 7/29/76, Collingswood, N.J. BR/TR, 6'2", 185 lbs. Deb: 10/6/15																												
1915	Phi-A	1	0	1.000	1	1	1	1	0	9	2	0	0	0	5	12	7.0	0.00	—	.074	.219	0	.000	-0	3	3	-0	0.2
1916	Phi-A	14	23	.378	44	35	31	2	1	315	280	169	7	14	168	182	13.2	3.66	78	.248	.353	27	.214	2	-29	-28	5	-2.3
1917	Phi-A	9	16	.360	38	23	13	2	3	201^2	221	122	2	5	79	88	13.6	4.42	62	.283	.353	18	.247	2	-39	-36	1	-4.0
1918	Phi-A	4	8	.333	18	15	5	1	1	95^1	101	66	4	4	42	17	13.9	4.63	63	.283	.365	5	.143	-2	-20	-17	2	-2.1
1919	Cle-A	8	7	.533	23	15	6	1	1	134^2	134	68	3	10	43	38	12.5	3.74	89	.264	.334	11	.239	2	-8	-6	1	-0.3
1920	Cle-A	2	4	.333	16	7	2	0	1	71^2	93	52	1	4	23	16	15.1	4.77	80	.316	.374	6	.240	0	-8	-8	0	-0.6
	Bos-A	9	1	.900	12	10	9	1	0	97	90	30	1	2	24	34	10.8	2.13	171	.249	.299	12	.316	3	18	17	-1	1.9
	Yr	11	5	.688	28	17	11	1	1	168^2	183	82	2	6	47	50	12.6	3.25	114	.279	.333	18	.286	3	10	9	-1	1.3
1921	Bos-A	8	12	.400	30	20	11	0	0	172	217	107	11	10	53	40	14.7	4.87	87	.315	.373	14	.215	-2	-11	-12	0	-1.3
1922	Bos-A	0	1	.000	3	1	0	0	0	5^2	10	11	1	2	3	1	23.8	17.47	24	.370	.469	0	.000	-0	-8	-8	0	-1.1
Total	8	55	72	.433	185	127	78	8	7	1102	1148	625	30	51	440	428	13.4	4.06	80	.275	.352	93	.226	4	-102	-96	8	-9.6
● HENRY MYERS Myers, Henry C. b: 5/1858, Philadelphia, Pa. d: 4/18/1895, Philadelphia, Pa. BR/TR, 5'9", 159 lbs. Deb: 8/20/1881 M◆																												
1882	Bal-a	0	2	.000	6	2	1	0	0	26	30	28	2		4	7	11.8	6.58	42	.270	.296	53	.180	-1	-11	-11	-0	-0.7
● JIMMY MYERS Myers, James Xavier b: 4/28/69, Oklahoma City, Okla. BR/TR, 6'1", 190 lbs. Deb: 4/6/96																												
1996	Bal-A	0	0	—	11	0	0	0	0	14	18	13	4	0	3	6	13.5	7.07	70	.305	.339	0	—	0	-3	-3	-0	-0.2
● JOSEPH MYERS Myers, Joseph William b: 3/18/1882, Wilmington, Del. d: 2/11/56, Delaware City, Del. BR/TR, 5'10.5", 205 lbs. Deb: 10/7/05																												
1905	Phi-A	0	0	—	1	1	1	0	0	5	3	3	0	1	3	5	12.6	3.60	74	.176	.333	0	.000	-0	-1	-1	-0	-0.1
● MIKE MYERS Myers, Michael Stanley b: 6/26/69, Cook County, Ill. BL/TL, 6'3", 200 lbs. Deb: 4/25/95																												
1995	Fla-N	0	0	—	2	0	0	0	0	2	1	0	0	0	3	0	18.0	0.00	—	.167	.444	0	—	0	1	1	-0	0.0
	Det-A	1	0	1.000	11	0	0	0	0	6^1	10	7	1	2	4	4	22.7	9.95	48	.385	.500	0	—	0	-4	-4	0	-0.5
1996	Det-A	1	5	.167	**83**	0	0	0	6	64^2	70	41	6	4	34	69	15.0	5.01	101	.272	.366	0	—	0	-0	0	2	0.2
1997	Det-A	0	4	.000	**88**	0	0	0	2	53^2	58	36	12	2	25	50	14.3	5.70	81	.274	.356	0	—	0	-7	-7	0	-0.4
1998	Mil-N	2	2	.500	70	0	0	0	1	50	44	19	5	6	22	40	13.0	2.70	158	.249	.351	0	—	0	9	9	1	0.7
1999	Mil-N	2	1	.667	71	0	0	0	0	41^1	46	24	7	3	13	35	13.5	5.23	87	.291	.356	0	.000	-0	-3	-3	-0	-0.1
2000	Col-N	0	1	.000	78	0	0	0	1	45^1	24	10	2	2	24	41	9.9	1.99	299	.160	.284	0	—	0	13	16	1	0.8
Total	6	6	13	.316	403	0	0	0	10	263^1	253	137	33	19	125	239	13.6	4.31	113	.257	.351	0	.000	-0	9	16	4	0.7
● RANDY MYERS Myers, Randall Kirk b: 9/19/62, Vancouver, Wash. BL/TL, 6'1", 215 lbs. Deb: 10/6/85																												
1985	NY-N	0	0	—	1	0	0	0	0	2	0	0	0	0	1	2	4.5	0.00	—	.000	.143	0	—	0	1	1	0	0.1
1986	NY-N	0	0	—	10	0	0	0	0	10^2	11	5	1	1	9	13	17.7	4.22	84	.256	.396	0	—	0	-1	-1	0	0.0
1987	NY-N	3	6	.333	54	0	0	0	6	75	61	36	6	0	30	92	10.9	3.96	96	.225	.302	2	.286	1	1	-2	0	-0.1
1988	*NY-N	7	3	.700	55	0	0	0	26	68	45	15	5	2	17	69	8.5	1.72	187	.190	.250	1	.250	1	13	12	-1	2.7
1989	NY-N	7	4	.636	65	0	0	0	24	84^1	62	23	4	0	40	88	10.9	2.35	139	.206	.299	0	.000	-1	11	9	0	1.6
1990	*Cin-N★	4	6	.400	66	0	0	0	31	86^2	59	24	6	3	38	98	10.4	2.08	190	.193	.288	1	.250	0	17	17	0	3.1
1991	Cin-N	6	13	.316	58	12	1	0	6	132	116	61	8	1	80	108	13.4	3.55	107	.242	.351	5	.172	0	2	4	-1	0.4
1992	SD-N	3	6	.333	66	0	0	0	38	79^2	84	38	7	1	34	66	13.4	4.29	83	.279	.354	1	.143	-0	-7	-6	-0	-1.3
1993	Chi-N	2	4	.333	73	0	0	0	**53**	75^1	65	26	7	1	26	86	11.0	3.11	129	.230	.297	1	.500	1	8	8	-1	1.5
1994	Chi-N★	1	5	.167	38	0	0	0	21	40^1	40	18	3	0	16	32	12.5	3.79	110	.260	.329	0	.000	-0	2	2	-1	0.2
1995	Chi-N★	1	2	.333	57	0	0	0	**38**	55^2	49	25	7	0	28	59	12.4	3.88	106	.237	.328	0	—	0	2	1	0	0.3
1996	*Bal-A	4	4	.500	62	0	0	0	31	58^2	60	24	7	1	29	74	13.8	3.53	140	.265	.352	0	—	0	10	9	-1	1.7
1997	*Bal-A★	2	3	.400	61	0	0	0	**45**	59^2	47	12	2	0	22	56	10.4	1.51	292	.217	.289	0	—	0	20	20	-1	3.8
1998	Tor-A	3	4	.429	41	0	0	0	28	42^1	44	21	4	2	19	32	13.8	4.46	105	.265	.348	0	.000	-0	1	1	-1	0.1
	*SD-N	1	3	.250	21	0	0	0	0	14^1	15	10	2	0	7	9	13.8	6.28	62	.273	.355	0	—	0	-3	-4	-0	-0.8
Total	14	44	63	.411	728	12	1	0	347	884^2	758	338	69	12	396	884	11.9	3.19	122	.233	.318	11	.183	2	76	71	-5	13.3
● RODNEY MYERS Myers, Rodney Luther b: 6/26/69, Rockford, Ill. BR/TR, 6'1", 200 lbs. Deb: 4/3/96																												
1996	Chi-N	2	1	.667	45	0	0	0	0	67^1	61	38	6	3	38	50	13.6	4.68	93	.243	.349	0	.000	-1	-3	-2	-1	-0.2
1997	Chi-N	0	0	—	5	1	0	0	0	9	12	6	1	1	7	6	20.0	6.00	72	.333	.455	0	—	0	-2	-2	-0	-0.1
1998	Chi-N	0	0	—	12	0	0	0	0	18	26	14	3	0	6	15	16.0	7.00	63	.342	.390	0	.000	-0	-6	-5	-0	-0.3
1999	Chi-N	3	1	.750	46	0	0	0	0	63^2	71	34	10	1	25	41	13.7	4.38	103	.289	.357	3	.429	1	1	1	-1	0.1
2000	SD-N	0	0	—	3	0	0	0	0	2	2	1	0	0	0	3	9.0	4.50	97	.250	.250	0	—	0	0	-0	0	0.0
Total	5	5	2	.714	111	1	0	0	0	160	172	93	20	5	76	115	14.2	4.89	90	.279	.362	3	.231	1	-9	-8	-2	-0.5
● AARON MYETTE Myette, Aaron Kenneth b: 9/26/77, New Westminster, B.C., Can. BR/TR, 6'4", 195 lbs. Deb: 9/7/99																												
1999	Chi-A	0	2	.000	4	3	0	0	0	15^2	17	11	2	2	14	11	19.0	6.32	77	.266	.412	0	—	0	-3	-2	-0	-0.3
2000	Chi-A	0	0	—	2	0	0	0	0	2^2	0	0	0	0	4	1	13.5	0.00	—	.000	.333	0	—	0	1	1	-0	0.1
Total	2	0	2	.000	6	3	0	0	0	18^1	17	11	2	2	18	12	18.2	5.40	91	.236	.402	0	—	0	-1	-1	-0	-0.2
● BOB MYRICK Myrick, Robert Howard b: 10/1/52, Hattiesburg, Miss. BR/TL, 6'1", 195 lbs. Deb: 5/28/76																												
1976	NY-N	1	1	.500	21	1	0	0	0	27^2	34	13	2	0	13	11	15.3	3.25	101	.306	.379	0	.000	-0	1	0	0	0.0
1977	NY-N	2	2	.500	44	4	0	0	2	87^1	86	39	5	1	33	49	12.4	3.61	104	.265	.334	2	.182	-0	3	1	0	0.1
1978	NY-N	0	3	.000	17	0	0	0	0	24^2	18	10	3	0	13	13	11.3	3.28	106	.207	.310	0	.000	-0	1	1	0	0.1
Total	3	3	6	.333	82	5	0	0	2	139^2	138	62	10	1	59	73	12.8	3.48	104	.264	.340	2	.125	-1	5	2	1	0.2
● CHRIS NABHOLZ Nabholz, Christopher William b: 1/5/67, Harrisburg, Pa. BL/TL, 6'5", 212 lbs. Deb: 6/11/90																												
1990	Mon-N	6	2	.750	11	11	1	1	0	70	43	23	6	2	32	53	9.9	2.83	129	.176	.276	0	.000	-2	8	7	-0	0.5
1991	Mon-N	8	7	.533	24	24	1	0	0	153^2	134	66	5	2	57	99	11.3	3.63	100	.237	.309	6	.115	-1	1	-0	1	0.0
1992	Mon-N	11	12	.478	32	32	1	1	0	195	176	80	11	5	74	130	11.8	3.32	104	.244	.318	8	.123	-1	4	3	3	0.6
1993	Mon-N	9	8	.529	26	21	1	0	0	116^2	100	57	9	8	63	74	13.2	4.09	102	.236	.346	5	.128	-1	-1	1	0	0.0
1994	Cle-A	0	1	.000	6	4	0	0	0	11	23	16	1	1	9	5	27.0	11.45	41	.418	.508	0	—	0	-8	-8	0	-0.6
	Bos-A	3	4	.429	8	8	0	0	0	42	44	32	5	2	29	23	16.1	6.64	76	.282	.401	0	—	0	-9	-7	0	-0.9
	Yr	3	5	.375	14	12	0	0	0	53	67	48	6	3	38	28	18.3	7.64	65	.318	.429	0	—	0	-17	-15	0	-1.5
1995	Chi-N	0	1	.000	34	0	0	0	0	23^1	22	15	4	0	14	21	13.9	5.40	76	.253	.356	0	.000	-0	-3	-3	0	-0.1
Total	6	37	35	.514	141	100	4	2	0	611^2	542	289	41	20	278	405	12.4	3.94	97	.240	.329	19	.107	-5	-8	-9	4	-0.5
● JACK NABORS Nabors, Herman John b: 11/19/1887, Montevallo, Ala. d: 11/20/23, Wilton, Ala. BR/TR, 6'3", 185 lbs. Deb: 8/9/15																												
1915	Phi-A	0	5	.000	10	7	2	0	0	54	58	46	1	5	35	18	16.3	5.50	53	.304	.424	2	.125	-1	-15	-16	-0	-1.4
1916	Phi-A	1	20	.048	40	30	11	0	1	212^2	206	110	2	3	95	74	12.9	3.47	82	.266	.349	7	.101	-4	-15	-14	-2	-2.1
1917	Phi-A	0	0	—	2	0	0	0	0	3	2	1	0	0	1	2	9.0	3.00	92	.200	.273	0	—	0	-0	-0	0	0.0
Total	3	1	25	.038	52	37	13	0	1	269^2	266	157	3	8	131	94	13.5	3.87	74	.273	.364	9	.106	-6	-31	-30	-2	-3.5
● BILL NAGEL Nagel, William Taylor b: 8/19/15, Memphis, Tenn. d: 10/8/81, Freehold, N.J. BR/TR, 6'1", 190 lbs. Deb: 4/20/39 ◆																												
1939	Phi-A	0	0	—	1	0	0	0	0	3	7	5	1	0	1	0	24.0	12.00	39	.438	.471	86	.252	0	-2	-2	-0	-0.1
● JUDGE NAGLE Nagle, Walter Harold "Lucky" b: 3/10/1880, Santa Rosa, Cal. d: 5/26/71, Santa Rosa, Cal. BR/TR, 6', 176 lbs. Deb: 4/26/11																												
1911	Pit-N	4	2	.667	8	3	1	0	1	27^1	33	16	3	1	6	11	13.2	3.62	95	.324	.367	1	.143	-0	-1	-1	0	-0.1
	Bos-A	1	1	.500	5	1	0	0	0	27	27	12	2	0	6	12	11.0	3.33	98	.262	.303	1	.100	-1	0	-0	-1	-0.2
Total	1	5	3	.625	13	4	1	0	1	54^1	60	28	5	1	12	23	12.1	3.48	97	.293	.335	2	.118	-1	-1	-1	-1	-0.3

YEAR	TM/L	W	L	PCT	G	GS	CG	SH	SV	IP	H	R	HR	HB	BB	SO	RAT	ERA	ERA+	OAV	OOB	BH	AVG	PB	PR	PR+	PD	TPI
● CHARLES NAGY Nagy, Charles Harrison b: 5/5/67, Bridgeport, Conn. BL/TR, 6'3", 200 lbs. Deb: 6/29/90																												
1990	Cle-A	2	4	.333	9	8	0	0	0	45^2	58	31	7	1	21	26	15.8	5.91	66	.315	.388	0	—	0	-10	-10	1	-1.1
1991	Cle-A	10	15	.400	33	33	6	1	0	211^1	228	103	15	6	66	109	12.8	4.13	101	.275	.333	0	—	0	-1	1	-1	-0.1
1992	Cle-A★	17	10	.630	33	33	10	3	0	252	245	91	11	2	57	169	10.9	2.96	132	.260	.303	0	—	0	28	27	3	3.1
1993	Cle-A	2	6	.250	9	9	1	0	0	48^2	66	38	6	2	13	30	15.0	6.29	69	.322	.368	0	—	0	-11	-11	2	-1.2
1994	Cle-A	10	8	.556	23	23	3	0	0	169^1	175	76	15	5	48	108	12.1	3.45	137	.265	.320	0	—	0	25	24	1	2.3
1995	*Cle-A	16	6	.727	29	29	2	1	0	178	194	95	20	6	61	139	13.2	4.55	103	.278	.342	0	—	0	3	3	3	0.6
1996	*Cle-A★	17	5	**.773**	32	32	5	0	0	222	217	89	21	3	61	167	11.4	3.41	144	.255	.307	0	—	0	39	37	3	3.5
1997	*Cle-A	15	11	.577	34	34	1	1	0	227	253	115	27	7	77	149	13.4	4.28	110	.282	.344	1	.200	0	7	10	3	1.3
1998	*Cle-A	15	10	.600	33	33	2	0	0	210^1	250	139	34	9	66	120	13.9	5.22	91	.297	.355	0	.000	-1	-13	-10	4	-0.7
1999	*Cle-A☆	17	11	.607	33	32	1	0	0	202	238	120	26	6	59	126	13.5	4.95	102	.293	.345	0	.000	-1	-2	2	2	0.4
2000	Cle-A	2	7	.222	11	11	0	0	0	57	71	53	15	2	21	41	14.8	8.21	61	.300	.362	0	—	0	-21	-20	2	-2.2
Total	11	123	93	.569	279	277	31	6	0	1823^1	1995	950	197	49	550	1184	12.8	4.32	106	.279	.334	1	.063	-1	46	52	23	5.9
● MIKE NAGY Nagy, Michael Timothy b: 3/25/48, Bronx, N.Y. BR/TR, 6'3", 200 lbs. Deb: 4/21/69																												
1969	Bos-A	12	2	.857	33	28	7	1	0	196^2	183	84	10	11	106	84	13.7	3.11	122	.245	.347	5	.077	-2	11	14	0	0.8
1970	Bos-A	6	5	.545	23	20	4	0	0	128^2	138	71	16	2	64	56	14.3	4.48	89	.275	.359	11	.250	2	-11	-7	-1	-0.4
1971	Bos-A	1	3	.250	12	7	0	0	0	38	46	29	4	0	20	9	15.6	6.63	56	.315	.398	1	.083	-1	-13	-12	-0	-1.2
1972	Bos-A	0	0	—	1	0	0	0	0	2	3	2	0	1	0	2	18.0	9.00	36	.375	.444	0	—	0	-1	-1	-0	-0.1
1973	StL-N	0	2	.000	9	7	0	0	0	40^2	44	21	4	1	15	14	13.3	4.20	87	.282	.349	1	.091	-1	-2	-3	-0	-0.2
1974	Hou-N	1	1	.500	9	0	0	0	0	12^2	17	13	3	1	5	5	16.3	8.53	41	.309	.377	0	.000	-0	-7	-7	-0	-1.0
Total	6	20	13	.606	87	62	11	1	0	418^2	431	220	37	16	210	170	14.1	4.15	92	.267	.357	18	.135	-2	-24	-15	-1	-2.1
● STEVE NAGY Nagy, Stephen b: 5/28/19, Franklin, N.J. BL/TL, 5'10", 170 lbs. Deb: 4/20/47																												
1947	Pit-N	1	3	.250	6	1	0	0	0	14	18	10	1	0	9	4	17.4	5.79	73	.310	.403	1	.250	0	-3	-2	0	-0.4
1950	Was-A	2	5	.286	9	9	2	0	0	53^1	69	50	5	0	29	17	16.5	6.58	68	.307	.386	5	.227	2	-12	-13	-0	-1.1
Total	2	3	8	.273	15	10	2	0	0	67^1	87	60	6	0	38	21	16.7	6.42	69	.307	.389	6	.231	2	-15	-15	-0	-1.5
● SAM NAHEM Nahem, Samuel Ralph "Subway Sam" b: 10/19/15, New York, N.Y. BR/TR, 6'1.5", 190 lbs. Deb: 10/2/38																												
1938	Bro-N	1	0	1.000	1	1	1	0	0	9	6	3	0	0	4	2	10.0	3.00	130	.194	.286	2	.400	0	1	1	-0	0.1
1941	StL-N	5	2	.714	26	8	2	0	1	81^2	76	35	2	2	38	31	12.8	2.98	126	.243	.329	4	.174	-1	6	7	1	0.6
1942	Phi-N	1	3	.250	35	2	0	0	0	74^2	72	48	2	2	40	38	13.7	4.94	67	.254	.350	2	.100	-1	-13	-14	1	-0.7
1948	Phi-N	3	3	.500	28	1	0	0	0	59	68	52	4	3	45	30	17.7	7.02	56	.288	.408	2	.154	-0	-20	-20	-1	-1.9
Total	4	10	8	.556	90	12	3	0	1	224^1	222	138	8	7	127	101	14.3	4.69	78	.257	.357	10	.164	-2	-27	-25	1	-1.9
● PETE NAKTENIS Naktenis, Peter Ernest b: 6/12/14, Aberdeen, Wash. BL/TL, 6'1", 185 lbs. Deb: 6/13/36																												
1936	Phi-A	0	1	.000	7	1	0	0	0	18^2	24	26	2	2	27	18	25.6	12.54	41	.324	.515	1	.200	-0	-16	-15	-1	-0.7
1939	Cin-N	0	0	—	3	0	0	0	0	4	2	1	0	2	0	1	9.0	2.25	170	.154	.267	0	—	0	1	1	0	0.1
Total	2	0	1	.000	10	1	0	0	0	22^2	26	27	2	4	27	19	22.6	10.72	45	.299	.483	1	.200	-0	-15	-15	-0	-0.6
● BUDDY NAPIER Napier, Skelton Le Roy b: 12/18/1889, Byromville, Ga. d: 3/29/68, Hutchins, Tex. BR/TR, 5'11", 165 lbs. Deb: 8/14/12																												
1912	StL-A	1	2	.333	7	2	0	0	0	25^1	33	21	0	3	5	10	14.6	4.97	67	.317	.366	0	.000	-1	-5	-5	-0	-0.6
1918	Chi-N	0	0	—	1	0	0	0	0	6^2	10	4	0	0	4	2	18.9	5.40	52	.357	.438	1	.333	0	-2	-2	-0	-0.1
1920	Cin-N	4	2	.667	9	5	5	1	0	49	47	12	0	1	7	17	10.1	1.29	236	.254	.285	3	.214	1	10	10	0	1.4
1921	Cin-N	0	2	.000	22	6	1	0	1	56^2	72	38	2	0	13	14	13.5	5.56	64	.329	.366	2	.143	1	-11	-13	1	-0.4
Total	4	5	6	.455	39	13	6	1	1	137^2	162	75	2	4	29	43	12.7	3.92	84	.302	.343	6	.158	1	-8	-10	1	0.3
● CHOLLY NARANJO Naranjo, Lazaro Ramon Gonzalo "Gonzalo" b: 11/25/34, Havana, Cuba BL/TR, 5'11.5", 165 lbs. Deb: 7/8/56																												
1956	Pit-N	1	2	.333	17	3	0	0	0	34^1	37	22	7	1	17	26	14.4	4.46	85	.282	.369	1	.143	0	-3	-3	1	-0.1
● RAY NARLESKI Narleski, Raymond Edmond b: 11/25/28, Camden, N.J. BR/TR, 6'1", 175 lbs. Deb: 4/17/54 F																												
1954	*Cle-A	3	3	.500	42	2	1	0	13	89	59	25	8	2	44	52	10.6	2.22	165	.189	.293	0	.000	-2	15	15	-1	1.1
1955	Cle-A	9	1	.900	**60**	1	1	0	**19**	111^2	91	47	11	0	52	94	11.5	3.71	108	.220	.308	7	.292	1	3	3	-2	0.3
1956	Cle-A†	3	2	.600	32	0	0	0	4	59^1	36	11	5	1	19	42	8.5	1.52	277	.170	.241	2	.250	0	**17**	**18**	-1	1.6
1957	Cle-A	11	5	.688	46	15	7	1	16	154^1	136	65	15	4	70	93	12.2	3.09	120	.235	.322	4	.093	-2	12	11	-4	0.7
1958	Cle-A★	13	10	.565	44	24	7	0	1	183^1	179	87	21	3	91	102	13.4	4.07	90	.255	.343	11	.204	1	-6	-9	-3	-1.3
1959	Det-A	4	12	.250	42	10	1	0	5	104^1	105	83	21	1	59	71	14.2	5.78	70	.254	.348	2	.095	-1	-22	-19	-2	-3.0
Total	6	43	33	.566	266	52	17	1	58	702	606	318	81	11	335	454	12.2	3.60	106	.230	.320	26	.157	-2	19	18	-12	-0.6
● BUSTER NARUM Narum, Leslie Ferdinand b: 11/16/40, Philadelphia, Pa. BR/TR, 6'1", 200 lbs. Deb: 4/14/63																												
1963	Bal-A	0	0	—	7	0	0	0	0	9	8	3	0	0	5	5	13.0	3.00	116	.242	.342	1	1.000	1	1	0	0	0.2
1964	Was-A	9	15	.375	38	32	7	2	0	199	195	104	31	5	73	121	12.3	4.30	86	.259	.328	4	.061	-5	-15	-13	-3	-2.2
1965	Was-A	4	12	.250	46	24	2	0	0	173^2	176	98	16	7	91	86	14.2	4.46	78	.267	.361	2	.043	-2	-19	-19	2	-1.6
1966	Was-A	0	0	—	3	0	0	0	0	3^1	11	9	2	0	4	0	40.5	21.60	16	.579	.652	0	—	0	-7	-7	-0	-0.3
1967	Was-A	1	0	1.000	2	2	0	0	0	11^2	8	4	1	0	4	8	9.3	3.09	103	.195	.267	0	.000	-1	0	0	-0	-0.1
Total	5	14	27	.341	96	58	9	2	0	396^2	398	218	50	12	177	220	13.3	4.45	80	.264	.346	7	.059	-6	-40	-38	-1	-4.0
● JIM NASH Nash, James Edwin b: 2/9/45, Hawthorne, Nev. BR/TR, 6'5", 230 lbs. Deb: 7/3/66																												
1966	KC-A	12	1	.923	18	17	5	0	1	127	95	32	6	0	47	98	10.1	2.06	165	.204	.277	5	.102	-2	19	19	-3	1.5
1967	KC-A	12	17	.414	37	34	8	2	0	222^1	200	103	21	4	87	186	11.8	3.76	85	.242	.317	7	.100	-2	-13	-15	-2	-2.2
1968	Oak-A	13	13	.500	34	33	12	6	0	228^2	185	63	18	3	55	169	9.6	2.28	123	.219	.270	5	.068	-2	18	14	-3	1.2
1969	Oak-A	8	8	.500	26	19	3	1	0	115^1	112	53	17	2	30	75	11.2	3.67	94	.247	.296	4	.111	-1	-1	-3	-1	-0.5
1970	Atl-N	13	9	.591	34	33	6	2	0	212^1	211	105	22	5	90	153	13.0	4.07	106	.257	.334	7	.087	-3	-0	5	0	0.2
1971	Atl-N	9	7	.563	32	19	2	0	2	133	166	81	17	0	50	65	14.6	4.94	75	.314	.374	7	.149	-1	-22	-17	-1	-2.2
1972	Atl-N	1	1	.500	11	4	0	0	1	31^1	35	20	2	0	25	10	17.2	5.46	70	.307	.432	2	.222	0	-7	-5	-0	-0.4
	Phi-N	0	8	.000	9	8	0	0	0	37^1	46	33	5	3	17	15	15.9	6.27	57	.311	.393	1	.100	-0	-12	-11	0	-2.0
	Yr	1	9	.100	20	12	0	0	1	68^2	81	53	7	3	42	25	16.5	5.90	62	.309	.410	3	.158	-0	-19	-16	-0	-2.4
Total	7	68	64	.515	201	167	36	11	4	1107^1	1050	490	108	17	401	771	11.9	3.58	96	.250	.318	38	.101	-11	-17	-16	-10	-4.4
● BILLY NASH Nash, William Mitchell b: 6/24/1865, Richmond, Va. d: 11/15/29, E.Orange, N.J. BR/TR, 5'8.5", 167 lbs. Deb: 8/5/1884 MU♦																												
1889	Bos-N	0	0	—	1	0	0	0	0	1	0	0	0	0	1	0	9.0	0.00	—	.000	.250	132	.274	0	0	0	-0	0.0
1890	Bos-P	0	0	—	1	0	0	0	0	0^1	1	0	0	0	0	0	27.0	0.00	—	.500	.500	130	.266	0	0	0	0	0.0
Total	2	0	0	—	2	0	0	0	0	1^1	1	0	0	0	1	0	13.5	0.00	—	.200	.333	1668	.282	1	1	1	-0	0.0
● PHILIP NASTU Nastu, Philip b: 3/8/55, Bridgeport, Conn. BL/TL, 6'2", 180 lbs. Deb: 9/15/78																												
1978	SF-N	0	1	.000	3	1	0	0	0	8	8	5	1	0	2	5	11.3	5.63	61	.258	.303	0	.000	-0	-2	-2	-0	-0.3
1979	SF-N	3	4	.429	25	14	1	0	0	100	105	51	14	2	41	47	13.3	4.32	81	.272	.345	1	.042	-1	-6	-10	0	-0.7
1980	SF-N	0	0	—	6	0	0	0	0	6	10	9	1	0	5	1	22.5	6.00	59	.357	.455	0	—	0	-2	-2	0	-0.1
Total	3	3	5	.375	34	15	1	0	0	114	123	65	16	2	48	53	13.7	4.50	78	.276	.349	1	.040	-1	-10	-13	0	-1.1
● JOE NATHAN Nathan, Joseph Michael b: 11/22/74, Houston, Tex. BR/TR, 6'4", 195 lbs. Deb: 4/21/99																												
1999	SF-N	7	4	.636	19	14	0	0	1	90^1	84	45	17	1	46	54	13.1	4.18	100	.243	.333	5	.179	1	4	0	-1	0.1
2000	SF-N	5	2	.714	20	15	0	0	0	93^1	89	63	12	4	63	61	15.0	5.21	81	.255	.375	5	.156	3	-6	-11	-0	-0.5
Total	2	12	6	.667	39	29	0	0	1	183^2	173	108	29	5	109	115	14.1	4.70	90	.249	.355	10	.167	4	-2	-11	-1	-0.4
● JOEY NATION Nation, Joseph Paul b: 9/28/78, Oklahoma City, Okla. BL/TL, 6'2", 175 lbs. Deb: 9/23/2000																												
2000	Chi-N	0	2	.000	2	2	0	0	0	11^2	12	9	2	2	8	8	17.0	6.94	66	.279	.415	2	.500	1	-3	-3	0	-0.3
● DAN NAULTY Naulty, Daniel Donovan b: 1/6/70, Los Angeles, Cal. BR/TR, 6'6", 210 lbs. Deb: 4/2/96																												
1996	Min-A	3	2	.600	49	0	0	0	4	57	43	26	5	0	35	56	12.3	3.79	135	.207	.321	0	—	0	8	8	0	0.7
1997	Min-A	1	1	.500	29	0	0	0	1	30^2	29	20	8	0	10	23	11.4	5.87	79	.254	.315	0	—	0	-4	-4	-1	-0.3
1998	Min-A	0	2	.000	19	0	0	0	0	23^2	25	16	3	0	10	15	13.3	4.94	97	.269	.340	0	—	0	-1	-0	-1	-0.1

YEAR	TM/L	W	L	PCT	G	GS	CG	SH	SV	IP	H	R	HR	HB	BB	SO	RAT	ERA	ERA+	OAV	OOB	BH	AVG	PB	PR	PR+	PD	TPI
1999	NY-A	1	0	1.000	33	0	0	0	0	49^1	40	24	8	4	22	25	12.0	4.38	108	.225	.324	0	—	0	3	2	0	0.1
Total	4	5	5	.500	130	0	0	0	5	160^2	137	86	24	4	77	119	12.2	4.54	107	.231	.323	0	—	0	5	6	-1	0.4
● JAIME NAVARRO	Navarro, Jaime (Cintron) b: 3/27/67, Bayamon, P.R. BR/TR, 6'4", 210 lbs. Deb: 6/20/89 F																											
1989	Mil-A	7	8	.467	19	17	1	0	0	109^2	119	47	6	1	32	56	12.5	3.12	123	.277	.328	0	—	0	9	9	-0	1.1
1990	Mil-A	8	7	.533	32	22	3	0	1	149^1	176	83	11	4	41	75	13.3	4.46	87	.293	.343	0	—	0	-9	-10	-0	-0.9
1991	Mil-A	15	12	.556	34	34	10	2	0	234	237	117	18	6	73	114	12.2	3.92	101	.261	.320	0	—	0	5	1	-1	0.0
1992	Mil-A	17	11	.607	34	34	5	3	0	246	224	98	14	6	64	100	10.8	3.33	116	.246	.299	0	—	0	17	14	-3	1.2
1993	Mil-A	11	12	.478	35	34	5	1	0	214^1	254	135	21	11	73	114	14.2	5.33	80	.300	.363	0	—	0	-24	-26	-2	-2.5
1994	Mil-A	4	9	.308	29	10	0	0	0	89^2	115	71	10	4	35	65	15.5	6.62	76	.314	.380	0	—	0	-18	-15	-1	-1.8
1995	Chi-N	14	6	.700	29	29	1	1	0	200^1	194	79	19	3	56	128	11.4	3.28	125	.251	.304	12	.185	2	20	19	-3	1.5
1996	Chi-N	15	12	.556	35	35	4	1	0	236^2	244	116	25	10	72	158	12.4	3.92	111	.269	.329	10	.130	-2	8	11	-3	0.6
1997	Chi-A	9	14	.391	33	33	2	0	0	209^2	267	155	22	3	73	142	14.7	5.79	76	.309	.365	0	.000	-0	-28	-34	-3	-3.3
1998	Chi-A	8	16	.333	37	27	1	0	1	172^2	223	135	30	7	77	71	16.0	6.36	72	.315	.388	0	.000	-0	-33	-35	-2	-4.1
1999	Chi-A	8	13	.381	32	27	0	0	0	159^2	206	126	29	11	71	74	16.2	6.09	80	.313	.389	0	.000	-0	-22	-21	-2	-2.4
2000	Mil-N	0	5	.000	5	5	0	0	0	18^2	34	31	6	0	18	7	25.1	12.54	36	.410	.515	0	.000	-1	-16	-17	-1	-2.5
	Cle-A	0	1	.000	7	2	0	0	0	14^2	20	13	3	1	5	9	16.0	7.98	63	.328	.388	0	—	0	-5	-5	-1	-0.3
Total	12	116	126	.479	361	309	32	8	2	2055^1	2313	1206	214	67	690	1113	13.4	4.72	90	.285	.346	22	.145	-2	-96	-109	-21	-13.4
● JULIO NAVARRO	Navarro, Julio (Ventura) "Whiplash" b: 1/9/36, Vieques, P.R. BR/TR, 5'11", 190 lbs. Deb: 9/3/62 F																											
1962	LA-A	1	1	.500	9	0	0	0	0	15^1	20	9	2	0	4	11	14.1	4.70	82	.317	.358	1	.500	0	-1	-1	-0	-0.2
1963	LA-A	4	5	.444	57	0	0	0	12	90^1	75	36	7	2	32	53	10.9	2.89	119	.228	.300	3	.200	1	7	6	1	0.9
1964	LA-A	0	0	—	5	0	0	0	1	9^1	5	2	0	2	5	8	11.6	1.93	170	.167	.324	0	.000	-0	2	2	0	0.1
	Det-A	2	1	.667	26	0	0	0	2	41	40	19	9	2	16	36	12.7	3.95	93	.250	.326	0	.000	-1	-1	-1	-0	-0.2
	Yr	2	1	.667	31	0	0	0	3	50^1	45	21	9	4	21	44	12.5	3.58	100	.237	.326	0	.000	-1	0	0	0	-0.1
1965	Det-A	0	2	.000	15	1	0	0	1	30	25	16	5	0	12	22	11.1	4.20	83	.238	.316	0	.000	-0	-2	-2	0	-0.2
1966	Det-A	0	0	—	1	0	0	0	0	0	2	2	1	0	—	—	∞	—	1.000	1.000	101	—	0	-3	-3	0	-0.3	
1970	Atl-N	0	0	—	17	0	0	0	1	26^1	24	12	7	1	1	21	8.9	4.10	105	.233	.248	1	.167	-0	-0	1	0	0.0
Total	6	7	9	.438	130	1	0	0	17	212^1	191	97	32	8	70	151	11.4	3.65	99	.241	.309	5	.147	-0	1	-1	1	0.1
● EARL NAYLOR	Naylor, Earl Eugene b: 5/19/19, Kansas City, Mo. d: 1/16/90, Winter Haven, Fla. BR/TR, 6', 190 lbs. Deb: 4/15/42 ♦																											
1942	Phi-N	0	5	.000	20	4	1	0	0	60^1	68	43	5	0	29	19	14.5	6.12	54	.286	.363	33	.196	1	-19	-19	-0	-1.4
● ROLLIE NAYLOR	Naylor, Roleine Cecil b: 2/4/1892, Krum, Tex. d: 6/18/66, Fort Worth, Tex. BR/TR, 6'1.5", 180 lbs. Deb: 9/14/17																											
1917	Phi-A	2	2	.500	5	5	3	0	0	33	30	10	1	1	11	11	11.5	1.64	168	.265	.336	1	.091	-1	4	4	1	0.5
1919	Phi-A	5	18	.217	31	23	17	0	0	204^2	210	109	2	4	64	68	12.2	3.34	103	.280	.339	12	.169	-2	-3	2	-0	-0.1
1920	Phi-A	10	23	.303	42	36	20	0	0	251^1	306	147	7	6	86	90	14.3	3.47	116	.312	.371	14	.163	-6	9	15	2	1.3
1921	Phi-A	3	13	.188	32	19	6	0	0	169^1	214	106	10	3	55	39	14.5	4.84	92	.315	.369	6	.115	-4	-10	-7	-2	-1.0
1922	Phi-A	10	15	.400	35	26	11	0	0	171^1	212	115	7	3	51	37	14.0	4.73	90	.309	.359	11	.200	1	-13	-9	1	-0.9
1923	Phi-A	12	7	.632	26	20	9	2	0	143	149	68	5	0	59	27	13.1	3.46	119	.273	.344	11	.244	1	8	10	-2	1.1
1924	Phi-A	0	5	.000	10	7	1	0	0	38^1	53	29	2	0	20	10	17.1	6.34	68	.333	.408	3	.375	1	-9	-9	0	-0.8
Total	7	42	83	.336	181	136	67	2	0	1011	1174	584	34	17	346	282	13.7	3.93	102	.300	.359	58	.177	-11	-14	7	1	0.1
● MIKE NAYMICK	Naymick, Michael John b: 9/6/17, Berlin, Pa. BR/TR, 6'8", 225 lbs. Deb: 9/24/39																											
1939	Cle-A	0	1	.000	2	1	1	0	0	4^2	3	1	0	0	5	3	15.4	1.93	228	.188	.381	0	.000	-0	1	1	-0	0.2
1940	Cle-A	1	2	.333	13	4	0	0	0	30	36	17	1	3	17	15	16.8	5.10	83	.290	.389	1	.167	0	-2	-3	1	-0.2
1943	Cle-A	4	4	.500	29	4	0	0	2	62^2	32	23	3	3	47	41	11.8	2.30	135	.160	.328	3	.188	-0	7	6	1	0.8
1944	Cle-A	0	0	—	7	0	0	0	0	13	16	15	1	0	10	4	18.0	9.69	34	.314	.426	0	.000	-0	-9	-10	0	-0.5
	StL-N	0	0	—	1	0	0	0	0	2	2	1	0	0	1	1	13.5	4.50	78	.333	.429	0	—	0	-0	-0	0	0.0
Total	4	5	7	.417	52	9	1	0	2	112^1	89	57	5	6	80	64	14.0	3.93	89	.224	.362	4	.154	-1	-3	-6	1	0.3
● DENNY NEAGLE	Neagle, Dennis Edward b: 9/13/68, Gambrills, Md. BL/TL, 6'2", 217 lbs. Deb: 7/27/91																											
1991	Min-A	0	1	.000	7	3	0	0	0	20	28	9	3	0	7	14	15.7	4.05	106	.329	.380	0	—	0	0	0	-0	0.0
1992	*Pit-N	4	6	.400	55	6	0	0	2	86^1	81	46	9	2	43	77	13.1	4.48	77	.247	.338	0	.000	-1	-9	-10	-0	-1.4
1993	Pit-N	3	5	.375	50	7	0	0	1	81^1	82	49	10	3	37	73	13.5	5.31	76	.258	.341	0	.000	-2	-11	-11	-1	-1.3
1994	Pit-N	9	10	.474	24	24	2	0	0	137	135	80	18	3	49	122	12.3	5.12	84	.259	.326	8	.190	1	-14	-12	0	-1.3
1995	Pit-N★	13	8	.619	31	31	5	1	0	**209**^{2}	221	91	20	3	45	150	11.5	3.43	125	.273	.314	9	.122	-0	17	20	1	1.9
1996	Pit-N	14	6	.700	27	27	1	0	0	182^2	186	67	21	3	34	131	11.0	3.05	143	.267	.304	10	.182	0	24	26	-0	2.6
	*Atl-N	2	3	.400	6	6	1	0	0	38^2	40	26	5	0	14	18	12.6	5.59	79	.268	.331	2	.143	-0	-6	-5	-1	-0.6
	Yr	16	9	.640	33	33	2	0	0	221^1	226	93	26	3	48	149	11.3	3.50	125	.267	.309	12	.174	-0	18	21	-1	2.0
1997	*Atl-N☆	**20**	5	.800	34	34	4	4	0	233^1	204	87	18	6	49	172	10.0	2.97	142	.233	.279	11	.153	1	32	32	-0	3.3
1998	*Atl-N	16	11	.593	32	31	5	2	0	210^1	196	91	25	6	60	165	11.2	3.55	117	.250	.308	11	.175	1	16	14	-3	1.5
1999	Cin-N	9	5	.643	20	19	0	0	0	111^2	95	54	23	4	40	76	11.2	4.27	109	.229	.303	6	.162	-0	4	5	-2	0.3
2000	Cin-N	8	2	.800	18	18	0	0	0	117^2	111	48	15	3	50	88	12.5	3.52	136	.247	.326	7	.189	1	15	16	-1	1.2
	*NY-A	7	7	.500	16	15	1	0	0	91^1	99	61	16	2	31	58	13.0	5.81	82	.278	.339	0	—	0	-9	-11	0	-1.3
Total	10	105	69	.603	320	221	19	7	3	1520	1478	709	183	35	459	1144	11.7	3.92	110	.255	.314	64	.153	0	58	65	-9	4.9
● JACK NEAGLE	Neagle, John Henry b: 1/2/1858, Syracuse, N.Y. d: 9/20/04, Syracuse, N.Y. BR/TR, 5'6", 155 lbs. Deb: 7/8/1879 ♦																											
1879	Cin-N	0	1	.000	2	2	1	0	0	13	13	12	0		5	4	12.5	3.46	67	.241	.305	2	.167	-0	-1	-2	-0	-0.2
1883	Phi-N	1	7	.125	8	7	6	0	0	61^1	88	77	0		21	13	16.0	6.90	45	.315	.363	12	.164	-2	-26	-26	-1	-2.5
	Bal-a	1	4	.200	6	5	4	0	0	46	48	48	1		20	9	13.3	4.89	71	.251	.322	10	.286	1	-8	-7	-0	-0.5
	Pit-a	3	12	.200	16	16	12	0	0	114	156	123	9		25	41	14.3	5.84	56	.306	.338	19	.188	-1	-32	-33	-1	-3.3
	Yr	4	16	.200	22	21	16	0	0	160	204	171	10		45	50	14.0	5.57	60	.291	.334	29	.213	-0	-40	-40	-1	-3.8
1884	Pit-a	11	26	.297	38	38	37	2	0	326	354	219	6	18	70	85	12.2	3.73	89	.255	.300	22	.149	-5	-17	-15	-3	-2.1
Total	3	16	50	.242	70	68	60	2	0	560^1	659	479	16	18	141	152	13.1	4.59	71	.272	.317	65	.176	-8	-85	-82	-5	-8.6
● JOE NEALE	Neale, Joseph Hunt b: 5/7/1866, Wadsworth, Ohio d: 12/30/13, Akron, Ohio BR/TR, 5'8", 153 lbs. Deb: 6/21/1886 ♦																											
1886	Lou-a	0	1	.000	1	1	0	0	0	7	11	12	0	1	7	0	24.4	7.71	47	.393	.528	0	.000	-0	-3	-3	-0	-0.3
1887	Lou-a	1	4	.200	5	4	4	0	0	41^1	75	50	4	2	15	11	16.8	6.97	63	.377	.383	4	.182	-2	-12	-12	0	-1.1
1890	StL-a	5	3	.625	10	9	8	0	0	69	53	37	4	4	15	23	9.4	3.39	127	.206	.261	2	.067	-3	4	6	-2	0.2
1891	StL-a	6	4	.600	15	11	9	1	1	110^1	109	73	4	7	36	24	12.4	4.24	99	.249	.317	6	.118	-3	-6	-0	2	-0.2
Total	4	12	12	.500	31	25	21	1	1	227^2	248	172	12	14	73	58	12.7	4.59	93	.269	.322	12	.111	-9	-18	-8	1	-1.4
● RON NECCIAI	Necciai, Ronald Andrew b: 6/18/32, Gallatin, Pa. BR/TR, 6'5", 185 lbs. Deb: 8/10/52																											
1952	Pit-N	1	6	.143	12	9	0	0	0	54^2	63	45	5	1	32	31	15.8	7.08	56	.296	.390	1	.059	-1	-20	-18	-0	-2.0
● RON NEGRAY	Negray, Ronald Alvin b: 2/26/30, Akron, Ohio BR/TR, 6'1", 185 lbs. Deb: 9/14/52																											
1952	Bro-N	0	0	—	4	1	0	0	0	13	15	5	0	0	5	5	13.8	3.46	105	.294	.357	0	.000	-0	0	0	-0	0.0
1955	Phi-N	4	3	.571	19	10	2	0	0	71^2	71	31	13	0	21	30	11.6	3.52	113	.257	.310	0	.000	-3	4	4	-0	0.0
1956	Phi-N	2	3	.400	39	4	0	0	3	66^2	72	36	6	1	24	44	13.1	4.18	89	.280	.344	3	.429	1	-3	-3	0	-0.1
1958	LA-N	0	0	—	4	0	0	0	0	11^1	12	9	4	0	7	2	15.1	7.15	57	.279	.380	0	.000	-0	-4	-4	-0	-0.2
Total	4	6	6	.500	66	15	2	0	3	162^2	170	81	23	1	57	81	12.6	4.04	95	.271	.333	3	.086	-3	-3	-3	-1	-0.3
● JIM NEHER	Neher, James Gilmore b: 2/5/1889, Rochester, N.Y. d: 11/11/51, Buffalo, N.Y. BR/TR, 5'11", 185 lbs. Deb: 9/10/12																											
1912	Cle-A	0	0	—	1	0	0	0	0	1	0	0	0	0	0	0	0.0	0.00	—	.000	.000	0	—	0	0	0	-0	0.0
● ART NEHF	Nehf, Arthur Neukom b: 7/31/1892, Terre Haute, Ind. d: 12/18/60, Phoenix, Ariz. BL/TL, 5'9.5", 176 lbs. Deb: 8/13/15																											
1915	Bos-N	5	4	.556	12	10	6	4	0	78^1	60	29	0	3	21	39	9.7	2.53	103	.214	.276	4	.143	-1	2	1	-0	0.0
1916	Bos-N	7	5	.583	22	13	6	1	0	121	110	40	1	3	20	36	9.9	2.01	124	.244	.281	5	.125	-0	8	7	-1	0.6
1917	Bos-N	17	8	.680	38	23	16	4	0	233^1	197	78	4	4	39	101	9.3	2.16	118	.231	.268	12	.171	5	14	11	-0	1.8
1918	Bos-N	15	15	.500	32	31	**28**	2	0	284^1	274	107	2	6	76	96	11.3	2.69	100	.259	.312	16	.168	1	2	-0	3	0.6
1919	Bos-N	8	9	.471	22	19	13	1	0	168^2	151	66	6	6	40	53	10.5	3.09	92	.242	.294	13	.206	2	-3	-5	1	-0.1

YEAR	TM/L	W	L	PCT	G	GS	CG	SH	SV	IP	H	R	HR	HB	BB	SO	RAT	ERA	ERA+	OAV	OOB	BH	AVG	PB	PR	PR+	PD	TPI
	NY-N	9	2	.818	13	12	9	2	0	102	70	23	2	2	19	24	8.0	1.50	187	.196	.240	8	.229	3	16	15	-1	2.1
	Yr	17	11	.607	35	31	22	3	0	270^{2}	221	89	8	8	59	77	9.6	2.49	114	.225	.275	21	.214	5	13	11	0	2.0
1920	NY-N	21	12	.636	40	33	22	4	0	280^{2}	273	113	8	1	45	79	10.2	3.08	97	.260	.291	26	.268	5	2	-3	3	0.5
1921	*NY-N	20	10	.667	41	34	18	2	1	260^{2}	266	116	18	2	55	67	11.2	3.63	101	.271	.311	18	.202	0	5	1	3	0.4
1922	*NY-N	19	13	.594	37	35	20	2	1	268^{1}	286	122	15	4	64	60	11.9	3.29	122	.276	.321	25	.255	4	24	22	1	2.6
1923	*NY-N	13	10	.565	34	27	7	1	2	196	219	112	14	2	49	50	12.4	4.50	85	.281	.326	12	.190	1	-11	-15	1	-1.4
1924	*NY-N	14	4	.778	30	20	11	0	2	171^{2}	167	75	14	2	42	72	11.1	3.62	101	.254	.301	13	.228	6	5	1	2	0.9
1925	NY-N	11	9	.550	29	20	8	1	1	155	193	86	7	1	50	63	14.2	3.77	107	.308	.360	11	.216	1	9	5	2	0.8
1926	NY-N	0	0	—	2	0	0	0	0	1^{2}	2	2	0	0	1	0	16.2	10.80	35	.286	.375	0	.000	-0	-1	-1	0	-0.1
	Cin-N	0	1	.000	7	1	0	0	0	17	25	10	0	1	5	4	16.4	3.71	100	.379	.431	1	.200	-0	0	-0	1	0.0
	Yr	0	1	.000	9	1	0	0	0	18^{2}	27	12	0	1	6	4	16.4	4.34	85	.370	.425	1	.167	-0	-1	-1	1	-0.1
1927	Cin-N	3	5	.375	21	5	1	0	4	45^{1}	59	33	2	0	14	21	14.5	5.56	68	.319	.367	1	.077	-1	-8	-9	1	-1.6
	Chi-N	1	1	.500	8	2	2	1	1	26^{1}	25	5	0	0	9	12	11.6	1.37	283	.260	.324	3	.429	1	7	7	-0	0.7
	Yr	4	6	.400	29	7	3	1	5	71^{2}	84	38	2	0	23	33	13.4	4.02	95	.299	.352	4	.200	0	-1	-2	1	-0.9
1928	Chi-N	13	7	.650	31	21	10	2	0	176^{2}	190	62	3	1	52	40	12.4	2.65	145	.281	.334	11	.190	2	26	24	1	2.9
1929	*Chi-N	8	5	.615	32	14	4	0	1	120^{2}	148	85	11	2	39	27	14.1	5.59	83	.310	.365	13	.289	4	-12	-13	1	-0.8
Total	15	184	120	.605	451	320	181	27	13	2707^{2}	2715	1164	107	40	640	844	11.3	3.20	105	.265	.310	192	.210	34	85	47	16	9.9
● GARY NEIBAUER	Neibauer, Gary Wayne b: 10/29/44, Billings, Mont. BR/TR, 6'3", 200 lbs. Deb: 4/12/69																											
1969	*Atl-N	1	2	.333	29	0	0	0	0	57^{2}	42	28	9	1	31	42	11.5	3.90	92	.204	.311	0	.000	-1	-2	-2	-0	-0.2
1970	Atl-N	0	3	.000	7	0	0	0	0	12^{2}	11	7	0	0	8	9	13.5	4.97	86	.239	.352	0	.000	-0	-1	-1	-0	-0.2
1971	Atl-N	1	0	1.000	6	1	0	0	1	21	14	5	3	1	9	6	10.3	2.14	173	.187	.282	0	.000	-1	3	3	0	0.1
1972	Atl-N	0	0	—	8	0	0	0	0	17^{1}	27	15	6	1	6	8	17.7	7.27	52	.360	.415	0	.000	-0	-7	-6	-0	-0.4
	Phi-N	0	2	.000	9	2	0	0	0	18^{2}	17	12	1	1	14	7	15.4	5.30	68	.239	.372	1	.250	0	-4	-3	-0	-0.4
	Yr	0	2	.000	17	2	0	0	0	36	44	27	7	2	20	15	16.5	6.25	59	.301	.393	1	.125	-0	-11	-10	-1	-0.8
1973	Atl-N	2	1	.667	16	1	0	0	0	21^{1}	24	19	3	2	19	9	19.0	7.17	55	.282	.425	1	.250	1	-8	-7	-1	-0.9
Total	5	4	8	.333	75	4	0	0	1	148^{2}	135	86	22	6	87	81	13.8	4.78	78	.242	.350	2	.069	-1	-20	-16	-2	-2.0
● JIM NEIDLINGER	Neidlinger, James Llewellyn b: 9/24/64, Vallejo, Cal. BB/TR, 6'4", 180 lbs. Deb: 8/1/90																											
1990	LA-N	5	3	.625	12	12	0	0	0	74	67	30	4	1	15	46	10.1	3.28	112	.241	.282	3	.120	-0	4	3	-1	0.2
● AL NEIGER	Neiger, Alvin Edward b: 3/26/39, Wilmington, Del. BL/TL, 6', 195 lbs. Deb: 7/30/60																											
1960	Phi-N	0	0	—	6	0	0	0	0	12^{2}	16	8	2	2	4	3	15.6	5.68	68	.340	.415	1	.500	0	-3	-2	-0	-0.1
● ERNIE NEITZKE	Neitzke, Ernest Fredrich b: 11/13/1894, Toledo, Ohio d: 4/27/77, Sylvania, Ohio BR/TR, 5'10", 180 lbs. Deb: 6/2/21 ♦																											
1921	Bos-A	0	0	—	2	0	0	0	0	7^{1}	8	5	0	0	4	1	14.7	6.14	69	.333	.429	6	.240	0	-2	-2	0	0.0
● BOTS NEKOLA	Nekola, Francis Joseph b: 12/10/06, New York, N.Y. d: 3/11/87, Rockville, Md. BL/TL, 5'11.5", 175 lbs. Deb: 7/19/29																											
1929	NY-A	0	0	—	9	1	0	0	0	18^{2}	21	10	0	0	15	2	17.4	4.34	89	.296	.419	2	.500	1	-0	-1	1	0.1
1933	Det-A	0	0	—	2	0	0	0	0	1^{1}	4	4	1	0	1	0	33.8	27.00	16	.500	.556	0	—	0	-3	-3	-0	-0.2
Total	2	0	0	—	11	1	0	0	0	20	25	14	1	0	16	2	18.4	5.85	66	.316	.432	2	.500	1	-4	-5	1	-0.1
● RED NELSON	Nelson, Albert Francis (b: Albert W. Horazdovsky) b: 5/19/1886, Cleveland, Ohio d: 10/26/56, St.Petersburg, Fla BR/TR, 5'11", 190 lbs. Deb: 9/9/10																											
1910	StL-A	5	1	.833	7	6	6	1	0	60	57	26	0	4	14	30	11.3	2.55	97	.261	.318	6	.261	2	-0	-1	4	0.6
1911	StL-A	3	9	.250	16	13	6	0	0	81	103	68	1	7	44	24	17.1	5.22	65	.324	.417	3	.111	-2	-17	-16	-1	-2.3
1912	StL-A	0	2	.000	8	3	0	0	1	18	21	14	0	0	13	9	17.0	7.00	47	.318	.430	1	.333	1	-7	-7	-1	-0.8
	Phi-N	2	0	1.000	4	2	1	0	0	19^{1}	25	10	2	2	6	2	15.4	3.72	97	.305	.367	1	.100	-1	-1	-0	-0	-0.1
1913	Phi-N	0	0	—	2	0	0	0	0	8^{1}	9	2	0	0	4	3	14.0	2.16	154	.290	.371	1	.333	0	1	1	0	0.1
	Cin-N	0	0	—	2	0	0	0	0	1^{2}	6	7	1	1	4	0	59.4	37.80	9	.667	.786	0	—	0	-6	-6	-0	-0.3
	Yr	0	0	—	4	0	0	0	0	10	15	9	1	1	8	3	21.6	8.10	41	.375	.490	1	.333	0	-5	-5	0	-0.2
Total	4	10	12	.455	39	24	13	1	1	188^{1}	221	127	4	14	85	68	15.3	4.54	68	.305	.389	12	.182	0	-31	-30	2	-2.8
● ANDY NELSON	Nelson, Andrew "Peaches" b: 11/30/1884, St.Paul, Minn. TL, Deb: 5/26/08																											
1908	Chi-A	0	0	—	2	1	0	0	0	9	11	4	0	1	4	1	16.0	2.00	116	.282	.364	0	.000	0	0	0	-1	0.0
● EMMETT NELSON	Nelson, George Emmett "Ramrod" b: 2/26/05, Viborg, S.Dak. d: 8/25/67, Sioux Falls, S.D. BR/TR, 6'3", 180 lbs. Deb: 6/24/35																											
1935	Cin-N	4	4	.500	19	7	3	1	1	60^{1}	70	31	2	2	23	14	14.2	4.33	92	.295	.363	2	.133	-1	-2	-2	1	-0.3
1936	Cin-N	1	0	1.000	6	1	0	0	0	17	24	8	1	1	4	3	15.4	3.18	120	.333	.377	1	.167	-0	2	1	-0	0.0
Total	2	5	4	.556	25	8	3	1	1	77^{1}	94	39	3	3	27	17	14.4	4.07	97	.304	.366	3	.143	-1	-0	-1	1	-0.3
● JIM NELSON	Nelson, James Lorin b: 7/4/47, Birmingham, Ala. BR/TR, 6', 180 lbs. Deb: 5/30/70																											
1970	Pit-N	4	2	.667	15	10	1	1	0	68^{1}	64	32	5	3	38	42	13.8	3.42	114	.255	.360	4	.200	0	5	4	-1	0.2
1971	Pit-N	2	2	.500	17	2	0	0	0	34^{2}	27	9	0	5	26	11	15.1	2.34	145	.225	.384	3	.500	2	4	4	-0	0.6
Total	2	6	4	.600	32	12	1	1	0	103	91	41	5	8	64	53	14.2	3.06	122	.245	.368	7	.269	2	9	8	-1	0.8
● JEFF NELSON	Nelson, Jeffrey Allan b: 11/17/66, Baltimore, Md. BR/TR, 6'8", 235 lbs. Deb: 4/16/92																											
1992	Sea-A	1	7	.125	66	0	0	0	6	81	71	34	7	6	44	46	13.4	3.44	116	.245	.356	0	—	0	5	5	0	0.5
1993	Sea-A	5	3	.625	71	0	0	0	1	60	57	30	5	8	34	61	14.9	4.35	102	.258	.376	0	—	0	-0	0	1	0.2
1994	Sea-A	0	0	—	28	0	0	0	0	42^{1}	35	18	3	8	20	44	13.4	2.76	177	.226	.344	0	—	0	10	10	-0	0.4
1995	*Sea-A	7	3	.700	62	0	0	0	2	78^{2}	58	21	4	6	27	96	10.4	2.17	218	.209	.294	0	—	0	22	22	0	2.6
1996	*NY-A	4	4	.500	73	0	0	0	2	74^{1}	75	38	6	2	36	91	13.7	4.36	113	.262	.349	0	—	0	5	5	2	0.6
1997	*NY-A	3	7	.300	77	0	0	0	2	78^{2}	53	32	7	4	37	81	10.8	2.86	156	.191	.296	0	—	0	15	14	2	1.8
1998	*NY-A	5	3	.625	45	0	0	0	3	40^{1}	44	18	1	8	22	35	16.5	3.79	116	.278	.394	0	.000	-0	4	3	1	0.6
1999	*NY-A	2	1	.667	39	0	0	0	1	30^{1}	27	14	2	3	22	35	15.4	4.15	114	.245	.385	0	—	0	2	2	1	0.2
2000	*NY-A	8	4	.667	73	0	0	0	0	69^{2}	44	24	2	2	45	71	11.8	2.45	195	.183	.316	0	.000	-0	19	19	0	2.7
Total	9	35	32	.522	534	0	0	0	17	555^{1}	464	229	37	47	287	560	12.9	3.29	139	.230	.340	0	.000	-0	82	80	6	9.6
● LUKE NELSON	Nelson, Luther Martin b: 12/4/1893, Cable, Ill. d: 11/14/85, Moline, Ill. BR/TR, 6', 180 lbs. Deb: 5/25/19																											
1919	NY-A	3	0	1.000	9	1	0	0	0	24^{1}	22	9	1	1	11	11	12.6	2.96	108	.244	.333	1	.143	-0	1	1	-0	0.0
● LYNN NELSON	Nelson, Lynn Bernard "Line Drive" b: 2/24/05, Sheldon, N.Dak. d: 2/15/55, Kansas City, Mo. BL/TR, 5'10.5", 170 lbs. Deb: 4/18/30 ♦																											
1930	Chi-N	3	2	.600	37	3	0	0	0	81^{1}	97	52	10	6	28	29	14.5	5.09	96	.300	.367	4	.222	0	-1	-2	1	0.1
1933	Chi-N	5	5	.500	24	3	3	0	1	75^{2}	65	34	2	0	30	20	11.3	3.21	102	.232	.306	5	.238	2	1	1	1	0.3
1934	Chi-N	0	1	.000	2	1	0	0	0	1	4	4	1	0	1	0	45.0	36.00	11	.667	.714	0	—	0	-4	-4	-0	-0.6
1937	Phi-A	4	9	.308	30	4	1	0	2	116	140	78	12	2	51	49	15.0	5.90	80	.300	.371	40	.354	6	-16	-15	-2	-0.5
1938	Phi-A	10	11	.476	32	23	13	0	2	191	215	142	29	5	79	75	14.1	5.65	85	.277	.347	31	.277	4	-18	-17	-0	-1.1
1939	Phi-A	10	13	.435	35	24	12	2	1	197^{2}	233	117	27	3	64	75	13.7	4.78	98	.292	.347	15	.188	-2	-4	-2	-1	-0.4
1940	Det-A	1	1	.500	6	2	0	0	0	14	23	19	5	0	9	7	20.6	10.93	44	.371	.451	8	.348	2	-10	-9	0	-0.8
Total	7	33	42	.440	166	60	29	2	6	676^{2}	777	446	86	16	262	255	14.0	5.25	88	.287	.353	103	.281	13	-52	-49	-1	-3.0
● MEL NELSON	Nelson, Melvin Frederick b: 5/30/36, San Diego, Cal. BR/TL, 6', 185 lbs. Deb: 9/27/60																											
1960	StL-N	0	1	.000	2	1	0	0	0	8	7	3	1	0	2	7	10.1	3.38	121	.226	.273	1	.500	0	0	1	-0	0.1
1963	LA-A	2	3	.400	36	3	0	0	1	52^{2}	55	34	7	2	32	41	15.2	5.30	65	.263	.366	1	.091	-1	-10	-12	1	-1.0
1965	Min-A	0	4	.000	28	3	0	0	3	54^{2}	57	29	7	2	23	31	13.5	4.12	86	.261	.337	1	.111	-0	-4	-3	-0	-0.4
1967	Min-A	0	0	—	1	0	0	0	0	0^{1}	3	2	1	0	0	0	81.0	54.00	6	.750	.750	0	—	0	-2	-2	0	-0.1
1968	*StL-N	2	1	.667	18	4	1	0	1	52^{2}	49	20	3	0	9	16	9.9	2.91	100	.254	.287	2	.167	0	0	-0	-0	0.0
1969	StL-N	0	1	.000	8	0	0	0	0	5^{1}	13	7	0	0	3	3	27.0	11.81	30	.520	.571	0	—	0	-5	-5	-0	-0.8
Total	6	4	10	.286	93	11	1	0	5	173^{2}	184	95	19	4	69	98	13.3	4.40	76	.271	.341	5	.147	-1	-20	-21	0	-2.2
● ROGER NELSON	Nelson, Roger Eugene "Spider" b: 6/7/44, Altadena, Cal. BR/TR, 6'3", 205 lbs. Deb: 9/9/67																											
1967	Chi-A	0	1	.000	5	0	0	0	0	7	4	1	1	2	0	4	7.7	1.29	241	.182	.250	0	—	0	2	1	0	0.3
1968	Bal-A	4	3	.571	19	6	0	0	1	71	49	21	3	1	26	70	9.6	2.41	121	.192	.270	1	.063	-0	5	4	-0	0.4

YEAR TM/L	W	L	PCT	G	GS	CG	SH	SV	IP	H	R	HR	HB	BB	SO	RAT	ERA	ERA+	OAV	OOB	BH	AVG	PB	PR	PR+	PD	TPI
1969 KC-A	7	13	.350	29	29	8	1	0	193^1	170	78	12	6	65	82	11.2	3.31	112	.243	.313	8	.138	-1	7	8	-1	0.6
1970 KC-A	0	2	.000	4	2	0	0	0	9	18	10	3	1	0	3	19.0	10.00	37	.419	.432	0	—	0	-6	-6	0	-1.1
1971 KC-A	0	1	.000	13	1	0	0	0	34	35	20	1	0	5	29	10.6	5.29	65	.269	.296	2	.333	1	-7	-7	1	-0.2
1972 KC-A	11	6	.647	34	19	10	6	2	173^1	120	41	13	1	31	120	**7.9**	2.08	146	.196	**.236**	5	.093	-2	19	19	1	1.9
1973 *Cin-N	3	2	.600	14	8	1	0	0	54^2	49	25	4	3	24	17	12.5	3.46	99	.246	.336	2	.111	-1	0	-0	1	0.0
1974 Cin-N	4	4	.500	14	12	1	0	1	85^1	67	36	7	1	35	42	10.9	3.38	104	.213	.293	5	.179	0	2	1	-1	0.1
1976 KC-A	0	0	—	3	0	0	0	0	8^2	4	2	0	2	4	4	10.4	2.08	169	.138	.286	0	—	0	1	1	0	0.1
Total 9	29	32	.475	135	77	20	7	4	636^1	516	234	44	17	190	371	10.2	3.06	110	.224	.288	23	.128	-3	24	22	2	2.1

● **GENE NELSON** Nelson, Wayland Eugene b: 12/3/60, Tampa, Fla. BR/TR, 6', 174 lbs. Deb: 5/4/81

YEAR TM/L	W	L	PCT	G	GS	CG	SH	SV	IP	H	R	HR	HB	BB	SO	RAT	ERA	ERA+	OAV	OOB	BH	AVG	PB	PR	PR+	PD	TPI
1981 NY-A	3	1	.750	8	7	0	0	0	39^1	40	24	5	1	23	16	14.6	4.81	74	.261	.362	0	—	0	-5	-5	-0	-0.5
1982 Sea-A	6	9	.400	22	19	2	1	0	122^2	133	70	16	2	60	71	14.3	4.62	92	.279	.362	0	—	0	-7	-5	1	-0.4
1983 Sea-A	0	3	.000	10	5	1	0	0	32	38	29	6	1	21	11	16.9	7.88	54	.295	.397	0	—	0	-14	-12	1	-0.9
1984 Chi-A	3	5	.375	20	9	2	0	1	74^2	72	38	9	1	17	36	10.8	4.46	93	.254	.299	0	—	0	-4	-2	0	-0.2
1985 Chi-A	10	10	.500	46	18	1	0	2	145^2	144	74	23	7	67	101	13.5	4.26	101	.258	.345	0	.000	-0	-2	1	0	0.1
1986 Chi-A	6	6	.500	54	1	0	0	6	114^2	118	52	7	3	41	70	12.7	3.85	112	.271	.338	0	—	0	4	6	1	0.7
1987 Oak-A	6	5	.545	54	6	0	0	3	123^2	120	58	12	5	35	94	11.6	3.93	105	.249	.307	0	—	0	7	3	-1	0.2
1988 *Oak-A	9	6	.600	54	1	0	0	3	111^2	93	42	9	3	38	67	10.8	3.06	124	.228	.298	0	—	0	11	9	-1	1.1
1989 *Oak-A	3	5	.375	50	0	0	0	3	80	60	33	5	2	30	70	10.3	3.26	113	.203	.280	0	—	0	6	4	-1	0.3
1990 *Oak-A	3	3	.500	51	0	0	0	5	74^2	55	14	5	3	17	38	9.0	1.57	238	.208	.263	0	—	0	20	19	-1	1.5
1991 Oak-A	1	5	.167	44	0	0	0	0	48^2	60	38	12	3	23	23	15.9	6.84	56	.306	.387	0	—	0	-15	-17	-1	-1.9
1992 Oak-A	3	1	.750	28	2	0	0	0	51^2	68	37	5	0	22	23	15.7	6.45	58	.335	.400	0	—	0	-14	-16	-1	-1.2
1993 Cal-A	0	5	.000	46	0	0	0	4	52^2	50	25	3	2	23	31	12.8	3.08	147	.251	.335	0	—	0	7	8	0	0.8
Tex-A	0	0	—	6	0	0	0	1	8	10	3	0	0	1	4	12.4	3.38	123	.303	.324	0	—	0	1	1	-0	0.0
Yr	0	5	.000	52	0	0	0	5	60^2	60	28	3	2	24	35	12.8	3.12	144	.259	.333	0	—	0	8	9	0	0.8
Total 13	53	64	.453	493	68	6	1	28	1080	1061	537	117	33	418	655	12.6	4.13	98	.258	.331	0	.000	-0	-4	-8	-3	-0.4

● **BILL NELSON** Nelson, William F. b: 9/28/1863, Terre Haute, Ind. d: 6/23/41, Terre Haute, Ind. TR, Deb: 9/3/1884

YEAR TM/L	W	L	PCT	G	GS	CG	SH	SV	IP	H	R	HR	HB	BB	SO	RAT	ERA	ERA+	OAV	OOB	BH	AVG	PB	PR	PR+	PD	TPI
1884 Pit-a	1	2	.333	3	3	3	0	0	26	26	21	1	4	8	6	13.2	4.50	73	.252	.330	2	.167	-1	-4	-3	-0	-0.4

● **ROBB NEN** Nen, Robert Allen b: 11/28/69, San Pedro, Cal. BR/TR, 6'4", 200 lbs. Deb: 4/10/93 F

YEAR TM/L	W	L	PCT	G	GS	CG	SH	SV	IP	H	R	HR	HB	BB	SO	RAT	ERA	ERA+	OAV	OOB	BH	AVG	PB	PR	PR+	PD	TPI
1993 Tex-A	1	1	.500	9	3	0	0	0	22^2	28	17	1	0	26	12	21.4	6.35	66	.326	.482	0	—	0	-5	-6	0	-0.4
Fla-N	1	0	1.000	15	1	0	0	0	33^1	35	28	5	0	20	27	14.9	7.02	62	.255	.350	0	.000	-0	-11	-9	-0	-0.5
1994 Fla-N	5	5	.500	44	0	0	0	15	58	46	20	6	0	17	60	9.8	2.95	148	.222	.281	0	.000	-0	8	9	-0	1.7
1995 Fla-N	0	7	.000	62	0	0	0	23	65^2	62	26	6	1	23	68	11.8	3.29	128	.244	.309	0	—	0	7	7	0	1.1
1996 Fla-N	5	1	.833	75	0	0	0	35	83	67	21	2	1	21	92	9.7	1.95	209	.225	.278	0	.000	-0	**21**	**20**	-0	2.8
1997 *Fla-N	9	3	.750	73	0	0	0	35	74	72	35	7	0	40	81	13.6	3.89	104	.250	.341	0	—	0	3	1	0	0.3
1998 SF-N★	7	7	.500	78	0	0	0	40	88^2	59	21	4	1	25	110	8.6	1.52	261	.180	.241	0	.000	-0	**27**	**26**	-0	5.2
1999 SF-N†	3	8	.273	72	0	0	0	37	72^1	79	36	8	0	27	77	13.2	3.98	106	.275	.338	0	—	0	5	2	0	0.4
2000 *SF-N	4	3	.571	68	0	0	0	41	66	37	15	4	2	19	92	7.9	1.50	282	.162	.233	0	—	0	**23**	22	-0	4.2
Total 8	35	35	.500	496	4	0	0	226	563^2	485	219	43	5	218	619	11.3	3.08	135	.230	.303	0	.000	-1	77	70	-1	14.8

● **HAL NEUBAUER** Neubauer, Harold Charles b: 5/13/02, Hoboken, N.J. d: 9/9/49, Providence, R.I. BR/TR, 6'0.5", 185 lbs. Deb: 6/12/25

YEAR TM/L	W	L	PCT	G	GS	CG	SH	SV	IP	H	R	HR	HB	BB	SO	RAT	ERA	ERA+	OAV	OOB	BH	AVG	PB	PR	PR+	PD	TPI
1925 Bos-A	1	0	1.000	7	0	0	0	0	10^1	17	18	2	0	11	4	24.4	12.19	37	.378	.500	0	—	0	-9	-8	0	-0.6

● **TEX NEUER** Neuer, John S. b: 6/8/1877, Fremont, Ohio d: 1/14/66, Northumberland, Pa TL, Deb: 8/28/07

YEAR TM/L	W	L	PCT	G	GS	CG	SH	SV	IP	H	R	HR	HB	BB	SO	RAT	ERA	ERA+	OAV	OOB	BH	AVG	PB	PR	PR+	PD	TPI
1907 NY-A	4	2	.667	7	6	6	3	0	54	40	21	1	0	19	22	9.8	2.17	129	.208	.280	2	.095	-2	2	3	-1	0.1

● **DAN NEUMEIER** Neumeier, Daniel George b: 3/9/48, Shawano, Wis. BR/TR, 6'5", 205 lbs. Deb: 9/8/72

YEAR TM/L	W	L	PCT	G	GS	CG	SH	SV	IP	H	R	HR	HB	BB	SO	RAT	ERA	ERA+	OAV	OOB	BH	AVG	PB	PR	PR+	PD	TPI
1972 Chi-A	0	0	—	3	0	0	0	0	3	2	3	0	0	3	0	15.0	9.00	35	.200	.385	0	.000	-0	-2	-2	-0	-0.1

● **ERNIE NEVEL** Nevel, Ernie Wyre b: 8/17/18, Charleston, Mo. d: 7/10/88, Springfield, Mo. BR/TR, 6'1", 200 lbs. Deb: 9/26/50

YEAR TM/L	W	L	PCT	G	GS	CG	SH	SV	IP	H	R	HR	HB	BB	SO	RAT	ERA	ERA+	OAV	OOB	BH	AVG	PB	PR	PR+	PD	TPI
1950 NY-A	0	1	.000	3	1	0	0	0	6^1	10	7	0	0	6	3	22.7	9.95	43	.345	.457	0	.000	-0	-4	-4	0	-0.5
1951 NY-A	0	0	—	1	0	0	0	1	4	1	0	0	0	1	1	4.5	0.00	—	.083	.154	0	.000	-0	2	2	-0	0.1
1953 Cin-N	0	0	—	10	0	0	0	0	10^1	16	7	0	0	1	5	14.8	6.10	71	.390	.405	0	—	0	-2	-2	0	-0.1
Total 3	0	1	.000	14	1	0	0	1	20^2	27	14	0	0	8	9	15.2	6.10	69	.329	.389	0	.000	-0	-4	-4	0	-0.5

● **ERNIE NEVERS** Nevers, Ernest Alonzo b: 6/11/02, Willow River, Minn. d: 5/3/76, San Rafael, Cal. BR/TR, 6', 205 lbs. Deb: 4/26/26

YEAR TM/L	W	L	PCT	G	GS	CG	SH	SV	IP	H	R	HR	HB	BB	SO	RAT	ERA	ERA+	OAV	OOB	BH	AVG	PB	PR	PR+	PD	TPI
1926 StL-A	2	4	.333	11	7	4	0	0	74^2	82	41	4	1	24	16	12.9	4.46	96	.290	.347	5	.185	-1	-4	-1	2	0.0
1927 StL-A	3	8	.273	27	5	2	0	2	94^2	105	61	8	2	35	22	13.5	4.94	88	.311	.379	7	.219	-1	-8	-6	1	-0.6
1928 StL-A	1	0	1.000	6	0	0	0	0	9	9	4	1	0	2	1	11.0	3.00	140	.281	.324	0	.000	-0	1	1	0	0.1
Total 3	6	12	.333	44	12	6	0	2	178^1	196	106	13	3	61	39	13.1	4.64	93	.300	.363	12	.200	-2	-11	-6	3	-0.5

● **DON NEWCOMBE** Newcombe, Donald "Newk" b: 6/14/26, Madison, N.J. BL/TR, 6'4", 225 lbs. Deb: 5/20/49 ◆

YEAR TM/L	W	L	PCT	G	GS	CG	SH	SV	IP	H	R	HR	HB	BB	SO	RAT	ERA	ERA+	OAV	OOB	BH	AVG	PB	PR	PR+	PD	TPI
1949 *Bro-N★	17	8	.680	38	31	19	**5**	1	244^1	223	89	17	3	73	149	11.0	3.17	129	.243	.301	22	.229	3	24	25	1	2.7
1950 Bro-N★	19	11	.633	40	35	20	4	3	267^1	258	120	22	2	75	130	11.3	3.70	111	.254	.306	24	.247	7	13	12	-0	1.9
1951 Bro-N★	20	9	.690	40	36	18	3	0	272	235	115	19	6	91	**164**	11.0	3.28	120	.230	.297	23	.223	5	21	20	1	2.5
1954 Bro-N	9	8	.529	29	25	6	0	0	144^1	158	81	24	5	49	82	13.2	4.55	90	.274	.337	15	.319	4	-8	-7	-1	-0.5
1955 *Bro-N★	20	5	**.800**	34	31	17	1	0	233^2	222	103	35	1	38	143	**10.1**	3.20	127	.249	.280	42	.359	20	22	22	-2	**4.1**
1956 *Bro-N	**27**	7	**.794**	38	36	18	5	0	268	219	101	33	3	46	139	**9.0**	3.06	130	**.221**	**.257**	26	.234	8	21	26	0	**4.1**
1957 Bro-N	11	12	.478	28	28	12	4	0	198^2	199	86	28	1	33	90	10.6	3.49	119	.258	.290	17	.230	5	9	14	1	2.1
1958 LA-N	0	6	.000	11	8	1	0	0	34^1	53	37	11	0	8	16	16.0	7.86	52	.346	.379	5	.417	2	-15	-14	0	-1.8
Cin-N	7	7	.500	20	18	7	0	1	133^1	159	61	20	1	28	53	12.7	3.85	108	.298	.335	21	.350	8	2	4	-2	1.0
Yr	7	13	.350	31	26	8	0	1	167^2	212	98	31	1	36	69	13.4	4.67	89	.309	.344	26	.361	10	-13	-10	-2	-0.8
1959 Cin-N	13	8	.619	30	29	17	2	1	222	216	87	25	5	27	100	10.1	3.16	128	.253	.280	32	.305	15	19	21	-1	3.4
1960 Cin-N	4	6	.400	16	15	1	0	0	82^2	99	48	12	3	14	36	12.6	4.57	84	.304	.338	5	.139	-0	-7	-7	-1	-0.9
Cle-A	2	3	.400	20	2	0	0	1	54	61	28	6	0	8	27	11.5	4.33	86	.289	.315	6	.300	2	-3	-4	-1	-0.2
Total 10	149	90	.623	344	294	136	24	7	2154^2	2102	956	252	30	490	1129	11.0	3.56	114	.254	.299	238	.271	79	97	113	-6	18.4

● **TOM NEWELL** Newell, Thomas Dean b: 5/17/63, Monrovia, Cal. BR/TR, 6'1", 185 lbs. Deb: 9/9/87

YEAR TM/L	W	L	PCT	G	GS	CG	SH	SV	IP	H	R	HR	HB	BB	SO	RAT	ERA	ERA+	OAV	OOB	BH	AVG	PB	PR	PR+	PD	TPI
1987 Phi-N	0	0	—	2	0	0	0	0	1	4	4	1	0	3	1	63.0	36.00	12	.571	.700	0	—	0	-4	-3	0	-0.2

● **DON NEWHAUSER** Newhauser, Donald Louis b: 11/7/47, Miami, Fla. BR/TR, 6'4", 200 lbs. Deb: 6/15/72

YEAR TM/L	W	L	PCT	G	GS	CG	SH	SV	IP	H	R	HR	HB	BB	SO	RAT	ERA	ERA+	OAV	OOB	BH	AVG	PB	PR	PR+	PD	TPI
1972 Bos-A	4	2	.667	31	0	0	0	4	37	30	11	2	2	25	27	13.9	2.43	133	.226	.356	0	.000	-0	3	3	-0	0.6
1973 Bos-A	0	0	—	9	0	0	0	1	12	9	2	0	1	13	8	17.3	0.00	—	.205	.397	0	—	0	5	5	-0	0.2
1974 Bos-A	0	1	.000	2	0	0	0	0	3^2	5	4	0	0	4	2	22.1	9.82	39	.357	.500	0	—	0	-3	-2	0	-0.4
Total 3	4	3	.571	42	0	0	0	5	52^2	44	17	2	3	42	37	15.2	2.39	144	.230	.377	0	.000	-0	5	6	-0	0.4

● **HAL NEWHOUSER** Newhouser, Harold "Prince Hal" b: 5/20/21, Detroit, Mich. d: 11/10/98, Detroit, Mich. BL/TL, 6'2", 192 lbs. Deb: 9/29/39 H

YEAR TM/L	W	L	PCT	G	GS	CG	SH	SV	IP	H	R	HR	HB	BB	SO	RAT	ERA	ERA+	OAV	OOB	BH	AVG	PB	PR	PR+	PD	TPI
1939 Det-A	0	1	.000	1	1	1	0	0	5	3	3	0	0	4	4	12.6	5.40	91	.188	.350	0	.000	-0	-0	-0	0	-0.1
1940 Det-A	9	9	.500	28	20	7	0	0	133^1	149	81	12	2	76	89	15.3	4.86	98	.282	.374	8	.200	-1	-7	-1	2	-0.1
1941 Det-A	9	11	.450	33	27	5	1	0	173	166	109	6	1	137	106	15.8	4.79	95	.249	.378	9	.150	-2	-12	-4	2	-0.5
1942 Det-A☆	8	14	.364	38	23	11	1	5	183^2	137	73	4	2	114	103	12.4	2.45	161	**.207**	.325	8	.154	-1	25	28	2	3.7
1943 Det-A★	8	17	.320	37	25	10	1	1	195^2	163	88	3	0	111	144	12.6	3.04	116	.224	.327	12	.185	-1	6	10	3	1.5
1944 Det-A★	**29**	9	.763	47	34	25	6	2	312^1	264	94	6	1	102	**187**	10.6	2.22	161	.230	.293	29	.242	3	42	45	1	6.2
1945 *Det-A†	**25**	9	**.735**	40	36	**29**	**8**	2	**313^1**	239	73	5	0	110	**212**	10.0	**1.81**	**194**	**.211**	.281	28	.257	4	**54**	**57**	3	**7.5**
1946 Det-A★	**26**	9	.743	37	34	29	6	1	292^2	215	77	10	1	98	275	**9.7**	**1.94**	**189**	**.201**	**.269**	13	.126	-1	51	54	2	**6.8**
1947 Det-A★	17	17	.500	40	36	**24**	3	2	285	268	105	9	2	110	176	12.0	2.87	131	.249	.320	19	.198	2	26	28	3	**3.9**
1948 Det-A★	**21**	12	.636	39	35	19	2	1	272^1	249	109	10	1	99	143	11.5	3.01	145	.242	.309	19	.207	1	39	40	2	4.8
1949 Det-A	18	11	.621	38	35	22	3	1	292	277	118	19	0	111	144	12.0	3.36	124	.251	.319	18	.198	2	27	26	3	2.8
1950 Det-A	15	13	.536	35	30	15	1	3	213^2	232	110	23	4	81	87	13.4	4.34	108	.279	.346	13	.176	-2	6	8	-0	0.7
1951 Det-A	6	6	.500	15	14	7	1	0	96^1	98	47	9	3	19	37	11.2	3.92	106	.268	.310	9	.310	2	2	3	1	0.6

YEAR	TM/L	W	L	PCT	G	GS	CG	SH	SV	IP	H	R	HR	HB	BB	SO	RAT	ERA	ERA+	OAV	OOB	BH	AVG	PB	PR	PR+	PD	TPI
1952	Det-A	9	9	.500	25	19	8	0	0	154	148	72	13	0	47	57	11.4	3.74	102	.254	.310	10	.217	3	-1	1	1	0.5
1953	Det-A	0	1	.000	7	4	0	0	1	21^{2}	31	22	4	2	8	6	17.0	7.06	58	.348	.414	4	.500	2	-7	-7	0	-0.2
1954	*Cle-A	7	2	.778	26	1	0	0	7	46^{2}	34	16	3	0	18	25	10.0	2.51	147	.209	.287	2	.154	-0	6	6	-0	1.2
1955	Cle-A	0	0	—	2	0	0	0	0	2^{1}	1	0	0	0	4	1	19.3	0.00	—	.125	.417	0	—	0	1	1	-0	0.0
Total	17	207	150	.580	488	374	212	33	26	2993	2674	1197	136	19	1249	1796	11.9	3.06	130	.239	.316	201	.201	12	257	294	22	39.3

● FLOYD NEWKIRK

Newkirk, Floyd Elmo "Three-Finger" b: 7/16/08, Norris City, Ill. d: 4/15/76, Clayton, Mo. BR/TR, 5'11", 178 lbs. Deb: 8/21/34 F

YEAR	TM/L	W	L	PCT	G	GS	CG	SH	SV	IP	H	R	HR	HB	BB	SO	RAT	ERA	ERA+	OAV	OOB	BH	AVG	PB	PR	PR+	PD	TPI
1934	NY-A	0	0	—	1	0	0	0	0	1	1	0	0	0	1	0	18.0	0.00	—	.333	.500	0	—	0	0	0	0	0.1

● JOEL NEWKIRK

Newkirk, Joel Inez "Sailor" b: 5/1/1896, Kyana, Ind. d: 1/22/66, Eldorado, Ill. BR/TR, 6', 180 lbs. Deb: 8/20/19 F

YEAR	TM/L	W	L	PCT	G	GS	CG	SH	SV	IP	H	R	HR	HB	BB	SO	RAT	ERA	ERA+	OAV	OOB	BH	AVG	PB	PR	PR+	PD	TPI
1919	Chi-N	0	0	—	1	0	0	0	0	2	2	3	0	1	3	1	27.0	13.50	21	.286	.545	0	.000	-0	-2	-2	0	-0.1
1920	Chi-N	0	1	.000	2	1	0	0	0	6^{2}	8	6	1	0	6	2	18.9	5.40	59	.333	.467	0	.000	-0	-2	-2	-1	-0.3
Total	2	0	1	.000	3	1	0	0	0	8^{2}	10	9	1	1	9	3	20.8	7.27	43	.323	.488	0	.000	-1	-4	-4	-0	-0.4

● MAURY NEWLIN

Newlin, Maurice Milton b: 6/22/14, Bloomingdale, Ind d: 8/14/78, Houston, Tex. BR/TR, 6', 176 lbs. Deb: 9/20/40

YEAR	TM/L	W	L	PCT	G	GS	CG	SH	SV	IP	H	R	HR	HB	BB	SO	RAT	ERA	ERA+	OAV	OOB	BH	AVG	PB	PR	PR+	PD	TPI
1940	StL-A	1	0	1.000	1	1	0	0	0	6	4	4	1	0	2	3	9.0	6.00	76	.190	.261	1	.500	0	-1	-1	-0	-0.1
1941	StL-A	0	2	.000	14	0	0	0	1	27^{2}	43	24	4	0	12	10	17.9	6.51	66	.361	.420	0	.000	-1	-7	-7	1	-0.5
Total	2	1	2	.333	15	1	0	0	1	33^{2}	47	28	5	0	14	13	16.3	6.42	68	.336	.396	1	.125	-1	-8	-7	0	-0.6

● ALAN NEWMAN

Newman, Alan Spencer b: 10/2/69, LaHabra, Cal. BL/TL, 6'6", 240 lbs. Deb: 5/14/99

YEAR	TM/L	W	L	PCT	G	GS	CG	SH	SV	IP	H	R	HR	HB	BB	SO	RAT	ERA	ERA+	OAV	OOB	BH	AVG	PB	PR	PR+	PD	TPI
1999	TB-A	2	2	.500	18	0	0	0	0	15^{2}	22	12	2	1	9	20	18.4	6.89	72	.333	.421	0	—	0	-4	-3	-0	-0.6
2000	Cle-A	0	0	—	1	0	0	0	0	1^{1}	6	3	1	0	1	0	47.3	20.25	25	.667	.700	0	—	0	-2	-2	0	-0.1
Total	2	2	2	.500	19	0	0	0	0	17	28	15	3	1	10	20	20.6	7.94	63	.373	.453	0	—	0	-6	-5	-0	-0.7

● FRED NEWMAN

Newman, Frederick William b: 2/21/42, Boston, Mass. d: 6/24/87, Framingham, Mass. BR/TR, 6'3", 190 lbs. Deb: 9/16/62

YEAR	TM/L	W	L	PCT	G	GS	CG	SH	SV	IP	H	R	HR	HB	BB	SO	RAT	ERA	ERA+	OAV	OOB	BH	AVG	PB	PR	PR+	PD	TPI
1962	LA-A	0	1	.000	4	1	0	0	0	6^{1}	11	7	0	0	3	4	19.9	9.95	39	.393	.452	0	.000	-0	-4	-4	-0	-0.6
1963	LA-A	1	5	.167	12	8	0	0	0	44	56	27	6	2	15	16	14.9	5.32	64	.316	.376	4	.250	1	-8	-10	-0	-1.2
1964	LA-A	13	10	.565	32	28	7	2	0	190	177	68	9	7	39	83	10.6	2.75	120	.246	.291	11	.180	2	19	12	4	2.2
1965	Cal-A	14	16	.467	36	36	10	2	0	260^{2}	225	94	15	1	64	109	10.0	2.93	116	.234	.282	7	.095	-0	15	14	8	2.4
1966	Cal-A	4	7	.364	21	19	1	0	0	102^{2}	112	54	7	6	31	42	13.1	4.73	71	.289	.351	6	.200	1	-15	-16	1	-1.4
1967	Cal-A	1	0	1.000	3	1	0	0	0	6^{1}	8	5	1	1	2	0	15.6	1.42	221	.320	.393	0	.000	-0	1	1	-0	0.2
Total	6	33	39	.458	108	93	18	4	0	610	589	255	38	17	154	254	11.2	3.41	99	.256	.308	28	.153	3	8	-3	12	1.6

● JEFF NEWMAN

Newman, Jeffrey Lynn b: 9/11/48, Fort Worth, Tex. BR/TR, 6'2", 218 lbs. Deb: 6/30/76 MC♦

YEAR	TM/L	W	L	PCT	G	GS	CG	SH	SV	IP	H	R	HR	HB	BB	SO	RAT	ERA	ERA+	OAV	OOB	BH	AVG	PB	PR	PR+	PD	TPI
1977	Oak-A	0	0	—	1	0	0	0	0	1	1	0	0	1	0	0	18.0	0.00	—	.250	.400	36	.222	0	0	0	0	0.0

● RAY NEWMAN

Newman, Raymond Francis b: 6/20/45, Evansville, Ind. BL/TL, 6'5", 205 lbs. Deb: 5/16/71

YEAR	TM/L	W	L	PCT	G	GS	CG	SH	SV	IP	H	R	HR	HB	BB	SO	RAT	ERA	ERA+	OAV	OOB	BH	AVG	PB	PR	PR+	PD	TPI
1971	Chi-N	1	2	.333	30	0	0	0	2	38^{1}	30	15	4	0	17	35	11.0	3.52	112	.219	.305	0	.000	-1	-0	2	0	0.1
1972	Mil-A	0	0	—	4	0	0	0	1	7	4	0	0	0	2	1	7.7	0.00	—	.182	.250	1	1.000	0	2	2	0	0.2
1973	Mil-A	2	1	.667	11	0	0	0	1	18^{1}	19	6	2	0	5	10	11.8	2.95	128	.260	.308	0	—	0	2	2	1	0.3
Total	3	3	3	.500	45	0	0	0	4	63^{2}	53	21	6	0	24	46	10.9	2.97	128	.228	.301	1	.143	-0	4	5	1	0.6

● BOBO NEWSOM

Newsom, Louis Norman "Buck" b: 8/11/07, Hartsville, S.C. d: 12/7/62, Orlando, Fla. BR/TR, 6'2", 220 lbs. Deb: 9/11/29

YEAR	TM/L	W	L	PCT	G	GS	CG	SH	SV	IP	H	R	HR	HB	BB	SO	RAT	ERA	ERA+	OAV	OOB	BH	AVG	PB	PR	PR+	PD	TPI
1929	Bro-N	0	3	.000	3	2	0	0	0	9^{1}	15	12	0	0	5	6	19.3	10.61	44	.375	.444	0	.000	-0	-6	-6	0	-1.0
1930	Bro-N	0	0	—	2	0	0	0	0	3	2	2	0	0	2	1	12.0	0.00	—	.167	.286	0	—	0	2	2	-0	0.1
1932	Chi-N	0	0	—	1	0	0	0	0	1	1	0	0	0	0	0	9.0	0.00	—	.333	.333	0	—	0	0	0	0	0.0
1934	StL-A	16	20	.444	47	32	15	2	5	262^{1}	259	138	15	1	149	135	14.0	4.01	124	.261	.358	17	.183	-3	14	26	0	2.9
1935	StL-A	0	6	.000	7	6	1	0	1	42^{2}	54	29	2	0	13	22	14.1	4.85	99	.303	.351	1	.091	-1	-2	-0	0	-0.1
	Was-A	11	12	.478	28	23	17	2	2	198^{1}	222	108	9	4	84	65	14.1	4.45	97	.288	.361	22	.301	4	0	-3	-3	-0.1
	Yr	11	18	.379	35	29	18	2	3	241	276	137	11	4	97	87	14.1	4.52	97	.291	.359	23	.274	3	-2	-3	-2	-0.2
1936	Was-A	17	15	.531	43	38	24	4	2	285^{2}	294	160	13	3	146	156	14.0	4.32	111	.268	.355	23	.213	0	23	15	1	1.5
1937	Was-A	3	4	.429	11	10	3	0	0	67^{2}	76	49	4	3	48	39	16.9	5.85	76	.287	.402	3	.120	-1	-9	-11	0	-1.0
	Bos-A	13	10	.565	30	27	14	1	0	207^{2}	193	114	14	3	119	127	13.7	4.46	106	.243	.344	19	.253	2	4	6	-2	0.6
	Yr	16	14	.533	41	37	17	1	0	275^{1}	269	163	18	6	167	166	14.4	4.81	97	.254	.359	22	.220	1	-6	-4	-1	-0.4
1938	StL-A☆	20	16	.556	44	40	**31**	0	1	**329^{2}**	334	205	30	5	192	226	14.5	5.08	98	.265	.364	31	.250	1	-11	-4	-3	-0.4
1939	StL-A	3	1	.750	6	6	3	0	0	45^{2}	50	26	5	1	22	28	14.4	4.73	103	.266	.346	4	.222	-0	-1	1	0	0.0
	Det-A☆	17	10	.630	35	31	21	3	2	246	222	100	14	2	104	164	12.0	3.37	145	.238	.316	18	.186	-4	34	39	-1	3.4
	Yr	20	11	.645	41	37	**24**	3	2	291^{2}	272	126	19	3	126	192	12.4	3.58	136	.243	.321	22	.191	-4	34	40	-1	3.4
1940	*Det-A★	21	5	.808	36	34	20	3	0	264	235	110	19	3	100	164	11.5	2.83	**168**	.238	.310	23	.215	-1	46	52	-3	4.2
1941	Det-A	12	20	.375	43	36	12	2	2	250^{1}	265	140	15	3	118	175	13.9	4.60	99	.264	.343	9	.102	-6	-13	-1	-2	-0.9
1942	Was-A	11	17	.393	30	29	15	2	0	213^{2}	236	135	5	3	92	**113**	13.9	4.93	74	.280	.353	12	.160	-2	-30	-30	-3	-3.8
	Bro-N	2	2	.500	6	5	2	1	0	32	28	13	1	1	14	21	12.1	3.38	97	.235	.321	0	.000	-1	-0	-0	-1	-0.3
1943	Bro-N	9	4	.692	22	12	6	1	1	125	113	51	4	2	57	75	12.4	3.02	111	.244	.329	11	.250	1	5	5	0	0.6
	StL-A	1	6	.143	10	9	0	0	0	52^{1}	69	45	7	1	35	37	18.1	7.39	45	.318	.415	5	.333	1	-24	-23	-1	-2.6
	Was-A	3	3	.500	6	6	2	0	0	40	38	22	1	2	21	11	13.7	3.82	84	.247	.345	2	.133	-1	-2	-3	-1	-0.6
	Yr	4	9	.308	16	15	2	0	0	92^{1}	107	67	8	3	56	48	16.2	5.85	56	.288	.386	7	.233	0	-26	-27	-2	-3.2
1944	Phi-A★	13	15	.464	37	33	18	2	1	265	243	100	11	4	82	142	11.2	2.82	123	.244	.304	10	.114	-6	18	19	-1	1.2
1945	Phi-A	8	20	.286	36	34	16	3	0	257^{1}	255	111	12	3	103	127	12.6	3.29	104	.260	.332	14	.163	-4	2	4	-4	-0.4
1946	Phi-A	3	5	.375	10	9	3	1	0	58^{2}	61	27	2	5	30	32	14.7	3.38	105	.266	.364	2	.105	-1	1	1	-1	0.0
	Was-A	11	8	.579	24	22	14	2	1	178	163	63	5	2	60	82	11.4	2.78	120	.242	.306	10	.161	-2	14	12	-3	0.7
	Yr	14	13	.519	34	31	17	3	1	236^{2}	224	90	7	7	90	114	12.2	2.93	116	.248	.321	12	.148	-3	15	13	-4	0.7
1947	Was-A	4	6	.400	14	13	1	0	0	83^{2}	99	44	2	1	37	40	14.7	4.09	91	.296	.368	7	.241	1	-4	-3	-2	-0.5
	*NY-A	7	5	.583	17	15	6	2	0	115^{2}	109	38	8	2	30	42	11.0	2.80	126	.250	.301	4	.095	-3	12	10	-2	0.4
	Yr	11	11	.500	31	28	7	2	0	199^{1}	208	82	10	3	67	82	12.6	3.34	108	.270	.331	11	.155	-3	8	6	-3	-0.1
1948	NY-N	0	4	.000	11	4	0	0	0	25^{2}	35	16	1	0	13	9	16.8	4.21	94	.330	.403	3	.429	1	-1	-1	-0	-0.1
1952	Was-A	1	1	.500	10	0	0	0	2	12^{2}	16	7	2	0	9	5	17.8	4.97	72	.302	.403	0	.000	-0	-2	-2	0	-0.4
	Phi-A	3	3	.500	14	5	1	0	1	47^{2}	38	19	2	2	23	22	11.9	3.59	110	.220	.318	2	.133	-1	0	2	0	0.2
	Yr	4	4	.500	24	5	1	0	3	60^{1}	54	26	4	2	32	27	13.1	3.88	100	.239	.338	2	.118	-1	-1	-0	1	-0.2
1953	Phi-A	2	1	.667	17	2	1	0	0	38^{2}	44	24	3	5	24	16	17.0	4.89	88	.282	.395	1	.167	-0	-4	-2	0	-0.2
Total	20	211	222	.487	600	483	246	31	21	3759^{1}	3769	1908	206	61	1732	2082	13.3	3.98	107	.261	.342	253	.189	-26	67	107	-29	3.4

● DICK NEWSOME

Newsome, Heber Hampton b: 12/13/09, Ahoskie, N.C. d: 12/15/65, Ahoskie, N.C. BR/TR, 6', 185 lbs. Deb: 4/25/41

YEAR	TM/L	W	L	PCT	G	GS	CG	SH	SV	IP	H	R	HR	HB	BB	SO	RAT	ERA	ERA+	OAV	OOB	BH	AVG	PB	PR	PR+	PD	TPI
1941	Bos-A	19	10	.655	36	29	17	2	0	213^{2}	235	115	13	7	79	58	13.5	4.13	101	.277	.344	19	.244	3	0	1	3	0.7
1942	Bos-A	8	10	.444	24	23	11	0	0	158	174	98	11	0	67	40	13.7	5.01	74	.278	.348	13	.236	2	-24	-22	1	-2.0
1943	Bos-A	8	13	.381	25	22	8	2	0	154^{1}	166	83	8	5	68	40	13.9	4.49	74	.274	.352	7	.146	-1	-20	-20	-2	-2.8
Total	3	35	33	.515	85	74	36	4	0	526	575	296	32	12	214	138	13.7	4.50	84	.276	.347	39	.215	3	-44	-41	2	-4.1

● DOC NEWTON

Newton, Eustace James b: 10/26/1877, Indianapolis, Ind. d: 5/14/31, Memphis, Tenn. BL/TL, 6', 185 lbs. Deb: 4/27/00

YEAR	TM/L	W	L	PCT	G	GS	CG	SH	SV	IP	H	R	HR	HB	BB	SO	RAT	ERA	ERA+	OAV	OOB	BH	AVG	PB	PR	PR+	PD	TPI
1900	Cin-N	9	15	.375	35	27	22	1	0	234^{2}	255	146	4	12	100	88	14.1	4.14	89	.276	.355	17	.198	-1	-12	-12	-2	-1.3
1901	Cin-N	4	13	.235	20	18	17	0	0	168^{1}	190	117	6	14	59	65	14.1	4.12	78	.282	.353	9	.130	-4	-15	-18	1	-1.8
	Bro-N	6	5	.545	13	12	9	0	0	105	110	42	1	7	30	45	12.6	2.83	119	.268	.328	9	.220	1	6	6	-0	0.6
	Yr	10	18	.357	33	30	26	0	0	273^{1}	300	159	7	21	89	110	13.5	3.62	90	.277	.343	18	.164	-4	-9	-11	1	-1.2
1902	Bro-N	15	14	.517	31	28	26	4	2	264^{1}	208	95	2	11	87	107	10.4	2.42	114	**.217**	.289	19	.174	-1	11	10	-2	0.8
1905	NY-A	2	2	.500	11	7	2	0	0	59^{2}	61	23	1	2	24	15	13.1	2.11	139	.266	.341	3	.136	-1	4	5	-1	0.1
1906	NY-A	7	5	.583	21	15	6	2	0	125	118	53	3	7	33	52	11.4	3.17	94	.252	.311	9	.220	-0	-7	-3	2	-0.1
1907	NY-A	7	10	.412	19	15	10	0	0	133	132	66	0	7	31	70	11.5	3.18	88	.261	.313	4	.108	-1	-9	-5	1	-0.7
1908	NY-A	4	5	.444	23	13	6	1	1	88^{1}	78	52	0	7	41	49	12.8	2.95	84	.242	.341	4	.160	-0	-6	-5	0	-0.5
1909	NY-A	0	3	.000	4	4	1	0	0	22^{1}	27	17	0	3	11	11	16.5	2.82	90	.300	.394	1	.167	0	-1	-1	1	0.0
Total	8	54	72	.429	177	139	99	8	3	1200^{2}	1179	611	17	70	416	502	12.5	3.22	95	.257	.329	75	.172	-9	-29	-19	-2	-2.9

● KID NICHOLS

Nichols, Charles Augustus b: 9/14/1869, Madison, Wis. d: 4/11/53, Kansas City, Mo. BB/TR, 5'10.5", 175 lbs. Deb: 4/23/1890 MH

YEAR	TM/L	W	L	PCT	G	GS	CG	SH	SV	IP	H	R	HR	HB	BB	SO	RAT	ERA	ERA+	OAV	OOB	BH	AVG	PB	PR	PR+	PD	TPI
1890	Bos-N	27	19	.587	48	47	47	**7**	0	424	374	175	8	11	112	222	10.5	2.23	168	.229	.284	43	.247	1	63	68	0	6.3

YEAR	TM/L	W	L	PCT	G	GS	CG	SH	SV	IP	H	R	HR	HB	BB	SO	RAT	ERA	ERA+	OAV	OOB	BH	AVG	PB	PR	PR+	PD	TPI
1891	Bos-N	30	17	.638	52	48	45	5	**3**	425^1	413	219	15	17	103	240	11.3	2.39	**153**	.245	.295	36	.197	-3	**45**	**55**	6	**5.3**
1892	*Bos-N	35	16	.686	53	51	49	5	0	453	404	211	15	10	121	192	10.6	2.84	124	.229	.283	40	.203	1	22	32	-1	3.0
1893	Bos-N	34	14	.708	52	44	43	1	1	425	426	222	15	15	118	94	11.8	3.52	140	.253	.308	39	.220	-2	54	63	-2	5.1
1894	Bos-N	32	13	.711	50	46	40	**3**	0	407	488	308	23	9	121	113	13.7	4.75	120	.294	.345	50	.294	3	26	39	0	3.3
1895	Bos-N	26	16	.619	48	43	43	1	**3**	389^2	429	220	15	5	90	147	12.1	3.37	151	.275	.317	37	.230	-5	61	**70**	-0	5.4
1896	Bos-N	**30**	14	.682	49	43	37	3	1	372^1	387	211	14	7	101	102	12.0	2.83	161	.266	.316	28	.190	-3	**64**	**68**	2	**6.4**
1897	*Bos-N	**31**	11	.738	46	40	37	2	**3**	**368**	362	152	9	3	68	127	**10.6**	2.64	**169**	.255	**.291**	39	.265	4	**68**	**72**	-2	**7.0**
1898	Bos-N	**31**	12	.721	**50**	42	40	5	**4**	388	316	136	7	14	85	138	**9.6**	2.13	173	**.221**	**.272**	38	.241	3	**64**	**66**	-2	**6.7**
1899	Bos-N	21	19	.525	42	37	37	4	1	343^1	326	155	11	6	82	108	10.9	2.99	139	.250	.298	26	.191	-5	33	41	-1	3.6
1900	Bos-N	13	16	.448	29	27	25	**4**	0	231^1	215	116	11	11	72	53	11.6	3.07	134	.246	.311	18	.200	-2	16	24	-1	2.3
1901	Bos-N	19	16	.543	38	34	33	4	0	321	306	146	8	10	90	143	11.4	3.22	112	.250	.306	46	.282	9	4	13	-1	2.2
1904	StL-N	21	13	.618	36	35	35	3	1	317	268	97	3	5	50	134	9.2	2.02	134	.222	.256	17	.156	-1	25	24	-1	2.5
1905	StL-N	1	5	.167	7	7	5	0	0	51^2	64	47	1	0	18	16	14.3	5.40	55	.296	.350	5	.227	0	-14	-14	-1	-1.5
	Phi-N	10	6	.625	17	16	15	1	0	138^2	129	47	1	4	28	50	10.4	2.27	129	.250	.294	10	.189	0	11	10	-4	0.7
	Yr	11	11	.500	24	23	20	1	0	190^1	193	94	2	4	46	66	11.5	3.12	94	.264	.311	15	.200	0	-2	-4	-5	-0.8
1906	Phi-N	0	1	.000	4	2	1	0	0	11	17	16	0	2	13	1	26.2	9.82	27	.386	.542	0	.000	-0	-9	-9	-1	-0.8
Total	15	361	208	.634	621	562	532	48	17	5066^1	4924	2478	156	129	1272	1880	11.2	2.95	139	.250	.300	472	.226	-0	534	621	-8	57.5

● CHET NICHOLS

Nichols, Chester Raymond Jr. b: 2/22/31, Pawtucket, R.I. d: 3/27/95, Lincoln, R.I. BB/TL, 6′1.5″, 195 lbs. Deb: 4/19/51 F

YEAR	TM/L	W	L	PCT	G	GS	CG	SH	SV	IP	H	R	HR	HB	BB	SO	RAT	ERA	ERA+	OAV	OOB	BH	AVG	PB	PR	PR+	PD	TPI
1951	Bos-N	11	8	.579	33	19	12	3	2	156	142	61	4	1	69	71	12.2	**2.88**	127	.246	.327	7	.137	-2	19	15	2	1.7
1954	Mil-N	9	11	.450	35	20	5	1	1	122^1	132	68	5	4	65	55	14.8	4.41	84	.286	.379	3	.086	-3	-5	-10	1	-1.6
1955	Mil-N	9	8	.529	34	21	6	0	1	144	139	79	20	1	67	44	12.9	4.00	94	.253	.335	8	.154	-2	1	-4	2	-0.5
1956	Mil-N	0	1	.000	2	0	0	0	0	4	9	3	1	0	3	2	27.0	6.75	51	.563	.632	0	.000	-0	-1	-2	0	-0.3
1960	Bos-A	0	2	.000	6	1	0	0	0	12^2	12	6	0	0	4	11	11.4	4.26	95	.240	.296	0	.000	-0	-1	-0	0	0.0
1961	Bos-A	3	2	.600	26	2	0	0	3	51^2	40	12	3	0	26	20	11.5	2.09	199	.221	.319	1	.111	-0	11	12	3	1.4
1962	Bos-A	1	1	.500	29	1	0	0	3	57	61	25	3	0	22	33	13.1	3.00	138	.276	.342	0	.000	-1	6	7	1	0.4
1963	Bos-A	1	3	.250	21	7	0	0	0	52^2	61	30	8	0	24	27	14.5	4.78	79	.298	.371	3	.231	0	-7	-6	-0	-0.4
1964	Cin-N	0	0	—	3	0	0	0	0	3	4	2	1	0	0	3	12.0	6.00	60	.308	.308	0	—	0	-1	-1	-0	-0.1
Total	9	34	36	.486	189	71	23	4	10	603^1	600	286	45	6	280	266	13.2	3.64	105	.264	.346	22	.127	-8	22	12	8	0.6

● CHET NICHOLS

Nichols, Chester Raymond Sr. "Nick" b: 7/3/1897, Woonsocket, R.I. d: 7/11/82, Pawtucket, R.I. BR/TR, 5′11″, 160 lbs. Deb: 7/30/26 F

YEAR	TM/L	W	L	PCT	G	GS	CG	SH	SV	IP	H	R	HR	HB	BB	SO	RAT	ERA	ERA+	OAV	OOB	BH	AVG	PB	PR	PR+	PD	TPI
1926	Pit-N	0	0	—	3	0	0	0	0	7^2	13	11	0	0	5	2	21.1	8.22	48	.342	.419	1	.333	0	-4	-4	0	-0.1
1927	Pit-N	0	3	.000	8	0	0	0	0	27^2	34	19	1	1	17	9	16.9	5.86	70	.309	.406	1	.111	-0	-6	-5	-0	-0.5
1928	NY-N	0	0	—	3	0	0	0	0	2^2	11	13	0	1	3	1	50.6	23.63	17	.611	.682	0	—	0	-6	-6	0	-0.3
1930	Phi-N	1	2	.333	16	5	1	0	0	59^2	76	51	8	2	16	15	14.2	6.79	80	.306	.353	6	.300	0	-12	-8	1	-0.2
1931	Phi-N	0	1	.000	3	0	0	0	0	5^2	10	6	0	0	1	1	17.5	9.53	45	.435	.458	0	.000	-0	-4	-3	0	-0.5
1932	Phi-N	0	2	.000	11	0	0	0	1	19^1	23	16	2	0	14	5	17.2	6.98	63	.299	.407	0	.000	-1	-7	-5	0	-0.5
Total	6	1	8	.111	44	5	1	0	1	122^2	167	116	11	4	56	33	16.7	7.19	67	.325	.395	8	.211	-1	-38	-30	1	-2.1

● DOLAN NICHOLS

Nichols, Dolan Levon "Nick" b: 2/28/30, Tishomingo, Miss. d: 11/20/89, Tupelo, Miss. BR/TR, 6′, 195 lbs. Deb: 4/15/58

YEAR	TM/L	W	L	PCT	G	GS	CG	SH	SV	IP	H	R	HR	HB	BB	SO	RAT	ERA	ERA+	OAV	OOB	BH	AVG	PB	PR	PR+	PD	TPI
1958	Chi-N	0	4	.000	24	0	0	0	1	41^1	46	27	1	1	16	9	13.7	5.01	78	.295	.364	0	.000	-1	-5	-5	1	-0.4

● TRICKY NICHOLS

Nichols, Frederick C. b: 7/26/1850, Bridgeport, Conn. d: 8/22/1897, Bridgeport, Conn. BR/TR, 5′7.5″, 150 lbs. Deb: 4/21/1875

YEAR	TM/L	W	L	PCT	G	GS	CG	SH	SV	IP	H	R	HR	HB	BB	SO	RAT	ERA	ERA+	OAV	OOB	BH	AVG	PB	PR	PR+	PD	TPI
1875	NH-n	4	29	.121	34	33	30	0	0	288	321	245	2		9	48	10.3	2.38	87	.242	.248	23	.193	-2	-5	-10		-0.3
1876	Bos-N	1	0	1.000	1	1	1	0	0	9	7	5	0		0	0	7.0	1.00	226	.200	.200	0	.000	-1	1	1	0	0.1
1877	StL-N	18	23	.439	42	39	35	1	0	350	376	195	2		53	80	11.0	2.60	100	.263	.289	31	.167	-6	8	0	-0	-0.6
1878	Pro-N	4	7	.364	11	10	10	0	0	98	157	98	0		8	21	15.2	4.22	52	.344	.356	9	.184	-0	-21	-23	2	-1.9
1880	Wor-N	0	2	.000	2	2	2	0	0	17^2	29	16	0		4	4	16.8	4.08	64	.358	.388	0	.000	-1	-3	-3	-1	-0.4
1882	Bal-a	1	12	.077	16	13	12	0	0	118^1	155	113	2		17	21	13.1	5.02	55	.296	.319	15	.158	-2	-31	-29	-2	-2.6
Total	5	24	44	.353	72	65	60	1	0	593	724	427	4		82	126	12.2	3.37	76	.287	.309	55	.161	-10	-45	-56	-1	-5.4

● ROD NICHOLS

Nichols, Rodney Lea b: 12/29/64, Burlington, Iowa BR/TR, 6′2″, 200 lbs. Deb: 7/30/88

YEAR	TM/L	W	L	PCT	G	GS	CG	SH	SV	IP	H	R	HR	HB	BB	SO	RAT	ERA	ERA+	OAV	OOB	BH	AVG	PB	PR	PR+	PD	TPI
1988	Cle-A	1	7	.125	11	10	3	0	0	69^1	73	41	5	2	23	31	12.7	5.06	81	.272	.334	0	—	0	-8	-7	-0	-0.7
1989	Cle-A	4	6	.400	15	11	0	0	0	71^2	81	42	9	2	24	42	13.4	4.40	90	.285	.345	0	—	0	-4	-3	-0	-0.5
1990	Cle-A	0	3	.000	4	2	0	0	0	16	24	14	5	2	6	3	18.0	7.88	50	.343	.410	0	—	0	-7	-7	0	-1.0
1991	Cle-A	2	11	.154	31	16	3	1	1	137^1	145	63	6	6	30	76	11.9	3.54	118	.273	.319	0	—	0	9	9	-1	0.7
1992	Cle-A	4	3	.571	30	9	0	0	0	105^1	114	58	13	2	31	56	12.6	4.53	86	.273	.327	0	—	0	-7	-7	-0	-0.5
1993	LA-N	0	1	.000	4	0	0	0	0	6^1	9	5	1	0	2	3	15.6	5.68	67	.360	.407	0	—	0	-1	-1	0	-0.2
1995	Atl-N	0	0	—	5	0	0	0	0	6^2	14	11	3	0	5	3	25.7	5.40	79	.424	.500	0	—	0	-1	-1	0	0.0
Total	7	11	31	.262	100	48	6	1	1	412^2	460	234	42	14	121	214	13.0	4.43	91	.282	.337	0	—	0	-20	-17	-1	-2.2

● FRANK NICHOLSON

Nicholson, Frank Collins b: 8/29/1889, Berlin, Pa. d: 11/10/72, Jersey Shore, Pa. BR/TR, 6′2″, 175 lbs. Deb: 9/6/12

YEAR	TM/L	W	L	PCT	G	GS	CG	SH	SV	IP	H	R	HR	HB	BB	SO	RAT	ERA	ERA+	OAV	OOB	BH	AVG	PB	PR	PR+	PD	TPI
1912	Phi-N	0	0	—	2	0	0	0	0	4	8	3	1	0	2	1	22.5	6.75	54	.471	.526	0	—	0	-1	-1	0	-0.1

● CHRIS NICHTING

Nichting, Christopher Thomas b: 5/13/66, Cincinnati, Ohio BR/TR, 6′1″, 205 lbs. Deb: 5/15/95

YEAR	TM/L	W	L	PCT	G	GS	CG	SH	SV	IP	H	R	HR	HB	BB	SO	RAT	ERA	ERA+	OAV	OOB	BH	AVG	PB	PR	PR+	PD	TPI
1995	Tex-A	0	0	—	13	0	0	0	0	24^1	36	19	1	1	13	6	18.5	7.03	69	.343	.420	0	—	0	-6	-6	1	-0.2
2000	Cle-A	0	0	—	7	0	0	0	0	9	13	7	0	2	5	7	20.0	7.00	71	.342	.444	0	—	0	-2	-2	0	-0.1
Total	2	0	0	—	20	0	0	0	0	33^1	49	26	1	3	18	13	18.9	7.02	69	.343	.427	0	—	0	-8	-8	1	-0.3

● DOUG NICKLE

Nickle, Douglas Alan b: 10/2/74, Sonoma, Cal. BR/TR, 6′4″, 210 lbs. Deb: 9/18/2000

YEAR	TM/L	W	L	PCT	G	GS	CG	SH	SV	IP	H	R	HR	HB	BB	SO	RAT	ERA	ERA+	OAV	OOB	BH	AVG	PB	PR	PR+	PD	TPI
2000	Phi-N	0	0	—	4	0	0	0	0	2^2	5	4	0	1	2	0	27.0	13.50	35	.417	.533	0	—	0	-3	-3	0	-0.1

● GEORGE NICOL

Nicol, George Edward b: 10/17/1870, Barry, Ill. d: 8/10/24, Milwaukee, Wis. TL, 5′7″, 155 lbs. Deb: 9/23/1890 ♦

YEAR	TM/L	W	L	PCT	G	GS	CG	SH	SV	IP	H	R	HR	HB	BB	SO	RAT	ERA	ERA+	OAV	OOB	BH	AVG	PB	PR	PR+	PD	TPI
1890	StL-a	2	1	.667	3	3	2	0	0	17	11	13	1	2	19	16	16.9	4.76	91	.180	.390	2	.286	1	-2	-1	-0	0.0
1891	Chi-N	0	1	.000	3	2	0	0	0	11	14	20	0	1	10	12	20.5	4.91	68	.298	.431	2	.333	1	-2	-2	-1	-0.1
1894	Pit-N	3	4	.429	9	5	3	0	0	46^1	58	38	2	5	39	13	19.8	6.22	84	.304	.434	9	.409	2	-5	-5	-1	-0.5
	Lou-N	0	1	.000	2	2	2	0	0	17^1	35	35	4	1	16	4	27.0	10.90	47	.412	.510	38	.339	1	-11	-12	0	-0.4
	Yr	3	5	.375	11	7	5	0	0	63^2	93	73	6	6	55	17	21.8	7.49	69	.337	.457	47	.351	2	-15	-17	-1	-0.9
Total	3	5	7	.417	17	12	7	0	0	91^2	118	106	7	9	84	45	20.7	6.68	73	.307	.442	51	.347	4	-19	-19	-2	-1.0

● DAVID NIED

Nied, David Glen b: 12/22/68, Dallas, Texas BR/TR, 6′2″, 188 lbs. Deb: 9/1/92

YEAR	TM/L	W	L	PCT	G	GS	CG	SH	SV	IP	H	R	HR	HB	BB	SO	RAT	ERA	ERA+	OAV	OOB	BH	AVG	PB	PR	PR+	PD	TPI
1992	Atl-N	3	0	1.000	6	2	0	0	0	23	10	3	0	0	5	19	5.9	1.17	312	.130	.183	2	.286	0	6	6	-0	0.8
1993	Col-N	5	9	.357	16	16	1	0	0	87	99	53	8	1	42	46	14.7	5.17	92	.296	.376	4	.174	0	-11	-3	1	-0.4
1994	Col-N	9	7	.563	22	22	2	1	0	122	137	70	15	4	47	74	13.9	4.80	104	.287	.356	4	.100	-2	-8	2	-2	-0.1
1995	Col-N	0	0	—	2	0	0	0	0	4^1	11	10	2	0	3	3	29.1	20.77	26	.458	.519	0	—	0	-8	-6	-0	-0.3
1996	Col-N	0	2	.000	6	1	0	0	0	5^1	5	8	1	0	8	4	21.9	13.50	39	.250	.464	0	.000	-0	-5	-4	-0	-0.7
Total	5	17	18	.486	52	41	3	1	0	241^2	262	144	26	5	105	146	13.9	5.06	94	.281	.357	10	.141	-2	-26	-6	-2	-0.7

● TOM NIEDENFUER

Niedenfuer, Thomas Edward b: 8/13/59, St.Louis Park, Minn. BR/TR, 6′5″, 225 lbs. Deb: 8/15/81

YEAR	TM/L	W	L	PCT	G	GS	CG	SH	SV	IP	H	R	HR	HB	BB	SO	RAT	ERA	ERA+	OAV	OOB	BH	AVG	PB	PR	PR+	PD	TPI
1981	*LA-N	3	1	.750	17	0	0	0	2	26	25	11	1	1	6	12	11.1	3.81	87	.258	.308	0	—	0	-1	-1	-0	-0.3
1982	LA-N	3	4	.429	55	0	0	0	9	69^2	71	22	3	2	25	60	12.7	2.71	128	.269	.337	0	.000	-0	7	6	-1	0.7
1983	*LA-N	8	3	.727	66	0	0	0	11	94^2	55	22	6	1	29	66	8.1	1.90	189	.170	.240	0	.000	-0	18	18	-1	2.3
1984	LA-N	2	5	.286	33	0	0	0	11	47^1	39	14	3	2	23	45	12.2	2.47	143	.227	.325	0	.000	-0	6	6	-0	1.0
1985	*LA-N	7	9	.438	64	0	0	0	19	106^1	86	32	6	1	24	102	9.4	2.71	129	.223	.270	1	.111	-0	11	9	-1	1.6
1986	LA-N	6	6	.500	60	0	0	0	11	80	86	35	11	1	29	55	13.0	3.71	93	.280	.344	2	.500	1	0	-2	0	-0.3
1987	LA-N	1	0	1.000	15	0	0	0	1	16^1	13	5	1	1	9	10	12.7	2.76	144	.220	.333	0	—	0	2	2	0	0.2
	Bal-A	3	5	.375	45	0	0	0	13	52^1	55	32	11	1	22	37	13.4	4.99	89	.266	.339	0	—	0	-3	-3	-1	-0.7
1988	Bal-A	3	4	.429	52	0	0	0	18	59	59	23	8	2	19	40	12.2	3.51	111	.259	.321	0	—	0	3	3	-1	0.4
1989	Sea-A	0	3	.000	25	0	0	0	0	36^1	46	29	7	1	15	15	15.4	6.69	60	.309	.376	0	—	0	-11	-10	0	-0.8
1990	StL-N	0	6	.000	52	0	0	0	2	65	66	26	3	0	25	32	12.6	3.46	110	.269	.337	0	.000	-0	2	3	-1	0.1
Total	10	36	46	.439	484	0	0	0	97	653	601	251	60	13	226	474	11.6	3.29	112	.247	.314	3	.115	-1	34	29	-5	4.2

● DICK NIEHAUS

Niehaus, Richard J. b: 10/24/1892, Covington, Ky. d: 3/12/57, Atlanta, Ga. BL/TL, 5'11", 165 lbs. Deb: 9/9/13

YEAR	TM/L	W	L	PCT	G	GS	CG	SH	SV	IP	H	R	HR	HB	BB	SO	RAT	ERA	ERA+	OAV	OOB	BH	AVG	PB	PR	PR+	PD	TPI
1913	StL-N	0	2	.000	3	3	2	0	0	24	20	17	1	0	13	4	12.4	4.13	78	.241	.344	2	.286	1	-2	-2	0	-0.1
1914	StL-N	1	0	1.000	8	1	1	0	0	17^1	18	11	1	0	8	6	13.5	3.12	90	.269	.347	1	.250	1	-1	-1	-1	0.0
1915	StL-N	2	1	.667	15	2	0	0	0	45^1	48	35	2	1	22	21	14.1	3.97	70	.281	.366	1	.071	-1	-6	-6	0	-0.4
1920	Cle-A	1	2	.333	19	3	0	0	2	40	42	21	0	1	16	12	13.3	3.60	106	.269	.341	4	.444	2	1	1	-1	0.1
Total	4	4	5	.444	45	9	3	0	2	126^2	128	84	4	2	59	43	13.4	3.77	85	.268	.351	8	.235	2	-8	-8	-1	-0.4

● JOE NIEKRO

Niekro, Joseph Franklin b: 11/7/44, Martins Ferry, Ohio BR/TR, 6'1", 190 lbs. Deb: 4/16/67 F

YEAR	TM/L	W	L	PCT	G	GS	CG	SH	SV	IP	H	R	HR	HB	BB	SO	RAT	ERA	ERA+	OAV	OOB	BH	AVG	PB	PR	PR+	PD	TPI
1967	Chi-N	10	7	.588	36	22	7	2	0	169^2	171	68	15	2	32	77	10.9	3.34	106	.257	.293	9	.196	1	1	4	-1	0.4
1968	Chi-N	14	10	.583	34	29	2	1	2	177	204	93	18	3	59	65	13.5	4.32	73	.294	.351	6	.100	-2	-26	-22	0	-3.1
1969	Chi-N	0	1	.000	4	3	0	0	0	19^1	24	9	3	0	6	7	14.0	3.72	108	.304	.353	1	.200	0	-0	1	1	0.1
	SD-N	8	17	.320	37	31	8	3	0	202	213	91	15	0	45	55	11.5	3.70	96	.273	.312	6	.118	0	-2	-4	-1	-0.5
	Yr	8	18	.308	41	34	8	3	0	221^1	237	100	18	0	51	62	11.7	3.70	97	.276	.316	7	.125	0	-3	-3	-1	-0.4
1970	Det-A	12	13	.480	38	34	6	2	0	213	221	107	28	3	72	101	12.5	4.06	92	.266	.327	13	.197	4	-8	-8	1	-0.4
1971	Det-A	6	7	.462	31	15	0	0	1	122^1	136	62	13	2	49	43	13.8	4.49	80	.283	.352	4	.133	-0	-14	-12	1	-1.1
1972	*Det-A	3	2	.600	18	7	1	0	1	47	62	20	3	1	8	24	13.6	3.83	82	.330	.360	3	.250	1	-4	-3	-0	-0.3
1973	Atl-N	2	4	.333	20	0	0	0	3	24	23	11	2	0	11	12	12.8	4.13	96	.277	.362	1	.333	0	-1	-0	1	0.0
1974	Atl-N	3	2	.600	27	2	0	0	0	43	36	19	5	2	18	31	11.7	3.56	107	.237	.326	0	.000	-1	0	1	1	0.1
1975	Hou-N	6	4	.600	40	4	1	1	4	88	79	32	3	2	39	54	12.3	3.07	110	.240	.324	3	.214	1	6	3	0	0.5
1976	Hou-N	4	8	.333	36	13	0	0	0	118	107	60	8	1	56	77	12.5	3.36	95	.238	.324	5	.185	2	2	-2	-1	-0.1
1977	Hou-N	13	8	.619	44	14	9	2	5	180^2	155	66	14	1	64	101	11.0	3.04	117	.237	.306	7	.140	-1	18	12	1	1.4
1978	Hou-N	14	14	.500	35	29	10	1	0	202^2	190	97	13	9	73	97	12.1	3.86	86	.248	.321	9	.138	-1	-6	-13	-1	-1.9
1979	Hou-N☆	**21**	11	.656	38	38	11	**5**	0	263^2	221	102	17	7	107	119	11.4	3.00	117	.228	.309	10	.120	-2	22	16	0	1.7
1980	*Hou-N	20	12	.625	37	36	11	2	0	256	268	119	12	4	79	127	12.3	3.55	93	.270	.326	22	.275	8	2	-8	-1	-0.2
1981	*Hou-N	9	9	.500	24	24	5	2	0	166	150	60	8	0	47	77	10.7	2.82	117	.243	.297	9	.176	1	12	9	-1	1.0
1982	Hou-N	17	12	.586	35	35	16	5	0	270	224	79	12	5	64	130	9.8	2.47	135	.229	.279	8	.090	-4	34	28	0	2.5
1983	Hou-N	15	14	.517	38	38	9	1	0	263^2	238	115	15	3	101	152	11.7	3.48	98	.241	.313	8	.094	-3	5	-2	-2	-0.8
1984	Hou-N	16	12	.571	38	38	6	1	0	248^1	223	104	16	4	89	127	11.5	3.04	109	.241	.310	11	.133	-2	15	8	1	0.8
1985	Hou-N	9	12	.429	32	32	4	1	0	213	197	100	21	5	99	117	12.7	3.72	93	.247	.333	17	.250	4	-3	-6	0	-0.2
	NY-A	2	1	.667	3	3	0	0	0	12^1	14	8	3	0	8	4	16.1	5.84	69	.280	.379	0	—	0	-2	-3	0	-0.5
1986	NY-A	9	10	.474	25	25	0	0	0	125^2	139	84	15	1	63	59	14.5	4.87	84	.275	.356	0	—	0	-10	-11	-1	-1.5
1987	NY-A	3	4	.429	8	8	1	0	0	50^2	40	25	4	4	19	30	11.2	3.55	124	.215	.301	0	—	0	5	5	-0	0.6
	*Min-A	4	9	.308	19	18	0	0	0	96^1	115	76	11	6	45	54	15.5	6.26	74	.296	.378	0	—	0	-19	-17	-1	-1.9
	Yr	7	13	.350	27	26	1	0	0	147	155	101	15	10	64	84	14.0	5.33	85	.270	.353	0	—	0	-14	-12	-1	-1.3
1988	Min-A	1	1	.500	5	2	0	0	0	11^2	16	13	2	0	9	7	19.3	10.03	41	.320	.424	0	—	0	-8	-8	1	-1.0
Total	22	221	204	.520	702	500	107	29	16	3584	3466	1620	276	65	1262	1747	12.0	3.59	97	.255	.321	152	.156	6	17	-37	-3	-4.4

● PHIL NIEKRO

Niekro, Philip Henry b: 4/1/39, Blaine, Ohio BR/TR, 6'1", 180 lbs. Deb: 4/15/64 FH

YEAR	TM/L	W	L	PCT	G	GS	CG	SH	SV	IP	H	R	HR	HB	BB	SO	RAT	ERA	ERA+	OAV	OOB	BH	AVG	PB	PR	PR+	PD	TPI
1964	Mil-N	0	0	—	10	0	0	0	0	15	15	10	1	1	7	8	13.8	4.80	73	.273	.365	0	—	0	-2	-2	-0	-0.1
1965	Mil-N	2	3	.400	41	1	0	0	6	74^2	73	32	5	3	26	49	12.3	2.89	122	.258	.327	1	.100	-0	5	5	1	0.5
1966	Atl-N	4	3	.571	28	0	0	0	2	50^1	48	32	4	2	23	17	13.1	4.11	88	.249	.335	0	.000	-1	-3	-3	2	-0.3
1967	Atl-N	11	9	.550	46	20	10	1	9	207	164	64	9	7	55	129	9.8	**1.87**	**178**	.218	.277	7	.123	-0	35	34	1	3.8
1968	Atl-N	14	12	.538	37	34	15	5	2	257	228	83	16	5	45	140	9.7	2.59	116	.239	.277	8	.104	-1	11	11	3	1.5
1969	*Atl-N★	23	13	.639	40	35	21	4	1	284^1	235	93	21	5	57	193	9.4	2.56	141	.221	.264	20	.211	3	33	33	2	4.8
1970	Atl-N	12	18	.400	34	32	10	3	0	229^2	222	124	40	6	68	168	11.6	4.27	101	.248	.305	12	.152	-1	-6	1	2	0.1
1971	Atl-N	15	14	.517	42	36	18	4	2	268^2	248	112	27	3	70	173	10.8	2.98	125	.245	.296	14	.152	-2	15	21	2	2.1
1972	Atl-N	16	12	.571	38	36	17	1	0	282^1	254	112	22	5	53	164	9.9	3.06	124	.236	.275	18	.194	1	12	21	1	2.3
1973	Atl-N	13	10	.565	42	30	9	1	4	245	214	103	21	5	89	131	11.3	3.31	119	.234	.306	10	.122	-1	10	16	2	1.6
1974	Atl-N	**20**	13	.606	41	39	**18**	6	1	**302^1**	249	91	19	6	88	195	10.2	2.38	159	.225	.286	20	.192	-0	**42**	**45**	0	**5.1**
1975	Atl-N☆	15	15	.500	39	37	13	1	0	275^2	285	115	29	11	72	144	12.0	3.20	118	.269	.322	17	.172	-0	13	17	1	1.9
1976	Atl-N	17	11	.607	38	37	10	2	0	270^2	249	116	18	8	101	173	11.9	3.29	115	.242	.315	18	.191	1	6	14	1	1.6
1977	Atl-N	16	20	.444	44	43	**20**	2	0	**330^1**	315	166	26	8	164	**262**	13.3	4.03	110	.255	.346	19	.174	-3	-4	14	2	1.3
1978	Atl-N★	19	18	.514	44	42	**22**	4	1	**334^1**	295	129	16	13	102	248	11.0	2.88	141	.235	.299	27	.225	2	26	**39**	4	**5.1**
1979	Atl-N	**21**	20	.512	44	44	**23**	1	0	**342**	311	160	41	11	113	208	11.4	3.39	120	.241	.307	24	.195	1	13	23	3	3.2
1980	Atl-N	15	18	.455	40	38	11	3	1	275	256	119	30	3	85	176	11.3	3.63	103	.249	.308	12	.133	-2	-1	3	1	0.3
1981	Atl-N	7	7	.500	22	22	3	3	0	139^1	120	56	6	1	56	62	11.4	3.10	116	.233	.310	4	.077	-4	6	7	0	0.3
1982	*Atl-N☆	17	4	**.810**	35	35	4	2	0	234^1	225	106	23	3	73	144	11.6	3.61	104	.255	.314	17	.195	2	-0	3	1	0.6
1983	Atl-N	11	10	.524	34	33	2	0	0	201^2	212	94	18	2	105	128	14.2	3.97	98	.276	.364	12	.185	0	-8	-2	0	-0.1
1984	NY-A☆	16	8	.667	32	31	5	1	0	215^2	219	85	15	3	76	136	12.4	3.09	123	.267	.331	0	—	0	22	18	2	2.1
1985	NY-A	16	12	.571	33	33	7	1	0	220	203	110	29	2	120	149	13.3	4.09	98	.245	.342	0	—	0	1	-2	-2	-0.4
1986	Cle-A	11	11	.500	34	32	5	0	0	210^1	241	126	24	6	95	81	14.6	4.32	96	.287	.363	0	—	0	-3	-4	-1	-0.4
1987	Tor-A	0	2	.000	3	3	0	0	0	12	15	11	4	0	7	7	16.5	8.25	55	.306	.393	0	—	0	-5	-5	-0	-0.7
	Cle-A	7	11	.389	22	22	2	0	0	123^2	142	83	18	4	53	57	14.5	5.89	77	.286	.359	0	—	0	-20	-18	0	-2.2
	Yr	7	13	.350	25	25	2	0	0	135^2	157	94	22	4	60	64	14.7	6.10	74	.288	.362	0	—	0	-25	-23	-0	-2.9
	Atl-N	0	0	—	1	1	0	0	0	3	6	5	0	0	6	0	36.0	15.00	29	.429	.600	0	.000	-0	-4	-3	-0	-0.2
Total	24	318	274	.537	864	716	245	45	29	5404^1	5044	2337	482	123	1809	3342	11.6	3.35	115	.247	.312	260	.169	-6	196	289	28	33.8

● JERRY NIELSEN

Nielsen, Gerald Arthur b: 8/5/66, Sacramento, Cal. BL/TL, 6'3", 185 lbs. Deb: 7/12/92

YEAR	TM/L	W	L	PCT	G	GS	CG	SH	SV	IP	H	R	HR	HB	BB	SO	RAT	ERA	ERA+	OAV	OOB	BH	AVG	PB	PR	PR+	PD	TPI
1992	NY-A	1	0	1.000	20	0	0	0	0	19^2	17	10	1	0	18	12	16.0	4.58	86	.243	.398	0	—	0	-1	-1	0	0.0
1993	Cal-A	0	0	—	10	0	0	0	0	12^1	18	13	1	1	4	8	16.8	8.03	56	.340	.397	0	—	0	-5	-5	-0	-0.2
Total	2	1	0	1.000	30	0	0	0	0	32	35	23	2	1	22	20	16.3	5.91	70	.285	.397	0	—	0	-6	-6	0	-0.2

● SCOTT NIELSEN

Nielsen, Jeffrey Scott b: 12/18/58, Salt Lake City, Ut. BR/TR, 6'1", 190 lbs. Deb: 7/7/86

YEAR	TM/L	W	L	PCT	G	GS	CG	SH	SV	IP	H	R	HR	HB	BB	SO	RAT	ERA	ERA+	OAV	OOB	BH	AVG	PB	PR	PR+	PD	TPI
1986	NY-A	4	4	.500	10	9	2	2	0	56	66	29	12	2	12	20	12.9	4.02	102	.299	.340	0	—	0	1	1	-1	0.0
1987	Chi-A	3	5	.375	19	7	1	1	2	66^1	83	48	9	1	25	23	14.8	6.24	74	.307	.368	0	—	0	-13	-12	-1	-1.3
1988	NY-A	1	2	.333	7	2	0	0	0	19^2	27	16	5	0	13	4	18.3	6.86	58	.333	.426	0	—	0	-6	-6	0	-0.8
1989	NY-A	1	0	1.000	2	0	0	0	0	0^2	2	1	0	0	1	0	40.5	13.50	29	.500	.600	0	—	0	-1	-1	0	-0.1
Total	4	9	11	.450	38	18	3	3	2	142^2	178	94	26	3	51	47	14.6	5.49	78	.309	.368	0	—	0	-19	-19	-1	-2.2

● RANDY NIEMANN

Niemann, Randal Harold b: 11/15/55, Scotia, Cal. BL/TL, 6'4", 200 lbs. Deb: 5/20/79 C

YEAR	TM/L	W	L	PCT	G	GS	CG	SH	SV	IP	H	R	HR	HB	BB	SO	RAT	ERA	ERA+	OAV	OOB	BH	AVG	PB	PR	PR+	PD	TPI
1979	Hou-N	3	2	.600	26	7	3	2	1	67	68	32	1	1	22	24	12.2	3.76	94	.272	.333	2	.133	-0	-0	-2	-1	-0.3
1980	Hou-N	0	1	.000	22	1	0	0	1	33	40	21	2	0	12	18	14.2	5.45	60	.299	.356	2	.333	1	-7	-9	1	-0.3
1982	Pit-N	1	1	.500	20	0	0	0	1	35^1	34	22	1	2	17	26	13.5	5.09	73	.254	.346	2	1.000	1	-6	-5	1	-0.2
1983	Pit-N	0	1	.000	8	1	0	0	0	13^2	20	14	2	1	7	8	18.4	9.22	40	.357	.438	0	.000	-0	-8	-8	0	-0.5
1984	Chi-A	0	0	—	5	0	0	0	0	5^1	5	1	0	0	5	5	16.9	1.69	247	.263	.417	0	—	0	1	1	0	0.1
1985	NY-N	0	0	—	4	0	0	0	0	4^2	5	0	0	0	0	2	9.6	0.00	—	.278	.278	0	—	0	2	2	0	0.1
1986	NY-N	2	3	.400	31	1	0	0	0	35^2	44	17	2	0	12	18	14.1	3.79	94	.308	.361	2	.333	1	-0	-1	1	0.0
1987	Min-A	1	0	1.000	6	0	0	0	0	5^1	3	5	0	2	7	1	20.3	8.44	55	.158	.429	0	—	0	-2	-2	0	-0.3
Total	8	7	8	.467	122	10	3	2	3	200	219	112	8	6	82	102	13.8	4.64	77	.283	.357	8	.267	2	-21	-24	2	-1.4

● JACK NIEMES

Niemes, Jacob Leland b: 10/19/19, Cincinnati, Ohio d: 3/4/66, Hamilton, Ohio BR/TL, 6'1", 180 lbs. Deb: 5/30/43

YEAR	TM/L	W	L	PCT	G	GS	CG	SH	SV	IP	H	R	HR	HB	BB	SO	RAT	ERA	ERA+	OAV	OOB	BH	AVG	PB	PR	PR+	PD	TPI
1943	Cin-N	0	0	—	3	0	0	0	0	3	5	3	0	0	2	1	21.0	6.00	55	.385	.467	0	—	0	-1	-1	-0	-0.1

● CHUCK NIESON

Nieson, Charles Bassett b: 9/24/42, Hanford, Cal. BR/TR, 6'2", 185 lbs. Deb: 9/18/64

YEAR	TM/L	W	L	PCT	G	GS	CG	SH	SV	IP	H	R	HR	HB	BB	SO	RAT	ERA	ERA+	OAV	OOB	BH	AVG	PB	PR	PR+	PD	TPI
1964	Min-A	0	0	—	2	0	0	0	0	2	1	1	1	0	1	5	9.0	4.50	79	.143	.250	0	—	0	-0	-0	0	0.0

● JUAN NIEVES

Nieves, Juan Manuel (Cruz) b: 1/5/65, Las Lomas, P.R. BL/TL, 6'3", 175 lbs. Deb: 4/10/86

YEAR	TM/L	W	L	PCT	G	GS	CG	SH	SV	IP	H	R	HR	HB	BB	SO	RAT	ERA	ERA+	OAV	OOB	BH	AVG	PB	PR	PR+	PD	TPI
1986	Mil-A	11	12	.478	35	33	4	3	0	184^2	224	124	17	1	77	116	14.7	4.92	88	.299	.366	0	—	0	-15	-12	-2	-1.5
1987	Mil-A	14	8	.636	34	33	3	1	0	195^2	199	112	24	2	100	163	13.8	4.88	94	.264	.351	0	—	0	-9	-6	-1	-0.7
1988	Mil-A	7	5	.583	25	15	1	1	1	110^1	84	53	13	1	50	73	11.0	4.08	98	.208	.297	0	—	0	-1	-1	-0	-0.2
Total	3	32	25	.561	94	81	8	5	1	490^2	507	289	54	4	227	352	13.5	4.71	92	.266	.345	0	—	0	-25	-19	-4	-2.4

YEAR	TM/L	W	L	PCT	G	GS	CG	SH	SV	IP	H	R	HR	HB	BB	SO	RAT	ERA	ERA+	OAV	OOB	BH	AVG	PB	PR	PR+	PD	TPI
● JOHNNY NIGGELING Niggeling, John Arnold b: 7/10/03, Remsen, Iowa d: 9/16/63, LeMars, Iowa BR/TR, 6′, 170 lbs. Deb: 4/30/38																												
1938	Bos-N	1	0	1.000	2	0	0	0	0	2	4	2	0	0	1	1	22.5	9.00	38	.400	.455	0	—	0	-1	-1	-0	-0.2
1939	Cin-N	2	1	.667	10	5	2	1	0	40^1	51	28	2	2	13	20	14.7	5.80	66	.309	.367	2	.154	-0	-8	-9	-0	-0.7
1940	StL-A	7	11	.389	28	20	10	0	0	153^2	148	88	9	5	69	82	13.0	4.45	103	.250	.333	9	.176	-1	-1	2	-0	0.1
1941	StL-A	7	9	.438	24	20	13	1	0	168^1	168	83	17	1	63	68	12.4	3.80	113	.255	.320	10	.167	-1	7	9	-1	0.5
1942	StL-A	15	11	.577	28	27	16	3	0	206^1	173	76	10	11	93	107	12.1	2.66	139	.226	.319	10	.139	-2	23	24	-2	2.5
1943	StL-A	6	8	.429	20	20	7	0	0	150^1	122	61	7	6	57	73	11.1	3.17	105	.220	.299	3	.061	-4	2	3	-0	-0.3
	Was-A	4	2	.667	6	6	5	3	0	51	27	6	0	0	17	24	7.8	0.88	363	.153	.227	5	.278	1	14	14	0	2.1
	Yr	10	10	.500	26	26	12	3	0	201^1	149	67	7	6	74	97	10.2	2.59	127	.204	.282	8	.119	-3	16	16	0	1.8
1944	Was-A	10	8	.556	24	24	14	2	0	206	164	65	5	4	88	121	11.2	2.32	141	.221	.307	9	.130	-2	25	23	-1	1.6
1945	Was-A	7	12	.368	26	25	8	2	0	176^2	161	80	7	3	73	90	12.1	3.16	98	.240	.318	7	.119	-4	4	-1	-2	-0.7
1946	Was-A	3	2	.600	8	6	3	0	0	38	39	22	1	1	21	10	14.4	4.03	83	.265	.361	2	.182	0	-2	-3	-0	-0.3
	Bos-N	2	5	.286	8	8	3	0	0	58	54	23	2	1	21	24	11.8	3.26	105	.243	.311	2	.111	-1	1	1	0	0.0
Total	9	64	69	.481	184	161	81	12	0	1250^2	1111	534	60	34	516	620	12.0	3.22	113	.236	.316	59	.140	-14	63	59	-7	4.6
● AL NIPPER Nipper, Albert Samuel b: 4/2/59, San Diego, Cal. BR/TR, 6′, 194 lbs. Deb: 9/6/83 C																												
1983	Bos-A	1	1	.500	3	2	1	0	0	16	17	4	0	1	7	5	14.1	2.25	194	.293	.379	0	—	0	3	4	-0	0.4
1984	Bos-A	11	6	.647	29	24	6	0	0	182^2	183	86	18	7	52	84	11.9	3.89	107	.257	.313	0	—	0	2	5	3	0.7
1985	Bos-A	9	12	.429	25	25	5	0	0	162	157	83	14	9	82	85	13.8	4.06	106	.256	.352	0	—	0	2	4	2	0.7
1986	*Bos-A	10	12	.455	26	26	3	0	0	159	186	108	24	4	47	79	13.4	5.38	78	.290	.342	0	—	0	-21	-21	3	-2.2
1987	Bos-A	11	12	.478	30	30	6	0	0	174	196	115	30	7	62	89	13.7	5.43	84	.284	.349	0	—	0	-19	-17	1	-1.7
1988	Chi-N	2	4	.333	22	12	0	0	1	80	72	37	9	3	34	27	12.3	3.04	119	.238	.322	2	.087	-1	4	5	-2	0.1
1990	Cle-A	2	3	.400	9	5	0	0	0	24	35	19	2	2	19	12	21.0	6.75	58	.354	.467	0	—	0	-8	-7	-0	-1.4
Total	7	46	50	.479	144	124	21	0	1	797^2	846	452	97	33	303	381	13.3	4.52	93	.271	.342	2	.087	-1	-36	-26	7	-3.4
● MERLIN NIPPERT Nippert, Merlin Lee b: 9/1/38, Mangum, Okla. BR/TR, 6′1″, 175 lbs. Deb: 9/12/62																												
1962	Bos-A	0	0	—	4	0	0	0	0	6	4	3	1	0	4	3	12.0	4.50	92	.200	.333	0	—	0	-0	-0	-0	0.0
● RON NISCHWITZ Nischwitz, Ronald Lee b: 7/1/37, Dayton, Ohio BB/TL, 6′3″, 205 lbs. Deb: 9/4/61																												
1961	Det-A	0	1	.000	6	1	0	0	0	11^1	13	12	2	0	8	8	16.7	5.56	74	.295	.404	0	.000	-0	-2	-2	-0	-0.2
1962	Det-A	4	5	.444	48	0	0	0	4	64^2	73	30	5	1	26	28	13.9	3.90	104	.285	.353	5	.417	2	1	1	0	0.4
1963	Cle-A	0	2	.000	14	0	0	0	1	16^2	17	13	3	0	8	10	13.5	6.48	56	.262	.342	0	.000	-0	-5	-5	0	-0.7
1965	Det-A	1	0	1.000	20	0	0	0	1	22^2	21	10	2	0	6	12	10.7	2.78	125	.259	.310	0	.000	-0	2	2	-0	0.0
Total	4	5	8	.385	88	1	0	0	6	115^1	124	65	12	1	48	58	13.5	4.21	92	.278	.349	5	.278	1	-5	-4	0	-0.5
● OTHO NITCHOLAS Nitcholas, Otho James b: 9/13/08, McKinney, Tex. d: 9/11/86, McKinney, Tex. BR/TR, 6′, 190 lbs. Deb: 4/18/45																												
1945	Bro-N	1	0	1.000	7	0	0	0	0	18^2	19	14	4	0	1	4	9.6	5.30	71	.257	.267	1	.250	0	-3	-3	-0	-0.2
● C. J. NITKOWSKI Nitkowski, Christopher John b: 3/9/73, Suffern, N.Y. BL/TL, 6′2″, 185 lbs. Deb: 6/3/95																												
1995	Cin-N	1	3	.250	9	7	0	0	0	32^1	41	25	4	2	15	18	16.1	6.12	67	.306	.384	2	.200	0	-7	-7	-1	-0.8
	Det-A	1	4	.200	11	11	0	0	0	39^1	53	32	7	3	20	13	17.4	7.09	67	.335	.420	0	—	0	-10	-10	-0	-1.0
1996	Det-A	2	3	.400	11	8	0	0	0	45^2	62	44	7	7	38	36	21.1	8.08	63	.332	.461	0	—	0	-16	-15	-0	-1.3
1998	Hou-N	3	3	.500	43	0	0	0	3	59^2	49	27	4	6	23	44	11.8	3.77	108	.228	.320	0	.000	-0	3	2	0	0.2
1999	Det-A	4	5	.444	68	7	0	0	0	81^2	63	44	11	3	45	66	12.2	4.30	113	.213	.323	0	.000	-0	5	5	1	0.6
2000	Det-A	4	9	.308	67	11	0	0	0	109^2	124	79	13	4	49	81	14.5	5.25	91	.286	.364	0	—	0	-4	-6	2	-0.4
Total	5	15	27	.357	209	44	0	0	3	368^1	392	251	46	25	190	258	14.8	5.42	86	.275	.371	2	.133	-1	-29	-32	2	-2.7
● WILLARD NIXON Nixon, Willard Lee b: 6/17/28, Taylorsville, Ga. BL/TR, 6′2″, 195 lbs. Deb: 7/7/50																												
1950	Bos-A	8	6	.571	22	15	2	0	2	101^1	126	75	7	2	58	57	16.5	6.04	81	.310	.398	5	.139	-1	-16	-12	-0	-1.5
1951	Bos-A	7	4	.636	33	14	2	1	1	125	136	79	12	7	56	70	14.3	4.90	91	.285	.368	13	.289	3	-11	-6	-0	-0.2
1952	Bos-A	5	4	.556	23	13	5	0	0	103^2	115	64	12	4	61	50	15.6	4.86	81	.290	.390	11	.208	1	-14	-10	1	-0.6
1953	Bos-A	4	8	.333	23	15	5	1	0	116^2	114	57	6	1	59	57	13.4	3.93	107	.254	.343	8	.190	0	1	3	-0	0.3
1954	Bos-A	11	12	.478	31	30	8	2	0	199^2	182	102	16	9	87	102	12.5	4.06	101	.248	.335	18	.265	5	-7	1	1	0.7
1955	Bos-A	12	10	.545	31	31	7	3	0	208	207	102	10	3	85	95	12.8	4.07	105	.259	.333	18	.261	5	-2	5	2	1.2
1956	Bos-A	9	8	.529	23	22	9	1	0	145^1	142	79	9	8	57	74	12.8	4.21	110	.255	.333	11	.204	-1	-1	6	2	0.7
1957	Bos-A	12	13	.480	29	29	11	1	0	191	207	86	10	7	56	96	12.7	3.68	108	.280	.337	22	.293	5	2	6	-1	1.2
1958	Bos-A	1	7	.125	10	8	2	0	0	43^1	48	30	7	0	11	15	12.3	6.02	67	.281	.324	5	.294	1	-11	-9	0	-1.4
Total	9	69	72	.489	225	177	51	9	3	1234	1277	674	89	41	530	616	13.5	4.39	97	.270	.349	111	.242	17	-59	-15	5	0.4
● JUNIOR NOBOA Noboa, Milciades Arturo (Diaz) b: 11/10/64, Azua, D.R. BR/TR, 5′10″, 160 lbs. Deb: 8/22/84 ♦																												
1990	Mon-N	0	0	—	1	0	0	0	0	0^2	0	0	0	0	1	0	13.5	0.00	—	.000	.500	42	.266	0	0	0	0	0.0
● THE ONLY NOLAN Nolan, Edward Sylvester b: 11/7/1857, Paterson, N.J. d: 5/18/13, Paterson, N.J. BL/TR, 5′8″, 171 lbs. Deb: 5/1/1878																												
1878	Ind-N	13	22	.371	38	38	37	1	0	347	357	208	1		56	125	10.7	2.57	79	.253	.281	37	.243	6	-10	-23	2	-1.2
1881	Cle-N	8	14	.364	22	21	20	0	0	180	183	111	3		38	54	11.1	3.05	86	.251	.288	41	.244	1	-6	-9	-1	-0.9
1883	Pit-a	0	7	.000	7	7	6	0	0	55	81	44	0		10	23	14.9	4.25	76	.321	.347	8	.308	1	-6	-6	-0	-0.5
1884	Wil-U	1	4	.200	5	5	5	0	0	40	44	28	1		7	52	11.5	2.93	91	.262	.291	9	.273	-0	-2	-1	1	0.0
1885	Phi-N	1	5	.167	7	7	6	0	0	54	55	43	1		24	20	13.2	4.17	67	.256	.331	2	.077	-2	-8	-8	-1	-0.9
Total	5	23	52	.307	79	78	74	1	0	676	720	434	6		135	274	11.4	2.98	80	.259	.294	97	.240	6	-32	-49	1	-3.5
● GARY NOLAN Nolan, Gary Lynn b: 5/27/48, Herlong, Cal. BR/TR, 6′2.5″, 197 lbs. Deb: 4/15/67																												
1967	Cin-N	14	8	.636	33	32	8	5	0	226^2	193	73	18	5	62	206	10.3	2.58	145	.228	.284	7	.104	-1	20	26	-1	2.3
1968	Cin-N	9	4	.692	23	22	4	2	0	150	105	48	10	3	49	111	9.4	2.40	132	.196	.267	6	.130	2	10	12	-2	1.1
1969	Cin-N	8	8	.500	16	15	2	1	0	108^2	102	45	11	0	40	83	11.8	3.56	106	.247	.313	8	.229	3	0	2	-2	0.5
1970	*Cin-N	18	7	.720	37	37	4	2	0	250^2	226	102	25	1	96	181	11.6	3.27	124	.240	.311	13	.159	1	22	22	-1	1.9
1971	Cin-N	12	15	.444	35	35	9	0	0	244^2	208	91	12	2	59	146	9.9	3.16	106	.227	.275	11	.147	-1	8	6	1	0.6
1972	*Cin-N†	15	5	**.750**	25	25	6	2	0	176	147	48	13	1	30	90	9.1	1.99	161	.227	.262	7	.117	-1	29	26	-1	2.8
1973	Cin-N	0	1	.000	2	2	0	0	0	10^1	6	4	1	0	7	3	11.3	3.48	98	.167	.302	0	.000	0	0	-0	-0	0.0
1975	*Cin-N	15	9	.625	32	32	5	1	0	210^2	202	75	18	1	29	74	9.9	3.16	114	.251	.278	12	.176	2	11	10	-2	1.1
1976	*Cin-N	15	9	.625	34	34	7	1	0	239^1	232	96	28	1	27	113	9.8	3.46	101	.254	.276	8	.101	-3	1	1	-4	-0.6
1977	Cin-N	4	1	.800	8	8	0	0	0	39^1	53	22	5	0	12	28	14.9	4.81	82	.321	.367	1	.067	-1	-4	-4	-0	-0.6
	Cal-A	0	3	.000	5	5	0	0	0	18^1	31	19	5	0	2	4	16.2	8.84	44	.365	.379	0	—	0	-10	-10	-0	-1.3
Total	10	110	70	.611	250	247	45	14	0	1674^2	1505	623	146	14	413	1039	10.4	3.08	116	.239	.287	73	.138	0	88	93	-12	7.8
● DICK NOLD Nold, Richard Louis b: 5/4/43, San Francisco, Cal. BR/TR, 6′2″, 190 lbs. Deb: 8/19/67																												
1967	Was-A	0	2	.000	7	3	0	0	0	20^1	19	13	1	0	13	10	14.2	4.87	65	.241	.348	0	.000	-0	-4	-4	-0	-0.4
● DICKIE NOLES Noles, Dickie Ray b: 11/19/56, Charlotte, N.C. BR/TR, 6′2″, 190 lbs. Deb: 7/5/79																												
1979	Phi-N	3	4	.429	14	14	0	0	0	90	80	40	6	2	38	42	12.0	3.80	101	.246	.329	3	.100	-1	-1	0	1	0.0
1980	*Phi-N	1	4	.200	48	3	0	0	6	81	80	42	5	1	42	57	13.7	3.89	98	.254	.344	4	.308	1	-3	-1	-0	0.0
1981	*Phi-N	2	2	.500	13	8	0	0	0	58^1	57	30	2	3	23	34	12.8	4.17	87	.260	.339	2	.105	-1	-4	-3	-1	-0.5
1982	Chi-N	10	13	.435	31	30	2	2	0	171	180	99	11	5	61	85	12.9	4.42	85	.274	.340	6	.107	-2	-15	-12	-0	-1.7
1983	Chi-N	5	10	.333	24	18	1	1	0	116^1	133	69	9	1	37	59	13.2	4.72	81	.287	.341	9	.237	1	-14	-11	-0	-1.2
1984	Chi-N	2	2	.500	21	1	0	0	0	50^2	60	29	4	1	16	14	13.7	5.15	76	.305	.360	0	.000	-1	-9	-6	-1	-0.7
	Tex-A	2	3	.400	18	6	0	0	0	57^2	60	38	6	5	30	39	14.8	5.15	81	.262	.360	0	—	0	-7	-6	-1	-0.6
1985	Tex-A	4	8	.333	28	13	0	0	1	110^1	129	67	11	6	33	59	13.7	5.06	84	.289	.346	0	—	0	-11	-10	1	-0.9
1986	Cle-A	3	2	.600	32	0	0	0	0	54^2	56	33	9	5	30	32	15.0	5.10	81	.269	.374	0	—	0	-6	-6	0	-0.4
1987	Chi-N	4	2	.667	41	1	0	0	2	64^1	59	31	1	5	27	33	12.7	3.50	122	.239	.326	0	.000	-1	4	5	1	0.5
	Det-A	0	0	—	4	0	0	0	2	2	2	1	0	0	1	0	13.5	4.50	94	.250	.333	0	—	0	-0	-0	0	0.0
1988	Bal-A	0	2	.000	2	2	0	0	0	3^1	11	10	2	1	0	1	32.4	24.30	16	.500	.522	0	—	0	-8	-8	-0	-1.1

YEAR	TM/L	W	L	PCT	G	GS	CG	SH	SV	IP	H	R	HR	HB	BB	SO	RAT	ERA	ERA+	OAV	OOB	BH	AVG	PB	PR	PR+	PD	TPI
1990	Phi-N	0	1	.000	1	0	0	0	0	0^1	2	1	0	0	0	0	54.0	27.00	14	.667	.667	0	—	0	-1	-1	0	-0.2
Total	11	36	53	.404	277	96	3	3	11	860	909	490	66	35	338	455	13.4	4.56	86	.272	.345	24	.136	-3	-74	-58	-2	-6.8
● **ERIC NOLTE** Nolte, Eric Carl b: 4/28/64, Canoga Park, Cal. BL/TL, 6'3", 205 lbs. Deb: 8/1/87																												
1987	SD-N	2	6	.250	12	12	1	0	0	67^1	57	28	6	2	36	44	12.7	3.21	123	.226	.328	2	.095	-1	7	6	-1	0.5
1988	SD-N	0	0	—	2	0	0	0	0	3	3	2	1	0	2	1	15.0	6.00	57	.273	.385	0	—	0	-1	-1	-0	-0.1
1989	SD-N	0	0	—	3	1	0	0	0	9	15	12	1	0	7	8	22.0	11.00	32	.375	.468	0	.000	-0	-7	-7	0	-0.4
1991	SD-N	3	2	.600	6	6	0	0	0	22	37	27	6	0	10	15	19.2	11.05	34	.378	.435	1	.111	-0	-18	-17	-0	-2.8
	Tex-A	0	0	—	3	0	0	0	0	2^2	3	1	0	0	3	1	20.3	3.38	120	.273	.429	0	—	0	0	0	-0	0.0
Total	4	5	8	.385	26	19	1	0	0	104	115	70	14	2	58	69	15.1	5.63	69	.279	.371	3	.094	-1	-20	-20	-1	-2.8
● **HIDEO NOMO** Nomo, Hideo b: 8/31/68, Osaka, Japan BR/TR, 6'2", 210 lbs. Deb: 5/2/95																												
1995	*LA-N★	13	6	.684	28	28	4	**3**	0	191^1	124	63	14	5	78	**236**	9.7	2.54	149	**.182**	.271	6	.091	-4	35	29	-2	2.1
1996	*LA-N	16	11	.593	33	33	3	2	0	228^1	180	93	23	2	85	234	10.5	3.19	121	.218	.292	10	.133	-0	26	19	-1	1.9
1997	LA-N	14	12	.538	33	33	1	0	0	207^1	193	104	23	9	92	233	12.8	4.25	91	.243	.328	11	.159	2	-1	-10	-3	-1.2
1998	LA-N	2	7	.222	12	12	2	0	0	67^2	57	39	8	3	38	73	13.0	5.05	78	.228	.337	1	.050	-1	-6	-9	-1	-1.1
	NY-N	4	5	.444	17	16	1	0	0	89^2	73	49	11	1	56	94	13.0	4.82	86	.224	.339	8	.267	2	-6	-7	0	-0.4
	Yr	6	12	.333	29	28	3	0	0	157^1	130	88	19	4	94	167	13.0	4.92	83	.226	.338	9	.180	1	-12	-16	-1	-1.5
1999	Mil-N	12	8	.600	28	28	0	0	0	176^1	173	96	27	3	78	161	13.0	4.54	100	.256	.336	12	.214	2	0	-0	-2	0.1
2000	Det-A	8	12	.400	32	31	1	0	0	190	191	102	31	3	89	181	13.4	4.74	101	.263	.346	0	.000	-1	4	1	-1	0.0
Total	6	69	61	.531	183	181	12	5	0	1150^2	991	546	137	26	516	1212	12.0	3.97	104	.231	.318	48	.149	0	52	21	-10	1.4
● **JERRY NOPS** Nops, Jeremiah H. b: 6/23/1875, Toledo, Ohio d: 3/26/37, Camden, N.J. BL/TL, 5'8.5", 168 lbs. Deb: 9/7/1896																												
1896	Phi-N	1	0	1.000	1	1	1	0	0	7	11	5	0	0	1	1	15.4	5.14	84	.355	.375	0	.000	-1	-1	-1	-0	-0.2
	Bal-N	2	1	.667	3	3	3	0	0	22	29	15	0	0	2	8	12.7	6.14	70	.315	.330	1	.111	-1	-4	-5	-0	-0.5
	Yr	3	1	.750	4	4	4	0	0	29	40	20	0	0	3	9	13.3	5.90	73	.325	.341	1	.077	-2	-5	-5	-0	-0.7
1897	*Bal-N	20	6	.769	30	25	23	1	0	220^2	235	107	5	9	52	69	12.1	2.81	148	.270	.318	18	.196	-3	37	34	-2	2.8
1898	Bal-N	16	9	.640	33	29	23	2	0	235	241	130	5	16	78	91	12.8	3.56	101	.263	.332	20	.220	2	1	0	-4	-0.2
1899	Bal-N	17	11	.607	33	33	26	2	0	259	296	156	1	11	71	60	13.1	4.03	98	.287	.339	29	.276	-1	-5	-2	-3	-0.3
1900	Bro-N	4	4	.500	9	8	6	1	0	68	79	45	1	2	18	22	13.1	3.84	100	.289	.338	4	.160	-1	-1	0	-1	-0.2
1901	Bal-A	12	10	.545	27	23	17	1	1	176^2	192	123	5	13	59	43	13.4	4.08	95	.274	.341	13	.220	-0	-8	-4	-4	-0.8
Total	6	72	41	.637	136	122	99	7	1	988^1	1083	581	17	51	281	294	12.9	3.70	106	.277	.333	85	.221	-2	19	23	-15	0.6
● **WAYNE NORDHAGEN** Nordhagen, Wayne Oren b: 7/4/48, Thief River Falls, Minn. BR/TR, 6'2", 205 lbs. Deb: 7/16/76 ♦																												
1979	Chi-A	0	0	—	2	0	0	0	0	2	2	2	0	0	1	2	13.5	9.00	47	.286	.375	54	.280	1	-1	-1	-0	0.0
● **JOHN NORIEGA** Noriega, John Alan b: 12/20/43, Ogden, Utah BR/TR, 6'4", 185 lbs. Deb: 5/1/69																												
1969	Cin-N	0	0	—	5	0	0	0	0	7^2	12	6	1	0	3	4	17.6	5.87	64	.400	.455	0	—	0	-2	-2	-0	-0.1
1970	Cin-N	0	0	—	8	0	0	0	0	18	25	17	0	2	10	6	18.5	8.00	51	.333	.425	1	.250	0	-8	-8	1	-0.3
Total	2	0	0	—	13	0	0	0	0	25^2	37	23	1	2	13	10	18.2	7.36	54	.352	.433	1	.250	0	-10	-10	1	-0.4
● **FRED NORMAN** Norman, Fredie Hubert b: 8/20/42, San Antonio, Tex. BB/TL, 5'8", 160 lbs. Deb: 9/21/62																												
1962	KC-A	0	0	—	2	0	0	0	0	4	4	1	0	0	1	2	11.3	2.25	188	.250	.294	0	—	0	1	1	-0	0.0
1963	KC-A	0	1	.000	2	2	0	0	0	6^1	9	9	1	0	7	6	22.7	11.37	34	.346	.485	0	.000	-0	-5	-5	0	-0.6
1964	Chi-N	0	4	.000	8	5	0	0	0	31^2	34	25	9	1	21	20	15.9	6.54	57	.279	.389	1	.091	-1	-11	-9	-0	-1.1
1966	Chi-N	0	0	—	2	0	0	0	0	4	5	2	0	0	2	6	15.8	4.50	82	.313	.389	0	—	0	-0	-0	-0	0.0
1967	Chi-N	0	0	—	1	0	0	0	0	1	0	0	0	0	0	3	0.0	0.00	—	.000	.000	0	—	0	0	0	0	0.0
1970	LA-N	2	0	1.000	30	0	0	0	1	62	65	40	8	2	33	47	14.5	5.23	73	.273	.366	1	.143	0	-8	-10	-1	-0.5
	StL-N	0	0	—	1	0	0	0	0	1	1	0	0	0	0	0	9.0	0.00	—	.333	.333	0	—	0	0	0	0	0.0
	Yr	2	0	1.000	31	0	0	0	1	63	66	40	8	2	33	47	14.4	5.14	75	.274	.366	1	.143	0	-8	-10	-1	-0.5
1971	StL-N	0	0	—	4	0	0	0	0	3^2	7	5	0	0	7	4	34.4	12.27	29	.438	.609	0	—	0	-4	-3	-0	-0.2
	SD-N	3	12	.200	20	18	5	0	0	127^1	114	48	7	2	56	77	12.2	3.32	99	.240	.323	9	.237	2	2	-0	-1	0.1
	Yr	3	12	.200	24	18	5	0	0	131	121	53	8	2	63	81	12.8	3.57	93	.246	.335	9	.237	2	-1	-4	-1	-0.1
1972	SD-N	9	11	.450	42	28	10	6	2	211^2	195	88	18	2	88	167	12.1	3.44	96	.244	.321	8	.125	1	0	-4	-1	-0.4
1973	SD-N	1	7	.125	12	11	1	0	0	74	72	35	9	1	29	49	12.4	4.26	82	.262	.334	3	.136	-0	-5	-7	1	-0.6
	*Cin-N	12	6	.667	24	24	7	3	0	166^1	136	67	18	1	72	112	11.3	3.30	103	.224	.307	3	.052	-4	7	2	-1	-0.3
	Yr	13	13	.500	36	35	8	3	0	240^1	208	102	27	2	101	161	11.6	3.60	95	.236	.315	6	.075	-4	2	-5	-0	-0.9
1974	Cin-N	13	12	.520	35	26	8	2	0	186^1	170	69	15	2	68	141	11.6	3.14	111	.241	.309	8	.131	-2	10	8	-3	0.4
1975	*Cin-N	12	4	.750	34	26	2	0	0	188	163	85	23	0	84	119	11.8	3.73	97	.235	.318	7	.117	-2	-2	-3	-2	-0.6
1976	*Cin-N	12	7	.632	33	24	8	3	0	180^1	153	71	10	3	70	126	11.3	3.09	113	.231	.308	7	.140	-1	8	7	-3	0.4
1977	Cin-N	14	13	.519	35	34	8	1	0	221^1	200	97	28	3	98	160	12.2	3.38	117	.241	.324	8	.110	-2	13	14	-0	1.2
1978	Cin-N	11	9	.550	36	31	0	0	1	177^1	173	86	19	3	82	111	13.1	3.70	96	.255	.338	7	.140	-1	-2	-3	-1	-0.5
1979	*Cin-N	11	13	.458	34	31	5	0	0	195^1	193	86	14	0	57	95	11.5	3.64	103	.258	.311	9	.153	0	2	2	-2	0.1
1980	Mon-N	4	4	.500	48	8	2	0	4	98	96	50	8	3	40	58	12.8	4.13	86	.259	.337	1	.050	-2	-6	-6	-1	-0.8
Total	16	104	103	.502	403	268	56	15	8	1939^2	1790	864	188	23	815	1303	12.2	3.64	98	.246	.324	72	.125	-11	2	-16	-15	-3.4
● **MIKE NORRIS** Norris, Michael Kelvin b: 3/19/55, San Francisco, Cal. BR/TR, 6'2", 175 lbs. Deb: 4/10/75																												
1975	Oak-A	1	0	1.000	4	3	1	1	0	16^2	6	2	0	0	8	5	7.6	0.00	—	.107	.219	0	—	0	7	7	0	0.4
1976	Oak-A	4	5	.444	24	19	1	1	0	96	91	53	10	2	56	44	14.0	4.78	70	.250	.353	0	—	0	-13	-16	3	-1.1
1977	Oak-A	2	7	.222	16	12	1	1	0	77^1	77	45	14	4	31	35	13.0	4.77	85	.260	.338	0	.000	-0	-6	-6	1	-0.5
1978	Oak-A	0	5	.000	14	5	1	0	0	49	46	35	2	3	35	36	15.4	5.51	66	.249	.377	0	—	0	-9	-10	-0	-1.0
1979	Oak-A	5	8	.385	29	18	3	0	0	146^1	146	87	11	9	94	96	15.3	4.80	85	.265	.381	0	—	0	-9	-13	1	-1.1
1980	Oak-A	22	9	.710	33	33	24	1	0	284^1	215	88	18	6	83	180	9.6	2.53	149	**.209**	.272	0	—	0	**48**	**42**	3	**4.8**
1981	*Oak-A★	12	9	.571	23	23	12	2	0	172^2	145	77	17	10	63	78	11.4	3.75	93	.228	.308	0	—	0	-2	-5	-0	-0.9
1982	Oak-A	7	11	.389	28	28	7	1	0	166^1	154	103	25	6	84	83	13.2	4.76	82	.242	.336	0	—	0	-13	-16	1	-1.5
1983	Oak-A	4	5	.444	16	16	2	0	0	88^2	68	42	11	3	36	63	10.9	3.76	103	.213	.299	0	—	0	3	1	-2	-0.1
1990	Oak-A	1	0	1.000	14	0	0	0	0	27	24	10	0	2	9	16	11.7	3.00	124	.242	.318	0	—	0	3	2	0	0.1
Total	10	58	59	.496	201	157	52	7	0	1124^1	972	542	108	45	499	636	12.1	3.89	97	.233	.322	0	.000	-0	8	-16	5	-0.6
● **LOU NORTH** North, Louis Alexander b: 6/15/1891, Elgin, Ill. d: 5/15/74, Shelton, Conn. BR/TR, 5'11", 175 lbs. Deb: 8/22/13																												
1913	Det-A	0	1	.000	1	1	0	0	0	6	10	11	1	0	9	3	28.5	15.00	19	.357	.514	0	.000	-0	-8	-8	-0	-0.8
1917	StL-N	0	0	—	5	0	0	0	0	11^1	14	5	1	0	4	4	14.3	3.97	68	.350	.409	0	.000	-0	-2	-2	-0	-0.1
1920	StL-N	3	2	.600	24	6	3	0	1	88	90	42	3	2	32	37	12.7	3.27	91	.278	.346	7	.226	0	-1	-3	-1	-0.3
1921	StL-N	4	4	.500	40	0	0	0	**7**	86^1	81	39	5	1	32	28	11.9	3.54	103	.256	.327	3	.158	-1	**2**	**1**	-2	-0.2
1922	StL-N	10	3	.769	**53**	10	4	0	4	149^2	164	90	4	6	64	84	14.1	4.45	87	.283	.361	11	.234	2	-6	-10	4	-0.2
1923	StL-N	3	4	.429	34	3	0	0	1	71^2	90	50	8	3	31	24	15.6	5.15	76	.308	.380	4	.182	-1	-9	-10	1	-0.9
1924	StL-N	0	0	—	6	1	0	0	0	14^2	15	12	1	0	9	8	14.7	6.75	56	.273	.375	1	.250	-0	-5	-5	-0	-0.3
	Bos-N	1	2	.333	9	4	1	0	0	35^1	45	25	1	0	19	11	16.3	5.35	71	.321	.403	1	.111	-1	-6	-6	1	-0.6
	Yr	1	2	.333	15	5	1	0	0	50	60	37	2	0	28	19	15.8	5.76	66	.308	.395	2	.154	-1	-11	-11	-1	-0.9
Total	7	21	16	.568	172	25	8	0	13	463	509	274	24	12	200	199	14.0	4.43	82	.287	.363	27	.197	-1	-34	-43	0	-3.4
● **JAKE NORTHROP** Northrop, George Howard "Jerky" b: 3/5/1888, Monroeton, Pa. d: 11/16/45, Monroeton, Pa. BL/TR, 5'11", 170 lbs. Deb: 7/29/18																												
1918	Bos-N	5	1	.833	7	4	4	1	0	40	26	9	0	0	3	4	6.5	1.35	199	.183	.200	2	.154	-1	6	6	0	0.9
1919	Bos-N	1	5	.167	11	3	2	0	0	37^1	43	22	2	1	10	9	13.0	4.58	62	.301	.351	4	.500	3	-7	-7	1	-0.7
Total	2	6	6	.500	18	7	6	1	0	77^1	69	31	2	1	13	13	9.7	2.91	95	.242	.278	6	.286	2	-1	-1	1	0.2
● **EFFIE NORTON** Norton, Elisha Strong "Leiter" b: 8/17/1873, Conneaut, Ohio d: 3/5/50, Aspinwall, Pa. BR/TR, Deb: 8/8/1896																												
1896	Was-N	3	1	.750	8	5	2	0	0	44	49	25	2	6	14	13	14.1	3.07	144	.280	.354	4	.211	-0	6	6	-0	0.4
1897	Was-N	2	1	.667	4	2	1	0	0	17	31	18	0	0	11	3	22.2	6.88	63	.387	.462	5	.278	1	-5	-5	-0	-0.6
Total	2	5	2	.714	12	7	3	0	0	61	80	43	2	6	25	16	16.4	4.13	106	.314	.388	9	.243	0	1	2	-1	-0.2

YEAR	TM/L	W	L	PCT	G	GS	CG	SH	SV	IP	H	R	HR	HB	BB	SO	RAT	ERA	ERA+	OAV	OOB	BH	AVG	PB	PR	PR+	PD	TPI
● PHIL NORTON	Norton, Phillip Douglas b: 2/1/76, Texarkana, Tex. BR/TL, 6'1", 190 lbs. Deb: 8/3/2000																											
2000	Chi-N	0	1	.000	2	2	0	0	0	8^2	14	10	5	0	7	6	21.8	9.35	49	.350	.447	2	.667	1	-5	-5	0	-0.3
● TOM NORTON	Norton, Thomas John b: 4/26/50, Elyria, Ohio BR/TR, 6'1", 200 lbs. Deb: 4/18/72																											
1972	Min-A	0	1	.000	21	0	0	0	0	32^1	31	14	1	1	14	22	12.8	2.78	116	.252	.333	0	—	0	1	1	1	0.2
● RANDY NOSEK	Nosek, Randall William b: 1/8/67, Omaha, Neb. BR/TR, 6'4", 215 lbs. Deb: 5/27/89																											
1989	Det-A	0	2	.000	2	2	0	0	0	5^1	7	8	2	0	10	4	28.7	13.50	28	.333	.548	0	—	0	-6	-6	-0	-0.9
1990	Det-A	1	1	.500	3	2	0	0	0	7	7	7	1	0	9	3	20.6	7.71	51	.280	.471	0	—	0	-3	-3	-0	-0.5
Total	2	1	3	.250	5	4	0	0	0	12^1	14	15	3	0	19	7	24.1	10.22	38	.304	.508	0	—	0	-9	-9	-0	-1.4
● DON NOTTEBART	Nottebart, Donald Edward b: 1/23/36, West Newton, Mass. BR/TR, 6'1", 190 lbs. Deb: 7/1/60																											
1960	Mil-N	1	0	1.000	5	1	0	0	1	15^1	14	10	0	0	15	8	17.0	4.11	83	.233	.387	0	.000	-1	-1	-1	1	-0.1
1961	Mil-N	6	7	.462	38	11	2	0	3	126^1	117	61	11	2	48	66	11.9	4.06	92	.251	.323	7	.184	0	-0	-5	2	-0.3
1962	Mil-N	2	2	.500	39	0	0	0	2	64	64	30	4	4	20	36	12.4	3.23	117	.258	.324	2	.333	1	5	4	2	0.5
1963	Hou-N	11	8	.579	31	27	9	2	0	193	170	80	10	1	39	118	9.8	3.17	99	.234	.275	11	.167	0	3	-0	-0	0.0
1964	Hou-N	6	11	.353	28	24	2	0	0	157	165	76	12	1	37	90	11.6	3.90	88	.275	.319	3	.064	-2	-6	-9	4	-0.7
1965	Hou-N	4	15	.211	29	25	3	0	0	158	166	99	14	5	55	77	12.9	4.67	72	.273	.338	5	.104	-1	-20	-24	2	-2.5
1966	Cin-N	5	4	.556	59	1	0	0	11	111^1	97	45	11	2	43	69	11.5	3.07	127	.235	.311	4	.167	-0	7	9	1	1.0
1967	Cin-N	0	3	.000	47	0	0	0	4	79^1	75	25	4	2	19	48	10.9	1.93	194	.253	.303	0	.000	-0	13	14	1	0.8
1969	NY-A	0	0	—	4	0	0	0	0	6	6	3	1	1	0	5	10.5	4.50	77	.261	.292	0	—	0	-1	-1	0	0.0
	Chi-N	1	1	.500	16	0	0	0	0	18	28	14	2	0	7	8	17.5	7.00	58	.350	.402	0	.000	0	-7	-5	0	-0.5
Total	9	36	51	.414	296	89	16	2	21	928^1	902	443	69	18	283	525	11.7	3.65	96	.256	.315	32	.134	-3	-8	-14	11	-1.8
● CHET NOURSE	Nourse, Chester Linwood b: 8/7/1887, Ipswich, Mass. d: 4/20/58, Clearwater, Fla. BR/TR, 6'3", 185 lbs. Deb: 7/27/09																											
1909	Bos-A	0	0	—	3	0	0	0	0	5	5	5	0	0	5	3	18.0	7.20	35	.263	.417	0	.000	-0	-3	-3	0	-0.2
● RAFAEL NOVOA	Novoa, Rafael Angel b: 10/26/67, New York, N.Y. BL/TL, 6', 180 lbs. Deb: 7/31/90																											
1990	SF-N	0	1	.000	7	2	0	0	1	18^2	21	14	3	0	13	14	16.4	6.75	54	.284	.391	1	.200	0	-6	-7	-1	-0.4
1993	Mil-A	0	3	.000	15	7	2	0	0	56	58	32	7	4	22	17	13.5	4.50	95	.267	.346	0	—	0	-1	-2	-1	-0.1
Total	2	0	4	.000	22	9	2	0	1	74^2	79	46	10	4	35	31	14.2	5.06	81	.271	.358	1	.200	0	-7	-8	-1	-0.5
● WIN NOYES	Noyes, Winfield Charles b: 6/16/1889, Pleasanton, Neb. d: 4/8/69, Cashmere, Wash. BR/TR, 6', 180 lbs. Deb: 5/19/13																											
1913	Bos-N	0	0	—	11	0	0	0	0	20^2	22	18	1	4	6	5	13.9	4.79	69	.289	.372	1	.250	0	-4	-3	0	-0.2
1917	Phi-A	10	10	.500	27	22	11	1	1	171	156	74	5	4	77	64	12.5	2.95	93	.258	.345	6	.115	-2	-5	-4	-1	-0.8
1919	Phi-A	1	5	.167	10	6	3	0	0	49	66	34	1	1	15	20	15.1	5.69	60	.332	.381	2	.125	-1	-13	-12	0	-1.3
	Chi-A	0	0	—	1	1	0	0	0	6	10	5	0	0	0	4	15.0	7.50	42	.385	.385	1	.500	0	-3	-3	-0	-0.1
	Yr	1	5	.167	11	7	3	0	0	55	76	39	1	1	15	24	15.1	5.89	58	.338	.382	3	.167	-1	-16	-14	0	-1.4
Total	3	11	15	.423	49	29	14	1	1	246^2	254	131	7	9	98	93	13.2	3.76	78	.280	.356	10	.135	-3	-25	-22	-1	-2.4
● EDWIN NUNEZ	Nunez, Edwin (Martinez) b: 5/27/63, Humacao, P.R. BR/TR, 6'5", 237 lbs. Deb: 4/7/82																											
1982	Sea-A	1	2	.333	8	5	0	0	0	35^1	36	18	7	0	16	27	13.2	4.58	93	.269	.347	0	—	0	-2	-1	0	-0.1
1983	Sea-A	0	4	.000	14	5	0	0	0	37	40	21	3	3	22	35	15.8	4.38	98	.278	.385	0	—	0	-1	-0	0	0.0
1984	Sea-A	2	2	.500	37	0	0	0	7	67^2	55	26	8	3	21	57	10.5	3.19	125	.218	.286	0	—	0	6	6	-1	0.4
1985	Sea-A	7	3	.700	70	0	0	0	16	90^1	79	36	13	0	34	58	11.3	3.09	136	.234	.305	0	—	0	11	11	0	1.5
1986	Sea-A	1	2	.333	14	1	0	0	0	21^2	25	15	5	0	5	17	12.5	5.82	73	.284	.323	0	—	0	-4	-4	-0	-0.5
1987	Sea-A	3	4	.429	48	0	0	0	12	47^1	45	20	7	1	18	34	12.2	3.80	125	.262	.335	0	—	0	4	5	-0	0.8
1988	Sea-A	1	4	.200	14	3	0	0	0	29^1	45	33	4	2	14	19	18.7	7.98	52	.366	.439	0	—	0	-13	-12	1	-1.6
	NY-N	1	0	1.000	10	0	0	0	0	14	21	7	1	0	3	8	15.4	4.50	72	.339	.369	0	—	0	-2	-2	-0	-0.2
1989	Det-A	3	4	.429	27	0	0	0	1	54	49	33	6	0	36	41	14.2	4.17	92	.254	.371	0	—	0	-2	-2	1	-0.2
1990	Det-A	3	1	.750	42	0	0	0	6	80^1	65	26	4	2	37	66	11.7	2.24	177	.218	.309	0	—	0	15	15	-1	0.8
1991	Mil-A	2	1	.667	23	0	0	0	8	25^1	28	20	6	0	13	24	14.6	6.04	66	.277	.360	0	—	0	-5	-6	-0	-0.9
1992	Mil-A	1	1	.500	10	0	0	0	0	13^2	12	5	1	0	6	10	11.9	2.63	146	.231	.310	0	—	0	2	2	-0	0.2
	Tex-A	0	2	.000	39	0	0	0	3	45^2	51	29	5	2	16	39	13.6	5.52	69	.279	.343	0	—	0	-8	-9	-1	-0.5
	Yr	1	3	.250	49	0	0	0	3	59^1	63	34	6	2	22	49	13.2	4.85	79	.268	.336	0	—	0	-6	-7	-1	-0.3
1993	Oak-A	3	6	.333	56	0	0	0	1	75^2	89	36	2	6	29	58	14.7	3.81	107	.298	.371	0	—	0	4	3	-0	0.3
1994	Oak-A	0	0	—	15	0	0	0	0	15	26	20	2	0	10	15	21.6	12.00	37	.382	.462	0	—	0	-12	-14	0	-0.6
Total	13	28	36	.438	427	14	0	0	54	652^1	666	345	74	19	280	508	13.3	4.19	98	.266	.344	0	—	0	-7	-7	-1	-0.6
● JOSE NUNEZ	Nunez, Jose (Jimenez) b: 1/13/64, Jarabacoa, D.R. BR/TR, 6'3", 175 lbs. Deb: 4/9/87																											
1987	Tor-A	5	2	.714	37	9	0	0	0	97	91	57	12	0	58	99	13.8	5.01	90	.256	.360	0	—	0	-6	-5	-1	-0.4
1988	Tor-A	0	1	.000	13	2	0	0	0	29^1	28	11	3	1	17	18	14.1	3.07	128	.259	.365	0	—	0	3	3	0	0.1
1989	Tor-A	0	0	—	6	1	0	0	0	10^2	8	3	0	0	2	14	8.4	2.53	149	.200	.238	0	—	0	2	2	-0	0.0
1990	Chi-N	4	7	.364	21	10	0	0	0	60^2	61	47	5	0	34	40	14.1	6.53	63	.270	.365	0	.000	-1	-18	-15	0	-2.5
Total	4	9	10	.474	77	22	0	0	0	197^2	188	118	20	1	111	171	13.7	5.05	84	.258	.356	0	.000	-1	-20	-17	-1	-2.8
● VLADIMIR NUNEZ	Nunez, Vladimir (Zarabaza) b: 3/15/75, Havana, Cuba BR/TR, 6'4", 235 lbs. Deb: 9/11/98																											
1998	Ari-N	0	0	—	4	0	0	0	0	5^1	7	6	0	0	2	2	15.2	10.13	42	.318	.375	0	—	0	-3	-4	-0	-0.2
1999	Ari-N	3	2	.600	27	0	0	0	1	34	29	15	2	1	20	28	13.2	2.91	157	.242	.355	0	.000	-0	6	6	0	0.8
	Fla-N	4	8	.333	17	12	0	0	0	74^2	66	48	9	3	34	58	12.4	4.58	95	.243	.333	4	.160	-0	-0	-2	1	-0.2
	Yr	7	10	.412	44	12	0	0	1	108^2	95	63	11	4	54	86	12.7	4.06	109	.242	.340	4	.143	-1	6	5	1	0.6
2000	Fla-N	0	6	.000	17	12	0	0	0	68^1	88	63	12	2	34	45	16.3	7.90	56	.319	.397	2	.118	0	-25	-28	1	-1.9
Total	3	7	16	.304	65	24	0	0	1	182^1	190	132	23	6	90	133	14.1	5.68	78	.275	.364	6	.133	-1	-22	-26	1	-1.5
● HOWIE NUNN	Nunn, Howard Ralph b: 10/18/35, Westfield, N.C. BR/TR, 6', 173 lbs. Deb: 4/11/59																											
1959	StL-N	2	2	.500	16	0	0	0	0	21^1	23	18	3	0	15	20	16.0	7.59	56	.291	.404	0	.000	-0	-9	-7	1	-1.2
1961	Cin-N	2	1	.667	24	0	0	0	0	37^2	35	17	0	1	24	26	14.3	3.58	113	.252	.366	2	.250	0	2	2	-0	0.1
1962	Cin-N	0	0	—	6	0	0	0	0	9^2	15	6	0	0	3	4	16.8	5.59	72	.375	.419	0	.000	-0	-2	-2	0	-0.1
Total	3	4	3	.571	46	0	0	0	0	68^2	73	41	3	1	42	50	15.2	5.11	80	.283	.385	2	.200	-0	-9	-7	1	-1.2
● JOE NUXHALL	Nuxhall, Joseph Henry b: 7/30/28, Hamilton, Ohio BL/TL, 6'3", 219 lbs. Deb: 6/10/44																											
1944	Cin-N	0	0	—	1	0	0	0	0	0^2	2	5	0	0	5	0	94.5	67.50	5	.500	.778	0	—	0	-5	-5	-0	-0.2
1952	Cin-N	1	4	.200	37	5	2	0	1	92^1	83	33	4	3	42	52	12.5	3.22	117	.246	.334	2	.087	-1	5	6	2	0.3
1953	Cin-N	9	11	.450	30	17	5	1	2	141^2	136	77	13	8	69	52	13.5	4.32	101	.252	.345	16	.327	7	-1	1	-2	0.6
1954	Cin-N	12	5	.706	35	14	5	1	0	166^2	188	77	11	6	59	85	13.7	3.89	108	.292	.357	9	.173	4	3	5	0	0.9
1955	Cin-N★	17	12	.586	50	33	14	**5**	3	257	240	108	25	5	78	98	11.3	3.47	122	.249	.309	17	.198	4	16	21	-2	2.4
1956	Cin-N☆	13	11	.542	44	32	10	2	3	200^2	196	96	18	6	87	120	13.0	3.72	107	.257	.338	11	.186	3	1	5	-1	0.8
1957	Cin-N	10	10	.500	39	28	6	2	1	174^1	192	104	24	7	53	99	13.0	4.75	87	.275	.332	14	.237	3	-17	-12	-2	-1.2
1958	Cin-N	12	11	.522	36	26	5	0	0	175^2	169	78	15	1	63	111	11.9	3.79	109	.257	.323	13	.210	0	3	7	-0	0.7
1959	Cin-N	9	9	.500	28	21	6	1	1	131^2	155	76	10	1	35	75	13.1	4.24	96	.292	.337	11	.250	3	-4	-3	-1	-0.1
1960	Cin-N	1	8	.111	38	6	0	0	0	112	130	58	8	4	27	72	12.9	4.42	86	.297	.344	2	.077	-1	-8	-7	2	-0.5
1961	KC-A	5	8	.385	37	13	1	0	1	128	135	81	12	3	65	81	14.3	5.34	78	.268	.355	19	.292	7	-19	-16	-1	-0.8
1962	LA-A	0	0	—	5	0	0	0	0	5^1	7	6	0	1	5	2	21.9	10.13	38	.304	.448	0	—	0	-4	-4	0	-0.2
	Cin-N	5	0	1.000	12	9	1	0	1	66	59	20	4	1	25	57	11.6	2.45	164	.240	.313	7	.269	3	11	11	-0	1.1
1963	Cin-N	15	8	.652	35	29	14	2	2	217^1	194	73	14	6	39	169	9.9	2.61	128	.237	.277	12	.158	0	16	17	-1	1.7
1964	Cin-N	9	8	.529	32	22	7	4	2	154^2	146	73	19	6	51	111	11.8	4.07	89	.250	.317	7	.130	-1	-9	-8	-2	-1.1
1965	Cin-N	11	4	.733	32	16	5	1	2	148^2	142	57	18	3	31	117	10.7	3.45	109	.252	.295	8	.178	1	1	5	-3	0.2
1966	Cin-N	6	8	.429	35	16	2	1	0	130	136	71	14	9	42	71	12.9	4.50	87	.270	.338	4	.100	-2	-13	-8	-1	-1.1
Total	16	135	117	.536	526	287	83	20	19	2302^2	2310	1093	209	70	776	1372	12.3	3.90	102	.262	.327	152	.198	28	-21	16	-12	3.5
● RICH NYE	Nye, Richard Raymond b: 8/4/44, Oakland, Cal. BL/TL, 6'4", 185 lbs. Deb: 9/16/66																											
1966	Chi-N	0	2	.000	3	2	0	0	0	17	16	4	1	0	7	9	12.2	2.12	174	.254	.329	1	.250	0	3	3	-1	0.3

YEAR	TM/L	W	L	PCT	G	GS	CG	SH	SV	IP	H	R	HR	HB	BB	SO	RAT	ERA	ERA+	OAV	OOB	BH	AVG	PB	PR	PR+	PD	TPI
1967	Chi-N	13	10	.565	35	30	7	0	0	205	179	82	15	2	52	119	10.2	3.20	111	.234	.284	16	.213	3	4	7	-0	1.1
1968	Chi-N	7	12	.368	27	20	6	1	1	132^2	145	65	16	1	34	74	12.2	3.80	83	.276	.321	8	.182	-0	-12	-9	-0	-1.3
1969	Chi-N	3	5	.375	34	5	1	0	3	68^2	72	43	13	1	21	39	12.3	5.11	79	.271	.326	1	.063	-1	-12	-7	-1	-1.1
1970	StL-N	0	0	—	6	0	0	0	0	8	13	5	2	0	6	5	21.4	4.50	92	.371	.463	1	.500	1	-0	-0	0	0.0
	Mon-N	3	2	.600	8	6	2	0	0	46^1	47	23	3	0	20	21	13.0	4.08	101	.260	.333	3	.176	0	-0	0	0	0.0
	Yr	3	2	.600	14	6	2	0	0	54^1	60	28	5	0	26	26	14.2	4.14	99	.278	.355	4	.211	1	-1	-0	0	0.0
Total	5	26	31	.456	113	63	16	1	4	477^2	472	222	50	4	140	267	11.6	3.71	96	.257	.311	30	.190	2	-17	-7	-2	-1.0
● RYAN NYE	Nye, Ryan Craig b: 6/24/73, Biloxi, Miss. BR/TR, 6'2", 195 lbs. Deb: 6/7/97																											
1997	Phi-N	0	2	.000	4	2	0	0	0	12	20	11	2	2	9	7	23.3	8.25	51	.392	.500	0	.000	-0	-5	-5	0	-0.7
1998	Phi-N	0	0	—	1	0	0	0	0	1	3	3	1	0	0	3	27.0	27.00	16	.500	.500	0	—	0	-3	-2	0	-0.1
Total	2	0	2	.000	5	2	0	0	0	13	23	14	3	2	9	10	23.5	9.69	44	.404	.500	0	.000	-0	-8	-8	0	-0.8
● JERRY NYMAN	Nyman, Gerald Smith b: 11/23/42, Logan, Utah BL/TL, 5'10", 165 lbs. Deb: 8/24/68																											
1968	Chi-A	2	1	.667	8	7	1	1	0	40^1	38	13	1	0	16	27	12.0	2.01	151	.247	.318	2	.154	-0	4	4	-0	0.3
1969	Chi-A	4	4	.500	20	10	2	1	0	64^2	58	40	7	0	39	40	13.5	5.29	73	.244	.350	1	.050	-1	-12	-10	-1	-1.2
1970	SD-N	0	2	.000	2	2	0	0	0	5^1	8	9	1	0	2	2	16.9	15.19	26	.364	.417	0	—	0	-7	-7	-0	-1.0
Total	3	6	7	.462	30	19	3	2	0	110^1	104	62	9	0	57	69	13.1	4.57	78	.251	.342	3	.091	-1	-14	-12	-1	-1.9
● PRINCE OANA	Oana, Henry Kauhane b: 1/22/08, Waipahu, Hawaii d: 6/19/76, Austin, Tex. BR/TR, 6'2", 193 lbs. Deb: 4/22/34 ◆																											
1943	Det-A	3	2	.600	10	0	0	0	0	34	34	21	4	2	19	15	14.6	4.50	78	.262	.364	10	.385	4	-5	-3	-0	-0.1
1945	Det-A	0	0	—	3	1	0	0	1	11^1	3	2	0	0	7	3	7.9	1.59	221	.086	.238	1	.200	-0	2	2	-0	0.1
Total	2	3	2	.600	13	1	0	0	1	45^1	37	23	4	2	26	18	12.9	3.77	93	.224	.337	16	.308	4	-2	-1	-1	0.0
● HENRY OBERBECK	Oberbeck, Henry A. b: 5/17/1858, Missouri d: 8/26/21, St.Louis, Mo. Deb: 5/7/1883 ◆																											
1884	Bal-U	0	0	—	2	1	0	0	0	6	9	3	0		2	1	16.5	3.00	89	.321	.367	23	.184	-1	-0	-0	-0	-0.1
	KC-U	0	5	.000	6	4	3	0	0	29^2	47	35	0		3	6	15.2	5.76	39	.338	.352	17	.189	-1	-11	-13	-1	-1.6
	Yr	0	5	.000	8	5	3	0	0	35^2	56	38	0		5	7	15.4	5.30	44	.335	.355	40	.186	-2	-11	-13	-1	-1.7
● DOC OBERLANDER	Oberlander, Hartman Louis b: 5/12/1864, Waukegan, Ill. d: 11/14/22, Pryor, Montana TL, Deb: 5/16/1888																											
1888	Cle-a	1	2	.333	3	3	3	0	0	25^2	27	33	2	1	18	23	16.1	5.26	59	.260	.374	3	.214	0	-6	-6	-0	-0.5
● FRANK OBERLIN	Oberlin, Frank Rufus "Flossie" b: 3/29/1876, Elsie, Mich. d: 1/6/52, Ashley, Ind. BR/TR, 6'1", 165 lbs. Deb: 9/20/06																											
1906	Bos-A	1	3	.250	4	4	4	0	0	34	38	20	0	2	13	13	14.0	3.18	87	.286	.358	2	.154	-0	-2	-2	1	-0.1
1907	Bos-A	1	5	.167	12	4	2	0	0	46	48	31	2	2	24	18	14.5	4.30	60	.271	.365	2	.154	-0	-9	-9	-1	-1.1
	Was-A	2	6	.250	11	8	3	0	0	48^2	57	38	0	2	12	18	13.1	4.62	52	.294	.341	1	.056	-2	-11	-13	-1	-2.1
	Yr	3	11	.214	23	12	5	0	0	94^2	105	69	2	4	36	36	13.8	4.47	56	.283	.353	3	.097	-2	-20	-21	-2	-3.2
1909	Was-A	1	4	.200	9	4	1	0	0	41	41	22	1	6	16	13	13.8	3.73	65	.266	.358	2	.143	-1	-6	-6	-1	-0.9
1910	Was-A	0	6	.000	8	6	6	0	0	57^1	52	32	0	2	23	18	12.1	2.98	84	.259	.341	1	.053	-2	-3	-3	-1	-0.6
Total	4	5	24	.172	44	26	16	0	0	227	236	143	3	14	88	80	13.4	3.77	67	.275	.352	8	.104	-4	-31	-32	-3	-4.8
● DAN O'BRIEN	O'Brien, Daniel Jogues b: 4/22/54, St.Petersburg, Fla. BR/TR, 6'4", 215 lbs. Deb: 9/4/78																											
1978	StL-N	0	2	.000	7	2	0	0	0	18	22	12	1	2	8	12	16.0	4.50	78	.301	.386	0	.000	-0	-2	-2	-0	-0.3
1979	StL-N	1	1	.500	6	0	0	0	0	11	21	10	0	0	3	5	19.6	8.18	46	.420	.453	0	.000	-0	-5	-5	-0	-0.9
Total	2	1	3	.250	13	2	0	0	0	29	43	22	1	2	11	17	17.4	5.90	61	.350	.412	0	.000	-1	-7	-7	-1	-1.2
● EDDIE O'BRIEN	O'Brien, Edward Joseph b: 12/11/30, S.Amboy, N.J. BR/TR, 5'9", 165 lbs. Deb: 4/25/53 FC◆																											
1956	Pit-N	0	0	—	1	0	0	0	0	2	1	0	0	1	0	0	9.0	0.00	—	.167	.286	14	.264	0	1	1	-0	0.0
1957	Pit-N	1	0	1.000	3	1	1	0	0	12^1	11	3	2	0	3	10	10.2	2.19	173	.229	.275	0	.000	-1	2	2	0	0.1
1958	Pit-N	0	0	—	1	0	0	0	0	2	4	3	1	0	1	1	22.5	13.50	29	.444	.500	0	—	0	-2	-2	-0	-0.1
Total	3	1	0	1.000	5	1	1	0	0	16^1	16	6	3	1	4	11	11.6	3.31	115	.254	.309	131	.236	-0	1	1	-0	0.0
● DARBY O'BRIEN	O'Brien, John F. b: 4/15/1867, Troy, N.Y. d: 3/11/1892, W.Troy, N.Y. BR/TR, 5'10", 165 lbs. Deb: 6/23/1888																											
1888	Cle-a	11	19	.367	30	30	30	1	0	259	245	162	5	12	99	135	12.4	3.30	94	.241	.315	20	.183	-3	-7	-6	2	-0.6
1889	Cle-N	22	17	.564	41	41	39	1	0	346^2	345	216	9	24	167	122	13.9	4.15	97	.251	.343	35	.250	4	-5	-5	2	0.1
1890	Cle-P	8	16	.333	25	25	22	0	0	206^1	229	171	9	19	93	54	14.9	3.40	117	.269	.354	15	.156	-6	19	14	-1	0.6
1891	Bos-a	18	13	.581	40	30	22	0	**2**	268^2	300	197	13	20	127	87	15.0	3.65	95	.273	.359	30	.234	1	2	-5	-3	-0.7
Total	4	59	65	.476	136	126	113	2	2	1080^2	1119	746	36	75	486	398	14.0	3.68	100	.258	.343	100	.211	-4	9	-2	0	-0.6
● JOHNNY O'BRIEN	O'Brien, John Thomas b: 12/11/30, S.Amboy, N.J. BR/TR, 5'9", 170 lbs. Deb: 4/19/53 F◆																											
1956	Pit-N	1	0	1.000	8	0	0	0	0	19	8	6	2	2	9	9	9.0	2.84	133	.133	.268	18	.173	-0	2	2	-1	0.0
1957	Pit-N	0	3	.000	16	1	0	0	0	40	46	32	7	1	24	19	16.0	6.07	62	.293	.390	11	.314	2	-10	-10	-1	-0.6
1958	StL-N	0	0	—	1	0	0	0	0	2	7	5	0	0	2	2	40.5	22.50	18	.538	.600	0	.000	0	-4	-4	-0	-0.2
Total	3	1	3	.250	25	1	0	0	0	61	61	43	9	3	35	30	14.6	5.61	68	.265	.369	204	.250	2	-12	-12	-2	-0.8
● BOB O'BRIEN	O'Brien, Robert Allen b: 4/23/49, Pittsburgh, Pa. BL/TL, 5'10", 170 lbs. Deb: 4/11/71																											
1971	LA-N	2	2	.500	14	4	1	1	0	42	42	18	4	1	13	15	12.0	3.00	108	.262	.322	1	.111	-0	2	1	-1	0.0
● TOM O'BRIEN	O'Brien, Thomas H. b: 6/22/1860, Salem, Mass. d: 4/21/21, Worcester, Mass. BR/TR, 6'1", 185 lbs. Deb: 6/14/1882 ◆																											
1887	NY-a	0	0	—	1	0	0	0	0	3^2	9	5	0	0	5	0	22.1	7.36	58	.375	.375	27	.206	-0	-1	-1	-0	-0.1
● BUCK O'BRIEN	O'Brien, Thomas Joseph b: 5/9/1882, Brockton, Mass. d: 7/25/59, Boston, Mass. BR/TR, 5'10", 188 lbs. Deb: 9/9/11																											
1911	Bos-A	5	1	.833	6	5	5	2	0	47^2	30	9	0	1	21	31	9.8	0.38	868	.180	.275	2	.125	-1	16	16	1	2.1
1912	*Bos-A	20	13	.606	37	34	25	2	0	275^2	237	107	3	10	90	115	11.0	2.58	132	.237	.306	13	.138	-5	23	25	0	2.4
1913	Bos-A	4	9	.308	15	12	6	0	0	90^1	103	42	0	0	35	54	13.7	3.69	80	.305	.370	5	.167	0	-8	-7	1	-0.9
	Chi-A	0	2	.000	6	3	0	0	0	18^1	21	14	0	0	13	4	16.7	3.93	74	.318	.430	0	.000	-0	-2	-2	-0	-0.3
	Yr	4	11	.267	21	15	6	0	0	108^2	124	56	0	0	48	58	14.2	3.73	79	.307	.381	5	.152	-0	-10	-9	0	-1.2
Total	3	29	25	.537	64	54	36	4	0	432	391	172	3	11	159	204	11.7	2.63	125	.249	.322	20	.140	-6	29	31	2	3.3
● DARBY O'BRIEN	O'Brien, William D. b: 9/1/1863, Peoria, Ill. d: 6/15/1893, Peoria, Ill. BR/TR, 6'1", 186 lbs. Deb: 4/16/1887 ◆																											
1887	NY-a	0	0	—	1	0	0	0	0	1	2	0	0	0	1	0	18.0	0.00	—	.500	.500	197	.351	0	0	0	-0	0.0
● BILLY O'BRIEN	O'Brien, William Smith b: 3/14/1860, Albany, N.Y. d: 5/26/11, Kansas City, Mo. BR/TR, 6', 185 lbs. Deb: 9/27/1884 ◆																											
1884	StP-U	1	0	1.000	2	0	0	0	0	10	8	5	0		3	7	9.9	1.80	74	.205	.262	7	.233	-0	1	-1	0	0.0
● WALTER OCKEY	Ockey, Walter Andrew "Footie" (b: Walter Andrew Okpych) b: 1/4/20, New York, N.Y. d: 12/4/71, Staten Island, N.Y. BR/TR, 6', 175 lbs. Deb: 5/3/44																											
1944	NY-N	0	0	—	2	0	0	0	0	2^2	2	1	1	0	2	1	13.5	3.38	109	.200	.333	0	—	0	0	0	0	0.0
● PAT O'CONNELL	O'Connell, Patrick H. b: 6/10/1861, Bangor, Me. d: 1/24/43, Lewiston, Maine BR/TR, 5'10", 175 lbs. Deb: 7/22/1886 ◆																											
1886	Bal-a	0	0	—	1	0	0	0	0	3	4	3	0	0	2	1	18.0	6.00	57	.333	.429	30	.181	-0	-1	-1	-0	0.0
● ANDY O'CONNOR	O'Connor, Andrew James b: 9/14/1884, Roxbury, Mass. d: 9/26/80, Norwood, Mass. BR/TR, 6', 160 lbs. Deb: 10/6/08																											
1908	NY-A	0	1	.000	1	1	1	0	0	8	15	11	0	3	7	5	28.1	10.13	24	.429	.556	0	.000	-0	-7	-7	-0	-0.6
● BRIAN O'CONNOR	O'Connor, Brian Michael b: 1/4/77, Cincinnati, Ohio BL/TL, 6'2", 190 lbs. Deb: 5/13/2000																											
2000	Pit-N	0	0	—	6	1	0	0	0	12^1	12	11	2	1	11	7	17.5	5.11	90	.250	.400	1	.500	0	-1	-1	-0	0.0
● FRANK O'CONNOR	O'Connor, Frank Henry b: 9/15/1870, Keeseville, N.Y. d: 12/26/13, Brattleboro, Vt. BL/TL, 6', 185 lbs. Deb: 8/3/1893																											
1893	Phi-N	0	0	—	3	1	0	0	1	4	2	5	0	0	9	0	24.8	11.25	41	.143	.478	2	1.000	2	-3	-3	0	0.0
● JACK O'CONNOR	O'Connor, Jack William b: 6/2/58, Twentynine Palms, Cal. BL/TL, 6'3", 215 lbs. Deb: 4/9/81																											
1981	Min-A	3	2	.600	28	0	0	0	0	35^1	46	27	3	2	30	16	19.9	5.86	67	.336	.462	0	—	0	-9	-7	1	-0.9
1982	Min-A	8	9	.471	23	19	6	1	0	126	122	63	13	2	57	56	12.9	4.29	99	.255	.337	0	—	0	-3	-0	-3	-0.3

YEAR	TM/L	W	L	PCT	G	GS	CG	SH	SV	IP	H	R	HR	HB	BB	SO	RAT	ERA	ERA+	OAV	OOB	BH	AVG	PB	PR	PR+	PD	TPI
1983	Min-A	2	3	.400	27	8	0	0	0	83	107	59	13	0	36	56	15.5	5.86	73	.315	.380	0	—	0	-16	-14	-1	-0.9
1984	Min-A	0	0	—	2	0	0	0	0	4^2	1	1	1	0	4	0	9.6	1.93	218	.067	.263	0	—	0	1	1	-0	0.0
1985	Mon-N	0	2	.000	20	1	0	0	0	23^2	21	14	1	0	13	16	12.9	4.94	69	.239	.337	0	—	0	-4	-4	-1	-0.4
1987	Bal-A	1	1	.500	29	0	0	0	2	46	46	23	5	0	23	33	13.5	4.30	103	.263	.348	0	—	0	1	1	-1	-0.1
Total	6	14	17	.452	129	28	6	1	2	318^2	343	187	36	4	163	177	14.4	4.89	86	.278	.364	0	—	0	-29	-24	-5	-2.6

● **HANK O'DAY** O'Day, Henry Francis b: 7/8/1862, Chicago, Ill. d: 7/2/35, Chicago, Ill. TR, 6', 180 lbs. Deb: 5/2/1884 MU

YEAR	TM/L	W	L	PCT	G	GS	CG	SH	SV	IP	H	R	HR	HB	BB	SO	RAT	ERA	ERA+	OAV	OOB	BH	AVG	PB	PR	PR+	PD	TPI
1884	Tol-a	9	28	.243	41	40	35	2	**1**	326^2	335	241	6	18	66	163	11.5	3.75	91	.252	.297	51	.211	-1	-18	-11	4	-0.8
1885	Pit-a	5	7	.417	12	12	10	0	0	103	110	77	4	7	16	36	11.6	3.67	88	.258	.296	12	.245	1	-5	-5	0	-0.3
1886	Was-N	2	2	.500	6	6	6	0	0	49	41	17	1		17	47	10.7	1.65	199	.219	.284	1	.053	-2	9	9	1	0.5
1887	Was-N	8	20	.286	30	30	29	0	0	254^2	364	197	15	9	109	86	13.2	4.17	97	.327	.332	30	.244	-3	-3	-3	1	-0.5
1888	Was-N	16	29	.356	46	46	46	2	0	403	359	208	19	16	117	186	11.0	3.10	90	.232	.293	23	.139	-7	-11	-14	-3	-2.3
1889	Was-N	2	10	.167	13	13	11	0	0	108	117	88	7	6	57	23	15.0	4.33	91	.268	.360	8	.182	-1	-4	-5	0	-0.4
	*NY-N	9	1	.900	10	10	8	0	0	78	83	51	2	7	35	28	14.4	4.27	92	.264	.351	3	.097	-1	-2	-3	-1	-0.5
	Yr	11	11	.500	23	23	19	0	0	186	200	139	9	13	92	51	14.8	4.31	92	.266	.356	11	.147	-2	-6	-8	-0	-0.9
1890	NY-P	22	13	.629	43	35	32	1	**3**	329	355	249	11	18	161	94	14.6	4.21	108	.264	.350	34	.227	-3	1	11	-4	0.4
Total	7	73	110	.399	201	192	177	5	4	1651^1	1764	1128	65	81	578	663	12.6	3.74	97	.263	.319	162	.197	-17	-33	-21	-0	-3.9

● **PAUL O'DEA** O'Dea, Paul "Lefty" b: 7/3/20, Cleveland, Ohio d: 12/11/78, Cleveland, Ohio BL/TL, 6', 200 lbs. Deb: 4/19/44 ♦

YEAR	TM/L	W	L	PCT	G	GS	CG	SH	SV	IP	H	R	HR	HB	BB	SO	RAT	ERA	ERA+	OAV	OOB	BH	AVG	PB	PR	PR+	PD	TPI
1944	Cle-A	0	0	—	3	0	0	0	0	4^1	5	1	0	0	6	0	22.8	2.08	159	.333	.524	55	.318	1	1	1	-0	0.0
1945	Cle-A	0	0	—	1	0	0	0	0	2	4	3	0	0	2	0	27.0	13.50	24	.400	.500	52	.235	0	-2	-2	0	-0.1
Total	2	0	0	—	4	0	0	0	0	6^1	9	4	0	0	8	0	24.2	5.68	58	.360	.515	107	.272	1	-2	-2	-0	-0.1

● **BILLY O'DELL** O'Dell, William Oliver b: 2/10/32, Whitmire, S.C. BB/TL, 5'11", 170 lbs. Deb: 6/20/54

YEAR	TM/L	W	L	PCT	G	GS	CG	SH	SV	IP	H	R	HR	HB	BB	SO	RAT	ERA	ERA+	OAV	OOB	BH	AVG	PB	PR	PR+	PD	TPI
1954	Bal-A	1	1	.500	7	2	1	0	0	16^1	15	7	0	0	5	6	11.0	2.76	130	.242	.299	0	.000	-0	2	2	0	0.2
1956	Bal-A	0	0	—	4	1	0	0	0	8	6	1	0	0	6	6	13.5	1.13	349	.222	.364	0	.000	-0	3	3	-0	0.1
1957	Bal-A	4	10	.286	35	15	2	1	4	140^1	107	48	12	5	39	97	9.7	2.69	133	.212	.276	5	.147	-1	17	15	-2	1.2
1958	Bal-A★	14	11	.560	41	25	12	3	8	221^1	201	83	13	4	51	137	10.4	2.97	121	.241	.288	8	.111	-1	20	16	-0	1.8
1959	Bal-A★	10	12	.455	38	24	6	2	1	199^1	163	74	18	1	67	88	10.4	2.93	129	.220	.286	5	.083	-3	21	19	1	1.8
1960	SF-N	8	13	.381	43	24	6	1	2	202^2	198	80	16	2	72	145	12.1	3.20	109	.252	.317	6	.107	1	13	7	-1	0.6
1961	SF-N	7	5	.583	46	14	4	1	2	130^1	132	63	10	1	33	110	11.5	3.59	106	.260	.306	4	.103	-2	6	3	-1	0.0
1962	*SF-N	19	14	.576	43	39	20	2	0	280^2	282	126	18	7	66	195	11.4	3.53	108	.258	.304	12	.133	-1	13	9	-2	0.6
1963	SF-N	14	10	.583	36	33	10	3	1	222^1	218	90	14	7	70	116	11.9	3.16	101	.253	.314	16	.205	4	3	1	-4	0.0
1964	SF-N	8	7	.533	36	8	1	0	2	85	82	55	10	4	35	54	12.8	5.40	66	.252	.332	0	.000	-2	-18	-17	-1	-3.1
1965	Mil-N	10	6	.625	62	1	0	0	18	111^1	87	35	10	2	30	78	9.6	2.18	161	.215	.272	4	.174	1	17	17	-0	3.0
1966	Atl-N	2	3	.400	24	0	0	0	6	41^1	44	14	3	2	18	20	13.9	2.40	152	.272	.352	2	.250	0	6	6	-0	0.8
	Pit-N	3	2	.600	37	2	0	0	4	71^1	74	24	3	4	23	47	12.7	2.78	129	.275	.341	1	.063	-1	7	6	-1	0.3
	Yr	5	5	.500	61	2	0	0	10	112^2	118	38	6	6	41	67	13.2	2.64	136	.274	.345	3	.125	-1	12	12	-1	1.1
1967	Pit-N	5	6	.455	27	11	1	0	0	86^2	88	58	10	3	41	34	13.7	5.82	58	.265	.351	3	.115	-0	-24	-24	-1	-2.9
Total	13	105	100	.512	479	199	63	13	48	1817	1697	758	137	42	556	1133	11.4	3.29	109	.246	.306	66	.125	-7	85	61	-12	4.4

● **TED ODENWALD** Odenwald, Theodore Joseph "Lefty" b: 1/4/02, Hudson, Wis. d: 10/23/65, Shakopee, Minn. BR/TL, 5'10", 147 lbs. Deb: 4/13/21

YEAR	TM/L	W	L	PCT	G	GS	CG	SH	SV	IP	H	R	HR	HB	BB	SO	RAT	ERA	ERA+	OAV	OOB	BH	AVG	PB	PR	PR+	PD	TPI
1921	Cle-A	1	0	1.000	10	0	0	0	0	17^1	16	5	0	1	6	4	11.9	1.56	274	.262	.338	0	.000	-1	5	5	0	0.2
1922	Cle-A	0	0	—	1	0	0	0	0	1^1	6	6	0	0	2	2	54.0	40.50	10	.600	.667	0	—	0	-5	-5	0	-0.2
Total	2	1	0	1.000	11	0	0	0	0	18^2	22	11	0	1	8	6	14.9	4.34	98	.310	.387	0	.000	-1	-0	-0	0	0.0

● **DAVE ODOM** Odom, David Everett "Blimp" or "Porky" b: 6/5/18, Dinuba, Cal. d: 11/19/87, Myrtle Beach, S.C. BR/TR, 6'1", 220 lbs. Deb: 5/31/43

YEAR	TM/L	W	L	PCT	G	GS	CG	SH	SV	IP	H	R	HR	HB	BB	SO	RAT	ERA	ERA+	OAV	OOB	BH	AVG	PB	PR	PR+	PD	TPI
1943	Bos-N	0	3	.000	22	3	1	0	2	54^2	54	32	3	4	30	17	14.5	5.27	65	.269	.374	0	.000	-2	-11	-11	-1	-1.0

● **BLUE MOON ODOM** Odom, Johnny Lee b: 5/29/45, Macon, Ga. BR/TR, 6', 185 lbs. Deb: 9/5/64 ♦

YEAR	TM/L	W	L	PCT	G	GS	CG	SH	SV	IP	H	R	HR	HB	BB	SO	RAT	ERA	ERA+	OAV	OOB	BH	AVG	PB	PR	PR+	PD	TPI
1964	KC-A	1	2	.333	5	5	1	1	0	17	29	21	5	0	11	10	21.2	10.06	38	.363	.440	0	.000	-0	-12	-11	0	-1.6
1965	KC-A	0	0	—	1	0	0	0	0	1	2	1	0	0	2	0	36.0	9.00	39	.400	.571	0	—	0	-1	-1	0	0.0
1966	KC-A	5	5	.500	14	14	4	2	0	90^1	70	31	1	2	53	47	12.5	2.49	136	.215	.328	3	.097	-1	9	9	2	1.2
1967	KC-A	3	8	.273	29	17	0	0	0	103^2	94	67	9	3	68	67	14.3	5.04	63	.243	.360	8	.286	2	-21	-22	0	-1.9
1968	Oak-A★	16	10	.615	32	31	9	4	0	231^1	179	74	9	7	98	143	11.0	2.45	115	.216	.304	17	.218	6	14	10	1	2.1
1969	Oak-A★	15	6	.714	32	32	10	3	0	231^1	179	87	15	6	112	150	11.6	2.92	118	.215	.312	21	.266	11	18	14	1	2.6
1970	Oak-A	9	8	.529	29	29	4	1	0	156^1	128	77	14	8	100	88	13.6	3.80	93	.227	.351	13	.241	6	-1	-5	2	0.4
1971	Oak-A	10	12	.455	25	25	3	1	0	140^2	147	78	13	0	71	69	13.9	4.29	78	.271	.355	8	.160	1	-13	-15	-1	-2.1
1972	*Oak-A	15	6	.714	31	30	4	2	0	194^1	164	62	10	3	87	86	11.8	2.50	114	.234	.321	8	.121	0	12	8	0	1.0
1973	*Oak-A	5	12	.294	30	24	3	0	0	150^1	153	86	14	2	67	83	13.3	4.49	79	.263	.341	0	.000	-0	-11	-17	-1	-1.8
1974	*Oak-A	1	5	.167	34	5	1	0	1	87^1	85	39	4	3	52	52	14.4	3.81	87	.267	.375	0	—	0	-2	-5	1	-0.3
1975	Oak-A	0	2	.000	7	2	0	0	0	11	19	15	1	1	11	4	25.4	12.27	30	.422	.544	0	—	0	-10	-11	0	-1.6
	Cle-A	1	0	1.000	3	1	1	1	0	10^1	4	3	1	0	8	10	10.5	2.61	145	.118	.286	0	—	0	1	1	-0	0.1
	Yr	1	2	.333	10	3	1	1	0	21^1	23	18	2	1	19	14	18.1	7.59	49	.291	.434	0	—	0	-9	-9	-0	-1.5
	Atl-N	1	7	.125	15	10	0	0	0	56	78	46	5	0	28	30	17.0	7.07	54	.342	.414	1	.077	-1	-21	-20	0	-2.4
1976	Chi-A	2	2	.500	8	4	0	0	0	28	31	21	2	1	20	18	16.7	5.79	62	.282	.397	0	—	0	-7	-7	-1	-0.9
Total	13	84	85	.497	295	229	40	15	1	1509	1362	708	103	36	788	857	13.0	3.70	89	.244	.341	79	.195	26	-45	-74	5	-5.2

● **GEORGE O'DONNELL** O'Donnell, George Dana b: 5/27/29, Winchester, Ill. BR/TR, 6'3", 175 lbs. Deb: 4/18/54

YEAR	TM/L	W	L	PCT	G	GS	CG	SH	SV	IP	H	R	HR	HB	BB	SO	RAT	ERA	ERA+	OAV	OOB	BH	AVG	PB	PR	PR+	PD	TPI
1954	Pit-N	3	9	.250	21	10	3	0	1	87^1	105	50	4	2	21	8	13.2	4.53	92	.315	.360	2	.087	-1	-4	-3	1	-0.4

● **JOHN O'DONOGHUE** O'Donoghue, John Eugene b: 10/7/39, Kansas City, Mo. BR/TL, 6'3", 210 lbs. Deb: 9/29/63 F

YEAR	TM/L	W	L	PCT	G	GS	CG	SH	SV	IP	H	R	HR	HB	BB	SO	RAT	ERA	ERA+	OAV	OOB	BH	AVG	PB	PR	PR+	PD	TPI
1963	KC-A	0	1	.000	1	1	0	0	0	6	6	2	0	0	2	1	12.0	1.50	260	.286	.348	0	.000	-0	1	1	-0	0.2
1964	KC-A	10	14	.417	39	32	2	1	0	173^2	202	104	24	3	65	79	14.0	4.92	78	.286	.349	13	.236	2	-25	-20	-1	-2.4
1965	KC-A☆	9	18	.333	34	30	4	1	0	177^2	183	92	15	1	66	82	12.7	3.95	88	.267	.332	12	.218	3	-10	-9	0	-1.0
1966	Cle-A	6	8	.429	32	13	2	0	0	108	109	50	13	2	23	49	11.2	3.83	90	.264	.306	5	.152	-0	-5	-5	1	-0.5
1967	Cle-A	8	9	.471	33	17	5	2	2	130^2	120	52	10	2	33	81	10.7	3.24	101	.247	.298	4	.100	-0	-0	0	3	0.4
1968	Bal-A	0	0	—	16	0	0	0	2	22	34	15	2	0	7	11	16.8	6.14	48	.374	.418	0	.000	-0	-8	-8	0	-0.5
1969	Sea-A	2	2	.500	55	0	0	0	6	70	58	28	5	3	37	48	12.6	2.96	123	.230	.336	1	.077	-1	5	5	-0	0.3
1970	Mil-A	2	0	1.000	25	0	0	0	0	23^1	29	15	4	0	9	13	14.7	5.01	76	.299	.358	0	.000	-0	-3	-3	1	-0.2
	Mon-N	2	3	.400	9	3	0	0	0	22^1	20	14	2	2	11	6	13.3	5.24	79	.263	.371	0	.000	-0	-3	-3	0	-0.5
1971	Mon-N	0	0	—	13	0	0	0	0	17^1	19	10	3	0	7	7	13.5	4.67	76	.271	.338	0	—	0	-2	-2	-0	-0.1
Total	9	39	55	.415	257	96	13	4	10	751	780	382	78	13	260	377	12.6	4.07	87	.269	.332	35	.170	2	-49	-43	4	-4.3

● **JOHN O'DONOGHUE** O'Donoghue, John Preston b: 5/26/69, Wilmington, Del. BL/TL, 6'6", 198 lbs. Deb: 6/27/93 F

YEAR	TM/L	W	L	PCT	G	GS	CG	SH	SV	IP	H	R	HR	HB	BB	SO	RAT	ERA	ERA+	OAV	OOB	BH	AVG	PB	PR	PR+	PD	TPI
1993	Bal-A	0	1	.000	11	1	0	0	0	19^2	22	12	4	1	10	16	15.1	4.58	98	.278	.367	0	—	0	-1	-0	-0	0.0

● **LEFTY O'DOUL** O'Doul, Francis Joseph b: 3/4/1897, San Francisco, Cal. d: 12/7/69, San Francisco, Cal. BL/TL, 6', 180 lbs. Deb: 4/29/19 ♦

YEAR	TM/L	W	L	PCT	G	GS	CG	SH	SV	IP	H	R	HR	HB	BB	SO	RAT	ERA	ERA+	OAV	OOB	BH	AVG	PB	PR	PR+	PD	TPI
1919	NY-A	0	0	—	3	0	0	0	0	5	7	6	0	0	4	2	19.8	3.60	89	.304	.407	4	.250	0	-0	-0	-0	0.0
1920	NY-A	0	0	—	2	0	0	0	0	3^2	4	2	0	1	2	2	17.2	4.91	78	.286	.412	2	.167	-0	-0	-0	-0	-0.1
1922	NY-A	0	0	—	6	0	0	0	0	16	24	13	0	0	12	5	20.3	3.38	119	.353	.450	3	.333	1	1	1	0	0.1
1923	Bos-A	1	1	.500	23	1	0	0	0	53	69	50	2	4	31	10	17.7	5.43	76	.337	.433	5	.143	-1	-9	-8	1	-0.4
Total	4	1	1	.500	34	1	0	0	0	77^2	104	71	2	5	49	19	18.3	4.87	83	.335	.434	1140	.349	-1	-8	-7	1	-0.4

● **BRYAN OELKERS** Oelkers, Bryan Alois b: 3/11/61, Zaragoza, Spain BL/TL, 6'3", 192 lbs. Deb: 4/9/83

YEAR	TM/L	W	L	PCT	G	GS	CG	SH	SV	IP	H	R	HR	HB	BB	SO	RAT	ERA	ERA+	OAV	OOB	BH	AVG	PB	PR	PR+	PD	TPI
1983	Min-A	0	5	.000	10	8	0	0	0	34^1	56	34	7	0	17	13	19.1	8.65	49	.376	.440	0	—	0	-17	-16	-1	-2.0
1986	Cle-A	3	3	.500	35	4	0	0	1	69	70	38	13	6	40	33	15.1	4.70	88	.262	.371	0	—	0	-4	-4	-1	-0.4
Total	2	3	8	.273	45	12	0	0	1	103^1	126	72	20	6	57	46	16.5	6.01	70	.303	.395	0	—	0	-21	-21	-2	-2.4

● **JOE OESCHGER** Oeschger, Joseph Carl b: 5/24/1892, Chicago, Ill. d: 7/28/86, Rohnert Park, Cal BR/TR, 6' ", 190 lbs. Deb: 4/21/14

YEAR	TM/L	W	L	PCT	G	GS	CG	SH	SV	IP	H	R	HR	HB	BB	SO	RAT	ERA	ERA+	OAV	OOB	BH	AVG	PB	PR	PR+	PD	TPI
1914	Phi-N	4	8	.333	32	12	5	0	1	124	129	74	5	10	54	47	14.0	3.77	78	.279	.366	3	.075	-4	-14	-11	-1	-1.5
1915	Phi-N	1	0	1.000	6	1	1	0	0	23^2	21	13	1	0	9	8	11.4	3.42	80	.247	.319	0	.000	-1	-2	-2	-0	-0.2

YEAR TM/L	W	L	PCT	G	GS	CG	SH	SV	IP	H	R	HR	HB	BB	SO	RAT	ERA	ERA+	OAV	OOB	BH	AVG	PB	PR	PR+	PD	TPI
1916 Phi-N	1	0	1.000	14	0	0	0	0	30^{1}	18	8	2	1	14	17	9.8	2.37	112	.184	.292	0	.000	-1	1	1	1	0.1
1917 Phi-N	15	14	.517	42	30	18	5	1	262	241	108	7	6	72	123	11.0	2.75	102	.249	.305	10	.114	-4	-1	2	-3	-0.6
1918 Phi-N	6	18	.250	30	23	13	2	**3**	184	159	87	3	7	83	60	12.2	3.03	99	.238	.328	5	.083	-4	-6	-1	-2	-0.7
1919 Phi-N	0	1	.000	5	4	2	0	0	38	52	29	1	2	16	5	16.6	5.92	54	.340	.409	0	.000	-2	-13	-10	-0	-0.8
NY-N	0	1	.000	5	1	0	0	0	8	12	4	0	0	2	3	15.8	4.50	62	.400	.438	0	.000	-0	-1	-2	0	-0.2
Bos-N	4	2	.667	7	7	4	1	0	56^{2}	63	19	0	1	21	16	13.5	2.54	112	.300	.366	2	.091	-1	2	2	-1	-0.1
Yr	4	4	.500	17	12	6	1	0	102^{2}	127	52	1	3	39	24	14.8	3.94	76	.323	.389	2	.053	-4	-12	-11	-2	-1.1
1920 Bos-N	15	13	.536	38	30	20	5	0	299	294	124	10	8	99	80	12.1	3.46	88	.265	.329	18	.178	-3	-11	-14	-3	-1.8
1921 Bos-N	20	14	.588	46	36	19	**3**	0	299	303	128	11	15	97	68	12.5	3.52	104	.274	.341	28	.255	2	9	4	2	0.9
1922 Bos-N	6	21	.222	46	23	10	1	1	195^{2}	234	137	8	8	81	51	14.9	5.06	79	.303	.375	12	.190	-0	-21	-24	1	-2.6
1923 Bos-N	5	15	.250	44	19	6	1	2	166^{1}	227	117	4	5	54	33	15.5	5.68	70	.330	.383	12	.231	-0	-31	-31	0	-3.2
1924 NY-N	2	0	1.000	10	2	0	0	0	29	35	17	1	0	14	10	15.2	3.10	118	.287	.360	3	.429	1	2	2	-1	0.1
Phi-N	2	7	.222	19	8	0	0	0	65^{1}	88	44	6	3	16	8	14.7	4.41	101	.333	.378	5	.250	-1	-4	0	-0	0.0
Yr	4	7	.364	29	10	0	0	0	94^{1}	123	61	7	3	30	18	14.9	4.01	105	.319	.372	8	.296	0	-1	2	-1	0.1
1925 Bro-N	1	2	.333	21	3	1	0	0	37	60	38	2	1	19	6	19.5	6.08	69	.382	.452	1	.125	-0	-7	-8	-0	-0.6
Total 12	82	116	.414	365	199	99	18	8	1818	1936	947	61	67	651	535	13.1	3.81	88	.281	.349	99	.165	-18	-96	-88	-8	-11.2

● JACK OGDEN Ogden, John Mahlon b: 11/5/1897, Ogden, Pa. d: 11/9/77, Philadelphia, Pa. BR/TR, 6', 190 lbs. Deb: 6/22/18 F

YEAR TM/L	W	L	PCT	G	GS	CG	SH	SV	IP	H	R	HR	HB	BB	SO	RAT	ERA	ERA+	OAV	OOB	BH	AVG	PB	PR	PR+	PD	TPI
1918 NY-N	0	0	—	5	0	0	0	0	8^{2}	8	4	0	2	3	1	13.5	3.12	84	.296	.406	0	.000	-0	-0	-0	-0	-0.1
1928 StL-A	15	16	.484	38	31	18	1	2	242^{2}	257	121	23	1	80	67	12.5	4.15	101	.274	.331	17	.200	-1	-3	1	-4	-0.3
1929 StL-A	4	8	.333	34	14	7	0	0	131^{1}	154	83	8	0	44	32	13.6	4.93	90	.301	.357	11	.244	0	-10	-7	0	-0.5
1931 Cin-N	4	8	.333	22	9	3	1	1	89	79	42	3	0	32	24	11.2	2.93	127	.242	.310	4	.148	-1	9	8	-1	0.8
1932 Cin-N	2	2	.500	24	3	1	0	0	57	72	40	5	0	22	20	14.8	5.21	74	.310	.370	2	.167	0	-8	-9	1	-0.5
Total 5	25	34	.424	123	57	29	2	3	528^{2}	570	290	39	3	181	144	12.8	4.24	97	.280	.340	34	.200	-1	-13	-7	-4	-0.6

● CURLY OGDEN Ogden, Warren Harvey b: 1/24/01, Ogden, Pa. d: 8/6/64, Upland, Pa. BR/TR, 6'1.5", 180 lbs. Deb: 7/18/22 F

YEAR TM/L	W	L	PCT	G	GS	CG	SH	SV	IP	H	R	HR	HB	BB	SO	RAT	ERA	ERA+	OAV	OOB	BH	AVG	PB	PR	PR+	PD	TPI
1922 Phi-A	1	4	.200	15	6	4	0	0	72^{1}	59	29	4	5	33	20	12.1	3.11	137	.237	.338	7	.241	-0	8	9	-0	0.5
1923 Phi-A	1	2	.333	18	2	0	0	0	46^{1}	63	39	2	3	32	14	19.0	5.63	73	.330	.434	5	.294	1	-8	-8	0	-0.3
1924 Phi-A	0	3	.000	5	1	0	0	0	12^{2}	14	9	1	1	7	4	15.6	4.97	86	.275	.373	0	.000	-1	-1	-1	-0	-0.3
*Was-A	9	5	.643	16	16	9	3	0	108	83	36	3	2	51	23	11.3	2.58	156	.221	.317	13	.277	2	20	18	-0	2.3
Yr	9	8	.529	21	17	9	3	0	120^{2}	97	45	4	3	58	27	11.8	2.83	143	.227	.324	13	.260	1	19	17	-1	2.0
1925 Was-A	3	1	.750	17	4	2	1	0	42	45	24	1	2	18	6	13.9	4.50	94	.288	.369	3	.250	-0	-0	-1	-0	-0.1
1926 Was-A	4	4	.500	22	9	4	0	0	96^{1}	114	55	2	5	45	21	15.3	4.30	90	.305	.387	5	.185	-1	-3	-5	-1	-0.5
Total 5	18	19	.486	93	38	19	4	0	377^{2}	378	192	13	18	186	88	13.9	3.79	108	.271	.364	33	.244	1	14	12	-2	1.6

● CHAD OGEA Ogea, Chad Wayne b: 11/9/70, Lake Charles, La. BR/TR, 6'2", 200 lbs. Deb: 5/3/94

YEAR TM/L	W	L	PCT	G	GS	CG	SH	SV	IP	H	R	HR	HB	BB	SO	RAT	ERA	ERA+	OAV	OOB	BH	AVG	PB	PR	PR+	PD	TPI
1994 Cle-A	0	1	.000	4	1	0	0	0	16^{1}	21	11	2	1	10	11	17.6	6.06	78	.304	.400	0	—	0	-2	-2	-0	-0.1
1995 *Cle-A	8	3	.727	20	14	1	0	0	106^{1}	95	38	11	1	29	57	10.6	3.05	154	.233	.286	0	—	0	20	20	-1	1.7
1996 *Cle-A	10	6	.625	29	21	1	1	0	146^{2}	151	82	22	5	42	101	12.1	4.79	102	.266	.322	0	—	0	3	2	-1	0.0
1997 *Cle-A	8	9	.471	21	21	1	0	0	126^{1}	139	79	13	5	47	80	13.6	4.99	94	.283	.351	0	.000	-0	-6	-4	-0	-0.5
1998 *Cle-A	5	4	.556	19	9	0	0	0	69	74	44	9	7	25	43	13.8	5.61	85	.273	.350	0	—	0	-7	-6	-0	-0.7
1999 Phi-N	6	12	.333	36	28	0	0	0	168	192	110	36	4	61	77	13.8	5.63	84	.288	.351	4	.091	-2	-20	-16	-2	-1.8
Total 6	37	35	.514	129	94	3	1	0	632^{2}	672	364	93	23	214	369	12.9	4.88	98	.272	.335	4	.087	-2	-12	-8	-5	-1.4

● JOE OGRODOWSKI Ogrodowski, Joseph Anthony b: 11/20/06, Hoytville, Pa. d: 6/24/59, Elmira, N.Y. BR/TR, 5'11", 165 lbs. Deb: 4/27/25

YEAR TM/L	W	L	PCT	G	GS	CG	SH	SV	IP	H	R	HR	HB	BB	SO	RAT	ERA	ERA+	OAV	OOB	BH	AVG	PB	PR	PR+	PD	TPI
1925 Bos-N	0	0	—	1	0	0	0	0	1	6	8	0	0	3	0	81.0	54.00	7	.600	.692	0	—	0	-6	-6	-0	-0.2

● BILL O'HARA O'Hara, William Alexander b: 8/14/1883, Toronto, Ont., Can. d: 6/13/31, Jersey City, N.J. BL/TR, 5'10", Deb: 4/15/09 ♦

YEAR TM/L	W	L	PCT	G	GS	CG	SH	SV	IP	H	R	HR	HB	BB	SO	RAT	ERA	ERA+	OAV	OOB	BH	AVG	PB	PR	PR+	PD	TPI
1910 StL-N	0	0	—	1	0	0	0	0	1	0	0	0	0	0	0	0.0	0.00	—	.000	.000	3	.150	-0	0	0	-0	0.0

● TOMOKAZU OHKA Ohka, Tomokazu b: 3/18/76, Kyoto, Japan BR/TR, 6'1", 180 lbs. Deb: 7/19/99

YEAR TM/L	W	L	PCT	G	GS	CG	SH	SV	IP	H	R	HR	HB	BB	SO	RAT	ERA	ERA+	OAV	OOB	BH	AVG	PB	PR	PR+	PD	TPI
1999 Bos-A	1	2	.333	8	2	0	0	0	13	21	12	2	0	6	8	18.7	6.23	80	.362	.422	0	—	0	-2	-2	0	-0.3
2000 Bos-A	3	6	.333	13	12	0	0	0	69^{1}	70	25	7	2	26	40	12.7	3.12	163	.263	.333	0	—	0	14	15	0	1.7
Total 2	4	8	.333	21	14	0	0	0	82^{1}	91	37	9	2	32	48	13.7	3.61	141	.281	.349	0	—	0	12	13	0	1.4

● JOE OHL Ohl, Joseph Earl (b: Joseph Earl Von Ohl) b: 1/10/1888, Jobstown, N.J. d: 12/18/51, Camden, N.J. BL/TL, Deb: 7/29/09

YEAR TM/L	W	L	PCT	G	GS	CG	SH	SV	IP	H	R	HR	HB	BB	SO	RAT	ERA	ERA+	OAV	OOB	BH	AVG	PB	PR	PR+	PD	TPI
1909 Was-A	0	0	—	4	0	0	0	0	8^{2}	7	4	0	1	1	2	9.3	2.08	117	.194	.237	0	.000	-0	0	0	-0	0.0

● WILL OHMAN Ohman, William McDaniel b: 8/13/77, Frankfurt, West Germany BL/TL, 6'2", 195 lbs. Deb: 9/19/2000

YEAR TM/L	W	L	PCT	G	GS	CG	SH	SV	IP	H	R	HR	HB	BB	SO	RAT	ERA	ERA+	OAV	OOB	BH	AVG	PB	PR	PR+	PD	TPI
2000 Chi-N	1	0	1.000	6	0	0	0	0	3^{1}	4	3	0	0	4	2	21.6	8.10	56	.308	.471	0	—	0	-1	-1	0	-0.2

● KIRT OJALA Ojala, Kirt Stanley b: 12/24/68, Kalamazoo, Mich. BL/TL, 6'2", 200 lbs. Deb: 8/18/97

YEAR TM/L	W	L	PCT	G	GS	CG	SH	SV	IP	H	R	HR	HB	BB	SO	RAT	ERA	ERA+	OAV	OOB	BH	AVG	PB	PR	PR+	PD	TPI
1997 Fla-N	1	2	.333	7	5	0	0	0	28^{2}	28	10	4	0	18	19	14.4	3.14	128	.252	.357	0	.000	-1	3	3	0	0.2
1998 Fla-N	2	7	.222	41	13	1	0	0	125	128	71	14	4	59	75	13.8	4.25	96	.267	.352	4	.154	1	-0	-3	1	0.0
1999 Fla-N	0	1	.000	8	1	0	0	0	10^{2}	21	17	1	0	6	5	22.8	14.34	30	.438	.500	0	—	0	-12	-12	-0	-1.0
Total 3	3	10	.231	56	19	1	0	0	164^{1}	177	98	19	4	83	99	14.5	4.71	86	.277	.364	4	.121	0	-8	-12	1	-0.8

● BOB OJEDA Ojeda, Robert Michael b: 12/17/57, Los Angeles, Cal. BL/TL, 6'1", 190 lbs. Deb: 7/13/80

YEAR TM/L	W	L	PCT	G	GS	CG	SH	SV	IP	H	R	HR	HB	BB	SO	RAT	ERA	ERA+	OAV	OOB	BH	AVG	PB	PR	PR+	PD	TPI
1980 Bos-A	1	1	.500	7	7	0	0	0	26	39	20	2	0	14	12	18.3	6.92	61	.361	.434	0	—	0	-8	-7	-0	-0.5
1981 Bos-A	6	2	.750	10	10	2	0	0	66^{1}	50	25	6	2	25	28	10.4	3.12	124	.212	.293	0	—	0	4	5	-0	0.6
1982 Bos-A	4	6	.400	22	14	0	0	0	78^{1}	95	53	13	1	29	52	14.4	5.63	77	.296	.356	0	—	0	-13	-11	-1	-1.3
1983 Bos-A	12	7	.632	29	28	5	0	0	173^{2}	173	85	15	3	73	94	12.9	4.04	108	.265	.342	0	—	0	6	6	0	0.6
1984 Bos-A	12	12	.500	33	32	8	**5**	0	216^{2}	211	106	17	2	96	137	12.8	3.99	105	.259	.338	0	—	0	0	4	1	0.5
1985 Bos-A	9	11	.450	39	22	5	0	1	157^{2}	166	74	11	2	48	102	12.3	4.00	107	.273	.328	0	—	0	3	5	0	0.6
1986 *NY-N	18	5	**.783**	32	30	7	2	0	217^{1}	185	72	15	2	52	148	9.9	2.57	138	.230	.279	8	.113	-2	28	25	1	2.4
1987 NY-N	3	5	.375	10	7	0	0	0	46^{1}	45	23	5	0	10	21	10.7	3.88	97	.253	.293	1	.071	-0	1	-1	0	-0.1
1988 NY-N	10	13	.435	29	29	5	5	0	190^{1}	158	74	6	4	33	133	9.2	2.88	112	.225	.264	10	.164	1	12	8	2	1.2
1989 NY-N	13	11	.542	31	31	5	2	0	192	179	83	16	2	78	95	12.1	3.47	94	.245	.319	7	.106	-2	1	-5	2	-0.5
1990 NY-N	7	6	.538	38	12	0	0	0	118	123	53	10	2	40	62	12.6	3.66	102	.272	.334	4	.133	-0	2	1	3	0.4
1991 LA-N	12	9	.571	31	31	2	1	0	189^{1}	181	78	15	3	70	120	12.1	3.18	113	.257	.326	9	.161	1	11	9	1	1.2
1992 LA-N	6	9	.400	29	29	2	1	0	166^{1}	169	80	8	1	81	94	13.6	3.63	95	.268	.352	5	.102	-1	-2	-3	2	-0.2
1993 Cle-A	2	1	.667	9	7	0	0	0	43	48	22	5	0	21	27	14.4	4.40	99	.289	.369	0	—	0	-0	-0	1	0.1
1994 NY-A	0	0	—	2	2	0	0	0	3	11	8	1	0	6	3	51.0	24.00	19	.611	.708	0	—	0	-6	-7	0	-0.3
Total 15	115	98	.540	351	291	41	16	1	1884^{1}	1833	856	145	24	676	1128	12.1	3.65	103	.257	.323	44	.127	-4	31	26	10	4.7

● FRANK OKRIE Okrie, Frank Anthony "Lefty" b: 10/28/1896, Detroit, Mich. d: 10/16/59, Detroit, Mich. BL/TL, 5'11", 175 lbs. Deb: 4/20/20 F

YEAR TM/L	W	L	PCT	G	GS	CG	SH	SV	IP	H	R	HR	HB	BB	SO	RAT	ERA	ERA+	OAV	OOB	BH	AVG	PB	PR	PR+	PD	TPI
1920 Det-A	1	2	.333	21	1	1	0	0	41	44	29	2	5	18	9	14.7	5.27	71	.295	.390	1	.200	-0	-7	-7	6	0.1

● RED OLDHAM Oldham, John Cyrus b: 7/15/1893, Zion, Md. d: 1/28/61, Costa Mesa, Cal. BB/TL (BL 1922, 25-26), 6' ", 176 lbs. Deb: 8/19/14

YEAR TM/L	W	L	PCT	G	GS	CG	SH	SV	IP	H	R	HR	HB	BB	SO	RAT	ERA	ERA+	OAV	OOB	BH	AVG	PB	PR	PR+	PD	TPI
1914 Det-A	2	4	.333	9	7	3	0	0	45^{1}	42	22	1	3	8	23	10.5	3.38	83	.243	.288	4	.267	1	-3	-3	-1	-0.4
1915 Det-A	3	0	1.000	17	2	1	0	4	57^{2}	52	22	1	4	17	17	11.4	2.81	108	.243	.311	2	.143	-0	1	1	-1	0.0
1920 Det-A	8	13	.381	39	22	10	1	1	215^{1}	248	132	5	6	91	62	14.4	3.85	97	.302	.376	12	.174	-1	-1	-3	4	0.0
1921 Det-A	11	14	.440	40	28	12	1	1	229^{1}	258	129	11	6	81	67	13.5	4.24	101	.288	.351	19	.224	2	1	1	1	0.4
1922 Det-A	10	13	.435	43	28	9	0	3	212	256	130	14	11	59	72	13.8	4.67	83	.305	.358	19	.260	4	-15	-19	1	-1.4
1925 *Pit-N	3	2	.600	11	4	3	0	1	53	66	27	2	2	18	10	14.6	3.91	114	.313	.372	6	.333	2	2	3	0	0.5
1926 Pit-N	2	2	.500	17	2	0	0	2	41^{2}	56	27	1	1	18	16	16.2	5.62	70	.359	.429	2	.222	0	-8	-8	0	-0.5
Total 7	39	48	.448	176	93	38	2	12	854^{1}	978	489	35	33	292	267	13.7	4.15	93	.295	.358	64	.226	9	-23	-26	4	-1.6

● STEVE OLIN Olin, Steven Robert b: 10/4/65, Portland, Ore. d: 3/22/93, Little Lake Nellie, Fla. BR/TR, 6'3", 185 lbs. Deb: 7/29/89

YEAR TM/L	W	L	PCT	G	GS	CG	SH	SV	IP	H	R	HR	HB	BB	SO	RAT	ERA	ERA+	OAV	OOB	BH	AVG	PB	PR	PR+	PD	TPI
1989 Cle-A	1	4	.200	25	0	0	0	1	36	35	16	0	1	14	24	12.3	3.75	106	.255	.325	0	—	0	1	1	0	0.1
1990 Cle-A	4	4	.500	50	1	0	0	1	92^{1}	96	41	3	6	26	64	12.5	3.41	115	.270	.331	0	—	0	5	5	2	0.6
1991 Cle-A	3	6	.333	48	0	0	0	17	56^{1}	61	26	2	1	23	38	13.6	3.36	124	.274	.344	0	—	0	5	5	0	1.0

YEAR	TM/L	W	L	PCT	G	GS	CG	SH	SV	IP	H	R	HR	HB	BB	SO	RAT	ERA	ERA+	OAV	OOB	BH	AVG	PB	PR	PR+	PD	TPI
1992	Cle-A	8	5	.615	72	0	0	0	29	88^1	80	25	8	4	27	47	11.3	2.34	167	.248	.314	0	—	0	16	16	1	3.1
Total	4	16	19	.457	195	1	0	0	48	273	272	108	14	11	90	173	12.3	3.10	128	.262	.328	0	—	0	26	27	3	4.8
● OMAR OLIVARES Olivares, Omar (Palqu) b: 7/6/67, Mayaguez, P.R. BR/TR, 6'1", 193 lbs. Deb: 8/18/90 F																												
1990	StL-N	1	1	.500	9	6	0	0	0	49^1	45	17	2	2	17	20	11.7	2.92	131	.249	.320	3	.176	1	5	5	1	0.4
1991	StL-N	11	7	.611	28	24	0	0	1	167^1	148	72	13	5	61	91	11.5	3.71	100	.243	.317	12	.226	3	-0	0	2	0.5
1992	StL-N	9	9	.500	32	30	1	0	0	197	189	84	20	4	63	124	11.7	3.84	88	.257	.319	16	.235	4	-7	-10	3	-0.2
1993	StL-N	5	3	.625	58	9	0	0	1	118^2	134	60	10	9	54	63	14.9	4.17	95	.288	.372	7	.269	2	-2	-3	4	0.4
1994	StL-N	3	4	.429	14	12	1	0	1	73^2	84	53	10	4	37	26	15.3	5.74	72	.294	.382	6	.214	2	-12	-13	1	-0.9
1995	Col-N	1	3	.250	11	6	0	0	0	31^2	44	28	4	2	21	15	19.0	7.39	73	.349	.450	1	.143	0	-11	-5	0	-0.6
	Phi-N	0	1	.000	5	0	0	0	0	10	11	6	1	1	2	7	12.6	5.40	78	.282	.333	1	.500	1	-1	-1	0	0.0
	Yr	1	4	.200	16	6	0	0	0	41^2	55	34	5	3	23	22	17.5	6.91	74	.333	.424	2	.222	1	-13	-7	1	-0.6
1996	Det-A	7	11	.389	25	25	4	0	0	160	169	90	16	9	75	81	14.2	4.89	103	.275	.362	0	—	0	2	3	0	0.3
1997	Det-A	5	6	.455	19	19	3	2	0	115	110	68	8	9	53	74	13.5	4.70	98	.253	.347	2	.667	1	-2	-1	1	0.1
	Sea-A	1	4	.200	13	12	0	0	0	62^1	81	41	10	4	28	29	16.3	5.49	82	.315	.391	1	.500	0	-6	-7	-1	-0.5
	Yr	6	10	.375	32	31	3	2	0	177^1	191	109	18	13	81	103	14.5	4.97	92	.276	.363	3	.600	2	-8	-8	0	-0.4
1998	Ana-A	9	9	.500	37	26	1	0	0	183	189	92	19	5	91	112	14.0	4.03	116	.270	.358	0	.000	0	13	13	3	1.5
1999	Ana-A	8	9	.471	20	20	3	0	0	131	135	62	11	6	49	49	13.1	4.05	120	.273	.345	2	.333	1	12	12	1	1.5
	Oak-A	7	2	.778	12	12	1	0	0	74^2	82	43	8	3	32	36	14.1	4.34	107	.283	.360	0	—	0	4	3	1	0.3
	Yr	15	11	.577	32	32	4	0	0	205^2	217	105	19	9	81	85	13.4	4.16	115	.276	.351	2	.333	1	16	15	2	1.8
2000	Oak-A	4	8	.333	21	16	1	0	0	108	134	86	10	7	60	57	16.8	6.75	71	.309	.401	1	1.000	0	-22	-25	0	-2.1
Total	11	71	77	.480	304	217	15	2	3	1481^2	1555	802	142	70	643	784	13.8	4.53	96	.274	.355	52	.242	16	-29	-30	16	0.7
● DARREN OLIVER Oliver, Darren Christopher b: 10/6/70, Rio Linda, Cal. BR/TL, 6'2", 200 lbs. Deb: 9/1/93 F																												
1993	Tex-A	0	0	—	2	0	0	0	0	3^1	2	1	1	0	1	4	8.1	2.70	154	.154	.214	0	—	0	1	1	0	0.0
1994	Tex-A	4	0	1.000	43	0	0	0	2	50	40	24	4	6	35	50	14.6	3.42	141	.223	.368	0	—	0	8	8	2	0.8
1995	Tex-A	4	2	.667	17	7	0	0	0	49	47	25	3	1	32	39	14.7	4.22	114	.257	.370	0	—	0	3	3	1	0.4
1996	*Tex-A	14	6	.700	30	30	1	1	0	173^2	190	97	20	10	76	112	14.3	4.66	112	.279	.359	0	—	0	6	11	-1	1.0
1997	Tex-A	13	12	.520	32	32	3	1	0	201^1	213	111	29	11	82	104	13.7	4.20	114	.271	.348	1	.500	1	8	13	-2	1.3
1998	Tex-A	6	7	.462	19	19	2	0	0	103^1	140	84	11	10	43	58	16.8	6.53	74	.325	.399	1	.167	0	-22	-19	-0	-1.9
	StL-N	4	4	.500	10	10	0	0	0	57	64	31	7	0	23	29	13.7	4.26	98	.283	.349	2	.087	-1	-0	-0	0	-0.1
1999	StL-N	9	9	.500	30	30	2	1	0	196^1	197	96	16	11	74	119	12.9	4.26	107	.265	.341	20	.274	5	7	7	1	1.1
2000	Tex-A	2	9	.182	21	21	0	0	0	108	151	95	16	4	42	49	16.4	7.42	69	.339	.400	0	.000	0	-30	-27	0	-2.1
Total	8	56	49	.533	204	149	8	3	2	942	1044	564	107	53	408	564	14.4	4.88	99	.283	.363	24	.226	6	-19	-5	1	0.5
● FRANCISCO OLIVERAS Oliveras, Francisco Javier (Noa) b: 1/31/63, Santurce, P.R. BR/TR, 5'10", 170 lbs. Deb: 5/3/89																												
1989	Min-A	3	4	.429	12	8	1	0	0	55^2	64	28	8	1	15	24	12.9	4.53	92	.288	.336	0	—	0	-4	-2	-1	-0.3
1990	SF-N	2	2	.500	33	2	0	0	2	55^1	47	22	5	2	21	41	11.4	2.77	132	.230	.308	0	.000	-1	6	6	-1	0.3
1991	SF-N	6	6	.500	55	1	0	0	3	79^1	69	36	12	1	22	48	10.4	3.86	93	.242	.299	2	.200	0	-1	-2	-0	-0.4
1992	SF-N	0	3	.000	16	7	0	0	0	44^2	41	19	11	1	10	17	10.5	3.63	91	.250	.297	1	.143	0	-1	-2	-0	-0.1
Total	4	11	15	.423	116	18	1	0	5	235	221	105	36	5	68	130	11.3	3.71	99	.253	.310	3	.136	-0	0	-1	-2	-0.5
● DIOMEDES OLIVO Olivo, Diomedes Antonio (Maldonado) b: 1/22/19, Guayubin, D.R. d: 2/15/77, Santo Domingo, D.R. BL/TL, 6'1", 195 lbs. Deb: 9/5/60 F																												
1960	Pit-N	0	0	—	4	0	0	0	0	9^2	8	3	1	0	5	10	12.1	2.79	134	.216	.310	0	.000	-0	1	1	-0	0.0
1962	Pit-N	5	1	.833	62	1	0	0	7	84^1	88	30	5	0	25	66	12.1	2.77	142	.277	.329	3	.188	1	11	11	-1	0.9
1963	StL-N	0	5	.000	19	0	0	0	0	13^1	16	9	1	1	9	9	17.6	5.40	66	.296	.406	0	—	0	-3	-3	0	-0.5
Total	3	5	6	.455	85	1	0	0	7	107^1	112	42	7	1	39	85	12.7	3.10	125	.274	.339	3	.176	0	9	9	-0	0.4
● CHI-CHI OLIVO Olivo, Federico Emilio (Maldonado) b: 3/18/28, Guayubin, D.R. d: 2/3/77, Guayubin, D.R. BR/TR, 6'2", 215 lbs. Deb: 6/5/61 F																												
1961	Mil-N	0	0	—	3	0	0	0	0	2	3	4	1	0	5	1	36.0	18.00	21	.500	.727	0	—	0	-3	-3	-0	-0.2
1964	Mil-N	2	1	.667	38	0	0	0	5	60	55	25	7	0	21	45	11.4	3.75	94	.247	.311	1	.250	0	-1	-2	1	0.0
1965	Mil-N	0	1	.000	8	0	0	0	0	13	12	2	1	0	5	11	11.8	1.38	254	.267	.340	0	—	0	3	3	-0	0.2
1966	Atl-N	5	4	.556	47	0	0	0	7	66	59	34	4	1	19	41	10.8	4.23	86	.240	.297	1	.111	-0	-5	-4	-1	-0.8
Total	4	7	6	.538	96	0	0	0	12	141	129	65	13	1	50	98	11.5	3.96	90	.248	.315	2	.154	-0	-6	-6	-1	-0.8
● JIM OLLOM Ollom, James Donald b: 7/8/45, Snohomish, Wash. BR/TL, 6'4", 210 lbs. Deb: 9/3/66																												
1966	Min-A	0	0	—	3	1	0	0	0	10	6	4	1	1	1	11	7.2	3.60	100	.167	.211	0	.000	-0	-0	-0	-0	0.0
1967	Min-A	0	1	.000	21	2	0	0	0	35	33	24	4	4	11	17	12.3	5.40	64	.258	.336	1	.200	0	-8	-7	-0	-0.4
Total	2	0	1	.000	24	3	0	0	0	45	39	28	5	5	12	28	11.2	5.00	70	.258	.309	1	.143	-0	-9	-7	-0	-0.4
● FRED OLMSTEAD Olmstead, Frederic William b: 7/3/1881, Grand Rapids, Mich. d: 10/22/36, Muskogee, Okla. BR/TR, 5'11", 170 lbs. Deb: 7/2/08																												
1908	Chi-A	0	0	—	1	0	0	0	0	2	6	3	0	0	1	1	31.5	13.50	17	.600	.636	0	.000	1	-2	-3	-0	-0.1
1909	Chi-A	3	2	.600	8	6	5	0	0	54^2	52	17	1	1	12	21	10.7	1.81	129	.277	.323	2	.095	-0	4	3	-0	0.2
1910	Chi-A	10	12	.455	32	20	14	4	0	184^1	174	64	1	4	50	68	11.1	1.95	123	.260	.316	10	.154	-2	12	10	1	1.0
1911	Chi-A	6	6	.500	25	11	7	1	2	117^2	146	78	3	6	30	45	13.9	4.21	77	.309	.358	7	.189	-0	-11	-13	-1	-1.3
Total	4	19	20	.487	66	37	26	5	2	358^2	378	162	5	11	93	135	12.1	2.74	97	.283	.334	19	.153	-3	2	-3	-0	-0.2
● AL OLMSTED Olmsted, Alan Ray b: 3/18/57, St.Louis, Mo. BR/TL, 6'2", 195 lbs. Deb: 9/12/80																												
1980	StL-N	1	1	.500	5	5	0	0	0	34^2	32	13	2	1	14	14	12.2	2.86	130	.244	.322	2	.182	-0	3	3	1	0.2
● HANK OLMSTED Olmsted, Henry Theodore b: 1/12/1879, Sac Bay, Mich. d: 1/6/69, Bradenton, Fla. BR/TR, 5'8.5", 147 lbs. Deb: 7/15/05																												
1905	Bos-A	1	2	.333	3	3	3	0	0	25	18	10	0	0	12	6	10.8	3.24	83	.205	.300	1	.125	-0	-2	-1	-1	-0.3
● OLE OLSEN Olsen, Arthur Ole b: 9/12/1894, S.Norwalk, Conn. d: 9/12/80, Norwalk, Conn. BR/TR, 5'10", 163 lbs. Deb: 4/12/22																												
1922	Det-A	7	6	.538	37	15	5	0	3	137	147	84	8	14	40	52	13.2	4.53	86	.281	.348	7	.179	-1	-7	-10	1	-0.9
1923	Det-A	1	1	.500	17	2	1	0	0	41^1	42	30	1	5	17	12	13.9	6.31	61	.290	.383	1	.125	-1	-11	-12	-1	-0.7
Total	2	8	7	.533	54	17	6	0	3	178^1	189	114	9	19	57	64	13.4	4.95	78	.283	.356	8	.170	-2	-18	-22	-0	-1.6
● VERN OLSEN Olsen, Vern Jarl b: 3/16/18, Hillsboro, Ore. d: 7/13/89, Maywood, Ill. BR/TL, 6'0.5", 175 lbs. Deb: 9/8/39																												
1939	Chi-N	1	0	1.000	4	0	0	0	0	7^2	2	0	0	0	7	3	10.6	0.00	—	.087	.300	0	.000	0	3	3	-0	0.4
1940	Chi-N	13	9	.591	34	20	9	4	0	172^2	172	64	5	2	62	71	12.3	2.97	126	.260	.325	15	.263	3	17	15	4	2.6
1941	Chi-N	10	8	.556	37	23	10	2	1	185^2	202	84	7	1	59	73	12.7	3.15	111	.276	.331	15	.238	3	10	8	2	1.3
1942	Chi-N	6	9	.400	32	17	4	1	1	140^1	161	75	6	1	55	46	13.9	4.49	71	.283	.347	9	.188	1	-18	-21	1	-1.8
1946	Chi-N	0	0	—	5	0	0	0	0	9^2	10	3	0	0	9	8	17.7	2.79	119	.294	.442	0	—	0	1	1	0	0.0
Total	5	30	26	.536	112	60	23	7	2	516	547	226	18	4	192	201	13.0	3.40	103	.271	.335	39	.231	8	12	6	7	2.5
● GREGG OLSON Olson, Greggory William b: 10/11/66, Scribner, Neb. BR/TR, 6'4", 206 lbs. Deb: 9/2/88																												
1988	Bal-A	1	1	.500	10	0	0	0	0	11	10	4	1	0	10	9	16.4	3.27	120	.244	.392	0	—	0	1	1	0	0.2
1989	Bal-A	5	2	.714	64	0	0	0	27	85	57	17	1	1	46	90	11.0	1.69	224	.188	.296	0	—	0	21	20	0	2.8
1990	Bal-A☆	6	5	.545	64	0	0	0	37	74^1	57	20	3	3	31	74	11.0	2.42	157	.213	.301	0	—	0	12	12	-1	2.4
1991	Bal-A	4	6	.400	72	0	0	0	31	73^2	74	28	1	1	29	72	12.7	3.18	125	.261	.332	0	—	0	8	7	0	1.3
1992	Bal-A	1	5	.167	60	0	0	0	36	61^1	46	14	3	0	24	58	10.3	2.05	196	.211	.289	0	—	0	13	13	1	2.6
1993	Bal-A	0	2	.000	50	0	0	0	29	45	37	9	1	0	18	44	11.0	1.60	280	.223	.299	0	.000	-0	14	14	0	2.1
1994	Atl-N	0	2	.000	16	0	0	0	1	14^2	19	15	1	1	13	10	20.3	9.20	46	.317	.446	0	.000	-0	-8	-8	-1	-1.1
1995	Cle-A	0	0	—	3	0	0	0	0	2^2	5	4	1	0	2	0	23.6	13.50	35	.417	.500	0	—	0	-3	-3	-0	-0.1
	KC-A	3	3	.500	20	0	0	0	3	30^1	23	11	3	0	17	21	11.9	3.26	147	.215	.323	0	—	0	5	5	0	1.0
	Yr	3	3	.500	23	0	0	0	3	33	28	15	4	0	19	21	12.8	4.09	117	.235	.341	0	—	0	2	3	0	0.9
1996	Det-A	3	0	1.000	43	0	0	0	8	43	43	25	6	1	28	29	15.1	5.02	101	.259	.369	0	—	0	-0	0	-1	0.0
	Hou-N	1	0	1.000	9	0	0	0	0	9^1	12	5	1	0	7	8	18.3	4.82	80	.308	.413	0	—	0	-1	-1	0	-0.1
1997	Min-A	0	0	—	11	0	0	0	0	8^1	19	17	0	0	11	6	32.4	18.36	25	.432	.545	0	—	0	-13	-12	0	-0.6
	KC-A	4	3	.571	34	0	0	0	1	41^2	39	18	3	1	17	28	12.3	3.02	156	.260	.339	0	—	0	7	8	-0	1.1
	Yr	4	3	.571	45	0	0	0	1	50	58	35	3	1	28	34	15.7	5.58	84	.299	.390	0	—	0	-6	-5	-0	0.5

YEAR	TM/L	W	L	PCT	G	GS	CG	SH	SV	IP	H	R	HR	HB	BB	SO	RAT	ERA	ERA+	OAV	OOB	BH	AVG	PB	PR	PR+	PD	TPI
1998	Ari-N	3	4	.429	64	0	0	0	30	68^{2}	56	25	4	1	25	55	10.7	3.01	140	.223	.296	1	.500	1	9	9	-1	1.6
1999	*Ari-N	9	4	.692	61	0	0	0	14	60^{2}	54	28	9	2	25	45	12.0	3.71	123	.238	.319	0	—	0	6	6	0	1.2
2000	LA-N	0	1	.000	13	0	0	0	0	17^{2}	21	11	4	1	7	15	14.8	5.09	86	.296	.367	0	—	0	-1	-1	0	-0.1
Total	13	40	38	.513	594	0	0	0	217	647^{1}	572	251	42	12	310	564	12.4	3.28	129	.238	.328	1	.250	1	70	69	0	14.3

● **TED OLSON** Olson, Theodore Otto b: 8/27/12, Quincy, Mass. d: 12/9/80, Weymouth, Mass. BR/TR, 6'2.5", 185 lbs. Deb: 6/21/36

YEAR	TM/L	W	L	PCT	G	GS	CG	SH	SV	IP	H	R	HR	HB	BB	SO	RAT	ERA	ERA+	OAV	OOB	BH	AVG	PB	PR	PR+	PD	TPI
1936	Bos-A	1	1	.500	5	3	1	0	0	18^{1}	24	16	3	0	8	5	15.7	7.36	72	.324	.390	1	.143	-0	-5	-4	0	-0.3
1937	Bos-A	0	0	—	11	0	0	0	0	32^{1}	42	28	4	0	15	11	15.9	7.24	66	.318	.388	3	.300	1	-9	-9	1	-0.2
1938	Bos-A	0	0	—	2	0	0	0	0	7	9	5	0	0	2	2	14.1	6.43	77	.310	.355	0	.000	-0	-1	-1	-0	-0.1
Total	3	1	1	.500	18	3	1	0	0	57^{2}	75	49	7	0	25	18	15.6	7.18	69	.319	.385	4	.222	1	-15	-14	1	-0.6

● **ED OLWINE** Olwine, Edward R. b: 5/28/58, Greenville, Ohio BL/TL, 6'2", 165 lbs. Deb: 6/2/86

YEAR	TM/L	W	L	PCT	G	GS	CG	SH	SV	IP	H	R	HR	HB	BB	SO	RAT	ERA	ERA+	OAV	OOB	BH	AVG	PB	PR	PR+	PD	TPI
1986	Atl-N	0	0	—	37	0	0	0	1	47^{2}	35	20	5	1	17	37	10.0	3.40	117	.207	.283	1	.333	1	2	3	-0	0.2
1987	Atl-N	0	1	.000	27	0	0	0	1	23^{1}	25	16	4	1	8	12	13.1	5.01	87	.269	.333	0	—	0	-2	-2	-0	-0.1
1988	Atl-N	0	0	—	16	0	0	0	1	18^{2}	22	15	4	1	4	5	13.0	6.75	55	.286	.329	0	—	0	-7	-6	-1	-0.4
Total	3	0	1	.000	80	0	0	0	3	89^{2}	82	51	13	3	29	54	11.4	4.52	89	.242	.307	1	.333	1	-8	-5	-1	-0.3

● **SKINNY O'NEAL** O'Neal, Oran Herbert b: 5/2/1899, Gatewood, Mo. d: 6/2/81, Springfield, Mo. BR/TR, 5'11", 160 lbs. Deb: 4/18/25

YEAR	TM/L	W	L	PCT	G	GS	CG	SH	SV	IP	H	R	HR	HB	BB	SO	RAT	ERA	ERA+	OAV	OOB	BH	AVG	PB	PR	PR+	PD	TPI
1925	Phi-N	0	0	—	11	1	0	0	0	20^{1}	35	23	2	0	12	6	20.8	9.30	51	.407	.480	1	.167	-0	-11	-9	-0	-0.5
1927	Phi-N	0	0	—	2	0	0	0	0	5	9	5	0	0	2	2	19.8	9.00	46	.409	.458	0	.000	-0	-3	-3	1	-0.1
Total	2	0	0	—	13	1	0	0	0	25^{1}	44	28	2	0	14	8	20.6	9.24	50	.407	.475	1	.143	-0	-14	-12	0	-0.6

● **RANDY O'NEAL** O'Neal, Randall Jeffrey b: 8/30/60, Ashland, Ky. BR/TR, 6'2", 195 lbs. Deb: 9/12/84

YEAR	TM/L	W	L	PCT	G	GS	CG	SH	SV	IP	H	R	HR	HB	BB	SO	RAT	ERA	ERA+	OAV	OOB	BH	AVG	PB	PR	PR+	PD	TPI
1984	Det-A	2	1	.667	4	3	0	0	0	18^{2}	16	7	0	0	6	12	10.6	3.38	116	.222	.282	0	—	0	1	1	-0	0.1
1985	Det-A	5	5	.500	28	12	1	0	1	94^{1}	82	42	8	2	36	52	11.4	3.24	126	.240	.316	0	—	0	9	9	1	1.0
1986	Det-A	3	7	.300	37	11	1	0	2	122^{2}	121	69	13	3	44	68	12.3	4.33	95	.260	.327	0	—	0	-2	-3	1	-0.1
1987	Atl-N	4	2	.667	16	10	0	0	0	61	79	41	12	2	24	33	15.5	5.61	78	.316	.380	2	.105	-1	-10	-8	1	-0.6
	StL-N	0	0	—	1	1	0	0	0	5	2	1	0	0	2	4	7.2	1.80	231	.111	.200	1	1.000	0	1	1	0	0.1
	Yr	4	2	.667	17	11	0	0	0	66	81	42	12	2	26	37	14.9	5.32	82	.302	.368	3	.150	-0	-9	-7	1	-0.5
1988	StL-N	2	3	.400	10	8	0	0	0	53	57	29	7	2	10	20	11.7	4.58	76	.274	.314	0	.000	-2	-7	-6	1	-0.7
1989	Phi-N	0	1	.000	20	1	0	0	0	39	46	28	5	0	9	29	12.7	6.23	57	.301	.340	0	.000	-1	-12	-11	1	-0.6
1990	SF-N	1	0	1.000	26	0	0	0	0	47	58	23	3	0	18	30	14.6	3.83	95	.314	.374	1	.167	-0	-0	-1	0	0.0
Total	7	17	19	.472	142	46	2	0	3	440^{2}	461	240	48	9	149	248	12.6	4.35	91	.272	.334	4	.080	-3	-19	-19	5	-0.8

● **ED O'NEIL** O'Neil, Edward J. b: 3/11/1859, Fall River, Mass. d: 9/30/1892, Fall River, Mass. TR, 5'11", 180 lbs. Deb: 6/20/1890

YEAR	TM/L	W	L	PCT	G	GS	CG	SH	SV	IP	H	R	HR	HB	BB	SO	RAT	ERA	ERA+	OAV	OOB	BH	AVG	PB	PR	PR+	PD	TPI
1890	Tol-a	0	2	.000	2	2	2	0	0	16	27	18	0	0	13	2	22.5	7.88	50	.365	.460	0	.000	-2	-7	-7	0	-0.7
	Phi-a	0	6	.000	6	6	6	0	0	52	84	77	0	7	32	17	21.3	9.69	40	.353	.444	5	.161	-1	-34	-34	1	-2.5
	Yr	0	8	.000	8	8	8	0	0	68	111	95	0	7	45	19	21.6	9.26	42	.356	.448	5	.125	-2	-41	-40	1	-3.2

● **J. O'NEILL** O'Neill, J. b: Brooklyn, N.Y. Deb: 8/20/1875

YEAR	TM/L	W	L	PCT	G	GS	CG	SH	SV	IP	H	R	HR	HB	BB	SO	RAT	ERA	ERA+	OAV	OOB	BH	AVG	PB	PR	PR+	PD	TPI
1875	Atl-n	0	4	.000	5	4	3	0	0	34	59	45	3		0	0	15.6	5.03	41	.343	.343	2	.077	-2	-11	-12		-1.1

● **TIP O'NEILL** O'Neill, James Edward b: 5/25/1858, Woodstock, Ont., Canada d: 12/31/15, Montreal, Que., Can BR/TR, 6'1.5", 167 lbs. Deb: 5/5/1883 ♦

YEAR	TM/L	W	L	PCT	G	GS	CG	SH	SV	IP	H	R	HR	HB	BB	SO	RAT	ERA	ERA+	OAV	OOB	BH	AVG	PB	PR	PR+	PD	TPI
1883	NY-N	5	12	.294	19	19	15	0	0	148	182	129	5		64	55	15.0	4.07	76	.289	.354	15	.197	-1	-15	-16	-1	-1.6
1884	StL-a	11	4	.733	17	14	14	0	0	141	125	95	3	4	51	36	11.5	2.68	122	.219	.288	82	.276	5	9	9	0	1.2
Total	2	16	16	.500	36	33	29	0	0	289	307	224	8	4	115	91	13.3	3.39	94	.256	.323	1435	.334	3	-6	-7	-1	-0.4

● **HARRY O'NEILL** O'Neill, Joseph Henry b: 2/20/1897, Ridgetown, Ont., Canada d: 9/5/69, Ridgetown, Ont., Can. BR/TR, 6', 180 lbs. Deb: 9/15/22

YEAR	TM/L	W	L	PCT	G	GS	CG	SH	SV	IP	H	R	HR	HB	BB	SO	RAT	ERA	ERA+	OAV	OOB	BH	AVG	PB	PR	PR+	PD	TPI
1922	Phi-A	0	0	—	1	0	0	0	0	3	2	1	0	1	1	0	12.0	3.00	142	.200	.333	0	.000	-0	0	0	0	0.0
1923	Phi-A	0	0	—	3	0	0	0	0	2	1	0	0	0	3	2	18.0	0.00	—	.167	.444	0	—	0	1	1	-0	0.0
Total	2	0	0	—	4	0	0	0	0	5	3	1	0	1	4	2	14.4	1.80	233	.188	.381	0	.000	-0	1	1	0	0.0

● **MIKE O'NEILL** O'Neill, Michael Joyce (a.k.a. Michael Joyce In 1901)
b: 9/7/1877, Maam, Ireland d: 8/12/59, Scranton, Pa. BL/TL, 5'11", 185 lbs. Deb: 9/20/01 F♦

YEAR	TM/L	W	L	PCT	G	GS	CG	SH	SV	IP	H	R	HR	HB	BB	SO	RAT	ERA	ERA+	OAV	OOB	BH	AVG	PB	PR	PR+	PD	TPI
1901	StL-N	2	2	.500	5	4	4	1	0	41	29	12	2	5	10	16	9.7	1.32	242	.197	.272	6	.400	3	9	9	-1	1.1
1902	StL-N	16	15	.516	36	32	29	2	2	288^{1}	297	136	3	12	66	105	11.7	2.90	94	.266	.314	43	.319	9	-4	-5	0	0.8
1903	StL-N	4	13	.235	19	17	12	0	0	145	184	124	2	6	43	39	14.5	3.79	86	.304	.356	25	.227	2	-8	-8	-0	-0.6
1904	StL-N	10	14	.417	25	24	23	1	0	220	229	86	1	3	50	68	11.5	2.09	129	.262	.304	21	.231	5	16	15	1	2.4
Total	4	32	44	.421	85	77	68	4	2	694^{1}	739	358	8	26	169	228	12.1	2.73	105	.269	.318	97	.255	19	13	10	0	3.7

● **PAUL O'NEILL** O'Neill, Paul Andrew b: 2/25/63, Columbus, Ohio BL/TL, 6'4", 215 lbs. Deb: 9/3/85 ♦

YEAR	TM/L	W	L	PCT	G	GS	CG	SH	SV	IP	H	R	HR	HB	BB	SO	RAT	ERA	ERA+	OAV	OOB	BH	AVG	PB	PR	PR+	PD	TPI
1987	Cin-N	0	0	—	1	0	0	0	0	2	2	3	1	0	4	2	27.0	13.50	31	.286	.545	41	.256	0	-2	-2	-0	-0.1

● **EMMETT O'NEILL** O'Neill, Robert Emmett "Pinky" b: 1/13/18, San Mateo, Cal. d: 10/11/93, Sparks, Nevada BR/TR, 6'2.5", 180 lbs. Deb: 8/3/43

YEAR	TM/L	W	L	PCT	G	GS	CG	SH	SV	IP	H	R	HR	HB	BB	SO	RAT	ERA	ERA+	OAV	OOB	BH	AVG	PB	PR	PR+	PD	TPI
1943	Bos-A	1	4	.200	11	5	1	0	0	57^{2}	56	31	3	1	46	20	16.1	4.53	73	.256	.387	3	.188	1	-8	-8	0	-0.6
1944	Bos-A	6	11	.353	28	22	8	1	0	151^{2}	154	88	6	2	89	68	14.5	4.63	73	.265	.365	10	.182	-0	-20	-21	-2	-2.4
1945	Bos-A	8	11	.421	24	22	10	1	0	141^{2}	134	87	5	5	117	55	16.3	5.15	66	.258	.399	9	.180	2	-28	-27	1	-3.0
1946	Chi-N	0	0	—	1	0	0	0	0	1	0	0	0	0	3	1	27.0	0.00	—	.000	.500	0	—	0	0	0	0	0.0
	Chi-A	0	0	—	2	0	0	0	0	3^{2}	4	2	0	0	5	0	22.1	0.00	—	.333	.529	0	.000	-0	1	1	0	0.1
Total	4	15	26	.366	66	49	19	2	0	355^{2}	348	208	14	8	260	144	15.6	4.76	71	.261	.385	22	.180	2	-54	-54	-2	-5.9

● **STEVE ONTIVEROS** Ontiveros, Steven b: 3/5/61, Tularosa, N.Mex. BR/TR, 6', 190 lbs. Deb: 6/14/85

YEAR	TM/L	W	L	PCT	G	GS	CG	SH	SV	IP	H	R	HR	HB	BB	SO	RAT	ERA	ERA+	OAV	OOB	BH	AVG	PB	PR	PR+	PD	TPI
1985	Oak-A	1	3	.250	39	0	0	0	8	74^{2}	45	17	4	2	19	36	8.0	1.93	200	.174	.236	0	—	0	18	17	1	1.3
1986	Oak-A	2	2	.500	46	0	0	0	10	72^{2}	72	40	10	1	25	54	12.1	4.71	82	.265	.329	0	—	0	-4	-7	0	-0.5
1987	Oak-A	10	8	.556	35	22	2	1	1	150^{2}	141	78	19	4	50	97	11.6	4.00	103	.242	.306	0	—	0	8	3	2	0.4
1988	Oak-A	3	4	.429	10	10	0	0	0	54^{2}	57	32	4	0	21	30	12.8	4.61	82	.265	.331	0	—	0	-4	-5	1	-0.5
1989	Phi-N	2	1	.667	6	5	0	0	0	30^{2}	34	15	2	0	15	12	14.4	3.82	93	.288	.368	1	.083	-0	-1	-1	1	0.0
1990	Phi-N	0	0	—	5	0	0	0	0	10	9	3	1	0	3	6	10.8	2.70	142	.225	.279	0	—	0	1	1	1	0.1
1993	Sea-A	0	2	.000	14	0	0	0	0	18	18	3	0	0	6	13	12.0	1.00	442	.277	.338	0	—	0	7	7	-0	0.7
1994	Oak-A	6	4	.600	27	13	2	0	0	115^{1}	93	39	7	6	26	56	**9.8**	**2.65**	167	.217	**.272**	0	—	0	28	25	2	2.1
1995	Oak-A★	9	6	.600	22	22	2	1	0	129^{2}	144	75	12	4	38	77	12.9	4.37	102	.283	.338	0	—	0	5	2	3	0.4
2000	Bos-A	1	1	.500	3	1	0	0	0	5^{1}	9	6	1	0	4	1	21.9	10.13	50	.375	.464	0	—	0	-3	-3	-0	-0.5
Total	10	34	31	.523	207	73	6	2	19	661^{2}	622	308	60	17	207	382	11.5	3.67	113	.248	.309	1	.083	-0	55	38	10	3.5

● **JOSE OQUENDO** Oquendo, Jose Manuel (Contreras) b: 7/4/63, Rio Piedras, P.R. BB/TR, 5'10", 160 lbs. Deb: 5/2/83 C♦

YEAR	TM/L	W	L	PCT	G	GS	CG	SH	SV	IP	H	R	HR	HB	BB	SO	RAT	ERA	ERA+	OAV	OOB	BH	AVG	PB	PR	PR+	PD	TPI
1987	*StL-N	0	0	—	1	0	0	0	0	1	4	3	0	1	1	0	54.0	27.00	15	.571	.667	71	.286	0	-3	-2	-0	-0.1
1988	StL-N	0	1	.000	1	0	0	0	0	4	4	2	0	0	6	1	22.5	4.50	77	.267	.476	125	.277	0	-0	-0	-0	-0.1
1991	StL-N	0	0	—	1	0	0	0	0	1	2	3	0	0	2	1	36.0	27.00	14	.400	.571	88	.240	0	-3	-3	0	-0.1
Total	3	0	1	.000	3	0	0	0	0	6	10	8	0	1	9	2	30.0	12.00	30	.370	.541	821	.256	1	-6	-6	-0	-0.3

● **MIKE OQUIST** Oquist, Michael Lee b: 5/30/68, LaJunta, Colo. BR/TR, 6'2", 170 lbs. Deb: 8/14/93

YEAR	TM/L	W	L	PCT	G	GS	CG	SH	SV	IP	H	R	HR	HB	BB	SO	RAT	ERA	ERA+	OAV	OOB	BH	AVG	PB	PR	PR+	PD	TPI
1993	Bal-A	0	0	—	5	0	0	0	0	11^{2}	12	5	0	0	4	8	12.3	3.86	116	.261	.320	0	—	0	1	1	-0	0.0
1994	Bal-A	3	3	.500	15	9	0	0	0	58^{1}	75	41	7	6	30	39	17.1	6.17	81	.319	.410	0	—	0	-9	-7	0	-0.6
1995	Bal-A	2	1	.667	27	0	0	0	0	54	51	27	6	2	41	27	15.7	4.17	114	.246	.376	0	—	0	3	4	-0	0.1
1996	SD-N	0	0	—	8	0	0	0	0	7^{2}	6	2	0	0	4	4	11.7	2.35	169	.231	.333	0	—	0	2	1	-0	0.1
1997	Oak-A	4	6	.400	19	17	1	0	0	107^{2}	111	62	15	6	43	72	13.4	5.02	90	.266	.343	1	.250	0	-5	-6	-1	-0.5
1998	Oak-A	7	11	.389	31	29	0	0	0	175	210	125	27	5	57	112	14.0	6.22	73	.298	.355	0	.000	-0	-30	-33	-2	-2.9
1999	Oak-A	9	10	.474	28	24	0	0	0	140^{2}	158	86	18	2	64	89	14.3	5.37	87	.283	.358	0	.000	-0	-8	-12	-1	-1.4
Total	7	25	31	.446	133	79	1	0	0	555	623	348	73	21	243	351	14.4	5.46	85	.284	.361	1	.143	-0	-47	-52	-4	-5.2

● **DON O'RILEY** O'Riley, Donald Lee b: 3/12/45, Topeka, Kan. d: 5/2/97, Kansas City, Mo. BR/TR, 6'3", 205 lbs. Deb: 6/20/69

YEAR	TM/L	W	L	PCT	G	GS	CG	SH	SV	IP	H	R	HR	HB	BB	SO	RAT	ERA	ERA+	OAV	OOB	BH	AVG	PB	PR	PR+	PD	TPI
1969	KC-A	1	1	.500	18	0	0	0	1	23^{1}	32	23	0	0	15	10	18.1	6.94	53	.311	.398	0	.000	-0	-9	-8	-0	-0.8

YEAR	TM/L	W	L	PCT	G	GS	CG	SH	SV	IP	H	R	HR	HB	BB	SO	RAT	ERA	ERA+	OAV	OOB	BH	AVG	PB	PR	PR+	PD	TPI
1970	KC-A	0	0	—	9	2	0	0	0	23^1	26	15	5	1	9	13	13.9	5.40	69	.277	.346	0	.000	-0	-4	-4	-0	-0.3
Total	2	1	1	.500	27	2	0	0	1	46^2	58	38	5	1	24	23	16.0	6.17	60	.294	.374	0	.000	-1	-13	-13	-1	-1.1
● **JESSE OROSCO** Orosco, Jesse Russell b: 4/21/57, Santa Barbara, Cal. BR/TL, 6'2", 185 lbs. Deb: 4/5/79																												
1979	NY-N	1	2	.333	18	2	0	0	0	35	33	20	4	2	22	22	14.7	4.89	75	.260	.377	0	.000	-1	-4	-5	1	-0.4
1981	NY-N	0	1	.000	8	0	0	0	1	17^1	13	4	2	0	6	18	9.9	1.56	224	.213	.284	0	.000	-0	4	4	0	0.2
1982	NY-N	4	10	.286	54	2	0	0	4	109^1	92	37	7	2	40	89	11.0	2.72	134	.230	.303	2	.143	-0	11	11	0	1.4
1983	NY-N★	13	7	.650	62	0	0	0	17	110	76	27	3	1	38	84	9.4	1.47	247	.197	.271	4	.333	1	**26**	**26**	1	**5.8**
1984	NY-N☆	10	6	.625	60	0	0	0	31	87	58	29	7	2	34	85	9.7	2.59	137	.185	.269	1	.250	1	10	9	-0	2.1
1985	NY-N	8	6	.571	54	0	0	0	17	79	66	26	6	0	34	68	11.4	2.73	127	.224	.304	3	.429	1	8	7	-1	1.5
1986	*NY-N	8	6	.571	58	0	0	0	21	81	64	23	6	3	35	62	11.3	2.33	152	.217	.306	0	.000	0	13	11	-1	2.4
1987	NY-N	3	9	.250	58	0	0	0	16	77	78	41	5	2	31	78	13.0	4.44	85	.266	.340	0	.000	-1	-3	-6	-0	-1.1
1988	*LA-N	3	2	.600	55	0	0	0	9	53	41	18	4	2	30	43	12.4	2.72	123	.215	.327	0	.000	-0	4	4	0	0.5
1989	Cle-A	3	4	.429	69	0	0	0	3	78	54	20	7	2	26	79	9.5	2.08	191	.198	.272	0	—	0	16	16	1	1.6
1990	Cle-A	5	4	.556	55	0	0	0	2	64^2	58	35	9	0	38	55	13.4	3.90	101	.239	.342	0	—	0	0	0	1	0.1
1991	Cle-A	2	0	1.000	47	0	0	0	0	45^2	52	20	4	1	15	36	13.4	3.74	111	.286	.343	0	—	0	2	2	-1	0.1
1992	Mil-A	3	1	.750	59	0	0	0	1	39	33	15	5	1	13	40	10.8	3.23	119	.232	.301	0	—	0	3	3	-0	0.2
1993	Mil-A	3	5	.375	57	0	0	0	8	56^2	47	25	2	3	17	67	10.6	3.18	134	.224	.291	0	.000	-0	7	7	3	1.3
1994	Mil-A	3	1	.750	40	0	0	0	0	39	32	26	4	2	26	36	13.8	5.08	99	.222	.349	0	—	0	-1	-0	-0	0.0
1995	Bal-A	2	4	.333	**65**	0	0	0	3	49^2	28	19	4	1	27	58	10.1	3.26	146	.169	.289	0	—	0	8	8	1	1.0
1996	*Bal-A	3	1	.750	66	0	0	0	0	55^2	42	22	5	2	28	52	11.6	3.40	145	.207	.309	0	—	0	10	10	0	0.6
1997	*Bal-A	6	3	.667	71	0	0	0	0	50^1	29	13	6	0	30	46	10.5	2.32	190	.169	.292	0	—	0	13	12	0	1.9
1998	Bal-A	4	1	.800	69	0	0	0	7	56^2	46	20	6	1	28	50	11.9	3.18	143	.221	.316	0	—	0	9	9	-1	0.8
1999	Bal-A	0	2	.000	65	0	0	0	1	32	28	21	5	2	20	35	14.1	5.34	88	.239	.360	0	—	0	-2	-2	0	-0.1
2000	StL-N	0	0	—	6	0	0	0	0	2^1	3	3	1	2	3	4	30.9	3.86	120	.273	.500	0	—	0	0	0	0	0.0
Total	21	84	75	.528	1096	4	0	0	141	1218^1	973	464	102	31	541	1107	11.4	3.03	130	.220	.309	10	.169	2	133	127	5	19.9
● **O'ROURKE** O'Rourke Deb: 7/9/1872																												
1872	Eck-n	0	1	.000	1	1	1	0	0	9	16	15	0		2	0	18.0	8.00	42	.327	.353	0	.000	-1	-4	-5		-0.3
● **JIM O'ROURKE** O'Rourke, James Henry "Orator Jim" b: 9/1/1850, Bridgeport, Conn. d: 1/8/19, Bridgeport, Conn. BR/TR, 5'8", 185 lbs. Deb: 4/26/1872 FMUH♦																												
1883	Buf-N	0	0	—	2	0	0	0	1	7	10	9	0		1	1	14.1	6.43	49	.357	.379	143	.328	1	-3	-3	-0	-0.1
1884	Buf-N	0	1	.000	4	0	0	0	1	12^2	7	5	0		1	3	5.7	2.84	111	.175	.195	162	.347	2	0	0	-0	0.1
Total	2	0	1	.000	6	0	0	0	2	19^2	17	14	0		2	4	8.7	4.12	77	.250	.271	2340	.313	2	-2	-2	-1	0.0
● **MIKE O'ROURKE** O'Rourke, Michael J. Deb: 9/1/1890																												
1890	Bal-a	1	2	.333	5	5	5	0	0	41	45	19	0	3	10	8	12.7	3.95	103	.271	.324	3	.115	-1	-0	0	1	0.0
● **DAVE ORR** Orr, David L. b: 9/29/1859, New York, N.Y. d: 6/2/15, Richmond Hill, N.Y. BR/TR, 5'11", 250 lbs. Deb: 5/17/1883 M♦																												
1885	NY-a	0	0	—	3	0	0	0	0	10	11	13	2	0	5	1	14.4	7.20	41	.229	.302	152	.342	2	-4	-5	-0	-0.2
● **JOE ORRELL** Orrell, Forrest Gordon b: 10/6/17, National City, Cal. d: 1/12/93, Chula Vista, Cal. BR/TR, 6'4", 210 lbs. Deb: 8/12/43																												
1943	Det-A	0	0	—	10	0	0	0	1	19^1	18	9	0	2	11	2	14.4	3.72	95	.257	.373	1	.250	0	-1	-0	-0	0.0
1944	Det-A	2	1	.667	10	2	0	0	0	22^1	26	13	0	1	11	10	15.3	2.42	147	.286	.369	1	.250	0	3	3	1	0.5
1945	Det-A	2	3	.400	12	5	1	0	0	48	46	18	1	2	24	14	13.5	3.00	117	.260	.355	2	.133	-1	2	3	-0	0.1
Total	3	4	4	.500	32	7	1	0	1	89^2	90	40	1	5	46	26	14.2	3.01	117	.266	.362	4	.174	-1	4	5	0	0.6
● **PHIL ORTEGA** Ortega, Filomeno Coronado "Kemo" b: 10/7/39, Gilbert, Ariz. BR/TR, 6'2", 175 lbs. Deb: 9/10/60																												
1960	LA-N	0	0	—	3	1	0	0	0	6^1	12	12	1	0	5	4	24.2	17.05	23	.400	.486	0	.000	-0	-9	-9	0	-0.4
1961	LA-N	0	2	.000	4	2	1	0	0	13	10	9	6	0	2	15	8.3	5.54	78	.208	.240	1	.250	0	-2	-2	-0	-0.2
1962	LA-N	0	2	.000	24	3	0	0	1	53^2	60	43	8	3	39	30	17.1	6.88	53	.276	.394	0	.000	-1	-17	-21	-1	-1.2
1963	LA-N	0	0	—	1	0	0	0	0	1	2	2	1	0	0	1	18.0	18.00	17	.400	.400	0	—	0	-2	-2	0	-0.1
1964	LA-N	7	9	.438	34	25	4	3	1	157^1	149	74	22	6	56	107	12.1	4.00	81	.249	.320	6	.136	-0	-8	-15	-2	-1.7
1965	Was-A	12	15	.444	35	29	4	2	0	179^2	176	107	33	5	97	88	13.9	5.11	68	.262	.359	11	.208	4	-33	-32	-1	-4.1
1966	Was-A	12	12	.500	33	31	5	1	0	197^1	158	91	29	5	53	121	9.9	3.92	88	.218	.276	3	.056	-2	-11	-10	-1	-1.5
1967	Was-A	10	10	.500	34	34	5	2	0	219^2	189	77	16	6	57	122	10.3	3.03	104	.231	.286	4	.061	-3	5	3	-1	-0.1
1968	Was-A	5	12	.294	31	16	1	1	0	115^2	115	70	12	5	62	57	14.2	4.98	59	.263	.361	4	.167	1	-26	-27	-0	-3.7
1969	Cal-A	0	0	—	5	0	0	0	0	8	13	13	3	0	7	4	22.5	10.13	34	.333	.435	0	—	0	-6	-6	0	-0.3
Total	10	46	62	.426	204	141	20	9	2	951^2	884	498	131	30	378	549	12.2	4.43	75	.246	.323	29	.115	-1	-109	-120	-6	-13.3
● **AL ORTH** Orth, Albert Lewis "Smiling Al" or "The Curveless Wonder" b: 9/5/1872, Tipton, Ind. d: 10/8/48, Lynchburg, Va. BL/TR, 6', 200 lbs. Deb: 8/15/1895 U♦																												
1895	Phi-N	8	1	.889	11	10	9	0	1	88	103	50	0	2	22	25	13.0	3.89	123	.288	.332	16	.356	4	9	9	-1	0.9
1896	Phi-N	15	10	.600	25	23	19	0	0	196	244	128	10	3	46	23	13.5	4.41	98	.302	.342	21	.256	3	-1	-2	1	0.1
1897	Phi-N	14	19	.424	36	34	29	2	0	282^1	349	194	12	6	82	64	13.9	4.62	91	.301	.350	50	.329	7	-10	-14	1	-0.4
1898	Phi-N	15	13	.536	32	28	25	1	0	250	290	131	2	8	53	52	12.6	3.02	114	.288	.329	36	.293	8	16	12	0	2.0
1899	Phi-N	14	3	.824	21	15	13	3	1	144^2	149	67	0	3	19	35	10.6	**2.49**	148	.266	.294	13	.210	1	22	20	-4	1.7
1900	Phi-N	14	14	.500	33	30	24	2	1	262	302	145	4	13	60	68	12.9	3.78	96	.288	.335	40	.310	7	-2	-5	1	0.3
1901	Phi-N	20	12	.625	35	33	30	**6**	1	281^2	250	101	3	8	32	92	**9.3**	2.27	150	.237	**.264**	36	.281	5	33	35	3	**4.7**
1902	Was-A	19	18	.514	38	37	36	1	0	324	367	181	18	9	40	76	11.6	3.97	93	.286	.312	38	.217	1	-14	-9	1	-0.6
1903	Was-A	10	22	.313	36	32	30	2	**2**	279^2	326	174	8	7	62	88	12.7	4.34	72	.290	.331	49	.302	9	-43	-36	-0	-2.6
1904	Was-A	3	4	.429	10	7	7	0	0	73^2	88	49	2	3	15	23	13.0	4.76	56	.297	.338	22	.216	0	-18	-17	0	-1.4
	NY-A	11	6	.647	20	18	11	2	0	137^2	122	47	0	3	19	47	9.4	2.68	101	.238	.270	19	.297	3	-1	0	1	0.5
	Yr	14	10	.583	30	25	18	2	0	211^1	210	96	2	6	34	70	10.6	3.41	79	.260	.295	41	.247	3	-19	-16	1	-0.9
1905	NY-A	18	16	.529	40	37	26	6	0	305^1	273	122	8	7	61	121	10.1	2.86	103	.241	.284	24	.183	-1	-7	2	-0	0.1
1906	NY-A	**27**	17	.614	45	39	**36**	3	0	**338^2**	317	115	2	1	66	133	10.2	2.34	127	.251	.289	37	.274	6	13	21	-1	3.5
1907	NY-A	14	21	.400	36	33	21	2	0	248^2	244	134	2	6	53	78	11.0	2.61	107	.259	.303	34	.324	7	-2	5	2	1.8
1908	NY-A	2	13	.133	21	17	8	1	0	139^1	134	62	4	4	30	22	10.9	3.42	72	.255	.300	20	.290	5	-16	-14	-1	-1.1
1909	NY-A	0	0	—	1	1	0	0	0	3	6	4	0	0	1	1	21.0	12.00	21	.429	.467	9	.265	0	-3	-3	-0	-0.2
Total	15	204	189	.519	440	394	324	31	6	3354^2	3564	1704	75	83	661	948	11.6	3.37	101	.272	.311	464	.273	63	-24	14	2	9.3
● **RAMON ORTIZ** Ortiz, Diogenes Ramon (Ortiz) b: 3/23/76, Cotui, D.R. BR/TR, 6', 165 lbs. Deb: 8/19/99																												
1999	Ana-A	2	3	.400	9	9	0	0	0	48^1	50	35	7	2	25	44	14.3	6.52	75	.265	.356	0	—	0	-9	-9	0	-0.7
2000	Ana-A	8	6	.571	18	18	2	0	0	111^1	96	69	18	2	55	73	12.4	5.09	98	.236	.330	0	—	0	-2	-1	-1	-0.2
Total	2	10	9	.526	27	27	2	0	0	159^2	146	104	25	4	80	117	13.0	5.52	89	.245	.338	0	—	0	-11	-10	-1	-0.9
● **BABY ORTIZ** Ortiz, Oliverio (Nunez) b: 12/5/19, Camaguey, Cuba d: 3/27/84, Central Senado, Camaguey, Cuba BR/TR, 6', 190 lbs. Deb: 9/23/44 F																												
1944	Was-A	0	2	.000	2	2	1	0	0	13	13	11	0	0	6	4	13.2	6.23	52	.255	.333	1	.167	-0	-4	-5	-1	-0.6
● **RUSS ORTIZ** Ortiz, Russell Reid b: 6/5/74, Van Nuys, Cal. BR/TR, 6'1", 200 lbs. Deb: 4/2/98																												
1998	SF-N	4	4	.500	22	13	0	0	0	88^1	90	51	11	4	46	75	14.3	4.99	80	.269	.364	7	.280	3	-7	-11	1	-0.5
1999	SF-N	18	9	.667	33	33	3	0	0	207^2	189	109	24	6	125	164	13.9	3.81	110	.244	.354	14	.197	3	17	10	1	1.6
2000	*SF-N	14	12	.538	33	32	0	0	0	195^2	192	117	28	7	112	167	14.3	5.01	84	.261	.364	12	.197	4	-8	-19	2	-1.5
Total	3	36	25	.590	88	78	3	0	0	491^2	471	277	63	17	283	406	14.1	4.50	93	.255	.359	33	.210	11	2	-19	4	-0.4
● **OSSIE ORWOLL** Orwoll, Oswald Christian b: 11/17/1900, Portland, Ore. d: 5/8/67, Decorah, Iowa BL/TL, 6', 174 lbs. Deb: 4/13/28 ♦																												
1928	Phi-A	6	5	.545	27	8	3	0	2	106	110	59	7	2	50	53	13.8	4.58	87	.274	.358	52	.306	7	-6	-7	-0	-0.3
1929	Phi-A	0	2	.000	12	0	0	0	1	30	32	23	6	0	6	12	11.4	4.80	88	.278	.314	13	.255	1	-2	-2	-0	-0.1
Total	2	6	7	.462	39	8	3	0	3	136	142	82	13	2	56	65	13.2	4.63	88	.275	.348	65	.294	7	-8	-9	-1	-0.4
● **OZZIE OSBORN** Osborn, Danny Leon b: 6/19/46, Springfield, Mo. BR/TR, 6'2", 195 lbs. Deb: 4/26/75																												
1975	Chi-A	3	0	1.000	24	0	0	0	0	58	57	29	2	2	37	38	14.9	4.50	86	.265	.378	0	—	0	-5	-4	-1	-0.3

YEAR	TM/L	W	L	PCT	G	GS	CG	SH	SV	IP	H	R	HR	HB	BB	SO	RAT	ERA	ERA+	OAV	OOB	BH	AVG	PB	PR	PR+	PD	TPI
● BOB OSBORN Osborn, John Bode b: 4/17/03, San Diego, Tex. d: 4/19/60, Paris, Ark. BR/TR, 6'1", 175 lbs. Deb: 9/16/25																												
1925	Chi-N	0	0	—	1	0	0	0	0	2	6	2	0	0	0	0	27.0	0.00	—	.600	.600	0	—	0	1	1	0	0.1
1926	Chi-N	6	5	.545	31	15	6	0	1	136^1	157	64	3	0	58	43	14.2	3.63	106	.301	.371	6	.146	-3	3	3	2	0.2
1927	Chi-N	5	5	.500	24	12	2	0	0	107^2	125	54	2	1	48	45	14.5	4.18	92	.294	.367	8	.205	-0	-3	-4	-1	-0.4
1929	Chi-N	0	0	—	3	1	0	0	0	9	8	3	0	0	2	1	10.0	3.00	154	.242	.286	1	.250	0	2	2	-0	0.1
1930	Chi-N	10	6	.625	35	13	3	0	1	126^2	147	74	9	1	53	42	14.3	4.97	98	.300	.369	4	.095	-5	-0	-1	2	-0.4
1931	Pit-N	6	1	.857	27	2	0	0	0	64^2	85	43	3	1	20	9	14.8	5.01	77	.316	.366	3	.167	-0	-8	-8	-1	-0.9
Total	6	27	17	.614	121	43	11	0	2	446^1	528	240	17	3	181	140	14.4	4.32	97	.302	.368	22	.153	-8	-6	-7	2	-1.3
● DONOVAN OSBORNE Osborne, Donovan Alan b: 6/21/69, Roseville, Cal. BB/TL, 6'2", 195 lbs. Deb: 4/9/92																												
1992	StL-N	11	9	.550	34	29	0	0	0	179	193	91	14	2	38	104	11.7	3.77	90	.275	.314	7	.121	-1	-5	-8	-3	-1.2
1993	StL-N	10	7	.588	26	26	1	0	0	155^2	153	73	18	7	47	83	12.0	3.76	106	.257	.319	10	.204	2	5	4	0	0.6
1995	StL-N	4	6	.400	19	19	0	0	0	113^1	112	58	17	2	34	82	11.8	3.81	110	.260	.318	5	.161	2	5	5	-0	0.5
1996	*StL-N	13	9	.591	30	30	2	1	0	198^2	191	87	22	1	57	134	11.3	3.53	119	.254	.307	13	.220	4	15	15	-2	1.7
1997	StL-N	3	7	.300	14	14	0	0	0	80^1	84	46	10	1	23	51	12.1	4.93	84	.274	.326	5	.208	1	-6	-7	-0	-0.7
1998	StL-N	5	4	.556	14	14	1	1	0	83^2	84	42	11	1	22	60	11.5	4.09	103	.256	.305	1	.040	-1	-1	1	-1	-0.1
1999	StL-N	1	3	.250	6	6	0	0	0	29^1	34	18	4	2	10	21	14.1	5.52	83	.298	.365	1	.100	-0	-3	-3	1	-0.3
Total	7	47	45	.511	143	138	4	2	0	840	851	415	96	16	231	535	11.8	3.92	102	.263	.316	42	.164	6	12	6	-6	0.5
● TINY OSBORNE Osborne, Earnest Preston b: 4/9/1893, Porterdale, Ga. d: 1/5/69, Atlanta, Ga. BL/TR, 6'4.5", 215 lbs. Deb: 4/15/22 F																												
1922	Chi-N	9	5	.643	41	14	7	1	3	184	183	113	7	12	95	81	14.2	4.50	93	.271	.370	9	.134	-4	-8	-6	-3	-1.0
1923	Chi-N	8	15	.348	37	25	8	1	1	179^2	174	117	14	2	89	69	13.3	4.56	88	.255	.342	12	.200	-1	-11	-11	-1	-1.4
1924	Chi-N	0	0	—	2	0	0	0	1	3	3	1	0	0	2	2	15.0	3.00	130	.300	.417	0	—	0	0	0	0	0.0
	Bro-N	6	5	.545	21	13	6	0	0	104^1	123	67	1	4	54	52	15.6	5.09	74	.298	.384	9	.250	1	-14	-16	-1	-1.5
	Yr	6	5	.545	23	13	6	0	1	107^1	126	68	1	4	56	54	15.6	5.03	75	.298	.385	9	.250	1	-14	-16	-1	-1.5
1925	Bro-N	8	15	.348	41	22	10	0	1	175	210	111	9	4	75	59	14.9	4.94	85	.304	.375	14	.246	1	-13	-15	-2	-1.7
Total	4	31	40	.437	142	74	31	2	6	646	693	409	31	22	315	263	14.3	4.72	86	.280	.367	44	.200	-3	-46	-47	-6	-5.6
● FRED OSBORNE Osborne, Frederick W. b: Hampton, Iowa TL, Deb: 7/14/1890 ♦																												
1890	Pit-N	0	5	.000	8	5	5	0	0	58	82	87	6	7	45	14	20.8	8.38	39	.323	.438	40	.238	1	-31	-35	-0	-2.1
● WAYNE OSBORNE Osborne, Wayne Harold "Ossie" or "Fish Hook" b: 10/11/12, Watsonville, Cal. d: 3/13/87, Vancouver, Wash. BL/TR, 6'2.5", 172 lbs. Deb: 4/18/35																												
1935	Pit-N	0	0	—	2	0	0	0	0	1^1	1	1	0	0	0	1	6.8	6.75	61	.250	.250	0	—	0	-0	-0	0	0.0
1936	Bos-N	1	1	.500	5	3	0	0	0	20	31	13	1	0	9	8	18.0	5.85	66	.352	.412	2	.250	0	-4	-5	0	-0.4
Total	2	1	1	.500	7	3	0	0	0	21^1	32	14	1	0	9	9	17.3	5.91	65	.348	.406	2	.250	0	-4	-5	0	-0.4
● PAT OSBURN Osburn, Larry Patrick b: 5/4/49, Murray, Ky. BL/TL, 6'4", 195 lbs. Deb: 4/13/74																												
1974	Cin-N	0	0	—	6	0	0	0	0	9	11	9	2	0	4	4	15.0	8.00	44	.297	.366	0	.000	-0	-4	-5	0	-0.2
1975	Mil-A	0	1	.000	6	1	0	0	0	11^2	19	9	2	2	9	1	23.1	5.40	71	.404	.517	0	—	0	-2	-2	0	-0.1
Total	2	0	1	.000	12	1	0	0	0	20^2	30	18	4	2	13	5	19.6	6.53	57	.357	.455	0	.000	-0	-6	-7	1	-0.3
● CHARLIE OSGOOD Osgood, Charles Benjamin b: 11/23/26, Somerville, Mass. BR/TR, 5'10", 180 lbs. Deb: 6/18/44																												
1944	Bro-N	0	0	—	1	0	0	0	0	3	2	1	0	1	3	0	18.0	3.00	118	.222	.462	0	—	0	0	0	-0	0.0
● KEITH OSIK Osik, Keith Richard b: 10/22/68, Port Jefferson, N.Y. BR/TR, 6', 185 lbs. Deb: 4/5/96 ♦																												
1999	Pit-N	0	0	—	1	0	0	0	0	1	2	4	0	1	2	1	45.0	36.00	13	.400	.625	31	.186	0	-3	-3	0	-0.2
2000	Pit-N	0	0	—	1	0	0	0	0	1	5	5	1	2	0	1	63.0	45.00	10	.625	.700	36	.293	0	-4	-5	0	-0.2
Total	2	0	0	—	2	0	0	0	0	2	7	9	1	3	2	2	54.0	40.50	11	.538	.667	156	.246	1	-8	-8	0	-0.4
● DAN OSINSKI Osinski, Daniel b: 11/17/33, Chicago, Ill. BR/TR, 6'2", 195 lbs. Deb: 4/11/62																												
1962	KC-A	0	0	—	4	0	0	0	0	4^2	8	9	1	0	8	4	30.9	17.36	24	.381	.552	0	—	0	-7	-6	0	-0.3
	LA-A	6	4	.600	33	0	0	0	4	54^1	45	22	3	0	30	44	12.4	2.82	137	.223	.323	0	.000	-1	7	6	0	1.1
	Yr	6	4	.600	37	0	0	0	4	59	53	31	4	0	38	48	13.9	3.97	98	.238	.349	0	.000	-1	0	-1	0	0.8
1963	LA-A	8	8	.500	47	16	4	1	0	159^1	145	66	15	2	80	100	12.8	3.28	105	.242	.333	5	.111	-2	6	3	-1	-0.1
1964	LA-A	3	3	.500	47	4	1	1	2	93	87	47	8	2	39	88	12.4	3.48	94	.244	.322	1	.056	-1	1	-2	1	-0.1
1965	Mil-N	0	3	.000	61	0	0	0	6	83	81	28	4	1	40	54	13.2	2.82	125	.261	.348	1	.167	-0	7	7	-0	0.3
1966	Bos-A	4	3	.571	44	1	0	0	2	67^1	68	33	8	1	28	44	13.0	3.61	105	.274	.350	2	.333	0	-1	1	-1	0.1
1967	*Bos-A	3	1	.750	34	0	0	0	2	63^2	61	19	5	0	14	38	10.6	2.54	137	.243	.283	3	.333	1	5	6	-0	0.5
1969	Chi-A	5	5	.500	51	0	0	0	2	60^2	56	28	3	0	23	27	11.7	3.56	108	.251	.321	0	.000	-0	0	2	2	0.5
1970	Hou-N	0	1	.000	3	0	0	0	0	3^2	5	4	0	0	2	1	17.2	9.82	40	.357	.438	0	—	0	-2	-3	-0	-0.5
Total	8	29	28	.509	324	21	5	2	18	589^2	556	256	47	6	264	400	12.6	3.34	107	.250	.331	12	.122	-3	16	15	1	1.5
● CLAUDE OSTEEN Osteen, Claude Wilson b: 8/9/39, Caney Spring, Tenn. BL/TL, 5'11", 173 lbs. Deb: 7/6/57 C																												
1957	Cin-N	0	0	—	3	0	0	0	0	4	4	1	0	0	3	3	15.8	2.25	183	.250	.368	0	.000	-0	1	1	-0	0.0
1959	Cin-N	0	0	—	2	0	0	0	0	7^2	11	10	2	0	9	3	23.5	7.04	58	.333	.476	0	.000	-0	-3	-2	-0	-0.2
1960	Cin-N	0	1	.000	20	3	0	0	0	48^1	53	29	4	1	30	15	15.6	5.03	76	.293	.396	1	.083	-1	-7	-6	0	-0.4
1961	Cin-N	0	0	—	1	0	0	0	0	0^1	0	0	0	0	0	0	0.0	0.00	—	.000	.000	0	—	0	0	0	0	0.0
	Was-A	1	1	.500	3	3	0	0	0	18^1	14	11	3	1	9	14	11.8	4.91	82	.219	.324	1	.143	-0	-2	-2	0	-0.2
1962	Was-A	8	13	.381	28	22	7	2	1	150^1	140	62	12	4	47	59	11.4	3.65	111	.246	.309	10	.208	1	5	6	0	1.0
1963	Was-A	9	14	.391	40	29	8	2	0	212^1	222	101	23	1	60	109	12.0	3.35	111	.270	.320	12	.171	1	7	8	-1	0.8
1964	Was-A	15	13	.536	37	36	13	0	0	257	256	107	20	3	64	133	11.3	3.33	111	.259	.306	14	.156	1	8	10	2	1.4
1965	*LA-N	15	15	.500	40	40	9	1	0	287	253	95	19	3	78	162	10.5	2.79	117	.236	.290	12	.121	-1	24	16	6	2.2
1966	*LA-N	17	14	.548	39	38	8	3	0	240^1	238	92	6	2	65	137	11.4	2.85	116	.261	.312	16	.211	6	20	13	1	2.4
1967	LA-N☆	17	17	.500	39	39	14	5	0	288^1	298	116	19	2	52	152	11.0	3.22	96	.270	.304	18	.178	6	5	-4	-0	0.2
1968	LA-N	12	18	.400	39	36	5	3	0	253^2	267	109	14	5	54	119	11.6	3.09	90	.275	.316	15	.179	2	-3	-10	1	-0.8
1969	LA-N	20	15	.571	41	41	16	7	0	321	293	103	17	6	74	183	10.5	2.66	125	.245	.293	24	.216	6	33	26	3	3.8
1970	LA-N★	16	14	.533	37	37	11	4	0	258^2	280	121	24	4	52	114	11.7	3.83	100	.276	.313	19	.204	5	6	0	-1	0.4
1971	LA-N	14	11	.560	38	38	11	4	0	259	262	108	25	3	63	109	11.4	3.51	92	.266	.312	16	.186	2	-1	-8	6	0.1
1972	LA-N	20	11	.645	33	33	14	4	0	252	232	82	16	4	69	100	10.9	2.64	126	.245	.299	24	.273	10	23	20	-0	3.6
1973	LA-N★	16	11	.593	33	33	12	3	0	236^2	227	97	20	2	61	86	11.0	3.31	104	.258	.307	12	.154	-1	9	4	2	0.6
1974	Hou-N	9	9	.500	23	21	7	2	0	138^1	158	67	8	2	47	45	13.5	3.71	94	.292	.351	13	.283	3	-1	-4	0	-0.1
	StL-N	0	2	.000	8	2	0	0	0	22^2	26	14	1	0	11	6	14.7	4.37	82	.286	.363	0	.000	-1	-2	-2	0	-0.2
	Yr	9	11	.450	31	23	7	2	0	161	184	81	9	2	58	51	13.6	3.80	92	.291	.353	13	.245	3	-3	-6	0	-0.3
1975	Chi-A	7	16	.304	37	37	5	0	0	204^1	237	110	16	2	92	63	14.6	4.36	89	.294	.367	0	—	0	-13	-11	1	-0.9
Total	18	196	195	.501	541	488	140	40	1	3460^1	3471	1435	249	45	940	1612	11.6	3.30	104	.263	.314	207	.188	38	111	53	20	13.7
● DARRELL OSTEEN Osteen, Milton Darrell b: 2/14/43, Oklahoma City, Okla. BR/TR, 6'1", 170 lbs. Deb: 9/2/65																												
1965	Cin-N	0	0	—	3	0	0	0	0	3	2	0	0	0	4	1	18.0	0.00	—	.200	.429	0	—	0	1	1	0	0.1
1966	Cin-N	0	2	.000	13	0	0	0	1	15	26	21	3	0	9	17	21.0	12.00	33	.371	.443	1	.500	0	-14	-12	-0	-1.6
1967	Cin-N	0	2	.000	10	0	0	0	2	14^1	10	10	1	3	13	13	16.3	6.28	60	.196	.388	0	.000	-0	-5	-4	0	-0.6
1970	Oak-A	1	0	1.000	3	1	0	0	0	5^2	9	4	0	0	3	3	19.1	6.35	56	.346	.414	0	.000	-0	-2	-2	-0	-0.3
Total	4	1	4	.200	29	1	0	0	3	38	47	35	4	3	29	34	18.7	8.05	47	.299	.418	1	.200	-0	-19	-17	-0	-2.4
● FRED OSTENDORF Ostendorf, Frederick K. b: 8/5/1890, Baltimore, Md. d: 3/2/65, Kecoughtan, Va. BL/TL, 6'0.5", 169 lbs. Deb: 7/16/14																												
1914	Ind-F	0	0	—	1	0	0	0	0	2	5	5	0	1	2	0	36.0	22.50	14	.500	.615	0	.000	-0	-4	-4	0	-0.2
● BILL OSTER Oster, William Charles b: 1/2/33, New York, N.Y. BL/TL, 6'3", 198 lbs. Deb: 8/23/54																												
1954	Phi-A	0	1	.000	8	1	0	0	0	15^2	19	15	2	0	12	5	17.8	6.32	62	.311	.425	1	.333	0	-5	-4	-0	-0.2
● FRITZ OSTERMUELLER Ostermueller, Frederick Raymond b: 9/15/07, Quincy, Ill. d: 12/17/57, Quincy, Ill. BL/TL, 5'11", 175 lbs. Deb: 4/21/34																												
1934	Bos-A	10	13	.435	33	23	10	0	3	198^2	200	93	7	1	99	75	13.6	3.49	138	.262	.348	13	.167	-2	22	27	3	2.9

YEAR	TM/L	W	L	PCT	G	GS	CG	SH	SV	IP	H	R	HR	HB	BB	SO	RAT	ERA	ERA+	OAV	OOB	BH	AVG	PB	PR	PR+	PD	TPI
1935	Bos-A	7	8	.467	22	19	10	0	1	137^2	135	67	0	3	78	41	14.1	3.92	121	.257	.356	14	.286	1	8	12	-0	1.2
1936	Bos-A	10	16	.385	43	23	7	1	2	180^2	210	115	8	3	84	90	14.8	4.88	109	.288	.364	15	.234	0	3	8	3	1.2
1937	Bos-A	3	7	.300	25	7	2	0	1	86^2	101	64	2	1	44	29	15.2	4.98	95	.286	.367	11	.333	3	-4	-2	0	0.1
1938	Bos-A	13	5	.722	31	18	10	1	2	176^2	199	98	15	3	58	46	13.2	4.58	108	.275	.331	16	.216	2	4	7	-0	0.7
1939	Bos-A	11	7	.611	34	20	8	0	4	159^1	173	86	6	2	58	61	13.2	4.24	112	.277	.341	9	.161	-2	7	8	-1	0.6
1940	Bos-A	5	9	.357	31	16	5	0	0	143^2	166	86	7	0	70	80	14.8	4.95	91	.284	.361	17	.315	4	-9	-7	-1	-0.3
1941	StL-A	0	3	.000	15	2	0	0	0	46	45	26	3	0	23	20	13.3	4.50	96	.257	.343	3	.214	0	-2	-1	0	0.0
1942	StL-A	3	1	.750	10	4	2	0	0	43^2	46	22	4	0	17	21	13.0	3.71	100	.266	.332	3	.188	-0	-0	-0	-1	-0.1
1943	StL-A	0	2	.000	11	3	0	0	0	28^2	36	16	1	0	13	4	15.4	5.02	66	.321	.392	2	.286	0	-5	-5	0	-0.3
	Bro-N	1	1	.500	7	1	0	0	0	27^1	21	11	0	0	12	15	10.9	3.29	102	.212	.297	0	.000	-1	0	0	-0	-0.1
1944	Bro-N	2	1	.667	10	4	3	0	1	41^2	46	17	3	0	12	17	12.5	3.24	110	.267	.315	2	.154	-0	2	1	-0	0.0
	Pit-N	11	7	.611	28	24	14	1	1	204^2	201	79	7	1	65	80	11.7	2.73	136	.260	.318	20	.250	2	20	22	-1	2.0
	Yr	13	8	.619	38	28	17	1	2	246^1	247	96	10	1	77	97	11.9	2.81	131	.261	.317	22	.237	2	22	23	-1	2.0
1945	Pit-N	5	4	.556	14	11	4	1	0	80^2	74	45	6	2	37	29	12.6	4.57	86	.236	.321	9	.321	2	-7	-5	0	-0.3
1946	Pit-N	13	10	.565	27	25	16	2	0	193^1	193	70	5	3	56	57	11.7	2.84	124	.263	.318	21	.328	6	12	14	-2	2.3
1947	Pit-N	12	10	.545	26	24	12	3	0	183	181	94	18	1	68	66	12.3	3.84	110	.254	.320	12	.188	0	5	8	-1	0.7
1948	Pit-N	8	11	.421	23	22	10	2	0	134^1	143	73	13	1	41	43	12.4	4.42	92	.262	.315	8	.182	-0	-7	-5	-1	-0.8
Total	15	114	115	.498	390	246	113	11	15	2066^2	2170	1062	105	21	835	774	13.2	3.99	109	.268	.337	175	.234	16	49	82	-3	9.8

● JOE OSTROWSKI Ostrowski, Joseph Paul "Professor" or "Specs" b: 11/15/16, W.Wyoming, Pa. BL/TL, 6′, 180 lbs. Deb: 7/18/48

YEAR	TM/L	W	L	PCT	G	GS	CG	SH	SV	IP	H	R	HR	HB	BB	SO	RAT	ERA	ERA+	OAV	OOB	BH	AVG	PB	PR	PR+	PD	TPI
1948	StL-A	4	6	.400	26	9	3	0	3	78^1	108	54	6	0	17	20	14.4	5.97	76	.333	.367	4	.222	1	-15	-12	2	-1.1
1949	StL-A	8	8	.500	40	13	4	0	2	141	185	94	16	0	27	34	13.5	4.79	95	.307	.337	7	.189	2	-9	-4	-1	-0.2
1950	StL-A	2	4	.333	9	7	2	0	0	57^1	57	22	2	0	7	15	10.0	2.51	197	.251	.274	4	.222	1	13	14	-1	1.5
	NY-A	1	1	.500	21	4	1	0	3	43^2	50	26	11	0	15	15	13.4	5.15	83	.294	.351	1	.111	-0	-3	-4	0	-0.2
	Yr	3	5	.375	30	11	3	0	3	101	107	48	13	0	22	30	11.5	3.65	128	.270	.308	5	.185	1	10	11	-1	1.3
1951	*NY-A	6	4	.600	34	3	2	0	5	95^1	103	44	4	1	18	30	11.5	3.49	110	.279	.314	3	.107	-2	7	4	-1	0.2
1952	NY-A	2	2	.500	20	1	0	0	2	40	56	31	5	1	14	17	16.0	5.62	59	.327	.382	0	.000	-1	-9	-11	-1	-1.3
Total	5	23	25	.479	150	37	12	0	15	455^2	559	271	44	2	98	131	13.0	4.54	95	.300	.336	19	.161	1	-16	-12	-1	-1.1

● AL OSUNA Osuna, Alfonso b: 8/10/65, Inglewood, Cal. BR/TL, 6′3″, 200 lbs. Deb: 9/2/90

YEAR	TM/L	W	L	PCT	G	GS	CG	SH	SV	IP	H	R	HR	HB	BB	SO	RAT	ERA	ERA+	OAV	OOB	BH	AVG	PB	PR	PR+	PD	TPI
1990	Hou-N	2	0	1.000	12	0	0	0	0	11^1	10	6	1	3	6	6	15.1	4.76	78	.270	.413	0	—	0	-1	-1	-0	-0.2
1991	Hou-N	7	6	.538	71	0	0	0	12	81^2	59	39	5	3	46	68	11.9	3.42	103	.201	.316	0	.000	-0	2	1	-0	0.1
1992	Hou-N	6	3	.667	66	0	0	0	0	61^2	52	29	8	1	38	37	13.3	4.23	80	.236	.351	0	—	0	-5	-6	0	-0.9
1993	Hou-N	1	1	.500	44	0	0	0	2	25^1	17	10	3	1	13	21	11.0	3.20	121	.200	.313	0	—	0	2	2	-1	0.1
1994	LA-N	2	0	1.000	15	0	0	0	0	8^2	13	6	0	0	4	7	17.7	6.23	63	.333	.395	0	—	0	-2	-2	-0	-0.5
1996	SD-N	0	0	—	10	0	0	0	0	4	5	1	0	1	2	4	18.0	2.25	177	.313	.421	0	.000	-0	1	1	0	0.0
Total	6	18	10	.643	218	0	0	0	14	192^2	156	91	17	9	109	143	12.8	3.83	93	.226	.339	0	.000	-0	-2	-6	-1	-1.4

● ANTONIO OSUNA Osuna, Antonio Pedro b: 4/12/73, Sinaloa, Mexico BR/TR, 5′11″, 160 lbs. Deb: 4/25/95

YEAR	TM/L	W	L	PCT	G	GS	CG	SH	SV	IP	H	R	HR	HB	BB	SO	RAT	ERA	ERA+	OAV	OOB	BH	AVG	PB	PR	PR+	PD	TPI
1995	*LA-N	2	4	.333	39	0	0	0	0	44^2	39	22	5	1	20	46	12.1	4.43	86	.241	.328	0	.000	-0	-1	-3	0	-0.4
1996	*LA-N	9	6	.600	73	0	0	0	4	84	65	33	6	2	32	85	10.6	3.00	129	.220	.300	0	.000	0	11	9	0	1.5
1997	LA-N	3	4	.429	48	0	0	0	0	61^2	46	15	6	1	19	68	9.6	2.19	176	.209	.275	1	.500	0	14	12	1	1.4
1998	LA-N	7	1	.875	54	0	0	0	6	64^2	50	26	8	2	32	72	11.7	3.06	129	.214	.313	0	.000	-0	8	7	0	0.9
1999	LA-N	0	0	—	5	0	0	0	0	4^2	4	5	0	1	3	5	15.4	7.71	56	.222	.364	0	—	0	-2	-2	0	-0.1
2000	LA-N	3	6	.333	46	0	0	0	0	67^1	57	30	7	2	35	70	12.6	3.74	117	.229	.329	0	.000	-0	7	5	-0	0.5
Total	6	24	21	.533	265	0	0	0	10	327	261	131	32	9	141	346	11.3	3.28	122	.221	.309	1	.111	-0	38	28	1	3.8

● BILL OTEY Otey, William Tilford "Steamboat Bill" b: 12/16/1886, Dayton, Ohio d: 4/23/31, Dayton, Ohio BL/TL, 6′2″, 181 lbs. Deb: 9/27/07

YEAR	TM/L	W	L	PCT	G	GS	CG	SH	SV	IP	H	R	HR	HB	BB	SO	RAT	ERA	ERA+	OAV	OOB	BH	AVG	PB	PR	PR+	PD	TPI
1907	Pit-N	0	1	.000	3	2	1	0	0	16^1	23	11	1	1	4	5	15.4	4.41	55	.319	.364	1	.250	0	-4	-4	-0	-0.3
1910	Was-A	0	1	.000	9	1	1	0	0	34^2	40	17	1	1	6	12	12.2	3.38	74	.301	.336	5	.385	2	-3	-3	-1	-0.1
1911	Was-A	1	3	.250	12	2	0	0	0	49^2	68	44	2	3	15	16	15.6	6.34	52	.333	.387	1	.059	-2	-17	-17	1	-1.3
Total	3	1	5	.167	24	5	2	0	0	100^2	131	72	4	5	25	33	14.4	5.01	57	.320	.367	7	.206	0	-23	-24	-1	-1.7

● HARRY OTIS Otis, Harry George "Cannonball" b: 10/5/1886, W.New York, N.J. d: 1/29/76, Teaneck, N.J. BR/TL, 6′ ″, 180 lbs. Deb: 9/5/09

YEAR	TM/L	W	L	PCT	G	GS	CG	SH	SV	IP	H	R	HR	HB	BB	SO	RAT	ERA	ERA+	OAV	OOB	BH	AVG	PB	PR	PR+	PD	TPI
1909	Cle-A	2	2	.500	5	3	0	0	0	26^1	26	11	0	3	18	6	16.1	1.37	187	.283	.416	1	.111	-0	3	3	-0	0.5

● DENNIS O'TOOLE O'Toole, Dennis Joseph b: 3/13/49, Chicago, Ill. BR/TR, 6′3″, 195 lbs. Deb: 9/8/69 F

YEAR	TM/L	W	L	PCT	G	GS	CG	SH	SV	IP	H	R	HR	HB	BB	SO	RAT	ERA	ERA+	OAV	OOB	BH	AVG	PB	PR	PR+	PD	TPI
1969	Chi-A	0	0	—	2	0	0	0	0	4	5	3	0	0	2	4	15.8	6.75	57	.333	.412	0	—	0	-1	-1	-0	-0.1
1970	Chi-A	0	0	—	3	0	0	0	0	3^1	5	1	0	0	2	3	18.9	2.70	144	.357	.438	0	—	0	0	0	-0	0.0
1971	Chi-A	0	0	—	1	0	0	0	0	2	0	0	0	0	1	2	4.5	0.00	—	.000	.143	0	—	0	1	1	-0	0.0
1972	Chi-A	0	0	—	3	0	0	0	0	5	10	3	0	0	2	5	21.6	5.40	58	.417	.462	0	—	0	-1	-1	0	-0.1
1973	Chi-A	0	0	—	6	0	0	0	0	16	23	11	3	0	3	8	14.6	5.63	70	.329	.356	0	—	0	-3	-3	0	-0.1
Total	5	0	0	—	15	0	0	0	0	30^1	43	18	3	0	10	22	15.7	5.04	75	.333	.381	0	—	0	-5	-4	-0	-0.3

● JIM O'TOOLE O'Toole, James Jerome b: 1/10/37, Chicago, Ill. BB/TL, 6′, 198 lbs. Deb: 9/26/58 F

YEAR	TM/L	W	L	PCT	G	GS	CG	SH	SV	IP	H	R	HR	HB	BB	SO	RAT	ERA	ERA+	OAV	OOB	BH	AVG	PB	PR	PR+	PD	TPI
1958	Cin-N	0	1	.000	1	1	0	0	0	7	4	2	0	0	5	4	11.6	1.29	322	.154	.290	0	.000	-0	2	2	-0	0.3
1959	Cin-N	5	8	.385	28	19	3	1	0	129^1	144	78	14	4	73	68	15.4	5.15	79	.287	.382	5	.135	-0	-17	-15	1	-1.3
1960	Cin-N	12	12	.500	34	31	7	2	1	196^1	198	94	14	4	66	124	12.3	3.80	100	.263	.325	7	.106	-3	-1	0	-3	-0.6
1961	*Cin-N	19	9	.679	39	35	11	3	2	252^2	229	101	16	3	93	178	11.6	3.10	131	.240	.310	16	.172	-1	26	**27**	-0	2.7
1962	Cin-N	16	13	.552	36	34	11	3	0	251^2	222	115	20	5	87	170	11.2	3.50	115	.238	.307	10	.110	-5	12	14	-2	0.8
1963	Cin-N★	17	14	.548	33	32	12	5	0	234^1	208	85	13	3	57	146	10.3	2.88	116	.239	.288	11	.149	-1	11	12	-3	1.2
1964	Cin-N	17	7	.708	30	30	9	3	0	220	194	71	8	0	51	145	10.0	2.66	136	.235	.279	7	.100	-1	21	23	-2	2.1
1965	Cin-N	3	10	.231	29	22	2	0	1	127^2	154	98	14	3	47	71	14.4	5.92	63	.294	.355	4	.089	-2	-34	-29	-2	-3.0
1966	Cin-N	5	7	.417	25	24	2	0	0	142	139	65	16	3	49	96	12.1	3.55	110	.254	.318	6	.128	-2	1	5	-1	0.1
1967	Chi-A	4	3	.571	15	10	1	1	0	54^1	53	21	4	1	18	37	11.9	2.82	110	.251	.313	1	.077	-1	3	2	-1	0.1
Total	10	98	84	.538	270	238	58	18	4	1615^1	1545	730	119	26	546	1039	11.8	3.57	106	.251	.315	67	.125	-15	24	39	-12	2.4

● MARTY O'TOOLE O'Toole, Martin James b: 11/27/1888, Wm.Penn, Pa. d: 2/18/49, Aberdeen, Wash. BR/TR, 5′11″, 175 lbs. Deb: 9/21/08

YEAR	TM/L	W	L	PCT	G	GS	CG	SH	SV	IP	H	R	HR	HB	BB	SO	RAT	ERA	ERA+	OAV	OOB	BH	AVG	PB	PR	PR+	PD	TPI
1908	Cin-N	1	0	1.000	3	2	1	0	0	15	15	8	0	0	7	5	13.2	2.40	96	.273	.355	1	.200	-0	-0	-0	-0	0.0
1911	Pit-N	3	2	.600	5	5	3	0	0	38	28	17	1	0	20	34	11.4	2.37	145	.215	.320	5	.357	2	4	4	0	0.8
1912	Pit-N	15	17	.469	37	36	17	**6**	0	275^1	237	110	4	2	159	150	13.0	2.71	120	.241	.348	22	.222	2	21	18	1	2.1
1913	Pit-N	6	8	.429	26	16	7	0	1	144^2	148	69	3	3	55	58	12.8	3.30	92	.271	.341	7	.132	-2	-1	-5	-0	-0.7
1914	Pit-N	1	8	.111	19	9	1	0	1	92^1	92	56	3	0	47	36	13.5	4.68	57	.270	.358	5	.167	0	-19	-22	-1	-2.1
	NY-N	1	1	.500	10	5	2	0	0	34	34	17	0	0	12	13	12.2	4.24	63	.262	.324	3	.300	1	-5	-6	-0	-0.3
	Yr	2	9	.182	29	14	3	0	1	126^1	126	73	3	0	59	49	13.2	4.56	58	.268	.349	8	.200	1	-25	-28	-1	-2.4
Total	5	27	36	.429	100	73	31	6	2	599^1	554	277	11	5	300	296	12.9	3.21	95	.254	.345	43	.204	2	-1	-11	-0	-0.2

● JIM OTTEN Otten, James Edward b: 7/1/51, Lewistown, Mont. BR/TR, 6′2″, 195 lbs. Deb: 7/31/74

YEAR	TM/L	W	L	PCT	G	GS	CG	SH	SV	IP	H	R	HR	HB	BB	SO	RAT	ERA	ERA+	OAV	OOB	BH	AVG	PB	PR	PR+	PD	TPI
1974	Chi-A	0	1	.000	5	1	0	0	0	16^1	22	11	0	1	12	11	19.3	5.51	68	.324	.432	0	—	0	-3	-3	-0	-0.2
1975	Chi-A	0	0	—	2	0	0	0	0	5^1	4	5	1	0	7	3	18.6	6.75	58	.235	.458	0	—	0	-2	-2	0	-0.1
1976	Chi-A	0	0	—	2	0	0	0	0	6	9	6	0	0	2	3	16.5	4.50	79	.333	.379	0	—	0	-1	-1	-0	-0.1
1980	StL-N	0	5	.000	31	4	0	0	0	55^1	71	38	3	2	26	38	16.1	5.53	67	.323	.399	1	.200	-0	-12	-11	1	-0.9
1981	StL-N	1	0	1.000	24	0	0	0	0	35^2	44	23	3	0	20	20	16.1	5.30	67	.321	.408	0	.000	-0	-7	-7	-1	-0.5
Total	5	1	6	.143	64	5	0	0	0	118^2	150	83	7	3	67	75	16.7	5.46	67	.320	.408	1	.143	-0	-25	-23	-1	-1.8

● DAVE OTTO Otto, David Alan b: 11/12/64, Chicago, Ill. BL/TL, 6′7″, 210 lbs. Deb: 9/8/87

YEAR	TM/L	W	L	PCT	G	GS	CG	SH	SV	IP	H	R	HR	HB	BB	SO	RAT	ERA	ERA+	OAV	OOB	BH	AVG	PB	PR	PR+	PD	TPI
1987	Oak-A	0	0	—	3	0	0	0	0	6	7	6	1	0	1	3	12.0	9.00	46	.304	.333	0	—	0	-3	-3	-0	-0.2
1988	Oak-A	0	0	—	3	2	0	0	0	10	9	2	0	0	6	7	13.5	1.80	210	.243	.349	0	—	0	2	2	0	0.1
1989	Oak-A	0	0	—	1	1	0	0	0	6^2	6	2	0	0	2	4	10.8	2.70	137	.261	.320	0	—	0	1	1	-0	0.0
1990	Oak-A	0	0	—	2	0	0	0	0	2^1	3	3	0	0	3	2	23.1	7.71	48	.300	.462	0	—	0	-1	-1	0	0.0
1991	Cle-A	2	8	.200	18	14	1	0	0	100	108	52	7	4	27	47	12.5	4.23	98	.283	.337	0	—	0	-1	-1	-0	-0.1
1992	Cle-A	5	9	.357	18	16	0	0	0	80^1	110	64	12	1	33	32	16.1	7.06	55	.333	.396	0	—	0	-28	-28	0	-4.0

YEAR	TM/L	W	L	PCT	G	GS	CG	SH	SV	IP	H	R	HR	HB	BB	SO	RAT	ERA	ERA+	OAV	OOB	BH	AVG	PB	PR	PR+	PD	TPI
1993	Pit-N	3	4	.429	28	8	0	0	0	68	85	40	9	3	28	30	15.4	5.03	81	.317	.388	4	.222	1	-7	-7	1	-0.5
1994	Chi-N	0	1	.000	36	0	0	0	0	45	49	20	4	1	22	19	14.4	3.80	109	.283	.367	0	.000	-0	2	2	-1	0.0
Total	8	10	22	.313	109	41	1	0	0	318^{1}	377	189	33	9	122	144	14.4	5.06	80	.303	.369	4	.200	1	-35	-36	0	-4.7

● ORVAL OVERALL Overall, Orval b: 2/2/1881, Farmersville, Cal. d: 7/14/47, Fresno, Cal. BB/TR, 6'2", 214 lbs. Deb: 4/16/05

YEAR	TM/L	W	L	PCT	G	GS	CG	SH	SV	IP	H	R	HR	HB	BB	SO	RAT	ERA	ERA+	OAV	OOB	BH	AVG	PB	PR	PR+	PD	TPI
1905	Cin-N	18	23	.439	42	39	32	2	0	318	290	146	4	14	147	173	12.8	2.86	116	.252	.343	17	.145	-2	5	14	-1	1.4
1906	Cin-N	4	5	.444	13	10	6	0	0	82^{1}	77	52	1	4	46	33	13.9	4.26	65	.253	.359	6	.194	0	-15	-13	-1	-1.5
	*Chi-N	12	3	.800	18	14	13	2	1	144	116	43	1	4	51	94	10.7	1.88	141	.217	.290	9	.170	-1	12	12	0	1.2
	Yr	16	8	.667	31	24	19	2	1	226^{1}	193	95	2	8	97	127	11.8	2.74	98	.230	.316	15	.179	-1	-3	-2	-1	-0.3
1907	*Chi-N	23	7	.767	36	30	26	**8**	3	268^{1}	201	62	3	11	69	141	9.4	1.68	149	.208	.268	20	.213	3	24	24	2	3.5
1908	*Chi-N	15	11	.577	37	27	16	4	4	225	165	74	3	2	78	167	9.8	1.92	123	.208	.280	9	.129	-0	11	11	-1	1.2
1909	Chi-N	20	11	.645	38	32	23	**9**	3	285	204	66	1	8	80	**205**	9.2	1.42	179	**.198**	.262	22	.229	8	37	36	0	5.2
1910	*Chi-N	12	6	.667	23	21	11	4	1	144^{2}	106	44	2	1	54	92	10.0	2.68	108	.212	.291	5	.122	-1	6	3	1	0.5
1913	Chi-N	4	5	.444	11	9	6	1	0	68	73	33	1	1	26	30	13.2	3.31	96	.284	.352	6	.250	2	-1	-1	1	0.2
Total	7	108	71	.603	218	182	133	30	12	1535^{1}	1232	520	16	45	551	935	10.7	2.23	123	.223	.298	94	.179	9	79	85	1	11.7

● STUBBY OVERMIRE Overmire, Frank W. b: 5/16/19, Moline, Mich. d: 3/3/77, Lakeland, Fla. BR/TL, 5'7", 170 lbs. Deb: 4/25/43 C

YEAR	TM/L	W	L	PCT	G	GS	CG	SH	SV	IP	H	R	HR	HB	BB	SO	RAT	ERA	ERA+	OAV	OOB	BH	AVG	PB	PR	PR+	PD	TPI
1943	Det-A	7	6	.538	29	18	8	3	1	147	135	56	5	1	38	48	10.7	3.18	111	.243	.293	7	.167	0	2	5	-1	0.3
1944	Det-A	11	11	.500	32	28	11	3	1	199^{2}	214	84	2	2	41	57	11.6	3.07	116	.271	.309	11	.175	1	8	11	2	1.4
1945	*Det-A	9	9	.500	31	22	9	0	4	162^{1}	189	81	6	3	42	36	13.0	3.88	91	.294	.341	10	.189	0	-9	-6	0	-0.7
1946	Det-A	5	7	.417	24	13	3	0	1	97^{1}	106	54	6	0	29	34	12.5	4.62	79	.274	.325	5	.152	-1	-12	-10	1	-1.1
1947	Det-A	11	5	.688	28	17	7	3	0	140^{2}	142	62	9	1	44	33	12.0	3.77	100	.259	.315	7	.149	-1	-1	-0	-0	-0.1
1948	Det-A	3	4	.429	37	4	0	0	3	66^{1}	89	48	5	0	31	14	16.3	5.97	73	.326	.395	1	.071	-1	-12	-12	1	-1.2
1949	Det-A	1	3	.250	14	1	0	0	0	17^{1}	29	21	2	1	9	3	20.3	9.87	42	.377	.448	1	.333	0	-11	-11	0	-2.0
1950	StL-A	9	12	.429	31	19	8	2	0	161	200	89	11	1	45	39	13.8	4.19	118	.298	.343	8	.167	1	7	13	-2	1.3
1951	StL-A	1	6	.143	8	7	3	0	0	53^{1}	61	26	5	0	21	13	13.8	3.54	124	.281	.345	1	.071	-1	3	5	-1	0.4
	NY-A	1	1	.500	15	4	1	0	0	44^{2}	50	27	2	2	18	14	14.1	4.63	83	.287	.361	1	.143	0	-3	-4	0	-0.2
	Yr	2	7	.222	23	11	4	0	0	98	111	53	7	2	39	27	14.0	4.04	102	.284	.352	2	.095	-0	1	1	-1	0.2
1952	StL-A	0	3	.000	17	4	0	0	0	41	44	21	3	0	7	10	11.2	3.73	105	.270	.300	2	.182	-0	-0	1	1	0.1
Total	10	58	67	.464	266	137	50	11	10	1130^{2}	1259	569	56	11	325	301	12.7	3.96	98	.280	.330	54	.161	-1	-28	-8	1	-1.8

● MIKE OVERY Overy, Harry Michael b: 1/27/51, Clinton, Ill. BR/TR, 6'2", 190 lbs. Deb: 8/14/76

YEAR	TM/L	W	L	PCT	G	GS	CG	SH	SV	IP	H	R	HR	HB	BB	SO	RAT	ERA	ERA+	OAV	OOB	BH	AVG	PB	PR	PR+	PD	TPI
1976	Cal-A	0	2	.000	5	0	0	0	0	7^{1}	6	5	1	1	3	8	12.3	6.14	54	.214	.313	0	—	0	-2	-2	0	-0.5

● ERNIE OVITZ Ovitz, Ernest Gayhart b: 10/7/1885, Mineral Point, Wis. d: 9/11/80, Green Bay, Wis. BR/TR, 5'8.5", 156 lbs. Deb: 6/22/11

YEAR	TM/L	W	L	PCT	G	GS	CG	SH	SV	IP	H	R	HR	HB	BB	SO	RAT	ERA	ERA+	OAV	OOB	BH	AVG	PB	PR	PR+	PD	TPI
1911	Chi-N	0	0	—	1	0	0	0	0	2	3	2	0	0	3	0	27.0	4.50	74	.375	.545	0	—	0	-0	-0	-0	0.0

● BOB OWCHINKO Owchinko, Robert Dennis b: 1/1/55, Detroit, Mich. BL/TL, 6'2", 195 lbs. Deb: 9/25/76

YEAR	TM/L	W	L	PCT	G	GS	CG	SH	SV	IP	H	R	HR	HB	BB	SO	RAT	ERA	ERA+	OAV	OOB	BH	AVG	PB	PR	PR+	PD	TPI
1976	SD-N	0	2	.000	2	2	0	0	0	4^{1}	11	8	0	0	3	4	29.1	16.62	20	.478	.538	0	.000	-0	-6	-7	0	-1.1
1977	SD-N	9	12	.429	30	28	3	2	0	170	191	93	20	0	67	101	13.7	4.45	80	.287	.352	4	.082	-2	-10	-19	-2	-2.4
1978	SD-N	10	13	.435	36	33	4	1	0	202^{1}	198	87	14	1	78	94	12.3	3.56	94	.263	.333	11	.175	1	1	-5	-1	-0.5
1979	SD-N	6	12	.333	42	20	2	0	0	149^{1}	144	73	16	2	55	66	12.1	3.74	95	.259	.328	4	.121	-0	0	-4	-0	-0.5
1980	Cle-A	2	9	.182	29	14	1	1	0	114^{1}	138	71	13	2	47	66	14.7	5.27	77	.301	.368	0	—	0	-16	-15	-0	-1.3
1981	*Oak-A	4	3	.571	29	0	0	0	2	39^{1}	34	15	2	1	19	26	12.4	3.20	109	.245	.340	0	—	0	2	1	-0	0.2
1982	Oak-A	2	4	.333	54	0	0	0	3	102	111	60	11	0	52	67	14.4	5.21	75	.275	.358	0	—	0	-13	-15	-1	-1.0
1983	Pit-N	0	0	—	1	0	0	0	0	0	2	1	0	0	—	—	∞	—	1.000	1.000	102	—	0	-1	-1	0	-0.1	
1984	Cin-N	3	5	.375	49	4	0	0	2	94	91	47	10	0	39	60	12.4	4.12	92	.253	.327	2	.167	1	-5	-3	-1	-0.3
1986	Mon-N	1	0	1.000	3	3	0	0	0	15	17	6	1	0	3	6	12.0	3.60	103	.288	.323	1	.200	0	0	0	-0	0.0
Total	10	37	60	.381	275	104	10	4	7	890^{2}	937	461	88	6	363	490	13.2	4.28	85	.274	.345	22	.135	-0	-48	-68	-5	-7.0

● FRANK OWEN Owen, Frank Malcolm "Yip" b: 12/23/1879, Ypsilanti, Mich. d: 11/24/42, Dearborn, Mich. BB/TR, 5'11", 160 lbs. Deb: 4/29/01

YEAR	TM/L	W	L	PCT	G	GS	CG	SH	SV	IP	H	R	HR	HB	BB	SO	RAT	ERA	ERA+	OAV	OOB	BH	AVG	PB	PR	PR+	PD	TPI
1901	Det-A	1	3	.250	8	5	3	0	0	56	70	43	1	4	30	17	16.7	4.34	89	.302	.391	1	.050	-2	-4	-3	2	-0.2
1903	Chi-A	8	12	.400	26	20	15	1	1	167^{1}	167	85	1	7	44	66	11.7	3.50	80	.259	.314	7	.123	-1	-10	-13	4	-1.2
1904	Chi-A	21	15	.583	37	36	34	4	1	315	243	95	2	11	61	103	9.0	1.94	126	.214	.261	23	.215	5	23	19	6	3.7
1905	Chi-A	21	13	.618	42	38	32	3	0	334	276	110	6	9	56	125	9.2	2.10	117	.227	.266	18	.145	-4	21	15	3	1.4
1906	*Chi-A	22	13	.629	42	36	27	7	0	293	289	114	4	4	54	66	10.7	2.33	109	.261	.298	14	.136	-2	12	7	4	1.1
1907	Chi-A	2	3	.400	11	4	2	0	0	47	43	22	1	0	13	15	10.7	2.49	96	.246	.298	4	.250	0	0	-1	1	0.0
1908	Chi-A	6	7	.462	25	14	5	1	0	140	142	79	2	3	37	48	11.7	3.41	68	.260	.310	9	.180	1	-16	-18	2	-1.4
1909	Chi-A	1	1	.500	3	2	1	0	0	16	19	8	0	1	3	3	12.9	4.50	52	.279	.319	1	.167	-0	-4	-4	-0	-0.5
Total	8	82	67	.550	194	155	119	16	2	1368^{1}	1249	556	17	39	298	443	10.4	2.55	100	.244	.290	77	.159	-3	22	1	22	2.9

● JIM OWENS Owens, James Philip "Bear" b: 1/16/34, Gifford, Pa. BR/TR, 5'11", 190 lbs. Deb: 4/19/55 C

YEAR	TM/L	W	L	PCT	G	GS	CG	SH	SV	IP	H	R	HR	HB	BB	SO	RAT	ERA	ERA+	OAV	OOB	BH	AVG	PB	PR	PR+	PD	TPI
1955	Phi-N	0	2	.000	3	2	0	0	0	8^{2}	13	8	2	0	7	6	20.8	8.31	48	.382	.488	0	.000	-0	-4	-4	-0	-0.8
1956	Phi-N	0	4	.000	10	5	0	0	0	29^{2}	35	26	3	2	22	22	17.9	7.28	51	.313	.434	1	.167	0	-12	-12	0	-1.3
1958	Phi-N	1	0	1.000	1	1	0	0	0	7	4	4	1	0	5	3	11.6	2.57	154	.154	.290	0	.000	0	1	1	-0	0.1
1959	Phi-N	12	12	.500	31	30	11	1	1	221^{1}	203	97	14	4	73	135	11.4	3.21	128	.244	.308	9	.120	-1	18	21	-0	2.0
1960	Phi-N	4	14	.222	31	22	6	0	0	150	182	95	21	1	64	83	14.8	5.04	77	.299	.367	3	.068	-3	-21	-19	-1	-2.4
1961	Phi-N	5	10	.333	20	17	3	0	0	106^{2}	119	62	8	0	32	38	12.7	4.47	91	.287	.339	2	.074	-1	-5	-5	-2	-0.8
1962	Phi-N	2	4	.333	23	12	1	0	0	69^{2}	90	53	12	0	33	21	15.9	6.33	61	.318	.389	2	.143	0	-18	-19	-1	-1.6
1963	Cin-N	0	2	.000	19	3	0	0	4	42^{1}	42	28	6	0	24	29	14.0	5.31	63	.259	.355	1	.125	0	-10	-9	1	-0.6
1964	Hou-N	8	7	.533	48	11	0	0	6	118	115	48	7	0	32	88	11.2	3.28	104	.262	.312	3	.103	-1	3	2	-1	0.0
1965	Hou-N	6	5	.545	50	0	0	0	8	71^{1}	64	28	4	0	29	53	11.7	3.28	102	.238	.312	1	.125	-0	2	1	-0	0.1
1966	Hou-N	4	7	.364	40	0	0	0	2	50	53	29	5	1	17	32	12.8	4.68	73	.273	.335	0	.000	-0	-6	-7	1	-1.5
1967	Hou-N	0	1	.000	10	0	0	0	0	10^{2}	12	5	1	0	2	6	11.8	4.22	78	.308	.341	0	—	0	-1	-1	-0	-0.1
Total	12	42	68	.382	286	103	21	1	21	885^{1}	932	483	84	8	340	516	13.0	4.31	88	.273	.340	22	.101	-7	-53	-51	-5	-6.9

● RICK OWNBEY Ownbey, Richard Wayne b: 10/20/57, Corona, Cal. BR/TR, 6'3", 185 lbs. Deb: 8/17/82

YEAR	TM/L	W	L	PCT	G	GS	CG	SH	SV	IP	H	R	HR	HB	BB	SO	RAT	ERA	ERA+	OAV	OOB	BH	AVG	PB	PR	PR+	PD	TPI
1982	NY-N	1	2	.333	8	8	2	0	0	50^{1}	44	23	3	0	43	28	15.6	3.75	97	.242	.387	3	.200	1	-1	-1	-1	0.0
1983	NY-N	1	3	.250	10	4	0	0	0	34^{2}	31	19	4	1	21	19	13.8	4.67	78	.240	.351	1	.111	-0	-4	-4	0	-0.5
1984	StL-N	0	3	.000	4	4	0	0	0	19	23	13	1	0	8	11	14.7	4.74	73	.303	.369	0	.000	-0	-2	-3	-0	-0.5
1986	StL-N	1	3	.250	17	3	0	0	0	42^{2}	47	20	4	2	19	25	14.3	3.80	96	.294	.376	0	.000	-1	-0	-1	-1	-0.2
Total	4	3	11	.214	39	19	2	0	0	146^{2}	145	75	12	3	91	83	14.7	4.11	88	.265	.373	4	.114	-1	-8	-8	-2	-1.2

● DOC OZMER Ozmer, Horace Robert b: 5/25/01, Atlanta, Ga. d: 12/28/70, Atlanta, Ga. BR/TR, 5'10.5", 185 lbs. Deb: 5/11/23

YEAR	TM/L	W	L	PCT	G	GS	CG	SH	SV	IP	H	R	HR	HB	BB	SO	RAT	ERA	ERA+	OAV	OOB	BH	AVG	PB	PR	PR+	PD	TPI
1923	Phi-A	0	0	—	1	0	0	0	0	2	1	1	0	0	1	1	9.0	4.50	91	.167	.286	0	—	0	-0	-0	0	0.0

● CHARLIE PABOR Pabor, Charles Henry b: 9/24/1846, New York, N.Y. d: 4/23/13, New Haven, Conn. BL/TL, 5'8", 155 lbs. Deb: 5/4/1871 M♦

YEAR	TM/L	W	L	PCT	G	GS	CG	SH	SV	IP	H	R	HR	HB	BB	SO	RAT	ERA	ERA+	OAV	OOB	BH	AVG	PB	PR	PR+	PD	TPI
1871	Cle-n	0	2	.000	7	1	1	0	0	29^{1}	50	53	4		6	0	17.2	6.75	61	.325	.350	42	.296	0	-8	-9		-0.3
1872	Cle-n	1	1	.500	2	2	2	0	0	18	20	15	0		3	0	11.5	4.00	89	.247	.274	19	.207	-0	-1	-1		-0.1
1875	Atl-n	0	1	.000	1	1	0	0	0	4	11	12	0		1	0	27.0	9.00	23	.407	.429	36	.235	0	-3	-3		-0.5
Total	3 n	1	4	.200	10	4	3	0	0	51^{1}	81	80	4		10	0	16.0	5.96	35	.309	.335	204	.285	-0	-21	-24		-0.9

● JOHN PACELLA Pacella, John Lewis b: 9/15/56, Brooklyn, N.Y. BR/TR, 6'3", 195 lbs. Deb: 9/15/77

YEAR	TM/L	W	L	PCT	G	GS	CG	SH	SV	IP	H	R	HR	HB	BB	SO	RAT	ERA	ERA+	OAV	OOB	BH	AVG	PB	PR	PR+	PD	TPI
1977	NY-N	0	0	—	3	0	0	0	0	4	2	2	0	0	2	1	9.0	0.00	—	.133	.235	0	—	0	2	2	-0	0.1
1979	NY-N	0	2	.000	4	3	0	0	0	16^{1}	16	8	0	0	4	12	11.0	4.41	83	.246	.290	0	.000	-0	-1	-1	-0	-0.2
1980	NY-N	3	4	.429	32	15	0	0	0	84	89	51	5	2	59	68	16.1	5.14	69	.280	.396	2	.100	-1	-14	-15	-0	-1.3
1982	NY-A	0	1	.000	3	1	0	0	0	10	13	8	0	1	9	2	20.7	7.20	55	.342	.479	0	—	0	-3	-4	-0	-0.3
	Min-A	1	2	.333	21	1	0	0	2	51^{2}	61	48	14	0	37	20	17.1	7.32	58	.299	.407	0	—	0	-19	-17	-1	-1.1
	Yr	1	3	.250	24	2	0	0	2	61^{2}	74	56	14	1	46	22	17.7	7.30	58	.306	.419	0	—	0	-22	-21	-2	-1.4
1984	Bal-A	0	1	.000	6	1	0	0	0	14^{2}	15	13	2	0	9	8	14.7	6.75	57	.268	.369	0	—	0	-4	-5	-0	-0.3
1986	Det-A	0	0	—	5	0	0	0	1	11	10	5	0	0	13	5	18.8	4.09	101	.294	.489	0	—	0	0	0	1	0.1
Total	6	4	10	.286	74	21	0	0	3	191^{2}	206	135	21	3	133	116	16.1	5.73	67	.282	.395	2	.083	-1	-40	-40	-2	-3.0

YEAR TM/L	W	L	PCT	G	GS	CG	SH	SV	IP	H	R	HR	HB	BB	SO	RAT	ERA	ERA+	OAV	OOB	BH	AVG	PB	PR	PR+	PD	TPI
● ALEX PACHECO Pacheco, Alexander Melchor (Lara) b: 7/19/73, Caracas, Venez. BR/TR, 6'3", 200 lbs. Deb: 4/17/96																											
1996 Mon-N	0	0	—	5	0	0	0	0	5^{2}	8	7	2	0	1	7	14.3	11.12	39	.320	.346	0	—	0	-4	-4	-0	-0.2
● PAT PACILLO Pacillo, Patrick Michael b: 7/23/63, Jersey City, N.J. BR/TR, 6'2", 205 lbs. Deb: 5/23/87																											
1987 Cin-N	3	3	.500	12	7	0	0	0	39^{2}	41	30	7	1	19	23	13.8	6.13	69	.270	.355	1	.091	-0	-9	-8	-0	-1.1
1988 Cin-N	1	0	1.000	6	0	0	0	0	10^{2}	14	7	2	0	4	11	15.2	5.06	71	.318	.375	0	.000	-0	-2	-2	-0	-0.2
Total 2	4	3	.571	18	7	0	0	0	50^{1}	55	37	9	1	23	34	14.1	5.90	70	.281	.359	1	.083	-0	-11	-10	-1	-1.3
● GENE PACKARD Packard, Eugene Milo b: 7/13/1887, Colorado Springs, Colorado d: 5/18/59, Riverside, Cal. BL/TL, 5'10", 155 lbs. Deb: 9/27/12																											
1912 Cin-N	1	0	1.000	1	1	1	0	0	9	7	3	0	0	4	2	11.0	3.00	112	.206	.289	1	.250	1	0	0	0	0.1
1913 Cin-N	7	11	.389	39	21	9	2	0	190^{2}	208	97	2	8	64	73	13.2	2.97	109	.286	.350	11	.180	-0	5	6	-1	0.4
1914 KC-F	20	14	.588	42	34	24	4	5	302	282	127	5	3	88	154	11.1	2.89	96	.246	.301	28	.241	2	-0	-4	9	0.7
1915 KC-F	20	12	.625	42	31	21	5	2	281^{2}	250	111	3	9	74	108	10.6	2.68	98	.242	.298	22	.232	2	1	-2	7	0.7
1916 Chi-N	10	6	.625	37	16	5	2	5	155^{1}	154	60	4	3	38	36	11.3	2.78	105	.256	.304	7	.130	-1	-3	2	5	0.7
1917 Chi-N	0	0	—	2	0	0	0	0	1^{2}	3	2	1	0	0	1	16.2	10.80	27	.375	.375	0	—	0	-1	-1	0	-0.1
StL-N	9	6	.600	34	11	6	0	2	153^{1}	138	48	4	3	25	44	9.7	2.47	109	.246	.281	15	.288	3	4	4	-1	0.7
Yr	9	6	.600	36	11	6	0	2	155	141	50	5	3	25	45	9.8	2.55	105	.247	.283	15	.288	3	3	2	-0	0.6
1918 StL-N	12	12	.500	30	23	10	1	2	182^{1}	184	84	6	5	33	46	11.0	3.50	77	.266	.304	12	.174	-1	-15	-16	-1	-2.3
1919 Phi-N	6	8	.429	21	16	10	1	1	134^{1}	167	70	3	4	30	24	13.5	4.15	78	.321	.363	7	.137	-2	-19	-13	-0	-1.5
Total 8	85	69	.552	248	153	86	15	17	1410^{1}	1393	602	28	35	356	488	11.4	3.01	95	.262	.312	103	.205	4	-27	-24	17	-0.6
● JOE PACTWA Pactwa, Joseph Martin b: 6/2/48, Hammond, Ind. BL/TL, 5'11", 185 lbs. Deb: 9/15/75																											
1975 Cal-A	1	0	1.000	4	3	0	0	0	16^{1}	23	7	0	0	10	3	18.2	3.86	92	.343	.429	0	—	0	-0	-1	-0	-0.1
● VICENTE PADILLA Padilla, Vicente De La Cruz b: 9/27/77, Chinandega, Nic. BR/TR, 6'2", 200 lbs. Deb: 6/29/99																											
1999 Ari-N	0	1	.000	5	0	0	0	0	2^{2}	7	5	1	0	3	0	33.8	16.88	27	.467	.556	0	—	0	-4	-4	-0	-0.7
2000 Ari-N	2	1	.667	27	0	0	0	0	35	32	10	0	0	10	30	10.8	2.31	199	.242	.296	1	1.000	0	9	9	-0	0.7
Phi-N	2	6	.250	28	0	0	0	2	30^{1}	40	23	3	1	18	21	17.5	5.34	88	.328	.418	0	—	0	-2	-2	-2	-0.6
Yr	4	7	.364	55	0	0	0	2	65^{1}	72	33	3	1	28	51	13.9	3.72	125	.283	.357	1	1.000	0	7	7	-2	0.1
Total 2	4	8	.333	60	0	0	0	2	68	79	38	4	1	31	51	14.7	4.24	110	.294	.369	1	1.000	0	3	3	-3	-0.6
● DAVE PAGAN Pagan, David Percy b: 9/15/49, Nipawin, Sask., Canada BR/TR, 6'2", 175 lbs. Deb: 7/1/73																											
1973 NY-A	0	0	—	4	1	0	0	0	12^{2}	16	4	1	0	1	9	12.1	2.84	129	.320	.333	0	—	0	1	1	0	0.1
1974 NY-A	1	3	.250	16	6	1	0	0	49^{1}	49	29	1	0	28	39	14.0	5.11	69	.265	.362	0	—	0	-8	-9	-0	-0.7
1975 NY-A	0	0	—	13	0	0	0	1	31	30	16	2	2	13	18	13.1	4.06	91	.256	.341	0	—	0	-1	-1	-1	-0.1
1976 NY-A	1	1	.500	7	2	1	0	0	23^{2}	18	7	0	0	4	13	8.4	2.28	150	.222	.259	0	—	0	3	3	-1	0.2
Bal-A	1	4	.200	20	5	0	0	1	46^{2}	54	33	2	1	23	34	15.0	5.98	55	.298	.380	0	—	0	-13	-15	-1	-1.6
Yr	2	5	.286	27	7	1	0	1	70^{1}	72	40	2	1	27	47	12.8	4.73	70	.275	.345	0	—	0	-9	-12	-2	-1.4
1977 Sea-A	1	1	.500	24	4	1	1	2	66	86	52	3	2	26	30	15.5	6.14	67	.323	.388	0	—	0	-15	-15	-0	-0.7
Pit-N	0	0	—	1	0	0	0	0	3	1	0	0	0	0	4	3.0	0.00	—	.100	.100	0	—	0	1	1	0	0.1
Total 5	4	9	.308	85	18	3	1	4	232^{1}	254	141	9	5	95	147	13.7	4.96	74	.285	.358	0	—	0	-31	-34	-2	-2.7
● JOE PAGE Page, Joseph Francis "Fireman" b: 10/28/17, Cherry Valley, Pa. d: 4/21/80, Latrobe, Pa. BL/TL, 6'2", 205 lbs. Deb: 4/19/44																											
1944 NY-A☆	5	7	.417	19	16	4	0	0	102^{2}	100	65	3	3	52	63	13.6	4.56	76	.258	.351	5	.156	-0	-13	-12	-1	-1.4
1945 NY-A	6	3	.667	20	9	4	0	0	102	95	43	1	0	46	50	12.4	2.82	123	.246	.326	9	.250	1	6	7	-2	0.5
1946 NY-A	9	8	.529	31	17	6	1	3	136	126	66	7	4	72	77	13.4	3.57	97	.252	.351	7	.163	-0	-1	-2	-1	-0.3
1947 *NY-A★	14	8	.636	56	2	0	0	**17**	141^{1}	105	41	5	1	72	116	11.3	2.48	142	.208	.308	10	.217	1	**19**	**17**	-1	3.2
1948 NY-A☆	7	8	.467	**55**	1	0	0	16	107^{2}	116	59	6	1	66	77	15.3	4.26	96	.275	.374	7	.292	3	0	-2	-1	-0.1
1949 *NY-A	13	8	.619	**60**	0	0	0	**27**	135^{1}	103	44	8	5	75	99	12.2	2.59	156	.215	.328	7	.175	-1	**24**	**23**	-2	3.9
1950 NY-A	3	7	.300	37	0	0	0	13	55^{1}	66	34	8	0	31	33	15.8	5.04	85	.295	.380	2	.250	1	-3	-5	-1	-0.9
1954 Pit-N	0	0	—	7	0	0	0	0	9^{2}	16	17	4	1	7	4	22.3	11.17	37	.364	.462	0	—	0	-8	-7	0	-0.4
Total 8	57	49	.538	285	45	14	1	76	790	727	369	42	15	421	519	13.2	3.53	106	.247	.344	47	.205	5	25	18	-7	4.5
● PHIL PAGE Page, Philippe Rausac b: 8/23/05, Springfield, Mass. d: 7/27/58, Springfield, Mass BR/TL, 6'2", 175 lbs. Deb: 9/18/28 C																											
1928 Det-A	2	0	1.000	3	2	2	0	0	22	21	9	1	0	10	3	12.7	2.45	167	.256	.337	2	.222	-0	4	4	1	0.4
1929 Det-A	0	2	.000	10	4	1	0	0	25^{1}	29	24	1	1	19	6	17.4	8.17	53	.296	.415	1	.125	-1	-11	-11	-1	-0.8
1930 Det-A	0	1	.000	12	0	0	0	0	12	23	16	1	0	9	2	24.0	9.75	49	.434	.516	0	—	0	-7	-6	0	-0.4
1934 Bro-N	1	0	1.000	6	0	0	0	0	10	13	7	1	0	6	4	17.1	5.40	72	.342	.432	0	.000	-0	-1	-2	1	-0.1
Total 4	3	3	.500	31	6	3	0	0	69^{1}	86	56	4	1	44	15	17.0	6.23	68	.317	.415	3	.167	-1	-15	-15	1	-0.9
● SAM PAGE Page, Samuel Walter b: 2/11/16, Woodruff, S.C. BL/TR, 6', 172 lbs. Deb: 9/11/39																											
1939 Phi-A	0	3	.000	4	3	1	0	0	22	34	27	1	0	15	11	20.0	6.95	68	.343	.430	3	.429	1	-6	-5	1	-0.4
● VANCE PAGE Page, Vance Linwood b: 9/15/05, Elm City, N.C. d: 7/14/51, Wilson, N.C. BR/TR, 6', 180 lbs. Deb: 8/6/38																											
1938 *Chi-N	5	4	.556	13	9	3	0	1	68	90	33	4	0	13	18	13.6	3.84	100	.323	.353	4	.154	-1	-0	-0	3	0.1
1939 Chi-N	7	7	.500	27	17	8	1	1	139^{1}	169	77	8	1	37	43	13.4	3.88	102	.298	.342	12	.255	3	1	1	1	0.4
1940 Chi-N	1	3	.250	30	1	0	0	2	59	65	38	1	0	26	22	13.9	4.42	85	.271	.342	4	.308	2	-4	-5	0	-0.1
1941 Chi-N	2	2	.500	25	3	1	0	1	48^{1}	48	24	2	2	30	17	14.9	4.28	82	.254	.362	2	.286	1	-3	-4	0	-0.2
Total 4	15	16	.484	95	30	12	1	5	314^{2}	372	172	15	3	106	100	13.8	4.03	95	.292	.348	22	.237	4	-7	-8	4	0.2
● PAT PAIGE Paige, George Lynn "Piggy" b: 5/5/1882, Paw Paw, Mich. d: 6/8/39, Berlin, Wis. BL/TR, 5'10", 175 lbs. Deb: 5/20/11																											
1911 Cle-A	1	0	1.000	2	1	1	0	0	16	21	12	0	0	7	6	15.8	4.50	76	.339	.406	1	.143	-0	-2	-2	1	-0.1
● SATCHEL PAIGE Paige, Leroy Robert b: 7/7/06, Mobile, Ala. d: 6/8/82, Kansas City, Mo. BR/TR, 6'3.5", 180 lbs. Deb: 7/9/48 CH																											
1948 *Cle-A	6	1	.857	21	7	3	2	1	72^{2}	61	21	2	1	22	43	10.4	2.48	164	.228	.290	2	.087	-2	15	13	-0	1.0
1949 Cle-A	4	7	.364	31	5	1	0	5	83	70	29	4	1	33	54	11.3	3.04	131	.230	.308	1	.063	-1	11	9	-1	1.0
1951 StL-A	3	4	.429	23	3	0	0	5	62	67	39	6	1	29	48	14.1	4.79	92	.276	.355	2	.125	-2	-5	-3	-1	-0.5
1952 StL-A☆	12	10	.545	46	6	3	2	10	138	116	51	5	3	57	91	11.5	3.07	128	.226	.307	5	.128	-2	9	12	0	1.9
1953 StL-A★	3	9	.250	57	4	0	0	11	117^{1}	114	51	12	1	39	51	11.8	3.53	119	.257	.319	2	.069	-3	6	8	-2	0.5
1965 KC-A	0	0	—	1	1	0	0	0	3	1	0	0	0	0	1	3.0	0.00	—	.100	.100	0	.000	-0	1	1	-0	0.0
Total 6	28	31	.475	179	26	7	4	32	476	429	191	29	7	180	288	11.6	3.29	124	.241	.313	12	.097	-10	37	41	-3	3.9
● PHIL PAINE Paine, Phillips Steere "Flip" b: 6/8/30, Chepachet, R.I. d: 2/19/78, Lebanon, Pa. BR/TR, 6'2", 181 lbs. Deb: 7/14/51																											
1951 Bos-N	2	0	1.000	21	0	0	0	0	35^{1}	36	15	2	4	20	17	15.3	3.06	120	.271	.382	0	.000	-1	4	3	-0	0.1
1954 Mil-N	1	0	1.000	11	0	0	0	0	14	14	9	1	1	12	11	17.4	3.86	97	.292	.443	0	—	0	0	-0	-0	-0.1
1955 Mil-N	2	0	1.000	15	0	0	0	0	25^{1}	20	8	2	0	14	26	12.1	2.49	151	.225	.330	1	.333	0	4	4	0	0.3
1956 Mil-N	0	0	—	1	0	0	0	0	0	3	0	0	0	—	—	∞	—	1.000	1.000	92	—	0	-2	-2	0	-0.2	
1957 Mil-N	0	0	—	1	0	0	0	0	2	1	0	0	0	3	2	18.0	0.00	—	.143	.400	0	—	0	1	1	0	0.1
1958 StL-N	5	1	.833	46	0	0	0	1	73^{1}	70	33	7	5	31	45	13.0	3.56	116	.256	.343	2	.286	0	3	4	0	0.4
Total 6	10	1	.909	95	0	0	0	1	150	144	67	12	10	80	101	14.0	3.36	116	.260	.364	3	.214	-0	10	9	-0	0.6
● LANCE PAINTER Painter, Lance Telford b: 7/21/67, Bedford, England BL/TL, 6'1", 195 lbs. Deb: 5/19/93																											
1993 Col-N	2	2	.500	10	6	1	0	0	39	52	26	5	0	9	16	14.1	6.00	80	.333	.370	3	.300	1	-8	-4	0	-0.3
1994 Col-N	4	6	.400	15	14	0	0	0	73^{2}	91	51	9	1	26	41	14.4	6.11	81	.302	.360	3	.143	-1	-15	-8	0	-1.0
1995 *Col-N	3	0	1.000	33	1	0	0	1	45^{1}	55	23	9	2	10	36	13.3	4.37	124	.296	.338	1	.111	-0	-1	4	0	0.2
1996 Col-N	4	2	.667	34	1	0	0	0	50^{2}	56	37	12	3	25	48	14.9	5.86	89	.280	.368	2	.133	-1	-9	-3	-0	-0.4
1997 StL-N	1	1	.500	14	0	0	0	0	17	13	9	1	0	8	11	11.1	4.76	87	.213	.304	0	.000	-0	-1	-1	1	-0.1
1998 StL-N	4	0	1.000	65	0	0	0	1	47^{1}	42	24	5	4	28	39	14.1	3.99	105	.249	.368	1	1.000	0	1	1	2	0.3
1999 StL-N	4	5	.444	56	4	0	0	1	63^{1}	63	37	6	2	25	56	12.8	4.83	95	.265	.340	0	.000	-1	-2	-2	1	-0.2
2000 Tor-A	2	0	1.000	42	2	0	0	0	66^{2}	69	37	9	2	22	53	12.6	4.72	106	.271	.333	0	—	0	1	2	2	0.3
Total 8	24	16	.600	269	28	1	0	3	403	441	244	56	14	153	300	13.6	5.14	95	.282	.351	10	.156	-1	-34	-11	5	-1.2

● VICENTE PALACIOS

Palacios, Vicente (Diaz) b: 7/19/63, Veracruz, Mex. BR/TR, 6'3", 195 lbs. Deb: 9/4/87

YEAR TM/L	W	L	PCT	G	GS	CG	SH	SV	IP	H	R	HR	HB	BB	SO	RAT	ERA	ERA+	OAV	OOB	BH	AVG	PB	PR	PR+	PD	TPI
1987 Pit-N	2	1	.667	6	4	0	0	0	29^1	27	14	1	1	9	13	11.4	4.30	96	.250	.314	1	.111	-0	-1	-1	-1	-0.2
1988 Pit-N	1	2	.333	7	3	0	0	0	24^1	28	18	3	0	15	15	15.9	6.66	51	.295	.391	0	.000	-0	-9	-9	0	-1.0
1990 Pit-N	0	0	—	7	0	0	0	3	15	4	0	0	0	2	8	3.6	0.00	—	.083	.120	0	.000	-0	6	6	0	0.3
1991 Pit-N	6	3	.667	36	7	1	1	3	81^2	69	34	12	1	38	64	11.9	3.75	95	.228	.316	1	.071	-1	-1	-2	-1	-0.3
1992 Pit-N	3	2	.600	20	8	0	0	0	53	56	25	1	0	27	33	14.1	4.25	81	.280	.366	1	.071	-1	-4	-5	-0	-0.5
1994 StL-N	3	8	.273	31	17	1	1	1	117^2	104	60	16	3	43	95	11.5	4.44	94	.245	.319	0	.000	-4	-3	-4	-0	-0.7
1995 StL-N	2	3	.400	20	5	0	0	0	40^1	48	29	7	2	19	34	15.4	5.80	72	.300	.381	1	.167	-0	-7	-7	-0	-0.8
2000 SD-N	0	1	.000	7	0	0	0	0	10^2	12	10	4	0	5	8	14.3	6.75	65	.308	.386	0	—	0	-3	-3	0	-0.2
Total 8	17	20	.459	134	44	2	2	7	372	348	190	44	7	158	270	12.4	4.43	87	.253	.333	4	.045	-6	-20	-24	-1	-3.4

● MIKE PALAGYI

Palagyi, Michael Raymond b: 7/4/17, Conneaut, Ohio BR/TR, 6'2", 185 lbs. Deb: 8/18/39

YEAR TM/L	W	L	PCT	G	GS	CG	SH	SV	IP	H	R	HR	HB	BB	SO	RAT	ERA	ERA+	OAV	OOB	BH	AVG	PB	PR	PR+	PD	TPI
1939 Was-A	0	0	—	1	0	0	0	0	0	0	0	1	3	—	—	∞	—	—	1.000	94	—	0	-3	-3		0	-0.3

● ERV PALICA

Palica, Ervin Martin (b: Ervin Martin Pavliecivich)
b: 2/9/28, Lomita, Cal. d: 5/29/82, Huntington Beach, Cal. BR/TR, 6'1.5", 180 lbs. Deb: 4/21/45 ♦

YEAR TM/L	W	L	PCT	G	GS	CG	SH	SV	IP	H	R	HR	HB	BB	SO	RAT	ERA	ERA+	OAV	OOB	BH	AVG	PB	PR	PR+	PD	TPI
1947 Bro-N	0	1	.000	3	0	0	0	0	3	2	1	0	1	2	1	15.0	3.00	138	.182	.357	0	—	0	0	0	-0	0.1
1948 Bro-N	6	6	.500	41	10	3	0	3	125^1	111	63	13	3	58	74	12.4	4.45	90	.239	.327	5	.128	0	-7	-6	-1	-0.7
1949 *Bro-N	8	9	.471	49	1	0	0	6	97	93	43	6	1	49	44	13.3	3.62	113	.261	.352	3	.158	0	5	5	-0	0.9
1950 Bro-N	13	8	.619	43	19	10	2	1	201^1	176	89	13	2	98	131	12.3	3.58	115	.237	.327	15	.221	2	13	12	-4	0.9
1951 Bro-N	2	6	.250	19	8	0	0	0	53	55	28	10	0	20	15	12.7	4.75	83	.259	.323	2	.154	0	-5	-5	1	-0.6
1953 Bro-N	0	0	—	4	0	0	0	0	6	10	8	1	0	8	3	27.0	12.00	36	.370	.514	1	1.000	0	-5	-5	-0	-0.2
1954 Bro-N	3	3	.500	25	3	0	0	0	67^2	77	45	9	1	31	25	14.5	5.32	77	.285	.361	4	.250	1	-9	-9	-2	-0.8
1955 Bal-A	5	11	.313	33	25	5	1	2	169^2	165	91	10	2	83	68	13.3	4.14	92	.260	.348	13	.236	2	-3	-6	-1	-0.4
1956 Bal-A	4	11	.267	29	14	2	0	0	116^1	117	64	10	1	50	62	13.0	4.49	87	.264	.339	5	.156	-2	-4	-8	-0	-1.0
Total 9	41	55	.427	246	80	20	3	12	839^1	806	432	72	11	399	423	13.0	4.22	94	.255	.340	48	.198	5	-16	-22	-7	-1.8

● DONN PALL

Pall, Donn Steven b: 1/11/62, Chicago, Ill. BR/TR, 6'1", 183 lbs. Deb: 8/1/88

YEAR TM/L	W	L	PCT	G	GS	CG	SH	SV	IP	H	R	HR	HB	BB	SO	RAT	ERA	ERA+	OAV	OOB	BH	AVG	PB	PR	PR+	PD	TPI
1988 Chi-A	0	2	.000	17	0	0	0	0	28^2	39	11	1	0	8	16	14.8	3.45	115	.328	.370	0	—	0	2	2	1	0.2
1989 Chi-A	4	5	.444	53	0	0	0	6	87	90	35	9	8	19	58	12.1	3.31	115	.270	.325	0	—	0	6	5	-1	0.4
1990 Chi-A	3	5	.375	56	0	0	0	2	76	63	33	7	4	24	39	10.8	3.32	116	.232	.303	0	—	0	5	4	-0	0.4
1991 Chi-A	7	2	.778	51	0	0	0	0	71	59	22	7	3	20	40	10.4	2.41	165	.231	.295	0	—	0	13	13	-1	1.4
1992 Chi-A	5	2	.714	39	0	0	0	1	73	79	43	9	2	27	27	13.3	4.93	78	.272	.339	0	—	0	-8	-9	-1	-0.9
1993 Chi-A	2	3	.400	39	0	0	0	1	58^2	62	25	5	2	11	29	11.5	3.22	130	.268	.307	0	—	0	7	7	0	0.6
Phi-N	1	0	1.000	8	0	0	0	0	17^2	15	7	1	0	3	11	9.2	2.55	156	.231	.265	0	—	0	3	3	-0	0.1
1994 NY-A	1	2	.333	26	0	0	0	0	35	43	18	3	1	9	21	13.6	3.60	127	.295	.340	0	—	0	5	4	0	0.3
Chi-N	0	0	—	2	0	0	0	0	4	8	2	1	0	1	2	20.3	4.50	92	.444	.474	0	—	0	-0	-0	-0	0.0
1996 Fla-N	1	1	.500	12	0	0	0	0	18^2	16	15	3	0	9	9	12.1	5.79	70	.232	.321	0	.000	0	-3	-4	-0	-0.4
1997 Fla-N	0	0	—	2	0	0	0	0	2^1	3	1	1	0	1	0	15.4	3.86	105	.300	.364	0	.000	-0	0	0	-0	0.0
1998 Fla-N	0	1	.000	23	0	0	0	0	33^1	42	19	5	1	7	26	13.5	5.13	79	.326	.365	0	.000	-0	-3	-4	0	-0.2
Total 10	24	23	.511	328	0	0	0	10	505^1	519	231	52	21	139	278	12.1	3.63	110	.268	.324	0	.000	-0	26	21	-2	1.9

● MIKE PALM

Palm, Richard Paul b: 2/13/25, Boston, Mass. BR/TR, 6'3.5", 190 lbs. Deb: 7/11/48

YEAR TM/L	W	L	PCT	G	GS	CG	SH	SV	IP	H	R	HR	HB	BB	SO	RAT	ERA	ERA+	OAV	OOB	BH	AVG	PB	PR	PR+	PD	TPI
1948 Bos-A	0	0	—	3	0	0	0	0	3	6	2	0	0	5	1	33.0	6.00	73	.400	.550	0	.000	-0	-1	-1	-0	-0.1

● PALMER

Palmer b: St.Louis, Mo. Deb: 5/28/1885

YEAR TM/L	W	L	PCT	G	GS	CG	SH	SV	IP	H	R	HR	HB	BB	SO	RAT	ERA	ERA+	OAV	OOB	BH	AVG	PB	PR	PR+	PD	TPI
1885 StL-N	0	4	.000	4	4	4	0	0	34	46	33	2		20	9	17.5	3.44	80	.311	.393	1	.091	-0	-2	-3	-1	-0.4

● DAVID PALMER

Palmer, David William b: 10/19/57, Glens Falls, N.Y. BR/TR, 6'1", 205 lbs. Deb: 9/9/78

YEAR TM/L	W	L	PCT	G	GS	CG	SH	SV	IP	H	R	HR	HB	BB	SO	RAT	ERA	ERA+	OAV	OOB	BH	AVG	PB	PR	PR+	PD	TPI
1978 Mon-N	0	1	.000	5	1	0	0	0	9^2	9	4	1	0	2	7	10.2	2.79	126	.243	.282	0	.000	-0	1	1	1	0.1
1979 Mon-N	10	2	.833	36	11	2	1	2	122^2	110	41	10	2	30	72	10.4	2.64	139	.237	.286	1	.032	-3	15	14	-0	1.1
1980 Mon-N	8	6	.571	24	19	3	1	0	129^2	124	53	11	2	30	73	10.8	2.98	120	.255	.301	9	.200	1	9	9	1	1.2
1982 Mon-N	6	4	.600	13	13	1	0	0	73^2	60	34	3	2	36	46	12.0	3.18	115	.224	.320	1	.042	-2	4	4	0	0.3
1984 Mon-N	7	3	.700	20	19	1	0	0	105^1	101	45	5	0	44	66	12.4	3.84	89	.256	.331	5	.152	1	-3	-5	-0	-0.3
1985 Mon-N	7	10	.412	24	23	0	0	0	135^2	128	60	5	3	67	106	13.1	3.71	91	.250	.341	4	.111	-1	-2	-5	2	-0.5
1986 Atl-N	11	10	.524	35	35	2	0	0	209^2	181	98	17	5	102	170	12.4	3.65	109	.234	.327	12	.182	1	2	7	2	1.0
1987 Atl-N	8	11	.421	28	28	0	0	0	152^1	169	94	17	7	64	111	14.2	4.90	89	.281	.357	6	.125	-0	-14	-9	1	-0.9
1988 Phi-N	7	9	.438	22	22	1	1	0	129	129	67	8	0	48	85	12.3	4.47	80	.261	.327	10	.256	5	-15	-12	-1	-1.0
1989 Det-A	0	3	.000	5	5	0	0	0	17^1	25	19	1	0	11	12	18.7	7.79	49	.342	.429	0	—	0	-8	-8	-0	-1.1
Total 10	64	59	.520	212	176	10	4	2	1085	1036	515	78	21	434	748	12.4	3.78	99	.252	.327	48	.149	2	-10	-5	5	-0.1

● JIM PALMER

Palmer, James Alvin b: 10/15/45, New York, N.Y. BR/TR, 6'3", 196 lbs. Deb: 4/17/65 H

YEAR TM/L	W	L	PCT	G	GS	CG	SH	SV	IP	H	R	HR	HB	BB	SO	RAT	ERA	ERA+	OAV	OOB	BH	AVG	PB	PR	PR+	PD	TPI
1965 Bal-A	5	4	.556	27	6	0	0	1	92	75	49	6	2	56	75	13.0	3.72	93	.229	.345	5	.192	1	-3	-3	0	-0.1
1966 *Bal-A	15	10	.600	30	30	6	0	0	208^1	176	83	21	0	91	147	11.5	3.46	96	.231	.313	7	.096	-2	-0	-3	-1	-0.7
1967 Bal-A	3	1	.750	9	9	2	1	0	49	34	18	6	0	20	23	9.9	2.94	107	.199	.283	1	.077	0	2	1	0	0.1
1969 *Bal-A	16	4	**.800**	26	23	11	6	0	181	131	48	11	1	64	123	9.7	2.34	153	.200	.272	13	.203	2	26	25	-4	2.6
1970 *Bal-A★	20	10	.667	39	39	17	**5**	0	**305**	263	98	21	1	100	199	10.7	2.71	134	.231	.294	17	.150	-1	**34**	32	-0	2.9
1971 *Bal-A★	20	9	.690	37	37	20	3	0	282	231	94	19	4	106	184	10.9	2.68	125	.221	.295	20	.196	2	25	22	0	2.5
1972 Bal-A★	21	10	.677	36	36	18	3	0	274^1	219	73	21	1	70	184	9.5	2.07	149	.217	.269	22	.224	4	31	31	-1	4.2
1973 *Bal-A	22	9	.710	38	37	19	6	1	296^1	225	86	16	3	113	158	10.4	**2.40**	156	.211	.289	0	—	0	47	45	-1	4.5
1974 *Bal-A	7	12	.368	26	26	5	2	0	178^2	176	78	12	3	69	84	12.5	3.27	106	.257	.328	0	—	0	7	4	2	0.6
1975 Bal-A☆	**23**	11	.676	39	38	25	**10**	1	323	253	87	20	2	80	193	9.3	**2.09**	**168**	.216	.267	0	—	0	**61**	**55**	2	**6.1**
1976 Bal-A	**22**	13	.629	40	40	23	6	0	**315**	255	101	20	8	84	159	9.9	2.51	130	.224	.282	0	—	0	35	29	1	3.3
1977 Bal-A★	**20**	11	.645	39	39	**22**	3	0	**319**	263	106	24	3	99	193	10.3	2.91	131	.229	.292	0	—	0	41	34	0	3.1
1978 Bal-A★	21	12	.636	38	38	19	6	0	**296**	246	94	19	1	97	138	10.5	2.46	142	.227	.291	0	—	0	43	37	1	4.2
1979 *Bal-A	10	6	.625	23	22	7	0	0	155^2	144	66	12	0	43	67	10.8	3.30	122	.246	.297	0	—	0	16	13	-0	1.2
1980 Bal-A	16	10	.615	34	33	4	0	0	224	238	108	26	3	74	109	12.7	3.98	100	.275	.334	0	—	0	2	-0	1	0.1
1981 Bal-A	7	8	.467	22	22	5	0	0	127^1	117	60	14	2	46	35	11.7	3.75	97	.247	.316	0	—	0	-1	-2	1	0.0
1982 Bal-A	15	5	**.750**	36	32	8	2	1	227	195	85	22	4	63	103	**10.4**	3.13	129	.231	**.287**	0	—	0	24	23	1	2.0
1983 *Bal-A	5	4	.556	14	11	0	0	0	76^2	86	42	11	0	19	34	12.3	4.23	94	.281	.323	0	—	0	-1	-2	1	-0.3
1984 Bal-A	0	3	.000	5	3	0	0	0	17^2	22	19	2	0	17	4	19.9	9.17	42	.319	.453	0	—	0	-10	-11	0	-1.4
Total 19	268	152	.638	558	521	211	53	4	3948	3349	1395	303	38	1311	2212	10.7	2.86	125	.230	.296	85	.174	7	378	330	3	34.9

● LOWELL PALMER

Palmer, Lowell Raymond b: 8/18/47, Sacramento, Cal. BR/TR, 6'1", 190 lbs. Deb: 6/21/69

YEAR TM/L	W	L	PCT	G	GS	CG	SH	SV	IP	H	R	HR	HB	BB	SO	RAT	ERA	ERA+	OAV	OOB	BH	AVG	PB	PR	PR+	PD	TPI
1969 Phi-N	2	8	.200	26	9	1	1	0	90	91	54	12	6	47	68	14.4	5.20	68	.264	.362	3	.136	1	-16	-17	-0	-1.6
1970 Phi-N	1	2	.333	38	5	0	0	0	102	98	66	15	5	55	85	13.9	5.47	73	.255	.355	4	.148	1	-16	-17	-1	-0.8
1971 Phi-N	0	0	—	3	1	0	0	0	15	13	11	3	4	13	6	18.0	6.00	59	.236	.417	1	.200	-0	-4	-4	-0	-0.2
1972 StL-N	0	3	.000	16	2	0	0	0	34^2	30	16	2	1	26	25	14.8	3.89	87	.244	.380	0	.000	-1	-2	-2	0	-0.2
Cle-A	0	0	—	1	0	0	0	0	2	2	1	0	0	2	3	18.0	4.50	72	.222	.364	0	—	0	-0	-0	-0	0.0
1974 SD-N	2	5	.286	22	8	1	0	0	73	68	48	9	7	59	52	16.5	5.67	63	.256	.404	2	.087	-1	-17	-17	-1	-1.7
Total 5	5	18	.217	106	25	2	1	0	316^2	302	196	41	23	202	239	15.0	5.29	70	.255	.374	10	.122	-0	-55	-57	-1	-4.5

● EMILIO PALMERO

Palmero, Emilio Antonio "Pal"
b: 6/13/1895, Guanabacoa, Cuba d: 7/15/70, Toledo, Ohio BL/TL (BB 1915-16), 5'11", 157 lbs. Deb: 9/21/15

YEAR TM/L	W	L	PCT	G	GS	CG	SH	SV	IP	H	R	HR	HB	BB	SO	RAT	ERA	ERA+	OAV	OOB	BH	AVG	PB	PR	PR+	PD	TPI
1915 NY-N	0	2	.000	3	2	1	0	0	11^2	10	4	0	3	9	8	17.0	3.09	83	.233	.400	1	.250	0	-0	-1	0	-0.1
1916 NY-N	0	3	.000	4	2	0	0	0	15^2	17	14	2	1	8	8	14.9	8.04	30	.288	.382	0	.000	-0	-9	-11	1	-1.6
1921 StL-A	4	7	.364	24	9	4	0	0	90	109	63	1	6	49	26	16.4	5.00	90	.319	.413	8	.216	1	-3	-5	1	-0.3
1926 Was-A	2	2	.500	7	3	0	0	0	17	22	15	1	1	15	6	20.1	4.76	81	.344	.475	1	.333	0	-1	-2	-0	-0.3
1928 Bos-N	0	1	.000	3	1	0	0	0	6^2	14	8	0	0	2	0	21.6	5.40	72	.452	.485	0	.000	-0	-1	-1	-0	-0.2
Total 5	6	15	.286	41	17	5	0	0	141	172	104	4	11	83	48	17.0	5.17	77	.319	.420	10	.208	1	-19	-19	2	-2.5

YEAR TM/L	W	L	PCT	G	GS	CG	SH	SV	IP	H	R	HR	HB	BB	SO	RAT	ERA	ERA+	OAV	OOB	BH	AVG	PB	PR	PR+	PD	TPI
● ED PALMQUIST Palmquist, Edwin Lee b: 6/10/33, Los Angeles, Cal. BR/TR, 6'3", 195 lbs. Deb: 6/10/60																											
1960 LA-N	0	1	.000	22	0	0	0	0	39	34	16	6	1	16	23	11.8	2.54	156	.243	.325	0	.000	-1	5	6	0	0.2
1961 LA-N	0	1	.000	5	0	0	0	1	8^{2}	10	8	0	2	7	5	19.7	6.23	70	.333	.487	0	—	0	-2	-2	-0	-0.2
Min-A	1	1	.500	9	2	0	0	0	21	33	23	7	3	13	13	21.0	9.43	45	.359	.454	0	.000	-0	-13	-11	0	-0.9
Total 2	1	3	.250	36	2	0	0	1	68^{2}	77	47	13	6	36	41	15.6	5.11	80	.294	.391	0	.000	-1	-9	-7	0	-0.9
● JOSE PANIAGUA Paniagua, Jose Luis (Sanchez) b: 8/20/73, San Jose De Ocoa, D.R. BR/TR, 6'2", 185 lbs. Deb: 4/4/96																											
1996 Mon-N	2	4	.333	13	11	0	0	0	51	55	24	7	3	23	27	14.3	3.53	123	.282	.367	0	.000	-1	4	4	0	0.4
1997 Mon-N	1	2	.333	9	3	0	0	0	18	29	24	2	4	16	8	24.5	12.00	35	.372	.500	0	.000	-1	-16	-16	-0	-2.1
1998 Sea-A	2	0	1.000	18	0	0	0	1	22	15	5	3	3	5	16	9.4	2.05	227	.200	.277	0	—	0	6	6	1	0.6
1999 Sea-A	6	11	.353	59	0	0	0	3	77^{2}	75	37	5	7	52	74	15.5	4.06	117	.264	.391	0	—	0	7	6	-1	1.1
2000 *Sea-A	3	0	1.000	69	0	0	0	5	80^{1}	68	31	6	7	38	71	12.7	3.47	138	.234	.336	0	.000	-0	13	12	0	0.6
Total 5	14	17	.452	168	14	0	0	9	249	242	121	23	24	134	196	14.5	4.16	111	.262	.370	0	.000	-1	15	13	1	0.6
● JIM PANTHER Panther, James Edward b: 3/1/45, Burlington, Iowa BR/TR, 6'1", 190 lbs. Deb: 4/5/71																											
1971 Oak-A	0	1	.000	4	0	0	0	0	5^{2}	10	9	1	0	5	4	23.8	11.12	30	.385	.484	0	.000	-0	-5	-5	0	-0.8
1972 Tex-A	5	9	.357	58	4	0	0	0	93^{2}	101	55	8	5	46	44	14.6	4.13	73	.277	.365	1	.125	0	-11	-12	0	-1.7
1973 Atl-N	2	3	.400	23	0	0	0	0	30^{2}	45	26	3	0	9	8	15.8	7.63	52	.363	.406	0	—	0	-13	-12	-1	-1.8
Total 3	7	13	.350	85	4	0	0	0	130	156	90	12	5	60	56	15.3	5.26	62	.303	.381	1	.111	-0	-29	-29	-1	-4.3
● JOHN PAPA Papa, John Paul b: 12/5/40, Bridgeport, Conn. BR/TR, 5'11", 190 lbs. Deb: 4/11/61																											
1961 Bal-A	0	0	—	2	0	0	0	0	1	2	2	1	0	3	3	45.0	18.00	21	.400	.625	0	—	0	-2	-2	0	-0.1
1962 Bal-A	0	0	—	1	0	0	0	0	1	3	3	0	0	1	0	36.0	27.00	14	.600	.667	0	—	0	-3	-3	-0	-0.1
Total 2	0	0	—	3	0	0	0	0	2	5	5	1	0	4	3	40.5	22.50	17	.500	.643	0	—	0	-4	-4	-0	-0.2
● AL PAPAI Papai, Alfred Thomas b: 5/7/17, Divernon, Ill. d: 9/7/95, Springfield, Ill. BR/TR, 6'3", 185 lbs. Deb: 4/24/48																											
1948 StL-N	0	1	.000	10	0	0	0	0	16	14	10	3	0	7	8	11.8	5.06	81	.241	.323	0	.000	-0	-2	-2	0	-0.1
1949 StL-A	4	11	.267	42	15	6	0	2	142^{1}	175	103	8	1	81	31	16.3	5.06	90	.298	.384	3	.079	-2	-14	-8	3	-0.6
1950 Bos-A	4	2	.667	16	3	2	0	2	50^{2}	61	41	5	0	28	19	15.8	6.75	73	.293	.377	3	.176	-0	-12	-10	-1	-1.1
StL-N	1	0	1.000	13	0	0	0	0	19	21	12	0	0	14	7	16.6	5.21	82	.300	.417	0	.000	-0	-2	-2	0	-0.1
1955 Chi-A	0	0	—	7	0	0	0	0	11^{2}	10	5	1	0	8	5	13.9	3.86	102	.244	.367	0	.000	-0	0	0	1	0.1
Total 4	9	14	.391	88	18	8	0	4	239^{2}	281	171	17	1	138	70	15.8	5.37	84	.291	.381	6	.097	-3	-30	-21	4	-1.8
● LARRY PAPE Pape, Laurence Albert b: 7/21/1883, Norwood, Ohio d: 7/21/18, Swissvale, Pa. BR/TR, 5'11", 175 lbs. Deb: 7/6/09																											
1909 Bos-A	2	0	1.000	11	3	2	1	2	57^{1}	46	17	0	5	12	18	9.9	2.04	123	.221	.280	3	.143	-1	3	3	-3	-0.2
1911 Bos-A	10	8	.556	27	19	10	1	0	176^{1}	167	68	3	4	63	49	11.9	2.45	134	.264	.335	13	.203	-1	18	17	5	1.9
1912 Bos-A	1	1	.500	13	2	1	0	1	48^{2}	74	36	0	2	16	17	17.0	4.99	68	.366	.418	4	.235	1	-9	-8	0	-0.3
Total 3	13	9	.591	51	24	13	2	3	282^{1}	287	121	3	11	91	84	12.4	2.81	112	.275	.340	20	.196	-1	11	11	2	1.4
● FRANK PAPISH Papish, Frank Richard "Pap" b: 10/21/17, Pueblo, Colo. d: 8/30/65, Pueblo, Colo. BR/TL, 6'2", 192 lbs. Deb: 5/8/45																											
1945 Chi-A	4	4	.500	19	5	3	0	1	84^{1}	75	36	3	0	40	45	12.3	3.74	89	.241	.328	6	.231	1	-3	-4	1	-0.1
1946 Chi-A	7	5	.583	31	15	6	2	0	138	122	52	7	1	63	66	12.1	2.74	125	.243	.328	8	.186	-0	12	11	0	0.9
1947 Chi-A	12	12	.500	38	26	6	1	3	199	185	82	6	2	98	79	12.9	3.26	112	.245	.333	5	.086	-5	10	9	-1	0.4
1948 Chi-A	2	8	.200	32	14	2	0	4	95^{1}	97	65	7	3	75	41	16.5	5.00	85	.265	.394	5	.185	-1	-8	-8	-1	-0.9
1949 Cle-A	1	0	1.000	25	3	1	0	1	62	54	24	2	0	39	23	13.5	3.19	125	.240	.352	1	.125	0	7	6	0	0.3
1950 Pit-N	0	0	—	4	1	0	0	0	2^{1}	8	7	1	0	4	1	46.3	27.00	16	.533	.632	0	—	0	-6	-6	0	-0.3
Total 6	26	29	.473	149	64	18	3	9	581	541	266	26	6	319	255	13.4	3.58	103	.249	.346	25	.154	-5	12	7	0	0.3
● JOHN PAPPALAU Pappalau, John Joseph b: 4/3/1875, Albany, N.Y. d: 5/12/44, Albany, N.Y. BR/TR, 6', 175 lbs. Deb: 6/9/1897																											
1897 Cle-N	0	1	.000	2	1	1	0	0	12	22	16	0	2	6	3	22.5	10.50	43	.393	.469	0	.000	-0	-8	-8	0	-0.5
● MILT PAPPAS Pappas, Milton Stephen "Gimpy" (b: Miltiades Stergios Papastegios) b: 5/11/39, Detroit, Mich. BR/TR, 6'3", 190 lbs. Deb: 8/10/57																											
1957 Bal-A	0	0	—	4	0	0	0	0	9	6	1	0	0	3	3	9.0	1.00	359	.200	.273	0	.000	-0	3	3	0	0.1
1958 Bal-A	10	10	.500	31	21	3	0	0	135^{1}	135	67	8	2	48	72	12.3	4.06	89	.262	.327	6	.143	-0	-4	-7	1	-0.9
1959 Bal-A	15	9	.625	33	27	15	4	3	209^{1}	175	82	8	4	75	120	10.9	3.27	116	.226	.298	11	.139	-3	14	12	-1	0.9
1960 Bal-A	15	11	.577	30	27	11	3	0	205^{2}	184	81	15	6	83	126	11.9	3.37	113	.243	.323	3	.043	-5	12	10	1	0.7
1961 Bal-A	13	9	.591	26	23	11	4	1	177^{2}	134	67	16	7	78	89	11.1	3.04	127	.208	.301	9	.136	1	19	17	2	2.3
1962 Bal-A★	12	10	.545	35	32	9	1	0	205^{1}	200	105	31	2	75	130	12.1	4.03	92	.257	.324	6	.087	-0	-1	-8	2	-0.6
1963 Bal-A	16	9	.640	34	32	11	4	0	216^{2}	186	80	21	5	69	120	10.8	3.03	115	.233	.298	9	.127	-0	14	11	3	1.5
1964 Bal-A	16	7	.696	37	36	13	7	0	251^{2}	225	89	21	7	48	157	10.0	2.97	120	.239	.281	12	.129	-2	18	17	-1	1.2
1965 Bal-A★	13	9	.591	34	34	9	3	0	221^{1}	192	81	22	3	52	127	10.0	2.60	133	.233	.281	5	.071	-3	21	21	-3	1.3
1966 Cin-N	12	11	.522	33	32	6	2	0	209^{2}	224	106	23	3	39	133	11.4	4.29	91	.275	.310	8	.107	-2	-16	-8	0	-1.1
1967 Cin-N	16	13	.552	34	32	5	3	0	217^{2}	218	88	19	5	38	129	10.8	3.35	112	.259	.295	7	.097	-2	1	9	0	0.9
1968 Cin-N	2	5	.286	15	11	0	0	0	62^{2}	70	41	9	2	10	43	11.8	5.60	56	.275	.307	1	.063	-1	-18	-16	-0	-1.8
Atl-N	10	8	.556	22	19	3	1	0	121^{1}	111	36	8	3	22	75	10.1	2.37	126	.246	.285	6	.162	2	8	8	-1	1.5
Yr	12	13	.480	37	30	3	1	0	184	181	77	17	5	32	118	10.7	3.47	88	.256	.293	7	.132	1	-10	-8	-1	-0.3
1969 *Atl-N	6	10	.375	26	24	1	0	0	144	149	66	14	4	44	72	12.3	3.63	100	.267	.325	7	.156	3	-0	-0	-0	0.2
1970 Atl-N	2	2	.500	11	3	1	0	0	35^{2}	44	25	6	2	7	25	13.4	6.06	71	.293	.333	0	.000	-1	-8	-7	0	-0.7
Chi-N	10	8	.556	21	20	6	2	0	144^{2}	135	53	14	0	36	80	10.6	2.68	168	.248	.294	12	.240	4	22	26	-1	3.6
Yr	12	10	.545	32	23	7	2	0	180^{1}	179	78	20	2	43	105	11.2	3.34	134	.258	.303	12	.200	3	14	20	-1	2.9
1971 Chi-N	17	14	.548	35	35	14	**5**	0	261^{1}	279	109	25	5	62	99	11.9	3.51	112	.274	.319	14	.154	-1	-1	11	-2	0.9
1972 Chi-N	17	7	.708	29	28	10	3	0	195	187	72	18	8	29	80	10.3	2.77	138	.251	.287	13	.191	1	15	20	0	2.8
1973 Chi-N	7	12	.368	30	29	1	1	0	162	192	82	20	4	40	48	13.1	4.28	92	.299	.344	3	.063	-3	-11	-5	-1	-0.9
Total 17	209	164	.560	520	465	129	43	4	3186	3046	1331	298	72	858	1728	11.2	3.40	110	.252	.306	132	.123	-14	87	117	-0	11.9
● CHAN HO PARK Park, Chan Ho b: 6/30/73, Kongju, South Korea BR/TR, 6'2", 185 lbs. Deb: 4/8/94																											
1994 LA-N	0	0	—	2	0	0	0	0	4	5	5	1	1	5	6	24.8	11.25	35	.294	.478	0	—	0	-3	-3	-0	-0.2
1995 LA-N	0	0	—	2	1	0	0	0	4	2	2	1	0	2	7	9.0	4.50	84	.143	.250	0	.000	-0	-0	-0	-0	0.0
1996 LA-N	5	5	.500	48	10	0	0	0	108^{2}	82	48	7	4	71	119	13.0	3.64	106	.209	.335	1	.053	-1	7	3	2	0.4
1997 LA-N	14	8	.636	32	29	2	0	0	192	149	80	24	8	70	166	10.6	3.38	114	.213	.292	9	.176	3	18	11	-0	1.5
1998 LA-N	15	9	.625	34	34	2	0	0	220^{2}	199	101	16	11	97	191	12.5	3.71	107	.244	.332	14	.194	3	13	7	1	1.0
1999 LA-N	13	11	.542	33	33	0	0	0	194^{1}	208	120	31	14	100	174	14.9	5.23	82	.276	.371	9	.153	0	-14	-22	3	-1.9
2000 LA-N	18	10	.643	34	34	3	1	0	226	173	92	21	12	124	217	12.3	3.27	135	.214	.327	15	.214	5	34	30	3	4.2
Total 7	65	43	.602	185	141	7	1	0	949^{2}	818	448	101	50	469	880	12.7	3.88	106	.233	.332	48	.176	10	54	25	9	5.0
● JIM PARK Park, James b: 11/10/1892, Richmond, Ky. d: 12/17/70, Lexington, Ky. BR/TR, 6'2", 175 lbs. Deb: 9/7/15																											
1915 StL-A	2	0	1.000	3	3	1	0	0	22^{2}	18	8	1	0	9	5	10.7	1.19	240	.214	.290	4	.400	1	4	4	-1	0.5
1916 StL-A	1	4	.200	26	6	1	0	0	79	69	28	2	1	25	26	10.8	2.62	105	.244	.307	2	.100	-2	2	1	-2	-0.3
1917 StL-A	1	1	.500	13	0	0	0	0	20^{1}	27	20	1	0	12	9	17.3	6.64	39	.333	.419	0	.000	-0	-9	-9	0	-0.9
Total 3	4	5	.444	42	9	2	0	0	122	114	56	4	1	46	40	11.9	3.02	91	.254	.325	6	.188	-0	-3	-4	-2	-0.7
● DOC PARKER Parker, Harley Park b: 6/14/1872, Theresa, N.Y. d: 3/3/41, Chicago, Ill. BR/TR, 6'2", 200 lbs. Deb: 7/11/1893 F																											
1893 Chi-N	0	0	—	1	0	0	0	1	2	5	3	0	0	1	0	27.0	13.50	34	.455	.500	0	.000	-0	-2	-2	-0	-0.2
1895 Chi-N	4	2	.667	7	6	5	1	0	51^{1}	65	30	1	3	9	9	13.5	3.68	138	.304	.341	7	.318	1	6	8	0	0.8
1896 Chi-N	1	5	.167	9	7	7	0	0	73	100	71	3	3	27	15	16.0	6.16	74	.323	.382	10	.278	0	-15	-13	1	-0.7
1901 Cin-N	0	1	.000	1	1	1	0	0	8	26	21	1	0	2	0	31.5	15.75	20	.531	.549	0	.000	-0	-11	-12	-0	-0.9
Total 4	5	8	.385	18	14	13	1	1	134^{1}	196	125	5	6	39	24	16.1	5.90	79	.336	.383	17	.274	0	-21	-18	1	-1.0
● HARRY PARKER Parker, Harry William b: 9/14/47, Highland, Ill. BR/TR, 6'3", 190 lbs. Deb: 8/8/70																											
1970 StL-N	1	1	.500	7	4	0	0	0	22^{1}	24	13	0	0	15	9	15.7	3.22	128	.276	.382	2	.250	0	2	2	0	0.2
1971 StL-N	0	0	—	4	0	0	0	0	5	6	4	2	0	2	2	14.4	7.20	50	.286	.348	0	—	0	-2	-2	-0	-0.1
1973 *NY-N	8	4	.667	38	9	0	0	5	96^{2}	79	40	7	3	36	63	11.0	3.35	108	.217	.293	4	.174	-0	3	3	-0	0.3

YEAR	TM/L	W	L	PCT	G	GS	CG	SH	SV	IP	H	R	HR	HB	BB	SO	RAT	ERA	ERA+	OAV	OOB	BH	AVG	PB	PR	PR+	PD	TPI
1974	NY-N	4	12	.250	40	16	1	0	4	131	145	64	10	3	46	58	13.3	3.92	91	.281	.343	0	.000	-4	-4	-5	-2	-1.2
1975	NY-N	2	3	.400	18	1	0	0	2	34^2	37	17	2	0	19	22	14.5	4.41	78	.272	.361	0	.000	1	-3	-4	-0	-0.5
	StL-N	0	1	.000	14	0	0	0	1	18^2	21	13	3	0	10	13	14.9	6.27	60	.288	.373	0	.000	0	-5	-5	1	-0.2
	Yr	2	4	.333	32	1	0	0	3	53^1	58	30	5	0	29	35	14.7	5.06	70	.278	.366	0	.000	1	-8	-9	0	-0.7
1976	Cle-A	0	0	—	3	0	0	0	0	7	3	0	0	0	0	5	3.9	0.00	—	.136	.136	0	—	0	3	3	0	0.2
Total	6	15	21	.417	124	30	1	0	12	315^1	315	151	24	6	128	172	12.8	3.85	94	.258	.332	6	.086	-3	-7	-8	-1	-1.3
● CLAY PARKER	Parker, James Clayton b: 12/19/62, Columbia, La. BR/TR, 6'1", 185 lbs. Deb: 9/14/87																											
1987	Sea-A	0	0	—	3	1	0	0	0	7^2	15	10	2	1	4	8	23.5	10.57	45	.405	.476	0	—	0	-5	-5	0	-0.2
1989	NY-A	4	5	.444	22	17	2	0	0	120	123	53	12	2	31	53	11.7	3.68	105	.264	.313	0	—	0	3	3	0	0.2
1990	NY-A	1	1	.500	5	2	0	0	0	22	19	11	5	0	7	20	10.6	4.50	88	.229	.289	0	—	0	-1	-1	-0	-0.1
	Det-A	2	2	.500	24	1	0	0	0	51	45	18	6	1	25	20	12.5	3.18	125	.242	.335	0	—	0	4	4	0	0.4
	Yr	3	3	.500	29	3	0	0	0	73	64	29	11	1	32	40	12.0	3.58	111	.238	.321	0	—	0	3	3	0	0.3
1992	Sea-A	0	2	.000	8	6	0	0	0	33^1	47	28	6	2	11	20	16.2	7.56	53	.338	.395	0	—	0	-13	-13	-0	-0.7
Total	4	7	10	.412	62	27	2	0	0	234	249	120	31	6	78	121	12.8	4.42	89	.273	.335	0	—	0	-13	-12	0	-0.4
● JAY PARKER	Parker, Jay b: 7/8/1874, Theresa, N.Y. d: 6/8/35, Hartford, Mich. BR/TR, 5'11", 185 lbs. Deb: 9/27/1899 F																											
1899	Pit-N	0	0	—	1	1	0	0	0	0	0	0	1	2	—	—	∞	—	—	1.000	99	—	0	-2	-2	0	-0.2	
● ROY PARKER	Parker, Roy William b: 2/29/1896, Union, Mo. d: 5/17/54, Tulsa, Okla. BR/TR, 6'3", 200 lbs. Deb: 9/10/19																											
1919	StL-N	0	0	—	2	0	0	0	0	2	6	7	0	1	1	0	36.0	31.50	9	.333	.400	0	—	0	-6	-7	0	-0.3
● SLICKER PARKS	Parks, Vernon Henry b: 11/10/1895, Dallas, Mich. d: 2/21/78, Royal Oak, Mich. BR/TR, 5'10", 158 lbs. Deb: 7/11/21																											
1921	Det-A	3	2	.600	10	1	0	0	0	25^1	33	17	2	1	16	10	17.8	5.68	75	.306	.400	1	.111	-1	-4	-4	-1	-0.8
● BILL PARKS	Parks, William Robert b: 6/4/1849, Easton, Pa. d: 10/10/11, Easton, Pa. BR/TR, 5'8", 150 lbs. Deb: 4/26/1875 M◆																											
1875	Was-n	4	8	.333	14	11	9	0	0	106^2	144	120	3		5	3	12.6	3.29	72	.280	.287	20	.180	-3	-13	-10		-1.0
	Phi-n	0	0	—	2	0	0	0	0	5^1	13	11	0		1	0	23.6	8.44	27	.419	.438	1	.167	-0	-4	-4		-0.2
	Yr	4	8	.333	16	11	9	0	0	112	157	131	3		6	3	13.1	3.54	67	.288	.295	21	.179	-3	-16	-14		-1.2
● ROY PARMELEE	Parmelee, Le Roy Earl "Tarzan" b: 4/25/07, Lambertville, Mich d: 8/31/81, Monroe, Mich. BR/TR, 6'1", 190 lbs. Deb: 9/28/29																											
1929	NY-N	1	0	1.000	2	1	0	0	0	7	13	7	1	1	3	1	21.9	9.00	51	.481	.548	1	.500	0	-3	-4	0	-0.3
1930	NY-N	0	1	.000	11	1	0	0	0	21	18	26	3	0	26	19	18.9	9.43	50	.228	.419	1	.250	1	-10	-12	0	-0.4
1931	NY-N	2	2	.500	13	5	4	0	0	58^2	47	25	1	3	33	30	12.7	3.68	100	.223	.336	4	.200	-0	1	0	0	0.0
1932	NY-N	0	3	.000	8	3	0	0	0	25^1	25	18	0	2	14	23	14.6	3.91	95	.250	.353	2	.400	1	-0	-1	0	0.1
1933	NY-N	13	8	.619	32	32	14	3	0	218^1	191	94	9	14	77	132	11.6	3.17	101	.232	.309	19	.235	4	4	1	0	0.5
1934	NY-N	10	6	.625	22	21	7	2	0	152^2	134	59	6	6	60	83	11.8	3.42	113	**.238**	.318	11	.200	2	11	8	2	1.1
1935	NY-N	14	10	.583	34	31	13	0	0	226	214	117	20	9	97	79	12.7	4.22	91	.249	.332	18	.209	3	-5	-10	2	-0.5
1936	StL-N	11	11	.500	37	28	9	0	2	221	226	125	13	10	107	79	14.0	4.56	86	.270	.360	15	.197	-0	-13	-15	-1	-1.4
1937	Chi-N	7	8	.467	33	18	8	0	0	145^2	165	93	13	7	79	55	15.5	5.13	78	.286	.379	9	.173	0	-20	-18	1	-1.6
1939	Phi-A	1	6	.143	14	5	0	0	1	44^2	42	41	2	3	35	13	16.1	6.45	73	.235	.369	2	.133	-1	-9	-8	0	-1.1
Total	10	59	55	.518	206	145	55	5	3	1120^1	1075	605	68	55	531	514	13.3	4.27	89	.253	.343	82	.207	9	-45	-60	5	-3.6
● MEL PARNELL	Parnell, Melvin Lloyd "Dusty" b: 6/13/22, New Orleans, La. BL/TL, 6', 180 lbs. Deb: 4/20/47																											
1947	Bos-A	2	3	.400	15	5	1	0	0	50^2	60	41	1	1	27	23	15.6	6.39	61	.296	.381	1	.056	-2	-15	-13	-1	-1.4
1948	Bos-A	15	8	.652	35	27	16	1	0	212	205	87	7	4	90	77	12.7	3.14	140	.252	.330	13	.162	-4	27	29	2	2.6
1949	Bos-A★	**25**	7	.781	39	33	**27**	4	2	**295^1**	258	102	8	5	134	122	12.1	2.77	157	.237	.324	29	.254	2	**47**	**50**	-0	5.3
1950	Bos-A	18	10	.643	40	31	21	2	3	249	244	116	17	7	106	93	12.9	3.61	136	.259	.338	19	.194	-1	27	33	5	3.7
1951	Bos-A★	18	11	.621	36	29	11	3	2	221	229	99	11	0	77	77	12.5	3.26	137	.272	.333	25	.309	4	21	27	-0	**3.8**
1952	Bos-A	12	12	.500	33	29	15	3	2	214	207	94	13	5	89	107	12.7	3.62	109	.255	.332	8	.095	-3	1	7	1	0.5
1953	Bos-A	21	8	.724	38	34	12	5	0	241	217	98	15	4	116	136	12.6	3.06	137	.239	.328	21	.223	1	25	29	-2	3.2
1954	Bos-A	3	7	.300	19	15	4	1	0	92^1	104	45	7	1	35	38	13.6	3.70	111	.287	.352	3	.088	-2	0	4	0	0.2
1955	Bos-A	2	3	.400	13	9	0	0	1	46	62	44	12	1	25	18	17.2	7.83	55	.318	.398	6	.316	1	-20	-17	0	-1.5
1956	Bos-A	7	6	.538	21	20	6	1	0	131^1	129	71	13	0	59	41	12.9	3.77	123	.256	.335	7	.152	-2	6	11	-1	0.7
Total	10	123	75	.621	289	232	113	20	10	1752^2	1715	797	104	28	758	732	12.8	3.50	125	.257	.336	132	.198	-7	119	160	3	17.1
● RUBE PARNHAM	Parnham, James Arthur b: 2/1/1894, Heidelberg, Pa. d: 11/25/63, McKeesport, Pa. BR/TR, 6'3", 185 lbs. Deb: 9/20/16																											
1916	Phi-A	2	1	.667	4	3	2	0	0	24^2	27	14	0	0	13	8	14.6	4.01	71	.300	.388	3	.273	1	-3	-3	1	-0.2
1917	Phi-A	0	1	.000	2	2	0	0	0	11	12	6	1	0	9	4	17.2	4.09	67	.316	.447	0	.000	-0	-2	-2	0	-0.2
Total	2	2	2	.500	6	5	2	0	0	35^2	39	20	1	0	22	12	15.4	4.04	70	.305	.407	3	.214	0	-5	-5	1	-0.4
● JIM PARQUE	Parque, Jim Vo b: 2/8/75, Norwalk, Cal. BL/TL, 5'11", 165 lbs. Deb: 5/26/98																											
1998	Chi-A	7	5	.583	21	21	0	0	0	113	135	72	14	6	49	77	15.1	5.10	89	.299	.375	0	.000	-0	-6	-7	0	-0.6
1999	Chi-A	9	15	.375	31	30	1	0	0	173^2	210	111	23	10	79	111	15.5	5.13	95	.299	.378	2	.400	1	-5	-5	-1	-0.6
2000	*Chi-A	13	6	.684	33	32	0	0	0	187	208	105	21	11	71	111	14.0	4.28	116	.283	.355	0	.000	-0	13	14	-1	1.1
Total	3	29	26	.527	85	83	1	0	0	473^2	553	288	58	27	199	299	14.8	4.79	101	.293	.368	2	.200	0	3	3	-2	-0.1
● JOSE PARRA	Parra, Jose Miguel b: 11/28/72, Jacagua, D.R. BR/TR, 5'11", 160 lbs. Deb: 5/7/95																											
1995	LA-N	0	0	—	8	0	0	0	0	10^1	10	8	2	1	6	7	14.8	4.35	87	.256	.370	0	—	0	-0	-1	-0	0.0
	Min-A	1	5	.167	12	12	0	0	0	61^2	83	59	11	2	22	29	15.6	7.59	63	.313	.370	0	—	0	-20	-19	-0	-1.5
1996	Min-A	5	5	.500	27	5	0	0	0	70	88	48	15	3	27	50	15.2	6.04	85	.308	.373	0	—	0	-8	-7	-0	-0.8
2000	Pit-N	0	1	.000	6	2	0	0	0	11^2	17	9	3	1	7	9	19.3	6.94	66	.354	.446	0	—	1	-3	-3	0	-0.1
Total	3	6	11	.353	53	19	0	0	0	153^2	198	124	31	7	62	95	15.6	6.62	73	.310	.378	0	—	1	-31	-30	-0	-2.4
● JEFF PARRETT	Parrett, Jeffrey Dale b: 8/26/61, Indianapolis, Ind. BR/TR, 6'3", 193 lbs. Deb: 4/11/86																											
1986	Mon-N	0	1	.000	12	0	0	0	0	20^1	19	11	3	0	13	21	14.2	4.87	76	.247	.356	1	.500	0	-3	-3	0	-0.1
1987	Mon-N	7	6	.538	45	0	0	0	6	62	53	33	8	0	30	56	12.0	4.21	100	.229	.318	0	.000	-1	-1	-0	0	-0.1
1988	Mon-N	12	4	.750	61	0	0	0	6	91^2	66	29	8	1	45	62	11.0	2.65	136	.214	.316	0	—	0	8	9	-1	1.6
1989	Phi-N	12	6	.667	72	0	0	0	6	105^2	90	43	6	0	44	98	11.4	2.98	119	.232	.310	0	.000	-1	6	7	-1	1.0
1990	Phi-N	4	9	.308	47	5	0	0	1	81^2	92	51	10	1	36	69	14.2	5.18	74	.293	.368	0	.000	-1	-13	-12	-0	-1.9
	Atl-N	1	1	.500	20	0	0	0	1	27	27	11	1	1	19	17	15.7	3.00	135	.281	.405	1	1.000	0	2	3	0	0.3
	Yr	5	10	.333	67	5	0	0	2	108^2	119	62	11	2	55	86	14.6	4.64	84	.290	.377	1	.091	-1	-10	-9	0	-1.6
1991	Atl-N	1	2	.333	18	0	0	0	1	21^1	31	18	2	0	12	14	18.1	6.33	61	.326	.402	0	—	0	-6	-5	1	-0.7
1992	*Oak-A	9	1	.900	66	0	0	0	0	98^1	81	35	7	2	42	78	11.4	3.02	124	.226	.311	0	—	0	10	8	-1	0.7
1993	Col-N	3	3	.500	40	6	0	0	1	73^2	78	47	6	2	45	66	15.3	5.38	89	.274	.377	1	.091	-1	-11	-4	-0	-0.4
1995	StL-N	4	7	.364	59	0	0	0	0	76^2	71	33	8	1	28	71	11.7	3.64	115	.243	.312	1	.500	0	5	5	-1	0.6
1996	StL-N	2	2	.500	33	0	0	0	0	42^1	40	20	2	1	20	42	13.0	4.25	99	.245	.332	0	.000	0	-0	-0	1	0.0
	Phi-N	1	1	.500	18	0	0	0	0	24	24	5	0	0	11	22	13.1	1.88	230	.270	.350	0	—	0	6	6	-0	0.4
	Yr	3	3	.500	51	0	0	0	0	66^1	64	25	2	1	31	64	13.0	3.39	125	.254	.338	0	.000	0	6	6	0	0.4
Total	10	56	43	.566	491	11	0	0	22	724^2	672	336	61	9	345	616	12.7	3.80	104	.249	.336	4	.105	-1	4	12	-3	1.4
● STEVE PARRIS	Parris, Steven Michael b: 12/17/67, Joliet, Ill. BR/TR, 6', 190 lbs. Deb: 6/21/95																											
1995	Pit-N	6	6	.500	15	15	1	1	0	82	89	49	12	7	33	61	14.2	5.38	80	.283	.363	7	.250	1	-11	-9	-0	-1.1
1996	Pit-N	0	3	.000	8	4	0	0	0	26^1	35	22	4	1	11	27	16.1	7.18	61	.321	.388	1	.167	0	-9	-8	0	-0.7
1998	Cin-N	6	5	.545	18	16	1	1	0	99	89	44	9	4	32	77	11.4	3.73	115	.236	.303	4	.138	-1	6	6	1	0.6
1999	Cin-N	11	4	.733	22	21	2	1	0	128^2	124	59	16	6	52	86	12.7	3.50	133	.260	.340	6	.158	-1	15	16	0	1.6
2000	Cin-N	12	17	.414	33	33	0	0	0	192^2	227	109	30	4	71	117	14.1	4.81	99	.294	.356	7	.127	-1	-4	-1	-1	-0.3
Total	5	35	35	.500	96	89	4	3	0	528^2	564	283	71	22	199	368	13.4	4.49	101	.275	.346	25	.160	-2	-2	4	1	0.1
● JOHN PARRISH	Parrish, John Henry b: 11/26/77, Lancaster, Pa. BL/TL, 5'11", 180 lbs. Deb: 7/24/2000																											
2000	Bal-A	2	4	.333	8	8	0	0	0	36^1	40	32	6	1	35	28	18.8	7.18	67	.288	.434	0	—	0	-9	-10	-0	-1.3

YEAR	TM/L	W	L	PCT	G	GS	CG	SH	SV	IP	H	R	HR	HB	BB	SO	RAT	ERA	ERA+	OAV	OOB	BH	AVG	PB	PR	PR+	PD	TPI
● MIKE PARROTT	Parrott, Michael Everett Arch b: 12/6/54, Oxnard, Cal. BR/TR, 6'4", 210 lbs. Deb: 9/5/77																											
1977	Bal-A	0	0	—	3	0	0	0	0	4^1	4	1	0	0	2	2	12.5	2.08	183	.250	.333	0	—	0	1	1	-0	0.0
1978	Sea-A	1	5	.167	27	10	0	0	1	82^1	108	59	8	3	32	41	15.6	5.14	74	.316	.379	0	—	0	-12	-12	0	-0.8
1979	Sea-A	14	12	.538	38	30	13	2	0	229^1	231	104	17	6	86	127	12.7	3.77	116	.267	.338	0	—	0	12	15	3	1.8
1980	Sea-A	1	16	.059	27	16	1	0	3	94	136	83	16	1	42	53	17.1	7.28	57	.348	.412	0	—	0	-34	-32	4	-4.6
1981	Sea-A	3	6	.333	24	12	0	0	1	85	102	51	3	1	28	43	13.9	5.08	76	.299	.354	0	—	0	-13	-11	0	-1.1
Total	5	19	39	.328	119	68	14	2	5	495	581	298	44	11	190	266	14.2	4.87	85	.297	.363	0	—	0	-47	-39	6	-4.7
● TOM PARROTT	Parrott, Thomas William "Tacky Tom" b: 4/10/1868, Portland, Ore. d: 1/1/32, Dundee, Ore. BR/TR, 5'10.5", 170 lbs. Deb: 6/18/1893 F♦																											
1893	Chi-N	0	3	.000	4	3	2	0	0	27	35	30	1	0	17	7	17.3	6.67	69	.304	.394	7	.259	-0	-6	-6	-1	-0.5
	Cin-N	10	7	.588	22	17	11	1	0	154	174	95	1	9	70	33	14.8	4.09	117	.276	.357	13	.191	-3	10	12	2	0.8
	Yr	10	10	.500	26	20	13	1	0	181	209	125	2	9	87	40	15.2	4.48	106	.281	.363	20	.211	-3	4	6	1	0.3
1894	Cin-N	17	19	.472	41	36	31	1	1	308^2	402	268	19	11	126	61	15.7	5.60	99	.311	.377	74	.323	8	-9	-1	3	0.7
1895	Cin-N	11	18	.379	41	31	23	0	**3**	263^1	382	228	8	5	76	57	15.8	5.47	91	.334	.378	69	.343	10	-20	-14	3	-0.2
1896	StL-N	1	1	.500	7	2	2	0	0	42	62	39	4	3	18	8	17.8	6.21	70	.339	.407	138	.291	1	-9	-9	-0	-0.3
Total	4	39	48	.448	115	89	69	2	4	795	1055	660	33	28	307	166	15.7	5.33	96	.314	.376	301	.301	16	-34	-18	6	0.5
● JIGGS PARSON	Parson, William Edwin b: 12/28/1885, Parker, S.Dak. d: 5/19/67, Los Angeles, Cal. BR/TR, 6'2", 180 lbs. Deb: 5/16/10																											
1910	Bos-N	0	2	.000	10	4	0	0	0	35^1	35	23	2	2	26	7	16.0	3.82	87	.278	.409	1	.083	-1	-3	-2	-0	-0.2
1911	Bos-N	0	1	.000	7	0	0	0	0	25	36	30	2	4	15	7	19.8	6.48	59	.375	.478	2	.200	-0	-9	-7	-1	-0.4
Total	2	0	3	.000	17	4	0	0	0	60^1	71	53	4	6	41	14	17.6	4.92	72	.320	.439	3	.136	-2	-12	-8	-1	-0.6
● CHARLIE PARSONS	Parsons, Charles James b: 7/18/1863, Cherry Flats, Pa. d: 3/24/36, Mansfield, Pa. BL/TL, 5'10", 160 lbs. Deb: 5/29/1886																											
1886	Bos-N	0	2	.000	2	2	2	0	0	16	20	13	0		4	5	13.5	3.94	81	.308	.348	3	.375	1	-1	-1	-1	-0.1
1887	NY-a	1	1	.500	4	4	4	0	0	34	57	36	0	1	6	5	15.4	4.50	94	.343	.347	4	.250	-1	-1	-1	0	-0.1
1890	Cle-N	0	1	.000	2	1	0	0	0	9	12	11	0	4	6	2	22.0	6.00	60	.308	.449	3	.750	1	-2	-2	0	-0.1
Total	3	1	4	.200	8	7	6	0	0	59	89	60	0	5	16	12	15.9	4.58	84	.330	.365	10	.357	2	-4	-5	-1	-0.3
● TOM PARSONS	Parsons, Thomas Anthony b: 9/13/39, Lakeville, Conn. BR/TR, 6'7", 210 lbs. Deb: 9/5/63																											
1963	Pit-N	0	1	.000	1	1	0	0	0	4^1	7	6	1	0	2	2	18.7	8.31	40	.368	.429	0	.000	-0	-2	-2	0	-0.4
1964	NY-N	1	2	.333	4	2	1	0	0	19^1	20	9	1	0	6	10	12.1	4.19	85	.274	.329	0	.000	-1	-1	-1	-0	-0.3
1965	NY-N	1	10	.091	35	11	1	1	1	90^2	108	53	17	0	17	58	12.4	4.67	76	.290	.321	1	.056	-1	-11	-11	1	-1.3
Total	3	2	13	.133	40	14	2	1	1	114^1	135	68	19	0	25	70	12.6	4.72	75	.291	.327	1	.037	-2	-15	-15	1	-2.0
● BILL PARSONS	Parsons, William Raymond b: 8/17/48, Riverside, Cal. BR/TR, 6'6", 195 lbs. Deb: 4/13/71																											
1971	Mil-A	13	17	.433	36	35	12	4	0	244^2	219	95	19	4	93	139	11.6	3.20	109	.241	.315	12	.167	3	7	7	0	1.3
1972	Mil-A	13	13	.500	33	30	10	2	0	214	194	102	27	3	68	111	11.1	3.91	78	.240	.301	11	.164	0	-20	-21	-3	-2.7
1973	Mil-A	3	6	.333	20	17	0	0	0	59^2	59	50	6	0	67	30	19.0	6.79	55	.257	.424	0	—	0	-20	-20	-0	-2.6
1974	Oak-A	0	0	—	4	0	0	0	0	2	1	0	0	0	3	2	18.0	0.00	—	.143	.400	0	—	0	1	1	-0	0.0
Total	4	29	36	.446	93	82	22	6	0	520^1	473	247	52	7	231	282	12.3	3.89	86	.242	.325	23	.165	3	-32	-33	-3	-4.0
● STAN PARTENHEIMER	Partenheimer, Stanwood Wendell "Party" b: 10/21/22, Chicopee Falls, Mass. d: 1/28/89, Wilson, N.C. BR/TL, 5'11", 175 lbs. Deb: 5/27/44 F																											
1944	Bos-A	0	0	—	1	1	0	0	0	1	3	2	0	0	2	0	45.0	18.00	19	.500	.625	0	.000	-0	-2	-2	-0	-0.1
1945	StL-N	0	0	—	8	2	0	0	0	13^1	12	9	2	0	16	6	18.9	6.08	62	.250	.438	0	.000	-0	-3	-4	0	-0.2
Total	2	0	0	—	9	3	0	0	0	14^1	15	11	2	0	18	6	20.7	6.91	54	.278	.458	0	.000	-1	-5	-5	0	-0.3
● BILL PASCHALL	Paschall, William Herbert b: 4/22/54, Norfolk, Va. BR/TR, 6', 175 lbs. Deb: 9/20/78																											
1978	KC-A	0	1	.000	2	0	0	0	1	8	6	3	0	1	0	5	7.9	3.38	114	.207	.233	0	—	0	0	0	-0	0.0
1979	KC-A	0	1	.000	7	0	0	0	0	13^2	18	11	2	2	5	3	16.5	6.59	65	.300	.373	0	—	0	-4	-3	-0	-0.2
1981	KC-A	0	0	—	2	0	0	0	0	2	2	1	0	0	0	1	9.0	4.50	80	.286	.286	0	—	0	-0	-0	-0	0.0
Total	3	0	2	.000	11	0	0	0	1	23^2	26	15	2	3	5	9	12.9	5.32	76	.271	.327	0	—	0	-3	-3	-1	-0.2
● CAMILO PASCUAL	Pascual, Camilo Alberto (Lus) b: 1/20/34, Havana, Cuba BR/TR, 5'11", 185 lbs. Deb: 4/15/54 FC																											
1954	Was-A	4	7	.364	48	4	1	0	3	119^1	126	65	7	6	61	60	14.6	4.22	84	.276	.368	4	.133	-0	-7	-9	3	-0.6
1955	Was-A	2	12	.143	43	16	1	0	3	129	158	94	5	6	70	82	16.3	6.14	62	.311	.401	7	.219	0	-31	-34	2	-3.1
1956	Was-A	6	18	.250	39	27	6	0	2	188^2	194	131	33	6	89	162	13.8	5.87	74	.261	.345	8	.138	-2	-36	-31	1	-3.4
1957	Was-A	8	17	.320	29	26	8	2	0	175^2	168	85	11	3	76	113	12.7	4.10	95	.258	.338	7	.140	-2	-6	-4	2	-0.5
1958	Was-A	8	12	.400	31	27	6	2	0	177^1	166	66	14	3	60	146	11.6	3.15	121	.248	.313	9	.158	-1	12	13	1	1.4
1959	Was-A†	17	10	.630	32	30	**17**	**6**	0	238^2	202	80	10	3	69	185	10.3	2.64	148	.226	.284	26	.302	6	32	33	5	**5.0**
1960	Was-A†	12	8	.600	26	22	8	3	2	151^2	139	65	11	2	53	143	11.5	3.03	128	.240	.306	9	.176	3	14	14	0	2.2
1961	Min-A★	15	16	.484	35	33	15	**8**	0	252^1	205	114	26	3	100	**221**	11.0	3.46	123	.217	.294	14	.165	-0	16	21	1	2.4
1962	Min-A★	20	11	.645	34	33	**18**	**5**	0	257^2	236	100	25	2	59	**206**	10.4	3.32	123	.241	.286	26	.268	8	19	21	0	3.3
1963	Min-A	21	9	.700	31	31	**18**	3	0	248^1	205	76	21	3	81	**202**	10.5	2.46	148	.224	.289	23	.250	6	32	32	-1	4.6
1964	Min-A★	15	12	.556	36	36	14	1	0	267^1	245	121	30	3	98	213	11.6	3.30	108	.241	.309	17	.181	4	10	8	0	1.2
1965	*Min-A	9	3	.750	27	27	5	1	0	156	126	67	12	5	63	96	11.2	3.35	106	.217	.299	12	.200	3	2	4	2	0.7
1966	Min-A	8	6	.571	21	19	2	0	0	103	113	63	9	2	30	56	12.7	4.89	73	.278	.330	8	.216	1	-17	-14	2	-1.5
1967	Was-A	12	10	.545	28	27	5	1	0	164^2	147	73	15	3	43	106	10.5	3.28	96	.237	.289	9	.176	1	-1	-2	-0	-0.2
1968	Was-A	13	12	.520	31	31	8	4	0	201	181	72	11	4	59	111	10.9	2.69	109	.239	.298	12	.185	1	7	5	1	0.9
1969	Was-A	2	5	.286	14	13	0	0	0	55^1	49	42	12	5	38	34	15.0	6.83	51	.239	.371	4	.235	0	-20	-22	-0	-2.3
	Cin-N	0	0	—	5	1	0	0	0	7^1	14	7	2	0	4	3	22.1	8.59	44	.424	.486	0	—	0	-4	-4	-0	-0.2
1970	LA-N	0	0	—	10	0	0	0	0	14	12	4	2	1	5	8	11.6	2.57	149	.231	.310	0	—	0	2	2	0	0.1
1971	Cle-A	2	2	.500	9	1	0	0	0	23^1	17	9	0	1	11	20	11.2	3.09	124	.205	.305	3	.600	1	1	2	1	0.5
Total	18	174	170	.506	529	404	132	36	10	2930^2	2703	1334	256	61	1069	2167	11.8	3.63	103	.244	.314	198	.205	29	26	37	18	10.5
● CARLOS PASCUAL	Pascual, Carlos Alberto (Lus) "Little Potato" b: 3/13/31, Havana, Cuba BR/TR, 5'6", 165 lbs. Deb: 9/24/50 F																											
1950	Was-A	1	1	.500	2	2	2	0	0	17	12	5	0	1	8	3	11.1	2.12	212	.194	.296	1	.250	0	5	5	-1	0.4
● LARRY PASHNICK	Pashnick, Larry John b: 4/25/56, Lincoln Park, Mich. BR/TR, 6'3", 205 lbs. Deb: 4/10/82																											
1982	Det-A	4	4	.500	28	13	1	0	0	94^1	110	46	17	1	25	19	13.0	4.01	102	.297	.343	0	—	0	1	1	-1	0.0
1983	Det-A	1	3	.250	12	6	0	0	0	37^2	48	27	5	3	18	17	16.5	5.26	75	.308	.390	0	—	0	-5	-6	1	-0.5
1984	Min-A	2	1	.667	13	1	0	0	0	38^1	38	19	3	2	11	10	12.0	3.52	120	.260	.321	0	—	0	2	3	0	0.2
Total	3	7	8	.467	53	20	1	0	0	170^1	196	92	25	6	54	46	13.5	4.17	98	.292	.350	0	—	0	-2	-2	0	-0.3
● CLAUDE PASSEAU	Passeau, Claude William b: 4/9/09, Waynesboro, Miss. BR/TR, 6'3", 198 lbs. Deb: 9/29/35																											
1935	Pit-N	0	1	.000	1	1	0	0	0	3	7	4	0	0	2	1	27.0	12.00	34	.500	.563	0	.000	-0	-3	-3	0	-0.4
1936	Phi-N	11	15	.423	49	21	8	2	3	217^1	247	118	7	4	55	85	12.7	3.48	130	.280	.325	22	.282	3	13	23	1	3.0
1937	Phi-N	14	18	.438	50	34	18	1	2	**292^1**	348	158	16	5	79	135	13.3	4.34	100	.296	.343	21	.196	-0	-14	-0	0	0.0
1938	Phi-N	11	18	.379	44	33	15	0	1	239	281	147	8	8	93	100	14.4	4.52	86	.287	.354	13	.162	-2	-19	-16	3	-1.7
1939	Phi-N	2	4	.333	8	8	4	1	0	53^1	54	26	1	1	25	29	13.5	4.22	95	.263	.346	4	.200	-0	-2	-1	0	-0.2
	Chi-N	13	9	.591	34	27	13	1	3	221	215	86	8	4	48	108	10.9	3.05	129	.254	.297	12	.156	-1	21	22	1	2.0
	Yr	15	13	.536	42	35	17	2	3	274^1	269	112	9	5	73	**137**	11.4	3.28	120	.256	.307	16	.165	-2	19	20	1	1.8
1940	Chi-N	20	13	.606	46	31	20	4	5	280^2	259	97	8	4	59	124	10.3	2.50	150	.237	.278	20	.204	6	42	40	1	**5.5**
1941	Chi-N★	14	14	.500	34	30	20	3	0	231	262	99	10	1	52	80	12.3	3.35	105	.281	.320	19	.221	5	7	4	-1	0.9
1942	Chi-N★	19	14	.576	35	34	24	3	0	278^1	284	116	13	3	74	89	11.7	2.68	119	.260	.309	19	.181	1	20	17	1	2.1
1943	Chi-N☆	15	12	.556	35	31	18	1	1	257	245	96	10	4	66	93	11.0	2.91	115	.249	.299	19	.198	1	14	12	1	1.5
1944	Chi-N	15	9	.625	34	27	18	2	3	227	234	80	8	1	50	89	11.3	2.89	122	.266	.306	13	.162	-1	18	16	1	1.7
1945	*Chi-N†	17	9	.654	34	27	19	**5**	1	227	205	70	4	2	59	98	10.5	2.46	149	.238	.289	17	.187	2	34	**31**	3	**3.9**
1946	Chi-N★	9	8	.529	21	21	10	2	0	129^1	118	53	5	1	42	47	11.2	3.13	106	.237	.298	10	.204	3	4	3	1	0.7
1947	Chi-N	2	6	.250	19	6	1	1	2	63^1	97	54	7	1	24	26	17.3	6.25	63	.353	.407	0	.000	-2	-15	-17	-1	-2.1
Total	13	162	150	.519	444	331	188	26	21	2719^2	2856	1204	105	39	728	1104	12.0	3.32	113	.267	.316	189	.192	13	120	127	11	16.9

● FRANK PASTORE Pastore, Frank Enrico b: 8/21/57, Alhambra, Cal. BR/TR, 6'3", 205 lbs. Deb: 4/4/79

YEAR	TM/L	W	L	PCT	G	GS	CG	SH	SV	IP	H	R	HR	HB	BB	SO	RAT	ERA	ERA+	OAV	OOB	BH	AVG	PB	PR	PR+	PD	TPI
1979	*Cin-N	6	7	.462	30	9	2	1	4	95^1	102	47	8	1	23	63	11.9	4.25	88	.271	.315	4	.160	-0	-5	-5	0	-0.8
1980	Cin-N	13	7	.650	27	27	9	2	0	184^2	161	72	13	0	42	110	9.9	3.27	110	.233	.277	10	.156	-1	7	7	-1	0.5
1981	Cin-N	4	9	.308	22	22	2	1	0	132	125	73	11	3	35	81	11.1	4.02	88	.247	.300	5	.114	-2	-8	-7	-2	-1.0
1982	Cin-N	8	13	.381	31	29	3	2	0	188^1	210	86	13	4	57	94	13.0	3.97	93	.286	.341	10	.172	1	-7	-5	-2	-0.6
1983	Cin-N	9	12	.429	36	29	4	1	0	184^1	207	104	20	1	64	93	13.3	4.88	78	.290	.349	11	.186	2	-26	-21	-1	-2.1
1984	Cin-N	3	8	.273	24	16	1	0	0	98^1	110	74	10	3	40	53	14.0	6.50	58	.285	.357	2	.071	-2	-32	-28	0	-2.9
1985	Cin-N	2	1	.667	17	6	1	0	0	54	60	23	1	1	16	29	12.8	3.83	99	.287	.341	2	.143	-0	-1	-0	0	0.0
1986	Min-A	3	1	.750	33	1	0	0	2	49^1	54	28	4	0	24	18	14.2	4.01	108	.283	.363	0	—	0	1	2	-1	0.1
Total	8	48	58	.453	220	139	22	7	6	986^1	1029	507	80	13	301	541	12.3	4.29	87	.270	.326	44	.151	-2	-71	-60	-5	-6.8

● JIM PASTORIUS Pastorius, James W. "Sunny Jim" b: 7/12/1881, Pittsburgh, Pa. d: 5/10/41, Pittsburgh, Pa. BL/TL, 5'9", 165 lbs. Deb: 4/15/06

YEAR	TM/L	W	L	PCT	G	GS	CG	SH	SV	IP	H	R	HR	HB	BB	SO	RAT	ERA	ERA+	OAV	OOB	BH	AVG	PB	PR	PR+	PD	TPI
1906	Bro-N	10	14	.417	29	24	16	3	0	211^2	225	111	4	3	69	58	12.6	3.61	70	.274	.333	10	.141	-0	-23	-27	-1	-3.0
1907	Bro-N	16	12	.571	28	26	20	4	0	222	218	74	2	6	77	70	12.2	2.35	100	.264	.331	15	.205	3	3	-0	-1	0.2
1908	Bro-N	4	20	.167	28	25	16	2	0	213^2	171	88	5	7	74	54	10.6	2.44	96	.216	.288	8	.129	-0	-2	-2	0	-0.3
1909	Bro-N	1	9	.100	12	9	5	1	0	79^2	91	65	4	1	58	23	16.9	5.76	45	.313	.429	2	.080	-1	-28	-28	1	-3.1
Total	4	31	55	.360	97	84	57	10	0	727	705	338	15	17	278	205	12.4	3.12	78	.258	.330	35	.152	1	-50	-58	-1	-6.2

● JOE PATE Pate, Joseph William b: 6/6/1892, Alice, Tex. d: 12/26/48, Fort Worth, Tex. BL/TL, 5'10", 184 lbs. Deb: 4/15/26

YEAR	TM/L	W	L	PCT	G	GS	CG	SH	SV	IP	H	R	HR	HB	BB	SO	RAT	ERA	ERA+	OAV	OOB	BH	AVG	PB	PR	PR+	PD	TPI
1926	Phi-A	9	0	1.000	47	2	0	0	6	113	109	38	3	2	51	24	12.9	2.71	154	.262	.345	4	.148	-0	**16**	**18**	3	1.8
1927	Phi-A	0	3	.000	32	0	0	0	6	53^2	67	36	3	1	21	14	14.9	5.20	82	.318	.382	3	.300	1	-6	-5	0	-0.3
Total	2	9	3	.750	79	2	0	0	12	166^2	176	74	6	3	72	38	13.6	3.51	120	.281	.358	7	.189	1	10	12	4	1.5

● BRONSWELL PATRICK Patrick, Bronswell Dante b: 9/16/70, Greenville, N.C. BR/TR, 6'1", 220 lbs. Deb: 5/18/98

YEAR	TM/L	W	L	PCT	G	GS	CG	SH	SV	IP	H	R	HR	HB	BB	SO	RAT	ERA	ERA+	OAV	OOB	BH	AVG	PB	PR	PR+	PD	TPI
1998	Mil-N	4	1	.800	32	3	0	0	0	78^2	83	43	9	0	29	49	12.8	4.69	91	.279	.343	3	.200	2	-4	-4	-1	-0.2
1999	SF-N	1	0	1.000	6	0	0	0	1	5^1	9	7	1	0	3	6	20.3	10.13	42	.375	.444	0	.000	-0	-3	-4	0	-0.7
Total	2	5	1	.833	38	3	0	0	1	84	92	50	10	0	32	55	13.3	5.04	85	.286	.350	3	.188	1	-7	-7	-1	-0.9

● CASE PATTEN Patten, Case Lyman "Casey" b: 5/7/1876, Westport, N.Y. d: 5/31/35, Rochester, N.Y. BB/TL, 6', 175 lbs. Deb: 5/4/01

YEAR	TM/L	W	L	PCT	G	GS	CG	SH	SV	IP	H	R	HR	HB	BB	SO	RAT	ERA	ERA+	OAV	OOB	BH	AVG	PB	PR	PR+	PD	TPI
1901	Was-A	18	10	.643	32	30	26	4	0	254^1	285	163	8	17	74	109	13.3	3.93	93	.280	.339	13	.135	-5	-7	-7	0	-1.1
1902	Was-A	18	17	.514	36	34	33	1	0	299^2	331	186	11	11	89	92	12.9	4.05	91	.281	.337	12	.096	-10	-16	-11	-1	-2.1
1903	Was-A	11	22	.333	36	34	32	0	1	300	313	163	11	4	80	133	11.9	3.60	87	.268	.317	14	.132	-6	-21	-15	1	-2.0
1904	Was-A	14	23	.378	45	39	37	2	**3**	357^2	367	162	2	20	79	150	11.7	3.07	87	.266	.315	16	.127	-5	-19	-16	1	-2.1
1905	Was-A	14	21	.400	42	36	29	2	0	309^2	300	145	3	10	86	113	11.5	3.14	84	.256	.312	16	.155	-2	-17	-17	-2	-2.3
1906	Was-A	19	16	.543	38	32	28	7	0	282^2	253	106	2	6	79	96	10.8	2.17	122	.242	.299	11	.117	-4	17	15	-1	1.3
1907	Was-A	12	16	.429	36	29	20	1	0	237^1	272	135	3	6	63	58	12.9	3.56	68	.290	.339	11	.126	-3	-27	-32	-5	-4.2
1908	Was-A	0	2	.000	4	3	1	0	0	18	25	14	0	0	6	6	15.5	3.50	65	.333	.383	1	.200	-0	-2	-3	-0	-0.3
	Bos-A	0	1	.000	1	1	0	0	0	3	8	5	0	0	1	0	27.0	15.00	16	.533	.563	0	.000	-0	-4	-4	0	-0.6
	Yr	0	3	.000	5	4	1	0	0	21	33	19	0	0	7	6	17.1	5.14	45	.367	.412	1	.167	-0	-6	-7	-0	-0.9
Total	8	106	128	.453	270	238	206	17	4	2062^1	2154	1079	40	74	557	757	12.2	3.36	88	.270	.323	94	.127	-35	-97	-90	-7	-13.4

● DANNY PATTERSON Patterson, Danny Shane b: 2/17/71, San Gabriel, Cal. BR/TR, 6', 170 lbs. Deb: 7/26/96

YEAR	TM/L	W	L	PCT	G	GS	CG	SH	SV	IP	H	R	HR	HB	BB	SO	RAT	ERA	ERA+	OAV	OOB	BH	AVG	PB	PR	PR+	PD	TPI
1996	*Tex-A	0	0	—	7	0	0	0	0	8^2	10	4	0	0	3	5	13.5	0.00	—	.286	.342	0	—	0	5	5	0	0.2
1997	Tex-A	10	6	.625	54	0	0	0	1	71	70	29	3	0	23	69	11.8	3.42	140	.263	.322	0	—	0	9	10	-0	2.0
1998	Tex-A	2	5	.286	56	0	0	0	2	60^2	64	31	11	2	19	33	12.6	4.45	108	.274	.333	0	—	0	1	2	-0	0.2
1999	*Tex-A	2	0	1.000	53	0	0	0	0	60^1	77	38	5	1	19	43	14.5	5.67	90	.304	.355	0	.000	-0	-5	-4	-0	-0.2
2000	Det-A	5	1	.833	58	0	0	0	0	56^2	69	26	4	2	14	29	13.5	3.97	120	.309	.356	0	—	0	6	5	0	0.5
Total	5	19	12	.613	228	0	0	0	3	257^1	290	128	23	5	78	179	13.0	4.20	116	.287	.341	0	.000	-0	16	19	-0	2.7

● DARYL PATTERSON Patterson, Daryl Alan b: 11/21/43, Coalinga, Cal. BL/TR, 6'4", 195 lbs. Deb: 4/10/68

YEAR	TM/L	W	L	PCT	G	GS	CG	SH	SV	IP	H	R	HR	HB	BB	SO	RAT	ERA	ERA+	OAV	OOB	BH	AVG	PB	PR	PR+	PD	TPI
1968	*Det-A	2	3	.400	38	1	0	0	7	68	53	19	3	4	27	49	11.1	2.12	142	.213	.300	0	.000	-1	7	7	-0	0.5
1969	Det-A	0	2	.000	18	0	0	0	0	22^1	15	8	2	0	19	12	13.7	2.82	132	.205	.370	0	.000	-0	2	2	-1	0.1
1970	Det-A	7	1	.875	43	0	0	0	2	78	81	47	9	5	39	55	14.4	4.85	77	.269	.362	0	.000	-1	-10	-10	-1	-1.2
1971	Det-A	0	1	.000	12	0	0	0	0	9^1	14	7	1	1	6	5	20.3	4.82	75	.359	.457	0	—	0	-1	-1	-0	-0.1
	Oak-A	0	0	—	4	0	0	0	0	5^2	5	5	3	1	4	2	15.9	7.94	42	.238	.385	0	.000	-0	-3	-3	-0	-0.2
	Yr	0	1	.000	16	0	0	0	0	15	19	12	4	2	10	7	18.6	6.00	58	.317	.431	0	.000	-0	-4	-4	-0	-0.3
	StL-N	0	1	.000	13	2	0	0	1	26^2	20	14	3	0	15	11	11.8	4.39	82	.211	.318	0	.000	-0	-3	-2	-1	-0.2
1974	Pit-N	2	1	.667	14	0	0	0	1	21	35	19	3	0	9	8	18.9	7.29	47	.376	.431	0	.000	-1	-9	-9	0	-1.3
Total	5	11	9	.550	142	3	0	0	11	231	223	119	24	11	119	142	13.8	4.09	85	.256	.353	0	.000	-3	-17	-16	-3	-2.4

● DAVE PATTERSON Patterson, David Glenn b: 7/25/56, Springfield, Mo. BR/TR, 6', 170 lbs. Deb: 6/9/79

YEAR	TM/L	W	L	PCT	G	GS	CG	SH	SV	IP	H	R	HR	HB	BB	SO	RAT	ERA	ERA+	OAV	OOB	BH	AVG	PB	PR	PR+	PD	TPI
1979	LA-N	4	1	.800	36	0	0	0	6	53	62	35	5	0	22	34	14.3	5.26	69	.292	.359	1	.143	-0	-9	-10	-0	-1.1

● GIL PATTERSON Patterson, Gilbert Thomas b: 9/5/55, Philadelphia, Pa. BR/TR, 6'1", 185 lbs. Deb: 4/19/77

YEAR	TM/L	W	L	PCT	G	GS	CG	SH	SV	IP	H	R	HR	HB	BB	SO	RAT	ERA	ERA+	OAV	OOB	BH	AVG	PB	PR	PR+	PD	TPI
1977	NY-A	1	2	.333	10	6	0	0	1	33^1	38	20	3	3	20	29	16.5	5.40	73	.290	.396	0	—	0	-5	-6	1	-0.4

● JEFF PATTERSON Patterson, Jeffrey Simmons b: 10/1/68, Anaheim, Cal. BR/TR, 6'2", 200 lbs. Deb: 4/30/95

YEAR	TM/L	W	L	PCT	G	GS	CG	SH	SV	IP	H	R	HR	HB	BB	SO	RAT	ERA	ERA+	OAV	OOB	BH	AVG	PB	PR	PR+	PD	TPI
1995	NY-A	0	0	—	3	0	0	0	0	3^1	3	1	1	0	3	3	16.2	2.70	171	.231	.375	0	—	0	1	1	-0	0.0

● KEN PATTERSON Patterson, Kenneth Brian b: 7/8/64, Costa Mesa, Cal. BL/TL, 6'4", 210 lbs. Deb: 7/9/88

YEAR	TM/L	W	L	PCT	G	GS	CG	SH	SV	IP	H	R	HR	HB	BB	SO	RAT	ERA	ERA+	OAV	OOB	BH	AVG	PB	PR	PR+	PD	TPI
1988	Chi-A	0	2	.000	9	2	0	0	1	20^2	25	11	2	0	7	8	13.9	4.79	83	.294	.348	0	—	0	-2	-2	-0	-0.2
1989	Chi-A	6	1	.857	50	1	0	0	0	65^2	64	37	11	2	28	43	12.9	4.52	84	.257	.337	0	—	0	-5	-5	-1	-0.6
1990	Chi-A	2	1	.667	43	0	0	0	2	66^1	58	27	6	2	34	40	12.8	3.39	113	.242	.341	0	—	0	4	3	0	0.2
1991	Chi-A	3	0	1.000	43	0	0	0	1	63^2	48	22	5	1	35	32	11.9	2.83	141	.214	.323	0	—	0	9	8	-1	0.3
1992	Chi-N	2	3	.400	32	1	0	0	0	41^2	41	25	7	1	27	23	14.9	3.89	93	.268	.381	0	.000	-0	-2	-1	-0	-0.2
1993	Cal-A	1	1	.500	46	0	0	0	1	59	54	30	7	0	35	36	13.6	4.58	99	.249	.353	0	—	0	-2	-0	-0	-0.1
1994	Cal-A	0	0	—	1	0	0	0	0	0^2	0	0	0	0	0	1	0.0	0.00	—	.000	.000	0	—	0	0	0	0	0.0
Total	7	14	8	.636	224	4	0	0	5	317^2	290	152	38	6	166	183	13.1	3.88	102	.248	.344	0	.000	-0	3	3	-3	-0.6

● REGGIE PATTERSON Patterson, Reginald Allen b: 11/7/58, Birmingham, Ala. BR/TR, 6'4", 180 lbs. Deb: 8/13/81

YEAR	TM/L	W	L	PCT	G	GS	CG	SH	SV	IP	H	R	HR	HB	BB	SO	RAT	ERA	ERA+	OAV	OOB	BH	AVG	PB	PR	PR+	PD	TPI
1981	Chi-A	0	1	.000	6	1	0	0	0	7^1	14	11	1	0	6	2	24.5	13.50	27	.412	.500	0	—	0	-8	-8	0	-0.9
1983	Chi-N	1	2	.333	5	2	0	0	0	18^2	17	12	3	2	6	10	12.1	4.82	79	.246	.325	0	.000	-1	-2	-2	-0	-0.4
1984	Chi-N	0	1	.000	3	1	0	0	0	6	10	7	1	0	2	5	18.0	10.50	37	.357	.400	0	.000	-0	-5	-4	0	-0.6
1985	Chi-N	3	0	1.000	8	5	1	0	0	39	36	13	2	0	10	17	10.6	3.00	133	.250	.299	1	.100	-0	3	4	-0	0.2
Total	4	4	4	.500	22	9	1	0	0	71	77	43	7	2	24	34	13.1	5.20	75	.280	.342	1	.056	-1	-12	-10	0	-1.7

● BOB PATTERSON Patterson, Robert Chandler b: 5/16/59, Jacksonville, Fla. BR/TL, 6'2", 192 lbs. Deb: 9/2/85

YEAR	TM/L	W	L	PCT	G	GS	CG	SH	SV	IP	H	R	HR	HB	BB	SO	RAT	ERA	ERA+	OAV	OOB	BH	AVG	PB	PR	PR+	PD	TPI
1985	SD-N	0	0	—	3	0	0	0	0	4	13	11	2	0	3	1	36.0	24.75	14	.565	.615	0	—	0	-9	-10	-0	-0.5
1986	Pit-N	2	3	.400	11	5	0	0	0	36^1	49	20	0	0	5	20	13.4	4.95	78	.322	.344	1	.125	-0	-5	-4	1	-0.5
1987	Pit-N	1	4	.200	15	7	0	0	0	43	49	34	5	1	22	27	15.1	6.70	61	.290	.375	1	.083	-1	-12	-12	-0	-1.3
1989	Pit-N	4	3	.571	12	3	0	0	1	26^2	23	13	3	0	8	20	10.5	4.05	83	.232	.290	0	.000	0	-2	-2	-0	-0.5
1990	*Pit-N	8	5	.615	55	5	0	0	5	94^2	88	33	9	3	21	70	10.6	2.95	123	.249	.296	1	.053	-1	9	7	-0	0.9
1991	*Pit-N	4	3	.571	54	1	0	0	2	65^2	67	32	7	0	15	57	11.2	4.11	87	.267	.308	1	.250	0	-3	-4	0	-0.4
1992	*Pit-N	6	3	.667	60	0	0	0	9	64^2	59	22	7	0	23	43	11.4	2.92	118	.246	.312	2	.333	1	4	4	-1	0.7
1993	Tex-A	2	4	.333	52	0	0	0	1	52^2	59	28	8	1	11	46	12.1	4.78	87	.282	.321	0	—	0	-3	-4	0	-0.4
1994	Cal-A	2	3	.400	47	0	0	0	1	42	35	21	6	2	15	30	11.1	4.07	120	.229	.306	0	—	0	3	4	-1	0.3
1995	Cal-A	5	2	.714	62	0	0	0	0	53^1	48	18	6	1	13	41	10.5	3.04	155	.246	.297	0	—	0	10	10	-1	1.0
1996	Chi-N	3	3	.500	79	0	0	0	8	54^2	46	19	6	1	22	53	11.4	3.13	139	.229	.308	1	.333	0	7	7	-1	0.8
1997	Chi-N	1	6	.143	76	0	0	0	0	59^1	47	23	9	0	10	58	8.6	3.34	129	.222	.257	0	.000	-0	6	6	0	0.7
1998	Chi-N	1	1	.500	33	0	0	0	1	20^1	36	20	2	0	12	17	21.2	7.52	59	.391	.462	0	—	0	-7	-7	-0	-0.7
Total	13	39	40	.494	559	21	0	0	28	617^1	619	294	70	9	180	483	11.8	4.08	98	.263	.318	7	.125	-1	-3	-5	-4	0.1

YEAR	TM/L	W	L	PCT	G	GS	CG	SH	SV	IP	H	R	HR	HB	BB	SO	RAT	ERA	ERA+	OAV	OOB	BH	AVG	PB	PR	PR+	PD	TPI
● ROY PATTERSON Patterson, Roy Lewis "Boy Wonder" b: 12/17/1876, Stoddard, Wis. d: 4/14/53, St.Croix Falls, Wis. BR/TR, 6', 185 lbs. Deb: 4/24/01																												
1901	Chi-A	20	15	.571	41	35	30	4	0	312^1	345	164	11	11	62	127	12.0	3.37	103	.277	.317	26	.222	1	10	4	0	0.4
1902	Chi-A	19	14	.576	34	30	26	2	0	268	262	111	5	3	67	61	11.1	3.06	111	.256	.304	20	.190	-2	15	10	1	1.0
1903	Chi-A	15	15	.500	34	30	26	2	1	293	275	119	5	11	69	89	10.9	2.70	104	.248	.298	11	.105	-6	8	4	2	0.0
1904	Chi-A	9	9	.500	22	17	14	4	0	165	148	52	1	7	24	64	9.8	2.29	107	.241	.277	6	.103	-4	6	3	-1	-0.2
1905	Chi-A	4	6	.400	13	9	7	0	0	88^2	73	34	0	0	16	29	9.0	1.83	135	.226	.263	8	.267	2	8	7	1	1.1
1906	Chi-A	10	7	.588	21	18	12	3	1	142	119	46	1	4	17	45	8.9	2.09	121	.231	.261	3	.061	-5	9	8	0	0.4
1907	Chi-A	4	6	.400	19	13	4	1	0	96	105	42	0	2	18	27	11.7	2.63	91	.280	.316	3	.097	-3	-1	-3	1	-0.4
Total	7	81	72	.529	184	152	119	16	2	1365	1327	568	23	38	273	442	10.8	2.75	107	.255	.297	77	.156	-16	57	33	5	2.3
● MARTY PATTIN Pattin, Martin William b: 4/6/43, Charleston, Ill. BR/TR, 5'11", 180 lbs. Deb: 5/14/68 C																												
1968	Cal-A	4	4	.500	52	4	0	0	3	84	67	27	7	2	37	66	11.4	2.79	104	.221	.310	1	.083	-1	2	1	-1	-0.1
1969	Sea-A	7	12	.368	34	27	2	1	0	158^2	166	104	29	2	71	126	13.6	5.62	65	.268	.345	9	.155	-1	-35	-35	-1	-3.9
1970	Mil-A	14	12	.538	37	29	11	0	0	233^1	204	91	20	6	71	161	10.8	3.39	112	.235	.298	9	.129	-2	8	10	2	1.1
1971	Mil-A☆	14	14	.500	36	36	9	5	0	264^2	225	100	29	4	73	169	10.3	3.13	111	.235	.292	7	.084	-3	10	10	-1	0.7
1972	Bos-A	17	13	.567	38	35	13	4	0	253	232	102	19	9	65	168	10.9	3.24	100	.243	.297	12	.140	0	-5	-0	1	0.0
1973	Bos-A	15	15	.500	34	30	11	2	1	219^1	238	112	31	8	69	119	12.9	4.31	93	.277	.337	0	—	0	-12	-7	1	-0.7
1974	KC-A	3	7	.300	25	11	2	0	0	117^1	121	55	10	2	28	50	11.6	3.99	96	.264	.309	0	—	0	-5	-2	-1	-0.3
1975	KC-A	10	10	.500	44	15	5	1	5	177	173	77	13	3	45	89	11.2	3.25	119	.253	.302	0	—	0	11	12	-1	1.2
1976	*KC-A	8	14	.364	44	15	4	1	5	141	114	51	9	3	38	65	9.9	2.49	141	.216	.273	0	—	0	16	16	-0	2.6
1977	*KC-A	10	3	.769	31	10	4	0	0	128^1	115	56	16	2	37	55	10.8	3.58	113	.242	.300	0	—	0	7	7	-1	0.6
1978	*KC-A	3	3	.500	32	5	2	0	4	78^2	72	41	8	2	25	30	11.3	3.32	116	.248	.312	0	—	0	4	4	-2	0.2
1979	KC-A	5	2	.714	31	7	1	0	3	94^1	109	50	11	1	21	41	12.5	4.58	93	.293	.332	0	—	0	-4	-3	-1	-0.3
1980	*KC-A	4	0	1.000	37	0	0	0	4	89	97	39	7	1	23	40	12.2	3.64	112	.277	.324	0	—	0	4	4	-1	0.1
Total	13	114	109	.511	475	224	64	14	25	2038^2	1933	905	209	45	603	1179	11.4	3.62	102	.250	.309	38	.123	-7	2	17	-6	1.2
● JIMMY PATTISON Pattison, James Wells b: 12/18/08, Bronx, N.Y. d: 2/22/91, Melbourne, Fla. BL/TL, 6', 185 lbs. Deb: 4/18/29																												
1929	Bro-N	0	1	.000	6	0	0	0	0	11^2	9	6	1	0	4	5	10.0	4.63	100	.231	.302	1	.500	0	0	-0	-0	0.0
● HARRY PATTON Patton, Harry Claude b: 6/29/1884, Gillespie, Ill. d: 6/9/30, St.Louis, Mo. Deb: 8/22/10																												
1910	StL-N	0	0	—	1	0	0	0	0	4	4	2	0	0	2	2	13.5	2.25	132	.267	.353	0	—	0	0	0	0	0.1
● MIKE PAUL Paul, Michael George b: 4/18/45, Detroit, Mich. BL/TL, 6', 183 lbs. Deb: 5/27/68 C																												
1968	Cle-A	5	8	.385	36	7	0	0	3	91^2	72	42	11	5	35	87	11.0	3.93	75	.213	.296	4	.167	0	-10	-10	-1	-1.6
1969	Cle-A	5	10	.333	47	12	0	0	2	117^1	104	48	12	2	54	98	12.3	3.61	105	.241	.328	0	.000	-3	0	2	-1	-0.1
1970	Cle-A	2	8	.200	30	15	1	0	0	88	91	51	13	0	45	70	13.9	4.81	82	.271	.357	4	.154	-1	-11	-8	-2	-1.0
1971	Cle-A	2	7	.222	17	12	1	0	0	62	78	42	8	5	14	33	14.1	5.95	64	.318	.367	1	.053	-1	-17	-13	-1	-1.9
1972	Tex-A	8	9	.471	49	20	2	1	1	161^2	149	50	4	2	52	108	11.3	2.17	139	.246	.308	8	.167	1	16	16	-1	1.7
1973	Tex-A	5	4	.556	36	10	1	0	2	87^1	104	55	9	5	36	49	14.9	4.95	75	.295	.368	0	—	0	-11	-12	1	-1.1
	Chi-N	0	1	.000	11	1	0	0	0	18^1	17	7	2	0	9	6	12.8	3.44	115	.258	.347	0	.000	-0	0	1	0	0.0
1974	Chi-N	0	1	.000	2	0	0	0	0	1^1	4	4	1	0	1	1	33.8	27.00	14	.500	.556	0	—	0	-3	-3	0	-0.6
Total	7	27	48	.360	228	77	5	1	8	627^2	619	299	60	19	246	452	12.7	3.91	89	.260	.334	17	.115	-4	-35	-29	-4	-4.6
● GENE PAULETTE Paulette, Eugene Edward b: 5/26/1891, Centralia, Ill. d: 2/8/66, Little Rock, Ark. BR/TR, 6', 150 lbs. Deb: 6/16/11 ♦																												
1918	StL-N	0	0	—	1	0	0	0	0	0^1	1	0	0	0	0	0	27.0	0.00	—	.500	.500	126	.273	0	0	0	0	0.0
● GIL PAULSEN Paulsen, Guilford Paul Hans b: 11/14/02, Graettinger, Iowa d: 4/2/94, Harlan, Iowa BR/TR, 6'2.5", 190 lbs. Deb: 10/3/25																												
1925	StL-N	0	0	—	1	0	0	0	0	2	1	0	0	0	0	1	4.5	0.00	—	.125	.125	0	—	0	1	1	0	0.1
● CARL PAVANO Pavano, Carl Anthony b: 1/8/76, New Britain, Conn. BR/TR, 6'5", 228 lbs. Deb: 5/23/98																												
1998	Mon-N	6	9	.400	24	23	0	0	0	134^2	130	70	18	8	43	83	12.1	4.21	100	.251	.318	6	.158	-0	0	-0	-1	-0.1
1999	Mon-N	6	8	.429	19	18	1	1	0	104	117	66	8	4	35	70	13.5	5.63	80	.285	.347	2	.061	-2	-12	-13	2	-1.5
2000	Mon-N	8	4	.667	15	15	0	0	0	97	89	40	8	8	34	64	12.2	3.06	154	.248	.327	5	.143	-1	17	18	0	1.9
Total	3	20	21	.488	58	56	1	1	0	335^2	336	176	34	20	112	217	12.5	4.32	103	.261	.330	13	.123	-4	5	5	2	0.3
● DAVE PAVLAS Pavlas, David Lee b: 8/12/62, Frankfurt, W.Germany BR/TR, 6'7", 180 lbs. Deb: 8/21/90																												
1990	Chi-N	2	0	1.000	13	0	0	0	0	21^1	23	7	2	0	6	12	12.2	2.11	194	.271	.319	0	.000	0	4	4	-0	0.4
1991	Chi-N	0	0	—	1	0	0	0	0	1	3	2	1	0	0	0	27.0	18.00	22	.750	.750	0	—	0	-2	-1	-0	-0.1
1995	NY-A	0	0	—	4	0	0	0	0	5^2	8	2	0	0	0	3	12.7	3.18	145	.333	.333	0	—	0	1	1	-0	0.0
1996	NY-A	0	0	—	16	0	0	0	1	23	23	7	0	1	7	18	12.1	2.35	211	.264	.326	0	—	0	7	7	0	0.3
Total	4	2	0	1.000	34	0	0	0	1	51	57	18	3	1	13	33	12.5	2.65	172	.285	.332	0	.000	0	10	11	-0	0.6
● ROGER PAVLIK Pavlik, Roger Allen b: 10/4/67, Houston, Tex. BB/TR, 6'2", 220 lbs. Deb: 5/2/92																												
1992	Tex-A	4	4	.500	13	12	1	0	0	62	66	32	3	3	34	45	15.0	4.21	90	.280	.377	0	—	0	-2	-3	-1	-0.4
1993	Tex-A	12	6	.667	26	26	2	0	0	166^1	151	67	18	5	80	131	12.8	3.41	122	.245	.336	0	—	0	17	14	1	1.5
1994	Tex-A	2	5	.286	11	11	0	0	0	50^1	61	45	8	4	30	31	17.0	7.69	63	.300	.401	0	—	0	-16	-16	0	-1.7
1995	Tex-A	10	10	.500	31	31	2	1	0	191^2	174	96	19	4	90	149	12.6	4.37	111	.243	.331	0	—	0	7	10	3	1.1
1996	*Tex-A★	15	8	.652	34	34	7	0	0	201	216	120	28	5	81	127	13.5	5.19	101	.276	.347	0	—	0	-4	1	-3	-0.2
1997	Tex-A	3	5	.375	11	11	0	0	0	57^2	59	29	7	1	31	35	14.2	4.37	110	.267	.360	0	—	0	1	3	-1	0.2
1998	Tex-A	1	1	.500	5	0	0	0	1	14	16	8	2	1	5	8	14.1	3.86	125	.286	.355	0	—	0	1	1	-0	0.2
Total	7	47	39	.547	131	125	12	1	1	743	743	397	85	23	351	526	13.5	4.58	103	.262	.348	0	—	0	5	9	-1	0.7
● JOHN PAWLOWSKI Pawlowski, John b: 9/6/63, Johnson City, N.Y. BR/TR, 6'2", 175 lbs. Deb: 9/19/87																												
1987	Chi-A	0	0	—	2	0	0	0	0	3^2	7	2	0	0	3	2	24.5	4.91	94	.438	.526	0	—	0	-0	-0	-0	0.0
1988	Chi-A	1	0	1.000	6	0	0	0	0	14	20	14	2	0	3	10	14.8	8.36	48	.328	.359	0	—	0	-7	-7	0	-0.4
Total	2	1	0	1.000	8	0	0	0	0	17^2	27	16	2	0	6	12	16.8	7.64	54	.351	.398	0	—	0	-7	-7	-0	-0.4
● MIKE PAXTON Paxton, Michael De Wayne b: 9/3/53, Memphis, Tenn. BR/TR, 5'11", 190 lbs. Deb: 5/25/77																												
1977	Bos-A	10	5	.667	29	12	2	1	0	108	134	53	7	3	25	58	13.5	3.83	118	.311	.353	0	—	0	3	7	-0	0.9
1978	Cle-A	12	11	.522	33	27	5	2	1	191	179	89	13	8	63	96	11.8	3.86	97	.247	.314	0	—	0	-2	-2	-1	-0.4
1979	Cle-A	8	8	.500	33	24	3	0	0	159^2	210	118	14	2	52	70	14.9	5.92	72	.315	.366	0	—	0	-30	-29	0	-2.5
1980	Cle-A	0	0	—	4	0	0	0	0	7^2	13	11	4	0	6	6	22.3	12.91	32	.394	.487	0	—	0	-8	-7	-0	-0.4
Total	4	30	24	.556	99	63	10	3	1	466^1	536	271	38	13	146	230	13.4	4.71	87	.289	.345	0	—	0	-36	-31	-2	-2.4
● GEORGE PAYNE Payne, George Washington b: 5/23/1890, Mt.Vernon, Ky. d: 1/24/59, Bellflower, Cal. BR/TR, 5'11", 172 lbs. Deb: 5/8/20																												
1920	Chi-A	1	1	.500	12	0	0	0	0	29^2	39	24	2	0	9	7	14.6	5.46	69	.312	.358	1	.125	-0	-5	-6	-1	-0.5
● HARLEY PAYNE Payne, Harley Fenwick "Lady" b: 1/9/1868, Windsor, Ont., Can. d: 12/29/35, Orwell, Ohio BB/TL, 6', 160 lbs. Deb: 4/18/1896																												
1896	Bro-N	14	16	.467	34	28	24	2	0	241^2	284	129	4	8	58	52	13.0	3.39	122	.290	.335	21	.214	0	26	21	3	2.3
1897	Bro-N	14	17	.452	40	38	30	1	0	280	350	215	8	17	71	86	14.1	4.63	89	.303	.353	26	.236	-0	-10	-17	1	-1.4
1898	Bro-N	1	0	1.000	1	1	1	0	0	9	11	8	0	0	3	2	14.0	4.00	90	.297	.350	3	.750	1	-0	-0	0	0.1
1899	Pit-N	1	3	.250	5	5	2	0	0	26^1	33	19	2	2	4	8	13.3	3.76	101	.306	.342	1	.100	-1	0	0	2	0.1
Total	4	30	36	.455	80	72	57	3	0	557	678	371	14	27	136	148	13.6	4.04	101	.298	.345	51	.230	0	16	3	7	1.1
● MIKE PAYNE Payne, Michael Earl b: 11/15/61, Woonsocket, R.I. BR/TR, 5'11", 165 lbs. Deb: 8/22/84																												
1984	Atl-N	0	1	.000	3	1	0	0	0	5^2	7	4	0	0	3	3	15.9	6.35	61	.333	.417	0	.000	-0	-2	-1	0	-0.2
● MIKE PAZIK Pazik, Michael Joseph b: 1/26/50, Lynn, Mass. BL/TL, 6'2", 195 lbs. Deb: 5/11/75 C																												
1975	Min-A	0	4	.000	5	3	0	0	0	19^2	28	20	5	0	10	8	17.4	8.24	47	.329	.400	0	—	0	-10	-10	-1	-1.6
1976	Min-A	0	0	—	5	0	0	0	0	9	13	9	0	1	4	6	18.0	7.00	51	.342	.419	0	—	0	-3	-3	-0	-0.2
1977	Min-A	1	0	1.000	3	3	0	0	0	18	18	5	1	0	6	6	12.0	2.50	160	.265	.324	0	—	0	3	3	0	0.2
Total	3	1	4	.200	13	6	0	0	0	46^2	59	34	6	1	20	20	15.4	5.79	67	.309	.377	0	—	0	-10	-10	-1	-1.6

YEAR	TM/L	W	L	PCT	G	GS	CG	SH	SV	IP	H	R	HR	HB	BB	SO	RAT	ERA	ERA+	OAV	OOB	BH	AVG	PB	PR	PR+	PD	TPI
● FRANK PEARCE	Pearce, Franklin Johnson b: 3/30/1860, Jefferson County, Ky. d: 11/13/26, Louisville, Ky. Deb: 10/4/1876																											
1876	Lou-N	0	0	—	1	0	0	0	0	4	5	4	0	1	1	1	13.5	4.50	60	.250	.300	0	.000	-0	-1	-1	-0	-0.1
● FRANK PEARCE	Pearce, Franklin Thomas b: 8/31/05, Middletown, Ky. d: 9/3/50, Van Buren, N.Y. BR/TR, 6', 170 lbs. Deb: 4/20/33																											
1933	Phi-N	5	4	.556	20	7	3	1	0	82	78	41	5	0	29	18	11.7	3.62	105	.251	.315	5	.192	-1	-3	2	0	0.1
1934	Phi-N	0	2	.000	7	1	0	0	0	20	25	16	4	0	5	4	13.5	7.20	66	.301	.341	2	.667	1	-7	-5	-1	-0.4
1935	Phi-N	0	0	—	5	0	0	0	0	13	22	15	0	0	6	7	19.4	8.31	55	.361	.418	2	.500	1	-6	-5	0	-0.1
Total	3	5	6	.455	32	8	3	1	0	115	125	72	9	0	40	29	12.9	4.77	85	.275	.333	9	.273	1	-16	-8	-0	-0.4
● GEORGE PEARCE	Pearce, George Thomas "Filbert" b: 1/10/1888, Aurora, Ill. d: 10/11/35, Joliet, Ill. BL/TL, 5'10.5", 175 lbs. Deb: 4/16/12																											
1912	Chi-N	0	0	—	3	2	0	0	0	14^2	15	13	0	0	12	9	16.6	5.52	60	.185	.290	1	.167	0	-3	-4	1	-0.1
1913	Chi-N	13	5	.722	25	21	14	3	0	164	137	60	4	3	59	73	10.9	2.30	138	.234	.308	4	.073	-3	16	16	-0	1.3
1914	Chi-N	9	12	.429	30	17	4	0	1	141	122	82	3	2	65	78	12.1	3.51	79	.239	.327	4	.089	-3	-11	-11	2	-1.8
1915	Chi-N	13	9	.591	36	20	8	2	0	176	158	83	1	4	77	96	12.2	3.32	84	.244	.328	11	.196	1	-11	-11	-0	-1.2
1916	Chi-N	0	0	—	4	1	0	0	0	4^1	6	5	0	0	1	0	14.5	2.08	140	.300	.333	0	—	0	0	0	-0	0.0
1917	StL-N	1	1	.500	5	0	0	0	0	10^1	7	7	0	1	3	4	9.6	3.48	77	.184	.262	0	.000	-1	-1	-1	0	-0.2
Total	6	36	27	.571	103	61	26	5	1	510^1	445	250	8	10	217	260	11.9	3.10	94	.236	.318	20	.120	-6	-10	-10	2	-2.0
● JIM PEARCE	Pearce, James Madison b: 6/9/25, Zebulon, N.C. BR/TR, 6'6", 180 lbs. Deb: 9/8/49																											
1949	Was-A	0	1	.000	2	1	0	0	0	5^1	9	10	1	0	5	1	23.6	8.44	50	.375	.483	0	.000	-0	-3	-2	1	-0.3
1950	Was-A	2	1	.667	20	3	1	0	0	56^2	58	40	2	1	37	18	15.2	6.04	74	.270	.379	2	.154	-1	-9	-10	-0	-0.6
1953	Was-A	0	1	.000	4	1	0	0	0	9^1	15	10	3	0	6	0	20.3	7.71	51	.405	.488	0	.000	-0	-4	-4	-0	-0.4
1954	Cin-N	1	0	1.000	2	1	1	0	0	11	7	1	0	1	5	3	10.6	0.00	—	.194	.310	0	.000	-0	5	5	0	0.4
1955	Cin-N	0	1	.000	2	1	0	0	0	3^1	8	5	0	0	0	0	21.6	10.80	39	.471	.471	0	—	0	-3	-2	0	-0.4
Total	5	3	4	.429	30	7	2	0	0	85^2	97	66	6	2	53	22	16.0	5.78	76	.295	.396	2	.105	-2	-13	-14	0	-1.3
● DICKEY PEARCE	Pearce, Richard J. b: 2/29/1836, Brooklyn, N.Y. d: 10/12/08, Wareham, Mass. BR/TR, 5'3.5", 161 lbs. Deb: 5/18/1871 MU♦																											
1875	StL-n	0	0	—	2	0	0	0	0	5^1	10	11	0		0	0	16.9	3.38	60	.333	.333	77	.248	0	-1	-1		0.0
● FRANK PEARS	Pears, Frank H. b: 8/30/1866, Kentucky d: 11/29/23, St.Louis, Mo. TR, 5'9", 145 lbs. Deb: 10/6/1889 U																											
1889	KC-a	0	2	.000	3	2	2	0	0	22	21	16	2	1	9	5	12.7	4.91	85	.244	.323	1	.091	-1	-3	-2	-0	-0.2
1893	StL-N	0	0	—	1	0	0	0	0	4	9	7	0	1	2	0	27.0	13.50	35	.429	.500	0	.000	-0	-4	-4	0	-0.2
Total	2	0	2	.000	4	2	2	0	0	26	30	23	2	2	11	5	14.9	6.23	69	.280	.358	1	.077	-2	-7	-5	-0	-0.4
● ALEX PEARSON	Pearson, Alexander Franklin b: 3/9/1877, Greensboro, Pa. d: 10/30/66, Rochester, Pa. BR/TR, 5'10.5", 160 lbs. Deb: 8/1/02																											
1902	StL-N	2	6	.250	11	10	8	0	0	82	90	47	0	3	22	24	12.6	3.95	69	.279	.330	9	.265	0	-11	-11	-0	-0.9
1903	Cle-A	1	2	.333	4	3	2	0	0	30^1	34	15	1	1	3	12	11.3	3.56	80	.281	.304	1	.083	-1	-2	-2	0	-0.3
Total	2	3	8	.273	15	13	10	0	0	112^1	124	62	1	4	25	36	12.3	3.85	72	.279	.323	10	.217	-0	-13	-14	-0	-1.2
● IKE PEARSON	Pearson, Issac Overton b: 3/1/17, Grenada, Miss. d: 3/17/85, Sarasota, Fla. BR/TR, 6'1", 180 lbs. Deb: 6/6/39																											
1939	Phi-N	2	13	.133	26	13	4	0	0	125	144	84	15	5	56	29	14.8	5.76	70	.296	.374	2	.054	-3	-26	-24	1	-2.7
1940	Phi-N	3	14	.176	29	20	5	1	1	145^1	160	91	13	3	57	43	13.6	5.45	72	.275	.343	9	.205	1	-26	-25	1	-2.3
1941	Phi-N	4	14	.222	46	10	0	0	6	136	139	75	8	8	70	38	14.4	3.57	104	.266	.361	5	.125	-2	1	2	0	0.0
1942	Phi-N	1	6	.143	35	7	0	0	0	85^1	87	48	4	4	50	21	14.9	4.54	73	.271	.376	1	.043	-2	-12	-12	-0	-1.2
1946	Phi-N	1	0	1.000	5	2	1	1	0	14^1	16	8	1	1	8	6	15.7	3.77	91	.271	.368	1	.200	1	-1	-1	0	0.1
1948	Chi-A	2	3	.400	23	2	0	0	1	53	62	32	8	2	27	12	15.5	4.92	87	.292	.378	2	.200	-0	-4	-4	1	-0.3
Total	6	13	50	.206	164	54	10	2	8	559	608	338	49	23	268	149	14.5	4.83	79	.279	.363	20	.126	-6	-66	-63	2	-6.4
● MONTE PEARSON	Pearson, Montgomery Marcellus "Hoot" b: 9/2/09, Oakland, Cal. d: 1/27/78, Fresno, Cal. BR/TR, 6', 175 lbs. Deb: 4/22/32																											
1932	Cle-A	0	0	—	8	0	0	0	0	8	10	9	1	0	11	5	23.6	10.13	47	.323	.500	0	—	0	-5	-5	1	-0.1
1933	Cle-A	10	5	.667	19	16	10	0	0	135^1	111	45	5	0	55	54	11.0	**2.33**	191	.221	.297	13	.260	1	29	31	-1	3.2
1934	Cle-A	18	13	.581	39	33	19	0	2	254^2	257	144	16	1	130	140	13.7	4.52	101	.260	.346	25	.272	6	-1	1	1	0.7
1935	Cle-A	8	13	.381	30	24	10	1	0	181^2	199	117	9	0	103	90	15.0	4.90	92	.279	.371	11	.177	-0	-9	-8	2	-0.6
1936	*NY-A☆	19	7	**.731**	33	31	15	1	1	223	191	99	13	3	135	118	13.3	3.71	125	**.233**	.343	23	.253	6	33	25	1	3.1
1937	*NY-A	9	3	.750	22	20	7	1	1	144^2	145	60	6	1	64	71	13.1	3.17	140	.261	.339	11	.216	1	23	21	-1	1.5
1938	*NY-A	16	7	.696	28	27	17	1	0	202	198	107	12	0	113	98	13.9	3.97	114	.258	.354	13	.171	1	18	13	2	1.5
1939	*NY-A	12	5	.706	22	20	8	0	0	146^1	151	77	9	1	70	76	13.7	4.49	97	.272	.354	17	.321	6	2	-2	1	0.4
1940	NY-A☆	7	5	.583	16	16	7	1	0	109^2	108	48	8	0	44	43	12.5	3.69	109	.262	.333	4	.121	-1	8	4	2	0.5
1941	Cin-N	1	3	.250	7	4	1	0	0	24^1	22	15	3	0	15	8	13.7	5.18	69	.242	.349	0	.000	-1	-4	-4	-0	-0.7
Total	10	100	61	.621	224	191	94	5	4	1429^2	1392	721	82	6	740	703	13.5	4.00	112	.256	.346	117	.228	19	95	77	8	9.5
● MARV PEASLEY	Peasley, Marvin Warren b: 7/16/1888, Jonesport, Me. d: 12/27/48, San Francisco, Cal BL/TL, 6'1", 175 lbs. Deb: 9/27/10																											
1910	Det-A	0	1	.000	2	1	0	0	0	10	13	14	0	1	11	4	22.5	8.10	32	.295	.446	0	.000	0	-6	-6	-0	-0.5
● GEORGE PECHINEY	Pechiney, George Adolphe "Pisch" b: 9/20/1861, Cincinnati, Ohio d: 7/14/43, Cincinnati, Ohio BR/TR, 5'9", 184 lbs. Deb: 8/4/1885																											
1885	Cin-a	7	4	.636	11	11	11	1	0	98	95	45	1	6	30	49	12.0	2.02	161	.247	.311	6	.150	-2	13	13	1	1.2
1886	Cin-a	15	21	.417	40	40	35	2	0	330^1	355	230	4	14	133	110	13.7	4.14	85	.266	.339	30	.208	-1	-25	-22	-3	-2.3
1887	Cle-a	1	9	.100	10	10	10	0	0	86	162	124	8	3	44	24	17.3	7.12	61	.374	.378	11	.289	-0	-27	-26	0	-2.0
Total	3	23	34	.404	61	61	56	3	0	514^1	612	399	13	23	207	183	14.0	4.23	85	.284	.341	47	.212	-3	-39	-35	-2	-3.1
● BILL PECOTA	Pecota, William Joseph b: 2/16/60, Redwood City, Cal. BR/TR, 6'2", 190 lbs. Deb: 9/19/86 ♦																											
1991	KC-A	0	0	—	1	0	0	0	0	2	4	1	0	0	0	0	18.0	4.50	92	.444	.444	114	.286	0	-0	-0	-0	0.0
1992	NY-N	0	0	—	1	0	0	0	0	1	1	1	1	0	0	0	9.0	9.00	39	.250	.250	61	.227	0	-1	-1	-0	0.0
Total	2	0	0	—	2	0	0	0	0	3	5	2	1	0	0	0	15.0	6.00	65	.385	.385	380	.249	0	-1	-1	-0	0.0
● STEVE PEEK	Peek, Stephen George b: 7/30/14, Springfield, Mass d: 9/20/91, Syracuse, N.Y. BB/TR, 6'2", 195 lbs. Deb: 4/16/41																											
1941	NY-A	4	2	.667	17	8	2	0	0	80	85	48	6	0	39	18	13.9	5.06	78	.276	.357	1	.036	-3	-8	-11	0	-0.9
● RED PEERY	Peery, George Allan b: 8/15/06, Payson, Utah d: 5/6/85, Salt Lake City, Ut. BL/TL, 5'11", 160 lbs. Deb: 9/22/27																											
1927	Pit-N	0	0	—	1	0	0	0	0	1	0	1	0	0	1	0	9.0	0.00	—	.000	.200	0	—	0	0	0	0	0.0
1929	Bos-N	0	1	.000	9	1	0	0	0	44	53	28	1	0	9	3	12.7	5.11	91	.305	.339	3	.214	1	-2	-2	-0	0.0
Total	2	0	1	.000	10	1	0	0	0	45	53	29	1	0	10	3	12.6	5.00	93	.298	.335	3	.214	1	-2	-2	0	0.0
● HEINIE PEITZ	Peitz, Henry Clement b: 11/28/1870, St.Louis, Mo. d: 10/23/43, Cincinnati, Ohio BR/TR, 5'11", 165 lbs. Deb: 10/15/1892 FC♦																											
1894	StL-N	0	0	—	1	0	0	0	0	3	7	7	0	1	2	0	30.0	9.00	60	.438	.526	89	.263	0	-1	-1	-0	-0.1
1897	Cin-N	0	1	.000	2	1	1	0	0	8	9	8	0	2	4	0	16.9	7.88	58	.281	.395	78	.293	0	-3	-3	1	-0.2
1899	Cin-N	0	0	—	1	0	0	0	0	5	6	3	0	0	1	3	12.6	5.40	73	.300	.333	79	.270	0	-1	-1	0	0.0
Total	3	0	1	.000	4	1	1	0	0	16	22	18	0	3	7	3	18.0	7.31	62	.324	.410	1117	.271	1	-5	-5	1	-0.3
● BARNEY PELTY	Pelty, Barney b: 9/10/1880, Farmington, Mo. d: 5/24/39, Farmington, Mo. BR/TR, 5'9", 175 lbs. Deb: 8/20/03																											
1903	StL-A	3	3	.500	7	6	5	0	1	48^2	49	25	1	2	15	20	12.2	2.40	121	.261	.322	3	.150	-0	3	3	-1	0.2
1904	StL-A	15	18	.455	39	35	31	2	0	301	270	121	7	20	77	126	11.0	2.84	87	.241	.301	15	.127	-6	-8	-13	-1	-2.2
1905	StL-A	14	14	.500	31	28	27	1	0	258^2	222	106	3	12	68	114	10.5	2.75	93	.233	.293	15	.153	-3	-3	-6	3	-0.7
1906	StL-A	16	11	.593	34	30	25	4	2	260^2	189	77	1	18	59	92	9.2	1.59	163	**.206**	.267	15	.165	-3	**32**	**30**	4	3.5
1907	StL-A	12	21	.364	36	31	29	5	1	273	234	101	1	18	64	85	10.4	2.57	98	.234	.292	16	.168	-2	-1	-2	2	-0.2
1908	StL-A	7	4	.636	20	13	7	1	0	122	104	44	0	10	32	36	10.8	1.99	120	.241	.309	5	.119	-3	5	5	1	0.3
1909	StL-A	11	11	.500	27	23	17	5	0	199^1	158	63	2	5	53	88	9.8	2.30	105	.222	.281	15	.165	0	4	3	4	0.8
1910	StL-A	5	11	.313	27	19	13	3	0	165^1	157	81	3	8	70	48	12.8	3.48	71	.263	.348	5	.089	-4	-18	-19	4	-1.8
1911	StL-A	7	15	.318	28	22	18	1	0	197	197	87	4	4	69	59	12.3	2.97	114	.265	.331	9	.138	-3	8	9	1	0.7
1912	StL-A	1	5	.167	6	6	2	0	0	38^2	43	27	0	3	15	10	14.2	5.59	59	.297	.374	0	.000	-2	-10	-10	0	-1.4
	Was-A	1	4	.200	11	4	1	0	0	43^2	40	18	0	4	10	15	11.1	3.30	101	.250	.310	2	.222	0	0	0	-1	0.0

YEAR	TM/L	W	L	PCT	G	GS	CG	SH	SV	IP	H	R	HR	HB	BB	SO	RAT	ERA	ERA+	OAV	OOB	BH	AVG	PB	PR	PR+	PD	TPI
	Yr	2	9	.182	17	10	3	0	0	82^1	83	45	0	7	25	25	12.6	4.37	76	.272	.341	2	.095	-2	-10	-10	-1	-1.4
Total	10	92	117	.440	266	217	175	22	4	1908	1663	750	22	104	532	693	10.8	2.63	100	.239	.302	100	.143	-25	14	0	16	-0.8
● ALEJANDRO PENA Pena, Alejandro (Vasquez) b: 6/25/59, Cambiaso, D.R. BR/TR, 6'1", 205 lbs. Deb: 9/14/81																												
1981	*LA-N	1	1	.500	14	0	0	0	2	25^1	18	8	2	0	11	14	10.3	2.84	117	.194	.279	0	.000	-1	2	1	0	0.1
1982	LA-N	0	2	.000	29	0	0	0	0	35^2	37	24	2	1	21	20	14.9	4.79	72	.272	.373	0	—	0	-5	-5	1	-0.2
1983	*LA-N	12	9	.571	34	26	4	3	1	177	152	67	7	1	51	120	10.4	2.75	131	.229	.285	6	.100	-2	18	17	2	1.9
1984	LA-N	12	6	.667	28	28	8	**4**	0	199^1	186	67	7	3	46	135	10.6	**2.48**	**142**	.246	.292	8	.121	-1	**25**	**24**	-1	1.9
1985	LA-N	0	1	.000	2	1	0	0	0	4^1	7	5	1	0	3	2	20.8	8.31	42	.350	.435	0	.000	-0	-2	-2	-0	-0.5
1986	LA-N	1	2	.333	24	10	0	0	1	70	74	40	6	1	30	46	13.5	4.89	71	.270	.344	3	.176	0	-9	-12	-1	-0.7
1987	LA-N	2	7	.222	37	7	0	0	11	87^1	82	41	9	2	37	76	12.5	3.50	113	.251	.331	1	.077	-1	6	5	-2	0.2
1988	*LA-N	6	7	.462	60	0	0	0	12	94^1	75	29	4	1	27	83	9.8	1.91	175	.218	.277	0	.000	-1	16	15	-0	2.4
1989	LA-N	4	3	.571	53	0	0	0	5	76	62	20	6	2	18	75	9.7	2.13	160	.220	.272	1	1.000	0	12	11	-1	1.1
1990	NY-N	3	3	.500	52	0	0	0	5	76	71	31	4	1	22	76	11.1	3.20	117	.245	.300	1	.167	0	5	5	-1	0.3
1991	NY-N	6	1	.857	44	0	0	0	4	63	63	20	5	0	19	49	11.7	2.71	134	.267	.322	0	—	0	7	7	-0	0.7
	*Atl-N	2	0	1.000	15	0	0	0	11	19^1	11	3	1	0	3	13	6.5	1.40	279	.167	.203	0	.000	-0	5	5	-0	1.0
	Yr	8	1	.889	59	0	0	0	15	82^1	74	23	6	0	22	62	10.5	2.40	154	.245	.296	0	.000	-0	12	12	-0	1.7
1992	Atl-N	1	6	.143	41	0	0	0	15	42	40	19	7	0	13	34	11.4	4.07	90	.255	.312	0	.000	-0	-3	-2	-1	-0.5
1994	Pit-N	3	2	.600	22	0	0	0	7	28^2	22	16	4	1	10	27	10.4	5.02	86	.206	.280	0	.000	-0	-3	-2	-1	-0.5
1995	Bos-A	1	1	.500	17	0	0	0	0	24^1	33	23	5	0	12	25	16.6	7.40	66	.314	.385	0	—	0	-7	-7	-0	-0.5
	Fla-N	2	0	1.000	13	0	0	0	0	18	11	3	2	0	3	21	7.0	1.50	281	.169	.206	0	.000	-0	5	5	-1	0.5
	*Atl-N	0	0	—	14	0	0	0	0	13	11	6	1	0	4	18	10.4	4.15	103	.224	.283	0	—	0	0	0	0	0.0
	Yr	2	0	1.000	27	0	0	0	0	31	22	9	3	0	7	39	8.4	2.61	162	.193	.240	0	.000	-0	5	6	-0	0.5
1996	Fla-N	0	1	.000	4	0	0	0	0	4	4	5	2	0	1	5	11.3	4.50	91	.235	.278	0	—	0	-0	-0	-0	0.0
Total	15	56	52	.519	503	72	12	7	74	1057^2	959	427	75	13	331	839	11.1	3.11	118	.240	.301	20	.110	-5	71	65	-8	7.2
● HIPOLITO PENA Pena, Hipolito (Concepcion) b: 1/30/64, Fantino, D.R. BL/TL, 6'3", 165 lbs. Deb: 9/1/86																												
1986	Pit-N	0	3	.000	10	1	0	0	1	8^1	7	10	3	1	3	6	11.9	8.64	44	.206	.289	0	—	0	-5	-4	-0	-0.9
1987	Pit-N	0	3	.000	16	1	0	0	1	25^2	16	14	2	0	26	16	14.7	4.56	90	.184	.372	1	.167	-0	-1	-1	-0	-0.1
1988	NY-A	1	1	.500	16	0	0	0	0	14^1	10	8	1	0	9	10	11.9	3.14	126	.192	.311	0	—	0	1	1	0	0.2
Total	3	1	7	.125	42	2	0	0	2	48^1	33	32	6	1	38	32	13.4	4.84	83	.191	.340	1	.167	-0	-5	-4	0	-0.8
● JIM PENA Pena, James Patrick b: 9/17/64, Los Angeles, Cal. BL/TL, 6', 175 lbs. Deb: 7/7/92																												
1992	SF-N	1	1	.500	25	2	0	0	0	44	49	19	4	1	20	32	14.3	3.48	95	.282	.359	1	.200	0	0	-1	1	0.0
● JESUS PENA Pena, Jesus b: 3/8/75, Santo Domingo, D.R. BL/TL, 6', 170 lbs. Deb: 8/7/99																												
1999	Chi-A	0	0	—	26	0	0	0	0	20^1	21	15	3	1	23	20	19.9	5.31	92	.259	.429	0	—	0	-1	-1	0	0.0
2000	Chi-A	2	1	.667	20	0	0	0	1	23^1	25	18	6	1	16	19	16.2	5.40	92	.278	.393	0	—	0	-1	-1	0	-0.1
	Bos-A	0	0	—	2	0	0	0	0	3	3	1	1	0	3	1	18.0	3.00	170	.273	.429	0	—	0	1	1	-0	0.0
	Yr	2	1	.667	22	0	0	0	1	26^1	28	19	7	1	19	20	16.4	5.13	97	.277	.397	0	—	0	-1	-0	0	-0.1
Total	2	2	1	.667	48	0	0	0	1	46^2	49	34	10	2	42	40	17.9	5.21	95	.269	.412	0	—	0	-2	-1	1	-0.1
● JOSE PENA Pena, Jose (Gutierrez) b: 12/3/42, Ciudad Juarez, Mex. BR/TR, 6'2", 190 lbs. Deb: 6/1/69																												
1969	Cin-N	1	1	.500	6	0	0	0	0	5	10	10	0	0	5	3	27.0	18.00	21	.400	.500	0	—	0	-8	-8	0	-1.4
1970	LA-N	4	3	.571	29	0	0	0	4	57	51	32	8	3	29	31	13.1	4.42	87	.241	.340	1	.125	0	-2	-4	1	-0.4
1971	LA-N	2	0	1.000	21	0	0	0	1	43	32	18	7	1	18	44	10.7	3.56	91	.211	.298	2	.667	1	-0	-2	-1	0.0
1972	LA-N	0	0	—	5	0	0	0	0	7^1	13	8	1	0	6	4	23.3	8.59	39	.371	.463	0	—	0	-4	-4	-0	-0.2
Total	4	7	4	.636	61	0	0	0	5	112^1	106	68	16	4	58	82	13.5	4.97	72	.250	.346	3	.273	1	-15	-18	0	-2.0
● JUAN PENA Pena, Juan Francisco b: 6/27/77, Santo Domingo, D.R. BR/TR, 6'5", 210 lbs. Deb: 5/8/99																												
1999	Bos-A	2	0	1.000	2	2	0	0	0	13	9	1	0	0	3	15	8.3	0.69	719	.196	.245	0	—	0	6	6	0	1.0
● ORLANDO PENA Pena, Orlando Gregorio (Quevara) b: 11/17/33, Victoria De Las Tunas, Cuba BR/TR, 5'11", 154 lbs. Deb: 8/24/58																												
1958	Cin-N	1	0	1.000	9	0	0	0	3	15	10	1	0	0	4	11	8.4	0.60	691	.185	.241	0	—	0	6	6	-0	0.6
1959	Cin-N	5	9	.357	46	8	1	0	5	136	150	80	26	0	39	76	12.5	4.76	85	.280	.329	3	.088	-0	-12	-11	-1	-1.2
1960	Cin-N	0	1	.000	4	0	0	0	0	9^1	8	3	0	0	3	9	10.6	2.89	132	.222	.282	0	.000	-0	1	1	-0	0.1
1962	KC-A	6	4	.600	13	12	6	1	0	89^2	71	31	9	1	27	56	9.9	3.01	140	.213	.274	5	.161	-0	10	11	-1	1.0
1963	KC-A	12	20	.375	35	33	9	3	0	217	218	93	24	5	53	128	11.4	3.69	106	.260	.308	9	.145	0	-1	5	-2	0.5
1964	KC-A	12	14	.462	40	32	5	0	0	219^1	231	126	40	8	73	184	12.8	4.43	86	.268	.331	12	.160	0	-20	-14	-2	-1.7
1965	KC-A	0	6	.000	12	5	0	0	0	35^1	42	30	4	2	13	24	14.5	6.88	51	.302	.370	1	.111	-0	-13	-13	-0	-2.0
	Det-A	4	6	.400	30	0	0	0	4	57^1	54	18	5	1	20	55	11.8	2.51	138	.252	.319	2	.250	1	6	6	-1	1.1
	Yr	4	12	.250	42	5	0	0	4	92^2	96	48	9	3	33	79	12.8	4.18	83	.272	.339	3	.176	1	-7	-7	-1	-0.9
1966	Det-A	4	2	.667	54	0	0	0	7	108	105	47	16	5	35	79	12.1	3.08	113	.252	.317	2	.111	-1	4	5	2	0.5
1967	Det-A	0	1	.000	2	0	0	0	0	2	5	3	0	1	0	2	27.0	13.50	24	.500	.545	0	—	0	-2	-2	-0	-0.4
	Cle-A	0	3	.000	48	1	0	0	8	88^1	67	34	8	1	22	72	9.2	3.36	97	.208	.261	0	.000	-1	-1	-1	-0	-0.2
	Yr	0	4	.000	50	1	0	0	8	90^1	72	37	8	2	22	74	9.6	3.59	91	.217	.270	0	.000	-1	-4	-3	-1	-0.6
1970	Pit-N	2	1	.667	23	0	0	0	2	37^2	38	21	6	1	7	25	11.0	4.78	82	.268	.307	0	.000	-1	-3	-4	1	-0.3
1971	Bal-A	0	1	.000	5	0	0	0	0	14^2	16	7	0	0	5	4	12.9	3.07	109	.281	.339	0	.000	-0	1	0	0	0.0
1973	Bal-A	1	1	.500	11	2	0	0	1	44^2	36	20	10	2	8	23	9.3	4.03	93	.218	.263	0	—	0	-1	-1	-0	-0.1
	StL-N	4	4	.500	42	0	0	0	6	62	60	17	3	0	14	38	10.7	2.18	168	.251	.292	1	.143	-0	10	10	0	1.5
1974	StL-N	5	2	.714	42	0	0	0	1	45	45	15	0	1	20	23	13.2	2.60	138	.269	.351	1	.500	0	5	5	-0	0.8
	Cal-A	0	0	—	4	0	0	0	3	8	6	0	0	0	1	5	7.9	0.00	—	.214	.241	0	—	0	3	3	0	0.3
1975	Cal-A	0	2	.000	7	0	0	0	0	12^2	13	3	0	0	8	4	14.9	2.13	167	.283	.389	0	—	0	2	2	-1	0.3
Total	14	56	77	.421	427	93	21	4	40	1202	1175	549	151	28	352	818	11.6	3.71	102	.255	.312	36	.136	-3	-7	8	-6	0.8
● RAMON PENA Pena, Ramon Arturo (Padilla) b: 5/5/62, Santiago, D.R. BR/TR, 5'10", 155 lbs. Deb: 4/27/89 F																												
1989	Det-A	0	0	—	8	0	0	0	0	18	26	13	0	2	8	12	18.0	6.00	64	.338	.414	0	—	0	-4	-4	1	-0.2
● RUSTY PENCE Pence, Russell William b: 3/11/1900, Marine, Ill. d: 8/11/71, Hot Springs, Ark. BR/TR, 6', 185 lbs. Deb: 5/13/21																												
1921	Chi-A	0	0	—	4	0	0	0	0	5^1	6	5	0	1	7	2	23.6	8.44	50	.286	.483	0	.000	-0	-2	-3	0	-0.1
● KEN PENNER Penner, Kenneth William b: 4/24/1896, Boonville, Ind. d: 5/28/59, Sacramento, Cal. BL/TR, 5'11.5", 170 lbs. Deb: 9/11/16																												
1916	Cle-A	1	1	.500	4	2	0	0	0	12^2	14	6	0	0	4	5	12.8	4.26	71	.304	.360	0	.000	-0	-2	-2	1	-0.2
1929	Chi-N	0	1	.000	5	0	0	0	0	12^2	14	11	1	0	6	3	14.2	2.84	162	.280	.357	1	.250	0	3	3	-0	0.2
Total	2	1	2	.333	9	2	0	0	0	25^1	28	17	1	0	10	8	13.5	3.55	108	.292	.358	1	.167	-0	1	1	1	0.0
● BRAD PENNINGTON Pennington, Brad Lee b: 4/14/69, Salem, Ind. BL/TL, 6'5", 205 lbs. Deb: 4/17/93																												
1993	Bal-A	3	2	.600	34	0	0	0	4	33	34	25	7	2	25	39	16.6	6.55	69	.266	.394	0	—	0	-8	-7	-0	-1.1
1994	Bal-A	0	1	.000	8	0	0	0	0	6	9	8	2	0	8	7	25.5	12.00	42	.346	.500	0	—	0	-5	-4	-0	-0.6
1995	Bal-A	0	1	.000	8	0	0	0	0	6^2	3	7	1	0	11	10	18.9	8.10	59	.136	.424	0	—	0	-3	-2	-0	-0.3
	Cin-N	0	0	—	6	0	0	0	0	9^2	9	8	0	1	11	7	19.6	5.59	74	.273	.467	0	.000	-0	-2	-2	-0	-0.1
1996	Bos-A	0	2	.000	14	0	0	0	0	13	6	5	1	0	15	13	14.5	2.77	183	.140	.362	0	—	0	3	3	0	0.4
	Cal-A	0	0	—	8	0	0	0	0	7^1	5	10	1	0	16	7	25.8	12.27	41	.185	.488	0	—	0	-6	-6	-0	-0.3
	Yr	0	2	.000	22	0	0	0	0	20^1	11	15	2	0	31	20	18.6	6.20	82	.157	.416	0	—	0	-3	-3	-0	0.1
1998	TB-A	0	0	—	1	0	0	0	0	0	1	0	0	3	—	—	∞	—	1.000	1.000	103	—	0	-1	-1	0		-0.1
Total	5	3	6	.333	79	0	0	0	4	75^2	67	64	12	3	89	83	18.9	7.02	66	.239	.427	0	.000	-0	-21	-19	-1	-2.1
● KEWPIE PENNINGTON Pennington, George Louis b: 9/24/1896, New York, N.Y. d: 5/3/53, Newark, N.J. BR/TR, 5'8.5", 168 lbs. Deb: 4/14/17																												
1917	StL-A	0	0	—	1	0	0	0	0	1	1	0	0	0	0	0	9.0	0.00	—	.250	.250	0	—	0	0	0	-0	0.0

YEAR TM/L	W	L	PCT	G	GS	CG	SH	SV	IP	H	R	HR	HB	BB	SO	RAT	ERA	ERA+	OAV	OOB	BH	AVG	PB	PR	PR+	PD	TPI
● **HERB PENNOCK** Pennock, Herbert Jefferis "The Knight Of Kennett Square" b: 2/10/1894, Kennett Square, Pa d: 1/30/48, New York, N.Y. BB/TL, 6', 160 lbs. Deb: 5/14/12 CH																											
1912 Phi-A	1	2	.333	17	2	1	0	2	50	48	31	1	3	30	38	14.6	4.50	68	.262	.375	2	.133	-1	-7	-9	1	-0.6
1913 Phi-A	2	1	.667	14	3	1	0	0	33^1	30	24	4	0	22	17	14.0	5.13	54	.221	.329	1	.111	-0	-8	-9	-0	-0.8
1914 *Phi-A	11	4	.733	28	14	8	3	3	151^2	136	56	1	2	65	90	12.0	2.79	94	.248	.330	12	.214	2	-1	-3	-1	-0.1
1915 Phi-A	3	6	.333	11	8	3	1	1	44	46	34	2	2	29	24	15.8	5.32	55	.266	.377	5	.278	1	-12	-12	1	-2.0
Bos-A	0	0	—	5	1	0	0	0	14	23	16	0	0	10	7	21.2	9.64	29	.390	.478	1	.167	0	-10	-11	-1	-0.6
Yr	3	6	.333	16	9	3	1	1	58	69	50	2	2	39	31	17.1	6.36	45	.297	.403	6	.250	1	-22	-23	-0	-2.6
1916 Bos-A	0	2	.000	9	2	0	0	1	26^2	23	11	0	1	8	12	10.8	3.04	91	.245	.311	1	.125	-0	-1	-1	-1	-0.1
1917 Bos-A	5	5	.500	24	5	4	1	1	100^2	90	49	2	3	23	35	10.4	3.31	78	.243	.292	4	.167	2	-7	-8	-0	-0.7
1919 Bos-A	16	8	.667	32	26	16	5	0	219	223	78	2	3	48	70	11.3	2.71	111	.274	.316	13	.173	1	13	8	-2	0.7
1920 Bos-A	16	13	.552	37	31	19	4	2	242^1	244	108	9	4	61	68	11.5	3.68	99	.264	.312	20	.260	4	3	-1	-3	0.1
1921 Bos-A	13	14	.481	32	31	15	1	0	222^2	268	121	7	2	59	91	13.3	4.04	105	.307	.352	18	.212	2	6	5	1	0.8
1922 Bos-A	10	17	.370	32	26	15	1	1	202	230	108	7	1	74	59	13.6	4.32	95	.297	.359	9	.138	-3	-6	-5	1	-0.7
1923 *NY-A	19	6	**.760**	35	27	21	1	3	238^1	235	86	11	2	68	93	11.5	3.13	126	.261	.314	16	.193	0	23	22	1	2.2
1924 NY-A	21	9	.700	40	34	25	4	3	286^1	302	104	13	1	64	101	11.5	2.83	147	.273	.314	16	.158	-2	45	**43**	-1	3.8
1925 NY-A	16	17	.485	47	31	21	2	2	**277**	267	117	11	2	71	88	**11.0**	2.96	144	.254	**.303**	20	.202	-3	**44**	**41**	-3	3.8
1926 *NY-A	23	11	.676	40	33	19	1	2	266^1	294	133	11	4	43	78	**11.5**	3.62	107	.282	**.313**	18	.212	3	12	7	1	1.2
1927 *NY-A	19	8	.704	34	26	18	1	2	209^2	225	89	5	2	48	51	11.8	3.00	128	.283	.325	15	.217	-0	26	21	-2	2.2
1928 NY-A	17	6	.739	28	24	18	**5**	3	211	215	71	2	0	40	53	10.9	2.56	147	.267	.302	15	.203	-1	35	30	2	3.2
1929 NY-A	9	11	.450	27	23	8	1	2	157^1	205	101	11	3	28	49	13.5	4.92	78	.318	.349	9	.176	-1	-12	-20	-1	-2.3
1930 NY-A	11	7	.611	25	19	11	1	0	156^1	194	95	8	0	20	46	12.3	4.32	100	.301	.322	11	.183	-2	6	-0	-2	-0.4
1931 NY-A	11	6	.647	25	25	12	1	0	189^1	247	96	7	1	30	65	13.2	4.28	93	.315	.342	10	.152	1	2	-7	-1	-0.5
1932 *NY-A	9	5	.643	22	21	9	1	0	146^2	191	94	8	0	38	54	14.1	4.60	89	.310	.350	8	.151	0	-2	-9	-1	-0.8
1933 NY-A	7	4	.636	23	5	2	1	4	65	96	46	4	0	21	22	16.2	5.54	70	.342	.387	5	.238	0	-9	-13	-0	-2.0
1934 Bos-A	2	0	1.000	30	2	1	0	1	62	68	31	2	0	16	16	12.2	3.05	158	.276	.321	3	.214	-0	**10**	**11**	-1	0.4
Total 22	241	162	.598	617	419	247	35	33	3571^2	3900	1699	128	36	916	1227	12.2	3.60	106	.281	.328	232	.191	3	150	85	-11	6.8
● **BRAD PENNY** Penny, Bradley Wayne b: 5/24/78, Broken Arrow, Okla. BR/TR, 6'4", 200 lbs. Deb: 4/7/2000																											
2000 Fla-N	8	7	.533	23	22	0	0	0	119^2	120	70	13	5	60	80	13.9	4.81	92	.263	.355	5	.111	-2	-2	-5	0	-0.7
● **PAUL PENSON** Penson, Paul Eugene b: 7/12/31, Kansas City, Kan. BR/TR, 6'1", 185 lbs. Deb: 4/21/54																											
1954 Phi-N	1	1	.500	5	3	0	0	0	16	14	11	1	0	14	3	15.8	4.50	90	.237	.384	0	.000	-1	-1	-1	-1	-0.2
● **GENE PENTZ** Pentz, Eugene David b: 6/21/53, Johnstown, Pa. BR/TR, 6'1", 200 lbs. Deb: 7/29/75																											
1975 Det-A	0	4	.000	13	0	0	0	0	25^1	27	14	0	0	20	21	16.7	3.20	126	.293	.420	0	—	0	2	2	-0	0.3
1976 Hou-N	3	3	.500	40	0	0	0	5	63^2	62	26	5	1	31	36	13.3	2.97	108	.259	.347	1	.200	0	4	2	1	0.3
1977 Hou-N	5	2	.714	41	4	0	0	2	87	76	41	8	1	44	51	12.5	3.83	93	.236	.330	0	.000	-2	1	-3	0	-0.4
1978 Hou-N	0	0	—	10	0	0	0	0	15	12	13	1	1	13	8	15.6	6.00	55	.214	.371	0	.000	-0	-4	-5	1	-0.2
Total 4	8	9	.471	104	4	0	0	7	191	177	94	14	3	108	116	13.6	3.63	96	.250	.351	1	.053	-1	2	-3	1	0.0
● **JIMMY PEOPLES** Peoples, James Elsworth b: 10/8/1863, Big Beaver, Mich. d: 8/29/20, Detroit, Mich. TR, 5'8", 200 lbs. Deb: 5/29/1884 U◆																											
1885 Cin-a	0	2	.000	2	2	1	0	0	15	30	28	0	3	2	4	21.0	12.00	27	.390	.427	4	.182	-0	-15	-15	1	-1.2
● **LAURIN PEPPER** Pepper, Hugh McLaurin b: 1/18/31, Vaughan, Miss. BR/TR, 5'11", 190 lbs. Deb: 7/4/54																											
1954 Pit-N	1	5	.167	14	8	0	0	0	50^2	63	53	4	0	43	17	18.8	7.99	52	.315	.436	4	.235	0	-22	-21	1	-1.9
1955 Pit-N	0	1	.000	14	1	0	0	0	20	30	24	5	2	25	7	25.6	10.35	40	.370	.528	0	.000	0	-14	-14	-0	-0.7
1956 Pit-N	1	1	.500	11	7	0	0	0	30	30	17	1	0	25	12	16.5	3.00	126	.256	.387	0	.000	-0	3	3	-1	0.0
1957 Pit-N	0	1	.000	5	1	0	0	0	9	11	8	1	0	5	4	16.0	8.00	47	.297	.381	0	—	0	-4	-4	-0	-0.4
Total 4	2	8	.200	44	17	0	0	0	109^2	134	102	11	2	98	40	19.2	7.06	57	.308	.437	4	.160	-0	-38	-36	0	-3.0
● **BOB PEPPER** Pepper, Robert Ernest b: 5/3/1895, Rosston, Pa. d: 4/8/68, Ford Cliff, Pa. BR/TR, 6'2", 178 lbs. Deb: 7/23/15																											
1915 Phi-A	0	0	—	1	0	0	0	0	5	6	5	0	1	4	0	19.8	1.80	163	.333	.478	0	.000	-0	1	1	-0	0.0
● **HARRISON PEPPERS** Peppers, Harrison (b: William Harrison Pepper) b: 9/1866, Kentucky d: 11/5/03, Webb City, Mo. BL, Deb: 6/30/1894																											
1894 Lou-N	0	1	.000	2	1	0	0	0	8	10	7	0	0	4	0	15.8	6.75	76	.303	.378	0	.000	-1	-1	-2	-0	-0.2
● **LUIS PERAZA** Peraza, Luis (Rios) b: 6/17/42, Rio Piedras, P.R. BR/TR, 5'11", 185 lbs. Deb: 4/9/69																											
1969 Phi-N	0	0	—	8	0	0	0	0	9	12	6	1	0	2	7	14.0	6.00	59	.364	.400	0	.000	-0	-2	-2	-0	-0.2
● **OSWALDO PERAZA** Peraza, Oswald Jose b: 10/19/62, Puerto Cabello, Venez. BR/TR, 6'4", 172 lbs. Deb: 4/4/88																											
1988 Bal-A	5	7	.417	19	15	1	0	0	86	98	62	10	2	37	61	14.3	5.55	71	.282	.355	0	—	0	-15	-16	0	-1.9
● **TROY PERCIVAL** Percival, Troy Eugene b: 8/9/69, Fontana, Cal. BR/TR, 6'3", 200 lbs. Deb: 4/26/95																											
1995 Cal-A	3	2	.600	62	0	0	0	3	74	37	19	6	1	26	94	7.8	1.95	242	.147	.229	0	—	0	23	23	-1	1.4
1996 Cal-A★	0	2	.000	62	0	0	0	36	74	38	20	8	2	31	100	8.6	2.31	217	.149	.247	0	.000	-0	22	22	-1	2.3
1997 Ana-A	5	5	.500	55	0	0	0	27	52	40	20	6	4	22	72	11.4	3.46	132	.205	.299	0	—	0	6	6	-1	1.2
1998 Ana-A★	2	7	.222	67	0	0	0	42	66^2	45	31	5	3	37	87	11.5	3.65	129	.186	.301	0	—	0	7	8	-1	1.4
1999 Ana-A☆	4	6	.400	60	0	0	0	31	57	38	24	9	3	22	58	9.9	3.79	128	.186	.275	0	—	0	7	7	-1	1.2
2000 Ana-A	5	5	.500	54	0	0	0	32	50	42	27	7	2	30	49	13.3	4.50	110	.228	.343	0	—	0	2	3	-1	0.4
Total 6	19	27	.413	360	0	0	0	171	373^2	240	141	41	15	168	460	10.2	3.16	152	.180	.279	0	.000	-0	68	68	-5	7.9
● **HUB PERDUE** Perdue, Herbert Rodney "The Gallatin Squash" b: 6/7/1882, Bethpage, Tenn. d: 10/31/68, Gallatin, Tex. BR/TR, 5'10.5", 192 lbs. Deb: 4/19/11																											
1911 Bos-N	6	10	.375	24	19	9	0	1	137^1	180	100	10	4	41	40	14.7	4.98	77	.321	.372	10	.208	-1	-24	-16	-0	-1.7
1912 Bos-N	13	16	.448	37	30	20	1	3	249	295	135	11	2	54	101	12.7	3.80	94	.303	.341	12	.138	-5	-11	-6	-4	-1.5
1913 Bos-N	16	13	.552	38	32	16	3	1	212^1	201	107	7	4	39	91	10.3	3.26	101	.249	.287	7	.104	-5	-1	0	-7	-1.1
1914 Bos-N	2	5	.286	9	9	2	0	0	51	60	35	5	3	11	13	13.1	5.82	47	.311	.357	1	.071	-0	-17	-18	0	-2.1
StL-N	8	8	.500	22	19	12	0	1	153^1	160	60	3	5	35	43	11.7	2.82	99	.290	.338	8	.167	-1	-0	-0	-4	-0.6
Yr	10	13	.435	31	28	14	0	1	204^1	220	95	8	8	46	56	12.1	3.57	78	.296	.343	9	.145	-1	-18	-18	-4	-2.7
1915 StL-N	6	12	.333	31	13	5	1	1	115^1	141	66	7	2	19	29	12.6	4.21	66	.311	.341	4	.111	-1	-19	-18	-1	-2.9
Total 5	51	64	.443	161	122	64	5	7	918^1	1037	503	43	20	199	317	12.3	3.85	85	.293	.334	42	.140	-13	-73	-58	-15	-9.9
● **CARLOS PEREZ** Perez, Carlos Gross (b: Carlos Gross (Perez)) b: 4/14/71, Nigua, D.R. BL/TL, 6'3", 195 lbs. Deb: 4/27/95 F																											
1995 Mon-N★	10	8	.556	28	23	2	1	0	141^1	142	61	18	5	28	106	11.1	3.69	116	.257	.299	6	.133	1	8	9	0	1.2
1997 Mon-N	12	13	.480	33	32	8	**5**	0	206^2	206	109	21	4	48	110	11.2	3.88	108	.260	.305	11	.172	2	8	7	2	1.1
1998 Mon-N	7	10	.412	23	23	3	0	0	163^1	177	79	12	3	33	82	11.7	3.75	112	.277	.315	9	.191	2	9	8	1	1.0
LA-N	4	4	.500	11	11	4	2	0	77^2	67	30	9	0	30	46	11.2	3.24	122	.234	.307	2	.083	-0	9	7	1	0.6
Yr	11	14	.440	34	34	7	2	0	241	244	109	21	3	63	128	11.6	3.59	115	.263	.313	11	.155	1	17	15	1	1.6
1999 LA-N	2	10	.167	17	16	0	0	0	89^2	116	77	23	6	39	40	16.2	7.43	58	.317	.392	8	.296	4	-29	-33	-0	-3.1
2000 LA-N	5	8	.385	30	22	0	0	0	144	192	95	25	8	33	64	14.6	5.56	79	.324	.368	2	.047	-3	-15	-20	-0	-1.8
Total 5	40	53	.430	142	127	17	8	0	822^2	900	451	108	26	211	448	12.4	4.44	96	.279	.328	38	.152	6	-11	-19	3	-1.0
● **GEORGE PEREZ** Perez, George Thomas b: 12/29/37, San Fernando, Cal. BR/TR, 6'2.5", 200 lbs. Deb: 4/17/58																											
1958 Pit-N	0	1	.000	4	0	0	0	1	8^1	9	5	1	0	4	2	14.0	5.40	72	.300	.382	0	.000	-0	-1	-1	-0	-0.2
● **MELIDO PEREZ** Perez, Melido Turpen Gross (b: Melido Turpen Gross (Perez)) b: 2/15/66, San Cristobal, D.R. BR/TR, 6'4", 180 lbs. Deb: 9/4/87 F																											
1987 KC-A	1	1	.500	3	3	0	0	0	10^1	18	12	2	0	5	5	20.0	7.84	58	.375	.434	0	—	0	-4	-4	-1	-0.6
1988 Chi-A	12	10	.545	32	32	3	1	0	197	186	105	26	2	72	138	11.9	3.79	105	.248	.316	0	—	0	4	4	-2	0.2
1989 Chi-A	11	14	.440	31	31	2	0	0	183^1	187	106	23	3	90	141	13.7	5.01	76	.264	.350	0	—	0	-23	-25	-1	-3.0
1990 Chi-A	13	14	.481	35	35	3	3	0	197	177	111	14	2	86	161	12.1	4.61	83	.241	.322	0	—	0	-15	-18	-2	-2.3
1991 Chi-A	8	7	.533	49	8	0	0	1	135^2	111	49	15	1	52	128	10.9	3.12	128	.224	.299	0	—	0	15	13	1	1.4
1992 NY-A	13	16	.448	33	33	10	1	0	247^2	212	94	16	5	93	218	11.3	2.87	137	.235	.310	0	—	0	30	29	-1	3.2

YEAR TM/L	W	L	PCT	G	GS	CG	SH	SV	IP	H	R	HR	HB	BB	SO	RAT	ERA	ERA+	OAV	OOB	BH	AVG	PB	PR	PR+	PD	TPI
1993 NY-A	6	14	.300	25	25	0	0	0	163	173	103	22	1	64	148	13.1	5.19	80	.267	.334	0	—	0	-15	-19	-1	-2.1
1994 NY-A	9	4	.692	22	22	1	0	0	151^1	134	74	16	3	58	109	11.6	4.10	112	.238	.313	0	—	0	12	8	-0	0.6
1995 NY-A	5	5	.500	13	12	1	0	0	69^1	70	46	10	1	31	44	13.2	5.58	83	.261	.340	0	—	0	-7	-8	-1	-1.0
Total 9	78	85	.479	243	201	20	5	1	1354^2	1268	700	144	18	551	1092	12.2	4.17	97	.248	.323	0	—	0	-4	-17	-8	-3.6
● MIKE PEREZ	Perez, Michael Irvin (Ortega) b: 10/19/64, Yauco, P.R. BR/TR, 6', 187 lbs. Deb: 9/5/90																										
1990 StL-N	1	0	1.000	13	0	0	0	1	13^2	12	6	0	0	3	5	9.9	3.95	97	.240	.283	0	.000	-0	-0	-0	0	0.0
1991 StL-N	0	2	.000	14	0	0	0	0	17	19	11	1	1	7	7	14.3	5.82	64	.288	.365	0	—	0	-4	-4	-0	-0.5
1992 StL-N	9	3	.750	77	0	0	0	0	93	70	23	4	1	32	46	10.0	1.84	185	.210	.281	0	.000	-0	17	17	0	2.1
1993 StL-N	7	2	.778	65	0	0	0	7	72^2	65	24	4	1	20	58	10.7	2.48	160	.243	.299	0	.000	0	13	12	0	1.7
1994 StL-N	2	3	.400	36	0	0	0	12	31	52	32	5	3	10	20	18.9	8.71	48	.391	.445	0	—	0	-15	-16	-0	-3.0
1995 Chi-N	2	6	.250	68	0	0	0	2	71^1	72	30	8	4	27	49	13.0	3.66	112	.268	.343	0	.000	0	4	4	-1	0.3
1996 Chi-N	1	0	1.000	24	0	0	0	0	27	29	14	2	3	13	22	15.0	4.67	93	.264	.357	0	.000	-0	-1	-1	-0	-0.1
1997 KC-A	2	0	1.000	16	0	0	0	0	20^1	15	8	2	1	8	17	10.6	3.54	133	.214	.304	0	—	0	2	3	0	0.2
Total 8	24	16	.600	313	0	0	0	22	346	334	148	26	14	120	224	12.2	3.56	110	.257	.327	0	.000	-0	15	14	0	0.7
● ODALIS PEREZ	Perez, Odalis Amadol b: 6/7/78, Las Matas De Farfan, D.R. BL/TL, 6', 175 lbs. Deb: 9/1/98																										
1998 *Atl-N	0	1	.000	10	0	0	0	0	10^2	10	5	1	0	4	5	11.8	4.22	99	.244	.311	0	—	0	0	-0	-0	0.0
1999 Atl-N	4	6	.400	18	17	0	0	0	93	100	65	12	1	53	82	14.9	6.00	75	.275	.369	4	.133	-1	-15	-16	1	-1.4
Total 2	4	7	.364	28	17	0	0	0	103^2	110	70	13	1	57	87	14.6	5.82	77	.272	.364	4	.133	-1	-15	-16	1	-1.4
● PASCUAL PEREZ	Perez, Pascual Gross (b: Pascual Gross (Perez)) b: 5/17/57, San Cristobal, D.R. BR/TR, 6'2", 163 lbs. Deb: 5/7/80 F																										
1980 Pit-N	0	1	.000	2	2	0	0	0	12	15	6	0	2	2	7	14.3	3.75	97	.341	.396	1	.250	0	-0	-0	-0	0.0
1981 Pit-N	2	7	.222	17	13	2	0	0	86^1	92	50	5	3	34	46	13.4	3.96	91	.273	.345	3	.136	-0	-5	-3	-0	-0.4
1982 *Atl-N	4	4	.500	16	11	0	0	0	79^1	85	35	4	0	17	29	11.6	3.06	122	.276	.314	3	.167	1	5	6	0	0.7
1983 Atl-N★	15	8	.652	33	33	7	1	0	215^1	213	88	20	4	51	144	11.2	3.43	113	.260	.307	12	.160	-1	5	10	1	1.1
1984 Atl-N	14	8	.636	30	30	4	1	0	211^2	208	96	26	3	51	145	11.1	3.74	103	.260	.307	5	.076	-2	-3	3	3	0.4
1985 Atl-N	1	13	.071	22	22	0	0	0	95^1	115	72	10	1	57	57	16.3	6.14	63	.297	.389	3	.120	-0	-27	-23	-1	-3.0
1987 Mon-N	7	0	1.000	10	10	2	0	0	70^1	52	21	5	1	16	58	8.8	2.30	183	.206	.257	1	.042	-2	14	14	1	1.3
1988 Mon-N	12	8	.600	27	27	4	2	0	188	133	59	15	7	44	131	**8.8**	2.44	148	.196	**.253**	2	.037	-3	21	23	2	2.4
1989 Mon-N	9	13	.409	33	28	2	0	0	198^1	178	85	15	4	45	152	10.3	3.31	107	.237	.283	11	.204	2	4	5	0	0.8
1990 NY-A	1	2	.333	3	3	0	0	0	14	8	3	0	0	3	12	7.1	1.29	310	.163	.212	0	—	0	4	4	-0	0.9
1991 NY-A	2	4	.333	14	14	0	0	0	73^2	68	26	7	0	24	41	11.2	3.18	131	.250	.311	0	—	0	8	8	-0	0.5
Total 11	67	68	.496	207	193	21	4	0	1244^1	1167	541	107	25	344	822	11.1	3.44	110	.249	.303	41	.120	-5	26	46	6	4.7
● YORKIS PEREZ	Perez, Yorkis Miguel Vargas (b: Yorkis Miguel Vargas (Perez)) b: 9/30/67, Bajos De Haina, D.R. BL/TL, 6', 180 lbs. Deb: 9/30/91																										
1991 Chi-N	1	0	1.000	3	0	0	0	0	4^1	2	1	0	0	2	3	8.3	2.08	187	.167	.286	0	—	0	1	1	0	0.2
1994 Fla-N	3	0	1.000	44	0	0	0	0	40^2	33	18	4	1	14	41	10.6	3.54	124	.220	.291	0	.000	-0	3	4	-1	0.2
1995 Fla-N	2	6	.250	69	0	0	0	1	46^2	35	29	6	2	28	47	12.5	5.21	81	.203	.322	0	.000	-0	-5	-5	-1	-0.9
1996 Fla-N	3	4	.429	64	0	0	0	0	47^2	51	28	2	1	31	47	15.7	5.29	77	.274	.381	0	.000	-0	-6	-7	0	-0.8
1997 NY-N	0	1	.000	9	0	0	0	0	8^2	15	8	2	0	4	7	19.7	8.31	49	.375	.432	0	.000	-0	-4	-4	-0	-0.5
1998 Phi-N	0	2	.000	57	0	0	0	0	52	40	23	3	0	25	42	11.3	3.81	114	.209	.301	0	.000	-0	2	3	-0	0.1
1999 Phi-N	3	1	.750	35	0	0	0	0	32	29	15	4	0	15	26	12.4	3.94	120	.244	.328	0	.000	-0	2	3	-1	0.2
2000 Hou-N	2	1	.667	33	0	0	0	0	22^2	25	18	4	0	14	21	15.5	5.16	95	.266	.361	0	.000	-0	-1	-1	-0	-0.1
Total 8	14	15	.483	314	0	0	0	1	254^2	230	140	25	4	133	234	13.0	4.56	95	.239	.333	0	.000	-1	-8	-6	-2	-1.6
● MATT PERISHO	Perisho, Matthew Alan b: 6/8/75, Burlington, Ia. BL/TL, 6', 175 lbs. Deb: 5/27/97																										
1997 Ana-A	0	2	.000	11	8	0	0	0	45	59	34	6	3	28	35	18.0	6.00	76	.324	.423	0	.000	-0	-7	-7	0	-0.3
1998 Tex-A	0	2	.000	2	2	0	0	0	5	15	17	2	2	8	2	45.0	27.00	18	.500	.625	0	—	0	-12	-12	-0	-1.5
1999 Tex-A	0	0	—	4	1	0	0	0	10^1	8	3	0	0	2	17	8.7	2.61	195	.211	.250	0	—	0	3	3	0	0.1
2000 Tex-A	2	7	.222	34	13	0	0	0	105	136	99	20	6	67	74	17.9	7.37	69	.316	.415	0	.000	-0	-29	-26	-1	-1.9
Total 4	2	11	.154	51	24	0	0	0	165^1	218	153	28	11	105	128	18.2	7.29	68	.320	.419	0	.000	-1	-46	-42	-1	-3.6
● CECIL PERKINS	Perkins, Cecil Boyce b: 12/1/40, Baltimore, Md. BR/TR, 6', 175 lbs. Deb: 7/5/67																										
1967 NY-A	0	1	.000	2	1	0	0	0	5	6	5	1	0	2	1	14.4	9.00	35	.316	.381	0	.000	-0	-3	-3	0	-0.6
● CHARLIE PERKINS	Perkins, Charles Sullivan "Lefty" b: 9/9/05, Ensley, Ala. d: 5/25/88, Salem, Ore. BR/TL, 6'1", 175 lbs. Deb: 5/1/30																										
1930 Phi-A	0	0	—	8	1	0	0	0	23^2	25	20	0	0	15	15	15.2	6.46	72	.313	.421	1	.125	-1	-5	-5	0	-0.3
1934 Bro-N	0	3	.000	11	2	0	0	0	24^1	37	25	3	2	14	5	19.6	8.51	46	.336	.421	2	.286	0	-12	-13	-1	-1.3
Total 2	0	3	.000	19	3	0	0	0	48	62	45	3	2	29	20	17.4	7.50	57	.326	.421	3	.200	-1	-17	-17	-1	-1.6
● DAN PERKINS	Perkins, Daniel Lee b: 3/15/75, Miami, Fla. BR/TR, 6'2", 193 lbs. Deb: 4/7/99																										
1999 Min-A	1	7	.125	29	12	0	0	0	86^2	117	69	14	5	43	44	17.1	6.54	78	.326	.405	1	.500	0	-16	-13	-1	-1.0
● JOHN PERKOVICH	Perkovich, John Joseph "Perky" b: 3/10/24, Chicago, Ill. BR/TR, 5'11", 170 lbs. Deb: 5/6/50																										
1950 Chi-A	0	0	—	1	0	0	0	0	5	7	4	3	0	1	3	14.4	7.20	62	.318	.348	0	.000	-0	-1	-2	-0	-0.1
● HARRY PERKOWSKI	Perkowski, Harry Walter b: 9/6/22, Dante, Va. BL/TL, 6'2.5", 196 lbs. Deb: 9/13/47																										
1947 Cin-N	0	0	—	3	1	0	0	0	7^1	12	3	1	0	3	2	18.4	3.68	111	.375	.429	0	.000	0	0	0	-0	0.0
1949 Cin-N	1	1	.500	5	3	2	0	0	23^2	21	14	2	0	14	3	13.3	4.56	92	.236	.340	3	.333	1	-1	-1	-1	-0.1
1950 Cin-N	0	0	—	22	0	0	0	0	34^1	36	21	6	1	23	19	15.7	5.24	81	.286	.400	7	.318	2	-4	-4	1	0.1
1951 Cin-N	3	6	.333	35	7	1	0	1	102	96	42	2	1	46	56	12.6	2.82	144	.251	.333	1	.040	-3	13	14	1	0.9
1952 Cin-N	12	10	.545	33	24	11	1	0	194	197	91	9	3	89	86	13.4	3.80	99	.265	.347	12	.160	-0	-2	-1	1	0.0
1953 Cin-N	12	11	.522	33	25	7	2	2	193	204	107	26	1	62	70	12.5	4.52	96	.271	.327	14	.203	1	-5	-4	-0	-0.2
1954 Cin-N	2	8	.200	28	12	3	1	0	95^2	100	71	16	1	62	32	15.3	6.11	69	.276	.384	4	.160	0	-22	-20	-1	-1.9
1955 Chi-N	3	4	.429	25	4	0	0	2	47^2	53	32	3	0	25	28	14.7	5.29	77	.283	.368	2	.154	-0	-7	-6	1	-0.8
Total 8	33	40	.452	184	76	24	4	5	697^2	719	381	65	7	324	296	13.5	4.37	94	.269	.350	43	.180	1	-27	-21	2	-2.0
● JON PERLMAN	Perlman, Jonathan Samuel b: 12/13/56, Dallas, Tex. BL/TR, 6'3", 185 lbs. Deb: 9/6/85																										
1985 Chi-N	1	0	1.000	6	0	0	0	0	8^2	10	11	3	0	8	4	18.7	11.42	35	.313	.450	0	.000	-0	-8	-6	0	-0.7
1987 SF-N	0	0	—	10	0	0	0	0	11^1	11	7	1	1	4	3	12.7	3.97	97	.256	.333	0	—	0	0	-0	-0	0.0
1988 Cle-A	0	2	.000	10	0	0	0	0	19^2	25	12	0	0	11	10	16.5	5.49	75	.309	.391	0	—	0	-3	-3	1	-0.2
Total 3	1	2	.333	26	0	0	0	0	39^2	46	30	4	1	23	17	15.9	6.35	63	.295	.389	0	.000	-0	-11	-10	1	-0.9
● LEN PERME	Perme, Leonard John b: 11/25/17, Cleveland, Ohio BL/TL, 6', 170 lbs. Deb: 9/8/42																										
1942 Chi-A	0	1	.000	4	1	1	0	0	13	5	2	0	1	4	4	6.9	1.38	260	.119	.213	1	.333	0	3	3	-0	0.3
1946 Chi-A	0	0	—	4	0	0	0	0	4^1	6	4	0	0	7	2	27.0	8.31	41	.316	.500	0	—	0	-2	-2	0	-0.1
Total 2	0	1	.000	8	1	1	0	0	17^1	11	6	0	1	11	6	11.9	3.12	114	.180	.315	1	.333	0	1	1	0	0.2
● HUB PERNOLL	Pernoll, Henry Hubbard b: 3/14/1888, Grants Pass, Ore. d: 2/18/44, Grants Pass, Ore. BR/TL, 5'8", 175 lbs. Deb: 4/25/10																										
1910 Det-A	4	3	.571	11	5	4	0	0	54^2	54	20	1	5	14	25	12.0	2.96	89	.270	.333	1	.063	-2	-3	-2	3	-0.1
1912 Det-A	0	0	—	3	0	0	0	0	9	9	6	0	0	4	3	13.0	6.00	54	.265	.342	0	.000	-0	-3	-3	0	-0.2
Total 2	4	3	.571	14	5	4	0	0	63^2	63	26	1	5	18	28	12.2	3.39	80	.269	.335	1	.053	-2	-5	-5	3	-0.3
● RON PERRANOSKI	Perranoski, Ronald Peter (b: Ronald Peter Perzanowski) b: 4/1/36, Paterson, N.J. BL/TL, 6', 192 lbs. Deb: 4/14/61 C																										
1961 LA-N	7	5	.583	53	1	0	0	6	91^2	82	31	5	4	41	56	12.5	2.65	164	.244	.333	1	.083	-0	14	16	0	2.1
1962 LA-N	6	6	.500	**70**	0	0	0	20	107^1	103	40	1	0	36	68	11.7	2.85	127	.255	.316	1	.071	-1	13	10	-1	1.3
1963 *LA-N	16	3	**.842**	**69**	0	0	0	21	129	112	30	7	4	43	75	11.1	1.67	180	.231	.299	3	.125	0	**23**	**21**	0	4.0
1964 LA-N	5	7	.417	72	0	0	0	14	125^1	128	62	5	1	46	79	12.6	3.09	105	.263	.328	2	.105	-0	6	2	2	0.4
1965 *LA-N	6	6	.500	59	0	0	0	17	104^2	85	28	2	3	40	53	11.0	2.24	146	.226	.305	3	.158	1	15	13	-1	1.9
1966 *LA-N	6	7	.462	55	0	0	0	7	82	82	32	4	1	31	50	12.5	3.18	104	.269	.338	2	.250	1	4	1	2	0.6
1967 LA-N	6	7	.462	**70**	0	0	0	16	110	97	36	4	3	45	75	11.9	2.45	126	.240	.320	1	.100	-0	11	9	1	1.4

YEAR	TM/L	W	L	PCT	G	GS	CG	SH	SV	IP	H	R	HR	HB	BB	SO	RAT	ERA	ERA+	OAV	OOB	BH	AVG	PB	PR	PR+	PD	TPI
1968	Min-A	8	7	.533	66	0	0	0	6	87	86	36	5	0	38	65	12.8	3.10	100	.252	.327	0	.000	-1	-1	-0	-0	-0.1
1969	*Min-A	9	10	.474	75	0	0	0	**31**	119^2	85	32	4	1	52	62	10.4	2.11	174	.205	.295	2	.083	-1	20	20	1	**4.4**
1970	*Min-A	7	8	.467	67	0	0	0	**34**	111	108	38	7	1	42	55	12.2	2.43	153	.259	.328	1	.042	-2	16	16	-1	2.7
1971	Min-A	1	4	.200	36	0	0	0	5	42^2	60	39	2	3	28	21	19.2	6.75	53	.337	.435	0	.000	-0	-16	-15	-0	-2.1
	Det-A	0	1	.000	11	0	0	0	2	18	16	9	2	1	3	8	10.0	2.50	144	.254	.299	0	.000	-0	2	2	-0	0.1
	Yr	1	5	.167	47	0	0	0	7	60^2	76	48	4	4	31	29	16.5	5.49	65	.315	.402	0	.000	-1	-14	-13	-1	-2.0
1972	Det-A	0	1	.000	17	0	0	0	0	18^2	23	16	2	1	8	10	15.4	7.71	41	.307	.381	0	.000	-0	-10	-9	-1	-0.6
	LA-N	2	0	1.000	9	0	0	0	0	16^2	19	8	0	0	8	5	14.6	2.70	124	.292	.370	0	—	0	1	1	-0	0.1
1973	Cal-A	0	2	.000	8	0	0	0	0	11	11	5	0	1	7	5	15.5	4.09	87	.282	.404	0	—	0	-0	-1	-0	-0.1
Total	13	79	74	.516	737	1	0	0	179	1174^2	1097	442	50	24	468	687	12.2	2.79	123	.250	.325	16	.096	-4	99	86	2	16.1
● BILL PERRIN Perrin, William Joseph "Lefty" b: 6/23/10, New Orleans, La. d: 6/30/74, New Orleans, La. BR/TL, 5'11", 172 lbs. Deb: 9/30/34																												
1934	Cle-A	0	1	.000	1	1	0	0	0	5	13	9	0	1	2	3	28.8	14.40	32	.520	.571	0	.000	-0	-6	-5	0	-0.7
● GEORGE PERRING Perring, George Wilson b: 8/13/1884, Sharon, Wis. d: 8/20/60, Beloit, Wis. BR/TR (BB 1909 (1 game)), 6', 190 lbs. Deb: 4/25/08 ♦																												
1914	KC-F	0	0	—	1	0	0	0	0	0^2	2	1	0	0	1	0	40.5	13.50	21	1.000	1.000	138	.278	0	-1	-1	-0	0.0
● POL PERRITT Perritt, William Dayton b: 8/30/1892, Arcadia, La. d: 10/15/47, Shreveport, La. BR/TR, 6'2", 168 lbs. Deb: 9/7/12																												
1912	StL-N	1	1	.500	6	3	1	0	0	31	25	16	0	0	10	13	10.2	3.19	107	.243	.310	2	.222	-0	1	1	0	0.0
1913	StL-N	6	14	.300	36	21	8	0	0	175	205	123	9	8	64	64	14.2	5.25	62	.300	.367	12	.203	-1	-40	-39	1	-3.9
1914	StL-N	16	13	.552	41	32	18	3	2	286	248	106	7	15	93	115	11.2	2.36	118	.245	.318	13	.141	-2	14	14	-3	0.8
1915	NY-N	12	18	.400	35	29	16	4	0	220	226	95	6	12	59	91	12.1	2.66	96	.266	.323	11	.162	-1	2	-3	-5	-1.0
1916	NY-N	18	11	.621	40	29	17	5	2	251	243	82	11	7	56	115	11.0	2.62	93	.257	.304	7	.084	-4	0	-6	-2	-1.3
1917	*NY-N	17	7	.708	35	26	14	5	1	215	186	61	3	7	45	72	10.0	1.88	135	.237	.284	11	.157	-2	20	17	1	1.8
1918	NY-N	18	13	.581	35	31	19	6	0	233	212	82	5	1	38	60	9.7	2.74	96	.246	.278	14	.175	-1	1	-3	-3	-0.9
1919	NY-N	1	1	.500	11	3	0	0	1	19	27	18	0	2	12	2	19.4	7.11	39	.386	.488	0	.000	-1	-9	-9	0	-1.1
1920	NY-N	0	0	—	8	0	0	0	2	15	9	3	0	0	4	3	7.8	1.80	167	.167	.224	0	.000	-1	2	2	0	0.1
1921	NY-N	2	0	1.000	5	1	0	0	0	11^2	17	9	0	0	2	5	14.7	3.86	95	.321	.345	0	.000	-0	-0	-0	-1	-0.1
	Det-A	1	0	1.000	4	2	0	0	0	13	18	9	0	1	7	3	18.0	4.85	88	.383	.473	2	.400	0	-1	-1	-0	0.0
Total	10	92	78	.541	256	177	93	23	8	1469^2	1416	604	41	53	390	543	11.4	2.89	94	.259	.315	72	.151	-13	-10	-29	-11	-5.6
● GAYLORD PERRY Perry, Gaylord Jackson b: 9/15/38, Williamston, N.C. BR/TR, 6'4", 215 lbs. Deb: 4/14/62 FH																												
1962	SF-N	3	1	.750	13	7	1	0	0	43	54	29	3	0	14	20	14.2	5.23	73	.310	.362	3	.231	0	-6	-7	-1	-0.6
1963	SF-N	1	6	.143	31	4	0	0	2	76	84	41	10	2	29	52	13.6	4.03	79	.279	.346	4	.222	1	-6	-7	-0	-0.6
1964	SF-N	12	11	.522	44	19	5	2	5	206^1	179	65	16	5	43	155	9.9	2.75	130	.232	.278	3	.054	-3	18	19	-2	1.6
1965	SF-N	8	12	.400	47	26	6	0	1	195^2	194	105	21	6	70	170	12.4	4.19	86	.256	.324	10	.156	-0	-14	-13	3	-0.9
1966	SF-N★	21	8	.724	36	35	13	3	0	255^2	242	92	15	5	40	201	10.1	2.99	123	.247	.280	16	.186	-0	17	19	1	2.1
1967	SF-N	15	17	.469	39	37	18	3	1	293	231	98	20	4	84	230	9.8	2.61	126	.214	.274	13	.143	-1	25	23	4	2.8
1968	SF-N	16	15	.516	39	38	19	3	1	291	240	93	10	4	59	173	9.4	2.44	120	.222	.265	11	.113	-3	18	16	4	2.0
1969	SF-N	19	14	.576	40	39	26	3	0	**325^1**	290	115	23	11	91	233	10.8	2.49	141	.237	.295	14	.120	-2	40	38	3	4.0
1970	SF-N★	**23**	13	.639	41	41	23	**5**	0	**328^2**	292	138	27	8	84	214	10.5	3.20	124	.237	.290	14	.117	-4	31	29	5	3.1
1971	*SF-N	16	12	.571	37	37	14	2	0	280	255	116	20	5	67	158	10.5	2.76	123	.242	.290	10	.102	-3	22	20	0	1.7
1972	Cle-A★	**24**	16	.600	41	40	**29**	5	1	342^2	253	79	17	12	82	234	9.1	1.92	168	.205	.261	17	.155	0	**44**	**48**	2	**6.7**
1973	Cle-A	19	19	.500	41	41	**29**	7	0	344	315	143	34	5	115	238	11.4	3.38	116	.246	.311	0	—	0	17	20	1	2.3
1974	Cle-A★	21	13	.618	37	37	28	4	0	322^1	230	98	25	6	99	216	9.4	2.51	**144**	.204	.272	0	—	0	40	**40**	1	4.4
1975	Cle-A	6	9	.400	15	15	10	1	0	121^2	120	57	16	1	34	85	11.5	3.55	107	.256	.308	0	—	0	3	3	1	0.5
	Tex-A	12	8	.600	22	22	15	4	0	184	157	70	12	3	36	148	9.6	3.03	124	.227	.268	0	—	0	15	15	-1	1.5
	Yr	18	17	.514	37	37	25	5	0	305^2	277	127	28	4	70	233	10.3	3.24	117	.239	.284	0	—	0	19	18	1	2.0
1976	Tex-A	15	14	.517	32	32	21	2	0	250^1	232	93	14	0	52	143	10.2	3.24	111	.247	.287	0	—	0	8	10	-3	0.8
1977	Tex-A	15	12	.556	34	34	13	4	0	238	239	108	21	5	56	177	11.3	3.37	122	.262	.308	0	—	0	19	19	-1	1.9
1978	SD-N	**21**	6	**.778**	37	37	5	2	0	260^2	241	96	9	2	66	154	10.7	2.73	122	.248	.298	8	.092	-3	25	19	0	1.6
1979	SD-N★	12	11	.522	32	32	10	0	0	232^2	225	90	12	4	67	140	11.4	3.06	116	.257	.313	6	.085	-2	18	13	1	1.2
1980	Tex-A	6	9	.400	24	24	6	2	0	155	159	74	12	7	46	107	12.3	3.43	114	.268	.328	0	—	0	11	9	1	0.9
	NY-A	4	4	.500	10	8	0	0	0	50^2	65	33	2	1	18	28	14.9	4.44	89	.320	.378	0	—	0	-2	-3	-0	-0.4
	Yr	10	13	.435	34	32	6	2	0	205^2	224	107	14	8	64	135	13.0	3.68	106	.281	.341	0	—	0	8	6	1	0.5
1981	Atl-N	8	9	.471	23	23	3	0	0	150^2	182	70	9	4	24	60	12.5	3.94	91	.304	.335	12	.250	3	-8	-6	-1	-0.5
1982	Sea-A	10	12	.455	32	32	6	0	0	216^2	245	117	27	4	54	116	12.6	4.40	97	.287	.332	0	—	0	-8	-4	0	-0.3
1983	Sea-A	3	10	.231	16	16	2	0	0	102	116	60	18	3	23	42	12.5	4.94	86	.286	.329	0	—	0	-10	-7	0	-0.8
	KC-A	4	4	.500	14	14	1	1	0	84^1	98	48	6	1	26	40	13.3	4.27	96	.292	.344	0	—	0	-2	-2	0	-0.1
	Yr	7	14	.333	30	30	3	1	0	186^1	214	108	24	4	49	82	12.9	4.64	90	.289	.336	0	—	0	-12	-9	1	-0.9
Total	22	314	265	.542	777	690	303	53	11	5350^1	4938	2128	399	108	1379	3534	10.8	3.11	117	.245	.297	141	.131	-16	315	310	21	34.9
● SCOTT PERRY Perry, Herbert Scott b: 4/17/1891, Denison, Tex. d: 10/27/59, Kansas City, Mo. BR/TR, 6', 175 lbs. Deb: 5/13/15																												
1915	StL-A	0	0	—	1	1	0	0	0	2	5	3	0	1	1	0	31.5	13.50	21	.455	.538	0	—	0	-2	-2	-0	-0.1
1916	Chi-N	2	1	.667	4	3	2	1	0	28^1	30	9	0	0	3	10	10.5	2.54	115	.291	.311	3	.273	1	0	1	0	0.2
1917	Cin-N	0	0	—	4	1	0	0	0	13^1	17	15	0	1	8	4	17.6	6.75	39	.321	.419	0	.000	-1	-6	-6	-0	-0.4
1918	Phi-A	20	19	.513	44	36	**30**	3	2	**332^1**	295	97	1	2	111	81	11.0	1.98	148	.247	.312	15	.134	-6	30	33	2	3.7
1919	Phi-A	4	17	.190	25	21	12	0	1	183^2	193	92	4	2	72	38	13.1	3.58	96	.282	.352	8	.136	-3	-7	-3	6	0.1
1920	Phi-A	11	25	.306	42	34	20	1	1	263^2	310	151	14	7	65	79	13.0	3.62	111	.300	.345	13	.157	-4	5	11	0	1.0
1921	Phi-A	3	6	.333	12	8	5	0	1	70	77	36	4	1	24	19	13.1	4.11	108	.288	.349	1	.038	-4	1	3	1	0.0
Total	7	40	68	.370	132	104	69	5	5	893^1	927	403	23	14	284	231	12.3	3.07	113	.277	.336	40	.135	-17	21	38	9	4.5
● JIM PERRY Perry, James Evan b: 10/30/35, Williamston, N.C. BB/TR, 6'4", 200 lbs. Deb: 4/23/59 F																												
1959	Cle-A	12	10	.545	44	13	8	2	4	153	122	54	10	2	55	79	10.5	2.65	139	.225	.298	15	.300	3	21	18	-0	3.0
1960	Cle-A	**18**	10	**.643**	41	36	10	**4**	1	261^1	257	118	35	4	91	120	12.1	3.62	103	.260	.324	22	.242	3	7	4	0	0.6
1961	Cle-A☆	10	17	.370	35	35	6	1	0	223^2	238	132	28	6	87	90	13.3	4.71	84	.273	.343	12	.164	-1	-17	-20	-0	-2.1
1962	Cle-A	12	12	.500	35	27	7	3	0	193^2	213	94	21	2	59	74	12.7	4.14	94	.285	.339	11	.183	0	-4	-6	1	-0.5
1963	Cle-A	0	0	—	5	0	0	0	0	10^1	12	6	0	0	2	7	12.2	5.23	69	.293	.326	0	.000	-0	-2	-2	0	-0.1
	Min-A	9	9	.500	35	25	5	1	1	168^1	167	77	17	2	57	65	12.1	3.74	97	.256	.318	11	.216	3	-2	-2	-1	0.0
	Yr	9	9	.500	40	25	5	1	1	178^2	179	83	17	2	59	72	12.1	3.83	95	.258	.318	11	.208	3	-4	-4	-1	-0.1
1964	Min-A	6	3	.667	42	1	0	0	2	65^1	61	26	7	1	23	55	11.7	3.44	104	.245	.311	2	.154	-0	1	1	-0	0.1
1965	*Min-A	12	7	.632	36	19	4	2	0	167^2	142	57	18	3	47	88	10.3	2.63	135	.232	.290	9	.170	1	15	17	-1	1.9
1966	Min-A	11	7	.611	33	25	8	1	0	184^1	149	61	17	5	53	122	10.1	2.54	142	.222	.284	13	.220	4	18	21	-2	2.3
1967	Min-A	8	7	.533	37	11	3	2	0	130^2	123	51	8	3	50	94	12.1	3.03	114	.255	.328	8	.190	1	3	6	-1	0.6
1968	Min-A	8	6	.571	32	18	3	2	1	139	113	37	8	5	26	69	9.3	2.27	136	.219	.263	6	.143	2	11	12	1	1.6
1969	*Min-A	20	6	.769	46	36	12	3	0	261^2	244	87	18	9	66	153	11.0	2.82	130	.247	.300	16	.172	1	23	24	-2	2.2
1970	*Min-A★	**24**	12	.667	40	40	13	4	0	278^2	258	112	20	9	57	168	10.5	3.04	123	.243	.287	24	.247	5	21	21	1	3.3
1971	Min-A☆	17	17	.500	40	39	8	0	1	270	263	135	39	5	102	126	12.3	4.23	84	.259	.329	17	.185	1	-23	-20	0	-2.2
1972	Min-A	13	16	.448	35	35	5	2	0	217^2	191	93	14	8	60	85	10.7	3.35	96	.236	.295	11	.155	-1	-7	-3	-1	-0.6
1973	Det-A	14	13	.519	35	34	7	1	0	203	225	96	22	4	55	66	12.6	4.03	101	.282	.331	0	—	0	-5	1	-0	0.1
1974	Cle-A	17	12	.586	36	36	8	3	0	252	242	94	11	5	64	71	11.1	2.96	122	.254	.304	0	—	0	18	18	-1	2.0
1975	Cle-A	1	6	.143	8	6	0	0	0	37^2	46	34	8	0	18	11	15.3	6.69	57	.309	.383	0	—	0	-12	-12	0	-1.8
	Oak-A	3	4	.429	15	11	2	1	0	67^2	61	43	7	7	26	33	12.5	4.66	78	.237	.324	0	—	0	-7	-8	-1	-0.8
	Yr	4	10	.286	23	17	2	1	0	105^1	107	77	15	7	44	44	13.5	5.38	69	.264	.346	0	—	0	-19	-20	-1	-2.6
Total	17	215	174	.553	630	447	109	32	10	3285^2	3127	1407	308	80	998	1576	11.5	3.45	106	.252	.312	177	.199	23	62	75	-7	9.6
● PAT PERRY Perry, William Patrick b: 2/4/59, Taylorville, Ill. BL/TL, 6'1", 170 lbs. Deb: 9/12/85																												
1985	StL-N	1	0	1.000	6	0	0	0	0	12^1	3	0	0	0	3	6	4.4	0.00	—	.077	.143	1	.500	0	5	5	-0	0.4
1986	StL-N	2	3	.400	46	0	0	0	2	68^2	59	31	5	0	34	29	12.2	3.80	96	.239	.331	0	.000	-1	-1	-1	1	-0.1
1987	StL-N	4	2	.667	45	0	0	0	1	65^2	54	34	7	2	21	33	10.6	4.39	95	.222	.289	1	.143	-0	-2	-2	0	-0.1
	Cin-N	1	0	1.000	12	0	0	0	1	15^1	6	0	0	1	4	6	6.5	0.00	—	.122	.204	0	—	0	7	7	0	0.5

YEAR	TM/L	W	L	PCT	G	GS	CG	SH	SV	IP	H	R	HR	HB	BB	SO	RAT	ERA	ERA+	OAV	OOB	BH	AVG	PB	PR	PR+	PD	TPI
	Yr	5	2	.714	57	0	0	0	2	81	60	34	7	3	25	39	9.8	3.56	117	.205	.275	1	.143	-0	5	5	1	0.4
1988	Cin-N	2	2	.500	12	0	0	0	0	20^2	21	17	4	0	9	11	13.1	5.66	63	.262	.337	0	.000	-0	-5	-5	-0	-0.9
	Chi-N	2	2	.500	35	0	0	0	1	38	40	15	5	1	7	24	11.4	3.32	109	.270	.308	1	1.000	1	1	1	-0	0.3
	Yr	4	4	.500	47	0	0	0	1	58^2	61	32	9	1	16	35	12.0	4.14	87	.268	.318	1	.333	1	-4	-3	-0	-0.6
1989	Chi-N	0	1	.000	19	0	0	0	1	35^2	23	8	2	0	16	20	9.8	1.77	213	.187	.281	1	.167	-0	7	7	-1	0.3
1990	LA-N	0	0	—	7	0	0	0	0	6^2	9	7	0	1	5	2	20.3	8.10	45	.310	.429	0	.000	-0	-3	-3	-0	-0.2
Total	6	12	10	.545	182	0	0	0	6	263	215	112	23	5	99	131	10.9	3.46	110	.224	.300	4	.148	0	8	10	-0	0.2

● PARSON PERRYMAN Perryman, Emmett Key b: 10/24/1888, Everett Springs, Ga. d: 9/12/66, Starke, Fla. BR/TR, 6'4.5", 193 lbs. Deb: 4/14/15

YEAR	TM/L	W	L	PCT	G	GS	CG	SH	SV	IP	H	R	HR	HB	BB	SO	RAT	ERA	ERA+	OAV	OOB	BH	AVG	PB	PR	PR+	PD	TPI
1915	StL-A	2	4	.333	24	3	0	0	0	50^1	52	27	2	1	16	19	12.3	3.93	73	.281	.342	0	.000	-1	-6	-6	1	-0.7

● ROBERT PERSON Person, Robert Alan b: 10/6/69, Lowell, Mass. BR/TR, 5'11", 180 lbs. Deb: 9/18/95

YEAR	TM/L	W	L	PCT	G	GS	CG	SH	SV	IP	H	R	HR	HB	BB	SO	RAT	ERA	ERA+	OAV	OOB	BH	AVG	PB	PR	PR+	PD	TPI
1995	NY-N	1	0	1.000	3	1	0	0	0	12	5	1	1	0	2	10	5.3	0.75	540	.119	.159	2	.667	1	5	5	-0	0.4
1996	NY-N	4	5	.444	27	13	0	0	0	89^2	86	50	16	2	35	76	12.3	4.52	89	.247	.319	3	.143	-0	-3	-5	-2	-0.6
1997	Tor-A	5	10	.333	23	22	0	0	0	128^1	125	86	19	5	60	99	13.3	5.61	82	.255	.342	0	.000	-0	-15	-14	-2	-1.6
1998	Tor-A	3	1	.750	27	0	0	0	6	38^1	45	31	9	2	22	31	16.2	7.04	66	.294	.390	0	—	0	-10	-10	-1	-1.2
1999	Tor-A	0	2	.000	11	0	0	0	2	11	9	12	1	4	15	12	22.9	9.82	50	.231	.483	0	—	0	-6	-6	-0	-1.0
	Phi-N	10	5	.667	31	22	0	0	0	137	130	72	23	2	70	127	13.3	4.27	111	.252	.344	3	.073	-2	5	7	-1	0.3
2000	Phi-N	9	7	.563	28	28	1	1	0	173^1	144	73	13	6	95	164	12.7	3.63	130	.229	.336	7	.132	-0	19	21	0	1.6
Total	6	32	30	.516	150	86	1	1	8	589^2	544	325	82	21	299	519	13.2	4.62	99	.245	.340	15	.123	-2	-6	-3	-6	-2.1

● BILL PERTICA Pertica, William Andrew b: 3/5/1897, Santa Barbara, Cal. d: 12/28/67, Los Angeles, Cal. BR/TR, 5'9", 165 lbs. Deb: 8/7/18

YEAR	TM/L	W	L	PCT	G	GS	CG	SH	SV	IP	H	R	HR	HB	BB	SO	RAT	ERA	ERA+	OAV	OOB	BH	AVG	PB	PR	PR+	PD	TPI
1918	Bos-A	0	0	—	1	0	0	0	0	3	3	1	0	0	0	1	9.0	3.00	89	.273	.273	0	.000	-0	-0	-0	0	0.0
1921	StL-N	14	10	.583	38	31	15	2	2	208^1	212	104	9	10	70	67	12.6	3.37	109	.267	.334	10	.143	-3	10	7	-3	0.1
1922	StL-N	8	8	.500	34	15	2	0	0	117^1	153	94	5	3	65	30	17.0	5.91	65	.333	.419	6	.182	-0	-24	-28	1	-3.1
1923	StL-N	0	0	—	1	1	0	0	0	2^1	2	2	0	1	3	0	23.1	3.86	101	.250	.500	0	.000	-0	0	0	0	0.0
Total	4	22	18	.550	74	47	17	2	2	331	370	201	14	14	138	98	14.2	4.27	87	.291	.367	16	.152	-4	-14	-21	-2	-3.0

● STAN PERZANOWSKI Perzanowski, Stanley b: 8/25/50, East Chicago, Ind. BB/TR, 6'2", 170 lbs. Deb: 6/20/71

YEAR	TM/L	W	L	PCT	G	GS	CG	SH	SV	IP	H	R	HR	HB	BB	SO	RAT	ERA	ERA+	OAV	OOB	BH	AVG	PB	PR	PR+	PD	TPI
1971	Chi-A	0	1	.000	5	0	0	0	1	6	14	10	1	0	3	5	25.5	12.00	30	.412	.459	0	.000	-0	-6	-5	-0	-1.0
1974	Chi-A	0	0	—	2	1	0	0	0	2^1	8	7	1	0	2	2	38.6	19.29	19	.533	.588	0	—	0	-4	-4	0	-0.2
1975	Tex-A	3	3	.500	12	8	1	0	0	66	59	25	1	5	25	26	12.1	3.00	126	.246	.330	0	—	0	6	6	1	0.6
1976	Tex-A	0	0	—	5	0	0	0	0	11^2	20	15	3	2	4	6	20.1	10.03	36	.385	.448	0	—	0	-8	-8	0	-0.4
1978	Min-A	2	7	.222	13	7	1	0	1	56^2	59	37	1	4	26	31	14.1	5.24	73	.276	.365	0	—	0	-9	-9	1	-1.2
Total	5	5	11	.313	37	16	2	0	2	142^2	160	94	7	11	60	70	14.6	5.11	74	.288	.369	0	.000	-0	-22	-21	2	-2.2

● JEFF PETEREK Peterek, Jeffrey Allen b: 9/22/63, Michigan City, Ind. BR/TR, 6'2", 195 lbs. Deb: 8/14/89

YEAR	TM/L	W	L	PCT	G	GS	CG	SH	SV	IP	H	R	HR	HB	BB	SO	RAT	ERA	ERA+	OAV	OOB	BH	AVG	PB	PR	PR+	PD	TPI
1989	Mil-A	0	2	.000	7	4	0	0	0	31^1	31	14	3	0	14	16	12.9	4.02	96	.252	.328	0	—	0	-0	-1	0	0.0

● CHRIS PETERS Peters, Christopher Michael b: 1/28/72, Fort Thomas, Ky. BL/TL, 6'1", 170 lbs. Deb: 7/19/96

YEAR	TM/L	W	L	PCT	G	GS	CG	SH	SV	IP	H	R	HR	HB	BB	SO	RAT	ERA	ERA+	OAV	OOB	BH	AVG	PB	PR	PR+	PD	TPI
1996	Pit-N	2	4	.333	16	10	0	0	0	64	72	43	9	1	25	28	13.8	5.63	78	.287	.354	4	.211	0	-10	-9	-0	-0.7
1997	Pit-N	2	2	.500	31	1	0	0	0	37^1	38	23	6	3	21	17	14.9	4.58	94	.277	.385	1	.250	0	-2	-1	0	-0.1
1998	Pit-N	8	10	.444	39	21	1	0	1	148	142	63	13	3	55	103	12.2	3.47	124	.252	.322	9	.231	1	13	14	-2	1.5
1999	Pit-N	5	4	.556	19	11	0	0	0	71	98	59	17	4	27	46	16.4	6.59	69	.322	.385	6	.273	2	-16	-16	1	-1.4
2000	Pit-N	0	1	.000	18	0	0	0	1	28^1	23	9	2	1	14	16	12.1	2.86	161	.221	.319	1	.167	-0	6	6	0	0.3
Total	5	17	21	.447	123	43	1	0	2	348^2	373	197	47	12	142	210	13.6	4.57	96	.274	.348	21	.233	3	-9	-7	-1	-0.4

● GARY PETERS Peters, Gary Charles b: 4/21/37, Grove City, Pa. BL/TL, 6'2", 200 lbs. Deb: 9/10/59

YEAR	TM/L	W	L	PCT	G	GS	CG	SH	SV	IP	H	R	HR	HB	BB	SO	RAT	ERA	ERA+	OAV	OOB	BH	AVG	PB	PR	PR+	PD	TPI
1959	Chi-A	0	0	—	2	0	0	0	0	1	2	0	0	0	2	1	36.0	0.00	—	.400	.571	0	—	0	0	0	0	0.0
1960	Chi-A	0	0	—	2	0	0	0	0	3^1	4	1	0	0	1	4	13.5	2.70	140	.286	.333	0	—	0	0	0	-0	0.0
1961	Chi-A	0	0	—	3	0	0	0	1	10^1	10	2	0	0	2	6	10.5	1.74	225	.270	.308	1	.333	0	3	3	1	0.3
1962	Chi-A	0	1	.000	5	0	0	0	0	6^1	8	5	0	1	1	4	14.2	5.68	69	.308	.357	0	—	0	-1	-1	0	-0.2
1963	Chi-A	19	8	.704	41	30	13	4	1	243	192	69	9	8	68	189	9.9	**2.33**	**150**	.216	.278	21	.259	9	**35**	**33**	-1	4.6
1964	Chi-A☆	**20**	8	.714	37	36	11	3	0	273^2	217	89	20	7	104	205	10.8	2.50	138	.219	.297	25	.208	8	34	30	0	4.1
1965	Chi-A	10	12	.455	33	30	1	0	0	176^1	181	76	19	4	63	95	12.7	3.62	88	.265	.331	13	.181	2	-3	-9	0	-0.8
1966	Chi-A	12	10	.545	30	27	11	4	0	204^2	156	54	11	3	45	129	**9.0**	**1.98**	**160**	.212	**.261**	19	.235	6	**33**	**29**	1	**4.2**
1967	Chi-A★	16	11	.593	38	36	11	3	0	260	187	81	15	11	91	215	10.0	2.28	136	**.199**	.277	21	.212	7	27	25	3	**3.8**
1968	Chi-A	4	13	.235	31	25	6	1	1	162^2	146	79	7	7	60	110	11.8	3.76	80	.242	.318	15	.208	7	-14	-13	-0	-0.7
1969	Chi-A	10	15	.400	36	32	7	3	0	218^2	238	118	21	5	78	140	13.2	4.53	85	.283	.347	12	.169	2	-22	-15	-2	-1.6
1970	Bos-A	16	11	.593	34	34	10	4	0	221^2	221	114	20	7	83	155	12.6	4.06	98	.257	.328	20	.244	6	-8	-2	-1	0.2
1971	Bos-A	14	11	.560	34	32	9	1	1	214	241	111	25	6	70	100	13.3	4.37	85	.288	.347	26	.271	8	-22	-15	-2	-1.0
1972	Bos-A	3	3	.500	33	4	0	0	1	85^1	91	48	10	3	38	67	13.9	4.32	75	.279	.360	6	.200	1	-12	-10	-1	-0.7
Total	14	124	103	.546	359	286	79	23	5	2081	1894	847	157	62	706	1420	11.5	3.25	106	.243	.311	179	.222	57	51	47	-1	12.2

● JOHN PETERS Peters, John Paul b: 4/8/1850, Louisiana, Mo. d: 1/4/24, St.Louis, Mo. BR/TR, 5'7", 180 lbs. Deb: 5/23/1874 ♦

YEAR	TM/L	W	L	PCT	G	GS	CG	SH	SV	IP	H	R	HR	HB	BB	SO	RAT	ERA	ERA+	OAV	OOB	BH	AVG	PB	PR	PR+	PD	TPI
1876	Chi-N	0	0	—	1	0	0	0	1	1	1	1	0		1	0	18.0	0.00	—	.200	.400	111	.348	0	0	0	0	0.0

● RUBE PETERS Peters, Oscar Casper b: 3/15/1885, Grantfork, Ill. d: 2/7/65, Pequannock, N.J. BR/TR, 6'1", 195 lbs. Deb: 4/13/12

YEAR	TM/L	W	L	PCT	G	GS	CG	SH	SV	IP	H	R	HR	HB	BB	SO	RAT	ERA	ERA+	OAV	OOB	BH	AVG	PB	PR	PR+	PD	TPI
1912	Chi-A	5	6	.455	28	11	4	0	0	108^2	134	73	2	6	33	39	14.3	4.14	77	.309	.366	6	.194	-1	-10	-12	4	-0.7
1914	Bro-F	2	2	.500	11	3	1	0	0	37^2	52	27	1	0	16	13	16.2	3.82	75	.335	.398	1	.091	-1	-4	-4	0	-0.5
Total	2	7	8	.467	39	14	5	0	0	146^1	186	100	3	6	49	52	14.8	4.06	77	.316	.374	7	.167	-1	-14	-16	4	-1.2

● RAY PETERS Peters, Raymond James b: 8/27/46, Buffalo, N.Y. BR/TR, 6'5.5", 210 lbs. Deb: 6/4/70

YEAR	TM/L	W	L	PCT	G	GS	CG	SH	SV	IP	H	R	HR	HB	BB	SO	RAT	ERA	ERA+	OAV	OOB	BH	AVG	PB	PR	PR+	PD	TPI
1970	Mil-A	0	2	.000	2	2	0	0	0	2	7	7	0	0	5	1	54.0	31.50	12	.583	.706	0	—	0	-6	-6	0	-0.9

● STEVE PETERS Peters, Steven Bradley b: 11/14/62, Oklahoma City, Okla BL/TL, 5'10", 170 lbs. Deb: 8/11/87

YEAR	TM/L	W	L	PCT	G	GS	CG	SH	SV	IP	H	R	HR	HB	BB	SO	RAT	ERA	ERA+	OAV	OOB	BH	AVG	PB	PR	PR+	PD	TPI
1987	StL-N	0	0	—	12	0	0	0	1	15	17	3	1	0	6	11	13.8	1.80	231	.298	.365	0	.000	-0	4	4	1	0.2
1988	StL-N	3	3	.500	44	0	0	0	0	45	57	34	8	0	22	30	15.8	6.40	54	.313	.387	0	.000	-0	-15	-14	-1	-1.9
Total	2	3	3	.500	56	0	0	0	1	60	74	37	9	0	28	41	15.3	5.25	70	.310	.382	0	.000	-1	-11	-11	0	-1.7

● ADAM PETERSON Peterson, Adam Charles b: 12/11/65, Long Beach, Cal. BR/TR, 6'3", 190 lbs. Deb: 9/19/87

YEAR	TM/L	W	L	PCT	G	GS	CG	SH	SV	IP	H	R	HR	HB	BB	SO	RAT	ERA	ERA+	OAV	OOB	BH	AVG	PB	PR	PR+	PD	TPI
1987	Chi-A	0	0	—	1	1	0	0	0	4	8	6	1	0	3	1	24.8	13.50	34	.444	.524	0	—	0	-4	-4	-0	-0.2
1988	Chi-A	0	1	.000	2	2	0	0	0	6	6	9	0	0	6	5	18.0	13.50	29	.240	.387	0	—	0	-6	-6	-0	-0.8
1989	Chi-A	0	1	.000	3	2	0	0	0	5^1	13	9	1	0	2	3	25.3	15.19	25	.464	.500	0	—	0	-7	-7	-0	-1.0
1990	Chi-A	2	5	.286	20	11	2	0	0	85	90	46	12	2	26	29	12.5	4.55	84	.278	.335	0	—	0	-6	-7	-1	-0.7
1991	SD-N	3	4	.429	13	11	0	0	0	54^2	50	33	10	0	28	37	12.8	4.45	86	.242	.332	0	.000	-1	-5	-4	-0	-0.6
Total	5	5	11	.313	39	27	2	0	0	155	167	103	24	2	65	75	13.6	5.46	71	.277	.350	0	.000	-1	-28	-28	-2	-3.3

● FRITZ PETERSON Peterson, Fritz Fred (b: Fred Ingels Peterson) b: 2/8/42, Chicago, Ill. BB/TL, 6', 200 lbs. Deb: 4/15/66

YEAR	TM/L	W	L	PCT	G	GS	CG	SH	SV	IP	H	R	HR	HB	BB	SO	RAT	ERA	ERA+	OAV	OOB	BH	AVG	PB	PR	PR+	PD	TPI
1966	NY-A	12	11	.522	34	32	11	2	0	215	196	89	15	3	40	96	10.0	3.31	101	.241	.279	15	.224	4	3	0	-0	0.4
1967	NY-A	8	14	.364	36	30	6	1	0	181^1	179	88	11	3	43	102	11.2	3.47	90	.256	.302	7	.146	1	-5	-7	1	-0.6
1968	NY-A	12	11	.522	36	27	6	2	0	212^1	187	72	13	4	29	115	9.3	2.63	110	.241	.272	5	.079	-2	8	7	4	1.0
1969	NY-A	17	16	.515	37	37	16	4	0	272	228	95	15	3	43	150	**9.1**	2.55	137	.229	.263	9	.112	-0	33	29	2	3.8
1970	NY-A★	20	11	.645	39	37	8	2	0	260^1	247	102	24	3	40	127	**10.0**	2.90	121	.248	**.280**	20	.222	5	24	19	2	3.0
1971	NY-A	15	13	.536	37	35	16	4	1	274	269	106	25	4	42	139	10.3	3.05	106	.258	.289	7	.082	-3	13	6	2	0.5
1972	NY-A	17	15	.531	35	35	12	3	0	250^1	270	98	17	5	44	100	11.5	3.24	91	.276	.310	19	.232	4	-5	-8	1	-0.5
1973	NY-A	8	15	.348	31	31	6	0	0	184^1	207	93	18	7	49	59	12.8	3.95	93	.286	.337	0	—	0	-3	-6	0	-0.7
1974	NY-A	0	0	—	3	1	0	0	0	7^2	13	4	1	0	2	5	17.6	4.70	75	.361	.395	0	—	0	-1	-1	-0	-0.1
	Cle-A	9	14	.391	29	29	3	0	0	152^2	187	89	16	4	37	52	13.4	4.36	83	.305	.349	0	—	0	-13	-13	1	-1.6
	Yr	9	14	.391	32	30	3	0	0	160^1	200	93	17	4	39	57	13.6	4.38	83	.308	.351	0	—	0	-13	-14	1	-1.7
1975	Cle-A	14	8	.636	25	25	6	2	0	146^1	154	73	15	6	40	47	12.3	3.94	96	.275	.331	0	—	0	-2	-2	1	-0.3
1976	Cle-A	0	3	.000	9	9	0	0	0	47	59	31	3	0	10	19	13.2	5.55	63	.309	.343	0	—	0	-11	-11	-0	-0.6

YEAR	TM/L	W	L	PCT	G	GS	CG	SH	SV	IP	H	R	HR	HB	BB	SO	RAT	ERA	ERA+	OAV	OOB	BH	AVG	PB	PR	PR+	PD	TPI
	Tex-A	1	0	1.000	4	2	0	0	0	15	21	7	0	0	7	4	16.8	3.60	100	.344	.412	0	—	0	-0	-0	0	0.0
	Yr	1	3	.250	13	11	0	0	0	62	80	38	3	0	17	23	14.1	5.08	69	.317	.361	0	—	0	-11	-11	0	-0.6
Total	11	133	131	.504	355	330	90	20	1	2218^1	2217	947	173	42	426	1015	10.9	3.30	101	.261	.300	82	.159	8	41	12	15	4.3
● JIM PETERSON	Peterson, James Niels b: 8/18/08, Philadelphia, Pa. d: 4/8/75, Palm Beach, Fla. BR/TR, 6'0.5", 200 lbs. Deb: 7/9/31																											
1931	Phi-A	0	1	.000	6	1	1	0	0	13	18	10	0	0	4	7	15.2	6.23	72	.321	.367	1	.500	1	-3	-2	-0	-0.1
1933	Phi-A	2	5	.286	32	5	0	0	0	90^2	114	64	6	0	36	18	14.9	4.96	86	.305	.366	4	.148	-1	-7	-7	2	-0.3
1937	Bro-N	0	0	—	3	0	0	0	0	5^2	8	5	3	0	2	4	15.9	7.94	51	.333	.385	0	—	0	-3	-2	1	-0.1
Total	3	2	6	.250	41	6	1	0	0	109^1	140	79	9	0	42	29	15.0	5.27	82	.308	.367	5	.172	0	-12	-12	3	-0.5
● KENT PETERSON	Peterson, Kent Franklin "Pete" b: 12/21/25, Goshen, Utah d: 4/27/95, Highland, Utah BR/TL, 5'10", 175 lbs. Deb: 7/15/44																											
1944	Cin-N	0	0	—	1	0	0	0	0	1	0	0	0	0	0	0	0.0	0.00	—	.000	.000	0	—	0	0	0	-0	0.0
1947	Cin-N	6	13	.316	37	17	3	1	2	152^1	156	74	8	3	62	78	13.1	4.25	96	.265	.338	3	.068	-3	-3	-3	-2	-0.8
1948	Cin-N	2	15	.118	43	17	2	0	1	137	146	82	10	6	59	64	13.9	4.60	85	.271	.350	5	.139	-2	-10	-11	0	-1.3
1949	Cin-N	4	5	.444	30	7	2	0	0	66^1	66	54	8	4	46	28	15.7	6.24	67	.261	.383	1	.056	-2	-16	-15	-1	-1.9
1950	Cin-N	0	3	.000	9	2	0	0	0	20	25	20	4	0	17	6	18.9	7.20	59	.305	.424	1	.333	0	-7	-6	-1	-0.9
1951	Cin-N	1	1	.500	9	0	0	0	0	9^2	13	8	0	1	8	5	20.5	6.52	63	.317	.440	0	.000	-0	-3	-3	0	-0.5
1952	Phi-N	0	0	—	3	0	0	0	2	7	2	0	0	0	2	7	5.1	0.00	—	.091	.167	0	.000	-0	3	3	-0	0.2
1953	Phi-N	0	1	.000	15	0	0	0	0	27	26	20	3	1	21	20	16.0	6.67	63	.252	.384	0	.000	-1	-7	-8	-0	-0.5
Total	8	13	38	.255	147	43	7	1	5	420^1	434	258	33	15	215	208	14.2	4.95	82	.266	.357	10	.091	-8	-43	-41	-4	-5.7
● KYLE PETERSON	Peterson, Kyle Jonathan b: 4/5/76, Elkhorn, Neb. BL/TR, 6'3", 215 lbs. Deb: 7/19/99																											
1999	Mil-N	4	7	.364	17	12	0	0	0	77	87	46	3	4	25	34	13.6	4.56	100	.285	.347	3	.136	-0	0	-0	-1	-0.2
● SID PETERSON	Peterson, Sidney Herbert b: 1/31/18, Havelock, N.Dak. BR/TR, 6'3", 220 lbs. Deb: 5/4/43																											
1943	StL-A	2	0	1.000	3	0	0	0	0	10	15	3	0	1	3	0	17.1	2.70	123	.341	.396	0	.000	-0	1	1	-0	0.1
● MARK PETKOVSEK	Petkovsek, Mark Joseph b: 11/18/65, Beaumont, Tex. BR/TR, 6', 185 lbs. Deb: 6/8/91																											
1991	Tex-A	0	1	.000	4	1	0	0	0	9^1	21	16	4	0	4	6	24.1	14.46	28	.438	.481	0	—	0	-11	-11	-0	-0.9
1993	Pit-N	3	0	1.000	26	0	0	0	0	32^1	43	25	7	0	9	14	14.5	6.96	58	.328	.371	0	—	0	-10	-10	1	-0.8
1995	StL-N	6	6	.500	26	21	1	1	0	137^1	136	71	11	6	35	71	11.6	4.00	105	.262	.316	3	.081	-1	3	3	-1	0.1
1996	*StL-N	11	2	.846	48	6	0	0	0	88^2	83	37	9	5	35	45	12.5	3.55	118	.251	.332	3	.188	0	7	6	0	0.9
1997	StL-N	4	7	.364	55	2	0	0	2	96	109	61	14	6	31	51	13.7	5.06	82	.292	.356	1	.091	-0	-9	-10	1	-0.9
1998	StL-N	7	4	.636	48	10	0	0	0	105^2	131	63	9	8	36	55	14.9	4.77	88	.312	.377	7	.318	2	-6	-7	-1	-0.5
1999	Ana-A	10	4	.714	64	0	0	0	1	83	85	37	6	2	21	43	11.7	3.47	140	.269	.319	0	—	0	13	13	1	1.9
2000	Ana-A	4	2	.667	64	1	0	0	2	81	86	39	8	3	23	31	12.4	4.30	118	.277	.333	0	—	0	6	7	0	0.4
Total	8	45	26	.634	335	41	1	1	5	633^1	694	349	68	30	194	316	13.0	4.49	97	.283	.343	14	.163	1	-8	-9	1	0.2
● DAN PETRY	Petry, Daniel Joseph b: 11/13/58, Palo Alto, Cal. BR/TR, 6'4", 200 lbs. Deb: 7/8/79																											
1979	Det-A	6	5	.545	15	15	2	0	0	98	90	46	11	4	33	43	11.7	3.95	110	.254	.325	0	—	0	3	4	-1	0.3
1980	Det-A	10	9	.526	27	25	4	3	0	164^2	156	82	9	1	83	88	13.1	3.94	105	.253	.342	0	—	0	2	3	2	0.5
1981	Det-A	10	9	.526	23	22	7	2	0	141	115	53	10	1	57	79	11.0	3.00	126	.224	.302	0	—	0	10	12	2	1.8
1982	Det-A	15	9	.625	35	35	8	1	0	246	220	98	15	4	100	132	11.9	3.22	126	.241	.319	0	—	0	24	23	4	2.6
1983	Det-A	19	11	.633	38	38	9	2	0	266^1	256	126	37	6	99	122	12.2	3.92	100	.256	.327	0	—	0	5	0	3	0.3
1984	*Det-A	18	8	.692	35	35	7	2	0	233^1	231	94	21	3	66	144	11.6	3.24	121	.259	.312	0	—	0	20	18	3	2.2
1985	Det-A★	15	13	.536	34	34	8	0	0	238^2	190	98	24	3	81	109	10.3	3.36	121	.217	.285	0	—	0	21	19	0	2.1
1986	Det-A	5	10	.333	20	20	2	0	0	116	122	78	15	5	53	56	14.0	4.66	89	.268	.350	0	—	0	-6	-7	1	-0.7
1987	*Det-A	9	7	.563	30	21	0	0	0	134^2	148	101	22	10	76	93	15.6	5.61	75	.279	.379	0	—	0	-17	-22	1	-2.0
1988	Cal-A	3	9	.250	22	22	4	1	0	139^2	139	70	18	6	59	64	13.1	4.38	88	.263	.344	0	—	0	-6	-8	2	-0.4
1989	Cal-A	3	2	.600	19	4	0	0	0	51	53	32	8	1	23	21	13.6	5.47	70	.275	.355	0	—	0	-9	-10	0	-0.8
1990	Det-A	10	9	.526	32	23	1	0	0	149^2	148	78	14	1	77	73	13.6	4.45	89	.263	.353	0	—	0	-9	-8	2	-0.7
1991	Det-A	2	3	.400	17	6	0	0	0	54^2	66	35	9	0	19	18	14.0	4.94	84	.300	.356	0	—	0	-5	-5	2	-0.2
	Atl-N	0	0	—	10	0	0	0	0	24^1	29	17	2	1	14	9	16.3	5.55	70	.296	.389	1	.200	0	-5	-4	0	-0.2
	Bos-A	0	0	—	13	0	0	0	1	22^1	21	17	3	1	12	12	13.7	4.43	97	.250	.351	0	—	0	-1	-0	0	0.0
Total	13	125	104	.546	370	300	52	11	1	2080^1	1984	1025	218	47	852	1063	12.5	3.95	102	.253	.330	1	.200	0	26	18	22	4.8
● JAY PETTIBONE	Pettibone, Harry Jonathan b: 6/21/57, Mt.Clemens, Mich. BR/TR, 6'4", 182 lbs. Deb: 9/11/83																											
1983	Min-A	0	4	.000	4	4	1	0	0	27	28	16	8	2	8	10	12.7	5.33	80	.280	.345	0	—	0	-4	-3	0	-0.4
● PAUL PETTIT	Pettit, George William Paul "Lefty" b: 11/29/31, Los Angeles, Cal. BL/TL, 6'2", 195 lbs. Deb: 5/4/51																											
1951	Pit-N	0	0	—	2	0	0	0	0	2^2	2	1	1	0	1	0	10.1	3.38	125	.200	.273	0	.000	-0	0	0	-0	0.0
1953	Pit-N	1	2	.333	10	5	0	0	0	28	33	27	1	0	20	14	17.0	7.71	58	.297	.405	2	.250	1	-11	-10	0	-0.8
Total	2	1	2	.333	12	5	0	0	0	30^2	35	28	2	0	21	14	16.4	7.34	61	.289	.394	2	.222	1	-10	-9	0	-0.8
● LEON PETTIT	Pettit, Leon Arthur "Lefty" b: 6/23/02, Waynesburg, Pa. d: 11/21/74, Columbia, Tenn. BL/TL, 5'10.5", 165 lbs. Deb: 4/18/35																											
1935	Was-A	8	5	.615	41	7	1	0	3	109	129	65	6	4	58	45	15.8	4.95	87	.301	.390	2	.080	0	-6	-8	-0	-0.8
1937	Phi-N	0	1	.000	3	1	0	0	0	4	6	5	1	0	4	0	22.5	11.25	39	.353	.476	0	—	0	-3	-3	0	-0.5
Total	2	8	6	.571	44	8	1	0	3	113	135	70	7	4	62	45	16.0	5.18	84	.303	.393	2	.080	0	-9	-11	-0	-1.3
● BOB PETTIT	Pettit, Robert Henry b: 7/19/1861, Williamstown, Mass. d: 11/1/10, Derby, Conn. BL/TR, 5'9", 160 lbs. Deb: 9/3/1887 ♦																											
1887	Chi-N	0	0	—	1	0	0	0	**1**	1	5	8	0	0	2	0	45.0	0.00	—	.500	.500	44	.301	0	0	0	0	0.1
● ANDY PETTITTE	Pettitte, Andrew Eugene b: 6/15/72, Baton Rouge, La. BL/TL, 6'5", 235 lbs. Deb: 4/29/95																											
1995	*NY-A	12	9	.571	31	26	3	0	0	175	183	86	15	1	63	114	12.7	4.17	111	.272	.336	0	—	0	11	9	0	0.9
1996	*NY-A☆	**21**	8	.724	35	34	2	0	0	221	229	105	23	3	72	162	12.4	3.87	128	.271	.331	0	—	0	28	27	1	3.1
1997	*NY-A	18	7	.720	35	35	4	1	0	240^1	233	86	7	3	65	166	11.3	2.88	154	.256	.308	0	—	0	45	43	2	4.3
1998	*NY-A	16	11	.593	33	32	5	0	0	216^1	226	110	20	6	87	146	13.3	4.24	103	.274	.347	0	.000	-0	10	4	2	0.5
1999	*NY-A	14	11	.560	31	31	0	0	0	191^2	216	105	20	3	89	121	14.5	4.70	101	.289	.367	1	.200	0	4	1	2	0.3
2000	*NY-A	19	9	.679	32	32	3	1	0	204^2	219	111	17	4	80	125	13.3	4.35	110	.271	.340	0	.000	-0	13	10	2	1.3
Total	6	100	55	.645	197	190	17	2	0	1249	1306	603	102	20	456	834	12.8	3.99	116	.272	.337	1	.071	-0	110	94	9	10.4
● CHARLIE PETTY	Petty, Charles E. b: 6/28/1866, Nashville, Tenn. TR, Deb: 7/30/1889																											
1889	Cin-a	2	3	.400	5	5	5	0	0	44	44	29	3	6	20	10	14.3	5.52	71	.253	.350	6	.300	1	-8	-8	0	-0.6
1893	NY-N	5	2	.714	9	6	4	0	0	54	66	36	0	1	28	12	15.8	3.33	140	.292	.373	7	.318	3	8	8	-0	1.0
1894	Was-N	3	8	.273	16	12	8	0	0	103	156	114	4	9	32	14	17.2	5.59	94	.344	.399	8	.195	-2	-3	-4	-1	-0.5
	Cle-N	0	2	.000	4	3	2	0	0	27	42	37	4	3	14	4	19.7	8.67	63	.350	.431	1	.083	-2	-10	-9	-1	-0.6
	Yr	3	10	.231	20	15	10	0	0	130	198	151	8	12	46	18	17.7	6.23	85	.346	.406	9	.170	-4	-13	-13	-1	-1.1
Total	3	10	15	.400	34	26	19	0	0	228	308	216	11	19	94	40	16.6	5.41	90	.317	.388	22	.232	-0	-13	-13	-2	-0.7
● JESSE PETTY	Petty, Jesse Lee "The Silver Fox" b: 11/23/1894, Orr, Okla. d: 10/23/71, St.Paul, Minn. BR/TL, 6', 195 lbs. Deb: 4/14/21																											
1921	Cle-A	0	0	—	4	0	0	0	0	9	10	2	0	0	0	0	10.0	2.00	213	.345	.345	0	.000	-0	2	2	1	0.2
1925	Bro-N	9	9	.500	28	21	7	0	0	153	188	97	15	2	47	39	13.9	4.88	86	.304	.355	7	.140	-3	-10	-12	-2	-1.6
1926	Bro-N	17	17	.500	38	33	23	1	1	275^2	246	118	9	3	79	101	10.7	2.84	135	**.240**	.296	17	.175	-3	30	30	-4	2.7
1927	Bro-N	13	18	.419	42	33	19	2	1	271^2	263	108	13	4	53	101	10.6	2.98	133	.254	.293	9	.099	-7	28	29	-3	2.1
1928	Bro-N	15	15	.500	40	31	15	2	1	234	264	119	18	5	56	74	12.5	4.04	98	.289	.334	9	.111	-5	-1	-2	-4	-1.1
1929	Pit-N	11	10	.524	36	25	12	1	0	184^1	197	100	12	0	42	58	11.7	3.71	129	.277	.317	7	.104	-5	21	21	-2	1.4
1930	Pit-N	1	6	.143	10	7	0	0	1	41^1	67	43	8	2	13	16	17.9	8.27	60	.362	.410	1	.083	-1	-15	-15	-0	-2.0
	Chi-N	1	3	.250	9	3	0	0	0	39^1	51	18	2	0	6	18	13.0	2.97	164	.317	.341	3	.231	0	9	9	-0	0.7
	Yr	2	9	.182	19	10	0	0	1	80^2	118	61	10	2	19	34	15.5	5.69	87	.341	.379	4	.160	-1	-6	-7	-0	-1.3
Total	7	67	78	.462	207	153	76	6	4	1208^1	1286	605	77	16	296	407	11.9	3.68	113	.275	.320	53	.128	-25	63	63	-14	2.4

● PRETZEL PEZZULLO Pezzullo, John b: 12/10/10, Bridgeport, Conn. d: 5/16/90, Dallas, Tex. BL/TL, 5'11.5", 180 lbs. Deb: 4/18/35

YEAR	TM/L	W	L	PCT	G	GS	CG	SH	SV	IP	H	R	HR	HB	BB	SO	RAT	ERA	ERA+	OAV	OOB	BH	AVG	PB	PR	PR+	PD	TPI
1935	Phi-N	3	5	.375	41	7	2	0	1	84^1	115	74	5	7	45	24	17.8	6.40	71	.321	.407	6	.250	0	-22	-16	-2	-1.5
1936	Phi-N	0	0	—	1	0	0	0	0	2	1	1	0	0	6	0	31.5	4.50	101	.167	.583	0	—	0	-0	0	-0	0.0
Total	2	3	5	.375	42	7	2	0	1	86^1	116	75	5	7	51	24	18.1	6.36	71	.319	.412	6	.250	0	-22	-16	-2	-1.5

● BILL PFANN Pfann, William F. b: 6/1863, Hamilton, Ont., Can. d: 6/3/04, Hamilton, Ont., Can 6', 205 lbs. Deb: 6/16/1894

YEAR	TM/L	W	L	PCT	G	GS	CG	SH	SV	IP	H	R	HR	HB	BB	SO	RAT	ERA	ERA+	OAV	OOB	BH	AVG	PB	PR	PR+	PD	TPI
1894	Cin-N	0	1	.000	1	1	0	0	0	3	10	10	1	0	4	0	42.0	27.00	21	.526	.609	0	.000	-0	-7	-7	0	-0.8

● JEFF PFEFFER Pfeffer, Edward Joseph b: 3/4/1888, Seymour, Ill. d: 8/15/72, Chicago, Ill. BR/TR, 6'3", 210 lbs. Deb: 4/16/11 F

YEAR	TM/L	W	L	PCT	G	GS	CG	SH	SV	IP	H	R	HR	HB	BB	SO	RAT	ERA	ERA+	OAV	OOB	BH	AVG	PB	PR	PR+	PD	TPI
1911	StL-A	0	0	—	2	0	0	0	0	10	11	11	0	0	4	4	13.5	7.20	47	.297	.366	0	.000	-1	-4	-4	-0	-0.3
1913	Bro-N	0	1	.000	5	2	1	0	0	24^1	28	16	0	4	13	13	16.6	3.33	99	.311	.421	0	.000	-1	-0	-0	0	-0.1
1914	Bro-N	23	12	.657	43	34	27	3	4	315	264	99	9	7	91	135	10.3	1.97	145	.232	.293	23	.198	-1	29	30	-4	3.0
1915	Bro-N	19	14	.576	40	34	26	6	3	291^2	243	93	8	17	76	84	10.4	2.10	132	.231	.293	27	.255	5	21	22	-4	2.6
1916	*Bro-N	25	11	.694	41	36	30	6	1	328^2	274	91	5	17	63	128	9.7	1.92	140	.230	.278	34	.279	7	26	27	-5	3.5
1917	Bro-N	11	15	.423	30	30	24	3	0	266	225	84	4	16	66	115	10.4	2.23	125	.234	.294	13	.130	-4	14	16	-2	0.9
1918	Bro-N	1	0	1.000	1	1	1	1	0	9	2	0	0	0	3	1	5.0	0.00	—	.071	.161	1	.250	0	3	3	0	0.5
1919	Bro-N	17	13	.567	30	30	26	4	0	267	270	95	7	12	49	92	11.2	2.66	112	.267	.308	20	.206	1	7	9	1	1.1
1920	*Bro-N	16	9	.640	30	28	20	2	0	215	225	81	5	5	45	80	11.5	3.01	106	.273	.314	18	.243	1	3	4	-3	0.2
1921	Bro-N	1	5	.167	6	5	2	0	0	31^2	36	19	0	1	9	8	13.1	4.55	86	.310	.365	0	.000	-2	-3	-2	-0	-0.5
	StL-N	9	3	.750	18	13	7	1	0	98^2	115	51	3	5	28	22	13.5	4.29	86	.305	.361	4	.138	-1	-6	-7	-2	-1.0
	Yr	10	8	.556	24	18	9	1	0	130^1	151	70	3	6	37	30	13.4	4.35	86	.306	.362	4	.100	-2	-8	-9	-1	-1.5
1922	StL-N	19	12	.613	44	32	19	1	2	261^1	286	126	12	11	58	83	12.2	3.58	108	.279	.324	24	.245	4	15	9	1	1.4
1923	StL-N	8	9	.471	26	18	7	1	0	152^1	171	80	8	9	40	32	13.0	4.02	97	.287	.341	7	.127	-4	-0	-2	-1	-0.7
1924	StL-N	4	5	.444	16	12	3	0	0	78	102	52	3	1	30	20	15.3	5.31	71	.318	.378	3	.115	-2	-12	-14	-1	-1.6
	Pit-N	5	3	.625	15	4	1	0	0	58^2	68	23	3	0	17	19	13.0	3.07	125	.293	.341	6	.240	-0	5	5	-1	0.5
	Yr	9	8	.529	31	16	4	0	0	136^2	170	75	6	1	47	39	14.4	4.35	88	.307	.363	9	.176	-3	-7	-8	-2	-1.1
Total	13	158	112	.585	347	279	194	28	10	2407^1	2320	921	67	105	592	836	11.3	2.77	114	.258	.311	180	.206	2	97	102	-21	9.5

● BIG JEFF PFEFFER Pfeffer, Francis Xavier b: 3/31/1882, Champaign, Ill. d: 12/19/54, Kankakee, Ill. BR/TR, 6'1", 185 lbs. Deb: 4/15/05 F

YEAR	TM/L	W	L	PCT	G	GS	CG	SH	SV	IP	H	R	HR	HB	BB	SO	RAT	ERA	ERA+	OAV	OOB	BH	AVG	PB	PR	PR+	PD	TPI
1905	Chi-N	4	4	.500	15	11	9	0	0	101	84	36	2	4	36	56	11.0	2.50	120	.240	.318	8	.200	1	6	6	-1	0.4
1906	Bos-N	13	22	.371	36	36	33	4	0	302^1	270	138	4	16	114	158	11.9	2.95	91	.246	.325	31	.196	3	-11	-8	2	-0.3
1907	Bos-N	6	8	.429	19	16	12	1	0	144	129	62	3	7	61	65	12.3	3.00	85	.253	.341	15	.250	3	-8	-7	-0	-0.4
1908	Bos-N	0	0	—	4	0	0	0	0	10	18	16	1	0	8	3	23.4	12.60	19	.383	.473	0	.000	-0	-11	-11	-0	-0.7
1910	Chi-N	1	0	1.000	13	1	1	0	0	41^1	43	31	1	1	16	11	13.1	3.27	88	.281	.353	3	.176	1	-1	-2	-1	-0.1
1911	Bos-N	7	5	.583	26	6	4	1	2	97	116	74	3	0	57	24	16.1	4.73	81	.301	.391	9	.196	1	-14	-9	-0	-0.8
Total	6	31	39	.443	113	70	59	6	2	695^2	660	357	14	28	292	317	12.7	3.30	87	.260	.342	66	.204	8	-40	-33	-0	-1.9

● FRED PFEFFER Pfeffer, Nathaniel Frederick "Fritz" or "Dandelion"
b: 3/17/1860, Louisville, Ky. d: 4/10/32, Chicago, Ill. BR/TR, 5'10.5", 184 lbs. Deb: 5/1/1882 M♦

YEAR	TM/L	W	L	PCT	G	GS	CG	SH	SV	IP	H	R	HR	HB	BB	SO	RAT	ERA	ERA+	OAV	OOB	BH	AVG	PB	PR	PR+	PD	TPI
1884	Chi-N	0	0	—	1	0	0	0	0	1	3	2	0		1	0	36.0	9.00	35	.333	.400	135	.289	0	-1	-1	-0	0.0
1885	*Chi-N	2	1	.667	5	2	2	0	**2**	31^2	26	15	1		8	13	9.7	2.56	118	.222	.272	113	.241	1	1	1	-0	0.1
1892	Lou-N	0	0	—	1	0	0	0	0	5	4	3	0	0	5	0	16.2	1.80	170	.211	.375	121	.257	0	1	1	0	0.1
1894	Lou-N	0	0	—	1	0	0	0	0	7	8	6	0	1	6	0	19.3	2.57	198	.286	.429	128	.309	0	2	2	-0	0.1
Total	4	2	1	.667	8	2	2	0	2	44^2	41	26	1	1	20	13	12.5	2.62	129	.237	.320	1707	.259	1	3	4	-1	0.3

● JACK PFIESTER Pfiester, John Albert "Jack The Giant Killer" (b: John Albert Hagenbush)
b: 5/24/1878, Cincinnati, Ohio d: 9/3/53, Loveland, Ohio BR/TL, 5'11", 180 lbs. Deb: 9/8/03

YEAR	TM/L	W	L	PCT	G	GS	CG	SH	SV	IP	H	R	HR	HB	BB	SO	RAT	ERA	ERA+	OAV	OOB	BH	AVG	PB	PR	PR+	PD	TPI
1903	Pit-N	0	3	.000	3	3	2	0	0	19	26	21	0	2	10	15	18.0	6.16	53	.321	.409	0	.000	-1	-6	-6	-0	-0.8
1904	Pit-N	1	1	.500	3	2	1	0	0	20	28	18	0	0	9	6	16.6	7.20	38	.318	.381	2	.286	1	-10	-10	-0	-0.7
1906	*Chi-N	20	8	.714	31	29	20	4	0	250^2	173	63	3	13	63	153	8.9	1.51	175	.194	.258	4	.048	-7	31	31	-1	2.8
1907	*Chi-N	14	9	.609	30	22	13	3	0	195	143	61	1	5	48	90	9.0	**1.15**	**216**	.207	.263	6	.094	-3	29	29	-2	3.1
1908	*Chi-N	12	10	.545	33	29	18	3	0	252	204	82	1	11	70	117	10.2	2.00	118	.223	.287	8	.101	-4	10	10	-3	0.1
1909	Chi-N	17	6	.739	29	25	13	5	0	196^2	179	67	1	5	49	73	10.7	2.43	105	.240	.291	11	.169	0	4	3	3	0.6
1910	*Chi-N	6	3	.667	14	13	5	2	0	100^1	82	28	0	1	26	34	9.8	1.79	161	.225	.279	3	.091	-2	14	13	-0	0.8
1911	Chi-N	1	4	.200	6	5	3	0	0	33^2	34	25	0	2	18	15	14.4	4.01	83	.262	.360	2	.182	0	-2	-3	1	-0.3
Total	8	71	44	.617	149	128	75	17	0	1067^1	869	365	6	39	293	503	10.1	2.02	128	.223	.284	36	.103	-15	69	67	-3	5.6

● DAN PFISTER Pfister, Daniel Albin b: 12/20/36, Plainfield, N.J. BR/TR, 6', 187 lbs. Deb: 9/9/61

YEAR	TM/L	W	L	PCT	G	GS	CG	SH	SV	IP	H	R	HR	HB	BB	SO	RAT	ERA	ERA+	OAV	OOB	BH	AVG	PB	PR	PR+	PD	TPI
1961	KC-A	0	0	—	2	0	0	0	0	2^1	5	4	2	0	4	3	34.7	15.43	27	.417	.563	0	—	0	-3	-3	-0	-0.1
1962	KC-A	4	14	.222	41	25	2	0	1	196^1	175	112	27	9	106	123	13.3	4.54	93	.238	.341	12	.185	-1	-12	-6	1	-0.6
1963	KC-A	1	0	1.000	3	1	0	0	0	9^1	8	2	1	1	3	9	11.6	1.93	202	.229	.308	0	.000	-0	2	2	0	0.2
1964	KC-A	1	5	.167	19	3	0	0	0	41^1	50	32	10	6	29	21	18.5	6.53	58	.311	.434	0	.000	-0	-13	-12	-0	-1.6
Total	4	6	19	.240	65	29	2	0	1	249^1	238	150	40	16	142	156	14.3	4.87	85	.252	.359	12	.162	-2	-27	-19	1	-2.1

● LEE PFUND Pfund, Le Roy Herbert b: 10/10/18, Oak Park, Ill. BR/TR, 6'1", 185 lbs. Deb: 4/21/45

YEAR	TM/L	W	L	PCT	G	GS	CG	SH	SV	IP	H	R	HR	HB	BB	SO	RAT	ERA	ERA+	OAV	OOB	BH	AVG	PB	PR	PR+	PD	TPI
1945	Bro-N	3	2	.600	15	10	2	0	0	62^1	69	51	4	5	35	27	15.7	5.20	72	.274	.373	4	.182	0	-10	-10	1	-0.6

● BILL PHEBUS Phebus, Raymond William b: 8/2/09, Cherryvale, Kan. d: 10/11/89, Bartow, Fla. BR/TR, 5'9", 170 lbs. Deb: 9/6/36

YEAR	TM/L	W	L	PCT	G	GS	CG	SH	SV	IP	H	R	HR	HB	BB	SO	RAT	ERA	ERA+	OAV	OOB	BH	AVG	PB	PR	PR+	PD	TPI
1936	Was-A	0	0	—	2	1	0	0	0	7^1	4	6	1	1	4	4	11.0	2.45	195	.114	.225	0	.000	0	2	2	-0	0.1
1937	Was-A	3	2	.600	6	5	4	1	1	40^2	33	13	2	2	24	12	13.1	2.21	200	.232	.351	0	.000	1	11	10	-1	1.2
1938	Was-A	0	0	—	5	0	0	0	1	6^1	9	9	1	0	7	2	22.7	11.37	40	.346	.485	0	.000	-0	-5	-5	0	-0.2
Total	3	3	2	.600	13	6	4	1	2	54^1	46	28	4	3	35	18	13.9	3.31	135	.227	.349	0	.000	1	8	7	-1	1.1

● RAY PHELPS Phelps, Raymond Clifford b: 12/11/03, Dunlap, Tenn. d: 7/7/71, Fort Pierce, Fla. BR/TR, 6'2", 200 lbs. Deb: 4/23/30

YEAR	TM/L	W	L	PCT	G	GS	CG	SH	SV	IP	H	R	HR	HB	BB	SO	RAT	ERA	ERA+	OAV	OOB	BH	AVG	PB	PR	PR+	PD	TPI
1930	Bro-N	14	7	.667	36	24	11	2	0	179^2	198	98	21	3	52	64	12.7	4.11	120	.280	.332	10	.147	-2	17	16	2	1.5
1931	Bro-N	7	9	.438	28	26	3	1	0	149^1	184	88	3	4	44	50	14.0	5.00	76	.306	.357	8	.157	-1	-19	-20	0	-2.0
1932	Bro-N	4	5	.444	20	9	4	1	0	79^1	101	58	5	3	27	21	14.9	5.90	65	.323	.382	2	.087	-1	-18	-19	0	-1.9
1935	Chi-A	4	8	.333	27	17	4	0	1	125	126	77	10	3	55	38	13.2	4.82	96	.262	.341	5	.122	-4	-5	-3	2	-0.4
1936	Chi-A	4	6	.400	15	4	2	0	0	68^2	91	54	9	2	42	17	17.7	6.03	86	.331	.423	6	.231	1	-8	-6	1	-0.6
Total	5	33	35	.485	126	80	24	4	1	602	700	375	48	15	220	190	14.0	4.93	90	.294	.358	31	.148	-8	-32	-31	5	-3.4

● DEACON PHILLIPPE Phillippe, Charles Louis b: 5/23/1872, Rural Retreat, Va. d: 3/30/52, Avalon, Pa. BR/TR, 6'0.5", 180 lbs. Deb: 4/21/1899

YEAR	TM/L	W	L	PCT	G	GS	CG	SH	SV	IP	H	R	HR	HB	BB	SO	RAT	ERA	ERA+	OAV	OOB	BH	AVG	PB	PR	PR+	PD	TPI
1899	Lou-N	21	17	.553	42	38	33	2	1	321	331	178	10	7	64	68	11.3	3.17	122	.266	.306	26	.203	-1	24	25	-0	2.3
1900	*Pit-N	20	13	.606	38	33	29	1	0	279	274	127	7	7	42	75	**10.4**	2.84	128	.257	**.289**	19	.181	-2	27	25	-2	2.0
1901	Pit-N	22	12	.647	37	32	30	1	2	296	274	115	7	10	38	103	9.8	2.22	147	.244	.275	26	.230	5	**36**	35	3	4.5
1902	Pit-N	20	9	.690	31	30	29	5	0	272	265	90	1	4	26	122	9.8	2.05	134	.255	.276	25	.221	3	22	21	-2	2.2
1903	*Pit-N	25	9	.735	36	33	31	4	2	289^1	269	116	4	4	29	123	**9.4**	2.43	133	.241	**.263**	26	.210	2	27	26	-2	2.7
1904	Pit-N	10	10	.500	21	19	17	3	1	166^2	183	82	1	3	26	82	11.4	3.24	85	.272	.302	8	.123	-4	-9	-9	-0	-1.4
1905	Pit-N	20	13	.606	38	33	25	5	0	279	235	95	0	10	48	133	9.5	2.19	137	.233	.274	9	.093	-4	25	25	-1	2.2
1906	Pit-N	15	10	.600	33	24	19	3	0	218^2	216	78	3	2	26	90	10.0	2.47	108	.252	.276	20	.244	3	4	5	-1	0.8
1907	Pit-N	14	11	.560	35	26	17	1	2	214	214	83	2	5	36	61	10.7	2.61	93	.264	.300	12	.185	1	-3	-4	-2	-0.6
1908	Pit-N	0	0	—	5	0	0	0	0	12	20	15	0	0	3	1	17.3	11.25	20	.357	.390	1	.250	0	-12	-12	-1	-0.7
1909	*Pit-N	8	3	.727	22	13	7	1	0	131^2	121	41	2	4	14	38	9.5	2.32	117	.253	.280	3	.071	-3	4	6	-2	-0.1
1910	Pit-N	14	2	.875	31	8	5	1	4	121^2	111	46	4	3	9	30	9.1	2.29	135	.239	.258	9	.220	1	10	11	-3	1.2
1911	Pit-N	0	0	—	3	0	0	0	0	6	5	5	0	0	2	3	10.5	7.50	46	.238	.304	1	1.000	1	-3	-3	-0	0.0
Total	13	189	109	.634	372	289	242	27	12	2607	2518	1071	41	59	363	929	10.1	2.59	120	.253	.283	185	.189	2	153	150	-14	15.1

● BUZ PHILLIPS Phillips, Albert Abernathy b: 5/25/04, Newton, N.C. d: 11/6/64, Baltimore, Md. BR/TR, 5'11.5", 185 lbs. Deb: 8/5/30

YEAR	TM/L	W	L	PCT	G	GS	CG	SH	SV	IP	H	R	HR	HB	BB	SO	RAT	ERA	ERA+	OAV	OOB	BH	AVG	PB	PR	PR+	PD	TPI
1930	Phi-N	0	0	—	14	1	0	0	0	43^2	68	44	6	1	18	9	17.9	8.04	68	.354	.412	6	.462	2	-15	-11	-1	-0.4

● RED PHILLIPS Phillips, Clarence Lemuel b: 11/3/08, Pauls Valley, Okla. d: 2/1/88, Wichita, Kan. BR/TR, 6'3.5", 195 lbs. Deb: 7/24/34

YEAR	TM/L	W	L	PCT	G	GS	CG	SH	SV	IP	H	R	HR	HB	BB	SO	RAT	ERA	ERA+	OAV	OOB	BH	AVG	PB	PR	PR+	PD	TPI
1934	Det-A	2	0	1.000	7	1	1	0	1	23^1	31	17	1	0	16	3	18.1	6.17	71	.316	.412	3	.250	1	-4	-5	-1	-0.3

YEAR	TM/L	W	L	PCT	G	GS	CG	SH	SV	IP	H	R	HR	HB	BB	SO	RAT	ERA	ERA+	OAV	OOB	BH	AVG	PB	PR	PR+	PD	TPI
1936	Det-A	2	4	.333	22	6	3	0	0	87^1	124	67	12	0	22	15	15.0	6.49	76	.332	.370	10	.303	2	-14	-15	-0	-0.7
Total	2	4	4	.500	29	7	4	0	1	110^2	155	84	13	0	38	18	15.7	6.42	75	.329	.379	13	.289	3	-18	-20	-1	-1.0
● **JACK PHILLIPS**	Phillips, Jack Dorn "Stretch" b: 9/6/21, Clarence, N.Y. BR/TR, 6'4", 193 lbs. Deb: 8/22/47 ♦																											
1950	Pit-N	0	0	—	1	0	0	0	0	5	7	4	0	0	1	2	14.4	7.20	61	.333	.364	61	.293	0	-2	-1	0	0.0
● **JASON PHILLIPS**	Phillips, Jason Charles b: 3/22/74, Williamsport, Pa. BR/TR, 6'6", 225 lbs. Deb: 4/5/99																											
1999	Pit-N	0	0	—	6	0	0	0	0	7	11	9	2	0	6	7	21.9	11.57	39	.393	.500	0	—	0	-5	-5	0	-0.2
● **JACK PHILLIPS**	Phillips, John Stephen b: 5/24/19, St.Louis, Mo. d: 6/16/58, St.Louis, Mo. BR/TR, 6'1", 185 lbs. Deb: 7/13/45 ♦																											
1945	NY-N	0	0	—	1	0	0	0	0	4^1	5	5	1	1	4	0	20.8	10.38	38	.294	.455	1	.500	0	-3	-3	-0	-0.1
● **ED PHILLIPS**	Phillips, Norman Edwin b: 9/20/44, Ardmore, Okla. BR/TR, 6'1", 190 lbs. Deb: 4/9/70																											
1970	Bos-A	0	2	.000	18	0	0	0	0	23^2	29	14	4	2	10	23	15.6	5.32	74	.312	.390	0	.000	-0	-4	-3	-1	-0.4
● **TOM PHILLIPS**	Phillips, Thomas Gerald b: 4/5/1889, Philipsburg, Pa. d: 4/12/29, Philipsburg, Pa. BR/TR, 6'2", 190 lbs. Deb: 9/13/15																											
1915	StL-A	1	3	.250	5	4	1	0	0	27^1	28	13	0	2	12	5	13.8	2.96	97	.283	.372	1	.111	-1	-0	-0	-1	-0.2
1919	Cle-A	3	2	.600	22	3	1	0	0	55	55	27	2	3	34	18	15.1	2.95	114	.272	.385	4	.364	1	**2**	**2**	-1	0.2
1921	Was-A	1	0	1.000	1	1	1	0	0	9	9	2	0	0	3	2	12.0	2.00	206	.290	.353	0	.000	-1	2	2	-0	0.1
1922	Was-A	3	7	.300	17	7	2	1	0	70	72	43	2	4	22	19	12.6	4.89	79	.273	.338	3	.150	-1	-7	-8	-1	-1.1
Total	4	8	12	.400	45	15	5	1	0	161^1	164	85	4	9	71	44	13.6	3.74	95	.275	.361	8	.186	-1	-3	-3	-3	-1.0
● **BILL PHILLIPS**	Phillips, William Corcoran "Whoa Bill" or "Silver Bill" b: 11/9/1868, Allenport, Pa. d: 10/25/41, Charleroi, Pa. BR/TR, 5'11", 180 lbs. Deb: 8/11/1890 M																											
1890	Pit-N	1	9	.100	10	10	9	0	0	82	123	97	8	1	29	25	16.8	7.57	44	.336	.386	11	.239	1	-36	-42	0	-3.4
1895	Cin-N	6	7	.462	18	9	6	0	2	109	126	90	6	7	44	15	14.6	6.03	82	.285	.359	15	.313	2	-15	-12	1	-0.9
1899	Cin-N	17	9	.654	33	27	18	1	1	227^2	234	121	3	14	71	43	12.6	3.32	118	.266	.330	12	.130	-5	13	15	-0	0.9
1900	Cin-N	9	11	.450	29	24	17	3	0	208^1	229	140	5	13	67	51	13.3	4.28	86	.279	.343	13	.165	-4	-13	-14	6	-0.9
1901	Cin-N	14	18	.438	37	36	29	1	0	281^1	364	196	7	12	67	109	14.2	4.64	69	.311	.354	22	.202	2	-41	-47	5	-3.8
1902	Cin-N	16	16	.500	33	33	30	0	0	269	267	121	3	9	55	85	11.1	2.51	119	.259	.302	39	.342	10	8	14	3	3.0
1903	Cin-N	7	6	.538	16	13	11	1	0	118^1	134	74	0	7	30	46	13.0	3.35	106	.279	.330	10	.175	-1	-1	3	2	0.3
Total	7	70	76	.479	176	152	120	6	3	1295^2	1477	839	32	63	363	374	13.2	4.09	87	.284	.339	122	.224	4	-85	-76	16	-4.8
● **TAYLOR PHILLIPS**	Phillips, William Taylor "Tay" b: 6/18/33, Atlanta, Ga. BL/TL, 5'11", 185 lbs. Deb: 6/8/56																											
1956	Mil-N	5	3	.625	23	6	3	0	2	87^2	69	25	6	7	33	36	11.2	2.26	153	.223	.311	0	.000	-2	15	13	2	1.2
1957	Mil-N	3	2	.600	27	6	0	0	2	73	82	46	3	1	40	36	15.2	5.55	63	.300	.392	2	.100	-1	-14	-18	0	-1.3
1958	Chi-N	7	10	.412	39	27	5	1	1	170^1	178	102	22	6	79	102	13.9	4.76	82	.266	.349	3	.056	-4	-15	-16	1	-1.7
1959	Chi-N	0	2	.000	7	2	0	0	0	16^2	22	14	3	2	11	5	18.9	7.56	52	.319	.427	0	.000	-0	-7	-7	0	-0.7
	Phi-N	1	4	.200	32	3	1	0	1	63	72	35	4	4	31	35	15.3	5.00	82	.303	.392	1	.091	-1	-7	-6	0	-0.5
	Yr	1	6	.143	39	5	1	0	1	79^2	94	49	7	6	42	40	16.0	5.54	74	.306	.400	1	.067	-1	-14	-13	1	-1.2
1960	Phi-N	0	1	.000	10	1	0	0	0	14	21	13	2	1	4	6	16.7	8.36	46	.356	.406	0	.000	-0	-7	-7	-0	-0.5
1963	Chi-A	0	0	—	9	0	0	0	0	14	16	16	2	1	13	13	19.3	10.29	34	.302	.448	0	.000	-0	-10	-11	0	-0.6
Total	6	16	22	.421	147	45	9	1	6	438^2	460	251	42	22	211	233	14.2	4.82	78	.275	.364	6	.053	-9	-46	-53	4	-4.1
● **TOM PHOEBUS**	Phoebus, Thomas Harold b: 4/7/42, Baltimore, Md. BR/TR, 5'8", 185 lbs. Deb: 9/15/66																											
1966	Bal-A	2	1	.667	3	3	2	2	0	22	16	3	0	0	6	17	9.0	1.23	271	.213	.272	1	.167	0	5	5	-0	0.8
1967	Bal-A	14	9	.609	33	33	7	4	0	208	177	84	16	0	114	179	12.6	3.33	95	.227	.326	11	.145	1	-2	-4	-2	-0.6
1968	Bal-A	15	15	.500	36	36	9	3	0	240^2	186	81	10	4	105	193	11.0	2.62	112	.212	.299	15	.183	3	10	8	-0	1.4
1969	Bal-A	14	7	.667	35	33	6	2	0	202	180	89	23	4	87	117	12.1	3.52	101	.241	.324	15	.200	2	2	1	-1	0.2
1970	*Bal-A	5	5	.500	27	21	3	0	0	135	106	58	11	6	62	72	11.6	3.07	119	.219	.315	7	.163	-0	10	9	0	0.6
1971	SD-N	3	11	.214	29	21	2	0	0	133^1	144	67	14	3	64	80	14.2	4.45	74	.280	.363	6	.167	1	-15	-18	-1	-1.7
1972	SD-N	0	1	.000	1	1	0	0	0	5^2	3	5	2	0	6	8	14.3	7.94	41	.150	.346	0	.000	-0	-3	-3	0	-0.4
	Chi-N	3	3	.500	37	1	0	0	6	83^1	76	40	9	2	45	59	13.3	3.78	101	.247	.346	2	.133	-1	-3	0	1	0.0
	Yr	3	4	.429	38	2	0	0	6	89	79	45	11	2	51	67	13.3	4.04	93	.241	.346	2	.118	-1	-6	-2	1	-0.4
Total	7	56	52	.519	201	149	29	11	6	1030	888	427	85	19	489	725	12.2	3.33	100	.233	.324	57	.170	6	4	-1	-3	0.3
● **STEVE PHOENIX**	Phoenix, Steven Robert b: 1/31/68, Phoenix, Ariz. BR/TR, 6'2", 175 lbs. Deb: 7/30/94																											
1994	Oak-A	0	0	—	2	0	0	0	0	4^1	4	3	0	0	2	3	12.5	6.23	71	.235	.316	0	—	0	-1	-1	-0	-0.1
1995	Oak-A	0	0	—	1	0	0	0	0	1^2	3	6	1	0	3	3	32.4	32.40	14	.429	.600	0	—	0	-5	-5	0	-0.2
Total	2	0	0	—	3	0	0	0	0	6	7	9	1	0	5	6	18.0	13.50	33	.292	.414	0	—	0	-6	-6	-0	-0.3
● **BILL PHYLE**	Phyle, William Joseph b: 6/25/1875, Duluth, Minn. d: 8/6/53, Los Angeles, Cal. TR, Deb: 9/17/1898 ♦																											
1898	Chi-N	2	1	.667	3	3	3	2	0	23	24	15	0	2	6	4	12.5	0.78	458	.267	.327	1	.111	-0	7	7	-1	0.8
1899	Chi-N	1	8	.111	10	9	9	0	1	83^2	92	58	2	4	29	10	13.4	4.20	89	.279	.344	6	.176	-2	-3	-4	1	-0.5
1901	NY-N	7	10	.412	24	19	16	0	1	168^2	208	121	2	6	54	62	14.3	4.27	77	.301	.356	12	.182	-1	-18	-18	1	-1.5
Total	3	10	19	.345	37	31	28	2	2	275^1	324	194	4	12	89	76	13.9	3.96	88	.291	.350	32	.176	-4	-14	-15	2	-1.2
● **DOUG PIATT**	Piatt, Douglas William b: 9/26/65, Beaver, Pa. BL/TR, 6'1", 185 lbs. Deb: 6/11/91																											
1991	Mon-N	0	0	—	21	0	0	0	0	34^2	29	11	3	0	17	29	11.9	2.60	139	.230	.322	0	.000	-0	4	4	0	0.2
● **WILEY PIATT**	Piatt, Wiley Harold "Iron Man" b: 7/13/1874, Blue Creek, Ohio d: 9/20/46, Cincinnati, Ohio BL/TL, 5'10", 175 lbs. Deb: 4/22/1898																											
1898	Phi-N	24	14	.632	39	37	33	**6**	0	306	285	156	2	19	97	121	11.8	3.18	108	.245	.314	32	.262	4	15	9	-2	1.1
1899	Phi-N	23	15	.605	39	38	31	2	0	305	323	173	6	23	86	89	12.7	3.45	107	.271	.333	33	.270	4	14	8	-5	0.8
1900	Phi-N	9	10	.474	22	20	16	1	0	160^2	194	120	5	16	71	47	15.7	4.71	77	.298	.380	17	.250	2	-18	-20	-3	-2.0
1901	Phi-A	5	12	.294	18	16	15	0	1	140	176	112	4	3	60	45	15.4	4.63	82	.303	.372	13	.224	0	-15	-13	-4	-1.6
	Chi-A	4	2	.667	7	6	4	1	0	51^2	42	29	2	4	14	19	10.5	2.79	125	.220	.287	2	.118	-1	5	4	-1	0.2
	Yr	9	14	.391	25	22	19	1	1	191^2	218	141	6	7	74	64	14.0	4.13	89	.283	.351	15	.200	-1	-10	-9	-5	-1.4
1902	Chi-A	12	12	.500	32	30	22	2	0	246	263	129	3	9	66	96	12.4	3.51	96	.274	.327	17	.200	2	2	-4	-3	-0.5
1903	Bos-N	9	14	.391	25	23	18	0	0	181	198	107	5	4	61	100	13.1	3.18	101	.280	.340	16	.225	2	2	1	-3	0.0
Total	6	86	79	.521	182	170	139	12	1	1390^1	1481	826	27	78	455	517	13.0	3.61	97	.272	.337	130	.239	13	4	-15	-20	-2.0
● **HIPOLITO PICHARDO**	Pichardo, Hipolito Antonio (Balbina) b: 8/22/69, Jicome Esperanza, D.R. BR/TR, 6'1", 185 lbs. Deb: 4/21/92																											
1992	KC-A	9	6	.600	31	24	1	1	0	143^2	148	71	9	3	49	59	12.5	3.95	103	.267	.330	0	—	0	0	2	0	0.2
1993	KC-A	7	8	.467	30	25	2	0	0	165	183	85	10	6	53	70	13.2	4.04	114	.282	.341	0	—	0	5	10	2	0.9
1994	KC-A	5	3	.625	45	0	0	0	3	67^2	82	42	4	7	24	36	15.0	4.92	102	.308	.380	0	—	0	-1	1	1	0.2
1995	KC-A	8	4	.667	44	0	0	0	1	64	66	34	4	4	30	43	14.1	4.36	110	.265	.353	0	.000	-0	3	3	1	0.5
1996	KC-A	3	5	.375	57	0	0	0	3	68	74	41	5	2	26	43	13.5	5.43	92	.284	.353	0	—	0	-3	-3	1	-0.2
1997	KC-A	3	5	.375	47	0	0	0	11	49	51	24	7	1	24	34	14.0	4.22	112	.271	.357	0	—	0	2	3	2	0.6
1998	KC-A	7	8	.467	27	18	0	0	1	112^1	126	73	11	4	43	55	13.9	5.13	94	.280	.348	0	.000	-0	-6	-4	1	-0.3
2000	Bos-A	6	3	.667	38	1	0	0	1	65	63	29	1	3	26	37	12.7	3.46	147	.260	.339	0	.000	-0	11	11	1	1.4
Total	8	48	42	.533	319	68	3	1	20	734^2	793	399	51	30	275	377	13.5	4.39	107	.277	.347	0	.000	-1	11	23	8	3.3
● **RON PICHE**	Piche, Ronald Jacques b: 5/22/35, Verdun, Que., Canada BR/TR, 5'11", 165 lbs. Deb: 5/30/60 C																											
1960	Mil-N	3	5	.375	37	0	0	0	9	48	48	26	3	3	23	38	13.9	3.56	96	.258	.349	0	.000	-0	1	-1	-1	-0.2
1961	Mil-N	2	2	.500	12	1	1	0	1	23^1	20	12	1	0	16	16	13.9	3.47	108	.238	.360	0	.000	-1	1	1	0	0.1
1962	Mil-N	3	2	.600	14	8	2	0	0	52	54	32	6	3	29	28	14.9	4.85	78	.273	.374	1	.056	-1	-5	-6	1	-0.6
1963	Mil-N	1	1	.500	37	1	0	0	0	53	53	32	4	0	25	40	13.2	3.40	95	.256	.336	0	.000	-1	-1	-1	1	0.0
1965	Cal-A	0	3	.000	14	1	0	0	0	19^2	20	15	5	0	12	14	14.6	6.86	50	.267	.368	0	.000	-0	-7	-8	0	-1.1
1966	StL-N	1	3	.250	20	0	0	0	2	25^1	21	13	4	1	18	21	14.2	4.26	84	.214	.342	0	.000	-0	-2	-2	-0	-0.4
Total	6	10	16	.385	134	11	3	0	12	221^1	216	130	23	7	123	157	14.1	4.19	84	.255	.354	1	.024	-3	-13	-17	1	-2.2
● **RICKY PICKETT**	Pickett, Cecil Lee b: 1/19/70, Fort Worth, Tex. BL/TL, 6'1", 220 lbs. Deb: 4/28/98																											
1998	Ari-N	0	0	—	2	0	0	0	0	0^2	3	6	0	0	4	2	94.5	81.00	5	.600	.778	0	—	0	-6	-6	0	-0.3

● CHARLIE PICKETT Pickett, Charles Albert b: 3/1/1883, Delaware, Ohio d: 5/20/69, Springfield, Ohio BR/TR, 6′1″, 175 lbs. Deb: 6/21/10

YEAR	TM/L	W	L	PCT	G	GS	CG	SH	SV	IP	H	R	HR	HB	BB	SO	RAT	ERA	ERA+	OAV	OOB	BH	AVG	PB	PR	PR+	PD	TPI
1910	StL-N	0	0	—	2	0	0	0	0	6	7	2	0	0	2	2	13.5	1.50	199	.280	.333	0	—	0	1	1	-0	0.1

● CLARENCE PICKREL Pickrel, Clarence Douglas b: 3/28/11, Gretna, Va. d: 11/4/83, Rocky Mount, Va. BR/TR, 6′1″, 180 lbs. Deb: 4/22/33

YEAR	TM/L	W	L	PCT	G	GS	CG	SH	SV	IP	H	R	HR	HB	BB	SO	RAT	ERA	ERA+	OAV	OOB	BH	AVG	PB	PR	PR+	PD	TPI
1933	Phi-N	1	0	1.000	9	0	0	0	0	13^2	20	7	0	1	3	6	15.8	3.95	97	.357	.400	0	.000	-0	-1	-0	-1	-0.1
1934	Bos-N	0	0	—	10	1	0	0	0	16	24	9	0	0	7	9	17.4	5.06	76	.333	.392	0	.000	-0	-2	-2	-1	-0.2
Total	2	1	0	1.000	19	1	0	0	0	29^2	44	16	0	1	10	15	16.7	4.55	85	.344	.396	0	.000	-0	-3	-2	-1	-0.3

● JEFF PICO Pico, Jeffrey Mark b: 2/12/66, Antioch, Cal. BR/TR, 6′1″, 190 lbs. Deb: 5/31/88

YEAR	TM/L	W	L	PCT	G	GS	CG	SH	SV	IP	H	R	HR	HB	BB	SO	RAT	ERA	ERA+	OAV	OOB	BH	AVG	PB	PR	PR+	PD	TPI
1988	Chi-N	6	7	.462	29	13	3	2	1	112^2	108	57	6	0	37	57	11.6	4.15	87	.252	.312	5	.147	-0	-9	-6	-0	-0.8
1989	Chi-N	3	1	.750	53	5	0	0	2	90^2	99	43	8	0	31	38	12.9	3.77	100	.278	.336	1	.100	-1	-3	-0	1	0.1
1990	Chi-N	4	4	.500	31	8	0	0	2	92	120	53	7	1	37	37	15.5	4.79	85	.321	.383	6	.273	2	-10	-7	1	-0.2
Total	3	13	12	.520	113	26	3	2	5	295^1	327	153	21	1	105	132	13.2	4.24	90	.282	.343	12	.182	1	-22	-13	2	-0.9

● MARIO PICONE Picone, Mario Peter "Babe" b: 7/5/26, Brooklyn, N.Y. BR/TR, 5′11″, 180 lbs. Deb: 9/27/47

YEAR	TM/L	W	L	PCT	G	GS	CG	SH	SV	IP	H	R	HR	HB	BB	SO	RAT	ERA	ERA+	OAV	OOB	BH	AVG	PB	PR	PR+	PD	TPI
1947	NY-N	0	0	—	2	1	0	0	0	7	10	6	1	0	2	1	15.4	7.71	53	.345	.387	1	.500	1	-3	-3	0	-0.1
1952	NY-N	0	1	.000	2	1	0	0	0	9	11	8	2	0	5	3	16.0	7.00	53	.306	.390	0	.000	-0	-3	-3	0	-0.3
1954	NY-N	0	0	—	5	0	0	0	0	13^2	13	8	1	0	11	6	15.8	5.27	77	.283	.421	0	.000	0	-2	-2	-0	-0.1
	Cin-N	0	1	.000	4	1	0	0	0	10^1	9	7	3	0	7	1	13.9	6.10	69	.243	.364	0	.000	0	-2	-2	0	-0.1
	Yr	0	1	.000	9	1	0	0	0	24	22	15	4	0	18	7	15.0	5.63	73	.265	.396	0	.000	0	-4	-4	0	-0.2
Total	3	0	2	.000	13	3	0	0	0	40	43	29	7	0	25	11	15.3	6.30	64	.291	.393	1	.167	1	-10	-10	1	-0.6

● AL PIECHOTA Piechota, Aloysius Edward "Pie" b: 1/19/14, Chicago, Ill. d: 6/13/96, Chicago, Ill. BR/TR, 6′, 195 lbs. Deb: 5/7/40

YEAR	TM/L	W	L	PCT	G	GS	CG	SH	SV	IP	H	R	HR	HB	BB	SO	RAT	ERA	ERA+	OAV	OOB	BH	AVG	PB	PR	PR+	PD	TPI
1940	Bos-N	2	5	.286	21	8	2	0	0	61	68	45	6	0	41	18	16.1	5.75	65	.278	.381	4	.200	1	-13	-14	-0	-1.4
1941	Bos-N	0	0	—	1	0	0	0	0	1	0	0	0	0	1	0	9.0	0.00	—	.000	.250	0	—	0	0	0	-0	0.0
Total	2	2	5	.286	22	8	2	0	0	62	68	45	6	0	42	18	16.0	5.66	66	.274	.379	4	.200	1	-13	-14	-0	-1.4

● CY PIEH Pieh, Edwin John b: 9/29/1886, Waunakee, Wis. d: 9/12/45, Jacksonville, Fla BR/TR, 6′2″, 190 lbs. Deb: 9/6/13

YEAR	TM/L	W	L	PCT	G	GS	CG	SH	SV	IP	H	R	HR	HB	BB	SO	RAT	ERA	ERA+	OAV	OOB	BH	AVG	PB	PR	PR+	PD	TPI
1913	NY-A	1	0	1.000	4	0	0	0	0	10^1	10	8	0	0	7	6	14.8	4.35	69	.250	.362	1	.250	0	-2	-2	1	0.0
1914	NY-A	3	4	.429	18	4	1	0	0	62^1	68	41	6	0	29	24	14.0	5.05	55	.289	.367	2	.118	-0	-16	-16	-1	-1.8
1915	NY-A	4	5	.444	21	8	3	2	0	94	78	40	2	5	39	46	11.7	2.87	102	.234	.324	2	.067	-3	1	1	-0	-0.3
Total	3	8	9	.471	43	12	4	2	0	166^2	156	89	8	5	75	76	12.7	3.78	76	.257	.343	5	.098	-3	-17	-17	-0	-2.1

● ED PIERCE Pierce, Edward John b: 10/6/68, Arcadia, Cal. BL/TL, 6′1″, 185 lbs. Deb: 9/6/92

YEAR	TM/L	W	L	PCT	G	GS	CG	SH	SV	IP	H	R	HR	HB	BB	SO	RAT	ERA	ERA+	OAV	OOB	BH	AVG	PB	PR	PR+	PD	TPI
1992	KC-A	0	0	—	2	1	0	0	0	5^1	9	2	1	0	4	3	21.9	3.38	120	.429	.520	0	—	0	0	0	0	0.0

● JEFF PIERCE Pierce, Jeffrey Charles b: 6/7/69, Poughkeepsie, N.Y. BR/TR, 6′1″, 190 lbs. Deb: 4/26/95

YEAR	TM/L	W	L	PCT	G	GS	CG	SH	SV	IP	H	R	HR	HB	BB	SO	RAT	ERA	ERA+	OAV	OOB	BH	AVG	PB	PR	PR+	PD	TPI
1995	Bos-A	0	3	.000	12	0	0	0	0	15	16	12	0	0	14	12	18.0	6.60	74	.286	.429	0	—	0	-3	-3	-0	-0.5

● RAY PIERCE Pierce, Raymond Lester "Lefty" b: 6/6/1897, Emporia, Kan. d: 5/4/63, Denver, Colo. BL/TL, 5′7″, 156 lbs. Deb: 5/12/24

YEAR	TM/L	W	L	PCT	G	GS	CG	SH	SV	IP	H	R	HR	HB	BB	SO	RAT	ERA	ERA+	OAV	OOB	BH	AVG	PB	PR	PR+	PD	TPI
1924	Chi-N	0	0	—	6	0	0	0	0	7^1	7	6	2	0	4	2	13.5	7.36	53	.269	.367	0	—	0	-3	-3	-0	-0.2
1925	Phi-N	5	4	.556	23	8	4	0	0	90	134	67	7	1	24	18	15.9	5.50	87	.356	.397	5	.179	-0	-12	-7	0	-0.5
1926	Phi-N	2	7	.222	37	7	1	0	0	84^2	128	71	3	1	35	18	17.4	5.63	74	.348	.406	3	.125	-2	-17	-13	-1	-1.4
Total	3	7	11	.389	66	15	5	0	0	182	269	144	12	2	63	38	16.5	5.64	79	.349	.400	8	.154	-2	-32	-22	-1	-2.1

● TONY PIERCE Pierce, Tony Michael b: 1/29/46, Brunswick, Ga. BR/TL, 6′1″, 190 lbs. Deb: 4/14/67

YEAR	TM/L	W	L	PCT	G	GS	CG	SH	SV	IP	H	R	HR	HB	BB	SO	RAT	ERA	ERA+	OAV	OOB	BH	AVG	PB	PR	PR+	PD	TPI
1967	KC-A	3	4	.429	49	6	0	0	7	97^2	79	42	6	5	30	61	10.5	3.04	105	.221	.290	0	.000	-2	2	2	-1	-0.2
1968	Oak-A	1	2	.333	17	3	0	0	1	32^2	39	16	3	1	10	16	13.8	3.86	73	.295	.350	0	.000	-1	-3	-4	1	-0.4
Total	2	4	6	.400	66	9	0	0	8	130^1	118	58	9	6	40	77	11.3	3.25	95	.241	.306	0	.000	-3	-1	-2	-1	-0.6

● BILLY PIERCE Pierce, Walter William b: 4/2/27, Detroit, Mich. BL/TL, 5′10″, 160 lbs. Deb: 6/1/45

YEAR	TM/L	W	L	PCT	G	GS	CG	SH	SV	IP	H	R	HR	HB	BB	SO	RAT	ERA	ERA+	OAV	OOB	BH	AVG	PB	PR	PR+	PD	TPI
1945	Det-A	0	0	—	5	0	0	0	0	10	6	2	1	1	10	10	15.3	1.80	195	.182	.386	0	.000	-0	2	2	0	0.1
1948	Det-A	3	0	1.000	22	5	0	0	0	55^1	47	40	5	1	51	36	16.1	6.34	69	.234	.391	5	.294	2	-13	-12	0	-0.4
1949	Chi-A	7	15	.318	32	26	8	0	0	171^2	145	89	11	0	112	95	13.5	3.88	108	.228	.344	9	.176	-1	6	6	1	0.7
1950	Chi-A	12	16	.429	33	29	15	1	1	219^1	189	112	11	2	137	118	13.5	3.98	113	.228	.339	20	.260	4	15	13	-2	1.6
1951	Chi-A	15	14	.517	37	28	18	1	2	240^1	237	93	14	1	73	113	11.6	3.03	133	.258	.313	16	.203	-0	29	27	-1	3.0
1952	Chi-A	15	12	.556	33	32	14	4	1	255^1	214	76	12	3	79	144	10.4	2.57	142	.227	.289	17	.187	0	31	31	0	3.2
1953	Chi-A★	18	12	.600	40	33	19	7	3	271^1	216	94	20	3	102	**186**	10.6	2.72	148	**.218**	.292	11	.126	-4	**38**	**39**	-2	3.5
1954	Chi-A	9	10	.474	36	26	12	4	3	188^2	179	86	15	3	86	148	12.8	3.48	107	.249	.332	11	.193	0	5	5	-2	0.3
1955	Chi-A★	15	10	.600	33	26	16	6	1	205^2	162	50	16	3	64	157	**10.0**	**1.97**	**200**	.213	**.277**	12	.171	-1	**45**	**45**	-1	**5.3**
1956	Chi-A★	20	9	.690	35	33	**21**	1	1	276^1	261	108	24	3	100	192	11.9	3.32	123	.249	.316	16	.157	-4	26	24	-3	1.6
1957	Chi-A★	**20**	12	.625	37	34	**16**	4	2	257	228	98	18	1	71	171	10.5	3.26	115	.234	.287	17	.172	-2	15	14	0	1.5
1958	Chi-A☆	17	11	.607	35	32	**19**	3	2	245	204	83	33	1	66	144	10.0	2.68	136	.227	.280	17	.205	2	30	27	-3	3.0
1959	*Chi-A☆	14	15	.483	34	33	12	2	0	224	217	98	26	3	62	114	11.3	3.62	104	.253	.306	13	.191	3	6	4	0	0.7
1960	Chi-A	14	7	.667	32	30	8	1	0	196^1	201	81	24	0	46	108	11.3	3.62	104	.266	.308	12	.179	1	5	4	-1	0.3
1961	Chi-A☆	10	9	.526	39	28	5	1	3	180	190	85	17	1	54	106	12.3	3.80	103	.275	.328	8	.143	-2	4	2	-0	0.0
1962	*SF-N	16	6	.727	30	23	7	2	1	162^1	147	67	19	3	35	76	10.3	3.49	109	.239	.284	12	.214	2	8	6	-1	0.7
1963	SF-N	3	11	.214	38	13	3	1	8	99	106	49	12	1	20	52	11.5	4.27	75	.272	.309	4	.129	-0	-11	-12	0	-1.8
1964	SF-N	3	0	1.000	34	1	0	0	4	49	40	14	6	0	10	29	9.2	2.20	162	.222	.263	3	.333	1	7	7	-1	0.6
Total	18	211	169	.555	585	432	193	38	32	3306^2	2989	1325	284	30	1178	1999	11.4	3.27	119	.240	.307	203	.184	0	250	232	-15	23.9

● BILL PIERCY Piercy, William Benton "Wild Bill" b: 5/2/1896, ElMonte, Cal. d: 8/28/51, Long Beach, Cal. BR/TR, 6′1″, 185 lbs. Deb: 10/3/17

YEAR	TM/L	W	L	PCT	G	GS	CG	SH	SV	IP	H	R	HR	HB	BB	SO	RAT	ERA	ERA+	OAV	OOB	BH	AVG	PB	PR	PR+	PD	TPI
1917	NY-A	0	1	.000	1	1	1	0	0	9	9	3	0	0	2	4	11.0	3.00	90	.257	.297	0	.000	0	-0	-0	-0	0.0
1921	*NY-A	5	4	.556	14	10	5	1	0	81^2	82	40	4	7	28	35	12.9	2.98	142	.263	.337	6	.214	0	12	12	-0	1.1
1922	Bos-A	3	9	.250	29	12	7	1	0	121^1	140	77	2	6	62	24	15.4	4.67	88	.304	.394	5	.147	-1	-8	-7	2	-0.5
1923	Bos-A	8	17	.320	30	24	11	0	0	187^1	193	105	5	14	73	51	13.5	3.41	121	.277	.357	7	.132	-3	12	14	3	1.7
1924	Bos-A	5	7	.417	23	18	3	0	0	121	156	87	4	10	66	20	17.3	5.95	73	.335	.429	6	.154	-2	-23	-21	1	-1.7
1926	Chi-N	6	5	.545	19	5	1	0	0	90^1	96	52	1	6	37	31	13.8	4.48	86	.280	.360	9	.257	1	-7	-6	0	-0.6
Total	6	27	43	.386	116	70	28	2	0	610^2	676	364	16	43	268	165	14.5	4.26	97	.292	.376	33	.173	-5	-15	-9	7	0.0

● MARINO PIERETTI Pieretti, Marino Paul "Chick" b: 9/23/20, Lucca, Italy d: 1/30/81, San Francisco, Cal. BR/TR, 5′7″, 158 lbs. Deb: 4/19/45

YEAR	TM/L	W	L	PCT	G	GS	CG	SH	SV	IP	H	R	HR	HB	BB	SO	RAT	ERA	ERA+	OAV	OOB	BH	AVG	PB	PR	PR+	PD	TPI
1945	Was-A	14	13	.519	44	27	14	3	2	233^1	235	114	3	1	91	66	12.6	3.32	94	.257	.325	18	.222	2	1	-6	1	-0.4
1946	Was-A	2	2	.500	30	2	1	0	0	62	70	48	9	2	40	20	16.3	5.95	56	.292	.397	3	.214	0	-17	-19	1	-1.0
1947	Was-A	2	4	.333	23	10	2	1	0	83^1	97	50	3	2	47	32	15.8	4.21	88	.287	.377	6	.231	-0	-5	-5	-0	-0.3
1948	Was-A	0	2	.000	8	1	0	0	0	11^2	18	14	1	0	7	6	19.3	10.80	40	.375	.455	0	.000	-0	-8	-8	-0	-1.2
	Chi-A	8	10	.444	21	18	4	0	1	120	117	70	6	0	52	28	12.7	4.95	86	.262	.339	7	.179	-1	-9	-9	1	-1.1
	Yr	8	12	.400	29	19	4	0	1	131^2	135	84	7	0	59	34	13.3	5.47	78	.273	.351	7	.171	-1	-17	-18	1	-2.3
1949	Chi-A	4	6	.400	39	9	0	0	4	116	131	77	10	0	54	25	14.4	5.51	76	.289	.364	9	.237	1	-17	-17	2	-1.2
1950	Cle-A	0	1	.000	29	1	0	0	1	47^1	45	24	2	0	30	11	14.3	4.18	104	.253	.361	2	.286	0	2	1	1	0.1
Total	6	30	38	.441	194	68	21	4	8	673^2	713	397	34	5	321	188	13.9	4.53	81	.272	.353	45	.217	2	-52	-65	5	-5.1

● AL PIEROTTI Pierotti, Albert Felix b: 10/24/1895, Boston, Mass. d: 2/12/64, Everett, Mass. BR/TR, 5′10.5″, 195 lbs. Deb: 8/9/20

YEAR	TM/L	W	L	PCT	G	GS	CG	SH	SV	IP	H	R	HR	HB	BB	SO	RAT	ERA	ERA+	OAV	OOB	BH	AVG	PB	PR	PR+	PD	TPI
1920	Bos-N	1	1	.500	6	2	2	0	0	25	23	9	2	0	9	12	11.5	2.88	106	.250	.317	2	.250	0	1	0	-0	0.0
1921	Bos-N	0	1	.000	2	0	0	0	0	1^2	3	4	0	0	3	1	32.4	21.60	17	.375	.545	0	.000	-0	-3	-3	0	-0.6
Total	2	1	2	.333	8	2	2	0	0	26^2	26	13	2	0	12	13	12.8	4.05	76	.260	.339	2	.222	-0	-3	-3	-0	-0.6

● BILL PIERRO Pierro, William Leonard "Wild Bill" b: 4/15/26, Brooklyn, N.Y. BR/TR, 6′1″, 155 lbs. Deb: 7/17/50

YEAR	TM/L	W	L	PCT	G	GS	CG	SH	SV	IP	H	R	HR	HB	BB	SO	RAT	ERA	ERA+	OAV	OOB	BH	AVG	PB	PR	PR+	PD	TPI
1950	Pit-N	0	2	.000	12	3	0	0	0	29	33	34	2	2	28	13	19.6	10.55	42	.289	.438	2	.222	-0	-21	-19	-1	-1.1

● DAVE PIERSON Pierson, David P. b: 8/20/1855, Wilkes-Barre, Pa. d: 11/11/22, Newark, N.J. BR/TR, 5′7″, 142 lbs. Deb: 4/25/1876 F♦

YEAR	TM/L	W	L	PCT	G	GS	CG	SH	SV	IP	H	R	HR	HB	BB	SO	RAT	ERA	ERA+	OAV	OOB	BH	AVG	PB	PR	PR+	PD	TPI
1876	Cin-N	0	1	.000	1	1	0	0	0	0	2	1		0	—	—	∞	—	1.000	1.000	95	.235	-0	-2	-2	0	-0.2	

● **WILLIAM PIERSON** Pierson, William Morris b: 6/14/1899, Atlantic City, N.J. d: 2/20/59, Atlantic City, N.J BL/TL, 6'2", 180 lbs. Deb: 7/4/18

YEAR	TM/L	W	L	PCT	G	GS	CG	SH	SV	IP	H	R	HR	HB	BB	SO	RAT	ERA	ERA+	OAV	OOB	BH	AVG	PB	PR	PR+	PD	TPI
1918	Phi-A	0	1	.000	8	1	0	0	0	21^2	20	10	0	2	20	6	17.4	3.32	88	.286	.457	1	.250	-0	-1	-1	-1	-0.2
1919	Phi-A	0	0	—	2	1	0	0	0	7^2	9	3	0	0	8	4	20.0	3.52	97	.333	.486	1	.333	0	-0	-0	0	0.1
1924	Phi-A	0	0	—	1	0	0	0	0	2^2	3	1	0	0	3	0	20.3	3.38	127	.300	.462	0	—	0	0	0	0	0.0
Total	3	0	1	.000	11	2	0	0	0	32	32	14	0	2	31	10	18.3	3.38	94	.299	.464	2	.286	0	-1	-1	-1	-0.1

● **GEORGE PIKTUZIS** Piktuzis, George Richard b: 1/3/32, Chicago, Ill. d: 11/28/93, Long Beach, Cal. BR/TL, 6'2", 200 lbs. Deb: 4/25/56

YEAR	TM/L	W	L	PCT	G	GS	CG	SH	SV	IP	H	R	HR	HB	BB	SO	RAT	ERA	ERA+	OAV	OOB	BH	AVG	PB	PR	PR+	PD	TPI
1956	Chi-N	0	0	—	2	0	0	0	0	5	6	4	1	0	2	3	14.4	7.20	52	.333	.400	0	—	0	-2	-2	-0	-0.1

● **DUANE PILLETTE** Pillette, Duane Xavier "Dee" b: 7/24/22, Detroit, Mich. BR/TR, 6'3", 205 lbs. Deb: 7/19/49 F

YEAR	TM/L	W	L	PCT	G	GS	CG	SH	SV	IP	H	R	HR	HB	BB	SO	RAT	ERA	ERA+	OAV	OOB	BH	AVG	PB	PR	PR+	PD	TPI
1949	NY-A	2	4	.333	12	3	2	0	0	37^1	43	20	6	0	19	9	14.9	4.34	93	.299	.380	0	.000	-1	-1	-1	1	-0.2
1950	NY-A	0	0	—	4	0	0	0	0	7	9	3	0	0	3	4	15.4	1.29	334	.321	.387	0	—	0	3	2	-0	0.1
	StL-A	3	5	.375	24	7	1	0	2	73^2	104	62	6	2	44	18	18.3	7.09	70	.337	.423	3	.136	-1	-21	-16	-0	-1.6
	Yr	3	5	.375	28	7	1	0	2	80^2	113	65	6	2	47	22	18.1	6.58	74	.335	.420	3	.136	-1	-18	-14	-1	-1.5
1951	StL-A	6	14	.300	35	24	6	1	0	191	205	113	14	5	115	65	15.3	4.99	88	.276	.376	8	.136	-3	-19	-12	-1	-1.5
1952	StL-A	10	13	.435	30	30	9	1	0	205^1	222	94	14	7	55	62	12.4	3.59	109	.274	.325	12	.182	0	2	7	-2	0.5
1953	StL-A	7	13	.350	31	25	5	1	0	166^2	181	90	16	2	62	58	13.2	4.48	94	.277	.341	7	.132	-1	-9	-5	-1	-0.7
1954	Bal-A	10	14	.417	25	25	11	1	0	179	158	79	9	1	67	66	11.4	3.12	115	.234	.305	7	.132	-1	12	10	3	1.5
1955	Bal-A	0	3	.000	7	5	0	0	0	20^2	31	16	0	0	14	13	19.6	6.53	58	.344	.433	1	.167	0	-6	-6	0	-0.8
1956	Phi-N	0	0	—	20	0	0	0	0	23^1	32	21	2	0	12	10	17.0	6.56	57	.330	.404	0	.000	-0	-7	-7	-0	-0.4
Total	8	38	66	.365	188	119	34	4	2	904	985	498	67	17	391	305	13.9	4.40	93	.277	.352	38	.140	-7	-45	-31	-1	-3.1

● **HERMAN PILLETTE** Pillette, Herman Polycarp "Old Folks"
b: 12/26/1895, St.Paul, Ore. d: 4/30/60, Sacramento, Cal. BR/TR, 6'2", 190 lbs. Deb: 7/30/17 F

YEAR	TM/L	W	L	PCT	G	GS	CG	SH	SV	IP	H	R	HR	HB	BB	SO	RAT	ERA	ERA+	OAV	OOB	BH	AVG	PB	PR	PR+	PD	TPI
1917	Cin-N	0	0	—	1	0	0	0	0	1	4	2	0	0	0	0	36.0	18.00	15	.571	.571	0	—	0	-2	-2	-0	-0.1
1922	Det-A	19	12	.613	40	37	18	4	1	274^2	270	110	6	15	95	71	12.5	2.85	136	.258	.328	17	.172	-3	36	33	3	3.3
1923	Det-A	14	19	.424	47	36	14	0	1	250^1	280	138	7	6	83	64	13.3	3.85	100	.288	.347	21	.247	4	4	1	4	0.8
1924	Det-A	1	1	.500	19	3	1	0	1	37^2	46	30	1	3	14	13	15.1	4.78	86	.297	.366	4	.364	1	-2	-3	0	0.0
Total	4	34	32	.515	107	76	33	4	3	563^2	600	280	14	24	192	148	13.0	3.45	113	.275	.340	42	.215	2	36	28	7	4.0

● **SQUIZ PILLION** Pillion, Cecil Randolph b: 4/13/1894, Hartford, Conn. d: 9/30/62, Pittsburgh, Pa. BL/TL, 6', 178 lbs. Deb: 8/20/15

YEAR	TM/L	W	L	PCT	G	GS	CG	SH	SV	IP	H	R	HR	HB	BB	SO	RAT	ERA	ERA+	OAV	OOB	BH	AVG	PB	PR	PR+	PD	TPI
1915	Phi-A	0	0	—	2	0	0	0	0	5^1	10	5	0	1	2	0	21.9	6.75	43	.400	.464	0	.000	-0	-2	-2	0	-0.1

● **HORACIO PINA** Pina, Horacio (Garcia) b: 3/12/45, Coahuila, Mexico BR/TR, 6'2", 177 lbs. Deb: 8/14/68

YEAR	TM/L	W	L	PCT	G	GS	CG	SH	SV	IP	H	R	HR	HB	BB	SO	RAT	ERA	ERA+	OAV	OOB	BH	AVG	PB	PR	PR+	PD	TPI
1968	Cle-A	1	1	.500	12	3	0	0	2	31^1	24	7	0	1	15	24	11.5	1.72	172	.218	.317	0	.000	-1	4	4	-0	0.3
1969	Cle-A	4	2	.667	31	4	0	0	1	46^2	44	29	6	5	27	32	14.7	5.21	72	.256	.373	3	.500	1	-8	-7	0	-0.7
1970	Was-A	5	3	.625	61	0	0	0	6	71	66	25	4	3	35	41	13.2	2.79	128	.250	.344	0	.000	-0	7	6	1	0.8
1971	Was-A	1	1	.500	56	0	0	0	2	57^2	47	26	2	4	31	38	12.8	3.59	92	.227	.339	0	.000	-0	-1	-2	1	0.0
1972	Tex-A	2	7	.222	60	0	0	0	15	76	61	33	3	8	43	60	13.3	3.20	94	.228	.352	1	.200	0	-1	-2	3	0.1
1973	*Oak-A	6	3	.667	47	0	0	0	8	88	58	31	8	8	34	41	10.2	2.76	129	.193	.292	0	—	0	10	8	3	1.3
1974	Chi-N	3	4	.429	34	0	0	0	4	47^1	49	22	4	2	28	32	15.0	3.99	96	.268	.371	1	.200	-0	-2	-1	1	-0.1
	Cal-A	1	2	.333	11	0	0	0	0	11^2	9	3	1	0	3	6	9.3	2.31	149	.209	.261	0	—	0	2	2	1	0.4
1978	Phi-N	0	0	—	2	0	0	0	0	2^1	0	0	0	0	0	4	0.0	0.00	—	.000	.000	0	.000	-0	1	1	0	0.0
Total	8	23	23	.500	314	7	0	0	38	432	358	176	28	31	216	278	12.6	3.25	106	.231	.336	5	.185	0	13	9	9	2.1

● **JOEL PINEIRO** Pineiro, Joel Alberto b: 9/25/78, Rio Piedras, P.R. BR/TR, 6'1", 180 lbs. Deb: 8/8/2000

YEAR	TM/L	W	L	PCT	G	GS	CG	SH	SV	IP	H	R	HR	HB	BB	SO	RAT	ERA	ERA+	OAV	OOB	BH	AVG	PB	PR	PR+	PD	TPI
2000	Sea-A	1	0	1.000	8	1	0	0	0	19^1	25	13	3	0	13	10	17.7	5.59	86	.316	.413	0	—	0	-1	-2	-0	-0.1

● **ED PINKHAM** Pinkham, Edward b: 1849, Brooklyn, N.Y. TL, 5'7", 142 lbs. Deb: 5/8/1871 ♦

YEAR	TM/L	W	L	PCT	G	GS	CG	SH	SV	IP	H	R	HR	HB	BB	SO	RAT	ERA	ERA+	OAV	OOB	BH	AVG	PB	PR	PR+	PD	TPI
1871	Chi-n	1	0	1.000	3	0	0	0	1	10^1	10	8	0		3	0	11.3	3.48	132	.208	.255	25	.263	1	**1**	**1**		0.1

● **GEORGE PINKNEY** Pinkney, George Burton b: 1/11/1862, Orange Prairie, Ill. d: 11/10/26, Peoria, Ill. BR/TR, 5'7", 160 lbs. Deb: 8/16/1884 ♦

YEAR	TM/L	W	L	PCT	G	GS	CG	SH	SV	IP	H	R	HR	HB	BB	SO	RAT	ERA	ERA+	OAV	OOB	BH	AVG	PB	PR	PR+	PD	TPI
1886	Bro-a	0	0	—	1	0	0	0	0	2	2	1	0	0	0	0	9.0	4.50	78	.400	.400	156	.261	0	-0	-0	-0	0.0

● **ED PINNANCE** Pinnance, Edward D. "Peanuts"
b: 10/22/1879, Walpole Island, Ont., Canada d: 12/12/44, Walpole Island, Ontario, Canada BL/TR, 6'1", 180 lbs. Deb: 9/14/03

YEAR	TM/L	W	L	PCT	G	GS	CG	SH	SV	IP	H	R	HR	HB	BB	SO	RAT	ERA	ERA+	OAV	OOB	BH	AVG	PB	PR	PR+	PD	TPI
1903	Phi-A	0	0	—	2	1	0	0	1	7	5	2	0	0	2	2	9.0	2.57	119	.200	.259	0	.000	-0	0	0	-0	0.0

● **LERTON PINTO** Pinto, William Lerton b: 4/8/1899, Chillicothe, Ohio d: 5/13/83, Oxnard, Cal. BL/TL, 6', 190 lbs. Deb: 5/23/22

YEAR	TM/L	W	L	PCT	G	GS	CG	SH	SV	IP	H	R	HR	HB	BB	SO	RAT	ERA	ERA+	OAV	OOB	BH	AVG	PB	PR	PR+	PD	TPI
1922	Phi-N	0	1	.000	9	0	0	0	0	24^2	31	20	1	0	14	4	16.4	5.11	91	.320	.405	1	.111	-1	-3	-1	-1	-0.1
1924	Phi-N	0	0	—	3	0	0	0	0	4	7	4	1	0	0	1	15.8	9.00	50	.467	.467	0	.000	-0	-2	-2	0	-0.1
Total	2	0	1	.000	12	0	0	0	0	28^2	38	24	2	0	14	5	16.3	5.65	82	.339	.413	1	.100	-1	-5	-3	-1	-0.2

● **ED PIPGRAS** Pipgras, Edward John b: 6/15/04, Schleswig, Iowa d: 4/13/64, Currie, Minn. BR/TR, 6'2.5", 175 lbs. Deb: 8/25/32 F

YEAR	TM/L	W	L	PCT	G	GS	CG	SH	SV	IP	H	R	HR	HB	BB	SO	RAT	ERA	ERA+	OAV	OOB	BH	AVG	PB	PR	PR+	PD	TPI
1932	Bro-N	0	1	.000	5	1	0	0	0	10	16	11	2	0	6	5	19.8	5.40	71	.348	.423	0	.000	-0	-2	-2	0	-0.2

● **GEORGE PIPGRAS** Pipgras, George William b: 12/20/1899, Ida Grove, Iowa d: 10/19/86, Gainesville, Fla. BR/TR, 6'1.5", 185 lbs. Deb: 6/9/23 FU

YEAR	TM/L	W	L	PCT	G	GS	CG	SH	SV	IP	H	R	HR	HB	BB	SO	RAT	ERA	ERA+	OAV	OOB	BH	AVG	PB	PR	PR+	PD	TPI
1923	NY-A	1	3	.250	8	2	2	0	0	33^1	34	22	2	1	25	12	16.2	5.94	66	.276	.403	0	.000	-1	-7	-7	-0	-0.9
1924	NY-A	0	1	.000	9	1	0	0	1	15^1	20	18	0	4	18	4	24.7	9.98	42	.351	.532	1	.333	0	-10	-10	1	-0.6
1927	*NY-A	10	3	.769	29	21	9	1	0	166^1	148	81	2	1	77	81	12.2	4.11	94	.247	.334	16	.239	2	1	-5	-1	-0.3
1928	*NY-A	**24**	13	.649	46	38	22	4	3	**300^2**	314	132	4	3	103	139	12.6	3.38	111	.272	.333	18	.157	-4	22	14	-4	0.7
1929	NY-A	18	12	.600	39	33	13	3	0	225^1	229	132	16	5	95	125	13.1	4.23	91	.264	.340	12	.143	-4	0	-10	-3	-1.8
1930	NY-A	15	15	.500	44	30	15	**3**	4	221	230	133	9	8	70	111	12.5	4.11	105	.263	.324	12	.150	-2	13	5	-2	0.1
1931	NY-A	7	6	.538	36	14	6	1	3	137^2	134	73	8	2	58	59	12.7	3.79	105	.251	.327	1	.024	-6	9	3	-2	-0.5
1932	*NY-A	16	9	.640	32	27	14	2	0	219	235	120	15	6	87	111	13.5	4.19	97	.269	.340	18	.220	1	7	-3	-2	-0.4
1933	NY-A	2	2	.500	4	4	3	0	0	33	32	13	1	0	12	14	12.0	3.27	119	.252	.317	1	.091	-1	4	2	1	0.3
	Bos-A	9	8	.529	22	17	9	2	1	128^1	140	65	5	2	45	56	13.1	4.07	108	.276	.337	9	.196	-1	3	4	-2	0.3
	Yr	11	10	.524	26	21	12	2	1	161^1	172	78	6	2	57	70	12.9	3.90	110	.271	.333	10	.175	-1	7	7	-1	0.6
1934	Bos-A	0	0	—	2	1	0	0	0	3^1	4	3	1	0	3	0	18.9	8.10	59	.308	.438	0	.000	-0	-1	-1	0	0.0
1935	Bos-A	0	1	.000	5	1	0	0	0	5	9	9	3	1	5	2	27.0	14.40	33	.391	.517	0	—	0	-6	-5	0	-0.8
Total	11	102	73	.583	276	189	93	16	12	1488^1	1529	801	66	33	598	714	13.1	4.09	98	.266	.339	88	.163	-15	35	-15	-15	-3.9

● **COTTON PIPPEN** Pippen, Henry Harold b: 4/2/11, Cisco, Tex. d: 2/15/81, Williams, Cal. BR/TR, 6'2", 180 lbs. Deb: 8/28/36

YEAR	TM/L	W	L	PCT	G	GS	CG	SH	SV	IP	H	R	HR	HB	BB	SO	RAT	ERA	ERA+	OAV	OOB	BH	AVG	PB	PR	PR+	PD	TPI
1936	StL-N	0	2	.000	6	3	0	0	0	21	37	18	5	2	8	8	20.1	7.71	51	.402	.461	1	.167	0	-9	-9	1	-0.6
1939	Phi-A	4	11	.267	25	17	5	0	1	118^2	169	97	13	1	40	33	15.9	5.99	79	.329	.378	3	.086	-2	-18	-17	2	-1.8
	Det-A	0	1	.000	3	2	0	0	0	14	18	13	1	0	6	5	15.4	7.07	69	.310	.375	2	.400	0	-4	-3	-0	-0.2
	Yr	4	12	.250	28	19	5	0	1	132^2	187	110	14	1	46	38	15.9	6.11	77	.327	.378	5	.125	-2	-22	-20	1	-2.0
1940	Det-A	1	2	.333	4	3	0	0	0	21^1	29	16	3	1	10	9	16.9	6.75	70	.326	.400	0	.000	-1	-6	-4	0	-0.6
Total	3	5	16	.238	38	25	5	0	1	175	253	144	22	4	64	55	16.5	6.38	73	.336	.391	6	.111	-3	-36	-33	2	-3.2

● **GERRY PIRTLE** Pirtle, Gerald Eugene b: 12/3/47, Tulsa, Okla. BR/TR, 6'1", 185 lbs. Deb: 7/2/78

YEAR	TM/L	W	L	PCT	G	GS	CG	SH	SV	IP	H	R	HR	HB	BB	SO	RAT	ERA	ERA+	OAV	OOB	BH	AVG	PB	PR	PR+	PD	TPI
1978	Mon-N	0	2	.000	19	0	0	0	0	25^2	33	24	5	2	23	14	20.3	5.96	59	.314	.446	0	—	0	-7	-7	-0	-0.5

● **MARC PISCIOTTA** Pisciotta, Marc George b: 8/7/70, Edison, N.J. BR/TR, 6'5", 240 lbs. Deb: 6/30/97

YEAR	TM/L	W	L	PCT	G	GS	CG	SH	SV	IP	H	R	HR	HB	BB	SO	RAT	ERA	ERA+	OAV	OOB	BH	AVG	PB	PR	PR+	PD	TPI
1997	Chi-N	3	1	.750	24	0	0	0	0	28^1	20	10	1	1	16	21	11.8	3.18	136	.200	.316	0	.000	-0	3	3	0	0.4
1998	Chi-N	1	2	.333	43	0	0	0	0	44	44	21	4	2	32	31	16.0	4.09	108	.259	.382	1	.333	0	1	1	-0	0.1
1999	KC-A	0	2	.000	8	0	0	0	0	8^1	9	8	1	0	10	3	20.5	8.64	58	.281	.452	0	—	0	-3	-3	0	-0.6
Total	3	4	5	.444	75	0	0	0	0	80^2	73	39	6	3	58	55	15.0	4.24	105	.242	.369	1	.250	0	0	2	-0	-0.1

● **SKIP PITLOCK** Pitlock, Lee Patrick Thomas b: 11/6/47, Hillside, Ill. BL/TL, 6'2", 180 lbs. Deb: 6/12/70

YEAR	TM/L	W	L	PCT	G	GS	CG	SH	SV	IP	H	R	HR	HB	BB	SO	RAT	ERA	ERA+	OAV	OOB	BH	AVG	PB	PR	PR+	PD	TPI
1970	SF-N	5	5	.500	18	15	1	0	0	87	92	48	13	4	48	56	14.9	4.66	85	.274	.371	2	.080	-0	-6	-7	0	-0.7
1974	Chi-A	3	3	.500	40	5	0	0	1	105^2	103	58	7	7	55	68	14.1	4.43	84	.257	.356	0	—	0	-9	-8	-1	-0.6

YEAR	TM/L	W	L	PCT	G	GS	CG	SH	SV	IP	H	R	HR	HB	BB	SO	RAT	ERA	ERA+	OAV	OOB	BH	AVG	PB	PR	PR+	PD	TPI
1975	Chi-A	0	0	—	1	0	0	0	0	0	1	0	0	0	—	—	—	—	1.000	1.000	103	—	0	0	0	0	0.0	
Total	3	8	8	.500	59	20	1	0	1	192^2	196	106	20	11	103	124	14.5	4.53	85	.266	.364	2	.080	-0	-15	-14	-1	-1.3

● TOGIE PITTINGER

Pittinger, Charles Reno b: 1/12/1872, Greencastle, Pa. d: 1/14/09, Greencastle, Pa. BL/TR, 6'2", 175 lbs. Deb: 4/26/00

YEAR	TM/L	W	L	PCT	G	GS	CG	SH	SV	IP	H	R	HR	HB	BB	SO	RAT	ERA	ERA+	OAV	OOB	BH	AVG	PB	PR	PR+	PD	TPI
1900	Bos-N	2	9	.182	18	13	8	0	0	114	135	97	7	8	54	27	15.6	5.13	80	.293	.377	6	.130	-4	-18	-11	-1	-1.3
1901	Bos-N	13	16	.448	34	33	27	1	0	281^1	288	135	7	8	76	129	11.9	3.01	120	.263	.316	11	.110	-8	10	18	3	1.1
1902	Bos-N	27	16	.628	46	40	36	7	0	389^1	360	139	4	16	128	174	11.7	2.52	112	.245	.313	20	.136	-8	11	13	-2	0.2
1903	Bos-N	18	22	.450	44	39	35	3	1	351^2	396	205	12	17	143	140	14.2	3.48	92	.294	.369	14	.109	-9	-8	-11	-3	-2.1
1904	Bos-N	15	21	.417	38	37	35	5	0	335^1	298	149	1	14	144	146	12.2	2.66	104	.242	.329	13	.107	-9	3	4	5	0.0
1905	Phi-N	23	14	.622	**46**	37	29	4	2	337^1	311	155	3	16	104	136	11.5	3.09	94	.247	.313	19	.156	-3	-3	-7	-3	-1.3
1906	Phi-N	8	10	.444	20	16	9	2	0	129^2	128	62	2	12	50	43	13.2	3.40	77	.252	.334	4	.091	-1	-11	-11	-1	-1.8
1907	Phi-N	9	5	.643	16	12	8	1	0	102	101	43	3	5	35	37	12.4	3.00	81	.261	.330	5	.139	-1	-6	-7	-1	-1.0
Total	8	115	113	.504	262	227	187	23	3	2040^2	2017	985	39	96	734	832	12.6	3.10	98	.260	.332	92	.124	-43	-22	-13	-3	-6.2

● JIM PITTSLEY

Pittsley, James Michael b: 4/3/74, DuBois, Pa. BR/TR, 6'7", 215 lbs. Deb: 5/23/95

YEAR	TM/L	W	L	PCT	G	GS	CG	SH	SV	IP	H	R	HR	HB	BB	SO	RAT	ERA	ERA+	OAV	OOB	BH	AVG	PB	PR	PR+	PD	TPI
1995	KC-A	0	0	—	1	1	0	0	0	3^1	7	5	3	0	1	0	21.6	13.50	35	.438	.471	0	—	0	-3	-3	-0	-0.1
1997	KC-A	5	8	.385	21	21	0	0	0	112	120	72	15	6	54	52	14.5	5.46	86	.277	.365	1	.500	1	-11	-9	-2	-0.9
1998	KC-A	1	1	.500	39	2	0	0	0	68^1	88	56	13	2	37	44	16.7	6.59	73	.322	.407	0	.000	-0	-15	-13	0	-0.6
1999	KC-A	1	2	.333	5	5	0	0	0	23^1	33	22	2	1	15	7	18.9	6.94	72	.337	.430	0	—	0	-5	-5	0	-0.5
	Mil-N	0	1	.000	15	0	0	0	0	18^2	20	12	3	1	10	13	14.9	4.82	94	.274	.369	0	.000	0	-1	-1	0	0.0
Total	4	7	12	.368	81	29	0	0	0	225^2	268	167	36	10	117	116	15.8	6.02	79	.300	.387	1	.200	1	-35	-31	-1	-2.1

● STAN PITULA

Pitula, Stanley b: 3/23/31, Hackensack, N.J. d: 8/15/65, Hackensack, N.J. BR/TR, 5'10", 170 lbs. Deb: 4/24/57

YEAR	TM/L	W	L	PCT	G	GS	CG	SH	SV	IP	H	R	HR	HB	BB	SO	RAT	ERA	ERA+	OAV	OOB	BH	AVG	PB	PR	PR+	PD	TPI
1957	Cle-A	2	2	.500	23	5	1	0	0	59^2	67	37	8	2	32	17	15.2	4.98	75	.296	.388	3	.200	0	-8	-9	-1	-0.6

● JUAN PIZARRO

Pizarro, Juan Ramon (Cordova) b: 2/7/37, Santurce, P.R. BL/TL, 5'11", 190 lbs. Deb: 5/4/57

YEAR	TM/L	W	L	PCT	G	GS	CG	SH	SV	IP	H	R	HR	HB	BB	SO	RAT	ERA	ERA+	OAV	OOB	BH	AVG	PB	PR	PR+	PD	TPI
1957	*Mil-N	5	6	.455	24	10	3	0	0	99^1	99	58	16	1	51	68	13.7	4.62	76	.261	.350	9	.250	3	-8	-14	-1	-1.1
1958	*Mil-N	6	4	.600	16	10	7	1	1	96^2	75	36	12	4	47	84	11.7	2.70	130	.212	.312	8	.250	3	13	10	1	1.3
1959	Mil-N	6	2	.750	29	14	6	2	0	133^2	117	61	13	8	70	126	13.1	3.77	94	.237	.342	5	.122	-0	3	-4	0	-0.2
1960	Mil-N	6	7	.462	21	17	3	0	0	114^2	105	63	13	4	72	88	14.2	4.55	75	.244	.357	11	.275	3	-10	-16	-1	-1.4
1961	Chi-A	14	7	.667	39	25	12	1	2	194^2	164	73	17	4	89	188	11.9	3.05	128	.226	.314	17	.246	5	21	19	-1	2.4
1962	Chi-A	12	14	.462	36	32	9	1	1	203^1	182	97	16	1	97	173	12.4	3.81	103	.236	.322	11	.159	-0	4	2	-2	0.1
1963	Chi-A★	16	8	.667	32	28	10	3	1	214^2	177	69	14	3	63	163	10.2	2.39	147	.224	.284	13	.178	3	30	28	-3	3.1
1964	Chi-A☆	19	9	.679	33	33	11	4	0	239	193	78	23	3	55	162	9.5	2.56	135	.219	.267	19	.211	5	28	25	-1	3.3
1965	Chi-A	6	3	.667	18	18	2	1	0	97	96	42	9	1	37	65	12.4	3.43	93	.254	.322	8	.235	3	0	-3	-0	0.1
1966	Chi-A	8	6	.571	34	9	1	0	3	88^2	91	49	9	1	39	42	13.3	3.76	84	.269	.347	4	.154	0	-3	-6	1	-0.9
1967	Pit-N	8	10	.444	50	9	1	1	9	107	99	55	10	2	52	96	12.9	3.95	85	.245	.334	7	.259	2	-7	-7	-1	-1.2
1968	Pit-N	1	1	.500	12	0	0	0	0	11	14	7	2	1	10	6	20.5	3.27	89	.311	.446	0	.000	-0	-0	-0	-0	-0.2
	Bos-A	6	8	.429	19	12	6	0	2	107^2	97	46	15	0	44	84	11.8	3.59	88	.242	.317	5	.161	1	-7	-5	2	-0.4
1969	Bos-A	0	1	.000	6	0	0	0	2	9	14	7	2	0	6	4	20.0	6.00	63	.359	.444	1	.333	0	-2	-2	0	-0.3
	Cle-A	3	3	.500	48	4	1	0	4	82^2	67	34	6	2	49	44	12.8	3.16	119	.229	.343	3	.200	0	4	5	0	0.5
	Oak-A	1	1	.500	3	0	0	0	1	7^2	3	2	1	0	3	4	7.0	2.35	147	.125	.222	1	.500	0	1	1	-0	0.2
	Yr	4	5	.444	57	4	1	0	7	99^1	84	43	9	2	58	52	13.0	3.35	112	.236	.346	5	.250	1	3	4	0	0.4
1970	Chi-N	0	0	—	12	0	0	0	1	15^2	16	9	2	1	9	14	14.9	4.60	98	.262	.366	0	.000	-0	-1	-0	0	0.0
1971	Chi-N	7	6	.538	16	14	6	3	0	101^1	78	43	10	2	40	67	10.7	3.46	114	.209	.289	6	.176	1	0	5	0	0.7
1972	Chi-N	4	5	.444	16	7	1	0	1	59^1	66	28	7	1	32	24	15.0	3.94	97	.293	.384	3	.143	-0	-3	-1	1	0.0
1973	Chi-N	0	1	.000	2	0	0	0	0	4	6	5	1	1	1	3	18.0	11.25	35	.353	.421	0	.000	-0	-3	-3	0	-0.5
	Hou-N	2	2	.500	15	1	0	0	0	23^1	28	17	1	1	11	10	15.4	6.56	56	.301	.381	0	.000	-0	-7	-8	1	-1.1
	Yr	2	3	.400	17	1	0	0	0	27^1	34	22	2	2	12	13	15.8	7.24	51	.309	.387	0	.000	-0	-11	-11	1	-1.6
1974	*Pit-N	1	1	.500	7	2	0	0	0	24	20	11	2	0	11	7	11.6	1.88	184	.220	.304	2	.333	0	5	4	-0	0.4
Total	18	131	105	.555	488	245	79	17	28	2034^1	1807	890	201	41	888	1522	12.1	3.43	104	.237	.320	133	.202	29	56	34	-5	4.8

● GORDIE PLADSON

Pladson, Gordon Cecil b: 7/31/56, New Westminster, B.C., Canada BR/TR, 6'4", 210 lbs. Deb: 9/7/79

YEAR	TM/L	W	L	PCT	G	GS	CG	SH	SV	IP	H	R	HR	HB	BB	SO	RAT	ERA	ERA+	OAV	OOB	BH	AVG	PB	PR	PR+	PD	TPI
1979	Hou-N	0	0	—	4	0	0	0	0	4	9	2	1	0	2	2	24.8	4.50	78	.450	.500	0	—	0	-0	-0	-0	0.0
1980	Hou-N	0	4	.000	12	6	0	0	0	41^1	38	23	3	0	16	13	11.8	4.35	76	.244	.314	0	.000	-1	-3	-5	0	-0.5
1981	Hou-N	0	0	—	2	0	0	0	0	4	9	4	0	0	3	3	27.0	9.00	37	.429	.500	0	—	0	-2	-3	-0	-0.2
1982	Hou-N	0	0	—	2	0	0	0	0	1^1	10	8	0	0	2	0	81.0	54.00	6	.769	.800	0	—	0	-7	-8	-0	-0.4
Total	4	0	4	.000	20	6	0	0	0	50^2	66	37	4	0	23	18	15.8	6.04	55	.314	.382	0	.000	-1	-14	-17	-0	-1.1

● EMIL PLANETA

Planeta, Emil Joseph b: 1/31/09, Higganum, Conn. d: 2/2/63, Rocky Hill, Conn. BR/TR, 6', 190 lbs. Deb: 9/20/31

YEAR	TM/L	W	L	PCT	G	GS	CG	SH	SV	IP	H	R	HR	HB	BB	SO	RAT	ERA	ERA+	OAV	OOB	BH	AVG	PB	PR	PR+	PD	TPI
1931	NY-N	0	0	—	2	0	0	0	0	5^1	7	7	0	0	4	0	18.6	10.13	36	.292	.393	0	.000	-0	-4	-4	-0	-0.2

● ED PLANK

Plank, Edward Arthur b: 4/9/52, Chicago, Ill. BR/TR, 6'1", 205 lbs. Deb: 9/6/78

YEAR	TM/L	W	L	PCT	G	GS	CG	SH	SV	IP	H	R	HR	HB	BB	SO	RAT	ERA	ERA+	OAV	OOB	BH	AVG	PB	PR	PR+	PD	TPI
1978	SF-N	0	0	—	5	0	0	0	0	6^2	6	3	1	0	2	1	10.8	4.05	85	.273	.333	0	—	0	-0	-0	-0	-0.1
1979	SF-N	0	0	—	4	0	0	0	0	3^2	9	5	0	0	2	1	27.0	7.36	48	.450	.500	0	—	0	-1	-2	-0	-0.1
Total	2	0	0	—	9	0	0	0	0	10^1	15	8	1	0	4	2	16.5	5.23	66	.357	.413	0	—	0	-2	-2	-1	-0.2

● EDDIE PLANK

Plank, Edward Stewart "Gettysburg Eddie" b: 8/31/1875, Gettysburg, Pa. d: 2/24/26, Gettysburg, Pa. BL/TL, 5'11.5", 175 lbs. Deb: 5/13/01 H

YEAR	TM/L	W	L	PCT	G	GS	CG	SH	SV	IP	H	R	HR	HB	BB	SO	RAT	ERA	ERA+	OAV	OOB	BH	AVG	PB	PR	PR+	PD	TPI
1901	Phi-A	17	13	.567	33	32	28	1	0	260^2	254	133	2	7	68	90	11.4	3.31	114	.252	.304	18	.182	-3	10	13	-2	0.7
1902	Phi-A	20	15	.571	36	32	31	1	0	300	319	140	5	18	61	107	11.9	3.30	111	.273	.319	35	.292	6	9	12	-2	1.6
1903	Phi-A	23	16	.590	**43**	40	33	3	0	336	317	128	5	23	65	176	10.8	2.38	128	.249	.297	25	.187	-1	22	24	-1	2.5
1904	Phi-A	26	17	.605	44	43	37	7	0	357^1	311	111	2	19	86	201	10.5	2.17	124	.235	.292	31	.240	3	17	20	-0	2.7
1905	*Phi-A	24	12	.667	41	41	**35**	4	0	346^2	287	113	3	24	75	210	10.0	2.26	118	.227	.283	29	.230	3	15	15	-3	1.6
1906	Phi-A	19	6	**.760**	26	25	21	5	0	211^2	173	70	1	15	51	108	10.2	2.25	121	.226	.288	17	.233	2	10	11	-2	1.2
1907	Phi-A	24	16	.600	43	40	33	**8**	0	343^2	282	115	5	17	85	183	10.1	2.20	118	.226	.285	26	.211	2	13	15	-1	1.9
1908	Phi-A	14	16	.467	34	28	21	4	1	244^2	202	71	1	9	46	135	9.5	2.17	118	.224	.269	16	.180	-1	6	10	-4	0.6
1909	Phi-A	19	10	.655	34	33	24	3	0	265^1	215	74	1	8	62	132	9.7	1.76	136	.224	.277	21	.219	4	21	20	1	2.7
1910	Phi-A	16	10	.615	38	32	22	1	2	250^1	218	89	3	8	55	123	10.1	2.01	118	.237	.286	11	.128	-3	14	11	-3	0.4
1911	*Phi-A	23	8	.742	40	30	24	**6**	**4**	256^2	237	85	2	14	77	149	11.5	2.10	150	.255	.322	18	.191	-1	35	32	1	3.6
1912	Phi-A	26	6	.813	37	30	23	5	2	259^2	234	90	1	6	83	110	11.2	2.22	139	.245	.309	24	.267	4	32	27	-2	3.5
1913	*Phi-A	18	10	.643	41	30	18	7	4	242^2	211	87	3	5	57	151	10.1	2.60	106	.234	.283	8	.105	-0	9	5	-1	0.3
1914	*Phi-A	15	7	.682	34	22	12	4	3	185^1	178	68	2	6	42	110	11.0	2.87	91	.266	.315	9	.150	0	-3	-5	-3	-1.0
1915	StL-F	21	11	.656	42	31	23	6	3	268^1	212	75	1	3	54	147	**9.0**	2.08	**138**	.218	**.262**	24	.258	3	19	23	-3	**2.8**
1916	StL-A	16	15	.516	37	26	17	3	3	235^2	203	78	2	6	67	88	10.5	2.33	118	.237	.297	15	.185	-0	13	11	-4	1.1
1917	StL-A	5	6	.455	20	14	8	1	1	131	105	39	2	2	38	26	10.0	1.79	145	.225	.287	4	.105	-1	13	12	-2	0.7
Total	17	326	194	.627	623	529	410	69	23	4495^2	3958	1566	41	190	1072	2246	10.5	2.35	122	.239	.293	331	.206	17	257	255	-32	26.9

● ERIK PLANTENBERG

Plantenberg, Erik John b: 10/30/68, Renton, Wash. BB/TL, 6'1", 180 lbs. Deb: 7/31/93

YEAR	TM/L	W	L	PCT	G	GS	CG	SH	SV	IP	H	R	HR	HB	BB	SO	RAT	ERA	ERA+	OAV	OOB	BH	AVG	PB	PR	PR+	PD	TPI
1993	Sea-A	0	0	—	20	0	0	0	1	9^2	11	7	0	1	12	3	22.3	6.52	68	.282	.462	0	—	0	-2	-2	0	-0.1
1994	Sea-A	0	0	—	6	0	0	0	0	7	4	0	0	1	7	1	15.4	0.00	—	.174	.387	0	—	0	4	4	0	0.2
1997	Phi-N	0	0	—	35	0	0	0	0	25^2	25	14	1	1	12	12	13.3	4.91	87	.255	.342	0	—	0	-2	-2	-1	-0.1
Total	3	0	0	—	61	0	0	0	1	42^1	40	21	1	3	31	16	15.7	4.46	98	.250	.381	0	—	0	-1	-0	-0	0.0

● BILL PLEIS

Pleis, William b: 8/5/37, St.Louis, Mo. BL/TL, 5'10", 175 lbs. Deb: 4/16/61

YEAR	TM/L	W	L	PCT	G	GS	CG	SH	SV	IP	H	R	HR	HB	BB	SO	RAT	ERA	ERA+	OAV	OOB	BH	AVG	PB	PR	PR+	PD	TPI
1961	Min-A	4	2	.667	37	0	0	0	2	56^1	59	35	4	4	34	32	15.5	4.95	86	.266	.373	1	.111	-1	-6	-4	-1	-0.6
1962	Min-A	2	5	.286	21	4	0	0	3	45	46	27	7	1	14	31	12.2	4.40	93	.264	.323	4	.286	1	-2	-2	-1	-0.2
1963	Min-A	6	2	.750	36	4	1	0	0	68	67	37	10	0	16	37	11.0	4.37	83	.258	.301	2	.125	0	-6	-5	-0	-0.6
1964	Min-A	4	1	.800	47	0	0	0	4	50^2	43	23	6	1	31	42	13.3	3.91	92	.232	.346	1	.250	0	-2	-2	0	-0.1
1965	*Min-A	4	4	.500	41	2	0	0	4	51^1	49	20	3	0	27	33	13.3	2.98	119	.250	.341	0	.000	-1	3	3	-0	0.4
1966	Min-A	1	2	.333	8	0	0	0	0	9^1	5	6	1	0	4	9	8.7	1.93	186	.152	.243	0	—	0	2	2	-0	0.3
Total	6	21	16	.568	190	10	1	0	13	280^2	269	148	31	6	126	184	12.9	4.07	93	.251	.334	8	.160	0	-11	-8	-3	-0.8

YEAR	TM/L	W	L	PCT	G	GS	CG	SH	SV	IP	H	R	HR	HB	BB	SO	RAT	ERA	ERA+	OAV	OOB	BH	AVG	PB	PR	PR+	PD	TPI
● **DAN PLESAC**	Plesac, Daniel Thomas b: 2/4/62, Gary, Ind. BL/TL, 6'5", 215 lbs. Deb: 4/11/86																											
1986	Mil-A	10	7	.588	51	0	0	0	14	91	81	34	5	0	29	75	10.9	2.97	146	.240	.301	0	—	0	12	13	-1	2.6
1987	Mil-A★	5	6	.455	57	0	0	0	23	79^1	63	30	8	3	23	89	10.1	2.61	176	.213	.276	0	—	0	16	17	0	3.1
1988	Mil-A★	1	2	.333	50	0	0	0	30	52^1	46	14	2	0	12	52	10.0	2.41	166	.234	.278	0	—	0	9	9	-0	1.4
1989	Mil-A★	3	4	.429	52	0	0	0	33	61^1	47	16	6	0	17	52	9.4	2.35	164	.213	.269	0	—	0	11	10	-0	2.1
1990	Mil-A	3	7	.300	66	0	0	0	24	69	67	36	5	3	31	65	13.2	4.43	88	.257	.342	0	—	0	-4	-4	-0	-0.8
1991	Mil-A	2	7	.222	45	10	0	0	8	92^1	92	49	12	3	39	61	13.1	4.29	93	.263	.342	0	—	0	-2	-3	-2	-0.5
1992	Mil-A	5	4	.556	44	4	0	0	1	79	64	28	5	3	35	54	11.6	2.96	130	.229	.321	0	—	0	9	8	-1	0.8
1993	Chi-N	2	1	.667	57	0	0	0	0	62^2	74	37	10	0	21	47	13.6	4.74	84	.298	.353	0	.000	-0	-5	-5	-0	-0.3
1994	Chi-N	2	3	.400	54	0	0	0	1	54^2	61	30	9	1	13	53	12.3	4.61	90	.279	.322	0	.000	-0	-2	-3	-1	-0.4
1995	Pit-N	4	4	.500	58	0	0	0	3	60^1	53	26	3	1	27	57	12.1	3.58	120	.237	.321	1	.250	0	4	5	0	0.6
1996	Pit-N	6	5	.545	73	0	0	0	11	70^1	67	35	4	0	24	76	11.6	4.09	107	.247	.308	0	.000	-1	1	2	-2	0.1
1997	Tor-A	2	4	.333	73	0	0	0	1	50^1	47	22	8	0	19	61	11.8	3.58	128	.244	.311	0	—	0	6	6	-1	0.5
1998	Tor-A	4	3	.571	78	0	0	0	4	50	41	23	4	1	16	55	10.4	3.78	124	.224	.290	0	—	0	5	5	-1	0.5
1999	Tor-A	0	3	.000	30	0	0	0	0	22^2	28	21	4	0	9	26	14.7	8.34	59	.308	.370	0	—	0	-9	-8	-0	-0.9
	*Ari-N	2	1	.667	34	0	0	0	1	21^2	22	9	3	0	8	27	12.5	3.32	138	.259	.323	0	.000	-0	3	3	0	0.4
2000	Ari-N	5	1	.833	62	0	0	0	0	40	34	21	4	0	26	45	13.5	3.15	147	.228	.343	0	—	0	7	7	-1	0.8
Total	15	56	62	.475	884	14	0	0	154	957	887	431	92	15	349	895	11.8	3.65	116	.246	.315	1	.067	-1	60	61	-9	10.0
● **NORMAN PLITT**	Plitt, Norman William b: 2/21/1893, York, Pa. d: 2/1/54, New York, N.Y. BR/TR, 5'11", 180 lbs. Deb: 4/26/18																											
1918	Bro-N	0	0	—	1	0	0	0	0	2	3	1	0	0	1	0	18.0	4.50	62	.429	.500	1	1.000	0	-0	-0	-0	0.0
1927	Bro-N	2	6	.250	19	8	1	0	0	62^1	73	40	3	1	36	9	15.9	4.91	81	.303	.396	4	.222	-0	-7	-6	0	-0.7
	NY-N	1	0	1.000	3	0	0	0	0	7^1	9	3	0	1	1	0	13.5	3.68	105	.310	.355	0	.000	-0	0	0	0	0.0
	Yr	3	6	.333	22	8	1	0	0	69^2	82	43	3	2	37	9	15.6	4.78	83	.304	.392	4	.211	-0	-7	-6	1	-0.7
Total	2	3	6	.333	23	8	1	0	0	71^2	85	44	3	2	38	9	15.7	4.77	82	.307	.394	5	.250	0	-7	-7	1	-0.7
● **TIM PLODINEC**	Plodinec, Timothy Alfred b: 1/27/47, Aliquippa, Pa. BR/TR, 6'4", 190 lbs. Deb: 6/2/72																											
1972	StL-N	0	0	—	1	0	0	0	0	0^1	3	1	0	0	0	0	81.0	27.00	13	.750	.750	0	—	0	-1	-1	0	0.0
● **ERIC PLUNK**	Plunk, Eric Vaughn b: 9/3/63, Wilmington, Cal. BR/TR, 6'5", 217 lbs. Deb: 5/12/86																											
1986	Oak-A	4	7	.364	26	15	0	0	0	120^1	91	75	14	5	102	98	14.8	5.31	73	.214	.372	0	—	0	-15	-21	-2	-1.8
1987	Oak-A	4	6	.400	32	11	0	0	2	95	91	53	8	2	62	90	14.7	4.74	87	.253	.366	0	—	0	-3	-7	-1	-0.7
1988	*Oak-A	7	2	.778	49	0	0	0	5	78	62	27	6	1	39	79	11.8	3.00	126	.217	.313	0	—	0	8	7	-1	0.7
1989	Oak-A	1	1	.500	23	0	0	0	1	28^2	17	7	1	1	12	24	9.4	2.20	168	.172	.268	0	—	0	5	5	-0	0.3
	NY-A	7	5	.583	27	7	0	0	0	75^2	65	36	9	0	52	61	13.9	3.69	105	.237	.359	0	—	0	2	2	-2	0.1
	Yr	8	6	.571	50	7	0	0	1	104^1	82	43	10	1	64	85	12.7	3.28	117	.220	.336	0	—	0	7	6	-2	0.4
1990	NY-A	6	3	.667	47	0	0	0	0	72^2	58	27	6	2	43	67	12.8	2.72	146	.225	.340	0	—	0	10	10	2	1.3
1991	NY-A	2	5	.286	43	8	0	0	0	111^2	128	69	18	1	62	103	15.4	4.76	87	.286	.374	0	—	0	-8	-7	-2	-0.6
1992	Cle-A	9	6	.600	58	0	0	0	4	71^2	61	31	5	0	38	50	12.4	3.64	107	.229	.326	0	—	0	2	2	-0	0.4
1993	Cle-A	4	5	.444	70	0	0	0	15	71	61	29	5	0	30	77	11.5	2.79	156	.226	.303	0	—	0	12	12	-1	1.7
1994	Cle-A	7	2	.778	41	0	0	0	3	71	61	25	3	2	37	73	12.7	2.54	186	.231	.330	0	—	0	18	18	-1	2.0
1995	*Cle-A	6	2	.750	56	0	0	0	2	64	48	19	5	4	27	71	11.1	2.67	176	.211	.305	0	—	0	15	14	0	1.6
1996	*Cle-A	3	2	.600	56	0	0	0	2	77^2	56	21	6	3	34	85	10.8	2.43	201	.203	.297	0	—	0	22	22	-0	1.2
1997	*Cle-A	4	5	.444	55	0	0	0	0	65^2	62	37	12	1	36	66	13.6	4.66	101	.245	.341	0	.000	-0	-1	0	-1	-0.1
1998	Cle-A	3	1	.750	37	0	0	0	0	41	44	23	6	2	15	38	13.4	4.83	99	.282	.353	0	—	0	-1	-0	-0	-0.1
	Mil-N	1	2	.333	26	0	0	0	1	31^2	33	14	3	3	15	36	14.5	3.69	115	.270	.364	0	.000	0	2	2	-1	0.1
1999	Mil-N	4	4	.500	68	0	0	0	0	75^1	71	44	15	5	43	63	14.2	5.02	90	.251	.360	0	—	0	-4	-4	-1	-0.5
Total	14	72	58	.554	714	41	0	0	35	1151	1009	537	122	32	647	1081	13.2	3.82	111	.236	.341	0	.000	0	65	57	-11	5.6
● **JEFF PLYMPTON**	Plympton, Jeffrey Hunter b: 11/24/65, Framingham, Mass. BR/TR, 6'2", 205 lbs. Deb: 6/15/91																											
1991	Bos-A	0	0	—	4	0	0	0	0	5^1	5	0	0	0	4	2	15.2	0.00	—	.263	.391	0	—	0	2	2	-0	0.1
● **RAY POAT**	Poat, Raymond Willis b: 12/19/17, Chicago, Ill. d: 4/29/90, Oak Lawn, Ill. BR/TR, 6'2", 200 lbs. Deb: 4/15/42																											
1942	Cle-A	1	3	.250	4	4	1	1	0	18^1	24	11	1	1	9	8	16.7	5.40	64	.296	.374	0	.000	-0	-4	-4	0	-0.8
1943	Cle-A	2	5	.286	17	4	1	0	0	45	44	22	3	0	20	31	12.8	4.40	71	.259	.337	2	.154	-1	-6	-7	-0	-1.1
1944	Cle-A	4	8	.333	36	6	1	0	1	80^2	82	50	9	0	37	40	13.3	5.13	64	.265	.343	0	.000	-2	-15	-17	-0	-2.6
1947	NY-N	4	3	.571	7	7	5	0	0	60	53	18	8	0	13	25	9.9	2.55	160	.238	.280	4	.190	2	10	10	-0	1.3
1948	NY-N	11	10	.524	39	24	7	3	0	157^2	162	95	21	3	67	57	13.2	4.34	91	.262	.337	7	.125	-1	-7	-7	-2	-1.2
1949	NY-N	0	0	—	2	0	0	0	0	2^1	8	6	0	0	1	0	34.7	19.29	21	.615	.643	0	—	0	-4	-4	-0	-0.2
	Pit-N	0	1	.000	11	2	0	0	0	36	52	29	6	0	15	17	16.8	6.25	67	.335	.394	1	.100	-1	-9	-8	-0	-0.5
	Yr	0	1	.000	13	2	0	0	0	38^1	60	35	6	0	16	17	17.8	7.04	59	.357	.413	1	.100	-1	-13	-12	-0	-0.7
Total	6	22	30	.423	116	47	15	4	1	400	425	231	48	4	162	178	13.3	4.55	82	.271	.340	14	.115	-3	-34	-37	-3	-5.1
● **BUD PODBIELAN**	Podbielan, Clarence Anthony b: 3/6/24, Curlew, Wash. d: 10/26/82, Syracuse, N.Y. BR/TR, 6'1.5", 170 lbs. Deb: 4/25/49																											
1949	Bro-N	0	1	.000	7	1	0	0	0	12^1	9	9	1	1	9	5	13.9	3.65	112	.205	.352	0	.000	-0	1	1	1	0.1
1950	Bro-N	5	4	.556	20	10	2	0	1	72^2	93	47	10	2	29	28	15.4	5.33	77	.307	.371	3	.107	-1	-10	-10	1	-1.2
1951	Bro-N	2	2	.500	27	5	1	0	0	79^2	67	32	9	2	36	26	11.9	3.50	112	.233	.322	7	.304	1	4	4	0	0.3
1952	Bro-N	0	0	—	3	0	0	0	0	2	4	5	1	0	3	1	31.5	18.00	20	.444	.583	0	—	0	-3	-3	-0	-0.2
	Cin-N	4	5	.444	24	7	4	1	1	86^2	78	30	8	1	26	22	10.9	2.80	135	.245	.304	4	.160	0	9	9	-1	0.8
	Yr	4	5	.444	27	7	4	1	1	88^2	82	35	9	1	29	23	11.4	3.15	120	.251	.314	4	.160	0	6	6	-1	0.6
1953	Cin-N	6	16	.273	36	24	8	1	1	186^1	214	112	21	8	67	74	14.0	4.73	92	.290	.356	7	.125	-3	-9	-8	-0	-1.1
1954	Cin-N	7	10	.412	27	24	4	0	0	131	157	92	20	2	58	42	14.9	5.36	78	.300	.372	6	.143	-1	-19	-16	-2	-2.1
1955	Cin-N	1	2	.333	17	2	0	0	0	42	36	16	4	1	11	26	10.3	3.21	132	.234	.289	2	.400	1	4	5	0	0.4
1957	Cin-N	0	1	.000	5	3	1	0	0	16	18	11	4	0	4	13	12.4	6.19	66	.290	.333	0	.000	-1	-4	-3	-1	-0.3
1959	Cle-A	0	1	.000	6	0	0	0	0	12^1	17	8	1	0	2	5	13.9	5.84	63	.354	.380	0	.000	-0	-3	-3	0	-0.2
Total	9	25	42	.373	172	76	20	2	3	641	693	362	79	17	245	242	13.4	4.49	92	.279	.348	29	.154	-4	-30	-26	-2	-3.5
● **JOHNNY PODGAJNY**	Podgajny, John Sigmund "Specs" b: 6/10/20, Chester, Pa. d: 3/2/71, Chester, Pa. BR/TR, 6'2", 173 lbs. Deb: 9/15/40																											
1940	Phi-N	1	3	.250	4	4	3	0	0	35	33	14	0	1	1	12	9.0	2.83	138	.250	.261	2	.167	-0	4	4	0	0.5
1941	Phi-N	9	12	.429	34	24	8	0	0	181^1	191	96	8	4	70	53	13.2	4.62	80	.270	.339	8	.129	-3	-20	-18	1	-2.0
1942	Phi-N	6	14	.300	43	23	6	0	0	186^2	191	95	9	11	63	40	12.8	3.91	85	.268	.337	11	.183	-0	-12	-12	-1	-1.4
1943	Phi-N	4	4	.500	13	5	3	0	0	64	77	32	4	0	16	13	13.1	4.22	80	.310	.352	5	.250	1	-6	-6	1	-0.5
	Pit-N	0	4	.000	15	5	0	0	0	34^1	37	28	1	0	13	7	13.1	4.72	74	.266	.329	1	.143	-0	-5	-5	2	-0.4
	Yr	4	8	.333	28	10	3	0	0	98^1	114	60	5	0	29	20	13.1	4.39	78	.295	.344	6	.222	0	-11	-11	3	-0.9
1946	Cle-A	0	0	—	6	0	0	0	0	9	13	8	0	0	2	4	15.0	5.00	66	.302	.333	0	—	0	-1	-2	0	-0.1
Total	5	20	37	.351	115	61	20	0	0	510^1	542	273	22	16	165	129	12.8	4.20	84	.273	.334	27	.168	-3	-41	-39	3	-3.9
● **JOHNNY PODRES**	Podres, John Joseph b: 9/30/32, Witherbee, N.Y. BL/TL, 5'11", 192 lbs. Deb: 4/17/53 C																											
1953	*Bro-N	9	4	.692	33	18	3	1	0	115	126	62	12	1	64	82	14.9	4.23	101	.282	.373	11	.306	2	1	0	-0	0.2
1954	Bro-N	11	7	.611	29	21	6	2	0	151^2	147	77	13	1	53	79	11.9	4.27	96	.255	.319	17	.283	5	-3	-3	-2	0.0
1955	*Bro-N	9	10	.474	27	24	5	2	0	159^1	160	80	15	4	57	114	12.5	3.95	103	.259	.326	11	.183	-0	1	2	-1	0.0
1957	Bro-N	12	9	.571	31	27	10	**6**	3	196	168	64	15	1	44	109	**9.8**	**2.66**	**156**	.230	**.274**	15	.208	1	26	30	-0	3.3
1958	LA-N☆	13	15	.464	39	31	10	2	1	210^1	208	96	27	2	78	143	12.3	3.72	110	.261	.328	9	.127	-3	5	8	-2	0.5
1959	*LA-N	14	9	.609	34	29	6	2	0	195	192	93	23	3	74	145	12.4	4.11	103	.261	.331	16	.246	3	-3	2	1	0.7
1960	LA-N★	14	12	.538	34	33	8	1	0	227^2	217	88	25	1	71	159	11.4	3.08	129	.250	.308	9	.136	-1	17	21	-2	2.0
1961	LA-N	18	5	**.783**	32	29	6	1	0	182^2	192	81	27	4	51	124	12.2	3.74	116	.271	.324	16	.232	1	6	11	-2	1.2
1962	LA-N★	15	13	.536	40	40	8	0	0	255	270	121	20	3	71	178	12.1	3.81	95	.272	.323	14	.159	1	4	-6	-4	-0.8
1963	*LA-N	14	12	.538	37	34	10	5	1	198^1	196	91	16	3	64	134	11.9	3.54	85	.257	.316	9	.141	1	-6	-12	-1	-1.5
1964	LA-N	0	2	.000	2	2	0	0	0	2^2	5	5	1	0	3	0	27.0	16.88	19	.417	.533	0	—	0	-4	-4	-0	-0.7
1965	LA-N	7	6	.538	27	22	2	1	1	134	126	57	17	2	39	63	11.2	3.43	95	.247	.303	8	.178	1	2	-3	-3	-0.4
1966	LA-N	0	0	—	1	0	0	0	0	1^2	2	0	0	0	1	1	16.2	0.00	—	.400	.500	0	—	0	1	1	0	0.0

YEAR TM/L	W	L	PCT	G	GS	CG	SH	SV	IP	H	R	HR	HB	BB	SO	RAT	ERA	ERA+	OAV	OOB	BH	AVG	PB	PR	PR+	PD	TPI
Det-A	4	5	.444	36	13	2	1	4	107^2	106	48	12	1	34	53	11.8	3.43	102	.259	.317	7	.233	2	0	1	-1	0.2
1967 Det-A	3	1	.750	21	8	0	0	1	63^1	58	29	12	1	11	34	9.9	3.84	85	.244	.280	2	.100	-1	-4	-4	-1	-0.4
1969 SD-N	5	6	.455	17	9	1	0	0	64^2	66	34	7	1	28	17	13.2	4.31	82	.264	.341	1	.063	-1	-5	-6	-1	-1.1
Total 15	148	116	.561	440	340	77	24	11	2265	2239	1026	242	28	743	1435	12.0	3.68	105	.259	.319	145	.190	12	37	45	-17	3.2
● JOE POETZ	Poetz, Joseph Frank "Bull Montana" b: 6/22/1900, St.Louis, Mo. d: 2/7/42, St.Louis, Mo. BR/TR, 5'10.5", 175 lbs. Deb: 9/14/26																										
1926 NY-N	0	1	.000	2	1	0	0	0	8	5	3	2	1	8	0	15.8	3.38	111	.192	.400	0	.000	0	0	0	0	0.1
● BOOTS POFFENBERGER	Poffenberger, Cletus Elwood b: 7/1/15, Williamsport, Md. d: 9/1/99, Williamsport, Md. BR/TR, 5'10", 178 lbs. Deb: 6/11/37																										
1937 Det-A	10	5	.667	29	16	5	0	3	137^1	147	83	8	4	79	35	15.1	4.65	100	.277	.375	11	.216	-0	-1	0	1	0.1
1938 Det-A	6	7	.462	25	15	8	1	1	125	147	74	8	2	66	28	15.5	4.82	104	.297	.382	8	.182	-1	-1	2	-2	-0.1
1939 Bro-N	0	0	—	3	1	0	0	0	5	7	3	1	0	4	2	19.8	5.40	75	.318	.423	0	.000	-0	-1	-1	0	0.0
Total 3	16	12	.571	57	32	13	1	4	267^1	301	160	17	6	149	65	15.4	4.75	101	.287	.379	19	.198	-2	-2	2	-0	0.0
● TOM POHOLSKY	Poholsky, Thomas George b: 8/26/29, Detroit, Mich. BR/TR, 6'3", 205 lbs. Deb: 4/20/50																										
1950 StL-N	0	0	—	5	1	0	0	0	14^2	16	6	2	0	3	2	11.7	3.68	117	.281	.317	0	.000	-0	1	1	-0	0.0
1951 StL-N	7	13	.350	38	26	10	1	1	195	204	106	15	0	68	70	12.6	4.43	89	.271	.331	14	.209	0	-10	-10	1	-0.8
1954 StL-N	5	7	.417	25	13	4	0	0	106	101	43	11	4	20	55	10.6	3.06	135	.254	.296	4	.148	-1	12	12	0	1.2
1955 StL-N	9	11	.450	30	24	8	2	0	151	143	71	26	2	35	66	10.7	3.81	106	.244	.289	8	.182	-0	4	4	-1	0.4
1956 StL-N	9	14	.391	33	29	7	2	0	203	210	100	27	5	44	95	11.5	3.59	105	.268	.311	11	.159	-1	4	4	0	0.4
1957 Chi-N	1	7	.125	28	11	1	0	0	84	117	55	9	2	22	28	15.1	4.93	79	.330	.372	2	.105	-1	-10	-10	0	-0.9
Total 6	31	52	.373	159	104	30	5	1	753^2	791	381	90	13	192	316	11.9	3.93	101	.270	.317	39	.171	-3	1	2	1	0.3
● JENNINGS POINDEXTER	Poindexter, Chester Jennings "Jinx" b: 9/30/10, Pauls Valley, Okla. d: 3/3/83, Norman, Okla. BL/TL, 5'10", 165 lbs. Deb: 9/15/36																										
1936 Bos-A	0	2	.000	3	3	0	0	0	10^2	13	11	0	0	16	2	24.5	6.75	79	.302	.492	0	.000	-1	-2	-2	-0	-0.3
1939 Phi-N	0	0	—	11	1	0	0	0	30^1	29	19	0	0	15	12	13.1	4.15	96	.250	.336	2	.200	-0	-1	-0	-0	-0.1
Total 2	0	2	.000	14	4	0	0	0	41	42	30	0	0	31	14	16.0	4.83	90	.264	.384	2	.143	-1	-3	-2	-0	-0.4
● LOU POLCHOW	Polchow, Louis William b: 3/14/1881, Mankato, Minn. d: 8/15/12, Good Thunder, Minn 5'9", Deb: 9/14/02																										
1902 Cle-A	0	1	.000	1	1	1	0	0	8	9	5	0	0	4	2	14.6	5.63	61	.281	.361	0	.000	-1	-2	-2	-0	-0.2
● DICK POLE	Pole, Richard Henry b: 10/13/50, Trout Creek, Mich. BR/TR, 6'3", 210 lbs. Deb: 8/3/73 C																										
1973 Bos-A	3	2	.600	12	7	0	0	0	54^2	70	35	4	0	18	24	14.5	5.60	72	.318	.370	0	—	0	-11	-9	-0	-0.8
1974 Bos-A	1	1	.500	15	2	0	0	1	45	55	28	6	1	13	32	13.8	4.20	92	.304	.354	0	—	0	-3	-2	1	0.0
1975 *Bos-A	4	6	.400	18	11	2	1	0	89^2	102	46	11	2	32	42	13.7	4.42	92	.290	.352	0	—	0	-6	-3	0	-0.3
1976 Bos-A	6	5	.545	31	15	1	0	0	120^2	131	62	8	2	48	49	13.5	4.33	90	.279	.348	0	.000	-0	-11	-5	-1	-0.6
1977 Sea-A	7	12	.368	25	24	3	0	0	122^1	127	76	16	6	57	51	14.0	5.15	80	.270	.356	0	—	0	-15	-14	-3	-2.1
1978 Sea-A	4	11	.267	21	18	2	0	0	98^2	122	82	16	3	41	41	15.1	6.48	59	.306	.375	0	—	0	-30	-29	-1	-3.7
Total 6	25	37	.403	122	77	8	1	1	531	607	329	61	14	209	239	14.1	5.05	79	.290	.359	0	.000	-0	-75	-60	-5	-7.5
● CLIFF POLITTE	Politte, Clifford Anthony b: 2/27/74, Kirkwood, Mo. BR/TR, 5'11", 185 lbs. Deb: 4/2/98																										
1998 StL-N	2	3	.400	8	8	0	0	0	37	45	32	6	1	18	22	15.6	6.32	66	.302	.381	1	.071	-1	-9	-9	-0	-1.1
1999 Phi-N	1	0	1.000	13	0	0	0	0	17^2	19	14	2	0	15	15	17.3	7.13	66	.275	.405	0	—	0	-5	-5	-0	-0.2
2000 Phi-N	4	3	.571	12	8	0	0	0	59	55	24	8	0	27	50	12.5	3.66	129	.248	.329	2	.133	0	6	7	0	0.7
Total 3	7	6	.538	33	16	0	0	0	113^2	119	70	16	1	60	87	14.3	5.07	90	.270	.359	3	.103	-1	-7	-6	-0	-0.6
● KEN POLIVKA	Polivka, Kenneth Lyle "Soup" b: 1/21/21, Chicago, Ill. d: 7/23/88, Aurora, Ill. BL/TL, 5'10.5", 175 lbs. Deb: 4/18/47																										
1947 Cin-N	0	0	—	2	0	0	0	0	3	3	1	0	0	3	1	18.0	3.00	137	.250	.400	0	—	0	0	0	0	0.0
● HOWIE POLLET	Pollet, Howard Joseph b: 6/26/21, New Orleans, La. d: 8/8/74, Houston, Tex. BL/TL, 6'1.5", 175 lbs. Deb: 8/20/41 C																										
1941 StL-N	5	2	.714	9	8	6	2	0	70	55	18	1	1	27	37	10.7	1.93	195	.212	.289	5	.179	-0	13	14	1	1.4
1942 *StL-N	7	5	.583	27	13	5	2	0	109^1	102	43	7	2	39	42	11.8	2.88	119	.242	.309	7	.226	3	5	6	-2	0.8
1943 StL-N†	8	4	.667	16	14	12	5	0	118^1	83	26	2	2	32	61	8.9	**1.75**	192	.200	.261	7	.163	-1	21	21	-2	1.9
1946 *StL-N☆	**21**	10	.677	40	32	22	4	5	**266**	228	84	12	5	86	107	10.8	**2.10**	**165**	.234	.300	14	.161	-0	**39**	**40**	1	5.0
1947 StL-N	9	11	.450	37	24	9	0	2	176^1	195	96	11	3	87	73	14.5	4.34	95	.286	.369	15	.231	2	-5	-4	0	-0.2
1948 StL-N	13	8	.619	36	26	11	0	0	186^1	216	102	10	2	67	80	13.8	4.54	90	.289	.349	8	.118	-3	-12	-9	2	-1.0
1949 StL-N★	20	9	.690	39	28	17	**5**	1	230^2	228	80	9	2	59	108	11.3	2.77	150	.256	.304	16	.195	1	33	35	-2	4.1
1950 StL-N	14	13	.519	37	30	14	2	2	232^1	228	103	19	1	68	117	11.5	3.29	130	.256	.310	12	.143	-2	22	25	0	2.5
1951 StL-N	0	3	.000	6	2	0	0	1	12^1	10	10	1	0	8	10	13.1	4.38	91	.208	.321	0	.000	1	-1	-1	0	0.0
Pit-N	6	10	.375	21	21	4	1	0	128^2	149	81	24	1	51	47	14.1	5.04	84	.294	.360	5	.139	-0	-15	-11	-0	-1.2
Yr	6	13	.316	27	23	4	1	1	141	159	91	25	1	59	57	14.0	4.98	84	.287	.357	5	.135	0	-16	-11	-0	-1.2
1952 Pit-N	7	16	.304	31	30	9	1	0	214	217	111	22	3	71	90	12.2	4.12	97	.266	.327	13	.191	2	-9	-3	1	0.0
1953 Pit-N	1	1	.500	5	2	0	0	0	12^2	27	15	2	0	6	8	23.4	10.66	42	.482	.532	1	.333	0	-9	-8	-0	-1.0
Chi-N	5	6	.455	25	17	2	0	1	111^1	120	62	6	1	44	45	13.3	4.12	108	.271	.338	4	.129	-1	2	4	-1	0.2
Yr	6	7	.462	30	19	2	0	1	124	147	77	8	1	50	53	14.4	4.79	93	.295	.360	5	.147	-1	-7	-4	-1	-0.8
1954 Chi-N	8	10	.444	20	20	4	2	0	128^1	131	60	4	0	54	58	13.0	3.58	117	.263	.335	13	.277	2	7	9	-0	1.4
1955 Chi-N	4	3	.571	24	7	1	1	5	61	62	41	11	0	27	27	13.1	5.61	73	.265	.341	6	.400	3	-11	-10	1	-0.8
1956 Chi-A	3	1	.750	11	4	0	0	0	26^1	27	15	2	0	11	14	13.0	4.10	100	.252	.322	3	.375	1	0	-0	-0	0.1
Pit-N	0	4	.000	19	0	0	0	3	23^1	18	10	3	0	8	10	10.0	3.09	122	.212	.280	0	.000	0	2	2	0	0.4
Total 14	131	116	.530	403	278	116	25	20	2107^1	2096	957	146	23	745	934	12.2	3.51	113	.260	.324	129	.185	7	82	107	0	13.6
● DALE POLLEY	Polley, Ezra Dale b: 8/9/65, Georgetown, Ky. BR/TL, 6', 165 lbs. Deb: 6/23/96																										
1996 NY-A	1	3	.250	32	0	0	0	0	21^2	23	20	5	3	11	14	15.4	7.89	63	.264	.366	0	—	0	-7	-7	0	-1.1
● LOU POLLI	Polli, Louis Americo "Crip" b: 7/9/01, Baveno, Italy BR/TR, 5'10.5", 165 lbs. Deb: 4/18/32																										
1932 StL-A	0	0	—	5	0	0	0	0	6^2	13	8	0	0	3	5	21.6	5.40	90	.406	.457	1	.500	0	-1	-0	-0	0.0
1944 NY-N	0	2	.000	19	0	0	0	3	35^2	42	25	3	0	20	6	15.6	4.54	81	.294	.380	0	.000	-1	-4	-3	-0	-0.3
Total 2	0	2	.000	24	0	0	0	3	42^1	55	33	3	0	23	11	16.6	4.68	82	.314	.394	1	.125	-1	-4	-4	-1	-0.3
● JOHN POLONI	Poloni, John Paul b: 2/28/54, Dearborn, Mich. BL/TL, 6'5", 210 lbs. Deb: 9/16/77																										
1977 Tex-A	1	0	1.000	2	1	0	0	0	7	8	5	1	0	1	5	11.6	6.43	64	.286	.310	0	—	0	-2	-2	-0	-0.2
● JOHN POMORSKI	Pomorski, John Leon b: 12/30/05, Brooklyn, N.Y. d: 12/6/77, Brampton, Ont., Can. BR/TR, 6', 178 lbs. Deb: 4/17/34																										
1934 Chi-A	0	0	—	3	0	0	0	0	1^2	1	2	0	0	2	0	16.2	5.40	88	.143	.333	0	—	0	-0	-0	0	0.0
● ARLIE POND	Pond, Erasmus Arlington b: 1/19/1872, Rutland, Vt. d: 9/19/30, Cebu, Philippines BR/TR, 5'10", 160 lbs. Deb: 7/4/1895																										
1895 Bal-N	0	1	.000	6	1	1	0	2	13^2	10	13	0	1	12	13	15.1	5.93	80	.200	.365	2	.333	1	-2	-2	0	-0.1
1896 Bal-N	16	8	.667	28	26	21	2	0	214^1	232	133	4	6	57	80	12.4	3.49	123	.274	.324	19	.235	0	21	19	-2	1.5
1897 Bal-N	18	9	.667	32	28	23	0	0	248	267	131	4	15	72	59	12.8	3.52	118	.273	.332	22	.244	2	22	18	-1	1.7
1898 Bal-N	1	1	.500	3	2	1	1	0	20	8	4	0	2	9	4	8.5	0.45	796	.123	.250	2	.286	1	7	7	-1	0.7
Total 4	35	19	.648	69	57	46	3	2	496	517	281	8	24	150	156	12.5	3.45	122	.266	.327	45	.245	3	48	43	-3	3.8
● ELMER PONDER	Ponder, Charles Elmer b: 6/26/1893, Reed, Okla. d: 4/20/74, Albuquerque, N.Mex BR/TR, 6', 178 lbs. Deb: 9/18/17																										
1917 Pit-N	1	1	.500	3	2	1	1	0	21^1	12	5	0	1	6	11	8.0	1.69	168	.167	.241	0	.000	-1	2	3	-1	0.0
1919 Pit-N	0	5	.000	9	5	0	0	0	47^1	55	26	0	3	6	6	12.2	3.99	76	.297	.330	2	.133	-1	-6	-5	-1	-0.7
1920 Pit-N	11	15	.423	33	23	13	2	0	196	182	76	3	2	40	62	10.3	2.62	123	.246	.286	7	.119	-4	11	13	1	1.3
1921 Pit-N	2	0	1.000	8	1	1	0	0	24^2	29	8	1	0	3	3	11.7	2.19	175	.305	.327	0	.000	-2	4	4	0	0.2
Chi-N	3	6	.333	16	11	5	0	0	89^1	117	58	7	3	17	31	13.8	4.74	81	.321	.356	4	.121	-2	-9	-9	2	-0.9
Yr	5	6	.455	24	12	6	0	0	114	146	66	8	3	20	34	13.3	4.18	91	.317	.356	4	.093	-4	-5	-5	2	-0.7
Total 4	17	27	.386	69	42	20	3	0	378^2	395	173	11	9	72	113	11.3	3.21	105	.271	.309	13	.105	-10	3	6	0	-0.1

YEAR TM/L	W	L	PCT	G	GS	CG	SH	SV	IP	H	R	HR	HB	BB	SO	RAT	ERA	ERA+	OAV	OOB	BH	AVG	PB	PR	PR+	PD	TPI
● SIDNEY PONSON Ponson, Sidney Alton b: 11/2/76, Noord, Aruba BR/TR, 6'1", 220 lbs. Deb: 4/19/98																											
1998 Bal-A	8	9	.471	31	20	0	0	1	135	157	82	19	3	42	85	13.5	5.27	87	.293	.348	2	.500	1	-9	-11	-1	-1.2
1999 Bal-A	12	12	.500	32	32	6	0	0	210	227	118	35	1	80	112	13.2	4.71	100	.282	.348	0	.000	-0	4	-0	-0	-0.1
2000 Bal-A	9	13	.409	32	32	6	1	0	222	223	125	30	1	83	152	12.4	4.82	99	.258	.324	0	.000	-0	2	-1	-1	-0.2
Total 3	29	34	.460	95	84	12	1	1	567	607	325	84	5	205	349	13.0	4.89	96	.275	.338	2	.250	0	-3	-12	-3	-1.5
● ED POOLE Poole, Edward I. b: 9/7/1874, Canton, Ohio d: 3/11/19, Malvern, Ohio BR/TR, 5'10", 175 lbs. Deb: 10/6/00 ♦																											
1900 Pit-N	1	0	1.000	1	0	0	0	0	7	4	1	0	0	0	3	5.1	1.29	283	.167	.167	2	.500	1	2	2	0	0.4
1901 Pit-N	5	4	.556	12	10	8	1	0	80	78	45	3	6	30	26	12.8	3.60	91	.254	.332	16	.205	1	-2	-3	0	-0.2
1902 Pit-N	0	0	—	1	0	0	0	0	8	7	4	0	0	3	2	11.3	1.13	244	.233	.303	1	.250	0	1	1	-0	0.1
Cin-N	12	4	.750	16	16	16	2	0	138	129	47	2	8	54	55	12.5	2.15	139	.248	.328	7	.115	-4	10	12	-0	0.9
Yr	12	4	.750	17	16	16	2	0	146	136	51	2	8	57	57	12.4	2.10	142	.247	.326	8	.123	-4	11	13	-0	1.0
1903 Cin-N	7	13	.350	25	21	18	1	0	184	188	105	4	12	77	73	13.5	3.28	109	.270	.352	17	.243	0	-0	5	2	0.7
1904 Bro-N	8	14	.364	25	23	19	1	1	178	178	86	4	8	74	67	13.1	3.39	81	.268	.349	8	.129	-3	-13	-13	3	-1.5
Total 5	33	35	.485	80	70	61	5	1	595	584	288	13	34	238	226	12.9	3.04	103	.260	.340	51	.183	-6	-2	6	6	0.4
● JIM POOLE Poole, James Richard b: 4/28/66, Rochester, N.Y. BL/TL, 6'2", 203 lbs. Deb: 6/15/90																											
1990 LA-N	0	0	—	16	0	0	0	0	10^2	7	5	1	0	8	6	12.7	4.22	87	.184	.326	0	—	0	-0	-1	-0	-0.1
1991 Tex-A	0	0	—	5	0	0	0	1	6	10	4	0	0	3	4	19.5	4.50	90	.370	.433	0	—	0	-0	-0	-0	0.0
Bal-A	3	2	.600	24	0	0	0	0	36	19	10	3	0	9	34	7.0	2.00	198	.157	.215	0	—	0	8	8	0	1.1
Yr	3	2	.600	29	0	0	0	1	42	29	14	3	0	12	38	8.8	2.36	168	.196	.256	0	—	0	8	8	0	1.1
1992 Bal-A	0	0	—	6	0	0	0	0	3^1	3	3	0	0	1	3	10.8	0.00	—	.231	.286	0	—	0	1	1	0	0.1
1993 Bal-A	2	1	.667	55	0	0	0	2	50^1	30	18	2	0	21	29	9.1	2.15	209	.175	.266	0	—	0	12	13	0	0.8
1994 Bal-A	1	0	1.000	38	0	0	0	0	20^1	32	15	4	0	11	18	19.0	6.64	75	.372	.443	0	—	0	-4	-4	1	-0.1
1995 *Cle-A	3	3	.500	42	0	0	0	0	50^1	40	22	7	2	17	41	10.5	3.75	125	.217	.291	0	—	0	5	5	0	0.6
1996 Cle-A	4	0	1.000	32	0	0	0	0	26^2	29	15	3	0	14	19	14.5	3.04	161	.274	.358	0	—	0	6	6	1	0.7
SF-N	2	1	.667	35	0	0	0	0	23^2	15	7	2	1	13	19	11.0	2.66	154	.188	.309	0	.000	-0	4	4	1	0.5
1997 SF-N	3	1	.750	63	0	0	0	0	49^1	73	44	6	4	25	26	18.6	7.11	57	.353	.432	0	—	0	-16	-17	-1	-1.3
1998 SF-N	1	3	.250	26	0	0	0	0	32^1	38	20	5	0	9	16	13.1	5.29	75	.302	.348	1	.250	1	-4	-5	0	-0.5
*Cle-A	0	0	—	12	0	0	0	0	7	9	4	0	1	3	11	16.7	5.14	93	.300	.382	0	—	0	-0	-0	0	0.0
1999 Phi-N	1	1	.500	51	0	0	0	1	35^1	48	20	3	3	15	22	16.8	4.33	109	.327	.400	0	.000	-0	1	1	-1	0.0
Cle-A	1	0	1.000	3	0	0	0	0	1	2	2	0	0	3	0	45.0	18.00	28	.667	.833	0	—	0	-1	-1	0	-0.2
2000 Det-A	1	0	1.000	18	0	0	0	0	8^2	13	8	4	1	1	5	15.6	7.27	66	.361	.395	0	—	0	-2	-2	0	-0.2
Mon-N	0	0	—	5	0	0	0	0	2	8	6	1	0	3	3	49.5	27.00	17	.571	.647	0	—	0	-5	-5	-0	-0.2
Total 11	22	12	.647	431	0	0	0	4	363	376	203	41	12	156	256	13.5	4.31	102	.271	.349	1	.125	0	5	3	1	1.2
● TOM POORMAN Poorman, Thomas Iverson b: 10/14/1857, Lock Haven, Pa. d: 2/18/05, Lock Haven, Pa. BL/TR, 5'7", 135 lbs. Deb: 5/5/1880 ♦																											
1880 Buf-N	1	8	.111	11	9	9	0	1	85	117	90	3		19	13	14.4	4.13	59	.307	.340	11	.157	-3	-17	-15	1	-1.5
Chi-N	2	0	1.000	2	1	0	0	0	15	12	5	0		8	0	12.0	2.40	101	.203	.299	5	.200	0	-0	0	-1	-0.1
Yr	3	8	.273	13	10	9	0	1	100	129	95	3		27	13	14.0	3.87	63	.293	.334	16	.168	-3	-17	-15	0	-1.6
1884 Tol-a	0	1	.000	1	1	1	0	0	9	13	11	1	0	2	0	15.0	3.00	114	.310	.341	89	.233	0	0	0	0	0.0
1887 Phi-a	0	0	—	1	0	0	0	0	0^2	6	4	1	0	1	1	81.0	40.50	11	.750	.750	190	.306	0	-3	-3	0	-0.1
Total 3	3	9	.250	15	11	10	0	1	109^2	148	110	5	0	30	14	14.5	4.02	63	.302	.341	533	.256	-2	-19	-17	0	-1.7
● BILL POPP Popp, William Peter b: 6/7/1877, St.Louis, Mo. d: 9/5/09, St.Louis, Mo. TR, 5'10.5", 170 lbs. Deb: 4/19/02																											
1902 StL-N	2	6	.250	9	7	5	0	0	60^1	87	60	2	5	26	20	17.6	4.92	56	.337	.408	1	.048	-3	-14	-15	1	-1.8
● ED PORRAY Porray, Edmund Joseph b: 12/5/1888, AtSea On Atlantic Ocean d: 7/13/54, Lackawaxen, Pa. BR/TR, 5'11", 170 lbs. Deb: 4/17/14																											
1914 Buf-F	0	1	.000	3	3	0	0	0	10^1	18	9	2	0	7	0	21.8	4.35	68	.391	.472	0	.000	-1	-2	-2	1	-0.2
● CHUCK PORTER Porter, Charles William b: 1/12/56, Baltimore, Md. BR/TR, 6'3", 188 lbs. Deb: 9/14/81																											
1981 Mil-A	0	0	—	3	0	0	0	0	4^1	6	2	0	0	1	1	14.5	4.15	83	.316	.350	0	—	0	-0	-0	-0	0.0
1982 Mil-A	0	0	—	3	0	0	0	0	3^2	3	2	0	0	1	3	9.8	4.91	77	.250	.308	0	—	0	-0	-0	-0	0.0
1983 Mil-A	7	9	.438	25	21	6	1	0	134	162	72	9	2	38	76	13.6	4.50	83	.298	.346	0	—	0	-6	-12	0	-1.2
1984 Mil-A	6	4	.600	17	12	1	0	0	81^1	92	37	8	0	12	48	11.5	3.87	100	.284	.310	0	—	0	1	-0	0	0.0
1985 Mil-A	0	0	—	6	1	0	0	0	13^2	15	8	1	0	2	8	11.2	1.98	211	.273	.298	0	—	0	3	3	-0	0.1
Total 5	13	13	.500	54	34	7	1	0	237	278	121	18	2	54	136	12.7	4.14	92	.291	.331	0	—	0	-2	-9	-0	-1.1
● HENRY PORTER Porter, Henry b: 6/1858, Vergennes, Vt. d: 12/30/06, Brockton, Mass. BR/TR, Deb: 9/27/1884																											
1884 Mil-U	3	3	.500	6	6	6	1	0	51	32	25	1		9	71	7.2	3.00	44	.168	.205	11	.275	1	-3	-18	1	-1.2
1885 Bro-a	33	21	.611	54	54	53	2	0	481^2	427	261	11	16	107	197	10.3	2.78	118	.223	.270	40	.205	-2	25	27	3	2.6
1886 Bro-a	27	19	.587	48	48	48	1	0	424	439	277	8	5	120	163	12.0	3.42	102	.252	.303	33	.179	-9	2	3	-2	-0.7
1887 Bro-a	15	24	.385	40	40	38	1	0	339^2	512	264	7	7	96	74	13.8	4.21	102	.342	.345	39	.250	-3	3	3	-2	-0.1
1888 KC-a	18	37	.327	55	54	53	4	0	474	527	336	16	23	120	145	12.7	4.16	83	.272	.321	28	.144	-13	-58	-34	4	-3.9
1889 KC-a	0	3	.000	4	4	3	0	0	23	52	46	0	1	14	9	26.2	12.52	33	.433	.496	1	.100	-1	-22	-20	0	-1.7
Total 6	96	107	.473	207	206	201	9	0	1793^1	1989	1209	43	52	466	659	12.1	3.70	95	.269	.308	152	.195	-27	-53	-34	3	-5.0
● NED PORTER Porter, Ned Swindell b: 5/6/05, Apalachicola, Fla. d: 6/30/68, Gainesville, Fla. BR/TR, 6', 173 lbs. Deb: 8/7/26																											
1926 NY-N	0	0	—	2	0	0	0	0	2	2	1	1	0	0	1	9.0	4.50	83	.250	.250	0	—	0	-0	-0	-0	0.0
1927 NY-N	0	0	—	1	0	0	0	0	2	3	1	0	0	1	0	18.0	0.00	—	.333	.400	0	—	0	1	1	-0	0.0
Total 2	0	0	—	3	0	0	0	0	4	5	2	1	0	1	1	13.5	2.25	169	.294	.333	0	—	0	1	1	-0	0.0
● ODIE PORTER Porter, Odie Oscar b: 5/24/1877, Borden, Ind. d: 5/2/03, Borden, Ind. TL, Deb: 6/16/02																											
1902 Phi-A	0	1	.000	1	1	1	0	0	8	12	10	0	0	5	2	19.1	3.38	109	.343	.425	0	.000	-0	0	0	0	0.0
● BOB PORTERFIELD Porterfield, Erwin Coolidge b: 8/10/23, Newport, Va. d: 4/28/80, Sealy, Tex. BR/TR, 6', 190 lbs. Deb: 8/8/48																											
1948 NY-A	5	3	.625	16	12	2	1	0	78	85	42	5	0	34	30	13.7	4.50	91	.273	.345	6	.250	0	-2	-4	-1	-0.4
1949 NY-A	2	5	.286	12	8	3	0	0	57^2	53	26	3	1	29	25	13.0	4.06	100	.251	.344	1	.053	-2	1	-0	-1	-0.2
1950 NY-A	1	1	.500	10	2	0	0	1	19^2	28	19	2	0	8	9	16.5	8.69	49	.341	.400	1	.333	1	-9	-10	-0	-0.9
1951 NY-A	0	0	—	2	0	0	0	0	3	5	6	0	0	3	2	24.0	15.00	26	.385	.500	0	—	0	-4	-4	0	-0.2
Was-A	9	8	.529	19	19	10	3	0	133^1	109	51	8	0	54	53	11.0	3.24	126	.224	.302	6	.130	-3	13	13	-0	1.2
Yr	9	8	.529	21	19	10	3	0	136^1	114	57	8	0	57	55	11.3	3.50	117	.228	.308	6	.130	-3	9	9	-0	1.0
1952 Was-A	13	14	.481	31	29	15	3	0	231^1	222	80	7	4	85	80	12.1	2.72	131	.254	.323	15	.190	0	24	22	-3	2.3
1953 Was-A	**22**	10	.688	34	32	**24**	**9**	0	255	243	99	19	1	73	77	11.2	3.35	116	.257	.310	25	.255	8	18	16	2	3.0
1954 Was-A★	13	15	.464	32	31	**21**	2	0	244	249	104	14	3	77	82	12.1	3.32	107	.266	.324	9	.102	-3	11	7	3	0.7
1955 Was-A	10	17	.370	30	27	8	2	0	178	197	103	14	2	54	74	12.8	4.45	86	.282	.335	12	.190	1	-10	-13	-1	-1.6
1956 Bos-A	3	12	.200	25	18	4	1	0	126	127	82	21	1	64	53	13.7	5.14	90	.260	.347	14	.326	3	-14	-7	-2	-0.6
1957 Bos-A	4	4	.500	28	9	3	1	1	102^1	107	54	8	1	30	28	12.1	4.05	99	.272	.325	5	.172	-0	-3	-1	1	0.0
1958 Bos-A	0	0	—	2	0	0	0	0	4	3	2	1	0	0	1	6.8	4.50	89	.214	.214	0	—	0	-0	-0	-0	0.0
Pit-N	4	6	.400	37	6	2	1	5	87^2	78	33	7	1	19	39	10.1	3.29	118	.241	.285	1	.050	-1	6	6	-0	0.6
1959 Pit-N	0	0	—	6	0	0	0	0	5^1	6	2	1	0	2	1	13.5	1.69	229	.286	.348	0	—	0	1	1	-0	0.0
Chi-N	0	0	—	4	0	0	0	0	6^1	14	9	1	0	3	0	24.2	11.37	35	.424	.472	0	.000	-0	-5	-5	0	-0.2
Pit-N	1	2	.333	30	0	0	0	1	36	45	20	2	0	17	18	15.5	4.75	81	.321	.395	0	.000	-0	-3	-4	1	-0.2
Yr	1	2	.333	40	0	0	0	1	47^2	65	31	4	0	22	19	16.4	5.29	73	.335	.403	0	.000	-0	-7	-8	1	-0.4
Total 12	87	97	.473	318	193	92	23	8	1567^2	1571	732	113	14	552	572	12.3	3.79	102	.263	.327	95	.184	4	26	16	0	3.5
● AL PORTO Porto, Alfred "Lefty" b: 6/27/26, Heilwood, Pa. BL/TL, 5'11", 176 lbs. Deb: 4/22/48																											
1948 Phi-N	0	0	—	3	0	0	0	0	4	2	0	0	0	1	1	6.8	0.00	—	.143	.200	0	—	0	2	2	-0	0.1
● ARNIE PORTOCARRERO Portocarrero, Arnold Mario b: 7/5/31, New York, N.Y. d: 6/21/86, Kansas City, Kan. BR/TR, 6'3", 196 lbs. Deb: 4/18/54																											
1954 Phi-A	9	18	.333	34	33	16	1	0	248	233	124	25	5	114	132	12.8	4.06	96	.249	.334	8	.107	-2	-9	-4	-4	-1.0
1955 KC-A	5	9	.357	24	20	4	1	0	111^1	109	66	12	4	67	34	14.6	4.77	88	.259	.366	4	.108	-1	-10	-7	-1	-1.0

YEAR TM/L	W	L	PCT	G	GS	CG	SH	SV	IP	H	R	HR	HB	BB	SO	RAT	ERA	ERA+	OAV	OOB	BH	AVG	PB	PR	PR+	PD	TPI
1956 KC-A	0	1	.000	3	1	0	0	0	8	9	9	2	0	7	2	18.0	10.13	43	.300	.432	0	.000	-0	-5	-5	-0	-0.5
1957 KC-A	4	9	.308	33	17	1	0	0	114^2	103	55	10	3	34	42	11.0	3.92	101	.240	.300	3	.107	-1	-2	0	-1	-0.2
1958 Bal-A	15	11	.577	32	27	10	3	2	204^2	173	81	17	3	57	90	10.2	3.25	110	.229	.286	11	.164	0	12	8	-3	0.7
1959 Bal-A	2	7	.222	27	14	1	0	0	90	107	73	10	2	32	23	14.1	6.80	56	.294	.354	0	.000	-3	-29	-31	1	-2.8
1960 Bal-A	3	2	.600	13	5	1	0	0	40^2	44	23	6	0	9	15	11.7	4.43	86	.275	.314	0	.000	-1	-2	-3	-1	-0.5
Total 7	38	57	.400	166	117	33	5	2	817^1	778	431	82	17	320	338	12.3	4.32	89	.252	.325	26	.108	-9	-47	-41	-9	-5.3

● MARK PORTUGAL

Portugal, Mark Steven b: 10/30/62, Los Angeles, Cal. BR/TR, 6', 190 lbs. Deb: 8/14/85

YEAR TM/L	W	L	PCT	G	GS	CG	SH	SV	IP	H	R	HR	HB	BB	SO	RAT	ERA	ERA+	OAV	OOB	BH	AVG	PB	PR	PR+	PD	TPI
1985 Min-A	1	3	.250	6	4	0	0	0	24^1	24	16	3	0	14	12	14.1	5.55	79	.270	.369	0	—	0	-4	-3	1	-0.3
1986 Min-A	6	10	.375	27	15	3	0	1	112^2	112	56	10	1	50	67	13.0	4.31	100	.265	.345	0	—	0	-2	0	-0	0.0
1987 Min-A	1	3	.250	13	7	0	0	0	44	58	40	13	1	24	28	17.0	7.77	60	.326	.409	0	—	0	-16	-15	0	-1.1
1988 Min-A	3	3	.500	26	0	0	0	3	57^2	60	30	11	1	17	31	12.2	4.53	90	.274	.329	0	—	0	-4	-3	-2	-0.5
1989 Hou-N	7	1	.875	20	15	2	1	0	108	91	34	7	2	37	86	10.8	2.75	123	.232	.302	7	.206	3	9	8	0	0.9
1990 Hou-N	11	10	.524	32	32	1	0	0	196^2	187	90	21	4	67	136	11.8	3.62	103	.250	.315	9	.136	-1	4	2	-0	0.1
1991 Hou-N	10	12	.455	32	27	1	0	1	168^1	163	91	19	2	59	120	12.0	4.49	78	.256	.321	9	.196	3	-15	-19	-1	-2.1
1992 Hou-N	6	3	.667	18	16	1	1	0	101^1	76	32	7	1	41	62	10.5	2.66	126	.213	.296	3	.107	-1	10	8	0	0.6
1993 Hou-N	18	4	**.818**	33	33	1	1	0	208	194	75	10	4	77	131	11.9	2.77	140	.248	.319	15	.231	4	30	27	1	3.1
1994 SF-N	10	8	.556	21	21	1	0	0	137^1	135	68	17	6	45	87	12.2	3.93	102	.260	.326	17	.354	8	4	1	-2	0.8
1995 SF-N	5	5	.500	17	17	1	0	0	104	106	56	10	2	34	63	12.3	4.15	98	.262	.323	3	.103	-0	0	-1	-1	-0.2
*Cin-N	6	5	.545	14	14	0	0	0	77^2	79	35	7	2	22	33	11.9	3.82	108	.262	.317	5	.172	2	3	3	-1	0.4
Yr	11	10	.524	31	31	1	0	0	181^2	185	91	17	4	56	96	12.1	4.01	102	.262	.320	8	.138	1	3	2	-2	0.2
1996 Cin-N	8	9	.471	27	26	1	1	0	156	146	77	20	2	42	93	11.0	3.98	106	.248	.300	8	.167	-0	4	4	-2	0.3
1997 Phi-N	0	2	.000	3	3	0	0	0	13^2	17	8	0	0	5	2	14.5	4.61	92	.321	.379	0	.000	-0	-1	-1	-0	-0.1
1998 Phi-N	10	5	.667	26	26	3	0	0	166^1	186	88	26	4	32	104	12.0	4.44	98	.283	.320	13	.260	4	-4	-2	-0	0.3
1999 Bos-A	7	12	.368	31	27	1	0	0	150^1	179	100	28	4	41	79	13.4	5.51	90	.292	.340	0	.000	-0	-11	-9	-0	-0.9
Total 15	109	95	.534	346	283	16	4	5	1826^1	1813	896	209	36	607	1134	12.1	4.03	100	.261	.323	89	.198	20	9	-1	-6	1.3

● MIKE PORZIO

Porzio, Lawrence Michael b: 8/20/72, Waterbury, Conn. BL/TL, 6'3", 190 lbs. Deb: 7/9/99

YEAR TM/L	W	L	PCT	G	GS	CG	SH	SV	IP	H	R	HR	HB	BB	SO	RAT	ERA	ERA+	OAV	OOB	BH	AVG	PB	PR	PR+	PD	TPI
1999 Col-N	0	0	—	16	0	0	0	0	14^2	21	14	5	0	10	10	19.0	8.59	68	.328	.419	0	—	0	-7	-4	0	-0.2

● BILL POSEDEL

Posedel, William John "Sailor Bill" or "Barnacle Bill"
b: 8/2/06, San Francisco, Cal. d: 11/28/89, Livermore, Cal. BR/TR, 5'11", 175 lbs. Deb: 4/23/38 C

YEAR TM/L	W	L	PCT	G	GS	CG	SH	SV	IP	H	R	HR	HB	BB	SO	RAT	ERA	ERA+	OAV	OOB	BH	AVG	PB	PR	PR+	PD	TPI
1938 Bro-N	8	9	.471	33	17	6	1	1	140	178	96	14	2	46	49	14.5	5.66	69	.311	.365	10	.227	1	-29	-26	-1	-2.9
1939 Bos-N	15	13	.536	33	29	18	5	0	220^2	221	103	8	0	78	73	12.2	3.92	94	.268	.331	8	.110	-4	0	-6	-1	-1.1
1940 Bos-N	12	17	.414	35	32	18	0	1	233	263	118	16	1	81	86	13.3	4.13	90	.288	.346	14	.171	1	-7	-11	-0	-1.1
1941 Bos-N	4	4	.500	18	9	3	0	0	57^1	61	36	6	1	30	10	14.4	4.87	73	.279	.368	8	.320	2	-8	-8	-0	-0.8
1946 Bos-N	2	0	1.000	19	0	0	0	4	28^1	34	24	4	0	13	9	14.9	6.99	49	.304	.376	0	.000	-0	-11	-11	-0	-1.2
Total 5	41	43	.488	138	87	45	6	6	679^1	757	377	48	4	248	227	13.4	4.56	82	.286	.349	40	.176	0	-55	-64	-4	-7.1

● BOB POSER

Poser, John Falk b: 3/16/10, Columbus, Wis. BL/TR, 6', 173 lbs. Deb: 4/17/32

YEAR TM/L	W	L	PCT	G	GS	CG	SH	SV	IP	H	R	HR	HB	BB	SO	RAT	ERA	ERA+	OAV	OOB	BH	AVG	PB	PR	PR+	PD	TPI
1932 Chi-A	0	0	—	1	0	0	0	0	0^2	3	2	0	0	2	1	67.5	27.00	16	.600	.714	0	.000	-0	-2	-2	0	-0.1
1935 StL-A	1	1	.500	4	1	0	0	0	13^2	26	15	0	0	4	1	19.8	9.22	52	.400	.435	1	.250	0	-7	-6	-1	-0.7
Total 2	1	1	.500	5	1	0	0	0	14^1	29	17	0	0	6	2	22.0	10.05	47	.414	.461	1	.143	0	-9	-8	-1	-0.8

● LOU POSSEHL

Possehl, Louis Thomas b: 4/12/26, Chicago, Ill. d: 10/7/97, Sarasota, Fla. BR/TR, 6'2", 180 lbs. Deb: 8/25/46 F

YEAR TM/L	W	L	PCT	G	GS	CG	SH	SV	IP	H	R	HR	HB	BB	SO	RAT	ERA	ERA+	OAV	OOB	BH	AVG	PB	PR	PR+	PD	TPI
1946 Phi-N	1	2	.333	4	4	0	0	0	13^2	19	9	0	1	10	4	19.8	5.93	58	.339	.448	0	.000	-0	-4	-4	0	-0.7
1947 Phi-N	0	0	—	2	0	0	0	0	4^1	5	2	0	1	0	1	12.5	4.15	96	.385	.429	0	—	0	-0	-0	0	0.1
1948 Phi-N	1	1	.500	3	2	1	0	0	14^2	17	8	3	0	4	7	12.9	4.91	80	.304	.350	1	.250	0	-2	-2	0	-0.2
1951 Phi-N	0	1	.000	2	1	0	0	0	6	9	5	0	0	3	6	18.0	6.00	64	.333	.400	0	.000	-0	-1	-1	0	-0.2
1952 Phi-N	0	1	.000	4	1	0	0	0	12^2	12	9	3	0	7	4	13.5	4.97	73	.235	.328	0	.000	-0	-2	-2	-0	-0.2
Total 5	2	5	.286	15	8	1	0	0	51^1	62	33	6	2	24	22	15.4	5.26	71	.305	.384	1	.100	-0	-9	-9	0	-1.2

● LOU POTE

Pote, Louis William b: 8/27/71, Evergreen Park, Ill. BR/TR, 6'3", 190 lbs. Deb: 8/11/99

YEAR TM/L	W	L	PCT	G	GS	CG	SH	SV	IP	H	R	HR	HB	BB	SO	RAT	ERA	ERA+	OAV	OOB	BH	AVG	PB	PR	PR+	PD	TPI
1999 Ana-A	1	1	.500	20	0	0	0	3	29^1	23	9	1	0	12	20	10.7	2.15	226	.219	.299	0	—	0	9	9	0	0.7
2000 Ana-A	1	1	.500	32	1	0	0	1	50^1	52	23	4	0	17	44	12.3	3.40	146	.267	.325	0	—	0	9	9	1	0.5
Total 2	2	2	.500	52	1	0	0	4	79^2	75	32	5	0	29	64	11.7	2.94	168	.250	.316	0	—	0	17	18	1	1.2

● NELLIE POTT

Pott, Nelson Adolph "Lefty" b: 7/16/1899, Cincinnati, Ohio d: 12/3/63, Cincinnati, Ohio BL/TL, 6', 185 lbs. Deb: 4/19/22

YEAR TM/L	W	L	PCT	G	GS	CG	SH	SV	IP	H	R	HR	HB	BB	SO	RAT	ERA	ERA+	OAV	OOB	BH	AVG	PB	PR	PR+	PD	TPI
1922 Cle-A	0	0	—	2	0	0	0	0	2	7	7	1	0	2	0	40.5	31.50	13	.583	.643	0	—	0	-6	-6	-0	-0.3

● DYKES POTTER

Potter, Maryland Dykes b: 9/7/10, Ashland, Ky. BR/TR, 6', 185 lbs. Deb: 4/26/38 F

YEAR TM/L	W	L	PCT	G	GS	CG	SH	SV	IP	H	R	HR	HB	BB	SO	RAT	ERA	ERA+	OAV	OOB	BH	AVG	PB	PR	PR+	PD	TPI
1938 Bro-N	0	0	—	2	0	0	0	0	2	4	1	1	0	0	1	18.0	4.50	87	.400	.400	0	—	0	-0	-0	-0	0.0

● NELS POTTER

Potter, Nelson Thomas "Nellie" b: 8/23/11, Mt.Morris, Ill. d: 9/30/90, Mt.Morris, Ill. BL/TR, 5'11", 180 lbs. Deb: 4/25/36

YEAR TM/L	W	L	PCT	G	GS	CG	SH	SV	IP	H	R	HR	HB	BB	SO	RAT	ERA	ERA+	OAV	OOB	BH	AVG	PB	PR	PR+	PD	TPI
1936 StL-N	0	0	—	1	0	0	0	0	1	0	0	0	0	0	0	0.0	0.00	—	.000	.000	0	—	0	0	0	-0	0.0
1938 Phi-A	2	12	.143	35	9	4	0	5	111^1	139	95	15	2	49	43	15.4	6.47	75	.306	.376	10	.256	1	-21	-20	-1	-2.1
1939 Phi-A	8	12	.400	41	25	9	0	2	196^1	258	163	26	5	88	60	16.1	6.60	71	.321	.391	12	.179	-1	-43	-41	-0	-3.4
1940 Phi-A	9	14	.391	31	25	13	0	0	200^2	213	115	18	1	71	73	12.8	4.44	100	.269	.330	18	.254	2	-1	0	-0	0.2
1941 Phi-A	1	1	.500	10	3	1	0	2	23^1	35	26	3	0	16	7	19.7	9.26	45	.337	.425	1	.167	0	-13	-13	0	-1.1
Bos-A	2	0	1.000	10	0	0	0	0	20	21	10	0	0	16	6	16.6	4.50	93	.284	.411	0	.000	-0	-1	-1	-0	-0.1
Yr	3	1	.750	20	3	1	0	2	43^1	56	36	3	0	32	13	18.3	7.06	59	.315	.419	1	.111	0	-14	-14	-0	-1.2
1943 StL-A	10	5	.667	33	13	8	0	1	168^1	146	56	11	3	54	80	10.9	2.78	120	.235	.299	8	.145	-1	10	10	1	0.9
1944 *StL-A	19	7	.731	32	29	16	3	0	232	211	79	6	1	70	91	10.9	2.83	127	.244	.301	13	.159	-2	25	19	2	2.0
1945 StL-A	15	11	.577	32	32	21	3	0	255^1	212	75	10	1	68	129	9.9	2.47	143	.226	.279	28	.304	4	25	29	-1	3.3
1946 StL-A	8	9	.471	23	19	10	0	0	145	152	72	9	3	59	72	13.3	3.72	100	.268	.340	12	.231	2	-4	0	-1	0.2
1947 StL-A	4	10	.286	32	10	3	0	2	122^2	130	61	13	2	44	65	12.9	4.04	96	.277	.342	9	.257	3	-5	-2	1	0.2
1948 StL-A	1	1	.500	2	2	0	0	0	10^1	11	7	1	2	4	4	14.8	5.23	87	.262	.354	2	.500	1	-1	-1	0	0.0
Phi-A	2	2	.500	8	0	0	0	1	18	17	8	1	0	5	13	11.0	4.00	107	.250	.301	1	.250	0	1	1	-0	0.1
Yr	3	3	.500	10	2	0	0	1	28^1	28	15	2	2	9	17	12.4	4.45	99	.255	.322	3	.375	1	-0	-0	0	0.1
*Bos-N	5	2	.714	18	7	3	0	2	85	77	27	4	0	8	47	9.0	2.33	165	.245	.264	11	.379	3	15	15	1	1.7
1949 Bos-N	6	11	.353	41	3	1	0	7	96^2	99	49	6	1	30	57	12.1	4.19	90	.265	.321	3	.130	-0	-2	-5	1	-0.8
Total 12	92	97	.487	349	177	89	6	22	1686	1721	843	123	21	582	747	12.4	3.99	99	.265	.328	128	.228	11	-23	-6	3	1.1

● SQUIRE POTTER

Potter, Robert b: 3/18/02, Flatwoods, Ky. d: 1/27/83, Ashland, Ky. BR/TR, 6'1", 185 lbs. Deb: 8/7/23 F

YEAR TM/L	W	L	PCT	G	GS	CG	SH	SV	IP	H	R	HR	HB	BB	SO	RAT	ERA	ERA+	OAV	OOB	BH	AVG	PB	PR	PR+	PD	TPI
1923 Was-A	0	0	—	1	0	0	0	0	3	11	9	0	0	4	1	45.0	21.00	18	.688	.750	0	—	0	-6	-6	-0	-0.3

● MIKE POTTS

Potts, Michael Larry b: 9/5/70, Langdale, Ala. BL/TL, 5'9", 179 lbs. Deb: 4/6/96

YEAR TM/L	W	L	PCT	G	GS	CG	SH	SV	IP	H	R	HR	HB	BB	SO	RAT	ERA	ERA+	OAV	OOB	BH	AVG	PB	PR	PR+	PD	TPI
1996 Mil-A	1	2	.333	24	0	0	0	1	45^1	58	39	7	0	30	21	17.5	7.15	73	.319	.415	0	—	0	-11	-9	-1	-0.6

● BILL POUNDS

Pounds, Jeared Wells b: 3/11/1878, Paterson, N.J. d: 7/7/36, Paterson, N.J. BR/TR, 5'10.5", 178 lbs. Deb: 5/2/03

YEAR TM/L	W	L	PCT	G	GS	CG	SH	SV	IP	H	R	HR	HB	BB	SO	RAT	ERA	ERA+	OAV	OOB	BH	AVG	PB	PR	PR+	PD	TPI
1903 Cle-A	0	0	—	1	0	0	0	0	5	8	7	0	0	0	2	14.4	10.80	26	.364	.364	1	.500	1	-4	-5	-0	-0.2
Bro-N	0	0	—	1	0	0	0	0	6	8	5	1	0	2	2	15.0	6.00	53	.348	.400	2	.667	1	-2	-2	-0	0.0
Total 1	0	0	—	2	0	0	0	0	11	16	12	1	0	2	4	14.7	8.18	37	.356	.383	3	.600	1	-6	-6	0	-0.2

● ABNER POWELL

Powell, Charles Abner "Ab" b: 12/15/1860, Shenandoah, Pa. d: 8/7/53, New Orleans, La. BL/TR, 5'7", 160 lbs. Deb: 8/4/1884 ♦

YEAR TM/L	W	L	PCT	G	GS	CG	SH	SV	IP	H	R	HR	HB	BB	SO	RAT	ERA	ERA+	OAV	OOB	BH	AVG	PB	PR	PR+	PD	TPI
1884 Was-U	6	12	.333	18	17	14	1	0	134	135	107	3		19	78	10.3	3.43	70	.245	.270	54	.283	0	-15	-16	2	-1.4
1886 Bal-a	2	5	.286	7	7	7	0	0	60	66	51	2	1	26	15	14.0	5.10	67	.264	.336	7	.179	-1	-11	-11	2	-0.9
Cin-a	0	1	.000	4	1	1	0	0	15^1	16	13	0	0	9	4	14.7	4.70	75	.271	.368	17	.230	-0	-2	-2	-0	-0.1
Yr	2	6	.250	11	8	8	0	0	75^1	82	64	2	1	35	19	14.1	5.02	69	.265	.342	24	.212	-1	-13	-13	1	-1.0
Total 2	8	18	.308	29	25	22	1	0	209^1	217	171	5	1	54	97	11.7	4.00	69	.252	.297	78	.257	-1	-28	-29	3	-2.4

● DENNIS POWELL

Powell, Dennis Clay b: 8/13/63, Moultrie, Ga. BR/TL, 6'3", 200 lbs. Deb: 7/7/85

YEAR TM/L	W	L	PCT	G	GS	CG	SH	SV	IP	H	R	HR	HB	BB	SO	RAT	ERA	ERA+	OAV	OOB	BH	AVG	PB	PR	PR+	PD	TPI
1985 LA-N	1	1	.500	16	2	0	0	1	29^1	30	19	7	1	13	19	13.5	5.22	67	.263	.344	0	.000	-0	-5	-6	0	-0.4

YEAR	TM/L	W	L	PCT	G	GS	CG	SH	SV	IP	H	R	HR	HB	BB	SO	RAT	ERA	ERA+	OAV	OOB	BH	AVG	PB	PR	PR+	PD	TPI
1986	LA-N	2	7	.222	27	6	0	0	0	65^1	65	32	5	1	25	31	12.5	4.27	81	.272	.343	3	.214	1	-4	-6	-1	-0.7
1987	Sea-A	1	3	.250	16	3	0	0	0	34^1	32	13	3	0	15	17	12.3	3.15	151	.250	.329	0	—	0	5	6	0	0.6
1988	Sea-A	1	3	.250	12	2	0	0	0	18^2	29	20	2	2	11	15	20.3	8.68	48	.363	.452	0	—	0	-10	-9	0	-1.6
1989	Sea-A	2	2	.500	43	1	0	0	2	45	49	25	6	2	21	27	14.4	5.00	81	.285	.369	0	—	0	-6	-5	1	-0.3
1990	Sea-A	0	0	—	2	0	0	0	0	3	5	3	0	1	2	0	24.0	9.00	44	.357	.471	0	—	0	-2	-2	-0	-0.1
	Mil-A	0	4	.000	9	7	0	0	0	39^1	59	37	0	1	19	23	18.1	6.86	57	.341	.409	0	—	0	-13	-13	1	-1.1
	Yr	0	4	.000	11	7	0	0	0	42^1	64	40	0	2	21	23	18.5	7.02	55	.342	.414	0	—	0	-15	-15	1	-1.2
1992	Sea-A	4	2	.667	49	0	0	0	0	57	49	30	5	3	29	35	12.8	4.58	87	.238	.340	0	—	0	-4	-4	-0	-0.4
1993	Sea-A	0	0	—	33	2	0	0	0	47^2	42	22	7	1	24	32	12.7	4.15	106	.255	.353	0	—	0	1	1	-0	0.0
Total	8	11	22	.333	207	23	0	0	3	339^2	360	201	35	12	159	199	14.1	4.95	80	.279	.363	3	.176	1	-37	-37	1	-4.0
● **GROVER POWELL**	Powell, Grover David b: 10/10/40, Sayre, Pa. d: 5/21/85, Raleigh, N.C. BL/TL, 5'10", 175 lbs. Deb: 7/13/63																											
1963	NY-N	1	1	.500	20	4	1	1	0	49^2	37	23	2	1	32	39	12.7	2.72	128	.202	.324	2	.200	1	3	4	0	0.3
● **JAY POWELL**	Powell, James Willard b: 1/9/72, Meridian, Miss. BR/TR, 6'4", 220 lbs. Deb: 9/10/95																											
1995	Fla-N	0	0	—	9	0	0	0	0	8^1	7	2	0	2	6	4	16.2	1.08	391	.241	.405	0	—	0	3	3	0	0.2
1996	Fla-N	4	3	.571	67	0	0	0	2	71^1	71	41	5	4	36	52	14.0	4.54	90	.255	.349	0	.000	-1	-3	-4	-1	-0.5
1997	*Fla-N	7	2	.778	74	0	0	0	2	79^2	71	35	3	4	30	65	11.9	3.28	123	.242	.321	2	.500	1	8	7	1	0.9
1998	Fla-N	4	4	.500	33	0	0	0	3	36^1	36	19	5	2	22	24	14.9	4.21	96	.263	.373	0	—	0	0	-1	0	-0.1
	*Hou-N	3	3	.500	29	0	0	0	4	34	22	9	1	1	15	38	10.1	2.38	170	.182	.277	0	.000	-0	7	7	-1	1.1
	Yr	7	7	.500	62	0	0	0	7	70^1	58	28	6	3	37	62	12.5	3.33	122	.225	.329	0	.000	-0	7	6	-1	1.0
1999	*Hou-N	5	4	.556	67	0	0	0	4	75	82	38	3	3	40	77	15.0	4.32	102	.282	.374	0	—	0	2	1	-1	0.0
2000	Hou-N	1	1	.500	29	0	0	0	0	27	29	18	1	0	19	16	16.0	5.67	86	.271	.381	0	.000	-0	-3	-2	-0	-0.2
Total	6	24	17	.585	308	0	0	0	15	331^2	318	162	18	16	168	276	13.6	3.93	107	.253	.349	2	.182	-0	15	10	-1	1.4
● **JEREMY POWELL**	Powell, Jeremy Robert b: 6/18/76, Bellflower, Cal. BR/TR, 6'5", 230 lbs. Deb: 7/23/98																											
1998	Mon-N	1	5	.167	7	6	0	0	0	25	27	25	5	4	11	14	15.1	7.92	53	.290	.389	0	.000	-1	-10	-10	-0	-1.8
1999	Mon-N	4	8	.333	17	17	0	0	0	97	113	60	14	8	44	44	15.3	4.73	95	.302	.387	4	.133	0	-2	-3	-0	-0.3
2000	Mon-N	0	3	.000	11	4	0	0	0	26	35	27	6	0	9	19	15.2	7.96	59	.321	.373	3	.600	1	-10	-9	0	-0.7
Total	3	5	16	.238	35	27	0	0	0	148	175	112	25	12	64	77	15.3	5.84	77	.304	.385	7	.171	1	-22	-23	-0	-2.8
● **JACK POWELL**	Powell, John Joseph "Red" b: 7/9/1874, Bloomington, Ill. d: 10/17/44, Chicago, Ill. BR/TR, 5'11", 195 lbs. Deb: 6/23/1897																											
1897	Cle-N	15	10	.600	27	26	24	2	0	225	245	117	2	9	62	61	12.6	3.16	142	.275	.328	20	.206	-4	29	32	-1	2.4
1898	Cle-N	23	15	.605	42	41	36	**6**	0	342	328	154	8	16	112	93	12.0	3.00	121	.251	.317	18	.132	-7	23	23	-2	1.4
1899	StL-N	23	19	.548	48	43	**40**	2	0	373	433	197	15	15	85	87	12.9	3.52	113	.290	.334	27	.201	-1	14	18	-3	1.3
1900	StL-N	17	16	.515	38	37	28	3	0	287^2	325	194	9	3	77	77	12.7	4.44	82	.284	.331	31	.284	10	-24	-26	0	-1.6
1901	StL-N	19	19	.500	**45**	37	33	2	**3**	338^1	351	168	14	12	50	133	11.0	3.54	90	.266	.299	21	.176	1	-8	-14	-5	-1.7
1902	StL-A	22	17	.564	42	39	36	3	**2**	328^1	320	144	12	9	93	137	11.6	3.21	110	.256	.312	26	.205	4	13	12	-5	1.1
1903	StL-A	15	19	.441	38	34	33	4	**2**	306^1	294	131	11	5	58	169	10.5	2.91	100	.252	.290	25	.208	2	2	0	-1	0.2
1904	NY-A	23	19	.548	47	45	38	3	0	390^1	340	154	15	10	92	202	10.2	2.44	111	.235	.286	26	.178	-3	7	11	-6	0.3
1905	NY-A	8	13	.381	37	23	13	1	1	203	214	107	4	6	57	84	12.3	3.50	84	.272	.326	12	.185	-0	-19	-12	-6	-1.9
	StL-A	2	1	.667	3	3	3	0	0	28	22	6	0	1	5	12	9.0	1.61	158	.218	.262	1	.100	-0	3	3	-1	0.2
	Yr	10	14	.417	40	26	16	1	1	231	236	113	4	7	62	96	11.9	3.27	88	.266	.319	13	.173	-1	-16	-9	-7	-1.7
1906	StL-A	13	14	.481	28	26	25	3	1	244	196	77	2	8	55	132	9.6	1.77	146	.223	.275	21	.231	3	25	23	-4	2.6
1907	StL-A	13	16	.448	32	31	27	4	1	255^2	229	104	4	5	62	96	10.4	2.68	94	.242	.292	12	.132	-3	-4	-5	-3	-1.2
1908	StL-A	16	13	.552	33	32	23	5	1	256	208	73	1	6	47	85	9.2	2.11	113	.231	.274	21	.236	3	8	8	-6	0.5
1909	StL-A	12	16	.429	34	27	18	4	3	239	221	83	1	4	42	82	10.1	2.11	115	.250	.287	14	.179	0	10	8	-4	0.6
1910	StL-A	7	11	.389	21	18	8	3	0	129^1	121	45	0	1	28	52	10.4	2.30	108	.250	.292	7	.163	-1	3	3	-3	-0.2
1911	StL-A	8	19	.296	31	27	18	1	1	207^2	224	120	7	7	44	52	11.9	3.29	102	.262	.304	12	.164	-3	1	2	-5	-0.5
1912	StL-A	9	17	.346	32	27	19	0	0	235^1	248	117	5	3	52	67	11.6	3.10	107	.276	.318	15	.183	0	6	6	-4	0.3
Total	16	245	254	.491	578	516	422	46	15	4389	4319	1991	110	120	1021	1621	11.2	2.97	106	.258	.305	309	.192	-1	89	93	-58	3.8
● **JACK POWELL**	Powell, Reginald Bertrand b: 8/17/1891, Holcomb, Mo. d: 3/12/30, Memphis, Tenn. TR, 6'2", Deb: 6/14/13																											
1913	StL-A	0	0	—	2	0	0	0	0	2	1	3	0	0	2	0	13.5	0.00	—	.143	.333	0	—	0	1	1	1	0.1
● **ROSS POWELL**	Powell, Ross John b: 1/24/68, Grand Rapids, Mich. BL/TL, 6', 180 lbs. Deb: 9/5/93																											
1993	Cin-N	0	3	.000	9	1	0	0	0	16^1	13	8	1	0	6	17	10.5	4.41	91	.224	.297	0	.000	-0	-1	-1	-0	-0.1
1994	Hou-N	0	0	—	12	0	0	0	0	7^1	6	1	0	1	5	5	14.7	1.23	322	.240	.387	0	—	0	2	2	0	0.1
1995	Hou-N	0	0	—	15	0	0	0	0	9	16	12	1	0	11	8	27.0	11.00	35	.381	.509	0	—	0	-7	-8	0	-0.4
	Pit-N	0	2	.000	12	3	0	0	0	20^2	20	14	5	2	10	12	13.9	5.23	82	.253	.352	0	.000	-0	-2	-2	0	-0.2
	Yr	0	2	.000	27	3	0	0	0	29^2	36	26	6	2	21	20	17.9	6.98	60	.298	.410	0	.000	-0	-9	-9	0	-0.6
Total	3	0	5	.000	48	4	0	0	0	53^1	55	35	7	3	32	42	15.2	5.40	76	.270	.377	0	.000	-0	-7	-8	0	-0.6
● **BRIAN POWELL**	Powell, William Brian b: 10/10/73, Bainbridge, Ga. BR/TR, 6'2", 205 lbs. Deb: 6/27/98																											
1998	Det-A	3	8	.273	18	16	0	0	0	83^2	101	67	17	2	36	46	15.0	6.35	74	.294	.365	0	.000	-0	-16	-15	-1	-1.7
2000	Hou-N	2	1	.667	9	5	0	0	0	31^1	34	21	8	1	13	14	13.8	5.74	85	.279	.353	2	.222	1	-4	-3	-0	-0.2
Total	2	5	9	.357	27	21	0	0	0	115	135	88	25	3	49	60	14.6	6.18	77	.290	.362	2	.200	1	-20	-18	-1	-1.9
● **BILL POWELL**	Powell, William Burris "Big Bill" b: 5/8/1885, Taylor County, W.Va. d: 9/28/67, E.Liverpool, Ohio BR/TR, 6'2.5", 182 lbs. Deb: 4/16/09																											
1909	Pit-N	0	1	.000	3	1	0	0	0	7^1	7	6	0	1	6	2	17.2	3.68	74	.292	.452	1	.333	0	-1	-1	0	-0.1
1910	Pit-N	4	6	.400	12	9	4	2	0	75	65	32	0	5	34	23	12.5	2.40	129	.242	.338	6	.261	1	5	6	2	1.0
1912	Chi-N	0	0	—	1	0	0	0	0	2	2	2	0	0	1	0	13.5	9.00	37	.250	.333	0	—	0	-1	-1	0	-0.1
1913	Cin-N	0	1	.000	1	1	0	0	0	0^1	2	2	0	0	2	0	108.0	54.00	6	1.000	1.000	0	—	0	-2	-2	0	-0.3
Total	4	4	8	.333	17	11	4	2	0	84^2	76	42	0	6	43	25	13.3	2.87	107	.251	.355	7	.269	1	1	2	2	0.5
● **TED POWER**	Power, Ted Henry b: 1/31/55, Guthrie, Okla. BR/TR, 6'4", 225 lbs. Deb: 9/9/81																											
1981	LA-N	1	3	.250	5	2	0	0	0	14^1	16	6	0	1	7	7	15.1	3.14	106	.286	.375	0	.000	-0	1	0	-1	0.0
1982	LA-N	1	1	.500	12	4	0	0	0	33^2	38	27	4	0	23	15	16.3	6.68	52	.288	.394	0	.000	-1	-11	-12	-0	-0.7
1983	Cin-N	5	6	.455	49	6	1	0	2	111	120	62	10	1	49	57	13.8	4.54	84	.286	.362	0	.000	-1	-11	-9	-2	-1.2
1984	Cin-N	9	7	.563	**78**	0	0	0	11	108^2	93	37	4	0	46	81	11.5	2.82	134	.237	.317	0	.000	-0	9	11	0	1.8
1985	Cin-N	8	6	.571	64	0	0	0	27	80	65	27	2	1	45	42	12.5	2.70	141	.227	.334	0	—	0	8	9	-2	1.8
1986	Cin-N	10	6	.625	56	10	0	0	1	129	115	59	13	1	52	95	11.7	3.70	105	.245	.322	3	.125	0	0	2	-0	0.3
1987	Cin-N	10	13	.435	34	34	2	1	0	204	213	115	28	3	71	133	12.7	4.50	94	.267	.329	7	.119	0	-9	-5	-3	-0.9
1988	KC-A	5	6	.455	22	12	2	2	0	80^1	98	54	7	3	30	44	14.7	5.94	67	.305	.370	0	—	0	-18	-17	-0	-2.1
	Det-A	1	1	.500	4	2	0	0	0	18^2	23	13	1	0	8	13	14.9	5.79	66	.307	.373	0	—	0	-4	-4	0	-0.4
	Yr	6	7	.462	26	14	2	2	0	99	121	67	8	3	38	57	14.7	5.91	67	.306	.371	0	—	0	-21	-21	-0	-2.5
1989	StL-N	7	7	.500	23	15	0	0	0	97	96	47	7	1	21	43	10.9	3.71	98	.255	.296	3	.091	-2	-2	-1	-2	-0.5
1990	*Pit-N	1	3	.250	40	0	0	0	7	51^2	50	23	5	0	17	42	11.7	3.66	99	.255	.315	1	.125	0	1	-0	-1	-0.1
1991	Cin-N	5	3	.625	68	0	0	0	3	87	87	37	6	2	31	51	12.4	3.62	105	.265	.332	0	.000	-0	1	2	-0	0.1
1992	Cle-A	3	3	.500	64	0	0	0	6	99^1	88	33	7	4	35	51	11.5	2.54	154	.248	.322	0	—	0	16	15	0	1.0
1993	Cle-A	0	2	.000	20	0	0	0	0	20	30	17	2	0	8	11	17.1	7.20	60	.333	.388	0	—	0	-6	-6	-1	-0.6
	Sea-A	2	2	.500	25	0	0	0	13	25^1	27	11	1	0	9	16	12.8	3.91	113	.287	.350	0	—	0	1	1	0	0.3
	Yr	2	4	.333	45	0	0	0	13	45^1	57	28	3	0	17	27	14.7	5.36	82	.310	.368	0	—	0	-5	-5	-1	-0.3
Total	13	68	69	.496	564	85	5	3	70	1160	1159	568	97	17	452	701	12.6	4.00	98	.264	.335	14	.089	-4	-25	-12	-11	-1.2
● **JIM POWERS**	Powers, James T. b: 1868, New York, N.Y. 5'10", 150 lbs. Deb: 4/18/1890																											
1890	Bro-a	1	2	.333	4	2	2	0	0	30	38	29	1	1	16	3	16.5	5.70	68	.299	.382	2	.154	-0	-6	-6	-0	-0.5
● **IKE POWERS**	Powers, John Lloyd b: 3/13/06, Hancock, Md. d: 12/22/68, Hancock, Md. BR/TR, 6'0.5", 188 lbs. Deb: 7/26/27																											
1927	Phi-A	1	1	.500	11	1	0	0	0	26	26	16	1	0	7	3	11.4	4.50	95	.271	.320	2	.400	1	-1	-1	-0	0.0
1928	Phi-A	1	0	1.000	9	0	0	0	2	12	8	6	1	1	10	4	14.3	4.50	89	.222	.404	0	—	0	-1	-1	1	0.0
Total	2	2	1	.667	20	1	0	0	2	38	34	22	2	1	17	7	12.3	4.50	93	.258	.347	2	.400	1	-2	-1	1	0.0

● WILLIE PRALL
Prall, Wilfred Anthony b: 4/20/50, Hackensack, N.J. BL/TL, 6'3", 200 lbs. Deb: 9/3/75

YEAR TM/L	W	L	PCT	G	GS	CG	SH	SV	IP	H	R	HR	HB	BB	SO	RAT	ERA	ERA+	OAV	OOB	BH	AVG	PB	PR	PR+	PD	TPI
1975 Chi-N	0	2	.000	3	3	0	0	0	14^2	21	15	1	0	8	7	17.8	8.59	45	.339	.414	0	.000	-0	-8	-7	0	-0.8

● AL PRATT
Pratt, Albert George "Uncle Al" b: 11/19/1848, Allegheny, Pa. d: 11/21/37, Pittsburgh, Pa. TR, 5'7", 140 lbs. Deb: 5/4/1871 MU

YEAR TM/L	W	L	PCT	G	GS	CG	SH	SV	IP	H	R	HR	HB	BB	SO	RAT	ERA	ERA+	OAV	OOB	BH	AVG	PB	PR	PR+	PD	TPI
1871 Cle-n	10	17	.370	28	28	22	0	0	224^2	296	288	9		47	**34**	13.7	3.77	110	.277	.307	34	.262	2	11	9		1.0
1872 Cle-n	2	9	.182	15	12	8	0	0	105^2	150	133	3		14	7	14.0	5.79	61	.286	.305	18	.277	0	-25	-27		-1.6
Total 2 n	12	26	.316	43	40	30	0	0	330^1	446	421	12		61	41	13.8	4.41	81	.280	.306	52	.267	3	-28	-32		-0.6

● JOHN PREGENZER
Pregenzer, John Arthur b: 8/2/35, Burlington, Wis. BR/TR, 6'5", 220 lbs. Deb: 4/20/63

YEAR TM/L	W	L	PCT	G	GS	CG	SH	SV	IP	H	R	HR	HB	BB	SO	RAT	ERA	ERA+	OAV	OOB	BH	AVG	PB	PR	PR+	PD	TPI
1963 SF-N	0	0	—	6	0	0	0	1	9^1	8	5	0	1	8	5	16.4	4.82	66	.242	.405	0	—	0	-2	-2	0	-0.1
1964 SF-N	2	0	1.000	13	0	0	0	0	18^1	21	15	1	1	11	8	16.2	4.91	73	.296	.398	0	—	0	-3	-3	-0	-0.3
Total 2	2	0	1.000	19	0	0	0	1	27^2	29	20	1	2	19	13	16.3	4.88	70	.279	.400	0	—	0	-4	-4	-0	-0.4

● JIM PRENDERGAST
Prendergast, James Bartholomew b: 8/23/17, Brooklyn, N.Y. d: 8/23/94, Amherst, N.Y. BL/TL, 6'1", 208 lbs. Deb: 4/25/48

YEAR TM/L	W	L	PCT	G	GS	CG	SH	SV	IP	H	R	HR	HB	BB	SO	RAT	ERA	ERA+	OAV	OOB	BH	AVG	PB	PR	PR+	PD	TPI
1948 Bos-N	1	1	.500	10	2	0	0	1	16^2	30	20	1	0	5	3	18.9	10.26	37	.380	.417	0	.000	-1	-12	-12	0	-1.4

● MIKE PRENDERGAST
Prendergast, Michael Thomas b: 12/15/1888, Arlington, Ill. d: 11/18/67, Omaha, Neb. BR/TR, 5'9.5", 165 lbs. Deb: 4/26/14

YEAR TM/L	W	L	PCT	G	GS	CG	SH	SV	IP	H	R	HR	HB	BB	SO	RAT	ERA	ERA+	OAV	OOB	BH	AVG	PB	PR	PR+	PD	TPI
1914 Chi-F	5	9	.357	30	19	7	1	0	136	131	53	6	3	40	71	11.5	2.38	111	.255	.313	4	.108	-3	8	4	-2	0.0
1915 Chi-F	14	12	.538	42	30	16	3	0	253^2	220	93	6	4	67	95	10.3	2.48	101	.240	.295	6	.075	-9	7	1	-3	-1.1
1916 Chi-N	6	11	.353	35	10	4	2	2	152	127	53	5	1	23	56	8.9	2.31	126	.228	.260	7	.152	-2	5	9	-1	0.8
1917 Chi-N	3	6	.333	35	8	1	0	1	99^1	112	42	6	0	21	43	12.1	3.35	86	.302	.339	7	.250	1	-7	-5	-1	-0.4
1918 Phi-N	13	14	.481	33	30	20	0	1	252^1	257	102	6	1	46	41	10.8	2.89	104	.273	.308	7	.082	-8	-4	3	-2	-0.7
1919 Phi-N	0	1	.000	5	1	0	0	0	15	20	15	0	1	10	5	18.6	8.40	38	.351	.456	1	.333	0	-9	-8	0	-0.4
Total 6	41	53	.436	180	98	48	6	4	908^1	867	358	29	10	207	311	10.7	2.74	102	.258	.304	32	.115	-19	0	5	-8	-1.8

● GEORGE PRENTISS
Prentiss, George Pepper (a.k.a. George Pepper Wilson In 1901) b: 6/10/1876, Wilmington, Del. d: 9/8/02, Wilmington, Del. BB/TR, 5'11", 175 lbs. Deb: 9/23/01

YEAR TM/L	W	L	PCT	G	GS	CG	SH	SV	IP	H	R	HR	HB	BB	SO	RAT	ERA	ERA+	OAV	OOB	BH	AVG	PB	PR	PR+	PD	TPI
1901 Bos-A	1	0	1.000	2	1	1	0	0	10	7	4	0	0	6	0	11.7	1.80	196	.194	.310	1	.333	1	2	2	-0	0.2
1902 Bos-A	2	2	.500	7	4	3	0	0	41	55	31	0	0	10	9	14.3	5.27	68	.322	.359	5	.313	1	-8	-8	-0	-0.6
Bal-A	0	1	.000	2	2	0	0	0	6^2	14	10	1	0	5	1	25.7	10.80	35	.424	.500	0	.000	-1	-5	-5	-0	-0.6
Yr	2	3	.400	9	6	3	0	0	47^2	69	41	1	0	15	10	15.9	6.04	60	.338	.384	5	.250	-0	-13	-13	-0	-1.2
Total 2	3	3	.500	11	7	4	0	0	57^2	76	45	1	0	21	10	15.1	5.31	68	.317	.372	6	.261	1	-11	-11	-0	-1.0

● JOE PRESKO
Presko, Joseph Edward "Baby Joe" b: 10/7/28, Kansas City, Mo. BR/TR, 6', 170 lbs. Deb: 5/3/51

YEAR TM/L	W	L	PCT	G	GS	CG	SH	SV	IP	H	R	HR	HB	BB	SO	RAT	ERA	ERA+	OAV	OOB	BH	AVG	PB	PR	PR+	PD	TPI
1951 StL-N	7	4	.636	15	12	5	0	2	88^2	86	36	9	2	20	38	11.0	3.45	115	.251	.296	6	.162	-1	5	5	-1	0.4
1952 StL-N	7	10	.412	28	18	5	1	0	146^2	140	74	16	1	57	63	12.1	4.05	92	.247	.317	4	.093	-2	-5	-6	-1	-0.9
1953 StL-N	6	13	.316	34	25	4	0	1	161^2	165	95	19	5	65	56	13.1	5.01	85	.261	.335	13	.220	1	-13	-14	-1	-1.4
1954 StL-N	4	9	.308	37	6	1	1	0	71^2	97	56	14	5	41	36	18.0	6.91	60	.327	.417	4	.250	0	-23	-22	-0	-3.4
1957 Det-A	1	1	.500	7	0	0	0	0	11	10	3	0	1	4	3	12.3	1.64	236	.278	.366	0	.000	-0	3	3	-0	0.4
1958 Det-A	0	0	—	7	0	0	0	2	10^2	13	4	0	0	1	6	11.8	3.38	120	.317	.333	0	—	0	0	1	-0	0.1
Total 6	25	37	.403	128	61	15	2	5	490^1	511	268	58	14	188	202	13.1	4.61	87	.267	.337	27	.173	-1	-33	-33	-4	-4.8

● TOT PRESSNELL
Pressnell, Forest Charles b: 8/8/06, Findlay, Ohio BR/TR, 5'10", 175 lbs. Deb: 4/21/38

YEAR TM/L	W	L	PCT	G	GS	CG	SH	SV	IP	H	R	HR	HB	BB	SO	RAT	ERA	ERA+	OAV	OOB	BH	AVG	PB	PR	PR+	PD	TPI
1938 Bro-N	11	14	.440	43	19	6	1	3	192	209	86	11	8	56	57	12.8	3.56	110	.276	.332	9	.143	-1	5	7	-1	0.7
1939 Bro-N	9	7	.563	31	18	10	2	2	156^2	171	76	8	1	33	43	11.8	4.02	100	.273	.311	10	.196	-1	-2	0	0	-0.1
1940 Bro-N	6	5	.545	24	4	1	1	2	68^1	58	31	4	2	17	21	10.1	3.69	108	.221	.274	0	.000	-2	1	2	-1	0.0
1941 Chi-N	5	3	.625	29	1	0	0	1	70	69	26	2	4	23	27	12.3	3.09	114	.253	.320	3	.200	0	**4**	**3**	-1	0.3
1942 Chi-N	1	1	.500	27	0	0	0	4	39^1	40	28	5	5	5	9	11.4	5.49	58	.260	.305	2	.667	1	-10	-10	-0	-0.6
Total 5	32	30	.516	154	42	17	4	12	526^1	547	247	30	20	134	157	12.0	3.80	101	.264	.315	24	.161	-3	-1	3	-3	0.3

● JOE PRICE
Price, Joseph Walter b: 11/29/56, Inglewood, Cal. BR/TL, 6'4", 220 lbs. Deb: 6/14/80

YEAR TM/L	W	L	PCT	G	GS	CG	SH	SV	IP	H	R	HR	HB	BB	SO	RAT	ERA	ERA+	OAV	OOB	BH	AVG	PB	PR	PR+	PD	TPI
1980 Cin-N	7	3	.700	24	13	2	0	0	111^1	95	45	10	1	37	44	10.8	3.56	101	.236	.302	5	.128	-2	1	0	-1	-0.2
1981 Cin-N	6	1	.857	41	0	0	0	4	53^2	42	19	3	0	18	41	10.1	2.52	141	.222	.290	0	.000	-0	6	6	1	0.9
1982 Cin-N	3	4	.429	59	1	0	0	3	72^2	73	26	7	4	32	71	13.5	2.85	130	.263	.347	1	.333	0	6	7	-1	0.6
1983 Cin-N	10	6	.625	21	21	5	0	0	144	118	46	12	0	46	83	10.3	2.88	133	.225	.287	4	.098	-1	12	14	-0	1.4
1984 Cin-N	7	13	.350	30	30	3	1	0	171^2	176	91	19	2	61	129	12.5	4.19	90	.261	.324	7	.146	-1	-11	-7	-3	-1.1
1985 Cin-N	2	2	.500	26	8	0	0	1	64^2	59	35	10	0	23	52	11.4	3.90	97	.242	.307	0	.000	-1	-2	-1	-1	-0.3
1986 Cin-N	1	2	.333	25	2	0	0	0	41^2	49	30	5	0	22	30	15.3	5.40	72	.293	.376	1	.143	0	-8	-7	-1	-0.5
1987 *SF-N	2	2	.500	20	0	0	0	1	35	19	10	5	1	13	42	8.5	2.57	150	.154	.241	1	.167	-0	6	5	-1	0.5
1988 SF-N	1	6	.143	38	3	0	0	4	61^2	59	33	5	1	27	49	12.7	3.94	83	.249	.328	0	.000	-0	-3	-5	-0	-0.7
1989 SF-N	1	1	.500	7	1	0	0	0	14	16	9	3	0	4	10	12.9	5.79	58	.314	.364	0	.000	0	-4	-4	0	-0.5
Bos-A	2	5	.286	31	5	0	0	0	70^1	71	35	8	0	30	52	12.9	4.35	94	.262	.336	0	—	0	-4	-2	-1	-0.3
1990 Bal-A	3	4	.429	50	0	0	0	0	65^1	62	29	8	0	24	54	11.8	3.58	106	.253	.320	0	—	0	2	2	-0	0.1
Total 11	45	49	.479	372	84	10	1	13	906	839	408	95	9	337	657	11.8	3.65	103	.246	.316	19	.111	-5	1	9	-8	-0.1

● BILL PRICE
Price, William b: Philadelphia, Pa. Deb: 4/27/1890

YEAR TM/L	W	L	PCT	G	GS	CG	SH	SV	IP	H	R	HR	HB	BB	SO	RAT	ERA	ERA+	OAV	OOB	BH	AVG	PB	PR	PR+	PD	TPI
1890 Phi-a	1	0	1.000	1	1	1	0	0	9	6	3	0	1	7	1	14.0	2.00	194	.182	.341	1	.250	-0	2	2	0	0.2

● BOB PRIDDY
Priddy, Robert Simpson b: 12/10/39, Pittsburgh, Pa. BR/TR, 6'1", 200 lbs. Deb: 9/20/62

YEAR TM/L	W	L	PCT	G	GS	CG	SH	SV	IP	H	R	HR	HB	BB	SO	RAT	ERA	ERA+	OAV	OOB	BH	AVG	PB	PR	PR+	PD	TPI
1962 Pit-N	1	0	1.000	2	0	0	0	0	3	4	1	0	0	1	1	15.0	3.00	131	.308	.357	0	—	0	0	0	-0	0.0
1964 Pit-N	1	2	.333	19	0	0	0	1	34^1	35	16	2	1	15	23	13.4	3.93	89	.282	.364	0	.000	0	-2	-2	-1	-0.2
1965 SF-N	1	0	1.000	8	0	0	0	1	10^1	6	2	1	0	2	7	7.0	1.74	207	.176	.222	0	.000	-0	2	2	0	0.2
1966 SF-N	6	3	.667	38	3	0	0	1	91	88	45	8	3	28	51	11.8	3.96	93	.259	.321	3	.176	0	-4	-3	-1	-0.4
1967 Was-A	3	7	.300	46	8	1	0	4	110	98	48	12	0	33	57	10.7	3.44	92	.240	.297	4	.182	1	-3	-3	1	-0.1
1968 Chi-A	3	11	.214	35	18	2	0	0	114	106	50	14	4	41	66	11.9	3.63	83	.244	.315	1	.042	-1	-8	-8	-2	-1.2
1969 Chi-A	0	0	—	4	0	0	0	0	8	10	5	2	0	2	5	13.5	4.50	86	.303	.343	0	—	0	-1	-1	0	0.0
Cal-A	0	1	.000	15	0	0	0	0	26^1	24	14	4	0	7	15	10.6	4.78	73	.242	.292	0	.000	0	-3	-4	0	-0.2
Yr	0	1	.000	19	0	0	0	0	34^1	34	19	6	0	9	20	11.3	4.72	76	.258	.305	0	.000	0	-4	-4	0	-0.2
Atl-N	0	0	—	1	0	0	0	0	2	1	0	0	0	1	1	9.0	0.00	—	.143	.250	0	—	0	1	1	-0	0.0
1970 Atl-N	5	5	.500	41	0	0	0	8	73	75	46	9	3	24	32	12.6	5.42	79	.269	.333	3	.200	0	-11	-9	1	-1.2
1971 Atl-N	4	9	.308	40	0	0	0	4	64	71	36	8	1	44	36	16.3	4.22	88	.289	.399	2	.182	0	-5	-3	1	-0.6
Total 9	24	38	.387	249	29	3	0	18	536	518	263	60	12	198	294	12.2	4.00	88	.257	.327	13	.137	1	-33	-29	-2	-3.7

● EDDIE PRIEST
Priest, Eddie Lee b: 4/8/74, Boaz, Ala. BR/TL, 6'1", 200 lbs. Deb: 5/27/98

YEAR TM/L	W	L	PCT	G	GS	CG	SH	SV	IP	H	R	HR	HB	BB	SO	RAT	ERA	ERA+	OAV	OOB	BH	AVG	PB	PR	PR+	PD	TPI
1998 Cin-N	0	1	.000	2	2	0	0	0	6	12	8	2	0	1	1	19.5	10.50	41	.444	.464	0	.000	-0	-4	-4	-0	-0.6

● ARIEL PRIETO
Prieto, Ariel b: 10/22/69, Havana, Cuba BR/TR, 6'3", 225 lbs. Deb: 7/2/95

YEAR TM/L	W	L	PCT	G	GS	CG	SH	SV	IP	H	R	HR	HB	BB	SO	RAT	ERA	ERA+	OAV	OOB	BH	AVG	PB	PR	PR+	PD	TPI
1995 Oak-A	2	6	.250	14	9	1	0	0	58	57	35	4	5	32	37	14.6	4.97	90	.264	.372	0	—	0	-2	-3	-0	-0.4
1996 Oak-A	6	7	.462	21	21	2	0	0	125^2	130	66	9	7	54	75	13.7	4.15	119	.273	.356	0	—	0	12	11	0	1.0
1997 Oak-A	6	8	.429	22	22	0	0	0	125	155	84	16	5	70	90	16.6	5.04	90	.306	.396	0	—	0	-7	-7	0	-0.6
1998 Oak-A	0	1	.000	2	2	0	0	0	8^1	17	11	2	1	5	8	24.8	11.88	38	.415	.489	0	—	0	-7	-7	0	-0.6
2000 Oak-A	1	2	.333	8	6	0	0	0	31^2	42	21	3	1	13	19	15.9	5.12	93	.321	.386	0	.000	-0	-1	0	-0	-0.1
Total 5	15	24	.385	67	60	3	0	0	348^2	401	217	34	19	174	229	15.3	4.88	96	.293	.380	0	.000	-0	-4	-8	1	-0.7

● RAY PRIM
Prim, Raymond Lee "Pop" b: 12/30/06, Salitpa, Ala. d: 4/29/95, Monte Rio, Cal. BR/TL, 6', 178 lbs. Deb: 9/24/33

YEAR TM/L	W	L	PCT	G	GS	CG	SH	SV	IP	H	R	HR	HB	BB	SO	RAT	ERA	ERA+	OAV	OOB	BH	AVG	PB	PR	PR+	PD	TPI
1933 Was-A	0	1	.000	2	1	0	0	0	14^1	13	6	0	0	2	6	9.4	3.14	133	.232	.259	0	.000	-1	2	2	1	0.1
1934 Was-A	0	2	.000	8	2	0	0	0	14^2	19	11	1	0	8	3	16.6	6.75	64	.339	.422	0	.000	-0	-4	-4	0	-0.4
1935 Phi-N	3	4	.429	29	6	1	0	0	73^1	110	54	4	0	15	27	15.3	5.77	79	.340	.369	2	.083	-2	-14	-9	-0	-1.0
1943 Chi-N	4	3	.571	29	5	0	0	1	60	67	24	2	1	14	27	12.2	2.55	131	.282	.321	2	.167	-0	6	5	2	0.8
1945 *Chi-N	13	8	.619	34	19	9	2	2	165^1	142	58	9	0	23	88	**9.0**	2.40	**153**	**.228**	**.256**	13	.255	3	26	24	1	3.2
1946 Chi-N	2	3	.400	14	2	0	1	0	23^1	28	17	5	0	10	10	14.7	5.79	57	.289	.355	1	.200	0	-6	-7	1	-1.2
Total 6	22	21	.512	116	34	10	2	4	351	379	170	21	1	72	161	11.6	3.56	107	.272	.308	18	.180	-0	9	9	3	1.5

YEAR	TM/L	W	L	PCT	G	GS	CG	SH	SV	IP	H	R	HR	HB	BB	SO	RAT	ERA	ERA+	OAV	OOB	BH	AVG	PB	PR	PR+	PD	TPI
● DON PRINCE Prince, Donald Mark b: 4/5/38, Clarkton, N.C. BR/TR, 6'4", 200 lbs. Deb: 9/21/62																												
1962	Chi-N	0	0	—	1	0	0	0	0	1	0	0	0	1	1	0	18.0	0.00	—	.000	.500	0	—	0	0	0	0	0.0
● JIM PROCTOR Proctor, James Arthur b: 9/9/35, Brandywine, Md. BR/TR, 6', 165 lbs. Deb: 9/14/59																												
1959	Det-A	0	1	.000	2	1	0	0	0	2^2	8	5	0	0	3	0	37.1	16.88	24	.533	.611	0	—	0	-4	-4	0	-0.6
● RED PROCTOR Proctor, Noah Richard b: 10/27/1900, Williamsburg, Va. d: 12/17/54, Richmond, Va. BR/TR, 6'1", 165 lbs. Deb: 8/6/23																												
1923	Chi-A	0	0	—	2	0	0	0	0	4	11	8	0	0	2	0	29.3	13.50	29	.550	.591	0	—	0	-4	-4	-0	-0.2
● GEORGE PROESER Proeser, George "Yatz" b: 5/30/1864, Cincinnati, Ohio d: 10/13/41, New Burlington, O. BL/TL, 5'10", 190 lbs. Deb: 9/15/1888 ♦																												
1888	Cle-a	3	4	.429	7	7	7	1	0	59	53	39	4	7	30	20	13.7	3.81	81	.231	.338	7	.304	2	-5	-5	-1	-0.4
● LUKE PROKOPEC Prokopec, Kenneth Luke b: 2/23/78, Blackwood, Australia BL/TR, 5'11", 166 lbs. Deb: 9/4/2000																												
2000	LA-N	1	1	.500	5	3	0	0	0	21	19	10	2	2	9	12	12.9	3.00	146	.253	.349	0	.000	-1	4	3	0	0.2
● MIKE PROLY Proly, Michael James b: 12/15/50, Jamaica, N.Y. BR/TR, 6', 185 lbs. Deb: 4/10/76																												
1976	StL-N	1	0	1.000	14	0	0	0	0	17	21	9	0	0	6	4	14.3	3.71	96	.328	.386	0	—	0	-0	-0	0	0.0
1978	Chi-A	5	2	.714	14	6	2	0	1	65^2	63	24	4	0	12	19	10.3	2.74	139	.250	.284	0	—	0	8	8	-1	0.8
1979	Chi-A	3	8	.273	38	6	0	0	9	88^1	89	43	6	1	40	32	13.2	3.87	110	.260	.339	0	—	0	4	4	1	0.6
1980	Chi-A	5	10	.333	62	3	0	0	8	146^2	136	67	7	3	58	56	12.1	3.07	132	.253	.329	0	—	0	16	16	2	1.8
1981	Phi-N	2	1	.667	35	2	0	0	2	63	66	29	6	1	19	19	12.3	3.86	94	.282	.339	0	.000	-1	-3	-2	1	-0.1
1982	Chi-N	5	3	.625	44	1	0	0	1	82	77	22	5	2	22	24	11.1	2.30	162	.257	.312	4	.286	1	12	13	0	1.4
1983	Chi-N	1	5	.167	60	0	0	0	1	83	79	35	5	1	38	31	12.8	3.58	106	.259	.343	1	.091	-0	1	2	0	0.1
Total	7	22	29	.431	267	18	2	0	22	545^2	531	229	33	8	195	185	12.1	3.23	121	.261	.328	5	.156	-0	36	40	4	4.6
● BILL PROUGH Prough, Herschel Clinton "Clint" b: 11/28/1887, Markle, Ind. d: 12/29/36, Richmond, Ind. BR/TR, 6'3", 185 lbs. Deb: 4/27/12																												
1912	Cin-N	0	0	—	1	0	0	0	0	3	7	5	0	0	1	1	24.0	6.00	56	.538	.571	0	.000	-0	-1	-1	-0	-0.1
● AUGIE PRUDHOMME Prudhomme, John Olgus b: 11/20/02, Frierson, La. d: 10/4/92, Shreveport, La. BR/TR, 6'2", 186 lbs. Deb: 4/19/29																												
1929	Det-A	1	6	.143	34	6	2	0	1	94	119	78	7	2	53	26	16.7	6.22	69	.322	.410	5	.238	1	-21	-20	1	-1.1
● HUB PRUETT Pruett, Hubert Shelby "Shucks" b: 9/1/1900, Malden, Mo. d: 1/28/82, Ladue, Mo. BL/TL, 5'10.5", 165 lbs. Deb: 4/26/22																												
1922	StL-A	7	7	.500	39	8	4	0	7	119^2	99	48	2	5	59	70	12.3	2.33	178	.235	.336	5	.147	-1	23	24	2	2.9
1923	StL-A	4	7	.364	32	8	3	0	2	104^1	109	57	3	3	64	59	15.2	4.31	97	.279	.385	3	.130	-1	-4	-2	-0	-0.1
1924	StL-A	3	4	.429	33	1	0	0	0	65	64	42	1	4	42	27	15.2	4.57	99	.270	.389	3	.200	-1	-2	-0	1	0.0
1927	Phi-N	7	17	.292	31	28	12	1	1	186	238	147	6	12	89	90	16.4	6.05	68	.314	.395	13	.217	1	-44	-38	3	-3.7
1928	Phi-N	2	4	.333	13	9	4	0	0	71^1	78	49	2	3	49	35	16.4	4.54	94	.291	.406	5	.208	-0	-4	-2	0	-0.1
1930	NY-N	5	4	.556	45	8	1	0	3	135^2	152	83	11	4	63	49	14.5	4.78	99	.287	.367	5	.135	-1	3	-1	1	-0.1
1932	Bos-N	1	5	.167	18	7	4	0	0	63	76	42	3	6	30	27	16.0	5.14	73	.308	.396	2	.105	-1	-9	-10	2	-0.7
Total	7	29	48	.377	211	69	28	1	13	745	816	468	28	37	396	357	15.1	4.63	92	.286	.380	36	.170	-3	-38	-28	10	-1.8
● TEX PRUIETT Pruiett, Charles Le Roy b: 4/10/1883, Osgood, Ind. d: 3/6/53, Ventura, Cal. BL/TR, Deb: 4/26/07																												
1907	Bos-A	3	11	.214	35	17	6	2	3	173^2	166	77	1	8	59	54	12.1	3.11	83	.254	.323	8	.157	-1	-11	-10	1	-0.8
1908	Bos-A	1	7	.125	13	6	1	1	2	58^2	55	26	1	2	21	28	12.0	1.99	123	.275	.350	1	.063	-2	3	3	0	0.3
Total	2	4	18	.182	48	23	7	3	5	232^1	221	103	2	10	80	82	12.0	2.83	90	.259	.329	9	.134	-2	-8	-7	1	-0.5
● TROY PUCKETT Puckett, Troy Levi b: 12/10/1889, Winchester, Ind. d: 4/13/71, Winchester, Ind. BL/TR, 6'2", 186 lbs. Deb: 10/4/11																												
1911	Phi-N	0	0	—	1	0	0	0	0	2	4	3	0	1	2	1	31.5	13.50	26	.444	.583	0	—	0	-2	-2	0	-0.1
● MIGUEL PUENTE Puente, Miguel Antonio (Aguilar) b: 5/8/48, San Luis Potosi, Mex BR/TR, 6', 160 lbs. Deb: 5/3/70																												
1970	SF-N	1	3	.250	6	4	1	0	0	18^2	25	18	5	0	11	14	17.4	8.20	49	.325	.409	0	.000	-1	-9	-9	0	-1.5
● TIM PUGH Pugh, Timothy Dean b: 1/26/67, S.Lake Tahoe, Cal. BR/TR, 6'6", 230 lbs. Deb: 9/1/92																												
1992	Cin-N	4	2	.667	7	7	0	0	0	45^1	47	15	2	1	13	18	12.1	2.58	140	.276	.332	1	.077	-0	5	5	-0	0.6
1993	Cin-N	10	15	.400	31	27	3	1	0	164^1	200	102	19	7	59	94	14.6	5.26	77	.303	.366	12	.222	2	-22	-22	-0	-2.8
1994	Cin-N	3	3	.500	10	9	1	0	0	47^2	60	37	5	3	26	24	16.8	6.04	68	.314	.405	5	.357	2	-10	-10	0	-0.9
1995	Cin-N	6	5	.545	28	12	0	0	0	98^1	100	46	13	1	32	38	12.2	3.84	107	.266	.325	4	.143	0	4	3	-1	0.2
1996	Cin-N	1	0	1.000	9	0	0	0	0	15^1	20	18	3	1	11	9	18.8	10.57	40	.317	.427	0	—	0	-11	-11	1	-0.5
	KC-A	0	1	.000	19	1	0	0	0	36^1	42	24	9	2	12	27	13.9	5.45	92	.282	.344	0	—	0	-2	-2	0	-0.1
	Cin-N	0	1	.000	1	0	0	0	0	0^1	4	2	0	0	0	0	108.0	54.00	8	.800	.800	0	—	0	-2	-2	0	-0.3
1997	Det-A	1	1	.500	2	2	0	0	0	9	6	5	0	0	5	4	11.0	5.00	92	.188	.297	0	—	0	-0	-0	0	-0.1
Total	6	25	28	.472	107	58	4	1	0	416^2	479	249	51	15	158	214	14.1	4.97	83	.291	.358	22	.202	4	-38	-39	-1	-3.9
● CHARLIE PULEO Puleo, Charles Michael b: 2/7/55, Glen Ridge, N.J. BR/TR, 6'3", 200 lbs. Deb: 9/16/81																												
1981	NY-N	0	0	—	4	1	0	0	0	13^1	8	1	0	0	8	8	10.8	0.00	—	.182	.308	0	.000	-0	5	5	0	0.3
1982	NY-N	9	9	.500	36	24	1	1	1	171	179	99	13	2	90	98	14.3	4.47	81	.275	.364	6	.125	-1	-16	-16	3	-1.4
1983	Cin-N	6	12	.333	27	24	0	0	0	143^2	145	86	18	5	91	71	15.1	4.89	78	.269	.379	5	.100	-2	-20	-16	-2	-2.1
1984	Cin-N	1	2	.333	5	4	0	0	0	22	27	15	2	0	15	6	17.2	5.73	66	.297	.396	1	.200	0	-5	-5	-1	-0.6
1986	Atl-N	1	2	.333	5	3	1	0	0	24^1	13	10	4	1	12	18	9.6	2.96	135	.160	.277	2	.333	0	2	3	-0	0.3
1987	Atl-N	6	8	.429	35	16	1	0	0	123^1	122	63	11	3	40	99	12.0	4.23	103	.262	.325	5	.179	1	-2	2	-2	0.1
1988	Atl-N	5	5	.500	53	3	0	0	1	106^1	101	46	9	3	47	70	12.8	3.47	106	.251	.333	3	.231	0	-0	2	-0	0.2
1989	Atl-N	1	1	.500	15	1	0	0	0	29	26	15	2	0	16	17	13.0	4.66	79	.245	.344	0	.000	-0	-4	-3	-1	-0.3
Total	8	29	39	.426	180	76	3	1	2	633	621	335	59	14	319	387	13.6	4.25	90	.261	.351	22	.144	-1	-40	-28	-2	-3.5
● ALFONSO PULIDO Pulido, Alfonso (Manzo) b: 1/23/57, Veracruz, Mexico BL/TL, 5'11", 170 lbs. Deb: 9/5/83																												
1983	Pit-N	0	0	—	1	1	0	0	0	2	4	3	2	0	1	1	22.5	9.00	41	.400	.455	0	—	0	-1	-1	-0	-0.1
1984	Pit-N	0	0	—	1	0	0	0	0	2	3	2	0	0	1	2	18.0	9.00	40	.333	.400	0	—	0	-1	-1	-0	-0.1
1986	NY-A	1	1	.500	10	3	0	0	1	30^2	38	17	8	0	9	13	13.8	4.70	87	.306	.353	0	—	0	-2	-2	-0	-0.1
Total	3	1	1	.500	12	4	0	0	1	34^2	45	22	10	0	11	16	14.5	5.19	78	.315	.364	0	—	0	-4	-4	-0	-0.3
● CARLOS PULIDO Pulido, Juan Carlos (Valera) b: 8/5/71, Caracas, Venez. BL/TL, 6', 195 lbs. Deb: 4/9/94																												
1994	Min-A	3	7	.300	19	14	0	0	0	84^1	87	57	17	1	40	32	13.7	5.98	82	.273	.356	0	—	0	-11	-10	-1	-1.0
● BILL PULSIPHER Pulsipher, William Thomas b: 10/9/73, Fort Benning, Ga. BL/TL, 6'3", 210 lbs. Deb: 6/17/95																												
1995	NY-N	5	7	.417	17	17	2	0	0	126^2	122	58	11	4	45	81	12.2	3.98	102	.255	.324	4	.105	0	3	1	-0	0.1
1998	NY-N	0	0	—	15	1	0	0	0	14^1	23	11	2	0	5	13	17.6	6.91	60	.371	.418	0	.000	-0	-4	-5	1	-0.2
	Mil-N	3	4	.429	11	10	0	0	0	58	63	30	6	1	26	38	14.0	4.66	92	.289	.367	3	.158	-0	-3	-2	-1	-0.4
	Yr	3	4	.429	26	11	0	0	0	72^1	86	41	8	1	31	51	14.7	5.10	83	.307	.378	3	.150	-1	-7	-7	0	-0.6
1999	Mil-N	5	6	.455	19	16	0	0	0	87^1	100	65	19	2	36	42	14.2	5.98	76	.286	.356	3	.143	-1	-14	-14	1	-1.4
2000	NY-N	0	2	.000	2	2	0	0	0	6^2	12	9	1	1	6	7	25.7	12.15	36	.387	.500	0	.000	-0	-6	-6	0	-0.9
Total	4	13	19	.406	64	46	2	0	0	293	320	173	39	8	118	181	13.7	5.04	84	.281	.353	10	.123	-1	-23	-26	1	-2.8
● SPENCER PUMPELLY Pumpelly, Spencer Armstrong b: 4/11/1893, Owego, N.Y. d: 12/5/73, Sayre, Pa. TR, 5'11", 175 lbs. Deb: 7/11/25																												
1925	Was-A	0	0	—	1	0	0	0	0	1	1	1	1	0	1	0	18.0	9.00	47	.333	.500	0	—	0	-1	-1	-0	0.0
● BLONDIE PURCELL Purcell, William Aloysius b: Paterson, N.J. BR/TR, 5'9.5", 159 lbs. Deb: 5/1/1879 M♦																												
1879	Syr-N	4	15	.211	22	17	15	0	0	179^2	245	165	1		19	28	13.2	3.76	63	.303	.319	72	.260	3	-25	-29	-3	-2.4
	Cin-N	0	2	.000	2	2	2	0	0	18	27	15	0		2	3	14.5	4.00	58	.355	.372	11	.220	0	-3	-4	0	-0.3
	Yr	4	17	.190	24	19	17	0	0	197^2	272	180	1		21	31	13.3	3.78	63	.308	.324	83	.254	3	-28	-33	-2	-2.7
1880	Cin-N	3	17	.150	25	21	21	0	0	196	235	149	1		32	47	12.3	3.21	77	.271	.297	95	.292	4	-18	-15	-0	-0.9
1881	Buf-N	4	1	.800	9	5	5	0	0	61^2	62	37	2		9	15	10.4	2.77	100	.248	.274	33	.292	2	0	0	1	0.2
1882	Buf-N	2	1	.667	6	3	2	0	0	31	44	30	2		4	9	13.9	4.94	59	.338	.358	105	.276	1	-7	-7	1	-0.4
1883	Phi-N	2	6	.250	11	9	7	0	0	80	110	71	0		12	30	13.7	4.39	70	.306	.329	114	.268	2	-11	-12	1	-0.6

YEAR	TM/L	W	L	PCT	G	GS	CG	SH	SV	IP	H	R	HR	HB	BB	SO	RAT	ERA	ERA+	OAV	OOB	BH	AVG	PB	PR	PR+	PD	TPI
1884	Phi-N	0	0	—	1	0	0	0	0	4	3	1	0	0	0	1	6.8	2.25	133	.188	.188	108	.252	0	0	0	-0	0.0
1885	Phi-a	0	1	.000	1	0	0	0	0	6	11	9	0	0	2	3	19.5	6.00	57	.423	.464	90	.296	0	-2	-2	0	-0.2
1886	Bal-a	0	0	—	1	0	0	0	0	1	1	1	0	0	0	0	9.0	9.00	38	.200	.200	19	.224	0	-1	-1	0	0.0
1887	Bal-a	0	0	—	1	0	0	0	0	4	12	8	0	1	4	2	29.3	15.75	26	.480	.500	188	.307	0	-5	-5	-0	-0.2
Total	9	15	43	.259	79	57	52	0	0	581^1	750	486	6	1	84	138	12.9	3.73	70	.293	.314	1263	.274	12	-72	-73	-1	-4.8

● JOHN PURDIN Purdin, John Nolan b: 7/16/42, Lynx, Ohio BR/TR, 6'2", 185 lbs. Deb: 9/16/64

YEAR	TM/L	W	L	PCT	G	GS	CG	SH	SV	IP	H	R	HR	HB	BB	SO	RAT	ERA	ERA+	OAV	OOB	BH	AVG	PB	PR	PR+	PD	TPI
1964	LA-N	2	0	1.000	3	2	1	1	0	16	6	1	1	0	6	8	6.8	0.56	576	.115	.207	1	.200	0	5	5	-0	0.7
1965	LA-N	2	1	.667	11	2	0	0	0	22^2	26	19	8	0	13	16	15.5	6.75	48	.283	.371	0	.000	-0	-8	-10	-1	-1.2
1968	LA-N	2	3	.400	35	1	0	0	2	55^2	42	22	2	0	21	38	10.2	3.07	90	.206	.280	3	.500	1	-1	-2	-0	-0.1
1969	LA-N	0	0	—	9	0	0	0	0	16^1	19	11	7	0	12	6	17.1	6.06	55	.292	.403	0	.000	-0	-4	-5	0	-0.3
Total	4	6	4	.600	58	5	1	1	2	110^2	93	53	18	0	52	68	11.8	3.90	77	.225	.312	4	.250	1	-8	-12	-1	-0.9

● BOB PURKEY Purkey, Robert Thomas b: 7/14/29, Pittsburgh, Pa. BR/TR, 6'2", 195 lbs. Deb: 4/14/54

YEAR	TM/L	W	L	PCT	G	GS	CG	SH	SV	IP	H	R	HR	HB	BB	SO	RAT	ERA	ERA+	OAV	OOB	BH	AVG	PB	PR	PR+	PD	TPI
1954	Pit-N	3	8	.273	36	11	0	0	0	131^1	145	78	3	7	62	38	14.7	5.07	83	.293	.379	2	.077	-1	-15	-13	5	-0.5
1955	Pit-N	2	7	.222	14	10	2	0	1	67^2	77	47	5	2	25	24	13.8	5.32	77	.287	.353	6	.316	2	-10	-9	1	-0.8
1956	Pit-N	0	0	—	2	0	0	0	0	4	2	1	1	0	0	1	4.5	2.25	168	.143	.143	0	—	0	1	1	0	0.0
1957	Pit-N	11	14	.440	48	21	6	1	2	179^2	194	84	10	7	38	51	12.0	3.86	98	.278	.322	5	.111	-0	0	-1	-1	-0.2
1958	Cin-N☆	17	11	.607	37	34	17	3	0	250	259	106	25	4	49	70	11.2	3.60	115	.268	.306	9	.111	-2	10	14	2	1.5
1959	Cin-N	13	18	.419	38	33	9	1	1	218	241	118	25	6	43	78	12.0	4.25	95	.279	.318	11	.167	3	-7	-5	-0	-0.3
1960	Cin-N	17	11	.607	41	33	11	1	0	252^2	259	114	23	9	59	97	11.6	3.60	106	.265	.312	11	.133	-2	5	6	2	0.7
1961	*Cin-N★	16	12	.571	36	34	13	1	1	246^1	245	118	27	6	51	116	11.0	3.73	109	.255	.297	8	.100	-3	8	9	6	1.2
1962	Cin-N★	23	5	**.821**	37	37	18	2	0	288^1	260	109	28	14	64	141	10.6	2.81	143	.240	.291	11	.103	-2	36	**38**	3	3.5
1963	Cin-N	6	10	.375	21	21	4	1	0	137	143	60	12	2	33	55	11.7	3.55	94	.272	.318	4	.098	-1	-4	-3	1	-0.3
1964	Cin-N	11	9	.550	34	25	9	2	1	195^2	181	77	16	7	49	78	10.9	3.04	119	.246	.299	3	.052	-4	11	12	2	1.0
1965	StL-N	10	9	.526	32	17	3	1	2	124^1	148	83	20	7	33	39	13.6	5.79	66	.294	.346	1	.029	-3	-31	-25	1	-3.7
1966	Pit-N	0	1	.000	10	0	0	0	1	19^2	16	3	0	0	4	5	9.2	1.37	260	.235	.278	0	.000	-0	5	5	1	0.4
Total	13	129	115	.529	386	276	92	13	9	2114^2	2170	998	195	71	510	793	11.7	3.79	103	.266	.315	71	.110	-13	9	29	21	2.5

● OSCAR PURNER Purner, Oscar E. b: 12/9/1873, Washington, D.C. Deb: 9/2/1895

YEAR	TM/L	W	L	PCT	G	GS	CG	SH	SV	IP	H	R	HR	HB	BB	SO	RAT	ERA	ERA+	OAV	OOB	BH	AVG	PB	PR	PR+	PD	TPI
1895	Was-N	0	0	—	1	0	0	0	0	2	4	2	1	0	3	0	31.5	9.00	53	.400	.538	0	.000	-0	-1	-1	-0	-0.1

● AMBROSE PUTTMANN Puttmann, Ambrose Nicholas "Putty" or "Brose" b: 9/9/1880, Cincinnati, Ohio d: 6/21/36, Jamaica, N.Y. TL, 6'4", 185 lbs. Deb: 9/4/03

YEAR	TM/L	W	L	PCT	G	GS	CG	SH	SV	IP	H	R	HR	HB	BB	SO	RAT	ERA	ERA+	OAV	OOB	BH	AVG	PB	PR	PR+	PD	TPI
1903	NY-A	2	0	1.000	3	2	1	0	0	19	16	9	0	1	4	8	9.9	0.95	330	.229	.280	1	.143	-0	4	4	1	0.6
1904	NY-A	2	0	1.000	9	3	2	1	0	49^1	40	21	0	0	17	26	10.4	2.74	99	.222	.289	5	.278	2	-1	-0	0	0.2
1905	NY-A	2	7	.222	17	9	5	1	1	86^1	79	50	2	5	37	39	12.6	4.27	69	.245	.332	10	.313	3	-16	-12	-0	-1.0
1906	StL-N	2	2	.500	4	4	0	0	0	18^2	23	13	2	2	9	12	16.4	5.30	50	.303	.391	2	.333	0	-6	-6	0	-1.0
Total	4	8	9	.471	33	18	8	2	1	173^1	158	93	4	8	67	85	12.1	3.58	80	.244	.322	18	.286	4	-18	-13	1	-1.2

● JOHN PYECHA Pyecha, John Nicholas b: 11/25/31, Aliquippa, Pa. BR/TR, 6'5", 200 lbs. Deb: 4/24/54

YEAR	TM/L	W	L	PCT	G	GS	CG	SH	SV	IP	H	R	HR	HB	BB	SO	RAT	ERA	ERA+	OAV	OOB	BH	AVG	PB	PR	PR+	PD	TPI
1954	Chi-N	0	1	.000	1	0	0	0	0	2^2	4	3	1	0	2	2	20.3	10.13	41	.333	.429	0	.000	-0	-2	-2	-0	-0.3

● HARLAN PYLE Pyle, Harlan Albert "Firpo" b: 11/29/05, Burchard, Neb. d: 1/13/93, Beatrice, Neb. BR/TR, 6'2", 180 lbs. Deb: 9/21/28

YEAR	TM/L	W	L	PCT	G	GS	CG	SH	SV	IP	H	R	HR	HB	BB	SO	RAT	ERA	ERA+	OAV	OOB	BH	AVG	PB	PR	PR+	PD	TPI
1928	Cin-N	0	0	—	2	1	0	0	0	1^1	1	3	0	0	4	1	33.8	20.25	20	.143	.455	0	.000	-0	-2	-2	0	-0.1

● SHADOW PYLE Pyle, Harry Thomas b: 11/29/1861, Reading, Pa. d: 12/26/08, Reading, Pa. TL, 5'8", 136 lbs. Deb: 10/15/1884

YEAR	TM/L	W	L	PCT	G	GS	CG	SH	SV	IP	H	R	HR	HB	BB	SO	RAT	ERA	ERA+	OAV	OOB	BH	AVG	PB	PR	PR+	PD	TPI
1884	Phi-N	0	1	.000	1	1	1	0	0	9	9	8	0		6	4	15.0	4.00	75	.257	.366	0	.000	-1	-1	-1	-0	-0.2
1887	Chi-N	1	3	.250	4	4	3	0	0	26^2	53	27	1	2	21	5	18.6	4.73	95	.405	.414	3	.188	-0	-2	-1	1	0.0
Total	2	1	4	.200	5	5	4	0	0	35^2	62	35	1	2	27	9	17.7	4.54	90	.373	.402	3	.150	-1	-3	-2	1	-0.2

● EWALD PYLE Pyle, Herbert Ewald "Lefty" b: 8/27/10, St.Louis, Mo. BL/TL, 6'0.5", 175 lbs. Deb: 4/23/39

YEAR	TM/L	W	L	PCT	G	GS	CG	SH	SV	IP	H	R	HR	HB	BB	SO	RAT	ERA	ERA+	OAV	OOB	BH	AVG	PB	PR	PR+	PD	TPI
1939	StL-A	0	2	.000	6	1	0	0	0	8^1	17	15	3	0	11	5	30.2	12.96	38	.405	.528	0	.000	-0	-8	-7	1	-1.2
1942	StL-A	0	0	—	2	0	0	0	0	5^1	6	4	0	0	4	1	16.9	6.75	55	.286	.400	0	.000	-0	-2	-2	-0	-0.1
1943	Was-A	4	8	.333	18	11	2	1	1	72^2	70	38	0	1	45	25	14.4	4.09	78	.254	.360	2	.100	-1	-6	-7	-1	-1.4
1944	NY-N	7	10	.412	31	21	3	0	0	164	152	89	12	6	68	79	12.4	4.34	85	.241	.321	8	.157	-0	-13	-12	0	-1.1
1945	NY-N	0	0	—	6	1	0	0	0	6^1	16	12	0	0	4	2	28.4	17.05	23	.457	.513	0	.000	-0	-9	-9	1	-0.4
	Bos-N	0	1	.000	4	2	0	0	0	13^2	16	15	1	0	18	10	22.4	7.24	53	.302	.479	2	.333	1	-5	-5	-0	-0.3
	Yr	0	1	.000	10	3	0	0	0	20	32	27	1	0	22	12	24.3	10.35	37	.364	.491	2	.250	0	-15	-14	0	-0.7
Total	5	11	21	.344	67	36	5	1	1	270^1	277	173	16	7	150	122	14.4	5.03	71	.262	.357	12	.143	-2	-44	-43	-0	-4.5

● TOM QUALTERS Qualters, Thomas Francis "Money Bags" b: 4/1/35, McKeesport, Pa. BR/TR, 6'0.5", 190 lbs. Deb: 9/13/53

YEAR	TM/L	W	L	PCT	G	GS	CG	SH	SV	IP	H	R	HR	HB	BB	SO	RAT	ERA	ERA+	OAV	OOB	BH	AVG	PB	PR	PR+	PD	TPI
1953	Phi-N	0	0	—	1	0	0	0	0	0^1	4	6	1	1	1	0	162.0	162.00	3	.800	.857	0	—	0	-6	-6	0	-0.3
1957	Phi-N	0	0	—	6	0	0	0	0	7^1	12	6	0	0	4	6	19.6	7.36	52	.400	.471	0	—	0	-3	-3	0	-0.1
1958	Phi-N	0	0	—	1	0	0	0	0	2	2	1	0	0	0	0	13.5	4.50	88	.222	.300	0	—	0	-0	-0	-0	0.0
	Chi-A	0	0	—	26	0	0	0	0	43	45	22	1	0	20	14	13.6	4.19	87	.281	.361	0	.000	0	-2	-3	1	0.0
Total	3	0	0	—	34	0	0	0	0	52^2	63	35	2	1	26	20	15.4	5.64	65	.309	.390	0	.000	0	-11	-12	1	-0.4

● PAUL QUANTRILL Quantrill, Paul John b: 11/3/68, London, Ont., Canada BL/TR, 6'1", 185 lbs. Deb: 7/20/92

YEAR	TM/L	W	L	PCT	G	GS	CG	SH	SV	IP	H	R	HR	HB	BB	SO	RAT	ERA	ERA+	OAV	OOB	BH	AVG	PB	PR	PR+	PD	TPI
1992	Bos-A	2	3	.400	27	0	0	0	1	49^1	55	18	1	1	15	24	13.0	2.19	193	.288	.343	0	—	0	10	10	-0	1.0
1993	Bos-A	6	12	.333	49	14	1	1	1	138	151	73	13	2	44	66	12.8	3.91	118	.279	.335	0	—	0	6	10	-1	1.1
1994	Bos-A	1	1	.500	17	0	0	0	0	23	25	10	4	2	5	15	12.5	3.52	143	.278	.330	0	—	0	3	4	-0	0.2
	Phi-N	2	2	.500	18	1	0	0	1	30	39	21	3	3	10	13	15.6	6.00	72	.331	.397	0	.000	-0	-6	-6	0	-0.7
1995	Phi-N	11	12	.478	33	29	0	0	0	179^1	212	102	20	6	44	103	13.1	4.67	91	.295	.341	6	.105	-2	-10	-9	1	-1.1
1996	Tor-A	5	14	.263	38	20	0	0	0	134^1	172	90	27	2	51	86	15.1	5.43	92	.316	.377	0	—	0	-6	-6	1	-0.7
1997	Tor-A	6	7	.462	77	0	0	0	5	88	103	25	5	1	17	56	12.4	1.94	236	.297	.332	0	.000	-0	**26**	**26**	1	3.7
1998	Tor-A	3	4	.429	82	0	0	0	7	80	88	26	5	3	22	59	12.7	2.59	180	.285	.338	0	—	0	18	18	1	1.7
1999	Tor-A	3	2	.600	41	0	0	0	0	48^2	53	19	5	4	17	28	13.7	3.33	148	.282	.354	0	—	0	8	9	1	0.8
2000	Tor-A	2	5	.286	68	0	0	0	1	83^2	100	45	7	2	25	47	13.7	4.52	110	.298	.350	0	—	0	4	4	-1	0.3
Total	9	41	62	.398	450	64	1	1	16	854^1	998	429	90	26	250	497	13.4	3.97	117	.295	.348	6	.098	-2	54	62	2	6.3

● BILL QUARLES Quarles, William H. b: 1869, Petersburg, Va. d: 3/25/1897, Petersburg, Va. 6'3", Deb: 5/21/1891

YEAR	TM/L	W	L	PCT	G	GS	CG	SH	SV	IP	H	R	HR	HB	BB	SO	RAT	ERA	ERA+	OAV	OOB	BH	AVG	PB	PR	PR+	PD	TPI
1891	Was-a	1	1	.500	3	2	2	0	0	22	32	27	1	2	12	10	18.8	8.18	46	.330	.414	0	.000	-2	-11	-11	-0	-0.8
1893	Bos-N	2	1	.667	3	3	3	0	0	27	31	20	2	2	5	6	12.7	4.67	106	.279	.322	2	.222	0	-0	1	-0	0.0
Total	2	3	2	.600	6	5	5	0	0	49	63	47	3	4	17	16	15.4	6.24	70	.303	.367	2	.100	-2	-11	-10	-1	-0.8

● MEL QUEEN Queen, Melvin Douglas b: 3/26/42, Johnson City, N.Y. BL/TR, 6'1", 197 lbs. Deb: 4/13/64 FMC◆

YEAR	TM/L	W	L	PCT	G	GS	CG	SH	SV	IP	H	R	HR	HB	BB	SO	RAT	ERA	ERA+	OAV	OOB	BH	AVG	PB	PR	PR+	PD	TPI
1966	Cin-N	0	0	—	7	0	0	0	0	7	11	5	0	0	6	9	21.9	6.43	61	.367	.472	7	.127	0	-2	-2	0	-0.1
1967	Cin-N	14	8	.636	31	24	6	2	0	195^2	155	69	17	6	52	154	9.8	2.76	136	.215	.273	17	.210	3	13	19	-2	2.3
1968	Cin-N	0	1	.000	5	4	0	0	0	18^1	25	15	7	0	6	20	15.2	5.89	54	.333	.383	1	.125	0	-6	-5	0	-0.3
1969	Cin-N	1	0	1.000	2	2	0	0	0	12	7	3	2	1	3	7	8.3	2.25	167	.163	.234	1	.167	-0	2	2	-0	0.1
1970	Cal-A	3	6	.333	34	3	0	0	9	60	58	28	5	5	28	44	13.7	4.20	86	.261	.357	4	.250	1	-3	-4	-1	-0.7
1971	Cal-A	2	2	.500	44	0	0	0	4	65^2	49	17	3	8	29	53	11.8	1.78	182	.212	.321	0	.000	-1	12	11	-1	0.7
1972	Cal-A	0	0	—	17	0	0	0	0	31	31	17	2	3	19	19	15.4	4.35	67	.265	.381	0	.000	-0	-4	-5	-0	-0.3
Total	7	20	17	.541	140	33	6	2	14	389^2	336	154	36	23	143	306	11.6	3.14	113	.233	.313	49	.179	3	12	17	-4	1.7

● MEL QUEEN Queen, Melvin Joseph b: 3/4/18, Maxwell, Pa. d: 4/4/82, Fort Smith, Ark. BR/TR, 6'0.5", 204 lbs. Deb: 4/18/42 F

YEAR	TM/L	W	L	PCT	G	GS	CG	SH	SV	IP	H	R	HR	HB	BB	SO	RAT	ERA	ERA+	OAV	OOB	BH	AVG	PB	PR	PR+	PD	TPI
1942	NY-A	1	0	1.000	4	0	0	0	0	5^2	6	0	0	2	3	0	17.5	0.00	—	.300	.440	0	—	0	2	2	0	0.4
1944	NY-A	6	3	.667	10	10	4	1	0	81^2	68	32	7	1	34	30	11.4	3.31	105	.227	.308	6	.194	0	1	2	-2	0.0
1946	NY-A	1	1	.500	14	3	1	0	0	30^1	40	28	2	0	21	26	18.1	6.53	53	.315	.412	1	.143	-0	-10	-11	-0	-0.7
1947	NY-A	0	0	—	5	0	0	0	0	6^2	9	7	2	1	4	2	18.9	9.45	37	.321	.424	0	.000	-0	-4	-5	-0	-0.3
	Pit-N	3	7	.300	14	12	2	0	0	74	70	39	8	1	51	34	14.8	4.01	105	.244	.360	2	.077	-2	0	2	-1	-0.1

YEAR	TM/L	W	L	PCT	G	GS	CG	SH	SV	IP	H	R	HR	HB	BB	SO	RAT	ERA	ERA+	OAV	OOB	BH	AVG	PB	PR	PR+	PD	TPI
1948	Pit-N	4	4	.500	25	8	0	0	1	66^1	82	51	8	3	40	34	17.0	6.65	61	.308	.405	1	.059	-2	-20	-18	-1	-2.2
1950	Pit-N	5	14	.263	33	21	4	1	0	120^1	135	95	18	2	73	76	15.7	5.98	73	.284	.381	2	.057	-3	-25	-20	-1	-3.1
1951	Pit-N	7	9	.438	39	21	4	1	0	168^1	149	90	21	1	99	123	13.3	4.44	95	.233	.337	5	.106	-3	-9	-4	-3	-0.9
1952	Pit-N	0	2	.000	2	2	0	0	0	3^1	8	12	2	0	4	3	32.4	29.70	13	.381	.480	0	—	0	-10	-9	-0	-1.3
Total	8	27	40	.403	146	77	15	3	1	556^2	567	354	68	11	329	328	14.7	5.09	80	.262	.362	17	.104	-10	-74	-61	-9	-8.2

● RUBEN QUEVEDO Quevedo, Ruben Eduardo b: 1/5/79, Valencia, Venez. BR/TR, 6'1", 190 lbs. Deb: 4/14/2000

YEAR	TM/L	W	L	PCT	G	GS	CG	SH	SV	IP	H	R	HR	HB	BB	SO	RAT	ERA	ERA+	OAV	OOB	BH	AVG	PB	PR	PR+	PD	TPI
2000	Chi-N	3	10	.231	21	15	1	0	0	88	96	81	21	3	54	65	15.6	7.47	61	.271	.372	4	.133	-1	-28	-29	-0	-3.4

● EDDIE QUICK Quick, Edward b: 12/1881, Baltimore, Md. d: 6/19/13, Rocky Ford, Colo. TR, 5'11", Deb: 9/28/03

YEAR	TM/L	W	L	PCT	G	GS	CG	SH	SV	IP	H	R	HR	HB	BB	SO	RAT	ERA	ERA+	OAV	OOB	BH	AVG	PB	PR	PR+	PD	TPI
1903	NY-A	0	0	—	1	1	0	0	0	2	5	5	0	0	1	0	27.0	9.00	35	.455	.500	0	.000	-0	-1	-1	0	-0.1

● TAD QUINN Quinn, Clarence Carr b: 9/21/1882, Torrington, Conn. d: 8/6/46, Waterbury, Conn. TR, 6'1", 210 lbs. Deb: 9/27/02

YEAR	TM/L	W	L	PCT	G	GS	CG	SH	SV	IP	H	R	HR	HB	BB	SO	RAT	ERA	ERA+	OAV	OOB	BH	AVG	PB	PR	PR+	PD	TPI
1902	Phi-A	0	1	.000	1	1	1	0	0	8	12	9	1	0	1	3	14.6	4.50	82	.343	.361	0	.000	-0	-1	-1	-0	-0.1
1903	Phi-A	0	0	—	2	0	0	0	0	9	11	6	0	1	5	1	17.0	5.00	61	.297	.395	2	.667	1	-2	-2	1	0.1
Total	2	0	1	.000	3	1	1	0	0	17	23	15	1	1	6	4	15.9	4.76	70	.319	.380	2	.333	1	-3	-3	0	0.0

● FRANK QUINN Quinn, Frank William b: 11/27/27, Springfield, Mass. d: 1/11/93, Boynton Beach, Fla. BR/TR, 6'2", 180 lbs. Deb: 5/29/49

YEAR	TM/L	W	L	PCT	G	GS	CG	SH	SV	IP	H	R	HR	HB	BB	SO	RAT	ERA	ERA+	OAV	OOB	BH	AVG	PB	PR	PR+	PD	TPI
1949	Bos-A	0	0	—	8	0	0	0	0	22	18	7	2	1	9	4	11.5	2.86	152	.222	.308	1	.167	-0	3	4	-0	0.1
1950	Bos-A	0	0	—	1	0	0	0	0	2	2	2	0	0	1	0	13.5	9.00	54	.250	.333	0	—	0	-1	-1	0	0.0
Total	2	0	0	—	9	0	0	0	0	24	20	9	2	1	10	4	11.6	3.38	131	.225	.310	1	.167	-0	2	3	0	0.1

● JACK QUINN Quinn, John Picus (b: John Quinn Picus) b: 7/5/1883, Janesville, Pa. d: 4/17/46, Pottsville, Pa. BR/TR, 6', 196 lbs. Deb: 4/15/09

YEAR	TM/L	W	L	PCT	G	GS	CG	SH	SV	IP	H	R	HR	HB	BB	SO	RAT	ERA	ERA+	OAV	OOB	BH	AVG	PB	PR	PR+	PD	TPI
1909	NY-A	9	5	.643	23	11	8	0	1	118^2	110	45	1	4	24	36	10.5	1.97	128	.252	.297	7	.156	0	7	7	3	1.3
1910	NY-A	18	12	.600	35	31	20	0	0	235^2	214	88	2	6	58	82	10.6	2.37	112	.247	.299	19	.232	4	4	7	7	2.1
1911	NY-A	8	10	.444	40	16	7	0	2	174^2	203	111	2	4	41	71	12.8	3.76	96	.297	.341	10	.164	-1	-8	-3	3	-0.1
1912	NY-A	5	7	.417	18	11	7	0	0	102^2	139	89	4	4	23	47	14.6	5.79	62	.325	.365	8	.205	-1	-28	-23	2	-2.1
1913	Bos-N	4	3	.571	8	7	6	1	0	56^1	55	22	1	1	7	33	10.1	2.40	137	.261	.288	4	.200	1	5	5	2	1.1
1914	Bal-F	26	14	.650	46	42	27	4	1	342^2	335	129	3	8	65	164	10.7	2.60	117	.266	.307	33	.273	6	11	16	1	2.6
1915	Bal-F	9	22	.290	44	31	21	0	1	273^2	289	137	9	8	63	118	11.8	3.45	83	.278	.325	29	.264	3	-22	-17	3	-1.1
1918	Chi-A	5	1	.833	6	5	5	0	0	51	38	13	0	0	7	22	7.9	2.29	119	.216	.246	4	.222	1	3	3	0	0.5
1919	NY-A	15	14	.517	38	31	18	4	0	266	242	96	8	6	65	97	10.6	2.61	123	.244	.295	19	.209	1	18	18	1	2.0
1920	NY-A	18	10	.643	41	32	17	2	3	253^1	271	110	8	2	48	101	11.4	3.20	119	.273	.308	8	.091	-5	17	17	3	1.5
1921	*NY-A	8	7	.533	33	13	6	0	0	119	158	61	2	5	32	44	14.7	3.78	112	.327	.375	9	.220	1	7	6	1	0.8
1922	Bos-A	13	16	.448	40	32	16	4	0	256	263	119	9	3	59	67	11.4	3.48	118	.267	.311	9	.099	-5	16	18	5	1.8
1923	Bos-A	13	17	.433	42	28	16	1	7	243	302	125	6	6	53	71	13.4	3.89	106	.316	.356	18	.225	0	3	6	-1	0.6
1924	Bos-A	12	13	.480	44	25	13	2	7	228^2	241	109	10	12	52	64	12.0	3.27	134	.273	.322	14	.179	-4	24	27	4	2.8
1925	Bos-A	7	8	.467	19	15	8	0	0	105	140	68	3	3	26	24	14.5	4.37	104	.315	.357	3	.094	-2	0	2	2	0.2
	Phi-A	6	3	.667	18	13	4	0	0	99^2	119	56	3	3	16	19	12.5	3.88	120	.296	.328	3	.097	-3	6	8	1	0.5
	Yr	13	11	.542	37	28	12	0	0	204^2	259	124	6	6	42	43	13.5	4.13	111	.306	.343	6	.095	-5	6	10	3	0.7
1926	Phi-A	10	11	.476	31	21	8	3	1	163^2	191	74	4	1	36	58	12.5	3.41	122	.296	.334	8	.174	-0	11	13	1	1.6
1927	Phi-A	15	10	.600	34	26	11	3	1	201^1	211	82	8	4	37	43	11.3	3.26	131	.273	.315	6	.091	-7	20	22	-1	1.6
1928	Phi-A	18	7	.720	31	28	18	4	1	211^1	239	92	3	7	34	43	11.9	2.90	139	.286	.320	13	.165	-3	27	26	1	2.6
1929	*Phi-A	11	9	.550	35	18	7	0	2	161	182	87	8	1	39	41	12.4	3.97	107	.290	.332	8	.133	-4	5	5	0	0.1
1930	*Phi-A	9	7	.563	35	6	7	0	6	89^2	109	51	6	1	22	28	13.2	4.42	106	.302	.344	9	.265	1	**2**	**3**	2	0.6
1931	Bro-N	5	4	.556	39	1	0	0	**15**	64^1	65	28	1	1	24	25	12.6	2.66	143	.266	.335	3	.200	0	9	8	1	1.6
1932	Bro-N	3	7	.300	42	0	0	0	**8**	87^1	102	36	1	1	24	28	13.1	3.30	116	.296	.343	4	.200	0	**6**	**5**	0	0.7
1933	Cin-N	0	1	.000	14	0	0	0	1	15^2	20	9	0	0	5	3	14.4	4.02	84	.323	.373	0	.000	-0	-1	-1	1	0.0
Total	23	247	218	.531	756	443	243	28	57	3920^1	4238	1837	102	91	860	1329	11.9	3.29	113	.280	.323	248	.184	-16	140	177	40	23.3

● WIMPY QUINN Quinn, Wellington Hunt b: 5/12/18, Birmingham, Ala. d: 9/1/54, Santa Monica, Cal. BR/TR, 6'2", 187 lbs. Deb: 6/8/41

YEAR	TM/L	W	L	PCT	G	GS	CG	SH	SV	IP	H	R	HR	HB	BB	SO	RAT	ERA	ERA+	OAV	OOB	BH	AVG	PB	PR	PR+	PD	TPI
1941	Chi-N	0	0	—	3	0	0	0	0	5	3	4	0	0	3	2	10.8	7.20	49	.158	.273	1	.500	0	-2	-2	-0	-0.1

● LUIS QUINTANA Quintana, Luis Joaquin (Santos) b: 12/25/51, Vega Baja, P.R. BL/TL, 6'2", 175 lbs. Deb: 7/9/74

YEAR	TM/L	W	L	PCT	G	GS	CG	SH	SV	IP	H	R	HR	HB	BB	SO	RAT	ERA	ERA+	OAV	OOB	BH	AVG	PB	PR	PR+	PD	TPI
1974	Cal-A	2	1	.667	18	0	0	0	0	12^2	17	6	0	0	14	11	22.0	4.26	81	.327	.470	0	—	0	-1	-1	-0	-0.3
1975	Cal-A	0	2	.000	4	0	0	0	0	7	13	6	2	0	6	5	24.4	6.43	55	.394	.487	0	—	0	-2	-2	-0	-0.5
Total	2	2	3	.400	22	0	0	0	0	19^2	30	12	2	0	20	16	22.9	5.03	69	.353	.476	0	—	0	-3	-4	-0	-0.8

● RAFAEL QUIRICO Quirico, Rafael Octavio (Dottin) b: 9/7/69, Santo Domingo, D.R. BL/TL, 6'3", 170 lbs. Deb: 6/25/96

YEAR	TM/L	W	L	PCT	G	GS	CG	SH	SV	IP	H	R	HR	HB	BB	SO	RAT	ERA	ERA+	OAV	OOB	BH	AVG	PB	PR	PR+	PD	TPI
1996	Phi-N	0	1	.000	1	1	0	0	0	1^2	4	7	1	0	5	1	48.6	37.80	11	.444	.643	0	—	0	-6	-6	0	-0.8

● ART QUIRK Quirk, Arthur Lincoln b: 4/11/38, Providence, R.I. BR/TL, 5'11", 170 lbs. Deb: 4/17/62

YEAR	TM/L	W	L	PCT	G	GS	CG	SH	SV	IP	H	R	HR	HB	BB	SO	RAT	ERA	ERA+	OAV	OOB	BH	AVG	PB	PR	PR+	PD	TPI
1962	Bal-A	2	2	.500	7	5	0	0	0	27^1	36	20	3	0	18	18	17.8	5.93	62	.308	.400	1	.143	0	-6	-7	1	-0.8
1963	Was-A	1	0	1.000	7	3	0	0	0	21	23	13	3	0	8	12	13.3	4.29	87	.280	.344	1	.250	0	-2	-1	-0	-0.1
Total	2	3	2	.600	14	8	0	0	0	48^1	59	33	6	0	26	30	15.8	5.21	71	.296	.378	2	.182	0	-7	-8	0	-0.9

● DAN QUISENBERRY Quisenberry, Daniel Raymond b: 2/7/53, Santa Monica, Cal. d: 9/30/98, Leawood, Kan. BR/TR, 6'2", 180 lbs. Deb: 7/8/79

YEAR	TM/L	W	L	PCT	G	GS	CG	SH	SV	IP	H	R	HR	HB	BB	SO	RAT	ERA	ERA+	OAV	OOB	BH	AVG	PB	PR	PR+	PD	TPI
1979	KC-A	3	2	.600	32	0	0	0	5	40	42	16	5	0	7	13	11.0	3.15	136	.278	.310	0	—	0	5	5	1	0.7
1980	*KC-A	12	7	.632	**75**	0	0	0	**33**	128^1	129	47	5	1	27	37	11.0	3.09	132	.265	.305	0	—	0	14	14	3	3.0
1981	*KC-A	1	4	.200	40	0	0	0	18	62^1	59	16	1	1	15	20	10.8	1.73	208	.258	.306	0	—	0	13	13	3	2.3
1982	KC-A★	9	7	.563	72	0	0	0	**35**	136^2	126	43	12	0	12	46	9.1	2.57	159	.252	.270	0	—	0	23	23	6	**4.5**
1983	KC-A★	5	3	.625	**69**	0	0	0	**45**	139	118	35	6	0	11	48	8.4	1.94	211	.229	.245	0	—	0	**33**	**33**	2	4.2
1984	*KC-A☆	6	3	.667	72	0	0	0	**44**	129^1	121	39	10	0	12	41	9.3	2.64	153	.247	.265	0	—	0	19	20	3	2.9
1985	*KC-A	8	9	.471	**84**	0	0	0	**37**	129	142	41	8	1	16	54	11.1	2.37	175	.280	.303	0	—	0	25	26	1	4.6
1986	KC-A	3	7	.300	62	0	0	0	12	81^1	92	30	2	3	24	36	13.2	2.77	154	.291	.347	0	—	0	13	13	2	2.1
1987	KC-A	4	1	.800	47	0	0	0	8	49	58	15	3	1	10	17	12.7	2.76	166	.287	.324	0	—	0	9	10	2	1.3
1988	KC-A	0	1	.000	20	0	0	0	1	25^1	32	11	0	0	5	9	13.1	3.55	112	.305	.336	0	—	0	1	1	1	0.2
	StL-N	2	0	1.000	33	0	0	0	0	38	54	26	4	0	6	19	14.2	6.16	57	.344	.368	0	.000	0	-11	-11	0	-0.5
1989	StL-N	3	1	.750	63	0	0	0	6	78^1	78	25	2	0	14	37	10.6	2.64	138	.261	.294	1	.250	0	7	8	2	0.8
1990	SF-N	0	1	.000	5	0	0	0	0	6^2	13	12	1	0	3	2	21.6	13.50	27	.419	.471	0	.000	-0	-7	-8	-0	-1.0
Total	12	56	46	.549	674	0	0	0	244	1043^1	1064	356	59	7	162	379	10.6	2.76	146	.267	.297	1	.167	0	145	147	25	25.1

● CHARLIE RABE Rabe, Charles Henry b: 5/6/32, Boyce, Tex. BL/TL, 6'1", 180 lbs. Deb: 9/21/57

YEAR	TM/L	W	L	PCT	G	GS	CG	SH	SV	IP	H	R	HR	HB	BB	SO	RAT	ERA	ERA+	OAV	OOB	BH	AVG	PB	PR	PR+	PD	TPI
1957	Cin-N	0	1	.000	2	1	0	0	0	8^1	5	2	2	0	0	6	5.4	2.16	190	.167	.167	0	.000	-0	2	2	-0	0.1
1958	Cin-N	0	3	.000	9	1	0	0	0	18^2	25	10	3	0	9	10	16.4	4.34	96	.321	.391	0	.000	-1	-1	-0	0	-0.1
Total	2	0	4	.000	11	2	0	0	0	27	30	12	5	0	9	16	13.0	3.67	113	.278	.333	0	.000	-1	1	1	0	0.0

● STEVE RACHUNOK Rachunok, Stephen Stepanovich "The Mad Russian" b: 12/5/16, Rittman, Ohio BR/TR, 6'4.5", 205 lbs. Deb: 9/17/40

YEAR	TM/L	W	L	PCT	G	GS	CG	SH	SV	IP	H	R	HR	HB	BB	SO	RAT	ERA	ERA+	OAV	OOB	BH	AVG	PB	PR	PR+	PD	TPI
1940	Bro-N	0	1	.000	2	1	1	0	0	10	9	5	0	0	5	10	12.6	4.50	89	.243	.333	0	.000	0	-1	-1	0	0.0

● MIKE RACZKA Raczka, Michael b: 11/16/62, New Britain, Conn. BL/TL, 6', 200 lbs. Deb: 8/15/92

YEAR	TM/L	W	L	PCT	G	GS	CG	SH	SV	IP	H	R	HR	HB	BB	SO	RAT	ERA	ERA+	OAV	OOB	BH	AVG	PB	PR	PR+	PD	TPI
1992	Oak-A	0	0	—	8	0	0	0	0	6^1	8	7	0	0	5	2	18.5	8.53	44	.308	.419	0	—	0	-3	-4	-0	-0.2

● DICK RADATZ Radatz, Richard Raymond "The Monster" b: 4/2/37, Detroit, Mich. BR/TR, 6'5", 235 lbs. Deb: 4/10/62

YEAR	TM/L	W	L	PCT	G	GS	CG	SH	SV	IP	H	R	HR	HB	BB	SO	RAT	ERA	ERA+	OAV	OOB	BH	AVG	PB	PR	PR+	PD	TPI
1962	Bos-A	9	6	.600	**62**	0	0	0	**24**	124^2	95	32	9	4	40	144	10.0	2.24	184	.211	.281	3	.097	-2	**24**	**25**	-2	3.6
1963	Bos-A★	15	6	.714	66	0	0	0	25	132^1	94	31	9	5	51	162	10.2	1.97	192	.201	.286	2	.069	-2	**24**	**26**	-2	**4.8**
1964	Bos-A★	16	9	.640	79	0	0	0	**29**	157	103	44	13	7	58	181	9.6	2.29	168	.186	.271	6	.162	-0	23	26	-2	4.8
1965	Bos-A	9	11	.450	63	0	0	0	22	124^1	104	57	11	5	53	121	11.7	3.91	95	.227	.314	5	.185	1	-6	-2	-1	-0.4
1966	Bos-A	0	2	.000	16	0	0	0	4	19	24	10	3	0	11	19	16.6	4.74	80	.304	.389	0	.000	-0	-3	-2	-1	-0.3
	Cle-A	0	3	.000	39	0	0	0	10	56^2	49	33	6	3	34	49	13.7	4.61	75	.233	.348	1	.111	-0	-7	-7	-1	-0.8
	Yr	0	5	.000	55	0	0	0	14	75^2	73	43	9	3	45	68	14.4	4.64	76	.253	.359	1	.091	-1	-10	-9	-2	-1.1
1967	Cle-A	0	0	—	3	0	0	0	0	3	5	2	1	0	2	1	21.0	6.00	54	.357	.438	0	—	0	-1	-1	-0	-0.1

YEAR	TM/L	W	L	PCT	G	GS	CG	SH	SV	IP	H	R	HR	HB	BB	SO	RAT	ERA	ERA+	OAV	OOB	BH	AVG	PB	PR	PR+	PD	TPI
	Chi-N	1	0	1.000	20	0	0	0	5	23^{1}	12	21	4	5	24	18	15.8	6.56	54	.154	.383	1	.250	0	-8	-7	-0	-0.7
1969	Det-A	2	2	.500	11	0	0	0	0	18^{2}	14	8	3	0	5	18	9.2	3.38	111	.212	.268	0	.000	-0	1	1	0	0.1
	Mon-N	0	4	.000	22	0	0	0	3	34^{2}	32	22	6	1	18	32	13.2	5.71	64	.244	.340	1	.250	0	-8	-8	-1	-1.0
Total	7	52	43	.547	381	0	0	0	122	693^{2}	532	260	65	30	296	745	11.1	3.13	122	.212	.303	19	.131	-3	38	50	-9	10.0
● CHARLEY RADBOURN Radbourn, Charles Gardner "Old Hoss" b: 12/11/1854, Rochester, N.Y. d: 2/5/1897, Bloomington, Ill. BR/TR (BB 1886 (part)), 5'9", 168 lbs. Deb: 5/5/1880 H ◆																												
1881	Pro-N	25	11	**.694**	41	36	34	3	0	325^{1}	309	162	1		64	117	10.3	2.43	109	**.235**	.270	59	.219	-1	12	8	3	0.9
1882	Pro-N	33	19	.635	54	51	50	**6**	0	466	422	213	6		51	**201**	9.1	2.11	134	.226	.247	78	.239	-1	**41**	**38**	1	**3.4**
1883	Pro-N	**48**	25	.658	**76**	68	66	4	1	632^{1}	563	275	7		56	315	**8.8**	2.05	151	.227	**.244**	108	.283	14	**76**	**74**	5	**8.5**
1884	*Pro-N	**59**	12	**.831**	**75**	73	**73**	11	1	**678^{2}**	528	216	18		98	**441**	8.3	**1.38**	**206**	.205	.234	83	.230	5	121	116	-4	**10.4**
1885	Pro-N	28	21	.571	49	49	49	2	0	445^{2}	423	209	4		83	154	10.2	2.20	122	.241	.275	58	.233	11	31	25	4	3.8
1886	Bos-N	27	31	.466	58	58	57	3	0	509^{1}	521	300	18		111	218	11.2	3.00	106	.254	.292	60	.237	8	17	11	2	1.9
1887	Bos-N	24	23	.511	50	50	48	1	0	425	638	305	20	14	133	87	13.8	4.55	89	.336	.340	58	.301	2	-23	-23	-3	-2.1
1888	Bos-N	7	16	.304	24	24	24	1	0	207	187	110	8	8	45	64	10.4	2.87	99	.234	.282	17	.215	1	-0	-0	-1	-0.1
1889	Bos-N	20	11	.645	33	31	28	1	0	277	282	151	14	8	72	99	11.8	3.67	113	.256	.306	23	.189	-1	11	15	2	1.4
1890	Bos-P	27	12	.692	41	38	36	1	0	343	352	183	8	11	100	80	12.1	3.31	133	.254	.309	39	.253	0	35	40	2	3.5
1891	Cin-N	11	13	.458	26	24	23	2	0	218	236	149	13	13	62	54	12.8	4.25	79	.266	.323	17	.177	-1	-22	-21	-3	-2.1
Total	11	309	194	.614	527	502	488	35	2	4527^{1}	4461	2273	117	54	875	1830	10.5	2.68	120	.246	.278	603	.241	39	300	275	7	29.5
● GEORGE RADBOURN Radbourn, George B. "Dordy" b: 4/8/1856, Bloomington, Ill. d: 1/1/04, Bloomington, Ill. 160 lbs. Deb: 5/30/1883																												
1883	Det-N	1	2	.333	3	3	2	0	0	22	38	28	1		7	2	18.4	6.55	47	.345	.385	2	.167	-1	-8	-8	-0	-0.8
● ROY RADEBAUGH Radebaugh, Roy b: 2/22/1884, Champaign, Ill. d: 1/17/45, Cedar Rapids, Iowa BR/TR, 5'7", 160 lbs. Deb: 9/22/11																												
1911	StL-N	0	0	—	2	1	0	0	0	10	6	3	0	0	4	1	9.0	2.70	125	.176	.263	0	.000	-0	1	1	0	0.0
● DREW RADER Rader, Drew Leon "Lefty" b: 5/14/01, Elmira, N.Y. d: 6/5/75, Catskill, N.Y. BR/TL, 6'2", 187 lbs. Deb: 7/18/21																												
1921	Pit-N	0	0	—	1	0	0	0	0	2	2	0	0	0	0	0	9.0	0.00	—	.286	.286	0	.000	-0	1	1	-0	0.0
● PAUL RADFORD Radford, Paul Revere "Shorty" b: 10/14/1861, Roxbury, Mass. d: 2/21/45, Boston, Mass. BR/TR, 5'6", 148 lbs. Deb: 5/1/1883 ◆																												
1884	*Pro-N	0	2	.000	2	2	1	0	0	13	27	19	0		3	2	20.8	7.62	37	.403	.429	70	.197	0	-7	-7	-0	-0.8
1885	Pro-N	0	2	.000	3	2	2	0	0	18^{1}	34	27	1		8	3	20.6	7.85	34	.378	.429	90	.243	1	-10	-11	0	-0.9
1887	NY-a	0	0	—	2	0	0	0	0	5	18	16	1	0	3	4	32.4	18.00	24	.818	.818	235	.397	1	-8	-8	-0	-0.3
1890	Cle-P	0	0	—	1	0	0	0	0	5	7	5	1	0	1	3	14.4	3.60	110	.318	.348	136	.292	0	0	0	1	0.1
1891	Bos-a	0	0	—	1	0	0	0	0	1	0	0	0	0	0	0	0.0	0.00	—	.000	.000	118	.259	0	0	0	-0	0.0
1893	Was-N	0	0	—	1	0	0	0	0	1	2	2	2	0	2	1	36.0	18.00	26	.400	.571	106	.228	0	-1	-1	-0	-0.1
Total	6	0	4	.000	10	4	3	0	0	43^{1}	88	69	5	0	17	13	21.2	8.52	37	.421	.457	1312	.258	2	-25	-27	0	-2.0
● SCOTT RADINSKY Radinsky, Scott David b: 3/3/68, Glendale, Cal. BL/TL, 6'3", 204 lbs. Deb: 4/9/90																												
1990	Chi-A	6	1	.857	62	0	0	0	4	52^{1}	47	29	1	2	36	46	14.6	4.82	80	.241	.365	0	—	0	-5	-6	0	-0.8
1991	Chi-A	5	5	.500	67	0	0	0	8	71^{1}	53	18	4	1	23	49	9.7	2.02	197	.206	.274	0	—	0	17	16	1	2.4
1992	Chi-A	3	7	.300	68	0	0	0	15	59^{1}	54	21	3	2	34	48	13.7	2.73	142	.243	.349	0	—	0	8	8	0	1.6
1993	*Chi-A	8	2	.800	73	0	0	0	4	54^{2}	61	33	3	1	19	44	13.3	4.28	98	.268	.327	0	—	0	0	-1	0	-0.1
1995	Chi-A	2	1	.667	46	0	0	0	1	38	46	23	7	0	17	14	14.9	5.45	82	.309	.380	0	—	0	-3	-4	0	-0.3
1996	*LA-N	5	1	.833	58	0	0	0	1	52^{1}	52	19	2	0	17	48	11.9	2.41	161	.264	.322	0	.000	-0	11	9	0	1.0
1997	LA-N	5	1	.833	75	0	0	0	3	62^{1}	54	22	4	1	21	44	11.0	2.89	134	.236	.303	0	.000	-0	9	7	-0	0.6
1998	LA-N	6	6	.500	62	0	0	0	13	61^{2}	63	21	5	4	20	45	12.7	2.63	151	.272	.340	0	—	0	11	10	-0	1.9
1999	StL-N	2	1	.667	43	0	0	0	3	27^{2}	27	16	2	1	18	17	15.0	4.88	94	.270	.387	0	—	0	-1	-1	-0	-0.1
2000	StL-N	0	0	—	1	0	0	0	0	0	0	0	0	1	—	—	—	—	—	1.000	100	—		0	0	0		0.0
Total	10	42	25	.627	555	0	0	0	52	479^{2}	457	202	31	12	206	355	12.7	3.34	120	.253	.333	0	.000	-1	46	38	1	6.2
● BRAD RADKE Radke, Brad William b: 10/27/72, Eau Claire, Wis. BR/TR, 6'2", 180 lbs. Deb: 4/29/95																												
1995	Min-A	11	14	.440	29	28	2	1	0	181	195	112	32	4	47	75	12.2	5.32	90	.275	.323	0	—	0	-12	-11	-1	-1.3
1996	Min-A	11	16	.407	35	35	3	0	0	232	231	125	40	4	57	148	11.3	4.46	115	.256	.304	0	—	0	14	17	-3	1.4
1997	Min-A	20	10	.667	35	35	4	1	0	239^{2}	238	114	28	3	48	174	10.9	3.87	120	.257	.296	0	.000	-0	19	21	1	2.3
1998	Min-A★	12	14	.462	32	32	5	1	0	213^{2}	238	109	23	9	43	146	12.2	4.30	111	.283	.325	0	.000	-0	9	11	1	1.2
1999	Min-A	12	14	.462	33	33	4	0	0	218^{2}	239	97	28	1	44	121	11.7	3.75	136	.280	.316	0	.000	-1	27	31	3	3.5
2000	Min-A	12	16	.429	34	34	4	1	0	226^{2}	261	119	27	5	51	141	12.6	4.45	118	.286	.328	0	.000	-0	12	19	1	2.1
Total	6	78	84	.481	198	197	22	4	0	1311^{2}	1402	676	178	26	290	805	11.8	4.32	114	.273	.315	0	.000	-1	68	88	2	9.2
● ROB RADLOSKY Radlosky, Robert Vincent b: 1/7/74, W.Palm Beach, Fla. BR/TR, 6'2", 192 lbs. Deb: 5/25/99																												
1999	Min-A	0	1	.000	7	0	0	0	0	8^{2}	15	12	7	1	4	3	20.8	12.46	41	.375	.444	0	—	0	-7	-7	-0	-0.6
● HAL RAETHER Raether, Harold Herman "Bud" b: 10/10/32, Lake Mills, Wis. BR/TR, 6'1", 185 lbs. Deb: 7/4/54																												
1954	Phi-A	0	0	—	1	0	0	0	0	2	1	1	0	0	4	0	22.5	4.50	87	.200	.556	0	—	0	-0	-0	0	0.0
1957	KC-A	0	0	—	1	0	0	0	0	2	2	2	1	0	0	0	9.0	9.00	44	.250	.250	0	—	0	-1	-1	-0	-0.1
Total	2	0	0	—	2	0	0	0	0	4	3	3	1	0	4	0	15.8	6.75	58	.231	.412	0	—	0	-1	-1	0	-0.1
● KEN RAFFENSBERGER Raffensberger, Kenneth David b: 8/8/17, York, Pa. BR/TL, 6'2", 185 lbs. Deb: 4/25/39																												
1939	StL-N	0	0	—	1	0	0	0	0	1	2	0	0	0	0	1	18.0	0.00	—	.400	.400	0	—	0	0	0	0	0.0
1940	Chi-N	7	9	.438	43	10	3	0	3	114^{2}	120	54	10	2	29	55	11.9	3.38	111	.271	.319	5	.167	-1	6	5	-1	0.5
1941	Chi-N	0	1	.000	10	1	0	0	0	18	17	9	0	0	7	5	12.0	4.50	78	.262	.333	0	.000	-1	-2	-2	1	-0.1
1943	Phi-N	0	1	.000	1	1	1	0	0	8	7	3	0	0	2	3	10.1	1.13	300	.241	.290	0	.000	-0	2	2	-0	0.2
1944	Phi-N★	13	20	.394	37	31	18	3	0	258^{2}	257	101	9	2	45	136	10.6	3.06	118	.252	.285	11	.138	-3	16	16	-3	1.3
1945	Phi-N	0	3	.000	5	4	1	0	0	24^{1}	28	19	3	0	14	6	15.5	4.44	86	.283	.372	0	.000	-1	-2	-2	0	-0.3
1946	Phi-N	8	15	.348	39	23	14	2	**6**	196	203	89	10	1	39	73	11.2	3.63	95	.265	.302	10	.167	-1	-5	-4	-3	-0.8
1947	Phi-N	2	6	.250	10	7	3	1	0	41	50	30	4	1	8	16	13.0	5.49	73	.307	.343	4	.267	0	-7	-7	1	-1.0
	Cin-N	6	5	.545	19	15	7	0	1	106^{2}	132	54	11	0	29	38	13.6	4.13	99	.305	.348	6	.162	-1	-1	-0	-1	-0.2
	Yr	8	11	.421	29	22	10	1	1	147^{2}	182	84	15	1	37	54	13.4	4.51	90	.305	.347	10	.192	-0	-7	-7	0	-1.2
1948	Cin-N	11	12	.478	40	24	7	4	0	180^{1}	187	88	15	1	37	57	11.2	3.84	102	.259	.296	7	.113	-3	2	1	-2	-0.3
1949	Cin-N	18	17	.514	41	38	20	**5**	0	284	289	129	23	2	80	103	11.8	3.39	123	.264	.315	16	.178	0	21	24	-3	2.5
1950	Cin-N	14	19	.424	38	35	18	4	0	239	271	127	34	2	40	87	11.8	4.26	100	.279	.308	11	.134	-2	-3	-1	-2	-0.4
1951	Cin-N	16	17	.485	42	33	14	5	5	248^{2}	232	108	29	6	38	81	**10.0**	3.44	119	.246	.279	10	.122	-3	14	17	-1	1.4
1952	Cin-N	17	13	.567	38	33	18	**6**	1	247	247	85	18	2	45	93	10.7	2.81	134	.261	.295	8	.107	-2	25	26	-2	2.6
1953	Cin-N	7	14	.333	26	26	9	1	0	174	200	87	23	0	33	47	12.1	3.93	111	.289	.322	8	.140	-1	7	8	2	0.9
1954	Cin-N	0	2	.000	6	1	1	0	0	10^{1}	15	10	2	0	3	5	15.7	7.84	53	.333	.375	1	.500	0	-4	-4	-0	-0.7
Total	15	119	154	.436	396	282	133	31	16	2151^{2}	2257	993	191	19	449	806	11.4	3.60	110	.267	.306	97	.141	-17	71	81	-18	5.6
● AL RAFFO Raffo, Albert Martin b: 11/27/41, San Francisco, Cal. BR/TR, 6'5", 210 lbs. Deb: 4/29/69																												
1969	Phi-N	1	3	.250	45	0	0	0	1	72^{1}	81	35	6	4	25	38	13.7	4.11	86	.286	.353	1	.167	0	-4	-5	1	-0.2
● PAT RAGAN Ragan, Don Carlos Patrick b: 11/15/1888, Blanchard, Iowa d: 9/4/56, Los Angeles, Cal. BR/TR, 5'10.5", 185 lbs. Deb: 4/21/09 C																												
1909	Cin-N	0	1	.000	2	0	0	0	0	8	7	4	0	0	4	2	12.4	3.38	77	.259	.355	1	.500	0	-1	-1	-0	-0.1
	Chi-N	0	0	—	2	0	0	0	0	3^{2}	4	2	0	0	1	2	12.3	2.45	104	.286	.333	0	.000	-0	0	0	-0	0.0
	Yr	0	1	.000	4	0	0	0	0	11^{2}	11	6	0	0	5	4	12.3	3.09	84	.268	.348	1	.250	0	-1	-1	-0	-0.1
1911	Bro-N	4	3	.571	22	7	5	1	1	93^{2}	81	32	0	2	31	39	11.0	2.11	158	.252	.321	4	.138	-1	13	13	-1	0.7
1912	Bro-N	7	18	.280	36	26	12	1	0	208	211	101	7	4	65	101	12.1	3.63	92	.270	.329	4	.060	-7	-5	-7	-1	-1.5
1913	Bro-N	15	18	.455	44	32	14	0	0	264^{2}	284	145	10	4	64	109	12.0	3.77	87	.281	.327	15	.165	-2	-17	-14	2	-1.7
1914	Bro-N	10	15	.400	38	25	14	1	3	208^{1}	214	104	5	3	85	106	13.0	2.98	96	.270	.343	10	.133	-3	-4	-3	0	-0.7
1915	Bro-N	1	0	1.000	5	0	0	0	0	19^{2}	11	2	0	0	8	7	8.7	0.92	304	.164	.253	1	.167	-0	4	4	0	0.2
	Bos-N	16	12	.571	33	26	13	3	0	227	208	71	2	7	59	81	10.9	2.46	105	.255	.311	12	.150	-0	7	4	-3	0.0
	Yr	17	12	.586	38	26	13	3	0	246^{2}	219	77	2	7	67	88	10.7	2.34	112	.248	.306	13	.151	-1	11	8	-2	0.2

YEAR	TM/L	W	L	PCT	G	GS	CG	SH	SV	IP	H	R	HR	HB	BB	SO	RAT	ERA	ERA+	OAV	OOB	BH	AVG	PB	PR	PR+	PD	TPI
1916	Bos-N	9	9	.500	28	23	14	3	0	182	143	53	3	0	47	94	9.4	2.08	120	.218	.270	13	.217	3	11	9	1	1.3
1917	Bos-N	6	9	.400	30	13	5	1	1	147^2	138	59	6	1	35	61	10.6	2.93	87	.250	.295	6	.125	-1	-4	-7	0	-0.8
1918	Bos-N	8	17	.320	30	25	15	2	0	206^1	212	95	4	4	54	68	11.8	3.23	83	.270	.320	13	.183	-2	-11	-13	-0	-1.7
1919	Bos-N	0	2	.000	4	3	0	0	0	12^2	16	13	0	0	3	3	13.5	7.11	40	.281	.317	1	.250	0	-6	-6	0	-0.8
	NY-N	1	0	1.000	7	1	1	0	0	22^2	19	7	0	0	14	7	13.1	1.59	177	.247	.363	3	.429	1	3	3	0	0.3
	Yr	1	2	.333	11	4	1	0	0	35^1	35	20	0	0	17	10	13.2	3.57	79	.261	.344	4	.364	1	-3	-3	0	-0.5
	Chi-A	0	0	—	1	0	0	0	0	1	1	0	0	0	0	0	9.0	0.00	—	.250	.250	0	—	0	0	0	0	0.0
1923	Phi-N	0	0	—	1	0	0	0	0	3	6	2	1	0	0	0	18.0	6.00	77	.400	.400	1	.500	0	-1	-0	-0	0.0
Total	11	77	104	.425	283	181	93	12	6	1608^1	1555	694	38	25	470	680	11.5	2.99	97	.260	.317	84	.154	-13	-8	-19	-3	-4.8
● BRADY RAGGIO	Raggio, Brady John b: 9/17/72, Los Angeles, Cal. BR/TR, 6'4", 210 lbs. Deb: 4/15/97																											
1997	StL-N	1	2	.333	15	4	0	0	0	31^1	44	24	1	1	16	21	17.5	6.89	60	.336	.412	0	.000	-0	-9	-10	0	-0.8
1998	StL-N	1	1	.500	4	1	0	0	0	7	22	12	1	1	3	3	33.4	15.43	27	.579	.619	0	.000	-0	-9	-9	0	-1.4
Total	2	2	3	.400	19	5	0	0	0	38^1	66	36	2	2	19	24	20.4	8.45	49	.391	.458	0	.000	-0	-18	-19	0	-2.2
● FRANK RAGLAND	Ragland, Frank Roland b: 5/26/04, Water Valley, Miss. d: 7/28/59, Paris, Miss. BR/TR, 6'1", 186 lbs. Deb: 4/17/32																											
1932	Was-A	1	0	1.000	12	1	0	0	0	37^2	54	33	5	3	21	11	18.6	7.41	58	.346	.433	3	.273	1	-12	-13	0	-0.5
1933	Phi-N	0	4	.000	11	5	0	0	0	38^1	51	32	1	1	10	4	14.6	6.81	56	.317	.360	2	.200	-0	-15	-11	1	-1.0
Total	2	1	4	.200	23	6	0	0	0	76	105	65	6	4	31	15	16.6	7.11	58	.331	.398	5	.238	1	-27	-24	1	-1.5
● ERIC RAICH	Raich, Eric James b: 11/1/51, Detroit, Mich. BR/TR, 6'4", 225 lbs. Deb: 5/24/75																											
1975	Cle-A	7	8	.467	18	17	2	0	0	92^2	118	61	12	1	31	34	14.6	5.54	69	.320	.374	0	—	0	-18	-18	-1	-2.6
1976	Cle-A	0	0	—	1	0	0	0	0	2^2	7	5	1	0	0	1	23.6	16.88	21	.467	.467	0	—	0	-4	-4	-0	-0.2
Total	2	7	8	.467	19	17	2	0	0	95^1	125	66	13	1	31	35	14.8	5.85	65	.326	.377	0	—	0	-22	-22	-1	-2.8
● STEVE RAIN	Rain, Steven Nicholas b: 6/2/75, Los Angeles, Cal. BR/TR, 6'6", 250 lbs. Deb: 7/17/99																											
1999	Chi-N	0	1	.000	16	0	0	0	0	14^2	28	17	1	1	7	12	22.1	9.20	49	.418	.480	0	—	0	-8	-8	0	-0.4
2000	Chi-N	3	4	.429	37	0	0	0	0	49^2	46	25	10	1	27	54	13.4	4.35	105	.250	.349	0	.000	0	2	1	-1	0.1
Total	2	3	5	.375	53	0	0	0	0	64^1	74	42	11	2	34	66	15.4	5.46	84	.295	.383	0	.000	0	-6	-7	-0	-0.3
● CHUCK RAINEY	Rainey, Charles David b: 7/14/54, San Diego, Cal. BR/TR, 5'11", 190 lbs. Deb: 4/8/79																											
1979	Bos-A	8	5	.615	20	16	4	1	1	103^2	97	47	7	3	41	41	12.2	3.82	116	.250	.326	0	—	0	5	7	1	0.8
1980	Bos-A	8	3	.727	16	13	2	1	0	87	92	49	7	2	41	43	14.0	4.86	87	.273	.355	0	—	0	-8	-6	-1	-0.7
1981	Bos-A	0	1	.000	11	2	0	0	0	40	39	21	2	0	13	20	11.7	2.70	144	.252	.310	0	—	0	4	5	1	0.3
1982	Bos-A	7	5	.583	27	25	3	3	0	129	146	75	14	2	63	57	14.7	5.02	86	.294	.376	0	—	0	-13	-10	1	-0.7
1983	Chi-N	14	13	.519	34	34	1	1	0	191	219	109	17	3	74	84	13.9	4.48	85	.295	.361	9	.161	1	-18	-14	3	-1.4
1984	Chi-N	5	7	.417	17	16	0	0	0	88^1	102	55	4	2	38	45	14.5	4.28	91	.290	.362	3	.097	-1	-7	-3	1	-0.5
	Oak-A	1	1	.500	16	0	0	0	1	30^2	43	27	2	0	17	10	17.6	6.75	56	.333	.411	0	—	0	-9	-11	-0	-0.7
Total	6	43	35	.551	141	106	10	6	2	669^2	738	383	53	12	287	300	13.9	4.50	90	.284	.358	12	.138	-1	-46	-31	5	-2.9
● DAVE RAJSICH	Rajsich, David Christopher b: 9/28/51, Youngstown, Ohio BL/TL, 6'5", 175 lbs. Deb: 7/2/78 F																											
1978	NY-A	0	0	—	4	2	0	0	0	13^1	16	6	0	0	6	9	14.9	4.05	90	.320	.393	0	—	0	-0	-1	-0	-0.1
1979	Tex-A	1	3	.250	27	3	0	0	0	53^2	56	25	7	0	18	32	12.4	3.52	118	.267	.325	0	—	0	4	4	1	0.3
1980	Tex-A	2	1	.667	24	1	0	0	2	48^1	56	34	7	3	22	35	15.1	5.96	65	.295	.377	0	—	0	-10	-11	0	-0.7
Total	3	3	4	.429	55	6	0	0	2	115^1	128	65	14	3	46	76	13.8	4.60	87	.284	.355	0	—	0	-6	-8	1	-0.5
● JASON RAKERS	Rakers, Jason Paul b: 6/29/73, Pittsburgh, Pa. BR/TR, 6'2", 197 lbs. Deb: 5/6/98																											
1998	Cle-A	0	0	—	1	0	0	0	0	1	0	1	0	0	3	0	27.0	9.00	53	.000	.600	0	—	0	-0	-0	0	0.0
1999	Cle-A	0	0	—	1	0	0	0	0	2	2	1	1	0	1	0	13.5	4.50	112	.250	.333	0	—	0	0	0	-0	0.0
2000	KC-A	2	0	1.000	11	0	0	0	0	21^2	33	22	5	0	7	16	16.6	9.14	55	.351	.396	0	—	0	-10	-10	-1	-0.8
Total	3	2	0	1.000	13	0	0	0	0	24^2	35	24	6	0	11	16	16.8	8.76	57	.337	.400	0	—	0	-11	-10	-1	-0.8
● ED RAKOW	Rakow, Edward Charles "Rock" b: 5/30/36, Pittsburgh, Pa. BB/TR, 5'11", 178 lbs. Deb: 4/22/60																											
1960	LA-N	0	1	.000	9	2	0	0	0	22	30	19	5	0	11	9	16.8	7.36	54	.323	.394	2	.333	0	-9	-8	-0	-0.4
1961	KC-A	2	8	.200	45	11	1	0	1	124^2	131	80	14	8	49	81	13.6	4.76	88	.269	.346	3	.103	-2	-10	-8	1	-0.7
1962	KC-A	14	17	.452	42	35	11	2	1	235^1	232	126	31	4	98	159	12.8	4.25	99	.260	.336	8	.098	-5	-7	-1	2	-0.4
1963	KC-A	9	10	.474	34	26	7	1	0	174^1	173	85	18	5	61	104	12.3	3.92	99	.261	.328	6	.105	-2	-6	-0	1	-0.1
1964	Det-A	8	9	.471	42	13	1	0	3	152^1	155	70	14	6	59	96	13.0	3.72	98	.266	.340	0	.000	-4	-2	-1	2	-0.3
1965	Det-A	0	0	—	6	0	0	0	0	13^1	14	11	2	0	11	10	16.9	6.08	57	.280	.410	0	.000	-0	-4	-4	-1	-0.3
1967	Atl-N	3	2	.600	17	3	0	0	0	39^1	36	23	4	1	15	25	11.9	5.26	63	.240	.313	0	.000	-1	-8	-9	-1	-1.2
Total	7	36	47	.434	195	90	20	3	5	761^1	771	414	88	24	304	484	13.0	4.33	92	.264	.339	19	.084	-13	-46	-30	4	-3.4
● JOHN RALEIGH	Raleigh, John Austin b: 4/21/1890, Elkhorn, Wis. d: 8/24/55, Escondido, Cal. BR/TL, Deb: 8/4/09																											
1909	StL-N	1	10	.091	15	10	3	0	0	80^2	85	42	0	3	21	26	12.2	3.79	67	.285	.339	2	.087	-2	-11	-12	0	-1.7
1910	StL-N	0	0	—	3	1	0	0	0	5	8	5	0	0	0	2	14.4	9.00	33	.364	.364	0	.000	-0	-3	-3	0	-0.2
Total	2	1	10	.091	18	11	3	0	0	85^2	93	47	0	3	21	28	12.3	4.10	62	.291	.340	2	.083	-2	-14	-15	0	-1.9
● PEP RAMBERT	Rambert, Elmer Donald b: 8/1/16, Cleveland, Ohio d: 11/16/74, W.Palm Beach, Fla. BR/TR, 6', 175 lbs. Deb: 9/23/39																											
1939	Pit-N	0	0	—	2	0	0	0	0	3^2	7	4	0	0	1	4	19.6	9.82	39	.389	.421	0	—	0	-2	-2	0	-0.1
1940	Pit-N	0	1	.000	3	1	0	0	0	8^1	12	8	0	3	4	0	20.5	7.56	50	.333	.442	0	.000	0	-3	-4	0	-0.4
Total	2	0	1	.000	5	1	0	0	0	12	19	12	0	3	5	4	20.3	8.25	46	.352	.435	0	.000	0	-6	-6	0	-0.5
● PETE RAMBO	Rambo, Warren Dawson b: 11/1/06, Thorofare, N.J. d: 6/19/91, Camden, N.J. BR/TR, 5'9", 150 lbs. Deb: 9/15/26																											
1926	Phi-N	0	0	—	1	0	0	0	0	3^2	6	8	0	0	4	4	24.5	14.73	28	.353	.476	1	1.000	0	-4	-4	0	-0.1
● ALLAN RAMIREZ	Ramirez, Daniel Allan b: 5/1/57, Victoria, Tex. BR/TR, 5'10", 180 lbs. Deb: 6/8/83																											
1983	Bal-A	4	4	.500	11	10	1	0	0	57	46	22	6	0	30	20	12.0	3.47	114	.229	.329	0	—	0	4	3	0	0.4
● HECTOR RAMIREZ	Ramirez, Hector Bienvenido b: 12/15/71, ElSeibo, D.R. BR/TR, 6'3", 218 lbs. Deb: 8/28/99																											
1999	Mil-N	1	2	.333	15	0	0	0	0	21	19	8	1	0	11	9	12.9	3.43	132	.247	.341	0	.000	-0	3	3	-0	0.3
2000	Mil-N	0	1	.000	6	0	0	0	0	9	11	10	1	0	5	4	16.0	10.00	46	.289	.372	1	1.000	0	-5	-6	-0	-0.5
Total	2	1	3	.250	21	0	0	0	0	30	30	18	2	0	16	13	13.8	5.40	84	.261	.351	1	.250	0	-3	-3	-1	-0.2
● ROBERTO RAMIREZ	Ramirez, Roberto Sanchez b: 8/17/72, Veracruz, Mexico BL/TL, 6', 171 lbs. Deb: 6/12/98																											
1998	SD-N	1	0	1.000	21	0	0	0	0	14^2	12	13	4	0	12	17	14.7	6.14	64	.211	.348	0	—	0	-3	-4	-0	-0.3
1999	Col-N	1	5	.167	32	4	0	0	1	40^1	68	42	8	0	22	32	20.1	8.26	70	.368	.435	1	.143	-0	-17	-9	0	-1.1
Total	2	2	5	.286	53	4	0	0	1	55	80	55	12	0	34	49	18.7	7.69	69	.331	.413	1	.143	-0	-20	-12	-0	-1.4
● EDGAR RAMOS	Ramos, Edgar Jose (Malave) b: 3/6/75, Cumana, Venezuela BR/TR, 6'4", 190 lbs. Deb: 5/21/97																											
1997	Phi-N	0	2	.000	4	2	0	0	0	14	15	9	3	1	6	4	14.1	5.14	83	.288	.373	0	.000	-0	-1	-1	-0	-0.2
● PEDRO RAMOS	Ramos, Pedro (Guerra) "Pete" b: 4/28/35, Pinar Del Rio, Cuba BB/TR, 6', 185 lbs. Deb: 4/11/55 ♦																											
1955	Was-A	5	11	.313	45	9	3	1	5	130	121	62	13	11	39	34	11.8	3.88	99	.253	.323	3	.079	-3	1	-1	-1	-0.4
1956	Was-A	12	10	.545	37	18	4	0	0	152	178	95	23	3	76	54	15.2	5.27	82	.299	.381	9	.205	0	-19	-15	-0	-1.9
1957	Was-A	12	16	.429	43	30	7	1	0	231	251	131	43	7	69	91	12.7	4.79	81	.271	.327	13	.171	-1	-26	-22	-0	-2.5
1958	Was-A	14	18	.438	43	37	10	4	3	259^1	277	133	38	5	77	132	12.5	4.23	90	.273	.327	21	.239	1	-13	-12	-1	-1.3
1959	Was-A☆	13	19	.406	37	35	11	0	0	233^2	233	127	30	9	52	95	11.3	4.16	94	.257	.304	11	.147	-0	-8	-6	-1	-0.8
1960	Was-A	11	18	.379	43	36	14	1	2	274	254	126	24	7	99	160	11.8	3.45	113	.245	.315	10	.116	-2	13	13	0	1.2
1961	Min-A	11	20	.355	42	34	9	3	2	264^1	265	134	39	4	79	174	11.8	3.95	107	.258	.313	16	.172	1	2	8	-3	0.7
1962	Cle-A	10	12	.455	37	27	7	2	1	201^1	189	104	28	5	85	96	12.5	3.71	104	.246	.326	10	.147	2	6	4	0	0.6
1963	Cle-A	9	8	.529	36	22	5	0	0	184^2	156	74	29	4	41	169	9.8	3.12	116	.226	.273	6	.109	1	10	10	-2	0.8
1964	Cle-A	7	10	.412	36	19	3	1	0	133	144	84	18	4	26	98	11.8	5.14	70	.273	.312	7	.179	2	-22	-23	-1	-2.5
	NY-A	1	0	1.000	13	0	0	0	8	21^2	13	3	1	0	0	21	5.4	1.25	291	.183	.183	0	.000	-1	6	6	-1	0.6

YEAR	TM/L	W	L	PCT	G	GS	CG	SH	SV	IP	H	R	HR	HB	BB	SO	RAT	ERA	ERA+	OAV	OOB	BH	AVG	PB	PR	PR+	PD	TPI
	Yr	8	10	.444	49	19	3	1	8	154^2	157	87	19	4	26	119	10.9	4.60	78	.263	.298	7	.159	1	-17	-17	-2	-1.9
1965	NY-A	5	5	.500	65	0	0	0	19	92^1	80	34	7	1	27	68	10.5	2.92	116	.237	.296	1	.083	-1	5	5	-1	0.6
1966	NY-A	3	9	.250	52	1	0	0	13	89^2	98	43	10	1	18	58	11.7	3.61	92	.283	.321	2	.154	-0	-2	-3	-0	-0.5
1967	Phi-N	0	0	—	6	0	0	0	0	8	14	8	1	2	8	1	27.0	9.00	38	.412	.545	0	.000	-0	-5	-5	1	-0.2
1969	Pit-N	0	1	.000	5	0	0	0	0	6	8	4	2	0	0	4	12.0	6.00	58	.320	.320	0	.000	-0	-2	-2	0	-0.3
	Cin-N	4	3	.571	38	0	0	0	2	66^1	73	41	8	5	24	40	13.8	5.16	73	.284	.357	0	.000	-1	-11	-10	-0	-1.1
	Yr	4	4	.500	43	0	0	0	2	72^1	81	45	10	5	24	44	13.7	5.23	72	.287	.354	0	.000	-1	-13	-11	-0	-1.4
1970	Was-A	0	0	—	4	0	0	0	0	8^1	10	7	2	0	4	10	15.1	7.56	47	.294	.368	0	.000	0	-4	-4	0	-0.2
Total	15	117	160	.422	582	268	73	13	55	2355^2	2364	1210	316	68	724	1305	12.1	4.08	95	.261	.320	109	.155	-0	-68	-58	-9	-7.2

● ROBERT RAMSAY Ramsay, Robert Arthur b: 12/3/73, Vancouver, Wash. BL/TL, 6'5", 230 lbs. Deb: 8/27/99

YEAR	TM/L	W	L	PCT	G	GS	CG	SH	SV	IP	H	R	HR	HB	BB	SO	RAT	ERA	ERA+	OAV	OOB	BH	AVG	PB	PR	PR+	PD	TPI
1999	Sea-A	0	2	.000	6	3	0	0	0	18^1	23	13	3	0	9	11	15.7	6.38	74	.324	.400	0	—	0	-3	-3	-0	-0.3
2000	*Sea-A	1	1	.500	37	1	0	0	0	50^1	43	22	3	1	40	32	15.0	3.40	141	.234	.373	0	—	0	9	8	0	0.4
Total	2	1	3	.250	43	4	0	0	0	68^2	66	35	6	1	49	43	15.2	4.19	114	.259	.380	0	—	0	5	5	-0	0.1

● WILLIE RAMSDELL Ramsdell, James Willard "The Knuck" b: 4/4/16, Williamsburg, Kan. d: 10/8/69, Wichita, Kan. BR/TR, 5'10", 180 lbs. Deb: 9/24/47

YEAR	TM/L	W	L	PCT	G	GS	CG	SH	SV	IP	H	R	HR	HB	BB	SO	RAT	ERA	ERA+	OAV	OOB	BH	AVG	PB	PR	PR+	PD	TPI
1947	Bro-N	1	1	.500	2	0	0	0	0	2^2	4	6	0	1	3	3	27.0	6.75	61	.333	.500	1	1.000	0	-1	-1	0	-0.1
1948	Bro-N	4	4	.500	27	1	0	0	4	50^1	48	35	6	3	41	34	16.5	5.19	77	.251	.391	1	.091	-1	-7	-7	1	-1.0
1950	Bro-N	1	2	.333	5	0	0	0	1	6^1	7	3	0	1	2	2	14.2	2.84	144	.292	.370	0	.000	-0	1	1	0	0.2
	Cin-N	7	12	.368	27	22	8	1	0	157^1	151	77	17	2	75	83	13.0	3.72	114	.255	.341	10	.200	1	7	9	-1	0.9
	Yr	8	14	.364	32	22	8	1	1	163^2	158	80	17	3	77	85	13.1	3.68	115	.257	.342	10	.189	0	8	10	-1	1.1
1951	Cin-N	9	17	.346	31	31	10	1	0	196	204	103	18	8	70	88	12.9	4.04	101	.266	.333	9	.155	-1	-2	1	-2	-0.2
1952	Chi-N	2	3	.400	19	4	0	0	0	67	41	22	5	5	24	30	9.4	2.42	159	.173	.263	1	.056	-1	10	10	-1	0.6
Total	5	24	39	.381	111	58	18	2	5	479^2	455	246	46	20	215	240	12.9	3.83	107	.250	.335	22	.156	-2	9	14	-2	0.4

● TOAD RAMSEY Ramsey, Thomas A. b: 8/8/1864, Indianapolis, Ind. d: 3/27/06, Indianapolis, Ind. BR/TL, Deb: 9/5/1885

YEAR	TM/L	W	L	PCT	G	GS	CG	SH	SV	IP	H	R	HR	HB	BB	SO	RAT	ERA	ERA+	OAV	OOB	BH	AVG	PB	PR	PR+	PD	TPI
1885	Lou-a	3	6	.333	9	9	9	0	0	79	44	38	1	1	28	83	8.3	1.94	167	.150	.227	4	.129	-2	12	11	-0	0.9
1886	Lou-a	38	27	.585	67	67	**66**	3	0	**588**^{2}	447	297	3	12	207	499	10.2	2.45	149	**.198**	.269	58	.241	-3	66	74	-3	6.2
1887	Lou-a	37	27	.578	65	64	61	0	0	561	711	358	9	16	167	**355**	11.7	3.43	128	.295	.299	62	.254	-10	54	58	-9	3.4
1888	Lou-a	8	30	.211	40	40	37	1	0	342^1	362	278	10	11	86	228	12.1	3.42	90	.262	.310	17	.120	-7	-13	-13	-4	-2.1
1889	Lou-a	1	16	.059	18	18	15	0	0	140	175	152	7	2	71	60	15.9	5.59	69	.297	.374	15	.263	0	-27	-27	-2	-2.5
	StL-a	3	1	.750	5	3	3	0	0	41	44	29	0	1	10	33	12.1	3.95	107	.265	.311	5	.294	0	-0	1	-1	0.1
	Yr	4	17	.190	23	21	18	0	0	181	219	181	7	3	81	93	15.1	5.22	75	.290	.361	20	.270	1	-28	-25	-2	-2.4
1890	StL-a	24	17	.585	44	40	34	1	0	348^2	325	221	10	8	102	257	11.2	3.69	117	.239	.296	33	.228	-1	7	22	-7	1.3
Total	6	114	124	.479	248	241	225	5	0	2100^2	2108	1373	40	51	671	1515	11.4	3.29	117	.249	.295	194	.221	-22	97	128	-25	7.3

● RIBS RANEY Raney, Frank Robert Donald (b: Frank Robert Donald Raniszewski) b: 2/16/23, Detroit, Mich. BR/TR, 6'4", 190 lbs. Deb: 9/18/49

YEAR	TM/L	W	L	PCT	G	GS	CG	SH	SV	IP	H	R	HR	HB	BB	SO	RAT	ERA	ERA+	OAV	OOB	BH	AVG	PB	PR	PR+	PD	TPI
1949	StL-A	1	2	.333	3	3	1	0	0	16^1	23	15	2	0	12	5	19.3	7.71	59	.333	.432	0	.000	-1	-6	-5	-0	-0.8
1950	StL-A	0	1	.000	1	0	0	0	0	2	2	2	0	0	2	2	18.0	4.50	110	.250	.400	0	.000	-0	0	0	0	0.0
Total	2	1	3	.250	4	3	1	0	0	18^1	25	17	2	0	14	7	19.1	7.36	62	.325	.429	0	.000	-1	-6	-5	-0	-0.8

● PAT RAPP Rapp, Patrick Leland b: 7/13/67, Jennings, La. BR/TR, 6'3", 215 lbs. Deb: 7/10/92

YEAR	TM/L	W	L	PCT	G	GS	CG	SH	SV	IP	H	R	HR	HB	BB	SO	RAT	ERA	ERA+	OAV	OOB	BH	AVG	PB	PR	PR+	PD	TPI
1992	SF-N	0	2	.000	3	2	0	0	0	10	8	8	0	1	6	3	13.5	7.20	46	.235	.366	0	.000	-0	-4	-5	0	-0.8
1993	Fla-N	4	6	.400	16	16	1	0	0	94	101	49	7	2	39	57	13.6	4.02	108	.281	.355	6	.194	0	0	3	0	0.3
1994	Fla-N	7	8	.467	24	23	2	1	0	133^1	132	67	13	7	69	75	14.0	3.85	114	.266	.364	5	.122	-2	5	8	-1	0.5
1995	Fla-N	14	7	.667	28	28	3	2	0	167^1	158	72	10	7	76	102	13.0	3.44	123	.253	.340	6	.107	-3	14	14	-1	1.3
1996	Fla-N	8	16	.333	30	29	0	0	0	162^1	184	95	12	3	91	86	15.4	5.10	80	.301	.394	7	.121	-2	-16	-19	0	-2.6
1997	Fla-N	4	6	.400	19	19	1	1	0	108^2	121	59	11	3	51	64	14.5	4.47	90	.286	.367	5	.143	0	-3	-6	-0	-0.4
	SF-N	1	2	.333	8	6	0	0	0	33	37	24	5	2	21	28	16.4	6.00	68	.294	.403	0	.000	-1	-7	-7	-0	-0.7
	Yr	5	8	.385	27	25	1	1	0	141^2	158	83	16	5	72	92	14.9	4.83	84	.288	.375	5	.106	-1	-10	-13	-0	-1.1
1998	KC-A	12	13	.480	32	32	1	1	0	188^1	208	117	24	10	107	132	15.5	5.30	91	.285	.384	0	.000	-0	-14	-10	0	-1.1
1999	*Bos-A	6	7	.462	37	26	0	0	0	146^1	147	78	13	7	69	90	13.7	4.12	121	.263	.351	0	.000	-0	12	14	-1	0.9
2000	Bal-A	9	12	.429	31	30	0	0	0	174	203	125	18	5	83	106	15.1	5.90	81	.289	.368	0	.000	-0	-19	-22	0	-2.1
Total	9	65	79	.451	228	211	8	5	0	1217^1	1299	694	113	47	612	743	14.5	4.67	96	.279	.368	29	.120	-8	-30	-27	-2	-4.7

● VIC RASCHI Raschi, Victor John Angelo b: 3/28/19, W.Springfield, Mass. d: 10/14/88, Groveland, N.Y. BR/TR, 6'1", 205 lbs. Deb: 9/23/46

YEAR	TM/L	W	L	PCT	G	GS	CG	SH	SV	IP	H	R	HR	HB	BB	SO	RAT	ERA	ERA+	OAV	OOB	BH	AVG	PB	PR	PR+	PD	TPI
1946	NY-A	2	0	1.000	2	2	2	0	0	16	14	7	0	0	5	11	10.7	3.94	88	.230	.288	1	.250	0	-1	-1	0	-0.1
1947	*NY-A	7	2	.778	15	14	6	1	0	104^2	89	47	11	1	38	51	11.0	3.87	91	.226	.296	10	.250	2	-2	-4	-0	-0.2
1948	NY-A★	19	8	.704	36	31	18	6	1	222^2	208	103	15	3	74	124	11.5	3.84	106	.247	.310	19	.235	2	11	6	-1	0.7
1949	*NY-A★	21	10	.677	38	37	21	3	0	274^2	247	120	16	6	138	124	12.8	3.34	121	.241	.334	13	.157	1	26	22	1	2.4
1950	*NY-A★	21	8	**.724**	33	32	17	2	1	256^2	232	120	19	3	116	155	12.3	4.00	107	.243	.327	17	.198	1	17	9	-3	0.7
1951	*NY-A	21	10	.677	35	34	15	4	0	258^1	233	110	20	5	103	**164**	11.9	3.27	117	.242	.319	15	.176	-2	24	17	-3	1.4
1952	*NY-A★	16	6	.727	31	31	13	4	0	223	174	78	12	6	91	127	10.9	2.78	119	.216	.300	13	.188	3	22	15	-4	1.3
1953	*NY-A	13	6	.684	28	26	7	4	1	181	150	74	11	1	55	76	**10.2**	3.33	111	.224	**.283**	9	.143	-2	13	8	-2	0.4
1954	StL-N	8	9	.471	30	29	6	2	0	179	182	99	24	0	71	73	12.7	4.73	87	.268	.337	9	.141	-2	-13	-12	1	-1.1
1955	StL-N	0	1	.000	1	1	0	0	0	1^2	5	4	0	0	1	1	32.4	21.60	19	.556	.600	0	—	0	-3	-3	-0	-0.5
	KC-A	4	6	.400	20	18	1	0	0	101^1	132	66	10	1	35	38	14.9	5.42	77	.312	.366	6	.182	-0	-16	-13	1	-1.1
Total	10	132	66	.667	269	255	106	26	3	1819	1666	828	138	26	727	944	12.0	3.72	105	.244	.319	112	.184	3	78	40	-9	3.9

● DENNIS RASMUSSEN Rasmussen, Dennis Lee b: 4/18/59, Los Angeles, Cal. BL/TL, 6'7", 230 lbs. Deb: 9/16/83 F

YEAR	TM/L	W	L	PCT	G	GS	CG	SH	SV	IP	H	R	HR	HB	BB	SO	RAT	ERA	ERA+	OAV	OOB	BH	AVG	PB	PR	PR+	PD	TPI
1983	SD-N	0	0	—	4	1	0	0	0	13^2	10	5	1	0	8	13	11.9	1.98	177	.200	.310	0	.000	-0	3	2	1	0.1
1984	NY-A	9	6	.600	24	24	1	0	0	147^2	127	79	16	4	60	110	11.6	4.57	83	.234	.315	0	—	0	-9	-13	-1	-1.3
1985	NY-A	3	5	.375	22	16	2	0	0	101^2	97	56	10	1	42	63	12.4	3.98	101	.255	.331	0	—	0	2	0	0	0.0
1986	NY-A	18	6	.750	31	31	3	1	0	202	160	91	28	2	74	131	10.5	3.88	106	.217	.290	0	—	0	7	5	-1	0.5
1987	NY-A	9	7	.563	26	25	2	0	0	146	145	78	31	4	55	89	12.6	4.75	93	.260	.331	0	—	0	-4	-6	-0	-0.5
	Cin-N	4	1	.800	7	7	0	0	0	45^1	39	22	5	1	12	39	10.3	3.97	107	.229	.284	1	.067	-1	1	1	0	0.1
1988	Cin-N	2	6	.250	11	11	1	1	0	56^1	68	36	8	2	22	27	14.7	5.75	62	.300	.367	5	.227	1	-14	-13	0	-1.6
	SD-N	14	4	.778	20	20	6	0	0	148^1	131	48	9	2	36	85	10.3	2.55	133	.238	.287	9	.188	2	15	14	2	2.3
	Yr	16	10	.615	31	31	7	1	0	204^2	199	84	17	4	58	112	11.5	3.43	101	.256	.311	14	.200	3	1	1	2	0.7
1989	SD-N	10	10	.500	33	33	1	0	0	183^2	190	100	18	3	72	87	13.0	4.26	82	.270	.340	11	.169	1	-16	-16	-1	-1.6
1990	SD-N	11	15	.423	32	32	3	1	0	187^2	217	110	28	3	62	86	13.5	4.51	85	.292	.349	18	.290	5	-15	-14	0	-1.3
1991	SD-N	6	13	.316	24	24	1	1	0	146^2	155	74	12	2	49	75	12.6	3.74	102	.271	.331	6	.136	1	1	1	2	0.4
1992	Chi-N	0	0	—	3	1	0	0	0	5	7	6	2	1	2	0	18.0	10.80	33	.350	.435	0	—	0	-4	-4	0	-0.2
	KC-A	4	1	.800	5	5	1	1	0	37^2	25	7	0	0	6	12	7.4	1.43	283	.197	.233	0	—	0	11	11	1	1.7
1993	KC-A	1	2	.333	9	4	0	0	0	29	40	25	4	1	14	12	17.1	7.45	62	.328	.401	0	—	0	-10	-9	-0	-0.8
1995	KC-A	0	1	.000	5	1	0	0	0	10	13	10	3	0	8	6	18.9	9.00	53	.302	.412	0	—	0	-5	-5	-0	-0.4
Total	12	91	77	.542	256	235	21	5	0	1460^2	1424	747	175	26	522	835	12.2	4.15	93	.257	.324	50	.193	8	-41	-44	2	-2.6

● ERIC RASMUSSEN Rasmussen, Eric Ralph (Born Harold Ralph Rasmussen) b: 3/22/52, Racine, Wis. BR/TR, 6'3", 205 lbs. Deb: 7/21/75

YEAR	TM/L	W	L	PCT	G	GS	CG	SH	SV	IP	H	R	HR	HB	BB	SO	RAT	ERA	ERA+	OAV	OOB	BH	AVG	PB	PR	PR+	PD	TPI
1975	StL-N	5	5	.500	14	13	2	1	0	81	86	44	8	0	20	59	11.8	3.78	100	.264	.306	4	.154	-0	-1	-0	-0	-0.1
1976	StL-N	6	12	.333	43	17	2	1	0	150^1	139	67	10	2	54	76	11.7	3.53	100	.247	.315	4	.105	-1	-0	0	3	0.2
1977	StL-N	11	17	.393	34	34	11	3	0	233	223	103	24	5	63	120	11.2	3.48	111	.254	.308	10	.139	0	11	10	-1	1.0
1978	StL-N	2	5	.286	10	10	2	1	0	60^1	61	32	4	0	20	32	12.1	4.18	84	.270	.329	2	.111	-1	-4	-4	0	-0.6
	SD-N	12	10	.545	27	24	3	2	0	146^1	154	72	16	1	43	59	12.2	4.06	82	.277	.331	7	.152	-1	-8	-13	1	-1.7
	Yr	14	15	.483	37	34	5	3	0	206^2	215	104	20	1	63	91	12.1	4.09	83	.275	.330	9	.141	-2	-12	-17	1	-2.3
1979	SD-N	6	9	.400	45	20	5	3	3	156^2	142	59	9	0	42	54	10.6	3.27	108	.244	.295	2	.056	-2	8	5	-1	0.2
1980	SD-N	4	11	.267	40	14	0	0	1	111^1	130	60	9	3	33	50	13.4	4.37	79	.295	.349	2	.095	-1	-9	-12	-0	-1.6
1982	StL-N	1	2	.333	8	3	0	0	0	18^1	21	13	2	0	8	15	14.2	4.42	82	.288	.358	0	.000	-0	-2	-2	0	-0.2
1983	StL-N	0	0	—	6	0	0	0	1	7^2	16	11	1	0	4	6	23.5	11.74	31	.444	.500	0	—	0	-7	-7	0	-0.3
	KC-A	3	6	.333	11	9	2	1	0	52^2	61	28	4	0	22	18	14.2	4.78	85	.289	.356	0	—	0	-4	-4	-0	-0.6
Total	8	50	77	.394	238	144	27	12	5	1017^2	1033	489	87	11	309	489	12.0	3.85	94	.266	.321	31	.119	-5	-16	-27	2	-3.7

YEAR	TM/L	W	L	PCT	G	GS	CG	SH	SV	IP	H	R	HR	HB	BB	SO	RAT	ERA	ERA+	OAV	OOB	BH	AVG	PB	PR	PR+	PD	TPI
● HANS RASMUSSEN	Rasmussen, Henry Florian b: 4/18/1895, Chicago, Ill. d: 1/1/49, Chicago, Ill. BR/TR, 6'6", 220 lbs. Deb: 8/11/15																											
1915	Chi-F	0	0	—	2	0	0	0	0	2	3	3	0	0	2	2	22.5	13.50	19	.600	.714	0	.000	-0	-2	-3	0	-0.1
● GARY RATH	Rath, Alfred Gary b: 1/10/73, Gulfport, Miss. BL/TL, 6'2", 185 lbs. Deb: 6/2/98																											
1998	LA-N	0	0	—	3	0	0	0	0	3^1	3	4	1	0	2	4	13.5	10.80	37	.250	.357	0	—	0	-2	-3	-0	-0.1
1999	Min-A	0	1	.000	5	1	0	0	0	4^2	6	6	1	0	5	1	21.2	11.57	44	.300	.440	0	—	0	-3	-3	0	-0.5
Total	2	0	1	.000	8	1	0	0	0	8	9	10	2	0	7	5	18.0	11.25	41	.281	.410	0	—	0	-6	-6	-0	-0.6
● FRED RATH	Rath, Frederick Helsher Jr. b: 1/5/73, Dallas, Tex. BR/TR, 6'3", 220 lbs. Deb: 7/29/98 F																											
1998	Col-N	0	0	—	2	0	0	0	0	5^1	6	1	0	0	2	2	13.5	1.69	306	.300	.364	0	.000	-0	2	2	-0	0.0
● FRED RATH	Rath, Frederick Helsher Sr. b: 9/1/43, Little Rock, Ark. BR/TR, 6'3", 200 lbs. Deb: 9/10/68 F																											
1968	Chi-A	0	0	—	5	0	0	0	0	11^1	8	5	0	1	3	3	9.5	1.59	191	.182	.250	0	—	0	2	2	0	0.1
1969	Chi-A	0	2	.000	3	2	0	0	0	11^2	11	10	4	0	8	4	14.7	7.71	50	.256	.373	0	.000	-0	-5	-5	0	-0.7
Total	2	0	2	.000	8	2	0	0	0	23	19	15	4	1	11	7	12.1	4.70	73	.218	.313	0	.000	-0	-4	-3	0	-0.6
● JON RATLIFF	Ratliff, Jon Charles b: 12/22/71, Syracuse, N.Y. BR/TR, 6'4", 195 lbs. Deb: 9/15/2000																											
2000	Oak-A	0	0	—	1	0	0	0	0	1	0	0	0	0	0	0	0.0	0.00	—	.000	.000	0	—	0	1	1	0	0.0
● STEVE RATZER	Ratzer, Steven Wayne b: 9/9/53, Paterson, N.J. BR/TR, 6'1", 192 lbs. Deb: 10/5/80																											
1980	Mon-N	0	0	—	1	1	0	0	0	4	9	5	0	0	2	0	24.8	11.25	32	.450	.500	0	.000	-0	-3	-3	0	-0.1
1981	Mon-N	1	1	.500	12	0	0	0	0	17^1	23	14	2	0	7	4	15.6	6.23	56	.311	.370	0	.000	-0	-5	-5	1	-0.5
Total	2	1	1	.500	13	1	0	0	0	21^1	32	19	2	0	9	4	17.3	7.17	49	.340	.398	0	.000	-0	-9	-9	1	-0.6
● DOUG RAU	Rau, Douglas James b: 12/15/48, Columbus, Tex. BL/TL, 6'2", 175 lbs. Deb: 9/2/72																											
1972	LA-N	2	2	.500	7	3	2	0	0	32^2	18	11	1	1	11	19	8.3	2.20	151	.159	.240	1	.143	1	5	4	0	0.6
1973	LA-N	4	2	.667	31	3	0	0	3	63^2	64	28	5	1	28	51	13.1	3.96	87	.259	.337	1	.091	-1	-2	-4	-0	-0.5
1974	*LA-N	13	11	.542	36	35	3	1	0	198^1	191	90	20	4	70	126	12.0	3.72	92	.251	.318	9	.141	-1	-2	-7	-0	-0.9
1975	LA-N	15	9	.625	38	38	8	2	0	257^2	227	96	18	3	61	151	10.2	3.11	110	.236	.283	17	.195	2	15	9	-1	0.9
1976	LA-N	16	12	.571	34	32	8	3	0	231	221	71	18	7	69	98	11.6	2.57	132	.258	.318	9	.150	1	24	22	-0	2.7
1977	*LA-N	14	8	.636	32	32	4	2	0	212^1	232	87	15	6	49	126	12.2	3.43	112	.282	.327	10	.141	-0	11	10	-1	0.7
1978	*LA-N	15	9	.625	30	30	7	2	0	199	219	82	17	2	68	95	13.1	3.26	108	.284	.344	9	.143	-1	7	6	-2	0.3
1979	LA-N	1	5	.167	11	11	1	1	0	56	73	37	3	4	22	28	15.9	5.30	69	.320	.390	2	.143	1	-10	-11	0	-0.9
1981	Cal-A	1	2	.333	3	3	0	0	0	10^1	14	10	2	0	4	3	15.7	8.71	42	.341	.400	0	—	0	-6	-6	-0	-1.0
Total	9	81	60	.574	222	187	33	11	3	1261	1259	512	99	28	382	697	11.9	3.35	105	.262	.320	58	.154	2	43	23	-6	1.9
● BOB RAUCH	Rauch, Robert John b: 6/16/49, Brookings, S.D. BR/TR, 6'4", 200 lbs. Deb: 6/29/72																											
1972	NY-N	0	1	.000	19	0	0	0	1	27	27	16	3	0	21	23	16.0	5.00	67	.273	.400	0	.000	-0	-5	-5	0	-0.3
● LANCE RAUTZHAN	Rautzhan, Clarence George b: 8/20/52, Pottsville, Pa. BR/TL, 6'1", 195 lbs. Deb: 7/23/77																											
1977	*LA-N	4	1	.800	25	0	0	0	2	20^2	25	10	0	0	7	13	13.9	4.35	88	.313	.368	0	.000	-0	-1	-1	0	-0.2
1978	*LA-N	2	1	.667	43	0	0	0	4	61^1	61	22	1	1	19	25	11.9	2.93	120	.263	.321	0	.000	-0	4	4	2	0.4
1979	LA-N	0	2	.000	12	0	0	0	1	9^2	9	9	0	1	11	5	19.6	7.45	49	.273	.467	0	—	0	-4	-4	0	-0.8
	Mil-A	0	0	—	3	0	0	0	0	3	3	3	0	0	10	2	39.0	9.00	46	.300	.650	0	—	0	-2	-2	0	-0.1
Total	3	6	4	.600	83	0	0	0	7	94^2	98	44	1	2	47	45	14.0	3.90	93	.276	.364	0	.000	-1	-2	-3	2	-0.7
● SHANE RAWLEY	Rawley, Shane William b: 7/27/55, Racine, Wis. BR/TL, 6', 180 lbs. Deb: 4/6/78																											
1978	Sea-A	4	9	.308	52	2	0	0	4	111^1	114	57	7	5	51	66	13.7	4.12	93	.275	.362	0	—	0	-4	-4	1	-0.3
1979	Sea-A	5	9	.357	48	3	0	0	11	84^1	88	40	2	1	40	48	13.8	3.84	114	.278	.361	0	—	0	4	5	1	0.9
1980	Sea-A	7	7	.500	59	0	0	0	13	113^2	103	44	3	3	63	68	13.4	3.33	125	.257	.363	0	—	0	9	10	2	1.6
1981	Sea-A	4	6	.400	46	0	0	0	8	68^1	64	31	1	1	38	35	13.6	3.95	98	.257	.358	0	—	0	-2	-1	0	-0.1
1982	NY-A	11	10	.524	47	17	3	0	3	164	165	79	10	2	54	111	12.1	4.06	98	.267	.328	0	—	0	0	-1	1	-0.1
1983	NY-A	14	14	.500	34	33	13	2	1	238^1	246	111	19	3	79	124	12.4	3.78	103	.269	.329	0	—	0	8	4	0	0.4
1984	NY-A	2	3	.400	11	10	0	0	0	42	46	33	0	0	27	24	15.6	6.21	61	.272	.372	0	—	0	-10	-12	-0	-1.2
	Phi-N	10	6	.625	18	18	3	0	0	120^1	117	55	13	1	27	58	10.8	3.81	95	.257	.300	5	.116	-2	-3	-2	-1	-0.6
1985	Phi-N	13	8	.619	36	31	6	2	0	198^2	188	82	16	2	81	106	12.3	3.31	112	.249	.323	8	.138	0	6	8	1	1.0
1986	Phi-N☆	11	7	.611	23	23	7	1	0	157^2	166	67	13	1	50	73	12.4	3.54	109	.270	.326	9	.173	0	3	5	-0	0.6
1987	Phi-N	17	11	.607	36	36	4	1	0	229^2	250	118	23	5	86	123	13.4	4.39	97	.279	.346	12	.152	-0	-8	-4	-1	-0.5
1988	Phi-N	8	16	.333	32	32	4	1	0	198	220	111	27	4	78	87	13.7	4.18	85	.286	.355	6	.105	-1	-16	-13	-0	-1.7
1989	Min-A	5	12	.294	27	25	1	0	0	145	167	89	19	0	60	68	14.1	5.21	80	.293	.361	0	—	0	-21	-16	-1	-1.8
Total	12	111	118	.485	469	230	41	7	40	1871^1	1934	917	153	28	734	991	13.0	4.02	98	.271	.341	40	.138	-3	-34	-20	2	-1.8
● CARL RAY	Ray, Carl Grady b: 1/31/1889, Danbury, N.C. d: 4/3/70, Walnut Cove, N.C. BL/TL, 5'11", 170 lbs. Deb: 9/25/15																											
1915	Phi-A	0	1	.000	2	1	0	0	0	7^1	11	7	0	4	6	6	25.8	4.91	60	.333	.488	0	.000	0	-2	-2	-0	-0.2
1916	Phi-A	0	1	.000	3	1	0	0	0	9^1	9	8	0	1	14	5	23.1	4.82	59	.257	.480	0	.000	-0	-2	-2	-0	-0.3
Total	2	0	2	.000	5	2	0	0	0	16^2	20	15	0	5	20	11	24.3	4.86	59	.294	.484	0	.000	-0	-4	-4	-1	-0.5
● JIM RAY	Ray, James Francis "Sting" b: 12/1/44, Rock Hill, S.C. BR/TR, 6'1", 195 lbs. Deb: 9/16/65																											
1965	Hou-N	0	2	.000	3	2	0	0	0	7^2	11	9	1	0	6	7	20.0	10.57	32	.355	.459	0	.000	-0	-6	-6	0	-1.1
1966	Hou-N	0	0	—	1	0	0	0	0	0	0	0	0	1	—	—	∞	—	—	1.000	95	—	0	-1	-1	0	-0.1	
1968	Hou-N	2	3	.400	41	2	1	0	1	80^2	65	26	5	1	25	71	10.2	2.68	110	.220	.283	1	.067	-1	3	3	-1	0.0
1969	Hou-N	8	2	.800	40	13	0	0	0	115	105	55	11	2	48	115	12.1	3.91	91	.245	.324	3	.115	-1	-4	-5	-1	-0.6
1970	Hou-N	6	3	.667	52	2	0	0	5	105	97	39	13	0	49	67	12.5	3.26	119	.251	.336	5	.185	-0	9	8	0	0.6
1971	Hou-N	10	4	.714	47	1	0	0	3	97^2	72	27	3	2	31	46	9.7	2.12	159	.211	.281	3	.167	0	15	14	-2	1.9
1972	Hou-N	10	9	.526	54	0	0	0	8	90^1	77	50	10	3	44	50	12.4	4.28	79	.227	.321	1	.063	-1	-8	-9	-1	-2.3
1973	Hou-N	6	4	.600	42	0	0	0	6	69	65	37	5	3	38	25	13.8	4.43	82	.253	.356	3	.231	0	-6	-6	-1	-1.0
1974	Det-A	1	3	.250	28	0	0	0	2	52^1	49	27	4	1	29	26	13.6	4.47	85	.254	.354	0	—	0	-5	-4	0	-0.3
Total	9	43	30	.589	308	20	1	0	25	617^2	541	271	52	12	271	407	12.0	3.61	97	.238	.323	16	.137	-3	-3	-8	-6	-2.9
● KEN RAY	Ray, Kenneth Alan b: 11/27/74, Atlanta, Ga. BR/TR, 6'2", 200 lbs. Deb: 7/10/99																											
1999	KC-A	1	0	1.000	13	0	0	0	0	11^1	23	12	2	1	6	0	23.8	8.74	57	.460	.526	0	—	0	-5	-5	0	-0.3
● FARMER RAY	Ray, Robert Henry b: 9/17/1886, Ft.Lyon, Colo. d: 3/11/63, Electra, Tex. BL/TR, 5'11", 160 lbs. Deb: 6/13/10																											
1910	StL-A	4	10	.286	21	16	11	0	0	140^2	146	77	3	7	49	35	12.9	3.58	69	.285	.356	7	.175	0	-17	-18	-3	-2.0
● CURT RAYDON	Raydon, Curtis Lowell b: 11/18/33, Bloomington, Ill. BR/TR, 6'4", 190 lbs. Deb: 4/15/58																											
1958	Pit-N	8	4	.667	31	20	2	1	1	134^1	118	64	18	5	61	85	12.3	3.62	107	.236	.326	1	.026	-2	5	4	-3	-0.2
● BUGS RAYMOND	Raymond, Arthur Lawrence b: 2/24/1882, Chicago, Ill. d: 9/7/12, Chicago, Ill. BR/TR, 5'10", 180 lbs. Deb: 9/23/04																											
1904	Det-A	0	1	.000	5	2	1	0	0	14^2	14	9	0	2	6	7	13.5	3.07	83	.250	.344	0	.000	-1	-1	-1	1	0.0
1907	StL-N	2	4	.333	8	6	6	1	0	64^2	56	34	3	1	21	34	10.9	1.67	150	.230	.294	2	.091	-0	6	6	0	0.6
1908	StL-N	15	25	.375	48	37	23	5	2	324^1	236	116	2	14	95	145	9.6	2.03	116	.207	.277	17	.189	1	12	12	3	2.1
1909	NY-N	18	12	.600	39	30	18	2	0	270	239	98	7	6	87	121	11.1	2.47	104	.245	.311	13	.146	0	4	3	2	0.5
1910	NY-N	4	11	.267	19	11	6	0	0	99^1	106	63	2	8	40	55	14.0	3.81	78	.280	.362	5	.156	-1	-9	-9	2	-1.2
1911	NY-N	6	4	.600	17	9	4	1	0	81^2	73	40	1	2	33	39	11.9	3.31	102	.248	.328	5	.200	-0	1	1	1	0.1
Total	6	45	57	.441	136	95	58	9	2	854^2	724	360	15	33	282	401	10.9	2.49	105	.235	.306	42	.160	-0	13	11	9	2.1
● HARRY RAYMOND	Raymond, Harry H. "Jack" b: 2/20/1862, Utica, N.Y. d: 3/21/25, San Diego, Cal. 5'9", 179 lbs. Deb: 9/9/1888 ♦																											
1889	Lou-a	1	0	1.000	1	1	1	0	0	9	8	2	0	0	11	1	19.0	1.00	385	.229	.413	123	.239	0	3	3	-0	0.2
● CLAUDE RAYMOND	Raymond, Joseph Claude Marc "Frenchy" b: 5/7/37, St.Jean, Que., Canada BR/TR, 5'10", 175 lbs. Deb: 4/15/59																											
1959	Chi-A	0	0	—	3	0	0	0	0	4	5	4	2	0	2	1	15.8	9.00	42	.333	.412	0	—	0	-2	-2	0	-0.1
1961	Mil-N	1	0	1.000	13	0	0	0	2	20^1	22	9	2	1	9	13	14.2	3.98	94	.275	.356	0	.000	-0	0	-1	0	0.0

YEAR	TM/L	W	L	PCT	G	GS	CG	SH	SV	IP	H	R	HR	HB	BB	SO	RAT	ERA	ERA+	OAV	OOB	BH	AVG	PB	PR	PR+	PD	TPI
1962	Mil-N	5	5	.500	26	0	0	0	10	42^2	37	15	5	2	15	40	11.4	2.74	138	.236	.310	0	.000	-1	6	5	-1	0.9
1963	Mil-N	4	6	.400	45	0	0	0	5	53^1	57	36	12	4	27	44	14.9	5.40	60	.268	.361	2	.500	2	-13	-13	1	-2.3
1964	Hou-N	5	5	.500	38	0	0	0	0	79^2	64	28	3	3	22	56	10.1	2.82	121	.229	.292	1	.071	-0	6	5	1	0.8
1965	Hou-N	7	4	.636	33	7	2	0	5	96^1	87	35	6	5	16	79	10.1	2.90	116	.244	.286	3	.115	-1	7	5	-0	0.6
1966	Hou-N☆	7	5	.583	62	0	0	0	16	92	85	39	10	4	25	73	11.2	3.13	109	.242	.300	1	.111	-0	5	3	-2	0.3
1967	Hou-N	0	4	.000	21	0	0	0	5	31	31	12	5	2	7	17	11.6	3.19	104	.256	.308	1	.200	0	1	0	-0	0.1
	Atl-N	4	1	.800	28	0	0	0	5	34^1	33	11	2	0	11	14	11.5	2.62	127	.260	.319	0	.000	-0	3	3	0	0.5
	Yr	4	5	.444	49	0	0	0	10	65^1	64	23	7	2	18	31	11.6	2.89	115	.258	.313	1	.143	0	4	3	-0	0.6
1968	Atl-N	3	5	.375	36	0	0	0	10	60^1	56	21	4	1	18	37	11.2	2.83	106	.256	.315	1	.143	-0	1	1	0	0.2
1969	Atl-N	2	2	.500	33	0	0	0	1	48	56	34	4	2	13	15	13.3	5.25	69	.298	.350	2	.286	0	-9	-9	-1	-0.8
	Mon-N	1	2	.333	15	0	0	0	1	22	21	12	2	2	8	11	12.7	4.09	90	.256	.337	0	.000	-0	-1	-1	-1	-0.1
	Yr	3	4	.429	48	0	0	0	2	70	77	46	6	4	21	26	13.1	4.89	74	.285	.346	2	.182	-0	-10	-10	-0	-0.9
1970	Mon-N	6	7	.462	59	0	0	0	23	83^1	76	48	13	2	27	68	11.3	4.43	93	.240	.303	0	.000	-1	-3	-3	-1	-0.8
1971	Mon-N	1	7	.125	37	0	0	0	0	53^2	81	34	5	0	25	29	17.8	4.70	75	.373	.438	0	.000	-0	-7	-7	1	-0.9
Total	12	46	53	.465	449	7	2	0	83	721	711	338	75	28	225	497	12.0	3.66	96	.261	.324	11	.109	-2	-7	-13	-0	-1.6

● BARRY RAZIANO Raziano, Barry John b: 2/5/47, New Orleans, La. BB/TR, 5'10", 175 lbs. Deb: 8/18/73

YEAR	TM/L	W	L	PCT	G	GS	CG	SH	SV	IP	H	R	HR	HB	BB	SO	RAT	ERA	ERA+	OAV	OOB	BH	AVG	PB	PR	PR+	PD	TPI
1973	KC-A	0	0	—	2	0	0	0	0	5	6	3	1	1	1	0	14.4	5.40	76	.316	.381	0	—	0	-1	-1	0	0.0
1974	Cal-A	1	2	.333	13	0	0	0	1	16^2	15	14	1	0	8	9	12.4	6.48	53	.246	.333	0	—	0	-5	-6	-0	-1.1
Total	2	1	2	.333	15	0	0	0	1	21^2	21	17	2	1	9	9	12.9	6.23	58	.262	.344	0	—	0	-6	-6	-0	-1.1

● RIP REAGAN Reagan, Arthur (b: Arthur Edgar Ragan) b: 6/5/1878, Lincoln, Ill. d: 6/8/53, Kansas City, Mo. BR/TR, 5'11", 170 lbs. Deb: 9/19/03

YEAR	TM/L	W	L	PCT	G	GS	CG	SH	SV	IP	H	R	HR	HB	BB	SO	RAT	ERA	ERA+	OAV	OOB	BH	AVG	PB	PR	PR+	PD	TPI
1903	Cin-N	0	2	.000	3	2	2	0	0	18	40	30	0	1	7	7	24.0	6.00	59	.455	.500	2	.250	0	-5	-4	-0	-0.4

● BRITT REAMES Reames, William Britt b: 8/19/73, Seneca, S.C. BR/TR, 5'11", 175 lbs. Deb: 8/20/2000

YEAR	TM/L	W	L	PCT	G	GS	CG	SH	SV	IP	H	R	HR	HB	BB	SO	RAT	ERA	ERA+	OAV	OOB	BH	AVG	PB	PR	PR+	PD	TPI
2000	*StL-N	2	1	.667	8	7	0	0	0	40^2	30	17	4	1	23	31	12.0	2.88	161	.207	.320	2	.167	-0	8	8	0	0.5

● JEFF REARDON Reardon, Jeffrey James b: 10/1/55, Dalton, Mass. BR/TR, 6'1", 195 lbs. Deb: 8/25/79

YEAR	TM/L	W	L	PCT	G	GS	CG	SH	SV	IP	H	R	HR	HB	BB	SO	RAT	ERA	ERA+	OAV	OOB	BH	AVG	PB	PR	PR+	PD	TPI
1979	NY-N	1	2	.333	18	0	0	0	2	20^2	12	7	2	0	9	10	9.1	1.74	209	.174	.269	0	—	0	5	4	-0	0.7
1980	NY-N	8	7	.533	61	0	0	0	6	110^1	96	36	10	0	47	101	11.7	2.61	136	.231	.310	0	.000	-1	12	12	-2	1.4
1981	NY-N	1	0	1.000	18	0	0	0	2	28^2	27	11	2	1	12	28	12.6	3.45	101	.245	.325	0	.000	-0	0	0	-1	-0.1
	*Mon-N	2	0	1.000	25	0	0	0	6	41^2	21	6	3	1	9	21	6.7	1.30	270	.148	.204	0	.000	-0	10	10	-1	0.6
	Yr	3	0	1.000	43	0	0	0	8	70^1	48	17	5	2	21	49	9.1	2.18	160	.190	.258	0	.000	-1	10	10	-2	0.5
1982	Mon-N	7	4	.636	75	0	0	0	26	109	87	28	6	2	36	86	10.3	2.06	177	.221	.289	1	.100	-0	19	19	-1	2.6
1983	Mon-N	7	9	.438	66	0	0	0	21	92	87	34	7	1	44	78	12.9	3.03	119	.250	.336	1	.125	-0	6	6	-2	1.0
1984	Mon-N	7	7	.500	68	0	0	0	23	87	70	31	5	3	37	79	11.4	2.90	118	.220	.307	0	.000	-1	7	5	-2	0.8
1985	Mon-N★	2	8	.200	63	0	0	0	**41**	87^2	68	31	7	1	26	67	9.8	3.18	107	.209	.270	2	.286	0	4	2	-1	0.4
1986	Mon-N☆	7	9	.438	62	0	0	0	35	89	83	42	12	1	26	67	11.1	3.94	94	.251	.307	1	.125	-0	-2	-2	-0	-0.6
1987	*Min-A	8	8	.500	63	0	0	0	31	80^1	70	41	14	3	28	83	11.3	4.48	103	.232	.303	0	—	0	-0	1	-1	0.2
1988	Min-A☆	2	4	.333	63	0	0	0	42	73	68	21	6	2	15	56	10.5	2.47	165	.245	.289	0	—	0	12	13	-2	2.2
1989	Min-A	5	4	.556	65	0	0	0	31	73	68	33	8	3	12	46	10.2	4.07	102	.246	.285	0	—	0	-1	1	-2	-0.1
1990	*Bos-A	5	3	.625	47	0	0	0	21	51^1	39	19	5	1	19	33	10.3	3.16	129	.206	.282	0	—	0	4	5	-1	1.0
1991	Bos-A★	1	4	.200	57	0	0	0	40	59^1	54	21	9	1	16	44	10.8	3.03	142	.236	.289	0	—	0	7	8	-2	1.4
1992	Bos-A	2	2	.500	46	0	0	0	27	42^1	53	20	6	1	7	32	13.0	4.25	99	.308	.339	0	—	0	-1	-0	-0	-0.1
	*Atl-N	3	0	1.000	14	0	0	0	3	15^2	14	2	0	1	2	7	9.8	1.15	319	.241	.279	0	—	0	4	4	-0	0.9
1993	Cin-N	4	6	.400	58	0	0	0	8	61^2	66	34	4	5	10	35	11.8	4.09	99	.270	.313	0	.000	-0	-0	-0	-1	-0.2
1994	NY-A	1	0	1.000	11	0	0	0	2	9^2	17	9	3	0	3	4	18.6	8.38	55	.386	.426	0	—	0	-4	-4	-0	-0.5
Total	16	73	77	.487	880	0	0	0	367	1132^1	1000	426	109	27	358	877	11.0	3.16	121	.236	.299	5	.088	-3	81	84	-19	11.6

● JEREMIAH REARDON Reardon, Jeremiah J. b: 9/1868, d: 4/22/07, St.Louis, Mo. Deb: 7/17/1886

YEAR	TM/L	W	L	PCT	G	GS	CG	SH	SV	IP	H	R	HR	HB	BB	SO	RAT	ERA	ERA+	OAV	OOB	BH	AVG	PB	PR	PR+	PD	TPI
1886	StL-N	0	1	.000	1	1	1	0	0	8	10	8	1		5	0	16.9	6.75	48	.323	.417	1	.250	0	-3	-3	-0	-0.3
	Cin-a	0	1	.000	1	1	0	0	0	2	5	4	0	0	4	0	40.5	18.00	20	.500	.643	0	.000	-1	-3	-3	0	-0.5
Total	1	0	2	.000	2	2	1	0	0	10	15	12	1	0	9	0	21.6	9.00	36	.366	.480	1	.143	-1	-6	-6	-0	-0.8

● FRANK REBERGER Reberger, Frank Beall "Crane" b: 6/7/44, Caldwell, Idaho BL/TR, 6'5", 200 lbs. Deb: 6/6/68 C

YEAR	TM/L	W	L	PCT	G	GS	CG	SH	SV	IP	H	R	HR	HB	BB	SO	RAT	ERA	ERA+	OAV	OOB	BH	AVG	PB	PR	PR+	PD	TPI
1968	Chi-N	0	1	.000	3	1	0	0	0	6	9	4	1	0	2	3	16.5	4.50	70	.346	.393	0	—	0	-1	-1	0	-0.1
1969	SD-N	1	2	.333	67	0	0	0	6	87^2	83	38	6	2	41	65	12.9	3.59	99	.258	.345	1	.200	0	0	-1	2	0.2
1970	SF-N	7	8	.467	45	18	3	0	2	152	178	108	13	7	98	117	16.8	5.57	72	.293	.397	11	.234	1	-26	-27	-0	-2.3
1971	SF-N	3	0	1.000	13	7	0	0	0	43^2	37	20	5	2	19	21	12.0	3.92	87	.228	.317	3	.231	0	-2	-3	0	-0.1
1972	SF-N	3	4	.429	20	11	2	0	0	99^1	97	49	10	5	37	52	12.6	3.99	87	.257	.332	8	.229	2	-6	-5	1	0.0
Total	5	14	15	.483	148	37	5	0	8	388^2	404	219	35	16	197	258	14.3	4.52	81	.270	.361	23	.230	4	-35	-36	4	-2.3

● JOHN RECCIUS Reccius, John b: 10/29/1859, Louisville, Ky. d: 9/1/30, Louisville, Ky. 5'6.5", Deb: 5/2/1882 F♦

YEAR	TM/L	W	L	PCT	G	GS	CG	SH	SV	IP	H	R	HR	HB	BB	SO	RAT	ERA	ERA+	OAV	OOB	BH	AVG	PB	PR	PR+	PD	TPI
1882	Lou-a	4	6	.400	13	10	9	1	0	95	106	70	3		22	31	12.1	3.03	82	.264	.303	63	.237	3	-4	-6	-1	-0.5
1883	Lou-a	0	0	—	1	0	0	0	0	4	10	3	0		0	0	22.5	2.25	133	.455	.455	9	.143	-0	0	0	0	0.0
Total	2	4	6	.400	14	10	9	1	0	99	116	73	3		22	31	12.5	3.00	83	.274	.310	72	.219	3	-3	-6	-1	-0.5

● PHIL RECCIUS Reccius, Phillip b: 6/7/1862, Louisville, Ky. d: 2/15/03, Louisville, Ky. 5'9", 163 lbs. Deb: 9/25/1882 F♦

YEAR	TM/L	W	L	PCT	G	GS	CG	SH	SV	IP	H	R	HR	HB	BB	SO	RAT	ERA	ERA+	OAV	OOB	BH	AVG	PB	PR	PR+	PD	TPI
1884	Lou-a	6	7	.462	18	11	11	0	0	129^1	118	80	2	4	19	46	9.8	2.71	114	.228	.261	63	.240	2	8	6	0	0.7
1885	Lou-a	0	4	.000	7	5	4	0	1	40	46	35	0	1	11	10	13.0	3.82	84	.253	.299	97	.241	1	-3	-3	1	-0.1
1886	Lou-a	0	1	.000	1	1	0	0	0	3	7	6	0	0	3	0	30.0	9.00	40	.467	.556	4	.308	0	-2	-2	-0	-0.3
1887	Cle-a	0	0	—	1	0	0	0	0	7	13	7	0	0	5	0	16.7	7.71	56	.433	.433	71	.281	-0	-3	-3	0	-0.1
Total	4	6	12	.333	27	17	15	0	1	179^1	184	128	2	5	38	56	11.1	3.26	97	.247	.284	257	.255	4	1	-2	1	0.2

● PHIL REDDING Redding, Philip Hayden b: 1/28/1889, Crystal Springs, Miss. d: 3/31/28, Greenwood, Miss. BL/TR, 5'11.5", 190 lbs. Deb: 9/14/12

YEAR	TM/L	W	L	PCT	G	GS	CG	SH	SV	IP	H	R	HR	HB	BB	SO	RAT	ERA	ERA+	OAV	OOB	BH	AVG	PB	PR	PR+	PD	TPI
1912	StL-N	2	1	.667	3	3	2	0	0	25^1	31	17	2	0	11	9	14.9	4.97	69	.313	.382	0	.000	-1	-4	-4	0	-0.5
1913	StL-N	0	0	—	1	0	0	0	0	2^2	2	2	0	0	1	1	10.1	6.75	48	.286	.375	0	.000	-0	-1	-1	0	-0.1
Total	2	2	1	.667	4	3	2	0	0	28	33	19	2	0	12	10	14.5	5.14	66	.311	.381	0	.000	-1	-5	-5	-0	-0.6

● PETE REDFERN Redfern, Peter Irvine b: 8/25/54, Glendale, Cal. BR/TR, 6'2", 195 lbs. Deb: 5/15/76

YEAR	TM/L	W	L	PCT	G	GS	CG	SH	SV	IP	H	R	HR	HB	BB	SO	RAT	ERA	ERA+	OAV	OOB	BH	AVG	PB	PR	PR+	PD	TPI
1976	Min-A	8	8	.500	23	23	1	1	0	118	105	61	6	3	63	74	13.0	3.51	102	.241	.341	0	—	0	0	1	-1	0.1
1977	Min-A	6	9	.400	30	28	1	0	0	137^1	164	89	13	4	66	73	15.3	5.18	77	.304	.384	0	—	0	-17	-18	1	-1.7
1978	Min-A	0	2	.000	3	2	0	0	0	9^2	10	12	2	0	6	4	14.9	6.52	59	.294	.400	0	—	0	-3	-3	0	-0.5
1979	Min-A	7	3	.700	40	6	0	0	1	108^1	106	45	8	1	35	85	11.8	3.49	126	.258	.318	0	—	0	9	10	-1	0.8
1980	Min-A	7	7	.500	23	16	2	0	2	104^2	117	58	11	0	33	73	12.9	4.56	96	.283	.336	0	—	0	-6	-2	-1	-0.3
1981	Min-A	9	8	.529	24	23	3	0	0	141^2	140	70	12	2	52	77	12.3	4.07	97	.261	.328	0	—	0	-6	-2	-1	-0.3
1982	Min-A	5	11	.313	27	13	2	0	0	94^1	122	74	16	1	51	40	16.6	6.58	65	.322	.404	0	—	0	-26	-23	0	-3.3
Total	7	42	48	.467	170	111	9	1	3	714	764	409	68	11	306	426	13.6	4.54	90	.278	.353	0	—	0	-49	-36	-2	-5.2

● MARK REDMAN Redman, Mark Allen b: 1/5/74, San Diego, Cal. BL/TL, 6'5", 220 lbs. Deb: 7/24/99

YEAR	TM/L	W	L	PCT	G	GS	CG	SH	SV	IP	H	R	HR	HB	BB	SO	RAT	ERA	ERA+	OAV	OOB	BH	AVG	PB	PR	PR+	PD	TPI
1999	Min-A	1	0	1.000	5	1	0	0	0	12^2	17	13	3	1	7	11	17.8	8.53	60	.298	.385	0	—	0	-5	-5	-0	-0.3
2000	Min-A	12	9	.571	32	24	0	0	0	151^1	168	81	22	3	45	117	12.8	4.76	111	.281	.334	0	.000	-0	3	8	-1	0.8
Total	2	13	9	.591	37	25	0	0	0	164	185	94	25	4	52	128	13.2	5.05	104	.282	.339	0	.000	-0	-2	3	-1	0.5

● HOWIE REED Reed, Howard Dean "Diz" b: 12/21/36, Dallas, Tex. d: 12/7/84, Corpus Christi, Tex. BR/TR, 6'1", 210 lbs. Deb: 9/13/58

YEAR	TM/L	W	L	PCT	G	GS	CG	SH	SV	IP	H	R	HR	HB	BB	SO	RAT	ERA	ERA+	OAV	OOB	BH	AVG	PB	PR	PR+	PD	TPI
1958	KC-A	1	0	1.000	3	1	1	0	0	10^1	5	1	0	0	4	5	7.8	0.87	449	.132	.214	0	.000	0	3	3	-0	0.3
1959	KC-A	0	3	.000	6	3	0	0	0	20^2	26	19	3	0	10	11	15.7	7.40	54	.313	.387	0	.000	-0	-8	-8	-1	-1.0
1960	KC-A	0	0	—	1	0	0	0	0	1^2	2	1	1	0	0	1	10.8	0.00	—	.286	.286	0	—	0	1	1	-0	0.0
1964	LA-N	3	4	.429	26	7	0	0	1	90	79	34	4	0	36	52	11.5	3.20	101	.236	.310	2	.100	-0	3	0	1	0.1
1965	*LA-N	7	5	.583	38	5	0	0	1	78	73	31	6	3	27	47	11.9	3.12	105	.243	.312	0	.000	0	4	1	1	0.3
1966	LA-N	0	0	—	1	0	0	0	0	1^2	1	0	0	0	0	0	5.4	0.00	—	.167	.167	0	.000	-0	1	1	0	0.0
	Cal-A	0	1	.000	19	1	0	0	1	43	39	14	5	0	15	17	11.3	2.93	115	.247	.312	0	.000	-1	2	2	-0	0.0

YEAR	TM/L	W	L	PCT	G	GS	CG	SH	SV	IP	H	R	HR	HB	BB	SO	RAT	ERA	ERA+	OAV	OOB	BH	AVG	PB	PR	PR+	PD	TPI
1967	Hou-N	1	1	.500	4	2	0	0	0	18^1	19	8	0	0	2	9	10.3	3.44	96	.268	.288	0	.000	-0	-0	-0	-0	-0.1
1969	Mon-N	6	7	.462	31	15	2	1	1	106	119	59	7	2	50	59	14.5	4.84	76	.290	.369	4	.125	1	-15	-13	2	-1.2
1970	Mon-N	6	5	.545	57	1	0	0	5	89	81	34	7	2	40	42	12.4	3.13	131	.252	.339	0	.000	-0	9	10	0	1.2
1971	Mon-N	2	3	.400	43	0	0	0	0	56^2	66	28	8	0	24	25	14.3	4.29	82	.296	.364	0	.000	-0	-5	-5	0	-0.4
Total	10	26	29	.473	229	35	3	1	9	515^1	510	229	41	7	208	268	12.7	3.72	96	.261	.334	6	.066	-1	-5	-9	3	-0.8

● JERRY REED Reed, Jerry Maxwell b: 10/8/55, Bryson City, N.C. BR/TR, 6'1", 190 lbs. Deb: 9/11/81

YEAR	TM/L	W	L	PCT	G	GS	CG	SH	SV	IP	H	R	HR	HB	BB	SO	RAT	ERA	ERA+	OAV	OOB	BH	AVG	PB	PR	PR+	PD	TPI
1981	Phi-N	0	1	.000	4	0	0	0	0	4^2	7	4	0	0	6	5	25.1	7.71	47	.333	.481	0	—	0	-2	-2	0	-0.4
1982	Phi-N	1	0	1.000	7	0	0	0	0	8^2	11	6	0	1	3	1	15.6	5.19	71	.324	.395	0	—	0	-2	-1	-0	-0.2
	Cle-A	1	1	.500	6	1	0	0	0	15^2	15	6	1	0	3	10	10.3	3.45	119	.250	.286	0	—	0	1	1	0	0.1
1983	Cle-A	0	0	—	7	0	0	0	0	21^1	26	19	4	0	9	11	14.8	7.17	59	.310	.376	0	—	0	-7	-7	1	-0.2
1985	Cle-A	3	5	.375	33	5	0	0	8	72^1	67	41	12	3	19	37	11.1	4.11	101	.245	.302	0	—	0	0	0	1	0.1
1986	Sea-A	4	0	1.000	11	4	0	0	0	34^2	38	13	3	0	13	16	13.2	3.12	136	.273	.336	0	—	0	4	4	-0	0.4
1987	Sea-A	1	2	.333	39	1	0	0	7	81^2	79	32	7	3	24	51	11.7	3.42	139	.255	.315	0	—	0	10	11	-0	0.5
1988	Sea-A	1	1	.500	46	0	0	0	1	86^1	82	42	8	2	33	48	12.2	3.96	105	.256	.330	0	—	0	0	2	1	0.2
1989	Sea-A	7	7	.500	52	1	0	0	0	101^2	89	44	10	1	43	50	11.8	3.19	127	.235	.314	0	—	0	8	9	-0	1.2
1990	Sea-A	0	1	.000	4	0	0	0	0	7^1	8	4	1	0	3	2	13.5	4.91	81	.286	.355	0	—	0	-1	-1	0	-0.1
	Bos-A	2	1	.667	29	0	0	0	2	45	55	27	1	0	16	17	14.2	4.80	85	.302	.359	0	—	0	-4	-3	-0	-0.2
	Yr	2	2	.500	33	0	0	0	2	52^1	63	31	2	0	19	19	14.1	4.82	85	.300	.358	0	—	0	-5	-4	0	-0.3
Total	9	20	19	.513	238	12	0	0	18	479^1	477	238	47	10	172	248	12.4	3.94	107	.261	.328	0	—	0	7	14	2	1.4

● RICK REED Reed, Richard Allen b: 8/16/64, Huntington, W.Va. BR/TR, 6', 205 lbs. Deb: 8/8/88

YEAR	TM/L	W	L	PCT	G	GS	CG	SH	SV	IP	H	R	HR	HB	BB	SO	RAT	ERA	ERA+	OAV	OOB	BH	AVG	PB	PR	PR+	PD	TPI
1988	Pit-N	1	0	1.000	2	2	0	0	0	12	10	4	1	0	2	6	9.0	3.00	114	.233	.267	0	.000	-0	1	1	0	0.0
1989	Pit-N	1	4	.200	15	7	0	0	0	54^2	62	35	5	2	11	34	12.3	5.60	60	.290	.330	1	.077	-0	-13	-14	-0	-1.2
1990	Pit-N	2	3	.400	13	8	1	1	1	53^2	62	32	6	1	12	27	12.6	4.36	83	.279	.319	4	.250	1	-3	-5	-1	-0.4
1991	Pit-N	0	0	—	1	1	0	0	0	4^1	8	6	1	0	1	2	18.7	10.38	34	.400	.429	1	.500	1	-3	-3	-0	-0.1
1992	KC-A	3	7	.300	19	18	1	1	0	100^1	105	47	10	5	20	49	11.7	3.68	110	.271	.316	0	—	0	3	4	1	0.5
1993	KC-A	0	0	—	1	0	0	0	0	3^2	6	4	0	1	1	3	19.6	9.82	47	.375	.444	0	—	0	-2	-2	0	-0.1
	Tex-A	1	0	1.000	2	0	0	0	0	4	6	1	1	1	1	2	18.0	2.25	185	.375	.444	0	—	0	1	1	0	0.2
	Yr	1	0	1.000	3	0	0	0	0	7^2	12	5	1	2	2	5	18.8	5.87	74	.375	.444	0	—	0	-1	-1	0	0.1
1994	Tex-A	1	1	.500	4	3	0	0	0	16^2	17	13	3	1	7	12	13.5	5.94	81	.254	.333	0	—	0	-2	-2	0	-0.2
1995	Cin-N	0	0	—	4	3	0	0	0	17	18	12	5	0	3	10	11.1	5.82	71	.273	.304	0	.000	-0	-3	-3	-0	-0.2
1997	NY-N	13	9	.591	33	31	2	0	0	208^1	186	76	19	5	31	113	9.6	2.89	140	.239	.273	10	.175	4	30	28	-0	3.0
1998	NY-N☆	16	11	.593	31	31	2	1	0	212^1	208	84	30	6	29	153	10.3	3.48	119	.261	.292	8	.125	-1	18	16	1	2.0
1999	*NY-N	11	5	.688	26	26	1	1	0	149^1	163	77	23	1	47	104	12.7	4.58	96	.281	.336	11	.244	2	-0	-3	2	0.1
2000	*NY-N	11	5	.688	30	30	0	0	0	184	192	90	28	5	34	121	11.3	4.11	107	.266	.304	10	.204	1	11	7	-3	0.4
Total	12	60	45	.571	181	160	7	4	1	1020^1	1043	481	132	28	199	636	11.2	3.93	105	.266	.306	45	.178	7	37	23	1	4.0

● BOB REED Reed, Robert Edward b: 1/12/45, Boston, Mass. BR/TR, 5'10", 175 lbs. Deb: 9/5/69

YEAR	TM/L	W	L	PCT	G	GS	CG	SH	SV	IP	H	R	HR	HB	BB	SO	RAT	ERA	ERA+	OAV	OOB	BH	AVG	PB	PR	PR+	PD	TPI
1969	Det-A	0	0	—	8	1	0	0	0	14^2	9	3	0	0	8	9	10.4	1.84	203	.184	.298	1	.500	0	3	3	0	0.2
1970	Det-A	2	4	.333	16	4	0	0	2	46^1	54	25	5	0	14	26	13.2	4.86	77	.292	.342	1	.083	-0	-6	-6	-1	-0.8
Total	2	2	4	.333	24	5	0	0	2	61	63	28	5	0	22	35	12.5	4.13	90	.269	.332	2	.143	-0	-3	-3	-0	-0.6

● RON REED Reed, Ronald Lee b: 11/2/42, LaPorte, Ind. BR/TR, 6'6", 215 lbs. Deb: 9/26/66

YEAR	TM/L	W	L	PCT	G	GS	CG	SH	SV	IP	H	R	HR	HB	BB	SO	RAT	ERA	ERA+	OAV	OOB	BH	AVG	PB	PR	PR+	PD	TPI
1966	Atl-N	1	1	.500	2	2	0	0	0	8^1	8	2	1	0	4	6	11.9	2.16	168	.226	.314	0	.000	-0	1	1	-0	0.2
1967	Atl-N	1	1	.500	3	3	0	0	0	21^1	21	8	1	2	3	11	11.0	2.95	112	.262	.306	0	.000	-1	1	1	1	0.1
1968	Atl-N★	11	10	.524	35	28	6	1	0	201^2	189	87	10	6	49	111	10.9	3.35	89	.246	.297	10	.161	1	-8	-8	-0	-0.7
1969	*Atl-N	18	10	.643	36	33	7	1	0	241^1	227	103	24	6	56	160	10.8	3.47	104	.246	.294	10	.125	-2	3	4	-1	0.1
1970	Atl-N	7	10	.412	21	18	6	0	0	134^2	140	69	16	2	39	68	12.1	4.41	97	.266	.319	4	.091	-2	-5	-2	1	-0.3
1971	Atl-N	13	14	.481	32	32	8	1	0	222^1	221	105	26	2	54	129	11.2	3.72	100	.261	.306	11	.149	-3	-6	-0	-1	-0.4
1972	Atl-N	11	15	.423	31	30	11	1	0	213	222	109	18	6	60	111	12.2	3.93	97	.270	.325	13	.178	-1	-11	-3	1	-0.3
1973	Atl-N	4	11	.267	20	19	2	0	1	116^1	133	71	7	3	31	64	12.9	4.41	89	.287	.335	9	.200	-0	-10	-6	1	-0.6
1974	Atl-N	10	11	.476	28	28	6	2	0	186	171	76	16	2	41	78	10.4	3.39	112	.243	.286	6	.105	-3	5	8	-2	0.3
1975	Atl-N	4	5	.444	10	10	1	0	0	74^2	93	39	1	0	16	40	13.1	4.22	90	.304	.339	6	.231	1	-5	-3	-0	-0.3
	StL-N	9	8	.529	24	24	7	2	0	175^2	181	79	4	4	37	99	11.4	3.23	117	.263	.305	9	.161	-0	8	10	-1	0.8
	Yr	13	13	.500	34	34	8	2	0	250^1	274	118	5	4	53	139	11.9	3.52	107	.276	.315	15	.183	1	3	7	-1	0.5
1976	*Phi-N	8	7	.533	59	4	1	0	14	128	88	39	8	2	32	96	8.6	2.46	144	.193	.249	4	.167	-0	15	15	-1	2.0
1977	*Phi-N	7	5	.583	60	3	0	0	15	124^1	101	41	9	1	37	84	10.1	2.75	146	.223	.283	2	.111	-0	16	17	-1	1.8
1978	*Phi-N	3	4	.429	66	0	0	0	17	108^2	87	32	6	5	23	85	9.5	2.24	160	.223	.275	0	.000	-0	16	16	-2	1.4
1979	Phi-N	13	8	.619	61	0	0	0	5	102	110	52	9	2	32	58	12.7	4.15	92	.278	.335	3	.300	1	-5	-3	-0	-0.6
1980	*Phi-N	7	5	.583	55	0	0	0	9	91^1	88	45	4	1	30	54	11.7	4.04	94	.253	.314	3	.300	1	-4	-2	1	-0.1
1981	*Phi-N	5	3	.625	39	0	0	0	8	61^1	54	26	6	1	17	40	10.6	3.08	118	.237	.293	3	.500	1	3	4	1	0.6
1982	Phi-N	5	5	.500	57	2	0	0	14	98	85	30	4	3	24	57	10.3	2.66	138	.235	.289	4	.333	2	10	11	2	1.7
1983	*Phi-N	9	1	.900	61	0	0	0	8	95^2	89	42	5	1	34	73	11.7	3.48	103	.248	.315	1	.167	-0	2	1	-2	-0.1
1984	Chi-A	0	6	.000	51	0	0	0	12	73	67	29	7	1	14	57	10.1	3.08	135	.248	.288	0	.000	-0	7	8	0	0.9
Total	19	146	140	.510	751	236	55	8	103	2477^2	2374	1084	182	50	633	1481	11.1	3.46	107	.252	.303	98	.158	-6	34	67	-3	6.5

● STEVE REED Reed, Steven Vincent b: 3/11/66, Los Angeles, Cal. BR/TR, 6'2", 202 lbs. Deb: 8/30/92

YEAR	TM/L	W	L	PCT	G	GS	CG	SH	SV	IP	H	R	HR	HB	BB	SO	RAT	ERA	ERA+	OAV	OOB	BH	AVG	PB	PR	PR+	PD	TPI
1992	SF-N	1	0	1.000	18	0	0	0	0	15^2	13	5	2	1	3	11	9.8	2.30	144	.220	.270	0	—	0	2	2	1	0.2
1993	Col-N	9	5	.643	64	0	0	0	3	84^1	80	47	13	3	30	51	12.1	4.48	107	.259	.330	0	.000	-1	-4	2	0	0.3
1994	Col-N	3	2	.600	**61**	0	0	0	3	64	79	33	9	6	26	51	15.6	3.94	126	.306	.383	0	.000	-0	2	6	-1	0.4
1995	*Col-N	5	2	.714	71	0	0	0	3	84	61	24	8	1	21	79	8.9	2.14	252	.203	.257	1	.333	0	19	**24**	1	2.0
1996	Col-N	4	3	.571	70	0	0	0	0	75	66	38	11	6	19	51	10.9	3.96	132	.239	.302	1	.333	0	2	9	-1	0.7
1997	Col-N	4	6	.400	63	0	0	0	6	62^1	49	28	10	5	27	43	11.7	4.04	128	.219	.316	0	.000	-0	1	6	0	1.0
1998	SF-N	2	1	.667	50	0	0	0	1	54^2	30	10	4	4	19	50	8.7	1.48	268	.160	.251	1	.333	0	17	16	-1	0.8
	*Cle-A	2	2	.500	20	0	0	0	0	25^2	26	19	4	1	8	23	12.3	6.66	72	.260	.321	0	—	0	-6	-5	0	-0.7
1999	*Cle-A	3	2	.600	63	0	0	0	0	61^2	69	33	10	3	20	44	13.4	4.23	119	.285	.347	0	—	0	4	5	0	0.4
2000	Cle-A	2	0	1.000	57	0	0	0	0	56	58	30	7	1	21	39	12.9	4.34	115	.269	.336	0	—	0	4	4	0	0.2
Total	9	35	23	.603	537	0	0	0	16	583^1	531	267	78	31	194	442	11.7	3.69	134	.244	.315	3	.143	-1	41	71	0	5.3

● BILL REEDER Reeder, William Edgar b: 2/20/22, Dike, Texas BR/TR, 6'5", 205 lbs. Deb: 4/23/49

YEAR	TM/L	W	L	PCT	G	GS	CG	SH	SV	IP	H	R	HR	HB	BB	SO	RAT	ERA	ERA+	OAV	OOB	BH	AVG	PB	PR	PR+	PD	TPI
1949	StL-N	1	1	.500	21	1	0	0	0	33^2	33	22	2	1	30	21	17.1	5.08	82	.270	.418	0	.000	-0	-4	-3	-0	-0.2

● STAN REES Rees, Stanley Milton "Nellie" b: 2/25/1899, Cynthiana, Ky. d: 8/30/37, Lexington, Ky. BL/TL, 6'3", 190 lbs. Deb: 6/12/18

YEAR	TM/L	W	L	PCT	G	GS	CG	SH	SV	IP	H	R	HR	HB	BB	SO	RAT	ERA	ERA+	OAV	OOB	BH	AVG	PB	PR	PR+	PD	TPI
1918	Was-A	1	0	1.000	2	0	0	0	0	2	3	0	0	0	4	1	31.5	0.00	—	.500	.700	0	—	0	1	1	0	0.2

● BOBBY REEVES Reeves, Robert Edwin "Gunner" b: 6/24/04, Hill City, Tenn. d: 6/4/93, Chattanooga, Tenn. BR/TR, 5'11", 170 lbs. Deb: 6/9/26 ♦

YEAR	TM/L	W	L	PCT	G	GS	CG	SH	SV	IP	H	R	HR	HB	BB	SO	RAT	ERA	ERA+	OAV	OOB	BH	AVG	PB	PR	PR+	PD	TPI
1931	Bos-A	0	0	—	1	0	0	0	0	7^1	6	3	0	0	1	0	8.6	3.68	117	.214	.241	14	.167	0	1	1	0	0.0

● MIKE REGAN Regan, Michael John b: 11/19/1888, Phoenix, N.Y. d: 5/22/61, Albany, N.Y. BR/TR, 5'10", 160 lbs. Deb: 5/13/17

YEAR	TM/L	W	L	PCT	G	GS	CG	SH	SV	IP	H	R	HR	HB	BB	SO	RAT	ERA	ERA+	OAV	OOB	BH	AVG	PB	PR	PR+	PD	TPI
1917	Cin-N	11	10	.524	32	26	16	1	0	216	228	106	4	4	41	50	11.4	2.71	97	.273	.310	15	.200	1	0	-2	3	0.2
1918	Cin-N	5	5	.500	22	6	4	3	2	80	77	38	0	0	29	15	11.9	3.26	82	.262	.328	8	.296	2	-4	-5	-1	-0.6
1919	Cin-N	0	0	—	1	0	0	0	0	2^1	1	1	0	0	0	1	3.9	0.00	—	.143	.143	0	.000	-0	1	1	-0	0.0
Total	3	16	15	.516	55	32	20	4	2	298^1	306	145	4	4	70	66	11.5	2.84	93	.269	.314	23	.223	3	-4	-7	2	-0.4

● PHIL REGAN Regan, Philip Raymond "The Vulture" b: 4/6/37, Otsego, Mich. BR/TR, 6'3", 200 lbs. Deb: 7/19/60 MC

YEAR	TM/L	W	L	PCT	G	GS	CG	SH	SV	IP	H	R	HR	HB	BB	SO	RAT	ERA	ERA+	OAV	OOB	BH	AVG	PB	PR	PR+	PD	TPI
1960	Det-A	0	4	.000	17	7	0	0	1	68	70	39	11	2	25	38	12.8	4.50	88	.267	.336	1	.059	-1	-5	-4	-1	-0.4
1961	Det-A	10	7	.588	32	16	6	0	2	120	134	70	19	1	41	46	13.2	5.25	78	.281	.339	3	.075	-2	-16	-15	-3	-2.3
1962	Det-A	11	9	.550	35	23	6	0	0	171^1	169	89	23	1	64	87	12.3	4.04	101	.254	.320	13	.206	1	-1	0	-2	-0.1
1963	Det-A	15	9	.625	38	27	5	1	1	189	179	95	33	7	59	115	11.7	3.86	97	.245	.308	9	.143	-1	-5	-2	-3	-0.6
1964	Det-A	5	10	.333	32	21	2	0	1	146^2	162	87	21	5	49	91	13.3	5.03	73	.282	.344	13	.317	5	-23	-22	-0	-1.6
1965	Det-A	1	5	.167	16	7	1	0	0	51^2	57	31	6	0	20	37	13.4	5.05	69	.282	.347	1	.083	-0	-9	-9	-0	-1.0

YEAR	TM/L	W	L	PCT	G	GS	CG	SH	SV	IP	H	R	HR	HB	BB	SO	RAT	ERA	ERA+	OAV	OOB	BH	AVG	PB	PR	PR+	PD	TPI
1966	*LA-N☆	14	1	.933	65	0	0	0	**21**	116^2	85	24	6	0	24	88	8.4	1.62	203	.207	.251	3	.143	0	**26**	**24**	1	4.1
1967	LA-N	6	9	.400	55	3	0	0	6	96^1	108	38	2	2	32	53	13.3	2.99	104	.284	.343	1	.100	-0	4	1	1	0.3
1968	LA-N	2	0	1.000	5	0	0	0	0	7^2	10	3	1	0	1	7	12.9	3.52	78	.313	.333	0	.000	-0	-0	-1	-0	-0.2
	Chi-N	10	5	.667	68	0	0	0	25	127	109	36	9	2	24	60	9.6	2.20	144	.232	.272	3	.150	0	11	13	0	2.3
	Yr	12	5	.706	73	0	0	0	**25**	134^2	119	39	10	2	25	67	9.8	2.27	138	.237	.276	3	.143	0	11	12	-0	2.1
1969	Chi-N	12	6	.667	71	0	0	0	17	112	120	49	6	2	35	56	12.6	3.70	109	.282	.339	1	.067	-0	-1	4	0	0.7
1970	Chi-N	5	9	.357	54	0	0	0	12	75^2	81	43	8	1	32	31	13.6	4.76	95	.287	.362	0	.000	-1	-6	-2	2	-0.3
1971	Chi-N	5	5	.500	48	1	0	0	6	73^1	84	37	4	2	33	28	14.6	3.93	100	.301	.379	0	.000	-1	-4	0	1	0.0
1972	Chi-N	0	1	.000	5	0	0	0	0	4	6	1	0	0	2	2	18.0	2.25	169	.400	.471	0	—	0	1	1	-0	0.1
	Chi-A	0	1	.000	10	0	0	0	0	13^1	18	7	1	1	6	4	16.9	4.05	77	.346	.424	1	1.000	0	-1	-1	0	0.0
Total	13	96	81	.542	551	105	20	1	92	1372^2	1392	649	150	26	447	743	12.2	3.84	97	.265	.325	49	.153	1	-31	-15	-4	1.0
● DAN REICHERT	Reichert, Daniel Robert b: 7/12/76, Monterey, Cal. BR/TR, 6'3", 175 lbs. Deb: 7/16/99																											
1999	KC-A	2	2	.500	8	8	0	0	0	36^2	48	38	2	2	32	20	20.1	9.08	55	.327	.453	1	.333	0	-17	-16	-0	-1.3
2000	KC-A	8	10	.444	44	18	1	1	2	153^1	157	92	15	7	91	94	15.0	4.70	107	.271	.376	0	.000	-0	4	5	0	0.5
Total	2	10	12	.455	52	26	1	1	2	190	205	130	17	9	123	114	16.0	5.54	90	.282	.392	1	.250	0	-13	-11	-0	-0.8
● EARL REID	Reid, Earl Percy b: 6/8/13, Bangor, Ala. d: 5/11/84, Cullman, Ala. BL/TR, 6'3", 190 lbs. Deb: 5/8/46																											
1946	Bos-N	1	0	1.000	2	0	0	0	0	3	4	3	0	0	3	2	21.0	3.00	114	.308	.438	0	—	0	0	0	-0	0.0
● BILL REIDY	Reidy, William Joseph b: 10/9/1873, Cleveland, Ohio d: 10/14/15, Cleveland, Ohio BR/TR, 5'10", 175 lbs. Deb: 7/21/1896																											
1896	NY-N	0	1	.000	2	1	1	0	0	13	24	11	0	3	2	1	20.1	7.62	55	.393	.439	0	.000	-1	-5	-5	0	-0.4
1899	Bro-N	1	0	1.000	2	1	1	0	1	7	9	2	0	0	2	2	14.1	2.57	152	.310	.355	0	.000	-1	1	1	0	0.1
1901	Mil-A	16	20	.444	37	33	28	2	0	301^1	364	183	14	9	62	50	13.0	4.21	85	.295	.333	16	.143	-6	-18	-21	-3	-2.8
1902	StL-A	3	5	.375	12	9	7	0	0	95	111	52	0	7	13	16	12.4	4.45	79	.292	.327	8	.195	-0	-9	-10	1	-0.6
1903	StL-A	1	4	.200	5	5	5	0	0	43	53	31	1	3	7	8	13.2	3.98	73	.301	.339	1	.067	-2	-5	-5	-1	-0.8
	Bro-N	6	7	.462	15	13	11	0	0	104	130	54	0	6	14	21	13.0	3.46	92	.315	.346	9	.243	1	-2	-3	-1	-0.4
1904	Bro-N	0	4	.000	6	4	2	0	1	38^1	49	33	0	2	6	11	13.4	4.46	62	.293	.326	5	.156	-0	-7	-7	-1	-0.8
Total	6	27	41	.397	79	66	55	3	2	601^2	740	366	15	30	106	109	13.1	4.17	82	.301	.337	39	.159	-9	-46	-51	-5	-5.7
● ART REINHART	Reinhart, Arthur Conrad b: 5/29/1899, Ackley, Iowa d: 11/11/46, Houston, Tex. BL/TL, 6'1", 170 lbs. Deb: 4/26/19																											
1919	StL-N	0	0	—	1	0	0	0	0	0	0	0	1	0	—	—	—	—	—	1.000	96	—	0	0	0	0	0.0	
1925	StL-N	11	5	.688	20	16	15	1	0	144^2	149	61	7	4	47	26	12.4	3.05	142	.278	.341	22	.328	5	20	20	-0	2.4
1926	*StL-N	10	5	.667	27	11	9	0	0	143	159	75	5	3	47	26	13.2	4.22	93	.295	.355	20	.317	4	-6	-5	1	0.0
1927	StL-N	5	2	.714	21	9	4	2	1	81^2	82	47	5	0	36	15	13.0	4.19	94	.267	.344	10	.313	2	-2	-2	-1	-0.1
1928	StL-N	4	6	.400	23	9	3	1	2	75^1	80	39	3	0	27	12	12.8	2.87	140	.272	.333	4	.167	-0	9	9	-1	1.1
Total	5	30	18	.625	92	45	31	4	3	444^2	470	222	20	8	157	79	12.9	3.60	113	.280	.345	56	.301	10	20	23	-1	3.4
● JACK REIS	Reis, Harrie Crane b: 6/14/1890, Cincinnati, Ohio d: 7/20/39, Cincinnati, Ohio BR/TR, 5'10.5", 160 lbs. Deb: 9/9/11																											
1911	StL-N	0	0	—	3	0	0	0	0	9^1	5	3	0	0	8	4	12.5	0.96	350	.156	.325	0	.000	-0	3	3	0	0.1
● LAURIE REIS	Reis, Lawrence P. b: 11/20/1858, Illinois d: 1/24/21, Chicago, Ill. BR/TR, 160 lbs. Deb: 10/1/1877																											
1877	Chi-N	3	1	.750	4	4	4	1	0	36	29	8	1		6	11	8.8	0.75	396	.213	.246	2	.125	-2	8	8	-0	0.6
1878	Chi-N	1	3	.250	4	4	4	0	0	36	55	34	0		4	8	14.8	3.25	75	.335	.351	3	.150	-1	-4	-3	-1	-0.5
Total	2	4	4	.500	8	8	8	1	0	72	84	42	1		10	19	11.8	2.00	135	.280	.303	5	.139	-2	4	5	-2	0.1
● BOBBY REIS	Reis, Robert Joseph Thomas b: 1/2/09, Woodside, N.Y. d: 5/1/73, St.Paul, Minn. BR/TR, 6'1", 175 lbs. Deb: 9/19/31 ◆																											
1935	Bro-N	3	2	.600	14	2	1	0	2	41^1	46	26	0	1	24	7	15.5	2.83	140	.277	.372	21	.247	1	5	5	1	0.8
1936	Bos-N	6	5	.545	35	5	3	0	0	138^2	152	77	7	5	74	25	15.0	4.48	86	.283	.375	13	.217	1	-7	-10	4	-0.3
1937	Bos-N	0	0	—	4	0	0	0	0	5	3	1	0	0	5	0	14.4	1.80	199	.158	.333	21	.244	1	1	1	-0	0.1
1938	Bos-N	1	6	.143	16	2	1	0	0	57^2	61	35	5	6	41	20	16.9	4.99	69	.271	.397	9	.184	-0	-8	-11	0	-1.1
Total	4	10	13	.435	69	9	5	0	2	242^2	262	139	12	12	144	52	15.5	4.27	88	.277	.379	70	.233	3	-8	-14	5	-0.5
● TOMMY REIS	Reis, Thomas Edward b: 8/6/14, Newport, Ky. BR/TR, 6'2", 180 lbs. Deb: 4/27/38																											
1938	Phi-N	0	1	.000	4	0	0	0	0	4^2	8	11	0	0	8	2	30.9	19.29	20	.364	.533	0	.000	-0	-8	-8	0	-1.3
	Bos-N	0	0	—	4	0	0	0	0	6^1	8	5	1	0	1	4	12.8	7.11	48	.296	.321	0	—	0	-2	-3	-0	-0.2
	Yr	0	1	.000	8	0	0	0	0	11	16	16	1	0	9	6	20.5	12.27	30	.327	.431	0	.000	-0	-10	-11	-0	-1.5
● BUGS REISIGL	Reisigl, Jacob b: 12/12/1887, Brooklyn, N.Y. d: 2/24/57, Amsterdam, N.Y. BR/TR, 5'10.5", 175 lbs. Deb: 9/20/11																											
1911	Cle-A	0	1	.000	2	1	1	0	0	13	13	9	1	0	3	6	11.1	6.23	55	.271	.314	0	.000	-1	-4	-4	-0	-0.3
● DOC REISLING	Reisling, Frank Carl b: 7/25/1874, Martins Ferry, O. d: 3/4/55, Tulsa, Okla. BR/TR, 5'10", 180 lbs. Deb: 9/10/04																											
1904	Bro-N	3	4	.429	7	7	6	1	0	51	45	16	0	9	10	19	11.3	2.12	130	.238	.308	2	.154	0	4	4	0	0.5
1905	Bro-N	0	1	.000	2	0	0	0	0	3	3	1	0	0	4	2	21.0	3.00	96	.273	.467	0	.000	0	0	-0	0	0.0
1909	Was-A	2	4	.333	10	6	6	1	0	66^2	70	29	0	0	17	22	11.7	2.43	100	.270	.315	4	.167	0	0	0	-1	-0.1
1910	Was-A	10	10	.500	30	20	13	2	1	191	185	77	3	5	44	57	11.0	2.54	98	.264	.312	12	.200	2	-1	-1	0	0.1
Total	4	15	19	.441	49	33	25	4	1	311^2	303	123	3	14	75	100	11.3	2.45	103	.261	.314	18	.184	2	3	2	-1	0.5
● BRYAN REKAR	Rekar, Bryan Robert b: 6/3/72, Oak Lawn, Ill. BR/TR, 6'3", 205 lbs. Deb: 7/19/95																											
1995	Col-N	4	6	.400	15	14	1	0	0	85	95	51	11	3	24	60	12.9	4.98	108	.282	.335	1	.038	-2	-7	3	1	0.2
1996	Col-N	2	4	.333	14	11	0	0	0	58^1	87	61	11	5	26	25	18.2	8.95	58	.345	.417	4	.267	1	-31	-20	-0	-1.6
1997	Col-N	1	0	1.000	2	2	0	0	0	9^1	11	7	3	0	6	4	16.4	5.79	89	.282	.378	1	.250	0	-2	-1	-0	0.0
1998	TB-A	2	8	.200	16	15	1	0	0	86^2	95	56	16	2	21	55	12.3	4.98	96	.282	.328	0	—	0	-3	-2	-1	-0.2
1999	TB-A	6	6	.500	27	12	0	0	0	94^2	121	68	14	5	41	55	15.9	5.80	86	.313	.387	1	.200	0	-10	-8	0	-0.9
2000	TB-A	7	10	.412	30	27	2	0	0	173^1	200	92	22	4	39	95	12.6	4.41	112	.291	.332	1	.333	1	10	10	-0	0.9
Total	6	22	34	.393	104	81	4	0	0	507^1	609	335	77	19	157	294	13.9	5.41	94	.299	.354	8	.151	-1	-43	-17	0	-1.6
● MIKE REMLINGER	Remlinger, Michael John b: 3/23/66, Middletown, N.Y. BL/TL, 6', 195 lbs. Deb: 6/15/91																											
1991	SF-N	2	1	.667	8	6	1	1	0	35	36	17	5	0	20	19	14.4	4.37	82	.271	.366	0	.000	-0	-3	-3	-0	-0.3
1994	NY-N	1	5	.167	10	9	0	0	0	54^2	55	30	9	1	35	33	15.0	4.61	91	.261	.368	0	.000	-1	-2	-3	-1	-0.5
1995	NY-N	0	1	.000	5	0	0	0	0	5^2	7	5	1	0	2	6	14.3	6.35	64	.292	.346	0	.000	-0	-1	-1	-0	-0.3
	Cin-N	0	0	—	2	0	0	0	0	1	2	1	0	0	3	1	45.0	9.00	46	.500	.714	0	—	0	-1	-1	0	0.0
	Yr	0	1	.000	7	0	0	0	0	6^2	9	6	1	0	5	7	18.9	6.75	60	.321	.424	0	.000	-0	-2	-2	-0	-0.3
1996	Cin-N	0	1	.000	19	4	0	0	0	27^1	24	17	4	3	19	19	15.1	5.60	76	.242	.380	1	.143	0	-4	-4	0	-0.2
1997	Cin-N	8	8	.500	69	12	2	0	2	124	100	61	11	7	60	145	12.1	4.14	103	.223	.324	2	.095	0	1	2	1	0.3
1998	Cin-N	8	15	.348	35	28	1	1	0	164^1	164	96	23	5	87	144	14.0	4.82	89	.266	.362	5	.106	-2	-11	-10	-2	-1.5
1999	*Atl-N	10	1	.909	73	0	0	0	1	83^2	66	24	9	1	35	81	11.0	2.37	190	.215	.297	0	.000	-0	20	20	-0	2.3
2000	*Atl-N	5	3	.625	71	0	0	0	12	72^2	55	29	6	3	37	72	11.8	3.47	131	.207	.310	0	.000	-0	9	9	-0	1.0
Total	8	34	35	.493	292	59	4	2	15	568^1	509	280	68	20	298	520	13.1	4.15	103	.241	.341	8	.077	-4	9	9	-2	0.8
● WIN REMMERSWAAL	Remmerswaal, Wilhelmus Abraham b: 3/8/54, The Hague, Netherlands BR/TR, 6'2", 160 lbs. Deb: 8/3/79																											
1979	Bos-A	1	0	1.000	8	0	0	0	0	20^1	26	16	1	1	12	16	17.3	7.08	63	.317	.411	0	—	0	-6	-6	-0	-0.3
1980	Bos-A	2	1	.667	14	0	0	0	0	35^1	39	18	4	0	9	20	12.2	4.58	92	.295	.340	0	—	0	-2	-1	-1	-0.2
Total	2	3	1	.750	22	0	0	0	0	55^2	65	34	5	1	21	36	14.1	5.50	78	.304	.369	0	—	0	-9	-7	-1	-0.5
● ALEX REMNEAS	Remneas, Alexander Norman b: 2/21/1886, Minneapolis, Minn. d: 8/27/75, Phoenix, Ariz. BR/TR, 6'1", 180 lbs. Deb: 4/15/12																											
1912	Det-A	0	0	—	1	0	0	0	0	1^2	5	5	0	0	0	0	27.0	27.00	12	.455	.455	0	—	0	-4	-4	0	-0.2
1915	StL-A	0	0	—	2	0	0	0	0	6	3	4	0	1	3	5	10.5	1.50	191	.136	.269	0	.000	-0	1	1	0	0.0
Total	2	0	0	—	3	0	0	0	0	7^2	8	9	0	1	3	5	14.1	7.04	42	.242	.324	0	.000	0	-3	-4	0	-0.2
● ERWIN RENFER	Renfer, Erwin Arthur b: 12/11/1891, Elgin, Ill. d: 10/26/57, Sycamore, Ill. BR/TR, 6', 180 lbs. Deb: 9/18/13																											
1913	Det-A	0	1	.000	1	1	0	0	0	6	5	5	0	1	3	1	13.5	6.00	49	.227	.346	0	.000	-0	-2	-2	0	-0.3

● **LADDIE RENFROE** Renfroe, Cohen Williams b: 5/9/62, Natchez, Miss. BB/TR, 5'11", 200 lbs. Deb: 7/3/91

YEAR	TM/L	W	L	PCT	G	GS	CG	SH	SV	IP	H	R	HR	HB	BB	SO	RAT	ERA	ERA+	OAV	OOB	BH	AVG	PB	PR	PR+	PD	TPI
1991	Chi-N	0	1	.000	4	0	0	0	0	4^2	11	7	1	0	2	4	25.1	13.50	29	.440	.481	0	.000	-0	-5	-5	0	-0.8

● **MARSHALL RENFROE** Renfroe, Marshall Daniel b: 5/25/36, Century, Fla. d: 12/10/70, Pensacola, Fla. BL/TL, 6', 180 lbs. Deb: 9/27/59

YEAR	TM/L	W	L	PCT	G	GS	CG	SH	SV	IP	H	R	HR	HB	BB	SO	RAT	ERA	ERA+	OAV	OOB	BH	AVG	PB	PR	PR+	PD	TPI
1959	SF-N	0	0	—	1	1	0	0	0	2	3	6	1	0	3	3	27.0	27.00	14	.333	.500	0	.000	-0	-5	-5	-0	-0.2

● **HAL RENIFF** Reniff, Harold Eugene "Porky" b: 7/2/38, Warren, Ohio BR/TR, 6', 215 lbs. Deb: 6/8/61

YEAR	TM/L	W	L	PCT	G	GS	CG	SH	SV	IP	H	R	HR	HB	BB	SO	RAT	ERA	ERA+	OAV	OOB	BH	AVG	PB	PR	PR+	PD	TPI
1961	NY-A	2	0	1.000	25	0	0	0	2	45^1	31	14	1	0	31	21	12.3	2.58	144	.197	.330	0	.000	-1	7	6	-1	0.2
1962	NY-A	0	0	—	2	0	0	0	0	3^2	6	3	0	1	5	1	29.5	7.36	51	.400	.571	0	—	0	-1	-2	-0	-0.1
1963	*NY-A	4	3	.571	48	0	0	0	18	89^1	63	31	3	2	42	56	10.8	2.62	134	.202	.301	0	.000	-1	10	9	3	1.3
1964	*NY-A	6	4	.600	41	0	0	0	9	69^1	47	26	3	0	30	38	10.0	3.12	116	.199	.289	1	.100	-1	4	4	0	0.6
1965	NY-A	3	4	.429	51	0	0	0	3	85^1	74	40	4	5	48	74	13.4	3.80	90	.232	.341	0	.000	-0	-3	-4	-0	-0.4
1966	NY-A	3	7	.300	56	0	0	0	9	95^1	80	37	2	5	49	79	12.7	3.21	104	.229	.333	4	.286	-1	2	1	-1	0.2
1967	NY-A	0	2	.000	24	0	0	0	0	40	40	22	0	3	14	24	12.8	4.27	73	.256	.329	0	.000	-0	-5	-5	-1	-0.4
	NY-N	3	3	.500	29	0	0	0	4	43	42	20	1	1	23	21	13.8	3.35	101	.266	.363	0	.000	-0	0	0	-1	-0.1
Total	7	21	23	.477	276	0	0	0	45	471^1	383	193	14	17	242	314	12.3	3.27	106	.225	.327	5	.096	-2	14	10	-0	1.3

● **JIM RENINGER** Reninger, James David b: 3/7/15, Aurora, Ill. d: 8/23/93, N.Fort Myers, Fla. BR/TR, 6'3", 210 lbs. Deb: 9/17/38

YEAR	TM/L	W	L	PCT	G	GS	CG	SH	SV	IP	H	R	HR	HB	BB	SO	RAT	ERA	ERA+	OAV	OOB	BH	AVG	PB	PR	PR+	PD	TPI
1938	Phi-A	0	2	.000	4	4	1	0	0	22^2	28	18	3	0	14	9	16.7	7.15	68	.295	.385	0	.000	-0	-6	-6	0	-0.4
1939	Phi-A	0	2	.000	4	2	0	0	0	16^1	24	15	3	0	12	3	19.8	7.71	61	.369	.468	1	.167	-0	-6	-5	0	-0.5
Total	2	0	4	.000	8	6	1	0	0	39	52	33	6	0	26	12	18.0	7.38	65	.325	.419	1	.077	-1	-12	-11	0	-0.9

● **STEVE RENKO** Renko, Steven b: 12/10/44, Kansas City, Kan. BR/TR, 6'5", 230 lbs. Deb: 6/27/69

YEAR	TM/L	W	L	PCT	G	GS	CG	SH	SV	IP	H	R	HR	HB	BB	SO	RAT	ERA	ERA+	OAV	OOB	BH	AVG	PB	PR	PR+	PD	TPI
1969	Mon-N	6	7	.462	18	15	4	0	0	103^1	94	54	14	2	50	68	12.7	4.01	92	.243	.333	6	.167	1	-5	-4	-1	-0.4
1970	Mon-N	13	11	.542	41	33	7	1	1	222^2	203	121	27	6	104	142	12.7	4.32	95	.241	.329	16	.200	2	-7	-5	-0	-0.3
1971	Mon-N	15	14	.517	40	37	9	3	0	275^2	256	128	24	3	135	129	12.9	3.75	94	.247	.336	21	.210	4	-9	-7	-2	-0.3
1972	Mon-N	1	10	.091	30	12	0	0	0	97	96	60	11	0	67	66	15.1	5.20	68	.262	.376	7	.292	1	-19	-17	1	-1.6
1973	Mon-N	15	11	.577	36	34	9	0	1	249^2	201	94	26	1	108	164	11.2	2.81	136	.218	.300	24	.273	7	24	27	-2	3.5
1974	Mon-N	12	16	.429	37	35	8	1	0	227^2	222	115	17	0	81	138	12.0	4.03	96	.257	.321	17	.210	3	-10	-4	3	0.2
1975	Mon-N	6	12	.333	31	25	3	1	1	170^1	175	89	20	1	76	99	13.3	4.07	94	.265	.341	15	.278	5	-8	-4	-0	0.1
1976	Mon-N	0	1	.000	5	1	0	0	0	13	15	8	1	0	3	4	12.5	5.54	67	.288	.327	1	.333	0	-3	-2	-1	-0.2
	Chi-N	8	11	.421	28	27	4	1	0	163^1	164	79	12	0	43	112	11.4	3.86	100	.258	.305	5	.094	-3	-6	0	-1	-0.5
	Yr	8	12	.400	33	28	4	1	0	176^1	179	87	14	0	46	116	11.5	3.98	97	.260	.307	6	.107	-3	-9	-2	-2	-0.7
1977	Chi-N	2	2	.500	13	8	0	0	1	51^1	51	32	10	1	21	34	12.8	4.56	96	.258	.332	2	.167	-0	-4	-1	-1	-0.2
	Chi-A	5	0	1.000	8	8	0	0	0	53^1	55	23	3	1	17	36	12.3	3.54	116	.274	.333	0	—	0	3	3	0	0.3
1978	Oak-A	6	12	.333	27	25	3	1	0	151	152	77	10	2	67	89	13.2	4.29	85	.265	.344	0	—	0	-9	-11	-0	-1.2
1979	Bos-A	11	9	.550	27	27	4	1	0	171	174	86	22	2	53	99	12.1	4.11	108	.260	.317	0	—	0	2	6	-1	0.5
1980	Bos-A	9	9	.500	32	23	1	0	0	165^1	180	86	17	1	56	90	12.9	4.19	101	.281	.340	0	—	0	-3	1	-1	0.0
1981	Cal-A	8	4	.667	22	15	0	0	1	102	93	40	7	1	42	50	12.0	3.44	106	.250	.328	0	—	0	3	2	-2	0.1
1982	Cal-A	11	6	.647	31	23	4	0	0	156	163	78	17	1	51	81	12.4	4.44	91	.269	.327	0	—	0	-6	-7	-2	-0.8
1983	KC-A	6	11	.353	25	17	1	0	1	121^1	144	63	9	0	36	54	13.4	4.30	95	.293	.341	0	—	0	-3	-3	-1	-0.4
Total	15	134	146	.479	451	365	57	9	6	2494	2438	1233	248	22	1010	1455	12.5	3.99	98	.256	.329	114	.215	21	-59	-24	-9	-1.2

● **ANDY REPLOGLE** Replogle, Andrew David b: 10/7/53, South Bend, Ind. BR/TR, 6'5", 205 lbs. Deb: 4/11/78

YEAR	TM/L	W	L	PCT	G	GS	CG	SH	SV	IP	H	R	HR	HB	BB	SO	RAT	ERA	ERA+	OAV	OOB	BH	AVG	PB	PR	PR+	PD	TPI
1978	Mil-A	9	5	.643	32	18	3	2	0	149^1	177	75	14	1	47	41	13.6	3.92	96	.301	.353	0	—	0	-2	-2	-2	-0.4
1979	Mil-A	0	0	—	3	0	0	0	0	8	13	5	0	0	2	2	16.9	5.63	74	.382	.417	0	—	0	-1	-1	0	-0.1
Total	2	9	5	.643	35	18	3	2	0	157^1	190	80	14	1	49	43	13.7	4.00	95	.305	.357	0	—	0	-4	-4	-2	-0.5

● **XAVIER RESCIGNO** Rescigno, Xavier Frederick "Mr. X" b: 10/13/13, New York, N.Y. BR/TR, 5'10.5", 175 lbs. Deb: 4/22/43

YEAR	TM/L	W	L	PCT	G	GS	CG	SH	SV	IP	H	R	HR	HB	BB	SO	RAT	ERA	ERA+	OAV	OOB	BH	AVG	PB	PR	PR+	PD	TPI
1943	Pit-N	6	9	.400	37	14	5	1	2	132^2	125	52	6	2	45	41	11.7	2.98	117	.252	.317	5	.143	0	6	7	-2	0.6
1944	Pit-N	10	8	.556	48	6	2	0	5	124	146	69	9	1	34	45	13.1	4.35	85	.291	.337	2	.091	-1	-10	-9	-0	-1.3
1945	Pit-N	3	5	.375	44	1	0	0	9	78^2	95	57	6	1	34	29	14.9	5.72	69	.303	.372	2	.133	-0	-17	-15	-0	-1.8
Total	3	19	22	.463	129	21	7	1	16	335^1	366	178	21	4	113	115	13.0	4.13	89	.279	.338	9	.125	-1	-21	-17	-3	-2.5

● **GEORGE RETTGER** Rettger, George Edward b: 7/29/1868, Cleveland, Ohio d: 6/5/21, Lakewood, Ohio BR/TR, 5'11", 175 lbs. Deb: 8/13/1891

YEAR	TM/L	W	L	PCT	G	GS	CG	SH	SV	IP	H	R	HR	HB	BB	SO	RAT	ERA	ERA+	OAV	OOB	BH	AVG	PB	PR	PR+	PD	TPI
1891	StL-a	7	3	.700	14	12	10	1	1	92^2	85	63	4	8	51	49	14.0	3.40	123	.235	.343	3	.071	-3	3	7	-1	0.3
1892	Cle-N	1	3	.250	6	5	3	0	0	38	32	27	2	1	31	12	15.2	4.26	80	.219	.360	2	.133	-0	-4	-4	-0	-0.4
	Cin-N	1	0	1.000	1	1	1	0	0	9	8	5	0	1	10	1	19.0	4.00	82	.229	.413	1	.125	-0	-1	-1	-0	-0.1
	Yr	2	3	.400	7	6	4	0	0	47	40	32	2	2	41	13	15.9	4.21	80	.221	.371	3	.130	-0	-5	-4	-0	-0.5
Total	2	9	6	.600	21	18	14	1	1	139^2	125	95	6	10	92	62	14.6	3.67	106	.231	.352	6	.092	-3	-2	3	-1	-0.2

● **OTTO RETTIG** Rettig, Adolph John b: 1/29/1894, New York, N.Y. d: 6/16/77, Stuart, Fla. BR/TR, 5'11", 165 lbs. Deb: 7/19/22

YEAR	TM/L	W	L	PCT	G	GS	CG	SH	SV	IP	H	R	HR	HB	BB	SO	RAT	ERA	ERA+	OAV	OOB	BH	AVG	PB	PR	PR+	PD	TPI
1922	Phi-A	1	2	.333	4	4	1	0	0	18^1	18	11	0	1	12	3	15.2	4.91	87	.265	.383	0	.000	-1	-2	-1	0	-0.3

● **ED REULBACH** Reulbach, Edward Marvin "Big Ed" b: 12/1/1882, Detroit, Mich. d: 7/17/61, Glens Falls, N.Y. BR/TR, 6'1", 190 lbs. Deb: 5/16/05

YEAR	TM/L	W	L	PCT	G	GS	CG	SH	SV	IP	H	R	HR	HB	BB	SO	RAT	ERA	ERA+	OAV	OOB	BH	AVG	PB	PR	PR+	PD	TPI
1905	Chi-N	18	14	.563	34	29	28	5	1	291^2	208	71	1	18	73	152	9.2	1.42	210	**.201**	.266	14	.127	-6	51	51	-1	4.9
1906	*Chi-N	19	4	**.826**	33	24	20	6	3	218	129	51	2	13	92	94	9.7	1.65	160	**.175**	.278	13	.157	-2	24	24	3	2.8
1907	*Chi-N	17	4	**.810**	27	22	16	4	0	192	147	48	1	9	64	96	10.3	1.69	148	.217	.294	11	.175	0	17	17	1	2.1
1908	*Chi-N	24	7	**.774**	46	35	25	7	1	297^2	227	81	4	12	106	133	10.4	2.03	116	.214	.292	23	.232	7	11	11	-1	1.7
1909	Chi-N	19	10	.655	35	32	23	6	0	262^2	194	69	1	11	82	105	9.8	1.78	143	.212	.285	12	.140	-1	24	23	4	2.9
1910	*Chi-N	12	8	.600	24	23	14	1	0	173^1	161	76	1	9	49	55	11.4	3.12	92	.250	.312	6	.107	-3	-2	-5	1	-0.8
1911	Chi-N	16	9	.640	33	29	15	2	0	221^2	191	97	3	4	103	79	12.1	2.96	112	.236	.325	6	.090	-1	11	9	3	1.1
1912	Chi-N	10	6	.625	39	19	8	0	4	169	161	86	7	8	60	75	12.2	3.78	88	.259	.332	6	.109	-3	-7	-9	4	-0.7
1913	Chi-N	1	3	.250	10	3	1	0	0	38^2	41	27	1	1	21	10	14.7	4.42	72	.281	.375	3	.250	0	-5	-5	0	-0.5
	Bro-N	7	6	.538	15	12	8	2	0	110	77	34	3	4	34	46	9.4	2.05	161	.202	.274	3	.103	0	14	15	-1	1.7
	Yr	8	9	.471	25	15	9	2	0	148^2	118	61	4	5	55	56	10.8	2.66	123	.223	.303	6	.146	0	9	10	-1	1.2
1914	Bro-N	11	18	.379	44	29	14	3	3	256	228	108	5	10	83	119	11.3	2.64	108	.242	.310	9	.122	-0	4	6	1	0.8
1915	New-F	21	10	.677	33	30	23	4	1	270	233	88	3	3	69	117	10.2	2.23	115	.236	.287	18	.196	-2	15	10	1	1.1
1916	Bos-N	7	6	.538	21	11	6	0	0	109^1	99	38	1	4	41	47	11.9	2.47	101	.251	.328	3	.091	-1	2	0	5	0.5
1917	Bos-N	0	1	.000	5	2	0	0	0	22^1	21	13	0	1	15	9	14.9	2.82	90	.256	.378	0	.000	1	-0	-1	1	0.2
Total	13	182	106	.632	399	300	201	40	13	2632^1	2117	887	33	107	892	1137	10.7	2.28	122	.224	.299	127	.147	-11	159	148	22	17.8

● **PAUL REUSCHEL** Reuschel, Paul Richard b: 1/12/47, Quincy, Ill. BR/TR, 6'4", 225 lbs. Deb: 7/25/75 F

YEAR	TM/L	W	L	PCT	G	GS	CG	SH	SV	IP	H	R	HR	HB	BB	SO	RAT	ERA	ERA+	OAV	OOB	BH	AVG	PB	PR	PR+	PD	TPI
1975	Chi-N	1	3	.250	28	0	0	0	5	36	44	15	1	1	13	12	14.5	3.50	110	.312	.374	0	.000	-0	1	1	0	0.2
1976	Chi-N	4	2	.667	50	2	0	0	3	87	94	46	12	1	33	55	13.2	4.55	85	.278	.344	2	.154	-0	-10	-6	1	-0.3
1977	Chi-N	5	6	.455	69	0	0	0	4	107	105	58	9	0	40	62	12.2	4.37	100	.262	.329	0	.000	-1	-5	0	2	0.1
1978	Chi-N	2	0	1.000	16	0	0	0	0	28	29	16	4	1	13	13	13.8	5.14	78	.269	.352	0	.000	-0	-5	-3	-0	-0.3
	Cle-A	2	4	.333	18	6	1	0	0	89^2	95	33	5	2	22	24	11.9	3.11	121	.271	.318	0	—	0	7	6	1	0.5
1979	Cle-A	2	1	.667	17	1	0	0	1	45^1	73	43	7	0	11	22	16.7	7.94	54	.365	.398	0	—	0	-19	-18	1	-1.1
Total	5	16	16	.500	198	9	1	0	13	393	440	211	38	5	132	188	13.2	4.51	90	.286	.344	2	.063	-2	-32	-19	5	-0.9

● **RICK REUSCHEL** Reuschel, Rickey Eugene b: 5/16/49, Quincy, Ill. BR/TR, 6'3", 235 lbs. Deb: 6/19/72 F

YEAR	TM/L	W	L	PCT	G	GS	CG	SH	SV	IP	H	R	HR	HB	BB	SO	RAT	ERA	ERA+	OAV	OOB	BH	AVG	PB	PR	PR+	PD	TPI
1972	Chi-N	10	8	.556	21	18	5	4	0	129	127	46	3	2	29	87	11.0	2.93	130	.259	.303	6	.136	-1	8	11	-0	1.5
1973	Chi-N	14	15	.483	36	36	7	3	0	237	244	95	15	5	62	168	11.8	3.00	132	.263	.312	9	.123	-3	18	23	4	2.9
1974	Chi-N	13	12	.520	41	38	8	2	0	240^2	262	130	18	6	83	160	13.1	4.30	89	.276	.338	19	.221	2	-18	-12	5	-0.5
1975	Chi-N	11	17	.393	38	37	6	0	1	234	244	116	17	7	67	155	12.2	3.73	103	.268	.323	16	.208	2	-3	3	3	0.9
1976	Chi-N	14	12	.538	38	37	9	2	1	260	260	117	17	8	64	146	11.5	3.46	112	.265	.315	19	.229	4	1	11	3	1.8
1977	Chi-N★	20	10	.667	39	37	8	4	1	252	233	84	13	5	74	166	11.1	2.79	158	.247	.305	18	.207	1	32	40	3	5.2
1978	Chi-N	14	15	.483	35	35	9	1	0	242^2	235	98	16	5	54	115	10.9	3.41	118	.254	.299	10	.137	-1	5	15	2	1.8
1979	Chi-N	18	12	.600	36	36	5	1	0	239	251	104	16	10	75	125	12.7	3.62	114	.274	.335	13	.165	1	3	12	5	2.1
1980	Chi-N	11	13	.458	38	38	6	0	0	257	281	111	13	4	76	140	12.6	3.40	115	.286	.340	13	.159	-1	6	14	5	1.7

YEAR	TM/L	W	L	PCT	G	GS	CG	SH	SV	IP	H	R	HR	HB	BB	SO	RAT	ERA	ERA+	OAV	OOB	BH	AVG	PB	PR	PR+	PD	TPI
1981	Chi-N	4	7	.364	13	13	1	0	0	85^2	87	40	4	4	23	53	12.0	3.47	107	.267	.323	2	.080	-1	0	2	2	0.3
	*NY-A	4	4	.500	12	11	3	0	0	70^2	75	24	4	1	10	22	11.0	2.67	134	.280	.308	0	—	0	8	7	1	0.9
1983	Chi-N	1	1	.500	4	4	0	0	0	20^2	18	9	1	0	10	9	12.2	3.92	97	.234	.322	1	.143	-0	-1	-0	1	0.1
1984	Chi-N	5	5	.500	19	14	1	0	0	92^1	123	57	7	3	23	43	14.5	5.17	76	.339	.383	7	.241	2	-16	-12	1	-0.9
1985	Pit-N	14	8	.636	31	26	9	1	1	194	153	58	7	3	52	138	9.6	2.27	158	.215	.272	10	.169	2	29	28	4	4.0
1986	Pit-N	9	16	.360	35	34	4	2	0	215^2	232	106	20	8	57	125	12.4	3.96	97	.274	.326	11	.157	0	-6	-3	3	0.0
1987	Pit-N★	8	6	.571	25	25	9	3	0	177	163	63	12	6	35	80	10.4	2.75	150	.246	.290	9	.150	2	26	27	1	2.3
	*SF-N	5	3	.625	9	8	3	1	0	50	44	28	1	2	7	27	9.5	4.32	89	.230	.265	2	.105	-0	-1	-3	0	-0.4
	Yr	13	9	.591	34	33	**12**	**4**	0	227	207	91	13	8	42	107	**10.2**	3.09	131	.242	.284	11	.139	2	25	24	1	1.9
1988	SF-N	19	11	.633	36	36	7	2	0	245	242	88	11	6	42	92	10.7	3.12	105	.260	.297	8	.110	-1	9	4	-2	0.1
1989	*SF-N★	17	8	.680	32	32	2	0	0	208^1	195	75	18	2	54	111	10.8	2.94	115	.247	.297	10	.164	1	13	11	-0	1.3
1990	SF-N	3	6	.333	15	13	0	0	1	87	102	40	8	1	31	49	13.9	3.93	93	.297	.357	4	.154	0	-1	-3	0	-0.2
1991	SF-N	0	2	.000	4	1	0	0	0	10^2	17	5	0	0	7	4	20.3	4.22	85	.370	.453	0	.000	-0	-1	-1	-0	-0.2
Total	19	214	191	.528	557	529	102	26	5	3548^1	3588	1494	221	88	935	2015	11.7	3.37	114	.264	.316	187	.168	8	111	177	39	24.7
● **JERRY REUSS** Reuss, Jerry b: 6/19/49, St.Louis, Mo. BL/TL, 6'5", 217 lbs. Deb: 9/27/69																												
1969	StL-N	1	0	1.000	1	1	0	0	0	7	2	0	0	2	3	3	9.0	0.00	—	.091	.259	1	.333	0	3	3	0	0.6
1970	StL-N	7	8	.467	20	20	5	2	0	127^1	132	62	9	1	49	74	12.9	4.10	101	.271	.339	2	.050	-3	-1	0	-0	-0.2
1971	StL-N	14	14	.500	36	35	7	2	0	211	228	125	15	7	109	131	14.7	4.78	75	.279	.368	8	.123	0	-31	-26	-2	-3.4
1972	Hou-N	9	13	.409	33	30	4	1	1	192	177	101	14	10	83	174	12.7	4.17	81	.246	.332	7	.106	-1	-15	-18	-1	-2.1
1973	Hou-N	16	13	.552	41	40	12	3	0	279^1	271	123	17	3	117	177	12.6	3.74	97	.256	.332	13	.137	-1	-2	-3	-2	-0.6
1974	*Pit-N	16	11	.593	35	35	14	1	0	260	259	115	20	1	101	105	12.5	3.50	99	.261	.329	13	.151	0	4	-1	-2	-0.3
1975	*Pit-N★	18	11	.621	32	32	15	6	0	237^1	224	73	10	0	78	131	11.5	2.54	140	.253	.314	14	.197	2	29	27	2	3.8
1976	Pit-N	14	9	.609	31	29	11	3	2	209^1	209	98	16	2	51	108	11.3	3.53	99	.256	.301	16	.242	6	-0	-1	-2	0.3
1977	Pit-N	10	13	.435	33	33	8	2	0	208	225	109	11	4	71	116	13.0	4.11	97	.280	.341	12	.171	1	-5	-3	1	-0.1
1978	Pit-N	3	2	.600	23	12	3	1	0	82^2	97	48	5	3	23	42	13.4	4.90	76	.297	.348	5	.185	0	-12	-11	-0	-0.6
1979	LA-N	7	14	.333	39	21	4	1	3	160	178	88	4	3	60	83	13.6	3.54	103	.282	.347	7	.167	1	4	2	1	0.5
1980	LA-N★	18	6	.750	37	29	10	**6**	3	229^1	193	74	12	0	40	111	9.1	2.51	140	.227	.261	6	.088	-1	28	26	1	2.8
1981	*LA-N	10	4	.714	22	22	8	2	0	152^2	138	44	6	4	27	51	10.0	2.30	144	.243	.282	10	.196	0	20	18	3	2.0
1982	LA-N	18	11	.621	39	37	8	4	0	254^2	232	98	11	2	50	138	10.0	3.11	112	.240	.278	17	.221	3	14	11	2	1.7
1983	*LA-N	12	11	.522	32	31	7	0	0	223^1	233	94	12	2	50	143	11.5	2.94	122	.271	.313	20	.282	5	17	16	4	2.7
1984	LA-N	5	7	.417	30	15	2	0	1	99	102	51	4	0	31	44	12.1	3.82	93	.266	.321	4	.167	1	-2	-3	-0	-0.3
1985	*LA-N	14	10	.583	34	33	5	3	0	212^2	210	78	13	3	58	84	11.5	2.92	119	.260	.312	10	.135	1	16	14	-2	1.1
1986	LA-N	2	6	.250	19	13	0	0	1	74	96	57	13	2	17	29	14.0	5.84	59	.313	.353	5	.250	2	-17	-21	1	-1.8
1987	LA-N	0	0	—	1	0	0	0	0	2	2	1	0	0	0	2	9.0	4.50	88	.333	.333	0	—	0	-0	-0	-0	0.0
	Cin-N	0	5	.000	7	7	0	0	0	34^2	52	31	2	1	12	10	16.9	7.79	55	.351	.404	1	.125	0	-14	-13	-1	-1.6
	Yr	0	5	.000	8	7	0	0	0	36^2	54	32	2	1	12	12	16.4	7.61	56	.351	.401	1	.125	0	-14	-13	-1	-1.6
	Cal-A	4	5	.444	17	16	1	1	0	82^1	112	60	16	2	17	37	14.3	5.25	82	.327	.362	0	—	0	-7	-9	2	-0.7
1988	Chi-A	13	9	.591	32	29	2	0	0	183	183	79	15	3	43	73	11.3	3.44	116	.263	.309	0	—	0	11	11	0	1.2
1989	Chi-A	8	5	.615	23	19	1	1	0	106^2	135	65	12	3	21	27	13.4	5.06	75	.308	.344	0	—	0	-14	-15	-2	-1.8
	Mil-A	1	4	.200	7	7	0	0	0	33^2	36	23	7	1	13	13	13.4	5.35	72	.273	.342	0	—	0	-5	-6	-0	-0.7
	Yr	9	9	.500	30	26	1	1	0	140^1	171	88	19	4	34	40	13.4	5.13	74	.300	.344	0	—	0	-19	-21	-2	-2.5
1990	Pit-N	0	0	—	4	1	0	0	0	7^2	8	3	1	0	3	1	12.9	3.52	103	.267	.333	0	—	0	0	0	0	0.0
Total	22	220	191	.535	628	547	127	39	11	3669^2	3734	1700	245	59	1127	1907	12.1	3.64	100	.265	.322	171	.167	15	19	-4	2	2.5
● **TODD REVENIG** Revenig, Todd Michael b: 6/28/69, Brainerd, Minn. BR/TR, 6'1", 185 lbs. Deb: 8/24/92																												
1992	Oak-A	0	0	—	2	0	0	0	0	2	2	0	0	0	0	1	9.0	0.00	—	.286	.286	0	—	0	1	1	-0	0.0
● **CARLOS REYES** Reyes, Carlos Alberto b: 4/4/69, Miami, Fla. BB/TR, 6'1", 190 lbs. Deb: 4/7/94																												
1994	Oak-A	0	3	.000	27	9	0	0	1	78	71	38	10	2	44	57	13.5	4.15	107	.242	.345	0	—	0	6	3	-1	0.0
1995	Oak-A	4	6	.400	40	1	0	0	0	69	71	43	10	5	28	48	13.6	5.09	88	.264	.344	0	—	0	-3	-5	-1	-0.5
1996	Oak-A	7	10	.412	46	10	0	0	0	122^1	134	71	19	2	61	78	14.5	4.78	103	.281	.365	0	—	0	3	2	-1	0.1
1997	Oak-A	3	4	.429	37	6	0	0	0	77^1	101	52	13	2	25	43	14.9	5.82	78	.316	.369	0	—	0	-11	-11	0	-0.8
1998	SD-N	2	2	.500	22	0	0	0	1	27^2	23	11	4	2	6	24	10.1	3.58	109	.235	.292	0	—	0	2	1	0	0.2
	Bos-A	1	1	.500	24	0	0	0	0	38^1	35	15	2	1	14	23	11.7	3.52	134	.246	.318	0	—	0	5	5	0	0.2
1999	SD-N	2	4	.333	65	0	0	0	1	77^1	76	38	11	0	24	57	11.6	3.72	113	.254	.310	0	.000	-0	7	4	1	0.4
2000	Phi-N	0	2	.000	10	0	0	0	0	10^1	10	6	2	0	5	4	13.1	5.23	90	.270	.357	0	—	0	-1	-1	-0	-0.1
	SD-N	1	1	.500	12	0	0	0	1	18	15	12	5	1	8	13	12.0	6.00	73	.221	.312	0	.000	-0	-3	-3	-0	-0.4
	Yr	1	3	.250	22	0	0	0	1	28^1	25	18	7	1	13	17	12.4	5.72	79	.238	.328	0	.000	-0	-3	-4	-1	-0.5
Total	7	20	33	.377	283	26	0	0	4	518^1	536	286	76	15	215	347	13.3	4.62	98	.268	.343	0	.000	-0	6	-5	-1	-0.9
● **DENNYS REYES** Reyes, Dennys (Valarde) b: 4/19/77, Higuera De Zaragoza, Mex. BL/TL, 6'3", 246 lbs. Deb: 7/13/97																												
1997	LA-N	2	3	.400	14	5	0	0	0	47	51	21	4	1	18	36	13.4	3.83	101	.280	.348	0	.000	-1	2	0	2	0.1
1998	LA-N	0	4	.000	11	3	0	0	0	28^2	27	17	1	0	20	33	14.8	4.71	84	.255	.373	0	.000	-1	-2	-3	0	-0.3
	Cin-N	3	1	.750	8	7	0	0	0	38^2	35	19	2	1	27	44	14.7	4.42	97	.255	.382	1	.083	-0	-1	-1	0	-0.1
	Yr	3	5	.375	19	10	0	0	0	67^1	62	36	3	1	47	77	14.7	4.54	91	.255	.378	1	.059	-1	-2	-3	0	-0.4
1999	Cin-N	2	2	.500	65	1	0	0	2	61^2	53	30	5	3	39	72	13.9	3.79	123	.232	.352	0	.000	-0	5	6	-1	0.2
2000	Cin-N	2	1	.667	62	0	0	0	0	43^2	43	31	5	1	29	36	15.0	4.53	105	.262	.376	0	.000	0	1	1	-0	0.1
Total	4	9	11	.450	160	16	0	0	2	219^2	209	118	17	6	133	221	14.3	4.18	104	.256	.364	1	.031	-2	5	4	1	-0.0
● **AL REYES** Reyes, Rafael Alberto b: 4/10/71, San Cristobal, D.R. BR/TR, 6'1", 195 lbs. Deb: 4/27/95																												
1995	Mil-A	1	1	.500	27	0	0	0	1	33^1	19	9	3	3	18	29	10.8	2.43	205	.167	.296	0	—	0	8	9	0	0.5
1996	Mil-A	1	0	1.000	5	0	0	0	0	5^2	8	5	1	0	2	2	15.9	7.94	65	.320	.370	0	—	0	-2	-2	-0	-0.3
1997	Mil-A	1	2	.333	19	0	0	0	1	29^2	32	19	4	3	9	28	13.3	5.46	85	.274	.341	0	—	0	-3	-3	0	-0.2
1998	Mil-N	5	1	.833	50	0	0	0	0	57	55	26	9	2	31	58	13.9	3.95	108	.253	.352	1	.200	0	2	2	-0	0.1
1999	Mil-N	2	0	1.000	26	0	0	0	0	36	27	17	5	3	25	39	13.8	4.25	107	.206	.346	0	.000	-0	1	1	-0	0.0
	Bal-A	2	3	.400	27	0	0	0	0	29^2	23	16	4	3	16	28	12.7	4.85	97	.225	.347	0	—	0	0	-1	0	-0.1
2000	Bal-A	1	0	1.000	13	0	0	0	0	13	13	10	2	0	11	10	16.6	6.92	69	.271	.407	0	—	0	-3	-3	0	-0.2
	LA-N	0	0	—	6	0	0	0	0	6^2	2	0	0	0	1	8	4.1	0.00	—	.087	.125	0	—	0	3	3	0	0.2
Total	6	13	7	.650	173	0	0	0	2	211	179	102	28	14	113	202	13.1	4.27	108	.230	.338	1	.143	-0	7	8	0	-0.0
● **ALLIE REYNOLDS** Reynolds, Allie Pierce "Superchief" b: 2/10/15, Bethany, Okla. d: 12/26/94, Oklahoma City, Okla. BR/TR, 6', 195 lbs. Deb: 9/17/42																												
1942	Cle-A	0	0	—	2	0	0	0	0	5	5	1	0	0	4	2	16.2	0.00	—	.250	.375	0	.000	-0	2	2	-0	0.1
1943	Cle-A	11	12	.478	34	21	11	3	3	198^2	140	72	3	7	109	**151**	11.6	2.99	104	**.202**	.316	10	.149	-1	7	3	-0	0.1
1944	Cle-A	11	8	.579	28	21	5	1	1	158	141	63	2	4	91	84	13.4	3.30	100	.240	.346	7	.123	-3	2	-0	-1	-0.4
1945	Cle-A†	18	12	.600	44	30	16	2	4	247^1	227	102	7	5	130	112	13.2	3.20	101	.247	.343	8	.094	-7	5	1	-1	-0.7
1946	Cle-A	11	15	.423	31	28	9	3	0	183^1	180	93	10	1	108	107	14.2	3.88	85	.259	.359	14	.222	1	-8	-12	-1	-1.6
1947	*NY-A	19	8	**.704**	34	30	17	4	2	241^2	207	94	23	4	123	129	12.4	3.20	110	.227	.322	13	.146	-2	13	9	-2	0.6
1948	NY-A	16	7	.696	39	31	11	1	3	236^1	240	108	17	4	111	101	13.5	3.77	108	.268	.351	16	.193	0	14	9	-3	0.5
1949	*NY-A☆	17	6	.739	35	31	4	2	1	213^2	200	102	15	4	123	105	13.8	4.00	101	.250	.353	17	.218	6	5	1	-0	0.6
1950	*NY-A★	16	12	.571	35	29	14	2	2	240^2	215	108	12	8	138	160	13.5	3.74	115	.242	.349	15	.185	1	22	16	-1	1.6
1951	*NY-A	17	8	.680	40	26	16	**7**	7	221	171	84	12	5	100	126	11.2	3.05	125	**.213**	.304	14	.184	0	26	20	-3	2.0
1952	*NY-A☆	20	8	.714	35	29	24	**6**	6	244^1	194	70	10	7	97	**160**	11.0	**2.06**	**161**	.218	.300	13	.153	-1	**44**	38	-1	4.4
1953	*NY-A★	13	7	.650	41	15	5	1	13	145	140	64	9	5	61	86	12.8	3.41	108	.253	.333	5	.122	1	9	5	-2	0.5
1954	NY-A†	13	4	.765	36	18	5	4	7	157^1	133	65	13	3	66	100	11.6	3.32	104	.233	.316	8	.160	-0	7	2	-0	0.2
Total	13	182	107	.630	434	309	137	36	49	2492^1	2193	1026	133	57	1261	1423	12.7	3.30	110	.238	.333	140	.163	-5	149	92	-16	7.9
● **ARCHIE REYNOLDS** Reynolds, Archie Edward b: 1/3/46, Glendale, Cal. BR/TR, 6'2", 205 lbs. Deb: 8/15/68																												
1968	Chi-N	0	1	.000	7	1	0	0	0	13^1	14	10	1	1	7	6	14.9	6.75	47	.259	.355	1	.500	1	-6	-5	-0	-0.4
1969	Chi-N	0	1	.000	2	2	0	0	0	7^1	11	5	1	0	7	4	22.1	2.45	164	.379	.500	0	.000	0	1	1	0	0.2
1970	Chi-N	0	2	.000	7	1	0	0	0	15	17	11	2	1	9	9	16.2	6.60	68	.298	.403	0	.000	0	-4	-3	-0	-0.4

YEAR TM/L	W	L	PCT	G	GS	CG	SH	SV	IP	H	R	HR	HB	BB	SO	RAT	ERA	ERA+	OAV	OOB	BH	AVG	PB	PR	PR+	PD	TPI
1971 Cal-A	0	3	.000	15	1	0	0	0	27^1	32	15	2	0	18	15	16.5	4.61	70	.305	.407	0	.000	-0	-3	-4	0	-0.5
1972 Mil-A	0	1	.000	5	2	0	0	0	18^2	26	18	2	0	8	13	16.4	7.23	42	.338	.400	2	.500	1	-9	-9	-1	-0.5
Total 5	0	8	.000	36	7	0	0	0	81^2	100	59	8	2	49	47	16.6	5.73	61	.311	.405	3	.273	2	-21	-20	-1	-1.6
● **CHARLIE REYNOLDS**	Reynolds, Charles E. b: 7/31/1857, Allegany, N.Y. d: 5/1/13, Buffalo, N.Y. Deb: 5/18/1882																										
1882 Phi-a	1	1	.500	2	2	1	0	0	12	18	11	0		3	4	15.8	5.25	57	.327	.362	1	.125	-1	-3	-3	-1	-0.4
● **CRAIG REYNOLDS**	Reynolds, Gordon Craig b: 12/27/52, Houston, Tex. BL/TR, 6'1", 175 lbs. Deb: 8/1/75 ♦																										
1986 *Hou-N	0	0	—	1	0	0	0	0	1	3	3	0	0	2	1	45.0	27.00	13	.500	.625	78	.249	0	-3	-3	0	-0.1
1989 *Hou-N	0	0	—	1	0	0	0	0	1	3	4	0	1	1	0	45.0	27.00	13	.500	.625	38	.201	0	-3	-3	0	-0.1
Total 2	0	0	—	2	0	0	0	0	2	6	7	0	1	3	1	45.0	27.00	13	.500	.625	1142	.256	0	-5	-5	0	-0.2
● **KEN REYNOLDS**	Reynolds, Kenneth Lee b: 1/4/47, Trevose, Pa. BL/TL, 6', 180 lbs. Deb: 9/5/70																										
1970 Phi-N	0	0	—	4	0	0	0	0	2^1	3	0	0	0	4	1	27.0	0.00	—	.333	.538	0	—	0	1	1	0	0.1
1971 Phi-N	5	9	.357	35	25	2	1	0	162^1	163	89	11	6	82	81	13.9	4.49	79	.269	.361	10	.200	2	-18	-17	-1	-1.3
1972 Phi-N	2	15	.118	33	23	2	0	0	154^1	149	76	17	1	60	87	12.2	4.26	84	.258	.329	8	.200	1	-14	-11	-0	-1.0
1973 Mil-A	0	1	.000	2	1	0	0	0	7^1	5	7	1	1	10	3	19.6	7.36	51	.200	.444	0	—	0	-3	-3	1	-0.3
1975 StL-N	0	1	.000	10	0	0	0	0	17	12	4	0	0	11	7	12.2	1.59	237	.214	.343	0	.000	-0	4	4	1	0.3
1976 SD-N	0	3	.000	19	2	0	0	1	32^1	38	27	0	0	29	18	18.6	6.40	51	.309	.441	0	.000	-1	-10	-12	-0	-1.2
Total 6	7	29	.194	103	51	4	1	1	375^2	370	203	29	8	196	197	13.8	4.46	80	.265	.358	18	.186	2	-41	-37	0	-3.4
● **SHANE REYNOLDS**	Reynolds, Richard Shane b: 3/26/68, Bastrop, La. BR/TR, 6'3", 210 lbs. Deb: 7/20/92																										
1992 Hou-N	1	3	.250	8	5	0	0	0	25^1	42	22	2	0	6	10	17.1	7.11	47	.385	.417	2	.500	1	-10	-11	0	-1.4
1993 Hou-N	0	0	—	5	1	0	0	0	11	11	4	0	0	6	10	13.9	0.82	474	.256	.347	1	.500	0	4	4	-0	0.2
1994 Hou-N	8	5	.615	33	14	1	1	0	124	128	46	10	6	21	110	11.3	3.05	130	.263	.302	3	.091	-2	16	13	0	1.1
1995 Hou-N	10	11	.476	30	30	3	2	0	189^1	196	87	15	2	37	175	11.2	3.47	112	.263	.300	8	.127	-2	15	9	3	1.1
1996 Hou-N	16	10	.615	35	35	4	1	0	239	227	103	20	8	44	204	10.5	3.65	106	.249	.290	14	.184	4	15	6	-1	1.0
1997 *Hou-N	9	10	.474	30	30	2	0	0	181	189	92	19	3	47	152	11.9	4.23	95	.267	.315	6	.113	-0	-0	-5	1	-0.4
1998 *Hou-N	19	8	.704	35	35	3	1	0	233^1	257	99	25	2	53	209	12.0	3.51	115	.280	.320	13	.159	1	19	15	4	2.0
1999 *Hou-N	16	14	.533	35	35	4	2	0	231^2	250	108	23	1	37	197	11.2	3.85	115	.275	.304	11	.167	1	19	15	3	2.2
2000 Hou-N☆	7	8	.467	22	22	0	0	0	131	150	86	20	6	45	93	13.8	5.22	94	.287	.350	9	.225	2	-8	-5	1	-0.2
Total 9	86	69	.555	233	207	17	7	0	1365^2	1450	647	134	28	296	1160	11.7	3.85	107	.271	.312	67	.160	7	69	40	11	5.6
● **BOB REYNOLDS**	Reynolds, Robert Allen b: 1/21/47, Seattle, Wash. BR/TR, 6', 205 lbs. Deb: 9/19/69																										
1969 Mon-N	0	0	—	1	1	0	0	0	1^1	3	6	0	0	3	2	40.5	20.25	18	.429	.600	0	—	0	-2	-2	0	-0.1
1971 StL-N	0	0	—	4	0	0	0	0	7	15	8	2	1	6	4	28.3	10.29	35	.441	.537	0	.000	-0	-5	-5	-0	-0.3
Mil-A	0	1	.000	3	0	0	0	0	6	4	2	0	0	3	4	10.5	3.00	116	.222	.333	0	.000	-0	0	0	0	0.0
1972 Bal-A	0	0	—	3	0	0	0	0	9^2	8	2	0	0	7	5	14.0	1.86	166	.258	.395	0	.000	-0	1	1	-0	0.0
1973 *Bal-A	7	5	.583	42	1	0	0	9	111	88	27	3	0	31	77	9.6	1.95	192	.219	.275	0	—	0	23	23	-2	2.5
1974 *Bal-A	7	5	.583	54	0	0	0	7	69^1	75	23	4	1	14	43	11.7	2.73	127	.278	.316	0	—	0	7	6	-0	1.1
1975 Bal-A	0	1	.000	7	0	0	0	0	6	11	6	1	0	1	1	18.0	9.00	39	.423	.444	0	—	0	-3	-4	-0	-0.6
Det-A	0	2	.000	21	0	0	0	3	34^2	40	20	8	1	14	26	14.3	4.67	86	.288	.357	0	—	0	-3	-2	0	-0.2
Cle-A	0	2	.000	5	0	0	0	2	9^2	11	7	0	0	3	5	13.0	4.66	81	.289	.341	0	—	0	-1	-1	-0	-0.2
Yr	0	5	.000	33	0	0	0	5	50^1	62	33	9	1	18	32	14.5	5.19	76	.305	.365	0	—	0	-8	-7	-0	-1.0
Total 6	14	16	.467	140	2	0	0	21	254^2	255	101	18	3	82	167	12.0	3.15	116	.264	.324	0	.000	-0	16	15	-3	2.2
● **ROSS REYNOLDS**	Reynolds, Ross Ernest "Doc" b: 8/20/1887, Barksdale, Tex. d: 6/23/70, Ada, Okla. BR/TR, 6'2", 185 lbs. Deb: 5/2/14																										
1914 Det-A	5	3	.625	26	7	3	1	0	78	62	26	0	6	39	31	12.3	2.08	135	.230	.340	1	.048	-2	6	6	-1	0.3
1915 Det-A	0	1	.000	4	2	0	0	0	11^1	17	9	0	1	5	2	18.3	6.35	48	.378	.451	0	.000	-0	-4	-4	0	-0.3
Total 2	5	4	.556	30	9	3	1	0	89^1	79	35	0	7	44	33	13.1	2.62	108	.251	.355	1	.042	-2	1	2	-1	0.0
● **ARMANDO REYNOSO**	Reynoso, Armando Martin (Gutierrez) b: 5/1/66, San Luis Potosi, Mex. BR/TR, 6', 196 lbs. Deb: 8/11/91																										
1991 Atl-N	2	1	.667	6	5	0	0	0	23^1	26	18	4	3	10	10	15.0	6.17	63	.299	.390	0	.000	-0	-6	-6	2	-0.5
1992 Atl-N	1	0	1.000	3	1	0	0	1	7^2	11	4	2	1	2	2	16.4	4.70	78	.393	.452	0	.000	-0	-1	-1	0	-0.1
1993 Col-N	12	11	.522	30	30	4	0	0	189	206	101	22	9	63	117	13.2	4.00	119	.277	.340	8	.127	-1	1	14	2	1.7
1994 Col-N	3	4	.429	9	9	1	0	0	52^1	54	30	5	6	22	25	14.1	4.82	103	.278	.369	3	.176	-0	-3	1	2	0.3
1995 *Col-N	7	7	.500	20	18	0	0	0	93	116	61	12	5	36	40	15.2	5.32	101	.316	.385	4	.133	-2	-12	1	3	0.2
1996 Col-N	8	9	.471	30	30	0	0	0	168^2	195	97	27	9	49	88	13.5	4.96	105	.291	.348	9	.173	-1	-14	4	2	0.5
1997 NY-N	6	3	.667	16	16	1	1	0	91^1	95	47	7	6	29	47	12.8	4.53	89	.275	.342	7	.241	3	-3	-5	1	-0.1
1998 NY-N	7	3	.700	11	11	0	0	0	68^1	64	31	4	5	32	40	13.3	3.82	108	.256	.352	5	.167	0	3	2	3	0.6
1999 Ari-N	10	6	.625	31	27	0	0	0	167	178	90	20	6	67	79	13.5	4.37	105	.276	.350	8	.163	-0	4	4	1	0.4
2000 Ari-N	11	12	.478	31	30	2	0	0	170^2	179	102	22	6	52	89	12.5	5.27	88	.273	.332	5	.104	-2	-12	-13	2	-1.4
Total 10	67	56	.545	187	177	8	1	1	1031^1	1124	581	125	56	362	537	13.5	4.68	101	.282	.350	49	.150	-3	-44	6	18	1.6
● **FLINT RHEM**	Rhem, Charles Flint "Shad" b: 1/24/01, Rhems, S.C. d: 7/30/69, Columbia, S.C. BR/TR, 6'2", 180 lbs. Deb: 9/6/24																										
1924 StL-N	2	2	.500	6	3	3	0	1	32^1	31	18	1	0	17	20	13.4	4.45	85	.254	.345	2	.167	-0	-2	-2	0	-0.3
1925 StL-N	8	13	.381	30	24	8	1	1	170	204	114	16	4	58	66	14.1	4.92	88	.299	.357	14	.237	1	-12	-11	0	-1.0
1926 *StL-N	**20**	7	.741	34	34	20	1	0	258	241	121	12	1	75	72	11.1	3.21	122	.250	.305	18	.188	-2	18	20	1	1.8
1927 StL-N	10	12	.455	27	26	9	2	0	169^1	189	102	6	4	54	51	13.1	4.41	90	.285	.342	4	.068	-5	-9	-9	-3	-1.7
1928 *StL-N	11	8	.579	28	22	9	0	3	169^2	199	91	13	3	71	47	14.5	4.14	97	.296	.365	11	.164	-1	-3	-3	2	-0.3
1930 *StL-N	12	8	.600	26	19	9	0	0	139^2	173	90	11	3	37	47	13.7	4.45	113	.306	.352	12	.231	-1	8	9	-3	0.7
1931 *StL-N	11	10	.524	33	26	10	2	1	207^1	214	100	17	3	60	72	12.0	3.56	111	.268	.321	9	.130	-4	7	9	-2	0.2
1932 StL-N	4	2	.667	6	6	5	1	0	50	48	19	3	0	10	18	10.4	3.06	129	.257	.294	3	.188	0	5	5	0	0.5
Phi-N	11	7	.611	26	20	10	0	0	168^2	177	79	13	0	49	35	12.1	3.74	118	.269	.319	7	.113	-5	3	11	-0	0.6
Yr	15	9	.625	32	26	15	1	1	218^2	225	98	16	0	59	53	11.7	3.58	120	.266	.314	10	.128	-5	7	16	-0	1.1
1933 Phi-N	5	14	.263	28	19	3	0	2	125	182	109	10	2	33	27	15.6	6.62	58	.340	.381	4	.087	-4	-46	-34	-0	-4.9
1934 StL-N	1	0	1.000	5	1	0	0	1	15^2	26	12	0	0	7	6	19.0	4.60	92	.394	.452	0	.000	-0	-1	-1	-0	-0.1
Bos-N	8	8	.500	25	20	5	1	0	152^2	164	71	5	0	38	56	11.9	3.60	106	.273	.317	3	.058	-5	8	4	1	0.0
Yr	9	8	.529	30	21	5	1	1	168^1	190	83	5	0	45	62	12.6	3.69	105	.285	.331	3	.056	-5	7	3	1	-0.1
1935 Bos-N	0	5	.000	10	6	0	0	0	40^1	61	37	4	0	11	10	16.1	5.36	71	.341	.379	0	.000	-1	-6	-7	0	-0.9
1936 StL-N	2	1	.667	10	4	0	0	0	26^2	49	26	2	0	9	7	19.6	6.75	58	.405	.446	1	.125	-0	-8	-8	-1	-0.9
Total 12	105	97	.520	294	230	91	8	10	1725^1	1958	989	113	20	529	534	13.1	4.20	98	.287	.340	88	.144	-28	-39	-19	-3	-6.3
● **BILLY RHINES**	Rhines, William Pearl "Bunker" b: 3/14/1869, Ridgway, Pa. d: 1/30/22, Ridgway, Pa. BR/TR, 5'11", 168 lbs. Deb: 4/22/1890																										
1890 Cin-N	28	17	.622	46	45	45	6	0	401^1	337	163	6	15	113	182	**10.4**	**1.95**	**182**	.221	**.281**	29	.188	-5	**72**	**72**	1	6.5
1891 Cin-N	17	24	.415	48	43	40	1	0	372^2	364	224	4	22	124	138	12.3	2.87	117	.246	.314	18	.122	-9	20	21	3	1.3
1892 Cin-N	3	7	.300	11	9	6	0	0	74^2	102	71	0	4	36	10	17.1	5.42	60	.313	.388	5	.185	1	-18	-18	-2	-1.9
1893 Lou-N	1	4	.200	5	5	3	0	0	31	49	37	3	3	19	0	20.6	8.71	51	.348	.436	1	.091	-2	-14	-16	0	-1.7
1895 Cin-N	19	10	.655	38	33	25	0	0	267^2	322	195	4	21	76	72	14.1	4.81	103	.293	.351	25	.221	-4	-1	5	-0	0.0
1896 Cin-N	8	6	.571	19	17	11	3	0	143	128	52	1	9	48	32	**11.6**	**2.45**	**188**	**.238**	**.311**	10	.192	-3	30	32	0	2.3
1897 Cin-N	21	15	.583	41	32	26	1	0	288^2	311	175	4	17	86	65	12.9	4.08	111	.273	.333	17	.159	-6	7	14	-2	0.6
1898 Pit-N	12	16	.429	31	29	27	2	0	258	289	143	0	13	61	48	12.7	3.52	101	.281	.329	15	.150	-4	2	1	5	0.2
1899 Pit-N	4	4	.500	9	9	4	0	0	54	59	42	3	4	13	6	12.7	6.00	63	.277	.330	10	.435	4	-13	-13	-1	-1.3
Total 9	113	103	.523	248	222	187	13	1	1891	1961	1102	25	108	576	553	12.6	3.48	114	.262	.324	130	.177	-27	86	98	3	6.0
● **BOB RHOADS**	Rhoads, Robert Barton "Dusty" b: 10/4/1879, Wooster, Ohio d: 2/12/67, San Bernardino, Cal. BR/TR, 6'1", 215 lbs. Deb: 4/19/02																										
1902 Chi-N	4	8	.333	16	12	12	1	1	118	131	66	1	6	42	43	13.7	3.20	84	.281	.348	10	.222	0	-5	-7	-1	-0.7
1903 StL-N	5	8	.385	17	13	12	1	0	129	154	88	3	3	47	52	14.2	4.60	71	.303	.366	7	.140	-2	-19	-19	-1	-1.9
Cle-A	2	3	.400	5	5	5	0	0	41	55	34	2	2	3	21	13.2	5.27	54	.320	.339	2	.118	-1	-10	-11	-0	-1.2
1904 Cle-A	10	9	.526	22	19	18	0	0	175^1	175	72	1	5	48	72	11.7	2.87	88	.261	.315	18	.196	0	-5	-7	-1	-0.8
1905 Cle-A	16	9	.640	28	26	24	4	0	235	219	96	4	10	55	61	10.9	2.83	93	.249	.300	21	.221	4	-5	-5	0	-0.1
1906 Cle-A	22	10	.688	38	34	31	7	0	315	259	95	5	5	92	89	10.2	1.80	145	.227	.288	19	.161	-3	31	29	-2	2.5

YEAR TM/L	W	L	PCT	G	GS	CG	SH	SV	IP	H	R	HR	HB	BB	SO	RAT	ERA	ERA+	OAV	OOB	BH	AVG	PB	PR	PR+	PD	TPI
1907 Cle-A	15	14	.517	35	31	23	5	1	275	258	105	0	14	84	76	11.7	2.29	109	.250	.316	17	.185	-1	8	7	-1	0.4
1908 Cle-A	18	12	.600	37	30	20	1	0	270	229	82	2	7	73	62	10.3	1.77	135	.239	.298	20	.222	4	19	19	2	2.9
1909 Cle-A	5	9	.357	20	15	9	2	0	133^1	124	63	1	6	50	46	12.2	2.90	88	.281	.361	7	.163	-0	-6	-5	1	-0.5
Total 8	97	82	.542	218	185	154	21	2	1691^2	1604	701	19	58	494	522	11.5	2.61	100	.256	.316	121	.188	-0	6	0	-3	0.6

● RICK RHODEN
Rhoden, Richard Alan b: 5/16/53, Boynton Beach, Fla. BR/TR, 6'3", 195 lbs. Deb: 7/5/74

YEAR TM/L	W	L	PCT	G	GS	CG	SH	SV	IP	H	R	HR	HB	BB	SO	RAT	ERA	ERA+	OAV	OOB	BH	AVG	PB	PR	PR+	PD	TPI
1974 LA-N	1	0	1.000	4	0	0	0	0	9	5	2	1	0	4	7	9.0	2.00	171	.161	.257	1	.500	0	2	2	-0	0.2
1975 LA-N	3	3	.500	26	11	1	0	0	99^1	94	40	8	1	32	40	11.5	3.08	111	.253	.314	2	.071	-2	6	4	0	0.0
1976 LA-N★	12	3	.800	27	26	10	3	0	181	165	66	17	1	53	77	10.9	2.98	114	.242	.298	20	.308	7	11	8	-2	1.2
1977 *LA-N	16	10	.615	31	31	4	1	0	216^1	223	98	20	2	63	122	12.0	3.74	102	.270	.323	18	.231	5	4	2	-3	0.5
1978 *LA-N	10	8	.556	30	23	6	3	0	164^2	160	77	13	3	51	79	11.7	3.66	96	.255	.314	7	.135	-0	-1	-3	-1	-0.5
1979 Pit-N	0	1	.000	1	1	0	0	0	5	5	4	0	0	2	2	12.6	7.20	54	.263	.333	1	1.000	0	-2	-2	0	-0.2
1980 Pit-N	7	5	.583	20	19	2	0	0	126^2	133	58	9	3	40	70	12.5	3.84	95	.273	.332	15	.375	6	-3	-3	0	0.5
1981 Pit-N	9	4	.692	21	21	4	2	0	136^1	147	66	6	2	53	76	13.3	3.89	92	.283	.352	9	.188	1	-6	-4	1	-0.2
1982 Pit-N	11	14	.440	35	35	6	1	0	230^1	239	115	14	2	70	128	12.2	4.14	90	.267	.321	22	.265	8	-14	-11	2	0.0
1983 Pit-N	13	13	.500	36	35	7	2	1	244^1	256	95	13	2	68	153	12.0	3.09	120	.276	.327	13	.151	-2	15	16	1	1.6
1984 Pit-N	14	9	.609	33	33	6	3	0	238^1	216	81	13	1	62	136	10.5	2.72	133	.243	.293	28	.333	10	23	23	2	3.5
1985 Pit-N	10	15	.400	35	35	2	0	0	213^1	254	119	18	6	69	128	13.9	4.47	80	.296	.352	14	.189	2	-21	-21	-0	-2.1
1986 Pit-N☆	15	12	.556	34	34	12	1	0	253^2	211	82	17	2	76	159	10.3	2.84	135	.228	.288	25	.278	9	25	27	1	4.0
1987 NY-A	16	10	.615	30	29	4	0	0	181^2	184	84	22	3	61	107	12.3	3.86	114	.268	.330	0	—	0	12	11	-0	1.4
1988 NY-A	12	12	.500	30	30	5	1	0	197	206	107	20	8	56	94	12.3	4.29	92	.269	.325	0	.000	-0	-7	-8	-1	-0.9
1989 Hou-N	2	6	.250	20	17	0	0	0	96^2	108	49	7	3	41	41	14.2	4.28	79	.289	.364	6	.207	1	-8	-10	1	-0.6
Total 16	151	125	.547	413	380	69	17	1	2593^2	2606	1143	198	39	801	1419	12.0	3.59	103	.264	.321	181	.238	45	35	34	1	8.4

● ARTHUR RHODES
Rhodes, Arthur Lee b: 10/24/69, Waco, Tex. BL/TL, 6'2", 206 lbs. Deb: 8/21/91

YEAR TM/L	W	L	PCT	G	GS	CG	SH	SV	IP	H	R	HR	HB	BB	SO	RAT	ERA	ERA+	OAV	OOB	BH	AVG	PB	PR	PR+	PD	TPI
1991 Bal-A	0	3	.000	8	8	0	0	0	36	47	35	4	0	23	23	17.5	8.00	49	.320	.412	0	—	0	-16	-17	-1	-1.2
1992 Bal-A	7	5	.583	15	15	2	1	0	94^1	87	39	6	1	38	77	12.0	3.63	111	.249	.325	0	—	0	3	4	0	0.5
1993 Bal-A	5	6	.455	17	17	0	0	0	85^2	91	62	16	1	49	49	14.8	6.51	69	.274	.369	0	—	0	-21	-19	-1	-2.1
1994 Bal-A	3	5	.375	10	10	3	2	0	52^2	51	34	8	2	30	47	14.2	5.81	86	.254	.356	0	—	0	-6	-4	-0	-0.7
1995 Bal-A	2	5	.286	19	9	0	0	0	75^1	68	53	13	0	48	77	13.9	6.21	77	.239	.349	0	—	0	-13	-12	-1	-1.0
1996 *Bal-A	9	1	.900	28	2	0	0	1	53	48	28	6	0	23	62	12.1	4.08	121	.241	.320	0	—	0	5	5	-1	0.7
1997 *Bal-A	10	3	.769	53	0	0	0	1	95^1	75	32	9	4	26	102	9.9	3.02	146	.218	.281	0	.000	-0	16	15	1	1.9
1998 Bal-A	4	4	.500	45	0	0	0	4	77	65	30	8	1	34	83	11.7	3.51	130	.233	.318	1	.500	0	10	9	-1	0.8
1999 Bal-A	3	4	.429	43	0	0	0	3	53	43	37	9	0	45	59	14.9	5.43	86	.221	.367	0	—	0	-3	-5	-0	-0.5
2000 *Sea-A	5	8	.385	72	0	0	0	0	69^1	51	34	6	0	29	77	10.4	4.28	112	.205	.288	0	—	0	5	4	0	0.6
Total 10	48	44	.522	310	61	5	3	9	691^2	626	384	85	9	345	656	12.8	4.80	95	.243	.334	1	.333	0	-18	-20	-5	-1.0

● CHARLIE RHODES
Rhodes, Charles Anderson "Dusty" b: 4/7/1885, Caney, Kan. d: 10/26/18, Caney, Kan. BR/TR, 5'7", 180 lbs. Deb: 7/26/06

YEAR TM/L	W	L	PCT	G	GS	CG	SH	SV	IP	H	R	HR	HB	BB	SO	RAT	ERA	ERA+	OAV	OOB	BH	AVG	PB	PR	PR+	PD	TPI
1906 StL-N	3	4	.429	9	6	3	0	0	45	37	21	0	6	20	32	12.6	3.40	77	.223	.328	3	.188	-0	-4	-4	0	-0.6
1908 Cin-N	0	0	—	1	0	0	0	0	4	1	2	0	1	2	4	9.0	0.00	—	.077	.250	0	.000	-0	1	1	0	0.1
StL-N	1	2	.333	4	4	3	0	0	33	23	14	2	1	12	15	9.8	3.00	79	.200	.281	3	.250	1	-2	-2	1	-0.1
Yr	1	2	.333	5	4	3	0	0	37	24	16	2	2	14	19	9.7	2.68	88	.188	.278	3	.231	1	-1	-1	1	0.0
1909 StL-N	3	5	.375	12	10	4	0	0	61	55	36	0	2	33	25	13.3	3.98	63	.256	.360	4	.211	1	-9	-10	2	-0.9
Total 3	7	11	.389	26	20	10	0	0	143	116	73	2	10	67	76	12.1	3.46	73	.228	.329	10	.208	2	-15	-15	4	-1.5

● GORDON RHODES
Rhodes, John Gordon "Dusty" b: 8/11/07, Winnemucca, Nev. d: 3/24/60, Long Beach, Cal. BR/TR, 6', 187 lbs. Deb: 4/29/29

YEAR TM/L	W	L	PCT	G	GS	CG	SH	SV	IP	H	R	HR	HB	BB	SO	RAT	ERA	ERA+	OAV	OOB	BH	AVG	PB	PR	PR+	PD	TPI
1929 NY-A	0	4	.000	10	4	0	0	0	42^2	57	32	3	2	16	13	15.8	4.85	80	.333	.397	3	.300	1	-3	-5	-1	-0.4
1930 NY-A	0	0	—	3	0	0	0	0	2	3	3	0	1	4	1	31.5	9.00	48	.500	.700	0	—	0	-1	-1	0	0.0
1931 NY-A	6	3	.667	18	11	4	0	0	87	82	49	3	0	52	36	13.9	3.41	116	.235	.334	6	.214	1	9	6	0	0.6
1932 NY-A	1	2	.333	10	2	1	0	0	24	25	22	0	0	21	15	17.3	7.88	52	.275	.411	2	.286	0	-9	-11	1	-0.9
Bos-A	1	8	.111	12	11	4	0	0	79^1	79	46	5	0	31	22	12.5	5.11	88	.261	.329	2	.074	-2	-6	-5	-0	-0.7
Yr	2	10	.167	22	13	5	0	0	103^1	104	68	5	0	52	37	13.6	5.75	76	.264	.350	4	.118	-2	-15	-16	1	-1.6
1933 Bos-A	12	15	.444	34	29	14	0	0	232	242	126	13	1	93	85	13.0	4.03	109	.265	.334	23	.267	4	6	9	-1	1.3
1934 Bos-A	12	12	.500	44	31	10	0	2	219	247	133	10	4	98	79	14.3	4.56	105	.285	.360	10	.133	-3	-2	5	1	0.2
1935 Bos-A	2	10	.167	34	19	1	0	2	146^1	195	103	14	1	60	44	15.7	5.41	88	.324	.387	7	.146	-4	-16	-10	-1	-1.1
1936 Phi-A	9	20	.310	35	28	13	1	1	216^1	266	162	26	2	102	61	15.4	5.74	89	.304	.378	16	.213	-2	-17	-15	-3	-1.9
Total 8	43	74	.368	200	135	47	1	5	1048^2	1196	676	74	10	477	356	14.4	4.85	95	.286	.361	69	.194	-5	-37	-27	-3	-2.9

● BILL RHODES
Rhodes, William Clarence b: Pottstown, Pa. Deb: 6/14/1893

YEAR TM/L	W	L	PCT	G	GS	CG	SH	SV	IP	H	R	HR	HB	BB	SO	RAT	ERA	ERA+	OAV	OOB	BH	AVG	PB	PR	PR+	PD	TPI
1893 Lou-N	5	12	.294	20	19	17	0	0	151^2	244	173	10	10	66	22	19.0	7.60	58	.352	.416	9	.129	-4	-49	-57	-2	-4.7

● DENNIS RIBANT
Ribant, Dennis Joseph b: 9/20/41, Detroit, Mich. BR/TR, 5'11", 175 lbs. Deb: 8/9/64

YEAR TM/L	W	L	PCT	G	GS	CG	SH	SV	IP	H	R	HR	HB	BB	SO	RAT	ERA	ERA+	OAV	OOB	BH	AVG	PB	PR	PR+	PD	TPI
1964 NY-N	1	5	.167	14	7	1	1	1	57^2	65	35	8	0	9	35	11.5	5.15	69	.281	.308	2	.100	-0	-10	-10	-1	-1.1
1965 NY-N	1	3	.250	19	1	0	0	3	35^1	29	16	5	0	6	13	8.9	3.82	92	.228	.263	0	.000	-1	-1	-1	-0	-0.3
1966 NY-N	11	9	.550	39	26	10	1	3	188^1	184	78	20	1	40	84	10.8	3.20	114	.254	.294	12	.197	0	8	9	0	1.1
1967 Pit-N	9	8	.529	38	22	2	0	0	172	186	78	16	3	40	75	12.0	4.08	82	.280	.324	16	.267	5	-14	-14	2	-0.6
1968 Det-A	2	2	.500	14	0	0	0	1	24^1	20	7	1	1	10	7	11.5	2.22	136	.217	.301	1	.200	0	2	2	-1	0.4
Chi-A	0	2	.000	17	0	0	0	1	31^1	42	24	3	2	17	20	17.5	6.03	50	.318	.404	0	.000	-1	-11	-10	-0	-0.8
Yr	2	4	.333	31	0	0	0	2	55^2	62	31	4	3	27	27	14.9	4.37	69	.277	.362	1	.083	-0	-9	-8	-0	-0.4
1969 StL-N	0	0	—	1	0	0	0	0	1^1	4	2	1	0	1	0	33.8	13.50	26	.571	.625	0	—	0	-1	-1	-0	-0.1
Cin-N	0	0	—	7	0	0	0	0	8^1	6	1	1	0	3	7	9.7	1.08	349	.188	.257	0	—	0	2	2	-0	0.1
Yr	0	0	—	8	0	0	0	0	9^2	10	7	2	0	4	7	13.0	2.79	134	.256	.326	0	—	0	1	1	-0	0.0
Total 6	24	29	.453	149	56	13	2	9	518^2	536	245	55	7	126	241	11.6	3.87	90	.267	.312	31	.195	4	-24	-23	0	-1.3

● FRANK RICCELLI
Riccelli, Frank Joseph b: 2/24/53, Syracuse, N.Y. BL/TL, 6'3", 205 lbs. Deb: 9/11/76

YEAR TM/L	W	L	PCT	G	GS	CG	SH	SV	IP	H	R	HR	HB	BB	SO	RAT	ERA	ERA+	OAV	OOB	BH	AVG	PB	PR	PR+	PD	TPI
1976 SF-N	1	1	.500	4	3	0	0	0	16	16	10	1	0	5	11	11.8	5.63	65	.258	.313	1	.167	-0	-4	-3	-0	-0.4
1978 Hou-N	0	0	—	2	0	0	0	0	3	1	0	0	0	0	1	3.0	0.00	—	.100	.100	0	—	0	1	1	-0	0.1
1979 Hou-N	2	2	.500	11	2	0	0	0	22	22	11	0	0	18	20	16.4	4.09	86	.262	.392	2	.333	1	-1	-1	-1	-0.1
Total 3	3	3	.500	17	5	0	0	0	41	39	21	1	0	23	32	13.6	4.39	81	.250	.346	3	.250	1	-3	-4	0	-0.4

● CHUCK RICCI
Ricci, Charles Mark b: 11/20/68, Abington, Pa. BR/TR, 6'2", 180 lbs. Deb: 9/8/95

YEAR TM/L	W	L	PCT	G	GS	CG	SH	SV	IP	H	R	HR	HB	BB	SO	RAT	ERA	ERA+	OAV	OOB	BH	AVG	PB	PR	PR+	PD	TPI
1995 Phi-N	1	0	1.000	7	0	0	0	0	10	9	2	0	1	3	9	11.7	1.80	235	.273	.351	0	—	0	3	3	-0	0.2

● SAM RICE
Rice, Edgar Charles b: 2/20/1890, Morocco, Ind. d: 10/13/74, Rossmoor, Md. BL/TR, 5'9", 150 lbs. Deb: 8/7/15 H♦

YEAR TM/L	W	L	PCT	G	GS	CG	SH	SV	IP	H	R	HR	HB	BB	SO	RAT	ERA	ERA+	OAV	OOB	BH	AVG	PB	PR	PR+	PD	TPI
1915 Was-A	1	0	1.000	4	2	1	0	0	18	13	8	0	0	9	9	11.0	2.00	148	.213	.314	3	.375	1	2	2	0	0.2
1916 Was-A	0	1	.000	5	1	0	0	0	21^1	18	10	0	0	10	3	11.8	2.95	95	.237	.326	59	.299	2	-0	-0	0	0.1
Total 2	1	1	.500	9	3	1	0	0	39^1	31	18	0	0	19	12	11.4	2.52	114	.226	.321	2987	.322	2	2	2	0	0.3

● PAT RICE
Rice, Patrick Edward b: 11/2/63, Rapid City, S.Dak. BR/TR, 6'2", 200 lbs. Deb: 5/18/91

YEAR TM/L	W	L	PCT	G	GS	CG	SH	SV	IP	H	R	HR	HB	BB	SO	RAT	ERA	ERA+	OAV	OOB	BH	AVG	PB	PR	PR+	PD	TPI
1991 Sea-A	1	1	.500	7	2	0	0	0	21	18	10	3	1	10	12	12.4	3.00	138	.234	.330	0	—	0	3	3	-0	0.2

● WOODY RICH
Rich, Woodrow Earl b: 3/9/16, Morganton, N.C. d: 4/18/83, Morganton, N.C. BL/TR, 6'2", 185 lbs. Deb: 4/22/39

YEAR TM/L	W	L	PCT	G	GS	CG	SH	SV	IP	H	R	HR	HB	BB	SO	RAT	ERA	ERA+	OAV	OOB	BH	AVG	PB	PR	PR+	PD	TPI
1939 Bos-A	4	3	.571	21	12	3	0	1	77	78	46	2	5	35	24	13.8	4.91	96	.264	.352	7	.259	0	-2	-2	1	0.0
1940 Bos-A	1	0	1.000	3	1	1	0	0	11^2	9	3	2	0	1	8	7.7	0.77	583	.214	.233	0	.000	-1	5	5	-0	0.3
1941 Bos-A	0	0	—	2	1	0	0	0	3^2	8	7	1	0	2	4	24.5	17.18	24	.421	.476	0	—	0	-5	-5	0	-0.2
1944 Bos-N	1	1	.500	7	2	1	0	0	25	32	17	3	3	12	6	16.9	5.76	66	.327	.416	1	.125	-1	-6	-5	0	-0.4
Total 4	6	4	.600	33	16	5	0	1	117^1	127	73	8	8	50	42	14.2	5.06	89	.280	.361	8	.205	-1	-9	-7	2	-0.3

● J.R. RICHARD
Richard, James Rodney b: 3/7/50, Vienna, La. BR/TR, 6'8", 222 lbs. Deb: 9/5/71

YEAR TM/L	W	L	PCT	G	GS	CG	SH	SV	IP	H	R	HR	HB	BB	SO	RAT	ERA	ERA+	OAV	OOB	BH	AVG	PB	PR	PR+	PD	TPI
1971 Hou-N	2	1	.667	4	4	1	0	0	21	17	9	1	0	16	29	14.1	3.43	98	.215	.347	0	.000	-1	0	-0	0	-0.1
1972 Hou-N	1	0	1.000	4	1	0	0	0	6	10	9	0	2	8	8	30.0	13.50	25	.385	.556	0	—	0	-7	-7	0	-0.9
1973 Hou-N	6	2	.750	16	10	2	1	0	72	54	37	2	1	38	75	11.6	4.00	91	.210	.314	5	.179	-0	-3	-3	-1	-0.4

YEAR	TM/L	W	L	PCT	G	GS	CG	SH	SV	IP	H	R	HR	HB	BB	SO	RAT	ERA	ERA+	OAV	OOB	BH	AVG	PB	PR	PR+	PD	TPI
1974	Hou-N	2	3	.400	15	9	0	0	0	64^2	58	31	3	1	36	42	13.2	4.18	83	.243	.344	3	.143	0	-4	-5	-1	-0.4
1975	Hou-N	12	10	.545	33	31	7	1	0	203	178	107	8	4	138	176	14.2	4.39	77	.238	.359	15	.203	4	-17	-25	-2	-2.2
1976	Hou-N	20	15	.571	39	39	14	3	0	291	221	105	14	4	151	214	11.6	2.75	116	**.212**	.314	14	.140	0	24	16	-1	1.8
1977	Hou-N	18	12	.600	36	36	13	3	0	267	212	94	18	0	104	214	10.7	2.97	120	.218	.293	20	.230	6	28	20	3	3.1
1978	Hou-N	18	11	.621	36	36	16	3	0	275^1	192	104	12	2	141	**303**	11.0	3.11	107	**.196**	.299	18	.178	1	15	7	2	1.1
1979	Hou-N	18	13	.581	38	38	19	4	0	292^1	220	98	13	3	98	**313**	9.9	**2.71**	130	**.209**	.278	12	.126	-0	**34**	**28**	-1	2.8
1980	Hou-N★	10	4	.714	17	17	4	4	0	113^2	65	31	2	0	40	119	8.3	1.90	173	.166	.244	6	.154	1	22	19	-1	2.5
Total	10	107	71	.601	238	221	76	19	0	1606	1227	625	73	17	770	1493	11.3	3.15	108	.212	.306	93	.168	12	92	49	0	7.3

● **DUANE RICHARDS** Richards, Duane Lee b: 12/16/36, Spartanburg, Ind. BR/TR, 6'3", 200 lbs. Deb: 9/25/60

YEAR	TM/L	W	L	PCT	G	GS	CG	SH	SV	IP	H	R	HR	HB	BB	SO	RAT	ERA	ERA+	OAV	OOB	BH	AVG	PB	PR	PR+	PD	TPI
1960	Cin-N	0	0	—	2	0	0	0	0	3	5	4	0	0	2	2	21.0	9.00	42	.385	.467	0	—	0	-2	-2	0	-0.1

● **RUSTY RICHARDS** Richards, Russell Earl b: 1/27/65, Houston, Tex. BL/TR, 6'4", 200 lbs. Deb: 9/20/89

YEAR	TM/L	W	L	PCT	G	GS	CG	SH	SV	IP	H	R	HR	HB	BB	SO	RAT	ERA	ERA+	OAV	OOB	BH	AVG	PB	PR	PR+	PD	TPI
1989	Atl-N	0	0	—	2	2	0	0	0	9^1	10	5	2	1	6	4	16.4	4.82	76	.278	.395	0	.000	-0	-1	-1	0	-0.1
1990	Atl-N	0	0	—	1	0	0	0	0	1	2	3	1	0	1	0	27.0	27.00	15	.400	.500	0	—	0	-3	-2	0	-0.1
Total	2	0	0	—	3	2	0	0	0	10^1	12	8	3	1	7	4	17.4	6.97	53	.293	.408	0	.000	-0	-4	-4	0	-0.2

● **HARDY RICHARDSON** Richardson, Abram Harding "Old True Blue" b: 4/21/1855, Clarksboro, N.J. d: 1/14/31, Utica, N.Y. BR/TR, 5'9.5", 170 lbs. Deb: 5/1/1879 ♦

YEAR	TM/L	W	L	PCT	G	GS	CG	SH	SV	IP	H	R	HR	HB	BB	SO	RAT	ERA	ERA+	OAV	OOB	BH	AVG	PB	PR	PR+	PD	TPI
1885	Buf-N	0	0	—	1	0	0	0	0	4	5	2	0		3	1	18.0	2.25	133	.294	.400	136	.319	0	0	0	0	0.1
1886	Det-N	3	0	1.000	4	0	0	0	0	12	11	8	1		10	5	15.8	4.50	74	.208	.333	189	.351	2	-2	-2	-0	-0.2
Total	2	3	0	1.000	5	0	0	0	0	16	16	10	1		13	6	16.3	3.94	82	.229	.349	1719	.303	3	-1	-1	0	-0.1

● **DANNY RICHARDSON** Richardson, Daniel b: 1/25/1863, Elmira, N.Y. d: 9/12/26, New York, N.Y. BR/TR, 5'8", 165 lbs. Deb: 5/22/1884 M♦

YEAR	TM/L	W	L	PCT	G	GS	CG	SH	SV	IP	H	R	HR	HB	BB	SO	RAT	ERA	ERA+	OAV	OOB	BH	AVG	PB	PR	PR+	PD	TPI
1885	NY-N	7	1	.875	9	8	7	1	0	75	58	30	0		18	21	9.1	2.40	111	.205	.252	52	.263	2	4	2	-1	0.3
1886	NY-N	0	2	.000	5	1	1	0	0	25	33	24	1		11	17	15.8	5.76	56	.320	.386	55	.232	1	-7	-7	1	-0.3
1887	NY-N	0	0	—	1	0	0	0	0	0	1	0	0	1	—	—	—	—	1.000	1.000	93	.331	0	0	0	0	0.0	
Total	3	7	3	.700	15	9	8	1	0	100	92	54	1	0	30	38	10.9	3.24	87	.238	.291	1165	.260	3	-3	-5	-0	0.0

● **GORDIE RICHARDSON** Richardson, Gordon Clark b: 7/19/38, Colquitt, Ga. BR/TL, 6', 185 lbs. Deb: 7/26/64

YEAR	TM/L	W	L	PCT	G	GS	CG	SH	SV	IP	H	R	HR	HB	BB	SO	RAT	ERA	ERA+	OAV	OOB	BH	AVG	PB	PR	PR+	PD	TPI
1964	*StL-N	4	2	.667	19	6	1	0	1	47	40	18	2	1	15	28	10.7	2.30	166	.231	.296	1	.077	-0	6	7	-1	0.8
1965	NY-N	2	2	.500	35	0	0	0	2	52^1	41	27	5	2	16	43	10.1	3.78	93	.224	.294	0	.000	-1	-1	-1	-0	-0.2
1966	NY-N	0	2	.000	15	1	0	0	1	18^2	24	19	7	0	6	15	14.5	9.16	40	.312	.361	0	.000	-0	-12	-11	-0	-1.2
Total	3	6	6	.500	69	7	1	0	4	118	105	64	14	3	37	86	11.1	4.04	90	.242	.307	1	.048	-1	-6	-5	-2	-0.6

● **JEFF RICHARDSON** Richardson, Jeffrey Scott b: 8/29/63, Wichita, Kan. BR/TR, 6'3", 185 lbs. Deb: 9/19/90

YEAR	TM/L	W	L	PCT	G	GS	CG	SH	SV	IP	H	R	HR	HB	BB	SO	RAT	ERA	ERA+	OAV	OOB	BH	AVG	PB	PR	PR+	PD	TPI
1990	Cal-A	0	0	—	1	0	0	0	0	0^1	1	0	0	0	0	0	27.0	0.00	—	.500	.500	0	—	0	0	0	0	0.0

● **JACK RICHARDSON** Richardson, John William b: 10/3/1891, Central City, Ill. d: 1/18/70, Marion, Ill. BB/TR, 6'3", 197 lbs. Deb: 9/17/15

YEAR	TM/L	W	L	PCT	G	GS	CG	SH	SV	IP	H	R	HR	HB	BB	SO	RAT	ERA	ERA+	OAV	OOB	BH	AVG	PB	PR	PR+	PD	TPI
1915	Phi-A	0	1	.000	3	3	2	0	0	24	21	13	0	1	14	11	13.5	2.63	111	.253	.367	0	.000	-1	1	1	-0	-0.1
1916	Phi-A	0	0	—	1	0	0	0	0	0^2	2	3	0	0	1	1	40.5	40.50	7	.667	.750	0	—	0	-3	-3	-0	-0.1
Total	2	0	1	.000	4	3	2	0	0	24^2	23	16	0	1	15	12	14.2	3.65	80	.267	.382	0	.000	-1	-2	-2	-0	-0.2

● **PETE RICHERT** Richert, Peter Gerard b: 10/29/39, Floral Park, N.Y. BL/TL, 6', 184 lbs. Deb: 4/12/62

YEAR	TM/L	W	L	PCT	G	GS	CG	SH	SV	IP	H	R	HR	HB	BB	SO	RAT	ERA	ERA+	OAV	OOB	BH	AVG	PB	PR	PR+	PD	TPI
1962	LA-N	5	4	.556	19	12	1	0	0	81^1	77	35	6	1	45	75	13.6	3.87	94	.249	.346	2	.080	-1	1	-2	1	-0.3
1963	LA-N	5	3	.625	20	12	1	0	0	78	80	40	7	1	28	54	12.6	4.50	67	.262	.326	4	.182	1	-11	-14	-1	-1.4
1964	LA-N	2	3	.400	8	6	1	1	0	34^2	38	17	2	2	18	25	15.1	4.15	78	.271	.363	1	.091	0	-2	-4	1	-0.5
1965	Was-A★	15	12	.556	34	29	6	0	0	194	146	64	18	2	84	161	10.8	2.60	134	.210	.297	10	.156	-0	19	19	-0	2.6
1966	Was-A★	14	14	.500	36	34	7	0	0	245^2	196	106	36	1	69	195	9.7	3.37	103	.215	.271	14	.163	2	2	2	-2	0.2
1967	Was-A	2	6	.250	11	10	1	1	0	54^1	49	29	5	1	15	41	10.8	4.64	68	.237	.291	1	.059	-1	-8	-9	-1	-1.5
	Bal-A	7	10	.412	26	19	5	1	2	132^1	107	53	11	1	41	90	10.1	2.99	105	.220	.282	4	.108	-1	4	2	1	0.3
	Yr	9	16	.360	37	29	6	2	2	186^2	156	82	16	2	56	131	10.3	3.47	91	.225	.285	5	.093	-2	-5	-7	-1	-1.2
1968	Bal-A	6	3	.667	36	0	0	0	6	62^1	51	25	7	3	12	47	9.5	3.47	84	.225	.273	2	.200	0	-3	-4	1	-0.5
1969	*Bal-A	7	4	.636	44	0	0	0	12	57^1	42	17	7	0	14	54	8.8	2.20	162	.202	.252	1	.125	-0	9	9	-1	1.8
1970	*Bal-A	7	2	.778	50	0	0	0	13	54^2	36	14	5	1	24	66	10.0	1.98	185	.194	.289	0	.000	-0	11	10	0	2.1
1971	*Bal-A	3	5	.375	35	0	0	0	4	36^1	26	15	3	1	22	35	12.1	3.47	97	.205	.327	0	.000	-0	0	-0	0	-0.1
1972	LA-N	2	3	.400	37	0	0	0	6	52	42	17	3	1	18	38	10.6	2.25	148	.219	.289	3	.500	1	7	6	-0	0.9
1973	LA-N	3	3	.500	39	0	0	0	7	51	44	18	5	1	19	31	11.3	3.18	108	.234	.308	1	.200	0	3	2	1	0.3
1974	StL-N	0	0	—	13	0	0	0	1	11^1	10	7	1	0	11	4	16.7	2.38	151	.244	.404	0	—	0	2	2	-0	0.0
	Phi-N	2	1	.667	21	0	0	0	0	20^1	15	6	0	0	4	9	8.4	2.21	171	.205	.247	0	—	0	3	3	-0	0.5
	Yr	2	1	.667	34	0	0	0	1	31^2	25	13	1	0	15	13	11.4	2.27	163	.219	.310	0	—	0	5	5	-1	0.5
Total	13	80	73	.523	429	122	22	3	51	1165^2	959	463	116	16	424	925	10.8	3.19	106	.223	.295	43	.145	-1	34	25	-3	4.4

● **LEW RICHIE** Richie, Lewis A. b: 8/23/1883, Ambler, Pa. d: 8/15/36, South Mountain, Pa. BR/TR, 5'8", 165 lbs. Deb: 5/8/06

YEAR	TM/L	W	L	PCT	G	GS	CG	SH	SV	IP	H	R	HR	HB	BB	SO	RAT	ERA	ERA+	OAV	OOB	BH	AVG	PB	PR	PR+	PD	TPI
1906	Phi-N	9	11	.450	33	22	14	3	0	205^2	170	86	3	6	79	65	11.2	2.41	109	.230	.309	3	.050	-3	5	5	-3	-0.2
1907	Phi-N	6	6	.500	25	12	9	2	0	117	88	37	0	5	38	40	10.1	1.77	137	.215	.290	7	.163	0	9	9	-1	0.8
1908	Phi-N	7	10	.412	25	15	13	2	1	157^2	125	50	1	6	49	58	10.3	1.83	133	.233	.304	11	.212	2	9	10	-1	1.2
1909	Phi-N	1	1	.500	11	1	0	0	1	45	40	14	0	2	18	11	12.0	2.00	130	.263	.349	4	.250	1	3	3	-1	0.2
	Bos-N	7	7	.500	22	13	9	2	2	131^2	118	58	2	1	44	42	11.1	2.32	121	.247	.312	5	.114	-2	4	7	-3	0.1
	Yr	8	8	.500	33	14	9	2	3	176^2	158	72	2	3	62	53	11.4	2.24	123	.251	.321	9	.150	-1	7	10	-4	0.3
1910	Bos-N	0	3	.000	4	2	0	0	0	16^1	20	11	0	0	9	7	16.0	2.76	121	.317	.403	0	.000	-1	1	1	1	0.2
	*Chi-N	11	4	.733	30	11	8	3	4	130	117	45	1	3	51	53	11.8	2.70	107	.257	.336	9	.225	3	5	3	1	0.6
	Yr	11	7	.611	34	13	8	3	4	146^1	137	56	1	3	60	60	12.3	2.71	108	.264	.344	9	.205	2	5	4	1	0.8
1911	Chi-N	15	11	.577	36	29	18	4	1	253	213	88	6	2	103	78	11.3	2.31	143	.235	.315	14	.154	-3	31	29	0	2.5
1912	Chi-N	16	8	.667	39	27	15	4	0	238	222	102	5	6	74	69	11.4	2.95	113	.261	.324	10	.132	-3	12	10	-2	0.3
1913	Chi-N	2	4	.333	16	5	1	0	0	65	77	53	3	1	30	15	15.0	5.82	55	.304	.380	2	.118	-0	-19	-19	-1	-1.7
Total	8	74	65	.532	241	137	87	20	9	1359^1	1190	544	21	32	495	438	11.4	2.54	115	.246	.320	65	.147	-7	60	58	-11	4.0

● **BERYL RICHMOND** Richmond, Beryl Justice b: 8/24/07, Glen Easton, W.Va. d: 4/24/80, Cameron, W.Va. BB/TL (BR 1933), 6'1", 185 lbs. Deb: 4/21/33

YEAR	TM/L	W	L	PCT	G	GS	CG	SH	SV	IP	H	R	HR	HB	BB	SO	RAT	ERA	ERA+	OAV	OOB	BH	AVG	PB	PR	PR+	PD	TPI
1933	Chi-N	0	0	—	4	0	0	0	0	4^2	10	1	0	0	2	2	23.1	1.93	170	.455	.500	0	.000	-0	1	1	-0	0.0
1934	Cin-N	1	2	.333	6	2	1	0	0	19^1	23	11	0	0	10	9	15.4	3.72	110	.303	.384	0	.000	-1	1	1	-0	0.0
Total	2	1	2	.333	10	2	1	0	0	24	33	12	0	0	12	11	16.9	3.38	116	.337	.409	0	.000	-1	1	1	-0	0.0

● **LEE RICHMOND** Richmond, J Lee b: 5/5/1857, Sheffield, Ohio d: 10/1/29, Toledo, Ohio TL, 5'10", 155 lbs. Deb: 9/27/1879 ♦

YEAR	TM/L	W	L	PCT	G	GS	CG	SH	SV	IP	H	R	HR	HB	BB	SO	RAT	ERA	ERA+	OAV	OOB	BH	AVG	PB	PR	PR+	PD	TPI
1879	Bos-N	1	0	1.000	1	1	1	0	0	9	4	6	0		1	11	5.0	2.00	124	.114	.139	2	.333	0	0	0	0	0.1
1880	Wor-N	32	32	.500	**74**	66	57	5	**3**	590^2	541	278	7		74	243	9.4	2.15	121	.232	.255	70	.227	-4	15	27	-6	1.7
1881	Wor-N	25	26	.490	53	52	50	3	0	462^1	547	302	7		68	156	12.0	3.39	89	.284	.309	63	.250	-1	-31	-18	2	-1.4
1882	Wor-N	14	33	.298	48	46	44	0	0	411	525	343	11		88	123	13.4	3.74	83	.294	.327	64	.281	7	-39	-27	3	-1.5
1883	Pro-N	3	7	.300	12	12	8	0	0	92	122	67	2		27	13	14.6	3.33	93	.314	.358	55	.284	3	-2	-3	-0	0.0
1886	Cin-a	0	2	.000	3	2	1	0	0	18	24	22	0	2	11	6	18.5	8.00	44	.308	.407	8	.276	0	-9	-9	-0	-0.7
Total	6	75	100	.429	191	179	161	8	3	1583	1763	1018	27	2	269	552	11.6	3.06	95	.269	.298	262	.257	7	-66	-26	-1	-1.8

● **RAY RICHMOND** Richmond, Raymond Sinclair b: 6/15/1896, Fillmore, Ill. d: 10/21/69, DeSoto, Mo. BR/TR, 6', 175 lbs. Deb: 9/25/20

YEAR	TM/L	W	L	PCT	G	GS	CG	SH	SV	IP	H	R	HR	HB	BB	SO	RAT	ERA	ERA+	OAV	OOB	BH	AVG	PB	PR	PR+	PD	TPI
1920	StL-A	2	0	1.000	2	2	1	0	0	17	18	12	0	0	9	4	14.3	6.35	62	.273	.360	1	.167	-0	-5	-4	0	-0.4
1921	StL-A	0	1	.000	6	2	0	0	0	14^1	21	19	1	3	13	6	23.2	11.30	40	.362	.500	0	.000	-1	-11	-10	0	-0.6
Total	2	2	1	.667	8	4	1	0	0	31^1	39	31	1	3	22	10	18.4	8.62	48	.315	.430	1	.100	-1	-16	-15	0	-1.0

● **REGGIE RICHTER** Richter, Emil Henry b: 9/14/1888, Dusseldorf, Germany d: 8/2/34, Winfield, Ill. BR/TR, 6'2", 180 lbs. Deb: 5/30/11

YEAR	TM/L	W	L	PCT	G	GS	CG	SH	SV	IP	H	R	HR	HB	BB	SO	RAT	ERA	ERA+	OAV	OOB	BH	AVG	PB	PR	PR+	PD	TPI
1911	Chi-N	1	3	.250	22	5	0	0	2	54^2	62	30	1	3	20	34	14.0	3.13	106	.307	.378	1	.100	-1	**2**	1	-0	0.0

● **DICK RICKETTS** Ricketts, Richard James b: 12/4/33, Pottstown, Pa. d: 3/6/88, Rochester, N.Y. BL/TR, 6'7", 215 lbs. Deb: 6/14/59 F

YEAR	TM/L	W	L	PCT	G	GS	CG	SH	SV	IP	H	R	HR	HB	BB	SO	RAT	ERA	ERA+	OAV	OOB	BH	AVG	PB	PR	PR+	PD	TPI
1959	StL-N	1	6	.143	12	9	0	0	0	55^2	68	42	7	0	30	25	15.8	5.82	73	.301	.383	1	.056	-2	-12	-9	-2	-1.3

● ELMER RIDDLE Riddle, Elmer Ray b: 7/31/14, Columbus, Ga. d: 5/14/84, Columbus, Ga. BR/TR, 5′11.5″, 170 lbs. Deb: 10/1/39 F

YEAR	TM/L	W	L	PCT	G	GS	CG	SH	SV	IP	H	R	HR	HB	BB	SO	RAT	ERA	ERA+	OAV	OOB	BH	AVG	PB	PR	PR+	PD	TPI
1939	Cin-N	0	0	—	1	0	0	0	0	2	1	0	0	0	0	0	4.5	0.00	—	.143	.143	0	—	0	1	1	-0	0.0
1940	*Cin-N	1	2	.333	15	1	1	0	2	33^2	30	12	0	0	17	9	12.6	1.87	202	.250	.343	1	.143	0	7	7	0	0.7
1941	Cin-N	19	4	**.826**	33	22	15	4	1	216^2	180	68	8	5	59	80	10.1	**2.24**	**160**	.224	.282	16	.225	3	33	33	-1	3.7
1942	Cin-N	7	11	.389	29	19	7	1	0	158^1	157	74	7	4	79	78	13.6	3.69	89	.260	.349	15	.259	3	-7	-7	-1	-0.6
1943	Cin-N	**21**	11	.656	36	33	19	5	3	260^1	235	87	6	2	107	69	11.9	2.63	126	.245	.322	18	.194	1	22	20	-1	2.5
1944	Cin-N	2	2	.500	4	4	2	0	0	26^2	25	12	0	0	12	6	12.5	4.05	86	.250	.330	1	.125	-0	-1	-2	1	-0.2
1945	Cin-N	1	4	.200	12	3	0	0	0	29^2	39	27	4	0	27	5	20.0	8.19	46	.333	.458	3	.273	1	-14	-15	0	-2.0
1947	Cin-N	1	0	1.000	16	3	0	0	0	30^1	42	30	5	1	31	8	22.0	8.31	49	.333	.468	0	.000	-0	-14	-14	-1	-0.8
1948	Pit-N☆	12	10	.545	28	27	12	3	1	191	184	83	20	3	81	63	12.6	3.49	117	.250	.327	12	.188	1	10	12	0	1.4
1949	Pit-N	1	8	.111	16	12	1	0	1	74^1	81	45	9	4	45	24	15.7	5.33	79	.281	.386	3	.136	-1	-11	-9	-2	-1.2
Total	10	65	52	.556	190	124	57	13	8	1023	974	438	59	19	458	342	12.8	3.40	107	.252	.335	69	.204	7	26	26	-4	3.5

● DENNY RIDDLEBERGER Riddleberger, Dennis Michael b: 11/22/45, Clifton Forge, Va. BR/TL, 6′3″, 195 lbs. Deb: 9/15/70

YEAR	TM/L	W	L	PCT	G	GS	CG	SH	SV	IP	H	R	HR	HB	BB	SO	RAT	ERA	ERA+	OAV	OOB	BH	AVG	PB	PR	PR+	PD	TPI
1970	Was-A	0	0	—	8	0	0	0	0	9^1	7	2	1	0	2	5	8.7	0.96	369	.219	.265	0	—	0	3	3	-0	0.1
1971	Was-A	3	1	.750	57	0	0	0	1	69^2	67	27	9	1	32	56	12.9	3.23	103	.260	.344	0	.000	0	2	1	-0	0.1
1972	Cle-A	1	3	.250	38	0	0	0	0	54	45	23	5	2	22	34	11.5	2.50	129	.237	.322	0	.000	-0	3	4	-0	0.2
Total	3	4	4	.500	103	0	0	0	1	133	119	52	15	3	56	95	12.0	2.77	119	.248	.330	0	.000	-0	8	8	-1	0.4

● DORSEY RIDDLEMOSER Riddlemoser, Dorsey Lee b: 3/25/1875, Frederick, Md. d: 5/11/54, Frederick, Md. BR/TR, Deb: 8/22/1899

YEAR	TM/L	W	L	PCT	G	GS	CG	SH	SV	IP	H	R	HR	HB	BB	SO	RAT	ERA	ERA+	OAV	OOB	BH	AVG	PB	PR	PR+	PD	TPI
1899	Was-N	0	0	—	1	0	0	0	0	2	7	4	0	0	2	0	40.5	18.00	22	.538	.600	0	.000	-0	-3	-3	0	-0.1

● JACK RIDGWAY Ridgway, Jacob A. b: 7/23/1889, Philadelphia, Pa. d: 2/23/28, Philadelphia, Pa. BL/TR, 5′11″, 174 lbs. Deb: 5/20/14

YEAR	TM/L	W	L	PCT	G	GS	CG	SH	SV	IP	H	R	HR	HB	BB	SO	RAT	ERA	ERA+	OAV	OOB	BH	AVG	PB	PR	PR+	PD	TPI
1914	Bal-F	0	1	.000	4	1	0	0	0	9	20	11	1	1	3	2	24.0	11.00	28	.444	.490	0	.000	-0	-8	-8	0	-0.7

● STEVE RIDZIK Ridzik, Stephen George b: 4/29/29, Yonkers, N.Y. BR/TR, 5′11″, 170 lbs. Deb: 9/4/50

YEAR	TM/L	W	L	PCT	G	GS	CG	SH	SV	IP	H	R	HR	HB	BB	SO	RAT	ERA	ERA+	OAV	OOB	BH	AVG	PB	PR	PR+	PD	TPI
1950	Phi-N	0	0	—	1	0	0	0	0	3	3	2	1	0	1	2	12.0	6.00	67	.300	.364	0	—	0	-1	-1	-0	0.0
1952	Phi-N	4	2	.667	24	9	2	0	0	92^2	74	37	11	1	37	43	10.9	3.01	121	.218	.297	3	.136	0	7	7	-2	0.2
1953	Phi-N	9	6	.600	42	12	1	0	0	124	119	61	15	5	48	53	12.5	3.77	112	.256	.332	7	.194	2	7	6	-1	0.8
1954	Phi-N	4	5	.444	35	6	0	0	0	80^2	72	42	7	0	44	45	12.9	4.13	98	.233	.329	5	.227	1	-1	-1	0	0.0
1955	Phi-N	0	1	.000	3	1	0	0	0	11	7	9	1	3	8	6	14.7	2.45	162	.179	.360	0	.000	-1	2	2	-0	0.1
	Cin-N	0	3	.000	13	2	0	0	0	30	35	16	4	1	14	6	15.0	4.50	94	.299	.379	1	.167	-0	-2	-1	-1	-0.2
	Yr	0	4	.000	16	3	0	0	0	41	42	25	5	4	22	12	14.9	3.95	105	.269	.374	1	.100	-1	0	1	-1	-0.1
1956	NY-N	6	2	.750	41	5	1	1	0	92^1	80	42	7	5	65	53	14.6	3.80	99	.240	.371	7	.250	1	-0	-0	-0	0.0
1957	NY-N	0	2	.000	15	0	0	0	0	26^2	19	14	3	2	19	13	13.5	4.73	83	.213	.364	1	.200	-0	-3	-2	0	-0.1
1958	Cle-A	0	2	.000	6	0	0	0	0	8^2	9	7	1	0	5	6	14.5	2.08	176	.257	.350	0	.000	-0	2	2	0	0.3
1963	Was-A	5	6	.455	20	10	0	0	1	89^2	82	53	16	5	35	47	12.2	4.82	77	.240	.319	5	.172	0	-12	-11	-0	-1.2
1964	Was-A	5	5	.500	49	3	0	0	2	112	96	46	10	7	31	60	10.8	2.89	128	.236	.301	6	.222	1	9	10	-1	0.9
1965	Was-A	6	4	.600	63	0	0	0	8	109^2	108	61	18	7	43	72	13.0	4.02	86	.257	.335	3	.167	0	-7	-7	0	-0.6
1966	Phi-N	0	0	—	2	0	0	0	0	2^1	5	2	0	0	1	0	23.1	7.71	47	.455	.500	0	—	0	-1	-1	-0	-0.1
Total	12	39	38	.506	314	48	4	1	11	782^2	709	392	94	36	351	406	12.6	3.79	101	.243	.332	38	.192	4	2	3	-4	0.1

● JOHN RIEDLING Riedling, John Richard b: 8/29/75, Ft.Lauderdale, Fla. BR/TR, 5′11″, 190 lbs. Deb: 8/30/2000

YEAR	TM/L	W	L	PCT	G	GS	CG	SH	SV	IP	H	R	HR	HB	BB	SO	RAT	ERA	ERA+	OAV	OOB	BH	AVG	PB	PR	PR+	PD	TPI
2000	Cin-N	3	1	.750	13	0	0	0	1	15^1	11	7	1	1	8	18	11.7	2.35	203	.208	.323	0	.000	-0	4	4	-0	0.7

● ELMER RIEGER Rieger, Elmer Jay b: 2/25/1889, Perris, Cal. d: 10/21/59, Los Angeles, Cal. BB/TR, 6′, 175 lbs. Deb: 4/20/10

YEAR	TM/L	W	L	PCT	G	GS	CG	SH	SV	IP	H	R	HR	HB	BB	SO	RAT	ERA	ERA+	OAV	OOB	BH	AVG	PB	PR	PR+	PD	TPI
1910	StL-N	0	2	.000	13	1	0	0	0	21^1	26	16	1	1	7	9	14.3	5.48	54	.325	.386	0	.000	0	-6	-6	0	-0.5

● BRAD RIGBY Rigby, Bradley Kenneth b: 5/14/73, Milwaukee, Wis. BR/TR, 6′6″, 203 lbs. Deb: 6/28/97

YEAR	TM/L	W	L	PCT	G	GS	CG	SH	SV	IP	H	R	HR	HB	BB	SO	RAT	ERA	ERA+	OAV	OOB	BH	AVG	PB	PR	PR+	PD	TPI
1997	Oak-A	1	7	.125	14	14	0	0	0	77^2	92	44	14	2	22	34	13.4	4.87	93	.302	.353	0	.000	-0	-3	-3	1	-0.2
1999	Oak-A	3	4	.429	29	0	0	0	0	62^1	69	31	5	5	26	26	14.4	4.33	107	.284	.365	0	—	0	4	2	-1	0.1
	KC-A	1	2	.333	20	0	0	0	0	21^1	33	20	6	2	5	10	16.9	7.17	70	.351	.396	0	—	0	-5	-5	-1	-0.6
	Yr	4	6	.400	49	0	0	0	0	83^2	102	51	11	7	31	36	15.1	5.06	94	.303	.373	0	—	0	-2	-3	-2	-0.5
2000	KC-A	0	0	—	4	0	0	0	1	8^1	19	16	6	1	5	3	27.0	16.20	31	.422	.490	0	—	0	-10	-10	0	-0.4
	Mon-N	0	0	—	6	0	0	0	1	5^1	8	5	0	1	3	2	20.3	5.06	93	.348	.444	0	.000	-0	-0	-0	-0	0.0
Total	3	5	13	.278	73	14	0	0	2	175	221	116	31	11	61	75	15.1	5.50	85	.311	.375	0	.000	-0	-15	-17	-2	-1.1

● PAUL RIGDON Rigdon, Paul David b: 11/2/75, Jacksonville, Fla. BR/TR, 6′5″, 210 lbs. Deb: 5/21/2000

YEAR	TM/L	W	L	PCT	G	GS	CG	SH	SV	IP	H	R	HR	HB	BB	SO	RAT	ERA	ERA+	OAV	OOB	BH	AVG	PB	PR	PR+	PD	TPI
2000	Cle-A	1	1	.500	5	4	0	0	0	17^2	21	15	4	0	9	15	15.3	7.64	65	.300	.380	0	—	0	-5	-5	-0	-0.5
	Mil-N	4	4	.500	12	12	0	0	0	69^2	68	37	14	1	26	48	12.3	4.52	101	.255	.323	3	.188	2	1	0	-0	0.2
Total	1	5	5	.500	17	16	0	0	0	87^1	89	52	18	1	35	63	12.9	5.15	90	.264	.335	3	.188	2	-4	-5	-0	-0.3

● JERROD RIGGAN Riggan, Jerrod Ashley b: 5/16/74, Brewster, Wash. BR/TR, 6′3″, 200 lbs. Deb: 8/29/2000

YEAR	TM/L	W	L	PCT	G	GS	CG	SH	SV	IP	H	R	HR	HB	BB	SO	RAT	ERA	ERA+	OAV	OOB	BH	AVG	PB	PR	PR+	PD	TPI
2000	NY-N	0	0	—	1	0	0	0	0	2	3	2	0	0	0	1	13.5	0.00	—	.300	.300	0	—	0	1	1	-0	0.0

● DAVE RIGHETTI Righetti, David Allan b: 11/28/58, San Jose, Cal. BL/TL, 6′3″, 198 lbs. Deb: 9/16/79 C

YEAR	TM/L	W	L	PCT	G	GS	CG	SH	SV	IP	H	R	HR	HB	BB	SO	RAT	ERA	ERA+	OAV	OOB	BH	AVG	PB	PR	PR+	PD	TPI
1979	NY-A	0	1	.000	3	3	0	0	0	17^1	10	7	2	0	10	13	10.4	3.63	112	.182	.308	0	—	0	1	1	0	0.1
1981	*NY-A	8	4	.667	15	15	2	0	0	105^1	75	25	1	0	38	89	9.7	2.05	175	.196	.269	0	—	0	19	18	-1	2.0
1982	NY-A	11	10	.524	33	27	4	0	1	183	155	88	11	6	108	163	13.2	3.79	105	.229	.340	0	—	0	6	4	-2	0.3
1983	NY-A	14	8	.636	31	31	7	2	0	217	194	96	12	2	67	169	10.9	3.44	113	.237	.297	0	—	0	15	12	-1	0.9
1984	NY-A	5	6	.455	64	0	0	0	31	96^1	79	29	5	0	37	90	10.8	2.34	163	.223	.296	0	—	0	18	16	-0	2.8
1985	NY-A	12	7	.632	74	0	0	0	29	107	96	36	5	0	45	92	11.9	2.78	144	.241	.318	0	—	0	16	15	-1	3.0
1986	NY-A★	8	8	.500	74	0	0	0	**46**	106^2	88	31	4	2	35	83	10.5	2.45	167	.226	.293	0	—	0	21	20	-1	3.9
1987	NY-A★	8	6	.571	60	0	0	0	31	95	95	45	9	2	44	77	13.4	3.51	126	.262	.346	0	—	0	10	10	-0	1.8
1988	NY-A	5	4	.556	60	0	0	0	25	87	86	35	5	1	37	70	12.8	3.52	112	.257	.332	0	—	0	4	4	-1	0.5
1989	NY-A	2	6	.250	55	0	0	0	25	69	73	32	3	1	26	51	13.0	3.00	129	.277	.344	0	—	0	7	7	-0	1.1
1990	NY-A	1	1	.500	53	0	0	0	36	53	48	24	8	2	26	43	12.9	3.57	112	.234	.326	0	—	0	2	2	-1	0.2
1991	SF-N	2	7	.222	61	0	0	0	24	71^2	64	29	4	3	28	51	11.9	3.39	106	.240	.319	0	.000	-0	2	2	1	0.3
1992	SF-N	2	7	.222	54	4	0	0	3	78^1	79	47	4	0	36	47	13.2	5.06	65	.269	.348	1	.143	-0	-13	-16	-2	-2.1
1993	SF-N	1	1	.500	51	0	0	0	1	47^1	58	31	11	1	17	31	14.5	5.70	69	.305	.365	1	1.000	0	-9	-10	-0	-0.5
1994	Oak-A	0	0	—	7	0	0	0	0	7	13	13	3	1	9	4	29.6	16.71	27	.419	.561	0	—	0	-9	-10	0	-0.5
	Tor-A	0	1	.000	13	0	0	0	0	13^1	9	10	2	0	10	10	12.8	6.75	71	.188	.328	0	—	0	-3	-3	0	-0.2
	Yr	0	1	.000	20	0	0	0	0	20^1	22	23	5	1	19	14	18.6	10.18	46	.278	.424	0	—	0	-12	-13	0	-0.7
1995	Chi-A	3	2	.600	10	9	0	0	0	49^1	65	24	6	0	18	29	15.1	4.20	106	.325	.381	0	—	0	3	2	-1	0.1
Total	16	82	79	.509	718	89	13	2	252	1403^2	1287	602	95	21	591	1112	12.2	3.46	113	.244	.323	2	.182	0	91	75	-10	13.7

● RON RIGHTNOWAR Rightnowar, Ronald Gene b: 9/5/64, Toledo, Ohio BR/TR, 6′3″, 190 lbs. Deb: 5/20/95

YEAR	TM/L	W	L	PCT	G	GS	CG	SH	SV	IP	H	R	HR	HB	BB	SO	RAT	ERA	ERA+	OAV	OOB	BH	AVG	PB	PR	PR+	PD	TPI
1995	Mil-A	2	1	.667	34	0	0	0	1	36^2	35	23	3	5	18	22	14.2	5.40	92	.271	.382	0	—	0	-3	-2	1	-0.1

● JOHNNY RIGNEY Rigney, John Dungan b: 10/28/14, Oak Park, Ill. d: 10/21/84, Lombard, Ill. BR/TR, 6′2″, 190 lbs. Deb: 4/21/37

YEAR	TM/L	W	L	PCT	G	GS	CG	SH	SV	IP	H	R	HR	HB	BB	SO	RAT	ERA	ERA+	OAV	OOB	BH	AVG	PB	PR	PR+	PD	TPI
1937	Chi-A	2	5	.286	22	4	0	0	1	90^2	107	65	10	3	46	38	15.5	4.96	93	.290	.373	5	.167	-0	-3	-4	-1	-0.3
1938	Chi-A	9	9	.500	38	12	7	1	1	167	164	74	16	2	72	84	12.8	3.56	138	.256	.333	8	.145	-3	23	24	0	2.0
1939	Chi-A	15	8	.652	35	29	11	2	0	218^2	208	103	10	2	84	119	12.1	3.70	128	.247	.316	16	.200	-1	22	24	-2	1.9
1940	Chi-A	14	18	.438	39	33	19	2	3	280^2	240	117	22	2	90	141	10.6	3.11	142	.230	.292	20	.215	1	40	41	-1	4.2
1941	Chi-A	13	13	.500	30	29	18	3	0	237	224	116	21	2	92	119	12.1	3.84	107	.249	.320	17	.202	2	8	7	-0	0.8
1942	Chi-A	3	3	.500	7	7	6	0	0	59	40	23	2	1	16	34	8.7	3.20	112	.185	.245	1	.053	-1	3	3	0	0.1
1946	Chi-A	5	5	.500	15	11	3	2	0	82^2	76	37	6	2	35	51	12.3	4.03	85	.240	.319	4	.154	-1	-5	-6	-1	-0.8
1947	Chi-A	2	3	.400	11	7	2	0	0	50^2	42	15	3	0	15	19	10.1	1.95	187	.228	.286	0	.000	-2	10	10	1	0.9
Total	8	63	64	.496	197	132	66	10	5	1186^1	1101	550	90	14	450	605	11.9	3.59	121	.244	.314	71	.177	-6	98	99	-3	8.8

● JOSE RIJO Rijo, Jose Antonio (Abreu) b: 5/13/65, San Cristobal, D.R. BR/TR, 6′2″, 200 lbs. Deb: 4/5/84

YEAR	TM/L	W	L	PCT	G	GS	CG	SH	SV	IP	H	R	HR	HB	BB	SO	RAT	ERA	ERA+	OAV	OOB	BH	AVG	PB	PR	PR+	PD	TPI
1984	NY-A	2	8	.200	24	5	0	0	2	62^1	74	40	5	1	33	47	15.6	4.76	80	.298	.383	0	—	0	-5	-7	1	-1.0

YEAR TM/L	W	L	PCT	G	GS	CG	SH	SV	IP	H	R	HR	HB	BB	SO	RAT	ERA	ERA+	OAV	OOB	BH	AVG	PB	PR	PR+	PD	TPI
1985 Oak-A	6	4	.600	12	9	0	0	0	63^2	57	26	6	1	28	65	12.2	3.53	109	.239	.322	0	—	0	4	2	-1	0.3
1986 Oak-A	9	11	.450	39	26	4	0	1	193^2	172	116	24	4	108	176	13.2	4.65	83	.237	.339	0	—	0	-10	-18	-1	-1.7
1987 Oak-A	2	7	.222	21	14	1	0	0	82^1	106	67	10	2	41	67	16.3	5.90	70	.305	.381	0	—	0	-13	-17	0	-1.5
1988 Cin-N	13	8	.619	49	19	0	0	0	162	120	47	7	3	63	160	10.3	2.39	150	.209	.291	2	.054	-2	19	21	0	2.5
1989 Cin-N	7	6	.538	19	19	1	1	0	111	101	39	6	2	48	86	12.2	2.84	127	.249	.332	8	.211	1	8	9	-0	1.2
1990 *Cin-N	14	8	.636	29	29	7	1	0	197	151	65	10	2	78	152	10.6	2.70	147	.212	.292	10	.161	-0	24	26	1	3.0
1991 Cin-N	15	6	**.714**	30	30	3	1	0	204^1	165	69	8	3	55	172	**9.8**	2.51	152	.219	**.274**	14	.209	1	27	28	-0	3.0
1992 Cin-N	15	10	.600	33	33	2	0	0	211	185	67	15	3	44	171	9.9	2.56	141	.238	.282	14	.194	1	22	24	1	3.1
1993 Cin-N	14	9	.609	36	36	2	1	0	257^1	218	76	19	2	62	**227**	9.9	2.48	162	.230	.278	22	.268	7	45	44	3	4.9
1994 Cin-N†	9	6	.600	26	26	2	0	0	172^1	177	73	16	4	52	171	12.2	3.08	134	.265	.322	10	.204	2	22	21	2	2.0
1995 Cin-N	5	4	.556	14	14	0	0	0	69	76	33	6	0	22	62	12.8	4.17	99	.285	.339	3	.136	-0	0	-0	0	-0.1
Total 12	111	87	.561	332	260	22	4	3	1786	1602	718	132	27	634	1556	11.4	3.16	123	.240	.309	83	.193	10	143	142	5	15.7
● **GEORGE RILEY** Riley, George Michael b: 10/6/56, Philadelphia, Pa. BL/TL, 6'2", 210 lbs. Deb: 9/15/79																											
1979 Chi-N	0	1	.000	4	1	0	0	0	13	16	9	1	2	6	5	16.6	5.54	75	.320	.414	0	.000	-0	-3	-2	0	-0.1
1980 Chi-N	0	4	.000	22	0	0	0	0	36	41	29	2	2	20	18	15.8	5.75	68	.293	.389	0	.000	-0	-9	-7	1	-0.6
1984 SF-N	1	0	1.000	5	4	0	0	0	29^1	39	14	1	2	7	12	14.7	3.99	88	.315	.361	1	.100	-0	-1	-2	-0	-0.2
1986 Mon-N	0	0	—	10	0	0	0	0	8^2	7	4	0	1	8	5	16.6	4.15	89	.212	.381	0	—	0	-0	-0	-0	-0.1
Total 4	1	5	.167	41	5	0	0	0	87	103	56	4	7	41	40	15.6	4.97	76	.297	.382	1	.077	-1	-13	-11	1	-1.0
● **MATT RILEY** Riley, Matthew Paul b: 8/2/79, Antioch, Cal. BL/TL, 6'1", 205 lbs. Deb: 9/9/99																											
1999 Bal-A	0	0	—	3	3	0	0	0	11	17	9	4	0	13	6	24.5	7.36	64	.378	.517	0	—	0	-3	-3	0	-0.1
● **ANDY RINCON** Rincon, Andrew John b: 3/5/59, Monterey Park, Cal. BR/TR, 6'3", 195 lbs. Deb: 9/15/80																											
1980 StL-N	3	1	.750	4	4	1	0	0	31	23	9	1	0	7	22	8.7	2.61	142	.215	.263	3	.250	0	3	4	0	0.6
1981 StL-N	3	1	.750	5	5	1	1	0	35^2	27	8	0	2	5	13	8.6	1.77	201	.214	.256	3	.231	1	7	7	-0	0.9
1982 StL-N	2	3	.400	11	6	1	0	0	40	35	22	1	0	25	11	13.5	4.72	77	.241	.353	1	.100	-0	-5	-5	-1	-0.6
Total 3	8	5	.615	20	15	3	1	0	106^2	85	39	2	2	37	46	10.5	3.12	116	.225	.297	7	.200	1	5	6	-1	0.9
● **RICARDO RINCON** Rincon, Ricardo (Espinoza) b: 4/13/70, Veracruz, Mexico BL/TL, 6', 190 lbs. Deb: 4/3/97																											
1997 Pit-N	4	8	.333	62	0	0	0	4	60	51	26	5	2	24	71	11.6	3.45	124	.230	.310	0	.000	-0	5	5	-0	1.0
1998 Pit-N	0	2	.000	60	0	0	0	14	65	50	31	6	0	29	64	10.9	2.91	148	.208	.294	0	.000	-0	10	10	0	0.6
1999 *Cle-A	2	3	.400	59	0	0	0	0	44^2	41	22	6	1	24	30	13.3	4.43	114	.248	.347	0	—	0	2	3	1	0.3
2000 Cle-A	2	0	1.000	35	0	0	0	0	20	17	7	1	1	13	20	13.9	2.70	185	.224	.344	0	—	0	5	5	0	0.4
Total 4	8	13	.381	216	0	0	0	18	189^2	159	86	18	4	90	185	12.0	3.42	133	.226	.317	0	.000	-0	22	23	1	2.3
● **JEFF RINEER** Rineer, Jeffrey Alan b: 7/3/55, Lancaster, Pa. BL/TL, 6'4", 205 lbs. Deb: 9/30/79																											
1979 Bal-A	0	0	—	1	0	0	0	0	1	0	0	0	0	0	0	0.0	0.00	—	.000	.000	0	—	0	0	0	0	0.0
● **JIMMY RING** Ring, James Joseph b: 2/15/1895, Brooklyn, N.Y. d: 7/6/65, Queens, N.Y. BR/TR, 6'1", 170 lbs. Deb: 4/13/17																											
1917 Cin-N	3	7	.300	24	7	3	0	2	88	90	47	2	1	35	33	12.9	4.40	60	.272	.343	2	.077	-2	-16	-18	0	-2.2
1918 Cin-N	9	5	.643	21	18	13	4	0	142^1	130	57	5	3	48	26	11.4	2.85	94	.247	.314	6	.120	-3	-1	-3	-3	-0.9
1919 *Cin-N	10	9	.526	32	18	12	2	3	183	150	53	1	3	51	61	10.0	2.26	123	.232	.291	6	.097	-5	13	11	3	1.0
1920 Cin-N	17	16	.515	42	33	18	1	1	266^2	268	134	4	5	92	73	12.3	3.54	86	.264	.329	19	.198	-0	-12	-15	1	-1.8
1921 Phi-N	10	19	.345	34	30	21	0	1	246	258	161	8	5	88	88	12.8	4.24	100	.274	.340	12	.145	-4	-13	-0	3	-0.2
1922 Phi-N	12	18	.400	40	33	17	0	1	249^1	292	160	19	3	103	116	14.4	4.58	102	.297	.365	13	.148	-5	-13	2	4	0.2
1923 Phi-N	18	16	.529	39	36	23	0	0	304^1	336	151	13	1	115	112	13.4	3.87	119	.283	.347	12	.106	-9	4	21	3	1.5
1924 Phi-N	10	12	.455	32	31	16	1	0	215^1	236	123	9	4	108	72	14.5	3.97	112	.286	.371	17	.230	-1	-2	10	2	1.1
1925 Phi-N	14	16	.467	38	37	21	1	0	270	325	166	14	1	119	93	14.8	4.37	109	.297	.367	11	.109	-7	-3	11	2	0.5
1926 NY-N	11	10	.524	39	23	5	0	2	183^1	207	114	12	1	74	76	13.8	4.57	82	.290	.357	8	.143	-3	-15	-17	-1	-2.1
1927 StL-N	0	4	.000	13	3	1	0	0	33	39	28	3	1	17	13	15.5	6.55	60	.300	.385	3	.375	1	-10	-9	1	-0.8
1928 Phi-N	4	17	.190	35	25	4	0	1	176	220	135	14	2	103	70	16.6	6.44	66	.320	.410	11	.183	-2	-48	-40	1	-4.0
Total 12	118	149	.442	389	294	154	9	11	2357^1	2551	1329	104	30	953	833	13.5	4.13	95	.281	.351	120	.147	-40	-116	-48	16	-7.7
● **DANNY RIOS** Rios, Daniel b: 11/11/72, Madrid, Spain BR/TR, 6'2", 190 lbs. Deb: 5/30/97																											
1997 NY-A	0	0	—	2	0	0	0	0	2^1	9	5	3	1	2	1	46.3	19.29	23	.563	.632	0	—	0	-4	-4	0	-0.2
1998 KC-A	0	1	.000	5	0	0	0	0	7^1	9	9	1	1	6	6	19.6	6.14	79	.300	.432	0	—	0	-1	-1	-0	-0.1
Total 2	0	1	.000	7	0	0	0	0	9^2	18	14	4	2	8	7	26.1	9.31	51	.391	.500	0	—	0	-5	-5	-0	-0.3
● **ALLEN RIPLEY** Ripley, Allen Stevens b: 10/18/52, Norwood, Mass. BR/TR, 6'3", 190 lbs. Deb: 4/10/78 F																											
1978 Bos-A	2	5	.286	15	11	1	0	0	73	92	49	10	3	22	26	14.4	5.55	74	.311	.364	0	—	0	-14	-11	-1	-1.0
1979 Bos-A	3	1	.750	16	3	0	0	1	64^2	77	42	9	3	25	34	14.6	5.15	86	.295	.363	0	—	0	-7	-5	-1	-0.4
1980 SF-N	9	10	.474	23	20	2	0	0	112^2	119	59	10	4	36	65	12.7	4.15	85	.274	.335	6	.150	-0	-7	-8	-0	-1.2
1981 SF-N	4	4	.500	19	14	1	0	0	90^2	103	45	5	3	27	47	13.2	4.07	84	.289	.345	4	.133	-1	-6	-7	1	-0.6
1982 Chi-N	5	7	.417	28	19	0	0	0	122^2	130	61	12	2	38	57	12.5	4.26	88	.285	.343	5	.132	-1	-9	-7	1	-0.7
Total 5	23	27	.460	101	67	4	0	1	463^2	521	256	46	15	148	229	13.3	4.52	84	.289	.348	15	.139	-3	-42	-37	-0	-3.9
● **WALT RIPLEY** Ripley, Walter Franklin b: 11/26/16, Worcester, Mass. d: 10/7/90, Attleboro, Mass. BR/TR, 6', 168 lbs. Deb: 8/17/35 F																											
1935 Bos-A	0	0	—	2	0	0	0	0	4	7	4	0	0	3	0	22.5	9.00	53	.412	.500	0	—	0	-2	-2	-0	-0.1
● **RAY RIPPELMEYER** Rippelmeyer, Raymond Roy b: 7/9/33, Valmeyer, Ill. BR/TR, 6'3", 200 lbs. Deb: 4/14/62 C																											
1962 Was-A	1	2	.333	18	1	0	0	0	39^1	47	24	7	0	17	17	14.6	5.49	74	.294	.362	3	.500	2	-7	-6	2	0.0
● **CHARLIE RIPPLE** Ripple, Charles Dawson b: 12/1/21, Bolton, N.C. d: 5/6/79, Wilmington, N.C. BL/TL, 6'2", 210 lbs. Deb: 9/25/44																											
1944 Phi-N	0	0	—	1	1	0	0	0	2^1	6	4	0	0	4	2	38.6	15.43	23	.500	.625	1	1.000	0	-3	-3	-0	-0.1
1945 Phi-N	0	1	.000	4	0	0	0	0	7^2	7	6	0	0	10	5	20.0	7.04	54	.241	.436	0	.000	-0	-3	-3	-0	-0.3
1946 Phi-N	1	0	1.000	6	0	0	0	0	3^1	5	4	0	0	6	3	29.7	10.80	32	.385	.579	0	—	0	-3	-3	-0	-0.6
Total 3	1	1	.500	11	1	0	0	0	13^1	18	14	0	0	20	10	25.7	9.45	39	.333	.514	1	.500	0	-9	-8	-0	-1.0
● **DAVID RISKE** Riske, David Richard b: 10/23/76, Renton, Wash. BR/TR, 6'2", 175 lbs. Deb: 8/14/99																											
1999 Cle-A	1	1	.500	12	0	0	0	0	14	20	15	2	0	6	16	16.7	8.36	60	.333	.394	0	—	0	-5	-5	0	-0.6
● **BILL RISLEY** Risley, William Charles b: 5/29/67, Chicago, Ill. BR/TR, 6'2", 215 lbs. Deb: 7/8/92																											
1992 Mon-N	1	0	1.000	1	1	0	0	0	5	4	1	0	0	1	2	9.0	1.80	193	.235	.278	0	.000	-0	1	1	0	0.2
1993 Mon-N	0	0	—	2	0	0	0	0	3	2	3	1	1	2	2	15.0	6.00	70	.200	.385	0	—	0	-1	-1	0	0.0
1994 Sea-A	9	6	.600	37	0	0	0	0	52^1	31	20	7	0	19	61	8.6	3.44	142	.170	.249	0	—	0	8	8	-0	1.5
1995 *Sea-A	2	1	.667	45	0	0	0	1	60^1	55	21	7	1	18	65	11.0	3.13	151	.244	.303	0	—	0	11	11	-1	0.4
1996 Tor-A	0	1	.000	25	0	0	0	0	41^2	33	20	7	0	25	29	12.5	3.89	129	.221	.333	0	—	0	5	5	-1	0.2
1997 Tor-A	0	1	.000	3	0	0	0	0	4^1	3	4	2	0	2	2	10.4	8.31	55	.188	.278	0	—	0	-2	-2	-0	-0.3
1998 Tor-A	3	4	.429	44	0	0	0	0	54^2	52	37	7	4	34	42	14.8	5.27	89	.259	.377	0	—	0	-4	-4	-1	-0.5
Total 7	15	13	.536	157	1	0	0	1	221^1	180	106	31	6	101	203	11.7	3.98	120	.225	.316	0	.000	-0	19	19	-3	1.5
● **JAY RITCHIE** Ritchie, Jay Seay b: 11/20/36, Salisbury, N.C. BR/TR, 6'4", 190 lbs. Deb: 8/4/64																											
1964 Bos-A	1	1	.500	21	0	0	0	0	46	43	21	4	0	14	35	11.2	2.74	141	.249	.305	1	.111	-1	5	5	-0	0.2
1965 Bos-A	1	2	.333	44	0	0	0	2	71	83	30	3	1	26	55	13.9	3.17	118	.302	.364	1	.200	0	2	4	0	0.3
1966 Atl-N	0	1	.000	22	0	0	0	4	35^1	32	17	3	0	12	33	11.2	4.08	89	.241	.303	2	.500	1	-2	-2	0	0.0
1967 Atl-N	4	6	.400	52	0	0	0	2	82^1	75	32	6	4	29	57	11.8	3.17	105	.245	.319	3	.300	1	2	1	1	0.4
1968 Cin-N	2	3	.400	28	2	0	0	0	56^2	68	32	7	1	13	32	13.0	4.61	69	.293	.333	0	.000	-1	-10	-9	-1	-0.9
Total 5	8	13	.381	167	2	0	0	8	291^1	301	132	23	6	94	212	12.4	3.49	101	.269	.329	7	.200	1	-3	1	0	0.0
● **TODD RITCHIE** Ritchie, Todd Everett b: 11/7/71, Portsmouth, Va. BR/TR, 6'3", 205 lbs. Deb: 4/3/97																											
1997 Min-A	2	3	.400	42	0	0	0	0	74^2	87	41	11	2	28	44	14.1	4.58	102	.290	.355	0	.000	-0	-0	1	-0	0.0
1998 Min-A	0	0	—	15	0	0	0	0	24	30	17	1	0	9	21	14.6	5.63	85	.288	.345	0	—	0	-3	-2	-1	-0.2

YEAR	TM/L	W	L	PCT	G	GS	CG	SH	SV	IP	H	R	HR	HB	BB	SO	RAT	ERA	ERA+	OAV	OOB	BH	AVG	PB	PR	PR+	PD	TPI
1999	Pit-N	15	9	.625	28	26	2	0	0	172^2	169	79	17	4	54	107	11.8	3.49	131	.259	.319	8	.151	-1	21	21	0	2.5
2000	Pit-N	9	8	.529	31	31	1	1	0	187	208	111	26	3	51	124	12.6	4.81	96	.282	.331	13	.217	2	-4	-4	2	0.0
Total	4	26	20	.565	116	57	3	1	0	458^1	494	248	55	9	142	296	12.7	4.32	107	.275	.332	21	.183	1	14	15	1	2.3
● WALLY RITCHIE Ritchie, Wallace Reid b: 7/12/65, Glendale, Cal. BL/TL, 6′2″, 180 lbs. Deb: 5/1/87																												
1987	Phi-N	3	2	.600	49	0	0	0	3	62^1	60	27	8	1	29	45	13.0	3.75	113	.254	.338	1	.250	0	2	3	-0	0.3
1988	Phi-N	0	0	—	19	0	0	0	0	26	19	14	1	1	17	8	12.8	3.12	114	.207	.336	0	—	0	1	1	-0	0.0
1991	Phi-N	1	2	.333	39	0	0	0	0	50^1	44	17	4	2	17	26	11.3	2.50	147	.234	.304	0	.000	-0	7	7	-0	0.3
1992	Phi-N	2	1	.667	40	0	0	0	1	39	44	17	3	0	17	19	14.1	3.00	117	.288	.359	0	.000	0	2	2	-0	0.2
Total	4	6	5	.545	147	0	0	0	4	177^2	167	75	16	4	80	98	12.7	3.14	121	.250	.333	1	.125	0	12	13	-1	0.8
● REGGIE RITTER Ritter, Reggie Blake b: 1/23/60, Malvern, Ark. BL/TR, 6′2″, 195 lbs. Deb: 5/17/86																												
1986	Cle-A	0	0	—	5	0	0	0	0	10	14	10	1	1	4	6	17.1	6.30	66	.341	.413	0	—	0	-2	-2	0	-0.1
1987	Cle-A	1	1	.500	14	0	0	0	0	26^2	33	21	5	0	16	11	16.5	6.08	75	.300	.389	0	—	0	-5	-4	0	-0.3
Total	2	1	1	.500	19	0	0	0	0	36^2	47	31	6	1	20	17	16.7	6.14	72	.311	.395	0	—	0	-7	-7	1	-0.4
● HANK RITTER Ritter, William Herbert b: 10/12/1893, McCoysville, Pa. d: 9/3/64, Akron, Ohio BR/TR, 6′, 180 lbs. Deb: 8/3/12																												
1912	Phi-N	0	0	—	3	0	0	0	0	6	5	5	0	0	5	1	15.0	4.50	81	.192	.323	0	.000	-0	-1	-1	-0	-0.1
1914	NY-N	1	0	1.000	1	0	0	0	0	8	4	1	0	0	4	4	9.0	1.13	236	.160	.276	0	.000	-0	1	1	-0	0.1
1915	NY-N	2	1	.667	22	1	0	0	2	58^1	66	38	4	5	15	35	13.3	4.63	55	.291	.348	2	.125	-1	-12	-14	-0	-1.0
1916	NY-N	1	0	1.000	3	0	0	0	0	5	3	0	0	1	0	3	7.2	0.00	—	.200	.250	0	—	0	1	1	0	0.3
Total	4	4	1	.800	29	1	0	0	2	77^1	78	44	4	6	24	43	12.6	3.96	67	.266	.334	2	.100	-1	-10	-12	-1	-0.7
● JIM RITTWAGE Rittwage, James Michael b: 10/23/44, Cleveland, Ohio BR/TR, 6′3″, 190 lbs. Deb: 9/7/70																												
1970	Cle-A	1	1	.500	8	3	1	0	0	26	18	12	0	0	21	16	13.5	4.15	95	.194	.342	3	.375	1	-1	-1	0	0.1
● KEVIN RITZ Ritz, Kevin D b: 6/8/65, Eatontown, N.J. BR/TR, 6′4″, 220 lbs. Deb: 7/15/89																												
1989	Det-A	4	6	.400	12	12	1	0	0	74	75	41	2	1	44	56	14.6	4.38	87	.265	.366	0	—	0	-4	-5	0	-0.6
1990	Det-A	0	4	.000	4	4	0	0	0	7^1	14	12	0	0	14	3	34.4	11.05	36	.400	.571	0	—	0	-6	-6	1	-1.0
1991	Det-A	0	3	.000	11	5	0	0	0	15^1	17	22	1	2	22	9	24.1	11.74	35	.288	.494	0	—	0	-13	-13	0	-2.0
1992	Det-A	2	5	.286	23	11	0	0	0	80^1	88	52	4	3	44	57	15.1	5.60	71	.278	.372	0	—	0	-15	-15	0	-1.1
1994	Col-N	5	6	.455	15	15	0	0	0	73^2	88	49	5	4	35	53	15.5	5.62	89	.303	.386	0	.000	-2	-11	-4	1	-0.7
1995	*Col-N	11	11	.500	31	28	0	0	2	173^1	171	91	16	6	65	120	12.6	4.21	128	.259	.332	9	.188	-1	-0	18	3	2.3
1996	Col-N	17	11	.607	35	35	2	0	0	213	236	135	24	12	105	105	14.9	5.28	99	.282	.370	15	.231	2	-25	-1	4	0.5
1997	Col-N	6	8	.429	18	18	1	0	0	107^1	142	72	16	1	46	56	15.8	5.87	88	.330	.396	2	.057	-2	-20	-7	1	-0.9
1998	Col-N	0	2	.000	2	2	0	0	0	9	17	11	1	1	2	3	20.0	11.00	47	.395	.435	1	.333	0	-7	-5	0	-0.7
Total	9	45	56	.446	151	130	4	0	2	753^1	848	485	69	30	377	462	15.0	5.35	92	.287	.374	27	.158	-3	-101	-31	10	-4.2
● BEN RIVERA Rivera, Bienvenido Santana b: 1/11/68, San Pedro De Macoris, D.R. BR/TR, 6′6″, 210 lbs. Deb: 4/9/92																												
1992	Atl-N	0	1	.000	8	0	0	0	0	15^1	21	8	1	2	13	11	21.1	4.70	78	.339	.468	0	.000	-0	-2	-2	0	-0.1
	Phi-N	7	3	.700	20	14	4	1	0	102	78	32	8	2	32	66	9.9	2.82	124	.211	.278	3	.094	-1	8	8	-0	0.6
	Yr	7	4	.636	28	14	4	1	0	117^1	99	40	9	4	45	77	11.4	3.07	115	.230	.308	3	.091	-1	6	6	0	0.5
1993	*Phi-N	13	9	.591	30	28	1	1	0	163	175	99	16	6	85	123	14.7	5.02	79	.273	.363	5	.098	-2	-18	-19	-2	-2.6
1994	Phi-N	3	4	.429	9	7	0	0	0	38	40	29	7	1	22	19	14.9	6.87	63	.274	.373	0	.000	-1	-11	-11	0	-1.6
Total	3	23	17	.575	67	49	5	2	0	318^1	314	168	32	11	152	219	13.5	4.52	85	.258	.345	8	.086	-3	-23	-24	-2	-3.7
● LUIS RIVERA Rivera, Luis (Gutierrez) b: 6/21/78, Chihuahua, Mex. BR/TR, 6′3″, 163 lbs. Deb: 4/4/2000																												
2000	Atl-N	1	0	1.000	5	0	0	0	0	6^2	4	1	0	0	5	5	12.2	1.35	335	.190	.346	0	—	0	2	2	0	0.3
	Bal-A	0	0	—	1	0	0	0	0	0^2	1	0	0	0	1	0	27.0	0.00	—	.333	.500	0	—	0	0	0	0	0.0
Total	1	1	0	1.000	6	0	0	0	0	7^1	5	1	0	0	6	5	13.5	1.23	371	.208	.367	0	—	0	3	3	0	0.3
● MARIANO RIVERA Rivera, Mariano b: 11/29/69, Panama City, Panama BR/TR, 6′4″, 170 lbs. Deb: 5/23/95																												
1995	*NY-A	5	3	.625	19	10	0	0	0	67	71	43	11	2	30	51	13.8	5.51	84	.266	.344	0	—	0	-6	-7	1	-0.6
1996	*NY-A	8	3	.727	61	0	0	0	5	107^2	73	25	1	2	34	130	9.1	2.09	237	.189	.258	0	—	0	**35**	**35**	0	3.3
1997	*NY-A★	6	4	.600	66	0	0	0	43	71^2	65	17	5	0	20	68	10.7	1.88	236	.237	.289	0	—	0	21	21	1	4.2
1998	*NY-A	3	0	1.000	54	0	0	0	36	61^1	48	13	3	1	17	36	9.7	1.91	230	.215	.274	0	—	0	19	18	1	2.6
1999	*NY-A†	4	3	.571	66	0	0	0	**45**	69	43	15	2	3	18	52	8.3	1.83	260	.176	.241	0	—	0	23	23	1	4.5
2000	*NY-A★	7	4	.636	66	0	0	0	36	75^2	58	26	4	0	25	58	9.9	2.85	168	.208	.273	0	—	0	17	17	2	3.3
Total	6	33	17	.660	332	10	0	0	165	452^1	358	139	26	8	144	395	10.1	2.63	178	.214	.279	0	—	0	110	106	6	17.3
● ROBERTO RIVERA Rivera, Roberto (Diaz) b: 1/1/69, Bayamon, P.R. BL/TL, 6′, 175 lbs. Deb: 9/3/95																												
1995	Chi-N	0	0	—	7	0	0	0	0	5	8	3	1	0	2	2	18.0	5.40	76	.381	.435	0	—	0	-1	-1	0	0.0
1999	SD-N	1	2	.333	12	0	0	0	0	7	6	4	1	0	3	3	11.6	3.86	109	.240	.321	0	—	0	1	0	0	0.1
Total	2	1	2	.333	19	0	0	0	0	12	14	7	2	0	5	5	14.3	4.50	93	.304	.373	0	—	0	-0	-0	0	0.1
● TINK RIVIERE Riviere, Arthur Bernard b: 8/2/1899, Liberty, Tex. d: 9/27/65, Liberty, Tex. BR/TR, 5′10″, 167 lbs. Deb: 4/15/21																												
1921	StL-N	1	0	1.000	18	2	0	0	0	38^1	45	30	2	2	20	15	15.7	6.10	60	.280	.366	3	.375	2	-10	-11	-2	-0.5
1925	Chi-A	0	0	—	3	0	0	0	0	4^2	6	7	0	1	7	1	27.0	13.50	31	.429	.636	0	.000	-0	-5	-5	1	-0.2
Total	2	1	0	1.000	21	2	0	0	0	43	51	37	2	3	27	16	17.0	6.91	54	.291	.395	3	.333	2	-15	-16	-1	-0.7
● EPPA RIXEY Rixey, Eppa "Jeptha" b: 5/3/1891, Culpeper, Va. d: 2/28/63, Cincinnati, Ohio BR/TL, 6′5″, 210 lbs. Deb: 6/21/12 H																												
1912	Phi-N	10	10	.500	23	20	10	3	0	162	147	57	2	2	54	59	11.3	2.50	145	.256	.322	9	.170	-2	16	19	-1	1.9
1913	Phi-N	9	5	.643	35	19	9	1	2	155^2	148	67	4	6	56	75	12.1	3.12	107	.258	.331	9	.191	-0	1	4	-0	0.2
1914	Phi-N	2	11	.154	24	15	2	0	0	103	124	73	0	3	45	41	15.0	4.37	67	.313	.387	1	.038	-1	-18	-16	0	-1.9
1915	*Phi-N	11	12	.478	29	22	10	2	1	176^2	163	67	2	2	64	88	11.7	2.39	115	.250	.319	9	.164	-0	7	7	0	0.9
1916	Phi-N	22	10	.688	38	33	20	3	0	287	239	91	2	7	74	134	10.0	1.85	143	.229	.284	15	.155	-2	25	25	3	3.2
1917	Phi-N	16	21	.432	39	36	23	4	1	281^1	249	102	1	5	67	121	10.3	2.27	124	.241	.290	18	.191	-1	14	16	4	2.5
1919	Phi-N	6	12	.333	23	18	11	1	0	154	160	88	4	3	50	63	12.4	3.97	81	.278	.339	7	.149	-2	-18	-12	2	-1.3
1920	Phi-N	11	22	.333	41	34	25	0	2	284^1	288	137	5	4	69	109	11.4	3.48	98	.274	.321	25	.248	1	-11	-2	3	0.3
1921	Cin-N	19	18	.514	40	37	21	2	1	301	324	128	1	5	66	76	11.8	2.78	129	.282	.324	13	.129	-5	**34**	28	3	3.0
1922	Cin-N	**25**	13	.658	40	38	26	2	0	**313^1**	337	146	13	4	45	80	11.1	3.53	113	.275	.303	21	.193	-1	20	16	-0	1.6
1923	Cin-N	20	15	.571	42	37	23	3	1	309	334	124	3	4	65	97	11.7	2.80	138	.280	.320	17	.159	-5	41	38	2	3.6
1924	Cin-N	15	14	.517	35	29	15	**4**	1	238^1	219	86	3	2	47	57	10.1	2.76	137	.246	.285	18	.214	1	29	27	-1	3.2
1925	Cin-N	21	11	.656	39	36	22	2	1	287^1	302	109	8	7	47	69	11.2	2.88	143	.273	.307	22	.214	-1	44	41	-2	3.8
1926	Cin-N	14	8	.636	37	29	14	3	0	233	231	104	12	2	58	61	11.2	3.40	109	.265	.313	19	.226	0	11	8	-2	0.5
1927	Cin-N	12	10	.545	34	29	11	1	1	219^2	240	106	3	3	43	42	11.7	3.48	109	.287	.325	20	.247	4	11	8	-1	1.0
1928	Cin-N	19	18	.514	43	37	17	3	2	291^1	317	127	4	3	67	58	12.0	3.43	115	.288	.330	18	.173	-1	18	17	-0	1.8
1929	Cin-N	10	13	.435	35	24	11	0	1	201	235	102	6	3	60	37	13.3	4.16	110	.296	.348	15	.231	0	12	9	-1	0.8
1930	Cin-N	9	13	.409	32	21	5	0	0	164	207	103	11	7	47	37	14.3	5.10	95	.317	.370	11	.200	-1	-2	-5	0	-0.6
1931	Cin-N	4	7	.364	22	17	4	0	0	126^2	143	71	4	0	30	22	12.3	3.91	96	.291	.332	6	.150	-1	-1	-3	4	0.1
1932	Cin-N	5	5	.500	25	11	6	2	0	111^2	108	50	3	4	16	14	10.3	2.66	145	.254	.288	9	.265	1	15	15	1	1.4
1933	Cin-N	6	3	.667	16	12	5	1	0	94^1	118	48	1	0	12	10	12.4	3.15	108	.298	.319	9	.257	2	2	3	1	0.6
Total	21	266	251	.515	692	554	290	37	14	4494^2	4633	1986	92	76	1082	1350	11.6	3.15	116	.272	.318	291	.191	-15	251	248	16	26.6
● TODD RIZZO Rizzo, Todd Michael b: 5/24/71, Media, Pa. BR/TL, 6′3″, 220 lbs. Deb: 4/2/98																												
1998	Chi-A	0	0	—	9	0	0	0	0	6^2	12	12	0	0	6	3	24.3	13.50	34	.387	.486	0	—	0	-7	-7	-0	-0.3
1999	Chi-A	0	2	.000	3	0	0	0	0	1^1	4	2	0	0	3	2	47.3	6.75	72	.500	.636	0	—	0	-0	-0	0	-0.1
Total	2	0	2	.000	12	0	0	0	0	8	16	14	0	0	9	5	28.1	12.38	37	.410	.521	0	—	0	-7	-7	-0	-0.4
● JOE ROA Roa, Joseph Rodger b: 10/11/71, Southfield, Mich. BR/TR, 6′1″, 194 lbs. Deb: 9/20/95																												
1995	Cle-A	0	1	.000	1	1	0	0	0	6	9	4	1	0	2	0	16.5	6.00	78	.360	.407	0	—	0	-1	-1	0	-0.1
1996	Cle-A	0	0	—	1	0	0	0	0	1^2	4	2	0	0	3	0	37.8	10.80	45	.500	.636	0	—	0	-1	-1	-0	-0.1

YEAR TM/L	W	L	PCT	G	GS	CG	SH	SV	IP	H	R	HR	HB	BB	SO	RAT	ERA	ERA+	OAV	OOB	BH	AVG	PB	PR	PR+	PD	TPI
1997 SF-N	2	5	.286	28	3	0	0	0	65^2	86	40	8	2	20	34	14.8	5.21	78	.333	.386	2	.133	-0	-7	-8	2	-0.6
Total 3	2	6	.250	30	4	0	0	0	73^1	99	46	9	2	25	34	15.5	5.40	77	.340	.396	2	.133	-0	-9	-10	2	-0.8

● JOHN ROACH
Roach, John F. b: Farrandsville, Pa. BR/TR, 5'9", 175 lbs. Deb: 5/14/1887

YEAR TM/L	W	L	PCT	G	GS	CG	SH	SV	IP	H	R	HR	HB	BB	SO	RAT	ERA	ERA+	OAV	OOB	BH	AVG	PB	PR	PR+	PD	TPI
1887 NY-N	0	1	.000	1	1	1	0	0	8	22	17	0	1	4	3	25.9	11.25	33	.468	.479	1	.250	-0	-6	-7	-0	-0.5

● SKEL ROACH
Roach, Rudolph Charles (b: Rudolph Charles Weichbrodt) b: 10/20/1871, Danzig, Germany d: 3/9/58, Oak Park, Ill. BR/TR, 6'2", Deb: 8/9/1899

YEAR TM/L	W	L	PCT	G	GS	CG	SH	SV	IP	H	R	HR	HB	BB	SO	RAT	ERA	ERA+	OAV	OOB	BH	AVG	PB	PR	PR+	PD	TPI
1899 Chi-N	1	0	1.000	1	1	1	0	0	9	13	3	0	0	1	0	14.0	3.00	125	.333	.350	0	.000	-1	1	1	-0	0.0

● BRUCE ROBBINS
Robbins, Bruce Duane b: 9/10/59, Portland, Ind. BL/TL, 6'1", 190 lbs. Deb: 7/28/79

YEAR TM/L	W	L	PCT	G	GS	CG	SH	SV	IP	H	R	HR	HB	BB	SO	RAT	ERA	ERA+	OAV	OOB	BH	AVG	PB	PR	PR+	PD	TPI
1979 Det-A	3	3	.500	10	8	0	0	0	46	45	21	3	0	21	22	12.9	3.91	111	.265	.346	0	—	0	2	2	-1	0.2
1980 Det-A	4	2	.667	15	6	0	0	0	51^2	60	40	12	0	28	23	15.3	6.62	62	.287	.371	0	—	0	-15	-14	0	-1.4
Total 2	7	5	.583	25	14	0	0	0	97^2	105	61	15	0	49	45	14.2	5.34	79	.277	.360	0	—	0	-13	-12	-0	-1.2

● BERT ROBERGE
Roberge, Bertrand Roland b: 10/3/54, Lewiston, Maine BR/TR, 6'4", 190 lbs. Deb: 5/28/79

YEAR TM/L	W	L	PCT	G	GS	CG	SH	SV	IP	H	R	HR	HB	BB	SO	RAT	ERA	ERA+	OAV	OOB	BH	AVG	PB	PR	PR+	PD	TPI
1979 Hou-N	3	0	1.000	26	0	0	0	4	32	20	6	0	0	17	13	10.4	1.69	209	.196	.311	0	.000	-0	7	7	-0	0.7
1980 Hou-N	2	0	1.000	14	0	0	0	0	24^1	24	16	2	2	10	9	13.3	5.92	56	.261	.346	0	.000	-0	-6	-8	0	-0.6
1982 Hou-N	1	2	.333	22	0	0	0	3	25^2	29	12	0	0	6	18	12.3	4.21	79	.284	.324	0	.000	-0	-2	-3	0	-0.4
1984 Chi-A	3	3	.500	21	0	0	0	0	40^2	36	18	2	3	15	25	12.0	3.76	111	.240	.321	0	—	0	1	2	1	0.3
1985 Mon-N	3	3	.500	42	0	0	0	2	68	58	28	5	2	22	34	10.9	3.44	99	.232	.299	0	.000	-0	1	-0	0	0.0
1986 Mon-N	0	4	.000	21	0	0	0	1	28^2	33	20	2	1	10	20	13.8	6.28	59	.295	.358	0	.000	-0	-8	-8	-0	-1.1
Total 6	12	12	.500	146	0	0	0	10	219^1	200	100	11	8	80	119	11.8	3.98	90	.248	.321	0	.000	-1	-7	-10	1	-1.1

● SID ROBERSON
Roberson, Sidney Dean b: 9/9/71, Jacksonville, Fla. BL/TL, 5'9", 170 lbs. Deb: 5/20/95

YEAR TM/L	W	L	PCT	G	GS	CG	SH	SV	IP	H	R	HR	HB	BB	SO	RAT	ERA	ERA+	OAV	OOB	BH	AVG	PB	PR	PR+	PD	TPI
1995 Mil-A	6	4	.600	26	13	0	0	0	84^1	102	55	16	8	37	40	15.7	5.76	87	.307	.390	0	—	0	-10	-7	-2	-0.9

● DALE ROBERTS
Roberts, Dale "Mountain Man" b: 4/12/42, Owenton, Ky. BR/TL, 6'4", 180 lbs. Deb: 9/9/67

YEAR TM/L	W	L	PCT	G	GS	CG	SH	SV	IP	H	R	HR	HB	BB	SO	RAT	ERA	ERA+	OAV	OOB	BH	AVG	PB	PR	PR+	PD	TPI
1967 NY-A	0	0	—	2	0	0	0	0	2	3	2	0	2	2	0	31.5	9.00	35	.429	.636	0	—	0	-1	-1	0	-0.1

● DAVE ROBERTS
Roberts, David Arthur b: 9/11/44, Gallipolis, Ohio BL/TL, 6'2", 197 lbs. Deb: 7/6/69

YEAR TM/L	W	L	PCT	G	GS	CG	SH	SV	IP	H	R	HR	HB	BB	SO	RAT	ERA	ERA+	OAV	OOB	BH	AVG	PB	PR	PR+	PD	TPI
1969 SD-N	0	3	.000	22	5	0	0	1	48^2	65	30	5	3	19	19	16.1	4.81	74	.322	.388	4	.267	1	-7	-7	0	-0.3
1970 SD-N	8	14	.364	43	21	3	2	1	181^2	182	80	16	1	43	102	11.2	3.81	104	.261	.305	9	.153	1	5	3	-0	0.5
1971 SD-N	14	17	.452	37	34	14	2	0	269^2	238	79	9	5	61	135	10.1	2.10	157	.240	.288	19	.221	2	41	38	1	4.9
1972 Hou-N	12	7	.632	35	28	7	3	2	192	227	100	18	2	57	111	13.4	4.50	75	.296	.346	16	.239	6	-22	-25	-1	-1.9
1973 Hou-N	17	11	.607	39	36	12	6	0	249^1	264	92	15	2	62	119	11.8	2.85	128	.271	.316	11	.129	-3	23	22	-1	2.0
1974 Hou-N	10	12	.455	34	30	8	2	1	204	216	83	6	3	65	72	12.5	3.40	102	.276	.333	16	.219	5	5	2	2	1.0
1975 Hou-N	8	14	.364	32	27	7	0	1	198^1	182	98	16	2	73	101	11.7	4.27	79	.244	.313	9	.143	-0	-14	-21	1	-2.0
1976 Det-A	16	17	.485	36	36	18	4	0	252	254	122	16	4	63	79	11.5	4.00	93	.264	.312	0	—	0	-13	-8	2	-0.8
1977 Det-A	4	10	.286	22	22	5	0	0	129^1	143	88	20	2	41	46	12.9	5.15	84	.274	.330	0	—	0	-15	-12	-0	-1.1
Chi-N	1	1	.500	17	6	1	0	1	53	55	22	1	1	12	23	11.5	3.23	136	.275	.319	1	.059	-2	4	6	2	0.3
1978 Chi-N	6	8	.429	35	20	2	1	1	142^1	159	87	17	3	56	54	13.8	5.25	77	.288	.357	17	.327	6	-26	-17	1	-0.9
1979 SF-N	0	2	.000	26	1	0	0	3	42	42	15	3	1	18	23	13.1	2.57	136	.262	.341	0	.000	-1	5	5	1	0.3
*Pit-N	5	2	.714	21	3	0	0	1	38^2	47	18	1	1	12	15	14.0	3.26	119	.318	.373	0	.000	-1	2	3	0	0.4
Yr	5	4	.556	47	4	0	0	4	80^2	89	33	4	2	30	38	13.5	2.90	127	.289	.356	0	.000	-1	8	7	1	0.7
1980 Pit-N	0	1	.000	2	0	0	0	0	2^1	2	1	0	0	1	1	11.6	3.86	95	.250	.333	0	—	0	-0	-0	-0	0.0
Sea-A	2	3	.400	37	4	0	0	3	80^1	86	46	7	1	27	47	12.8	4.37	95	.270	.329	0	—	0	-3	-2	-1	-0.3
1981 NY-N	0	3	.000	7	4	0	0	0	15^1	26	18	5	0	5	10	18.2	9.39	37	.366	.408	1	.250	0	-10	-10	0	-1.6
Total 13	103	125	.452	445	277	77	20	15	2099	2188	979	155	31	615	957	12.2	3.78	97	.270	.324	103	.194	15	-26	-26	7	0.5

● GRANT ROBERTS
Roberts, Grant William b: 9/13/77, ElCajon, Cal. BR/TR, 6'3", 205 lbs. Deb: 7/27/2000

YEAR TM/L	W	L	PCT	G	GS	CG	SH	SV	IP	H	R	HR	HB	BB	SO	RAT	ERA	ERA+	OAV	OOB	BH	AVG	PB	PR	PR+	PD	TPI
2000 NY-N	0	0	—	4	1	0	0	0	7	11	10	0	0	4	6	19.3	11.57	38	.344	.417	0	—	0	-5	-6	-0	-0.3

● JIM ROBERTS
Roberts, James Newson "Big Jim" b: 10/13/1895, Artesia, Miss. d: 6/24/84, Columbus, Miss. BR/TR, 6'3", 205 lbs. Deb: 7/27/24

YEAR TM/L	W	L	PCT	G	GS	CG	SH	SV	IP	H	R	HR	HB	BB	SO	RAT	ERA	ERA+	OAV	OOB	BH	AVG	PB	PR	PR+	PD	TPI
1924 Bro-N	0	3	.000	11	5	0	0	0	25^1	41	28	1	2	8	10	18.1	7.46	50	.360	.411	1	.143	-0	-10	-11	-0	-1.1
1925 Bro-N	0	0	—	1	0	0	0	0	1	1	1	0	0	0	0	9.0	0.00	—	.500	.500	0	—	0	0	0	0	0.0
Total 2	0	3	.000	12	5	0	0	0	26^1	42	29	1	2	8	10	17.8	7.18	52	.362	.413	1	.143	-0	-10	-10	-0	-1.1

● LEON ROBERTS
Roberts, Leon Kauffman b: 1/22/51, Vicksburg, Mich. BR/TR, 6'3", 200 lbs. Deb: 9/3/74 C◆

YEAR TM/L	W	L	PCT	G	GS	CG	SH	SV	IP	H	R	HR	HB	BB	SO	RAT	ERA	ERA+	OAV	OOB	BH	AVG	PB	PR	PR+	PD	TPI
1984 KC-A	0	0	—	1	0	0	0	0	1	4	3	1	0	1	1	45.0	27.00	15	.571	.625	10	.222	0	-3	-3	0	-0.1

● RAY ROBERTS
Roberts, Raymond b: 8/25/1895, Cruger, Miss. d: 1/30/62, Cruger, Miss. BL/TR, 5'11", 180 lbs. Deb: 9/12/19

YEAR TM/L	W	L	PCT	G	GS	CG	SH	SV	IP	H	R	HR	HB	BB	SO	RAT	ERA	ERA+	OAV	OOB	BH	AVG	PB	PR	PR+	PD	TPI
1919 Phi-A	0	2	.000	3	2	0	0	0	14	21	14	0	0	3	2	15.4	7.71	44	.368	.400	1	.250	-0	-7	-6	-0	-0.8

● ROBIN ROBERTS
Roberts, Robin Evan b: 9/30/26, Springfield, Ill. BB/TR, 6', 190 lbs. Deb: 6/18/48 H

YEAR TM/L	W	L	PCT	G	GS	CG	SH	SV	IP	H	R	HR	HB	BB	SO	RAT	ERA	ERA+	OAV	OOB	BH	AVG	PB	PR	PR+	PD	TPI
1948 Phi-N	7	9	.438	20	20	9	0	0	146^2	148	63	10	4	61	84	13.1	3.19	124	.278	.356	11	.250	4	12	12	-2	1.5
1949 Phi-N	15	15	.500	43	31	11	3	4	226^2	229	101	15	5	75	95	12.3	3.69	107	.273	.337	5	.075	-3	9	6	-3	0.1
1950 *Phi-N★	20	11	.645	40	39	21	**5**	1	304^1	282	112	29	2	77	146	10.7	3.02	134	.248	.297	12	.118	-4	**38**	36	0	3.0
1951 Phi-N★	21	15	.583	44	39	22	6	2	**315**	284	115	20	3	64	127	10.0	3.03	127	.237	**.278**	15	.172	5	33	30	-3	**3.5**
1952 Phi-N☆	**28**	7	.800	39	37	**30**	3	2	**330**	292	104	22	5	45	148	9.3	2.59	141	.234	.263	14	.125	2	**42**	**40**	-3	4.1
1953 Phi-N★	**23**	16	.590	44	41	**33**	5	2	**346^2**	324	119	30	2	61	**198**	10.0	2.75	153	.242	.276	22	.179	2	59	57	-1	6.2
1954 Phi-N★	**23**	15	.605	45	38	**29**	4	4	**336^2**	289	116	35	5	56	**185**	**9.4**	2.97	136	.231	**.267**	15	.123	-3	41	40	-4	3.7
1955 Phi-N★	**23**	14	.622	41	38	**26**	1	3	**305**	292	137	41	2	53	160	10.2	3.28	121	.246	**.280**	27	.252	14	26	24	-5	3.8
1956 Phi-N☆	19	18	.514	43	37	**22**	1	3	297^1	328	155	46	2	40	157	11.2	4.45	84	.282	.307	20	.200	4	-22	-24	-0	-2.4
1957 Phi-N	10	22	.313	39	32	14	2	2	249^2	246	122	40	1	43	128	10.5	4.07	93	.252	.284	13	.162	0	-5	-8	0	-0.8
1958 Phi-N	17	14	.548	35	34	21	1	0	269^2	270	112	30	2	51	130	10.8	3.24	122	.259	.294	20	.202	4	21	22	-2	2.5
1959 Phi-N	15	17	.469	35	35	19	2	0	257^1	267	137	34	5	35	137	10.7	4.27	96	.263	.291	17	.191	3	-9	-4	0	-0.2
1960 Phi-N	12	16	.429	35	33	13	2	1	237^1	256	113	31	2	34	122	11.1	4.02	97	.275	.302	12	.152	-1	-7	-4	-3	-0.7
1961 Phi-N	1	10	.091	26	18	2	0	0	117	154	85	19	2	23	54	13.8	5.85	70	.326	.360	3	.091	-2	-24	-23	-2	-2.1
1962 Bal-A	10	9	.526	27	25	6	0	0	191^1	176	63	17	4	41	102	10.4	2.78	133	.244	.289	10	.192	2	25	21	-1	2.1
1963 Bal-A	14	13	.519	35	35	9	2	0	251^1	230	100	35	3	40	124	9.8	3.33	104	.240	**.272**	16	.203	2	8	4	-2	0.5
1964 Bal-A	13	7	.650	31	31	8	4	0	204	203	69	18	3	52	109	11.4	2.91	123	.261	.310	9	.132	-1	16	15	-2	1.2
1965 Bal-A	5	7	.417	20	15	5	1	0	114^2	110	51	17	1	20	63	10.3	3.38	103	.252	.286	6	.171	1	1	1	-1	0.1
Hou-N	5	2	.714	10	10	3	2	0	76	61	22	1	0	10	34	8.4	1.89	177	.216	.243	5	.238	3	14	13	-2	1.4
1966 Hou-N	3	5	.375	13	12	1	1	1	63^2	79	31	7	1	10	26	12.7	3.82	90	.307	.336	1	.063	-1	-1	-3	-1	-0.5
Chi-N	2	3	.400	11	9	1	0	0	48^1	62	35	8	0	11	28	13.6	6.14	60	.313	.349	2	.200	1	-14	-13	0	-1.1
Yr	5	8	.385	24	21	2	1	1	112	141	66	15	1	21	54	13.1	4.82	73	.310	.342	3	.115	-0	-15	-16	-0	-1.6
Total 19	286	245	.539	676	609	305	45	25	4688^2	4582	1962	505	54	902	2357	10.6	3.41	113	.255	.293	255	.167	34	264	239	-35	25.9

● WILLIS ROBERTS
Roberts, Willis Augusto (De Leon) b: 6/19/75, San Cristobal, D.R. BR/TR, 6'3", 175 lbs. Deb: 7/2/99

YEAR TM/L	W	L	PCT	G	GS	CG	SH	SV	IP	H	R	HR	HB	BB	SO	RAT	ERA	ERA+	OAV	OOB	BH	AVG	PB	PR	PR+	PD	TPI
1999 Det-A	0	0	—	1	0	0	0	0	1^1	3	4	0	1	0	0	27.0	13.50	36	.500	.571	0	—	0	-1	-1	0	-0.1

● CHARLIE ROBERTSON
Robertson, Charles Culbertson b: 1/31/1896, Dexter, Tex. d: 8/23/84, Fort Worth, Tex. BL/TR, 6', 175 lbs. Deb: 5/13/19

YEAR TM/L	W	L	PCT	G	GS	CG	SH	SV	IP	H	R	HR	HB	BB	SO	RAT	ERA	ERA+	OAV	OOB	BH	AVG	PB	PR	PR+	PD	TPI
1919 Chi-A	0	1	.000	1	1	0	0	0	2	5	2	0	0	0	1	22.5	9.00	35	.556	.556	0	—	0	-1	-1	-0	-0.2
1922 Chi-A	14	15	.483	37	34	21	3	0	272	294	124	9	4	89	83	12.8	3.64	112	.286	.345	16	.184	-2	12	13	-5	0.6
1923 Chi-A	13	18	.419	38	34	18	1	0	255	262	126	8	5	104	91	13.1	3.81	104	.272	.346	21	.247	0	5	4	-2	0.3
1924 Chi-A	4	10	.286	17	14	5	0	0	97^1	108	65	2	0	54	29	15.0	4.99	83	.293	.383	6	.182	-1	-8	-10	-2	-1.4
1925 Chi-A	8	12	.400	24	23	6	2	0	137	181	96	8	2	47	27	15.1	5.26	79	.327	.381	10	.222	0	-13	-18	-2	-2.2
1926 StL-A	1	2	.333	8	7	1	0	0	28	38	27	4	2	21	13	19.6	8.36	51	.333	.445	3	.300	1	-13	-12	0	-1.0
1927 Bos-N	7	17	.292	28	21	6	0	0	154^1	188	90	2	4	46	49	13.9	4.72	79	.308	.360	12	.240	1	-14	-18	-1	-2.5
1928 Bos-N	2	5	.286	13	7	3	0	1	59^1	73	40	5	0	16	17	13.5	5.31	74	.308	.352	0	.000	-1	-9	-9	-1	-1.1
Total 8	49	80	.380	166	141	60	6	1	1005	1149	570	38	17	377	310	13.8	4.44	90	.296	.361	68	.208	-2	-42	-50	-13	-7.5

YEAR	TM/L	W	L	PCT	G	GS	CG	SH	SV	IP	H	R	HR	HB	BB	SO	RAT	ERA	ERA+	OAV	OOB	BH	AVG	PB	PR	PR+	PD	TPI
● **JERRY ROBERTSON** Robertson, Jerry Lee b: 10/13/43, Winchester, Kan. d: 3/24/96, Burlington, Kan. BB/TR, 6'2", 205 lbs. Deb: 4/8/69																												
1969	Mon-N	5	16	.238	38	27	3	0	1	179^2	186	87	17	4	81	133	13.6	3.96	93	.272	.352	5	.089	-3	-7	-5	-3	-1.1
1970	Det-A	0	0	—	11	0	0	0	0	14^2	19	8	1	0	5	11	14.7	3.68	101	.306	.358	0	—	0	0	0	-0	0.0
Total	2	5	16	.238	49	27	3	0	1	194^1	205	95	18	4	86	144	13.7	3.94	94	.274	.352	5	.089	-3	-7	-5	-3	-1.1
● **DICK ROBERTSON** Robertson, Preston b: 1891, Washington, D.C. d: 10/2/44, New Orleans, La. BR/TR, 5'9", 160 lbs. Deb: 9/16/13																												
1913	Cin-N	0	1	.000	2	1	1	0	0	10	13	9	0	0	9	1	19.8	7.20	45	.342	.468	0	.000	-0	-4	-4	-0	-0.4
1918	Bro-N	3	6	.333	13	9	7	1	0	87	87	34	0	0	28	18	11.9	2.59	108	.272	.330	9	.300	2	2	2	-0	0.4
1919	Was-A	0	1	.000	7	4	0	0	0	27^2	25	11	1	0	9	7	11.1	2.28	141	.253	.315	0	.000	-1	3	3	0	0.1
Total	3	3	8	.273	22	14	8	1	0	124^2	125	54	1	0	46	26	12.3	2.89	101	.274	.340	9	.225	0	0	0	-1	0.1
● **RICH ROBERTSON** Robertson, Richard Paul b: 10/14/44, Albany, Cal. BR/TR, 6'2", 210 lbs. Deb: 9/10/66																												
1966	SF-N	0	0	—	1	0	0	0	0	2^1	3	3	0	0	2	2	19.3	7.71	48	.300	.417	0	—	0	-1	-1	-0	-0.1
1967	SF-N	0	0	—	1	0	0	0	0	2	3	1	0	0	0	1	13.5	4.50	73	.333	.333	0	—	0	-0	-0	0	0.0
1968	SF-N	2	0	1.000	3	1	0	0	0	9	9	6	0	0	3	8	12.0	6.00	49	.265	.324	1	.500	0	-3	-3	0	-0.6
1969	SF-N	1	3	.250	17	7	1	1	0	44^1	53	32	4	1	21	20	15.2	5.48	64	.298	.375	0	.000	-1	-9	-10	0	-0.9
1970	SF-N	8	9	.471	41	26	6	0	1	183^2	199	113	22	1	96	121	14.5	4.85	82	.277	.363	6	.102	-1	-16	-18	-0	-1.6
1971	SF-N	2	2	.500	23	6	1	0	1	61	66	40	5	2	31	32	14.6	4.57	74	.267	.354	1	.067	-1	-7	-8	-1	-0.8
Total	6	13	14	.481	86	40	8	1	2	302^1	333	195	31	4	153	184	14.6	4.94	76	.278	.362	8	.093	-2	-37	-41	-1	-4.0
● **RICH ROBERTSON** Robertson, Richard Wayne b: 9/15/68, Nacogdoches, Tex. BL/TL, 6'4", 175 lbs. Deb: 4/30/93																												
1993	Pit-N	0	1	.000	9	0	0	0	0	9	15	6	0	0	4	5	19.0	6.00	68	.385	.442	0	—	0	-2	-2	-0	-0.2
1994	Pit-N	0	0	—	8	0	0	0	0	15^2	20	12	2	0	10	8	17.2	6.89	63	.313	.405	1	.250	0	-5	-4	-0	-0.2
1995	Min-A	2	0	1.000	25	4	1	0	0	51^2	48	28	4	0	31	38	13.8	3.83	125	.253	.357	0	—	0	5	5	-1	0.2
1996	Min-A	7	17	.292	36	31	5	**3**	0	186^1	197	113	22	9	116	114	15.6	5.12	100	.273	.380	0	—	0	-3	-0	2	0.2
1997	Min-A	8	12	.400	31	26	0	0	0	147	169	105	19	6	70	69	15.0	5.69	82	.292	.374	1	.200	0	-18	-17	-2	-2.0
1998	Ana-A	0	0	—	5	0	0	0	0	5^2	11	11	3	0	2	3	20.6	15.88	30	.393	.433	0	—	0	-7	-7	1	-0.3
Total	6	17	30	.362	114	61	6	3	0	415^1	460	275	50	15	233	237	15.3	5.40	90	.284	.379	2	.222	0	-29	-25	-1	-2.3
● **DEWEY ROBINSON** Robinson, Dewey Everett b: 4/28/55, Evanston, Ill. BR/TR, 6', 180 lbs. Deb: 4/6/79 C																												
1979	Chi-A	0	1	.000	11	0	0	0	0	14^1	11	12	1	0	9	5	12.6	6.28	68	.212	.328	0	—	0	-3	-3	-0	-0.2
1980	Chi-A	1	1	.500	15	0	0	0	0	35	26	13	2	0	16	28	10.8	3.09	131	.215	.307	0	—	0	4	4	0	0.2
1981	Chi-A	1	0	1.000	4	0	0	0	0	4	5	2	1	0	3	2	18.0	4.50	80	.357	.471	0	—	0	-0	-0	-0	-0.1
Total	3	2	2	.500	30	0	0	0	0	53^1	42	27	4	0	28	35	11.8	4.05	100	.225	.326	0	—	0	0	0	-0	-0.1
● **DON ROBINSON** Robinson, Don Allen b: 6/8/57, Ashland, Ky. BR/TR, 6'4", 231 lbs. Deb: 4/10/78																												
1978	Pit-N	14	6	.700	35	32	9	1	1	228^1	203	98	20	3	57	135	10.4	3.47	107	.236	.286	20	.235	2	3	6	-1	0.6
1979	*Pit-N	8	8	.500	29	25	4	0	0	160^2	171	74	12	4	52	96	12.7	3.87	101	.277	.337	10	.204	1	-2	0	-3	-0.2
1980	Pit-N	7	10	.412	29	24	3	2	1	160^1	157	74	14	5	45	103	11.6	3.99	92	.257	.314	19	.333	6	-7	-6	0	0.1
1981	Pit-N	0	3	.000	16	2	0	0	2	38^1	47	27	4	0	23	17	16.4	5.87	61	.313	.405	3	.250	1	-10	-9	1	-0.6
1982	Pit-N	15	13	.536	38	30	6	0	0	227	213	123	26	3	103	165	12.6	4.28	87	.250	.333	24	.282	8	-17	-14	-2	-0.9
1983	Pit-N	2	2	.500	9	6	0	0	0	36^1	43	21	5	0	21	28	15.9	4.46	83	.297	.386	2	.154	1	-3	-3	0	-0.2
1984	Pit-N	5	6	.455	51	1	0	0	10	122	99	45	6	0	49	110	10.9	3.02	119	.226	.304	9	.290	4	8	8	1	1.3
1985	Pit-N	5	11	.313	44	6	0	0	3	95^1	95	49	6	2	42	65	13.1	3.87	93	.255	.334	5	.238	3	-3	-3	-0	-0.3
1986	Pit-N	3	4	.429	50	0	0	0	14	69^1	61	27	5	2	27	53	11.7	3.38	114	.237	.315	4	.667	2	3	3	0	0.7
1987	Pit-N	6	6	.500	42	0	0	0	12	65^1	66	29	6	0	22	53	12.1	3.86	107	.267	.327	1	.143	0	2	2	0	0.4
	*SF-N	5	1	.833	25	0	0	0	7	42^2	39	13	1	0	18	26	12.0	2.74	140	.239	.315	3	.273	2	6	6	-1	1.0
	Yr	11	7	.611	67	0	0	0	19	108	105	42	7	0	40	79	12.1	3.42	117	.256	.322	4	.222	2	8	7	-1	1.4
1988	SF-N	10	5	.667	51	19	3	2	6	176^2	152	63	11	3	49	122	10.4	2.45	134	.231	.287	9	.173	3	20	17	-2	1.7
1989	*SF-N	12	11	.522	34	32	5	1	0	197	184	80	22	2	37	96	10.2	3.43	99	.248	.285	15	.185	4	2	-1	-4	-0.2
1990	SF-N	10	7	.588	26	25	4	0	0	157^2	173	84	18	1	41	78	12.3	4.57	80	.280	.326	9	.143	1	-13	-17	-2	-1.7
1991	SF-N	5	9	.357	34	16	0	0	1	121^1	123	64	12	1	50	78	12.9	4.38	82	.265	.337	6	.150	0	-9	-11	-0	-1.2
1992	Cal-A	1	0	1.000	3	3	0	0	0	16^1	19	4	1	0	3	9	12.1	2.20	181	.292	.324	0	—	0	3	3	-1	0.1
	Phi-N	1	4	.200	8	8	0	0	0	43^2	49	32	6	1	4	17	11.1	6.18	57	.290	.310	7	.389	3	-13	-13	-1	-1.1
Total	15	109	106	.507	524	229	34	6	57	1958^1	1894	907	175	27	643	1251	11.8	3.79	96	.255	.317	146	.231	41	-32	-33	-14	-0.5
● **HUMBERTO ROBINSON** Robinson, Humberto Valentino b: 6/25/30, Colon, Panama BR/TR, 6'1", 155 lbs. Deb: 4/20/55																												
1955	Mil-N	3	1	.750	13	2	1	0	2	38	31	13	1	4	25	19	14.2	3.08	122	.235	.373	1	.077	-1	4	3	0	0.2
1956	Mil-N	0	0	—	1	0	0	0	0	2	1	0	0	0	2	0	13.5	0.00	—	.167	.375	0	—	0	1	1	0	0.1
1958	Mil-N	2	4	.333	19	0	0	0	1	41^2	30	15	4	2	13	26	9.7	3.02	116	.203	.276	1	.167	1	4	3	1	0.5
1959	Cle-A	1	0	1.000	5	0	0	0	0	8^2	9	4	0	0	4	6	13.5	4.15	89	.281	.361	0	—	0	-0	-0	0	0.0
	Phi-N	2	4	.333	31	4	1	0	1	73	70	36	6	0	24	32	11.6	3.33	123	.251	.310	3	.231	1	5	6	0	0.6
1960	Phi-N	0	4	.000	33	1	0	0	0	49^2	48	24	6	0	22	31	12.7	3.44	113	.255	.333	1	.167	-0	2	2	0	0.2
Total	5	8	13	.381	102	7	2	0	4	213	189	92	17	6	90	114	12.0	3.25	119	.241	.323	6	.158	0	16	14	2	1.6
● **JEFF ROBINSON** Robinson, Jeffrey Daniel b: 12/13/60, Santa Ana, Cal. BR/TR, 6'4", 200 lbs. Deb: 4/7/84																												
1984	SF-N	7	15	.318	34	33	1	1	0	171^2	195	99	12	7	52	102	13.3	4.56	77	.288	.345	7	.115	-2	-18	-20	0	-2.6
1985	SF-N	0	0	—	8	0	0	0	0	12^1	16	11	2	0	10	8	19.0	5.11	67	.333	.448	0	—	0	-2	-2	-0	-0.2
1986	SF-N	6	3	.667	64	1	0	0	8	104^1	92	46	8	1	32	90	10.8	3.36	105	.234	.293	1	.067	-1	4	2	-1	0.0
1987	SF-N	6	8	.429	63	0	0	0	10	96^2	69	34	10	1	48	82	11.0	2.79	138	.207	.309	2	.111	-1	14	12	1	1.8
	Pit-N	2	1	.667	18	0	0	0	4	26^2	20	9	1	0	6	19	8.8	3.04	135	.215	.263	1	.250	1	3	3	0	0.6
	Yr	8	9	.471	81	0	0	0	14	123^1	89	43	11	1	54	101	10.5	2.85	137	.209	.299	3	.136	0	17	15	1	2.4
1988	Pit-N	11	5	.688	75	0	0	0	9	124^2	113	44	6	3	39	87	11.2	3.03	112	.244	.307	3	.188	0	6	5	0	0.8
1989	Pit-N	7	13	.350	50	19	0	0	4	141^1	161	92	14	1	59	95	14.1	4.58	73	.283	.351	8	.229	2	-17	-20	1	-2.4
1990	NY-A	3	6	.333	54	4	1	0	0	88^2	82	35	8	1	34	43	11.9	3.45	115	.248	.320	0	—	0	5	5	2	0.7
1991	Cal-A	0	3	.000	39	0	0	0	3	57	56	34	9	2	29	57	13.7	5.37	77	.259	.352	0	—	0	-8	-8	0	-0.4
1992	Chi-N	4	3	.571	49	5	0	0	1	78	76	29	5	2	40	46	13.6	3.00	120	.263	.356	0	.000	-1	4	5	1	0.4
Total	9	46	57	.447	454	62	2	1	39	901^1	880	433	75	18	349	629	12.5	3.79	95	.258	.330	22	.137	-1	-10	-18	4	-1.3
● **JEFF ROBINSON** Robinson, Jeffrey Mark b: 12/14/61, Ventura, Cal. BR/TR, 6'6", 240 lbs. Deb: 4/12/87																												
1987	*Det-A	9	6	.600	29	21	2	1	0	127^1	132	86	16	7	54	98	13.6	5.37	79	.262	.342	0	—	0	-13	-17	-1	-1.7
1988	Det-A	13	6	.684	24	23	6	2	0	172	121	61	19	3	72	114	10.3	2.98	128	**.197**	.284	0	—	0	19	17	-0	1.7
1989	Det-A	4	5	.444	16	16	1	1	0	78	76	47	10	1	46	40	14.2	4.73	81	.259	.361	0	—	0	-7	-8	-1	-0.9
1990	Det-A	10	9	.526	27	27	1	1	0	145	141	101	23	6	88	76	14.6	5.96	67	.255	.364	0	—	0	-33	-32	-1	-3.6
1991	Bal-A	4	9	.308	21	19	0	0	0	104^1	119	62	12	6	51	65	15.2	5.18	76	.289	.375	0	—	0	-12	-15	-1	-1.7
1992	Tex-A	4	4	.500	16	4	0	0	0	45^2	50	30	6	0	21	18	14.0	5.72	67	.281	.357	0	—	0	-9	-10	-0	-1.6
	Pit-N	3	1	.750	8	7	0	0	0	36^1	33	18	2	1	15	14	12.1	4.46	77	.244	.325	1	.091	-1	-4	-4	0	-0.5
Total	6	47	40	.540	141	117	10	5	0	708^2	672	405	88	24	347	425	13.2	4.79	82	.250	.341	1	.091	-1	-59	-69	-4	-8.3
● **JACK ROBINSON** Robinson, John Edward b: 2/20/21, Orange, N.J. d: 3/2/2000, Ormond Beach, Fla. BR/TR, 6', 175 lbs. Deb: 5/4/49																												
1949	Bos-A	0	0	—	3	0	0	0	0	4	4	1	0	1	1	1	13.5	2.25	194	.267	.353	0	—	0	1	1	0	0.1
● **HANK ROBINSON** Robinson, John Henry "Rube" (b: John Henry Roberson) b: 8/16/1889, Floyd, Ark. d: 7/3/65, N.Little Rock, Ark BR/TL, 5'11.5", 160 lbs. Deb: 9/2/11																												
1911	Pit-N	0	1	.000	5	0	0	0	0	13	13	7	0	1	5	8	13.2	2.77	124	.283	.365	0	.000	-0	1	1	1	0.1
1912	Pit-N	12	7	.632	33	16	11	0	2	175	146	54	3	10	30	79	**9.6**	2.26	144	.237	.284	15	.254	3	22	20	-1	2.2
1913	Pit-N	14	9	.609	43	22	8	1	0	196^1	184	72	1	7	41	50	10.6	2.38	127	.255	.301	11	.180	-1	18	15	-2	1.4
1914	StL-N	7	8	.467	26	16	6	1	0	126	128	61	1	4	32	30	11.7	3.00	93	.274	.325	6	.171	-0	-3	-3	2	-0.2
1915	StL-N	7	8	.467	32	15	6	1	0	143	128	54	1	7	35	57	10.7	2.45	114	.245	.301	5	.106	-2	5	5	1	0.4
1918	NY-A	2	4	.333	11	3	1	0	0	48	47	21	0	3	16	14	12.4	3.00	94	.269	.340	0	.000	-2	-1	-1	-0	-0.3
Total	6	42	37	.532	150	72	32	3	2	701^1	646	269	6	32	159	238	10.7	2.53	118	.253	.305	37	.170	-3	42	37	1	3.6

YEAR	TM/L	W	L	PCT	G	GS	CG	SH	SV	IP	H	R	HR	HB	BB	SO	RAT	ERA	ERA+	OAV	OOB	BH	AVG	PB	PR	PR+	PD	TPI
● KENNY ROBINSON	Robinson, Kenneth Neal b: 11/3/69, Barberton, Ohio d: 2/28/99, Tucson, Ariz. BR/TR, 5'7", 175 lbs. Deb: 7/20/95																											
1995	Tor-A	1	2	.333	21	0	0	0	0	39	25	21	7	2	22	31	11.3	3.69	128	.179	.299	0	—	0	4	4	-1	0.2
1996	KC-A	1	0	1.000	5	0	0	0	0	6	9	4	0	0	3	5	18.0	6.00	84	.346	.414	0	—	0	-1	-1	-0	-0.1
1997	Tor-A	0	0	—	3	0	0	0	0	3^{1}	1	1	1	0	1	4	5.4	2.70	170	.100	.182	0	—	0	1	1	1	0.1
Total	3	2	2	.500	29	0	0	0	0	48^{1}	35	26	8	2	26	40	11.7	3.91	121	.199	.309	0	—	0	4	4	-0	0.2
● RON ROBINSON	Robinson, Ronald Dean b: 3/24/62, Exeter, Cal. BR/TR, 6'4", 235 lbs. Deb: 8/14/84																											
1984	Cin-N	1	2	.333	12	5	1	0	0	39^{2}	35	18	3	0	13	24	10.9	2.72	139	.232	.293	0	.000	-1	4	4	0	0.2
1985	Cin-N	7	7	.500	33	12	0	0	1	108^{1}	107	53	11	1	32	76	11.6	3.99	95	.259	.314	2	.091	-1	-5	-2	1	-0.3
1986	Cin-N	10	3	.769	70	0	0	0	14	116^{2}	110	44	10	2	43	117	12.0	3.24	120	.253	.323	1	.071	-1	6	8	1	1.1
1987	Cin-N	7	5	.583	48	18	0	0	4	154	148	71	14	1	43	99	11.2	3.68	115	.256	.308	7	.194	0	7	9	-2	0.5
1988	Cin-N	3	7	.300	17	16	0	0	0	78^{2}	88	47	5	2	26	38	13.3	4.12	87	.285	.344	5	.200	1	-6	-4	-0	-0.5
1989	Cin-N	5	3	.625	15	15	0	0	0	83^{1}	80	36	8	2	28	36	11.9	3.35	108	.252	.317	6	.214	1	1	2	-0	0.3
1990	Cin-N	2	2	.500	6	5	0	0	0	31^{1}	36	18	2	0	14	14	14.4	4.88	81	.295	.368	1	.091	-1	-4	-3	-0	-0.4
	Mil-A	12	5	.706	22	22	7	2	0	148^{1}	158	60	5	6	37	57	12.2	2.91	133	.275	.326	0	—	0	17	16	-0	1.7
1991	Mil-A	0	1	.000	1	1	0	0	0	4^{1}	6	3	0	1	3	0	20.8	6.23	64	.353	.476	0	—	0	-1	-1	0	-0.2
1992	Mil-A	1	4	.200	8	8	0	0	0	35^{1}	51	26	3	2	14	12	17.1	5.86	66	.331	.394	0	—	0	-8	-8	-0	-1.0
Total	9	48	39	.552	232	102	8	2	19	800	819	376	61	17	253	473	12.3	3.63	107	.267	.326	22	.153	-2	12	21	-1	1.4
● BILL ROBINSON	Robinson, William (b: William Anderson) b: Taylorsville, Ky. Deb: 8/12/1889																											
1889	Lou-a	0	1	.000	1	1	1	0	0	8	10	10	2	0	6	2	18.0	10.13	38	.294	.400	1	.333	0	-6	-6	0	-0.4
● YANK ROBINSON	Robinson, William H. b: 9/19/1859, Philadelphia, Pa. d: 8/25/1894, St.Louis, Mo. BR/TR, 5'6.5", 170 lbs. Deb: 8/24/1882 ◆																											
1882	Det-N	0	0	—	1	0	0	0	0	2	0	0	0	0	1	0	4.5	0.00	—	.000	.125	7	.179	-0	1	1	0	0.0
1884	Bal-U	3	3	.500	11	3	3	0	0	75	96	61	1	1	18	61	13.7	3.48	77	.292	.329	111	.267	-0	-9	-6	-3	-0.6
1886	*StL-a	0	1	.000	1	1	1	0	0	9	10	11	0	0	7	1	17.0	3.00	115	.286	.405	132	.274	0	0	0	-0	0.1
1887	*StL-a	0	0	—	1	0	0	0	1	3	6	2	0	1	3	0	21.0	3.00	151	.500	.538	223	.427	0	0	0	-0	0.0
Total	4	3	4	.429	14	4	4	0	1	89	112	74	1	1	29	62	14.1	3.34	85	.292	.339	917	.261	0	-7	-5	-3	-0.5
● CHICK ROBITAILLE	Robitaille, Joseph Anthony b: 3/2/1879, Whitehall, N.Y. d: 7/30/47, Waterford, N.Y. BR/TR, 5'8", 150 lbs. Deb: 9/2/04																											
1904	Pit-N	4	3	.571	9	8	8	0	0	66	52	22	1	1	13	34	9.0	1.91	144	.208	.250	2	.095	-2	6	6	-1	0.3
1905	Pit-N	8	5	.615	17	12	10	0	0	120^{1}	126	54	1	3	28	32	11.7	2.92	103	.276	.322	6	.133	-2	1	1	-0	-0.1
Total	2	12	8	.600	26	20	18	0	0	186^{1}	178	76	2	4	41	66	10.8	2.56	114	.252	.297	8	.121	-4	7	7	-1	0.2
● ARMANDO ROCHE	Roche, Armando (Baez) b: 12/7/26, Havana, Cuba d: 6/26/97, Chicago, Ill. BR/TR, 6', 190 lbs. Deb: 5/10/45																											
1945	Was-A	0	0	—	2	0	0	0	0	6	10	4	0	0	2	0	18.0	6.00	52	.400	.444	0	.000	-0	-2	-2	0	-0.1
● MIKE ROCHFORD	Rochford, Michael Joseph b: 3/14/63, Methuen, Mass. BL/TL, 6'4", 205 lbs. Deb: 9/3/88																											
1988	Bos-A	0	0	—	2	0	0	0	0	2^{1}	4	0	0	0	1	1	19.3	0.00	—	.364	.417	0	—	0	1	1	0	0.1
1989	Bos-A	0	0	—	4	0	0	0	0	4	4	7	1	0	4	1	18.0	6.75	61	.267	.421	0	—	0	-1	-1	-0	-0.1
1990	Bos-A	0	1	.000	2	1	0	0	0	4	10	10	1	0	4	0	31.5	18.00	23	.526	.609	0	—	0	-6	-6	-0	-0.9
Total	3	0	1	.000	8	1	0	0	0	10^{1}	18	17	2	0	9	2	23.5	9.58	43	.400	.500	0	—	0	-6	-6	0	-0.9
● JOHN ROCKER	Rocker, John Loy b: 10/17/74, Statesboro, Ga. BR/TL, 6'4", 210 lbs. Deb: 5/5/98																											
1998	*Atl-N	1	3	.250	47	0	0	0	2	38	22	10	4	3	22	42	11.1	2.13	195	.172	.307	0	—	0	9	9	0	0.9
1999	*Atl-N	4	5	.444	74	0	0	0	38	72^{1}	47	24	5	1	37	104	10.6	2.49	181	.180	.284	0	—	0	17	16	1	3.2
2000	*Atl-N	1	2	.333	59	0	0	0	24	53	42	25	5	2	48	77	15.6	2.89	157	.210	.368	0	—	0	10	10	0	1.3
Total	3	6	10	.375	180	0	0	0	64	163^{1}	111	59	14	6	107	223	12.3	2.53	175	.188	.319	0	—	0	36	35	1	5.4
● RICH RODAS	Rodas, Richard Martin b: 11/7/59, Roseville, Cal. BL/TL, 6'1", 180 lbs. Deb: 9/6/83																											
1983	LA-N	0	0	—	7	0	0	0	0	4^{2}	4	1	0	0	3	5	13.5	1.93	187	.222	.333	0	—	0	1	1	-0	0.0
1984	LA-N	0	0	—	3	0	0	0	0	5	5	3	2	0	1	1	10.8	5.40	65	.250	.286	0	.000	-0	-1	-1	0	-0.1
Total	2	0	0	—	10	0	0	0	0	9^{2}	9	4	2	0	4	6	12.1	3.72	96	.237	.310	0	.000	-0	-0	-0	0	-0.1
● EDUARDO RODRIGUEZ	Rodriguez, Eduardo (Reyes) b: 3/6/52, Barceloneta, P.R. BR/TR, 6', 185 lbs. Deb: 6/20/73																											
1973	Mil-A	9	7	.563	30	6	2	0	5	76^{1}	71	33	6	2	47	49	14.1	3.30	114	.247	.357	1	1.000	1	4	4	-0	0.9
1974	Mil-A	7	4	.636	43	6	0	0	4	111^{2}	97	49	7	5	51	58	12.3	3.63	100	.241	.333	0	—	0	-0	-0	0	0.0
1975	Mil-A	7	0	1.000	43	1	0	0	7	87^{2}	77	37	9	5	44	65	12.9	3.49	110	.235	.334	0	—	0	3	3	-2	0.2
1976	Mil-A	5	13	.278	45	12	3	0	8	136	124	68	10	3	65	77	12.7	3.64	96	.249	.339	0	—	0	-2	-2	-1	-0.4
1977	Mil-A	5	6	.455	42	5	1	1	4	142^{2}	126	70	15	3	56	104	11.7	4.35	94	.236	.311	0	—	0	-4	-4	-1	-0.4
1978	Mil-A	5	5	.500	32	8	0	0	2	105^{1}	107	49	9	2	26	51	11.5	3.93	96	.262	.310	0	—	0	-2	-2	-0	-0.2
1979	KC-A	4	1	.800	29	1	1	0	2	74^{1}	79	42	9	3	34	26	14.0	4.84	88	.276	.359	0	—	0	-5	-5	-1	-0.4
Total	7	42	36	.538	264	39	7	1	32	734	681	348	65	23	323	430	12.6	3.89	98	.248	.332	1	1.000	1	-6	-6	-5	-0.3
● FELIX RODRIGUEZ	Rodriguez, Felix Antonio b: 12/5/72, Monte Cristi, D.R. BR/TR, 6'1", 170 lbs. Deb: 5/13/95																											
1995	LA-N	1	1	.500	11	0	0	0	0	10^{2}	11	3	2	0	5	5	13.5	2.53	150	.275	.356	0	—	0	2	2	-0	0.3
1997	Cin-N	0	0	—	26	1	0	0	0	46	48	23	2	6	28	34	16.0	4.30	99	.271	.389	0	.000	-0	-1	-0	-1	-0.2
1998	Ari-N	0	2	.000	43	0	0	0	5	44	44	31	5	1	29	36	15.1	6.14	69	.259	.370	0	—	0	-9	-9	1	-0.5
1999	SF-N	2	3	.400	47	0	0	0	0	66^{1}	67	32	6	2	29	55	13.3	3.80	111	.262	.341	2	.333	2	6	3	1	0.5
2000	*SF-N	4	2	.667	76	0	0	0	3	81^{2}	65	29	5	3	42	95	12.1	2.64	160	.220	.323	0	.000	-0	18	16	-2	0.9
Total	5	7	8	.467	203	1	0	0	8	248^{2}	235	118	20	12	133	225	13.8	3.87	109	.250	.351	2	.154	1	16	10	-1	1.0
● FREDDY RODRIGUEZ	Rodriguez, Fernando Pedro (Borrego) b: 4/29/24, Havana, Cuba BR/TR, 6', 180 lbs. Deb: 4/18/58																											
1958	Chi-N	0	0	—	7	0	0	0	2	7^{1}	8	6	2	1	5	5	17.2	7.36	53	.267	.389	0	.000	-0	-3	-3	-0	-0.2
1959	Phi-N	0	0	—	1	0	0	0	0	2	4	3	1	1	0	1	22.5	13.50	30	.400	.455	0	—	0	-2	-2	-0	-0.1
Total	2	0	0	—	8	0	0	0	2	9^{1}	12	9	3	2	5	6	18.3	8.68	46	.300	.404	0	.000	-0	-5	-5	-0	-0.3
● FRANK RODRIGUEZ	Rodriguez, Francisco b: 12/11/72, Brooklyn, N.Y. BR/TR, 6', 190 lbs. Deb: 4/26/95																											
1995	Bos-A	0	2	.000	9	2	0	0	0	15^{1}	21	19	3	0	10	14	18.2	10.57	46	.323	.413	0	—	0	-10	-9	1	-0.9
	Min-A	5	6	.455	16	16	0	0	0	90^{1}	93	64	8	5	47	45	14.4	5.38	89	.269	.364	0	—	0	-7	-6	2	-0.4
	Yr	5	8	.385	25	18	0	0	0	105^{2}	114	83	11	5	57	59	15.0	6.13	78	.277	.372	0	—	0	-17	-16	3	-1.3
1996	Min-A	13	14	.481	38	33	3	0	2	206^{2}	218	129	27	5	78	110	13.1	5.05	101	.272	.340	0	—	0	-1	1	1	0.3
1997	Min-A	3	6	.333	43	15	0	0	0	142^{1}	147	82	12	4	60	65	13.3	4.62	101	.271	.348	0	.000	-0	-1	1	1	0.1
1998	Min-A	4	6	.400	20	11	0	0	0	70	88	58	6	3	30	62	15.6	6.56	73	.303	.375	0	—	0	-15	-14	0	-1.6
1999	Sea-A	2	4	.333	28	5	0	0	3	73^{1}	94	47	11	4	30	47	15.7	5.65	84	.314	.384	1	.333	0	-6	-8	1	-0.4
2000	Sea-A	2	1	.667	23	0	0	0	0	47^{1}	60	33	8	0	22	19	15.6	6.27	76	.317	.389	0	.000	-0	-7	-8	1	-0.4
Total	6	29	39	.426	177	82	3	0	5	645^{1}	721	432	75	21	277	362	14.2	5.45	89	.285	.360	1	.200	0	-47	-42	6	-3.3
● JOSE RODRIGUEZ	Rodriguez, Jose (Jose) b: 12/18/74, Cayey, P.R. BL/TL, 6'1", 205 lbs. Deb: 5/18/2000																											
2000	StL-N	0	0	—	6	0	0	0	0	4	2	2	0	1	3	2	13.5	0.00	—	.143	.333	0	.000	-0	2	2	-0	0.1
● NERIO RODRIGUEZ	Rodriguez, Nerio b: 3/22/73, San Pedro De Macoris, D.R. BR/TR, 6'1", 195 lbs. Deb: 8/16/96																											
1996	Bal-A	0	1	.000	8	1	0	0	0	16^{2}	18	11	2	1	7	12	14.0	4.32	114	.265	.342	0	—	0	1	1	-1	0.0
1997	Bal-A	2	1	.667	6	2	0	0	0	22	21	15	2	1	8	11	12.3	4.91	90	.250	.323	0	—	0	-1	-1	0	-0.1
1998	Bal-A	1	3	.250	6	4	0	0	0	19	25	17	0	0	9	8	16.1	8.05	57	.321	.391	0	—	0	-7	-8	-1	-1.3
	Tor-A	1	0	1.000	7	0	0	0	0	8^{1}	10	9	1	1	8	3	20.5	9.72	48	.286	.432	0	—	0	-5	-5	-0	-0.5
	Yr	2	3	.400	13	4	0	0	0	27^{1}	35	26	1	1	17	11	17.5	8.56	54	.310	.405	0	—	0	-12	-12	-1	-1.8
1999	Tor-A	0	1	.000	2	0	0	0	0	2	2	3	2	0	2	2	18.0	13.50	37	.250	.400	0	—	0	-2	-2	-0	-0.3
Total	4	4	6	.400	29	7	0	0	0	68	76	55	7	3	34	36	15.0	6.49	71	.278	.365	0	—	0	-13	-14	-1	-2.2
● RICK RODRIGUEZ	Rodriguez, Ricardo b: 9/21/60, Oakland, Cal. BR/TR, 6'3", 190 lbs. Deb: 9/17/86																											
1986	Oak-A	1	2	.333	3	3	0	0	0	16^{1}	17	12	4	0	7	2	13.2	6.61	59	.262	.333	0	—	0	-4	-5	0	-0.7

YEAR	TM/L	W	L	PCT	G	GS	CG	SH	SV	IP	H	R	HR	HB	BB	SO	RAT	ERA	ERA+	OAV	OOB	BH	AVG	PB	PR	PR+	PD	TPI
1987	Oak-A	1	0	1.000	15	0	0	0	0	24^1	32	8	1	1	15	9	17.8	2.96	140	.337	.432	0	—	0	4	3	1	0.2
1988	Cle-A	1	2	.333	10	5	0	0	0	33	43	28	4	1	17	9	16.6	7.09	58	.323	.404	0	—	0	-11	-10	1	-0.7
1990	SF-N	0	0	—	3	0	0	0	0	3^1	5	3	0	0	2	2	18.9	8.10	45	.357	.438	0	—	0	-2	-2	0	-0.1
Total	4	3	4	.429	31	8	0	0	0	77	97	51	9	2	41	22	16.4	5.73	71	.316	.400	0	—	0	-13	-15	2	-1.3

● RICH RODRIGUEZ Rodriguez, Richard Anthony b: 3/1/63, Downey, Cal. BL/TL, 6', 200 lbs. Deb: 6/30/90

YEAR	TM/L	W	L	PCT	G	GS	CG	SH	SV	IP	H	R	HR	HB	BB	SO	RAT	ERA	ERA+	OAV	OOB	BH	AVG	PB	PR	PR+	PD	TPI
1990	SD-N	1	1	.500	32	0	0	0	1	47^2	52	17	2	1	16	22	13.0	2.83	135	.287	.348	0	.000	-0	5	5	1	0.3
1991	SD-N	3	1	.750	64	1	0	0	0	80	66	31	8	0	44	40	12.4	3.26	117	.234	.337	0	.000	-1	4	5	-0	0.2
1992	SD-N	6	3	.667	61	1	0	0	0	91	77	28	4	0	29	64	10.5	2.37	151	.229	.290	0	.000	-0	11	12	1	1.2
1993	SD-N	2	3	.400	34	0	0	0	2	30	34	15	2	1	9	22	13.2	3.30	125	.281	.336	0	—	0	2	3	-1	0.4
	Fla-N	0	1	.000	36	0	0	0	1	46	39	23	8	1	24	21	12.5	4.11	105	.229	.328	0	.000	-0	-0	1	1	0.1
	Yr	2	4	.333	70	0	0	0	3	76	73	38	10	2	33	43	12.8	3.79	112	.251	.331	0	.000	-0	2	4	0	0.5
1994	StL-N	3	5	.375	56	0	0	0	0	60^1	62	30	6	1	26	43	13.3	4.03	103	.270	.346	0	.000	-0	1	1	-1	0.0
1995	StL-N	0	0	—	1	0	0	0	0	1^2	0	0	0	0	0	0	0.0	0.00	—	.000	.000	0	—	0	1	1	-0	0.0
1997	*SF-N	4	3	.571	71	0	0	0	1	65^1	65	24	7	1	21	32	12.0	3.17	129	.264	.325	1	.333	1	8	7	1	0.9
1998	SF-N	4	0	1.000	68	0	0	0	2	65^2	69	28	7	0	20	44	12.2	3.70	107	.272	.325	1	.167	-0	4	2	1	0.2
1999	SF-N	3	0	1.000	62	0	0	0	0	56^2	60	33	8	1	28	44	14.1	5.24	80	.274	.359	1	1.000	1	-4	-7	1	-0.2
2000	NY-N	0	1	.000	32	0	0	0	0	37	59	40	7	3	15	18	18.7	7.78	57	.364	.428	0	.000	-0	-13	-15	0	-0.7
Total	10	26	18	.591	517	2	0	0	7	581^1	583	269	59	9	232	350	12.8	3.75	107	.264	.337	3	.107	-0	19	17	3	2.4

● ROSARIO RODRIGUEZ Rodriguez, Rosario Isabel (Echavarria) b: 7/8/69, Los Mochis, Mexico BR/TL, 6', 185 lbs. Deb: 9/1/89

YEAR	TM/L	W	L	PCT	G	GS	CG	SH	SV	IP	H	R	HR	HB	BB	SO	RAT	ERA	ERA+	OAV	OOB	BH	AVG	PB	PR	PR+	PD	TPI
1989	Cin-N	1	1	.500	7	0	0	0	0	4^1	3	2	0	0	3	0	12.5	4.15	87	.188	.316	0	—	0	-0	-0	0	0.0
1990	Cin-N	0	0	—	9	0	0	0	0	10^1	15	7	3	1	2	8	15.7	6.10	65	.357	.400	0	—	0	-3	-2	0	-0.1
1991	*Pit-N	1	1	.500	18	0	0	0	6	15^1	14	7	1	1	8	10	13.5	4.11	87	.246	.348	0	.000	-0	-1	-1	0	-0.2
Total	3	2	2	.500	34	0	0	0	6	30	32	16	4	2	13	18	14.1	4.80	77	.278	.362	0	.000	-0	-4	-4	1	-0.3

● ROBERTO RODRIQUEZ Rodriquez, Roberto (Munoz) b: 11/29/41, Caracas, Venez. BR/TR, 6'3", 185 lbs. Deb: 5/13/67

YEAR	TM/L	W	L	PCT	G	GS	CG	SH	SV	IP	H	R	HR	HB	BB	SO	RAT	ERA	ERA+	OAV	OOB	BH	AVG	PB	PR	PR+	PD	TPI
1967	KC-A	1	1	.500	15	5	0	0	2	40^1	42	17	4	1	14	29	12.7	3.57	89	.268	.331	0	.000	-1	-2	-2	-0	-0.3
1970	Oak-A	0	0	—	6	0	0	0	0	12^1	10	5	2	0	3	8	9.5	2.92	121	.227	.277	0	.000	-0	1	1	-0	0.0
	SD-N	0	0	—	10	0	0	0	3	16^1	26	16	1	0	5	8	17.1	6.61	60	.366	.408	0	.000	-0	-5	-5	0	-0.3
	Chi-N	3	2	.600	26	0	0	0	2	43^1	50	33	6	0	15	46	13.5	5.82	78	.289	.346	1	.125	1	-8	-6	0	-0.6
	Yr	3	2	.600	36	0	0	0	5	59^2	76	49	7	0	20	54	14.5	6.03	72	.311	.364	1	.091	0	-13	-10	0	-0.9
Total	2	4	3	.571	57	5	0	0	7	112^1	128	71	13	1	37	91	13.3	4.81	80	.288	.344	1	.048	-1	-14	-12	-0	-1.2

● PREACHER ROE Roe, Elwin Charles b: 2/26/15, Ash Flat, Ark. BR/TL, 6'2", 170 lbs. Deb: 8/22/38

YEAR	TM/L	W	L	PCT	G	GS	CG	SH	SV	IP	H	R	HR	HB	BB	SO	RAT	ERA	ERA+	OAV	OOB	BH	AVG	PB	PR	PR+	PD	TPI
1938	StL-N	0	0	—	1	0	0	0	0	2^2	6	4	0	0	2	1	27.0	13.50	29	.429	.500	0	.000	-0	-3	-3	-0	-0.2
1944	Pit-N	13	11	.542	39	25	7	1	1	185^1	182	82	7	2	59	88	11.8	3.11	120	.253	.311	7	.132	-2	10	12	-1	1.1
1945	Pit-N†	14	13	.519	33	31	15	3	1	235	228	77	11	1	46	**148**	10.5	2.87	137	.259	.296	8	.107	-3	24	27	1	2.7
1946	Pit-N	3	8	.273	21	10	1	0	2	70	83	50	5	2	25	28	14.1	5.14	69	.294	.356	1	.067	-1	-13	-12	-0	-1.9
1947	Pit-N	4	15	.211	38	22	4	1	2	144	156	93	19	0	63	59	13.7	5.25	80	.276	.348	5	.125	-2	-19	-16	-1	-2.1
1948	Bro-N	12	8	.600	34	22	8	2	2	177^2	156	60	14	2	33	86	9.7	2.63	152	.233	.271	5	.098	-2	26	27	-1	2.6
1949	*Bro-N★	15	6	**.714**	30	27	13	3	1	212^2	201	69	25	2	44	109	10.5	2.79	147	.252	.293	8	.114	-2	29	30	-2	2.4
1950	Bro-N☆	19	11	.633	36	32	16	2	1	250^2	245	96	34	4	66	125	11.3	3.30	124	.257	.308	14	.154	-3	23	22	-2	1.9
1951	Bro-N☆	22	3	**.880**	34	33	19	2	0	257^2	247	91	30	0	64	113	10.9	3.04	129	.258	.304	10	.112	-5	26	26	-1	1.7
1952	*Bro-N†	11	2	.846	27	25	8	2	0	158^2	163	59	16	3	39	83	11.6	3.12	117	.270	.317	4	.070	-3	11	9	-1	0.2
1953	*Bro-N	11	3	.786	25	24	9	1	0	157	171	78	27	1	40	85	12.2	4.36	98	.278	.323	3	.053	-4	-1	-2	1	-0.5
1954	Bro-N	3	4	.429	15	10	1	0	0	63	69	40	11	0	23	31	13.1	5.00	82	.279	.341	3	.143	-0	-7	-6	-0	-0.7
Total	12	127	84	.602	333	261	101	17	10	1914^1	1907	799	199	17	504	956	11.4	3.43	116	.261	.310	68	.110	-27	108	114	-9	7.2

● CLAY ROE Roe, James Clay "Shad" b: 1/7/04, Greenbriar, Tenn. d: 4/4/56, Cleveland, Miss. BL/TL, 6'1", 180 lbs. Deb: 10/3/23

YEAR	TM/L	W	L	PCT	G	GS	CG	SH	SV	IP	H	R	HR	HB	BB	SO	RAT	ERA	ERA+	OAV	OOB	BH	AVG	PB	PR	PR+	PD	TPI
1923	Was-A	0	1	.000	1	1	0	0	0	1^2	0	4	0	0	6	2	32.4	0.00	—	.000	.500	0	—	0	1	1	-0	0.1

● ED ROEBUCK Roebuck, Edward Jack b: 7/3/31, East Millsboro, Pa. BR/TR, 6'2", 185 lbs. Deb: 4/18/55

YEAR	TM/L	W	L	PCT	G	GS	CG	SH	SV	IP	H	R	HR	HB	BB	SO	RAT	ERA	ERA+	OAV	OOB	BH	AVG	PB	PR	PR+	PD	TPI
1955	*Bro-N	5	6	.455	47	0	0	0	12	84	96	51	14	3	24	33	13.2	4.71	86	.288	.342	2	.111	-1	-6	-6	1	-0.9
1956	*Bro-N	5	4	.556	43	0	0	0	1	89^1	83	49	15	2	29	60	11.5	3.93	101	.251	.315	6	.333	2	-2	0	1	0.3
1957	Bro-N	8	2	.800	44	1	0	0	8	96^1	70	37	9	2	46	73	11.0	2.71	154	.205	.303	5	.238	2	13	**15**	2	2.2
1958	LA-N	0	1	.000	32	0	0	0	5	44	45	22	9	2	15	26	12.7	3.48	118	.271	.339	2	.500	1	2	3	-0	0.2
1960	LA-N	8	3	.727	58	0	0	0	8	116^2	109	42	13	0	38	77	11.3	2.78	143	.256	.317	4	.167	-0	13	15	2	1.7
1961	LA-N	2	0	1.000	5	0	0	0	0	9	12	5	1	0	2	9	14.0	5.00	87	.324	.359	0	.000	-0	-1	-1	0	-0.1
1962	LA-N	10	2	.833	64	0	0	0	9	119^1	102	60	11	6	54	72	12.2	3.09	117	.232	.325	6	.214	1	11	8	0	0.9
1963	LA-N	2	4	.333	29	0	0	0	0	40^1	54	25	4	2	21	26	17.2	4.24	71	.321	.403	1	.250	0	-4	-6	1	-0.8
	Was-A	2	1	.667	26	0	0	0	4	57^1	63	27	5	2	29	25	14.8	3.30	113	.284	.372	2	.182	0	2	3	1	0.2
1964	Was-A	0	0	—	2	0	0	0	0	1	0	1	0	0	2	0	18.0	9.00	41	.000	.333	0	—	0	-1	-1	0	0.0
	Phi-N	5	3	.625	60	0	0	0	12	77^1	55	21	7	4	25	42	9.8	2.21	157	.196	.272	0	.000	-1	11	11	1	1.5
1965	Phi-N	5	3	.625	44	0	0	0	3	50^1	55	27	2	5	15	29	13.4	3.40	102	.288	.355	0	.000	-0	1	0	-1	-0.1
1966	Phi-N	0	2	.000	6	0	0	0	0	6	9	7	0	0	2	5	16.5	6.00	60	.333	.379	0	—	0	-2	-2	-0	-0.3
Total	11	52	31	.627	460	1	0	0	62	791	753	374	90	28	302	477	12.3	3.35	114	.254	.329	28	.204	3	38	40	7	4.8

● MIKE ROESLER Roesler, Michael Joseph b: 9/12/63, Fort Wayne, Ind. BR/TR, 6'5", 195 lbs. Deb: 8/9/89

YEAR	TM/L	W	L	PCT	G	GS	CG	SH	SV	IP	H	R	HR	HB	BB	SO	RAT	ERA	ERA+	OAV	OOB	BH	AVG	PB	PR	PR+	PD	TPI
1989	Cin-N	0	1	.000	17	0	0	0	0	25	22	11	4	0	9	14	11.2	3.96	91	.239	.307	0	—	0	-1	-1	-1	-0.1
1990	Pit-N	1	0	1.000	5	0	0	0	0	6	5	2	1	0	2	4	10.5	3.00	121	.217	.280	0	.000	-0	1	0	-0	0.0
Total	2	1	1	.500	22	0	0	0	0	31	27	13	5	0	11	18	11.0	3.77	96	.235	.302	0	.000	-0	-1	-1	-1	-0.1

● OSCAR ROETTGER Roettger, Oscar Frederick Louis "Okkie" b: 2/19/1900, St.Louis, Mo. d: 7/4/86, St.Louis, Mo. BR/TR, 6', 170 lbs. Deb: 7/7/23 F♦

YEAR	TM/L	W	L	PCT	G	GS	CG	SH	SV	IP	H	R	HR	HB	BB	SO	RAT	ERA	ERA+	OAV	OOB	BH	AVG	PB	PR	PR+	PD	TPI
1923	NY-A	0	0	—	5	0	0	0	1	11^2	16	15	3	1	12	7	22.4	8.49	46	.340	.483	0	.000	-0	-6	-6	0	-0.3
1924	NY-A	0	0	—	1	0	0	0	0	0	1	0	0	2	—	—	—	—	1.000	1.000	98	—	0	0	0	0	0.0	
Total	2	0	0	—	6	0	0	0	1	11^2	17	15	3	1	14	7	24.7	8.49	46	.354	.508	14	.212	-0	-6	-6	0	-0.3

● JOE ROGALSKI Rogalski, Joseph Anthony b: 7/16/15, Ashland, Wis. d: 11/20/51, Ashland, Wis. BR/TR, 6'2", 187 lbs. Deb: 9/14/38

YEAR	TM/L	W	L	PCT	G	GS	CG	SH	SV	IP	H	R	HR	HB	BB	SO	RAT	ERA	ERA+	OAV	OOB	BH	AVG	PB	PR	PR+	PD	TPI
1938	Det-A	0	0	—	2	0	0	0	0	7	12	4	0	0	0	2	15.4	2.57	194	.400	.400	0	.000	-0	2	2	-0	0.0

● KEVIN ROGERS Rogers, Charles Kevin b: 8/20/68, Cleveland, Miss. BB/TL, 6'2", 190 lbs. Deb: 9/4/92

YEAR	TM/L	W	L	PCT	G	GS	CG	SH	SV	IP	H	R	HR	HB	BB	SO	RAT	ERA	ERA+	OAV	OOB	BH	AVG	PB	PR	PR+	PD	TPI
1992	SF-N	0	2	.000	6	6	0	0	0	34	37	17	4	1	13	26	13.5	4.24	78	.280	.349	2	.222	0	-3	-4	-1	-0.2
1993	SF-N	2	2	.500	64	0	0	0	0	80^2	71	28	3	4	28	62	11.5	2.68	146	.236	.309	0	.000	-0	12	11	-1	0.4
1994	SF-N	0	0	—	9	0	0	0	0	10^1	10	4	1	0	6	7	13.9	3.48	115	.250	.348	0	—	0	1	1	-0	0.0
Total	3	2	4	.333	79	6	0	0	0	125	118	49	8	5	47	95	12.2	3.17	119	.249	.324	2	.167	-0	10	9	-2	0.2

● JIMMY ROGERS Rogers, James Randall b: 1/3/67, Tulsa, Okla. BR/TR, 6'2", 190 lbs. Deb: 7/30/95

YEAR	TM/L	W	L	PCT	G	GS	CG	SH	SV	IP	H	R	HR	HB	BB	SO	RAT	ERA	ERA+	OAV	OOB	BH	AVG	PB	PR	PR+	PD	TPI
1995	Tor-A	2	4	.333	19	0	0	0	0	23^2	21	15	4	0	18	13	14.8	5.70	83	.239	.368	0	—	0	-3	-3	-0	-0.5

● KENNY ROGERS Rogers, Kenneth Scott b: 11/10/64, Savannah, Ga. BL/TL, 6'1", 205 lbs. Deb: 4/6/89

YEAR	TM/L	W	L	PCT	G	GS	CG	SH	SV	IP	H	R	HR	HB	BB	SO	RAT	ERA	ERA+	OAV	OOB	BH	AVG	PB	PR	PR+	PD	TPI
1989	Tex-A	3	4	.429	73	0	0	0	2	73^2	60	28	2	4	42	63	13.0	2.93	135	.232	.348	0	—	0	8	8	2	1.0
1990	Tex-A	10	6	.625	69	3	0	0	15	97^2	93	40	6	1	42	74	12.5	3.13	125	.249	.326	0	—	0	9	9	2	1.7
1991	Tex-A	10	10	.500	63	9	0	0	5	109^2	121	80	14	6	61	73	15.4	5.42	75	.281	.378	0	—	0	-16	-17	-0	-2.9
1992	Tex-A	3	6	.333	**81**	0	0	0	6	78^2	80	32	7	0	26	70	12.1	3.09	123	.261	.319	0	—	0	8	6	1	0.9
1993	Tex-A	16	10	.615	35	33	5	0	0	208^1	210	108	18	4	71	140	12.3	4.10	101	.263	.326	0	—	0	5	1	4	0.6
1994	Tex-A	11	8	.579	24	24	6	2	0	167^1	169	93	24	3	52	120	12.0	4.46	108	.260	.318	0	—	0	6	7	2	0.9
1995	Tex-A★	17	7	.708	31	31	3	1	0	208	192	87	26	2	76	140	11.7	3.38	143	.243	.311	0	—	0	31	33	1	3.5
1996	*NY-A	12	8	.600	30	30	2	1	0	179	179	97	16	8	83	92	13.6	4.68	106	.261	.347	0	—	0	6	5	2	0.7
1997	NY-A	6	7	.462	31	22	1	0	0	145	161	100	18	7	62	78	14.3	5.65	79	.280	.357	0	.000	-0	-17	-20	5	-1.1
1998	Oak-A	16	8	.667	34	34	7	1	0	238^2	215	96	19	7	67	138	10.9	3.17	144	.242	.301	0	.000	-0	39	38	7	4.1
1999	Oak-A	5	3	.625	19	19	3	0	0	119^1	135	66	8	9	41	68	14.0	4.30	108	.288	.357	0	.000	-0	8	5	5	0.7

YEAR	TM/L	W	L	PCT	G	GS	CG	SH	SV	IP	H	R	HR	HB	BB	SO	RAT	ERA	ERA+	OAV	OOB	BH	AVG	PB	PR	PR+	PD	TPI
	*NY-N	5	1	.833	12	12	2	1	0	76	71	35	8	4	28	58	12.2	4.03	109	.253	.329	3	.120	-0	5	3	2	0.4
2000	Tex-A	13	13	.500	34	34	2	0	0	227^1	257	126	20	11	78	127	13.7	4.55	112	.285	.349	2	.500	1	9	13	4	1.8
Total	12	127	91	.583	536	251	31	6	28	1928^2	1943	988	186	66	729	1241	12.8	4.11	111	.262	.334	5	.128	-1	101	93	38	12.3

● LEE ROGERS

Rogers, Lee Otis "Buck" b: 10/8/13, Tuscaloosa, Ala. d: 11/23/95, Little Rock, Ark. BR/TL, 5'11", 170 lbs. Deb: 4/27/38

YEAR	TM/L	W	L	PCT	G	GS	CG	SH	SV	IP	H	R	HR	HB	BB	SO	RAT	ERA	ERA+	OAV	OOB	BH	AVG	PB	PR	PR+	PD	TPI
1938	Bos-A	1	1	.500	14	2	0	0	0	27^2	32	24	4	0	18	7	16.3	6.51	76	.302	.403	0	.000	-0	-5	-5	1	-0.2
	Bro-N	0	2	.000	12	2	0	0	0	23^2	23	16	0	1	10	11	12.9	5.70	68	.256	.337	0	.000	0	-5	-5	1	-0.2
Total	1	1	3	.250	26	4	0	0	0	51^1	55	40	4	1	28	18	14.7	6.14	73	.281	.373	0	.000	0	-10	-9	2	-0.4

● BUCK ROGERS

Rogers, Orlin Woodrow "Lefty" b: 11/5/12, Spring Garden, Va. d: 2/20/99, Winston-Salem, N.C BR/TL, 5'8.5", 164 lbs. Deb: 9/15/35

YEAR	TM/L	W	L	PCT	G	GS	CG	SH	SV	IP	H	R	HR	HB	BB	SO	RAT	ERA	ERA+	OAV	OOB	BH	AVG	PB	PR	PR+	PD	TPI
1935	Was-A	0	1	.000	2	1	0	0	0	10	16	15	0	0	6	7	19.8	7.20	60	.340	.415	0	.000	-1	-3	-3	-0	-0.3

● STEVE ROGERS

Rogers, Stephen Douglas b: 10/26/49, Jefferson City, Mo. BR/TR, 6'1", 182 lbs. Deb: 7/18/73

YEAR	TM/L	W	L	PCT	G	GS	CG	SH	SV	IP	H	R	HR	HB	BB	SO	RAT	ERA	ERA+	OAV	OOB	BH	AVG	PB	PR	PR+	PD	TPI
1973	Mon-N	10	5	.667	17	17	7	3	0	134	93	28	5	1	49	64	9.6	1.54	247	.199	.276	4	.098	-1	32	33	1	3.9
1974	Mon-N☆	15	22	.405	38	38	11	1	0	253^2	255	139	19	5	80	154	12.1	4.47	86	.265	.324	11	.139	-1	-24	-16	3	-2.1
1975	Mon-N	11	12	.478	35	35	12	3	0	251^2	248	104	13	4	88	137	12.2	3.29	117	.260	.325	13	.169	1	10	14	0	1.5
1976	Mon-N	7	17	.292	33	32	8	4	1	230	212	93	10	4	69	150	11.2	3.21	116	.250	.309	11	.149	-2	8	12	5	1.6
1977	Mon-N	17	16	.515	40	40	17	4	0	301^2	272	122	16	5	81	206	10.7	3.10	123	.242	.296	10	.104	-5	27	24	4	2.4
1978	Mon-N★	13	10	.565	30	29	11	1	1	219	186	64	12	2	64	126	10.4	2.47	143	.235	.294	8	.113	-2	27	26	1	2.7
1979	Mon-N★	13	12	.520	37	37	13	**5**	0	248^2	232	97	14	4	78	143	11.4	3.00	122	.251	.312	12	.156	1	20	19	2	2.1
1980	Mon-N	16	11	.593	37	37	**14**	4	0	281	247	101	16	3	85	147	10.7	2.98	120	.238	.298	13	.160	1	20	19	-1	1.8
1981	*Mon-N	12	8	.600	22	22	7	3	0	160^2	149	64	7	2	41	87	10.8	3.42	102	.248	.298	8	.145	-1	1	1	-1	0.0
1982	Mon-N★	19	8	.704	35	35	14	4	0	277	245	84	12	6	65	179	10.3	**2.40**	**152**	.237	.286	11	.129	0	**37**	**38**	0	3.7
1983	Mon-N☆	17	12	.586	36	36	13	**5**	0	273	258	108	14	5	78	146	11.2	3.23	111	.252	.308	12	.146	-1	12	11	-2	0.9
1984	Mon-N	6	15	.286	31	28	1	0	0	169^1	171	93	12	2	78	64	13.3	4.31	80	.267	.348	7	.143	1	-13	-17	0	-1.9
1985	Mon-N	2	4	.333	8	7	1	0	0	38	51	25	1	0	20	18	16.8	5.68	60	.329	.406	2	.143	0	-9	-10	1	-1.3
Total	13	158	152	.510	399	393	129	37	2	2837^2	2619	1122	151	43	876	1621	11.2	3.17	116	.248	.308	122	.138	-8	148	156	14	15.3

● TOM ROGERS

Rogers, Thomas Andrew "Shotgun" b: 2/12/1892, Sparta, Tenn. d: 3/7/36, Nashville, Tenn. BR/TR, 6'0.5", 180 lbs. Deb: 4/14/17

YEAR	TM/L	W	L	PCT	G	GS	CG	SH	SV	IP	H	R	HR	HB	BB	SO	RAT	ERA	ERA+	OAV	OOB	BH	AVG	PB	PR	PR+	PD	TPI
1917	StL-A	3	6	.333	24	8	3	0	0	108^2	112	58	2	3	44	27	13.2	3.89	67	.277	.352	5	.172	-1	-15	-16	-0	-1.4
1918	StL-A	8	10	.444	29	16	11	0	2	154	148	66	3	3	49	29	11.7	3.27	84	.267	.330	13	.245	2	-8	-9	2	-0.7
1919	StL-A	0	1	.000	2	0	0	0	0	1	7	6	0	0	0	1	63.0	27.00	12	.700	.700	0	—	0	-3	-3	0	-0.5
	Phi-A	4	12	.250	23	18	7	1	0	140	152	82	9	3	60	37	13.8	4.31	80	.292	.369	11	.224	-0	-17	-13	4	-0.9
	Yr	4	13	.235	25	18	7	1	0	141	159	88	9	3	60	38	14.2	4.47	77	.300	.374	11	.224	-0	-19	-15	4	-1.4
1921	*NY-A	0	1	.000	5	0	0	0	1	11	12	9	1	1	9	0	18.0	7.36	58	.300	.440	1	.333	0	-4	-4	1	-0.3
Total	4	15	30	.333	83	42	21	1	3	414^2	431	221	15	10	162	94	13.1	3.95	75	.282	.354	30	.224	1	-46	-45	6	-3.8

● CLINT ROGGE

Rogge, Francis Clinton b: 7/19/1889, Memphis, Mich. d: 1/6/69, Mt.Clemens, Mich. BL/TR, 5'10", 185 lbs. Deb: 4/11/15

YEAR	TM/L	W	L	PCT	G	GS	CG	SH	SV	IP	H	R	HR	HB	BB	SO	RAT	ERA	ERA+	OAV	OOB	BH	AVG	PB	PR	PR+	PD	TPI
1915	Pit-F	17	11	.607	37	31	17	5	0	254^1	240	96	6	9	93	93	12.1	2.55	106	.257	.330	14	.173	-1	5	5	1	0.5
1921	Cin-N	1	2	.333	6	2	0	0	0	35^1	43	19	2	0	9	12	13.2	4.08	88	.307	.349	1	.100	0	-1	-2	0	-0.1
Total	2	18	13	.581	43	33	17	5	0	289^2	283	115	8	9	102	105	12.2	2.73	103	.264	.332	15	.165	-1	4	3	1	0.4

● GARRY ROGGENBURK

Roggenburk, Garry Earl b: 4/16/40, Cleveland, Ohio BR/TL, 6'6", 195 lbs. Deb: 4/20/63

YEAR	TM/L	W	L	PCT	G	GS	CG	SH	SV	IP	H	R	HR	HB	BB	SO	RAT	ERA	ERA+	OAV	OOB	BH	AVG	PB	PR	PR+	PD	TPI
1963	Min-A	2	4	.333	36	2	0	0	4	50	47	26	3	5	22	24	13.3	2.16	169	.253	.347	1	.143	0	8	8	1	1.2
1965	Min-A	1	0	1.000	12	0	0	0	2	21	21	10	1	0	12	6	14.1	3.43	104	.266	.363	0	.000	-0	0	0	-1	0.0
1966	Min-A	1	2	.333	12	0	0	0	1	12^1	14	8	4	0	10	3	17.5	5.84	62	.292	.414	0	—	0	-3	-3	0	-0.6
	Bos-A	0	0	—	1	0	0	0	0	0^1	1	0	0	0	1	0	54.0	0.00	—	.500	.667	0	—	0	0	0	0	0.0
	Yr	1	2	.333	13	0	0	0	1	12^2	15	8	4	0	11	3	18.5	5.68	63	.300	.426	0	—	0	-3	-3	0	-0.6
1968	Bos-A	0	0	—	4	0	0	0	0	8^1	9	2	0	0	3	4	13.0	2.16	146	.257	.316	0	—	0	1	1	-0	0.0
1969	Bos-A	0	1	.000	7	0	0	0	0	9^2	13	9	1	1	5	8	17.7	8.38	45	.342	.432	0	.000	-0	-5	-5	0	-0.4
	Sea-A	2	2	.500	7	4	1	0	0	24^1	27	12	6	1	11	11	14.4	4.44	82	.276	.355	1	.125	-0	-2	-2	-0	-0.4
	Yr	2	3	.400	14	4	1	0	0	34	40	21	7	2	16	19	15.4	5.56	66	.294	.377	1	.100	-1	-7	-7	0	-0.8
Total	5	6	9	.400	79	6	1	0	7	126	132	67	15	7	64	56	14.5	3.64	99	.272	.364	2	.100	-1	-1	-0	0	-0.2

● SAUL ROGOVIN

Rogovin, Saul Walter b: 10/10/23, Brooklyn, N.Y. d: 1/23/95, New York, N.Y. BR/TR, 6'2", 205 lbs. Deb: 4/28/49

YEAR	TM/L	W	L	PCT	G	GS	CG	SH	SV	IP	H	R	HR	HB	BB	SO	RAT	ERA	ERA+	OAV	OOB	BH	AVG	PB	PR	PR+	PD	TPI
1949	Det-A	0	1	.000	5	0	0	0	0	5^2	13	9	1	0	7	2	31.8	14.29	29	.464	.571	0	—	0	-6	-6	-0	-0.9
1950	Det-A	2	1	.667	11	5	1	0	0	40	39	21	5	2	26	11	15.1	4.50	104	.258	.374	3	.188	0	0	1	-1	0.0
1951	Det-A	1	1	.500	5	4	0	0	0	24	23	15	4	0	7	5	11.3	5.25	80	.247	.300	2	.286	1	-3	-3	0	-0.1
	Chi-A	11	7	.611	22	22	17	3	0	192^2	166	64	11	1	67	77	10.9	2.48	163	.234	.301	15	.203	-0	35	34	-1	2.9
	Yr	12	8	.600	27	26	17	3	0	216^2	189	79	15	1	74	82	11.0	**2.78**	**146**	.235	.301	17	.210	1	32	**31**	-0	2.8
1952	Chi-A	14	9	.609	33	30	12	3	1	231^2	224	104	14	3	79	121	11.9	3.85	95	.255	.318	17	.202	3	-4	-5	-0	-0.2
1953	Chi-A	7	12	.368	22	19	4	1	1	131	151	82	17	2	48	62	13.8	5.22	77	.289	.351	5	.135	-0	-18	-17	-0	-2.2
1955	Bal-A	1	8	.111	14	12	1	0	0	71	79	42	5	2	27	35	13.7	4.56	84	.288	.356	2	.091	-1	-5	-6	-0	-0.9
	Phi-N	5	3	.625	12	11	5	2	0	73	60	25	3	0	17	27	9.5	3.08	129	.230	.277	6	.250	2	8	7	-1	0.9
1956	Phi-N	7	6	.538	22	18	3	0	0	106^2	122	65	22	0	27	48	12.6	4.98	75	.282	.325	4	.111	-2	-14	-15	-1	-1.9
1957	Phi-N	0	0	—	4	0	0	0	0	8	11	8	1	0	3	0	15.8	9.00	42	.333	.389	0	—	0	-5	-5	-0	-0.3
Total	8	48	48	.500	150	121	43	9	2	883^2	888	435	83	10	308	388	12.3	4.06	96	.262	.326	54	.180	2	-12	-16	-4	-2.7

● LES ROHR

Rohr, Leslie Norvin b: 3/5/46, Lowestoft, England BL/TL, 6'5", 205 lbs. Deb: 9/19/67

YEAR	TM/L	W	L	PCT	G	GS	CG	SH	SV	IP	H	R	HR	HB	BB	SO	RAT	ERA	ERA+	OAV	OOB	BH	AVG	PB	PR	PR+	PD	TPI
1967	NY-N	2	1	.667	3	3	0	0	0	17	13	7	1	0	9	15	11.6	2.12	160	.224	.328	0	.000	-1	2	2	-1	0.3
1968	NY-N	0	2	.000	2	1	0	0	0	6	9	4	0	0	7	5	24.0	4.50	67	.333	.471	0	—	0	-1	-1	0	-0.2
1969	NY-N	0	0	—	1	0	0	0	0	1^1	5	4	0	0	1	0	40.5	20.25	18	.625	.667	0	—	0	-2	-2	-0	-0.1
Total	3	2	3	.400	6	4	0	0	0	24^1	27	15	1	0	17	20	16.3	3.70	90	.290	.400	0	.000	-0	-1	-1	-1	0.0

● BILLY ROHR

Rohr, William Joseph b: 7/1/45, San Diego, Cal. BL/TL, 6'3", 170 lbs. Deb: 4/14/67

YEAR	TM/L	W	L	PCT	G	GS	CG	SH	SV	IP	H	R	HR	HB	BB	SO	RAT	ERA	ERA+	OAV	OOB	BH	AVG	PB	PR	PR+	PD	TPI
1967	Bos-A	2	3	.400	10	8	2	1	0	42^1	43	27	4	2	22	16	14.2	5.10	68	.256	.349	0	.000	-1	-9	-7	-0	-0.9
1968	Cle-A	1	0	1.000	17	0	0	0	1	18^1	18	16	5	0	10	5	13.7	6.87	43	.265	.359	0	.000	-0	-8	-8	0	-0.6
Total	2	3	3	.500	27	8	2	1	1	60^2	61	43	9	2	32	21	14.1	5.64	59	.258	.352	0	.000	-1	-17	-15	-0	-1.5

● MEL ROJAS

Rojas, Melquiades (Medrano) b: 12/10/66, Haina, D.R. BR/TR, 5'11", 185 lbs. Deb: 8/1/90

YEAR	TM/L	W	L	PCT	G	GS	CG	SH	SV	IP	H	R	HR	HB	BB	SO	RAT	ERA	ERA+	OAV	OOB	BH	AVG	PB	PR	PR+	PD	TPI
1990	Mon-N	3	1	.750	23	0	0	0	1	40	34	17	5	2	24	26	13.5	3.60	101	.234	.351	0	.000	-0	1	0	-0	-0.1
1991	Mon-N	3	3	.500	37	0	0	0	6	48	42	21	4	1	13	37	10.5	3.75	97	.228	.283	0	.000	-0	-0	-1	-0	-0.2
1992	Mon-N	7	1	.875	68	0	0	0	10	100^2	71	17	2	2	34	70	9.6	1.43	243	.199	.272	1	.067	-1	**23**	**23**	-0	2.1
1993	Mon-N	5	8	.385	66	0	0	0	10	88^1	80	39	6	4	30	48	11.6	2.95	141	.242	.313	1	.083	-1	11	12	-1	1.6
1994	Mon-N	3	2	.600	58	0	0	0	16	84	71	35	11	4	21	84	10.3	3.32	127	.227	.284	2	.200	0	8	8	0	0.8
1995	Mon-N	1	4	.200	59	0	0	0	30	67^2	69	32	2	7	29	61	14.0	4.12	104	.262	.351	0	.000	-1	0	1	-0	0.1
1996	Mon-N	7	4	.636	74	0	0	0	36	81	56	30	5	2	28	92	9.6	3.22	134	.193	.269	3	.375	1	9	10	1	2.1
1997	Chi-N	0	4	.000	54	0	0	0	13	59	54	30	11	5	30	61	13.6	4.42	97	.244	.348	0	.000	-0	-1	-1	-1	-0.2
	NY-N	0	2	.000	23	0	0	0	2	26^1	24	17	4	2	6	32	10.9	5.13	79	.235	.291	0	—	0	-3	-3	-0	-0.3
	Yr	0	6	.000	77	0	0	0	15	85^1	78	47	15	7	36	93	12.8	4.64	91	.241	.331	0	.000	-0	-4	-4	-1	-0.5
1998	NY-N	5	2	.714	50	0	0	0	2	58	68	39	9	3	30	41	15.7	6.05	68	.305	.395	0	—	0	-12	-13	1	-1.3
1999	LA-N	0	0	—	5	0	0	0	0	5	5	7	3	0	3	3	14.4	12.60	34	.250	.348	0	—	0	-4	-5	0	-0.2
	Det-A	0	0	—	5	0	0	0	0	6^1	12	16	3	3	4	6	27.0	22.74	21	.387	.500	0	—	0	-13	-13	0	-0.5
	Mon-N	0	0	—	3	0	0	0	0	2^2	5	5	0	2	2	1	30.4	16.88	27	.417	.563	0	—	0	-4	-4	0	-0.2
Total	10	34	31	.523	525	0	0	0	126	667	591	305	65	37	254	562	11.9	3.82	106	.237	.317	7	.119	-2	16	17	-1	3.7

● MINNIE ROJAS

Rojas, Minervino Alejandro (Landin) b: 11/26/38, Remidios, Las Villas, Cuba BR/TR, 6'1", 170 lbs. Deb: 5/30/66

YEAR	TM/L	W	L	PCT	G	GS	CG	SH	SV	IP	H	R	HR	HB	BB	SO	RAT	ERA	ERA+	OAV	OOB	BH	AVG	PB	PR	PR+	PD	TPI
1966	Cal-A	7	4	.636	47	2	0	0	10	84^1	83	28	9	1	15	37	10.6	2.88	117	.262	.297	1	.071	-0	5	5	-1	0.5
1967	Cal-A	12	9	.571	72	0	0	0	**27**	121^2	106	45	7	3	38	83	10.9	2.52	125	.232	.296	1	.059	-1	10	9	-2	1.6
1968	Cal-A	4	3	.571	38	0	0	0	6	55	55	29	11	0	15	33	11.5	4.25	68	.252	.300	1	.100	-0	-8	-8	-1	-1.5
Total	3	23	16	.590	157	2	0	0	43	261	244	102	27	4	68	153	10.9	3.00	105	.246	.297	3	.073	-2	7	5	-4	0.6

YEAR	TM/L	W	L	PCT	G	GS	CG	SH	SV	IP	H	R	HR	HB	BB	SO	RAT	ERA	ERA+	OAV	OOB	BH	AVG	PB	PR	PR+	PD	TPI
● COOKIE ROJAS	Rojas, Octavio Victor (Rivas) b: 3/6/39, Havana, Cuba BR/TR, 5'10", 170 lbs. Deb: 4/10/62 MC ♦																											
1967	Phi-N	0	0	—	1	0	0	0	0	1	1	0	0	0	0	0	9.0	0.00	—	.200	.200	137	.259	0	0	0	-0	0.0
● JIM ROLAND	Roland, James Ivan b: 12/14/42, Franklin, N.C. BR/TL, 6'3", 190 lbs. Deb: 9/20/62																											
1962	Min-A	0	0	—	1	0	0	0	0	2	1	0	0	0	0	1	4.5	0.00	—	.143	.143	0	—	0	1	1	-0	0.0
1963	Min-A	4	1	.800	10	7	2	1	0	49	32	17	4	0	27	34	10.8	2.57	142	.185	.295	0	.000	-2	6	6	0	0.4
1964	Min-A	2	6	.250	30	13	1	0	3	94^1	76	48	12	4	55	63	12.9	4.10	87	.218	.332	4	.148	-1	-5	-6	-1	-0.7
1966	Min-A	0	0	—	1	0	0	0	0	2	0	0	0	0	0	1	0.0	0.00	—	.000	.000	0	—	0	1	1	-0	0.0
1967	Min-A	0	1	.000	25	0	0	0	2	35^2	33	12	3	0	17	16	12.6	3.03	114	.244	.329	0	.000	-0	1	2	-0	0.0
1968	Min-A	4	1	.800	28	4	1	0	0	61^2	55	33	3	2	24	36	11.8	3.50	88	.238	.315	0	.000	-1	-4	-3	1	-0.2
1969	Oak-A	5	1	.833	39	3	2	0	1	86^1	59	24	2	6	46	48	11.6	2.19	157	.197	.316	2	.095	-1	14	13	0	0.8
1970	Oak-A	3	3	.500	28	2	0	0	2	43^1	28	14	2	0	23	26	10.6	2.70	131	.181	.287	0	.000	-0	5	4	1	0.6
1971	Oak-A	1	3	.250	31	0	0	0	1	45^1	34	18	4	5	19	30	11.5	3.18	105	.214	.317	0	.000	-0	1	1	-1	0.0
1972	Oak-A	0	0	—	2	0	0	0	0	2^1	5	2	0	0	0	0	19.3	3.86	74	.455	.455	0	—	0	-0	-0	0	0.0
	NY-A	0	1	.000	16	0	0	0	0	25	27	14	3	1	16	13	15.8	5.04	59	.287	.396	0	.000	-0	-5	-6	-0	-0.4
	Tex-A	0	0	—	5	0	0	0	0	3^1	7	3	1	1	2	4	27.0	8.10	37	.412	.500	0	—	0	-2	-2	-0	-0.1
	Yr	0	1	.000	23	0	0	0	0	30^2	39	19	4	2	18	17	17.3	5.28	56	.320	.415	0	.000	-0	-8	-8	-0	-0.5
Total	10	19	17	.528	216	29	6	1	9	450^1	357	185	34	19	229	272	12.1	3.22	106	.218	.321	6	.071	-5	12	10	-1	0.4
● JOSE ROMAN	Roman, Jose Rafael (Sarita) b: 5/21/63, Santo Domingo, D.R. BR/TR, 6', 175 lbs. Deb: 9/5/84																											
1984	Cle-A	0	2	.000	3	2	0	0	0	6	9	12	1	0	11	3	30.0	18.00	23	.391	.588	0	—	0	-9	-9	-0	-1.4
1985	Cle-A	0	4	.000	5	3	0	0	0	16^1	13	17	3	0	14	12	14.9	6.61	63	.200	.342	0	—	0	-4	-5	-0	-0.8
1986	Cle-A	1	2	.333	6	5	0	0	0	22	23	20	3	1	17	9	16.8	6.55	63	.280	.410	0	—	0	-6	-6	-1	-0.7
Total	3	1	8	.111	14	10	0	0	0	44^1	45	49	7	1	42	24	17.9	8.12	51	.265	.413	0	—	0	-20	-20	-1	-2.9
● RON ROMANICK	Romanick, Ronald James b: 11/6/60, Burley, Idaho BR/TR, 6'4", 195 lbs. Deb: 4/5/84																											
1984	Cal-A	12	12	.500	33	33	8	2	0	229^2	240	107	23	4	61	87	12.0	3.76	106	.270	.320	0	—	0	6	5	-2	0.3
1985	Cal-A	14	9	.609	31	31	6	1	0	195	210	101	29	4	62	64	12.7	4.11	100	.280	.338	0	—	0	1	0	-3	-0.3
1986	Cal-A	5	8	.385	18	18	1	1	0	106^1	124	68	13	0	44	38	14.2	5.50	75	.297	.364	0	—	0	-16	-17	-1	-1.8
Total	3	31	29	.517	82	82	15	4	0	531	574	276	65	8	167	189	12.7	4.24	96	.279	.336	0	—	0	-9	-11	-6	-1.8
● JIM ROMANO	Romano, James King b: 4/6/27, Brooklyn, N.Y. d: 9/12/90, New York, N.Y. BR/TR, 6'4", 190 lbs. Deb: 9/21/50																											
1950	Bro-N	0	0	—	3	1	0	0	0	6^1	8	6	0	0	2	8	14.2	5.68	72	.296	.345	0	.000	-0	-1	-1	0	0.0
● MIKE ROMANO	Romano, Michael Desport b: 3/3/72, New Orleans, La. BR/TR, 6'2", 195 lbs. Deb: 9/5/99																											
1999	Tor-A	0	0	—	3	0	0	0	0	5^1	8	8	1	0	5	3	21.9	11.81	42	.364	.481	0	—	0	-4	-4	-0	-0.2
● DUTCH ROMBERGER	Romberger, Allen Isaiah b: 5/26/27, Klingerstown, Pa. d: 5/26/83, Weikert, Pa. BR/TR, 6', 185 lbs. Deb: 5/31/54																											
1954	Phi-A	1	1	.500	10	0	0	0	0	15^2	28	20	3	0	12	6	23.0	11.49	34	.406	.494	0	.000	0	-14	-13	-0	-1.4
● J.C. ROMERO	Romero, Juan Carlos b: 6/4/76, Rio Pedras, P.R. BB/TL, 5'11", 193 lbs. Deb: 9/15/99																											
1999	Min-A	0	0	—	5	0	0	0	0	9^2	13	4	0	0	0	4	12.1	3.72	137	.333	.333	0	—	0	1	1	-0	0.1
2000	Min-A	2	7	.222	12	11	0	0	0	57^2	72	51	8	1	30	50	16.1	7.02	75	.312	.393	0	—	0	-13	-11	1	-1.2
Total	2	2	7	.222	17	11	0	0	0	67^1	85	55	8	1	30	54	15.5	6.55	80	.315	.385	0	—	0	-12	-9	1	-1.1
● RAMON ROMERO	Romero, Ramon (De Los Santos) b: 1/8/59, San Pedro De Macoris, D.R. BL/TL, 6'4", 170 lbs. Deb: 9/18/84																											
1984	Cle-A	0	0	—	1	0	0	0	0	3	0	0	0	1	0	3	3.0	0.00	—	.000	.111	0	—	0	1	1	-0	0.1
1985	Cle-A	2	3	.400	19	10	0	0	0	64^1	69	48	13	5	38	38	15.7	6.58	63	.276	.382	0	—	0	-17	-17	-1	-1.3
Total	2	2	3	.400	20	10	0	0	0	67^1	69	48	13	6	38	41	15.1	6.28	66	.267	.374	0	—	0	-16	-16	-1	-1.2
● EDDIE ROMMEL	Rommel, Edwin Americus b: 9/13/1897, Baltimore, Md. d: 8/26/70, Baltimore, Md. BR/TR, 6'2", 197 lbs. Deb: 4/19/20 CU																											
1920	Phi-A	7	7	.500	33	12	8	2	1	173^2	165	68	5	4	43	43	11.0	2.85	141	.259	.309	11	.216	-0	18	21	5	2.1
1921	Phi-A	16	23	.410	46	32	20	0	3	285^1	312	155	21	1	87	71	12.6	3.94	113	.284	.337	18	.191	-2	11	16	3	1.9
1922	Phi-A	**27**	13	.675	**51**	33	22	3	2	294	294	128	21	5	63	54	11.1	3.28	130	.267	.309	17	.181	-3	25	30	3	3.8
1923	Phi-A	18	19	.486	**56**	31	19	3	5	297^2	306	141	14	3	108	76	12.6	3.27	126	.271	.336	24	.238	1	24	27	6	**3.9**
1924	Phi-A	18	15	.545	43	34	21	3	1	278	302	139	8	3	94	72	12.9	3.95	108	.284	.344	15	.158	-6	9	10	8	1.2
1925	Phi-A	**21**	10	.677	52	28	14	1	3	261	285	127	10	7	95	67	13.3	3.69	126	.281	.346	15	.185	-1	20	26	5	3.1
1926	Phi-A	11	11	.500	37	26	12	3	0	219	225	91	10	2	54	52	11.5	3.08	135	.268	.314	6	.098	-4	23	25	2	2.2
1927	Phi-A	11	3	.786	30	17	8	2	1	146^2	166	83	6	3	48	33	13.3	4.36	98	.286	.343	8	.157	-2	-4	-1	3	-0.1
1928	Phi-A	13	5	.722	43	11	6	0	4	173^2	177	70	11	2	26	37	10.6	3.06	131	.266	.295	12	.255	3	19	19	3	2.3
1929	*Phi-A	12	2	.857	32	6	4	0	4	113^2	135	52	10	1	34	25	13.5	2.85	148	.294	.344	8	.205	-0	18	18	1	2.0
1930	Phi-A	9	4	.692	35	9	5	0	3	130^1	142	66	11	1	27	35	11.7	4.28	109	.277	.315	10	.263	3	5	6	1	0.9
1931	*Phi-A	7	5	.583	25	10	8	1	0	118	136	50	5	1	27	18	12.5	2.97	151	.291	.331	14	.259	2	18	19	-0	1.9
1932	Phi-A	1	2	.333	17	0	0	0	2	65^1	84	43	6	0	18	16	14.1	5.51	82	.315	.358	6	.300	2	-7	-7	2	0.0
Total	13	171	119	.590	500	249	147	18	29	2556^1	2729	1213	138	33	724	599	12.3	3.54	122	.277	.329	164	.199	-7	179	210	42	25.2
● ENRIQUE ROMO	Romo, Enrique (Navarro) b: 7/15/47, Santa Rosalia, Mex BR/TR, 5'11", 185 lbs. Deb: 4/7/77 F																											
1977	Sea-A	8	10	.444	58	3	0	0	16	114^1	93	40	8	5	39	105	10.8	2.83	146	.227	.302	0	—	0	16	16	1	3.0
1978	Sea-A	11	7	.611	56	0	0	0	10	107^1	88	46	12	5	39	62	11.1	3.69	104	.227	.306	0	—	0	1	2	-1	0.2
1979	*Pit-N	10	5	.667	84	0	0	0	5	129^1	122	50	11	3	43	106	11.7	2.99	130	.253	.318	2	.167	-0	11	12	2	1.6
1980	Pit-N	5	5	.500	74	0	0	0	11	123^2	117	53	10	1	28	82	10.6	3.27	111	.252	.296	5	.455	3	5	5	1	0.9
1981	Pit-N	1	3	.250	33	0	0	0	9	41^2	47	27	5	0	18	23	14.0	4.54	79	.288	.359	0	.000	-0	-5	-4	-0	-0.7
1982	Pit-N	9	3	.750	45	0	0	0	1	86^2	81	43	11	1	36	58	12.3	4.36	85	.245	.322	3	.300	1	-7	-6	-0	-0.7
Total	6	44	33	.571	350	3	0	0	52	603	548	259	57	15	203	436	11.4	3.45	111	.245	.312	10	.270	4	20	25	2	4.3
● VICENTE ROMO	Romo, Vicente (Navarro) "Huevo" b: 4/12/43, Santa Rosalia, Mex. BR/TR, 6'1", 195 lbs. Deb: 4/11/68 F																											
1968	LA-N	0	0	—	1	0	0	0	0	1	1	1	0	0	0	0	9.0	0.00	—	.250	.250	0	—	0	0	0	-0	0.0
	Cle-A	5	3	.625	40	1	0	0	12	83^1	43	15	5	2	32	54	8.3	1.62	183	.154	.245	2	.143	-0	13	12	-0	1.7
1969	Cle-A	1	1	.500	3	0	0	0	0	8	7	3	0	0	3	7	11.3	2.25	168	.233	.303	1	.500	0	1	1	-0	0.3
	Bos-A	7	9	.438	52	11	4	1	11	127^1	116	51	14	1	50	89	11.8	3.18	120	.247	.321	4	.129	-1	6	8	0	1.1
	Yr	8	10	.444	55	11	4	1	11	135^1	123	54	14	1	53	96	11.8	3.13	122	.246	.320	5	.152	-0	8	10	0	1.4
1970	Bos-A	7	3	.700	48	10	0	0	6	108	115	51	14	0	43	71	13.2	4.08	97	.273	.340	4	.148	0	-4	-1	1	0.0
1971	Chi-A	1	7	.125	45	2	0	0	5	72	52	27	5	0	37	48	11.1	3.38	107	.202	.303	4	.364	1	1	2	1	0.5
1972	Chi-A	3	0	1.000	28	0	0	0	1	51^2	47	19	5	1	18	46	11.5	3.31	95	.246	.314	0	.000	-1	-1	-1	1	-0.1
1973	SD-N	2	3	.400	49	1	0	0	7	87^2	85	43	11	0	46	51	13.4	3.70	94	.260	.351	2	.125	-0	-0	-2	0	-0.1
1974	SD-N	5	5	.500	54	1	0	0	9	71	78	47	6	2	37	26	14.8	4.56	78	.290	.380	0	.000	-1	-7	-8	2	-1.2
1982	LA-N	1	2	.333	15	6	0	0	1	35^2	25	12	1	2	14	24	10.3	3.03	115	.195	.285	1	.200	0	2	2	1	0.2
Total	8	32	33	.492	335	32	4	1	52	645^2	569	269	61	8	280	416	11.9	3.36	106	.239	.322	18	.149	-1	10	14	5	2.4
● JOHN ROMONOSKY	Romonosky, John b: 7/7/29, Harrisburg, Ill. BR/TR, 6'2", 195 lbs. Deb: 9/6/53																											
1953	StL-N	0	0	—	2	2	0	0	0	7^2	9	6	1	1	4	3	16.4	4.70	91	.281	.378	0	.000	-0	-0	-0	-0	-0.1
1958	Was-A	2	4	.333	18	5	1	0	0	55^1	52	42	6	0	28	38	13.0	6.51	59	.243	.331	4	.308	2	-17	-16	0	-1.3
1959	Was-A	1	0	1.000	12	2	0	0	0	38^1	36	15	4	3	19	22	13.6	3.29	119	.254	.354	2	.182	0	2	3	-0	0.2
Total	3	3	4	.429	32	9	1	0	0	101^1	97	63	11	4	51	63	13.5	5.15	75	.250	.343	6	.231	2	-15	-14	-0	-1.2
● GILBERTO RONDON	Rondon, Gilberto b: 11/18/53, Bronx, N.Y. BR/TR, 6'2", 200 lbs. Deb: 4/10/76 F																											
1976	Hou-N	2	2	.500	19	7	0	0	0	53^2	70	37	6	0	39	21	18.3	5.70	56	.315	.418	4	.286	1	-13	-16	-1	-1.1
1979	Chi-A	0	0	—	4	0	0	0	0	9^2	11	5	2	0	6	3	15.8	3.72	114	.282	.378	0	—	0	1	1	-0	0.0
Total	2	2	2	.500	23	7	0	0	0	63^1	81	42	8	0	45	24	17.9	5.40	62	.310	.412	4	.286	1	-13	-16	-1	-1.1
● JIM ROOKER	Rooker, James Phillip b: 9/23/42, Lakeview, Ore. BR/TL, 6', 201 lbs. Deb: 6/30/68																											
1968	Det-A	0	0	—	2	0	0	0	0	4^2	4	2	0	0	1	4	9.6	3.86	78	.235	.278	0	.000	-0	-0	-0	0	0.0

YEAR	TM/L	W	L	PCT	G	GS	CG	SH	SV	IP	H	R	HR	HB	BB	SO	RAT	ERA	ERA+	OAV	OOB	BH	AVG	PB	PR	PR+	PD	TPI
1969	KC-A	4	16	.200	28	22	8	1	0	158^1	136	80	13	1	73	108	11.9	3.75	98	.229	.315	16	.281	8	-2	-1	-1	0.6
1970	KC-A	10	15	.400	38	29	6	3	1	203^2	190	99	11	1	102	117	12.9	3.54	106	.252	.341	14	.200	3	4	5	-0	0.9
1971	KC-A	2	7	.222	20	7	1	1	0	54	59	35	2	1	24	31	14.0	5.33	64	.284	.361	0	.000	-1	-11	-11	-1	-1.9
1972	KC-A	5	6	.455	18	10	4	2	0	72	78	37	3	1	24	44	12.9	4.38	70	.280	.339	2	.100	-1	-10	-11	1	-1.6
1973	Pit-N	10	6	.625	41	18	6	3	5	170^1	143	59	12	2	52	122	10.4	2.85	124	.229	.290	12	.245	3	15	13	1	1.6
1974	*Pit-N	15	11	.577	33	33	15	1	0	262^2	228	93	11	4	83	139	10.8	2.78	125	.238	.301	29	.305	11	25	21	1	3.3
1975	*Pit-N	13	11	.542	28	28	7	1	0	196^2	177	80	16	3	76	102	11.7	2.97	119	.238	.311	6	.095	-3	14	13	0	1.2
1976	Pit-N	15	8	.652	30	29	10	1	1	198^2	201	83	12	2	72	92	12.5	3.35	104	.263	.328	16	.216	3	3	3	-1	0.6
1977	Pit-N	14	9	.609	30	30	7	2	0	204^1	196	87	24	0	64	89	11.5	3.08	129	.253	.310	13	.186	0	19	20	-2	2.0
1978	Pit-N	9	11	.450	28	28	1	0	0	163^1	160	94	13	3	81	76	13.4	4.24	87	.259	.348	9	.161	0	-12	-9	1	-1.0
1979	*Pit-N	4	7	.364	19	17	1	0	0	103^2	106	58	11	0	39	44	12.6	4.60	84	.266	.331	4	.121	-1	-10	-8	1	-0.9
1980	Pit-N	2	2	.500	4	4	0	0	0	18	16	7	0	0	12	8	14.0	3.50	104	.262	.384	1	.143	1	0	0	0	0.2
Total	13	103	109	.486	319	255	66	15	7	1810^1	1694	814	128	18	703	976	12.0	3.46	105	.249	.321	122	.201	23	35	32	-2	5.0

● CHARLIE ROOT Root, Charles Henry "Chinski" b: 3/17/1899, Middletown, Ohio d: 11/5/70, Hollister, Cal. BR/TR, 5'10.5", 190 lbs. Deb: 4/18/23 C

YEAR	TM/L	W	L	PCT	G	GS	CG	SH	SV	IP	H	R	HR	HB	BB	SO	RAT	ERA	ERA+	OAV	OOB	BH	AVG	PB	PR	PR+	PD	TPI
1923	StL-A	0	4	.000	27	2	0	0	0	60	68	45	4	6	18	27	13.8	5.70	73	.302	.369	1	.077	-1	-11	-10	-1	-0.7
1926	Chi-N	18	17	.514	42	32	21	2	2	271^1	267	104	10	6	62	127	11.1	2.82	136	.264	.310	13	.143	-4	30	31	-1	3.2
1927	Chi-N	**26**	15	.634	**48**	36	21	4	2	**309**	296	148	16	9	117	145	12.3	3.76	103	.254	.326	27	.221	3	6	4	-4	0.3
1928	Chi-N	14	18	.438	40	30	13	1	2	237	214	109	15	7	73	122	11.2	3.57	108	.242	.305	13	.178	-0	11	8	-3	0.6
1929	*Chi-N	19	6	**.760**	43	31	19	4	5	272	286	120	12	3	83	124	12.3	3.47	133	.275	.330	15	.156	0	38	35	-4	2.5
1930	Chi-N	16	14	.533	37	30	15	**4**	3	220^1	247	122	17	7	63	124	12.9	4.33	113	.281	.334	21	.262	5	16	14	-3	1.7
1931	Chi-N	17	14	.548	39	31	19	3	2	251	240	109	7	7	71	131	11.4	3.48	111	.252	.309	20	.222	3	11	11	-3	1.2
1932	*Chi-N	15	10	.600	39	24	11	0	3	216^1	211	99	10	5	55	96	11.3	3.58	105	.253	.303	13	.171	-1	7	5	-3	0.1
1933	Chi-N	15	10	.600	35	30	20	2	0	242^1	232	85	14	10	61	86	11.3	2.60	126	.252	.306	8	.094	-4	20	18	-3	1.1
1934	Chi-N	4	7	.364	34	9	2	0	0	117^2	141	62	8	5	53	46	15.2	4.28	90	.298	.375	7	.175	2	-3	-6	-1	-0.4
1935	*Chi-N	15	8	.652	38	18	11	1	2	201^1	193	85	15	3	47	94	10.9	3.08	127	.252	.298	14	.203	2	21	19	-3	1.9
1936	Chi-N	3	6	.333	33	4	0	0	1	73^2	81	34	3	2	20	32	12.6	4.15	96	.280	.331	5	.333	1	-1	-1	-0	-0.1
1937	Chi-N	13	5	.722	43	15	5	0	5	178^2	173	71	18	4	32	74	10.5	3.38	118	.253	.290	12	.179	0	11	12	-1	1.1
1938	*Chi-N	8	7	.533	44	11	5	0	8	160^2	163	62	10	2	30	70	10.9	2.86	134	.258	.294	8	.167	-0	17	17	-2	1.4
1939	Chi-N	8	8	.500	35	16	8	0	4	167^1	189	83	11	2	34	65	12.1	4.03	98	.286	.323	10	.175	2	-2	-2	-3	-0.3
1940	Chi-N	2	4	.333	36	8	1	0	2	112	118	61	9	1	33	50	12.2	3.86	97	.265	.317	4	.129	-1	-0	-1	-0	-0.2
1941	Chi-N	8	7	.533	19	15	6	0	0	106^2	133	68	8	0	37	46	14.3	5.40	65	.306	.360	5	.152	2	-21	-23	1	-2.7
Total	17	201	160	.557	632	342	177	21	40	3197^1	3252	1467	187	79	889	1459	11.9	3.59	110	.264	.318	196	.180	8	148	131	-35	10.7

● JOHN ROPER Roper, John Christopher b: 11/21/71, Southern Pines, N.C. BR/TR, 6', 175 lbs. Deb: 5/16/93

YEAR	TM/L	W	L	PCT	G	GS	CG	SH	SV	IP	H	R	HR	HB	BB	SO	RAT	ERA	ERA+	OAV	OOB	BH	AVG	PB	PR	PR+	PD	TPI
1993	Cin-N	2	5	.286	16	15	0	0	0	80	92	51	10	4	36	54	14.8	5.62	72	.295	.375	5	.179	-0	-14	-14	-0	-1.1
1994	Cin-N	6	2	.750	16	15	0	0	0	92	90	49	16	4	30	51	12.1	4.50	92	.255	.320	6	.182	0	-3	-4	-0	-0.2
1995	Cin-N	0	0	—	2	2	0	0	0	7	13	9	3	0	4	6	21.9	10.29	40	.406	.472	0	.000	-0	-5	-5	0	-0.2
	SF-N	0	0	—	1	0	0	0	0	1	2	3	0	0	2	0	36.0	27.00	15	.500	.667	0	—	0	-3	-3	-0	-0.1
	Yr	0	0	—	3	2	0	0	0	8	15	12	3	0	6	6	23.6	12.38	33	.417	.500	0	.000	-0	-7	-7	-0	-0.3
Total	3	8	7	.533	35	32	0	0	0	180	197	112	29	8	72	111	13.9	5.35	76	.281	.355	11	.177	0	-24	-26	-1	-1.7

● RAFAEL ROQUE Roque, Rafael Antonio b: 1/1/72, Cotui, D.R. BL/TL, 6'4", 186 lbs. Deb: 8/1/98

YEAR	TM/L	W	L	PCT	G	GS	CG	SH	SV	IP	H	R	HR	HB	BB	SO	RAT	ERA	ERA+	OAV	OOB	BH	AVG	PB	PR	PR+	PD	TPI
1998	Mil-N	4	2	.667	9	9	0	0	0	48	42	28	9	1	24	34	12.6	4.88	88	.237	.332	1	.077	-1	-3	-3	1	-0.4
1999	Mil-N	1	6	.143	43	9	0	0	1	84^1	96	52	16	4	42	66	15.2	5.34	85	.286	.372	1	.059	-1	-8	-8	0	-0.6
2000	Mil-N	0	0	—	4	0	0	0	0	5^1	7	6	1	0	7	4	23.6	10.13	45	.333	.500	0	—	0	-3	-3	-0	-0.2
Total	3	5	8	.385	56	18	0	0	1	137^2	145	86	26	5	73	104	14.6	5.36	83	.272	.364	2	.067	-2	-14	-14	1	-1.2

● JOSE ROSADO Rosado, Jose Antonio b: 11/9/74, Newark, N.J. BL/TL, 6', 175 lbs. Deb: 6/12/96

YEAR	TM/L	W	L	PCT	G	GS	CG	SH	SV	IP	H	R	HR	HB	BB	SO	RAT	ERA	ERA+	OAV	OOB	BH	AVG	PB	PR	PR+	PD	TPI
1996	KC-A	8	6	.571	16	16	2	1	0	106^2	101	39	7	4	26	64	11.1	3.21	156	.249	.300	0	—	0	21	21	-0	2.4
1997	KC-A★	9	12	.429	33	33	2	0	0	203^1	208	117	26	4	73	129	12.6	4.69	101	.264	.330	0	.000	-0	-3	1	-1	0.0
1998	KC-A	8	11	.421	38	25	2	1	1	174^2	180	106	25	5	57	135	12.5	4.69	103	.260	.321	1	.500	0	-1	3	1	0.3
1999	KC-A★	10	14	.417	33	33	5	0	0	208	197	103	24	5	72	141	11.9	3.85	130	.248	.315	0	.000	-1	24	26	-1	2.5
2000	KC-A	2	2	.500	5	5	0	0	0	27^2	29	18	4	4	9	15	13.7	5.86	86	.271	.350	0	—	0	-3	-3	0	-0.3
Total	5	37	45	.451	125	112	11	2	1	720^1	715	383	86	22	237	484	12.2	4.27	114	.257	.320	1	.111	-0	39	48	-1	4.9

● BRIAN ROSE Rose, Brian Leonard b: 2/13/76, New Bedford, Mass. BR/TR, 6'3", 215 lbs. Deb: 7/25/97

YEAR	TM/L	W	L	PCT	G	GS	CG	SH	SV	IP	H	R	HR	HB	BB	SO	RAT	ERA	ERA+	OAV	OOB	BH	AVG	PB	PR	PR+	PD	TPI
1997	Bos-A	0	0	—	1	1	0	0	0	3	5	4	0	0	2	3	21.0	12.00	39	.357	.438	0	—	0	-2	-2	-0	-0.1
1998	Bos-A	1	4	.200	8	8	0	0	0	37^2	43	32	9	2	14	18	14.1	6.93	68	.285	.353	0	—	0	-10	-9	-0	-1.0
1999	Bos-A	7	6	.538	22	18	0	0	0	98	112	59	19	2	29	51	13.1	4.87	102	.280	.332	0	.000	-0	0	1	1	0.2
2000	Bos-A	3	5	.375	15	12	0	0	0	53	58	37	11	3	21	24	13.9	6.11	83	.274	.347	0	.000	-0	-7	-6	-1	-0.8
	Col-N	4	5	.444	12	12	0	0	0	63^2	72	41	10	3	30	40	14.8	5.51	108	.281	.363	1	.048	-2	-6	2	0	0.1
Total	4	15	20	.429	58	51	0	0	0	255^1	290	173	49	10	96	136	14.0	5.67	92	.281	.348	1	.038	-2	-25	-12	0	-1.6

● CHUCK ROSE Rose, Charles Alfred b: 9/1/1885, Macon, Mo. d: 8/4/61, Salina, Kan. BL/TL, 5'8.5", 158 lbs. Deb: 9/13/09

YEAR	TM/L	W	L	PCT	G	GS	CG	SH	SV	IP	H	R	HR	HB	BB	SO	RAT	ERA	ERA+	OAV	OOB	BH	AVG	PB	PR	PR+	PD	TPI
1909	StL-A	1	2	.333	3	3	3	0	0	25	32	17	1	3	7	6	15.1	5.40	45	.330	.393	0	.000	-1	-8	-9	-1	-1.0

● DON ROSE Rose, Donald Gary b: 3/19/47, Covina, Cal. BR/TR, 6'3", 195 lbs. Deb: 9/15/71

YEAR	TM/L	W	L	PCT	G	GS	CG	SH	SV	IP	H	R	HR	HB	BB	SO	RAT	ERA	ERA+	OAV	OOB	BH	AVG	PB	PR	PR+	PD	TPI
1971	NY-N	0	0	—	1	0	0	0	0	2	2	0	0	0	0	1	9.0	0.00	—	.286	.286	0	—	0	1	1	-0	0.0
1972	Cal-A	1	4	.200	16	4	0	0	0	42^2	49	25	9	0	19	39	14.3	4.22	69	.283	.354	2	.200	1	-5	-6	-0	-0.6
1974	SF-N	0	0	—	2	0	0	0	0	1	4	1	0	0	1	0	45.0	9.00	42	.667	.714	0	—	0	-1	-1	0	0.0
Total	3	1	4	.200	19	4	0	0	0	45^2	55	26	9	0	20	40	14.8	4.14	72	.296	.364	2	.200	1	-5	-6	-1	-0.6

● ZEKE ROSEBRAUGH Rosebraugh, Eli Ethelbert b: 9/8/1870, Charleston, Ill. d: 7/16/30, Fresno, Cal. TL, Deb: 9/21/1898

YEAR	TM/L	W	L	PCT	G	GS	CG	SH	SV	IP	H	R	HR	HB	BB	SO	RAT	ERA	ERA+	OAV	OOB	BH	AVG	PB	PR	PR+	PD	TPI
1898	Pit-N	0	2	.000	4	2	2	0	0	21^2	23	14	0	3	9	6	14.5	3.32	107	.271	.361	3	.375	1	-0	1	0	0.1
1899	Pit-N	0	1	.000	2	2	0	0	0	6	14	8	0	1	3	2	27.0	9.00	42	.452	.514	0	.000	-0	-3	-3	-0	-0.5
Total	2	0	3	.000	6	4	2	0	0	27^2	37	22	0	4	12	8	17.2	4.55	79	.319	.402	3	.300	1	-3	-3	-0	-0.4

● CHIEF ROSEMAN Roseman, James John b: 1856, New York, N.Y. d: 7/4/38, Brooklyn, N.Y. BR/TR, 5'7", 167 lbs. Deb: 5/1/1882 M♦

YEAR	TM/L	W	L	PCT	G	GS	CG	SH	SV	IP	H	R	HR	HB	BB	SO	RAT	ERA	ERA+	OAV	OOB	BH	AVG	PB	PR	PR+	PD	TPI
1885	NY-a	0	1	.000	1	1	0	0	0	1	3	5	0	0	2	0	45.0	27.00	11	.333	.455	114	.278	0	-3	-3	0	-0.4
1886	NY-a	0	0	—	1	0	0	0	0	7	6	6	0	0	0	0	7.7	5.14	66	.240	.240	127	.227	0	-1	-1	0	0.0
1887	NY-a	0	0	—	2	0	0	0	0	8	16	14	0	2	5	1	20.3	7.88	54	.500	.529	64	.256	-0	-3	-3	-0	-0.1
Total	3	0	1	.000	4	1	0	0	0	16	25	25	0	2	7	1	16.3	7.88	48	.379	.414	745	.268	0	-7	-7	-0	-0.5

● STEVE ROSENBERG Rosenberg, Steven Allen b: 10/31/64, Brooklyn, N.Y. BL/TL, 6', 186 lbs. Deb: 6/4/88

YEAR	TM/L	W	L	PCT	G	GS	CG	SH	SV	IP	H	R	HR	HB	BB	SO	RAT	ERA	ERA+	OAV	OOB	BH	AVG	PB	PR	PR+	PD	TPI
1988	Chi-A	0	1	.000	33	0	0	0	1	46	53	22	5	0	19	28	14.1	4.30	92	.298	.365	0	—	0	-2	-2	-0	-0.1
1989	Chi-A	4	13	.235	38	21	2	0	0	142	148	92	14	1	58	77	13.1	4.94	77	.273	.344	0	—	0	-17	-18	0	-1.9
1990	Chi-A	1	0	1.000	6	0	0	0	0	10	10	6	2	0	5	4	13.5	5.40	71	.256	.341	0	—	0	-2	-2	0	-0.1
1991	SD-N	1	1	.500	10	0	0	0	0	11^2	11	9	3	0	5	6	12.3	6.94	55	.250	.327	0	.000	-0	-4	-4	-0	-0.6
Total	4	6	15	.286	87	21	2	0	1	209^2	222	129	24	1	87	115	13.3	4.94	78	.276	.348	0	.000	-0	-24	-26	-0	-2.7

● WAYNE ROSENTHAL Rosenthal, Wayne Scott b: 2/19/65, Brooklyn, N.Y. BR/TR, 6'5", 220 lbs. Deb: 6/26/91

YEAR	TM/L	W	L	PCT	G	GS	CG	SH	SV	IP	H	R	HR	HB	BB	SO	RAT	ERA	ERA+	OAV	OOB	BH	AVG	PB	PR	PR+	PD	TPI
1991	Tex-A	1	4	.200	36	0	0	0	1	70^1	72	43	9	1	36	61	13.9	5.25	77	.257	.344	0	—	0	-9	-10	-1	-0.7
1992	Tex-A	0	0	—	6	0	0	0	0	4^2	7	4	1	0	2	1	17.4	7.71	49	.333	.391	0	—	0	-2	-2	0	-0.1
Total	2	1	4	.200	42	0	0	0	1	75	79	47	10	1	38	62	14.2	5.40	74	.262	.347	0	—	0	-11	-12	-1	-0.8

● STEVE ROSER Roser, Emerson Corey b: 1/25/18, Rome, N.Y. BR/TR, 6'4", 220 lbs. Deb: 5/5/44

YEAR	TM/L	W	L	PCT	G	GS	CG	SH	SV	IP	H	R	HR	HB	BB	SO	RAT	ERA	ERA+	OAV	OOB	BH	AVG	PB	PR	PR+	PD	TPI
1944	NY-A	4	3	.571	16	6	1	0	1	84	80	39	3	0	34	34	12.2	3.86	90	.256	.329	3	.100	-2	-4	-3	-1	-0.5
1945	NY-A	0	0	—	11	0	0	0	0	27	27	15	1	0	8	11	11.7	3.67	94	.262	.315	1	.125	-0	-1	-1	0	0.0
1946	NY-A	1	1	.500	4	1	0	0	0	3^1	7	6	0	0	4	1	29.7	16.20	21	.438	.550	0	—	0	-5	-5	-0	-0.9
	Bos-N	1	1	.500	14	1	0	0	1	35	33	15	1	0	18	18	13.1	3.60	95	.250	.340	0	.000	-1	-1	-1	-0	-0.1
Total	3	6	5	.545	45	8	1	0	2	149^1	147	75	5	0	64	64	12.7	4.04	86	.261	.336	4	.093	-3	-10	-9	-1	-1.5

● BUSTER ROSS Ross, Chester Franklin b: 3/11/03, Kuttawa, Ky. d: 4/24/82, Mayfield, Ky. BL/TL, 6'1", 195 lbs. Deb: 6/15/24

YEAR	TM/L	W	L	PCT	G	GS	CG	SH	SV	IP	H	R	HR	HB	BB	SO	RAT	ERA	ERA+	OAV	OOB	BH	AVG	PB	PR	PR+	PD	TPI
1924	Bos-A	4	3	.571	30	2	1	1	1	93^1	109	49	3	0	30	16	13.4	3.47	126	.307	.361	5	.200	-0	8	9	-1	0.5
1925	Bos-A	3	8	.273	33	8	0	0	0	94^1	119	86	9	5	40	15	15.6	6.20	73	.313	.386	3	.125	-1	-19	-17	-1	-1.8
1926	Bos-A	0	1	.000	1	0	0	0	0	2^2	5	7	0	0	4	0	30.4	16.88	24	.385	.529	0	.000	-0	-4	-4	-0	-0.6
Total	3	7	12	.368	64	10	1	1	1	190^1	233	142	12	5	74	31	14.8	5.01	89	.311	.377	8	.160	-2	-15	-11	-2	-1.9

● CLIFF ROSS Ross, Clifford Davis b: 8/3/28, Philadelphia, Pa. d: 4/13/99, Philadelphia, Pa. BL/TL, 6'4", 195 lbs. Deb: 9/11/54

YEAR	TM/L	W	L	PCT	G	GS	CG	SH	SV	IP	H	R	HR	HB	BB	SO	RAT	ERA	ERA+	OAV	OOB	BH	AVG	PB	PR	PR+	PD	TPI
1954	Cin-N	0	0	—	4	0	0	0	1	2^2	0	0	0	0	0	1	0.0	0.00	—	.000	.000	0	—	0	1	1	0	0.1

● ERNIE ROSS Ross, Ernest Bertram "Curly" b: 3/31/1880, Toronto, Ont., Can. d: 3/28/50, Toronto, Ont., Can. BL/TL, 5'8", 150 lbs. Deb: 9/17/02

YEAR	TM/L	W	L	PCT	G	GS	CG	SH	SV	IP	H	R	HR	HB	BB	SO	RAT	ERA	ERA+	OAV	OOB	BH	AVG	PB	PR	PR+	PD	TPI
1902	Bal-A	1	1	.500	2	2	2	0	0	17	20	18	0	1	12	2	17.5	7.41	51	.294	.407	0	.000	-1	-7	-7	-1	-0.7

● BOB ROSS Ross, Floyd Robert b: 11/2/28, Fullerton, Cal. BR/TL, 6', 165 lbs. Deb: 6/16/50

YEAR	TM/L	W	L	PCT	G	GS	CG	SH	SV	IP	H	R	HR	HB	BB	SO	RAT	ERA	ERA+	OAV	OOB	BH	AVG	PB	PR	PR+	PD	TPI
1950	Was-A	0	1	.000	6	2	0	0	0	12^2	15	12	1	0	15	2	21.3	8.53	53	.300	.462	0	.000	-0	-6	-6	0	-0.4
1951	Was-A	0	1	.000	11	1	0	0	0	31^2	36	25	3	0	21	23	16.2	6.54	63	.295	.399	1	.111	-0	-8	-9	-1	-0.5
1956	Phi-N	0	0	—	3	0	0	0	0	3^1	4	3	1	0	2	4	16.2	8.10	46	.333	.429	0	—	0	-2	-2	0	-0.1
Total	3	0	2	.000	20	3	0	0	0	47^2	55	40	5	0	38	29	17.6	7.17	58	.299	.419	1	.083	-1	-16	-16	-0	-1.0

● GARY ROSS Ross, Gary Douglas b: 9/16/47, McKeesport, Pa. BR/TR, 6'1", 190 lbs. Deb: 6/28/68

YEAR	TM/L	W	L	PCT	G	GS	CG	SH	SV	IP	H	R	HR	HB	BB	SO	RAT	ERA	ERA+	OAV	OOB	BH	AVG	PB	PR	PR+	PD	TPI
1968	Chi-N	1	1	.500	13	5	1	0	0	41	44	22	1	0	25	31	15.1	4.17	76	.288	.388	1	.091	-1	-5	-4	0	-0.3
1969	Chi-N	0	0	—	2	1	0	0	0	2	1	3	0	0	2	2	13.5	13.50	30	.143	.333	0	—	0	-2	-2	-0	-0.1
	SD-N	3	12	.200	46	7	0	0	3	109^2	104	58	5	5	56	58	13.5	4.19	85	.252	.348	0	.000	-2	-7	-8	2	-1.1
	Yr	3	12	.200	48	8	0	0	3	111^2	105	61	5	5	58	60	13.5	4.35	82	.250	.348	0	.000	-2	-9	-10	2	-1.2
1970	SD-N	2	3	.400	33	2	0	0	1	62^1	72	37	8	3	36	39	16.0	5.20	77	.305	.404	4	.500	2	-8	-9	1	-0.4
1971	SD-N	1	3	.250	13	0	0	0	0	24^1	27	10	0	1	11	13	14.4	2.96	112	.300	.382	0	.000	-0	1	1	0	0.1
1972	SD-N	4	3	.571	60	0	0	0	3	91^2	87	35	2	4	49	46	13.7	2.45	134	.261	.363	2	.154	-0	10	9	1	0.8
1973	SD-N	4	4	.500	58	0	0	0	0	76^1	93	51	8	4	33	44	15.3	5.42	64	.304	.379	0	.000	-0	-15	-17	0	-1.7
1974	SD-N	0	0	—	9	0	0	0	0	18	23	10	1	0	6	11	14.5	4.50	79	.315	.367	0	.000	-0	-2	-2	0	-0.1
1975	Cal-A	0	1	.000	1	1	0	0	0	5	6	3	1	0	1	4	12.6	5.40	66	.273	.304	0	—	0	-1	-1	-0	-0.2
1976	Cal-A	8	16	.333	34	31	7	2	0	225	224	89	12	5	58	100	11.5	3.00	111	.258	.308	0	—	0	13	9	5	1.4
1977	Cal-A	2	4	.333	14	12	0	0	0	58^1	83	41	10	2	11	30	14.8	5.55	71	.337	.371	0	—	0	-10	-11	1	-0.9
Total	10	25	47	.347	283	59	8	2	7	713^2	764	359	48	24	288	378	13.6	3.92	89	.278	.352	7	.115	-2	-25	-36	9	-2.5

● GEORGE ROSS Ross, George Sidney b: 6/27/1892, San Rafael, Cal. d: 4/22/35, Amityville, N.Y. BL/TL, 5'10.5", 175 lbs. Deb: 6/27/18

YEAR	TM/L	W	L	PCT	G	GS	CG	SH	SV	IP	H	R	HR	HB	BB	SO	RAT	ERA	ERA+	OAV	OOB	BH	AVG	PB	PR	PR+	PD	TPI
1918	NY-N	0	0	—	1	0	0	0	1	2^1	2	0	0	0	3	2	19.3	0.00	—	.222	.417	0	.000	-0	1	1	0	0.1

● BUCK ROSS Ross, Lee Ravon b: 2/2/15, Norwood, N.C. d: 11/23/78, Charlotte, N.C. BR/TR, 6'2", 170 lbs. Deb: 5/7/36

YEAR	TM/L	W	L	PCT	G	GS	CG	SH	SV	IP	H	R	HR	HB	BB	SO	RAT	ERA	ERA+	OAV	OOB	BH	AVG	PB	PR	PR+	PD	TPI
1936	Phi-A	9	14	.391	30	27	12	1	0	200^2	253	146	17	0	83	47	15.1	5.83	88	.304	.367	12	.169	-1	-18	-16	-2	-1.7
1937	Phi-A	5	10	.333	28	22	7	1	0	147^1	183	102	12	2	63	37	15.1	4.89	96	.306	.373	5	.102	-3	-4	-3	0	-0.5
1938	Phi-A	9	16	.360	29	28	10	0	0	184^1	218	132	23	0	80	54	14.5	5.32	91	.289	.357	12	.190	-0	-11	-10	-0	-1.1
1939	Phi-A	6	14	.300	29	28	6	1	0	174	216	143	17	0	95	43	16.1	6.00	78	.302	.384	12	.207	-1	-27	-25	-2	-2.5
1940	Phi-A	5	10	.333	24	19	10	0	1	156^1	160	91	15	0	60	43	12.7	4.38	102	.256	.322	7	.132	-2	0	1	-1	-0.2
1941	Phi-A	0	1	.000	1	1	0	0	0	4	10	10	2	0	2	0	27.0	18.00	23	.435	.480	0	.000	-0	-6	-6	0	-0.8
	Chi-A	3	8	.273	20	11	7	0	0	108^1	99	51	6	1	43	30	11.9	3.16	130	.239	.312	7	.219	1	12	11	-2	1.0
	Yr	3	9	.250	21	12	7	0	0	112^1	109	60	8	1	45	30	12.4	3.69	111	.249	.321	7	.212	1	6	5	-2	0.2
1942	Chi-A	5	7	.417	22	14	4	2	1	113^1	118	63	6	0	39	37	12.5	5.00	72	.264	.323	6	.158	0	-17	-18	-3	-1.9
1943	Chi-A	11	7	.611	21	21	7	1	0	149^1	140	61	6	2	56	41	11.9	3.19	105	.253	.324	4	.087	-1	2	2	-1	0.0
1944	Chi-A	2	7	.222	20	9	2	0	0	90^1	97	56	7	2	35	20	13.4	5.18	66	.280	.350	2	.077	-2	-18	-18	-2	-2.0
1945	Chi-A	1	1	.500	13	2	0	0	0	37^1	51	28	3	0	17	8	16.4	5.79	57	.327	.393	2	.182	-0	-10	-10	-1	-0.6
Total	10	56	95	.371	237	182	65	6	2	1365^1	1545	882	114	7	573	360	14.0	4.94	88	.283	.351	69	.154	-11	-97	-91	-13	-10.3

● MARK ROSS Ross, Mark Joseph b: 8/8/57, Galveston, Tex. BR/TR, 6', 195 lbs. Deb: 9/12/82

YEAR	TM/L	W	L	PCT	G	GS	CG	SH	SV	IP	H	R	HR	HB	BB	SO	RAT	ERA	ERA+	OAV	OOB	BH	AVG	PB	PR	PR+	PD	TPI
1982	Hou-N	0	0	—	4	0	0	0	0	6	3	1	0	0	0	4	4.5	1.50	222	.143	.143	0	—	0	1	1	0	0.1
1984	Hou-N	1	0	1.000	2	0	0	0	0	2^1	1	0	0	0	0	1	3.9	0.00	—	.125	.125	0	—	0	1	1	0	0.2
1985	Hou-N	0	2	.000	8	0	0	0	1	13	12	7	2	0	2	3	9.7	4.85	72	.240	.269	0	.000	-0	-2	-2	0	-0.3
1987	Pit-N	0	0	—	1	0	0	0	0	1	1	1	1	0	0	0	9.0	9.00	46	.250	.250	0	—	0	-1	-1	0	0.0
1988	Tor-A	0	0	—	3	0	0	0	0	7^1	5	6	0	0	4	4	11.0	4.91	80	.185	.290	0	—	0	-1	-1	-0	-0.1
1990	Pit-N	1	0	1.000	9	0	0	0	0	12^2	11	5	2	0	4	5	10.7	3.55	102	.244	.306	0	.000	-0	0	0	0	0.0
Total	6	2	2	.500	27	0	0	0	1	42^1	33	20	5	0	10	17	9.1	3.83	94	.213	.261	0	.000	-0	-0	-1	0	-0.1

● JOE ROSSELLI Rosselli, Joseph Donald b: 5/28/72, Burbank, Cal. BR/TL, 6'1", 170 lbs. Deb: 4/30/95

YEAR	TM/L	W	L	PCT	G	GS	CG	SH	SV	IP	H	R	HR	HB	BB	SO	RAT	ERA	ERA+	OAV	OOB	BH	AVG	PB	PR	PR+	PD	TPI
1995	SF-N	2	1	.667	9	5	0	0	0	30	39	29	5	0	20	7	17.7	8.70	47	.342	.440	2	.200	0	-15	-16	-0	-1.3

● FRANK ROSSO Rosso, Francis James b: 3/1/21, Agawam, Mass. d: 1/26/80, Springfield, Mass. BR/TR, 5'11", 180 lbs. Deb: 9/15/44

YEAR	TM/L	W	L	PCT	G	GS	CG	SH	SV	IP	H	R	HR	HB	BB	SO	RAT	ERA	ERA+	OAV	OOB	BH	AVG	PB	PR	PR+	PD	TPI
1944	NY-N	0	0	—	2	0	0	0	0	4	11	5	0	0	3	1	31.5	9.00	41	.550	.609	0	—	0	-2	-2	0	-0.1

● MARV ROTBLATT Rotblatt, Marvin "Rotty" b: 10/18/27, Chicago, Ill. BB/TL, 5'7", 160 lbs. Deb: 7/4/48

YEAR	TM/L	W	L	PCT	G	GS	CG	SH	SV	IP	H	R	HR	HB	BB	SO	RAT	ERA	ERA+	OAV	OOB	BH	AVG	PB	PR	PR+	PD	TPI
1948	Chi-A	0	1	.000	7	2	0	0	0	18^1	19	16	0	1	23	4	21.1	7.85	54	.271	.457	0	.000	-0	-7	-7	-1	-0.4
1950	Chi-A	0	0	—	2	0	0	0	0	8^2	11	7	2	0	5	6	16.6	6.23	72	.344	.432	0	.000	-0	-2	-2	0	-0.1
1951	Chi-A	4	2	.667	26	2	0	0	2	47^2	44	21	4	1	23	20	12.8	3.40	119	.244	.333	0	.000	-2	4	3	1	0.3
Total	3	4	3	.571	35	4	0	0	2	74^2	74	44	6	2	51	30	15.3	4.82	86	.262	.379	0	.000	-2	-5	-6	1	-0.2

● JACK ROTHROCK Rothrock, John Huston b: 3/14/05, Long Beach, Cal. d: 2/2/80, San Bernardino, Cal BB/TR, 5'11.5", 165 lbs. Deb: 7/28/25 ♦

YEAR	TM/L	W	L	PCT	G	GS	CG	SH	SV	IP	H	R	HR	HB	BB	SO	RAT	ERA	ERA+	OAV	OOB	BH	AVG	PB	PR	PR+	PD	TPI
1928	Bos-A	0	0	—	1	0	0	0	0	1	0	0	0	0	0	0	0.0	0.00	—	.000	.000	92	.267	0	0	0	0	0.1

● LARRY ROTHSCHILD Rothschild, Lawrence Lee b: 3/12/54, Chicago, Ill. BL/TR, 6'2", 180 lbs. Deb: 9/11/81 MC

YEAR	TM/L	W	L	PCT	G	GS	CG	SH	SV	IP	H	R	HR	HB	BB	SO	RAT	ERA	ERA+	OAV	OOB	BH	AVG	PB	PR	PR+	PD	TPI
1981	Det-A	0	0	—	5	0	0	0	1	5^2	4	1	0	0	6	1	15.9	1.59	238	.200	.385	0	—	0	1	1	0	0.1
1982	Det-A	0	0	—	2	0	0	0	0	2^2	4	4	1	0	2	0	20.3	13.50	30	.333	.429	0	—	0	-3	-3	-0	-0.1
Total	2	0	0	—	7	0	0	0	1	8^1	8	5	1	0	8	1	17.3	5.40	72	.250	.400	0	—	0	-1	-1	0	0.0

● GENE ROUNSAVILLE Rounsaville, Virle Gene b: 9/27/44, Konawa, Okla. BR/TR, 6'3", 205 lbs. Deb: 4/7/70

YEAR	TM/L	W	L	PCT	G	GS	CG	SH	SV	IP	H	R	HR	HB	BB	SO	RAT	ERA	ERA+	OAV	OOB	BH	AVG	PB	PR	PR+	PD	TPI
1970	Chi-A	0	1	.000	8	0	0	0	0	6^1	10	8	1	0	2	3	17.1	9.95	39	.357	.400	0	—	0	-4	-4	-0	-0.6

● JACK ROWAN Rowan, John Albert b: 6/16/1887, New Castle, Pa. d: 9/29/66, Dayton, Ohio BR/TR, 6'1", 210 lbs. Deb: 9/6/06

YEAR	TM/L	W	L	PCT	G	GS	CG	SH	SV	IP	H	R	HR	HB	BB	SO	RAT	ERA	ERA+	OAV	OOB	BH	AVG	PB	PR	PR+	PD	TPI
1906	Det-A	0	1	.000	1	1	1	0	0	9	15	13	0	0	6	0	21.0	11.00	25	.375	.457	1	.250	0	-8	-8	-0	-0.6
1908	Cin-N	3	3	.500	8	7	4	1	0	49^1	46	17	0	0	16	24	11.3	1.82	126	.253	.313	1	.071	-0	3	3	1	0.4
1909	Cin-N	11	12	.478	38	23	14	0	0	225^2	185	86	0	3	104	81	11.6	2.79	93	.233	.324	6	.092	-1	-5	-5	-5	-1.1
1910	Cin-N	14	13	.519	42	30	18	4	1	261	242	122	4	9	105	108	12.3	2.93	99	.254	.334	19	.229	3	3	-0	-4	-0.2
1911	Phi-N	2	4	.333	12	6	2	0	0	45^2	59	35	3	1	20	17	15.8	4.73	73	.316	.385	1	.077	-1	-7	-6	1	-0.8
	Chi-N	0	0	—	1	0	0	0	0	2	1	4	0	1	2	0	18.0	4.50	74	.143	.400	0	.000	-0	-0	-0	0	0.0
	Yr	2	4	.333	13	6	2	0	0	47^2	60	39	3	2	22	17	15.9	4.72	73	.309	.385	1	.071	-1	-7	-7	1	-0.8
1913	Cin-N	0	4	.000	5	5	0	0	0	39	37	14	0	1	9	21	10.8	3.00	108	.264	.313	2	.182	1	1	1	-0	0.2
1914	Cin-N	1	3	.250	12	2	0	0	2	39	38	22	1	0	10	16	11.1	3.46	85	.262	.310	0	.000	-1	-3	-2	-1	-0.4
Total	7	31	40	.437	119	74	44	5	3	670^2	623	313	8	15	272	267	12.2	3.07	92	.255	.333	30	.151	1	-16	-19	-9	-2.5

● DAVE ROWE Rowe, David Elwood b: 10/9/1854, Harrisburg, Pa. d: 12/9/30, Glendale, Cal. BR/TR, 5'9", 180 lbs. Deb: 5/30/1877 FM♦

YEAR	TM/L	W	L	PCT	G	GS	CG	SH	SV	IP	H	R	HR	HB	BB	SO	RAT	ERA	ERA+	OAV	OOB	BH	AVG	PB	PR	PR+	PD	TPI
1877	Chi-N	0	1	.000	1	1	1	0	0	4	13	12	0		2	0	45.0	18.00	17	.600	.714	2	.286	0	-2	-2	0	-0.3
1882	Cle-N	0	1	.000	1	1	1	0	0	9	29	35	3		7	0	36.0	12.00	23	.492	.545	25	.258	0	-9	-10	-0	-0.6
1883	Bal-a	0	0	—	1	0	0	0	0	4	12	11	1		2	1	31.5	20.25	17	.500	.538	80	.313	0	-8	-7	-0	-0.3
1884	StL-U	1	0	1.000	1	1	1	0	0	9	10	3	0		0	2	10.0	2.00	120	.263	.263	142	.293	0	0	0	0	0.1
Total	4	1	2	.333	4	3	2	0	0	23	54	51	4		11	3	25.4	9.78	28	.429	.474	383	.263	0	-18	-18	-0	-1.1

YEAR	TM/L	W	L	PCT	G	GS	CG	SH	SV	IP	H	R	HR	HB	BB	SO	RAT	ERA	ERA+	OAV	OOB	BH	AVG	PB	PR	PR+	PD	TPI
● DON ROWE	Rowe, Donald Howard b: 4/3/36, Brawley, Cal. BL/TL, 6', 180 lbs. Deb: 4/9/63 C																											
1963	NY-N	0	0	—	26	1	0	0	0	54^2	59	27	6	1	21	27	13.3	4.28	81	.280	.348	3	.231	0	-6	-5	-1	-0.3
● KEN ROWE	Rowe, Kenneth Darrell b: 12/31/33, Ferndale, Mich. BR/TR, 6'2", 185 lbs. Deb: 4/14/63 C																											
1963	LA-N	1	1	.500	14	0	0	0	1	27^2	28	16	2	1	11	12	13.0	2.93	103	.264	.339	0	.000	-1	1	0	-0	-0.1
1964	Bal-A	1	0	1.000	6	0	0	0	0	4^1	10	10	1	0	1	4	22.8	8.31	43	.455	.478	0	—	0	-2	-2	0	-0.4
1965	Bal-A	0	0	—	6	0	0	0	0	13^1	17	5	0	0	2	3	12.8	3.38	103	.321	.345	1	1.000	0	0	0	-1	0.0
Total	3	2	1	.667	26	0	0	0	1	45^1	55	31	3	1	14	19	13.9	3.57	90	.304	.357	1	.167	-0	-1	-2	-1	-0.5
● SCHOOLBOY ROWE	Rowe, Lynwood Thomas b: 1/11/10, Waco, Tex. d: 1/8/61, ElDorado, Ark. BR/TR, 6'4.5", 210 lbs. Deb: 4/15/33 C♦																											
1933	Det-A	7	4	.636	19	15	8	1	0	123^1	129	60	7	1	31	75	11.7	3.58	121	.269	.315	11	.220	-0	10	10	2	0.9
1934	*Det-A	24	8	.750	45	30	20	3	1	266	259	110	12	1	81	149	11.5	3.45	127	.256	.312	33	.303	12	31	28	-0	4.1
1935	*Det-A☆	19	13	.594	42	34	21	**6**	3	275^2	272	121	11	2	68	140	11.2	3.69	113	.255	**.301**	34	.312	14	23	16	-2	2.7
1936	Det-A★	19	10	.655	41	35	19	4	3	245^1	266	134	15	2	64	115	12.2	4.51	110	.275	.321	23	.256	7	14	12	2	2.0
1937	Det-A	1	4	.200	10	2	1	0	0	31^1	49	32	7	1	9	6	16.9	8.62	54	.350	.393	2	.200	-0	-14	-14	0	-1.6
1938	Det-A	0	2	.000	4	3	0	0	0	21	20	11	1	0	11	4	13.3	3.00	167	.256	.348	1	.167	-0	4	4	1	0.4
1939	Det-A	10	12	.455	28	24	8	1	0	164	192	113	17	2	61	51	14.0	4.99	98	.291	.353	15	.246	2	-7	-2	0	0.0
1940	*Det-A	16	3	**.842**	27	23	11	1	0	169	170	68	15	1	43	61	11.4	3.46	137	.259	.305	18	.269	5	17	22	-0	2.7
1941	Det-A	8	6	.571	27	14	4	0	1	139	155	70	6	0	33	54	12.2	4.14	110	.278	.318	15	.273	5	0	6	1	1.1
1942	Det-A	1	0	1.000	2	1	0	0	0	10^1	9	2	0	0	2	7	9.6	0.00	—	.220	.256	0	.000	-1	4	4	0	0.4
	Bro-N	1	0	1.000	9	2	0	0	0	30^1	36	19	2	1	12	6	14.5	5.34	61	.288	.355	4	.211	0	-7	-7	0	-0.3
1943	Phi-N	14	8	.636	27	25	11	3	1	199	196	73	7	3	29	52	10.3	2.94	115	.249	.279	36	.300	16	10	10	0	3.1
1946	Phi-N	11	4	.733	17	16	9	2	0	136	112	39	3	6	21	51	9.2	2.12	162	.224	.263	11	.180	2	20	20	-2	2.3
1947	Phi-N★	14	10	.583	31	28	15	1	1	195^2	232	106	22	3	45	74	12.9	4.32	93	.292	.333	22	.278	10	-6	-7	-1	0.1
1948	Phi-N	10	10	.500	30	20	8	0	2	148	167	74	5	2	31	46	12.2	4.07	97	.281	.319	10	.192	2	-2	-2	1	0.0
1949	Phi-N	3	7	.300	23	6	2	0	0	65^1	68	43	2	2	17	22	12.0	4.82	82	.300	.354	4	.235	2	-6	-7	1	-0.6
Total	15	158	101	.610	382	278	137	22	12	2219^1	2332	1075	132	27	558	913	11.8	3.87	110	.269	.315	239	.263	76	93	96	2	17.3
● MIKE ROWLAND	Rowland, Michael Evan b: 1/31/53, Chicago, Ill. BR/TR, 6'3", 205 lbs. Deb: 7/25/80																											
1980	SF-N	1	1	.500	19	0	0	0	0	27	20	8	2	1	8	8	9.7	2.33	152	.206	.274	0	—	0	4	4	-0	0.2
1981	SF-N	0	1	.000	9	1	0	0	0	15^2	13	7	1	1	6	8	11.5	3.45	100	.232	.317	1	1.000	0	0	-0	-0	0.0
Total	2	1	2	.333	28	1	0	0	0	42^2	33	15	3	2	14	16	10.3	2.74	128	.216	.290	1	1.000	0	4	4	-0	0.2
● CHARLIE ROY	Roy, Charles Robert b: 6/22/1884, Beaulieu, Minn. d: 2/10/50, Blackfoot, Idaho BR/TR, 5'10", 190 lbs. Deb: 6/27/06 F																											
1906	Phi-N	0	1	.000	7	1	0	0	0	18^1	24	12	0	1	5	6	14.7	4.91	53	.316	.366	0	.000	-1	-5	-5	-0	-0.4
● EMIL ROY	Roy, Emil Arthur b: 5/26/07, Brighton, Mass. d: 1/5/97, Crystal River, Fla. BR/TR, 5'11", 180 lbs. Deb: 9/30/33																											
1933	Phi-A	0	1	.000	1	1	0	0	0	2^1	4	7	0	0	4	3	30.9	27.00	16	.364	.533	0	—	0	-6	-6	-0	-0.8
● JEAN-PIERRE ROY	Roy, Jean-Pierre b: 6/26/20, Montreal, Que., Can. BB/TR, 5'10", 160 lbs. Deb: 5/5/46																											
1946	Bro-N	0	0	—	3	1	0	0	0	6^1	5	7	2	0	5	6	14.2	9.95	34	.200	.333	0	.000	-0	-5	-5	-0	-0.3
● LUTHER ROY	Roy, Luther Franklin b: 7/29/02, Ooltewah, Tenn. d: 7/24/63, Grand Rapids, Mich. BR/TR, 5'10.5", 161 lbs. Deb: 6/12/24 F																											
1924	Cle-A	0	5	.000	16	5	2	0	0	48^2	62	48	3	0	31	14	17.2	7.77	55	.318	.412	4	.267	-0	-19	-19	1	-1.5
1925	Cle-A	0	0	—	6	1	0	0	0	10	14	7	1	0	11	1	22.5	3.60	123	.368	.510	0	.000	-0	1	1	-0	0.0
1927	Chi-N	3	1	.750	11	0	0	0	0	19^2	14	9	0	1	11	5	11.9	2.29	169	.209	.329	1	.333	0	4	3	0	0.7
1929	Phi-N	3	6	.333	21	11	1	0	0	88^2	137	91	11	3	37	16	18.0	8.42	62	.350	.411	9	.281	2	-37	-29	1	-2.0
	Bro-N	0	0	—	2	0	0	0	0	3^2	4	2	0	0	2	0	14.7	4.91	94	.286	.375	0	.000	-0	-0	-0	0	0.0
	Yr	3	6	.333	23	11	1	0	0	92^1	141	93	11	3	39	16	17.8	8.29	62	.348	.409	9	.273	2	-37	-29	1	-2.0
Total	4	6	12	.333	56	17	3	0	0	170^2	231	157	15	4	92	36	17.2	7.17	66	.328	.408	14	.264	2	-51	-44	1	-2.8
● NORMIE ROY	Roy, Norman Brooks "Jumbo" b: 11/15/28, Newton, Mass. BR/TR, 6', 200 lbs. Deb: 4/23/50																											
1950	Bos-N	4	3	.571	19	6	2	0	1	59^2	72	38	6	2	39	25	17.0	5.13	75	.305	.408	3	.167	0	-7	-9	0	-0.9
● DICK ROZEK	Rozek, Richard Louis b: 3/27/27, Cedar Rapids, Iowa BL/TL, 6'0.5", 190 lbs. Deb: 4/29/50																											
1950	Cle-A	0	0	—	12	2	0	0	0	25^1	28	15	3	0	19	14	16.7	4.97	87	.283	.398	0	.000	-1	-1	-2	-1	-0.2
1951	Cle-A	0	0	—	7	1	0	0	0	15^1	18	12	1	1	11	5	17.6	2.93	129	.286	.400	1	.333	0	2	2	-1	0.0
1952	Cle-A	1	0	1.000	10	1	0	0	0	12^2	11	8	0	0	13	5	17.1	4.97	67	.224	.387	0	.000	-0	-2	-3	-0	-0.2
1953	Phi-A	0	0	—	2	0	0	0	0	10^2	8	6	3	0	9	2	14.3	5.06	85	.222	.378	0	.000	-0	-1	-1	-0	-0.1
1954	Phi-A	0	0	—	2	0	0	0	0	1^1	0	1	0	1	3	0	27.0	6.75	58	.000	.571	0	—	0	-0	-0	-0	0.0
Total	5	1	0	1.000	33	4	0	0	0	65^1	65	42	7	2	55	26	16.8	4.55	88	.260	.397	1	.083	-1	-3	-4	-2	-0.5
● DAVE ROZEMA	Rozema, David Scott b: 8/5/56, Grand Rapids, Mich. BR/TR, 6'4", 200 lbs. Deb: 4/11/77																											
1977	Det-A	15	7	.682	28	28	16	1	0	218^1	222	87	25	7	34	92	10.8	3.09	139	.265	.299	0	—	0	24	28	0	2.7
1978	Det-A	9	12	.429	28	28	11	2	0	209^1	205	83	17	2	41	57	10.7	3.14	124	.260	.298	0	—	0	15	17	-1	1.5
1979	Det-A	4	4	.500	16	16	4	1	0	97^1	101	52	12	6	30	33	12.7	3.51	124	.270	.334	0	—	0	8	9	0	0.7
1980	Det-A	6	9	.400	42	13	2	1	4	144^2	152	68	11	5	49	49	12.8	3.92	105	.277	.342	0	—	0	2	3	1	0.4
1981	Det-A	5	5	.500	28	9	2	2	3	104	99	42	12	3	25	46	11.0	3.63	104	.256	.306	0	—	0	0	2	-1	0.1
1982	Det-A	3	0	1.000	8	2	0	0	1	27^2	17	5	2	1	7	15	8.1	1.63	250	.179	.243	0	—	0	8	8	1	0.9
1983	Det-A	8	3	.727	29	16	1	0	2	105	100	50	10	1	29	63	11.1	3.43	114	.248	.300	0	—	0	8	6	1	0.7
1984	Det-A	7	6	.538	29	16	0	0	0	101	110	49	13	2	18	48	11.6	3.74	105	.274	.309	0	—	0	3	2	1	0.3
1985	Tex-A	3	7	.300	34	4	0	0	7	88	100	45	10	2	22	42	12.7	4.19	101	.287	.333	0	—	0	-0	0	1	0.1
1986	Tex-A	0	0	—	6	0	0	0	0	10^2	19	9	1	0	3	3	18.6	5.91	73	.404	.440	0	—	0	-2	-2	0	-0.1
Total	10	60	53	.531	248	132	36	7	17	1106	1125	490	113	29	258	448	11.5	3.47	117	.266	.313	0	—	0	64	73	3	7.3
● JORGE RUBIO	Rubio, Jorge Jesus (Chavez) b: 4/23/45, Mexicali, Mexico BR/TR, 6'3", 200 lbs. Deb: 4/21/66																											
1966	Cal-A	2	1	.667	7	4	1	1	0	27^1	22	10	2	1	16	27	12.8	2.96	113	.220	.333	0	.000	-1	1	1	-0	0.0
1967	Cal-A	0	2	.000	3	3	0	0	0	15	18	7	2	4	9	4	18.6	3.60	87	.316	.443	1	.333	1	-1	-1	0	0.0
Total	2	2	3	.400	10	7	1	1	0	42^1	40	17	4	5	25	31	14.9	3.19	103	.255	.374	1	.091	-0	1	0	-0	0.0
● DAVE RUCKER	Rucker, David Michael b: 9/1/57, San Bernardino, Cal BL/TL, 6'1", 190 lbs. Deb: 4/12/81																											
1981	Det-A	0	0	—	2	0	0	0	0	4	3	4	0	1	1	2	11.3	6.75	56	.188	.278	0	—	0	-1	-1	-0	-0.1
1982	Det-A	5	6	.455	27	4	1	0	0	64	62	26	4	2	23	31	12.2	3.38	121	.251	.320	0	—	0	5	5	0	0.8
1983	Det-A	1	2	.333	4	3	0	0	0	9	18	17	2	1	8	6	27.0	17.00	23	.419	.519	0	—	0	-13	-14	0	-2.0
	StL-N	5	3	.625	34	0	0	0	0	37	36	14	1	1	18	22	13.4	2.43	149	.263	.353	0	.000	-0	5	5	0	1.0
1984	StL-N	2	3	.400	50	0	0	0	0	73	62	23	0	1	34	38	12.0	2.10	166	.237	.327	1	.143	-0	12	12	-1	0.7
1985	Phi-N	3	2	.600	39	3	0	0	1	79^1	83	42	6	2	40	41	14.2	4.31	86	.279	.368	4	.333	2	-6	-5	0	-0.1
1986	Phi-N	0	2	.000	19	0	0	0	0	25	34	19	4	0	14	14	17.3	5.76	67	.340	.421	0	.000	-0	-6	-5	0	-0.4
1988	Pit-N	0	2	.000	31	0	0	0	0	28^1	39	19	2	0	9	16	15.2	4.76	72	.328	.375	0	.000	-0	-4	-4	-0	-0.3
Total	7	16	20	.444	206	10	1	0	1	319^2	337	164	19	8	147	170	13.9	3.94	94	.276	.357	5	.192	1	-8	-8	0	-0.4
● NAP RUCKER	Rucker, George b: 9/30/1884, Crabapple, Ga. d: 12/19/70, Alpharetta, Ga. BR/TL, 5'11", 190 lbs. Deb: 4/15/07																											
1907	Bro-N	15	13	.536	37	30	26	4	0	275^1	242	94	3	8	80	131	10.8	2.06	114	.242	.303	15	.155	-1	13	9	-1	0.8
1908	Bro-N	17	19	.472	42	37	30	6	1	333^1	265	107	1	19	125	199	11.0	2.08	113	.231	.317	21	.179	-1	11	10	4	1.5
1909	Bro-N	13	19	.406	38	33	28	6	1	309^1	245	95	6	14	101	201	10.5	2.24	116	.228	.303	12	.119	-5	12	12	-2	0.5
1910	Bro-N	17	18	.486	41	39	**27**	**6**	0	**320**^{1}	293	112	5	9	84	147	10.8	2.58	117	.251	.306	23	.209	-1	16	16	-2	1.3
1911	Bro-N	22	18	.550	48	33	23	5	4	315^2	255	102	12	8	110	190	10.6	2.71	123	.226	.300	21	.202	2	24	22	2	3.1
1912	Bro-N	18	21	.462	45	34	23	**6**	4	297^2	272	101	6	3	72	151	10.5	2.21	152	.250	.298	25	.245	2	40	38	2	**5.3**
1913	Bro-N	14	15	.483	41	33	16	4	3	260	236	99	3	7	67	111	10.7	2.87	115	.249	.304	21	.241	2	10	12	-4	1.1
1914	Bro-N	7	6	.538	16	16	5	0	0	103^2	113	57	2	2	27	35	12.3	3.39	84	.275	.323	9	.265	2	-7	-6	0	-0.5
1915	Bro-N	9	4	.692	19	15	7	1	1	122^2	134	42	3	2	28	38	12.0	2.42	115	.279	.322	9	.214	1	4	5	1	0.8

YEAR	TM/L	W	L	PCT	G	GS	CG	SH	SV	IP	H	R	HR	HB	BB	SO	RAT	ERA	ERA+	OAV	OOB	BH	AVG	PB	PR	PR+	PD	TPI
1916	*Bro-N	2	1	.667	9	3	1	0	0	37^1	34	14	0	1	7	14	10.1	1.69	159	.241	.282	1	.091	-1	4	4	0	0.2
Total	10	134	134	.500	336	273	186	38	14	2375^1	2089	823	41	73	701	1217	10.8	2.42	119	.243	.306	157	.195	1	127	122	1	14.1

● ERNIE RUDOLPH Rudolph, Ernest William b: 2/13/09, Black River Falls, Wis. BL/TR, 5'8", 165 lbs. Deb: 6/16/45

YEAR	TM/L	W	L	PCT	G	GS	CG	SH	SV	IP	H	R	HR	HB	BB	SO	RAT	ERA	ERA+	OAV	OOB	BH	AVG	PB	PR	PR+	PD	TPI
1945	Bro-N	1	0	1.000	7	0	0	0	0	8^2	12	10	1	0	7	3	19.7	5.19	72	.333	.442	0	—	1	-1	-1	0	-0.1

● DON RUDOLPH Rudolph, Frederick Donald b: 8/16/31, Baltimore, Md. d: 9/12/68, Granada Hills, Cal BL/TL, 5'11", 195 lbs. Deb: 9/21/57

YEAR	TM/L	W	L	PCT	G	GS	CG	SH	SV	IP	H	R	HR	HB	BB	SO	RAT	ERA	ERA+	OAV	OOB	BH	AVG	PB	PR	PR+	PD	TPI
1957	Chi-A	1	0	1.000	5	0	0	0	0	12	6	3	2	0	2	2	6.0	2.25	166	.146	.186	1	.500	1	2	2	-0	0.2
1958	Chi-A	1	0	1.000	7	0	0	0	1	7	4	2	0	0	5	2	11.6	2.57	141	.190	.346	0	—	0	1	1	0	0.2
1959	Chi-A	0	0	—	4	0	0	0	1	3	4	0	0	0	2	0	18.0	0.00	—	.333	.429	0	—	0	1	1	0	0.1
	Cin-N	0	0	—	5	0	0	0	0	7^1	13	4	1	0	3	8	19.6	4.91	83	.394	.444	0	.000	-0	-1	-1	0	0.0
1962	Cle-A	0	0	—	1	0	0	0	0	0^1	1	0	0	0	0	0	27.0	0.00	—	1.000	1.000	0	—	0	0	0	0	0.0
	Was-A	8	10	.444	37	23	6	2	0	176^1	187	84	13	3	42	68	11.8	3.62	111	.274	.319	10	.175	1	7	8	-1	0.8
	Yr	8	10	.444	38	23	6	2	0	176^2	188	84	13	3	42	68	11.9	3.62	112	.275	.320	10	.175	1	7	8	-1	0.8
1963	Was-A	7	19	.269	37	26	4	0	1	174	189	98	28	6	36	70	11.9	4.55	82	.275	.317	8	.178	2	-18	-16	-1	-2.1
1964	Was-A	1	3	.250	28	8	0	0	0	70^1	81	36	10	0	12	32	11.9	4.09	90	.290	.320	1	.067	-1	-4	-3	-0	-0.3
Total	6	18	32	.360	124	57	10	2	3	450^1	485	227	54	9	102	182	11.9	4.00	96	.276	.319	20	.167	3	-11	-8	-1	-1.1

● DICK RUDOLPH Rudolph, Richard "Baldy" b: 8/25/1887, New York, N.Y. d: 10/20/49, Bronx, N.Y. BR/TR (BB 1919-27), 5'9.5", 160 lbs. Deb: 9/30/10 MC

YEAR	TM/L	W	L	PCT	G	GS	CG	SH	SV	IP	H	R	HR	HB	BB	SO	RAT	ERA	ERA+	OAV	OOB	BH	AVG	PB	PR	PR+	PD	TPI
1910	NY-N	0	1	.000	3	1	1	0	2	12	21	11	0	0	2	9	17.3	7.50	40	.350	.371	1	.250	0	-6	-6	-0	-0.7
1911	NY-N	0	0	—	1	0	0	0	0	2	2	2	0	0	0	0	9.0	9.00	37	.250	.250	1	1.000	0	-1	-1	-0	0.0
1913	Bos-N	14	13	.519	33	22	17	2	0	249^1	258	101	4	2	59	109	11.5	2.92	112	.276	.320	21	.239	4	8	10	5	1.9
1914	*Bos-N	26	10	.722	42	36	31	6	0	336^1	288	105	9	4	61	138	**9.4**	2.35	117	.238	.276	15	.125	-1	16	15	2	1.7
1915	Bos-N	22	19	.537	44	43	30	3	1	341^1	304	125	4	6	64	147	9.9	2.37	109	.242	.282	23	.198	6	14	9	0	1.8
1916	Bos-N	19	12	.613	41	38	27	5	3	312	266	93	7	3	38	133	**8.9**	2.16	115	.235	**.261**	16	.158	1	16	12	6	2.0
1917	Bos-N	13	14	.481	31	30	22	5	0	242^2	252	104	1	4	54	96	11.5	3.41	75	.272	.314	20	.230	3	-19	-25	1	-2.3
1918	Bos-N	9	10	.474	21	20	15	3	0	154	144	63	2	0	30	48	10.2	2.57	104	.255	.292	10	.185	-1	3	2	1	0.3
1919	Bos-N	13	18	.419	37	32	24	2	2	273^2	282	95	2	3	54	76	11.1	2.17	132	.276	.314	17	.193	3	23	21	0	3.0
1920	Bos-N	4	8	.333	18	11	3	0	0	89	104	57	4	4	24	24	13.3	4.04	75	.294	.346	5	.185	-0	-9	-10	0	-1.3
1922	Bos-N	0	2	.000	3	3	1	0	0	16	22	10	2	0	5	3	15.2	5.06	79	.328	.375	2	.400	1	-2	-2	0	-0.2
1923	Bos-N	1	2	.333	4	4	1	1	0	19^1	27	12	0	1	10	3	17.7	3.72	107	.333	.413	0	.000	-1	1	1	0	0.0
1927	Bos-N	0	0	—	1	0	0	0	0	1^1	1	0	0	0	1	0	13.5	0.00	—	.200	.333	0	—	0	1	1	-0	0.0
Total	13	121	109	.526	279	240	172	27	8	2049	1971	778	35	27	402	786	10.5	2.66	104	.258	.298	131	.188	14	44	26	15	6.2

● MATT RUEBEL Ruebel, Matthew Alexander b: 10/16/69, Cincinnati, Ohio BL/TL, 6'2", 180 lbs. Deb: 5/21/96

YEAR	TM/L	W	L	PCT	G	GS	CG	SH	SV	IP	H	R	HR	HB	BB	SO	RAT	ERA	ERA+	OAV	OOB	BH	AVG	PB	PR	PR+	PD	TPI
1996	Pit-N	1	1	.500	26	7	0	0	1	58^2	64	38	7	6	25	22	14.6	4.60	95	.277	.363	3	.231	1	-2	-1	0	0.0
1997	Pit-N	3	2	.600	44	0	0	0	0	62^2	77	50	8	5	27	50	15.7	6.32	68	.301	.378	0	.000	-1	-15	-14	-0	-1.1
1998	TB-A	0	2	.000	7	1	0	0	0	8^2	11	7	3	0	4	6	15.6	6.23	77	.314	.385	0	—	0	-2	-1	-0	-0.3
Total	3	4	5	.444	77	8	0	0	1	130	152	95	18	11	56	78	15.2	5.54	79	.291	.372	3	.150	-0	-19	-17	-1	-1.4

● KIRK RUETER Rueter, Kirk Wesley b: 12/1/70, Hoyleton, Ill. BL/TL, 6'3", 195 lbs. Deb: 7/7/93

YEAR	TM/L	W	L	PCT	G	GS	CG	SH	SV	IP	H	R	HR	HB	BB	SO	RAT	ERA	ERA+	OAV	OOB	BH	AVG	PB	PR	PR+	PD	TPI
1993	Mon-N	8	0	1.000	14	14	1	0	0	85^2	85	33	5	0	18	31	10.8	2.73	153	.264	.303	2	.077	-1	13	13	2	1.2
1994	Mon-N	7	3	.700	20	20	0	0	0	92^1	106	60	11	2	23	50	12.8	5.17	82	.294	.340	4	.118	-1	-10	-10	0	-1.0
1995	Mon-N	5	3	.625	9	9	1	1	0	47^1	38	17	3	1	9	28	9.1	3.23	133	.224	.267	0	.000	-2	5	5	1	0.8
1996	Mon-N	5	6	.455	16	16	0	0	0	78^2	91	44	12	2	22	30	13.2	4.58	95	.294	.345	3	.120	-1	-3	-2	2	-0.1
	SF-N	1	2	.333	4	3	0	0	0	23^1	18	6	0	0	5	16	8.9	1.93	212	.207	.250	1	.143	0	6	6	-0	0.7
	Yr	6	8	.429	20	19	0	0	0	102	109	50	12	2	27	46	12.2	3.97	108	.275	.325	4	.125	-1	3	3	2	0.6
1997	*SF-N	13	6	.684	32	32	0	0	0	190^2	194	83	17	1	51	115	11.6	3.45	119	.264	.313	9	.138	-1	16	14	5	1.7
1998	SF-N	16	9	.640	33	33	1	0	0	187^2	193	100	27	7	57	102	12.3	4.36	91	.265	.324	14	.209	1	-3	-9	2	-0.7
1999	SF-N	15	10	.600	33	33	1	0	0	184^2	219	118	28	2	55	94	13.5	5.41	78	.297	.348	9	.155	1	-17	-27	1	-2.8
2000	*SF-N	11	9	.550	32	31	0	0	0	184	205	92	23	2	62	71	13.2	3.96	107	.290	.349	12	.200	2	14	6	3	1.1
Total	8	81	48	.628	193	191	4	1	0	1074^1	1149	553	126	17	302	537	12.3	4.16	100	.277	.328	54	.151	-1	21	0	16	0.9

● DUTCH RUETHER Ruether, Walter Henry b: 9/13/1893, Alameda, Cal. d: 5/16/70, Phoenix, Ariz. BL/TL, 6'1.5", 180 lbs. Deb: 4/13/17 ♦

YEAR	TM/L	W	L	PCT	G	GS	CG	SH	SV	IP	H	R	HR	HB	BB	SO	RAT	ERA	ERA+	OAV	OOB	BH	AVG	PB	PR	PR+	PD	TPI
1917	Chi-N	2	0	1.000	10	4	1	0	0	36^1	37	12	0	3	12	23	12.9	2.48	117	.285	.359	12	.273	2	1	2	1	0.4
	Cin-N	1	2	.333	7	4	1	1	0	35^2	43	17	0	2	14	12	14.9	3.53	74	.323	.396	5	.208	1	-3	-4	-0	-0.2
	Yr	3	2	.600	17	8	2	1	0	72	80	29	0	5	26	35	13.9	3.00	92	.304	.378	17	.250	3	-2	-2	0	0.2
1918	Cin-N	0	1	.000	2	2	1	0	0	10	10	9	0	1	3	10	12.6	2.70	99	.244	.311	0	.000	-0	0	-0	-0	-0.1
1919	*Cin-N	19	6	**.760**	33	29	20	3	0	242^2	195	69	1	7	83	78	10.6	1.82	153	.223	.295	24	.261	6	30	27	-3	3.3
1920	Cin-N	16	12	.571	37	33	23	5	3	265^2	235	87	2	9	96	99	11.5	2.47	123	.247	.321	20	.192	-1	20	17	0	1.8
1921	Bro-N	10	13	.435	36	27	12	1	2	211^1	247	116	7	7	67	78	13.7	4.26	91	.299	.356	34	.351	11	-11	-8	-1	0.2
1922	Bro-N	21	12	.636	35	35	26	2	0	267^1	290	123	11	6	92	89	13.1	3.53	115	.282	.345	26	.208	6	17	16	-0	2.2
1923	Bro-N	15	14	.517	34	34	20	0	0	275	308	157	11	6	86	87	13.1	4.22	92	.287	.343	32	.274	4	-7	-11	-2	-0.6
1924	Bro-N	8	13	.381	30	21	13	2	3	168	190	92	4	5	45	63	12.9	3.91	96	.282	.332	15	.242	2	-1	-3	1	0.0
1925	*Was-A	18	7	.720	30	29	16	1	0	223^1	241	105	5	8	105	68	14.3	3.87	109	.281	.365	36	.333	6	13	9	-3	1.7
1926	Was-A	12	6	.667	23	23	9	0	0	169^1	214	100	5	4	66	48	15.1	4.84	80	.311	.375	23	.250	4	-15	-19	-2	-1.5
	*NY-A	2	3	.400	5	5	1	0	0	36	32	14	0	1	18	8	12.8	3.50	110	.248	.345	2	.095	-2	2	1	-1	-0.1
	Yr	14	9	.609	28	28	10	0	0	205^1	246	114	5	5	84	56	14.7	4.60	84	.301	.370	25	.221	3	-13	-17	-3	-1.6
1927	NY-A	13	6	.684	27	26	12	3	0	184	202	88	8	7	52	45	12.8	3.38	114	.287	.343	21	.262	5	16	11	0	1.4
Total	11	137	95	.591	309	272	155	18	8	2124^2	2244	989	54	66	739	708	12.9	3.50	104	.277	.342	250	.258	45	60	37	-9	8.5

● SCOTT RUFFCORN Ruffcorn, Scott Patrick b: 12/29/69, Austin, Tex. BR/TR, 6'4", 210 lbs. Deb: 6/19/93

YEAR	TM/L	W	L	PCT	G	GS	CG	SH	SV	IP	H	R	HR	HB	BB	SO	RAT	ERA	ERA+	OAV	OOB	BH	AVG	PB	PR	PR+	PD	TPI
1993	Chi-A	0	2	.000	3	2	0	0	0	10	9	11	2	0	10	2	17.1	8.10	52	.265	.432	0	—	0	-4	-4	-1	-0.7
1994	Chi-A	0	2	.000	2	2	0	0	0	6^1	15	11	1	0	5	3	28.4	12.79	37	.455	.526	0	—	0	-6	-6	-0	-0.9
1995	Chi-A	0	0	—	4	0	0	0	0	8	10	7	0	2	13	5	28.1	7.88	57	.333	.556	0	—	0	-3	-3	0	-0.1
1996	Chi-A	0	1	.000	3	1	0	0	0	6^1	10	8	1	0	6	3	22.7	11.37	42	.370	.485	0	—	0	-4	-5	-0	-0.6
1997	Phi-N	0	3	.000	18	4	0	0	0	39^2	42	40	4	7	36	33	19.3	7.71	55	.275	.434	0	.000	-0	-15	-15	-1	-1.1
Total	5	0	8	.000	30	9	0	0	0	70^1	86	77	8	9	70	46	21.1	8.57	51	.310	.463	0	.000	-0	-33	-33	-1	-3.4

● BRUCE RUFFIN Ruffin, Bruce Wayne b: 10/4/63, Lubbock, Tex BB/TL, 6'2", 209 lbs. Deb: 6/28/86

YEAR	TM/L	W	L	PCT	G	GS	CG	SH	SV	IP	H	R	HR	HB	BB	SO	RAT	ERA	ERA+	OAV	OOB	BH	AVG	PB	PR	PR+	PD	TPI
1986	Phi-N	9	4	.692	21	21	6	0	0	146^1	138	53	6	1	44	70	11.3	2.46	157	.251	.308	4	.073	-3	21	22	-1	1.4
1987	Phi-N	11	14	.440	35	35	3	1	0	204^2	236	118	17	2	73	93	13.7	4.35	98	.298	.359	4	.055	-5	-6	-2	-1	-0.8
1988	Phi-N	6	10	.375	55	15	3	0	3	144^1	151	86	7	3	80	82	14.6	4.43	81	.275	.370	4	.121	-0	-16	-13	1	-1.4
1989	Phi-N	6	10	.375	24	23	1	0	0	125^2	152	69	10	0	62	70	15.3	4.44	80	.301	.377	6	.176	2	-13	-12	2	-1.0
1990	Phi-N	6	13	.316	32	25	2	1	0	149	178	99	14	1	62	79	14.6	5.38	71	.297	.364	3	.068	-2	-26	-25	0	-3.0
1991	Phi-N	4	7	.364	31	15	1	1	0	119	125	52	6	1	38	85	12.4	3.78	97	.272	.329	0	.000	-1	-1	-2	-0	-0.3
1992	Mil-A	1	6	.143	25	6	1	0	0	58	66	43	7	0	41	45	16.6	6.67	58	.293	.402	0	—	0	-18	-19	-0	-2.0
1993	Col-N	6	5	.545	59	12	0	0	2	139^2	145	71	10	1	69	126	13.9	3.87	124	.269	.352	2	.080	-1	3	12	-0	0.8
1994	Col-N	4	5	.444	56	0	0	0	16	55^2	55	28	6	1	30	65	13.9	4.04	123	.253	.347	1	.250	0	1	5	1	1.1
1995	*Col-N	0	1	.000	37	0	0	0	11	34	26	8	1	0	19	23	11.9	2.12	255	.222	.331	0	.000	-0	8	10	0	0.8
1996	Col-N	7	5	.583	71	0	0	0	24	69^2	55	35	5	0	29	74	10.9	4.00	130	.212	.291	0	.000	0	2	8	0	1.5
1997	Col-N	0	2	.000	23	0	0	0	7	22	18	15	3	0	18	31	14.7	5.32	97	.220	.360	0	—	0	-3	-0	0	0.0
Total	12	60	82	.423	469	152	17	3	63	1268	1345	677	92	10	565	843	13.6	4.19	98	.275	.351	24	.081	-10	-48	-11	1	-2.9

● JOHNNY RUFFIN Ruffin, Johnny Renando b: 7/29/71, Butler, Ala. BR/TR, 6'3", 172 lbs. Deb: 8/8/93

YEAR	TM/L	W	L	PCT	G	GS	CG	SH	SV	IP	H	R	HR	HB	BB	SO	RAT	ERA	ERA+	OAV	OOB	BH	AVG	PB	PR	PR+	PD	TPI
1993	Cin-N	2	1	.667	21	0	0	0	2	37^2	36	16	4	1	11	30	11.5	3.58	112	.247	.304	1	.333	0	2	2	0	0.2
1994	Cin-N	7	2	.778	51	0	0	0	1	70	57	26	7	0	27	44	10.8	3.09	134	.223	.297	0	.000	-1	9	8	-1	0.8
1995	Cin-N	0	0	—	10	0	0	0	0	13^1	4	3	0	0	11	11	10.1	1.35	305	.093	.278	0	.000	-0	4	4	0	0.2
1996	Cin-N	1	3	.250	49	0	0	0	0	62^1	71	42	10	2	37	69	15.9	5.49	77	.292	.390	2	.500	1	-9	-9	-0	-0.5
2000	Ari-N	0	0	—	5	0	0	0	0	9	14	9	4	0	3	5	17.0	9.00	51	.350	.395	0	—	0	-4	-4	0	-0.2
Total	5	10	6	.625	136	0	0	0	3	192^1	182	96	25	3	89	159	12.8	4.12	101	.250	.334	3	.176	-0	2	1	-1	0.5

● RED RUFFING

Ruffing, Charles Herbert b: 5/3/04, Granville, Ill. d: 2/17/86, Mayfield Hts., O. BR/TR, 6'1.5", 205 lbs. Deb: 5/31/24 CH♦

YEAR	TM/L	W	L	PCT	G	GS	CG	SH	SV	IP	H	R	HR	HB	BB	SO	RAT	ERA	ERA+	OAV	OOB	BH	AVG	PB	PR	PR+	PD	TPI
1924	Bos-A	0	0	—	8	2	0	0	0	23	29	17	0	3	9	10	16.0	6.65	66	.333	.414	1	.143	-0	-6	-6	-1	-0.3
1925	Bos-A	9	18	.333	37	27	13	3	1	217^1	253	135	10	2	75	64	13.7	5.01	91	.299	.357	17	.215	-0	-15	-11	-1	-1.2
1926	Bos-A	6	15	.286	37	22	6	0	2	166	169	96	4	5	68	58	13.1	4.39	93	.274	.351	10	.196	0	-7	-6	-1	-0.7
1927	Bos-A	5	13	.278	26	18	10	0	2	158^1	160	94	7	4	87	77	14.3	4.66	91	.277	.375	14	.255	1	-9	-8	0	-0.6
1928	Bos-A	10	25	.286	42	34	**25**	1	2	289^1	303	147	8	10	96	118	12.7	3.89	106	.275	.339	38	.314	11	5	7	-3	1.7
1929	Bos-A	9	22	.290	35	32	18	1	1	244^1	280	162	17	2	118	109	14.7	4.86	88	.297	.376	35	.307	5	-17	-16	-1	-1.0
1930	Bos-A	0	3	.000	4	3	1	0	0	24	32	19	1	1	6	14	14.6	6.38	72	.323	.368	3	.273	1	-5	-5	-1	-0.5
	NY-A	15	5	.750	34	25	12	2	1	197^2	200	106	10	2	62	117	12.0	4.14	104	.260	.317	37	.374	17	11	4	-2	1.6
	Yr	15	8	.652	38	28	13	2	1	221^2	232	125	11	3	68	131	12.3	4.38	99	.268	.323	40	.364	18	7	-1	-3	1.1
1931	NY-A	16	14	.533	37	30	19	1	2	237	240	130	11	6	87	132	12.6	4.41	90	.256	.323	36	.330	11	-1	-13	-3	-0.5
1932	*NY-A	18	7	.720	35	29	22	3	2	259	219	102	16	3	115	**190**	11.7	3.09	132	**.226**	.311	38	.306	14	40	31	-2	3.8
1933	NY-A	9	14	.391	35	28	18	0	3	235	230	118	7	4	93	122	12.5	3.91	99	.258	.330	29	.252	8	10	-1	-0	0.7
1934	NY-A★	19	11	.633	36	31	19	5	0	256^1	232	134	18	1	104	149	11.8	3.93	103	.236	.310	28	.248	7	16	4	-3	0.7
1935	NY-A	16	11	.593	30	29	19	2	0	222	201	88	17	1	76	81	11.3	3.12	130	.239	.303	37	.339	14	33	25	-2	3.8
1936	*NY-A	20	12	.625	33	33	25	3	0	271	274	133	22	3	90	102	12.2	3.85	121	.263	.323	37	.291	16	36	26	2	4.1
1937	*NY-A	20	7	.741	31	31	22	4	0	256^1	242	101	17	1	68	131	10.9	2.98	149	.247	.296	26	.202	3	47	43	-4	3.8
1938	*NY-A☆	**21**	7	**.750**	31	31	22	3	0	247^1	246	104	16	0	82	127	11.9	3.31	137	.258	.317	24	.224	10	**41**	35	-2	**4.2**
1939	*NY-A★	21	7	.750	28	28	22	**5**	0	233^1	211	88	15	2	75	95	11.1	2.93	149	.240	.301	35	.307	9	44	39	-2	4.9
1940	NY-A★	15	12	.556	30	30	20	3	0	226	218	98	24	3	76	97	11.8	3.38	119	.252	.314	11	.124	-3	25	18	-3	1.3
1941	*NY-A☆	15	6	.714	23	23	13	2	0	185^2	177	87	13	1	54	60	11.2	3.54	111	.252	.306	27	.303	12	13	9	-3	1.7
1942	*NY-A☆	14	7	.667	24	24	16	4	0	193^2	183	72	10	3	41	80	10.5	3.21	107	.250	.292	20	.250	7	10	5	-2	1.0
1945	NY-A	7	3	.700	11	11	8	1	0	87^1	85	32	2	1	20	24	10.9	2.89	120	.251	.294	10	.217	1	5	5	-2	0.5
1946	NY-A	5	1	.833	8	8	4	2	0	61	37	13	2	0	23	19	8.9	1.77	195	.171	.251	3	.120	-1	12	12	-1	0.9
1947	Chi-A	3	5	.375	9	9	1	0	0	53	63	39	7	0	16	11	13.4	6.11	60	.290	.339	5	.208	-0	-14	-15	-0	-1.9
Total	22	273	225	.548	624	538	335	45	16	4344	4284	2115	254	58	1541	1987	12.2	3.80	109	.258	.323	521	.269	143	272	182	-34	28.0

● VERN RUHLE

Ruhle, Vernon Gerald b: 1/25/51, Coleman, Mich. BR/TR, 6'1", 187 lbs. Deb: 9/9/74 C

YEAR	TM/L	W	L	PCT	G	GS	CG	SH	SV	IP	H	R	HR	HB	BB	SO	RAT	ERA	ERA+	OAV	OOB	BH	AVG	PB	PR	PR+	PD	TPI
1974	Det-A	2	0	1.000	5	3	1	0	0	33	35	13	1	1	6	10	11.5	2.73	140	.273	.311	0	—	0	3	4	-1	0.2
1975	Det-A	11	12	.478	32	31	8	3	0	190	199	104	17	7	65	67	12.8	4.03	100	.266	.330	0	—	0	-5	0	-2	-0.2
1976	Det-A	9	12	.429	32	32	5	1	0	199^2	227	99	19	4	59	88	13.1	3.92	95	.288	.340	0	—	0	-9	-4	-0	-0.5
1977	Det-A	3	5	.375	14	10	0	0	0	66^1	83	44	9	3	15	27	13.7	5.70	75	.305	.348	0	—	0	-12	-10	-1	-1.1
1978	Hou-N	3	3	.500	13	10	2	2	0	68	57	17	0	1	20	27	10.3	2.12	156	.224	.283	1	.056	-1	11	10	-1	0.7
1979	Hou-N	2	6	.250	13	10	2	2	0	66^1	64	33	9	2	8	33	10.0	4.07	86	.249	.277	1	.053	-1	-2	-4	-1	-0.7
1980	*Hou-N	12	4	.750	28	22	6	2	0	159^1	148	51	7	3	29	55	10.2	2.37	139	.251	.289	12	.245	4	22	18	-2	2.1
1981	*Hou-N	4	6	.400	20	15	1	0	1	102	97	36	6	1	20	39	10.4	2.91	113	.250	.289	6	.250	3	7	5	-2	0.6
1982	Hou-N	9	13	.409	31	21	3	2	1	149	169	81	12	4	24	56	11.9	3.93	85	.289	.321	4	.098	-0	-5	-11	-1	-1.6
1983	Hou-N	8	5	.615	41	9	0	0	3	114^2	107	49	13	3	36	43	11.5	3.69	92	.249	.312	2	.105	0	-1	-4	0	-0.4
1984	Hou-N	1	9	.100	40	6	0	0	2	90^1	112	58	5	3	29	60	14.3	4.58	73	.309	.365	1	.083	0	-10	-14	1	-1.4
1985	Cle-A	2	10	.167	42	16	1	0	3	125	139	65	16	2	30	54	12.3	4.32	96	.283	.326	0	—	0	-2	-3	-0	-0.3
1986	*Cal-A	1	3	.250	16	3	0	0	1	47^2	46	25	5	1	7	23	10.2	4.15	99	.247	.278	0	—	0	0	-0	1	0.0
Total	13	67	88	.432	327	188	29	12	11	1411^1	1483	675	119	35	348	582	11.9	3.73	97	.270	.318	27	.148	6	-4	-15	-8	-2.6

● SEAN RUNYAN

Runyan, Sean David b: 6/21/74, Fort Smith, Ark. BL/TL, 6'3", 200 lbs. Deb: 3/31/98

YEAR	TM/L	W	L	PCT	G	GS	CG	SH	SV	IP	H	R	HR	HB	BB	SO	RAT	ERA	ERA+	OAV	OOB	BH	AVG	PB	PR	PR+	PD	TPI
1998	Det-A	1	4	.200	**88**	0	0	0	1	50^1	47	23	7	2	28	39	13.8	3.58	132	.255	.360	0	—	0	6	6	-1	0.4
1999	Det-A	0	1	.000	12	0	0	0	0	10^2	9	4	2	1	3	6	11.0	3.38	144	.237	.310	0	—	0	2	2	0	0.2
2000	Det-A	0	0	—	3	0	0	0	0	3	2	2	0	0	2	1	12.0	6.00	80	.222	.364	0	—	0	-0	-0	0	0.0
Total	3	1	5	.167	103	0	0	0	1	64	58	29	9	3	33	46	13.2	3.66	130	.251	.352	0	—	0	7	8	-1	0.6

● RYAN RUPE

Rupe, Ryan Kittman b: 3/31/75, Houston, Tex. BR/TR, 6'6", 240 lbs. Deb: 5/5/99

YEAR	TM/L	W	L	PCT	G	GS	CG	SH	SV	IP	H	R	HR	HB	BB	SO	RAT	ERA	ERA+	OAV	OOB	BH	AVG	PB	PR	PR+	PD	TPI
1999	TB-A	8	9	.471	24	24	0	0	0	142^1	136	81	17	12	57	97	13.0	4.55	109	.253	.338	0	.000	-0	5	7	-1	0.5
2000	TB-A	5	6	.455	18	18	0	0	0	91	121	75	19	9	31	61	15.9	6.92	72	.321	.386	0	.000	-0	-20	-20	-1	-1.9
Total	2	13	15	.464	42	42	0	0	0	233^1	257	156	36	21	88	158	14.1	5.48	91	.281	.358	0	.000	-1	-15	-13	-2	-1.4

● GLENDON RUSCH

Rusch, Glendon James b: 11/7/74, Seattle, Wash. BL/TL, 6'2", 170 lbs. Deb: 4/6/97

YEAR	TM/L	W	L	PCT	G	GS	CG	SH	SV	IP	H	R	HR	HB	BB	SO	RAT	ERA	ERA+	OAV	OOB	BH	AVG	PB	PR	PR+	PD	TPI
1997	KC-A	6	9	.400	30	27	1	0	0	170^1	206	111	28	7	52	116	14.0	5.50	86	.301	.357	0	.000	-0	-17	-14	-2	-1.3
1998	KC-A	6	15	.286	29	24	1	1	1	154^2	191	104	22	4	50	94	14.3	5.88	82	.304	.359	0	.000	-0	-21	-17	0	-2.0
1999	KC-A	0	1	.000	3	0	0	0	0	4	7	7	1	1	3	4	24.8	15.75	32	.368	.478	0	—	0	-5	-5	-0	-0.8
	NY-N	0	0	—	1	0	0	0	0	1	1	0	0	0	0	0	9.0	0.00	—	.333	.333	0	—	0	1	1	0	0.0
2000	*NY-N	11	11	.500	31	30	2	0	0	190^2	196	91	18	6	44	157	11.6	4.01	110	.267	.313	3	.060	-3	13	9	-0	0.6
Total	4	23	36	.390	94	81	4	1	1	520^2	601	313	69	18	149	371	13.3	5.13	90	.290	.343	3	.054	-4	-30	-28	-2	-3.5

● ANDY RUSH

Rush, Jesse Howard b: 12/26/1889, Longton, Kan. d: 3/16/69, Fresno, Cal. BR/TR, 6'3", 180 lbs. Deb: 4/16/25

YEAR	TM/L	W	L	PCT	G	GS	CG	SH	SV	IP	H	R	HR	HB	BB	SO	RAT	ERA	ERA+	OAV	OOB	BH	AVG	PB	PR	PR+	PD	TPI
1925	Bro-N	0	1	.000	4	2	0	0	0	9^2	16	14	3	0	5	4	19.6	9.31	45	.364	.429	0	.000	-0	-5	-6	0	-0.5

● BOB RUSH

Rush, Robert Ransom b: 12/21/25, Battle Creek, Mich BR/TR, 6'4", 205 lbs. Deb: 4/22/48

YEAR	TM/L	W	L	PCT	G	GS	CG	SH	SV	IP	H	R	HR	HB	BB	SO	RAT	ERA	ERA+	OAV	OOB	BH	AVG	PB	PR	PR+	PD	TPI
1948	Chi-N	5	11	.313	36	16	4	0	0	133^1	153	70	8	1	37	72	12.9	3.92	100	.287	.335	5	.128	-2	1	-0	1	-0.1
1949	Chi-N	10	18	.357	35	27	9	1	4	201	197	104	10	0	79	80	12.4	4.07	99	.255	.324	2	.032	-7	-1	-1	1	-0.7
1950	Chi-N☆	13	20	.394	39	34	19	1	1	254^2	261	124	11	6	93	93	12.7	3.71	113	.265	.332	15	.167	-1	12	14	2	1.8
1951	Chi-N	11	12	.478	37	29	12	2	2	211^1	212	108	16	3	68	129	12.1	3.83	107	.254	.312	13	.191	-0	3	6	1	0.7
1952	Chi-N★	17	13	.567	34	32	17	4	0	250^1	205	99	14	6	81	157	10.5	2.70	143	.216	.282	28	.292	7	29	31	2	**4.8**
1953	Chi-N	9	14	.391	29	28	8	1	0	166^2	177	97	17	5	66	84	13.4	4.54	98	.270	.341	6	.111	-2	-5	-2	1	-0.3
1954	Chi-N	13	15	.464	33	32	11	0	0	236^1	213	102	12	5	103	124	12.2	3.77	111	.243	.326	23	.277	7	8	11	3	2.3
1955	Chi-N	13	11	.542	33	33	14	3	0	234	204	95	19	2	73	130	10.7	3.50	117	.234	.295	9	.110	-3	14	15	1	1.2
1956	Chi-N	13	10	.565	32	32	13	1	0	239^2	210	101	30	2	59	104	10.2	3.19	118	.233	.282	8	.098	-3	15	15	-2	0.9
1957	Chi-N	6	16	.273	31	29	5	0	0	205^1	211	111	16	2	66	103	12.2	4.38	88	.265	.323	14	.203	2	-12	-12	-2	-1.1
1958	*Mil-N	10	6	.625	28	20	5	2	0	147^1	142	59	13	1	31	84	10.6	3.42	103	.253	.293	9	.200	2	9	2	-2	0.2
1959	Mil-N	5	6	.455	31	9	1	1	0	101^1	102	39	5	1	23	64	11.2	2.40	148	.257	.299	6	.188	0	17	14	-1	1.4
1960	Mil-N	2	0	1.000	10	0	0	0	1	15	24	9	2	0	5	8	17.4	4.20	82	.369	.414	1	.333	1	-1	-1	-0	-0.1
	Chi-A	0	0	—	9	0	0	0	0	14^1	16	10	4	0	5	12	13.2	5.65	67	.302	.362	1	1.000	0	-3	-3	0	-0.1
Total	13	127	152	.455	417	321	118	16	8	2410^2	2327	1128	177	34	789	1244	11.8	3.65	109	.251	.313	140	.173	0	88	90	7	10.9

● AMOS RUSIE

Rusie, Amos Wilson "The Hoosier Thunderbolt" b: 5/30/1871, Mooresville, Ind. d: 12/6/42, Seattle, Wash. BR/TR, 6'1", 200 lbs. Deb: 5/9/1889 H

YEAR	TM/L	W	L	PCT	G	GS	CG	SH	SV	IP	H	R	HR	HB	BB	SO	RAT	ERA	ERA+	OAV	OOB	BH	AVG	PB	PR	PR+	PD	TPI
1889	Ind-N	12	10	.545	33	22	19	1	0	225	246	181	12	9	116	109	14.8	5.32	78	.270	.358	18	.175	-3	-33	-28	-2	-2.4
1890	NY-N	29	34	.460	67	62	56	4	1	548^2	436	300	3	26	289	**341**	12.3	2.56	137	**.212**	.316	79	.278	10	62	59	6	**7.0**
1891	NY-N	33	20	.623	61	57	52	**6**	1	500^1	391	244	6	18	262	**337**	12.1	2.55	125	**.207**	.310	54	.245	4	44	38	2	3.8
1892	NY-N	32	31	.508	65	62	59	2	0	541	410	290	7	12	270	304	11.5	2.84	113	.202	.299	55	.215	0	27	23	6	2.8
1893	NY-N	33	21	.611	**56**	52	**50**	**4**	1	**482**	451	260	15	16	218	**208**	12.8	3.23	144	**.240**	.324	57	.269	3	**77**	**76**	3	**7.2**
1894	*NY-N	**36**	13	.735	54	50	45	**3**	1	444	426	228	10	5	200	**195**	**12.8**	**2.78**	**189**	**.250**	**.331**	52	.280	2	126	124	8	**11.1**
1895	NY-N	23	23	.500	49	47	42	**4**	0	393^1	384	248	9	7	159	**201**	12.6	3.73	124	.252	.325	44	.246	-5	46	41	3	3.4
1897	NY-N	28	10	.737	38	37	35	2	0	322^1	314	143	6	10	87	135	11.5	**2.54**	163	.253	.308	40	.278	3	63	60	2	6.3
1898	NY-N	20	11	.645	37	36	33	4	1	300	288	149	6	9	103	114	12.0	3.03	115	.251	.317	29	.210	-1	19	16	-0	1.2
1901	Cin-N	0	1	.000	3	2	2	0	0	22	43	25	1	0	3	6	18.8	8.59	37	.406	.422	1	.125	-0	-13	-14	0	-0.6
Total	10	246	174	.586	463	427	393	30	5	3778^2	3389	2068	75	112	1707	1950	12.4	3.07	130	.234	.319	429	.248	13	418	391	27	39.8

● SCOTT RUSKIN

Ruskin, Scott Drew b: 6/8/63, Jacksonville, Fla. BR/TL, 6'2", 185 lbs. Deb: 4/9/90

YEAR	TM/L	W	L	PCT	G	GS	CG	SH	SV	IP	H	R	HR	HB	BB	SO	RAT	ERA	ERA+	OAV	OOB	BH	AVG	PB	PR	PR+	PD	TPI
1990	Pit-N	2	2	.500	44	0	0	0	2	47^2	50	21	2	2	28	34	15.1	3.02	120	.269	.370	2	.333	2	4	3	0	0.5
	Mon-N	1	0	1.000	23	0	0	0	0	27^2	25	7	2	0	10	23	11.4	2.28	160	.243	.310	0	.000	-0	5	4	0	0.3
	Yr	3	2	.600	67	0	0	0	2	75^1	75	28	4	2	38	57	13.7	2.75	132	.260	.350	2	.250	1	9	8	0	0.8
1991	Mon-N	4	4	.500	64	0	0	0	6	63^2	57	31	4	3	30	46	12.7	4.24	85	.241	.333	0	.000	0	-4	-4	-0	-0.6
1992	Cin-N	4	3	.571	57	0	0	0	0	53^2	56	31	6	1	20	43	12.9	5.03	72	.275	.342	0	.000	-0	-9	-8	0	-1.0

YEAR TM/L	W	L	PCT	G	GS	CG	SH	SV	IP	H	R	HR	HB	BB	SO	RAT	ERA	ERA+	OAV	OOB	BH	AVG	PB	PR	PR+	PD	TPI
1993 Cin-N	0	0	—	4	0	0	0	0	1	3	2	1	0	2	0	45.0	18.00	22	.500	.625	0	—	0	-2	-2	0	-0.1
Total 4	11	9	.550	192	0	0	0	8	193^2	191	92	15	6	90	146	13.3	3.95	92	.260	.345	2	.154	1	-6	-7	1	-0.9
● JOHN RUSS Russ, John b: 4/1/1858, Cannelton, Ind. d: 1/18/12, Louisville, Ky. Deb: 7/4/1882 ♦																											
1882 Bal-a	0	0	—	1	0	0	0	0	3	3	1	0		1	0	12.0	3.00	92	.250	.308	1	.333	0	-0	-0	-0	0.0
● ALLAN RUSSELL Russell, Allan E. "Rubberarm" b: 7/31/1893, Baltimore, Md. d: 10/20/72, Baltimore, Md. BB/TR, 5'11", 165 lbs. Deb: 9/13/15 F																											
1915 NY-A	1	2	.333	5	3	1	0	0	27	21	10	1	1	21	21	14.3	2.67	110	.228	.377	2	.250	0	1	1	-0	0.1
1916 NY-A	6	10	.375	34	19	8	1	6	171^1	138	83	8	7	75	104	11.6	3.20	90	.232	.324	2	.044	-3	-7	-6	0	-0.9
1917 NY-A	7	8	.467	25	10	6	0	2	104^1	89	42	3	7	39	55	11.6	2.24	120	.236	.319	10	.323	3	5	5	-1	1.1
1918 NY-A	7	11	.389	27	18	7	2	4	141	139	68	6	5	73	54	13.9	3.26	87	.267	.363	7	.167	-1	-7	-7	-1	-1.1
1919 NY-A	5	5	.500	23	9	4	1	1	90^2	89	48	6	2	32	50	12.2	3.47	92	.251	.317	7	.233	0	-2	-3	0	-0.2
Bos-A	10	4	.714	21	11	9	1	4	121^1	105	38	0	1	39	63	10.8	2.52	120	.246	.310	5	.122	-1	10	7	-1	0.6
Yr	15	9	.625	44	20	13	2	**5**	212	194	86	6	3	71	113	11.4	2.93	106	.248	.313	12	.169	-1	7	4	-0	0.4
1920 Bos-A	5	6	.455	16	10	7	0	1	107^2	100	44	3	3	38	53	11.8	3.01	121	.251	.321	5	.122	-2	9	8	1	0.6
1921 Bos-A	6	11	.353	39	14	7	0	3	173	204	92	10	9	77	60	15.1	4.11	103	.303	.382	7	.123	-5	3	2	0	-0.3
1922 Bos-A	6	7	.462	34	11	1	0	2	125^2	152	81	6	5	57	34	15.3	5.01	82	.314	.392	3	.079	-3	-14	-12	2	-1.2
1923 Was-A	10	7	.588	52	5	4	0	**9**	181^1	177	81	9	2	77	67	12.7	3.03	124	.270	.348	10	.200	2	19	16	-3	1.3
1924 *Was-A	5	1	.833	37	0	0	0	8	82^1	83	49	1	1	45	17	14.1	4.37	92	.282	.379	5	.278	2	-1	-3	-0	-0.1
1925 Was-A	2	4	.333	32	2	0	0	2	68^2	85	57	6	1	37	25	16.1	5.77	73	.315	.399	2	.143	-1	-10	-12	2	-0.9
Total 11	70	76	.479	345	112	54	5	42	1394^1	1382	693	59	44	610	603	13.1	3.52	99	.269	.351	65	.157	-10	5	-4	-0	-1.0
● LEFTY RUSSELL Russell, Clarence Dickson b: 7/8/1890, Baltimore, Md. d: 1/22/62, Baltimore, Md. BL/TL, 6'1", 165 lbs. Deb: 10/1/10 F																											
1910 Phi-A	1	0	1.000	1	1	1	1	0	9	8	0	0	0	2	5	10.0	0.00	—	.258	.303	0	.000	-0	3	3	0	0.3
1911 Phi-A	0	3	.000	7	2	0	0	0	31^2	45	32	1	5	18	7	19.3	7.67	41	.357	.456	5	.385	1	-15	-17	1	-1.1
1912 Phi-A	0	2	.000	5	2	1	0	0	17^1	18	18	1	3	14	9	18.2	7.27	42	.265	.412	0	.000	-0	-8	-9	0	-0.8
Total 3	1	5	.167	13	5	2	1	0	58	71	50	2	8	34	21	17.5	6.36	47	.316	.423	5	.250	0	-20	-23	1	-1.6
● REB RUSSELL Russell, Ewell Albert b: 4/12/1889, Jackson, Miss. d: 9/30/73, Indianapolis, Ind BL/TL, 5'11", 185 lbs. Deb: 4/18/13 ♦																											
1913 Chi-A	22	16	.579	**52**	36	26	8	4	316^2	250	89	2	7	79	122	9.5	1.90	154	.219	.273	20	.189	3	36	36	-5	4.2
1914 Chi-A	7	12	.368	38	23	8	1	1	167^1	168	80	3	3	33	79	11.0	2.90	92	.268	.308	17	.266	4	-3	-4	0	-0.1
1915 Chi-A	11	10	.524	41	25	10	3	2	229^1	215	90	0	6	47	90	10.5	2.59	115	.249	.292	21	.244	4	9	10	-2	1.1
1916 Chi-A	18	11	.621	56	25	16	5	3	264^1	207	88	1	1	42	112	**8.5**	2.42	114	.220	**.254**	13	.143	-4	12	10	-2	0.6
1917 *Chi-A	15	5	**.750**	35	24	11	5	3	189^1	170	61	1	1	32	54	9.6	1.95	136	.245	.279	19	.279	5	15	15	-1	2.2
1918 Chi-A	7	5	.583	19	15	10	2	0	124^2	117	45	0	0	33	38	10.8	2.60	105	.252	.302	7	.140	-1	2	2	-1	-0.2
1919 Chi-A	0	0	—	1	0	0	0	0	0	1	0	0	1		—	—	—	1.000	1.000	99	—	0	0	0	0	0.0	
Total 7	80	59	.576	242	148	81	24	13	1291^2	1128	453	7	18	267	495	9.8	2.33	120	.238	.281	262	.268	10	72	69	-11	7.8
● JACK RUSSELL Russell, Jack Erwin b: 10/24/05, Paris, Tex. d: 11/3/90, Clearwater, Fla. BR/TR, 6'1.5", 178 lbs. Deb: 5/5/26																											
1926 Bos-A	0	5	.000	36	5	1	0	0	98	94	40	2	1	24	17	10.9	3.58	114	.268	.316	4	.190	-0	5	5	4	0.6
1927 Bos-A	4	9	.308	34	15	4	1	0	147	172	80	5	5	40	25	13.3	4.10	103	.298	.348	6	.125	-3	1	2	1	0.0
1928 Bos-A	11	14	.440	32	26	10	2	0	201^1	233	102	6	4	41	27	12.4	3.84	107	.294	.332	13	.210	-0	4	6	1	0.7
1929 Bos-A	6	18	.250	35	32	13	0	0	227^1	263	132	12	3	40	37	12.1	3.92	109	.290	.322	9	.129	-4	8	9	4	0.8
1930 Bos-A	9	20	.310	35	30	15	0	0	229^2	302	162	11	3	53	35	14.0	5.45	85	.321	.359	14	.177	-3	-20	-22	2	-2.2
1931 Bos-A	10	18	.357	36	31	13	0	0	232	298	145	7	2	65	45	14.2	5.16	83	.310	.355	16	.195	-0	-20	-22	3	-1.9
1932 Bos-A	1	7	.125	11	6	1	0	0	39^2	61	35	2	0	15	7	17.2	6.81	66	.343	.394	1	.091	-1	-10	-10	0	-1.7
Cle-A	5	7	.417	18	11	6	0	1	113	146	67	5	1	27	27	13.9	4.70	101	.310	.349	12	.300	2	-3	1	1	0.4
Yr	6	14	.300	29	17	7	0	1	152^2	207	102	7	1	42	34	14.7	5.25	89	.319	.361	13	.255	1	-13	-9	2	-1.3
1933 *Was-A	12	6	.667	50	3	2	0	**13**	124	119	45	3	1	32	28	11.0	2.69	156	.255	.305	5	.147	-1	**22**	**21**	4	3.5
1934 Was-A☆	5	10	.333	**54**	9	3	0	**7**	157^2	179	86	6	2	56	38	13.5	4.17	104	.287	.348	7	.159	3	6	3	3	0.8
1935 Was-A	4	9	.308	43	7	2	0	3	126	170	88	10	2	37	30	14.9	5.71	76	.324	.371	7	.200	1	-18	-20	3	-1.5
1936 Was-A	3	2	.600	18	5	1	0	3	49^2	66	46	3	0	25	6	16.5	6.34	75	.317	.391	0	.000	-2	-7	-9	1	-0.9
Bos-A	0	3	.000	23	2	0	0	0	40	57	27	2	0	16	9	16.4	5.62	94	.345	.403	2	.286	0	-3	-1	2	0.1
Yr	3	5	.375	41	7	1	0	3	89^2	123	73	5	0	41	15	16.5	6.02	83	.330	.396	2	.091	-2	-10	-10	3	-0.8
1937 Det-A	2	5	.286	25	0	0	0	4	40^1	63	35	4	1	20	10	18.7	7.59	62	.362	.431	0	.000	-0	-13	-13	1	-2.0
1938 *Chi-N	6	1	.857	42	0	0	0	3	102^1	100	43	1	1	30	29	11.5	3.34	115	.258	.313	7	.219	1	5	5	3	0.8
1939 Chi-N	4	3	.571	39	0	0	0	3	68^2	78	32	3	0	24	32	13.4	3.67	107	.282	.339	0	.000	-2	**2**	2	2	0.1
1940 StL-N	3	4	.429	26	0	0	0	1	54	53	22	1	0	26	16	13.2	2.50	160	.252	.335	0	.000	-2	8	9	1	1.0
Total 15	85	141	.376	557	182	71	3	38	2050^2	2454	1187	83	26	571	418	13.4	4.46	97	.299	.346	103	.167	-11	-33	-33	36	-1.4
● JEFF RUSSELL Russell, Jeffrey Lee b: 9/2/61, Cincinnati, Ohio BR/TR, 6'3", 210 lbs. Deb: 8/13/83																											
1983 Cin-N	4	5	.444	10	10	2	0	0	68^1	58	30	7	0	22	40	10.5	3.03	126	.233	.295	3	.143	1	5	6	-0	0.8
1984 Cin-N	6	18	.250	33	30	4	2	0	181^2	186	97	15	4	65	101	12.6	4.26	89	.263	.329	8	.140	-0	-13	-9	1	-1.0
1985 Tex-A	3	6	.333	13	13	0	0	0	62	85	55	10	2	27	44	16.5	7.55	56	.324	.392	0	—	0	-23	-22	1	-2.5
1986 Tex-A	5	2	.714	37	0	0	0	2	82	74	40	11	1	31	54	11.6	3.40	127	.244	.316	0	—	0	7	8	2	0.8
1987 Tex-A	5	4	.556	52	2	0	0	3	97^1	109	56	9	2	52	56	15.1	4.44	101	.285	.373	0	—	0	0	1	1	0.2
1988 Tex-A★	10	9	.526	34	24	5	0	0	188^2	183	86	15	7	66	88	12.2	3.82	107	.257	.326	0	.000	-0	3	6	2	0.7
1989 Tex-A★	6	4	.600	71	0	0	0	**38**	72^2	45	21	4	3	24	77	8.9	1.98	200	.182	.263	0	—	0	15	16	2	3.5
1990 Tex-A	1	5	.167	27	0	0	0	10	25^1	23	15	1	0	16	16	13.9	4.26	92	.253	.364	0	—	0	-1	-1	0	-0.2
1991 Tex-A	6	4	.600	68	0	0	0	30	79^1	71	36	11	1	26	52	11.1	3.29	123	.235	.298	0	—	0	7	7	2	1.3
1992 Tex-A	2	3	.400	51	0	0	0	28	56^2	51	14	3	2	22	43	11.9	1.91	199	.238	.315	0	—	0	13	12	1	2.2
*Oak-A	2	0	1.000	8	0	0	0	2	9^2	4	0	0	0	3	5	6.5	0.00	—	.125	.200	0	—	0	4	4	-0	0.9
Yr	4	3	.571	59	0	0	0	30	66^1	55	14	3	2	25	48	11.1	1.63	233	.224	.300	0	—	0	17	17	0	3.1
1993 Bos-A	1	4	.200	51	0	0	0	33	46^2	39	16	1	1	14	45	10.4	2.70	171	.231	.293	0	—	0	8	9	1	1.9
1994 Bos-A	0	5	.000	29	0	0	0	12	28	30	17	3	1	13	18	14.1	5.14	98	.270	.352	0	—	0	-1	-0	-1	-0.1
Cle-A	1	1	.500	13	0	0	0	5	12^2	13	8	2	0	3	10	11.4	4.97	95	.265	.308	0	—	0	-0	-0	-0	-0.1
Yr	1	6	.143	42	0	0	0	17	40^2	43	25	5	1	16	28	13.3	5.09	97	.269	.339	0	—	0	-1	-1	-1	-0.2
1995 Tex-A	1	0	1.000	37	0	0	0	20	32^2	36	12	3	0	9	21	12.4	3.03	159	.277	.324	0	—	0	6	6	-1	0.8
1996 *Tex-A	3	3	.500	55	0	0	0	3	56	58	22	5	4	22	23	13.5	3.38	155	.269	.347	0	—	0	10	11	-0	1.1
Total 14	56	73	.434	589	79	11	2	186	1099^2	1065	525	100	28	415	693	12.3	3.75	112	.255	.326	11	.139	1	41	52	9	10.3
● JOHN RUSSELL Russell, John Albert b: 10/20/1894, San Mateo, Cal. d: 11/19/30, Ely, Nev. BL/TL, 6'2", 195 lbs. Deb: 7/4/17																											
1917 Bro-N	0	1	.000	5	1	1	0	0	16	12	8	1	0	6	1	10.1	4.50	62	.222	.300	1	.250	0	-3	-3	-0	-0.2
1918 Bro-N	0	0	—	1	0	0	0	0	1	2	2	0	0	1	0	27.0	18.00	15	.500	.600	0	—	0	-2	-2	-0	-0.1
1921 Chi-A	2	5	.286	11	9	4	0	0	66^1	82	42	3	1	35	15	16.0	5.29	80	.314	.397	10	.400	3	-7	-8	-1	-0.4
1922 Chi-A	0	1	.000	4	1	0	0	1	6^2	7	5	0	0	4	3	14.9	6.75	60	.280	.379	0	.000	-0	-2	-2	0	-0.3
Total 4	2	7	.222	21	11	5	0	1	90	103	57	4	1	46	19	15.0	5.40	73	.299	.384	11	.367	3	-14	-14	-1	-1.0
● JOHN RUSSELL Russell, John William b: 1/5/61, Oklahoma City, Okla. BR/TR, 6', 200 lbs. Deb: 6/22/84 ♦																											
1989 Atl-N	0	0	—	1	0	0	0	0	0^1	0	0	0	0	0	0	0.0	0.00	—	.000	.000	29	.182	0	0	0	0	0.0
● MARIUS RUSSO Russo, Marius Ugo "Lefty" b: 7/19/14, Brooklyn, N.Y. BR/TL, 6'1", 190 lbs. Deb: 6/6/39																											
1939 NY-A	8	3	.727	21	11	9	2	2	116	86	37	6	1	41	55	9.9	2.41	181	.210	.283	10	.244	1	29	27	2	2.7
1940 NY-A	14	8	.636	30	24	15	0	1	189^1	181	79	17	1	55	87	11.3	3.28	123	.249	.303	12	.188	2	23	17	3	2.3
1941 *NY-A☆	14	10	.583	28	27	17	3	1	209^2	195	85	8	1	87	105	12.1	3.09	127	.247	.322	18	.231	3	25	21	2	2.6
1942 NY-A	4	1	.800	9	5	2	0	0	45^1	41	15	2	1	14	15	11.1	2.78	124	.244	.306	4	.235	1	4	4	0	0.5
1943 *NY-A	5	10	.333	24	14	5	1	1	101^2	89	53	7	2	45	42	12.0	3.72	87	.235	.319	6	.194	1	-5	-6	0	-0.7
1946 NY-A	0	2	.000	8	3	0	0	0	18^2	26	9	1	0	11	7	17.8	4.34	80	.333	.416	0	.000	-1	-2	-2	0	-0.2
Total 6	45	34	.570	120	84	48	6	5	680^2	618	278	41	6	253	311	11.6	3.13	124	.242	.312	50	.213	8	74	60	8	7.2
● DICK RUSTECK Rusteck, Richard Frank b: 7/12/41, Chicago, Ill. BR/TL, 6'1", 175 lbs. Deb: 6/10/66																											
1966 NY-N	1	2	.333	8	3	1	1	0	24	24	10	1	0	8	9	12.0	3.00	121	.276	.337	0	.000	-1	2	2	-0	0.1

YEAR	TM/L	W	L	PCT	G	GS	CG	SH	SV	IP	H	R	HR	HB	BB	SO	RAT	ERA	ERA+	OAV	OOB	BH	AVG	PB	PR	PR+	PD	TPI
● BABE RUTH Ruth, George Herman "The Bambino" or "The Sultan Of Swat" b: 2/6/1895, Baltimore, Md. d: 8/16/48, New York, N.Y. BL/TL (BB 1923 (part)), 6'2", 215 lbs. Deb: 7/11/14 CH♦																												
1914	Bos-A	2	1	.667	4	3	1	0	0	23	21	12	1	0	7	3	11.0	3.91	69	.236	.292	2	.200	0	-3	-3	-0	-0.4
1915	*Bos-A	18	8	.692	32	28	16	1	0	217^2	166	80	3	6	85	112	10.6	2.44	114	.212	.294	29	.315	16	12	9	1	2.8
1916	*Bos-A	23	12	.657	44	41	23	**9**	1	323^2	230	83	0	8	118	170	9.9	**1.75**	**158**	**.201**	.280	37	.272	14	**39**	**37**	0	**6.0**
1917	Bos-A	24	13	.649	41	38	**35**	6	2	326^1	244	93	2	11	108	128	10.0	2.01	128	.211	.284	40	.325	17	24	21	2	4.8
1918	*Bos-A	13	7	.650	20	19	18	1	0	166^1	125	51	1	2	49	40	9.5	2.22	121	.214	.277	95	.300	12	10	9	4	3.0
1919	Bos-A	9	5	.643	17	15	12	0	1	133^1	148	59	2	2	58	30	14.0	2.97	102	.290	.365	139	.322	14	4	1	0	1.5
1920	NY-A	1	0	1.000	1	1	0	0	0	4	3	4	0	0	2	0	11.3	4.50	85	.200	.294	172	.376	1	-0	-0	-0	0.0
1921	*NY-A	2	0	1.000	2	1	0	0	0	9	14	10	1	0	9	2	23.0	9.00	47	.350	.469	204	.378	2	-5	-5	0	-0.7
1930	NY-A	1	0	1.000	1	1	1	0	0	9	11	3	0	0	2	3	13.0	3.00	143	.306	.342	186	.359	1	2	1	1	0.3
1933	NY-A★	1	0	1.000	1	1	1	0	0	9	12	5	0	0	3	0	15.0	5.00	78	.308	.357	138	.301	1	-1	-1	-0	-0.1
Total	10	94	46	.671	163	148	107	17	4	1221^1	974	400	10	29	441	488	10.6	2.28	122	.221	.297	2873	.342	78	81	70	8	17.2
● JOHNNY RUTHERFORD Rutherford, John William "Doc" b: 5/5/25, Belleville, Ont., Canada BL/TR, 5'10.5", 170 lbs. Deb: 4/30/52																												
1952	*Bro-N	7	7	.500	22	11	4	0	2	97^1	97	51	9	2	29	29	11.8	4.25	86	.262	.319	9	.290	2	-6	-7	1	-0.6
● DICK RUTHVEN Ruthven, Richard David b: 3/27/51, Sacramento, Cal. BR/TR, 6'3", 190 lbs. Deb: 4/17/73																												
1973	Phi-N	6	9	.400	25	23	3	1	1	128^1	125	69	10	3	75	98	14.2	4.21	90	.257	.360	5	.132	-1	-8	-6	1	-0.6
1974	Phi-N	9	13	.409	35	35	6	0	0	212^2	182	106	11	3	116	153	12.7	4.02	94	.231	.332	13	.191	-1	-9	-5	-1	-0.7
1975	Phi-N	2	2	.500	11	7	0	0	0	40^2	37	22	2	1	22	26	13.3	4.20	89	.243	.343	2	.154	-0	-3	-2	-0	-0.3
1976	Atl-N☆	14	17	.452	36	36	8	4	0	240^1	255	112	14	8	90	142	13.2	4.19	90	.275	.345	13	.171	-0	-18	-10	2	-1.0
1977	Atl-N	7	13	.350	25	23	6	2	0	151	158	86	14	1	62	84	13.2	4.23	105	.267	.338	12	.267	3	-5	3	-2	0.5
1978	Atl-N	2	6	.250	13	13	2	1	0	81	78	43	8	0	28	45	11.8	4.11	99	.257	.319	2	.083	-2	-5	-0	-0	-0.2
	*Phi-N	13	5	.722	20	20	9	2	0	150^2	136	52	13	1	28	75	9.9	2.99	120	.248	.285	15	.283	4	10	10	-0	1.6
	Yr	15	11	.577	33	33	11	3	0	231^2	214	95	21	1	56	120	10.5	3.38	111	.251	.298	17	.221	3	5	9	-1	1.4
1979	Phi-N	7	5	.583	20	20	3	2	0	122^1	121	59	10	2	37	58	11.8	4.27	90	.256	.313	6	.146	-0	-7	-6	-2	-0.7
1980	*Phi-N	17	10	.630	33	33	6	1	0	223^1	241	99	9	3	74	86	12.8	3.55	107	.283	.342	16	.235	4	2	6	-0	1.0
1981	*Phi-N★	12	7	.632	23	22	5	0	0	146^2	162	94	10	3	54	80	13.4	5.15	70	.281	.346	7	.140	-0	-27	-24	-1	-2.9
1982	Phi-N	11	11	.500	33	31	8	2	0	204^1	189	99	18	6	59	115	11.2	3.79	97	.246	.305	7	.109	-2	-4	-3	-2	-0.8
1983	Phi-N	1	3	.250	7	7	0	0	0	33^2	46	23	5	0	10	26	15.0	5.61	64	.333	.378	1	.111	-0	-7	-8	0	-0.8
	Chi-N	12	9	.571	25	25	5	2	0	149^1	156	78	17	3	28	73	11.3	4.10	93	.269	.306	12	.226	2	-8	-5	2	-0.2
	Yr	13	12	.520	32	32	5	2	0	183	202	101	22	3	38	99	12.0	4.38	86	.281	.320	13	.210	2	-15	-12	2	-1.0
1984	Chi-N	6	10	.375	23	22	0	0	0	126^2	154	75	14	4	41	55	14.1	5.04	78	.302	.359	7	.159	0	-20	-15	-0	-1.7
1985	Chi-N	4	7	.364	20	15	0	0	0	87^1	103	49	6	0	37	26	14.4	4.53	88	.299	.367	5	.208	0	-9	-5	-1	-0.7
1986	Chi-N	0	0	—	6	0	0	0	0	10^2	12	9	4	0	6	3	15.2	5.06	80	.293	.383	0	.000	-0	-2	-1	-0	-0.1
Total	14	123	127	.492	355	332	61	17	1	2109	2155	1075	165	38	767	1145	12.6	4.14	92	.267	.333	123	.183	6	-121	-69	-4	-7.6
● CYCLONE RYAN Ryan, Daniel R. b: 1866, Cappagh White, Ireland d: 1/30/17, Medfield, Mass. TR, 6', 200 lbs. Deb: 8/8/1887 ♦																												
1887	NY-a	0	1	.000	2	1	0	0	0	2^1	11	9	1	0	6	0	42.4	23.14	18	.647	.647	10	.286	-0	-5	-5	-0	-0.7
1891	Bos-N	0	0	—	1	0	0	0	0	3	2	0	0	0	1	0	9.0	0.00	—	.182	.250	0	.000	-0	1	1	0	0.0
Total	2	0	1	.000	3	1	0	0	0	5^1	13	9	1	0	7	0	23.6	10.13	39	.464	.483	10	.278	-0	-4	-4	0	-0.7
● JACK RYAN Ryan, Jack "Gulfport" b: 9/19/1884, Lawrenceville, Ill. d: 10/16/49, Handsboro, Miss. BR/TR, 5'10", 165 lbs. Deb: 7/2/08																												
1908	Cle-A	1	1	.500	8	1	1	0	1	35^2	27	12	3	1	2	7	7.6	2.27	105	.220	.238	1	.091	0	0	0	-0	0.1
1909	Bos-A	3	3	.500	13	8	2	0	0	59^1	64	34	0	4	20	24	13.3	3.34	75	.288	.358	4	.211	0	-6	-5	-1	-0.6
1911	Bro-N	0	1	.000	3	1	0	0	0	6	9	7	1	1	4	1	21.0	3.00	111	.375	.483	0	.000	-0	0	0	0	0.0
Total	3	4	5	.444	24	10	3	0	1	101	100	53	4	6	26	32	11.8	2.94	85	.271	.329	5	.161	1	-5	-5	-0	-0.5
● JIMMY RYAN Ryan, James Edward "Pony" b: 2/11/1863, Clinton, Mass. d: 10/26/23, Chicago, Ill. BR/TL, 5'9", 162 lbs. Deb: 10/8/1885 ♦																												
1886	*Chi-N	0	0	—	5	0	0	0	1	23^1	19	13	2		13	15	12.3	4.63	78	.257	.368	100	.306	1	-3	-2	0	0.0
1887	Chi-N	2	1	.667	8	3	2	0	0	45	70	36	3	6	17	14	15.2	4.20	107	.366	.386	198	.353	2	-1	1	2	0.3
1888	Chi-N	4	0	1.000	8	2	1	0	0	38^1	47	29	2	0	12	11	13.9	3.05	99	.297	.347	182	.332	4	-1	-0	0	0.2
1891	Chi-N	0	0	—	2	0	0	0	1	5^2	11	7	0	0	2	2	20.6	1.59	210	.393	.433	140	.277	1	1	1	-0	0.0
1893	Chi-N	0	0	—	1	0	0	0	0	4^2	3	0	0	0	0	1	5.8	0.00	—	.176	.176	102	.299	0	2	2	0	0.1
Total	5	6	1	.857	24	5	3	0	2	117	150	85	7	6	44	43	14.1	3.62	105	.321	.365	2556	.311	9	-1	2	2	0.6
● JAY RYAN Ryan, Jason Paul b: 1/21/76, Long Branch, N.J. BB/TR, 6'3", 185 lbs. Deb: 8/24/99																												
1999	Min-A	1	4	.200	8	8	1	0	0	40^2	46	23	9	3	17	15	14.6	4.87	105	.286	.365	0	—	0	0	1	-0	0.1
2000	Min-A	0	1	.000	16	1	0	0	0	26	37	24	8	1	10	19	16.6	7.62	69	.330	.390	0	—	0	-8	-6	-1	-0.3
Total	2	1	5	.167	24	9	1	0	0	66^2	83	47	17	4	27	34	15.4	5.94	87	.304	.375	0	—	0	-8	-5	-1	-0.2
● JOHN RYAN Ryan, John A. b: Birmingham, Mich. TR, Deb: 4/19/1884																												
1884	Bal-U	3	2	.600	6	6	5	0	0	51	61	42	1		16	33	13.6	3.35	80	.277	.326	2	.080	-3	-5	-3	-0	-0.6
● JOHNNY RYAN Ryan, John Joseph b: 10/1853, Philadelphia, Pa. d: 3/22/02, Philadelphia, Pa. 5'7.5", 150 lbs. Deb: 8/19/1873 ♦																												
1874	Bal-n	0	0	—	1	0	0	0	0	3^1	13	8	0		0	0	35.1	16.20	14	.565	.565	35	.193	-0	-5	-5		-0.2
1875	NH-n	1	5	.167	10	6	4	0	0	59^1	70	55	1		9	1	12.0	3.19	65	.255	.279	23	.158	-1	-6	-8		-0.7
1876	Lou-N	0	0	—	1	0	0	0	0	8	22	20	0		0	1	24.8	5.63	48	.449	.449	61	.247	-0	-3	-2	-0	-0.1
Total	2 n	1	5	.167	11	6	4	0	0	62^2	83	63	1		9	1	13.2	3.88	54	.279	.301	60	.179	-1	-12	-13		-0.9
● KEN RYAN Ryan, Kenneth Frederick b: 10/24/68, Pawtucket, R.I. BR/TR, 6'3", 230 lbs. Deb: 8/31/92																												
1992	Bos-A	0	0	—	7	0	0	0	1	7	4	5	2	0	5	5	11.6	6.43	66	.174	.321	0	—	0	-2	-2	0	-0.1
1993	Bos-A	7	2	.778	47	0	0	0	1	50	43	23	2	3	29	49	13.5	3.60	129	.235	.349	0	—	0	4	5	0	0.9
1994	Bos-A	2	3	.400	42	0	0	0	13	48	46	14	1	1	17	32	12.0	2.44	207	.256	.323	0	—	0	13	13	-1	1.8
1995	Bos-A	0	4	.000	28	0	0	0	7	32^2	34	20	4	1	24	34	16.3	4.96	98	.268	.388	0	—	0	-1	-0	-1	-0.1
1996	Phi-N	3	5	.375	62	0	0	0	8	89	71	32	4	1	45	70	11.8	2.43	178	.223	.321	1	.143	-0	18	18	0	1.7
1997	Phi-N	1	0	1.000	22	0	0	0	0	20^2	31	23	5	2	13	10	20.0	9.58	44	.344	.438	0	—	0	-12	-12	-0	-0.6
1998	Phi-N	0	0	—	17	1	0	0	0	22^2	21	12	1	1	20	16	16.7	4.37	99	.253	.404	0	.000	-0	-0	-0	0	0.0
1999	Phi-N	1	2	.333	15	0	0	0	0	15^2	16	11	2	0	11	9	15.5	6.32	75	.267	.380	0	—	0	-3	-3	0	-0.4
Total	8	14	16	.467	240	1	0	0	30	285^2	266	140	21	9	164	225	13.8	3.91	117	.250	.355	1	.125	-0	16	20	-0	3.2
● NOLAN RYAN Ryan, Lynn Nolan b: 1/31/47, Refugio, Tex. BR/TR, 6'2", 195 lbs. Deb: 9/11/66 H																												
1966	NY-N	0	1	.000	2	1	0	0	0	3	5	5	1	0	3	6	24.0	15.00	24	.357	.471	0	—	0	-4	-4	0	-0.6
1968	NY-N	6	9	.400	21	18	3	0	0	134	93	50	12	4	75	133	11.6	3.09	98	.200	.317	5	.114	-1	-2	-1	-2	-0.5
1969	*NY-N	6	3	.667	25	10	2	0	1	89^1	60	38	3	1	53	92	11.5	3.53	104	.189	.307	3	.103	-1	1	1	-2	-0.3
1970	NY-N	7	11	.389	27	19	5	2	1	131^2	86	59	10	4	97	125	12.8	3.42	118	.188	.335	8	.178	-1	9	9	-1	1.0
1971	NY-N	10	14	.417	30	26	3	0	0	152	125	78	8	15	116	137	15.2	3.97	86	.219	.365	6	.128	-0	-8	-10	-1	-1.6
1972	Cal-A☆	19	16	.543	39	39	20	**9**	0	284	166	80	14	10	157	**329**	10.6	2.28	128	**.171**	.292	13	.135	0	25	21	-2	2.6
1973	Cal-A★	21	16	.568	41	39	26	4	1	326	238	113	18	7	162	**383**	11.2	2.87	124	.203	.304	0	—	0	34	26	-2	2.7
1974	Cal-A	22	16	.579	42	41	26	3	0	**332^2**	221	127	18	9	202	**367**	11.7	2.89	119	**.190**	.314	0	—	0	27	21	2	2.5
1975	Cal-A☆	14	12	.538	28	28	10	5	0	198	152	90	13	7	132	186	13.2	3.45	103	.213	.342	0	—	0	7	2	-2	0.1
1976	Cal-A	17	18	.486	39	39	21	**7**	0	284^1	193	117	13	5	183	**327**	12.1	3.36	99	**.195**	.323	0	—	0	5	-1	0	-0.1
1977	Cal-A†	19	16	.543	37	37	**22**	4	0	299	198	110	12	9	204	**341**	12.4	2.77	142	**.193**	.331	0	—	0	**43**	**40**	0	4.5
1978	Cal-A	10	13	.435	31	31	14	3	0	234^2	183	106	12	3	148	**260**	12.8	3.72	97	.220	.340	0	—	0	1	-3	1	-0.1
1979	*Cal-A★	16	14	.533	34	34	17	**5**	0	222^2	169	104	15	6	114	**223**	11.7	3.60	114	**.212**	.314	0	—	0	16	13	-0	1.5
1980	*Hou-N	11	10	.524	35	35	4	2	0	233^2	205	100	10	3	98	200	11.8	3.35	98	.236	.316	6	.086	-1	7	-2	-1	-0.4
1981	*Hou-N★	11	5	.688	21	21	5	3	0	149	99	34	2	1	68	140	10.1	**1.69**	**195**	**.188**	.281	11	.216	3	**30**	**28**	-1	**3.5**
1982	Hou-N	16	12	.571	35	35	10	3	0	250^1	196	100	20	8	109	245	11.3	3.16	105	**.213**	.302	10	.120	-1	12	5	-0	0.3
1983	Hou-N	14	9	.609	29	29	5	2	0	196^1	134	74	9	4	101	183	11.0	2.98	114	**.195**	.302	5	.072	-4	14	10	-0	0.7
1984	Hou-N	12	11	.522	30	30	5	2	0	183^2	143	78	12	4	69	197	10.6	3.04	109	.211	.288	6	.098	-2	11	6	-3	0.3

YEAR	TM/L	W	L	PCT	G	GS	CG	SH	SV	IP	H	R	HR	HB	BB	SO	RAT	ERA	ERA+	OAV	OOB	BH	AVG	PB	PR	PR+	PD	TPI
1985	Hou-N★	10	12	.455	35	35	4	0	0	232	205	108	12	9	95	209	12.0	3.80	91	.239	.322	7	.111	-1	-5	-9	-3	-1.2
1986	*Hou-N	12	8	.600	30	30	1	0	0	178	119	72	14	4	82	194	10.4	3.34	108	.188	.285	6	.102	-2	8	6	-1	0.2
1987	Hou-N	8	16	.333	34	34	0	0	0	211^2	154	75	14	4	87	**270**	10.4	**2.76**	**142**	**.199**	.284	4	.062	-3	**31**	**28**	-1	2.6
1988	Hou-N	12	11	.522	33	33	4	1	0	220	186	98	18	7	87	**228**	11.5	3.52	95	.227	.307	4	.057	-3	-2	-5	-3	-1.1
1989	Tex-A★	16	10	.615	32	32	6	2	0	239^1	162	96	17	9	98	**301**	10.1	3.20	124	**.187**	.276	0	—	0	18	20	-1	1.9
1990	Tex-A	13	9	.591	30	30	5	2	0	204	137	86	18	7	74	**232**	**9.6**	3.44	114	**.188**	**.269**	0	—	0	11	11	-2	0.9
1991	Tex-A	12	6	.667	27	27	2	2	0	173	102	58	12	5	72	203	**9.3**	2.91	139	**.172**	**.267**	0	—	0	23	22	-1	2.1
1992	Tex-A	5	9	.357	27	27	2	0	0	157^1	138	75	9	12	69	157	12.5	3.72	102	.238	.331	0	—	0	4	2	-1	0.0
1993	Tex-A	5	5	.500	13	13	0	0	0	66^1	54	47	5	1	40	46	12.9	4.88	85	.220	.331	0	—	0	-4	-6	-2	-0.8
Total	27	324	292	.526	807	773	222	61	3	5386	3923	2178	321	158	2795	5714	11.5	3.19	112	.204	.309	94	.110	-17	314	233	-29	20.7

● B.J. RYAN Ryan, Robert Victor b: 12/28/75, Bossier City, La. BL/TL, 6'6", 230 lbs. Deb: 7/28/99

YEAR	TM/L	W	L	PCT	G	GS	CG	SH	SV	IP	H	R	HR	HB	BB	SO	RAT	ERA	ERA+	OAV	OOB	BH	AVG	PB	PR	PR+	PD	TPI
1999	Cin-N	0	0	—	1	0	0	0	0	2	4	1	0	0	1	1	22.5	4.50	104	.500	.556	0	—	0	0	0	-0	0.0
	Bal-A	1	0	1.000	13	0	0	0	0	18^1	9	6	0	0	12	28	10.3	2.95	159	.150	.292	0	—	0	4	4	-0	0.2
2000	Bal-A	2	3	.400	42	0	0	0	0	42^2	36	29	7	0	31	41	14.1	5.91	81	.225	.351	0	—	0	-5	-5	-0	-0.6
Total	2	3	3	.500	56	0	0	0	0	63	49	36	7	0	44	70	13.3	5.00	95	.215	.342	0	—	0	-1	-2	-1	-0.4

● ROSY RYAN Ryan, Wilfred Patrick Dolan b: 3/15/1898, Worcester, Mass. d: 12/10/80, Scottsdale, Ariz. BL/TR, 6', 185 lbs. Deb: 9/7/19

YEAR	TM/L	W	L	PCT	G	GS	CG	SH	SV	IP	H	R	HR	HB	BB	SO	RAT	ERA	ERA+	OAV	OOB	BH	AVG	PB	PR	PR+	PD	TPI
1919	NY-N	1	2	.333	4	3	1	0	0	20^1	20	9	0	1	9	7	13.3	3.10	91	.260	.345	0	.000	-1	-0	-1	-1	-0.2
1920	NY-N	0	1	.000	3	1	1	0	0	15^1	14	6	1	0	4	5	10.6	1.76	170	.259	.310	0	.000	-1	2	2	0	0.1
1921	NY-N	7	10	.412	36	16	5	0	3	147^1	140	72	6	1	32	58	10.6	3.73	98	.255	.297	9	.200	1	1	-1	-1	-0.2
1922	*NY-N	17	12	.586	46	22	12	1	3	191^2	194	87	5	2	74	75	12.7	3.01	133	.269	.338	12	.194	1	23	22	-1	2.9
1923	*NY-N	16	5	.762	**45**	15	7	0	4	172^2	169	77	8	2	46	58	11.3	3.49	109	.257	.308	11	.208	0	10	7	0	0.8
1924	*NY-N	8	6	.571	37	9	2	0	5	124^2	137	64	1	2	37	36	12.7	4.26	86	.285	.339	5	.139	-1	-5	-9	-2	-1.2
1925	Bos-N	2	8	.200	37	7	1	0	2	122^2	152	103	7	0	52	48	15.0	6.31	64	.303	.368	11	.282	3	-28	-33	-1	-2.1
1926	Bos-N	0	2	.000	7	2	0	0	0	19	29	19	1	0	7	1	17.1	7.58	47	.392	.444	1	.200	-0	-8	-9	-0	-0.8
1928	NY-A	0	0	—	3	0	0	0	0	6	17	11	1	0	1	5	27.0	16.50	23	.486	.500	0	.000	-1	-8	-9	-0	-0.5
1933	Bro-N	1	1	.500	30	0	0	0	2	61^1	69	38	3	3	16	22	12.9	4.55	71	.276	.327	2	.154	0	-8	-9	-0	-0.5
Total	10	52	47	.525	248	75	29	1	19	881	941	486	33	11	278	315	12.6	4.14	91	.277	.333	51	.190	1	-22	-39	-5	-1.7

● MIKE RYBA Ryba, Dominic Joseph b: 6/9/03, DeLancey, Pa. d: 12/13/71, Brookline Station, Mo. BR/TR, 5'11.5", 195 lbs. Deb: 9/22/35 C

YEAR	TM/L	W	L	PCT	G	GS	CG	SH	SV	IP	H	R	HR	HB	BB	SO	RAT	ERA	ERA+	OAV	OOB	BH	AVG	PB	PR	PR+	PD	TPI
1935	StL-N	1	1	.500	2	1	1	0	0	16	15	6	0	0	1	6	9.0	3.38	121	.242	.254	2	.400	1	1	1	0	0.2
1936	StL-N	5	1	.833	14	0	0	0	0	45	55	33	3	2	16	25	14.6	5.40	73	.294	.356	3	.167	-0	-7	-7	-1	-1.0
1937	StL-N	9	6	.600	38	8	5	0	0	135	152	76	8	2	40	57	12.9	4.13	96	.284	.336	15	.313	4	-3	-2	0	0.2
1938	StL-N	1	1	.500	3	0	0	0	0	5	8	3	0	0	1	0	16.2	5.40	73	.348	.375	0	—	0	-1	-1	0	-0.1
1941	Bos-A	7	3	.700	40	3	0	0	6	121	143	72	14	0	42	54	13.8	4.46	93	.297	.353	8	.216	1	-4	-4	2	0.0
1942	Bos-A	3	3	.500	18	0	0	0	3	44^1	49	25	5	1	13	16	12.8	3.86	97	.278	.332	5	.294	1	-1	-1	1	0.1
1943	Bos-A	7	5	.583	40	8	4	1	2	143^2	142	57	4	0	57	50	12.5	3.26	102	.262	.333	8	.186	0	1	1	-1	0.0
1944	Bos-A	12	7	.632	42	7	2	0	2	138	119	57	7	0	39	50	10.3	3.33	102	.233	.287	6	.146	-0	2	1	3	0.4
1945	Bos-A	7	6	.538	34	9	4	1	2	123	122	45	5	2	33	44	11.5	2.49	137	.259	.310	9	.250	2	12	12	-1	1.5
1946	*Bos-A	0	1	.000	9	0	0	0	1	12^2	12	7	1	0	5	5	12.1	3.55	103	.261	.333	2	1.000	1	-0	0	-0	0.1
Total	10	52	34	.605	240	36	16	2	16	783^2	817	381	47	7	247	307	12.3	3.66	100	.269	.326	58	.235	9	-1	1	3	1.4

● GARY RYERSON Ryerson, Gary Lawrence b: 6/7/48, Los Angeles, Cal. BR/TL, 6'1", 175 lbs. Deb: 6/28/72

YEAR	TM/L	W	L	PCT	G	GS	CG	SH	SV	IP	H	R	HR	HB	BB	SO	RAT	ERA	ERA+	OAV	OOB	BH	AVG	PB	PR	PR+	PD	TPI
1972	Mil-A	3	8	.273	20	14	4	1	0	102	119	48	9	0	21	45	12.4	3.62	84	.290	.324	1	.042	-1	-6	-7	-1	-1.0
1973	Mil-A	0	1	.000	9	4	0	0	0	23	32	23	0	0	7	10	15.3	7.83	48	.327	.371	0	—	0	-10	-11	0	-0.5
Total	2	3	9	.250	29	18	4	1	0	125	151	71	9	0	28	55	12.9	4.39	72	.297	.333	1	.042	-1	-16	-17	-1	-1.5

● ERIK SABEL Sabel, Erik Douglas b: 10/14/74, Lafayette, Ind. BR/TR, 6'3", 193 lbs. Deb: 7/9/99

YEAR	TM/L	W	L	PCT	G	GS	CG	SH	SV	IP	H	R	HR	HB	BB	SO	RAT	ERA	ERA+	OAV	OOB	BH	AVG	PB	PR	PR+	PD	TPI
1999	Ari-N	0	0	—	7	0	0	0	0	9^2	12	7	1	2	6	6	18.6	6.52	70	.300	.417	0	.000	-0	-2	-2	0	-0.1

● BRET SABERHAGEN Saberhagen, Bret William b: 4/11/64, Chicago Heights, Ill. BR/TR, 6'1", 195 lbs. Deb: 4/4/84

YEAR	TM/L	W	L	PCT	G	GS	CG	SH	SV	IP	H	R	HR	HB	BB	SO	RAT	ERA	ERA+	OAV	OOB	BH	AVG	PB	PR	PR+	PD	TPI
1984	*KC-A	10	11	.476	38	18	2	1	1	157^2	138	71	13	2	36	73	10.0	3.48	116	.237	.283	0	—	0	9	10	0	1.2
1985	*KC-A	20	6	.769	32	32	10	1	0	235^1	211	79	19	1	38	158	**9.6**	2.87	145	.241	**.273**	0	—	0	33	34	2	3.8
1986	KC-A	7	12	.368	30	25	4	2	0	156	165	77	15	2	29	112	11.3	4.15	103	.268	.303	0	—	0	1	2	1	0.3
1987	KC-A★	18	10	.643	33	33	15	4	0	257	246	99	27	6	53	163	10.7	3.36	136	.252	.295	0	—	0	32	34	1	3.4
1988	KC-A	14	16	.467	35	35	9	0	0	260^2	271	122	18	4	59	171	11.5	3.80	105	.269	.312	0	—	0	5	6	0	0.6
1989	KC-A	**23**	6	**.793**	36	35	**12**	4	0	**262^1**	209	74	13	2	43	193	**8.7**	**2.16**	**178**	.217	**.252**	0	—	0	**50**	**50**	0	**5.5**
1990	KC-A★	5	9	.357	20	20	5	0	0	135	146	52	9	1	28	87	11.7	3.27	118	.279	.316	0	—	0	10	9	3	1.2
1991	KC-A	13	8	.619	28	28	7	2	0	196^1	165	76	12	9	45	136	10.0	3.07	134	.228	.281	0	—	0	22	23	1	2.5
1992	NY-N	3	5	.375	17	15	1	1	0	97^2	84	39	6	4	27	81	10.6	3.50	99	.233	.294	3	.107	-1	0	-0	3	0.2
1993	NY-N	7	7	.500	19	19	4	1	0	139^1	131	55	11	3	17	93	9.8	3.29	112	.250	.278	5	.111	-0	12	11	3	1.3
1994	NY-N☆	14	4	**.778**	24	24	4	0	0	177^1	169	58	13	4	13	143	9.4	2.74	153	.254	.273	10	.172	1	29	29	2	3.1
1995	NY-N	5	5	.500	16	16	3	0	0	110	105	45	13	5	20	71	10.6	3.35	121	.251	.293	4	.114	-1	10	9	2	0.9
	*Col-N	2	1	.667	9	9	0	0	0	43	60	33	8	5	13	29	16.3	6.28	86	.323	.382	1	.071	-1	-3	-3	-0	-0.3
	Yr	7	6	.538	25	25	3	0	0	153	165	78	21	10	33	100	12.2	4.18	106	.273	.321	5	.102	-2	0	4	2	0.6
1997	Bos-A	0	1	.000	6	6	0	0	0	26	30	20	5	2	10	14	14.5	6.58	71	.288	.362	0	.000	-0	-6	-6	-0	-0.3
1998	*Bos-A	15	8	.652	31	31	0	0	0	175	181	82	22	6	29	100	11.1	3.96	119	.264	.300	0	.000	-1	14	15	-1	1.5
1999	*Bos-A	10	6	.625	22	22	0	0	0	119	122	43	11	2	11	81	10.2	2.95	169	.265	.285	0	.000	-0	25	26	0	3.2
Total	15	166	115	.591	396	368	76	16	1	2547^2	2433	1025	215	58	471	1705	10.5	3.33	126	.252	.290	23	.121	-2	237	244	18	28.1

● BRIAN SACKINSKY Sackinsky, Brian Walter b: 6/22/71, Pittsburgh, Pa. BR/TR, 6'4", 220 lbs. Deb: 4/20/96

YEAR	TM/L	W	L	PCT	G	GS	CG	SH	SV	IP	H	R	HR	HB	BB	SO	RAT	ERA	ERA+	OAV	OOB	BH	AVG	PB	PR	PR+	PD	TPI
1996	Bal-A	0	0	—	3	0	0	0	0	4^2	6	2	1	0	3	2	17.4	3.86	128	.316	.409	0	—	0	1	1	-0	0.0

● RAY SADECKI Sadecki, Raymond Michael b: 12/26/40, Kansas City, Kan. BL/TL, 5'11", 180 lbs. Deb: 5/19/60

YEAR	TM/L	W	L	PCT	G	GS	CG	SH	SV	IP	H	R	HR	HB	BB	SO	RAT	ERA	ERA+	OAV	OOB	BH	AVG	PB	PR	PR+	PD	TPI
1960	StL-N	9	9	.500	26	26	7	1	0	157^1	148	76	15	1	86	95	13.4	3.78	109	.249	.345	12	.211	-0	-0	5	-2	0.4
1961	StL-N	14	10	.583	31	31	13	0	0	222^2	196	100	28	3	102	114	12.2	3.72	118	.238	.324	22	.253	2	8	15	-5	1.2
1962	StL-N	6	8	.429	22	17	4	1	1	102^1	121	74	13	3	43	50	14.7	5.54	77	.296	.367	3	.081	-2	-18	-13	-2	-1.9
1963	StL-N	10	10	.500	36	28	4	1	1	193^1	198	100	25	4	78	136	13.0	4.10	87	.266	.339	9	.141	-1	-17	-11	-3	-1.5
1964	*StL-N	20	11	.645	37	32	9	2	1	220	232	104	16	1	60	119	12.0	3.68	103	.273	.322	12	.160	2	-4	3	-3	0.3
1965	StL-N	6	15	.286	36	28	4	0	1	172^2	192	107	26	0	64	122	13.3	5.21	74	.284	.346	11	.200	2	-32	-24	-2	-2.7
1966	StL-N	2	1	.667	5	3	1	0	0	24^1	16	9	2	0	9	21	9.2	2.22	162	.188	.266	3	.429	2	4	4	0	0.7
	SF-N	3	7	.300	26	19	3	1	0	105	125	82	20	4	39	62	14.4	5.40	68	.293	.358	11	.324	5	-21	-20	-2	-1.4
	Yr	5	8	.385	31	22	4	1	0	129^1	141	91	22	4	48	83	13.4	4.80	76	.276	.343	14	.341	7	-17	-16	-2	-0.7
1967	SF-N	12	6	.667	35	24	10	2	0	188	165	65	8	4	58	145	10.9	2.78	118	.238	.301	18	.247	4	13	11	-1	1.5
1968	SF-N	12	18	.400	38	36	13	6	0	254	225	94	14	3	70	206	10.6	2.91	101	.237	.292	8	.094	-1	2	1	-2	-0.3
1969	SF-N	5	8	.385	29	17	4	3	0	138^1	137	73	18	2	53	104	12.5	4.23	83	.259	.329	5	.125	2	-10	-11	2	-0.7
1970	NY-N	8	4	.667	28	19	4	0	0	138^2	134	67	18	0	52	89	12.1	3.89	103	.255	.322	8	.205	1	2	2	-2	0.0
1971	NY-N	7	7	.500	34	20	5	2	0	163^1	139	56	10	4	44	120	10.3	2.92	117	.229	.285	10	.200	1	10	9	-2	0.7
1972	NY-N	2	1	.667	34	2	0	0	0	75^2	73	33	3	2	31	38	12.6	3.09	109	.257	.334	2	.154	-0	3	2	-1	0.0
1973	*NY-N	5	4	.556	31	11	1	0	1	116^2	109	47	11	1	41	87	11.6	3.39	107	.248	.314	7	.226	1	4	3	-3	0.1
1974	NY-N	8	8	.500	34	10	3	1	0	103	107	49	7	2	35	46	12.6	3.41	105	.274	.337	7	.259	1	3	2	-0	0.4
1975	StL-N	1	0	1.000	8	0	0	0	0	11	13	7	0	0	7	8	16.4	3.27	115	.289	.385	0	—	0	0	1	-0	0.0
	Atl-N	2	3	.400	25	5	0	0	1	66^1	73	39	3	4	21	24	13.3	4.21	90	.286	.350	3	.200	0	-4	-3	-1	-0.3
	Yr	3	3	.500	33	5	0	0	1	77^1	86	46	3	4	28	32	13.7	4.07	93	.287	.355	3	.200	0	-4	-2	-1	-0.3
	KC-A	1	0	1.000	5	0	0	0	0	3	5	1	0	0	3	0	24.0	3.00	129	.333	.444	0	—	0	0	0	-0	0.0
1976	KC-A	0	0	—	3	0	0	0	0	4^2	7	0	0	0	3	1	19.3	0.00	—	.368	.455	0	—	0	2	2	-0	0.1
	Mil-A	2	0	1.000	36	0	0	0	1	37^1	38	20	2	3	20	27	14.7	4.34	81	.262	.363	0	—	0	-3	-4	-1	-0.3
	Yr	2	0	1.000	39	0	0	0	1	42	45	20	2	3	23	28	15.2	3.86	91	.274	.374	0	—	0	-2	-2	-1	-0.2
1977	NY-N	0	1	.000	4	0	0	0	0	3	3	2	1	0	3	0	18.0	6.00	62	.300	.462	0	—	0	-1	-1	-0	-0.2
Total	18	135	131	.508	563	328	85	20	7	2500^2	2456	1206	240	41	922	1614	12.3	3.78	97	.258	.326	151	.191	19	-60	-30	-30	-3.9

YEAR	TM/L	W	L	PCT	G	GS	CG	SH	SV	IP	H	R	HR	HB	BB	SO	RAT	ERA	ERA+	OAV	OOB	BH	AVG	PB	PR	PR+	PD	TPI
● **JIM SADOWSKI**	Sadowski, James Michael b: 8/7/51, Pittsburgh, Pa. BR/TR, 6'3", 195 lbs. Deb: 4/27/74																											
1974	Pit-N	0	1	.000	4	0	0	0	0	9	7	6	1	0	9	1	16.0	6.00	58	.233	.410	0	.000	0	-2	-3	1	-0.2
● **BOB SADOWSKI**	Sadowski, Robert b: 2/19/38, Pittsburgh, Pa. BR/TR, 6'2", 195 lbs. Deb: 6/19/63 F																											
1963	Mil-N	5	7	.417	19	18	5	1	0	116^2	99	36	8	5	30	72	10.3	2.62	123	.231	.289	2	.057	-2	9	8	1	0.7
1964	Mil-N	9	10	.474	51	18	5	0	5	166^2	159	85	18	7	56	96	12.0	4.10	86	.251	.319	8	.154	0	-11	-11	3	-1.0
1965	Mil-N	5	9	.357	34	13	3	0	3	123	117	62	11	3	35	78	11.3	4.32	82	.250	.306	3	.086	-2	-11	-11	-1	-1.5
1966	Bos-A	1	1	.500	11	5	0	0	0	33^1	41	26	4	1	9	11	13.8	5.40	70	.311	.359	0	.000	-1	-7	-5	-0	-0.4
Total	4	20	27	.426	115	54	13	1	8	439^2	416	209	41	16	130	257	11.5	3.87	90	.250	.311	13	.101	-4	-20	-20	2	-2.2
● **TED SADOWSKI**	Sadowski, Theodore b: 4/1/36, Pittsburgh, Pa. d: 7/18/93, Shaler Twsp., Pa. BR/TR, 6'1.5", 190 lbs. Deb: 9/2/60 F																											
1960	Was-A	1	0	1.000	9	1	0	0	1	17^1	17	10	4	1	9	12	14.0	5.19	75	.258	.355	0	.000	-0	-3	-3	-0	-0.2
1961	Min-A	0	2	.000	15	1	0	0	0	33	49	29	6	1	11	12	16.6	6.82	62	.348	.399	0	.000	-1	-10	-9	1	-0.5
1962	Min-A	1	1	.500	19	0	0	0	0	34	37	19	6	1	11	15	13.0	5.03	81	.301	.363	2	.500	1	-4	-3	0	-0.1
Total	3	2	3	.400	43	2	0	0	1	84^1	103	58	16	3	31	39	14.6	5.76	71	.312	.376	2	.154	-0	-17	-15	1	-0.8
● **A. J. SAGER**	Sager, Anthony Joseph b: 3/3/65, Columbus, Ohio BR/TR, 6'4", 220 lbs. Deb: 4/4/94																											
1994	SD-N	1	4	.200	22	3	0	0	0	46^2	62	34	4	2	16	26	15.4	5.98	69	.325	.383	1	.100	0	-9	-10	2	-0.7
1995	Col-N	0	0	—	10	0	0	0	0	14^2	19	16	1	0	7	10	16.0	7.36	73	.311	.382	0	.000	-0	-5	-2	1	-0.1
1996	Det-A	4	5	.444	22	9	0	0	0	79	91	46	10	2	29	52	13.9	5.01	101	.294	.358	0	—	0	-0	0	-0	0.0
1997	Det-A	3	4	.429	38	1	0	0	3	84	81	43	10	1	24	53	11.4	4.18	110	.258	.313	0	—	0	4	4	0	0.3
1998	Det-A	4	2	.667	31	3	0	0	2	59^1	79	47	7	1	23	23	15.6	6.52	72	.325	.386	0	.000	-0	-12	-12	1	-1.0
Total	5	12	15	.444	123	16	0	0	5	283^2	332	186	32	6	99	164	13.9	5.36	88	.297	.357	1	.071	-0	-23	-20	4	-1.5
● **JOHNNY SAIN**	Sain, John Franklin b: 9/25/17, Havana, Ark. BR/TR, 6'2", 200 lbs. Deb: 4/24/42 C																											
1942	Bos-N	4	7	.364	40	3	0	0	6	97	79	54	8	5	63	68	13.6	3.90	86	.228	.354	2	.074	-2	-6	-6	1	-0.8
1946	Bos-N	20	14	.588	37	34	**24**	3	2	265	225	80	8	2	87	129	10.7	2.21	155	.230	.294	28	.298	5	35	36	3	**5.9**
1947	Bos-N★	21	12	.636	38	35	22	3	1	266	265	117	19	4	79	132	11.8	3.52	111	.255	.310	37	.346	12	16	12	1	2.7
1948	*Bos-N★	**24**	15	.615	42	39	**28**	4	1	**314^2**	297	105	19	5	83	137	11.0	2.60	147	.245	.296	25	.217	3	**47**	44	-2	**5.4**
1949	Bos-N	10	17	.370	37	36	16	1	0	243	285	150	15	4	75	73	13.5	4.81	78	.291	.344	20	.206	1	-21	-30	-2	-2.9
1950	Bos-N	20	13	.606	37	37	25	3	0	278^1	294	139	34	2	70	96	11.8	3.94	98	.269	.314	21	.206	4	6	-3	-2	-0.2
1951	Bos-N	5	13	.278	26	22	6	1	1	160^1	195	88	16	3	45	63	13.6	4.21	87	.299	.347	11	.212	3	-4	-10	0	-0.7
	*NY-A	2	1	.667	7	4	1	0	1	37	41	17	5	0	8	21	11.9	4.14	93	.281	.318	4	.286	1	-0	-1	1	0.0
1952	*NY-A	11	6	.647	35	16	8	0	7	148^1	149	70	15	2	38	57	11.5	3.46	96	.261	.310	19	.268	7	4	-2	-1	0.2
1953	*NY-A☆	14	7	.667	40	19	10	1	9	189	189	68	16	3	45	84	11.3	3.00	123	.262	.308	17	.250	5	21	16	-0	2.2
1954	NY-A	6	6	.500	45	0	0	0	**22**	77	66	27	11	0	15	33	9.5	3.16	109	.229	.267	6	.353	3	5	3	-0	0.8
1955	NY-A	0	0	—	3	0	0	0	0	5^1	6	4	4	0	1	5	11.8	6.75	55	.300	.333	0	.000	-0	-2	-2	0	-0.1
	KC-A	2	5	.286	25	0	0	0	1	44^2	54	28	10	0	10	12	12.9	5.44	77	.297	.333	0	.000	-1	-7	-6	-1	-1.0
	Yr	2	5	.286	28	0	0	0	1	50	60	32	14	0	11	17	12.8	5.58	74	.297	.333	0	.000	-1	-9	-8	-1	-1.1
Total	11	139	116	.545	412	245	140	16	51	2125^2	2145	947	180	30	619	910	11.8	3.49	106	.261	.315	190	.245	40	94	53	-2	11.5
● **RANDY ST.CLAIRE**	St.Claire, Randy Anthony b: 8/23/60, Glens Falls, N.Y. BR/TR, 6'2", 190 lbs. Deb: 9/11/84 F																											
1984	Mon-N	0	0	—	4	0	0	0	0	8	11	4	0	1	2	4	15.8	4.50	76	.344	.400	0	—	0	-1	-1	-0	-0.1
1985	Mon-N	5	3	.625	42	0	0	0	0	68^2	69	32	3	1	26	25	12.6	3.93	86	.265	.334	1	.200	1	-3	-4	0	-0.4
1986	Mon-N	2	0	1.000	11	0	0	0	1	19	13	5	2	0	6	21	9.0	2.37	156	.186	.250	0	.000	-0	3	3	1	0.4
1987	Mon-N	3	3	.500	44	0	0	0	7	67	64	31	9	1	20	43	11.4	4.03	104	.249	.306	2	.333	0	0	1	-0	0.1
1988	Mon-N	0	0	—	6	0	0	0	0	7^1	11	5	2	0	5	6	19.6	6.14	59	.344	.432	0	—	0	-2	-2	0	-0.1
	Cin-N	1	0	1.000	10	0	0	0	0	13^2	13	8	3	0	5	8	11.9	2.63	136	.241	.305	0	.000	-0	1	1	-0	0.1
	Yr	1	0	1.000	16	0	0	0	0	21	24	13	5	0	10	14	14.6	3.86	93	.279	.354	0	.000	-0	-1	-1	0	0.0
1989	Min-A	1	0	1.000	14	0	0	0	1	22^1	19	13	4	2	10	14	12.5	5.24	79	.226	.323	0	—	0	-3	-3	0	-0.1
1991	*Atl-N	0	0	—	19	0	0	0	0	28^2	31	17	4	0	9	30	12.6	4.08	95	.282	.336	1	.500	0	-1	-1	0	0.0
1992	Atl-N	0	0	—	10	0	0	0	0	15^1	17	11	1	0	8	7	14.7	5.87	62	.283	.368	0	—	0	-4	-4	0	-0.2
1994	Tor-A	0	0	—	2	0	0	0	0	2	4	4	0	0	2	2	27.0	9.00	54	.444	.545	0	—	0	-1	-1	0	0.0
Total	9	12	6	.667	162	0	0	0	9	252	252	130	28	5	93	160	12.5	4.14	92	.260	.328	4	.267	1	-11	-10	2	-0.3
● **JIM ST.VRAIN**	St.Vrain, James Marcellin b: 6/6/1883, Ralls County, Mo. d: 6/12/37, Butte, Montana BR/TL, 5'9", 175 lbs. Deb: 4/20/02																											
1902	Chi-N	4	6	.400	12	11	10	1	0	95	88	36	0	5	25	51	11.2	2.08	130	.246	.304	3	.097	-2	7	7	0	0.5
● **MIKE SAIPE**	Saipe, Michael Eric b: 9/10/73, San Diego, Cal. BR/TR, 6'1", 190 lbs. Deb: 6/25/98																											
1998	Col-N	0	1	.000	2	2	0	0	0	10	22	12	5	2	0	2	21.6	10.80	48	.431	.453	0	.000	0	-7	-5	0	-0.4
● **LUIS SALAZAR**	Salazar, Luis Ernesto (Garcia) b: 5/19/56, Barcelona, Venez. BR/TR, 5'9", 180 lbs. Deb: 8/15/80 ◆																											
1987	SD-N	0	0	—	2	0	0	0	0	2	2	1	0	0	1	0	13.5	4.50	88	.250	.333	48	.254	0	-0	-0	0	0.0
● **FREDDY SALE**	Sale, Frederick Link b: 5/2/02, Chester, S.C. d: 5/27/56, Hermosa Beach, Cal BR/TR, 5'9", 160 lbs. Deb: 6/30/24																											
1924	Pit-N	0	0	—	1	0	0	0	0	1	2	0	0	0	0	0	18.0	0.00	—	.500	.500	0	—	0	0	0	-0	0.0
● **HARRY SALISBURY**	Salisbury, Henry H. b: 5/15/1855, Providence, R.I. d: 3/29/33, Chicago, Ill. BL, 5'8.5", 162 lbs. Deb: 8/28/1879																											
1879	Tro-N	4	6	.400	10	10	9	0	0	89	103	72	0		11	31	11.5	2.22	112	.265	.285	2	.056	-4	3	3	2	0.0
1882	Pit-a	20	18	.526	38	38	38	1	0	335	315	188	1		37	135	9.5	2.63	99	.232	.253	22	.152	-6	2	-1	-2	-0.8
Total	2	24	24	.500	48	48	47	1	0	424	418	260	1		48	166	9.9	2.55	102	.239	.260	24	.133	-10	5	2	-1	-0.8
● **BILL SALISBURY**	Salisbury, William Ansel "Solly" b: 11/12/1876, Algona, Iowa d: 1/17/52, Rowena, Ore. BR/TR, 6', 180 lbs. Deb: 4/19/02																											
1902	Phi-N	0	0	—	2	1	0	0	0	6	15	10	1	1	2	0	27.0	13.50	21	.469	.514	0	.000	-0	-7	-7	-1	-0.4
● **ROGER SALKELD**	Salkeld, Roger William b: 3/6/71, Burbank, Cal. BR/TR, 6'5", 215 lbs. Deb: 9/8/93 F																											
1993	Sea-A	0	0	—	3	2	0	0	0	14^1	13	4	0	1	4	13	11.3	2.51	176	.232	.295	0	—	0	3	3	0	0.1
1994	Sea-A	2	5	.286	13	13	0	0	0	59	76	47	7	1	45	46	18.6	7.17	68	.314	.424	0	—	0	-15	-15	-1	-1.5
1996	Cin-N	8	5	.615	29	19	1	1	0	116	114	69	18	6	54	82	13.5	5.20	82	.261	.351	1	.031	-3	-13	-12	-0	-1.5
Total	3	10	10	.500	45	34	1	1	0	189^1	203	120	25	8	103	141	14.9	5.61	79	.277	.372	1	.031	-3	-25	-24	-1	-2.9
● **SLIM SALLEE**	Sallee, Harry Franklin "Scatter" b: 2/3/1885, Higginsport, Ohio d: 3/23/50, Higginsport, Ohio BL/TL, 6'3", 180 lbs. Deb: 4/16/08																											
1908	StL-N	3	8	.273	25	12	7	1	0	128^2	144	65	1	3	36	39	12.8	3.15	75	.274	.324	2	.049	-3	-11	-11	-0	-1.3
1909	StL-N	10	11	.476	32	27	12	1	0	219	223	107	3	5	59	55	11.8	2.42	104	.264	.315	8	.113	-2	4	3	-0	0.0
1910	StL-N	7	8	.467	18	13	9	1	2	115	112	44	4	1	24	46	10.7	2.97	100	.251	.290	4	.108	-2	1	0	0	-0.2
1911	StL-N	15	9	.625	36	30	18	1	3	245	234	102	6	5	64	74	11.1	2.76	123	.257	.309	15	.169	-2	18	17	-3	1.1
1912	StL-N	16	17	.485	48	32	20	3	**6**	294	289	122	6	6	72	108	11.2	2.60	132	.266	.315	14	.136	-4	26	27	-2	2.3
1913	StL-N	19	15	.559	50	29	18	3	5	276	257	98	11	5	60	106	10.5	2.71	119	.255	.301	20	.211	2	15	16	1	2.2
1914	StL-N	18	17	.514	46	29	18	3	**6**	282^1	252	92	5	9	72	105	10.6	2.10	133	.246	.302	21	.231	2	22	22	-2	2.9
1915	StL-N	13	17	.433	46	33	17	2	3	275^1	245	121	6	3	57	91	10.0	2.84	98	.238	.280	11	.120	-3	-3	-2	-1	-0.7
1916	StL-N	5	5	.500	16	7	4	2	1	70	75	28	2	2	23	28	12.9	3.47	76	.290	.352	3	.167	-0	-7	-6	-1	-1.1
	NY-N	9	4	.692	15	11	7	2	0	111^2	96	24	2	0	10	35	8.5	1.37	178	.234	.252	9	.257	2	15	14	-3	1.8
	Yr	14	9	.609	31	18	11	4	1	181^2	171	52	4	2	33	63	10.2	2.18	115	.256	.293	12	.226	2	9	7	-4	0.7
1917	*NY-N	18	7	.720	34	24	18	1	**4**	215^2	199	70	4	1	34	54	9.8	2.17	118	.249	.280	17	.221	1	13	10	-4	0.9
1918	NY-N	8	8	.500	18	16	12	1	2	132	122	44	3	0	12	33	**9.1**	2.25	117	.241	**.259**	5	.122	-2	8	6	-2	0.3
1919	*Cin-N	21	7	.750	29	28	22	4	0	227^2	221	63	4	1	20	24	9.6	2.06	135	.258	.276	14	.189	2	22	19	-5	2.1
1920	Cin-N	5	6	.455	21	12	6	0	2	116	129	57	4	2	16	13	11.4	3.34	91	.293	.320	6	.171	-1	-3	-4	-3	-0.8
	NY-N	1	0	1.000	5	2	1	0	0	17	16	7	0	0	0	2	8.5	1.59	189	.239	.239	1	.333	1	3	3	-0	0.2
	Yr	6	6	.500	26	14	7	0	2	133	145	64	4	2	16	15	11.0	3.11	97	.285	.310	7	.184	-0	0	-1	-4	-0.6
1921	NY-N	6	4	.600	37	0	0	0	2	96^1	115	48	7	0	14	23	12.1	3.64	101	.307	.332	8	.364	2	1	0	-2	0.1
Total	14	174	143	.549	476	305	189	25	36	2821^2	2729	1092	68	43	573	836	10.7	2.56	114	.258	.299	158	.171	-8	125	111	-26	9.8

YEAR	TM/L	W	L	PCT	G	GS	CG	SH	SV	IP	H	R	HR	HB	BB	SO	RAT	ERA	ERA+	OAV	OOB	BH	AVG	PB	PR	PR+	PD	TPI
● **ROGER SALMON**	Salmon, Roger Elliott b: 5/11/1891, Newark, N.J. d: 6/17/74, Belfast, Me. BL/TL, 6'2", 170 lbs. Deb: 5/3/12																											
1912	Phi-A	1	0	1.000	2	1	0	0	0	5	7	7	0	0	4	5	19.8	9.00	34	.318	.423	0	.000	-0	-3	-4	-0	-0.6
● **GUS SALVE**	Salve, Augustus William b: 12/29/1885, Boston, Mass. d: 3/29/71, Providence, R.I. BL/TL, 6', 190 lbs. Deb: 9/14/08																											
1908	Phi-A	0	1	.000	2	1	1	0	0	15^1	17	7	1	1	9	6	15.8	4.11	62	.266	.365	0	.000	-1	-3	-2	-1	-0.3
● **JACK SALVESON**	Salveson, John Theodore b: 1/5/14, Fullerton, Cal. d: 12/28/74, Norwalk, Cal. BR/TR, 6'0.5", 180 lbs. Deb: 6/3/33																											
1933	NY-N	0	2	.000	8	2	2	0	0	30^2	30	17	4	0	14	8	12.9	3.82	84	.252	.331	1	.111	-1	-2	-2	0	-0.2
1934	NY-N	3	1	.750	12	4	0	0	0	38^1	43	16	2	0	13	18	13.1	3.52	110	.281	.337	3	.300	0	2	2	1	0.2
1935	Pit-N	0	1	.000	5	0	0	0	0	7	11	12	1	1	5	2	21.9	9.00	46	.306	.405	0	.000	-0	-4	-4	1	-0.4
	Chi-A	1	2	.333	20	2	2	0	1	66^2	79	39	6	0	23	22	13.8	4.86	95	.298	.354	6	.300	2	-3	-2	-0	0.1
1943	Cle-A	5	3	.625	23	11	4	3	3	86	87	36	5	1	26	24	11.9	3.35	93	.266	.322	6	.231	2	-0	-2	0	0.0
1945	Cle-A	0	0	—	19	0	0	0	0	44	52	23	3	1	6	11	12.1	3.68	88	.294	.321	4	.400	3	-2	-2	1	0.3
Total	5	9	9	.500	87	19	8	3	4	272^2	302	143	21	3	87	85	12.9	3.99	91	.280	.336	20	.260	7	-8	-11	2	0.0
● **MANNY SALVO**	Salvo, Manuel "Gyp" b: 6/30/12, Sacramento, Cal. d: 2/7/97, Vallejo, Cal. BR/TR, 6'4", 210 lbs. Deb: 4/22/39																											
1939	NY-N	4	10	.286	32	18	4	0	1	136	150	84	11	5	75	69	15.2	4.63	85	.285	.380	4	.098	-2	-11	-11	1	-1.0
1940	Bos-N	10	9	.526	21	20	14	**5**	0	160^2	151	63	9	2	43	60	11.0	3.08	121	.248	.300	6	.103	-3	14	12	-1	0.9
1941	Bos-N	7	16	.304	35	27	11	2	0	195	192	103	9	4	93	67	13.3	4.06	88	.255	.340	7	.113	-0	-9	-11	-0	-1.2
1942	Bos-N	7	8	.467	25	14	6	1	0	130^2	129	52	7	4	41	25	12.0	3.03	110	.260	.322	5	.122	-1	4	4	-1	0.2
1943	Bos-N	0	1	.000	1	1	0	0	0	5	5	4	0	0	6	1	19.8	7.20	47	.250	.423	2	1.000	2	-2	-2	-0	-0.2
	Phi-N	0	0	—	1	0	0	0	0	0^1	2	1	0	0	1	0	81.0	27.00	12	.667	.750	0	—	0	-1	-1	0	0.0
	Bos-N	5	6	.455	20	13	5	1	0	93^2	94	45	6	1	25	25	11.5	3.27	105	.261	.311	6	.214	0	1	2	-1	0.2
	Yr	5	7	.417	22	14	5	1	0	99	101	50	6	1	32	26	12.2	3.55	96	.264	.322	8	.267	2	-2	-1	-1	0.0
Total	5	33	50	.398	135	93	40	9	1	721^1	723	352	42	16	284	247	12.8	3.69	98	.261	.334	30	.129	-4	-4	-7	-3	-1.1
● **JOE SAMBITO**	Sambito, Joseph Charles b: 6/28/52, Brooklyn, N.Y. BL/TL, 6'1", 190 lbs. Deb: 7/20/76																											
1976	Hou-N	3	2	.600	20	4	1	1	1	53^1	45	21	4	0	14	26	10.0	3.54	90	.237	.289	2	.222	1	-0	-2	1	0.0
1977	Hou-N	5	5	.500	54	1	0	0	7	89	77	34	6	0	24	67	10.2	2.33	154	.235	.287	2	.154	-0	16	13	1	1.7
1978	Hou-N	4	9	.308	62	0	0	0	11	88	85	32	5	0	32	96	12.0	3.07	108	.260	.326	1	.167	0	5	3	1	0.6
1979	Hou-N★	8	7	.533	63	0	0	0	22	91^1	80	20	8	4	23	83	10.5	1.77	198	.235	.292	2	.286	2	**20**	19	1	**4.3**
1980	*Hou-N	8	4	.667	64	0	0	0	17	90^1	65	26	3	2	22	75	8.9	2.19	150	.200	.255	0	.000	-1	14	12	0	2.0
1981	*Hou-N	5	5	.500	49	0	0	0	10	63^2	43	17	4	2	22	41	9.5	1.84	179	.192	.270	0	.000	-1	12	11	1	2.1
1982	Hou-N	0	0	—	9	0	0	0	4	12^2	7	2	0	0	2	7	6.4	0.71	468	.159	.196	0	.000	-0	4	4	0	0.3
1984	Hou-N	0	0	—	32	0	0	0	0	47^2	39	16	5	0	16	26	10.4	3.02	110	.228	.294	0	.000	-0	3	2	-1	0.0
1985	NY-N	0	0	—	8	0	0	0	0	10^2	21	18	1	0	8	3	24.5	12.66	27	.420	.500	0	—	0	-11	-11	0	-0.5
1986	*Bos-A	2	0	1.000	53	0	0	0	12	44^2	54	26	4	2	16	30	14.5	4.84	86	.298	.362	0	—	0	-3	-3	0	-0.3
1987	Bos-A	2	6	.250	47	0	0	0	0	37^2	46	29	8	0	16	35	14.8	6.93	66	.301	.367	0	—	0	-10	-10	-0	-1.8
Total	11	37	38	.493	461	5	1	1	84	629	562	241	48	10	195	489	11.0	3.03	115	.241	.302	7	.135	2	49	35	4	8.4
● **BILL SAMPEN**	Sampen, William Albert b: 1/18/63, Lincoln, Ill. BR/TR, 6'2", 195 lbs. Deb: 4/10/90																											
1990	Mon-N	12	7	.632	59	4	0	0	2	90^1	94	34	7	2	33	69	12.9	2.99	122	.268	.334	0	.000	-1	8	7	-1	1.3
1991	Mon-N	9	5	.643	43	8	0	0	0	92^1	96	49	13	3	46	52	14.1	4.00	91	.273	.362	3	.231	0	-3	-4	-1	-0.6
1992	Mon-N	1	4	.200	44	1	0	0	0	63^1	62	22	4	1	29	23	13.1	3.13	111	.268	.352	0	.000	-1	3	2	1	0.2
	KC-A	0	2	.000	8	1	0	0	0	19^2	21	10	0	3	3	14	12.4	3.66	111	.292	.346	0	—	0	1	1	0	0.1
1993	KC-A	2	2	.500	18	0	0	0	0	18^1	25	12	1	4	9	9	18.7	5.89	78	.338	.437	0	—	0	-3	-2	0	-0.5
1994	Cal-A	1	1	.500	10	0	0	0	0	15^1	14	11	1	3	13	9	17.6	6.46	76	.241	.405	0	—	0	-3	-3	0	-0.3
Total	5	25	21	.543	182	14	0	0	2	299^1	312	138	26	16	133	176	13.9	3.73	101	.274	.358	3	.111	-1	2	1	-1	0.2
● **BENJ SAMPSON**	Sampson, Benjamin Damon b: 4/27/75, Des Moines, Iowa BR/TL, 6'2", 210 lbs. Deb: 9/9/98																											
1998	Min-A	1	0	1.000	5	2	0	0	0	17^1	10	3	0	1	6	16	8.8	1.56	306	.172	.262	0	—	0	6	6	-0	0.3
1999	Min-A	3	2	.600	30	4	0	0	0	71	107	65	17	0	34	56	17.9	8.11	63	.351	.416	0	.000	-0	-26	-23	-1	-1.4
Total	2	4	2	.667	35	6	0	0	0	88^1	117	68	17	1	40	72	16.1	6.83	74	.322	.391	0	.000	-0	-20	-17	-1	-1.1
● **JOE SAMUELS**	Samuels, Joseph Jonas "Skabotch" b: 3/21/05, Scranton, Pa. d: 10/28/96, Bath, N.Y. BR/TR, 6'1.5", 196 lbs. Deb: 4/23/30																											
1930	Det-A	0	0	—	2	0	0	0	0	6	10	11	1	0	6	1	24.0	16.50	29	.417	.533	0	.000	-0	-8	-8	-0	-0.3
● **ROGER SAMUELS**	Samuels, Roger Howard b: 1/5/61, San Jose, Cal. BL/TL, 6'5", 210 lbs. Deb: 7/20/88																											
1988	SF-N	1	2	.333	15	0	0	0	0	23^1	17	10	4	1	7	22	9.6	3.47	94	.202	.272	0	.000	-0	-0	-1	0	-0.1
1989	Pit-N	0	0	—	5	0	0	0	0	3^2	9	4	1	0	4	2	31.9	9.82	34	.474	.565	0	—	0	-3	-3	-0	-0.2
Total	2	1	2	.333	20	0	0	0	0	27	26	14	5	1	11	24	12.7	4.33	76	.252	.330	0	.000	-0	-3	-3	0	-0.3
● **ALEX SANCHEZ**	Sanchez, Alex Anthony b: 4/8/66, Concord, Cal. BR/TR, 6'2", 185 lbs. Deb: 5/23/89																											
1989	Tor-A	0	1	.000	4	3	0	0	0	11^2	16	13	1	0	14	4	23.1	10.03	38	.356	.508	0	—	0	-8	-8	1	-0.5
● **ISRAEL SANCHEZ**	Sanchez, Israel (Matos) b: 8/20/63, Falcon Lasvias, Cuba BL/TL, 5'9", 170 lbs. Deb: 7/7/88																											
1988	KC-A	3	2	.600	19	1	0	0	1	35^2	36	20	0	0	18	14	13.6	4.54	88	.265	.351	0	—	0	-2	-2	0	-0.3
1990	KC-A	0	0	—	11	0	0	0	0	9^2	16	9	1	1	3	5	18.6	8.38	46	.381	.435	0	—	0	-5	-5	-0	-0.3
Total	2	3	2	.600	30	1	0	0	1	45^1	52	29	1	1	21	19	14.7	5.36	74	.292	.370	0	—	0	-7	-7	0	-0.6
● **JESUS SANCHEZ**	Sanchez, Jesus Paulino b: 10/11/74, Nizao Bani, D.R. BL/TL, 5'10", 153 lbs. Deb: 3/31/98																											
1998	Fla-N	7	9	.438	35	29	0	0	0	173	178	98	18	4	91	137	14.2	4.47	91	.272	.364	7	.135	-1	-5	-8	2	-0.6
1999	Fla-N	5	7	.417	59	10	0	0	0	76^1	84	53	16	4	60	62	17.4	6.01	73	.291	.419	1	.083	-0	-12	-15	0	-2.0
2000	Fla-N	9	12	.429	32	32	2	2	0	182	197	118	32	4	76	123	13.7	5.34	83	.280	.353	13	.232	2	-14	-19	0	-1.7
Total	3	21	28	.429	126	71	2	2	0	431^1	459	269	66	12	227	322	14.6	5.11	83	.279	.370	21	.175	1	-31	-42	2	-4.3
● **LUIS SANCHEZ**	Sanchez, Luis Mercedes (b: Luis Mercedes Escoba (Sanchez)) b: 8/24/53, Cariaco, Ven. BR/TR, 6'2", 210 lbs. Deb: 4/10/81																											
1981	Cal-A	0	2	.000	17	0	0	0	2	33^2	39	16	4	1	11	13	13.6	2.94	124	.287	.345	0	—	0	3	3	-0	0.2
1982	*Cal-A	7	4	.636	46	0	0	0	5	92^2	89	36	3	7	34	58	12.6	3.21	127	.259	.339	0	—	0	9	9	1	1.2
1983	Cal-A	10	8	.556	56	1	0	0	7	98^1	92	42	6	3	40	49	12.4	3.66	110	.254	.333	0	—	0	5	4	2	0.9
1984	Cal-A	9	7	.563	49	0	0	0	11	83^2	84	34	10	3	33	62	12.9	3.33	119	.268	.343	0	—	0	6	6	-0	1.2
1985	Cal-A	2	0	1.000	26	0	0	0	2	61^1	67	41	9	1	27	34	13.9	5.72	72	.283	.358	0	—	0	-11	-11	0	-0.5
Total	5	28	21	.571	194	1	0	0	27	369^2	371	169	32	15	145	216	12.9	3.75	107	.267	.342	0	—	0	12	11	2	3.0
● **RAUL SANCHEZ**	Sanchez, Raul Guadalupe (Rodriguez) b: 12/12/30, Marianao, Cuba BR/TR, 6', 150 lbs. Deb: 4/17/52																											
1952	Was-A	1	1	.500	3	2	1	1	0	12^2	13	5	0	0	7	6	14.2	3.55	100	.260	.351	0	.000	-1	0	0	0	-0.1
1957	Cin-N	3	2	.600	38	0	0	0	5	62^1	61	37	7	4	25	37	13.0	4.76	86	.262	.344	2	.286	1	-6	-4	1	-0.3
1960	Cin-N	1	0	1.000	8	0	0	0	0	14^2	12	9	1	3	11	5	16.0	4.91	78	.226	.388	1	.500	0	-2	-2	0	-0.1
Total	3	5	3	.625	49	2	1	1	5	89^2	86	51	8	7	43	48	13.7	4.62	86	.256	.352	3	.214	0	-8	-6	1	-0.5
● **BEN SANDERS**	Sanders, Alexander Bennett b: 2/16/1865, Catharpin, Va. d: 8/29/30, Memphis, Tenn. BR/TR, 6', 210 lbs. Deb: 6/6/1888 ♦																											
1888	Phi-N	19	10	.655	31	29	28	**8**	0	275^1	240	100	3	3	33	121	9.0	1.90	157	.228	.253	58	.246	5	29	32	4	4.0
1889	Phi-N	19	18	.514	44	39	34	1	1	349^2	406	217	9	4	96	123	13.0	3.55	122	.282	.328	47	.278	6	18	29	-2	2.8
1890	Phi-P	19	18	.514	43	40	37	2	1	346^2	412	237	13	10	69	107	12.7	3.76	114	.283	.320	59	.312	9	18	19	1	2.4
1891	Phi-a	11	5	.688	19	18	15	0	0	145	157	85	3	8	37	40	12.5	3.79	100	.267	.319	39	.250	2	-1	0	-1	0.1
1892	Lou-N	12	19	.387	31	31	30	3	0	268^1	281	150	6	2	62	77	11.6	3.22	95	.259	.300	54	.273	10	2	-5	-1	0.4
Total	5	80	70	.533	168	157	144	14	2	1385	1496	789	34	27	297	468	11.8	3.24	116	.266	.306	257	.271	33	66	76	1	9.7
● **DEE SANDERS**	Sanders, Dee Wilma b: 4/8/21, Quitman, Tex. BR/TR, 6'3", 195 lbs. Deb: 8/12/45																											
1945	StL-A	0	0	—	2	0	0	0	0	1^1	7	7	0	0	1	1	54.0	40.50	9	.700	.727	0	—	0	-6	-5	0	-0.2
● **KEN SANDERS**	Sanders, Kenneth George "Daffy" b: 7/8/41, St.Louis, Mo. BR/TR, 5'11", 185 lbs. Deb: 8/6/64																											
1964	KC-A	0	2	.000	21	0	0	0	1	27	23	12	2	1	17	18	13.7	3.67	104	.232	.350	0	—	0	-0	0	1	0.1

YEAR	TM/L	W	L	PCT	G	GS	CG	SH	SV	IP	H	R	HR	HB	BB	SO	RAT	ERA	ERA+	OAV	OOB	BH	AVG	PB	PR	PR+	PD	TPI
1966	Bos-A	3	6	.333	24	0	0	0	2	47^1	36	22	2	2	28	33	12.5	3.80	100	.214	.333	0	.000	-0	-2	0	-0	0.0
	KC-A	3	4	.429	38	1	0	0	1	65^1	59	28	8	1	48	41	14.9	3.72	91	.250	.379	2	.250	0	-2	-2	1	-0.2
	Yr	6	10	.375	62	1	0	0	3	112^2	95	50	10	3	76	74	13.9	3.75	95	.235	.360	2	.143	0	-4	-2	1	-0.2
1968	Oak-A	0	1	.000	7	0	0	0	0	10^2	8	5	1	0	8	6	13.5	3.38	84	.229	.372	0	—	0	-0	-1	0	-0.1
1970	Mil-A	5	2	.714	50	0	0	0	13	92^1	64	19	1	4	25	64	9.1	1.75	216	.201	.268	3	.231	1	20	20	1	2.3
1971	Mil-A	7	12	.368	**83**	0	0	0	**31**	136^1	111	35	9	4	34	80	9.8	1.91	182	.227	.282	0	.000	-1	**24**	**24**	2	4.7
1972	Mil-A	2	9	.182	62	0	0	0	17	92^1	88	38	10	2	31	51	11.8	3.12	98	.245	.309	1	.143	0	-0	-1	1	0.0
1973	Min-A	2	4	.333	27	0	0	0	8	44^1	53	31	4	2	21	19	15.4	6.09	65	.299	.380	0	—	0	-11	-10	0	-1.6
	Cle-A	5	1	.833	15	0	0	0	5	27^1	18	6	2	0	9	14	8.9	1.65	238	.188	.257	0	—	0	7	7	0	1.5
	Yr	7	5	.583	42	0	0	0	13	71^2	71	37	6	2	30	33	12.9	4.40	90	.260	.338	0	—	0	-5	-3	0	-0.1
1974	Cle-A	0	1	.000	9	0	0	0	1	11	21	12	5	0	5	4	21.3	9.82	37	.404	.456	0	—	0	-8	-8	0	-0.8
	Cal-A	0	0	—	9	0	0	0	1	9^2	10	5	0	0	3	4	12.1	2.79	123	.278	.333	0	—	0	1	1	1	0.1
	Yr	0	1	.000	18	0	0	0	2	20^2	31	17	5	0	8	8	17.0	6.53	54	.352	.406	0	—	0	-7	-7	1	-0.7
1975	NY-N	1	1	.500	29	0	0	0	5	43	31	11	2	0	14	8	9.4	2.30	150	.205	.273	0	.000	-0	6	6	-0	0.4
1976	NY-N	1	2	.333	31	0	0	0	1	47	39	16	4	1	12	16	10.0	2.87	115	.231	.286	0	.000	-0	3	2	1	0.2
	KC-A	0	0	—	3	0	0	0	0	3	3	0	0	0	3	2	18.0	0.00	—	.273	.429	0	—	0	1	1	-0	0.1
Total	10	29	45	.392	408	1	0	0	86	656^2	564	240	50	17	258	360	11.5	2.97	118	.235	.314	6	.115	-0	38	39	7	6.7

● ROY SANDERS Sanders, Roy Garvin "Butch" or "Pepe" b: 8/1/1892, Stafford, Kan. d: 1/17/50, Kansas City, Mo. BR/TR, 6'0.5", 195 lbs. Deb: 4/16/17

YEAR	TM/L	W	L	PCT	G	GS	CG	SH	SV	IP	H	R	HR	HB	BB	SO	RAT	ERA	ERA+	OAV	OOB	BH	AVG	PB	PR	PR+	PD	TPI
1917	Cin-N	0	1	.000	2	2	1	0	0	14	12	7	0	1	16	3	18.6	4.50	58	.273	.475	0	.000	-1	-3	-3	1	-0.2
1918	Pit-N	7	9	.438	28	14	6	1	1	156	135	59	1	2	52	55	10.9	2.60	111	.239	.305	8	.151	-1	3	5	2	0.6
Total	2	7	10	.412	30	16	7	1	1	170	147	66	1	3	68	58	11.5	2.75	104	.241	.321	8	.136	-2	0	2	2	0.4

● ROY SANDERS Sanders, Roy Lee "Simon" b: 6/10/1894, Missouri d: 7/8/63, Louisville, Ky. BR/TR, 6', 185 lbs. Deb: 8/6/18

YEAR	TM/L	W	L	PCT	G	GS	CG	SH	SV	IP	H	R	HR	HB	BB	SO	RAT	ERA	ERA+	OAV	OOB	BH	AVG	PB	PR	PR+	PD	TPI
1918	NY-A	0	2	.000	6	2	0	0	0	25^2	28	15	0	2	16	8	16.1	4.21	67	.301	.414	0	.000	-1	-4	-4	-1	-0.5
1920	StL-A	1	1	.500	8	1	0	0	0	17^1	20	10	1	1	17	2	19.7	5.19	75	.313	.463	0	.000	-1	-3	-2	-1	-0.4
Total	2	1	3	.250	14	3	0	0	0	43	48	25	1	3	33	10	17.6	4.60	71	.306	.435	0	.000	-2	-7	-6	-1	-0.9

● SCOTT SANDERS Sanders, Scott Gerald b: 3/25/69, Hannibal, Mo. BR/TR, 6'4", 220 lbs. Deb: 8/6/93

YEAR	TM/L	W	L	PCT	G	GS	CG	SH	SV	IP	H	R	HR	HB	BB	SO	RAT	ERA	ERA+	OAV	OOB	BH	AVG	PB	PR	PR+	PD	TPI
1993	SD-N	3	3	.500	9	9	0	0	0	52^1	54	32	4	1	23	37	13.4	4.13	100	.265	.342	1	.063	-1	-0	0	-1	-0.2
1994	SD-N	4	8	.333	23	20	0	0	1	111	103	63	10	5	48	109	12.6	4.78	86	.245	.329	4	.125	-0	-7	-8	1	-0.8
1995	SD-N	5	5	.500	17	15	1	0	0	90	79	46	14	2	31	88	11.2	4.30	94	.228	.296	8	.296	2	-1	-3	-2	-0.2
1996	*SD-N	9	5	.643	46	16	0	0	0	144	117	58	10	2	48	157	10.4	3.38	118	.221	.288	7	.194	2	14	10	-1	0.9
1997	Sea-A	3	6	.333	33	6	0	0	2	65^1	73	48	16	3	38	62	15.7	6.47	70	.280	.377	0	—	0	-14	-15	-2	-1.9
	Det-A	3	8	.273	14	14	1	1	0	74^1	79	44	14	1	24	58	12.6	5.33	86	.276	.334	0	—	0	-6	-6	-0	-0.8
	Yr	6	14	.300	47	20	1	1	2	139^2	152	92	30	4	62	120	14.0	5.86	78	.278	.356	0	—	0	-20	-20	-2	-2.7
1998	Det-A	0	2	.000	3	2	0	0	0	9^2	24	19	1	0	6	6	27.9	17.69	27	.471	.526	0	—	0	-14	-14	0	-1.8
	SD-N	3	1	.750	23	0	0	0	0	30^2	33	20	5	0	5	26	11.2	4.11	95	.270	.299	0	—	0	0	-1	0	-0.1
1999	Chi-N	4	7	.364	67	6	0	0	2	104^1	112	69	19	0	53	89	14.2	5.52	82	.277	.360	5	.278	2	-11	-12	-0	-1.0
Total	7	34	45	.430	235	88	2	1	5	681^2	674	399	93	14	276	632	12.7	4.86	87	.257	.331	25	.194	4	-40	-49	-5	-5.9

● WAR SANDERS Sanders, Warren Williams b: 8/2/1877, Maynardville, Tenn. d: 8/3/62, Chattanooga, Tenn. BR/TL, 5'10", 160 lbs. Deb: 4/18/03

YEAR	TM/L	W	L	PCT	G	GS	CG	SH	SV	IP	H	R	HR	HB	BB	SO	RAT	ERA	ERA+	OAV	OOB	BH	AVG	PB	PR	PR+	PD	TPI
1903	StL-N	1	6	.143	8	6	3	0	0	40	48	37	0	2	21	9	16.0	6.07	54	.286	.372	1	.067	-2	-12	-13	-1	-1.9
1904	StL-N	1	2	.333	4	3	1	0	0	19	25	15	1	1	1	11	12.8	4.74	57	.298	.314	0	.000	-1	-4	-4	0	-0.6
Total	2	2	8	.200	12	9	4	0	0	59	73	52	1	3	22	20	14.9	5.64	55	.290	.354	1	.048	-2	-17	-17	-0	-2.5

● SCOTT SANDERSON Sanderson, Scott Douglas b: 7/22/56, Dearborn, Mich. BR/TR, 6'5", 200 lbs. Deb: 8/6/78

YEAR	TM/L	W	L	PCT	G	GS	CG	SH	SV	IP	H	R	HR	HB	BB	SO	RAT	ERA	ERA+	OAV	OOB	BH	AVG	PB	PR	PR+	PD	TPI
1978	Mon-N	4	2	.667	10	9	1	1	0	61	52	20	3	1	21	50	10.9	2.51	141	.232	.301	2	.105	-1	7	7	-1	0.5
1979	Mon-N	9	8	.529	34	24	5	3	1	168	148	69	16	3	54	138	11.0	3.43	107	.236	.300	8	.160	-0	6	5	-2	0.2
1980	Mon-N	16	11	.593	33	33	7	3	0	211^1	206	76	18	3	56	125	11.3	3.11	115	.257	.308	5	.078	-3	12	11	-2	0.8
1981	*Mon-N	9	7	.563	22	22	4	1	0	137^1	122	50	10	1	31	77	10.1	2.95	119	.236	.281	4	.114	2	8	8	-2	1.0
1982	Mon-N	12	12	.500	32	32	7	0	0	224	212	98	24	3	58	158	11.0	3.46	106	.251	.301	8	.140	1	4	5	-3	0.2
1983	Mon-N	6	7	.462	18	16	0	0	1	81^1	98	50	12	0	20	55	13.1	4.65	77	.303	.344	4	.143	-0	-9	-10	-1	-1.5
1984	*Chi-N	8	5	.615	24	24	3	0	0	140^2	140	54	5	2	24	76	10.6	3.14	125	.264	.298	5	.119	-1	7	11	1	1.0
1985	Chi-N	5	6	.455	19	19	2	0	0	121	100	49	13	0	27	80	9.4	3.12	128	.228	.273	2	.065	-2	6	11	1	0.9
1986	Chi-N	9	11	.450	37	28	1	1	1	169^2	165	85	21	2	37	124	10.8	4.19	97	.255	.297	3	.059	-3	-9	-2	-1	-0.7
1987	Chi-N	8	9	.471	32	22	0	0	2	144^2	156	72	23	3	50	106	13.0	4.29	100	.274	.336	3	.075	-1	-3	-0	-1	-0.2
1988	Chi-N	1	2	.333	11	0	0	0	0	15^1	13	9	1	0	3	6	9.4	5.28	68	.232	.271	0	—	0	-3	-3	-0	-0.5
1989	*Chi-N	11	9	.550	37	23	2	0	0	146^1	155	69	16	2	31	86	11.6	3.94	96	.273	.313	2	.047	-2	-7	-3	-2	-0.7
1990	*Oak-A	17	11	.607	34	34	2	1	0	206^1	205	99	27	4	66	128	12.0	3.88	96	.255	.315	0	—	0	1	-4	-2	-0.7
1991	NY-A☆	16	10	.615	34	34	2	2	0	208	200	95	22	3	29	130	10.0	3.81	109	.252	.281	0	—	0	7	8	-3	0.6
1992	NY-A	12	11	.522	33	33	2	1	0	193^1	220	116	28	4	64	104	13.4	4.93	80	.286	.344	0	—	0	-21	-22	-2	-2.5
1993	Cal-A	7	11	.389	21	21	4	1	0	135^1	153	77	15	5	27	66	12.3	4.46	101	.289	.329	0	—	0	-2	1	-1	0.0
	SF-N	4	2	.667	11	8	0	0	0	48^2	48	20	12	1	7	36	10.4	3.51	111	.255	.286	0	.000	-1	3	2	0	0.1
1994	Chi-A	8	4	.667	18	14	1	0	0	92	110	57	20	2	12	36	12.1	5.09	92	.296	.322	0	—	0	-3	-4	1	-0.4
1995	Cal-A	1	3	.250	7	7	0	0	0	39^1	48	23	6	2	4	23	12.4	4.12	114	.298	.323	0	—	0	3	3	-0	0.2
1996	Cal-A	0	2	.000	5	4	0	0	0	18	39	21	5	2	4	7	22.5	7.50	67	.433	.469	0	—	0	-5	-5	0	-0.4
Total	19	163	143	.533	472	407	43	14	5	2561^2	2590	1209	297	43	625	1611	11.4	3.84	102	.263	.310	46	.097	-12	1	21	-21	-2.1

● FRED SANFORD Sanford, John Frederick b: 8/9/19, Garfield, Utah BB/TR (BR 1948), 6'1", 200 lbs. Deb: 5/5/43

YEAR	TM/L	W	L	PCT	G	GS	CG	SH	SV	IP	H	R	HR	HB	BB	SO	RAT	ERA	ERA+	OAV	OOB	BH	AVG	PB	PR	PR+	PD	TPI
1943	StL-A	0	0	—	3	0	0	0	0	9^1	7	2	0	0	4	2	10.6	1.93	172	.219	.306	0	—	0	1	1	0	0.1
1946	StL-A	2	1	.667	3	3	2	2	0	22	19	7	0	0	9	8	11.5	2.05	182	.235	.311	2	.286	1	4	4	-0	0.7
1947	StL-A	7	16	.304	34	23	9	0	4	186^2	186	89	17	0	76	62	12.6	3.71	104	.261	.332	11	.204	-0	-0	3	-1	0.2
1948	StL-A	12	21	.364	42	33	9	1	2	227	250	123	19	2	91	79	13.6	4.64	98	.279	.347	11	.151	-2	-9	-2	1	-0.4
1949	NY-A	7	3	.700	29	11	3	0	0	95^1	100	53	9	0	57	51	14.8	3.87	105	.270	.367	4	.118	-2	3	2	-0	-0.1
1950	NY-A	5	4	.556	26	12	2	0	0	112^2	103	60	9	1	79	54	14.6	4.55	94	.252	.374	8	.229	1	0	-3	3	0.1
1951	NY-A	0	3	.000	11	2	0	0	0	26^2	15	11	2	0	25	10	13.5	3.71	103	.169	.351	0	.000	-1	1	0	1	0.0
	Was-A	2	3	.400	7	7	0	0	0	37	51	27	5	0	27	12	19.0	6.57	62	.329	.429	1	.071	-1	-10	-10	-1	-1.3
	StL-A	2	4	.333	9	7	1	0	0	27^1	37	33	6	0	23	7	19.8	10.21	43	.308	.420	2	.286	1	-18	-17	-0	-2.7
	Yr	4	10	.286	27	16	1	0	0	91	103	71	13	0	75	29	17.6	6.82	60	.283	.405	3	.115	-1	-27	-28	-0	-4.0
Total	7	37	55	.402	164	98	26	3	6	744	768	405	67	3	391	285	14.1	4.45	94	.268	.357	39	.170	-4	-28	-21	2	-3.4

● JACK SANFORD Sanford, John Stanley b: 5/18/29, Wellesley Hills, Mass. d: 3/7/2000, Beckley, W.Va. BR/TR, 6', 190 lbs. Deb: 9/16/56 C

YEAR	TM/L	W	L	PCT	G	GS	CG	SH	SV	IP	H	R	HR	HB	BB	SO	RAT	ERA	ERA+	OAV	OOB	BH	AVG	PB	PR	PR+	PD	TPI
1956	Phi-N	1	0	1.000	3	1	0	0	0	13	7	2	0	1	13	6	14.5	1.38	269	.184	.404	1	.333	0	3	3	0	0.3
1957	Phi-N★	19	8	.704	33	33	15	3	0	236^2	194	94	22	3	94	**188**	11.1	3.08	124	**.221**	.298	15	.169	-1	21	19	-1	1.9
1958	Phi-N	10	13	.435	38	27	7	2	0	186^1	197	103	15	3	81	106	13.6	4.44	89	.274	.350	10	.169	1	-10	-10	-2	-1.1
1959	SF-N	15	12	.556	36	31	10	0	1	222^1	198	90	22	7	70	132	11.1	3.16	121	.235	.300	8	.111	-1	20	17	-1	1.7
1960	SF-N	12	14	.462	37	34	11	**6**	0	219	199	111	11	2	99	125	12.3	3.82	91	.243	.326	13	.176	1	-1	-9	-1	-0.9
1961	SF-N	13	9	.591	38	33	6	0	0	217^1	203	114	22	5	87	112	12.2	4.22	90	.249	.325	16	.216	6	-5	-11	-1	-0.5
1962	*SF-N	24	7	.774	39	38	13	2	0	265^1	233	110	23	3	92	147	11.1	3.43	111	.234	.301	15	.153	0	15	11	2	1.4
1963	SF-N	16	13	.552	42	42	11	0	0	284^1	273	123	21	5	76	158	11.2	3.51	91	.251	.303	13	.138	3	-7	-10	3	-0.4
1964	SF-N	5	7	.417	18	17	3	1	1	106^1	91	44	7	4	37	64	11.2	3.30	108	.228	.300	4	.133	1	3	3	1	0.4
1965	SF-N	4	5	.444	23	16	0	0	2	91	92	50	11	7	30	43	12.8	3.96	91	.256	.325	3	.120	-0	-4	-4	-1	-0.4
	Cal-A	1	2	.333	9	5	0	0	1	29^1	35	16	2	0	10	13	13.8	4.60	74	.324	.381	1	.143	-0	-4	-4	1	-0.4
1966	Cal-A	13	7	.650	50	6	0	0	5	108	108	51	11	4	27	54	11.6	3.83	88	.271	.323	3	.136	1	-5	-6	1	-0.9
1967	Cal-A	3	2	.600	12	9	0	0	1	48^1	53	26	6	0	7	21	11.2	4.47	70	.288	.314	3	.200	1	-7	-7	1	-0.5
	KC-A	1	2	.333	10	1	0	0	0	22	24	18	1	2	14	13	16.4	6.55	49	.296	.412	0	.000	-0	-8	-8	1	-1.0
	Yr	4	4	.500	22	10	0	0	1	70^1	77	44	7	2	21	34	12.8	5.12	62	.291	.347	3	.167	1	-15	-16	2	-1.5
Total	12	137	101	.576	388	293	76	14	11	2049^1	1907	952	174	46	737	1182	11.8	3.69	98	.247	.316	105	.158	12	11	-14	3	-0.4

YEAR	TM/L	W	L	PCT	G	GS	CG	SH	SV	IP	H	R	HR	HB	BB	SO	RAT	ERA	ERA+	OAV	OOB	BH	AVG	PB	PR	PR+	PD	TPI
● **MO SANFORD** Sanford, Meredith Leroy b: 12/24/66, Americus, Ga. BR/TR, 6'6", 220 lbs. Deb: 8/9/91																												
1991	Cin-N	1	2	.333	5	5	0	0	0	28	19	14	3	1	15	31	11.3	3.86	99	.186	.297	0	.000	-1	-1	-0	-0	-0.1
1993	Col-N	1	2	.333	11	6	0	0	0	35^2	37	25	4	0	27	36	16.1	5.30	90	.278	.400	0	.000	-1	-5	-2	-1	-0.3
1995	Min-A	0	0	—	11	0	0	0	0	18^2	16	11	7	2	16	17	16.4	5.30	90	.225	.382	0	—	0	-1	-1	-1	-0.1
Total	3	2	4	.333	27	11	0	0	0	82^1	72	50	14	3	58	84	14.5	4.81	93	.235	.362	0	.000	-2	-7	-3	-2	-0.5
● **JOHAN SANTANA** Santana, Johan Alexander b: 3/13/79, Tovar, Venez. BL/TL, 6', 195 lbs. Deb: 4/3/2000																												
2000	Min-A	2	3	.400	30	5	0	0	0	86	102	64	11	2	54	64	16.5	6.49	81	.302	.401	0	.000	-0	-15	-11	1	-0.5
● **JULIO SANTANA** Santana, Julio Franklin b: 1/20/73, San Pedro De Macoris, D.R. BR/TR, 6', 175 lbs. Deb: 4/6/97																												
1997	Tex-A	4	6	.400	30	14	0	0	0	104	141	86	16	4	49	64	16.8	6.75	71	.323	.396	1	.500	0	-25	-22	1	-1.6
1998	Tex-A	0	0	—	3	0	0	0	0	5^1	7	5	0	0	4	1	18.6	8.44	57	.304	.407	0	—	0	-2	-2	0	-0.1
	TB-A	5	6	.455	32	19	1	0	0	140^1	144	72	18	5	58	60	13.3	4.23	113	.270	.347	0	.000	-0	7	9	-3	0.3
	Yr	5	6	.455	35	19	1	0	0	145^2	151	77	18	5	62	61	13.5	4.39	109	.272	.350	0	.000	-0	4	6	-3	0.2
1999	TB-A	1	4	.200	22	5	0	0	0	55^1	66	49	10	7	32	34	17.1	7.32	68	.300	.405	1	1.000	0	-15	-14	-1	-1.0
2000	Mon-N	1	5	.167	36	4	0	0	0	66^2	69	45	11	2	33	58	14.0	5.67	83	.271	.359	0	.000	-1	-8	-7	0	-0.6
Total	4	11	21	.344	123	42	1	0	0	371^2	427	257	55	18	176	217	15.0	5.71	84	.291	.374	2	.143	-0	-44	-36	-2	-3.0
● **MARINO SANTANA** Santana, Marino (Castro) b: 5/10/72, San Jose De Los Llanos, D.R. BR/TR, 6'1", 175 lbs. Deb: 9/4/98																												
1998	Det-A	0	0	—	7	0	0	0	0	7^1	9	3	1	1	8	10	22.1	3.68	128	.310	.474	0	—	0	1	1	0	0.0
1999	Bos-A	0	0	—	3	0	0	0	0	4	8	7	3	0	3	4	24.8	15.75	32	.444	.524	0	—	0	-5	-5	0	-0.2
Total	2	0	0	—	10	0	0	0	0	11^1	17	10	4	1	11	14	23.0	7.94	61	.362	.492	0	—	0	-4	-4	0	-0.2
● **JOSE SANTIAGO** Santiago, Jose Guillermo (Guzman) "Pants" b: 9/4/28, Coamo, P.R. BR/TR, 5'10", 175 lbs. Deb: 4/17/54																												
1954	Cle-A	0	0	—	1	0	0	0	0	1^2	0	1	0	0	2	1	10.8	0.00	—	.000	.286	0	—	0	1	1	-0	0.0
1955	Cle-A	2	0	1.000	17	0	0	0	0	32^2	31	11	1	5	14	19	13.8	2.48	161	.256	.357	2	.500	1	5	5	0	0.4
1956	KC-A	1	2	.333	9	5	0	0	0	21^2	36	26	8	5	17	9	24.1	8.31	52	.387	.504	2	.400	0	-10	-9	0	-1.0
Total	3	3	2	.600	27	5	0	0	0	56	67	38	9	10	33	29	17.7	4.66	88	.306	.420	4	.444	2	-4	-3	0	-0.6
● **JOSE SANTIAGO** Santiago, Jose Rafael (Alfonso) b: 8/15/40, Juana Diaz, P.R. BR/TR, 6'2", 185 lbs. Deb: 9/9/63																												
1963	KC-A	1	0	1.000	4	0	0	0	0	7	8	7	4	0	2	6	12.9	9.00	43	.276	.323	0	—	0	-4	-4	0	-0.5
1964	KC-A	0	6	.000	34	8	0	0	0	83^2	84	53	9	4	35	64	13.2	4.73	81	.258	.337	0	.000	-2	-10	-8	-1	-0.8
1965	KC-A	0	0	—	4	0	0	0	0	5	8	5	1	0	4	8	21.6	9.00	39	.364	.462	0	—	0	-3	-3	0	-0.1
1966	Bos-A	12	13	.480	35	28	7	1	2	172	155	87	17	2	58	119	11.3	3.66	104	.238	.302	11	.196	0	-4	2	-1	0.3
1967	*Bos-A	12	4	.750	50	11	2	0	5	145^1	138	61	15	2	47	109	11.6	3.59	97	.251	.313	8	.190	2	-6	-2	0	0.1
1968	Bos-A†	9	4	.692	18	18	7	2	0	124	96	34	9	3	42	86	10.2	2.25	140	.215	.287	7	.163	1	10	12	-0	1.4
1969	Bos-A	0	0	—	10	0	0	0	0	7^2	11	5	2	0	4	4	17.6	3.52	108	.324	.395	0	—	0	0	0	-0	0.0
1970	Bos-A	0	2	.000	8	0	0	0	1	11^1	18	13	0	0	8	8	20.6	10.32	38	.353	.441	2	.667	1	-8	-8	-0	-1.2
Total	8	34	29	.540	163	65	16	3	8	556	518	265	57	11	200	404	11.8	3.74	96	.246	.314	28	.173	2	-26	-9	-2	-0.8
● **JOSE SANTIAGO** Santiago, Jose Rafael (Fuentes) b: 11/5/74, Fajardo, P.R. BR/TR, 6'3", 200 lbs. Deb: 6/7/97																												
1997	KC-A	0	0	—	4	0	0	0	0	4^2	7	2	0	1	2	1	19.3	1.93	245	.333	.417	0	—	0	1	1	-0	0.0
1998	KC-A	0	0	—	2	0	0	0	0	2	4	2	0	0	0	2	18.0	9.00	54	.444	.444	0	—	0	-1	-1	0	0.0
1999	KC-A	3	4	.429	34	0	0	0	2	47^1	46	23	7	2	14	15	11.8	3.42	147	.251	.312	0	—	0	8	8	-1	1.0
2000	KC-A	8	6	.571	45	0	0	0	2	69	70	33	7	3	26	44	12.9	3.91	128	.260	.332	0	—	0	8	8	0	1.5
Total	4	11	10	.524	85	0	0	0	4	123	127	60	14	6	42	62	12.8	3.73	134	.263	.330	0	—	0	16	17	-1	2.5
● **AL SANTORINI** Santorini, Alan Joel b: 5/19/48, Irvington, N.J. BR/TR, 6', 190 lbs. Deb: 9/10/68																												
1968	Atl-N	0	1	.000	1	1	0	0	0	3	4	4	1	0	0	0	12.0	0.00	—	.286	.286	0	—	0	1	1	-0	0.3
1969	SD-N	8	14	.364	32	30	2	1	0	184^2	194	95	11	7	73	111	13.4	3.95	90	.270	.343	7	.111	-1	-7	-9	1	-1.0
1970	SD-N	1	8	.111	21	12	0	0	1	75^2	91	56	11	3	43	41	16.3	6.07	66	.294	.385	0	.000	-2	-17	-18	-1	-2.1
1971	SD-N	0	2	.000	18	3	0	0	0	38^1	43	19	4	0	11	21	12.7	3.76	88	.285	.333	2	.400	1	-1	-2	-1	-0.1
	StL-N	0	2	.000	19	5	0	0	2	49^2	51	21	2	1	19	21	12.9	3.81	95	.270	.340	3	.300	1	-2	-1	-0	0.0
	Yr	0	4	.000	37	8	0	0	2	88	94	40	6	1	30	42	12.8	3.78	92	.276	.337	5	.333	1	-3	-3	-1	-0.1
1972	StL-N	8	11	.421	30	19	3	3	0	133^2	136	63	6	1	46	72	12.3	4.11	83	.263	.324	3	.075	-2	-10	-11	-1	-1.7
1973	StL-N	0	0	—	6	0	0	0	0	8^1	14	5	1	1	2	2	18.4	5.40	68	.400	.447	0	.000	-0	-2	-2	-0	-0.1
Total	6	17	38	.309	127	70	5	4	3	493^1	533	263	36	13	194	268	13.5	4.29	83	.276	.346	15	.109	-4	-37	-40	-3	-4.7
● **MANNY SARMIENTO** Sarmiento, Manuel Eduardo (Aponte) b: 2/2/56, Cagua, Venez. BR/TR, 6', 170 lbs. Deb: 7/30/76																												
1976	*Cin-N	5	1	.833	22	0	0	0	0	43^2	36	14	1	1	12	20	10.1	2.06	170	.222	.280	0	.000	-1	7	7	-1	0.7
1977	Cin-N	0	0	—	24	0	0	0	1	40^1	28	13	6	0	11	23	8.7	2.45	160	.196	.253	0	.000	-0	7	7	-1	0.2
1978	Cin-N	9	7	.563	63	4	0	0	5	127^1	109	65	16	1	54	72	11.6	4.38	81	.234	.315	0	.000	-1	-11	-12	-1	-1.7
1979	Cin-N	0	4	.000	23	1	0	0	0	38^2	47	21	2	1	7	23	12.8	4.66	80	.311	.346	0	.000	-1	-4	-4	-0	-0.5
1980	Sea-A	0	1	.000	9	0	0	0	1	14^2	14	7	2	0	6	15	12.3	3.68	112	.255	.328	0	—	0	1	1	-0	0.0
1982	Pit-N	9	4	.692	35	17	4	0	1	164^2	153	69	7	0	46	81	10.9	3.39	110	.246	.298	9	.191	1	4	6	-2	0.3
1983	Pit-N	3	5	.375	52	0	0	0	4	84^1	74	35	8	0	36	49	11.7	2.99	124	.243	.324	0	.000	-1	6	7	-1	0.5
Total	7	26	22	.542	228	22	4	0	12	513^2	461	224	42	3	172	283	11.1	3.49	106	.242	.306	9	.103	-3	9	11	-6	-0.5
● **KAZUHIRO SASAKI** Sasaki, Kazuhiro b: 2/22/68, Tokyo, Japan BR/TR, 6'4", 209 lbs. Deb: 4/5/2000																												
2000	*Sea-A	2	5	.286	63	0	0	0	37	62^2	42	25	10	2	31	78	10.8	3.16	152	.184	.287	0	—	0	12	12	-1	2.1
● **KEVIN SAUCIER** Saucier, Kevin Andrew b: 8/9/56, Pensacola, Fla. BR/TL, 6'1", 196 lbs. Deb: 10/1/78																												
1978	Phi-N	0	1	.000	1	0	0	0	0	2	4	4	0	1	1	2	27.0	18.00	20	.400	.500	0	—	0	-3	-3	-0	-0.5
1979	Phi-N	1	4	.200	29	2	0	0	1	62^1	68	31	4	3	33	21	15.0	4.19	92	.291	.385	1	.100	-1	-2	-2	0	-0.2
1980	*Phi-N	7	3	.700	40	0	0	0	0	50	50	21	2	4	20	25	13.3	3.42	111	.281	.366	0	.000	-1	1	2	0	0.3
1981	Det-A	4	2	.667	38	0	0	0	13	49	26	11	1	5	21	23	9.6	1.65	228	.160	.277	0	—	0	11	11	0	2.1
1982	Det-A	3	1	.750	31	1	0	0	5	40^1	35	15	0	2	29	23	14.7	3.12	130	.254	.391	0	—	0	4	4	0	0.5
Total	5	15	11	.577	139	3	0	0	19	203^2	183	82	7	15	104	94	13.3	3.31	116	.253	.359	1	.056	-2	10	12	1	2.2
● **SCOTT SAUERBECK** Sauerbeck, Scott William b: 11/9/71, Cincinnati, Ohio BR/TL, 6'3", 190 lbs. Deb: 4/5/99																												
1999	Pit-N	4	1	.800	65	0	0	0	2	67^2	53	19	6	4	38	55	12.6	2.00	229	.220	.336	0	.000	-0	19	19	0	1.3
2000	Pit-N	5	4	.556	75	0	0	0	1	75^2	76	36	4	1	61	83	16.4	4.04	114	.270	.402	0	.000	-0	5	5	1	0.5
Total	2	9	5	.643	140	0	0	0	3	143^1	129	55	10	5	99	138	14.6	3.08	149	.247	.372	0	.000	-0	24	24	1	1.8
● **TONY SAUNDERS** Saunders, Anthony Scott b: 4/29/74, Baltimore, Md. BL/TL, 6'2", 205 lbs. Deb: 4/5/97																												
1997	*Fla-N	4	6	.400	22	21	0	0	0	111^1	99	62	12	2	64	102	13.3	4.61	88	.244	.350	3	.081	-1	-5	-7	-1	-0.8
1998	TB-A	6	15	.286	31	31	2	0	0	192^1	191	95	15	7	111	172	14.5	4.12	116	.265	.368	2	1.000	1	12	14	-1	1.3
1999	TB-A	3	3	.500	9	9	0	0	0	42	53	39	6	4	29	30	18.4	6.43	77	.315	.428	0	—	0	-7	-7	0	-0.8
Total	3	13	24	.351	62	61	2	0	0	345^2	343	196	33	13	204	304	14.6	4.56	100	.265	.371	5	.128	0	-1	0	-2	-0.3
● **DENNIS SAUNDERS** Saunders, Dennis James b: 1/4/49, Alhambra, Cal. BB/TR, 6'3", 195 lbs. Deb: 5/21/70																												
1970	Det-A	1	1	.500	8	0	0	0	1	14	16	5	1	1	5	8	14.1	3.21	116	.286	.355	0	.000	-1	1	1	1	0.1
● **RICH SAUVEUR** Sauveur, Richard Daniel b: 11/23/63, Arlington, Va. BL/TL, 6'4", 170 lbs. Deb: 7/1/86																												
1986	Pit-N	0	0	—	3	3	0	0	0	12	17	8	3	2	6	6	18.8	6.00	64	.354	.446	1	.333	0	-3	-3	1	0.0
1988	Mon-N	0	0	—	4	0	0	0	0	3	3	2	1	0	2	3	15.0	6.00	60	.250	.357	0	—	0	-1	-1	0	0.0
1991	NY-N	0	0	—	6	0	0	0	0	3^1	7	4	1	0	2	4	24.3	10.80	34	.467	.529	0	—	0	-3	-3	0	-0.1
1992	KC-A	0	1	.000	8	0	0	0	0	14^1	15	7	1	2	8	7	15.7	4.40	92	.273	.385	0	—	0	-1	-1	-0	-0.1
1996	Chi-A	0	0	—	3	0	0	0	0	3	3	5	1	1	5	1	27.0	15.00	32	.333	.600	0	—	0	-3	-4	0	-0.1
2000	Oak-A	0	0	—	10	0	0	0	0	10^1	13	5	3	0	1	7	12.2	4.35	109	.310	.326	0	—	0	1	0	-0	0.0
Total	6	0	1	.000	34	3	0	0	0	46	58	31	10	5	24	28	17.0	6.07	69	.320	.414	1	.333	0	-10	-10	1	-0.3

YEAR	TM/L	W	L	PCT	G	GS	CG	SH	SV	IP	H	R	HR	HB	BB	SO	RAT	ERA	ERA+	OAV	OOB	BH	AVG	PB	PR	PR+	PD	TPI
● JACK SAVAGE	Savage, John Joseph b: 4/22/64, Louisville, Ky. BR/TR, 6'3", 190 lbs. Deb: 9/14/87																											
1987	LA-N	0	0	—	3	0	0	0	0	3^1	4	1	0	0	0	0	10.8	2.70	147	.286	.286	0	—	0	1	0	-0	0.0
1990	Min-A	0	2	.000	17	0	0	0	1	26	37	26	3	0	11	12	16.6	8.31	50	.339	.400	0	—	0	-13	-11	-0	-0.8
Total	2	0	2	.000	20	0	0	0	1	29^1	41	27	3	0	11	12	16.0	7.67	54	.333	.388	0	—	0	-12	-11	-0	-0.8
● BOB SAVAGE	Savage, John Robert b: 12/1/21, Manchester, N.H. BR/TR, 6'2", 180 lbs. Deb: 6/24/42																											
1942	Phi-A	0	1	.000	8	3	0	0	0	30^2	24	16	0	0	31	10	16.1	3.23	117	.220	.393	1	.111	0	1	2	-0	0.1
1946	Phi-A	3	15	.167	40	19	7	1	2	164	164	80	5	2	93	78	14.2	4.06	87	.259	.355	5	.122	1	-10	-9	-3	-1.2
1947	Phi-A	8	10	.444	44	8	2	1	2	146	135	71	8	0	55	56	11.7	3.76	101	.245	.314	2	.050	-4	-1	1	-2	-0.5
1948	Phi-A	5	1	.833	33	1	1	0	5	75^1	98	55	9	0	33	26	15.7	6.21	69	.318	.384	1	.077	-1	-16	-16	-1	-1.4
1949	StL-A	0	0	—	4	0	0	0	0	7	12	5	1	0	3	1	19.3	6.43	70	.400	.455	0	.000	-0	-2	-1	0	-0.1
Total	5	16	27	.372	129	31	10	2	9	423	433	227	23	2	215	171	13.8	4.32	88	.265	.352	9	.087	-3	-27	-24	-6	-3.1
● DON SAVIDGE	Savidge, Donald Snyder b: 8/28/08, Berwick, Pa. d: 3/22/83, Santa Barbara, Cal BR/TR, 6'1", 180 lbs. Deb: 8/6/29 F																											
1929	Was-A	0	0	—	3	0	0	0	0	6	12	7	1	0	2	2	21.0	9.00	47	.414	.452	0	—	0	-3	-3	0	-0.1
● RALPH SAVIDGE	Savidge, Ralph Austin "The Human Whipcord" b: 2/3/1879, Jerseytown, Pa. d: 7/22/59, Berwick, Pa. BR/TR, 6'2", 210 lbs. Deb: 9/22/08 F																											
1908	Cin-N	0	1	.000	4	1	1	0	0	21	18	9	0	0	8	7	11.1	2.57	90	.247	.321	0	.000	-1	-0	-1	-1	-0.2
1909	Cin-N	0	0	—	1	0	0	0	0	4	10	12	1	1	3	2	31.5	22.50	12	.588	.667	0	.000	-0	-9	-9	0	-0.4
Total	2	0	1	.000	5	1	1	0	0	25	28	21	1	1	11	9	14.4	5.76	41	.311	.392	0	.000	-1	-9	-10	-1	-0.6
● MOE SAVRANSKY	Savransky, Morris b: 1/13/29, Cleveland, Ohio BL/TL, 5'11", 175 lbs. Deb: 4/23/54																											
1954	Cin-N	0	2	.000	16	0	0	0	0	24	23	13	6	2	8	7	12.4	4.88	86	.247	.320	1	.500	1	-2	-2	1	0.0
● RICK SAWYER	Sawyer, Richard Clyde b: 4/7/48, Bakersfield, Cal. BR/TR, 6'2", 205 lbs. Deb: 4/28/74																											
1974	NY-A	0	0	—	1	0	0	0	0	1^2	2	3	0	0	1	1	16.2	16.20	22	.500	.600	0	—	0	-2	-2	0	-0.1
1975	NY-A	0	0	—	4	0	0	0	0	6	7	4	0	0	2	3	13.5	3.00	123	.304	.360	0	—	0	1	0	-0	0.0
1976	SD-N	5	3	.625	13	11	4	2	0	81^2	84	24	2	1	38	33	13.6	2.53	129	.272	.353	5	.208	1	9	7	-0	0.8
1977	SD-N	7	6	.538	56	9	0	0	0	111	136	77	15	7	55	45	16.1	5.84	61	.316	.402	3	.150	1	-24	-31	1	-3.0
Total	4	12	9	.571	74	20	4	2	0	200^1	229	108	17	8	96	82	15.0	4.49	77	.299	.382	8	.182	2	-17	-25	1	-2.3
● WILL SAWYER	Sawyer, Willard Newton b: 7/29/1864, Brimfield, Ohio d: 1/5/36, Kent, Ohio BL/TL, Deb: 7/21/1883																											
1883	Cle-N	4	10	.286	17	15	15	0	0	141	119	79	1		47	76	10.6	2.36	133	**.217**	.279	1	.021	-7	12	12	-3	0.1
● BILL SAYLES	Sayles, William Nisbeth b: 7/27/17, Portland, Ore. d: 11/20/96, Lincoln City, Ore. BR/TR, 6'2", 175 lbs. Deb: 7/17/39																											
1939	Bos-A	0	0	—	5	0	0	0	0	14	14	13	1	0	13	9	17.4	7.07	67	.264	.409	1	.143	-0	-4	-4	0	-0.2
1943	NY-N	1	3	.250	18	3	1	0	0	53	60	29	1	0	23	38	14.1	4.75	72	.284	.355	4	.308	1	-8	-8	-0	-0.5
	Bro-N	0	0	—	5	0	0	0	0	11^2	13	14	0	0	10	5	17.7	7.71	44	.271	.397	1	.500	0	-6	-6	-0	-0.3
	Yr	1	3	.250	23	3	1	0	0	64^2	73	43	1	0	33	43	14.8	5.29	65	.282	.363	5	.333	1	-14	-13	-1	-0.8
Total	2	1	3	.250	28	3	1	0	0	78^2	87	56	2	0	46	52	15.2	5.61	65	.279	.372	6	.273	1	-17	-17	-0	-1.0
● PHIL SAYLOR	Saylor, Philip Andrew "Lefty" b: 1/2/1871, Van Wert Co., Ohio d: 7/23/37, W.Alexandria, Ohio TL, Deb: 7/11/1891																											
1891	Phi-N	0	0	—	1	0	0	0	0	3	2	2	1	0	0	0	6.0	6.00	57	.182	.182	0	.000	-0	-1	-1	-0	-0.1
● FRANK SCANLAN	Scanlan, Frank Aloysius b: 4/28/1890, Syracuse, N.Y. d: 4/9/69, Brooklyn, N.Y. BL/TL, 6'1.5", 175 lbs. Deb: 8/6/09 F																											
1909	Phi-N	0	0	—	6	0	0	0	1	11	8	3	0	0	5	5	10.6	1.64	159	.211	.302	0	.000	-1	1	1	-0	0.0
● BOB SCANLAN	Scanlan, Robert Guy b: 8/9/66, Los Angeles, Cal. BR/TR, 6'8", 210 lbs. Deb: 5/7/91																											
1991	Chi-N	7	8	.467	40	13	0	0	1	111	114	60	5	3	40	44	12.7	3.89	100	.268	.335	1	.042	-2	-3	-0	-0	-0.2
1992	Chi-N	3	6	.333	69	0	0	0	14	87^1	76	32	4	1	30	42	11.0	2.89	125	.235	.302	0	.000	-0	6	7	1	1.0
1993	Chi-N	4	5	.444	70	0	0	0	0	75^1	79	41	6	3	28	44	13.1	4.54	88	.278	.349	1	.500	0	-4	-5	-1	-0.6
1994	Mil-A	2	6	.250	30	12	0	0	2	103	117	53	11	4	28	65	13.0	4.11	123	.288	.340	0	—	0	8	10	-0	0.7
1995	Mil-A	4	7	.364	17	14	0	0	0	83^1	101	66	9	7	44	29	16.4	6.59	76	.304	.397	0	—	0	-17	-14	0	-1.5
1996	Det-A	0	0	—	8	0	0	0	0	11	16	15	1	1	9	3	21.3	10.64	48	.348	.464	0	—	0	-7	-7	-0	-0.3
	KC-A	0	1	.000	9	0	0	0	0	11^1	13	4	1	1	3	3	13.5	3.18	158	.295	.354	0	—	0	2	2	-0	0.1
	Yr	0	1	.000	17	0	0	0	0	22^1	29	19	2	2	12	6	17.3	6.85	73	.322	.413	0	—	0	-5	-4	-0	-0.2
1998	Hou-N	0	1	.000	27	0	0	0	0	26^1	24	12	4	1	13	9	13.0	3.08	132	.245	.339	0	—	0	3	3	-1	0.1
2000	Mil-N	0	0	—	2	0	0	0	0	1^2	6	6	0	1	0	1	37.8	27.00	17	.600	.636	0	—	0	-4	-4	-0	-0.2
Total	8	20	34	.370	272	39	0	0	17	510^1	546	289	41	22	195	240	13.5	4.46	97	.277	.349	2	.067	-2	-15	-7	-1	-0.9
● DOC SCANLAN	Scanlan, William Dennis b: 3/7/1881, Syracuse, N.Y. d: 5/29/49, Brooklyn, N.Y. BL/TR, 5'8", 165 lbs. Deb: 9/24/03 F																											
1903	Pit-N	0	1	.000	1	1	1	0	0	9	5	7	0	0	6	0	11.0	4.00	81	.167	.306	0	.000	0	-1	-1	-0	-0.1
1904	Pit-N	1	3	.250	4	3	1	0	0	22	21	18	0	2	20	10	17.6	4.91	56	.236	.387	0	.000	-1	-5	-5	-0	-0.9
	Bro-N	6	6	.500	13	12	11	3	0	104	94	39	0	2	40	40	11.8	2.16	127	.242	.316	5	.143	-2	7	7	-2	0.4
	Yr	7	9	.438	17	15	12	3	0	126	115	57	0	4	60	50	12.8	2.64	104	.241	.331	5	.122	-2	1	1	-2	-0.5
1905	Bro-N	14	12	.538	33	28	22	2	0	249^2	220	119	4	8	104	135	12.0	2.92	99	.237	.319	16	.167	-2	2	-1	-2	-0.4
1906	Bro-N	18	13	.581	38	33	28	6	2	288	230	128	5	6	127	120	11.3	3.19	79	.214	.301	18	.186	3	-18	-22	-7	-2.8
1907	Bro-N	6	8	.429	17	15	10	2	0	107	90	50	1	3	61	59	13.0	3.20	73	.239	.349	9	.265	5	-9	-11	-2	-1.0
1909	Bro-N	8	7	.533	19	17	12	2	0	141^1	125	53	2	4	65	72	12.4	2.93	88	.252	.343	12	.273	5	-5	-5	-1	-0.1
1910	Bro-N	9	11	.450	34	25	14	0	2	217^1	175	76	1	5	116	103	12.3	2.61	116	.234	.341	14	.203	1	10	10	-2	0.8
1911	Bro-N	3	10	.231	22	15	3	0	1	113^2	101	67	2	6	69	45	13.9	3.64	92	.256	.374	4	.121	-2	-3	-4	-1	-0.7
Total	8	65	71	.478	181	149	102	15	5	1252	1061	557	15	36	608	584	12.3	3.00	93	.234	.330	78	.188	8	-21	-31	-17	-4.8
● PAT SCANTLEBURY	Scantlebury, Patricio Athelstan b: 11/11/17, Gatun, Canal Zone d: 5/24/91, Glen Ridge, N.J. BL/TL, 6'1", 180 lbs. Deb: 4/19/56																											
1956	Cin-N	0	1	.000	6	2	0	0	0	19	24	14	5	0	5	10	13.7	6.63	60	.293	.333	0	.000	-0	-6	-5	-0	-0.3
● RANDY SCARBERY	Scarbery, Randy James b: 6/22/52, Fresno, Cal. BB/TR, 6'1", 185 lbs. Deb: 4/16/79																											
1979	Chi-A	2	8	.200	45	5	0	0	4	101^1	102	56	9	3	34	45	12.3	4.62	92	.262	.326	0	—	0	-4	-4	0	-0.4
1980	Chi-A	1	2	.333	15	0	0	0	2	28^2	24	14	1	2	7	18	10.4	4.08	99	.238	.300	0	—	0	-0	-0	-0	-0.1
Total	2	3	10	.231	60	5	0	0	6	130	126	70	10	5	41	63	11.9	4.50	94	.257	.320	0	—	0	-4	-4	-0	-0.5
● RAY SCARBOROUGH	Scarborough, Ray Wilson (b: Rae Wilson Scarborough) b: 7/23/17, Mt.Gilead, N.C. d: 7/1/82, Mount Olive, N.C. BR/TR, 6', 185 lbs. Deb: 6/26/42 C																											
1942	Was-A	2	1	.667	17	5	1	1	0	63^1	68	32	2	0	32	16	14.2	4.12	89	.272	.355	4	.190	0	-3	-3	1	-0.1
1943	Was-A	4	4	.500	24	6	2	0	3	86	93	42	2	0	46	43	14.5	2.83	113	.273	.359	8	.333	2	5	4	0	0.6
1946	Was-A	7	11	.389	32	20	6	1	1	155^2	176	85	8	1	74	46	14.5	4.05	83	.286	.364	7	.140	-2	-9	-13	2	-1.4
1947	Was-A	6	13	.316	33	18	8	2	0	161	165	74	5	1	67	63	13.0	3.41	109	.267	.339	6	.120	-3	5	6	-0	0.3
1948	Was-A	15	8	.652	31	26	9	0	1	185^1	166	71	10	3	72	76	11.7	2.82	154	.233	.307	14	.219	-0	30	31	1	3.8
1949	Was-A	13	11	.542	34	27	11	1	0	199^2	204	115	10	7	88	81	13.5	4.60	93	.265	.346	13	.194	-0	-9	-7	1	-0.7
1950	Was-A	3	5	.375	8	8	4	2	0	58^1	62	30	2	2	22	24	13.3	4.01	112	.276	.345	2	.100	-1	4	3	1	0.3
	Chi-A☆	10	13	.435	27	23	8	1	1	149^1	160	95	10	4	62	70	13.6	5.30	85	.274	.347	8	.174	-1	-12	-14	-1	-1.9
	Yr	13	18	.419	35	31	12	3	1	207^2	222	125	12	6	84	94	13.5	4.94	91	.274	.347	10	.152	-3	-8	-11	-0	-1.6
1951	Bos-A	12	9	.571	37	22	8	0	0	184	201	106	21	14	61	71	13.5	5.09	88	.275	.342	13	.191	-2	-20	-12	1	-1.4
1952	Bos-A	1	5	.167	28	8	1	1	4	76^2	79	47	8	4	35	29	13.9	4.81	82	.266	.351	4	.222	0	-10	-7	0	-0.5
	*NY-A	5	1	.833	9	4	1	0	0	34	27	11	4	1	15	13	11.4	2.91	114	.223	.314	5	.357	2	3	2	-0	0.4
	Yr	6	6	.500	37	12	2	1	4	110^2	106	58	12	5	50	42	13.1	4.23	89	.254	.340	9	.281	2	-7	-6	0	-0.1
1953	NY-A	2	2	.500	25	1	0	0	2	54^2	52	23	4	4	26	20	13.5	3.29	112	.250	.345	1	.083	-0	4	3	0	0.2
	Det-A	0	2	.000	13	0	0	0	2	20^2	34	24	3	3	11	12	20.9	8.27	49	.354	.436	0	.000	-0	-10	-9	-0	-1.1
	Yr	2	4	.333	38	1	0	0	4	75^1	86	47	7	7	37	32	15.5	4.66	81	.283	.374	1	.071	-0	-6	-8	-0	-0.9
Total	10	80	85	.485	318	168	59	9	14	1428^2	1487	755	89	44	611	564	13.5	4.13	97	.267	.344	85	.186	-6	-22	-19	4	-1.5

YEAR	TM/L	W	L	PCT	G	GS	CG	SH	SV	IP	H	R	HR	HB	BB	SO	RAT	ERA	ERA+	OAV	OOB	BH	AVG	PB	PR	PR+	PD	TPI
● **MAC SCARCE**	Scarce, Guerrant McCurdy b: 4/8/49, Danville, Va. BL/TL, 6'3", 200 lbs. Deb: 7/10/72																											
1972	Phi-N	1	2	.333	31	0	0	0	4	36^2	30	14	6	2	20	40	12.8	3.44	105	.222	.331	0	.000	-1	0	1	1	0.1
1973	Phi-N	1	8	.111	52	0	0	0	12	70^2	54	23	3	1	47	57	13.0	2.42	157	.220	.347	0	.000	-1	10	10	-1	1.5
1974	Phi-N	3	8	.273	58	0	0	0	5	70^1	72	40	6	2	35	50	13.9	4.99	76	.275	.365	0	.000	-1	-11	-9	-1	-1.7
1975	NY-N	0	0	—	1	0	0	0	0	0	1	0	0	0	—	—	—	—	1.000	1.000	95	—	0	0	0		0	0.0
1978	Min-A	1	1	.500	17	0	0	0	0	32	35	19	5	3	15	17	14.9	3.94	97	.292	.384	0	—	0	-1	-0	-1	-0.1
Total	5	6	19	.240	159	0	0	0	21	209^2	192	96	20	8	117	164	13.6	3.69	102	.251	.357	0	.000	-2	-1	2	-2	-0.2
● **AL SCHACHT**	Schacht, Alexander b: 11/11/1892, New York, N.Y. d: 7/14/84, Waterbury, Conn. BR/TR, 5'11", 142 lbs. Deb: 9/18/19 C																											
1919	Was-A	2	0	1.000	2	2	1	0	0	15	14	5	0	0	4	4	10.8	2.40	134	.233	.281	0	.000	0	1	1	-0	0.2
1920	Was-A	6	4	.600	22	11	5	1	1	99^1	130	60	2	1	30	19	14.6	4.44	84	.319	.367	5	.192	1	-7	-8	2	-0.5
1921	Was-A	6	6	.500	29	5	2	0	1	82^2	110	59	2	2	27	15	15.1	4.90	84	.332	.386	5	.227	1	-6	-7	-3	-1.2
Total	3	14	10	.583	53	18	8	1	2	197	254	124	4	3	61	38	14.5	4.48	86	.318	.368	10	.196	2	-11	-14	-2	-1.5
● **SID SCHACHT**	Schacht, Sidney b: 2/3/18, Bogota, N.J. d: 3/30/91, Ft.Lauderdale, Fla. BR/TR, 5'11", 170 lbs. Deb: 4/23/50																											
1950	StL-A	0	0	—	8	1	0	0	0	10^2	24	22	5	0	14	7	32.1	16.03	31	.429	.543	0	.000	-0	-14	-12	-0	-0.6
1951	StL-A	0	0	—	6	0	0	0	1	6	14	15	1	0	5	4	28.5	21.00	21	.452	.528	0	—	0	-11	-10	-0	-0.5
	Bos-N	0	2	.000	5	0	0	0	0	4^2	6	4	0	0	2	1	15.4	1.93	191	.300	.364	0	—	0	1	1	-0	0.2
Total	2	0	2	.000	19	1	0	0	1	21^1	44	41	6	0	21	12	27.4	14.34	31	.411	.508	0	.000	-0	-24	-22	-1	-0.9
● **HAL SCHACKER**	Schacker, Harold b: 4/6/25, Brooklyn, N.Y. BR/TR, 6', 190 lbs. Deb: 5/9/45																											
1945	Bos-N	0	1	.000	6	0	0	0	0	15^1	14	12	2	0	9	6	13.5	5.28	73	.241	.343	0	.000	0	-3	-2	-0	-0.2
● **GERMANY SCHAEFER**	Schaefer, Herman A. b: 2/4/1877, Chicago, Ill. d: 5/16/19, Saranac Lake, N.Y. BR/TR, 5'9", 175 lbs. Deb: 10/5/01 ♦																											
1912	Was-A	0	0	—	1	0	0	0	0	0^2	1	0	0	0	0	0	13.5	0.00	—	.333	.333	41	.247	0	0	0	-0	0.0
1913	Was-A	0	0	—	1	0	0	0	0	0^1	2	2	1	0	0	0	54.0	54.00	5	.667	.667	32	.320	0	-2	-2	0	-0.1
Total	2	0	0	—	2	0	0	0	0	1	3	2	1	0	0	0	27.0	18.00	18	.500	.500	972	.257	0	-2	-2	0	-0.1
● **HARRY SCHAEFFER**	Schaeffer, Harry Edward "Lefty" b: 6/23/24, Reading, Pa. BL/TL, 6'2.5", 175 lbs. Deb: 7/28/52																											
1952	NY-A	0	1	.000	5	2	0	0	0	17	18	14	2	0	18	15	19.1	5.29	63	.265	.419	0	.000	-0	-3	-4	0	-0.2
● **MARK SCHAEFFER**	Schaeffer, Mark Philip b: 6/5/48, Santa Monica, Cal. BL/TL, 6'5", 215 lbs. Deb: 4/18/72																											
1972	SD-N	2	0	1.000	41	0	0	0	1	41	52	21	3	2	28	25	18.0	4.61	71	.319	.425	0	.000	-0	-5	-6	1	-0.3
● **JOE SCHAFFERNOTH**	Schaffernoth, Joseph Arthur b: 8/6/37, Trenton, N.J. BR/TR, 6'4.5", 195 lbs. Deb: 4/15/59																											
1959	Chi-N	1	0	1.000	5	1	0	0	0	7^2	11	7	1	0	4	3	17.6	8.22	48	.355	.429	0	.000	-0	-4	-4	-0	-0.5
1960	Chi-N	2	3	.400	33	0	0	0	3	55	46	21	2	1	17	33	10.5	2.78	136	.235	.299	2	.286	0	6	6	0	0.7
1961	Chi-N	0	4	.000	21	0	0	0	0	38^1	43	29	7	1	18	23	14.6	6.34	66	.293	.373	0	.000	-1	-10	-9	-0	-0.9
	Cle-A	0	1	.000	15	0	0	0	0	17	16	11	2	1	14	9	16.4	4.76	83	.242	.383	0	.000	-0	-1	-2	1	0.0
Total	3	3	8	.273	74	1	0	0	3	118	116	68	12	3	53	68	13.1	4.58	86	.264	.347	2	.125	-1	-9	-8	1	-0.7
● **ART SCHALLOCK**	Schallock, Arthur Lawrence b: 4/25/24, Mill Valley, Cal. BL/TL, 5'9", 160 lbs. Deb: 7/16/51																											
1951	NY-A	3	1	.750	11	6	1	0	0	46^1	50	20	3	1	20	19	13.8	3.88	99	.272	.346	5	.294	1	1	-0	0	0.1
1952	NY-A	0	0	—	2	0	0	0	0	2	3	2	0	0	2	1	22.5	9.00	37	.375	.500	0	—	0	-1	-1	-0	-0.1
1953	*NY-A	0	0	—	7	1	0	0	1	21^1	30	12	2	1	15	13	19.4	2.95	125	.345	.447	2	.333	0	2	2	-0	0.1
1954	NY-A	0	1	.000	6	1	1	0	0	17^1	20	10	3	1	11	9	16.6	4.15	83	.282	.386	0	.000	-0	-1	-1	-0	-0.2
1955	NY-A	0	0	—	2	0	0	0	0	3	4	2	1	0	1	2	15.0	6.00	62	.333	.385	0	—	0	-1	-1	0	0.0
	Bal-A	3	5	.375	30	6	1	0	0	80^1	92	52	2	2	42	33	15.2	4.15	92	.294	.381	2	.105	-1	-2	-3	-1	-0.4
	Yr	3	5	.375	32	6	1	0	0	83^1	96	54	3	2	43	35	15.2	4.21	90	.295	.381	2	.105	-1	-2	-4	-1	-0.4
Total	5	6	7	.462	58	14	3	0	1	170^1	199	98	11	5	91	77	15.6	4.02	94	.295	.383	9	.200	1	-1	-5	-1	-0.5
● **CHARLEY SCHANZ**	Schanz, Charles Murrell b: 6/8/19, Anacortes, Wash. d: 5/28/92, Sacramento, Cal. BR/TR, 6'3.5", 215 lbs. Deb: 4/20/44																											
1944	Phi-N	13	16	.448	40	30	13	1	3	241^1	231	108	6	6	103	84	12.7	3.32	109	.254	.334	12	.148	-1	8	8	-0	0.8
1945	Phi-N	4	15	.211	35	21	5	1	5	144^2	165	99	5	9	87	56	16.2	4.35	88	.285	.387	6	.154	-0	-9	-8	1	-1.0
1946	Phi-N	6	6	.500	32	15	4	0	4	116^1	130	82	8	5	71	47	15.9	5.80	59	.286	.389	3	.083	-2	-31	-30	1	-3.2
1947	Phi-N	2	4	.333	34	6	1	0	2	101^2	107	59	7	3	47	42	13.9	4.16	96	.295	.380	4	.148	-1	-1	-2	0	-0.2
1950	Bos-A	3	2	.600	14	0	0	0	0	22^2	25	21	3	1	24	14	19.9	8.34	59	.281	.439	1	.091	-1	-9	-8	0	-1.5
Total	5	28	43	.394	155	72	23	2	14	626^2	658	369	29	24	332	243	14.6	4.34	86	.275	.369	26	.134	-5	-43	-41	1	-5.1
● **JOHN SCHAPPERT**	Schappert, John b: Brooklyn, N.Y. d: 7/29/16, Rockaway Beach, N.Y. BR/TR, 5'10", 170 lbs. Deb: 5/3/1882																											
1882	StL-a	8	7	.533	15	14	13	0	0	128	131	99	2		32	38	11.5	3.52	80	.248	.291	9	.180	0	-12	-10	-2	-1.1
● **BILL SCHARDT**	Schardt, Wilburt "Big Bill" b: 1/20/1886, Cleveland, Ohio d: 7/20/64, Vermilion, Ohio BR/TR, 6'4", 210 lbs. Deb: 4/14/11																											
1911	Bro-N	5	15	.250	39	22	10	1	4	195^1	190	102	4	8	91	77	13.3	3.59	93	.266	.355	10	.169	0	-4	-6	0	-0.5
1912	Bro-N	0	1	.000	7	0	0	0	1	20^2	25	13	1	2	6	7	14.4	4.35	77	.321	.384	0	.000	-1	-2	-2	2	0.0
Total	2	5	16	.238	46	22	10	1	5	216	215	115	5	10	97	84	13.4	3.67	91	.271	.358	10	.154	-1	-6	-8	2	-0.5
● **JEFF SCHATTINGER**	Schattinger, Jeffrey Charles b: 10/25/55, Fresno, Cal. BL/TR, 6'5", 200 lbs. Deb: 9/21/81																											
1981	KC-A	0	0	—	1	0	0	0	0	3	2	0	0	2	1	1	15.0	0.00	—	.182	.357	0	—	0	1	1	-0	0.1
● **DAN SCHATZEDER**	Schatzeder, Daniel Ernest b: 12/1/54, Elmhurst, Ill. BL/TL, 6', 195 lbs. Deb: 9/4/77																											
1977	Mon-N	2	1	.667	6	3	1	1	0	21^2	16	6	0	0	13	14	12.0	2.49	153	.203	.315	2	.333	0	3	3	-0	0.5
1978	Mon-N	7	7	.500	29	18	2	0	0	143^2	108	54	10	2	68	69	11.2	3.07	115	.213	.308	10	.222	3	8	7	-2	0.9
1979	Mon-N	10	5	.667	32	21	3	0	1	162	136	57	17	1	59	106	10.9	2.83	130	.225	.295	11	.216	4	16	15	-3	1.5
1980	Det-A	11	13	.458	32	26	9	2	0	192^2	178	88	23	3	58	94	11.2	4.02	103	.246	.304	0	—	0	1	2	-2	0.0
1981	Det-A	6	8	.429	17	14	1	0	0	71^1	74	49	13	2	29	20	13.2	6.06	62	.265	.339	0	—	0	-19	-18	-0	-3.0
1982	SF-N	1	4	.200	13	3	0	0	0	33^1	47	30	3	0	12	18	15.9	7.29	49	.333	.386	1	.125	-0	-14	-14	0	-1.8
	Mon-N	0	2	.000	26	1	0	0	0	36	37	16	1	2	12	15	12.8	3.50	104	.276	.345	2	.400	1	0	1	-0	0.1
	Yr	1	6	.143	39	4	0	0	0	69^1	84	46	4	2	24	33	14.3	5.32	68	.305	.365	3	.231	1	-13	-13	0	-1.7
1983	Mon-N	5	2	.714	58	2	0	0	2	87	88	34	3	5	25	48	12.2	3.21	112	.265	.326	2	.200	0	4	4	-1	0.2
1984	Mon-N	7	7	.500	36	14	1	1	1	136	112	44	13	2	36	89	9.9	2.71	126	.224	.278	11	.314	5	13	11	-3	1.4
1985	Mon-N	3	5	.375	24	15	1	0	0	104^1	101	52	13	0	31	64	11.4	3.80	90	.259	.314	6	.194	3	-2	-5	0	0.0
1986	Mon-N	3	2	.600	30	1	0	0	1	59	53	29	6	0	19	33	11.0	3.20	116	.240	.300	9	.429	6	3	3	-1	0.9
	Phi-N	3	3	.500	25	0	0	0	1	29^1	28	14	3	0	16	14	13.5	3.38	114	.252	.346	1	.200	0	1	2	-0	0.3
	Yr	6	5	.545	55	1	0	0	2	88^1	81	43	9	0	35	47	11.8	3.26	115	.244	.316	10	.385	7	5	5	-1	1.2
1987	Phi-N	3	1	.750	26	0	0	0	0	37^2	40	21	4	0	14	28	12.9	4.06	105	.278	.342	2	.167	0	0	1	-1	0.0
	*Min-A	3	1	.750	30	1	0	0	0	43^2	64	37	8	1	18	30	17.1	6.39	73	.342	.403	0	—	0	-9	-8	-0	-0.7
1988	Cle-A	0	2	.000	15	0	0	0	3	16	26	19	6	1	2	10	16.3	9.56	43	.351	.377	0	—	0	-10	-9	-0	-1.3
	Min-A	0	1	.000	10	0	0	0	0	10^1	8	2	1	1	5	7	12.2	1.74	234	.216	.326	0	—	0	3	3	0	0.2
	Yr	0	3	.000	25	0	0	0	3	26^1	34	21	7	2	7	17	14.7	6.49	63	.306	.358	0	—	0	-7	-7	-0	-1.1
1989	Hou-N	4	1	.800	36	0	0	0	1	56^2	64	33	2	3	28	46	15.1	4.45	76	.287	.374	0	.000	-1	-6	-7	0	-0.7
1990	Hou-N	1	3	.250	45	2	0	0	0	64	61	23	2	0	23	37	11.8	2.39	156	.261	.327	1	.250	0	10	10	-0	0.6
	NY-N	0	0	—	6	0	0	0	0	5^2	5	0	0	0	0	2	7.9	0.00	—	.263	.263	0	—	0	2	2	-0	0.1
	Yr	1	3	.250	51	2	0	0	0	69^2	66	23	2	0	23	39	11.5	2.20	169	.261	.322	1	.250	0	12	12	-0	0.7
1991	KC-A	0	0	—	8	0	0	0	0	6^2	11	9	0	0	7	4	24.3	9.45	44	.367	.486	0	—	0	-4	-4	-0	-0.2
Total	15	69	68	.504	504	121	18	4	10	1317	1257	617	128	23	475	748	12.0	3.74	100	.253	.321	58	.240	22	2	-3	-13	-1.0
● **RUBE SCHAUER**	Schauer, Alexander John (b: Dimitri Ivanovich Dimitrihoff) b: 3/19/1891, Odessa, Russia d: 4/15/57, Minneapolis, Minn. BR/TR, 6'2", 192 lbs. Deb: 8/27/13																											
1913	NY-N	0	1	.000	3	1	1	0	0	12	14	11	0	0	9	7	17.3	7.50	42	.292	.404	0	.000	-0	-6	-6	0	-0.4
1914	NY-N	0	0	—	6	0	0	0	0	22^1	16	10	2	0	8	6	9.7	3.22	82	.205	.279	1	.143	-0	-1	-1	-1	-0.2
1915	NY-N	2	8	.200	32	7	4	0	0	105^1	101	56	4	2	35	65	11.8	3.50	73	.258	.322	2	.077	-2	-9	-12	-1	-1.3

YEAR	TM/L	W	L	PCT	G	GS	CG	SH	SV	IP	H	R	HR	HB	BB	SO	RAT	ERA	ERA+	OAV	OOB	BH	AVG	PB	PR	PR+	PD	TPI
1916	NY-N	1	4	.200	19	3	1	0	0	45^2	44	22	0	2	16	24	12.2	2.96	82	.257	.328	2	.222	0	-2	-3	-0	-0.3
1917	Phi-A	7	16	.304	33	21	10	0	1	215	209	116	6	3	69	62	11.8	3.14	88	.263	.324	11	.145	-2	-11	-9	0	-1.2
Total	5	10	29	.256	93	32	16	0	1	400^1	384	215	12	7	137	164	11.9	3.35	80	.259	.324	16	.132	-4	-29	-30	-1	-3.4

● OWEN SCHEETZ

Scheetz, Owen Franklin b: 12/24/13, New Bedford, Ohio d: 9/28/94, Kirkersville, O. BR/TR, 6'1", 200 lbs. Deb: 4/22/43

YEAR	TM/L	W	L	PCT	G	GS	CG	SH	SV	IP	H	R	HR	HB	BB	SO	RAT	ERA	ERA+	OAV	OOB	BH	AVG	PB	PR	PR+	PD	TPI
1943	Was-A	0	0	—	6	0	0	0	1	9	16	7	0	0	4	5	20.0	7.00	46	.381	.435	0	.000	-0	-4	-4	0	-0.2

● AARON SCHEFFER

Scheffer, Aaron Alvin Marcus b: 10/15/75, Ypsilanti, Mich. BL/TR, 6'2", 165 lbs. Deb: 6/13/99

YEAR	TM/L	W	L	PCT	G	GS	CG	SH	SV	IP	H	R	HR	HB	BB	SO	RAT	ERA	ERA+	OAV	OOB	BH	AVG	PB	PR	PR+	PD	TPI
1999	Sea-A	0	0	—	4	0	0	0	0	4^2	6	5	0	1	3	4	19.3	1.93	246	.353	.476	0	—	0	2	1	-0	0.0

● LEFTY SCHEGG

Schegg, Gilbert Eugene (b: Gilbert Eugene Price)
b: 8/28/1889, Leesville, Ohio d: 2/27/63, Niles, Ohio BL/TL, 5'11", 180 lbs. Deb: 8/20/12

YEAR	TM/L	W	L	PCT	G	GS	CG	SH	SV	IP	H	R	HR	HB	BB	SO	RAT	ERA	ERA+	OAV	OOB	BH	AVG	PB	PR	PR+	PD	TPI
1912	Was-A	0	0	—	2	1	0	0	0	5^1	7	5	0	0	4	3	18.6	3.38	99	.333	.440	0	.000	-0	-0	-0	-1	-0.1

● CARL SCHEIB

Scheib, Carl Alvin b: 1/1/27, Gratz, Pa. BR/TR, 6'1", 192 lbs. Deb: 9/6/43

YEAR	TM/L	W	L	PCT	G	GS	CG	SH	SV	IP	H	R	HR	HB	BB	SO	RAT	ERA	ERA+	OAV	OOB	BH	AVG	PB	PR	PR+	PD	TPI
1943	Phi-A	0	1	.000	6	0	0	0	0	18^2	24	14	4	1	3	3	13.5	4.34	78	.308	.341	0	.000	-1	-2	-2	-1	-0.2
1944	Phi-A	0	0	—	15	0	0	0	0	36^1	36	18	1	4	11	13	12.6	4.21	83	.257	.329	3	.300	1	-3	-3	1	0.1
1945	Phi-A	0	0	—	4	0	0	0	0	8^2	6	3	0	0	4	2	10.4	3.12	110	.207	.303	0	.000	-0	0	0	0	0.0
1947	Phi-A	4	6	.400	21	12	6	2	0	116	121	68	11	2	55	26	13.8	5.04	76	.274	.357	6	.133	-2	-17	-15	-2	-1.6
1948	Phi-A	14	8	.636	32	24	15	1	0	198^2	219	90	14	1	76	44	13.4	3.94	109	.286	.351	31	.298	7	8	8	1	1.9
1949	Phi-A	9	12	.429	38	23	11	2	0	182^2	191	117	16	2	118	43	15.3	5.12	80	.275	.382	17	.236	3	-19	-21	-3	-2.0
1950	Phi-A	3	10	.231	43	8	1	0	3	106	138	96	13	0	70	37	17.7	7.22	63	.317	.411	13	.250	2	-31	-32	-1	-3.2
1951	Phi-A	1	12	.077	46	11	3	0	10	143	132	78	7	8	71	49	13.3	4.47	96	.250	.347	21	.396	8	-6	-3	4	1.0
1952	Phi-A	11	7	.611	30	19	8	1	2	158	153	82	21	4	50	42	11.8	4.39	90	.253	.314	18	.220	-1	-12	-7	0	-0.8
1953	Phi-A	3	7	.300	28	8	3	0	2	96	99	57	9	7	29	25	12.7	4.88	88	.261	.325	8	.195	-1	-9	-6	-0	-0.7
1954	Phi-A	0	1	.000	1	1	0	0	0	2	5	5	0	1	1	1	31.5	22.50	17	.500	.583	0	—	0	-4	-4	-0	-0.6
	StL-N	0	1	.000	3	1	0	0	0	4^2	6	6	3	0	5	5	21.2	11.57	36	.300	.440	0	.000	-0	-4	-4	0	-0.7
Total	11	45	65	.409	267	107	47	6	17	1070^2	1130	634	99	30	493	290	13.9	4.88	85	.274	.355	117	.250	16	-100	-87	0	-6.8

● FRANK SCHEIBECK

Scheibeck, Frank S. b: 6/28/1865, Detroit, Mich. d: 10/22/56, Detroit, Mich. BR/TR, 5'7", 145 lbs. Deb: 5/9/1887 ♦

YEAR	TM/L	W	L	PCT	G	GS	CG	SH	SV	IP	H	R	HR	HB	BB	SO	RAT	ERA	ERA+	OAV	OOB	BH	AVG	PB	PR	PR+	PD	TPI
1887	Cle-a	0	1	.000	1	1	1	0	0	9	21	18	1	1	4	3	22.0	12.00	36	.412	.423	4	.364	0	-8	-8	-0	-0.5

● JACK SCHEIBLE

Scheible, John G. b: 2/16/1866, Youngstown, Ohio d: 8/9/1897, Youngstown, Ohio TL, Deb: 9/8/1893

YEAR	TM/L	W	L	PCT	G	GS	CG	SH	SV	IP	H	R	HR	HB	BB	SO	RAT	ERA	ERA+	OAV	OOB	BH	AVG	PB	PR	PR+	PD	TPI
1893	Cle-N	1	1	.500	2	2	2	1	0	18	15	9	0	0	11	1	13.0	2.00	244	.221	.329	1	.143	-0	5	6	-0	0.4
1894	Phi-N	0	1	.000	1	1	0	0	0	0^1	6	10	0	1	2	0	243.0	189.00	3	.857	.900	0	—	0	-7	-7	-0	-0.8
Total	2	1	2	.333	3	3	2	1	0	18^1	21	19	0	1	13	1	17.2	5.40	91	.280	.393	1	.143	-0	-1	-1	-0	-0.4

● RICH SCHEID

Scheid, Richard Paul b: 2/3/65, Staten Island, N.Y. BL/TL, 6'3", 185 lbs. Deb: 9/11/92

YEAR	TM/L	W	L	PCT	G	GS	CG	SH	SV	IP	H	R	HR	HB	BB	SO	RAT	ERA	ERA+	OAV	OOB	BH	AVG	PB	PR	PR+	PD	TPI
1992	Hou-N	0	1	.000	7	1	0	0	0	12	14	8	2	0	6	8	15.0	6.00	56	.280	.357	0	.000	-0	-3	-4	-0	-0.3
1994	Fla-N	1	3	.250	8	5	0	0	0	32^1	35	18	6	2	8	17	12.5	3.34	131	.269	.321	0	.000	-1	3	4	-1	0.3
1995	Fla-N	0	0	—	6	0	0	0	0	10^1	14	7	1	0	7	10	18.3	6.10	69	.341	.438	0	.000	-0	-2	-2	1	0.0
Total	3	1	4	.200	21	6	0	0	0	54^2	63	33	9	2	21	35	14.2	4.45	93	.285	.352	0	.000	-1	-2	-2	0	0.0

● JIM SCHELLE

Schelle, Gerard Anthony b: 4/13/17, Baltimore, Md. d: 5/4/90, Weymouth, Mass. BR/TR, 6'3", 204 lbs. Deb: 7/23/39

YEAR	TM/L	W	L	PCT	G	GS	CG	SH	SV	IP	H	R	HR	HB	BB	SO	RAT	ERA	ERA+	OAV	OOB	BH	AVG	PB	PR	PR+	PD	TPI
1939	Phi-A	0	0	—	1	0	0	0	0	0	1	0	1	3	—	—	∞	—	1.000	1.000	102	—	0	-3	-3	0	-0.2	

● FRED SCHEMANSKE

Schemanske, Frederick George "Buck" b: 4/28/03, Detroit, Mich. d: 2/18/60, Detroit, Mich. BR/TR, 6'2", 190 lbs. Deb: 9/15/23 ♦

YEAR	TM/L	W	L	PCT	G	GS	CG	SH	SV	IP	H	R	HR	HB	BB	SO	RAT	ERA	ERA+	OAV	OOB	BH	AVG	PB	PR	PR+	PD	TPI
1923	Was-A	0	0	—	1	0	0	0	0	1	3	3	0	0	0	0	27.0	27.00	14	.600	.600	2	1.000	1	-3	-3	-0	0.0

● BILL SCHENCK

Schenck, William G. b: 7/1854, Brooklyn, N.Y. d: 1/29/34, Brooklyn, N.Y. 5'7", 171 lbs. Deb: 5/29/1882 ♦

YEAR	TM/L	W	L	PCT	G	GS	CG	SH	SV	IP	H	R	HR	HB	BB	SO	RAT	ERA	ERA+	OAV	OOB	BH	AVG	PB	PR	PR+	PD	TPI
1882	Lou-a	1	0	1.000	2	1	1	0	0	10	6	2	0		1	4	6.3	0.90	275	.162	.184	60	.260	0	2	2	-0	0.1

● JOHN SCHENEBERG

Scheneberg, John Bluford b: 11/20/1887, Guyandotte, W.Va. d: 9/26/50, Huntington, W.Va. BB/TR, 6'1", 180 lbs. Deb: 9/23/13

YEAR	TM/L	W	L	PCT	G	GS	CG	SH	SV	IP	H	R	HR	HB	BB	SO	RAT	ERA	ERA+	OAV	OOB	BH	AVG	PB	PR	PR+	PD	TPI
1913	Pit-N	0	1	.000	1	1	0	0	0	6	10	5	0	0	2	1	18.0	6.00	50	.400	.444	1	.500	0	-2	-2	0	-0.2
1920	StL-A	0	0	—	1	0	0	0	0	2	7	7	0	0	1	0	36.0	27.00	15	.583	.615	0	—	0	-5	-5	-0	-0.2
Total	2	0	1	.000	2	1	0	0	0	8	17	12	0	0	3	1	22.5	11.25	29	.459	.500	1	.500	0	-7	-7	0	-0.4

● FRED SCHERMAN

Scherman, Frederick John b: 7/25/44, Dayton, Ohio BL/TL, 6'1", 195 lbs. Deb: 4/26/69

YEAR	TM/L	W	L	PCT	G	GS	CG	SH	SV	IP	H	R	HR	HB	BB	SO	RAT	ERA	ERA+	OAV	OOB	BH	AVG	PB	PR	PR+	PD	TPI
1969	Det-A	1	0	1.000	4	0	0	0	0	4	6	3	2	0	0	3	13.5	6.75	55	.333	.333	0	—	0	-1	-1	0	-0.3
1970	Det-A	4	4	.500	48	0	0	0	1	69^2	61	28	5	1	28	58	11.6	3.23	115	.237	.315	2	.167	-0	4	4	0	0.4
1971	Det-A	11	6	.647	69	1	1	0	20	113	91	38	11	5	49	46	11.5	2.71	133	.226	.318	5	.208	1	10	11	1	2.3
1972	*Det-A	7	3	.700	57	3	0	0	12	94	91	43	5	5	53	53	14.3	3.64	87	.269	.376	2	.091	-1	-6	-5	-1	-0.9
1973	Det-A	2	2	.500	34	0	0	0	1	61^2	59	30	6	3	30	28	13.4	4.23	97	.258	.351	0	—	0	-3	-1	-1	-0.2
1974	Hou-N	2	5	.286	53	0	0	0	4	61^1	67	33	5	7	26	35	14.7	4.11	85	.284	.372	0	.000	-0	-3	-5	-0	-0.6
1975	Hou-N	0	1	.000	16	0	0	0	0	16^1	21	11	4	1	4	13	14.3	4.96	68	.318	.366	0	.000	-0	-2	-3	0	-0.2
	Mon-N	4	3	.571	34	7	0	0	0	76^1	84	37	3	5	41	43	15.3	3.54	108	.283	.379	1	.063	-1	1	2	1	0.2
	Yr	4	4	.500	50	7	0	0	0	92^2	105	48	7	6	45	56	15.2	3.79	99	.289	.377	1	.059	-1	-2	-0	1	0.0
1976	Mon-N	2	2	.500	31	0	0	0	1	40	42	25	5	3	14	18	13.3	4.95	75	.261	.331	1	.250	0	-6	-5	-1	-0.6
Total	8	33	26	.559	346	11	1	0	39	536^1	522	248	46	30	245	297	13.4	3.66	99	.260	.350	11	.134	-1	-8	-2	-1	0.1

● BILL SCHERRER

Scherrer, William Joseph b: 1/20/58, Tonawanda, N.Y. BL/TL, 6'4", 180 lbs. Deb: 9/7/82

YEAR	TM/L	W	L	PCT	G	GS	CG	SH	SV	IP	H	R	HR	HB	BB	SO	RAT	ERA	ERA+	OAV	OOB	BH	AVG	PB	PR	PR+	PD	TPI
1982	Cin-N	0	1	.000	5	2	0	0	0	17^1	17	7	0	0	0	7	8.8	2.60	143	.250	.250	1	.500	1	2	2	-0	0.2
1983	Cin-N	2	3	.400	73	0	0	0	10	92	73	31	6	0	33	57	10.4	2.74	139	.225	.296	1	.091	-0	9	10	1	0.8
1984	Cin-N	1	1	.500	36	0	0	0	1	52^1	64	31	6	0	15	35	13.6	4.99	76	.300	.346	0	.000	-0	-8	-7	0	-0.3
	*Det-A	1	0	1.000	18	0	0	0	0	19	14	4	1	0	8	16	10.4	1.89	207	.206	.289	0	—	0	4	4	-0	0.2
1985	Det-A	3	2	.600	48	0	0	0	0	66	62	35	10	1	41	46	14.2	4.36	93	.248	.356	0	—	0	-2	-2	1	-0.1
1986	Det-A	0	1	.000	13	0	0	0	0	21	19	19	3	1	22	16	18.0	7.29	57	.244	.416	0	—	0	-7	-7	0	-0.4
1987	Cin-N	1	1	.500	23	0	0	0	0	33	43	17	3	0	16	24	16.1	4.36	97	.328	.401	0	.000	-0	-1	-0	-0	-0.1
1988	Bal-A	0	1	.000	4	0	0	0	0	4	8	6	2	0	3	3	24.8	13.50	29	.400	.478	0	—	0	-4	-4	-0	-0.8
	Phi-N	0	0	—	8	0	0	0	0	6^2	7	4	0	0	2	3	12.2	5.40	66	.269	.321	0	—	0	-1	-1	0	-0.1
Total	7	8	10	.444	228	2	0	0	11	311^1	307	154	31	2	140	207	13.0	4.08	97	.260	.340	2	.118	-0	-8	-5	1	-0.6

● DUTCH SCHESLER

Schesler, Charles b: 6/1/1900, Frankfurt, Germany d: 11/19/53, Harrisburg, Pa. BR/TR, 6'2", 185 lbs. Deb: 4/16/31

YEAR	TM/L	W	L	PCT	G	GS	CG	SH	SV	IP	H	R	HR	HB	BB	SO	RAT	ERA	ERA+	OAV	OOB	BH	AVG	PB	PR	PR+	PD	TPI
1931	Phi-N	0	0	—	17	0	0	0	0	38^1	65	39	4	4	18	14	20.4	7.28	58	.385	.455	1	.111	-0	-15	-12	0	-0.6

● LOU SCHETTLER

Schettler, Louis Martin b: 6/12/1886, Pittsburgh, Pa. d: 5/1/60, Youngstown, Ohio BR/TR, 5'11", 160 lbs. Deb: 4/25/10

YEAR	TM/L	W	L	PCT	G	GS	CG	SH	SV	IP	H	R	HR	HB	BB	SO	RAT	ERA	ERA+	OAV	OOB	BH	AVG	PB	PR	PR+	PD	TPI
1910	Phi-N	2	6	.250	27	7	3	0	1	107	96	53	2	2	51	62	12.5	3.20	98	.247	.337	7	.171	-1	-2	-1	-1	-0.3

● CURT SCHILLING

Schilling, Curtis Montague b: 11/14/66, Anchorage, Alaska BR/TR, 6'4", 215 lbs. Deb: 9/7/88

YEAR	TM/L	W	L	PCT	G	GS	CG	SH	SV	IP	H	R	HR	HB	BB	SO	RAT	ERA	ERA+	OAV	OOB	BH	AVG	PB	PR	PR+	PD	TPI
1988	Bal-A	0	3	.000	4	4	0	0	0	14^2	22	19	3	1	10	4	20.3	9.82	40	.355	.452	0	—	0	-10	-10	-1	-1.5
1989	Bal-A	0	1	.000	5	1	0	0	0	8^2	10	6	2	0	3	6	13.5	6.23	61	.286	.342	0	—	0	-2	-2	-0	-0.3
1990	Bal-A	1	2	.333	35	0	0	0	3	46	38	13	1	0	19	32	11.2	2.54	150	.229	.308	0	—	0	7	7	-1	0.4
1991	Hou-N	3	5	.375	56	0	0	0	8	75^2	79	35	2	0	39	71	14.0	3.81	92	.271	.358	1	.333	0	-1	-3	-1	-0.4
1992	Phi-N	14	11	.560	42	26	10	4	2	226^1	165	67	11	1	59	147	**8.9**	2.35	149	**.201**	**.256**	10	.156	-0	29	29	-3	3.0
1993	*Phi-N	16	7	.696	34	34	7	2	0	235^1	234	114	23	4	57	186	11.3	4.02	99	.259	.305	11	.147	-1	1	-1	0	-0.2
1994	Phi-N	2	8	.200	13	13	1	0	0	82^1	87	42	10	3	28	58	12.9	4.48	96	.270	.334	3	.107	-1	-2	-2	-1	-0.3
1995	Phi-N	7	5	.583	17	17	1	0	0	116	96	52	12	3	26	114	9.7	3.57	119	.220	.268	7	.175	0	8	8	-2	0.6
1996	Phi-N	9	10	.474	26	26	**8**	2	0	183^1	149	69	16	3	50	182	9.9	3.19	135	.223	.280	11	.175	-0	21	22	-3	1.8
1997	Phi-N★	17	11	.607	35	35	7	2	0	254^1	208	96	25	5	58	**319**	9.6	2.97	143	.224	.273	14	.173	-0	35	36	1	3.8
1998	Phi-N☆	15	14	.517	35	35	**15**	2	0	**268^2**	236	101	23	6	61	**300**	10.2	3.25	133	.236	.284	10	.132	-1	29	32	1	3.1
1999	Phi-N★	15	6	.714	24	24	8	1	0	180^1	159	74	25	5	44	152	10.4	3.54	133	.237	.288	5	.100	0	20	23	-1	2.3
2000	Phi-N	6	6	.500	16	16	4	1	0	112^2	110	49	17	1	32	96	11.4	3.91	121	.253	.306	5	.167	0	9	10	-1	0.8
	Ari-N	5	6	.455	13	13	4	1	0	97^2	94	41	10	0	13	72	9.9	3.69	125	.257	.282	8	.258	2	10	10	-1	1.1

YEAR	TM/L	W	L	PCT	G	GS	CG	SH	SV	IP	H	R	HR	HB	BB	SO	RAT	ERA	ERA+	OAV	OOB	BH	AVG	PB	PR	PR+	PD	TPI
Yr		11	12	.478	29	29	**8**	2	0	210^{1}	204	90	27	1	45	168	10.7	3.81	123	.255	.295	13	.213	2	19	20	-2	1.9
Total	13	110	95	.537	355	244	65	15	13	1902	1687	778	180	32	499	1739	10.5	3.43	122	.237	.290	85	.157	-2	155	160	-11	14.2

● RED SCHILLINGS Schillings, Elbert Isaiah b: 3/29/1900, Deport, Tex. d: 1/7/54, Oklahoma City, Okla BR/TR, 5'10", 180 lbs. Deb: 9/11/22

YEAR	TM/L	W	L	PCT	G	GS	CG	SH	SV	IP	H	R	HR	HB	BB	SO	RAT	ERA	ERA+	OAV	OOB	BH	AVG	PB	PR	PR+	PD	TPI
1922	Phi-A	0	0	—	4	0	0	0	0	8	10	6	1	0	11	4	23.6	6.75	63	.313	.488	0	.000	-0	-2	-2	-0	-0.1

● CALVIN SCHIRALDI Schiraldi, Calvin Drew b: 6/16/62, Houston, Tex. BR/TR, 6'4", 200 lbs. Deb: 9/1/84

YEAR	TM/L	W	L	PCT	G	GS	CG	SH	SV	IP	H	R	HR	HB	BB	SO	RAT	ERA	ERA+	OAV	OOB	BH	AVG	PB	PR	PR+	PD	TPI
1984	NY-N	0	2	.000	5	3	0	0	0	17^{1}	20	13	3	0	10	16	15.6	5.71	62	.286	.375	0	.000	-0	-4	-4	0	-0.5
1985	NY-N	2	1	.667	10	4	0	0	0	26^{1}	43	27	4	3	11	21	19.5	8.89	39	.368	.435	1	.125	-0	-15	-16	0	-1.6
1986	*Bos-A	4	2	.667	25	0	0	0	9	51	36	8	5	1	15	55	9.2	1.41	296	.201	.267	0	—	0	16	16	1	2.2
1987	Bos-A	8	5	.615	62	1	0	0	6	83^{2}	75	45	15	1	40	93	12.5	4.41	103	.240	.328	0	—	0	1	1	-0	0.2
1988	Chi-N	9	13	.409	29	27	2	1	1	166^{1}	166	87	13	2	63	140	12.5	4.38	82	.257	.325	6	.100	-2	-17	-14	-2	-2.1
1989	Chi-N	3	6	.333	54	0	0	0	4	78^{2}	60	34	7	1	50	54	12.7	3.78	100	.209	.328	0	.000	-1	-2	-0	-1	-0.2
	SD-N	3	1	.750	5	4	0	0	0	21^{1}	12	6	1	0	13	17	10.5	2.53	138	.162	.287	1	.143	1	2	2	-0	0.5
	Yr	6	7	.462	59	4	0	0	4	100	72	40	8	1	63	71	12.2	3.51	106	.199	.320	1	.063	0	-0	2	-2	0.3
1990	SD-N	3	8	.273	42	8	0	0	1	104	105	59	11	1	60	74	14.4	4.41	87	.264	.362	4	.190	2	-7	-7	-1	-0.6
1991	Tex-A	0	1	.000	3	0	0	0	0	4^{2}	5	6	3	0	5	1	19.3	11.57	35	.263	.417	0	—	0	-4	-4	0	-0.7
Total	8	32	39	.451	235	47	2	1	21	553^{1}	522	285	62	9	267	471	13.0	4.28	90	.248	.336	12	.111	-1	-32	-25	-5	-2.8

● BIFF SCHLITZER Schlitzer, Victor Joseph b: 12/4/1884, Rochester, N.Y. d: 1/4/48, Wellesley Hills, Mass. BR/TR, 5'11", 175 lbs. Deb: 4/17/08

YEAR	TM/L	W	L	PCT	G	GS	CG	SH	SV	IP	H	R	HR	HB	BB	SO	RAT	ERA	ERA+	OAV	OOB	BH	AVG	PB	PR	PR+	PD	TPI
1908	Phi-A	6	8	.429	24	18	11	2	0	131	110	56	1	2	45	57	10.8	3.16	81	.234	.303	9	.196	-1	-11	-8	-2	-1.2
1909	Phi-A	0	3	.000	4	3	0	0	0	13^{1}	18	9	0	3	7	6	15.5	5.40	45	.245	.365	1	.250	0	-4	-5	1	-0.8
	Bos-A	4	4	.500	13	8	5	0	1	69^{2}	68	34	0	1	17	23	11.1	3.49	72	.234	.279	5	.185	0	-8	-8	1	-0.8
	Yr	4	7	.364	17	11	5	0	1	83	81	43	0	4	24	29	11.8	3.80	65	.236	.294	6	.194	1	-12	-12	1	-1.6
1914	Buf-F	0	0	—	3	0	0	0	0	3^{1}	7	8	3	0	2	1	24.3	16.20	18	.438	.500	1	1.000	0	-5	-5	0	-0.2
Total	3	10	15	.400	44	29	16	2	1	217^{1}	198	107	4	6	71	87	11.4	3.60	71	.239	.303	16	.205	0	-28	-25	-1	-3.0

● GEORGE SCHMEES Schmees, George Edward "Rocky" b: 9/6/24, Cincinnati, Ohio d: 10/30/98, San Jose, Cal. BL/TL, 6', 190 lbs. Deb: 4/15/52 ♦

YEAR	TM/L	W	L	PCT	G	GS	CG	SH	SV	IP	H	R	HR	HB	BB	SO	RAT	ERA	ERA+	OAV	OOB	BH	AVG	PB	PR	PR+	PD	TPI
1952	Bos-A	0	0	—	2	1	0	0	0	6	9	2	0	0	2	2	16.5	3.00	131	.346	.393	13	.203	0	0	1	1	0.1

● AL SCHMELZ Schmelz, Alan George b: 11/12/43, Whittier, Cal. BR/TR, 6'4", 210 lbs. Deb: 9/7/67

YEAR	TM/L	W	L	PCT	G	GS	CG	SH	SV	IP	H	R	HR	HB	BB	SO	RAT	ERA	ERA+	OAV	OOB	BH	AVG	PB	PR	PR+	PD	TPI
1967	NY-N	0	0	—	2	0	0	0	0	3	4	1	1	0	1	2	15.0	3.00	113	.364	.417	0	—	0	0	0	0	0.0

● BUTCH SCHMIDT Schmidt, Charles John "Butcher Boy" b: 7/19/1886, Baltimore, Md. d: 9/4/52, Baltimore, Md. BL/TL, 6'1.5", 200 lbs. Deb: 5/11/09 ♦

YEAR	TM/L	W	L	PCT	G	GS	CG	SH	SV	IP	H	R	HR	HB	BB	SO	RAT	ERA	ERA+	OAV	OOB	BH	AVG	PB	PR	PR+	PD	TPI
1909	NY-A	0	0	—	1	0	0	0	0	5	10	8	0	0	1	2	19.8	7.20	35	.435	.458	0	.000	-0	-3	-3	-0	-0.2

● CURT SCHMIDT Schmidt, Curtis Allen b: 3/16/70, Miles City, Mont. BR/TR, 6'6", 200 lbs. Deb: 4/28/95

YEAR	TM/L	W	L	PCT	G	GS	CG	SH	SV	IP	H	R	HR	HB	BB	SO	RAT	ERA	ERA+	OAV	OOB	BH	AVG	PB	PR	PR+	PD	TPI
1995	Mon-N	0	0	—	11	0	0	0	0	10^{1}	15	8	1	2	9	7	22.6	6.97	62	.357	.491	0	—	0	-3	-3	-0	-0.2

● DAVE SCHMIDT Schmidt, David Joseph b: 4/22/57, Niles, Mich. BR/TR, 6'1", 185 lbs. Deb: 5/1/81

YEAR	TM/L	W	L	PCT	G	GS	CG	SH	SV	IP	H	R	HR	HB	BB	SO	RAT	ERA	ERA+	OAV	OOB	BH	AVG	PB	PR	PR+	PD	TPI
1981	Tex-A	0	1	.000	14	1	0	0	1	31^{2}	31	11	1	1	11	13	12.2	3.13	111	.258	.326	0	—	0	2	1	0	0.1
1982	Tex-A	4	6	.400	33	8	0	0	6	109^{2}	118	45	5	5	25	69	12.1	3.20	121	.279	.327	0	—	0	11	9	-0	0.8
1983	Tex-A	3	3	.500	31	0	0	0	2	46^{1}	42	20	3	1	14	29	11.1	3.88	103	.241	.302	0	—	0	1	1	0	0.1
1984	Tex-A	6	6	.500	43	0	0	0	12	70^{1}	69	30	3	0	20	46	11.4	2.56	162	.262	.314	0	—	0	11	12	1	2.4
1985	Tex-A	7	6	.538	51	4	1	1	5	85^{2}	81	36	6	0	22	46	10.8	3.15	134	.246	.293	0	—	0	9	10	1	1.6
1986	Chi-A	3	6	.333	49	1	0	0	8	92^{1}	94	37	10	5	27	67	12.3	3.31	130	.264	.325	0	—	0	9	10	-1	0.9
1987	Bal-A	10	5	.667	35	14	2	2	1	124	128	57	13	1	26	70	11.3	3.77	117	.263	.302	0	—	0	10	9	-1	0.9
1988	Bal-A	8	5	.615	41	9	0	0	2	129^{2}	129	58	14	3	38	67	11.8	3.40	115	.262	.319	0	—	0	8	7	2	0.9
1989	Bal-A	10	13	.435	38	26	2	0	0	156^{2}	196	102	24	2	36	46	13.4	5.69	67	.310	.349	0	—	0	-31	-34	1	-4.1
1990	Mon-N	3	3	.500	34	0	0	0	13	48	58	26	3	0	13	22	13.3	4.31	85	.297	.341	0	.000	-0	-3	-4	0	-0.6
1991	Mon-N	0	1	.000	4	0	0	0	0	4^{1}	9	5	2	0	2	3	22.8	10.38	35	.429	.478	0	—	0	-3	-3	0	-0.6
1992	Sea-A	0	0	—	3	0	0	0	0	3^{1}	7	7	1	0	1	1	27.0	18.90	21	.438	.526	0	—	0	-6	-5	0	-0.3
Total	12	54	55	.495	376	63	5	3	50	902	962	434	85	18	237	479	12.1	3.88	104	.274	.323	0	.000	-0	18	14	3	2.1

● FREDDY SCHMIDT Schmidt, Frederick Albert b: 2/9/16, Hartford, Conn. BR/TR, 6'1", 185 lbs. Deb: 4/25/44

YEAR	TM/L	W	L	PCT	G	GS	CG	SH	SV	IP	H	R	HR	HB	BB	SO	RAT	ERA	ERA+	OAV	OOB	BH	AVG	PB	PR	PR+	PD	TPI
1944	*StL-N	7	3	.700	37	9	3	2	5	114^{1}	94	48	5	1	58	58	12.0	3.15	112	.222	.317	7	.206	-0	6	5	-1	0.3
1946	StL-N	1	0	1.000	16	0	0	0	0	27^{1}	27	11	0	3	15	14	14.8	3.29	105	.276	.388	0	.000	-0	1	1	-0	0.0
1947	StL-N	0	0	—	2	0	0	0	0	4	5	2	1	0	1	2	13.5	2.25	184	.333	.375	0	—	0	1	1	0	0.0
	Phi-N	5	8	.385	29	5	0	0	0	76^{2}	76	44	4	4	43	24	14.4	4.70	85	.285	.392	1	.050	-2	-5	-6	-1	-1.1
	Chi-N	0	0	—	1	1	0	0	0	3	4	3	0	0	5	0	27.0	9.00	44	.333	.529	0	.000	-0	-2	-2	0	-0.1
	Yr	5	8	.385	32	6	0	0	0	83^{2}	85	49	5	4	49	26	14.8	4.73	85	.289	.398	1	.045	-2	-6	-7	-1	-1.2
Total	3	13	11	.542	85	15	3	2	5	225^{1}	206	108	10	8	122	98	13.4	3.75	98	.252	.355	8	.140	-2	-0	-1	-1	-0.9

● PETE SCHMIDT Schmidt, Friedrich Christoph Herman b: 7/23/1890, Lowden, Iowa d: 3/11/73, Pembroke, Ont., Can BR/TR, 5'11", 175 lbs. Deb: 7/14/13

YEAR	TM/L	W	L	PCT	G	GS	CG	SH	SV	IP	H	R	HR	HB	BB	SO	RAT	ERA	ERA+	OAV	OOB	BH	AVG	PB	PR	PR+	PD	TPI
1913	StL-A	0	0	—	1	0	0	0	1	2	3	1	0	0	2	0	22.5	4.50	65	.333	.455	0	—	0	-0	-0	-0	-0.1

● HENRY SCHMIDT Schmidt, Henry Martin b: 6/26/1873, Brownsville, Tex. d: 4/23/26, Nashville, Tenn. BR/TR, 5'11", 170 lbs. Deb: 4/17/03

YEAR	TM/L	W	L	PCT	G	GS	CG	SH	SV	IP	H	R	HR	HB	BB	SO	RAT	ERA	ERA+	OAV	OOB	BH	AVG	PB	PR	PR+	PD	TPI
1903	Bro-N	22	13	.629	40	36	29	5	2	301	321	167	5	21	120	96	13.8	3.83	83	.280	.359	21	.196	3	-19	-22	6	-1.3

● JASON SCHMIDT Schmidt, Jason David b: 1/29/73, Kelso, Wash. BR/TR, 6'5", 185 lbs. Deb: 4/28/95

YEAR	TM/L	W	L	PCT	G	GS	CG	SH	SV	IP	H	R	HR	HB	BB	SO	RAT	ERA	ERA+	OAV	OOB	BH	AVG	PB	PR	PR+	PD	TPI
1995	Atl-N	2	2	.500	9	2	0	0	0	25	27	17	2	1	18	19	16.6	5.76	74	.287	.407	1	.200	0	-4	-4	0	-0.5
1996	Atl-N	3	4	.429	13	11	0	0	0	58^{2}	69	48	8	0	32	48	15.5	6.75	65	.296	.381	0	.000	-2	-16	-15	-1	-1.7
	Pit-N	2	2	.500	6	6	1	0	0	37^{2}	39	19	2	2	21	26	14.8	4.06	108	.271	.371	1	.083	-1	1	1	-0	0.0
	Yr	5	6	.455	19	17	1	0	0	96^{1}	108	67	10	2	53	74	15.2	5.70	77	.286	.377	1	.032	-2	-16	-13	-1	-1.7
1997	Pit-N	10	9	.526	32	32	2	0	0	187^{2}	193	106	16	9	76	136	13.3	4.60	93	.265	.342	6	.107	-1	-8	-6	-1	-0.8
1998	Pit-N	11	14	.440	33	33	0	0	0	214^{1}	228	106	24	4	71	158	12.7	4.07	106	.275	.336	6	.097	-2	4	5	-4	0.0
1999	Pit-N	13	11	.542	33	33	2	0	0	212^{2}	219	110	24	3	85	148	13.0	4.19	109	.262	.333	5	.083	-2	9	9	-3	0.4
2000	Pit-N	2	5	.286	11	11	0	0	0	63^{1}	71	43	6	1	41	51	16.1	5.40	85	.284	.387	0	.000	-2	-5	-6	-0	-0.7
Total	6	43	47	.478	137	128	5	0	0	799^{1}	846	449	82	20	344	586	13.6	4.58	96	.272	.348	19	.082	-10	-21	-16	-9	-3.3

● JEFF SCHMIDT Schmidt, Jeffrey Thomas b: 2/21/71, Northfield, Minn. BR/TR, 6'5", 205 lbs. Deb: 5/17/96

YEAR	TM/L	W	L	PCT	G	GS	CG	SH	SV	IP	H	R	HR	HB	BB	SO	RAT	ERA	ERA+	OAV	OOB	BH	AVG	PB	PR	PR+	PD	TPI
1996	Cal-A	2	0	1.000	9	0	0	0	0	8	13	9	2	0	8	2	23.6	7.88	64	.394	.512	0	—	0	-3	-3	-0	-0.5

● WILLARD SCHMIDT Schmidt, Willard Raymond b: 5/29/28, Hays, Kan. BR/TR, 6'1", 187 lbs. Deb: 4/19/52

YEAR	TM/L	W	L	PCT	G	GS	CG	SH	SV	IP	H	R	HR	HB	BB	SO	RAT	ERA	ERA+	OAV	OOB	BH	AVG	PB	PR	PR+	PD	TPI
1952	StL-N	2	3	.400	18	3	0	0	1	34^{2}	36	20	6	2	18	30	14.5	5.19	72	.267	.361	1	.125	-0	-6	-6	1	-0.7
1953	StL-N	0	2	.000	6	2	0	0	0	17^{2}	21	20	1	1	13	11	17.8	9.17	46	.288	.402	0	.000	-1	-10	-10	-0	-0.9
1955	StL-N	7	6	.538	20	15	8	1	0	129^{2}	89	40	7	3	57	86	10.3	2.78	146	.197	.291	5	.119	-3	18	18	1	1.5
1956	StL-N	6	8	.429	33	21	2	0	1	147^{2}	131	69	18	1	78	52	12.8	3.84	99	.246	.344	10	.233	1	-1	-1	2	0.2
1957	StL-N	10	3	.769	40	8	1	0	0	116^{2}	146	67	13	2	49	63	15.2	4.78	83	.312	.380	7	.212	0	-12	-10	1	-1.0
1958	Cin-N	3	5	.375	41	2	0	0	0	69^{1}	60	29	8	1	33	41	12.2	2.86	145	.235	.325	1	.091	-1	8	9	1	1.1
1959	Cin-N	3	2	.600	36	4	0	0	0	70^{2}	80	36	4	1	30	40	14.1	3.95	103	.296	.369	1	.083	0	-0	1	1	0.2
Total	7	31	29	.517	194	55	11	1	2	586^{1}	563	281	57	11	278	323	13.1	3.93	101	.258	.344	25	.163	-2	-1	2	6	0.4

● CRAZY SCHMIT Schmit, Frederick M. "Germany" b: 2/13/1866, Chicago, Ill. d: 10/5/40, Chicago, Ill. BL/TL, 5'10.5", 165 lbs. Deb: 4/21/1890

YEAR	TM/L	W	L	PCT	G	GS	CG	SH	SV	IP	H	R	HR	HB	BB	SO	RAT	ERA	ERA+	OAV	OOB	BH	AVG	PB	PR	PR+	PD	TPI
1890	Pit-N	1	9	.100	11	10	9	1	0	83^{1}	108	98	3	8	42	35	17.1	5.83	57	.304	.390	2	.061	-3	-21	-25	-0	-2.4
1892	Bal-N	1	4	.200	6	6	6	0	0	47^{1}	37	26	0	0	26	17	12.0	3.23	106	.207	.307	2	.105	-1	0	1	1	0.1
1893	Bal-N	3	2	.600	9	6	4	0	0	49	67	51	1	2	22	10	16.7	6.61	72	.316	.386	5	.238	-0	-11	-10	-1	-0.8
	NY-N	0	2	.000	4	4	1	0	0	20^{2}	30	25	0	2	17	5	21.3	7.40	63	.330	.445	4	.444	2	-6	-6	0	-0.3
	Yr	3	4	.429	13	10	5	0	0	69^{2}	97	76	1	4	39	15	18.1	6.85	69	.320	.405	9	.300	1	-17	-16	-1	-1.1
1899	Cle-N	2	17	.105	20	19	16	0	0	138^{1}	197	138	3	14	62	24	17.8	5.86	63	.334	.410	11	.157	-2	-31	-35	2	-3.6
1901	Bal-A	0	2	.000	4	3	1	0	0	22^{2}	25	20	0	0	16	2	16.3	1.99	195	.278	.387	2	.222	0	4	4	1	0.4
Total	5	7	36	.163	54	48	37	1	0	361^{1}	464	358	7	26	185	93	16.8	5.45	69	.306	.391	26	.161	-4	-64	-69	2	-6.6

YEAR	TM/L	W	L	PCT	G	GS	CG	SH	SV	IP	H	R	HR	HB	BB	SO	RAT	ERA	ERA+	OAV	OOB	BH	AVG	PB	PR	PR+	PD	TPI
● **JOHNNY SCHMITZ**	Schmitz, John Albert "Bear Tracks" b: 11/27/20, Wausau, Wis. BR/TL, 6', 170 lbs. Deb: 9/6/41																											
1941	Chi-N	2	0	1.000	5	3	1	0	0	20^{2}	12	5	0	1	9	11	9.6	1.31	269	.182	.289	4	.571	2	5	5	1	0.8
1942	Chi-N	3	7	.300	23	10	1	0	2	86^{2}	70	41	3	3	45	51	12.3	3.43	93	.230	.335	4	.154	-1	-1	-2	4	0.1
1946	Chi-N☆	11	11	.500	41	31	14	2	2	224^{1}	184	77	6	2	94	**135**	11.2	2.61	127	**.221**	.302	9	.129	-2	20	18	2	1.8
1947	Chi-N	13	18	.419	38	28	10	3	4	207	209	91	8	2	80	97	12.7	3.22	123	.262	.330	9	.132	-2	19	17	2	2.4
1948	Chi-N★	18	13	.581	34	30	18	2	1	242	186	92	11	2	97	100	10.6	2.64	148	**.215**	.295	11	.131	-2	35	34	5	4.7
1949	Chi-N	11	13	.458	36	31	9	3	3	207	227	117	11	2	92	75	14.0	4.35	93	.287	.363	10	.143	-1	-7	-7	5	-0.3
1950	Chi-N	10	16	.385	39	27	8	3	0	193	217	122	23	4	91	75	14.5	4.99	84	.284	.363	8	.119	-3	-18	-17	5	-1.7
1951	Chi-N	1	2	.333	8	3	0	0	0	18	22	16	1	0	15	6	18.5	8.00	51	.301	.420	1	.167	-0	-8	-8	1	-0.9
	Bro-N	1	4	.200	16	7	0	0	0	55^{2}	55	37	4	2	28	20	13.7	5.34	74	.259	.351	4	.222	2	-9	-9	1	-0.5
	Yr	2	6	.250	24	10	0	0	0	73^{2}	77	53	5	2	43	26	14.9	5.99	66	.270	.370	5	.208	1	-17	-17	2	-1.4
1952	Bro-N	1	1	.500	10	3	1	0	0	33^{1}	29	16	3	1	18	11	13.0	4.32	84	.238	.340	1	.125	-0	-2	-3	1	0.0
	NY-A	1	1	.500	5	2	1	0	1	15	15	7	0	1	9	3	15.0	3.60	92	.263	.373	3	.600	2	0	-1	0	0.2
	Cin-N	1	0	1.000	3	0	0	0	0	5	3	0	0	0	3	3	10.8	0.00	—	.188	.316	0	—	0	2	2	0	0.4
1953	NY-A	0	0	—	3	0	0	0	0	4^{1}	2	1	1	0	3	0	10.4	2.08	178	.143	.294	0	—	0	1	1	0	0.1
	Was-A	2	7	.222	24	13	5	0	4	107^{2}	118	52	9	4	37	39	13.3	3.68	106	.286	.351	2	.059	-4	4	3	1	-0.1
	Yr	2	7	.222	27	13	5	0	4	112	120	53	10	4	40	39	13.2	3.62	108	.282	.349	2	.059	-4	5	3	1	0.0
1954	Was-A	11	8	.579	29	23	12	2	1	185^{1}	176	66	6	3	64	56	11.8	2.91	122	.255	.321	7	.117	-3	17	14	2	1.3
1955	Was-A	7	10	.412	32	21	6	1	1	165	187	76	8	7	54	49	13.5	3.71	103	.291	.352	10	.185	0	5	2	2	0.5
1956	Bos-A	0	0	—	2	0	0	0	0	4^{1}	5	2	0	0	4	0	18.7	0.00	—	.278	.409	0	.000	-0	2	2	0	0.1
	Bal-A	0	3	.000	18	3	0	0	0	38^{1}	49	23	3	1	14	15	15.0	3.99	98	.318	.379	0	.000	-1	1	-0	1	-0.1
	Yr	0	3	.000	20	3	0	0	0	42^{2}	54	25	3	1	18	15	15.4	3.59	111	.314	.382	0	.000	-2	3	2	1	0.0
Total	13	93	114	.449	366	235	86	16	19	1812^{2}	1766	841	97	35	757	746	12.7	3.55	107	.258	.335	83	.141	-14	66	51	35	8.8
● **CHARLIE SCHMUTZ**	Schmutz, Charles Otto "King" b: 1/1/1890, San Diego, Cal. d: 6/27/62, Seattle, Wash. BR/TR, 6'1.5", 195 lbs. Deb: 5/13/14																											
1914	Bro-N	1	3	.250	18	5	1	0	0	57^{1}	57	29	1	1	13	21	11.1	3.30	87	.265	.310	3	.188	1	-3	-3	0	-0.1
1915	Bro-N	0	0	—	1	0	0	0	0	4	7	5	0	0	1	1	18.0	6.75	41	.438	.471	0	.000	-0	-2	-2	0	-0.1
Total	2	1	3	.250	19	5	1	0	0	61^{1}	64	34	1	1	14	22	11.6	3.52	81	.277	.321	3	.176	0	-5	-4	1	-0.2
● **FRANK SCHNEIBERG**	Schneiberg, Frank Frederick b: 3/12/1882, Milwaukee, Wis. d: 5/18/48, Milwaukee, Wis. TR, Deb: 6/8/10																											
1910	Bro-N	0	0	—	1	0	0	0	0	1	5	8	0	0	4	0	81.0	63.00	5	.625	.750	0	—	0	-7	-7	-0	-0.3
● **DAN SCHNEIDER**	Schneider, Daniel Louis b: 8/29/42, Evansville, Ind. BL/TL, 6'3", 170 lbs. Deb: 5/12/63																											
1963	Mil-N	1	0	1.000	30	3	0	0	0	43^{2}	36	20	2	0	20	19	11.5	3.09	104	.225	.311	0	.000	-1	1	1	-1	-0.2
1964	Mil-N	1	2	.333	13	5	0	0	0	36^{1}	38	25	6	0	13	14	12.6	5.45	65	.270	.331	0	.000	-1	-8	-8	1	-0.6
1966	Atl-N	0	0	—	14	0	0	0	0	26^{1}	35	13	1	1	5	11	14.0	3.42	106	.324	.360	4	.500	1	1	1	-0	0.1
1967	Hou-N	0	2	.000	54	0	0	0	2	52^{2}	60	33	5	2	27	39	15.2	4.96	67	.296	.384	1	.200	0	-9	-10	1	-0.4
1969	Hou-N	0	1	.000	6	0	0	0	0	7^{1}	16	12	2	0	5	3	25.8	13.50	26	.485	.553	0	.000	-0	-8	-8	0	-1.0
Total	5	2	5	.286	117	8	0	0	2	166^{1}	185	103	16	3	70	86	14.0	4.71	72	.287	.359	5	.172	-0	-24	-25	1	-2.1
● **JEFF SCHNEIDER**	Schneider, Jeffrey Theodore b: 12/6/52, Bremerton, Wash. BB/TL, 6'3", 195 lbs. Deb: 8/12/81																											
1981	Bal-A	0	0	—	11	0	0	0	1	24	27	15	4	1	12	17	15.0	4.88	74	.290	.377	0	—	0	-3	-3	-0	-0.2
● **PETE SCHNEIDER**	Schneider, Peter Joseph b: 8/20/1895, Los Angeles, Cal. d: 6/1/57, Los Angeles, Cal. BR/TR, 6'1", 194 lbs. Deb: 6/20/14																											
1914	Cin-N	5	13	.278	29	15	11	1	1	144^{1}	143	71	1	7	56	62	12.8	2.81	104	.269	.347	8	.178	1	-0	2	-1	0.2
1915	Cin-N	14	19	.424	48	35	16	5	2	275^{2}	254	110	4	7	104	108	11.9	2.48	115	.251	.325	23	.245	5	8	11	-1	1.9
1916	Cin-N	10	19	.345	44	31	16	2	1	274^{1}	259	112	4	13	82	117	11.6	2.69	96	.255	.319	21	.236	2	-2	-3	-3	-0.3
1917	Cin-N	20	19	.513	46	42	24	0	0	333^{2}	311	128	4	11	117	138	11.8	2.10	124	.255	.326	19	.167	0	23	20	-5	1.9
1918	Cin-N	10	15	.400	33	30	17	2	0	217	213	106	2	11	117	51	14.1	3.53	76	.272	.374	24	.289	6	-18	-21	-3	-2.0
1919	NY-A	0	1	.000	7	4	0	0	0	29	19	14	1	3	22	11	13.7	3.41	94	.192	.355	1	.111	-1	-1	-1	-1	-0.2
Total	6	59	86	.407	207	157	84	10	4	1274	1199	541	16	52	498	487	12.4	2.66	102	.257	.336	96	.221	14	9	8	-13	1.5
● **KARL SCHNELL**	Schnell, Karl Otto b: 9/20/1899, Los Angeles, Cal. d: 5/31/92, Palo Alto, Cal. BR/TR, 6'1", 176 lbs. Deb: 4/24/22																											
1922	Cin-N	0	0	—	10	0	0	0	0	20	21	10	0	0	18	5	17.5	2.70	148	.300	.443	1	.250	0	3	3	0	0.2
1923	Cin-N	0	0	—	1	0	0	0	0	1	2	4	0	0	2	0	36.0	36.00	11	.667	.800	0	—	0	-4	-4	-0	-0.2
Total	2	0	0	—	11	0	0	0	0	21	23	14	0	0	20	5	18.4	4.29	93	.315	.462	1	.250	0	-0	-1	0	0.0
● **GERRY SCHOEN**	Schoen, Gerald Thomas b: 1/15/47, New Orleans, La. BR/TR, 6'3", 215 lbs. Deb: 9/14/68																											
1968	Was-A	0	1	.000	1	1	0	0	0	3^{2}	6	3	1	0	1	1	17.2	7.36	40	.400	.438	0	.000	-0	-2	-2	-0	-0.4
● **JUMBO SCHOENECK**	Schoeneck, Louis N. b: 3/3/1862, Chicago, Ill. d: 1/20/30, Chicago, Ill. BR/TR, 6'3", 223 lbs. Deb: 4/20/1884 ♦																											
1888	Ind-N	0	0	—	2	0	0	0	0	4^{1}	5	4	0	0	1	1	12.5	0.00	—	.227	.261	40	.237	0	1	1	-0	0.1
● **SCOTT SCHOENEWEIS**	Schoeneweis, Scott David b: 10/2/73, Long Branch, N.J. BL/TL, 6', 186 lbs. Deb: 4/7/99																											
1999	Ana-A	1	1	.500	31	0	0	0	0	39^{1}	47	27	4	0	14	22	14.0	5.49	88	.294	.351	0	—	0	-3	-3	1	0.0
2000	Ana-A	7	10	.412	27	27	1	1	0	170	183	112	21	6	67	78	13.6	5.45	91	.276	.348	1	.333	0	-10	-9	0	-0.7
Total	2	8	11	.421	58	27	1	1	0	209^{1}	230	139	25	6	81	100	13.6	5.46	91	.280	.349	1	.333	0	-13	-12	1	-0.7
● **MIKE SCHOOLER**	Schooler, Michael Ralph b: 8/10/62, Anaheim, Cal. BR/TR, 6'3", 220 lbs. Deb: 6/10/88																											
1988	Sea-A	5	8	.385	40	0	0	0	15	48^{1}	45	21	4	1	24	54	13.0	3.54	118	.245	.335	0	—	0	2	3	-0	0.6
1989	Sea-A	1	7	.125	67	0	0	0	33	77	81	27	2	2	19	69	11.9	2.81	144	.266	.314	0	—	0	9	10	1	1.9
1990	Sea-A	1	4	.200	49	0	0	0	30	56	47	18	5	1	16	45	10.3	2.25	176	.227	.286	0	.000	-0	10	11	0	1.8
1991	Sea-A	3	3	.500	34	0	0	0	7	34^{1}	25	14	2	0	10	31	9.2	3.67	112	.198	.257	0	—	0	2	2	-0	0.3
1992	Sea-A	2	7	.222	53	0	0	0	13	51^{2}	55	29	7	1	24	33	13.9	4.70	85	.275	.356	0	—	0	-4	-4	1	-0.8
1993	Tex-A	3	0	1.000	17	0	0	0	0	24^{1}	30	17	3	0	10	16	14.8	5.55	75	.303	.367	0	—	0	-3	-4	-0	-0.4
Total	6	15	29	.341	260	0	0	0	98	291^{2}	283	126	23	5	103	248	12.1	3.49	116	.253	.318	0	.000	-0	16	18	1	3.4
● **ED SCHORR**	Schorr, Edward Walter b: 2/14/1891, Bremen, Ohio d: 9/12/69, Atlantic City, N.J. BR/TR, 6'2.5", 180 lbs. Deb: 4/26/15																											
1915	Chi-N	0	0	—	2	0	0	0	0	6	9	5	0	0	5	3	21.0	7.50	37	.409	.519	1	.500	0	-3	-3	0	-0.1
● **GENE SCHOTT**	Schott, Arthur Eugene b: 7/14/13, Batavia, Ohio d: 11/16/92, Sun City Center, Fla. BR/TR, 6'2", 185 lbs. Deb: 4/16/35 ♦																											
1935	Cin-N	8	11	.421	33	19	9	1	0	159	153	84	5	1	64	49	12.3	3.91	102	.253	.326	12	.200	1	2	1	3	0.5
1936	Cin-N	11	11	.500	31	22	8	0	1	180	184	93	7	4	73	65	13.1	3.80	101	.262	.335	18	.300	7	4	0	1	0.9
1937	Cin-N	4	13	.235	37	16	7	2	1	154^{1}	150	69	2	1	48	56	11.6	2.97	125	.253	.310	7	.143	-1	16	14	1	1.4
1938	Cin-N	5	5	.500	31	4	0	0	2	83	89	47	8	1	32	21	13.2	4.45	82	.279	.347	3	.125	-1	-6	-8	1	-0.9
1939	Phi-N	0	1	.000	4	0	0	0	0	11	14	7	0	2	5	1	17.2	4.91	82	.326	.420	2	.333	1	-1	-1	-1	0.0
Total	5	28	41	.406	136	61	24	3	4	587^{1}	590	300	22	9	222	192	12.6	3.72	103	.261	.329	42	.211	6	15	7	6	1.9
● **PETE SCHOUREK**	Schourek, Peter Alan b: 5/10/69, Austin, Tex. BL/TL, 6'5", 205 lbs. Deb: 4/9/91																											
1991	NY-N	5	4	.556	35	8	1	1	2	86^{1}	82	49	7	2	43	67	13.2	4.27	85	.248	.338	3	.136	0	-6	-6	1	-0.5
1992	NY-N	6	8	.429	22	21	0	0	0	136	137	60	9	2	44	60	12.1	3.64	96	.261	.321	2	.048	-3	-2	-2	-2	-0.8
1993	NY-N	5	12	.294	41	18	0	0	0	128^{1}	168	90	13	3	45	72	15.1	5.96	67	.319	.376	7	.219	2	-27	-28	-0	-3.1
1994	Cin-N	7	2	.778	22	10	0	0	0	81^{1}	90	39	11	3	29	69	13.5	4.09	101	.287	.353	4	.174	1	1	0	0	0.2
1995	*Cin-N	18	7	.720	29	29	2	0	0	190^{1}	158	72	17	8	45	160	10.0	3.22	128	.228	.283	13	.220	2	21	19	0	2.6
1996	Cin-N	4	5	.444	12	12	0	0	0	67^{1}	79	48	7	3	24	54	14.2	6.01	70	.293	.357	5	.263	1	-13	-13	0	-1.4
1997	Cin-N	5	8	.385	18	17	0	0	0	84^{2}	78	59	18	4	38	59	12.8	5.42	79	.241	.328	4	.167	1	-11	-11	-1	-1.4
1998	Hou-N	7	6	.538	15	15	0	0	0	80	82	43	10	4	36	59	13.7	4.50	90	.269	.354	4	.211	1	-2	-4	-1	-0.6
	*Bos-A	1	3	.250	10	8	0	0	0	44	45	21	7	1	14	36	12.3	4.30	110	.273	.333	0	—	0	2	2	-1	0.1
1999	Pit-N	4	7	.364	30	17	0	0	0	113	128	75	20	5	49	94	14.5	5.34	86	.287	.364	0	.000	-2	-10	-10	-0	-1.0
2000	Bos-A	3	10	.231	21	21	0	0	0	107^{1}	116	67	17	3	38	63	13.2	5.11	100	.278	.342	2	.500	1	-2	-0	0	0.1
Total	10	65	72	.474	255	176	3	1	2	1118^{2}	1163	623	136	38	405	793	12.9	4.59	91	.269	.337	44	.164	3	-51	-53	-4	-5.8

YEAR	TM/L	W	L	PCT	G	GS	CG	SH	SV	IP	H	R	HR	HB	BB	SO	RAT	ERA	ERA+	OAV	OOB	BH	AVG	PB	PR	PR+	PD	TPI
● BARNEY SCHREIBER Schreiber, David Henry b: 5/8/1882, Waverly, Ohio d: 10/6/64, Chillicothe, Ohio BL/TL, 6′, 185 lbs. Deb: 5/15/11																												
1911	Cin-N	0	0	—	3	0	0	0	1	10	19	11	2	0	2	5	18.9	5.40	61	.413	.438	0	.000	-0	-2	-2	-0	-0.2
● PAUL SCHREIBER Schreiber, Paul Frederick "Von" b: 10/8/02, Jacksonville, Fla. d: 1/28/82, Sarasota, Fla. BR/TR, 6′2″, 180 lbs. Deb: 9/2/22 C																												
1922	Bro-N	0	0	—	1	0	0	0	0	1	2	0	0	0	0	0	18.0	0.00	—	.500	.500	0	—	0	0	0	0	0.0
1923	Bro-N	0	0	—	9	0	0	0	1	15	16	9	1	2	8	4	15.6	4.20	92	.276	.382	0	.000	-0	-0	-1	-0	-0.1
1945	NY-A	0	0	—	2	0	0	0	0	4^1	4	2	0	0	2	1	12.5	4.15	83	.267	.353	0	.000	-0	-0	-0	1	0.0
Total	3	0	0	—	12	0	0	0	1	20^1	22	11	1	2	10	5	15.0	3.98	96	.286	.382	0	.000	-0	-0	-0	1	-0.1
● STEVE SCHRENK Schrenk, Steven Wayne b: 11/20/68, Chicago, Ill. BR/TR, 6′3″, 185 lbs. Deb: 7/3/99																												
1999	Phi-N	1	3	.250	32	2	0	0	1	50^1	41	24	6	7	14	36	11.1	4.29	110	.223	.302	0	.000	-0	2	2	0	0.2
2000	Phi-N	2	3	.400	20	0	0	0	0	23^1	25	20	3	1	13	19	15.0	7.33	64	.269	.364	0	—	0	-7	-7	-0	-1.2
Total	2	3	6	.333	52	2	0	0	1	73^2	66	44	9	8	27	55	12.3	5.25	90	.238	.324	0	.000	-0	-5	-4	0	-1.0
● AL SCHROLL Schroll, Albert Bringhurst "Bull" b: 3/22/32, New Orleans, La. d: 11/30/99, Alexandria, La. BR/TR, 6′2″, 210 lbs. Deb: 4/20/58																												
1958	Bos-A	0	0	—	5	0	0	0	0	10	6	5	1	0	4	7	9.0	4.50	89	.176	.263	1	1.000	0	-1	-1	0	0.0
1959	Phi-N	1	1	.500	3	0	0	0	0	9^1	12	9	1	0	6	4	17.4	8.68	47	.353	.450	1	.250	0	-5	-5	0	-0.7
	Bos-A	1	4	.200	14	5	1	0	0	46	47	29	3	1	22	26	13.7	4.70	86	.269	.354	1	.111	0	-4	-3	-1	-0.3
1960	Chi-N	0	0	—	2	0	0	0	0	2^2	3	3	1	0	5	2	27.0	10.13	37	.273	.500	1	1.000	0	-2	-2	-0	-0.1
1961	Min-A	4	4	.500	11	8	2	0	0	50	53	36	5	2	27	24	14.8	5.22	81	.266	.360	5	.278	2	-7	-5	-0	-0.5
Total	4	6	9	.400	35	13	3	0	0	118	121	82	11	3	64	63	14.3	5.34	77	.267	.362	9	.273	4	-19	-15	-1	-1.6
● KEN SCHROM Schrom, Kenneth Marvin b: 11/23/54, Grangeville, Idaho BR/TR, 6′2″, 195 lbs. Deb: 8/8/80																												
1980	Tor-A	1	0	1.000	17	0	0	0	1	31	32	18	2	0	19	13	14.8	5.23	82	.274	.375	0	—	0	-4	-3	0	-0.1
1982	Tor-A	1	0	1.000	6	0	0	0	0	15^1	13	11	3	0	15	8	16.4	5.87	76	.232	.394	0	—	0	-3	-2	-1	-0.2
1983	Min-A	15	8	.652	33	28	6	1	0	196^1	196	92	14	9	80	80	13.1	3.71	115	.266	.345	0	—	0	8	12	-3	0.9
1984	Min-A	5	11	.313	25	21	3	0	0	137	156	75	15	1	41	49	13.0	4.47	94	.285	.336	0	—	0	-7	-4	-2	-0.6
1985	Min-A	9	12	.429	29	26	6	0	0	160^2	164	95	28	0	59	74	12.5	4.99	88	.272	.337	0	—	0	-15	-10	1	-1.0
1986	Cle-A☆	14	7	.667	34	33	3	1	0	206	217	118	34	12	49	87	12.1	4.54	91	.271	.322	0	—	0	-8	-9	-3	-1.1
1987	Cle-A	6	13	.316	32	29	4	1	0	153^2	185	126	29	3	57	61	14.3	6.50	70	.298	.360	0	—	0	-35	-33	-2	-3.5
Total	7	51	51	.500	176	137	22	3	1	900	963	535	125	25	320	372	13.1	4.81	90	.276	.342	0	—	0	-64	-48	-10	-5.6
● RON SCHUELER Schueler, Ronald Richard b: 4/18/48, Catharine, Kan. BR/TR, 6′4″, 205 lbs. Deb: 4/16/72 C																												
1972	Atl-N	5	8	.385	37	18	3	0	2	144^2	122	68	16	2	60	96	11.4	3.67	103	.227	.307	8	.190	0	-3	2	-1	0.1
1973	Atl-N	8	7	.533	39	20	4	2	2	186	179	91	24	0	66	124	11.9	3.87	102	.255	.319	11	.177	-1	-4	1	-1	0.0
1974	Phi-N	11	16	.407	44	27	5	0	1	203^1	202	91	17	4	98	109	13.5	3.72	102	.264	.351	6	.118	-2	-2	2	-2	-0.3
1975	Phi-N	4	4	.500	46	6	1	0	0	92^2	88	55	6	1	40	69	12.5	5.24	71	.258	.338	2	.154	-0	-17	-15	1	-1.1
1976	Phi-N	1	0	1.000	35	0	0	0	3	49^2	44	18	4	2	16	43	11.2	2.90	123	.243	.312	0	.000	-0	3	4	-1	0.1
1977	Min-A	8	7	.533	52	7	0	0	3	134^2	131	74	16	6	61	77	13.2	4.41	91	.260	.347	0	—	0	-5	-6	2	-0.5
1978	Chi-A	3	5	.375	30	7	0	0	0	81^2	76	50	10	7	39	39	13.4	4.30	89	.251	.350	0	—	0	-5	-4	0	-0.4
1979	Chi-A	0	1	.000	8	1	0	0	0	19^2	19	16	3	2	13	6	15.6	7.32	58	.264	.391	0	—	0	-7	-7	-0	-0.3
Total	8	40	48	.455	291	86	13	2	11	912^1	861	463	96	24	393	563	12.6	4.08	94	.253	.334	27	.159	-3	-39	-23	-2	-2.4
● DAVE SCHULER Schuler, David Paul b: 10/4/53, Framingham, Mass. BR/TL, 6′4″, 210 lbs. Deb: 9/17/79																												
1979	Cal-A	0	0	—	1	0	0	0	0	1^2	2	2	1	0	0	0	10.8	10.80	38	.333	.333	0	—	0	-1	-1	-0	-0.1
1980	Cal-A	0	1	.000	8	0	0	0	0	12^2	13	5	3	0	2	7	10.7	3.55	111	.271	.300	0	—	0	1	1	-0	0.0
1985	Atl-N	0	0	—	9	0	0	0	0	10^2	19	8	4	0	3	10	18.6	6.75	57	.404	.440	0	—	0	-4	-3	-0	-0.2
Total	3	0	1	.000	18	0	0	0	0	25	34	15	8	0	5	17	14.0	5.40	73	.337	.368	0	—	0	-4	-4	-1	-0.3
● ERIK SCHULLSTROM Schullstrom, Erik Paul b: 3/25/69, San Diego, Cal. BR/TR, 6′5″, 220 lbs. Deb: 7/18/94																												
1994	Min-A	0	0	—	9	0	0	0	1	13	13	7	0	1	5	13	13.2	2.77	176	.260	.339	0	—	0	3	3	-0	0.1
1995	Min-A	0	0	—	37	0	0	0	0	47	66	36	8	1	22	21	17.0	6.89	69	.332	.401	0	—	0	-11	-11	-0	-0.5
Total	2	0	0	—	46	0	0	0	1	60	79	43	8	2	27	34	16.2	6.00	80	.317	.388	0	—	0	-8	-8	-1	-0.4
● BUDDY SCHULTZ Schultz, Charles Budd b: 9/19/50, Cleveland, Ohio BR/TL, 6′, 175 lbs. Deb: 9/3/75																												
1975	Chi-N	2	0	1.000	6	0	0	0	0	5^2	11	6	0	0	5	4	25.4	6.35	61	.367	.457	0	—	0	-2	-1	-0	-0.3
1976	Chi-N	1	1	.500	29	0	0	0	2	23^2	37	19	3	0	9	15	17.5	6.08	64	.356	.407	0	.000	-0	-7	-5	1	-0.5
1977	StL-N	6	1	.857	40	3	0	0	1	85^1	76	26	5	0	24	66	10.5	2.32	166	.245	.299	2	.167	0	15	15	-1	1.1
1978	StL-N	2	4	.333	62	0	0	0	6	83	68	36	6	0	36	70	11.3	3.80	93	.226	.309	1	.200	1	-2	-3	-1	-0.2
1979	StL-N	4	3	.571	31	0	0	0	3	42^1	40	21	7	0	14	38	11.5	4.46	84	.256	.318	0	.000	-0	-3	-3	-0	-0.6
Total	5	15	9	.625	168	3	0	0	12	240	232	108	21	0	88	193	12.0	3.68	101	.257	.324	3	.120	0	1	1	-1	-0.5
● BARNEY SCHULTZ Schultz, George Warren b: 8/15/26, Beverly, N.J. BR/TR, 6′2″, 200 lbs. Deb: 4/12/55 C																												
1955	StL-N	1	2	.333	19	0	0	0	4	29^2	28	27	5	4	15	19	14.3	7.89	52	.259	.370	0	.000	-1	-13	-13	1	-1.4
1959	Det-A	1	2	.333	13	0	0	0	0	18^1	17	12	1	1	14	17	15.7	4.42	92	.254	.390	2	1.000	1	-1	-1	-0	0.0
1961	Chi-N	7	6	.538	41	0	0	0	7	66^2	57	32	6	4	25	59	11.6	2.70	155	.228	.308	1	.100	-1	10	11	-0	2.0
1962	Chi-N	5	5	.500	51	0	0	0	5	77^2	66	36	8	4	23	58	10.8	3.82	108	.231	.297	0	.000	-0	1	3	0	0.3
1963	Chi-N	1	0	1.000	15	0	0	0	2	27^1	25	11	5	0	9	18	11.2	3.62	97	.263	.327	0	.000	-0	-1	-0	0	0.0
	StL-N	2	0	1.000	24	0	0	0	1	35^1	36	15	5	2	8	26	11.7	3.57	99	.263	.313	0	—	0	-1	-0	-0	0.0
	Yr	3	0	1.000	39	0	0	0	3	62^2	61	26	10	2	17	44	11.5	3.59	98	.263	.319	0	.000	-0	-2	-0	0	0.0
1964	*StL-N	1	3	.250	30	0	0	0	14	49^1	35	14	1	0	11	29	8.4	1.64	232	.201	.249	1	.167	-0	10	11	-1	1.5
1965	StL-N	2	2	.500	34	0	0	0	2	42^1	39	22	8	0	11	38	10.6	3.83	100	.242	.291	0	.000	-0	-1	0	0	0.0
Total	7	20	20	.500	227	0	0	0	35	346^2	303	169	39	15	116	264	11.3	3.63	109	.237	.308	4	.121	-1	4	12	-0	2.4
● BOB SCHULTZ Schultz, Robert Duffy b: 11/27/23, Louisville, Ky. d: 3/31/79, Nashville, Tenn. BR/TL, 6′3″, 200 lbs. Deb: 4/20/51																												
1951	Chi-N	3	6	.333	17	10	2	0	0	77^1	75	51	9	2	51	27	14.9	5.24	78	.251	.364	4	.138	-1	-11	-9	-1	-1.2
1952	Chi-N	6	3	.667	29	5	1	0	0	74	63	34	3	2	51	31	14.1	4.01	96	.232	.357	4	.222	0	-2	-1	-2	-0.3
1953	Chi-N	0	2	.000	7	2	0	0	0	11^2	13	10	2	1	11	4	19.3	5.40	82	.289	.439	0	.000	-0	-1	-1	-1	-0.3
	Pit-N	0	2	.000	11	2	0	0	0	18^2	26	19	3	2	10	5	18.3	8.20	55	.321	.409	0	.000	0	-8	-7	-0	-0.7
	Yr	0	4	.000	18	4	0	0	0	30^1	39	29	5	3	21	9	18.7	7.12	63	.310	.420	0	.000	-0	-10	-9	-1	-1.0
1955	Det-A	0	0	—	1	0	0	0	0	1^1	2	3	0	0	2	0	27.0	20.25	19	.333	.500	0	—	0	-2	-3	-0	-0.1
Total	4	9	13	.409	65	19	3	0	0	183	179	117	17	7	125	67	15.3	5.16	79	.255	.372	8	.154	-1	-25	-22	-4	-2.6
● WEBB SCHULTZ Schultz, Webb Carl b: 1/31/1898, Wautoma, Wis. d: 7/26/86, Delavan, Wis. BR/TR, 5′11″, 172 lbs. Deb: 8/3/24																												
1924	Chi-A	0	0	—	1	0	0	0	0	1	1	1	0	0	0	0	9.0	9.00	46	.250	.250	0	—	0	-1	-1	-0	0.0
● MIKE SCHULTZ Schultz, William Michael b: 12/17/20, Syracuse, N.Y. BL/TL, 6′1″, 175 lbs. Deb: 4/20/47																												
1947	Cin-N	0	0	—	1	0	0	0	0	2	4	2	0	0	2	0	27.0	4.50	91	.444	.545	0	—	0	-0	-0	-0	0.0
● JOHN SCHULTZE Schultze, John F. b: Burlington, N.J. 6′0.5″, 165 lbs. Deb: 5/6/1891																												
1891	Phi-N	0	1	.000	6	1	0	0	0	15	18	15	1	0	11	4	17.4	6.60	52	.286	.392	1	.167	-0	-5	-5	-1	-0.3
● AL SCHULZ Schulz, Albert Christopher b: 5/12/1889, Toledo, Ohio d: 12/13/31, Gallipolis, Ohio BR/TL, 6′, 182 lbs. Deb: 9/25/12																												
1912	NY-A	1	1	.500	3	1	1	0	0	16^1	11	8	0	0	11	8	12.1	2.20	163	.183	.310	0	.000	-0	2	2	1	0.3
1913	NY-A	7	14	.333	38	22	9	0	0	193	197	110	4	5	69	77	12.6	3.73	80	.266	.333	11	.175	0	-17	-16	-1	-1.7
1914	NY-A	1	3	.250	6	4	1	0	0	28^1	27	17	0	2	10	18	12.4	4.76	58	.237	.310	0	.000	-0	-6	-6	1	-0.8
	Buf-F	9	12	.429	27	23	10	0	2	171	160	80	3	2	77	87	12.6	3.37	88	.259	.343	10	.179	-1	-9	-8	2	-0.8
1915	Buf-F	21	14	.600	42	38	25	5	0	309^2	264	125	8	6	149	160	12.2	3.08	91	.238	.332	18	.165	-4	-12	-9	1	-1.3
1916	Cin-N	8	19	.296	44	22	10	0	2	215	208	100	4	5	93	95	12.8	3.14	83	.268	.350	8	.125	-3	-12	-13	0	-2.1
Total	5	47	63	.427	160	110	56	5	4	933^1	867	440	19	20	409	445	12.5	3.32	85	.254	.337	47	.155	-9	-55	-49	3	-6.4

YEAR	TM/L	W	L	PCT	G	GS	CG	SH	SV	IP	H	R	HR	HB	BB	SO	RAT	ERA	ERA+	OAV	OOB	BH	AVG	PB	PR	PR+	PD	TPI
● WALT SCHULZ	Schulz, Walter Frederick b: 4/16/1900, St.Louis, Mo. d: 2/27/28, Prescott, Ark. BR/TR, 6', 170 lbs. Deb: 9/24/20																											
1920	StL-N	0	0	—	2	0	0	0	0	6	10	5	0	0	2	0	18.0	6.00	50	.370	.414	0	.000	-0	-2	-2	0	-0.1
● DON SCHULZE	Schulze, Donald Arthur b: 9/27/62, Roselle, Ill. BR/TR, 6'3", 225 lbs. Deb: 9/13/83																											
1983	Chi-N	0	1	.000	4	3	0	0	0	14	19	11	1	1	7	8	17.4	7.07	54	.322	.403	0	.000	0	-5	-5	0	-0.3
1984	Chi-N	0	0	—	1	1	0	0	0	3	8	4	0	0	1	2	27.0	12.00	33	.571	.600	0	—	0	-3	-2	0	-0.1
	Cle-A	3	6	.333	19	14	2	0	0	85^2	105	53	9	0	27	39	13.9	4.83	85	.302	.352	0	—	0	-8	-7	-0	-0.7
1985	Cle-A	4	10	.286	19	18	1	0	0	94^1	128	75	10	4	19	37	14.4	6.01	69	.322	.360	0	—	0	-20	-20	1	-2.4
1986	Cle-A	4	4	.500	19	13	1	0	0	84^2	88	48	9	5	34	33	13.5	5.00	83	.266	.343	0	—	0	-8	-8	-1	-0.8
1987	NY-N	1	2	.333	5	4	0	0	0	21^2	24	15	4	1	6	5	12.9	6.23	61	.296	.352	0	.000	0	-5	-6	1	-0.6
1989	NY-A	1	1	.500	2	2	0	0	0	11	12	5	1	1	5	5	14.7	4.09	95	.300	.391	0	—	0	-0	-0	-0	-0.1
	SD-N	2	1	.667	7	4	0	0	0	24^1	38	20	6	0	6	15	16.3	5.55	63	.352	.386	0	.000	-0	-6	-6	1	-0.6
Total	6	15	25	.375	76	59	4	0	0	338^2	422	231	40	12	105	144	14.3	5.47	74	.306	.361	0	.000	0	-54	-54	1	-5.6
● HAL SCHUMACHER	Schumacher, Harold Henry "Prince Hal" b: 11/23/10, Hinckley, N.Y. d: 4/21/93, Cooperstown, N.Y. BR/TR, 6', 190 lbs. Deb: 4/15/31																											
1931	NY-N	1	1	.500	8	2	1	0	1	18^1	31	23	3	0	14	11	22.1	10.80	34	.387	.479	1	.143	-0	-14	-15	1	-1.5
1932	NY-N	5	6	.455	27	13	2	1	0	101^1	119	60	3	2	39	38	14.2	3.55	104	.288	.352	7	.226	1	4	2	2	0.5
1933	*NY-N☆	19	12	.613	35	33	21	7	1	258^2	199	71	9	1	84	96	9.9	2.16	149	**.214**	.280	21	.214	1	34	32	3	4.4
1934	NY-N	23	10	.697	41	36	18	2	0	297	299	131	16	2	89	112	11.8	3.18	122	.259	.313	28	.239	10	29	24	3	3.7
1935	NY-N★	19	9	.679	33	33	19	3	0	261^2	235	100	11	5	70	79	10.7	2.89	133	.238	.292	21	.196	2	33	29	7	3.8
1936	*NY-N	11	13	.458	35	30	9	2	1	215^1	234	103	15	1	69	75	12.7	3.47	112	.280	.336	16	.216	2	13	11	4	1.6
1937	*NY-N	13	12	.520	38	29	10	1	1	217^2	222	100	12	0	89	100	12.9	3.60	108	.264	.335	18	.222	3	8	7	1	1.1
1938	NY-N	13	8	.619	28	28	12	3	0	185	178	81	12	2	50	54	11.2	3.50	108	.248	.299	16	.239	4	6	5	2	1.2
1939	NY-N	13	10	.565	29	27	8	0	0	181^2	199	106	14	3	89	58	14.4	4.81	82	.276	.358	14	.203	1	-18	-18	-0	-1.9
1940	NY-N	13	13	.500	34	30	12	1	1	227	218	93	14	0	96	123	12.4	3.25	119	.251	.325	15	.192	2	15	16	4	2.4
1941	NY-N	12	10	.545	30	26	12	3	1	206	187	81	11	5	79	63	11.8	3.36	110	.243	.317	10	.152	-1	6	7	-1	0.6
1942	NY-N	12	13	.480	29	29	12	3	0	216	208	81	12	3	82	49	12.2	3.04	111	.251	.321	13	.173	1	7	8	2	1.2
1946	NY-N	4	4	.500	24	13	2	0	1	96^2	95	50	8	0	52	48	13.7	3.91	88	.255	.347	1	.038	-2	-5	-5	3	-0.4
Total	13	158	121	.566	391	329	138	26	7	2482^1	2424	1080	140	24	902	906	12.1	3.36	111	.255	.321	181	.202	24	117	102	30	16.7
● HACK SCHUMANN	Schumann, Carl J. b: 8/13/1884, Buffalo, N.Y. d: 3/25/46, Mill Grove, N.Y. TR, 6'2", 230 lbs. Deb: 9/19/06																											
1906	Phi-A	0	2	.000	4	2	1	0	0	18	21	13	0	2	8	9	15.5	4.00	68	.296	.383	0	.000	-1	-3	-3	-0	-0.4
● FERDIE SCHUPP	Schupp, Ferdinand Maurice b: 1/16/1891, Louisville, Ky. d: 12/16/71, Los Angeles, Cal. BR/TR, 5'10", 150 lbs. Deb: 4/19/13																											
1913	NY-N	0	0	—	5	1	0	0	0	12	10	3	0	0	3	2	9.8	0.75	416	.244	.295	1	.333	1	3	3	-0	0.2
1914	NY-N	0	0	—	8	0	0	0	1	17	19	11	0	2	9	9	15.9	5.82	46	.306	.411	0	.000	-0	-6	-6	-0	-0.4
1915	NY-N	1	0	1.000	23	1	0	0	0	54^2	57	37	1	3	29	28	14.7	5.10	50	.281	.379	2	.200	0	-14	-17	0	-0.9
1916	NY-N	9	3	.750	30	11	8	4	1	140^1	79	22	1	5	37	86	7.8	0.90	271	.167	.235	4	.098	-2	27	26	-3	1.8
1917	*NY-N	21	7	**.750**	36	32	25	6	0	272	202	69	7	4	70	147	9.1	1.95	131	**.209**	.265	15	.161	1	23	19	-3	1.8
1918	NY-N	0	1	.000	10	2	1	0	0	33^1	42	34	1	3	27	22	19.4	7.56	35	.328	.456	1	.111	-0	-18	-19	0	-1.0
1919	NY-N	1	3	.250	9	4	0	0	1	32	32	24	2	0	18	17	14.1	5.63	50	.269	.365	2	.333	0	-10	-10	-1	-1.3
	StL-N	4	4	.500	10	10	6	0	0	69^2	55	31	2	1	30	37	11.1	3.75	75	.221	.307	1	.050	-0	-6	-8	-1	-1.0
	Yr	5	7	.417	19	14	6	0	1	101^2	87	55	4	1	48	54	12.0	4.34	64	.236	.326	3	.115	-0	-16	-18	-2	-2.3
1920	StL-N	16	13	.552	38	37	17	0	0	250^2	246	118	5	9	127	119	13.7	3.52	85	.265	.358	22	.256	6	-11	-16	-2	-1.4
1921	StL-N	2	0	1.000	9	4	1	0	1	37^1	42	26	5	2	21	22	15.7	4.10	89	.276	.371	4	.286	0	-1	-2	-0	-0.1
	Bro-N	3	4	.429	20	7	1	0	2	61	75	34	2	2	27	26	15.3	4.57	85	.310	.384	1	.083	-1	-5	-5	-0	-0.5
	Yr	5	4	.556	29	11	2	0	3	98^1	117	60	7	4	48	48	15.5	4.39	87	.297	.379	5	.192	-0	-7	-6	-0	-0.6
1922	Chi-A	4	4	.500	18	12	3	1	0	74	79	61	4	2	66	38	17.9	6.08	67	.284	.425	5	.217	1	-17	-16	-0	-1.5
Total	10	61	39	.610	216	121	62	11	6	1054	938	470	30	33	464	553	12.3	3.32	87	.244	.331	58	.182	5	-35	-53	-10	-4.3
● WAYNE SCHURR	Schurr, Wayne Allen b: 8/6/37, Garrett, Ind. BR/TR, 6'4", 185 lbs. Deb: 4/15/64																											
1964	Chi-N	0	0	—	26	0	0	0	0	48^1	57	22	3	0	11	29	12.7	3.72	100	.298	.337	0	.000	-0	-1	-0	-0	-0.1
● CARL SCHUTZ	Schutz, Carl James b: 8/22/71, Hammond, La. BL/TL, 5'11", 208 lbs. Deb: 9/3/96																											
1996	Atl-N	0	0	—	3	0	0	0	0	3^1	3	1	0	0	2	5	13.5	2.70	163	.273	.385	0	—	0	1	1	-0	0.0
● MIKE SCHWABE	Schwabe, Michael Scott b: 7/12/64, Ft.Dodge, Iowa BR/TR, 6'4", 200 lbs. Deb: 5/27/89																											
1989	Det-A	2	4	.333	13	4	0	0	0	44^2	58	33	6	1	16	13	15.1	6.04	63	.307	.364	0	—	0	-11	-11	1	-1.2
1990	Det-A	0	0	—	1	0	0	0	0	3^2	5	1	0	0	0	1	12.3	2.45	162	.357	.357	0	—	0	1	1	0	0.1
Total	2	2	4	.333	14	4	0	0	0	48^1	63	34	6	1	16	14	14.9	5.77	66	.310	.364	0	—	0	-10	-11	1	-1.1
● DON SCHWALL	Schwall, Donald Bernard b: 3/2/36, Wilkes-Barre, Pa. BR/TR, 6'6", 200 lbs. Deb: 5/21/61																											
1961	Bos-A★	15	7	.682	25	25	10	2	0	178^2	167	76	8	6	110	91	14.3	3.22	129	.255	.368	11	.180	-0	16	18	1	2.1
1962	Bos-A	9	15	.375	33	32	5	1	0	182^1	180	118	18	10	121	89	15.4	4.94	84	.260	.378	9	.136	-2	-20	-16	0	-2.0
1963	Pit-N	6	12	.333	33	24	3	2	0	167^2	158	72	13	6	74	86	12.8	3.33	99	.255	.340	8	.160	-0	-1	-1	2	0.1
1964	Pit-N	4	3	.571	15	9	0	0	0	49^2	53	28	1	0	15	36	12.3	4.35	81	.269	.321	5	.263	2	-4	-5	0	-0.4
1965	Pit-N	9	6	.600	43	1	0	0	4	77^2	77	37	5	2	30	55	12.7	2.92	120	.269	.343	0	.000	-2	5	5	2	1.0
1966	Pit-N	3	2	.600	11	4	0	0	0	41^2	31	13	3	1	21	24	11.4	2.16	165	.209	.312	1	.100	-0	7	7	0	0.8
	Atl-N	3	3	.500	11	8	0	0	0	45^1	44	23	2	2	19	27	12.9	4.37	83	.256	.337	0	.000	-2	-4	-4	-0	-0.6
	Yr	6	5	.545	22	12	0	0	0	87	75	36	5	3	40	51	12.2	3.31	109	.234	.325	1	.043	-2	3	3	-0	0.2
1967	Atl-N	0	0	—	1	0	0	0	0	0^2	0	0	0	0	1	0	13.5	0.00	—	.000	.500	0	—	0	0	0	-0	0.0
Total	7	49	48	.505	172	103	18	5	4	743	710	367	50	27	391	408	13.7	3.72	102	.257	.354	34	.145	-5	-1	5	4	1.0
● BLACKIE SCHWAMB	Schwamb, Ralph Richard b: 8/6/26, Lancaster, Cal. d: 12/21/89, Los Angeles, Cal. BR/TR, 6'5.5", 198 lbs. Deb: 7/25/48																											
1948	StL-A	1	1	.500	12	5	0	0	0	31^2	44	34	3	0	21	7	18.5	8.53	53	.331	.422	3	.300	1	-15	-13	0	-0.6
● JEFF SCHWARZ	Schwarz, Jeffrey William b: 5/20/64, Fort Pierce, Fla. BR/TR, 6'5", 190 lbs. Deb: 4/24/93																											
1993	Chi-A	2	2	.500	41	0	0	0	0	51	35	21	1	3	38	41	13.4	3.71	113	.201	.353	0	—	0	4	3	-1	0.1
1994	Chi-A	0	0	—	9	0	0	0	0	11^1	9	10	0	0	16	14	19.9	6.35	74	.205	.417	0	—	0	-2	-2	-0	-0.1
	Cal-A	0	0	—	4	0	0	0	0	6^2	5	3	0	0	6	4	14.9	4.05	121	.250	.423	0	—	0	1	1	0	0.0
	Yr	0	0	—	13	0	0	0	0	18	14	13	0	0	22	18	18.0	5.50	86	.219	.419	0	—	0	-1	-2	-0	-0.1
Total	2	2	2	.500	54	0	0	0	0	69	49	34	1	3	60	59	14.6	4.17	104	.206	.372	0	—	0	2	1	-2	0.0
● RUDY SCHWENCK	Schwenck, Rudolph Christian b: 4/6/1884, Louisville, Ky. d: 11/27/41, Anchorage, Ky. BL/TL, 6', 174 lbs. Deb: 9/23/09																											
1909	Chi-N	1	1	.500	3	2	0	0	0	4	16	7	0	1	3	3	45.0	13.50	19	.308	.357	1	.250	0	-5	-5	1	-0.8
● HAL SCHWENK	Schwenk, Harold Edward b: 8/23/1890, Schuylkill Haven, Pa. d: 9/3/55, Kansas City, Mo. BL/TL, 6', 185 lbs. Deb: 9/4/13																											
1913	StL-A	1	0	1.000	1	1	1	0	0	11	12	4	0	0	4	3	13.1	3.27	90	.333	.400	1	.333	1	-0	-0	-0	0.0
● JIM SCOGGINS	Scoggins, Lynn J. "Lefty" b: 7/19/1891, Killeen, Tex. d: 8/16/23, Columbia, S.C. BL/TL, 5'11", 165 lbs. Deb: 8/26/13																											
1913	Chi-A	0	1	.000	1	1	0	0	0	0	0	0	0	1	—	—	—	—	.000	.500	100	—	0	0	0	0	0.0	
● HERB SCORE	Score, Herbert Jude b: 6/7/33, Rosedale, N.Y. BL/TL, 6'2", 185 lbs. Deb: 4/15/55																											
1955	Cle-A☆	16	10	.615	33	32	11	2	0	227^1	158	85	18	1	154	**245**	12.4	2.85	140	.194	.323	10	.119	-4	28	29	-4	2.2
1956	Cle-A★	20	9	.690	35	33	16	**5**	0	249^1	162	82	18	2	129	**263**	**10.6**	2.53	**166**	**.186**	.292	16	.184	1	**45**	**46**	-4	4.8
1957	Cle-A	2	1	.667	5	5	3	1	0	36	18	9	0	1	26	39	11.3	2.00	186	.149	.304	1	.091	-0	7	7	0	0.6
1958	Cle-A	2	3	.400	12	5	2	1	3	41	29	19	1	0	34	48	13.8	3.95	92	.197	.348	1	.091	-0	-1	-1	-1	-0.3
1959	Cle-A	9	11	.450	30	25	9	1	0	160^2	123	93	28	1	115	147	13.4	4.71	78	**.210**	.341	5	.096	-3	-15	-19	-3	-2.6
1960	Chi-A	5	10	.333	23	22	5	1	0	113^2	91	54	10	2	87	78	14.3	3.72	102	.226	.366	3	.100	-0	2	1	-1	0.0
1961	Chi-A	1	2	.333	8	5	1	0	0	24^1	22	19	3	0	24	14	17.0	6.66	59	.259	.422	0	.000	-1	-7	-8	0	-0.8
1962	Chi-A	0	0	—	4	0	0	0	0	6	6	3	1	0	4	3	15.0	4.50	87	.261	.370	0	—	0	-0	-0	0	0.0
Total	8	55	46	.545	150	127	47	11	3	858^1	609	364	79	7	573	837	12.5	3.36	117	.200	.328	36	.128	-8	59	56	-12	3.9

YEAR	TM/L	W	L	PCT	G	GS	CG	SH	SV	IP	H	R	HR	HB	BB	SO	RAT	ERA	ERA+	OAV	OOB	BH	AVG	PB	PR	PR+	PD	TPI
● DICK SCOTT Scott, Amos Richard b: 2/5/1883, Bethel, Ohio d: 1/18/11, Chicago, Ill. BR/TR, 6', 180 lbs. Deb: 6/26/01																												
1901	Cin-N	0	2	.000	3	2	2	0	0	21	26	15	2	3	9	7	16.3	5.14	62	.302	.388	0	.000	-1	-4	-5	-1	-0.5
● DARRYL SCOTT Scott, Darryl Nelson b: 8/6/68, Fresno, Cal. BR/TR, 6'1", 185 lbs. Deb: 5/31/93																												
1993	Cal-A	1	2	.333	16	0	0	0	0	20	19	13	1	1	11	13	13.9	5.85	77	.250	.352	0	—	0	-3	-3	-1	-0.4
● ED SCOTT Scott, Edward b: 8/12/1870, Walbridge, Ohio d: 11/1/33, Toledo, Ohio BR/TR, 6'3", Deb: 4/19/00																												
1900	Cin-N	17	20	.459	42	35	31	0	1	315	370	192	10	14	65	87	12.8	3.86	95	.292	.334	19	.154	-5	-6	-6	9	-0.2
1901	Cle-A	6	6	.500	17	16	11	0	1	124^2	149	82	2	7	38	23	14.0	4.40	81	.293	.350	10	.208	1	-10	-12	2	-0.7
Total	2	23	26	.469	59	51	42	0	2	439^2	519	274	12	21	103	110	13.2	4.01	91	.292	.338	29	.170	-4	-16	-18	11	-0.9
● GEORGE SCOTT Scott, George William b: 11/17/1896, Trenton, Mo. BR/TR, 6'1", 175 lbs. Deb: 9/13/20																												
1920	StL-N	0	0	—	2	0	0	0	0	6	4	3	0	0	3	1	10.5	4.50	66	.200	.304	0	.000	-0	-1	-1	-0	-0.1
● JIM SCOTT Scott, James "Death Valley Jim" b: 4/23/1888, Deadwood, S.Dak. d: 4/7/57, Jacumba, Cal. BR/TR, 6'1", 235 lbs. Deb: 4/25/09 U																												
1909	Chi-A	12	12	.500	36	29	20	4	0	250^1	194	86	0	16	93	135	10.9	2.30	102	.223	.310	9	.106	-1	5	1	-1	-0.2
1910	Chi-A	8	18	.308	41	23	14	2	1	229^2	182	99	5	4	86	135	10.7	2.43	99	.226	.303	15	.203	2	2	-1	3	0.4
1911	Chi-A	14	11	.560	39	26	13	3	0	222	195	82	3	4	81	128	11.4	2.39	135	.240	.311	11	.155	-2	24	21	-4	1.6
1912	Chi-A	2	2	.500	6	4	2	1	0	37^2	36	16	0	1	15	23	12.4	2.15	149	.265	.342	0	.000	-2	5	5	-0	0.2
1913	Chi-A	20	21	.488	48	38	25	4	1	312^1	252	96	2	9	86	158	10.0	1.90	154	.221	.281	7	.072	-7	36	36	-1	3.9
1914	Chi-A	14	18	.438	43	33	12	2	1	253^1	228	109	5	5	75	138	10.9	2.84	94	.246	.306	14	.163	-0	-3	-5	3	-0.4
1915	Chi-A	24	11	.686	48	35	23	**7**	2	296^1	256	98	3	5	78	120	10.3	2.03	146	.238	.292	12	.126	-5	30	31	2	3.4
1916	Chi-A	7	14	.333	32	21	8	1	3	165^1	155	63	3	3	53	71	11.5	2.72	101	.258	.321	6	.115	-3	2	1	-0	0.4
1917	Chi-A	6	7	.462	24	17	6	2	1	125	126	37	0	6	42	37	12.5	1.87	142	.272	.341	5	.119	-2	11	11	0	1.0
Total	9	107	114	.484	317	226	123	26	9	1892	1624	686	21	53	609	945	10.9	2.30	120	.238	.305	79	.129	-21	111	101	3	9.5
● JACK SCOTT Scott, John William b: 4/18/1892, Ridgeway, N.C. d: 11/30/59, Durham, N.C. BL/TR, 6'2.5", 199 lbs. Deb: 9/6/16																												
1916	Pit-N	0	0	—	1	0	0	0	0	5	5	6	1	0	3	4	14.4	10.80	25	.278	.381	0	.000	0	-5	-4	0	-0.2
1917	Bos-N	1	2	.333	7	3	3	0	0	39^2	36	12	0	3	5	21	10.0	1.82	141	.255	.295	2	.125	-1	4	3	-1	0.1
1919	Bos-N	6	6	.500	19	12	7	0	1	103^2	109	47	3	1	39	44	12.9	3.13	91	.275	.341	7	.175	-1	-2	-3	-3	-0.8
1920	Bos-N	10	21	.323	44	33	22	3	1	291	308	148	6	13	85	94	12.6	3.53	87	.277	.336	21	.212	0	-13	-16	-4	-2.0
1921	Bos-N	15	13	.536	**47**	28	16	2	3	233^2	258	108	9	7	57	83	12.4	3.70	99	.283	.330	30	.341	10	2	-1	-1	0.8
1922	Cin-N	0	0	—	1	0	0	0	0	1	2	1	0	0	1	0	27.0	9.00	44	.500	.600	0	.000	-0	-1	-1	-0	0.0
	*NY-N	8	2	.800	17	10	5	0	2	79^2	83	42	7	2	23	37	12.2	4.41	91	.265	.320	8	.267	1	-3	-4	-1	-0.4
	Yr	8	2	.800	18	10	5	0	2	80^2	85	43	7	2	24	37	12.4	4.46	90	.268	.324	8	.258	1	-3	-4	-1	-0.4
1923	*NY-N	16	7	.696	40	25	9	3	1	220	223	104	15	4	65	79	11.9	3.89	98	.267	.323	25	.316	7	3	-2	-2	0.3
1925	NY-N	14	15	.483	36	28	18	2	3	239^2	251	98	10	4	55	87	11.6	3.15	128	.269	.313	21	.241	6	30	25	2	3.5
1926	NY-N	13	15	.464	**50**	22	13	0	5	226	242	118	13	3	53	82	11.9	4.34	86	.276	.319	28	.337	9	-13	-15	-1	-0.9
1927	Phi-N	9	21	.300	**48**	25	17	1	1	233^1	304	154	15	4	69	69	14.5	5.09	81	.330	.379	33	.289	8	-30	-24	-0	-1.8
1928	NY-N	4	1	.800	16	3	3	0	1	50^1	59	22	3	2	11	17	12.9	3.58	109	.295	.338	4	.267	1	2	2	0	0.3
1929	NY-N	7	6	.538	30	6	2	0	1	91^2	89	44	12	0	27	40	11.4	3.53	130	.260	.314	8	.308	3	12	11	1	1.7
Total	12	103	109	.486	356	195	115	11	19	1814^2	1969	904	94	43	493	657	12.4	3.85	96	.281	.332	187	.275	44	-13	-31	-9	0.6
● LEFTY SCOTT Scott, Marshall b: 7/15/15, Roswell, N.Mex. d: 3/3/64, Houston, Tex. BR/TL, 6'0.5", 165 lbs. Deb: 6/15/45																												
1945	Phi-N	0	2	.000	8	2	0	0	0	22^1	29	13	1	0	12	5	16.5	4.43	86	.312	.390	0	.000	-0	-2	-1	-1	-0.2
● MIKE SCOTT Scott, Michael Warren b: 4/26/55, Santa Monica, Cal. BR/TR, 6'3", 215 lbs. Deb: 4/18/79																												
1979	NY-N	1	3	.250	18	9	0	0	0	52^1	59	35	4	0	20	21	13.6	5.33	68	.289	.353	0	.000	-1	-9	-10	-0	-0.8
1980	NY-N	1	1	.500	6	6	1	1	0	29^1	40	14	1	0	8	13	14.7	4.30	83	.331	.372	1	.111	0	-2	-2	-0	-0.1
1981	NY-N	5	10	.333	23	23	1	0	0	136	130	65	11	1	34	54	10.9	3.90	89	.261	.309	3	.073	-2	-6	-6	3	-0.5
1982	NY-N	7	13	.350	37	22	1	0	3	147	185	100	13	2	60	63	15.1	5.14	71	.321	.387	7	.146	0	-25	-24	4	-2.7
1983	Hou-N	10	6	.625	24	24	2	2	0	145	143	67	8	5	46	73	12.0	3.72	92	.258	.320	8	.167	1	-1	-5	0	-0.4
1984	Hou-N	5	11	.313	31	29	0	0	0	154	179	96	7	3	43	83	13.1	4.68	71	.293	.343	6	.128	-0	-19	-25	-0	-2.4
1985	Hou-N	18	8	.692	36	35	4	2	0	221^2	194	91	20	3	80	137	11.2	3.29	106	.235	.304	11	.153	2	8	5	-2	0.6
1986	*Hou-N★	18	10	.643	37	37	7	**5**	0	**275^1**	182	73	17	2	72	**306**	**8.4**	**2.22**	**162**	**.186**	**.244**	12	.126	-2	**46**	**44**	2	**4.5**
1987	Hou-N★	16	13	.552	36	36	8	3	0	247^2	199	94	21	4	79	233	10.2	3.23	121	.217	**.282**	10	.125	-1	23	20	0	2.0
1988	Hou-N	14	8	.636	32	32	8	5	0	218^2	162	74	19	8	53	190	9.2	2.92	114	.204	.261	6	.085	-3	13	10	-1	0.6
1989	Hou-N†	**20**	10	.667	33	32	9	2	0	229	180	87	23	3	62	172	9.6	3.10	109	.212	.268	10	.133	-0	10	8	-2	0.7
1990	Hou-N	9	13	.409	32	32	4	2	0	205^2	194	102	27	1	66	121	11.4	3.81	98	.246	.305	7	.130	-0	-0	-2	-2	-0.4
1991	Hou-N	0	2	.000	2	2	0	0	0	7	11	10	2	1	4	3	20.6	12.86	27	.367	.457	0	.000	-0	-7	-8	-0	-1.2
Total	13	124	108	.534	347	319	45	22	3	2068^2	1858	908	173	33	627	1469	11.0	3.54	100	.240	.300	81	.124	-6	30	2	3	-0.1
● MILT SCOTT Scott, Milton Parker "Mikado Milt" b: 1/17/1866, Chicago, Ill. d: 11/3/38, Baltimore, Md. BR, 5'9", 160 lbs. Deb: 9/30/1882 ♦																												
1886	Bal-a	0	0	—	1	0	0	0	0	3	2	2	0	1	2	0	15.0	3.00	114	.125	.263	92	.190	-0	0	0	-0	0.0
● MICKEY SCOTT Scott, Ralph Robert b: 7/25/47, Weimar, Germany BL/TL, 6'1", 165 lbs. Deb: 5/6/72																												
1972	Bal-A	0	1	.000	15	0	0	0	0	23	23	7	2	1	5	11	11.3	2.74	113	.277	.326	0	.000	1	1	1	-0	0.1
1973	Bal-A	0	0	—	1	0	0	0	0	1^2	2	1	1	0	2	2	21.6	5.40	69	.286	.444	0	—	0	-0	-0	-0	0.0
	Mon-N	1	2	.333	22	0	0	0	0	24	27	14	3	2	9	11	14.3	5.25	73	.287	.362	0	.000	-0	-4	-4	0	-0.4
1975	Cal-A	4	2	.667	50	0	0	0	1	68^1	59	34	8	1	18	31	10.3	3.29	108	.233	.287	0	—	0	4	2	-1	0.1
1976	Cal-A	3	0	1.000	33	0	0	0	3	39	47	17	3	0	12	10	13.6	3.23	103	.307	.358	0	—	0	1	0	-1	0.0
1977	Cal-A	0	2	.000	12	0	0	0	0	16	19	16	1	0	4	5	12.9	5.63	70	.302	.343	0	—	0	-3	-3	-0	-0.3
Total	5	8	7	.533	133	0	0	0	4	172	177	89	18	4	50	70	12.1	3.72	95	.271	.327	0	.000	0	-1	-4	-1	-0.5
● DICK SCOTT Scott, Richard Lewis b: 3/15/33, Portsmouth, N.H. BR/TL, 6'2", 185 lbs. Deb: 5/8/63																												
1963	LA-N	0	0	—	9	0	0	0	2	12	17	10	6	0	3	6	15.0	6.75	45	.340	.377	0	—	0	-5	-5	0	-0.3
1964	Chi-N	0	0	—	3	0	0	0	0	4^1	10	6	2	0	1	1	22.8	12.46	30	.417	.440	0	—	0	-4	-4	0	-0.2
Total	2	0	0	—	12	0	0	0	2	16^1	27	16	8	0	4	7	17.1	8.27	39	.365	.397	0	—	0	-9	-10	0	-0.5
● TIM SCOTT Scott, Timothy Dale b: 11/16/66, Hanford, Cal. BR/TR, 6'2", 205 lbs. Deb: 6/25/91																												
1991	SD-N	0	0	—	2	0	0	0	0	1	2	2	0	0	0	1	18.0	9.00	42	.400	.400	0	—	0	-1	-1	0	0.0
1992	SD-N	4	1	.800	34	0	0	0	0	37^2	39	24	4	1	21	30	14.6	5.26	68	.267	.363	0	—	0	-7	-7	-1	-0.9
1993	SD-N	2	0	1.000	24	0	0	0	0	37^2	38	13	1	4	15	30	13.6	2.39	173	.260	.345	0	.000	-0	7	7	0	0.3
	Mon-N	5	2	.714	32	0	0	0	1	34	31	15	3	0	19	35	13.2	3.71	113	.242	.340	0	.000	-0	1	2	-0	0.3
	Yr	7	2	.778	56	0	0	0	1	71^2	69	28	4	4	34	65	13.4	3.01	138	.252	.343	0	.000	-0	8	9	-0	0.6
1994	Mon-N	5	2	.714	40	0	0	0	1	53^1	51	17	0	2	18	37	12.0	2.70	157	.251	.318	0	.000	-0	9	9	-2	0.9
1995	Mon-N	2	0	1.000	62	0	0	0	2	63^1	52	30	6	6	23	57	11.5	3.98	108	.222	.308	1	.250	0	1	2	-1	0.0
1996	Mon-N	3	5	.375	45	0	0	0	1	46^1	41	18	3	2	21	37	12.4	3.11	139	.238	.328	0	.000	-0	6	6	-1	0.8
	SF-N	2	2	.500	20	0	0	0	0	19^2	24	18	5	1	9	10	15.6	8.24	50	.316	.395	0	.000	-0	-9	-9	1	-1.6
	Yr	5	7	.417	65	0	0	0	1	66	65	36	8	3	30	47	13.4	4.64	92	.262	.349	0	.000	-1	-3	-3	-0	-0.8
1997	SD-N	1	1	.500	14	0	0	0	0	18^1	25	17	2	3	5	14	16.2	7.85	49	.321	.384	0	—	0	-7	-9	1	-0.8
	Col-N	0	0	—	3	0	0	0	0	2^2	5	3	0	0	2	2	23.6	10.13	51	.455	.538	0	—	0	-2	-1	-0	0.0
	Yr	1	1	.500	17	0	0	0	0	21	30	20	2	3	7	16	17.1	8.14	50	.337	.404	0	—	0	-9	-10	1	-0.8
Total	7	24	13	.649	276	0	0	0	5	314	308	157	24	19	133	253	13.2	4.13	100	.257	.340	1	.067	-1	-1	1	-3	-1.0
● SCOTT SCUDDER Scudder, William Scott b: 2/14/68, Paris, Tex. BR/TR, 6'2", 185 lbs. Deb: 6/6/89																												
1989	Cin-N	4	9	.308	23	17	0	0	0	100^1	91	54	14	1	61	66	13.7	4.49	80	.239	.346	4	.167	1	-11	-10	-1	-1.2
1990	*Cin-N	5	5	.500	21	10	0	0	0	71^2	74	41	12	3	30	42	13.4	4.90	81	.265	.343	1	.056	-1	-9	-7	-1	-1.1
1991	Cin-N	6	9	.400	27	14	0	0	1	101^1	91	52	6	6	56	51	13.6	4.35	87	.246	.354	3	.103	-0	-7	-6	-1	-0.9
1992	Cle-A	6	10	.375	23	22	0	0	0	109	134	80	10	2	55	66	15.8	5.28	74	.303	.383	0	.000	-0	-16	-17	0	-2.1
1993	Cle-A	0	1	.000	2	1	0	0	0	4	5	4	0	1	4	1	22.5	9.00	48	.333	.500	0	—	0	-2	-2	-0	-0.4
Total	5	21	34	.382	96	64	0	0	1	386^1	395	231	42	13	206	226	14.3	4.80	80	.266	.360	8	.113	-0	-45	-41	-3	-5.7

● ROD SCURRY
Scurry, Rodney Grant b: 3/17/56, Sacramento, Cal. d: 11/5/92, Reno, Nev. BL/TL, 6'2", 180 lbs. Deb: 4/17/80

YEAR	TM/L	W	L	PCT	G	GS	CG	SH	SV	IP	H	R	HR	HB	BB	SO	RAT	ERA	ERA+	OAV	OOB	BH	AVG	PB	PR	PR+	PD	TPI
1980	Pit-N	0	2	.000	20	0	0	0	0	37^{2}	23	12	2	2	17	28	10.0	2.15	170	.176	.280	1	.250	0	6	6	-0	0.3
1981	Pit-N	4	5	.444	27	7	0	0	7	74	74	33	6	3	40	65	14.2	3.77	95	.261	.358	3	.158	0	-2	-1	-1	-0.3
1982	Pit-N	4	5	.444	76	0	0	0	14	103^{2}	79	26	3	4	64	94	12.8	1.74	214	.212	.334	5	.238	1	22	22	-1	2.5
1983	Pit-N	4	9	.308	61	0	0	0	7	68	63	45	6	4	53	67	15.9	5.56	67	.249	.387	0	.000	-1	-15	-14	-0	-2.7
1984	Pit-N	5	6	.455	43	0	0	0	4	46^{1}	28	14	1	0	22	48	9.7	2.53	143	.175	.275	0	.000	-0	6	6	0	1.2
1985	Pit-N	0	1	.000	30	0	0	0	2	47^{2}	42	22	4	0	28	43	13.2	3.21	112	.236	.340	0	.000	-0	2	2	0	0.1
	NY-A	1	0	1.000	5	0	0	0	1	12^{2}	5	4	2	0	10	17	10.7	2.84	141	.125	.300	0	—	0	2	2	-0	0.1
1986	NY-A	1	2	.333	31	0	0	0	2	39^{1}	38	18	1	2	22	36	14.2	3.66	112	.252	.354	0	—	0	2	2	0	0.2
1988	Sea-A	0	2	.000	39	0	0	0	2	31^{1}	32	16	6	4	18	33	15.5	4.02	104	.258	.370	0	—	0	-0	0	0	0.1
Total	8	19	32	.373	332	7	0	0	39	460^{2}	384	190	31	19	274	431	13.2	3.24	115	.227	.341	9	.164	0	22	25	-0	1.5

● JOHNNIE SEALE
Seale, Johnny Ray "Durango Kid" b: 11/14/38, Edgewater, Colo. BL/TL, 5'10", 155 lbs. Deb: 9/20/64

YEAR	TM/L	W	L	PCT	G	GS	CG	SH	SV	IP	H	R	HR	HB	BB	SO	RAT	ERA	ERA+	OAV	OOB	BH	AVG	PB	PR	PR+	PD	TPI
1964	Det-A	1	0	1.000	4	0	0	0	0	10	6	4	1	0	4	5	9.0	3.60	102	.171	.256	0	.000	-0	0	0	-0	0.0
1965	Det-A	0	0	—	4	0	0	0	0	3	7	4	1	0	2	3	27.0	12.00	29	.500	.563	0	—	0	-3	-3	-0	-0.2
Total	2	1	0	1.000	8	0	0	0	0	13	13	8	2	0	6	8	13.2	5.54	65	.265	.345	0	.000	-0	-3	-3	-0	-0.2

● KIM SEAMAN
Seaman, Kim Michael b: 5/6/57, Pascagoula, Miss. BL/TL, 6'4", 205 lbs. Deb: 9/28/79

YEAR	TM/L	W	L	PCT	G	GS	CG	SH	SV	IP	H	R	HR	HB	BB	SO	RAT	ERA	ERA+	OAV	OOB	BH	AVG	PB	PR	PR+	PD	TPI
1979	StL-N	0	0	—	1	0	0	0	0	2	0	0	0	0	2	3	9.0	0.00	—	.000	.250	0	—	0	1	1	0	0.0
1980	StL-N	3	2	.600	26	0	0	0	4	23^{2}	16	9	2	0	13	10	11.0	3.42	108	.188	.296	0	.000	-0	0	1	-0	0.1
Total	2	3	2	.600	27	0	0	0	4	25^{2}	16	9	2	0	15	13	10.9	3.16	117	.176	.292	0	.000	-0	1	2	-0	0.1

● RUDY SEANEZ
Seanez, Rudy Caballero b: 10/20/68, Brawley, Cal. BR/TR, 5'10", 185 lbs. Deb: 9/7/89

YEAR	TM/L	W	L	PCT	G	GS	CG	SH	SV	IP	H	R	HR	HB	BB	SO	RAT	ERA	ERA+	OAV	OOB	BH	AVG	PB	PR	PR+	PD	TPI
1989	Cle-A	0	0	—	5	0	0	0	0	5	1	2	0	0	4	7	9.0	3.60	110	.071	.278	0	—	0	0	0	-0	0.0
1990	Cle-A	2	1	.667	24	0	0	0	0	27^{1}	22	17	2	1	25	24	15.8	5.60	70	.220	.381	0	—	0	-5	-5	-1	-0.5
1991	Cle-A	0	0	—	5	0	0	0	0	5	10	12	2	0	7	7	30.6	16.20	26	.385	.515	0	—	0	-7	-7	-0	-0.3
1993	SD-N	0	0	—	3	0	0	0	0	3^{1}	8	6	1	0	2	1	27.0	13.50	31	.471	.526	0	—	0	-4	-3	0	-0.2
1994	LA-N	1	1	.500	17	0	0	0	0	23^{2}	24	7	2	1	9	18	12.9	2.66	148	.273	.347	0	.000	-0	4	4	0	0.3
1995	LA-N	1	3	.250	37	0	0	0	3	34^{2}	39	27	5	1	18	29	15.1	6.75	56	.285	.372	0	.000	-0	-10	-13	-0	-1.5
1998	*Atl-N	4	1	.800	34	0	0	0	2	36	25	13	2	1	16	50	10.5	2.75	151	.195	.290	0	.000	-0	6	6	-0	0.7
1999	Atl-N	6	1	.857	56	0	0	0	3	53^{2}	47	21	3	1	21	41	11.6	3.35	134	.234	.309	0	.000	0	7	7	-0	0.8
2000	Atl-N	2	4	.333	23	0	0	0	2	21	15	11	3	1	9	20	10.7	4.29	106	.192	.284	0	—	0	1	1	-0	0.1
Total	9	16	11	.593	204	0	0	0	10	209^{2}	191	116	20	6	111	197	13.2	4.59	91	.242	.340	0	.000	-0	-7	-10	-2	-0.6

● RAY SEARAGE
Searage, Raymond Mark b: 5/1/55, Freeport, N.Y. BL/TL, 6'1", 180 lbs. Deb: 6/11/81

YEAR	TM/L	W	L	PCT	G	GS	CG	SH	SV	IP	H	R	HR	HB	BB	SO	RAT	ERA	ERA+	OAV	OOB	BH	AVG	PB	PR	PR+	PD	TPI
1981	NY-N	1	0	1.000	26	0	0	0	1	36^{2}	34	16	2	0	17	16	12.5	3.68	95	.252	.336	1	1.000	0	-1	-1	-0	0.0
1984	Mil-A	2	1	.667	21	0	0	0	6	38^{1}	20	3	0	1	16	29	8.7	0.70	547	.155	.253	0	—	0	14	14	-0	1.5
1985	Mil-A	1	4	.200	33	0	0	0	1	38^{1}	54	27	2	0	24	36	18.5	5.92	70	.338	.424	0	—	0	-7	-7	-1	-1.0
1986	Mil-A	0	1	.000	17	0	0	0	1	22	29	17	6	1	9	10	16.0	6.95	62	.315	.382	0	—	0	-7	-6	0	-0.3
	Chi-A	1	0	1.000	29	0	0	0	0	29	15	3	1	0	19	26	10.6	0.62	696	.156	.296	0	—	0	11	12	0	0.6
	Yr	1	1	.500	46	0	0	0	1	51	44	20	7	1	28	36	12.9	3.35	129	.234	.336	0	—	0	5	5	0	0.3
1987	Chi-A	2	3	.400	58	0	0	0	2	55^{2}	56	28	9	1	24	33	13.1	4.20	109	.264	.342	0	—	0	2	2	0	0.2
1989	LA-N	3	4	.429	41	0	0	0	0	35^{2}	29	15	1	0	18	24	11.9	3.53	97	.225	.320	0	—	0	-0	-0	1	0.0
1990	LA-N	1	0	1.000	29	0	0	0	0	32^{1}	30	11	1	0	10	19	11.1	2.78	132	.250	.308	0	.000	-0	4	3	1	0.2
Total	7	11	13	.458	254	0	0	0	11	287^{2}	267	120	22	3	137	193	12.7	3.50	114	.249	.336	1	.333	0	16	16	0	1.2

● STEVE SEARCY
Searcy, William Steven b: 6/4/64, Knoxville, Tenn. BL/TL, 6'1", 185 lbs. Deb: 8/29/88

YEAR	TM/L	W	L	PCT	G	GS	CG	SH	SV	IP	H	R	HR	HB	BB	SO	RAT	ERA	ERA+	OAV	OOB	BH	AVG	PB	PR	PR+	PD	TPI
1988	Det-A	0	2	.000	2	2	0	0	0	8	8	6	3	0	4	5	13.5	5.63	68	.242	.324	0	—	0	-1	-2	-0	-0.3
1989	Det-A	1	1	.500	8	2	0	0	0	22^{1}	27	16	3	0	12	11	15.7	6.04	63	.307	.390	0	—	0	-5	-6	-0	-0.5
1990	Det-A	2	7	.222	16	12	1	0	0	75^{1}	76	44	9	0	51	66	15.2	4.66	85	.270	.381	0	—	0	-6	-6	-0	-0.7
1991	Det-A	1	2	.333	16	5	0	0	0	40^{2}	52	40	8	0	30	32	18.1	8.41	49	.313	.418	0	—	0	-19	-19	-0	-1.2
	Phi-N	2	1	.667	18	0	0	0	0	30^{1}	29	16	2	0	14	21	12.8	4.15	88	.252	.333	0	.000	-0	-2	-2	-0	-0.2
1992	Phi-N	0	0	—	10	0	0	0	0	10^{1}	13	9	0	0	8	5	18.3	6.10	57	.325	.438	0	—	0	-3	-3	0	-0.2
Total	5	6	13	.316	70	21	1	0	0	187	205	131	25	0	119	140	15.6	5.68	69	.283	.384	0	.000	-0	-37	-37	-1	-3.1

● TOM SEATON
Seaton, Thomas Gordon b: 8/30/1887, Blair, Neb. d: 4/10/40, ElPaso, Tex. BB/TR, 6', 175 lbs. Deb: 4/13/12

YEAR	TM/L	W	L	PCT	G	GS	CG	SH	SV	IP	H	R	HR	HB	BB	SO	RAT	ERA	ERA+	OAV	OOB	BH	AVG	PB	PR	PR+	PD	TPI
1912	Phi-N	16	12	.571	44	27	16	2	2	255	246	126	8	9	106	118	12.7	3.28	111	.261	.342	18	.217	-0	4	9	-2	0.7
1913	Phi-N	**27**	12	.692	52	35	21	5	1	**322^{1}**	262	117	6	10	136	**168**	11.4	2.60	128	.226	.313	12	.109	-5	22	25	2	2.6
1914	Bro-F	25	14	.641	44	38	26	7	2	302^{2}	299	130	6	13	102	172	12.3	3.03	95	.259	.326	22	.206	2	-5	-5	0	-0.4
1915	Bro-F	11	11	.500	32	24	13	0	3	189^{1}	199	123	6	3	99	86	14.3	4.42	62	.273	.362	16	.242	3	-36	-36	1	-3.5
	New-F	2	6	.250	12	10	7	0	1	75	61	26	1	2	21	28	10.1	2.28	112	.224	.285	4	.154	-0	4	2	1	0.4
	Yr	13	17	.433	44	34	20	0	4	264^{1}	260	149	7	5	120	114	13.1	3.81	70	.260	.342	20	.217	3	-32	-34	2	-3.1
1916	Chi-N	6	6	.500	31	12	4	0	1	121	108	54	3	4	43	45	11.5	3.27	89	.246	.319	7	.184	0	-9	-4	1	-0.4
1917	Chi-N	5	4	.556	16	9	3	1	1	74^{2}	60	30	0	1	23	27	10.1	2.53	115	.227	.292	5	.238	1	1	3	1	0.6
Total	6	92	65	.586	231	155	90	15	11	1340	1235	606	30	42	530	644	12.1	3.12	99	.249	.327	84	.186	0	-19	-5	4	-0.0

● TOM SEATS
Seats, Thomas Edward b: 9/24/10, Farmington, N.C. d: 5/10/92, San Ramon, Cal. BR/TL (BB 1940), 5'11", 190 lbs. Deb: 5/4/40

YEAR	TM/L	W	L	PCT	G	GS	CG	SH	SV	IP	H	R	HR	HB	BB	SO	RAT	ERA	ERA+	OAV	OOB	BH	AVG	PB	PR	PR+	PD	TPI
1940	Det-A	2	2	.500	26	2	0	0	1	55^{2}	67	43	4	0	21	25	14.2	4.69	101	.290	.349	1	.083	-1	-2	0	0	-0.1
1945	Bro-N	10	7	.588	31	18	6	2	0	121^{2}	127	71	8	5	37	44	12.5	4.36	86	.261	.320	9	.209	0	-8	-8	0	-1.0
Total	2	12	9	.571	57	20	6	2	1	177^{1}	194	114	12	5	58	69	13.0	4.47	91	.271	.329	10	.182	-1	-10	-8	0	-1.1

● TOM SEAVER
Seaver, George Thomas "Tom Terrific" b: 11/17/44, Fresno, Cal. BR/TR, 6'1", 206 lbs. Deb: 4/13/67 H

YEAR	TM/L	W	L	PCT	G	GS	CG	SH	SV	IP	H	R	HR	HB	BB	SO	RAT	ERA	ERA+	OAV	OOB	BH	AVG	PB	PR	PR+	PD	TPI
1967	NY-N★	16	13	.552	35	34	18	2	0	251	224	85	19	5	78	170	11.0	2.76	123	.241	.303	11	.143	2	17	17	0	2.3
1968	NY-N★	16	12	.571	36	35	14	5	1	277^{2}	224	73	15	8	48	205	9.1	2.20	137	.222	.262	15	.158	0	24	25	2	3.0
1969	*NY-N☆	**25**	7	**.781**	36	35	18	5	0	273^{1}	202	75	24	7	82	208	9.6	2.21	166	**.207**	.273	11	.121	-0	42	43	2	5.5
1970	NY-N★	18	12	.600	37	36	19	2	0	290^{2}	230	103	21	4	83	**283**	9.8	**2.82**	**143**	.214	.273	17	.179	4	**40**	**39**	2	**4.5**
1971	NY-N☆	20	10	.667	36	35	21	4	0	286^{1}	210	61	18	4	61	**289**	**8.6**	**1.76**	**194**	.206	**.253**	18	.196	4	**54**	**53**	1	**6.6**
1972	NY-N☆	21	12	.636	35	35	13	3	0	262	215	92	23	5	77	249	10.2	2.92	115	.224	.285	13	.146	4	16	13	2	2.3
1973	*NY-N★	19	10	.655	36	36	**18**	3	0	290	219	74	23	4	64	**251**	**8.9**	**2.08**	**174**	**.206**	**.254**	15	.161	3	**51**	**50**	-0	**5.5**
1974	NY-N	11	11	.500	32	32	12	5	0	236	199	89	19	3	75	201	10.6	3.20	112	.230	.293	7	.099	-2	11	10	2	0.9
1975	NY-N★	**22**	9	.710	36	36	15	5	0	280^{1}	217	81	11	4	88	**243**	9.9	2.38	146	.214	.280	17	.179	3	39	36	2	4.5
1976	NY-N★	14	11	.560	35	34	13	5	0	271	211	83	14	4	77	**235**	9.7	2.59	127	.213	.273	7	.085	-2	**28**	23	1	2.0
1977	NY-N	7	3	.700	13	13	5	3	0	96	79	33	7	0	28	72	10.0	3.00	125	.221	.277	5	.161	-0	10	8	1	0.9
	Cin-N★	14	3	.824	20	20	14	4	0	165^{1}	120	45	12	0	38	124	8.6	2.34	168	.201	.249	12	.218	4	29	29	-1	3.3
	Yr	21	6	.778	33	33	19	**7**	0	261^{1}	199	78	19	0	66	196	**9.1**	2.58	150	**.209**	**.260**	17	.198	4	39	38	-0	4.2
1978	Cin-N☆	16	14	.533	36	36	8	1	0	259^{2}	218	97	26	0	89	226	10.6	2.88	124	.227	.292	9	.122	-0	20	20	-2	2.0
1979	*Cin-N	16	6	**.727**	32	32	9	**5**	0	215	187	85	16	0	61	131	10.4	3.14	119	.236	.291	12	.158	2	14	14	0	1.6
1980	Cin-N	10	8	.556	26	26	5	1	0	168	140	74	24	1	59	101	10.7	3.64	98	.225	.293	6	.130	1	-1	-1	1	0.1
1981	Cin-N★	**14**	2	**.875**	23	23	6	1	0	166^{1}	120	51	10	3	66	87	10.2	2.54	140	.205	.289	11	.200	4	18	18	-1	2.1
1982	Cin-N	5	13	.278	21	21	0	0	0	111^{1}	136	75	14	3	44	62	14.8	5.50	67	.302	.368	6	.176	1	-23	-22	-1	-3.1
1983	NY-N	9	14	.391	34	34	5	2	0	231	201	104	18	4	86	135	11.3	3.55	103	.235	.308	10	.156	2	2	2	-1	0.3
1984	Chi-A	15	11	.577	34	33	10	4	0	236^{2}	216	108	27	2	61	131	10.6	3.95	105	.240	.290	0	—	0	1	5	1	0.7
1985	Chi-A	16	11	.593	35	33	6	1	0	238^{2}	223	103	22	8	69	134	11.3	3.17	136	.248	.307	0	—	0	26	29	2	3.4
1986	Chi-A	2	6	.250	12	12	1	0	0	72	66	37	9	5	27	31	12.3	4.38	99	.242	.321	0	—	0	-2	-0	-1	-0.1
	Bos-A	5	7	.417	16	16	1	0	0	104^{1}	114	46	8	2	29	72	12.5	3.80	110	.278	.329	0	—	0	5	4	-0	0.4
	Yr	7	13	.350	28	28	2	0	0	176^{1}	180	83	17	7	56	103	12.4	4.03	105	.264	.326	0	—	0	3	4	-1	0.3
Total	20	311	205	.603	656	647	231	61	1	4782^{2}	3971	1674	380	76	1390	3640	10.2	2.86	127	.226	.285	202	.154	28	422	416	13	48.7

● BOB SEBRA
Sebra, Robert Bush b: 12/11/61, Ridgewood, N.J. BR/TR, 6'2", 200 lbs. Deb: 6/26/85

YEAR	TM/L	W	L	PCT	G	GS	CG	SH	SV	IP	H	R	HR	HB	BB	SO	RAT	ERA	ERA+	OAV	OOB	BH	AVG	PB	PR	PR+	PD	TPI
1985	Tex-A	0	2	.000	7	4	0	0	0	20^{1}	26	17	4	1	14	13	18.1	7.52	56	.306	.410	0	—	0	-8	-7	-0	-0.6
1986	Mon-N	5	5	.500	17	13	3	1	0	91^{1}	82	39	9	3	25	66	10.8	3.55	104	.239	.296	6	.207	1	2	2	-1	0.2

YEAR	TM/L	W	L	PCT	G	GS	CG	SH	SV	IP	H	R	HR	HB	BB	SO	RAT	ERA	ERA+	OAV	OOB	BH	AVG	PB	PR	PR+	PD	TPI
1987	Mon-N	6	15	.286	36	27	4	1	0	177^1	184	99	15	3	67	156	12.9	4.42	95	.272	.340	8	.157	0	-6	-4	-1	-0.5
1988	Phi-N	1	2	.333	3	3	0	0	0	11^1	15	11	0	0	10	7	19.9	7.94	45	.333	.455	0	.000	-0	-6	-5	-0	-1.0
1989	Phi-N	2	3	.400	6	5	0	0	0	34^1	41	20	6	4	10	21	14.4	4.46	80	.295	.359	0	.000	-0	-4	-3	-0	-0.5
	Cin-N	0	0	—	15	0	0	0	1	21	24	16	2	3	18	14	19.3	6.43	56	.296	.441	0	.000	-0	-7	-6	-0	-0.4
	Yr	2	3	.400	21	5	0	0	1	55^1	65	36	8	7	28	35	16.3	5.20	69	.295	.392	0	.000	-1	-10	-10	-0	-0.9
1990	Mil-A	1	2	.333	10	0	0	0	0	11	20	10	1	1	5	4	21.3	8.18	47	.408	.473	0	—	0	-5	-5	1	-1.0
Total	6	15	29	.341	94	52	7	2	1	366^2	392	212	37	15	149	281	13.6	4.71	84	.276	.351	14	.146	-0	-34	-30	-2	-3.8
● **DOC SECHRIST**	Sechrist, Theodore O'Hara b: 2/10/1876, Williamstown, Ky. d: 4/2/50, Louisville, Ky. BR/TR, 5'9", 160 lbs. Deb: 4/28/1899																											
1899	NY-N	0	0	—	1	0	0	0	0	0	0	0	0	2	—	—	—	—	—	1.000	97	—	0	0	0	0	0.0	
● **DON SECRIST**	Secrist, Donald Laverne b: 2/26/44, Seattle, Wash. BL/TL, 6'2", 195 lbs. Deb: 4/11/69																											
1969	Chi-A	0	1	.000	19	0	0	0	0	40	35	28	7	1	14	23	11.2	6.07	64	.227	.296	1	.143	0	-11	-9	0	-0.5
1970	Chi-A	0	0	—	9	0	0	0	0	14^2	19	9	2	0	12	9	19.0	5.52	71	.333	.449	0	—	0	-3	-3	-0	-0.1
Total	2	0	1	.000	28	0	0	0	0	54^2	54	37	9	1	26	32	13.3	5.93	65	.256	.340	1	.143	0	-14	-12	0	-0.6
● **DUKE SEDGWICK**	Sedgwick, Henry Kenneth b: 6/1/1898, Martins Ferry, O. d: 12/4/82, Clearwater, Fla. BR/TR, 6', 175 lbs. Deb: 7/12/21																											
1921	Phi-N	1	3	.250	16	5	1	0	0	71^1	81	48	3	4	32	21	14.8	4.92	86	.283	.363	5	.208	-1	-9	-5	-1	-0.4
1923	Was-A	0	1	.000	5	2	1	0	0	16	27	17	1	0	6	4	18.6	7.88	48	.415	.465	0	.000	-1	-7	-8	1	-0.4
Total	2	1	4	.200	21	7	2	0	0	87^1	108	65	4	4	38	25	15.5	5.46	76	.308	.382	5	.172	-2	-16	-12	-0	-0.8
● **CHARLIE SEE**	See, Charles Henry "Chad" b: 10/13/1896, Pleasantville, N.Y d: 7/19/48, Bridgeport, Conn. BL/TR, 5'10.5", 175 lbs. Deb: 8/6/19 ♦																											
1920	Cin-N	0	0	—	1	0	0	0	0	6	6	8	0	0	4	3	15.0	6.00	51	.286	.400	25	.305	0	-2	-2	-0	-0.1
● **CHUCK SEELBACH**	Seelbach, Charles Frederick b: 3/20/48, Lakewood, Ohio BR/TR, 6', 180 lbs. Deb: 6/29/71																											
1971	Det-A	0	0	—	5	0	0	0	0	4	6	6	2	1	7	1	31.5	13.50	27	.375	.583	0	—	0	-4	-4	-0	-0.2
1972	*Det-A	9	8	.529	61	3	0	0	14	112	96	39	6	3	39	76	11.1	2.89	109	.238	.310	3	.143	1	2	3	-1	0.7
1973	Det-A	1	0	1.000	5	0	0	0	0	7	7	3	1	0	2	2	11.6	3.86	106	.250	.300	0	—	0	-0	0	1	0.1
1974	Det-A	0	0	—	4	0	0	0	0	7^2	9	4	2	1	3	0	15.3	4.70	81	.300	.382	0	—	0	-1	-1	-0	-0.1
Total	4	10	8	.556	75	3	0	0	14	130^2	118	52	11	5	51	79	12.0	3.38	97	.247	.326	3	.143	1	-3	-2	-0	0.5
● **CHRIS SEELBACH**	Seelbach, Christopher Don b: 12/18/72, Lufkin, Tex. BR/TR, 6'4", 180 lbs. Deb: 9/9/2000																											
2000	Atl-N	0	1	.000	2	0	0	0	0	1^2	3	2	0	0	0	1	16.2	10.80	42	.500	.500	0	—	0	-1	-1	-0	-0.2
● **EMMETT SEERY**	Seery, John Emmett b: 2/13/1861, Princeville, Ill. d: 8/7/30, Saranac Lake, N.Y. BL/TR, Deb: 4/17/1884 ♦																											
1886	StL-N	0	0	—	2	0	0	0	0	7	8	7	1		3	2	14.1	7.71	42	.320	.393	108	.238	0	-3	-4	-0	-0.2
● **HERMAN SEGELKE**	Segelke, Herman Neils b: 4/24/58, San Mateo, Cal. BR/TR, 6'4", 200 lbs. Deb: 4/7/82																											
1982	Chi-N	0	0	—	3	0	0	0	0	4^1	6	4	1	0	6	4	24.9	8.31	45	.316	.480	0	—	0	-2	-2	0	-0.1
● **DIEGO SEGUI**	Segui, Diego Pablo (Gonzalez) b: 8/17/37, Holguin, Cuba BR/TR, 6', 190 lbs. Deb: 4/12/62 F																											
1962	KC-A	8	5	.615	37	13	2	0	6	116^2	89	53	16	1	46	71	10.5	3.86	109	.211	.291	8	.235	2	1	4	0	0.7
1963	KC-A	9	6	.600	38	23	4	1	0	167	173	84	17	2	73	116	13.4	3.77	103	.267	.343	12	.218	1	-3	2	1	0.4
1964	KC-A	8	17	.320	40	35	5	2	0	217	219	118	30	1	94	155	13.0	4.56	84	.260	.335	11	.155	0	-23	-17	2	-1.6
1965	KC-A	5	15	.250	40	25	5	1	0	163	166	102	18	2	67	119	13.0	4.64	75	.261	.334	9	.191	2	-21	-21	-1	-2.2
1966	Was-A	3	7	.300	21	13	1	1	0	72	82	42	8	0	24	54	13.3	5.00	69	.291	.346	2	.111	-1	-13	-12	-1	-1.7
1967	KC-A	3	4	.429	36	3	0	0	1	70	62	30	4	2	31	52	12.2	3.09	103	.238	.324	0	.000	-1	1	1	-0	-0.1
1968	Oak-A	6	5	.545	52	0	0	0	6	83	51	25	7	0	32	72	9.0	2.39	118	.173	.255	1	.111	0	5	4	-1	0.6
1969	Sea-A	12	6	.667	66	8	2	0	12	142^1	127	62	14	2	61	113	12.0	3.35	109	.238	.319	4	.148	-0	4	5	1	0.7
1970	Oak-A	10	10	.500	47	19	3	2	2	162	130	54	9	2	68	95	11.1	**2.56**	**139**	.222	.305	5	.116	-2	21	19	-1	1.9
1971	*Oak-A	10	8	.556	26	21	5	0	0	146^1	122	59	13	4	63	81	11.6	3.14	106	.229	.316	4	.085	-1	5	3	-1	0.2
1972	Oak-A	0	1	.000	7	3	0	0	0	22^2	25	10	2	0	7	11	12.7	3.57	80	.287	.340	1	.143	-0	-1	-2	-0	-0.2
	StL-N	3	1	.750	33	0	0	0	9	55^2	47	23	2	0	32	54	12.8	3.07	111	.229	.333	1	.143	0	2	2	1	0.3
1973	StL-N	7	6	.538	65	0	0	0	17	100^1	78	35	6	0	53	93	11.8	2.78	131	.211	.310	0	.000	-1	10	10	-1	1.3
1974	Bos-A	6	8	.429	58	0	0	0	10	108	106	54	9	1	49	76	13.0	4.00	96	.257	.337	0	—	0	-5	-2	-1	-0.3
1975	*Bos-A	2	5	.286	33	1	1	0	6	71	71	41	10	0	43	45	14.5	4.82	85	.270	.373	0	—	0	-8	-5	-1	-0.6
1977	Sea-A	0	7	.000	40	7	0	0	2	110^2	108	75	20	1	43	91	12.4	5.69	72	.251	.321	0	—	0	-20	-19	0	-1.1
Total	15	92	111	.453	639	171	28	7	71	1807^2	1656	867	185	18	786	1298	12.2	3.81	96	.243	.323	58	.151	-1	-42	-31	-3	-1.7
● **JOSE SEGURA**	Segura, Jose Altagracia (Mota) b: 1/26/63, Fundacion, D.R. BR/TR, 5'11", 180 lbs. Deb: 4/10/88																											
1988	Chi-A	0	0	—	4	0	0	0	0	8^2	19	17	1	0	8	2	28.0	13.50	29	.432	.519	0	—	0	-9	-9	0	-0.4
1989	Chi-A	0	1	.000	7	0	0	0	0	6	13	11	2	0	3	4	24.0	15.00	25	.464	.516	0	—	0	-7	-8	0	-1.0
1991	SF-N	0	1	.000	11	0	0	0	0	16^1	20	11	1	0	5	10	13.8	4.41	81	.303	.352	0	—	0	-1	-2	-0	-0.1
Total	3	0	2	.000	22	0	0	0	0	31	52	39	4	0	16	16	19.7	9.00	42	.377	.442	0	—	0	-18	-18	0	-1.5
● **SOCKS SEIBOLD**	Seibold, Harry b: 4/3/1896, Philadelphia, Pa. d: 9/21/65, Philadelphia, Pa. BR/TR, 5'8.5", 162 lbs. Deb: 9/18/15 ♦																											
1916	Phi-A	1	1	.500	3	2	1	1	0	21^2	22	12	0	0	9	5	12.9	4.15	69	.272	.344	2	.167	-0	-3	-3	1	-0.2
1917	Phi-A	4	16	.200	33	15	9	1	1	160	141	86	1	3	85	55	12.9	3.94	70	.243	.343	13	.220	2	-23	-20	-1	-2.4
1919	Phi-A	2	3	.400	14	4	1	0	0	45^2	58	34	2	4	26	19	17.3	5.32	64	.322	.419	2	.154	-1	-11	-9	0	-1.0
1929	Bos-N	12	17	.414	33	27	16	1	1	205^2	228	119	17	2	80	54	13.6	4.73	99	.285	.352	20	.286	4	-0	-1	-1	0.2
1930	Bos-N	15	16	.484	36	33	20	1	2	251	288	135	16	2	85	70	13.4	4.12	120	.290	.348	19	.211	0	24	23	-3	2.1
1931	Bos-N	10	18	.357	33	29	10	3	0	206^1	226	122	12	3	65	50	12.8	4.67	81	.279	.335	9	.129	-4	-18	-21	0	-2.8
1932	Bos-N	3	10	.231	28	20	6	1	0	136^2	173	91	12	2	41	33	14.2	4.68	80	.309	.358	7	.152	-2	-12	-14	2	-1.1
1933	Bos-N	1	4	.200	11	5	1	0	1	36^2	43	18	0	0	14	10	14.0	3.68	83	.295	.356	1	.111	0	-1	-3	0	-0.3
Total	8	48	85	.361	191	135	64	8	5	1063^2	1179	617	60	16	405	296	13.5	4.43	91	.284	.350	76	.192	-0	-45	-48	-1	-5.5
● **KEVIN SEITZER**	Seitzer, Kevin Lee b: 3/26/62, Springfield, Ill. BR/TR, 5'11", 190 lbs. Deb: 9/3/86 ♦																											
1993	Oak-A	0	0	—	1	0	0	0	0	0^1	0	0	0	0	0	1	0.0	0.00	—	.000	.000	65	.255	0	0	0	0	0.0
● **AARON SELE**	Sele, Aaron Helmer b: 6/25/70, Golden Valley, Minn. BR/TR, 6'5", 218 lbs. Deb: 6/23/93																											
1993	Bos-A	7	2	.778	18	18	0	0	0	111^2	100	42	5	7	48	93	12.5	2.74	169	.237	.325	0	—	0	20	22	-2	1.4
1994	Bos-A	8	7	.533	22	22	2	0	0	143^1	140	68	13	9	60	105	13.1	3.83	131	.261	.345	0	—	0	16	18	-1	1.6
1995	Bos-A	3	1	.750	6	6	0	0	0	32^1	32	14	3	3	14	21	13.6	3.06	159	.252	.340	0	—	0	6	6	-0	0.7
1996	Bos-A	7	11	.389	29	29	1	0	0	157^1	192	110	14	8	67	137	15.3	5.32	95	.303	.377	0	—	0	-6	-4	-0	-0.4
1997	Bos-A	13	12	.520	33	33	1	0	0	177^1	196	115	25	15	80	122	14.8	5.38	86	.279	.365	0	.000	-0	-16	-14	0	-1.7
1998	*Tex-A☆	19	11	.633	33	33	3	2	0	212^2	239	116	14	13	84	167	14.2	4.23	114	.283	.357	1	.250	0	10	14	-1	1.6
1999	*Tex-A	18	9	.667	33	33	2	2	0	205	244	115	21	12	70	186	14.3	4.79	106	.293	.356	0	.000	-0	2	7	1	0.8
2000	*Sea-A★	17	10	.630	34	34	2	2	0	211^2	221	110	17	5	74	137	12.8	4.51	106	.271	.335	0	.000	-0	10	7	2	0.9
Total	8	92	63	.594	208	208	11	6	0	1251^1	1364	690	112	72	497	968	13.9	4.46	109	.277	.352	1	.077	-0	42	57	-1	4.9
● **EPP SELL**	Sell, Lester Elwood b: 4/26/1897, Llewellyn, Pa. d: 2/19/61, Reading, Pa. BR/TR, 6', 175 lbs. Deb: 9/1/22																											
1922	StL-N	4	2	.667	7	5	0	0	0	33	47	26	2	2	6	5	15.0	6.82	57	.338	.374	4	.333	1	-10	-12	1	-1.4
1923	StL-N	0	1	.000	5	1	0	0	0	15	16	10	1	0	8	2	14.4	6.00	65	.291	.381	0	.000	-1	-3	-4	-0	-0.3
Total	2	4	3	.571	12	6	0	0	0	48	63	36	3	2	14	7	14.8	6.56	59	.325	.376	4	.211	0	-13	-15	0	-1.7
● **JEFF SELLERS**	Sellers, Jeffrey Doyle b: 5/11/64, Compton, Cal. BR/TR, 6'1", 175 lbs. Deb: 9/15/85																											
1985	Bos-A	2	0	1.000	4	4	1	0	0	22^1	24	10	1	0	7	6	12.5	3.63	118	.273	.326	0	—	0	1	2	-0	0.1
1986	Bos-A	3	7	.300	14	13	1	0	0	82	90	56	13	3	40	51	14.6	4.94	84	.282	.367	0	—	0	-7	-7	0	-0.7
1987	Bos-A	7	8	.467	25	22	4	2	0	139^2	161	85	10	3	61	99	14.5	5.28	86	.298	.373	0	—	0	-13	-11	1	-1.0
1988	Bos-A	1	7	.125	18	12	1	0	0	85^2	89	49	9	3	56	70	15.5	4.83	85	.268	.379	0	—	0	-8	-7	-0	-0.6
Total	4	13	22	.371	61	51	7	2	0	329^2	364	200	33	9	164	226	14.7	4.97	87	.285	.370	0	—	0	-26	-23	0	-2.2

● **DAVE SELLS** Sells, David Wayne b: 9/18/46, Vacaville, Cal. BR/TR, 5'11", 175 lbs. Deb: 8/2/72

YEAR	TM/L	W	L	PCT	G	GS	CG	SH	SV	IP	H	R	HR	HB	BB	SO	RAT	ERA	ERA+	OAV	OOB	BH	AVG	PB	PR	PR+	PD	TPI
1972	Cal-A	2	0	1.000	10	0	0	0	0	16	11	6	0	0	5	2	9.0	2.81	104	.196	.262	0	—	0	0	0	0	0.1
1973	Cal-A	7	2	.778	51	0	0	0	10	68	72	30	2	5	35	25	14.8	3.71	96	.277	.373	0	—	0	1	-1	0	-0.2
1974	Cal-A	2	3	.400	20	0	0	0	2	39	48	19	3	3	16	14	15.5	3.69	93	.312	.387	0	—	0	-0	-1	0	-0.1
1975	Cal-A	0	0	—	4	0	0	0	0	8^1	9	10	3	0	8	7	18.4	8.64	41	.250	.386	0	—	0	-4	-5	0	-0.2
	LA-N	0	2	.000	5	0	0	0	0	7	6	3	2	0	3	1	11.6	3.86	88	.222	.300	1	1.000	1	-0	-0	0	0.0
Total	4	11	7	.611	90	0	0	0	12	138^1	146	68	10	8	67	49	14.4	3.90	88	.274	.363	1	1.000	1	-4	-8	1	-0.4

● **DICK SELMA** Selma, Richard Jay b: 11/4/43, Santa Ana, Cal. BR/TR, 5'11", 175 lbs. Deb: 9/2/65

YEAR	TM/L	W	L	PCT	G	GS	CG	SH	SV	IP	H	R	HR	HB	BB	SO	RAT	ERA	ERA+	OAV	OOB	BH	AVG	PB	PR	PR+	PD	TPI
1965	NY-N	2	1	.667	4	4	1	1	0	26^2	22	11	2	1	9	26	10.8	3.71	95	.229	.302	2	.222	0	-1	-1	1	0.0
1966	NY-N	4	6	.400	30	7	0	0	1	80^2	84	47	11	3	39	58	14.1	4.24	86	.274	.361	1	.071	0	-6	-5	2	-0.4
1967	NY-N	2	4	.333	38	4	0	0	2	81^1	71	29	3	2	36	52	12.1	2.77	122	.241	.328	2	.091	-1	6	6	1	0.4
1968	NY-N	9	10	.474	33	23	4	3	0	169^2	148	63	11	5	54	117	11.0	2.76	110	.233	.298	12	.207	2	4	5	2	1.0
1969	SD-N	2	2	.500	4	3	1	0	0	22	19	10	3	0	9	20	11.5	4.09	87	.229	.304	2	.286	0	-1	-1	0	-0.2
	Chi-N	10	8	.556	36	25	4	2	1	168^2	137	74	13	3	72	161	11.3	3.63	111	.222	.307	8	.154	-0	-1	7	-1	0.6
	Yr	12	10	.545	40	28	5	2	1	190^2	156	84	16	3	81	181	11.3	3.68	108	.223	.307	10	.169	-0	-2	6	-1	0.4
1970	Phi-N	8	9	.471	73	0	0	0	22	134^1	108	42	8	4	59	153	11.5	2.75	145	.226	.317	3	.150	0	**19**	**19**	2	3.1
1971	Phi-N	0	2	.000	17	0	0	0	1	24^2	21	9	2	2	8	15	11.3	3.28	107	.231	.307	1	1.000	0	1	1	0	0.1
1972	Phi-N	2	9	.182	46	10	1	0	3	98^2	91	67	13	5	73	58	15.4	5.56	65	.249	.381	4	.200	1	-23	-21	1	-2.2
1973	Phi-N	1	1	.500	6	0	0	0	0	8	6	5	1	0	5	4	12.4	5.63	68	.240	.367	0	—	0	-2	-2	1	-0.3
1974	Cal-A	2	2	.500	18	0	0	0	1	23	22	13	2	1	17	15	15.7	5.09	68	.272	.404	0	—	0	-4	-4	1	-0.7
	Mil-A	0	0	—	2	0	0	0	0	2^1	5	5	0	1	0	2	23.1	19.29	19	.455	.500	0	—	0	-4	-4	-0	-0.2
	Yr	2	2	.500	20	0	0	0	1	25^1	27	18	2	2	17	17	16.3	6.39	54	.293	.414	0	—	0	-8	-9	1	-0.9
Total	10	42	54	.438	307	76	11	6	31	840	734	375	69	27	381	681	12.2	3.62	100	.238	.327	35	.172	2	-11	-1	8	1.2

● **FRANK SELMAN** Selman, Frank C. (a.k.a. Frank C. Williams 1871-75) b: Baltimore, Md. Deb: 5/4/1871 ♦

YEAR	TM/L	W	L	PCT	G	GS	CG	SH	SV	IP	H	R	HR	HB	BB	SO	RAT	ERA	ERA+	OAV	OOB	BH	AVG	PB	PR	PR+	PD	TPI
1873	Mar-n	0	1	.000	1	1	1	0	0	9	21	26	0		0	0	21.0	8.00	40	.350	.350	1	.333	0	-5	-5		-0.3

● **CARROLL SEMBERA** Sembera, Carroll William b: 7/26/41, Shiner, Tex. BR/TR, 6', 155 lbs. Deb: 9/28/65

YEAR	TM/L	W	L	PCT	G	GS	CG	SH	SV	IP	H	R	HR	HB	BB	SO	RAT	ERA	ERA+	OAV	OOB	BH	AVG	PB	PR	PR+	PD	TPI
1965	Hou-N	0	1	.000	2	1	0	0	0	7^1	5	3	0	0	3	4	9.8	3.68	91	.185	.267	0	.000	-0	-0	-0	0	0.0
1966	Hou-N	1	2	.333	24	0	0	0	1	33	36	11	3	0	16	21	14.2	3.00	114	.288	.369	0	.000	-0	2	2	0	0.1
1967	Hou-N	2	6	.250	45	0	0	0	3	59^2	66	39	7	1	19	48	13.0	4.83	69	.269	.325	1	.143	-0	-10	-10	1	-1.3
1969	Mon-N	0	2	.000	23	0	0	0	2	33	28	14	1	2	24	15	14.7	3.55	104	.246	.386	1	.250	0	0	0	-0	0.0
1970	Mon-N	0	0	—	5	0	0	0	0	6^2	14	14	2	1	11	6	35.1	18.90	22	.424	.578	0	—	0	-11	-11	0	-0.5
Total	5	3	11	.214	99	1	0	0	6	139^2	149	81	13	4	73	94	14.6	4.70	74	.274	.364	2	.133	-0	-18	-20	1	-1.7

● **FRANK SEMINARA** Seminara, Frank Peter b: 5/16/67, Brooklyn, N.Y. BR/TR, 6'2", 205 lbs. Deb: 6/2/92

YEAR	TM/L	W	L	PCT	G	GS	CG	SH	SV	IP	H	R	HR	HB	BB	SO	RAT	ERA	ERA+	OAV	OOB	BH	AVG	PB	PR	PR+	PD	TPI
1992	SD-N	9	4	.692	19	18	0	0	0	100^1	98	46	5	3	46	61	13.2	3.68	97	.257	.342	4	.118	-1	-2	-1	2	0.0
1993	SD-N	3	3	.500	18	7	0	0	0	46^1	53	30	5	3	21	22	15.0	4.47	93	.294	.377	2	.200	0	-2	-2	0	-0.2
1994	NY-N	0	2	.000	10	1	0	0	0	17	20	12	2	0	8	7	14.8	5.82	72	.303	.378	0	.000	-0	-3	-3	-1	-0.4
Total	3	12	9	.571	47	26	0	0	0	163^2	171	88	12	6	75	90	13.9	4.12	92	.273	.356	6	.128	-1	-7	-6	1	-0.6

● **RAY SEMPROCH** Semproch, Roman Anthony "Baby" b: 1/7/31, Cleveland, Ohio BR/TR, 5'11", 180 lbs. Deb: 4/15/58

YEAR	TM/L	W	L	PCT	G	GS	CG	SH	SV	IP	H	R	HR	HB	BB	SO	RAT	ERA	ERA+	OAV	OOB	BH	AVG	PB	PR	PR+	PD	TPI
1958	Phi-N	13	11	.542	36	30	12	2	0	204^1	211	105	25	6	58	92	12.1	3.92	101	.264	.319	7	.095	-5	1	1	-1	-0.4
1959	Phi-N	3	10	.231	30	18	2	0	3	111^2	119	76	12	3	59	54	14.6	5.40	76	.277	.368	6	.176	-0	-18	-15	1	-1.6
1960	Det-A	3	0	1.000	17	0	0	0	0	27	29	17	2	0	16	9	15.0	4.00	99	.269	.363	0	.000	-0	-0	-0	1	0.1
1961	LA-A	0	0	—	2	0	0	0	0	1	2	2	0	0	3	1	36.0	9.00	50	.333	.667	0	—	0	-1	-0	0	0.0
Total	4	19	21	.475	85	48	14	2	3	344	360	200	39	9	136	156	13.2	4.42	91	.269	.340	13	.116	-5	-18	-16	1	-1.9

● **STEVE SENTENEY** Senteney, Stephen Leonard b: 8/7/55, Indianapolis, Ind. d: 6/19/89, Colusa, Cal. BR/TR, 6'2", 205 lbs. Deb: 6/6/82

YEAR	TM/L	W	L	PCT	G	GS	CG	SH	SV	IP	H	R	HR	HB	BB	SO	RAT	ERA	ERA+	OAV	OOB	BH	AVG	PB	PR	PR+	PD	TPI
1982	Tor-A	0	0	—	11	0	0	0	0	22	23	16	5	0	6	20	11.9	4.91	91	.247	.293	0	—	0	-2	-1	-0	-0.1

● **MANNY SEOANE** Seoane, Manuel Modesto b: 6/26/55, Tampa, Fla. BR/TR, 6'3", 187 lbs. Deb: 9/18/77

YEAR	TM/L	W	L	PCT	G	GS	CG	SH	SV	IP	H	R	HR	HB	BB	SO	RAT	ERA	ERA+	OAV	OOB	BH	AVG	PB	PR	PR+	PD	TPI
1977	Phi-N	0	0	—	2	1	0	0	0	6	11	4	0	0	3	4	21.0	6.00	67	.407	.467	1	.500	0	-1	-1	-0	-0.1
1978	Chi-N	1	0	1.000	7	1	0	0	0	8^1	11	6	0	0	6	5	18.4	5.40	75	.297	.395	0	—	0	-2	-1	-0	-0.2
Total	2	1	0	1.000	9	2	0	0	0	14^1	22	10	0	0	9	9	19.5	5.65	71	.344	.425	1	.500	0	-3	-2	-1	-0.3

● **BILLY SERAD** Serad, William I. b: 1863, Philadelphia, Pa. d: 11/1/25, Chester, Pa. BR/TR, 5'7", 156 lbs. Deb: 5/5/1884

YEAR	TM/L	W	L	PCT	G	GS	CG	SH	SV	IP	H	R	HR	HB	BB	SO	RAT	ERA	ERA+	OAV	OOB	BH	AVG	PB	PR	PR+	PD	TPI
1884	Buf-N	16	20	.444	37	37	34	2	0	308	373	285	21		111	150	14.1	4.27	74	.281	.336	24	.175	-7	-44	-36	-3	-4.0
1885	Buf-N	7	21	.250	30	29	27	0	0	241^1	299	194	5		80	90	14.1	4.10	73	.293	.344	16	.154	-6	-34	-28	-3	-3.4
1887	Cin-a	10	11	.476	22	21	20	2	1	187^1	281	139	7	8	80	34	13.9	4.08	106	.337	.343	17	.207	-4	4	5	-1	0.1
1888	Cin-a	2	3	.400	6	5	5	0	0	50^2	62	43	1	6	19	4	15.5	3.55	89	.291	.366	3	.130	-1	-3	-2	-1	-0.3
Total	4	35	55	.389	95	92	86	4	1	787^1	1015	661	34	14	290	278	14.2	4.13	82	.299	.342	60	.173	-17	-77	-61	-7	-7.6

● **DAN SERAFINI** Serafini, Daniel Joseph b: 1/25/74, San Francisco, Cal. BB/TL, 6'1", 185 lbs. Deb: 6/25/96

YEAR	TM/L	W	L	PCT	G	GS	CG	SH	SV	IP	H	R	HR	HB	BB	SO	RAT	ERA	ERA+	OAV	OOB	BH	AVG	PB	PR	PR+	PD	TPI
1996	Min-A	0	1	.000	1	1	0	0	0	4^1	7	5	1	1	2	1	20.8	10.38	49	.368	.455	0	—	0	-3	-2	-0	-0.4
1997	Min-A	2	1	.667	6	4	1	0	0	26^1	27	11	1	0	11	15	13.0	3.42	136	.273	.345	0	—	0	3	4	-1	0.3
1998	Min-A	7	4	.636	28	9	0	0	0	75	95	58	10	1	29	46	15.0	6.48	74	.310	.372	0	.000	-0	-15	-14	-1	-1.8
1999	Chi-N	3	2	.600	42	4	0	0	1	62^1	86	51	9	1	32	17	17.2	6.93	65	.333	.409	1	.083	0	-16	-17	-1	-1.3
2000	SD-N	0	0	—	3	0	0	0	0	3	9	6	2	0	2	3	33.0	18.00	24	.500	.550	0	—	0	-4	-5	0	-0.2
	Pit-N	2	5	.286	11	11	0	0	0	62^1	70	35	9	4	26	32	14.4	4.91	94	.292	.370	2	.083	-2	-2	-2	-1	-0.4
	Yr	2	5	.286	14	11	0	0	0	65^1	79	41	11	4	28	35	15.3	5.51	83	.306	.383	2	.083	-2	-6	-7	-1	-0.6
Total	5	14	13	.519	91	29	1	0	1	233^1	294	166	32	7	102	114	15.5	6.06	77	.313	.384	3	.081	-2	-37	-36	-4	-3.8

● **GARY SERUM** Serum, Gary Wayne b: 10/24/56, Fargo, N.D. BR/TR, 6'1", 180 lbs. Deb: 7/22/77

YEAR	TM/L	W	L	PCT	G	GS	CG	SH	SV	IP	H	R	HR	HB	BB	SO	RAT	ERA	ERA+	OAV	OOB	BH	AVG	PB	PR	PR+	PD	TPI
1977	Min-A	0	0	—	8	0	0	0	0	22^2	22	11	4	2	10	14	13.5	4.37	92	.268	.362	0	—	0	-1	-1	-0	-0.1
1978	Min-A	9	9	.500	34	23	6	1	1	184^1	188	88	14	3	44	80	11.5	4.10	93	.266	.311	0	—	0	-7	-5	0	-0.5
1979	Min-A	1	3	.250	20	5	0	0	0	64	93	47	10	0	20	31	15.9	6.61	66	.354	.399	0	—	0	-17	-15	0	-0.8
Total	3	10	12	.455	62	28	6	1	1	271	303	146	28	5	74	125	12.7	4.72	84	.288	.337	0	—	0	-24	-22	-0	-1.4

● **SCOTT SERVICE** Service, Scott David b: 2/26/67, Cincinnati, Ohio BR/TR, 6'6", 226 lbs. Deb: 9/5/88

YEAR	TM/L	W	L	PCT	G	GS	CG	SH	SV	IP	H	R	HR	HB	BB	SO	RAT	ERA	ERA+	OAV	OOB	BH	AVG	PB	PR	PR+	PD	TPI
1988	Phi-N	0	0	—	5	0	0	0	0	5^1	7	1	0	1	1	6	15.2	1.69	211	.333	.391	0	—	0	1	1	-0	0.0
1992	Mon-N	0	0	—	5	0	0	0	0	7	15	11	1	0	5	11	25.7	14.14	25	.417	.488	0	.000	-0	-8	-8	-0	-0.5
1993	Col-N	0	0	—	3	0	0	0	0	4^2	8	5	1	1	1	3	19.3	9.64	50	.400	.455	0	—	0	-3	-2	0	-0.1
	Cin-N	2	2	.500	26	0	0	0	2	41^1	36	19	5	1	15	40	11.3	3.70	109	.235	.308	1	.143	-0	2	2	-0	0.1
	Yr	2	2	.500	29	0	0	0	2	46	44	24	6	2	16	43	12.1	4.30	95	.254	.325	1	.143	-0	-1	-1	0	0.0
1994	Cin-N	1	2	.333	6	0	0	0	0	7^1	8	9	2	0	3	5	13.5	7.36	56	.267	.333	0	—	0	-3	-3	0	-0.5
1995	SF-N	3	1	.750	28	0	0	0	0	31	18	11	4	2	20	30	11.6	3.19	128	.176	.323	0	.000	-0	3	3	-0	0.3
1996	Cin-N	1	0	1.000	34	1	0	0	0	48	51	21	7	6	18	46	14.1	3.94	108	.277	.361	0	.000	-1	2	2	0	0.1
1997	Cin-N	0	0	—	4	0	0	0	0	5^1	11	7	1	0	1	3	20.3	11.81	36	.458	.480	0	—	0	-5	-4	0	-0.2
	KC-A	0	3	.000	12	0	0	0	0	17	17	9	1	0	5	19	11.6	4.76	99	.274	.328	0	—	0	-0	-0	-0	0.0
1998	KC-A	6	4	.600	73	0	0	0	4	82^2	70	35	7	9	34	95	12.3	3.48	139	.231	.327	0	.000	-0	11	12	-0	1.4
1999	KC-A	5	5	.500	68	0	0	0	8	75^1	87	51	13	3	42	68	15.8	6.09	82	.294	.387	0	—	0	-10	-9	-1	-1.2
2000	Oak-A	1	2	.333	20	0	0	0	1	36^2	45	31	5	1	19	35	16.0	6.38	75	.302	.385	0	—	0	-6	-7	-0	-0.5
Total	10	19	19	.500	284	1	0	0	15	361^2	373	210	47	24	164	361	14.0	4.90	93	.270	.358	1	.063	-1	-16	-14	-0	-1.1

● **MERLE SETTLEMIRE** Settlemire, Edgar Merle "Lefty" b: 1/19/03, Santa Fe, Ohio d: 6/12/88, Russells Point, Ohio BL/TL, 5'9", 156 lbs. Deb: 4/13/28

YEAR	TM/L	W	L	PCT	G	GS	CG	SH	SV	IP	H	R	HR	HB	BB	SO	RAT	ERA	ERA+	OAV	OOB	BH	AVG	PB	PR	PR+	PD	TPI
1928	Bos-A	0	6	.000	30	9	0	0	0	82^1	116	62	2	6	34	12	17.1	5.47	75	.345	.415	3	.176	-1	-13	-12	2	-0.6

● **AL SEVERINSEN** Severinsen, Albert Henry b: 11/9/44, Brooklyn, N.Y. BR/TR, 6'3", 220 lbs. Deb: 7/1/69

YEAR	TM/L	W	L	PCT	G	GS	CG	SH	SV	IP	H	R	HR	HB	BB	SO	RAT	ERA	ERA+	OAV	OOB	BH	AVG	PB	PR	PR+	PD	TPI
1969	Bal-A	1	1	.500	12	0	0	0	0	19^2	14	6	2	0	10	13	11.0	2.29	156	.206	.308	1	.333	0	3	3	0	0.3
1971	SD-N	2	5	.286	59	0	0	0	8	70	77	30	4	2	30	31	14.0	3.47	95	.292	.368	0	.000	-0	-0	-1	1	0.0

YEAR	TM/L	W	L	PCT	G	GS	CG	SH	SV	IP	H	R	HR	HB	BB	SO	RAT	ERA	ERA+	OAV	OOB	BH	AVG	PB	PR	PR+	PD	TPI
1972	SD-N	0	1	.000	17	0	0	0	1	21^1	13	8	1	2	7	9	9.3	2.53	130	.173	.262	0	.000	-0	2	2	0	0.1
Total	3	3	7	.300	88	0	0	0	9	111	104	44	7	4	47	53	12.6	3.08	109	.256	.338	1	.200	0	5	3	2	0.4

● **ED SEWARD** Seward, Edward William (b: Edward William Sourhardt)
b: 6/29/1867, Cleveland, Ohio d: 7/30/47, Cleveland, Ohio TR, 5'7", 175 lbs. Deb: 9/30/1885 U♦

YEAR	TM/L	W	L	PCT	G	GS	CG	SH	SV	IP	H	R	HR	HB	BB	SO	RAT	ERA	ERA+	OAV	OOB	BH	AVG	PB	PR	PR+	PD	TPI
1885	Pro-N	0	0	—	1	0	0	0	0	6	2	0	0		0	1	3.0	0.00	—	.100	.100	0	.000	-0	2	2	1	0.1
1887	Phi-a	25	25	.500	55	52	52	3	0	470^2	585	293	7	24	140	155	11.6	4.13	104	.298	.306	66	.234	-4	9	8	-2	0.1
1888	Phi-a	35	19	.648	57	57	57	**6**	0	518^2	388	203	4	22	127	**272**	9.3	2.01	149	.200	.258	32	.142	-4	61	58	3	5.0
1889	Phi-a	21	15	.583	39	38	35	3	0	320	353	212	8	13	101	102	13.1	3.97	95	.271	.330	31	.217	6	-4	-7	-2	-0.2
1890	Phi-a	6	12	.333	21	19	15	1	0	154	165	105	4	7	72	55	14.3	4.73	82	.266	.349	10	.139	-1	-15	-15	-0	-1.5
1891	Cle-N	2	1	.667	3	3	0	0	0	16^1	16	10	0	0	11	4	14.9	3.86	90	.246	.355	4	.211	0	-1	-1	-1	-0.1
Total	6	89	72	.553	176	169	159	13	0	1485^2	1509	823	23	66	451	589	11.4	3.40	108	.255	.300	143	.192	-4	51	44	-2	3.4

● **FRANK SEWARD** Seward, Frank Martin b: 4/7/21, Pennsauken, N.J. BR/TR, 6'3", 200 lbs. Deb: 9/28/43

YEAR	TM/L	W	L	PCT	G	GS	CG	SH	SV	IP	H	R	HR	HB	BB	SO	RAT	ERA	ERA+	OAV	OOB	BH	AVG	PB	PR	PR+	PD	TPI
1943	NY-N	0	1	.000	1	1	1	0	0	9	12	3	0	0	5	2	17.0	3.00	115	.324	.405	0	.000	-1	0	0	-0	-0.1
1944	NY-N	3	2	.600	25	7	2	0	0	78^1	98	51	8	2	32	16	15.2	5.40	68	.306	.373	2	.083	-2	-16	-15	-1	-1.2
Total	2	3	3	.500	26	8	3	0	0	87^1	110	54	8	2	37	18	15.4	5.15	71	.308	.376	2	.071	-2	-15	-14	-2	-1.3

● **RIP SEWELL** Sewell, Truett Banks b: 5/11/07, Decatur, Ala. d: 9/3/89, Plant City, Fla. BL/TR, 6'1", 180 lbs. Deb: 6/14/32 C

YEAR	TM/L	W	L	PCT	G	GS	CG	SH	SV	IP	H	R	HR	HB	BB	SO	RAT	ERA	ERA+	OAV	OOB	BH	AVG	PB	PR	PR+	PD	TPI
1932	Det-A	0	0	—	5	0	0	0	0	10^2	19	15	2	0	8	2	22.8	12.66	37	.388	.474	1	.500	0	-10	-9	0	-0.4
1938	Pit-N	0	1	.000	17	0	0	0	1	38^1	41	27	3	2	21	17	15.0	4.23	90	.275	.372	1	.083	-1	-2	-2	1	-0.1
1939	Pit-N	10	9	.526	52	12	5	1	2	176^1	177	93	10	1	73	69	12.8	4.08	94	.265	.339	11	.200	1	-3	-5	3	-0.1
1940	Pit-N	16	5	.762	33	23	14	2	1	189^2	169	71	6	3	67	60	11.3	2.80	136	.238	.307	14	.192	2	22	22	2	2.7
1941	Pit-N	14	17	.452	39	32	18	2	2	249	225	126	18	3	84	76	11.3	3.72	97	.235	.299	16	.174	0	-2	-3	2	-0.1
1942	Pit-N	17	15	.531	40	33	18	5	2	248	259	117	13	2	72	69	12.1	3.41	99	.265	.317	13	.149	-2	-3	-1	-0	-0.3
1943	Pit-N★	**21**	9	.700	35	31	**25**	2	3	265^1	267	94	6	2	75	65	11.7	2.54	137	.260	.312	30	.286	6	25	27	1	**3.9**
1944	Pit-N★	21	12	.636	38	33	24	3	2	286	263	112	15	3	99	87	11.5	3.18	117	.240	.304	25	.223	3	14	17	-1	2.0
1945	Pit-N†	11	9	.550	33	24	9	1	1	188	212	116	9	2	91	60	14.6	4.07	97	.279	.357	20	.313	6	-6	-2	-0	0.3
1946	Pit-N★	8	12	.400	25	20	11	2	0	149^1	140	68	6	1	53	33	11.7	3.68	96	.245	.310	9	.180	0	-4	-2	-1	-0.4
1947	Pit-N	6	4	.600	24	12	4	1	0	121	121	58	11	3	36	36	11.9	3.57	118	.263	.321	5	.125	-1	7	8	1	0.6
1948	Pit-N	13	3	.813	21	17	7	0	0	121^2	126	51	9	1	37	36	12.1	3.48	117	.262	.317	6	.143	1	6	8	-0	1.0
1949	Pit-N	6	1	.857	28	6	2	1	1	76	82	35	8	0	32	26	13.5	3.91	108	.280	.351	1	.063	-0	1	2	-1	0.1
Total	13	143	97	.596	390	243	137	20	15	2119^1	2101	983	116	23	748	636	12.2	3.48	107	.256	.320	152	.203	16	45	59	7	9.2

● **ELMER SEXAUER** Sexauer, Elmer George b: 5/21/26, St.Louis Co., Mo. BR/TR, 6'4", 220 lbs. Deb: 9/6/48

YEAR	TM/L	W	L	PCT	G	GS	CG	SH	SV	IP	H	R	HR	HB	BB	SO	RAT	ERA	ERA+	OAV	OOB	BH	AVG	PB	PR	PR+	PD	TPI
1948	Bro-N	0	0	—	2	0	0	0	0	0^2	0	1	0	0	2	0	27.0	13.50	30	.000	.500	0	—	0	-1	-1	-0	0.0

● **FRANK SEXTON** Sexton, Frank Joseph b: 7/8/1872, Brockton, Mass. d: 1/4/38, Brighton, Mass. 160 lbs. Deb: 6/21/1895

YEAR	TM/L	W	L	PCT	G	GS	CG	SH	SV	IP	H	R	HR	HB	BB	SO	RAT	ERA	ERA+	OAV	OOB	BH	AVG	PB	PR	PR+	PD	TPI
1895	Bos-N	1	5	.167	7	5	4	0	0	49	59	39	2	2	22	14	15.2	5.69	90	.294	.369	7	.269	-1	-5	-3	-1	-0.4

● **GORDON SEYFRIED** Seyfried, Gordon Clay b: 7/4/37, Long Beach, Cal. BR/TR, 6', 185 lbs. Deb: 9/13/63

YEAR	TM/L	W	L	PCT	G	GS	CG	SH	SV	IP	H	R	HR	HB	BB	SO	RAT	ERA	ERA+	OAV	OOB	BH	AVG	PB	PR	PR+	PD	TPI
1963	Cle-A	0	1	.000	3	1	0	0	0	7^1	9	2	0	0	3	1	14.7	1.23	295	.300	.364	0	.000	-0	2	2	0	0.3
1964	Cle-A	0	0	—	2	0	0	0	0	2^1	4	0	0	0	0	0	15.4	0.00	—	.444	.444	0	—	0	1	1	-0	0.0
Total	2	0	1	.000	5	1	0	0	0	9^2	13	2	0	0	3	1	14.9	0.93	388	.333	.381	0	.000	-0	3	3	0	0.3

● **JAKE SEYMOUR** Seymour, Jacob (b: Jacob Semer) b: 1854, Pittsburgh, Pa. d: 8/1/1897, Allegheny, Pa. Deb: 9/23/1882

YEAR	TM/L	W	L	PCT	G	GS	CG	SH	SV	IP	H	R	HR	HB	BB	SO	RAT	ERA	ERA+	OAV	OOB	BH	AVG	PB	PR	PR+	PD	TPI
1882	Pit-a	0	1	.000	1	1	1	0	0	8	16	13	0		2	2	20.3	7.88	33	.390	.419	0	.000	-1	-5	-5	-0	-0.5

● **CY SEYMOUR** Seymour, James Bentley b: 12/9/1872, Albany, N.Y. d: 9/20/19, New York, N.Y. BL/TL, 6', 200 lbs. Deb: 4/22/1896 ♦

YEAR	TM/L	W	L	PCT	G	GS	CG	SH	SV	IP	H	R	HR	HB	BB	SO	RAT	ERA	ERA+	OAV	OOB	BH	AVG	PB	PR	PR+	PD	TPI
1896	NY-N	2	4	.333	11	8	4	0	0	70^1	75	75	8	3	51	33	16.5	6.40	66	.271	.390	7	.219	-1	-16	-18	1	-1.2
1897	NY-N	18	14	.563	39	34	29	2	1	286^2	257	162	4	22	168	**156**	14.0	3.27	127	**.238**	.352	34	.241	1	33	29	8	3.4
1898	NY-N	25	19	.568	45	43	39	4	0	356^2	313	199	4	32	213	**239**	14.1	3.18	109	.234	.353	82	.276	7	17	12	8	2.7
1899	NY-N	14	18	.438	32	32	31	0	0	268^1	247	139	5	20	170	142	14.7	3.56	106	.245	.364	52	.327	8	9	6	5	1.9
1900	NY-N	2	1	.667	13	7	2	0	0	53	58	54	4	10	54	19	20.7	6.96	52	.278	.447	12	.300	1	-19	-20	1	-0.7
1902	Cin-N	0	0	—	1	0	0	0	0	3	4	3	0	0	3	2	21.0	9.00	33	.308	.438	83	.340	0	-2	-2	-0	-0.1
Total	6	61	56	.521	141	124	105	6	1	1038	954	632	25	87	659	591	14.7	3.73	102	.243	.364	1724	.303	16	22	8	24	6.0

● **JOHN SHAFFER** Shaffer, John W. "Cannon Ball" b: 2/18/1864, Lock Haven, Pa. d: 11/21/26, Endicott, N.Y. Deb: 9/13/1886

YEAR	TM/L	W	L	PCT	G	GS	CG	SH	SV	IP	H	R	HR	HB	BB	SO	RAT	ERA	ERA+	OAV	OOB	BH	AVG	PB	PR	PR+	PD	TPI
1886	NY-a	5	3	.625	8	8	8	1	0	69	40	29	0	1	29	36	9.1	1.96	174	.164	.255	6	.240	1	11	11	-1	1.1
1887	NY-a	2	11	.154	13	13	13	0	0	112	201	119	3	11	53	22	17.0	6.19	69	.379	.391	9	.184	-3	-24	-24	2	-2.0
Total	2	7	14	.333	21	21	21	1	0	181	241	148	3	12	82	58	14.0	4.57	86	.311	.346	15	.203	-2	-12	-13	1	-0.9

● **GUS SHALLIX** Shallix, August (b: August Schallick)
b: 3/29/1858, Paderborn, Westphalia, Germany d: 10/28/37, Cincinnati, Ohio BR/TR, 5'11", 165 lbs. Deb: 6/22/1884

YEAR	TM/L	W	L	PCT	G	GS	CG	SH	SV	IP	H	R	HR	HB	BB	SO	RAT	ERA	ERA+	OAV	OOB	BH	AVG	PB	PR	PR+	PD	TPI
1884	Cin-a	11	10	.524	23	23	23	0	0	199^2	163	113	6	26	53	78	10.9	3.70	90	.212	.286	3	.036	-10	-10	-8	1	-1.5
1885	Cin-a	6	4	.600	13	12	7	0	0	91^1	95	59	1	13	33	15	13.9	3.25	100	.265	.349	5	.128	-2	-0	0	1	-0.1
Total	2	17	14	.548	36	35	30	0	0	291	258	172	7	39	86	93	11.8	3.56	93	.229	.306	8	.065	-12	-10	-8	2	-1.6

● **GREG SHANAHAN** Shanahan, Paul Gregory b: 12/11/47, Eureka, Cal. BR/TR, 6'2", 190 lbs. Deb: 9/4/73

YEAR	TM/L	W	L	PCT	G	GS	CG	SH	SV	IP	H	R	HR	HB	BB	SO	RAT	ERA	ERA+	OAV	OOB	BH	AVG	PB	PR	PR+	PD	TPI
1973	LA-N	0	0	—	7	0	0	0	1	15^2	14	6	2	0	4	11	10.3	3.45	100	.230	.277	0	.000	0	0	-0	-0	0.0
1974	LA-N	0	0	—	4	0	0	0	0	7	7	3	1	0	5	2	15.4	3.86	88	.259	.375	0	—	0	-0	-0	0	0.0
Total	2	0	0	—	11	0	0	0	1	22^2	21	9	3	0	9	13	11.9	3.57	96	.239	.309	0	.000	0	0	-0	0	0.0

● **HARVEY SHANK** Shank, Harvey Tillman b: 7/29/46, Toronto, Ont., Can. BR/TR, 6'4", 220 lbs. Deb: 5/16/70

YEAR	TM/L	W	L	PCT	G	GS	CG	SH	SV	IP	H	R	HR	HB	BB	SO	RAT	ERA	ERA+	OAV	OOB	BH	AVG	PB	PR	PR+	PD	TPI
1970	Cal-A	0	0	—	1	0	0	0	0	3	2	0	0	0	2	1	12.0	0.00	—	.182	.308	0	—	0	1	1	-0	0.1

● **BILL SHANNER** Shanner, Wilfred William b: 11/4/1894, Oakland City, Ind. d: 12/18/86, Evansville, Ind. BL/TR, Deb: 10/1/20

YEAR	TM/L	W	L	PCT	G	GS	CG	SH	SV	IP	H	R	HR	HB	BB	SO	RAT	ERA	ERA+	OAV	OOB	BH	AVG	PB	PR	PR+	PD	TPI
1920	Phi-A	0	0	—	1	0	0	0	0	4	6	4	2	0	1	1	15.8	6.75	60	.353	.389	0	.000	-0	-1	-1	0	-0.1

● **BOBBY SHANTZ** Shantz, Robert Clayton b: 9/26/25, Pottstown, Pa. BR/TL, 5'6", 142 lbs. Deb: 5/1/49 F

YEAR	TM/L	W	L	PCT	G	GS	CG	SH	SV	IP	H	R	HR	HB	BB	SO	RAT	ERA	ERA+	OAV	OOB	BH	AVG	PB	PR	PR+	PD	TPI
1949	Phi-A	6	8	.429	33	7	4	1	2	127	100	50	9	3	74	58	12.5	3.40	121	.221	.334	7	.189	1	11	10	4	1.5
1950	Phi-A	8	14	.364	36	23	6	1	0	214^2	251	122	18	7	85	93	14.4	4.61	99	.294	.362	11	.167	-0	-1	-1	4	0.2
1951	Phi-A☆	18	10	.643	32	25	13	3	0	205^1	213	96	15	5	70	77	12.6	3.94	108	.270	.333	18	.250	2	4	7	3	1.4
1952	Phi-A★	**24**	7	**.774**	33	33	27	5	0	279^2	230	87	21	4	63	152	**9.6**	2.48	160	.225	**.272**	19	.198	2	37	**43**	2	**5.2**
1953	Phi-A	5	9	.357	16	16	6	0	0	105^2	107	52	10	0	26	58	11.3	4.09	105	.263	.307	9	.237	1	-1	2	2	0.6
1954	Phi-A	1	0	1.000	2	1	0	0	0	8	12	7	2	1	3	3	18.0	7.88	50	.364	.432	1	.333	0	-4	-3	0	-0.3
1955	KC-A	5	10	.333	23	17	4	1	0	125	124	70	8	1	66	58	13.8	4.54	92	.264	.356	6	.146	-2	-8	-5	1	-0.5
1956	KC-A	2	7	.222	45	2	1	0	9	101^1	95	51	12	3	37	67	12.0	4.35	99	.248	.319	2	.091	-1	-2	-0	1	0.0
1957	*NY-A☆	11	5	.688	30	21	9	1	5	173	157	58	15	6	40	72	10.6	**2.45**	**147**	.248	.299	10	.179	2	26	23	6	3.2
1958	NY-A	7	6	.538	33	13	3	0	0	126	127	52	8	2	35	80	11.7	3.36	105	.262	.315	8	.229	2	6	3	3	0.8
1959	NY-A	7	3	.700	33	4	2	2	3	94^2	64	33	4	0	33	66	9.2	2.38	153	.189	.261	5	.217	2	16	14	1	1.8
1960	*NY-A	5	4	.556	42	0	0	0	11	67^2	57	24	5	2	24	54	11.0	2.79	128	.235	.309	1	.100	-0	8	6	1	1.1
1961	Pit-N	6	3	.667	43	6	2	1	2	89^1	91	38	5	4	26	61	12.2	3.32	120	.271	.331	7	.438	3	7	7	2	1.1
1962	Hou-N	1	1	.500	3	3	1	0	0	20^2	15	4	1	0	5	14	8.7	1.31	286	.208	.260	0	.000	-1	6	6	2	0.7
	StL-N	5	3	.625	28	0	0	0	4	57^2	45	22	7	1	20	47	10.3	2.18	195	.211	.282	2	.154	-0	11	12	1	1.9
	Yr	6	4	.600	31	3	1	0	4	78^1	60	26	8	1	25	61	9.9	1.95	211	.211	.277	2	.095	-1	17	18	3	2.6
1963	StL-N	6	4	.600	55	0	0	0	11	79^1	55	28	6	2	17	70	8.4	2.61	136	.192	.243	1	.143	0	6	8	3	1.5
1964	StL-N	1	3	.250	16	0	0	0	0	17^1	14	6	2	0	7	12	10.9	3.12	122	.226	.304	0	—	0	1	1	1	0.4
	Chi-N	0	1	.000	20	0	0	0	1	11^1	15	7	2	0	6	12	16.7	5.56	67	.319	.396	0	—	0	-3	-2	0	-0.2
	Phi-N	1	1	.500	14	0	0	0	0	32	23	10	1	0	6	18	8.2	2.25	154	.204	.244	0	.000	-0	5	4	2	0.5
	Yr	2	5	.286	50	0	0	0	1	60^2	52	23	5	0	19	42	10.5	3.12	116	.234	.295	0	.000	0	3	3	4	0.7
Total	16	119	99	.546	537	171	78	15	48	1935^2	1795	817	151	41	643	1072	11.5	3.38	119	.248	.313	107	.195	11	125	135	39	20.9

● **GEORGE SHARROTT** Sharrott, George Oscar b: 11/2/1869, Staten Island, N.Y. d: 1/6/32, Jamaica, N.Y. BL/TL, 5'8", 164 lbs. Deb: 7/27/1893

YEAR	TM/L	W	L	PCT	G	GS	CG	SH	SV	IP	H	R	HR	HB	BB	SO	RAT	ERA	ERA+	OAV	OOB	BH	AVG	PB	PR	PR+	PD	TPI
1893	Bro-N	4	6	.400	13	10	10	0	1	95	114	80	3	8	58	24	17.1	5.87	75	.289	.390	9	.231	0	-13	-16	-1	-1.3
1894	Bro-N	0	1	.000	3	3	2	0	0	18^{1}	25	21	0	5	8	7	18.7	6.87	72	.321	.418	3	.429	1	-3	-4	0	-0.1
Total	2	4	7	.364	16	13	12	0	1	113^{1}	139	101	3	13	66	31	17.3	6.04	75	.294	.395	12	.261	1	-16	-20	-1	-1.4

● **JACK SHARROTT** Sharrott, John Henry b: 8/13/1869, Bangor, Me. d: 12/31/27, Los Angeles, Cal. BR/TR, 5'9", 165 lbs. Deb: 4/22/1890 ◆

YEAR	TM/L	W	L	PCT	G	GS	CG	SH	SV	IP	H	R	HR	HB	BB	SO	RAT	ERA	ERA+	OAV	OOB	BH	AVG	PB	PR	PR+	PD	TPI
1890	NY-N	11	10	.524	25	19	18	0	0	184	162	107	3	9	88	84	12.7	2.89	121	.229	.322	22	.202	-2	14	13	3	1.2
1891	NY-N	5	5	.500	10	9	6	0	1	69^{1}	47	32	2	4	35	41	11.2	2.60	123	.185	.294	10	.333	4	6	5	1	1.0
1892	NY-N	0	0	—	1	0	0	0	0	2	2	1	0	0	1	1	13.5	4.50	72	.250	.333	1	.125	-0	-0	-0	-0	0.0
1893	Phi-N	4	2	.667	12	4	2	0	0	56	53	43	1	4	33	11	14.5	4.50	102	.242	.352	38	.250	0	1	0	0	0.1
Total	4	20	17	.541	48	32	26	0	1	311^{1}	264	183	6	17	157	137	12.7	3.12	116	.222	.322	71	.237	2	21	18	3	2.3

● **JOE SHAUTE** Shaute, Joseph Benjamin "Lefty" b: 8/1/1899, Peckville, Pa. d: 2/21/70, Scranton, Pa. BL/TL, 6', 190 lbs. Deb: 7/6/22

YEAR	TM/L	W	L	PCT	G	GS	CG	SH	SV	IP	H	R	HR	HB	BB	SO	RAT	ERA	ERA+	OAV	OOB	BH	AVG	PB	PR	PR+	PD	TPI
1922	Cle-A	0	0	—	2	0	0	0	0	3^{2}	7	8	2	0	3	3	24.5	19.64	20	.389	.476	0	.000	-0	-6	-6	-0	-0.3
1923	Cle-A	10	8	.556	33	16	7	0	0	172	176	93	4	1	53	61	12.0	3.51	113	.275	.332	11	.162	-4	9	9	-2	0.3
1924	Cle-A	20	17	.541	46	34	21	2	2	283	317	138	8	6	83	68	12.9	3.75	114	.287	.340	34	.318	9	15	16	-2	2.6
1925	Cle-A	4	12	.250	26	17	10	1	4	131	160	91	6	1	44	34	14.1	5.43	81	.304	.358	16	.302	3	-15	-15	-2	-1.4
1926	Cle-A	14	10	.583	34	25	15	1	1	206^{2}	215	92	9	3	65	47	12.3	3.53	115	.278	.337	20	.274	4	11	12	-5	1.1
1927	Cle-A	9	16	.360	45	28	14	0	2	230^{1}	255	140	9	2	75	63	13.0	4.22	100	.286	.343	27	.325	6	-2	-0	-2	0.3
1928	Cle-A	13	17	.433	36	31	21	1	2	253^{2}	295	145	9	6	68	81	13.1	4.04	102	.299	.348	21	.228	3	-0	3	1	0.7
1929	Cle-A	8	8	.500	26	24	8	0	0	162	211	100	6	1	52	43	14.7	4.28	104	.320	.370	17	.293	3	-1	3	-3	0.3
1930	Cle-A	0	0	—	4	0	0	0	0	4^{2}	8	10	0	0	4	2	23.1	15.43	31	.333	.429	0	—	0	-6	-5	0	-0.2
1931	Bro-N	11	8	.579	25	19	6	0	0	128^{2}	162	87	9	1	32	50	13.6	4.83	79	.305	.346	8	.178	-0	-14	-15	0	-1.9
1932	Bro-N	7	7	.500	34	9	1	0	4	117	147	67	8	2	21	32	13.1	4.54	84	.301	.333	9	.200	1	-9	-10	-2	-1.1
1933	Bro-N	3	4	.429	41	4	0	0	2	108^{1}	125	63	4	1	31	26	13.0	3.49	92	.287	.336	6	.222	1	-2	-3	1	0.0
1934	Cin-N	0	2	.000	8	1	0	0	1	17^{1}	19	9	1	0	3	2	11.4	4.15	98	.268	.297	1	.250	0	-0	-0	-1	-0.1
Total	13	99	109	.476	360	208	103	5	18	1818^{1}	2097	1043	75	24	534	512	13.1	4.15	99	.293	.345	170	.258	25	-18	-12	-14	0.3

● **JEFF SHAVER** Shaver, Jeffrey Thomas b: 7/30/63, Beaver, Pa. BR/TR, 6'3", 195 lbs. Deb: 7/6/88

YEAR	TM/L	W	L	PCT	G	GS	CG	SH	SV	IP	H	R	HR	HB	BB	SO	RAT	ERA	ERA+	OAV	OOB	BH	AVG	PB	PR	PR+	PD	TPI
1988	Oak-A	0	0	—	1	0	0	0	0	1	0	0	0	1	0	0	9.0	0.00	—	.000	.333	0	—	0	0	0	0	0.0

● **DON SHAW** Shaw, Donald Wellington b: 2/23/44, Pittsburgh, Pa. BL/TL, 6', 185 lbs. Deb: 4/11/67

YEAR	TM/L	W	L	PCT	G	GS	CG	SH	SV	IP	H	R	HR	HB	BB	SO	RAT	ERA	ERA+	OAV	OOB	BH	AVG	PB	PR	PR+	PD	TPI
1967	NY-N	4	5	.444	40	0	0	0	3	51^{1}	40	19	5	0	23	44	11.0	2.98	114	.219	.306	0	.000	0	2	2	-1	0.4
1968	NY-N	0	0	—	7	0	0	0	0	12^{1}	3	1	1	0	5	11	5.8	0.73	414	.086	.200	0	—	0	3	3	0	0.2
1969	Mon-N	2	5	.286	35	1	0	0	1	65^{2}	61	43	9	2	37	45	13.7	5.21	71	.254	.358	0	.000	-0	-12	-11	1	-1.1
1971	StL-N	7	2	.778	45	0	0	0	2	51	45	19	1	1	31	19	13.6	2.65	136	.237	.347	0	.000	-0	5	5	-0	0.9
1972	StL-N	0	1	.000	8	0	0	0	0	3	5	3	1	0	3	0	24.0	9.00	38	.417	.533	0	.000	-0	-2	-2	-0	-0.4
	Oak-A	0	1	.000	3	0	0	0	0	5^{1}	12	10	2	0	2	4	23.6	16.88	17	.500	.538	0	—	0	-8	-9	-0	-1.3
Total	5	13	14	.481	138	1	0	0	6	188^{2}	166	95	19	3	101	123	12.9	4.01	88	.243	.343	0	.000	-0	-12	-10	-0	-1.3

● **DUPEE SHAW** Shaw, Frederick Lander b: 5/31/1859, Charlestown, Mass. d: 6/11/38, Wakefield, Mass. BL/TL, 5'8", 165 lbs. Deb: 6/18/1883

YEAR	TM/L	W	L	PCT	G	GS	CG	SH	SV	IP	H	R	HR	HB	BB	SO	RAT	ERA	ERA+	OAV	OOB	BH	AVG	PB	PR	PR+	PD	TPI
1883	Det-N	10	15	.400	26	25	23	1	0	227	238	135	3		44	73	11.2	2.50	124	.256	.290	29	.206	-3	16	16	0	1.2
1884	Det-N	9	18	.333	28	28	25	0	0	227^{2}	219	153	8		72	142	11.5	3.04	95	.237	.292	26	.191	-1	-2	-4	2	-0.3
	Bos-U	21	15	.583	39	38	35	5	0	315^{2}	227	128	1		37	309	7.5	1.77	135	.188	.212	37	.242	-5	**24**	22	-0	1.5
1885	Pro-N	23	26	.469	49	49	47	6	0	399^{2}	343	209	7		99	194	10.0	2.57	105	.209	.254	22	.133	-10	11	6	-2	-0.6
1886	Was-N	13	31	.295	45	44	43	1	0	385^{2}	384	224	12		91	177	11.1	3.34	98	.250	.291	13	.088	-10	-1	-2	-1	-1.2
1887	Was-N	7	13	.350	21	20	20	0	0	181^{1}	309	177	8	3	46	47	15.5	6.45	63	.364	.366	21	.269	-2	-48	-48	-2	-4.0
1888	Was-N	0	3	.000	3	3	3	0	0	25	36	24	2	0	7	8	15.5	6.48	43	.333	.374	0	.000	-1	-10	-10	-1	-1.1
Total	6	83	121	.407	211	207	196	13	0	1762	1756	1050	41	3	396	950	10.8	3.10	96	.244	.279	148	.178	-32	-9	-23	-5	-4.5

● **JIM SHAW** Shaw, James Aloysius "Grunting Jim" b: 8/19/1893, Pittsburgh, Pa. d: 1/27/62, Washington, D.C. BR/TR, 6', 180 lbs. Deb: 9/15/13

YEAR	TM/L	W	L	PCT	G	GS	CG	SH	SV	IP	H	R	HR	HB	BB	SO	RAT	ERA	ERA+	OAV	OOB	BH	AVG	PB	PR	PR+	PD	TPI
1913	Was-A	0	1	.000	2	1	0	0	0	13	8	4	0	1	7	14	11.1	2.08	142	.205	.340	0	.000	-0	1	1	1	0.2
1914	Was-A	15	17	.469	48	31	15	5	**4**	257	198	99	3	8	137	164	12.0	2.70	104	.216	.324	10	.118	-3	1	3	1	0.2
1915	Was-A	6	11	.353	25	18	7	1	1	133	102	50	2	2	76	78	12.2	2.50	119	.220	.333	10	.233	1	6	7	-1	0.9
1916	Was-A	3	8	.273	26	9	5	2	1	106^{1}	86	36	1	2	50	44	11.7	2.62	106	.227	.320	5	.156	-0	2	2	-3	-0.1
1917	Was-A	15	14	.517	47	31	15	2	1	266^{1}	233	118	1	1	123	118	12.1	3.21	82	.242	.328	14	.154	-2	-16	-18	-3	-2.4
1918	Was-A	16	12	.571	41	30	14	4	1	241^{1}	201	88	2	1	90	129	10.9	2.42	113	.228	.300	11	.133	-5	9	8	-5	-0.1
1919	Was-A	17	17	.500	**45**	37	23	3	**5**	**306^{2}**	274	118	5	5	101	128	11.2	2.73	118	.244	.309	17	.160	-1	17	16	-6	1.1
1920	Was-A	11	18	.379	38	32	17	0	1	236^{1}	285	127	12	4	87	88	14.3	4.27	87	.314	.376	14	.189	0	-12	-14	-4	-1.9
1921	Was-A	1	0	1.000	15	5	0	0	3	40^{1}	59	37	2	0	17	4	17.0	7.36	56	.345	.404	5	.417	2	-14	-15	0	-0.5
Total	9	84	98	.462	287	194	96	17	17	1600^{1}	1446	677	28	24	688	767	12.1	3.07	99	.247	.329	86	.163	-8	-4	-7	-19	-2.6

● **JEFF SHAW** Shaw, Jeffrey Lee b: 7/7/66, Washington Court House, Ohio BR/TR, 6'2", 200 lbs. Deb: 4/30/90

YEAR	TM/L	W	L	PCT	G	GS	CG	SH	SV	IP	H	R	HR	HB	BB	SO	RAT	ERA	ERA+	OAV	OOB	BH	AVG	PB	PR	PR+	PD	TPI
1990	Cle-A	3	4	.429	12	9	0	0	0	48^{2}	73	38	11	0	20	25	17.2	6.66	59	.356	.413	0	—	0	-15	-15	0	-1.8
1991	Cle-A	0	5	.000	29	1	0	0	1	72^{1}	72	34	6	4	27	31	12.8	3.36	124	.262	.337	0	—	0	6	6	0	0.4
1992	Cle-A	0	1	.000	2	1	0	0	0	7^{2}	7	7	2	0	4	3	12.9	8.22	48	.259	.355	0	—	0	-4	-4	0	-0.4
1993	Mon-N	2	7	.222	55	8	0	0	0	95^{2}	91	47	12	7	32	50	12.2	4.14	101	.254	.327	1	.067	-1	-1	0	1	0.0
1994	Mon-N	5	2	.714	46	0	0	0	1	67^{1}	67	32	8	2	15	47	11.2	3.88	109	.254	.299	2	.286	1	3	3	1	0.4
1995	Mon-N	1	6	.143	50	0	0	0	3	62^{1}	58	35	4	3	26	45	12.6	4.62	93	.250	.333	0	.000	-0	-3	-2	1	-0.2
	Chi-A	0	0	—	9	0	0	0	0	9^{2}	12	7	2	1	1	6	13.0	6.52	68	.316	.350	0	—	0	-2	-2	0	-0.1
1996	Cin-N	8	6	.571	78	0	0	0	4	104^{2}	99	34	8	2	29	69	11.2	2.49	170	.252	.307	0	.000	-0	20	20	1	2.6
1997	Cin-N	4	2	.667	78	0	0	0	**42**	94^{2}	79	26	7	1	12	74	8.7	2.38	180	.227	.255	0	.000	-0	**19**	**20**	1	2.7
1998	Cin-N	2	4	.333	39	0	0	0	23	49^{2}	40	11	2	1	12	29	9.6	1.81	236	.231	.285	0	.000	-0	13	13	0	2.6
	LA-N★	1	4	.200	34	0	0	0	25	35^{1}	35	11	6	0	7	26	10.7	2.55	156	.252	.288	0	—	0	7	6	1	1.3
	Yr	3	8	.273	73	0	0	0	48	85	75	22	8	1	19	55	10.1	2.12	196	.240	.286	0	.000	-0	20	20	1	3.9
1999	LA-N	2	4	.333	64	0	0	0	34	68	64	25	6	1	15	43	10.6	2.78	154	.242	.285	0	—	0	13	12	-0	1.9
2000	LA-N	3	4	.429	60	0	0	0	27	57^{1}	61	29	7	1	16	39	12.2	4.24	104	.265	.316	0	—	0	3	1	1	0.3
Total	11	31	49	.387	556	19	0	0	160	773^{1}	758	336	81	23	216	487	11.6	3.54	119	.257	.313	3	.079	-1	60	59	6	9.7

● **BOB SHAW** Shaw, Robert John b: 6/29/33, Bronx, N.Y. BR/TR, 6'2", 195 lbs. Deb: 8/11/57 C

YEAR	TM/L	W	L	PCT	G	GS	CG	SH	SV	IP	H	R	HR	HB	BB	SO	RAT	ERA	ERA+	OAV	OOB	BH	AVG	PB	PR	PR+	PD	TPI
1957	Det-A	0	1	.000	7	0	0	0	0	9^{2}	11	9	2	0	7	4	16.8	7.45	52	.289	.400	0	.000	-0	-4	-4	-0	-0.4
1958	Det-A	1	2	.333	11	2	0	0	0	26^{2}	32	16	2	0	13	17	15.2	5.06	80	.302	.378	3	.375	1	-4	-3	1	-0.1
	Chi-A	4	2	.667	29	3	0	0	1	64	67	33	8	2	28	18	13.6	4.64	78	.271	.350	0	.000	-1	-6	-7	2	-0.6
	Yr	5	4	.556	40	5	0	0	1	90^{2}	99	49	10	2	41	35	14.1	4.76	79	.280	.359	3	.136	-0	-10	-10	2	-0.7
1959	*Chi-A	18	6	**.750**	47	26	8	3	3	230^{2}	217	72	15	6	54	89	10.8	2.69	140	.249	.297	9	.123	-2	30	28	1	2.7
1960	Chi-A	13	13	.500	36	32	7	1	0	192^{2}	221	97	16	3	62	46	13.4	4.06	93	.292	.348	8	.138	-0	-4	-6	-1	-0.9
1961	Chi-A	3	4	.429	14	10	3	0	0	71^{1}	85	40	11	1	20	31	13.4	3.79	103	.302	.351	0	.000	-1	2	1	-0	-0.1
	KC-A	9	10	.474	26	24	6	0	0	150^{1}	165	87	14	7	58	60	13.8	4.31	97	.281	.352	11	.200	-1	-5	-2	0	-0.3
	Yr	12	14	.462	40	34	9	0	0	221^{2}	250	127	25	8	78	91	13.6	4.14	99	.288	.352	11	.151	-2	-3	-1	-0	-0.4
1962	Mil-N★	15	9	.625	38	29	12	3	2	225	223	80	20	12	44	124	11.2	2.80	136	.260	.305	10	.137	1	29	26	-0	2.7
1963	Mil-N	7	11	.389	48	16	3	3	13	159	144	51	10	4	55	105	11.5	2.66	121	.243	.312	5	.122	0	11	10	-2	1.2
1964	SF-N	7	6	.538	61	1	0	0	11	93^{1}	105	43	5	5	31	57	13.6	3.76	95	.286	.350	0	.000	-1	-2	-2	-2	-0.6
1965	SF-N	16	9	.640	42	33	6	1	2	235	213	85	17	3	53	148	10.3	2.64	136	.236	.280	8	.101	-3	23	25	1	2.4
1966	SF-N	1	4	.200	13	6	0	0	0	31^{2}	45	23	9	0	7	21	14.8	6.25	59	.324	.356	0	.000	-1	-9	-9	-1	-1.4
	NY-N	11	10	.524	26	25	7	2	0	167^{2}	171	85	12	7	42	104	11.8	3.92	93	.261	.313	13	.260	3	-6	-5	1	-0.2
	Yr	12	14	.462	39	31	7	2	0	199^{1}	216	108	21	7	49	125	12.3	4.29	85	.272	.320	13	.232	2	-15	-14	0	-1.6
1967	NY-N	3	9	.250	23	13	3	1	0	98^{2}	105	54	9	2	28	49	12.3	4.29	79	.273	.326	1	.040	-2	-10	-10	-1	-1.4
	Chi-N	0	2	.000	9	3	0	0	0	22^{1}	33	16	0	4	9	7	18.5	6.04	59	.351	.430	1	.250	0	-7	-6	-1	-0.6
	Yr	3	11	.214	32	16	3	1	0	121	138	70	9	6	37	56	13.5	4.61	74	.289	.347	2	.069	-1	-17	-16	-2	-2.0
Total	11	108	98	.524	430	223	55	14	32	1778	1837	791	150	56	511	880	12.2	3.52	105	.267	.323	69	.133	-7	38	34	-2	2.4

YEAR	TM/L	W	L	PCT	G	GS	CG	SH	SV	IP	H	R	HR	HB	BB	SO	RAT	ERA	ERA+	OAV	OOB	BH	AVG	PB	PR	PR+	PD	TPI
● SAM SHAW	Shaw, Samuel E. b: 5/1864, Baltimore, Md. BR/TR, 5'5", 140 lbs. Deb: 5/3/1888																											
1888	Bal-a	2	4	.333	6	6	6	0	0	53	65	37	2	4	15	22	14.3	3.40	88	.291	.347	3	.150	-1	-2	-3	-1	-0.4
1893	Chi-N	1	0	1.000	2	2	1	0	0	16	12	12	2	9	13	1	19.1	5.63	82	.203	.420	2	.286	-0	-2	-2	-0	-0.1
Total	2	3	4	.429	8	8	7	0	0	69	77	49	4	13	28	23	15.4	3.91	86	.273	.365	5	.185	-1	-4	-4	-1	-0.5
● BOB SHAWKEY	Shawkey, James Robert b: 12/4/1890, Sigel, Pa. d: 12/31/80, Syracuse, N.Y. BR/TR, 5'11", 168 lbs. Deb: 7/16/13 MC																											
1913	Phi-A	6	5	.545	18	15	8	1	0	111^1	92	41	2	3	50	52	11.7	2.34	118	.207	.291	6	.136	-2	7	6	1	0.5
1914	*Phi-A	15	8	.652	38	31	18	5	2	237	223	88	4	2	75	89	11.4	2.73	96	.262	.323	17	.205	2	0	-3	-2	-0.3
1915	Phi-A	6	6	.500	17	13	7	1	0	100	103	57	3	1	38	56	12.8	4.05	72	.278	.346	4	.129	-1	-12	-13	0	-1.4
	NY-A	4	7	.364	16	9	5	1	0	85^2	78	38	2	2	35	31	12.1	3.26	90	.265	.347	7	.241	1	-3	-3	-1	-0.3
	Yr	10	13	.435	33	22	12	2	0	185^2	181	95	5	3	73	87	12.5	3.68	80	.272	.347	11	.183	1	-15	-16	-1	-1.7
1916	NY-A	24	14	.632	53	27	21	4	**8**	276^2	204	78	4	6	81	122	9.5	2.21	131	.209	.273	17	.183	-1	19	20	0	2.9
1917	NY-A	13	15	.464	32	26	16	2	0	236^1	207	81	2	6	72	97	10.9	2.44	110	.243	.306	16	.190	-0	6	6	3	1.1
1918	NY-A	1	1	.500	3	2	1	1	0	16	7	2	0	0	10	3	9.6	1.13	251	.143	.288	3	.750	2	3	3	0	0.7
1919	NY-A	20	11	.645	41	27	22	3	**5**	261^1	218	94	7	5	92	122	10.8	2.72	117	.231	.303	22	.234	-0	15	14	-1	1.5
1920	NY-A	20	13	.606	38	31	20	5	2	267^2	246	88	10	1	85	126	11.2	**2.45**	**156**	.248	.308	23	.230	-0	40	40	-3	4.3
1921	*NY-A	18	12	.600	38	31	18	3	2	245	245	131	15	7	86	126	12.4	4.08	104	.263	.329	27	.300	4	6	4	-4	0.4
1922	*NY-A	20	12	.625	39	34	22	3	1	299^2	286	112	16	0	98	130	11.5	2.91	138	.256	.316	21	.183	-3	38	37	-0	3.2
1923	*NY-A	16	11	.593	36	31	17	1	1	258^2	232	114	17	4	102	125	11.8	3.51	112	**.246**	.322	20	.202	-3	14	12	-1	0.8
1924	NY-A	16	11	.593	38	25	10	1	0	207^2	226	107	11	3	74	114	13.1	4.12	101	.286	.350	22	.319	8	3	1	-1	0.7
1925	NY-A	6	14	.300	33	19	9	1	0	186	209	101	12	5	67	81	13.6	4.11	104	.294	.359	10	.147	-4	6	3	-1	-0.2
1926	*NY-A	8	7	.533	29	10	3	1	3	104^1	102	49	8	2	37	63	12.2	3.62	106	.263	.330	9	.257	2	5	3	-0	0.5
1927	NY-A	2	3	.400	19	2	0	0	4	43^2	44	19	1	1	16	23	12.6	2.89	134	.262	.330	1	.091	-1	6	5	0	0.5
Total	15	195	150	.565	488	333	197	33	28	2937	2722	1200	114	48	1018	1360	11.6	3.09	114	.251	.319	225	.214	4	151	138	-10	14.9
● SPEC SHEA	Shea, Francis Joseph "The Naugatuck Nuggett" (b: Francis Joseph O'shea) b: 10/2/20, Naugatuck, Conn. BR/TR, 6', 195 lbs. Deb: 4/19/47																											
1947	*NY-A★	14	5	.737	27	23	13	3	1	178^2	127	63	10	4	89	89	11.1	3.07	115	**.200**	.303	11	.196	2	13	10	-3	0.9
1948	NY-A	9	10	.474	28	22	8	3	1	155^2	117	66	10	2	87	71	11.9	3.41	120	**.208**	.316	7	.149	1	15	12	-2	1.1
1949	NY-A	1	1	.500	20	3	0	0	1	52^1	48	36	5	0	43	22	15.6	5.33	76	.250	.387	3	.250	1	-7	-8	-0	-0.3
1951	NY-A	5	5	.500	25	11	2	2	0	95^2	112	59	11	4	50	38	15.6	4.33	88	.300	.389	6	.214	1	-2	-6	-0	-0.5
1952	Was-A	11	7	.611	22	21	12	2	0	169	144	62	6	2	92	65	12.7	2.93	121	.231	.331	15	.238	2	14	12	-1	1.4
1953	Was-A	12	7	.632	23	23	11	1	0	164^2	151	82	11	4	75	38	12.6	3.94	99	.244	.329	11	.177	-1	1	-1	-1	-0.3
1954	Was-A	2	9	.182	23	11	1	0	0	71^1	97	54	9	2	34	22	16.8	6.18	58	.340	.414	1	.050	-2	-19	-22	1	-3.0
1955	Was-A	2	2	.500	27	4	1	1	2	56^1	53	31	4	1	27	16	12.9	3.99	96	.251	.339	4	.400	2	-0	-1	-1	0.0
Total	8	56	46	.549	195	118	48	12	5	943^2	849	453	66	19	497	361	13.0	3.80	99	.243	.340	58	.195	6	14	-3	-8	-0.7
● JOHN SHEA	Shea, John Michael Joseph "Lefty" b: 12/27/04, Everett, Mass. d: 11/30/56, Malden, Mass. BL/TL, 5'10.5", 171 lbs. Deb: 6/30/28																											
1928	Bos-A	0	0	—	1	0	0	0	0	1	1	2	0	0	1	0	18.0	18.00	23	.250	.400	0	—	0	-2	-2	0	-0.1
● MIKE SHEA	Shea, Michael Joseph b: 3/10/1867, New Orleans, La. d: 8/22/27, New Orleans, La. TR, 5'10", 170 lbs. Deb: 4/20/1887																											
1887	Cin-a	1	1	.500	2	2	2	0	0	16^2	36	25	0	0	10	0	19.4	7.02	62	.409	.409	3	.333	0	-5	-5	1	-0.3
● RED SHEA	Shea, Patrick Henry b: 11/29/1898, Ware, Mass. d: 11/17/81, Stafford Springs, Conn. BR/TR, 6', 165 lbs. Deb: 5/6/18																											
1918	Phi-A	0	0	—	3	0	0	0	0	9	14	8	0	0	2	2	16.0	4.00	73	.378	.410	0	.000	-0	-1	-1	-0	-0.1
1921	NY-N	5	2	.714	9	2	1	0	0	32	28	13	2	3	2	10	9.3	3.09	119	.239	.270	1	.111	-1	2	2	-1	0.3
1922	NY-N	0	3	.000	11	2	0	0	0	23	22	14	2	0	11	5	12.9	4.70	85	.256	.340	0	.000	-1	-2	-2	1	-0.2
Total	3	5	5	.500	23	4	1	0	0	64	64	35	4	3	15	17	11.5	3.80	97	.267	.318	1	.053	-2	-0	-1	-0	0.0
● STEVE SHEA	Shea, Steven Francis b: 12/5/42, Worcester, Mass. BR/TR, 6'3", 215 lbs. Deb: 7/14/68																											
1968	Hou-N	4	4	.500	30	0	0	0	6	34^2	27	14	0	3	11	15	10.6	3.38	88	.229	.311	0	.000	-1	-2	-2	1	-0.4
1969	Mon-N	0	0	—	10	0	0	0	0	15^2	18	8	2	0	8	11	14.9	2.87	128	.300	.382	0	—	0	1	1	0	0.1
Total	2	4	4	.500	40	0	0	0	6	50^1	45	22	2	3	19	26	12.0	3.22	99	.253	.335	0	.000	-1	-0	-0	1	-0.3
● AL SHEALY	Shealy, Albert Berley b: 3/20/1900, Chapin, S.C. d: 3/7/67, Hagerstown, Md. BR/TR, 5'11", 175 lbs. Deb: 4/13/28																											
1928	NY-A	8	6	.571	23	12	3	0	2	96	124	64	4	1	42	39	15.7	5.06	74	.308	.375	9	.237	2	-11	-15	0	-1.7
1930	Chi-N	0	0	—	24	0	0	0	0	27	37	24	2	0	14	14	17.0	8.00	61	.327	.402	3	.600	1	-9	-10	-0	-0.3
Total	2	8	6	.571	47	12	3	0	2	123	161	88	6	1	56	53	16.0	5.71	70	.313	.381	12	.279	4	-20	-25	-0	-2.0
● JOHN SHEARON	Shearon, John M. b: 1870, Pittsburgh, Pa. d: 2/1/23, Bradford, Pa. Deb: 7/28/1891 ♦																											
1891	Cle-N	1	3	.250	6	5	4	0	0	46	57	39	2	1	24	19	16.0	3.52	98	.292	.373	30	.242	-0	-1	-0	-0	0.0
● GEORGE SHEARS	Shears, George Penfield b: 4/13/1890, Marshall, Mo. d: 11/12/78, Loveland, Colo. BR/TL, 6'3", 180 lbs. Deb: 4/24/12																											
1912	NY-A	0	0	—	4	0	0	0	0	15	24	18	1	0	11	9	21.0	5.40	67	.364	.455	1	.167	0	-3	-3	0	-0.1
● TOM SHEEHAN	Sheehan, Thomas Clancy b: 3/31/1894, Grand Ridge, Ill. d: 10/29/82, Chillicothe, Ohio BR/TR, 6'2.5", 190 lbs. Deb: 7/14/15 MC																											
1915	Phi-A	4	9	.308	15	13	8	1	0	102	131	73	1	1	38	22	15.0	4.15	71	.335	.395	4	.118	-3	-14	-14	-1	-1.9
1916	Phi-A	1	16	.059	38	17	8	0	0	188	197	111	2	2	94	54	14.0	3.69	78	.287	.374	7	.125	-2	-18	-17	3	-1.3
1921	NY-A	1	0	1.000	12	1	0	0	1	33	43	23	1	1	19	7	17.2	5.45	78	.326	.414	5	.625	2	-4	-5	2	0.1
1924	Cin-N	9	11	.450	39	14	8	2	1	166^2	170	72	5	1	54	52	12.1	3.24	116	.269	.328	18	.310	4	12	10	-2	1.3
1925	Cin-N	1	0	1.000	10	3	1	0	1	29	37	31	3	0	12	5	15.2	8.07	51	.298	.360	1	.200	1	-12	-13	-1	-0.6
	Pit-N	1	1	.500	23	0	0	0	2	57^1	63	25	2	0	13	13	11.9	2.67	167	.286	.326	3	.150	-1	10	11	0	0.4
	Yr	2	1	.667	33	3	1	0	3	86^1	100	56	5	0	25	18	13.0	4.48	97	.291	.339	4	.160	-0	-2	-1	-1	-0.2
1926	Pit-N	0	2	.000	9	2	1	0	0	31	36	24	0	2	12	16	14.5	6.68	59	.298	.370	1	.111	-1	-10	-9	-0	-0.6
Total	6	17	39	.304	146	50	26	3	5	607	677	359	14	7	242	169	13.7	4.00	86	.294	.362	39	.205	0	-36	-37	1	-2.6
● ROLLIE SHELDON	Sheldon, Roland Frank b: 12/17/36, Putnam, Conn. BR/TR, 6'4", 190 lbs. Deb: 4/23/61																											
1961	NY-A	11	5	.688	35	21	6	2	0	162^2	149	70	17	2	55	84	11.4	3.60	103	.246	.311	7	.125	-2	8	2	1	0.1
1962	NY-A	7	8	.467	34	16	2	0	1	118	136	78	12	1	28	54	12.6	5.49	68	.289	.331	2	.077	0	-20	-24	-2	-2.9
1964	*NY-A	5	2	.714	19	12	3	0	1	102^1	92	43	18	1	18	57	9.8	3.61	100	.243	.279	3	.088	-2	0	0	1	-0.1
1965	NY-A	0	0	—	3	0	0	0	0	6^1	5	1	0	0	1	7	8.5	1.42	240	.238	.273	0	.000	-0	1	1	0	0.1
	KC-A	10	8	.556	32	29	4	1	0	186^2	180	86	22	7	56	105	11.7	3.95	88	.251	.312	4	.078	-3	-10	-10	-0	-1.2
	Yr	10	8	.556	35	29	4	1	0	193	185	87	22	7	57	112	11.6	3.87	90	.251	.311	4	.077	-3	-9	-8	0	-1.1
1966	KC-A	4	7	.364	14	13	1	1	0	69	73	31	3	1	26	26	13.0	3.13	109	.275	.342	2	.087	-1	2	2	0	0.2
	Bos-A	1	6	.143	23	10	1	0	0	79^2	106	49	15	2	23	38	14.8	4.97	77	.320	.368	2	.111	-1	-14	-9	0	-0.8
	Yr	5	13	.278	37	23	2	1	0	148^2	179	80	18	3	49	64	14.0	4.12	88	.300	.356	4	.098	-2	-11	-8	1	-0.6
Total	5	38	36	.514	160	101	17	4	2	724^2	741	358	87	14	207	371	11.9	4.09	89	.266	.320	20	.096	-9	-32	-37	0	-4.6
● SCOTT SHELDON	Sheldon, Scott Patrick b: 11/28/68, Hammond, Ind. BR/TR, 6'3", 185 lbs. Deb: 5/18/97 ♦																											
2000	Tex-A	0	0	—	1	0	0	0	0	0^1	0	0	0	0	0	1	0.0	0.00	—	.000	.000	35	.282	0	0	0	0	0.0
● FRANK SHELLENBACK	Shellenback, Frank Victor b: 12/16/1898, Joplin, Mo. d: 8/17/69, Newton, Mass. BR/TR, 6'2", 192 lbs. Deb: 5/8/18 C																											
1918	Chi-A	9	12	.429	28	21	10	2	2	182^2	180	77	1	4	74	47	12.7	2.66	103	.262	.338	7	.130	-1	2	2	-5	-0.5
1919	Chi-A	1	3	.250	8	4	2	0	0	35	40	24	1	0	16	10	14.4	5.14	62	.303	.378	1	.091	-0	-7	-8	-0	-0.8
Total	2	10	15	.400	36	25	12	2	2	217^2	220	101	2	4	90	57	13.0	3.06	92	.269	.344	8	.123	-1	-5	-6	-5	-1.3
● JIM SHELLENBACK	Shellenback, James Philip b: 11/18/43, Riverside, Cal. BL/TL, 6'2", 200 lbs. Deb: 9/15/66 C																											
1966	Pit-N	0	0	—	2	0	0	0	0	3	3	3	2	0	3	0	18.0	9.00	40	.300	.462	0	—	0	-2	-2	0	-0.1
1967	Pit-N	1	1	.500	6	2	1	0	0	23^1	23	12	1	1	12	11	13.9	2.70	125	.250	.343	1	.167	-0	2	2	-0	0.1
1969	Pit-N	0	0	—	8	0	0	0	0	16^2	14	8	1	0	4	7	9.7	3.24	108	.233	.281	0	.000	-0	1	0	1	0.2
	Was-A	4	7	.364	30	11	2	0	1	84^2	87	43	8	1	48	50	14.5	4.04	86	.268	.364	5	.185	-0	-4	-6	2	-0.5
1970	Was-A	6	7	.462	39	14	2	1	0	117^1	107	57	6	0	51	57	12.1	3.68	97	.246	.325	2	.067	-2	0	-2	-1	-0.4
1971	Was-A	3	11	.214	40	15	3	1	0	120	123	56	10	3	49	47	13.1	3.53	94	.267	.342	5	.167	0	-1	-3	1	-0.2

YEAR	TM/L	W	L	PCT	G	GS	CG	SH	SV	IP	H	R	HR	HB	BB	SO	RAT	ERA	ERA+	OAV	OOB	BH	AVG	PB	PR	PR+	PD	TPI
1972	Tex-A	2	4	.333	22	6	0	0	1	57	46	24	6	2	16	30	10.1	3.47	87	.221	.283	1	.100	-0	-3	-3	-1	-0.4
1973	Tex-A	0	0	—	2	0	0	0	0	1^2	0	0	0	0	0	3	0.0	0.00	—	.000	.000	0	—	0	1	1	0	0.1
1974	Tex-A	0	0	—	11	0	0	0	0	24^2	30	18	5	1	12	14	15.7	5.84	61	.306	.387	0	—	0	-6	-6	0	-0.3
1977	Min-A	0	0	—	5	0	0	0	0	5^2	10	7	1	0	5	3	23.8	7.94	50	.385	.484	0	—	0	-2	-3	0	-0.1
Total	9	16	30	.348	165	48	8	2	2	454	443	228	40	8	200	222	12.9	3.81	89	.258	.338	14	.135	-2	-14	-21	3	-1.6

● BERT SHEPARD
Shepard, Bert Robert b: 6/28/20, Dana, Ind. BL/TL, 5'11", 185 lbs. Deb: 8/4/45

YEAR	TM/L	W	L	PCT	G	GS	CG	SH	SV	IP	H	R	HR	HB	BB	SO	RAT	ERA	ERA+	OAV	OOB	BH	AVG	PB	PR	PR+	PD	TPI
1945	Was-A	0	0	—	1	0	0	0	0	5^1	3	1	0	1	1	2	8.4	1.69	184	.167	.250	0	.000	-0	1	1	0	0.0

● KEITH SHEPHERD
Shepherd, Keith Wayne b: 1/21/68, Wabash, Ind. BR/TR, 6'2", 205 lbs. Deb: 9/6/92

YEAR	TM/L	W	L	PCT	G	GS	CG	SH	SV	IP	H	R	HR	HB	BB	SO	RAT	ERA	ERA+	OAV	OOB	BH	AVG	PB	PR	PR+	PD	TPI
1992	Phi-N	1	1	.500	12	0	0	0	2	22	19	10	0	0	6	10	10.2	3.27	107	.244	.298	0	—	0	1	1	0	0.1
1993	Col-N	1	3	.250	14	1	0	0	1	19^1	26	16	4	1	4	7	14.4	6.98	68	.333	.373	0	.000	-0	-6	-4	-0	-0.8
1995	Bos-A	0	0	—	2	0	0	0	0	1	4	4	0	0	2	0	54.0	36.00	14	.571	.667	0	—	0	-3	-3	0	-0.1
1996	Bal-A	0	1	.000	13	0	0	0	0	20^2	31	27	6	0	18	17	21.3	8.71	57	.341	.450	0	—	0	-9	-9	-0	-0.4
Total	4	2	5	.286	41	1	0	0	3	63	80	57	10	1	30	34	15.9	6.71	65	.315	.389	0	.000	-0	-18	-15	0	-1.2

● BILL SHERDEL
Sherdel, William Henry "Wee Willie" b: 8/15/1896, McSherrystown, Pa d: 11/14/68, McSherrystown, Pa BL/TL, 5'10", 160 lbs. Deb: 4/22/18

YEAR	TM/L	W	L	PCT	G	GS	CG	SH	SV	IP	H	R	HR	HB	BB	SO	RAT	ERA	ERA+	OAV	OOB	BH	AVG	PB	PR	PR+	PD	TPI
1918	StL-N	6	12	.333	35	16	9	1	0	182^1	174	78	3	3	49	40	11.2	2.71	100	.259	.313	15	.242	3	1	-0	-2	0.2
1919	StL-N	5	9	.357	36	11	7	0	1	137^1	137	66	3	2	42	52	11.9	3.47	80	.270	.328	13	.271	2	-9	-11	1	-0.7
1920	StL-N	11	10	.524	43	7	4	0	**6**	170	183	72	1	11	40	74	12.4	3.28	91	.297	.350	14	.222	2	-3	-6	1	-0.4
1921	StL-N	9	8	.529	38	8	5	1	1	144^1	137	62	7	3	38	57	11.1	3.18	115	.247	.299	5	.114	-2	10	8	1	0.7
1922	StL-N	17	13	.567	47	31	15	3	2	242	298	132	12	5	62	79	13.6	3.87	100	.303	.348	17	.193	1	6	-0	-3	-0.3
1923	StL-N	15	13	.536	39	26	14	0	2	225	270	127	15	6	59	78	13.4	4.32	90	.296	.343	28	.337	9	-8	-11	-3	-0.7
1924	StL-N	8	9	.471	35	10	6	0	1	168^2	188	77	9	5	38	57	12.3	3.42	111	.291	.335	15	.200	2	8	7	-2	0.7
1925	StL-N	15	6	**.714**	32	21	17	2	1	200	216	77	8	3	42	53	11.7	3.11	139	.277	.316	15	.205	2	26	27	-1	2.6
1926	*StL-N	16	12	.571	34	29	17	3	0	234^2	255	103	15	5	49	59	11.9	3.49	112	.278	.318	22	.244	2	9	11	-3	1.0
1927	StL-N	17	12	.586	39	28	18	0	**6**	232^1	241	109	17	3	48	59	11.3	3.53	112	.269	.308	14	.194	1	10	11	-4	1.0
1928	*StL-N	21	10	.677	38	27	20	0	**5**	248^2	251	96	17	2	56	72	11.2	2.86	140	.261	.303	19	.226	4	31	31	-5	3.7
1929	StL-N	10	15	.400	33	22	11	1	0	195^2	278	144	14	2	58	69	15.5	5.93	79	.337	.382	16	.229	2	-26	-28	-2	-2.9
1930	StL-N	3	2	.600	13	7	1	0	0	64	86	34	5	1	13	29	14.1	4.64	108	.325	.358	2	.105	-1	2	3	-1	0.0
	Bos-N	6	5	.545	21	14	7	0	1	119^1	131	73	10	2	30	26	12.3	4.75	104	.283	.329	4	.095	-4	3	2	-1	-0.2
	Yr	9	7	.563	34	21	8	0	1	183^1	217	107	15	3	43	55	12.9	4.71	105	.298	.340	6	.098	-5	5	5	-1	-0.2
1931	Bos-N	6	10	.375	27	16	8	0	0	137^2	163	70	13	1	35	34	13.0	4.25	89	.294	.337	14	.304	4	-6	-7	-2	-0.6
1932	Bos-N	0	0	—	1	0	0	0	0	1^2	3	3	0	0	1	0	21.6	0.00	—	.375	.444	0	—	0	1	1	-0	0.0
	StL-N	0	0	—	3	0	0	0	0	5^2	7	3	0	0	1	1	12.7	4.76	83	.304	.333	1	1.000	1	-1	-1	0	0.1
	Yr	0	0	—	4	0	0	0	0	7^1	10	6	0	0	2	1	14.7	3.68	106	.323	.364	1	1.000	1	0	0	0	0.1
Total	15	165	146	.531	514	273	159	11	26	2709^1	3018	1326	149	54	661	839	12.4	3.72	103	.285	.330	214	.223	27	55	38	-25	4.2

● ROY SHERID
Sherid, Royden Richard b: 1/25/07, Norristown, Pa. d: 2/28/82, Parker Ford, Pa. BR/TR, 6'2", 185 lbs. Deb: 5/11/29

YEAR	TM/L	W	L	PCT	G	GS	CG	SH	SV	IP	H	R	HR	HB	BB	SO	RAT	ERA	ERA+	OAV	OOB	BH	AVG	PB	PR	PR+	PD	TPI
1929	NY-A	6	6	.500	33	15	9	0	1	154^2	165	81	6	5	55	51	13.1	3.61	107	.277	.343	9	.180	-1	11	5	-1	0.2
1930	NY-A	12	13	.480	37	21	8	0	4	184	214	122	13	5	87	59	15.0	5.23	82	.289	.368	7	.101	-6	-12	-21	-1	-2.9
1931	NY-A	5	5	.500	17	8	3	0	2	74^1	94	52	4	3	24	39	14.7	5.69	70	.306	.362	10	.333	2	-11	-16	0	-1.6
Total	3	23	24	.489	87	44	20	0	7	413	473	255	23	13	166	149	14.2	4.71	87	.288	.358	26	.174	-4	-12	-32	-2	-4.3

● JOE SHERMAN
Sherman, Joel Powers b: 11/4/1890, Yarmouth, Mass. d: 12/21/87, Cape Coral, Fla. BR/TR, 6', 165 lbs. Deb: 9/24/15

YEAR	TM/L	W	L	PCT	G	GS	CG	SH	SV	IP	H	R	HR	HB	BB	SO	RAT	ERA	ERA+	OAV	OOB	BH	AVG	PB	PR	PR+	PD	TPI
1915	Phi-A	1	0	1.000	2	1	1	0	0	15	15	4	0	2	1	5	10.8	2.40	122	.259	.295	2	.333	1	1	1	-0	0.1

● DAN SHERMAN
Sherman, Lester Daniel "Babe" b: 5/9/1890, Hubbardsville, N.Y. d: 9/16/55, Highland Park, Mich. BR/TR, 5'6", 145 lbs. Deb: 6/4/14

YEAR	TM/L	W	L	PCT	G	GS	CG	SH	SV	IP	H	R	HR	HB	BB	SO	RAT	ERA	ERA+	OAV	OOB	BH	AVG	PB	PR	PR+	PD	TPI
1914	Chi-F	0	1	.000	1	1	0	0	0	0^1	0	2	0	0	2	0	54.0	0.00	—	.000	.667	0	—	0	0	0	0	0.0

● TIM SHERRILL
Sherrill, Timothy Shawn b: 9/10/65, Harrison, Ark. BL/TL, 5'11", 170 lbs. Deb: 8/14/90

YEAR	TM/L	W	L	PCT	G	GS	CG	SH	SV	IP	H	R	HR	HB	BB	SO	RAT	ERA	ERA+	OAV	OOB	BH	AVG	PB	PR	PR+	PD	TPI
1990	StL-N	0	0	—	8	0	0	0	0	4^1	10	5	0	0	3	3	27.0	6.23	61	.476	.542	0	—	0	-1	-1	0	-0.1
1991	StL-N	0	0	—	10	0	0	0	0	14^1	20	13	2	2	3	4	15.7	8.16	46	.339	.391	0	—	0	-7	-7	0	-0.3
Total	2	0	0	—	18	0	0	0	0	18^2	30	18	2	2	6	7	18.3	7.71	49	.375	.432	0	—	0	-8	-8	0	-0.4

● FRED SHERRY
Sherry, Fred Peter (b: Fred Peter Schuerholz) b: 1/13/1889, Honesdale, Pa. d: 7/27/75, Honesdale, Pa. BR/TR, 6', 170 lbs. Deb: 4/25/11

YEAR	TM/L	W	L	PCT	G	GS	CG	SH	SV	IP	H	R	HR	HB	BB	SO	RAT	ERA	ERA+	OAV	OOB	BH	AVG	PB	PR	PR+	PD	TPI
1911	Was-A	0	4	.000	10	3	2	0	0	52^1	63	40	1	0	19	20	14.1	4.30	76	.310	.369	3	.158	-1	-6	-6	0	-0.4

● LARRY SHERRY
Sherry, Lawrence b: 7/25/35, Los Angeles, Cal. BR/TR, 6'2", 204 lbs. Deb: 4/17/58 FC

YEAR	TM/L	W	L	PCT	G	GS	CG	SH	SV	IP	H	R	HR	HB	BB	SO	RAT	ERA	ERA+	OAV	OOB	BH	AVG	PB	PR	PR+	PD	TPI
1958	LA-N	0	0	—	5	0	0	0	0	4^1	10	7	0	1	7	2	37.4	12.46	33	.476	.621	0	—	0	-4	-4	0	-0.2
1959	*LA-N	7	2	.778	23	9	1	1	3	94^1	75	27	9	2	43	72	11.4	2.19	193	.218	.308	7	.219	2	18	20	-1	2.1
1960	LA-N	14	10	.583	57	3	1	0	7	142^1	125	65	14	6	82	114	13.5	3.79	105	.238	.347	6	.162	1	3	3	1	0.6
1961	LA-N	4	4	.500	53	1	0	0	15	94^2	90	48	10	4	39	79	12.6	3.90	111	.252	.333	2	.154	-0	1	4	-2	0.3
1962	LA-N	7	3	.700	58	0	0	0	11	90	81	40	8	6	44	71	13.1	3.20	113	.241	.339	2	.118	-0	7	5	-0	0.5
1963	LA-N	2	6	.250	36	3	0	0	3	79^2	82	43	8	4	24	47	12.4	3.73	81	.265	.325	1	.111	-0	-4	-7	-0	-0.7
1964	Det-A	7	5	.583	38	0	0	0	11	66^1	52	29	7	3	37	58	12.5	3.66	100	.216	.327	0	.000	-2	-0	-0	-0	-0.2
1965	Det-A	3	6	.333	39	0	0	0	5	78^1	71	30	5	1	40	46	12.9	3.10	112	.254	.349	3	.300	2	3	3	0	0.6
1966	Det-A	8	5	.615	55	0	0	0	20	77^2	66	38	8	3	36	63	12.2	3.82	91	.232	.325	4	.400	2	-3	-3	-1	-0.5
1967	Det-A	0	1	.000	20	0	0	0	1	28	35	22	3	1	7	20	13.8	6.43	51	.289	.333	0	.000	-0	-10	-10	0	-0.5
	Hou-N	1	2	.333	29	0	0	0	6	40^2	53	26	4	1	13	32	14.8	4.87	68	.327	.381	0	.000	-1	-7	-7	1	-0.7
1968	Cal-A	0	0	—	3	0	0	0	0	3	7	2	2	0	2	2	27.0	6.00	49	.467	.529	0	—	0	-1	-1	-0	-0.1
Total	11	53	44	.546	416	16	2	1	82	799^1	747	377	78	32	374	606	13.0	3.67	101	.249	.339	25	.169	4	0	4	-2	1.2

● BEN SHIELDS
Shields, Benjamin Cowan "Big Ben" or "Lefty"
b: 6/17/03, Huntersville, N.C d: 1/24/82, Woodruff, S.C. BR/TL (BB 1930-31), 6'1.5", 195 lbs. Deb: 4/17/24

YEAR	TM/L	W	L	PCT	G	GS	CG	SH	SV	IP	H	R	HR	HB	BB	SO	RAT	ERA	ERA+	OAV	OOB	BH	AVG	PB	PR	PR+	PD	TPI
1924	NY-A	0	0	—	2	0	0	0	0	2	6	6	0	0	2	3	36.0	27.00	15	.545	.615	0	—	0	-5	-5	-0	-0.2
1925	NY-A	3	0	1.000	4	2	2	0	0	24	24	13	2	2	12	5	14.3	4.88	87	.267	.365	1	.125	-1	-1	-2	-1	-0.3
1930	Bos-A	0	0	—	3	0	0	0	0	10	16	11	0	0	6	1	19.8	9.00	51	.400	.478	0	.000	-1	-5	-5	0	-0.3
1931	Phi-N	1	0	1.000	4	0	0	0	0	5^1	9	9	1	0	7	0	27.0	15.19	28	.391	.533	0	.000	-0	-7	-6	0	-0.9
Total	4	4	0	1.000	13	2	2	0	0	41^1	55	39	3	2	27	9	18.3	8.27	53	.335	.435	1	.077	-2	-18	-18	-1	-1.7

● CHARLIE SHIELDS
Shields, Charles Jessamine b: 12/10/1879, Jackson, Tenn. d: 8/27/53, Memphis, Tenn. BL/TL, Deb: 4/23/02

YEAR	TM/L	W	L	PCT	G	GS	CG	SH	SV	IP	H	R	HR	HB	BB	SO	RAT	ERA	ERA+	OAV	OOB	BH	AVG	PB	PR	PR+	PD	TPI
1902	Bal-A	4	11	.267	23	15	10	1	1	142^1	201	102	7	2	32	28	14.9	4.24	89	.333	.368	8	.167	-1	-10	-7	-4	-1.1
	StL-A	3	0	1.000	4	4	3	0	0	30	37	16	1	0	7	6	13.2	3.30	107	.303	.341	6	.462	2	1	1	-1	0.3
	Yr	7	11	.389	27	19	13	1	1	172^1	238	118	8	2	39	34	14.6	4.07	92	.328	.364	14	.230	1	-10	-6	-5	-0.8
1907	StL-N	0	2	.000	3	2	0	0	0	6^2	12	11	0	2	7	1	28.4	9.45	26	.444	.583	0	.000	-0	-5	-5	0	-1.0
Total	2	7	13	.350	30	21	13	1	1	179	250	129	8	4	46	35	15.1	4.27	86	.332	.374	14	.222	1	-15	-11	-4	-1.8

● STEVE SHIELDS
Shields, Stephen Mack b: 11/30/58, Gadsden, Ala. BR/TR, 6'5", 230 lbs. Deb: 6/1/85

YEAR	TM/L	W	L	PCT	G	GS	CG	SH	SV	IP	H	R	HR	HB	BB	SO	RAT	ERA	ERA+	OAV	OOB	BH	AVG	PB	PR	PR+	PD	TPI
1985	Atl-N	1	2	.333	23	6	0	0	0	68	86	46	9	1	32	29	15.8	5.16	75	.320	.394	2	.111	-1	-12	-9	-1	-0.6
1986	Atl-N	0	0	—	6	0	0	0	0	12^2	13	10	4	0	7	6	14.2	7.11	56	.271	.364	0	.000	-0	-5	-4	-0	-0.2
	KC-A	0	0	—	3	0	0	0	0	8^2	3	3	1	0	4	2	7.3	2.08	205	.111	.226	0	—	0	2	2	-0	0.1
1987	Sea-A	2	0	1.000	20	0	0	0	3	30	43	25	7	0	12	22	16.5	6.60	72	.333	.390	0	—	0	-7	-6	0	-0.4
1988	NY-A	5	5	.500	39	0	0	0	0	82^1	96	44	8	2	30	55	14.0	4.37	90	.298	.362	0	—	0	-4	-4	0	-0.4
1989	Min-A	0	1	.000	11	0	0	0	0	17^1	28	18	3	0	6	12	17.7	7.79	53	.354	.400	0	—	0	-8	-7	0	-0.3
Total	5	8	8	.500	102	6	0	0	3	219	269	146	32	3	91	126	14.9	5.26	77	.308	.375	2	.105	-1	-33	-28	-1	-1.8

● VINCE SHIELDS
Shields, Vincent William
b: 11/18/1900, Fredericton, N.B., Canada d: 10/17/52, Plaster Rock, N.B., Canada BL/TR, 5'11", 185 lbs. Deb: 9/20/24

YEAR	TM/L	W	L	PCT	G	GS	CG	SH	SV	IP	H	R	HR	HB	BB	SO	RAT	ERA	ERA+	OAV	OOB	BH	AVG	PB	PR	PR+	PD	TPI
1924	StL-N	1	1	.500	2	1	0	0	0	12	10	5	1	3	3	4	12.0	3.00	126	.227	.320	2	.400	0	1	1	-1	0.2

● GARLAND SHIFFLETT
Shifflett, Garland Jessie "Duck" b: 3/28/35, Elkton, Va. BR/TR, 5'10.5", 165 lbs. Deb: 4/22/57

YEAR	TM/L	W	L	PCT	G	GS	CG	SH	SV	IP	H	R	HR	HB	BB	SO	RAT	ERA	ERA+	OAV	OOB	BH	AVG	PB	PR	PR+	PD	TPI
1957	Was-A	0	0	—	6	1	0	0	0	8	6	9	0	0	10	2	18.0	10.13	38	.222	.432	0	—	0	-6	-5	-0	-0.3

YEAR	TM/L	W	L	PCT	G	GS	CG	SH	SV	IP	H	R	HR	HB	BB	SO	RAT	ERA	ERA+	OAV	OOB	BH	AVG	PB	PR	PR+	PD	TPI
1964	Min-A	0	2	.000	10	0	0	0	1	17^2	22	9	1	1	7	8	15.3	4.58	78	.297	.366	0	.000	-0	-2	-2	0	-0.2
Total	2	0	2	.000	16	1	0	0	1	25^2	28	18	1	1	17	10	16.1	6.31	58	.277	.387	0	.000	-0	-8	-8	0	-0.5
● **STEVE SHIFFLETT**	Shifflett, Stephen Earl b: 1/5/66, Kansas City, Mo. BR/TR, 6'1", 205 lbs. Deb: 7/3/92																											
1992	KC-A	1	4	.200	34	0	0	0	0	52	55	15	6	2	17	25	12.8	2.60	156	.279	.343	0	—	0	8	8	0	0.7
● **ZAK SHINALL**	Shinall, Zakary Sebastien b: 10/14/68, St.Louis, Mo. BR/TR, 6'3", 215 lbs. Deb: 5/12/93																											
1993	Sea-A	0	0	—	1	0	0	0	0	2^2	4	1	1	0	2	0	20.3	3.38	131	.333	.429	0	—	0	0	0	0	0.0
● **RAZOR SHINES**	Shines, Anthony Raymond "Ray" b: 7/18/56, Durham, N.C. BB/TR, 6'1", 210 lbs. Deb: 9/9/83 ♦																											
1985	Mon-N	0	0	—	1	0	0	0	0	1	1	0	0	0	0	0	9.0	0.00	—	.250	.250	6	.120	-0	0	0	-0	0.0
● **DAVE SHIPANOFF**	Shipanoff, David Noel b: 11/13/59, Edmonton, Alberta, Can. BR/TR, 6'2", 185 lbs. Deb: 8/9/85																											
1985	Phi-N	1	2	.333	26	0	0	0	3	36^1	33	15	3	1	16	26	12.4	3.22	115	.231	.313	0	.000	-0	2	2	-0	0.1
● **JOE SHIPLEY**	Shipley, Joseph Clark "Moses" b: 5/9/35, Morristown, Tenn. BR/TR, 6'4", 210 lbs. Deb: 7/14/58																											
1958	SF-N	0	0	—	1	0	0	0	0	1^1	3	5	0	2	3	0	54.0	33.75	11	.429	.667	0	—	0	-4	-5	-0	-0.2
1959	SF-N	0	0	—	10	1	0	0	0	18	16	11	2	1	17	11	17.0	4.50	85	.239	.400	0	.000	-0	-1	-1	-0	-0.1
1960	SF-N	0	0	—	15	0	0	0	0	20	20	13	2	3	9	9	14.4	5.40	64	.274	.376	0	—	0	-4	-5	1	-0.2
1963	Chi-A	0	1	.000	3	0	0	0	0	4^2	9	7	0	0	6	3	28.9	5.79	61	.409	.536	0	.000	-0	-1	-1	0	-0.3
Total	4	0	1	.000	29	1	0	0	0	44	48	36	4	6	35	23	18.2	5.93	61	.284	.424	0	.000	-1	-10	-12	0	-0.8
● **DUKE SHIREY**	Shirey, Clair Lee b: 6/20/1898, Jersey Shore, Pa. d: 9/1/62, Hagerstown, Md. BR/TR, 6'1", 175 lbs. Deb: 9/28/20																											
1920	Was-A	0	1	.000	2	1	0	0	0	4	5	4	0	1	2	0	18.0	6.75	55	.313	.421	0	.000	-0	-1	-1	-0	-0.3
● **TEX SHIRLEY**	Shirley, Alvis Newman b: 4/25/18, Birthright, Tex. d: 11/7/93, DeSoto, Tex. BB/TR (BR 1941-42), 6'1", 175 lbs. Deb: 9/6/41																											
1941	Phi-A	0	1	.000	5	0	0	0	1	7^1	8	4	1	0	6	1	17.2	2.45	171	.286	.412	0	.000	-0	1	1	0	0.2
1942	Phi-A	0	1	.000	15	1	0	0	1	35^2	37	30	0	2	22	10	15.4	5.30	71	.272	.381	0	.000	-1	-7	-6	-1	-0.5
1944	*StL-A	5	4	.556	23	11	2	1	0	80^1	59	45	4	1	64	35	13.9	4.15	87	.203	.348	4	.143	-2	-6	-5	-1	-0.8
1945	StL-A	8	12	.400	32	24	10	2	0	183^2	191	79	8	1	93	77	14.0	3.63	97	.274	.360	20	.286	2	-5	-2	-1	-0.1
1946	StL-A	6	12	.333	27	18	7	0	0	139^2	148	89	7	1	105	45	16.4	4.96	75	.273	.391	10	.196	-0	-23	-18	-1	-2.2
Total	5	19	30	.388	102	54	19	3	2	446^2	443	247	20	5	290	168	14.9	4.25	85	.261	.371	34	.214	-1	-39	-29	-3	-3.4
● **BOB SHIRLEY**	Shirley, Robert Charles b: 6/25/54, Cushing, Okla. BR/TL, 5'11", 185 lbs. Deb: 4/10/77																											
1977	SD-N	12	18	.400	39	35	1	0	0	214	215	107	22	4	100	146	13.4	3.70	96	.259	.341	9	.122	-2	5	-4	1	-0.6
1978	SD-N	8	11	.421	50	20	2	0	5	166	164	75	10	3	61	102	12.4	3.69	90	.262	.330	5	.125	-0	-2	-7	2	-0.6
1979	SD-N	8	16	.333	49	25	4	1	0	205	196	89	15	6	59	117	11.5	3.38	105	.257	.316	5	.091	-2	8	4	0	0.2
1980	SD-N	11	12	.478	59	12	3	0	7	137	143	58	12	0	54	67	12.9	3.55	97	.276	.344	1	.033	-2	1	-2	2	-0.3
1981	StL-N	6	4	.600	28	11	1	0	1	79^1	78	42	6	1	34	36	12.8	4.08	87	.260	.337	3	.136	-1	-5	-5	-1	-0.8
1982	Cin-N	8	13	.381	41	20	1	0	0	152^2	138	74	17	3	73	89	12.6	3.60	103	.248	.338	6	.143	-1	0	2	1	0.2
1983	NY-A	5	8	.385	25	17	1	1	0	108	122	71	10	0	36	53	13.2	5.08	77	.293	.350	0	—	0	-12	-15	1	-1.5
1984	NY-A	3	3	.500	41	7	1	0	0	114^1	119	47	8	0	38	48	12.4	3.38	112	.274	.333	0	—	0	8	6	0	0.3
1985	NY-A	5	5	.500	48	8	2	0	2	109	103	34	5	0	26	55	10.7	2.64	152	.251	.295	0	—	0	18	17	-1	1.4
1986	NY-A	0	4	.000	39	6	0	0	3	105^1	108	60	13	3	40	64	12.9	5.04	81	.271	.342	0	—	0	-10	-11	1	-0.5
1987	NY-A	1	0	1.000	12	1	0	0	0	34	36	20	4	0	16	12	13.8	4.50	98	.277	.356	0	—	0	-0	-0	-1	-0.1
	KC-A	0	0	—	3	0	0	0	0	7^1	10	12	5	0	6	1	19.6	14.73	31	.323	.432	0	—	0	-8	-8	-0	-0.4
	Yr	1	0	1.000	15	1	0	0	0	41^1	46	32	9	0	22	13	14.8	6.31	70	.286	.372	0	—	0	-8	-9	-1	-0.5
Total	11	67	94	.416	434	162	16	2	18	1432	1432	689	127	20	543	790	12.5	3.82	96	.264	.334	29	.110	-8	3	-24	5	-2.7
● **STEVE SHIRLEY**	Shirley, Steven Brian b: 10/12/56, San Francisco, Cal. BL/TL, 6', 185 lbs. Deb: 6/21/82																											
1982	LA-N	1	1	.500	11	0	0	0	0	12^2	15	6	0	0	7	8	15.6	4.26	82	.300	.386	1	1.000	0	-1	-1	0	-0.1
● **GEORGE SHOCH**	Shoch, George Quintus b: 1/6/1859, Philadelphia, Pa. d: 9/30/37, Philadelphia, Pa. BR/TR, 5'6", 158 lbs. Deb: 9/10/1886 ♦																											
1888	Was-N	0	0	—	1	0	0	0	0	3	2	0	0	0	1	0	9.0	0.00	—	.167	.231	58	.183	0	1	1	-0	0.0
● **URBAN SHOCKER**	Shocker, Urban James (b: Urbain Jacques Shockcor) b: 9/22/1892, Cleveland, Ohio d: 9/9/28, Denver, Colo. BR/TR, 5'10", 170 lbs. Deb: 4/24/16																											
1916	NY-A	4	3	.571	12	9	4	1	0	82^1	67	25	2	6	32	43	11.5	2.62	110	.230	.319	4	.190	1	2	2	-0	0.3
1917	NY-A	8	5	.615	26	13	7	0	1	145	124	59	4	0	46	68	10.6	2.61	103	.241	.303	8	.178	-1	1	1	2	0.2
1918	StL-A	6	5	.545	14	9	7	0	2	94^2	69	26	0	1	40	33	10.5	1.81	152	.209	.296	11	.324	4	10	10	1	1.8
1919	StL-A	13	11	.542	30	25	14	5	0	211	193	75	6	4	55	86	10.7	2.69	123	.244	.296	8	.138	-0	13	14	-1	1.4
1920	StL-A	20	10	.667	38	28	22	5	**5**	245^2	224	97	10	4	70	107	10.9	2.71	145	.248	.305	18	.225	2	30	32	-0	3.9
1921	StL-A	**27**	12	.692	47	38	30	4	4	326^2	345	151	21	6	86	132	12.0	3.55	126	.270	.319	27	.260	5	26	32	3	4.2
1922	StL-A	24	17	.585	48	38	29	2	3	348	365	141	22	4	57	**149**	11.0	2.97	139	.272	.304	22	.191	2	41	44	-3	4.7
1923	StL-A	20	12	.625	43	35	24	3	5	277^1	292	122	12	3	49	109	**11.2**	3.41	122	.272	**.306**	16	.200	2	18	22	-3	2.3
1924	StL-A	16	13	.552	40	33	17	4	1	246^1	270	128	11	3	52	88	11.9	4.20	107	.277	.315	16	.239	5	1	8	-2	1.1
1925	NY-A	12	12	.500	41	30	15	2	2	244^1	278	108	17	3	58	74	12.5	3.65	117	.294	.336	11	.172	5	20	17	-2	1.8
1926	*NY-A	19	11	.633	41	32	18	0	2	258^1	272	113	13	2	71	59	12.0	3.38	114	.269	.318	13	.171	1	18	14	-2	1.4
1927	NY-A	18	6	.750	31	27	13	2	0	200	207	86	8	1	41	35	11.2	2.84	136	.268	.306	13	.241	3	29	24	-2	2.7
1928	NY-A	0	0	—	1	0	0	0	0	2	3	0	0	0	0	0	13.5	0.00	—	.429	.429	0	—	0	1	1	-0	0.0
Total	13	187	117	.615	412	317	200	28	25	2681^2	2709	1131	126	37	657	983	11.4	3.17	124	.265	.311	167	.209	28	210	223	-9	25.8
● **MILT SHOFFNER**	Shoffner, Milburn James b: 11/13/05, Sherman, Tex. d: 1/19/78, Madison, Ohio BL/TL, 6'1.5", 184 lbs. Deb: 7/20/29																											
1929	Cle-A	2	3	.400	11	3	1	0	0	44^2	46	28	4	3	22	15	14.3	5.04	88	.284	.380	0	.000	-2	-4	-3	0	-0.5
1930	Cle-A	3	4	.429	24	10	1	0	0	84^2	129	86	8	1	50	17	19.1	7.97	61	.362	.442	7	.212	1	-31	-29	-0	-1.8
1931	Cle-A	2	3	.400	12	4	1	0	0	41	55	34	4	2	26	12	18.2	7.24	64	.320	.415	1	.077	-1	-13	-11	-0	-1.2
1937	Bos-N	3	1	.750	6	5	3	1	1	42^2	38	14	1	1	9	13	10.1	2.53	142	.239	.284	2	.125	1	7	5	1	0.7
1938	Bos-N	8	7	.533	26	15	9	1	1	139^2	147	60	7	2	36	49	11.9	3.54	97	.270	.317	12	.211	3	4	-2	-2	-0.1
1939	Bos-N	4	6	.400	25	11	7	0	1	132^1	133	56	4	1	42	51	12.0	3.13	118	.265	.324	7	.159	-0	12	9	0	0.6
	Cin-N	2	2	.500	10	3	0	0	0	37^2	43	18	3	2	11	6	13.4	3.35	115	.289	.346	1	.091	-1	2	2	-0	0.1
	Yr	6	8	.429	35	14	7	0	1	170	176	74	7	3	53	57	12.3	3.18	117	.271	.329	8	.145	-1	14	11	0	0.7
1940	Cin-N	1	0	1.000	20	0	0	0	0	54^1	56	35	3	0	18	17	12.3	5.63	67	.268	.326	2	.125	-1	-11	-11	-1	-0.7
Total	7	25	26	.490	134	51	22	2	3	577	647	331	34	12	214	180	13.6	4.59	85	.287	.352	32	.156	-0	-35	-44	-2	-2.9
● **ERNIE SHORE**	Shore, Ernest Grady b: 3/24/1891, East Bend, N.C. d: 9/24/80, Winston-Salem, N.C. BR/TR, 6'4", 220 lbs. Deb: 6/20/12																											
1912	NY-N	0	0	—	1	0	0	0	1	1	8	10	1	0	1	1	81.0	27.00	13	.667	.692	0	—	0	-3	-3	-0	-0.4
1914	Bos-A	10	5	.667	20	16	10	1	1	139^2	103	45	1	5	34	51	9.2	2.00	135	.204	.261	5	.102	-3	12	11	2	1.1
1915	*Bos-A	19	8	.704	38	32	17	4	0	247	207	75	3	4	66	102	10.1	1.64	169	.228	.283	8	.101	-3	36	33	4	3.7
1916	*Bos-A	16	10	.615	38	28	10	3	1	225^2	221	83	1	4	49	62	10.9	2.63	105	.259	.302	7	.091	-5	5	4	5	0.4
1917	Bos-A	13	10	.565	29	27	14	1	1	226^2	201	76	1	12	55	57	10.6	2.22	116	.240	.297	13	.167	-1	11	9	3	1.1
1919	NY-A	5	8	.385	20	13	3	0	0	95	105	50	4	1	44	24	14.2	4.17	77	.288	.366	4	.143	-2	-10	-10	0	-1.4
1920	NY-A	2	2	.500	14	5	2	0	1	44^1	61	31	1	1	21	12	16.8	4.87	78	.333	.405	2	.182	0	-5	-5	1	-0.4
Total	7	65	43	.602	160	121	56	9	5	979^1	906	370	12	27	270	309	11.1	2.47	113	.247	.304	39	.121	-14	45	37	14	4.1
● **RAY SHORE**	Shore, Raymond Everett b: 6/9/21, Cincinnati, Ohio d: 8/13/96, St.Louis, Mo. BR/TR, 6'3", 210 lbs. Deb: 9/21/46 C																											
1946	StL-A	0	0	—	1	0	0	0	0	1	3	2	0	0	1	1	36.0	18.00	21	.500	.571	0	—	0	-2	-1	0	-0.1
1948	StL-A	1	2	.333	17	4	0	0	0	38	40	30	2	4	35	12	18.7	6.39	71	.270	.422	0	.000	-1	-9	-7	0	-0.6
1949	StL-A	0	1	.000	13	0	0	0	0	23^1	27	30	3	2	31	13	23.1	10.80	42	.297	.484	0	.000	-1	-17	-15	1	-0.7
Total	3	1	3	.250	31	4	0	0	0	62^1	70	62	5	6	67	26	20.6	8.23	55	.286	.450	0	.000	-2	-28	-24	1	-1.4
● **BILL SHORES**	Shores, William David b: 5/26/04, Abilene, Tex. d: 2/19/84, Purcell, Okla. BR/TR, 6', 185 lbs. Deb: 4/11/28																											
1928	Phi-A	1	1	.500	3	2	1	0	0	14	13	7	0	0	7	5	12.9	3.21	125	.250	.339	0	.000	-1	1	1	-0	0.0
1929	Phi-A	11	6	.647	39	13	5	1	7	152^2	150	71	9	3	59	49	12.5	3.60	118	.262	.334	5	.125	-2	11	11	-1	0.9

YEAR	TM/L	W	L	PCT	G	GS	CG	SH	SV	IP	H	R	HR	HB	BB	SO	RAT	ERA	ERA+	OAV	OOB	BH	AVG	PB	PR	PR+	PD	TPI
1930	*Phi-A	12	4	.750	31	19	7	1	0	159	169	86	11	3	70	48	13.7	4.19	112	.276	.353	11	.193	-2	8	9	0	0.5
1931	Phi-A	0	3	.000	6	2	0	0	0	16	26	18	3	0	10	2	20.3	5.06	89	.361	.439	1	.333	0	-1	-1	0	-0.1
1933	NY-N	2	1	.667	8	3	1	0	0	36^2	41	18	4	0	14	20	13.5	3.93	82	.291	.355	3	.273	1	-2	-3	1	0.0
1936	Chi-A	0	0	—	9	0	0	0	0	17	26	18	1	0	8	5	18.0	9.53	55	.356	.420	1	.200	-0	-8	-8	0	-0.3
Total	6	26	15	.634	96	39	14	2	7	395^1	425	218	28	6	168	129	13.6	4.17	105	.279	.353	21	.174	-4	8	8	1	1.0

● CHRIS SHORT Short, Christopher Joseph b: 9/19/37, Milford, Del. d: 8/1/91, Wilmington, Del. BR/TL, 6'4", 205 lbs. Deb: 4/19/59

YEAR	TM/L	W	L	PCT	G	GS	CG	SH	SV	IP	H	R	HR	HB	BB	SO	RAT	ERA	ERA+	OAV	OOB	BH	AVG	PB	PR	PR+	PD	TPI
1959	Phi-N	0	0	—	3	2	0	0	0	14^1	19	13	3	1	10	8	18.8	8.16	50	.317	.423	0	.000	-1	-7	-6	-0	-0.4
1960	Phi-N	6	9	.400	42	10	2	0	3	107^1	101	55	8	3	52	54	13.1	3.94	99	.249	.339	0	.000	-3	-2	-1	0	-0.4
1961	Phi-N	6	12	.333	39	16	1	0	1	127^1	157	94	12	3	71	80	16.3	5.94	69	.304	.391	6	.162	-1	-27	-26	-1	-3.3
1962	Phi-N	11	9	.550	47	12	4	0	3	142	149	66	13	8	56	91	13.5	3.42	113	.272	.348	8	.222	1	8	7	0	1.1
1963	Phi-N	9	12	.429	38	27	6	3	0	198	185	77	12	3	69	160	11.7	2.95	109	.248	.315	7	.106	-2	7	6	4	0.8
1964	Phi-N★	17	9	.654	42	31	12	4	2	220^2	174	63	10	4	51	181	9.3	2.20	158	.217	.268	7	.108	-1	33	32	-1	3.5
1965	Phi-N	18	11	.621	47	40	15	5	2	297^1	260	102	18	5	89	237	10.7	2.82	123	.235	.295	13	.131	-2	24	22	-3	1.6
1966	Phi-N	20	10	.667	42	39	19	4	0	272	257	120	28	9	68	177	11.1	3.54	102	.250	.302	22	.208	1	2	2	0	0.3
1967	Phi-N★	9	11	.450	29	26	8	2	1	199^1	163	55	9	4	74	142	10.9	2.39	142	.225	.300	6	.091	-2	22	22	0	2.1
1968	Phi-N	19	13	.594	42	36	9	2	1	269^2	236	99	25	9	81	202	10.9	2.94	102	.236	.299	12	.152	0	1	2	-1	0.2
1969	Phi-N	0	0	—	2	2	0	0	0	10	11	8	2	1	4	5	14.4	7.20	49	.282	.364	0	.000	-0	-4	-4	0	-0.2
1970	Phi-N	9	16	.360	36	34	7	2	1	199	211	100	13	6	66	133	12.8	4.30	93	.272	.334	3	.049	-5	-5	-7	-2	-1.5
1971	Phi-N	7	14	.333	31	26	5	2	1	173	182	85	22	3	63	95	12.9	3.85	92	.274	.339	4	.083	-1	-7	-6	-1	-0.9
1972	Phi-N	1	1	.500	19	0	0	0	1	23	24	12	3	0	8	20	12.5	3.91	92	.267	.327	0	—	0	-1	-1	-0	-0.1
1973	Mil-A	3	5	.375	42	7	0	0	2	72	86	42	5	2	44	44	16.5	5.13	73	.299	.395	0	—	0	-10	-11	0	-1.2
Total	15	135	132	.506	501	308	88	24	18	2325	2215	991	183	61	806	1629	11.9	3.43	103	.252	.319	88	.126	-17	33	30	-4	1.6

● BILL SHORT Short, William Ross b: 11/27/37, Kingston, N.Y. BL/TL, 5'9", 170 lbs. Deb: 4/23/60

YEAR	TM/L	W	L	PCT	G	GS	CG	SH	SV	IP	H	R	HR	HB	BB	SO	RAT	ERA	ERA+	OAV	OOB	BH	AVG	PB	PR	PR+	PD	TPI
1960	NY-A	3	5	.375	10	10	2	0	0	47	49	25	5	1	30	14	15.3	4.79	75	.282	.390	3	.200	1	-5	-7	-1	-1.0
1962	Bal-A	0	0	—	5	0	0	0	0	4	8	7	0	1	6	3	33.8	15.75	23	.381	.536	0	.000	-0	-5	-6	0	-0.3
1966	Bal-A	2	3	.400	6	6	1	1	0	37^2	34	15	2	0	10	27	10.5	2.87	116	.239	.289	1	.091	-1	2	2	1	0.2
	Bos-A	0	0	—	8	0	0	0	0	8^1	10	6	1	0	2	2	13.0	4.32	88	.294	.333	0	.000	-0	-1	-0	0	0.0
	Yr	2	3	.400	14	6	1	1	0	46	44	21	3	0	12	29	11.0	3.13	109	.250	.298	1	.083	-1	2	1	1	0.2
1967	Pit-N	0	0	—	6	0	0	0	1	2^1	1	1	0	0	1	1	7.7	3.86	87	.143	.250	0	.000	-0	-0	-0	0	0.0
1968	NY-N	0	3	.000	34	0	0	0	1	30^1	24	17	0	1	14	24	11.6	4.75	64	.220	.315	0	.000	-0	-6	-6	1	-0.5
1969	Cin-N	0	0	—	4	0	0	0	0	2^1	4	4	0	0	1	0	19.3	15.43	24	.400	.455	0	.000	-0	-3	-3	-0	-0.2
Total	6	5	11	.313	73	16	3	1	2	132	130	75	8	3	64	71	13.4	4.70	73	.262	.349	4	.125	-1	-18	-19	2	-1.8

● CLYDE SHOUN Shoun, Clyde Mitchell "Hardrock" b: 3/20/12, Mountain City, Tenn. d: 3/20/68, Mountain Home, Tenn. BL/TL, 6'1", 188 lbs. Deb: 8/7/35

YEAR	TM/L	W	L	PCT	G	GS	CG	SH	SV	IP	H	R	HR	HB	BB	SO	RAT	ERA	ERA+	OAV	OOB	BH	AVG	PB	PR	PR+	PD	TPI
1935	Chi-N	1	0	1.000	5	1	0	0	0	12^2	14	4	2	0	5	5	13.5	2.84	138	.298	.365	0	.000	-0	2	2	-0	0.0
1936	Chi-N	0	0	—	4	0	0	0	0	4^1	3	6	0	0	6	1	18.7	12.46	32	.200	.429	0	—	0	-4	-4	0	-0.2
1937	Chi-N	7	7	.500	37	9	2	0	0	93	118	65	9	0	45	43	15.8	5.61	71	.309	.382	4	.138	-1	-18	-17	-1	-2.3
1938	StL-N	6	6	.500	40	12	3	0	1	117^1	130	58	8	1	43	37	13.3	4.14	96	.283	.345	8	.258	0	-5	-2	-1	-0.3
1939	StL-N	3	1	.750	**53**	2	0	0	**9**	103	98	51	4	2	42	50	12.4	3.76	109	.248	.323	3	.115	-1	2	**4**	-1	0.1
1940	StL-N	13	11	.542	**54**	19	13	1	5	197^1	193	96	13	2	46	82	11.0	3.92	102	.255	.299	12	.190	-1	-2	1	-0	0.0
1941	StL-N	3	5	.375	26	6	0	0	0	70	98	48	9	0	20	34	15.2	5.66	67	.337	.379	4	.182	0	-16	-14	1	-1.3
1942	StL-N	0	0	—	2	0	0	0	0	1^2	1	0	0	0	0	0	5.4	0.00	—	.167	.167	0	—	0	1	1	-0	0.0
	Cin-N	1	3	.250	34	0	0	0	0	72^2	55	23	2	0	24	32	9.8	2.23	147	.216	.283	4	.308	1	9	9	1	0.6
	Yr	1	3	.250	36	0	0	0	0	74^1	56	23	2	0	24	32	9.7	2.18	151	.215	.281	4	.308	1	9	9	1	0.6
1943	Cin-N	14	5	.737	45	5	2	0	7	147	131	52	5	0	46	61	10.8	3.06	108	.241	.300	13	.310	4	5	4	1	1.0
1944	Cin-N	13	10	.565	38	21	12	1	2	202^2	193	83	10	3	42	55	10.6	3.02	116	.248	.290	15	.224	1	13	11	-3	1.0
1946	Cin-N	1	6	.143	27	5	0	0	0	79	87	42	3	1	26	20	13.0	4.10	82	.292	.351	2	.095	-1	-6	-7	-2	-0.9
1947	Cin-N	0	0	—	10	0	0	0	0	14^1	16	8	2	1	5	7	13.8	5.02	82	.320	.393	0	—	0	-2	-1	0	0.0
	Bos-N	5	3	.625	26	3	1	1	1	73^2	73	41	6	0	21	23	11.5	4.40	89	.254	.305	3	.158	-1	-3	-4	-1	-0.6
	Yr	5	3	.625	36	3	1	1	1	88	89	49	8	1	26	30	11.9	4.50	87	.264	.319	3	.158	-1	-4	-6	-1	-0.6
1948	Bos-N	5	1	.833	36	2	1	0	4	74	77	37	7	0	20	25	11.8	4.01	96	.267	.315	4	.190	0	-0	-2	-2	-0.3
1949	Bos-N	0	0	—	1	0	0	0	0	1	1	0	0	0	0	0	9.0	0.00	—	.250	.250	0	—	0	0	0	-0	0.0
	Chi-A	1	1	.500	16	0	0	0	0	23^1	37	17	1	0	13	8	19.3	5.79	72	.370	.442	1	.200	0	-4	-4	0	-0.3
Total	14	73	59	.553	454	85	34	3	29	1287	1325	631	81	10	404	483	12.2	3.91	96	.267	.324	73	.202	1	-27	-25	-9	-3.5

● BRIAN SHOUSE Shouse, Brian Douglas b: 9/26/68, Effingham, Ill. BL/TL, 5'11", 180 lbs. Deb: 7/31/93

YEAR	TM/L	W	L	PCT	G	GS	CG	SH	SV	IP	H	R	HR	HB	BB	SO	RAT	ERA	ERA+	OAV	OOB	BH	AVG	PB	PR	PR+	PD	TPI
1993	Pit-N	0	0	—	6	0	0	0	0	4	7	4	1	0	2	3	20.3	9.00	45	.368	.429	0	—	0	-2	-2	0	-0.1
1998	Bos-A	0	1	.000	7	0	0	0	0	8	9	5	2	0	4	5	14.6	5.63	84	.281	.361	0	—	0	-1	-1	0	-0.1
Total	2	0	1	.000	13	0	0	0	0	12	16	9	3	0	6	8	16.5	6.75	67	.314	.386	0	—	0	-3	-3	0	-0.2

● ERIC SHOW Show, Eric Vaughn b: 5/19/56, Riverside, Cal. d: 3/16/94, Dulzura, Cal. BR/TR, 6'1", 185 lbs. Deb: 9/2/81

YEAR	TM/L	W	L	PCT	G	GS	CG	SH	SV	IP	H	R	HR	HB	BB	SO	RAT	ERA	ERA+	OAV	OOB	BH	AVG	PB	PR	PR+	PD	TPI
1981	SD-N	1	3	.250	15	0	0	0	3	23	17	9	2	1	9	22	10.6	3.13	104	.213	.300	0	—	0	1	0	0	0.1
1982	SD-N	10	6	.625	47	14	2	2	3	150	117	49	10	5	48	88	10.2	2.64	130	.217	.287	6	.146	-1	16	14	2	1.6
1983	SD-N	15	12	.556	35	33	4	2	0	200^2	201	97	25	6	74	120	12.6	4.17	84	.263	.333	11	.172	1	-12	-16	-2	-2.0
1984	*SD-N	15	9	.625	32	32	3	1	0	206^2	175	88	18	4	88	104	11.6	3.40	105	.234	.317	17	.246	6	5	4	-1	1.1
1985	SD-N	12	11	.522	35	35	5	2	0	233	212	95	27	5	87	141	11.7	3.09	115	.243	.316	10	.127	-1	13	12	-3	0.7
1986	SD-N	9	5	.643	24	22	2	0	0	136^1	109	47	11	4	69	94	12.0	2.97	123	.225	.326	7	.163	1	11	11	-2	0.9
1987	SD-N	8	16	.333	34	34	5	3	0	206^1	188	99	26	9	85	117	12.3	3.84	103	.241	.323	5	.071	-4	6	3	-1	-0.2
1988	SD-N	16	11	.593	32	32	13	1	0	234^2	201	86	22	6	53	144	10.0	3.26	104	.231	.280	12	.148	-0	5	4	-4	-0.1
1989	SD-N	8	6	.571	16	16	1	0	0	106^1	113	59	9	2	39	66	13.0	4.23	83	.274	.340	8	.235	2	-9	-9	-1	-1.0
1990	SD-N	6	8	.429	39	12	0	0	1	106^1	131	74	16	4	41	55	14.9	5.76	67	.306	.372	5	.200	1	-23	-23	-1	-2.7
1991	Oak-A	1	2	.333	23	5	0	0	0	51^2	62	36	5	0	17	20	13.8	5.92	65	.298	.351	0	—	0	-10	-13	-1	-0.8
Total	11	101	89	.532	332	235	35	11	7	1655	1526	739	171	46	610	971	11.9	3.66	98	.247	.319	81	.160	3	3	-12	-13	-2.4

● LEV SHREVE Shreve, Leven Lawrence b: 1/14/1869, Louisville, Ky. d: 10/18/42, Detroit, Mich. BR/TR, 5'11", 150 lbs. Deb: 5/2/1887

YEAR	TM/L	W	L	PCT	G	GS	CG	SH	SV	IP	H	R	HR	HB	BB	SO	RAT	ERA	ERA+	OAV	OOB	BH	AVG	PB	PR	PR+	PD	TPI
1887	Bal-a	3	1	.750	5	5	4	1	0	38	52	26	0	1	19	13	12.6	3.79	108	.317	.321	5	.200	-1	2	1	0	0.0
	Ind-N	5	9	.357	14	14	14	1	0	122	206	100	5	4	65	22	15.5	4.72	88	.349	.365	16	.308	0	-9	-8	-2	-0.8
1888	Ind-N	11	24	.314	35	35	34	1	0	297^2	352	208	23	8	93	101	13.7	4.63	64	.288	.342	21	.183	-1	-59	-53	0	-5.2
1889	Ind-N	0	3	.000	3	3	1	0	0	15^2	25	27	3	1	12	5	21.8	13.79	30	.352	.452	0	.000	-1	-17	-16	0	-1.8
Total	3	19	37	.339	57	57	53	3	0	473^1	635	361	31	14	189	141	14.3	4.89	70	.313	.351	42	.211	-3	-82	-76	-1	-7.8

● HARRY SHRIVER Shriver, Harry Graydon "Pop" b: 9/2/1896, Wadestown, W.Va. d: 1/21/70, Morgantown, W.Va. BR/TR, 6'2", 180 lbs. Deb: 4/14/22

YEAR	TM/L	W	L	PCT	G	GS	CG	SH	SV	IP	H	R	HR	HB	BB	SO	RAT	ERA	ERA+	OAV	OOB	BH	AVG	PB	PR	PR+	PD	TPI
1922	Bro-N	4	6	.400	25	13	4	2	0	108^1	114	49	5	2	48	38	13.6	2.99	136	.287	.367	1	.037	-3	13	13	-2	0.5
1923	Bro-N	0	0	—	1	1	0	0	0	4	8	3	0	0	0	1	18.0	6.75	58	.444	.444	0	.000	-0	-1	-1	-0	-0.1
Total	2	4	6	.400	26	14	4	2	0	112^1	122	52	5	2	48	39	13.8	3.12	130	.294	.370	1	.036	-3	12	12	-3	0.4

● PAUL SHUEY Shuey, Paul Kenneth b: 9/16/70, Lima, Ohio BR/TR, 6'3", 215 lbs. Deb: 5/8/94

YEAR	TM/L	W	L	PCT	G	GS	CG	SH	SV	IP	H	R	HR	HB	BB	SO	RAT	ERA	ERA+	OAV	OOB	BH	AVG	PB	PR	PR+	PD	TPI
1994	Cle-A	0	1	.000	14	0	0	0	5	11^2	14	11	1	0	12	16	20.1	8.49	56	.280	.419	0	—	0	-5	-5	-0	-0.7
1995	Cle-A	0	2	.000	7	0	0	0	0	6^1	5	4	0	0	5	5	14.2	4.26	110	.238	.385	0	—	0	0	0	0	0.1
1996	*Cle-A	5	2	.714	42	0	0	0	4	53^2	45	19	6	0	26	44	11.9	2.85	172	.231	.321	0	—	0	13	12	-0	1.5
1997	Cle-A	4	2	.667	40	0	0	0	2	45	52	31	5	1	28	46	16.2	6.20	76	.294	.393	0	.000	-0	-8	-7	1	-0.8
1998	*Cle-A	5	4	.556	43	0	0	0	2	51	44	19	6	3	25	58	12.7	3.00	159	.229	.327	0	.000	-0	9	10	-0	1.5
1999	*Cle-A	8	5	.615	72	0	0	0	6	81^2	68	37	8	1	40	103	12.0	3.53	143	.223	.315	0	—	0	12	13	0	2.0
2000	Cle-A	4	2	.667	57	0	0	0	0	63^2	51	25	4	3	30	69	11.9	3.39	147	.219	.316	0	—	0	11	11	1	0.9
Total	7	26	18	.591	275	0	0	0	19	313	279	146	30	8	166	341	13.0	3.88	126	.238	.336	0	.000	-0	33	35	1	4.5

● TOOTS SHULTZ Shultz, Wallace Luther b: 10/10/1888, Homestead, Pa. d: 1/30/59, McKeesport, Pa. BR/TR, 5'10", 175 lbs. Deb: 5/5/11

YEAR	TM/L	W	L	PCT	G	GS	CG	SH	SV	IP	H	R	HR	HB	BB	SO	RAT	ERA	ERA+	OAV	OOB	BH	AVG	PB	PR	PR+	PD	TPI
1911	Phi-N	0	3	.000	5	3	2	0	0	25	30	28	5	4	15	9	17.6	9.36	37	.300	.412	2	.250	0	-17	-16	0	-1.5

YEAR	TM/L	W	L	PCT	G	GS	CG	SH	SV	IP	H	R	HR	HB	BB	SO	RAT	ERA	ERA+	OAV	OOB	BH	AVG	PB	PR	PR+	PD	TPI
1912	Phi-N	1	4	.200	22	4	1	0	1	59	75	44	2	3	35	20	17.2	4.58	79	.333	.430	5	.238	0	-8	-6	0	-0.4
Total	2	1	7	.125	27	7	3	0	1	84	105	72	7	7	50	29	17.4	6.00	60	.323	.424	7	.241	0	-24	-22	1	-1.9

● ANTHONY SHUMAKER Shumaker, Anthony Warren b: 5/14/73, Tucson, Ariz. BL/TL, 6'5", 225 lbs. Deb: 7/23/99

YEAR	TM/L	W	L	PCT	G	GS	CG	SH	SV	IP	H	R	HR	HB	BB	SO	RAT	ERA	ERA+	OAV	OOB	BH	AVG	PB	PR	PR+	PD	TPI
1999	Phi-N	0	3	.000	8	4	0	0	0	22^2	23	17	3	1	14	17	15.1	5.96	79	.261	.369	1	.200	0	-4	-3	0	-0.3

● HARRY SHUMAN Shuman, Harry b: 3/5/15, Philadelphia, Pa. d: 10/25/96, Philadelphia, Pa. BR/TR, 6'2", 195 lbs. Deb: 9/14/42

YEAR	TM/L	W	L	PCT	G	GS	CG	SH	SV	IP	H	R	HR	HB	BB	SO	RAT	ERA	ERA+	OAV	OOB	BH	AVG	PB	PR	PR+	PD	TPI
1942	Pit-N	0	0	—	1	0	0	0	0	2	0	0	0	0	1	1	4.5	0.00	—	.000	.167	0	—	0	1	1	-0	0.0
1943	Pit-N	0	0	—	11	0	0	0	0	22	30	20	0	2	8	5	16.4	5.32	65	.337	.404	0	.000	-0	-5	-4	0	-0.2
1944	Phi-N	0	0	—	18	0	0	0	0	26^2	26	15	1	0	11	4	12.5	4.05	89	.245	.316	0	.000	-0	-1	-1	0	-0.1
Total	3	0	0	—	30	0	0	0	0	50^2	56	35	1	2	20	10	13.9	4.44	80	.280	.351	0	.000	-0	-5	-5	0	-0.3

● PAUL SIEBERT Siebert, Paul Edward b: 6/5/53, Minneapolis, Minn. BL/TL, 6'2", 205 lbs. Deb: 9/7/74 F

YEAR	TM/L	W	L	PCT	G	GS	CG	SH	SV	IP	H	R	HR	HB	BB	SO	RAT	ERA	ERA+	OAV	OOB	BH	AVG	PB	PR	PR+	PD	TPI
1974	Hou-N	1	1	.500	5	5	1	1	0	25^1	21	12	3	0	11	10	11.4	3.55	98	.236	.320	0	.000	-1	0	-0	1	0.0
1975	Hou-N	0	2	.000	7	2	0	0	2	18^1	20	7	0	1	6	6	13.3	2.95	115	.294	.360	0	.000	-0	1	1	0	0.1
1976	Hou-N	0	2	.000	19	0	0	0	2	25^2	29	10	0	1	18	10	16.8	3.16	101	.296	.410	0	.000	-0	1	0	-1	-0.1
1977	SD-N	0	0	—	4	0	0	0	0	3^2	3	4	1	0	4	1	17.2	2.45	144	.214	.389	0	—	0	1	0	-0	0.0
	NY-N	2	1	.667	25	0	0	0	0	28	27	12	0	1	13	20	13.2	3.86	97	.257	.345	0	.000	-0	0	-0	-0	-0.1
	Yr	2	1	.667	29	0	0	0	0	31^2	30	16	1	1	17	21	13.6	3.69	101	.252	.350	0	.000	-0	1	0	-0	-0.1
1978	NY-N	0	2	.000	27	0	0	0	1	28	30	16	2	1	21	12	16.7	5.14	68	.283	.406	0	.000	-0	-5	-5	0	-0.4
Total	5	3	8	.273	87	7	1	1	3	129	130	61	6	4	73	59	14.4	3.77	92	.271	.372	0	.000	-2	-1	-5	0	-0.5

● SONNY SIEBERT Siebert, Wilfred Charles b: 1/14/37, St.Marys, Mo. BR/TR, 6'3", 198 lbs. Deb: 4/26/64 C

YEAR	TM/L	W	L	PCT	G	GS	CG	SH	SV	IP	H	R	HR	HB	BB	SO	RAT	ERA	ERA+	OAV	OOB	BH	AVG	PB	PR	PR+	PD	TPI
1964	Cle-A	7	9	.438	41	14	3	1	3	156	142	61	15	2	57	144	11.6	3.23	111	.243	.313	13	.265	5	7	6	-2	1.1
1965	Cle-A	16	8	.667	39	27	4	1	1	188^2	139	58	14	5	46	191	9.1	2.43	143	.206	**.262**	7	.106	-2	22	22	1	2.7
1966	Cle-A★	16	8	**.667**	34	32	11	1	1	241	193	89	25	6	62	163	9.7	2.80	123	.221	.278	11	.129	-2	17	17	2	1.7
1967	Cle-A	10	12	.455	34	26	7	1	4	185^1	136	59	17	6	54	136	9.5	2.38	137	.202	.268	7	.135	1	18	18	-2	2.2
1968	Cle-A	12	10	.545	31	30	8	4	0	206	145	76	12	8	88	146	10.5	2.97	100	.198	.290	11	.157	1	0	-0	1	0.2
1969	Cle-A	0	1	.000	2	2	0	0	0	14	10	5	1	0	8	6	11.6	3.21	117	.196	.305	1	.250	0	1	1	-0	0.1
	Bos-A	14	10	.583	43	22	2	0	5	163^1	151	93	21	4	68	127	12.3	3.80	100	.245	.324	8	.151	1	-3	0	2	0.3
	Yr	14	11	.560	45	24	2	0	5	177^1	161	98	22	4	76	133	12.2	3.76	101	.241	.322	9	.158	1	-3	1	2	0.4
1970	Bos-A	15	8	.652	33	33	7	2	0	222^2	207	98	29	6	60	142	11.0	3.44	115	.248	.303	10	.130	-2	7	12	0	1.0
1971	Bos-A☆	16	10	.615	32	32	12	4	0	235^1	220	84	20	3	60	131	10.8	2.91	127	.245	.294	21	.266	10	15	19	1	3.4
1972	Bos-A	12	12	.500	32	30	7	3	0	196^1	204	105	17	7	59	123	12.4	3.80	85	.264	.322	17	.236	6	-16	-12	1	-0.7
1973	Bos-A	0	1	.000	2	0	0	0	0	2^1	5	2	1	0	1	5	23.1	7.71	52	.417	.462	0	—	0	-1	-1	0	-0.2
	Tex-A	7	11	.389	25	20	1	1	2	119^2	120	68	11	3	37	76	12.0	3.99	93	.258	.317	0	—	0	-2	-4	2	-0.3
	Yr	7	12	.368	27	20	1	1	2	122	125	70	12	3	38	81	12.2	4.06	92	.262	.320	0	—	0	-3	-5	2	-0.5
1974	StL-N	8	8	.500	28	20	5	3	0	133^2	150	66	8	3	51	68	13.7	3.84	93	.288	.355	5	.114	-2	-3	-4	-1	-0.7
1975	SD-N	3	2	.600	6	6	0	0	0	26^2	37	15	2	1	10	10	16.2	4.39	79	.330	.390	3	.375	2	-2	-3	0	-0.3
	Oak-A	4	4	.500	17	13	0	0	0	61	60	28	4	0	31	44	13.4	3.69	99	.252	.338	0	.000	-0	1	-0	-1	-0.1
Total	12	140	114	.551	399	307	67	21	16	2152	1919	907	197	54	692	1512	11.1	3.21	110	.238	.303	114	.173	18	58	73	5	10.4

● DWIGHT SIEBLER Siebler, Dwight Leroy b: 8/5/37, Columbus, Neb. BR/TR, 6'2", 184 lbs. Deb: 8/26/63

YEAR	TM/L	W	L	PCT	G	GS	CG	SH	SV	IP	H	R	HR	HB	BB	SO	RAT	ERA	ERA+	OAV	OOB	BH	AVG	PB	PR	PR+	PD	TPI
1963	Min-A	2	1	.667	7	5	2	0	0	38^2	25	13	6	1	12	22	8.8	2.79	130	.182	.253	2	.133	-0	4	4	-1	0.1
1964	Min-A	0	0	—	9	0	0	0	0	11	10	6	1	0	6	10	13.1	4.91	73	.256	.356	0	—	0	-2	-2	-0	-0.1
1965	Min-A	0	0	—	7	1	0	0	0	15	11	7	2	0	11	15	13.2	4.20	85	.193	.324	0	.000	-0	-1	-1	0	-0.1
1966	Min-A	2	2	.500	23	2	0	0	1	49^2	47	26	6	1	14	24	11.2	3.44	104	.253	.308	0	.000	-1	-0	1	-1	-0.1
1967	Min-A	0	0	—	2	0	0	0	0	3	4	1	0	0	1	0	15.0	3.00	115	.364	.417	0	—	0	0	0	-0	0.0
Total	5	4	3	.571	48	8	2	0	1	117^1	97	53	15	2	44	71	11.0	3.45	104	.226	.300	2	.074	-1	1	2	-2	-0.2

● CANDY SIERRA Sierra, Ulises (Pizarro) b: 3/27/67, Rio Piedras, P.R. BR/TR, 6'2", 190 lbs. Deb: 4/6/88

YEAR	TM/L	W	L	PCT	G	GS	CG	SH	SV	IP	H	R	HR	HB	BB	SO	RAT	ERA	ERA+	OAV	OOB	BH	AVG	PB	PR	PR+	PD	TPI
1988	SD-N	0	1	.000	15	0	0	0	0	23^2	36	15	2	0	11	20	17.9	5.70	60	.379	.443	0	.000	-0	-6	-6	-0	-0.4
	Cin-N	0	0	—	1	0	0	0	0	4	5	2	0	0	1	4	13.5	4.50	80	.294	.333	0	.000	-0	-0	-0	0	0.0
	Yr	0	1	.000	16	0	0	0	0	27^2	41	17	2	0	12	24	17.2	5.53	62	.366	.427	0	.000	-0	-6	-7	-0	-0.4

● ED SIEVER Siever, Edward Tilden b: 4/2/1877, Goddard, Kan. d: 2/4/20, Detroit, Mich. BL/TL, 5'11.5", 190 lbs. Deb: 4/26/01

YEAR	TM/L	W	L	PCT	G	GS	CG	SH	SV	IP	H	R	HR	HB	BB	SO	RAT	ERA	ERA+	OAV	OOB	BH	AVG	PB	PR	PR+	PD	TPI
1901	Det-A	18	14	.563	38	33	30	2	0	288^2	334	166	9	8	65	85	12.7	3.24	119	.286	.328	18	.168	-5	14	19	-1	1.1
1902	Det-A	8	11	.421	25	23	17	4	1	188^1	166	73	0	2	32	36	9.6	**1.91**	**191**	.237	.272	10	.152	-4	35	36	-4	2.5
1903	StL-A	13	14	.481	31	27	24	1	0	254	245	102	6	5	39	90	10.2	2.48	117	.253	.285	13	.140	-4	14	12	2	1.1
1904	StL-A	10	15	.400	29	24	19	2	0	217	235	112	3	3	65	77	12.6	2.65	93	.277	.330	11	.155	-1	-1	-4	1	-0.6
1906	Det-A	14	11	.560	30	25	20	1	0	222^2	240	95	5	10	45	71	11.9	2.71	102	.278	.321	12	.156	-3	-0	1	-2	-0.4
1907	*Det-A	18	11	.621	39	33	22	3	1	274^2	256	89	1	11	52	88	10.5	2.16	120	.249	.293	15	.160	-3	12	13	-3	0.7
1908	Det-A	2	6	.250	11	9	4	1	0	61^2	74	37	0	0	13	23	12.7	3.50	69	.302	.337	3	.167	-1	-8	-7	-1	-1.1
Total	7	83	82	.503	203	174	136	14	2	1507	1550	674	24	39	311	470	11.3	2.60	116	.266	.308	82	.156	-21	64	69	-8	3.3

● WALTER SIGNER Signer, Walter Donald Aloysius b: 10/12/10, New York, N.Y. d: 7/23/74, Greenwich, Conn. BR/TR, 6', 185 lbs. Deb: 9/18/43

YEAR	TM/L	W	L	PCT	G	GS	CG	SH	SV	IP	H	R	HR	HB	BB	SO	RAT	ERA	ERA+	OAV	OOB	BH	AVG	PB	PR	PR+	PD	TPI
1943	Chi-N	2	1	.667	4	2	1	0	0	25	24	8	3	0	4	5	10.1	2.88	116	.245	.275	2	.250	0	1	1	-0	0.2
1945	Chi-N	0	0	—	6	0	0	0	1	8	11	6	1	0	5	0	18.0	3.38	108	.256	.333	0	.000	-0	0	0	-0	0.0
Total	2	2	1	.667	10	2	1	0	1	33	35	14	4	0	9	5	12.0	3.00	114	.248	.293	2	.222	0	2	2	-0	0.2

● SETH SIGSBY Sigsby, Seth De Witt (b: Seth De Witt) b: 4/30/1874, Cobleskill, N.Y. d: 9/15/53, Schenectady, N.Y 6', 175 lbs. Deb: 6/27/1893

YEAR	TM/L	W	L	PCT	G	GS	CG	SH	SV	IP	H	R	HR	HB	BB	SO	RAT	ERA	ERA+	OAV	OOB	BH	AVG	PB	PR	PR+	PD	TPI
1893	NY-N	0	0	—	1	0	0	0	0	3	1	4	0	1	4	2	18.0	9.00	52	.100	.400	0	.000	-0	-1	-1	-0	-0.1

● BRIAN SIKORSKI Sikorski, Brian Patrick b: 7/27/74, Detroit, Mich. BR/TR, 6'1", 190 lbs. Deb: 8/16/2000

YEAR	TM/L	W	L	PCT	G	GS	CG	SH	SV	IP	H	R	HR	HB	BB	SO	RAT	ERA	ERA+	OAV	OOB	BH	AVG	PB	PR	PR+	PD	TPI
2000	Tex-A	1	3	.250	10	5	0	0	0	37^2	46	31	9	3	25	32	17.2	5.73	89	.287	.387	0	—	0	-3	-3	-1	-0.3

● JOSE SILVA Silva, Jose Leonel b: 12/19/73, Tijuana, Mex. BR/TR, 6'5", 210 lbs. Deb: 9/10/96

YEAR	TM/L	W	L	PCT	G	GS	CG	SH	SV	IP	H	R	HR	HB	BB	SO	RAT	ERA	ERA+	OAV	OOB	BH	AVG	PB	PR	PR+	PD	TPI
1996	Tor-A	0	0	—	2	0	0	0	0	2	5	3	1	0	0	0	22.5	13.50	37	.455	.455	0	—	0	-2	-2	0	-0.1
1997	Pit-N	2	1	.667	11	4	0	0	0	36^1	52	26	4	1	16	30	17.1	5.94	72	.347	.413	1	.143	-0	-7	-7	-1	-0.6
1998	Pit-N	6	7	.462	18	18	1	0	0	100^1	104	55	7	1	30	64	12.1	4.40	98	.271	.325	1	.037	-1	-2	-1	0	-0.2
1999	Pit-N	2	8	.200	34	12	0	0	4	97^1	108	70	10	3	39	77	13.9	5.73	80	.281	.351	2	.100	-1	-13	-13	1	-1.2
2000	Pit-N	11	9	.550	51	19	1	0	0	136	178	96	16	5	50	98	15.4	5.56	83	.317	.378	6	.176	0	-14	-15	-1	-1.9
Total	5	21	25	.457	116	53	2	0	4	372	447	250	38	10	135	269	14.3	5.37	84	.300	.362	10	.114	-2	-37	-36	-0	-4.0

● AL SIMA Sima, Albert b: 10/7/21, Mahwah, N.J. d: 8/17/93, Suffern, N.Y. BR/TL, 6', 187 lbs. Deb: 6/28/50

YEAR	TM/L	W	L	PCT	G	GS	CG	SH	SV	IP	H	R	HR	HB	BB	SO	RAT	ERA	ERA+	OAV	OOB	BH	AVG	PB	PR	PR+	PD	TPI
1950	Was-A	4	5	.444	17	9	1	0	0	77	89	49	9	1	26	23	13.6	4.79	94	.291	.348	3	.115	-2	-2	-3	-1	-0.6
1951	Was-A	3	7	.300	18	8	1	0	0	77	79	51	5	0	41	26	14.0	4.79	85	.261	.349	3	.176	1	-6	-6	-1	-0.6
1953	Was-A	2	3	.400	31	5	1	0	1	68^1	63	31	7	3	31	25	12.8	3.42	114	.249	.338	2	.118	-1	4	4	1	0.3
1954	Chi-A	0	1	.000	5	1	0	0	1	7	11	5	1	0	2	1	16.7	5.14	73	.393	.433	0	.000	-0	-1	-1	0	-0.2
	Phi-A	2	5	.286	29	7	1	0	2	79^1	101	51	9	0	32	36	15.1	5.22	75	.309	.370	1	.050	-2	-13	-11	-1	-1.2
	Yr	2	6	.250	34	8	1	0	3	86^1	112	56	10	0	34	37	15.2	5.21	75	.315	.375	1	.045	-2	-14	-12	-1	-1.4
Total	4	11	21	.344	100	30	4	0	4	308^2	343	187	31	4	132	111	14.0	4.61	89	.282	.354	9	.110	-5	-18	-17	-2	-2.3

● BILL SIMAS Simas, William Anthony b: 11/28/71, Hanford, Cal. BL/TR, 6'3", 220 lbs. Deb: 8/15/95

YEAR	TM/L	W	L	PCT	G	GS	CG	SH	SV	IP	H	R	HR	HB	BB	SO	RAT	ERA	ERA+	OAV	OOB	BH	AVG	PB	PR	PR+	PD	TPI
1995	Chi-A	1	1	.500	14	0	0	0	0	14	15	5	1	1	10	16	16.7	2.57	173	.273	.394	0	—	0	3	3	-0	0.3
1996	Chi-A	2	8	.200	64	0	0	0	2	72^2	75	39	5	3	39	65	14.5	4.58	104	.265	.360	0	—	0	3	1	-0	0.1
1997	Chi-A	3	1	.750	40	0	0	0	1	41^1	46	23	6	2	24	38	15.7	4.14	106	.279	.377	0	—	0	2	1	-0	0.1
1998	Chi-A	4	3	.571	60	0	0	0	18	70^2	54	29	12	1	22	56	9.8	3.57	128	.206	.270	0	—	0	9	8	-0	1.0
1999	Chi-A	6	3	.667	70	0	0	0	2	72	73	36	6	6	32	41	13.9	3.75	130	.263	.351	0	—	0	9	9	-0	1.0
2000	*Chi-A	2	3	.400	60	0	0	0	0	67^2	69	27	9	1	22	49	12.2	3.46	144	.276	.337	0	—	0	11	11	-0	0.7
Total	6	18	19	.486	308	0	0	0	23	338^1	332	159	39	14	149	265	13.2	3.83	123	.257	.340	0	—	0	37	34	-2	3.2

● CURT SIMMONS Simmons, Curtis Thomas b: 5/19/29, Egypt, Pa. BL/TL, 6', 187 lbs. Deb: 9/28/47

YEAR	TM/L	W	L	PCT	G	GS	CG	SH	SV	IP	H	R	HR	HB	BB	SO	RAT	ERA	ERA+	OAV	OOB	BH	AVG	PB	PR	PR+	PD	TPI
1947	Phi-N	1	0	1.000	1	1	1	0	0	9	5	1	0	0	6	9	11.0	1.00	401	.161	.297	1	.500	0	3	3	-0	0.4
1948	Phi-N	7	13	.350	31	22	7	0	0	170	169	110	8	2	108	86	14.8	4.87	81	.266	.374	7	.137	-1	-17	-18	1	-1.8
1949	Phi-N	4	10	.286	38	14	2	0	1	131^1	133	72	7	1	55	83	13.0	4.59	86	.275	.350	7	.171	-1	-8	-10	-0	-1.0
1950	Phi-N	17	8	.680	31	27	11	2	1	214^2	178	93	19	2	88	146	11.2	3.40	119	.223	.302	12	.156	-1	18	16	-0	1.6
1952	Phi-N★	14	8	.636	28	28	15	**6**	0	201^1	170	72	11	1	70	141	10.8	2.82	130	.227	.294	11	.164	2	20	19	-3	2.0
1953	Phi-N★	16	13	.552	32	30	19	4	0	238	211	102	17	3	82	138	11.2	3.21	131	.236	.302	13	.140	-3	28	27	-3	2.4
1954	Phi-N	14	15	.483	34	33	21	3	1	253	226	101	14	5	98	125	11.7	2.81	144	.239	.314	16	.176	-1	35	35	-3	3.3
1955	Phi-N	8	8	.500	25	22	3	0	0	130	148	76	15	3	50	58	13.9	4.92	81	.290	.356	8	.174	-1	-13	-14	-1	-1.6
1956	Phi-N	15	10	.600	33	27	14	0	0	198	186	95	17	3	65	88	11.5	3.36	111	.248	.311	17	.236	3	9	8	-1	1.3
1957	Phi-N★	12	11	.522	32	29	9	2	0	212	214	92	11	2	50	92	11.3	3.44	111	.264	.309	17	.239	4	10	9	-3	1.0
1958	Phi-N	7	14	.333	29	27	7	1	1	168^1	196	92	11	3	40	78	12.8	4.38	90	.293	.336	12	.203	0	-8	-8	-1	-1.0
1959	Phi-N	0	0	—	7	0	0	0	0	10	16	5	2	1	0	4	15.3	4.50	91	.400	.415	0	—	0	-1	-0	0	0.0
1960	Phi-N	0	0	—	4	2	0	0	0	4	13	8	3	0	6	4	42.8	18.00	22	.542	.633	0	—	0	-6	-6	1	-0.3
	StL-N	7	4	.636	23	17	3	1	0	152	149	50	11	0	31	63	10.7	2.66	154	.257	.295	10	.213	1	19	22	0	1.7
	Yr	7	4	.636	27	19	3	1	0	156	162	58	14	0	37	67	11.5	3.06	134	.269	.311	10	.213	1	12	16	1	1.4
1961	StL-N	9	10	.474	30	29	6	2	0	195^2	203	91	14	4	64	99	12.5	3.13	**141**	.269	.329	20	.303	5	20	25	-0	2.8
1962	StL-N	10	10	.500	31	22	9	4	0	154	167	78	18	3	32	74	11.8	3.51	122	.280	.320	8	.160	0	7	12	-1	1.4
1963	StL-N	15	9	.625	32	32	11	6	0	232^2	209	82	13	6	48	127	10.2	2.48	143	.239	.283	13	.160	0	21	26	-4	2.3
1964	*StL-N	18	9	.667	34	34	12	3	0	244	233	106	24	5	49	104	10.6	3.43	111	.249	.290	10	.106	-3	3	9	-1	0.6
1965	StL-N	9	15	.375	34	32	5	0	0	203	229	104	19	4	54	96	12.7	4.08	94	.283	.331	3	.047	-5	-12	-5	-2	-1.2
1966	StL-N	1	1	.500	10	5	1	0	0	33^1	35	17	3	0	14	14	13.2	4.59	78	.269	.340	1	.125	0	-4	-4	-1	-0.2
	Chi-N	4	7	.364	19	10	3	1	0	77^1	79	39	7	1	21	24	11.8	4.07	90	.268	.319	2	.111	-0	-4	-3	2	-0.4
	Yr	5	8	.385	29	15	4	1	0	110^2	114	56	10	1	35	38	12.2	4.23	86	.268	.325	3	.115	-0	-8	-7	1	-0.6
1967	Chi-N	3	7	.300	17	14	3	0	0	82	100	54	10	2	23	31	13.7	4.94	72	.300	.349	4	.143	-1	-14	-12	-0	-1.5
	Cal-A	2	1	.667	14	4	1	1	1	34^2	44	11	1	2	9	13	14.3	2.60	121	.321	.372	2	.222	1	2	2	-1	0.2
Total	20	193	183	.513	569	461	163	36	5	3348^1	3313	1551	255	53	1063	1697	11.9	3.54	111	.259	.319	194	.171	1	109	139	-21	12.0

● PAT SIMMONS Simmons, Patrick Clement (b: Patrick Clement Simoni) b: 11/29/08, Watervliet, N.Y. d: 7/3/68, Albany, N.Y. BR/TR, 5'11", 172 lbs. Deb: 4/18/28

YEAR	TM/L	W	L	PCT	G	GS	CG	SH	SV	IP	H	R	HR	HB	BB	SO	RAT	ERA	ERA+	OAV	OOB	BH	AVG	PB	PR	PR+	PD	TPI
1928	Bos-A	0	2	.000	31	3	0	0	1	69	69	38	4	1	38	16	14.1	4.04	102	.271	.367	2	.133	-1	0	**1**	-0	-0.1
1929	Bos-A	0	0	—	2	0	0	0	1	7	6	0	0	0	3	2	11.6	0.00	—	.231	.310	0	.000	-0	3	3	0	0.1
Total	2	0	2	.000	33	3	0	0	2	76	75	38	4	1	41	18	13.9	3.67	112	.267	.362	2	.125	-1	3	4	-0	0.0

● DOUG SIMONS Simons, Douglas Eugene b: 9/15/66, Bakersfield, Cal. BL/TL, 6', 170 lbs. Deb: 4/9/91

YEAR	TM/L	W	L	PCT	G	GS	CG	SH	SV	IP	H	R	HR	HB	BB	SO	RAT	ERA	ERA+	OAV	OOB	BH	AVG	PB	PR	PR+	PD	TPI
1991	NY-N	2	3	.400	42	1	0	0	1	60^2	55	40	5	2	19	38	11.3	5.19	70	.246	.310	0	.000	-0	-10	-11	2	-0.7
1992	Mon-N	0	0	—	7	0	0	0	0	5^1	15	14	3	1	2	6	30.4	23.63	15	.500	.545	0	—	0	-12	-12	-0	-0.6
Total	2	2	3	.400	49	1	0	0	1	66	70	54	8	3	21	44	12.8	6.68	54	.276	.338	0	.000	-0	-22	-23	2	-1.3

● JOE SIMPSON Simpson, Joe Allen b: 12/31/51, Purcell, Okla. BL/TL, 6'3", 175 lbs. Deb: 9/2/75 ♦

YEAR	TM/L	W	L	PCT	G	GS	CG	SH	SV	IP	H	R	HR	HB	BB	SO	RAT	ERA	ERA+	OAV	OOB	BH	AVG	PB	PR	PR+	PD	TPI
1983	KC-A	0	0	—	2	0	0	0	0	3	4	1	0	0	2	1	18.0	3.00	136	.308	.400	20	.168	0	0	0	-0	0.0

● STEVE SIMPSON Simpson, Steven Edward b: 8/30/48, St.Joseph, Mo. d: 11/2/89, Omaha, Neb. BR/TR, 6'3", 200 lbs. Deb: 9/10/72

YEAR	TM/L	W	L	PCT	G	GS	CG	SH	SV	IP	H	R	HR	HB	BB	SO	RAT	ERA	ERA+	OAV	OOB	BH	AVG	PB	PR	PR+	PD	TPI
1972	SD-N	0	2	.000	9	0	0	0	2	11^1	10	6	0	0	8	9	14.3	4.76	69	.238	.360	0	—	0	-2	-2	-0	-0.4

● DUKE SIMPSON Simpson, Thomas Leo b: 9/15/27, Columbus, Ohio BR/TR, 6'1.5", 190 lbs. Deb: 5/6/53

YEAR	TM/L	W	L	PCT	G	GS	CG	SH	SV	IP	H	R	HR	HB	BB	SO	RAT	ERA	ERA+	OAV	OOB	BH	AVG	PB	PR	PR+	PD	TPI
1953	Chi-N	1	2	.333	30	1	0	0	0	45	60	47	8	1	25	21	17.2	8.00	56	.314	.396	2	.250	0	-19	-17	-0	-1.0

● WAYNE SIMPSON Simpson, Wayne Kirby b: 12/2/48, Los Angeles, Cal. BR/TR, 6'3", 220 lbs. Deb: 4/9/70

YEAR	TM/L	W	L	PCT	G	GS	CG	SH	SV	IP	H	R	HR	HB	BB	SO	RAT	ERA	ERA+	OAV	OOB	BH	AVG	PB	PR	PR+	PD	TPI
1970	Cin-N☆	14	3	.824	26	26	10	2	0	176	125	73	15	9	81	119	11.0	3.02	134	**.198**	.298	6	.094	-4	20	20	2	1.6
1971	Cin-N	4	7	.364	22	21	1	0	0	117^1	106	66	9	3	77	61	14.3	4.76	71	.244	.361	1	.031	-2	-17	-19	2	-1.6
1972	Cin-N	8	5	.615	24	22	1	0	0	130^1	124	63	17	2	49	70	12.1	4.14	78	.247	.316	3	.063	-3	-10	-14	-3	-1.9
1973	KC-A	3	4	.429	16	10	1	0	0	59^2	66	39	1	1	35	29	15.4	5.73	72	.284	.381	0	—	0	-13	-10	-0	-1.1
1975	Phi-N	1	0	1.000	7	5	0	0	0	30^2	31	11	1	1	11	19	12.6	3.23	116	.263	.331	2	.222	0	1	2	0	0.2
1977	Cal-A	6	12	.333	27	23	0	0	0	122	154	90	14	7	62	55	16.5	5.83	67	.308	.392	0	—	0	-24	-27	-1	-3.4
Total	6	36	31	.537	122	107	13	2	0	636	606	342	57	23	315	353	13.4	4.37	85	.251	.343	12	.078	-8	-41	-48	0	-6.2

● PETE SIMS Sims, Clarence b: 5/24/1891, Crown City, Ohio d: 12/2/68, Dallas, Tex. BR/TR, 5'11.5", 165 lbs. Deb: 9/16/15

YEAR	TM/L	W	L	PCT	G	GS	CG	SH	SV	IP	H	R	HR	HB	BB	SO	RAT	ERA	ERA+	OAV	OOB	BH	AVG	PB	PR	PR+	PD	TPI
1915	StL-A	1	0	1.000	3	2	0	0	0	8^1	6	4	0	0	6	4	13.0	4.32	66	.214	.353	1	1.000	1	-1	-1	-0	-0.1

● STEVE SINCLAIR Sinclair, Steven Scott b: 8/2/71, Victoria, B.C., Canada BL/TL, 6'2", 190 lbs. Deb: 4/25/98

YEAR	TM/L	W	L	PCT	G	GS	CG	SH	SV	IP	H	R	HR	HB	BB	SO	RAT	ERA	ERA+	OAV	OOB	BH	AVG	PB	PR	PR+	PD	TPI
1998	Tor-A	0	2	.000	24	0	0	0	0	15	13	7	0	0	5	8	10.8	3.60	130	.232	.295	0	—	0	2	2	0	0.2
1999	Tor-A	0	0	—	3	0	0	0	0	5^2	7	8	4	1	4	3	19.1	12.71	39	.304	.429	0	—	0	-5	-5	-0	-0.2
	Sea-A	0	1	.000	18	0	0	0	0	13^2	15	8	1	1	10	15	17.1	3.95	120	.268	.388	0	—	0	1	1	-0	0.1
	Yr	0	1	.000	21	0	0	0	0	19^1	22	16	5	2	14	18	17.7	6.52	74	.278	.400	0	—	0	-4	-4	-0	-0.1
Total	2	0	3	.000	45	0	0	0	0	34^1	35	23	5	2	19	26	14.7	5.24	90	.259	.359	0	—	0	-2	-2	0	0.1

● BERT SINCOCK Sincock, Herbert Sylvester b: 9/8/1887, Barkerville, B.C., Canada d: 8/1/46, Houghton, Mich. BL/TL, 5'10.5", 165 lbs. Deb: 6/25/08

YEAR	TM/L	W	L	PCT	G	GS	CG	SH	SV	IP	H	R	HR	HB	BB	SO	RAT	ERA	ERA+	OAV	OOB	BH	AVG	PB	PR	PR+	PD	TPI
1908	Cin-N	0	0	—	1	0	0	0	0	4^2	3	2	0	0	0	1	5.8	3.86	60	.176	.176	0	.000	-0	-1	-1	-0	-0.1

● BILL SINGER Singer, William Robert "The Singer Throwing Machine" b: 4/24/44, Los Angeles, Cal. BR/TR, 6'4", 200 lbs. Deb: 9/24/64

YEAR	TM/L	W	L	PCT	G	GS	CG	SH	SV	IP	H	R	HR	HB	BB	SO	RAT	ERA	ERA+	OAV	OOB	BH	AVG	PB	PR	PR+	PD	TPI
1964	LA-N	0	1	.000	2	2	0	0	0	14	11	5	0	0	12	3	14.8	3.21	101	.216	.365	1	.167	0	1	0	-0	0.0
1965	LA-N	0	0	—	2	0	0	0	0	1	2	0	0	0	2	1	36.0	0.00	—	.400	.571	0	—	0	0	0	0	0.0
1966	LA-N	0	0	—	3	0	0	0	0	4	4	0	0	0	2	4	13.5	0.00	—	.286	.375	0	—	0	2	2	0	0.1
1967	LA-N	12	8	.600	32	29	7	3	0	204^1	185	68	5	8	61	169	11.2	2.64	117	.239	.301	6	.090	-3	17	11	1	0.8
1968	LA-N	13	17	.433	37	36	12	6	0	256^1	227	97	14	5	78	227	10.9	2.88	96	.237	.298	12	.148	3	3	-4	0	0.0
1969	LA-N★	20	12	.625	41	40	16	2	1	315^2	244	96	22	10	74	247	9.4	2.34	142	.210	.263	11	.102	-4	44	38	-2	3.2
1970	LA-N	8	5	.615	16	16	5	3	0	106^1	79	39	10	2	32	93	9.6	3.13	123	.203	.267	5	.132	-0	11	9	-1	0.9
1971	LA-N	10	17	.370	31	31	8	1	0	203^1	195	103	19	4	71	144	12.0	4.16	78	.252	.318	6	.103	-0	-16	-22	-1	-2.9
1972	LA-N	6	16	.273	26	25	4	3	0	169^1	148	84	8	5	60	101	11.3	3.67	91	.237	.309	4	.073	-3	-4	-6	1	-1.0
1973	Cal-A★	20	14	.588	40	40	19	2	0	315^2	280	124	15	9	130	241	11.9	3.22	110	.235	.314	0	—	0	21	12	-2	1.1
1974	Cal-A	7	4	.636	14	14	8	0	0	108^2	102	48	3	1	43	77	12.1	2.98	115	.250	.323	0	—	0	8	6	0	0.6
1975	Cal-A	7	15	.318	29	27	8	0	1	179	171	107	18	6	81	78	13.0	4.98	71	.257	.343	0	—	0	-24	-30	-1	-3.3
1976	Tex-A	4	1	.800	10	10	2	1	0	64^2	56	31	4	5	27	34	12.2	3.48	103	.239	.331	0	—	0	0	1	-1	0.0
	Min-A	9	9	.500	26	26	5	3	0	172	177	88	9	6	69	63	13.2	3.77	95	.274	.349	0	—	0	-5	-4	-2	-0.5
	Yr	13	10	.565	36	36	7	4	0	236^2	233	119	13	11	96	97	12.9	3.69	97	.264	.344	0	—	0	-4	-3	-2	-0.5
1977	Tor-A	2	8	.200	13	12	0	0	0	59^2	71	54	5	2	39	33	16.9	6.79	62	.296	.399	0	—	0	-18	-17	-0	-2.3
Total	14	118	127	.482	322	308	94	24	2	2174	1952	944	132	63	781	1515	11.6	3.39	99	.240	.311	45	.109	-7	40	-7	-7	-3.3

● ELMER SINGLETON Singleton, Bert Elmer "Smoky" b: 6/26/18, Ogden, Utah d: 1/5/96, Ogden, Utah BR/TR (BB 1957-58), 6'2", 174 lbs. Deb: 8/20/45

YEAR	TM/L	W	L	PCT	G	GS	CG	SH	SV	IP	H	R	HR	HB	BB	SO	RAT	ERA	ERA+	OAV	OOB	BH	AVG	PB	PR	PR+	PD	TPI
1945	Bos-N	1	4	.200	7	5	1	0	0	37^1	35	22	1	1	14	14	12.1	4.82	79	.248	.321	0	.000	-1	-4	-4	-0	-0.6
1946	Bos-N	0	1	.000	15	2	0	0	1	33^2	27	20	3	1	21	17	13.1	3.74	92	.221	.340	0	.000	-1	-1	-1	0	-0.1
1947	Pit-N	2	2	.500	36	3	0	0	1	67	70	49	9	2	39	24	14.9	6.31	67	.267	.366	4	.308	1	-17	-15	0	-0.7
1948	Pit-N	4	6	.400	38	5	1	0	2	92^1	90	52	11	1	40	53	12.8	4.97	82	.253	.330	2	.087	-2	-10	-9	1	-0.9
1950	Was-A	1	2	.333	21	1	0	0	0	36^1	39	23	4	0	17	19	13.9	5.20	86	.291	.371	3	.429	1	-3	-3	1	0.0
1957	Chi-N	0	1	.000	5	2	0	0	0	13^1	20	11	3	0	2	6	14.9	6.75	57	.333	.355	0	.000	-0	-4	-4	0	-0.3
1958	Chi-N	1	0	1.000	2	0	0	0	0	4^2	1	0	0	0	1	2	3.9	0.00	—	.071	.133	0	.000	-0	2	2	-0	0.4
1959	Chi-N	2	1	.667	21	1	0	0	0	43	40	15	2	0	12	25	10.9	2.72	145	.252	.304	0	.000	-1	6	6	1	0.4
Total	8	11	17	.393	145	19	2	0	4	327^2	322	192	33	5	146	160	13.0	4.83	83	.258	.338	9	.132	-3	-32	-29	3	-1.8

● JOHN SINGLETON Singleton, John Edward "Sheriff" b: 11/27/1896, Gallipolis, Ohio d: 10/23/37, Dayton, Ohio BR/TR, 5'11", 171 lbs. Deb: 6/8/22

YEAR	TM/L	W	L	PCT	G	GS	CG	SH	SV	IP	H	R	HR	HB	BB	SO	RAT	ERA	ERA+	OAV	OOB	BH	AVG	PB	PR	PR+	PD	TPI
1922	Phi-N	1	10	.091	22	9	3	1	0	93	127	80	6	5	38	27	16.5	5.90	79	.346	.415	5	.139	-2	-19	-11	-1	-1.4

YEAR	TM/L	W	L	PCT	G	GS	CG	SH	SV	IP	H	R	HR	HB	BB	SO	RAT	ERA	ERA+	OAV	OOB	BH	AVG	PB	PR	PR+	PD	TPI
● MIKE SIROTKA Sirotka, Michael Robert b: 5/13/71, Houston, Tex. BL/TL, 6'1", 190 lbs. Deb: 7/19/95																												
1995	Chi-A	1	2	.333	6	6	0	0	0	34^1	39	16	2	0	17	19	14.7	4.19	106	.298	.378	0	—	0	2	1	-0	0.1
1996	Chi-A	1	2	.333	15	4	0	0	0	26^1	34	27	3	0	12	11	15.7	7.18	66	.315	.383	0	—	0	-6	-7	-1	-0.7
1997	Chi-A	3	0	1.000	7	4	0	0	0	32	36	9	4	1	5	24	11.8	2.25	195	.290	.323	0	.000	-0	8	8	-0	0.6
1998	Chi-A	14	15	.483	33	33	5	0	0	211^2	255	137	30	2	47	128	12.9	5.06	90	.300	.338	0	.000	-0	-9	-12	0	-1.4
1999	Chi-A	11	13	.458	32	32	3	1	0	209	236	108	24	3	57	125	12.7	4.00	122	.283	.331	2	.250	0	20	20	-2	1.9
2000	*Chi-A	15	10	.600	32	32	1	0	0	197	203	101	23	1	69	128	12.5	3.79	131	.269	.331	0	.000	-0	25	25	-2	2.6
Total	6	45	42	.517	125	111	9	1	0	710^1	803	398	86	7	207	435	12.9	4.31	110	.286	.337	2	.118	0	39	36	-4	3.1
● DOUG SISK Sisk, Douglas Randall b: 9/26/57, Renton, Wash. BR/TR, 6'2", 210 lbs. Deb: 9/6/82																												
1982	NY-N	0	1	.000	8	0	0	0	1	8^2	5	1	1	1	4	4	10.4	1.04	350	.172	.294	0	—	0	2	2	0	0.3
1983	NY-N	5	4	.556	67	0	0	0	11	104^1	88	38	1	4	59	33	13.0	2.24	162	.235	.346	3	.500	1	16	16	-1	1.7
1984	NY-N	1	3	.250	50	0	0	0	15	77^2	57	24	1	3	54	32	13.2	2.09	170	.215	.354	1	.091	-0	13	13	0	1.1
1985	NY-N	4	5	.444	42	0	0	0	2	73	86	48	3	2	40	26	15.8	5.30	65	.291	.379	0	.000	-1	-14	-15	1	-1.9
1986	*NY-N	4	2	.667	41	0	0	0	1	70^2	77	31	0	5	31	31	14.4	3.06	116	.282	.366	0	.000	-0	5	4	-1	0.2
1987	NY-N	3	1	.750	55	0	0	0	3	78	83	38	5	3	22	37	12.5	3.46	109	.270	.325	0	.000	-1	5	3	1	0.2
1988	Bal-A	3	3	.500	52	0	0	0	0	94^1	109	43	3	2	45	26	14.9	3.72	105	.306	.387	0	—	0	3	2	1	0.2
1990	Atl-N	0	0	—	3	0	0	0	0	2^1	1	1	0	0	4	1	19.3	3.86	105	.143	.455	0	—	0	-0	0	0	0.0
1991	Atl-N	2	1	.667	14	0	0	0	0	14^1	21	14	1	0	8	5	18.2	5.02	77	.333	.408	0	—	0	-2	-2	0	-0.3
Total	9	22	20	.524	332	0	0	0	33	523^1	527	238	15	20	267	195	14.0	3.27	112	.268	.361	4	.105	-1	29	24	2	1.5
● TOMMIE SISK Sisk, Tommie Wayne b: 4/12/42, Ardmore, Okla. BR/TR, 6'3", 195 lbs. Deb: 7/19/62																												
1962	Pit-N	0	2	.000	5	3	1	0	0	17^2	18	9	1	1	8	6	13.8	4.08	97	.257	.342	1	.200	0	-0	-0	-0	-0.1
1963	Pit-N	1	3	.250	57	4	1	0	1	108	85	42	6	1	45	73	10.9	2.92	113	.222	.305	1	.063	-0	4	5	1	0.3
1964	Pit-N	1	4	.200	42	1	0	0	0	61^1	91	47	4	3	29	35	18.0	6.16	57	.364	.436	0	.000	-1	-18	-18	2	-1.3
1965	Pit-N	7	3	.700	38	12	1	2	0	111^1	103	48	6	1	50	66	12.4	3.40	103	.248	.330	2	.061	-2	2	1	-1	-0.2
1966	Pit-N	10	5	.667	34	23	4	1	1	150	146	74	14	4	52	60	12.1	4.14	86	.256	.323	5	.098	-1	-9	-10	0	-1.0
1967	Pit-N	13	13	.500	37	31	11	2	1	207^2	196	88	6	3	78	85	12.0	3.34	101	.253	.324	7	.101	-2	1	1	-1	-0.1
1968	Pit-N	5	5	.500	33	11	0	0	1	96	101	40	3	3	35	41	13.0	3.28	89	.282	.351	2	.083	-1	-3	-4	0	-0.5
1969	SD-N	2	13	.133	53	13	1	0	6	143	160	81	11	1	48	59	13.2	4.78	74	.285	.342	3	.120	0	-19	-20	0	-2.1
1970	Chi-A	1	1	.500	17	1	0	0	0	33^1	37	28	6	0	13	16	13.5	5.40	72	.276	.340	1	.250	0	-6	-5	1	-0.2
Total	9	40	49	.449	316	99	19	4	10	928^1	937	457	57	17	358	441	12.7	3.92	88	.266	.337	22	.094	-7	-48	-51	3	-5.2
● DAVE SISLER Sisler, David Michael b: 10/16/31, St.Louis, Mo. BR/TR, 6'4", 200 lbs. Deb: 4/21/56 F																												
1956	Bos-A	9	8	.529	39	14	3	0	3	142^1	120	81	13	7	72	93	12.6	4.62	100	.227	.328	5	.119	-2	-7	0	0	-0.2
1957	Bos-A	7	8	.467	22	19	5	0	1	122^1	135	68	15	2	61	55	14.6	4.71	85	.280	.363	7	.167	-0	-12	-9	-1	-1.0
1958	Bos-A	8	9	.471	30	25	4	1	0	149^1	157	94	22	1	79	71	14.3	4.94	81	.276	.366	9	.196	0	-19	-15	-1	-1.6
1959	Bos-A	0	0	—	3	0	0	0	0	6^2	9	5	3	0	1	3	13.5	6.75	60	.310	.333	1	.500	0	-2	-2	-0	-0.1
	Det-A	1	3	.250	32	0	0	0	7	51^2	46	28	4	1	36	29	14.5	4.01	101	.242	.366	1	.200	-0	-1	0	-1	0.0
	Yr	1	3	.250	35	0	0	0	7	58^1	55	33	7	1	37	32	14.3	4.32	94	.251	.362	2	.286	0	-3	-2	-1	-0.1
1960	Det-A	7	5	.583	41	0	0	0	6	80	56	23	3	2	45	47	11.6	2.47	160	.199	.314	2	.125	-0	12	13	-0	2.1
1961	Was-A	2	8	.200	45	1	0	0	11	60^1	55	34	6	3	48	30	15.8	4.18	96	.251	.393	0	.000	0	-1	-1	0	-0.2
1962	Cin-N	4	3	.571	35	0	0	0	1	43^2	44	19	4	0	26	27	14.4	3.92	103	.270	.370	0	—	0	0	1	-1	0.0
Total	7	38	44	.463	247	59	12	1	29	656^1	622	352	70	16	368	355	13.8	4.33	95	.253	.354	25	.157	-2	-31	-14	1	-1.0
● GEORGE SISLER Sisler, George Harold "Georgeous George" b: 3/24/1893, Manchester, Ohio d: 3/26/73, Richmond Heights, Mo. BL/TL, 5'11", 170 lbs. Deb: 6/28/15 FMCH♦																												
1915	StL-A	4	4	.500	15	8	6	0	0	70	62	26	0	4	38	41	13.4	2.83	101	.247	.355	78	.285	3	1	0	0	0.3
1916	StL-A	1	2	.333	3	3	3	1	0	27	18	4	0	1	6	12	8.3	1.00	275	.198	.255	177	.305	1	5	5	1	1.0
1918	StL-A	0	0	—	2	1	0	0	1	8	10	6	0	1	4	4	16.9	4.50	61	.286	.375	154	.341	1	-2	-2	0	0.0
1920	StL-A	0	0	—	1	0	0	0	1	1	0	0	0	0	0	2	0.0	0.00	—	.000	.000	257	.407	1	0	0	0	0.1
1925	StL-A	0	0	—	1	0	0	0	0	2	1	0	0	0	1	1	9.0	0.00	—	.167	.286	224	.345	0	1	1	0	0.1
1926	StL-A	0	0	—	1	0	0	0	1	2	0	0	0	0	2	3	9.0	0.00	—	.000	.286	178	.290	0	1	1	0	0.1
1928	Bos-N	0	0	—	1	0	0	0	0	1	0	0	0	0	1	0	9.0	0.00	—	.000	.333	167	.340	0	0	0	-0	0.0
Total	7	5	6	.455	24	12	9	1	3	111	91	36	0	6	52	63	12.1	2.35	123	.231	.330	2812	.340	7	8	7	1	1.6
● CARL SITTON Sitton, Carl Vetter b: 9/22/1882, Pendleton, S.C. d: 9/11/31, Valdosta, Ga. BR/TR, 5'10.5", 170 lbs. Deb: 4/24/09																												
1909	Cle-A	3	2	.600	14	5	3	0	0	50	50	22	1	2	16	16	12.2	2.88	89	.263	.327	2	.154	0	-2	-2	-1	-0.2
● PETE SIVESS Sivess, Peter b: 9/23/13, South River, N.J. BR/TR, 6'3.5", 195 lbs. Deb: 6/13/36																												
1936	Phi-N	3	4	.429	17	6	2	0	0	65	84	40	6	1	36	22	16.8	4.57	99	.310	.393	3	.120	-2	-4	-0	-2	-0.4
1937	Phi-N	1	1	.500	6	2	1	0	0	23	30	18	5	0	11	4	16.0	7.04	62	.330	.402	0	.000	-1	-8	-6	-1	-0.6
1938	Phi-N	3	6	.333	39	8	2	0	3	116	143	78	12	1	69	32	16.5	5.51	71	.306	.397	6	.188	-1	-22	-20	-1	-1.6
Total	3	7	11	.389	62	16	5	0	3	204	257	136	23	2	116	58	16.5	5.38	77	.310	.396	9	.143	-4	-34	-26	-3	-2.6
● JIM SIWY Siwy, James Gerard b: 9/20/58, Central Falls, R.I BR/TR, 6'4", 200 lbs. Deb: 8/20/82																												
1982	Chi-A	0	0	—	2	1	0	0	0	7	10	8	1	0	5	3	19.3	10.29	39	.385	.484	0	—	0	-5	-5	-0	-0.3
1984	Chi-A	0	0	—	1	0	0	0	0	4^1	3	1	0	0	2	1	10.4	2.08	201	.231	.333	0	—	0	1	1	0	0.1
Total	2	0	0	—	3	1	0	0	0	11^1	13	9	1	0	7	4	15.9	7.15	57	.333	.435	0	—	0	-4	-4	-0	-0.2
● JOE SKALSKI Skalski, Joseph Douglas b: 9/26/64, Burnham, Ill. BR/TR, 6'3", 190 lbs. Deb: 4/10/89																												
1989	Cle-A	0	2	.000	2	1	0	0	0	6^2	7	6	0	2	4	3	17.6	6.75	59	.259	.394	0	—	0	-2	-2	-0	-0.4
● DAVE SKAUGSTAD Skaugstad, David Wendell b: 1/10/40, Algona, Iowa BL/TL, 6'1", 179 lbs. Deb: 9/25/57																												
1957	Cin-N	0	0	—	2	0	0	0	0	5^2	4	1	0	0	6	4	15.9	1.59	259	.190	.370	0	.000	0	1	1	0	0.1
● DAVE SKEELS Skeels, David b: 12/29/1892, Addy, Wash. d: 12/2/26, Spokane, Wash. BL/TR, 6'1", 187 lbs. Deb: 9/14/10																												
1910	Det-A	0	0	—	1	1	0	0	0	6	9	8	0	1	4	2	21.0	12.00	22	.333	.438	0	.000	-0	-6	-6	0	-0.3
● CRAIG SKOK Skok, Craig Richard b: 9/1/47, Dobbs Ferry, N.Y. BR/TL, 6', 190 lbs. Deb: 5/4/73																												
1973	Bos-A	0	1	.000	11	0	0	0	1	28^2	35	22	2	0	11	22	14.4	6.28	64	.304	.365	0	—	0	-8	-7	-0	-0.4
1976	Tex-A	0	1	.000	9	0	0	0	0	5	13	7	2	0	3	5	28.8	12.60	28	.481	.533	0	—	0	-5	-5	0	-0.9
1978	Atl-N	3	2	.600	43	0	0	0	2	62	64	38	8	0	27	28	13.2	4.35	93	.266	.340	2	.250	0	-5	-2	-0	-0.1
1979	Atl-N	1	3	.250	44	0	0	0	2	54^1	58	26	7	3	17	30	12.9	3.98	102	.282	.345	0	.000	-0	-1	0	0	0.1
Total	4	4	7	.364	107	0	0	0	5	150	170	93	19	3	58	85	13.9	4.86	83	.289	.355	2	.182	0	-20	-13	-0	-1.3
● JOHN SKOPEC Skopec, John S. "Buckshot" b: 5/8/1880, Chicago, Ill. d: 10/20/12, Chicago, Ill. BR/TL, 5'10", 190 lbs. Deb: 4/25/01																												
1901	Chi-A	6	3	.667	9	9	6	0	0	68^1	62	39	1	8	45	24	15.1	3.16	110	.239	.369	10	.333	3	4	3	3	0.8
1903	Det-A	2	2	.500	6	5	3	0	0	39^1	46	22	0	2	13	14	14.0	3.43	85	.291	.353	2	.154	-0	-2	-2	-0	-0.2
Total	2	8	5	.615	15	14	9	0	0	107^2	108	61	1	10	58	38	14.7	3.26	101	.259	.363	12	.279	3	2	0	3	0.6
● MATT SKRMETTA Skrmetta, Matthew Leland b: 11/6/72, Biloxi, Miss. BB/TR, 6'3", 220 lbs. Deb: 6/6/2000																												
2000	Mon-N	0	0	—	6	0	0	0	0	5^1	6	10	1	0	6	4	20.3	15.19	31	.273	.429	0	—	0	-6	-6	-0	-0.3
	Pit-N	2	2	.500	8	0	0	0	0	9^1	13	12	2	1	3	7	16.4	9.64	48	.333	.395	0	.000	-0	-5	-5	-0	-1.0
	Yr	2	2	.500	14	0	0	0	0	14^2	19	22	3	1	9	11	17.8	11.66	40	.311	.408	0	.000	-0	-11	-11	-0	-1.3
● JOHN SLAGLE Slagle, John A. b: Lawrence, Ind. BL/TR, Deb: 4/30/1891																												
1891	Cin-a	0	0	—	1	0	0	0	1	1^1	3	0	0	0	1	1	27.0	0.00	—	.429	.500	0	.000	-0	1	1	0	0.1
● ROGER SLAGLE Slagle, Roger Lee b: 11/4/53, Wichita, Kan. BR/TR, 6'3", 190 lbs. Deb: 9/7/79																												
1979	NY-A	0	0	—	1	0	0	0	0	2	0	0	0	0	0	2	0.0	0.00	—	.000	.000	0	—	0	1	1	0	0.1

YEAR	TM/L	W	L	PCT	G	GS	CG	SH	SV	IP	H	R	HR	HB	BB	SO	RAT	ERA	ERA+	OAV	OOB	BH	AVG	PB	PR	PR+	PD	TPI
● **WALT SLAGLE** Slagle, Walter Jennings b: 12/15/1878, Kenton, Ohio d: 6/17/74, San Gabriel, Cal. BB/TR, 6', 165 lbs. Deb: 5/4/10																												
1910	Cin-N	0	0	—	1	0	0	0	0	1	0	1	0	1	3	0	36.0	9.00	32	.000	.571	0	—	0	-1	-1	-0	0.0
● **CY SLAPNICKA** Slapnicka, Cyril Charles b: 3/23/1886, Cedar Rapids, Iowa d: 10/20/79, Cedar Rapids, Iowa BB/TR, 5'10", 165 lbs. Deb: 9/26/11																												
1911	Chi-N	0	2	.000	3	2	1	0	0	24	21	12	0	3	7	10	11.6	3.38	98	.236	.313	2	.222	-0	0	-0	1	0.1
1918	Pit-N	1	4	.200	7	6	4	0	1	49^{1}	50	34	2	5	22	3	14.0	4.74	61	.269	.362	1	.071	-1	-11	-10	-0	-1.1
Total	2	1	6	.143	10	8	5	0	1	73^{1}	71	46	2	8	29	13	13.3	4.30	70	.258	.346	3	.130	-1	-11	-10	0	-1.0
● **JOHN SLAPPEY** Slappey, John Henry b: 8/8/1898, Albany, Ga. d: 6/10/57, Marietta, Ga. BL/TL, 6'4", 170 lbs. Deb: 8/23/20																												
1920	Phi-A	0	1	.000	3	1	0	0	0	6^{1}	15	12	0	0	4	1	27.0	7.11	57	.441	.500	1	.500	1	-2	-2	-0	-0.2
● **JIM SLATON** Slaton, James Michael b: 6/19/50, Long Beach, Cal. BR/TR, 6', 185 lbs. Deb: 4/14/71																												
1971	Mil-A	10	8	.556	26	23	5	4	0	147^{2}	140	67	16	1	71	63	12.9	3.78	92	.253	.339	5	.109	-1	-5	-5	-2	-0.9
1972	Mil-A	1	6	.143	9	8	0	0	0	44	50	31	3	1	21	17	14.7	5.52	55	.287	.367	1	.091	-1	-12	-12	1	-1.8
1973	Mil-A	13	15	.464	38	38	13	3	0	276^{1}	266	127	30	1	99	134	11.9	3.71	101	.251	.316	0	—	0	3	2	-3	-0.2
1974	Mil-A	13	16	.448	40	35	10	3	0	250	255	117	22	3	102	126	13.0	3.92	92	.268	.341	0	—	0	-8	-8	0	-0.9
1975	Mil-A	11	18	.379	37	33	10	3	0	217	238	129	28	2	90	119	13.7	4.52	85	.276	.346	0	—	0	-18	-16	1	-1.9
1976	Mil-A	14	15	.483	38	38	12	2	0	292^{2}	287	126	14	6	94	138	11.9	3.44	102	.259	.320	0	—	0	3	2	-0	0.1
1977	Mil-A☆	10	14	.417	32	31	7	1	0	221	223	104	25	11	77	104	12.7	3.58	114	.266	.336	0	—	0	12	12	0	1.2
1978	Det-A	17	11	.607	35	34	11	2	0	233^{2}	235	117	27	8	85	92	12.6	4.12	94	.263	.332	0	—	0	-9	-6	-1	-0.8
1979	Mil-A	15	9	.625	32	31	12	3	0	213	229	95	15	2	54	80	12.0	3.63	115	.278	.323	0	—	0	14	13	1	1.4
1980	Mil-A	1	1	.500	3	3	0	0	0	16^{1}	17	10	3	0	5	4	12.1	4.41	88	.270	.324	0	—	0	-1	-1	0	-0.1
1981	*Mil-A	5	7	.417	24	21	0	0	0	117^{1}	120	60	10	2	50	47	13.2	4.37	78	.273	.350	0	—	0	-9	-13	-0	-1.2
1982	*Mil-A	10	6	.625	39	7	0	0	6	117^{2}	117	48	14	1	41	59	12.2	3.29	115	.264	.327	0	—	0	10	7	-0	0.9
1983	Mil-A	14	6	.700	46	0	0	0	5	112^{1}	112	57	12	3	56	38	13.7	4.33	87	.272	.363	0	—	0	-3	-8	-0	-1.3
1984	Cal-A	7	10	.412	32	22	5	1	0	163	192	95	22	2	56	67	13.8	4.97	80	.295	.353	0	—	0	-18	-18	0	-1.6
1985	Cal-A	6	10	.375	29	24	1	0	1	148^{1}	162	82	22	2	63	60	13.8	4.37	94	.284	.357	0	—	0	-4	-4	-0	-0.4
1986	Cal-A	4	6	.400	14	12	0	0	0	73^{1}	84	52	9	2	29	31	14.1	5.65	73	.295	.364	0	—	0	-12	-13	1	-1.4
	Det-A	0	0	—	22	0	0	0	2	40	46	18	5	1	11	12	13.0	4.05	102	.287	.337	0	—	0	1	0	0	0.1
	Yr	4	6	.400	36	12	0	0	2	113^{1}	130	70	14	3	40	43	13.7	5.08	81	.292	.355	0	—	0	-11	-12	1	-1.3
Total	16	151	158	.489	496	360	86	22	14	2683^{2}	2773	1335	277	48	1004	1191	12.8	4.03	94	.270	.337	6	.105	-2	-55	-68	-4	-8.8
● **PHIL SLATTERY** Slattery, Philip Ryan b: 2/25/1893, Harper, Iowa d: 3/2/68, Long Beach, Cal. BR/TL, 5'11", 160 lbs. Deb: 9/16/15																												
1915	Pit-N	0	0	—	3	0	0	0	0	8	5	0	0	2	1	1	9.0	0.00	—	.185	.267	0	.000	-0	2	2	-1	0.1
● **BARNEY SLAUGHTER** Slaughter, Byron Atkins b: 10/6/1884, Smyrna, Del. d: 5/17/61, Philadelphia, Pa. BR/TR, 5'11.5", 165 lbs. Deb: 8/9/10																												
1910	Phi-N	0	1	.000	8	1	0	0	1	18	21	12	0	0	11	7	16.0	5.50	57	.318	.416	1	.200	0	-5	-5	0	-0.3
● **STERLING SLAUGHTER** Slaughter, Sterling Feore b: 11/18/41, Danville, Ill. BR/TR, 5'11", 165 lbs. Deb: 4/19/64																												
1964	Chi-N	2	4	.333	20	6	1	0	0	51^{2}	64	35	8	0	32	32	16.7	5.75	65	.305	.397	1	.083	-0	-13	-11	-1	-1.3
● **BILL SLAYBACK** Slayback, William Grover b: 2/21/48, Hollywood, Cal. BR/TR, 6'4", 200 lbs. Deb: 6/26/72																												
1972	Det-A	5	6	.455	23	13	3	1	0	81^{2}	74	36	4	1	25	65	11.0	3.20	99	.239	.298	4	.174	-0	-1	-0	1	0.0
1973	Det-A	0	0	—	3	0	0	0	0	2	5	4	0	1	0	1	27.0	4.50	91	.417	.462	0	—	0	-0	-0	-0	0.0
1974	Det-A	1	3	.250	16	4	0	0	0	54^{2}	57	34	1	3	26	23	14.2	4.77	80	.273	.361	0	—	0	-7	-6	-0	-0.4
Total	3	6	9	.400	42	17	3	1	0	138^{1}	136	74	5	5	51	89	12.5	3.84	89	.256	.327	4	.174	-0	-8	-6	0	-0.4
● **STEVE SLAYTON** Slayton, Foster Herbert b: 4/26/02, Barre, Vt. d: 12/20/84, Manchester, N.H. BR/TR, 6', 163 lbs. Deb: 7/21/28																												
1928	Bos-A	0	0	—	3	0	0	0	0	7	6	3	0	0	3	2	11.6	3.86	107	.240	.321	0	.000	-0	0	0	-0	0.0
● **LOU SLEATER** Sleater, Louis Mortimer b: 9/8/26, St.Louis, Mo. BL/TL, 5'10", 185 lbs. Deb: 4/25/50																												
1950	StL-A	0	0	—	1	0	0	0	0	1	0	0	0	0	0	1	0.0	0.00	—	.000	.000	0	—	0	1	1	0	0.0
1951	StL-A	1	9	.100	20	8	4	0	1	81	88	53	7	5	53	33	16.2	5.11	86	.271	.381	7	.226	0	-9	-6	-1	-0.7
1952	StL-A	0	1	.000	4	2	0	0	0	8^{2}	9	8	1	0	5	1	14.5	7.27	54	.265	.359	0	.000	-0	-3	-3	0	-0.3
	Was-A	4	2	.667	14	9	3	1	0	57	56	29	4	2	30	22	13.9	3.63	98	.260	.356	1	.050	-2	0	-0	-1	-0.4
	Yr	4	3	.571	18	11	3	1	0	65^{2}	65	37	5	2	35	23	14.0	4.11	88	.261	.357	1	.045	-2	-3	-4	-1	-0.7
1955	KC-A	1	1	.500	16	1	0	0	0	25^{2}	33	22	3	0	21	11	18.9	7.71	54	.324	.439	2	.154	-1	-11	-10	-0	-0.7
1956	Mil-N	2	2	.500	25	1	0	0	2	45^{2}	42	22	6	0	27	32	13.6	3.15	110	.240	.342	5	.500	2	3	2	1	0.5
1957	Det-A	3	3	.500	41	0	0	0	2	69^{1}	61	33	9	1	28	43	11.7	3.76	102	.237	.315	5	.250	3	0	1	-0	0.4
1958	Det-A	0	0	—	4	0	0	0	0	5^{1}	3	4	2	0	6	4	15.2	6.75	60	.158	.360	1	1.000	1	-2	-2	0	0.1
	Bal-A	1	0	1.000	6	0	0	0	0	7	14	10	0	0	2	5	20.6	12.86	28	.438	.471	0	.000	-1	-7	-8	0	-1.0
	Yr	1	0	1.000	10	0	0	0	0	12^{1}	17	14	2	0	8	9	18.2	10.22	37	.333	.424	1	.143	0	-9	-9	0	-0.9
Total	7	12	18	.400	131	21	7	1	5	300^{2}	306	181	32	8	172	152	14.5	4.70	83	.263	.362	21	.204	3	-28	-26	-2	-2.1
● **LEFTY SLOAT** Sloat, Dwain Clifford b: 12/1/18, Nokomis, Ill. BR/TL, 6', 168 lbs. Deb: 4/24/48																												
1948	Bro-N	0	1	.000	4	1	0	0	0	7^{1}	7	5	0	0	8	1	18.4	6.14	65	.280	.455	0	.000	-0	-2	-2	1	-0.2
1949	Chi-N	0	0	—	5	1	0	0	0	9	14	7	0	0	3	3	17.0	7.00	58	.400	.447	0	—	0	-3	-3	0	-0.1
Total	2	0	1	.000	9	2	0	0	0	16^{1}	21	12	0	0	11	4	17.6	6.61	61	.350	.451	0	.000	-0	-5	-5	1	-0.3
● **HEATHCLIFF SLOCUMB** Slocumb, Heath b: 6/7/66, Jamaica, N.Y. BR/TR, 6'3", 220 lbs. Deb: 4/11/91																												
1991	Chi-N	2	1	.667	52	0	0	0	1	62^{2}	53	29	3	3	30	34	12.4	3.45	113	.231	.328	0	.000	-0	2	3	0	0.1
1992	Chi-N	0	3	.000	30	0	0	0	1	36	52	27	3	1	21	27	18.5	6.50	56	.351	.435	0	.000	-0	-12	-11	-0	-1.0
1993	Chi-N	1	0	1.000	10	0	0	0	0	10^{2}	7	5	0	0	4	4	9.3	3.38	118	.189	.268	0	.000	-0	1	1	0	0.1
	Cle-A	3	1	.750	20	0	0	0	0	27^{1}	28	14	3	0	16	18	14.5	4.28	101	.272	.370	0	—	0	0	0	-0	0.0
1994	Phi-N	5	1	.833	52	0	0	0	0	72^{1}	75	32	0	2	28	58	13.1	2.86	150	.262	.332	1	.250	0	11	11	0	0.9
1995	Phi-N★	5	6	.455	61	0	0	0	32	65^{1}	64	26	2	1	35	63	13.8	2.89	146	.257	.351	0	.000	-0	9	10	2	2.1
1996	Bos-A	5	5	.500	75	0	0	0	31	83^{1}	68	31	2	3	55	88	13.6	3.02	168	.222	.346	0	—	0	18	19	1	3.2
1997	Bos-A	0	5	.000	49	0	0	0	17	46^{2}	58	32	4	3	34	36	18.3	5.79	80	.312	.426	0	—	0	-6	-6	-0	-0.9
	*Sea-A	0	4	.000	27	0	0	0	10	28^{1}	26	13	2	1	15	28	13.3	4.13	109	.241	.339	0	—	0	1	1	-0	0.2
	Yr	0	9	.000	76	0	0	0	27	75	84	45	6	4	49	64	16.4	5.16	89	.286	.395	0	—	0	-5	-5	-0	-0.7
1998	Sea-A	2	5	.286	57	0	0	0	3	67^{2}	72	40	5	1	44	51	15.6	5.32	87	.275	.381	0	—	0	-5	-5	-0	-0.5
1999	Bal-A	0	0	—	10	0	0	0	0	8^{2}	15	12	2	2	9	12	27.0	12.46	38	.395	.531	0	—	0	-7	-8	-0	-0.4
	StL-N	3	2	.600	40	0	0	0	2	53^{1}	49	16	3	1	30	48	13.5	2.36	194	.243	.343	0	—	0	13	13	0	1.2
2000	StL-N	2	3	.400	43	0	0	0	1	49^{2}	50	32	9	1	24	34	13.6	5.44	85	.266	.352	0	.000	-0	-4	-4	-0	-0.4
	SD-N	0	1	.000	22	0	0	0	0	19	19	11	0	2	13	12	16.1	3.79	115	.264	.391	0	—	0	2	1	0	0.1
	Yr	2	4	.333	65	0	0	0	1	68^{2}	69	43	9	3	37	46	14.3	4.98	92	.265	.363	0	.000	-0	-3	-3	-0	-0.3
Total	10	28	37	.431	548	0	0	0	98	631	636	320	38	21	358	513	14.5	4.08	109	.263	.363	1	.083	-1	22	25	3	4.7
● **JOE SLUSARSKI** Slusarski, Joseph Andrew b: 12/19/66, Indianapolis, Ind. BR/TR, 6'4", 195 lbs. Deb: 4/11/91																												
1991	Oak-A	5	7	.417	20	19	1	0	0	109^{1}	121	69	14	4	52	60	14.6	5.27	73	.283	.366	0	—	0	-14	-19	-1	-1.8
1992	Oak-A	5	5	.500	15	14	0	0	0	76	85	52	15	6	27	38	14.0	5.45	69	.284	.355	0	—	0	-13	-15	-1	-1.8
1993	Oak-A	0	0	—	2	1	0	0	0	8^{2}	9	5	1	0	11	1	20.8	5.19	79	.300	.488	0	—	0	-1	-1	0	0.0
1995	Mil-A	1	1	.500	12	0	0	0	0	15	21	11	3	2	6	6	17.4	5.40	92	.333	.408	0	—	0	-1	-1	-0	-0.1
1999	Hou-N	0	0	—	3	0	0	0	0	3^{2}	1	0	0	0	3	3	9.8	0.00	—	.083	.267	0	—	0	2	2	-0	0.1
2000	Hou-N	2	7	.222	54	0	0	0	3	77	80	36	8	3	22	54	12.3	4.21	116	.268	.325	1	.111	-0	4	6	-1	0.5
Total	6	13	20	.394	106	34	1	0	3	289^{2}	317	173	41	15	121	162	14.1	4.97	84	.281	.358	1	.111	-0	-23	-27	-3	-3.1
● **AARON SMALL** Small, Aaron James b: 11/23/71, Oxnard, Cal. BR/TR, 6'5", 200 lbs. Deb: 6/11/94																												
1994	Tor-A	0	0	—	1	0	0	0	0	2	5	2	1	0	2	0	31.5	9.00	54	.500	.583	0	—	0	-1	-1	0	0.0
1995	Fla-N	1	0	1.000	7	0	0	0	0	6^{1}	7	2	1	0	6	5	18.5	1.42	297	.269	.406	0	—	0	2	2	0	0.3
1996	Oak-A	1	3	.250	12	3	0	0	0	28^{2}	37	28	3	1	22	17	18.8	8.16	60	.308	.420	0	—	0	-10	-10	0	-1.1
1997	Oak-A	9	5	.643	71	0	0	0	4	96^{2}	109	50	6	3	40	57	14.2	4.28	106	.294	.367	0	.000	-0	3	3	0	0.4

YEAR TM/L	W	L	PCT	G	GS	CG	SH	SV	IP	H	R	HR	HB	BB	SO	RAT	ERA	ERA+	OAV	OOB	BH	AVG	PB	PR	PR+	PD	TPI
1998 Oak-A	1	1	.500	24	0	0	0	0	36	51	34	3	3	14	19	17.0	7.25	63	.333	.400	0	.000	0	-10	-11	-1	-0.6
Ari-N	3	1	.750	23	0	0	0	0	31^{2}	32	14	5	1	8	14	11.7	3.69	114	.269	.320	0	—	0	2	2	-1	0.1
Total 5	15	10	.600	138	3	0	0	4	201^{1}	241	130	19	8	92	112	15.2	5.23	87	.302	.379	0	.000	-0	-14	-16	-1	-0.9
● MARK SMALL Small, Mark Allen b: 11/12/67, Portland, Ore. BR/TR, 6'3", 205 lbs. Deb: 4/5/96																											
1996 Hou-N	0	1	.000	16	0	0	0	0	24^{1}	33	23	1	1	13	16	17.4	5.92	65	.308	.388	0	.000	-0	-5	-6	-1	-0.4
● WALT SMALLWOOD Smallwood, Walter Clayton b: 4/24/1893, Dayton, Md. d: 4/29/67, Baltimore, Md. BR/TR, 6'2", 190 lbs. Deb: 9/19/17																											
1917 NY-A	0	0	—	2	0	0	0	0	2	1	0	0	0	1	1	9.0	0.00	—	.167	.286	0	—	0	1	1	0	0.0
1919 NY-A	0	0	—	6	0	0	0	0	21^{2}	20	12	1	2	9	6	12.9	4.98	64	.263	.356	0	.000	-1	-4	-4	-0	-0.3
Total 2	0	0	—	8	0	0	0	0	23^{2}	21	12	1	2	10	7	12.5	4.56	69	.256	.351	0	.000	-1	-4	-4	-0	-0.3
● J.D. SMART Smart, Jon David b: 11/12/73, San Saba, Tex. BR/TR, 6'2", 185 lbs. Deb: 4/6/99																											
1999 Mon-N	0	1	.000	29	0	0	0	0	52	56	30	4	0	17	21	12.6	5.02	89	.276	.332	0	.000	-0	-3	-3	-0	-0.2
● JOHN SMILEY Smiley, John Patrick b: 3/17/65, Phoenixville, Pa. BL/TL, 6'4", 200 lbs. Deb: 9/1/86																											
1986 Pit-N	1	0	1.000	12	0	0	0	0	11^{2}	4	6	2	0	4	9	6.2	3.86	100	.105	.190	0	—	0	-0	-0	0	0.0
1987 Pit-N	5	5	.500	63	0	0	0	4	75	69	49	7	0	50	58	14.3	5.76	71	.244	.357	1	.143	0	-14	-14	0	-1.7
1988 Pit-N	13	11	.542	34	32	5	1	0	205	185	81	15	3	46	129	10.3	3.25	105	.241	.287	5	.079	-2	5	4	-1	0.2
1989 Pit-N	12	8	.600	28	28	8	1	0	205^{1}	174	78	22	4	49	123	9.9	2.81	120	.226	.276	9	.138	1	16	13	-2	1.1
1990 *Pit-N	9	10	.474	26	25	2	0	0	149^{1}	161	83	15	2	36	86	12.0	4.64	78	.275	.319	6	.122	-0	-14	-18	0	-2.0
1991 *Pit-N★	**20**	8	**.714**	33	32	2	1	0	207^{2}	194	78	17	3	44	129	10.4	3.08	116	.251	.294	7	.100	-2	14	12	-0	1.3
1992 Min-A	16	9	.640	34	34	5	2	0	241	205	93	17	6	65	163	10.3	3.21	126	.231	.288	0	—	0	20	22	0	2.2
1993 Cin-N	3	9	.250	18	18	2	0	0	105^{2}	117	69	15	2	31	60	12.8	5.62	72	.286	.339	8	.250	2	-18	-19	0	-1.6
1994 Cin-N	11	10	.524	24	24	1	1	0	158^{2}	169	80	18	4	37	112	11.9	3.86	107	.275	.320	11	.200	3	6	5	-1	0.8
1995 *Cin-N★	12	5	.706	28	27	1	0	0	176^{2}	173	72	11	4	39	124	11.0	3.46	119	.263	.308	9	.164	2	14	13	-0	1.4
1996 Cin-N	13	14	.481	35	34	2	2	0	217^{1}	207	100	20	4	54	171	11.0	3.64	116	.256	.306	13	.191	2	14	14	-1	1.7
1997 Cin-N	9	10	.474	20	20	0	0	0	117	139	76	17	6	31	94	13.5	5.23	82	.296	.347	4	.100	-2	-13	-12	-2	-2.0
Cle-A	2	4	.333	6	6	0	0	0	37^{1}	45	23	9	1	10	26	13.5	5.54	85	.304	.352	0	—	0	-4	-3	-0	-0.5
Total 12	126	103	.550	361	280	28	8	4	1907^{2}	1842	888	185	39	496	1284	11.2	3.80	102	.255	.307	73	.145	3	25	17	-6	0.9
● SMITH Smith Deb: 6/5/1884																											
1884 Bal-U	0	0	—	1	1	0	0	0	6	12	11	0		2	2	21.0	9.00	30	.387	.424	1	.200	-1	-4	-4	-0	-0.2
● SMITH Smith Deb: 5/31/1886																											
1886 Cin-a	0	1	.000	1	1	1	0	0	9	8	8	0	0	10	1	18.0	4.00	88	.229	.400	1	.250	-0	-1	-0	-0	-0.1
● AL SMITH Smith, Alfred John b: 10/12/07, Belleville, Ill. d: 4/28/77, Brownsville, Tex. BL/TL, 5'11", 180 lbs. Deb: 5/5/34 C																											
1934 NY-N	3	5	.375	30	4	0	0	5	66^{2}	70	40	2	0	21	27	12.3	4.32	90	.266	.320	4	.286	1	-2	-4	-0	-0.4
1935 NY-N	10	8	.556	40	10	4	1	5	124	125	50	6	7	32	44	11.9	3.41	113	.263	.319	4	.118	-0	8	6	-1	0.8
1936 *NY-N	14	13	.519	43	30	9	**4**	2	209^{1}	217	116	16	4	69	89	12.5	3.78	103	.274	.335	10	.137	-1	6	3	-1	0.1
1937 *NY-N	5	4	.556	33	9	2	0	0	85^{2}	91	45	8	2	30	41	12.9	4.20	93	.275	.339	3	.120	-2	-3	-3	-1	-0.5
1938 Phi-N	1	4	.200	37	1	0	0	1	86	115	70	7	0	40	46	16.2	6.28	62	.320	.388	0	.000	-2	-24	-22	0	-1.4
1939 Phi-N	0	0	—	5	0	0	0	0	9	11	5	1	2	5	2	18.0	4.00	100	.314	.429	0	.000	-0	-0	0	0	0.0
1940 Cle-A	15	7	.682	31	24	11	1	2	183	187	79	12	6	55	46	12.2	3.44	122	.270	.329	19	.306	7	19	16	2	2.6
1941 Cle-A	12	13	.480	29	27	13	2	0	206^{2}	204	95	12	1	75	76	12.2	3.83	103	.256	.321	11	.155	2	7	3	2	0.7
1942 Cle-A	10	15	.400	30	24	7	1	0	168^{1}	163	96	9	5	71	66	12.8	3.96	87	.251	.329	15	.250	3	-6	-10	-1	-1.1
1943 Cle-A☆	17	7	.708	29	27	14	3	1	208^{1}	186	74	7	0	72	72	11.1	2.55	122	.239	.303	14	.206	3	17	14	-0	2.0
1944 Cle-A	7	13	.350	28	26	7	1	0	181^{2}	197	83	6	3	69	44	13.3	3.42	96	.280	.347	10	.156	-1	0	-3	1	-0.3
1945 Cle-A	5	12	.294	21	19	8	3	1	133^{2}	141	74	8	2	48	34	12.9	3.84	85	.275	.340	12	.293	4	-7	-9	2	-0.5
Total 12	99	101	.495	356	201	75	16	17	1662^{1}	1707	827	94	32	587	587	12.6	3.72	99	.267	.332	102	.191	14	17	-11	4	2.0
● AL SMITH Smith, Alfred Kendricks b: 12/13/03, Norristown, Pa. d: 8/11/95, San Diego, Cal. BR/TR, 6', 170 lbs. Deb: 6/18/26																											
1926 NY-N	0	0	—	1	0	0	0	0	2	4	2	0	0	2	0	27.0	9.00	42	.444	.545	0	—	0	-1	-1	-0	-0.1
● ART SMITH Smith, Arthur Laird b: 6/21/06, Boston, Mass. d: 11/22/95, Norwalk, Conn. BR/TR, 6', 175 lbs. Deb: 6/9/32																											
1932 Chi-A	0	1	.000	3	2	0	0	0	7	17	13	1	0	4	1	27.0	11.57	37	.500	.553	0	.000	-0	-6	-6	1	-0.6
● BILLY SMITH Smith, Billy Lavern b: 9/13/54, LaMarque, Tex. BR/TR, 6'7", 200 lbs. Deb: 6/9/81																											
1981 *Hou-N	1	1	.500	10	1	0	0	1	20^{2}	20	7	3	0	3	3	10.0	3.05	108	.263	.291	0	.000	-0	1	1	0	0.0
● BRYN SMITH Smith, Bryn Nelson b: 8/11/55, Marietta, Ga. BR/TR, 6'2", 205 lbs. Deb: 9/8/81																											
1981 Mon-N	1	0	1.000	7	0	0	0	0	13	14	4	1	0	3	9	11.8	2.77	126	.280	.321	0	.000	-0	1	1	-0	0.0
1982 Mon-N	2	4	.333	47	1	0	0	3	79^{1}	81	43	5	0	23	50	11.8	4.20	87	.264	.315	0	.000	-0	-5	-5	0	-0.4
1983 Mon-N	6	11	.353	49	12	5	3	3	155^{1}	142	51	13	5	43	101	11.0	2.49	144	.248	.306	5	.167	0	20	19	0	2.2
1984 Mon-N	12	13	.480	28	28	4	2	0	179	178	72	15	3	51	101	11.7	3.32	103	.259	.313	7	.132	1	5	2	2	0.6
1985 Mon-N	18	5	.783	32	32	4	2	0	222^{1}	193	85	12	1	41	127	9.5	2.91	117	.232	.269	14	.194	3	17	13	-1	1.5
1986 Mon-N	10	8	.556	30	30	1	0	0	187^{1}	182	101	15	6	63	105	12.1	3.94	94	.251	.316	8	.138	1	-4	-5	3	0.0
1987 Mon-N	10	9	.526	26	26	2	0	0	150^{1}	164	81	16	2	31	94	11.8	4.37	96	.274	.312	6	.136	-0	-5	-3	-0	-0.3
1988 Mon-N	12	10	.545	32	32	1	0	0	198	179	79	15	10	32	122	10.0	3.00	120	.243	.284	6	.109	-1	10	13	-2	1.1
1989 Mon-N	10	11	.476	33	32	3	1	0	215^{2}	177	76	16	4	54	129	9.8	2.84	125	.223	.276	4	.065	-2	16	17	2	1.6
1990 StL-N	9	8	.529	26	25	0	0	0	141^{1}	160	81	11	4	30	78	12.4	4.27	90	.286	.327	10	.256	3	-7	-7	-1	-0.5
1991 StL-N	12	9	.571	31	31	3	0	0	198^{2}	188	95	16	7	45	94	10.9	3.85	97	.251	.300	16	.246	3	-4	-3	-1	-0.1
1992 StL-N	4	2	.667	13	1	0	0	0	21^{1}	20	11	3	3	5	9	11.8	4.64	73	.247	.315	0	.000	-0	-3	-3	0	-0.7
1993 Col-N	2	4	.333	11	5	0	0	0	29^{2}	47	29	2	3	11	9	18.5	8.49	56	.362	.424	0	.000	-0	-15	-10	1	-1.7
Total 13	108	94	.535	365	255	23	8	6	1791^{1}	1725	808	140	48	432	1028	11.1	3.53	104	.253	.302	76	.153	7	26	26	4	3.3
● CHUCK SMITH Smith, Charles Edward b: 10/21/69, Memphis, Tenn. BR/TR, 6'1", 185 lbs. Deb: 6/13/2000																											
2000 Fla-N	6	6	.500	19	19	1	0	0	122^{2}	111	53	6	3	54	118	12.3	3.23	137	.248	.333	4	.100	-2	19	17	0	1.3
● CHARLIE SMITH Smith, Charles Edwin b: 4/20/1880, Cleveland, Ohio d: 1/3/29, Wickliffe, Ohio BR/TR, 6'1", 185 lbs. Deb: 8/6/02 F																											
1902 Cle-A	2	1	.667	3	3	2	1	0	20	23	9	0	0	5	5	12.6	4.05	85	.287	.329	1	.125	-0	-1	-1	0	-0.2
1906 Was-A	9	16	.360	33	22	17	2	0	235^{1}	250	113	2	8	75	105	12.7	2.91	91	.275	.336	16	.184	-1	-6	-7	-3	-1.1
1907 Was-A	10	20	.333	36	31	21	3	0	258^{2}	254	103	0	1	51	119	10.6	2.61	93	.259	.297	12	.143	-3	-2	-6	3	-0.6
1908 Was-A	9	13	.409	26	23	14	1	0	183	166	76	2	3	60	83	11.3	2.41	95	.247	.311	8	.123	-2	-0	-3	-1	-0.7
1909 Was-A	3	12	.200	23	15	7	1	0	145^{2}	140	73	4	5	37	72	11.2	3.27	74	.250	.303	7	.156	-1	-13	-14	0	-1.5
Bos-A	3	0	1.000	3	3	2	0	0	25	23	6	2	1	2	11	9.4	2.16	116	.237	.260	3	.300	1	1	1	0	0.2
Yr	6	12	.333	26	18	9	1	0	170^{2}	163	79	6	6	39	83	11.0	3.11	78	.248	.297	10	.182	-0	-12	-13	1	-1.3
1910 Bos-A	11	6	.647	24	18	11	0	1	156^{1}	141	57	4	2	35	53	10.2	2.30	111	.248	.294	5	.114	-2	4	4	-2	-0.1
1911 Bos-A	0	0	—	1	1	0	0	0	2	2	3	1	0	1	0	13.5	9.00	36	.250	.333	0	—	0	-1	-1	0	0.0
Chi-N	3	2	.600	7	5	3	1	0	38	31	11	0	1	7	11	9.2	1.42	233	.228	.271	1	.077	-1	8	8	-1	0.8
1912 Chi-N	7	4	.636	20	5	1	0	1	94	92	56	2	3	31	47	12.1	4.21	79	.269	.335	9	.257	1	-8	-10	1	-0.8
1913 Chi-N	7	9	.438	20	17	8	1	0	137^{2}	138	53	2	4	34	47	11.5	2.55	125	.274	.325	4	.089	-3	10	10	0	0.7
1914 Chi-N	2	4	.333	16	5	1	0	0	53^{2}	49	27	3	1	15	17	10.9	3.86	72	.251	.308	1	.091	-1	-6	-6	-1	-0.9
Total 10	66	87	.431	212	148	87	10	3	1349^{1}	1309	587	22	29	353	570	11.3	2.81	94	.259	.311	67	.150	-13	-15	-25	-2	-4.2
● POP SMITH Smith, Charles Marvin b: 10/12/1856, Digby, N.S., Canada d: 4/18/27, Boston, Mass. BR/TR, 5'11", 170 lbs. Deb: 5/1/1880 U♦																											
1883 Col-a	0	0	—	3	0	0	0	0	5^{2}	10	7	0		0	0	15.9	6.35	48	.357	.357	106	.262	1	-2	-2	-0	-0.1
● POP-BOY SMITH Smith, Clarence Ossie b: 5/23/1892, Newport, Tenn. d: 2/16/24, Sweetwater, Tex. BR/TR, 6'1", 176 lbs. Deb: 4/19/13																											
1913 Chi-A	0	1	.000	15	2	0	0	0	32	31	15	0	3	11	13	12.7	3.38	87	.261	.338	0	.000	-1	-2	-2	1	-0.1
1916 Cle-A	1	2	.333	5	3	0	0	1	25^{2}	25	15	1	1	11	4	13.0	3.86	78	.253	.333	2	.286	0	-3	-2	-0	-0.3

YEAR	TM/L	W	L	PCT	G	GS	CG	SH	SV	IP	H	R	HR	HB	BB	SO	RAT	ERA	ERA+	OAV	OOB	BH	AVG	PB	PR	PR+	PD	TPI
1917	Cle-A	0	1	.000	6	0	0	0	0	8^2	14	11	0	1	4	3	19.7	8.31	34	.368	.442	0	.000	-0	-5	-5	1	-0.4
Total	3	1	4	.200	26	5	0	0	1	66^1	70	41	1	5	26	20	13.7	4.21	70	.273	.352	2	.154	-1	-10	-9	2	-0.8

● CLAY SMITH
Smith, Clay Jamieson b: 9/11/14, Cambridge, Kan. BR/TR, 6'2", 190 lbs. Deb: 9/13/38

YEAR	TM/L	W	L	PCT	G	GS	CG	SH	SV	IP	H	R	HR	HB	BB	SO	RAT	ERA	ERA+	OAV	OOB	BH	AVG	PB	PR	PR+	PD	TPI
1938	Cle-A	0	0	—	4	0	0	0	0	11	18	10	1	0	2	3	16.4	6.55	71	.367	.392	0	.000	-0	-2	-2	0	-0.1
1940	*Det-A	1	1	.500	14	1	0	0	0	28^1	32	18	3	1	13	14	14.6	5.08	94	.283	.362	0	.000	-1	-2	-1	1	-0.1
Total	2	1	1	.500	18	1	0	0	0	39^1	50	28	4	1	15	17	15.1	5.49	86	.309	.371	0	.000	-1	-4	-3	1	-0.2

● DAN SMITH
Smith, Daniel Charles b: 9/15/75, Flemington, N.J. BR/TR, 6'3", 210 lbs. Deb: 6/8/99

YEAR	TM/L	W	L	PCT	G	GS	CG	SH	SV	IP	H	R	HR	HB	BB	SO	RAT	ERA	ERA+	OAV	OOB	BH	AVG	PB	PR	PR+	PD	TPI
1999	Mon-N	4	9	.308	20	17	0	0	0	89^2	104	64	12	4	39	72	14.8	6.02	75	.293	.369	2	.083	-1	-15	-16	-1	-2.0
2000	Bos-A	0	0	—	2	0	0	0	0	3^1	2	3	0	0	3	1	13.5	8.10	63	.250	.455	0	—	0	-1	-1	-0	-0.1
Total	2	4	9	.308	22	17	0	0	0	93	106	67	12	4	42	73	14.7	6.10	74	.292	.372	2	.083	-1	-16	-17	-1	-2.1

● DAN SMITH
Smith, Daniel Scott b: 4/20/69, St.Paul, Minn. BL/TL, 6'5", 190 lbs. Deb: 9/12/92

YEAR	TM/L	W	L	PCT	G	GS	CG	SH	SV	IP	H	R	HR	HB	BB	SO	RAT	ERA	ERA+	OAV	OOB	BH	AVG	PB	PR	PR+	PD	TPI
1992	Tex-A	0	3	.000	4	2	0	0	0	14^1	18	8	1	0	8	5	16.3	5.02	76	.321	.406	0	—	0	-2	-2	-0	-0.4
1994	Tex-A	1	2	.333	13	0	0	0	0	14^2	18	11	2	0	12	9	18.4	4.30	112	.281	.395	0	—	0	1	1	-0	0.1
Total	2	1	5	.167	17	2	0	0	0	29	36	19	3	0	20	14	17.4	4.66	93	.300	.400	0	—	0	-1	-1	-1	-0.3

● DARYL SMITH
Smith, Daryl Clinton b: 7/29/60, Baltimore, Md. BR/TR, 6'4", 185 lbs. Deb: 9/18/90

YEAR	TM/L	W	L	PCT	G	GS	CG	SH	SV	IP	H	R	HR	HB	BB	SO	RAT	ERA	ERA+	OAV	OOB	BH	AVG	PB	PR	PR+	PD	TPI
1990	KC-A	0	1	.000	2	1	0	0	0	6^2	5	3	0	0	4	6	12.2	4.05	95	.238	.360	0	—	0	-0	-0	-0	0.0

● DAVE SMITH
Smith, David Merwin b: 12/17/14, Sellers, S.C. d: 4/1/98, Whiteville, N.C. BR/TR, 5'10", 170 lbs. Deb: 6/16/38

YEAR	TM/L	W	L	PCT	G	GS	CG	SH	SV	IP	H	R	HR	HB	BB	SO	RAT	ERA	ERA+	OAV	OOB	BH	AVG	PB	PR	PR+	PD	TPI
1938	Phi-A	2	1	.667	21	0	0	0	0	44^1	50	29	0	1	28	13	16.0	5.08	95	.284	.385	0	.000	-1	-1	-1	-0	-0.2
1939	Phi-A	0	0	—	1	0	0	0	0	0	1	0	0	2	—	—	—	—	1.000	1.000	102	—	0	0	0	0	0.0	
Total	2	2	1	.667	22	0	0	0	0	44^1	51	29	0	1	30	13	16.6	5.08	95	.288	.394	0	.000	-1	-1	-1	-0	-0.2

● DAVE SMITH
Smith, David Stanley b: 1/21/55, Richmond, Cal. BR/TR, 6'1", 195 lbs. Deb: 4/11/80 C

YEAR	TM/L	W	L	PCT	G	GS	CG	SH	SV	IP	H	R	HR	HB	BB	SO	RAT	ERA	ERA+	OAV	OOB	BH	AVG	PB	PR	PR+	PD	TPI
1980	*Hou-N	7	5	.583	57	0	0	0	10	102^2	90	24	1	4	32	85	11.0	1.93	171	.237	.304	0	.000	-1	19	17	-1	2.0
1981	*Hou-N	5	3	.625	42	0	0	0	8	75	54	26	2	2	23	52	9.5	2.76	119	.198	.265	2	.250	0	6	5	-0	0.6
1982	Hou-N	5	4	.556	49	1	0	0	11	63^1	69	30	4	0	31	28	14.2	3.84	87	.285	.366	0	.000	-0	-2	-4	-1	-0.8
1983	Hou-N	3	1	.750	42	0	0	0	6	72^2	72	32	2	0	36	41	13.4	3.10	110	.258	.343	0	.000	-1	4	3	-2	-0.1
1984	Hou-N	5	4	.556	53	0	0	0	5	77^1	60	22	5	1	20	45	9.4	2.21	150	.214	.269	0	.000	-0	12	10	-1	1.2
1985	Hou-N	9	5	.643	64	0	0	0	27	79^1	69	26	3	1	17	40	9.9	2.27	153	.235	.280	0	.000	0	12	11	-1	2.2
1986	*Hou-N☆	4	7	.364	54	0	0	0	33	56	39	17	5	1	22	46	10.0	2.73	132	.200	.284	0	.000	-0	6	6	0	1.2
1987	Hou-N	2	3	.400	50	0	0	0	24	60	39	13	0	1	21	73	9.2	1.65	238	.182	.258	1	.500	1	16	16	-0	2.4
1988	Hou-N	4	5	.444	51	0	0	0	27	57^1	60	26	1	1	19	38	12.6	2.67	125	.268	.328	0	.000	-0	5	4	-0	0.9
1989	Hou-N	3	4	.429	52	0	0	0	25	58	49	20	1	1	19	31	10.7	2.64	129	.233	.300	0	.000	-0	6	5	1	1.1
1990	Hou-N★	6	6	.500	49	0	0	0	23	60^1	45	18	4	0	20	50	9.7	2.39	156	.210	.278	0	.000	0	9	9	-1	1.8
1991	Chi-N	0	6	.000	35	0	0	0	17	33	39	22	6	1	19	16	16.1	6.00	65	.302	.396	0	.000	-0	-8	-7	-0	-1.5
1992	Chi-N	0	0	—	11	0	0	0	0	14^1	15	4	0	0	4	3	11.9	2.51	144	.273	.322	0	—	0	2	2	-0	0.1
Total	13	53	53	.500	609	1	0	0	216	809^1	700	280	34	13	283	548	11.1	2.67	130	.234	.303	3	.068	-2	87	75	-7	11.1

● DAVE SMITH
Smith, David Wayne b: 8/30/57, Tomball, Tex. BR/TR, 6'1", 190 lbs. Deb: 9/18/84

YEAR	TM/L	W	L	PCT	G	GS	CG	SH	SV	IP	H	R	HR	HB	BB	SO	RAT	ERA	ERA+	OAV	OOB	BH	AVG	PB	PR	PR+	PD	TPI
1984	Cal-A	0	0	—	1	0	0	0	0	1	4	2	1	0	0	0	36.0	18.00	22	.571	.571	0	—	0	-2	-2	0	-0.1
1985	Cal-A	0	0	—	4	0	0	0	0	5	5	4	1	0	1	3	10.8	7.20	57	.278	.316	0	—	0	-2	-2	0	-0.1
Total	2	0	0	—	5	0	0	0	0	6	9	6	2	0	1	3	15.0	9.00	45	.360	.385	0	—	0	-3	-3	0	-0.2

● DOUG SMITH
Smith, Douglass Weldon b: 5/25/1892, Millers Falls, Mass. d: 9/18/73, Greenfield, Mass. BL/TL, 5'10", 168 lbs. Deb: 7/10/12

YEAR	TM/L	W	L	PCT	G	GS	CG	SH	SV	IP	H	R	HR	HB	BB	SO	RAT	ERA	ERA+	OAV	OOB	BH	AVG	PB	PR	PR+	PD	TPI
1912	Bos-A	0	0	—	1	0	0	0	0	3	4	1	0	0	0	1	12.0	3.00	113	.364	.364	0	—	0	0	0	-0	0.0

● ED SMITH
Smith, Ed Deb: 4/18/1884

YEAR	TM/L	W	L	PCT	G	GS	CG	SH	SV	IP	H	R	HR	HB	BB	SO	RAT	ERA	ERA+	OAV	OOB	BH	AVG	PB	PR	PR+	PD	TPI
1884	Bal-U	3	4	.429	9	8	5	0	0	62	86	61	2		17	13	15.0	3.48	77	.308	.348	5	.147	-4	-7	-5	-1	-0.8

● EDDIE SMITH
Smith, Edgar b: 12/14/13, Mansfield, N.J. d: 1/2/94, Willingboro, N.J. BB/TL, 5'10", 174 lbs. Deb: 9/20/36

YEAR	TM/L	W	L	PCT	G	GS	CG	SH	SV	IP	H	R	HR	HB	BB	SO	RAT	ERA	ERA+	OAV	OOB	BH	AVG	PB	PR	PR+	PD	TPI
1936	Phi-A	1	1	.500	2	2	2	0	0	19	22	10	3	0	8	7	14.2	1.89	269	.275	.341	1	.125	-1	7	7	0	0.6
1937	Phi-A	4	17	.190	38	23	14	1	5	196^2	178	100	18	4	90	79	12.4	3.94	120	.242	.327	17	.233	1	15	17	-2	1.6
1938	Phi-A	3	10	.231	43	7	0	0	4	130^2	151	102	13	4	76	78	15.9	5.92	82	.287	.381	12	.286	3	-16	-16	0	-1.1
1939	Phi-A	1	0	1.000	3	0	0	0	0	3^2	7	4	0	0	2	3	22.1	9.82	48	.412	.474	0	—	0	-2	-2	-0	-0.4
	Chi-A	9	11	.450	29	22	7	1	0	176^2	161	83	11	4	90	67	13.0	3.67	129	.247	.342	6	.115	-1	19	20	-2	1.7
	Yr	10	11	.476	32	22	7	1	0	180^1	168	87	11	4	92	70	13.2	3.79	125	.251	.346	6	.115	-1	17	18	-2	1.3
1940	Chi-A	14	9	.609	32	28	12	0	0	207^1	179	92	16	3	95	119	12.0	3.21	138	.228	.313	15	.217	2	27	28	-1	2.9
1941	Chi-A★	13	17	.433	34	33	21	1	1	263^1	243	107	13	5	114	111	12.4	3.18	129	.246	.328	19	.216	4	28	27	0	3.3
1942	Chi-A☆	7	20	.259	29	28	18	2	1	215	223	112	17	4	86	78	13.1	3.98	90	.269	.341	9	.123	-2	-8	-9	2	-1.1
1943	Chi-A	11	11	.500	25	25	14	2	0	187^2	197	85	2	5	76	66	13.3	3.69	90	.277	.351	11	.159	-1	-8	-7	1	-0.8
1946	Chi-A	8	11	.421	24	21	3	1	1	145^1	135	71	9	4	60	59	12.3	2.85	120	.246	.325	8	.178	0	11	9	-0	1.2
1947	Chi-A	1	3	.250	15	5	0	0	0	33^1	40	36	1	0	24	12	17.3	7.29	50	.299	.405	1	.167	-0	-13	-14	-1	-1.5
	Bos-A	1	3	.250	8	3	0	0	0	17	18	14	3	0	18	15	19.1	7.41	52	.269	.424	1	.167	0	-7	-6	-0	-1.2
	Yr	2	6	.250	23	8	0	0	0	50^1	58	50	4	0	42	27	17.9	7.33	51	.289	.412	2	.167	-0	-20	-20	-1	-2.7
Total	10	73	113	.392	282	197	91	8	12	1595^2	1554	816	106	33	739	694	13.1	3.82	108	.256	.340	100	.188	5	51	53	-3	5.2

● EDGAR SMITH
Smith, Edgar Eugene b: 6/12/1862, Providence, R.I. d: 11/3/1892, Providence, R.I. BR/TR, 5'10", 160 lbs. Deb: 5/25/1883 ♦

YEAR	TM/L	W	L	PCT	G	GS	CG	SH	SV	IP	H	R	HR	HB	BB	SO	RAT	ERA	ERA+	OAV	OOB	BH	AVG	PB	PR	PR+	PD	TPI
1883	Phi-N	0	1	.000	1	1	0	0	0	7	18	17	0		3	2	27.0	15.43	20	.409	.447	3	.750	1	-10	-10	-0	-0.7
1884	Was-a	0	2	.000	3	2	2	0	0	22	27	23	0	1	5	4	13.5	4.91	62	.276	.317	5	.088	-1	-4	-5	-0	-0.4
1885	Pro-N	1	0	1.000	1	1	1	0	0	9	9	3	0		0	1	9.0	1.00	269	.273	.273	1	.250	0	2	2	0	0.2
1890	Cle-N	1	4	.200	6	6	5	0	0	44	42	24	1	1	10	11	10.8	4.30	83	.244	.290	7	.292	2	-4	-3	2	0.0
Total	4	2	7	.222	11	10	8	0	0	82	96	67	1	2	18	18	12.7	5.05	65	.277	.316	18	.184	2	-15	-16	1	-0.9

● ELMER SMITH
Smith, Elmer Ellsworth b: 3/23/1868, Pittsburgh, Pa. d: 11/3/45, Pittsburgh, Pa. BL/TL, 5'11", 178 lbs. Deb: 9/10/1886 ♦

YEAR	TM/L	W	L	PCT	G	GS	CG	SH	SV	IP	H	R	HR	HB	BB	SO	RAT	ERA	ERA+	OAV	OOB	BH	AVG	PB	PR	PR+	PD	TPI
1886	Cin-a	4	4	.500	9	9	8	0	0	72^2	57	54	1	3	44	40	12.9	3.72	95	.211	.328	8	.286	4	-2	-2	-2	0.0
1887	Cin-a	34	17	.667	52	52	49	3	0	447^1	526	224	5	9	126	176	**10.8**	**2.94**	**148**	.282	**.286**	58	.294	5	68	69	-5	5.9
1888	Cin-a	22	17	.564	40	40	37	5	0	348^1	309	167	1	19	89	154	10.8	2.74	116	.229	.286	29	.225	4	13	16	-5	1.4
1889	Cin-a	9	12	.429	29	22	16	0	0	203	253	171	11	7	101	104	16.0	4.88	80	.296	.375	23	.277	6	-23	-22	-4	-1.6
1892	Pit-N	6	7	.462	17	13	12	1	0	134	140	94	2	1	58	51	13.4	3.63	91	.258	.331	140	.274	6	-5	-5	-1	-0.1
1894	Pit-N	0	0	—	1	0	0	0	0	4	6	2	0	1	1	0	18.0	4.50	117	.333	.400	175	.357	0	0	0	-0	0.0
1898	Cin-N	0	0	—	1	0	0	0	0	1	2	2	0	0	3	0	45.0	18.00	21	.400	.625	166	.342	0	-2	-1	-0	-0.1
Total	7	75	57	.568	149	136	122	9	0	1210^1	1293	714	20	40	422	525	12.1	3.35	113	.264	.311	1467	.312	25	48	57	-19	5.5

● BILL SMITH
Smith, F. William b: 1863, New Orleans, La. TR, 5'8", 152 lbs. Deb: 7/6/1886

YEAR	TM/L	W	L	PCT	G	GS	CG	SH	SV	IP	H	R	HR	HB	BB	SO	RAT	ERA	ERA+	OAV	OOB	BH	AVG	PB	PR	PR+	PD	TPI
1886	Det-N	5	4	.556	9	9	9	0	0	77	81	47	0		30	36	13.0	4.09	81	.259	.324	7	.184	-1	-7	-7	-1	-0.8

● FRANK SMITH
Smith, Frank Elmer "Nig" or "Piano Mover" (b: Frank Elmer Schmidt)
b: 10/28/1879, Pittsburgh, Pa. d: 11/3/52, Pittsburgh, Pa. BR/TR, 5'10.5", 194 lbs. Deb: 4/22/04

YEAR	TM/L	W	L	PCT	G	GS	CG	SH	SV	IP	H	R	HR	HB	BB	SO	RAT	ERA	ERA+	OAV	OOB	BH	AVG	PB	PR	PR+	PD	TPI
1904	Chi-A	16	9	.640	26	23	22	4	0	202^1	157	62	0	12	58	107	10.1	2.09	117	.215	.284	18	.250	4	11	9	-2	1.4
1905	Chi-A	19	13	.594	39	31	27	4	0	291^2	215	97	0	8	107	171	10.2	2.13	116	.208	.287	24	.226	7	17	12	0	2.0
1906	Chi-A	5	5	.500	20	13	8	1	1	122	124	58	3	5	37	53	12.2	3.39	75	.267	.327	12	.293	5	-10	-12	1	-0.4
1907	Chi-A	23	10	.697	41	37	29	3	0	310	280	105	3	2	111	139	11.4	2.47	97	.243	.311	18	.196	5	3	-3	3	0.6
1908	Chi-A	16	17	.485	41	35	24	3	1	297^2	213	92	2	2	73	129	8.7	2.03	114	.203	.256	20	.189	2	12	10	3	1.7
1909	Chi-A	25	17	.595	**51**	40	**37**	7	1	**365**	278	104	1	6	70	**177**	8.7	1.80	130	.214	.257	22	.173	6	27	23	10	**4.7**
1910	Chi-A	4	9	.308	19	15	9	3	0	128^2	91	43	1	2	40	50	9.3	2.03	118	.204	.272	8	.186	2	7	6	4	1.2
	Bos-A	1	2	.333	4	3	2	0	0	28	22	19	0	1	11	8	10.9	4.82	53	.234	.321	1	.111	-0	-7	-7	-0	-0.7
	Yr	5	11	.313	23	18	11	3	0	156^2	113	62	1	3	51	58	9.6	2.53	96	.209	.281	9	.173	2	-0	-2	4	0.5
1911	Bos-A	0	0	—	1	1	0	0	0	2^1	6	4	0	0	3	1	34.7	15.43	21	.500	.600	0	—	0	-3	-3	0	-0.1
	Cin-N	10	14	.417	34	18	10	0	1	176^1	198	112	1	3	55	67	13.1	3.98	83	.289	.345	12	.214	3	-11	-14	4	-1.0

YEAR	TM/L	W	L	PCT	G	GS	CG	SH	SV	IP	H	R	HR	HB	BB	SO	RAT	ERA	ERA+	OAV	OOB	BH	AVG	PB	PR	PR+	PD	TPI
1912	Cin-N	1	1	.500	7	3	1	0	0	22^{2}	34	25	1	0	15	5	19.5	6.35	53	.370	.458	0	.000	-0	-7	-8	-0	-0.6
1914	Bal-F	10	8	.556	39	22	9	1	2	174^{2}	180	86	8	0	47	83	11.7	2.99	101	.259	.306	12	.203	0	-2	1	2	0.3
1915	Bal-F	4	4	.500	17	9	2	0	0	88^{2}	108	53	5	0	31	37	14.1	4.67	61	.312	.369	5	.172	0	-19	-17	0	-1.3
	Bro-F	5	2	.714	15	5	4	1	0	63	69	31	2	0	18	24	12.4	3.14	87	.290	.340	4	.200	0	-3	-3	1	-0.2
	Yr	9	6	.600	32	14	6	1	0	151^{2}	177	84	7	0	49	61	13.4	4.04	70	.303	.357	9	.184	1	-22	-20	1	-1.5
Total	11	139	111	.556	354	255	184	27	6	2273	1975	891	27	41	676	1051	10.7	2.59	99	.237	.297	156	.204	35	15	-10	26	7.6
● FRANK SMITH	Smith, Frank Thomas b: 4/4/28, Pierrepont Manor, N.Y. BR/TR, 6'3", 200 lbs. Deb: 4/18/50																											
1950	Cin-N	2	7	.222	38	4	0	0	3	90^{2}	73	43	12	8	39	55	11.9	3.87	109	.216	.312	2	.095	-2	3	4	-1	0.1
1951	Cin-N	5	5	.500	50	0	0	0	11	76	65	33	7	4	22	34	10.8	3.20	128	.230	.295	0	.000	-1	6	7	0	1.0
1952	Cin-N	12	11	.522	53	2	1	0	7	122^{1}	109	56	13	7	41	77	11.6	3.75	101	.242	.315	5	.172	0	-0	0	-2	-0.1
1953	Cin-N	8	1	.889	50	1	0	0	2	83^{2}	89	64	15	3	25	42	12.6	5.49	79	.272	.330	2	.154	-1	-11	-10	1	-1.0
1954	Cin-N	5	8	.385	50	0	0	0	20	81	60	29	15	3	29	51	10.2	2.67	157	.211	.291	1	.100	1	13	13	0	2.8
1955	StL-N	3	1	.750	28	0	0	0	1	39	27	18	3	5	23	17	12.7	3.23	126	.205	.344	0	.000	-1	3	4	-0	0.3
1956	Cin-N	0	0	—	2	0	0	0	0	3	3	4	2	0	2	1	15.0	12.00	33	.300	.417	0	—	0	-3	-3	-0	-0.1
Total	7	35	33	.515	271	7	1	0	44	495^{2}	426	247	67	30	181	277	11.6	3.81	107	.234	.313	10	.115	-3	11	15	-2	3.0
● FRED SMITH	Smith, Frederick b: 11/24/1878, New Diggings, Wis. d: 2/4/64, Los Angeles, Cal. BL/TR, 6', 186 lbs. Deb: 6/14/07																											
1907	Cin-N	2	7	.222	18	9	5	0	1	85^{1}	90	44	3	4	24	19	12.4	2.85	91	.274	.331	3	.107	-2	-4	-2	0	-0.4
● FRED SMITH	Smith, Frederick C. b: 3/25/1863, Greene, N.Y. d: 1/9/41, Syracuse, N.Y. BL/TR, 5'11", 156 lbs. Deb: 4/18/1890																											
1890	Tol-a	19	13	.594	35	34	31	2	0	286	273	155	13	13	90	116	11.8	3.27	121	.244	.307	21	.167	-2	19	21	3	1.9
● GEORGE SMITH	Smith, George Allen "Columbia George" b: 5/31/1892, Byram, Conn. d: 1/7/65, Greenwich, Conn. BR/TR, 6'2", 163 lbs. Deb: 8/9/16																											
1916	NY-N	3	0	1.000	9	1	0	0	0	20^{2}	14	8	0	1	6	9	9.1	2.61	93	.197	.269	0	.000	-0	0	-0	0	0.0
1917	NY-N	0	3	.000	14	1	1	0	0	38	38	13	1	1	11	16	11.8	2.84	90	.270	.327	0	.000	-1	-1	-1	-0	-0.3
1918	Cin-N	2	3	.400	10	6	4	1	0	55^{1}	71	36	3	0	11	19	13.3	4.07	66	.329	.361	0	.000	-2	-8	-9	1	-0.9
	NY-N	2	3	.400	5	2	1	0	0	26^{2}	26	12	0	1	6	4	11.1	4.05	65	.255	.303	2	.250	0	-4	-4	-1	-0.9
	Bro-N	4	1	.800	8	5	4	0	0	50	43	14	0	2	5	18	9.0	2.34	119	.249	.278	3	.200	0	2	2	1	0.4
	Yr	8	7	.533	23	13	9	1	0	132	140	62	3	3	22	41	11.3	3.41	79	.285	.320	5	.125	-2	-9	-11	0	-1.4
1919	NY-N	0	2	.000	3	2	0	0	0	11	18	8	1	0	4	0	18.0	5.73	49	.383	.431	0	.000	-0	-3	-4	-0	-0.7
	Phi-N	5	11	.313	31	19	11	1	0	184^{2}	194	94	7	3	46	42	11.8	3.22	100	.278	.326	8	.133	-3	-6	0	-1	-0.4
	Yr	5	13	.278	34	21	11	1	0	195^{2}	212	102	8	3	50	42	12.2	3.36	95	.285	.332	8	.127	-4	-10	-3	-1	-1.1
1920	Phi-N	13	18	.419	43	28	10	1	2	250^{2}	265	115	10	6	51	51	11.6	3.45	99	.283	.324	7	.097	-6	-9	-1	-2	-0.9
1921	Phi-N	4	20	.167	39	28	12	1	1	221^{1}	303	166	12	3	52	45	14.6	4.76	89	.335	.373	4	.056	-8	-24	-12	-2	-2.0
1922	Phi-N	5	14	.263	42	16	6	1	0	194	250	124	16	6	35	44	13.5	4.78	98	.316	.350	5	.076	-7	-15	-2	-2	-1.0
1923	Bro-N	3	6	.333	25	7	3	0	1	91	99	53	4	3	28	15	12.9	3.66	106	.278	.336	5	.192	-1	3	2	-2	-0.1
Total	8	41	81	.336	229	115	52	5	4	1143^{1}	1321	643	54	26	255	263	12.6	3.89	94	.298	.340	34	.097	-29	-63	-29	-8	-6.8
● HEINIE SMITH	Smith, George Henry b: 10/24/1871, Pittsburgh, Pa. d: 6/25/39, Buffalo, N.Y. BR/TR, 5'9.5", 160 lbs. Deb: 9/8/1897 M◆																											
1901	NY-N	0	1	.000	2	1	1	0	0	13^{1}	24	13	0	3	5	5	21.6	8.10	41	.387	.457	6	.207	0	-7	-7	-0	-0.4
● GERMANY SMITH	Smith, George J. b: 4/21/1863, Pittsburgh, Pa. d: 12/1/27, Altoona, Pa. BR/TR, 6', 175 lbs. Deb: 4/17/1884 ◆																											
1884	Alt-U	0	0	—	1	0	0	0	0	1	3	2	0		0	1	27.0	9.00	30	.500	.500	34	.315	0	-1	-1	0	0.0
● GEORGE SMITH	Smith, George Shelby b: 10/27/01, Louisville, Ky. d: 5/26/81, Richmond, Va. BR/TR, 6'1", 175 lbs. Deb: 4/21/26																											
1926	Det-A	1	2	.333	23	1	0	0	0	44	55	37	3	2	33	15	18.4	6.95	58	.318	.433	0	.000	-0	-14	-14	-1	-0.9
1927	Det-A	4	1	.800	29	0	0	0	0	71^{1}	62	38	3	2	50	32	14.4	3.91	108	.240	.368	7	.368	3	2	2	-1	0.4
1928	Det-A	1	1	.500	39	2	0	0	3	106	103	55	3	0	50	54	13.0	4.42	93	.263	.346	3	.111	-2	-4	-4	-2	-0.5
1929	Det-A	3	2	.600	14	2	1	0	0	35^{2}	42	33	1	0	36	13	19.7	5.80	74	.307	.451	5	.417	2	-6	-6	1	-0.4
1930	Bos-A	1	2	.333	27	2	0	0	0	73^{2}	92	62	7	1	49	21	17.3	6.60	70	.317	.418	8	.333	2	-16	-16	0	-0.5
Total	5	10	8	.556	132	7	1	0	3	330^{2}	354	225	17	5	218	135	15.7	5.28	81	.283	.392	23	.264	4	-39	-37	-2	-1.9
● HAL SMITH	Smith, Harold Laverne b: 6/30/02, Creston, Iowa d: 9/27/92, Ft.Lauderdale, Fla. BR/TR, 6'3", 195 lbs. Deb: 9/14/32																											
1932	Pit-N	1	0	1.000	2	1	1	1	0	12	9	1	0	0	2	4	8.3	0.75	508	.209	.244	0	.000	-0	4	4	0	0.3
1933	Pit-N	8	7	.533	28	19	8	2	1	145	149	66	5	5	31	40	11.5	2.86	116	.261	.305	6	.128	-2	8	8	-2	0.4
1934	Pit-N	3	4	.429	20	5	1	0	0	50	72	44	3	4	18	15	16.9	7.20	57	.343	.405	1	.059	-2	-17	-17	-0	-2.2
1935	Pit-N	0	0	—	1	0	0	0	0	3	2	1	0	0	1	0	9.0	3.00	137	.200	.273	0	—	0	0	0	-0	0.0
Total	4	12	11	.522	51	25	10	3	1	210	232	112	8	9	52	59	12.6	3.77	94	.279	.328	7	.104	-4	-5	-5	-2	-1.5
● HARRY SMITH	Smith, Harrison Morton b: 8/15/1889, Union, Neb. d: 7/26/64, Dunbar, Neb. BR/TR, 5'9", 160 lbs. Deb: 10/6/12																											
1912	Chi-A	1	0	1.000	1	1	0	0	0	5	6	1	0	0	0	1	10.8	1.80	178	.333	.333	0	.000	-0	1	1	-0	0.1
● JACK SMITH	Smith, Jack Hatfield b: 11/15/35, Pikeville, Ky. BR/TR, 6', 185 lbs. Deb: 9/10/62																											
1962	LA-N	0	0	—	8	0	0	0	1	10	10	6	0	0	4	7	12.6	4.50	81	.263	.333	0	.000	-0	-1	-1	-0	-0.1
1963	LA-N	0	0	—	4	0	0	0	0	8^{1}	10	7	2	2	2	5	15.1	7.56	40	.303	.378	0	.000	-0	-4	-5	0	-0.2
1964	Mil-N	2	2	.500	22	0	0	0	0	31	28	15	3	0	11	19	11.3	3.77	93	.237	.302	1	.333	0	-1	-1	1	0.0
Total	3	2	2	.500	34	0	0	0	1	49^{1}	48	28	5	2	17	31	12.2	4.56	76	.254	.322	1	.167	-0	-5	-6	1	-0.3
● JAKE SMITH	Smith, Jacob (b: Jacob Schmidt) b: 6/10/1887, Dravosburg, Pa d: 11/7/48, E.McKeesport, Pa. BB/TL, 6'5", 200 lbs. Deb: 10/3/11																											
1911	Phi-N	0	0	—	2	0	0	0	0	5	3	0	0	0	2	1	9.0	0.00	—	.176	.263	0	.000	-0	2	2	0	0.1
● PHENOMENAL SMITH	Smith, John Francis (b: John Francis Gammon) b: 12/12/1864, Philadelphia, Pa. d: 4/3/52, Manchester, N.H. BL/TL, 5'6.5", 161 lbs. Deb: 8/14/1884																											
1884	Phi-a	0	1	.000	1	1	1	0	0	9	14	6	0	0	1	3	15.0	4.00	85	.368	.385	1	.250	-0	-1	-1	0	0.0
	Pit-a	0	1	.000	1	1	1	0	0	8	11	10	0	1	2	4	15.8	9.00	37	.306	.359	0	.000	-1	-5	-5	0	-0.5
	Yr	0	2	.000	2	2	2	0	0	17	25	16	0	1	3	7	15.4	6.35	53	.338	.372	1	.125	-1	-6	-6	0	-0.5
1885	Bro-a	0	1	.000	1	1	1	0	0	8	12	18	0	1	6	2	21.4	12.38	27	.300	.404	1	.333	0	-8	-8	0	-0.6
	Phi-a	0	1	.000	1	1	0	0	0	4	7	9	0	1	4	7	27.0	9.00	38	.368	.500	0	.000	-0	-3	-2	0	-0.4
	Yr	0	2	.000	2	2	1	0	0	12	19	27	0	2	10	9	23.3	11.25	30	.322	.437	1	.200	-0	-11	-10	0	-1.0
1886	Det-N	1	1	.500	3	3	3	0	0	25	16	9	0		8	15	8.6	2.16	153	.174	.240	1	.111	-1	3	3	-1	0.1
1887	Bal-a	25	30	.455	58	55	54	1	0	491^{1}	702	369	7	14	176	206	13.1	3.79	108	.321	.325	74	.320	8	28	18	-1	2.1
1888	Bal-a	14	19	.424	35	32	31	0	0	292	249	170	5	24	137	152	12.6	3.61	83	.222	.320	27	.248	8	-18	-21	-4	-1.6
	Phi-a	2	1	.667	3	3	3	0	0	22	21	15	0	0	10	19	12.7	2.86	104	.241	.320	3	.333	1	0	0	-0	0.1
	Yr	16	20	.444	38	35	34	0	0	314	270	185	5	24	147	171	12.6	3.55	84	.224	.320	30	.254	9	-17	-21	-4	-1.5
1889	Phi-a	2	3	.400	5	5	5	0	0	43	53	31	2	3	25	12	17.0	4.40	86	.294	.389	3	.188	0	-3	-3	-1	-0.3
1890	Phi-N	8	12	.400	24	20	19	1	0	204	209	125	5	8	89	81	13.5	4.28	85	.257	.336	24	.279	4	-16	-14	-2	-0.9
	Pit-N	1	3	.250	5	5	5	0	0	44	39	25	0	1	13	15	10.8	3.07	107	.231	.290	7	.412	2	2	1	-0	0.3
	Yr	9	15	.375	29	25	24	1	0	248	248	150	5	9	102	96	13.0	4.06	88	.253	.328	31	.301	6	-14	-13	-3	-0.6
1891	Phi-N	1	1	.500	3	2	0	0	0	19	20	15	1	0	8	3	13.3	4.26	80	.260	.329	3	.375	1	-2	-2	-1	-0.1
Total	8	54	74	.422	140	129	123	2	0	1169^{1}	1353	802	20	53	479	519	13.2	3.89	93	.278	.328	144	.289	23	-21	-34	-9	-1.8
● CHICK SMITH	Smith, John William (b: Jan Smadt) b: 12/2/1892, Dayton, Ky. d: 10/11/35, Dayton, Ky. BL/TL, 5'8", 165 lbs. Deb: 4/12/13																											
1913	Cin-N	0	1	.000	5	1	0	0	0	17^{2}	15	8	1	0	11	11	13.2	3.57	91	.238	.351	0	.000	-1	-1	-1	0	-0.1
● LEE SMITH	Smith, Lee Arthur b: 12/4/57, Shreveport, La. BR/TR, 6'6", 225 lbs. Deb: 9/1/80																											
1980	Chi-N	2	0	1.000	18	0	0	0	0	21^{2}	21	9	0	0	14	17	14.5	2.91	135	.259	.368	0	—	0	2	2	-0	0.2
1981	Chi-N	3	6	.333	40	1	0	0	1	66^{2}	57	31	2	1	31	50	12.0	3.51	105	.239	.330	0	.000	-1	-0	1	-0	0.0
1982	Chi-N	2	5	.286	72	5	0	0	17	117	105	38	5	3	37	99	11.2	2.69	139	.245	.309	1	.063	-0	12	13	-1	1.0
1983	Chi-N★	4	10	.286	66	0	0	0	**29**	103^{1}	70	23	5	1	41	91	9.8	1.65	230	.194	.279	1	.111	-0	23	24	-1	4.4
1984	*Chi-N	9	7	.563	69	0	0	0	33	101	98	42	6	0	35	86	11.9	3.65	107	.255	.317	1	.077	-1	-1	3	0	0.5
1985	Chi-N	7	4	.636	65	0	0	0	33	97^{2}	87	35	9	1	32	112	11.1	3.04	132	.242	.305	0	.000	-0	6	9	-1	1.6
1986	Chi-N	9	9	.500	66	0	0	0	31	90^{1}	69	32	7	0	42	93	11.1	3.09	131	.215	.306	0	.000	-1	6	9	-0	1.8

YEAR	TM/L	W	L	PCT	G	GS	CG	SH	SV	IP	H	R	HR	HB	BB	SO	RAT	ERA	ERA+	OAV	OOB	BH	AVG	PB	PR	PR+	PD	TPI
1987	Chi-N★	4	10	.286	62	0	0	0	36	83^2	84	30	4	0	32	96	12.5	3.12	137	.259	.326	0	.000	-0	9	10	-1	2.0
1988	*Bos-A	4	5	.444	64	0	0	0	29	83^2	72	34	7	1	37	96	11.8	2.80	147	.225	.307	0	—	0	11	12	-1	1.8
1989	Bos-A	6	1	.857	64	0	0	0	25	70^2	53	30	6	0	33	96	11.0	3.57	115	.209	.301	0	—	0	3	4	-1	0.5
1990	Bos-A	2	1	.667	11	0	0	0	4	14^1	13	4	0	0	9	17	13.8	1.88	217	.236	.344	0	—	0	3	3	0	0.7
	StL-N	3	4	.429	53	0	0	0	27	68^2	58	20	3	0	20	70	10.2	2.10	182	.227	.284	0	.000	-0	13	13	-2	2.1
1991	StL-N☆	6	3	.667	67	0	0	0	**47**	73	70	19	5	0	13	67	10.2	2.34	159	.249	.282	0	—	0	11	11	-1	2.3
1992	StL-N☆	4	9	.308	70	0	0	0	**43**	75	62	28	4	0	26	60	10.6	3.12	109	.221	.287	0	—	0	3	2	-1	0.4
1993	StL-N☆	2	4	.333	55	0	0	0	43	50	49	25	11	0	9	49	10.4	4.50	88	.251	.284	0	.000	-0	-3	-3	-1	-0.7
	NY-A	0	0	—	8	0	0	0	3	8	4	0	0	0	5	11	10.1	0.00	—	.148	.281	0	—	0	4	4	0	0.2
1994	Bal-A★	1	4	.200	41	0	0	0	**33**	38^1	34	16	6	0	11	42	10.6	3.29	153	.239	.294	0	—	0	6	7	-1	1.3
1995	Cal-A☆	0	5	.000	52	0	0	0	37	49^1	42	19	3	1	25	43	12.4	3.47	136	.237	.335	0	—	0	7	7	-1	1.2
1996	Cal-A	0	0	—	11	0	0	0	0	11	8	4	0	0	3	6	9.0	2.45	204	.205	.262	0	—	0	3	3	-0	0.1
	Cin-N	3	4	.429	43	0	0	0	2	44^1	49	20	4	1	23	35	14.8	4.06	104	.277	.363	0	—	0	1	1	-0	0.1
1997	Mon-N	0	1	.000	25	0	0	0	5	21^2	28	16	2	1	8	15	15.4	5.82	72	.308	.370	0	—	0	-4	-4	0	-0.3
Total	18	71	92	.436	1022	6	0	0	478	1289^1	1133	475	89	10	486	1251	11.4	3.03	132	.237	.308	3	.047	-4	116	133	-11	21.2

● ROY SMITH

Smith, Le Roy Purdy b: 9/6/61, Mt.Vernon, N.Y. BR/TR, 6'3", 200 lbs. Deb: 6/23/84

YEAR	TM/L	W	L	PCT	G	GS	CG	SH	SV	IP	H	R	HR	HB	BB	SO	RAT	ERA	ERA+	OAV	OOB	BH	AVG	PB	PR	PR+	PD	TPI
1984	Cle-A	5	5	.500	22	14	0	0	0	86^1	91	49	14	1	40	55	13.8	4.59	89	.270	.349	0	—	0	-6	-5	-2	-0.6
1985	Cle-A	1	4	.200	12	11	1	0	0	62^1	84	40	8	1	17	28	14.7	5.34	77	.321	.364	0	—	0	-8	-8	-1	-0.7
1986	Min-A	0	2	.000	5	0	0	0	0	10^1	13	8	1	1	5	8	16.5	6.97	62	.295	.380	0	—	0	-3	-3	-0	-0.5
1987	Min-A	1	0	1.000	7	1	0	0	0	16^1	20	10	3	2	6	8	15.4	4.96	93	.290	.364	0	—	0	-1	-1	-0	0.0
1988	Min-A	3	0	1.000	9	4	0	0	0	37	29	12	3	1	12	17	10.2	2.68	152	.210	.278	0	—	0	5	6	-1	0.4
1989	Min-A	10	6	.625	32	26	2	0	1	172^1	180	82	22	5	51	92	12.3	3.92	106	.269	.326	0	—	0	-0	4	-3	0.1
1990	Min-A	5	10	.333	32	23	1	1	0	153^1	191	91	20	0	47	87	14.0	4.81	87	.313	.362	0	—	0	-15	-10	-2	-1.1
1991	Bal-A	5	4	.556	17	14	0	0	0	80^1	99	52	9	1	24	25	13.9	5.60	71	.311	.362	0	—	0	-13	-15	-1	-1.5
Total	8	30	31	.492	136	93	4	1	1	618^1	707	344	80	12	202	320	13.4	4.60	90	.289	.346	0	—	0	-42	-31	-9	-3.9

● MARK SMITH

Smith, Mark Christopher b: 11/23/55, Arlington, Va. BR/TR, 6'2", 215 lbs. Deb: 8/12/83

YEAR	TM/L	W	L	PCT	G	GS	CG	SH	SV	IP	H	R	HR	HB	BB	SO	RAT	ERA	ERA+	OAV	OOB	BH	AVG	PB	PR	PR+	PD	TPI
1983	Oak-A	1	0	1.000	8	1	0	0	0	14^2	24	11	0	1	6	10	19.0	6.75	57	.387	.449	0	—	0	-4	-5	-0	-0.3

● MIKE SMITH

Smith, Michael Anthony b: 2/23/61, Jackson, Miss. BR/TR, 6'1", 195 lbs. Deb: 4/6/84

YEAR	TM/L	W	L	PCT	G	GS	CG	SH	SV	IP	H	R	HR	HB	BB	SO	RAT	ERA	ERA+	OAV	OOB	BH	AVG	PB	PR	PR+	PD	TPI
1984	Cin-N	1	0	1.000	8	0	0	0	0	10^1	12	6	1	0	5	7	14.8	5.23	72	.286	.362	0	—	0	-2	-2	-0	-0.2
1985	Cin-N	0	0	—	2	0	0	0	0	3^1	2	2	2	0	1	2	8.1	5.40	70	.167	.231	0	—	0	-1	-1	0	0.0
1986	Cin-N	0	0	—	2	1	0	0	0	3^1	7	5	0	0	1	1	21.6	13.50	29	.412	.444	0	—	0	-4	-3	-0	-0.2
1988	Mon-N	0	0	—	5	0	0	0	1	8^2	6	3	0	0	5	4	11.4	3.12	116	.207	.324	0	.000	-0	0	0	-0	0.0
1989	Pit-N	0	1	.000	16	0	0	0	0	24	28	12	1	0	10	12	14.3	3.75	90	.301	.369	0	.000	-0	-1	-1	1	0.0
Total	5	1	1	.500	33	1	0	0	1	49^2	55	28	4	0	22	26	14.0	4.71	75	.285	.358	0	.000	-1	-6	-6	0	-0.4

● MIKE SMITH

Smith, Michael Anthony b: 10/31/63, San Antonio, Tex. BR/TR, 6'3", 180 lbs. Deb: 6/30/89

YEAR	TM/L	W	L	PCT	G	GS	CG	SH	SV	IP	H	R	HR	HB	BB	SO	RAT	ERA	ERA+	OAV	OOB	BH	AVG	PB	PR	PR+	PD	TPI
1989	Bal-A	2	0	1.000	13	1	0	0	0	20	25	19	3	0	14	12	17.5	7.65	50	.313	.415	0	—	0	-8	-9	0	-0.8
1990	Bal-A	0	0	—	2	0	0	0	0	3	4	4	2	0	1	2	15.0	12.00	32	.308	.357	0	—	0	-3	-3	-0	-0.1
Total	2	2	0	1.000	15	1	0	0	0	23	29	23	5	0	15	14	17.2	8.22	46	.312	.407	0	—	0	-11	-12	0	-0.9

● PETE SMITH

Smith, Peter John b: 2/27/66, Abington, Mass. BR/TR, 6'2", 200 lbs. Deb: 9/8/87

YEAR	TM/L	W	L	PCT	G	GS	CG	SH	SV	IP	H	R	HR	HB	BB	SO	RAT	ERA	ERA+	OAV	OOB	BH	AVG	PB	PR	PR+	PD	TPI
1987	Atl-N	1	2	.333	6	6	0	0	0	31^2	39	21	3	0	14	11	15.1	4.83	90	.307	.376	1	.091	-1	-3	-2	-1	-0.3
1988	Atl-N	7	15	.318	32	32	5	3	0	195^1	183	89	15	1	88	124	12.5	3.69	100	.250	.331	6	.113	-1	-5	-0	-3	-0.4
1989	Atl-N	5	14	.263	28	27	1	0	0	142	144	83	13	0	57	115	12.7	4.75	77	.263	.333	4	.098	-0	-20	-17	-1	-2.2
1990	Atl-N	5	6	.455	13	13	3	0	0	77	77	45	11	0	24	56	11.8	4.79	84	.260	.316	2	.087	-1	-9	-6	-1	-1.0
1991	Atl-N	1	3	.250	14	10	0	0	0	48	48	33	5	0	22	29	13.1	5.06	77	.262	.341	2	.167	0	-7	-6	1	-0.3
1992	*Atl-N	7	0	1.000	12	11	2	1	0	79	63	19	3	0	28	43	10.4	2.05	179	.217	.286	1	.038	-1	13	14	-0	1.0
1993	Atl-N	4	8	.333	20	14	0	0	0	90^2	92	45	15	2	36	53	12.9	4.37	92	.270	.343	6	.222	1	-3	-4	0	-0.3
1994	NY-N	4	10	.286	21	21	1	0	0	131^1	145	83	25	2	42	62	13.0	5.55	75	.285	.342	5	.135	0	-19	-20	1	-1.7
1995	Cin-N	1	2	.333	11	2	0	0	0	24^1	30	19	8	1	7	14	14.1	6.66	62	.319	.373	0	.000	0	-7	-7	0	-0.7
1997	SD-N	7	6	.538	37	15	0	0	1	118	120	66	16	1	52	68	13.2	4.81	81	.267	.345	5	.167	1	-8	-13	1	-1.1
1998	SD-N	3	2	.600	10	8	0	0	0	43^1	45	23	5	3	18	36	13.7	4.78	82	.266	.347	1	.071	-0	-3	-4	0	-0.5
	Bal-A	2	3	.400	27	4	0	0	0	45	57	31	7	0	16	29	14.6	6.20	74	.311	.367	0	.000	-0	-8	-8	1	-0.7
Total	11	47	71	.398	231	163	12	4	1	1025^2	1043	557	126	10	404	640	12.8	4.55	86	.266	.336	33	.118	-2	-78	-70	-1	-8.2

● PETE SMITH

Smith, Peter Luke b: 3/19/40, Natick, Mass. BR/TR, 6'2", 190 lbs. Deb: 9/13/62

YEAR	TM/L	W	L	PCT	G	GS	CG	SH	SV	IP	H	R	HR	HB	BB	SO	RAT	ERA	ERA+	OAV	OOB	BH	AVG	PB	PR	PR+	PD	TPI
1962	Bos-A	0	1	.000	1	1	0	0	0	3^2	7	8	3	0	2	1	22.1	19.64	21	.438	.500	0	.000	-0	-6	-6	0	-0.8
1963	Bos-A	0	0	—	6	1	0	0	0	15	11	6	2	0	6	6	10.2	3.60	105	.212	.293	0	.000	-0	0	0	0	0.0
Total	2	0	1	.000	7	2	0	0	0	18^2	18	14	5	0	8	7	12.5	6.75	57	.265	.342	0	.000	-0	-6	-6	0	-0.8

● BRIAN SMITH

Smith, Randall Brian b: 7/19/72, Salisbury, N.C. BR/TR, 5'11", 185 lbs. Deb: 9/11/2000

YEAR	TM/L	W	L	PCT	G	GS	CG	SH	SV	IP	H	R	HR	HB	BB	SO	RAT	ERA	ERA+	OAV	OOB	BH	AVG	PB	PR	PR+	PD	TPI
2000	Pit-N	0	0	—	3	0	0	0	0	4^1	6	5	1	0	2	3	16.6	10.38	44	.375	.444	0	—	0	-3	-3	0	-0.1

● REX SMITH

Smith, Rex (b: Henry W. Schmidt) b: 1864, Louisville, Ky. d: 6/21/1895, Louisville, Ky. Deb: 7/11/1886

YEAR	TM/L	W	L	PCT	G	GS	CG	SH	SV	IP	H	R	HR	HB	BB	SO	RAT	ERA	ERA+	OAV	OOB	BH	AVG	PB	PR	PR+	PD	TPI
1886	Phi-a	0	1	.000	1	1	1	0	0	9	15	13	0	0	5	4	20.0	7.00	50	.385	.455	0	.000	-1	-4	-3	-0	-0.3

● ED SMITH

Smith, Rhesa Edward b: 2/21/1879, Mentone, Ind. d: 3/20/55, Tarpon Springs, Fla. BR/TR, 5'11", 170 lbs. Deb: 4/27/06

YEAR	TM/L	W	L	PCT	G	GS	CG	SH	SV	IP	H	R	HR	HB	BB	SO	RAT	ERA	ERA+	OAV	OOB	BH	AVG	PB	PR	PR+	PD	TPI
1906	StL-A	8	11	.421	19	18	13	0	0	154^2	153	90	3	8	53	45	12.5	3.72	69	.261	.331	11	.204	2	-18	-20	1	-2.0

● BOB SMITH

Smith, Robert Ashley (a.k.a. Robert M. Brown In 1914)
b: 7/20/1890, Woodbury, Vt. d: 12/27/65, West Los Angeles, Cal. BR/TR, 5'11", 160 lbs. Deb: 4/19/13

YEAR	TM/L	W	L	PCT	G	GS	CG	SH	SV	IP	H	R	HR	HB	BB	SO	RAT	ERA	ERA+	OAV	OOB	BH	AVG	PB	PR	PR+	PD	TPI
1913	Chi-A	0	0	—	1	0	0	0	0	2	3	3	0	0	3	1	27.0	13.50	22	.273	.429	0	—	0	-2	-2	-0	-0.1
1914	Buf-F	0	0	—	15	1	0	0	3	36^2	39	16	3	2	16	13	14.0	3.44	86	.281	.363	2	.222	0	-2	-2	1	0.0
1915	Buf-F	0	0	—	1	0	0	0	0	1	1	2	0	1	2	0	36.0	18.00	16	.333	.667	0	—	0	-2	-2	0	-0.1
Total	3	0	0	—	17	1	0	0	3	39^2	43	21	3	3	21	14	15.2	4.31	69	.281	.379	2	.222	0	-6	-6	1	-0.2

● BOB SMITH

Smith, Robert Eldridge b: 4/22/1895, Rogersville, Tenn. d: 7/19/87, Waycross, Ga. BR/TR, 5'10", 175 lbs. Deb: 4/19/23 ♦

YEAR	TM/L	W	L	PCT	G	GS	CG	SH	SV	IP	H	R	HR	HB	BB	SO	RAT	ERA	ERA+	OAV	OOB	BH	AVG	PB	PR	PR+	PD	TPI
1925	Bos-N	5	3	.625	13	10	6	0	0	92^2	110	51	6	0	36	19	14.2	4.47	90	.304	.367	49	.282	3	-2	-5	-0	-0.1
1926	Bos-N	10	13	.435	33	23	14	4	1	201^1	199	91	10	0	75	44	12.2	3.75	94	.269	.336	25	.298	7	2	-5	2	0.4
1927	Bos-N	10	18	.357	41	31	16	1	3	260^2	297	132	9	2	75	81	12.9	3.76	99	.301	.351	27	.248	4	4	-2	2	0.6
1928	Bos-N	13	17	.433	38	26	14	0	2	244^1	274	138	11	2	74	59	12.9	3.87	101	.289	.342	23	.250	3	3	1	3	0.7
1929	Bos-N	11	17	.393	34	29	19	1	3	231	256	135	20	1	71	65	12.8	4.68	100	.285	.338	17	.172	-1	1	0	1	0.1
1930	Bos-N	10	14	.417	38	24	14	2	5	219^2	247	115	25	3	85	84	13.7	4.26	116	.290	.357	19	.235	-1	17	17	2	1.6
1931	Chi-N	15	12	.556	36	29	18	2	2	240^1	239	101	10	1	62	63	11.3	3.22	120	.256	.303	19	.218	2	17	17	1	2.0
1932	*Chi-N	4	3	.571	34	11	4	1	2	119	148	64	4	3	36	35	14.1	4.61	82	.303	.355	10	.238	2	-10	-12	1	-0.4
1933	Cin-N	4	4	.500	16	6	4	0	0	73^2	75	27	3	0	11	18	10.5	2.20	154	.260	.287	5	.200	0	9	10	-0	1.0
	Bos-N	4	3	.571	14	4	3	1	1	58^2	68	24	3	0	7	16	11.5	3.22	95	.296	.316	4	.200	1	1	-1	1	0.0
	Yr	8	7	.533	30	10	7	1	1	132^1	143	51	6	0	18	34	10.9	2.65	123	.276	.300	9	.200	1	10	9	1	1.0
1934	Bos-N	6	9	.400	39	5	3	0	5	121^2	133	69	9	0	36	26	12.5	4.66	82	.277	.328	9	.250	1	-8	-12	1	-1.2
1935	Bos-N	8	18	.308	46	20	8	2	5	203^1	232	105	13	3	61	58	13.1	3.94	96	.285	.337	17	.270	2	2	-4	-1	-0.2
1936	Bos-N	6	7	.462	35	11	5	2	8	136	142	65	3	1	35	36	11.8	3.77	102	.264	.311	10	.222	0	4	1	1	0.2
1937	Bos-N	0	1	.000	18	0	0	0	3	44	52	22	6	2	6	14	12.3	4.09	88	.295	.326	2	.200	0	-1	-3	-1	-0.2
Total	13	106	139	.433	435	229	128	16	40	2246^1	2472	1139	132	18	670	618	12.7	3.94	100	.283	.335	409	.242	23	40	4	12	4.5

● BOB SMITH

Smith, Robert Gilchrist b: 2/1/31, Woodsville, N.H. BR/TL, 6'1.5", 190 lbs. Deb: 4/29/55

YEAR	TM/L	W	L	PCT	G	GS	CG	SH	SV	IP	H	R	HR	HB	BB	SO	RAT	ERA	ERA+	OAV	OOB	BH	AVG	PB	PR	PR+	PD	TPI
1955	Bos-A	0	0	—	1	0	0	0	0	1^2	1	0	0	0	1	1	10.8	0.00	—	.200	.333	0	—	0	1	1	-0	0.0
1957	StL-N	0	0	—	6	0	0	0	1	9^2	12	10	0	1	6	11	17.7	4.66	85	.267	.365	0	.000	-0	-1	-1	0	-0.1
	Pit-N	2	4	.333	20	4	2	0	0	55	48	22	3	1	25	35	12.1	3.11	122	.229	.314	1	.077	-1	5	4	-1	0.2
	Yr	2	4	.333	26	4	2	0	1	64^2	60	32	3	2	31	46	12.9	3.34	114	.235	.323	1	.067	-1	4	3	-1	0.1

YEAR	TM/L	W	L	PCT	G	GS	CG	SH	SV	IP	H	R	HR	HB	BB	SO	RAT	ERA	ERA+	OAV	OOB	BH	AVG	PB	PR	PR+	PD	TPI
1958	Pit-N	2	2	.500	35	4	0	0	1	61	61	39	6	2	31	24	13.9	4.43	87	.262	.353	1	.091	-1	-3	-4	1	-0.3
1959	Pit-N	0	0	—	20	0	0	0	0	28^1	32	16	1	0	17	12	15.6	3.49	111	.291	.386	0	.000	-0	1	1	-0	0.0
	Det-A	0	3	.000	9	0	0	0	0	11	20	15	5	0	3	10	18.8	8.18	50	.417	.451	0	.000	-0	-5	-5	0	-0.9
Total	4	4	9	.308	91	8	2	0	2	166^2	174	102	15	4	83	93	14.1	4.05	95	.267	.354	2	.069	-2	-2	-3	-0	-1.1

● BOB SMITH
Smith, Robert Walkup "Riverboat" b: 5/13/27, Clarence, Mo. BR/TL (BB 1959), 6', 185 lbs. Deb: 4/22/58

YEAR	TM/L	W	L	PCT	G	GS	CG	SH	SV	IP	H	R	HR	HB	BB	SO	RAT	ERA	ERA+	OAV	OOB	BH	AVG	PB	PR	PR+	PD	TPI
1958	Bos-A	4	3	.571	17	7	1	0	0	66^2	61	32	4	0	45	43	14.3	3.78	106	.248	.364	2	.105	-1	-0	2	1	0.1
1959	Chi-N	0	0	—	1	0	0	0	0	0^2	5	6	0	0	2	0	94.5	81.00	5	.833	.875	0	—	0	-6	-6	0	-0.2
	Cle-A	0	1	.000	12	3	0	0	0	29^1	31	19	2	0	12	17	13.2	5.22	71	.282	.352	0	.000	-1	-4	-5	0	-0.3
Total	2	4	4	.500	30	10	1	0	0	96^2	97	57	6	0	59	60	14.5	4.75	82	.268	.371	2	.080	-2	-10	-9	1	-0.4

● RUFUS SMITH
Smith, Rufus Frazier "Shirt" b: 1/24/05, Guilford College, N.C. d: 8/21/84, Aiken, S.C. BR/TL, 5'8", 165 lbs. Deb: 10/2/27

YEAR	TM/L	W	L	PCT	G	GS	CG	SH	SV	IP	H	R	HR	HB	BB	SO	RAT	ERA	ERA+	OAV	OOB	BH	AVG	PB	PR	PR+	PD	TPI
1927	Det-A	0	0	—	1	1	0	0	0	8	8	4	0	1	3	2	13.5	3.38	125	.242	.324	0	.000	-1	1	1	-0	0.0

● SHERRY SMITH
Smith, Sherrod Malone b: 2/18/1891, Monticello, Ga. d: 9/12/49, Reidsville, Ga. BR/TL, 6'1", 170 lbs. Deb: 5/11/11

YEAR	TM/L	W	L	PCT	G	GS	CG	SH	SV	IP	H	R	HR	HB	BB	SO	RAT	ERA	ERA+	OAV	OOB	BH	AVG	PB	PR	PR+	PD	TPI
1911	Pit-N	0	0	—	1	0	0	0	0	0^2	4	5	0	0	1	0	67.5	54.00	6	.667	.714	0	—	0	-4	-4	-0	-0.2
1912	Pit-N	0	0	—	3	0	0	0	1	4	6	3	0	0	1	3	15.8	6.75	48	.600	.636	0	—	0	-1	-2	-0	-0.1
1915	Bro-N	14	8	.636	29	20	11	2	2	173^2	169	71	3	5	42	52	11.2	2.59	107	.264	.315	14	.246	3	3	4	-0	0.7
1916	*Bro-N	14	10	.583	36	25	15	4	1	219	193	76	5	3	45	67	9.9	2.34	114	.239	.282	21	.273	5	7	8	0	1.6
1917	Bro-N	12	12	.500	38	23	15	0	3	211^1	210	103	5	2	51	58	11.2	3.32	84	.265	.311	15	.195	2	-14	-12	3	-0.8
1919	Bro-N	7	12	.368	30	19	13	2	1	173	181	63	3	4	29	40	11.1	2.24	133	.278	.313	8	.148	-2	13	14	3	1.7
1920	*Bro-N	11	9	.550	33	13	6	2	3	136^1	134	42	1	2	27	33	10.8	1.85	173	.264	.304	10	.233	2	19	20	5	4.0
1921	Bro-N	7	11	.389	35	17	9	0	4	175^1	232	95	4	1	34	36	13.7	3.90	100	.319	.350	13	.228	1	-2	-0	5	0.5
1922	Bro-N	4	8	.333	28	8	3	1	2	108^2	128	71	6	7	35	15	14.1	4.56	89	.309	.373	9	.257	2	-5	-6	1	-0.3
	Cle-A	1	0	1.000	2	2	1	0	0	15^2	18	7	0	0	3	4	12.1	3.45	116	.295	.328	2	.333	1	1	1	0	0.1
1923	Cle-A	9	6	.600	30	16	10	1	1	124	129	62	4	2	37	23	12.2	3.27	121	.269	.324	11	.244	1	10	10	2	1.4
1924	Cle-A	12	14	.462	39	27	20	2	1	247^2	267	110	5	7	42	34	11.5	3.02	142	.277	.312	18	.202	-1	33	34	3	3.4
1925	Cle-A	11	14	.440	31	30	**22**	1	1	237	296	151	11	5	48	30	13.3	4.86	91	.306	.342	28	.304	7	-12	-12	-0	-0.4
1926	Cle-A	11	10	.524	27	24	16	1	0	188^1	214	80	8	4	31	25	11.9	3.73	109	.292	.324	14	.215	2	6	7	3	1.2
1927	Cle-A	1	4	.200	11	2	1	0	1	38	53	25	2	0	14	8	15.9	5.45	77	.342	.396	2	.167	-0	-6	-5	0	-0.6
Total	14	114	118	.491	373	226	142	16	21	2052^2	2234	964	57	42	440	428	11.9	3.32	108	.282	.324	165	.233	22	48	58	26	12.2

● TOM SMITH
Smith, Thomas Edward b: 12/5/1871, Boston, Mass. d: 3/2/29, Dorchester, Mass. BR/TR, 5'7.5", 165 lbs. Deb: 6/6/1894

YEAR	TM/L	W	L	PCT	G	GS	CG	SH	SV	IP	H	R	HR	HB	BB	SO	RAT	ERA	ERA+	OAV	OOB	BH	AVG	PB	PR	PR+	PD	TPI
1894	Bos-N	0	0	—	2	0	0	0	1	6	8	14	2	4	6	2	27.0	15.00	38	.320	.514	0	.000	-0	-6	-6	-0	-0.2
1895	Phi-N	2	3	.400	11	7	4	0	0	68	76	67	1	7	53	21	18.0	6.88	70	.278	.408	8	.242	-0	-16	-16	-1	-0.9
1896	Lou-N	2	3	.400	11	5	4	0	0	55	73	55	2	4	25	14	16.7	5.40	80	.316	.392	8	.205	-0	-6	-7	1	-0.4
1898	StL-N	0	1	.000	1	1	1	0	0	9	9	8	0	2	5	1	16.0	2.00	189	.257	.381	1	.500	1	2	2	0	0.3
Total	4	4	7	.364	25	13	9	0	1	138	166	144	5	17	89	38	17.7	6.33	72	.294	.406	17	.224	-0	-27	-27	-0	-1.2

● TRAVIS SMITH
Smith, Travis William b: 11/7/72, Springfield, Ore. BR/TR, 5'10", 170 lbs. Deb: 6/21/98

YEAR	TM/L	W	L	PCT	G	GS	CG	SH	SV	IP	H	R	HR	HB	BB	SO	RAT	ERA	ERA+	OAV	OOB	BH	AVG	PB	PR	PR+	PD	TPI
1998	Mil-N	0	0	—	1	0	0	0	0	2	1	0	0	0	0	1	4.5	0.00	—	.143	.143	0	.000	-0	1	1	-0	0.0

● BILL SMITH
Smith, William Garland b: 6/8/34, Washington, D.C. d: 3/30/97, Clinton, Md. BL/TL, 6', 190 lbs. Deb: 9/13/58

YEAR	TM/L	W	L	PCT	G	GS	CG	SH	SV	IP	H	R	HR	HB	BB	SO	RAT	ERA	ERA+	OAV	OOB	BH	AVG	PB	PR	PR+	PD	TPI
1958	StL-N	0	1	.000	2	1	0	0	0	9^2	12	7	0	0	4	4	14.9	6.52	63	.324	.390	0	.000	-0	-3	-2	0	-0.2
1959	StL-N	0	0	—	6	0	0	0	1	8^1	11	3	0	0	3	4	15.1	1.08	393	.333	.389	0	.000	-0	3	3	-0	0.1
1962	Phi-N	1	5	.167	24	5	0	0	0	50^1	59	32	8	1	10	26	12.5	4.29	90	.295	.332	2	.182	1	-2	-2	-0	-0.2
Total	3	1	6	.143	32	6	0	0	1	68^1	82	42	8	1	17	34	13.2	4.21	94	.304	.347	2	.143	0	-2	-2	-0	-0.3

● WILLIE SMITH
Smith, Willie b: 2/11/39, Anniston, Ala. BL/TL, 6', 190 lbs. Deb: 6/18/63 ♦

YEAR	TM/L	W	L	PCT	G	GS	CG	SH	SV	IP	H	R	HR	HB	BB	SO	RAT	ERA	ERA+	OAV	OOB	BH	AVG	PB	PR	PR+	PD	TPI
1963	Det-A	1	0	1.000	11	2	0	0	2	21^2	24	13	2	0	13	16	15.4	4.57	82	.300	.398	1	.125	-0	-2	-2	0	-0.2
1964	LA-A	1	4	.200	15	1	0	0	0	31^2	34	13	5	1	10	20	12.8	2.84	116	.293	.354	108	.301	6	3	2	0	0.5
1968	Cle-A	0	0	—	2	0	0	0	0	5	2	0	0	0	0	1	5.4	0.00	—	.125	.176	6	.143	0	2	2	0	0.1
	Chi-N	0	0	—	1	0	0	0	0	2^2	0	0	0	0	0	2	0.0	0.00	—	.000	.000	39	.275	0	1	1	0	0.1
Total	3	2	4	.333	29	3	0	0	2	61	60	26	7	1	24	39	12.5	3.10	110	.273	.347	410	.248	6	3	2	1	0.5

● WILLIE SMITH
Smith, Willie Everett b: 8/27/67, Savannah, Ga. BR/TR, 6'6", 250 lbs. Deb: 4/25/94

YEAR	TM/L	W	L	PCT	G	GS	CG	SH	SV	IP	H	R	HR	HB	BB	SO	RAT	ERA	ERA+	OAV	OOB	BH	AVG	PB	PR	PR+	PD	TPI
1994	StL-N	1	1	.500	8	0	0	0	0	7	9	7	4	0	3	7	15.4	9.00	46	.300	.364	0	—	0	-4	-4	-0	-0.7

● ZANE SMITH
Smith, Zane William b: 12/28/60, Madison, Wis. BL/TL, 6'2", 195 lbs. Deb: 9/10/84

YEAR	TM/L	W	L	PCT	G	GS	CG	SH	SV	IP	H	R	HR	HB	BB	SO	RAT	ERA	ERA+	OAV	OOB	BH	AVG	PB	PR	PR+	PD	TPI
1984	Atl-N	1	0	1.000	3	3	0	0	0	20	16	7	1	0	13	16	13.0	2.25	172	.219	.337	5	.556	2	3	3	0	0.4
1985	Atl-N	9	10	.474	42	18	2	2	0	147	135	70	4	3	80	85	13.3	3.80	102	.254	.355	6	.162	-0	-3	1	2	0.3
1986	Atl-N	8	16	.333	38	32	3	1	1	204^2	209	109	8	5	105	139	14.0	4.05	98	.275	.367	5	.085	-3	-7	-1	3	-0.2
1987	Atl-N	15	10	.600	36	36	9	3	0	242	245	130	19	5	91	130	12.7	4.09	106	.266	.335	10	.132	-1	-0	7	1	0.7
1988	Atl-N	5	10	.333	23	22	3	0	0	140^1	159	72	8	3	44	59	13.2	4.30	86	.292	.348	7	.167	0	-13	-9	3	-0.6
1989	Atl-N	1	12	.077	17	17	0	0	0	99	102	65	5	2	33	58	12.5	4.45	82	.267	.329	5	.179	-0	-10	-8	2	-0.8
	Mon-N	0	1	.000	31	0	0	0	2	48	39	11	2	1	19	35	11.1	1.50	236	.220	.299	1	.250	0	11	11	1	0.7
	Yr	1	13	.071	48	17	0	0	2	147	141	76	7	3	52	93	12.0	3.49	104	.252	.319	6	.188	0	0	2	3	-0.1
1990	Mon-N	6	7	.462	22	21	1	0	0	139^1	141	57	11	3	41	80	11.9	3.23	113	.266	.322	7	.175	1	9	7	1	0.8
	*Pit-N	6	2	.750	11	10	3	2	0	76	55	20	4	0	9	50	7.6	1.30	278	.203	.229	4	.143	1	21	21	-0	2.3
	Yr	12	9	.571	33	31	4	2	0	215^1	196	77	15	3	50	130	10.4	2.55	143	.245	.292	11	.162	2	30	27	1	3.1
1991	*Pit-N	16	10	.615	35	35	6	3	0	228	234	95	15	2	29	120	10.5	3.20	112	.268	.293	13	.183	3	12	10	1	1.4
1992	Pit-N	8	8	.500	23	22	4	3	0	141	138	56	8	2	19	56	10.1	3.06	113	.261	.289	6	.122	-0	7	6	1	0.8
1993	Pit-N	3	7	.300	14	14	1	0	0	83	97	43	5	0	22	32	12.9	4.55	89	.298	.343	2	.080	-2	-5	-5	-1	-0.7
1994	Pit-N	10	8	.556	25	24	2	1	0	157	162	67	18	0	34	57	11.2	3.27	132	.270	.309	12	.211	1	17	18	3	2.3
1995	*Bos-A	8	8	.500	24	21	0	0	0	110^2	144	78	7	1	23	47	13.7	5.61	87	.316	.351	0	—	0	-11	-9	0	-1.0
1996	Pit-N	4	6	.400	16	16	1	1	0	83^1	104	53	7	4	21	47	13.9	5.08	86	.309	.356	4	.154	-1	-8	-6	-0	-0.8
Total	13	100	115	.465	360	291	35	16	3	1919^1	1980	933	122	31	583	1011	12.2	3.74	105	.271	.327	87	.158	0	22	41	17	5.6

● ROGER SMITHBERG
Smithberg, Roger Craig b: 3/21/66, Elgin, Ill. BR/TR, 6'3", 205 lbs. Deb: 9/1/93

YEAR	TM/L	W	L	PCT	G	GS	CG	SH	SV	IP	H	R	HR	HB	BB	SO	RAT	ERA	ERA+	OAV	OOB	BH	AVG	PB	PR	PR+	PD	TPI
1993	Oak-A	1	2	.333	13	0	0	0	3	19^2	13	7	2	1	7	4	9.6	2.75	149	.197	.284	0	—	0	3	3	1	0.6
1994	Oak-A	0	0	—	2	0	0	0	0	2^1	6	4	1	0	1	3	27.0	15.43	29	.500	.538	0	—	0	-3	-3	0	-0.1
Total	2	1	2	.333	15	0	0	0	3	22	19	11	3	1	8	7	11.5	4.09	101	.244	.322	0	—	0	1	0	1	0.5

● MIKE SMITHSON
Smithson, Billy Mike b: 1/21/55, Centerville, Tenn. BL/TR, 6'8", 215 lbs. Deb: 8/27/82

YEAR	TM/L	W	L	PCT	G	GS	CG	SH	SV	IP	H	R	HR	HB	BB	SO	RAT	ERA	ERA+	OAV	OOB	BH	AVG	PB	PR	PR+	PD	TPI
1982	Tex-A	3	4	.429	8	8	3	0	0	46^2	51	26	5	3	13	24	12.9	5.01	77	.282	.340	0	—	0	-5	-6	-1	-0.9
1983	Tex-A	10	14	.417	33	33	10	0	0	223^1	233	102	14	8	71	135	12.6	3.91	103	.269	.330	0	—	0	4	3	1	0.4
1984	Min-A	15	13	.536	36	36	10	1	0	252	246	113	35	8	54	144	11.0	3.68	114	.252	.296	0	—	0	9	14	-1	1.4
1985	Min-A	15	14	.517	37	37	8	3	0	257	264	134	25	15	78	127	12.5	4.34	102	.270	.333	0	—	0	-6	2	-2	0.0
1986	Min-A	13	14	.481	34	33	8	1	0	198	234	123	26	14	57	114	13.9	4.77	90	.294	.352	0	—	0	-13	-10	1	-1.1
1987	Min-A	4	7	.364	21	20	0	0	0	109	126	76	17	9	38	53	14.3	5.94	78	.286	.355	0	—	0	-18	-15	-1	-1.4
1988	*Bos-A	9	6	.600	31	18	1	0	1	126^2	149	87	25	6	37	73	13.6	5.97	69	.292	.347	0	—	0	-28	-25	-1	-2.7
1989	Bos-A	7	14	.333	40	19	1	1	2	143^2	170	84	21	10	35	61	13.5	4.95	83	.297	.348	0	—	0	-17	-13	-1	-1.7
Total	8	76	86	.469	240	204	41	6	2	1356^1	1473	745	168	73	383	731	12.8	4.58	93	.277	.334	0	—	0	-73	-50	-4	-6.0

● LEFTY SMOLL
Smoll, Clyde Hetrick b: 4/17/14, Quakertown, Pa. d: 8/31/85, Quakertown, Pa. BB/TL, 5'10", 175 lbs. Deb: 4/26/40

YEAR	TM/L	W	L	PCT	G	GS	CG	SH	SV	IP	H	R	HR	HB	BB	SO	RAT	ERA	ERA+	OAV	OOB	BH	AVG	PB	PR	PR+	PD	TPI
1940	Phi-N	2	8	.200	33	9	0	0	0	109	145	77	6	4	36	31	15.3	5.37	73	.322	.378	5	.161	-1	-18	-18	-2	-1.7

● JOHN SMOLTZ
Smoltz, John Andrew b: 5/15/67, Detroit, Mich. BR/TR, 6'3", 210 lbs. Deb: 7/23/88

YEAR	TM/L	W	L	PCT	G	GS	CG	SH	SV	IP	H	R	HR	HB	BB	SO	RAT	ERA	ERA+	OAV	OOB	BH	AVG	PB	PR	PR+	PD	TPI
1988	Atl-N	2	7	.222	12	12	0	0	0	64	74	40	10	2	33	37	15.3	5.48	67	.285	.369	2	.118	-0	-14	-12	-1	-1.6
1989	Atl-N★	12	11	.522	29	29	5	0	0	208	160	79	15	2	72	168	10.1	2.94	124	.212	.282	7	.113	1	13	16	2	2.0
1990	Atl-N	14	11	.560	34	34	6	2	0	231^1	206	109	20	1	90	170	11.6	3.85	105	.240	.313	12	.162	1	-1	5	1	0.7
1991	*Atl-N	14	13	.519	36	36	5	0	0	229^2	206	101	16	3	77	148	11.2	3.80	102	.243	.308	7	.108	-1	-3	2	0	0.2

YEAR	TM/L	W	L	PCT	G	GS	CG	SH	SV	IP	H	R	HR	HB	BB	SO	RAT	ERA	ERA+	OAV	OOB	BH	AVG	PB	PR	PR+	PD	TPI
1992	*Atl-N★	15	12	.556	35	35	9	3	0	246^2	206	90	17	5	80	**215**	10.6	2.85	129	.224	.289	12	.160	2	18	21	-1	2.5
1993	*Atl-N★	15	11	.577	35	35	3	1	0	243^2	208	104	23	6	100	208	11.6	3.62	111	.230	.311	13	.183	3	12	11	-0	1.3
1994	Atl-N	6	10	.375	21	21	1	0	0	134^2	120	69	15	4	48	113	11.5	4.14	103	.239	.310	6	.162	2	1	2	0	0.3
1995	*Atl-N	12	7	.632	29	29	2	1	0	192^2	166	76	15	4	72	193	11.3	3.18	134	.232	.306	6	.107	-1	22	23	-1	1.8
1996	*Atl-N★	**24**	8	**.750**	35	35	6	2	0	**253**^{2}	199	93	19	2	55	**276**	**9.1**	2.94	150	.216	**.261**	17	.218	4	36	40	1	5.2
1997	*Atl-N	15	12	.556	35	35	7	2	0	**256**	234	97	21	1	63	241	10.5	3.02	139	.242	.289	18	.228	6	34	34	1	4.0
1998	*Atl-N	17	3	**.850**	26	26	2	2	0	167^2	145	58	10	4	44	173	10.4	2.90	144	.231	.286	10	.196	3	25	24	0	3.1
1999	*Atl-N	11	8	.579	29	29	1	1	0	186^1	168	70	14	4	40	156	10.2	3.19	141	.245	.290	17	.274	7	29	28	1	3.4
Total	12	157	113	.581	356	356	47	14	0	2414^1	2092	986	195	38	774	2098	10.8	3.35	122	.233	.297	127	.175	26	170	192	4	22.9

● HARRY SMYTHE Smythe, William Henry b: 10/24/04, Augusta, Ga. d: 8/28/80, Augusta, Ga. BL/TL, 5'10.5", 179 lbs. Deb: 7/21/29

YEAR	TM/L	W	L	PCT	G	GS	CG	SH	SV	IP	H	R	HR	HB	BB	SO	RAT	ERA	ERA+	OAV	OOB	BH	AVG	PB	PR	PR+	PD	TPI
1929	Phi-N	4	6	.400	19	9	2	0	1	68^2	94	47	3	1	15	12	14.4	5.24	99	.330	.365	5	.192	-1	-4	-0	2	0.0
1930	Phi-N	0	3	.000	25	3	0	0	2	49^2	84	60	3	3	31	9	21.4	7.79	70	.368	.450	4	.286	-0	-16	-12	-1	-0.7
1934	NY-A	0	2	.000	8	0	0	0	1	15	24	16	1	0	8	7	19.2	7.80	52	.381	.451	1	.200	-0	-6	-7	1	-0.8
	Bro-N	1	1	.500	8	0	0	0	0	21^1	30	19	3	1	8	5	16.5	5.91	66	.337	.398	3	.333	1	-4	-5	1	-0.2
Total	3	5	12	.294	60	12	2	0	4	154^2	232	142	10	5	62	33	17.4	6.40	78	.349	.408	13	.241	0	-29	-23	2	-1.7

● NATE SNELL Snell, Nathaniel b: 9/2/52, Orangeburg, S.C. BR/TR, 6'4", 190 lbs. Deb: 9/20/84

YEAR	TM/L	W	L	PCT	G	GS	CG	SH	SV	IP	H	R	HR	HB	BB	SO	RAT	ERA	ERA+	OAV	OOB	BH	AVG	PB	PR	PR+	PD	TPI
1984	Bal-A	1	1	.500	5	0	0	0	0	7^2	8	2	1	0	1	7	10.6	2.35	165	.258	.281	0	—	0	1	1	-0	0.3
1985	Bal-A	3	2	.600	43	0	0	0	5	100^1	100	44	4	1	30	41	11.8	2.69	150	.260	.315	0	—	0	16	15	1	1.0
1986	Bal-A	2	1	.667	34	0	0	0	0	72^1	69	36	9	1	22	29	11.4	3.86	107	.257	.316	0	—	0	3	2	1	0.2
1987	Det-A	1	2	.333	22	2	0	0	0	38^2	39	20	5	0	19	19	13.5	3.96	107	.267	.352	0	—	0	2	1	-1	0.0
Total	4	7	6	.538	104	2	0	0	5	219	216	102	19	2	72	96	11.9	3.29	125	.260	.321	0	—	0	23	20	1	1.5

● FRANK SNOOK Snook, Frank Walter b: 3/28/49, Somerville, N.J. BR/TR, 6'2", 180 lbs. Deb: 7/13/73

YEAR	TM/L	W	L	PCT	G	GS	CG	SH	SV	IP	H	R	HR	HB	BB	SO	RAT	ERA	ERA+	OAV	OOB	BH	AVG	PB	PR	PR+	PD	TPI
1973	SD-N	0	2	.000	18	0	0	0	1	27^1	19	15	4	0	18	13	12.2	3.62	96	.200	.327	0	.000	-0	0	-0	1	0.0

● COLONEL SNOVER Snover, Colonel Lester "Bosco" b: 5/16/1895, Hallstead, Pa. d: 4/30/69, Rochester, N.Y. BL/TL, 6'0.5", 200 lbs. Deb: 9/18/19

YEAR	TM/L	W	L	PCT	G	GS	CG	SH	SV	IP	H	R	HR	HB	BB	SO	RAT	ERA	ERA+	OAV	OOB	BH	AVG	PB	PR	PR+	PD	TPI
1919	NY-N	0	1	.000	2	1	0	0	0	9	7	5	0	1	3	4	11.0	1.00	281	.212	.297	0	.000	0	2	2	-0	0.2

● BRIAN SNYDER Snyder, Brian Robert b: 2/20/58, Flemington, N.J. BL/TL, 6'3", 185 lbs. Deb: 5/25/85

YEAR	TM/L	W	L	PCT	G	GS	CG	SH	SV	IP	H	R	HR	HB	BB	SO	RAT	ERA	ERA+	OAV	OOB	BH	AVG	PB	PR	PR+	PD	TPI
1985	Sea-A	1	2	.333	15	6	0	0	1	35^1	44	28	2	1	19	23	16.3	6.37	66	.306	.390	0	—	0	-9	-8	1	-0.6
1989	Oak-A	0	0	—	2	0	0	0	0	0^2	2	2	1	0	2	1	54.0	27.00	14	.500	.667	0	—	0	-2	-2	0	-0.1
Total	2	1	2	.333	17	6	0	0	1	36	46	30	3	1	21	24	17.0	6.75	62	.311	.400	0	—	0	-10	-10	1	-0.7

● GENE SNYDER Snyder, Gene Walter b: 3/31/31, York, Pa. d: 6/2/96, York, Pa. BR/TL, 5'11", 175 lbs. Deb: 4/26/59

YEAR	TM/L	W	L	PCT	G	GS	CG	SH	SV	IP	H	R	HR	HB	BB	SO	RAT	ERA	ERA+	OAV	OOB	BH	AVG	PB	PR	PR+	PD	TPI
1959	LA-N	1	1	.500	11	2	0	0	0	26^1	32	19	1	0	20	20	17.8	5.47	77	.299	.409	0	.000	-0	-4	-3	-0	-0.3

● GEORGE SNYDER Snyder, George T. b: 8/1848, Philadelphia, Pa. d: 8/2/05, Philadelphia, Pa. Deb: 9/30/1882

YEAR	TM/L	W	L	PCT	G	GS	CG	SH	SV	IP	H	R	HR	HB	BB	SO	RAT	ERA	ERA+	OAV	OOB	BH	AVG	PB	PR	PR+	PD	TPI
1882	Phi-a	1	0	1.000	1	1	1	0	0	9	4	3	0		2	0	6.0	0.00	—	.125	.176	1	.333	0	3	3	0	0.3

● JOHN SNYDER Snyder, John Michael b: 8/16/74, Southfield, Mich. BR/TR, 6'3", 185 lbs. Deb: 6/30/98

YEAR	TM/L	W	L	PCT	G	GS	CG	SH	SV	IP	H	R	HR	HB	BB	SO	RAT	ERA	ERA+	OAV	OOB	BH	AVG	PB	PR	PR+	PD	TPI
1998	Chi-A	7	2	.778	15	14	1	0	0	86^1	96	49	14	2	23	52	12.6	4.80	95	.286	.335	0	—	0	-1	-2	1	-0.2
1999	Chi-A	9	12	.429	25	25	1	0	0	129^1	167	103	27	6	49	67	15.4	6.68	73	.311	.375	0	—	0	-26	-26	-0	-3.3
2000	Mil-N	3	10	.231	23	23	0	0	0	127	147	95	8	9	77	69	16.5	6.17	74	.296	.400	3	.079	-1	-22	-23	0	-2.0
Total	3	19	24	.442	63	62	2	0	0	342^2	410	247	49	17	149	188	15.1	6.01	78	.299	.375	3	.079	-1	-49	-51	1	-5.5

● BILL SNYDER Snyder, William Nicholas b: 1/28/1898, Mansfield, Ohio d: 10/8/34, Vicksburg, Mich. BR/TR, Deb: 9/4/19

YEAR	TM/L	W	L	PCT	G	GS	CG	SH	SV	IP	H	R	HR	HB	BB	SO	RAT	ERA	ERA+	OAV	OOB	BH	AVG	PB	PR	PR+	PD	TPI
1919	Was-A	0	1	.000	2	1	0	0	0	8	6	4	0	0	3	5	10.1	1.13	285	.200	.273	0	.000	-0	2	2	-0	0.2
1920	Was-A	2	1	.667	16	4	1	0	1	54	59	33	1	6	28	17	15.5	4.17	90	.280	.380	6	.316	1	-2	-3	-1	-0.1
Total	2	2	2	.500	18	5	1	0	1	62	65	37	1	6	31	22	14.8	3.77	97	.270	.367	6	.286	1	-0	-1	-1	0.1

● STEVE SODERSTROM Soderstrom, Stephen Andrew b: 4/3/72, Turlock, Cal. BR/TR, 6'3", 215 lbs. Deb: 9/17/96

YEAR	TM/L	W	L	PCT	G	GS	CG	SH	SV	IP	H	R	HR	HB	BB	SO	RAT	ERA	ERA+	OAV	OOB	BH	AVG	PB	PR	PR+	PD	TPI
1996	SF-N	2	0	1.000	3	3	0	0	0	13^2	16	11	1	2	6	9	15.8	5.27	78	.302	.393	0	.000	-1	-2	-2	-0	-0.3

● CLINT SODOWSKY Sodowsky, Clint Rea b: 7/13/72, Ponca City, Okla. BL/TR, 6'3", 180 lbs. Deb: 9/4/95

YEAR	TM/L	W	L	PCT	G	GS	CG	SH	SV	IP	H	R	HR	HB	BB	SO	RAT	ERA	ERA+	OAV	OOB	BH	AVG	PB	PR	PR+	PD	TPI
1995	Det-A	2	2	.500	6	6	0	0	0	23^1	24	15	4	0	18	14	16.2	5.01	95	.258	.378	0	—	0	-1	-1	-0	-0.1
1996	Det-A	1	3	.250	7	7	0	0	0	24^1	40	34	5	3	20	9	23.3	11.84	43	.370	.481	0	—	0	-18	-18	-0	-2.1
1997	Pit-N	2	2	.500	45	0	0	0	0	52	49	22	6	2	34	51	14.7	3.63	118	.249	.365	1	.500	0	3	4	-0	0.3
1998	Ari-N	3	6	.333	45	6	0	0	0	77^2	86	56	5	7	39	42	15.3	5.68	74	.283	.377	3	.300	1	-12	-13	-0	-1.2
1999	StL-N	0	1	.000	3	1	0	0	0	6^1	15	11	1	0	6	2	29.8	15.63	29	.455	.538	0	.000	-0	-8	-8	-0	-0.9
Total	5	8	14	.364	106	20	0	0	0	183^2	214	138	21	12	117	118	16.8	6.17	72	.291	.397	4	.308	1	-36	-35	-1	-4.0

● RAY SOFF Soff, Raymond John b: 10/31/58, Adrian, Mich. BR/TR, 6', 185 lbs. Deb: 7/17/86

YEAR	TM/L	W	L	PCT	G	GS	CG	SH	SV	IP	H	R	HR	HB	BB	SO	RAT	ERA	ERA+	OAV	OOB	BH	AVG	PB	PR	PR+	PD	TPI
1986	StL-N	4	2	.667	30	0	0	0	0	38^1	37	17	4	0	13	22	11.7	3.29	111	.255	.316	0	.000	-0	2	2	0	0.3
1987	StL-N	1	0	1.000	12	0	0	0	0	15^1	18	11	3	1	5	9	14.1	6.46	64	.295	.358	0	.000	-0	-4	-4	-0	-0.2
Total	2	5	2	.714	42	0	0	0	0	53^2	55	28	7	1	18	31	12.4	4.19	90	.267	.329	0	.000	-0	-2	-2	0	0.1

● JULIO SOLANO Solano, Julio Cesar b: 1/8/60, Agua Blanca, D.R. BR/TR, 6'1", 160 lbs. Deb: 4/5/83

YEAR	TM/L	W	L	PCT	G	GS	CG	SH	SV	IP	H	R	HR	HB	BB	SO	RAT	ERA	ERA+	OAV	OOB	BH	AVG	PB	PR	PR+	PD	TPI
1983	Hou-N	0	2	.000	4	0	0	0	0	6	5	5	1	0	4	3	13.5	6.00	57	.217	.333	0	—	0	-2	-2	0	-0.4
1984	Hou-N	1	3	.250	31	0	0	0	0	50^2	31	13	3	0	18	33	8.7	1.95	170	.179	.257	1	.333	0	9	8	-1	0.6
1985	Hou-N	2	2	.500	20	0	0	0	0	33^2	34	13	5	0	13	17	12.6	3.48	100	.262	.329	0	.000	-0	0	-0	-1	-0.1
1986	Hou-N	3	1	.750	16	1	0	0	0	32	39	28	5	3	22	21	18.0	7.59	47	.310	.424	0	.000	-1	-14	-15	-0	-1.7
1987	Hou-N	0	0	—	11	0	0	0	0	20	25	17	5	0	9	12	15.3	7.65	51	.298	.366	0	.000	-0	-8	-9	0	-0.4
1988	Sea-A	0	0	—	17	0	0	0	3	22	22	13	3	0	12	10	13.9	4.09	102	.268	.362	0	—	0	-0	0	0	0.0
1989	Sea-A	0	0	—	7	0	0	0	0	9^2	6	8	1	1	4	6	10.2	5.59	72	.176	.282	0	—	0	-2	-2	0	0.0
Total	7	6	8	.429	106	1	0	0	3	174	162	97	23	4	82	102	12.8	4.55	79	.248	.336	1	.077	-1	-16	-19	-2	-2.0

● MARCELINO SOLIS Solis, Marcelino b: 7/19/30, San Luis Potosi, Mexico BL/TL, 6'1", 185 lbs. Deb: 7/16/58

YEAR	TM/L	W	L	PCT	G	GS	CG	SH	SV	IP	H	R	HR	HB	BB	SO	RAT	ERA	ERA+	OAV	OOB	BH	AVG	PB	PR	PR+	PD	TPI
1958	Chi-N	3	3	.500	15	4	0	0	0	52	74	41	5	4	20	15	17.0	6.06	65	.339	.405	5	.250	1	-12	-12	-0	-1.2

● EDDIE SOLOMON Solomon, Eddie "Buddy" b: 2/9/51, Perry, Ga. d: 1/12/86, Macon, Ga. BR/TR, 6'3", 190 lbs. Deb: 9/2/73

YEAR	TM/L	W	L	PCT	G	GS	CG	SH	SV	IP	H	R	HR	HB	BB	SO	RAT	ERA	ERA+	OAV	OOB	BH	AVG	PB	PR	PR+	PD	TPI
1973	LA-N	0	0	—	4	0	0	0	0	6^1	10	5	3	1	4	6	21.3	7.11	48	.357	.455	0	.000	-0	-2	-3	-0	-0.2
1974	*LA-N	0	0	—	4	0	0	0	1	6	5	1	1	0	2	2	10.5	1.50	227	.217	.280	0	—	0	1	1	0	0.1
1975	Chi-N	0	0	—	6	0	0	0	0	6^2	7	6	1	0	6	3	17.6	1.35	286	.269	.406	0	—	0	2	2	0	0.1
1976	StL-N	1	1	.500	26	2	0	0	0	37	45	24	2	1	16	19	15.1	4.86	73	.306	.378	2	.400	1	-6	-5	1	-0.1
1977	Atl-N	6	6	.500	18	16	0	0	0	88^2	110	64	10	2	34	54	14.8	4.57	98	.305	.368	4	.129	-1	-6	-1	-0	-0.2
1978	Atl-N	4	6	.400	37	8	0	0	2	106	98	52	12	2	50	64	12.7	4.08	99	.247	.335	4	.138	-1	-6	-0	-0	-0.1
1979	Atl-N	7	14	.333	31	30	4	0	0	186	184	98	19	6	51	96	11.7	4.21	96	.254	.308	13	.203	1	-10	-3	-1	-0.3
1980	Pit-N	7	3	.700	26	12	2	0	0	100^1	96	44	8	4	37	35	12.3	2.69	136	.253	.325	7	.219	1	10	11	-0	1.1
1981	Pit-N	8	6	.571	22	17	2	0	1	127	133	49	10	3	27	38	11.6	3.12	115	.278	.321	7	.163	-1	5	7	-1	0.5
1982	Pit-N	2	6	.250	11	10	0	0	0	46^2	69	38	9	1	18	18	17.0	6.75	55	.347	.404	2	.133	-1	-16	-15	-2	-2.4
	Chi-A	1	0	1.000	6	0	0	0	0	7^1	7	5	1	0	2	2	11.0	3.68	110	.241	.290	0	—	0	0	0	-0	0.0
Total	10	36	42	.462	191	95	8	0	4	718	764	386	76	20	247	337	12.9	4.00	98	.274	.337	39	.177	-1	-27	-7	-3	-1.5

● JOE SOMMER Sommer, Joseph John b: 11/20/1858, Covington, Ky. d: 1/16/38, Cincinnati, Ohio BR/TR, Deb: 7/8/1880 ♦

YEAR	TM/L	W	L	PCT	G	GS	CG	SH	SV	IP	H	R	HR	HB	BB	SO	RAT	ERA	ERA+	OAV	OOB	BH	AVG	PB	PR	PR+	PD	TPI
1883	Cin-a	0	0	—	1	0	0	0	0	5	9	6	0		1	2	18.0	5.40	60	.360	.385	115	.278	0	-1	-1	-0	-0.1
1885	Bal-a	0	0	—	2	0	0	0	1	3	6	3	0	0	0	0	18.0	9.00	36	.429	.429	118	.251	0	-2	-2	-0	-0.1
1886	Bal-a	0	0	—	1	0	0	0	0	4	14	12	0	0	3	1	38.3	18.00	19	.519	.567	117	.209	-0	-6	-7	-0	-0.3
1887	Bal-a	0	0	—	1	0	0	0	0	1	3	1	0	0	1	0	27.0	9.00	46	.429	.429	186	.354	0	-1	-1	-0	0.0
1890	Cle-N	0	0	—	1	0	0	0	0	1	2	3	1	0	2	0	36.0	0.00	—	.400	.571	8	.229	-0	0	0	-0	0.0
Total	5	0	0	—	6	0	0	0	1	14	34	25	1	0	7	3	25.7	9.64	35	.436	.476	974	.261	1	-10	-10	-1	-0.5

YEAR	TM/L	W	L	PCT	G	GS	CG	SH	SV	IP	H	R	HR	HB	BB	SO	RAT	ERA	ERA+	OAV	OOB	BH	AVG	PB	PR	PR+	PD	TPI
● **RUDY SOMMERS**	Sommers, Rudolph b: 10/30/1886, Cincinnati, Ohio d: 3/18/49, Louisville, Ky. BB/TL, 5'11", 165 lbs. Deb: 9/8/12																											
1912	Chi-N	0	1	.000	1	0	0	0	0	3	4	1	0	0	2	2	18.0	3.00	111	.333	.429	0	.000	0	0	0	-0	0.0
1914	Bro-F	2	7	.222	23	8	2	0	2	82	88	54	2	3	34	40	13.7	4.06	71	.282	.358	6	.250	2	-11	-11	-1	-1.0
1926	Bos-A	0	0	—	2	0	0	0	0	2	3	3	0	0	3	0	27.0	13.50	30	.333	.500	0	—	0	-2	-2	0	-0.1
1927	Bos-A	0	0	—	7	0	0	0	0	14	18	15	2	0	14	2	20.6	8.36	51	.353	.492	1	.500	0	-7	-6	1	-0.2
Total	4	2	8	.200	33	8	2	0	2	101	113	73	4	3	53	44	15.1	4.81	64	.294	.384	7	.259	2	-19	-19	-0	-1.3
● **ANDY SOMMERVILLE**	Sommerville, Andrew Henry (b: Henry Travers Summersgill) b: 2/6/1876, Brooklyn, N.Y. d: 6/16/31, Richmond Hill, N.Y. Deb: 8/8/1894																											
1894	Bro-N	0	1	.000	1	1	0	0	0	0^1	1	6	0	0	5	0	162.0	162.00	3	.500	.857	0	—	0	-6	-6	0	-0.7
● **DON SONGER**	Songer, Donald C. b: 1/31/1900, Walnut, Kan. d: 10/3/62, Kansas City, Mo. BL/TL, 6', 165 lbs. Deb: 9/21/24																											
1924	Pit-N	0	0	—	4	1	0	0	1	9^1	14	7	1	0	3	3	16.4	6.75	57	.333	.378	0	.000	-0	-3	-3	0	-0.2
1925	Pit-N	0	1	.000	8	0	0	0	0	11^2	14	7	0	0	8	4	17.0	2.31	193	.298	.400	0	.000	-0	3	3	-0	0.2
1926	Pit-N	7	8	.467	35	15	5	1	2	126^1	118	60	4	11	52	27	12.9	3.13	126	.252	.340	4	.105	-2	10	11	1	1.0
1927	Pit-N	0	0	—	2	0	0	0	0	4^2	10	10	0	1	4	1	28.9	11.57	36	.526	.625	0	.000	-0	-4	-4	-0	-0.2
	NY-N	3	5	.375	22	1	0	0	1	50^1	48	22	4	1	31	9	14.3	2.86	135	.261	.370	3	.300	1	6	6	1	1.0
	Yr	3	5	.375	24	1	0	0	1	55	58	32	4	2	35	10	15.5	3.60	108	.286	.396	3	.273	1	2	2	1	0.8
Total	4	10	14	.417	71	17	5	1	4	202^1	204	106	9	13	98	44	14.0	3.38	117	.268	.361	7	.132	-2	11	12	2	1.8
● **LARY SORENSEN**	Sorensen, Lary Alan b: 10/4/55, Detroit, Mich. BR/TR, 6'2", 210 lbs. Deb: 6/7/77																											
1977	Mil-A	7	10	.412	23	20	9	0	0	142^1	147	72	10	1	36	57	11.6	4.36	94	.270	.316	0	—	0	-5	-4	1	-0.4
1978	Mil-A★	18	12	.600	37	36	17	3	1	280^2	277	111	14	5	50	78	10.6	3.21	118	.259	.295	0	—	0	18	18	1	1.9
1979	Mil-A	15	14	.517	34	34	16	2	0	235^1	250	113	30	4	42	63	11.3	3.98	105	.275	.310	0	—	0	7	5	1	0.6
1980	Mil-A	12	10	.545	35	29	8	2	1	195^2	242	91	13	2	45	54	13.3	3.68	105	.311	.351	0	—	0	8	4	1	0.5
1981	StL-N	7	7	.500	23	23	3	1	0	140^1	149	59	3	1	26	52	11.3	3.27	109	.271	.305	3	.065	-3	3	4	0	0.1
1982	Cle-A	10	15	.400	32	30	6	1	0	189^1	251	130	19	3	55	62	14.7	5.61	73	.322	.369	0	—	0	-32	-32	-1	-3.6
1983	Cle-A	12	11	.522	36	34	8	1	0	222^2	238	112	21	2	65	76	12.3	4.24	100	.276	.328	0	—	0	-4	0	2	0.2
1984	Oak-A	6	13	.316	46	21	2	0	1	183^1	240	117	21	6	44	63	14.2	4.91	76	.317	.359	0	—	0	-19	-25	-1	-2.4
1985	Chi-N	3	7	.300	45	3	0	0	0	82^1	86	44	8	4	24	34	12.5	4.26	94	.274	.333	0	.000	-0	-6	-2	-0	-0.3
1987	Mon-N	3	4	.429	23	5	0	0	1	47^2	56	32	7	3	12	21	13.4	4.72	89	.286	.336	0	.000	-1	-3	-3	-1	-0.5
1988	SF-N	0	0	—	12	0	0	0	2	16^2	24	13	1	0	3	9	14.6	4.86	67	.329	.355	0	.000	-0	-3	-3	-0	-0.2
Total	11	93	103	.474	346	235	69	10	6	1736^1	1960	894	147	31	402	569	12.4	4.15	96	.287	.329	3	.049	-4	-36	-36	1	-4.1
● **VIC SORRELL**	Sorrell, Victor Garland b: 4/9/01, Morrisville, N.C. d: 5/4/72, Raleigh, N.C. BR/TR, 5'10", 180 lbs. Deb: 4/22/28																											
1928	Det-A	8	11	.421	29	23	8	0	0	171	182	106	9	5	83	67	14.2	4.79	86	.277	.363	6	.109	-5	-14	-13	-3	-1.9
1929	Det-A	14	15	.483	36	31	13	1	1	226	270	152	15	2	106	81	15.1	5.18	83	.302	.377	12	.145	-6	-23	-22	-1	-3.0
1930	Det-A	16	11	.593	35	30	14	2	1	233^1	245	116	13	0	106	97	13.5	3.86	124	.274	.351	15	.188	-3	21	24	-3	1.8
1931	Det-A	13	14	.481	35	32	19	1	1	245	267	131	8	1	114	99	14.0	4.15	110	.278	.355	14	.159	-4	6	11	1	0.8
1932	Det-A	14	14	.500	32	31	13	1	0	234^1	234	124	11	3	77	84	12.1	4.03	117	.259	.319	9	.118	-4	12	17	-2	1.2
1933	Det-A	11	15	.423	36	28	13	1	1	232^2	233	112	18	2	78	75	12.1	3.79	114	.260	.321	11	.149	-2	13	13	-0	1.0
1934	Det-A	6	9	.400	28	19	6	1	2	129^2	146	76	13	3	45	46	13.5	4.79	92	.283	.345	4	.108	-1	-4	-6	2	-0.6
1935	Det-A	4	3	.571	12	6	4	0	0	51^1	65	28	2	2	25	22	16.1	4.03	103	.319	.398	0	.000	-3	2	1	0	-0.2
1936	Det-A	6	7	.462	30	14	5	1	3	131^1	153	86	9	2	64	37	15.0	5.28	94	.294	.373	6	.154	1	-3	-5	2	-0.2
1937	Det-A	0	2	.000	7	2	0	0	1	17	25	18	3	0	8	11	17.5	9.00	52	.338	.402	0	.000	-0	-8	-8	0	-0.9
Total	10	92	101	.477	280	216	95	8	10	1671^2	1820	949	101	20	706	619	13.7	4.43	102	.279	.351	77	.139	-27	-0	14	-4	-2.0
● **ELIAS SOSA**	Sosa, Elias (Martinez) b: 6/10/50, LaVega, D.R. BR/TR, 6'2", 190 lbs. Deb: 9/8/72																											
1972	SF-N	0	1	.000	8	0	0	0	3	15^2	10	4	0	0	12	10	12.6	2.30	152	.189	.338	0	.000	-0	2	2	-0	0.2
1973	SF-N	10	4	.714	71	1	0	0	18	107	95	42	7	4	41	70	11.8	3.28	117	.241	.318	1	.071	-0	5	6	-1	0.9
1974	SF-N	9	7	.563	68	0	0	0	6	101	94	54	8	1	45	48	12.5	3.48	110	.252	.334	1	.067	-1	2	4	-1	0.4
1975	StL-N	0	3	.000	14	1	0	0	0	27^1	22	14	3	1	14	15	12.2	3.95	95	.227	.330	1	.125	-0	-1	-1	-0	-0.1
	Atl-N	2	2	.500	43	0	0	0	2	62^1	70	35	3	3	29	31	14.7	4.48	85	.294	.378	1	.143	-0	-6	-5	-0	-0.3
	Yr	2	5	.286	57	1	0	0	2	89^2	92	49	6	4	43	46	14.0	4.32	88	.275	.364	2	.133	-1	-7	-5	-0	-0.4
1976	Atl-N	4	4	.500	21	0	0	0	3	35^1	41	26	3	1	13	32	14.0	5.35	71	.287	.350	1	.143	-0	-7	-6	-0	-1.2
	LA-N	2	4	.333	24	0	0	0	1	33^2	30	16	0	0	12	20	11.2	3.48	97	.242	.309	0	—	0	0	-0	0	-0.1
	Yr	6	8	.429	45	0	0	0	4	69	71	42	3	1	25	52	12.7	4.43	81	.266	.331	1	.143	-0	-7	-6	-0	-1.3
1977	*LA-N	2	2	.500	44	0	0	0	1	63^2	42	15	7	1	12	47	7.8	1.98	193	.189	.234	1	.250	0	14	13	-0	0.8
1978	Oak-A	8	2	.800	68	0	0	0	14	109	106	37	5	1	44	61	12.5	2.64	138	.264	.338	0	—	0	14	13	0	1.5
1979	Mon-N	8	7	.533	62	0	0	0	18	96^2	77	24	2	2	37	59	10.8	1.96	188	.219	.297	2	.154	0	19	19	-1	3.4
1980	Mon-N	9	6	.600	67	0	0	0	9	93^2	104	33	5	1	19	58	11.9	3.07	116	.286	.323	1	.091	-1	6	5	-0	0.8
1981	*Mon-N	1	2	.333	32	0	0	0	3	39^1	46	16	3	1	8	18	12.6	3.66	95	.297	.335	2	1.000	1	-1	-1	0	0.1
1982	Det-A	3	3	.500	38	0	0	0	4	61	64	31	11	2	18	24	12.4	4.43	92	.270	.327	0	—	0	-2	-2	1	-0.2
1983	SD-N	1	4	.200	41	1	0	0	1	72^1	72	41	7	3	30	45	13.1	4.35	80	.268	.348	1	.143	-0	-6	-7	-1	-0.6
Total	12	59	51	.536	601	3	0	0	83	918	873	388	64	21	334	538	12.0	3.32	112	.255	.325	12	.130	-3	38	39	-3	5.6
● **JOSE SOSA**	Sosa, Jose Ynocencio (b: Jose Ynocencio (Sosa)) b: 12/28/52, Santo Domingo, D.R. BR/TR, 5'11", 158 lbs. Deb: 7/22/75																											
1975	Hou-N	1	3	.250	25	2	0	0	1	47	51	21	5	1	23	31	14.4	4.02	84	.291	.377	3	.333	2	-2	-4	-1	-0.2
1976	Hou-N	0	0	—	9	0	0	0	0	11^2	16	9	0	3	6	5	19.3	6.94	46	.340	.446	0	—	0	-4	-5	1	-0.2
Total	2	1	3	.250	34	2	0	0	1	58^2	67	30	5	4	29	36	15.3	4.60	73	.302	.392	3	.333	2	-6	-9	-0	-0.4
● **ALLEN SOTHORON**	Sothoron, Allen Sutton b: 4/27/1893, Bradford, Ohio d: 6/17/39, St.Louis, Mo. BB/TR (BR 1924-26), 5'11", 182 lbs. Deb: 9/17/14 MC																											
1914	StL-A	0	0	—	1	0	0	0	0	6	6	4	0	0	4	3	15.0	6.00	45	.261	.370	0	.000	-0	-2	-2	-0	-0.2
1915	StL-A	0	1	.000	3	1	0	0	0	3^2	8	10	0	0	5	2	31.9	7.36	39	.400	.520	0	.000	-0	-2	-2	0	-0.4
1917	StL-A	14	19	.424	48	32	17	3	4	276^2	259	135	2	9	96	85	11.8	2.83	92	.251	.320	20	.217	3	-5	-7	-1	-0.6
1918	StL-A	12	12	.500	29	24	14	2	0	209	152	64	3	3	67	71	9.6	1.94	141	**.205**	.274	10	.159	-2	20	19	-3	1.6
1919	StL-A	20	12	.625	40	30	21	3	3	270	256	101	4	10	87	106	11.8	2.20	151	.246	.311	17	.175	-2	31	33	-7	2.8
1920	StL-A	8	15	.348	36	26	12	1	2	218^1	263	151	6	6	89	81	14.8	4.70	83	.307	.376	16	.222	-1	-22	-18	-2	-2.0
1921	StL-A	1	2	.333	5	4	1	0	0	27^2	33	19	0	1	8	9	13.7	5.20	86	.314	.368	1	.111	-1	-3	-2	-0	-0.3
	Bos-A	0	2	.000	2	2	0	0	0	6	15	10	0	0	5	2	30.0	13.50	31	.455	.526	1	.500	1	-6	-6	0	-0.9
	Cle-A	12	4	.750	22	16	10	2	0	144^2	146	60	0	7	58	61	13.1	3.24	132	.279	.358	16	.276	2	17	17	-2	1.5
	Yr	13	8	.619	29	22	11	2	0	178^1	194	89	0	8	71	72	13.8	3.89	111	.293	.368	18	.261	2	8	8	-2	0.3
1922	Cle-A	1	3	.250	6	4	2	0	0	25^1	26	22	1	2	14	8	14.9	6.39	63	.274	.378	4	.444	1	-7	-7	-0	-0.8
1924	StL-N	10	16	.385	29	28	16	**4**	0	196^2	209	102	9	10	84	62	13.9	3.57	106	.275	.354	14	.194	-2	7	5	-3	0.1
1925	StL-N	10	10	.500	28	22	8	2	0	155^2	173	86	7	6	63	67	14.0	4.05	107	.280	.353	11	.196	-1	4	5	-4	0.0
1926	StL-N	3	3	.500	15	4	1	0	0	42^2	37	22	2	0	16	19	11.2	4.22	93	.247	.319	3	.231	0	-2	-1	-1	-0.3
Total	11	91	99	.479	264	193	102	17	9	1582^1	1583	786	34	54	596	576	12.7	3.31	105	.264	.336	113	.207	-2	29	30	-24	0.5
● **MARIO SOTO**	Soto, Mario Melvin b: 7/12/56, Bani, D.R. BR/TR, 6', 185 lbs. Deb: 7/21/77																											
1977	Cin-N	2	6	.250	12	10	2	1	0	60^2	60	38	12	3	26	44	13.2	5.34	74	.258	.340	1	.077	-0	-10	-9	0	-1.1
1978	Cin-N	1	0	1.000	5	1	0	0	0	18	13	5	1	0	13	13	13.0	2.50	142	.197	.329	0	.000	-0	2	2	-0	0.0
1979	*Cin-N	3	2	.600	25	0	0	0	0	37^1	33	25	2	1	30	32	15.4	5.30	71	.243	.383	4	.571	2	-6	-6	-1	-0.7
1980	Cin-N	10	8	.556	53	12	3	1	4	190^1	126	72	11	2	84	182	10.0	3.07	117	**.187**	.279	2	.043	-4	11	11	0	0.6
1981	Cin-N	12	9	.571	25	25	10	3	0	175	142	69	13	3	61	151	10.6	3.29	108	.220	.290	4	.068	-4	4	5	-1	0.0
1982	Cin-N★	14	13	.519	35	34	13	2	0	257^2	202	88	19	4	71	274	**9.7**	2.79	133	.215	**.273**	14	.167	1	23	25	-1	2.6
1983	Cin-N★	17	13	.567	34	34	**18**	3	0	273^2	207	96	28	5	95	242	10.1	2.70	141	.208	.280	11	.125	-2	29	32	-1	3.1
1984	Cin-N★	18	7	.720	33	33	**13**	0	0	237^1	181	102	26	5	87	185	10.4	3.53	107	.209	.286	18	.207	3	2	6	-3	0.7
1985	Cin-N	12	15	.444	36	36	9	1	0	256^2	196	109	30	2	104	214	10.6	3.58	106	.211	.292	11	.133	-2	1	6	-1	0.3
1986	Cin-N	5	10	.333	19	19	1	1	0	105	113	61	15	1	46	67	13.7	4.71	82	.280	.355	3	.111	-1	-12	-9	-1	-1.3
1987	Cin-N	3	2	.600	6	6	0	0	0	31^2	34	18	7	0	12	11	13.1	5.12	83	.279	.343	1	.083	-1	-4	-3	0	-0.5

YEAR	TM/L	W	L	PCT	G	GS	CG	SH	SV	IP	H	R	HR	HB	BB	SO	RAT	ERA	ERA+	OAV	OOB	BH	AVG	PB	PR	PR+	PD	TPI
1988	Cin-N	3	7	.300	14	14	3	1	0	87	88	49	8	2	28	34	12.2	4.66	77	.267	.328	1	.045	-1	-12	-10	-1	-1.2
Total	12	100	92	.521	297	224	72	13	4	1730^1	1395	732	172	28	657	1449	10.8	3.47	108	.220	.296	70	.132	-10	29	50	-8	2.5
● MARK SOUZA	Souza, Kenneth Mark b: 2/1/55, Redwood City, Cal. BL/TL, 6', 180 lbs. Deb: 4/22/80																											
1980	Oak-A	0	0	—	5	0	0	0	0	7	9	6	1	0	5	2	18.0	7.71	49	.310	.412	0	—	0	-3	-3	-0	-0.2
● JOHN SOWDERS	Sowders, John b: 12/10/1866, Louisville, Ky. d: 7/29/39, Indianapolis, Ind BR/TL, 6', Deb: 6/28/1887 F♦																											
1887	Ind-N	0	0	—	1	0	0	0	0	3	16	13	0	0	5	0	48.0	21.00	20	.593	.593	0	.000	-0	-6	-6	-0	-0.3
1889	KC-a	6	16	.273	25	23	20	0	1	185	204	181	9	7	105	104	15.4	4.82	87	.271	.366	19	.218	-2	-20	-12	-2	-1.3
1890	Bro-P	19	16	.543	39	37	28	1	0	309	358	233	3	11	161	91	15.4	3.82	117	.278	.363	25	.189	-5	14	21	-2	1.2
Total	3	25	32	.439	65	60	48	1	1	497	578	427	12	18	271	195	15.6	4.29	102	.279	.366	44	.199	-7	-11	3	-4	-0.4
● BILL SOWDERS	Sowders, William Jefferson "Little Bill" b: 11/29/1864, Louisville, Ky. d: 2/2/51, Indianapolis, Ind. BR/TR, 6', 155 lbs. Deb: 4/24/1888 F																											
1888	Bos-N	19	15	.559	36	35	34	2	0	317	278	155	3	9	73	132	10.2	2.07	138	.226	.275	18	.148	-4	27	27	1	2.3
1889	Bos-N	1	2	.333	7	4	3	0	3	42	53	35	3	2	23	10	16.7	5.14	81	.299	.386	4	.235	-0	-5	-4	1	-0.2
	Pit-N	6	5	.545	13	11	9	0	0	52^2	94	55	1	4	29	33	21.7	7.35	51	.376	.449	13	.271	2	-19	-23	2	-2.9
	Yr	7	7	.500	20	15	12	0	**3**	94^2	147	90	4	6	52	43	19.5	6.37	62	.344	.423	17	.262	2	-25	-26	3	-3.1
1890	Pit-N	3	8	.273	15	11	9	0	0	106	117	77	1	2	24	30	12.1	4.42	75	.271	.313	9	.180	-2	-10	-14	-2	-1.5
Total	3	29	30	.492	71	61	55	2	3	517^2	542	322	8	17	149	205	12.3	3.34	94	.260	.314	44	.186	-4	-7	-11	2	-2.3
● BOB SPADE	Spade, Robert b: 1/4/1877, Akron, Ohio d: 9/7/24, Cincinnati, Ohio BR/TR, 5'10", 190 lbs. Deb: 9/22/07																											
1907	Cin-N	1	2	.333	3	3	3	1	0	27	21	5	0	1	9	7	10.3	1.00	260	.219	.292	2	.286	1	4	5	-1	0.7
1908	Cin-N	17	12	.586	35	28	22	2	1	249^1	230	111	2	5	85	74	11.6	2.74	84	.250	.317	17	.195	1	-11	-12	-4	-1.8
1909	Cin-N	5	5	.500	14	13	8	0	0	98	91	38	0	4	39	31	12.3	2.85	91	.236	.313	10	.294	4	-3	-3	-4	-0.3
1910	Cin-N	1	2	.333	3	3	1	0	0	17^1	35	19	1	1	9	1	23.4	6.75	43	.479	.542	0	.000	-1	-7	-8	-0	-1.1
	StL-A	1	3	.250	7	5	2	1	0	34^2	34	24	1	1	17	8	13.5	4.41	56	.270	.361	3	.273	2	-7	-8	-1	-0.7
Total	4	25	24	.510	62	52	36	4	1	426^1	411	197	4	12	159	121	12.3	2.96	82	.257	.329	32	.222	7	-23	-25	-9	-3.2
● WARREN SPAHN	Spahn, Warren Edward b: 4/23/21, Buffalo, N.Y. BL/TL, 6', 175 lbs. Deb: 4/19/42 CH																											
1942	Bos-N	0	0	—	4	2	1	0	0	15^2	25	15	0	0	11	7	20.7	5.74	58	.368	.456	1	.167	-0	-4	-4	-0	-0.3
1946	Bos-N	8	5	.615	24	16	8	0	1	125^2	107	46	6	1	36	67	10.3	2.94	117	.228	.285	7	.163	-1	7	7	-2	0.4
1947	Bos-N★	21	10	.677	40	35	22	**7**	3	**289^2**	245	87	15	1	84	123	**10.3**	**2.33**	**167**	.226	**.283**	16	.163	1	**56**	**52**	-2	**5.3**
1948	*Bos-N	15	12	.556	36	35	16	3	1	257	237	115	19	1	77	114	11.0	3.71	103	.242	.298	15	.167	2	7	4	0	0.5
1949	Bos-N★	**21**	14	.600	38	38	**25**	4	0	**302^1**	283	125	27	3	86	**151**	11.1	3.07	123	.245	.299	18	.162	-0	33	26	-2	2.5
1950	Bos-N☆	**21**	17	.553	41	39	25	1	1	293	248	123	22	1	111	**191**	11.1	3.16	122	.227	.299	23	.217	4	32	24	0	3.3
1951	Bos-N☆	22	14	.611	39	36	**26**	**7**	0	310^2	278	111	20	1	109	**164**	11.2	2.98	123	.238	.304	22	.190	5	34	26	-2	3.1
1952	Bos-N☆	14	19	.424	40	35	19	5	3	290	263	109	19	6	73	**183**	10.6	2.98	121	.240	.291	18	.161	2	24	21	1	2.8
1953	Mil-N★	**23**	7	.767	35	32	24	5	3	265^2	211	75	14	1	70	148	**9.6**	**2.10**	**187**	**.217**	**.270**	23	.219	5	**65**	**59**	2	**7.3**
1954	Mil-N★	21	12	.636	39	34	23	1	3	283^1	262	107	24	1	86	136	11.1	3.14	118	.245	.302	21	.208	6	29	20	1	2.9
1955	Mil-N	17	14	.548	39	32	16	1	1	245^2	249	99	25	2	65	110	11.6	3.26	115	.265	.314	17	.210	5	21	15	0	2.3
1956	Mil-N★	20	11	.645	39	35	20	3	3	281^1	249	92	25	3	52	128	9.7	2.78	124	.238	.276	22	.210	6	**31**	23	-1	3.1
1957	*Mil-N☆	**21**	11	.656	39	35	**18**	4	3	271	241	94	23	2	78	111	10.7	2.69	130	.237	.293	13	.138	1	**36**	27	0	3.3
1958	*Mil-N★	**22**	11	**.667**	38	36	**23**	2	1	**290**	257	106	29	2	76	150	**10.4**	3.07	115	.237	.288	36	.333	18	28	16	4	**4.1**
1959	Mil-N☆	**21**	15	.583	40	36	**21**	**4**	0	**292**	282	106	21	1	70	143	10.9	2.96	120	.253	.298	24	.231	7	32	21	-1	3.1
1960	Mil-N	**21**	10	.677	40	33	**18**	4	2	267^2	254	114	24	4	74	154	11.2	3.50	98	.250	.303	14	.147	3	8	-2	3	0.3
1961	Mil-N★	**21**	13	.618	38	34	**21**	**4**	0	262^2	236	96	24	4	64	115	**10.4**	**3.02**	124	.243	**.293**	21	.223	10	**30**	23	3	**4.2**
1962	Mil-N☆	18	14	.563	34	34	**22**	0	0	269^1	248	97	25	3	55	118	10.2	3.04	125	.246	.287	18	.184	4	27	23	1	3.2
1963	Mil-N☆	23	7	.767	33	33	**22**	7	0	259^2	241	85	23	0	49	102	10.1	2.60	124	.248	.284	16	.178	5	20	18	4	3.2
1964	Mil-N	6	13	.316	38	25	4	1	4	173^2	204	110	23	2	52	78	13.4	5.29	67	.297	.348	11	.186	2	-34	-34	-1	-3.4
1965	NY-N	4	12	.250	20	19	5	0	0	126	140	70	18	2	35	56	12.6	4.36	81	.281	.331	4	.114	1	-11	-12	0	-1.2
	SF-N	3	4	.429	16	11	3	0	0	71^2	70	34	8	1	21	34	11.6	3.39	106	.256	.312	3	.143	0	1	2	1	0.2
	Yr	7	16	.304	36	30	8	0	0	197^2	210	104	26	3	56	90	12.2	4.01	89	.272	.324	7	.125	2	-10	-10	1	-1.0
Total	21	363	245	.597	750	665	382	63	29	5243^2	4830	2016	434	42	1434	2583	10.8	3.09	118	.244	.297	363	.194	88	470	351	9	50.2
● AL SPALDING	Spalding, Albert Goodwill b: 9/2/1850, Byron, Ill. d: 9/9/15, San Diego, Cal. BR/TR, 6'1", 170 lbs. Deb: 5/5/1871 MH♦																											
1871	Bos-n	**19**	10	.655	31	31	22	**1**	0	257^1	333	272	2		38	23	13.0	3.36	124	.268	.290	39	.271	2	25	23		1.6
1872	Bos-n	**38**	8	**.826**	48	48	41	**3**	0	404^2	417	224	0		27	27	9.9	1.87	195	.244	.255	84	.354	18	**80**	**80**		**7.1**
1873	Bos-n	**41**	14	**.745**	**60**	55	47	1	2	**497^2**	643	414	5		28	31	12.1	2.46	135	.283	.292	106	.329	21	**44**	**46**		**5.4**
1874	Bos-n	**52**	16	**.765**	**71**	69	**65**	**4**	0	**617^1**	755	402	1		19	31	11.3	1.92	113	.273	.278	119	.329	21	18	17		**3.0**
1875	Bos-n	**54**	5	**.915**	**72**	62	52	**7**	**9**	570^2	573	241	1		18	75	9.3	1.59	135	.245	.251	107	.312	22	**40**	**36**		**4.8**
1876	Chi-N	**47**	12	**.797**	61	60	53	8	0	528^2	542	226	6		26	39	9.7	1.75	139	.244	.256	91	.305	9	33	38	4	4.4
1877	Chi-N	1	0	1.000	4	1	0	0	1	11	17	12	0		0	2	13.9	3.27	91	.321	.321	65	.256	0	-1	-0	1	0.0
Total	5 n	204	53	.794	282	265	227	16	11	2347^2	2721	1553	9		130	187	10.9	2.10	136	.264	.273	455	.323	85	206	202		21.9
Total	2	48	12	.800	65	61	53	8	1	539^2	559	238	6		26	41	9.8	1.78	138	.246	.257	158	.284	9	32	38	5	4.4
● BILL SPANSWICK	Spanswick, William Henry b: 7/8/38, Springfield, Mass. BL/TL, 6'3", 195 lbs. Deb: 4/18/64																											
1964	Bos-A	2	3	.400	29	7	0	0	0	65^1	75	51	9	3	44	55	16.8	6.89	56	.306	.418	4	.286	1	-24	-21	1	-1.3
● JEFF SPARKS	Sparks, James Jeffrey b: 4/4/72, Houston, Tex. BR/TR, 6'3", 220 lbs. Deb: 9/12/99																											
1999	TB-A	0	0	—	8	0	0	0	1	10	6	6	1	1	12	17	17.1	5.40	92	.171	.396	0	—	0	-1	-0	-0	0.0
2000	TB-A	0	1	.000	15	0	0	0	0	20^1	13	8	2	2	18	24	14.6	3.54	140	.186	.367	0	—	0	3	3	-0	0.1
Total	2	0	1	.000	23	0	0	0	1	30^1	19	14	3	3	30	41	15.4	4.15	120	.181	.377	0	—	0	3	3	-1	0.1
● STEVE SPARKS	Sparks, Stephen Lanier b: 3/28/75, Mobile, Ala. BR/TR, 6'4", 210 lbs. Deb: 7/19/2000																											
2000	Pit-N	0	0	—	3	0	0	0	0	4	4	3	0	0	5	2	20.3	6.75	68	.267	.450	0	—	0	-1	-1	0	0.0
● STEVE SPARKS	Sparks, Steven William b: 7/2/65, Tulsa, Okla. BR/TR, 6', 180 lbs. Deb: 4/28/95																											
1995	Mil-A	9	11	.450	33	27	3	0	0	202	210	111	17	5	86	96	13.4	4.63	108	.274	.351	0	—	0	2	8	4	1.0
1996	Mil-A	4	7	.364	20	13	1	0	0	88^2	103	66	19	3	52	21	16.0	6.60	79	.297	.393	0	—	0	-16	-13	2	-1.1
1998	Ana-A	9	4	.692	22	20	0	0	0	128^2	130	66	14	5	58	90	13.5	4.34	108	.263	.346	0	.000	0	5	5	3	0.8
1999	Ana-A	5	11	.313	28	26	0	0	0	147^2	165	101	21	9	82	73	15.6	5.42	90	.281	.378	1	.333	1	-9	-9	3	-0.5
2000	Det-A	7	5	.583	20	15	1	1	1	104	108	55	7	4	29	53	12.2	4.07	118	.263	.318	0	—	0	10	8	1	1.0
Total	5	34	38	.472	123	101	5	1	1	671	716	399	78	26	307	333	14.1	4.92	100	.275	.357	1	.250	1	-8	-2	13	1.2
● TULLY SPARKS	Sparks, Thomas Frank b: 12/12/1874, Etna, Ga. d: 7/15/37, Anniston, Ala. BR/TR, 5'10", 160 lbs. Deb: 9/15/1897																											
1897	Phi-N	0	1	.000	1	1	1	0	0	8	12	9	0	0	4	0	18.0	10.13	41	.343	.410	0	.000	-1	-5	-5	0	-0.5
1899	Pit-N	8	6	.571	28	17	8	0	0	170	180	101	1	10	82	53	14.4	3.86	99	.271	.360	8	.129	-2	-0	-1	-1	-0.3
1901	Mil-A	7	17	.292	29	26	18	0	0	210	228	157	5	14	93	62	14.4	3.51	102	.273	.356	12	.169	-1	4	2	-0	0.1
1902	NY-N	4	10	.286	16	14	12	0	1	123^1	142	72	2	4	41	42	13.6	4.16	68	.288	.348	6	.150	-1	-19	-18	3	-1.7
	Bos-A	7	9	.438	17	15	15	1	0	142^2	151	83	4	7	40	37	12.5	3.47	103	.272	.329	8	.154	-1	2	2	0	0.0
1903	Phi-N	11	15	.423	28	28	27	0	0	248	248	109	3	8	56	88	11.3	2.72	120	.263	.310	10	.109	-5	15	15	-2	0.7
1904	Phi-N	7	16	.304	26	25	19	3	0	200^2	208	109	1	5	43	67	11.5	2.65	101	.260	.302	8	.105	-5	2	1	-4	-0.8
1905	Phi-N	14	11	.560	34	26	20	3	1	259^2	217	86	2	9	73	98	10.4	2.18	134	.236	.298	12	.128	-2	24	22	-6	1.2
1906	Phi-N	19	16	.543	42	37	29	6	3	316^2	244	99	4	10	62	114	9.0	2.16	121	.211	.257	16	.154	0	17	16	-4	1.4
1907	Phi-N	22	8	.733	33	31	24	3	1	265	221	78	2	7	51	90	9.5	2.00	121	.228	.271	3	.034	-8	14	13	-5	0.0
1908	Phi-N	16	15	.516	33	31	24	2	2	263^1	251	98	3	8	51	85	10.6	2.60	93	.257	.300	4	.052	-5	-7	-5	-2	-1.5
1909	Phi-N	6	11	.353	24	16	6	1	0	121^2	126	54	4	3	32	40	11.9	2.96	88	.280	.332	5	.139	-1	-5	-5	-1	-0.9
1910	Phi-N	0	2	.000	3	3	0	0	0	15	22	12	2	2	2	4	15.6	6.00	52	.324	.361	0	.000	-1	-5	-5	0	-0.6
Total	12	121	137	.469	314	270	203	19	8	2344	2250	1067	33	87	630	780	11.4	2.82	104	.254	.310	92	.115	-32	36	30	-20	-2.9

● JOE SPARMA
Sparma, Joseph Blase b: 2/4/42, Massillon, Ohio d: 5/14/86, Columbus, Ohio BR/TR, 6', 195 lbs. Deb: 5/20/64

YEAR TM/L	W	L	PCT	G	GS	CG	SH	SV	IP	H	R	HR	HB	BB	SO	RAT	ERA	ERA+	OAV	OOB	BH	AVG	PB	PR	PR+	PD	TPI
1964 Det-A	5	6	.455	21	11	3	2	0	84	62	33	4	3	45	71	11.8	3.00	122	.207	.316	4	.160	1	6	6	1	1.0
1965 Det-A	13	8	.619	30	28	6	0	0	167	142	69	13	3	75	127	11.9	3.18	109	.228	.314	7	.135	-0	5	5	-1	0.6
1966 Det-A	2	7	.222	29	13	0	0	0	91^2	103	57	14	3	52	61	15.5	5.30	66	.288	.383	5	.217	1	-19	-18	-2	-1.8
1967 Det-A	16	9	.640	37	37	11	5	0	217^2	186	103	20	8	85	153	11.5	3.76	87	.227	.306	4	.054	-5	-13	-12	-2	-2.1
1968 *Det-A	10	10	.500	34	31	7	1	0	182^1	169	81	14	7	77	110	12.5	3.70	81	.246	.328	8	.133	-1	-15	-14	-2	-1.9
1969 Det-A	6	8	.429	23	16	3	2	0	92^2	78	55	5	1	77	41	15.2	4.76	79	.231	.375	4	.138	-1	-12	-10	-1	-1.6
1970 Mon-N	0	4	.000	9	6	1	0	0	29^1	34	25	7	2	25	23	18.7	7.06	58	.296	.430	0	.000	-0	-10	-9	-0	-1.1
Total 7	52	52	.500	183	142	31	10	0	864^2	774	423	77	27	436	586	12.9	3.94	86	.239	.334	32	.119	-6	-57	-53	-7	-6.9

● TRIS SPEAKER
Speaker, Tristram E "The Grey Eagle" b: 4/4/1888, Hubbard, Tex. d: 12/8/58, Lake Whitney, Tex. BL/TL, 5'11.5", 193 lbs. Deb: 9/14/07 MH♦

YEAR TM/L	W	L	PCT	G	GS	CG	SH	SV	IP	H	R	HR	HB	BB	SO	RAT	ERA	ERA+	OAV	OOB	BH	AVG	PB	PR	PR+	PD	TPI
1914 Bos-A	0	0	—	1	0	0	0	0	1	2	1	0	0	0	0	18.0	9.00	30	.500	.500	193	.338	1	-1	-1	0	0.0

● CLIFF SPECK
Speck, Robert Clifford b: 8/8/56, Portland, Ore. BR/TR, 6'4", 195 lbs. Deb: 7/30/86

YEAR TM/L	W	L	PCT	G	GS	CG	SH	SV	IP	H	R	HR	HB	BB	SO	RAT	ERA	ERA+	OAV	OOB	BH	AVG	PB	PR	PR+	PD	TPI
1986 Atl-N	2	1	.667	13	1	0	0	0	28^1	25	13	2	1	15	21	13.0	4.13	96	.238	.339	0	.000	-0	-1	-0	0	0.0

● BY SPEECE
Speece, Byron Franklin b: 1/6/1897, West Baden, Ind. d: 9/29/74, Elgin, Ore. BR/TR, 5'11", 170 lbs. Deb: 4/21/24

YEAR TM/L	W	L	PCT	G	GS	CG	SH	SV	IP	H	R	HR	HB	BB	SO	RAT	ERA	ERA+	OAV	OOB	BH	AVG	PB	PR	PR+	PD	TPI
1924 *Was-A	2	1	.667	21	1	0	0	0	54^1	60	30	0	2	27	15	14.7	2.65	152	.303	.392	3	.150	-1	**10**	**9**	1	0.5
1925 Cle-A	3	5	.375	28	3	3	0	1	90^1	106	48	0	3	28	26	13.6	4.28	103	.297	.353	5	.161	-2	1	1	0	0.0
1926 Cle-A	0	0	—	2	0	0	0	0	3	1	1	0	0	2	1	9.0	0.00	—	.125	.300	0	—	0	1	1	0	0.1
1930 Phi-N	0	0	—	11	0	0	0	0	19^2	41	30	1	0	4	9	20.6	13.27	41	.432	.455	1	.333	0	-18	-16	-0	-0.7
Total 4	5	6	.455	62	4	3	0	1	167^1	208	109	1	5	61	51	14.7	4.73	93	.316	.378	9	.167	-2	-6	-6	2	-0.1

● FLOYD SPEER
Speer, Floyd Vernie b: 1/27/13, Booneville, Ark. d: 3/22/69, Little Rock, Ark. BR/TR, 6', 180 lbs. Deb: 4/25/43

YEAR TM/L	W	L	PCT	G	GS	CG	SH	SV	IP	H	R	HR	HB	BB	SO	RAT	ERA	ERA+	OAV	OOB	BH	AVG	PB	PR	PR+	PD	TPI
1943 Chi-A	0	0	—	1	0	0	0	0	1	1	1	0	0	2	1	27.0	9.00	37	.250	.500	0	—	0	-1	-1	0	0.0
1944 Chi-A	0	0	—	2	0	0	0	0	2	4	2	0	0	0	1	18.0	9.00	38	.500	.500	0	—	0	-1	-1	-0	-0.1
Total 2	0	0	—	3	0	0	0	0	3	5	3	0	0	2	2	21.0	9.00	38	.417	.500	0	—	0	-2	-2	0	-0.1

● KID SPEER
Speer, George Nathan b: 6/16/1886, Corning, Mo. d: 1/13/46, Edmonton, Alberta, Canada BL/TL, 5'9", 152 lbs. Deb: 4/24/09

YEAR TM/L	W	L	PCT	G	GS	CG	SH	SV	IP	H	R	HR	HB	BB	SO	RAT	ERA	ERA+	OAV	OOB	BH	AVG	PB	PR	PR+	PD	TPI
1909 Det-A	4	4	.500	12	8	4	0	1	76^1	88	39	2	4	13	12	12.4	2.83	89	.293	.331	3	.120	-0	-3	-3	1	-0.2

● JUSTIN SPEIER
Speier, Justin James b: 11/6/73, Daly City, Cal. BR/TR, 6'4", 200 lbs. Deb: 5/27/98 F

YEAR TM/L	W	L	PCT	G	GS	CG	SH	SV	IP	H	R	HR	HB	BB	SO	RAT	ERA	ERA+	OAV	OOB	BH	AVG	PB	PR	PR+	PD	TPI
1998 Chi-N	0	0	—	1	0	0	0	0	1^1	2	2	0	0	1	2	20.3	13.50	33	.333	.429	0	—	0	-1	-1	0	-0.1
Fla-N	0	3	.000	18	0	0	0	0	19^1	25	18	7	0	12	15	17.2	8.38	48	.325	.416	0	—	0	-9	-10	-0	-1.3
Yr	0	3	.000	19	0	0	0	0	20^2	27	20	7	0	13	17	17.4	8.71	47	.325	.417	0	—	0	-10	-11	-0	-1.4
1999 Atl-N	0	0	—	19	0	0	0	0	28^2	28	18	8	0	13	22	12.9	5.65	80	.248	.325	1	.333	0	-3	-4	0	-0.2
2000 Cle-A	5	2	.714	47	0	0	0	0	68^1	57	27	9	4	28	69	11.7	3.29	152	.226	.313	1	.500	0	12	13	-1	1.1
Total 3	5	5	.500	85	0	0	0	0	117^2	112	65	24	4	54	108	13.0	4.82	98	.250	.336	2	.400	1	-1	-1	-1	-0.5

● HACK SPENCER
Spencer, Fred Calvin b: 4/25/1885, St.Cloud, Minn. d: 2/5/69, St.Anthony, Minn. BR/TR, 5'10.5", 172 lbs. Deb: 4/18/12

YEAR TM/L	W	L	PCT	G	GS	CG	SH	SV	IP	H	R	HR	HB	BB	SO	RAT	ERA	ERA+	OAV	OOB	BH	AVG	PB	PR	PR+	PD	TPI
1912 StL-A	0	0	—	1	0	0	0	0	1^2	2	2	0	0	0	0	10.8	0.00	—	.286	.286	0	—	0	1	1	0	0.0

● GEORGE SPENCER
Spencer, George Elwell b: 7/7/26, Columbus, Ohio BR/TR, 6'1", 215 lbs. Deb: 8/17/50

YEAR TM/L	W	L	PCT	G	GS	CG	SH	SV	IP	H	R	HR	HB	BB	SO	RAT	ERA	ERA+	OAV	OOB	BH	AVG	PB	PR	PR+	PD	TPI
1950 NY-N	1	0	1.000	10	1	1	0	0	25^1	12	7	3	0	7	5	6.8	2.49	165	.141	.207	0	.000	-1	5	5	0	0.2
1951 *NY-N	10	4	.714	57	4	2	0	6	132	125	62	21	1	56	36	12.4	3.75	104	.254	.332	4	.125	-1	3	2	1	0.3
1952 NY-N	3	5	.375	35	4	0	0	3	60	57	39	13	3	21	27	12.2	5.55	67	.251	.323	2	.200	0	-12	-12	-0	-1.6
1953 NY-N	0	0	—	1	0	0	0	0	2^1	3	2	0	0	1	1	19.3	7.71	56	.300	.417	0	—	0	-1	-1	-0	0.0
1954 NY-N	1	0	1.000	6	0	0	0	0	12^1	9	5	1	0	8	4	12.4	3.65	111	.209	.333	0	.000	-0	1	1	0	0.1
1955 NY-N	0	0	—	1	0	0	0	0	1^2	1	1	1	0	3	0	21.6	5.40	75	.167	.444	0	—	0	-0	-0	0	0.0
1958 Det-A	1	0	1.000	7	0	0	0	0	10	11	4	0	0	4	5	13.5	2.70	149	.289	.357	0	—	0	1	1	0	0.2
1960 Det-A	0	1	.000	5	0	0	0	0	7^2	10	3	1	0	5	4	17.6	3.52	112	.323	.417	0	.000	0	0	-0	0	0.0
Total 8	16	10	.615	122	9	3	0	9	251^1	228	123	40	4	106	82	12.1	4.05	96	.245	.324	6	.120	-2	-3	-4	2	-0.8

● GLENN SPENCER
Spencer, Glenn Edward b: 9/11/05, Corning, N.Y. d: 12/30/58, Binghamton, N.Y. BR/TR, 5'11", 155 lbs. Deb: 4/11/28

YEAR TM/L	W	L	PCT	G	GS	CG	SH	SV	IP	H	R	HR	HB	BB	SO	RAT	ERA	ERA+	OAV	OOB	BH	AVG	PB	PR	PR+	PD	TPI
1928 Pit-N	0	0	—	4	0	0	0	0	5^2	4	3	0	0	3	2	11.1	1.59	256	.200	.304	0	.000	-0	2	2	-0	0.0
1930 Pit-N	8	9	.471	41	11	5	0	4	156^2	185	110	16	2	63	60	14.4	5.40	92	.305	.372	6	.113	-4	-7	-7	-2	-1.2
1931 Pit-N	11	12	.478	38	18	11	1	3	186^2	180	83	8	5	65	51	12.1	3.42	112	.260	.328	5	.096	-3	9	9	-0	0.7
1932 Pit-N	4	8	.333	39	13	5	1	1	137^2	167	104	10	3	44	35	14.0	4.97	77	.288	.341	6	.162	-1	-17	-18	-1	-1.6
1933 NY-N	0	2	.000	17	3	1	0	0	47^1	52	33	3	1	26	14	15.0	5.13	63	.284	.376	2	.167	-0	-9	-11	0	-0.5
Total 5	23	31	.426	139	45	22	2	8	534	588	333	37	11	201	162	13.5	4.53	91	.282	.349	19	.123	-9	-23	-25	-3	-2.6

● SEAN SPENCER
Spencer, Sean James b: 5/29/75, Seattle, Wash. BL/TL, 5'11", 185 lbs. Deb: 5/6/99

YEAR TM/L	W	L	PCT	G	GS	CG	SH	SV	IP	H	R	HR	HB	BB	SO	RAT	ERA	ERA+	OAV	OOB	BH	AVG	PB	PR	PR+	PD	TPI
1999 Sea-A	0	0	—	2	0	0	0	0	1^2	5	4	0	0	3	2	43.2	21.60	22	.556	.667	0	—	0	-3	-3	-0	-0.1
2000 Mon-N	0	0	—	8	0	0	0	0	6^2	7	4	2	0	3	6	13.5	5.40	87	.292	.370	0	—	0	-1	-0	-0	0.0
Total 2	0	0	—	10	0	0	0	0	8^1	12	8	2	0	6	8	19.4	8.64	55	.364	.462	0	—	0	-4	-4	-0	-0.1

● STAN SPENCER
Spencer, Stanley Roger b: 8/2/68, Vancouver, Wash. BR/TR, 6'4", 205 lbs. Deb: 8/27/98

YEAR TM/L	W	L	PCT	G	GS	CG	SH	SV	IP	H	R	HR	HB	BB	SO	RAT	ERA	ERA+	OAV	OOB	BH	AVG	PB	PR	PR+	PD	TPI
1998 SD-N	1	0	1.000	6	5	0	0	0	30^2	29	16	5	1	4	31	10.0	4.70	83	.244	.274	1	.111	-0	-2	-3	-1	-0.2
1999 SD-N	0	7	.000	9	8	0	0	0	38^1	56	44	11	1	11	36	16.0	9.16	46	.335	.380	0	.000	-1	-20	-23	-1	-3.1
2000 SD-N	2	2	.500	8	8	0	0	0	49^2	44	22	7	2	19	40	11.8	3.26	134	.239	.317	4	.333	1	8	7	-0	0.6
Total 3	3	9	.250	23	21	0	0	0	118^2	129	82	23	4	34	107	12.7	5.54	76	.274	.329	5	.161	1	-14	-19	-1	-2.7

● BOB SPICER
Spicer, Robert Oberton b: 4/11/25, Richmond, Va. BL/TR, 5'10", 173 lbs. Deb: 4/17/55

YEAR TM/L	W	L	PCT	G	GS	CG	SH	SV	IP	H	R	HR	HB	BB	SO	RAT	ERA	ERA+	OAV	OOB	BH	AVG	PB	PR	PR+	PD	TPI
1955 KC-A	0	0	—	2	0	0	0	0	2^2	9	10	2	1	4	2	47.3	33.75	12	.529	.636	0	.000	-0	-9	-8	-0	-0.4
1956 KC-A	0	0	—	2	0	0	0	0	2^1	6	5	1	1	1	0	30.9	19.29	22	.545	.615	0	—	0	-4	-4	0	-0.2
Total 2	0	0	—	4	0	0	0	0	5	15	15	3	2	5	2	39.6	27.00	16	.536	.629	0	.000	0	-13	-12	0	-0.6

● DAN SPILLNER
Spillner, Daniel Ray b: 11/27/51, Casper, Wyo. BR/TR, 6'1", 190 lbs. Deb: 5/21/74

YEAR TM/L	W	L	PCT	G	GS	CG	SH	SV	IP	H	R	HR	HB	BB	SO	RAT	ERA	ERA+	OAV	OOB	BH	AVG	PB	PR	PR+	PD	TPI
1974 SD-N	9	11	.450	30	25	5	2	0	148	153	78	15	0	70	95	13.6	4.01	89	.267	.346	1	.023	-4	-6	-7	-1	-1.5
1975 SD-N	5	13	.278	37	25	3	0	1	166^2	194	93	14	2	63	104	14.0	4.27	82	.293	.356	6	.133	1	-12	-15	-0	-1.4
1976 SD-N	2	11	.154	32	14	0	0	0	106^2	120	70	11	0	55	57	14.8	5.06	65	.291	.374	1	.040	-1	-18	-23	1	-2.5
1977 SD-N	7	6	.538	76	0	0	0	6	123	130	61	12	1	60	74	14.0	3.73	95	.280	.363	2	.118	1	3	-3	-2	-0.5
1978 SD-N	1	0	1.000	17	0	0	0	0	25^2	32	15	2	0	7	16	13.7	4.56	73	.317	.361	0	—	0	-3	-4	-0	-0.2
Cle-A	3	1	.750	36	0	0	0	3	56^1	54	26	2	1	21	48	12.1	3.67	102	.254	.323	0	—	0	1	0	-1	-0.1
1979 Cle-A	9	5	.643	49	13	3	0	3	157^2	153	82	16	3	64	97	12.6	4.62	92	.256	.331	0	—	0	-7	-6	-1	-0.6
1980 Cle-A	16	11	.593	34	30	7	1	0	194^1	225	122	23	3	74	100	14.0	5.28	77	.288	.352	0	—	0	-27	-26	-2	-3.3
1981 Cle-A	4	4	.500	32	5	1	0	7	97^1	86	41	3	0	39	59	11.6	3.14	115	.240	.314	0	—	0	6	5	0	0.5
1982 Cle-A	12	10	.545	65	0	0	0	21	133^2	117	44	9	0	45	90	10.9	2.49	164	.235	.299	0	—	0	**24**	**24**	-3	4.2
1983 Cle-A	2	9	.182	60	0	0	0	8	92^1	117	54	7	2	38	48	15.3	5.07	84	.315	.382	0	—	0	-10	-8	-1	-1.1
1984 Cle-A	0	5	.000	14	8	0	0	1	51	70	36	3	0	22	23	16.2	5.65	73	.332	.395	0	—	0	-9	-9	1	-0.7
Chi-A	1	0	1.000	22	0	0	0	1	48^1	51	25	7	1	14	26	12.3	4.10	102	.276	.330	0	—	0	-1	0	-0	0.0
Yr	1	5	.167	36	8	0	0	2	99^1	121	61	10	1	36	49	14.3	4.89	84	.306	.365	0	—	0	-10	-8	1	-0.7
1985 Chi-A	4	3	.571	52	3	0	0	1	91^2	83	39	10	0	33	41	11.4	3.44	126	.245	.312	0	—	0	7	9	-3	0.4
Total 12	75	89	.457	556	123	19	3	50	1492^2	1585	786	134	13	605	878	13.3	4.21	91	.275	.345	10	.077	-3	-53	-61	-12	-6.8

● SCIPIO SPINKS
Spinks, Scipio Ronald b: 7/12/47, Chicago, Ill. BR/TR, 6'1", 185 lbs. Deb: 9/16/69

YEAR TM/L	W	L	PCT	G	GS	CG	SH	SV	IP	H	R	HR	HB	BB	SO	RAT	ERA	ERA+	OAV	OOB	BH	AVG	PB	PR	PR+	PD	TPI
1969 Hou-N	0	0	—	1	0	0	0	0	2	1	1	0	0	1	4	9.0	0.00	—	.143	.250	0	—	0	1	1	0	0.0
1970 Hou-N	0	1	.000	5	2	0	0	0	13^2	17	15	5	0	9	6	17.1	9.88	39	.293	.388	0	.000	-0	-9	-10	-1	-0.7
1971 Hou-N	1	0	1.000	5	3	1	0	0	29^1	22	12	2	1	13	26	11.0	3.68	92	.210	.303	2	.222	0	-1	-1	-0	0.0
1972 StL-N	5	5	.500	16	16	6	0	0	118	96	39	5	2	59	93	12.0	2.67	128	.221	.317	7	.167	-1	10	10	1	0.8
1973 StL-N	1	5	.167	8	8	0	0	0	38^2	39	25	4	0	25	25	14.9	4.89	75	.269	.376	2	.182	1	-5	-5	1	-0.6
Total 5	7	11	.389	35	29	7	0	0	201^2	175	92	16	3	107	154	12.7	3.70	94	.234	.332	11	.169	0	-4	-5	1	-0.5

● PAUL SPLITTORFF Splittorff, Paul William b: 10/8/46, Evansville, Ind. BL/TL, 6'3", 210 lbs. Deb: 9/23/70

YEAR	TM/L	W	L	PCT	G	GS	CG	SH	SV	IP	H	R	HR	HB	BB	SO	RAT	ERA	ERA+	OAV	OOB	BH	AVG	PB	PR	PR+	PD	TPI
1970	KC-A	0	1	.000	2	1	0	0	0	8^2	16	9	1	0	5	10	21.8	7.27	51	.390	.457	1	.500	0	-3	-3	0	-0.3
1971	KC-A	8	9	.471	22	22	6	3	0	144^1	129	49	4	4	35	80	10.5	2.68	128	.243	.295	5	.104	-1	13	12	2	1.5
1972	KC-A	12	12	.500	35	33	12	2	0	216	189	81	11	4	67	140	10.8	3.13	97	.241	.304	16	.225	4	-1	-2	4	0.6
1973	KC-A	20	11	.645	38	38	12	3	0	262	279	135	19	5	78	110	12.4	3.98	103	.272	.327	0	—	0	-5	4	1	0.5
1974	KC-A	13	19	.406	36	36	8	1	0	226	252	122	23	1	75	90	13.1	4.10	93	.285	.342	0	—	0	-12	-7	0	-0.8
1975	KC-A	9	10	.474	35	23	6	3	1	159	156	75	10	1	56	76	12.1	3.17	122	.255	.319	0	—	0	11	12	2	1.6
1976	*KC-A	11	8	.579	26	23	5	1	0	158^2	169	79	11	3	59	59	13.1	3.97	88	.277	.343	0	—	0	-8	-8	1	-0.8
1977	*KC-A	16	6	**.727**	37	37	6	2	0	229	243	104	11	2	83	99	12.9	3.69	110	.278	.342	0	—	0	10	9	-0	0.8
1978	*KC-A	19	13	.594	39	38	13	2	0	262	244	113	22	3	60	76	10.5	3.40	113	.247	.293	0	—	0	11	13	1	1.5
1979	KC-A	15	17	.469	36	35	11	0	0	240	248	137	25	5	77	77	12.4	4.24	101	.268	.328	0	—	0	-0	1	-2	-0.1
1980	*KC-A	14	11	.560	34	33	4	0	0	204	236	101	17	1	43	53	12.4	4.15	98	.296	.333	0	—	0	-2	-2	-0	-0.2
1981	KC-A	5	5	.500	21	15	1	0	0	99	111	48	12	1	23	48	12.3	4.36	83	.294	.337	0	—	0	-8	-8	1	-0.7
1982	KC-A	10	10	.500	29	28	0	0	0	162	166	83	14	3	57	74	12.6	4.28	96	.266	.330	0	—	0	-4	-3	0	-0.4
1983	KC-A	13	8	.619	27	27	4	0	0	156	159	77	9	1	52	61	12.2	3.63	113	.262	.322	0	—	0	8	8	0	1.0
1984	KC-A	1	3	.250	12	3	0	0	0	28	47	30	3	0	10	4	18.3	7.71	52	.376	.422	0	—	0	-12	-11	1	-1.3
Total	15	166	143	.537	429	392	88	17	1	2554^2	2644	1243	192	34	780	1057	12.2	3.81	101	.270	.326	22	.182	3	-3	13	10	2.9

● PAUL SPOLJARIC Spoljaric, Paul Nikola b: 9/24/70, Kelowna, B.C., Canada BR/TL, 6'3", 205 lbs. Deb: 4/6/94

YEAR	TM/L	W	L	PCT	G	GS	CG	SH	SV	IP	H	R	HR	HB	BB	SO	RAT	ERA	ERA+	OAV	OOB	BH	AVG	PB	PR	PR+	PD	TPI
1994	Tor-A	0	1	.000	2	1	0	0	0	2^1	5	10	3	0	9	2	54.0	38.57	13	.417	.667	0	—	0	-9	-9	-0	-1.2
1996	Tor-A	2	2	.500	28	0	0	0	1	38	30	17	6	2	19	38	12.1	3.08	163	.214	.317	0	—	0	8	8	0	0.8
1997	Tor-A	0	3	.000	37	0	0	0	3	48	37	17	3	2	21	43	11.3	3.19	144	.215	.308	0	.000	-0	7	7	1	0.6
	*Sea-A	0	0	—	20	0	0	0	0	22^2	24	13	1	1	15	27	15.9	4.76	95	.276	.388	0	—	0	-0	-1	-0	0.0
	Yr	0	3	.000	57	0	0	0	3	70^2	61	30	4	3	36	70	12.7	3.69	124	.236	.336	0	.000	-0	7	7	1	0.6
1998	Sea-A	4	6	.400	53	6	0	0	0	83^1	85	67	14	1	55	89	15.2	6.48	72	.263	.372	0	—	0	-17	-17	-0	-1.7
1999	Phi-N	0	3	.000	5	3	0	0	0	11^1	23	24	1	1	7	10	24.6	15.09	31	.426	.500	0	.000	-0	-13	-13	-0	-2.0
	Tor-A	2	2	.500	37	2	0	0	0	62	62	41	9	2	32	63	13.9	4.65	106	.258	.350	0	—	0	2	2	-0	0.1
2000	KC-A	0	0	—	13	0	0	0	0	9^2	9	7	4	0	5	6	13.0	6.52	77	.265	.359	0	—	0	-2	-2	1	0.0
Total	6	8	17	.320	195	12	0	0	4	277^1	275	196	41	9	163	278	14.5	5.52	86	.259	.362	0	.000	-0	-24	-23	1	-3.4

● CARL SPONGBERG Spongberg, Carl Gustav b: 5/21/1884, Idaho Falls, Idaho d: 7/21/38, Los Angeles, Cal. BR/TR, 6'2", 208 lbs. Deb: 8/1/08

YEAR	TM/L	W	L	PCT	G	GS	CG	SH	SV	IP	H	R	HR	HB	BB	SO	RAT	ERA	ERA+	OAV	OOB	BH	AVG	PB	PR	PR+	PD	TPI
1908	Chi-N	0	0	—	1	0	0	0	0	7	9	7	1	2	6	4	21.9	9.00	26	.321	.472	2	.667	1	-5	-5	0	-0.2

● KARL SPOONER Spooner, Karl Benjamin b: 6/23/31, Oriskany Falls, N.Y. d: 4/10/84, Vero Beach, Fla. BR/TL, 6', 185 lbs. Deb: 9/22/54

YEAR	TM/L	W	L	PCT	G	GS	CG	SH	SV	IP	H	R	HR	HB	BB	SO	RAT	ERA	ERA+	OAV	OOB	BH	AVG	PB	PR	PR+	PD	TPI
1954	Bro-N	2	0	1.000	2	2	2	2	0	18	7	0	0	0	6	27	6.5	0.00	—	.113	.191	1	.167	0	8	8	-0	1.1
1955	*Bro-N	8	6	.571	29	14	2	1	2	98^2	79	50	8	5	41	78	11.4	3.65	111	.215	.302	8	.286	3	4	5	-0	0.8
Total	2	10	6	.625	31	16	4	3	2	116^2	86	50	8	5	47	105	10.6	3.09	132	.200	.286	9	.265	3	12	13	-1	1.9

● JERRY SPRADLIN Spradlin, Jerry Carl b: 6/14/67, Fullerton, Cal. BB/TR, 6'7", 230 lbs. Deb: 7/2/93

YEAR	TM/L	W	L	PCT	G	GS	CG	SH	SV	IP	H	R	HR	HB	BB	SO	RAT	ERA	ERA+	OAV	OOB	BH	AVG	PB	PR	PR+	PD	TPI
1993	Cin-N	2	1	.667	37	0	0	0	2	49	44	20	4	0	9	24	9.7	3.49	116	.249	.285	0	.000	-0	3	3	-1	0.0
1994	Cin-N	0	0	—	6	0	0	0	0	8	12	11	2	0	2	4	15.8	10.13	41	.353	.389	0	—	0	-5	-5	0	-0.3
1996	Cin-N	0	0	—	1	0	0	0	0	0^1	0	0	0	0	0	0	0.0	0.00	—	.000	.000	0	—	0	0	0	0	0.0
1997	Phi-N	4	8	.333	76	0	0	0	1	81^2	86	45	9	1	27	67	12.6	4.74	90	.274	.333	0	.000	-0	-5	-4	-1	-0.7
1998	Phi-N	4	4	.500	69	0	0	0	1	81^2	63	34	9	2	20	76	9.4	3.53	123	.216	.272	1	1.000	1	6	7	-0	0.7
1999	Cle-A	0	0	—	4	0	0	0	0	3	6	6	1	0	3	2	27.0	18.00	28	.400	.500	0	—	0	-4	-4	-0	-0.2
	SF-N	3	1	.750	59	0	0	0	0	58	59	31	4	10	29	52	15.2	4.19	100	.259	.367	0	.000	-0	2	0	-1	-0.1
2000	KC-A	4	4	.500	50	0	0	0	7	75	81	49	9	3	27	54	13.3	5.52	91	.283	.351	0	—	0	-5	-4	-0	-0.5
	Chi-N	0	1	.000	8	0	0	0	0	15	20	15	2	1	5	13	15.6	8.40	54	.328	.388	0	.000	-0	-6	-6	-0	-0.4
Total	7	17	19	.472	310	1	0	0	11	371^2	371	211	40	17	122	292	12.3	4.75	93	.264	.330	1	.167	0	-14	-14	-4	-1.5

● HOMER SPRAGINS Spragins, Homer Franklin b: 11/9/20, Grenada, Miss. BR/TR, 6'1", 190 lbs. Deb: 9/13/47

YEAR	TM/L	W	L	PCT	G	GS	CG	SH	SV	IP	H	R	HR	HB	BB	SO	RAT	ERA	ERA+	OAV	OOB	BH	AVG	PB	PR	PR+	PD	TPI
1947	Phi-N	0	0	—	4	0	0	0	0	5^1	3	4	0	0	3	3	10.1	6.75	59	.158	.273	0	—	0	-2	-2	0	-0.1

● CHARLIE SPRAGUE Sprague, Charles Wellington b: 10/10/1864, Cleveland, Ohio d: 12/31/12, Des Moines, Iowa BL/TL, 5'11", 150 lbs. Deb: 9/17/1887 ♦

YEAR	TM/L	W	L	PCT	G	GS	CG	SH	SV	IP	H	R	HR	HB	BB	SO	RAT	ERA	ERA+	OAV	OOB	BH	AVG	PB	PR	PR+	PD	TPI
1887	Chi-N	1	0	1.000	3	3	2	0	0	22	37	16	1	4	13	9	16.8	4.91	91	.370	.394	2	.154	-1	-2	-1	-1	-0.2
1889	Cle-N	0	2	.000	2	2	2	0	0	17	27	31	0	2	10	8	20.6	8.47	48	.351	.438	1	.143	-0	-8	-8	1	-0.6
1890	Tol-a	9	5	.643	19	12	9	0	0	122^2	111	83	0	18	78	59	15.2	3.89	102	.234	.363	47	.236	3	-0	1	-2	0.1
Total	3	10	7	.588	24	17	13	0	0	161^2	175	130	1	24	101	76	16.0	4.51	89	.269	.376	50	.228	1	-11	-8	-2	-0.7

● ED SPRAGUE Sprague, Edward Nelson Sr. b: 9/16/45, Boston, Mass. BR/TR, 6'4", 195 lbs. Deb: 4/10/68 F

YEAR	TM/L	W	L	PCT	G	GS	CG	SH	SV	IP	H	R	HR	HB	BB	SO	RAT	ERA	ERA+	OAV	OOB	BH	AVG	PB	PR	PR+	PD	TPI
1968	Oak-A	3	4	.429	47	1	0	0	4	68^2	51	29	5	2	34	34	11.4	3.28	86	.209	.311	0	.000	-1	-2	-4	1	-0.4
1969	Oak-A	1	1	.500	27	0	0	0	2	46^1	47	24	4	2	31	20	15.5	4.47	77	.267	.383	1	.200	0	-4	-6	2	0.0
1971	Cin-N	1	0	1.000	7	0	0	0	0	11	8	2	0	0	1	7	7.4	0.00	—	.195	.214	0	.000	-0	4	4	-1	0.3
1972	Cin-N	3	3	.500	33	1	0	0	0	56^2	55	33	6	3	26	25	13.3	4.13	78	.261	.350	0	.000	-1	-4	-6	-1	-0.8
1973	Cin-N	1	3	.250	28	0	0	0	1	38^2	35	22	3	2	22	19	13.7	5.12	67	.246	.355	0	.000	-0	-6	-8	0	-0.8
	StL-N	0	0	—	8	0	0	0	0	8	8	2	1	0	4	2	13.5	2.25	162	.276	.364	0	—	0	1	1	0	0.1
	Yr	1	3	.250	36	0	0	0	1	46^2	43	24	4	2	26	21	13.7	4.63	75	.251	.357	0	.000	-0	-5	-6	1	-0.7
	Mil-A	0	1	.000	7	0	0	0	1	9^2	13	11	0	2	14	3	27.0	9.31	40	.317	.509	0	—	0	-6	-6	-0	-0.7
1974	Mil-A	7	2	.778	20	10	3	0	0	94	94	32	3	4	31	57	12.4	2.39	151	.266	.332	0	—	0	13	13	-1	1.1
1975	Mil-A	1	7	.125	18	11	0	0	1	67^1	81	46	5	2	40	21	16.4	4.68	82	.297	.390	0	—	0	-7	-6	-1	-0.7
1976	Mil-A	0	2	.000	3	0	0	0	0	7^2	14	7	0	0	3	0	20.0	7.04	50	.438	.486	0	—	0	-3	-3	1	-0.5
Total	8	17	23	.425	198	23	3	0	9	408	406	208	27	17	206	188	13.9	3.84	89	.263	.356	1	.045	-1	-14	-20	2	-2.4

● JACK SPRING Spring, Jack Russell b: 3/11/33, Spokane, Wash. BR/TL, 6'1", 180 lbs. Deb: 4/16/55

YEAR	TM/L	W	L	PCT	G	GS	CG	SH	SV	IP	H	R	HR	HB	BB	SO	RAT	ERA	ERA+	OAV	OOB	BH	AVG	PB	PR	PR+	PD	TPI
1955	Phi-N	0	1	.000	2	0	0	0	0	2^2	2	2	2	0	1	2	10.1	6.75	59	.200	.273	0	.000	-0	-1	-1	-0	-0.2
1957	Bos-A	0	0	—	1	0	0	0	0	1	0	0	0	0	0	2	0.0	0.00	—	.000	.000	0	—	0	0	0	0	0.0
1958	Was-A	0	0	—	3	1	0	0	0	7	16	11	0	0	7	1	29.6	14.14	27	.457	.548	0	.000	-0	-8	-8	0	-0.4
1961	LA-A	3	0	1.000	18	4	0	0	0	38	35	19	4	3	15	27	12.6	4.26	106	.243	.327	0	.000	-1	-1	1	-0	0.0
1962	LA-A	4	2	.667	57	0	0	0	6	65	66	32	7	2	30	31	13.6	4.02	96	.270	.355	1	.091	-1	-0	-1	-0	-0.1
1963	LA-A	3	0	1.000	45	0	0	0	2	38^1	40	18	3	0	9	13	11.5	3.05	112	.268	.310	1	.333	0	2	2	1	0.2
1964	LA-A	1	0	1.000	6	0	0	0	0	3^1	3	1	1	0	3	0	16.2	2.70	122	.273	.429	0	—	0	0	0	-0	0.0
	Chi-N	0	0	—	7	0	0	0	0	6	4	5	0	0	2	1	9.0	6.00	62	.200	.273	0	—	0	-2	-1	-0	0.0
	StL-N	0	0	—	2	0	0	0	0	3	8	9	1	0	1	0	27.0	3.00	127	.471	.500	0	—	0	0	0	0	0.0
	Yr	0	0	—	9	0	0	0	0	9	12	14	1	0	3	1	15.0	5.00	75	.324	.375	0	—	0	-1	-1	-0	0.0
1965	Cle-A	1	2	.333	14	0	0	0	0	21^2	21	9	2	0	10	9	12.9	3.74	93	.259	.341	1	.333	0	-1	-1	-1	-0.1
Total	8	12	5	.706	155	5	0	0	8	186	195	106	21	5	78	86	13.5	4.26	90	.273	.349	3	.107	-1	-9	-9	1	-0.6

● BRAD SPRINGER Springer, Bradford Louis b: 5/9/04, Detroit, Mich. d: 1/4/70, Birmingham, Mich. BL/TL, 6', 155 lbs. Deb: 5/1/25

YEAR	TM/L	W	L	PCT	G	GS	CG	SH	SV	IP	H	R	HR	HB	BB	SO	RAT	ERA	ERA+	OAV	OOB	BH	AVG	PB	PR	PR+	PD	TPI
1925	StL-A	0	0	—	2	0	0	0	0	3	1	2	0	0	7	0	24.0	3.00	156	.200	.667	0	—	0	0	1	0	0.0
1926	Cin-N	0	0	—	1	0	0	0	0	1^1	2	3	0	1	2	1	33.8	6.75	55	.286	.500	0	.000	-0	-0	-0	0	0.0
Total	2	0	0	—	3	0	0	0	0	4^1	3	5	0	1	9	1	27.0	4.15	105	.250	.591	0	.000	-0	0	0	0	0.0

● DENNIS SPRINGER Springer, Dennis Leroy b: 2/12/65, Fresno, Cal. BR/TR, 5'10", 185 lbs. Deb: 9/14/95

YEAR	TM/L	W	L	PCT	G	GS	CG	SH	SV	IP	H	R	HR	HB	BB	SO	RAT	ERA	ERA+	OAV	OOB	BH	AVG	PB	PR	PR+	PD	TPI
1995	Phi-N	0	3	.000	4	4	0	0	0	22^1	21	15	3	1	9	15	12.5	4.84	87	.256	.337	1	.125	-0	-2	-1	-1	-0.2
1996	Cal-A	5	6	.455	20	15	2	1	0	94^2	91	65	24	6	43	64	13.3	5.51	91	.251	.340	0	—	0	-5	-5	-1	-0.6
1997	Ana-A	9	9	.500	32	28	3	1	0	194^2	199	118	32	10	73	75	13.0	5.18	88	.267	.340	0	.000	-0	-13	-13	-1	-1.1
1998	TB-A	3	11	.214	29	17	1	0	0	115^2	120	77	21	12	60	46	14.9	5.45	88	.271	.374	0	.000	-0	-10	-8	-1	-0.9
1999	Fla-N	6	16	.273	38	29	3	2	1	196^1	231	121	23	7	64	83	13.8	4.86	90	.303	.363	6	.120	-2	-6	-11	0	-1.2
2000	NY-N	0	1	.000	2	2	0	0	0	11^1	20	11	2	1	8	5	20.6	8.74	51	.377	.441	0	.000	-0	-5	-6	0	-0.4
Total	6	23	46	.333	125	95	9	4	1	635	682	407	105	37	254	288	13.8	5.23	88	.279	.355	7	.106	-3	-42	-45	-4	-4.4

YEAR TM/L	W	L	PCT	G	GS	CG	SH	SV	IP	H	R	HR	HB	BB	SO	RAT	ERA	ERA+	OAV	OOB	BH	AVG	PB	PR	PR+	PD	TPI
● ED SPRINGER Springer, Edward H. b: 2/9/1861, California d: 4/24/26, Los Angeles Co., Cal. 6'2", 187 lbs. Deb: 7/12/1889																											
1889 Lou-a	0	1	.000	1	1	1	0	0	5	8	8	0	2	2	1	21.6	9.00	43	.348	.444	0	.000	-0	-3	-3	-0	-0.4
● RUSS SPRINGER Springer, Russell Paul b: 11/7/68, Alexandria, La. BR/TR, 6'4", 195 lbs. Deb: 4/17/92																											
1992 NY-A	0	0	—	14	0	0	0	0	16	18	11	0	1	10	12	16.3	6.19	63	.281	.387	0	—	0	-4	-4	-0	-0.2
1993 Cal-A	1	6	.143	14	9	1	0	0	60	73	48	11	3	32	31	16.2	7.20	63	.303	.391	0	—	0	-19	-17	-1	-1.8
1994 Cal-A	2	2	.500	18	5	0	0	2	45^2	53	28	9	0	14	28	13.2	5.52	89	.291	.342	0	—	0	-4	-3	-1	-0.3
1995 Cal-A	1	2	.333	19	6	0	0	1	51^2	60	37	11	5	25	38	15.7	6.10	77	.290	.380	0	—	0	-8	-8	-0	-0.5
Phi-N	0	0	—	14	0	0	0	0	26^2	22	11	5	2	10	32	11.5	3.71	114	.227	.312	0	.000	-0	1	2	1	0.1
1996 Phi-N	3	10	.231	51	7	0	0	0	96^2	106	60	12	1	38	94	13.5	4.66	93	.272	.338	1	.059	-1	-5	-4	-1	-0.6
1997 *Hou-N	3	3	.500	54	0	0	0	3	55^1	48	28	4	4	27	74	12.8	4.23	95	.232	.332	0	.000	-0	-0	-1	0	-0.2
1998 Ari-N	4	3	.571	26	0	0	0	0	32^2	29	16	4	1	14	37	12.1	4.13	102	.232	.314	0	.000	-0	0	0	-1	0.0
Atl-N	1	1	.500	22	0	0	0	0	20	22	10	0	0	16	19	17.1	4.05	103	.301	.427	0	—	0	0	0	-0	0.0
Yr	5	4	.556	48	0	0	0	0	52^2	51	26	4	1	30	56	14.0	4.10	102	.258	.358	0	.000	-0	1	1	-1	0.0
1999 *Atl-N	2	1	.667	49	0	0	0	1	47^1	31	20	5	2	22	49	10.5	3.42	131	.185	.286	0	—	0	6	6	-0	0.3
2000 Ari-N	2	4	.333	52	0	0	0	0	62	63	36	11	2	34	59	14.4	5.08	91	.261	.357	1	.200	0	-3	-3	-1	-0.4
Total 9	19	32	.373	333	27	1	0	7	514	525	305	72	21	242	473	13.8	5.01	88	.263	.349	2	.080	-2	-34	-34	-5	-3.6
● CHARLIE SPROULL Sproull, Charles William b: 1/9/19, Taylorsville, Ga. d: 1/13/80, Rockford, Ill. BR/TR, 6'3", 185 lbs. Deb: 4/19/45																											
1945 Phi-N	4	10	.286	34	19	2	0	1	130^1	158	102	10	0	80	47	16.4	5.94	65	.298	.390	5	.143	-1	-31	-30	-1	-3.0
● BOB SPROUT Sprout, Robert Samuel b: 12/5/41, Florin, Pa. BL/TL, 6', 165 lbs. Deb: 9/27/61																											
1961 LA-A	0	0	—	1	1	0	0	0	4	4	3	0	0	3	2	15.8	4.50	100	.267	.389	0	—	0	-0	0	-0	0.0
● BOBBY SPROWL Sprowl, Robert John b: 4/14/56, Sandusky, Ohio BL/TL, 6'2", 190 lbs. Deb: 9/5/78																											
1978 Bos-A	0	2	.000	3	3	0	0	0	12^2	12	10	3	0	10	10	15.6	6.39	65	.245	.373	0	—	0	-4	-3	-0	-0.4
1979 Hou-N	0	0	—	3	0	0	0	0	4	1	0	0	0	2	3	6.8	0.00	—	.083	.214	0	—	0	2	2	-0	0.1
1980 Hou-N	0	0	—	1	0	0	0	0	1	1	0	0	0	1	3	18.0	0.00	—	.250	.400	0	—	0	0	0	0	0.0
1981 Hou-N	0	1	.000	15	1	0	0	0	28^2	40	20	1	0	14	18	17.0	5.97	55	.333	.403	1	.167	-0	-8	-9	-0	-0.5
Total 4	0	3	.000	22	4	0	0	0	46^1	54	30	4	0	27	34	15.7	5.44	65	.292	.382	1	.167	-0	-9	-10	-1	-0.8
● JAY SPURGEON Spurgeon, Jay Aaron b: 7/5/76, West Covina, Cal. BR/TR, 6'6", 211 lbs. Deb: 8/15/2000																											
2000 Bal-A	1	1	.500	7	4	0	0	0	24	26	16	5	2	15	11	16.1	6.00	80	.283	.394	0	—	0	-3	-3	-1	-0.3
● MIKE SQUIRES Squires, Michael Lynn b: 3/5/52, Kalamazoo, Mich. BL/TL, 5'11", 185 lbs. Deb: 9/1/75 C♦																											
1984 Chi-A	0	0	—	1	0	0	0	0	0^1	0	0	0	0	0	0	0.0	0.00	—	.000	.000	15	.183	0	0	0	0	0.0
● GEORGE STABLEIN Stablein, George Charles b: 10/29/57, Inglewood, Cal. BR/TR, 6'4", 185 lbs. Deb: 9/20/80																											
1980 SD-N	0	1	.000	4	2	0	0	0	11^2	16	4	0	0	3	4	14.7	3.09	111	.340	.380	0	.000	-0	1	0	-0	0.0
● EDDIE STACK Stack, William Edward b: 10/24/1887, Chicago, Ill. d: 8/28/58, Chicago, Ill. BR/TR, 6', 175 lbs. Deb: 6/7/10																											
1910 Phi-N	6	7	.462	20	16	8	1	0	117	115	61	7	4	34	48	11.8	4.00	78	.266	.326	3	.083	-3	-13	-11	-1	-1.5
1911 Phi-N	5	5	.500	13	10	5	0	0	77^2	67	48	3	6	41	36	13.2	3.59	96	.234	.342	2	.083	-2	-2	-1	0	-0.3
1912 Bro-N	7	5	.583	28	17	4	0	1	142	139	80	3	9	55	45	12.9	3.36	100	.264	.343	7	.135	-3	1	-0	-1	-0.4
1913 Bro-N	4	4	.500	23	9	4	1	0	87	79	30	0	1	32	34	11.6	2.38	138	.250	.321	4	.160	-1	8	9	-2	0.4
Chi-N	4	2	.667	11	7	3	1	1	51	56	29	1	2	15	28	12.9	4.24	75	.280	.336	1	.063	-1	-6	-6	-1	-0.9
Yr	8	6	.571	34	16	7	2	1	138	135	59	1	3	47	62	12.1	3.07	106	.262	.327	5	.122	-2	2	3	-3	-0.5
1914 Chi-N	0	1	.000	7	1	0	0	0	16^1	13	11	0	0	11	9	13.2	4.96	56	.220	.343	0	.000	-0	-4	-4	0	-0.2
Total 5	26	24	.520	102	60	24	3	2	491	469	259	14	22	188	200	12.4	3.52	93	.258	.334	17	.108	-10	-15	-14	-4	-2.9
● GENERAL STAFFORD Stafford, James Joseph "Jamsey" b: 7/9/1868, Webster, Mass. d: 9/18/23, Worcester, Mass. BR/TR, 5'8", 165 lbs. Deb: 8/27/1890 F♦																											
1890 Buf-P	3	9	.250	12	12	11	0	0	98	123	89	8	4	43	21	15.6	5.14	80	.294	.366	7	.143	-2	-10	-12	-1	-1.1
● JOHN STAFFORD Stafford, John Henry "Doc" b: 4/8/1870, Dudley, Mass. d: 7/3/40, Worcester, Mass. BR/TR, 5'10", 170 lbs. Deb: 6/15/1893 F																											
1893 Cle-N	0	1	.000	2	0	0	0	0	7	12	15	1	0	7	4	24.4	14.14	35	.364	.475	0	.000	-1	-7	-7	-0	-0.7
● BILL STAFFORD Stafford, William Charles b: 8/13/39, Catskill, N.Y. BR/TR, 6'2", 193 lbs. Deb: 4/17/60																											
1960 *NY-A	3	1	.750	11	8	2	1	0	60	50	17	3	1	18	36	10.4	2.25	159	.226	.287	1	.045	-2	11	10	1	0.4
1961 *NY-A	14	9	.609	36	25	8	3	2	195	168	65	13	5	59	101	10.7	2.68	139	.232	.294	12	.179	2	29	24	-1	2.8
1962 *NY-A	14	9	.609	35	33	7	2	0	213^1	188	95	23	4	77	109	11.3	3.67	102	.233	.303	17	.218	3	7	2	-1	0.4
1963 NY-A	4	8	.333	28	14	0	0	3	89^2	104	64	16	3	42	52	15.0	6.02	58	.287	.366	7	.292	3	-24	-26	-0	-3.1
1964 NY-A	5	0	1.000	31	1	0	0	4	60^2	50	19	4	2	22	39	11.0	2.67	136	.231	.308	1	.077	-1	6	6	0	0.5
1965 NY-A	3	8	.273	22	15	1	0	0	111^1	93	45	16	2	31	71	10.2	3.56	96	.229	.286	0	.000	-3	-1	-2	-0	-0.5
1966 KC-A	0	4	.000	9	8	0	0	0	39^2	42	28	2	2	12	31	12.7	4.99	68	.273	.333	0	.000	-1	-7	-7	-1	-0.8
1967 KC-A	0	1	.000	14	0	0	0	0	16	12	4	0	0	9	10	11.8	1.69	189	.214	.323	0	.000	-0	3	3	0	0.2
Total 8	43	40	.518	186	104	18	6	9	785^2	707	337	77	19	270	449	11.4	3.52	103	.240	.308	38	.155	0	24	9	-2	-0.1
● CHICK STAHL Stahl, Charles Sylvester b: 1/10/1873, Avilla, Ind. d: 3/28/07, W.Baden, Ind. BL/TL, 5'10", 160 lbs. Deb: 4/19/1897 M♦																											
1899 Bos-N	0	0	—	1	0	0	0	0	2	2	2	0	0	3	0	22.5	9.00	46	.250	.455	202	.351	0	-1	-1	0	0.0
● GERRY STALEY Staley, Gerald Lee b: 8/21/20, Brush Prairie, Wash. BR/TR, 6', 195 lbs. Deb: 4/20/47																											
1947 StL-N	1	0	1.000	18	1	1	0	0	29^1	33	11	2	1	8	14	12.9	2.76	150	.287	.339	0	.000	-1	4	4	1	0.2
1948 StL-N	4	4	.500	31	3	0	0	0	52	61	44	5	0	21	23	14.2	6.92	59	.288	.352	2	.222	1	-17	-16	1	-1.9
1949 StL-N	10	10	.500	45	17	5	2	6	171^1	154	65	7	3	41	55	10.4	2.73	152	**.238**	.286	5	.122	-0	25	26	3	3.4
1950 StL-N	13	13	.500	42	22	7	1	3	169^2	201	101	14	7	61	62	14.3	4.99	86	.300	.365	8	.145	-1	-16	-13	3	-1.5
1951 StL-N	19	13	.594	42	30	10	4	3	227	244	108	14	8	74	67	12.9	3.81	104	.275	.337	13	.160	-1	4	4	2	0.6
1952 StL-N☆	17	14	.548	35	33	15	0	0	239^2	238	101	21	7	52	93	11.2	3.27	114	.256	.301	13	.153	-2	12	12	4	1.6
1953 StL-N☆	18	9	.667	40	32	10	1	4	230	243	118	31	17	54	88	12.3	3.99	107	.269	.322	8	.103	-5	8	7	2	0.5
1954 StL-N	7	13	.350	48	20	3	1	2	155^2	198	107	21	6	47	50	14.5	5.26	78	.308	.361	5	.139	-0	-21	-20	2	-2.0
1955 Cin-N	5	8	.385	30	18	2	0	0	119^2	146	72	22	3	28	40	13.3	4.66	91	.309	.351	2	.056	-4	-8	-5	1	-0.8
NY-A	0	0	—	2	0	0	0	0	2	5	5	1	0	1	0	27.0	13.50	28	.417	.462	0	—	0	-2	-2	0	-0.1
1956 NY-A	0	0	—	1	0	0	0	0	0^1	4	4	0	0	1	1	108.0	108.00	4	.800	.800	0	.000	-0	-4	-4	0	-0.2
Chi-A	8	3	.727	26	10	5	0	0	101^2	98	37	11	6	20	25	11.0	2.92	140	.251	.298	3	.094	-2	14	14	1	1.1
Yr	8	3	.727	27	10	5	0	0	102	102	41	11	6	20	26	11.3	3.26	126	.258	.304	3	.091	-3	10	10	1	0.9
1957 Chi-A	5	1	.833	47	0	0	0	7	105	95	27	7	0	27	44	10.5	2.06	182	.244	.293	1	.045	-1	**20**	**20**	2	1.5
1958 Chi-A	4	5	.444	50	0	0	0	8	85^1	81	36	10	0	24	27	11.1	3.16	115	.259	.312	0	.000	-1	6	5	3	0.7
1959 *Chi-A	8	5	.615	**67**	0	0	0	14	116^1	111	39	5	0	25	54	10.5	2.24	167	.259	.300	2	.154	0	**21**	**20**	-0	2.2
1960 Chi-A★	13	8	.619	64	0	0	0	10	115^1	94	40	8	3	25	52	9.5	2.42	156	.227	.276	4	.235	1	**19**	**18**	3	**3.8**
1961 Chi-A	0	3	.000	16	0	0	0	0	18	17	10	3	0	5	8	11.0	5.00	78	.246	.297	0	—	0	-2	-2	0	-0.3
KC-A	1	1	.500	23	0	0	0	2	30	32	15	4	2	10	16	13.2	3.60	116	.278	.346	0	.000	0	1	2	1	0.2
Det-A	1	1	.500	13	0	0	0	2	13^1	15	6	1	0	6	8	14.2	3.38	121	.288	.362	0	.000	-0	1	1	0	0.2
Yr	2	5	.286	52	0	0	0	4	61^1	64	31	8	2	21	32	12.8	3.96	103	.271	.336	0	.000	-0	0	1	1	0.1
Total 15	134	111	.547	640	186	58	9	61	1981^2	2070	946	187	63	529	727	12.1	3.70	108	.270	.322	66	.126	-16	65	68	29	9.7
● HARRY STALEY Staley, Henry Eli b: 11/3/1866, Jacksonville, Ill. d: 1/12/10, Battle Creek, Mich BR/TR, 5'10", 175 lbs. Deb: 6/23/1888																											
1888 Pit-N	12	12	.500	25	24	24	2	0	207^1	185	104	6	7	53	89	10.6	2.69	99	.235	.289	11	.129	-4	4	-1	-2	-0.5
1889 Pit-N	21	26	.447	49	47	46	1	1	420	433	254	11	8	116	159	11.9	3.51	107	.258	.309	30	.161	-7	23	12	2	0.7
1890 Pit-P	21	25	.457	46	46	44	3	0	387^2	392	246	5	11	74	145	**11.1**	3.23	121	.251	**.290**	34	.207	1	43	32	-2	2.7
1891 Pit-N	4	5	.444	9	7	6	0	0	71^2	77	49	4	2	11	25	11.3	2.89	114	.265	.296	7	.226	1	4	3	-0	0.4
Bos-N	20	8	.714	31	30	26	1	0	252^1	236	111	11	4	69	114	11.0	2.50	146	.238	.290	17	.167	-2	24	30	-1	2.5
Yr	24	13	.649	40	37	32	1	0	324	313	160	15	6	80	139	**11.1**	2.58	138	.244	**.292**	24	.180	-1	28	33	-1	2.9
1892 *Bos-N	22	10	.688	37	35	31	3	0	299^2	273	144	10	3	97	93	11.2	3.03	116	.233	.293	16	.131	-6	8	15	-2	0.6

YEAR	TM/L	W	L	PCT	G	GS	CG	SH	SV	IP	H	R	HR	HB	BB	SO	RAT	ERA	ERA+	OAV	OOB	BH	AVG	PB	PR	PR+	PD	TPI
1893	Bos-N	18	10	.643	36	31	23	0	0	263	344	224	22	6	81	61	14.7	5.13	96	.307	.356	30	.265	3	-14	-5	-1	-0.3
1894	Bos-N	12	10	.545	27	21	18	0	1	208^2	305	204	15	5	61	32	16.0	6.81	83	.337	.382	20	.235	0	-34	-25	-3	-2.0
1895	StL-N	6	13	.316	23	16	13	0	0	158^2	223	136	8	2	39	28	15.0	5.22	93	.327	.365	9	.134	-6	-8	-7	-2	-1.2
Total	8	136	119	.533	283	257	231	10	2	2269	2468	1472	92	48	601	746	12.4	3.80	105	.269	.317	174	.182	-19	51	51	-9	2.9
● TRACY STALLARD	Stallard, Evan Tracy b: 8/31/37, Coeburn, Va. BR/TR, 6'5", 205 lbs. Deb: 9/24/60																											
1960	Bos-A	0	0	—	4	0	0	0	0	4	0	0	0	0	2	6	4.5	0.00	—	.000	.133	0	—	0	2	2	0	0.1
1961	Bos-A	2	7	.222	43	14	1	0	2	132^2	110	75	15	1	96	109	14.0	4.88	85	.229	.359	3	.083	-2	-13	-10	-2	-1.0
1962	Bos-A	0	0	—	1	0	0	0	0	1	0	0	0	0	0	0	0.0	0.00	—	.000	.000	0	—	0	0	0	-0	0.0
1963	NY-N	6	17	.261	39	23	5	0	1	154^2	156	89	23	1	77	110	13.6	4.71	74	.262	.347	3	.063	-3	-24	-20	-1	-3.2
1964	NY-N	10	20	.333	36	34	11	2	0	225^2	213	111	20	6	73	118	11.6	3.79	94	.252	.316	15	.190	2	-6	-5	-2	-0.7
1965	StL-N	11	8	.579	40	26	4	1	0	194^1	172	83	25	6	70	99	11.5	3.38	114	.235	.307	6	.088	-4	3	9	-2	0.2
1966	StL-N	1	5	.167	20	7	0	0	1	52^1	65	40	9	2	25	35	15.8	5.68	63	.305	.383	0	.000	-2	-12	-12	0	-1.5
Total	7	30	57	.345	183	104	21	3	4	764^2	716	398	92	16	343	477	12.7	4.17	90	.248	.332	27	.110	-9	-50	-35	-7	-6.1
● CHARLEY STANCEU	Stanceu, Charles b: 1/9/16, Canton, Ohio d: 4/3/69, Canton, Ohio BR/TR, 6'2", 190 lbs. Deb: 4/16/41																											
1941	NY-A	3	3	.500	22	2	0	0	0	48	58	41	3	1	35	21	17.6	5.63	70	.296	.405	0	.000	-2	-8	-10	-1	-1.2
1946	NY-A	0	0	—	3	0	0	0	0	4	6	4	0	0	5	3	24.8	9.00	38	.316	.458	0	—	0	-2	-3	0	-0.1
	Phi-N	2	4	.333	14	11	1	0	0	70^1	71	35	4	0	39	23	14.1	4.22	81	.270	.364	0	.000	-2	-6	-6	-1	-0.8
Total	2	5	7	.417	39	13	1	0	0	122^1	135	80	7	1	79	47	15.8	4.93	74	.282	.385	0	.000	-4	-17	-18	-2	-2.1
● PETE STANDRIDGE	Standridge, Alfred Peter b: 4/25/1891, Black Diamond, Wash. d: 8/2/63, San Francisco, Cal. BR/TR, 5'10.5", 165 lbs. Deb: 9/19/11																											
1911	StL-N	0	0	—	2	0	0	0	0	4^2	10	10	0	1	4	3	28.9	9.64	35	.435	.536	0	.000	-0	-3	-3	0	-0.2
1915	Chi-N	4	1	.800	29	3	2	0	0	112^1	120	56	2	2	36	42	12.7	3.61	77	.274	.332	9	.225	3	-11	-10	0	-0.3
Total	2	4	1	.800	31	3	2	0	0	117	130	66	2	3	40	45	13.3	3.85	73	.282	.343	9	.220	3	-14	-13	0	-0.5
● AL STANEK	Stanek, Albert Wilfred "Lefty" b: 12/24/43, Springfield, Mass. BL/TL, 5'11.5", 190 lbs. Deb: 4/26/63																											
1963	SF-N	0	0	—	11	0	0	0	0	13^1	10	7	1	0	12	5	14.9	4.73	68	.217	.379	0	.000	-0	-2	-2	1	0.0
● KEVIN STANFIELD	Stanfield, Kevin Bruce b: 12/19/55, Huron, S.Dak. BL/TL, 6', 190 lbs. Deb: 9/14/79																											
1979	Min-A	0	0	—	3	0	0	0	0	3	2	2	0	0	0	0	6.0	6.00	73	.200	.200	0	—	0	-1	-1	0	0.0
● LEE STANGE	Stange, Albert Lee b: 10/27/36, Chicago, Ill. BR/TR, 5'10", 170 lbs. Deb: 4/15/61 C																											
1961	Min-A	1	0	1.000	7	0	0	0	0	12^1	15	6	1	0	10	10	18.2	2.92	145	.294	.410	0	.000	-0	2	2	0	0.1
1962	Min-A	4	3	.571	44	6	1	0	3	95	98	57	14	1	39	70	13.1	4.45	92	.271	.343	1	.059	-1	-5	-4	-0	-0.4
1963	Min-A	12	5	.706	32	20	7	2	0	164^2	145	53	21	0	43	100	10.3	2.62	139	.233	.283	5	.096	-1	18	19	-0	1.7
1964	Min-A	3	6	.333	14	11	2	0	0	79^2	78	45	13	0	19	54	11.0	4.74	75	.255	.298	1	.040	-1	-10	-10	1	-1.1
	Cle-A	4	8	.333	23	14	0	0	0	91^2	98	47	14	1	31	78	12.8	4.12	87	.270	.329	2	.080	-1	-5	-5	-0	-0.8
	Yr	7	14	.333	37	25	2	0	0	171^1	176	92	27	1	50	132	11.9	4.41	81	.263	.315	3	.060	-2	-15	-16	0	-1.9
1965	Cle-A	8	4	.667	41	12	4	2	0	132	122	50	13	1	26	80	10.2	3.34	104	.247	.286	3	.107	1	2	2	-2	0.1
1966	Cle-A	1	0	1.000	8	2	1	0	0	16	17	5	1	1	3	8	11.8	2.81	122	.279	.323	1	.250	0	1	1	-0	0.1
	Bos-A	7	9	.438	28	19	8	2	0	153^1	140	65	17	1	43	77	10.8	3.35	114	.246	.300	3	.063	-3	2	7	-1	0.2
	Yr	8	9	.471	36	21	9	2	0	169^1	157	70	18	2	46	85	10.9	3.30	114	.249	.302	4	.077	-3	3	8	-2	0.3
1967	*Bos-A	8	10	.444	35	24	6	2	1	181^2	171	64	14	2	32	101	10.2	2.77	126	.246	.282	3	.061	-3	9	13	-3	0.8
1968	Bos-A	5	5	.500	50	2	1	0	12	103	89	54	10	1	25	53	10.0	3.93	80	.237	.286	2	.133	0	-11	-8	-1	-1.2
1969	Bos-A	6	9	.400	41	15	2	0	3	137	137	70	14	6	56	59	13.1	3.68	104	.256	.333	3	.086	-2	-1	2	-2	-0.1
1970	Bos-A	2	2	.500	20	0	0	0	2	27^1	34	24	5	2	12	14	15.8	5.60	71	.301	.378	0	.000	-0	-6	-5	0	-0.7
	Chi-A	1	0	1.000	16	0	0	0	0	22^1	28	13	5	0	5	14	13.3	5.24	74	.295	.330	0	.000	-0	-4	-3	-0	-0.2
	Yr	3	2	.600	36	0	0	0	2	49^2	62	37	10	2	17	28	14.7	5.44	72	.298	.357	0	.000	-0	-9	-8	-0	-0.9
Total	10	62	61	.504	359	125	32	8	21	1216	1172	553	142	16	344	718	11.3	3.56	102	.252	.306	24	.079	-11	-8	11	-9	-1.5
● DON STANHOUSE	Stanhouse, Donald Joseph b: 2/12/51, DuQuoin, Ill. BR/TR, 6'2", 195 lbs. Deb: 4/19/72																											
1972	Tex-A	2	9	.182	24	16	1	0	0	104^2	83	48	8	1	73	78	13.5	3.78	80	.223	.351	4	.129	-0	-8	-9	2	-0.8
1973	Tex-A	1	7	.125	21	5	1	0	1	70	70	41	5	2	44	42	14.9	4.76	78	.262	.371	0	—	0	-7	-8	2	-0.6
1974	Tex-A	1	1	.500	18	0	0	0	0	31^1	38	20	4	2	17	26	16.4	4.88	73	.302	.393	0	—	0	-4	-5	1	-0.2
1975	Mon-N	0	0	—	4	3	0	0	0	13	19	12	1	0	11	5	20.8	8.31	46	.345	.455	1	.333	0	-7	-6	-0	-0.3
1976	Mon-N	9	12	.429	34	26	8	1	1	184	182	84	7	4	92	79	13.6	3.77	99	.263	.352	11	.212	2	-5	-1	3	0.4
1977	Mon-N	10	10	.500	47	16	1	1	10	158^1	147	72	12	4	84	89	13.4	3.41	112	.251	.349	9	.191	1	9	7	-1	1.0
1978	Bal-A	6	9	.400	56	0	0	0	24	74^2	60	28	0	0	52	42	13.5	2.89	121	.230	.358	0	—	0	7	6	0	1.2
1979	*Bal-A☆	7	3	.700	52	0	0	0	21	72^2	49	24	4	1	51	34	12.5	2.85	141	.202	.342	0	—	0	11	10	1	2.0
1980	LA-N	2	2	.500	21	0	0	0	7	25	30	14	4	0	16	5	16.6	5.04	70	.306	.404	0	.000	0	-4	-4	1	-0.8
1982	Bal-A	0	1	.000	17	0	0	0	0	26^2	29	16	3	2	15	8	15.5	5.40	75	.276	.377	0	—	0	-4	-4	0	-0.2
Total	10	38	54	.413	294	66	11	2	64	760^1	707	359	48	16	455	408	13.9	3.84	95	.252	.359	25	.185	4	-12	-15	8	1.7
● ROB STANIFER	Stanifer, Robert Wayne b: 3/10/72, Easley, S.C. BR/TR, 6'3", 205 lbs. Deb: 5/3/97																											
1997	Fla-N	1	2	.333	36	0	0	0	1	45	43	23	9	3	16	28	12.4	4.60	88	.261	.337	2	.667	2	-2	-3	-0	-0.1
1998	Fla-N	2	4	.333	38	0	0	0	1	48	54	33	5	0	22	30	14.3	5.63	72	.277	.350	0	.000	-1	-7	-9	-1	-1.1
2000	Bos-A	0	0	—	8	0	0	0	0	13	22	19	3	0	4	3	18.0	7.62	67	.355	.394	0	—	0	-4	-4	-0	-0.2
Total	3	3	6	.333	82	0	0	0	2	106	119	75	17	3	42	61	13.9	5.43	77	.282	.351	2	.250	1	-13	-15	-1	-1.4
● JOE STANKA	Stanka, Joe Donald b: 7/23/31, Hammon, Okla. BR/TR, 6'5", 201 lbs. Deb: 9/2/59																											
1959	Chi-A	1	0	1.000	2	0	0	0	0	5^1	2	2	1	0	4	3	10.1	3.38	111	.111	.273	1	.333	0	0	0	-0	0.0
● BUCK STANLEY	Stanley, John Leonard b: 11/13/1889, Washington, D.C. d: 8/13/40, Norfolk, Va. BL/TL, 5'10", 160 lbs. Deb: 9/12/11 F																											
1911	Phi-N	0	0	—	4	0	0	0	0	11^1	14	11	0	0	9	5	18.3	6.35	54	.326	.442	0	.000	-1	-4	-4	-1	-0.3
● JOE STANLEY	Stanley, Joseph Bernard b: 4/2/1881, Washington, D.C. d: 9/13/67, Detroit, Mich. BB/TR, 5'9.5", 150 lbs. Deb: 9/11/1897 F♦																											
1897	Was-N	0	0	—	1	0	0	0	0	0^2	0	0	0	0	0	0	0.0	0.00	—	.000	.000	0	.000	-0	0	0	-0	0.0
1903	Bos-N	0	0	—	1	0	0	0	0	4	4	4	0	1	4	4	20.3	9.00	36	.286	.474	77	.250	0	-3	-3	-0	-0.1
1906	Was-A	0	0	—	1	0	0	0	0	3	3	5	1	1	1	0	15.0	12.00	22	.273	.385	36	.163	-0	-3	-3	-0	-0.2
Total	3	0	0	—	3	0	0	0	0	7^2	7	9	1	2	5	4	16.4	9.39	33	.259	.412	148	.213	0	-5	-5	-1	-0.3
● BOB STANLEY	Stanley, Robert William b: 11/10/54, Portland, Maine BR/TR, 6'4", 215 lbs. Deb: 4/16/77																											
1977	Bos-A	8	7	.533	41	13	3	1	3	151	176	74	10	3	43	44	13.2	3.99	113	.294	.344	0	—	0	1	8	4	1.1
1978	Bos-A	15	2	.882	52	3	0	0	10	141^2	142	50	5	1	34	38	11.2	2.60	158	.266	.312	0	—	0	18	22	2	3.1
1979	Bos-A★	16	12	.571	40	30	9	4	1	216^2	250	110	14	4	44	56	12.4	3.99	111	.294	.332	0	—	0	6	10	2	1.4
1980	Bos-A	10	8	.556	52	17	5	1	14	175	186	75	11	7	52	71	12.6	3.39	125	.278	.337	0	—	0	13	15	3	2.1
1981	Bos-A	10	8	.556	35	1	0	0	0	98^2	110	46	3	6	38	28	14.0	3.83	101	.294	.368	0	—	0	-2	0	3	0.4
1982	Bos-A	12	7	.632	48	0	0	0	14	168^1	161	60	11	4	50	83	11.5	3.10	**139**	.255	.313	0	—	0	18	21	4	3.1
1983	Bos-A★	8	10	.444	64	0	0	0	33	145^1	145	56	7	3	38	65	11.5	2.85	153	.266	.317	0	—	0	20	23	-1	3.7
1984	Bos-A	9	10	.474	57	0	0	0	22	106^2	113	57	9	2	23	52	11.6	3.54	118	.267	.308	0	—	0	5	7	3	1.7
1985	Bos-A	6	6	.500	48	0	0	0	10	87^2	76	30	7	2	30	46	11.1	2.87	149	.237	.306	0	—	0	12	13	0	2.0
1986	*Bos-A	6	6	.500	66	1	0	0	16	82^1	109	48	9	0	22	54	14.3	4.37	95	.322	.364	0	—	0	-2	-2	1	-0.3
1987	Bos-A	4	15	.211	34	20	4	1	0	152^2	198	96	17	1	42	67	14.2	5.01	91	.321	.366	0	—	0	-9	-8	1	-0.8
1988	*Bos-A	6	4	.600	57	0	0	0	5	101^2	90	41	6	7	29	57	11.2	3.19	129	.242	.309	0	—	0	9	10	-0	1.0
1989	Bos-A	5	2	.714	43	0	0	0	4	79^1	102	54	4	1	26	32	14.6	4.88	84	.321	.374	0	—	0	-9	-6	1	-0.5
Total	13	115	97	.542	637	85	21	7	132	1707	1858	797	113	41	471	693	12.5	3.64	118	.282	.334	0	—	0	82	117	22	18.0
● MIKE STANTON	Stanton, Michael Thomas b: 9/25/52, Phenix City, Ala. BB/TR, 6'2", 205 lbs. Deb: 7/9/75																											
1975	Hou-N	0	2	.000	7	2	0	0	1	17^1	20	14	1	0	20	16	20.8	7.27	46	.290	.449	1	.250	0	-7	-8	0	-0.9
1980	Cle-A	1	3	.250	51	0	0	0	5	85^2	98	58	5	3	44	74	15.2	5.46	75	.297	.385	0	—	0	-14	-13	0	-0.6
1981	Cle-A	3	3	.500	24	0	0	0	2	43^1	43	21	4	0	18	34	12.7	4.36	83	.262	.335	0	—	0	-3	-4	-1	-0.6

YEAR	TM/L	W	L	PCT	G	GS	CG	SH	SV	IP	H	R	HR	HB	BB	SO	RAT	ERA	ERA+	OAV	OOB	BH	AVG	PB	PR	PR+	PD	TPI
1982	Sea-A	2	4	.333	56	1	0	0	7	71^1	70	37	5	0	21	49	11.5	4.16	102	.260	.314	0	—	0	-1	1	1	0.2
1983	Sea-A	2	3	.400	50	0	0	0	7	65	65	26	3	1	28	47	13.0	3.32	129	.273	.352	0	—	0	5	7	-0	0.6
1984	Sea-A	4	4	.500	54	0	0	0	8	61	55	28	3	2	22	55	11.7	3.54	113	.241	.313	0	—	0	3	3	-1	0.4
1985	Sea-A	1	2	.333	24	0	0	0	1	29	32	20	4	3	21	17	17.4	5.28	80	.278	.403	0	—	0	-4	-3	1	-0.3
	Chi-A	0	1	.000	11	0	0	0	0	11^2	15	14	2	0	8	12	17.7	9.26	47	.294	.390	0	—	0	-7	-6	-0	-0.5
	Yr	1	3	.250	35	0	0	0	1	40^2	47	34	6	3	29	29	17.5	6.42	66	.283	.399	0	—	0	-10	-10	1	-0.8
Total	7	13	22	.371	277	3	0	0	31	384^1	398	218	27	9	182	304	13.8	4.61	88	.272	.356	1	.250	0	-26	-23	1	-1.7
● **MIKE STANTON**	Stanton, William Michael b: 6/2/67, Houston, Tex. BL/TL, 6'1", 190 lbs. Deb: 8/24/89																											
1989	Atl-N	0	1	.000	20	0	0	0	7	24	17	4	0	0	8	27	9.4	1.50	244	.207	.278	0	—	0	5	6	-0	0.5
1990	Atl-N	0	3	.000	7	0	0	0	2	7	16	16	1	1	4	7	27.0	18.00	22	.444	.512	0	—	0	-11	-10	0	-1.8
1991	*Atl-N	5	5	.500	74	0	0	0	7	78	62	27	6	1	21	54	9.7	2.88	135	.217	.273	3	.500	2	7	8	1	1.4
1992	*Atl-N	5	4	.556	65	0	0	0	8	63^2	59	32	6	2	20	44	11.5	4.10	89	.247	.310	1	.500	0	-4	-3	0	-0.4
1993	*Atl-N	4	6	.400	63	0	0	0	27	52	51	35	4	0	29	43	13.8	4.67	86	.255	.349	0	—	0	-4	-4	0	-0.7
1994	Atl-N	3	1	.750	49	0	0	0	3	45^2	41	18	2	3	26	35	13.8	3.55	120	.248	.361	2	.667	1	3	4	1	0.5
1995	Atl-N	1	1	.500	26	0	0	0	1	19^1	31	14	3	1	6	13	17.7	5.59	76	.369	.418	0	—	0	-3	-3	-0	-0.2
	*Bos-A	1	0	1.000	22	0	0	0	0	21	17	9	3	0	8	10	10.7	3.00	162	.224	.298	0	—	0	4	4	-0	0.2
1996	Bos-A	4	3	.571	59	0	0	0	1	56^1	58	24	9	0	23	46	12.9	3.83	132	.275	.346	0	—	0	7	8	-0	0.8
	*Tex-A	0	1	.000	22	0	0	0	0	22^1	20	8	2	0	4	14	9.7	3.22	163	.241	.276	0	—	0	4	5	-1	0.2
	Yr	4	4	.500	81	0	0	0	1	78^2	78	32	11	0	27	60	12.0	3.66	140	.265	.327	0	—	0	12	12	-1	1.0
1997	*NY-A	6	1	.857	64	0	0	0	3	66^2	50	19	3	3	34	70	11.7	2.57	174	.205	.310	0	—	0	15	14	-0	1.4
1998	*NY-A	4	1	.800	67	0	0	0	6	79	71	51	13	4	26	69	11.5	5.47	80	.239	.309	0	.000	-0	-7	-10	-1	-0.7
1999	*NY-A	2	2	.500	73	1	0	0	0	62^1	71	30	5	1	18	59	13.0	4.33	109	.289	.340	0	.000	-0	4	3	-0	0.1
2000	*NY-A	2	3	.400	69	0	0	0	0	68	68	32	5	2	24	75	12.4	4.10	117	.263	.330	1	1.000	0	6	5	1	0.4
Total	12	37	32	.536	680	1	0	0	65	665^1	632	319	62	18	251	566	12.2	4.00	110	.252	.324	7	.500	3	27	28	1	1.7
● **DAVE STAPLETON**	Stapleton, David Earl b: 10/16/61, Miami, Ariz. BL/TL, 6'1", 185 lbs. Deb: 9/14/87																											
1987	Mil-A	2	0	1.000	4	0	0	0	0	14^2	13	3	0	0	3	14	9.8	1.84	249	.241	.281	0	—	0	4	4	-0	0.5
1988	Mil-A	0	0	—	6	0	0	0	0	13^2	20	9	1	1	9	6	19.8	5.93	67	.339	.435	0	—	0	-3	-3	-0	-0.2
Total	2	2	0	1.000	10	0	0	0	0	28^1	33	12	1	1	12	20	14.6	3.81	113	.292	.365	0	—	0	1	2	-0	0.3
● **DENNIS STARK**	Stark, Dennis James b: 10/27/74, Hicksville, Ohio BR/TR, 6'2", 210 lbs. Deb: 9/15/99																											
1999	Sea-A	0	0	—	5	0	0	0	0	6^1	10	8	0	0	4	4	19.9	9.95	48	.370	.452	0	—	0	-4	-4	-0	-0.2
● **CON STARKEL**	Starkel, Conrad b: 11/16/1880, Germany d: 1/19/33, Tacoma, Wash. BR/TR, 6', 200 lbs. Deb: 4/19/06																											
1906	Was-A	0	0	—	1	0	0	0	0	3	7	6	1	0	2	1	27.0	18.00	15	.467	.529	0	—	0	-5	-5	0	-0.2
● **RAY STARR**	Starr, Raymond Francis "Iron Man" b: 4/23/06, Nowata, Okla. d: 2/9/63, Baylis, Ill. BR/TR, 6'1", 178 lbs. Deb: 9/11/32																											
1932	StL-N	1	1	.500	3	2	1	1	0	20	19	7	2	1	10	6	13.5	2.70	146	.284	.385	1	.250	0	3	3	1	0.3
1933	NY-N	0	1	.000	6	2	0	0	0	13^1	19	11	0	1	10	2	20.3	5.40	59	.339	.448	0	.000	-0	-3	-3	-0	-0.3
	Bos-N	0	1	.000	9	1	0	0	0	28	32	15	4	1	9	15	13.5	3.86	79	.296	.356	1	.143	0	-2	-3	0	-0.1
	Yr	0	2	.000	15	3	0	0	0	41^1	51	26	4	2	19	17	15.7	4.35	71	.311	.389	1	.100	-0	-5	-6	0	-0.4
1941	Cin-N	3	2	.600	7	4	3	2	0	34	28	10	1	1	6	11	9.3	2.65	136	.219	.259	2	.182	-0	4	4	0	0.5
1942	Cin-N☆	15	13	.536	37	33	17	4	0	276^2	228	88	10	3	106	83	11.0	2.67	123	.226	.301	8	.091	-5	20	19	-2	1.2
1943	Cin-N	11	10	.524	36	33	9	2	1	217^1	201	93	9	5	91	42	12.3	3.64	91	.248	.328	9	.122	-4	-6	-8	-0	-1.2
1944	Pit-N	6	5	.545	27	12	5	0	3	89^2	116	60	6	1	36	25	15.4	5.02	74	.314	.377	3	.136	1	-14	-13	-1	-1.5
1945	Pit-N	0	2	.000	4	0	0	0	0	6^2	10	7	0	0	4	0	18.9	9.45	42	.370	.452	1	1.000	1	-4	-4	0	-0.6
	Chi-N	1	0	1.000	9	1	0	0	0	13^1	17	11	1	0	7	5	16.2	7.43	49	.298	.375	1	.500	0	-5	-6	0	-0.3
	Yr	1	2	.333	13	1	0	0	0	20	27	18	1	0	11	5	17.1	8.10	46	.321	.400	2	.667	1	-10	-10	0	-0.9
Total	7	37	35	.514	138	88	35	9	4	699	670	302	33	13	279	189	12.4	3.53	96	.255	.329	26	.123	-7	-8	-11	-1	-2.0
● **DICK STARR**	Starr, Richard Eugene b: 3/2/21, Kittanning, Pa. BR/TR, 6'3", 190 lbs. Deb: 9/5/47																											
1947	NY-A	1	0	1.000	4	1	1	0	0	12^1	12	4	1	0	8	1	14.6	1.46	242	.250	.357	1	.333	1	3	3	0	0.3
1948	NY-A	0	0	—	1	0	0	0	0	2	0	1	0	0	2	2	9.0	4.50	91	.000	.250	0	—	0	-0	-0	-0	0.0
1949	StL-A	1	7	.125	30	8	1	1	0	83^1	96	46	6	1	48	44	15.7	4.32	105	.292	.384	2	.087	-1	-1	2	-1	-0.1
1950	StL-A	7	5	.583	32	16	4	1	2	123^2	140	83	11	7	74	30	16.1	5.02	99	.287	.389	5	.139	-3	-6	-1	-1	-0.4
1951	StL-A	2	5	.286	15	9	0	0	0	62^2	66	55	10	2	42	26	16.0	7.40	59	.273	.385	4	.222	0	-23	-19	-1	-1.8
	Was-A	1	7	.125	11	11	1	0	0	61^1	76	41	12	0	24	17	14.7	5.58	73	.304	.365	3	.176	1	-10	-10	-2	-1.2
	Yr	3	12	.200	26	20	1	0	0	123^1	142	96	22	2	66	43	15.3	6.49	65	.289	.375	7	.200	1	-33	-30	-2	-3.0
Total	5	12	24	.333	93	45	7	2	2	344^2	390	230	40	10	198	120	15.6	5.25	86	.286	.381	15	.155	-2	-37	-26	-4	-3.2
● **HERMAN STARRETTE**	Starrette, Herman Paul b: 11/20/38, Statesville, N.C. BR/TR, 6', 175 lbs. Deb: 7/1/63 C																											
1963	Bal-A	0	1	.000	18	0	0	0	0	26	26	10	1	2	7	13	12.1	3.46	100	.271	.333	0	.000	0	0	0	1	0.1
1964	Bal-A	1	0	1.000	5	0	0	0	0	11	9	3	0	0	6	5	12.3	1.64	218	.250	.357	0	.000	-0	2	2	-0	0.1
1965	Bal-A	0	0	—	4	0	0	0	0	9	8	3	0	0	3	3	11.0	1.00	347	.258	.324	0	.000	-0	2	2	0	0.2
Total	3	1	1	.500	27	0	0	0	0	46	43	16	1	2	16	21	11.9	2.54	137	.264	.337	0	.000	-0	5	5	1	0.4
● **ED STAUFFER**	Stauffer, Charles Edward b: 1/10/1898, Emsworth, Pa. d: 7/2/79, St.Petersburg, Fla BR/TR, 5'11", 185 lbs. Deb: 4/26/23																											
1923	Chi-N	0	0	—	1	0	0	0	0	2	5	3	0	0	1	0	27.0	13.50	30	.556	.600	0	—	0	-2	-2	0	-0.1
1925	StL-A	0	1	.000	20	1	0	0	0	30^1	34	21	1	0	21	13	16.3	5.34	87	.283	.390	1	.250	-0	-3	-2	-1	-0.2
Total	2	0	1	.000	21	1	0	0	0	32^1	39	24	1	0	22	13	17.0	5.85	79	.302	.404	1	.250	-0	-5	-4	-1	-0.3
● **BILL STEARNS**	Stearns, William E. b: 3/20/1853, Washington, D.C. d: 12/30/1898, Washington, D.C. TR, Deb: 6/26/1871																											
1871	Oly-n	2	0	1.000	2	2	2	0	0	18	10	11	0		8	0	9.0	2.50	167	.149	.240	0	.000	-1	3	3		0.1
1872	Nat-n	0	11	.000	11	11	11	0	0	99	193	190	2		3	2	17.8	6.18	75	.339	.343	12	.267	-3	-28	-14		-1.0
1873	Was-n	7	25	.219	32	32	32	0	0	283	481	395	7		15	4	15.8	4.55	74	.330	.337	24	.180	-6	-41	-37		-3.1
1874	Har-n	3	14	.176	22	18	14	0	0	158^2	237	194	0		15	14	14.3	2.95	78	.297	.310	21	.159	-5	-13	-11		-1.3
1875	Was-n	1	14	.067	17	16	14	0	0	141	246	211	3		4	3	16.0	4.02	59	.332	.336	20	.256	-0	-28	-24		-2.1
Total	5 n	13	64	.169	84	79	73	0	0	699^2	1167	1001	12		45	23	15.6	4.26	56	.321	.330	77	.194	-16	-158	-138		-7.4
● **WILLIAM STECHER**	Stecher, William Theodore b: 10/20/1869, Riverside, N.J. d: 12/26/26, Riverside, N.J. Deb: 9/6/1890																											
1890	Phi-a	0	10	.000	10	10	9	0	0	68	111	110	1	14	60	18	24.5	10.32	38	.356	.479	7	.241	1	-49	-49	2	-4.4
● **GENE STECHSCHULTE**	Stechschulte, Gene Urban b: 8/12/73, Lima, Ohio BR/TR, 6'5", 210 lbs. Deb: 4/20/2000																											
2000	StL-N	1	0	1.000	20	0	0	0	0	25^2	24	22	6	0	17	12	14.4	6.31	73	.247	.360	0	—	0	-5	-5	-0	-0.2
● **ELMER STEELE**	Steele, Elmer Rae b: 5/17/1886, Poughkeepsie, N.Y. d: 3/9/66, Rhinebeck, N.Y. BB/TR, 5'11", 200 lbs. Deb: 9/12/07																											
1907	Bos-A	0	1	.000	4	1	0	0	0	11^1	11	7	0	0	1	10	9.5	1.59	162	.256	.273	0	.000	-1	1	1	0	0.1
1908	Bos-A	5	7	.417	16	13	9	1	0	118	85	34	1	3	13	37	7.7	1.83	134	.209	.239	2	.051	-4	7	8	-1	0.3
1909	Bos-A	4	4	.500	16	8	2	0	1	75^2	75	37	1	1	15	32	10.8	2.85	88	.255	.294	5	.227	1	-3	-3	1	-0.1
1910	Pit-N	0	3	.000	3	3	2	0	0	24	19	9	0	0	3	7	8.3	2.25	138	.221	.247	0	.000	-1	2	2	1	0.3
1911	Pit-N	9	9	.500	31	16	7	2	2	166	153	65	5	4	31	52	10.2	2.60	132	.256	.297	11	.180	-0	15	15	2	1.7
	Bro-N	0	0	—	5	2	0	0	0	23	24	10	0	1	5	9	11.3	3.13	107	.258	.296	0	.000	-1	0	1	0	0.0
	Yr	9	9	.500	36	18	7	2	2	189	177	75	5	2	36	61	10.3	2.67	128	.257	.297	11	.157	-1	15	16	2	1.7
Total	5	18	24	.429	75	43	20	3	3	418	367	162	7	8	68	147	9.5	2.41	122	.241	.278	18	.127	-6	23	25	3	2.3
● **BOB STEELE**	Steele, Robert Wesley b: 1/5/1894, Cassburn, Ont., Can. d: 1/27/62, Ocala, Fla. BB/TL, 5'10.5", 175 lbs. Deb: 4/17/16																											
1916	StL-N	5	15	.250	29	21	7	1	0	148	156	74	6	3	42	67	12.2	3.41	78	.285	.340	10	.196	-1	-13	-12	-3	-2.0
1917	StL-N	1	3	.250	12	6	1	0	0	42	33	17	1	0	19	23	11.1	3.21	84	.223	.311	5	.385	2	-2	-2	-1	-0.1
	Pit-N	5	11	.313	27	19	13	1	1	179^2	158	71	0	5	53	82	10.8	2.76	103	.237	.298	17	.224	1	-1	2	-2	0.0
	Yr	6	14	.300	39	25	14	1	1	221^2	191	88	1	5	72	105	10.9	2.84	99	.235	.301	22	.247	2	-3	-1	-2	-0.1
1918	Pit-N	2	3	.400	10	4	2	1	1	49	44	25	2	2	17	21	11.6	3.31	87	.240	.312	2	.125	-0	-3	-2	-0	-0.3

YEAR	TM/L	W	L	PCT	G	GS	CG	SH	SV	IP	H	R	HR	HB	BB	SO	RAT	ERA	ERA+	OAV	OOB	BH	AVG	PB	PR	PR+	PD	TPI
	NY-N	3	5	.375	12	7	5	1	1	66	56	29	1	3	11	24	9.5	2.59	101	.226	.267	6	.286	2	1	0	-2	0.0
	Yr	5	8	.385	22	11	7	2	2	115	100	54	3	5	28	45	10.4	2.90	94	.232	.287	8	.216	2	-2	-2	-3	-0.3
1919	NY-N	0	1	.000	1	0	0	0	0	3	3	3	0	0	2	0	15.0	6.00	47	.250	.357	0	.000	-0	-1	-1	-0	-0.2
Total	4	16	38	.296	91	57	28	4	3	487^{2}	450	219	10	13	144	217	11.2	3.05	90	.249	.310	40	.225	3	-19	-16	-8	-2.6
● BILL STEELE	Steele, William Mitchell "Big Bill" b: 10/5/1885, Milford, Pa. d: 10/19/49, Overland, Mo. BR/TR, 5'11", 200 lbs. Deb: 9/10/10																											
1910	StL-N	4	4	.500	9	8	8	0	1	71^{2}	71	35	1	6	24	25	12.7	3.27	91	.264	.338	8	.258	1	-2	-2	1	0.0
1911	StL-N	18	19	.486	43	34	23	1	3	287^{1}	287	153	8	10	113	115	12.8	3.73	91	.269	.345	21	.208	4	-10	-11	3	-0.6
1912	StL-N	9	13	.409	40	25	7	0	2	194	245	143	5	7	66	67	14.8	4.69	73	.322	.381	11	.180	1	-27	-27	4	-2.2
1913	StL-N	4	4	.500	12	9	2	0	0	54	58	31	3	3	18	10	13.2	5.00	65	.286	.353	1	.056	-1	-11	-11	-1	-1.5
1914	StL-N	1	2	.333	17	2	0	0	0	53^{1}	55	30	3	3	7	16	11.0	2.70	104	.274	.308	5	.294	2	1	1	1	0.3
	Bro-N	1	1	.500	8	1	0	0	1	16^{1}	17	16	1	0	7	3	13.2	5.51	52	.258	.329	1	.333	1	-5	-5	-0	-0.5
	Yr	2	3	.400	25	3	0	0	1	69^{2}	72	46	4	3	14	19	11.5	3.36	84	.270	.313	6	.300	2	-4	-4	1	-0.2
Total	5	37	43	.463	129	79	40	1	7	676^{2}	733	408	21	29	235	236	13.3	4.02	82	.286	.352	47	.203	8	-55	-55	8	-4.5
● BILL STEEN	Steen, William John b: 11/11/1887, Pittsburgh, Pa. d: 3/13/79, Signal Hill, Cal. BR/TR, 6'0.5", 180 lbs. Deb: 4/15/12																											
1912	Cle-A	9	8	.529	26	16	6	1	0	143^{1}	163	75	3	1	45	61	13.1	3.77	90	.298	.352	13	.271	2	-7	-6	-1	-0.5
1913	Cle-A	4	5	.444	22	13	7	2	2	128^{1}	113	52	3	4	49	57	11.6	2.45	124	.237	.313	7	.171	-0	7	8	-0	0.5
1914	Cle-A	9	14	.391	30	22	13	1	0	200^{2}	201	74	0	4	68	97	12.2	2.60	111	.272	.337	14	.200	1	3	6	0	0.8
1915	Cle-A	1	4	.200	10	7	2	0	0	45^{1}	51	30	1	2	15	22	13.5	4.96	61	.290	.352	3	.188	-0	-10	-9	2	-0.8
	Det-A	5	1	.833	20	7	3	0	4	79^{1}	83	35	0	1	22	28	12.0	2.72	111	.269	.319	5	.179	-1	2	3	2	0.3
	Yr	6	5	.545	30	14	5	0	4	124^{2}	134	65	1	3	37	50	12.6	3.54	86	.276	.331	8	.182	-1	-8	-7	4	-0.5
Total	4	28	32	.467	108	65	31	4	6	597	611	266	7	12	199	265	12.4	3.05	101	.272	.334	42	.207	1	-6	2	2	0.3
● MILT STEENGRAFE	Steengrafe, Milton Henry b: 5/26/1900, San Francisco, Cal d: 6/2/77, Oklahoma City, Okla. BR/TR, 6', 170 lbs. Deb: 5/5/24																											
1924	Chi-A	0	0	—	3	0	0	0	0	5^{2}	15	8	0	0	4	3	30.2	12.71	32	.484	.543	0	.000	-0	-5	-6	0	-0.3
1926	Chi-A	1	1	.500	13	1	0	0	0	38^{1}	43	22	1	2	19	10	15.0	3.99	97	.295	.383	0	.000	-2	0	-1	-1	-0.3
Total	2	1	1	.500	16	1	0	0	0	44	58	30	1	2	23	13	17.0	5.11	76	.328	.411	0	.000	-2	-5	-6	-1	-0.6
● KENNIE STEENSTRA	Steenstra, Kenneth Gregory b: 10/13/70, Springfield, Mo. BR/TR, 6'5", 220 lbs. Deb: 5/21/98																											
1998	Chi-N	0	0	—	4	0	0	0	0	3^{1}	7	4	2	0	1	4	21.6	10.80	41	.412	.444	0	—	0	-2	-2	-0	-0.1
● MORRIE STEEVENS	Steevens, Morris Dale b: 10/7/40, Salem, Ill. BL/TL, 6'2", 175 lbs. Deb: 4/13/62																											
1962	Chi-N	0	1	.000	12	1	0	0	0	15	10	4	0	1	11	5	13.2	2.40	173	.196	.349	0	.000	-0	3	3	0	0.2
1964	Phi-N	0	0	—	4	0	0	0	0	2^{2}	5	3	0	0	1	3	20.3	3.38	103	.385	.429	0	—	0	0	0	0	0.0
1965	Phi-N	0	1	.000	6	0	0	0	0	2^{2}	5	5	1	0	4	3	30.4	16.88	20	.417	.563	0	—	0	-4	-4	-0	-0.8
Total	3	0	2	.000	22	1	0	0	0	20^{1}	20	12	1	1	16	11	16.4	4.43	90	.263	.398	0	.000	-0	-1	-1	-0	-0.6
● ED STEIN	Stein, Edward F. b: 9/5/1869, Detroit, Mich. d: 5/10/28, Detroit, Mich. BR/TR, 5'11", 170 lbs. Deb: 7/24/1890																											
1890	Chi-N	12	6	.667	20	18	14	1	0	160^{2}	147	100	9	11	83	65	13.5	3.81	96	.236	.336	9	.153	-2	-4	-3	-1	-0.5
1891	Chi-N	7	6	.538	14	10	9	1	0	101	99	68	7	2	57	38	14.1	3.74	89	.247	.343	7	.163	-1	-4	-5	2	-0.4
1892	Bro-N	27	16	.628	48	42	38	6	1	377^{1}	310	166	6	15	150	190	11.3	2.84	111	.215	.296	31	.215	4	19	14	2	1.9
1893	Bro-N	19	15	.559	37	34	28	1	0	298^{1}	294	190	4	8	119	81	12.7	3.77	117	.250	.323	25	.212	-3	30	23	2	1.8
1894	Bro-N	26	14	.650	44	40	37	2	1	350	388	261	10	14	170	84	14.7	4.63	107	.278	.362	38	.259	5	27	13	-0	1.4
1895	Bro-N	15	13	.536	32	27	24	1	1	255^{1}	282	163	9	6	93	55	13.4	4.72	93	.276	.340	26	.250	2	2	-10	1	-0.6
1896	Bro-N	3	6	.333	17	10	6	0	0	90^{1}	130	79	6	2	51	16	18.2	4.88	84	.334	.414	10	.256	0	-5	-8	0	-0.6
1898	Bro-N	0	2	.000	3	2	2	0	0	23	39	21	0	0	9	6	18.8	5.48	65	.371	.421	4	.400	1	-5	-5	-0	-0.3
Total	8	109	78	.583	215	183	158	12	3	1656	1689	1048	51	58	732	535	13.5	3.97	103	.258	.338	150	.226	5	59	23	5	2.7
● IRV STEIN	Stein, Irvin Michael b: 5/21/11, Madisonville, La. d: 1/7/81, Covington, La. BR/TR, 6'2", 170 lbs. Deb: 7/7/32																											
1932	Phi-A	0	0	—	1	0	0	0	0	3	7	4	2	0	1	0	24.0	12.00	38	.500	.533	0	.000	-0	-3	-2	0	-0.1
● BLAKE STEIN	Stein, William Blake b: 8/3/73, McComb, Miss. BR/TR, 6'7", 210 lbs. Deb: 5/10/98																											
1998	Oak-A	5	9	.357	24	20	1	1	0	117^{1}	117	92	22	5	71	89	14.8	6.37	72	.255	.361	0	.000	-0	-22	-24	-1	-2.4
1999	Oak-A	0	0	—	1	1	0	0	0	2^{2}	6	5	1	0	6	4	40.5	16.88	28	.462	.632	0	—	0	-4	-4	-0	-0.2
	KC-A	1	2	.333	12	11	0	0	0	70^{1}	59	33	10	7	41	43	13.7	4.09	123	.230	.351	0	—	0	6	7	-1	0.2
	Yr	1	2	.333	13	12	0	0	0	73	65	38	11	7	47	47	14.7	4.56	110	.241	.367	0	—	0	3	3	-1	0.0
2000	KC-A	8	5	.615	17	17	1	0	0	107^{2}	98	57	19	3	57	78	13.2	4.68	107	.247	.346	0	.000	-0	3	4	-1	0.3
Total	3	14	16	.467	54	49	2	1	0	298	280	187	52	15	175	214	14.2	5.32	91	.249	.357	0	.000	-1	-17	-16	-3	-2.1
● RANDY STEIN	Stein, William Randolph b: 3/7/53, Pomona, Cal. BR/TR, 6'4", 210 lbs. Deb: 4/17/78																											
1978	Mil-A	3	2	.600	31	1	0	0	1	72^{2}	78	51	5	4	39	42	15.0	5.33	71	.280	.376	0	—	0	-13	-13	0	-0.8
1979	Sea-A	2	3	.400	23	1	0	0	0	41^{1}	48	29	7	1	27	39	16.5	5.88	74	.291	.394	0	—	0	-8	-7	-1	-0.8
1981	Sea-A	0	1	.000	5	0	0	0	0	9^{1}	18	12	1	0	8	6	25.1	10.61	36	.429	.520	0	—	0	-7	-7	-0	-0.6
1982	Chi-N	0	0	—	6	0	0	0	0	10^{1}	7	4	2	0	7	6	12.2	3.48	107	.200	.333	0	—	0	0	0	0	0.0
Total	4	5	6	.455	65	2	0	0	1	133^{2}	151	96	15	5	81	93	16.0	5.72	69	.290	.390	0	—	0	-27	-26	-1	-2.2
● RAY STEINEDER	Steineder, Raymond J. b: 11/13/1895, Salem, N.J. d: 8/25/82, Vineland, N.J. BR/TR, 6'0.5", 160 lbs. Deb: 7/16/23																											
1923	Pit-N	2	0	1.000	15	2	1	0	0	55	58	30	3	2	18	23	12.8	4.75	85	.278	.341	7	.467	3	-5	-4	-1	-0.1
1924	Pit-N	0	1	.000	5	0	0	0	0	2^{2}	6	6	0	0	5	0	37.1	13.50	28	.400	.550	0	—	0	-3	-3	-0	-0.5
	Phi-N	1	1	.500	9	0	0	0	0	28^{2}	31	15	1	0	16	11	14.8	4.40	101	.284	.376	3	.300	0	-2	0	0	0.1
	Yr	1	2	.333	14	0	0	0	0	31^{1}	37	21	1	0	21	11	16.7	5.17	85	.298	.400	3	.300	0	-5	-2	0	-0.4
Total	2	3	2	.600	29	2	1	0	0	86^{1}	95	51	4	2	39	34	14.2	4.90	85	.285	.364	10	.400	3	-9	-7	-1	-0.5
● RICK STEIRER	Steirer, Ricky Francis b: 8/27/56, Baltimore, Md. BR/TR, 6'4", 200 lbs. Deb: 8/5/82																											
1982	Cal-A	1	0	1.000	10	1	0	0	0	26^{1}	25	14	2	1	11	14	12.6	3.76	108	.243	.322	0	—	0	1	1	0	0.1
1983	Cal-A	3	2	.600	19	5	0	0	0	61^{2}	77	40	3	3	18	25	14.3	4.82	84	.302	.355	0	—	0	-5	-5	1	-0.3
1984	Cal-A	0	1	.000	1	1	0	0	0	2^{2}	6	5	0	0	2	2	27.0	16.88	24	.500	.571	0	—	0	-4	-4	0	-0.6
Total	3	4	3	.571	30	7	0	0	0	90^{2}	108	59	5	4	31	41	14.2	4.86	83	.292	.353	0	—	0	-8	-8	1	-0.8
● BILL STELLBERGER	Stellberger, William F. b: 4/22/1865, Detroit, Mich. d: 11/9/36, Detroit, Mich. BL/TL, Deb: 10/1/1885																											
1885	Pro-N	0	1	.000	1	1	1	0	0	8	14	10	0		4	0	20.3	7.88	34	.389	.450	0	.000	-1	-4	-5	0	-0.4
● JEFF STEMBER	Stember, Jeffrey Alan b: 3/2/58, Elizabeth, N.J. BR/TR, 6'5", 220 lbs. Deb: 8/5/80																											
1980	SF-N	0	0	—	1	1	0	0	0	3	2	3	1	0	2	0	12.0	3.00	118	.167	.286	0	.000	-0	0	0	-0	0.0
● BILL STEMMEYER	Stemmeyer, William "Cannon Ball" b: 5/6/1865, Cleveland, Ohio d: 5/3/45, Cleveland, Ohio BR/TR, 6'2", 190 lbs. Deb: 10/3/1885																											
1885	Bos-N	1	1	.500	2	2	2	1	0	11	7	7	0		11	8	14.7	0.00	—	.194	.383	3	.429	1	3	3	0	0.8
1886	Bos-N	22	18	.550	41	41	41	0	0	348^{2}	300	218	11		144	239	11.5	3.02	106	.218	.292	41	.277	9	11	7	-3	1.2
1887	Bos-N	6	8	.429	15	14	14	0	1	119^{1}	179	107	4	2	41	41	13.7	5.20	78	.328	.331	15	.300	2	-15	-15	-2	-1.3
1888	Cle-a	0	2	.000	2	2	2	0	0	16	37	42	0	1	9	7	26.4	9.00	34	.435	.495	4	.400	1	-11	-10	-0	-0.8
Total	4	29	29	.500	60	59	59	1	1	495	523	374	15	3	205	295	12.5	3.67	92	.256	.312	63	.293	14	-11	-16	-4	-0.1
● DAVE STENHOUSE	Stenhouse, David Rotchford b: 9/12/33, Westerly, R.I. BR/TR, 6', 195 lbs. Deb: 4/18/62 F																											
1962	Was-A★	11	12	.478	34	26	9	2	0	197	169	84	24	2	90	123	11.9	3.65	110	.234	.320	3	.052	-5	7	8	2	0.5
1963	Was-A	3	9	.250	16	16	2	1	0	87	90	46	12	1	45	47	14.1	4.55	82	.260	.347	2	.080	-1	-9	-8	0	-1.1
1964	Was-A	2	7	.222	26	14	1	0	1	88	80	54	12	1	39	44	12.3	4.81	77	.239	.320	6	.300	2	-12	-11	-0	-0.9
Total	3	16	28	.364	76	56	12	3	1	372	339	184	48	4	174	214	12.5	4.14	94	.241	.327	11	.107	-4	-14	-10	1	-1.5
● BUZZ STEPHEN	Stephen, Louis Roberts b: 7/13/44, Porterville, Cal. BR/TR, 6'4", 205 lbs. Deb: 9/20/68																											
1968	Min-A	1	1	.500	2	2	0	0	0	11^{1}	11	7	0	1	7	4	15.1	4.76	65	.275	.396	0	.000	-0	-2	-2	0	-0.4

YEAR	TM/L	W	L	PCT	G	GS	CG	SH	SV	IP	H	R	HR	HB	BB	SO	RAT	ERA	ERA+	OAV	OOB	BH	AVG	PB	PR	PR+	PD	TPI
● **BRYAN STEPHENS**	Stephens, Bryan Maris b: 7/14/20, Fayetteville, Ark d: 11/21/91, Santa Ana, Cal. BR/TR, 6'4", 175 lbs. Deb: 5/15/47																											
1947	Cle-A	5	10	.333	31	5	1	0	1	92	79	46	6	2	39	34	11.7	4.01	87	.230	.312	3	.111	-2	-3	-6	-1	-1.2
1948	StL-A	3	6	.333	43	12	2	0	3	122^{2}	141	94	14	4	67	35	15.6	6.02	76	.289	.379	4	.125	-1	-24	-19	-1	-1.4
Total	2	8	16	.333	74	17	3	0	4	214^{2}	220	140	20	6	106	69	13.9	5.16	79	.264	.352	7	.119	-3	-27	-25	-2	-2.6
● **CLARENCE STEPHENS**	Stephens, Clarence Wright b: 8/19/1863, Cincinnati, Ohio d: 2/28/45, Cincinnati, Ohio TR, Deb: 10/8/1886																											
1886	Cin-a	1	0	1.000	1	1	1	0	0	8	9	8	0	1	5	6	16.9	5.63	63	.273	.385	3	.600	1	-2	-2	0	-0.1
1891	Cin-N	0	1	.000	1	1	1	0	0	8	9	9	1	0	3	3	13.5	7.88	43	.273	.333	0	.000	-0	-4	-4	-0	-0.4
1892	Cin-N	0	1	.000	1	1	0	0	0	7	12	3	0	0	4	1	20.6	1.29	254	.364	.432	0	.000	-0	2	2	0	0.2
Total	3	1	2	.333	3	3	2	0	0	23	30	20	1	1	12	10	16.8	5.09	67	.303	.384	3	.300	0	-4	-4	0	-0.3
● **BEN STEPHENS**	Stephens, George Benjamin b: 9/28/1867, Romeo, Mich. d: 8/5/1896, Armada, Mich. 5'10.5", 170 lbs. Deb: 8/5/1892																											
1892	Bal-N	1	1	.500	5	2	2	0	1	29	37	22	2	1	9	7	14.6	2.79	123	.298	.351	0	.000	-2	2	2	-0	0.0
1893	Was-N	0	6	.000	9	6	6	0	0	63^{2}	83	58	1	4	31	14	16.7	5.80	80	.306	.386	3	.103	-4	-8	-8	1	-0.8
1894	Was-N	0	0	—	3	2	1	0	0	11	19	16	1	1	8	1	22.9	4.91	107	.373	.467	1	.250	-0	1	0	0	0.0
Total	3	1	7	.125	17	10	9	0	1	103^{2}	139	96	4	6	48	22	16.8	4.86	90	.312	.386	4	.087	-5	-6	-6	1	-0.8
● **EARL STEPHENSON**	Stephenson, Chester Earl b: 7/31/47, Benson, N.C. BL/TL, 6'3", 175 lbs. Deb: 4/7/71																											
1971	Chi-N	1	0	1.000	16	0	0	0	1	20^{1}	24	10	1	0	11	11	15.5	4.43	89	.316	.402	0	.000	-0	-2	-1	0	0.0
1972	Mil-A	3	5	.375	35	8	1	0	0	80^{1}	79	32	5	3	33	33	12.9	3.25	94	.262	.340	0	.000	-2	-2	-2	0	-0.4
1977	Bal-A	0	0	—	1	0	0	0	0	3	5	3	1	0	0	2	15.0	9.00	42	.357	.357	0	—	0	-2	-2	-0	-0.1
1978	Bal-A	0	0	—	2	0	0	0	0	9^{2}	10	3	0	0	5	4	14.0	2.79	126	.294	.385	0	—	0	1	1	-0	0.0
Total	4	4	5	.444	54	8	1	0	1	113^{1}	118	48	7	3	49	50	13.5	3.57	91	.277	.356	0	.000	-2	-4	-4	-0	-0.5
● **GARRETT STEPHENSON**	Stephenson, Garrett Charles b: 1/2/72, Takoma Park, Md. BR/TR, 6'4", 185 lbs. Deb: 7/25/96																											
1996	Bal-A	0	1	.000	3	0	0	0	0	6^{1}	13	9	1	1	3	3	24.2	12.79	39	.433	.500	0	—	0	-5	-6	0	-0.7
1997	Phi-N	8	6	.571	20	18	2	0	0	117	104	45	11	3	38	81	11.2	3.15	135	.244	.310	3	.094	-1	14	14	0	1.5
1998	Phi-N	0	2	.000	6	6	0	0	0	23	31	24	3	0	19	17	19.6	9.00	48	.316	.427	1	.167	0	-12	-12	-0	-0.8
1999	StL-N	6	3	.667	18	12	0	0	0	85^{1}	90	43	11	5	29	59	13.1	4.22	108	.275	.343	2	.074	-2	3	3	-0	0.1
2000	*StL-N	16	9	.640	32	31	3	2	0	200^{1}	209	105	31	7	63	123	12.5	4.49	103	.270	.330	3	.051	-4	3	3	-0	0.0
Total	5	30	21	.588	79	67	5	2	0	432	447	226	57	16	152	283	12.8	4.44	102	.270	.337	9	.073	-6	3	3	-1	0.1
● **JERRY STEPHENSON**	Stephenson, Jerry Joseph b: 10/6/43, Detroit, Mich. BL/TR, 6'2", 185 lbs. Deb: 4/14/63 F																											
1963	Bos-A	0	0	—	1	1	0	0	0	2^{1}	5	2	0	0	2	3	27.0	7.71	49	.556	.636	0	.000	-0	-1	-1	-0	-0.1
1965	Bos-A	1	5	.167	15	8	0	0	0	52	62	41	7	1	33	49	16.6	6.23	60	.287	.384	3	.231	0	-16	-13	0	-1.3
1966	Bos-A	2	5	.286	15	11	1	0	0	66^{1}	68	51	6	1	44	50	15.3	5.83	65	.264	.373	2	.118	-1	-18	-13	0	-1.4
1967	*Bos-A	3	1	.750	8	6	0	0	1	39^{2}	32	18	4	1	16	24	11.1	3.86	90	.227	.310	4	.250	0	-3	-2	0	-0.1
1968	Bos-A	2	8	.200	23	7	2	0	0	68^{2}	81	51	4	2	42	51	16.4	5.64	56	.295	.392	6	.353	2	-20	-18	1	-2.2
1969	Sea-A	0	0	—	2	0	0	0	0	2^{2}	6	4	0	1	3	1	33.8	10.13	36	.429	.556	0	—	0	-2	-2	0	-0.1
1970	LA-N	0	0	—	3	0	0	0	0	6^{2}	11	7	0	0	5	6	21.6	9.45	41	.379	.471	0	.000	-0	-4	-4	-0	-0.2
Total	7	8	19	.296	67	33	3	0	1	238^{1}	265	174	21	6	145	184	15.7	5.70	62	.281	.381	15	.231	2	-64	-53	1	-5.4
● **JOHN STERLING**	Sterling, John A. b: Philadelphia, Pa. Deb: 10/12/1890																											
1890	Phi-a	0	1	.000	1	1	1	0	0	5	16	12	1	1	4	1	37.8	21.60	18	.516	.583	0	.000	-0	-10	-10	-0	-1.0
● **RANDY STERLING**	Sterling, Randall Wayne b: 4/21/51, Key West, Fla. BB/TR, 6'2", 195 lbs. Deb: 9/16/74																											
1974	NY-N	1	1	.500	3	2	0	0	0	9^{1}	13	8	0	1	3	2	16.4	4.82	74	.351	.415	0	.000	0	-1	-1	0	-0.2
● **DAVE STEVENS**	Stevens, David James b: 3/4/70, Fullerton, Cal. BR/TR, 6'3", 210 lbs. Deb: 5/20/94																											
1994	Min-A	5	2	.714	24	0	0	0	0	45	55	35	6	1	23	24	15.8	6.80	72	.302	.383	0	—	0	-10	-10	-0	-1.2
1995	Min-A	5	4	.556	56	0	0	0	10	65^{2}	74	40	14	1	32	47	14.7	5.07	94	.285	.365	0	—	0	-3	-2	0	-0.3
1996	Min-A	3	3	.500	49	0	0	0	11	58	58	31	12	0	25	29	12.9	4.66	110	.264	.339	0	—	0	2	3	-0	0.3
1997	Min-A	1	3	.250	6	6	0	0	0	23	41	23	8	0	17	16	22.7	9.00	52	.383	.468	0	—	0	-11	-11	-0	-1.5
	Chi-N	0	2	.000	10	0	0	0	0	9^{1}	13	11	0	1	9	13	22.2	9.64	45	.333	.469	0	.000	-0	-6	-5	-0	-1.0
1998	Chi-N	1	2	.333	31	0	0	0	0	38	42	20	6	1	17	31	14.2	4.74	93	.288	.366	1	.250	0	-2	-1	-1	-0.2
1999	Cle-A	0	0	—	5	0	0	0	0	9	10	10	1	0	8	6	18.0	10.00	50	.286	.419	0	—	0	-5	-5	-0	-0.2
2000	Atl-N	0	0	—	2	0	0	0	0	3	5	4	2	0	1	4	18.0	12.00	38	.357	.400	0	.000	-0	-2	-3	0	-0.1
Total	7	15	16	.484	183	6	0	0	21	251	298	174	49	4	132	170	15.6	6.02	80	.297	.381	1	.167	-0	-37	-34	-2	-4.2
● **JIM STEVENS**	Stevens, James Arthur "Steve" b: 8/25/1889, Williamsburg, Md. d: 9/25/66, Baltimore, Md. BR/TR, 5'11", 180 lbs. Deb: 8/24/14																											
1914	Was-A	0	0	—	2	0	0	0	0	3	4	3	0	1	2	0	21.0	9.00	31	.364	.500	0	.000	-0	-2	-2	-0	-0.1
● **DAVE STEWART**	Stewart, David Keith b: 2/19/57, Oakland, Cal. BR/TR, 6'2", 200 lbs. Deb: 9/22/78 C																											
1978	LA-N	0	0	—	1	0	0	0	0	2	1	0	0	0	0	1	4.5	0.00	—	.167	.167	0	—	0	1	1	-0	0.0
1981	*LA-N	4	3	.571	32	0	0	0	6	43^{1}	40	13	3	0	14	29	11.2	2.49	133	.250	.310	2	.400	2	5	4	0	1.0
1982	LA-N	9	8	.529	45	14	0	0	1	146^{1}	137	72	14	2	49	80	11.6	3.81	91	.249	.313	7	.179	1	-3	-6	-1	-0.7
1983	LA-N	5	2	.714	46	1	0	0	8	76	67	28	4	2	33	54	12.1	2.96	122	.237	.321	1	.143	-0	6	5	-1	0.5
	Tex-A	5	2	.714	8	8	2	0	0	59	50	15	2	2	17	24	10.5	2.14	188	.233	.295	0	—	0	13	13	0	1.5
1984	Tex-A	7	14	.333	32	27	3	0	0	192^{1}	193	106	26	4	87	119	13.3	4.73	88	.258	.339	0	—	0	-16	-12	-1	-1.3
1985	Tex-A	0	6	.000	42	5	0	0	4	81^{1}	86	53	13	2	37	64	13.8	5.42	78	.273	.353	0	—	0	-12	-11	0	-0.8
	Phi-N	0	0	—	4	0	0	0	0	4^{1}	5	4	0	0	4	2	18.7	6.23	59	.278	.409	0	—	0	-1	-1	-0	-0.1
1986	Phi-N	0	0	—	8	0	0	0	0	12^{1}	15	9	1	0	4	9	13.9	6.57	59	.306	.358	0	—	0	-4	-4	-0	-0.2
	Oak-A	9	5	.643	29	17	4	1	0	149^{1}	137	67	15	3	65	102	12.4	3.74	104	.241	.322	0	—	0	7	2	-0	0.2
1987	Oak-A	**20**	13	.606	37	37	8	1	0	261^{1}	224	121	24	6	105	205	11.5	3.68	112	.229	.307	0	—	0	23	14	-3	1.3
1988	*Oak-A	21	12	.636	37	37	**14**	2	0	**275^{2}**	240	111	14	3	110	192	11.5	3.23	117	.234	.310	0	—	0	23	18	-3	1.6
1989	*Oak-A★	21	9	.700	36	36	8	0	0	257^{2}	260	105	23	6	69	155	11.7	3.32	111	.263	.315	0	—	0	16	11	-1	1.1
1990	*Oak-A	22	11	.667	36	36	**11**	**4**	0	**267**	226	84	16	5	83	166	10.6	2.56	145	.231	.294	0	—	0	40	36	-2	4.2
1991	Oak-A	11	11	.500	35	35	2	1	0	226	245	135	24	9	105	144	14.3	5.18	74	.278	.361	0	—	0	-27	-36	-2	-3.2
1992	*Oak-A	12	10	.545	31	31	2	0	0	199^{1}	175	96	25	8	79	130	11.8	3.66	103	.237	.318	0	—	0	6	2	-3	-0.1
1993	*Tor-A	12	8	.600	26	26	0	0	0	162	146	86	23	4	72	96	12.3	4.44	97	.242	.326	0	—	0	-2	-2	-2	-0.4
1994	Tor-A	7	8	.467	22	22	1	0	0	133^{1}	151	89	26	4	62	111	14.6	5.87	82	.285	.364	0	—	0	-16	-15	-2	-1.5
1995	Oak-A	3	7	.300	16	16	0	0	0	81	101	65	11	2	39	58	15.8	6.89	65	.305	.382	0	—	0	-20	-23	0	-2.2
Total	16	168	129	.566	523	348	55	9	19	2629^{2}	2499	1259	264	62	1034	1741	12.3	3.95	100	.251	.325	10	.196	2	40	-4	-21	0.9
● **FRANK STEWART**	Stewart, Frank "Stewy" b: 9/8/06, Minneapolis, Minn. BR/TR, 6'1.5", 180 lbs. Deb: 10/2/27																											
1927	Chi-A	0	1	.000	1	1	0	0	0	4	5	4	0	0	4	0	20.3	9.00	45	.357	.500	0	.000	-0	-2	-2	1	-0.3
● **JOE STEWART**	Stewart, Joseph Lawrence "Ace" b: 3/11/1879, Monroe, N.C. d: 2/9/13, Youngstown, Ohio TR, 5'11", 175 lbs. Deb: 6/9/04																											
1904	Bos-N	0	0	—	2	0	0	0	0	9^{1}	12	11	0	1	4	1	16.4	9.64	29	.286	.362	1	.200	-0	-7	-7	-0	-0.4
● **SAMMY STEWART**	Stewart, Samuel Lee b: 10/28/54, Asheville, N.C. BR/TR, 6'3", 208 lbs. Deb: 9/1/78																											
1978	Bal-A	1	1	.500	2	2	0	0	0	11^{1}	10	5	0	0	3	11	10.3	3.18	110	.238	.289	0	—	0	1	0	0	0.1
1979	*Bal-A	8	5	.615	31	3	1	0	1	117^{2}	96	47	11	5	71	71	13.2	3.52	114	.232	.351	0	—	0	9	7	3	0.9
1980	Bal-A	7	7	.500	33	3	2	0	3	118^{2}	103	51	9	2	60	78	12.5	3.56	111	.235	.330	0	—	0	6	5	-0	0.6
1981	Bal-A	4	8	.333	29	3	0	0	4	112^{1}	89	33	8	3	57	57	11.9	2.32	**156**	.225	.327	0	—	0	17	16	-0	1.9
1982	Bal-A	10	9	.526	38	12	1	1	5	139	140	68	9	2	62	69	13.2	4.14	98	.263	.342	0	—	0	-1	-2	1	-0.2
1983	*Bal-A	9	4	.692	58	1	0	0	7	144^{1}	138	60	7	1	67	95	12.8	3.62	110	.253	.336	0	—	0	7	6	-1	0.5
1984	Bal-A	7	4	.636	60	0	0	0	13	93	81	42	7	1	47	56	12.5	3.29	118	.241	.336	0	—	0	7	6	0	0.8
1985	Bal-A	5	7	.417	56	1	0	0	9	129^{2}	117	60	15	1	66	77	12.8	3.61	112	.246	.339	0	—	0	8	6	-1	0.5
1986	Bos-A	4	1	.800	27	0	0	0	0	63^{2}	64	33	7	0	48	47	15.8	4.38	95	.266	.388	0	—	0	-1	-1	-0	-0.1
1987	Cle-A	4	2	.667	25	0	0	0	3	27	25	22	4	1	21	25	15.7	5.67	80	.234	.364	0	—	0	-4	-3	0	-0.6
Total	10	59	48	.551	359	25	4	1	45	956^{2}	863	421	77	16	502	586	13.0	3.59	110	.245	.341	0	—	0	50	41	1	4.4

YEAR	TM/L	W	L	PCT	G	GS	CG	SH	SV	IP	H	R	HR	HB	BB	SO	RAT	ERA	ERA+	OAV	OOB	BH	AVG	PB	PR	PR+	PD	TPI
● **BUNKY STEWART** Stewart, Veston Goff b: 1/7/31, Jasper, N.C. BL/TL, 6', 155 lbs. Deb: 5/4/52																												
1952	Was-A	0	0	—	1	0	0	0	0	1	2	2	0	0	1	1	27.0	18.00	20	.500	.600	0	—	0	-2	-2	0	-0.1
1953	Was-A	0	2	.000	2	2	1	0	0	15^1	17	9	1	1	11	3	17.0	4.70	83	.283	.403	1	.200	-0	-1	-1	-0	-0.2
1954	Was-A	0	2	.000	29	2	0	0	1	50^2	67	52	3	4	27	27	17.4	7.64	47	.324	.412	0	.000	-0	-22	-24	1	-1.1
1955	Was-A	0	0	—	7	1	0	0	0	15^1	18	7	0	0	6	10	14.1	4.11	93	.295	.358	0	.000	-0	-0	-0	0	0.0
1956	Was-A	5	7	.417	33	9	1	0	2	105	111	77	15	5	82	36	17.0	5.57	78	.276	.405	7	.250	-0	-16	-14	1	-1.4
Total	5	5	11	.313	72	14	2	0	3	187^1	215	147	19	10	127	77	16.9	6.01	67	.293	.404	8	.211	-0	-42	-41	2	-2.8
● **LEFTY STEWART** Stewart, Walter Cleveland b: 9/23/1900, Sparta, Tenn. d: 9/26/74, Knoxville, Tenn. BR/TL, 5'10", 160 lbs. Deb: 4/20/21																												
1921	Det-A	0	0	—	5	0	0	0	1	9	20	12	0	0	5	4	25.0	12.00	36	.455	.510	0	.000	-0	-8	-8	0	-0.3
1927	StL-A	8	11	.421	27	19	11	0	1	155^2	187	83	7	2	43	43	13.4	4.28	102	.310	.357	15	.306	3	-2	1	2	0.5
1928	StL-A	7	9	.438	29	17	7	1	3	142^2	173	81	5	2	32	25	13.1	4.67	90	.310	.350	14	.275	3	-10	-7	-0	-0.5
1929	StL-A	9	6	.600	23	18	8	1	0	149^2	137	67	11	4	49	47	11.4	3.25	136	.246	.312	6	.118	-4	17	19	-0	1.2
1930	StL-A	20	12	.625	35	33	23	1	0	271	281	119	21	1	70	79	11.7	3.45	141	.268	.315	22	.244	2	36	41	0	4.4
1931	StL-A	14	17	.452	36	33	20	1	0	258	287	155	17	3	85	89	13.1	4.40	105	.277	.334	22	.250	6	-0	6	1	1.3
1932	StL-A	15	19	.441	41	32	18	2	1	259^2	269	148	22	3	99	86	12.9	4.61	105	.270	.338	12	.146	-2	-4	6	-1	0.5
1933	*Was-A	15	6	.714	34	31	11	1	0	230^2	227	116	19	1	60	69	11.2	3.82	109	.256	.304	11	.143	1	12	9	1	0.9
1934	Was-A	7	11	.389	24	22	7	1	0	152	184	74	8	1	36	36	13.1	4.03	107	.303	.343	7	.156	-1	8	5	-0	0.3
1935	Was-A	0	1	.000	1	1	0	0	0	2^2	8	9	1	0	2	1	33.8	13.50	32	.533	.588	0	.000	-0	-3	-3	-0	-0.4
	Cle-A	6	6	.500	24	10	2	0	2	91	122	68	6	1	17	24	13.8	5.44	83	.312	.342	6	.200	-1	-10	-9	-1	-1.3
	Yr	6	7	.462	25	11	2	0	2	93^2	130	77	7	1	19	25	14.4	5.67	79	.320	.352	6	.194	-1	-13	-12	-1	-1.7
Total	10	101	98	.508	279	216	107	8	8	1722	1895	932	117	18	498	503	12.6	4.19	108	.281	.332	115	.204	6	35	62	0	6.6
● **MACK STEWART** Stewart, William Macklin b: 9/23/14, Stevenson, Ala. d: 3/21/60, Macon, Ga. BR/TR, 6', 167 lbs. Deb: 7/7/44																												
1944	Chi-N	0	0	—	8	0	0	0	0	12^1	11	2	1	0	4	3	10.9	1.46	242	.239	.300	0	.000	-0	3	3	-0	0.1
1945	Chi-N	0	1	.000	16	1	0	0	0	28^1	37	16	0	0	14	9	16.2	4.76	77	.322	.395	1	.333	0	-3	-4	0	-0.1
Total	2	0	1	.000	24	1	0	0	0	40^2	48	18	1	0	18	12	14.6	3.76	96	.298	.369	1	.250	0	-0	-1	0	0.0
● **PHIL STIDHAM** Stidham, Phillip Wayne b: 11/18/68, Tulsa, Okla. BR/TR, 6', 180 lbs. Deb: 6/4/94																												
1994	Det-A	0	0	—	5	0	0	0	0	4^1	12	12	3	0	4	4	33.2	24.92	19	.571	.640	0	—	0	-10	-10	-0	-0.4
● **DAVE STIEB** Stieb, David Andrew b: 7/22/57, Santa Ana, Cal. BR/TR, 6'1", 195 lbs. Deb: 6/29/79																												
1979	Tor-A	8	8	.500	18	18	7	1	0	129^1	139	70	11	4	48	52	13.3	4.31	101	.276	.344	0	—	0	-1	1	3	0.3
1980	Tor-A★	12	15	.444	34	32	14	4	0	242^2	232	108	12	6	83	108	11.9	3.71	116	.260	.327	0	.000	-0	9	15	5	2.1
1981	Tor-A★	11	10	.524	25	25	11	2	0	183^2	148	70	10	11	61	89	10.8	3.19	124	.223	.299	0	—	0	10	14	2	1.8
1982	Tor-A	17	14	.548	38	38	**19**	**5**	0	**288^1**	271	116	27	5	75	141	11.0	3.25	138	.248	.299	0	—	0	27	**36**	4	4.1
1983	Tor-A★	17	12	.586	36	36	14	4	0	278	223	105	21	14	93	187	10.7	3.04	142	.219	.293	0	—	0	32	**37**	1	3.7
1984	Tor-A★	16	8	.667	35	35	11	2	0	**267**	215	87	19	11	88	198	10.6	2.83	**145**	**.221**	.293	0	—	0	35	**37**	1	3.3
1985	*Tor-A★	14	13	.519	36	36	8	2	0	265	206	89	22	9	96	167	10.6	**2.48**	**170**	**.213**	.290	0	—	0	**49**	**50**	5	**5.5**
1986	Tor-A	7	12	.368	37	34	1	1	1	205	239	128	29	15	87	127	15.0	4.74	89	.297	.376	0	—	0	-13	-12	1	-0.8
1987	Tor-A	13	9	.591	33	31	3	1	0	185	164	92	16	7	87	115	12.6	4.09	110	.239	.331	0	—	0	8	9	1	1.0
1988	Tor-A★	16	8	.667	32	31	8	4	0	207^1	157	76	15	13	79	147	10.8	3.04	130	.210	.296	0	—	0	22	21	1	2.4
1989	*Tor-A	17	8	.680	33	33	3	2	0	206^2	164	83	12	13	76	101	11.0	3.35	113	.219	.302	0	—	0	12	10	0	1.1
1990	Tor-A★	18	6	.750	33	33	2	2	0	208^2	179	73	11	10	64	125	10.9	2.93	135	.230	.297	0	—	0	23	23	3	3.0
1991	Tor-A	4	3	.571	9	9	1	0	0	59^2	52	22	4	2	23	29	11.6	3.17	133	.243	.322	0	—	0	6	7	1	0.8
1992	Tor-A	4	6	.400	21	14	1	0	0	96^1	98	58	9	4	43	45	13.5	5.04	81	.275	.359	0	—	0	-12	-10	2	-0.7
1993	Chi-A	1	3	.250	4	4	0	0	0	22^1	27	17	1	0	14	11	16.5	6.04	69	.300	.394	0	—	0	-4	-5	-0	-0.7
1998	Tor-A	1	2	.333	19	3	0	0	2	50^1	58	31	6	5	17	27	14.3	4.83	97	.284	.354	0	.000	-0	-1	-1	-0	-0.1
Total	16	176	137	.562	443	412	103	30	3	2895^1	2572	1225	225	129	1034	1669	11.6	3.44	122	.239	.314	0	.000	-0	201	235	29	26.8
● **FRED STIELY** Stiely, Fred Warren "Lefty" b: 6/1/01, Pillow, Pa. d: 1/6/81, Valley View, Pa. BL/TL, 5'8", 170 lbs. Deb: 10/6/29																												
1929	StL-A	1	0	1.000	1	1	1	0	0	9	11	2	0	1	3	2	15.0	0.00		.297	.366	2	.667	1	4	4	0	0.7
1930	StL-A	0	1	.000	4	2	1	0	0	19	27	21	4	1	8	5	17.1	8.53	57	.346	.414	3	.429	1	-8	-7	-0	-0.2
1931	StL-A	0	0	—	4	0	0	0	0	6^2	7	5	0	1	3	2	14.9	6.75	69	.269	.367	0	—	0	-2	-1	-0	-0.1
Total	3	1	1	.500	9	3	2	0	0	34^2	45	28	4	3	14	9	16.1	5.97	79	.319	.392	5	.500	2	-6	-5	-1	0.4
● **DICK STIGMAN** Stigman, Richard Lewis b: 1/24/36, Nimrod, Minn. BR/TL, 6'3", 200 lbs. Deb: 4/22/60																												
1960	Cle-A☆	5	11	.313	41	18	3	0	9	133^2	118	78	13	0	87	104	13.8	4.51	83	.238	.352	8	.222	2	-9	-12	-2	-1.4
1961	Cle-A	2	5	.286	22	6	0	0	0	64^1	65	35	9	0	25	48	12.6	4.62	85	.264	.332	2	.125	-1	-4	-5	-0	-0.5
1962	Min-A	12	5	.706	40	15	6	0	3	142^2	122	60	19	2	64	116	11.9	3.66	112	.233	.319	2	.044	-4	5	7	-2	0.1
1963	Min-A	15	15	.500	33	33	15	3	0	241	210	90	32	0	81	193	10.9	3.25	112	.231	.294	9	.107	-2	10	11	-4	0.6
1964	Min-A	6	15	.286	32	29	5	1	0	190	160	94	31	5	70	159	11.1	4.03	89	.225	.299	7	.101	-3	-8	-10	-3	-1.5
1965	Min-A	4	2	.667	33	8	0	0	4	70	59	34	14	0	33	70	11.8	4.37	81	.227	.314	2	.133	-0	-7	-6	-1	-0.7
1966	Bos-A	2	1	.667	34	10	1	0	0	81	85	51	15	1	46	65	14.7	5.44	70	.268	.363	2	.118	-1	-18	-13	-1	-0.9
Total	7	46	54	.460	235	119	30	5	16	922^2	819	442	133	8	406	755	12.0	4.03	93	.237	.318	32	.113	-8	-32	-29	-13	-4.3
● **ROLLIE STILES** Stiles, Rolland Mays "Lena" b: 11/17/06, Ratcliff, Ark. BR/TR, 6'1.5", 180 lbs. Deb: 6/19/30																												
1930	StL-A	3	6	.333	20	7	3	0	0	102	136	77	10	1	41	25	15.7	5.91	82	.337	.399	10	.270	0	-14	-11	-1	-0.8
1931	StL-A	3	1	.750	34	2	0	0	0	81	112	72	2	2	60	32	19.3	7.22	64	.352	.458	1	.045	-2	-26	-22	-0	-1.2
1933	StL-A	3	7	.300	31	9	6	1	1	115	154	83	4	2	47	29	15.9	5.01	93	.327	.390	2	.061	-3	-9	-4	-1	-0.7
Total	3	9	14	.391	85	18	9	1	1	298	402	232	16	5	148	86	16.8	5.92	80	.337	.412	13	.141	-5	-49	-37	-2	-2.7
● **ARCHIE STIMMEL** Stimmel, Archibald May "Lumbago" b: 5/30/1873, Woodsboro, Md. d: 8/18/58, Frederick, Md. BR/TR, 6', 175 lbs. Deb: 7/3/00																												
1900	Cin-N	1	1	.500	2	1	1	0	0	13	18	11	0	0	4	2	15.2	6.92	53	.327	.373	1	.200	-0	-5	-5	-0	-0.6
1901	Cin-N	4	14	.222	20	18	14	1	0	153^1	170	96	10	12	44	55	13.3	4.11	78	.279	.339	5	.081	-5	-13	-16	-3	-2.2
1902	Cin-N	0	4	.000	4	3	3	0	0	26	37	16	1	2	12	7	17.7	3.46	87	.333	.408	2	.200	-0	-2	-1	-0	-0.2
Total	3	5	19	.208	26	22	18	1	0	192^1	225	123	12	14	60	64	14.0	4.21	76	.290	.352	8	.104	-5	-20	-22	-3	-3.0
● **CARL STIMSON** Stimson, Carl Remus b: 7/18/1894, Hamburg, Iowa d: 11/9/36, Omaha, Neb. BB/TR, 6'5", 190 lbs. Deb: 6/6/23																												
1923	Bos-A	0	0	—	2	0	0	0	0	4	12	10	0	1	5	1	40.5	22.50	18	.750	.818	0	.000	-0	-8	-8	0	-0.4
● **HARRY STINE** Stine, Harry C. b: 2/20/1864, Shenandoah, Pa. d: 6/5/24, Niagara Falls, N.Y TL, 5'6", 150 lbs. Deb: 7/22/1890																												
1890	Phi-a	0	1	.000	1	1	1	0	0	8	17	9	0	0	4	1	23.6	9.00	43	.415	.467	0	.000	-0	-5	-5	-0	-0.4
● **LEE STINE** Stine, Lee Elbert b: 11/17/13, Stillwater, Okla. BR/TR, 5'11", 185 lbs. Deb: 4/17/34																												
1934	Chi-A	0	0	—	4	0	0	0	0	11	11	10	2	1	10	8	18.0	8.18	58	.268	.423	0	.000	0	-5	-4	-0	-0.2
1935	Chi-A	0	0	—	1	0	0	0	0	2	2	2	1	0	3	1	22.5	9.00	51	.286	.500	0	—	0	-1	-1	1	0.0
1936	Cin-N	3	8	.273	40	13	5	1	2	121^2	157	79	6	8	41	26	15.2	5.03	76	.318	.379	8	.296	3	-14	-17	2	-1.0
1938	NY-A	0	0	—	4	0	0	0	0	8^2	9	1	0	0	1	4	10.4	1.04	437	.333	.357	1	.500	0	4	4	-0	0.2
Total	4	3	8	.273	49	13	5	1	2	143^1	179	92	9	9	55	39	15.3	5.09	78	.315	.384	9	.300	4	-16	-19	2	-1.0
● **JACK STIVETTS** Stivetts, John Elmer "Happy Jack" b: 3/31/1868, Ashland, Pa. d: 4/18/30, Ashland, Pa. BR/TR, 6'2", 185 lbs. Deb: 6/26/1889 ♦																												
1889	StL-a	12	7	.632	26	20	18	2	2	191^2	153	85	4	5	68	143	**10.6**	**2.25**	**188**	**.212**	**.285**	18	.228	-1	34	38	0	3.0
1890	StL-a	27	21	.563	54	46	41	3	0	419^1	399	255	14	17	179	289	12.8	3.52	123	.243	.324	65	.288	14	16	33	3	4.5
1891	StL-a	33	22	.600	**64**	56	40	3	1	440	357	237	15	18	232	**259**	12.4	2.86	147	.214	.317	92	.305	9	42	**58**	3	**6.9**
1892	*Bos-N	35	16	.686	54	48	45	3	1	415^2	346	223	12	10	171	180	11.4	3.03	116	.217	.297	71	.296	15	12	21	1	3.6
1893	Bos-N	20	12	.625	38	34	29	1	1	283^2	315	194	17	10	115	61	14.0	4.41	112	.273	.344	51	.297	7	8	16	-2	1.7
1894	Bos-N	26	14	.650	45	39	30	0	0	338	429	278	27	13	127	76	15.2	4.90	116	.306	.369	80	.328	10	16	28	-3	2.9
1895	Bos-N	17	17	.500	38	34	30	0	0	291	341	219	15	12	89	111	13.7	4.64	110	.288	.344	30	.190	-7	5	14	-1	0.5
1896	Bos-N	22	14	.611	42	36	31	2	0	329	353	219	20	7	99	71	12.6	4.10	111	.272	.327	77	.347	12	10	15	-3	2.1
1897	*Bos-N	11	4	.733	18	15	10	0	0	129^1	147	75	5	5	43	27	13.6	3.41	131	.284	.345	73	.367	7	13	15	1	2.1
1898	Bos-N	0	1	.000	2	1	1	0	0	12	17	12	2	0	7	1	18.0	8.25	45	.333	.414	28	.252	0	-6	-6	0	-0.3

YEAR	TM/L	W	L	PCT	G	GS	CG	SH	SV	IP	H	R	HR	HB	BB	SO	RAT	ERA	ERA+	OAV	OOB	BH	AVG	PB	PR	PR+	PD	TPI
1899	Cle-N	0	4	.000	7	4	3	0	0	38	48	39	0	2	25	5	17.8	5.68	65	.308	.410	8	.205	1	-8	-9	2	-0.5
Total	11	203	132	.606	388	333	278	14	5	2887^2	2905	1836	131	99	1155	1223	13.0	3.74	121	.255	.329	593	.298	65	141	229	0	26.5
● CHUCK STOBBS	Stobbs, Charles Klein b: 7/2/29, Wheeling, W.Va. BL/TL, 6'1", 185 lbs. Deb: 9/15/47																											
1947	Bos-A	0	1	.000	4	1	0	0	0	9	10	6	0	0	10	5	20.0	6.00	65	.294	.455	0	.000	-0	-2	-2	-0	-0.2
1948	Bos-A	0	0	—	6	0	0	0	0	7	9	5	0	0	7	4	20.6	6.43	68	.321	.457	0	.000	-0	-2	-2	0	-0.1
1949	Bos-A	11	6	.647	26	19	10	0	0	152	145	72	10	2	75	70	13.1	4.03	108	.254	.343	11	.208	0	3	5	-1	0.5
1950	Bos-A	12	7	.632	32	21	6	0	1	169^1	158	104	17	5	88	78	13.3	5.10	96	.250	.346	14	.246	3	-10	-4	1	0.0
1951	Bos-A	10	9	.526	34	25	6	0	0	170	180	100	16	5	74	75	13.7	4.76	94	.271	.349	11	.180	-2	-12	-5	-2	-0.9
1952	Chi-A	7	12	.368	38	17	2	0	1	135	118	54	9	5	72	73	13.0	3.13	116	.237	.339	3	.079	-1	8	8	1	1.0
1953	Was-A	11	8	.579	27	20	8	0	0	153	146	64	11	1	44	67	11.2	3.29	118	.246	.299	10	.227	1	12	10	-0	1.3
1954	Was-A	11	11	.500	31	24	10	3	0	182	189	87	6	1	67	67	12.7	4.10	87	.270	.335	7	.137	0	-8	-12	1	-1.2
1955	Was-A	4	14	.222	41	16	2	0	3	140^1	169	90	13	1	57	60	14.6	5.00	77	.302	.368	6	.171	2	-16	-19	1	-1.9
1956	Was-A	15	15	.500	37	33	15	1	1	240	264	115	29	1	54	97	12.0	3.60	120	.279	.318	15	.179	-2	15	19	1	2.0
1957	Was-A	8	20	.286	42	31	5	2	1	211^2	235	140	28	5	80	114	13.6	5.36	73	.279	.345	16	.211	1	-37	-33	-3	-4.1
1958	Was-A	2	6	.250	19	8	0	0	0	56^2	87	44	7	2	16	23	16.7	6.04	63	.369	.413	0	.000	-2	-14	-14	0	-1.9
	StL-N	1	3	.250	17	0	0	0	1	39^2	40	16	4	0	14	25	12.3	3.63	114	.261	.323	1	.250	0	1	2	1	0.3
1959	Was-A	1	8	.111	41	7	0	0	7	90^2	82	42	13	2	24	50	10.7	2.98	131	.238	.291	2	.105	-1	9	9	-0	0.9
1960	Was-A	12	7	.632	40	13	1	1	2	119^1	115	54	13	3	38	72	11.8	3.32	117	.252	.313	3	.088	-2	7	8	-2	0.8
1961	Min-A	2	3	.400	24	3	0	0	2	44^2	56	37	8	2	15	17	14.7	7.46	57	.311	.371	3	.375	1	-17	-15	-1	-1.6
Total	15	107	130	.451	459	238	65	7	19	1920^1	2003	1030	184	35	735	897	13.0	4.29	95	.269	.338	102	.176	-1	-63	-45	-3	-5.1
● WES STOCK	Stock, Wesley Gay b: 4/10/34, Longview, Wash. BR/TR, 6'2", 188 lbs. Deb: 4/19/59 C																											
1959	Bal-A	0	0	—	7	0	0	0	1	12^2	16	6	1	0	2	8	12.8	3.55	107	.302	.327	0	.000	-0	0	0	-0	0.0
1960	Bal-A	2	2	.500	17	0	0	0	2	34^1	26	11	2	1	14	23	10.7	2.88	132	.218	.306	0	.000	-1	4	4	1	0.4
1961	Bal-A	5	0	1.000	35	1	0	0	3	71^2	58	24	3	2	27	47	10.9	3.01	128	.225	.303	0	.000	-1	8	7	2	0.6
1962	Bal-A	3	2	.600	53	0	0	0	3	65	50	33	7	1	36	34	12.0	4.43	83	.217	.326	0	.000	-0	-3	-6	3	-0.2
1963	Bal-A	7	0	1.000	47	0	0	0	1	75^1	69	41	11	0	31	55	11.9	3.94	88	.246	.321	0	.000	-1	-3	-4	1	-0.4
1964	Bal-A	2	0	1.000	14	0	0	0	0	20^2	17	9	5	0	8	14	10.9	3.92	91	.233	.309	0	.000	-0	-1	-1	0	-0.1
	KC-A	6	3	.667	50	0	0	0	5	93	69	21	10	4	34	101	10.4	1.94	197	.213	.296	3	.200	0	17	18	-1	1.9
	Yr	8	3	.727	64	0	0	0	5	113^2	86	30	15	4	42	115	10.5	2.30	164	.217	.298	3	.158	-0	17	18	-0	1.8
1965	KC-A	0	4	.000	62	2	0	0	4	99^2	96	62	18	4	40	52	12.6	5.24	67	.251	.328	0	.000	-1	-20	-19	2	-0.9
1966	KC-A	2	2	.500	35	0	0	0	3	44	30	15	3	3	21	31	11.0	2.66	128	.199	.309	0	.000	-0	4	4	-0	0.3
1967	KC-A	0	0	—	1	0	0	0	0	1	3	2	0	0	2	0	45.0	18.00	18	.500	.625	0	—	0	-2	-2	0	-0.1
Total	9	27	13	.675	321	3	0	0	22	517^1	434	224	60	15	215	365	11.6	3.60	101	.231	.315	3	.051	-4	6	3	7	1.5
● OTIS STOCKSDALE	Stocksdale, Otis Hinkley "Old Gray Fox" b: 8/7/1871, Arcadia, Md. d: 3/15/33, Pennsville, N.J. BL/TR, 5'10.5", 180 lbs. Deb: 7/24/1893																											
1893	Was-N	2	8	.200	11	11	7	0	0	69	111	82	4	5	32	12	19.3	8.22	56	.352	.420	12	.300	2	-27	-28	1	-2.5
1894	Was-N	5	9	.357	18	14	11	0	0	117^1	176	115	10	14	42	10	17.8	5.06	104	.342	.407	23	.324	1	3	3	1	0.4
1895	Was-N	6	11	.353	20	17	11	0	1	136	199	143	7	8	52	23	17.1	6.09	79	.336	.397	23	.311	2	-20	-19	-0	-1.5
	Bos-N	2	2	.500	4	4	1	0	0	23	31	22	2	0	8	2	15.3	5.87	87	.316	.368	4	.267	-0	-3	-2	-0	-0.3
	Yr	8	13	.381	24	21	12	0	1	159	230	165	9	8	60	25	16.9	6.06	80	.333	.393	27	.303	2	-23	-21	-1	-1.8
1896	Bal-N	0	1	.000	1	0	0	0	0	1^2	4	4	0	1	2	1	37.8	16.20	26	.444	.583	1	.333	1	-2	-2	-0	-0.3
Total	4	15	31	.326	54	46	30	0	1	347	521	366	23	28	136	48	17.8	6.20	80	.341	.405	63	.310	5	-49	-48	1	-4.2
● BOB STODDARD	Stoddard, Robert Lyle b: 3/8/57, San Jose, Cal. BR/TR, 6'1", 200 lbs. Deb: 9/4/81																											
1981	Sea-A	2	1	.667	5	5	1	0	0	34^2	35	10	3	1	9	22	11.7	2.60	149	.269	.321	0	—	0	4	5	-0	0.4
1982	Sea-A	3	3	.500	9	9	2	1	0	67^1	48	22	7	3	18	24	9.2	2.41	177	.205	.271	0	—	0	13	13	0	1.2
1983	Sea-A	9	17	.346	35	23	2	1	0	175^2	182	95	29	4	58	87	12.5	4.41	97	.274	.336	0	—	0	-6	-2	3	-0.1
1984	Sea-A	2	3	.400	27	6	0	0	0	79	86	51	10	2	37	39	14.2	5.13	78	.278	.359	0	—	0	-10	-10	1	-0.5
1985	Det-A	0	0	—	8	0	0	0	1	13^1	15	11	3	0	5	11	13.5	6.75	60	.268	.328	0	—	0	-4	-4	1	-0.1
1986	SD-N	1	0	1.000	18	0	0	0	1	23^1	20	7	1	1	11	17	12.3	2.31	158	.227	.320	0	.000	-0	4	4	-0	0.2
1987	KC-A	1	3	.250	17	2	0	0	1	40	51	26	3	3	22	23	17.1	4.27	107	.313	.404	0	—	0	1	1	1	0.2
Total	7	18	27	.400	119	45	5	2	3	433^1	437	222	56	14	160	223	12.7	4.03	104	.266	.336	0	.000	-0	1	7	5	1.3
● TIM STODDARD	Stoddard, Timothy Paul b: 1/24/53, E.Chicago, Ind. BR/TR, 6'7", 250 lbs. Deb: 9/7/75																											
1975	Chi-A	0	0	—	1	0	0	0	0	1	2	1	1	0	0	0	18.0	9.00	43	.400	.400	0	—	0	-1	-1	0	0.0
1978	Bal-A	0	1	.000	8	0	0	0	0	18	22	17	3	2	8	14	16.0	6.00	58	.301	.386	0	—	0	-4	-5	0	-0.3
1979	*Bal-A	3	1	.750	29	0	0	0	3	58	44	12	3	0	19	47	9.8	1.71	236	.212	.278	0	—	0	16	16	-0	1.1
1980	Bal-A	5	3	.625	64	0	0	0	26	86	72	27	2	1	38	64	11.6	2.51	158	.233	.319	0	—	0	15	14	-1	2.1
1981	Bal-A	4	2	.667	31	0	0	0	7	37^1	38	16	6	2	18	32	14.0	3.86	94	.268	.358	0	—	0	-1	-1	-0	-0.2
1982	Bal-A	3	4	.429	50	0	0	0	12	56	53	26	4	1	29	42	13.3	4.02	101	.249	.342	0	—	0	0	0	-0	0.0
1983	Bal-A	4	3	.571	47	0	0	0	9	57^2	65	39	10	1	29	50	14.8	6.09	65	.293	.377	0	—	0	-13	-14	0	-1.9
1984	*Chi-N	10	6	.625	58	0	0	0	7	92	77	41	9	1	57	87	13.2	3.82	103	.236	.352	1	.091	-1	-2	1	-1	0.0
1985	SD-N	1	6	.143	44	0	0	0	1	60	63	35	3	0	37	42	15.0	4.65	76	.269	.369	0	.000	-1	-7	-8	-1	-1.0
1986	SD-N	1	3	.250	30	0	0	0	0	45^1	33	20	6	0	34	47	13.3	3.77	97	.200	.337	1	.250	1	-0	-1	0	0.1
	NY-A	4	1	.800	24	0	0	0	0	49^1	41	23	6	0	23	34	11.7	3.83	107	.232	.320	0	—	0	2	1	0	0.1
1987	NY-A	4	3	.571	57	0	0	0	8	92^2	83	38	13	0	30	78	11.0	3.50	126	.235	.295	0	—	0	10	9	-1	0.7
1988	NY-A	2	2	.500	28	0	0	0	3	55	62	41	5	2	27	33	14.9	6.38	62	.286	.370	0	—	0	-15	-15	0	-1.1
1989	Cle-A	0	0	—	14	0	0	0	0	21^1	25	7	1	0	7	12	13.5	2.95	134	.313	.368	0	—	0	2	2	0	0.1
Total	13	41	35	.539	485	0	0	0	76	729^2	680	343	72	10	356	582	12.9	3.95	100	.250	.339	2	.100	-0	3	1	-3	-0.3
● ART STOKES	Stokes, Arthur Milton b: 9/13/1896, Emmitsburg, Md. d: 6/3/62, Titusville, Pa. BR/TR, 5'10.5", 155 lbs. Deb: 5/5/25																											
1925	Phi-A	1	1	.500	12	0	0	0	0	24^1	24	15	0	2	10	7	13.3	4.07	114	.270	.356	0	.000	-0	1	1	-0	0.0
● DICK STONE	Stone, Charles Richard b: 12/5/11, Oklahoma City, Okla d: 2/18/80, Oklahoma City, Okla. BL/TL, 5'9", 153 lbs. Deb: 8/26/45																											
1945	Was-A	0	0	—	3	0	0	0	0	5	6	0	0	0	2	0	14.4	0.00	—	.316	.381	0	—	0	2	2	0	0.1
● DEAN STONE	Stone, Darrah Dean b: 9/1/30, Moline, Ill. BL/TL, 6'4", 205 lbs. Deb: 9/13/53																											
1953	Was-A	0	1	.000	3	1	0	0	0	8^2	13	8	0	0	5	5	18.7	8.31	47	.361	.439	0	.000	-0	-4	-4	-0	-0.5
1954	Was-A★	12	10	.545	31	23	10	2	0	178^2	161	76	7	1	69	87	11.6	3.22	110	.240	.312	5	.096	-0	10	7	-3	0.5
1955	Was-A	6	13	.316	43	24	5	1	1	180	180	98	14	3	114	84	14.9	4.15	92	.267	.375	2	.043	-4	-4	-7	-2	-1.1
1956	Was-A	5	7	.417	41	21	2	0	3	132	148	107	10	7	93	86	16.9	6.27	69	.282	.397	3	.088	-1	-31	-27	-1	-2.4
1957	Was-A	0	0	—	3	0	0	0	0	3^1	5	3	0	0	2	3	18.9	8.10	48	.357	.438	0	—	0	-2	-2	-0	-0.1
	Bos-A	1	3	.250	17	8	0	0	1	51^1	56	42	5	0	35	32	16.0	5.08	78	.284	.392	0	.000	-1	-7	-6	1	-0.5
	Yr	1	3	.250	20	8	0	0	1	54^2	61	45	5	0	37	35	16.1	5.27	76	.289	.395	0	.000	-1	-9	-7	1	-0.6
1959	StL-N	0	1	.000	18	1	0	0	1	30	30	15	4	0	16	17	13.8	4.20	101	.273	.365	0	.000	-0	-1	0	-0	-0.1
1962	Hou-N	3	2	.600	15	7	2	2	0	52^1	61	31	4	1	20	31	14.1	4.47	84	.295	.360	4	.250	1	-3	-5	0	-0.3
	Chi-A	1	0	1.000	27	0	0	0	5	30^1	28	11	3	1	9	23	11.3	3.26	120	.255	.317	1	.500	1	2	2	-0	0.2
1963	Bal-A	1	2	.333	17	0	0	0	1	19^1	23	11	0	0	10	12	15.4	5.12	68	.307	.388	0	—	0	-3	-4	0	-0.5
Total	8	29	39	.426	215	85	19	5	12	686	705	402	47	13	373	380	14.3	4.47	86	.269	.363	15	.088	-6	-43	-47	-5	-4.8
● DWIGHT STONE	Stone, Dwight Ely b: 8/2/1886, Holt Co., Neb. d: 6/3/76, Glendale, Cal. BR/TR, 6'1.5", 170 lbs. Deb: 4/13/13																											
1913	StL-A	2	6	.250	18	7	4	1	0	91	94	45	0	7	46	37	14.5	3.56	82	.267	.363	9	.273	2	-6	-6	1	-0.2
1914	KC-F	8	14	.364	39	22	6	0	0	186^2	205	110	8	8	77	88	14.0	4.34	64	.281	.356	7	.121	-4	-30	-34	1	-3.8
Total	2	10	20	.333	57	29	10	1	0	277^2	299	155	8	15	123	125	14.2	4.08	69	.276	.358	16	.176	-2	-36	-40	2	-4.0
● ARNIE STONE	Stone, Edwin Arnold b: 10/9/1892, North Creek, N.Y. d: 7/29/48, Hudson Falls, N.Y BR/TL, 6', 180 lbs. Deb: 7/30/23																											
1923	Pit-N	0	1	.000	9	0	0	0	0	12^1	19	12	0	0	4	2	16.8	8.03	50	.352	.397	0	.000	-0	-6	-5	-1	-0.4
1924	Pit-N	4	2	.667	26	2	1	0	0	64	57	27	0	0	15	7	10.1	2.95	130	.259	.306	2	.133	-1	6	6	0	0.4
Total	2	4	3	.571	35	2	1	0	0	76^1	76	39	0	0	19	9	11.2	3.77	102	.277	.324	2	.125	-1	1	1	-0	0.0

● GEORGE STONE Stone, George Heard b: 7/9/46, Ruston, La. BL/TL, 6'3", 205 lbs. Deb: 9/15/67

YEAR	TM/L	W	L	PCT	G	GS	CG	SH	SV	IP	H	R	HR	HB	BB	SO	RAT	ERA	ERA+	OAV	OOB	BH	AVG	PB	PR	PR+	PD	TPI
1967	Atl-N	0	0	—	2	1	0	0	0	7^1	8	4	0	0	1	5	11.0	4.91	68	.267	.290	0	.000	-0	-1	-1	0	-0.1
1968	Atl-N	7	4	.636	17	10	2	0	0	75	63	27	9	0	19	52	9.8	2.76	108	.222	.271	9	.333	3	2	2	1	0.5
1969	*Atl-N	13	10	.565	36	20	3	0	3	165^1	166	82	20	5	48	102	11.9	3.65	99	.260	.317	11	.186	1	-1	-1	-1	0.0
1970	Atl-N	11	11	.500	35	30	9	2	0	207^1	218	111	27	6	50	131	11.9	3.86	111	.267	.314	17	.236	4	4	9	3	1.6
1971	Atl-N	6	8	.429	27	24	4	2	0	172^2	186	80	19	6	35	110	11.8	3.60	103	.274	.315	11	.177	-0	-2	2	-0	0.1
1972	Atl-N	6	11	.353	31	16	2	1	1	111	143	72	18	4	44	63	15.5	5.51	69	.315	.380	5	.200	1	-25	-19	1	-2.5
1973	*NY-N	12	3	.800	27	20	2	0	1	148	157	53	16	0	31	77	11.4	2.80	130	.274	.311	13	.271	2	14	14	1	1.7
1974	NY-N	2	7	.222	15	13	1	0	0	77	103	57	10	0	21	29	14.5	5.03	71	.322	.364	3	.115	-1	-12	-13	0	-1.4
1975	NY-N	3	3	.500	13	11	1	0	0	57	75	38	3	0	21	21	15.2	5.05	69	.323	.379	3	.167	0	-9	-11	1	-0.9
Total	9	60	57	.513	203	145	24	5	5	1020^2	1119	524	122	21	270	590	12.4	3.89	96	.278	.326	72	.212	10	-30	-17	4	-1.0

● ROCKY STONE Stone, John Vernon b: 8/23/18, Redding, Cal. d: 11/12/86, Fountain Valley, Cal. BR/TR, 6', 200 lbs. Deb: 5/2/43

YEAR	TM/L	W	L	PCT	G	GS	CG	SH	SV	IP	H	R	HR	HB	BB	SO	RAT	ERA	ERA+	OAV	OOB	BH	AVG	PB	PR	PR+	PD	TPI
1943	Cin-N	0	1	.000	13	0	0	0	0	24^2	23	14	0	0	8	11	11.3	4.38	76	.237	.295	1	.250	0	-3	-3	-1	-0.2

● STEVE STONE Stone, Steven Michael b: 7/14/47, Euclid, Ohio BR/TR, 5'10", 175 lbs. Deb: 4/8/71

YEAR	TM/L	W	L	PCT	G	GS	CG	SH	SV	IP	H	R	HR	HB	BB	SO	RAT	ERA	ERA+	OAV	OOB	BH	AVG	PB	PR	PR+	PD	TPI
1971	SF-N	5	9	.357	24	19	2	2	0	110^2	110	56	9	3	55	63	13.7	4.15	82	.259	.349	0	.000	-2	-8	-9	2	-1.2
1972	SF-N	6	8	.429	27	16	4	1	0	123^2	97	48	11	2	49	85	10.8	2.98	117	.218	.298	4	.118	-1	6	7	0	0.7
1973	Chi-A	6	11	.353	36	22	3	0	1	176^1	163	87	11	7	82	138	12.9	4.24	94	.245	.335	0	—	0	-8	-5	0	-0.4
1974	Chi-N	8	6	.571	38	23	1	0	0	169^2	185	92	19	4	64	90	13.4	4.14	92	.278	.345	7	.121	-3	-10	-6	1	-0.6
1975	Chi-N	12	8	.600	33	32	6	1	0	214^1	198	103	24	5	80	139	11.9	3.95	98	.245	.317	8	.111	-2	-7	-2	0	-0.4
1976	Chi-N	3	6	.333	17	15	1	1	0	75	70	36	6	3	21	33	11.3	4.08	95	.250	.309	3	.143	-1	-5	-2	-1	-0.4
1977	Chi-A	15	12	.556	31	31	8	0	0	207^1	228	115	25	5	80	124	13.6	4.51	91	.281	.350	0	—	0	-10	-10	-0	-1.1
1978	Chi-A	12	12	.500	30	30	6	1	0	212	196	110	19	3	84	118	12.0	4.37	87	.247	.321	0	—	0	-14	-13	-1	-1.4
1979	*Bal-A	11	7	.611	32	32	3	0	0	186	173	91	31	1	73	96	12.0	3.77	107	.248	.320	0	—	0	9	5	1	0.6
1980	Bal-A★	**25**	7	**.781**	37	37	9	1	0	250^2	224	103	22	6	101	149	11.9	3.23	123	.240	.319	0	—	0	23	21	-2	2.2
1981	Bal-A	4	7	.364	15	12	0	0	0	62^2	63	39	7	1	27	30	13.1	4.60	79	.266	.343	0	—	0	-6	-7	-0	-1.1
Total	11	107	93	.535	320	269	43	7	1	1788^1	1707	880	184	40	716	1065	12.4	3.97	97	.253	.328	22	.100	-9	-30	-20	-0	-3.1

● TIGE STONE Stone, William Arthur b: 9/18/01, Macon, Ga. d: 1/1/60, Jacksonville, Fla. BR/TR, 5'8", 145 lbs. Deb: 8/23/23 ◆

YEAR	TM/L	W	L	PCT	G	GS	CG	SH	SV	IP	H	R	HR	HB	BB	SO	RAT	ERA	ERA+	OAV	OOB	BH	AVG	PB	PR	PR+	PD	TPI
1923	StL-N	0	0	—	1	0	0	0	0	3	5	4	1	0	3	1	24.0	12.00	33	.455	.571	1	1.000	0	-3	-3	0	0.0

● BILL STONEMAN Stoneman, William Hambly b: 4/7/44, Oak Park, Ill. BR/TR, 5'10", 170 lbs. Deb: 7/16/67

YEAR	TM/L	W	L	PCT	G	GS	CG	SH	SV	IP	H	R	HR	HB	BB	SO	RAT	ERA	ERA+	OAV	OOB	BH	AVG	PB	PR	PR+	PD	TPI
1967	Chi-N	2	4	.333	28	2	0	0	4	63	51	24	7	0	22	52	10.4	3.29	108	.223	.291	0	.000	-1	1	2	-1	0.0
1968	Chi-N	0	1	.000	18	0	0	0	0	29^1	35	19	6	1	14	18	15.3	5.52	57	.310	.391	0	.000	-0	-8	-7	-0	-0.5
1969	Mon-N	11	19	.367	42	36	8	5	0	235^2	233	133	26	12	123	185	14.1	4.39	84	.261	.358	4	.055	-3	-21	-18	-1	-2.5
1970	Mon-N	7	15	.318	40	30	5	3	0	207^2	209	118	26	14	109	176	14.4	4.59	90	.263	.361	6	.100	-2	-12	-11	-1	-1.3
1971	Mon-N	17	16	.515	39	39	20	3	0	294^2	243	112	20	5	146	251	12.0	3.15	112	.225	.321	12	.129	-1	11	12	0	1.4
1972	Mon-N★	12	14	.462	36	35	13	4	0	250^2	213	93	15	3	102	171	11.4	2.98	119	.229	.308	6	.080	-4	13	16	0	1.1
1973	Mon-N	4	8	.333	29	17	0	0	1	96^2	120	77	12	6	55	48	16.9	6.80	56	.310	.404	1	.050	-1	-34	-31	0	-3.4
1974	Cal-A	1	8	.111	13	11	0	0	0	58^2	78	41	8	2	31	33	17.0	6.14	56	.322	.404	0	—	0	-16	-18	0	-2.4
Total	8	54	85	.388	245	170	46	15	5	1236^1	1182	617	120	43	602	934	13.3	4.08	90	.253	.344	29	.086	-13	-67	-55	-3	-7.6

● LIL STONER Stoner, Ulysses Simpson Grant b: 2/28/1899, Bowie, Tex. d: 6/26/66, Enid, Okla. BR/TR, 5'9.5", 180 lbs. Deb: 4/15/22

YEAR	TM/L	W	L	PCT	G	GS	CG	SH	SV	IP	H	R	HR	HB	BB	SO	RAT	ERA	ERA+	OAV	OOB	BH	AVG	PB	PR	PR+	PD	TPI
1922	Det-A	4	4	.500	17	7	2	0	0	62^2	76	53	3	3	35	18	16.4	7.04	55	.315	.409	2	.100	-1	-21	-23	1	-2.4
1924	Det-A	11	11	.500	36	25	10	1	0	215^2	271	130	13	5	65	66	14.2	4.72	87	.316	.367	15	.195	1	-12	-15	-1	-1.2
1925	Det-A	10	9	.526	34	18	8	0	1	152	166	79	6	9	53	51	13.5	4.26	101	.283	.352	16	.291	4	2	1	-3	0.2
1926	Det-A	7	10	.412	32	22	7	0	0	159^2	179	115	11	3	63	57	13.8	5.47	74	.291	.359	9	.170	-2	-26	-25	-0	-2.4
1927	Det-A	10	13	.435	38	24	13	0	5	215	251	118	9	3	77	63	13.9	3.98	106	.301	.362	8	.108	-6	4	5	-2	-0.2
1928	Det-A	5	8	.385	36	11	4	0	4	126^1	151	75	16	3	42	29	14.0	4.35	95	.296	.353	7	.179	-1	-4	-3	-2	-0.6
1929	Det-A	3	3	.500	24	3	1	0	4	53	57	37	2	2	31	12	15.3	5.26	82	.288	.390	1	.067	-2	-6	-6	2	-0.6
1930	Pit-N	0	0	—	5	0	0	0	0	5^2	7	3	2	0	3	1	15.9	4.76	105	.318	.400	0	—	0	0	0	0	0.0
1931	Phi-N	0	0	—	7	1	0	0	0	13^2	22	13	0	0	5	2	17.8	6.59	64	.373	.422	0	.000	-1	-4	-3	-0	-0.2
Total	9	50	58	.463	229	111	45	1	14	1003^2	1180	623	62	28	374	299	14.2	4.76	87	.301	.366	58	.172	-7	-66	-68	-5	-7.4

● JIM STOOPS Stoops, James Wellington b: 6/30/72, Edison, N.J. BR/TR, 6'2", 180 lbs. Deb: 9/9/98

YEAR	TM/L	W	L	PCT	G	GS	CG	SH	SV	IP	H	R	HR	HB	BB	SO	RAT	ERA	ERA+	OAV	OOB	BH	AVG	PB	PR	PR+	PD	TPI
1998	Col-N	1	0	1.000	3	0	0	0	0	4	5	1	1	1	3	0	20.3	2.25	230	.385	.529	0	—	0	1	1	0	0.2

● MEL STOTTLEMYRE Stottlemyre, Melvin Leon Jr. b: 12/28/63, Prosser, Wash. BR/TR, 6', 190 lbs. Deb: 7/17/90 F

YEAR	TM/L	W	L	PCT	G	GS	CG	SH	SV	IP	H	R	HR	HB	BB	SO	RAT	ERA	ERA+	OAV	OOB	BH	AVG	PB	PR	PR+	PD	TPI
1990	KC-A	0	1	.000	13	2	0	0	0	31^1	35	18	3	0	12	14	13.5	4.88	79	.280	.343	0	—	0	-3	-4	0	-0.2

● MEL STOTTLEMYRE Stottlemyre, Melvin Leon Sr. b: 11/13/41, Hazleton, Mo. BR/TR, 6'2", 190 lbs. Deb: 8/12/64 FC

YEAR	TM/L	W	L	PCT	G	GS	CG	SH	SV	IP	H	R	HR	HB	BB	SO	RAT	ERA	ERA+	OAV	OOB	BH	AVG	PB	PR	PR+	PD	TPI
1964	*NY-A	9	3	.750	13	12	5	2	0	96	77	26	3	2	35	49	10.7	2.06	176	.219	.294	9	.243	2	17	17	1	2.5
1965	NY-A☆	20	9	.690	37	37	**18**	4	0	**291**	250	99	18	7	88	155	10.7	2.63	129	.233	.295	13	.131	1	27	25	6	3.3
1966	NY-A★	12	20	.375	37	35	9	3	1	251	239	116	18	1	82	146	11.5	3.80	87	.253	.313	11	.138	1	-10	-14	4	-1.1
1967	NY-A	15	15	.500	36	36	10	4	0	255	235	96	20	2	88	151	11.5	2.96	105	.248	.313	8	.098	-3	8	5	6	0.8
1968	NY-A★	21	12	.636	36	36	19	6	0	278^2	243	86	21	3	65	140	10.0	2.45	118	.234	.281	13	.143	2	16	14	2	2.3
1969	NY-A★	20	14	.588	39	39	**24**	3	0	303	267	105	19	6	97	113	11.0	2.82	123	.239	.303	18	.178	5	27	23	8	4.0
1970	NY-A★	15	13	.536	37	37	14	0	0	271	262	110	23	6	84	126	11.7	3.09	114	.255	.315	16	.188	9	19	14	2	2.6
1971	NY-A	16	12	.571	35	35	19	7	0	269^2	234	100	16	4	69	132	10.2	2.87	113	.233	.285	16	.170	2	18	12	3	1.8
1972	NY-A	14	18	.438	36	36	9	7	0	260	250	99	13	4	85	110	11.7	3.22	92	.254	.316	16	.200	3	-4	-8	3	-0.3
1973	NY-A	16	16	.500	38	38	19	4	0	273	259	112	13	5	79	95	11.3	3.07	120	.253	.310	0	—	0	23	19	2	2.3
1974	NY-A	6	7	.462	16	15	6	0	0	113	119	54	7	4	37	40	12.7	3.58	98	.272	.335	0	—	0	1	-1	-1	-0.1
Total	11	164	139	.541	360	356	152	40	1	2661^1	2435	1003	171	44	809	1257	11.1	2.97	112	.245	.304	120	.160	21	140	107	36	18.1

● TODD STOTTLEMYRE Stottlemyre, Todd Vernon b: 5/20/65, Sunnyside, Wash. BL/TR, 6'3", 195 lbs. Deb: 4/6/88 F

YEAR	TM/L	W	L	PCT	G	GS	CG	SH	SV	IP	H	R	HR	HB	BB	SO	RAT	ERA	ERA+	OAV	OOB	BH	AVG	PB	PR	PR+	PD	TPI
1988	Tor-A	4	8	.333	28	16	0	0	0	98	109	70	15	4	46	67	14.6	5.69	69	.283	.366	0	—	0	-19	-19	-0	-2.1
1989	*Tor-A	7	7	.500	27	18	0	0	0	127^2	137	56	11	5	44	63	13.1	3.88	97	.282	.348	0	—	0	0	-1	-1	-0.3
1990	Tor-A	13	17	.433	33	33	4	0	0	203	214	101	18	8	69	115	12.9	4.34	91	.274	.339	0	—	0	-10	-9	1	-1.0
1991	*Tor-A	15	8	.652	34	34	1	0	0	219	194	97	21	12	75	116	11.5	3.78	111	.235	.308	0	—	0	8	10	-0	0.9
1992	*Tor-A	12	11	.522	28	27	6	2	0	174	175	99	20	10	63	98	12.8	4.50	91	.262	.334	0	—	0	-11	-8	-1	-1.0
1993	*Tor-A	11	12	.478	30	28	1	1	0	176^2	204	107	11	3	69	98	14.1	4.84	89	.292	.358	0	—	0	-10	-10	-1	-1.2
1994	Tor-A	7	7	.500	26	19	3	1	1	140^2	149	67	19	7	48	105	13.1	4.22	114	.275	.342	0	—	0	9	9	-1	0.7
1995	Oak-A	14	7	.667	31	31	2	0	0	209^2	228	117	26	6	80	205	13.5	4.55	98	.276	.344	0	.000	-0	4	-2	-1	-0.2
1996	*StL-N	14	11	.560	34	33	5	2	0	223^1	191	100	30	4	93	194	11.6	3.87	108	.231	.312	15	.227	4	9	8	1	1.3
1997	StL-N	12	9	.571	28	28	0	0	0	181	155	86	16	12	65	160	11.5	3.88	107	.231	.310	13	.236	6	7	6	-1	1.1
1998	StL-N	9	9	.500	23	23	3	0	0	161^1	146	74	20	4	51	147	11.2	3.51	119	.240	.303	12	.226	2	13	12	1	1.6
	*Tex-A	5	4	.556	10	10	0	0	0	60^1	68	33	5	0	30	57	14.6	4.33	112	.282	.362	0	—	0	2	3	-1	0.4
1999	*Ari-N	6	3	.667	17	17	0	0	0	101^1	106	51	12	6	40	74	13.5	4.09	112	.268	.344	4	.125	1	5	6	-0	0.5
2000	Ari-N	9	6	.600	18	18	0	0	0	95^1	98	55	18	2	36	76	12.8	4.91	94	.268	.337	6	.194	2	-3	-3	1	-0.1
Total	13	138	119	.537	367	335	25	6	1	2171^1	2174	1113	242	83	809	1575	12.7	4.25	100	.261	.333	50	.210	15	5	3	-2	0.6

● ALLYN STOUT Stout, Allyn McClelland "Fish Hook" b: 10/31/04, Peoria, Ill. d: 12/22/74, Sikeston, Mo. BR/TR, 5'10", 167 lbs. Deb: 5/16/31

YEAR	TM/L	W	L	PCT	G	GS	CG	SH	SV	IP	H	R	HR	HB	BB	SO	RAT	ERA	ERA+	OAV	OOB	BH	AVG	PB	PR	PR+	PD	TPI
1931	StL-N	6	0	1.000	30	3	1	0	3	72^2	87	40	2	1	34	40	15.1	4.21	93	.305	.381	2	.105	-1	-3	-2	1	-0.2
1932	StL-N	4	5	.444	36	3	1	0	1	73^2	87	40	5	4	28	32	14.5	4.40	89	.305	.375	2	.100	-1	-4	-4	1	-0.5
1933	StL-N	0	0	—	1	0	0	0	0	2	1	0	0	0	1	1	9.0	0.00	—	.167	.286	0	—	0	1	1	0	0.1
	Cin-N	2	3	.400	23	5	2	0	0	71^1	85	36	3	0	26	29	14.0	3.79	90	.295	.354	4	.182	-0	-4	-3	-1	-0.3
	Yr	2	3	.400	24	5	2	0	0	73^1	86	36	3	0	27	30	13.9	3.68	92	.293	.352	4	.182	-0	-3	-2	-1	-0.2
1934	Cin-N	6	8	.429	41	16	4	0	1	140^2	170	85	10	4	47	51	14.1	4.86	84	.297	.354	8	.186	0	-13	-12	-0	-1.1
1935	NY-N	1	4	.200	40	2	0	0	5	88	99	58	7	4	37	29	14.3	4.91	79	.289	.365	2	.133	0	-9	-11	-1	-0.7

YEAR	TM/L	W	L	PCT	G	GS	CG	SH	SV	IP	H	R	HR	HB	BB	SO	RAT	ERA	ERA+	OAV	OOB	BH	AVG	PB	PR	PR+	PD	TPI
1943	Bos-N	1	0	1.000	9	0	0	0	1	9^1	17	12	1	0	4	3	20.3	6.75	51	.378	.429	0	.000	-0	-3	-3	-0	-0.5
Total	6	20	20	.500	180	29	8	0	11	457^2	546	271	28	13	177	185	14.5	4.54	85	.299	.365	18	.149	-3	-35	-34	-1	-3.2
● JESSE STOVALL Stovall, Jesse Cramer "Scout" b: 7/24/1875, Leeds, Mo. d: 7/12/55, San Diego, Cal. BL/TR, 6', 175 lbs. Deb: 8/31/03 F																												
1903	Cle-A	5	1	.833	6	6	6	2	0	57	44	17	0	3	21	12	10.7	2.05	139	.213	.294	1	.045	-2	6	5	-1	0.2
1904	Det-A	2	13	.133	22	17	13	1	0	146^2	170	97	3	16	45	41	14.2	4.42	58	.291	.358	11	.196	0	-30	-31	0	-2.9
Total	2	7	14	.333	28	23	19	3	0	203^2	214	114	3	19	66	53	13.2	3.76	70	.270	.341	12	.154	-2	-24	-26	-0	-2.7
● HARRY STOVEY Stovey, Harry Duffield (b: Harry Duffield Stowe) b: 12/20/1856, Philadelphia, Pa. d: 9/20/37, New Bedford, Mass BR/TR, 5'11.5", 175 lbs. Deb: 5/1/1880 M◆																												
1880	Wor-N	0	0	—	2	0	0	0	0	6	8	4	0		3	3	16.5	4.50	58	.308	.379	94	.265	0	-1	-1	-0	-0.1
1883	Phi-a	0	0	—	1	0	0	0	0	3	5	3	0		0	4	15.0	9.00	39	.357	.357	128	.304	0	-2	-2	-0	-0.1
1886	Phi-a	0	0	—	1	0	0	0	0	0^1	2	2	0	0	0	0	54.0	27.00	13	.667	.667	144	.294	0	-1	-1	0	0.0
Total	3	0	0	—	4	0	0	0	0	9^1	15	9	0	0	3	7	17.4	6.75	44	.349	.391	1827	.295	1	-4	-4	-0	-0.2
● HAL STOWE Stowe, Harold Rudolph b: 8/29/37, Gastonia, N.C. BL/TL, 6', 170 lbs. Deb: 9/30/60																												
1960	NY-A	0	0	—	1	0	0	0	0	1	0	1	0	0	1	0	9.0	9.00	40	.000	.500	0	—	0	-1	-1	-0	0.0
● MIKE STRAHLER Strahler, Michael Wayne b: 3/14/47, Chicago, Ill. BR/TR, 6'4", 180 lbs. Deb: 9/12/70																												
1970	LA-N	1	1	.500	6	0	0	0	1	18^2	13	6	1	0	10	11	11.1	1.45	265	.194	.299	2	.250	0	5	5	0	0.6
1971	LA-N	0	0	—	6	0	0	0	0	12^2	10	4	1	0	8	7	12.8	2.84	114	.217	.333	0	.000	-0	1	1	-0	0.0
1972	LA-N	1	2	.333	19	2	1	0	0	47	42	25	5	1	22	25	12.4	3.26	102	.237	.325	2	.182	1	1	0	-0	0.1
1973	Det-A	4	5	.444	22	11	1	0	0	80^1	84	45	7	1	39	37	13.9	4.37	94	.273	.356	0	—	0	-5	-2	-1	-0.3
Total	4	6	8	.429	53	13	2	0	1	158^2	149	80	14	2	79	80	13.0	3.57	105	.249	.339	4	.200	1	2	3	-1	0.4
● DICK STRAHS Strahs, Richard Bernard b: 12/4/23, Evanston, Ill. d: 5/26/88, Las Vegas, Nev. BL/TR, 6', 192 lbs. Deb: 7/24/54																												
1954	Chi-A	0	0	—	9	0	0	0	1	14^1	16	10	0	0	8	8	15.1	5.65	66	.271	.358	0	.000	-0	-3	-3	0	-0.1
● LES STRAKER Straker, Lester Paul (Bolnalda) b: 10/10/59, Ciudad Bolivar, Venezuela BR/TR, 6'1", 193 lbs. Deb: 4/11/87																												
1987	*Min-A	8	10	.444	31	26	1	0	0	154^1	150	79	24	2	59	76	12.3	4.37	106	.257	.328	0	—	0	2	4	-2	0.3
1988	Min-A	2	5	.286	16	14	1	1	1	82^2	86	39	8	0	25	23	12.1	3.92	104	.276	.329	0	—	0	1	1	0	0.2
Total	2	10	15	.400	47	40	2	1	1	237	236	118	32	2	84	99	12.2	4.22	105	.264	.328	0	—	0	2	6	-1	0.5
● BOB STRAMPE Strampe, Robert Edwin b: 6/13/50, Janesville, Wis. BB/TR, 6'1", 185 lbs. Deb: 5/10/72																												
1972	Det-A	0	0	—	7	0	0	0	0	4^2	6	6	0	0	7	4	25.1	11.57	27	.300	.481	0	—	0	-4	-4	-0	-0.3
● PAUL STRAND Strand, Paul Edward b: 12/19/1893, Carbonado, Wash. d: 7/2/74, Salt Lake City, Utah BR/TL, 6'0.5", 190 lbs. Deb: 5/15/13 ◆																												
1913	Bos-N	0	0	—	7	0	0	0	0	17	22	9	1	0	12	6	18.0	2.12	155	.393	.500	1	.167	-0	2	2	0	0.1
1914	Bos-N	6	2	.750	16	3	1	0	0	55^1	47	23	1	1	23	33	11.5	2.44	113	.235	.317	8	.333	2	2	2	-0	0.5
1915	Bos-N	1	1	.500	6	2	2	0	1	22^2	26	12	0	0	3	13	11.5	2.38	109	.295	.319	2	.091	-0	1	1	-1	-0.1
Total	3	7	3	.700	29	5	3	0	1	95	95	44	2	1	38	52	12.7	2.37	119	.276	.350	49	.224	2	5	5	-1	0.5
● SCOTT STRATTON Stratton, C. Scott b: 10/2/1869, Campbellsburg, Ky. d: 3/8/39, Louisville, Ky. BL/TR, 6', 180 lbs. Deb: 4/21/1888 ◆																												
1888	Lou-a	10	17	.370	33	28	28	2	0	269^2	287	196	7	15	53	97	11.8	3.64	85	.263	.306	64	.257	5	-17	-17	-1	-1.0
1889	Lou-a	3	13	.188	19	17	13	0	1	133^2	157	126	6	7	42	42	13.9	3.23	119	.284	.342	66	.288	4	9	9	2	1.4
1890	*Lou-a	34	14	**.708**	50	49	44	4	0	431	398	186	3	13	61	207	**9.9**	**2.36**	**163**	.238	**.270**	61	.323	16	**72**	**72**	6	**9.0**
1891	Pit-N	0	2	.000	2	2	2	0	0	18^1	16	9	0	0	5	5	10.3	2.45	134	.225	.276	1	.125	-1	2	2	1	0.2
	Lou-a	6	13	.316	20	20	20	1	0	172	204	112	10	7	34	52	12.8	4.08	89	.285	.324	27	.235	1	-7	-8	3	-0.4
1892	Lou-N	21	19	.525	42	40	39	2	0	351^2	342	188	1	9	70	93	10.8	2.92	105	.245	.285	56	.256	10	14	6	2	1.8
1893	Lou-N	12	23	.343	37	35	34	1	0	314^2	445	253	8	8	100	43	15.8	5.43	81	.323	.373	50	.226	3	-27	-38	6	-2.3
1894	Lou-N	1	5	.167	7	5	4	0	0	43	72	50	3	3	13	3	18.4	8.37	61	.367	.415	12	.324	2	-15	-16	0	-1.3
	Chi-N	8	5	.615	16	13	12	0	0	128^1	205	131	5	3	42	24	17.5	5.82	97	.357	.403	37	.374	7	-7	-3	0	0.4
	Yr	9	10	.474	23	18	16	0	0	171^1	277	181	8	6	55	27	17.8	6.46	85	.359	.406	49	.360	9	-22	-18	1	-0.9
1895	Chi-N	2	3	.400	5	5	3	0	0	30	51	42	1	4	14	4	20.7	9.60	53	.370	.442	7	.292	1	-16	-14	1	-1.4
Total	8	97	114	.460	231	214	199	10	1	1892^1	2177	1293	44	69	434	570	12.7	3.86	99	.280	.323	381	.274	48	9	-8	20	6.4
● MONTY STRATTON Stratton, Monty Franklin Pierce "Gander" b: 5/21/12, Celeste, Tex. d: 9/29/82, Greenville, Tex. BR/TR, 6'5", 180 lbs. Deb: 6/2/34 C																												
1934	Chi-A	0	0	—	1	0	0	0	0	3^1	4	2	0	0	1	0	13.5	5.40	88	.333	.385	0	.000	-0	-0	-0	-0	-0.1
1935	Chi-A	1	2	.333	5	5	2	0	0	38	40	17	0	2	9	8	12.1	4.03	115	.274	.325	2	.143	-1	2	2	0	0.1
1936	Chi-A	5	7	.417	16	14	3	0	0	95	117	66	8	1	46	37	15.5	5.21	100	.305	.381	8	.216	1	-2	-0	2	0.2
1937	Chi-A†	15	5	.750	22	21	14	5	0	164^2	142	55	6	2	37	69	**9.9**	2.40	**191**	.234	**.280**	12	.200	-0	41	40	1	4.6
1938	Chi-A	15	9	.625	26	22	17	0	2	186^1	186	95	18	7	56	82	12.0	4.01	122	.255	.315	21	.266	5	16	18	0	2.5
Total	5	36	23	.610	70	62	36	5	2	487^1	489	235	32	12	149	196	12.0	3.71	130	.261	.319	43	.224	5	56	60	3	7.3
● ED STRATTON Stratton, William Edward b: Baltimore, Md. Deb: 5/14/1873																												
1873	Mar-n	0	3	.000	3	3	3	0	0	27	75	75	1		1	0	25.3	8.33	39	.412	.415	2	.125	-1	-15	-15		-1.0
● JOE STRAUSS Strauss, Joseph "Dutch" or "The Socker" (b: Joseph Strasser) b: 11/16/1858, Cincinnati, Ohio d: 6/24/06, Cincinnati, Ohio BR/TR, Deb: 7/27/1884 ◆																												
1886	Lou-a	0	0	—	2	0	0	0	1	4	6	4	0	0	3	0	20.3	4.50	81	.231	.310	64	.215	-0	-0	-0	-0	0.0
● OSCAR STREIT Streit, Oscar William b: 7/7/1873, Florence, Ala. d: 10/10/35, Birmingham, Ala. BL/TL, 6'5", 190 lbs. Deb: 4/21/1899																												
1899	Bos-N	1	0	1.000	2	1	1	0	0	14^2	15	17	1	2	15	0	19.6	6.75	62	.263	.432	0	.000	-1	-5	-4	0	-0.3
1902	Cle-A	0	7	.000	8	7	4	0	0	51^2	72	54	3	3	25	10	17.4	5.23	66	.330	.407	4	.211	1	-9	-11	-1	-1.1
Total	2	1	7	.125	10	8	5	0	0	66^1	87	71	4	5	40	10	17.9	5.56	65	.316	.412	4	.154	-0	-14	-15	-1	-1.4
● ED STRELECKI Strelecki, Edward Harold b: 4/10/05, Newark, N.J. d: 1/9/68, Newark, N.J. BR/TR, 5'11.5", 180 lbs. Deb: 4/16/28																												
1928	StL-A	0	2	.000	22	2	1	0	1	50^1	49	27	4	1	17	8	12.0	4.29	98	.269	.335	2	.200	0	-1	-0	-0	0.0
1929	StL-A	1	1	.500	7	0	0	0	0	11	12	8	1	1	6	2	15.5	4.91	90	.279	.380	0	.000	-0	-1	-1	-0	-0.1
1931	Cin-N	0	0	—	13	0	0	0	0	24^1	37	25	2	3	9	3	18.1	9.25	40	.394	.462	1	.200	0	-15	-15	0	-0.7
Total	3	1	3	.250	42	2	1	0	1	85^2	98	60	7	5	32	13	14.2	5.78	71	.307	.379	3	.176	0	-17	-16	1	-0.8
● PHIL STREMMEL Stremmel, Philip b: 4/16/1880, Zanesville, Ohio d: 12/26/47, Chicago, Ill. BR/TR, 6', 175 lbs. Deb: 9/16/09																												
1909	StL-A	0	2	.000	2	2	2	0	0	18	20	9	0	1	4	6	12.5	4.50	54	.308	.357	0	.000	-1	-4	-4	0	-0.5
1910	StL-A	0	2	.000	5	2	2	0	0	29	31	19	0	0	16	7	14.6	3.72	66	.287	.379	1	.125	-0	-4	-4	2	-0.1
Total	2	0	4	.000	7	4	4	0	0	47	51	28	0	1	20	13	13.8	4.02	61	.295	.371	1	.071	-1	-8	-8	2	-0.6
● CUB STRICKER Stricker, John A. (b: John A. Streaker) b: 2/15/1860, Philadelphia, Pa. d: 11/19/37, Philadelphia, Pa. BR/TR, 5'3", 138 lbs. Deb: 5/2/1882 M◆																												
1882	Phi-a	1	0	1.000	2	0	0	0	0	7	3	1	0		1	2	5.1	1.29	232	.120	.154	59	.217	-0	1	1	-0	0.1
1884	Phi-a	0	0	—	1	0	0	0	0	3	6	2	0	0	1	1	21.0	6.00	56	.333	.368	92	.231	0	-1	-1	-0	-0.1
1887	Cle-a	0	0	—	3	0	0	0	1	5^2	12	5	0	0	7	2	19.1	3.18	137	.429	.429	194	.330	0	1	1	0	0.1
1888	Cle-a	1	0	1.000	2	0	0	0	0	12	16	6	0	1	2	5	14.3	4.50	69	.308	.345	115	.233	0	-2	-2	-0	-0.1
Total	4	2	0	1.000	8	0	0	0	1	27^2	37	14	0	1	11	10	13.7	3.58	94	.301	.328	1159	.247	1	-1	-1	-0	0.0
● JIM STRICKLAND Strickland, James Michael b: 6/12/46, Los Angeles, Cal. BL/TL, 6', 175 lbs. Deb: 5/19/71																												
1971	Min-A	1	0	1.000	24	0	0	0	1	31^1	20	14	2	2	18	21	11.5	1.44	248	.183	.310	0	.000	0	7	7	0	0.4
1972	Min-A	3	1	.750	25	0	0	0	3	36	28	16	7	0	19	30	11.8	2.50	129	.214	.313	1	.333	1	2	3	0	0.5
1973	Min-A	0	1	.000	7	0	0	0	0	5^1	11	8	0	0	5	6	27.0	11.81	34	.440	.533	0	—	0	-5	-4	0	-0.7
1975	Cle-A	0	0	—	4	0	0	0	1	4^2	4	1	0	1	2	3	13.5	1.93	197	.222	.333	0	—	0	1	1	-0	0.0
Total	4	4	2	.667	60	0	0	0	5	77^1	63	39	9	3	44	60	12.8	2.68	129	.223	.333	1	.250	1	6	6	0	0.2
● SCOTT STRICKLAND Strickland, Scott Michael b: 4/26/76, Houston, Tex. BR/TR, 5'11", 180 lbs. Deb: 8/14/99																												
1999	Mon-N	0	1	.000	17	0	0	0	0	18	15	10	3	0	11	23	13.0	4.50	100	.231	.342	0	—	0	0	-0	0	0.0

YEAR	TM/L	W	L	PCT	G	GS	CG	SH	SV	IP	H	R	HR	HB	BB	SO	RAT	ERA	ERA+	OAV	OOB	BH	AVG	PB	PR	PR+	PD	TPI
2000	Mon-N	4	3	.571	49	0	0	0	9	48	38	18	3	1	16	48	10.3	3.00	157	.215	.284	0	.000	-0	9	9	0	1.4
Total	2	4	4	.500	66	0	0	0	9	66	53	28	6	1	27	71	11.0	3.41	137	.219	.300	0	.000	-0	9	9	1	1.4
● **BILL STRICKLAND**	Strickland, William Goss b: 3/29/08, Nashville, Ga. BR/TR, 6′2″, 170 lbs. Deb: 9/16/37																											
1937	StL-A	0	0	—	9	0	0	0	0	21^1	28	18	2	2	15	6	19.0	5.91	82	.341	.455	1	.167	-0	-3	-2	-0	-0.2
● **ELMER STRICKLETT**	Stricklett, Elmer Griffin "Spitball" b: 8/29/1876, Glasco, Kan. d: 6/7/64, Santa Cruz, Cal. BR/TR, 5′6″, 140 lbs. Deb: 4/22/04																											
1904	Chi-A	0	1	.000	1	1	0	0	0	7	12	10	0	0	2	3	18.0	10.29	24	.375	.412	0	.000	-0	-6	-6	0	-0.7
1905	Bro-N	9	18	.333	33	28	25	1	1	237^1	259	143	0	14	71	77	13.0	3.34	87	.282	.343	13	.148	-1	-9	-12	9	-0.5
1906	Bro-N	14	18	.438	41	35	28	5	5	291^2	273	128	2	5	77	88	11.0	2.72	93	.253	.306	20	.206	5	-3	-6	9	0.9
1907	Bro-N	12	14	.462	29	26	25	4	0	229^2	211	85	1	8	65	69	11.1	2.27	103	.255	.315	12	.148	1	5	2	7	1.1
Total	4	35	51	.407	104	90	78	10	6	765^2	755	366	3	27	215	237	11.7	2.84	91	.264	.322	45	.167	4	-12	-23	25	0.8
● **JOHN STRIKE**	Strike, John b: 1865, Pennsylvania Deb: 9/24/1886																											
1886	Phi-N	1	1	.500	2	2	1	0	0	15	19	10	1		7	11	15.6	4.80	69	.311	.382	0	.000	-1	-2	-3	-1	-0.4
● **JAKE STRIKER**	Striker, Wilbur Scott b: 10/23/33, New Washington, O. BL/TL, 6′2″, 200 lbs. Deb: 9/25/59																											
1959	Cle-A	1	0	1.000	1	1	0	0	0	6^2	8	2	0	0	4	5	16.2	2.70	136	.296	.387	0	.000	1	1	1	0	0.2
1960	Chi-A	0	0	—	2	0	0	0	0	3^2	5	3	1	1	1	1	17.2	4.91	77	.357	.438	0	—	0	-0	-0	-0	0.0
Total	2	1	0	1.000	3	1	0	0	0	10^1	13	5	1	1	5	6	16.5	3.48	107	.317	.404	0	.000	1	0	0	-0	0.2
● **NICK STRINCEVICH**	Strincevich, Nicholas "Jumbo" b: 3/1/15, Gary, Ind. BR/TR, 6′1″, 180 lbs. Deb: 4/23/40																											
1940	Bos-N	4	8	.333	32	14	5	0	1	128^2	142	89	17	8	63	54	14.9	5.53	67	.278	.367	5	.116	-2	-24	-27	-2	-2.6
1941	Bos-N	0	0	—	3	0	0	0	0	3^1	7	5	0	1	6	1	37.8	10.80	33	.412	.583	0	—	0	-3	-3	0	-0.1
	Pit-N	1	2	.333	12	3	0	0	0	31	35	23	4	1	13	12	14.2	5.23	69	.280	.353	3	.429	1	-5	-6	0	-0.4
	Yr	1	2	.333	15	3	0	0	0	34^1	42	28	4	2	19	13	16.5	5.77	63	.296	.387	3	.429	1	-8	-8	0	-0.5
1942	Pit-N	0	0	—	7	1	0	0	0	22^1	19	7	2	1	9	10	11.7	2.82	120	.229	.312	0	.000	-1	1	1	-0	0.0
1944	Pit-N	14	7	.667	40	26	11	0	2	190	190	86	5	4	37	47	10.9	3.08	121	.257	.296	9	.158	-1	11	13	5	1.8
1945	Pit-N	16	10	.615	36	29	18	1	2	228^1	235	94	7	3	49	74	11.3	3.31	119	.260	.301	17	.202	0	12	16	2	1.5
1946	Pit-N	10	15	.400	32	22	11	3	1	176	185	77	7	4	44	49	11.9	3.58	98	.268	.316	8	.154	1	-3	-1	-2	-0.3
1947	Pit-N	1	6	.143	32	7	1	0	0	89	111	59	9	2	37	22	15.2	5.26	80	.316	.385	1	.048	-2	-12	-10	-0	-0.8
1948	Pit-N	0	0	—	3	0	0	0	0	4^1	8	4	0	0	2	1	20.8	8.31	49	.444	.500	0	—	0	-2	-2	0	-0.1
	Phi-N	0	1	.000	6	1	0	0	0	16^2	26	18	1	0	10	4	19.4	9.18	43	.347	.424	0	.000	-1	-10	-10	-1	-0.6
	Yr	0	1	.000	9	1	0	0	0	21	34	22	1	0	12	5	19.7	9.00	44	.366	.438	0	.000	-1	-12	-12	-0	-0.7
Total	8	46	49	.484	203	103	46	4	6	889^2	958	462	52	24	270	274	12.7	4.05	93	.273	.329	43	.158	-4	-34	-26	-0	-1.6
● **JOHN STROHMAYER**	Strohmayer, John Emery b: 10/13/46, Belle Fourche, S.D. BR/TR, 6′1″, 181 lbs. Deb: 4/29/70																											
1970	Mon-N	3	1	.750	42	0	0	0	0	76	85	48	7	2	39	74	14.9	4.86	85	.279	.364	1	.167	-0	-7	-6	-0	-0.3
1971	Mon-N	7	5	.583	27	14	2	0	1	114	124	63	16	4	31	56	12.6	4.34	81	.281	.333	8	.229	1	-11	-10	-1	-1.0
1972	Mon-N	1	2	.333	48	0	0	0	3	76^2	73	32	6	1	31	50	12.3	3.52	101	.256	.331	0	.000	-0	-1	0	1	0.1
1973	Mon-N	0	1	.000	17	3	0	0	0	34^2	34	20	4	1	22	15	14.8	5.19	74	.260	.370	1	.200	0	-6	-5	-0	-0.3
	NY-N	0	0	—	7	0	0	0	0	10	13	10	2	0	4	5	15.3	8.10	45	.310	.370	0	—	0	-5	-5	0	-0.2
	Yr	0	1	.000	24	3	0	0	0	44^2	47	30	6	1	26	20	14.9	5.84	65	.272	.370	1	.200	0	-11	-10	-0	-0.5
1974	NY-N	0	0	—	1	0	0	0	0	1	0	0	0	0	1	0	9.0	0.00	—	.000	.250	0	—	0	0	0	0	0.0
Total	5	11	9	.550	142	17	2	0	4	312^1	329	173	35	8	128	200	13.4	4.47	83	.272	.346	10	.200	1	-29	-25	-0	-1.7
● **BRENT STROM**	Strom, Brent Terry b: 10/14/48, San Diego, Cal. BR/TL, 6′3″, 190 lbs. Deb: 7/31/72 C																											
1972	NY-N	0	3	.000	11	5	0	0	0	30^1	34	25	7	0	15	20	14.5	6.82	49	.296	.377	0	.000	-1	-11	-12	-1	-1.2
1973	Cle-A	2	10	.167	27	18	2	0	0	123	134	73	18	3	47	91	13.5	4.61	85	.278	.346	0	—	0	-11	-9	1	-0.7
1975	SD-N	8	8	.500	18	16	6	2	0	120^1	103	42	6	2	33	56	10.3	2.54	137	.233	.289	3	.100	-1	15	13	0	1.7
1976	SD-N	12	16	.429	36	33	8	1	0	210^2	188	100	15	2	73	103	11.2	3.29	100	.239	.305	4	.063	-2	5	-0	0	-0.3
1977	SD-N	0	2	.000	8	3	0	0	0	16^2	23	25	5	0	12	8	18.9	12.42	29	.329	.427	1	.333	0	-16	-18	-0	-1.7
Total	5	22	39	.361	100	75	16	3	0	501	482	265	51	7	180	278	12.0	3.95	88	.254	.321	8	.078	-3	-18	-26	0	-2.2
● **FLOYD STROMME**	Stromme, Floyd Marvin "Rock" b: 8/1/16, Cooperstown, N.Dak. d: 2/7/93, Wenatchee, Wash. BR/TR, 5′11″, 170 lbs. Deb: 7/5/39																											
1939	Cle-A	0	1	.000	5	0	0	0	0	13	13	8	1	0	13	4	18.0	4.85	91	.265	.419	1	.333	0	-0	-1	-0	0.0
● **JOE STRONG**	Strong, Joseph Benjamin b: 9/9/62, Fairfield, Cal. BB/TR, 6′, 200 lbs. Deb: 5/11/2000																											
2000	Fla-N	1	1	.500	18	0	0	0	1	19^2	26	16	3	2	12	18	18.3	7.32	60	.325	.426	0	.000	-0	-6	-7	0	-0.6
● **SAILOR STROUD**	Stroud, Ralph Vivian b: 5/15/1885, Ironia, N.J. d: 4/11/70, Stockton, Cal. BR/TR, 6′, 160 lbs. Deb: 4/29/10																											
1910	Det-A	5	9	.357	28	15	7	3	1	130^1	123	54	9	7	41	63	11.8	3.25	81	.257	.325	1	.026	-4	-11	-9	-4	-1.7
1915	NY-N	12	9	.571	32	22	8	0	1	184	194	76	3	6	35	62	11.5	2.79	92	.281	.321	9	.161	-1	-1	-5	0	-0.7
1916	NY-N	3	2	.600	10	4	0	0	1	46^2	47	18	1	1	9	16	11.0	2.70	90	.266	.305	1	.071	-1	-0	-1	-0	-0.3
Total	3	20	20	.500	70	41	15	3	3	361	364	148	13	14	85	141	11.5	2.94	88	.271	.321	11	.101	-6	-12	-15	-4	-2.7
● **STEAMBOAT STRUSS**	Struss, Clarence Herbert b: 2/24/09, Riverdale, Ill. d: 9/12/85, Grand Rapids, Mich. BR/TR, 5′11″, 163 lbs. Deb: 9/30/34																											
1934	Pit-N	0	1	.000	1	1	0	0	0	7	7	6	0	0	6	3	16.7	6.43	64	.250	.382	1	.333	0	-2	-2	0	-0.2
● **DUTCH STRYKER**	Stryker, Sterling Alpa b: 7/29/1895, Atlantic Highlands, N.J. d: 11/5/64, Red Bank, N.J. BR/TR, 5′11.5″, 180 lbs. Deb: 4/16/24																											
1924	Bos-N	3	8	.273	20	10	2	0	0	73^1	90	56	4	1	22	22	13.9	6.01	64	.314	.365	5	.217	-0	-17	-18	2	-2.1
1926	Bro-N	0	0	—	2	0	0	0	0	2	8	8	0	0	1	0	40.5	27.00	14	.571	.600	0	—	0	-5	-5	-0	-0.2
Total	2	3	8	.273	22	10	2	0	0	75^1	98	64	4	1	23	22	14.6	6.57	58	.326	.375	5	.217	-0	-23	-23	2	-2.3
● **JOHNNY STUART**	Stuart, John Davis "Stud" b: 4/27/01, Clinton, Tenn. d: 5/13/70, Charleston, W.Va. BR/TR, 5′11″, 170 lbs. Deb: 7/27/22																											
1922	StL-N	0	0	—	2	1	0	0	0	2	2	4	0	1	2	1	22.5	9.00	43	.222	.417	0	—	0	-1	-1	-0	-0.1
1923	StL-N	9	5	.643	37	10	7	1	3	149^2	139	82	11	9	70	55	13.1	4.27	91	.252	.345	14	.246	1	-4	-6	-1	-0.6
1924	StL-N	9	11	.450	28	22	13	0	0	159	167	100	12	5	60	54	13.1	4.75	80	.273	.343	11	.204	-1	-16	-18	-3	-2.3
1925	StL-N	2	2	.500	15	1	1	0	0	47	52	41	6	2	24	14	14.9	6.13	71	.278	.366	4	.250	1	-10	-9	-0	-0.6
Total	4	20	18	.526	82	34	21	1	3	357^2	360	227	29	17	156	124	13.4	4.76	82	.265	.348	29	.228	1	-31	-35	-5	-3.6
● **MARLIN STUART**	Stuart, Marlin Henry b: 8/8/18, Paragould, Ark. d: 6/16/94, Paragould, Ark. BL/TR, 6′2″, 185 lbs. Deb: 4/26/49																											
1949	Det-A	0	2	.000	14	2	0	0	0	29^2	39	33	3	0	35	14	22.4	9.10	46	.348	.503	2	.333	1	-16	-16	0	-0.9
1950	Det-A	3	1	.750	19	1	0	0	2	43^2	59	32	6	1	22	19	16.9	5.56	84	.330	.406	1	.083	-1	-5	-4	0	-0.4
1951	Det-A	4	6	.400	29	15	5	0	1	124	119	60	9	7	71	46	14.3	3.77	111	.258	.365	10	.233	1	5	5	0	0.6
1952	Det-A	3	2	.600	30	9	2	0	1	91^1	91	60	8	3	48	32	14.0	4.93	77	.265	.360	2	.087	-1	-13	-11	-0	-0.7
	StL-A	1	2	.333	12	2	0	0	1	26	26	18	3	0	9	13	12.1	4.15	94	.260	.321	0	.000	-1	-1	-1	-1	-0.2
	Yr	4	4	.500	42	11	2	0	2	117^1	117	78	11	3	57	45	13.6	4.76	81	.264	.352	2	.069	-2	-14	-12	-1	-0.9
1953	StL-A	8	2	.800	60	2	0	0	7	114^1	136	62	6	1	44	46	14.2	3.94	107	.300	.363	5	.192	-1	1	3	-0	0.2
1954	Bal-A	1	2	.333	22	0	0	0	2	38^1	46	23	2	2	15	13	14.8	4.46	80	.303	.373	0	.000	-0	-3	-4	0	-0.3
	NY-A	3	0	1.000	10	0	0	0	1	18^1	28	12	0	0	12	2	19.6	5.40	64	.350	.435	2	.333	0	-3	-4	0	-0.6
	Yr	4	2	.667	32	0	0	0	3	56^2	74	35	2	2	27	15	16.4	4.76	74	.319	.395	2	.222	0	-7	-8	1	-0.9
Total	6	23	17	.575	196	31	7	0	15	485^2	544	300	37	14	256	185	15.1	4.65	87	.289	.378	22	.176	-1	-36	-31	-0	-2.3
● **GEORGE STUELAND**	Stueland, George Anton b: 3/2/1899, Algona, Iowa d: 9/9/64, Onawa, Iowa BB/TR, 6′1.5″, 174 lbs. Deb: 9/15/21																											
1921	Chi-N	0	1	.000	2	1	0	0	0	11	11	7	0	0	7	4	14.7	5.73	67	.282	.391	1	.333	0	-2	-2	0	-0.2
1922	Chi-N	9	4	.692	35	11	4	0	0	113	129	81	9	5	49	44	14.6	5.81	72	.292	.369	4	.129	-2	-22	-20	-1	-2.2
1923	Chi-N	0	1	.000	6	0	0	0	0	8	11	7	0	0	5	2	18.0	5.63	71	.478	.571	0	—	0	-1	-1	0	-0.1
1925	Chi-N	0	0	—	2	0	0	0	0	3	2	1	0	0	3	2	15.0	3.00	144	.182	.357	1	1.000	0	0	0	0	0.1
Total	4	9	6	.600	45	12	4	0	0	135	153	96	9	5	64	52	14.8	5.73	73	.297	.380	6	.171	-1	-25	-23	-1	-2.4
● **PAUL STUFFEL**	Stuffel, Paul Harrington "Stu" b: 3/22/27, Canton, Ohio BR/TR, 6′2″, 185 lbs. Deb: 9/16/50																											
1950	Phi-N	0	0	—	3	0	0	0	0	5	4	1	0	1	1	3	10.8	1.80	225	.211	.286	0	—	0	1	1	0	0.1

YEAR TM/L	W	L	PCT	G	GS	CG	SH	SV	IP	H	R	HR	HB	BB	SO	RAT	ERA	ERA+	OAV	OOB	BH	AVG	PB	PR	PR+	PD	TPI
1952 Phi-N	1	0	1.000	2	1	0	0	0	6	5	3	0	0	7	3	18.0	3.00	122	.217	.400	0	.000	-0	0	0	0	0.1
1953 Phi-N	0	0	—	2	0	0	0	0	0	0	0	0	4	—	—	∞	—	—	1.000	98	—	0	-4	-4	0		-0.4
Total 3	1	0	1.000	7	1	0	0	0	11	9	8	0	1	12	6	18.0	5.73	67	.214	.400	0	.000	-0	-2	-2	0	-0.2
● EVERETT STULL Stull, Everett James b: 8/24/71, Fort Riley, Kan. BR/TR, 6'3", 200 lbs. Deb: 4/14/97																											
1997 Mon-N	0	1	.000	3	0	0	0	0	3^1	7	7	1	0	4	2	29.7	16.20	26	.438	.550	0	—	0	-4	-4	-0	-0.8
1999 Atl-N	0	0	—	1	0	0	0	0	0^2	2	3	0	0	2	0	54.0	13.50	33	.500	.667	0	—	0	-1	-1	0	0.0
2000 Mil-N	2	3	.400	20	4	0	0	0	43^1	41	30	7	4	30	33	15.6	5.82	78	.256	.387	0	.000	-1	-6	-6	0	-0.6
Total 3	2	4	.333	24	4	0	0	0	47^1	50	40	8	4	36	35	17.1	6.65	68	.278	.409	0	.000	-1	-11	-11	0	-1.4
● GEORGE STULTZ Stultz, George Irvin b: 6/30/1873, Louisville, Ky. d: 3/19/55, Louisville, Ky. 5'10", 150 lbs. Deb: 9/22/1894																											
1894 Bos-N	1	0	1.000	1	1	1	0	0	9	4	2	0	0	5	1	9.0	0.00	—	.133	.257	1	.333	-0	5	5	1	0.6
● JIM STUMP Stump, James Gilbert b: 2/10/32, Lansing, Mich. BR/TR, 6', 188 lbs. Deb: 8/29/57																											
1957 Det-A	1	0	1.000	6	0	0	0	0	13^1	11	4	0	0	8	2	12.8	2.03	190	.220	.328	1	.500	0	3	3	0	0.2
1959 Det-A	0	0	—	5	0	0	0	0	11^1	12	3	1	0	4	6	12.7	2.38	170	.279	.340	1	1.000	1	2	2	0	0.2
Total 2	1	0	1.000	11	0	0	0	0	24^2	23	7	1	0	12	8	12.8	2.19	180	.247	.333	2	.667	1	4	5	0	0.4
● JOHN STUPER Stuper, John Anton b: 5/9/57, Butler, Pa. BR/TR, 6'2", 200 lbs. Deb: 6/1/82																											
1982 *StL-N	9	7	.563	23	21	2	0	0	136^2	137	55	8	0	55	53	12.6	3.36	108	.266	.337	5	.119	-1	4	4	-3	0.1
1983 StL-N	12	11	.522	40	30	6	1	1	198	202	95	15	2	71	81	12.5	3.68	99	.265	.329	8	.136	-1	-1	-1	-1	-0.3
1984 StL-N	3	5	.375	15	12	0	0	0	61^1	73	39	4	2	20	19	13.9	5.28	66	.297	.354	1	.063	-1	-12	-13	0	-1.5
1985 Cin-N	8	5	.615	33	13	1	0	0	99	116	60	8	0	37	38	13.9	4.55	83	.303	.364	1	.059	-0	-10	-8	0	-1.0
Total 4	32	28	.533	111	76	9	1	1	495	528	249	35	4	183	191	13.0	3.96	92	.277	.341	15	.112	-3	-19	-18	-4	-2.7
● TOM STURDIVANT Sturdivant, Thomas Virgil "Snake" b: 4/28/30, Gordon, Kan. BL/TR, 6'1", 186 lbs. Deb: 4/14/55																											
1955 *NY-A	1	3	.250	33	1	0	0	0	68^1	48	24	6	2	42	48	12.1	3.16	118	.203	.329	1	.083	-1	6	5	-0	0.1
1956 *NY-A	16	8	.667	32	17	6	2	5	158^1	134	63	15	4	52	110	10.8	3.30	117	.224	**.291**	20	.313	4	15	11	-2	1.8
1957 *NY-A	16	6	**.727**	28	28	7	2	0	201^2	170	65	14	4	80	118	11.3	2.54	141	.232	.311	13	.183	1	28	25	-2	2.5
1958 NY-A	3	6	.333	15	10	0	0	0	70^2	77	37	6	3	38	41	15.0	4.20	84	.274	.366	4	.190	0	-3	-6	-2	-0.8
1959 NY-A	0	2	.000	7	3	0	0	0	25^1	20	16	4	0	9	16	10.3	4.97	73	.222	.293	0	.000	-1	-3	-4	0	-0.3
KC-A	2	6	.250	36	3	0	0	5	71^2	70	45	9	6	34	57	13.8	4.65	86	.258	.354	1	.059	-2	-6	-5	1	-0.6
Yr	2	8	.200	43	6	0	0	5	97	90	61	13	6	43	73	12.9	4.73	83	.249	.339	1	.043	-3	-9	-9	2	-0.9
1960 Bos-A	3	3	.500	40	3	0	0	1	101^1	106	58	16	2	45	67	13.6	4.97	81	.279	.358	4	.182	-1	-12	-10	-0	-0.6
1961 Was-A	2	6	.250	15	10	1	1	0	80	67	42	6	3	40	39	12.4	4.61	87	.233	.332	2	.077	-1	-5	-5	1	-0.5
Pit-N	5	2	.714	13	11	6	1	1	85^2	81	29	6	1	17	45	10.4	2.84	141	.249	.289	8	.250	1	11	11	-1	0.8
1962 Pit-N	9	5	.643	49	12	2	1	2	125^1	120	62	12	3	39	76	11.6	3.73	105	.260	.321	6	.182	0	3	3	0	0.3
1963 Pit-N	0	0	—	3	0	0	0	0	8^1	8	6	1	0	4	6	13.0	6.48	51	.267	.353	0	.000	-0	-3	-3	0	-0.2
Det-A	1	2	.333	28	0	0	0	2	55	43	26	7	1	24	36	11.1	3.76	99	.221	.309	0	.000	-1	-1	-0	1	-0.1
KC-A	1	2	.333	17	3	0	0	0	53	47	24	3	1	17	26	11.0	3.74	104	.237	.301	0	.000	-1	-1	1	0	-0.1
Yr	2	4	.333	45	3	0	0	2	108	90	50	10	2	41	62	11.1	3.75	102	.229	.305	0	.000	-2	-1	1	1	-0.2
1964 KC-A	0	0	—	3	0	0	0	0	3^2	4	4	0	2	1	1	17.2	9.82	39	.308	.438	1	1.000	0	-3	-2	-0	-0.1
NY-N	0	0	—	16	0	0	0	1	28^2	34	20	2	2	7	18	13.5	5.97	60	.306	.358	0	.000	-0	-8	-8	-0	-0.4
Total 10	59	51	.536	335	101	22	7	17	1137	1029	521	107	34	449	704	12.0	3.74	102	.244	.322	60	.183	-1	18	10	-4	1.8
● TANYON STURTZE Sturtze, Tanyon James b: 10/12/70, Worcester, Mass. BR/TR, 6'5", 190 lbs. Deb: 5/3/95																											
1995 Chi-N	0	0	—	2	0	0	0	0	2	2	2	1	0	1	0	13.5	9.00	46	.250	.333	0	—	0	-1	-1	-0	-0.1
1996 Chi-N	1	0	1.000	6	0	0	0	0	11	16	11	3	0	5	7	17.2	9.00	48	.348	.412	0	.000	-0	-6	-6	0	-0.4
1997 Tex-A	1	1	.500	9	5	0	0	0	32^2	45	30	6	0	18	18	17.4	8.27	58	.338	.417	0	—	0	-13	-12	-1	-0.7
1999 Chi-A	0	0	—	1	1	0	0	0	6	4	0	0	0	2	2	9.0	0.00	—	.200	.273	0	—	0	3	3	0	0.2
2000 Chi-A	1	2	.333	10	1	0	0	0	15^2	25	23	4	2	15	6	24.1	12.06	41	.379	.506	0	—	0	-12	-12	-1	-1.8
TB-A	4	0	1.000	19	5	0	0	0	52^2	47	16	4	1	14	38	10.6	2.56	193	.236	.290	0	—	0	14	14	-0	0.9
Yr	5	2	.714	29	6	0	0	0	68^1	72	39	8	3	29	44	13.7	4.74	105	.272	.350	0	—	0	1	2	-1	-0.9
Total 5	7	3	.700	47	12	0	0	0	120	139	82	18	3	55	71	14.8	5.93	82	.294	.372	0	.000	-0	-16	-14	-2	-1.9
● DICK SUCH Such, Richard Stanley b: 10/15/44, Sanford, N.C. BL/TR, 6'4", 190 lbs. Deb: 4/6/70 C																											
1970 Was-A	1	5	.167	21	5	0	0	0	50	48	42	8	3	45	41	17.3	7.56	47	.258	.410	3	.231	1	-21	-23	0	-2.3
● CHARLEY SUCHE Suche, Charles Morris b: 8/5/15, Cranes Mill, Tex. d: 2/11/84, San Antonio, Tex. BR/TL, 6'2", 190 lbs. Deb: 9/18/38																											
1938 Cle-A	0	0	—	1	0	0	0	0	1^1	4	4	0	0	3	1	47.3	27.00	17	.571	.700	1	1.000	1	-3	-3	0	-0.1
● JIM SUCHECKI Suchecki, James Joseph b: 8/25/26, Chicago, Ill. d: 7/20/2000, Crofton, Md. BR/TR, 5'11", 185 lbs. Deb: 5/20/50																											
1950 Bos-A	0	0	—	4	0	0	0	0	4	3	2	0	0	4	3	15.8	4.50	109	.231	.412	0	—	0	0	0	-0	0.0
1951 StL-A	0	6	.000	29	6	0	0	0	89^2	113	64	8	1	42	47	15.7	5.42	81	.299	.371	2	.100	-2	-13	-10	-1	-0.8
1952 Pit-N	0	0	—	5	0	0	0	0	10	14	7	1	1	4	6	17.1	5.40	74	.326	.396	0	.000	0	-2	-1	-0	-0.1
Total 3	0	6	.000	38	6	0	0	0	103^2	130	73	9	2	50	56	15.8	5.38	81	.300	.374	2	.091	-2	-15	-11	-1	-0.9
● WILLIE SUDHOFF Sudhoff, John William "Wee Willie" b: 9/17/1874, St.Louis, Mo. d: 5/25/17, St.Louis, Mo. BR/TR, 5'7", 165 lbs. Deb: 8/20/1897																											
1897 StL-N	2	7	.222	11	9	9	0	0	92^2	126	72	8	0	21	19	14.3	4.47	98	.321	.356	10	.238	-1	-2	-1	2	0.0
1898 StL-N	11	27	.289	41	38	35	0	1	315	355	205	11	27	102	65	13.8	4.34	87	.282	.349	19	.158	-6	-26	-18	8	-1.7
1899 Cle-N	3	8	.273	11	10	8	0	0	86^1	131	85	3	7	25	10	17.0	6.98	53	.347	.399	2	.065	-2	-30	-33	2	-3.0
StL-N	12	10	.545	25	23	16	0	0	178^1	193	109	6	15	62	29	13.6	4.04	99	.276	.347	13	.203	-0	-4	-1	4	0.3
Yr	15	18	.455	36	33	24	0	0	264^2	324	194	9	22	87	39	14.7	5.00	78	.301	.365	15	.158	-2	-34	-33	7	-2.7
1900 StL-N	6	8	.429	16	14	13	2	0	127	128	62	3	8	37	29	12.3	2.76	132	.261	.323	20	.189	-0	13	13	1	1.2
1901 StL-N	17	11	.607	38	26	25	1	2	276^1	281	142	4	18	92	78	12.7	3.52	90	.262	.331	19	.176	3	-6	-11	2	-0.5
1902 StL-A	12	12	.500	30	25	20	0	0	220	213	99	6	12	67	42	11.9	2.86	123	.254	.319	13	.169	-2	17	16	3	1.7
1903 StL-A	21	15	.583	38	35	30	5	0	293^2	262	100	4	9	56	104	10.0	2.27	128	.238	.281	20	.182	-1	23	21	3	2.8
1904 StL-A	8	15	.348	27	24	20	1	0	222^1	232	121	8	10	54	63	12.0	3.76	66	.269	.320	14	.165	0	-29	-33	5	-2.7
1905 StL-A	10	20	.333	32	30	23	1	0	244	222	121	8	13	78	70	11.5	2.99	85	.244	.313	16	.186	2	-9	-13	4	-0.9
1906 Was-A	0	2	.000	9	5	0	0	0	19^2	30	25	1	2	9	7	18.8	9.15	29	.353	.427	3	.429	1	-14	-15	1	-1.2
Total 10	102	135	.430	278	239	199	10	3	2075^1	2173	1141	62	121	603	516	12.6	3.60	91	.269	.329	149	.178	-7	-66	-75	35	-4.0
● JOE SUGDEN Sugden, Joseph b: 7/31/1870, Philadelphia, Pa. d: 6/28/59, Philadelphia, Pa. BB/TR, 5'10", 180 lbs. Deb: 7/20/1893 C♦																											
1902 StL-A	0	0	—	1	0	0	0	0	1	1	0	0	0	0	0	9.0	0.00	—	.250	.250	50	.250	0	0	0	0	0.0
● GEORGE SUGGS Suggs, George Franklin b: 7/7/1882, Kinston, N.C. d: 4/4/49, Kinston, N.C. BR/TR, 5'7.5", 168 lbs. Deb: 4/21/08																											
1908 Det-A	1	1	.500	6	1	1	0	1	27	32	8	0	0	2	8	11.3	1.67	145	.299	.312	2	.200	0	2	2	-1	0.1
1909 Det-A	1	3	.250	9	4	2	0	1	44^1	34	12	1	3	10	18	9.5	2.03	124	.228	.290	1	.067	-1	2	2	-0	0.1
1910 Cin-N	20	12	.625	35	30	23	2	3	266	248	96	6	14	48	91	10.5	2.40	121	.253	.297	14	.165	2	19	16	1	2.2
1911 Cin-N	15	13	.536	36	29	17	1	0	260^2	258	110	3	10	79	91	12.0	3.00	110	.268	.330	23	.256	6	12	9	3	1.9
1912 Cin-N	19	16	.543	42	36	25	5	3	303	320	132	6	11	56	104	11.5	2.94	114	.278	.318	17	.160	-1	16	14	1	1.5
1913 Cin-N	8	15	.348	36	22	9	2	2	199	220	110	6	7	35	73	11.8	4.03	81	.292	.329	17	.254	2	-18	-17	3	-1.3
1914 Bal-F	24	14	.632	46	38	26	6	4	319^1	322	118	6	10	57	132	11.0	2.90	104	.266	.304	21	.212	2	-1	4	6	1.3
1915 Bal-F	11	17	.393	35	25	12	0	3	232^2	288	134	12	7	68	71	14.0	4.14	69	.318	.370	17	.221	0	-36	-31	2	-3.3
Total 8	99	91	.521	245	185	115	16	17	1652	1722	720	40	62	355	588	11.7	3.11	100	.277	.322	112	.204	11	-5	-1	14	2.5
● ED SUKLA Sukla, Edward Anthony (b: Edward Anthony Suckla) b: 3/3/43, Long Beach, Cal. BR/TR, 5'11", 170 lbs. Deb: 9/17/64																											
1964 LA-A	0	1	.000	2	0	0	0	0	2^2	2	2	1	0	1	3	10.1	6.75	49	.200	.273	0	—	0	-1	-1	0	-0.2
1965 Cal-A	2	3	.400	25	0	0	0	3	32	32	16	3	1	10	15	12.1	4.50	76	.264	.326	0	—	0	-4	-4	1	-0.6
1966 Cal-A	1	1	.500	12	0	0	0	1	16^2	18	12	4	0	6	8	13.0	6.48	52	.281	.343	0	.000	-0	-6	-6	-1	-0.8
Total 3	3	5	.375	39	0	0	0	4	51^1	52	30	8	1	17	26	12.3	5.26	64	.267	.329	0	.000	-0	-10	-11	0	-1.6

YEAR	TM/L	W	L	PCT	G	GS	CG	SH	SV	IP	H	R	HR	HB	BB	SO	RAT	ERA	ERA+	OAV	OOB	BH	AVG	PB	PR	PR+	PD	TPI
● CHARLIE SULLIVAN Sullivan, Charles Edward b: 5/23/03, Yadkin Valley, N.C d: 5/28/35, Maiden, N.C. BL/TR, 6'1", 185 lbs. Deb: 4/21/28																												
1928	Det-A	0	2	.000	3	2	0	0	0	12^1	18	12	1	0	6	2	17.5	6.57	63	.360	.429	0	.000	-1	-3	-3	0	-0.5
1930	Det-A	1	5	.167	40	3	2	0	5	93^2	112	72	9	1	53	38	16.0	6.53	73	.311	.401	7	.292	2	-20	-17	1	-0.9
1931	Det-A	3	2	.600	31	4	2	0	0	95	109	60	6	1	46	28	14.8	4.93	93	.288	.366	4	.167	-1	-6	-3	-0	-0.3
Total	3	4	9	.308	74	9	4	0	5	201	239	144	16	2	105	68	15.5	5.78	81	.303	.386	11	.212	-0	-29	-24	1	-1.7
● FLEURY SULLIVAN Sullivan, Florence P. b: 1862, E.St.Louis, Ill. d: 2/15/1897, E.St.Louis, Ill. Deb: 5/3/1884																												
1884	Pit-a	16	35	.314	51	51	51	2	0	441	496	328	15	20	96	189	12.5	4.20	79	.268	.311	29	.153	-9	-47	-43	1	-4.6
● FRANK SULLIVAN Sullivan, Franklin Leal b: 1/23/30, Hollywood, Cal. BR/TR, 6'6.5", 215 lbs. Deb: 7/31/53																												
1953	Bos-A	1	1	.500	14	0	0	0	0	25^2	24	16	3	1	11	17	12.6	5.61	75	.264	.350	1	.250	0	-5	-4	-0	-0.3
1954	Bos-A	15	12	.556	36	26	11	3	1	206^1	185	81	19	6	66	124	11.2	3.14	131	.240	.305	7	.103	-3	13	20	1	2.4
1955	Bos-A★	**18**	13	.581	35	35	16	3	0	**260**	235	103	23	7	100	129	11.8	2.91	147	.241	.316	10	.112	-4	30	37	1	3.8
1956	Bos-A☆	14	7	.667	34	33	12	1	0	242	253	112	22	8	82	116	12.8	3.42	135	.268	.332	12	.141	-5	20	29	0	1.8
1957	Bos-A	14	11	.560	31	30	14	3	0	240^2	206	76	16	7	48	127	**9.8**	2.73	146	.230	**.275**	13	.165	-2	28	32	2	**3.3**
1958	Bos-A	13	9	.591	32	29	10	2	3	199^1	216	91	12	3	49	103	12.1	3.57	112	.278	.324	11	.164	-1	4	9	-1	0.8
1959	Bos-A	9	11	.450	30	26	5	2	1	177^2	172	86	17	7	67	107	12.5	3.95	103	.258	.332	12	.200	-1	-2	2	-1	0.0
1960	Bos-A	6	16	.273	40	22	4	0	1	153^2	164	94	12	6	52	98	13.0	5.10	79	.269	.332	5	.125	-1	-21	-17	-1	-2.4
1961	Phi-N	3	16	.158	49	18	1	1	6	159^1	161	93	19	5	55	114	12.5	4.29	95	.262	.327	5	.152	0	-5	-4	1	-0.3
1962	Phi-N	0	2	.000	19	0	0	0	0	23	38	21	2	2	12	12	20.3	6.26	62	.396	.473	0	—	0	-6	-6	0	-0.5
	Min-A	4	1	.800	21	0	0	0	5	33^1	33	17	3	0	13	10	12.4	3.24	126	.258	.326	0	.000	-0	3	3	0	0.5
1963	Min-A	0	1	.000	10	0	0	0	1	11	15	7	1	0	4	2	15.5	5.73	64	.349	.404	0	—	0	-3	-3	0	-0.2
Total	11	97	100	.492	351	219	73	15	18	1732	1702	797	149	52	559	959	12.0	3.60	116	.257	.320	76	.144	-17	59	102	3	8.9
● HARRY SULLIVAN Sullivan, Harry Andrew b: 4/12/1888, Rockford, Ill. d: 9/22/19, Rockford, Ill. BL/TL, Deb: 8/11/09																												
1909	StL-N	0	0	—	2	1	0	0	0	1	4	6	1	0	2	1	54.0	36.00	7	.500	.600	0	.000	-0	-4	-4	-0	-0.2
● JIM SULLIVAN Sullivan, James E. b: 4/25/1869, Charlestown, Mass. d: 11/30/01, Roxbury, Mass. BR/TR, 5'10", 155 lbs. Deb: 4/22/1891																												
1891	Bos-N	0	0	—	1	0	0	0	0	0^1	2	4	0	0	5	0	189.0	81.00	5	.667	.875	0	—	0	-3	-3	-0	-0.1
	Col-a	0	1	.000	1	1	1	0	0	9	10	9	1	1	5	1	16.0	4.00	86	.270	.372	0	.000	-1	-0	-1	1	-0.1
1895	Bos-N	11	9	.550	21	19	16	0	0	179^1	236	135	10	16	58	46	15.6	4.82	106	.312	.373	15	.176	-6	-1	5	-2	-0.2
1896	Bos-N	11	12	.478	31	26	21	1	1	225^1	268	148	12	6	68	33	13.7	4.03	113	.293	.346	19	.216	-2	8	12	-3	0.5
1897	*Bos-N	4	5	.444	13	9	8	1	2	89	91	56	1	2	26	17	12.0	3.94	113	.262	.317	6	.182	-3	4	5	-1	0.1
Total	4	26	27	.491	67	55	46	2	3	503	607	352	24	25	162	97	14.2	4.35	108	.295	.354	40	.190	-11	8	19	-6	0.2
● JIM SULLIVAN Sullivan, James Richard b: 4/5/1894, Mine Run, Va. d: 2/12/72, Burtonsville, Md. BR/TR, 5'11", 165 lbs. Deb: 9/27/21																												
1921	Phi-A	0	2	.000	2	2	2	0	0	17	20	13	0	0	7	8	14.3	3.18	140	.294	.360	0	.000	-1	2	2	-0	0.1
1922	Phi-A	0	2	.000	20	2	1	0	0	51^1	76	43	3	1	25	15	17.9	5.44	78	.373	.443	1	.091	-1	-8	-6	-0	-0.4
1923	Cle-A	0	1	.000	3	0	0	0	0	5	10	10	0	1	5	4	28.8	14.40	28	.476	.593	0	.000	-0	-6	-6	0	-0.9
Total	3	0	5	.000	25	4	3	0	0	73^1	106	66	3	2	37	27	17.8	5.52	78	.362	.437	1	.056	-2	-12	-10	-1	-1.2
● JOE SULLIVAN Sullivan, Joe b: 9/26/10, Mason City, Ill. d: 4/8/85, Sequim, Wash. BL/TL, 5'11", 175 lbs. Deb: 4/20/35																												
1935	Det-A	6	6	.500	25	12	5	0	0	125^2	119	66	4	3	71	53	13.8	3.51	119	.244	.344	7	.163	-1	13	10	-1	0.6
1936	Det-A	2	5	.286	26	4	1	0	1	79^2	111	70	4	2	40	32	17.3	6.78	73	.331	.406	5	.179	-1	-15	-16	-1	-1.3
1939	Bos-N	6	9	.400	31	11	7	0	2	113^2	114	57	3	2	50	46	13.1	3.64	101	.266	.346	12	.300	3	3	1	0	0.5
1940	Bos-N	10	14	.417	36	22	7	0	1	177^1	157	89	9	8	89	64	12.9	3.55	105	.240	.339	14	.197	-0	6	3	0	0.4
1941	Bos-N	2	2	.500	16	2	0	0	0	52^1	60	26	3	2	26	11	15.1	4.13	86	.290	.374	1	.067	-1	-3	-3	1	-0.3
	Pit-N	4	1	.800	16	4	0	0	1	39^1	40	26	2	0	22	10	14.2	2.97	121	.258	.350	4	.364	1	3	3	0	0.5
	Yr	6	3	.667	32	6	0	0	1	91^2	100	52	5	2	48	21	14.7	3.63	99	.276	.364	5	.192	-0	0	-0	1	0.2
Total	5	30	37	.448	150	55	20	0	5	588	601	334	25	17	298	216	14.0	4.01	99	.265	.355	43	.207	1	7	-4	0	0.4
● JOHN SULLIVAN Sullivan, John Jeremiah "Lefty" b: 5/31/1894, Chicago, Ill. d: 7/7/58, Chicago, Ill. BL/TL, 5'11", 165 lbs. Deb: 7/18/19																												
1919	Chi-A	0	1	.000	4	2	1	0	0	15	24	15	0	1	8	9	19.8	4.20	76	.364	.440	0	.000	-0	-2	-2	-1	-0.2
● MARTY SULLIVAN Sullivan, Martin C. b: 10/20/1862, Lowell, Mass. d: 1/6/1894, Lowell, Mass. BR/TR, Deb: 4/30/1887 ♦																												
1887	Chi-N	0	0	—	1	0	0	0	0	2^1	7	2	0	0	1	1	27.0	7.71	58	.538	.538	170	.335	0	-1	-1	-0	0.0
● MIKE SULLIVAN Sullivan, Michael Joseph "Big Mike" b: 10/23/1866, Boston, Mass. d: 6/14/06, Boston, Mass. BL, 6'1", 210 lbs. Deb: 6/17/1889																												
1889	Was-N	0	3	.000	9	3	3	0	0	41	47	47	2	3	32	15	18.0	7.24	54	.280	.404	1	.053	-2	-15	-15	-0	-1.0
1890	Chi-N	5	6	.455	12	12	10	0	0	96	108	77	3	4	58	33	15.9	4.59	80	.276	.374	5	.125	-3	-11	-10	-0	-1.1
1891	Phi-a	0	2	.000	2	2	2	0	0	18	17	13	2	3	10	7	15.0	3.50	108	.239	.357	0	.000	-1	0	1	-0	-0.1
	NY-N	1	2	.333	3	3	3	0	0	24	24	19	0	1	8	11	12.4	3.38	95	.250	.314	2	.200	-0	-0	-0	0	-0.1
1892	Cin-N	12	4	.750	21	16	15	0	0	166^1	179	90	8	9	74	56	14.2	3.08	106	.264	.344	13	.176	-2	4	3	-2	-0.1
1893	Cin-N	8	11	.421	27	18	14	0	1	183^2	200	146	5	17	103	40	15.7	5.05	95	.269	.370	16	.203	-3	-8	-5	-0	-0.7
1894	Was-N	2	10	.167	20	12	11	0	1	117^2	166	134	10	8	74	21	19.0	6.58	80	.329	.422	9	.158	-4	-16	-17	-0	-1.5
	Cle-N	6	5	.545	13	11	9	0	0	90^2	128	82	4	3	47	19	17.7	6.35	86	.329	.405	13	.295	0	-10	-9	-1	-0.8
	Yr	8	15	.348	33	23	20	0	1	208^1	294	216	14	11	121	40	18.4	6.48	83	.329	.415	22	.218	-4	-27	-26	-1	-2.3
1895	Cle-N	1	2	.333	4	3	2	0	0	31	42	34	1	1	16	5	17.1	8.42	59	.318	.396	2	.133	-2	-13	-11	-1	-0.9
1896	NY-N	10	13	.435	25	22	18	0	0	185^1	188	131	3	13	71	42	13.2	4.66	90	.261	.338	16	.208	-3	-6	-10	0	-1.2
1897	NY-N	8	7	.533	23	16	11	1	2	148^2	183	113	6	14	71	35	16.2	5.09	82	.300	.386	18	.273	0	-13	-16	1	-1.2
1898	Bos-N	0	1	.000	3	2	0	0	0	12	19	16	1	1	9	1	21.8	12.00	31	.358	.460	1	.333	0	-11	-11	-0	-0.7
1899	Bos-N	1	0	1.000	1	1	1	0	0	9	10	6	1	1	4	1	15.0	5.00	83	.278	.366	1	.333	0	-1	-1	-0	-0.1
Total	11	54	66	.450	163	121	99	1	4	1123^1	1311	908	46	78	577	286	15.8	5.11	84	.285	.375	97	.196	-21	-100	-102	-5	-9.5
● PAT SULLIVAN Sullivan, Patrick J. b: 12/22/1862, Milwaukee, Wis. TR, 5'11", 165 lbs. Deb: 8/30/1884 ♦																												
1884	KC-U	0	1	.000	1	1	0	0	0	7	15	17	1		5	1	25.7	11.57	19	.405	.476	22	.193	-0	-7	-8	-0	-0.7
● LEFTY SULLIVAN Sullivan, Paul Thomas b: 9/7/16, Nashville, Tenn. d: 11/1/88, Scottsdale, Ariz. BL/TL, 6'3", 204 lbs. Deb: 5/6/39																												
1939	Cle-A	0	1	.000	7	1	0	0	0	12^2	9	8	0	1	9	4	13.5	4.26	103	.214	.365	0	.000	-0	1	0	-1	-0.1
● SUTER SULLIVAN Sullivan, Suter G. b: 10/14/1872, Baltimore, Md. d: 4/19/25, Baltimore, Md. 6', 170 lbs. Deb: 7/24/1898 ♦																												
1898	StL-N	0	0	—	1	0	0	0	0	6	10	4	0	0	4	3	21.0	1.50	253	.370	.452	32	.222	0	1	1	-0	0.0
● TOM SULLIVAN Sullivan, Thomas b: 3/1/1860, New York, N.Y. d: 4/12/47, Cincinnati, Ohio Deb: 9/27/1884																												
1884	Col-a	2	2	.500	4	4	4	0	0	31	42	22	2	0	3	12	13.1	4.06	75	.318	.333	1	.091	-1	-3	-4	-1	-0.5
1886	Lou-a	2	7	.222	9	9	8	0	0	75	94	70	6	2	33	27	15.5	3.96	92	.305	.376	3	.111	-2	-4	-3	0	-0.4
1888	KC-a	8	16	.333	24	24	24	0	0	214^2	227	146	2	24	68	84	13.4	3.40	101	.262	.332	10	.109	-6	-8	1	5	0.0
1889	KC-a	2	8	.200	10	10	10	0	0	87^1	111	88	2	7	48	24	17.1	5.67	74	.300	.391	5	.152	-1	-18	-13	-1	-1.2
Total	4	14	33	.298	47	47	46	0	0	408	474	326	12	33	152	147	14.5	4.04	89	.282	.354	19	.117	-9	-33	-18	4	-2.1
● TOM SULLIVAN Sullivan, Thomas Augustin b: 10/18/1895, Boston, Mass. d: 9/23/62, Boston, Mass. BL/TL, 5'11", 178 lbs. Deb: 5/15/22																												
1922	Phi-N	0	0	—	3	0	0	0	0	8	16	11	0	1	5	2	24.8	11.25	41	.410	.489	1	.250	1	-6	-5	0	-0.2
● SLEEPER SULLIVAN Sullivan, Thomas Jefferson "Old Iron Hands" b: 1859, Ireland. d: 10/13/09, St.Louis, Mo. BR/TR, 175 lbs. Deb: 5/3/1881 ♦																												
1884	StL-U	1	0	1.000	1	1	0	0	0	6	10	6	0		0	3	15.0	4.50	53	.345	.345	1	.111	-1	-1	-1	-0	-0.2
● BILL SULLIVAN Sullivan, William F. b: 12/1868, Providence, R.I. d: 10/8/05, Providence, R.I. BR/TR, Deb: 4/19/1890																												
1890	Syr-a	1	4	.200	6	6	4	0	0	42	51	50	2	6	27	13	18.0	7.93	45	.291	.404	2	.091	-2	-19	-22	-0	-2.0
● SCOTT SULLIVAN Sullivan, William Scott b: 3/13/71, Tuscaloosa, Ala. BR/TR, 6'3", 210 lbs. Deb: 5/6/95																												
1995	Cin-N	0	0	—	3	0	0	0	0	3^2	4	2	0	0	2	2	14.7	4.91	84	.286	.375	0	.000	-0	-0	-0	0	0.0
1996	Cin-N	0	0	—	7	0	0	0	0	8	7	2	0	1	5	3	14.6	2.25	188	.250	.382	0	.000	-0	2	2	0	0.1
1997	Cin-N	5	3	.625	59	0	0	0	1	97^1	79	36	12	7	30	96	10.7	3.24	132	.220	.293	0	.000	-1	10	11	-1	0.7

YEAR	TM/L	W	L	PCT	G	GS	CG	SH	SV	IP	H	R	HR	HB	BB	SO	RAT	ERA	ERA+	OAV	OOB	BH	AVG	PB	PR	PR+	PD	TPI
1998	Cin-N	5	5	.500	67	0	0	0	1	102	98	62	14	9	36	86	12.6	5.21	82	.253	.330	1	.091	-1	-11	-10	-0	-1.0
1999	Cin-N	5	4	.556	79	0	0	0	3	113^{2}	88	41	10	8	47	78	11.3	3.01	155	.216	.310	0	.000	-2	20	20	-2	1.2
2000	Cin-N	3	6	.333	79	0	0	0	3	106^{1}	87	44	14	9	38	96	11.3	3.47	138	.226	.310	2	.286	0	14	15	-1	1.1
Total	6	18	18	.500	294	0	0	0	8	431	363	187	50	34	158	361	11.6	3.70	122	.230	.313	3	.071	-3	34	38	-3	2.1
● ED SUMMERS	Summers, Oron Edgar "Kickapoo Ed" or "Chief" b: 12/5/1884, Ladoga, Ind. d: 5/12/53, Indianapolis, Ind. BB/TR, 6'2", 180 lbs. Deb: 4/16/08																											
1908	*Det-A	24	12	.667	40	32	23	5	1	301	271	112	3	20	55	103	10.3	1.64	147	.242	.290	14	.124	-6	25	26	-1	2.4
1909	*Det-A	19	9	.679	35	32	24	3	1	281^{2}	243	91	4	10	52	107	9.7	2.24	113	.227	.269	10	.106	-4	8	9	1	0.5
1910	Det-A	13	12	.520	30	25	18	1	0	220^{1}	211	83	8	5	60	82	11.3	2.53	104	.254	.308	14	.184	-0	-0	2	1	0.3
1911	Det-A	11	11	.500	30	20	13	0	1	179^{1}	189	108	3	11	51	65	12.6	3.66	95	.274	.334	16	.254	1	-6	-4	-1	-0.4
1912	Det-A	1	1	.500	3	3	1	0	0	16^{2}	16	10	1	0	3	5	10.3	4.86	67	.250	.284	3	.500	1	-3	-3	0	-0.2
Total	5	68	45	.602	138	112	79	9	3	999	930	404	19	46	221	362	10.8	2.42	111	.246	.296	57	.162	-9	23	29	-0	2.6
● BILLY SUNDAY	Sunday, William Ashley "Parson" or "The Evangelist" b: 11/19/1862, Ames, Iowa d: 11/6/35, Chicago, Ill. BL/TR, 5'10", 160 lbs. Deb: 5/22/1883 ♦																											
1890	Pit-N	0	0	—	1	0	0	0	0	0	2	0	0	0	—	—	∞	—		1.000	1.000	92	.257	0	-2	-2	0	-0.2
● GORDIE SUNDIN	Sundin, Gordon Vincent b: 10/10/37, Minneapolis, Minn. BR/TR, 6'4", 215 lbs. Deb: 9/19/56																											
1956	Bal-A	0	0	—	1	0	0	0	0	0	0	0	0	2	—	—	∞	—		—	1.000	94	—	0	-1	-1	0	-0.1
● STEVE SUNDRA	Sundra, Stephen Richard "Smokey" b: 3/27/10, Luxor, Pa. d: 3/23/52, Cleveland, Ohio BR/TR (BB 1936-40), 6'2", 190 lbs. Deb: 4/17/36																											
1936	NY-A	0	0	—	1	0	0	0	0	2	2	0	0	0	2	1	18.0	0.00	—	.286	.444	0	.000	-0	1	1	-0	0.0
1938	NY-A	6	4	.600	25	8	3	0	0	93^{2}	107	61	7	0	43	33	14.4	4.80	94	.291	.365	6	.182	1	-0	-3	1	-0.1
1939	*NY-A	11	1	.917	24	11	8	1	0	120^{2}	110	43	7	0	56	27	12.4	2.76	158	.240	.323	13	.265	4	25	23	1	2.3
1940	NY-A	4	6	.400	27	8	2	0	2	99^{1}	121	68	11	1	42	26	14.9	5.53	73	.299	.366	4	.138	-1	-13	-18	0	-1.6
1941	Was-A	9	13	.409	28	23	11	0	0	168^{1}	203	108	11	1	61	50	14.2	5.29	76	.294	.352	13	.217	2	-21	-24	-1	-2.4
1942	Was-A	1	3	.250	6	4	2	0	0	33^{2}	43	24	1	1	15	5	15.8	5.61	65	.305	.376	2	.167	-0	-7	-7	-0	-0.8
	StL-A	8	3	.727	20	13	6	0	0	110^{2}	122	56	2	0	29	26	12.3	3.82	97	.275	.319	9	.225	3	-2	-1	-0	0.1
	Yr	9	6	.600	26	17	8	0	0	144^{1}	165	80	3	1	44	31	13.1	4.24	87	.282	.333	11	.212	2	-9	-9	-0	-0.7
1943	StL-A	15	11	.577	32	29	13	3	0	208	212	89	10	0	66	44	12.0	3.25	103	.266	.322	16	.219	1	1	2	-0	0.4
1944	StL-A	2	0	1.000	3	3	2	0	0	19	15	3	1	0	4	1	9.0	1.42	253	.211	.253	0	.000	-0	4	4	-0	0.4
1946	StL-A	0	0	—	2	0	0	0	0	4	9	9	0	0	3	1	27.0	11.25	33	.409	.480	0	—	0	-3	-3	0	-0.2
Total	9	56	41	.577	168	99	47	4	2	859^{1}	944	461	50	3	321	214	13.3	4.17	94	.277	.340	63	.209	10	-16	-25	1	-1.9
● TOM SUNKEL	Sunkel, Thomas Jacob "Lefty" b: 8/9/12, Paris, Ill. BL/TL, 6'1", 190 lbs. Deb: 8/26/37																											
1937	StL-N	0	0	—	9	1	0	0	1	29^{1}	24	11	0	0	11	9	10.7	2.76	144	.214	.285	1	.111	-1	4	4	-0	0.1
1939	StL-N	4	4	.500	20	11	2	1	0	85^{1}	79	47	4	1	56	54	14.3	4.22	98	.242	.354	9	.321	2	-3	-1	-1	0.0
1941	NY-N	1	1	.500	2	2	1	1	0	15^{1}	7	5	0	1	12	14	11.7	2.93	126	.140	.317	2	.333	0	1	1	-0	0.2
1942	NY-N	3	6	.333	19	11	3	0	0	63^{2}	65	40	5	0	41	29	15.0	4.81	70	.269	.375	2	.105	-1	-11	-10	-2	-1.6
1943	NY-N	0	1	.000	1	1	0	0	0	2^{2}	4	3	1	0	3	0	23.6	10.13	34	.308	.438	0	—	0	-2	-2	0	-0.3
1944	Bro-N	1	3	.250	12	3	0	0	1	24	39	20	1	0	10	6	18.4	7.50	47	.368	.422	0	.000	-1	-10	-11	-1	-1.8
Total	6	9	15	.375	63	29	6	2	2	220^{1}	218	126	11	2	133	112	14.4	4.53	83	.256	.358	14	.212	0	-21	-18	-4	-3.4
● JEFF SUPPAN	Suppan, Jeffrey Scot b: 1/2/75, Oklahoma City, Okla. BR/TR, 6'1", 200 lbs. Deb: 7/17/95																											
1995	Bos-A	1	2	.333	8	3	0	0	0	22^{2}	29	15	4	0	5	19	13.5	5.96	82	.312	.347	0	—	0	-3	-3	-0	-0.3
1996	Bos-A	1	1	.500	8	4	0	0	0	22^{2}	29	19	3	1	13	13	17.1	7.54	67	.330	.422	0	—	0	-6	-6	-0	-0.5
1997	Bos-A	7	3	.700	23	22	0	0	0	112^{1}	140	75	12	4	36	67	14.4	5.69	82	.305	.361	0	.000	-0	-14	-13	-2	-1.1
1998	Ari-N	1	7	.125	13	13	1	0	0	66	82	55	12	1	21	39	14.2	6.68	63	.301	.354	6	.273	1	-18	-18	1	-1.6
	KC-A	0	0	—	4	1	0	0	0	12^{2}	9	1	1	0	1	12	7.1	0.71	680	.200	.217	0	—	0	6	6	0	0.3
1999	KC-A	10	12	.455	32	32	4	1	0	208^{2}	222	113	28	3	62	103	12.4	4.53	111	.274	.328	1	.200	0	8	11	-0	1.0
2000	KC-A	10	9	.526	35	33	3	1	0	217	240	121	36	7	84	128	13.7	4.94	101	.284	.353	0	.000	-0	-0	2	-2	-0.1
Total	6	30	34	.469	123	108	8	2	0	662	751	399	96	16	222	381	13.4	5.15	94	.287	.347	7	.219	1	-28	-21	-2	-2.3
● RICK SURHOFF	Surhoff, Richard Clifford b: 10/3/62, Bronx, N.Y. BR/TR, 6'3", 210 lbs. Deb: 9/8/85 F																											
1985	Phi-N	1	0	1.000	2	0	0	0	0	1	2	0	0	0	0	1	18.0	0.00	—	.500	.500	0	—	0	0	0	0	0.1
	Tex-A	0	1	.000	7	0	0	0	2	8^{1}	12	7	2	0	3	8	16.2	7.56	56	.343	.395	0	—	0	-3	-3	-0	-0.5
Total	1	1	1	.500	9	0	0	0	2	9^{1}	14	7	2	0	3	9	16.4	6.75	62	.359	.405	0	—	0	-3	-3	-0	-0.4
● MAX SURKONT	Surkont, Matthew Constantine b: 6/16/22, Central Falls, R.I. d: 10/8/86, Largo, Fla. BR/TR, 6', 205 lbs. Deb: 4/19/49																											
1949	Chi-A	3	5	.375	44	2	0	0	4	96	92	61	9	3	60	38	14.5	4.78	87	.255	.366	1	.045	-1	-6	-7	-1	-0.8
1950	Bos-N	5	2	.714	9	6	2	0	0	55^{2}	63	29	5	2	20	21	13.7	3.23	119	.285	.350	10	.435	5	6	4	-1	1.0
1951	Bos-N	12	16	.429	37	33	11	2	1	237	230	119	21	7	89	110	12.4	3.99	92	.252	.323	11	.151	0	-1	-9	-3	-1.1
1952	Bos-N	12	13	.480	31	29	12	3	0	215	201	95	19	3	76	125	11.7	3.77	96	.245	.311	7	.111	-1	-1	-4	-1	-0.6
1953	Mil-N	11	5	.688	28	24	11	2	0	170	168	82	22	0	64	83	12.3	4.18	94	.255	.321	16	.286	7	2	-5	1	0.3
1954	Pit-N	9	18	.333	33	29	11	0	0	208^{1}	216	124	25	4	78	78	12.9	4.41	95	.268	.335	10	.167	0	-8	-5	0	-0.5
1955	Pit-N	7	14	.333	35	22	5	0	2	166^{1}	194	109	23	3	78	84	14.9	5.57	74	.298	.376	7	.140	-1	-28	-26	-2	-3.2
1956	Pit-N	0	0	—	1	0	0	0	0	2	2	1	0	0	3	1	22.5	4.50	84	.333	.556	0	—	0	-0	-0	0	0.0
	StL-N	0	0	—	5	0	0	0	0	5^{2}	10	6	3	0	2	5	19.1	9.53	40	.417	.462	0	.000	-0	-4	-4	-0	-0.2
	NY-N	2	2	.500	8	4	1	0	1	32	24	17	5	0	9	18	9.3	4.78	79	.202	.258	1	.111	-0	-4	-4	-0	-0.5
	Yr	2	2	.500	14	4	1	0	1	39^{2}	36	24	8	0	14	24	11.3	5.45	69	.242	.307	1	.100	-0	-7	-7	-1	-0.7
1957	NY-N	0	1	.000	5	0	0	0	0	6^{1}	9	7	2	0	2	8	15.6	9.95	40	.321	.367	0	—	0	-4	-4	0	-0.6
Total	9	61	76	.445	236	149	53	7	8	1194^{1}	1209	650	134	22	481	571	12.9	4.38	89	.262	.335	63	.176	8	-48	-65	-5	-6.2
● GEORGE SUSCE	Susce, George Daniel b: 9/13/31, Pittsburgh, Pa. BR/TR, 6'1", 180 lbs. Deb: 4/15/55 F																											
1955	Bos-A	9	7	.563	29	15	6	1	1	144^{1}	123	54	12	8	49	60	11.2	3.06	140	.232	.306	7	.143	-2	15	18	-0	1.7
1956	Bos-A	2	4	.333	21	6	0	0	0	69^{2}	71	54	14	4	44	26	15.4	6.20	74	.262	.373	4	.222	1	-16	-11	-0	-0.7
1957	Bos-A	7	3	.700	29	5	0	0	1	88^{1}	93	45	6	3	41	40	14.0	4.28	93	.274	.358	3	.120	-1	-5	-3	-1	-0.5
1958	Bos-A	0	0	—	2	0	0	0	0	2	6	4	1	0	1	0	31.5	18.00	22	.600	.636	0	—	0	-3	-3	-0	-0.2
	Det-A	4	3	.571	27	10	2	0	1	90^{2}	90	45	7	3	26	42	11.8	3.67	110	.259	.316	3	.125	-1	1	3	-2	0.0
	Yr	4	3	.571	29	10	2	0	1	92^{2}	96	49	8	3	27	42	12.2	3.98	101	.269	.326	3	.125	-1	-2	1	-2	-0.2
1959	Det-A	0	0	—	9	0	0	0	0	14^{2}	24	22	4	2	9	9	21.5	12.89	32	.358	.449	0	.000	-0	-15	-14	-0	-0.7
Total	5	22	17	.564	117	36	8	1	3	409^{2}	407	224	44	20	170	177	13.1	4.42	95	.260	.340	17	.145	-2	-23	-9	-4	-0.4
● RICK SUTCLIFFE	Sutcliffe, Richard Lee b: 6/21/56, Independence, Mo. BL/TR, 6'7", 215 lbs. Deb: 9/29/76																											
1976	LA-N	0	0	—	1	1	0	0	0	5	2	0	0	0	1	3	5.4	0.00	—	.125	.176	0	.000	-0	2	2	-0	0.1
1978	LA-N	0	0	—	2	0	0	0	0	1^{2}	2	0	0	1	1	0	21.6	0.00	—	.286	.444	0	—	0	1	1	0	0.1
1979	LA-N	17	10	.630	39	30	5	1	0	242	217	104	16	2	97	117	11.8	3.46	105	.243	.319	21	.247	5	8	5	-2	0.9
1980	LA-N	3	9	.250	42	10	1	1	5	110	122	73	10	1	55	59	14.6	5.56	63	.285	.368	4	.148	-0	-24	-26	-1	-2.9
1981	LA-N	2	2	.500	14	6	0	0	0	47	41	24	5	2	20	16	12.1	4.02	83	.238	.325	2	.182	1	-3	-4	0	-0.2
1982	Cle-A	14	8	.636	34	27	6	1	1	216	174	81	16	4	98	142	11.5	**2.96**	138	**.226**	.317	0	—	0	**27**	27	1	2.7
1983	Cle-A☆	17	11	.607	36	35	10	2	0	243^{1}	251	131	23	6	102	160	13.3	4.29	99	.268	.344	0	—	0	-6	-1	2	0.1
1984	Cle-A	4	5	.444	15	15	2	0	0	94^{1}	111	60	7	2	46	58	15.2	5.15	79	.298	.378	0	—	0	-12	-11	-0	-0.9
	*Chi-N	16	1	**.941**	20	20	7	3	0	150^{1}	123	53	9	1	39	155	9.8	2.69	145	.220	.272	14	.250	3	15	19	2	2.6
1985	Chi-N	8	8	.500	20	20	6	3	0	130	119	51	12	3	44	102	11.5	3.18	126	.240	.306	10	.233	2	6	11	1	1.7
1986	Chi-N	5	14	.263	28	27	4	1	0	176^{2}	166	92	18	1	96	122	13.4	4.64	87	.252	.348	11	.208	2	-18	-11	1	-0.7
1987	Chi-N★	**18**	10	.643	34	34	6	1	0	237^{1}	223	106	24	4	106	174	12.6	3.68	116	.252	.335	12	.148	2	11	15	4	2.3
1988	Chi-N	13	14	.481	32	32	12	2	0	226	232	97	18	2	70	144	12.1	3.86	94	.269	.325	12	.160	3	-10	-6	1	-0.3
1989	*Chi-N★	16	11	.593	35	34	5	1	0	229	202	98	18	2	69	153	10.7	3.66	103	.240	.299	10	.143	1	-4	3	1	0.6
1990	Chi-N	0	2	.000	5	5	0	0	0	21^{1}	25	14	2	0	12	7	15.6	5.91	69	.305	.394	0	.000	0	-5	-4	0	-0.3
1991	Chi-N	6	5	.545	19	18	0	0	0	96^{2}	96	52	4	0	45	52	13.1	4.10	95	.264	.345	3	.094	-1	-4	-2	0	-0.3
1992	Bal-A	16	15	.516	36	36	5	2	0	237^{1}	251	123	20	7	74	109	12.6	4.47	90	.273	.332	0	—	0	-14	-11	-2	-1.5
1993	Bal-A	10	10	.500	29	28	3	0	0	166	212	112	23	6	74	80	15.8	5.75	78	.314	.386	0	—	0	-26	-22	1	-2.2

YEAR	TM/L	W	L	PCT	G	GS	CG	SH	SV	IP	H	R	HR	HB	BB	SO	RAT	ERA	ERA+	OAV	OOB	BH	AVG	PB	PR	PR+	PD	TPI
1994	StL-N	6	4	.600	16	14	0	0	0	67^{2}	93	53	11	2	32	26	16.9	6.52	64	.331	.403	3	.130	-1	-17	-18	1	-2.1
Total	18	171	139	.552	457	392	72	18	6	2697^{2}	2662	1324	236	46	1081	1679	12.6	4.08	97	.260	.334	102	.181	17	-74	-31	10	-0.3

● HARRY SUTER

Suter, Harry Richard "Handsome Harry" or "Rube"
b: 9/15/1887, Independence, Mo. d: 7/24/71, Topeka, Kan. BL/TL, 5'10", 190 lbs. Deb: 4/16/09

YEAR	TM/L	W	L	PCT	G	GS	CG	SH	SV	IP	H	R	HR	HB	BB	SO	RAT	ERA	ERA+	OAV	OOB	BH	AVG	PB	PR	PR+	PD	TPI
1909	Chi-A	2	3	.400	18	7	3	1	1	87^{1}	72	34	2	4	28	53	10.7	2.47	95	.199	.264	3	.094	-1	0	-1	-1	-0.3

● DARRELL SUTHERLAND

Sutherland, Darrell Wayne b: 11/14/41, Glendale, Cal. BR/TR, 6'4", 169 lbs. Deb: 6/28/64 F

YEAR	TM/L	W	L	PCT	G	GS	CG	SH	SV	IP	H	R	HR	HB	BB	SO	RAT	ERA	ERA+	OAV	OOB	BH	AVG	PB	PR	PR+	PD	TPI
1964	NY-N	0	3	.000	10	4	0	0	0	26^{2}	32	26	1	2	12	9	15.5	7.76	46	.302	.383	1	.200	0	-13	-12	1	-1.1
1965	NY-N	3	1	.750	18	2	0	0	0	48	33	16	4	4	17	16	10.1	2.81	125	.199	.289	2	.154	0	4	4	2	0.5
1966	NY-N	2	0	1.000	31	0	0	0	1	44^{1}	60	25	6	2	25	23	17.7	4.87	75	.339	.426	2	.667	1	-6	-6	1	-0.1
1968	Cle-A	0	0	—	3	0	0	0	0	3^{1}	6	3	0	0	4	2	27.0	8.10	37	.375	.500	0	—	0	-2	-2	-0	-0.1
Total	4	5	4	.556	62	6	0	0	1	122^{1}	131	70	11	8	58	50	14.5	4.78	75	.282	.371	5	.238	1	-17	-17	3	-0.8

● SUDS SUTHERLAND

Sutherland, Harvey Scott b: 2/20/1894, Beaverton, Ore. d: 5/11/72, Portland, Ore. BR/TR, 6', 180 lbs. Deb: 4/14/21

YEAR	TM/L	W	L	PCT	G	GS	CG	SH	SV	IP	H	R	HR	HB	BB	SO	RAT	ERA	ERA+	OAV	OOB	BH	AVG	PB	PR	PR+	PD	TPI
1921	Det-A	6	2	.750	13	8	3	0	0	58	80	43	1	0	18	18	15.2	4.97	86	.328	.374	11	.407	2	-4	-4	2	-0.1

● DIZZY SUTHERLAND

Sutherland, Howard Alvin b: 4/9/22, Washington, D.C. d: 8/26/79, Washington, D.C. BL/TL, 6', 200 lbs. Deb: 9/20/49

YEAR	TM/L	W	L	PCT	G	GS	CG	SH	SV	IP	H	R	HR	HB	BB	SO	RAT	ERA	ERA+	OAV	OOB	BH	AVG	PB	PR	PR+	PD	TPI
1949	Was-A	0	1	.000	1	1	0	0	0	1	2	5	0	0	6	0	72.0	45.00	9	.400	.727	0	—	0	-5	-4	0	-0.6

● BRUCE SUTTER

Sutter, Howard Bruce b: 1/8/53, Lancaster, Pa. BR/TR, 6'2", 190 lbs. Deb: 5/9/76

YEAR	TM/L	W	L	PCT	G	GS	CG	SH	SV	IP	H	R	HR	HB	BB	SO	RAT	ERA	ERA+	OAV	OOB	BH	AVG	PB	PR	PR+	PD	TPI
1976	Chi-N	6	3	.667	52	0	0	0	10	83^{1}	63	27	4	0	26	73	9.6	2.70	143	.209	.272	0	.000	-1	7	10	-0	1.2
1977	Chi-N†	7	3	.700	62	0	0	0	31	107^{1}	69	21	5	1	23	129	7.8	1.34	327	.183	.232	3	.150	-0	31	32	1	5.0
1978	Chi-N★	8	10	.444	64	0	0	0	27	98^{2}	82	44	10	1	34	106	10.7	3.19	126	.220	.287	1	.077	-0	4	8	0	1.7
1979	Chi-N★	6	6	.500	62	0	0	0	**37**	101^{1}	67	29	3	0	32	110	8.8	2.22	186	.186	.252	3	.250	0	17	**19**	1	4.0
1980	Chi-N★	5	8	.385	60	0	0	0	**28**	102^{1}	90	35	5	1	34	76	11.0	2.64	149	.242	.307	1	.111	-1	11	13	-0	2.4
1981	StL-N★	3	5	.375	48	0	0	0	**25**	82^{1}	64	24	5	1	24	57	9.7	2.62	136	.218	.279	0	.000	-1	8	8	-1	1.2
1982	*StL-N	9	8	.529	70	0	0	0	**36**	102^{1}	88	38	8	3	34	61	11.0	2.90	125	.235	.303	1	.125	-0	8	8	0	1.7
1983	StL-N	9	10	.474	60	0	0	0	21	89^{1}	90	45	8	1	30	64	12.2	4.23	86	.262	.324	0	.000	-1	-6	-6	2	-1.1
1984	StL-N☆	5	7	.417	71	0	0	0	**45**	122^{2}	109	26	9	1	23	77	9.8	1.54	226	.245	.284	0	.000	-1	**28**	**27**	1	**4.6**
1985	Atl-N	7	7	.500	58	0	0	0	23	88^{1}	91	46	13	3	29	52	12.5	4.48	86	.267	.330	0	.000	-0	-9	-6	-0	-1.2
1986	Atl-N	2	0	1.000	16	0	0	0	3	18^{2}	17	9	3	0	9	16	12.5	4.34	92	.243	.329	0	.000	-0	-1	-1	0	-0.1
1988	Atl-N	1	4	.200	38	0	0	0	14	45^{1}	49	26	4	1	11	40	12.1	4.76	77	.275	.321	0	.000	0	-7	-5	-0	-0.8
Total	12	68	71	.489	661	0	0	0	300	1042	879	370	77	13	309	861	10.4	2.83	136	.230	.289	9	.088	-5	92	110	4	18.6

● JACK SUTTHOFF

Sutthoff, John Gerhard "Sunny Jack" b: 6/29/1873, Cincinnati, Ohio d: 8/3/42, Cincinnati, Ohio BL/TR, 5'9", 175 lbs. Deb: 9/15/1898

YEAR	TM/L	W	L	PCT	G	GS	CG	SH	SV	IP	H	R	HR	HB	BB	SO	RAT	ERA	ERA+	OAV	OOB	BH	AVG	PB	PR	PR+	PD	TPI
1898	Was-N	0	0	—	2	1	0	0	0	8^{1}	16	13	1	0	8	3	25.9	12.96	28	.400	.500	1	.333	0	-9	-8	0	-0.3
1899	StL-N	1	2	.333	3	3	3	0	0	24	29	25	0	0	15	8	16.5	4.13	96	.299	.393	1	.100	-1	-1	-0	0	-0.1
1901	Cin-N	1	6	.143	10	4	4	0	0	70^{1}	82	55	2	2	39	12	15.7	5.50	58	.289	.378	3	.107	-2	-17	-19	-1	-1.8
1903	Cin-N	16	9	.640	30	27	21	3	0	224^{2}	207	104	2	16	79	76	12.1	2.80	127	.246	.323	12	.143	-3	12	17	-1	1.3
1904	Cin-N	5	6	.455	12	10	8	0	0	90	83	49	1	3	43	27	12.9	2.30	127	.255	.348	6	.182	-0	4	6	-2	0.4
	Phi-N	6	13	.316	19	18	17	0	0	163^{2}	172	90	2	9	71	46	13.9	3.68	73	.272	.354	10	.164	-0	-17	-19	-1	-2.1
	Yr	11	19	.367	31	28	25	0	0	253^{2}	255	139	3	12	114	73	13.5	3.19	87	.266	.352	16	.170	-1	-13	-12	-3	-1.7
1905	Phi-N	3	4	.429	13	6	4	1	0	77^{2}	82	46	2	4	36	26	14.1	3.82	76	.290	.378	2	.080	-1	-7	-8	0	-0.7
Total	6	32	40	.444	89	69	57	4	0	658^{2}	671	382	10	34	291	198	13.6	3.54	89	.268	.352	35	.143	-7	-35	-27	-5	-3.3

● DON SUTTON

Sutton, Donald Howard b: 4/2/45, Clio, Ala. BR/TR, 6'1", 185 lbs. Deb: 4/14/66 H

YEAR	TM/L	W	L	PCT	G	GS	CG	SH	SV	IP	H	R	HR	HB	BB	SO	RAT	ERA	ERA+	OAV	OOB	BH	AVG	PB	PR	PR+	PD	TPI
1966	LA-N	12	12	.500	37	35	6	2	0	225^{2}	192	82	19	3	52	209	9.9	2.99	110	.228	.276	15	.183	1	15	8	-0	1.0
1967	LA-N	11	15	.423	37	34	11	3	1	232^{2}	223	106	18	6	57	169	11.1	3.95	79	.250	.300	10	.133	-0	-15	-24	-2	-2.7
1968	LA-N	11	15	.423	35	27	7	2	1	207^{2}	179	64	6	2	59	162	10.4	2.60	106	.232	.288	11	.177	1	9	4	-1	0.5
1969	LA-N	17	18	.486	41	41	11	4	0	293^{1}	269	123	25	3	91	217	11.1	3.47	96	.242	.301	15	.153	-1	4	-5	0	-0.6
1970	LA-N	15	13	.536	38	38	10	4	0	260^{1}	251	127	38	10	78	201	11.7	4.08	94	.249	.310	13	.155	3	-1	-7	-1	-0.5
1971	LA-N	17	12	.586	38	37	12	4	1	265^{1}	231	85	10	5	55	194	9.9	2.54	127	.238	.282	19	.216	3	27	22	-1	2.7
1972	LA-N★	19	9	.679	33	33	18	**9**	0	272^{2}	186	78	13	4	63	207	**8.4**	2.08	160	**.189**	**.240**	13	.143	-1	42	39	-0	4.0
1973	LA-N★	18	10	.643	33	33	14	3	0	256^{1}	196	78	18	5	56	200	9.0	2.42	142	.209	.258	10	.119	-2	35	31	-1	3.1
1974	*LA-N	19	9	.679	40	40	10	5	0	276	241	111	23	6	80	179	10.7	3.23	106	.229	.288	18	.184	1	12	6	-1	0.5
1975	LA-N★	16	13	.552	35	35	11	4	0	254^{1}	202	87	17	3	62	175	9.4	2.87	119	.213	**.264**	11	.138	-1	22	16	-1	1.6
1976	LA-N	21	10	.677	35	34	15	4	0	267^{2}	231	98	22	3	82	161	10.6	3.06	111	.234	.295	7	.083	-3	13	10	-3	0.5
1977	*LA-N★	14	8	.636	33	33	9	3	0	240^{1}	207	93	23	3	69	150	10.4	3.18	120	.233	.291	11	.151	1	20	18	-1	1.5
1978	*LA-N	15	11	.577	34	34	12	2	0	238^{1}	228	109	29	5	54	154	10.8	3.55	99	.250	.295	6	.083	-3	1	-1	-2	-0.7
1979	LA-N	12	15	.444	33	32	6	1	1	226	201	109	21	1	61	146	10.5	3.82	95	.239	.291	11	.143	-2	-2	-5	-1	-0.8
1980	LA-N	13	5	.722	32	31	4	2	1	212^{1}	163	56	20	2	47	128	**9.0**	**2.20**	159	.211	**.258**	5	.078	-4	33	32	-0	2.2
1981	Hou-N	11	9	.550	23	23	6	3	0	158^{2}	132	51	6	1	29	104	**9.2**	2.61	126	.230	**.268**	7	.137	0	16	13	0	1.7
1982	Hou-N	13	8	.619	27	27	4	0	0	195	169	75	10	1	46	139	10.0	3.00	111	.232	.279	11	.162	-0	13	8	-1	0.7
	*Mil-A	4	1	.800	7	7	2	1	0	54^{2}	55	21	8	0	18	36	12.0	3.29	115	.263	.322	0	—	0	5	3	1	0.3
1983	Mil-A	8	13	.381	31	31	4	0	0	220^{1}	209	109	21	5	54	134	10.9	4.08	92	.246	.295	0	—	0	-0	-9	-1	-0.9
1984	Mil-A	14	12	.538	33	33	1	0	0	212^{2}	224	103	24	3	51	143	11.8	3.77	102	.266	.310	0	—	0	5	2	-2	0.1
1985	Oak-A	13	8	.619	29	29	1	1	0	194^{1}	194	88	19	0	51	91	11.3	3.89	99	.256	.302	0	—	0	6	-1	-0	-0.1
	Cal-A	2	2	.500	5	5	0	0	0	31^{2}	27	13	6	0	8	16	9.9	3.69	111	.233	.282	0	—	0	2	1	-1	0.1
	Yr	15	10	.600	34	34	1	1	0	226	221	101	25	0	59	107	11.2	3.86	101	.253	.300	0	—	0	7	1	-1	0.0
1986	*Cal-A	15	11	.577	34	34	3	1	0	207	192	93	31	3	49	116	10.6	3.74	110	.242	.288	0	—	0	10	9	-3	0.7
1987	Cal-A	11	11	.500	35	34	1	0	0	191^{2}	199	101	38	7	41	99	11.6	4.70	92	.269	.313	0	—	0	-5	-8	-3	-1.0
1988	LA-N	3	6	.333	16	16	0	0	0	87^{1}	91	44	7	1	30	44	12.6	3.92	85	.270	.332	2	.087	-1	-4	-6	-1	-0.7
Total	23	324	256	.559	774	756	178	58	5	5282^{1}	4692	2104	472	82	1343	3574	10.4	3.26	108	.236	.287	195	.144	-7	263	158	-26	13.2

● EZRA SUTTON

Sutton, Ezra Ballou b: 9/17/1850, Palmyra, N.Y. d: 6/20/07, Braintree, Mass. BR/TR, 5'8.5", 153 lbs. Deb: 5/4/1871 ♦

YEAR	TM/L	W	L	PCT	G	GS	CG	SH	SV	IP	H	R	HR	HB	BB	SO	RAT	ERA	ERA+	OAV	OOB	BH	AVG	PB	PR	PR+	PD	TPI
1875	Ath-n	0	0	—	2	0	0	0	0	6	14	13	0	0	0	0	21.0	10.50	23	.412	.412	116	.324	1	-6	-5		-0.2

● JOHN SUTTON

Sutton, Johnny Ike b: 11/13/52, Dallas, Tex. BR/TR, 5'11", 185 lbs. Deb: 4/7/77

YEAR	TM/L	W	L	PCT	G	GS	CG	SH	SV	IP	H	R	HR	HB	BB	SO	RAT	ERA	ERA+	OAV	OOB	BH	AVG	PB	PR	PR+	PD	TPI
1977	StL-N	2	1	.667	14	0	0	0	0	24^{1}	28	10	1	0	9	9	13.7	2.59	149	.315	.378	0	.000	-0	4	3	0	0.4
1978	Min-A	0	0	—	17	0	0	0	0	44^{1}	46	19	3	1	15	18	12.6	3.45	111	.264	.326	0	—	0	2	2	-0	0.1
Total	2	2	1	.667	31	0	0	0	0	68^{2}	74	29	4	1	24	27	13.0	3.15	122	.281	.344	0	.000	-0	5	5	0	0.5

● MAC SUZUKI

Suzuki, Makoto b: 5/31/75, Kobe, Japan BR/TR, 6'3", 195 lbs. Deb: 7/7/96

YEAR	TM/L	W	L	PCT	G	GS	CG	SH	SV	IP	H	R	HR	HB	BB	SO	RAT	ERA	ERA+	OAV	OOB	BH	AVG	PB	PR	PR+	PD	TPI
1996	Sea-A	0	0	—	1	0	0	0	0	1^{1}	2	3	0	0	2	1	27.0	20.25	24	.333	.500	0	—	0	-2	-2	0	-0.1
1998	Sea-A	1	2	.333	6	5	0	0	0	26^{1}	34	23	3	0	15	19	16.7	7.18	65	.304	.386	0	—	0	-7	-7	-0	-0.7
1999	Sea-A	0	2	.000	16	4	0	0	0	42	47	47	7	4	34	32	18.2	9.43	50	.283	.417	0	—	0	-21	-22	-0	-1.0
	KC-A	2	3	.400	22	9	0	0	0	68	77	45	9	3	30	36	14.6	5.16	97	.287	.365	0	—	0	-2	-1	-1	-0.1
	Yr	2	5	.286	38	13	0	0	0	110	124	92	16	7	64	68	16.0	6.79	72	.286	.386	0	—	0	-23	-23	-1	-1.1
2000	KC-A	8	10	.444	32	29	1	1	0	188^{2}	195	100	26	3	94	135	13.9	4.34	115	.265	.350	1	.200	0	12	14	-1	1.1
Total	4	11	17	.393	77	47	1	1	0	326^{1}	355	218	45	10	175	223	14.9	5.46	91	.275	.366	1	.200	0	-21	-18	-2	-0.8

● BILL SWABACH

Swabach, William Deb: 7/9/1887

YEAR	TM/L	W	L	PCT	G	GS	CG	SH	SV	IP	H	R	HR	HB	BB	SO	RAT	ERA	ERA+	OAV	OOB	BH	AVG	PB	PR	PR+	PD	TPI
1887	NY-N	0	2	.000	2	2	2	0	0	16	33	23	1	1	6	6	19.1	5.06	74	.393	.400	0	.000	-1	-2	-2	0	-0.3

● BILL SWAGGERTY

Swaggerty, William David b: 12/5/56, Sanford, Fla. BR/TR, 6'2", 186 lbs. Deb: 8/13/83

YEAR	TM/L	W	L	PCT	G	GS	CG	SH	SV	IP	H	R	HR	HB	BB	SO	RAT	ERA	ERA+	OAV	OOB	BH	AVG	PB	PR	PR+	PD	TPI
1983	Bal-A	1	1	.500	7	2	0	0	0	21^{2}	23	8	1	0	6	7	12.0	2.91	136	.267	.315	0	—	0	3	3	1	0.3
1984	Bal-A	3	2	.600	23	6	0	0	0	57	68	41	7	0	21	18	14.1	5.21	74	.302	.362	0	—	0	-8	-9	-1	-0.7
1985	Bal-A	0	0	—	1	0	0	0	0	1^{2}	3	1	0	0	2	2	27.0	5.40	75	.375	.500	0	—	0	-0	-0	-0	0.0
1986	Bal-A	0	0	—	1	0	0	0	0	1	6	2	0	0	1	1	63.0	18.00	23	.750	.778	0	—	0	-2	-2	0	-0.1
Total	4	4	3	.571	32	8	0	0	0	81^{1}	100	52	8	0	30	28	14.4	4.76	82	.306	.364	0	—	0	-7	-8	0	-0.5

YEAR TM/L	W	L	PCT	G	GS	CG	SH	SV	IP	H	R	HR	HB	BB	SO	RAT	ERA	ERA+	OAV	OOB	BH	AVG	PB	PR	PR+	PD	TPI
● CY SWAIM Swaim, John Hillary b: 3/11/1874, Cadwallader, Ohio d: 12/27/45, Eustis, Fla. 6'6", 180 lbs. Deb: 5/3/1897																											
1897 Was-N	9	11	.450	26	19	14	0	0	184	219	129	5	10	59	52	14.1	4.60	94	.293	.353	16	.225	-3	-6	-5	-4	-1.0
1898 Was-N	3	11	.214	16	13	9	0	1	101^{1}	119	77	4	4	28	30	13.4	4.26	86	.290	.342	5	.143	-3	-7	-7	-1	-1.1
Total 2	12	22	.353	42	32	23	0	1	285^{1}	338	206	9	14	87	82	13.8	4.48	92	.292	.349	21	.198	-6	-13	-12	-5	-2.1
● CRAIG SWAN Swan, Craig Steven b: 11/30/50, Van Nuys, Cal. BR/TR, 6'3", 215 lbs. Deb: 9/3/73																											
1973 NY-N	0	1	.000	3	1	0	0	0	8^{1}	16	9	2	0	2	4	19.4	8.64	42	.432	.462	0	.000	-0	-5	-5	-0	-0.5
1974 NY-N	1	3	.250	7	5	0	0	0	30^{1}	28	19	1	0	21	10	14.5	4.45	80	.255	.374	4	.364	1	-3	-3	0	-0.2
1975 NY-N	1	3	.250	6	6	0	0	0	31	38	22	4	1	13	19	15.1	6.39	54	.302	.371	0	.000	-1	-9	-11	-1	-1.3
1976 NY-N	6	9	.400	23	22	2	1	0	132^{1}	129	64	11	5	44	89	12.1	3.54	93	.254	.320	4	.103	-1	-0	-4	-1	-0.5
1977 NY-N	9	10	.474	26	24	2	1	0	146^{2}	153	76	10	1	56	71	12.9	4.23	88	.268	.334	9	.188	-0	-5	-8	-2	-1.2
1978 NY-N	9	6	.600	29	28	5	1	0	207^{1}	164	62	12	2	58	125	**9.7**	**2.43**	**144**	.219	.277	10	.154	-0	27	25	1	1.8
1979 NY-N	14	13	.519	35	35	10	3	0	251^{1}	241	102	20	2	57	145	10.7	3.29	111	.255	.299	10	.123	-1	12	10	-1	0.8
1980 NY-N	5	9	.357	21	21	4	1	0	128^{1}	117	59	20	0	30	79	10.3	3.58	99	.247	.292	7	.219	2	0	-0	-2	-0.1
1981 NY-N	0	2	.000	5	3	0	0	0	13^{2}	10	6	0	0	1	9	7.2	3.29	106	.204	.220	0	.000	-0	0	0	-0	0.0
1982 NY-N	11	7	.611	37	21	2	0	1	166^{1}	165	70	13	0	37	67	10.9	3.35	108	.256	.297	8	.182	3	5	5	-1	0.7
1983 NY-N	2	8	.200	27	18	0	0	1	96^{1}	112	63	14	0	42	43	14.4	5.51	66	.299	.369	2	.077	-2	-20	-20	-1	-2.2
1984 NY-N	1	0	1.000	10	0	0	0	0	18^{2}	18	17	5	0	7	10	12.1	8.20	43	.247	.313	0	—	0	-10	-10	-0	-0.5
Cal-A	0	1	.000	2	1	0	0	0	5	8	6	3	0	0	2	14.4	10.80	37	.348	.348	0	—	0	-4	-4	0	-0.6
Total 12	59	72	.450	231	185	25	7	2	1235^{2}	1199	575	115	11	368	673	11.5	3.74	96	.256	.312	54	.151	1	-11	-24	-10	-3.8
● DUCKY SWAN Swan, Harry Gordon b: 8/11/1887, Lancaster, Pa. d: 5/8/46, Pittsburgh, Pa. BR/TR, 5'10", 165 lbs. Deb: 4/28/14																											
1914 KC-F	0	0	—	1	0	0	0	0	1	0	0	0	0	1	1	9.0	0.00	—	.000	.250	0	—	0	0	0	-0	0.0
● RUSS SWAN Swan, Russell Howard b: 1/3/64, Fremont, Cal. BL/TL, 6'4", 215 lbs. Deb: 8/3/89																											
1989 SF-N	0	2	.000	2	2	0	0	0	6^{2}	11	10	4	0	4	2	20.3	10.80	31	.393	.469	0	.000	-0	-5	-6	0	-0.9
1990 SF-N	0	1	.000	2	1	0	0	0	2^{1}	6	4	0	0	4	1	38.6	3.86	95	.429	.556	0	.000	-0	-0	-0	0	0.0
Sea-A	2	3	.400	11	8	0	0	0	47	42	22	3	0	18	15	11.5	3.64	109	.244	.316	0	—	0	1	2	0	0.2
1991 Sea-A	6	2	.750	63	0	0	0	2	78^{2}	81	35	8	0	28	33	12.5	3.43	120	.269	.331	0	—	0	6	6	1	0.6
1992 Sea-A	3	10	.231	55	9	1	0	9	104^{1}	104	60	8	3	45	45	13.1	4.74	84	.262	.342	0	—	0	-9	-9	2	-0.9
1993 Sea-A	3	3	.500	23	0	0	0	0	19^{2}	25	20	2	2	18	10	20.6	9.15	48	.316	.455	0	—	0	-11	-10	1	-1.8
1994 Cle-A	0	1	.000	12	0	0	0	0	8	13	11	1	0	7	2	22.5	11.25	42	.382	.488	0	—	0	-6	-6	0	-0.6
Total 6	14	22	.389	168	20	1	0	11	266^{2}	282	162	26	5	124	108	13.9	4.83	84	.275	.356	0	.000	-0	-24	-23	3	-3.4
● RED SWANSON Swanson, Arthur Leonard b: 10/15/36, Baton Rouge, La. BR/TR, 6'1.5", 175 lbs. Deb: 9/10/55																											
1955 Pit-N	0	0	—	1	0	0	0	0	2	2	4	1	0	3	0	22.5	18.00	23	.286	.500	0	—	0	-3	-3	-0	-0.1
1956 Pit-N	0	0	—	9	0	0	0	0	11^{2}	21	13	1	0	8	5	22.4	10.03	38	.438	.518	0	—	0	-8	-8	1	-0.3
1957 Pit-N	3	3	.500	32	8	1	0	0	72^{2}	68	35	9	1	31	29	12.4	3.72	102	.248	.327	0	.000	-1	1	1	-1	-0.2
Total 3	3	3	.500	42	8	1	0	0	86^{1}	91	52	11	1	42	34	14.0	4.90	77	.277	.360	0	.000	-1	-10	-11	-0	-0.6
● ED SWARTWOOD Swartwood, Cyrus Edward b: 1/12/1859, Rockford, Ill. d: 5/15/24, Pittsburgh, Pa. BL/TR, 5'11", 198 lbs. Deb: 8/11/1881 U♦																											
1884 Pit-a	0	0	—	1	0	0	0	0	2^{1}	6	5	0	0	1	0	27.0	11.57	29	.400	.438	115	.288	0	-2	-2	-0	-0.1
1890 Tol-a	0	0	—	1	0	0	0	0	3	2	1	0	0	0	1	6.0	3.00	132	.182	.182	151	.327	0	0	0	-0	0.0
Total 2	0	0	—	2	0	0	0	0	5^{1}	8	6	0	0	1	1	15.2	6.75	54	.308	.333	907	.310	1	-2	-2	-0	-0.1
● BUD SWARTZ Swartz, Sherwin Merle b: 6/13/29, Tulsa, Okla. d: 6/24/91, Los Angeles, Cal. BL/TL, 6'2.5", 180 lbs. Deb: 7/12/47																											
1947 StL-A	0	0	—	5	0	0	0	0	5^{1}	9	6	1	0	7	1	27.0	6.75	57	.360	.500	1	1.000	0	-2	-2	-0	-0.1
● MONTY SWARTZ Swartz, Vernon Monroe "Dazzy" b: 1/1/1897, Farmersville, Ohio d: 1/13/80, Germantown, Ohio BR/TR, 5'11", 182 lbs. Deb: 10/3/20																											
1920 Cin-N	0	1	.000	1	1	1	0	0	12	17	6	0	0	2	2	14.3	4.50	68	.333	.358	2	.500	1	-2	-2	0	-0.1
● DAVE SWARTZBAUGH Swartzbaugh, David Theodore b: 2/11/68, Middletown, Ohio BR/TR, 6'2", 195 lbs. Deb: 9/3/95																											
1995 Chi-N	0	0	—	7	0	0	0	0	7^{1}	5	2	0	0	3	5	9.8	0.00	—	.208	.296	0	—	0	3	3	-0	0.1
1996 Chi-N	0	2	.000	6	5	0	0	0	24	26	17	3	0	14	13	15.0	6.38	68	.277	.370	0	.000	-0	-6	-5	0	-0.4
1997 Chi-N	0	1	.000	2	2	0	0	0	8	12	8	1	1	7	4	22.5	9.00	48	.364	.488	0	.000	-0	-4	-4	-0	-0.4
Total 3	0	3	.000	15	7	0	0	0	39^{1}	43	27	4	1	24	22	15.6	5.72	75	.285	.386	0	.000	-1	-7	-6	0	-0.7
● PARK SWARTZEL Swartzel, Park B. b: 11/21/1865, Knightstown, Ind. d: 1/3/40, Los Angeles, Cal. BR/TR, 5'10", Deb: 4/17/1889																											
1889 KC-a	19	27	.413	48	47	45	0	1	410^{1}	481	334	21	23	117	147	13.6	4.32	97	.283	.338	25	.144	-9	-22	-6	9	-0.5
● CHARLIE SWEENEY Sweeney, Charles J. b: 4/13/1863, San Francisco, Cal d: 4/4/02, San Francisco, Cal. BR/TR, 5'10.5", 181 lbs. Deb: 5/11/1882 ♦																											
1883 Pro-N	7	7	.500	20	18	14	0	0	146^{2}	142	94	3		28	48	10.4	3.13	99	.237	.272	19	.218	-1	0	-1	1	-0.1
1884 Pro-N	17	8	.680	27	24	22	4	1	221	153	70	4		29	145	**7.4**	1.55	184	**.187**	**.215**	50	.298	8	35	33	1	4.2
StL-U	24	7	.774	33	32	31	2	0	271	207	112	2		13	192	7.3	1.83	131	.197	.207	54	.316	6	19	17	5	2.5
1885 StL-N	11	21	.344	35	35	32	2	0	275	276	175	6		50	84	10.7	3.93	70	.250	.282	55	.206	-0	-34	-37	0	-3.4
1886 StL-N	5	6	.455	11	11	11	0	0	93	108	73	9		39	28	14.2	4.16	78	.285	.352	16	.250	1	-9	-10	0	-0.8
1887 Cle-a	0	3	.000	3	3	3	0	0	24	55	36	0		13	8	20.6	8.25	53	.437	.437	51	.331	0	-11	-10	0	-0.8
Total 5	64	52	.552	129	123	113	8	1	1030^{2}	941	560	24	0	172	505	9.6	2.87	98	.231	.260	245	.268	14	1	-8	8	1.6
● BILL SWEENEY Sweeney, William J. b: Philadelphia, Pa. d: 8/2/03, Philadelphia, Pa. TR, Deb: 6/27/1882																											
1882 Phi-a	9	10	.474	20	20	18	0	0	170	178	119	4		42	48	11.6	2.91	102	.252	.294	14	.159	-3	-4	1	-1	-0.2
1884 Bal-U	**40**	21	.656	**62**	60	**58**	4	0	**538**	522	294	13		74	374	10.0	2.59	103	.238	.263	71	.240	-16	-9	5	0	-0.8
Total 2	49	31	.613	82	80	76	4	0	708	700	413	17		116	422	10.4	2.67	103	.241	.270	85	.221	-19	-13	6	1	-1.0
● LES SWEETLAND Sweetland, Lester Leo (Born Leo Sweetland) b: 8/15/01, St.Ignace, Mich. d: 3/4/74, Melbourne, Fla. BR/TL (BB 1930-31), 5'11.5", 155 lbs. Deb: 7/4/27																											
1927 Phi-N	2	10	.167	21	13	6	0	0	103^{2}	147	77	3	3	53	21	17.6	6.16	67	.348	.425	12	.316	3	-26	-22	5	-1.4
1928 Phi-N	3	15	.167	37	18	5	0	2	135^{1}	163	111	15	15	97	23	18.3	6.58	65	.306	.426	9	.191	1	-39	-32	2	-3.4
1929 Phi-N	13	11	.542	43	26	10	2	2	204^{1}	255	129	23	9	87	47	15.5	5.11	102	.316	.389	26	.292	3	-9	2	4	0.8
1930 Phi-N	7	15	.318	34	25	8	1	0	167	271	164	24	5	60	36	18.1	7.71	71	.373	.425	16	.281	4	-51	-38	1	-3.4
1931 Chi-N	8	7	.533	26	14	9	0	0	130^{1}	156	89	3	5	61	32	15.3	5.04	77	.297	.375	15	.268	5	-17	-17	0	-1.3
Total 5	33	58	.363	161	96	38	3	4	740^{2}	992	570	68	37	358	159	16.9	6.10	77	.329	.407	78	.272	16	-142	-109	12	-8.7
● STEVE SWETONIC Swetonic, Stephen Albert b: 8/13/03, Mt.Pleasant, Pa. d: 4/22/74, Canonsburg, Pa. BR/TR, 5'11", 185 lbs. Deb: 4/17/29 ♦																											
1929 Pit-N	8	10	.444	41	12	3	0	5	143^{2}	172	87	6	5	50	35	14.2	4.82	99	.299	.360	13	.271	3	-2	-1	2	0.3
1930 Pit-N	6	6	.500	23	6	3	1	5	96^{2}	107	53	7	0	27	35	12.5	4.47	111	.276	.323	4	.111	-3	5	5	-1	0.3
1931 Pit-N	0	2	.000	14	0	0	0	1	27^{2}	28	12	0	0	16	8	14.3	3.90	99	.264	.361	1	.143	-0	-0	-0	-0	0.0
1932 Pit-N	11	6	.647	24	19	11	**4**	0	162^{2}	134	57	11	0	55	39	10.5	2.82	135	**.221**	.286	5	.093	-4	19	18	-1	1.2
1933 Pit-N	12	12	.500	31	21	8	3	0	164^{2}	166	78	10	2	64	37	12.7	3.50	95	.260	.330	11	.200	1	-3	-3	-1	-0.5
Total 5	37	36	.507	133	58	25	8	11	595^{1}	607	287	34	7	212	154	12.5	3.81	107	.262	.326	34	.170	-3	20	19	-2	1.3
● BILL SWIFT Swift, William Charles b: 10/27/61, Portland, Maine BR/TR, 6', 180 lbs. Deb: 6/7/85																											
1985 Sea-A	6	10	.375	23	21	0	0	0	120^{2}	131	71	8	5	48	55	13.7	4.77	88	.279	.352	0	—	0	-8	-7	0	-0.8
1986 Sea-A	2	9	.182	29	17	1	0	0	115^{1}	148	85	5	7	55	55	16.4	5.46	78	.319	.399	0	—	0	-16	-15	1	-1.1
1988 Sea-A	8	12	.400	38	24	6	1	0	174^{2}	199	99	10	8	65	47	14.0	4.59	91	.294	.363	0	—	0	-12	-8	2	-0.6
1989 Sea-A	7	3	.700	37	16	0	0	1	130	140	72	7	2	38	45	12.5	4.43	91	.278	.331	0	—	0	-8	-6	5	0.1
1990 Sea-A	6	4	.600	55	8	0	0	6	128	135	46	4	7	21	42	11.5	2.39	166	.272	.311	0	—	0	22	22	0	1.8
1991 Sea-A	1	2	.333	71	0	0	0	17	90^{1}	74	22	3	1	26	48	10.1	1.99	207	.224	.283	0	—	0	21	21	3	1.6
1992 SF-N	10	4	.714	30	22	3	2	1	164^{2}	144	41	6	3	43	77	10.4	**2.08**	159	.239	.293	8	.157	1	26	24	2	2.5
1993 SF-N	21	8	.724	34	34	1	1	0	232^{2}	195	82	18	6	55	157	9.9	2.82	139	.226	.278	21	.262	6	32	29	2	4.4
1994 SF-N	8	7	.533	17	17	0	0	0	109^{1}	109	49	10	1	31	62	11.6	3.38	119	.262	.315	6	.188	2	10	8	-1	1.2
1995 *Col-N	9	3	.750	19	19	0	0	0	105^{2}	122	62	12	1	43	68	14.1	4.94	109	.296	.364	7	.194	0	-9	4	3	0.8

YEAR TM/L	W	L	PCT	G	GS	CG	SH	SV	IP	H	R	HR	HB	BB	SO	RAT	ERA	ERA+	OAV	OOB	BH	AVG	PB	PR	PR+	PD	TPI
1996 Col-N	1	1	.500	7	3	0	0	2	18^1	23	12	1	0	5	5	13.7	5.40	97	.307	.350	2	.333	0	-2	-0	0	0.0
1997 Col-N	4	6	.400	14	13	0	0	0	65^1	85	57	11	2	26	29	15.6	6.34	82	.317	.382	4	.211	1	-15	-7	2	-0.6
1998 Sea-A	11	9	.550	29	26	0	0	0	144^2	183	103	21	10	51	77	15.2	5.85	79	.306	.370	0	.000	-0	-19	-20	2	-2.0
Total 13	94	78	.547	403	220	11	4	27	1599^2	1688	801	116	53	507	767	12.6	3.95	106	.273	.334	48	.210	10	21	40	23	7.3
● BILL SWIFT Swift, William Vincent b: 1/10/08, Elmira, N.Y. d: 2/23/69, Bartow, Fla. BR/TR, 6'1.5", 192 lbs. Deb: 4/12/32																											
1932 Pit-N	14	10	.583	39	23	11	0	4	214^1	205	97	15	2	26	64	9.8	3.61	106	.248	.272	15	.192	-1	6	5	-4	0.0
1933 Pit-N	14	10	.583	37	29	13	2	0	218^1	214	96	11	4	36	64	10.5	3.13	106	.251	.285	20	.244	3	5	5	-2	0.6
1934 Pit-N	11	13	.458	37	25	13	1	0	212^2	244	107	15	8	46	81	12.6	3.98	103	.284	.326	18	.214	2	2	3	-1	0.3
1935 Pit-N	15	8	.652	39	22	11	3	1	203^2	193	76	6	1	37	74	10.2	2.70	152	.247	.282	19	.244	3	30	31	-4	3.1
1936 Pit-N	16	16	.500	45	31	17	0	2	262^1	275	132	18	5	63	92	11.8	4.01	101	.265	.310	31	.295	9	0	1	-5	0.5
1937 Pit-N	9	10	.474	36	17	9	0	3	164	160	79	14	3	34	84	10.8	3.95	98	.256	.297	9	.167	-1	-1	-2	-3	-0.5
1938 Pit-N	7	5	.583	36	9	2	0	4	150	155	65	9	4	40	77	11.9	3.24	117	.271	.323	10	.200	2	9	9	-1	0.8
1939 Pit-N	5	7	.417	36	8	2	1	4	129^2	150	60	6	3	28	56	12.6	3.89	99	.293	.333	10	.238	2	0	-1	-3	-0.2
1940 Bos-N	1	1	.500	4	0	0	0	1	9^1	12	7	0	0	7	7	18.3	2.89	129	.308	.413	0	.000	-0	1	1	0	0.1
1941 Bro-N	3	0	1.000	9	0	0	0	1	22	26	9	4	0	7	9	13.5	3.27	112	.289	.340	1	.200	-0	1	1	-0	0.1
1943 Chi-A	0	2	.000	18	1	0	0	0	51^1	48	25	5	6	27	28	14.2	4.21	79	.246	.355	1	.100	0	-5	-5	-2	-0.4
Total 11	95	82	.537	336	165	78	7	20	1637^2	1682	753	103	36	351	636	11.4	3.58	108	.263	.305	134	.227	18	49	49	-25	4.4
● OAD SWIGART Swigart, Oadis Vaughn b: 2/13/15, Archie, Mo. d: 8/8/97, St.Joseph, Mo. BL/TR, 6', 175 lbs. Deb: 9/14/39																											
1939 Pit-N	1	1	.500	3	3	1	1	0	24^1	27	14	1	0	6	8	12.2	4.44	87	.293	.337	2	.250	0	-1	-2	-0	-0.1
1940 Pit-N	0	2	.000	7	2	0	0	0	22^1	27	14	1	0	10	9	14.9	4.43	86	.297	.366	1	.200	-0	-1	-2	-0	-0.1
Total 2	1	3	.250	10	5	1	1	0	46^2	54	28	2	0	16	17	13.5	4.44	86	.295	.352	3	.231	0	-3	-3	-0	-0.2
● AD SWIGLER Swigler, Adam William "Doc" b: 9/21/1895, Philadelphia, Pa. d: 2/5/75, Philadelphia, Pa. BR/TR, 5'10", 180 lbs. Deb: 9/25/17																											
1917 NY-N	0	1	.000	1	1	0	0	0	6	7	4	0	0	8	4	22.5	6.00	43	.333	.517	0	.000	-0	-2	-2	0	-0.4
● GREG SWINDELL Swindell, Forest Gregory b: 1/2/65, Fort Worth, Tex. BR/TL, 6'3", 225 lbs. Deb: 8/21/86																											
1986 Cle-A	5	2	.714	9	9	1	0	0	61^2	57	35	9	1	15	46	10.7	4.23	98	.243	.291	0	—	0	-0	-1	1	0.0
1987 Cle-A	3	8	.273	16	15	4	1	0	102^1	112	62	18	1	37	97	13.2	5.10	89	.283	.346	0	—	0	-7	-6	-0	-0.6
1988 Cle-A	18	14	.563	33	33	12	4	0	242	234	97	18	1	45	180	10.4	3.20	129	.252	.287	0	—	0	21	24	-1	2.9
1989 Cle-A★	13	6	.684	28	28	5	2	0	184^1	170	71	16	0	51	129	10.8	3.37	118	.246	.298	0	—	0	11	12	-0	1.1
1990 Cle-A	12	9	.571	34	34	3	0	0	214^2	245	110	27	1	47	135	12.3	4.40	89	.288	.326	0	—	0	-12	-11	-2	-1.2
1991 Cle-A	9	16	.360	33	33	7	0	0	238	241	112	21	3	31	169	10.4	3.48	120	.263	.289	0	—	0	16	18	-1	1.6
1992 Cin-N	12	8	.600	31	30	5	3	0	213^2	210	72	14	2	41	138	10.7	2.70	134	.260	.297	10	.125	-2	19	21	-2	1.7
1993 Hou-N	12	13	.480	31	30	1	1	0	190^1	215	98	24	1	40	124	12.1	4.16	93	.283	.319	11	.183	0	-2	-6	0	-0.7
1994 Hou-N	8	9	.471	24	24	1	0	0	148^1	175	80	20	1	26	74	12.3	4.37	91	.302	.333	11	.250	3	-2	-7	-2	-0.7
1995 Hou-N	10	9	.526	33	26	1	1	0	153	180	86	21	2	39	96	13.0	4.47	87	.297	.342	12	.240	4	-5	-11	2	-0.7
1996 Hou-N	0	3	.000	8	4	0	0	0	23	35	25	5	1	11	15	18.4	7.83	49	.340	.409	2	.333	1	-9	-11	-0	-1.1
Cle-A	1	1	.500	13	2	0	0	0	28^2	31	21	8	0	8	21	12.2	6.59	74	.279	.328	0	—	0	-5	-6	0	-0.3
1997 Min-A	7	4	.636	65	1	0	0	1	115^2	102	46	12	2	25	75	10.0	3.58	130	.238	.284	0	—	0	13	14	0	1.1
1998 Min-A	3	3	.500	52	0	0	0	2	66^1	67	27	10	3	18	45	11.9	3.66	130	.263	.319	0	—	0	7	8	-0	0.6
*Bos-A	2	3	.400	29	0	0	0	0	24	25	13	3	0	13	18	14.3	3.38	140	.278	.369	0	—	0	3	4	0	0.7
Yr	5	6	.455	81	0	0	0	2	90^1	92	40	13	3	31	63	12.6	3.59	133	.267	.332	0	—	0	11	12	0	1.3
1999 *Ari-N	4	0	1.000	63	0	0	0	1	64^2	54	19	8	1	21	51	10.6	2.51	183	.230	.296	0	.000	-0	15	15	0	0.8
2000 Ari-N	2	6	.250	64	0	0	0	1	76	71	29	7	1	20	64	10.9	3.20	144	.247	.298	0	.000	-0	12	12	0	1.1
Total 15	121	114	.515	566	269	40	12	5	2146^2	2224	1003	241	21	488	1477	11.5	3.80	108	.269	.311	46	.188	6	75	73	-5	6.3
● JOSH SWINDELL Swindell, Joshua Ernest b: 7/5/1883, Rose Hill, Kan. d: 3/19/69, Fruita, Colo. BR/TR, 6', 180 lbs. Deb: 9/16/11 ♦																											
1911 Cle-A	0	1	.000	4	1	1	0	0	17^1	19	9	0	1	4	6	12.5	2.08	164	.257	.304	1	.250	-0	2	3	-0	0.1
● PAUL SWINGLE Swingle, Paul Christopher b: 12/21/66, Inglewood, Cal. BR/TR, 6', 185 lbs. Deb: 9/7/93																											
1993 Cal-A	0	1	.000	9	0	0	0	0	9^2	15	9	2	0	6	6	19.6	8.38	54	.357	.438	0	—	0	-4	-4	-0	-0.4
● LEN SWORMSTEDT Swormstedt, Leonard Jordan b: 10/6/1878, Cincinnati, Ohio d: 7/19/64, Salem, Mass. BR/TR, 5'11.5", 165 lbs. Deb: 9/29/01																											
1901 Cin-N	2	1	.667	3	3	3	0	0	26	19	8	2	2	5	13	9.0	1.73	185	.202	.257	0	.000	-1	5	4	0	0.3
1902 Cin-N	0	2	.000	2	2	2	0	0	18	22	11	1	0	5	3	13.5	4.00	75	.301	.346	0	.000	-1	-2	-2	-0	-0.3
1906 Bos-A	1	1	.500	3	2	2	0	0	21	17	6	0	1	0	6	7.7	1.29	214	.224	.234	1	.125	-1	3	3	0	0.2
Total 3	3	4	.429	8	7	7	0	0	65	58	25	3	3	10	22	9.8	2.22	136	.239	.277	1	.043	-3	5	6	-1	0.2
● BOB SYKES Sykes, Robert Joseph b: 12/11/54, Neptune, N.J. BB/TL, 6'2", 200 lbs. Deb: 4/9/77																											
1977 Det-A	5	7	.417	32	20	3	0	0	132^2	141	74	15	2	50	58	13.1	4.41	98	.271	.337	0	—	0	-5	-1	-0	-0.2
1978 Det-A	6	6	.500	22	10	3	2	2	93^2	99	43	14	1	34	58	12.9	3.94	98	.275	.339	0	—	0	-2	-1	-2	-0.3
1979 StL-N	4	3	.571	13	11	0	0	0	67	86	49	11	1	34	35	16.3	6.18	61	.315	.393	2	.095	-0	-18	-18	-1	-1.7
1980 StL-N	6	10	.375	27	19	4	3	0	126	134	67	12	0	54	50	13.4	4.64	80	.277	.350	4	.103	-2	-14	-13	-2	-1.8
1981 StL-N	2	0	1.000	22	1	0	0	0	37^1	37	20	2	1	18	14	13.5	4.58	78	.266	.354	0	.000	0	-5	-4	1	-0.2
Total 5	23	26	.469	116	61	10	5	2	456^2	497	253	54	5	190	215	13.6	4.65	84	.280	.351	6	.097	-2	-44	-37	-4	-4.2
● LOU SYLVESTER Sylvester, Louis J. b: 2/14/1855, Springfield, Ill. BR/TR, 5'3", 165 lbs. Deb: 4/18/1884 ♦																											
1884 Cin-U	0	1	.000	6	1	1	0	1	32^2	32	27	0	0	6	7	10.5	3.58	72	.239	.271	89	.267	-0	-4	-4	-1	-0.2
● JEFF TABAKA Tabaka, Jeffrey Jon b: 1/17/64, Barberton, Ohio BR/TL, 6'2", 195 lbs. Deb: 4/19/94																											
1994 Pit-N	0	0	—	5	0	0	0	0	4	4	8	1	0	8	2	27.0	18.00	24	.250	.500	0	—	0	-6	-6	-0	-0.3
SD-N	3	1	.750	34	0	0	0	1	37	28	21	0	0	19	30	11.4	3.89	106	.209	.307	1	1.000	1	1	1	-0	0.2
Yr	3	1	.750	39	0	0	0	1	41	32	29	1	0	27	32	13.0	5.27	78	.213	.333	1	1.000	1	-5	-5	-1	-0.1
1995 SD-N	0	0	—	10	0	0	0	0	6^1	10	5	1	0	5	6	21.3	7.11	57	.370	.469	0	—	0	-2	-2	-0	-0.1
Hou-N	1	0	1.000	24	0	0	0	0	24^1	17	6	1	0	12	19	10.7	2.22	174	.202	.302	0	.000	-0	5	5	-0	0.2
Yr	1	0	1.000	34	0	0	0	0	30^2	27	11	2	0	17	25	12.9	3.23	121	.243	.344	0	.000	-0	3	2	-0	0.1
1996 Hou-N	0	2	.000	18	0	0	0	1	20^1	28	18	5	3	14	18	19.9	6.64	58	.322	.433	0	.000	-0	-5	-7	-1	-0.7
1997 Cin-N	0	0	—	3	0	0	0	0	2	1	1	1	2	1	1	18.0	4.50	95	.143	.400	0	—	0	-0	-0	-0	0.0
1998 Pit-N	2	2	.500	37	0	0	0	0	50^2	37	19	6	5	22	40	11.4	3.02	142	.204	.308	0	.000	-0	7	7	0	0.5
Total 5	6	5	.545	131	0	0	0	2	144^2	125	78	15	10	81	116	13.4	4.23	97	.233	.344	1	.250	1	-0	-2	-1	-0.1
● LEFTY TABER Taber, Edward Timothy b: 1/11/1900, Rock Island, Ill. d: 11/5/83, Lincoln, Neb. BL/TL, 6', 180 lbs. Deb: 9/4/26																											
1926 Phi-N	0	0	—	6	0	0	0	0	8^1	8	7	0	2	5	0	16.2	7.56	55	.242	.375	0	.000	-0	-3	-3	-0	-0.2
1927 Phi-N	0	1	.000	3	1	0	0	0	3^1	8	9	0	1	5	0	37.8	18.90	22	.533	.667	0	.000	-0	-6	-5	0	-0.9
Total 2	0	1	.000	9	1	0	0	0	11^2	16	16	0	3	10	0	22.4	10.80	38	.333	.475	0	.000	-0	-9	-8	0	-1.1
● JOHN TABER Taber, John Pardon b: 6/28/1868, Acushnet, Mass. d: 2/21/40, Boston, Mass. BR/TR, 5'8", Deb: 4/30/1890																											
1890 Bos-N	0	1	.000	2	1	1	0	1	13	11	8	0	0	8	3	13.2	4.15	90	.220	.328	0	.000	-1	-1	-1	0	-0.1
● JEFF TACKETT Tackett, Jeffrey Wilson b: 12/1/65, Fresno, Cal. BR/TR, 6'2", 200 lbs. Deb: 9/11/91 ♦																											
1993 Bal-A	0	0	—	1	0	0	0	0	1	1	0	0	0	1	0	18.0	0.00	—	.250	.400	15	.172	0	0	0	0	0.0
● JOHN TAFF Taff, John Gallatin b: 6/3/1890, Austin, Tex. d: 5/15/61, Houston, Tex. BR/TR, 6', 170 lbs. Deb: 5/11/13																											
1913 Phi-A	0	1	.000	7	1	0	0	1	17^2	22	13	0	0	5	9	13.8	6.62	42	.293	.338	1	.200	-0	-7	-8	0	-0.5
● DOUG TAITT Taitt, Douglas John "Poco" b: 8/3/02, Bay City, Mich. d: 12/12/70, Portland, Ore. BL/TR, 6', 176 lbs. Deb: 4/10/28 ♦																											
1928 Bos-A	0	0	—	1	0	0	0	0	1	2	3	0	0	2	1	36.0	27.00	15	.400	.571	144	.299	0	-3	-3	0	-0.1
● FRED TALBOT Talbot, Frederick Lealand "Bubby" b: 6/28/41, Washington, D.C. BR/TR, 6'2", 195 lbs. Deb: 9/28/63																											
1963 Chi-A	0	0	—	1	0	0	0	0	3	2	1	0	0	4	2	18.0	3.00	117	.222	.462	0	.000	-0	0	0	0	0.0
1964 Chi-A	4	5	.444	17	12	3	2	0	75^1	83	31	7	4	20	34	12.8	3.70	93	.288	.343	5	.263	3	-1	-2	-1	0.0

YEAR	TM/L	W	L	PCT	G	GS	CG	SH	SV	IP	H	R	HR	HB	BB	SO	RAT	ERA	ERA+	OAV	OOB	BH	AVG	PB	PR	PR+	PD	TPI
1965	KC-A	10	12	.455	39	33	2	1	0	198	188	96	25	6	86	117	12.7	4.14	84	.251	.333	14	.200	3	-15	-14	-1	-1.2
1966	KC-A	4	4	.500	11	11	0	0	0	67^2	65	39	6	2	28	37	12.6	4.79	71	.248	.325	3	.150	0	-10	-11	-0	-1.1
	NY-A	7	7	.500	23	19	3	0	0	124^1	123	59	16	3	45	48	12.4	4.13	81	.262	.331	5	.143	1	-10	-11	-0	-1.1
	Yr	11	11	.500	34	30	3	0	0	192	188	98	22	5	73	85	12.5	4.36	77	.257	.329	8	.145	1	-20	-22	-0	-2.2
1967	NY-A	6	8	.429	29	22	2	0	0	138^2	132	78	20	6	54	61	12.5	4.22	74	.252	.329	6	.158	3	-15	-17	2	-1.1
1968	NY-A	1	9	.100	29	11	1	0	0	99	89	47	6	2	42	67	12.1	3.36	86	.241	.322	2	.118	1	-4	-5	1	-0.4
1969	NY-A	0	0	—	8	0	0	0	0	12^1	13	9	1	0	6	7	13.9	5.11	68	.283	.365	0	.000	-0	-2	-2	0	-0.1
	Sea-A	5	8	.385	25	16	1	1	0	114^2	125	58	12	4	41	67	13.3	4.16	87	.278	.343	6	.162	2	-7	-7	0	-0.5
	Oak-A	1	2	.333	12	2	0	0	1	19	22	11	2	0	7	9	13.7	5.21	66	.297	.358	1	.333	0	-3	-4	0	-0.6
	Yr	6	10	.375	45	18	1	1	1	146	160	78	15	4	54	83	13.4	4.38	82	.281	.347	7	.171	2	-12	-13	0	-1.2
1970	Oak-A	0	1	.000	1	0	0	0	0	1^2	2	2	1	0	1	0	16.2	10.80	33	.286	.375	0	—	0	-1	-1	0	-0.2
Total	8	38	56	.404	195	126	12	4	1	853^2	844	431	96	27	334	449	12.7	4.12	81	.260	.334	42	.174	13	-68	-75	2	-6.3

● ROY TALCOTT Talcott, Le Roy Everett b: 1/16/20, Brookline, Mass. d: 12/6/99, Miami, Fla. BR/TR, 6′1.5″, 180 lbs. Deb: 6/24/43

YEAR	TM/L	W	L	PCT	G	GS	CG	SH	SV	IP	H	R	HR	HB	BB	SO	RAT	ERA	ERA+	OAV	OOB	BH	AVG	PB	PR	PR+	PD	TPI
1943	Bos-N	0	0	—	1	0	0	0	0	0^2	1	2	0	0	2	0	40.5	27.00	13	.333	.600	0	—	0	-2	-2	0	-0.1

● JEFF TAM Tam, Jeffrey Eugene b: 8/19/70, Fullerton, Cal. BR/TR, 6′1″, 202 lbs. Deb: 6/30/98

YEAR	TM/L	W	L	PCT	G	GS	CG	SH	SV	IP	H	R	HR	HB	BB	SO	RAT	ERA	ERA+	OAV	OOB	BH	AVG	PB	PR	PR+	PD	TPI
1998	NY-N	1	1	.500	15	0	0	0	0	14^1	13	10	2	2	4	8	11.9	6.28	66	.241	.317	0	.000	-0	-3	-3	0	-0.4
1999	Cle-A	0	0	—	1	0	0	0	0	0^1	2	3	0	0	1	0	81.0	81.00	6	1.000	1.000	0	—	0	-3	-3	0	-0.1
	NY-N	0	0	—	9	0	0	0	0	11^1	6	4	3	0	3	8	7.1	3.18	138	.150	.209	0	—	0	2	2	0	0.1
2000	*Oak-A	3	3	.500	72	0	0	0	3	85^2	86	30	3	1	23	46	11.6	2.63	181	.268	.319	0	—	0	22	21	1	1.4
Total	3	4	4	.500	97	0	0	0	3	111^2	107	47	8	3	31	62	11.4	3.39	137	.257	.313	0	.000	-0	18	16	1	1.0

● VITO TAMULIS Tamulis, Vitautis Casimirus b: 7/11/11, Cambridge, Mass. d: 5/5/74, Nashville, Tenn. BL/TL, 5′9″, 170 lbs. Deb: 9/25/34

YEAR	TM/L	W	L	PCT	G	GS	CG	SH	SV	IP	H	R	HR	HB	BB	SO	RAT	ERA	ERA+	OAV	OOB	BH	AVG	PB	PR	PR+	PD	TPI
1934	NY-A	1	0	1.000	1	1	1	1	0	9	7	0	0	0	1	5	8.0	0.00	—	.219	.242	1	.250	0	4	4	0	0.6
1935	NY-A	10	5	.667	30	19	9	3	1	160^2	178	80	7	2	55	57	13.2	4.09	99	.280	.339	14	.246	4	7	-1	-1	0.2
1938	StL-A	0	3	.000	3	2	0	0	0	15^1	26	15	2	0	10	11	21.1	7.63	65	.366	.444	2	.400	1	-5	-4	0	-0.6
	Bro-N	12	6	.667	38	18	9	0	2	159^2	181	81	11	2	40	70	12.6	3.83	102	.288	.333	7	.127	-3	-1	1	-2	-0.3
1939	Bro-N	9	8	.529	39	17	8	1	4	158^2	177	81	10	8	45	83	13.0	4.37	92	.287	.343	10	.182	-1	-8	-6	0	-0.6
1940	Bro-N	8	5	.615	41	12	4	1	2	154^1	147	60	5	3	34	55	10.7	3.09	129	.244	.288	6	.130	-1	13	15	-1	1.0
1941	Phi-N	0	1	.000	6	1	0	0	0	12	21	13	1	1	7	5	21.8	9.00	41	.382	.460	0	.000	-0	-7	-7	0	-0.5
	Bro-N	0	0	—	12	0	0	0	1	22	21	10	1	0	10	8	12.7	3.68	100	.244	.323	0	.000	-1	-0	-0	0	-0.1
	Yr	0	1	.000	18	1	0	0	1	34	42	23	2	1	17	13	15.9	5.56	66	.298	.377	0	.000	-1	-7	-7	0	-0.6
Total	6	40	28	.588	170	70	31	6	10	691^2	758	340	37	16	202	294	12.7	3.97	101	.278	.331	40	.175	-1	3	4	-2	-0.3

● FRANK TANANA Tanana, Frank Daryl b: 7/3/53, Detroit, Mich. BL/TL, 6′3″, 195 lbs. Deb: 9/9/73

YEAR	TM/L	W	L	PCT	G	GS	CG	SH	SV	IP	H	R	HR	HB	BB	SO	RAT	ERA	ERA+	OAV	OOB	BH	AVG	PB	PR	PR+	PD	TPI
1973	Cal-A	2	2	.500	4	4	2	1	0	26^1	20	11	2	0	8	22	9.6	3.08	115	.200	.259	0	—	0	2	1	0	0.2
1974	Cal-A	14	19	.424	39	35	12	4	0	268^2	262	104	27	8	77	180	11.6	3.12	111	.255	.312	0	—	0	15	10	0	1.3
1975	Cal-A	16	9	.640	34	33	16	5	0	257^1	211	80	21	7	73	**269**	10.2	2.62	136	.226	.288	0	—	0	33	28	3	3.0
1976	Cal-A★	19	10	.655	34	34	23	2	0	288^1	212	88	24	9	73	261	**9.2**	2.43	137	.203	**.261**	0	—	0	35	30	1	3.2
1977	Cal-A†	15	9	.625	31	31	20	**7**	0	241^1	201	72	19	12	61	205	10.2	**2.54**	**155**	.227	.286	0	—	0	41	39	1	3.8
1978	Cal-A☆	18	12	.600	33	33	10	4	0	239	239	108	26	9	60	137	11.6	3.65	99	.258	.309	0	—	0	3	-1	-2	-0.3
1979	*Cal-A	7	5	.583	18	17	2	1	0	90^1	93	44	9	2	25	46	12.0	3.89	105	.264	.317	0	—	0	3	2	-1	0.2
1980	Cal-A	11	12	.478	32	31	7	0	0	204	223	107	18	8	45	113	12.2	4.15	95	.277	.322	0	—	0	-2	-5	-1	-0.6
1981	Bos-A	4	10	.286	24	23	5	2	0	141^1	142	70	17	4	43	78	12.0	4.01	97	.265	.324	0	—	0	-5	-2	1	-0.1
1982	Tex-A	7	18	.280	30	30	7	0	0	194^1	199	102	16	7	55	87	12.1	4.21	92	.264	.320	0	—	0	-3	-8	-0	-0.9
1983	Tex-A	7	9	.438	29	22	3	0	0	159^1	144	70	14	7	49	108	11.3	3.16	127	.240	.304	0	—	0	16	15	3	1.7
1984	Tex-A	15	15	.500	35	35	9	1	0	246^1	234	117	30	6	81	141	11.7	3.25	128	.245	.308	0	—	0	20	24	1	2.8
1985	Tex-A	2	7	.222	13	13	0	0	0	77^2	89	53	15	1	23	52	13.1	5.91	72	.287	.338	0	—	0	-15	-14	0	-1.4
	Det-A	10	7	.588	20	20	4	0	0	137^1	131	59	13	2	34	107	10.9	3.34	122	.250	.298	0	—	0	12	11	1	1.4
	Yr	12	14	.462	33	33	4	0	0	215	220	112	28	3	57	159	11.7	4.27	97	.264	.313	0	—	0	-3	-3	1	0.0
1986	Det-A	12	9	.571	32	31	3	1	0	188^1	196	95	23	3	65	119	12.6	4.16	99	.268	.330	0	—	0	1	-1	1	0.1
1987	*Det-A	15	10	.600	34	34	5	3	0	218^2	216	106	27	5	56	146	11.4	3.91	108	.256	.306	0	—	0	14	8	1	0.9
1988	Det-A	14	11	.560	32	32	2	0	0	203	213	105	25	4	64	127	12.5	4.21	91	.267	.324	0	—	0	-5	-9	1	-0.9
1989	Det-A	10	14	.417	33	33	6	1	0	223^2	227	105	21	8	74	147	12.4	3.58	107	.265	.329	0	—	0	8	6	2	0.9
1990	Det-A	9	8	.529	34	29	1	0	1	176^1	190	104	25	9	66	114	13.5	5.31	75	.280	.352	0	—	0	-27	-26	1	-2.2
1991	Det-A	13	12	.520	33	33	3	2	0	217^1	217	98	26	2	78	107	12.3	3.77	110	.265	.330	0	.000	-0	8	9	1	1.1
1992	Det-A	13	11	.542	32	31	3	0	0	186^2	188	102	22	7	90	91	13.7	4.39	90	.267	.356	0	—	0	-9	-9	1	-1.0
1993	NY-N	7	15	.318	29	29	0	0	0	183	198	100	26	9	48	104	12.5	4.48	90	.278	.332	9	.155	0	-9	-9	-1	-1.1
	NY-A	0	2	.000	3	3	0	0	0	19^2	18	10	2	0	7	12	11.4	3.20	130	.222	.284	0	—	0	2	2	-1	0.1
Total	21	240	236	.504	638	616	143	34	1	4188^1	4063	1910	448	129	1255	2773	11.7	3.66	106	.254	.314	9	.153	0	139	101	14	12.2

● JESSE TANNEHILL Tannehill, Jesse Niles "Powder"
b: 7/14/1874, Dayton, Ky. d: 9/22/56, Dayton, Ky. BB/TL (BL 1903), 5′8″, 150 lbs. Deb: 6/17/1894 FC◆

YEAR	TM/L	W	L	PCT	G	GS	CG	SH	SV	IP	H	R	HR	HB	BB	SO	RAT	ERA	ERA+	OAV	OOB	BH	AVG	PB	PR	PR+	PD	TPI
1894	Cin-N	1	1	.500	5	2	1	0	1	29	37	30	1	1	16	7	16.8	7.14	78	.306	.391	0	.000	-2	-6	-5	-1	-0.5
1897	Pit-N	9	9	.500	21	16	11	1	1	142	172	97	1	8	24	40	12.9	4.25	98	.297	.333	49	.266	3	1	-1	3	0.3
1898	Pit-N	25	13	.658	43	38	34	5	2	326^2	338	147	2	12	63	93	11.4	2.95	121	.265	.306	44	.289	7	24	22	3	3.5
1899	Pit-N	24	14	.632	41	36	33	3	1	322^1	361	139	4	14	52	65	11.9	2.82	135	.282	.318	34	.250	4	37	36	4	4.5
1900	Pit-N	20	6	.769	29	27	23	2	0	234	247	108	3	17	43	50	11.8	2.88	126	.271	.316	37	.336	8	21	20	1	2.7
1901	Pit-N	18	10	.643	32	30	25	4	1	252^1	240	94	1	10	36	118	10.2	**2.18**	150	.249	.283	33	.244	5	32	31	-3	3.3
1902	Pit-N	20	6	.769	26	24	23	2	0	231	203	78	0	10	25	100	9.3	1.95	141	.236	.266	43	.291	7	21	21	-0	3.2
1903	NY-A	15	15	.500	32	31	22	2	0	239^2	258	123	3	10	34	106	11.3	3.27	96	.274	.307	26	.234	5	-8	-4	2	0.4
1904	Bos-A	21	11	.656	33	31	30	4	0	281^2	256	89	5	13	33	116	9.6	2.04	131	.243	.275	24	.197	3	17	19	3	3.0
1905	Bos-A	22	9	.710	37	32	27	6	0	271^2	238	91	7	13	59	113	10.3	2.48	109	.237	.288	21	.226	6	5	6	2	1.6
1906	Bos-A	13	11	.542	27	26	18	2	0	196^1	207	91	9	10	39	82	11.7	3.16	87	.274	.318	22	.278	6	-10	-9	0	-0.4
1907	Bos-A	6	7	.462	18	16	10	2	1	131	131	59	3	5	20	29	10.7	2.47	104	.263	.298	10	.196	1	1	1	0	0.3
1908	Bos-A	0	0	—	1	1	0	0	0	5	4	2	0	0	3	2	12.6	3.60	68	.200	.304	1	.500	0	-1	-1	0	0.0
	Was-A	2	4	.333	10	9	5	0	0	71^2	77	36	0	6	23	14	13.3	3.77	61	.278	.346	11	.256	2	-11	-12	1	-0.6
	Yr	2	4	.333	11	10	5	0	0	76^2	81	38	0	6	26	16	13.3	3.76	61	.273	.343	12	.267	2	-12	-13	2	-0.6
1909	Was-A	1	1	.500	3	2	2	1	0	21	19	8	1	1	5	8	10.7	3.43	71	.268	.325	6	.167	0	-2	-2	1	-0.1
1911	Cin-N	0	0	—	1	0	0	0	0	4^1	6	7	0	0	3	1	18.7	6.23	53	.316	.409	0	.000	-0	-1	-1	0	-0.1
Total	15	197	117	.627	359	321	264	34	7	2759^2	2794	1199	40	130	478	944	11.1	2.80	114	.263	.303	361	.255	54	121	122	17	21.1

● BRUCE TANNER Tanner, Bruce Matthew b: 12/9/61, New Castle, Pa. BL/TR, 6′3″, 220 lbs. Deb: 6/12/85 F

YEAR	TM/L	W	L	PCT	G	GS	CG	SH	SV	IP	H	R	HR	HB	BB	SO	RAT	ERA	ERA+	OAV	OOB	BH	AVG	PB	PR	PR+	PD	TPI
1985	Chi-A	1	2	.333	10	4	0	0	0	27	34	17	1	2	13	9	16.3	5.33	81	.309	.392	0	—	0	-4	-3	1	-0.2

● KEVIN TAPANI Tapani, Kevin Ray b: 2/18/64, Des Moines, Iowa BR/TR, 6′, 187 lbs. Deb: 7/4/89

YEAR	TM/L	W	L	PCT	G	GS	CG	SH	SV	IP	H	R	HR	HB	BB	SO	RAT	ERA	ERA+	OAV	OOB	BH	AVG	PB	PR	PR+	PD	TPI
1989	NY-N	0	0	—	3	0	0	0	0	7^1	5	3	1	0	4	2	11.0	3.68	89	.192	.300	0	.000	-0	-0	-0	0	0.0
	Min-A	2	2	.500	5	5	0	0	0	32^2	34	15	2	0	8	21	11.6	3.86	108	.266	.309	0	—	0	0	1	-0	0.1
1990	Min-A	12	8	.600	28	28	1	1	0	159^1	164	75	12	2	29	101	11.0	4.07	102	.264	.299	0	—	0	-3	2	0	0.2
1991	*Min-A	16	9	.640	34	34	4	1	0	244	225	84	23	2	40	135	9.8	2.99	143	.245	.278	0	—	0	30	33	-0	3.2
1992	Min-A	16	11	.593	34	34	4	1	0	220	226	103	17	5	48	138	11.4	3.97	102	.269	.313	0	—	0	-0	2	-0	0.2
1993	Min-A	12	15	.444	36	35	3	1	0	225^2	243	123	21	6	57	150	12.2	4.43	99	.272	.320	0	—	0	-2	-1	1	-0.1
1994	Min-A	11	7	.611	24	24	4	1	0	156	181	86	13	4	39	91	12.9	4.62	106	.291	.337	0	—	0	3	4	1	0.6
1995	Min-A	6	11	.353	20	20	3	1	0	133^2	155	79	21	4	34	88	13.0	4.92	97	.290	.337	0	—	0	-3	-2	-1	-0.3
	*LA-N	4	2	.667	13	11	0	0	0	57	72	37	8	1	14	43	13.7	5.05	75	.306	.348	3	.176	0	-5	-9	0	-0.7
1996	Chi-A	13	10	.565	34	34	1	0	0	225^1	236	123	34	3	76	150	12.6	4.59	103	.268	.328	0	—	0	10	4	-1	0.3
1997	Chi-N	9	3	.750	13	13	1	1	0	85	77	33	7	2	23	55	10.8	3.39	127	.242	.297	3	.136	-0	8	8	-1	1.1
1998	*Chi-N	19	9	.679	35	34	2	2	0	219	244	120	30	5	62	136	12.8	4.85	91	.284	.336	10	.133	1	-15	-10	-1	-1.2
1999	Chi-N	6	12	.333	23	23	1	0	0	136	151	81	12	4	33	73	12.4	4.83	93	.280	.326	2	.051	-2	-4	-5	-1	-0.8

YEAR TM/L	W	L	PCT	G	GS	CG	SH	SV	IP	H	R	HR	HB	BB	SO	RAT	ERA	ERA+	OAV	OOB	BH	AVG	PB	PR	PR+	PD	TPI
2000 Chi-N	8	12	.400	30	30	2	0	0	195^2	208	113	35	8	47	150	12.1	5.01	91	.271	.320	10	.179	2	-8	-10	-1	-0.8
Total 12	134	111	.547	332	325	26	9	0	2096^2	2221	1075	236	46	514	1333	11.9	4.34	102	.272	.318	28	.133	1	10	22	-2	1.8
● RANDY TATE	Tate, Randall Lee b: 10/23/52, Florence, Ala. BR/TR, 6'3", 190 lbs. Deb: 4/14/75																										
1975 NY-N	5	13	.278	26	23	2	0	0	137^2	121	73	8	5	86	99	13.9	4.45	78	.240	.356	0	.000	-4	-12	-16	0	-2.3
● STU TATE	Tate, Stuart Douglas b: 6/17/62, Huntsville, Ala. BR/TR, 6'3", 205 lbs. Deb: 9/20/89																										
1989 SF-N	0	0	—	2	0	0	0	0	2^2	3	3	0	0	0	4	10.1	3.38	100	.250	.250	0	—	0	0	0	-0	0.0
● AL TATE	Tate, Walter Alvin b: 7/1/18, Coleman, Okla. d: 5/8/93, Bountiful, Utah BR/TR, 6', 180 lbs. Deb: 9/27/46																										
1946 Pit-N	0	1	.000	2	1	1	0	0	9	8	5	0	0	7	2	15.0	5.00	70	.267	.405	1	.333	0	-2	-1	0	-0.1
● RAMON TATIS	Tatis, Ramon Francisco (Medrano) b: 1/5/73, Guayubin, D.R. BL/TL, 6'2", 185 lbs. Deb: 4/6/97																										
1997 Chi-N	1	1	.500	56	0	0	0	0	55^2	66	36	13	3	29	33	15.8	5.34	81	.308	.398	0	.000	-0	-7	-6	1	-0.2
1998 TB-A	0	0	—	22	0	0	0	0	11^2	23	19	2	1	16	5	30.9	13.89	35	.418	.556	0	—	0	-12	-11	1	-0.5
Total 2	1	1	.500	78	0	0	0	0	67^1	89	55	15	4	45	38	18.4	6.82	64	.331	.434	0	.000	-0	-19	-18	1	-0.7
● KEN TATUM	Tatum, Kenneth Ray b: 4/25/44, Alexandria, La. BR/TR, 6'2", 205 lbs. Deb: 5/28/69																										
1969 Cal-A	7	2	.778	45	0	0	0	22	86^1	51	13	1	4	39	65	9.8	1.36	257	.172	.277	6	.286	4	**22**	**21**	-0	3.9
1970 Cal-A	7	4	.636	62	0	0	0	17	88^2	68	35	12	5	26	50	10.0	2.94	123	.208	.277	2	.182	1	8	7	0	1.2
1971 Bos-A	2	4	.333	36	1	0	0	9	53^2	50	27	3	8	25	21	13.9	4.19	88	.255	.362	3	.300	2	-4	-3	0	-0.2
1972 Bos-A	0	2	.000	22	0	0	0	4	29^1	32	12	3	2	15	15	15.0	3.07	105	.283	.377	0	.000	0	0	0	-0	0.0
1973 Bos-A	0	0	—	1	0	0	0	0	4	6	4	2	0	3	0	20.3	9.00	45	.462	.563	0	—	0	-2	-2	-0	-0.1
1974 Chi-A	0	0	—	10	1	0	0	0	20^2	23	12	3	0	9	5	13.9	4.79	78	.274	.344	0	.000	-0	-3	-2	1	-0.1
Total 6	16	12	.571	176	2	0	0	52	282^2	230	103	24	19	117	156	11.7	2.93	122	.224	.314	11	.244	7	20	20	0	4.7
● WALT TAUSCHER	Tauscher, Walter Edward b: 11/22/01, LaSalle, Ill. d: 11/27/92, Winter Park, Fla. BR/TR, 6'1", 186 lbs. Deb: 4/19/28																										
1928 Pit-N	0	0	—	17	0	0	0	1	29^1	28	20	0	3	12	7	13.2	4.91	83	.280	.374	1	.167	-0	-3	-3	-0	-0.2
1931 Was-A	1	0	1.000	6	0	0	0	0	12	24	16	2	0	4	5	21.0	7.50	57	.429	.467	0	—	0	-4	-4	2	-0.2
Total 2	1	0	1.000	23	0	0	0	1	41^1	52	36	2	3	16	12	15.5	5.66	73	.333	.406	1	.167	-0	-7	-7	1	-0.4
● JULIAN TAVAREZ	Tavarez, Julian (Carmen) b: 5/22/73, Santiago, D.R. BL/TR, 6'2", 165 lbs. Deb: 8/7/93																										
1993 Cle-A	2	2	.500	8	7	0	0	0	37	53	29	7	2	13	19	16.5	6.57	66	.340	.398	0	—	0	-9	-9	-0	-0.8
1994 Cle-A	0	1	.000	1	1	0	0	0	1^2	6	8	1	0	1	0	37.8	21.60	22	.500	.538	0	—	0	-3	-3	-0	-0.5
1995 *Cle-A	10	2	.833	57	0	0	0	0	85	76	36	7	3	21	68	10.6	2.44	193	.235	.287	0	—	0	22	21	0	2.6
1996 *Cle-A	4	7	.364	51	4	0	0	0	80^2	101	49	9	1	22	46	13.8	5.36	91	.315	.360	0	—	0	-3	-4	-1	-0.5
1997 *SF-N	6	4	.600	**89**	0	0	0	0	88^1	91	43	6	4	34	38	13.1	3.87	106	.277	.351	0	.000	-0	3	2	-0	0.2
1998 SF-N	5	3	.625	60	0	0	0	1	85^1	96	41	5	8	36	52	14.8	3.80	105	.298	.383	1	.111	-0	4	2	-1	0.0
1999 SF-N	2	0	1.000	47	0	0	0	0	54^2	65	38	7	8	25	33	16.1	5.93	71	.295	.387	1	.200	0	-8	-11	0	-0.5
2000 Col-N	11	5	.688	51	12	1	0	1	120	124	68	11	7	53	62	13.8	4.43	134	.268	.352	3	.086	-3	3	16	2	1.7
Total 8	40	24	.625	364	24	1	0	2	552^2	612	312	53	33	205	318	13.8	4.41	107	.285	.356	5	.100	-3	8	17	-0	2.2
● ARLAS TAYLOR	Taylor, Arlas Walter "Lefty" or "Foxy" b: 3/16/1896, Warrick County, Ind. d: 9/10/58, Dade City, Fla. BR/TL, 5'11", Deb: 9/15/21																										
1921 Phi-A	0	1	.000	1	1	0	0	0	2	7	5	1	0	2	1	40.5	22.50	20	.636	.692	0	—	0	-4	-4	-0	-0.6
● BEN TAYLOR	Taylor, Benjamin Harrison b: 4/2/1889, Paoli, Ind. d: 11/3/46, Martin County, Ind. BR/TR, 5'11", 163 lbs. Deb: 6/28/12																										
1912 Cin-N	0	0	—	2	0	0	0	0	5^2	9	7	0	1	3	2	20.6	3.18	106	.360	.448	0	.000	0	0	0	-0	0.0
● BRUCE TAYLOR	Taylor, Bruce Bell b: 4/16/53, Holden, Mass. BR/TR, 6', 178 lbs. Deb: 8/5/77																										
1977 Det-A	1	0	1.000	19	0	0	0	2	29^1	23	11	2	1	10	19	10.4	3.38	127	.219	.293	0	—	0	2	3	0	0.1
1978 Det-A	0	0	—	1	0	0	0	0	1	0	0	0	0	0	0	0.0	0.00	—	.000	.000	0	—	0	0	0	0	0.0
1979 Det-A	1	2	.333	10	0	0	0	0	18^2	16	13	1	2	7	8	12.1	4.82	90	.242	.333	0	—	0	-1	-1	0	-0.1
Total 3	2	2	.500	30	0	0	0	2	49	39	24	3	3	17	27	10.8	3.86	112	.224	.304	0	—	0	1	2	0	0.0
● CHUCK TAYLOR	Taylor, Charles Gilbert b: 4/18/42, Murfreesboro, Tenn. BR/TR, 6'2", 195 lbs. Deb: 5/27/69																										
1969 StL-N	7	5	.583	27	13	5	1	0	126^2	108	39	8	3	30	62	10.0	2.56	140	.235	.287	7	.179	1	15	14	-2	1.2
1970 StL-N	6	7	.462	56	7	1	1	8	124^1	116	47	5	2	31	64	10.8	3.11	132	.256	.306	3	.115	-1	13	14	1	1.5
1971 StL-N	3	1	.750	43	1	0	0	3	71^1	72	32	7	1	25	46	12.4	3.53	102	.267	.331	2	.167	0	-0	1	0	0.1
1972 NY-N	0	0	—	20	0	0	0	2	31	44	19	2	1	9	9	15.7	5.52	61	.341	.388	0	.000	-0	-7	-8	1	-0.3
Mil-A	0	0	—	5	0	0	0	1	11^2	8	2	0	1	3	5	9.3	1.54	197	.200	.273	1	.500	0	2	2	-0	0.2
1973 Mon-N	2	0	1.000	8	0	0	0	0	20^1	17	4	3	0	2	10	8.4	1.77	216	.230	.250	0	.000	-0	4	4	1	0.4
1974 Mon-N	6	2	.750	61	0	0	0	11	107^2	101	27	8	3	25	43	10.8	2.17	177	.256	.305	3	.300	1	17	19	-0	1.9
1975 Mon-N	2	2	.500	54	0	0	0	6	74	72	32	6	1	24	29	11.8	3.53	109	.264	.326	0	.000	-0	1	2	0	0.1
1976 Mon-N	2	3	.400	31	0	0	0	0	40	38	20	4	0	13	14	11.5	4.50	83	.273	.336	0	.000	-0	-3	-3	-0	-0.4
Total 8	28	20	.583	305	21	6	2	31	607	576	222	43	12	162	282	11.1	3.07	123	.258	.312	16	.158	0	40	46	1	4.7
● DORN TAYLOR	Taylor, Donald Clyde b: 8/11/58, Abington, Pa. BR/TR, 6'2", 180 lbs. Deb: 4/30/87																										
1987 Pit-N	2	3	.400	14	8	0	0	0	53^1	48	35	10	1	28	37	13.0	5.74	72	.247	.345	3	.167	-0	-10	-10	-1	-0.8
1989 Pit-N	1	1	.500	9	0	0	0	0	10^2	14	6	0	0	5	3	16.0	5.06	66	.333	.404	0	.000	-0	-2	-2	-0	-0.4
1990 Bal-A	0	1	.000	4	0	0	0	0	3^2	4	3	0	0	2	4	14.7	2.45	155	.250	.333	0	—	0	1	1	-0	0.1
Total 3	3	5	.375	27	8	0	0	0	67^2	66	44	10	1	35	44	13.6	5.45	73	.262	.354	3	.158	-0	-11	-11	-1	-1.1
● ED TAYLOR	Taylor, Edgar Ruben "Rube" b: 3/23/1877, Palestine, Tex. d: 1/31/12, Dallas, Tex. TL, Deb: 8/8/03																										
1903 StL-N	0	0	—	1	0	0	0	0	3	0	0	0	0	0	1	0.0	0.00	—	.000	.000	0	.000	-0	1	1	0	0.0
● GARY TAYLOR	Taylor, Gary William b: 10/19/45, Detroit, Mich. BR/TR, 6'2", 190 lbs. Deb: 9/2/69																										
1969 Det-A	0	1	.000	7	0	0	0	0	10^1	10	6	2	0	6	3	13.9	5.23	71	.244	.340	0	.000	-0	-2	-2	0	-0.2
● HARRY TAYLOR	Taylor, Harry Evans b: 12/2/35, San Angelo, Tex. BR/TR, 6', 185 lbs. Deb: 9/17/57																										
1957 KC-A	0	0	—	2	0	0	0	0	8^2	11	4	0	1	4	4	16.6	3.12	127	.314	.400	1	.250	0	1	1	-0	0.0
● HARRY TAYLOR	Taylor, James Harry b: 5/20/19, E.Glenn, Ind. BR/TR, 6'1", 175 lbs. Deb: 9/22/46																										
1946 Bro-N	0	0	—	4	0	0	0	1	4^2	5	2	0	0	1	6	11.6	3.86	88	.313	.353	0	—	0	-0	-0	0	0.0
1947 *Bro-N	10	5	.667	33	20	10	2	1	162	130	63	10	5	83	58	12.1	3.11	133	**.225**	.327	8	.129	-2	17	18	1	1.4
1948 Bro-N	2	7	.222	17	13	2	0	0	80^2	90	55	8	3	61	32	17.2	5.36	75	.288	.408	6	.273	1	-13	-12	2	-0.9
1950 Bos-A	2	0	1.000	3	2	2	1	0	19	13	3	0	0	8	8	9.9	1.42	345	.197	.284	2	.286	0	7	7	0	0.7
1951 Bos-A	4	9	.308	31	8	1	0	2	81^1	100	59	6	1	42	22	15.8	5.75	78	.307	.388	3	.103	-3	-15	-11	1	-1.7
1952 Bos-A	1	0	1.000	2	1	1	0	0	10	6	2	1	1	6	1	11.7	1.80	219	.176	.317	1	.250	0	2	2	0	0.2
Total 6	19	21	.475	90	44	16	3	4	357^2	344	184	25	10	201	127	14.0	4.10	102	.258	.359	20	.161	-3	-2	4	4	-0.3
● JACK TAYLOR	Taylor, John Budd "Brewery Jack" b: 5/23/1873, Staten Island, N.Y d: 2/7/1900, Staten Island, N.Y. BR/TR, 6'1", 190 lbs. Deb: 9/16/1891																										
1891 NY-N	0	1	.000	1	1	1	0	0	8	4	2	1	0	3	3	7.9	1.13	285	.143	.226	0	.000	0	2	2	-0	0.2
1892 Phi-N	1	0	1.000	3	3	2	0	0	26	28	19	2	0	10	7	13.2	1.38	234	.264	.328	2	.167	-0	5	5	-1	0.1
1893 Phi-N	10	9	.526	25	16	14	0	1	170	187	113	8	10	77	41	14.5	4.24	108	.271	.353	20	.215	-2	8	7	2	0.5
1894 Phi-N	23	13	.639	41	34	31	1	1	298	347	201	13	17	96	76	13.9	4.08	125	.286	.349	49	.338	9	41	35	2	3.9
1895 Phi-N	26	14	.650	41	37	33	1	1	335	403	233	7	15	83	93	13.5	4.49	107	.293	.340	45	.290	7	11	11	4	1.9
1896 Phi-N	20	21	.488	45	41	35	1	1	359	459	282	17	20	112	97	14.8	4.79	90	.308	.365	29	.185	-7	-17	-19	4	-1.9
1897 Phi-N	16	20	.444	40	37	35	2	2	317^1	376	204	5	28	76	88	13.6	4.23	99	.292	.345	35	.252	2	3	-1	3	0.3
1898 StL-N	15	29	.341	**50**	47	**42**	0	1	**397^1**	465	259	14	25	83	89	13.0	3.90	97	.290	.335	38	.242	3	-13	-4	8	0.7
1899 Cin-N	9	10	.474	25	19	16	2	2	180^1	207	110	7	11	43	35	13.0	3.94	99	.287	.337	17	.239	-1	-2	-0	-1	-0.2
Total 9	120	117	.506	271	235	209	7	9	2091	2476	1423	74	126	583	529	13.7	4.21	104	.291	.346	235	.252	12	39	37	21	5.5

YEAR	TM/L	W	L	PCT	G	GS	CG	SH	SV	IP	H	R	HR	HB	BB	SO	RAT	ERA	ERA+	OAV	OOB	BH	AVG	PB	PR	PR+	PD	TPI
● JACK TAYLOR	Taylor, John W. b: 1/14/1874, New Straitsville, Ohio d: 3/4/38, Columbus, Ohio BR/TR, 5'10", 170 lbs. Deb: 9/25/1898																											
1898	Chi-N	5	0	1.000	5	5	5	0	0	41	32	12	0	1	10	11	9.4	2.20	163	.213	.267	3	.200	1	6	6	-0	0.8
1899	Chi-N	18	21	.462	41	39	39	1	0	354^2	380	223	6	22	84	67	12.3	3.76	100	.274	.325	37	.266	10	4	-0	1	1.0
1900	Chi-N	10	17	.370	28	26	25	2	1	222^1	226	130	4	8	58	57	11.8	2.55	141	.263	.316	19	.235	2	28	27	-3	2.8
1901	Chi-N	13	19	.406	33	31	30	0	0	275^2	341	165	5	8	44	68	12.8	3.36	96	.302	.332	23	.217	2	-1	-4	2	-0.1
1902	Chi-N	23	11	.676	37	34	34	**8**	1	333^2	273	86	2	12	45	88	**8.9**	**1.29**	**209**	.224	**.258**	44	.233	3	**55**	**54**	4	**6.7**
1903	Chi-N	21	14	.600	37	33	33	1	1	312^1	277	137	2	5	57	83	9.8	2.45	128	.235	.273	28	.222	4	28	25	1	3.0
1904	StL-N	20	19	.513	41	39	**39**	2	1	352	297	133	5	13	82	103	10.0	2.22	121	.220	.271	28	.211	4	20	19	1	2.7
1905	StL-N	15	21	.417	37	34	34	3	1	309	302	155	10	11	85	102	11.6	3.44	87	.259	.315	23	.190	4	-15	-16	-2	-1.5
1906	StL-N	8	9	.471	17	17	17	1	0	155	133	50	3	7	47	27	10.9	2.15	122	.227	.292	11	.208	3	8	8	1	1.4
	Chi-N	12	3	.800	17	16	15	2	0	147^1	116	42	1	6	39	34	9.8	1.83	144	.223	.285	11	.208	2	13	13	-0	1.5
	Yr	20	12	.625	34	33	32	3	0	302^1	249	92	4	13	86	61	10.4	1.99	132	.225	.289	22	.208	5	21	21	0	2.9
1907	Chi-N	7	5	.583	18	13	8	0	0	123	127	62	3	1	33	22	11.8	3.29	76	.268	.318	9	.191	0	-11	-11	1	-1.0
Total	10	152	139	.522	311	287	279	20	5	2626	2504	1195	41	94	584	662	10.9	2.65	115	.250	.297	236	.222	34	137	121	6	17.3
● KERRY TAYLOR	Taylor, Kerry Thomas b: 1/25/71, Bemidji, Minn. BR/TR, 6'3", 200 lbs. Deb: 4/13/93																											
1993	SD-N	0	5	.000	36	7	0	0	0	68^1	72	53	5	4	49	45	16.5	6.45	64	.277	.399	0	.000	-1	-18	-17	-1	-1.3
1994	SD-N	0	0	—	1	1	0	0	0	4^1	9	4	1	1	1	3	22.8	8.31	50	.409	.458	0	.000	-0	-2	-2	-0	-0.1
Total	2	0	5	.000	37	8	0	0	0	72^2	81	57	6	5	50	48	16.8	6.56	63	.287	.404	0	.000	-2	-20	-19	-1	-1.4
● DUMMY TAYLOR	Taylor, Luther Haden b: 2/21/1875, Oskaloosa, Kan. d: 8/22/58, Jacksonville, Ill. BR/TR, 6'1", 160 lbs. Deb: 8/27/00																											
1900	NY-N	4	3	.571	11	7	6	0	0	62^1	74	31	0	5	24	16	14.9	2.45	147	.294	.367	3	.136	-1	9	8	-2	0.5
1901	NY-N	18	27	.400	**45**	43	37	4	0	353^1	377	193	8	16	112	136	12.9	3.18	104	.271	.333	18	.132	-8	5	5	1	-0.2
1902	Cle-A	1	3	.250	4	4	4	1	0	34	37	17	0	2	8	8	12.4	1.59	217	.278	.329	1	.100	-0	8	7	1	0.9
	NY-N	7	15	.318	26	25	18	0	0	200^2	194	98	4	15	55	87	11.8	2.29	123	.254	.317	6	.092	-5	11	12	-1	0.6
1903	NY-N	13	13	.500	33	31	18	1	0	244^2	306	143	6	4	89	94	14.7	4.23	79	.314	.374	12	.146	-2	-26	-23	-1	-2.4
1904	NY-N	21	15	.583	37	36	29	5	0	296^1	231	100	6	9	75	138	9.6	2.34	117	.214	.270	16	.157	-1	13	13	3	1.6
1905	NY-N	16	9	.640	32	28	18	4	0	213^1	200	85	5	8	51	91	10.9	2.66	110	.247	.298	9	.130	-1	8	7	1	0.6
1906	NY-N	17	9	.654	31	27	13	2	0	213	186	81	4	6	57	91	10.5	2.20	119	.233	.289	14	.184	0	10	10	-1	1.1
1907	NY-N	11	7	.611	28	21	11	3	1	171	145	66	1	3	46	56	10.2	2.42	102	.232	.288	6	.125	-1	1	1	-1	-0.1
1908	NY-N	8	5	.615	27	15	6	1	2	127^2	127	56	5	4	34	50	11.6	2.33	104	.253	.306	8	.229	2	1	1	-0	0.3
Total	9	116	106	.523	274	237	160	21	3	1916^1	1877	870	39	72	551	767	11.7	2.75	107	.256	.314	93	.144	-17	40	39	0	2.9
● WILEY TAYLOR	Taylor, Philip Wiley b: 3/18/1888, Wamego, Kan. d: 7/8/54, Westmoreland, Kan. BR/TR, 6'1", 175 lbs. Deb: 9/6/11																											
1911	Det-A	0	2	.000	3	2	1	0	0	19	18	11	0	1	10	9	13.7	3.79	91	.247	.345	0	.000	-1	-1	-1	-1	-0.2
1912	Chi-A	0	1	.000	3	3	0	0	0	20	21	12	0	0	14	4	15.7	4.95	65	.309	.427	0	.000	-1	-4	-4	0	-0.3
1913	StL-A	0	2	.000	5	4	1	0	0	31^2	33	19	0	0	16	12	13.9	4.83	61	.280	.366	0	.000	-1	-7	-7	0	-0.5
1914	StL-A	2	5	.286	16	8	2	1	0	50	41	24	0	2	25	20	12.2	3.42	79	.209	.305	2	.167	-0	-4	-4	-0	-0.6
Total	4	2	10	.167	27	17	4	1	0	120^2	113	66	0	3	65	45	13.5	4.10	72	.248	.346	2	.061	-3	-15	-15	-0	-1.6
● SCOTT TAYLOR	Taylor, Rodney Scott b: 8/2/67, Defiance, Ohio BL/TL, 6'1", 185 lbs. Deb: 9/17/92																											
1992	Bos-A	1	1	.500	4	1	0	0	0	14^2	13	8	4	0	4	7	10.4	4.91	86	.245	.298	0	—	0	-2	-1	0	-0.1
1993	Bos-A	0	1	.000	16	0	0	0	0	11	14	10	1	1	12	8	22.1	8.18	57	.311	.466	0	—	0	-5	-4	-0	-0.3
Total	2	1	2	.333	20	1	0	0	0	25^2	27	18	5	1	16	15	15.4	6.31	70	.276	.383	0	—	0	-6	-5	-0	-0.4
● RON TAYLOR	Taylor, Ronald Wesley b: 12/13/37, Toronto, Ont., Can. BR/TR, 6'1", 195 lbs. Deb: 4/11/62																											
1962	Cle-A	2	2	.500	8	4	1	0	0	33^1	36	23	6	1	13	15	13.5	5.94	65	.281	.352	3	.273	0	-7	-8	-0	-0.8
1963	StL-N	9	7	.563	54	9	2	0	11	133^1	119	44	10	4	30	91	10.3	2.84	125	.243	.293	1	.031	-3	7	10	-3	0.8
1964	*StL-N	8	4	.667	63	2	0	0	7	101^1	109	56	15	1	33	69	12.7	4.62	82	.274	.331	2	.133	-0	-12	-9	2	-1.0
1965	StL-N	2	1	.667	25	0	0	0	1	43^2	43	24	6	1	15	26	12.2	4.53	85	.261	.326	2	.400	1	-5	-3	0	-0.1
	Hou-N	1	5	.167	32	1	0	0	4	57^2	68	42	5	5	16	37	13.9	6.40	52	.305	.365	0	.000	-1	-18	-21	-1	-2.5
	Yr	3	6	.333	57	1	0	0	5	101^1	111	66	11	6	31	63	13.1	5.60	64	.286	.348	2	.111	-1	-23	-23	-1	-2.6
1966	Hou-N	2	3	.400	36	1	0	0	0	64^2	89	47	5	5	10	29	14.5	5.71	60	.333	.369	2	.167	0	-15	-17	-1	-1.3
1967	NY-N	4	6	.400	50	0	0	0	8	73	60	21	1	1	23	46	10.4	2.34	145	.230	.295	0	.000	-1	8	8	0	1.3
1968	NY-N	1	5	.167	58	0	0	0	13	76^2	64	24	4	1	18	49	9.7	2.70	112	.228	.277	0	.000	-1	2	3	1	0.3
1969	*NY-N	9	4	.692	59	0	0	0	13	76	61	23	7	1	24	42	10.2	2.72	134	.228	.294	1	.250	0	7	8	0	1.6
1970	NY-N	5	4	.556	57	0	0	0	13	66^1	65	31	5	0	16	28	11.0	3.93	102	.265	.310	0	.000	-0	1	1	0	0.1
1971	NY-N	2	2	.500	45	0	0	0	2	69	71	28	7	1	11	32	10.8	3.65	93	.269	.301	1	.250	0	-1	-2	-0	-0.1
1972	SD-N	0	0	—	4	0	0	0	0	5	9	7	5	0	0	0	16.2	12.60	26	.375	.375	0	—	0	-5	-5	0	-0.3
Total	11	45	43	.511	491	17	3	0	72	800	794	370	76	21	209	464	11.5	3.93	91	.264	.316	12	.103	-5	-38	-32	-2	-2.0
● SCOTT TAYLOR	Taylor, Scott Michael b: 10/3/66, Topeka, Kan. BR/TR, 6'3", 200 lbs. Deb: 7/28/95																											
1995	Tex-A	1	2	.333	3	3	0	0	0	15^1	25	16	6	0	5	10	17.6	9.39	51	.379	.423	0	—	0	-8	-8	0	-1.0
● TERRY TAYLOR	Taylor, Terry Derrell b: 7/28/64, Crestview, Fla. BR/TR, 6'1", 180 lbs. Deb: 8/19/88																											
1988	Sea-A	0	1	.000	5	5	0	0	0	23	26	17	2	0	11	9	14.5	6.26	67	.295	.374	0	—	0	-6	-5	-1	-0.3
● PETE TAYLOR	Taylor, Vernon Charles b: 11/26/27, Severn, Md. BR/TR, 6'1", 170 lbs. Deb: 5/2/52																											
1952	StL-A	0	0	—	1	0	0	0	0	2	4	3	0	0	3	0	31.5	13.50	29	.500	.636	0	—	0	-2	-2	0	-0.1
● WADE TAYLOR	Taylor, Wade Eric b: 10/19/65, Mobile, Ala. BR/TR, 6'1", 185 lbs. Deb: 6/2/91																											
1991	NY-A	7	12	.368	23	22	0	0	0	116^1	144	85	13	7	53	72	15.8	6.27	66	.314	.393	0	—	0	-28	-27	1	-3.6
● BILLY TAYLOR	Taylor, William Henry "Bollicky Bill" b: 1855, Washington, D.C. d: 5/14/1900, Jacksonville, Fla. BR/TR, 5'11.5", 204 lbs. Deb: 5/21/1881 ♦																											
1881	Wor-N	0	1	.000	1	1	1	0	0	8	15	13	0		6	0	23.6	7.88	38	.366	.447	3	.107	-0	-5	-4	-0	-0.4
	Cle-N	0	0	—	1	0	0	0	0	3	0	0	0		1	2	3.0	0.00	—	.000	.100	25	.243	-0	1	1	-0	0.0
	Yr	0	1	.000	2	1	1	0	0	11	15	13	0		7	2	18.0	5.73	51	.300	.386	28	.214	-0	-4	-3	-0	-0.4
1882	Pit-a	0	1	.000	1	0	0	0	0	5	11	10	0		4	1	27.0	16.20	16	.407	.484	84	.281	0	-8	-8	-0	-0.9
1883	Pit-a	4	7	.364	19	9	8	0	0	127	166	115	4		34	41	14.2	5.39	60	.296	.337	96	.260	3	-29	-31	-2	-1.9
1884	StL-U	25	4	.862	33	29	29	2	**4**	263	222	97	2		40	154	9.0	1.68	143	.213	.243	68	.366	13	22	21	-1	**2.8**
	Phi-a	18	12	.600	30	30	30	1	0	260	232	118	3	12	44	130	10.0	2.53	134	.219	.258	28	.252	3	21	24	2	2.8
1885	Phi-a	1	5	.167	6	6	6	0	0	52^1	68	35	0	1	9	11	13.4	3.27	105	.343	.375	4	.190	-1	-0	1	-1	-0.1
1886	Bal-a	1	6	.143	8	8	8	0	0	72^1	87	63	1	2	20	37	13.6	5.72	60	.284	.332	12	.308	1	-18	-19	-0	-1.2
1887	Phi-a	1	0	1.000	1	1	1	0	0	9	17	5	1	0	7	0	17.0	3.00	143	.405	.405	1	.250	-0	1	1	-0	0.1
Total	7	50	36	.581	100	84	83	3	4	799^2	818	456	11	15	165	376	11.2	3.17	96	.249	.287	323	.277	20	-14	-12	-4	1.2
● BILLY TAYLOR	Taylor, William Howell b: 10/16/61, Monticello, Fla. BR/TR, 6'8", 200 lbs. Deb: 4/5/94																											
1994	Oak-A	1	3	.250	41	0	0	0	1	46^1	38	24	4	2	18	48	11.3	3.50	127	.220	.301	0	—	0	7	5	-0	0.4
1996	Oak-A	6	3	.667	55	0	0	0	17	60^1	52	30	5	4	25	67	12.1	4.33	114	.231	.319	0	—	0	5	4	1	0.8
1997	Oak-A	3	4	.429	72	0	0	0	23	73	70	32	3	5	36	66	13.7	3.82	119	.254	.350	0	—	0	6	6	1	0.9
1998	Oak-A	4	9	.308	70	0	0	0	33	73	71	37	7	3	22	58	11.8	3.58	128	.255	.317	0	—	0	9	8	-0	1.6
1999	Oak-A	1	5	.167	43	0	0	0	26	43	48	23	3	2	14	38	13.4	3.98	117	.287	.350	0	—	0	4	3	-0	0.6
	NY-N	0	1	.000	18	0	0	0	0	13^1	20	12	2	0	9	14	19.6	8.10	54	.345	.433	0	—	0	-5	-6	0	-0.4
2000	TB-A	1	3	.250	17	0	0	0	0	13^2	13	13	2	2	9	13	15.8	8.56	58	.255	.387	0	—	0	-6	-5	-0	-1.0
Total	6	16	28	.364	316	0	0	0	100	322^2	312	171	26	18	133	304	12.9	4.21	110	.254	.336	0	—	0	20	15	1	2.9
● BUD TEACHOUT	Teachout, Arthur John b: 2/27/04, Los Angeles, Cal. d: 5/11/85, Laguna Beach, Cal BR/TL, 6'2", 183 lbs. Deb: 5/12/30																											
1930	Chi-N	11	4	.733	40	16	6	0	0	153	178	80	16	0	48	59	13.3	4.06	120	.296	.348	17	.270	3	16	14	-1	1.3
1931	Chi-N	1	2	.333	27	3	1	0	0	61^1	79	40	6	1	28	14	15.8	5.72	67	.305	.375	5	.238	0	-13	-13	1	-0.5
1932	StL-N	0	0	—	1	0	0	0	0	1	2	1	0	0	0	0	18.0	0.00	—	.400	.400	0	—	0	0	0	-0	0.0
Total	3	12	6	.667	68	19	7	0	0	215^1	259	121	22	1	76	73	14.0	4.51	102	.299	.356	22	.262	3	3	2	0	0.8

● **GEORGE TEBEAU** Tebeau, George E. "White Wings" b: 12/26/1861, St.Louis, Mo. d: 2/4/23, Denver, Colo. BR/TR, 5'9", 175 lbs. Deb: 4/16/1887 F♦

YEAR TM/L	W	L	PCT	G	GS	CG	SH	SV	IP	H	R	HR	HB	BB	SO	RAT	ERA	ERA+	OAV	OOB	BH	AVG	PB	PR	PR+	PD	TPI
1887 Cin-a	0	1	.000	1	1	1	0	0	8	24	16	0	1	3	1	28.1	13.50	32	.522	.532	125	.358	0	-8	-8	0	-0.5
1890 Tol-a	0	0	—	1	0	0	0	0	5	9	8	0	0	5	0	25.2	9.00	44	.375	.483	102	.268	0	-3	-3	-0	-0.1
Total 2	0	1	.000	2	1	1	0	0	13	33	24	0	1	8	1	27.0	11.77	36	.471	.513	654	.278	1	-11	-11	0	-0.6

● **PATSY TEBEAU** Tebeau, Oliver Wendell b: 12/5/1864, St.Louis, Mo. d: 5/15/18, St.Louis, Mo. BR/TR, 5'8", 163 lbs. Deb: 9/20/1887 FM♦

YEAR TM/L	W	L	PCT	G	GS	CG	SH	SV	IP	H	R	HR	HB	BB	SO	RAT	ERA	ERA+	OAV	OOB	BH	AVG	PB	PR	PR+	PD	TPI
1896 *Cle-N	0	0	—	1	0	0	0	0	0	1	0	0	0	—	—	—	—	1.000	1.000	104	.269	0	0	0	0	0.0	

● **AL TEDROW** Tedrow, Allen Seymour b: 12/14/1891, Westerville, Ohio d: 1/23/58, Westerville, Ohio BR/TL, 6', 180 lbs. Deb: 9/15/14

YEAR TM/L	W	L	PCT	G	GS	CG	SH	SV	IP	H	R	HR	HB	BB	SO	RAT	ERA	ERA+	OAV	OOB	BH	AVG	PB	PR	PR+	PD	TPI
1914 Cle-A	1	2	.333	4	3	1	0	0	22^1	19	6	0	3	14	4	14.5	1.21	239	.235	.367	1	.167	0	4	4	-0	0.6

● **MICHAEL TEJERA** Tejera, Michael b: 10/18/76, Havana, Cuba BL/TL, 5'9", 175 lbs. Deb: 9/8/99

YEAR TM/L	W	L	PCT	G	GS	CG	SH	SV	IP	H	R	HR	HB	BB	SO	RAT	ERA	ERA+	OAV	OOB	BH	AVG	PB	PR	PR+	PD	TPI
1999 Fla-N	0	0	—	3	1	0	0	0	6^1	10	8	1	0	5	7	21.3	11.37	38	.385	.484	0	—	0	-5	-5	1	-0.2

● **KENT TEKULVE** Tekulve, Kenton Charles b: 3/5/47, Cincinnati, Ohio BR/TR, 6'4", 180 lbs. Deb: 5/20/74

YEAR TM/L	W	L	PCT	G	GS	CG	SH	SV	IP	H	R	HR	HB	BB	SO	RAT	ERA	ERA+	OAV	OOB	BH	AVG	PB	PR	PR+	PD	TPI
1974 Pit-N	1	1	.500	8	0	0	0	0	9	12	6	1	1	5	6	18.0	6.00	58	.343	.439	0	—	0	-2	-3	1	-0.5
1975 *Pit-N	1	2	.333	34	0	0	0	5	56	43	20	2	1	23	28	10.8	2.25	158	.215	.299	1	.091	-0	9	8	2	0.8
1976 Pit-N	5	3	.625	64	0	0	0	9	102^2	91	30	3	0	25	68	10.2	2.45	142	.241	.288	0	.000	-1	12	12	2	1.2
1977 Pit-N	10	1	.909	72	0	0	0	7	103	89	41	5	1	33	59	10.7	3.06	130	.236	.299	3	.250	0	10	10	3	1.6
1978 Pit-N	8	7	.533	**91**	0	0	0	31	135^1	115	44	5	2	55	77	11.4	2.33	159	.228	.306	2	.095	-1	**19**	20	3	3.4
1979 *Pit-N	10	8	.556	**94**	0	0	0	31	134^1	109	46	5	2	49	75	10.7	2.75	142	.222	.296	2	.133	-0	15	16	2	3.0
1980 Pit-N☆	8	12	.400	78	0	0	0	21	93	96	39	6	1	40	47	13.3	3.39	108	.267	.342	0	.000	-1	2	3	1	0.6
1981 Pit-N	5	5	.500	45	0	0	0	3	65	61	19	1	1	17	34	10.9	2.49	144	.250	.302	0	.000	-0	7	8	1	1.4
1982 Pit-N	12	8	.600	**85**	0	0	0	20	128^2	113	47	7	3	46	66	11.3	2.87	129	.237	.309	1	.071	-1	11	12	2	2.2
1983 Pit-N	7	5	.583	76	0	0	0	18	99	78	27	1	0	36	52	10.4	1.64	227	.223	.296	0	.000	-1	22	22	1	3.4
1984 Pit-N	3	9	.250	72	0	0	0	13	88	86	30	4	1	33	36	12.3	2.66	136	.262	.331	0	.000	-1	9	9	3	1.6
1985 Pit-N	0	0	—	3	0	0	0	0	3^1	7	7	1	0	5	4	32.4	16.20	22	.467	.600	0	—	0	-5	-5	0	-0.2
Phi-N	4	10	.286	58	0	0	0	14	72^1	67	28	4	2	25	36	11.7	2.99	124	.246	.314	0	.000	-0	5	6	0	1.2
Yr	4	10	.286	61	0	0	0	14	75^2	74	35	5	2	30	40	12.6	3.57	103	.258	.332	0	.000	-0	0	1	0	1.0
1986 Phi-N	11	5	.688	73	0	0	0	4	110	99	35	2	0	25	57	10.1	2.54	152	.240	.283	0	.000	-0	15	16	0	2.3
1987 Phi-N	6	4	.600	**90**	0	0	0	3	105	96	38	8	0	29	60	10.7	3.09	138	.243	.295	0	.000	0	12	13	1	1.3
1988 Phi-N	3	7	.300	70	0	0	0	4	80	87	34	3	2	22	43	12.5	3.60	99	.276	.327	0	.000	-0	-1	-0	1	0.0
1989 Cin-N	0	3	.000	37	0	0	0	1	52	56	35	5	0	23	31	13.7	5.02	72	.272	.345	1	.500	0	-9	-8	0	-0.4
Total 16	94	90	.511	1050	0	0	0	184	1436^2	1305	526	63	17	491	779	11.4	2.85	131	.244	.309	10	.083	-6	129	140	22	22.9

● **AMAURY TELEMACO** Telemaco, Amaury (Regalado) b: 1/19/74, Higuey, D.R. BR/TR, 6'4", 220 lbs. Deb: 5/16/96

YEAR TM/L	W	L	PCT	G	GS	CG	SH	SV	IP	H	R	HR	HB	BB	SO	RAT	ERA	ERA+	OAV	OOB	BH	AVG	PB	PR	PR+	PD	TPI
1996 Chi-N	5	7	.417	25	17	0	0	0	97^1	108	67	20	3	31	64	13.1	5.46	80	.281	.339	3	.103	-1	-13	-12	-1	-1.4
1997 Chi-N	0	3	.000	10	5	0	0	0	38	47	26	4	0	11	29	13.7	6.16	70	.303	.349	2	.222	0	-8	-8	0	-0.5
1998 Chi-N	1	1	.500	14	0	0	0	0	27^2	23	12	5	0	13	18	11.7	3.90	113	.219	.305	1	.167	-0	1	1	0	0.1
Ari-N	6	9	.400	27	18	0	0	0	121	127	63	13	4	33	60	12.2	3.94	107	.271	.325	2	.069	-1	4	4	-1	0.3
Yr	7	10	.412	41	18	0	0	0	148^2	150	75	18	4	46	78	12.1	3.93	108	.262	.321	3	.086	-1	5	5	-1	0.4
1999 Ari-N	1	0	1.000	5	0	0	0	0	6	7	5	2	0	6	2	19.5	7.50	61	.333	.481	0	—	0	-2	-2	0	-0.3
Phi-N	3	0	1.000	44	0	0	0	0	47	45	29	8	2	20	41	12.8	5.55	85	.250	.332	0	—	0	-5	-4	0	-0.2
Yr	4	0	1.000	49	0	0	0	0	53	52	34	10	2	26	43	13.6	5.77	81	.259	.349	0	—	0	-7	-6	0	-0.5
2000 Phi-N	1	3	.250	13	2	0	0	0	24^1	25	22	6	0	14	22	14.4	6.66	71	.275	.371	0	.000	-0	-5	-5	-1	-0.8
Total 5	17	23	.425	138	42	0	0	0	361^1	382	224	58	9	128	236	12.9	5.03	87	.272	.337	8	.104	-2	-29	-26	-2	-2.8

● **ANTHONY TELFORD** Telford, Anthony Charles b: 3/6/66, San Jose, Cal. BR/TR, 6', 175 lbs. Deb: 8/19/90

YEAR TM/L	W	L	PCT	G	GS	CG	SH	SV	IP	H	R	HR	HB	BB	SO	RAT	ERA	ERA+	OAV	OOB	BH	AVG	PB	PR	PR+	PD	TPI
1990 Bal-A	3	3	.500	8	8	0	0	0	36^1	43	22	4	1	19	20	15.6	4.95	77	.295	.380	0	—	0	-4	-5	0	-0.7
1991 Bal-A	0	0	—	9	1	0	0	0	26^2	27	12	3	0	6	24	11.1	4.05	98	.265	.306	0	—	0	0	-0	-0	0.0
1993 Bal-A	0	0	—	3	0	0	0	0	7^1	11	8	3	1	1	6	16.0	9.82	46	.344	.382	0	—	0	-4	-4	0	-0.2
1997 Mon-N	4	6	.400	65	0	0	0	1	89	77	34	11	5	33	61	11.6	3.24	130	.236	.316	3	.200	0	10	10	2	1.2
1998 Mon-N	3	6	.333	77	0	0	0	1	91	85	45	9	4	36	59	12.4	3.86	109	.247	.326	1	.250	0	4	4	1	0.4
1999 Mon-N	5	4	.556	79	0	0	0	2	96	112	52	3	3	38	69	14.3	3.94	114	.295	.363	0	.000	0	7	6	1	0.6
2000 Mon-N	5	4	.556	64	0	0	0	3	78^1	76	38	10	5	23	68	11.9	3.79	125	.257	.321	0	.000	-0	7	8	0	0.8
Total 7	20	23	.465	305	9	0	0	7	424^2	431	211	43	19	156	307	12.8	3.94	109	.265	.336	4	.174	0	19	18	4	2.1

● **DAVE TELGHEDER** Telgheder, David William b: 11/11/66, Middletown, N.Y. BR/TR, 6'3", 212 lbs. Deb: 6/12/93

YEAR TM/L	W	L	PCT	G	GS	CG	SH	SV	IP	H	R	HR	HB	BB	SO	RAT	ERA	ERA+	OAV	OOB	BH	AVG	PB	PR	PR+	PD	TPI
1993 NY-N	6	2	.750	24	7	0	0	0	75^2	82	40	10	4	21	35	12.7	4.76	84	.276	.332	1	.067	-0	-6	-6	-1	-0.7
1994 NY-N	0	1	.000	6	0	0	0	0	10	11	8	2	0	8	4	17.1	7.20	58	.282	.404	0	—	0	-3	-3	-1	-0.3
1995 NY-N	1	2	.333	7	4	0	0	0	25^2	34	18	4	0	7	16	14.4	5.61	72	.318	.360	2	.333	1	-4	-5	1	-0.4
1996 Oak-A	4	7	.364	16	14	1	1	0	79^1	92	42	12	1	26	43	13.5	4.65	106	.292	.348	0	—	0	3	2	0	0.3
1997 Oak-A	4	6	.400	20	19	0	0	0	101	134	71	15	2	35	55	15.2	6.06	75	.324	.379	0	.000	-0	-17	-17	3	-1.2
1998 Oak-A	0	1	.000	8	2	0	0	0	20	19	12	4	2	6	5	12.1	3.60	127	.235	.303	0	—	0	2	2	-0	0.1
Total 6	15	19	.441	81	46	1	1	0	311^2	372	191	47	9	103	158	14.0	5.23	85	.297	.355	3	.130	-0	-25	-27	2	-2.2

● **TOM TELLMANN** Tellmann, Thomas John b: 3/29/54, Warren, Pa. BR/TR, 6'3", 195 lbs. Deb: 6/9/79

YEAR TM/L	W	L	PCT	G	GS	CG	SH	SV	IP	H	R	HR	HB	BB	SO	RAT	ERA	ERA+	OAV	OOB	BH	AVG	PB	PR	PR+	PD	TPI
1979 SD-N	0	0	—	1	0	0	0	0	2^2	7	5	1	0	0	1	23.6	16.88	21	.467	.467	0	.000	-0	-4	-4	0	-0.2
1980 SD-N	3	0	1.000	6	2	2	0	1	22^1	23	5	0	0	8	9	12.5	1.61	213	.264	.326	1	.125	-0	5	5	0	0.7
1983 Mil-A	9	4	.692	44	0	0	0	8	99^2	95	34	7	2	35	48	11.9	2.80	134	.259	.327	0	—	0	14	11	3	1.8
1984 Mil-A	6	3	.667	50	0	0	0	4	81	82	28	6	1	31	28	12.7	2.78	139	.272	.342	0	—	0	11	10	1	1.2
1985 Oak-A	0	0	—	11	0	0	0	0	21^1	33	12	3	1	9	8	18.1	5.06	76	.347	.410	0	—	0	-2	-3	0	-0.1
Total 5	18	7	.720	112	2	2	0	13	227	240	84	17	4	83	94	13.0	3.05	123	.277	.343	1	.111	-0	24	19	4	3.4

● **CHUCK TEMPLETON** Templeton, Charles Sherman b: 6/1/32, Detroit, Mich. d: 10/9/97, Irving, Tex. BR/TL, 6'3", 210 lbs. Deb: 9/9/55

YEAR TM/L	W	L	PCT	G	GS	CG	SH	SV	IP	H	R	HR	HB	BB	SO	RAT	ERA	ERA+	OAV	OOB	BH	AVG	PB	PR	PR+	PD	TPI
1955 Bro-N	0	1	.000	4	0	0	0	0	4^2	5	7	2	1	5	3	21.2	11.57	35	.294	.478	0	—	0	-4	-4	0	-0.7
1956 Bro-N	0	1	.000	6	2	0	0	0	16^1	20	13	2	0	10	8	16.5	6.61	60	.294	.385	0	.000	-0	-5	-5	-0	-0.3
Total 2	0	2	.000	10	2	0	0	0	21	25	20	4	1	15	11	17.6	7.71	52	.294	.406	0	.000	-0	-9	-8	-0	-1.0

● **JOHN TENER** Tener, John Kinley b: 7/25/1863, County Tyrone, Ireland d: 5/19/46, Pittsburgh, Pa. BR/TR, 6'4", 180 lbs. Deb: 6/8/1885 ♦

YEAR TM/L	W	L	PCT	G	GS	CG	SH	SV	IP	H	R	HR	HB	BB	SO	RAT	ERA	ERA+	OAV	OOB	BH	AVG	PB	PR	PR+	PD	TPI
1888 Chi-N	7	5	.583	12	12	11	1	0	102	90	59	6	8	25	39	10.9	2.74	111	.228	.288	9	.196	-0	1	3	1	0.3
1889 Chi-N	15	15	.500	35	30	28	1	0	287	302	192	16	7	105	105	13.0	3.64	114	.262	.328	41	.273	5	12	16	3	2.1
1890 Pit-P	3	11	.214	14	14	13	0	0	117	160	147	6	5	70	30	18.1	7.31	53	.312	.400	12	.190	2	-40	-48	4	-3.3
Total 3	25	31	.446	61	56	52	2	0	506	552	398	28	20	200	174	13.7	4.30	90	.268	.339	62	.236	6	-27	-23	8	-0.9

● **JIM TENNANT** Tennant, James McDonnell b: 3/3/07, Shepherdstown, W.Va d: 4/16/67, Trumbull, Conn. BR/TR, 6'1", 190 lbs. Deb: 9/28/29

YEAR TM/L	W	L	PCT	G	GS	CG	SH	SV	IP	H	R	HR	HB	BB	SO	RAT	ERA	ERA+	OAV	OOB	BH	AVG	PB	PR	PR+	PD	TPI
1929 NY-N	0	0	—	1	0	0	0	0	1	1	0	0	0	0	1	9.0	0.00	—	.333	.333	0	—	0	1	1	0	0.0

● **FRED TENNEY** Tenney, Fred Clay b: 7/9/1859, Marlborough, N.H. d: 6/15/19, Fall River, Mass. Deb: 4/28/1884 ♦

YEAR TM/L	W	L	PCT	G	GS	CG	SH	SV	IP	H	R	HR	HB	BB	SO	RAT	ERA	ERA+	OAV	OOB	BH	AVG	PB	PR	PR+	PD	TPI
1884 Bos-U	3	1	.750	4	4	4	0	0	35	31	21	0		5	18	9.3	2.31	103	.221	.248	2	.118	-3	0	0	-1	-0.3
Wil-U	0	1	.000	1	1	1	0	0	8	6	5	0		4	10	11.3	1.13	237	.194	.286	0	.000	-1	1	1	0	0.1
Yr	3	2	.600	5	5	5	0	0	43	37	26	0		9	28	9.6	2.09	116	.216	.256	2	.100	-3	2	2	-1	-0.2

● **FRED TENNEY** Tenney, Frederick b: 11/26/1871, Georgetown, Mass. d: 7/3/52, Boston, Mass. BL/TL, 5'9", 155 lbs. Deb: 6/16/1894 M♦

YEAR TM/L	W	L	PCT	G	GS	CG	SH	SV	IP	H	R	HR	HB	BB	SO	RAT	ERA	ERA+	OAV	OOB	BH	AVG	PB	PR	PR+	PD	TPI
1905 Bos-N	0	0	—	1	0	0	0	0	2	5	4	0	0	1	0	27.0	4.50	69	.417	.462	158	.288	0	-0	-0	0	0.0

● **BOB TERLECKI** Terlecki, Robert Joseph b: 2/14/45, Trenton, N.J. BR/TR, 5'8", 185 lbs. Deb: 8/16/72

YEAR TM/L	W	L	PCT	G	GS	CG	SH	SV	IP	H	R	HR	HB	BB	SO	RAT	ERA	ERA+	OAV	OOB	BH	AVG	PB	PR	PR+	PD	TPI
1972 Phi-N	0	0	—	9	0	0	0	0	13^1	16	9	2	0	10	5	17.6	4.73	76	.308	.419	0	—	0	-2	-2	0	-0.1

● **GREG TERLECKY** Terlecky, Gregory John b: 3/20/52, Culver City, Cal. BR/TR, 6'3", 200 lbs. Deb: 6/12/75

YEAR TM/L	W	L	PCT	G	GS	CG	SH	SV	IP	H	R	HR	HB	BB	SO	RAT	ERA	ERA+	OAV	OOB	BH	AVG	PB	PR	PR+	PD	TPI
1975 StL-N	0	1	.000	20	0	0	0	0	30^1	38	16	4	0	12	13	14.8	4.45	85	.306	.368	1	.333	0	-3	-2	0	-0.1

YEAR	TM/L	W	L	PCT	G	GS	CG	SH	SV	IP	H	R	HR	HB	BB	SO	RAT	ERA	ERA+	OAV	OOB	BH	AVG	PB	PR	PR+	PD	TPI
● JEFF TERPKO	Terpko, Jeffrey Michael b: 10/16/50, Sayre, Pa. BR/TR, 6', 180 lbs. Deb: 9/21/74																											
1974	Tex-A	0	0	—	3	0	0	0	0	7	6	1	0	0	4	3	12.9	1.29	278	.231	.333	0	—	0	2	2	-0	0.1
1976	Tex-A	3	3	.500	32	0	0	0	0	52^2	42	15	3	0	29	24	12.1	2.39	150	.223	.327	0	—	0	7	7	-0	0.7
1977	Mon-N	0	1	.000	13	0	0	0	0	20^2	28	13	2	0	15	14	18.7	5.66	67	.346	.448	0	.000	-0	-4	-4	-0	-0.3
Total	3	3	4	.429	48	0	0	0	0	80^1	76	29	5	0	48	41	13.9	3.14	116	.258	.362	0	.000	-0	4	5	-1	0.5
● WALT TERRELL	Terrell, Charles Walter b: 5/11/58, Jeffersonville, Ind BL/TR, 6'2", 205 lbs. Deb: 9/8/82																											
1982	NY-N	0	3	.000	3	3	0	0	0	21	22	12	2	0	14	8	15.4	3.43	106	.268	.375	2	.400	1	0	0	-0	0.1
1983	NY-N	8	8	.500	21	20	4	2	0	133^2	123	57	7	2	55	59	12.1	3.57	102	.251	.329	8	.182	3	1	1	-0	0.4
1984	NY-N	11	12	.478	33	33	3	1	0	215	232	99	16	4	80	114	13.2	3.52	101	.282	.348	6	.080	-4	2	1	0	-0.3
1985	Det-A	15	10	.600	34	34	5	3	0	229	221	107	9	4	95	130	12.6	3.85	106	.255	.332	0	—	0	8	6	3	0.9
1986	Det-A	15	12	.556	34	33	9	2	0	217^1	199	116	30	3	98	93	12.4	4.56	91	.245	.329	0	—	0	-9	-10	2	-1.0
1987	*Det-A	17	10	.630	35	35	10	1	0	244^2	254	123	30	3	94	143	12.9	4.05	105	.268	.336	0	—	0	12	5	-1	0.4
1988	Det-A	7	16	.304	29	29	11	1	0	206^1	199	101	20	2	78	84	12.2	3.97	96	.258	.328	0	—	0	0	-3	1	-0.3
1989	SD-N	5	13	.278	19	19	4	1	0	123^1	134	65	14	0	26	63	11.7	4.01	87	.277	.314	4	.100	-0	-7	-7	3	-0.7
	NY-A	6	5	.545	13	13	1	1	0	83	102	52	9	2	24	30	13.9	5.20	74	.307	.358	0	—	0	-12	-12	-0	-1.4
1990	Pit-N	2	7	.222	16	16	0	0	0	82^2	98	59	13	4	33	34	14.7	5.88	62	.295	.366	3	.107	-1	-19	-22	1	-2.0
	Det-A	6	4	.600	13	12	0	0	0	75^1	86	39	7	8	24	30	14.1	4.54	87	.290	.359	0	—	0	-5	-5	-1	-0.6
1991	Det-A	12	14	.462	35	33	8	2	0	218^2	257	115	16	2	79	80	13.9	4.24	98	.301	.361	0	—	0	-3	-2	-1	-0.3
1992	Det-A	7	10	.412	36	14	1	0	0	136^2	163	86	14	3	48	61	14.1	5.20	76	.298	.358	0	—	0	-19	-19	1	-2.0
Total	11	111	124	.472	321	294	56	14	0	1986^2	2090	1031	187	37	748	929	13.0	4.22	93	.274	.341	23	.120	-1	-52	-67	8	-6.8
● JERRY TERRELL	Terrell, Jerry Wayne b: 7/13/46, Waseca, Minn. BR/TR, 6', 170 lbs. Deb: 4/14/73 ♦																											
1979	KC-A	0	0	—	1	0	0	0	0	1	0	0	0	0	0	0	0.0	0.00	—	.000	.000	12	.300	0	0	0	0	0.0
1980	KC-A	0	0	—	1	0	0	0	0	1	1	0	0	0	1	0	18.0	0.00	—	.250	.400	1	.063	-0	0	0	0	0.0
Total	2	0	0	—	2	0	0	0	0	2	1	0	0	0	1	0	9.0	0.00	—	.143	.250	412	.253	0	1	1	0	0.0
● JOHN TERRY	Terry, John Burchard b: 11/1/1879, Waterbury, Conn. d: 4/27/33, Kansas City, Mo. Deb: 9/17/02																											
1902	Det-A	0	1	.000	1	1	1	0	0	5	8	3	0	0	1	0	16.2	3.60	101	.364	.391	0	.000	-0	-0	0	-0	-0.1
1903	StL-A	1	1	.500	3	1	1	0	0	17^2	21	6	0	3	4	2	14.3	2.55	114	.296	.359	0	.000	-1	1	1	-0	-0.1
Total	2	1	2	.333	4	2	2	0	0	22^2	29	9	0	3	5	2	14.7	2.78	111	.312	.366	0	.000	-2	1	1	-1	-0.2
● YANK TERRY	Terry, Lancelot Yank b: 2/11/11, Bedford, Ind. d: 11/4/79, Bloomington, Ind. BR/TR, 6'1", 180 lbs. Deb: 8/3/40																											
1940	Bos-A	1	0	1.000	4	1	0	0	0	19^1	24	19	2	0	11	9	16.3	8.84	51	.304	.389	2	.250	0	-10	-9	0	-0.4
1942	Bos-A	6	5	.545	20	11	3	0	1	85	82	48	5	2	43	37	13.4	3.92	95	.248	.339	3	.111	-1	-2	-2	-0	-0.4
1943	Bos-A	7	9	.438	30	22	7	0	1	163^2	147	70	8	1	63	63	11.6	3.52	94	.242	.314	3	.067	-3	-4	-4	0	-0.6
1944	Bos-A	6	10	.375	27	17	3	0	0	132^2	142	72	10	3	65	30	14.2	4.21	81	.276	.361	11	.234	1	-11	-12	0	-1.2
1945	Bos-A	0	4	.000	12	4	1	0	0	56^2	68	29	8	0	14	28	13.0	4.13	82	.296	.336	2	.111	-2	-5	-4	-1	-0.5
Total	5	20	28	.417	93	55	14	0	2	457^1	463	238	33	6	196	167	13.1	4.09	85	.263	.339	21	.145	-4	-32	-31	-1	-3.1
● RALPH TERRY	Terry, Ralph Willard b: 1/9/36, Big Cabin, Okla. BR/TR, 6'3", 195 lbs. Deb: 8/6/56																											
1956	NY-A	1	2	.333	3	3	0	0	0	13^1	17	15	2	0	11	8	18.9	9.45	41	.347	.467	1	.167	-0	-8	-9	-0	-1.4
1957	NY-A	1	1	.500	7	2	1	1	0	20^2	18	7	1	0	8	7	11.3	3.05	118	.240	.313	1	.250	0	2	1	0	0.2
	KC-A	4	11	.267	21	19	3	1	0	130^2	119	63	15	4	47	80	11.7	3.38	117	.239	.310	6	.143	-2	6	8	0	0.7
	Yr	5	12	.294	28	21	4	2	0	151^1	137	70	16	4	55	87	11.7	3.33	117	.239	.310	7	.152	-2	8	9	0	0.9
1958	KC-A	11	13	.458	40	33	8	3	2	216^2	217	111	29	2	61	134	11.6	4.24	92	.262	.314	14	.197	-0	-11	-8	-2	-1.0
1959	KC-A	2	4	.333	9	7	2	0	0	46^1	56	29	9	1	19	35	14.8	5.24	76	.308	.376	3	.176	-1	-7	-6	1	-0.7
	NY-A	3	7	.300	24	16	5	1	0	127^1	130	55	7	2	30	55	11.5	3.39	107	.270	.316	4	.098	-3	7	4	-0	0.0
	Yr	5	11	.313	33	23	7	1	0	173^2	186	84	16	3	49	90	12.3	3.89	96	.281	.333	7	.121	-3	-0	-3	0	-0.7
1960	*NY-A	10	8	.556	35	23	7	3	1	166^2	149	78	15	4	52	92	11.1	3.40	105	.237	.300	6	.122	-2	9	4	0	0.2
1961	*NY-A	16	3	.842	31	27	9	2	0	188^1	162	74	19	1	42	86	9.8	3.15	118	.232	.277	15	.227	2	18	13	1	1.4
1962	*NY-A☆	**23**	12	.657	43	39	14	3	2	**298**^{2}	257	123	40	3	57	176	**9.6**	3.19	117	.231	.270	20	.189	1	26	19	-4	1.8
1963	*NY-A	17	15	.531	40	37	**18**	3	1	268	246	103	29	4	39	114	**9.7**	3.22	109	.242	.273	7	.080	-6	12	9	-1	0.3
1964	*NY-A	7	11	.389	27	14	2	1	4	115	130	60	20	1	31	77	12.7	4.54	80	.283	.329	7	.200	1	-12	-12	-0	-1.7
1965	Cle-A	11	6	.647	30	26	6	2	0	165^2	154	77	22	1	23	84	9.7	3.69	94	.242	.269	7	.143	2	-4	-4	-4	-0.6
1966	KC-A	1	5	.167	15	10	0	0	0	64	65	35	7	1	15	33	11.4	3.80	89	.263	.308	3	.214	1	-3	-3	-1	-0.2
	NY-N	0	1	.000	11	1	0	0	1	24^2	27	14	1	0	11	14	13.9	4.74	77	.293	.369	1	.167	-0	-3	-3	-0	-0.2
1967	NY-N	0	0	—	2	0	0	0	0	3^1	1	0	0	0	0	5	2.7	0.00	—	.091	.091	0	—	0	1	1	0	0.1
Total	12	107	99	.519	338	257	75	20	11	1849^1	1748	844	216	24	446	1000	10.8	3.62	102	.249	.296	95	.160	-6	32	14	-11	-1.1
● SCOTT TERRY	Terry, Scott Ray b: 11/21/59, Hobbs, N.Mex. BR/TR, 5'11", 195 lbs. Deb: 4/9/86																											
1986	Cin-N	1	2	.333	28	3	0	0	0	55^2	66	40	8	0	32	32	15.8	6.14	63	.300	.389	1	.250	0	-15	-13	0	-0.7
1987	StL-N	0	0	—	11	0	0	0	0	13^1	13	5	0	0	8	9	14.2	3.38	123	.260	.362	0	.000	-0	1	1	0	0.1
1988	StL-N	9	6	.600	51	11	1	0	3	129^1	119	48	5	0	34	65	10.6	2.92	119	.247	.297	7	.250	2	8	8	0	1.2
1989	StL-N	8	10	.444	31	24	1	0	2	148^2	142	65	14	3	43	69	11.4	3.57	102	.253	.310	7	.156	2	-1	1	2	0.5
1990	StL-N	2	6	.250	50	2	0	0	2	72	75	45	7	4	27	35	13.3	4.75	80	.264	.337	5	.455	2	-8	-7	0	-0.5
1991	StL-N	4	4	.500	65	0	0	0	1	80^1	76	31	1	0	32	52	12.1	2.80	133	.249	.320	1	.143	-0	8	8	1	0.9
Total	6	24	28	.462	236	40	2	0	8	499^1	491	234	35	7	176	262	12.1	3.73	99	.258	.323	21	.216	6	-7	-3	4	1.5
● ADONIS TERRY	Terry, William H b: 8/7/1864, Westfield, Mass. d: 2/24/15, Milwaukee, Wis. BR/TR, 5'11.5", 168 lbs. Deb: 5/1/1884 U♦																											
1884	Bro-a	19	35	.352	56	55	54	2	0	476	486	308	10	8	72	230	10.7	3.55	93	.248	.277	55	.233	3	-16	-12	-3	-1.2
1885	Bro-a	6	17	.261	25	23	23	0	1	209	213	147	9	4	42	96	11.2	4.26	77	.262	.301	45	.170	-3	-24	-22	1	-2.1
1886	Bro-a	18	16	.529	34	34	32	5	0	288^1	263	177	1	16	115	162	12.3	3.09	113	.231	.310	71	.237	2	12	13	4	1.8
1887	Bro-a	16	16	.500	40	35	35	1	**3**	318	430	230	10	9	99	138	12.4	4.02	107	.315	.320	119	.323	7	10	10	5	1.6
1888	Bro-a	13	8	.619	23	23	20	2	0	195	145	79	2	9	67	138	10.2	2.03	147	**.199**	.275	29	.252	3	22	21	1	2.3
1889	*Bro-a	22	15	.595	41	39	35	2	0	326	285	189	6	16	126	186	11.8	3.29	113	.228	.307	48	.300	12	20	16	6	3.0
1890	*Bro-N	26	16	.619	46	44	38	1	0	370	362	200	3	15	133	185	12.4	2.94	117	.248	.318	101	.278	15	26	21	1	3.1
1891	Bro-N	6	16	.273	25	22	18	1	1	194	207	139	5	7	80	65	13.6	4.22	78	.263	.336	19	.209	3	-19	-20	-1	-1.6
1892	Bal-N	0	1	.000	1	1	1	0	0	9	7	7	0	0	7	3	14.0	4.00	86	.206	.341	0	.000	-1	-1	-1	0	-0.1
	Pit-N	18	7	.720	30	26	24	2	1	240	185	106	3	8	106	95	11.2	2.51	131	.204	.293	16	.160	1	21	21	1	2.1
	Yr	18	8	.692	31	27	25	2	1	249	192	113	3	8	113	98	11.3	2.57	129	.204	.295	16	.154	1	20	20	1	2.0
1893	Pit-N	12	8	.600	26	19	14	0	0	170	177	121	5	11	99	52	15.2	4.45	102	.260	.363	18	.254	2	4	2	0	0.4
1894	Pit-N	0	1	.000	1	1	0	0	0	0^2	2	5	0	0	4	0	81.0	67.50	8	.500	.750	0	—	0	-5	-5	0	-0.6
	Chi-N	5	11	.313	23	21	16	0	0	163^1	232	191	12	16	123	39	20.4	5.84	96	.330	.441	33	.347	4	-9	-4	-1	0.0
	Yr	5	12	.294	24	22	16	0	0	164	234	196	12	16	127	39	20.7	6.09	92	.331	.444	33	.347	4	-14	-8	-1	-0.6
1895	Chi-N	21	14	.600	38	34	31	0	0	311^1	346	228	4	17	131	88	14.3	4.80	106	.277	.354	30	.219	-6	-1	9	2	0.4
1896	Chi-N	15	14	.517	30	28	25	1	0	235^2	273	166	6	10	88	75	14.2	4.43	102	.288	.354	26	.263	2	-2	3	-2	0.3
1897	Chi-N	0	1	.000	1	1	1	0	0	8	11	10	0	2	6	1	21.4	10.13	44	.324	.452	0	.000	-1	-5	-5	0	-0.4
Total	14	197	196	.501	440	406	367	17	6	3514^1	3624	2303	76	148	1298	1553	12.7	3.74	103	.258	.323	610	.254	45	34	43	15	9.0
● DICK TERWILLIGER	Terwilliger, Richard Martin b: 6/27/06, Sand Lake, Mich. d: 1/21/69, Greenville, Mich. BR/TR, 5'11", 178 lbs. Deb: 8/18/32																											
1932	StL-N	0	0	—	1	0	0	0	0	3	1	0	0	1	2	2	12.0	0.00	—	.143	.400	0	.000	-0	1	1	0	0.1
● JEFF TESREAU	Tesreau, Charles Monroe b: 3/5/1889, Silver Mine, Mo. d: 9/24/46, Hanover, N.H. BR/TR, 6'2", 218 lbs. Deb: 4/12/12 C																											
1912	*NY-N	17	7	.708	36	28	19	3	1	243	177	90	2	10	106	119	10.9	**1.96**	**172**	**.204**	.298	12	.146	-2	39	39	1	3.4
1913	*NY-N	22	13	.629	41	38	17	1	0	282	222	98	7	7	119	167	11.1	2.17	144	**.220**	.306	21	.221	2	32	31	1	4.0
1914	NY-N	26	10	.722	42	41	26	**8**	1	322^1	238	104	8	7	128	189	10.4	2.37	112	**.209**	.293	28	.239	6	15	11	-2	1.6
1915	NY-N	19	16	.543	43	39	24	8	3	306	235	98	4	5	75	176	9.3	2.29	112	.215	.269	24	.233	6	16	10	1	1.9
1916	NY-N	14	14	.500	40	32	23	5	2	268^1	249	103	9	6	65	113	10.7	2.92	83	.250	.300	18	.191	2	-9	-16	-0	-1.5
1917	*NY-N	13	8	.619	33	20	11	1	2	183^2	168	71	6	3	58	85	11.2	3.09	83	.249	.312	14	.230	2	-8	-12	2	-1.1

YEAR	TM/L	W	L	PCT	G	GS	CG	SH	SV	IP	H	R	HR	HB	BB	SO	RAT	ERA	ERA+	OAV	OOB	BH	AVG	PB	PR	PR+	PD	TPI
1918	NY-N	4	4	.500	12	9	3	1	0	73^2	61	27	1	0	21	31	10.0	2.32	113	.227	.283	7	.318	2	4	3	1	0.6
Total	7	115	72	.615	247	207	123	27	9	1679	1350	591	37	38	572	880	10.5	2.43	114	.223	.295	124	.216	17	89	66	3	8.9
● **JAY TESSMER**	Tessmer, Jay Weldon b: 12/26/71, Meadville, Pa. BR/TR, 6'3", 190 lbs. Deb: 8/27/98																											
1998	NY-A	1	0	1.000	7	0	0	0	0	8^2	4	3	1	0	4	6	8.3	3.12	141	.143	.250	0	—	0	1	1	-0	0.1
1999	NY-A	0	0	—	6	0	0	0	0	6^2	16	11	1	1	4	3	28.4	14.85	32	.444	.512	0	—	0	-7	-8	-0	-0.4
2000	NY-A	0	0	—	7	0	0	0	0	6^2	9	6	3	0	1	5	13.5	6.75	71	.300	.323	0	—	0	-1	-1	-0	-0.1
Total	3	1	0	1.000	20	0	0	0	0	22	29	20	5	1	9	14	16.0	7.77	59	.309	.375	0	—	0	-7	-8	-1	-0.4
● **BOB TEWKSBURY**	Tewksbury, Robert Alan b: 11/30/60, Concord, N.H. BR/TR, 6'4", 200 lbs. Deb: 4/11/86																											
1986	NY-A	9	5	.643	23	20	2	0	0	130^1	144	58	8	5	31	49	12.4	3.31	124	.282	.329	0	—	0	13	12	2	1.3
1987	NY-A	1	4	.200	8	6	0	0	0	33^1	47	26	5	1	7	12	14.9	6.75	65	.338	.374	0	—	0	-8	-9	0	-1.0
	Chi-N	0	4	.000	7	3	0	0	0	18	32	15	1	0	13	10	22.5	6.50	66	.421	.506	0	.000	-1	-5	-4	-1	-0.9
1988	Chi-N	0	0	—	1	1	0	0	0	3^1	6	5	1	0	2	1	21.6	8.10	45	.400	.471	0	.000	-0	-2	-2	0	-0.1
1989	StL-N	1	0	1.000	7	4	1	1	0	30	25	12	2	2	10	17	11.1	3.30	110	.225	.301	1	.111	-0	1	1	-0	0.0
1990	StL-N	10	9	.526	28	20	3	2	1	145^1	151	67	7	3	15	50	10.5	3.47	110	.267	.290	7	.171	1	5	6	-1	0.8
1991	StL-N	11	12	.478	30	30	3	0	0	191	206	86	13	5	38	75	11.7	3.25	114	.281	.321	9	.155	1	9	10	0	1.3
1992	StL-N★	16	5	**.762**	33	32	5	0	0	233	217	63	15	3	20	91	9.3	2.16	157	.248	.267	6	.086	-2	35	33	0	2.9
1993	StL-N	17	10	.630	32	32	2	0	0	213^2	258	99	15	6	20	97	12.0	3.83	104	.301	.322	14	.203	2	5	3	3	0.9
1994	StL-N	12	10	.545	24	24	4	1	0	155^2	190	97	19	3	22	79	12.4	5.32	78	.304	.330	10	.185	1	-19	-20	2	-2.2
1995	Tex-A	8	7	.533	21	21	4	1	0	129^2	169	75	8	3	20	53	13.3	4.58	105	.319	.348	0	.000	-0	2	4	1	0.5
1996	SD-N	10	10	.500	36	33	1	0	0	206^2	224	116	17	3	43	126	11.8	4.31	92	.275	.314	2	.031	-5	-2	-8	4	-0.7
1997	Min-A	8	13	.381	26	26	5	2	0	168^2	200	83	12	1	31	92	12.4	4.22	111	.297	.329	1	.200	0	7	8	3	1.2
1998	Min-A	7	13	.350	26	25	1	0	0	148^1	174	82	19	6	20	60	12.1	4.79	100	.292	.322	0	.000	-0	-2	-0	2	0.1
Total	13	110	102	.519	302	277	31	7	1	1807	2043	884	142	41	292	812	11.8	3.92	104	.287	.319	50	.132	-3	38	32	17	4.1
● **GRANT THATCHER**	Thatcher, Ulysses Grant b: 2/23/1877, Maytown, Pa. d: 3/17/36, Lancaster, Pa. TR, 5'10.5", 180 lbs. Deb: 9/9/03																											
1903	Bro-N	3	1	.750	4	4	4	0	0	28	33	12	1	0	7	9	12.9	2.89	110	.292	.333	2	.182	0	1	1	-0	0.1
1904	Bro-N	1	0	1.000	1	0	0	0	0	9	9	6	0	0	2	4	11.0	4.00	69	.281	.324	1	.250	0	-1	-1	-0	-0.1
Total	2	4	1	.800	5	4	4	0	0	37	42	18	1	0	9	13	12.4	3.16	98	.290	.331	3	.200	0	-0	-0	-0	0.0
● **GREG THAYER**	Thayer, Gregory Allen b: 10/23/49, Cedar Rapids, Iowa BR/TR, 5'11", 182 lbs. Deb: 4/7/78																											
1978	Min-A	1	1	.500	20	0	0	0	0	45	40	19	5	3	30	30	14.6	3.80	101	.258	.388	0	—	0	-0	0	-0	0.0
● **JACK THEIS**	Theis, John Louis b: 7/23/1891, Georgetown, Ohio d: 7/6/41, Georgetown, Ohio BR/TR, 6', 190 lbs. Deb: 7/5/20																											
1920	Cin-N	0	0	—	1	0	0	0	0	2	1	0	0	0	3	0	18.0	0.00	—	.143	.400	0	—	0	1	1	-0	0.0
● **DUANE THEISS**	Theiss, Duane Charles b: 11/20/53, Zanesville, Ohio BR/TR, 6'3", 185 lbs. Deb: 8/5/77																											
1977	Atl-N	1	1	.500	17	0	0	0	0	20^2	26	16	1	1	16	7	18.7	6.53	68	.338	.457	0	.000	-0	-6	-4	0	-0.4
1978	Atl-N	0	0	—	3	0	0	0	0	6^1	3	1	0	1	3	3	9.9	1.42	285	.158	.304	0	.000	-0	2	2	0	0.1
Total	2	1	1	.500	20	0	0	0	0	27	29	17	1	2	19	10	16.7	5.33	82	.302	.427	0	.000	-0	-4	-3	0	-0.3
● **JUG THESENGA**	Thesenga, Arnold Joseph b: 4/27/14, Jefferson, S.Dak. BR/TR, 6', 200 lbs. Deb: 9/1/44																											
1944	Was-A	0	0	—	5	1	0	0	0	12^1	18	9	0	0	12	2	21.9	5.11	64	.340	.462	0	.000	-0	-2	-3	0	-0.2
● **BERT THIEL**	Thiel, Maynard Bert b: 5/4/26, Marion, Wis. BR/TR, 5'10", 185 lbs. Deb: 4/17/52																											
1952	Bos-N	1	1	.500	4	0	0	0	0	7	11	7	1	2	4	6	21.9	7.71	47	.344	.447	0	—	0	-3	-3	-0	-0.6
● **HENRY THIELMAN**	Thielman, Henry Joseph b: 10/3/1880, St.Cloud, Minn. d: 9/2/42, New York, N.Y. BR/TR, 5'11", 175 lbs. Deb: 4/17/02 F♦																											
1902	NY-N	0	1	.000	2	2	0	0	0	6	8	10	0	0	6	5	21.0	1.50	187	.320	.452	1	.111	-0	1	1	0	0.2
	Cin-N	9	15	.375	25	23	22	0	1	211	201	111	2	19	78	49	12.7	3.24	92	.251	.332	12	.132	-4	-11	-5	-1	-1.0
	Yr	9	16	.360	27	25	22	0	1	217	209	121	2	19	84	54	12.9	3.19	94	.253	.336	13	.130	-4	-10	-4	-0	-0.8
1903	Bro-N	0	3	.000	4	3	3	0	0	29	31	20	3	2	14	10	14.6	4.66	69	.330	.427	5	.217	1	-4	-5	1	-0.2
Total	2	9	19	.321	31	28	25	0	1	246	240	141	5	21	98	64	13.1	3.37	90	.261	.346	18	.146	-3	-14	-9	0	-1.0
● **JAKE THIELMAN**	Thielman, John Peter b: 5/20/1879, St.Cloud, Minn. d: 1/28/28, Minneapolis, Minn. BR/TR, 5'11", 175 lbs. Deb: 4/23/05 F																											
1905	StL-N	15	16	.484	32	29	26	0	0	242	265	138	4	12	62	87	12.6	3.50	85	.281	.333	21	.231	8	-13	-14	3	-0.5
1906	StL-N	0	1	.000	1	1	0	0	0	5	5	6	0	0	2	0	12.6	3.60	73	.263	.333	1	.500	0	-1	-1	-0	-0.1
1907	Cle-A	11	8	.579	20	18	18	3	0	166	151	60	2	7	34	56	10.4	2.33	107	.245	.292	12	.203	1	4	3	-3	0.2
1908	Cle-A	4	3	.571	11	8	5	0	0	61^2	59	26	2	4	9	15	10.5	3.65	65	.260	.300	8	.348	4	-9	-9	2	-0.4
	Bos-A	0	0	—	1	0	0	0	0	0^2	3	4	1	0	0	0	40.5	40.50	6	.600	.600	0	—	0	-3	-3	-0	-0.2
	Yr	4	3	.571	12	8	5	0	0	62^1	62	30	3	4	9	15	10.8	4.04	59	.267	.306	8	.348	4	-11	-11	1	-0.6
Total	4	30	28	.517	65	56	49	3	0	475^1	483	234	9	23	107	158	11.6	3.16	86	.267	.316	42	.240	13	-21	-23	2	-1.0
● **DAVE THIES**	Thies, David Robert b: 3/21/37, Minneapolis, Minn. BR/TR, 6'4", 205 lbs. Deb: 4/20/63																											
1963	KC-A	0	1	.000	9	2	0	0	0	25^1	26	15	2	2	12	9	14.2	4.62	84	.274	.367	2	.333	1	-3	-2	0	0.0
● **JAKE THIES**	Thies, Vernon Arthur b: 4/1/26, St.Louis, Mo. BR/TR, 5'11", 170 lbs. Deb: 4/24/54																											
1954	Pit-N	3	9	.250	33	18	3	1	0	130^1	120	70	13	3	49	57	11.9	3.87	108	.244	.317	1	.030	-2	3	5	0	0.2
1955	Pit-N	0	1	.000	1	1	0	0	0	3^2	5	5	0	1	3	0	22.1	4.91	84	.357	.500	0	—	0	-0	-0	-0	0.0
Total	2	3	10	.231	34	19	3	1	0	134	125	75	13	4	52	57	12.2	3.90	107	.248	.323	1	.030	-2	3	4	0	0.2
● **BOBBY THIGPEN**	Thigpen, Robert Thomas b: 7/17/63, Tallahassee, Fla. BR/TR, 6'3", 195 lbs. Deb: 8/6/86																											
1986	Chi-A	2	0	1.000	20	0	0	0	7	35^2	26	7	1	1	12	20	9.8	1.77	245	.205	.279	0	—	0	10	10	-0	0.9
1987	Chi-A	7	5	.583	51	0	0	0	16	89	86	30	10	3	24	52	11.4	2.73	168	.256	.311	0	—	0	17	18	0	2.9
1988	Chi-A	5	8	.385	68	0	0	0	34	90	96	38	6	4	33	62	13.3	3.30	121	.273	.342	0	—	0	7	7	0	1.4
1989	Chi-A	2	6	.250	61	0	0	0	34	79	62	34	10	1	40	47	11.7	3.76	101	.218	.316	0	—	0	1	0	-1	0.0
1990	Chi-A★	4	6	.400	**77**	0	0	0	**57**	88^2	60	20	5	1	32	70	9.4	1.83	210	.195	.274	0	—	0	21	20	0	4.2
1991	Chi-A	7	5	.583	67	0	0	0	30	69^2	63	32	10	4	38	47	13.6	3.49	114	.245	.351	0	—	0	5	4	1	0.9
1992	Chi-A	1	3	.250	55	0	0	0	22	55	58	29	4	3	33	45	15.4	4.75	82	.275	.381	0	—	0	-5	-5	1	-0.7
1993	Chi-A	0	0	—	25	0	0	0	1	34^2	51	25	5	5	12	19	17.7	5.71	73	.349	.417	0	—	0	-5	-6	-1	-0.4
	*Phi-N	3	1	.750	17	0	0	0	0	19^1	23	13	2	1	9	10	15.4	6.05	66	.307	.388	0	.000	-0	-4	-5	0	-0.8
1994	Sea-A	0	2	.000	7	0	0	0	0	7^2	12	9	3	0	5	4	20.0	9.39	52	.353	.436	0	—	0	-4	-4	-0	-0.7
Total	9	31	36	.463	448	0	0	0	201	568^2	537	237	56	23	238	376	12.6	3.43	118	.252	.334	0	.000	-0	42	40	0	7.7
● **J. J. THOBE**	Thobe, John Joseph b: 11/19/70, Covington, Ky. BR/TR, 6'6", 200 lbs. Deb: 9/18/95 F																											
1995	Mon-N	0	0	—	4	0	0	0	0	4	6	4	0	0	3	0	20.3	9.00	48	.333	.429	0	—	0	-2	-2	-0	-0.1
● **TOM THOBE**	Thobe, Thomas Neal b: 9/3/69, Covington, Ky. BL/TL, 6'6", 195 lbs. Deb: 9/12/95 F																											
1995	Atl-N	0	0	—	3	0	0	0	0	3^1	7	4	0	0	0	2	18.9	10.80	40	.412	.412	0	—	0	-2	-2	-0	-0.1
1996	Atl-N	0	1	.000	4	0	0	0	0	6	5	2	1	0	0	1	7.5	1.50	294	.217	.217	0	.000	-0	2	2	-1	0.2
Total	2	0	1	.000	7	0	0	0	0	9^1	12	6	1	0	0	3	11.6	4.82	90	.300	.300	0	.000	-0	-1	-0	-1	0.1
● **DICK THOENEN**	Thoenen, Richard Crispin b: 1/9/44, Mexico, Mo. BR/TR, 6'6", 215 lbs. Deb: 9/16/67																											
1967	Phi-N	0	0	—	1	0	0	0	0	1	2	1	0	0	0	0	18.0	9.00	38	.500	.500	0	—	0	-1	-1	0	0.0
● **TOMMY THOMAS**	Thomas, Alphonse b: 12/23/1899, Baltimore, Md. d: 4/27/88, Dallastown, Pa. BR/TR, 5'10", 175 lbs. Deb: 4/17/26																											
1926	Chi-A	15	12	.556	44	32	13	2	2	249	225	113	7	1	110	127	12.1	3.80	102	**.244**	.325	16	.186	-1	6	2	-3	-0.2
1927	Chi-A	19	16	.543	40	36	24	3	1	**307^2**	271	110	16	1	94	107	10.7	2.98	136	.244	.303	14	.147	-3	40	37	-4	3.0
1928	Chi-A	17	16	.515	36	32	24	3	2	283	277	114	14	4	76	129	11.4	3.08	131	.259	.310	21	.219	3	30	30	-3	3.3
1929	Chi-A	14	18	.438	36	31	**24**	2	1	259^2	270	127	17	0	60	62	11.4	3.19	134	.269	.310	25	.255	2	30	31	-3	3.4
1930	Chi-A	5	13	.278	34	27	7	0	0	169	229	125	13	1	44	58	14.6	5.22	89	.323	.364	7	.125	-4	-11	-11	0	-1.3
1931	Chi-A	10	14	.417	43	36	11	2	2	245^1	298	166	17	5	69	72	13.6	4.73	90	.292	.340	21	.241	1	-10	-13	-1	-1.0

YEAR	TM/L	W	L	PCT	G	GS	CG	SH	SV	IP	H	R	HR	HB	BB	SO	RAT	ERA	ERA+	OAV	OOB	BH	AVG	PB	PR	PR+	PD	TPI
1932	Chi-A	3	3	.500	12	3	1	0	0	43^{2}	55	33	6	1	15	11	14.6	6.18	70	.307	.364	1	.077	-1	-8	-9	-0	-1.1
	Was-A	8	7	.533	18	14	7	1	0	117	114	48	5	0	46	36	12.3	3.54	122	.255	.325	10	.238	1	12	10	-2	1.0
	Yr	11	10	.524	30	17	8	1	0	160^{2}	169	81	11	1	61	47	12.9	4.26	101	.270	.336	11	.200	0	4	1	-2	-0.1
1933	*Was-A	7	7	.500	35	14	2	0	3	135	149	87	9	2	49	35	13.3	4.80	87	.273	.336	10	.238	1	-8	-9	-2	-0.9
1934	Was-A	8	9	.471	33	18	7	1	1	133^{1}	154	87	9	3	58	42	14.5	5.47	79	.294	.368	7	.184	-0	-14	-18	-2	-2.1
1935	Was-A	0	0	—	1	0	0	0	0	0^{1}	3	2	0	0	0	0	81.0	54.00	8	.750	.750	0	—	0	-2	-2	0	-0.1
	Phi-N	0	1	.000	4	1	0	0	0	12	15	9	2	0	5	3	15.0	5.25	86	.313	.377	0	.000	-0	-2	-1	-0	-0.1
1936	StL-A	11	9	.550	36	21	8	1	0	179^{2}	219	132	25	4	72	40	14.8	5.26	102	.297	.362	8	.138	-3	-4	2	-2	-0.3
1937	StL-A	0	1	.000	17	2	0	0	0	30^{2}	46	26	2	1	10	10	16.7	7.04	69	.348	.399	0	.000	-1	-8	-7	0	-0.4
	Bos-A	0	2	.000	9	0	0	0	0	11	16	6	2	1	4	4	17.2	4.09	116	.340	.404	1	.250	-0	1	1	-0	0.1
	Yr	0	3	.000	26	2	0	0	0	41^{2}	62	32	4	2	14	14	16.8	6.26	77	.346	.400	1	.125	-1	-8	-6	-0	-0.3
Total	12	117	128	.478	398	267	128	15	12	2176^{1}	2341	1185	144	24	712	736	12.7	4.11	104	.275	.333	141	.195	-5	52	43	-22	3.3
● **BLAINE THOMAS** Thomas, Blaine M. "Baldy" b: 8/1888, Glendora, Cal. d: 8/21/15, Glendora, Cal. BR/TR, 5'10", 165 lbs. Deb: 8/25/11																												
1911	Bos-A	0	0	—	2	2	0	0	0	4^{2}	3	2	0	1	7	0	21.2	0.00	—	.273	.579	1	.500	0	2	2	0	0.1
● **CARL THOMAS** Thomas, Carl Leslie b: 5/28/32, Minneapolis, Minn. BR/TR, 6'5", 245 lbs. Deb: 4/19/60																												
1960	Cle-A	1	0	1.000	4	0	0	0	0	9^{2}	8	8	1	1	10	5	17.7	7.45	50	.229	.413	1	.333	1	-4	-4	0	-0.3
● **LEFTY THOMAS** Thomas, Clarence Fletcher b: 10/4/03, Glade Spring, Va. d: 3/21/52, Charlottesville, Va. BL/TL, 6', 183 lbs. Deb: 9/26/25																												
1925	Was-A	0	2	.000	2	2	1	0	0	13	14	8	0	0	7	10	14.5	2.08	204	.264	.350	0	.000	-1	3	3	0	0.4
1926	Was-A	0	0	—	6	0	0	0	0	8^{2}	8	7	0	0	10	3	18.7	5.19	74	.267	.450	0	.000	0	-1	-1	-1	-0.1
Total	2	0	2	.000	8	2	1	0	0	21^{2}	22	15	0	0	17	13	16.2	3.32	123	.265	.390	0	.000	-1	2	2	-1	0.3
● **CLAUDE THOMAS** Thomas, Claude Alfred "Lefty" b: 5/15/1890, Stanberry, Mo. d: 3/6/46, Sulphur, Okla. BL/TL, 6'1", 180 lbs. Deb: 9/14/16																												
1916	Was-A	1	2	.333	7	4	1	1	0	28^{1}	27	14	1	2	12	7	13.0	4.13	68	.265	.353	1	.100	-1	-4	-4	-0	-0.5
● **FAY THOMAS** Thomas, Fay Wesley "Scow" b: 10/10/04, Holyrood, Kan. d: 8/16/90, Chatsworth, Cal. BR/TR, 6'2", 195 lbs. Deb: 6/27/27																												
1927	NY-N	0	0	—	9	0	0	0	0	16^{1}	19	10	3	1	4	11	13.2	3.31	117	.302	.353	0	.000	-0	1	1	-0	0.0
1931	Cle-A	2	4	.333	16	2	1	0	0	48^{2}	63	34	2	1	32	25	17.8	5.18	89	.323	.421	2	.154	-1	-4	-3	-1	-0.4
1932	Bro-N	0	1	.000	7	2	0	0	0	17	22	15	0	0	8	9	15.9	7.41	51	.306	.375	0	.000	-0	-7	-7	0	-0.4
1935	StL-A	7	15	.318	49	19	4	0	1	147	165	95	11	3	89	67	15.7	4.78	100	.289	.388	4	.105	-3	-5	0	2	0.0
Total	4	9	20	.310	81	23	5	0	1	229	269	154	16	5	133	112	16.0	4.95	93	.299	.392	6	.107	-4	-15	-8	1	-0.8
● **FROSTY THOMAS** Thomas, Forrest b: 5/23/1881, Faucett, Mo. d: 3/18/70, St.Joseph, Mo. BR/TR, 6', 185 lbs. Deb: 5/1/05																												
1905	Det-A	0	1	.000	2	1	0	0	0	6	10	8	0	1	3	5	21.0	7.50	36	.370	.452	0	.000	0	-3	-3	0	-0.4
● **LARRY THOMAS** Thomas, Larry Wayne b: 10/25/69, Miami, Fla. BR/TL, 6'1", 190 lbs. Deb: 8/11/95																												
1995	Chi-A	0	0	—	17	0	0	0	0	13^{2}	8	2	1	0	6	12	9.2	1.32	339	.167	.259	0	—	0	5	5	-0	0.2
1996	Chi-A	2	3	.400	57	0	0	0	0	30^{2}	32	11	1	3	14	20	14.4	3.23	147	.281	.374	0	—	0	6	5	0	0.7
1997	Chi-A	0	0	—	5	0	0	0	0	3^{1}	3	3	1	0	2	0	13.5	8.10	54	.250	.357	0	—	0	-1	-1	0	-0.1
Total	3	2	3	.400	79	0	0	0	0	47^{2}	43	16	3	3	22	32	12.8	3.02	154	.247	.342	0	—	0	10	9	-0	0.8
● **BUD THOMAS** Thomas, Luther Baxter b: 9/9/10, Faber, Va. BR/TR, 6', 180 lbs. Deb: 9/13/32																												
1932	Was-A	0	0	—	2	0	0	0	0	3	1	0	0	0	2	1	9.0	0.00	—	.100	.250	0	—	0	1	1	0	0.1
1933	Was-A	0	0	—	2	0	0	0	0	4	11	8	1	1	2	1	31.5	15.75	27	.550	.609	0	.000	-0	-5	-5	0	-0.2
1937	Phi-A	8	15	.348	35	26	6	1	0	169^{2}	208	108	15	1	52	54	13.8	4.99	95	.295	.344	6	.128	-1	-7	-5	-3	-0.9
1938	Phi-A	9	14	.391	42	29	7	1	0	212^{1}	259	138	23	2	62	48	13.7	4.92	98	.299	.347	9	.130	-3	-3	-2	-1	-0.5
1939	Phi-A	0	1	.000	2	2	0	0	0	4	8	8	2	0	1	0	20.3	15.75	30	.421	.450	0	.000	-0	-5	-5	0	-0.8
	Was-A	0	0	—	4	0	0	0	0	9	11	7	0	0	2	0	13.0	6.00	72	.306	.342	0	.000	-0	-1	-2	0	-0.1
	Det-A	7	0	1.000	27	0	0	0	1	47^{1}	45	25	7	0	20	14	12.4	4.18	117	.254	.330	1	.111	-1	2	4	0	0.4
	Yr	7	1	.875	33	2	0	0	1	60^{1}	64	40	9	0	23	14	13.0	5.22	92	.276	.341	1	.071	-2	-4	-3	0	-0.5
1940	Det-A	0	1	.000	3	0	0	0	0	4	8	5	1	0	3	0	24.8	9.00	53	.421	.500	0	—	0	-2	-2	1	-0.3
1941	Det-A	1	3	.250	26	1	0	0	2	72^{2}	74	45	4	0	22	17	11.9	4.21	108	.260	.313	2	.105	-1	-1	2	2	0.2
Total	7	25	34	.424	143	58	13	2	3	526	625	344	53	4	166	135	13.6	4.96	96	.292	.345	18	.120	-7	-20	-12	-1	-2.1
● **MIKE THOMAS** Thomas, Michael Steven b: 9/2/69, Sacramento, Cal. BL/TL, 6'2", 205 lbs. Deb: 7/12/95																												
1995	Mil-A	0	0	—	1	0	0	0	0	1^{1}	2	0	0	0	1	0	20.3	0.00	—	.333	.429	0	—	0	1	1	0	0.0
● **MYLES THOMAS** Thomas, Myles Lewis b: 10/22/1897, State College, Pa. d: 12/12/63, Toledo, Ohio BR/TR, 5'9.5", 170 lbs. Deb: 4/18/26																												
1926	*NY-A	6	6	.500	33	13	3	0	0	140^{1}	140	79	6	3	65	38	13.3	4.23	91	.271	.356	5	.116	-3	-3	-6	1	-0.7
1927	NY-A	7	4	.636	21	9	1	0	0	88^{2}	111	58	4	1	43	25	15.7	4.87	79	.322	.398	9	.333	2	-7	-11	0	-1.0
1928	NY-A	1	0	1.000	12	1	0	0	0	31^{2}	33	19	3	0	9	10	11.9	3.41	110	.277	.328	4	.400	1	2	1	-0	0.1
1929	NY-A	0	2	.000	5	1	0	0	0	15	27	21	1	0	9	3	21.6	10.80	36	.409	.480	1	.143	-1	-11	-13	1	-1.3
	Was-A	7	8	.467	22	14	7	0	2	125^{1}	139	72	3	0	48	33	13.4	3.52	121	.288	.352	14	.292	2	10	10	0	1.3
	Yr	7	10	.412	27	15	7	0	2	140^{1}	166	93	4	0	57	36	14.3	4.30	98	.302	.368	15	.273	1	-1	-2	1	0.0
1930	Was-A	2	2	.500	12	2	0	0	0	33^{2}	49	35	3	0	15	12	17.1	8.29	55	.358	.421	2	.182	-1	-14	-14	-1	-1.4
Total	5	23	22	.511	105	40	11	0	2	434^{2}	499	284	20	4	189	121	14.3	4.64	87	.299	.372	35	.240	0	-23	-31	1	-3.0
● **ROY THOMAS** Thomas, Roy Allen b: 3/24/1874, Norristown, Pa. d: 11/20/59, Norristown, Pa. BL/TL, 5'11", 150 lbs. Deb: 4/14/1899 FC◆																												
1900	Phi-N	0	0	—	1	0	0	0	0	2^{2}	4	1	0	0	0	0	13.5	3.38	107	.333	.333	168	.316	0	0	0	-0	0.0
● **ROY THOMAS** Thomas, Roy Justin b: 6/22/53, Quantico, Va. BR/TR, 6'6", 200 lbs. Deb: 9/21/77																												
1977	Hou-N	0	0	—	4	0	0	0	0	6^{1}	5	2	0	0	3	4	11.4	2.84	126	.208	.296	0	—	0	1	1	0	0.0
1978	StL-N	1	1	.500	16	1	0	0	3	28^{1}	21	14	0	0	16	16	11.8	3.81	92	.216	.327	1	.250	0	-1	-1	1	0.0
1979	StL-N	3	4	.429	26	6	0	0	1	77	66	29	9	0	24	44	10.5	2.92	129	.237	.298	1	.059	-1	7	7	1	0.6
1980	StL-N	2	3	.400	24	5	0	0	0	55	59	32	3	3	25	22	14.2	4.75	78	.274	.358	2	.154	-0	-7	-6	1	-0.5
1983	Sea-A	3	1	.750	43	0	0	0	1	88^{2}	95	44	3	2	32	77	13.1	3.45	124	.275	.340	0	—	0	6	8	-0	0.4
1984	Sea-A	3	2	.600	21	1	0	0	1	49^{2}	52	33	8	4	37	42	16.9	5.26	76	.280	.410	0	—	0	-7	-7	0	-0.6
1985	Sea-A	7	0	1.000	40	0	0	0	1	93^{2}	66	37	8	2	48	70	11.1	3.36	125	.202	.309	0	—	0	8	9	-1	0.5
1987	Sea-A	1	0	1.000	8	0	0	0	0	20^{2}	23	12	2	1	11	14	15.2	5.23	91	.299	.393	0	—	0	-2	-1	-1	-0.1
Total	8	20	11	.645	182	13	0	0	7	419^{1}	387	203	33	12	196	289	12.8	3.82	105	.250	.339	4	.118	-1	6	9	1	0.3
● **STAN THOMAS** Thomas, Stanley Brown b: 7/11/49, Rumford, Me. BR/TR, 6'2", 185 lbs. Deb: 7/5/74																												
1974	Tex-A	0	0	—	12	0	0	0	0	13^{2}	22	10	1	0	6	8	18.4	6.59	54	.379	.438	0	—	0	-4	-5	0	-0.2
1975	Tex-A	4	4	.500	46	1	0	0	3	81^{1}	72	36	2	3	34	46	12.1	3.10	122	.239	.322	0	—	0	6	6	0	0.6
1976	Cle-A	4	4	.500	37	7	2	0	6	105^{2}	88	33	5	4	41	54	11.3	2.30	152	.229	.310	0	—	0	14	14	3	1.5
1977	Sea-A	2	6	.250	13	9	1	0	0	58^{1}	74	49	8	3	25	14	15.7	6.02	69	.310	.382	0	—	0	-13	-12	-0	-1.4
	NY-A	1	0	1.000	3	0	0	0	0	6^{1}	7	7	0	0	4	1	15.6	7.11	56	.280	.379	0	—	0	-2	-2	-0	-0.3
	Yr	3	6	.333	16	9	1	0	0	64^{2}	81	56	8	3	29	15	15.7	6.12	67	.307	.382	0	—	0	-15	-14	-1	-1.7
Total	4	11	14	.440	111	17	3	0	9	265^{1}	263	135	16	10	110	123	13.0	3.70	101	.261	.340	0	—	0	1	1	3	0.2
● **TOM THOMAS** Thomas, Thomas R. "Savage Tom" b: 12/27/1873, Shawnee, Ohio d: 9/23/42, Shawnee, Ohio BR/TR, 6'4", 195 lbs. Deb: 9/20/1894																												
1894	Cle-N	0	0	—	1	0	0	0	1	0^{1}	0	1	0	0	2	0	54.0	27.00	20	.000	.667	0	—	0	-1	-1	0	-0.1
1899	StL-N	1	1	.500	4	2	2	0	0	25	22	14	1	0	4	8	9.4	2.52	158	.237	.268	3	.250	0	4	4	0	0.3
1900	StL-N	2	2	.500	5	1	1	0	0	26^{1}	38	22	2	1	4	7	14.7	3.76	97	.336	.364	1	.091	-1	-0	-0	-1	-0.2
Total	3	3	3	.500	10	3	3	0	1	51^{2}	60	37	3	1	10	15	12.4	3.31	115	.290	.326	4	.174	-1	3	3	-1	0.0
● **ERSKINE THOMASON** Thomason, Melvin Erskine b: 8/13/48, Laurens, S.C. BR/TR, 6'1", 190 lbs. Deb: 9/18/74																												
1974	Phi-N	0	0	—	1	0	0	0	0	1	0	0	0	0	0	1	0.0	0.00	—	.000	.000	0	—	0	0	0	0	0.0
● **ART THOMPSON** Thompson, Arthur J. Deb: 6/17/1884																												
1884	Was-U	0	1	.000	1	1	1	0	0	8	10	11	0		3	8	14.6	6.75	36	.286	.342	0	.000	-1	-4	-4	0	-0.4

YEAR TM/L	W	L	PCT	G	GS	CG	SH	SV	IP	H	R	HR	HB	BB	SO	RAT	ERA	ERA+	OAV	OOB	BH	AVG	PB	PR	PR+	PD	TPI
● **FORREST THOMPSON** Thompson, David Forrest b: 3/3/18, Mooresville, N.C. d: 2/26/79, Charlotte, N.C. BL/TL, 5'11", 195 lbs. Deb: 4/26/48																											
1948 Was-A	6	10	.375	46	7	0	0	4	131^1	134	71	9	1	54	40	13.0	3.84	113	.262	.334	10	.286	2	7	7	-0	1.1
1949 Was-A	1	3	.250	9	1	1	0	0	16^1	22	11	1	1	9	8	17.6	4.41	97	.328	.416	3	.600	2	-0	-0	0	0.1
Total 2	7	13	.350	55	8	1	0	4	147^2	156	82	10	2	63	48	13.5	3.90	111	.270	.344	13	.325	4	6	7	-0	1.2
● **JUNIOR THOMPSON** Thompson, Eugene Earl b: 6/7/17, Latham, Ill. BR/TR, 6'1", 185 lbs. Deb: 4/26/39																											
1939 *Cin-N	13	5	.722	42	11	5	3	2	152^1	130	51	6	3	55	87	11.1	2.54	151	.236	.309	11	.229	0	23	22	-1	2.4
1940 *Cin-N	16	9	.640	33	31	17	3	0	225^1	197	90	10	2	96	103	11.8	3.32	114	.233	.313	18	.228	3	13	12	-1	1.4
1941 Cin-N	6	6	.500	27	15	4	0	1	109	117	65	6	3	57	46	14.6	4.87	74	.272	.361	7	.233	1	-15	-16	2	-1.3
1942 Cin-N	4	7	.364	29	10	1	0	0	101^2	86	61	5	2	53	35	12.5	3.36	98	.226	.324	8	.267	2	-1	-1	4	0.5
1946 NY-N	4	6	.400	39	1	0	0	4	62^2	36	18	5	0	40	31	10.9	1.29	266	.190	.332	1	.143	0	15	15	2	2.8
1947 NY-N	4	2	.667	15	0	0	0	0	35^2	36	20	3	1	27	13	16.1	4.29	95	.279	.408	0	.000	-1	-1	-1	1	-0.1
Total 6	47	35	.573	185	68	27	6	7	686^2	602	305	35	11	328	315	12.3	3.26	113	.239	.329	45	.225	6	35	32	6	5.7
● **FULLER THOMPSON** Thompson, Fuller Weidner b: 5/1/1889, Los Angeles, Cal. d: 2/19/72, Los Angeles, Cal. BR/TR, 5'11.5", 164 lbs. Deb: 8/19/11																											
1911 Bos-N	0	0	—	3	0	0	0	0	4^2	5	4	0	0	2	0	13.5	3.86	99	.294	.368	0	—	0	-0	-0	0	0.0
● **HARRY THOMPSON** Thompson, Harold b: 9/9/1889, Nanticoke, Pa. d: 2/14/51, Reno, Nev. BL/TL, 5'8", 150 lbs. Deb: 4/24/19																											
1919 Was-A	0	3	.000	12	2	0	0	1	43^1	48	21	0	2	8	10	12.0	3.53	91	.293	.333	8	.250	1	-1	-2	0	0.0
Phi-A	0	1	.000	3	0	0	0	0	12	16	9	4	0	3	1	14.3	6.75	51	.327	.365	0	.000	-1	-5	-4	0	-0.4
Yr	0	4	.000	15	2	0	0	1	55^1	64	30	4	2	11	11	12.5	4.23	77	.300	.341	8	.211	0	-6	-6	1	-0.4
● **LEE THOMPSON** Thompson, John Dudley "Lefty" b: 2/26/1898, Smithfield, Utah d: 2/17/63, Santa Barbara, Cal BL/TL, 6'1", 185 lbs. Deb: 9/4/21																											
1921 Chi-A	0	3	.000	4	4	0	0	0	20^2	32	21	0	0	6	4	16.5	8.27	51	.333	.373	2	.286	0	-9	-9	-1	-1.1
● **GUS THOMPSON** Thompson, John Gustav b: 6/22/1877, Humboldt, Iowa d: 3/28/58, Kalispell, Mont. 6'2", 185 lbs. Deb: 8/31/03																											
1903 *Pit-N	2	2	.500	5	4	3	0	0	43	52	30	1	1	16	22	14.4	3.56	91	.295	.358	4	.250	0	-1	-2	-1	-0.2
1906 StL-N	2	11	.154	17	12	8	0	0	103	111	61	2	5	25	36	12.3	4.28	61	.285	.336	6	.176	-1	-19	-19	1	-2.2
Total 2	4	13	.235	22	16	11	0	0	146	163	91	3	6	41	58	12.9	4.07	69	.288	.343	10	.200	-0	-20	-21	0	-2.4
● **JOCKO THOMPSON** Thompson, John Samuel b: 1/17/17, Beverly, Mass. d: 2/3/88, Olney, Md. BL/TL, 6', 185 lbs. Deb: 9/21/48																											
1948 Phi-N	1	0	1.000	2	2	1	0	0	13	10	4	0	0	9	7	13.2	2.77	142	.233	.365	0	.000	0	2	2	-0	0.1
1949 Phi-N	1	3	.250	8	5	1	0	0	31^1	38	24	6	0	11	12	14.1	6.89	57	.314	.371	2	.182	-0	-10	-11	-0	-1.1
1950 Phi-N	0	0	—	2	0	0	0	0	4	1	1	0	0	4	2	11.3	0.00	—	.077	.294	0	—	0	2	2	0	0.1
1951 Phi-N	4	8	.333	29	14	3	2	1	119^1	102	55	12	2	59	60	12.3	3.85	100	.231	.325	4	.103	-1	2	0	-1	-0.2
Total 4	6	11	.353	41	21	5	2	1	167^2	151	84	18	2	83	81	12.7	4.24	91	.244	.336	6	.113	-1	-5	-7	-1	-1.1
● **JUSTIN THOMPSON** Thompson, Justin Willard b: 3/8/73, San Antonio, Tex. BL/TL, 6'4", 215 lbs. Deb: 5/27/96																											
1996 Det-A	1	6	.143	11	11	0	0	0	59	62	35	7	2	31	44	14.5	4.58	111	.267	.358	0	—	0	3	3	1	0.4
1997 Det-A★	15	11	.577	32	32	4	0	0	223^1	188	82	20	2	66	151	10.3	3.02	152	.233	.292	0	.000	-0	38	39	0	4.2
1998 Det-A	11	15	.423	34	34	5	0	0	222	227	114	20	2	79	149	12.5	4.05	116	.267	.331	1	.143	-0	15	16	0	1.7
1999 Det-A	9	11	.450	24	24	0	0	0	142^2	152	85	24	4	59	83	13.6	5.11	95	.274	.348	0	.000	-1	-4	-4	-2	-0.7
Total 4	36	43	.456	101	101	9	0	0	647	629	316	71	10	235	427	12.2	3.98	119	.257	.325	1	.071	-1	52	54	-0	5.6
● **MARK THOMPSON** Thompson, Mark Radford b: 4/7/71, Russellville, Ky. BR/TR, 6'2", 205 lbs. Deb: 7/26/94																											
1994 Col-N	1	1	.500	2	2	0	0	0	9	16	9	2	1	8	5	25.0	9.00	55	.400	.510	0	.000	-0	-5	-3	-0	-0.6
1995 *Col-N	2	3	.400	21	5	0	0	0	51	73	42	7	1	22	30	16.9	6.53	83	.349	.414	5	.385	1	-13	-5	1	-0.3
1996 Col-N	9	11	.450	34	28	3	1	0	169^2	189	109	25	13	74	99	14.6	5.30	99	.285	.368	8	.138	-2	-20	-1	-1	-0.4
1997 Col-N	3	3	.500	6	6	0	0	0	29^2	40	27	8	4	13	9	17.3	7.89	66	.323	.404	2	.182	1	-12	-7	0	-1.1
1998 Col-N	1	2	.333	6	6	0	0	0	23^1	36	22	8	5	12	14	20.4	7.71	67	.379	.473	1	.143	-0	-9	-5	-0	-0.6
1999 StL-N	1	3	.250	5	5	0	0	0	29^1	26	12	1	2	17	22	13.8	2.76	166	.241	.354	0	.000	-1	6	6	0	0.7
2000 StL-N	1	1	.500	20	0	0	0	0	25	24	21	4	3	15	19	15.1	5.04	92	.250	.368	0	.000	-0	-1	-1	0	-0.1
Total 7	18	24	.429	94	52	3	1	0	337	404	242	55	29	161	198	15.9	5.74	90	.303	.390	16	.154	-3	-55	-18	-0	-2.4
● **MIKE THOMPSON** Thompson, Michael Wayne b: 9/6/49, Denver, Colo. BR/TR, 6'3", 190 lbs. Deb: 5/19/71																											
1971 Was-A	1	6	.143	16	12	0	0	0	66^2	53	39	3	3	54	41	14.9	4.86	68	.222	.372	2	.118	0	-10	-12	0	-1.1
1973 StL-N	0	0	—	2	2	0	0	0	4	1	0	0	0	5	3	13.5	0.00	—	.077	.333	0	.000	-0	2	2	-0	0.1
1974 StL-N	0	3	.000	19	4	0	0	0	38^1	37	24	1	2	35	25	17.4	5.63	64	.274	.430	0	.000	-1	-9	-9	0	-0.7
Atl-N	0	0	—	1	1	0	0	0	4	7	2	0	0	2	2	20.3	4.50	84	.412	.474	1	1.000	0	-0	-0	0	0.0
Yr	0	3	.000	20	5	0	0	0	42^1	44	26	1	2	37	27	17.6	5.53	65	.289	.435	1	.111	-1	-9	-9	0	-0.7
1975 Atl-N	0	6	.000	16	10	0	0	0	51^2	60	32	2	0	32	42	16.0	4.70	80	.305	.402	1	.071	-1	-6	-5	1	-0.6
Total 4	1	15	.063	54	29	0	0	0	164^2	158	97	6	5	128	113	15.9	4.86	73	.263	.396	4	.098	-1	-24	-24	1	-2.3
● **RICH THOMPSON** Thompson, Richard Neil b: 11/1/58, New York, N.Y. BR/TR, 6'3", 225 lbs. Deb: 4/28/85																											
1985 Cle-A	3	8	.273	57	0	0	0	5	80	95	63	8	6	48	30	16.8	6.30	66	.303	.405	0	—	0	-19	-19	-2	-2.7
1989 Mon-N	0	2	.000	19	1	0	0	0	33	27	11	2	2	11	15	10.9	2.18	162	.241	.320	0	.000	0	5	5	-0	0.3
1990 Mon-N	0	0	—	1	0	0	0	0	1	1	0	0	0	0	0	9.0	0.00	—	.250	.250	0	—	0	0	0	0	0.0
Total 3	3	10	.231	77	1	0	0	5	114	123	74	10	8	59	45	15.0	5.05	78	.286	.382	0	.000	0	-14	-14	-2	-2.4
● **TOMMY THOMPSON** Thompson, Thomas Carl b: 11/7/1889, Spring City, Tenn. d: 1/16/63, LaJolla, Cal. BR/TR, 5'9.5", 170 lbs. Deb: 6/5/12 F																											
1912 NY-A	0	2	.000	7	2	1	0	0	32^2	43	32	0	3	13	15	16.3	6.06	59	.341	.415	3	.300	1	-10	-8	-1	-0.4
● **WILL THOMPSON** Thompson, Will McLain b: 8/30/1870, Pittsburgh, Pa. d: 6/9/62, Pittsburgh, Pa. BR/TR, 5'11.5", 190 lbs. Deb: 7/9/1892																											
1892 Pit-N	0	1	.000	1	1	0	0	0	3	3	5	0	1	5	0	27.0	3.00	110	.250	.500	0	—	0	0	0	0	0.1
● **JOHN THOMSON** Thomson, John Carl b: 10/1/73, Vicksburg, Miss. BR/TR, 6'3", 175 lbs. Deb: 5/11/97																											
1997 Col-N	7	9	.438	27	27	2	1	0	166^1	193	94	15	5	51	106	13.5	4.71	110	.296	.352	10	.213	-0	-9	7	-0	0.6
1998 Col-N	8	11	.421	26	26	2	0	0	161	174	86	21	2	49	106	12.6	4.81	108	.282	.337	6	.120	-3	-10	5	-1	0.2
1999 Col-N	1	10	.091	14	13	1	0	0	62^2	85	62	11	1	36	34	17.5	8.04	72	.324	.408	3	.167	-0	-24	-12	1	-1.6
Total 3	16	30	.348	67	66	5	1	0	390	452	242	47	8	136	246	13.8	5.28	100	.295	.356	19	.165	-3	-44	-0	-0	-0.8
● **HANK THORMAHLEN** Thormahlen, Herbert Ehler "Lefty" b: 7/5/1896, Jersey City, N.J. d: 2/6/55, Los Angeles, Cal. BL/TL, 6', 180 lbs. Deb: 9/29/17																											
1917 NY-A	0	1	.000	1	1	0	0	0	8	9	3	0	1	4	5	15.8	2.25	119	.281	.378	0	.000	-0	0	0	-0	0.0
1918 NY-A	7	3	.700	16	12	5	2	0	112^2	85	39	1	6	52	22	11.4	2.48	114	.217	.318	3	.077	-3	4	4	0	0.0
1919 NY-A	12	8	.600	30	25	13	2	1	188^2	155	69	10	4	61	62	10.5	2.62	122	.228	.295	11	.186	-0	13	12	-1	1.0
1920 NY-A	9	6	.600	29	15	6	0	1	143^1	178	86	5	2	43	35	14.0	4.14	92	.312	.362	10	.222	1	-6	-5	1	-0.3
1921 Bos-A	1	7	.125	23	9	3	0	0	96^1	101	56	3	6	34	17	13.2	4.48	94	.277	.349	4	.174	-1	-2	-3	-0	-0.2
1925 Bro-N	0	3	.000	5	2	0	0	0	16	22	14	0	2	9	7	18.6	3.94	106	.333	.429	1	.200	0	1	0	0	0.2
Total 6	29	28	.509	104	64	27	4	2	565	550	267	19	21	203	148	12.3	3.33	105	.261	.332	29	.168	-3	10	9	0	0.7
● **PAUL THORMODSGARD** Thormodsgard, Paul Gayton b: 11/10/53, San Francisco, Cal. BR/TR, 6'2", 190 lbs. Deb: 4/10/77																											
1977 Min-A	11	15	.423	37	37	8	1	0	218	236	122	25	3	65	94	12.6	4.62	86	.280	.333	0	—	0	-13	-15	-1	-1.7
1978 Min-A	1	6	.143	12	12	1	0	0	66	81	40	7	1	17	23	13.5	5.05	76	.308	.352	0	—	0	-9	-9	-1	-0.9
1979 Min-A	0	0	—	1	0	0	0	0	1	3	1	1	0	0	1	27.0	9.00	49	.500	.500	0	—	0	-1	-0	0	0.0
Total 3	12	21	.364	50	49	9	1	0	285	320	163	33	4	82	118	12.8	4.74	84	.288	.339	0	—	0	-23	-25	-2	-2.6
● **JOHN THORNTON** Thornton, John b: 1870, Washington, D.C. 5'10.5", 175 lbs. Deb: 8/14/1889 ◆																											
1889 Was-N	0	1	.000	1	1	1	0	0	9	8	11	0	0	7	3	15.0	5.00	79	.229	.357	0	.000	-1	-1	-1	-0	-0.2
1891 Phi-N	15	16	.484	37	32	23	1	2	269	268	161	3	10	115	52	13.1	3.68	93	.250	.328	17	.138	-7	-10	-8	2	-1.3
1892 Phi-N	0	2	.000	3	2	1	0	0	12	16	19	1	0	17	2	24.8	12.75	25	.308	.478	5	.385	1	-13	-13	0	-1.4
Total 3	15	19	.441	41	35	25	1	2	290	292	191	4	10	139	57	13.7	4.10	83	.252	.337	22	.154	-7	-24	-22	2	-2.9

● WALTER THORNTON
Thornton, Walter Miller b: 2/18/1875, Lewiston, Maine d: 7/14/60, Los Angeles, Cal. BL/TL, 6'1", 180 lbs. Deb: 7/1/1895 ◆

YEAR	TM/L	W	L	PCT	G	GS	CG	SH	SV	IP	H	R	HR	HB	BB	SO	RAT	ERA	ERA+	OAV	OOB	BH	AVG	PB	PR	PR+	PD	TPI
1895	Chi-N	2	0	1.000	7	2	2	0	1	40	58	50	3	5	31	13	21.1	6.07	84	.333	.448	7	.318	2	-6	-4	-1	-0.1
1896	Chi-N	2	1	.667	5	5	2	0	0	23^{2}	30	26	1	0	13	10	16.4	5.70	80	.306	.387	8	.364	2	-4	-3	-1	-0.2
1897	Chi-N	6	7	.462	16	16	15	0	0	130^{1}	164	91	4	6	51	55	15.3	4.70	95	.305	.371	85	.321	4	-6	-3	0	0.1
1898	Chi-N	13	10	.565	28	25	21	2	0	215^{1}	226	116	4	18	56	56	12.5	3.34	107	.268	.327	62	.295	6	6	6	-1	0.9
Total	4	23	18	.561	56	48	40	2	1	409^{1}	478	283	12	29	151	134	14.5	4.18	97	.289	.359	162	.312	13	-9	-6	-2	0.7

● BOB THORPE
Thorpe, Robert Joseph b: 1/12/35, San Diego, Cal. d: 3/17/60, San Diego, Cal. BR/TR, 6'1", 170 lbs. Deb: 4/17/55

YEAR	TM/L	W	L	PCT	G	GS	CG	SH	SV	IP	H	R	HR	HB	BB	SO	RAT	ERA	ERA+	OAV	OOB	BH	AVG	PB	PR	PR+	PD	TPI
1955	Chi-N	0	0	—	2	0	0	0	0	3	4	2	0	0	0	0	12.0	3.00	136	.333	.333	0	—	0	0	0	0	0.0

● GEORGE THROOP
Throop, George Lynford b: 11/24/50, Pasadena, Cal. BR/TR, 6'7", 205 lbs. Deb: 9/7/75

YEAR	TM/L	W	L	PCT	G	GS	CG	SH	SV	IP	H	R	HR	HB	BB	SO	RAT	ERA	ERA+	OAV	OOB	BH	AVG	PB	PR	PR+	PD	TPI
1975	KC-A	0	0	—	7	0	0	0	2	9	8	5	1	0	2	8	10.0	4.00	97	.250	.294	0	—	0	-0	-0	0	0.0
1977	KC-A	0	0	—	4	0	0	0	1	5^{1}	1	2	1	0	4	1	8.4	3.38	120	.059	.238	0	—	0	0	0	0	0.0
1978	KC-A	1	0	1.000	1	0	0	0	0	3	2	0	0	0	3	2	15.0	0.00	—	.222	.417	0	—	0	1	1	0	0.3
1979	KC-A	0	0	—	4	0	0	0	0	2^{2}	7	4	0	0	5	1	40.5	13.50	32	.467	.600	0	—	0	-3	-3	-0	-0.1
	Hou-N	1	0	1.000	14	0	0	0	0	22^{1}	23	10	4	1	11	15	14.1	3.22	109	.271	.361	0	.000	-0	1	1	-0	0.0
Total	4	2	0	1.000	30	0	0	0	3	42^{1}	41	21	6	1	25	27	14.2	3.83	97	.259	.364	0	.000	-0	-0	-0	0	0.2

● LOU THUMAN
Thuman, Louis Charles Frank b: 12/13/16, Baltimore, Md. BR/TR, 6'2", 185 lbs. Deb: 9/8/39

YEAR	TM/L	W	L	PCT	G	GS	CG	SH	SV	IP	H	R	HR	HB	BB	SO	RAT	ERA	ERA+	OAV	OOB	BH	AVG	PB	PR	PR+	PD	TPI
1939	Was-A	0	0	—	3	0	0	0	0	4	5	6	0	0	2	1	15.8	9.00	48	.278	.350	0	—	0	-2	-2	0	-0.1
1940	Was-A	0	1	.000	2	0	0	0	0	5	10	11	0	0	7	0	30.6	14.40	29	.400	.531	0	.000	-0	-6	-6	0	-0.8
Total	2	0	1	.000	5	0	0	0	0	9	15	17	0	0	9	1	24.0	12.00	35	.349	.462	0	.000	-0	-8	-8	0	-0.9

● MIKE THURMAN
Thurman, Michael Richard b: 7/22/73, Corvallis, Ore. BR/TR, 6'4", 190 lbs. Deb: 9/2/97

YEAR	TM/L	W	L	PCT	G	GS	CG	SH	SV	IP	H	R	HR	HB	BB	SO	RAT	ERA	ERA+	OAV	OOB	BH	AVG	PB	PR	PR+	PD	TPI
1997	Mon-N	1	0	1.000	5	2	0	0	0	11^{2}	8	9	3	1	4	8	10.0	5.40	78	.186	.271	1	.500	0	-2	-2	0	0.0
1998	Mon-N	4	5	.444	14	13	0	0	0	67	60	38	7	3	26	32	12.0	4.70	89	.238	.317	0	.000	-2	-3	-4	-0	-0.6
1999	Mon-N	7	11	.389	29	27	0	0	0	146^{2}	140	84	17	7	52	85	12.2	4.05	111	.251	.323	1	.025	-3	8	7	-2	0.3
2000	Mon-N	4	9	.308	17	17	0	0	0	88^{1}	112	69	9	3	46	52	16.4	6.42	74	.315	.399	1	.042	-2	-17	-16	-1	-2.1
Total	4	16	25	.390	65	59	0	0	0	313^{2}	320	200	36	14	128	177	13.3	4.91	91	.265	.342	3	.034	-7	-14	-15	-2	-2.4

● MARK THURMOND
Thurmond, Mark Anthony b: 9/12/56, Houston, Tex. BL/TL, 6', 193 lbs. Deb: 5/14/83

YEAR	TM/L	W	L	PCT	G	GS	CG	SH	SV	IP	H	R	HR	HB	BB	SO	RAT	ERA	ERA+	OAV	OOB	BH	AVG	PB	PR	PR+	PD	TPI
1983	SD-N	7	3	.700	21	18	2	0	0	115^{1}	104	40	7	2	33	49	10.8	2.65	132	.248	.306	2	.054	-2	13	11	1	0.8
1984	*SD-N	14	8	.636	32	29	1	1	0	178^{2}	174	70	12	0	55	57	11.5	2.97	120	.256	.311	11	.190	1	12	12	2	1.8
1985	SD-N	7	11	.389	36	23	1	1	2	138^{1}	154	70	9	3	44	57	13.1	3.97	89	.291	.349	3	.088	-2	-6	-7	1	-0.9
1986	SD-N	3	7	.300	17	15	2	1	0	70^{2}	96	58	7	0	27	32	15.7	6.50	56	.325	.382	6	.250	1	-22	-23	0	-2.6
	Det-A	4	1	.800	25	4	0	0	3	51^{2}	44	13	7	0	17	17	10.6	1.92	216	.234	.298	0	—	0	13	13	-1	1.2
1987	*Det-A	0	1	.000	48	0	0	0	5	61^{2}	83	32	5	0	24	21	15.6	4.23	100	.331	.389	0	—	0	2	0	-0	0.0
1988	Bal-A	1	8	.111	43	6	0	0	3	74^{2}	80	43	10	2	27	29	13.1	4.58	85	.277	.343	0	—	0	-5	-6	-1	-0.7
1989	Bal-A	2	4	.333	49	2	0	0	4	90	102	43	6	1	17	34	12.0	3.90	97	.288	.323	0	—	0	-0	-1	-1	-0.2
1990	SF-N	2	3	.400	43	0	0	0	4	56^{2}	53	26	6	0	18	24	11.3	3.34	109	.257	.317	0	.000	-1	3	2	1	0.3
Total	8	40	46	.465	314	97	6	3	21	837^{2}	890	395	69	8	262	320	12.5	3.69	101	.277	.333	22	.139	-1	10	2	2	-0.3

● SLOPPY THURSTON
Thurston, Hollis John b: 6/2/1899, Fremont, Neb. d: 9/14/73, Los Angeles, Cal. BR/TR, 5'11", 165 lbs. Deb: 4/19/23

YEAR	TM/L	W	L	PCT	G	GS	CG	SH	SV	IP	H	R	HR	HB	BB	SO	RAT	ERA	ERA+	OAV	OOB	BH	AVG	PB	PR	PR+	PD	TPI
1923	StL-A	0	0	—	2	1	0	0	0	4	8	4	0	0	2	0	22.5	6.75	62	.421	.476	0	—	0	-1	-1	-0	-0.1
	Chi-A	7	8	.467	44	12	8	0	4	191^{2}	223	70	11	1	36	55	12.2	3.05	130	.308	.341	25	.316	6	20	19	-0	2.0
	Yr	7	8	.467	46	13	8	0	4	195^{2}	231	74	11	1	38	55	12.4	3.13	127	.310	.345	25	.316	6	19	18	-1	1.9
1924	Chi-A	20	14	.588	38	36	**28**	1	1	291	330	150	17	6	60	37	12.2	3.80	108	.290	.329	31	.254	4	14	10	1	1.7
1925	Chi-A	10	14	.417	36	25	9	0	1	183	250	140	14	5	47	35	14.9	5.95	70	.335	.378	24	.286	7	-32	-39	2	-3.3
1926	Chi-A	6	8	.429	31	13	6	1	3	134^{1}	164	85	10	1	36	35	13.5	5.02	77	.311	.356	19	.311	6	-15	-18	-1	-1.3
1927	Was-A	13	13	.500	29	28	13	2	0	205^{1}	254	118	16	2	60	38	13.9	4.47	91	.308	.356	29	.315	9	-8	-9	-1	-0.2
1930	Bro-N	6	4	.600	24	11	5	2	1	106	110	46	4	0	17	26	10.8	3.40	145	.266	.295	10	.200	-0	19	18	2	1.6
1931	Bro-N	9	9	.500	24	17	11	0	0	143	175	72	3	1	39	23	13.5	3.97	96	.301	.346	13	.217	2	-2	-2	-1	-0.1
1932	Bro-N	12	8	.600	28	19	10	2	0	153	174	81	14	1	38	35	12.5	4.06	94	.287	.330	17	.304	5	-3	-4	1	0.1
1933	Bro-N	6	8	.429	32	15	5	0	3	131^{1}	171	70	4	6	34	22	14.5	4.52	71	.319	.366	7	.159	-1	-17	-20	2	-2.0
Total	9	89	86	.509	288	177	95	8	13	1542^{2}	1859	836	93	23	369	306	13.1	4.24	94	.304	.346	175	.270	38	-25	-43	3	-1.6

● LUIS TIANT
Tiant, Luis Clemente (Vega) b: 11/23/40, Marianao, Cuba BR/TR, 5'11", 190 lbs. Deb: 7/19/64

YEAR	TM/L	W	L	PCT	G	GS	CG	SH	SV	IP	H	R	HR	HB	BB	SO	RAT	ERA	ERA+	OAV	OOB	BH	AVG	PB	PR	PR+	PD	TPI
1964	Cle-A	10	4	.714	19	16	9	3	1	127	94	41	13	2	47	105	10.1	2.83	127	.207	.284	5	.111	-1	11	11	0	1.1
1965	Cle-A	11	11	.500	41	30	10	2	1	196^{1}	166	88	20	3	66	152	10.8	3.53	99	.228	.295	6	.088	-2	-2	-1	-0	-0.3
1966	Cle-A	12	11	.522	46	16	7	**5**	8	155	121	50	16	2	50	145	10.0	2.79	123	.213	.279	4	.111	-1	11	11	-1	1.5
1967	Cle-A	12	9	.571	33	29	9	1	2	213^{2}	177	76	24	1	67	219	10.3	2.74	119	.221	.282	18	.254	5	12	12	-2	1.6
1968	Cle-A★	21	9	.700	34	32	19	**9**	0	258^{1}	152	53	16	4	73	264	8.0	**1.60**	**185**	**.168**	**.233**	7	.080	-5	**40**	**39**	-3	4.2
1969	Cle-A	9	20	.310	38	37	9	1	0	249^{2}	229	123	37	8	129	156	13.2	3.71	102	.246	.343	19	.235	6	-2	2	-1	0.7
1970	*Min-A	7	3	.700	18	17	2	1	0	92^{2}	84	36	12	2	41	50	12.3	3.40	110	.246	.330	13	.406	5	3	3	-0	0.9
1971	Bos-A	1	7	.125	21	10	1	0	0	72^{1}	73	42	8	1	32	59	13.2	4.85	76	.259	.337	3	.158	-0	-11	-9	-0	-1.0
1972	Bos-A	15	6	.714	43	19	12	6	3	179	128	45	7	0	65	123	9.7	**1.91**	**169**	.202	.277	6	.107	-2	23	25	-1	2.9
1973	Bos-A	20	13	.606	35	35	23	0	0	272	217	105	32	7	78	206	**10.0**	3.34	120	.219	**.281**	0	—	0	15	20	-1	2.2
1974	Bos-A★	22	13	.629	38	38	25	**7**	0	311^{1}	281	106	21	4	82	176	10.6	2.92	132	.241	.293	0	—	0	24	30	-3	3.1
1975	*Bos-A	18	14	.563	35	35	18	2	0	260	262	126	25	4	72	142	11.7	4.02	102	.264	.316	0	.000	-0	-7	2	-3	-0.1
1976	Bos-A★	21	12	.636	38	38	19	3	0	279	274	107	25	3	64	131	11.0	3.06	128	.260	.304	0	.000	-0	14	24	-2	2.5
1977	Bos-A	12	8	.600	32	32	3	3	0	188^{2}	210	98	26	2	51	124	12.5	4.53	99	.279	.327	0	—	0	-10	-0	-2	-0.2
1978	Bos-A	13	8	.619	32	31	12	5	0	212^{1}	185	80	26	5	57	114	10.5	3.31	125	.234	.290	0	—	0	11	18	-2	1.5
1979	NY-A	13	8	.619	30	30	5	1	0	195^{2}	190	94	22	0	53	104	11.2	3.91	105	.251	.300	0	—	0	7	4	-0	0.3
1980	NY-A	8	9	.471	25	25	3	0	0	136^{1}	139	79	10	1	50	84	12.5	4.89	80	.265	.330	0	—	0	-13	-15	1	-1.5
1981	Pit-N	2	5	.286	9	9	1	0	0	57^{1}	54	31	3	0	19	32	11.5	3.92	92	.243	.303	3	.188	1	-3	-2	-1	-0.2
1982	Cal-A	2	2	.500	6	5	0	0	0	29^{2}	39	20	3	0	8	30	14.3	5.76	70	.310	.351	0	—	0	-6	-6	-1	-0.7
Total	19	229	172	.571	573	484	187	49	15	3486^{1}	3075	1400	346	49	1104	2416	10.9	3.30	114	.236	.298	84	.164	5	119	168	-21	18.5

● JAY TIBBS
Tibbs, Jay Lindsey b: 1/4/62, Birmingham, Ala. BR/TR, 6'3", 185 lbs. Deb: 7/15/84

YEAR	TM/L	W	L	PCT	G	GS	CG	SH	SV	IP	H	R	HR	HB	BB	SO	RAT	ERA	ERA+	OAV	OOB	BH	AVG	PB	PR	PR+	PD	TPI
1984	Cin-N	6	2	.750	14	14	3	1	0	100^{2}	87	34	4	0	33	40	10.7	2.86	132	.238	.302	5	.139	-1	8	10	-1	0.5
1985	Cin-N	10	16	.385	35	34	5	2	0	218	216	111	14	0	83	98	12.3	3.92	97	.262	.329	6	.092	-3	-8	-3	1	-0.5
1986	Mon-N	7	9	.438	35	31	3	2	0	190^{1}	181	96	12	3	70	117	12.0	3.97	93	.256	.326	7	.130	-0	-5	-6	-1	-0.5
1987	Mon-N	4	5	.444	19	12	0	0	0	83	95	55	10	0	34	54	14.0	4.99	84	.289	.355	3	.120	0	-8	-7	-1	-0.7
1988	Bal-A	4	15	.211	30	24	1	0	0	158^{2}	184	103	18	3	63	82	14.2	5.39	73	.293	.360	0	—	0	-25	-26	0	-2.7
1989	Bal-A	5	0	1.000	10	8	1	0	0	54^{1}	62	17	2	0	20	30	13.6	2.82	135	.287	.347	0	—	0	6	6	-0	0.5
1990	Bal-A	2	7	.222	10	10	0	0	0	50^{2}	55	34	8	0	14	23	12.3	5.68	67	.279	.327	0	—	0	-10	-11	0	-1.6
	Pit-N	1	0	1.000	5	0	0	0	0	7	7	2	0	0	2	4	11.6	2.57	141	.259	.310	0	—	0	1	1	0	0.1
Total	7	39	54	.419	158	133	13	5	0	862^{2}	887	452	68	6	319	448	12.6	4.20	91	.269	.335	21	.117	-4	-41	-35	-1	-4.9

● DICK TIDROW
Tidrow, Richard William b: 5/14/47, San Francisco, Cal. BR/TR, 6'4", 213 lbs. Deb: 4/18/72

YEAR	TM/L	W	L	PCT	G	GS	CG	SH	SV	IP	H	R	HR	HB	BB	SO	RAT	ERA	ERA+	OAV	OOB	BH	AVG	PB	PR	PR+	PD	TPI
1972	Cle-A	14	15	.483	39	34	10	3	0	237^{1}	200	83	21	6	70	123	10.5	2.77	117	.230	.291	7	.100	-3	8	12	-4	0.7
1973	Cle-A	14	16	.467	42	40	13	2	0	274^{2}	289	150	31	8	95	138	12.8	4.42	89	.270	.334	0	—	0	-18	-15	-2	-1.6
1974	Cle-A	1	3	.250	4	4	0	0	0	19	21	17	4	2	13	8	17.1	7.11	51	.276	.396	0	—	0	-7	-7	0	-1.2
	NY-A	11	9	.550	33	25	5	0	1	190^{2}	205	99	14	4	53	100	12.4	3.87	91	.279	.331	0	—	0	-5	-7	-2	-0.9
	Yr	12	12	.500	37	29	5	0	1	209^{2}	226	116	18	6	66	108	12.8	4.16	85	.279	.338	0	—	0	-13	-15	-1	-2.1
1975	NY-A	6	3	.667	37	0	0	0	5	69^{1}	65	27	5	3	31	38	12.9	3.12	118	.256	.344	0	—	0	5	5	-1	0.5
1976	*NY-A	4	5	.444	47	2	0	0	10	92^{1}	80	29	5	1	24	65	10.2	2.63	130	.233	.285	0	—	0	9	8	-1	0.9
1977	*NY-A	11	4	.733	49	7	0	0	5	151	143	57	20	2	41	83	11.1	3.16	125	.250	.303	0	—	0	15	14	-1	1.3
1978	*NY-A	7	11	.389	31	25	4	0	0	185^{1}	191	87	13	5	53	73	12.1	3.84	95	.267	.322	0	—	0	-1	-4	-2	-0.6
1979	NY-A	2	1	.667	14	0	0	0	2	22^{2}	38	20	5	0	4	7	16.7	7.94	51	.409	.433	0	—	0	-9	-10	1	-1.2
	Chi-N	11	5	.688	63	0	0	0	4	102^{2}	86	35	5	2	42	68	11.4	2.72	152	.231	.313	2	.200	0	12	15	1	2.4

YEAR	TM/L	W	L	PCT	G	GS	CG	SH	SV	IP	H	R	HR	HB	BB	SO	RAT	ERA	ERA+	OAV	OOB	BH	AVG	PB	PR	PR+	PD	TPI
1980	Chi-N	6	5	.545	**84**	0	0	0	6	116	97	44	10	5	53	97	12.0	2.79	140	.229	.322	0	.000	-0	11	13	-1	1.2
1981	Chi-N	3	10	.231	51	0	0	0	9	74^{2}	73	45	6	1	30	39	12.5	5.06	73	.256	.329	0	.000	-1	-13	-11	-1	-2.2
1982	Chi-N	8	3	.727	65	0	0	0	6	103^{2}	106	45	6	3	29	62	12.0	3.39	111	.265	.319	0	.000	-1	3	4	-2	0.2
1983	*Chi-A	2	4	.333	50	1	0	0	7	91^{2}	86	50	13	1	34	66	11.9	4.22	100	.242	.310	0	—	0	-1	-0	1	0.1
1984	NY-N	0	0	—	11	0	0	0	0	15^{2}	25	19	5	0	7	8	18.4	9.19	39	.357	.416	0	—	0	-10	-10	0	-0.5
Total	13	100	94	.515	620	138	32	5	55	1746^{2}	1705	807	163	43	579	975	12.0	3.68	101	.257	.321	9	.095	-5	-3	9	-11	-0.9
● **BOBBY TIEFENAUER** Tiefenauer, Bobby Gene b: 10/10/29, Desloge, Mo. d: 6/13/2000, Desloge, Mo. BR/TR, 6'2", 185 lbs. Deb: 7/14/52 C																												
1952	StL-N	0	0	—	6	0	0	0	0	8	12	8	1	0	7	3	21.4	7.88	47	.343	.452	0	.000	-0	-4	-4	0	-0.2
1955	StL-N	1	4	.200	18	0	0	0	0	32^{2}	31	19	6	4	10	16	12.4	4.41	92	.261	.338	0	.000	-0	-1	-1	0	-0.2
1960	Cle-A	0	1	.000	6	0	0	0	0	9	8	2	0	0	3	2	11.0	2.00	187	.242	.306	0	.000	0	2	2	-0	0.2
1961	StL-N	0	0	—	3	0	0	0	0	4^{1}	9	4	0	0	4	3	27.0	6.23	71	.450	.542	0	—	0	-1	-1	-0	-0.1
1962	Hou-N	2	4	.333	43	0	0	0	1	85	91	42	6	2	21	60	12.1	4.34	86	.277	.324	1	.111	0	-4	-6	-2	-0.5
1963	Mil-N	1	1	.500	12	0	0	0	2	29^{2}	20	4	1	0	4	22	7.3	1.21	265	.194	.224	0	.000	-0	7	7	1	0.6
1964	Mil-N	4	6	.400	46	0	0	0	13	73	61	33	6	3	15	48	9.7	3.21	110	.225	.273	0	.000	-1	3	3	-1	0.2
1965	Mil-N	0	1	.000	6	0	0	0	0	7	8	7	1	1	3	7	15.4	7.71	46	.286	.375	0	—	0	-3	-3	0	-0.4
	NY-A	1	1	.500	10	0	0	0	2	20^{1}	19	10	3	1	5	15	11.1	3.54	96	.253	.309	0	.000	0	-0	-0	-0	0.0
	Cle-A	0	5	.000	15	0	0	0	4	22^{1}	24	17	3	1	10	13	14.1	4.84	72	.273	.354	0	.000	-0	-3	-3	-0	-0.7
	Yr	1	6	.143	25	0	0	0	6	42^{2}	43	27	6	2	15	28	12.7	4.22	82	.264	.333	0	.000	-0	-4	-4	-0	-0.7
1967	Cle-A	0	1	.000	5	0	0	0	0	11^{1}	9	3	0	0	3	6	9.5	0.79	411	.225	.279	0	—	0	3	3	-1	0.2
1968	Chi-N	0	1	.000	9	0	0	0	1	13^{1}	20	12	2	0	2	9	14.9	6.08	52	.351	.373	0	.000	-0	-5	-4	-0	-0.4
Total	10	9	25	.265	179	0	0	0	23	316	312	161	29	12	87	204	11.7	3.84	94	.260	.317	1	.026	-1	-7	-9	-2	-1.3
● **VERLE TIEFENTHALER** Tiefenthaler, Verle Matthew b: 7/11/37, Breda, Iowa BL/TR, 6'1", 190 lbs. Deb: 4/19/62																												
1962	Chi-A	0	0	—	3	0	0	0	0	3^{2}	6	4	1	0	7	1	31.9	9.82	40	.353	.542	0	—	0	-2	-2	-0	-0.1
● **EDDIE TIEMEYER** Tiemeyer, Edward Carl b: 5/9/1885, Cincinnati, Ohio d: 9/27/46, Cincinnati, Ohio BR/TR, 5'11.5", 185 lbs. Deb: 8/19/06 ♦																												
1906	Cin-N	0	0	—	1	0	0	0	0	1	1	0	0	0	1	1	18.0	0.00	—	.500	.667	2	.182	0	0	0	-0	0.0
● **MIKE TIERNAN** Tiernan, Michael Joseph "Silent Mike" b: 1/21/1867, Trenton, N.J. d: 11/9/18, New York, N.Y. BL/TL, 5'11", 165 lbs. Deb: 4/30/1887 ♦																												
1887	NY-N	1	2	.333	5	0	0	0	**1**	19^{2}	40	25	2	1	7	3	18.8	8.69	43	.444	.451	149	.339	2	-10	-12	-0	-1.3
● **LES TIETJE** Tietje, Leslie William "Toots" b: 9/11/11, Sumner, Iowa d: 10/2/96, Rochester, Minn. BR/TR, 6'0.5", 178 lbs. Deb: 9/18/33																												
1933	Chi-A	2	0	1.000	3	3	1	0	0	22^{1}	16	8	1	0	15	9	12.5	2.42	175	.203	.330	1	.125	0	5	5	0	0.4
1934	Chi-A	5	14	.263	34	22	6	1	0	176	174	106	20	2	96	81	13.9	4.81	98	.257	.351	1	.017	-7	-6	-1	2	-0.7
1935	Chi-A	9	15	.375	30	21	9	1	0	169^{2}	184	88	14	2	81	64	14.2	4.30	108	.277	.357	12	.197	-1	3	6	-2	0.4
1936	Chi-A	0	0	—	2	0	0	0	0	2^{1}	6	7	0	0	5	3	42.4	27.00	19	.462	.611	0	—	0	-6	-5	-0	-0.2
	StL-A	3	5	.375	14	7	2	0	0	50^{1}	65	44	2	2	30	16	17.3	6.62	81	.310	.401	1	.067	-1	-9	-7	1	-0.8
	Yr	3	5	.375	16	7	2	0	0	52^{2}	71	51	2	2	35	19	18.5	7.52	71	.318	.415	1	.067	-1	-15	-12	1	-1.0
1937	StL-A	1	2	.333	5	4	2	0	0	30	32	15	0	0	17	5	14.7	4.20	115	.283	.377	0	.000	-2	1	2	-1	0.0
1938	StL-A	2	5	.286	17	8	2	1	0	62	83	55	8	0	38	15	17.6	7.55	66	.327	.414	2	.111	-1	-19	-17	-0	-1.6
Total	6	22	41	.349	105	65	22	3	0	512^{2}	560	323	45	6	282	193	14.9	5.11	93	.279	.369	17	.099	-12	-31	-18	0	-2.5
● **RAY TIFT** Tift, Raymond Frank b: 6/21/1884, Fitchburg, Mass. d: 3/29/45, Verona, N.J. TL, Deb: 8/7/07																												
1907	NY-A	0	0	—	4	1	0	0	0	19	33	14	0	0	4	6	17.5	4.74	59	.384	.411	0	.000	-0	-5	-4	-1	-0.3
● **JOHNNY TILLMAN** Tillman, John Lawrence "Ducky" b: 10/6/1893, Bridgeport, Conn. d: 4/7/64, Harrisburg, Pa. BB/TR, 5'11", 170 lbs. Deb: 9/20/15																												
1915	StL-A	1	0	1.000	2	1	0	0	0	10	6	2	0	0	4	6	9.0	0.90	318	.176	.263	0	.000	-0	2	2	0	0.2
● **THAD TILLOTSON** Tillotson, Thaddeus Asa b: 12/20/40, Merced, Cal. BR/TR, 6'2.5", 195 lbs. Deb: 4/14/67																												
1967	NY-A	3	9	.250	43	5	1	0	2	98^{1}	99	52	9	2	39	62	12.8	4.03	78	.261	.333	1	.063	-0	-9	-10	0	-1.3
1968	NY-A	1	0	1.000	7	0	0	0	0	10^{1}	11	6	0	0	7	1	15.7	4.35	67	.282	.391	0	.000	-0	-2	-2	0	-0.1
Total	2	4	9	.308	50	5	1	0	2	108^{2}	110	58	9	2	46	63	13.1	4.06	77	.263	.339	1	.059	-1	-10	-12	1	-1.4
● **GARY TIMBERLAKE** Timberlake, Gary Dale b: 8/8/48, Laconia, Ind. BR/TL, 6'2", 205 lbs. Deb: 6/18/69																												
1969	Sea-A	0	0	—	2	2	0	0	0	6	7	6	0	0	9	4	24.0	7.50	49	.269	.457	0	.000	-0	-3	-3	-0	-0.2
● **MIKE TIMLIN** Timlin, Michael August b: 3/10/66, Midland, Tex. BR/TR, 6'4", 210 lbs. Deb: 4/8/91																												
1991	*Tor-A	11	6	.647	63	3	0	0	3	108^{1}	94	43	6	1	50	85	12.0	3.16	133	.233	.319	0	—	0	11	12	1	1.9
1992	*Tor-A	0	2	.000	26	0	0	0	1	43^{2}	45	23	0	1	20	35	13.6	4.12	99	.271	.353	0	—	0	-1	-0	0	0.0
1993	*Tor-A	4	2	.667	54	0	0	0	1	55^{2}	63	32	7	1	27	49	14.7	4.69	92	.284	.364	0	—	0	-2	-2	1	-0.1
1994	Tor-A	0	1	.000	34	0	0	0	2	40	41	25	5	2	20	38	14.2	5.17	93	.261	.352	0	—	0	-2	-2	0	0.0
1995	Tor-A	4	3	.571	31	0	0	0	5	42	38	13	1	2	17	36	12.2	2.14	220	.242	.324	0	—	0	12	12	1	2.1
1996	Tor-A	1	6	.143	59	0	0	0	31	56^{2}	47	25	4	2	18	52	10.6	3.65	137	.229	.298	0	—	0	8	9	-0	1.6
1997	Tor-A	3	2	.600	38	0	0	0	9	47	41	17	6	1	15	36	10.9	2.87	160	.243	.308	0	—	0	9	9	1	1.2
	*Sea-A	3	2	.600	26	0	0	0	1	25^{2}	28	13	2	0	5	9	11.6	3.86	117	.280	.314	0	—	0	2	2	0	0.3
	Yr	6	4	.600	64	0	0	0	10	72^{2}	69	30	8	1	20	45	11.1	3.22	142	.257	.310	0	—	0	11	11	1	1.5
1998	Sea-A	3	3	.500	70	0	0	0	19	79^{1}	78	26	5	3	16	60	11.0	2.95	157	.264	.308	0	—	0	15	15	1	1.7
1999	Bal-A	3	9	.250	62	0	0	0	27	63	51	30	9	5	23	50	11.3	3.57	132	.221	.305	0	—	0	9	8	0	1.5
2000	Bal-A	2	3	.400	37	0	0	0	11	35	37	22	6	2	15	26	13.9	4.89	98	.276	.358	0	—	0	0	-0	1	0.0
	*StL-N	3	1	.750	25	0	0	0	1	29^{2}	30	11	2	2	20	26	15.8	3.34	139	.265	.385	0	—	0	4	4	0	0.5
Total	10	37	40	.481	525	3	0	0	111	626	593	280	53	22	246	502	12.4	3.59	127	.252	.328	0	—	0	67	67	6	10.7
● **TOM TIMMERMANN** Timmermann, Thomas Henry b: 5/12/40, Breese, Ill. BR/TR, 6'4", 215 lbs. Deb: 6/18/69																												
1969	Det-A	4	3	.571	31	1	1	0	1	55^{2}	50	22	1	2	26	42	12.6	2.75	136	.238	.328	1	.111	-0	5	6	-1	0.6
1970	Det-A	6	7	.462	61	0	0	0	27	85^{1}	90	44	3	2	34	49	13.3	4.11	91	.273	.344	0	.000	-2	-4	-4	-0	-1.0
1971	Det-A	7	6	.538	52	2	0	0	4	84	82	36	6	3	37	51	13.1	3.86	93	.262	.346	1	.053	-1	-4	-2	0	-0.5
1972	Det-A	8	10	.444	34	25	3	2	0	149^{2}	121	57	12	5	41	88	10.0	2.89	109	.216	.276	6	.136	-0	3	4	-2	0.3
1973	Det-A	1	1	.500	17	1	0	0	1	39	39	17	4	0	11	21	11.5	3.69	111	.258	.309	0	—	0	1	2	-1	0.0
	Cle-A	8	7	.533	29	15	4	0	2	124^{1}	117	73	15	3	54	62	12.6	4.92	80	.251	.332	0	—	0	-15	-13	-0	-1.5
	Yr	9	8	.529	46	16	4	0	3	163^{1}	156	90	19	3	65	83	12.3	4.63	86	.252	.327	0	—	0	-15	-12	-1	-1.5
1974	Cle-A	1	1	.500	4	0	0	0	0	10	9	6	1	0	5	2	12.6	5.40	67	.250	.341	0	—	0	-2	-2	1	-0.3
Total	6	35	35	.500	228	44	8	2	35	548	508	255	42	15	208	315	12.0	3.78	96	.246	.319	8	.091	-4	-15	-9	-3	-2.4
● **BEN TINCUP** Tincup, Austin Ben b: 12/14/1890, Adair, Okla. d: 7/5/80, Claremore, Okla. BL/TR, 6'1", 180 lbs. Deb: 5/22/14 C♦																												
1914	Phi-N	8	10	.444	28	17	9	3	2	155	165	71	0	4	62	108	13.4	2.61	113	.286	.359	9	.170	-1	3	5	1	0.6
1915	Phi-N	0	0	—	10	0	0	0	0	31	26	8	1	0	9	10	10.2	2.03	135	.263	.324	0	.000	-1	2	2	0	0.0
1918	Phi-N	0	1	.000	8	1	0	0	0	16^{2}	24	20	0	0	6	6	16.2	7.56	40	.329	.380	1	.125	-0	-9	-8	1	-0.4
1928	Chi-N	0	0	—	2	0	0	0	0	9	14	7	0	0	1	3	15.0	7.00	55	.378	.395	0	.000	-0	-3	-3	0	-0.2
Total	4	8	11	.421	48	18	9	3	2	211^{2}	229	106	1	4	78	127	13.2	3.10	95	.291	.358	10	.135	-3	-6	-3	3	0.0
● **BUD TINNING** Tinning, Lyle Forrest b: 3/12/06, Pilger, Neb. d: 1/17/61, Evansville, Ind. BB/TR (BR 1934-35), 5'11", 198 lbs. Deb: 4/20/32																												
1932	*Chi-N	5	3	.625	24	7	2	0	0	93^{1}	93	34	3	2	24	30	11.5	2.80	135	.263	.313	2	.087	-1	11	10	0	0.7
1933	Chi-N	13	6	.684	32	21	10	3	1	175^{1}	169	73	3	4	60	59	12.0	3.18	103	.255	.320	14	.209	1	3	2	-2	0.0
1934	Chi-N	4	6	.400	39	7	1	1	3	129^{1}	134	59	9	1	46	44	12.6	3.34	116	.269	.332	7	.179	-1	10	8	-1	0.4
1935	StL-N	0	0	—	4	0	0	0	0	7^{2}	9	6	1	1	5	2	17.6	5.87	70	.300	.417	0	.000	-0	-2	-1	0	-0.1
Total	4	22	15	.595	99	35	13	4	4	405^{2}	405	172	16	8	135	135	12.2	3.19	113	.262	.325	23	.177	-1	23	19	-4	1.0
● **DAN TIPPLE** Tipple, Daniel E. "Big Dan" or "Rusty" b: 2/13/1890, Rockford, Ill. d: 3/26/60, Omaha, Neb. BR/TR, 6', 176 lbs. Deb: 9/18/15																												
1915	NY-A	1	1	.500	3	2	2	0	0	19	14	6	1	0	11	14	11.8	0.95	310	.203	.313	0	.000	-1	4	4	-1	0.2
● **JACK TISING** Tising, Johnnie Joseph b: 10/9/03, High Point, Mo. d: 9/5/67, Leadville, Colo. BL/TR, 6'2", 180 lbs. Deb: 4/24/36																												
1936	Pit-N	1	3	.250	10	6	1	0	0	47	52	26	5	0	24	27	14.6	4.21	96	.272	.353	3	.273	0	-1	-1	-0	-0.1

YEAR	TM/L	W	L	PCT	G	GS	CG	SH	SV	IP	H	R	HR	HB	BB	SO	RAT	ERA	ERA+	OAV	OOB	BH	AVG	PB	PR	PR+	PD	TPI
● **CANNONBALL TITCOMB** Titcomb, Ledell b: 8/21/1866, W.Baldwin, Me. d: 6/8/50, Kingston, N.H. BL/TL, 5'6", 157 lbs. Deb: 5/5/1886																												
1886	Phi-N	0	5	.000	5	5	5	0	0	41	43	45	1		24	24	14.7	3.73	88	.244	.335	1	.063	-2	-2	-2	1	-0.3
1887	Phi-a	1	2	.333	3	3	3	0	0	24	50	30	1	0	19	16	18.8	6.75	64	.407	.407	2	.167	-1	-7	-7	-1	-0.7
	NY-N	4	3	.571	9	9	9	0	0	72	105	50	3	1	37	34	13.3	3.88	97	.302	.321	3	.100	-4	2	-1	-1	-0.5
1888	*NY-N	14	8	.636	23	23	22	4	0	197	149	91	4	5	46	129	9.1	2.24	122	.201	.253	10	.122	-4	13	11	-4	0.3
1889	NY-N	1	2	.333	3	3	3	0	0	26	27	26	1	2	16	7	15.6	6.58	60	.260	.369	1	.083	-1	-7	-8	-0	-0.7
1890	Roc-a	10	9	.526	20	19	19	1	0	168^{2}	168	123	6	14	97	73	14.9	3.74	95	.251	.358	8	.107	-5	3	-3	-3	-1.0
Total	5	30	29	.508	63	62	61	5	0	528^{2}	542	365	16	22	239	283	12.7	3.47	96	.253	.318	25	.110	-18	2	-9	-8	-2.9
● **DAVE TOBIK** Tobik, David Vance b: 3/2/53, Euclid, Ohio BR/TR, 6'1", 195 lbs. Deb: 8/26/78																												
1978	Det-A	0	0	—	5	0	0	0	0	12	12	5	1	0	3	11	11.3	3.75	103	.261	.306	0	—	0	0	0	-0	0.0
1979	Det-A	3	5	.375	37	0	0	0	3	68^{2}	59	34	12	0	25	48	11.0	4.33	100	.231	.300	0	—	0	-1	0	-1	-0.1
1980	Det-A	1	0	1.000	17	1	0	0	0	61	61	27	7	0	21	34	12.1	3.98	103	.266	.328	0	—	0	0	1	-0	0.0
1981	Det-A	2	2	.500	27	0	0	0	1	60^{1}	47	19	7	0	33	32	11.9	2.69	141	.215	.317	0	—	0	7	7	-1	0.3
1982	Det-A	4	9	.308	51	1	0	0	9	98^{2}	86	45	8	1	38	63	11.4	3.56	114	.241	.316	0	—	0	6	6	-1	0.7
1983	Tex-A	2	1	.667	27	0	0	0	9	44	36	18	2	0	13	30	10.0	3.68	109	.222	.280	0	—	0	2	2	0	0.2
1984	Tex-A	1	6	.143	24	0	0	0	5	42^{1}	44	20	5	1	17	30	13.2	3.61	115	.265	.337	0	—	0	2	2	1	0.5
1985	Sea-A	1	0	1.000	8	0	0	0	1	9	10	8	2	0	3	8	13.0	6.00	70	.286	.342	0	—	0	-2	-2	-0	-0.2
Total	8	14	23	.378	196	2	0	0	28	396	355	176	44	2	153	256	11.6	3.70	110	.242	.314	0	—	0	14	16	-3	1.4
● **JIM TOBIN** Tobin, James Anthony "Abba Dabba" b: 12/27/12, Oakland, Cal. d: 5/19/69, Oakland, Cal. BR/TR, 6', 185 lbs. Deb: 4/30/37 F♦																												
1937	Pit-N	6	3	.667	20	8	7	0	1	87	74	38	1	1	28	37	10.7	3.00	129	.226	.289	15	.441	7	9	8	-2	1.4
1938	Pit-N	14	12	.538	40	33	14	2	0	241^{1}	254	109	17	6	66	70	12.2	3.47	109	.270	.321	25	.243	7	9	9	-2	1.3
1939	Pit-N	9	9	.500	25	19	8	0	0	145^{1}	194	84	7	2	33	43	14.2	4.52	85	.319	.356	18	.243	5	-10	-11	-1	-0.9
1940	Bos-N	7	3	.700	15	11	9	0	0	96^{1}	102	41	8	0	24	29	11.8	3.83	97	.264	.307	12	.279	3	0	-1	-1	0.2
1941	Bos-N	12	12	.500	33	26	20	3	0	238	229	91	12	0	60	61	10.9	3.10	115	.253	.300	19	.184	3	14	13	4	2.0
1942	Bos-N	12	21	.364	37	33	**28**	1	0	**287^{2}**	283	145	20	6	96	71	12.0	3.97	84	.257	.320	28	.246	14	-21	-20	6	-0.1
1943	Bos-N	14	14	.500	33	30	24	1	0	250	241	96	12	2	69	52	11.2	2.66	128	.251	.303	30	.280	6	20	21	2	3.5
1944	Bos-N★	18	19	.486	43	36	**28**	5	3	299^{1}	271	125	18	3	97	83	11.2	3.01	127	.240	.302	22	.190	5	20	26	7	4.5
1945	Bos-N	9	14	.391	27	25	16	0	0	196^{2}	220	101	10	5	56	38	12.9	3.84	100	.282	.334	11	.143	5	-1	-0	2	0.7
	*Det-A	4	5	.444	14	6	2	0	1	58^{1}	61	31	2	4	28	14	14.3	3.55	99	.274	.365	3	.120	0	-1	-0	1	0.1
Total	9	105	112	.484	287	227	156	12	5	1900	1929	861	107	29	557	498	11.9	3.44	106	.262	.316	183	.230	54	39	45	16	12.7
● **PAT TOBIN** Tobin, Marion Brooks b: 1/28/16, Hermitage, Ark. d: 1/21/75, Shreveport, La. BR/TR, 6'1", 198 lbs. Deb: 8/21/41																												
1941	Phi-A	0	0	—	1	0	0	0	0	1	4	5	0	0	2	0	54.0	36.00	12	.571	.667	0	—	0	-4	-3	0	-0.1
● **FRANK TODD** Todd, George Franklin b: 10/18/1869, Aberdeen, Md. d: 8/11/19, Havre De Grace, Md. TL, Deb: 7/14/1898																												
1898	Lou-N	0	2	.000	4	2	0	0	0	11	23	21	0	2	8	5	27.0	13.91	26	.418	.508	1	.200	0	-13	-13	-1	-1.6
● **JACKSON TODD** Todd, Jackson A b: 11/20/51, Tulsa, Okla. BR/TR, 6'2", 180 lbs. Deb: 5/5/77																												
1977	NY-N	3	6	.333	19	10	0	0	0	71^{2}	78	41	8	2	20	39	12.6	4.77	78	.273	.325	1	.059	-1	-7	-9	0	-1.1
1979	Tor-A	0	1	.000	12	1	0	0	0	32^{1}	40	26	7	1	7	14	13.4	5.85	75	.299	.338	0	—	0	-6	-5	0	-0.2
1980	Tor-A	5	2	.714	12	12	4	0	0	85	90	40	14	2	30	44	12.9	4.02	107	.276	.341	0	—	0	0	3	1	0.3
1981	Tor-A	2	7	.222	21	13	3	0	0	97^{2}	94	51	10	4	31	41	11.9	3.96	100	.251	.315	0	—	0	-3	-0	1	0.1
Total	4	10	16	.385	64	36	7	0	0	286^{2}	302	158	39	9	88	138	12.5	4.40	92	.270	.328	1	.059	-1	-16	-11	2	-0.9
● **JIM TODD** Todd, James Richard b: 9/21/47, Lancaster, Pa. BL/TR, 6'2", 190 lbs. Deb: 4/29/74																												
1974	Chi-N	4	2	.667	43	6	0	0	3	88	82	45	7	3	41	42	12.9	3.89	98	.252	.341	1	.063	-1	-3	-1	1	-0.1
1975	*Oak-A	8	3	.727	58	0	0	0	12	122	104	40	4	3	33	50	10.3	2.29	159	.234	.292	0	—	0	20	19	4	2.4
1976	Oak-A	7	8	.467	49	0	0	0	4	82^{2}	87	43	6	6	34	22	13.8	3.81	88	.276	.358	0	—	0	-3	-4	2	-0.6
1977	Chi-N	1	1	.500	20	0	0	0	0	30^{2}	47	37	1	2	19	17	20.0	9.10	48	.336	.422	0	.000	-0	-18	-14	0	-0.8
1978	Sea-A	3	4	.429	49	2	0	0	3	106^{2}	113	52	4	0	61	37	14.7	3.88	98	.280	.375	0	—	0	-1	-1	0	0.0
1979	Oak-A	2	5	.286	51	0	0	0	2	81	108	66	12	2	51	26	17.9	6.56	62	.329	.423	0	—	0	-21	-23	0	-1.8
Total	6	25	23	.521	270	8	0	0	24	511	541	283	34	16	239	194	14.0	4.23	89	.277	.360	1	.059	-2	-25	-26	7	-0.9
● **HAL TOENES** Toenes, William Harrel b: 10/8/17, Mobile, Ala. BR/TR, 5'11.5", 175 lbs. Deb: 9/17/47																												
1947	Was-A	0	1	.000	3	1	0	0	0	6^{2}	11	5	0	0	2	5	17.6	6.75	55	.379	.419	0	.000	0	-2	-2	-0	-0.3
● **KEVIN TOLAR** Tolar, Kevin Anthony b: 1/28/71, Panama City, Fla. BR/TL, 6'3", 225 lbs. Deb: 9/11/2000																												
2000	Det-A	0	0	—	5	0	0	0	0	3	1	1	0	0	1	3	6.0	3.00	159	.091	.167	0	—	0	1	1	-0	0.0
● **FREDDIE TOLIVER** Toliver, Freddie Lee b: 2/3/61, Natchez, Miss. BR/TR, 6'1", 170 lbs. Deb: 9/15/84																												
1984	Cin-N	0	0	—	3	1	0	0	0	10	7	2	0	0	7	4	12.6	0.90	420	.206	.341	0	.000	-0	3	3	-0	0.1
1985	Phi-N	0	4	.000	11	3	0	0	1	25	27	15	2	0	17	23	15.8	4.68	79	.273	.379	2	.500	1	-3	-3	-0	-0.4
1986	Phi-N	0	2	.000	5	5	0	0	0	25^{2}	28	14	0	0	11	20	13.7	3.51	110	.286	.358	0	.000	-0	1	1	0	0.1
1987	Phi-N	1	1	.500	10	4	0	0	0	30^{1}	34	19	2	1	17	25	15.4	5.64	75	.291	.385	0	.000	-1	-5	-5	0	-0.3
1988	Min-A	7	6	.538	21	19	0	0	0	114^{2}	116	57	8	1	52	69	13.3	4.24	96	.270	.350	0	—	0	-3	-2	0	-0.2
1989	Min-A	1	3	.250	7	5	0	0	0	29	39	26	2	1	15	11	17.1	7.76	53	.317	.396	0	—	0	-12	-11	1	-1.1
	SD-N	0	0	—	9	0	0	0	0	14	17	14	5	1	9	14	17.4	7.07	50	.321	.429	0	—	0	-6	-6	-0	-0.3
1993	Pit-N	1	0	1.000	12	0	0	0	0	21^{2}	20	10	2	2	8	14	12.5	3.74	108	.267	.353	0	.000	-0	1	1	-1	0.0
Total	7	10	16	.385	78	37	0	0	1	270^{1}	288	157	21	6	136	180	14.3	4.73	85	.280	.367	2	.111	-0	-25	-21	1	-2.1
● **BRIAN TOLLBERG** Tollberg, Brian Patrick b: 9/16/72, Tampa, Fla. BR/TR, 6'3", 195 lbs. Deb: 6/20/2000																												
2000	SD-N	4	5	.444	19	19	1	0	0	118	126	58	13	5	35	76	12.7	3.58	122	.274	.332	3	.094	-2	14	11	-0	0.5
● **DICK TOMANEK** Tomanek, Richard Carl "Bones" b: 1/6/31, Avon Lake, Ohio BL/TL, 6'1", 175 lbs. Deb: 9/25/53																												
1953	Cle-A	1	0	1.000	1	1	1	0	0	9	6	3	1	1	6	6	13.0	2.00	188	.176	.317	0	.000	-1	2	2	-0	0.1
1954	Cle-A	0	0	—	1	0	0	0	0	1^{2}	1	1	1	0	1	0	10.8	5.40	68	.167	.286	0	—	0	-0	-0	0	0.0
1957	Cle-A	2	1	.667	34	2	0	0	0	69^{2}	67	51	13	1	37	55	13.6	5.68	65	.248	.341	3	.231	0	-15	-16	0	-0.7
1958	Cle-A	2	3	.400	18	6	2	0	0	57^{2}	61	37	8	2	28	42	14.2	5.62	65	.276	.363	2	.118	0	-12	-13	0	-1.0
	KC-A	5	5	.500	36	2	1	0	5	72^{1}	69	34	5	0	28	50	12.1	3.61	108	.252	.321	3	.231	1	1	2	-0	0.4
	Yr	7	8	.467	54	8	3	0	5	130	130	71	13	2	56	92	13.0	4.50	84	.263	.340	5	.167	1	-11	-10	0	-0.6
1959	KC-A	0	1	.000	16	0	0	0	2	20^{2}	27	15	6	2	12	13	17.9	6.53	61	.310	.406	1	.500	0	-6	-6	0	-0.3
Total	5	10	10	.500	106	11	4	0	7	231	231	141	34	6	112	166	13.6	4.95	77	.259	.346	9	.180	1	-30	-30	1	-1.5
● **ANDY TOMASIC** Tomasic, Andrew John b: 12/10/19, Hokendauqua, Pa. BR/TR, 6', 175 lbs. Deb: 4/28/49																												
1949	NY-N	0	1	.000	2	0	0	0	0	5	9	10	2	0	5	2	25.2	18.00	22	.375	.483	0	.000	-0	-8	-8	-0	-1.1
● **ANDY TOMBERLIN** Tomberlin, Andy Lee b: 11/7/66, Monroe, N.C. BL/TL, 5'11", 160 lbs. Deb: 8/12/93 ♦																												
1994	Bos-A	0	0	—	1	0	0	0	0	2	1	0	0	0	1	1	9.0	0.00	—	.143	.250	7	.194	0	1	1	-0	0.1
● **BRETT TOMKO** Tomko, Brett Daniel b: 4/7/73, Cleveland, O. BR/TR, 6'4", 215 lbs. Deb: 5/27/97																												
1997	Cin-N	11	7	.611	22	19	0	0	0	126	106	50	14	4	47	95	11.2	3.43	125	.233	.311	5	.139	-0	11	12	-2	1.3
1998	Cin-N	13	12	.520	34	34	1	0	0	210^{2}	198	111	22	7	64	162	11.5	4.44	96	.247	.308	7	.108	-2	-5	-4	-1	-0.6
1999	Cin-N	5	7	.417	33	26	1	0	0	172	175	103	31	4	60	132	12.5	4.92	95	.263	.327	10	.213	2	-7	-5	-1	-0.2
2000	*Sea-A	7	5	.583	32	8	0	0	1	92^{1}	92	53	12	3	40	59	13.2	4.68	102	.264	.345	0	—	0	3	1	-1	0.0
Total	4	36	31	.537	121	87	2	0	1	601	571	317	79	18	211	448	12.0	4.40	102	.252	.320	22	.149	-0	2	4	-4	0.5
● **DAVE TOMLIN** Tomlin, David Allen b: 6/22/49, Maysville, Ky. BL/TL, 6'3", 185 lbs. Deb: 9/2/72																												
1972	Cin-N	0	0	—	3	0	0	0	0	4	7	4	2	0	1	2	18.0	9.00	36	.412	.444	0	—	0	-2	-3	0	-0.1
1973	*Cin-N	1	2	.333	16	0	0	0	1	27^{2}	24	15	5	0	15	20	12.7	4.88	70	.238	.336	0	.000	-0	-4	-5	0	-0.6
1974	SD-N	2	0	1.000	47	0	0	0	2	58	59	29	4	2	30	29	14.1	4.34	82	.271	.364	0	.000	-0	-5	-5	1	-0.2

YEAR	TM/L	W	L	PCT	G	GS	CG	SH	SV	IP	H	R	HR	HB	BB	SO	RAT	ERA	ERA+	OAV	OOB	BH	AVG	PB	PR	PR+	PD	TPI
1975	SD-N	4	2	.667	67	0	0	0	1	83	87	38	5	2	31	48	13.0	3.25	107	.275	.344	1	.200	1	4	2	3	0.6
1976	SD-N	0	1	.000	49	1	0	0	0	73	62	24	4	1	20	43	10.2	2.84	116	.235	.291	0	.000	-1	5	4	2	0.4
1977	SD-N	4	4	.500	76	0	0	0	3	101^2	98	38	3	2	32	55	11.7	3.01	118	.259	.320	2	.286	0	10	7	1	0.7
1978	Cin-N	9	1	.900	57	0	0	0	4	62^1	88	54	3	3	30	32	17.5	5.78	62	.326	.399	1	.200	0	-15	-16	1	-2.5
1979	*Cin-N	2	2	.500	53	0	0	0	1	58^1	59	29	3	1	18	30	12.0	2.62	143	.269	.328	1	.500	0	7	7	0	0.5
1980	Cin-N	3	0	1.000	27	0	0	0	0	26	38	17	2	0	11	6	17.0	5.54	65	.355	.415	0	—	0	-6	-6	0	-0.5
1982	Mon-N	0	0	—	1	0	0	0	0	2	1	1	0	0	1	2	9.0	4.50	81	.167	.286	0	—	0	-0	-0	-0	0.0
1983	Pit-N	0	0	—	5	0	0	0	0	4	6	4	0	0	1	5	15.8	6.75	55	.316	.350	0	—	0	-1	-1	-0	-0.1
1985	Pit-N	0	0	—	1	0	0	0	0	1	1	0	0	0	1	0	18.0	0.00	—	.333	.500	0	—	0	0	0	-0	0.0
1986	Mon-N	0	0	—	7	0	0	0	0	10^1	13	8	1	1	7	6	18.3	5.23	71	.317	.429	0	—	0	-2	-2	0	0.0
Total	13	25	12	.676	409	1	0	0	12	511^1	543	261	32	12	198	278	13.3	3.82	92	.277	.347	5	.147	1	-8	-18	9	-1.8

● RANDY TOMLIN

Tomlin, Randy Leon b: 6/14/66, Bainbridge, Md. BL/TL, 5'11", 170 lbs. Deb: 8/6/90

YEAR	TM/L	W	L	PCT	G	GS	CG	SH	SV	IP	H	R	HR	HB	BB	SO	RAT	ERA	ERA+	OAV	OOB	BH	AVG	PB	PR	PR+	PD	TPI
1990	Pit-N	4	4	.500	12	12	2	0	0	77^2	62	24	5	1	12	42	8.7	2.55	142	.221	.256	1	.040	-1	11	10	1	1.0
1991	*Pit-N	8	7	.533	31	27	4	2	0	175	170	75	9	6	54	104	11.8	2.98	120	.254	.316	10	.192	1	14	12	2	1.3
1992	*Pit-N	14	9	.609	35	33	1	1	0	208^2	226	85	11	5	42	90	11.8	3.41	101	.282	.322	9	.138	-0	2	1	3	0.4
1993	Pit-N	4	8	.333	18	18	1	0	0	98^1	109	57	11	5	15	44	11.8	4.85	84	.291	.327	6	.182	0	-9	-9	1	-0.8
1994	Pit-N	0	3	.000	10	4	0	0	0	20^2	23	9	1	0	10	17	14.4	3.92	110	.291	.371	3	.500	1	1	1	0	0.2
Total	5	30	31	.492	106	94	8	3	0	580^1	590	250	37	17	133	297	11.5	3.43	106	.268	.314	29	.160	1	19	14	7	2.1

● CHUCK TOMPKINS

Tompkins, Charles Herbert b: 9/1/1889, Prescott, Ark. d: 9/20/75, Prescott, Ark. BR/TR, 6', 185 lbs. Deb: 6/25/12

YEAR	TM/L	W	L	PCT	G	GS	CG	SH	SV	IP	H	R	HR	HB	BB	SO	RAT	ERA	ERA+	OAV	OOB	BH	AVG	PB	PR	PR+	PD	TPI
1912	Cin-N	0	0	—	1	0	0	0	0	3	5	1	0	0	0	1	15.0	0.00	—	.357	.357	1	1.000	0	1	1	-0	0.1

● RON TOMPKINS

Tompkins, Ronald Everett "Stretch" b: 11/27/44, San Diego, Cal. BR/TR, 6'4", 198 lbs. Deb: 9/9/65

YEAR	TM/L	W	L	PCT	G	GS	CG	SH	SV	IP	H	R	HR	HB	BB	SO	RAT	ERA	ERA+	OAV	OOB	BH	AVG	PB	PR	PR+	PD	TPI
1965	KC-A	0	0	—	5	1	0	0	0	10^1	9	4	0	1	3	4	11.3	3.48	100	.237	.310	0	.000	-0	-0	0	0	0.0
1971	Chi-N	0	2	.000	35	0	0	0	3	39^2	31	18	3	3	21	20	12.5	4.08	96	.214	.325	0	—	0	-3	-1	1	0.1
Total	2	0	2	.000	40	1	0	0	3	50	40	22	3	4	24	24	12.2	3.96	97	.219	.322	0	.000	-0	-3	-1	1	0.1

● TOMMY TOMS

Toms, Thomas Howard b: 10/15/51, Charlottesville, Va BR/TR, 6'4", 195 lbs. Deb: 5/4/75

YEAR	TM/L	W	L	PCT	G	GS	CG	SH	SV	IP	H	R	HR	HB	BB	SO	RAT	ERA	ERA+	OAV	OOB	BH	AVG	PB	PR	PR+	PD	TPI
1975	SF-N	0	1	.000	7	0	0	0	0	10^1	13	8	1	0	6	6	16.5	6.10	63	.317	.404	0	—	0	-3	-3	-0	-0.2
1976	SF-N	0	1	.000	7	0	0	0	1	8^2	13	7	1	0	1	4	14.5	6.23	58	.351	.368	0	—	0	-3	-2	0	-0.3
1977	SF-N	0	1	.000	4	0	0	0	0	4^1	7	5	0	0	2	2	18.7	2.08	189	.333	.391	0	—	0	1	1	-0	0.2
Total	3	0	3	.000	18	0	0	0	1	23^1	33	20	2	0	9	12	16.2	5.40	70	.333	.389	0	—	0	-5	-4	-0	-0.3

● FRED TONEY

Toney, Fred Alexandra b: 12/11/1888, Nashville, Tenn. d: 3/11/53, Nashville, Tenn. BR/TR, 6'1", 195 lbs. Deb: 4/15/11

YEAR	TM/L	W	L	PCT	G	GS	CG	SH	SV	IP	H	R	HR	HB	BB	SO	RAT	ERA	ERA+	OAV	OOB	BH	AVG	PB	PR	PR+	PD	TPI
1911	Chi-N	1	1	.500	18	4	1	0	0	67	55	36	2	5	35	27	12.8	2.42	137	.229	.339	2	.111	-1	7	7	1	0.3
1912	Chi-N	1	2	.333	9	2	0	0	0	24	21	19	0	1	11	9	12.4	5.25	63	.247	.340	0	.000	-0	-5	-5	-1	-0.6
1913	Chi-N	2	2	.500	7	5	2	0	0	39	52	29	1	1	22	12	17.3	6.00	53	.327	.412	3	.250	1	-12	-12	0	-1.0
1915	Cin-N	17	6	.739	36	23	18	6	2	222^2	160	46	1	3	73	108	9.5	1.58	181	.207	.278	7	.095	-5	29	31	1	2.9
1916	Cin-N	14	17	.452	41	38	21	3	1	300	247	98	7	8	78	146	10.0	2.28	114	.231	.288	12	.121	-4	11	11	-4	0.2
1917	Cin-N	24	16	.600	43	42	31	7	1	339^2	300	119	4	6	77	123	10.1	2.20	119	.238	.286	13	.112	-6	19	16	-5	0.8
1918	Cin-N	6	10	.375	21	19	9	1	2	136^2	148	61	2	0	31	32	11.8	2.90	92	.282	.322	9	.214	0	-2	-4	1	-0.3
	NY-N	6	2	.750	11	9	7	1	1	85^1	55	19	1	2	7	19	6.8	1.69	156	.192	.216	6	.188	-1	10	9	-1	0.8
	Yr	12	12	.500	32	28	16	2	**3**	222	203	80	3	2	38	51	9.9	2.43	109	.250	.285	15	.203	-0	8	6	0	0.5
1919	NY-N	13	6	.684	24	20	14	4	1	181	157	47	6	2	35	40	9.6	1.84	152	.235	.276	15	.227	1	22	20	-3	2.0
1920	NY-N	21	11	.656	42	37	17	4	1	278^1	266	101	8	6	57	81	10.6	2.65	113	.259	.302	23	.240	3	15	11	-2	1.3
1921	*NY-N	18	11	.621	42	32	16	1	3	249^1	274	112	14	4	65	63	12.4	3.61	102	.289	.338	18	.209	2	5	2	-1	0.2
1922	NY-N	5	6	.455	13	12	6	0	0	86^1	91	44	5	2	31	10	12.9	4.17	96	.277	.343	2	.067	-3	-1	-2	-2	-0.6
1923	StL-N	11	12	.478	29	28	16	1	0	196^2	211	104	8	6	61	48	12.7	3.84	102	.282	.341	8	.116	-5	3	1	3	0.0
Total	12	139	102	.577	336	271	158	28	12	2206	2037	835	59	46	583	718	10.9	2.69	113	.251	.305	118	.159	-18	102	87	-12	6.0

● DOC TONKIN

Tonkin, Harry Glenville b: 8/11/1881, Concord, N.H. d: 5/30/59, Miami, Fla. BL/TL, 5'9", 165 lbs. Deb: 8/19/07

YEAR	TM/L	W	L	PCT	G	GS	CG	SH	SV	IP	H	R	HR	HB	BB	SO	RAT	ERA	ERA+	OAV	OOB	BH	AVG	PB	PR	PR+	PD	TPI
1907	Was-A	0	0	—	1	0	0	0	0	2^2	6	3	0	0	5	0	37.1	6.75	36	.462	.611	2	1.000	1	-1	-1	0	0.1

● STEVE TOOLE

Toole, Stephen John b: 4/9/1859, New Orleans, La. d: 3/28/19, Pittsburgh, Pa. BR/TL, 6', 170 lbs. Deb: 4/20/1886 U

YEAR	TM/L	W	L	PCT	G	GS	CG	SH	SV	IP	H	R	HR	HB	BB	SO	RAT	ERA	ERA+	OAV	OOB	BH	AVG	PB	PR	PR+	PD	TPI
1886	Bro-a	6	6	.500	13	12	11	0	0	104	100	92	0	8	64	48	14.9	4.41	79	.246	.359	20	.351	4	-11	-11	2	-0.5
1887	Bro-a	14	10	.583	24	24	22	1	0	194	292	133	1	12	106	48	14.1	4.31	100	.348	.358	27	.255	-1	-0	-0	-1	-0.2
1888	KC-a	5	6	.455	12	10	10	0	0	91^2	124	99	4	5	50	35	17.6	6.68	51	.312	.395	10	.208	-0	-37	-30	0	-2.6
1890	Bro-a	2	4	.333	6	6	6	0	0	53^1	47	32	0	4	39	10	15.2	4.05	96	.229	.363	6	.300	2	-1	-1	0	0.1
Total	4	27	26	.509	55	52	49	1	0	443	563	356	5	29	259	141	15.1	4.79	81	.305	.367	63	.273	5	-49	-43	2	-3.2

● RUPE TOPPIN

Toppin, Ruperto b: 12/7/41, Panama City, Panama BR/TR, 6', 185 lbs. Deb: 7/28/62

YEAR	TM/L	W	L	PCT	G	GS	CG	SH	SV	IP	H	R	HR	HB	BB	SO	RAT	ERA	ERA+	OAV	OOB	BH	AVG	PB	PR	PR+	PD	TPI
1962	KC-A	0	0	—	2	0	0	0	0	2	1	3	0	0	5	1	27.0	13.50	31	.167	.545	1	1.000	0	-2	-2	-0	-0.1

● RED TORKELSON

Torkelson, Chester Leroy b: 3/19/1894, Chicago, Ill. d: 9/22/64, Chicago, Ill. BR/TR, 6', 175 lbs. Deb: 8/29/17

YEAR	TM/L	W	L	PCT	G	GS	CG	SH	SV	IP	H	R	HR	HB	BB	SO	RAT	ERA	ERA+	OAV	OOB	BH	AVG	PB	PR	PR+	PD	TPI
1917	Cle-A	2	1	.667	4	3	0	0	0	22^1	33	25	1	2	13	10	19.3	7.66	37	.333	.421	2	.222	-0	-12	-11	0	-1.2

● PABLO TORREALBA

Torrealba, Pablo Arnoldo (Torrealba) b: 4/28/48, Barquisimeto, Ven. BL/TL, 5'9", 175 lbs. Deb: 4/9/75

YEAR	TM/L	W	L	PCT	G	GS	CG	SH	SV	IP	H	R	HR	HB	BB	SO	RAT	ERA	ERA+	OAV	OOB	BH	AVG	PB	PR	PR+	PD	TPI
1975	Atl-N	0	1	.000	6	0	0	0	0	6^2	7	2	0	0	3	5	13.5	1.35	280	.250	.323	1	1.000	0	2	2	1	0.4
1976	Atl-N	0	2	.000	36	0	0	0	2	53	67	25	0	3	22	33	15.6	3.57	106	.315	.387	0	.000	-0	-0	1	1	0.1
1977	Oak-A	4	6	.400	41	10	3	0	2	116^2	127	45	5	2	38	51	12.9	2.62	154	.279	.337	0	—	0	19	19	2	1.7
1978	Chi-A	2	4	.333	25	3	1	1	1	57^1	69	37	6	3	39	23	17.4	4.71	81	.301	.410	0	—	0	-6	-6	-1	-0.7
1979	Chi-A	0	0	—	3	0	0	0	0	5^2	5	1	1	0	2	1	11.1	1.59	268	.250	.318	0	—	0	2	2	0	0.1
Total	5	6	13	.316	111	13	4	1	5	239^1	275	110	12	8	104	113	14.6	3.27	120	.291	.366	1	.200	-0	16	17	2	1.6

● ANGEL TORRES

Torres, Angel Rafael (Ruiz) b: 10/24/52, Las Ciengas, Azua, D.R. BL/TL, 5'11", 168 lbs. Deb: 9/12/77

YEAR	TM/L	W	L	PCT	G	GS	CG	SH	SV	IP	H	R	HR	HB	BB	SO	RAT	ERA	ERA+	OAV	OOB	BH	AVG	PB	PR	PR+	PD	TPI
1977	Cin-N	0	0	—	5	0	0	0	0	8^1	7	2	2	0	8	8	16.2	2.16	182	.233	.395	0	—	0	2	2	0	0.1

● DILSON TORRES

Torres, Dilson Dario b: 5/31/70, Sur Edo Aragua, Venez. BR/TR, 6'3", 200 lbs. Deb: 4/29/95

YEAR	TM/L	W	L	PCT	G	GS	CG	SH	SV	IP	H	R	HR	HB	BB	SO	RAT	ERA	ERA+	OAV	OOB	BH	AVG	PB	PR	PR+	PD	TPI
1995	KC-A	1	2	.333	24	2	0	0	0	44^1	56	30	6	1	17	28	15.0	6.09	79	.311	.374	0	—	0	-7	-6	2	-0.2

● GIL TORRES

Torres, Don Gilberto (Nunez) b: 8/23/15, Regla, Cuba d: 1/10/83, Regla, Cuba BR/TR, 6', 155 lbs. Deb: 4/25/40 F◆

YEAR	TM/L	W	L	PCT	G	GS	CG	SH	SV	IP	H	R	HR	HB	BB	SO	RAT	ERA	ERA+	OAV	OOB	BH	AVG	PB	PR	PR+	PD	TPI
1940	Was-A	0	0	—	2	0	0	0	0	2^2	3	1	0	0	0	1	10.1	0.00	—	.273	.273	0	—	0	1	1	0	0.1
1946	Was-A	0	0	—	3	0	0	0	1	7	9	6	0	0	3	2	15.4	7.71	43	.310	.375	47	.254	1	-3	-4	-0	-0.2
Total	2	0	0	—	5	0	0	0	1	9^2	12	7	0	0	3	3	14.0	5.59	64	.300	.349	320	.252	1	-2	-2	-0	-0.1

● HECTOR TORRES

Torres, Hector Epitacio (Marroquin) b: 9/16/45, Monterrey, Mexico BR/TR, 6', 175 lbs. Deb: 4/10/68 C◆

YEAR	TM/L	W	L	PCT	G	GS	CG	SH	SV	IP	H	R	HR	HB	BB	SO	RAT	ERA	ERA+	OAV	OOB	BH	AVG	PB	PR	PR+	PD	TPI
1972	Mon-N	0	0	—	1	0	0	0	0	0^2	5	2	0	0	0	0	67.5	27.00	13	.714	.714	28	.155	0	-2	-2	0	-0.1

● SALOMON TORRES

Torres, Salomon (Ramirez) b: 3/11/72, San Pedro De Macoris, D.R. BR/TR, 5'11", 165 lbs. Deb: 8/29/93

YEAR	TM/L	W	L	PCT	G	GS	CG	SH	SV	IP	H	R	HR	HB	BB	SO	RAT	ERA	ERA+	OAV	OOB	BH	AVG	PB	PR	PR+	PD	TPI
1993	SF-N	3	5	.375	8	8	0	0	0	44^2	37	21	5	1	27	23	13.1	4.03	97	.231	.346	3	.231	0	0	-1	1	0.0
1994	SF-N	2	8	.200	16	14	1	0	0	84^1	95	55	10	7	34	42	14.5	5.44	74	.292	.372	4	.154	-0	-11	-14	-2	-1.6
1995	SF-N	0	1	.000	4	1	0	0	0	8	13	8	4	0	7	2	22.5	9.00	45	.394	.500	0	.000	-0	-4	-4	0	-0.5
	Sea-A	3	8	.273	16	13	1	0	0	72	87	53	12	2	42	45	16.4	6.00	79	.291	.382	0	—	0	-10	-10	1	-1.1
1996	Sea-A	3	3	.500	10	7	1	1	0	49	44	27	5	3	23	36	12.9	4.59	108	.242	.337	0	—	0	2	2	-1	0.1
1997	Sea-A	0	0	—	2	0	0	0	0	3^1	7	10	0	1	3	0	29.7	27.00	17	.412	.524	0	—	0	-8	-8	0	-0.4
	Mon-N	0	0	—	12	0	0	0	0	22^1	25	19	2	2	12	11	15.7	7.25	58	.284	.382	0	.000	-1	-8	-8	1	-0.4
Total	5	11	25	.306	68	43	3	1	0	283^2	308	193	38	16	148	159	15.0	5.71	76	.279	.372	7	.152	-1	-40	-43	0	-3.9

● MIKE TORREZ

Torrez, Michael Augustine b: 8/28/46, Topeka, Kan. BR/TR, 6'5", 220 lbs. Deb: 9/10/67

YEAR	TM/L	W	L	PCT	G	GS	CG	SH	SV	IP	H	R	HR	HB	BB	SO	RAT	ERA	ERA+	OAV	OOB	BH	AVG	PB	PR	PR+	PD	TPI
1967	StL-N	0	1	.000	3	1	0	0	0	5^2	5	2	0	1	1	5	11.1	3.18	103	.238	.304	0	.000	-0	0	0	-0	0.0
1968	StL-N	2	1	.667	5	2	0	0	0	19^1	20	7	1	1	12	6	15.4	2.79	104	.286	.398	2	.286	0	0	0	0	0.1
1969	StL-N	10	4	.714	24	15	3	0	0	107^2	96	47	7	3	62	61	13.5	3.59	99	.240	.346	3	.073	-2	0	-0	0	-0.2

YEAR	TM/L	W	L	PCT	G	GS	CG	SH	SV	IP	H	R	HR	HB	BB	SO	RAT	ERA	ERA+	OAV	OOB	BH	AVG	PB	PR	PR+	PD	TPI
1970	StL-N	8	10	.444	30	28	5	1	0	179^1	168	96	12	4	103	100	13.8	4.22	98	.248	.350	17	.270	4	-3	-2	-0	0.2
1971	StL-N	1	2	.333	9	6	0	0	0	36	41	27	2	1	30	8	18.0	6.00	60	.304	.434	1	.143	1	-10	-9	0	-0.6
	Mon-N	0	0	—	1	0	0	0	0	3	4	0	0	0	1	2	15.0	0.00	—	.308	.357	0	—	0	1	1	0	0.1
	Yr	1	2	.333	10	6	0	0	0	39	45	27	2	1	31	10	17.8	5.54	65	.304	.428	1	.143	1	-9	-8	1	-0.5
1972	Mon-N	16	12	.571	34	33	13	0	0	243^1	215	97	15	6	103	112	12.0	3.33	107	.242	.325	15	.176	0	3	6	2	1.0
1973	Mon-N	9	12	.429	35	34	3	1	0	208	207	116	17	4	115	90	14.1	4.46	86	.262	.359	12	.174	-1	-18	-14	2	-1.2
1974	Mon-N	15	8	.652	32	30	6	1	0	186^1	184	90	10	3	84	92	13.1	3.57	108	.257	.337	8	.125	-3	1	5	5	0.9
1975	Bal-A	20	9	**.690**	36	36	16	2	0	270^2	238	103	15	5	133	119	12.5	3.06	115	.239	.332	0	—	0	22	15	1	1.6
1976	Oak-A	16	12	.571	39	39	13	4	0	266^1	231	93	15	6	87	115	10.9	2.50	134	.235	.301	0	—	0	30	27	-1	2.7
1977	Oak-A	3	1	.750	4	4	2	0	0	26^1	23	14	3	1	11	12	12.0	4.44	91	.242	.327	0	—	0	-1	-1	-0	-0.2
	*NY-A	14	12	.538	31	31	15	2	0	217	212	99	20	6	75	90	12.2	3.82	104	.259	.326	0	—	0	6	3	-2	0.2
	Yr	17	13	.567	35	35	17	2	0	243^1	235	113	23	7	86	102	12.1	3.88	102	.257	.326	0	—	0	5	2	-2	0.0
1978	Bos-A	16	13	.552	36	36	15	2	0	250	272	122	19	3	99	120	13.5	3.96	104	.281	.349	0	—	0	-5	4	-2	0.3
1979	Bos-A	16	13	.552	36	36	12	1	0	252^1	254	144	20	5	121	125	13.6	4.49	99	.264	.349	0	—	0	-7	-2	-0	-0.2
1980	Bos-A	9	16	.360	36	32	6	1	0	207^1	256	124	18	1	75	97	14.4	5.08	83	.313	.371	0	—	0	-24	-19	2	-1.8
1981	Bos-A	10	3	.769	22	22	2	0	0	127^1	130	61	10	0	51	54	12.8	3.68	105	.267	.337	0	—	0	-0	3	-1	0.1
1982	Bos-A	9	9	.500	31	31	1	0	0	175^2	196	107	20	6	74	84	14.1	5.23	83	.282	.356	0	—	0	-22	-17	-2	-1.7
1983	NY-N	10	17	.370	39	34	5	0	0	222^1	227	120	16	1	113	94	13.8	4.37	83	.271	.358	3	.046	-5	-18	-18	0	-2.5
1984	NY-N	1	5	.167	9	8	0	0	0	37^2	55	25	3	2	18	16	17.9	5.02	71	.369	.444	3	.300	1	-6	-6	0	-0.8
	Oak-A	0	0	—	2	0	0	0	0	2^1	9	7	0	0	3	2	46.3	27.00	14	.563	.632	0	—	0	-6	-6	-0	-0.3
Total	18	185	160	.536	494	458	117	15	0	3044	3043	1501	223	59	1371	1404	13.2	3.96	97	.264	.345	64	.155	-4	-57	-34	3	-2.3

● LOU TOST Tost, Louis Eugene b: 6/1/11, Cumberland, Wash. d: 2/22/67, Santa Clara, Cal. BL/TL, 6', 175 lbs. Deb: 4/20/42

YEAR	TM/L	W	L	PCT	G	GS	CG	SH	SV	IP	H	R	HR	HB	BB	SO	RAT	ERA	ERA+	OAV	OOB	BH	AVG	PB	PR	PR+	PD	TPI
1942	Bos-N	10	10	.500	35	22	5	1	0	147^2	146	66	12	4	52	43	12.3	3.53	94	.256	.322	9	.176	0	-4	-3	-1	-0.5
1943	Bos-N	0	1	.000	3	1	0	0	0	6^2	10	5	2	0	4	3	18.9	5.40	63	.357	.438	0	.000	-0	-1	-1	0	-0.2
1947	Pit-N	0	0	—	1	0	0	0	0	1	3	1	0	0	0	0	27.0	9.00	47	.600	.600	0	—	0	-1	-1	0	0.0
Total	3	10	11	.476	39	23	5	1	0	155^1	159	72	14	4	56	46	12.7	3.65	92	.263	.330	9	.173	-0	-6	-5	-1	-0.7

● PAUL TOTH Toth, Paul Louis b: 6/30/35, McRoberts, Ky. d: 3/20/99, Anaheim, Cal. BR/TR, 6'1", 175 lbs. Deb: 4/22/62

YEAR	TM/L	W	L	PCT	G	GS	CG	SH	SV	IP	H	R	HR	HB	BB	SO	RAT	ERA	ERA+	OAV	OOB	BH	AVG	PB	PR	PR+	PD	TPI
1962	StL-N	1	0	1.000	6	1	1	0	0	16^2	18	10	1	0	4	5	11.9	5.40	79	.295	.338	2	.400	0	-3	-2	-0	-0.1
	Chi-N	3	1	.750	6	4	1	0	0	34	29	17	2	2	10	11	10.9	4.24	98	.240	.308	2	.182	0	-1	-0	-0	0.0
	Yr	4	1	.800	12	5	2	0	0	50^2	47	27	3	2	14	16	11.2	4.62	91	.258	.318	4	.250	1	-4	-2	-1	-0.1
1963	Chi-N	5	9	.357	27	14	3	2	0	130^2	115	50	9	2	35	66	10.5	3.10	113	.240	.294	1	.026	-3	3	6	1	0.1
1964	Chi-N	0	2	.000	4	2	1	0	0	10^2	15	10	2	0	5	0	16.9	8.44	44	.341	.408	1	.333	0	-6	-5	1	-0.8
Total	3	9	12	.429	43	21	5	2	0	192	177	87	14	4	54	82	11.0	3.80	97	.251	.308	6	.103	-2	-7	-2	-1	-0.8

● CLAY TOUCHSTONE Touchstone, Clayland Maffitt b: 1/24/03, Moores, Pa. d: 4/28/49, Beaumont, Tex. BR/TR, 5'9", 175 lbs. Deb: 9/4/28

YEAR	TM/L	W	L	PCT	G	GS	CG	SH	SV	IP	H	R	HR	HB	BB	SO	RAT	ERA	ERA+	OAV	OOB	BH	AVG	PB	PR	PR+	PD	TPI
1928	Bos-N	0	0	—	5	0	0	0	0	8	15	8	0	1	2	1	20.3	4.50	87	.417	.462	0	.000	-0	-0	-1	0	0.0
1929	Bos-N	0	0	—	1	0	0	0	0	2^2	6	5	1	0	0	1	20.3	16.88	28	.429	.429	1	1.000	0	-4	-4	-0	-0.1
1945	Chi-A	0	0	—	6	0	0	0	0	10	14	10	1	1	6	4	18.9	5.40	61	.311	.404	0	.000	-0	-2	-2	0	-0.1
Total	3	0	0	—	12	0	0	0	0	20^2	35	23	2	2	8	6	19.6	6.53	57	.368	.429	1	.250	0	-6	-7	0	-0.2

● CESAR TOVAR Tovar, Cesar Leonardo "Pepito" (b: Cesar Leonard Perez (Tovar)) b: 7/3/40, Caracas, Venez. d: 7/14/94, Caracas, Venez. BR/TR, 5'9", 155 lbs. Deb: 4/12/65 ♦

YEAR	TM/L	W	L	PCT	G	GS	CG	SH	SV	IP	H	R	HR	HB	BB	SO	RAT	ERA	ERA+	OAV	OOB	BH	AVG	PB	PR	PR+	PD	TPI
1968	Min-A	0	0	—	1	1	0	0	0	1	0	0	0	0	1	1	9.0	0.00	—	.000	.250	167	.272	0	0	0	0	0.0

● IRA TOWNSEND Townsend, Ira Dance "Pat" b: 1/9/1894, Weimar, Tex. d: 7/21/65, Schulenburg, Tex. BR/TR, 6'1", 180 lbs. Deb: 8/25/20

YEAR	TM/L	W	L	PCT	G	GS	CG	SH	SV	IP	H	R	HR	HB	BB	SO	RAT	ERA	ERA+	OAV	OOB	BH	AVG	PB	PR	PR+	PD	TPI
1920	Bos-N	0	0	—	4	1	0	0	0	6^2	10	3	0	1	2	1	17.6	1.35	226	.370	.433	0	.000	-0	1	1	-0	0.0
1921	Bos-N	0	0	—	4	0	0	0	0	7^1	11	7	1	2	4	0	20.9	6.14	59	.344	.447	0	.000	-0	-2	-2	0	-0.1
Total	2	0	0	—	8	1	0	0	0	14	21	10	1	3	6	1	19.3	3.86	87	.356	.441	0	.000	-1	-1	-1	0	-0.1

● HAPPY TOWNSEND Townsend, John b: 4/9/1879, Townsend, Del. d: 12/21/63, Wilmington, Del. BR/TR, 6', 190 lbs. Deb: 4/19/01

YEAR	TM/L	W	L	PCT	G	GS	CG	SH	SV	IP	H	R	HR	HB	BB	SO	RAT	ERA	ERA+	OAV	OOB	BH	AVG	PB	PR	PR+	PD	TPI
1901	Phi-N	9	6	.600	19	16	14	2	0	143^2	118	73	3	5	64	72	11.7	3.45	99	**.223**	.312	7	.109	-4	-2	-1	-2	-0.7
1902	Was-A	8	16	.333	27	26	22	0	0	220^1	233	157	12	13	89	71	13.7	4.45	83	.272	.349	23	.264	3	-21	-18	-1	-1.4
1903	Was-A	2	11	.154	20	13	10	0	0	126^2	145	85	3	9	48	54	14.4	4.76	66	.287	.359	2	.045	-4	-25	-22	0	-2.3
1904	Was-A	5	26	.161	36	34	31	2	0	291^1	319	163	3	9	100	143	13.2	3.58	74	.279	.342	20	.168	-2	-32	-29	-1	-3.3
1905	Was-A	7	16	.304	34	24	22	0	0	263	247	117	2	15	84	102	11.8	2.63	100	.250	.318	15	.181	1	1	0	-3	-0.1
1906	Cle-A	3	7	.300	17	12	8	1	0	92^2	92	45	1	6	31	31	12.5	2.91	90	.262	.332	4	.133	-1	-2	-3	-0	-0.5
Total	6	34	82	.293	153	125	107	5	0	1137^2	1154	640	24	57	416	473	12.9	3.59	83	.264	.336	71	.166	-8	-82	-74	-7	-8.3

● LEO TOWNSEND Townsend, Leo Alphonse "Lefty" b: 1/15/1891, Mobile, Ala. d: 12/3/76, Mobile, Ala. BL/TL, 5'10", 160 lbs. Deb: 9/8/20

YEAR	TM/L	W	L	PCT	G	GS	CG	SH	SV	IP	H	R	HR	HB	BB	SO	RAT	ERA	ERA+	OAV	OOB	BH	AVG	PB	PR	PR+	PD	TPI
1920	Bos-N	2	2	.500	7	1	1	0	0	24^1	18	4	1	0	2	0	7.4	1.48	206	.220	.238	1	.167	0	4	4	0	0.7
1921	Bos-N	0	1	.000	1	1	0	0	0	1^1	2	4	0	0	3	0	33.8	27.00	14	.400	.625	0	—	0	-3	-4	0	-0.5
Total	2	2	3	.400	8	2	1	0	0	25^2	20	8	1	0	5	0	8.8	2.81	110	.230	.272	1	.167	0	1	1	0	0.2

● BILL TOZER Tozer, William Louis b: 7/3/1882, St.Louis, Mo. d: 2/23/55, Belmont, Cal. BR/TR, 6', 200 lbs. Deb: 4/16/08

YEAR	TM/L	W	L	PCT	G	GS	CG	SH	SV	IP	H	R	HR	HB	BB	SO	RAT	ERA	ERA+	OAV	OOB	BH	AVG	PB	PR	PR+	PD	TPI
1908	Cin-N	0	0	—	4	0	0	0	0	10^2	11	5	0	1	4	5	13.5	1.69	137	.268	.348	0	.000	-0	1	1	0	0.0

● STEVE TRACHSEL Trachsel, Stephen Christopher b: 10/31/70, Oxnard, Cal. BR/TR, 6'4", 205 lbs. Deb: 9/19/93

YEAR	TM/L	W	L	PCT	G	GS	CG	SH	SV	IP	H	R	HR	HB	BB	SO	RAT	ERA	ERA+	OAV	OOB	BH	AVG	PB	PR	PR+	PD	TPI
1993	Chi-N	0	2	.000	3	3	0	0	0	19^2	16	10	4	0	3	14	8.7	4.58	87	.219	.250	1	.167	0	-1	-1	0	0.0
1994	Chi-N	9	7	.563	22	22	1	0	0	146	133	57	19	3	54	108	11.7	3.21	130	.242	.314	8	.186	1	16	16	2	1.9
1995	Chi-N	7	13	.350	30	29	2	0	0	160^2	174	104	25	0	76	117	14.0	5.15	80	.277	.355	13	.265	3	-17	-19	-2	-1.9
1996	Chi-N★	13	9	.591	31	31	3	2	0	205	181	82	30	8	62	132	11.0	3.03	143	.235	.299	7	.106	-2	27	29	0	2.7
1997	Chi-N	8	12	.400	34	34	0	0	0	201^1	225	110	32	5	69	160	13.4	4.51	95	.287	.348	7	.117	-0	-7	-5	0	-0.4
1998	Chi-N	15	8	.652	33	33	1	0	0	208	204	107	27	8	84	149	12.8	4.46	99	.260	.337	17	.266	6	-5	-1	2	0.7
1999	Chi-N	8	18	.308	34	34	4	0	0	205^2	226	133	32	3	64	149	12.8	5.56	81	.280	.335	7	.111	-2	-23	-24	-1	-2.7
2000	TB-A	6	10	.375	23	23	3	1	0	137^2	160	76	16	6	49	78	14.1	4.58	108	.294	.359	1	.250	0	5	6	1	0.7
	Tor-A	2	5	.286	11	11	0	0	0	63	72	40	10	0	25	32	13.9	5.29	94	.293	.358	0	—	0	-3	-2	1	-0.1
	Yr	8	15	.348	34	34	3	1	0	200^2	232	116	26	6	74	110	14.0	4.80	103	.294	.359	1	.250	0	3	4	2	0.6
Total	8	68	84	.447	221	220	14	3	0	1347	1391	719	195	33	486	939	12.8	4.42	100	.268	.335	61	.172	7	-7	-0	4	0.9

● FRED TRAUTMAN Trautman, Frederick Orlando b: 3/24/1892, Bucyrus, Ohio d: 2/15/64, Bucyrus, Ohio BR/TR, 6'1", 175 lbs. Deb: 4/27/15

YEAR	TM/L	W	L	PCT	G	GS	CG	SH	SV	IP	H	R	HR	HB	BB	SO	RAT	ERA	ERA+	OAV	OOB	BH	AVG	PB	PR	PR+	PD	TPI
1915	New-F	0	0	—	1	0	0	0	0	3	4	3	0	1	1	2	18.0	6.00	43	.364	.462	0	.000	-0	-1	-1	-0	-0.1

● JOHN TRAUTWEIN Trautwein, John Howard b: 8/7/62, Lafayette Hill, Pa. BR/TR, 6'3", 205 lbs. Deb: 4/7/88

YEAR	TM/L	W	L	PCT	G	GS	CG	SH	SV	IP	H	R	HR	HB	BB	SO	RAT	ERA	ERA+	OAV	OOB	BH	AVG	PB	PR	PR+	PD	TPI
1988	Bos-A	0	1	.000	9	0	0	0	0	16	26	17	2	1	9	8	20.3	9.00	46	.382	.462	0	—	0	-9	-8	0	-0.5

● ALLAN TRAVERS Travers, Aloysius Joseph "Joe" b: 5/7/1892, Philadelphia, Pa. d: 4/19/68, Philadelphia, Pa. BR/TR, 6'1", 180 lbs. Deb: 5/18/12

YEAR	TM/L	W	L	PCT	G	GS	CG	SH	SV	IP	H	R	HR	HB	BB	SO	RAT	ERA	ERA+	OAV	OOB	BH	AVG	PB	PR	PR+	PD	TPI
1912	Det-A	0	1	.000	1	1	1	0	0	8	26	24	0	0	7	1	37.1	15.75	21	.605	.660	0	.000	-0	-11	-11	1	-0.8

● BILL TRAVERS Travers, William Edward b: 10/27/52, Norwood, Mass. BL/TL, 6'6", 200 lbs. Deb: 5/19/74

YEAR	TM/L	W	L	PCT	G	GS	CG	SH	SV	IP	H	R	HR	HB	BB	SO	RAT	ERA	ERA+	OAV	OOB	BH	AVG	PB	PR	PR+	PD	TPI
1974	Mil-A	2	3	.400	23	1	0	0	0	53	59	29	6	1	30	31	15.3	4.92	74	.296	.391	0	—	0	-8	-8	0	-0.7
1975	Mil-A	6	11	.353	28	23	5	0	1	136^1	130	78	15	11	60	57	13.3	4.29	90	.251	.342	0	—	0	-8	-7	-1	-0.8
1976	Mil-A☆	15	16	.484	34	34	15	3	0	240	211	92	21	8	95	120	11.8	2.81	124	.237	.316	0	—	0	19	18	-1	2.3
1977	Mil-A	4	12	.250	19	19	2	1	0	121^2	140	75	13	7	57	49	15.1	5.25	78	.291	.374	0	—	0	-16	-16	0	-1.7
1978	Mil-A	12	11	.522	28	28	8	3	0	175^2	184	93	20	6	58	66	12.7	4.41	86	.268	.331	0	—	0	-12	-12	1	-1.4
1979	Mil-A	14	8	.636	30	27	9	2	0	187^1	196	89	33	3	45	74	11.7	3.89	107	.270	.315	0	—	0	7	6	-2	0.5
1980	Mil-A	12	6	.667	29	25	7	1	0	154^1	147	76	20	6	47	62	11.7	3.91	99	.249	.311	0	—	0	2	-1	-1	-0.1
1981	Cal-A	0	1	.000	4	4	0	0	0	9^2	14	11	2	0	4	5	16.8	8.38	44	.333	.391	0	—	0	-5	-5	-0	-0.5
1983	Cal-A	0	3	.000	10	7	0	0	0	42^2	58	32	4	2	19	24	16.7	5.91	68	.331	.403	0	—	0	-9	-9	0	-0.5
Total	9	65	71	.478	205	168	46	10	1	1120^2	1139	575	134	44	415	488	12.8	4.10	94	.264	.335	0	—	0	-29	-33	-3	-2.9

● HARRY TREKELL Trekell, Harry Roy b: 11/18/1892, Buda, Ill. d: 11/4/65, Spokane, Wash. BR/TR, 6'1.5", 170 lbs. Deb: 8/16/13

YEAR	TM/L	W	L	PCT	G	GS	CG	SH	SV	IP	H	R	HR	HB	BB	SO	RAT	ERA	ERA+	OAV	OOB	BH	AVG	PB	PR	PR+	PD	TPI
1913	StL-N	0	1	.000	7	1	1	0	0	30	25	20	2	2	8	15	10.5	4.50	72	.221	.285	1	.111	-0	-4	-4	-0	-0.3

● BILL TREMEL Tremel, William Leonard "Mumbles" b: 7/4/29, Lilly, Pa. BR/TR, 5'11", 180 lbs. Deb: 6/12/54

YEAR	TM/L	W	L	PCT	G	GS	CG	SH	SV	IP	H	R	HR	HB	BB	SO	RAT	ERA	ERA+	OAV	OOB	BH	AVG	PB	PR	PR+	PD	TPI
1954	Chi-N	1	2	.333	33	0	0	0	4	51^1	45	27	3	0	28	21	12.8	4.21	100	.243	.343	2	.250	0	-1	-0	-1	-0.1
1955	Chi-N	3	0	1.000	23	0	0	0	2	38^2	33	18	2	0	18	13	11.9	3.72	110	.239	.327	2	.286	0	1	2	-1	0.1
1956	Chi-N	0	0	—	1	0	0	0	0	1	3	1	0	0	0	0	27.0	9.00	42	.600	.600	0	—	0	-1	-1	-0	0.0
Total	3	4	2	.667	57	0	0	0	6	91	81	46	5	0	46	34	12.6	4.05	102	.247	.340	4	.267	1	-0	1	-2	0.0

● BOB TRICE Trice, Robert Lee b: 8/28/26, Newton, Ga. d: 9/16/88, Weirton, W.Va. BR/TR, 6'3", 190 lbs. Deb: 9/13/53

YEAR	TM/L	W	L	PCT	G	GS	CG	SH	SV	IP	H	R	HR	HB	BB	SO	RAT	ERA	ERA+	OAV	OOB	BH	AVG	PB	PR	PR+	PD	TPI
1953	Phi-A	2	1	.667	3	3	1	0	0	23	25	14	4	0	6	4	12.1	5.48	78	.275	.320	1	.143	0	-4	-3	1	-0.2
1954	Phi-A	7	8	.467	19	18	8	1	0	119	146	86	14	0	48	22	14.7	5.60	70	.305	.369	12	.286	4	-25	-21	0	-1.9
1955	KC-A	0	0	—	4	0	0	0	0	10	14	13	4	0	6	2	18.0	9.00	46	.326	.408	2	.667	1	-6	-5	1	-0.1
Total	3	9	9	.500	26	21	9	1	0	152	185	113	22	0	60	28	14.5	5.80	69	.302	.365	15	.288	5	-34	-29	2	-2.2

● JOE TRIMBLE Trimble, Joseph Gerard b: 10/12/30, Providence, R.I. BR/TR, 6'1", 190 lbs. Deb: 4/29/55

YEAR	TM/L	W	L	PCT	G	GS	CG	SH	SV	IP	H	R	HR	HB	BB	SO	RAT	ERA	ERA+	OAV	OOB	BH	AVG	PB	PR	PR+	PD	TPI
1955	Bos-A	0	0	—	2	0	0	0	0	2	0	0	0	0	3	1	13.5	0.00	—	.000	.375	0	—	0	1	1	0	0.1
1957	Pit-N	0	2	.000	5	4	0	0	0	19^2	23	19	7	1	13	9	16.9	8.24	46	.291	.398	1	.143	-0	-10	-10	0	-0.8
Total	2	0	2	.000	7	4	0	0	0	21^2	23	19	7	1	16	10	16.6	7.48	51	.274	.396	1	.143	-0	-9	-91	0	-0.7

● KEN TRINKLE Trinkle, Kenneth Wayne b: 12/15/19, Paoli, Ind. d: 5/10/76, Paoli, Ind. BR/TR, 6'1.5", 175 lbs. Deb: 4/25/43

YEAR	TM/L	W	L	PCT	G	GS	CG	SH	SV	IP	H	R	HR	HB	BB	SO	RAT	ERA	ERA+	OAV	OOB	BH	AVG	PB	PR	PR+	PD	TPI
1943	NY-N	1	5	.167	11	6	1	0	0	45^2	51	23	3	1	15	10	13.2	3.74	92	.276	.333	3	.250	1	-2	-1	1	0.0
1946	NY-N	7	14	.333	**48**	13	2	0	2	151	146	77	8	2	74	49	13.2	3.87	89	.253	.340	3	.079	-2	-8	-7	-0	-1.2
1947	NY-N	8	4	.667	**62**	0	0	0	10	93^2	100	47	3	1	48	37	14.3	3.75	109	.278	.364	3	.188	-0	3	3	2	0.6
1948	NY-N	4	5	.444	53	0	0	0	7	70^2	66	28	6	3	41	20	14.0	3.18	124	.244	.350	2	.250	0	6	6	1	1.0
1949	Phi-N	1	1	.500	42	0	0	0	2	74^1	79	37	3	3	30	14	13.6	4.00	99	.299	.377	0	.000	-0	0	-0	1	0.1
Total	5	21	29	.420	216	19	3	0	21	435^1	442	212	23	10	208	130	13.6	3.74	100	.267	.352	11	.138	-2	0	0	6	0.5

● RICKY TRLICEK Trlicek, Richard Alan b: 4/26/69, Houston, Tex. BR/TR, 6'2", 200 lbs. Deb: 4/8/92

YEAR	TM/L	W	L	PCT	G	GS	CG	SH	SV	IP	H	R	HR	HB	BB	SO	RAT	ERA	ERA+	OAV	OOB	BH	AVG	PB	PR	PR+	PD	TPI
1992	Tor-A	0	0	—	2	0	0	0	0	1^2	2	2	0	0	2	1	21.6	10.80	38	.286	.444	0	—	0	-1	-1	-0	-0.1
1993	LA-N	1	2	.333	41	0	0	0	1	64	59	32	3	2	21	41	11.5	4.08	94	.244	.309	1	.250	0	-0	-2	1	0.0
1994	Bos-A	1	1	.500	12	1	0	0	0	22^1	32	21	5	0	16	7	19.3	8.06	62	.330	.425	0	—	0	-8	-7	-0	-0.5
1996	NY-N	0	1	.000	5	0	0	0	0	5^1	3	2	0	1	3	3	11.8	3.38	119	.214	.389	0	—	0	1	0	0	0.1
1997	Bos-A	3	4	.429	18	0	0	0	0	23^1	26	14	2	1	18	10	17.4	4.63	100	.289	.413	0	—	0	-0	0	0	0.0
	NY-N	0	0	—	9	0	0	0	0	9	10	9	2	0	5	4	15.0	8.00	50	.303	.395	0	—	0	-4	-4	0	-0.2
Total	5	5	8	.385	87	1	0	0	1	125^2	132	80	12	4	65	66	14.4	5.23	80	.273	.364	1	.250	0	-13	-15	1	-0.7

● RICH TROEDSON Troedson, Richard La Monte b: 5/1/50, Palo Alto, Cal. BL/TL, 6'1", 170 lbs. Deb: 4/9/73

YEAR	TM/L	W	L	PCT	G	GS	CG	SH	SV	IP	H	R	HR	HB	BB	SO	RAT	ERA	ERA+	OAV	OOB	BH	AVG	PB	PR	PR+	PD	TPI
1973	SD-N	7	9	.438	50	18	2	0	1	152^1	167	77	12	1	59	81	13.4	4.25	82	.284	.351	7	.175	0	-10	-14	2	-1.2
1974	SD-N	1	1	.500	15	1	0	0	1	18^2	24	18	6	1	8	11	15.9	8.68	41	.300	.371	0	.000	-0	-10	-11	0	-1.1
Total	2	8	10	.444	65	19	2	0	2	171	191	95	18	2	67	92	13.7	4.74	74	.286	.353	7	.171	-0	-20	-25	2	-2.3

● MIKE TROMBLEY Trombley, Michael Scott b: 4/14/67, Springfield, Mass. BR/TR, 6'2", 208 lbs. Deb: 8/19/92

YEAR	TM/L	W	L	PCT	G	GS	CG	SH	SV	IP	H	R	HR	HB	BB	SO	RAT	ERA	ERA+	OAV	OOB	BH	AVG	PB	PR	PR+	PD	TPI
1992	Min-A	3	2	.600	10	7	0	0	0	46^1	43	20	5	1	17	38	11.8	3.30	123	.247	.318	0	—	0	3	4	0	0.4
1993	Min-A	6	6	.500	44	10	0	0	2	114^1	131	72	15	3	41	85	13.8	4.88	90	.290	.353	0	—	0	-7	-6	1	-0.5
1994	Min-A	2	0	1.000	24	0	0	0	0	48^1	56	36	10	3	18	32	14.3	6.33	77	.287	.356	0	—	0	-8	-8	-1	-0.4
1995	Min-A	4	8	.333	20	18	0	0	0	97^2	107	68	18	3	42	68	14.0	5.62	85	.273	.348	0	—	0	-10	-9	-1	-1.0
1996	Min-A	5	1	.833	43	0	0	0	6	68^2	61	24	2	5	25	57	11.9	3.01	170	.236	.315	0	—	0	15	16	-0	1.4
1997	Min-A	2	3	.400	67	0	0	0	1	82^1	77	43	7	2	31	74	12.0	4.37	107	.248	.320	0	.000	-0	2	3	-0	0.1
1998	Min-A	6	5	.545	77	1	0	0	1	96^2	90	41	16	5	41	89	12.7	3.63	131	.247	.332	0	—	0	11	12	-1	1.1
1999	Min-A	2	8	.200	75	0	0	0	24	87^1	93	42	15	2	28	82	12.7	4.33	118	.272	.331	0	—	0	5	7	0	1.0
2000	Bal-A	4	5	.444	75	0	0	0	4	72	67	34	15	4	38	72	13.6	4.13	116	.247	.348	0	.000	-0	6	5	1	0.7
Total	9	34	38	.472	435	36	0	0	38	713^2	725	380	103	28	281	597	13.0	4.43	107	.263	.337	0	.000	-0	18	24	-1	2.8

● HAL TROSKY Trosky, Harold Arthur Jr. "Hoot" (b: Harold Arthur Troyavesky Jr.) b: 9/29/36, Cleveland, Ohio BR/TR, 6'3", 205 lbs. Deb: 9/25/58 F

YEAR	TM/L	W	L	PCT	G	GS	CG	SH	SV	IP	H	R	HR	HB	BB	SO	RAT	ERA	ERA+	OAV	OOB	BH	AVG	PB	PR	PR+	PD	TPI
1958	Chi-A	1	0	1.000	2	0	0	0	0	3	5	3	0	0	2	1	21.0	6.00	61	.385	.467	0	—	0	-1	-1	0	-0.2

● BILL TROTTER Trotter, William Felix b: 8/10/08, Cisne, Ill. d: 8/26/84, Arlington, Mass. BR/TR, 6'2", 195 lbs. Deb: 4/23/37

YEAR	TM/L	W	L	PCT	G	GS	CG	SH	SV	IP	H	R	HR	HB	BB	SO	RAT	ERA	ERA+	OAV	OOB	BH	AVG	PB	PR	PR+	PD	TPI
1937	StL-A	2	9	.182	34	12	3	0	1	122^1	150	88	14	7	50	37	15.2	5.81	83	.304	.376	1	.030	-3	-16	-13	-2	-1.3
1938	StL-A	0	1	.000	1	1	1	0	0	8	8	7	0	0	0	1	9.0	5.63	88	.242	.242	0	.000	-0	-1	-1	1	0.0
1939	StL-A	6	13	.316	41	13	4	0	0	156^2	205	120	16	5	54	61	15.2	5.34	91	.318	.376	4	.108	-1	-13	-8	1	-0.8
1940	StL-A	7	6	.538	36	4	1	0	2	98	117	56	5	1	31	29	13.7	3.77	122	.300	.353	1	.045	-2	7	9	1	0.9
1941	StL-A	4	2	.667	29	0	0	0	0	49^2	68	35	2	2	19	17	16.1	5.98	72	.332	.394	0	.000	-1	-10	-9	1	-0.9
1942	StL-A	0	1	.000	3	0	0	0	0	2	5	5	0	0	2	0	31.5	18.00	21	.385	.467	0	—	0	-3	-3	0	-0.6
	Was-A	3	1	.750	17	0	0	0	0	40^2	52	29	4	0	14	13	14.6	5.75	63	.304	.357	0	.000	-0	-9	-10	0	-0.8
	Yr	3	2	.600	20	0	0	0	0	42^2	57	34	4	0	16	13	15.4	6.33	58	.310	.365	0	.000	-0	-13	-13	1	-1.4
1944	StL-N	0	1	.000	2	1	0	0	0	6	14	14	5	0	4	0	27.0	13.50	26	.467	.529	0	.000	-0	-7	-7	0	-0.8
Total	7	22	34	.393	163	31	9	0	3	483^1	619	354	46	15	174	158	15.0	5.40	85	.313	.373	6	.055	-7	-52	-40	2	-4.3

● DIZZY TROUT Trout, Paul Howard b: 6/29/15, Sandcut, Ind. d: 2/28/72, Harvey, Ill. BR/TR, 6'2.5", 195 lbs. Deb: 4/25/39 F

YEAR	TM/L	W	L	PCT	G	GS	CG	SH	SV	IP	H	R	HR	HB	BB	SO	RAT	ERA	ERA+	OAV	OOB	BH	AVG	PB	PR	PR+	PD	TPI
1939	Det-A	9	10	.474	33	22	6	0	2	162	168	82	5	4	74	72	13.7	3.61	135	.270	.351	12	.211	-0	18	22	-1	2.1
1940	*Det-A	3	7	.300	33	10	1	0	2	100^2	125	60	4	3	54	64	16.3	4.47	106	.307	.392	4	.129	-2	-1	3	2	0.2
1941	Det-A	9	9	.500	37	18	6	1	2	151^2	144	76	7	2	84	88	13.6	3.74	122	.252	.350	9	.180	0	7	12	1	1.5
1942	Det-A	12	18	.400	35	29	13	1	0	223	214	98	15	4	89	91	12.4	3.43	115	.249	.322	16	.213	2	6	12	4	2.2
1943	Det-A	**20**	12	.625	44	30	18	**5**	6	246^2	204	83	6	0	101	111	11.1	2.48	142	.227	.305	20	.220	2	22	27	4	4.4
1944	Det-A☆	27	14	.659	49	40	**33**	**7**	0	**352^1**	314	104	9	4	83	144	10.2	**2.12**	**168**	.237	.284	36	.271	12	**51**	**54**	7	**8.8**
1945	*Det-A	18	15	.545	41	31	18	4	2	246^1	252	108	8	0	79	97	12.1	3.14	112	.267	.324	25	.245	4	6	10	3	2.1
1946	Det-A	17	13	.567	38	32	23	5	3	276^1	244	85	11	3	97	151	11.2	2.34	156	.238	.306	20	.194	3	36	39	4	5.1
1947	Det-A☆	10	11	.476	32	26	9	2	2	186^1	186	85	6	3	65	74	12.3	3.48	108	.261	.325	11	.162	3	5	6	3	1.4
1948	Det-A	10	14	.417	32	23	11	2	2	183^2	193	87	6	2	73	91	13.1	3.43	127	.269	.338	15	.217	2	18	19	2	2.6
1949	Det-A	3	6	.333	33	0	0	0	3	59^1	68	35	2	0	21	19	13.5	4.40	95	.292	.350	2	.143	0	-1	-2	1	-0.1
1950	Det-A	13	5	.722	34	20	11	1	4	184^2	190	84	13	5	64	88	12.6	3.75	125	.267	.332	12	.190	1	17	19	3	2.1
1951	Det-A	9	14	.391	42	22	7	0	5	191^2	172	98	13	1	75	89	11.6	4.04	103	.240	.312	14	.269	5	2	3	4	1.2
1952	Det-A	1	5	.167	10	2	0	0	1	27	30	16	4	0	19	20	16.3	5.33	71	.286	.395	3	.333	1	-5	-4	1	-0.7
	Bos-A	9	8	.529	26	17	2	0	1	133^2	133	62	3	3	68	57	13.7	3.64	108	.263	.354	6	.136	-1	1	4	1	0.5
	Yr	10	13	.435	36	19	2	0	2	160^2	163	78	7	3	87	77	14.2	3.92	100	.267	.361	9	.170	-1	-4	-0	2	-0.2
1957	Bal-A	0	0	—	2	0	0	0	0	0^1	4	3	0	0	0	0	108.0	81.00	4	.800	.800	0	—	0	-3	-3	0	-0.1
Total	15	170	161	.514	521	322	158	28	35	2725^2	2641	1166	112	34	1046	1256	12.3	3.23	124	.255	.325	205	.213	31	177	221	38	33.3

● STEVE TROUT Trout, Steven Russell b: 7/30/57, Detroit, Mich. BL/TL, 6'4", 195 lbs. Deb: 7/1/78 F

YEAR	TM/L	W	L	PCT	G	GS	CG	SH	SV	IP	H	R	HR	HB	BB	SO	RAT	ERA	ERA+	OAV	OOB	BH	AVG	PB	PR	PR+	PD	TPI
1978	Chi-A	3	0	1.000	4	3	1	0	0	22^1	19	10	0	0	11	11	12.1	4.03	95	.229	.319	0	—	0	-1	-1	-0	-0.1
1979	Chi-A	11	8	.579	34	18	6	2	4	155	165	77	10	5	59	76	13.3	3.89	110	.273	.343	0	—	0	6	6	2	0.9
1980	Chi-A	9	16	.360	32	30	7	2	0	199^2	229	102	14	9	49	89	12.9	3.70	109	.290	.338	0	—	0	8	8	3	1.1
1981	Chi-A	8	7	.533	20	18	3	0	0	124^2	122	53	7	4	38	54	11.8	3.47	103	.261	.322	0	—	0	3	2	0	0.2
1982	Chi-A	6	9	.400	25	19	2	0	0	120^1	130	76	9	2	50	62	13.6	4.26	95	.273	.344	0	—	0	-2	-3	0	-0.3
1983	Chi-N	10	14	.417	34	32	1	0	0	180	217	105	13	2	59	80	13.9	4.65	82	.305	.360	12	.194	1	-20	-16	2	-1.7
1984	*Chi-N	13	7	.650	32	31	6	2	0	190	205	80	7	2	59	81	12.6	3.41	115	.285	.341	8	.131	-1	4	10	4	1.2
1985	Chi-N	9	7	.563	24	24	3	1	0	140^2	142	57	8	1	63	44	13.2	3.39	118	.270	.350	5	.109	-2	3	9	2	1.0
1986	Chi-N	5	7	.417	37	25	0	0	0	161	184	88	6	1	78	69	14.7	4.75	85	.298	.378	9	.209	1	-18	-12	1	-0.7
1987	Chi-N	6	3	.667	11	11	3	2	0	75	72	27	3	1	27	32	12.0	3.00	143	.260	.328	4	.154	-1	9	10	0	1.1
	NY-A	0	4	.000	14	9	0	0	0	46^1	51	36	4	1	37	27	17.3	6.60	67	.274	.397	0	—	0	-11	-12	0	-0.8

YEAR TM/L	W	L	PCT	G	GS	CG	SH	SV	IP	H	R	HR	HB	BB	SO	RAT	ERA	ERA+	OAV	OOB	BH	AVG	PB	PR	PR+	PD	TPI
1988 Sea-A	4	7	.364	15	13	0	0	0	56^{1}	86	53	6	5	31	14	19.5	7.83	53	.361	.445	0	—	0	-24	-22	0	-3.4
1989 Sea-A	4	3	.571	19	3	0	0	0	30	43	27	3	0	17	17	18.0	6.60	61	.333	.411	0	—	0	-9	-8	0	-1.6
Total 12	88	92	.489	301	236	32	9	4	1501^{1}	1665	791	90	33	578	656	13.6	4.18	96	.286	.354	38	.160	-2	-53	-27	14	-3.1

● BOB TROWBRIDGE Trowbridge, Robert b: 6/27/30, Hudson, N.Y. d: 4/3/80, Hudson, N.Y. BR/TR, 6'1", 190 lbs. Deb: 4/22/56

YEAR TM/L	W	L	PCT	G	GS	CG	SH	SV	IP	H	R	HR	HB	BB	SO	RAT	ERA	ERA+	OAV	OOB	BH	AVG	PB	PR	PR+	PD	TPI
1956 Mil-N	3	2	.600	19	4	1	0	0	50^{2}	38	15	4	2	34	40	13.1	2.66	130	.210	.341	0	.000	-1	6	5	0	0.4
1957 *Mil-N	7	5	.583	32	16	3	1	1	126	118	57	9	1	52	75	12.2	3.64	96	.248	.323	4	.103	-2	3	-2	-1	-0.4
1958 Mil-N	1	3	.250	27	4	0	0	1	55	53	26	4	1	26	31	13.1	3.93	90	.252	.338	1	.111	-1	0	-3	-1	-0.3
1959 Mil-N	1	0	1.000	16	0	0	0	1	30^{1}	45	25	2	0	10	22	16.3	5.93	60	.344	.390	0	.000	-0	-7	-9	-0	-0.5
1960 KC-A	1	3	.250	22	1	0	0	2	68^{1}	70	41	6	1	34	33	13.8	4.61	86	.281	.370	1	.056	-1	-6	-5	0	-0.4
Total 5	13	13	.500	116	25	4	1	5	330^{1}	324	164	25	5	156	201	13.2	3.95	91	.260	.344	6	.078	-5	-3	-14	-1	-1.2

● BUN TROY Troy, Robert b: 8/27/1888, Bad Wurzach, Ger. d: 10/7/18, Petit Maujouym, France BR/TR, 6'4", 195 lbs. Deb: 9/15/12

YEAR TM/L	W	L	PCT	G	GS	CG	SH	SV	IP	H	R	HR	HB	BB	SO	RAT	ERA	ERA+	OAV	OOB	BH	AVG	PB	PR	PR+	PD	TPI
1912 Det-A	0	1	.000	1	1	0	0	0	6^{2}	9	4	0	1	3	1	17.6	5.40	60	.346	.433	0	.000	-0	-2	-2	-0	-0.2

● VIRGIL TRUCKS Trucks, Virgil Oliver "Fire" b: 4/26/17, Birmingham, Ala. BR/TR, 5'11", 198 lbs. Deb: 9/27/41 C

YEAR TM/L	W	L	PCT	G	GS	CG	SH	SV	IP	H	R	HR	HB	BB	SO	RAT	ERA	ERA+	OAV	OOB	BH	AVG	PB	PR	PR+	PD	TPI
1941 Det-A	0	0	—	1	0	0	0	0	2	4	2	0	0	0	3	18.0	9.00	50	.500	.500	0	—	0	-1	-1	0	0.0
1942 Det-A	14	8	.636	28	20	8	2	0	167^{2}	147	64	3	2	74	91	12.0	2.74	144	.231	.314	8	.123	-4	17	21	-2	2.1
1943 Det-A	16	10	.615	33	25	10	2	2	202^{2}	170	72	11	1	52	118	9.9	2.84	124	.225	.276	13	.181	-2	10	14	-2	1.4
1945 *Det-A	0	0	—	1	1	0	0	0	5^{1}	3	1	0	0	2	3	8.4	1.69	208	.176	.263	0	.000	-0	1	1	0	0.1
1946 Det-A	14	9	.609	32	29	15	2	0	236^{2}	217	94	23	3	75	161	11.2	3.23	113	.241	.302	17	.179	-1	7	11	-1	0.7
1947 Det-A	10	12	.455	36	26	8	2	2	180^{2}	186	105	14	2	79	108	13.3	4.53	83	.263	.339	19	.271	2	-17	-15	-1	-1.6
1948 Det-A	14	13	.519	43	26	7	0	2	211^{2}	190	97	14	2	85	123	11.8	3.78	115	.240	.315	13	.165	-3	12	13	-1	1.1
1949 Det-A★	19	11	.633	41	32	17	**6**	4	275	209	95	16	4	124	**153**	11.0	2.81	148	.211	.301	12	.120	-6	42	41	-3	3.3
1950 Det-A	3	1	.750	7	7	2	1	0	48^{1}	45	20	6	1	21	25	12.5	3.54	133	.243	.324	3	.150	-1	6	6	1	0.4
1951 Det-A	13	8	.619	37	18	6	1	1	153^{2}	153	81	9	5	75	89	13.6	4.33	96	.262	.350	13	.236	-0	-4	-3	2	-0.2
1952 Det-A	5	19	.208	35	29	8	3	1	197	190	99	12	7	82	129	12.7	3.97	96	.251	.330	12	.188	-0	-7	-4	2	-0.2
1953 StL-A	5	4	.556	16	12	4	2	2	88	83	37	4	4	32	47	12.2	3.07	137	.249	.322	4	.160	-1	9	11	-1	0.9
Chi-A	15	6	.714	24	21	13	3	1	176^{1}	151	60	14	3	67	102	11.3	2.86	141	.232	.306	15	.238	2	22	23	1	2.9
Yr	20	10	.667	40	33	17	5	3	264^{1}	234	97	18	7	99	149	11.6	2.93	139	.238	.312	19	.216	1	31	33	0	3.8
1954 Chi-A★	19	12	.613	40	33	16	**5**	3	264^{2}	224	87	13	1	95	152	10.9	2.79	134	.228	.297	17	.183	-1	27	28	1	3.2
1955 Chi-A	13	8	.619	32	26	7	3	0	175	176	78	19	2	61	91	12.3	3.96	100	.260	.323	8	.125	-3	0	-0	0	-0.3
1956 Det-A	6	5	.545	22	16	3	1	1	120	104	56	15	6	63	43	13.0	3.83	108	.239	.343	11	.244	1	4	4	-1	0.3
1957 KC-A	9	7	.563	48	7	0	0	7	116	106	45	12	2	62	55	13.2	3.03	131	.248	.346	4	.143	-1	10	11	0	1.5
1958 KC-A	0	1	.000	16	0	0	0	3	22	18	7	2	0	15	15	13.5	2.05	191	.222	.344	0	.000	-0	4	4	0	0.3
NY-A	2	1	.667	25	0	0	0	1	39^{2}	40	24	1	2	24	26	15.0	4.54	78	.265	.373	2	.250	0	-3	-5	-0	-0.4
Yr	2	2	.500	41	0	0	0	4	61^{2}	58	31	3	2	39	41	14.4	3.65	100	.250	.363	2	.222	0	1	0	-0	-0.1
Total 17	177	135	.567	517	328	124	33	30	2682^{1}	2416	1124	188	47	1088	1534	11.9	3.39	117	.240	.317	171	.180	-19	141	164	-5	15.5

● MIKE TRUJILLO Trujillo, Michael Andrew b: 1/12/60, Denver, Colo. BR/TR, 6'1", 180 lbs. Deb: 4/14/85

YEAR TM/L	W	L	PCT	G	GS	CG	SH	SV	IP	H	R	HR	HB	BB	SO	RAT	ERA	ERA+	OAV	OOB	BH	AVG	PB	PR	PR+	PD	TPI
1985 Bos-A	4	4	.500	27	7	1	0	1	84	112	55	7	3	23	19	14.8	4.82	89	.320	.367	0	—	0	-6	-5	2	-0.3
1986 Bos-A	0	0	—	3	0	0	0	0	5^{2}	7	6	0	0	6	4	20.6	9.53	44	.304	.448	0	—	0	-3	-3	1	-0.1
Sea-A	3	2	.600	11	4	1	1	1	41^{1}	32	11	5	0	15	19	10.2	2.40	178	.215	.287	0	—	0	8	8	-0	1.0
Yr	3	2	.600	14	4	1	1	1	47	39	17	5	0	21	23	11.5	3.26	130	.227	.311	0	—	0	5	5	0	0.9
1987 Sea-A	4	4	.500	28	7	0	0	1	65^{2}	70	46	12	2	26	36	13.4	6.17	77	.277	.349	0	—	0	-12	-10	-1	-1.1
1988 Det-A	0	0	—	6	0	0	0	0	12^{1}	11	7	2	0	5	5	11.7	5.11	75	.234	.308	0	—	0	-2	-2	-0	-0.1
1989 Det-A	1	2	.333	8	4	1	0	0	25^{2}	35	17	3	0	13	13	16.8	5.96	64	.333	.407	0	—	0	-6	-6	0	-0.6
Total 5	12	12	.500	83	22	3	1	3	234^{2}	267	142	29	5	88	96	13.8	5.02	86	.288	.353	0	—	0	-21	-18	2	-1.2

● ED TRUMBULL Trumbull, Edward J. (b: Edward J. Trembly) b: 11/3/1860, Chicopee, Mass. d: 1/14/37, Kingston, Pa. Deb: 5/10/1884 ♦

YEAR TM/L	W	L	PCT	G	GS	CG	SH	SV	IP	H	R	HR	HB	BB	SO	RAT	ERA	ERA+	OAV	OOB	BH	AVG	PB	PR	PR+	PD	TPI
1884 Was-a	1	9	.100	10	10	10	0	0	84	108	90	4	1	31	43	15.0	4.71	64	.295	.352	10	.116	-2	-14	-17	-1	-1.7

● GEORGE TSAMIS Tsamis, George Alex b: 6/14/67, Campbell, Cal. BR/TL, 6'2", 190 lbs. Deb: 4/26/93

YEAR TM/L	W	L	PCT	G	GS	CG	SH	SV	IP	H	R	HR	HB	BB	SO	RAT	ERA	ERA+	OAV	OOB	BH	AVG	PB	PR	PR+	PD	TPI
1993 Min-A	1	2	.333	41	0	0	0	1	68^{1}	86	51	9	3	27	30	15.3	6.19	71	.317	.385	0	—	0	-14	-14	1	-0.5

● JOHN TSITOURIS Tsitouris, John Philip b: 5/4/36, Monroe, N.C. BR/TR, 6', 175 lbs. Deb: 6/13/57

YEAR TM/L	W	L	PCT	G	GS	CG	SH	SV	IP	H	R	HR	HB	BB	SO	RAT	ERA	ERA+	OAV	OOB	BH	AVG	PB	PR	PR+	PD	TPI
1957 Det-A	1	0	1.000	2	0	0	0	0	3^{1}	8	3	0	0	2	2	27.0	8.10	48	.500	.556	0	.000	-0	-2	-2	0	-0.3
1958 KC-A	0	0	—	1	1	0	0	0	3	2	1	0	0	2	1	12.0	3.00	130	.182	.308	0	.000	-0	0	0	0	0.0
1959 KC-A	4	3	.571	24	10	0	0	0	83^{1}	90	52	3	3	35	50	13.8	4.97	81	.271	.346	3	.150	-1	-10	-9	-1	-0.8
1960 KC-A	0	2	.000	14	2	0	0	0	33	38	25	3	8	21	12	18.3	6.55	61	.297	.427	0	.000	-1	-10	-9	0	-0.6
1962 Cin-N	1	0	1.000	4	2	1	1	0	21^{1}	13	2	0	3	7	7	9.7	0.84	477	.181	.280	0	.000	-1	7	7	-0	0.3
1963 Cin-N	12	8	.600	30	21	8	3	0	191	167	73	20	11	38	113	10.2	3.16	106	.232	.281	5	.081	-3	3	4	-3	-0.3
1964 Cin-N	9	13	.409	37	24	6	1	2	175^{1}	178	90	20	5	75	146	13.2	3.80	95	.263	.340	11	.190	2	-5	-4	-1	-0.3
1965 Cin-N	6	9	.400	31	20	3	0	1	131	134	87	18	9	65	91	14.3	4.95	76	.265	.359	3	.070	-2	-20	-16	-1	-2.1
1966 Cin-N	0	0	—	1	0	0	0	0	1	3	2	0	0	1	0	36.0	18.00	22	.750	.800	0	—	0	-2	-1	-0	-0.1
1967 Cin-N	1	0	1.000	2	1	0	0	0	8	4	3	1	0	6	4	11.3	3.38	111	.154	.313	0	—	0	0	0	0	0.1
1968 Cin-N	0	3	.000	3	3	0	0	0	12^{2}	16	10	6	1	8	6	17.8	7.11	44	.302	.403	0	.000	0	-6	-5	0	-1.0
Total 11	34	38	.472	149	84	18	5	3	663	653	348	71	40	260	432	12.9	4.13	88	.257	.335	22	.111	-6	-44	-35	-5	-5.1

● T.J. TUCKER Tucker, Thomas John b: 8/20/78, Clearwater, Fla. BR/TR, 6'3", 245 lbs. Deb: 6/3/2000

YEAR TM/L	W	L	PCT	G	GS	CG	SH	SV	IP	H	R	HR	HB	BB	SO	RAT	ERA	ERA+	OAV	OOB	BH	AVG	PB	PR	PR+	PD	TPI
2000 Mon-N	0	1	.000	2	2	0	0	0	7	11	9	5	0	3	2	18.0	11.57	41	.344	.400	1	1.000	0	-5	-5	-0	-0.5

● TOMMY TUCKER Tucker, Thomas Joseph "Foghorn" b: 10/28/1863, Holyoke, Mass. d: 10/22/35, Montague, Mass. BB/TR, 5'11", 165 lbs. Deb: 4/16/1887 ♦

YEAR TM/L	W	L	PCT	G	GS	CG	SH	SV	IP	H	R	HR	HB	BB	SO	RAT	ERA	ERA+	OAV	OOB	BH	AVG	PB	PR	PR+	PD	TPI
1888 Bal-a	0	0	—	1	0	0	0	0	2^{1}	4	1	0	0	0	2	15.4	3.86	77	.364	.364	149	.287	0	-0	-0	-0	0.0
1891 Bos-N	0	0	—	1	0	0	0	0	1	3	2	0	0	0	0	27.0	9.00	41	.500	.500	148	.270	0	-1	-1	-0	0.0
Total 2	0	0	—	2	0	0	0	0	3^{1}	7	3	0	0	0	2	18.9	5.40	59	.412	.412	1911	.294	0	-1	-1	-0	0.0

● TOM TUCKEY Tuckey, Thomas H. "Tabasco Tom" b: 10/7/1883, Birmingham, England d: 10/17/50, New York, N.Y. 6'3", Deb: 8/11/08

YEAR TM/L	W	L	PCT	G	GS	CG	SH	SV	IP	H	R	HR	HB	BB	SO	RAT	ERA	ERA+	OAV	OOB	BH	AVG	PB	PR	PR+	PD	TPI
1908 Bos-N	3	3	.500	8	8	3	1	0	72	60	21	2	4	20	26	10.5	2.50	96	.265	.336	1	.050	-2	-1	-1	0	-0.2
1909 Bos-N	0	9	.000	17	10	4	0	0	90^{2}	104	59	1	3	22	16	12.8	4.27	66	.295	.342	4	.138	-1	-17	-13	1	-1.3
Total 2	3	12	.200	25	18	7	1	0	162^{2}	164	80	3	7	42	42	11.8	3.49	76	.284	.340	5	.102	-3	-18	-15	1	-1.5

● JOHN TUDOR Tudor, John Thomas b: 2/2/54, Schenectady, N.Y. BL/TL, 6', 185 lbs. Deb: 8/16/79

YEAR TM/L	W	L	PCT	G	GS	CG	SH	SV	IP	H	R	HR	HB	BB	SO	RAT	ERA	ERA+	OAV	OOB	BH	AVG	PB	PR	PR+	PD	TPI
1979 Bos-A	1	2	.333	6	6	1	0	0	28	39	23	2	0	9	11	15.4	6.43	69	.345	.393	0	—	0	-7	-6	1	-0.5
1980 Bos-A	8	5	.615	16	13	5	0	0	92^{1}	81	35	4	3	31	45	11.2	3.02	140	.238	.307	0	—	0	10	12	2	1.8
1981 Bos-A	4	3	.571	18	11	2	0	1	78^{2}	74	44	11	3	28	44	12.0	4.58	85	.252	.323	0	—	0	-8	-6	1	-0.4
1982 Bos-A	13	10	.565	32	30	6	1	0	195^{2}	215	90	20	8	59	146	13.0	3.63	119	.280	.338	0	—	0	10	14	2	1.8
1983 Bos-A	13	12	.520	34	34	7	2	0	242	236	122	32	4	81	136	11.9	4.09	107	.255	.317	0	—	0	-0	7	-1	0.5
1984 Pit-N	12	11	.522	32	32	6	1	0	212	200	81	19	1	56	117	10.9	3.27	110	.248	.297	16	.211	2	8	8	-1	1.0
1985 *StL-N	21	8	.724	36	36	14	**10**	0	275	209	68	14	5	49	169	**8.6**	1.93	183	.209	**.249**	13	.138	1	51	50	1	5.7
1986 StL-N	13	7	.650	30	30	3	0	0	219	197	81	22	1	53	107	10.3	2.92	125	.244	.291	11	.153	-0	20	18	1	1.6
1987 *StL-N	10	2	.833	16	16	0	0	0	96	100	43	11	1	32	54	12.5	3.84	108	.272	.333	7	.200	1	3	3	1	0.6
1988 StL-N	6	5	.545	21	21	4	1	0	145^{1}	131	44	5	1	31	55	10.1	2.29	152	.247	.290	5	.109	-1	19	19	0	1.5
*LA-N	4	3	.571	9	9	1	0	0	52^{1}	58	16	5	0	10	32	11.7	2.41	139	.284	.318	0	.000	-1	6	6	0	0.7
Yr	10	8	.556	30	30	5	1	0	197^{2}	189	60	10	1	41	87	10.5	2.32	148	.257	.297	5	.085	-2	25	25	1	2.2
1989 LA-N	0	0	—	6	3	0	0	0	14^{1}	17	5	1	0	6	9	14.4	3.14	109	.309	.377	0	.000	-0	1	0	0	0.0
1990 StL-N	12	4	.750	25	22	1	1	0	146^{1}	120	48	10	2	30	63	9.3	2.40	159	.225	.269	7	.152	0	23	23	2	2.7
Total 12	117	72	.619	281	263	50	16	1	1797	1677	700	156	29	475	988	10.9	3.12	124	.248	.301	59	.154	3	134	145	9	17.0

● OSCAR TUERO Tuero, Oscar (Monzon) (b: Oscar Tuero Monzon) b: 12/17/1898, Canada d: 10/21/60, Houston, Tex. BR/TR, 5'8.5", 158 lbs. Deb: 5/30/18

YEAR TM/L	W	L	PCT	G	GS	CG	SH	SV	IP	H	R	HR	HB	BB	SO	RAT	ERA	ERA+	OAV	OOB	BH	AVG	PB	PR	PR+	PD	TPI
1918 StL-N	1	2	.333	11	3	2	0	0	44^{1}	32	12	0	3	10	13	9.1	1.02	267	.208	.269	3	.250	0	9	9	-1	0.6
1919 StL-N	5	7	.417	**45**	16	4	0	**4**	154^{2}	137	71	4	10	42	45	11.0	3.20	87	.242	.306	8	.205	1	-5	-7	-0	-0.5

YEAR	TM/L	W	L	PCT	G	GS	CG	SH	SV	IP	H	R	HR	HB	BB	SO	RAT	ERA	ERA+	OAV	OOB	BH	AVG	PB	PR	PR+	PD	TPI
1920	StL-N	0	0	—	2	0	0	0	0	0^2	5	4	0	0	1	0	81.0	54.00	6	.833	.857	0	—	0	-4	-4	-0	-0.2
Total	3	6	9	.400	58	19	6	0	4	199^2	174	87	4	13	53	58	10.8	2.88	96	.240	.303	11	.216	1	-0	-2	-1	-0.1
● BOB TUFTS	Tufts, Robert Malcolm b: 11/2/55, Medford, Mass. BL/TL, 6'5", 215 lbs. Deb: 8/10/81																											
1981	SF-N	0	0	—	11	0	0	0	0	15^1	20	9	1	1	6	12	15.8	3.52	97	.308	.375	0	.000	-0	-0	-0	1	0.0
1982	KC-A	2	0	1.000	10	0	0	0	2	20	24	10	3	0	3	13	12.1	4.50	91	.293	.318	0	—	0	-1	-1	-1	-0.2
1983	KC-A	0	0	—	6	0	0	0	0	6^2	16	8	1	1	5	3	29.7	8.10	50	.444	.524	0	—	0	-3	-3	0	-0.1
Total	3	2	0	1.000	27	0	0	0	2	42	60	27	5	2	14	28	16.3	4.71	82	.328	.382	0	.000	-0	-4	-4	0	-0.3
● LEE TUNNELL	Tunnell, Byron Lee b: 10/30/60, Tyler, Tex. BR/TR, 6'1", 180 lbs. Deb: 9/4/82																											
1982	Pit-N	1	1	.500	5	3	0	0	0	18^1	17	8	1	2	5	4	11.8	3.93	95	.254	.324	0	.000	-0	-1	-0	0	-0.1
1983	Pit-N	11	6	.647	35	25	5	3	0	177^2	167	81	15	2	58	95	11.5	3.65	102	.252	.314	7	.121	-1	-0	1	2	0.2
1984	Pit-N	1	7	.125	26	6	0	0	1	68^1	81	44	6	0	40	51	15.9	5.27	68	.298	.388	1	.083	-1	-13	-13	1	-1.3
1985	Pit-N	4	10	.286	24	23	0	0	0	132^1	126	70	11	1	57	74	12.5	4.01	89	.251	.329	4	.085	-2	-6	-6	1	-0.8
1987	*StL-N	4	4	.500	32	9	0	0	0	74^1	90	45	5	1	34	49	15.1	4.84	86	.307	.381	4	.235	0	-6	-6	0	-0.4
1989	Min-A	1	0	1.000	10	0	0	0	0	12	18	8	1	0	6	7	18.0	6.00	69	.340	.407	0	—	0	-3	-2	-0	-0.2
Total	6	22	28	.440	132	66	5	3	1	483	499	256	39	6	200	280	13.1	4.23	88	.270	.343	16	.116	-4	-29	-26	4	-2.6
● GEORGE TURBEVILLE	Turbeville, George Elkins b: 8/24/14, Turbeville, S.C. d: 10/5/83, Salisbury, N.C. BR/TL, 6'1", 175 lbs. Deb: 7/20/35																											
1935	Phi-A	0	3	.000	19	6	2	0	0	63^2	74	58	2	0	69	20	20.2	7.63	60	.312	.467	2	.105	-2	-22	-21	-1	-1.2
1936	Phi-A	2	5	.286	12	6	2	0	0	43^2	42	36	6	6	32	10	16.5	6.39	80	.258	.398	2	.143	-1	-7	-6	-0	-0.8
1937	Phi-A	0	4	.000	31	3	0	0	0	77^1	80	50	2	0	56	17	15.8	4.77	99	.266	.381	6	.231	0	-1	-0	-1	-0.1
Total	3	2	12	.143	62	15	4	0	0	184^2	196	144	10	6	157	47	17.5	6.14	77	.280	.416	10	.169	-2	-30	-28	-2	-2.1
● LUCAS TURK	Turk, Lucas Newton "Harlem" or "Chief" b: 5/2/1898, Homer, Ga. d: 1/11/94, Homer, Ga. BR/TR, 6', 165 lbs. Deb: 6/7/22																											
1922	Was-A	0	0	—	5	0	0	0	0	11^2	16	10	0	0	5	1	16.2	6.94	56	.340	.404	1	.250	0	-4	-4	-1	-0.3
● BOB TURLEY	Turley, Robert Lee "Bullet Bob" b: 9/19/30, Troy, Ill. BR/TR, 6'2", 215 lbs. Deb: 9/29/51 C																											
1951	StL-A	0	1	.000	1	1	0	0	0	7^1	11	6	0	0	3	5	17.2	7.36	60	.355	.412	0	.000	-0	-3	-2	0	-0.3
1953	StL-A	2	6	.250	10	7	3	1	0	60^1	39	24	4	2	44	61	12.7	3.28	128	.184	.329	5	.278	1	5	6	-1	0.8
1954	Bal-A☆	14	15	.483	35	35	14	0	0	247^1	178	106	7	7	181	**185**	13.3	3.46	104	**.203**	.343	11	.136	-3	7	4	-1	0.1
1955	*NY-A☆	17	13	.567	36	34	13	6	1	246^2	168	92	16	7	177	210	12.8	3.06	122	**.193**	.333	11	.134	-0	25	20	-2	2.0
1956	*NY-A	8	4	.667	27	21	5	1	1	132	138	76	13	4	103	91	16.7	5.05	77	.273	.400	8	.174	-0	-13	-19	-1	-1.6
1957	*NY-A	13	6	.684	32	23	9	4	3	176^1	120	59	17	9	85	152	10.9	2.71	133	**.194**	.300	5	.088	-2	21	18	-0	1.7
1958	*NY-A★	**21**	7	**.750**	33	31	**19**	6	1	245^1	178	82	24	8	128	168	11.5	2.97	119	**.206**	.313	12	.136	-1	22	16	-2	1.5
1959	NY-A	8	11	.421	33	22	7	3	0	154^1	141	80	15	3	83	111	13.2	4.32	84	.245	.343	4	.087	-2	-8	-12	-1	-1.6
1960	*NY-A	9	3	.750	34	24	4	1	5	173^1	138	67	14	5	87	87	11.9	3.27	110	.222	.322	4	.073	-4	12	6	-1	0.0
1961	NY-A	3	5	.375	15	12	1	0	0	72	74	47	11	4	51	48	16.1	5.75	65	.269	.391	2	.095	-1	-14	-18	-1	-1.8
1962	NY-A	3	3	.500	24	8	0	0	1	69	68	45	8	4	47	42	15.5	4.57	82	.263	.384	0	.000	-1	-5	-7	1	-0.6
1963	LA-A	2	7	.222	19	12	3	2	0	87^1	71	41	5	2	51	70	12.8	3.30	104	.222	.332	4	.160	1	3	1	-0	0.2
	Bos-A	1	4	.200	11	7	0	0	0	41^1	42	28	6	1	28	35	15.5	6.10	62	.256	.368	3	.214	0	-11	-10	-0	-1.1
	Yr	3	11	.214	30	19	3	2	0	128^2	113	69	11	3	79	105	13.6	4.20	84	.233	.345	7	.179	1	-8	-10	-1	-0.9
Total	12	101	85	.543	310	237	78	24	12	1712^2	1366	753	140	56	1068	1265	13.1	3.64	101	.220	.340	69	.126	-12	41	4	-9	-0.7
● DERRICK TURNBOW	Turnbow, Thomas Derrick b: 1/25/78, Union City, Tenn. BR/TR, 6'3", 195 lbs. Deb: 4/17/2000																											
2000	Ana-A	0	0	—	24	1	0	0	0	38	36	21	7	2	36	25	17.5	4.74	105	.254	.411	0	—	0	1	1	-1	0.0
● TUCK TURNER	Turner, George A. b: 2/13/1873, W.New Brighton, N.Y. d: 7/16/45, Staten Island, N.Y. BB/TL, 5'6.5", 155 lbs. Deb: 8/18/1893 ♦																											
1894	Phi-N	0	0	—	1	0	0	0	0	6	9	5	1	1	2	3	18.0	7.50	68	.346	.414	145	.418	1	-1	-2	-0	0.0
● JIM TURNER	Turner, James Riley "Milkman Jim" b: 8/6/03, Antioch, Tenn. d: 11/29/98, Nashville, Tenn. BL/TR, 6', 185 lbs. Deb: 4/30/37 C																											
1937	Bos-N	20	11	.645	33	30	**24**	**5**	1	256^2	228	80	13	0	52	69	**9.8**	**2.38**	**150**	.235	**.274**	24	.250	4	**44**	**37**	-0	**4.9**
1938	Bos-N☆	14	18	.438	35	34	22	3	0	268	267	123	21	5	54	71	10.9	3.46	99	.259	.299	22	.229	4	10	-1	4	0.8
1939	Bos-N	4	11	.267	25	22	9	0	0	157^2	181	83	10	4	51	50	13.5	4.28	86	.293	.351	13	.236	2	-6	-11	1	-0.6
1940	*Cin-N	14	7	.667	24	23	11	0	0	187	187	70	9	0	32	53	10.5	2.89	131	.264	.296	18	.240	3	20	19	-1	2.3
1941	Cin-N	6	4	.600	23	10	3	0	0	113	120	49	5	1	24	34	11.5	3.11	116	.277	.317	6	.146	-1	7	6	2	0.6
1942	Cin-N	0	0	—	3	0	0	0	0	3^1	5	5	1	0	3	0	21.6	10.80	30	.333	.444	0	.000	-0	-3	-3	0	-0.1
	*NY-A	1	1	.500	5	0	0	0	1	7	4	1	0	0	1	2	6.4	1.29	268	.167	.200	0	.000	-0	2	2	0	0.4
1943	NY-A	3	0	1.000	18	0	0	0	1	43^1	44	22	1	0	13	15	11.8	3.53	91	.260	.313	1	.077	-1	-1	-2	-0	-0.3
1944	NY-A	4	4	.500	35	0	0	0	7	41^2	42	23	3	0	22	13	13.8	3.46	101	.264	.354	2	.200	0	-0	0	-1	0.0
1945	NY-A	3	4	.429	30	0	0	0	**10**	54^1	45	26	4	0	31	22	12.6	3.64	95	.225	.329	1	.091	-1	-2	-1	1	-0.2
Total	9	69	60	.535	231	119	69	8	20	1132	1123	482	67	10	283	329	11.3	3.22	111	.260	.307	87	.218	12	70	48	6	7.8
● KEN TURNER	Turner, Kenneth Charles b: 8/17/43, Framingham, Mass. BR/TL, 6'2", 190 lbs. Deb: 6/11/67																											
1967	Cal-A	1	2	.333	13	1	0	0	0	17^1	16	9	4	1	4	6	10.9	4.15	76	.239	.292	0	.000	-0	-2	-2	0	-0.3
● TED TURNER	Turner, Theodore Holhot b: 5/4/1892, Lawrenceburg, Ky. d: 2/4/58, Lexington, Ky. BR/TR, 6', 180 lbs. Deb: 4/20/20																											
1920	Chi-N	0	0	—	1	0	0	0	0	1^1	2	2	0	0	1	0	20.3	13.50	24	.400	.500	0	.000	-0	-2	-1	-0	-0.1
● TINK TURNER	Turner, Thomas Lovatt b: 2/20/1890, Swarthmore, Pa. d: 2/25/62, Philadelphia, Pa. BR/TR, 6'1", 190 lbs. Deb: 9/24/15																											
1915	Phi-A	0	1	.000	1	1	0	0	0	2	5	6	1	0	3	0	36.0	22.50	13	.500	.615	0	—	0	-4	-4	0	-0.6
● MATT TURNER	Turner, William Matthew b: 2/18/67, Lexington, Ky. BR/TR, 6'5", 215 lbs. Deb: 4/23/93																											
1993	Fla-N	4	5	.444	55	0	0	0	0	68	55	23	7	1	26	59	10.9	2.91	149	.227	.305	0	.000	-0	9	10	0	1.2
1994	Cle-A	1	0	1.000	9	0	0	0	1	12^2	13	6	0	3	7	5	16.3	2.13	222	.241	.359	0	—	0	4	4	-1	0.3
Total	2	5	5	.500	64	0	0	0	1	80^2	68	29	7	4	33	64	11.7	2.79	158	.230	.315	0	.000	-0	12	14	-0	1.5
● ELMER TUTWILER	Tutwiler, Elmer Strange b: 11/19/05, Carbon Hill, Ala. d: 5/3/76, Pensacola, Fla. BR/TR, 5'11", 158 lbs. Deb: 8/20/28																											
1928	Pit-N	0	0	—	2	0	0	0	0	3^2	4	2	0	0	0	1	9.8	4.91	83	.267	.267	0	.000	-0	-0	-0	-0	0.0
● TWINK TWINING	Twining, Howard Earle "Doc" b: 5/30/1894, Horsham, Pa. d: 6/14/73, Lansdale, Pa. BR/TR, 6', 168 lbs. Deb: 7/9/16																											
1916	Cin-N	0	0	—	1	0	0	0	0	2	4	3	1	1	1	0	27.0	13.50	19	.444	.545	0	—	0	-2	-2	0	-0.1
● LARRY TWITCHELL	Twitchell, Lawrence Grant b: 2/18/1864, Cleveland, Ohio d: 8/23/30, Cleveland, Ohio BR/TR, 6', 185 lbs. Deb: 4/30/1886 ♦																											
1886	Det-N	0	2	.000	4	4	2	0	0	25	35	22	1		12	6	16.9	6.48	51	.347	.416	1	.063	-2	-9	-9	1	-0.6
1887	*Det-N	11	1	.917	15	12	11	0	**1**	112^1	156	74	3	10	36	24	13.3	4.33	94	.322	.336	96	.353	4	-3	-3	-1	-0.2
1888	Det-N	0	0	—	2	0	0	0	1	4	6	3	1	0	0	3	13.5	6.75	41	.375	.375	128	.244	0	-2	-2	0	-0.1
1889	Cle-N	0	0	—	1	0	0	0	0	1	0	0	0	0	1	0	9.0	0.00	—	.000	.250	151	.275	0	0	0	-0	0.0
1890	Buf-P	5	7	.417	13	12	12	0	0	104^1	112	77	3	15	72	29	17.2	4.57	90	.262	.387	38	.221	1	-4	-6	2	-0.2
1891	Col-a	1	1	.500	6	1	1	0	0	31	29	22	1	3	13	8	13.1	4.06	85	.240	.328	62	.277	2	-1	-2	-0	0.0
1894	Lou-N	0	0	—	1	0	0	0	0	3	5	2	1	0	1	0	18.0	6.00	85	.357	.400	56	.267	0	-0	-0	0	0.0
Total	7	17	11	.607	42	29	26	0	2	280^2	343	200	10	28	135	70	15.1	4.62	85	.294	.363	684	.265	7	-19	-22	1	-1.1
● WAYNE TWITCHELL	Twitchell, Wayne Lee b: 3/10/48, Portland, Ore. BR/TR, 6'6", 220 lbs. Deb: 9/7/70																											
1970	Mil-A	0	0	—	2	0	0	0	0	1^2	3	2	0	0	1	5	21.6	10.80	35	.333	.400	0	—	0	-1	-1	0	-0.1
1971	Phi-N	1	0	1.000	6	1	0	0	0	16	8	4	1	1	10	15	10.7	0.00	—	.145	.288	0	.000	-0	6	6	-0	0.3
1972	Phi-N	5	9	.357	49	15	1	1	1	139^2	138	72	6	2	56	112	12.6	4.06	89	.259	.332	2	.071	-2	-9	-7	-1	-1.0
1973	Phi-N★	13	9	.591	34	28	10	5	0	223^1	172	71	16	10	99	169	11.3	2.50	152	.219	.314	7	.097	-4	29	31	-3	2.3
1974	Phi-N	6	9	.400	25	18	2	0	0	112^1	122	71	11	7	65	72	15.5	5.21	73	.276	.377	6	.171	-1	-20	-17	-2	-2.2
1975	Phi-N	5	10	.333	36	20	0	0	0	134^1	132	82	10	1	78	101	14.1	4.42	85	.261	.361	3	.088	-2	-12	-10	-3	-1.5
1976	Phi-N	3	1	.750	26	2	0	0	1	61^2	55	18	3	3	18	67	11.1	1.75	203	.241	.305	1	.167	0	12	12	0	0.9
1977	Phi-N	0	5	.000	12	8	0	0	0	45^2	50	27	3	0	25	37	14.8	4.53	88	.287	.377	1	.091	-0	-3	-3	1	-0.3
	Mon-N	6	5	.545	22	22	2	0	0	139	116	71	18	5	49	93	11.0	4.21	91	.230	.304	8	.205	2	-5	-6	-1	-0.3

YEAR	TM/L	W	L	PCT	G	GS	CG	SH	SV	IP	H	R	HR	HB	BB	SO	RAT	ERA	ERA+	OAV	OOB	BH	AVG	PB	PR	PR+	PD	TPI
	Yr	6	10	.375	34	30	2	0	0	184^2	166	98	21	5	74	130	11.9	4.29	90	.244	.323	9	.180	2	-8	-9	-0	-0.6
1978	Mon-N	4	12	.250	33	15	0	0	0	112	121	68	16	5	71	69	15.8	5.38	66	.286	.395	2	.083	-1	-22	-23	-1	-3.2
1979	NY-N	5	3	.625	33	2	0	0	0	63^2	55	44	6	4	55	44	16.1	5.23	70	.243	.400	3	.375	1	-11	-11	-0	-1.3
	Sea-A	0	2	.000	4	2	0	0	0	13^2	11	11	2	2	10	5	15.1	5.27	83	.220	.371	0	—	0	-2	-1	-0	-0.2
Total	10	48	65	.425	282	133	15	6	2	1063	983	541	92	40	537	789	13.2	3.98	94	.250	.346	33	.127	-6	-37	-29	-10	-6.6
● **JEFF TWITTY**	Twitty, Jeffrey Dean b: 11/10/57, Lancaster, S.C. BL/TL, 6'2", 185 lbs. Deb: 7/5/80																											
1980	KC-A	2	1	.667	13	0	0	0	0	22^1	33	17	4	0	7	9	16.1	6.04	67	.351	.396	0	—	0	-5	-5	0	-0.6
● **CY TWOMBLY**	Twombly, Edwin Parker b: 6/15/1897, Groveland, Mass. d: 12/3/74, Savannah, Ga. BR/TR, 5'10.5", 170 lbs. Deb: 6/25/21																											
1921	Chi-A	1	2	.333	7	4	0	0	0	27^2	26	21	1	2	25	7	17.2	5.86	72	.283	.445	0	.000	-2	-5	-5	1	-0.5
● **LEFTY TYLER**	Tyler, George Albert b: 12/14/1889, Derry, N.H. d: 9/29/53, Lowell, Mass. BL/TL, 6', 175 lbs. Deb: 9/20/10 F																											
1910	Bos-N	0	0	—	2	0	0	0	0	11^1	11	3	1	0	6	6	13.5	2.38	140	.275	.370	2	.500	1	1	1	-0	0.1
1911	Bos-N	7	10	.412	28	20	10	1	0	165^1	150	118	11	10	109	90	14.6	5.06	76	.243	.365	10	.164	-1	-31	-20	3	-1.6
1912	Bos-N	12	22	.353	42	31	15	1	0	256^1	262	150	8	10	126	144	14.0	4.18	86	.276	.367	19	.198	-1	-22	-16	4	-1.7
1913	Bos-N	16	17	.485	39	34	**28**	4	2	290^1	245	131	2	11	108	143	11.3	2.79	118	.235	.313	21	.206	4	13	16	7	2.9
1914	*Bos-N	16	13	.552	38	34	21	5	2	271^1	247	113	7	14	101	140	12.0	2.69	103	.249	.327	19	.202	1	3	2	-2	0.1
1915	Bos-N	10	9	.526	32	24	15	1	0	204^2	182	87	6	5	84	89	11.9	2.86	91	.243	.324	23	.261	8	-2	-6	-1	0.1
1916	Bos-N	17	9	.654	34	28	21	6	1	249^1	200	79	6	3	58	117	9.4	2.02	123	.226	.276	19	.204	7	17	14	2	2.6
1917	Bos-N	14	12	.538	32	28	22	4	1	239	203	81	1	6	86	98	11.1	2.52	101	.240	.314	31	.231	4	5	1	3	1.1
1918	*Chi-N	19	8	.704	33	30	22	6	1	269^1	218	72	1	5	67	102	9.7	2.00	139	.226	.279	21	.210	1	23	23	3	3.0
1919	Chi-N	2	2	.500	6	5	3	0	0	30	20	8	0	0	13	9	9.9	2.10	137	.196	.287	1	.143	1	3	3	1	0.6
1920	Chi-N	11	12	.478	27	27	18	2	0	193	193	83	6	3	57	57	11.8	3.31	97	.268	.324	17	.262	4	-4	-2	3	0.6
1921	Chi-N	3	2	.600	10	6	4	0	0	50	59	22	2	0	14	8	13.1	3.24	118	.294	.340	6	.231	1	3	3	-1	0.3
Total	12	127	116	.523	323	267	179	30	7	2230	1990	947	51	67	829	1003	11.6	2.95	101	.245	.320	189	.217	30	9	11	21	8.1
● **JIM TYNG**	Tyng, James Alexander b: 3/27/1856, Philadelphia, Pa. d: 10/30/31, New York, N.Y. 5'9", 155 lbs. Deb: 9/23/1879																											
1879	Bos-N	1	2	.333	3	3	3	0	0	27	35	25	0		6	7	13.7	5.00	50	.292	.325	5	.357	1	-8	-8	0	-0.5
1888	Phi-N	0	0	—	1	0	0	0	1	4	8	4	0	1	2	2	24.8	4.50	66	.381	.458	0	.000	-0	-1	-1	0	0.0
Total	2	1	2	.333	4	3	3	0	1	31	43	29	0	1	8	9	15.1	4.94	51	.305	.347	5	.333	1	-8	-8	0	-0.5
● **DAVE TYRIVER**	Tyriver, David Burton b: 10/31/37, Oshkosh, Wis. d: 10/28/88, Oshkosh, Wis. BR/TR, 6' ", 175 lbs. Deb: 8/21/62																											
1962	Cle-A	0	0	—	4	0	0	0	0	10^2	10	6	2	1	7	7	15.2	4.22	92	.250	.375	0	.000	-0	-0	-0	0	0.0
● **JIMMY UCHRINSCKO**	Uchrinscko, James Emerson b: 10/20/1900, W.Newton, Pa. d: 3/17/95, Mt.Pleasant, Pa. BL/TR, 6', 180 lbs. Deb: 7/20/26																											
1926	Was-A	0	0	—	3	0	0	0	0	8	13	9	0	0	8	0	23.6	10.13	38	.433	.553	0	.000	-0	-5	-6	0	-0.3
● **BOB UHL**	Uhl, Robert Ellwood "Lefty" b: 9/17/13, San Francisco, Cal. d: 8/21/90, Santa Rosa, Cal. BB/TL, 5'11", 175 lbs. Deb: 5/8/38																											
1938	Chi-A	0	0	—	1	0	0	0	0	2	1	0	0	0	0	0	4.5	0.00	—	.167	.167	0	—	0	1	1	-0	0.0
1940	Det-A	0	0	—	1	0	0	0	0	0	4	0	0	2	—	—	∞	—	1.000	1.000	109	—	0	-4	-4	0	-0.3	
Total	2	0	0	—	2	0	0	0	0	2	5	5	0	0	2	0	31.5	18.00	27	.500	.583	0	—	0	-3	-3	-0	-0.3
● **GEORGE UHLE**	Uhle, George Ernest "The Bull" b: 9/18/1898, Cleveland, Ohio d: 2/26/85, Lakewood, Ohio BR/TR, 6', 190 lbs. Deb: 4/30/19 C♦																											
1919	Cle-A	10	5	.667	26	12	7	1	0	127	129	52	1	7	43	50	12.7	2.91	115	.261	.329	13	.302	3	5	6	0	1.0
1920	*Cle-A	4	5	.444	27	6	2	0	1	84^2	98	52	3	8	29	27	14.4	5.21	73	.296	.367	11	.344	2	-13	-13	0	-1.0
1921	Cle-A	16	13	.552	41	28	13	2	2	238	288	132	9	4	63	63	13.4	4.01	106	.306	.352	23	.245	3	7	7	-3	0.7
1922	Cle-A	22	16	.579	50	40	23	**5**	3	287^1	328	147	6	13	89	82	13.5	4.07	98	.290	.348	29	.266	9	-1	-2	-3	0.2
1923	Cle-A	**26**	16	.619	54	44	**29**	1	5	**357^2**	378	167	8	12	102	109	12.4	3.77	105	.271	.326	52	.361	16	8	8	0	2.5
1924	Cle-A	9	15	.375	28	25	15	0	1	196^1	238	134	6	13	75	57	14.9	4.77	90	.306	.376	33	.308	7	-12	-11	1	-0.4
1925	Cle-A	13	11	.542	29	26	17	1	0	210^2	218	118	5	8	78	68	13.0	4.10	108	.268	.339	29	.287	6	7	7	-3	1.0
1926	Cle-A	**27**	11	**.711**	39	36	**32**	3	1	**318^1**	300	114	7	13	118	159	12.2	2.83	143	.253	.328	30	.227	4	42	43	-0	**5.2**
1927	Cle-A	8	9	.471	25	22	10	1	1	153^1	187	88	3	9	59	69	15.0	4.34	97	.310	.379	21	.266	4	-3	-2	-1	0.1
1928	Cle-A	12	17	.414	31	28	18	2	1	214^1	252	121	8	8	48	74	12.9	4.07	102	.300	.344	28	.286	7	-1	2	3	1.1
1929	Det-A	15	11	.577	32	30	23	1	0	249	283	141	9	2	58	100	12.4	4.08	105	.287	.328	37	.343	8	4	6	-3	1.0
1930	Det-A	12	12	.500	33	29	18	1	3	239	239	110	18	5	75	117	12.0	3.65	131	.264	.323	36	.308	8	26	29	-3	3.1
1931	Det-A	11	12	.478	29	18	15	2	2	193	190	88	10	4	49	63	11.3	3.50	131	.255	.304	22	.244	5	19	22	-1	2.8
1932	Det-A	6	6	.500	33	15	6	1	5	146^2	152	84	15	4	42	51	12.1	4.48	105	.266	.320	10	.182	1	-0	3	-1	0.2
1933	Det-A	0	0	—	1	0	0	0	0	0^2	2	2	1	0	0	1	27.0	27.00	16	.500	.500	0	—	0	-2	-2	0	-0.1
	NY-N	1	1	.500	6	1	0	0	0	13^2	16	12	1	0	6	4	14.5	7.90	41	.302	.373	0	.000	-0	-7	-7	0	-1.0
	NY-A	6	1	.857	12	6	4	0	0	61	63	42	4	3	20	26	12.7	5.16	75	.257	.321	8	.400	4	-6	-10	-1	-0.6
1934	NY-A	2	4	.333	10	2	0	0	0	16^1	30	19	3	0	7	10	20.4	9.92	41	.400	.451	3	.600	2	-10	-12	-0	-1.9
1936	Cle-A	0	1	.000	7	0	0	0	0	12^2	26	12	2	0	5	5	22.0	8.53	59	.419	.463	8	.381	4	-5	-5	-1	0.0
Total	17	200	166	.546	513	368	232	21	25	3119^2	3417	1635	119	113	966	1135	13.0	3.99	105	.281	.340	393	.289	92	60	74	-15	13.9
● **JERRY UJDUR**	Ujdur, Gerald Raymond b: 3/5/57, Duluth, Minn. BR/TR, 6'1", 195 lbs. Deb: 8/17/80																											
1980	Det-A	1	0	1.000	9	2	0	0	0	21^1	36	20	5	1	10	8	19.8	7.59	54	.383	.448	0	—	0	-8	-8	-1	-0.4
1981	Det-A	0	0	—	4	4	0	0	0	14	19	12	2	0	5	5	15.4	6.43	59	.322	.375	0	—	0	-4	-4	0	-0.2
1982	Det-A	10	10	.500	25	25	7	0	0	178	150	76	29	3	69	86	11.2	3.69	110	.230	.306	0	—	0	8	8	-1	0.7
1983	Det-A	0	4	.000	11	6	0	0	0	34	41	33	6	1	20	13	16.4	7.15	55	.293	.385	0	—	0	-12	-13	-1	-1.3
1984	Cle-A	1	2	.333	4	3	0	0	0	14^1	22	14	1	2	6	6	18.8	6.91	59	.355	.429	0	—	0	-5	-4	-1	-0.8
Total	5	12	16	.429	53	40	7	0	0	261^2	268	155	43	7	110	118	13.2	4.78	85	.266	.342	0	—	0	-21	-22	-3	-2.0
● **SANDY ULLRICH**	Ullrich, Carlos Santiago (Castello) b: 7/25/21, Havana, Cuba BR/TR, 6'1", 180 lbs. Deb: 5/3/44																											
1944	Was-A	0	0	—	3	0	0	0	0	9^2	17	10	2	1	4	2	20.5	9.31	35	.386	.449	1	.333	0	-6	-7	0	-0.3
1945	Was-A	3	3	.500	28	6	0	0	1	81^1	91	45	3	0	34	26	13.8	4.54	68	.276	.343	6	.273	1	-11	-14	1	-0.7
Total	2	3	3	.500	31	6	0	0	1	91	108	55	5	1	38	28	14.5	5.04	62	.289	.356	7	.280	1	-17	-21	2	-1.0
● **DUTCH ULRICH**	Ulrich, Frank W. b: 11/18/1899, Baltimore, Md. d: 2/11/29, Baltimore, Md. BR/TR, 6'2", 195 lbs. Deb: 4/18/25																											
1925	Phi-N	3	3	.500	21	4	2	1	0	65	73	30	6	1	12	29	11.9	3.05	157	.285	.320	2	.125	-1	9	11	1	0.9
1926	Phi-N	8	13	.381	45	16	8	1	1	147^2	178	85	9	1	37	52	13.2	4.08	101	.304	.347	12	.245	1	-4	1	-0	0.3
1927	Phi-N	8	11	.421	32	18	14	1	1	193^1	201	82	6	0	40	42	11.2	3.17	131	.271	.308	9	.123	-6	16	20	-2	1.0
Total	3	19	27	.413	98	38	24	3	2	406	452	197	21	2	89	123	12.0	3.48	122	.286	.324	23	.167	-5	21	32	-2	2.2
● **ARNOLD UMBACH**	Umbach, Arnold William b: 12/6/42, Williamsburg, Va. BR/TR, 6'1", 180 lbs. Deb: 10/3/64																											
1964	Mil-N	1	0	1.000	1	1	0	0	0	8^1	11	5	0	0	4	7	16.2	3.24	109	.333	.405	0	.000	0	0	0	-0	0.0
1966	Atl-N	0	2	.000	22	3	0	0	0	40^2	40	15	1	2	18	23	13.3	3.10	117	.256	.341	1	.200	0	2	2	-0	0.1
Total	2	1	2	.333	23	4	0	0	0	49	51	20	1	2	22	30	13.8	3.12	116	.270	.352	1	.125	0	3	3	-0	0.1
● **JIM UMBARGER**	Umbarger, James Harold b: 2/17/53, Burbank, Cal. BL/TL, 6'6", 200 lbs. Deb: 4/8/75																											
1975	Tex-A	8	7	.533	56	12	3	2	2	131	134	63	11	2	59	50	13.4	4.12	91	.276	.357	0	—	0	-5	-5	1	-0.5
1976	Tex-A	10	12	.455	30	30	10	3	0	197^1	208	86	12	2	54	105	12.0	3.15	114	.274	.324	0	—	0	8	10	-0	1.0
1977	Oak-A	1	5	.167	12	8	1	0	0	44	62	40	3	4	28	24	19.2	6.55	62	.354	.454	0	—	0	-12	-12	0	-1.4
	Tex-A	1	1	.500	3	2	0	0	0	13	14	8	2	0	4	5	12.5	5.54	74	.275	.327	0	—	0	-2	-2	-0	-0.3
	Yr	2	6	.250	15	10	1	0	0	57	76	48	5	4	32	29	17.7	6.32	64	.336	.427	0	—	0	-14	-14	0	-1.7
1978	Tex-A	5	8	.385	32	9	1	0	1	97^2	116	58	9	2	36	60	14.2	4.88	77	.299	.362	0	—	0	-12	-12	1	-1.4
Total	4	25	33	.431	133	61	15	5	3	483	534	255	37	10	181	244	13.5	4.14	90	.287	.354	0	—	0	-23	-22	2	-2.6
● **JIM UMBRICHT**	Umbricht, James b: 9/17/30, Chicago, Ill. d: 4/8/64, Houston, Tex. BR/TR, 6'4", 215 lbs. Deb: 9/26/59																											
1959	Pit-N	0	0	—	1	1	0	0	0	7	7	5	3	0	4	3	14.1	6.43	60	.259	.355	0	.000	-0	-2	-2	0	-0.1
1960	Pit-N	1	2	.333	17	3	0	0	1	40^2	40	23	5	0	27	26	14.8	5.09	74	.270	.383	2	.333	0	-6	-6	-1	-0.5
1961	Pit-N	0	0	—	1	0	0	0	0	3^1	5	2	0	0	2	1	18.9	2.70	148	.333	.412	1	1.000	0	0	0	-0	0.1

YEAR	TM/L	W	L	PCT	G	GS	CG	SH	SV	IP	H	R	HR	HB	BB	SO	RAT	ERA	ERA+	OAV	OOB	BH	AVG	PB	PR	PR+	PD	TPI
1962	Hou-N	4	0	1.000	34	0	0	0	2	67	51	19	3	2	17	55	9.4	2.01	185	.213	.270	1	.111	-0	14	14	1	0.8
1963	Hou-N	4	3	.571	35	3	0	0	0	76	52	23	6	1	21	48	8.8	2.61	121	.195	.256	1	.111	-0	6	5	1	0.5
Total	5	9	5	.643	88	7	0	0	3	194	155	72	17	3	71	133	10.6	3.06	115	.222	.297	5	.179	-0	13	10	0	0.8
● WILLIE UNDERHILL	Underhill, Willie Vern b: 9/6/04, Yowell, Tex. d: 10/26/70, Bay City, Tex. BR/TR, 6′2″, 185 lbs. Deb: 9/8/27																											
1927	Cle-A	0	2	.000	4	1	0	0	0	8^1	12	11	0	0	11	4	24.8	9.72	43	.375	.535	0	.000	-0	-5	-5	0	-0.9
1928	Cle-A	1	2	.333	11	3	1	0	0	28	33	23	0	1	20	16	17.4	4.50	92	.306	.419	4	.364	2	-1	-1	0	0.1
Total	2	1	4	.200	15	4	1	0	0	36^1	45	34	0	1	31	20	19.1	5.70	73	.321	.448	4	.333	1	-7	-6	0	-0.8
● FRED UNDERWOOD	Underwood, Frederick Theodore b: 10/14/1868, St.Louis Co., Mo. d: 1/26/06, Kansas City, Mo. 170 lbs. Deb: 7/18/1894																											
1894	Bro-N	2	4	.333	7	6	5	0	0	47	80	62	1	2	30	10	21.4	7.85	63	.372	.453	7	.389	2	-13	-16	-0	-1.2
● PAT UNDERWOOD	Underwood, Patrick John b: 2/9/57, Kokomo, Ind. BL/TL, 6′, 175 lbs. Deb: 5/31/79 F																											
1979	Det-A	6	4	.600	27	15	1	0	0	121^2	126	64	17	2	29	83	11.6	4.59	95	.269	.314	0	—	0	-5	-3	-1	-0.3
1980	Det-A	3	6	.333	49	7	0	0	5	112^2	121	51	12	2	35	60	12.6	3.59	115	.277	.333	0	—	0	6	6	-0	0.5
1982	Det-A	4	8	.333	33	12	2	0	3	99	108	66	17	0	22	43	11.8	4.73	86	.269	.307	0	—	0	-7	-7	1	-0.8
1983	Det-A	0	0	—	4	0	0	0	0	10^1	11	10	1	0	6	2	14.8	8.71	45	.289	.386	0	—	0	-5	-6	-0	-0.3
Total	4	13	18	.419	113	34	3	0	8	343^2	366	191	47	4	92	188	12.1	4.43	94	.272	.320	0	—	0	-12	-9	-1	-0.9
● TOM UNDERWOOD	Underwood, Thomas Gerald b: 12/22/53, Kokomo, Ind. BR/TL, 5′11″, 170 lbs. Deb: 8/19/74 F																											
1974	Phi-N	1	0	1.000	7	0	0	0	0	13	15	8	1	0	5	8	13.8	4.85	78	.313	.377	0	.000	-0	-2	-1	-0	-0.2
1975	Phi-N	14	13	.519	35	35	7	2	0	219^1	221	110	12	6	84	123	12.8	4.14	90	.262	.333	9	.122	-2	-12	-10	-4	-1.7
1976	*Phi-N	10	5	.667	33	25	3	0	2	155^2	154	63	9	1	63	94	12.6	3.53	101	.260	.332	5	.109	-1	-0	0	-2	-0.3
1977	Phi-N	3	2	.600	14	0	0	0	1	33^1	44	21	2	0	18	20	16.7	5.13	78	.328	.408	0	.000	-0	-5	-4	-0	-0.6
	StL-N	6	9	.400	19	17	1	0	0	100	104	61	7	1	57	66	14.6	4.95	78	.278	.375	4	.133	-0	-12	-12	-1	-1.7
	Yr	9	11	.450	33	17	1	0	1	133^1	148	82	9	1	75	86	15.1	4.99	78	.291	.384	4	.121	-0	-16	-16	-2	-2.3
1978	Tor-A	6	14	.300	31	30	7	1	0	197^2	201	105	23	2	87	139	13.2	4.10	96	.263	.340	0	—	0	-7	-3	-3	-0.6
1979	Tor-A	9	16	.360	33	32	12	1	0	227	213	113	23	9	95	127	12.6	3.69	118	.253	.335	0	—	0	14	16	-0	1.6
1980	*NY-A	13	9	.591	38	27	2	2	2	187	163	85	15	4	66	116	11.2	3.66	107	.237	.307	0	—	0	8	6	-0	0.6
1981	NY-A	1	4	.200	9	6	0	0	0	32^2	32	17	2	0	13	29	12.4	4.41	81	.262	.333	0	—	0	-3	-3	-0	-0.4
	*Oak-A	3	2	.600	16	5	1	0	1	51	37	21	4	2	25	46	11.3	3.18	110	.202	.305	0	—	0	3	2	0	0.2
	Yr	4	6	.400	25	11	1	0	1	83^2	69	38	6	2	38	75	11.7	3.66	96	.226	.316	0	—	0	0	-1	-0	-0.2
1982	Oak-A	10	6	.625	56	10	2	0	7	153	136	66	11	1	68	79	12.1	3.29	119	.241	.324	0	—	0	13	11	-2	0.9
1983	Oak-A	9	7	.563	51	15	0	0	4	144^2	156	69	13	2	50	62	12.9	4.04	96	.277	.338	0	—	0	1	-3	-3	-0.6
1984	Bal-A	1	0	1.000	37	1	0	0	1	71^2	78	33	8	0	31	39	13.7	3.52	110	.282	.354	0	—	0	4	3	1	0.2
Total	11	86	87	.497	379	203	35	6	18	1586	1554	772	130	28	662	948	12.7	3.89	100	.259	.336	18	.117	-4	2	2	-15	-2.6
● WOODY UPCHURCH	Upchurch, Jefferson Woodrow b: 4/13/11, Buies Creek, N.C. d: 10/23/71, Buies Creek, N.C. BR/TL, 6′, 180 lbs. Deb: 9/14/35																											
1935	Phi-A	0	2	.000	3	3	1	0	0	21^1	23	13	3	0	12	2	14.8	5.06	90	.271	.361	2	.286	0	-1	-1	-0	-0.1
1936	Phi-A	0	2	.000	7	2	1	0	0	22^1	36	27	7	0	14	6	20.1	9.67	53	.353	.431	1	.143	-0	-12	-11	-1	-0.8
Total	2	0	4	.000	10	5	2	0	0	43^2	59	40	10	0	26	8	17.5	7.42	65	.316	.399	3	.214	-0	-13	-12	-1	-0.9
● JOHN UPHAM	Upham, John Leslie b: 12/29/41, Windsor, Ont., Can. BL/TL, 6′, 180 lbs. Deb: 4/16/67 ♦																											
1967	Chi-N	0	1	.000	5	0	0	0	0	1^1	4	5	1	0	2	2	40.5	33.75	11	.571	.667	2	.667	1	-5	-4	0	-0.8
1968	Chi-N	0	0	—	2	0	0	0	0	7	2	0	0	1	3	2	7.7	0.00	—	.087	.222	2	.200	0	2	2	0	0.2
Total	2	0	1	.000	7	0	0	0	0	8^1	6	5	1	1	5	4	13.0	5.40	60	.200	.333	4	.308	1	-2	-2	0	-0.6
● BILL UPHAM	Upham, William Lawrence b: 4/4/1888, Akron, Ohio d: 9/14/59, Newark, N.J. BB/TR, 6′, 178 lbs. Deb: 4/10/15																											
1915	Bro-F	7	8	.467	33	11	4	2	4	121	129	61	0	0	40	46	12.6	3.35	81	.274	.331	4	.111	-2	-8	-8	2	-1.1
1918	Bos-N	1	1	.500	3	2	2	0	0	20^2	28	14	2	0	1	8	12.6	5.23	51	.326	.333	2	.222	0	-6	-6	-0	-0.5
Total	2	8	9	.471	36	13	6	2	4	141^2	157	75	2	0	41	54	12.6	3.62	75	.282	.332	6	.133	-2	-14	-14	2	-1.6
● JERRY UPP	Upp, George Henry b: 12/10/1883, Sandusky, Ohio d: 6/30/37, Sandusky, Ohio TL, Deb: 9/2/09																											
1909	Cle-A	2	1	.667	7	4	2	0	0	26^2	26	10	0	0	12	13	12.8	1.69	152	.260	.339	2	.222	0	2	2	1	0.4
● CECIL UPSHAW	Upshaw, Cecil Lee b: 10/22/42, Spearsville, La. d: 2/7/95, Lawrenceville, Ga. BR/TR, 6′6″, 205 lbs. Deb: 10/1/66																											
1966	Atl-N	0	0	—	1	0	0	0	0	3	0	0	0	0	3	2	9.0	0.00	—	.000	.273	1	1.000	0	1	1	-0	0.1
1967	Atl-N	2	3	.400	30	0	0	0	8	45^1	42	14	4	4	8	31	10.7	2.58	129	.247	.297	1	.167	1	4	4	0	0.6
1968	Atl-N	8	7	.533	52	0	0	0	13	116^2	98	41	6	4	24	74	9.7	2.47	121	.229	.276	4	.174	0	7	7	-0	1.1
1969	*Atl-N	6	4	.600	62	0	0	0	27	105^1	102	36	7	1	29	57	11.3	2.91	124	.259	.311	5	.238	2	8	8	1	1.5
1971	Atl-N	11	6	.647	49	0	0	0	17	82	95	33	5	2	28	56	13.7	3.51	106	.292	.352	0	.000	-2	-0	2	-1	0.1
1972	Atl-N	3	5	.375	42	0	0	0	13	53^2	50	22	5	1	19	23	11.7	3.69	103	.249	.317	1	.143	-0	-1	1	1	0.1
1973	Atl-N	0	1	.000	5	0	0	0	0	3^2	8	5	0	0	2	3	24.5	9.82	40	.444	.500	0	—	0	-3	-2	0	-0.4
	Hou-N	2	3	.400	35	0	0	0	1	38^1	38	21	3	1	15	21	12.7	4.46	82	.259	.331	0	.000	-0	-3	-4	1	-0.4
	Yr	2	4	.333	40	0	0	0	1	42	46	26	3	1	17	24	13.7	4.93	74	.279	.350	0	.000	-0	-6	-6	1	-0.8
1974	Cle-A	0	1	.000	7	0	0	0	0	8	10	4	1	0	4	7	15.8	3.38	107	.345	.424	0	—	0	0	0	-0	0.0
	NY-A	1	5	.167	36	0	0	0	6	59^2	53	25	1	3	24	27	12.1	3.02	117	.254	.339	0	—	0	4	3	1	0.5
	Yr	1	6	.143	43	0	0	0	6	67^2	63	29	2	3	28	34	12.5	3.06	116	.265	.349	0	—	0	4	4	1	0.5
1975	Chi-A	1	1	.500	29	0	0	0	1	47^1	49	19	5	4	21	22	14.1	3.23	120	.271	.359	0	—	0	3	3	-0	0.1
Total	9	34	36	.486	348	0	0	0	86	563	545	220	37	20	177	323	11.9	3.13	112	.258	.322	12	.160	1	20	23	2	3.3
● BILL UPTON	Upton, William Ray b: 6/18/29, Esther, Mo. d: 1/2/87, San Diego, Cal. BR/TR, 6′, 167 lbs. Deb: 4/13/54 F																											
1954	Phi-A	0	0	—	2	0	0	0	1	5	6	1	1	0	1	2	12.6	1.80	217	.300	.333	0	—	0	1	1	0	0.1
● JACK URBAN	Urban, Jack Elmer b: 12/5/28, Omaha, Neb. BR/TR, 5′8″, 155 lbs. Deb: 6/13/57																											
1957	KC-A	7	4	.636	31	13	3	0	0	129^1	111	55	7	1	45	55	10.9	3.34	118	.237	.305	11	.282	2	6	8	2	1.1
1958	KC-A	8	11	.421	30	24	5	1	1	132	150	92	17	2	51	54	13.8	5.93	66	.286	.351	7	.152	-2	-32	-29	-1	-3.9
1959	StL-N	0	0	—	8	0	0	0	0	10^2	18	11	1	0	7	4	21.1	9.28	46	.409	.490	0	.000	-0	-6	-6	-0	-0.3
Total	3	15	15	.500	69	37	8	1	1	272	279	158	25	3	103	113	12.7	4.83	82	.269	.337	18	.209	0	-32	-26	-0	-3.1
● TOM URBANI	Urbani, Thomas James b: 1/21/68, Santa Cruz, Cal. BL/TL, 6′1″, 190 lbs. Deb: 4/21/93																											
1993	StL-N	1	3	.250	18	9	0	0	0	62	73	44	4	0	26	33	14.4	4.65	85	.296	.363	3	.188	1	-4	-5	0	-0.2
1994	StL-N	3	7	.300	20	10	0	0	0	80^1	98	48	12	3	21	43	13.7	5.15	81	.302	.350	6	.250	1	-8	-9	0	-0.8
1995	StL-N	3	5	.375	24	13	0	0	0	82^2	99	40	11	2	21	52	13.3	3.70	113	.305	.351	6	.316	3	4	5	1	0.9
1996	StL-N	1	0	1.000	3	2	0	0	0	11^2	15	10	3	0	4	1	14.7	7.71	54	.319	.373	1	.167	-0	-5	-5	-1	-0.4
	Det-A	2	2	.500	16	2	0	0	0	23^2	31	22	8	2	14	20	17.9	8.37	60	.310	.405	0	—	0	-9	-9	0	-1.1
Total	4	10	17	.370	81	36	0	0	0	260^1	316	164	38	7	86	149	14.1	4.98	84	.303	.360	16	.246	6	-21	-22	1	-1.6
● UGUETH URBINA	Urbina, Ugueth Urtain (Villarreal) b: 2/15/74, Caracas, Venez. BR/TR, 6′2″, 185 lbs. Deb: 5/9/95																											
1995	Mon-N	2	2	.500	7	4	0	0	0	23^1	26	17	6	0	14	15	15.4	6.17	70	.280	.374	2	.333	0	-5	-5	1	-0.6
1996	Mon-N	10	5	.667	33	17	0	0	0	114	102	54	18	1	44	108	11.6	3.71	117	.234	.306	3	.103	-1	7	8	-1	0.7
1997	Mon-N	5	8	.385	63	0	0	0	27	64^1	52	29	9	1	29	84	11.5	3.78	111	.214	.300	0	.000	-1	3	3	0	0.6
1998	Mon-N★	6	3	.667	64	0	0	0	34	69^1	37	11	2	0	33	94	9.1	1.30	324	.157	.260	0	.000	-1	23	23	-1	4.5
1999	Mon-N	6	6	.500	71	0	0	0	**41**	75^2	59	35	6	0	36	100	11.3	3.69	122	.208	.297	0	.000	-1	7	7	-1	1.2
2000	Mon-N	0	1	.000	13	0	0	0	8	13^1	11	6	1	0	5	22	10.8	4.05	117	.224	.296	0	.000	-0	1	1	-0	0.1
Total	6	29	25	.537	251	21	0	0	110	360	287	152	42	2	161	423	11.3	3.43	126	.214	.299	5	.096	-2	35	36	-2	6.5
● JOHN URREA	Urrea, John Godoy b: 2/9/55, Los Angeles, Cal. BR/TR, 6′3″, 205 lbs. Deb: 4/10/77																											
1977	StL-N	7	6	.538	41	12	2	1	4	139^2	126	56	13	0	35	81	10.4	3.16	122	.244	.292	4	.138	2	12	11	1	1.2
1978	StL-N	4	9	.308	27	12	1	0	0	98^2	108	75	4	7	47	61	14.8	5.38	65	.284	.373	3	.125	-1	-20	-21	0	-2.5
1979	StL-N	0	0	—	3	2	0	0	0	11^1	13	7	0	0	9	5	17.5	3.97	95	.310	.431	1	.250	0	-0	-0	0	0.0
1980	StL-N	4	1	.800	30	1	0	0	3	64^2	57	28	2	2	41	36	13.9	3.48	106	.239	.356	3	.231	0	1	2	-1	0.0

YEAR	TM/L	W	L	PCT	G	GS	CG	SH	SV	IP	H	R	HR	HB	BB	SO	RAT	ERA	ERA+	OAV	OOB	BH	AVG	PB	PR	PR+	PD	TPI
1981	SD-N	2	2	.500	38	0	0	0	2	49	43	14	1	3	28	19	13.6	2.39	136	.239	.351	1	.250	0	6	5	-1	0.4
Total	5	17	18	.486	139	27	3	1	9	363^1	347	180	20	12	160	202	12.9	3.74	98	.256	.339	12	.162	2	-1	-4	-1	-0.9
● BOB VAIL Vail, Robert Garfield "Doc" b: 9/24/1881, Linneus, Maine d: 3/22/42, Philadelphia, Pa. BR/TR, 5'10", 165 lbs. Deb: 8/27/08																												
1908	Pit-N	1	2	.333	4	1	0	0	0	15	15	10	0	1	7	9	13.8	6.00	38	.268	.359	1	.333	1	-6	-6	-1	-1.1
● ISMAEL VALDES Valdes, Ismael (Alvarez) b: 8/21/73, Victoria, Mex. BR/TR, 6'3", 185 lbs. Deb: 6/15/94																												
1994	LA-N	3	1	.750	21	1	0	0	0	28^1	21	10	2	0	10	28	9.8	3.18	124	.206	.277	0	.000	-0	3	3	1	0.4
1995	*LA-N	13	11	.542	33	27	6	2	1	197^2	168	76	17	1	51	150	10.0	3.05	124	.228	.279	6	.097	-3	25	18	1	1.8
1996	*LA-N	15	7	.682	33	33	0	0	0	225	219	94	20	3	54	173	11.0	3.32	116	.251	.296	10	.143	-1	23	15	-0	1.2
1997	LA-N	10	11	.476	30	30	0	0	0	196^2	171	68	16	3	47	140	10.1	2.65	145	.234	.283	5	.088	-2	34	29	0	2.8
1998	LA-N	11	10	.524	27	27	2	2	0	174	171	82	17	2	66	122	12.4	3.98	100	.256	.324	8	.167	1	5	-0	-0	0.0
1999	LA-N	9	14	.391	32	32	2	1	0	203^1	213	97	32	6	58	143	12.3	3.98	108	.270	.324	5	.086	-3	13	7	1	0.5
2000	Chi-N	2	4	.333	12	12	0	0	0	67	71	40	17	2	27	45	13.4	5.37	85	.273	.346	4	.286	2	-5	-6	0	-0.3
	LA-N	0	3	.000	9	8	0	0	0	40	53	29	5	1	13	29	15.1	6.07	72	.327	.381	1	.091	0	-6	-8	-0	-0.5
	Yr	2	7	.222	21	20	0	0	0	107	124	69	22	3	40	74	14.0	5.64	80	.294	.359	5	.200	2	-12	-14	0	-0.8
Total	7	63	61	.508	197	170	10	5	1	1132	1087	496	126	18	326	830	11.4	3.59	111	.251	.306	39	.121	-6	91	55	3	5.9
● MARC VALDES Valdes, Marc Christopher b: 12/20/71, Dayton, Ohio BR/TR, 6', 170 lbs. Deb: 8/28/95																												
1995	Fla-N	0	0	—	3	3	0	0	0	7	17	13	1	1	9	2	34.7	14.14	30	.459	.574	0	.000	-0	-8	-8	-0	-0.4
1996	Fla-N	1	3	.250	11	8	0	0	0	48^2	63	32	5	1	23	13	16.1	4.81	85	.315	.388	0	.000	-1	-3	-4	-1	-0.5
1997	Mon-N	4	4	.500	48	7	0	0	2	95	84	36	2	8	39	54	12.4	3.13	134	.240	.330	2	.105	-1	11	11	-1	0.8
1998	Mon-N	1	3	.250	20	4	0	0	0	36^1	41	34	6	1	21	28	15.6	7.43	57	.285	.380	2	.400	1	-13	-13	0	-1.1
2000	Hou-N	5	5	.500	53	0	0	0	2	56^2	69	41	3	5	25	35	15.7	5.08	96	.301	.382	0	.000	-0	-3	-1	1	-0.2
Total	5	11	15	.423	135	22	0	0	4	243^2	274	156	17	16	117	132	15.0	4.88	89	.285	.372	4	.093	-1	-15	-15	-1	-1.4
● CARLOS VALDEZ Valdez, Carlos Luis (Lorenzo) b: 12/26/71, Nizao Bani, D.R. BR/TR, 5'11", 165 lbs. Deb: 7/18/95																												
1995	SF-N	0	1	.000	11	0	0	0	0	14^2	19	10	1	1	8	7	17.2	6.14	67	.322	.412	0	.000	-0	-3	-3	-0	-0.2
1998	Bos-A	1	0	1.000	4	0	0	0	0	3^1	1	0	0	0	5	4	16.2	0.00	—	.100	.400	0	—	0	2	2	-0	0.3
Total	2	1	1	.500	15	0	0	0	0	18	20	10	1	1	13	11	17.0	5.00	84	.290	.410	0	.000	-0	-1	-2	-0	0.1
● EFRAIN VALDEZ Valdez, Efrain Antonio b: 7/11/66, Nizao Bani, D.R. BL/TL, 5'11", 180 lbs. Deb: 8/13/90																												
1990	Cle-A	1	1	.500	13	0	0	0	0	23^2	20	10	2	0	14	13	12.9	3.04	129	.233	.340	0	—	0	2	2	-0	0.2
1991	Cle-A	0	0	—	7	0	0	0	0	6	5	1	0	1	3	1	13.5	1.50	277	.238	.360	0	—	0	2	2	0	0.1
1998	Ari-N	0	0	—	6	0	0	0	0	4^1	7	2	2	0	1	2	16.6	4.15	101	.368	.400	0	—	0	0	0	0	0.0
Total	3	1	1	.500	26	0	0	0	0	34	32	13	4	1	18	16	13.5	2.91	138	.254	.352	0	—	0	4	4	0	0.3
● RAFAEL VALDEZ Valdez, Rafael Emilio (Diaz) b: 12/17/67, Nizao Bani, D.R. BR/TR, 5'11", 165 lbs. Deb: 4/18/90																												
1990	SD-N	0	1	.000	3	0	0	0	0	5^2	11	7	4	0	2	3	20.6	11.12	34	.393	.433	0	.000	-0	-5	-5	-0	-0.7
● RENE VALDEZ Valdez, Rene Gutierrez (b: Rene Gutierrez (Valdez)) b: 6/2/29, Guanabacoa, Cuba BR/TR, 6'3", 175 lbs. Deb: 4/21/57																												
1957	Bro-N	1	1	.500	5	1	0	0	0	13	13	8	1	0	7	10	13.8	5.54	75	.265	.357	0	.000	0	-2	-2	-0	-0.3
● SERGIO VALDEZ Valdez, Sergio Sanchez (b: Sergio Sanchez (Valdez)) b: 9/7/64, Elias Pina, D.R. BR/TR, 6'1", 190 lbs. Deb: 9/10/86																												
1986	Mon-N	0	4	.000	5	5	0	0	0	25	39	20	2	1	11	20	18.4	6.84	54	.361	.425	1	.125	-0	-9	-9	-0	-1.2
1989	Atl-N	1	2	.333	19	1	0	0	0	32^2	31	24	5	0	17	26	13.2	6.06	60	.246	.336	1	1.000	0	-9	-8	-1	-0.7
1990	Atl-N	0	0	—	6	0	0	0	0	5^1	6	4	0	0	3	3	15.2	6.75	60	.273	.360	0	—	0	-2	-2	0	-0.1
	Cle-A	6	6	.500	24	13	0	0	0	102^1	109	62	17	1	35	63	12.8	4.75	83	.276	.336	0	—	0	-9	-9	-0	-1.0
1991	Cle-A	1	0	1.000	6	0	0	0	0	16^1	15	11	3	0	5	11	11.0	5.51	75	.238	.294	0	—	0	-3	-2	-1	-0.2
1992	Mon-N	0	2	.000	27	0	0	0	0	37^1	25	12	2	0	12	32	8.9	2.41	144	.185	.252	0	.000	-0	5	4	0	0.2
1993	Mon-N	0	0	—	4	0	0	0	0	3	4	4	1	0	1	2	15.0	9.00	46	.308	.357	0	—	0	-2	-2	-0	-0.1
1994	Bos-A	0	1	.000	12	1	0	0	0	14^1	25	14	4	0	8	4	20.7	8.16	62	.391	.458	0	—	0	-5	-5	0	-0.2
1995	SF-N	4	5	.444	13	11	1	0	0	66^1	78	43	12	3	17	29	13.3	4.75	86	.298	.348	2	.095	-1	-4	-5	0	-0.7
Total	8	12	20	.375	116	31	1	0	0	302^2	332	194	46	5	109	190	13.3	5.06	78	.279	.343	4	.121	-1	-38	-38	-1	-4.0
● CORKY VALENTINE Valentine, Harold Lewis b: 1/4/29, Troy, Ohio BR/TR, 6'1", 203 lbs. Deb: 4/17/54																												
1954	Cin-N	12	11	.522	36	28	7	3	1	194^1	211	98	24	4	60	73	12.7	4.45	94	.282	.339	9	.138	-2	-8	-5	-2	-0.9
1955	Cin-N	2	1	.667	10	5	0	0	0	26^2	29	23	5	1	16	14	15.5	7.43	57	.276	.377	0	.000	-1	-10	-9	1	-0.9
Total	2	14	12	.538	46	33	7	3	1	221	240	121	29	5	76	87	13.1	4.81	87	.282	.344	9	.125	-3	-18	-14	-1	-1.8
● JOHN VALENTINE Valentine, John Gill b: 11/21/1855, Brooklyn, N.Y. d: 10/10/03, Central Islip, N.Y Deb: 5/3/1883																												
1883	Col-a	2	10	.167	13	12	11	0	0	102	130	80	0		17	13	13.0	3.53	87	.291	.317	17	.283	3	-3	-5	1	-0.2
● VITO VALENTINETTI Valentinetti, Vito John b: 9/16/28, W.New York, N.J. BR/TR, 6', 195 lbs. Deb: 6/20/54																												
1954	Chi-A	0	0	—	1	0	0	0	0	1	4	6	1	0	2	1	54.0	54.00	7	.571	.667	0	—	0	-6	-6	0	-0.3
1956	Chi-N	6	4	.600	42	2	0	0	1	95^1	84	47	10	1	36	26	11.4	3.78	100	.243	.317	2	.100	-1	-0	-0	-1	-0.3
1957	Chi-N	0	0	—	9	0	0	0	0	12	12	5	1	0	7	8	14.3	2.25	172	.255	.352	0	.000	0	2	2	-0	0.1
	Cle-A	2	2	.500	11	2	1	0	0	23^2	26	14	3	1	13	9	15.2	4.94	75	.289	.385	1	.200	-0	-3	-3	0	-0.5
1958	Det-A	1	0	1.000	15	0	0	0	2	18^2	18	7	4	1	5	10	11.6	3.38	120	.257	.316	0	—	0	1	1	-0	0.1
	Was-A	4	6	.400	23	10	2	0	0	95^2	106	54	16	2	49	33	14.8	5.08	75	.286	.373	9	.321	2	-14	-13	2	-0.9
	Yr	5	6	.455	38	10	2	0	2	114^1	124	61	20	3	54	43	14.2	4.80	80	.282	.364	9	.321	2	-13	-12	1	-0.8
1959	Was-A	0	2	.000	7	1	0	0	0	10^2	16	12	0	1	10	7	22.8	10.13	39	.356	.482	0	—	0	-7	-7	0	-1.1
Total	5	13	14	.481	108	15	3	0	3	257	266	145	35	6	122	94	13.8	4.73	81	.273	.358	12	.218	1	-27	-26	0	-2.9
● FERNANDO VALENZUELA Valenzuela, Fernando (Anguamea) b: 11/1/60, Navojoa, Mexico BL/TL, 5'11", 195 lbs. Deb: 9/15/80																												
1980	LA-N	2	0	1.000	10	0	0	0	1	17^2	8	2	0	0	5	16	6.6	0.00	—	.136	.203	0	.000	-0	7	7	0	0.9
1981	*LA-N★	13	7	.650	25	25	**11**	**8**	0	**192^1**	140	55	11	1	61	**180**	9.5	2.48	134	.205	.271	16	.250	3	22	19	2	2.6
1982	LA-N★	19	13	.594	37	37	18	4	0	285	247	105	13	2	83	199	10.5	2.87	121	.236	.294	16	.168	1	23	20	5	2.8
1983	*LA-N☆	15	10	.600	35	35	9	4	0	257	245	122	16	3	99	189	12.2	3.75	96	.255	.327	17	.187	2	-3	-4	4	0.3
1984	LA-N★	12	17	.414	34	34	12	2	0	261	218	109	14	2	106	240	11.2	3.03	117	.229	.308	15	.190	4	16	15	4	2.5
1985	*LA-N★	17	10	.630	35	35	14	5	0	272^1	211	92	14	1	101	208	10.3	2.45	142	.214	.288	21	.216	4	35	32	2	3.8
1986	LA-N★	**21**	11	.656	34	34	**20**	3	0	269^1	226	104	18	1	85	242	10.4	3.14	110	.226	.288	24	.220	5	18	10	4	2.1
1987	LA-N	14	14	.500	34	34	**12**	1	0	251	254	120	25	4	124	190	13.7	3.98	100	.262	.349	13	.141	-1	3	-0	3	0.2
1988	LA-N	5	8	.385	23	22	3	0	1	142^1	142	71	11	0	76	64	13.8	4.24	79	.268	.360	8	.182	1	-12	-15	3	-0.9
1989	LA-N	10	13	.435	31	31	3	0	0	196^2	185	89	11	2	98	116	13.0	3.43	100	.251	.340	12	.182	1	2	-0	2	0.2
1990	LA-N	13	13	.500	33	33	5	2	0	204	223	112	19	0	77	115	13.2	4.59	80	.276	.339	21	.304	8	-18	-22	-0	-1.7
1991	Cal-A	0	2	.000	2	2	0	0	0	6^2	14	10	3	0	3	5	23.0	12.15	34	.452	.500	0	—	0	-6	-6	0	-0.9
1993	Bal-A	8	10	.444	32	31	5	2	0	178^2	179	104	18	4	79	78	13.2	4.94	91	.266	.346	0	—	0	-12	-9	2	-0.6
1994	Phi-N	1	2	.333	8	7	0	0	0	45	42	16	8	0	7	19	9.8	3.00	143	.247	.277	3	.250	1	6	6	0	0.5
1995	SD-N	8	3	.727	29	15	0	0	0	90^1	101	53	16	0	34	57	13.5	4.98	81	.289	.352	8	.250	3	-8	-10	3	-0.4
1996	*SD-N	13	8	.619	33	31	0	0	0	171^2	177	78	17	0	67	95	12.8	3.62	110	.269	.336	9	.143	-1	12	7	2	0.9
1997	SD-N	2	8	.200	13	13	1	0	0	66^1	84	42	10	4	32	51	16.3	4.75	82	.309	.390	3	.176	0	-4	-7	1	-0.8
	StL-N	0	4	.000	5	5	0	0	0	22^2	22	19	2	1	14	10	14.7	5.56	75	.253	.363	1	.200	0	-3	-4	1	-0.5
	Yr	2	12	.143	18	18	1	0	0	89	106	61	12	5	46	61	15.9	4.96	80	.295	.383	4	.182	0	-7	-11	2	-1.3
Total	17	173	153	.531	453	424	113	31	2	2930	2718	1303	226	25	1151	2074	12.0	3.54	103	.248	.321	187	.200	32	76	39	36	11.0
● JULIO VALERA Valera, Julio Enrique (Torres) b: 10/13/68, Aguadilla, P.R. BR/TR, 6'2", 215 lbs. Deb: 9/1/90																												
1990	NY-N	1	1	.500	3	3	0	0	0	13	20	11	1	0	7	4	18.7	6.92	54	.351	.422	1	.200	0	-5	-5	-1	-0.6
1991	NY-N	0	0	—	2	0	0	0	0	2	1	0	0	0	4	3	22.5	0.00	—	.143	.455	0	—	0	1	1	0	0.0
1992	Cal-A	8	11	.421	30	28	4	2	0	188	188	82	15	2	64	113	12.2	3.73	107	.262	.324	0	—	0	4	5	-2	0.3
1993	Cal-A	3	6	.333	19	5	0	0	4	53	77	44	8	2	15	28	16.0	6.62	68	.344	.390	0	—	0	-13	-12	-0	-1.9

YEAR TM/L		W	L	PCT	G	GS	CG	SH	SV	IP	H	R	HR	HB	BB	SO	RAT	ERA	ERA+	OAV	OOB	BH	AVG	PB	PR	PR+	PD	TPI
1996	KC-A	3	2	.600	31	2	0	0	1	61^1	75	44	7	2	27	31	15.3	6.46	78	.307	.381	0	—	0	-10	-10	-0	-0.7
Total	5	15	20	.429	85	38	4	2	5	317^1	361	181	31	6	117	179	13.7	4.85	88	.289	.353	1	.200	0	-23	-20	-4	-2.9

● CLAY Van ALSTYNE Van Alstyne, Clayton Emory "Spike" b: 5/24/1900, Stuyvesant, N.Y. d: 1/5/60, Hudson, N.Y. BR/TR, 5'11", 180 lbs. Deb: 8/20/27

YEAR TM/L		W	L	PCT	G	GS	CG	SH	SV	IP	H	R	HR	HB	BB	SO	RAT	ERA	ERA+	OAV	OOB	BH	AVG	PB	PR	PR+	PD	TPI
1927	Was-A	0	0	—	2	0	0	0	0	3	3	1	0	0	0	0	9.0	3.00	136	.250	.250	0	—	0	0	0	-0	0.0
1928	Was-A	0	0	—	4	0	0	0	0	21^1	26	14	0	1	13	5	16.9	5.48	73	.329	.430	2	.250	1	-3	-4	1	0.0
Total	2	0	0	—	6	0	0	0	0	24^1	29	15	0	1	13	5	15.9	5.18	78	.319	.410	2	.250	1	-3	-3	1	0.0

● RUSS Van ATTA Van Atta, Russell "Sheriff" b: 6/21/06, Augusta, N.J. d: 10/10/86, Andover, N.J. BL/TL, 6', 184 lbs. Deb: 4/25/33

YEAR TM/L		W	L	PCT	G	GS	CG	SH	SV	IP	H	R	HR	HB	BB	SO	RAT	ERA	ERA+	OAV	OOB	BH	AVG	PB	PR	PR+	PD	TPI
1933	NY-A	12	4	.750	26	22	10	2	1	157	160	81	8	1	63	76	12.8	4.18	93	.262	.332	17	.283	4	2	-6	0	-0.2
1934	NY-A	3	5	.375	28	9	0	0	0	88	107	69	3	2	46	39	15.9	6.34	64	.307	.390	6	.207	1	-18	-25	-1	-1.8
1935	NY-A	0	0	—	5	0	0	0	0	4^2	5	5	0	0	4	3	17.4	3.86	105	.263	.391	0	.000	-0	0	0	-0	0.0
	StL-A	9	16	.360	53	17	1	0	3	170^1	201	116	10	3	87	87	15.4	5.34	90	.292	.374	9	.214	-1	-17	-10	-1	-1.4
	Yr	9	16	.360	**58**	17	1	0	3	175	206	121	10	3	91	90	15.4	5.30	90	.291	.375	9	.209	-1	-16	-9	-2	-1.4
1936	StL-A	4	7	.364	**52**	9	2	0	2	122^2	164	101	9	2	68	59	17.2	6.60	81	.320	.401	5	.172	-1	-21	-16	1	-1.1
1937	StL-A	1	2	.333	16	6	1	0	0	58^2	74	41	2	0	32	34	16.3	5.52	87	.307	.388	6	.462	3	-6	-4	1	0.2
1938	StL-A	4	7	.364	25	12	3	1	0	104	118	75	7	1	61	35	15.6	6.06	82	.289	.382	4	.133	-1	-15	-12	0	-1.1
1939	StL-A	0	0	—	2	1	0	0	0	7	9	10	0	1	7	6	21.9	11.57	42	.310	.459	0	.000	-0	-5	-5	-0	-0.3
Total	7	33	41	.446	207	76	17	3	6	712^1	838	498	39	10	368	339	15.4	5.60	82	.293	.376	47	.228	5	-80	-77	-1	-5.7

● OZZIE Van BRABANT Van Brabant, Camille Oscar b: 9/28/26, Kingsville, Ont., Canada BR/TR, 6'1", 165 lbs. Deb: 4/13/54

YEAR TM/L		W	L	PCT	G	GS	CG	SH	SV	IP	H	R	HR	HB	BB	SO	RAT	ERA	ERA+	OAV	OOB	BH	AVG	PB	PR	PR+	PD	TPI
1954	Phi-A	0	2	.000	9	2	0	0	0	26^2	35	23	3	1	18	10	18.2	7.09	55	.347	.450	1	.200	0	-10	-9	1	-0.5
1955	KC-A	0	0	—	2	0	0	0	0	2	4	4	1	0	2	1	27.0	18.00	23	.400	.500	0	—	0	-3	-3	-0	-0.1
Total	2	0	2	.000	11	2	0	0	0	28^2	39	27	4	1	20	11	18.8	7.85	50	.351	.455	1	.200	0	-13	-12	1	-0.6

● DAZZY VANCE Vance, Clarence Arthur b: 3/4/1891, Orient, Iowa d: 2/16/61, Homosassa Springs, Fla. BR/TR, 6'2", 200 lbs. Deb: 4/16/15 H

YEAR TM/L		W	L	PCT	G	GS	CG	SH	SV	IP	H	R	HR	HB	BB	SO	RAT	ERA	ERA+	OAV	OOB	BH	AVG	PB	PR	PR+	PD	TPI
1915	Pit-N	0	1	.000	1	1	0	0	0	2^2	3	3	0	1	5	0	30.4	10.13	27	.375	.643	0	.000	-0	-2	-2	0	-0.4
	NY-A	0	3	.000	8	3	1	0	0	28	23	14	1	2	16	18	13.2	3.54	83	.232	.350	2	.667	2	-2	-2	-0	0.0
1918	NY-A	0	0	—	2	0	0	0	0	2^1	9	5	0	0	2	0	42.4	15.43	18	.692	.733	0	—	0	-3	-3	-0	-0.2
1922	Bro-N	18	12	.600	36	31	16	**5**	0	245^2	259	122	9	8	94	**134**	13.2	3.70	110	.276	.347	20	.225	1	11	10	0	1.3
1923	Bro-N	18	15	.545	37	35	21	3	0	280^1	263	127	10	11	100	**197**	12.0	3.50	111	.250	.322	7	.084	-3	16	12	0	1.0
1924	Bro-N	**28**	6	.824	35	34	**30**	3	0	308^1	238	89	11	9	77	**262**	**9.5**	**2.16**	**173**	**.213**	**.269**	16	.151	-2	**58**	**56**	1	**5.9**
1925	Bro-N	**22**	9	.710	31	31	26	**4**	0	265^1	247	115	8	10	66	**221**	11.0	3.53	118	.250	.304	14	.143	-0	22	20	1	2.1
1926	Bro-N	9	10	.474	24	22	12	0	1	169	172	80	7	1	58	**140**	12.3	3.89	98	.271	.333	10	.182	-1	-1	-1	2	-0.1
1927	Bro-N	16	15	.516	34	32	**25**	2	1	273^1	242	98	12	6	69	**184**	10.4	2.70	147	**.239**	.291	15	.167	-2	37	38	-2	3.8
1928	Bro-N	22	10	.688	38	32	24	**4**	2	280^1	226	79	11	7	72	**200**	**9.8**	**2.09**	**191**	**.221**	**.277**	17	.177	2	**59**	**59**	1	**7.0**
1929	Bro-N	14	13	.519	31	27	17	1	0	231^1	244	110	15	9	47	126	11.7	3.89	119	.274	.316	10	.135	-2	21	19	1	1.7
1930	Bro-N	17	15	.531	35	31	20	**4**	0	258^2	241	97	15	5	55	173	**10.5**	**2.61**	**188**	**.246**	**.289**	12	.135	-5	**68**	**67**	-1	**6.7**
1931	Bro-N	11	13	.458	30	29	12	2	0	218^2	221	99	12	0	53	150	11.3	3.38	113	.261	.304	9	.134	-2	12	11	1	0.9
1932	Bro-N	12	11	.522	27	24	9	1	1	175^2	171	90	10	1	57	103	11.7	4.20	91	.256	.315	5	.089	-4	-6	-8	-0	-1.2
1933	StL-N	6	2	.750	28	11	2	0	3	99	105	42	3	1	28	67	12.2	3.55	98	.267	.318	5	.179	-1	-2	-1	-1	-0.2
1934	Cin-N	0	2	.000	6	2	0	0	0	18	28	21	1	1	11	9	20.0	7.50	54	.350	.435	1	.250	0	-7	-7	0	-0.6
	*StL-N	1	1	.500	19	4	1	0	1	59	62	26	4	2	14	33	11.9	3.66	115	.271	.318	2	.133	-0	3	4	-0	0.1
	Yr	1	3	.250	25	6	1	0	1	77	90	47	5	3	25	42	13.8	4.56	92	.291	.350	3	.158	0	-4	-3	-0	-0.5
1935	Bro-N	3	2	.600	20	0	0	0	2	51	55	29	3	3	16	28	13.1	4.41	90	.268	.330	1	.059	-2	-2	-2	-0	-0.4
Total	16	197	140	.585	442	349	216	29	11	2966^2	2809	1246	132	77	840	2045	11.3	3.24	125	.251	.308	146	.150	-18	281	269	3	27.4

● SANDY VANCE Vance, Gene Covington b: 1/5/47, Lamar, Colo. BR/TR, 6'2", 180 lbs. Deb: 4/26/70

YEAR TM/L		W	L	PCT	G	GS	CG	SH	SV	IP	H	R	HR	HB	BB	SO	RAT	ERA	ERA+	OAV	OOB	BH	AVG	PB	PR	PR+	PD	TPI
1970	LA-N	7	7	.500	20	18	2	0	0	115	109	47	9	1	37	45	11.5	3.13	123	.248	.308	7	.189	1	12	10	-3	0.9
1971	LA-N	2	1	.667	10	3	0	0	0	26	38	21	1	0	9	11	16.3	6.92	47	.355	.405	0	.000	-0	-10	-11	-0	-1.2
Total	2	9	8	.529	30	21	2	0	0	141	147	68	10	1	46	56	12.4	3.83	97	.269	.327	7	.167	0	2	-2	-3	-0.3

● JOE VANCE Vance, Joseph Albert "Sandy" b: 9/16/05, Devine, Tex. d: 7/4/78, San Antonio, Tex. BR/TR, 6'1.5", 190 lbs. Deb: 4/18/35

YEAR TM/L		W	L	PCT	G	GS	CG	SH	SV	IP	H	R	HR	HB	BB	SO	RAT	ERA	ERA+	OAV	OOB	BH	AVG	PB	PR	PR+	PD	TPI
1935	Chi-A	2	2	.500	10	0	0	0	0	31	36	26	1	0	21	12	16.5	6.68	69	.295	.399	2	.182	-1	-8	-7	1	-0.7
1937	NY-A	1	0	1.000	2	2	0	0	0	15	11	5	2	0	9	3	12.0	3.00	148	.204	.317	0	.000	-1	3	3	1	0.1
1938	NY-A	0	0	—	3	1	0	0	0	11^1	20	9	2	0	4	2	19.1	7.15	63	.408	.453	3	.750	2	-3	-3	0	0.0
Total	3	3	2	.600	15	3	0	0	0	57^1	67	40	5	0	34	17	15.9	5.81	79	.298	.390	5	.250	1	-8	-8	1	-0.6

● CHRIS Van CUYK Van Cuyk, Christian Gerald b: 1/3/27, Kimberly, Wis. d: 11/3/92, Hudson, Fla. BL/TL, 6'6", 215 lbs. Deb: 7/16/50 F

YEAR TM/L		W	L	PCT	G	GS	CG	SH	SV	IP	H	R	HR	HB	BB	SO	RAT	ERA	ERA+	OAV	OOB	BH	AVG	PB	PR	PR+	PD	TPI
1950	Bro-N	1	3	.250	12	4	1	0	0	33^1	33	19	3	1	12	21	12.4	4.86	84	.266	.336	1	.100	-1	-3	-3	-1	-0.4
1951	Bro-N	1	2	.333	9	6	0	0	0	29^1	33	22	4	4	11	16	14.7	5.52	71	.295	.378	2	.250	0	-5	-5	-0	-0.4
1952	Bro-N	5	6	.455	23	16	4	0	1	97^2	104	58	12	5	40	66	13.7	5.16	71	.271	.347	8	.242	2	-16	-17	-1	-1.7
Total	3	7	11	.389	44	26	5	0	1	160^1	170	99	19	10	63	103	13.6	5.16	73	.274	.351	11	.216	1	-23	-25	-2	-2.5

● JOHNNY Van CUYK Van Cuyk, John Henry b: 7/7/21, Little Chute, Wis. BL/TL, 6'1", 190 lbs. Deb: 9/18/47 F

YEAR TM/L		W	L	PCT	G	GS	CG	SH	SV	IP	H	R	HR	HB	BB	SO	RAT	ERA	ERA+	OAV	OOB	BH	AVG	PB	PR	PR+	PD	TPI
1947	Bro-N	0	0	—	2	0	0	0	0	3^1	5	2	0	0	1	2	16.2	5.40	77	.357	.400	0	—	0	-0	-0	0	0.0
1948	Bro-N	0	0	—	3	0	0	0	0	5	4	3	1	0	1	1	9.0	3.60	111	.200	.238	0	—	0	0	0	0	0.0
1949	Bro-N	0	0	—	2	0	0	0	0	2	3	2	0	0	1	0	18.0	9.00	46	.429	.500	0	—	0	-1	-1	-0	-0.1
Total	3	0	0	—	7	0	0	0	0	10^1	12	7	1	0	3	3	13.1	5.23	78	.293	.341	0	—	0	-1	-1	0	-0.1

● ED VANDE BERG Vande Berg, Edward John b: 10/26/58, Redlands, Cal. BR/TL, 6'2", 180 lbs. Deb: 4/7/82

YEAR TM/L		W	L	PCT	G	GS	CG	SH	SV	IP	H	R	HR	HB	BB	SO	RAT	ERA	ERA+	OAV	OOB	BH	AVG	PB	PR	PR+	PD	TPI
1982	Sea-A	9	4	.692	**78**	0	0	0	5	76	54	21	5	2	32	60	10.4	2.37	179	.207	.298	0	—	0	14	15	2	2.8
1983	Sea-A	2	4	.333	68	0	0	0	5	64^1	59	32	6	1	22	49	11.5	3.36	127	.246	.312	0	—	0	5	6	0	0.6
1984	Sea-A	8	12	.400	50	17	2	0	7	130^1	165	76	18	0	50	71	14.8	4.76	84	.313	.373	0	—	0	-11	-11	-0	-1.7
1985	Sea-A	2	1	.667	76	0	0	0	3	67^2	71	30	4	1	31	34	13.7	3.72	113	.274	.354	0	—	0	3	4	1	0.3
1986	LA-N	1	5	.167	60	0	0	0	0	71^1	83	32	8	1	33	42	14.8	3.41	102	.290	.366	0	.000	-0	3	0	1	0.1
1987	Cle-A	1	0	1.000	55	0	0	0	0	72^1	96	42	9	0	21	40	14.6	5.10	89	.325	.370	0	—	0	-5	-4	0	-0.2
1988	Tex-A	2	2	.500	26	0	0	0	2	37	44	19	2	0	11	18	13.4	4.14	99	.308	.357	0	—	0	-1	-0	-1	-0.1
Total	7	25	28	.472	413	17	2	0	22	519	572	252	52	5	200	314	13.5	3.92	105	.284	.351	0	.000	-0	9	10	3	1.8

● HY VANDENBERG Vandenberg, Harold Harris b: 3/17/06, Abilene, Kan. d: 7/31/94, Bloomington, Minn. BR/TR, 6'4", 220 lbs. Deb: 6/8/35

YEAR TM/L		W	L	PCT	G	GS	CG	SH	SV	IP	H	R	HR	HB	BB	SO	RAT	ERA	ERA+	OAV	OOB	BH	AVG	PB	PR	PR+	PD	TPI
1935	Bos-A	0	0	—	3	0	0	0	0	5^1	15	12	1	0	4	2	32.1	20.25	23	.500	.559	1	1.000	0	-9	-9	0	-0.3
1937	NY-N	0	1	.000	1	1	1	0	0	8	10	7	0	0	6	2	18.0	7.88	49	.313	.421	0	.000	-1	-4	-4	1	-0.3
1938	NY-N	0	1	.000	6	1	0	0	0	18	28	16	2	0	12	7	20.0	7.50	50	.368	.455	0	.000	-1	-7	-8	1	-0.3
1939	NY-N	0	0	—	2	1	0	0	0	6^1	10	5	0	0	6	3	22.7	5.68	69	.345	.457	0	.000	-0	-1	-1	0	-0.1
1940	NY-N	1	1	.500	13	3	1	0	1	32^1	27	15	2	1	16	17	12.2	3.90	100	.227	.324	1	.125	-0	-0	-0	-0	-0.1
1944	Chi-N	7	4	.636	35	9	2	0	2	126^1	123	67	8	1	51	54	12.5	3.63	97	.255	.327	9	.237	1	-0	-1	0	-0.1
1945	*Chi-N	7	3	.700	30	7	3	1	2	95^1	91	44	4	4	33	35	12.1	3.49	105	.259	.330	4	.125	-1	3	2	0	0.1
Total	7	15	10	.600	90	22	7	1	5	291^2	304	166	17	6	128	120	13.5	4.32	85	.271	.349	15	.169	-1	-19	-22	2	-1.1

● JOHNNY VANDER MEER Vander Meer, John Samuel "Double No-Hit" or "The Dutch Master"
b: 11/2/14, Prospect Park, N.J. d: 10/6/97, Tampa, Fla. BB/TL, 6'1", 190 lbs. Deb: 4/22/37

YEAR TM/L		W	L	PCT	G	GS	CG	SH	SV	IP	H	R	HR	HB	BB	SO	RAT	ERA	ERA+	OAV	OOB	BH	AVG	PB	PR	PR+	PD	TPI
1937	Cin-N	3	5	.375	19	10	4	0	0	84^1	63	41	0	2	69	52	14.3	3.84	97	.209	.359	5	.217	1	1	-1	2	0.2
1938	Cin-N★	15	10	.600	32	29	16	3	0	225^1	177	89	12	3	103	125	11.3	3.12	117	**.213**	.302	15	.181	-2	17	14	-1	1.0
1939	Cin-N☆	5	9	.357	30	21	8	0	0	129	128	76	7	2	95	102	15.7	4.67	82	.264	.387	4	.111	-1	-11	-12	-1	-1.4
1940	*Cin-N	3	1	.750	10	7	2	0	1	48	38	24	3	1	41	41	15.0	3.75	101	.211	.360	6	.300	2	1	0	0	0.2
1941	Cin-N	16	13	.552	33	32	18	6	0	226^1	172	83	8	1	126	**202**	11.9	2.82	127	.214	.321	10	.132	-3	20	20	2	2.3
1942	Cin-N★	18	12	.600	33	33	21	4	0	244	188	78	6	1	102	**186**	10.7	2.43	135	.208	.290	11	.147	-1	24	23	1	2.9
1943	Cin-N★	15	16	.484	36	36	21	3	0	289	228	102	5	3	162	**174**	12.2	2.87	116	.224	.332	13	.137	-2	17	15	3	1.6
1946	Cin-N	10	12	.455	29	25	11	4	0	204^1	175	77	11	0	78	94	11.1	3.17	105	.233	.305	18	.247	2	5	4	-2	0.5
1947	Cin-N	9	14	.391	30	29	9	3	0	186	186	104	11	3	87	79	13.4	4.40	93	.261	.343	5	.088	-3	-7	-6	-1	-1.0
1948	Cin-N	17	14	.548	33	33	14	3	0	232	204	97	15	1	124	120	12.8	3.41	115	.239	.336	11	.141	0	14	13	-1	1.6

YEAR	TM/L	W	L	PCT	G	GS	CG	SH	SV	IP	H	R	HR	HB	BB	SO	RAT	ERA	ERA+	OAV	OOB	BH	AVG	PB	PR	PR+	PD	TPI
1949	Cin-N	5	10	.333	28	24	7	3	0	159^2	172	92	12	2	85	76	14.6	4.90	85	.281	.370	4	.077	-3	-15	-12	1	-1.2
1950	Chi-N	3	4	.429	32	6	0	0	1	73^2	60	46	10	2	59	41	14.8	3.79	111	.221	.363	2	.125	-0	3	3	-0	0.3
1951	Cle-A	0	1	.000	1	1	0	0	0	3	8	6	0	0	1	2	27.0	18.00	21	.500	.529	0	.000	-0	-5	-5	1	-0.7
Total	13	119	121	.496	346	286	131	29	2	2104^2	1799	915	100	21	1132	1294	12.6	3.44	107	.232	.332	104	.152	-9	63	54	3	6.3
● BEN Van DYKE	Van Dyke, Benjamin Harrison b: 8/15/1888, Clintonville, Pa. d: 10/22/73, Sarasota, Fla. BR/TL, 6'1", 150 lbs. Deb: 5/11/09																											
1909	Phi-N	0	0	—	2	0	0	0	0	7^1	7	3	0	0	4	5	13.5	3.68	71	.269	.367	0	.000	-0	-1	-1	-0	-0.1
1912	Bos-A	0	0	—	3	1	0	0	0	14^1	13	10	0	1	7	8	13.2	3.14	108	.245	.344	1	.250	-0	0	0	-1	0.0
Total	2	0	0	—	5	1	0	0	0	21^2	20	13	0	1	11	13	13.3	3.32	94	.253	.352	1	.143	-0	-1	-0	-1	-0.1
● TIM Van EGMOND	Van Egmond, Timothy Layne b: 5/31/69, Shreveport, La. BR/TR, 6'2", 185 lbs. Deb: 6/26/94																											
1994	Bos-A	2	3	.400	7	7	1	0	0	38^1	38	27	7	0	21	22	13.9	6.34	79	.255	.347	0	—	0	-7	-5	-1	-0.6
1995	Bos-A	0	1	.000	4	1	0	0	0	6^2	9	7	2	0	6	5	20.3	9.45	52	.310	.429	0	—	0	-4	-3	0	-0.4
1996	Mil-A	3	5	.375	12	9	0	0	0	54^2	58	35	6	1	23	33	13.5	5.27	99	.274	.347	0	—	0	-2	-0	0	0.0
Total	3	5	9	.357	23	17	1	0	0	99^2	105	69	15	1	50	60	14.1	5.96	86	.269	.354	0	—	0	-12	-9	-1	-1.0
● ELAM VANGILDER	Vangilder, Elam Russell b: 4/23/1896, Cape Girardeau, Mo d: 4/30/77, Cape Girardeau, Mo BR/TR, 6'1", 192 lbs. Deb: 9/18/19																											
1919	StL-A	1	0	1.000	3	1	1	0	0	13	15	4	0	0	3	6	12.5	2.08	160	.306	.346	2	.667	1	2	2	1	0.3
1920	StL-A	3	8	.273	24	13	4	0	0	104^2	131	83	7	3	40	25	15.0	5.50	71	.310	.373	4	.133	-2	-20	-18	-0	-1.8
1921	StL-A	11	12	.478	31	21	10	1	0	180^1	196	98	10	2	67	48	13.2	3.94	114	.278	.342	13	.200	-2	7	10	-0	0.9
1922	StL-A	19	13	.594	43	30	19	3	4	245	248	109	13	6	48	63	11.1	3.42	121	.270	.310	32	.344	13	17	19	-3	3.4
1923	StL-A	16	17	.485	41	35	20	4	1	282^1	276	129	11	6	120	74	12.8	3.06	136	.266	.345	24	.218	-0	29	**33**	-3	3.2
1924	StL-A	5	10	.333	43	18	5	0	1	145^1	183	114	10	9	55	49	15.3	5.64	80	.317	.385	13	.295	3	-23	-17	2	-1.1
1925	StL-A	14	8	.636	52	16	4	1	6	193^1	225	127	11	6	92	61	15.0	4.70	99	.303	.385	13	.183	-3	-7	-1	-0	-0.3
1926	StL-A	9	11	.450	42	19	8	1	1	181	196	121	12	2	98	40	14.7	5.17	83	.285	.376	11	.190	1	-23	-17	-2	-1.7
1927	StL-A	10	12	.455	44	23	12	3	1	203	245	136	13	5	102	62	15.6	4.79	91	.310	.392	19	.279	2	-15	-9	-4	-0.9
1928	Det-A	11	10	.524	38	11	7	0	5	156^1	163	82	4	3	68	43	13.5	3.91	105	.273	.350	15	.259	2	2	3	0	0.6
1929	Det-A	0	1	.000	6	0	0	0	0	11^1	16	11	1	0	7	3	18.3	6.35	68	.348	.434	0	.000	-0	-3	-3	1	-0.1
Total	11	99	102	.493	367	187	90	13	19	1715^2	1894	1014	92	42	700	474	13.8	4.28	100	.288	.360	146	.243	15	-33	3	-9	2.5
● GEORGE Van HALTREN	Van Haltren, George Edward Martin "Rip" b: 3/30/1866, St.Louis, Mo. d: 9/29/45, Oakland, Cal. BL/TL, 5'11", 170 lbs. Deb: 6/27/1887 M♦																											
1887	Chi-N	11	7	.611	20	18	18	1	**1**	161	243	113	7	16	66	76	14.5	3.86	116	.344	.359	50	.267	-2	4	10	-0	0.7
1888	Chi-N	13	13	.500	30	24	24	4	1	245^2	263	149	15	13	60	139	12.3	3.52	86	.267	.318	90	.283	11	-18	-13	2	0.0
1890	Bro-P	15	10	.600	28	25	23	0	2	223	272	190	8	21	89	48	15.4	4.28	104	.288	.362	126	.335	10	-1	4	3	1.3
1891	Bal-a	0	1	.000	6	1	0	0	0	23	38	34	1	4	10	7	20.3	5.09	73	.358	.433	180	.318	3	-4	-3	-0	-0.1
1892	Bal-N	0	0	—	4	0	0	0	0	14^2	28	17	1	0	7	5	21.5	9.20	37	.389	.443	168	.302	2	-10	-9	0	-0.3
1895	NY-N	0	0	—	1	0	0	0	0	5	13	12	0	2	2	1	30.6	12.60	37	.481	.548	177	.340	0	-4	-5	-0	-0.2
1896	NY-N	1	0	1.000	2	0	0	0	0	8	5	2	1	0	1	3	6.8	2.25	187	.179	.207	197	.351	1	2	2	-0	0.2
1900	NY-N	0	0	—	1	0	0	0	0	3	1	0	0	0	3	0	12.0	0.00	—	.100	.308	180	.315	0	1	1	-0	0.1
1901	NY-N	0	0	—	1	0	0	0	0	6	12	10	0	1	6	2	28.5	3.00	110	.414	.528	182	.335	0	0	0	1	0.1
Total	9	40	31	.563	93	68	65	5	4	689^1	875	527	33	57	244	281	14.5	4.05	96	.301	.353	2552	.317	25	-30	-11	6	1.8
● WILLIAM Van LANDINGHAM	Van Landingham, William Joseph b: 7/16/70, Columbia, Tenn. BR/TR, 6'2", 210 lbs. Deb: 5/21/94																											
1994	SF-N	8	2	.800	16	14	0	0	0	84	70	37	4	2	43	56	12.3	3.54	113	.223	.320	2	.065	-2	6	5	-0	0.2
1995	SF-N	6	3	.667	18	18	1	0	0	122^2	124	58	14	2	40	95	12.2	3.67	111	.264	.324	7	.152	0	7	6	0	0.5
1996	SF-N	9	14	.391	32	32	0	0	0	181^2	196	123	17	9	78	97	14.0	5.40	76	.276	.355	8	.131	-1	-24	-27	-3	-3.2
1997	SF-N	4	7	.364	18	17	0	0	0	89	80	56	11	0	59	52	14.1	4.96	83	.237	.351	3	.115	-0	-7	-9	-2	-1.1
Total	4	27	26	.509	84	81	1	0	0	477^1	470	274	46	13	220	300	13.3	4.54	90	.257	.340	20	.122	-3	-18	-25	-5	-3.6
● TODD Van POPPEL	Van Poppel, Todd Matthew b: 12/9/71, Hinsdale, Ill. BR/TR, 6'5", 210 lbs. Deb: 9/11/91																											
1991	Oak-A	0	0	—	1	1	0	0	0	4^2	7	5	1	0	2	6	17.4	9.64	40	.368	.429	0	—	0	-3	-3	0	-0.1
1993	Oak-A	6	6	.500	16	16	0	0	0	84	76	50	10	2	62	47	15.0	5.04	81	.243	.371	0	—	0	-7	-9	-1	-1.3
1994	Oak-A	7	10	.412	23	23	0	0	0	116^2	108	80	20	3	89	83	15.4	6.09	73	.250	.382	0	—	0	-17	-23	-1	-2.8
1995	Oak-A	4	8	.333	36	14	1	0	0	138^1	125	77	16	4	56	122	12.0	4.88	92	.244	.323	0	—	0	-2	-7	-2	-0.6
1996	Oak-A	1	5	.167	28	6	0	0	1	63	86	56	13	2	33	37	17.3	7.71	64	.333	.413	0	—	0	-19	-20	-1	-1.7
	Det-A	2	4	.333	9	9	1	1	0	36^1	53	51	11	1	29	16	20.6	11.39	44	.338	.444	0	—	0	-26	-25	0	-2.9
	Yr	3	9	.250	37	15	1	1	1	99^1	139	107	24	3	62	53	18.5	9.06	55	.335	.425	0	—	0	-45	-45	-1	-4.6
1998	Tex-A	1	2	.333	4	4	0	0	0	19^1	26	20	5	1	10	10	17.2	8.84	55	.313	.394	0	.000	-0	-9	-8	-1	-1.0
	Pit-N	1	2	.333	18	7	0	0	0	47	53	32	4	0	18	32	13.6	5.36	80	.286	.350	3	.250	1	-6	-5	-1	-0.3
2000	Chi-N	4	5	.444	51	2	0	0	2	86^1	80	38	10	2	48	77	13.6	3.75	122	.249	.350	0	.000	-1	8	8	1	0.7
Total	7	26	42	.382	186	82	2	1	3	595^2	614	409	90	15	347	430	14.7	5.88	77	.269	.369	3	.130	-0	-80	-95	-6	-10.0
● BEN Van RYN	Van Ryn, Benjamin Ashley b: 8/9/71, Fort Wayne, Ind. BL/TL, 6'5", 185 lbs. Deb: 5/9/96																											
1996	Cal-A	0	0	—	1	0	0	0	0	1	1	0	0	0	1	0	18.0	0.00	—	.250	.400	0	—	0	1	1	0	0.0
1998	Chi-N	0	0	—	9	0	0	0	0	8	9	3	0	1	6	6	18.0	3.38	131	.290	.421	0	.000	-0	1	1	-0	0.0
	SD-N	0	1	.000	6	0	0	0	0	2^2	3	3	0	1	4	1	27.0	10.13	39	.273	.500	0	—	0	-2	-2	-0	-0.4
	Yr	0	1	.000	15	0	0	0	0	10^2	12	6	0	2	10	7	20.3	5.06	85	.286	.444	0	.000	-0	-1	-1	-0	-0.4
	Tor-A	0	1	.000	10	0	0	0	0	4	6	4	0	0	2	3	18.0	9.00	52	.400	.471	0	—	0	-2	-2	-0	-0.4
Total	2	0	2	.000	26	0	0	0	0	15^2	19	10	0	2	13	10	19.5	5.74	77	.311	.447	0	.000	-0	-2	-2	-0	-0.8
● IKE Van ZANDT	Van Zandt, Charles Isaac b: 2/1876, Brooklyn, N.Y. d: 9/14/08, Nashua, N.H. BL, Deb: 8/5/01 ♦																											
1901	NY-N	0	0	—	2	0	0	0	0	12^2	16	15	0	1	8	2	17.8	7.11	47	.308	.410	1	.167	-0	-5	-5	-1	-0.3
1905	StL-A	0	0	—	1	0	0	0	0	6^2	2	0	0	1	2	3	6.8	0.00	—	.095	.208	75	.233	0	2	2	0	0.1
Total	2	0	0	—	3	0	0	0	0	19^1	18	15	0	2	10	5	14.0	4.66	65	.247	.353	76	.224	-0	-3	-4	-1	-0.2
● ANDY VARGA	Varga, Andrew William b: 12/11/30, Chicago, Ill. d: 11/4/92, Orlando, Fla. BR/TL, 6'4", 187 lbs. Deb: 9/9/50																											
1950	Chi-N	0	0	—	1	0	0	0	0	1	0	0	0	0	1	0	9.0	0.00	—	.000	.333	0	—	0	0	0	-0	0.0
1951	Chi-N	0	0	—	2	0	0	0	0	3	2	1	0	0	6	1	24.0	3.00	136	.200	.500	0	—	0	0	0	-0	0.0
Total	2	0	0	—	3	0	0	0	0	4	2	1	0	0	7	1	20.3	2.25	183	.167	.474	0	—	0	1	1	-0	0.0
● ROBERTO VARGAS	Vargas, Roberto Enrique (Velez) b: 5/29/29, Santurce, P.R. BL/TL, 5'11", 170 lbs. Deb: 4/17/55																											
1955	Mil-N	0	0	—	25	0	0	0	2	24^2	39	25	4	1	14	13	19.7	8.76	43	.355	.432	1	.500	0	-13	-15	1	-0.6
● BILL VARGUS	Vargus, William Fay b: 11/11/1899, N.Scituate, Mass. d: 2/12/79, Hyannis, Mass. BL/TL, 6', 165 lbs. Deb: 6/23/25																											
1925	Bos-N	1	1	.500	11	2	1	0	0	36^1	45	24	1	2	13	5	14.9	3.96	101	.302	.366	3	.250	0	1	0	0	0.0
1926	Bos-N	0	0	—	4	0	0	0	0	3	4	1	0	0	1	0	15.0	3.00	118	.333	.385	0	—	0	0	0	0	0.0
Total	2	1	1	.500	15	2	1	0	0	39^1	49	25	1	2	14	5	14.9	3.89	102	.304	.367	3	.250	0	2	0	0	0.0
● DIKE VARNEY	Varney, Lawrence Delano (b: Lawrence Delano De Varney) b: 8/9/1880, Dover, N.H. d: 4/23/50, Long Island City, N.Y. BL/TL, 6', 165 lbs. Deb: 7/3/02																											
1902	Cle-A	1	1	.500	3	3	0	0	0	14^2	14	15	0	5	12	7	19.0	6.14	56	.250	.425	1	.167	-0	-4	-5	0	-0.5
● CAL VASBINDER	Vasbinder, Moses Calhoun b: 7/19/1880, Scio, Ohio d: 12/22/50, Cadiz, Ohio BR/TR, 6'2", Deb: 4/27/02																											
1902	Cle-A	0	0	—	2	0	0	0	0	5	5	5	1	0	8	2	23.4	9.00	38	.263	.481	1	.500	0	-3	-3	0	-0.1
● RAFAEL VASQUEZ	Vasquez, Rafael b: 6/28/58, LaRomana, D.R. BR/TR, 6', 160 lbs. Deb: 4/6/79																											
1979	Sea-A	1	0	1.000	9	0	0	0	0	16	23	9	4	1	6	9	16.9	5.06	86	.354	.417	0	—	0	-1	-1	-0	-0.1
● PORTER VAUGHAN	Vaughan, Cecil Porter "Lefty" b: 5/11/19, Stevensville, Va. BR/TL, 6'1", 178 lbs. Deb: 6/16/40																											
1940	Phi-A	2	9	.182	18	15	5	0	2	99^1	104	74	9	3	61	46	15.2	5.35	83	.264	.367	8	.235	0	-11	-10	-1	-1.0
1941	Phi-A	0	2	.000	5	3	1	0	0	22^2	32	25	3	0	12	6	17.5	7.94	53	.327	.400	1	.143	-0	-10	-9	-0	-0.7

YEAR	TM/L	W	L	PCT	G	GS	CG	SH	SV	IP	H	R	HR	HB	BB	SO	RAT	ERA	ERA+	OAV	OOB	BH	AVG	PB	PR	PR+	PD	TPI
1946	Phi-A	0	0	—	1	0	0	0	0	0	1	0	0	1	—	—	—	—	1.000	1.000	101	—	0	0	0	0	0.0	
Total	3	2	11	.154	24	18	6	0	2	122	137	99	12	3	74	52	15.8	5.83	75	.278	.375	9	.220	-0	-20	-19	-1	-1.7
● CHARLIE VAUGHAN Vaughan, Charles Wayne b: 10/6/47, Mercedes, Tex. BR/TL, 6'1.5", 185 lbs. Deb: 9/3/66																												
1966	Atl-N	1	0	1.000	1	1	0	0	0	7	8	2	0	0	3	6	14.1	2.57	141	.296	.367	1	.250	0	1	1	0	0.1
1969	Atl-N	0	0	—	1	0	0	0	0	1	1	2	0	0	3	1	36.0	18.00	20	.250	.571	0	—	0	-2	-2	0	-0.1
Total	2	1	0	1.000	2	1	0	0	0	8	9	4	0	0	6	7	16.9	4.50	81	.290	.405	1	.250	0	-1	-1	0	0.0
● ROY VAUGHN Vaughn, Clarence Leroy b: 9/4/11, Sedalia, Mo. d: 3/1/37, Martinsville, Va. BB/TR, 6'0.5", 178 lbs. Deb: 7/1/34																												
1934	Phi-A	0	0	—	2	0	0	0	0	4^1	3	2	1	0	3	1	12.5	2.08	211	.176	.300	0	.000	-0	1	1	-0	0.0
● DE WAYNE VAUGHN Vaughn, De Wayne Mathew b: 7/22/59, Oklahoma City, Okla BR/TR, 5'11", 180 lbs. Deb: 4/17/88																												
1988	Tex-A	0	0	—	8	0	0	0	0	15^1	24	15	4	0	4	8	16.4	7.63	54	.348	.384	0	—	0	-6	-6	-1	-0.3
● FARMER VAUGHN Vaughn, Harry Francis b: 3/1/1864, Ruraldale, Ohio d: 2/21/14, Cincinnati, Ohio BR/TR, 6'3", 177 lbs. Deb: 10/7/1886 ♦																												
1891	Cin-a	0	0	—	1	0	0	0	0	7	12	9	0	1	1	0	18.0	3.86	106	.364	.400	45	.257	0	-0	0	-0	0.0
● HIPPO VAUGHN Vaughn, James Leslie b: 4/9/1888, Weatherford, Tex. d: 5/29/66, Chicago, Ill. BB/TL, 6'4", 215 lbs. Deb: 6/19/08																												
1908	NY-A	0	0	—	2	0	0	0	0	2^1	1	1	0	0	4	2	19.3	3.86	64	.167	.500	0	.000	-0	-0	-0	0	0.0
1910	NY-A	13	11	.542	30	25	18	5	1	221^2	190	76	1	10	58	107	10.5	1.83	146	.237	.297	10	.133	-2	17	19	-0	1.9
1911	NY-A	8	10	.444	26	19	10	0	0	145^2	158	92	2	7	54	74	13.5	4.39	82	.284	.354	7	.143	-1	-17	-12	1	-1.3
1912	NY-A	2	8	.200	15	10	5	1	0	63	66	48	1	1	37	46	14.9	5.14	70	.264	.361	2	.095	-2	-13	-10	1	-1.4
	Was-A	4	3	.571	12	8	4	0	0	81	75	33	0	4	43	49	13.6	2.89	115	.253	.356	6	.200	-1	4	4	2	0.4
	Yr	6	11	.353	27	18	9	1	0	144	141	81	1	5	80	95	14.1	3.88	89	.258	.358	8	.157	-2	-9	-7	3	-1.0
1913	Chi-N	5	1	.833	7	6	5	2	0	56	37	13	0	2	27	36	10.6	1.45	220	.182	.284	4	.190	-1	11	11	0	1.1
1914	Chi-N	21	13	.618	42	35	23	4	1	293^2	236	119	1	8	109	165	10.8	2.05	135	.222	.299	14	.144	-0	24	24	-0	2.7
1915	Chi-N	20	12	.625	41	34	18	4	1	269^2	240	105	4	11	77	148	10.9	2.87	97	.238	.299	14	.163	1	-4	-3	-1	-0.3
1916	Chi-N	17	15	.531	44	35	21	4	1	294	269	94	4	7	67	144	10.5	2.20	132	.250	.298	14	.135	-4	14	21	1	2.0
1917	Chi-N	23	13	.639	41	38	27	5	0	295^2	255	97	3	9	91	195	10.8	2.01	144	.235	.300	16	.160	-1	23	27	3	3.8
1918	*Chi-N	**22**	10	.688	35	33	27	**8**	0	**290**^{1}	216	75	4	7	76	**148**	9.3	**1.74**	**161**	**.208**	.266	23	.240	4	**33**	**34**	-1	**4.4**
1919	Chi-N	21	14	.600	38	37	25	4	1	**306**^{2}	264	83	3	6	62	**141**	9.7	1.79	161	.234	.278	17	.173	-0	**38**	**38**	-3	4.3
1920	Chi-N	19	16	.543	40	38	24	4	0	301	301	113	8	8	81	131	11.7	2.54	126	.264	.318	22	.216	4	20	22	-2	2.7
1921	Chi-N	3	11	.214	17	14	7	0	0	109^1	153	90	8	5	31	30	15.6	6.01	64	.341	.390	10	.244	2	-27	-26	-1	-2.7
Total	13	178	137	.565	390	332	214	41	5	2730	2461	1039	39	85	817	1416	11.1	2.49	120	.244	.306	159	.173	-1	123	147	-1	17.6
● JAVIER VAZQUEZ Vazquez, Javier Carlos b: 6/25/76, Ponce, P.R. BR/TR, 6'2", 180 lbs. Deb: 4/3/98																												
1998	Mon-N	5	15	.250	33	32	0	0	0	172^1	196	121	31	11	68	139	14.4	6.06	69	.292	.366	9	.173	1	-35	-36	1	-3.3
1999	Mon-N	9	8	.529	26	26	3	1	0	154^2	154	98	20	4	52	113	12.2	5.00	90	.255	.318	12	.286	4	-8	-9	3	-0.2
2000	Mon-N	11	9	.550	33	33	2	1	0	217^2	247	104	24	5	61	196	12.9	4.05	117	.286	.336	15	.231	2	14	16	1	1.6
Total	3	25	32	.439	92	91	5	2	0	544^2	597	323	75	20	181	448	13.2	4.96	91	.279	.341	36	.226	7	-28	-28	4	-1.9
● AL VEACH Veach, Alvis Lindel b: 8/6/09, Maylene, Ala. d: 9/6/90, Charlotte, N.C. BR/TR, 5'11", 178 lbs. Deb: 9/22/35																												
1935	Phi-A	0	2	.000	2	2	1	0	0	10	20	15	1	0	9	3	26.1	11.70	39	.417	.509	0	.000	-1	-8	-8	0	-1.0
● BOBBY VEACH Veach, Robert Hayes b: 6/29/1888, Island, Ky. d: 8/7/45, Detroit, Mich. BL/TR, 5'11", 160 lbs. Deb: 8/6/12 ♦																												
1918	Det-A	0	0	—	1	0	0	0	1	2	2	1	0	0	2	0	18.0	4.50	59	.286	.444	139	.279	0	-0	-0	-0	-0.1
● PEEK-A-BOO VEACH Veach, William Walter b: 6/15/1862, Indianapolis, Ind d: 11/12/37, Indianapolis, Ind. Deb: 8/24/1884 ♦																												
1884	KC-U	3	9	.250	12	12	12	0	0	104	95	57	1		10	62	9.1	2.42	92	.227	.245	11	.134	-3	0	-2	1	-0.5
1887	Lou-a	0	1	.000	1	1	1	0	0	9	13	6	1	0	8	2	13.0	4.00	110	.351	.351	1	.250	-0	0	0	-0	0.0
Total	2	3	10	.231	13	13	13	0	0	113	108	63	2	0	18	64	9.4	2.55	94	.237	.253	77	.218	-4	1	-2	1	-0.5
● BOB VEALE Veale, Robert Andrew b: 10/28/35, Birmingham, Ala. BB/TL, 6'6", 212 lbs. Deb: 4/16/62																												
1962	Pit-N	2	2	.500	11	6	2	0	1	45^2	39	25	2	0	25	42	12.6	3.74	105	.235	.335	4	.250	1	1	1	-0	0.1
1963	Pit-N	5	2	.714	34	7	3	2	3	77^2	59	15	1	1	40	68	11.6	1.04	316	.215	.317	2	.087	-0	19	19	0	1.9
1964	Pit-N	18	12	.600	40	38	14	1	0	279^2	222	100	8	3	124	**250**	11.2	2.74	128	.217	.303	15	.156	-0	25	24	-1	2.4
1965	Pit-N☆	17	12	.586	39	37	14	7	0	266	221	98	5	7	119	276	11.7	2.84	124	.225	.313	8	.086	-4	21	20	-2	1.5
1966	Pit-N☆	16	12	.571	38	37	12	3	0	268^1	228	99	18	5	102	229	11.2	3.02	118	.232	.307	13	.138	-2	18	17	-2	1.2
1967	Pit-N	16	8	.667	33	31	6	1	0	203	184	90	12	5	119	179	13.7	3.64	93	.245	.352	3	.043	-5	-6	-6	1	-1.1
1968	Pit-N	13	14	.481	36	33	13	4	0	245^1	187	67	13	2	94	171	10.4	2.05	142	.211	.288	9	.110	-2	25	24	-2	2.4
1969	Pit-N	13	14	.481	34	34	9	1	0	225^2	232	93	8	3	91	213	13.0	3.23	108	.267	.338	4	.051	-5	9	7	-0	0.2
1970	Pit-N	10	15	.400	34	32	5	1	0	202	189	99	15	3	94	178	12.7	3.92	100	.246	.331	11	.164	1	3	-0	-2	-0.1
1971	*Pit-N	6	0	1.000	37	0	0	0	2	46^1	59	38	5	0	24	40	16.1	6.99	48	.314	.392	3	.333	1	-18	-19	-2	-2.5
1972	Pit-N	0	0	—	5	0	0	0	0	9	10	7	0	0	7	6	17.0	6.00	55	.313	.436	0	.000	-0	-3	-3	-0	-0.2
	Bos-A	2	0	1.000	6	0	0	0	2	8	2	0	0	0	3	10	5.6	0.00	—	.083	.185	0	.000	-0	3	3	0	0.7
1973	Bos-A	2	3	.400	32	0	0	0	11	36^1	37	16	2	0	12	25	12.1	3.47	116	.268	.327	0	—	0	1	2	1	0.5
1974	Bos-A	0	1	.000	18	0	0	0	2	13	15	8	2	0	4	16	13.2	5.54	69	.283	.333	0	—	0	-3	-2	-0	-0.3
Total	13	120	95	.558	397	255	78	20	21	1926	1684	755	91	29	858	1703	12.0	3.07	113	.236	.320	72	.114	-17	96	87	-9	6.7
● LOU VEDDER Vedder, Louis Edward b: 4/20/1897, Oakville, Mich. d: 3/9/90, Lake Placid, Fla. BR/TR, 5'10.5", 175 lbs. Deb: 9/18/20																												
1920	Det-A	0	0	—	1	0	0	0	0	2	0	0	0	0	0	1	0.0	0.00	—	.000	.000	0	—	0	1	1	0	0.1
● AL VEIGEL Veigel, Allen Francis b: 1/30/17, Dover, Ohio BR/TR, 6'1", 180 lbs. Deb: 9/21/39																												
1939	Bos-N	0	1	.000	2	2	0	0	0	2^2	3	6	0	0	5	1	27.0	6.75	55	.250	.471	0	.000	-0	-1	-1	-0	-0.2
● BUCKY VEIL Veil, Frederick William b: 8/2/1881, Tyrone, Pa. d: 4/16/31, Altoona, Pa. BR/TR, 5'10", 165 lbs. Deb: 4/19/03																												
1903	*Pit-N	5	3	.625	12	6	4	0	0	70^2	70	35	1	2	36	20	13.8	3.82	85	.269	.362	6	.207	-0	-4	-5	-0	-0.5
1904	Pit-N	0	0	—	1	1	0	0	0	4^2	4	3	0	1	4	1	17.4	5.79	47	.250	.429	1	1.000	0	-2	-2	0	0.0
Total	2	5	3	.625	13	7	4	0	0	75^1	74	38	1	3	40	21	14.0	3.94	81	.268	.367	7	.233	0	-6	-6	-0	-0.5
● CARLOS VELAZQUEZ Velazquez, Carlos (Quinones) b: 3/22/48, Loiza, P.R. BR/TR, 5'11", 180 lbs. Deb: 7/20/73																												
1973	Mil-A	2	2	.500	18	0	0	0	2	38^1	46	15	5	0	10	12	13.1	2.58	146	.297	.339	0	—	0	5	5	0	0.6
● MIKE VENAFRO Venafro, Michael Robert b: 8/2/73, Takoma Park, Md. BL/TL, 5'10", 170 lbs. Deb: 4/24/99																												
1999	*Tex-A	3	2	.600	65	0	0	0	0	68^1	63	29	4	3	22	37	11.6	3.29	154	.251	.319	0	—	0	12	13	2	0.9
2000	Tex-A	3	1	.750	77	0	0	0	1	56^1	64	27	2	4	21	32	14.2	3.83	133	.295	.368	0	—	0	7	8	0	0.5
Total	2	6	3	.667	142	0	0	0	1	124^2	127	56	6	7	43	69	12.8	3.54	144	.271	.342	0	—	0	19	21	2	1.4
● DARIO VERAS Veras, Dario Antonio b: 3/13/73, Santiago, D.R. BR/TR, 6'2", 165 lbs. Deb: 7/31/96																												
1996	*SD-N	3	1	.750	23	0	0	0	0	29	24	10	3	1	10	23	10.9	2.79	142	.231	.304	0	—	0	5	4	0	0.5
1997	SD-N	2	1	.667	23	0	0	0	0	24^2	28	18	5	2	12	21	15.3	5.11	76	.280	.368	0	—	0	-2	-4	-1	-0.5
1998	Bos-A	0	1	.000	7	0	0	0	0	8	12	9	0	1	7	2	22.5	10.13	47	.343	.465	0	—	0	-5	-5	-0	-0.5
Total	3	5	3	.625	53	0	0	0	0	61^2	64	37	8	4	29	46	14.2	4.67	86	.268	.357	0	—	0	-3	-5	-1	-0.5
● JOE VERBANIC Verbanic, Joseph Michael b: 4/24/43, Washington, Pa. BR/TR, 6', 155 lbs. Deb: 7/22/66																												
1966	Phi-N	1	1	.500	17	0	0	0	0	14	12	9	2	0	10	7	14.1	5.14	70	.226	.349	0	—	0	-2	-2	-0	-0.3
1967	NY-A	4	3	.571	28	6	1	1	2	80^1	74	27	6	2	21	39	10.9	2.80	112	.249	.303	2	.111	-0	4	3	2	0.4
1968	NY-A	6	7	.462	40	11	2	1	4	97	104	36	6	6	41	40	14.0	3.15	92	.284	.366	2	.080	-1	-2	-3	1	-0.4
1970	NY-A	1	0	1.000	7	0	0	0	0	15^2	20	9	1	1	12	8	19.0	4.60	77	.323	.440	1	.333	0	-2	-2	1	0.0
Total	4	12	11	.522	92	17	3	2	6	207	210	81	15	9	84	94	13.2	3.26	95	.270	.348	5	.109	-1	-2	-4	4	-0.3
● AL VERDEL Verdel, Albert Alfred "Stumpy" b: 6/10/21, Punxsutawney, Pa. d: 4/16/91, Sarasota, Fla. BR/TR, 5'9.5", 186 lbs. Deb: 4/20/44																												
1944	Phi-N	0	0	—	1	0	0	0	0	1	0	0	0	0	0	0	0.0	0.00	—	.000	.000	0	—	0	0	0	-0	0.0

● TOMMY VEREKER Vereker, John James b: 12/2/1893, Baltimore, Md. d: 4/2/74, Baltimore, Md. 5'10", 185 lbs. Deb: 6/17/15

YEAR	TM/L	W	L	PCT	G	GS	CG	SH	SV	IP	H	R	HR	HB	BB	SO	RAT	ERA	ERA+	OAV	OOB	BH	AVG	PB	PR	PR+	PD	TPI
1915	Bal-F	0	0	—	2	0	0	0	0	3	3	5	1	1	2	1	18.0	15.00	19	.273	.429	0	—	0	-4	-4	0	-0.2

● DAVE VERES Veres, David Scott b: 10/19/66, Montgomery, Ala. BR/TR, 6'2", 195 lbs. Deb: 5/10/94

YEAR	TM/L	W	L	PCT	G	GS	CG	SH	SV	IP	H	R	HR	HB	BB	SO	RAT	ERA	ERA+	OAV	OOB	BH	AVG	PB	PR	PR+	PD	TPI
1994	Hou-N	3	3	.500	32	0	0	0	1	41	39	13	4	1	7	28	10.3	2.41	164	.247	.283	1	.500	1	8	7	-1	1.0
1995	Hou-N	5	1	.833	72	0	0	0	1	103^1	89	29	5	4	30	94	10.7	2.26	171	.241	.304	0	.000	-1	**22**	20	-1	0.9
1996	Mon-N	6	3	.667	68	0	0	0	4	77^2	85	39	10	6	32	81	14.3	4.17	104	.277	.357	3	.375	1	0	1	-0	0.2
1997	Mon-N	2	3	.400	53	0	0	0	1	62	68	28	5	2	27	47	14.1	3.48	120	.278	.354	1	1.000	0	5	5	-1	0.4
1998	Col-N	3	1	.750	63	0	0	0	8	76^1	67	26	6	2	27	74	11.3	2.83	183	.233	.303	1	.333	0	12	16	1	1.1
1999	Col-N	4	8	.333	73	0	0	0	31	77	88	46	14	2	37	71	14.8	5.14	113	.290	.371	0	.000	-0	-5	5	-1	0.8
2000	*StL-N	3	5	.375	71	0	0	0	29	75^2	65	26	6	6	25	67	11.4	2.85	162	.239	.317	0	.000	-0	15	15	-1	2.3
Total	7	26	24	.520	432	0	0	0	75	513	501	207	50	23	185	462	12.4	3.32	138	.258	.330	6	.286	2	58	68	-2	6.7

● RANDY VERES Veres, Randolph Ruhland b: 11/25/65, Sacramento, Cal. BR/TR, 6'3", 210 lbs. Deb: 7/1/89

YEAR	TM/L	W	L	PCT	G	GS	CG	SH	SV	IP	H	R	HR	HB	BB	SO	RAT	ERA	ERA+	OAV	OOB	BH	AVG	PB	PR	PR+	PD	TPI
1989	Mil-A	0	1	.000	3	1	0	0	0	8^1	9	5	0	0	4	8	14.0	4.32	89	.290	.371	0	—	0	-0	-0	0	-0.1
1990	Mil-A	0	3	.000	26	0	0	0	1	41^2	38	17	5	1	16	16	11.9	3.67	106	.247	.322	0	—	0	1	1	1	0.2
1994	Chi-N	1	1	.500	10	0	0	0	0	9^2	12	6	3	1	2	5	14.0	5.59	74	.308	.357	0	.000	-0	-1	-2	0	-0.3
1995	Fla-N	4	4	.500	47	0	0	0	1	48^2	46	25	6	1	22	31	12.8	3.88	109	.251	.335	0	.000	-0	2	2	-1	0.1
1996	Det-A	0	4	.000	25	0	0	0	0	30^1	38	29	6	2	23	28	18.7	8.31	61	.306	.423	0	—	0	-11	-11	-1	-1.2
1997	KC-A	4	0	1.000	24	0	0	0	1	35^1	36	17	4	3	7	28	11.7	3.31	142	.273	.324	0	—	0	5	5	0	0.6
Total	6	9	13	.409	135	1	0	0	3	174	179	99	24	8	74	116	13.5	4.60	95	.270	.350	0	.000	-0	-5	-5	-1	-0.7

● JOHN VERHOEVEN Verhoeven, John C b: 7/3/52, Long Beach, Cal. BR/TR, 6'5", 200 lbs. Deb: 7/6/76

YEAR	TM/L	W	L	PCT	G	GS	CG	SH	SV	IP	H	R	HR	HB	BB	SO	RAT	ERA	ERA+	OAV	OOB	BH	AVG	PB	PR	PR+	PD	TPI
1976	Cal-A	0	2	.000	21	0	0	0	4	37^1	35	15	2	0	14	23	11.8	3.38	99	.252	.320	0	—	0	1	-0	1	0.1
1977	Cal-A	0	2	.000	3	0	0	0	0	4^2	4	3	0	1	4	3	17.4	3.86	102	.222	.391	0	—	0	0	0	0	0.0
	Chi-A	0	0	—	6	0	0	0	0	10^1	9	3	0	0	2	6	9.6	2.61	157	.231	.268	0	—	0	2	2	1	0.1
	Yr	0	2	.000	9	0	0	0	0	15	13	6	0	1	6	9	12.0	3.00	135	.228	.313	0	—	0	2	2	1	0.1
1980	Min-A	3	4	.429	44	0	0	0	0	99^2	109	53	10	3	29	42	12.7	3.97	110	.289	.345	0	—	0	1	4	0	0.3
1981	Min-A	0	0	—	25	0	0	0	0	52	57	27	4	2	14	16	12.6	3.98	99	.288	.341	0	—	0	-2	-0	0	0.0
Total	4	3	8	.273	99	0	0	0	4	204	214	101	16	6	63	90	12.5	3.79	107	.278	.337	0	—	0	1	5	2	0.5

● JOE VERNON Vernon, Joseph Henry b: 11/25/1889, Mansfield, Mass. d: 3/13/55, Philadelphia, Pa. BR/TR, 5'11", 160 lbs. Deb: 7/20/12

YEAR	TM/L	W	L	PCT	G	GS	CG	SH	SV	IP	H	R	HR	HB	BB	SO	RAT	ERA	ERA+	OAV	OOB	BH	AVG	PB	PR	PR+	PD	TPI
1912	Chi-N	0	0	—	1	0	0	0	0	4	4	6	0	1	6	1	24.8	11.25	30	.286	.524	0	.000	-0	-3	-4	-0	-0.2
1914	Bro-F	0	0	—	1	1	0	0	0	3^1	4	4	0	0	5	0	24.3	10.80	27	.308	.500	0	.000	-0	-3	-3	0	-0.2
Total	2	0	0	—	2	1	0	0	0	7^1	8	10	0	1	11	1	24.5	11.05	28	.296	.513	0	.000	-0	-6	-7	-0	-0.4

● BOB VESELIC Veselic, Robert Michael b: 9/27/55, Pittsburgh, Pa. d: 12/26/95, Los Angeles, Cal. BR/TR, 6', 175 lbs. Deb: 9/18/80

YEAR	TM/L	W	L	PCT	G	GS	CG	SH	SV	IP	H	R	HR	HB	BB	SO	RAT	ERA	ERA+	OAV	OOB	BH	AVG	PB	PR	PR+	PD	TPI
1980	Min-A	0	0	—	1	0	0	0	0	4	3	2	1	0	1	2	9.0	4.50	97	.214	.267	0	—	0	-0	-0	-0	0.0
1981	Min-A	1	1	.500	5	0	0	0	0	22^2	22	8	1	0	12	13	13.5	3.18	124	.250	.340	0	—	0	1	2	-1	0.1
Total	2	1	1	.500	6	0	0	0	0	26^2	25	10	2	0	13	15	12.8	3.38	119	.245	.330	0	—	0	1	2	-1	0.1

● LEE VIAU Viau, Leon A. b: 7/5/1866, Corinth, Vt. d: 12/17/47, Hopewell, N.J. BR/TR, 5'4", 160 lbs. Deb: 4/22/1888

YEAR	TM/L	W	L	PCT	G	GS	CG	SH	SV	IP	H	R	HR	HB	BB	SO	RAT	ERA	ERA+	OAV	OOB	BH	AVG	PB	PR	PR+	PD	TPI
1888	Cin-a	27	14	.659	42	42	42	1	0	387^2	331	192	7	20	110	164	10.7	2.65	120	.222	.285	13	.087	-11	18	22	-2	0.7
1889	Cin-a	22	20	.524	47	42	38	1	1	373	379	224	8	10	136	152	12.7	3.79	103	.255	.322	21	.143	-9	3	5	-3	-0.6
1890	Cin-N	7	5	.583	13	10	7	1	0	90	97	69	8	1	39	41	13.7	4.50	79	.266	.339	5	.139	-2	-9	-9	1	-1.1
	Cle-N	4	9	.308	13	13	13	1	0	107	101	65	4	5	42	30	12.4	3.36	106	.242	.318	7	.163	-2	2	3	-1	0.0
	Yr	11	14	.440	26	23	20	2	0	197	198	134	12	6	81	71	13.0	3.88	92	.253	.328	12	.152	-4	-7	-7	0	-1.1
1891	Cle-N	18	17	.514	45	38	31	0	0	343^2	367	239	3	15	138	130	13.6	3.01	115	.263	.336	23	.160	-3	13	17	1	1.1
1892	Cle-N	0	1	.000	1	1	0	0	0	1	5	5	0	0	1	0	54.0	36.00	9	.625	.667	0	—	0	-4	-4	0	-0.5
	Lou-N	4	11	.267	16	15	14	1	0	130^2	156	86	7	0	56	36	14.6	3.99	77	.285	.351	13	.197	1	-10	-14	2	-1.0
	Bos-N	1	0	1.000	1	1	1	0	0	9	5	1	0	0	4	1	9.0	0.00	—	.156	.250	0	.000	-0	3	3	-0	0.3
	Yr	5	12	.294	18	17	15	1	0	140^2	166	92	7	0	61	37	14.5	3.97	78	.282	.350	13	.188	1	-11	-14	2	-1.2
Total	5	83	77	.519	178	162	146	5	1	1442	1441	881	37	51	526	554	12.6	3.33	105	.251	.320	82	.139	-27	16	24	-1	-1.1

● RUBE VICKERS Vickers, Harry Porter b: 5/17/1878, St.Marys, Ont., Can d: 12/9/58, Belleville, Mich. BL/TR, 6'2", 225 lbs. Deb: 9/21/02

YEAR	TM/L	W	L	PCT	G	GS	CG	SH	SV	IP	H	R	HR	HB	BB	SO	RAT	ERA	ERA+	OAV	OOB	BH	AVG	PB	PR	PR+	PD	TPI
1902	Cin-N	0	3	.000	3	3	3	0	0	21	31	20	0	1	8	6	17.1	6.00	50	.341	.400	4	.364	1	-8	-7	-1	-0.7
1903	Bro-N	0	1	.000	4	1	1	0	0	14	27	23	0	1	9	5	23.8	10.93	29	.415	.493	1	.100	-1	-12	-12	1	-0.7
1907	Phi-A	2	2	.500	10	4	3	1	0	50^1	44	27	1	1	12	21	10.2	3.40	77	.238	.288	3	.150	-1	-5	-4	0	-0.4
1908	Phi-A	18	19	.486	53	34	21	6	1	317	264	114	0	11	71	156	9.8	2.21	116	.231	.282	17	.160	-1	6	11	-3	0.9
1909	Phi-A	2	2	.500	18	3	1	0	1	55^2	60	32	0	2	19	25	13.1	3.40	71	.274	.338	1	.063	-1	-6	-6	-1	-0.8
Total	5	22	27	.449	88	45	29	7	2	458	426	216	1	16	119	213	11.0	2.93	88	.250	.305	26	.160	-3	-24	-16	-4	-1.7

● TOM VICKERY Vickery, Thomas Gill "Vinegar Tom" b: 5/5/1867, Milford, N.J. d: 3/21/21, Burlington, N.J. TR, 6', 170 lbs. Deb: 4/21/1890

YEAR	TM/L	W	L	PCT	G	GS	CG	SH	SV	IP	H	R	HR	HB	BB	SO	RAT	ERA	ERA+	OAV	OOB	BH	AVG	PB	PR	PR+	PD	TPI
1890	Phi-N	24	22	.522	46	46	41	2	0	382	405	250	8	29	184	162	14.6	3.44	106	.264	.353	33	.208	-4	6	9	-2	0.3
1891	Chi-N	6	5	.545	14	12	7	0	0	79^2	72	55	4	5	44	39	13.7	4.07	82	.232	.337	7	.179	-2	-6	-7	1	-0.8
1892	Bal-N	8	10	.444	24	21	17	0	0	176	189	134	3	10	87	49	14.6	3.53	97	.264	.351	18	.243	2	-5	-2	-2	-0.1
1893	Phi-N	4	5	.444	13	11	7	0	0	80	100	65	1	6	37	15	16.1	5.40	85	.297	.376	11	.314	1	-7	-7	2	-0.3
Total	4	42	42	.500	97	90	72	2	0	717^2	766	504	16	50	352	265	14.6	3.75	98	.264	.354	69	.225	-3	-12	-6	-1	-0.9

● BRANDON VILLAFUERTE Villafuerte, Brandon Paul b: 12/17/75, Hilo, Hawaii BR/TR, 5'11", 180 lbs. Deb: 5/23/2000

YEAR	TM/L	W	L	PCT	G	GS	CG	SH	SV	IP	H	R	HR	HB	BB	SO	RAT	ERA	ERA+	OAV	OOB	BH	AVG	PB	PR	PR+	PD	TPI
2000	Det-A	0	0	—	3	0	0	0	0	4^1	4	5	0	0	4	1	16.6	10.38	46	.250	.400	0	—	0	-3	-3	0	-0.1

● ISMAEL VILLEGAS Villegas, Ismael (Diaz) b: 8/12/76, Rio Piedras, P.R. BR/TR, 6'1", 188 lbs. Deb: 7/3/2000

YEAR	TM/L	W	L	PCT	G	GS	CG	SH	SV	IP	H	R	HR	HB	BB	SO	RAT	ERA	ERA+	OAV	OOB	BH	AVG	PB	PR	PR+	PD	TPI
2000	Atl-N	0	0	—	1	0	0	0	0	2^2	4	4	2	1	2	2	23.6	13.50	34	.333	.467	0	.000	-0	-3	-3	0	-0.1

● RON VILLONE Villone, Ronald Thomas b: 1/16/70, Englewood, N.J. BL/TL, 6'3", 230 lbs. Deb: 4/28/95

YEAR	TM/L	W	L	PCT	G	GS	CG	SH	SV	IP	H	R	HR	HB	BB	SO	RAT	ERA	ERA+	OAV	OOB	BH	AVG	PB	PR	PR+	PD	TPI
1995	Sea-A	0	2	.000	19	0	0	0	0	19^1	20	19	6	1	23	26	20.5	7.91	60	.270	.449	0	—	0	-7	-7	-0	-0.6
	SD-N	2	1	.667	19	0	0	0	1	25^2	24	12	5	0	11	37	12.3	4.21	96	.242	.318	0	.000	-0	-0	-1	-0	-0.1
1996	SD-N	1	1	.500	21	0	0	0	0	18^1	17	6	2	1	7	19	12.3	2.95	135	.243	.321	0	—	0	3	2	0	0.2
	Mil-A	0	0	—	23	0	0	0	2	24^2	14	9	4	4	18	19	13.1	3.28	158	.175	.353	0	—	0	5	5	-1	0.2
1997	Mil-A	1	0	1.000	50	0	0	0	0	52^2	54	23	4	1	36	40	15.6	3.42	135	.271	.386	0	.000	-0	7	7	0	0.3
1998	Cle-A	0	0	—	25	0	0	0	0	27	30	18	3	2	22	15	18.0	6.00	80	.297	.432	0	—	0	-4	-4	0	-0.2
1999	Cin-N	9	7	.563	29	22	0	0	2	142^2	114	70	8	5	73	97	12.1	4.23	110	.219	.321	3	.070	-3	5	7	1	0.5
2000	Cin-N	10	10	.500	35	23	2	0	0	141	154	95	22	9	78	77	15.4	5.43	88	.286	.386	7	.163	-1	-12	-10	-0	-1.3
Total	6	23	21	.523	221	45	2	0	5	451^1	427	252	54	23	268	330	14.3	4.67	100	.254	.364	10	.114	-4	-4	-0	0	-1.0

● BOB VINES Vines, Robert Earl b: 2/25/1897, Waxahachie, Tex. d: 10/18/82, Orlando, Fla. BR/TR, 6'4", 184 lbs. Deb: 9/3/24

YEAR	TM/L	W	L	PCT	G	GS	CG	SH	SV	IP	H	R	HR	HB	BB	SO	RAT	ERA	ERA+	OAV	OOB	BH	AVG	PB	PR	PR+	PD	TPI
1924	StL-N	0	0	—	2	0	0	0	0	10^2	23	13	1	0	0	0	19.4	9.28	41	.426	.426	0	.000	-1	-6	-7	-0	-0.4
1925	Phi-N	0	0	—	3	0	0	0	0	4	9	10	0	0	3	0	27.0	11.25	42	.450	.522	0	—	0	-3	-3	0	-0.1
Total	2	0	0	—	5	0	0	0	0	14^2	32	23	1	0	3	0	21.5	9.82	41	.432	.455	0	.000	-1	-10	-9	-0	-0.5

● DAVE VINEYARD Vineyard, David Kent b: 2/25/41, Clay, W.Va. BR/TR, 6'3", 195 lbs. Deb: 7/18/64

YEAR	TM/L	W	L	PCT	G	GS	CG	SH	SV	IP	H	R	HR	HB	BB	SO	RAT	ERA	ERA+	OAV	OOB	BH	AVG	PB	PR	PR+	PD	TPI
1964	Bal-A	2	5	.286	19	6	1	0	0	54	57	34	5	0	27	50	14.0	4.17	86	.274	.357	2	.167	0	-3	-4	-1	-0.5

● BILL VINTON Vinton, William Miller b: 4/27/1865, Winthrop, Mass. d: 9/3/1893, Pawtucket, R.I. BR/TR, 6'1", 160 lbs. Deb: 7/3/1884

YEAR	TM/L	W	L	PCT	G	GS	CG	SH	SV	IP	H	R	HR	HB	BB	SO	RAT	ERA	ERA+	OAV	OOB	BH	AVG	PB	PR	PR+	PD	TPI
1884	Phi-N	10	10	.500	21	21	20	0	0	182	166	131	6		35	105	9.9	2.23	134	.220	.255	9	.115	-6	15	15	3	1.1
1885	Phi-N	3	6	.333	9	9	8	0	0	77	90	59	0		23	21	13.2	3.04	92	.269	.317	2	.067	-3	-2	-2	0	-0.5
	Phi-a	4	3	.571	7	7	6	2	0	55	46	41	1	4	15	34	10.6	2.45	140	.200	.261	4	.154	-0	5	6	-0	0.5
Total	2	17	19	.472	37	37	34	2	0	314	302	231	7	4	73	160	10.9	2.46	122	.229	.272	15	.112	-10	18	19	3	1.1

● FRANK VIOLA Viola, Frank John b: 4/19/60, Hempstead, N.Y. BL/TL, 6'4", 209 lbs. Deb: 6/6/82

YEAR	TM/L	W	L	PCT	G	GS	CG	SH	SV	IP	H	R	HR	HB	BB	SO	RAT	ERA	ERA+	OAV	OOB	BH	AVG	PB	PR	PR+	PD	TPI
1982	Min-A	4	10	.286	22	22	3	1	0	126	152	77	22	0	38	84	13.6	5.21	82	.302	.351	0	—	0	-16	-13	-1	-1.4

YEAR	TM/L	W	L	PCT	G	GS	CG	SH	SV	IP	H	R	HR	HB	BB	SO	RAT	ERA	ERA+	OAV	OOB	BH	AVG	PB	PR	PR+	PD	TPI
1983	Min-A	7	15	.318	35	34	4	0	0	210	242	141	34	8	92	127	14.7	5.49	78	.287	.363	0	—	0	-33	-27	-1	-2.6
1984	Min-A	18	12	.600	35	35	10	4	0	257^2	225	101	28	4	73	149	10.5	3.21	131	.233	.290	0	—	0	22	27	-3	2.7
1985	Min-A	18	14	.563	36	36	9	0	0	250^2	262	136	26	2	68	135	11.9	4.09	108	.268	.316	0	—	0	2	8	-2	0.8
1986	Min-A	16	13	.552	37	37	7	1	0	245^2	257	136	37	3	83	191	12.6	4.51	96	.268	.329	0	—	0	-9	-5	-3	-0.8
1987	*Min-A	17	10	.630	36	36	7	1	0	251^2	230	91	29	6	66	197	10.8	2.90	160	.241	.294	0	—	0	44	47	-1	4.5
1988	Min-A★	**24**	7	**.774**	35	35	7	2	0	255^1	236	80	20	3	54	193	10.3	2.64	154	.245	.288	0	—	0	38	**40**	-1	**4.6**
1989	Min-A	8	12	.400	24	24	7	1	0	175^2	171	80	17	3	47	138	11.3	3.79	109	.256	.308	0	—	0	2	7	0	0.7
	NY-N	5	5	.500	12	12	2	1	0	85^1	75	35	5	1	27	73	10.9	3.38	97	.236	.298	3	.130	-0	1	-1	-1	-0.2
1990	NY-N★	20	12	.625	35	35	7	3	0	**249^2**	227	83	15	2	60	182	10.4	2.67	141	.242	.289	13	.153	-1	**31**	30	-0	**3.7**
1991	NY-N★	13	15	.464	35	35	3	0	0	231^1	259	112	25	1	54	132	12.2	3.97	92	.286	.327	9	.127	-1	-7	-8	-1	-1.2
1992	Bos-A	13	12	.520	35	35	6	1	0	238	214	99	13	7	89	121	11.7	3.44	123	.242	.316	0	—	0	13	19	3	2.2
1993	Bos-A	11	8	.579	29	29	2	1	0	183^2	180	76	12	6	72	91	12.6	3.14	148	.259	.334	0	—	0	24	29	0	2.8
1994	Bos-A	1	1	.500	6	6	0	0	0	31	34	17	2	0	17	9	14.8	4.65	108	.296	.386	0	—	0	1	1	-0	0.0
1995	Cin-N	0	1	.000	3	3	0	0	0	14^1	20	11	3	0	3	4	14.4	6.28	66	.333	.365	1	.167	0	-3	-3	-0	-0.2
1996	Tor-A	1	3	.250	6	6	0	0	0	30^1	43	28	6	2	21	18	19.6	7.71	65	.350	.452	0	—	0	-9	-9	-0	-0.9
Total	15	176	150	.540	421	420	74	16	0	2836^1	2827	1303	294	48	864	1844	11.9	3.73	112	.260	.317	26	.141	-2	102	141	-12	14.7

● JAKE VIRTUE

Virtue, Jacob Kitchline "Guesses" b: 3/2/1865, Philadelphia, Pa. d: 2/3/43, Camden, N.J. BB/TL, 5'9.5", 165 lbs. Deb: 7/21/1890 ♦

YEAR	TM/L	W	L	PCT	G	GS	CG	SH	SV	IP	H	R	HR	HB	BB	SO	RAT	ERA	ERA+	OAV	OOB	BH	AVG	PB	PR	PR+	PD	TPI
1893	Cle-N	0	0	—	1	0	0	0	0	5	3	3	0	0	3	2	10.8	1.80	271	.167	.286	100	.265	0	2	2	-0	0.1
1894	Cle-N	0	0	—	1	0	0	0	0	0	0	0	0	1	—	—	—	—	—	1.000	103	.258	0	0	0	0	0.0	
Total	2	0	0	—	2	0	0	0	0	5	3	3	0	0	4	2	12.6	1.80	271	.167	.318	483	.274	0	2	2	-0	0.1

● JOE VITELLI

Vitelli, Antonio Joseph b: 4/12/08, McKees Rocks, Pa. d: 2/7/67, Pittsburgh, Pa. BR/TR, 6'1", 195 lbs. Deb: 5/30/44 ♦

YEAR	TM/L	W	L	PCT	G	GS	CG	SH	SV	IP	H	R	HR	HB	BB	SO	RAT	ERA	ERA+	OAV	OOB	BH	AVG	PB	PR	PR+	PD	TPI
1944	Pit-N	0	0	—	4	0	0	0	0	7	5	6	1	1	7	2	16.7	2.57	145	.185	.371	0	.000	-0	1	1	0	0.0

● JOE VITKO

Vitko, Joseph John b: 2/1/70, Somerville, N.J. BR/TR, 6'8", 210 lbs. Deb: 9/18/92

YEAR	TM/L	W	L	PCT	G	GS	CG	SH	SV	IP	H	R	HR	HB	BB	SO	RAT	ERA	ERA+	OAV	OOB	BH	AVG	PB	PR	PR+	PD	TPI
1992	NY-N	0	1	.000	3	1	0	0	0	4^2	12	11	1	0	1	6	25.1	13.50	26	.444	.464	0	—	0	-5	-5	-0	-0.9

● LUIS VIZCAINO

Vizcaino, Luis (Arias) b: 6/10/77, Bani, D.R. BR/TR, 6'1", 170 lbs. Deb: 7/23/99

YEAR	TM/L	W	L	PCT	G	GS	CG	SH	SV	IP	H	R	HR	HB	BB	SO	RAT	ERA	ERA+	OAV	OOB	BH	AVG	PB	PR	PR+	PD	TPI
1999	Oak-A	0	0	—	1	0	0	0	0	3^1	3	2	1	0	3	2	16.2	5.40	86	.231	.375	0	—	0	-0	-0	-0	0.0
2000	Oak-A	0	1	.000	12	0	0	0	0	19^1	25	17	2	2	11	18	17.7	7.45	64	.305	.400	0	—	0	-5	-6	0	-0.3
Total	2	0	1	.000	13	0	0	0	0	22^2	28	19	3	2	14	20	17.5	7.15	66	.295	.396	0	—	0	-6	-6	0	-0.3

● RYAN VOGELSONG

Vogelsong, Ryan Andrew b: 7/22/77, Charlotte, N.C. BR/TR, 6'3", 195 lbs. Deb: 9/2/2000

YEAR	TM/L	W	L	PCT	G	GS	CG	SH	SV	IP	H	R	HR	HB	BB	SO	RAT	ERA	ERA+	OAV	OOB	BH	AVG	PB	PR	PR+	PD	TPI
2000	SF-N	0	0	—	4	0	0	0	0	6	4	0	0	0	2	6	9.0	0.00	—	.182	.250	0	—	0	3	3	-0	0.1

● OLLIE VOIGT

Voigt, Olen Edward "Ode" b: 1/29/1900, Wheaton, Ill. d: 4/7/70, Scottsdale, Ariz. BL/TR, 6'1", 170 lbs. Deb: 4/19/24

YEAR	TM/L	W	L	PCT	G	GS	CG	SH	SV	IP	H	R	HR	HB	BB	SO	RAT	ERA	ERA+	OAV	OOB	BH	AVG	PB	PR	PR+	PD	TPI
1924	StL-A	1	0	1.000	8	1	0	0	0	16^1	21	13	1	0	13	4	18.7	5.51	82	.356	.472	1	.250	1	-2	-2	1	0.1

● BILL VOISELLE

Voiselle, William Symmes "Big Bill" or "Ninety-Six" b: 1/29/19, Greenwood, S.C. BR/TR, 6'4", 200 lbs. Deb: 9/1/42

YEAR	TM/L	W	L	PCT	G	GS	CG	SH	SV	IP	H	R	HR	HB	BB	SO	RAT	ERA	ERA+	OAV	OOB	BH	AVG	PB	PR	PR+	PD	TPI
1942	NY-N	0	1	.000	2	1	0	0	0	9	6	4	1	0	4	5	10.0	2.00	168	.176	.263	0	.000	0	1	1	0	0.2
1943	NY-N	1	2	.333	4	4	3	0	0	31	18	10	1	0	14	19	9.3	2.03	170	.154	.244	1	.111	-1	5	5	-1	0.3
1944	NY-N☆	21	16	.568	43	41	25	1	0	**312^2**	276	138	31	4	118	**161**	11.5	3.02	121	.232	.303	22	.210	3	20	22	-3	2.4
1945	NY-N	14	14	.500	41	35	14	4	0	232^1	249	128	15	4	97	115	13.6	4.49	87	.273	.345	10	.127	-3	-18	-15	-0	-1.8
1946	NY-N	9	15	.375	36	25	10	2	0	178	171	88	14	0	85	89	12.9	3.74	92	.248	.330	9	.164	-1	-7	-6	-0	-0.9
1947	NY-N	1	4	.200	11	5	1	0	0	42^2	44	26	4	1	22	20	14.1	4.64	88	.284	.376	2	.133	-1	-3	-3	-0	-0.4
	Bos-N	8	7	.533	22	20	7	0	0	131^1	146	66	10	1	51	59	13.6	4.32	90	.280	.345	9	.170	-1	-4	-6	1	-0.6
	Yr	9	11	.450	33	25	8	0	0	174	190	92	14	2	73	79	13.7	4.40	90	.281	.352	11	.162	-1	-7	-9	1	-1.0
1948	*Bos-N	13	13	.500	37	30	9	2	2	215^2	226	93	18	3	90	89	13.3	3.63	106	.272	.345	7	.097	-4	8	5	-3	-0.1
1949	Bos-N	7	8	.467	30	22	5	4	1	169^1	170	84	14	1	78	63	13.2	4.04	94	.263	.343	7	.115	-2	0	-5	1	-0.5
1950	Chi-N	0	4	.000	19	7	0	0	0	51^1	64	39	7	1	29	25	16.5	5.79	73	.303	.390	1	.077	-1	-9	-9	-1	-0.8
Total	9	74	84	.468	245	190	74	13	3	1373^1	1370	676	115	15	588	645	12.9	3.83	98	.258	.334	68	.147	-10	-6	-10	-6	-2.2

● JAKE VOLZ

Volz, Jacob Phillip "Silent Jake" b: 4/4/1878, San Antonio, Tex. d: 8/11/62, San Antonio, Tex. BR/TR, 5'10", 175 lbs. Deb: 9/28/01

YEAR	TM/L	W	L	PCT	G	GS	CG	SH	SV	IP	H	R	HR	HB	BB	SO	RAT	ERA	ERA+	OAV	OOB	BH	AVG	PB	PR	PR+	PD	TPI
1901	Bos-A	1	0	1.000	1	1	1	0	0	7	6	9	2	0	9	5	19.3	9.00	39	.231	.429	0	.000	-1	-4	-4	-1	-0.5
1905	Bos-N	0	2	.000	3	2	0	0	0	8^2	12	11	0	1	8	1	21.8	10.38	30	.364	.500	0	.000	-0	-7	-7	-1	-1.2
1908	Cin-N	1	2	.333	7	4	1	0	0	22^2	16	9	1	2	12	6	11.9	3.57	65	.195	.313	1	.250	0	-3	-3	-1	-0.5
Total	3	2	4	.333	11	7	2	0	0	38^1	34	29	3	3	29	12	15.5	6.10	44	.241	.382	1	.100	-1	-14	-15	-2	-2.2

● TONY Von FRICKEN

Von Fricken, Anthony b: 5/30/1870, Brooklyn, N.Y. d: 3/22/47, Troy, N.Y. BB/TR, 5'11.5", 160 lbs. Deb: 5/9/1890

YEAR	TM/L	W	L	PCT	G	GS	CG	SH	SV	IP	H	R	HR	HB	BB	SO	RAT	ERA	ERA+	OAV	OOB	BH	AVG	PB	PR	PR+	PD	TPI
1890	Bos-N	0	1	.000	1	1	1	0	0	8	23	16	0	0	8	2	34.9	10.13	37	.489	.564	0	.000	-1	-6	-5	-0	-0.5

● BRUCE Von HOFF

Von Hoff, Bruce Frederick b: 11/17/43, Oakland, Cal. BR/TR, 6', 187 lbs. Deb: 9/28/65

YEAR	TM/L	W	L	PCT	G	GS	CG	SH	SV	IP	H	R	HR	HB	BB	SO	RAT	ERA	ERA+	OAV	OOB	BH	AVG	PB	PR	PR+	PD	TPI
1965	Hou-N	0	0	—	3	0	0	0	0	3	3	3	0	0	2	1	15.0	9.00	37	.250	.357	0	—	0	-2	-2	-0	-0.1
1967	Hou-N	0	3	.000	10	10	0	0	0	50^1	52	29	3	0	28	22	14.3	4.83	69	.268	.360	1	.067	-1	-8	-9	-1	-0.7
Total	2	0	3	.000	13	10	0	0	0	53^1	55	32	3	0	30	23	14.3	5.06	65	.267	.360	1	.067	-1	-10	-11	-1	-0.8

● DAVE Von OHLEN

Von Ohlen, David b: 10/25/58, Flushing, N.Y. BL/TL, 6'2", 200 lbs. Deb: 5/13/83

YEAR	TM/L	W	L	PCT	G	GS	CG	SH	SV	IP	H	R	HR	HB	BB	SO	RAT	ERA	ERA+	OAV	OOB	BH	AVG	PB	PR	PR+	PD	TPI
1983	StL-N	3	2	.600	46	0	0	0	2	68^1	71	27	3	3	25	21	13.0	3.29	110	.280	.351	1	.143	0	3	3	-0	0.2
1984	StL-N	1	0	1.000	27	0	0	0	1	34^2	39	13	0	0	8	19	12.2	3.12	112	.300	.341	1	1.000	0	2	1	1	0.2
1985	Cle-A	3	2	.600	26	0	0	0	0	43^1	47	20	3	0	20	12	13.9	2.91	142	.288	.366	0	—	0	6	6	1	0.7
1986	Oak-A	0	3	.000	24	0	0	0	1	15^1	18	7	0	0	7	4	14.7	3.52	110	.300	.373	0	—	0	1	1	0	0.2
1987	Oak-A	0	0	—	4	0	0	0	0	6	10	5	1	0	1	3	16.5	7.50	55	.400	.423	0	—	0	-2	-2	-0	-0.1
Total	5	7	7	.500	127	0	0	0	4	167^2	185	72	7	3	61	59	13.4	3.33	113	.293	.358	2	.250	1	10	8	1	1.2

● CY VORHEES

Vorhees, Henry Bert b: 9/30/1874, Lodi, Ohio d: 2/8/10, Perry, Ohio 6'3", 200 lbs. Deb: 4/17/02

YEAR	TM/L	W	L	PCT	G	GS	CG	SH	SV	IP	H	R	HR	HB	BB	SO	RAT	ERA	ERA+	OAV	OOB	BH	AVG	PB	PR	PR+	PD	TPI
1902	Phi-N	3	3	.500	10	5	3	1	0	53^2	63	33	1	1	20	24	14.1	3.86	73	.292	.354	7	.350	2	-6	-6	-1	-0.5
	Was-A	0	1	.000	1	1	1	0	0	8	10	6	0	0	2	1	13.5	4.50	82	.303	.343	2	.667	1	-1	-1	-0	0.0
Total	1	3	4	.429	11	6	4	1	0	61^2	73	39	1	1	22	25	14.0	3.94	74	.293	.353	9	.391	3	-7	-7	-1	-0.5

● ED VOSBERG

Vosberg, Edward John b: 9/28/61, Tucson, Ariz. BL/TL, 6'1", 190 lbs. Deb: 9/17/86

YEAR	TM/L	W	L	PCT	G	GS	CG	SH	SV	IP	H	R	HR	HB	BB	SO	RAT	ERA	ERA+	OAV	OOB	BH	AVG	PB	PR	PR+	PD	TPI
1986	SD-N	0	1	.000	5	3	0	0	0	13^2	17	11	1	0	9	8	17.1	6.59	56	.304	.400	0	.000	-0	-4	-5	-0	-0.4
1990	SF-N	1	1	.500	18	0	0	0	0	24^1	21	16	3	0	12	12	12.2	5.55	66	.233	.324	0	—	0	-5	-5	0	-0.4
1994	Oak-A	0	2	.000	16	0	0	0	0	13^2	16	7	2	0	5	12	13.8	3.95	112	.320	.382	0	—	0	1	1	1	0.2
1995	Tex-A	5	5	.500	44	0	0	0	4	36	32	15	3	0	16	36	12.0	3.00	161	.241	.322	0	—	0	7	7	-1	1.3
1996	*Tex-A	1	1	.500	52	0	0	0	8	44	51	17	4	0	21	32	14.7	3.27	160	.298	.375	0	—	0	8	9	1	0.7
1997	Tex-A	1	2	.333	42	0	0	0	0	41	44	23	3	2	15	29	13.4	4.61	104	.277	.347	0	—	0	-0	1	-1	0.0
	*Fla-N	1	1	.500	17	0	0	0	1	12	15	7	0	3	6	8	18.0	3.75	108	.313	.421	0	—	0	1	0	-0	0.0
1999	Ari-N	0	1	.000	4	0	0	0	0	2^2	6	1	0	0	0	2	20.3	3.38	136	.462	.462	0	—	0	0	0	-0	0.1
	SD-N	0	0	—	15	0	0	0	0	8^1	16	11	1	2	3	6	22.7	9.72	43	.421	.488	0	—	0	-5	-6	0	-0.2
	Yr	0	1	.000	19	0	0	0	0	11	22	12	1	2	3	8	22.1	8.18	52	.431	.482	0	—	0	-4	-5	0	-0.1
2000	Phi-N	1	1	.500	31	0	0	0	0	24	21	11	4	0	18	23	14.6	4.13	115	.241	.371	0	—	0	1	2	1	0.2
Total	8	10	15	.400	244	3	0	0	13	219^2	239	119	21	7	105	168	14.4	4.34	106	.283	.367	0	.000	-0	5	6	1	1.5

● ALEX VOSS

Voss, Alexander b: 5/16/1858, Roswell, Ga. d: 8/31/06, Cincinnati, Ohio BR/TR, 6'1", 180 lbs. Deb: 4/17/1884 ♦

YEAR	TM/L	W	L	PCT	G	GS	CG	SH	SV	IP	H	R	HR	HB	BB	SO	RAT	ERA	ERA+	OAV	OOB	BH	AVG	PB	PR	PR+	PD	TPI
1884	Was-U	5	14	.263	27	20	18	0	0	186^1	206	136	2		32	112	11.5	3.57	67	.262	.291	47	.192	-9	-23	-25	3	-2.3
	KC-U	0	6	.000	7	6	6	0	0	53	74	45	2		7	17	13.8	4.25	53	.310	.329	4	.089	-4	-11	-13	1	-1.3
	Yr	5	20	.200	34	26	24	0	0	239^1	280	181	4		39	129	12.0	3.72	63	.273	.300	51	.176	-13	-34	-37	3	-3.6

● RIP VOWINKEL

Vowinkel, John Henry b: 11/18/1884, Oswego, N.Y. d: 7/13/66, Oswego, N.Y. BR/TR, 5'10", 195 lbs. Deb: 9/5/05

YEAR	TM/L	W	L	PCT	G	GS	CG	SH	SV	IP	H	R	HR	HB	BB	SO	RAT	ERA	ERA+	OAV	OOB	BH	AVG	PB	PR	PR+	PD	TPI
1905	Cin-N	3	3	.500	6	6	4	0	0	45^1	52	31	2	1	10	7	12.5	4.17	79	.302	.344	1	.071	-0	-6	-4	-2	-0.7

YEAR	TM/L	W	L	PCT	G	GS	CG	SH	SV	IP	H	R	HR	HB	BB	SO	RAT	ERA	ERA+	OAV	OOB	BH	AVG	PB	PR	PR+	PD	TPI
● PETE VUCKOVICH	Vuckovich, Peter Dennis b: 10/27/52, Johnstown, Pa. BR/TR, 6'4", 220 lbs. Deb: 8/3/75 C																											
1975	Chi-A	0	1	.000	4	2	0	0	0	10^1	17	15	0	0	7	5	20.9	13.06	30	.386	.471	0	—	0	-11	-10	0	-0.8
1976	Chi-A	7	4	.636	33	7	1	0	0	110^1	122	59	3	4	60	62	15.2	4.65	77	.287	.380	0	—	0	-14	-13	0	-1.2
1977	Tor-A	7	7	.500	53	8	3	1	8	148	143	64	13	5	59	123	12.6	3.47	122	.257	.333	0	—	0	10	12	1	1.2
1978	StL-N	12	12	.500	45	23	6	2	1	198^1	187	65	9	2	59	149	11.3	2.54	139	.253	.310	8	.138	-1	23	22	2	2.7
1979	StL-N	15	10	.600	34	32	9	0	0	233	229	108	22	3	64	145	11.4	3.59	105	.260	.312	12	.152	-2	4	5	-1	0.2
1980	StL-N	12	9	.571	32	30	7	3	1	222^1	203	96	18	2	68	132	11.1	3.40	109	.247	.306	13	.183	1	5	7	-1	0.7
1981	*Mil-A	**14**	4	**.778**	24	23	2	1	0	149^2	137	61	9	4	57	84	11.9	3.55	97	.249	.324	0	—	0	2	-2	1	-0.1
1982	*Mil-A	18	6	**.750**	30	30	9	1	0	223^2	234	96	14	5	102	105	13.7	3.34	114	.275	.356	0	—	0	18	12	1	1.3
1983	Mil-A	0	2	.000	3	3	0	0	0	14^2	15	9	0	1	10	10	16.0	4.91	76	.259	.377	0	—	0	-1	-2	-0	-0.3
1985	Mil-A	6	10	.375	22	22	1	0	0	112^2	134	74	16	7	48	55	15.1	5.51	76	.298	.374	0	—	0	-17	-17	-1	-2.1
1986	Mil-A	2	4	.333	6	6	0	0	0	32^1	33	18	3	2	11	12	12.8	3.06	142	.273	.343	0	—	0	4	4	0	0.8
Total	11	93	69	.574	286	186	38	8	10	1455^1	1454	665	107	35	545	882	12.6	3.66	103	.264	.334	33	.159	-2	23	18	2	2.4
● PAUL WACHTEL	Wachtel, Paul Horine b: 4/30/1888, Myersville, Md. d: 12/15/64, San Antonio, Tex. BR/TR, 5'11", 175 lbs. Deb: 9/18/17																											
1917	Bro-N	0	0	—	2	0	0	0	0	6	9	7	0	0	4	3	19.5	10.50	27	.375	.464	1	.333	0	-5	-5	-0	-0.3
● CHARLIE WACKER	Wacker, Charles James b: 12/8/1883, Jeffersonville, Ind d: 8/7/48, Evansville, Ind. BL/TL, 5'9", Deb: 4/28/09																											
1909	Pit-N	0	0	—	1	0	0	0	0	2	2	2	0	0	1	0	13.5	0.00	—	.400	.500	0	—	0	1	1	0	0.0
● RUBE WADDELL	Waddell, George Edward b: 10/13/1876, Bradford, Pa. d: 4/1/14, San Antonio, Tex. BR/TL, 6'1.5", 196 lbs. Deb: 9/8/1897 H																											
1897	Lou-N	0	1	.000	2	1	1	0	0	14	17	6	0	1	6	5	15.4	3.21	132	.298	.375	0	.000	-1	2	2	0	0.0
1899	Lou-N	7	2	.778	10	9	9	1	1	79	69	38	4	8	14	44	10.4	3.08	125	.235	.288	8	.235	-0	7	7	-1	0.6
1900	*Pit-N	8	13	.381	29	22	16	2	0	208^2	176	96	3	13	55	130	10.5	**2.37**	**153**	**.229**	.291	14	.173	-2	31	30	1	2.5
1901	Pit-N	0	2	.000	2	2	0	0	0	7^2	10	12	0	1	9	4	23.5	9.39	35	.313	.476	0	.000	-0	-5	-5	0	-0.8
	Chi-N	14	14	.500	29	28	26	0	0	243^2	239	123	5	9	66	168	11.6	2.81	115	.255	.310	25	.255	6	14	12	3	2.3
	Yr	14	16	.467	31	30	26	0	0	251^1	249	135	5	10	75	172	12.0	3.01	108	.257	.317	25	.248	6	9	7	4	1.5
1902	Phi-A	24	7	.774	33	27	26	3	0	276^1	224	90	7	10	64	**210**	9.7	2.05	179	.222	.276	32	.286	7	47	48	-0	5.7
1903	Phi-A	21	16	.568	39	38	**34**	4	0	324	274	109	3	8	85	**302**	10.2	2.44	125	.229	.284	14	.122	-6	19	21	0	1.7
1904	Phi-A	25	19	.568	46	46	39	8	0	383	307	109	5	14	91	**349**	9.7	1.62	**165**	.221	.275	17	.122	-7	**42**	**44**	2	4.7
1905	Phi-A	**27**	10	**.730**	**46**	34	27	7	0	328^2	231	86	5	10	90	**287**	9.1	**1.48**	**180**	**.200**	.263	20	.172	-1	**43**	**43**	-0	4.9
1906	Phi-A	15	17	.469	43	34	22	8	0	272^2	221	89	1	10	92	**196**	10.7	2.21	123	.225	.297	14	.163	-0	15	15	-2	1.6
1907	Phi-A	19	13	.594	44	33	20	7	0	284^2	234	115	2	15	73	**232**	10.2	2.15	121	.227	.287	12	.119	-5	12	14	-2	0.8
1908	StL-A	19	14	.576	43	36	25	5	3	285^2	223	93	0	8	90	232	10.1	1.89	127	.213	.281	10	.110	-1	16	16	-1	1.7
1909	StL-A	11	14	.440	31	28	16	5	0	220^1	204	78	1	7	57	141	10.9	2.37	102	.267	.323	5	.067	-5	3	1	-1	-0.6
1910	StL-A	3	1	.750	10	2	0	0	1	33	31	19	1	1	11	16	11.7	3.55	70	.242	.307	1	.111	-0	-4	-4	-1	-0.7
Total	13	193	143	.574	407	340	261	50	5	2961^1	2460	1063	37	115	803	2316	10.3	2.16	135	.228	.288	172	.161	-17	240	245	-0	24.4
● TOM WADDELL	Waddell, Thomas David b: 9/17/58, Dundee, Scotland BR/TR, 6'1", 185 lbs. Deb: 4/15/84																											
1984	Cle-A	7	4	.636	58	0	0	0	6	97	68	35	12	1	37	59	9.8	3.06	134	.202	.283	0	—	0	10	11	-1	1.2
1985	Cle-A	8	6	.571	49	9	1	0	9	112^2	104	61	20	1	39	53	11.5	4.87	85	.246	.312	0	—	0	-9	-9	0	-1.1
1987	Cle-A	0	1	.000	6	0	0	0	0	5^2	7	10	1	1	7	6	23.8	14.29	32	.292	.469	0	—	0	-6	-6	-0	-0.9
Total	3	15	11	.577	113	9	1	0	15	215^1	179	106	33	3	83	118	11.1	4.30	96	.229	.305	0	—	0	-5	-4	-1	-0.8
● BEN WADE	Wade, Benjamin Styron b: 11/26/22, Morehead City, N.C BR/TR, 6'3", 205 lbs. Deb: 4/30/48 F																											
1948	Chi-N	0	1	.000	2	0	0	0	0	5	4	4	0	0	4	1	14.4	7.20	54	.211	.348	0	.000	-0	-2	-2	0	-0.3
1952	Bro-N	11	9	.550	37	24	5	1	3	180	166	81	19	2	94	118	13.1	3.60	101	.246	.340	7	.117	1	3	1	-2	0.0
1953	*Bro-N	7	5	.583	32	0	0	0	3	90^1	79	40	15	4	33	65	11.6	3.79	113	.232	.308	4	.167	0	5	5	-2	0.4
1954	Bro-N	1	1	.500	23	0	0	0	3	45	62	46	9	0	21	25	16.6	8.20	50	.339	.407	0	.000	-1	-21	-21	-1	-1.2
	StL-N	0	0	—	13	0	0	0	0	23	27	15	3	2	15	19	17.2	5.48	75	.303	.415	0	.000	-0	-4	-3	0	-0.2
	Yr	1	1	.500	36	0	0	0	3	68	89	61	12	2	36	44	16.8	7.28	56	.327	.410	0	.000	-1	-24	-24	-1	-1.4
1955	Pit-N	0	1	.000	11	1	0	0	1	28	26	12	3	1	14	7	13.2	3.21	128	.252	.347	0	.000	-0	3	3	-0	0.1
Total	5	19	17	.528	118	25	5	1	10	371^1	364	198	49	9	181	235	13.4	4.34	90	.259	.347	11	.112	-0	-16	-18	-5	-1.2
● TERRELL WADE	Wade, Hawatha Terrell b: 1/25/73, Rembert, S.C. BL/TL, 6'3", 205 lbs. Deb: 9/12/95																											
1995	Atl-N	0	1	.000	3	0	0	0	0	4	3	2	1	0	4	3	15.8	4.50	95	.214	.389	0	—	0	-0	-0	-0	0.0
1996	*Atl-N	5	0	1.000	44	8	0	0	1	69^2	57	28	9	1	47	79	13.6	2.97	148	.227	.351	2	.154	-0	10	11	0	0.7
1997	Atl-N	2	3	.400	12	9	0	0	0	42	60	31	6	2	16	35	16.7	5.36	79	.349	.411	3	.250	1	-5	-5	-0	-0.5
1998	TB-A	1	1	.500	2	2	0	0	0	10^2	14	6	3	0	2	8	13.5	5.06	95	.318	.348	0	—	0	-0	-0	-0	-0.1
Total	4	8	5	.615	61	19	0	0	1	126^1	134	67	19	3	69	125	14.7	3.99	110	.279	.373	5	.200	1	4	5	-1	0.1
● JAKE WADE	Wade, Jacob Fields "Whistling Jake" b: 4/1/12, Morehead City, N.C. BL/TL, 6'2", 175 lbs. Deb: 4/22/36 F																											
1936	Det-A	4	5	.444	13	11	4	1	0	78^1	93	60	7	1	52	30	16.8	5.29	94	.296	.398	5	.172	-0	-2	-3	-1	-0.4
1937	Det-A	7	10	.412	33	25	7	1	0	165^1	160	106	13	3	107	69	14.7	5.39	87	.257	.368	11	.186	-1	-14	-13	1	-1.2
1938	Det-A	3	2	.600	27	2	0	0	0	70	73	56	9	0	48	23	15.6	6.56	76	.268	.378	1	.048	-2	-14	-12	0	-0.9
1939	Bos-A	1	4	.200	20	6	1	0	0	47^2	68	34	1	0	37	21	19.8	6.23	76	.358	.463	0	.000	-2	-9	-8	-0	-0.8
	StL-A	0	2	.000	4	2	1	0	0	16^1	26	25	1	0	19	9	24.8	11.02	44	.356	.489	0	.000	-1	-12	-11	0	-1.0
	Yr	1	6	.143	24	8	2	0	0	64	94	59	2	0	56	30	21.1	7.45	64	.357	.470	0	.000	-3	-20	-19	0	-1.8
1942	Chi-A	5	5	.500	15	10	3	1	0	85^2	84	45	2	0	56	32	14.7	4.10	88	.255	.363	7	.241	1	-4	-5	1	-0.3
1943	Chi-A	3	7	.300	21	9	3	1	0	83^2	66	34	3	4	54	41	13.3	3.01	111	.222	.349	4	.148	-0	3	3	-1	0.2
1944	Chi-A	2	4	.333	19	5	1	0	2	74^2	75	46	3	0	41	35	14.0	4.82	71	.261	.354	7	.292	1	-12	-12	-2	-1.0
1946	NY-A	2	1	.667	13	1	0	0	1	35^1	33	9	2	1	14	22	12.2	2.29	151	.250	.327	1	.111	-0	5	5	0	0.4
	Was-A	0	0	—	6	0	0	0	0	11^1	12	6	1	0	12	9	19.1	4.76	70	.279	.436	0	.000	-0	-2	-2	0	-0.1
	Yr	2	1	.667	19	1	0	0	1	46^2	45	15	3	1	26	31	13.9	2.89	118	.257	.356	1	.100	-0	3	3	1	0.3
Total	8	27	40	.403	171	71	20	3	3	668^1	690	421	42	9	440	291	15.3	5.00	84	.269	.378	36	.167	-5	-60	-58	-1	-5.1
● JACK WADSWORTH	Wadsworth, John L. b: 12/17/1867, Wellington, Ohio d: 7/8/41, Elyria, Ohio BL/TR, 180 lbs. Deb: 5/1/1890																											
1890	Cle-N	2	16	.111	20	19	19	0	0	169^2	202	139	6	6	81	26	15.3	5.20	69	.287	.365	12	.176	-3	-31	-30	-1	-2.7
1893	Bal-N	0	3	.000	3	3	0	0	0	16	37	30	0	0	8	2	25.3	11.25	42	.440	.489	3	.429	1	-12	-11	-1	-1.3
1894	Lou-N	4	18	.182	22	22	20	0	0	173	261	204	10	4	103	57	19.1	7.60	67	.344	.425	19	.257	0	-44	-50	-0	-4.0
1895	Lou-N	0	1	.000	2	0	0	0	0	9	24	20	0	0	7	2	31.0	16.00	29	.480	.544	1	.250	-0	-11	-12	0	-0.8
Total	4	6	38	.136	47	44	39	0	0	367^2	524	393	16	10	199	87	17.9	6.85	64	.328	.406	35	.229	-2	-97	-103	-1	-8.8
● CHARLIE WAGNER	Wagner, Charles Thomas "Broadway" b: 12/3/12, Reading, Pa. BR/TR, 5'11", 170 lbs. Deb: 4/19/38 C																											
1938	Bos-A	1	3	.250	13	6	1	0	0	36^2	47	36	5	1	24	14	17.7	8.35	59	.309	.407	2	.167	-1	-14	-14	-1	-1.2
1939	Bos-A	3	1	.750	9	5	0	0	0	38^1	49	19	3	0	14	13	14.8	4.23	112	.320	.377	1	.071	-2	2	2	-0	0.0
1940	Bos-A	1	0	1.000	12	1	0	0	0	29^1	45	22	5	0	8	13	16.3	5.52	81	.344	.381	1	.200	-0	-4	-3	-0	-0.2
1941	Bos-A	12	8	.600	29	25	12	3	0	187^1	175	76	14	1	85	51	12.5	3.07	136	.245	.326	10	.159	-1	22	23	-0	2.0
1942	Bos-A	14	11	.560	29	26	17	2	0	205^1	184	87	5	5	95	52	12.4	3.29	113	.247	.336	5	.077	-5	8	10	1	0.7
1946	Bos-A	1	0	1.000	8	4	0	0	0	30^2	32	21	6	0	19	14	15.0	5.87	62	.276	.378	1	.091	-1	-8	-7	-0	-0.5
Total	6	32	23	.582	100	67	30	5	0	527^2	532	261	38	7	245	157	13.4	3.91	104	.264	.346	20	.118	-9	6	10	-1	0.8
● GARY WAGNER	Wagner, Gary Edward b: 6/28/40, Bridgeport, Ill. BR/TR, 6'4", 191 lbs. Deb: 4/18/65																											
1965	Phi-N	7	7	.500	59	0	0	0	7	105	87	43	6	2	49	91	11.8	3.00	115	.233	.325	1	.077	-0	6	5	1	0.9
1966	Phi-N	0	1	.000	5	1	0	0	0	6^1	8	6	1	0	5	2	18.5	8.53	42	.333	.448	0	—	0	-3	-3	-0	-0.5
1967	Phi-N	0	0	—	2	0	0	0	0	2	1	0	0	0	0	1	4.5	0.00	—	.167	.167	0	—	0	1	1	0	0.1
1968	Phi-N	4	4	.500	44	0	0	0	8	78	69	27	0	5	31	43	12.1	3.00	100	.243	.328	1	.083	-1	-0	0	1	0.0
1969	Phi-N	0	3	.000	9	2	0	0	0	19^1	31	22	3	0	7	8	17.7	7.91	45	.365	.413	0	.000	-0	-9	-10	-1	-1.4
	Bos-A	1	3	.250	6	1	0	0	0	16^1	18	11	1	0	15	9	18.2	6.06	63	.300	.440	0	.000	-0	-4	-4	0	-0.8
1970	Bos-A	3	1	.750	38	0	0	0	7	40^1	36	21	3	2	19	20	12.7	3.35	118	.232	.324	1	.167	-0	2	3	-1	0.3
Total	6	15	19	.441	162	4	0	0	22	267^1	250	130	14	9	126	174	13.0	3.70	93	.253	.343	3	.081	-2	-9	-8	1	-1.4

YEAR	TM/L	W	L	PCT	G	GS	CG	SH	SV	IP	H	R	HR	HB	BB	SO	RAT	ERA	ERA+	OAV	OOB	BH	AVG	PB	PR	PR+	PD	TPI
● HECTOR WAGNER	Wagner, Hector Raul Guerrero (b: Hector Raul Guerrero (Wagner)) b: 11/26/68, San Juan, D.R. BR/TR, 6'3", 185 lbs. Deb: 9/10/90																											
1990	KC-A	0	2	.000	5	5	0	0	0	23^1	32	24	4	0	11	14	16.6	8.10	47	.323	.391	0	—	0	-11	-11	0	-0.8
1991	KC-A	1	1	.500	2	2	0	0	0	10	16	10	2	0	3	5	17.1	7.20	57	.348	.388	0	—	0	-3	-3	-0	-0.6
Total	2	1	3	.250	7	7	0	0	0	33^1	48	34	6	0	14	19	16.7	7.83	50	.331	.390	0	—	0	-14	-15	0	-1.4
● HONUS WAGNER	Wagner, John Peter "The Flying Dutchman" b: 2/24/1874, Chartiers, Pa. d: 12/6/55, Carnegie, Pa. BR/TR (BB 1909 (part)), 5'11", 200 lbs. Deb: 7/19/1897 FMCH♦																											
1900	*Pit-N	0	0	—	1	0	0	0	0	3	3	3	0	0	4	1	21.0	0.00	—	.250	.438	201	.381	1	1	1	-0	0.1
1902	Pit-N	0	0	—	1	0	0	0	0	5^1	4	2	0	0	2	5	10.1	0.00	—	.211	.286	176	.330	1	2	2	-0	0.1
Total	2	0	0	—	2	0	0	0	0	8^1	7	5	0	0	6	6	14.0	0.00	—	.226	.351	3420	.328	1	3	3	-0	0.2
● MARK WAGNER	Wagner, Mark Duane b: 3/4/54, Conneaut, Ohio BR/TR, 6'1", 175 lbs. Deb: 8/20/76 ♦																											
1984	Oak-A	0	0	—	1	0	0	0	0	1^2	2	0	0	0	1	1	16.2	0.00	—	.400	.500	20	.230	0	1	1	-0	0.0
● MATT WAGNER	Wagner, Matthew William b: 4/4/72, Cedar Falls, Ia. BR/TR, 6'5", 215 lbs. Deb: 6/5/96																											
1996	Sea-A	3	5	.375	15	14	1	0	0	80	91	62	15	3	38	41	14.8	6.86	72	.285	.367	0	—	0	-17	-17	-1	-1.4
● PAUL WAGNER	Wagner, Paul Alan b: 11/14/67, Milwaukee, Wis. BR/TR, 6'1", 202 lbs. Deb: 7/26/92																											
1992	Pit-N	2	0	1.000	6	1	0	0	0	13	9	1	0	0	5	5	9.7	0.69	498	.191	.269	1	.333	0	4	4	0	0.7
1993	Pit-N	8	8	.500	44	17	1	1	2	141^1	143	72	15	1	42	114	11.8	4.27	95	.263	.317	8	.190	0	-3	-3	-1	-0.4
1994	Pit-N	7	8	.467	29	17	1	0	0	119^2	136	69	7	8	50	86	14.6	4.59	94	.293	.372	6	.162	-0	-5	-3	2	-0.2
1995	Pit-N	5	16	.238	33	25	3	1	1	165	174	96	18	7	72	120	13.8	4.80	90	.273	.353	9	.214	2	-11	-9	1	-0.8
1996	Pit-N	4	8	.333	16	15	1	0	0	81^2	86	49	10	3	39	81	14.1	5.40	81	.275	.361	1	.040	-2	-11	-9	1	-1.2
1997	Pit-N	0	0	—	14	0	0	0	0	16	17	7	3	0	13	9	16.9	3.94	109	.274	.400	0	.000	-0	0	1	0	0.0
	Mil-A	1	0	1.000	2	0	0	0	0	2	3	2	1	0	0	0	13.5	9.00	51	.375	.375	0	—	0	-1	-1	0	-0.2
1998	Mil-N	1	5	.167	13	9	0	0	0	55^2	67	49	10	1	31	37	16.0	7.11	60	.302	.390	3	.158	-0	-18	-17	-0	-1.6
1999	Cle-A	1	0	1.000	3	0	0	0	0	4^1	5	4	0	2	3	0	20.8	4.15	122	.263	.417	0	—	0	0	0	-0	0.1
Total	8	29	45	.392	160	84	6	2	3	598^2	640	349	64	22	255	452	13.8	4.83	88	.276	.354	28	.166	-0	-44	-38	3	-3.6
● BILLY WAGNER	Wagner, William Edward b: 7/25/71, Tannersville, Va. BL/TL, 5'10", 180 lbs. Deb: 9/13/95																											
1995	Hou-N	0	0	—	1	0	0	0	0	0^1	0	0	0	0	0	0	0.0	0.00	—	.000	.000	0	—	0	0	0	0	0.0
1996	Hou-N	2	2	.500	37	0	0	0	9	51^2	28	16	6	3	30	67	10.6	2.44	159	.165	.300	0	.000	-1	10	9	-1	0.8
1997	*Hou-N	7	8	.467	62	0	0	0	23	66^1	49	23	5	3	30	106	11.1	2.85	140	.204	.300	0	.000	-0	10	9	0	1.8
1998	*Hou-N	4	3	.571	58	0	0	0	30	60	46	19	6	0	25	97	10.7	2.70	150	.211	.292	0	.000	-0	10	9	-1	1.8
1999	*Hou-N★	4	1	.800	66	0	0	0	39	74^2	35	14	5	1	23	124	7.1	1.57	282	.135	.208	1	.333	0	**25**	**24**	-0	3.7
2000	Hou-N	2	4	.333	28	0	0	0	6	27^2	28	19	6	1	18	28	15.3	6.18	79	.255	.364	0	.000	-0	-5	-4	-0	-0.8
Total	6	19	18	.514	252	0	0	0	107	280^2	186	91	28	8	126	422	10.3	2.73	153	.186	.283	1	.091	-1	51	47	-2	7.3
● BULL WAGNER	Wagner, William George b: 12/25/1887, Lilley, Mich. d: 10/2/67, Muskegon, Mich. BR/TR, 6'0.5", 225 lbs. Deb: 6/2/13																											
1913	Bro-N	4	2	.667	18	1	0	0	0	70^2	77	49	5	3	30	11	14.0	5.48	60	.285	.363	6	.231	0	-18	-17	-2	-1.4
1914	Bro-N	0	1	.000	6	0	0	0	0	12^1	14	11	0	1	12	4	19.7	6.57	44	.311	.466	0	.000	-0	-5	-5	-0	-0.4
Total	2	4	3	.571	24	1	0	0	0	83	91	60	5	4	42	15	14.9	5.64	57	.289	.380	6	.222	0	-23	-22	-2	-1.8
● DAVID WAINHOUSE	Wainhouse, David Paul b: 11/7/67, Toronto, Ont., Can. BL/TR, 6'2", 190 lbs. Deb: 8/3/91																											
1991	Mon-N	0	1	.000	2	0	0	0	0	2^2	2	2	0	0	4	1	20.3	6.75	54	.222	.462	0	—	0	-1	-1	-0	-0.2
1993	Sea-A	0	0	—	3	0	0	0	0	2^1	7	7	1	1	5	2	50.1	27.00	16	.500	.650	0	—	0	-6	-6	-0	-0.3
1996	Pit-N	1	0	1.000	17	0	0	0	0	23^2	22	16	3	0	10	16	12.2	5.70	77	.250	.327	0	—	0	-4	-3	1	-0.1
1997	Pit-N	0	1	.000	25	0	0	0	0	28	34	28	2	3	17	21	17.4	8.04	53	.301	.406	0	.000	-0	-12	-11	-0	-0.6
1998	Col-N	1	0	1.000	10	0	0	0	0	11	15	6	1	2	5	3	18.0	4.91	105	.341	.431	0	.000	-0	-1	0	1	0.1
1999	Col-N	0	0	—	19	0	0	0	0	28^2	37	22	6	0	16	18	16.6	6.91	84	.330	.414	0	.000	-0	-7	-3	0	-0.1
2000	StL-N	0	1	.000	9	0	0	0	0	8^2	13	10	2	2	4	5	19.7	9.35	50	.351	.442	0	—	0	-5	-5	0	-0.4
Total	7	2	3	.400	85	0	0	0	0	105	130	91	15	8	61	66	17.1	7.37	65	.312	.409	0	.000	-1	-35	-27	2	-1.6
● RICK WAITS	Waits, Michael Richard b: 5/15/52, Atlanta, Ga. BL/TL, 6'3", 195 lbs. Deb: 9/17/73																											
1973	Tex-A	0	0	—	1	0	0	0	1	1	1	1	0	0	1	0	18.0	9.00	41	.333	.500	0	—	0	-1	-1	0	-0.1
1975	Cle-A	6	2	.750	16	7	3	0	1	70^1	57	25	3	1	25	34	10.6	2.94	129	.221	.292	0	—	0	7	7	0	0.8
1976	Cle-A	7	9	.438	26	22	4	2	0	123^2	143	60	7	0	54	65	14.3	4.00	87	.297	.368	0	—	0	-7	-7	1	-0.8
1977	Cle-A	9	7	.563	37	16	1	0	2	135^1	132	67	8	1	64	62	13.1	3.99	99	.262	.347	0	—	0	1	-1	-0	-0.1
1978	Cle-A	13	15	.464	34	33	15	2	0	230^1	206	97	16	2	86	97	11.5	3.20	117	.240	.310	0	—	0	15	14	3	2.0
1979	Cle-A	16	13	.552	34	34	8	3	0	231	230	123	26	4	91	91	12.7	4.44	96	.264	.336	0	—	0	-5	-4	2	-0.3
1980	Cle-A	13	14	.481	33	33	9	2	0	224^1	231	118	18	1	82	109	12.6	4.45	92	.270	.335	0	—	0	-10	-9	-1	-1.1
1981	Cle-A	8	10	.444	22	21	5	1	0	126^1	173	74	7	1	44	51	15.5	4.92	74	.330	.383	0	—	0	-18	-18	2	-2.1
1982	Cle-A	2	13	.133	25	21	2	0	0	115	128	74	13	1	57	44	14.6	5.40	76	.290	.372	0	—	0	-17	-17	1	-1.8
1983	Cle-A	0	1	.000	8	0	0	0	0	19^2	23	13	1	0	9	13	14.6	4.58	93	.307	.381	0	—	0	-1	-1	0	-0.1
	Mil-A	0	2	.000	10	2	0	0	0	30	39	20	1	0	11	20	15.0	5.10	74	.320	.376	0	—	0	-3	-5	-0	-0.3
	Yr	0	3	.000	18	2	0	0	0	49^2	62	33	2	0	20	33	14.9	4.89	81	.315	.378	0	—	0	-5	-5	-0	-0.3
1984	Mil-A	2	4	.333	47	1	0	0	3	73	84	32	7	0	24	49	13.3	3.58	108	.297	.352	0	—	0	3	2	0	0.2
1985	Mil-A	3	2	.600	24	0	0	0	1	47	67	37	3	0	20	24	16.7	6.51	64	.340	.401	1	.000	-0	-12	-12	0	-1.2
Total	12	79	92	.462	317	190	47	10	8	1427	1514	741	110	11	568	659	13.2	4.25	92	.277	.346	1	.000	-0	-48	-52	8	-4.8
● TIM WAKEFIELD	Wakefield, Timothy Stephen b: 8/2/66, Melbourne, Fla. BR/TR, 6'2", 204 lbs. Deb: 7/31/92																											
1992	*Pit-N	8	1	.889	13	13	4	1	0	92	76	26	3	1	35	51	11.0	2.15	160	.232	.309	2	.071	-1	14	13	1	1.3
1993	Pit-N	6	11	.353	24	20	3	2	0	128^1	145	83	14	9	75	59	16.1	5.61	72	.291	.393	7	.163	1	-22	-22	-1	-2.5
1995	*Bos-A	16	8	.667	27	27	6	1	0	195^1	163	76	22	9	68	119	11.1	2.95	165	.227	.302	0	—	0	38	40	-1	4.4
1996	Bos-A	14	13	.519	32	32	6	0	0	211^2	238	151	38	12	90	140	14.5	5.14	99	.280	.357	0	—	0	-3	-2	-2	-0.3
1997	Bos-A	12	15	.444	35	29	4	2	0	201^1	193	109	24	16	87	151	13.2	4.25	109	.256	.346	0	.000	-0	7	9	-1	0.9
1998	*Bos-A	17	8	.680	36	33	2	0	0	216	211	123	30	14	79	146	12.7	4.58	103	.252	.327	0	.000	0	2	3	-1	0.2
1999	*Bos-A	6	11	.353	49	17	0	0	15	140	146	93	19	5	72	104	14.3	5.08	98	.266	.356	0	.000	-0	-3	-2	-1	-0.3
2000	Bos-A	6	10	.375	51	17	0	0	0	159^1	170	107	31	4	65	102	13.5	5.48	93	.272	.344	0	.000	-0	-10	-7	-2	-0.7
Total	8	85	77	.525	267	188	25	6	15	1344	1342	768	181	70	571	872	13.3	4.47	105	.260	.342	9	.114	-1	23	34	-9	3.0
● BILL WAKEFIELD	Wakefield, William Sumner b: 5/24/41, Kansas City, Mo. BR/TR, 6', 175 lbs. Deb: 4/18/64																											
1964	NY-N	3	5	.375	62	4	0	0	2	119^2	103	57	10	9	61	61	13.0	3.61	99	.235	.341	4	.167	-0	-1	-0	0	0.0
● RUBE WALBERG	Walberg, George Elvin b: 7/27/1896, Pine City, Minn. d: 10/27/78, Tempe, Ariz. BL/TL, 6'1.5", 190 lbs. Deb: 4/29/23																											
1923	NY-N	0	0	—	2	0	0	0	0	5	4	2	0	0	1	1	9.0	1.80	212	.211	.250	0	.000	-0	1	1	-0	0.0
	Phi-A	4	8	.333	26	10	4	0	0	115	122	77	10	2	60	38	14.4	5.32	77	.280	.369	13	.317	3	-17	-15	1	-1.0
1924	Phi-A	0	0	—	6	2	0	0	0	7	10	10	0	0	10	3	25.7	12.86	33	.345	.513	1	.500	0	-7	-7	0	-0.3
1925	Phi-A	8	14	.364	53	20	7	0	7	191^2	197	99	11	2	77	82	13.0	3.99	117	.269	.340	10	.156	-4	9	13	1	1.1
1926	Phi-A	12	10	.545	40	19	5	2	2	151	168	67	4	6	60	72	13.9	2.80	149	.292	.365	7	.152	-2	20	22	-1	2.7
1927	Phi-A	16	12	.571	46	33	14	0	4	249^1	257	139	18	4	91	136	12.7	3.93	108	.271	.337	18	.207	3	6	9	-0	1.1
1928	Phi-A	17	12	.586	38	30	15	3	1	235^2	236	111	19	3	64	112	11.6	3.55	113	.265	.317	18	.209	1	13	12	1	1.5
1929	*Phi-A	18	11	.621	40	33	20	3	4	267^2	256	115	22	0	99	94	11.9	3.60	118	.254	.320	23	.223	-0	19	19	-2	1.6
1930	*Phi-A	13	12	.520	38	30	12	2	1	205^1	207	121	6	2	85	100	12.9	4.69	100	.262	.335	12	.164	-3	-1	-0	-1	-0.4
1931	*Phi-A	20	12	.625	44	35	19	1	3	**291**	298	133	16	0	109	106	12.6	3.74	120	.266	.331	13	.124	-6	21	24	-1	1.5
1932	Phi-A	17	10	.630	41	34	19	3	1	272	305	159	16	0	103	96	13.5	4.73	96	.282	.344	16	.170	-3	-8	-6	-0	-0.8
1933	Phi-A	9	13	.409	40	20	10	1	4	201	224	132	12	1	95	68	14.3	4.88	88	.278	.354	9	.132	-1	-13	-13	1	-1.4
1934	Bos-A	6	7	.462	30	10	2	0	1	104^2	118	62	5	1	41	38	13.8	4.04	119	.284	.350	6	.188	-1	5	8	1	0.9
1935	Bos-A	5	9	.357	44	10	4	0	3	142^2	152	71	10	2	54	44	13.1	3.91	121	.273	.340	6	.162	-2	9	12	-1	0.8
1936	Bos-A	5	4	.556	24	9	5	0	0	100^1	98	53	7	1	36	49	12.1	4.40	121	.257	.323	5	.156	-1	7	10	1	0.6
1937	Bos-A	5	7	.417	32	11	3	0	1	104^2	143	72	7	3	46	46	16.5	5.59	85	.332	.400	5	.147	-1	-11	-10	-0	-1.1
Total	15	155	141	.524	544	306	139	15	32	2644	2795	1423	163	27	1031	1085	13.1	4.16	107	.273	.341	162	.179	-18	53	80	-2	6.8

YEAR	TM/L	W	L	PCT	G	GS	CG	SH	SV	IP	H	R	HR	HB	BB	SO	RAT	ERA	ERA+	OAV	OOB	BH	AVG	PB	PR	PR+	PD	TPI

● DOC WALDBAUER
Waldbauer, Albert Charles b: 2/22/1892, Richmond, Va. d: 7/16/69, Yakima, Wash. BR/TR, 6', 172 lbs. Deb: 9/24/17

YEAR	TM/L	W	L	PCT	G	GS	CG	SH	SV	IP	H	R	HR	HB	BB	SO	RAT	ERA	ERA+	OAV	OOB	BH	AVG	PB	PR	PR+	PD	TPI
1917	Was-A	0	0	—	2	0	0	0	1	5	10	4	0	0	2	2	21.6	7.20	36	.476	.522	0	.000	-0	-3	-3	0	-0.1

● BOB WALK
Walk, Robert Vernon b: 11/26/56, Van Nuys, Cal. BR/TR, 6'4", 208 lbs. Deb: 5/26/80

YEAR	TM/L	W	L	PCT	G	GS	CG	SH	SV	IP	H	R	HR	HB	BB	SO	RAT	ERA	ERA+	OAV	OOB	BH	AVG	PB	PR	PR+	PD	TPI
1980	*Phi-N	11	7	.611	27	27	2	0	0	151^2	163	82	8	2	71	94	14.0	4.57	83	.276	.356	7	.140	-0	-16	-12	-1	-1.5
1981	Atl-N	1	4	.200	12	8	0	0	0	43^1	41	25	6	0	23	16	13.3	4.57	78	.250	.342	1	.143	-0	-5	-5	-1	-0.6
1982	*Atl-N	11	9	.550	32	27	3	1	0	164^1	179	101	19	6	59	84	13.4	4.87	77	.280	.347	10	.196	2	-23	-20	-2	-2.3
1983	Atl-N	0	0	—	1	1	0	0	0	3^2	7	3	0	0	2	4	22.1	7.36	53	.412	.474	0	.000	-0	-2	-1	0	0.0
1984	Pit-N	1	1	.500	2	2	0	0	0	10^1	8	5	1	0	4	10	10.5	2.61	138	.200	.273	0	.000	-0	1	1	-0	0.1
1985	Pit-N	2	3	.400	9	9	1	1	0	58^2	60	27	3	0	18	40	12.0	3.68	97	.265	.320	0	.000	-1	-1	-1	-1	-0.3
1986	Pit-N	7	8	.467	44	15	1	1	2	141^2	129	66	14	3	64	78	12.5	3.75	102	.251	.337	6	.154	0	-0	1	2	0.4
1987	Pit-N	8	2	.800	39	12	1	1	0	117	107	52	11	3	51	78	12.4	3.31	124	.245	.329	6	.231	1	10	10	1	1.0
1988	Pit-N★	12	10	.545	32	32	1	1	0	212^2	183	75	6	2	65	81	10.6	2.71	126	.230	.290	6	.087	-2	18	17	0	1.5
1989	Pit-N	13	10	.565	33	31	2	0	0	196	208	106	15	4	65	83	12.7	4.41	76	.271	.331	13	.186	3	-20	-24	1	-2.3
1990	*Pit-N	7	5	.583	26	24	1	1	1	129^2	136	59	17	4	36	73	12.2	3.75	97	.270	.324	6	.162	1	1	-2	-1	-0.2
1991	*Pit-N	9	2	.818	25	20	0	0	0	115	104	53	10	5	35	67	11.3	3.60	99	.240	.304	8	.205	2	1	-0	-0	0.2
1992	*Pit-N	10	6	.625	36	19	1	0	2	135	132	54	10	6	43	60	12.1	3.20	108	.258	.323	4	.093	-2	5	4	1	0.4
1993	Pit-N	13	14	.481	32	32	3	0	0	187	214	121	23	5	70	80	13.9	5.68	71	.294	.360	7	.121	-2	-34	-34	-1	-4.3
Total	14	105	81	.565	350	259	16	6	5	1666	1671	829	143	40	606	848	12.5	4.03	91	.263	.330	74	.145	1	-65	-66	-1	-7.9

● ED WALKER
Walker, Edward Harrison b: 8/11/1874, Cambois, England d: 9/29/47, Akron, Ohio BL/TL, 6'5", 242 lbs. Deb: 9/26/02

YEAR	TM/L	W	L	PCT	G	GS	CG	SH	SV	IP	H	R	HR	HB	BB	SO	RAT	ERA	ERA+	OAV	OOB	BH	AVG	PB	PR	PR+	PD	TPI
1902	Cle-A	0	1	.000	1	1	1	0	0	8	11	4	0	0	3	1	15.8	3.38	102	.324	.378	1	.333	0	0	0	0	0.0
1903	Cle-A	0	1	.000	3	3	0	0	0	12	13	12	0	0	10	4	17.3	5.25	54	.277	.404	0	.000	-0	-3	-3	-1	-0.3
Total	2	0	2	.000	4	4	1	0	0	20	24	16	0	0	13	5	16.6	4.50	69	.296	.394	1	.167	0	-3	-3	-1	-0.3

● DIXIE WALKER
Walker, Ewart Gladstone b: 6/1/1887, Brownsville, Pa. d: 11/14/65, Leeds, Ala. BL/TR, 6', 192 lbs. Deb: 9/17/09 F

YEAR	TM/L	W	L	PCT	G	GS	CG	SH	SV	IP	H	R	HR	HB	BB	SO	RAT	ERA	ERA+	OAV	OOB	BH	AVG	PB	PR	PR+	PD	TPI
1909	Was-A	3	1	.750	4	4	4	0	0	36	31	12	0	0	6	25	9.3	2.50	97	.217	.248	2	.154	-0	-0	-0	-0	-0.1
1910	Was-A	11	11	.500	29	26	16	3	0	199^1	177	83	2	8	68	84	11.4	3.30	76	.245	.317	9	.130	-3	-17	-18	-1	-2.3
1911	Was-A	8	13	.381	32	24	15	2	0	185^2	205	103	2	8	50	65	12.7	3.39	97	.286	.339	20	.303	4	-1	-2	-1	0.0
1912	Was-A	3	6	.333	9	8	5	0	0	60	72	40	2	4	18	29	14.1	5.25	64	.300	.359	2	.125	1	-13	-13	-0	-1.5
Total	4	25	31	.446	74	62	40	5	0	481	485	238	6	20	142	203	12.1	3.52	82	.266	.326	33	.201	2	-31	-33	-3	-3.9

● MYSTERIOUS WALKER
Walker, Frederick Mitchell b: 3/21/1884, Utica, Neb. d: 2/1/58, Oak Park, Ill. BR/TR, 5'10.5", 185 lbs. Deb: 6/28/10

YEAR	TM/L	W	L	PCT	G	GS	CG	SH	SV	IP	H	R	HR	HB	BB	SO	RAT	ERA	ERA+	OAV	OOB	BH	AVG	PB	PR	PR+	PD	TPI
1910	Cin-N	0	0	—	1	0	0	0	0	3	4	2	0	0	4	1	24.0	3.00	97	.333	.500	0	.000	-0	0	-0	0	0.0
1912	Cle-A	0	0	—	1	0	0	0	0	1	0	0	0	0	1	0	9.0	0.00	—	.000	.200	0		0	0	0	-0	0.0
1913	Bro-N	1	3	.250	11	8	3	0	0	58^1	44	26	3	5	35	35	13.0	3.55	93	.233	.367	3	.167	-0	-2	-2	2	0.0
1914	Pit-F	4	16	.200	35	21	12	0	0	169^1	197	108	3	3	74	79	14.6	4.31	67	.294	.367	6	.113	-3	-27	-27	3	-2.9
1915	Bro-F	2	4	.333	13	7	2	0	1	65^2	61	37	3	0	22	28	11.4	3.70	73	.242	.303	6	.222	0	-7	-7	1	-0.5
Total	5	7	23	.233	61	36	17	0	1	297^1	306	173	9	8	136	143	13.6	4.00	73	.272	.354	15	.152	-3	-36	-36	6	-3.4

● GEORGE WALKER
Walker, George A. b: 1863, Hamilton, Ontario, Canada TR, 5'9", 184 lbs. Deb: 8/1/1888

YEAR	TM/L	W	L	PCT	G	GS	CG	SH	SV	IP	H	R	HR	HB	BB	SO	RAT	ERA	ERA+	OAV	OOB	BH	AVG	PB	PR	PR+	PD	TPI
1888	Bal-a	1	3	.250	4	4	4	1	0	35	36	31	2	0	14	18	12.9	5.91	50	.257	.325	1	.077	-1	-11	-12	-0	-1.1

● LUKE WALKER
Walker, James Luke b: 9/2/43, DeKalb, Tex. BL/TL, 6'1.5", 192 lbs. Deb: 9/7/65

YEAR	TM/L	W	L	PCT	G	GS	CG	SH	SV	IP	H	R	HR	HB	BB	SO	RAT	ERA	ERA+	OAV	OOB	BH	AVG	PB	PR	PR+	PD	TPI
1965	Pit-N	0	0	—	2	0	0	0	0	5	2	0	0	0	1	5	5.4	0.00	—	.118	.167	0	—	0	2	2	0	0.1
1966	Pit-N	0	1	.000	10	1	0	0	0	10	8	9	0	1	15	7	21.6	4.50	79	.205	.436	0	.000	-0	-1	-1	-0	-0.1
1968	Pit-N	0	3	.000	39	2	0	0	3	61^2	42	18	1	1	39	66	12.0	2.04	143	.190	.314	0	.000	-1	6	6	1	0.4
1969	Pit-N	4	6	.400	31	15	3	1	0	118^2	98	51	5	2	57	96	11.9	3.64	96	.226	.319	0	.000	-3	-1	-2	1	-0.4
1970	*Pit-N	15	6	.714	42	19	5	3	3	163	129	56	6	1	89	124	12.1	3.04	129	.219	.323	6	.130	-1	18	16	-0	1.9
1971	*Pit-N	10	8	.556	28	24	4	2	0	159^2	157	69	9	2	53	86	11.9	3.55	95	.262	.324	1	.022	-3	-1	-3	-2	-0.8
1972	*Pit-N	4	6	.400	26	12	2	0	2	92^2	98	41	4	0	34	48	12.8	3.40	98	.278	.342	2	.083	-1	1	-1	-0	-0.3
1973	Pit-N	7	12	.368	37	18	2	1	1	122	129	75	9	1	66	74	14.5	4.65	76	.270	.360	2	.067	-2	-13	-16	-1	-2.6
1974	Det-A	5	5	.500	28	9	0	0	0	92	100	56	9	2	54	52	15.3	4.99	76	.278	.375	0	—	0	-14	-11	-0	-1.2
Total	9	45	47	.489	243	100	16	7	9	824^2	763	375	43	10	408	558	12.9	3.65	97	.247	.337	11	.059	-11	-3	-10	-2	-3.0

● JAMIE WALKER
Walker, James Ross b: 7/1/71, McMinnville, Tenn. BL/TL, 6'2", 190 lbs. Deb: 4/2/97

YEAR	TM/L	W	L	PCT	G	GS	CG	SH	SV	IP	H	R	HR	HB	BB	SO	RAT	ERA	ERA+	OAV	OOB	BH	AVG	PB	PR	PR+	PD	TPI
1997	KC-A	3	3	.500	50	0	0	0	0	43	46	28	6	3	20	24	14.4	5.44	87	.271	.358	0	—	0	-4	-3	0	-0.4
1998	KC-A	0	1	.000	6	2	0	0	0	17^1	30	20	5	2	3	15	18.2	9.87	49	.380	.417	0	—	0	-10	-9	1	-0.4
Total	2	3	4	.429	56	2	0	0	0	60^1	76	48	11	5	23	39	15.5	6.71	71	.305	.375	0	—	0	-14	-13	1	-0.8

● ROY WALKER
Walker, James Roy "Dixie" b: 4/13/1893, Lawrenceburg, Tenn d: 2/10/62, New Orleans, La. BR/TR (BB 1918, 22), 6'1.5", 180 lbs. Deb: 9/16/12

YEAR	TM/L	W	L	PCT	G	GS	CG	SH	SV	IP	H	R	HR	HB	BB	SO	RAT	ERA	ERA+	OAV	OOB	BH	AVG	PB	PR	PR+	PD	TPI
1912	Cle-A	0	0	—	1	0	0	0	0	2	0	0	0	0	2	1	9.0	0.00	—	.000	.250	0	—	0	1	1	-0	0.0
1915	Cle-A	4	9	.308	25	15	4	0	1	131	122	73	1	7	65	57	13.3	3.98	77	.261	.360	5	.132	-2	-15	-13	-2	-1.7
1917	Chi-N	0	1	.000	2	1	0	0	0	7	8	5	0	0	5	4	16.7	3.86	75	.286	.394	0	.000	-0	-1	-1	-0	-0.1
1918	Chi-N	1	3	.250	13	7	2	0	1	43^1	50	27	1	1	15	20	13.7	2.70	103	.298	.359	0	.000	-1	0	0	0	-0.1
1921	StL-N	11	12	.478	38	23	11	0	3	170^2	194	93	10	1	53	52	13.1	4.22	87	.293	.347	11	.204	-0	-8	-11	-1	-1.5
1922	StL-N	1	2	.333	12	2	0	0	0	32	34	20	1	0	15	14	13.8	4.78	81	.293	.374	1	.143	-0	-2	-3	-1	-0.4
Total	6	17	27	.386	91	48	17	0	5	386	408	218	13	9	155	148	13.3	3.99	85	.282	.355	17	.153	-4	-26	-26	-5	-3.8

● JERRY WALKER
Walker, Jerry Allen b: 2/12/39, Ada, Okla. BB/TR, 6'1", 195 lbs. Deb: 7/6/57 C

YEAR	TM/L	W	L	PCT	G	GS	CG	SH	SV	IP	H	R	HR	HB	BB	SO	RAT	ERA	ERA+	OAV	OOB	BH	AVG	PB	PR	PR+	PD	TPI
1957	Bal-A	1	0	1.000	13	3	1	1	1	27^2	24	9	1	0	14	13	12.4	2.93	123	.245	.339	0	.000	-1	3	2	-0	0.0
1958	Bal-A	0	0	—	6	0	0	0	0	10^1	16	8	2	0	5	6	18.3	6.97	52	.340	.404	0	.000	-0	-4	-4	-0	-0.2
1959	Bal-A★	11	10	.524	30	22	7	2	4	182	160	68	13	3	52	100	10.6	2.92	130	.240	.297	11	.169	-1	19	18	-0	2.0
1960	Bal-A	3	4	.429	29	18	1	0	5	118	107	53	15	3	56	48	12.7	3.74	102	.247	.337	14	.368	5	2	1	1	0.6
1961	KC-A	8	14	.364	36	24	4	0	2	168	161	100	23	10	96	56	14.3	4.82	87	.253	.359	16	.250	3	-15	-12	1	-1.0
1962	KC-A	8	9	.471	31	21	3	1	0	143^1	165	101	27	7	78	57	15.7	5.90	72	.288	.381	15	.263	5	-31	-25	1	-2.0
1963	Cle-A	6	6	.500	39	2	0	0	1	88	92	53	15	2	36	41	13.3	4.91	74	.265	.338	2	.105	-0	-13	-13	-0	-1.7
1964	Cle-A	0	1	.000	6	0	0	0	0	9^2	9	5	1	0	4	5	12.1	4.66	77	.257	.333	0	.000	-0	-1	-1	-0	-0.2
Total	8	37	44	.457	190	90	16	4	13	747	734	397	97	25	341	326	13.3	4.36	90	.259	.343	58	.230	10	-39	-36	1	-2.5

● KEVIN WALKER
Walker, Kevin Michael b: 9/20/76, Irving, Tex. BL/TL, 6'4", 190 lbs. Deb: 4/14/2000

YEAR	TM/L	W	L	PCT	G	GS	CG	SH	SV	IP	H	R	HR	HB	BB	SO	RAT	ERA	ERA+	OAV	OOB	BH	AVG	PB	PR	PR+	PD	TPI
2000	SD-N	7	1	.875	70	0	0	0	0	66^2	49	35	5	5	38	56	12.4	4.18	105	.206	.327	1	.250	0	3	1	-0	0.1

● MARTY WALKER
Walker, Martin Van Buren "Buddy" b: 3/27/1899, Philadelphia, Pa. d: 4/24/78, Philadelphia, Pa. BL/TL, 6', 170 lbs. Deb: 9/30/28

YEAR	TM/L	W	L	PCT	G	GS	CG	SH	SV	IP	H	R	HR	HB	BB	SO	RAT	ERA	ERA+	OAV	OOB	BH	AVG	PB	PR	PR+	PD	TPI
1928	Phi-N	0	1	.000	1	1	0	0	0	0	2	0	0	3	—	—	∞	—	1.000	1.000	107	—	0	-2	-2	0	-0.2	

● MIKE WALKER
Walker, Michael Aaron b: 6/23/65, Houston, Tex. BR/TR, 6'3", 205 lbs. Deb: 6/16/92

YEAR	TM/L	W	L	PCT	G	GS	CG	SH	SV	IP	H	R	HR	HB	BB	SO	RAT	ERA	ERA+	OAV	OOB	BH	AVG	PB	PR	PR+	PD	TPI
1992	Sea-A	0	3	.000	5	3	0	0	0	14^2	21	14	4	0	9	5	18.4	7.36	54	.333	.417	0	—	0	-6	-5	0	-0.9

● MIKE WALKER
Walker, Michael Charles b: 10/4/66, Chicago, Ill. BR/TR, 6'1", 195 lbs. Deb: 9/9/88

YEAR	TM/L	W	L	PCT	G	GS	CG	SH	SV	IP	H	R	HR	HB	BB	SO	RAT	ERA	ERA+	OAV	OOB	BH	AVG	PB	PR	PR+	PD	TPI
1988	Cle-A	0	1	.000	3	1	0	0	0	8^2	8	7	0	0	10	7	18.7	7.27	57	.258	.439	0	—	0	-3	-3	0	-0.3
1990	Cle-A	2	6	.250	18	11	0	0	0	75^2	82	49	6	6	42	34	15.5	4.88	81	.277	.378	0	—	0	-8	-8	-0	-0.8
1991	Cle-A	0	1	.000	5	0	0	0	0	4^1	6	1	0	1	2	2	18.7	2.08	200	.316	.409	0	—	0	1	1	0	0.2
1995	Chi-N	1	3	.250	42	0	0	0	1	44^2	45	22	2	0	24	20	13.9	3.22	127	.259	.348	0	.000	-0	5	4	-0	0.3
1996	Det-A	0	0	—	20	0	0	0	1	27^2	40	26	10	1	17	13	18.9	8.46	60	.351	.439	0	—	0	-11	-10	-1	-0.5
Total	5	3	11	.214	88	12	0	0	2	161	181	105	18	8	95	76	15.9	5.09	82	.285	.385	0	.000	-0	-16	-16	-1	-1.1

● PETE WALKER
Walker, Peter Brian b: 4/8/69, Beverly, Mass. BR/TR, 6'2", 195 lbs. Deb: 6/7/95

YEAR	TM/L	W	L	PCT	G	GS	CG	SH	SV	IP	H	R	HR	HB	BB	SO	RAT	ERA	ERA+	OAV	OOB	BH	AVG	PB	PR	PR+	PD	TPI
1995	NY-N	1	0	1.000	13	0	0	0	0	17^2	24	9	3	0	5	5	14.8	4.58	88	.329	.372	0	—	0	-1	-1	-0	-0.1
1996	SD-N	0	0	—	1	0	0	0	0	0^2	0	0	0	0	3	1	40.5	0.00	—	.000	.600	0	—	0	0	0	0	0.0
2000	Col-N	0	0	—	3	0	0	0	0	4^2	10	9	1	0	4	2	27.0	17.36	34	.435	.519	0	—	0	-7	-5	0	-0.2
Total	3	1	0	1.000	17	0	0	0	0	23	34	18	4	0	12	8	18.0	7.04	63	.347	.418	0	—	0	-7	-7	-0	-0.3

YEAR	TM/L	W	L	PCT	G	GS	CG	SH	SV	IP	H	R	HR	HB	BB	SO	RAT	ERA	ERA+	OAV	OOB	BH	AVG	PB	PR	PR+	PD	TPI
● TOM WALKER	Walker, Robert Thomas b: 11/7/48, Tampa, Fla. BR/TR, 6'1", 188 lbs. Deb: 4/23/72																											
1972	Mon-N	2	2	.500	46	0	0	0	2	74^{2}	71	27	4	1	22	42	11.3	2.89	123	.248	.304	0	.000	-0	5	5	-0	0.3
1973	Mon-N	7	5	.583	54	0	0	0	4	91^{2}	95	52	7	3	42	68	13.7	3.63	105	.274	.357	0	.000	-1	0	2	-0	0.2
1974	Mon-N	4	5	.444	33	8	1	0	2	91^{2}	96	45	7	2	28	70	12.4	3.83	101	.266	.322	3	.188	0	-2	0	-1	0.0
1975	Det-A	3	8	.273	36	9	1	0	0	115^{1}	116	69	16	5	40	60	12.6	4.45	91	.261	.329	0	—	0	-8	-5	-2	-0.6
1976	StL-N	1	2	.333	10	0	0	0	3	19^{2}	22	10	2	0	3	11	11.4	4.12	86	.265	.291	2	.400	1	-1	-1	-1	-0.2
1977	Mon-N	1	1	.500	11	0	0	0	0	19	15	10	2	0	7	10	10.4	4.74	81	.221	.293	0	.000	-0	-2	-2	-0	-0.2
	Cal-A	0	0	—	1	0	0	0	0	2	3	2	2	0	0	1	13.5	9.00	44	.375	.375	0	—	0	-1	-1	-0	-0.1
Total	6	18	23	.439	191	17	2	0	11	414	418	215	40	11	142	262	12.4	3.87	99	.262	.326	5	.152	-0	-10	-2	-3	-0.6
● TOM WALKER	Walker, Thomas William b: 8/1/1881, Philadelphia, Pa. d: 7/10/44, Woodbury Heights, N.J. BR/TR, 5'11", 170 lbs. Deb: 9/27/02																											
1902	Phi-A	0	1	.000	1	1	1	0	0	8	10	7	0	1	0	2	12.4	5.63	65	.303	.324	1	.250	-0	-2	-2	1	-0.1
1904	Cin-N	15	8	.652	24	24	22	2	0	217	196	76	2	18	53	64	11.1	2.24	131	.238	.299	9	.117	-4	12	16	-2	0.9
1905	Cin-N	9	7	.563	23	19	12	1	0	144^{2}	171	71	3	6	44	28	13.7	3.24	102	.305	.362	7	.137	-1	-4	1	-0	-0.1
Total	3	24	16	.600	48	44	35	3	0	369^{2}	377	154	5	25	97	94	12.1	2.70	114	.266	.325	17	.129	-6	6	15	-1	0.7
● BILL WALKER	Walker, William Henry b: 10/7/03, E.St.Louis, Ill. d: 6/14/66, E.St.Louis, Ill. BR/TL, 6', 175 lbs. Deb: 9/13/27																											
1927	NY-N	0	0	—	3	0	0	0	0	4	6	6	0	0	5	4	24.8	9.00	43	.429	.579	0	—	0	-2	-2	-0	-0.1
1928	NY-N	3	6	.333	22	8	1	0	0	76^{1}	79	43	9	1	31	39	13.1	4.72	83	.275	.348	2	.091	-2	-6	-7	-0	-0.9
1929	NY-N	14	7	.667	29	23	13	1	0	177^{2}	188	71	11	4	57	65	12.6	**3.09**	148	.274	.334	7	.115	-3	32	30	-3	2.4
1930	NY-N	17	15	.531	39	34	13	2	1	245^{1}	258	133	19	7	88	105	12.9	3.93	121	.268	.334	16	.186	-1	29	23	-1	2.3
1931	NY-N	16	9	.640	37	28	19	**6**	3	239^{1}	212	78	6	3	64	121	10.5	**2.26**	**164**	.231	.283	5	.065	-6	**43**	**40**	-4	3.0
1932	NY-N	8	12	.400	31	22	9	0	2	163	177	95	23	3	55	74	13.0	4.14	90	.274	.334	7	.135	-2	-5	-8	2	-0.9
1933	StL-N	9	10	.474	29	20	6	2	0	158	168	71	8	1	67	41	13.4	3.42	102	.273	.346	7	.132	-2	-1	1	1	0.0
1934	*StL-N	12	4	.750	24	19	10	1	0	153	160	59	11	2	66	76	13.4	3.12	136	.270	.345	5	.093	-4	16	18	-1	1.1
1935	StL-N★	13	8	.619	37	25	8	2	1	193^{1}	222	93	7	5	78	79	14.2	3.82	107	.288	.357	6	.102	-4	4	6	-1	0.1
1936	StL-N	5	6	.455	21	13	4	1	1	79^{2}	106	62	5	2	27	22	15.3	5.87	67	.318	.373	7	.280	2	-16	-17	1	-1.8
Total	10	97	77	.557	272	192	83	15	8	1489^{2}	1576	711	99	28	538	626	12.9	3.59	114	.271	.335	62	.127	-23	93	84	-7	5.2
● JIM WALKUP	Walkup, James Elton b: 12/14/09, Havana, Ark. d: 2/7/97, Danville, Ark. BR/TR, 6'1", 170 lbs. Deb: 9/22/34																											
1934	StL-A	0	0	—	3	0	0	0	0	8^{1}	6	4	0	0	5	6	11.9	2.16	231	.200	.314	1	.333	0	2	2	-0	0.1
1935	StL-A	6	9	.400	55	20	4	1	0	181^{1}	226	139	17	2	104	44	16.5	6.25	77	.305	.392	6	.128	-3	-36	-27	-1	-2.3
1936	StL-A	0	3	.000	5	2	0	0	0	15^{2}	20	17	0	0	6	5	14.9	8.04	67	.308	.366	0	.000	-1	-5	-4	1	-0.6
1937	StL-A	9	12	.429	27	18	6	0	0	150^{1}	218	127	16	0	83	46	18.0	7.36	66	.347	.423	14	.241	-1	-46	-41	2	-4.2
1938	StL-A	1	12	.077	18	13	1	0	0	94	127	83	13	3	53	28	17.5	6.80	73	.329	.414	4	.138	-2	-21	-18	0	-2.1
1939	StL-A	0	1	.000	1	0	0	0	0	0^{2}	2	1	0	0	1	0	40.5	0.00	—	.500	.600	0	—	0	0	0	0	0.1
	Det-A	0	1	.000	7	0	0	0	0	12	15	10	3	0	8	5	17.3	7.50	65	.319	.418	1	.500	0	-4	-3	0	-0.2
	Yr	0	2	.000	8	0	0	0	0	12^{2}	17	11	3	0	9	5	18.5	7.11	69	.333	.433	1	.500	0	-3	-3	0	-0.1
Total	6	16	38	.296	116	53	11	1	0	462^{1}	614	381	49	5	260	134	17.1	6.74	72	.323	.406	26	.182	-6	-110	-91	1	-9.2
● JIM WALKUP	Walkup, James Huey b: 11/3/1895, Havana, Ark. d: 6/12/90, Duncan, Okla. BR/TL, 5'8", 150 lbs. Deb: 4/30/27																											
1927	Det-A	0	0	—	2	0	0	0	0	1^{2}	3	1	0	0	0	0	16.2	5.40	78	.429	.429	0	.000	-0	-0	-0	0	0.0
● DONNE WALL	Wall, Donnell Lee b: 7/11/67, Potosi, Mo. BR/TR, 6'1", 180 lbs. Deb: 9/2/95																											
1995	Hou-N	3	1	.750	6	5	0	0	0	24^{1}	33	19	5	0	5	16	14.1	5.55	70	.320	.352	0	.000	-1	-4	-5	-0	-0.7
1996	Hou-N	9	8	.529	26	23	2	1	0	150	170	84	17	6	34	99	12.6	4.56	85	.286	.331	9	.205	2	-6	-12	-0	-1.1
1997	Hou-N	2	5	.286	8	8	0	0	0	41^{2}	53	31	8	2	16	25	15.3	6.26	64	.315	.382	1	.100	-0	-10	-11	-0	-1.5
1998	*SD-N	5	4	.556	46	1	0	0	1	70^{1}	50	20	6	1	32	56	10.6	2.43	161	.202	.295	2	.286	0	14	13	0	1.6
1999	SD-N	7	4	.636	55	0	0	0	0	70^{1}	58	31	11	0	23	53	10.4	3.07	137	.219	.281	0	.000	-0	12	10	1	1.4
2000	SD-N	5	2	.714	44	0	0	0	1	53^{2}	36	20	4	0	21	29	9.6	3.35	130	.193	.274	0	.000	-0	8	6	-1	0.6
Total	6	31	24	.564	185	37	2	1	2	410^{1}	400	205	51	9	131	278	11.8	4.01	100	.256	.317	12	.176	1	15	0	-0	0.3
● MURRAY WALL	Wall, Murray Wesley b: 9/19/26, Dallas, Tex. d: 10/8/71, Lone Oak, Tex. BR/TR, 6'3", 185 lbs. Deb: 7/4/50																											
1950	Bos-N	0	0	—	1	0	0	0	0	4	6	5	0	0	2	2	18.0	9.00	43	.333	.400	0	.000	-0	-2	-2	-0	-0.1
1957	Bos-A	3	0	1.000	11	0	0	0	1	24^{1}	21	11	3	0	2	13	8.5	3.33	120	.233	.250	2	.333	0	1	2	1	0.4
1958	Bos-A	8	9	.471	52	1	0	0	10	114^{1}	109	51	14	5	33	53	11.6	3.62	111	.255	.316	3	.107	-2	2	5	3	0.8
1959	Bos-A	1	4	.200	15	0	0	0	3	31^{2}	31	21	5	0	15	8	13.1	5.40	75	.267	.351	0	.000	-1	-5	-4	1	-0.7
	Was-A	0	0	—	1	0	0	0	0	1^{1}	3	1	1	0	0	0	20.3	6.75	58	.600	.600	0	.000	-0	-0	-0	0	0.0
	Bos-A	1	1	.500	11	0	0	0	0	17^{1}	26	11	2	1	11	6	19.7	5.71	71	.371	.463	0	.000	-0	-4	-3	-0	-0.4
	Yr	2	5	.286	27	0	0	0	3	50^{1}	60	33	8	1	26	14	15.6	5.54	73	.314	.399	0	.000	-1	-9	-8	1	-1.1
Total	4	13	14	.481	91	1	0	0	14	193	196	100	25	6	63	82	12.4	4.20	96	.270	.333	5	.109	-3	-8	-4	5	0.0
● STAN WALL	Wall, Stanley Arthur b: 6/16/51, Butler, Mo. BL/TL, 6'1", 175 lbs. Deb: 7/19/75																											
1975	LA-N	0	1	.000	10	0	0	0	0	16	12	6	0	1	7	6	11.3	1.69	202	.222	.323	0	—	0	3	3	0	0.2
1976	LA-N	2	2	.500	31	0	0	0	1	50	50	21	5	2	15	27	12.1	3.60	94	.269	.330	0	.000	-0	-1	-1	-1	-0.2
1977	LA-N	2	3	.400	25	0	0	0	0	32	36	20	3	1	13	22	14.1	5.34	72	.279	.350	0	.000	-0	-5	-6	-1	-0.8
Total	3	4	6	.400	66	0	0	0	1	98	98	47	8	4	35	55	12.6	3.86	92	.266	.336	0	.000	-1	-2	-4	-1	-0.8
● DAVE WALLACE	Wallace, David William b: 9/7/47, Waterbury, Conn. BR/TR, 5'10", 185 lbs. Deb: 7/18/73																											
1973	Phi-N	0	0	—	4	0	0	0	0	3^{2}	13	9	1	0	2	2	36.8	22.09	17	.591	.625	0	—	0	-8	-7	0	-0.3
1974	Phi-N	0	1	.000	3	0	0	0	0	3	4	4	2	0	3	3	21.0	9.00	42	.308	.438	0	—	0	-2	-2	0	-0.3
1978	Tor-A	0	0	—	6	0	0	0	0	14	12	6	1	0	11	7	14.8	3.86	102	.245	.383	0	—	0	-0	0	-0	0.0
Total	3	0	1	.000	13	0	0	0	0	20^{2}	29	19	4	0	16	12	19.6	7.84	50	.345	.450	0	—	0	-9	-9	0	-0.6
● DEREK WALLACE	Wallace, Derek Robert b: 9/1/71, Van Nuys, Cal. BR/TR, 6'3", 200 lbs. Deb: 8/13/96																											
1996	NY-N	2	3	.400	19	0	0	0	3	24^{2}	29	12	2	0	14	15	15.7	4.01	100	.290	.377	0	—	0	1	0	-0	0.0
1999	KC-A	0	1	.000	8	0	0	0	0	8^{1}	7	4	2	0	5	5	13.0	3.24	155	.259	.375	0	—	0	2	2	-0	0.1
Total	2	2	4	.333	27	0	0	0	3	33	36	16	4	0	19	20	15.0	3.82	112	.283	.377	0	—	0	2	2	-0	0.1
● HUCK WALLACE	Wallace, Harry Clinton "Lefty" b: 7/27/1882, Richmond, Ind. d: 7/6/51, Cleveland, Ohio BL/TL, 5'6", 160 lbs. Deb: 6/5/12																											
1912	Phi-N	0	0	—	4	0	0	0	0	4^{2}	7	5	0	0	4	4	21.2	0.00	—	.350	.458	0	—	0	2	2	0	0.1
● LEFTY WALLACE	Wallace, James Harold b: 8/12/21, Evansville, Ind. d: 7/28/82, Evansville, Ind. BL/TL, 5'11", 160 lbs. Deb: 5/5/42																											
1942	Bos-N	1	3	.250	19	3	1	0	0	49^{1}	39	21	3	2	24	20	11.9	3.83	87	.217	.316	2	.143	-0	-3	-3	-1	-0.3
1945	Bos-N	1	0	1.000	5	3	1	0	0	20	18	11	1	1	9	4	12.6	4.50	85	.240	.329	0	.000	-1	-2	-1	0	-0.1
1946	Bos-N	3	3	.500	27	8	2	0	0	75^{1}	76	41	5	1	31	27	12.9	4.18	82	.253	.325	1	.056	-1	-6	-6	2	-0.4
Total	3	5	6	.455	51	14	4	0	0	144^{2}	133	73	9	4	64	51	12.5	4.11	84	.240	.323	3	.079	-2	-11	-10	1	-0.8
● JEFF WALLACE	Wallace, Jeffrey Allen b: 4/12/76, Wheeling, W.Va. BL/TL, 6'2", 240 lbs. Deb: 8/21/97																											
1997	Pit-N	0	0	—	11	0	0	0	0	12	8	2	0	0	8	14	12.0	0.75	572	.200	.333	0	—	0	5	5	0	0.2
1999	Pit-N	1	0	1.000	41	0	0	0	0	39	26	17	2	0	38	41	14.8	3.69	124	.195	.374	0	—	0	4	4	-1	0.2
2000	Pit-N	2	0	1.000	38	0	0	0	0	35^{2}	42	32	5	4	34	27	20.2	7.07	65	.290	.437	0	.000	-0	-10	-10	-1	-0.5
Total	3	3	0	1.000	90	0	0	0	0	86^{2}	76	51	7	4	80	82	16.6	4.67	97	.239	.398	0	.000	0	-1	-1	-1	-0.1
● MIKE WALLACE	Wallace, Michael Sherman b: 2/3/51, Gastonia, N.C. BL/TL, 6'2", 204 lbs. Deb: 6/27/73																											
1973	Phi-N	1	1	.500	20	3	1	0	1	33^{1}	38	16	1	0	15	20	14.3	3.78	101	.304	.379	0	.000	-0	-0	0	-0	0.0
1974	Phi-N	1	0	1.000	8	0	0	0	0	8^{1}	12	6	0	0	2	1	15.1	5.40	70	.324	.359	0	—	0	-2	-1	-0	-0.2
	NY-A	6	0	1.000	23	1	0	0	0	52^{1}	42	18	3	0	35	34	13.2	2.41	147	.222	.344	0	—	0	7	7	-1	0.6
1975	NY-A	0	0	—	3	0	0	0	0	4^{1}	11	7	1	0	1	2	24.9	14.54	25	.458	.480	0	—	0	-5	-5	0	-0.3
	StL-N	0	0	—	9	0	0	0	0	8^{2}	9	2	0	0	5	6	14.5	2.08	181	.281	.378	0	—	0	1	2	0	0.1
1976	StL-N	3	2	.600	49	0	0	0	2	66^{1}	66	34	3	0	39	40	14.2	4.07	87	.264	.363	1	.333	0	-4	-4	0	-0.2

YEAR	TM/L	W	L	PCT	G	GS	CG	SH	SV	IP	H	R	HR	HB	BB	SO	RAT	ERA	ERA+	OAV	OOB	BH	AVG	PB	PR	PR+	PD	TPI
1977	Tex-A	0	0	—	5	0	0	0	0	8^1	10	7	1	0	10	2	21.6	7.56	54	.323	.488	0	—	0	-3	-3	0	-0.1
Total	5	11	3	.786	117	4	1	0	3	181^2	188	90	9	0	107	105	14.6	3.91	93	.273	.371	1	.143	0	-6	-6	-1	-0.1
● **BOBBY WALLACE** Wallace, Rhoderick John b: 11/4/1873, Pittsburgh, Pa. d: 11/3/60, Torrance, Cal. BR/TR, 5'8", 170 lbs. Deb: 9/15/1894 MUCH◆																												
1894	Cle-N	2	1	.667	4	3	2	0	0	26	28	25	1	1	20	10	17.0	5.19	105	.272	.395	2	.154	-1	0	1	1	0.0
1895	Cle-N	12	14	.462	30	28	22	1	1	228^2	271	166	3	8	87	63	14.4	4.09	122	.290	.356	21	.214	-3	17	22	3	1.9
1896	*Cle-N	10	7	.588	22	16	13	2	0	145^1	167	75	2	4	49	46	13.6	3.34	136	.286	.345	35	.235	0	16	19	-0	1.7
1902	StL-A	0	0	—	1	1	0	0	0	2	3	2	0	0	0	1	13.5	0.00	—	.333	.333	141	.285	0	1	1	0	0.1
Total	4	24	22	.522	57	48	37	3	1	402	469	268	6	13	156	120	14.3	3.87	125	.288	.355	2309	.268	-3	35	42	4	3.7
● **TIM WALLACH** Wallach, Timothy Charles b: 9/14/57, Huntington Park, Cal. BR/TR, 6'3", 200 lbs. Deb: 9/6/80 ◆																												
1987	Mon-N★	0	0	—	1	0	0	0	0	1	1	0	0	0	0	0	9.0	0.00	—	.333	.333	177	.298	1	0	0	-0	0.0
1989	Mon-N★	0	0	—	1	0	0	0	0	1	2	1	0	0	0	0	18.0	9.00	39	.500	.500	159	.277	0	-1	-1	0	0.0
Total	2	0	0	—	2	0	0	0	0	2	3	1	0	0	0	0	13.5	4.50	86	.429	.429	2085	.257	1	-0	-0	-0	0.0
● **RED WALLER** Waller, John Francis b: 6/16/1883, Washington, D.C. d: 2/9/15, Secaucus, N.J. Deb: 4/27/09																												
1909	NY-N	0	0	—	1	0	0	0	0	1	3	2	0	1	0	1	36.0	0.00	—	.429	.500	0	—	0	0	0	0	0.0
● **AUGIE WALSH** Walsh, August Sothley b: 8/17/04, Wilmington, Del. d: 11/12/85, San Rafael, Cal. BR/TR, 6', 175 lbs. Deb: 10/2/27																												
1927	Phi-N	0	1	.000	1	1	1	0	0	10	12	5	3	0	5	0	15.3	4.50	92	.333	.415	1	.250	-0	-1	-0	-0	-0.1
1928	Phi-N	4	9	.308	38	11	2	0	2	122^1	160	92	13	5	40	38	15.1	6.18	69	.321	.378	10	.256	2	-30	-24	-2	-2.3
Total	2	4	10	.286	39	12	3	0	2	132^1	172	97	16	5	45	38	15.1	6.05	70	.322	.380	11	.256	2	-30	-25	-2	-2.4
● **CONNIE WALSH** Walsh, Cornelius R. b: 4/23/1882, St.Louis, Mo. d: 4/5/53, St.Louis, Mo. Deb: 9/16/07																												
1907	Pit-N	0	0	—	1	0	0	0	0	1	1	1	0	0	1	0	18.0	9.00	27	.250	.400	0	—	0	-1	-1	-0	0.0
● **DAVE WALSH** Walsh, David Peter b: 9/25/60, Arlington, Mass. BL/TL, 6'1", 185 lbs. Deb: 8/13/90																												
1990	LA-N	1	0	1.000	20	0	0	0	1	16^1	15	12	1	0	6	15	11.6	3.86	95	.242	.309	0	—	0	-0	-0	0	0.0
● **ED WALSH** Walsh, Edward Arthur b: 2/11/05, Meriden, Conn. d: 10/31/37, Meriden, Conn. BR/TR, 6'1", 180 lbs. Deb: 7/4/28 F																												
1928	Chi-A	4	7	.364	14	10	3	0	0	78	86	45	2	5	42	32	15.3	4.96	82	.290	.387	3	.111	-2	-8	-8	-1	-1.2
1929	Chi-A	6	11	.353	24	20	7	0	0	129	156	94	9	4	64	31	15.6	5.65	76	.312	.394	10	.233	2	-20	-19	1	-1.9
1930	Chi-A	1	4	.200	37	4	0	0	0	103^2	131	67	8	4	30	37	14.3	5.38	86	.316	.367	9	.265	1	-8	-9	-0	-0.2
1932	Chi-A	0	2	.000	4	4	1	0	0	20^1	26	22	3	0	13	7	17.3	8.41	51	.299	.390	2	.286	0	-9	-10	-0	-0.7
Total	4	11	24	.314	79	38	11	0	0	331	399	228	22	13	149	107	15.3	5.57	78	.307	.384	24	.216	1	-45	-45	1	-4.0
● **ED WALSH** Walsh, Edward Augustine "Big Ed" b: 5/14/1881, Plains, Pa. d: 5/26/59, Pompano Beach, Fla BR/TR, 6'1", 193 lbs. Deb: 5/7/04 FMUCH																												
1904	Chi-A	6	3	.667	18	8	6	1	1	110^2	90	45	1	3	32	57	10.2	2.60	94	.223	.285	9	.220	3	-0	-2	0	0.2
1905	Chi-A	8	3	.727	22	13	9	1	0	136^2	121	53	0	3	29	71	10.1	2.17	113	.239	.284	9	.155	-0	7	5	0	0.4
1906	*Chi-A	17	13	.567	41	31	24	**10**	2	278^1	215	83	1	7	58	171	9.1	1.88	135	.217	.265	14	.141	-2	25	22	8	3.1
1907	Chi-A	24	18	.571	**56**	46	**37**	5	**4**	**422^1**	341	120	3	8	87	206	9.3	**1.60**	**150**	.223	.269	25	.162	-1	**44**	**40**	22	**6.7**
1908	Chi-A	**40**	15	**.727**	**66**	49	**42**	**11**	**6**	**464**	343	111	2	9	56	**269**	7.9	1.42	163	.203	.232	27	.172	2	**50**	**48**	14	**8.4**
1909	Chi-A	15	11	.577	31	28	20	**8**	2	230^1	166	52	0	4	50	127	**8.6**	1.41	166	.203	**.253**	18	.214	4	**27**	**25**	7	4.6
1910	Chi-A	18	20	.474	**45**	36	33	7	**5**	369^2	242	87	5	4	61	258	**7.5**	**1.27**	**189**	**.187**	**.226**	30	.217	4	**52**	**49**	10	**7.4**
1911	Chi-A	27	18	.600	**56**	37	33	5	**4**	**368^2**	327	125	4	7	72	**255**	9.9	2.22	145	.239	**.280**	34	.219	-1	46	43	15	6.4
1912	Chi-A	27	17	.614	**62**	41	32	6	**10**	**393**	332	125	6	1	94	254	9.8	2.15	149	.231	.279	33	.243	6	51	47	7	6.8
1913	Chi-A	8	3	.727	16	14	7	1	1	97^2	91	37	1	4	39	34	12.3	2.58	113	.243	.321	5	.156	-1	4	4	1	0.4
1914	Chi-A	2	3	.400	8	5	3	1	0	44^2	33	19	0	1	20	15	10.9	2.82	95	.212	.305	1	.063	-1	-0	-1	1	-0.1
1915	Chi-A	3	0	1.000	3	3	3	1	0	27	19	4	0	0	7	12	8.7	1.33	223	.202	.257	4	.364	1	5	5	-1	0.6
1916	Chi-A	0	1	.000	2	1	0	0	0	3^1	4	3	0	0	3	3	18.9	2.70	102	.286	.412	0	—	0	0	0	0	0.0
1917	Bos-N	0	1	.000	4	3	1	0	0	18	22	9	0	1	9	4	16.0	3.50	73	.314	.400	1	.250	1	-2	-2	0	0.0
Total	14	195	126	.607	430	315	250	57	35	2964^1	2346	873	23	52	617	1736	9.2	1.82	145	.218	.264	210	.194	15	310	282	83	44.9
● **JUNIOR WALSH** Walsh, James Gerald b: 3/7/19, Newark, N.J. d: 11/12/90, Olyphant, Pa. BR/TR, 5'11", 185 lbs. Deb: 9/14/46																												
1946	Pit-N	0	1	.000	4	2	0	0	0	10^1	9	6	0	1	10	2	17.4	5.23	67	.237	.408	0	.000	-1	-2	-2	-0	-0.2
1948	Pit-N	1	0	1.000	2	0	0	0	0	4^1	4	5	1	0	5	0	18.7	10.38	39	.235	.409	0	.000	-0	-3	-3	0	-0.5
1949	Pit-N	1	4	.200	9	7	1	1	0	42^2	40	27	5	0	16	24	11.8	5.06	83	.244	.311	0	.000	-1	-5	-4	-1	-0.6
1950	Pit-N	1	1	.500	38	2	0	0	2	62^1	56	36	6	1	34	33	13.1	5.05	87	.246	.346	1	.167	1	-6	-4	0	-0.1
1951	Pit-N	1	4	.200	36	1	0	0	0	73^1	92	66	9	1	46	32	17.1	6.87	61	.304	.397	1	.143	0	-24	-20	0	-1.2
Total	5	4	10	.286	89	12	1	1	2	193	201	140	21	3	111	91	14.7	5.88	72	.268	.365	2	.065	-1	-40	-33	-0	-2.6
● **JIM WALSH** Walsh, James Thomas b: 7/10/1894, Roxbury, Mass. d: 5/13/67, Boston, Mass. BL/TL, 5'11", 175 lbs. Deb: 8/25/21																												
1921	Det-A	0	0	—	3	0	0	0	0	4	2	1	0	0	1	3	6.8	2.25	190	.125	.176	0	—	0	1	1	-0	0.0
● **DEE WALSH** Walsh, Leo Thomas b: 3/28/1890, St.Louis, Mo. d: 7/14/71, St.Louis, Mo. BB/TR, 5'9.5", 165 lbs. Deb: 4/10/13 ◆																												
1915	StL-A	0	0	—	1	0	0	0	0	2	2	4	0	0	2	0	18.0	13.50	21	.222	.364	33	.220	0	-2	-2	-0	-0.1
● **JIMMY WALSH** Walsh, Michael Timothy "Runt" b: 3/25/1886, Lima, Ohio d: 1/21/47, Baltimore, Md. BR/TR, 5'9", 174 lbs. Deb: 4/25/10 ◆																												
1911	Phi-N	0	1	.000	1	0	0	0	0	2^2	7	8	1	0	1	1	27.0	13.50	26	.500	.533	78	.270	0	-3	-3	-0	-0.5
● **GENE WALTER** Walter, Gene Winston b: 11/22/60, Chicago, Ill. BL/TL, 6'4", 200 lbs. Deb: 8/9/85																												
1985	SD-N	0	2	.000	15	0	0	0	3	22	12	6	0	0	8	18	8.2	2.05	173	.158	.238	0	.000	0	4	4	0	0.5
1986	SD-N	2	2	.500	57	0	0	0	1	98	89	47	7	4	49	84	13.0	3.86	95	.247	.343	2	.200	1	-1	-2	1	0.1
1987	NY-N	1	2	.333	21	0	0	0	0	19^2	18	10	1	1	13	11	14.6	3.20	118	.243	.364	0	.000	0	2	1	-0	0.2
1988	NY-N	0	1	.000	19	0	0	0	0	16^2	21	9	0	0	11	14	17.3	3.78	85	.309	.405	0	—	0	-1	-1	-0	-0.1
	Sea-A	1	0	1.000	16	0	0	0	0	26^1	21	16	0	2	15	13	13.0	5.13	81	.216	.333	0	—	0	-3	-3	-0	-0.2
Total	4	4	7	.364	128	0	0	0	4	182^2	161	88	8	7	96	140	13.0	3.74	99	.238	.339	2	.167	1	0	-1	0	0.5
● **BERNIE WALTER** Walter, James Bernard b: 8/15/08, Dover, Tenn. d: 10/30/88, Nashville, Tenn. BR/TR, 6'1", 175 lbs. Deb: 8/16/30																												
1930	Pit-N	0	0	—	1	0	0	0	0	1	0	0	0	0	0	1	0.0	0.00	—	.000	.000	0	—	0	1	1	0	0.0
● **CHARLIE WALTERS** Walters, Charles Leonard b: 2/21/47, Minneapolis, Minn. BR/TR, 6'4", 190 lbs. Deb: 4/11/69																												
1969	Min-A	0	0	—	6	0	0	0	0	6^2	6	4	1	1	3	2	13.5	5.40	68	.240	.345	0	—	0	-1	-1	-0	-0.1
● **MIKE WALTERS** Walters, Michael Charles b: 10/18/57, St.Louis, Mo. BR/TR, 6'5", 203 lbs. Deb: 7/8/83																												
1983	Min-A	1	1	.500	23	0	0	0	2	59	52	31	4	2	20	21	11.3	4.12	104	.243	.314	0	—	0	-0	1	0	0.1
1984	Min-A	0	3	.000	23	0	0	0	2	29	31	14	1	1	14	10	14.3	3.72	113	.287	.374	0	—	0	1	1	-0	0.1
Total	2	1	4	.200	46	0	0	0	4	88	83	45	5	3	34	31	12.3	3.99	106	.258	.334	0	—	0	1	2	-0	0.2
● **BUCKY WALTERS** Walters, William Henry b: 4/19/09, Philadelphia, Pa. d: 4/20/91, Abington, Pa. BR/TR, 6'1", 180 lbs. Deb: 9/18/31 MC◆																												
1934	Phi-N	0	0	—	2	1	0	0	0	7	8	3	1	1	2	7	14.1	1.29	367	.296	.367	78	.260	0	2	2	1	0.2
1935	Phi-N	9	9	.500	24	22	8	2	0	151	168	86	9	7	68	40	14.5	4.17	109	.289	.370	24	.250	1	-3	5	2	1.0
1936	Phi-N	11	21	.344	40	33	15	**4**	0	258	284	146	11	5	115	66	14.1	4.26	107	.277	.353	29	.240	2	-7	7	9	2.1
1937	Phi-N★	14	15	.483	37	34	15	3	0	246^1	292	148	14	3	86	87	13.9	4.75	91	.295	.353	38	.277	4	-23	-10	5	-0.1
1938	Phi-N	4	8	.333	12	12	9	1	0	82^2	91	53	8	3	42	28	14.8	5.23	74	.276	.363	10	.286	3	-13	-12	0	-1.1
	Cin-N	11	6	.647	27	22	11	2	1	168^1	168	81	5	2	66	65	12.6	3.69	99	.255	.324	9	.141	-0	2	-1	2	0.1
	Yr	15	14	.517	39	34	20	3	1	251	259	134	13	5	108	93	13.3	4.20	89	.262	.337	19	.192	3	-11	-13	3	-1.0
1939	*Cin-N☆	**27**	11	.711	39	36	**31**	2	0	**319**	250	98	15	6	109	**137**	10.3	**2.29**	**168**	**.220**	.291	39	.325	13	**58**	**56**	4	**8.6**
1940	*Cin-N★	**22**	10	.688	36	36	**29**	3	0	**305**	241	95	19	5	92	115	10.0	**2.48**	**153**	**.220**	.283	24	.205	2	**46**	**45**	-1	4.7
1941	Cin-N★	19	15	.559	37	35	**27**	5	2	**302**	292	108	10	2	88	129	11.4	2.83	127	.255	.309	20	.189	2	27	26	2	3.3
1942	Cin-N★	15	14	.517	34	32	21	2	0	253^2	223	101	8	5	73	109	10.7	2.66	123	.231	.289	24	.242	6	18	18	1	3.0
1943	Cin-N	15	15	.500	34	34	21	5	0	246^1	244	105	8	1	109	80	12.9	3.54	94	.264	.342	24	.267	8	-4	-6	1	0.2
1944	Cin-N★	**23**	8	.742	34	32	27	6	1	285	233	92	10	4	87	77	10.2	2.40	145	**.219**	.281	30	.280	8	**38**	**36**	1	**4.9**

YEAR	TM/L	W	L	PCT	G	GS	CG	SH	SV	IP	H	R	HR	HB	BB	SO	RAT	ERA	ERA+	OAV	OOB	BH	AVG	PB	PR	PR+	PD	TPI
1945	Cin-N	10	10	.500	22	22	12	3	0	168	166	62	6	2	51	45	11.7	2.68	140	.259	.316	14	.230	5	21	20	-0	2.9
1946	Cin-N	10	7	.588	22	22	10	2	0	151^1	146	55	9	2	64	60	12.6	2.56	131	.258	.336	7	.127	-1	14	13	2	1.6
1947	Cin-N	8	8	.500	20	20	5	2	0	122	137	83	15	3	49	43	13.9	5.75	71	.278	.347	12	.267	3	-23	-22	-1	-2.3
1948	Cin-N	0	3	.000	7	5	1	0	0	35	42	25	6	0	18	19	15.4	4.63	84	.316	.397	4	.267	0	-3	-3	1	-0.1
1950	Bos-N	0	0	—	1	0	0	0	0	4	5	2	0	0	2	0	15.8	4.50	86	.313	.389	0	.000	-0	-0	-0	-0	0.0
Total	16	198	160	.553	428	398	242	42	4	3104^2	2990	1343	154	51	1121	1107	12.1	3.30	115	.253	.321	477	.243	57	152	166	27	29.0

● BRUCE WALTON

Walton, Bruce Kenneth b: 12/25/62, Bakersfield, Cal. BR/TR, 6'2", 195 lbs. Deb: 5/11/91

YEAR	TM/L	W	L	PCT	G	GS	CG	SH	SV	IP	H	R	HR	HB	BB	SO	RAT	ERA	ERA+	OAV	OOB	BH	AVG	PB	PR	PR+	PD	TPI
1991	Oak-A	1	0	1.000	12	0	0	0	0	13	11	9	3	1	6	10	12.5	6.23	62	.229	.327	0	—	0	-3	-4	-0	-0.3
1992	Oak-A	0	0	—	7	0	0	0	0	10	17	11	1	0	3	7	18.0	9.90	38	.378	.417	0	—	0	-7	-7	-0	-0.4
1993	Mon-N	0	0	—	4	0	0	0	0	5^2	11	6	1	0	3	0	22.2	9.53	44	.407	.467	0	.000	-0	-3	-3	0	-0.2
1994	Col-N	1	0	1.000	4	0	0	0	0	5^1	6	5	1	0	3	1	15.2	8.44	59	.273	.360	0	—	0	-3	-2	-0	-0.3
Total	4	2	0	1.000	27	0	0	0	0	34	45	31	6	1	15	18	16.1	8.21	49	.317	.386	0	.000	-0	-16	-16	-1	-1.2

● DICK WANTZ

Wantz, Richard Carter b: 4/11/40, South Gate, Cal. d: 5/13/65, Inglewood, Cal. BR/TR, 6'5", 175 lbs. Deb: 4/13/65

YEAR	TM/L	W	L	PCT	G	GS	CG	SH	SV	IP	H	R	HR	HB	BB	SO	RAT	ERA	ERA+	OAV	OOB	BH	AVG	PB	PR	PR+	PD	TPI
1965	Cal-A	0	0	—	1	0	0	0	0	1	3	2	0	0	0	2	27.0	18.00	19	.500	.500	0	—	0	-2	-2	0	-0.1

● STEVE WAPNICK

Wapnick, Steven Lee b: 9/25/65, Panorama City, Cal. BR/TR, 6'2", 200 lbs. Deb: 4/14/90

YEAR	TM/L	W	L	PCT	G	GS	CG	SH	SV	IP	H	R	HR	HB	BB	SO	RAT	ERA	ERA+	OAV	OOB	BH	AVG	PB	PR	PR+	PD	TPI
1990	Det-A	0	0	—	4	0	0	0	0	7	8	5	0	0	10	6	23.1	6.43	62	.296	.486	0	—	0	-2	-2	-0	-0.1
1991	Chi-A	0	1	.000	6	0	0	0	0	5	2	1	0	0	4	1	10.8	1.80	221	.111	.273	0	—	0	1	1	-0	0.2
Total	2	0	1	.000	10	0	0	0	0	12	10	6	0	0	14	7	18.0	4.50	88	.222	.407	0	—	0	-1	-1	-0	0.1

● BRYAN WARD

Ward, Bryan Matthew b: 1/25/72, Bristol, Pa. BL/TL, 6'2", 210 lbs. Deb: 7/3/98

YEAR	TM/L	W	L	PCT	G	GS	CG	SH	SV	IP	H	R	HR	HB	BB	SO	RAT	ERA	ERA+	OAV	OOB	BH	AVG	PB	PR	PR+	PD	TPI
1998	Chi-A	1	2	.333	28	0	0	0	1	27	30	13	4	0	7	17	12.3	3.33	137	.278	.322	0	—	0	4	4	-1	0.3
1999	Chi-A	0	1	.000	40	0	0	0	0	39^1	63	36	10	0	11	35	16.9	7.55	65	.368	.407	0	—	0	-12	-12	0	-0.5
2000	Phi-N	0	0	—	20	0	0	0	0	19^1	14	5	2	0	8	11	10.2	2.33	203	.206	.289	0	—	0	5	5	-0	0.2
	Ana-A	0	0	—	7	0	0	0	0	8	8	6	1	0	2	3	11.3	5.63	88	.235	.278	0	—	0	-1	-1	-0	-0.1
Total	3	1	3	.250	95	0	0	0	1	93^2	115	60	17	0	28	66	13.7	5.09	94	.302	.350	0	—	0	-3	-3	-1	-0.1

● COLIN WARD

Ward, Colin Norval b: 11/22/60, Los Angeles, Cal. BL/TL, 6'3", 190 lbs. Deb: 9/21/85

YEAR	TM/L	W	L	PCT	G	GS	CG	SH	SV	IP	H	R	HR	HB	BB	SO	RAT	ERA	ERA+	OAV	OOB	BH	AVG	PB	PR	PR+	PD	TPI
1985	SF-N	0	0	—	6	2	0	0	0	12^1	10	6	0	0	7	8	12.4	4.38	79	.233	.340	0	.000	-0	-1	-1	0	-0.1

● JOHNNY WARD

Ward, John b: East St.Louis, Ill. Deb: 9/19/1885

YEAR	TM/L	W	L	PCT	G	GS	CG	SH	SV	IP	H	R	HR	HB	BB	SO	RAT	ERA	ERA+	OAV	OOB	BH	AVG	PB	PR	PR+	PD	TPI
1885	Pro-N	0	1	.000	1	1	1	0	0	8	10	7	0		1	3	12.4	4.50	60	.286	.306	0	.000	-0	-1	-2	-0	-0.2

● JOHN WARD

Ward, John Montgomery b: 3/3/1860, Bellefonte, Pa. d: 3/4/25, Augusta, Ga. BL/TR (BB 1888), 5'9", 165 lbs. Deb: 7/15/1878 MH♦

YEAR	TM/L	W	L	PCT	G	GS	CG	SH	SV	IP	H	R	HR	HB	BB	SO	RAT	ERA	ERA+	OAV	OOB	BH	AVG	PB	PR	PR+	PD	TPI
1878	Pro-N	22	13	.629	37	37	37	6	0	334	308	151	3		34	116	9.2	**1.51**	**146**	.231	.251	27	.196	2	**30**	**27**	2	**2.7**
1879	Pro-N	**47**	19	**.712**	70	60	58	2	**1**	587	571	270	5		36	**239**	9.3	2.15	110	.239	.250	104	.286	17	23	14	4	3.0
1880	Pro-N	39	24	.619	70	67	59	**8**	1	595	501	230	5		45	230	8.3	1.74	127	.217	.232	81	.228	1	**42**	33	5	3.6
1881	Pro-N	18	18	.500	39	35	32	3	0	330	326	183	2		53	119	10.3	2.13	125	.242	.271	87	.244	3	24	20	5	2.6
1882	Pro-N	19	13	.594	34	33	30	4	**1**	286	268	143	6		36	72	9.6	2.55	111	.232	.255	87	.245	1	11	9	4	1.2
1883	NY-N	16	13	.552	34	25	24	1	0	277	278	165	3		31	121	10.0	2.70	115	.246	.267	97	.255	6	14	12	4	1.9
1884	NY-N	3	3	.500	9	5	5	0	0	60^2	72	43	2		18	23	13.4	3.41	87	.280	.327	122	.253	1	-3	-3	1	-0.1
Total	7	164	103	.614	293	262	245	24	3	2469^2	2324	1185	26		253	920	9.4	2.10	118	.234	.254	2136	.278	31	140	111	24	14.9

● DICK WARD

Ward, Richard Ole b: 5/21/09, Herrick, S.Dak. d: 5/30/66, Freeland, Wash. BR/TR, 6'1", 198 lbs. Deb: 5/3/34

YEAR	TM/L	W	L	PCT	G	GS	CG	SH	SV	IP	H	R	HR	HB	BB	SO	RAT	ERA	ERA+	OAV	OOB	BH	AVG	PB	PR	PR+	PD	TPI
1934	Chi-N	0	0	—	3	0	0	0	0	6	9	6	0	0	2	1	16.5	3.00	129	.375	.423	0	.000	-0	1	1	-0	0.0
1935	StL-N	0	0	—	1	0	0	0	0	0	0	0	0	1	—	—	—	—	—	1.000	102	—	0	0	0	0	0.0	
Total	2	0	0	—	4	0	0	0	0	6	9	7	0	0	3	1	18.0	3.00	129	.375	.444	0	.000	-0	1	1	-0	0.0

● COLBY WARD

Ward, Robert Colby b: 1/2/64, Lansing, Mich. BR/TR, 6'2", 185 lbs. Deb: 7/27/90

YEAR	TM/L	W	L	PCT	G	GS	CG	SH	SV	IP	H	R	HR	HB	BB	SO	RAT	ERA	ERA+	OAV	OOB	BH	AVG	PB	PR	PR+	PD	TPI
1990	Cle-A	1	3	.250	22	0	0	0	1	36	31	17	3	1	21	23	13.3	4.25	92	.238	.349	0	—	0	-1	-1	-0	-0.2

● DUANE WARD

Ward, Roy Duane b: 5/28/64, Park View, N.Mex. BR/TR, 6'4", 210 lbs. Deb: 4/12/86

YEAR	TM/L	W	L	PCT	G	GS	CG	SH	SV	IP	H	R	HR	HB	BB	SO	RAT	ERA	ERA+	OAV	OOB	BH	AVG	PB	PR	PR+	PD	TPI
1986	Atl-N	0	1	.000	10	0	0	0	0	16	22	13	2	0	8	8	16.9	7.31	54	.349	.423	0	.000	-0	-6	-6	1	-0.3
	Tor-A	0	1	.000	2	1	0	0	0	2	3	4	0	1	4	1	36.0	13.50	31	.300	.533	0	—	0	-2	-2	0	-0.4
1987	Tor-A	1	0	1.000	12	1	0	0	0	11^2	14	9	0	0	12	10	20.1	6.94	65	.326	.473	0	—	0	-3	-3	0	-0.2
1988	Tor-A	9	3	.750	64	0	0	0	15	111^2	101	46	5	5	60	91	13.4	3.30	119	.245	.347	0	—	0	8	8	-0	0.9
1989	*Tor-A	4	10	.286	66	0	0	0	15	114^2	94	55	4	5	58	122	12.3	3.77	100	.230	.333	0	—	0	2	0	2	0.2
1990	Tor-A	2	8	.200	73	0	0	0	11	127^2	101	51	9	1	42	112	10.2	3.45	114	.221	.288	0	—	0	7	7	1	0.7
1991	*Tor-A	7	6	.538	**81**	0	0	0	23	107^1	80	36	3	2	33	132	9.6	2.77	152	.207	.273	0	—	0	16	17	0	2.5
1992	*Tor-A	7	4	.636	79	0	0	0	12	101^1	76	27	5	1	39	103	10.3	1.95	209	.207	.285	0	—	0	**22**	**23**	-0	2.8
1993	*Tor-A★	2	3	.400	71	0	0	0	**45**	71^2	49	17	4	1	25	97	9.4	2.13	203	.193	.268	0	—	0	18	18	-1	2.9
1995	Tor-A	0	1	.000	4	0	0	0	0	2^2	11	10	0	1	5	3	57.4	27.00	17	.579	.680	0	—	0	-7	-7	-0	-1.1
Total	9	32	37	.464	462	2	0	0	121	666^2	551	268	32	17	286	679	11.5	3.28	123	.228	.314	0	.000	-0	54	56	2	8.0

● JON WARDEN

Warden, Jonathan Edgar "Warbler" b: 10/1/46, Columbus, Ohio BB/TL, 6', 205 lbs. Deb: 4/11/68

YEAR	TM/L	W	L	PCT	G	GS	CG	SH	SV	IP	H	R	HR	HB	BB	SO	RAT	ERA	ERA+	OAV	OOB	BH	AVG	PB	PR	PR+	PD	TPI
1968	Det-A	4	1	.800	28	0	0	0	3	37^1	30	15	5	0	15	25	10.8	3.62	83	.217	.294	0	.000	-0	-3	-2	-1	-0.5

● CURT WARDLE

Wardle, Curtis Ray b: 11/16/60, Downey, Cal. BL/TL, 6'5", 220 lbs. Deb: 8/30/84

YEAR	TM/L	W	L	PCT	G	GS	CG	SH	SV	IP	H	R	HR	HB	BB	SO	RAT	ERA	ERA+	OAV	OOB	BH	AVG	PB	PR	PR+	PD	TPI
1984	Min-A	0	0	—	2	0	0	0	0	4	3	2	2	0	0	5	6.8	4.50	94	.200	.200	0	—	0	-0	-0	0	0.0
1985	Min-A	1	3	.250	35	0	0	0	1	49	49	32	9	1	28	47	14.3	5.51	80	.266	.366	0	—	0	-7	-6	1	-0.3
	Cle-A	7	6	.538	15	12	0	0	0	66	78	51	11	1	34	37	15.4	6.68	62	.297	.379	0	—	0	-19	-19	-1	-3.1
	Yr	8	9	.471	50	12	0	0	1	115	127	83	20	2	62	84	14.9	6.18	69	.284	.374	0	—	0	-26	-24	-0	-3.4
Total	2	8	9	.471	52	12	0	0	1	119	130	85	22	2	62	89	14.7	6.13	69	.281	.369	0	—	0	-26	-24	0	-3.4

● JEFF WARE

Ware, Jeffrey Allan b: 11/11/70, Norfolk, Va. BR/TR, 6'3", 190 lbs. Deb: 9/2/95

YEAR	TM/L	W	L	PCT	G	GS	CG	SH	SV	IP	H	R	HR	HB	BB	SO	RAT	ERA	ERA+	OAV	OOB	BH	AVG	PB	PR	PR+	PD	TPI
1995	Tor-A	2	1	.667	5	5	0	0	0	26^1	28	18	2	1	21	18	17.1	5.47	86	.277	.407	0	—	0	-2	-2	0	-0.2
1996	Tor-A	1	5	.167	13	4	0	0	0	32^2	35	34	6	2	31	11	18.7	9.09	55	.271	.420	0	—	0	-15	-15	0	-2.0
Total	2	3	6	.333	18	9	0	0	0	59	63	52	8	3	52	29	18.0	7.47	65	.274	.414	0	—	0	-17	-17	0	-2.2

● JACK WARHOP

Warhop, John Milton "Chief" or "Crab" (b: John Milton Wauhop)
b: 7/4/1884, Hinton, W.Va. d: 10/4/60, Freeport, Ill. BR/TR, 5'9.5", 168 lbs. Deb: 9/19/08

YEAR	TM/L	W	L	PCT	G	GS	CG	SH	SV	IP	H	R	HR	HB	BB	SO	RAT	ERA	ERA+	OAV	OOB	BH	AVG	PB	PR	PR+	PD	TPI
1908	NY-A	1	2	.333	5	4	3	0	0	36^1	40	19	0	4	8	11	12.9	4.46	56	.292	.349	1	.063	-1	-8	-8	0	-0.7
1909	NY-A	13	15	.464	36	23	21	3	2	243^1	197	84	2	26	81	95	11.2	2.40	105	.233	.319	11	.128	-2	2	3	1	0.3
1910	NY-A	14	14	.500	37	27	20	0	2	243	219	108	1	18	79	75	11.7	3.00	89	.246	.320	14	.177	-1	-13	-9	-4	-1.5
1911	NY-A	12	13	.480	31	25	17	1	0	209^2	239	118	6	15	44	71	12.8	4.16	86	.286	.333	12	.156	-4	-19	-12	-2	-1.8
1912	NY-A	10	19	.345	39	22	16	0	3	258	256	121	3	16	59	110	11.5	2.86	126	.266	.319	19	.207	-1	13	19	-3	1.8
1913	NY-A	4	5	.444	15	7	1	0	0	62^1	69	42	1	12	33	11	16.5	3.75	80	.292	.406	3	.130	-0	-6	-5	-2	-0.9
1914	NY-A	8	15	.348	37	23	15	0	0	216^2	182	75	8	11	44	56	9.8	2.37	117	.235	.286	10	.141	-1	9	9	-2	0.7
1915	NY-A	7	9	.438	21	19	12	0	0	143^1	164	74	7	12	52	34	14.3	3.96	74	.309	.384	7	.137	-2	-16	-16	-3	-2.0
Total	8	69	92	.429	221	150	105	4	7	1412^2	1366	641	28	114	400	463	12.0	3.12	96	.262	.328	77	.156	-12	-38	-18	-13	-4.1

● CY WARMOTH

Warmoth, Wallace Walter b: 2/2/1893, Bone Gap, Ill. d: 6/20/57, Mt.Carmel, Ill. BL/TL, 5'11", 158 lbs. Deb: 8/31/16

YEAR	TM/L	W	L	PCT	G	GS	CG	SH	SV	IP	H	R	HR	HB	BB	SO	RAT	ERA	ERA+	OAV	OOB	BH	AVG	PB	PR	PR+	PD	TPI
1916	StL-N	0	0	—	3	0	0	0	0	5	12	10	0	1	4	1	30.6	14.40	18	.500	.586	0	.000	-0	-7	-6	-0	-0.4
1922	Was-A	1	0	1.000	5	1	1	0	0	19	15	6	0	0	9	8	11.4	1.42	272	.205	.293	1	.143	-0	6	5	-0	0.2
1923	Was-A	7	5	.583	21	13	3	0	0	105	103	64	4	1	76	45	15.4	4.29	88	.261	.381	8	.222	2	-4	-6	0	-0.4
Total	3	8	5	.615	29	14	4	0	0	129	130	80	4	2	89	54	15.4	4.26	88	.264	.379	9	.200	1	-5	-8	-0	-0.6

● LON WARNEKE

Warneke, Lonnie "The Arkansas Hummingbird" b: 3/28/09, Mt.Ida, Ark. d: 6/23/76, Hot Springs, Ark. BR/TR, 6'2", 185 lbs. Deb: 4/18/30 U

YEAR	TM/L	W	L	PCT	G	GS	CG	SH	SV	IP	H	R	HR	HB	BB	SO	RAT	ERA	ERA+	OAV	OOB	BH	AVG	PB	PR	PR+	PD	TPI
1930	Chi-N	0	0	—	1	0	0	0	0	1^1	2	5	0	0	5	0	47.3	33.75	14	.400	.700	0	—	0	-4	-4	0	-0.2
1931	Chi-N	2	4	.333	20	7	3	0	0	64^1	67	33	1	3	37	27	15.0	3.22	120	.269	.370	5	.263	1	5	5	-1	0.4
1932	*Chi-N	**22**	6	**.786**	35	32	25	**4**	0	277	247	84	12	2	64	106	10.2	**2.37**	**159**	.237	.283	19	.192	-0	**46**	**44**	-0	4.2

YEAR	TM/L	W	L	PCT	G	GS	CG	SH	SV	IP	H	R	HR	HB	BB	SO	RAT	ERA	ERA+	OAV	OOB	BH	AVG	PB	PR	PR+	PD	TPI
1933	Chi-N★	18	13	.581	36	34	**26**	4	1	287^1	262	83	8	3	75	133	10.6	2.00	163	.244	.295	30	.300	10	43	41	3	6.3
1934	Chi-N★	22	10	.688	43	35	23	3	3	291^1	273	116	16	2	66	143	10.5	3.21	121	.244	.287	22	.195	-1	27	22	0	2.2
1935	*Chi-N	20	13	.606	42	30	20	1	4	261^2	257	102	19	3	50	120	10.7	3.06	128	.257	.294	20	.220	1	28	26	-1	3.0
1936	Chi-N★	16	13	.552	40	29	13	**4**	1	240^1	246	108	10	4	76	113	12.2	3.45	116	.264	.322	17	.202	0	15	15	-1	1.5
1937	StL-N	18	11	.621	36	33	18	2	0	238^2	280	139	32	0	69	87	13.2	4.53	88	.287	.335	21	.262	4	-16	-14	-3	-1.4
1938	StL-N	13	8	.619	31	26	12	4	0	197	199	102	14	2	64	89	12.1	3.97	100	.256	.314	23	.324	5	-4	-0	-2	0.3
1939	StL-N☆	13	7	.650	34	21	6	2	2	162	160	73	14	2	49	59	11.7	3.78	109	.259	.316	10	.192	1	3	6	-0	0.7
1940	StL-N	16	10	.615	33	31	17	1	0	232	235	103	17	3	47	85	11.1	3.14	127	.257	.296	18	.209	2	18	21	1	2.6
1941	StL-N☆	17	9	.654	37	30	12	4	0	246	227	100	19	3	82	83	11.4	3.15	120	.249	.313	9	.117	-2	13	16	-2	1.2
1942	StL-N	6	4	.600	12	12	5	0	0	82	76	34	8	0	15	31	10.0	3.29	104	.238	.272	10	.333	3	0	1	-1	0.3
	Chi-N	5	7	.417	15	12	8	1	2	99	97	33	2	0	21	28	10.7	2.27	141	.259	.298	6	.188	-0	11	11	-0	1.3
	Yr	11	11	.500	27	24	13	1	2	181	173	67	10	0	36	59	10.4	2.73	121	.249	.286	16	.258	2	12	11	-1	1.6
1943	Chi-N	4	5	.444	21	10	4	0	0	88^1	82	40	3	0	18	30	10.2	3.16	106	.246	.285	5	.192	1	2	2	1	0.4
1945	Chi-N	0	1	.000	9	1	0	0	0	14	16	9	0	0	1	6	10.9	3.86	95	.267	.279	0	.000	0	-0	-0	0	0.0
Total	15	192	121	.613	445	343	192	30	13	2782^1	2726	1164	175	27	739	1140	11.3	3.18	119	.255	.304	215	.223	27	188	188	-5	22.8

● ED WARNER Warner, Edward Emory b: 6/20/1889, Fitchburg, Mass. d: 2/5/54, New York, N.Y. BR/TL, 5'10.5", 165 lbs. Deb: 7/2/12

YEAR	TM/L	W	L	PCT	G	GS	CG	SH	SV	IP	H	R	HR	HB	BB	SO	RAT	ERA	ERA+	OAV	OOB	BH	AVG	PB	PR	PR+	PD	TPI
1912	Pit-N	1	1	.500	11	3	1	1	0	45	40	20	0	3	18	13	12.2	3.60	91	.242	.328	2	.133	-1	-1	-2	1	-0.1

● JACK WARNER Warner, Jack Dyer b: 7/12/40, Brandywine, W.Va. BR/TR, 5'11", 190 lbs. Deb: 4/10/62

YEAR	TM/L	W	L	PCT	G	GS	CG	SH	SV	IP	H	R	HR	HB	BB	SO	RAT	ERA	ERA+	OAV	OOB	BH	AVG	PB	PR	PR+	PD	TPI
1962	Chi-N	0	0	—	7	0	0	0	0	7	9	7	3	0	0	3	11.6	7.71	54	.321	.321	0	—	0	-3	-3	0	-0.1
1963	Chi-N	0	1	.000	8	0	0	0	0	22^2	21	7	1	0	8	7	11.5	2.78	126	.256	.322	1	.250	0	1	2	-0	0.1
1964	Chi-N	0	0	—	7	0	0	0	0	9^1	12	3	0	0	4	6	15.4	2.89	128	.333	.400	0	—	0	1	1	0	0.1
1965	Chi-N	0	1	.000	11	0	0	0	0	15^2	22	16	1	0	9	7	17.8	8.62	43	.355	.437	0	.000	-0	-9	-8	0	-0.5
Total	4	0	2	.000	33	0	0	0	0	54^2	64	33	5	0	21	23	14.0	5.10	72	.308	.371	1	.200	0	-10	-8	0	-0.4

● MIKE WARREN Warren, Michael Bruce b: 3/26/61, Inglewood, Cal. BR/TR, 6'1", 175 lbs. Deb: 6/12/83

YEAR	TM/L	W	L	PCT	G	GS	CG	SH	SV	IP	H	R	HR	HB	BB	SO	RAT	ERA	ERA+	OAV	OOB	BH	AVG	PB	PR	PR+	PD	TPI
1983	Oak-A	5	3	.625	12	9	3	1	0	65^2	51	33	4	1	18	30	9.6	4.11	94	.215	.273	0	—	0	-0	-2	-1	-0.3
1984	Oak-A	3	6	.333	24	12	0	0	0	90	104	52	11	3	44	61	15.1	4.90	77	.291	.373	0	—	0	-9	-12	-2	-1.3
1985	Oak-A	1	4	.200	16	6	0	0	0	49	52	42	13	4	38	48	17.3	6.61	58	.261	.390	0	—	0	-13	-16	-1	-1.5
Total	3	9	13	.409	52	27	3	1	0	204^2	207	127	28	8	100	139	13.9	5.06	75	.261	.349	0	—	0	-23	-30	-4	-3.1

● TOMMY WARREN Warren, Thomas Gentry b: 7/5/17, Tulsa, Okla. d: 1/2/68, Tulsa, Okla. BB/TL, 6'1", 190 lbs. Deb: 4/18/44

YEAR	TM/L	W	L	PCT	G	GS	CG	SH	SV	IP	H	R	HR	HB	BB	SO	RAT	ERA	ERA+	OAV	OOB	BH	AVG	PB	PR	PR+	PD	TPI
1944	Bro-N	1	4	.200	22	4	2	0	0	68^2	74	52	4	0	40	18	14.9	4.98	71	.270	.363	11	.256	2	-10	-11	0	-0.6

● DAN WARTHEN Warthen, Daniel Dean b: 12/1/52, Omaha, Neb. BB/TL, 6', 200 lbs. Deb: 5/18/75 C

YEAR	TM/L	W	L	PCT	G	GS	CG	SH	SV	IP	H	R	HR	HB	BB	SO	RAT	ERA	ERA+	OAV	OOB	BH	AVG	PB	PR	PR+	PD	TPI
1975	Mon-N	8	6	.571	40	18	2	0	3	167^2	130	62	8	1	87	128	11.7	3.11	123	.217	.317	6	.118	-2	10	13	1	0.9
1976	Mon-N	2	10	.167	23	16	2	1	0	90	76	59	8	2	66	67	14.4	5.30	70	.232	.364	0	.000	-3	-18	-15	0	-2.1
1977	Mon-N	2	3	.400	12	6	1	0	0	35	33	34	7	0	38	26	18.3	7.97	48	.262	.433	1	.111	-0	-16	-17	1	-1.9
	Phi-N	0	1	.000	3	0	0	0	0	3^2	4	3	0	0	5	1	22.1	0.00	—	.267	.450	0	—	0	2	2	-0	0.3
	Yr	2	4	.333	15	6	1	0	0	38^2	37	37	7	0	43	27	18.6	7.22	53	.262	.435	1	.111	-0	-14	-15	0	-1.6
1978	Hou-N	0	1	.000	5	1	0	0	0	10^2	10	5	3	0	2	2	10.1	4.22	79	.250	.286	0	.000	-0	-1	-1	-0	-0.1
Total	4	12	21	.364	83	41	5	1	3	307	253	163	26	3	198	224	13.3	4.31	88	.228	.347	7	.079	-6	-23	-17	1	-2.9

● JOHN WASDIN Wasdin, John Truman b: 8/5/72, Fort Belvoir, Va. BR/TR, 6'2", 190 lbs. Deb: 8/24/95

YEAR	TM/L	W	L	PCT	G	GS	CG	SH	SV	IP	H	R	HR	HB	BB	SO	RAT	ERA	ERA+	OAV	OOB	BH	AVG	PB	PR	PR+	PD	TPI
1995	Oak-A	1	1	.500	5	2	0	0	0	17^1	14	9	4	1	3	6	9.3	4.67	96	.215	.261	0	—	0	0	-0	-1	-0.1
1996	Oak-A	8	7	.533	25	21	1	0	0	131^1	145	96	24	4	50	75	13.6	5.96	83	.283	.352	0	—	0	-14	-15	-1	-1.5
1997	Bos-A	4	6	.400	53	7	0	0	0	124^2	121	68	18	3	38	84	11.7	4.40	105	.251	.310	0	—	0	2	3	-2	0.1
1998	*Bos-A	6	4	.600	47	8	0	0	0	96	111	57	14	2	27	59	13.1	5.25	90	.288	.337	0	—	0	-6	-6	0	-0.4
1999	*Bos-A	8	3	.727	45	0	0	0	2	74^1	66	38	14	0	18	57	10.2	4.12	121	.236	.282	0	—	0	6	7	-1	0.8
2000	Bos-A	1	3	.250	25	1	0	0	1	44^2	48	25	8	2	15	36	13.1	5.04	101	.273	.337	0	—	0	-1	0	-1	0.0
	Col-N	0	3	.000	14	3	1	0	0	35^2	42	23	6	3	9	35	13.6	5.80	102	.302	.358	2	.250	-0	-5	0	-0	0.0
Total	6	28	27	.509	214	42	2	0	3	524	547	316	88	15	160	352	12.4	5.07	97	.268	.326	2	.250	0	-17	-10	-5	-1.1

● GEORGE WASHBURN Washburn, George Edward b: 10/6/14, Solon, Me. d: 1/5/79, Baton Rouge, La. BL/TR, 6'1", 175 lbs. Deb: 5/4/41

YEAR	TM/L	W	L	PCT	G	GS	CG	SH	SV	IP	H	R	HR	HB	BB	SO	RAT	ERA	ERA+	OAV	OOB	BH	AVG	PB	PR	PR+	PD	TPI
1941	NY-A	0	1	.000	1	1	0	0	0	2	2	4	0	0	5	1	31.5	13.50	29	.286	.583	0	.000	-0	-2	-2	0	-0.4

● GREG WASHBURN Washburn, Gregory James b: 12/3/46, Coal City, Ill. BR/TR, 6', 190 lbs. Deb: 6/7/69

YEAR	TM/L	W	L	PCT	G	GS	CG	SH	SV	IP	H	R	HR	HB	BB	SO	RAT	ERA	ERA+	OAV	OOB	BH	AVG	PB	PR	PR+	PD	TPI
1969	Cal-A	0	2	.000	8	2	0	0	0	11^1	21	11	0	1	5	4	21.4	7.94	44	.404	.466	0	—	0	-5	-6	0	-0.9

● JARROD WASHBURN Washburn, Jarrod Michael b: 8/13/74, LaCrosse, Wis. BL/TL, 6'1", 190 lbs. Deb: 6/2/98

YEAR	TM/L	W	L	PCT	G	GS	CG	SH	SV	IP	H	R	HR	HB	BB	SO	RAT	ERA	ERA+	OAV	OOB	BH	AVG	PB	PR	PR+	PD	TPI
1998	Ana-A	6	3	.667	15	11	0	0	0	74	70	40	11	3	27	48	12.2	4.62	102	.248	.321	0	.000	-0	0	1	-1	0.0
1999	Ana-A	4	5	.444	16	10	0	0	0	61^2	61	36	6	1	26	39	12.8	5.25	92	.261	.337	0	—	0	-3	-3	-1	-0.4
2000	Ana-A	7	2	.778	14	14	0	0	0	84^1	64	38	16	1	37	49	10.9	3.74	133	.215	.304	1	.333	1	11	11	0	1.1
Total	3	17	10	.630	45	35	0	0	0	220	195	114	33	5	90	136	11.9	4.46	109	.240	.319	1	.250	0	9	9	-1	0.7

● LIBE WASHBURN Washburn, Libeus b: 6/16/1874, Lyme, N.H. d: 3/22/40, Malone, N.Y. BB/TL, 5'10", 180 lbs. Deb: 5/30/02 ♦

YEAR	TM/L	W	L	PCT	G	GS	CG	SH	SV	IP	H	R	HR	HB	BB	SO	RAT	ERA	ERA+	OAV	OOB	BH	AVG	PB	PR	PR+	PD	TPI
1903	Phi-N	0	4	.000	4	4	4	0	0	35	44	23	0	0	11	9	14.1	4.37	75	.326	.377	3	.167	-0	-4	-4	-1	-0.5

● RAY WASHBURN Washburn, Ray Clark b: 5/31/38, Pasco, Wash. BR/TR, 6'1", 205 lbs. Deb: 9/20/61

YEAR	TM/L	W	L	PCT	G	GS	CG	SH	SV	IP	H	R	HR	HB	BB	SO	RAT	ERA	ERA+	OAV	OOB	BH	AVG	PB	PR	PR+	PD	TPI
1961	StL-N	1	1	.500	3	2	1	0	0	20^1	10	4	1	1	7	12	8.0	1.77	248	.152	.243	1	.125	-1	5	5	0	0.5
1962	StL-N	12	9	.571	34	25	2	1	0	175^2	187	90	25	3	58	109	12.7	4.10	104	.273	.332	10	.179	1	-3	3	1	0.5
1963	StL-N	5	3	.625	11	11	4	2	0	64^1	50	25	5	1	14	47	9.1	3.08	115	.212	.259	1	.053	-1	2	3	1	0.4
1964	StL-N	3	4	.429	15	10	0	0	2	60	60	29	7	5	17	28	12.3	4.05	94	.264	.329	2	.133	-0	-3	-2	1	-0.1
1965	StL-N	9	11	.450	28	16	1	1	2	119^1	114	57	15	1	28	67	10.8	3.62	106	.254	.300	5	.152	0	-1	3	-1	0.4
1966	StL-N	11	9	.550	27	26	4	1	0	170	183	75	15	1	44	98	12.1	3.76	95	.280	.326	5	.093	-1	-3	-3	1	-0.4
1967	*StL-N	10	7	.588	27	27	3	1	0	186^1	190	78	14	4	42	98	11.4	3.53	93	.265	.309	6	.091	-2	-3	-5	2	-0.5
1968	*StL-N	14	8	.636	31	30	8	4	0	215	191	67	9	1	47	124	10.0	2.26	128	.239	.283	5	.083	0	17	16	-2	1.5
1969	StL-N	3	8	.273	28	16	2	0	1	132^1	133	59	9	1	49	80	12.4	3.06	117	.261	.327	3	.081	-2	8	8	1	0.5
1970	*Cin-N	4	4	.500	35	3	0	0	0	66^1	90	61	7	0	48	37	18.7	6.92	58	.324	.423	0	.000	-1	-21	-21	1	-2.2
Total	10	72	64	.529	239	166	25	10	5	1209^2	1208	545	107	18	354	700	11.8	3.53	101	.261	.316	38	.105	-7	-3	6	4	0.6

● BUCK WASHER Washer, William b: 10/11/1882, Akron, Ohio d: 12/8/55, Akron, Ohio BR/TR, 5'10", 175 lbs. Deb: 4/25/05

YEAR	TM/L	W	L	PCT	G	GS	CG	SH	SV	IP	H	R	HR	HB	BB	SO	RAT	ERA	ERA+	OAV	OOB	BH	AVG	PB	PR	PR+	PD	TPI
1905	Phi-N	0	0	—	1	0	0	0	0	3	4	2	0	0	5	0	27.0	6.00	49	.333	.529	0	.000	-0	-1	-1	0	-0.1

● GARY WASLEWSKI Waslewski, Gary Lee b: 7/21/41, Meriden, Conn. BR/TR, 6'4", 195 lbs. Deb: 6/11/67

YEAR	TM/L	W	L	PCT	G	GS	CG	SH	SV	IP	H	R	HR	HB	BB	SO	RAT	ERA	ERA+	OAV	OOB	BH	AVG	PB	PR	PR+	PD	TPI
1967	*Bos-A	2	2	.500	12	8	0	0	0	42	34	18	3	1	20	20	11.8	3.21	108	.225	.320	1	.091	-1	0	1	0	0.1
1968	Bos-A	4	7	.364	34	11	2	0	2	105^1	108	50	9	6	40	59	13.2	3.67	86	.269	.344	1	.038	-2	-8	-6	2	-0.6
1969	StL-N	0	2	.000	12	0	0	0	1	20^2	19	9	3	1	8	16	12.2	3.92	91	.244	.322	0	.000	-0	-1	-1	0	0.0
	Mon-N	3	7	.300	30	14	3	1	1	109^1	102	53	5	8	63	63	14.2	3.29	112	.252	.364	1	.033	-2	4	5	1	0.2
	Yr	3	9	.250	42	14	3	1	2	130	121	62	8	9	71	79	13.9	3.39	108	.251	.358	1	.032	-2	3	4	1	0.2
1970	Mon-N	0	2	.000	6	4	0	0	0	24^2	23	14	3	0	15	19	13.9	5.11	81	.247	.352	0	.000	-0	-3	-3	1	-0.2
	NY-A	2	2	.500	26	5	0	0	0	55	42	20	4	4	27	27	11.9	3.11	113	.219	.327	1	.100	-1	4	3	1	0.2
1971	NY-A	0	1	.000	24	0	0	0	1	35^2	28	15	2	1	16	17	11.4	3.28	99	.214	.304	0	.000	-0	1	-0	-0	0.0
1972	Oak-A	0	3	.000	8	0	0	0	0	17^2	12	5	3	0	8	8	10.2	2.04	140	.190	.282	0	.000	-0	2	2	0	0.3
Total	6	11	26	.297	152	42	5	1	5	410^1	368	184	32	21	197	229	12.9	3.44	100	.243	.338	4	.045	-6	-2	1	4	0.0

● STEVE WATERBURY Waterbury, Steven Craig b: 4/6/52, Carbondale, Ill. BR/TR, 6'5", 190 lbs. Deb: 9/14/76

YEAR	TM/L	W	L	PCT	G	GS	CG	SH	SV	IP	H	R	HR	HB	BB	SO	RAT	ERA	ERA+	OAV	OOB	BH	AVG	PB	PR	PR+	PD	TPI
1976	StL-N	0	0	—	5	0	0	0	0	6	7	4	0	0	3	4	15.0	6.00	59	.304	.385	0	—	0	-2	-2	-0	-0.1

● FRED WATERS Waters, Fred Warren b: 2/2/27, Benton, Miss. d: 8/28/89, Pensacola, Fla. BL/TL, 5'11", 185 lbs. Deb: 9/20/55

YEAR	TM/L	W	L	PCT	G	GS	CG	SH	SV	IP	H	R	HR	HB	BB	SO	RAT	ERA	ERA+	OAV	OOB	BH	AVG	PB	PR	PR+	PD	TPI
1955	Pit-N	0	0	—	2	0	0	0	0	5	7	2	1	0	2	0	16.2	3.60	114	.318	.375	0	.000	-0	0	0	0	0.0

YEAR	TM/L	W	L	PCT	G	GS	CG	SH	SV	IP	H	R	HR	HB	BB	SO	RAT	ERA	ERA+	OAV	OOB	BH	AVG	PB	PR	PR+	PD	TPI
1956	Pit-N	2	2	.500	23	5	1	0	0	51	48	18	3	1	30	14	13.9	2.82	134	.258	.364	1	.050	-1	5	5	-1	0.1
Total	2	2	2	.500	25	5	1	0	0	56	55	20	4	1	32	14	14.1	2.89	131	.264	.365	1	.048	-1	6	6	-1	0.1
● BOB WATKINS	Watkins, Robert Cecil b: 3/12/48, San Francisco, Cal. BR/TR, 6'1", 170 lbs. Deb: 9/6/69																											
1969	Hou-N	0	0	—	5	0	0	0	0	15^2	13	9	1	0	13	11	14.9	5.17	69	.241	.388	0	.000	-0	-3	-3	-0	-0.2
● SCOTT WATKINS	Watkins, Scott Allen b: 5/15/70, Tulsa, Okla. BL/TL, 6'3", 180 lbs. Deb: 8/1/95																											
1995	Min-A	0	0	—	27	0	0	0	0	21^2	22	14	2	0	11	11	13.7	5.40	88	.278	.367	0	—	0	-2	-1	0	-0.1
● ALLEN WATSON	Watson, Allen Kenneth b: 11/18/70, Jamaica, N.Y. BL/TL, 6'3", 190 lbs. Deb: 7/8/93																											
1993	StL-N	6	7	.462	16	15	0	0	0	86	90	53	11	3	28	49	12.7	4.60	86	.271	.333	6	.231	2	-5	-6	-1	-0.7
1994	StL-N	6	5	.545	22	22	0	0	0	115^2	130	73	15	8	53	74	14.9	5.52	75	.286	.370	6	.158	1	-17	-18	-1	-1.5
1995	StL-N	7	9	.438	21	19	0	0	0	114^1	126	68	17	5	41	49	13.5	4.96	85	.285	.352	15	.417	6	-10	-10	1	-0.5
1996	SF-N	8	12	.400	29	29	2	0	0	185^2	189	105	28	5	69	128	12.7	4.61	89	.273	.343	15	.231	4	-8	-11	-2	-0.7
1997	Ana-A	12	12	.500	35	34	0	0	0	199	220	121	37	8	73	141	13.6	4.93	93	.279	.346	0	—	0	-8	-8	1	-0.7
1998	Ana-A	6	7	.462	28	14	1	0	0	92^1	122	67	12	3	34	64	15.5	6.04	78	.323	.383	0	—	0	-14	-14	0	-1.6
1999	NY-N	2	2	.500	14	4	0	0	1	39^2	36	18	5	1	22	32	13.4	4.08	107	.252	.355	3	.300	1	2	1	-1	0.2
	Sea-A	0	1	.000	3	0	0	0	0	3	6	9	5	0	3	2	27.0	12.00	40	.400	.500	0	—	0	-2	-2	0	-0.4
	*NY-A	4	0	1.000	21	0	0	0	0	34^1	30	8	3	0	10	30	10.5	2.10	226	.236	.292	0	—	0	11	10	-0	1.0
	Yr	4	1	.800	24	0	0	0	0	37^1	36	17	8	0	13	32	11.8	2.89	164	.254	.316	0	—	0	8	8	-0	0.6
2000	NY-A	0	0	—	17	0	0	0	0	22	30	25	6	2	18	20	20.5	10.23	47	.330	.450	0	—	0	-13	-14	-0	-0.6
Total	8	51	55	.481	206	137	3	0	1	892	979	547	139	35	351	589	13.8	5.03	86	.283	.355	45	.257	15	-65	-71	-3	-5.5
● DOC WATSON	Watson, Charles John b: 1/30/1886, Kensington, Ohio d: 12/30/49, San Diego, Cal. BR/TL, 6', 170 lbs. Deb: 9/3/13																											
1913	Chi-N	1	0	1.000	1	1	1	0	0	9	8	2	0	1	6	1	15.0	1.00	318	.242	.375	0	.000	0	2	2	-1	0.2
1914	Chi-F	9	8	.529	26	18	10	3	1	172	145	50	2	3	49	69	10.3	2.04	130	.236	.295	5	.093	-5	16	13	-1	0.6
	StL-F	3	4	.429	9	7	4	2	0	56	41	18	1	4	24	18	11.1	1.93	158	.211	.311	2	.125	-1	6	7	-1	0.6
	Yr	12	12	.500	35	25	14	5	1	228	186	68	3	7	73	87	10.5	2.01	137	.230	.299	7	.100	-6	22	20	-2	1.2
1915	StL-F	9	9	.500	33	20	6	0	0	135^2	132	66	1	4	58	45	12.9	3.98	72	.273	.355	5	.125	-3	-19	-16	-4	-2.7
Total	3	22	21	.512	69	46	21	5	1	372^2	326	136	4	12	137	133	11.5	2.70	104	.246	.322	12	.107	-9	5	4	-7	-1.3
● MULE WATSON	Watson, John Reeves b: 10/15/1896, Homer, La. d: 8/25/49, Shreveport, La. BR/TR, 6'1.5", 185 lbs. Deb: 7/4/18																											
1918	Phi-A	7	10	.412	21	19	11	3	0	141^2	139	74	0	2	44	30	11.8	3.37	87	.288	.350	6	.128	-3	-9	-6	-2	-1.3
1919	Phi-A	0	1	.000	4	2	0	0	0	14^1	17	11	2	0	7	6	15.1	6.91	50	.309	.387	0	.000	-1	-6	-5	1	-0.3
1920	Bos-N	0	0	—	1	0	0	0	0	3	0	0	0	0	0	0	0.0	0.00	—	.000	.000	0	.000	-0	1	1	0	0.1
	Pit-N	0	0	—	5	0	0	0	0	11^1	15	11	2	0	7	1	17.5	8.74	37	.326	.415	0	.000	-0	-7	-7	0	-0.4
	Bos-N	5	4	.556	12	10	4	2	0	71^2	79	33	0	1	17	16	12.2	3.77	81	.298	.343	3	.130	-1	-5	-6	-0	-0.8
	Yr	5	4	.556	18	10	4	2	0	86	94	44	2	1	24	17	12.5	4.29	72	.294	.345	3	.111	-2	-11	-12	-0	-1.1
1921	Bos-N	14	13	.519	44	31	15	1	2	259^1	269	128	11	7	57	48	11.6	3.85	95	.270	.314	12	.138	-4	-2	-6	-1	-1.0
1922	Bos-N	8	14	.364	41	27	8	1	1	201	262	140	9	5	59	53	14.6	4.70	85	.317	.366	13	.197	-0	-13	-16	-0	-1.5
1923	Bos-N	1	2	.333	11	4	1	0	1	31^1	42	26	2	0	20	10	17.8	5.17	77	.339	.431	2	.250	-0	-4	-4	0	-0.4
	*NY-N	8	5	.615	17	15	8	0	0	108^1	117	43	11	1	21	26	11.5	3.41	112	.280	.316	8	.174	-1	7	5	-1	0.3
	Yr	9	7	.563	28	19	9	0	1	139^2	159	69	13	1	41	36	13.0	3.80	101	.293	.344	10	.185	-1	3	1	-1	-0.1
1924	*NY-N	7	4	.636	22	16	6	1	0	99^2	122	54	7	1	24	18	13.3	3.79	97	.303	.343	9	.257	4	1	-1	-1	0.2
Total	7	50	53	.485	178	124	53	8	4	941^2	1062	520	44	17	256	208	12.8	4.03	89	.293	.342	53	.165	-8	-38	-45	-3	-5.1
● MARK WATSON	Watson, Mark Bradford b: 1/23/74, Atlanta, Ga. BR/TL, 6'4", 215 lbs. Deb: 5/19/2000																											
2000	Cle-A	0	1	.000	6	0	0	0	0	6^1	12	7	0	1	2	4	21.3	8.53	59	.400	.455	0	—	0	-3	-2	-0	-0.3
● MILT WATSON	Watson, Milton Wilson "Mule" b: 1/10/1890, Flovilla, Ga. d: 4/10/62, Pine Bluff, Ark. BR/TR, 6'1", 180 lbs. Deb: 7/26/16																											
1916	StL-N	4	6	.400	18	13	5	2	0	103	109	51	3	4	33	27	12.8	3.06	86	.283	.346	7	.219	0	-5	-5	-1	-0.5
1917	StL-N	10	13	.435	41	20	5	3	0	161^1	149	74	3	9	51	45	11.7	3.51	77	.252	.321	5	.098	-4	-14	-15	1	-2.4
1918	Phi-N	5	7	.417	23	11	6	0	0	112^2	126	51	1	2	36	29	13.1	3.43	87	.293	.350	3	.075	-4	-8	-5	-1	-1.1
1919	Phi-N	2	4	.333	8	4	3	0	0	47	51	30	3	2	19	12	13.8	5.17	62	.282	.356	1	.063	-2	-12	-9	0	-1.2
Total	4	21	30	.412	90	48	19	5	0	424	435	206	10	17	139	113	12.5	3.57	79	.274	.339	16	.115	-9	-40	-34	-0	-5.2
● MOTHER WATSON	Watson, Walter L. b: 1/27/1865, Middleport, Ohio d: 11/23/1898, Middleport, Ohio 5'9", 145 lbs. Deb: 5/19/1887																											
1887	Cin-a	0	1	.000	2	2	1	0	0	14	28	18	0	0	6	1	18.0	5.79	75	.384	.384	2	.222	-0	-2	-2	-1	-0.2
● EDDIE WATT	Watt, Edward Dean b: 4/4/41, Lamoni, Iowa BR/TR, 5'10", 197 lbs. Deb: 4/12/66																											
1966	Bal-A	9	7	.563	43	13	1	0	4	145^2	123	67	11	5	44	102	10.6	3.83	87	.230	.295	14	.304	6	-6	-8	-2	-0.5
1967	Bal-A	3	5	.375	49	0	0	0	8	103^2	67	26	5	3	37	93	9.3	2.26	140	.183	.263	4	.182	2	11	11	0	1.2
1968	Bal-A	5	5	.500	59	0	0	0	11	83^1	63	32	1	2	35	72	10.8	2.27	129	.209	.295	0	.000	-0	7	6	0	1.0
1969	*Bal-A	5	2	.714	56	0	0	0	16	71	49	18	3	2	26	46	9.8	1.65	217	.194	.274	0	.000	-0	16	15	-0	2.3
1970	*Bal-A	7	7	.500	53	0	0	0	12	55^1	44	20	3	5	29	33	12.7	3.25	112	.239	.358	1	.125	-0	3	2	0	0.5
1971	*Bal-A	3	1	.750	35	0	0	0	11	39^2	39	12	1	0	8	26	10.7	1.82	185	.260	.297	0	.000	-0	7	7	-1	1.1
1972	Bal-A	2	3	.400	38	0	0	0	7	45^2	30	12	2	2	20	23	10.2	2.17	142	.191	.291	0	.000	-0	5	5	-0	0.7
1973	*Bal-A	3	4	.429	30	0	0	0	5	71	62	26	8	2	21	38	10.8	3.30	113	.235	.296	0	—	0	4	4	-1	0.3
1974	Phi-N	1	1	.500	42	0	0	0	6	38^1	39	20	3	2	26	23	15.7	3.99	95	.275	.394	0	.000	-0	-2	-1	0	-0.1
1975	Chi-N	0	1	.000	6	0	0	0	0	6	14	11	0	1	8	6	34.5	13.50	29	.452	.575	0	—	0	-7	-6	0	-0.9
Total	10	38	36	.514	411	13	1	0	80	659^2	530	244	37	24	254	462	11.0	2.91	116	.222	.304	19	.190	6	38	34	-3	5.6
● FRANK WATT	Watt, Frank Marion "Kilo" b: 12/15/02, Washington, D.C. d: 8/31/56, Washington, D.C. BR/TR, 6'1", 205 lbs. Deb: 4/14/31 F																											
1931	Phi-N	5	5	.500	38	12	5	0	2	122^2	147	81	5	3	49	25	14.6	4.84	88	.296	.362	8	.205	0	-13	-7	-2	-0.7
● JIM WAUGH	Waugh, James Elden b: 11/25/33, Lancaster, Ohio BR/TR, 6'3", 185 lbs. Deb: 4/19/52																											
1952	Pit-N	1	6	.143	17	7	1	0	0	52^1	61	43	4	2	32	18	16.3	6.36	63	.285	.383	1	.100	-0	-15	-13	-0	-1.5
1953	Pit-N	4	5	.444	29	11	1	0	0	90^1	108	70	21	0	56	23	16.3	6.48	69	.295	.389	5	.227	0	-22	-19	-1	-1.7
Total	2	5	11	.313	46	18	2	0	0	142^2	169	113	25	2	88	41	16.3	6.43	67	.291	.387	6	.188	0	-37	-32	-1	-3.2
● FRANK WAYENBERG	Wayenberg, Frank b: 8/27/1898, Franklin, Kan. d: 4/16/75, Zanesville, Ohio BR/TR, 6'0.5", 172 lbs. Deb: 8/25/24																											
1924	Cle-A	0	0	—	2	1	0	0	0	6^2	7	4	0	1	5	3	17.6	5.40	79	.259	.394	1	.500	0	-1	-1	-0	0.0
● GARY WAYNE	Wayne, Gary Anthony b: 11/30/62, Dearborn, Mich. BL/TL, 6'3", 192 lbs. Deb: 4/7/89																											
1989	Min-A	3	4	.429	60	0	0	0	1	71	55	28	4	1	36	41	11.7	3.30	126	.212	.311	0	—	0	5	6	-0	0.6
1990	Min-A	1	1	.500	38	0	0	0	1	38^2	38	19	5	1	13	28	12.1	4.19	99	.255	.319	0	—	0	-1	-0	-0	0.0
1991	Min-A	1	0	1.000	8	0	0	0	1	12^1	11	7	1	1	4	7	11.7	5.11	84	.244	.320	0	—	0	-1	-1	-0	-0.1
1992	Min-A	3	3	.500	41	0	0	0	0	48	46	18	2	3	19	29	12.8	2.63	155	.260	.342	0	—	0	7	7	1	1.0
1993	Col-N	5	3	.625	65	0	0	0	1	62^1	68	40	8	1	26	49	13.7	5.05	94	.276	.348	1	1.000	0	-7	-2	-0	-0.2
1994	LA-N	1	3	.250	19	0	0	0	0	17^1	19	13	2	3	6	10	14.5	4.67	84	.279	.364	0	.000	-0	-1	-2	0	-0.3
Total	6	14	14	.500	231	0	0	0	4	249^2	237	125	22	10	104	164	12.7	3.93	109	.251	.332	1	.500	0	1	9	1	1.0
● KEN WEAFER	Weafer, Kenneth Albert "Al" b: 2/6/14, Woburn, Mass. BR/TR, 6'0.5", 183 lbs. Deb: 5/29/36																											
1936	Bos-N	0	0	—	1	0	0	0	0	3	6	4	1	0	3	0	27.0	12.00	32	.375	.474	0	.000	-0	-3	-3	-0	-0.2
● DAVE WEATHERS	Weathers, John David b: 9/25/69, Lawrenceburg, Tenn. BR/TR, 6'3", 205 lbs. Deb: 8/2/91																											
1991	Tor-A	1	0	1.000	15	0	0	0	0	14^2	15	9	1	2	17	13	20.9	4.91	86	.263	.447	0	—	0	-1	-1	-0	-0.1
1992	Tor-A	0	0	—	2	0	0	0	0	3^1	5	3	1	0	2	3	18.9	8.10	50	.385	.467	0	—	0	-2	-1	-0	-0.1
1993	Fla-N	2	3	.400	14	6	0	0	0	45^2	57	26	3	1	13	34	14.0	5.12	84	.306	.355	1	.100	-1	-5	-4	-0	-0.5
1994	Fla-N	8	12	.400	24	24	0	0	0	135	166	87	13	4	59	72	15.3	5.27	83	.306	.379	3	.068	-2	-16	-13	-1	-1.9
1995	Fla-N	4	5	.444	28	15	0	0	0	90^1	104	68	8	5	52	60	16.0	5.98	71	.295	.394	4	.154	-1	-18	-18	-1	-1.6
1996	Fla-N	2	2	.500	31	8	0	0	0	71^1	85	41	7	4	28	40	14.8	4.54	90	.302	.374	3	.158	1	-3	-4	-0	-0.1
	*NY-A	0	2	.000	11	4	0	0	0	17^1	23	19	1	2	14	13	20.3	9.35	53	.315	.438	0	—	0	-8	-9	0	-0.8

YEAR	TM/L	W	L	PCT	G	GS	CG	SH	SV	IP	H	R	HR	HB	BB	SO	RAT	ERA	ERA+	OAV	OOB	BH	AVG	PB	PR	PR+	PD	TPI
1997	NY-A	0	1	.000	10	0	0	0	0	9	15	10	1	0	7	4	22.0	10.00	45	.375	.468	0	—	0	-5	-6	-0	-0.5
	Cle-A	1	2	.333	9	1	0	0	0	16^2	23	14	2	1	8	14	17.3	7.56	62	.343	.421	0	—	0	-6	-5	-0	-0.8
	Yr	1	3	.250	19	1	0	0	0	25^2	38	24	3	1	15	18	18.9	8.42	55	.355	.439	0	—	0	-11	-11	-0	-1.3
1998	Cin-N	2	4	.333	16	9	0	0	0	62^1	86	47	3	1	27	51	16.5	6.21	69	.330	.394	1	.067	0	-14	-13	-1	-1.1
	Mil-N	4	1	.800	28	0	0	0	0	47^2	44	22	3	2	14	43	11.3	3.21	133	.246	.308	1	.125	-0	5	6	0	0.5
	Yr	6	5	.545	44	9	0	0	0	110	130	69	6	3	41	94	14.2	4.91	87	.295	.360	2	.087	0	-8	-8	-1	-0.6
1999	Mil-N	7	4	.636	63	0	0	0	2	93	102	49	14	2	38	74	13.7	4.65	98	.279	.350	1	.143	0	-1	-1	0	-0.1
2000	Mil-N	3	5	.375	69	0	0	0	1	76^1	73	29	7	2	32	50	12.6	3.07	149	.260	.340	0	.000	-0	13	13	-1	1.1
Total	10	34	41	.453	320	67	0	0	3	682^2	798	424	64	26	311	471	15.0	5.12	85	.296	.374	14	.108	-3	-60	-56	-3	-6.0
● **FLOYD WEAVER**	Weaver, David Floyd b: 5/12/41, Ben Franklin, Tex. BR/TR, 6′4″, 195 lbs. Deb: 9/30/62																											
1962	Cle-A	1	0	1.000	1	1	0	0	0	5	3	1	1	0	0	8	5.4	1.80	215	.167	.167	1	.500	0	1	1	-0	0.3
1965	Cle-A	2	2	.500	32	1	0	0	1	61^1	61	40	10	5	24	37	13.2	5.43	64	.265	.347	1	.091	0	-13	-13	-0	-0.9
1970	Chi-A	1	2	.333	31	3	0	0	0	61^2	52	33	7	2	31	51	12.4	4.38	89	.233	.332	0	.000	-1	-5	-3	-1	-0.3
1971	Mil-A	0	1	.000	21	0	0	0	0	27^1	33	22	3	1	18	12	17.1	7.24	48	.320	.426	0	—	0	-11	-11	0	-0.6
Total	4	4	5	.444	85	5	0	0	1	155^1	149	96	21	8	73	108	13.3	5.21	70	.260	.351	2	.100	-0	-28	-26	-1	-1.5
● **HARRY WEAVER**	Weaver, Harry Abraham b: 2/26/1892, Clarendon, Pa. d: 5/30/83, Rochester, N.Y. BR/TR, 5′11″, 160 lbs. Deb: 9/18/15																											
1915	Phi-A	0	2	.000	2	2	2	0	0	18	18	10	1	1	10	1	14.5	3.00	98	.290	.397	1	.167	0	-0	-0	1	0.1
1916	Phi-A	0	0	—	3	0	0	0	0	8	14	10	0	0	5	2	21.4	10.13	28	.424	.500	1	.500	0	-6	-6	0	-0.3
1917	Chi-N	1	1	.500	4	2	1	1	0	19^2	17	10	0	0	7	8	11.0	2.75	106	.230	.296	1	.200	-0	-0	0	1	0.1
1918	Chi-N	2	2	.500	8	3	1	1	1	32^2	27	13	1	0	7	9	9.4	2.20	126	.227	.270	2	.250	0	2	2	1	0.4
1919	Chi-N	0	1	.000	2	1	0	0	0	3^1	6	7	0	1	2	1	24.3	10.80	27	.375	.474	0	.000	-0	-3	-3	-0	-0.6
Total	5	3	6	.333	19	8	4	2	1	81^2	82	50	2	2	31	21	12.7	3.64	79	.270	.341	5	.227	0	-8	-7	2	-0.3
● **JIM WEAVER**	Weaver, James Brian "Fluff" b: 2/19/39, Lancaster, Pa. BL/TL, 6′, 178 lbs. Deb: 8/13/67																											
1967	Cal-A	3	0	1.000	13	2	0	0	1	30^1	26	11	2	1	9	20	10.7	2.67	118	.232	.295	0	.000	-1	2	2	2	0.3
1968	Cal-A	0	1	.000	14	0	0	0	0	22^2	22	7	4	0	10	8	12.7	2.38	122	.259	.337	0	.000	-0	2	1	-1	0.0
Total	2	3	1	.750	27	2	0	0	1	53	48	18	6	1	19	28	11.5	2.55	119	.244	.313	0	.000	-1	3	3	1	0.3
● **JIM WEAVER**	Weaver, James Dement "Big Jim" b: 11/25/03, Obion County, Tenn. d: 12/12/83, Lakeland, Fla. BR/TR, 6′6″, 230 lbs. Deb: 8/27/28																											
1928	Was-A	0	0	—	3	0	0	0	0	6	2	2	0	1	6	2	13.5	1.50	267	.143	.429	0	.000	-0	2	2	0	0.1
1931	NY-A	2	1	.667	17	5	2	0	0	57^2	66	37	1	1	29	28	15.0	5.31	75	.280	.361	1	.050	-3	-6	-9	0	-0.6
1934	StL-A	2	0	1.000	5	5	2	0	0	19^2	17	14	3	0	20	11	16.9	6.41	78	.236	.402	1	.143	-0	-4	-3	1	-0.2
	Chi-N	11	9	.550	27	20	8	1	0	159	163	77	5	4	54	98	12.5	3.91	99	.263	.326	3	.058	-5	3	-1	-1	-0.6
1935	Pit-N	14	8	.636	33	22	11	**4**	0	176^1	177	85	9	2	58	87	12.1	3.42	120	.254	.313	4	.071	-4	12	13	1	1.2
1936	Pit-N	14	8	.636	38	31	11	1	0	225^2	239	125	12	1	74	108	12.5	4.31	94	.272	.329	8	.101	-5	-7	-6	-2	-1.2
1937	Pit-N	8	5	.615	32	9	2	1	0	109^2	106	49	2	0	31	44	11.2	3.20	121	.255	.307	4	.148	-0	9	8	-2	0.7
1938	StL-A	0	1	.000	1	1	0	0	0	7	9	7	0	0	9	4	23.1	9.00	55	.321	.486	0	.000	-0	-3	-3	-0	-0.3
	Cin-N	6	4	.600	30	15	2	0	3	129^1	109	58	6	1	54	64	11.4	3.13	117	.227	.306	9	.205	0	9	8	-1	0.5
1939	Cin-N	0	0	—	3	0	0	0	0	3	3	1	0	0	1	3	12.0	3.00	128	.250	.308	0	.000	-0	0	0	0	0.0
Total	8	57	36	.613	189	108	38	7	3	893^1	891	455	38	10	336	449	12.5	3.88	102	.258	.326	30	.104	-17	14	9	-4	-0.4
● **ERIC WEAVER**	Weaver, James Eric b: 8/4/73, Springfield, Ill. BR/TR, 6′5″, 230 lbs. Deb: 5/30/98																											
1998	LA-N	2	0	1.000	7	0	0	0	0	9^2	5	1	1	0	6	5	10.2	0.93	426	.179	.324	0	.000	-0	4	3	-0	0.6
1999	Sea-A	0	1	.000	8	0	0	0	0	9^1	14	12	2	0	8	14	21.2	10.61	45	.318	.423	0	—	0	-6	-6	-0	-0.5
2000	Ana-A	0	2	.000	17	0	0	0	0	18^1	20	16	5	0	16	8	17.7	6.87	72	.267	.396	0	—	0	-4	-4	0	-0.3
Total	3	2	3	.400	32	0	0	0	0	37^1	39	29	8	0	30	27	16.6	6.27	74	.265	.390	0	.000	-0	-6	-7	0	-0.2
● **JEFF WEAVER**	Weaver, Jeffrey Charles b: 8/22/76, Northridge, Cal. BR/TR, 6′5″, 200 lbs. Deb: 4/14/99																											
1999	Det-A	9	12	.429	30	29	0	0	0	163^2	176	104	27	17	56	114	13.7	5.55	88	.278	.352	2	.500	1	-12	-12	-0	-1.2
2000	Det-A	11	15	.423	31	30	2	0	0	200	205	102	26	15	52	136	12.2	4.32	111	.266	.325	0	.000	-0	13	11	1	1.2
Total	2	20	27	.426	61	59	2	0	0	363^2	381	206	53	32	108	250	12.9	4.88	99	.271	.337	2	.286	1	1	-2	1	0.0
● **MONTE WEAVER**	Weaver, Montie Morton "Prof" b: 6/15/06, Helton, N.C. d: 6/14/94, Orlando, Fla. BL/TR, 6′, 170 lbs. Deb: 9/20/31																											
1931	Was-A	1	0	1.000	3	1	1	0	0	10	11	6	0	0	6	6	15.3	4.50	95	.268	.362	0	.000	-0	-0	-0	0	0.0
1932	Was-A	22	10	.688	43	30	13	1	2	234	236	126	9	0	112	83	13.4	4.08	106	.261	.342	27	.287	6	10	6	-2	1.1
1933	*Was-A	10	5	.667	23	21	12	1	0	152^1	147	57	3	1	53	45	11.9	3.25	129	.257	.322	7	.125	-3	17	16	-1	1.0
1934	Was-A	11	15	.423	31	31	11	0	0	204^2	255	127	16	0	63	51	14.0	4.79	90	.306	.355	13	.162	-2	-7	-11	-2	-1.5
1935	Was-A	1	1	.500	5	2	0	0	0	12	16	8	1	0	6	4	16.5	5.25	82	.320	.393	1	.333	0	-1	-1	0	-0.2
1936	Was-A	6	4	.600	26	5	3	0	1	91	92	57	3	0	38	15	12.9	4.35	110	.262	.334	5	.200	1	7	5	-0	0.4
1937	Was-A	12	9	.571	30	26	9	0	0	188^2	197	102	21	0	70	44	12.7	4.20	105	.266	.330	14	.206	1	9	5	1	0.6
1938	Was-A	7	6	.538	31	18	7	0	0	139	157	93	9	3	74	43	15.2	5.24	86	.282	.370	12	.267	4	-7	-12	-1	-0.6
1939	Bos-A	1	0	1.000	9	1	1	0	1	20^1	26	15	0	1	13	6	17.7	6.64	71	.321	.421	0	.000	-1	-5	-4	-1	-0.3
Total	9	71	50	.587	201	135	57	2	4	1052	1137	591	62	5	435	297	13.5	4.36	101	.276	.345	79	.209	5	24	3	-6	0.5
● **ORLIE WEAVER**	Weaver, Orville Forest b: 6/4/1886, Newport, Ky. d: 11/28/70, New Orleans, La. BR/TR, 6′, 180 lbs. Deb: 9/14/10																											
1910	Chi-N	1	1	.500	7	2	2	0	0	32	34	17	2	1	15	22	14.1	3.66	79	.270	.352	2	.154	-1	-2	-3	-1	-0.3
1911	Chi-N	2	2	.500	6	3	1	1	0	43^2	29	12	0	4	17	20	10.3	2.06	161	.196	.296	1	.059	-1	7	6	-0	0.3
	Bos-N	3	12	.200	27	17	4	0	0	121	140	102	9	7	84	50	17.2	6.47	59	.303	.418	5	.122	-2	-41	-32	-2	-3.7
	Yr	5	14	.263	33	20	5	1	0	164^2	169	114	9	11	101	70	15.4	5.30	70	.277	.389	6	.103	-4	-35	-27	-3	-3.4
Total	2	6	15	.286	40	22	7	1	0	196^2	203	131	11	12	116	92	15.1	5.03	71	.276	.383	8	.113	-4	-37	-30	-4	-3.7
● **ROGER WEAVER**	Weaver, Roger Edward b: 10/6/54, Amsterdam, N.Y. BR/TR, 6′3″, 190 lbs. Deb: 6/6/80																											
1980	Det-A	3	4	.429	19	6	0	0	0	63^2	56	32	5	1	34	42	12.9	4.10	101	.247	.347	0	—	0	-0	0	1	0.1
● **SAM WEAVER**	Weaver, Samuel H. b: 7/10/1855, Philadelphia, Pa. d: 2/1/14, Philadelphia, Pa. BR/TR, 5′10″, 175 lbs. Deb: 10/25/1875																											
1875	Phi-n	1	0	1.000	1	1	1	0	0	6	6	2	0		2	2	12.0	1.50	152	.240	.296	1	.250	0	0	1		0.1
1878	Mil-N	12	31	.279	45	43	39	1	0	383	371	214	2		21	95	**9.2**	1.95	135	.237	**.247**	34	.200	-3	15	25	0	2.3
1882	Phi-a	26	15	.634	42	41	41	2	0	371	374	182	6		35	104	9.9	2.74	109	.245	.262	36	.232	1	-2	9	1	1.0
1883	Lou-a	24	22	.522	46	46	45	4	0	400^2	451	261	3		35	105	10.9	3.71	81	.266	.281	37	.192	0	-18	-35	-1	-3.2
1884	Phi-U	5	10	.333	17	17	14	0	0	136	206	146	3		11	40	14.4	5.76	40	.328	.339	18	.214	-5	-50	-55	-1	-4.6
1886	Phi-a	0	2	.000	2	2	1	0	0	11	30	29	0	1	2	2	27.0	14.73	24	.423	.446	1	.143	-1	-14	-14	-0	-1.4
Total	5	67	80	.456	152	149	140	7	0	1301^2	1432	832	14	1	104	346	10.6	3.22	88	.261	.275	126	.207	-7	-69	-52	-1	-5.9
● **LEFTY WEBB**	Webb, Cleon Earl b: 3/1/1885, Mt.Gilead, Ohio d: 1/12/58, Circleville, Ohio BB/TL, 5′11″, 165 lbs. Deb: 5/23/10																											
1910	Pit-N	2	1	.667	7	3	2	0	0	27	29	17	0	2	9	6	13.3	5.67	55	.266	.333	2	.200	-0	-8	-8	-0	-0.8
● **HANK WEBB**	Webb, Henry Gaylon Matthew b: 5/21/50, Copiague, N.Y. BR/TR, 6′3″, 175 lbs. Deb: 9/5/72																											
1972	NY-N	0	0	—	6	2	0	0	0	18^1	18	9	1	0	9	15	13.3	4.42	76	.261	.346	0	.000	-1	-2	-2	1	-0.1
1973	NY-N	0	0	—	2	0	0	0	0	1^2	2	2	1	0	2	1	21.6	10.80	34	.286	.444	0	—	0	-1	-1	-0	-0.1
1974	NY-N	0	2	.000	3	2	0	0	0	10	15	9	1	1	10	8	23.4	7.20	50	.341	.473	0	.000	-0	-4	-4	-0	-0.7
1975	NY-N	7	6	.538	29	15	3	1	0	115	102	58	12	1	62	38	12.9	4.07	85	.236	.333	8	.258	2	-6	-8	-1	-0.8
1976	NY-N	0	1	.000	8	0	0	0	0	16	17	9	2	2	7	7	14.6	4.50	73	.274	.366	0	.000	0	-2	-2	0	-0.1
1977	LA-N	0	0	—	5	0	0	0	0	8	5	2	1	1	1	2	7.9	2.25	170	.192	.250	0	—	0	1	1	-0	0.1
Total	6	7	9	.438	53	19	3	1	0	169	159	89	18	5	91	71	13.6	4.31	80	.248	.346	8	.200	1	-13	-17	-1	-1.7
● **RED WEBB**	Webb, Samuel Henry b: 9/25/24, Washington, D.C. d: 2/7/96, Hyattsville, Md. BL/TR, 6′, 175 lbs. Deb: 9/15/48																											
1948	NY-N	2	1	.667	5	3	2	0	0	28	27	12	2	1	10	9	12.2	3.21	122	.248	.317	2	.222	0	2	2	0	0.2
1949	NY-N	1	1	.500	20	0	0	0	0	44^2	41	23	3	0	21	9	12.5	4.03	99	.248	.333	4	.400	2	0	-0	2	0.4
Total	2	3	2	.600	25	3	2	0	0	72^2	68	35	5	1	31	18	12.4	3.72	107	.248	.327	6	.316	2	2	2	2	0.6

YEAR	TM/L	W	L	PCT	G	GS	CG	SH	SV	IP	H	R	HR	HB	BB	SO	RAT	ERA	ERA+	OAV	OOB	BH	AVG	PB	PR	PR+	PD	TPI
● **BILL WEBB**	Webb, William Frederick b: 12/12/13, Atlanta, Ga. d: 6/1/94, Austell, Ga. BR/TR, 6'2", 180 lbs. Deb: 5/15/43																											
1943	Phi-N	0	0	—	1	0	0	0	0	1	1	1	1	0	1	0	18.0	9.00	37	.333	.500	0	—	0	-1	-1	-0	0.0
● **LES WEBBER**	Webber, Lester Elmer b: 5/6/15, Kelseyville, Cal. d: 11/13/86, Santa Maria, Cal. BR/TR, 6'0.5", 185 lbs. Deb: 5/17/42																											
1942	Bro-N	3	2	.600	19	3	1	0	1	51^{2}	46	17	2	0	22	23	11.8	2.96	110	.230	.306	1	.071	-1	2	2	1	0.1
1943	Bro-N	2	2	.500	54	0	0	0	**10**	115^{2}	112	54	6	5	69	24	14.5	3.81	88	.264	.373	3	.120	-1	-6	-6	2	-0.2
1944	Bro-N	7	8	.467	48	9	1	0	3	140^{1}	157	85	9	1	64	42	14.2	4.94	72	.282	.357	8	.205	1	-21	-22	4	-1.8
1945	Bro-N	7	3	.700	17	7	5	0	0	75^{1}	69	37	3	1	25	30	11.3	3.58	105	.237	.300	2	.091	-1	2	1	-1	0.0
1946	Bro-N	3	3	.500	11	4	0	0	0	43	34	11	5	0	15	16	10.3	2.30	147	.225	.295	1	.100	-1	5	5	-1	0.6
	Cle-A	1	1	.500	4	2	0	0	0	5^{1}	13	14	0	0	5	5	30.4	23.63	14	.464	.545	0	.000	0	-12	-13	0	-2.0
1948	Cle-A	0	0	—	1	0	0	0	0	0^{2}	3	3	0	0	1	1	54.0	40.50	10	.750	.800	0	—	0	-3	-3	0	-0.1
Total	6	23	19	.548	154	25	7	0	14	432	434	221	25	7	201	141	13.4	4.19	83	.262	.345	15	.135	-2	-32	-34	5	-3.4
● **BEN WEBER**	Weber, Benjamin Edward b: 11/17/69, Port Arthur, Tex. BR/TR, 6'4", 185 lbs. Deb: 4/3/2000																											
2000	SF-N	0	1	.000	9	0	0	0	0	8	16	13	0	0	4	6	22.5	14.63	29	.400	.455	0	—	0	-9	-10	-0	-1.0
	Ana-A	1	0	1.000	10	0	0	0	0	14^{2}	12	6	0	0	2	8	8.6	1.84	270	.214	.241	0	—	0	5	5	-0	0.3
Total	1	1	1	.500	19	0	0	0	0	22^{2}	28	19	0	0	6	14	13.5	6.35	74	.292	.333	0	—	0	-4	-4	-1	-0.7
● **CHARLIE WEBER**	Weber, Charles P. "Count" b: 10/22/1868, Cincinnati, Ohio d: 6/13/14, Beaumont, Tex. Deb: 7/30/1898																											
1898	Was-N	0	1	.000	1	1	0	0	0	4	9	9	0	2	1	0	27.0	15.75	23	.450	.522	0	.000	-0	-5	-5	-0	-0.7
● **NEIL WEBER**	Weber, Neil Aaron b: 12/6/72, Newport Beach, Cal. BL/TL, 6'5", 215 lbs. Deb: 9/11/98																											
1998	Ari-N	0	0	—	4	0	0	0	0	2^{1}	5	3	0	0	3	4	30.9	11.57	36	.417	.533	0	—	0	-2	-2	0	-0.1
● **MIKE WEGENER**	Wegener, Michael Denis b: 10/8/46, Denver, Colo. BR/TR, 6'4", 215 lbs. Deb: 4/9/69																											
1969	Mon-N	5	14	.263	32	26	4	1	0	165^{2}	150	92	10	4	96	124	13.6	4.40	84	.243	.349	13	.241	2	-15	-13	1	-1.0
1970	Mon-N	3	6	.333	25	16	1	0	0	104^{1}	100	70	16	4	56	35	13.8	5.26	78	.252	.350	4	.118	-2	-14	-13	-1	-1.2
Total	2	8	20	.286	57	42	5	1	0	270	250	162	26	8	152	159	13.7	4.73	81	.247	.349	17	.193	0	-29	-26	1	-2.2
● **BILL WEGMAN**	Wegman, William Edward b: 12/19/62, Cincinnati, Ohio BR/TR, 6'5", 220 lbs. Deb: 9/14/85																											
1985	Mil-A	2	0	1.000	3	3	0	0	0	17^{2}	17	8	3	0	3	6	10.2	3.57	117	.246	.278	0	—	0	1	1	-0	0.1
1986	Mil-A	5	12	.294	35	32	2	0	0	198^{1}	217	120	32	7	43	82	12.1	5.13	85	.279	.323	0	—	0	-21	-17	-1	-1.4
1987	Mil-A	12	11	.522	34	33	7	0	0	225	229	113	31	6	53	102	11.5	4.24	108	.265	.312	0	—	0	6	9	-0	0.7
1988	Mil-A	13	13	.500	32	31	4	1	0	199	207	104	24	4	50	84	11.8	4.12	97	.265	.313	0	—	0	-3	-3	-1	-0.4
1989	Mil-A	2	6	.250	11	8	0	0	0	51	69	44	6	0	21	27	15.9	6.71	57	.321	.381	0	—	0	-16	-16	1	-2.1
1990	Mil-A	2	2	.500	8	5	1	1	0	29^{2}	37	21	6	0	6	20	13.0	4.85	80	.298	.331	0	—	0	-3	-3	-1	-0.4
1991	Mil-A	15	7	.682	28	28	7	2	0	193^{1}	176	76	16	7	40	89	10.4	2.84	140	.242	.288	0	—	0	27	25	2	3.0
1992	Mil-A	13	14	.481	35	35	7	0	0	261^{2}	251	104	28	9	55	127	10.8	3.20	120	.250	.295	0	—	0	22	19	4	2.3
1993	Mil-A	4	14	.222	20	18	5	0	0	120^{2}	135	70	13	2	34	50	12.8	4.48	95	.291	.342	0	—	0	-2	-3	1	-0.3
1994	Mil-A	8	4	.667	19	19	0	0	0	115^{2}	140	64	14	2	26	59	13.1	4.51	112	.303	.343	0	—	0	4	6	2	0.7
1995	Mil-A	5	7	.417	37	4	0	0	2	70^{2}	89	45	14	3	21	50	14.4	5.35	93	.312	.366	0	—	0	-5	-3	-1	-0.4
Total	11	81	90	.474	262	216	33	4	2	1482^{2}	1567	769	187	40	352	696	11.9	4.16	102	.271	.318	0	—	0	10	13	6	1.8
● **BIGGS WEHDE**	Wehde, Wilbur b: 11/23/06, Holstein, Iowa d: 9/21/70, Sioux Falls, S.Dak. BR/TR, 5'10.5", 180 lbs. Deb: 9/15/30																											
1930	Chi-A	0	0	—	4	0	0	0	0	6^{1}	7	8	1	1	7	3	21.3	9.95	46	.304	.484	0	.000	-0	-4	-4	1	-0.1
1931	Chi-A	1	0	1.000	8	0	0	0	0	16	19	12	0	2	10	3	17.4	6.75	63	.333	.449	0	.000	-0	-4	-5	1	-0.2
Total	2	1	0	1.000	12	0	0	0	0	22^{1}	26	20	1	3	17	6	18.5	7.66	57	.325	.460	0	.000	-1	-8	-8	1	-0.3
● **HERM WEHMEIER**	Wehmeier, Herman Ralph b: 2/18/27, Cincinnati, Ohio d: 5/21/73, Dallas, Tex. BR/TR, 6'2", 200 lbs. Deb: 9/7/45																											
1945	Cin-N	0	1	.000	2	2	0	0	0	5	10	7	0	0	4	0	25.2	12.60	30	.435	.519	0	.000	-0	-5	-5	0	-0.7
1947	Cin-N	0	0	—	1	0	0	0	0	1	0	0	0	0	0	0	0.0	0.00	—	.000	.000	0	—	0	0	0	-0	0.0
1948	Cin-N	11	8	.579	33	24	6	0	0	147^{1}	179	105	21	2	75	56	15.6	5.86	67	.299	.379	5	.091	-3	-31	-32	-0	-3.9
1949	Cin-N	11	12	.478	33	29	11	1	0	213^{1}	202	119	20	7	117	80	13.8	4.68	89	.253	.353	20	.256	2	-15	-11	-2	-1.1
1950	Cin-N	10	18	.357	41	32	12	0	4	230	255	157	27	4	135	121	15.4	5.67	75	.281	.376	14	.152	-3	-39	-36	-3	-4.3
1951	Cin-N	7	10	.412	39	22	10	2	2	184^{2}	167	82	15	4	89	93	12.7	3.70	110	.241	.330	17	.288	3	5	7	-2	0.8
1952	Cin-N	9	11	.450	33	26	6	1	0	190^{1}	197	115	23	7	103	83	14.5	5.15	73	.269	.365	12	.188	2	-30	-29	-4	-2.9
1953	Cin-N	1	6	.143	28	10	2	0	0	81^{2}	100	71	20	0	47	32	16.2	7.16	61	.299	.385	4	.200	-0	-26	-25	-1	-1.9
1954	Cin-N	0	3	.000	12	3	0	0	2	33^{2}	36	29	6	1	21	13	15.5	6.68	63	.271	.374	0	.000	-1	-10	-9	1	-0.8
	Phi-N	10	8	.556	25	17	10	2	0	138	117	61	10	1	51	49	11.0	3.85	105	.231	.302	6	.120	-2	3	3	-0	0.1
	Yr	10	11	.476	37	20	10	2	2	171^{2}	153	90	16	2	72	62	11.9	4.40	92	.239	.318	6	.102	-3	-6	-6	1	-0.7
1955	Phi-N	10	12	.455	31	29	10	1	0	193^{2}	176	101	21	2	67	85	11.4	4.41	90	.241	.307	20	.278	4	-8	-10	-1	-0.7
1956	Phi-N	0	2	.000	3	3	0	0	0	20	18	9	2	0	11	8	13.0	4.05	92	.240	.337	0	.000	-1	-1	-1	-1	-0.2
	StL-N	12	9	.571	34	19	7	2	1	170^{2}	150	80	16	1	71	68	11.7	3.69	102	.240	.319	13	.224	4	2	2	-1	0.5
	Yr	12	11	.522	37	22	7	2	1	190^{2}	168	89	18	1	82	76	11.8	3.73	101	.240	.321	13	.197	3	1	1	-2	0.3
1957	StL-N	10	7	.588	36	18	5	0	0	165	165	91	25	2	54	91	12.1	4.31	92	.253	.312	12	.203	0	-8	-6	-0	-0.6
1958	StL-N	0	1	.000	3	3	0	0	0	6	13	9	2	0	2	4	22.5	13.50	31	.448	.484	1	.500	1	-6	-6	0	-0.7
	Det-A	1	0	1.000	7	3	0	0	0	22^{2}	21	8	2	0	5	11	10.3	2.38	169	.241	.283	0	.000	-1	3	4	-0	0.1
Total	13	92	108	.460	361	240	79	9	9	1803	1806	1044	210	31	852	794	13.4	4.80	84	.260	.344	124	.196	5	-165	-154	-14	-16.3
● **DAVE WEHRMEISTER**	Wehrmeister, David Thomas b: 11/9/52, Berwyn, Ill. BR/TR, 6'4", 195 lbs. Deb: 4/16/76																											
1976	SD-N	0	4	.000	7	4	0	0	0	19^{1}	27	17	0	0	11	10	17.7	7.45	44	.333	.413	0	.000	-1	-8	-10	0	-1.7
1977	SD-N	1	3	.250	30	6	0	0	0	69^{2}	81	53	8	3	44	32	16.5	6.07	58	.293	.396	2	.167	0	-17	-22	-0	-1.1
1978	SD-N	1	0	1.000	4	0	0	0	0	7^{1}	8	5	1	0	5	2	16.0	6.14	54	.276	.382	0	—	0	-2	-2	-0	-0.3
1981	NY-A	0	0	—	5	0	0	0	0	7	6	4	0	0	7	7	16.7	5.14	70	.240	.406	0	—	0	-1	-1	0	0.0
1984	Phi-N	0	0	—	7	0	0	0	0	15	18	12	1	1	7	13	15.6	7.20	51	.300	.382	0	.000	-0	-6	-6	0	-0.3
1985	Chi-A	2	2	.500	23	0	0	0	2	39^{1}	35	15	4	3	10	32	11.0	3.43	126	.241	.304	0	—	0	3	4	-0	0.3
Total	6	4	9	.308	76	10	0	0	2	157^{2}	175	106	14	7	84	96	15.2	5.65	65	.284	.376	2	.100	-1	-31	-36	0	-3.1
● **DICK WEIK**	Weik, Richard Henry "Legs" b: 11/17/27, Waterloo, Iowa d: 4/21/91, Harvey, Ill. BR/TR, 6'3.5", 184 lbs. Deb: 9/8/48 ♦																											
1948	Was-A	1	2	.333	3	3	0	0	0	12^{2}	14	8	1	0	22	8	25.6	5.68	76	.311	.537	3	.750	2	-2	-2	-0	-0.2
1949	Was-A	3	12	.200	27	14	2	2	1	95^{1}	78	61	5	0	103	58	17.1	5.38	79	.230	.410	5	.179	-1	-13	-12	1	-1.6
1950	Was-A	1	3	.250	14	5	1	0	0	44	38	27	2	0	47	26	17.4	4.30	105	.236	.409	2	.154	-1	1	1	-1	-0.1
	Cle-A	1	3	.250	11	2	0	0	0	26	18	17	1	1	26	16	15.6	3.81	114	.205	.391	1	.200	0	2	2	0	0.2
	Yr	2	6	.250	25	7	1	0	0	70	56	44	3	1	73	42	16.7	4.11	108	.225	.402	3	.167	-1	4	3	-1	0.1
1953	Det-A	0	1	.000	12	1	0	0	0	19^{1}	32	30	3	0	23	6	25.6	13.97	29	.386	.519	1	.500	1	-21	-21	0	-0.9
1954	Det-A	0	1	.000	9	1	0	0	0	16^{1}	23	14	3	1	16	9	22.0	7.16	52	.354	.488	0	.000	-0	-6	-6	-1	-0.4
Total	5	6	22	.214	76	26	3	2	1	213^{2}	203	157	15	2	237	123	18.6	5.90	72	.260	.433	12	.226	1	-39	-39	0	-3.0
● **ED WEILAND**	Weiland, Edwin Nicholas b: 11/26/14, Evanston, Ill. d: 7/12/71, Chicago, Ill. BL/TR, 5'11", 180 lbs. Deb: 5/1/40 F																											
1940	Chi-A	0	0	—	5	0	0	0	0	14^{1}	15	15	5	0	7	3	13.8	8.79	50	.263	.344	1	.200	-0	-7	-7	-0	-0.4
1942	Chi-A	0	0	—	5	0	0	0	0	9^{2}	18	11	0	0	3	4	19.6	7.45	48	.383	.420	0	.000	-0	-4	-4	-0	-0.3
Total	2	0	0	—	10	0	0	0	0	24	33	26	5	0	10	7	16.1	8.25	50	.317	.377	1	.143	-0	-11	-11	-1	-0.7
● **BOB WEILAND**	Weiland, Robert George "Lefty" b: 12/14/05, Chicago, Ill. d: 11/9/88, Chicago, Ill. BL/TL, 6'4", 215 lbs. Deb: 9/30/28 F																											
1928	Chi-A	1	0	1.000	1	1	1	1	0	9	7	0	0	1	5	9	13.0	0.00	—	.212	.333	1	.333	0	4	4	0	0.5
1929	Chi-A	2	4	.333	15	9	1	0	1	62	62	42	3	3	43	25	15.7	5.81	74	.268	.390	2	.111	-1	-11	-10	-1	-1.1
1930	Chi-A	0	4	.000	14	3	0	0	0	32^{2}	38	31	1	2	21	15	16.8	6.61	70	.297	.404	0	.000	-1	-7	-7	-0	-0.8
1931	Chi-A	2	7	.222	15	8	3	0	0	75	75	55	3	4	46	38	15.0	5.16	83	.259	.368	4	.182	1	-7	-8	1	-0.6
1932	Bos-A	6	16	.273	43	27	7	0	1	195^{2}	231	125	11	6	97	63	15.4	4.51	100	.295	.377	9	.148	-1	-1	-0	3	0.2
1933	Bos-A	8	14	.364	39	27	12	0	3	216^{1}	197	107	19	5	100	97	12.6	3.87	113	.244	.331	7	.108	-4	10	12	-2	0.6
1934	Bos-A	1	5	.167	11	7	2	0	0	55^{2}	63	41	4	0	27	29	14.6	5.50	87	.293	.372	2	.105	-1	-6	-4	0	-0.4
	Cle-A	1	5	.167	16	7	2	0	0	70	71	41	5	0	30	42	13.0	4.11	111	.262	.336	3	.125	-0	3	3	-1	0.2

YEAR	TM/L	W	L	PCT	G	GS	CG	SH	SV	IP	H	R	HR	HB	BB	SO	RAT	ERA	ERA+	OAV	OOB	BH	AVG	PB	PR	PR+	PD	TPI
	Yr	2	10	.167	27	14	4	0	0	125^2	134	82	9	0	57	71	13.7	4.73	99	.276	.352	5	.116	-1	-3	-1	-0	-0.2
1935	StL-A	0	2	.000	14	4	0	0	0	32	39	35	6	1	31	11	20.0	9.56	50	.298	.436	0	.000	-1	-18	-16	-1	-1.0
1937	StL-N	15	14	.517	41	34	21	2	0	264^1	283	127	14	5	94	105	13.0	3.54	112	.276	.339	15	.169	0	11	13	-2	1.1
1938	StL-N	16	11	.593	35	29	11	1	1	228^1	248	118	14	4	67	117	12.6	3.59	110	.272	.324	11	.138	-3	5	9	-1	0.6
1939	StL-N	10	12	.455	32	23	6	3	1	146^1	146	69	4	6	50	63	12.4	3.57	115	.264	.331	3	.065	-4	6	8	-1	0.6
1940	StL-N	0	0	—	1	0	0	0	0	1	3	3	1	0	0	0	27.0	27.00	15	.600	.600	0	—	0	-3	-2	-0	-0.1
Total	12	62	94	.397	277	179	66	7	7	1388^1	1463	794	85	37	611	614	13.7	4.24	100	.272	.350	57	.129	-16	-13	2	-4	-0.2

● CARL WEILMAN

Weilman, Carl Woolworth "Zeke" (b: Carl Woolworth Weilenmann)
b: 11/29/1889, Hamilton, Ohio d: 5/25/24, Hamilton, Ohio BL/TL, 6'5.5", 187 lbs. Deb: 8/24/12

YEAR	TM/L	W	L	PCT	G	GS	CG	SH	SV	IP	H	R	HR	HB	BB	SO	RAT	ERA	ERA+	OAV	OOB	BH	AVG	PB	PR	PR+	PD	TPI
1912	StL-A	2	4	.333	8	6	5	2	1	48^1	42	19	0	0	3	24	8.4	2.79	119	.227	.239	2	.118	-1	3	3	0	0.3
1913	StL-A	10	19	.345	39	28	17	2	0	251^2	262	122	2	4	60	79	11.7	3.40	86	.281	.328	12	.146	-3	-13	-13	1	-1.6
1914	StL-A	17	12	.586	44	36	20	3	1	299	260	96	1	11	84	119	10.7	2.08	130	.237	.298	15	.149	-1	22	21	1	2.1
1915	StL-A	18	19	.486	47	31	19	3	4	295^2	240	110	6	3	83	125	9.9	2.34	122	.229	.287	23	.230	2	19	18	-1	2.3
1916	StL-A	17	18	.486	46	31	19	1	2	276	237	90	3	8	76	91	10.5	2.15	128	.242	.301	14	.154	-1	21	19	-3	2.0
1917	StL-A	1	2	.333	5	3	0	0	0	19	19	9	1	0	6	9	11.8	1.89	137	.268	.325	0	.000	-1	2	2	1	0.3
1919	StL-A	10	6	.625	20	20	12	3	0	148	133	51	3	3	45	44	11.0	2.07	160	.244	.305	9	.191	0	19	20	-0	2.1
1920	StL-A	9	13	.409	30	24	13	1	2	183^1	201	103	6	3	61	45	13.0	4.47	88	.291	.351	11	.175	-2	-14	-11	1	-1.2
Total	8	84	93	.475	239	179	105	15	10	1521	1394	600	22	32	418	536	10.9	2.67	112	.251	.307	86	.170	-7	59	56	0	6.3

● JAKE WEIMER

Weimer, Jacob "Tornado Jake" b: 11/29/1873, Ottumwa, Iowa d: 6/19/28, Chicago, Ill. BR/TL, 5'11", 175 lbs. Deb: 4/17/03

YEAR	TM/L	W	L	PCT	G	GS	CG	SH	SV	IP	H	R	HR	HB	BB	SO	RAT	ERA	ERA+	OAV	OOB	BH	AVG	PB	PR	PR+	PD	TPI
1903	Chi-N	20	8	.714	35	33	27	3	0	282	241	111	4	11	104	128	11.4	2.30	136	**.225**	.301	21	.196	2	30	27	-1	2.5
1904	Chi-N	20	14	.588	37	37	31	5	0	307	229	96	1	7	97	177	9.8	1.91	140	.204	.272	21	.183	-1	28	27	3	3.0
1905	Chi-N	18	12	.600	33	30	26	2	1	250^1	212	84	1	12	80	107	10.9	2.26	132	.229	.299	19	.207	2	21	20	-1	2.4
1906	Cin-N	20	14	.588	41	39	31	6	1	304^2	263	105	0	13	99	141	11.1	2.22	124	.236	.306	29	.269	6	14	17	1	2.8
1907	Cin-N	11	14	.440	29	26	19	3	0	209	165	73	6	23	63	67	10.8	2.41	108	.226	.308	14	.194	2	1	4	2	1.0
1908	Cin-N	8	7	.533	15	15	9	2	0	116^2	110	38	2	6	50	36	12.8	2.39	96	.255	.341	11	.244	2	-0	-1	1	0.2
1909	NY-N	0	0	—	1	0	0	0	0	3	7	4	0	1	0	1	24.0	9.00	28	.467	.500	0	.000	-0	-2	-2	-0	-0.1
Total	7	97	69	.584	191	180	143	21	2	1472^2	1227	511	14	73	493	657	11.0	2.23	125	.227	.300	115	.213	11	92	93	5	11.8

● LEFTY WEINERT

Weinert, Phillip Walter b: 4/21/02, Philadelphia, Pa. d: 4/17/73, Rockledge, Fla. BL/TL, 6'1", 195 lbs. Deb: 9/24/19

YEAR	TM/L	W	L	PCT	G	GS	CG	SH	SV	IP	H	R	HR	HB	BB	SO	RAT	ERA	ERA+	OAV	OOB	BH	AVG	PB	PR	PR+	PD	TPI
1919	Phi-N	0	0	—	1	0	0	0	0	4	11	9	0	0	2	0	29.3	18.00	18	.478	.520	2	1.000	1	-7	-6	0	-0.2
1920	Phi-N	1	1	.500	10	2	0	0	0	22	27	17	1	1	19	10	19.2	6.14	56	.333	.465	0	.000	-1	-7	-6	-0	-0.6
1921	Phi-N	1	0	1.000	8	0	0	0	0	12^1	8	6	1	1	5	2	10.2	1.46	290	.216	.326	1	1.000	0	3	3	-1	0.2
1922	Phi-N	8	11	.421	34	22	10	0	1	166^2	189	103	10	5	70	58	14.3	3.40	137	.289	.362	14	.241	-0	13	21	-2	2.0
1923	Phi-N	4	17	.190	38	20	8	0	1	156	207	131	10	8	81	46	17.1	5.42	85	.327	.410	19	.322	2	-25	-12	-3	-1.4
1924	Phi-N	0	1	.000	8	1	0	0	0	14^2	10	7	0	0	11	7	12.9	2.45	182	.204	.350	0	.000	-1	2	3	0	0.1
1927	Chi-N	1	1	.500	5	3	1	0	0	19^2	21	13	2	0	6	5	12.4	4.58	84	.259	.310	1	.200	0	-1	-2	-0	-0.2
1928	Chi-N	1	0	1.000	10	1	0	0	0	17	24	10	0	1	9	8	18.0	5.29	73	.393	.479	0	.000	-0	-2	-3	-1	-0.3
1931	NY-A	2	2	.500	17	0	0	0	0	24^2	31	19	2	5	19	24	20.1	6.20	64	.316	.451	0	.000	-0	-5	-7	0	-0.9
Total	9	18	33	.353	131	49	19	0	2	437	528	315	26	21	222	160	15.9	4.59	97	.308	.393	37	.261	2	-29	-7	-6	-1.3

● ROY WEIR

Weir, William Franklin "Bill" b: 2/25/11, Portland, Maine d: 9/30/89, Anaheim, Cal. BL/TL, 5'8.5", 170 lbs. Deb: 6/25/36

YEAR	TM/L	W	L	PCT	G	GS	CG	SH	SV	IP	H	R	HR	HB	BB	SO	RAT	ERA	ERA+	OAV	OOB	BH	AVG	PB	PR	PR+	PD	TPI
1936	Bos-N	4	3	.571	12	7	3	2	0	57^1	53	23	0	0	24	29	12.1	2.83	136	.241	.316	5	.278	2	8	7	1	1.0
1937	Bos-N	1	1	.500	10	4	1	0	0	33	27	18	0	0	19	8	12.5	3.82	94	.227	.333	0	.000	-1	0	-1	1	-0.1
1938	Bos-N	1	0	1.000	5	0	0	0	0	13^1	14	10	4	0	6	3	13.5	6.75	51	.269	.345	1	.333	0	-4	-5	0	-0.3
1939	Bos-N	0	0	—	2	0	0	0	0	2^2	1	0	0	0	1	2	6.8	0.00	—	.125	.222	0	.000	-0	1	1	0	0.1
Total	4	6	4	.600	29	11	4	2	0	106^1	95	51	4	0	50	42	12.3	3.55	104	.238	.323	6	.188	1	5	2	2	0.7

● CURT WELCH

Welch, Curtis Benton b: 2/10/1862, Williamsport, O. d: 8/29/1896, E.Liverpool, Ohio BR/TR, 5'10", 175 lbs. Deb: 5/1/1884 ♦

YEAR	TM/L	W	L	PCT	G	GS	CG	SH	SV	IP	H	R	HR	HB	BB	SO	RAT	ERA	ERA+	OAV	OOB	BH	AVG	PB	PR	PR+	PD	TPI
1890	Phi-a	0	0	—	1	0	0	0	0	1	6	6	0	0	0	1	54.0	54.00	7	.667	.667	106	.268	0	-6	-6	0	-0.2

● TED WELCH

Welch, Floyd John b: 10/17/1892, Coyville, Kan. d: 1/6/43, Great Bend, Kan. BL/TR, 5'9.5", 160 lbs. Deb: 5/15/14

YEAR	TM/L	W	L	PCT	G	GS	CG	SH	SV	IP	H	R	HR	HB	BB	SO	RAT	ERA	ERA+	OAV	OOB	BH	AVG	PB	PR	PR+	PD	TPI
1914	StL-F	0	0	—	3	0	0	0	0	6	6	4	0	3	3	2	18.0	6.00	51	.273	.429	0	.000	-0	-2	-2	-0	-0.1

● JOHNNY WELCH

Welch, John Vernon b: 12/2/06, Washington, D.C. d: 9/2/40, St.Louis, Mo. BL/TR, 6'3", 184 lbs. Deb: 5/22/26

YEAR	TM/L	W	L	PCT	G	GS	CG	SH	SV	IP	H	R	HR	HB	BB	SO	RAT	ERA	ERA+	OAV	OOB	BH	AVG	PB	PR	PR+	PD	TPI
1926	Chi-N	0	0	—	3	0	0	0	0	4^1	5	2	0	0	1	0	12.5	2.08	185	.357	.400	1	1.000	0	1	1	-0	0.1
1927	Chi-N	0	0	—	1	0	0	0	0	1	0	1	0	0	3	1	27.0	9.00	43	.000	.500	0	—	0	-1	-1	0	0.0
1928	Chi-N	0	0	—	3	0	0	0	0	4	13	7	0	0	0	2	29.3	15.75	24	.591	.591	0	—	0	-5	-5	0	-0.3
1931	Chi-N	2	1	.667	8	3	1	0	0	33^2	39	16	2	1	10	7	13.4	3.74	103	.291	.345	5	.417	2	0	0	0	0.2
1932	Bos-A	4	6	.400	20	8	3	1	0	72^1	93	46	3	3	38	26	16.7	5.23	86	.312	.395	9	.250	2	-6	-6	0	-0.5
1933	Bos-A	4	9	.308	47	7	1	0	3	129	142	81	6	2	67	68	14.7	4.60	95	.283	.370	6	.162	-1	-5	-3	1	-0.3
1934	Bos-A	13	15	.464	41	22	8	1	0	206^1	223	112	14	8	76	91	13.4	4.49	107	.274	.342	15	.203	-1	0	7	1	0.7
1935	Bos-A	10	9	.526	31	19	10	1	2	143	155	82	4	4	53	48	13.3	4.47	106	.273	.339	9	.180	-0	-0	4	-0	0.4
1936	Bos-A	2	1	.667	9	3	1	0	0	32^2	43	24	4	0	8	9	14.1	5.51	96	.305	.342	3	.273	1	-2	-1	0	0.0
	Pit-N	0	0	—	9	1	0	0	1	22	22	12	3	0	6	5	11.5	4.50	90	.265	.315	2	.286	1	-1	-1	-1	0.0
Total	9	35	41	.461	172	63	24	3	6	648^1	735	383	36	18	262	257	14.1	4.66	99	.285	.355	50	.219	3	-18	-4	1	0.3

● MICKEY WELCH

Welch, Michael Francis "Smiling Mickey" (b: Michael Francis Walsh)
b: 7/4/1859, Brooklyn, N.Y. d: 7/30/41, Concord, N.H. BR/TR, 5'8", 160 lbs. Deb: 5/1/1880 H

YEAR	TM/L	W	L	PCT	G	GS	CG	SH	SV	IP	H	R	HR	HB	BB	SO	RAT	ERA	ERA+	OAV	OOB	BH	AVG	PB	PR	PR+	PD	TPI
1880	Tro-N	34	30	.531	65	64	64	4	0	574	575	321	7		80	123	10.3	2.54	99	.249	.274	72	.287	10	-11	-1	-7	0.3
1881	Tro-N	21	18	.538	40	40	40	4	0	368	371	186	7		78	104	11.0	2.67	111	.255	.293	30	.203	-4	4	11	-6	0.0
1882	Tro-N	14	16	.467	33	33	30	5	0	281	334	221	7		62	53	12.7	3.46	82	.280	.315	37	.245	1	-17	-20	-3	-1.9
1883	NY-N	25	23	.521	54	52	46	4	0	426	431	271	11		66	144	10.5	2.73	114	.244	.272	75	.234	3	20	18	-6	1.3
1884	NY-N	39	21	.650	65	65	62	4	0	557^1	528	275	12		146	345	10.9	2.50	119	.237	.284	60	.241	9	30	29	-5	2.9
1885	NY-N	44	11	**.800**	56	55	55	7	1	492	372	170	4		131	258	9.2	1.66	160	.203	.256	41	.206	5	63	58	-8	5.3
1886	NY-N	33	22	.600	59	59	56	1	0	500	514	279	13		163	272	12.2	2.99	108	.259	.315	46	.216	1	18	13	-2	0.8
1887	NY-N	22	15	.595	41	40	39	2	0	346	430	191	7	5	91	115	11.3	3.36	112	.300	.303	42	.273	4	28	17	-2	1.4
1888	*NY-N	26	19	.578	47	47	47	5	0	425^1	328	156	12	14	108	167	9.5	1.93	142	.207	.263	32	.189	1	44	40	-4	3.4
1889	*NY-N	27	12	.692	45	41	39	3	2	375	340	196	14	10	149	125	12.0	3.02	130	.234	.310	30	.192	-2	41	39	-3	2.9
1890	NY-N	17	14	.548	37	37	33	2	0	292^1	268	145	5	12	122	97	12.4	2.99	117	.236	.317	22	.179	-3	19	17	-3	0.8
1891	NY-N	5	9	.357	22	15	14	0	1	160	177	136	7	11	97	46	16.0	4.27	75	.270	.373	10	.141	-4	-16	-20	-3	-1.9
1892	NY-N	0	0	—	1	1	0	0	0	5	11	9	0	0	4	1	27.0	14.40	22	.423	.500	1	.333	0	-6	-6	-0	-0.2
Total	13	307	210	.594	565	549	525	41	4	4802	4679	2556	106	52	1297	1850	11.1	2.71	114	.246	.292	498	.226	21	216	198	-52	15.1

● MIKE WELCH

Welch, Michael Paul b: 8/25/72, Haverhill, Mass. BL/TR, 6'2", 210 lbs. Deb: 7/17/98

YEAR	TM/L	W	L	PCT	G	GS	CG	SH	SV	IP	H	R	HR	HB	BB	SO	RAT	ERA	ERA+	OAV	OOB	BH	AVG	PB	PR	PR+	PD	TPI
1998	Phi-N	0	2	.000	10	2	0	0	0	20^2	26	19	7	2	7	15	15.2	8.27	52	.310	.376	0	.000	-0	-9	-9	0	-0.8

● BOB WELCH

Welch, Robert Lynn b: 11/3/56, Detroit, Mich. BR/TR, 6'3", 190 lbs. Deb: 6/20/78

YEAR	TM/L	W	L	PCT	G	GS	CG	SH	SV	IP	H	R	HR	HB	BB	SO	RAT	ERA	ERA+	OAV	OOB	BH	AVG	PB	PR	PR+	PD	TPI
1978	*LA-N	7	4	.636	23	13	4	3	3	111^1	92	28	6	1	26	66	9.6	2.02	174	.229	.277	5	.172	0	19	19	-1	1.9
1979	LA-N	5	6	.455	25	12	1	0	5	81^1	82	42	7	3	32	64	12.9	3.98	91	.265	.340	3	.158	-0	-2	-3	-1	-0.5
1980	LA-N★	14	9	.609	32	32	3	2	0	213^2	190	85	15	3	79	141	11.5	3.29	107	.242	.314	17	.243	3	8	5	-1	0.8
1981	*LA-N	9	5	.643	23	23	2	1	0	141^1	141	56	11	3	41	88	11.8	3.44	97	.259	.315	10	.222	2	1	-2	-1	-0.1
1982	LA-N	16	11	.593	36	36	9	3	0	235^2	199	94	19	5	81	176	10.9	3.36	103	.229	.299	12	.141	-1	7	3	-1	0.1
1983	*LA-N	15	12	.556	31	31	4	3	0	204	164	73	13	3	72	156	10.5	2.65	136	.222	.294	7	.096	-2	22	22	-0	2.6
1984	LA-N	13	13	.500	31	29	3	1	0	178^2	191	86	11	2	58	126	12.6	3.78	94	.273	.331	4	.078	-3	-4	-5	2	-0.8
1985	*LA-N	14	4	.778	23	23	8	3	0	167^1	141	49	16	6	35	96	9.8	2.31	151	.225	.273	9	.180	1	24	23	1	2.7
1986	LA-N	7	13	.350	33	33	7	3	0	235^2	227	95	14	7	55	183	11.0	3.28	105	.251	.299	8	.105	-0	12	5	-1	0.3
1987	LA-N	15	9	.625	35	35	6	**4**	0	251^2	204	94	21	4	86	196	10.5	3.22	123	.221	.291	13	.157	1	24	22	-2	2.2
1988	*Oak-A	17	9	.654	36	36	4	2	0	244^2	237	107	22	10	81	158	12.1	3.64	104	.257	.323	0	—	0	9	4	0	0.4
1989	*Oak-A	17	8	.680	33	33	1	0	0	209^2	191	82	13	6	78	137	11.8	3.00	123	.241	.314	0	—	0	21	17	-1	1.8
1990	*Oak-A★	**27**	6	**.818**	35	35	2	2	0	238	214	90	26	5	77	127	11.2	2.95	126	.242	.306	0	—	0	26	22	0	2.9

YEAR TM/L	W	L	PCT	G	GS	CG	SH	SV	IP	H	R	HR	HB	BB	SO	RAT	ERA	ERA+	OAV	OOB	BH	AVG	PB	PR	PR+	PD	TPI
1991 Oak-A	12	13	.480	35	35	7	1	0	220	220	124	25	11	91	101	13.2	4.58	84	.263	.343	0	—	0	-12	-19	-1	-2.0
1992 *Oak-A	11	7	.611	20	20	0	0	0	123^{2}	114	47	13	2	43	47	11.6	3.27	115	.247	.314	0	—	0	9	7	-1	0.8
1993 Oak-A	9	11	.450	30	28	0	0	0	166^{2}	208	102	25	7	56	63	14.6	5.29	77	.310	.370	0	—	0	-18	-24	1	-2.3
1994 Oak-A	3	6	.333	25	8	0	0	0	68^{2}	79	56	10	1	43	44	16.1	7.08	63	.290	.389	0	.000	-0	-17	-22	-1	-2.3
Total 17	211	146	.591	506	462	61	28	8	3092	2894	1310	267	79	1034	1969	11.7	3.47	106	.249	.314	88	.151	2	128	76	-4	8.5

● DON WELCHEL

Welchel, Donald Ray b: 2/3/57, Atlanta, Tex. BR/TR, 6'4", 205 lbs. Deb: 9/15/82

YEAR TM/L	W	L	PCT	G	GS	CG	SH	SV	IP	H	R	HR	HB	BB	SO	RAT	ERA	ERA+	OAV	OOB	BH	AVG	PB	PR	PR+	PD	TPI
1982 Bal-A	1	0	1.000	2	0	0	0	0	4^{1}	6	6	0	0	2	3	16.6	8.31	49	.300	.364	0	—	0	-2	-2	-0	-0.4
1983 Bal-A	0	2	.000	11	0	0	0	0	26^{2}	33	18	1	0	10	16	14.5	5.40	73	.297	.355	0	—	0	-4	-4	-0	-0.3
Total 2	1	2	.333	13	0	0	0	0	31	39	24	1	0	12	19	14.8	5.81	69	.298	.357	0	—	0	-6	-6	-0	-0.7

● DAVID WELLS

Wells, David Lee "Boomer" b: 5/20/63, Torrance, Cal. BL/TL, 6'4", 225 lbs. Deb: 6/30/87

YEAR TM/L	W	L	PCT	G	GS	CG	SH	SV	IP	H	R	HR	HB	BB	SO	RAT	ERA	ERA+	OAV	OOB	BH	AVG	PB	PR	PR+	PD	TPI
1987 Tor-A	4	3	.571	18	2	0	0	1	29^{1}	37	14	0	0	12	32	15.0	3.99	113	.311	.374	0	—	0	2	2	0	0.4
1988 Tor-A	3	5	.375	41	0	0	0	4	64^{1}	65	36	12	2	31	56	13.7	4.62	85	.269	.356	0	—	0	-5	-5	-0	-0.6
1989 *Tor-A	7	4	.636	54	0	0	0	2	86^{1}	66	25	5	0	28	78	9.8	2.40	158	.207	.271	0	—	0	14	14	0	1.7
1990 Tor-A	11	6	.647	43	25	0	0	3	189	165	72	14	2	45	115	10.1	3.14	126	.235	.283	0	—	0	16	17	1	1.6
1991 *Tor-A	15	10	.600	40	28	2	0	1	198^{1}	188	88	24	2	49	106	10.8	3.72	113	.251	.299	0	—	0	8	11	1	1.3
1992 *Tor-A	7	9	.438	41	14	0	0	2	120	138	84	16	8	36	62	13.7	5.40	76	.289	.349	0	—	0	-19	-17	-0	-2.1
1993 Det-A	11	9	.550	32	30	0	0	0	187	183	93	26	7	42	139	11.2	4.19	103	.254	.301	0	—	0	3	2	-1	0.2
1994 Det-A	5	7	.417	16	16	5	1	0	111^{1}	113	54	13	2	24	71	11.2	3.96	122	.260	.302	0	—	0	10	11	-1	0.9
1995 Det-A★	10	3	.769	18	18	3	0	0	130^{1}	120	54	17	2	37	83	11.0	3.04	157	.242	.298	0	—	0	24	25	-0	2.2
*Cin-N	6	5	.545	11	11	3	0	0	72^{2}	74	34	6	0	16	50	11.1	3.59	115	.265	.305	4	.143	-1	5	4	-1	0.4
1996 *Bal-A	11	14	.440	34	34	3	0	0	224^{1}	247	132	32	7	51	130	12.2	5.14	96	.285	.330	0	—	0	-3	-5	2	-0.3
1997 *NY-A	16	10	.615	32	32	5	2	0	218	239	109	24	6	45	156	12.0	4.21	106	.278	.318	0	—	0	9	6	-1	0.6
1998 *NY-A★	18	4	**.818**	30	30	8	**5**	0	214^{1}	195	86	29	1	29	163	**9.4**	3.49	126	.239	**.266**	1	.250	0	28	23	-1	2.0
1999 Tor-A	17	10	.630	34	34	**7**	1	0	**231^{2}**	246	132	32	6	62	169	12.2	4.82	103	.271	.322	0	.000	-1	1	3	-0	0.2
2000 Tor-A★	**20**	8	.714	35	35	**9**	1	0	229^{2}	266	115	23	8	31	166	12.0	4.11	121	.289	.318	1	.167	-0	21	22	-3	2.0
Total 14	161	107	.601	479	309	45	10	13	2306^{2}	2342	1128	273	53	538	1576	11.4	4.06	111	.263	.309	6	.136	-1	115	111	-3	10.5

● ED WELLS

Wells, Edwin Lee "Satchelfoot" b: 6/7/1900, Ashland, Ohio d: 5/1/86, Montgomery, Ala. BL/TL, 6'1.5", 183 lbs. Deb: 6/16/23

YEAR TM/L	W	L	PCT	G	GS	CG	SH	SV	IP	H	R	HR	HB	BB	SO	RAT	ERA	ERA+	OAV	OOB	BH	AVG	PB	PR	PR+	PD	TPI
1923 Det-A	0	0	—	7	0	0	0	0	10	11	6	0	0	6	6	15.3	5.40	72	.306	.405	0	.000	-0	-2	-2	-0	-0.1
1924 Det-A	6	8	.429	29	15	5	0	4	102	117	58	2	1	42	33	14.1	4.06	101	.291	.360	7	.212	-1	2	1	1	0.1
1925 Det-A	6	9	.400	35	14	5	0	2	134^{1}	190	106	8	2	62	45	17.0	6.23	69	.345	.413	12	.279	3	-27	-29	1	-2.5
1926 Det-A	12	10	.545	36	26	9	**4**	0	178	201	101	7	2	76	58	14.1	4.15	98	.297	.370	15	.205	0	-2	-2	-3	-0.4
1927 Det-A	0	1	.000	8	1	0	0	1	20	28	16	3	0	5	5	14.8	6.75	62	.333	.371	2	.286	0	-6	-6	1	-0.2
1929 NY-A	13	9	.591	31	23	10	3	0	193^{1}	179	102	19	1	81	78	12.1	4.33	89	.248	.324	17	.230	2	-2	-11	-4	-1.3
1930 NY-A	12	3	.800	27	21	7	0	0	150^{2}	185	101	11	4	49	46	14.2	5.20	83	.302	.358	15	.259	0	-9	-16	-2	-1.4
1931 NY-A	9	5	.643	27	10	6	0	2	116^{2}	130	68	7	1	37	34	13.0	4.32	92	.286	.341	10	.222	1	1	-5	-2	-0.6
1932 NY-A	3	3	.500	22	0	0	0	2	31^{2}	38	19	1	0	12	13	14.2	4.26	96	.302	.362	0	.000	-1	1	-1	-0	-0.2
1933 StL-A	6	14	.300	36	22	10	0	1	203^{2}	230	113	13	1	63	58	13.0	4.20	111	.278	.330	14	.197	-1	2	9	-3	0.5
1934 StL-A	1	7	.125	33	8	2	0	1	92	108	60	7	0	35	27	14.0	4.79	104	.292	.353	1	.045	-2	-3	2	1	0.1
Total 11	68	69	.496	291	140	54	7	13	1232^{1}	1417	750	78	12	468	403	13.9	4.65	91	.291	.355	93	.215	1	-46	-56	-10	-6.0

● JOHN WELLS

Wells, John Frederick b: 11/25/22, Junction City, Kan. d: 10/23/93, Olean, N.Y. BR/TR, 5'11.5", 180 lbs. Deb: 9/14/44

YEAR TM/L	W	L	PCT	G	GS	CG	SH	SV	IP	H	R	HR	HB	BB	SO	RAT	ERA	ERA+	OAV	OOB	BH	AVG	PB	PR	PR+	PD	TPI
1944 Bro-N	0	2	.000	4	2	0	0	0	15	18	9	1	0	11	7	17.4	5.40	66	.316	.426	1	.250	0	-3	-3	-0	-0.4

● KIP WELLS

Wells, Robert Kip b: 4/21/77, Houston, Tex. BR/TR, 6'3", 195 lbs. Deb: 8/2/99

YEAR TM/L	W	L	PCT	G	GS	CG	SH	SV	IP	H	R	HR	HB	BB	SO	RAT	ERA	ERA+	OAV	OOB	BH	AVG	PB	PR	PR+	PD	TPI
1999 Chi-A	4	1	.800	7	7	0	0	0	35^{2}	33	17	2	3	15	29	12.9	4.04	121	.248	.338	0	—	0	3	3	-0	0.4
2000 Chi-A	6	9	.400	20	20	0	0	0	98^{2}	126	76	15	2	58	71	17.0	6.02	83	.312	.401	0	.000	-0	-12	-11	-2	-1.6
Total 2	10	10	.500	27	27	0	0	0	134^{1}	159	93	17	5	73	100	15.9	5.49	90	.296	.385	0	.000	-0	-9	-8	-2	-1.2

● BOB WELLS

Wells, Robert Lee b: 11/1/66, Yakima, Wash. BR/TR, 6', 180 lbs. Deb: 5/16/94

YEAR TM/L	W	L	PCT	G	GS	CG	SH	SV	IP	H	R	HR	HB	BB	SO	RAT	ERA	ERA+	OAV	OOB	BH	AVG	PB	PR	PR+	PD	TPI
1994 Phi-N	1	0	1.000	6	0	0	0	0	5	4	1	0	1	3	3	14.4	1.80	239	.235	.381	0	—	0	1	1	-0	0.2
Sea-A	1	0	1.000	1	0	0	0	0	4	4	1	0	0	1	3	11.3	2.25	217	.250	.294	0	—	0	1	1	-0	0.2
1995 *Sea-A	4	3	.571	30	4	0	0	0	76^{2}	88	51	11	3	39	38	15.3	5.75	82	.284	.369	0	—	0	-9	-9	-0	-0.7
1996 Sea-A	12	7	.632	36	16	1	1	0	130^{2}	141	78	25	6	46	94	13.3	5.30	93	.274	.340	0	—	0	-4	-5	-1	-0.7
1997 *Sea-A	2	0	1.000	46	1	0	0	2	67^{1}	88	49	11	3	18	51	14.6	5.75	78	.314	.362	0	—	0	-9	-9	-0	-0.4
1998 Sea-A	2	2	.500	30	0	0	0	0	51^{2}	54	38	12	2	16	29	12.5	6.10	76	.261	.320	0	—	0	-8	-8	-0	-0.6
1999 Min-A	8	3	.727	**76**	0	0	0	1	87^{1}	79	41	8	5	28	44	11.5	3.81	134	.245	.315	0	—	0	10	12	-1	1.2
2000 Min-A	0	7	.000	76	0	0	0	10	86^{1}	80	39	14	4	15	76	10.3	3.65	144	.247	.289	0	—	0	12	14	-0	1.2
Total 7	30	22	.577	301	21	1	1	13	509	538	298	81	24	166	338	12.9	4.92	100	.270	.334	0	—	0	-5	-1	-4	0.4

● TERRY WELLS

Wells, Terry b: 9/10/63, Kankakee, Ill. BL/TL, 6'3", 205 lbs. Deb: 7/3/90

YEAR TM/L	W	L	PCT	G	GS	CG	SH	SV	IP	H	R	HR	HB	BB	SO	RAT	ERA	ERA+	OAV	OOB	BH	AVG	PB	PR	PR+	PD	TPI
1990 LA-N	1	2	.333	5	5	0	0	0	20^{2}	25	23	4	0	14	18	17.0	7.84	47	.287	.386	0	.000	-1	-9	-10	-1	-1.3

● CHRIS WELSH

Welsh, Christopher Charles b: 4/14/55, Wilmington, Del. BL/TL, 6'2", 185 lbs. Deb: 4/12/81

YEAR TM/L	W	L	PCT	G	GS	CG	SH	SV	IP	H	R	HR	HB	BB	SO	RAT	ERA	ERA+	OAV	OOB	BH	AVG	PB	PR	PR+	PD	TPI
1981 SD-N	6	7	.462	22	19	4	2	0	123^{2}	122	55	9	1	41	51	11.9	3.78	86	.264	.325	6	.146	0	-4	-8	1	-0.6
1982 SD-N	8	8	.500	28	20	3	1	0	139^{1}	146	88	16	3	63	48	13.7	4.91	70	.268	.347	11	.262	4	-20	-24	1	-2.0
1983 SD-N	0	1	.000	7	1	0	0	0	14^{1}	13	5	2	0	2	5	9.4	2.51	139	.236	.263	0	.000	-0	2	2	-0	0.0
Mon-N	0	1	.000	16	5	0	0	0	44^{2}	46	30	5	4	18	17	13.7	5.04	71	.267	.351	4	.286	1	-7	-7	1	-0.1
Yr	0	2	.000	23	6	0	0	0	59	59	35	7	4	20	22	12.7	4.42	81	.260	.331	4	.222	1	-5	-6	1	-0.1
1985 Tex-A	2	5	.286	25	6	0	0	0	76^{1}	101	40	11	4	25	31	15.3	4.13	103	.316	.372	0	—	0	0	1	-1	0.0
1986 Cin-N	6	9	.400	24	24	1	0	0	139^{1}	163	79	9	3	40	40	13.3	4.78	81	.301	.353	5	.119	0	-16	-13	1	-1.3
Total 5	22	31	.415	122	75	8	3	0	537^{2}	591	297	52	15	189	192	13.3	4.45	82	.282	.346	26	.182	5	-45	-50	2	-4.0

● DICK WELTEROTH

Welteroth, Richard John b: 8/3/27, Williamsport, Pa. BR/TR, 5'11", 165 lbs. Deb: 5/16/48

YEAR TM/L	W	L	PCT	G	GS	CG	SH	SV	IP	H	R	HR	HB	BB	SO	RAT	ERA	ERA+	OAV	OOB	BH	AVG	PB	PR	PR+	PD	TPI
1948 Was-A	2	1	.667	33	2	0	0	1	65^{1}	73	43	6	1	50	16	17.1	5.51	79	.286	.405	1	.100	-1	-9	-8	-0	-0.5
1949 Was-A	2	5	.286	52	2	0	0	2	95^{1}	107	83	6	1	89	37	18.6	7.36	58	.296	.437	1	.059	-1	-34	-32	-0	-2.2
1950 Was-A	0	0	—	5	0	0	0	0	6	5	5	0	0	6	2	16.5	3.00	150	.217	.379	0	—	0	1	1	-0	0.1
Total 3	4	6	.400	90	4	0	0	3	166^{2}	185	131	12	2	145	55	17.9	6.48	66	.290	.422	2	.074	-2	-41	-40	-0	-2.6

● TONY WELZER

Welzer, Anton Frank b: 4/5/1899, Germany d: 3/18/71, Milwaukee, Wis. BR/TR, 5'11", 160 lbs. Deb: 4/13/26

YEAR TM/L	W	L	PCT	G	GS	CG	SH	SV	IP	H	R	HR	HB	BB	SO	RAT	ERA	ERA+	OAV	OOB	BH	AVG	PB	PR	PR+	PD	TPI
1926 Bos-A	4	3	.571	39	5	1	1	0	139	167	88	5	3	53	29	14.4	4.86	84	.308	.373	8	.211	2	-13	-12	4	0.0
1927 Bos-A	6	11	.353	37	19	8	0	1	171^{2}	214	109	10	4	71	56	15.2	4.72	89	.318	.386	4	.095	-2	-11	-9	1	-0.9
Total 2	10	14	.417	76	24	9	1	1	310^{2}	381	197	15	7	124	85	14.8	4.78	87	.313	.380	12	.150	-0	-24	-21	4	-0.9

● TURK WENDELL

Wendell, Steven John b: 5/19/67, Pittsfield, Mass. BB/TR, 6'2", 190 lbs. Deb: 6/17/93

YEAR TM/L	W	L	PCT	G	GS	CG	SH	SV	IP	H	R	HR	HB	BB	SO	RAT	ERA	ERA+	OAV	OOB	BH	AVG	PB	PR	PR+	PD	TPI
1993 Chi-N	1	2	.333	7	4	0	0	0	22^{2}	24	13	0	0	8	15	12.7	4.37	91	.273	.333	1	.143	-0	-1	-1	0	-0.1
1994 Chi-N	0	1	.000	6	2	0	0	0	14^{1}	22	20	3	0	10	9	20.1	11.93	35	.349	.438	0	.000	-0	-12	-13	-0	-0.7
1995 Chi-N	3	1	.750	43	0	0	0	0	60^{1}	71	35	11	2	24	50	14.5	4.92	83	.298	.367	0	.000	-0	-5	-6	1	-0.2
1996 Chi-N	4	5	.444	70	0	0	0	18	79^{1}	58	26	8	3	44	75	11.9	2.84	153	.201	.313	1	.500	1	12	13	0	1.9
1997 Chi-N	3	5	.375	52	0	0	0	4	60	53	32	4	1	39	54	14.0	4.20	103	.238	.354	0	.000	-0	0	1	0	0.1
NY-N	0	0	—	13	0	0	0	1	16^{1}	15	10	3	1	14	10	16.5	4.96	81	.250	.400	0	.000	-0	-1	-2	1	-0.1
Yr	3	5	.375	65	0	0	0	5	76^{1}	68	42	7	2	53	64	14.5	4.36	97	.240	.364	0	.000	-0	-1	-1	1	0.0
1998 NY-N	5	1	.833	66	0	0	0	4	76^{2}	62	25	4	2	33	58	11.4	2.93	141	.221	.307	0	.000	-0	11	10	0	0.8
1999 *NY-N	5	4	.556	80	0	0	0	3	85^{2}	80	31	9	2	37	77	12.5	3.05	144	.245	.325	0	.000	-0	14	13	-1	1.1
2000 *NY-N	8	6	.571	77	0	0	0	1	82^{2}	60	36	9	5	41	73	11.5	3.59	123	.206	.315	1	.250	0	10	8	0	1.2
Total 8	29	25	.537	414	6	0	0	31	498	445	228	51	16	250	421	12.8	3.83	111	.239	.335	3	.081	-1	28	25	2	4.0

● DON WENGERT

Wengert, Donald Paul b: 11/6/69, Sioux City, Iowa BR/TR, 6'2", 205 lbs. Deb: 4/30/95

YEAR TM/L	W	L	PCT	G	GS	CG	SH	SV	IP	H	R	HR	HB	BB	SO	RAT	ERA	ERA+	OAV	OOB	BH	AVG	PB	PR	PR+	PD	TPI
1995 Oak-A	1	1	.500	19	0	0	0	0	29^{2}	30	14	3	1	12	16	13.0	3.34	134	.263	.339	0	—	0	5	4	1	0.2
1996 Oak-A	7	11	.389	36	25	1	1	0	161^{1}	200	102	29	6	60	75	14.8	5.58	88	.307	.371	0	—	0	-10	-12	-2	-1.3

YEAR	TM/L	W	L	PCT	G	GS	CG	SH	SV	IP	H	R	HR	HB	BB	SO	RAT	ERA	ERA+	OAV	OOB	BH	AVG	PB	PR	PR+	PD	TPI
1997	Oak-A	5	11	.313	49	12	1	0	2	134	177	96	21	8	41	68	15.2	6.04	75	.321	.377	0		0	-22	-23	0	-2.3
1998	SD-N	0	0	—	10	0	0	0	1	13^{2}	21	9	2	0	5	5	17.1	5.93	66	.356	.406	0	.000	-0	-3	-3	-0	-0.2
	Chi-N	1	5	.167	21	6	0	0	0	49^{2}	55	29	8	3	23	41	14.7	5.07	87	.279	.363	0	.000	-1	-5	-4	-0	-0.5
	Yr	1	5	.167	31	6	0	0	1	63^{1}	76	38	10	3	28	46	15.2	5.26	82	.297	.373	0	.000	-2	-7	-7	-1	-0.7
1999	KC-A	0	1	.000	11	1	0	0	0	24^{1}	41	26	6	0	5	10	17.0	9.25	54	.376	.404	0	—	0	-12	-11	-0	-0.5
2000	Atl-N	0	1	.000	10	0	0	0	0	10	12	9	2	0	5	7	15.3	7.20	63	.286	.362	0	—	0	-3	-3	-0	-0.3
Total	6	14	30	.318	156	44	2	1	3	422^{2}	536	285	71	18	151	222	15.0	5.77	81	.311	.373	0	.000	-2	-50	-52	-4	-4.9
● BUTCH WENSLOFF Wensloff, Charles William b: 12/3/15, Sausalito, Cal. BR/TR, 5'11", 185 lbs. Deb: 5/2/43																												
1943	NY-A	13	11	.542	29	27	18	1	1	223^{1}	179	80	7	1	70	105	10.1	2.54	127	.219	.282	14	.177	-0	19	17	-1	1.7
1947	*NY-A	3	1	.750	11	5	1	0	0	51^{2}	41	17	3	0	22	18	11.0	2.61	135	.217	.299	5	.263	1	6	6	-1	0.4
1948	Cle-A	0	1	.000	1	0	0	0	0	1^{2}	2	2	1	0	3	2	27.0	10.80	38	.286	.500	0	—	0	-1	-1	-0	-0.2
Total	3	16	13	.552	41	32	19	1	1	276^{2}	222	99	11	1	95	125	10.3	2.60	126	.219	.287	19	.194	0	24	22	-2	1.9
● FRED WENZ Wenz, Frederick Charles "Fireball" b: 8/26/41, Bound Brook, N.J. BR/TR, 6'3", 214 lbs. Deb: 6/4/68																												
1968	Bos-A	0	0	—	1	0	0	0	0	1	0	0	0	0	2	3	18.0	0.00	—	.000	.400	0	—	0	0	0	0	0.0
1969	Bos-A	1	0	1.000	8	0	0	0	0	11	9	7	7	0	10	11	15.5	5.73	66	.225	.380	0	—	0	-3	-2	0	-0.2
1970	Phi-N	2	0	1.000	22	0	0	0	1	30^{1}	27	16	2	1	13	24	12.2	4.45	90	.237	.320	0	.000	-1	-1	-2	-1	-0.2
Total	3	3	0	1.000	31	0	0	0	1	42^{1}	36	23	9	1	25	38	13.2	4.68	84	.229	.339	0	.000	-0	-4	-3	-1	-0.4
● PERRY WERDEN Werden, Percival Wheritt b: 7/21/1865, St.Louis, Mo. d: 1/9/34, Minneapolis, Minn. BR/TR, 6'2", 220 lbs. Deb: 4/24/1884 ♦																												
1884	StL-U	12	1	.923	16	16	12	1	0	141^{1}	113	61	1		22	51	8.6	1.97	121	.204	.235	18	.237	-4	7	7	1	0.2
● BILL WERLE Werle, William George "Bugs" b: 12/21/20, Oakland, Cal. BL/TL, 6'2.5", 182 lbs. Deb: 4/22/49 C																												
1949	Pit-N	12	13	.480	35	29	10	2	0	221	243	117	22	8	51	106	12.3	4.24	99	.278	.324	9	.117	-3	-5	-1	1	-0.3
1950	Pit-N	8	16	.333	48	22	6	0	8	215^{1}	249	127	25	6	65	78	13.4	4.60	95	.290	.344	13	.194	1	-11	-5	4	0.0
1951	Pit-N	8	6	.571	59	9	2	0	6	149^{2}	181	102	20	6	51	57	14.3	5.65	75	.304	.364	12	.300	3	-28	-22	3	-1.4
1952	Pit-N	0	0	—	5	0	0	0	0	4	9	5	1	0	1	1	22.5	9.00	44	.429	.455	0	—	0	-2	-2	0	-0.1
	StL-N	1	2	.333	19	0	0	0	1	39	40	23	6	1	15	23	12.9	4.85	77	.268	.339	1	.111	-0	-5	-5	1	-0.3
	Yr	1	2	.333	24	0	0	0	1	43	49	28	7	1	16	24	13.8	5.23	71	.288	.353	1	.111	-0	-7	-7	1	-0.4
1953	Bos-A	0	1	.000	5	0	0	0	0	11^{2}	7	3	1	0	1	4	6.2	1.54	273	.179	.200	0	.000	-0	3	3	1	0.3
1954	Bos-A	0	1	.000	14	0	0	0	0	24^{2}	41	13	5	2	10	14	19.3	4.38	94	.376	.438	0	.000	-0	-2	-1	-0	-0.1
Total	6	29	39	.426	185	60	18	2	15	665^{1}	770	390	80	23	194	283	13.4	4.69	90	.291	.345	35	.176	1	-50	-32	10	-1.9
● GEORGE WERLEY Werley, George William b: 9/8/38, St.Louis, Mo. BR/TR, 6'2", 196 lbs. Deb: 9/29/56																												
1956	Bal-A	0	0	—	1	0	0	0	0	1	1	1	0	0	2	0	27.0	9.00	44	.250	.500	0	—	0	-1	-1	0	0.0
● JOHNNY WERTS Werts, Henry Levi b: 4/20/1898, Pomaria, S.C. d: 9/24/90, Newberry, S.C. BR/TR, 5'10", 180 lbs. Deb: 4/14/26																												
1926	Bos-N	11	9	.550	32	23	7	1	0	189^{1}	212	85	6	10	47	65	12.8	3.28	108	.287	.338	17	.266	4	11	6	2	1.2
1927	Bos-N	4	10	.286	42	15	4	0	1	164^{1}	204	95	5	4	52	39	14.2	4.55	82	.315	.369	7	.163	-0	-11	-16	-1	-1.3
1928	Bos-N	0	2	.000	10	2	0	0	0	18^{1}	31	22	2	0	8	5	19.1	10.31	38	.369	.424	1	.333	0	-13	-13	0	-1.2
1929	Bos-N	0	0	—	4	0	0	0	1	6	13	8	1	0	4	2	25.5	10.50	45	.433	.500	1	1.000	0	-4	-4	-0	-0.1
Total	4	15	21	.417	88	40	11	1	2	378	460	210	14	14	111	111	13.9	4.29	85	.307	.360	26	.234	4	-17	-28	1	-1.4
● BILL WERTZ Wertz, William Charles b: 1/15/67, Cleveland, Ohio BR/TR, 6'6", 220 lbs. Deb: 5/22/93																												
1993	Cle-A	2	3	.400	34	0	0	0	0	59^{2}	54	28	5	1	32	53	13.1	3.62	120	.238	.335	0	—	0	5	5	-2	0.2
1994	Cle-A	0	0	—	1	0	0	0	0	4^{1}	9	5	0	0	1	1	20.8	10.38	45	.409	.435	0	—	0	-3	-3	-0	-0.1
Total	2	2	3	.400	35	0	0	0	0	64	63	33	5	1	33	54	13.6	4.08	107	.253	.343	0	—	0	2	2	-2	0.1
● DAVID WEST West, David Lee b: 9/1/64, Memphis, Tenn. BL/TL, 6'6", 230 lbs. Deb: 9/24/88																												
1988	NY-N	1	0	1.000	2	1	0	0	0	6	6	2	0	0	3	3	13.5	3.00	108	.273	.360	2	1.000	1	0	0	-0	0.2
1989	NY-N	0	2	.000	11	2	0	0	0	24^{1}	25	20	4	1	14	19	14.8	7.40	44	.260	.360	1	.200	0	-11	-12	-1	-0.9
	Min-A	3	2	.600	10	5	0	0	0	39^{1}	48	29	5	2	19	31	15.8	6.41	65	.306	.388	0	—	0	-11	-9	-1	-1.1
1990	Min-A	7	9	.438	29	27	2	0	0	146^{1}	142	88	21	4	78	92	13.8	5.10	82	.256	.352	0	—	0	-19	-14	-1	-1.5
1991	*Min-A	4	4	.500	15	12	0	0	0	71^{1}	66	37	13	1	28	52	12.0	4.54	94	.244	.317	0	—	0	-3	-2	0	-0.2
1992	Min-A	1	3	.250	9	3	0	0	0	28^{1}	32	24	3	1	20	19	16.8	6.99	58	.276	.387	0	—	0	-10	-9	-0	-1.1
1993	*Phi-N	6	4	.600	76	0	0	0	3	86^{1}	60	37	6	5	51	87	12.1	2.92	136	.194	.318	2	.400	1	11	10	-2	1.1
1994	Phi-N	4	10	.286	31	14	0	0	0	99	74	44	7	1	61	83	12.4	3.55	121	.205	.322	2	.071	-2	7	8	-2	0.7
1995	Phi-N	3	2	.600	8	8	0	0	0	38	34	17	5	1	19	25	12.8	3.79	112	.241	.335	1	.125	1	2	2	-1	0.2
1996	Phi-N	2	2	.500	7	6	0	0	0	28^{1}	31	17	0	0	11	22	13.3	4.76	91	.272	.336	2	.286	1	-2	-1	-0	-0.1
1998	Bos-A	0	0	—	6	0	0	0	0	2	7	6	1	0	7	4	63.0	27.00	17	.538	.700	0	—	0	-5	-5	0	-0.2
Total	10	31	38	.449	204	78	2	0	3	569^{1}	525	321	65	16	311	437	13.5	4.66	89	.244	.343	10	.182	2	-40	-33	-7	-2.9
● FRANK WEST West, J. Franklin b: 1/1874, Johnstown, Pa. d: 9/6/32, Wilmerding, Pa. 180 lbs. Deb: 7/11/1894																												
1894	Bos-N	0	0	—	1	0	0	0	0	3	5	5	0	0	2	1	21.0	9.00	63	.357	.438	0	.000	-0	-1	-1	-0	-0.1
● HI WEST West, James Hiram b: 8/8/1884, Roseville, Ill. d: 5/25/63, Los Angeles, Cal. BR/TR, 6', 185 lbs. Deb: 9/8/05																												
1905	Cle-A	2	2	.500	6	4	4	1	0	33	43	23	0	3	10	15	15.3	4.09	64	.316	.376	1	.077	-1	-5	-5	-2	-0.9
1911	Cle-A	3	4	.429	13	8	3	0	1	64^{2}	84	35	1	3	18	17	14.6	3.76	91	.343	.395	3	.130	-2	-3	-2	-1	-0.5
Total	2	5	6	.455	19	12	7	1	1	97^{2}	127	58	1	6	28	32	14.8	3.87	81	.333	.388	4	.111	-3	-8	-8	-3	-1.4
● LEFTY WEST West, Weldon Edison b: 9/3/15, Gibsonville, N.C. d: 7/23/79, Hendersonville, N.C. BR/TL, 6', 165 lbs. Deb: 4/30/44																												
1944	StL-A	0	0	—	11	0	0	0	0	24^{1}	34	18	1	1	19	11	20.0	6.29	57	.366	.478	1	.143	-0	-8	-7	-0	-0.4
1945	StL-A	3	4	.429	24	8	1	0	0	74^{1}	71	37	2	0	31	38	12.3	3.63	97	.245	.318	2	.074	-3	-2	-1	-2	-0.5
Total	2	3	4	.429	35	8	1	0	0	98^{2}	105	55	3	1	50	49	14.2	4.29	83	.274	.359	3	.088	-3	-10	-8	-2	-0.9
● JAKE WESTBROOK Westbrook, Jacob Cauthen b: 9/29/77, Athens, Ga. BR/TR, 6'3", 190 lbs. Deb: 6/17/2000																												
2000	NY-A	0	2	.000	3	2	0	0	0	6^{2}	15	10	1	0	4	1	25.7	13.50	36	.469	.528	0	—	0	-6	-7	-0	-1.0
● HUYLER WESTERVELT Westervelt, Huyler b: 10/1/1870, Piermont, N.Y. 5'9", 170 lbs. Deb: 4/21/1894																												
1894	NY-N	7	10	.412	23	18	11	1	0	141	170	118	4	5	76	35	16.0	5.04	104	.295	.382	8	.143	-5	4	3	0	-0.1
● MICKEY WESTON Weston, Michael Lee b: 3/26/61, Flint, Mich. BR/TR, 6'1", 187 lbs. Deb: 6/18/89																												
1989	Bal-A	1	0	1.000	7	0	0	0	1	13	18	8	1	1	2	7	14.5	5.54	69	.346	.382	0	—	0	-2	-3	-0	-0.2
1990	Bal-A	0	1	.000	9	2	0	0	0	21	28	20	6	0	6	9	14.6	7.71	49	.322	.366	0	—	0	-9	-9	-0	-0.5
1991	Tor-A	0	0	—	2	0	0	0	0	2	1	0	0	0	1	1	9.0	0.00	—	.143	.250	0	—	0	1	1	0	0.0
1992	Phi-N	0	1	.000	1	1	0	0	0	3^{2}	7	5	1	1	1	0	22.1	12.27	28	.412	.474	0	.000	-0	-4	-4	-0	-0.6
1993	NY-N	0	0	—	4	0	0	0	0	5^{2}	11	5	0	1	1	2	20.6	7.94	51	.393	.433	0	—	0	-2	-2	0	-0.1
Total	5	1	2	.333	23	3	0	0	1	45^{1}	65	38	8	3	11	19	15.7	7.15	53	.340	.385	0	.000	-0	-16	-17	-1	-1.4
● JOHN WETTELAND Wetteland, John Karl b: 8/21/66, San Mateo, Cal. BR/TR, 6'2", 195 lbs. Deb: 5/31/89																												
1989	LA-N	5	8	.385	31	12	0	0	1	102^{2}	81	46	8	0	34	96	10.1	3.77	91	.218	.284	3	.143	-0	-3	-4	-1	-0.7
1990	LA-N	2	4	.333	22	5	0	0	0	43	44	28	6	4	17	36	13.6	4.81	76	.263	.346	1	.143	1	-5	-6	-1	-0.7
1991	LA-N	1	0	1.000	6	0	0	0	0	9	5	2	0	1	3	9	9.0	0.00	—	.161	.257	0	—	0	4	4	0	0.4
1992	Mon-N	4	4	.500	67	0	0	0	37	83^{1}	64	27	6	4	36	99	11.2	2.92	119	.213	.305	1	.200	0	6	5	-1	0.9
1993	Mon-N	9	3	.750	70	0	0	0	43	85^{1}	58	17	3	2	28	113	9.3	1.37	305	.188	.260	0	.000	-0	25	26	-1	5.2
1994	Mon-N	4	6	.400	52	0	0	0	25	63^{2}	46	22	5	3	21	68	9.9	2.83	149	.202	.278	1	.250	0	10	10	-1	1.9
1995	*NY-A	1	5	.167	60	0	0	0	31	61^{1}	40	22	6	0	14	66	7.9	2.93	157	.185	.235	0	—	0	12	12	-1	1.9
1996	*NY-A☆	2	3	.400	62	0	0	0	**43**	63^{2}	54	23	9	0	21	69	10.6	2.83	175	.224	.286	0	—	0	15	15	-0	2.8
1997	Tex-A	7	2	.778	61	0	0	0	31	65	43	18	5	0	21	63	8.9	1.94	247	.182	.249	1	1.000	1	19	20	-1	3.9
1998	*Tex-A★	3	1	.750	63	0	0	0	42	62	47	17	6	0	14	72	8.9	2.03	238	.203	.249	0	—	0	18	19	-0	3.1
1999	*Tex-A★	4	4	.500	62	0	0	0	43	66	67	30	9	0	19	60	11.7	3.68	138	.262	.313	0	—	0	9	10	-1	1.8

YEAR	TM/L	W	L	PCT	G	GS	CG	SH	SV	IP	H	R	HR	HB	BB	SO	RAT	ERA	ERA+	OAV	OOB	BH	AVG	PB	PR	PR+	PD	TPI
2000	Tex-A	6	5	.545	62	0	0	0	34	60	67	35	10	2	24	53	14.0	4.20	121	.285	.356	0	—	0	5	6	-0	1.0
Total	12	48	45	.516	618	17	0	0	330	765	616	287	73	16	252	804	10.4	2.93	147	.218	.286	7	.167	1	115	117	-8	21.5
● BUZZ WETZEL	Wetzel, Charles Edward b: 8/25/1894, Jay, Okla. d: 3/7/41, Globe, Ariz. BR/TR, 6'1", 162 lbs. Deb: 7/25/27																											
1927	Phi-A	0	0	—	2	1	0	0	0	4^2	8	5	0	0	5	0	25.1	7.71	55	.400	.520	1	1.000	0	-2	-2	0	0.0
● SHORTY WETZEL	Wetzel, George William b: 1868, Philadelphia, Pa. d: 2/25/1899, Dayton, Ohio Deb: 8/26/1885																											
1885	Bal-a	0	2	.000	2	2	1	0	0	17	27	26	0	3	9	6	20.6	8.47	38	.333	.419	0	.000	-1	-10	-10	1	-0.8
● STEFAN WEVER	Wever, Stefan Matthew b: 4/22/58, Marburg, W.Ger. BR/TR, 6'8", 245 lbs. Deb: 9/17/82																											
1982	NY-A	0	1	.000	1	1	0	0	0	2^2	6	9	1	0	3	2	30.4	27.00	15	.429	.529	0	—	0	-7	-7	-0	-0.9
● GUS WEYHING	Weyhing, August "Cannonball" b: 9/29/1866, Louisville, Ky. d: 9/4/55, Louisville, Ky. BR/TR, 5'10", 145 lbs. Deb: 5/2/1887 F																											
1887	Phi-a	26	28	.481	55	55	53	2	0	466^1	632	342	12	37	167	193	12.9	4.27	101	.315	.328	48	.223	-9	2	1	-2	-0.8
1888	Phi-a	28	18	.609	47	47	45	3	0	404	314	198	4	42	111	204	10.4	2.25	133	.207	.279	40	.217	4	36	34	1	3.8
1889	Phi-a	30	21	.588	54	53	50	4	0	449	382	271	15	34	212	213	12.6	2.95	128	.223	.321	25	.131	-15	45	42	-3	2.2
1890	Bro-P	30	16	.652	49	46	38	3	0	390	419	250	10	17	179	177	14.2	3.60	124	.263	.343	27	.164	-6	27	35	-9	1.8
1891	Phi-a	31	20	.608	52	51	51	3	0	450	428	231	12	31	161	219	12.4	3.18	119	.242	.316	22	.111	-16	27	30	-5	0.9
1892	Phi-N	32	21	.604	59	49	46	6	**3**	469^2	411	213	9	18	168	202	11.4	2.66	122	.226	.298	29	.136	-10	33	31	-9	1.1
1893	Phi-N	23	16	.590	42	40	33	2	0	345^1	399	235	10	20	145	101	14.7	4.74	96	.281	.356	22	.150	-9	-3	-7	-2	-1.5
1894	Phi-N	16	14	.533	40	36	26	2	1	279^1	379	224	12	16	120	83	16.6	5.70	90	.320	.390	21	.174	-9	-12	-19	-2	-2.3
1895	Phi-N	0	2	.000	2	2	0	0	0	9	23	22	0	0	13	5	36.0	20.00	24	.469	.581	0	.000	-1	-15	-15	0	-1.7
	Pit-N	1	0	1.000	1	1	1	0	0	9	10	7	0	0	5	3	15.0	1.00	452	.278	.366	1	.250	0	4	4	1	0.5
	Lou-N	7	19	.269	28	25	22	1	0	213	285	205	9	8	66	53	15.2	5.41	86	.316	.368	20	.225	-0	-15	-19	0	-1.6
	Yr	8	21	.276	31	28	23	1	0	231	318	234	9	8	84	61	16.0	5.81	80	.322	.380	21	.216	-1	-26	-31	1	-2.8
1896	Lou-N	2	3	.400	5	5	4	0	0	42	62	46	6	2	15	9	16.9	6.64	65	.339	.395	2	.133	-1	-11	-11	1	-0.9
1898	Was-N	15	26	.366	45	42	39	0	0	361	428	232	10	16	84	92	13.2	4.51	81	.292	.338	25	.177	-5	-36	-34	-2	-3.7
1899	Was-N	17	21	.447	43	38	34	2	0	334^2	414	223	8	28	76	96	13.9	4.54	86	.303	.352	26	.206	-1	-26	-23	-6	-2.7
1900	StL-N	3	2	.600	7	5	3	0	0	46^2	60	44	2	1	21	6	15.8	4.63	79	.311	.381	2	.095	-2	-5	-5	-1	-0.7
	Bro-N	3	4	.429	8	8	3	0	0	48	66	33	1	2	20	8	16.5	4.31	89	.325	.391	4	.222	-0	-3	-2	-1	-0.4
	Yr	6	6	.500	15	13	6	0	0	94^2	126	77	3	3	41	14	16.2	4.47	84	.318	.386	6	.154	-3	-8	-8	-1	-1.1
1901	Cle-A	0	0	—	2	1	0	0	0	11^1	20	11	0	4	5	0	23.0	7.94	45	.377	.468	0	.000	-1	-5	-6	-0	-0.3
	Cin-N	0	1	.000	1	1	1	0	0	9	11	9	0	2	2	3	15.0	3.00	107	.297	.366	0	.000	-0	0	0	-0	-0.1
Total	14	264	232	.532	540	505	449	28	4	4337^1	4743	2796	120	278	1570	1667	13.3	3.88	102	.271	.335	314	.169	-83	43	39	-38	-6.4
● JOHN WEYHING	Weyhing, John b: 6/24/1869, Louisville, Ky. d: 6/20/1890, Louisville, Ky. BL/TL, 6'2", 185 lbs. Deb: 7/13/1888 F																											
1888	Cin-a	3	4	.429	8	8	7	0	0	65^2	52	26	0	1	17	30	9.6	1.23	257	.210	.263	3	.130	-2	13	14	-1	1.1
1889	Col-a	0	0	—	1	0	0	0	0	1	1	3	0	0	4	0	45.0	27.00	13	.250	.625	0	—	0	-3	-3	-0	-0.1
Total	2	3	4	.429	9	8	7	0	0	66^2	53	29	0	1	21	30	10.1	1.62	196	.210	.274	3	.130	-2	11	11	-1	1.0
● LEE WHEAT	Wheat, Leroy William b: 9/15/29, Edwardsville, Ill BR/TR, 6'4", 200 lbs. Deb: 4/21/54																											
1954	Phi-A	0	2	.000	8	1	0	0	0	28^1	38	18	1	1	9	7	15.2	5.72	68	.304	.356	1	.125	-0	-6	-5	-0	-0.4
1955	KC-A	0	0	—	3	0	0	0	0	2	8	7	1	0	3	1	49.5	22.50	19	.533	.611	0	—	0	-4	-4	0	-0.2
Total	2	0	2	.000	11	1	0	0	0	30^1	46	25	2	1	12	8	17.5	6.82	57	.329	.386	1	.125	-0	-10	-9	-0	-0.6
● CHARLIE WHEATLEY	Wheatley, Charles b: 6/27/1893, Rosedale, Kan. d: 12/10/82, Tulsa, Okla. BR/TR, 5'11", 174 lbs. Deb: 9/6/12																											
1912	Det-A	1	4	.200	5	5	2	0	0	35	45	27	1	2	17	14	16.5	6.17	53	.331	.413	0	.000	-2	-11	-12	0	-1.4
● WOODY WHEATON	Wheaton, Elwood Pierce b: 10/3/14, Philadelphia, Pa. d: 12/11/95, Lancaster, Pa. BL/TL, 5'8.5", 160 lbs. Deb: 9/28/43 ♦																											
1944	Phi-A	0	1	.000	11	1	1	0	0	38	36	17	1	1	20	15	13.5	3.55	98	.255	.352	11	.186	0	-1	-0	-1	-0.1
● DAN WHEELER	Wheeler, Daniel Michael b: 12/10/77, Providence, R.I. BR/TR, 6'3", 215 lbs. Deb: 9/1/99																											
1999	TB-A	0	4	.000	6	6	0	0	0	30^2	35	20	7	0	13	32	14.1	5.87	85	.287	.356	0	—	0	-3	-3	-0	-0.3
2000	TB-A	1	1	.500	11	2	0	0	0	23	29	14	2	2	11	17	16.4	5.48	90	.302	.385	0	—	0	-1	-1	0	-0.1
Total	2	1	5	.167	17	8	0	0	0	53^2	64	34	9	2	24	49	15.1	5.70	87	.294	.369	0	—	0	-5	-4	0	-0.4
● RIP WHEELER	Wheeler, Floyd Clark b: 3/2/1898, Marion, Ky. d: 9/18/68, Marion, Ky. BR/TR, 6', 180 lbs. Deb: 9/30/21																											
1921	Pit-N	0	0	—	1	0	0	0	0	3	6	4	0	1	1	0	24.0	9.00	43	.500	.571	0	.000	-0	-2	-2	0	-0.1
1922	Pit-N	0	0	—	1	0	0	0	0	1	1	0	0	0	2	0	27.0	0.00	—	.333	.600	0	—	0	0	0	0	0.0
1923	Chi-N	1	2	.333	3	3	1	0	0	24	28	14	2	3	5	5	13.5	4.88	82	.298	.353	1	.111	-1	-2	-2	1	-0.2
1924	Chi-N	3	6	.333	29	4	0	0	0	101^1	103	53	8	0	21	16	11.0	3.91	100	.265	.303	7	.219	-1	-0	-0	0	-0.1
Total	4	4	8	.333	34	7	1	0	0	129^1	138	71	10	4	29	21	11.9	4.18	94	.278	.323	8	.190	-2	-4	-4	2	-0.4
● GEORGE WHEELER	Wheeler, George L. (b: George L. Heroux) b: 8/3/1869, Methuen, Mass. d: 3/23/46, Santa Ana, Cal. BB/TR, 5'9", 180 lbs. Deb: 9/18/1896																											
1896	Phi-N	1	1	.500	3	2	2	0	0	16^1	18	11	0	2	5	2	13.8	3.86	112	.277	.347	1	.111	-1	1	1	0	0.0
1897	Phi-N	11	10	.524	26	19	17	0	0	191	229	114	3	3	62	35	13.9	3.96	106	.295	.349	16	.203	-1	7	5	1	0.4
1898	Phi-N	6	8	.429	15	13	10	0	0	112^1	155	94	1	6	36	20	15.8	4.17	82	.325	.380	8	.186	-1	-7	-10	3	-0.8
1899	Phi-N	3	1	.750	6	5	3	0	0	39	44	30	1	3	13	3	13.8	6.00	61	.284	.351	4	.235	1	-9	-10	0	-0.7
Total	4	21	20	.512	50	39	32	0	0	358^2	446	249	5	14	116	60	14.5	4.24	92	.303	.359	29	.196	-2	-8	-14	4	-1.1
● HARRY WHEELER	Wheeler, Harry Eugene b: 3/3/1858, Versailles, Ind. d: 10/9/1900, Cincinnati, Ohio BR/TR, 5'11", 165 lbs. Deb: 6/19/1878 M♦																											
1878	Pro-N	6	1	.857	7	6	6	0	0	62	70	40	1		25	25	13.8	3.48	63	.275	.339	4	.148	-1	-8	-9	-2	-1.0
1879	Cin-N	0	1	.000	1	1	0	0	0	1	6	10	0		4	0	90.0	81.00	3	.667	.769	0	.000	-0	-9	-9	-0	-1.0
1882	Cin-a	1	2	.333	4	1	1	0	0	21^2	21	17	0		12	10	13.7	5.40	49	.239	.330	86	.250	1	-7	-7	-0	-0.7
1883	Col-a	0	1	.000	1	1	0	0	0	5	13	7	0		2	0	27.0	7.20	43	.448	.484	84	.226	0	-2	-2	-0	-0.3
1884	KC-U	0	1	.000	1	1	1	0	0	8	7	6	0		0	6	7.9	1.13	199	.219	.219	16	.258	-0	1	1	0	0.1
Total	5	7	6	.538	14	10	8	0	0	97^2	117	80	1		43	41	14.7	4.70	50	.283	.351	256	.228	-1	-24	-27	-2	-2.9
● GARY WHEELOCK	Wheelock, Gary Richard b: 11/29/51, Bakersfield, Cal. BR/TR, 6'3", 205 lbs. Deb: 9/17/76																											
1976	Cal-A	0	0	—	2	0	0	0	0	2	6	6	0	1	1	2	36.0	27.00	12	.500	.571	0	—	0	-5	-6	-0	-0.3
1977	Sea-A	6	9	.400	17	17	2	0	0	88^1	94	58	16	2	26	47	12.4	4.89	84	.268	.322	0	—	0	-8	-7	-1	-1.1
1980	Sea-A	0	0	—	1	1	0	0	0	3	4	2	0	0	1	1	15.0	6.00	69	.333	.385	0	—	0	-1	-1	0	0.0
Total	3	6	9	.400	20	18	2	0	0	93^1	104	66	16	3	28	50	13.0	5.40	76	.277	.333	0	—	0	-14	-13	-1	-1.4
● JACK WHILLOCK	Whillock, Jack Franklin b: 11/4/42, Clinton, Ark. BR/TR, 6'3", 195 lbs. Deb: 8/29/71																											
1971	Det-A	0	2	.000	7	0	0	0	1	8	10	5	0	0	2	6	13.5	5.63	64	.323	.364	0	.000	-0	-2	-2	0	-0.4
● MATT WHISENANT	Whisenant, Matthew Michael b: 6/8/71, Los Angeles, Cal. BR/TL, 6'3", 215 lbs. Deb: 7/4/97																											
1997	Fla-N	0	0	—	4	0	0	0	0	2^2	4	6	0	0	6	4	33.8	16.88	24	.333	.556	0	—	0	-4	-4	-0	-0.2
	KC-A	1	0	1.000	24	0	0	0	0	19	15	7	0	3	12	16	14.2	2.84	166	.211	.349	0	—	0	4	4	0	0.2
1998	KC-A	2	1	.667	70	0	0	0	2	60^2	61	37	3	3	33	45	14.4	4.90	99	.271	.372	0	—	0	-2	-0	0	0.0
1999	KC-A	4	4	.500	48	0	0	0	1	39^2	40	28	4	7	26	27	16.6	6.35	79	.267	.399	0	—	0	-7	-6	-0	-1.0
	SD-N	0	1	.000	19	0	0	0	0	14^2	10	6	0	0	10	10	12.3	3.68	114	.200	.333	0	—	0	1	1	0	0.1
2000	SD-N	2	2	.500	24	0	0	0	0	21^1	16	12	1	0	17	12	13.9	3.80	115	.213	.359	0	—	0	2	1	-0	0.2
Total	4	9	8	.529	189	0	0	0	3	158	146	96	8	13	104	114	15.0	4.96	95	.250	.376	0	—	0	-5	-4	0	-0.7
● PAT WHITAKER	Whitaker, William H. b: 11/1864, St.Louis, Mo. d: 7/15/02, St.Louis, Mo. TR, Deb: 10/11/1888																											
1888	Bal-a	1	1	.500	2	2	2	0	0	14	13	12	0	2	6	5	13.5	5.14	58	.236	.333	0	.000	-1	-3	-3	2	-0.3
1889	Bal-a	1	0	1.000	1	1	1	0	0	9	10	4	0	0	4	1	14.0	2.00	197	.270	.341	1	.250	-0	2	2	0	0.2
Total	2	2	1	.667	3	3	3	0	0	23	23	16	0	2	10	6	13.7	3.91	86	.250	.337	1	.100	-1	-1	-1	2	-0.1

YEAR	TM/L	W	L	PCT	G	GS	CG	SH	SV	IP	H	R	HR	HB	BB	SO	RAT	ERA	ERA+	OAV	OOB	BH	AVG	PB	PR	PR+	PD	TPI
● BILL WHITBY	Whitby, William Edward b: 7/29/43, Crewe, Va. BR/TR, 6'1", 190 lbs. Deb: 6/17/64																											
1964	Min-A	0	0	—	4	0	0	0	0	6^1	8	6	3	0	1	2	12.8	8.53	42	.308	.333	0	.000	-0	-3	-4	-0	-0.2
● BOB WHITCHER	Whitcher, Robert Arthur b: 4/29/17, Berlin, N.H. d: 5/8/97, Akron, Ohio BL/TL, 5'8", 165 lbs. Deb: 8/20/45																											
1945	Bos-N	0	2	.000	6	3	0	0	0	15^2	12	6	1	0	12	6	13.8	2.87	133	.235	.381	1	.333	0	2	2	-0	0.2
● ABE WHITE	White, Adel b: 5/16/04, Winder, Ga. d: 10/1/78, Atlanta, Ga. BR/TL, 6', 185 lbs. Deb: 7/10/37																											
1937	StL-N	0	1	.000	5	0	0	0	0	9^1	14	7	1	0	3	2	16.4	6.75	59	.341	.386	1	1.000	0	-3	-3	-0	-0.2
● ERNIE WHITE	White, Ernest Daniel b: 9/5/16, Pacolet Mills, S.C d: 5/22/74, Augusta, Ga. BR/TL, 5'11.5", 175 lbs. Deb: 5/9/40 C																											
1940	StL-N	1	1	.500	8	1	0	0	0	21^2	29	13	0	1	14	15	18.3	4.15	96	.315	.411	3	.429	1	-1	-0	1	0.1
1941	StL-N	17	7	.708	32	25	12	3	2	210	169	72	12	6	70	117	10.5	2.40	157	.217	.287	15	.190	0	29	31	-4	3.1
1942	*StL-N	7	5	.583	26	19	7	1	2	128^1	113	57	11	2	41	67	10.9	2.52	136	.232	.294	8	.195	0	11	12	-2	0.9
1943	*StL-N	5	5	.500	14	10	5	1	0	78^2	78	38	4	1	33	28	12.8	3.78	89	.257	.332	6	.214	0	-3	-4	-1	-0.5
1946	Bos-N	0	1	.000	12	1	0	0	0	23^2	22	11	1	0	12	8	12.9	4.18	82	.256	.347	1	.250	0	-2	-2	-1	-0.2
1947	Bos-N	0	0	—	1	1	0	0	0	4	1	0	0	0	1	1	4.5	0.00	—	.083	.154	1	1.000	0	2	2	-0	0.1
1948	Bos-N	0	2	.000	15	0	0	0	2	23	13	7	0	0	17	8	11.7	1.96	196	.167	.316	0	.000	-0	5	5	-1	0.4
Total	7	30	21	.588	108	57	24	5	6	489^1	425	198	28	10	188	244	11.5	2.78	130	.231	.306	34	.209	2	41	44	-8	3.9
● GABE WHITE	White, Gabriel Allen b: 11/20/71, Sebring, Fla. BL/TL, 6'2", 200 lbs. Deb: 5/27/94																											
1994	Mon-N	1	1	.500	7	5	0	0	1	23^2	24	16	4	1	11	17	13.7	6.08	69	.261	.346	0	.000	-0	-5	-5	-0	-0.4
1995	Mon-N	1	2	.333	19	1	0	0	0	25^2	26	21	7	1	9	25	12.6	7.01	61	.260	.327	0	.000	-0	-8	-8	-0	-0.8
1997	Cin-N	2	2	.500	12	6	0	0	1	41	39	20	6	1	8	25	10.5	4.39	97	.253	.294	1	.111	-0	-1	-1	-1	-0.2
1998	Cin-N	5	5	.500	69	3	0	0	9	98^2	86	46	17	1	27	83	10.4	4.01	107	.231	.285	1	.167	-0	2	3	-1	0.3
1999	Cin-N	1	2	.333	50	0	0	0	0	61	68	31	13	2	14	61	12.4	4.43	105	.281	.326	0	—	0	1	2	-1	0.0
2000	Cin-N	0	0	—	1	0	0	0	0	1	2	2	1	0	1	2	27.0	18.00	27	.400	.500	0	—	0	-1	-1	0	-0.1
	Col-N	11	2	.846	67	0	0	0	5	83	62	21	5	3	14	82	8.6	2.17	274	.208	.251	2	.222	1	23	27	-1	4.0
	Yr	11	2	.846	68	0	0	0	5	84	64	23	6	3	15	84	8.8	2.36	251	.211	.255	2	.222	1	21	**26**	-1	3.9
Total	6	21	14	.600	225	15	0	0	16	334	307	157	53	9	84	295	10.8	4.10	116	.243	.295	4	.129	-0	11	22	-4	2.8
● DEKE WHITE	White, George Frederick b: 9/8/1872, Albany, N.Y. d: 11/5/57, Ilion, N.Y. BB/TL, Deb: 9/14/1895																											
1895	Phi-N	1	0	1.000	3	1	1	0	1	17^1	17	23	1	2	13	6	16.6	9.87	49	.254	.390	1	.125	-1	-10	-10	-0	-0.6
● DOC WHITE	White, Guy Harris b: 4/9/1879, Washington, D.C. d: 2/19/69, Silver Spring, Md. BL/TL, 6'1", 150 lbs. Deb: 4/22/01 ♦																											
1901	Phi-N	14	13	.519	31	27	22	0	0	236^2	241	122	2	14	56	132	11.8	3.19	106	.262	.314	27	.276	5	3	5	3	1.3
1902	Phi-N	16	20	.444	36	35	34	3	1	306	277	126	3	13	72	185	10.6	2.53	111	.241	.294	47	.263	4	9	10	2	2.0
1903	Chi-A	17	16	.515	37	36	29	3	0	300	258	119	4	14	69	114	10.2	2.13	132	.232	.285	20	.202	6	28	24	3	3.5
1904	Chi-A	16	12	.571	30	30	23	7	0	228	201	82	6	9	68	115	11.0	1.78	138	.238	.301	12	.158	0	21	18	1	2.5
1905	Chi-A	17	13	.567	36	33	25	4	0	260^1	204	67	2	9	58	120	9.4	1.76	140	.218	.270	15	.167	0	26	22	1	2.7
1906	*Chi-A	18	6	.750	28	24	20	7	0	219^1	160	47	2	5	38	95	**8.3**	**1.52**	**167**	.207	**.249**	12	.185	4	29	26	2	**3.8**
1907	Chi-A	**27**	13	.675	46	35	24	6	1	291	270	93	3	6	38	141	9.7	2.26	106	.248	.278	20	.222	4	9	5	5	1.7
1908	Chi-A	18	13	.581	41	37	24	5	0	296	262	94	3	9	69	126	10.3	2.55	91	.240	.291	25	.229	4	-5	-8	7	0.4
1909	Chi-A	11	9	.550	24	21	14	3	0	177^2	149	56	1	7	31	77	9.5	1.72	136	.226	.269	45	.234	6	15	13	-1	2.2
1910	Chi-A	15	13	.536	33	29	20	2	1	236^2	219	84	2	12	50	111	10.7	2.66	90	.243	.291	25	.198	2	-4	-7	2	-0.3
1911	Chi-A	10	14	.417	34	29	16	4	2	214^1	219	91	2	9	35	72	11.0	2.98	108	.271	.309	20	.256	3	9	6	-1	0.8
1912	Chi-A	8	10	.444	32	19	9	1	0	172	172	81	1	8	47	57	11.9	3.24	99	.267	.325	7	.125	-1	1	-1	-1	-0.3
1913	Chi-A	2	4	.333	19	8	2	0	0	103	106	56	2	5	39	39	13.1	3.50	84	.278	.353	3	.120	-1	-6	-7	2	-0.2
Total	13	189	156	.548	427	363	262	45	5	3041	2738	1118	33	120	670	1384	10.4	2.39	112	.242	.292	278	.217	37	134	103	25	20.1
● HAL WHITE	White, Harold George b: 3/18/19, Utica, N.Y. BR/TR, 5'10", 170 lbs. Deb: 4/22/41																											
1941	Det-A	0	0	—	4	0	0	0	0	9	11	6	0	0	6	2	17.0	6.00	76	.306	.405	0	.000	-0	-2	-1	0	-0.1
1942	Det-A	12	12	.500	34	25	12	4	1	216^2	212	80	6	5	82	93	12.4	2.91	136	.252	.323	13	.169	-1	18	23	0	2.4
1943	Det-A	7	12	.368	32	24	7	2	2	177^2	150	84	6	1	71	58	11.2	3.39	104	.228	.304	8	.140	-1	-2	2	0	0.2
1946	Det-A	1	1	.500	11	1	1	0	0	27^1	34	20	5	0	15	12	16.1	5.60	65	.312	.395	0	.000	-1	-6	-6	1	-0.4
1947	Det-A	4	5	.444	35	5	0	0	2	84^2	91	43	5	2	47	33	14.9	3.61	104	.279	.373	3	.167	0	1	1	1	0.3
1948	Det-A	2	1	.667	27	0	0	0	1	42^2	46	31	2	1	26	17	15.4	6.12	71	.272	.372	2	.154	0	-9	-8	-1	-0.6
1949	Det-A	1	0	1.000	9	0	0	0	2	12	5	0	0	0	4	4	6.8	0.00	—	.125	.205	1	.333	0	6	6	1	0.7
1950	Det-A	9	6	.600	42	8	3	1	1	111	96	59	7	1	65	53	13.1	4.54	103	.239	.347	4	.121	-2	0	2	0	0.0
1951	Det-A	3	4	.429	38	4	0	0	4	76	74	45	7	2	49	23	14.8	4.74	88	.264	.378	4	.250	0	-5	-5	2	-0.3
1952	Det-A	1	8	.111	41	0	0	0	5	63^1	53	29	1	0	39	18	13.1	3.69	103	.237	.350	2	.182	-0	-0	1	1	0.2
1953	StL-A	0	0	—	10	0	0	0	0	10^1	8	3	1	1	3	2	10.5	2.61	161	.205	.279	0	.000	0	2	2	0	0.1
	StL-N	6	5	.545	49	0	0	0	7	84^2	84	32	5	0	39	32	13.1	2.98	143	.272	.353	0	.000	-2	12	12	1	1.5
1954	StL-N	0	0	—	4	0	0	0	0	5	11	11	2	1	4	2	28.8	19.80	21	.440	.533	0	.000	-0	-9	-9	-0	-0.4
Total	12	46	54	.460	336	67	23	7	25	920^1	875	443	47	14	450	349	13.1	3.78	106	.253	.342	37	.145	-7	6	22	6	3.6
● DEACON WHITE	White, James Laurie b: 12/7/1847, Caton, N.Y. d: 7/7/39, Aurora, Ill. BL/TR, 5'11", 175 lbs. Deb: 5/4/1871 FM♦																											
1876	Chi-N	0	0	—	1	0	0	0	1	2	1	0	0		0	3	4.5	0.00	—	.143	.143	104	.335	0	1	1	0	0.1
1890	Buf-P	0	0	—	1	0	0	0	0	8	18	15	0	0	2	0	22.5	9.00	46	.429	.455	114	.260	0	-4	-5	-1	-0.2
Total	2	0	0	—	2	0	0	0	1	10	19	15	0	0	2	3	18.9	7.20	53	.388	.412	1645	.306	1	-4	-4	-0	-0.1
● LARRY WHITE	White, Larry David b: 9/25/58, San Fernando, Cal. BR/TR, 6'5", 190 lbs. Deb: 9/20/83																											
1983	LA-N	0	0	—	4	0	0	0	0	7	4	1	0	0	3	5	9.0	1.29	280	.174	.269	0	—	0	2	2	0	0.1
1984	LA-N	0	1	.000	7	1	0	0	0	12	9	5	2	0	6	10	11.3	3.00	118	.209	.306	0	.000	-0	1	1	-0	0.0
Total	2	0	1	.000	11	1	0	0	0	19	13	6	2	0	9	15	10.4	2.37	150	.197	.293	0	.000	-0	3	3	-0	0.1
● KIRBY WHITE	White, Oliver Kirby "Red" or "Buck" b: 1/3/1884, Hillsboro, Ohio d: 4/22/43, Hillsboro, Ohio BL/TR, 6', 190 lbs. Deb: 5/4/09																											
1909	Bos-N	6	13	.316	23	19	11	1	0	148^1	134	73	5	1	80	53	13.0	3.22	88	.245	.343	8	.160	-1	-10	-6	-1	-0.9
1910	Bos-N	1	2	.333	3	3	3	0	0	26	15	7	2	3	12	6	10.4	1.38	240	.188	.316	2	.333	1	5	5	0	0.7
	Pit-N	10	9	.526	30	21	7	3	2	153^1	142	73	2	5	75	42	13.0	3.46	90	.258	.352	12	.261	3	-7	-6	-3	-0.7
	Yr	11	11	.500	33	24	10	3	2	179^1	157	80	4	8	87	48	12.6	3.16	99	.249	.347	14	.269	4	-3	-1	-3	0.0
1911	Pit-N	0	1	.000	2	1	0	0	0	3	3	4	1	0	1	1	12.0	9.00	38	.250	.308	0	.000	-0	-2	-2	0	-0.3
Total	3	17	25	.405	58	44	21	4	2	330^2	294	157	10	9	168	102	12.8	3.24	93	.247	.345	22	.214	3	-15	-8	-4	-1.2
● RICK WHITE	White, Richard Allen b: 12/23/68, Springfield, Ohio BR/TR, 6'4", 215 lbs. Deb: 4/6/94																											
1994	Pit-N	4	5	.444	43	5	0	0	6	75^1	79	35	9	6	17	38	12.2	3.82	113	.280	.334	1	.077	-1	3	4	-1	0.4
1995	Pit-N	2	3	.400	15	9	0	0	0	55	66	33	3	2	18	29	14.1	4.75	91	.299	.357	1	.067	-1	-3	-3	0	-0.3
1998	TB-A	2	6	.250	38	3	0	0	0	68^2	66	32	8	2	23	39	11.9	3.80	126	.253	.318	1	.333	0	7	7	0	0.8
1999	TB-A	5	3	.625	63	1	0	0	0	108	132	56	8	1	38	81	14.3	4.08	122	.304	.362	0	—	0	9	11	0	0.7
2000	TB-A	3	6	.333	44	0	0	0	2	71^1	57	30	7	5	26	47	11.1	3.41	146	.220	.303	0	—	0	12	12	-1	1.3
	*NY-N	2	3	.400	22	0	0	0	1	28^1	26	14	2	2	12	20	12.7	3.81	116	.232	.317	1	.200	0	3	2	-0	0.3
Total	5	18	26	.409	225	18	0	0	9	406^2	426	200	37	18	134	254	12.8	3.94	119	.272	.336	4	.111	-1	30	34	-1	3.2
● STEVE WHITE	White, Stephen Vincent b: 12/21/1884, Dorchester, Mass. d: 1/29/75, Braintree, Mass. BR/TR, 5'10", 160 lbs. Deb: 5/29/12																											
1912	Was-A	0	0	—	1	0	0	0	0	0^2	2	2	1	0	0	1	27.0	0.00	—	.667	.667	0	—	0	0	0	-0	0.0
	Bos-N	0	0	—	3	0	0	0	0	6	9	5	0	1	5	2	22.5	6.00	60	.429	.556	0	.000	-0	-2	-2	0	-0.1
Total	1	0	0	—	4	0	0	0	0	6^2	11	7	1	1	5	3	23.0	5.40	66	.458	.567	0	.000	-0	-1	-1	-0	-0.1
● BILL WHITE	White, William Dighton b: 5/1/1860, Bridgeport, Ohio d: 12/29/24, Bellaire, Ohio TR, Deb: 5/3/1884 ♦																											
1886	Lou-a	0	0	—	1	0	0	0	0	1	2	2	0	0	2	1	36.0	9.00	40	.400	.571	143	.257	0	-1	-1	0	0.0
● WILL WHITE	White, William Henry "Whoop-La" b: 10/11/1854, Caton, N.Y. d: 8/31/11, Port Carling, Ont., Canada BB/TR, 5'9.5", 175 lbs. Deb: 7/20/1877 FM																											
1877	Bos-N	2	1	.667	3	3	3	1	0	27	27	15	0		2	7	9.7	3.00	94	.243	.257	3	.200	-1	-1	-1	-1	-0.2

YEAR	TM/L	W	L	PCT	G	GS	CG	SH	SV	IP	H	R	HR	HB	BB	SO	RAT	ERA	ERA+	OAV	OOB	BH	AVG	PB	PR	PR+	PD	TPI
1878	Cin-N	30	21	.588	52	52	52	5	0	468	477	249	1		45	169	10.0	1.79	119	.252	.269	28	.142	-8	27	19	-2	0.8
1879	Cin-N	43	31	.581	**76**	75	**75**	4	0	**680**	676	404	10		68	232	9.8	1.99	117	.238	.256	40	.136	-17	**38**	28	-7	0.3
1880	Cin-N	18	42	.300	62	62	58	3	0	517^{1}	550	323	9		56	161	10.5	2.14	116	.255	.273	35	.169	-9	13	19	-7	0.4
1881	Det-N	0	2	.000	2	2	2	0	0	18	24	18	0		2	5	13.0	5.00	58	.296	.313	0	.000	-1	-4	-4	-1	-0.5
1882	Cin-a	**40**	12	**.769**	54	54	**52**	**8**	0	**480**	411	164	3		71	122	9.0	1.54	172	.216	.244	55	.266	6	**61**	**60**	13	**7.4**
1883	Cin-a	**43**	22	.662	65	64	64	**6**	0	577	473	255	16		104	141	9.0	**2.09**	155	.209	.244	54	.225	3	**78**	**75**	-3	**6.8**
1884	Cin-a	34	18	.654	52	52	52	**7**	0	456	479	224	16	35	74	118	11.6	3.32	101	.255	.296	35	.190	-2	-3	1	-6	-0.7
1885	Cin-a	18	15	.545	34	34	33	2	0	293^{1}	295	169	9	27	64	80	11.8	3.53	92	.255	.309	20	.169	-3	-9	-9	-3	-1.4
1886	Cin-a	1	2	.333	3	3	3	0	0	26	28	23	1	6	10	6	15.2	4.15	85	.280	.379	1	.111	-1	-2	-2	-0	-0.2
Total	10	229	166	.580	403	401	394	36	0	3542^{2}	3440	1844	65	68	496	1041	10.2	2.28	120	.239	.268	271	.183	-33	198	182	-18	12.7

● JOHN WHITEHEAD Whitehead, John Henderson "Silent John" b: 4/27/09, Coleman, Tex. d: 10/20/64, Bonham, Tex. BR/TR, 6'2", 195 lbs. Deb: 4/19/35

YEAR	TM/L	W	L	PCT	G	GS	CG	SH	SV	IP	H	R	HR	HB	BB	SO	RAT	ERA	ERA+	OAV	OOB	BH	AVG	PB	PR	PR+	PD	TPI
1935	Chi-A	13	13	.500	28	27	18	1	0	222^{1}	209	101	17	2	101	72	12.6	3.72	124	.250	.332	12	.146	-5	18	21	3	1.9
1936	Chi-A	13	13	.500	34	32	15	1	1	230^{2}	254	137	9	5	98	70	13.9	4.64	112	.276	.349	21	.241	1	10	14	3	1.7
1937	Chi-A	11	8	.579	26	24	8	4	0	165^{2}	191	84	14	5	56	45	13.7	4.07	113	.294	.354	13	.224	1	10	10	-1	0.9
1938	Chi-A	10	11	.476	32	24	10	2	2	183^{1}	218	108	12	3	80	38	14.8	4.76	103	.299	.370	6	.100	-4	1	3	-1	-0.1
1939	Chi-A	0	3	.000	7	4	0	0	0	32	60	30	4	0	5	9	18.3	8.16	58	.408	.428	0	.000	-1	-13	-12	0	-1.0
	StL-A	1	3	.250	26	4	0	0	1	66	88	49	10	2	17	9	14.6	5.86	83	.321	.365	1	.059	-1	-9	-7	1	-0.4
	Yr	1	6	.143	33	8	0	0	1	98	148	79	14	2	22	18	15.8	6.61	73	.352	.387	1	.038	-3	-22	-19	1	-1.4
1940	StL-A	1	3	.250	15	4	1	1	0	40	46	25	3	0	14	11	13.5	5.40	85	.286	.343	2	.167	-1	-5	-3	-1	-0.4
1942	StL-A	0	0	—	4	0	0	0	0	4	8	3	0	1	1	0	22.5	6.75	55	.421	.476	0	—	0	-1	-1	0	0.0
Total	7	49	54	.476	172	119	52	9	4	944	1074	537	69	18	372	254	14.0	4.60	105	.287	.355	55	.169	-11	11	24	5	2.6

● MILT WHITEHEAD Whitehead, Milton P. b: 1862, Canada d: 8/15/01, Highland, Cal. BB, Deb: 4/20/1884 ◆

YEAR	TM/L	W	L	PCT	G	GS	CG	SH	SV	IP	H	R	HR	HB	BB	SO	RAT	ERA	ERA+	OAV	OOB	BH	AVG	PB	PR	PR+	PD	TPI
1884	StL-U	0	1	.000	1	1	1	0	0	8	14	9	0		2	2	18.0	9.00	27	.359	.390	83	.211	-0	-6	-6	0	-0.5

● EARL WHITEHILL Whitehill, Earl Oliver b: 2/7/1900, Cedar Rapids, Iowa d: 10/22/54, Omaha, Neb. BL/TL, 5'9.5", 174 lbs. Deb: 9/15/23 C

YEAR	TM/L	W	L	PCT	G	GS	CG	SH	SV	IP	H	R	HR	HB	BB	SO	RAT	ERA	ERA+	OAV	OOB	BH	AVG	PB	PR	PR+	PD	TPI
1923	Det-A	2	0	1.000	8	3	1	0	0	33	22	14	2	3	15	19	10.9	2.73	142	.188	.296	4	.364	1	5	4	-0	0.3
1924	Det-A	17	9	.654	35	32	16	2	0	233	260	125	8	13	79	65	13.6	3.86	106	.288	.353	19	.213	1	10	7	-0	0.7
1925	Det-A	11	11	.500	35	33	15	1	2	239^{1}	267	135	13	10	88	83	13.7	4.66	92	.293	.361	19	.218	0	-7	-10	-1	-0.8
1926	Det-A	16	13	.552	36	34	13	0	0	252^{1}	271	136	7	8	79	109	12.8	3.99	102	.277	.336	23	.253	4	1	2	-1	0.5
1927	Det-A	16	14	.533	41	31	17	3	3	236	238	110	4	9	105	95	13.4	3.36	125	.267	.350	16	.205	-0	21	22	-3	2.2
1928	Det-A	11	16	.407	31	30	12	1	0	196^{1}	214	131	8	1	78	93	13.4	4.31	95	.277	.344	13	.194	-1	-6	-4	1	-0.6
1929	Det-A	14	15	.483	38	28	18	1	1	245^{1}	267	147	16	3	96	103	13.4	4.62	93	.280	.348	23	.256	5	-10	-9	-0	-0.5
1930	Det-A	17	13	.567	34	31	16	0	1	220^{2}	248	139	8	8	80	109	13.7	4.24	113	.285	.351	16	.193	-4	10	13	-2	1.0
1931	Det-A	13	16	.448	34	34	22	0	0	271^{1}	287	152	22	5	118	81	13.6	4.08	112	.274	.351	15	.155	-5	9	15	2	1.1
1932	Det-A	16	12	.571	33	31	17	3	0	244	255	136	17	5	93	81	13.0	4.54	104	.269	.337	22	.244	1	-2	4	-2	0.4
1933	*Was-A	22	8	.733	39	37	19	2	1	270	271	112	9	4	100	96	12.5	3.33	125	.262	.329	24	.222	2	28	26	-2	2.5
1934	Was-A	14	11	.560	32	31	15	0	0	235	269	129	10	3	94	96	14.0	4.52	96	.290	.357	17	.200	4	-1	-5	-0	-0.2
1935	Was-A	14	13	.519	34	34	19	1	0	279^{1}	318	149	16	7	104	102	13.8	4.29	101	.289	.354	19	.183	-1	5	1	1	0.1
1936	Was-A	14	11	.560	28	28	14	0	0	212^{1}	252	124	17	2	89	63	14.5	4.87	98	.294	.362	13	.169	-0	4	-2	-1	-0.3
1937	Cle-A	8	8	.500	33	22	6	1	2	147	189	111	9	6	80	53	16.8	6.49	71	.322	.409	11	.224	1	-31	-31	1	-2.5
1938	Cle-A	9	8	.529	26	23	4	0	0	160^{1}	187	109	18	9	83	60	15.7	5.56	83	.289	.378	7	.125	-2	-14	-17	-2	-1.7
1939	Chi-N	4	7	.364	24	11	2	1	1	89^{1}	102	59	8	5	50	42	15.8	5.14	77	.292	.389	3	.103	-2	-12	-12	-1	-1.5
Total	17	218	185	.541	541	473	226	16	11	3564^{2}	3917	2018	192	101	1431	1350	13.8	4.36	100	.282	.353	264	.204	4	10	6	-9	0.7

● CHARLIE WHITEHOUSE Whitehouse, Charles Evis "Lefty" b: 1/25/1894, Charleston, Ill. d: 7/19/60, Indianapolis, Ind BB/TL, 6', 152 lbs. Deb: 8/29/14

YEAR	TM/L	W	L	PCT	G	GS	CG	SH	SV	IP	H	R	HR	HB	BB	SO	RAT	ERA	ERA+	OAV	OOB	BH	AVG	PB	PR	PR+	PD	TPI
1914	Ind-F	2	0	1.000	8	2	2	0	0	26	34	14	0	1	5	10	13.8	4.85	64	.324	.360	0	.000	-1	-6	-5	-0	-0.5
1915	New-F	2	2	.500	11	3	1	0	0	39^{2}	46	29	0	5	17	18	15.4	4.31	59	.299	.386	0	.000	-1	-7	-8	-1	-0.9
1919	Was-A	0	1	.000	6	1	0	0	0	12	13	7	1	0	6	5	14.3	4.50	71	.283	.365	0	.000	-0	-2	-2	-0	-0.2
Total	3	4	3	.571	25	6	3	0	0	77^{2}	93	50	1	6	28	33	14.7	4.52	63	.305	.375	0	.000	-2	-14	-15	-1	-1.6

● GIL WHITEHOUSE Whitehouse, Gilbert Arthur b: 10/15/1893, Somerville, Mass. d: 2/14/26, Brewer, Me. BB/TR, 5'10", 170 lbs. Deb: 6/20/12 ◆

YEAR	TM/L	W	L	PCT	G	GS	CG	SH	SV	IP	H	R	HR	HB	BB	SO	RAT	ERA	ERA+	OAV	OOB	BH	AVG	PB	PR	PR+	PD	TPI
1915	New-F	0	0	—	1	0	0	0	0	1	0	0	0	0	1	0	9.0	0.00	—	.000	.250	27	.225	0	0	0	-0	0.0

● LEN WHITEHOUSE Whitehouse, Leonard Joseph b: 9/10/57, Burlington, Vt. BL/TL, 5'11", 175 lbs. Deb: 9/1/81

YEAR	TM/L	W	L	PCT	G	GS	CG	SH	SV	IP	H	R	HR	HB	BB	SO	RAT	ERA	ERA+	OAV	OOB	BH	AVG	PB	PR	PR+	PD	TPI
1981	Tex-A	0	1	.000	2	1	0	0	0	3^{1}	8	7	1	0	2	2	27.0	16.20	21	.500	.556	0	—	0	-5	-5	-0	-0.8
1983	Min-A	7	1	.875	60	0	0	0	2	73^{2}	70	34	6	2	44	44	14.2	4.15	103	.261	.369	0	—	0	-1	1	-1	0.0
1984	Min-A	2	2	.500	30	0	0	0	1	31^{1}	29	11	3	2	17	18	13.8	3.16	133	.254	.361	0	—	0	3	3	-0	0.4
1985	Min-A	0	0	—	5	0	0	0	1	7^{1}	12	9	4	0	2	4	17.2	11.05	40	.353	.389	0	—	0	-6	-5	-0	-0.3
Total	4	9	4	.692	97	1	0	0	4	115^{2}	119	61	14	4	65	68	14.6	4.67	91	.275	.375	0	—	0	-8	-5	-1	-0.7

● WALLY WHITEHURST Whitehurst, Walter Richard b: 4/11/64, Shreveport, La. BR/TR, 6'3", 195 lbs. Deb: 7/17/89

YEAR	TM/L	W	L	PCT	G	GS	CG	SH	SV	IP	H	R	HR	HB	BB	SO	RAT	ERA	ERA+	OAV	OOB	BH	AVG	PB	PR	PR+	PD	TPI
1989	NY-N	0	1	.000	9	1	0	0	0	14	17	7	2	0	5	9	14.1	4.50	73	.293	.349	0	.000	0	-2	-2	-0	-0.1
1990	NY-N	1	0	1.000	38	0	0	0	2	65^{2}	63	27	5	0	9	46	9.9	3.29	114	.251	.277	2	.250	0	4	3	0	0.2
1991	NY-N	7	12	.368	36	20	0	0	1	133^{1}	142	67	12	4	25	87	11.5	4.18	87	.274	.313	6	.182	1	-7	-8	1	-0.8
1992	NY-N	3	9	.250	44	11	0	0	0	97	99	45	4	4	33	70	12.6	3.62	96	.264	.330	4	.182	1	-1	-2	1	-0.1
1993	SD-N	4	7	.364	21	19	0	0	0	105^{2}	109	47	11	3	30	57	12.1	3.83	108	.276	.332	2	.083	-2	3	4	0	0.2
1994	SD-N	4	7	.364	13	13	0	0	0	64	84	37	8	1	26	43	15.6	4.92	84	.319	.383	2	.105	0	-5	-6	0	-0.9
1996	NY-A	1	1	.500	2	2	0	0	0	8	11	6	1	0	2	1	14.6	6.75	73	.324	.361	0	—	0	-2	-2	0	-0.3
Total	7	20	37	.351	163	66	0	0	3	487^{2}	525	236	43	12	130	313	12.3	4.02	95	.277	.328	16	.150	1	-10	-12	2	-1.8

● MARK WHITEN Whiten, Mark Anthony b: 11/25/66, Pensacola, Fla. BB/TR, 6'3", 215 lbs. Deb: 7/12/90 ◆

YEAR	TM/L	W	L	PCT	G	GS	CG	SH	SV	IP	H	R	HR	HB	BB	SO	RAT	ERA	ERA+	OAV	OOB	BH	AVG	PB	PR	PR+	PD	TPI
1998	*Cle-A	0	0	—	1	0	0	0	0	1	1	1	0	1	2	3	36.0	9.00	53	.250	.571	64	.283	0	-0	-0	0	0.0

● SEAN WHITESIDE Whiteside, David Sean b: 4/19/71, Lakeland, Fla. BL/TL, 6'4", 190 lbs. Deb: 4/29/95

YEAR	TM/L	W	L	PCT	G	GS	CG	SH	SV	IP	H	R	HR	HB	BB	SO	RAT	ERA	ERA+	OAV	OOB	BH	AVG	PB	PR	PR+	PD	TPI
1995	Det-A	0	0	—	2	0	0	0	0	3^{2}	7	6	1	0	4	2	27.0	14.73	32	.438	.550	0	—	0	-4	-4	-0	-0.2

● MATT WHITESIDE Whiteside, Matthew Christopher b: 8/8/67, Charleston, Mo. BR/TR, 6', 205 lbs. Deb: 8/5/92

YEAR	TM/L	W	L	PCT	G	GS	CG	SH	SV	IP	H	R	HR	HB	BB	SO	RAT	ERA	ERA+	OAV	OOB	BH	AVG	PB	PR	PR+	PD	TPI
1992	Tex-A	1	1	.500	20	0	0	0	4	28	26	8	1	0	11	13	11.9	1.93	197	.245	.316	0	—	0	6	6	-0	0.5
1993	Tex-A	2	1	.667	60	0	0	0	1	73	78	37	7	1	23	39	12.6	4.32	96	.281	.338	0	—	0	0	-1	-1	-0.1
1994	Tex-A	2	2	.500	47	0	0	0	1	61	68	40	6	1	28	37	14.3	5.02	96	.286	.363	0	—	0	-1	-1	-1	-0.1
1995	Tex-A	5	4	.556	40	0	0	0	3	53	48	24	5	1	19	46	11.5	4.08	119	.242	.312	0	—	0	4	4	-1	0.6
1996	Tex-A	0	1	.000	14	0	0	0	0	32^{1}	43	24	8	0	11	15	15.0	6.68	78	.321	.372	0	—	0	-6	-5	-0	-0.2
1997	Tex-A	4	1	.800	42	1	0	0	0	72^{2}	85	45	4	3	26	44	14.1	5.08	94	.296	.361	0	—	0	-4	-2	2	0.0
1998	Phi-N	1	1	.500	10	0	0	0	0	18	27	18	6	0	5	14	16.0	8.50	51	.338	.376	0	.000	-0	-9	-8	0	-0.8
1999	SD-N	1	0	1.000	10	0	0	0	0	11	19	17	1	0	5	9	19.6	13.91	30	.396	.453	0	—	0	-11	-13	0	-0.9
2000	SD-N	2	3	.400	28	0	0	0	0	37	32	21	6	1	17	27	12.2	4.14	106	.232	.321	0	—	0	2	1	1	0.2
Total	9	18	14	.563	271	1	0	0	9	386	426	234	44	7	145	244	13.5	5.01	91	.283	.348	0	.000	-0	-19	-19	0	-0.8

● JESSE WHITING Whiting, Jesse W. b: 5/30/1879, Philadelphia, Pa. d: 10/28/37, Philadelphia, Pa. Deb: 9/27/02

YEAR	TM/L	W	L	PCT	G	GS	CG	SH	SV	IP	H	R	HR	HB	BB	SO	RAT	ERA	ERA+	OAV	OOB	BH	AVG	PB	PR	PR+	PD	TPI
1902	Phi-N	0	1	.000	1	1	1	0	0	9	13	8	0	0	6	0	19.0	5.00	56	.333	.422	1	.333	0	-2	-2	0	-0.2
1906	Bro-N	1	1	.500	3	2	2	1	0	24^{2}	26	10	0	1	6	7	12.0	2.92	86	.286	.337	3	.300	1	-1	-1	1	0.1
1907	Bro-N	0	0	—	1	0	0	0	0	3	3	4	0	0	3	2	18.0	12.00	20	.273	.429	0	.000	-0	-3	-3	0	-0.2
Total	3	1	2	.333	5	3	3	1	0	36^{2}	42	22	0	1	15	9	14.2	4.17	62	.298	.369	4	.267	0	-6	-7	1	-0.3

● ART WHITNEY Whitney, Arthur Wilson b: 1/16/1858, Brockton, Mass. d: 8/15/43, Lowell, Mass. BR/TR, 5'8", 155 lbs. Deb: 5/1/1880 F◆

YEAR	TM/L	W	L	PCT	G	GS	CG	SH	SV	IP	H	R	HR	HB	BB	SO	RAT	ERA	ERA+	OAV	OOB	BH	AVG	PB	PR	PR+	PD	TPI
1882	Det-N	0	1	.000	3	2	1	0	0	18	31	17	1		8	11	19.5	6.00	49	.373	.429	21	.183	-1	-6	-6	-1	-0.3
1886	Pit-a	0	0	—	1	0	0	0	0	6	7	4	0	0	3	2	15.0	3.00	113	.304	.385	122	.239	0	0	0	-0	0.0
1889	*NY-N	0	1	.000	1	0	0	0	0	6	7	5	0	0	3	3	15.0	3.00	131	.280	.357	103	.218	0	1	1	-0	0.1
Total	3	0	2	.000	5	2	1	0	0	30	45	26	1	0	14	16	17.7	4.80	67	.344	.407	875	.234	-1	-5	-5	-1	-0.2

YEAR	TM/L	W	L	PCT	G	GS	CG	SH	SV	IP	H	R	HR	HB	BB	SO	RAT	ERA	ERA+	OAV	OOB	BH	AVG	PB	PR	PR+	PD	TPI
● **JIM WHITNEY**	Whitney, James Evans "Grasshopper Jim" b: 11/10/1857, Conklin, N.Y. d: 5/21/1891, Binghamton, N.Y. BL/TR, 6'2", 172 lbs. Deb: 5/2/1881 ◆																											
1881	Bos-N	**31**	33	.484	**66**	63	**57**	6	0	**552^1**	548	284	6		90	162	10.4	2.48	107	.248	.277	72	.255	11	18	12	-4	1.9
1882	Bos-N	24	21	.533	49	48	46	3	0	420	404	229	3		41	180	9.5	2.64	109	.237	.255	81	.323	23	12	11	1	3.1
1883	Bos-N	37	21	.638	62	56	54	1	**2**	514	492	258	7		35	**345**	9.2	2.24	138	.238	.251	115	.281	20	51	50	0	6.1
1884	Bos-N	23	14	.622	38	37	35	6	0	336	272	140	12		27	270	8.0	2.09	138	.207	.223	70	.259	10	33	31	4	4.1
1885	Bos-N	18	32	.360	51	50	50	2	0	441^1	503	286	14		37	200	11.0	2.98	90	.272	.286	68	.234	7	-8	-15	6	-0.3
1886	KC-N	12	32	.273	46	44	42	3	0	393	465	292	9		55	167	11.9	4.49	84	.284	.308	59	.239	5	-51	-27	6	-1.3
1887	Was-N	24	21	.533	47	47	46	2	0	404^2	472	253	16	16	42	146	10.9	3.22	126	.277	.284	71	.324	9	38	38	4	4.7
1888	Was-N	18	21	.462	39	39	37	3	0	325	317	184	7	9	54	79	10.5	3.05	92	.245	.280	24	.170	-1	-7	-9	-1	-1.2
1889	Ind-N	2	7	.222	9	8	7	0	0	70	106	73	4	2	19	16	16.3	6.81	61	.339	.380	12	.375	5	-22	-20	-1	-1.4
1890	Phi-a	2	2	.500	6	4	3	0	0	40	61	27	1	1	11	6	16.4	5.17	75	.341	.382	5	.238	-0	-6	-6	-0	-0.5
Total	10	191	204	.484	413	396	377	26	2	3496^1	3640	2026	79	28	411	1571	10.4	2.97	105	.255	.275	577	.267	89	60	55	15	15.2
● **BILL WHITROCK**	Whitrock, William Franklin b: 3/4/1870, Cincinnati, Ohio d: 7/26/35, Derby, Conn. TR, 5'7.5", 170 lbs. Deb: 5/3/1890																											
1890	StL-a	5	6	.455	16	11	10	0	1	105	104	62	2	7	40	39	12.9	3.51	123	.251	.327	7	.146	-3	4	8	0	0.5
1893	Lou-N	2	5	.286	8	8	5	0	0	46^2	64	53	3	4	19	8	16.8	8.10	54	.317	.387	6	.286	1	-18	-20	0	-1.9
1894	Lou-N	0	1	.000	1	1	0	0	0	4	8	8	0	0	2	0	22.5	9.00	57	.400	.455	0	.000	-0	-2	-2	-0	-0.3
	Cin-N	2	6	.250	11	9	9	0	0	79^1	121	88	7	9	46	10	20.0	6.24	89	.347	.436	15	.231	-2	-8	-6	1	-0.5
	Yr	2	7	.222	12	10	9	0	0	83^1	129	96	7	9	48	10	20.1	6.37	87	.350	.437	15	.224	-3	-10	-7	1	-0.8
1896	Phi-N	0	1	.000	2	1	1	0	0	9	10	5	0	0	3	1	13.0	3.00	144	.278	.333	0	.000	-0	1	1	-0	0.1
Total	4	9	19	.321	38	30	25	0	1	244	307	216	12	20	110	58	16.1	5.35	89	.300	.379	28	.201	-4	-22	-15	1	-2.1
● **ED WHITSON**	Whitson, Eddie Lee b: 5/19/55, Johnson City, Tenn. BR/TR, 6'3", 195 lbs. Deb: 9/4/77																											
1977	Pit-N	1	0	1.000	5	2	0	0	0	15^2	11	6	0	0	9	10	11.5	3.45	116	.204	.317	0	.000	-0	1	1	-0	0.0
1978	Pit-N	5	6	.455	43	0	0	0	4	74	66	31	5	2	37	64	12.8	3.28	113	.243	.338	2	.182	-0	2	3	-1	0.4
1979	Pit-N	2	3	.400	19	7	0	0	1	57^2	53	36	6	1	36	31	14.0	4.37	89	.238	.346	0	.000	-1	-4	-3	-1	-0.4
	SF-N	5	8	.385	18	17	2	0	0	100^1	98	47	5	4	39	62	12.6	3.95	89	.254	.329	5	.156	-1	-2	-5	-0	-0.7
	Yr	7	11	.389	37	24	2	0	1	158	151	83	11	5	75	93	13.2	4.10	89	.248	.335	5	.111	-2	-6	-8	-1	-1.1
1980	SF-N☆	11	13	.458	34	34	6	2	0	211^2	222	88	7	4	56	90	12.0	3.10	114	.271	.321	6	.091	-4	12	11	-2	0.5
1981	SF-N	6	9	.400	22	22	2	1	0	123	130	61	10	2	47	65	13.1	4.02	85	.273	.340	3	.091	-1	-7	-8	-2	-1.2
1982	Cle-A	4	2	.667	40	9	1	1	2	107^2	91	43	6	0	58	61	12.5	3.26	125	.231	.330	0	—	0	10	10	-2	0.4
1983	SD-N	5	7	.417	31	21	2	0	1	144^1	143	73	23	1	50	81	12.1	4.30	81	.256	.318	8	.182	1	-11	-13	-4	-1.3
1984	*SD-N	14	8	.636	31	31	1	0	0	189	181	72	16	3	42	103	10.8	3.24	110	.255	.299	3	.049	-5	7	7	1	0.4
1985	NY-A	10	8	.556	30	30	2	2	0	158^2	201	100	19	2	43	89	14.0	4.88	82	.309	.354	0	—	0	-13	-16	-2	-1.7
1986	NY-A	5	2	.714	14	4	0	0	0	37	54	37	5	0	23	27	18.7	7.54	54	.335	.418	0	—	0	-14	-14	-0	-2.2
	SD-N	1	7	.125	17	12	0	0	0	75^2	85	48	8	0	37	46	14.5	5.59	66	.287	.366	3	.167	-0	-16	-16	0	-1.5
1987	SD-N	10	13	.435	36	34	3	1	0	205^2	197	113	36	3	64	135	11.6	4.73	84	.251	.310	8	.123	-1	-15	-18	-2	-2.1
1988	SD-N	13	11	.542	34	33	3	1	0	205^1	202	93	17	1	45	118	10.9	3.77	90	.259	.301	11	.167	1	-7	-9	-1	-0.9
1989	SD-N	16	11	.593	33	33	5	1	0	227	198	77	22	5	48	117	10.0	2.66	132	.235	.281	10	.139	1	21	21	-2	2.4
1990	SD-N	14	9	.609	32	32	6	3	0	228^2	215	73	13	1	47	127	10.4	2.60	147	.251	.291	10	.149	1	30	**31**	3	3.4
1991	SD-N	4	6	.400	13	12	2	0	0	78^2	93	47	13	0	17	40	12.6	5.03	76	.299	.335	3	.125	-1	-12	-10	-1	-1.3
Total	15	126	123	.506	452	333	35	12	8	2240	2240	1045	211	29	698	1266	11.9	3.79	97	.261	.319	72	.125	-11	-16	-27	-14	-5.8
● **WALT WHITTAKER**	Whittaker, Walter Elton "Doc" b: 6/11/1894, Chelsea, Mass. d: 8/9/65, Pembroke, Mass. BL/TR, 5'9.5", 165 lbs. Deb: 7/6/16																											
1916	Phi-A	0	0	—	1	0	0	0	0	2	3	1	0	0	2	0	22.5	4.50	63	.375	.500	0	—	0	-0	-0	0	0.0
● **KEVIN WICKANDER**	Wickander, Kevin Dean b: 1/4/65, Fort Dodge, Iowa BL/TL, 6'2", 202 lbs. Deb: 8/10/89																											
1989	Cle-A	0	0	—	2	0	0	0	0	2^2	6	1	0	0	2	0	27.0	3.38	118	.462	.533	0	—	0	0	0	-0	0.0
1990	Cle-A	0	1	.000	10	0	0	0	0	12^1	14	6	0	1	4	10	13.9	3.65	108	.304	.373	0	—	0	0	0	-0	0.0
1992	Cle-A	2	0	1.000	44	0	0	0	1	41	39	14	1	4	28	38	15.6	3.07	127	.258	.388	0	—	0	4	4	0	0.2
1993	Cle-A	0	0	—	11	0	0	0	0	8^2	15	7	3	0	3	3	18.7	4.15	104	.366	.409	0	—	0	0	0	-0	0.0
	Cin-N	1	0	1.000	33	0	0	0	0	25^1	32	20	5	2	19	20	18.8	6.75	60	.308	.424	0	.000	-0	-8	-8	-0	-0.4
1995	Det-A	0	0	—	21	0	0	0	1	17^1	18	6	1	1	9	9	14.5	2.60	183	.273	.368	0	—	0	4	4	0	0.2
	Mil-A	0	0	—	8	0	0	0	0	6	1	0	0	0	3	2	6.0	0.00	—	.059	.200	0	—	0	3	3	-0	0.1
	Yr	0	0	—	29	0	0	0	1	23^1	19	6	1	1	12	11	12.3	1.93	250	.229	.333	0	—	0	7	7	0	0.3
1996	Mil-A	2	0	1.000	21	0	0	0	0	25^1	26	16	2	0	17	19	15.3	4.97	104	.265	.374	0	—	0	0	1	0	0.0
Total	6	5	1	.833	150	0	0	0	2	138^2	151	70	12	8	85	101	15.8	4.02	108	.282	.388	0	.000	-0	4	5	-1	0.1
● **KEMP WICKER**	Wicker, Kemp Caswell (b: Kemp Caswell Whicker) b: 8/13/06, Kernersville, N.C. d: 6/11/73, Kernersville, N.C BR/TL, 5'11", 182 lbs. Deb: 8/14/36																											
1936	NY-A	1	2	.333	7	0	0	0	0	20	31	18	2	0	11	5	18.9	7.65	61	.356	.429	1	.143	-0	-6	-7	0	-0.8
1937	*NY-A	7	3	.700	16	10	6	1	0	88	107	52	8	0	26	14	13.6	4.40	101	.296	.343	4	.114	-3	2	0	-2	-0.4
1938	NY-A	1	0	1.000	1	0	0	0	0	1	0	0	0	0	1	0	9.0	0.00	—	.000	.250	0	—	0	1	1	-0	0.1
1941	Bro-N	1	2	.333	16	2	0	0	1	32	30	14	3	0	14	8	12.4	3.66	100	.252	.331	1	.250	0	-0	0	-0	0.0
Total	4	10	7	.588	40	12	6	1	1	141	168	84	13	0	52	27	14.0	4.66	92	.294	.353	6	.130	-2	-3	-6	-2	-1.1
● **BOB WICKER**	Wicker, Robert Kitridge b: 5/25/1877, Bono, Ind. d: 1/22/55, Evanston, Ill. BL/TR, 5'11", 210 lbs. Deb: 8/11/01																											
1901	StL-N	0	0	—	1	0	0	0	0	3	4	3	0	0	1	2	15.0	0.00	—	.308	.357	1	.333	0	1	1	-0	0.1
1902	StL-N	5	12	.294	22	16	14	1	0	152^1	159	82	1	2	45	78	12.2	3.19	86	.269	.322	18	.234	1	-7	-8	3	-0.4
1903	StL-N	0	0	—	1	0	0	0	0	5	4	1	0	0	3	3	12.6	0.00	—	.174	.269	0	.000	-0	2	2	1	0.1
	Chi-N	20	9	.690	32	27	24	1	1	247	236	114	3	3	74	110	11.4	3.02	104	.253	.311	24	.245	6	7	3	-5	0.4
	Yr	20	9	.690	33	27	24	1	1	252	240	115	3	3	77	113	11.4	2.96	106	.252	.309	24	.240	6	9	5	-4	0.5
1904	Chi-N	17	9	.654	30	27	23	4	0	229	201	92	6	3	58	99	10.3	2.67	100	.232	.282	34	.219	1	2	-0	-5	-0.5
1905	Chi-N	13	6	.684	22	22	17	4	0	178	139	46	3	1	47	86	9.5	2.02	147	.221	.276	10	.139	-2	19	19	-3	1.4
1906	Chi-N	3	5	.375	10	8	5	0	0	72^1	70	36	0	0	19	25	11.1	2.99	88	.257	.306	2	.100	-1	-3	-3	-1	-0.5
	Cin-N	6	11	.353	20	17	14	0	0	150	150	69	3	1	46	69	11.8	2.70	102	.263	.319	9	.180	2	-1	1	-4	-0.1
	Yr	9	16	.360	30	25	19	0	0	222^1	220	105	3	1	65	94	11.6	2.79	97	.261	.315	11	.157	1	-4	-2	-5	-0.6
Total	6	64	52	.552	138	117	97	10	1	1036^2	963	443	16	10	293	472	11.0	2.73	105	.247	.301	98	.205	6	20	16	-15	0.5
● **DAVE WICKERSHAM**	Wickersham, David Clifford b: 9/27/35, Erie, Pa. BR/TR, 6'3", 190 lbs. Deb: 9/18/60																											
1960	KC-A	0	0	—	5	0	0	0	2	8^1	4	1	0	0	1	3	5.4	1.08	369	.148	.179	0	.000	-0	3	3	0	0.1
1961	KC-A	2	1	.667	17	0	0	0	2	21	25	12	0	2	5	10	13.7	5.14	81	.309	.364	2	.667	1	-3	-2	0	-0.2
1962	KC-A	11	4	.733	30	9	3	0	1	110	105	53	13	8	43	61	12.8	4.17	101	.257	.340	2	.057	-3	-2	1	1	-0.1
1963	KC-A	12	15	.444	38	34	4	1	1	237^2	244	116	21	9	79	118	12.6	4.09	95	.268	.333	11	.138	-3	-12	-5	1	-0.8
1964	Det-A	19	12	.613	40	36	11	1	1	254	224	108	28	12	81	164	11.2	3.44	106	.232	.299	6	.073	-5	5	6	-0	0.1
1965	Det-A	9	14	.391	34	27	8	3	0	195^1	179	91	12	11	61	109	11.6	3.78	92	.241	.308	4	.069	-4	-7	-7	1	-1.0
1966	Det-A	8	3	.727	38	14	3	0	1	140^2	139	64	14	8	54	93	12.9	3.20	109	.261	.338	2	.044	-3	4	4	1	0.1
1967	Det-A	4	5	.444	36	4	0	0	4	85^1	72	30	6	4	33	44	11.5	2.74	119	.235	.318	0	.000	-2	5	5	1	0.5
1968	Pit-N	1	0	1.000	11	0	0	0	1	20^2	21	12	0	0	13	9	14.8	3.48	84	.276	.382	1	.333	0	-1	-1	-0	-0.1
1969	KC-A	2	3	.400	34	0	0	0	5	50	58	27	6	2	14	27	13.3	3.96	93	.294	.347	0	.000	0	-2	-1	0	-0.1
Total	10	68	57	.544	283	124	29	5	18	1123	1071	514	100	56	384	638	12.1	3.66	100	.252	.323	28	.086	-18	-11	2	4	-1.5
● **BOB WICKMAN**	Wickman, Robert Joe b: 2/6/69, Green Bay, Wis. BR/TR, 6'1", 212 lbs. Deb: 8/24/92																											
1992	NY-A	6	1	.857	8	8	0	0	0	50^1	51	25	2	2	20	21	13.1	4.11	95	.273	.349	0	—	0	-1	-1	0	-0.1
1993	NY-A	14	4	.778	41	19	1	1	4	140	156	82	13	5	69	70	14.8	4.63	90	.284	.369	0	—	0	-5	-7	-1	-0.9
1994	NY-A	5	4	.556	**53**	0	0	0	6	70	54	26	3	1	27	56	10.5	3.09	148	.213	.292	0	—	0	13	12	-0	1.5
1995	*NY-A	2	4	.333	63	1	0	0	1	80	77	38	6	5	33	51	12.9	4.05	114	.253	.336	0	—	0	6	5	0	0.4
1996	NY-A	4	1	.800	58	0	0	0	0	79	94	41	7	5	34	61	15.2	4.67	106	.299	.377	0	—	0	3	2	3	0.4
	Mil-A	3	0	1.000	12	0	0	0	0	16^2	12	9	3	0	10	14	11.9	3.24	160	.200	.314	0	—	0	3	3	-0	0.5
	Yr	7	1	.875	70	0	0	0	0	95^2	106	50	10	5	44	75	14.6	4.42	113	.283	.366	0	—	0	6	6	3	0.9
1997	Mil-A	7	6	.538	74	0	0	0	1	95^2	89	32	8	3	41	78	12.5	2.73	169	.252	.335	0	—	0	20	20	1	2.5

YEAR	TM/L	W	L	PCT	G	GS	CG	SH	SV	IP	H	R	HR	HB	BB	SO	RAT	ERA	ERA+	OAV	OOB	BH	AVG	PB	PR	PR+	PD	TPI
1998	Mil-N	6	9	.400	72	0	0	0	25	82^1	79	38	5	4	39	71	13.3	3.72	115	.262	.355	0	.000	-0	5	5	1	1.1
1999	Mil-N	3	8	.273	71	0	0	0	37	74^1	75	31	6	2	38	60	13.9	3.39	134	.262	.353	0	.000	-0	10	10	1	1.9
2000	Mil-N★	2	2	.500	43	0	0	0	16	46	37	18	1	1	20	44	11.3	2.93	155	.215	.301	0	—	0	9	8	1	1.2
	Cle-A	1	3	.250	26	0	0	0	14	26^2	27	12	0	0	12	11	13.2	3.38	148	.270	.348	0	—	0	5	5	0	0.9
Total	9	53	42	.558	521	28	1	1	104	761	751	352	54	28	343	537	13.3	3.76	120	.261	.345	0	.000	-0	67	63	6	9.4
● AL WIDMAR	Widmar, Albert Joseph b: 3/20/25, Cleveland, Ohio BR/TR, 6'3", 185 lbs. Deb: 4/25/47 C																											
1947	Bos-A	0	0	—	2	0	0	0	0	1^1	1	2	1	0	2	1	20.3	13.50	29	.200	.429	0	—	0	-1	-1	0	-0.1
1948	StL-A	2	6	.250	49	0	0	0	1	82^2	88	42	4	0	48	34	14.8	4.46	102	.275	.370	3	.300	1	-2	1	2	0.3
1950	StL-A	7	15	.318	36	26	8	1	4	194^2	211	115	16	3	74	78	13.3	4.76	104	.271	.337	10	.149	-3	-4	4	1	0.1
1951	StL-A	4	9	.308	26	16	4	0	0	107^2	157	84	19	2	52	28	17.6	6.52	67	.344	.414	5	.167	-1	-29	-24	1	-2.4
1952	Chi-A	0	0	—	1	0	0	0	0	2	4	1	1	0	0	2	18.0	4.50	81	.444	.444	0	—	0	-0	-0	-0	0.0
Total	5	13	30	.302	114	42	12	1	5	388^1	461	244	41	5	176	143	14.9	5.21	90	.294	.367	18	.168	-4	-36	-21	3	-2.1
● WILD BILL WIDNER	Widner, William Waterfield b: 6/3/1867, Cincinnati, Ohio d: 12/10/08, Cincinnati, Ohio BR/TR, 6', 180 lbs. Deb: 6/8/1887																											
1887	Cin-a	1	0	1.000	1	1	1	0	0	9	13	8	2	1	2	0	14.0	5.00	87	.310	.326	1	.250	-0	-1	-1	0	0.0
1888	Was-N	5	7	.417	13	13	13	0	0	115	111	69	7	6	22	33	10.9	2.82	100	.247	.291	12	.200	-1	0	-0	-0	-0.1
1889	Col-a	12	20	.375	41	34	25	2	1	294	368	241	11	18	85	63	14.4	5.20	70	.297	.351	28	.211	-2	-44	-55	0	-4.5
1890	Col-a	4	8	.333	13	10	8	1	0	96	103	52	3	3	24	14	12.2	3.28	109	.266	.314	8	.195	-1	6	4	2	0.5
1891	Cin-a	0	1	.000	1	1	1	0	0	8	13	7	0	2	4	0	21.4	7.88	52	.351	.442	1	.250	-0	-4	-3	-0	-0.3
Total	5	22	36	.379	69	59	48	3	1	522	608	377	23	30	137	110	13.3	4.36	79	.282	.333	50	.207	-3	-42	-55	2	-4.4
● TED WIEAND	Wieand, Franklin Delano Roosevelt b: 4/4/33, Walnutport, Pa. BR/TR, 6'2", 195 lbs. Deb: 9/27/58																											
1958	Cin-N	0	0	—	1	0	0	0	0	2	4	2	1	0	0	2	18.0	9.00	46	.400	.400	0	—	0	-1	-1	-0	-0.1
1960	Cin-N	0	1	.000	5	0	0	0	0	4^1	4	5	2	0	5	3	18.7	10.38	37	.250	.429	0	—	0	-3	-3	0	-0.6
Total	2	0	1	.000	6	0	0	0	0	6^1	8	7	3	0	5	5	18.5	9.95	39	.308	.419	0	—	0	-4	-4	0	-0.7
● CHARLIE WIEDEMEYER	Wiedemeyer, Charles John "Chick" b: 1/31/14, Chicago, Ill. d: 10/27/79, Lake Geneva, Fla. BL/TL, 6'3", 180 lbs. Deb: 9/9/34																											
1934	Chi-N	0	0	—	4	1	0	0	0	8^1	16	10	0	1	4	2	22.7	9.72	40	.432	.500	0	.000	-0	-5	-6	0	-0.3
● STUMP WIEDMAN	Wiedman, George Edward b: 2/17/1861, Rochester, N.Y. d: 3/2/05, New York, N.Y. BR/TR, 5'7.5", 165 lbs. Deb: 8/26/1880 U♦																											
1880	Buf-N	0	9	.000	17	13	9	0	0	113^2	141	77	1		9	25	11.9	3.40	72	.291	.304	8	.103	-5	-13	-12	-1	-1.3
1881	Det-N	8	5	.615	13	13	13	1	0	115	108	48	1		12	26	**9.4**	**1.80**	**162**	.238	**.258**	12	.255	0	12	14	-2	1.2
1882	Det-N	25	20	.556	46	45	43	4	0	411	391	204	10		39	161	9.4	2.63	112	.236	.253	42	.218	-5	12	14	-0	0.7
1883	Det-N	20	24	.455	52	47	41	3	**2**	402^1	435	265	8		72	183	11.3	3.53	88	.257	.288	58	.185	-8	-18	-19	0	-2.2
1884	Det-N	4	21	.160	26	26	24	0	0	212^2	257	179	9		57	96	13.3	3.72	78	.273	.314	49	.163	-4	-18	-20	-1	-2.2
1885	Det-N	14	24	.368	38	38	37	3	0	330	343	198	7		63	149	11.1	3.14	91	.252	.286	24	.157	-4	-11	-11	-3	-1.7
1886	KC-N	12	36	.250	51	51	48	1	0	427^2	549	323	11		112	168	13.9	4.50	84	.303	.344	30	.168	-10	-57	-30	4	-3.1
1887	Det-N	13	7	.650	21	21	20	0	0	183	281	132	9	9	60	56	14.3	5.36	76	.349	.356	20	.235	-2	-26	-27	-0	-2.4
	NY-a	4	8	.333	12	12	11	1	0	97	147	84	3	1	25	37	13.7	4.64	92	.292	.333	11	.220	-2	-4	-4	1	-0.4
	NY-N	0	1	.000	1	1	1	0	0	8	12	6	0	0	2	4	13.5	1.13	335	.098	.324	1	.333	0	3	3	-0	0.3
1888	NY-N	1	1	.500	2	2	2	0	0	18	17	20	2	2	8	5	13.5	3.50	78	.230	.321	0	.000	-0	-1	-2	-0	-0.2
Total	9	101	156	.393	279	269	249	13	2	2318^1	2681	1536	61	12	459	910	11.9	3.60	89	.275	.302	255	.181	-41	-120	-95	-2	-11.3
● JACK WIENEKE	Wieneke, John b: 3/10/1894, Saltsburg, Pa. d: 3/16/33, Pleasant Ridge, Mich. BR/TL, 6', 182 lbs. Deb: 7/4/21																											
1921	Chi-A	0	1	.000	10	3	0	0	0	25^1	39	24	4	1	17	10	20.3	8.17	52	.351	.442	1	.111	-1	-11	-11	0	-0.6
● BOB WIESLER	Wiesler, Robert George b: 8/13/30, St.Louis, Mo. BB/TL, 6'2", 195 lbs. Deb: 8/3/51																											
1951	NY-A	0	2	.000	4	3	0	0	0	9^1	13	15	0	0	11	3	23.1	13.50	28	.361	.511	0	.000	-1	-10	-11	0	-1.7
1954	NY-A	3	2	.600	6	5	0	0	0	30^1	28	15	0	0	30	25	17.2	4.15	83	.259	.420	3	.273	1	-1	-3	-1	-0.4
1955	NY-A	0	2	.000	16	7	0	0	0	53	39	27	1	1	49	22	15.1	3.91	96	.212	.380	2	.143	-1	0	-1	1	0.0
1956	Was-A	3	12	.200	37	21	3	0	0	123	141	98	11	3	112	49	18.7	6.44	67	.300	.438	3	.091	-3	-31	-28	1	-3.0
1957	Was-A	1	1	.500	3	2	1	0	0	16^1	15	8	2	1	11	9	14.9	4.41	88	.250	.375	1	.167	0	-1	-1	0	-0.1
1958	Was-A	0	0	—	4	0	0	0	0	9^1	14	8	2	1	5	5	19.3	6.75	56	.359	.444	0	.000	-0	-3	-3	1	-0.1
Total	6	7	19	.269	70	38	4	0	0	241^1	250	171	16	6	218	113	17.7	5.74	70	.279	.423	9	.130	-3	-46	-46	3	-5.3
● WHITEY WIETELMANN	Wietelmann, William Frederick b: 3/15/19, Zanesville, Ohio BB/TR (BR 1939-41), 6', 170 lbs. Deb: 9/6/39 C♦																											
1945	Bos-N	0	0	—	1	0	0	0	0	1	6	6	0	0	2	0	72.0	54.00	7	.667	.727	116	.271	0	-6	-6	-0	-0.2
1946	Bos-N	0	0	—	3	0	0	0	0	6^2	9	8	1	1	4	2	18.9	8.10	42	.310	.412	16	.205	0	-3	-3	-0	-0.2
Total	2	0	0	—	4	0	0	0	0	7^2	15	14	1	1	6	2	25.8	14.09	25	.395	.489	409	.232	1	-9	-9	-0	-0.4
● JIMMY WIGGS	Wiggs, James Alvin "Big Jim" b: 9/1/1876, Trondheim, Norway d: 1/20/63, Xenia, Ohio BB/TR, 6'4", 200 lbs. Deb: 4/23/03																											
1903	Cin-N	0	1	.000	2	1	0	0	0	5	12	7	0	1	2	2	27.0	5.40	66	.500	.556	0	.000	-0	-1	-1	-0	-0.2
1905	Det-A	3	3	.500	7	7	4	0	0	41^1	30	25	0	1	29	37	13.1	3.27	84	.205	.341	2	.133	-0	-3	-2	-0	-0.4
1906	Det-A	0	0	—	4	1	0	0	0	10^1	11	9	1	2	7	7	17.4	5.23	53	.275	.408	1	.333	0	-3	-3	0	-0.1
Total	3	3	4	.429	13	9	4	0	0	56^2	53	41	1	4	38	46	15.1	3.81	74	.252	.377	3	.158	-0	-7	-6	0	-0.7
● BILL WIGHT	Wight, William Robert "Lefty" b: 4/12/22, Rio Vista, Cal. BL/TL, 6'1", 180 lbs. Deb: 4/17/46																											
1946	NY-A	2	2	.500	14	4	1	0	0	40^1	44	22	1	1	30	11	16.7	4.46	77	.289	.410	0	.000	-1	-4	-5	0	-0.5
1947	NY-A	1	0	1.000	1	1	1	0	0	9	8	3	0	0	2	3	10.0	1.00	353	.242	.286	0	.000	0	3	3	0	0.4
1948	Chi-A	9	20	.310	34	32	7	1	1	223^1	238	132	9	1	135	68	15.1	4.80	89	.278	.377	6	.082	-7	-13	-13	1	-2.0
1949	Chi-A	15	13	.536	35	33	14	3	1	245	254	106	9	0	96	78	12.9	3.31	126	.275	.343	14	.165	-1	24	24	0	2.4
1950	Chi-A	10	16	.385	30	28	13	3	0	206	213	89	10	0	79	62	12.8	3.58	125	.270	.336	0	.000	-9	23	21	2	1.6
1951	Bos-A	7	7	.500	34	17	4	2	0	118^1	128	77	5	0	63	38	14.5	5.10	88	.282	.369	3	.073	-4	-13	-8	1	-1.1
1952	Bos-A	2	1	.667	10	2	0	0	0	24^1	14	11	3	1	14	5	10.7	2.96	133	.169	.296	1	.143	-0	2	2	0	0.3
	Det-A	5	9	.357	23	19	8	3	0	143^2	167	71	7	0	55	65	13.9	3.88	98	.291	.354	11	.220	1	-3	-1	2	0.2
	Yr	7	10	.412	33	21	8	3	0	168	181	82	10	1	69	70	13.4	3.75	102	.276	.346	12	.211	1	-1	1	2	0.5
1953	Det-A	0	3	.000	13	4	0	0	0	25^1	35	33	4	0	14	10	17.4	8.88	46	.333	.412	3	.429	1	-14	-13	-1	-1.3
	Cle-A	2	1	.667	20	0	0	0	1	26^2	29	12	1	0	16	14	15.2	3.71	101	.282	.378	0	.000	-1	1	0	0	0.0
	Yr	2	4	.333	33	4	0	0	1	52	64	45	5	0	30	24	16.3	6.23	63	.308	.395	3	.250	0	-13	-14	-0	-1.3
1955	Cle-A	0	0	—	17	0	0	0	1	24	24	8	0	0	9	9	12.4	2.63	152	.261	.327	0	—	0	4	4	2	0.4
	Bal-A	6	8	.429	19	14	8	2	2	117^1	111	43	6	1	39	54	11.6	2.45	155	.252	.315	3	.083	-2	20	18	2	2.2
	Yr	6	8	.429	36	14	8	2	3	141^1	135	51	6	1	48	63	11.7	2.48	155	.254	.317	3	.083	-2	23	22	4	2.6
1956	Bal-A	9	12	.429	35	26	7	1	0	174^2	198	92	7	6	72	84	14.2	4.02	98	.289	.362	12	.200	-1	3	-2	-1	-0.4
1957	Bal-A	6	6	.500	27	17	2	0	0	121	122	53	4	4	54	50	13.4	3.64	99	.271	.354	1	.029	-3	2	-1	-1	-0.5
1958	Cin-N	0	1	.000	7	0	0	0	0	6^2	7	4	1	0	4	5	14.9	4.05	102	.292	.393	0	—	0	-0	0	0	0.0
	StL-N	3	0	1.000	28	1	1	0	2	57^1	64	35	7	0	32	18	15.1	5.02	82	.290	.379	1	.100	-0	-7	-5	1	-0.3
	Yr	3	1	.750	35	1	1	0	2	64	71	39	8	0	36	23	15.0	4.92	84	.290	.381	1	.100	-0	-7	-5	1	-0.3
Total	12	77	99	.438	347	198	66	15	8	1563	1656	791	74	14	714	574	13.7	3.95	103	.277	.355	55	.115	-28	27	22	9	1.4
● FRED WIGINGTON	Wigington, Fred Thomas b: 12/16/1897, Rogers, Neb. d: 5/8/80, Mesa, Ariz. BR/TR, 5'10", 168 lbs. Deb: 4/20/23																											
1923	StL-N	0	0	—	4	0	0	0	0	8^1	11	4	0	0	5	2	17.3	3.24	121	.367	.457	0	.000	-0	1	1	0	0.1
● SANDY WIHTOL	Wihtol, Alexander Ames b: 6/1/55, Palo Alto, Cal. BR/TR, 6'1", 195 lbs. Deb: 9/7/79																											
1979	Cle-A	0	0	—	5	0	0	0	0	10^2	10	4	0	0	3	6	11.0	3.38	126	.238	.289	0	—	0	1	1	0	0.1
1980	Cle-A	1	0	1.000	17	0	0	0	1	35^1	35	18	2	2	14	20	13.0	3.57	114	.257	.336	0	—	0	2	2	-1	0.0
1982	Cle-A	0	0	—	6	0	0	0	0	11^2	9	6	1	1	7	8	13.1	4.63	88	.220	.347	0	—	0	-1	-1	-0	-0.1
Total	3	1	0	1.000	28	0	0	0	1	57^2	54	28	3	3	24	34	12.6	3.75	110	.247	.329	0	—	0	2	2	-1	0.0
● MILT WILCOX	Wilcox, Milton Edward b: 4/20/50, Honolulu, Hawaii BR/TR, 6'2", 185 lbs. Deb: 9/5/70																											
1970	*Cin-N	3	1	.750	5	2	1	1	1	22^1	19	6	2	1	7	13	10.9	2.42	167	.229	.297	1	.200	0	4	4	0	0.8
1971	Cin-N	2	2	.500	18	3	0	0	1	43^1	43	22	2	2	17	21	12.9	3.32	101	.269	.346	0	.000	-1	1	0	0	-0.1

YEAR	TM/L	W	L	PCT	G	GS	CG	SH	SV	IP	H	R	HR	HB	BB	SO	RAT	ERA	ERA+	OAV	OOB	BH	AVG	PB	PR	PR+	PD	TPI
1972	Cle-A	7	14	.333	32	27	4	2	0	156	145	67	18	5	72	90	12.8	3.40	95	.251	.339	9	.200	1	-6	-3	-3	-0.5
1973	Cle-A	8	10	.444	26	19	4	0	0	134^1	143	90	14	8	68	82	14.7	5.83	67	.275	.367	0	—	0	-30	-28	1	-3.1
1974	Cle-A	2	2	.500	41	2	1	0	4	71^1	74	42	10	5	24	33	13.0	4.67	78	.271	.341	0	—	0	-8	-8	1	-0.5
1975	Chi-N	0	1	.000	25	0	0	0	0	38^1	50	27	4	1	17	21	16.0	5.63	68	.323	.393	1	.333	0	-9	-7	0	-0.3
1977	Det-A	6	2	.750	20	13	1	0	0	106^1	96	46	13	1	37	82	11.3	3.64	118	.241	.307	0	—	0	5	7	-0	0.5
1978	Det-A	13	12	.520	29	27	16	2	0	215^1	208	94	22	8	68	132	11.9	3.76	103	.255	.318	0	—	0	0	3	1	0.4
1979	Det-A	12	10	.545	33	29	7	0	0	196^1	201	105	18	11	73	109	13.1	4.35	100	.267	.341	0	—	0	-3	-0	3	0.3
1980	Det-A	13	11	.542	32	31	13	1	0	198^2	201	112	24	6	68	97	12.5	4.48	92	.262	.327	0	—	0	-10	-8	1	-0.7
1981	Det-A	12	9	.571	24	24	8	1	0	166^1	152	61	10	6	52	79	11.4	3.03	125	.247	.312	0	—	0	12	13	1	1.7
1982	Det-A	12	10	.545	29	29	9	1	0	193^2	187	91	18	7	85	112	13.0	3.62	112	.257	.340	0	—	0	10	10	3	1.3
1983	Det-A	11	10	.524	26	26	9	2	0	186	164	89	19	4	74	101	11.7	3.97	99	.237	.314	0	—	0	2	-1	3	0.2
1984	*Det-A	17	8	.680	33	33	0	0	0	193^2	183	99	13	8	66	119	11.9	4.00	98	.252	.321	0	—	0	0	-2	1	0.0
1985	Det-A	1	3	.250	8	8	0	0	0	39	51	24	6	0	14	20	15.0	4.85	84	.315	.369	0	—	0	-3	-3	1	-0.2
1986	Sea-A	0	8	.000	13	10	0	0	0	55^2	74	38	11	1	28	26	16.7	5.50	77	.327	.404	0	—	0	-8	-8	0	-0.9
Total	16	119	113	.513	394	283	73	10	6	2016^2	1991	1013	204	74	770	1137	12.7	4.07	97	.260	.334	11	.177	0	-42	-30	14	-1.1

● RANDY WILES Wiles, Randall E b: 9/10/51, Fort Belvoir, Va. BL/TL, 6′1″, 185 lbs. Deb: 8/7/77

YEAR	TM/L	W	L	PCT	G	GS	CG	SH	SV	IP	H	R	HR	HB	BB	SO	RAT	ERA	ERA+	OAV	OOB	BH	AVG	PB	PR	PR+	PD	TPI
1977	Chi-A	1	1	.500	5	0	0	0	0	2^2	5	3	1	0	3	0	27.0	10.13	40	.417	.533	0	—	0	-2	-2	0	-0.3

● MARK WILEY Wiley, Mark Eugene b: 2/28/48, National City, Cal. BR/TR, 6′1″, 200 lbs. Deb: 6/17/75 C

YEAR	TM/L	W	L	PCT	G	GS	CG	SH	SV	IP	H	R	HR	HB	BB	SO	RAT	ERA	ERA+	OAV	OOB	BH	AVG	PB	PR	PR+	PD	TPI
1975	Min-A	1	3	.250	15	3	1	0	2	38^2	50	30	4	1	13	15	14.9	6.05	63	.325	.381	0	—	0	-10	-9	-1	-1.0
1978	SD-N	1	0	1.000	4	1	0	0	0	7^2	11	6	1	0	1	1	14.1	5.87	57	.324	.343	0	.000	-0	-2	-2	-0	-0.3
	Tor-A	0	0	—	2	0	0	0	0	2^2	3	2	0	0	1	2	13.5	6.75	58	.273	.333	0	—	0	-1	-1	-0	-0.1
Total	2	2	3	.400	21	4	1	0	2	49	64	38	5	1	15	18	14.7	6.06	62	.322	.372	0	.000	-0	-13	-13	-1	-1.4

● HARRY WILHELM Wilhelm, Harry Lester b: 4/7/1874, Uniontown, Pa. d: 2/20/44, Republic, Pa. BR/TR, 5′7″, 155 lbs. Deb: 8/12/1899

YEAR	TM/L	W	L	PCT	G	GS	CG	SH	SV	IP	H	R	HR	HB	BB	SO	RAT	ERA	ERA+	OAV	OOB	BH	AVG	PB	PR	PR+	PD	TPI
1899	Lou-N	1	0	1.000	5	3	2	0	0	25	36	22	1	1	3	6	14.4	6.12	63	.336	.360	3	.250	2	-6	-6	0	-0.1

● KAISER WILHELM Wilhelm, Irvin Key b: 1/26/1874, Wooster, Ohio d: 5/22/36, Rochester, N.Y. BR/TR, 6′, 162 lbs. Deb: 4/18/03 MUC

YEAR	TM/L	W	L	PCT	G	GS	CG	SH	SV	IP	H	R	HR	HB	BB	SO	RAT	ERA	ERA+	OAV	OOB	BH	AVG	PB	PR	PR+	PD	TPI
1903	Pit-N	5	3	.625	12	9	7	1	0	86	88	51	0	3	25	20	12.1	3.24	100	.264	.321	3	.088	-2	0	-0	2	-0.1
1904	Bos-N	14	20	.412	39	36	30	3	0	288	316	150	8	7	74	73	12.4	3.69	75	.285	.333	7	.070	-8	-30	-30	1	-3.9
1905	Bos-N	3	23	.115	34	28	23	0	0	242^1	287	166	7	5	75	76	13.6	4.53	68	.295	.349	16	.160	-2	-41	-37	2	-3.6
1908	Bro-N	16	22	.421	42	36	33	6	0	332	266	105	3	6	83	99	9.6	1.87	125	.217	.271	12	.108	-4	18	18	3	1.9
1909	Bro-N	3	13	.188	22	17	14	1	0	163	176	92	3	2	59	45	13.1	3.26	80	.289	.353	13	.228	2	-12	-12	1	-0.8
1910	Bro-N	3	7	.300	15	5	0	0	0	68^1	88	45	3	1	18	17	14.1	4.74	64	.314	.358	6	.316	2	-13	-13	1	-1.4
1914	Bal-F	12	17	.414	47	27	11	1	5	243^2	263	141	10	0	81	113	12.7	4.03	75	.291	.349	21	.250	1	-31	-26	3	-2.5
1915	Bal-F	0	0	—	1	0	0	0	0	1	0	0	0	0	0	0	0.0	0.00	—	.000	.000	0	—	0	0	0	-0	0.0
1921	Phi-N	0	0	—	4	0	0	0	0	8	11	3	0	0	3	1	15.8	3.38	125	.393	.452	0	.000	-0	0	1	-0	0.0
Total	9	56	105	.348	216	158	118	12	5	1432^1	1495	753	34	24	418	444	12.2	3.44	81	.274	.328	78	.154	-12	-108	-101	11	-10.4

● HOYT WILHELM Wilhelm, James Hoyt b: 7/26/23, Huntersville, N.C. BR/TR, 6′, 195 lbs. Deb: 4/19/52 H

YEAR	TM/L	W	L	PCT	G	GS	CG	SH	SV	IP	H	R	HR	HB	BB	SO	RAT	ERA	ERA+	OAV	OOB	BH	AVG	PB	PR	PR+	PD	TPI
1952	NY-N	15	3	**.833**	**71**	0	0	0	11	159^1	127	60	12	5	57	108	10.7	**2.43**	**152**	.220	.296	6	.158	0	23	23	1	2.9
1953	NY-N☆	7	8	.467	**68**	0	0	0	15	145	127	61	13	4	77	71	12.9	3.04	141	.238	.339	5	.152	1	**20**	**20**	-1	2.3
1954	*NY-N	12	4	.750	57	0	0	0	7	111^1	77	32	5	5	52	64	10.8	2.10	192	.198	.300	1	.048	-2	**24**	**24**	1	3.4
1955	NY-N	4	1	.800	59	0	0	0	0	103	104	53	10	2	40	71	12.8	3.93	102	.266	.337	3	.158	-1	1	1	3	0.2
1956	NY-N	4	9	.308	64	0	0	0	8	89^1	97	45	7	2	43	71	14.3	3.83	99	.280	.362	2	.222	0	-1	-0	2	0.1
1957	StL-N	1	4	.200	40	0	0	0	11	55	52	28	7	3	21	29	12.4	4.25	93	.254	.332	0	.000	-1	-2	-2	-0	-0.3
	Cle-A	1	0	1.000	2	0	0	0	1	3^2	2	1	1	1	1	0	9.8	2.45	151	.154	.267	0	—	0	1	1	-0	0.1
1958	Cle-A	2	7	.222	30	6	1	0	5	90^1	70	32	4	1	35	57	10.6	2.49	146	.215	.294	2	.095	-1	13	12	1	1.2
	Bal-A	1	3	.250	9	4	3	1	0	40^2	25	9	2	1	10	35	8.0	1.99	180	.179	.238	1	.091	-1	8	8	-0	0.6
	Yr	3	10	.231	39	10	4	1	5	131	95	41	6	2	45	92	9.8	2.34	155	.204	.277	3	.094	-2	21	20	1	1.8
1959	Bal-A★	15	11	.577	32	27	13	3	0	226	178	64	13	10	77	139	10.6	**2.19**	**173**	.224	.301	4	.053	-6	**42**	**41**	-1	3.8
1960	Bal-A	11	8	.579	41	11	3	1	7	147	125	69	13	1	39	107	10.1	3.31	115	.228	.280	3	.071	-3	9	8	1	0.9
1961	Bal-A★	9	7	.563	51	1	0	0	18	109^2	89	35	5	4	41	87	11.0	2.30	167	.219	.296	1	.050	-1	21	20	1	3.4
1962	Bal-A†	7	10	.412	52	0	0	0	15	93	64	28	5	3	34	90	9.8	1.94	191	.197	.279	2	.125	-0	21	20	0	**4.1**
1963	Chi-A	5	8	.385	55	3	0	0	21	136^1	106	47	8	4	30	111	9.2	2.64	133	.215	.265	2	.069	-1	15	14	1	1.7
1964	Chi-A	12	9	.571	73	0	0	0	27	131^1	94	35	7	2	30	95	8.6	1.99	174	.202	.254	3	.143	-0	24	22	-1	4.4
1965	Chi-A	7	7	.500	66	0	0	0	20	144	88	34	11	2	32	106	7.6	1.81	176	.177	.229	0	.000	-2	**26**	**24**	-1	2.7
1966	Chi-A	5	2	.714	46	0	0	0	6	81^1	50	21	6	1	17	61	7.5	1.66	191	.178	.227	1	.125	0	16	15	-1	1.4
1967	Chi-A	8	3	.727	49	0	0	0	12	89	58	21	2	4	34	76	9.7	1.31	236	.183	.270	1	.077	-1	**19**	**18**	-1	2.7
1968	Chi-A	4	4	.500	72	0	0	0	12	93^2	69	20	4	2	24	72	9.1	1.73	175	.205	.262	0	.000	-0	13	13	-1	1.5
1969	Cal-A	5	7	.417	44	0	0	0	10	65^2	45	21	4	3	18	53	9.0	2.47	141	.194	.261	0	.000	-1	8	8	-0	1.5
	Atl-N	2	0	1.000	8	0	0	0	4	12^1	5	1	0	1	4	14	7.3	0.73	494	.119	.213	0	.000	-0	4	4	0	0.9
1970	Atl-N☆	6	4	.600	50	0	0	0	13	78^1	69	29	7	1	39	67	12.5	3.10	138	.234	.325	1	.091	-0	8	10	0	1.5
	Chi-N	0	1	.000	3	0	0	0	0	3^2	4	4	1	0	3	1	17.2	9.82	46	.286	.412	0	—	0	-2	-2	0	-0.3
	Yr	6	5	.545	53	0	0	0	13	82	73	33	8	1	42	68	12.7	3.40	127	.236	.330	1	.091	-0	6	8	1	1.2
1971	Atl-N	0	0	—	3	0	0	0	0	2^1	6	5	2	0	1	1	27.0	15.43	24	.500	.538	0	—	0	-3	-3	0	-0.1
	LA-N	0	1	.000	9	0	0	0	3	17^2	6	2	1	0	4	15	5.1	1.02	318	.111	.172	0	.000	-0	5	5	-0	0.4
	Yr	0	1	.000	12	0	0	0	3	20	12	7	3	0	5	16	7.6	2.70	122	.182	.239	0	.000	-0	2	1	0	0.3
1972	LA-N	0	1	.000	16	0	0	0	1	25^1	20	16	0	0	15	9	12.4	4.62	72	.217	.327	0	.000	-0	-3	-4	0	-0.2
Total	21	143	122	.540	1070	52	20	5	227	2254^1	1757	773	150	62	778	1610	10.4	2.52	146	.216	.290	38	.088	-21	310	295	5	40.8

● LEFTY WILKIE Wilkie, Aldon Jay b: 10/30/14, Zealandia, Sask., Canada d: 8/5/92, Tualatin, Ore. BL/TL, 5′11.5″, 175 lbs. Deb: 4/22/41

YEAR	TM/L	W	L	PCT	G	GS	CG	SH	SV	IP	H	R	HR	HB	BB	SO	RAT	ERA	ERA+	OAV	OOB	BH	AVG	PB	PR	PR+	PD	TPI
1941	Pit-N	2	4	.333	26	6	2	1	2	79	90	42	1	1	40	16	14.9	4.56	79	.289	.372	7	.292	1	-8	-8	1	-0.4
1942	Pit-N	6	7	.462	35	6	3	0	1	107^1	112	53	4	1	37	18	12.6	4.19	81	.269	.330	10	.263	2	-10	-9	2	-0.7
1946	Pit-N	0	0	—	7	0	0	0	0	7^2	13	9	0	0	3	3	18.8	10.57	33	.382	.432	0	—	0	-6	-6	-0	-0.3
Total	3	8	11	.421	68	12	5	1	3	194	215	104	5	2	80	37	13.8	4.59	76	.283	.352	17	.274	3	-25	-24	3	-1.4

● DEAN WILKINS Wilkins, Dean Allan b: 8/24/66, Blue Island, Ill. BR/TR, 6′1″, 170 lbs. Deb: 8/21/89

YEAR	TM/L	W	L	PCT	G	GS	CG	SH	SV	IP	H	R	HR	HB	BB	SO	RAT	ERA	ERA+	OAV	OOB	BH	AVG	PB	PR	PR+	PD	TPI
1989	Chi-N	1	0	1.000	11	0	0	0	0	15^2	13	9	2	0	9	14	12.6	4.60	82	.228	.333	0	.000	-0	-2	-1	0	-0.1
1990	Chi-N	0	0	—	7	0	0	0	1	7^1	11	8	1	1	7	3	23.3	9.82	42	.333	.463	0	—	0	-5	-4	-0	-0.2
1991	Hou-N	2	1	.667	7	0	0	0	1	8	16	14	0	0	10	4	29.3	11.25	31	.410	.531	0	.000	-0	-7	-7	-0	-1.4
Total	3	3	1	.750	25	0	0	0	2	31	40	31	3	1	26	21	19.5	7.55	50	.310	.429	0	.000	-0	-14	-12	-0	-1.7

● ERIC WILKINS Wilkins, Eric Lamoine b: 12/9/56, St.Louis, Mo. BR/TR, 6′1″, 190 lbs. Deb: 4/11/79

YEAR	TM/L	W	L	PCT	G	GS	CG	SH	SV	IP	H	R	HR	HB	BB	SO	RAT	ERA	ERA+	OAV	OOB	BH	AVG	PB	PR	PR+	PD	TPI
1979	Cle-A	2	4	.333	16	14	0	0	0	69^2	77	41	4	4	38	52	15.4	4.39	97	.289	.386	0	—	0	-1	-1	0	-0.1

● MARC WILKINS Wilkins, Marc Allen b: 10/21/70, Mansfield, Ohio BR/TR, 5′11″, 200 lbs. Deb: 5/11/96

YEAR	TM/L	W	L	PCT	G	GS	CG	SH	SV	IP	H	R	HR	HB	BB	SO	RAT	ERA	ERA+	OAV	OOB	BH	AVG	PB	PR	PR+	PD	TPI
1996	Pit-N	4	3	.571	47	2	0	0	1	75	75	36	6	6	36	62	14.0	3.84	114	.266	.361	2	.222	0	3	4	-0	0.4
1997	Pit-N	9	5	.643	70	0	0	0	2	75^2	65	33	7	4	33	47	12.1	3.69	116	.242	.333	0	.000	-0	4	5	-2	0.7
1998	Pit-N	0	0	—	16	0	0	0	0	15^1	13	6	1	2	9	17	14.1	3.52	122	.236	.364	0	—	0	1	1	-0	0.0
1999	Pit-N	2	3	.400	46	0	0	0	0	51	49	28	3	4	26	44	13.9	4.24	108	.257	.357	0	.000	-0	2	2	1	0.2
2000	Pit-N	4	2	.667	52	0	0	0	0	60^1	54	34	4	6	43	37	15.4	5.07	91	.248	.386	1	.167	-0	-3	-3	0	-0.3
Total	5	19	13	.594	231	2	0	0	3	277^1	256	137	21	22	147	207	13.8	4.12	108	.252	.359	3	.150	0	8	9	-1	1.0

● ROY WILKINSON Wilkinson, Roy Hamilton b: 5/8/1893, Canandaigua, N.Y. d: 7/2/56, Louisville, Ky. BR/TR, 6′1″, 170 lbs. Deb: 4/29/18

YEAR	TM/L	W	L	PCT	G	GS	CG	SH	SV	IP	H	R	HR	HB	BB	SO	RAT	ERA	ERA+	OAV	OOB	BH	AVG	PB	PR	PR+	PD	TPI
1918	Cle-A	0	0	—	1	0	0	0	0	1	0	0	0	0	0	0	0.0	0.00	—	.000	.000	0	—	0	0	0	-0	0.0
1919	*Chi-A	1	1	.500	4	1	1	1	0	22	21	9	0	0	10	5	12.7	2.05	156	.266	.348	3	.375	2	3	3	1	0.5
1920	Chi-A	7	9	.438	34	12	8	0	2	145	162	75	6	2	48	30	13.2	4.03	93	.297	.356	7	.146	-3	-4	-4	-3	-1.0
1921	Chi-A	4	20	.167	36	23	11	0	3	198^1	259	135	4	4	78	50	15.5	5.13	83	.334	.397	8	.123	-4	-19	-20	5	-1.9
1922	Chi-A	0	1	.000	4	1	0	0	1	14^1	24	15	1	1	6	3	19.5	8.79	46	.393	.456	0	.000	-0	-8	-7	-0	-0.6
Total	5	12	31	.279	79	37	20	1	6	380^2	466	234	11	7	142	88	14.5	4.66	86	.318	.381	18	.145	-5	-27	-29	4	-3.0

YEAR	TM/L	W	L	PCT	G	GS	CG	SH	SV	IP	H	R	HR	HB	BB	SO	RAT	ERA	ERA+	OAV	OOB	BH	AVG	PB	PR	PR+	PD	TPI
● **BILL WILKINSON** Wilkinson, William Carl b: 8/10/64, Greybull, Wyoming BR/TL, 5'10", 160 lbs. Deb: 6/13/85 F																												
1985	Sea-A	0	2	.000	2	2	0	0	0	6	8	9	2	0	6	5	21.0	13.50	31	.333	.467	0	—	0	-6	-6	0	-0.9
1987	Sea-A	3	4	.429	56	0	0	0	10	76^1	61	33	8	0	21	73	9.7	3.66	130	.223	.278	0	—	0	7	9	-1	0.8
1988	Sea-A	2	2	.500	30	0	0	0	2	31	28	14	3	0	15	25	12.5	3.48	120	.233	.319	0	—	0	2	2	-1	0.2
Total	3	5	8	.385	88	2	0	0	12	113^1	97	56	13	0	42	103	11.0	4.13	110	.232	.302	0	—	0	2	5	-1	0.1
● **TED WILKS** Wilks, Theodore "Cork" b: 11/13/15, Fulton, N.Y. d: 8/21/89, Houston, Tex. BR/TR, 5'9.5", 178 lbs. Deb: 4/25/44 C																												
1944	*StL-N	17	4	**.810**	36	21	16	4	0	207^2	173	61	12	1	49	70	**9.7**	2.64	133	.227	**.275**	9	.141	-1	22	21	-4	1.4
1945	StL-N	4	7	.364	18	16	4	1	0	98^1	103	39	9	1	29	28	12.2	2.93	128	.270	.324	4	.133	-0	10	9	-2	0.7
1946	*StL-N	8	0	1.000	40	4	0	0	1	95	88	41	13	2	38	40	12.1	3.41	101	.248	.324	5	.208	0	0	0	-1	0.0
1947	StL-N	4	0	1.000	37	0	0	0	5	50^1	57	33	10	2	11	28	12.5	5.01	83	.279	.323	1	.167	0	-5	-5	-0	-0.4
1948	StL-N	6	6	.500	57	2	1	0	13	130^2	113	40	5	0	39	71	10.5	2.62	156	.235	.293	5	.167	0	**19**	**21**	-1	2.2
1949	StL-N	10	3	.769	**59**	0	0	0	**9**	118^1	105	52	7	0	38	71	10.9	3.73	112	.240	.301	1	.037	-3	4	6	-2	0.1
1950	StL-N	2	0	1.000	18	0	0	0	0	24^1	27	18	4	1	9	15	13.7	6.66	65	.287	.356	0	.000	-1	-7	-6	0	-0.5
1951	StL-N	0	0	—	17	0	0	0	1	18	19	7	1	0	5	5	12.0	3.00	132	.279	.329	0	.000	-0	2	2	-1	0.0
	Pit-N	3	5	.375	48	1	1	0	12	82^2	69	31	6	2	24	43	10.3	2.83	149	.231	.292	1	.083	-1	10	12	1	1.5
	Yr	3	5	.375	**65**	1	1	0	**13**	100^2	88	38	7	2	29	48	10.6	2.86	146	.240	.299	1	.077	-1	12	14	0	1.5
1952	Pit-N	5	5	.500	44	0	0	0	4	72^1	65	32	9	2	31	24	12.2	3.61	111	.245	.329	1	.125	-0	1	3	-1	0.3
	Cle-A	0	0	—	7	0	0	0	1	11^2	8	6	0	0	7	6	11.6	3.86	87	.186	.300	0	—	0	-0	-1	0	0.0
1953	Cle-A	0	0	—	4	0	0	0	0	3^2	5	4	0	0	3	2	19.6	7.36	51	.278	.381	0	—	0	-1	-2	-0	-0.1
Total	10	59	30	.663	385	44	22	5	46	913	832	364	76	11	283	403	11.1	3.26	118	.244	.304	27	.131	-5	55	60	-11	5.2
● **ED WILLETT** Willett, Robert Edgar b: 3/7/1884, Norfolk, Va. d: 5/10/34, Wellington, Kan. BR/TR, 6', 183 lbs. Deb: 9/5/06																												
1906	Det-A	0	3	.000	3	3	3	0	0	25	24	12	0	2	8	16	12.2	3.96	70	.255	.327	0	.000	-1	-4	-3	1	-0.4
1907	Det-A	1	5	.167	10	6	1	0	0	48^2	47	31	0	2	20	27	12.8	3.70	70	.255	.335	1	.077	-1	-6	-6	1	-0.7
1908	Det-A	15	8	.652	30	23	18	2	1	197^1	186	67	2	14	60	77	11.9	2.28	106	.261	.331	11	.164	-2	2	3	5	0.6
1909	*Det-A	21	10	.677	41	34	25	3	1	292^2	239	112	5	15	76	89	10.1	2.34	108	.221	.281	22	.196	3	5	6	-1	0.8
1910	Det-A	16	11	.593	37	25	18	4	0	224^1	175	85	2	17	74	65	10.7	2.37	111	.217	.296	11	.133	-2	4	6	7	1.2
1911	Det-A	13	14	.481	38	27	15	2	1	231^1	261	136	5	14	80	86	13.8	3.66	95	.295	.363	22	.268	7	-8	-5	3	0.4
1912	Det-A	17	15	.531	37	31	28	1	0	284^1	281	144	3	17	84	89	12.1	3.29	99	.262	.326	19	.165	-2	1	-1	5	0.3
1913	Det-A	13	14	.481	34	30	19	0	0	242	237	117	0	11	89	59	12.5	3.09	95	.260	.333	26	.283	7	-4	-5	3	0.7
1914	StL-F	4	17	.190	27	22	14	0	0	175	208	102	5	10	56	73	14.1	4.27	71	.295	.355	15	.234	2	-27	-23	5	-1.8
1915	StL-F	2	3	.400	17	2	1	0	2	52^2	61	36	2	3	18	19	14.0	4.61	62	.295	.360	3	.200	0	-11	-10	0	-0.9
Total	10	102	100	.505	274	203	142	12	5	1773^1	1719	842	24	105	565	600	12.1	3.08	94	.258	.326	130	.199	11	-48	-37	28	0.2
● **CARL WILLEY** Willey, Carlton Francis b: 6/6/31, Cherryfield, Me. BR/TR, 6', 175 lbs. Deb: 4/30/58																												
1958	*Mil-N	9	7	.563	23	19	9	**4**	0	140	110	44	14	2	53	74	10.6	2.70	130	.215	.291	5	.104	-2	19	14	-2	1.1
1959	Mil-N	5	9	.357	26	15	5	2	0	117	126	60	12	2	31	51	12.2	4.15	85	.273	.322	4	.103	-1	-3	-9	-1	-1.1
1960	Mil-N	6	7	.462	28	21	2	1	0	144^2	136	78	19	7	65	109	12.9	4.35	79	.248	.335	7	.146	1	-10	-16	-1	-1.3
1961	Mil-N	6	12	.333	35	22	4	0	0	159^2	147	71	20	2	65	91	12.1	3.83	98	.247	.323	1	.019	-6	4	-2	3	-0.5
1962	Mil-N	2	5	.286	30	6	0	0	1	73^1	95	49	9	1	20	40	14.2	5.40	70	.319	.364	3	.273	1	-12	-14	-0	-1.1
1963	NY-N	9	14	.391	30	28	7	4	0	183	149	74	24	4	69	101	10.9	3.10	113	.220	.296	6	.111	-1	4	7	0	0.9
1964	NY-N	0	2	.000	14	3	0	0	0	30	37	19	5	1	8	14	13.8	3.60	99	.301	.348	0	.000	-0	-0	-0	-1	-0.2
1965	NY-N	1	2	.333	13	3	1	0	0	28	30	13	2	2	15	13	15.1	4.18	84	.270	.367	0	.000	-1	-2	-2	-0	-0.3
Total	8	38	58	.396	199	117	28	11	1	875^2	830	408	105	21	326	493	12.1	3.76	95	.250	.320	26	.099	-9	1	-18	-3	-2.5
● **NICK WILLHITE** Willhite, Jon Nicholas b: 1/27/41, Tulsa, Okla. BL/TL, 6'2", 195 lbs. Deb: 6/16/63																												
1963	LA-N	2	3	.400	8	8	1	1	0	38	44	19	5	0	10	28	12.8	3.79	80	.286	.329	3	.300	1	-2	-4	-1	-0.4
1964	LA-N	2	4	.333	10	7	2	0	0	43^2	43	19	4	0	13	24	11.5	3.71	87	.264	.318	0	.000	-0	-1	-2	1	-0.3
1965	Was-A	0	0	—	5	0	0	0	0	6^1	10	11	2	0	4	3	19.9	7.11	49	.345	.424	0	—	0	-3	-3	-0	-0.1
	LA-N	2	2	.500	15	6	0	0	1	42	47	26	7	2	22	28	15.2	5.36	61	.288	.380	4	.400	3	-8	-11	-0	-0.7
1966	LA-N	0	0	—	6	0	0	0	0	4^1	3	1	0	0	5	4	16.6	2.08	159	.214	.421	0	—	0	1	1	0	0.1
1967	Cal-A	0	2	.000	10	7	0	0	0	39^1	39	20	8	0	16	22	12.6	4.35	72	.258	.329	0	.000	-1	-5	-5	-0	-0.4
	NY-N	0	1	.000	4	1	0	0	0	8^1	9	8	1	0	5	9	15.1	8.64	39	.257	.350	0	.000	-0	-5	-5	0	-0.5
Total	5	6	12	.333	58	29	3	1	1	182	195	104	27	2	75	118	13.5	4.55	70	.275	.346	7	.163	2	-23	-29	0	-2.3
● **ALBERT WILLIAMS** Williams, Albert Hamilton (De Souza) b: 5/6/54, Laguna De Perlas, Nic. BR/TR, 6'4", 190 lbs. Deb: 5/7/80																												
1980	Min-A	6	2	.750	18	9	3	0	1	77	73	33	9	0	30	35	12.0	3.51	125	.253	.323	0	—	0	5	7	-1	0.6
1981	Min-A	6	10	.375	23	22	4	0	0	150	160	72	11	1	52	76	12.8	4.08	97	.276	.337	0	—	0	-7	-2	-2	-0.4
1982	Min-A	9	7	.563	26	26	3	0	0	153^2	166	74	18	0	55	61	12.9	4.22	101	.276	.337	0	—	0	-2	1	0	0.1
1983	Min-A	11	14	.440	36	29	4	1	1	193^1	196	105	21	4	68	68	12.5	4.14	103	.262	.327	0	—	0	-1	2	-2	0.1
1984	Min-A	3	5	.375	17	11	1	0	0	68^2	75	46	9	7	22	22	13.6	5.77	73	.284	.355	0	—	0	-13	-11	0	-1.1
Total	5	35	38	.479	120	97	15	1	2	642^2	670	330	68	12	227	262	12.7	4.24	99	.270	.334	0	—	0	-20	-3	-4	-0.7
● **AL WILLIAMS** Williams, Almon Edward b: 5/11/14, Valhermoso Springs, Ala. d: 7/19/69, Groves, Tex. BR/TR, 6'3", 200 lbs. Deb: 4/19/37																												
1937	Phi-A	4	1	.800	16	8	2	0	1	75^1	88	51	0	1	49	27	16.5	5.38	88	.300	.402	2	.083	-2	-6	-5	0	-0.5
1938	Phi-A	0	7	.000	30	8	1	0	0	93^1	128	93	6	1	54	25	17.6	6.94	70	.324	.407	1	.040	-3	-22	-22	-0	-1.5
Total	2	4	8	.333	46	16	3	0	1	168^2	216	144	6	2	103	52	17.1	6.24	77	.314	.405	3	.061	-5	-29	-27	0	-2.0
● **GUS WILLIAMS** Williams, Augustine H. b: 1870, New York, N.Y. d: 10/14/1890, New York, N.Y. 5'11", 170 lbs. Deb: 4/18/1890																												
1890	Bro-a	0	1	.000	2	2	1	0	0	12	13	15	0	0	12	2	18.8	7.50	52	.265	.410	2	.500	1	-5	-5	-1	-0.3
● **BRIAN WILLIAMS** Williams, Brian O'Neal b: 2/15/69, Lancaster, S.C. BR/TR, 6'2", 195 lbs. Deb: 9/16/91																												
1991	Hou-N	0	1	.000	2	2	0	0	0	12	11	5	2	1	4	4	12.0	3.75	94	.250	.327	0	.000	-0	-0	-0	0	-0.1
1992	Hou-N	7	6	.538	16	16	0	0	0	96^1	92	44	10	0	42	54	12.5	3.92	86	.255	.333	4	.133	-0	-4	-6	0	-0.8
1993	Hou-N	4	4	.500	42	5	0	0	3	82	76	48	7	4	38	56	13.0	4.83	80	.248	.338	2	.200	0	-7	-9	2	-0.6
1994	Hou-N	6	5	.545	20	13	0	0	0	78^1	112	64	9	4	41	49	18.0	5.74	69	.343	.422	6	.261	1	-13	-17	-1	-1.9
1995	SD-N	3	10	.231	44	6	0	0	0	72	79	54	3	8	38	75	15.6	6.00	67	.279	.380	1	.071	-1	-15	-16	0	-2.6
1996	Det-A	3	10	.231	40	17	2	1	2	121	145	107	21	6	85	72	17.6	6.77	75	.304	.415	0	—	0	-24	-23	-0	-2.0
1997	Bal-A	0	0	—	13	0	0	0	0	24	20	8	0	0	18	14	14.3	3.00	147	.220	.349	0	—	0	4	4	-0	0.2
1999	Hou-N	2	1	.667	50	0	0	0	0	67^1	69	35	4	5	35	53	14.6	4.41	100	.272	.371	1	.333	0	1	0	1	0.1
2000	Chi-N	1	1	.500	22	0	0	0	1	24^1	28	27	4	3	23	14	20.0	9.62	48	.304	.458	1	.500	1	-13	-14	-0	-1.0
	Cle-A	0	0	—	7	0	0	0	0	18	23	9	2	1	8	6	16.0	4.00	125	.324	.400	0	—	0	2	2	0	0.1
Total	9	26	38	.406	256	59	2	1	6	595^1	655	401	62	32	332	397	15.4	5.37	78	.284	.382	15	.176	1	-70	-80	1	-8.6
● **CHARLIE WILLIAMS** Williams, Charles Prosek b: 10/11/47, Flushing, N.Y. BR/TR, 6'2", 200 lbs. Deb: 4/23/71																												
1971	NY-N	5	6	.455	31	9	1	0	0	90^1	92	53	7	2	41	53	13.5	4.78	71	.267	.348	2	.087	-1	-13	-14	-1	-1.8
1972	SF-N	0	2	.000	3	2	0	0	0	9^1	14	10	3	0	3	3	16.4	8.68	40	.333	.378	0	.000	-0	-5	-5	-0	-1.0
1973	SF-N	3	0	1.000	12	2	0	0	0	23	32	19	2	0	7	11	15.3	6.65	58	.330	.375	1	.333	0	-8	-7	0	-0.8
1974	SF-N	1	3	.250	39	7	0	0	0	100^1	93	38	6	2	31	48	11.3	2.78	137	.250	.311	3	.136	-1	9	11	3	0.7
1975	SF-N	5	3	.625	55	2	0	0	3	98	94	41	2	4	66	45	15.1	3.49	109	.261	.381	2	.125	0	2	3	2	0.5
1976	SF-N	2	0	1.000	48	2	0	0	1	85	80	33	4	2	39	34	12.8	2.96	123	.256	.343	1	.125	-0	5	6	1	0.4
1977	SF-N	6	5	.545	55	8	1	0	0	119^1	116	62	9	3	60	41	13.5	4.00	98	.262	.354	4	.222	0	-1	-1	-0	-0.1
1978	SF-N	1	3	.250	25	1	0	0	0	48	60	31	5	1	28	22	16.7	5.44	64	.314	.405	0	.000	-1	-10	-11	0	-0.9
Total	8	23	22	.511	268	33	2	0	4	573^1	581	287	38	14	275	257	13.7	3.97	93	.269	.355	13	.134	-2	-21	-16	3	-3.0
● **LEFTY WILLIAMS** Williams, Claude Preston b: 3/9/1893, Aurora, Mo. d: 11/4/59, Laguna Beach, Cal. BR/TL, 5'9", 160 lbs. Deb: 9/17/13																												
1913	Det-A	1	3	.250	5	4	3	0	1	29	34	18	0	1	4	9	12.1	4.97	59	.286	.315	1	.100	-0	-7	-7	-1	-1.0
1914	Det-A	0	1	.000	1	1	0	0	0	1	3	5	0	0	2	0	45.0	0.00	—	.429	.556	0	—	0	0	0	-0	0.1
1916	Chi-A	13	7	.650	43	26	10	2	1	224^1	220	99	5	8	65	138	11.8	2.89	96	.267	.327	10	.135	-0	-1	-3	-4	-0.8
1917	*Chi-A	17	8	.680	45	29	8	1	1	230	221	94	3	9	81	85	12.2	2.97	89	.252	.321	6	.090	-3	-8	-8	-5	-1.7

YEAR	TM/L	W	L	PCT	G	GS	CG	SH	SV	IP	H	R	HR	HB	BB	SO	RAT	ERA	ERA+	OAV	OOB	BH	AVG	PB	PR	PR+	PD	TPI
1918	Chi-A	6	4	.600	15	14	7	2	1	105^2	76	32	0	5	47	30	10.9	2.73	100	.209	.308	5	.132	-2	1	0	-2	-0.5
1919	*Chi-A	23	11	.676	41	40	27	5	1	297	265	104	7	11	58	125	10.1	2.64	121	.244	.289	17	.181	1	20	18	-5	1.5
1920	Chi-A	22	14	.611	39	38	25	0	0	299	302	145	15	12	90	128	12.2	3.91	96	.271	.332	22	.218	0	-4	-5	-3	-0.8
Total	7	82	48	.631	189	152	80	10	5	1186	1121	497	30	46	347	515	11.5	3.13	99	.255	.316	61	.159	-4	1	-4	-21	-3.2

● MUTT WILLIAMS
Williams, David Carter b: 7/31/1891, Ozark, Ark. d: 3/30/62, Fayetteville, Ark. BR/TR, 6'3.5", 195 lbs. Deb: 10/4/13

YEAR	TM/L	W	L	PCT	G	GS	CG	SH	SV	IP	H	R	HR	HB	BB	SO	RAT	ERA	ERA+	OAV	OOB	BH	AVG	PB	PR	PR+	PD	TPI
1913	Was-A	1	0	1.000	1	1	0	0	0	4	4	3	1	0	2	1	13.5	4.50	66	.286	.375	1	.500	0	-1	-1	0	-0.1
1914	Was-A	0	0	—	5	0	0	0	1	7	5	5	0	0	4	3	11.6	5.14	55	.227	.346	0	—	0	-2	-2	-0	-0.1
Total	2	1	0	1.000	6	1	0	0	1	11	9	8	1	0	6	4	12.3	4.91	58	.250	.357	1	.500	0	-3	-2	-0	-0.2

● DAVE WILLIAMS
Williams, David Owen b: 2/7/1881, Scranton, Pa. d: 4/25/18, Hot Springs, Ark. BR/TL, 5'11.5", 167 lbs. Deb: 7/2/02

YEAR	TM/L	W	L	PCT	G	GS	CG	SH	SV	IP	H	R	HR	HB	BB	SO	RAT	ERA	ERA+	OAV	OOB	BH	AVG	PB	PR	PR+	PD	TPI
1902	Bos-A	0	0	—	3	0	0	0	0	18^2	22	18	0	1	11	7	16.4	5.30	67	.293	.391	3	.333	1	-4	-4	-1	-0.2

● DON WILLIAMS
Williams, Donald Fred b: 9/14/31, Floyd, Va. BR/TR, 6'2", 180 lbs. Deb: 9/12/58

YEAR	TM/L	W	L	PCT	G	GS	CG	SH	SV	IP	H	R	HR	HB	BB	SO	RAT	ERA	ERA+	OAV	OOB	BH	AVG	PB	PR	PR+	PD	TPI
1958	Pit-N	0	0	—	2	0	0	0	0	4	6	3	1	0	1	3	15.8	6.75	57	.375	.412	0	—	0	-1	-1	0	-0.1
1959	Pit-N	0	0	—	6	0	0	0	0	12	17	9	1	0	3	3	15.0	6.75	57	.362	.400	1	.333	1	-4	-4	-1	-0.2
1962	KC-A	0	0	—	3	0	0	0	0	4	6	4	0	1	0	1	15.8	9.00	47	.353	.389	0	.000	-0	-2	-2	-0	-0.1
Total	3	0	0	—	11	0	0	0	0	20	29	16	2	1	4	7	15.3	7.20	55	.363	.400	1	.250	1	-7	-7	-1	-0.4

● DON WILLIAMS
Williams, Donald Reid "Dino" b: 9/2/35, Los Angeles, Cal. d: 12/20/91, LaJolla, Cal. BR/TR, 6'5", 218 lbs. Deb: 8/4/63

YEAR	TM/L	W	L	PCT	G	GS	CG	SH	SV	IP	H	R	HR	HB	BB	SO	RAT	ERA	ERA+	OAV	OOB	BH	AVG	PB	PR	PR+	PD	TPI
1963	Min-A	0	0	—	3	0	0	0	0	4^1	8	5	1	0	6	2	29.1	10.38	35	.381	.519	0	—	0	-3	-3	0	-0.1

● DALE WILLIAMS
Williams, Elisha Alphonso b: 10/6/1855, Ludlow, Ky. d: 10/22/39, Covington, Ky. BR/TR, 5'9", 175 lbs. Deb: 8/12/1876

YEAR	TM/L	W	L	PCT	G	GS	CG	SH	SV	IP	H	R	HR	HB	BB	SO	RAT	ERA	ERA+	OAV	OOB	BH	AVG	PB	PR	PR+	PD	TPI
1876	Cin-N	1	8	.111	9	9	9	0	0	83	123	75	1		4	9	13.8	4.23	52	.335	.346	7	.200	-2	-18	-20	-0	-1.7

● FRANK WILLIAMS
Williams, Frank Lee b: 2/13/58, Seattle, Wash. BR/TR, 6'1", 190 lbs. Deb: 4/5/84

YEAR	TM/L	W	L	PCT	G	GS	CG	SH	SV	IP	H	R	HR	HB	BB	SO	RAT	ERA	ERA+	OAV	OOB	BH	AVG	PB	PR	PR+	PD	TPI
1984	SF-N	9	4	.692	61	1	1	1	3	106^1	88	49	2	3	51	91	12.0	3.55	99	.226	.321	4	.222	1	0	-0	4	0.5
1985	SF-N	2	4	.333	49	0	0	0	0	73	65	39	5	6	35	54	13.1	4.19	82	.242	.342	0	.000	-0	-5	-6	0	-0.5
1986	SF-N	3	1	.750	36	0	0	0	1	52^1	35	8	0	4	21	33	10.3	1.20	293	.212	.316	1	.500	0	15	14	1	1.2
1987	Cin-N	4	0	1.000	85	0	0	0	2	105^2	101	37	5	2	39	60	12.1	2.30	185	.254	.324	0	.000	-1	21	22	1	1.1
1988	Cin-N	3	2	.600	60	0	0	0	1	62^2	59	24	6	2	35	43	13.8	2.59	139	.252	.354	0	.000	-0	6	7	0	0.6
1989	Det-A	3	3	.500	42	0	0	0	1	71^2	70	37	5	3	46	33	14.9	3.64	105	.254	.366	0	—	0	2	1	-0	0.1
Total	6	24	14	.632	333	1	1	1	8	471^2	418	194	23	20	227	314	12.7	3.00	124	.242	.336	5	.172	1	39	38	5	3.0

● WOODY WILLIAMS
Williams, Gregory Scott b: 8/19/66, Houston, Tex. BR/TR, 6', 190 lbs. Deb: 5/14/93

YEAR	TM/L	W	L	PCT	G	GS	CG	SH	SV	IP	H	R	HR	HB	BB	SO	RAT	ERA	ERA+	OAV	OOB	BH	AVG	PB	PR	PR+	PD	TPI
1993	Tor-A	3	1	.750	30	0	0	0	0	37	40	18	2	1	22	24	15.3	4.38	99	.274	.373	0	—	0	-0	-0	1	0.0
1994	Tor-A	1	3	.250	38	0	0	0	0	59^1	44	24	5	2	33	56	12.0	3.64	133	.205	.316	0	—	0	8	8	-0	0.4
1995	Tor-A	1	2	.333	23	3	0	0	0	53^2	44	23	6	2	28	41	12.4	3.69	128	.220	.322	0	—	0	6	6	0	0.3
1996	Tor-A	4	5	.444	12	10	1	0	0	59	64	33	8	1	21	43	13.1	4.73	106	.278	.341	0	—	0	2	2	-0	0.2
1997	Tor-A	9	14	.391	31	31	0	0	0	194^2	201	98	31	5	66	124	12.6	4.35	106	.269	.332	1	.500	0	5	5	-4	0.2
1998	Tor-A	10	9	.526	32	32	1	1	0	209^2	196	112	36	2	81	151	12.0	4.46	105	.245	.316	2	.333	1	4	5	-2	0.2
1999	SD-N	12	12	.500	33	33	0	0	0	208^1	213	106	33	2	73	137	12.4	4.41	95	.268	.331	13	.178	2	4	-5	-2	-0.6
2000	SD-N	10	8	.556	23	23	4	0	0	168	152	74	23	3	54	111	11.2	3.75	117	.239	.302	15	.259	7	17	12	-3	1.6
Total	8	50	54	.481	222	132	6	1	0	989^2	954	488	144	18	378	687	12.3	4.23	107	.253	.324	31	.223	9	45	33	-11	2.3

● JEFF WILLIAMS
Williams, Jeffrey F. b: 6/6/72, Canberra, Australia BR/TL, 6', 180 lbs. Deb: 9/12/99

YEAR	TM/L	W	L	PCT	G	GS	CG	SH	SV	IP	H	R	HR	HB	BB	SO	RAT	ERA	ERA+	OAV	OOB	BH	AVG	PB	PR	PR+	PD	TPI
1999	LA-N	2	0	1.000	5	3	0	0	0	17^2	12	10	2	0	9	7	10.7	4.08	105	.190	.292	1	.200	0	1	0	0	0.1
2000	LA-N	0	0	—	7	0	0	0	0	5^2	12	11	1	0	8	3	31.8	15.88	28	.462	.588	0	—	0	-7	-8	-0	-0.4
Total	2	2	0	1.000	12	3	0	0	0	23^1	24	21	3	0	17	10	15.8	6.94	62	.270	.387	1	.200	0	-6	-7	-0	-0.3

● JOHNNIE WILLIAMS
Williams, John Brodie "Honolulu Johnnie"
b: 7/16/1889, Honolulu, Hawaii d: 9/8/63, Long Beach, Cal. BR/TR, 6', 180 lbs. Deb: 4/21/14

YEAR	TM/L	W	L	PCT	G	GS	CG	SH	SV	IP	H	R	HR	HB	BB	SO	RAT	ERA	ERA+	OAV	OOB	BH	AVG	PB	PR	PR+	PD	TPI
1914	Det-A	0	2	.000	4	3	1	0	0	11^1	17	12	0	0	5	4	17.5	6.35	44	.378	.440	0	.000	-0	-5	-4	-0	-0.8

● LEON WILLIAMS
Williams, Leon Theo "Lefty" b: 12/2/05, Macon, Ga. d: 11/20/84, Atlanta, Ga. BL/TL, 5'10.5", 154 lbs. Deb: 6/2/26

YEAR	TM/L	W	L	PCT	G	GS	CG	SH	SV	IP	H	R	HR	HB	BB	SO	RAT	ERA	ERA+	OAV	OOB	BH	AVG	PB	PR	PR+	PD	TPI
1926	Bro-N	0	0	—	8	0	0	0	0	8^1	16	6	0	0	2	3	19.4	5.40	71	.421	.450	1	.200	0	-1	-1	1	0.0

● MARSH WILLIAMS
Williams, Marshall McDiarmid "Cap" b: 2/21/1893, Faison, N.C. d: 2/22/35, Tucson, Ariz. BR/TR, 6', 180 lbs. Deb: 7/7/16

YEAR	TM/L	W	L	PCT	G	GS	CG	SH	SV	IP	H	R	HR	HB	BB	SO	RAT	ERA	ERA+	OAV	OOB	BH	AVG	PB	PR	PR+	PD	TPI
1916	Phi-A	0	6	.000	10	4	3	0	0	51^1	71	53	4	0	31	17	17.9	7.89	36	.350	.436	2	.105	-1	-29	-28	-1	-2.9

● MATT WILLIAMS
Williams, Matthew Evan b: 7/25/59, Houston, Tex. BR/TR, 6'1", 200 lbs. Deb: 8/2/83

YEAR	TM/L	W	L	PCT	G	GS	CG	SH	SV	IP	H	R	HR	HB	BB	SO	RAT	ERA	ERA+	OAV	OOB	BH	AVG	PB	PR	PR+	PD	TPI
1983	Tor-A	1	1	.500	4	3	0	0	0	8	13	13	5	1	7	5	23.6	14.63	30	.361	.477	0	—	0	-9	-9	0	-1.4
1985	Tex-A	2	1	.667	6	3	0	0	0	26	20	7	3	0	10	22	10.4	2.42	175	.211	.286	0	—	0	5	5	-1	0.5
Total	2	3	2	.600	10	6	0	0	0	34	33	20	8	1	17	27	13.5	5.29	80	.252	.342	0	—	0	-4	-4	-0	-0.9

● MATT WILLIAMS
Williams, Matthew Taylor b: 4/12/71, Virginia Beach, Va. BB/TL, 6', 185 lbs. Deb: 4/5/2000

YEAR	TM/L	W	L	PCT	G	GS	CG	SH	SV	IP	H	R	HR	HB	BB	SO	RAT	ERA	ERA+	OAV	OOB	BH	AVG	PB	PR	PR+	PD	TPI
2000	Mil-N	0	0	—	11	0	0	0	0	9	7	7	2	1	13	7	21.0	7.00	65	.219	.457	0	.000	-0	-2	-2	0	-0.1

● MIKE WILLIAMS
Williams, Michael Darren b: 7/29/68, Radford, Va. BR/TR, 6'2", 199 lbs. Deb: 6/30/92

YEAR	TM/L	W	L	PCT	G	GS	CG	SH	SV	IP	H	R	HR	HB	BB	SO	RAT	ERA	ERA+	OAV	OOB	BH	AVG	PB	PR	PR+	PD	TPI
1992	Phi-N	1	1	.500	5	5	1	0	0	28^2	29	20	3	0	7	5	11.3	5.34	66	.259	.303	4	.400	1	-6	-6	-0	-0.3
1993	Phi-N	1	3	.250	17	4	0	0	0	51	50	32	5	0	22	33	12.7	5.29	75	.253	.327	1	.083	-1	-7	-8	-0	-0.6
1994	Phi-N	2	4	.333	12	8	0	0	0	50^1	61	31	7	0	20	29	14.5	5.01	86	.310	.373	2	.167	0	-4	-4	0	-0.4
1995	Phi-N	3	3	.500	33	8	0	0	0	87^2	78	37	10	3	29	57	11.3	3.29	129	.239	.306	2	.125	-0	9	9	1	0.6
1996	Phi-N	6	14	.300	32	29	0	0	0	167	188	107	25	6	67	103	14.1	5.44	79	.290	.362	8	.157	-1	-23	-20	3	-1.9
1997	KC-A	0	2	.000	10	0	0	0	1	14	20	11	1	1	8	10	18.6	6.43	73	.333	.420	0	—	0	-3	-3	-0	-0.4
1998	Pit-N	4	2	.667	37	1	0	0	0	51	39	12	1	0	16	59	9.7	1.94	221	.211	.274	0	.000	-0	13	13	1	1.5
1999	Pit-N	3	4	.429	58	0	0	0	23	58^1	63	36	9	1	37	76	15.6	5.09	90	.276	.380	0	.000	-0	-3	-3	1	-0.5
2000	Pit-N	3	4	.429	72	0	0	0	24	72	56	34	8	4	40	71	12.5	3.50	131	.218	.332	0	.000	-0	9	9	1	1.3
Total	9	23	37	.383	276	55	1	0	48	580	584	320	69	15	246	443	13.1	4.50	96	.264	.342	17	.159	-1	-15	-13	6	-0.7

● MITCH WILLIAMS
Williams, Mitchell Steven "Wild Thing" b: 11/17/64, Santa Ana, Cal. BL/TL, 6'4", 205 lbs. Deb: 4/9/86

YEAR	TM/L	W	L	PCT	G	GS	CG	SH	SV	IP	H	R	HR	HB	BB	SO	RAT	ERA	ERA+	OAV	OOB	BH	AVG	PB	PR	PR+	PD	TPI
1986	Tex-A	8	6	.571	**80**	0	0	0	8	98	69	39	8	11	79	90	14.6	3.58	120	.202	.369	0	—	0	7	8	-1	1.0
1987	Tex-A	8	6	.571	85	1	0	0	6	108^2	63	47	9	7	94	129	13.6	3.23	139	.175	.355	0	—	0	15	15	1	1.9
1988	Tex-A	2	7	.222	67	0	0	0	18	68	48	38	4	6	47	61	13.4	4.63	88	.203	.349	0	—	0	-5	-4	0	-0.6
1989	*Chi-N★	4	4	.500	**76**	0	0	0	36	81^2	71	27	6	8	52	67	14.4	2.76	137	.238	.366	1	.200	1	7	9	-1	1.6
1990	Chi-N	1	8	.111	59	2	0	0	16	66^1	60	38	4	1	50	55	15.1	3.93	104	.239	.368	0	.000	-1	-1	1	-1	0.0
1991	Phi-N	12	5	.706	69	0	0	0	30	88^1	56	24	4	8	62	84	12.8	2.34	157	.182	.333	0	.000	0	13	13	-1	2.7
1992	Phi-N	5	8	.385	66	0	0	0	29	81	69	39	4	6	64	74	15.4	3.78	93	.240	.389	1	.250	0	-2	-3	-1	-0.6
1993	*Phi-N	3	7	.300	65	0	0	0	43	62	56	30	3	2	44	60	14.8	3.34	119	.245	.371	1	1.000	0	5	4	-1	0.8
1994	Hou-N	1	4	.200	25	0	0	0	6	20	21	17	4	1	24	21	20.7	7.65	52	.269	.447	0	—	0	-8	-9	-0	-1.7
1995	Cal-A	1	2	.333	20	0	0	0	0	10^2	13	10	1	2	21	9	30.4	6.75	70	.317	.563	0	—	0	-2	-2	0	-0.5
1997	KC-A	0	1	.000	7	0	0	0	0	6^2	11	8	2	0	7	10	24.3	10.80	44	.367	.486	0	—	0	-5	-4	-0	-0.6
Total	11	45	58	.437	619	3	0	0	192	691^1	537	317	49	52	544	660	14.7	3.65	110	.218	.371	3	.188	1	23	29	-6	4.0

● STEAMBOAT WILLIAMS
Williams, Rees Gephardt b: 1/31/1892, Cascade, Mont. d: 6/29/79, Deer River, Minn. BL/TR, 5'11", 170 lbs. Deb: 7/12/14

YEAR	TM/L	W	L	PCT	G	GS	CG	SH	SV	IP	H	R	HR	HB	BB	SO	RAT	ERA	ERA+	OAV	OOB	BH	AVG	PB	PR	PR+	PD	TPI
1914	StL-N	0	1	.000	5	1	0	0	0	11	13	8	1	0	6	2	15.5	6.55	43	.295	.380	0	.000	-0	-5	-5	-0	-0.4
1916	StL-N	6	7	.462	36	8	5	0	1	105	121	63	6	1	27	25	12.8	4.20	63	.291	.336	5	.208	1	-18	-18	-0	-2.2
Total	2	6	8	.429	41	9	5	0	1	116	134	71	7	1	33	27	13.0	4.42	60	.291	.340	5	.200	1	-23	-23	-0	-2.6

● RICK WILLIAMS
Williams, Richard Allen b: 11/9/52, Merced, Cal. BR/TR, 6'1", 180 lbs. Deb: 6/12/78

YEAR	TM/L	W	L	PCT	G	GS	CG	SH	SV	IP	H	R	HR	HB	BB	SO	RAT	ERA	ERA+	OAV	OOB	BH	AVG	PB	PR	PR+	PD	TPI
1978	Hou-N	1	2	.333	17	1	0	0	0	34^2	43	19	2	0	10	17	13.8	4.67	71	.301	.346	0	.000	-1	-4	-6	0	-0.5
1979	Hou-N	4	7	.364	31	16	2	2	0	121^1	122	45	6	2	30	37	11.4	3.26	108	.261	.308	8	.258	3	6	4	0	0.6
Total	2	5	9	.357	48	17	2	2	0	156	165	64	8	2	40	54	11.9	3.58	97	.270	.317	8	.222	2	2	-2	1	0.1

YEAR	TM/L	W	L	PCT	G	GS	CG	SH	SV	IP	H	R	HR	HB	BB	SO	RAT	ERA	ERA+	OAV	OOB	BH	AVG	PB	PR	PR+	PD	TPI
● **ACE WILLIAMS**	Williams, Robert Fulton b: 3/18/17, Montclair, N.J. d: 9/16/99, Fort Myers, Fla. BR/TL, 6'2", 174 lbs. Deb: 7/15/40																											
1940	Bos-N	0	0	—	5	0	0	0	0	9	21	17	0	1	12	5	34.0	16.00	23	.375	.493	0	.000	-0	-12	-13	0	-0.6
1946	Bos-N	0	0	—	1	0	0	0	0	0	1	0	0	1	—	—	—	—	1.000	1.000	101	—	0	0	0	0	0.0	
Total	2	0	0	—	6	0	0	0	0	9	22	17	0	1	13	5	36.0	16.00	23	.386	.507	0	.000	-0	-12	-13	0	-0.6
● **SHAD WILLIAMS**	Williams, Shad Clayton b: 3/10/71, Fresno, Cal. BR/TR, 6', 198 lbs. Deb: 5/18/96																											
1996	Cal-A	0	2	.000	13	2	0	0	0	28^1	42	34	7	2	21	26	20.6	8.89	56	.341	.445	0	—	0	-12	-12	-1	-0.8
1997	Ana-A	0	0	—	1	0	0	0	0	1	1	0	0	0	1	0	18.0	0.00	—	.250	.400	0	—	0	1	1	0	0.0
Total	2	0	2	.000	14	2	0	0	0	29^1	43	34	7	2	22	26	20.6	8.59	58	.339	.444	0	—	0	-12	-12	-1	-0.8
● **STAN WILLIAMS**	Williams, Stanley Wilson b: 9/14/36, Enfield, N.H. BR/TR, 6'5", 230 lbs. Deb: 5/17/58 C																											
1958	LA-N	9	7	.563	27	21	3	2	0	119	99	58	10	7	65	80	12.9	4.01	102	.228	.338	2	.050	-3	-1	1	0	-0.1
1959	*LA-N	5	5	.500	35	15	2	0	0	124^2	102	64	12	9	86	89	14.2	3.97	106	.228	.363	7	.194	1	-0	3	0	0.3
1960	LA-N★	14	10	.583	38	30	9	2	1	207^1	162	84	26	5	72	175	10.4	3.00	133	.210	.282	9	.141	0	18	21	1	2.5
1961	LA-N	15	12	.556	41	35	6	2	0	235^1	213	114	21	6	108	205	12.5	3.90	111	.242	.329	13	.167	-1	3	11	-1	1.0
1962	LA-N	14	12	.538	40	28	4	1	1	185^2	184	104	16	0	98	108	13.7	4.46	81	.253	.341	5	.076	-2	-11	-19	-1	-2.6
1963	*NY-A	9	8	.529	29	21	6	1	0	146	137	59	7	6	57	98	12.3	3.21	110	.249	.326	5	.102	-1	7	5	1	0.5
1964	NY-A	1	5	.167	21	10	1	0	0	82	76	39	7	0	38	54	12.5	3.84	94	.248	.330	3	.143	-0	-2	-2	1	-0.1
1965	Cle-A	0	0	—	3	0	0	0	0	4^1	6	4	1	0	3	1	18.7	6.23	56	.353	.450	0	—	0	-1	-1	0	-0.1
1967	Cle-A	6	4	.600	16	8	2	1	1	79	64	26	6	1	24	75	10.1	2.62	125	.218	.279	2	.091	-1	5	6	-2	0.4
1968	Cle-A	13	11	.542	44	24	6	2	9	194^1	163	64	14	10	51	147	10.4	2.50	118	.225	.285	9	.161	1	10	10	-1	1.5
1969	Cle-A	6	14	.300	61	15	3	0	12	178^1	155	86	25	12	67	139	11.8	3.94	96	.235	.317	4	.100	-1	-6	-3	-1	-0.5
1970	*Min-A	10	1	.909	68	0	0	0	15	113^1	85	34	8	5	32	76	9.7	1.99	188	.208	.274	0	.000	-2	22	22	-2	2.2
1971	Min-A	4	5	.444	46	1	0	0	4	78	63	44	7	8	44	47	13.3	4.15	86	.220	.340	0	.000	-1	-6	-5	-1	-0.8
	StL-N	3	0	1.000	10	0	0	0	0	12^2	13	2	0	2	2	8	12.1	1.42	254	.265	.321	0	.000	-0	3	3	0	0.7
1972	Bos-A	0	0	—	3	0	0	0	0	4^1	5	3	0	0	1	3	12.5	6.23	52	.294	.333	0	—	0	-2	-1	0	-0.1
Total	14	109	94	.537	482	208	42	11	43	1764^1	1527	785	160	71	748	1305	12.0	3.48	108	.232	.317	59	.118	-10	40	52	-4	4.8
● **TED WILLIAMS**	Williams, Theodore Samuel "The Kid', "The Thumper" or "The Splendid Splinter" b: 8/30/18, San Diego, Cal. BL/TR, 6'3", 205 lbs. Deb: 4/20/39 MH ♦																											
1940	Bos-A★	0	0	—	1	0	0	0	0	2	3	1	0	0	0	1	13.5	4.50	100	.333	.333	193	.344	1	-0	-0	0	0.0
● **TOM WILLIAMS**	Williams, Thomas C. b: 8/19/1870, Minersville, Ohio d: 7/27/40, Columbus, Ohio Deb: 5/1/1892																											
1892	Cle-N	1	0	1.000	2	1	1	0	0	9	9	4	1	0	1	3	10.0	3.00	113	.250	.270	1	.100	-1	0	0	-0	0.0
1893	Cle-N	1	1	.500	5	2	2	0	0	24	33	18	1	1	10	6	16.5	4.88	100	.317	.383	5	.278	0	-1	0	0	0.0
Total	2	2	1	.667	7	3	3	0	0	33	42	22	2	1	11	9	14.7	4.36	102	.300	.355	6	.214	-0	-0	0	-0	0.0
● **TODD WILLIAMS**	Williams, Todd Michael b: 2/13/71, Syracuse, N.Y. BR/TR, 6'3", 185 lbs. Deb: 4/29/95																											
1995	LA-N	2	2	.500	16	0	0	0	0	19^1	19	11	3	0	7	8	12.1	5.12	74	.264	.329	1	.500	0	-2	-3	1	-0.5
1998	Cin-N	0	1	.000	6	0	0	0	0	9^1	15	8	1	0	6	4	20.3	7.71	56	.341	.420	0	.000	-0	-4	-4	-0	-0.4
1999	Sea-A	0	0	—	13	0	0	0	0	9^2	11	5	1	1	7	7	17.7	4.66	102	.289	.413	0	—	0	0	0	-0	0.0
Total	3	2	3	.400	35	0	0	0	0	38^1	45	24	5	1	20	19	15.5	5.63	74	.292	.377	1	.250	0	-5	-7	0	-0.9
● **POP WILLIAMS**	Williams, Walter Merrill b: 5/19/1874, Bowdoinham, Me. d: 8/4/59, Topsham, Maine BL/TR, 5'11", 190 lbs. Deb: 9/14/1898																											
1898	Was-N	0	2	.000	2	2	2	0	0	17	32	18	0	0	7	3	20.6	8.47	43	.395	.443	3	.375	1	-9	-9	-1	-0.7
1902	Chi-N	11	16	.407	32	32	27	1	0	263^1	267	112	1	10	63	99	11.6	2.49	108	.263	.312	25	.208	3	8	6	3	1.3
1903	Chi-N	0	1	.000	1	1	1	0	0	5	9	3	0	0	0	2	16.2	5.40	58	.409	.409	0	.000	0	-1	-1	-0	-0.2
	Phi-N	1	1	.500	2	2	2	0	0	18	21	11	0	1	6	8	14.0	3.00	109	.304	.368	2	.286	0	1	1	1	0.2
	Bos-N	4	5	.444	10	10	9	1	0	83	97	60	3	9	37	20	15.5	4.12	78	.295	.381	10	.238	-0	-8	-9	-1	-0.8
	Yr	5	7	.417	13	13	12	1	0	106	127	74	3	10	43	30	15.3	3.99	81	.302	.381	12	.235	0	-8	-9	0	-0.8
Total	3	16	25	.390	47	47	41	2	0	386^1	426	204	4	20	113	132	13.0	3.17	91	.281	.339	40	.223	5	-9	-13	2	-0.2
● **WASH WILLIAMS**	Williams, Washington J. b: Philadelphia, Pa. d: 1/1890, Philadelphia, Pa. 5'11", 180 lbs. Deb: 8/5/1884 ♦																											
1885	Chi-N	0	0	—	1	1	0	0	0	2	2	5	0		5	0	31.5	13.50	22	.400	.700	1	.250	-0	-2	-2	0	-0.1
● **NED WILLIAMSON**	Williamson, Edward Nagle b: 10/24/1857, Philadelphia, Pa. d: 3/3/1894, Mountain Valley Springs, Ark BR/TR, 5'11", 210 lbs. Deb: 5/1/1878 ♦																											
1881	Chi-N	1	1	.500	3	1	1	0	0	18	14	9	0		0	2	7.0	2.00	137	.209	.209	92	.268	1	2	1	-0	0.1
1882	Chi-N	0	0	—	1	0	0	0	0	3	9	8	1		1	0	30.0	6.00	48	.500	.526	98	.282	0	-1	-1	0	0.0
1883	Chi-N	0	0	—	1	0	0	0	0	1	1	2	0		1	1	18.0	9.00	37	.167	.286	111	.276	0	-1	-1	0	0.0
1884	Chi-N	0	0	—	2	0	0	0	0	2	8	8	0		2	0	45.0	18.00	17	.500	.556	116	.278	1	-3	-3	0	-0.1
1885	*Chi-N	0	0	—	2	0	0	0	**2**	6	2	2	0		0	3	3.0	0.00	—	.080	.080	97	.238	0	2	2	0	0.2
1886	*Chi-N	0	0	—	2	0	0	0	1	3	2	2	0		0	1	6.0	0.00	—	.143	.143	93	.216	0	1	1	-0	0.1
1887	Chi-N	0	0	—	1	0	0	0	0	2	3	2	0	0	1	0	13.5	9.00	50	.300	.300	190	.371	0	-1	-1	0	0.0
Total	7	1	1	.500	12	1	1	0	3	35	39	31	1	0	5	7	11.1	3.34	90	.250	.269	1232	.266	3	-2	-1	0	0.3
● **MARK WILLIAMSON**	Williamson, Mark Alan b: 7/21/59, Corpus Christi, Tex. BR/TR, 6', 172 lbs. Deb: 4/8/87																											
1987	Bal-A	8	9	.471	61	2	0	0	3	125	122	59	12	3	41	73	12.0	4.03	109	.261	.324	0	—	0	6	5	1	0.7
1988	Bal-A	5	8	.385	37	10	2	0	2	117^2	125	70	14	2	40	69	12.8	4.90	80	.272	.333	0	—	0	-12	-13	-0	-1.3
1989	Bal-A	10	5	.667	65	0	0	0	9	107^1	105	35	4	2	30	55	11.5	2.93	130	.261	.315	0	—	0	11	11	-1	1.4
1990	Bal-A	8	2	.800	49	0	0	0	1	85^1	65	25	8	0	28	60	9.8	2.21	172	.215	.282	0	—	0	16	16	1	1.9
1991	Bal-A	5	5	.500	65	0	0	0	4	80^1	87	42	9	0	35	53	13.7	4.48	88	.275	.348	0	—	0	-3	-5	-0	-0.6
1992	Bal-A	0	0	—	12	0	0	0	1	18^2	16	3	1	0	10	14	12.5	0.96	418	.239	.338	0	—	0	6	6	-1	0.3
1993	Bal-A	7	5	.583	48	1	0	0	0	88	106	54	5	0	25	45	13.4	4.91	91	.304	.350	0	—	0	-6	-4	-0	-0.5
1994	Bal-A	3	1	.750	28	2	0	0	1	67^1	75	33	9	2	17	28	12.6	4.01	125	.278	.325	0	—	0	6	7	-1	0.3
Total	8	46	35	.568	365	15	2	0	21	689^2	701	321	62	9	226	397	12.2	3.86	108	.266	.326	0	—	0	25	23	-1	2.2
● **SCOTT WILLIAMSON**	Williamson, Scott Ryan b: 2/17/76, Fort Polk, La. BR/TR, 6', 185 lbs. Deb: 4/5/99																											
1999	Cin-N☆	12	7	.632	62	0	0	0	19	93^1	54	29	8	1	43	107	9.5	2.41	193	.171	.273	0	.000	-1	22	23	-1	4.3
2000	Cin-N	5	8	.385	48	10	0	0	6	112	92	45	7	3	75	136	13.7	3.29	145	.224	.348	1	.063	-1	17	18	-1	1.8
Total	2	17	15	.531	110	10	0	0	25	205^1	146	74	15	4	118	243	11.7	2.89	163	.201	.316	1	.043	-1	39	41	-1	6.1
● **AL WILLIAMSON**	Williamson, Silas Albert b: 2/20/1900, Buckville, Ark. d: 11/29/78, Hot Springs, Ark. BR/TR, 5'11", 160 lbs. Deb: 4/27/28																											
1928	Chi-A	0	0	—	1	0	0	0	0	2	1	0	0	0	0	0	4.5	0.00	—	.167	.167	0	—	0	1	1	0	0.0
● **CARL WILLIS**	Willis, Carl Blake b: 12/28/60, Danville, Va. BL/TR, 6'4", 213 lbs. Deb: 6/9/84																											
1984	Det-A	0	2	.000	10	2	0	0	0	16	25	13	1	0	5	4	16.9	7.31	54	.362	.405	0	—	0	-6	-6	0	-0.7
	Cin-N	0	1	.000	7	0	0	0	1	9^2	8	4	1	0	2	3	9.3	3.72	102	.222	.263	0	—	0	-0	0	0	0.0
1985	Cin-N	1	0	1.000	11	0	0	0	1	13^2	21	18	3	0	5	6	17.1	9.22	41	.344	.394	0	.000	0	-9	-8	-0	-0.7
1986	Cin-N	1	3	.250	29	0	0	0	0	52^1	54	29	4	1	32	24	15.0	4.47	87	.278	.383	1	.333	0	-4	-3	1	-0.1
1988	Chi-A	0	0	—	6	0	0	0	0	12	17	12	3	0	7	6	18.0	8.25	48	.362	.444	0	—	0	-6	-6	-0	-0.3
1991	*Min-A	8	3	.727	40	0	0	0	2	89	76	31	4	1	19	53	9.7	2.63	163	.232	.276	0	—	0	15	16	-1	1.7
1992	Min-A	7	3	.700	59	0	0	0	1	79^1	73	25	4	0	11	45	9.5	2.72	149	.246	.273	0	—	0	11	11	-1	1.3
1993	Min-A	3	0	1.000	53	0	0	0	5	58	56	23	2	0	17	44	11.3	3.10	141	.259	.313	0	—	0	8	8	-0	0.4
1994	Min-A	2	4	.333	49	0	0	0	3	59^1	89	48	6	0	12	37	15.3	5.92	82	.335	.363	0	—	0	-7	-7	-1	-0.7
1995	Min-A	0	0	—	3	0	0	0	0	0^2	5	7	0	0	5	0	135.0	94.50	5	.833	.909	0	—	0	-7	-7	0	-0.3
Total	9	22	16	.579	267	2	0	0	13	390	424	210	28	2	115	222	12.5	4.25	100	.279	.330	1	.250	0	-5	-0	-3	0.6
● **LEFTY WILLIS**	Willis, Charles William b: 11/4/05, Leetown, W.Va. d: 5/10/62, Bethesda, Md. BL/TL, 6'1", 175 lbs. Deb: 10/3/25																											
1925	Phi-A	0	0	—	1	1	0	0	0	5	9	7	2	0	2	3	19.8	10.80	43	.409	.458	0	.000	-1	-4	-3	0	-0.2
1926	Phi-A	0	0	—	13	1	0	0	1	32^1	31	9	0	1	12	13	12.2	1.39	300	.270	.344	2	.222	-0	9	10	-0	0.4

YEAR TM/L	W	L	PCT	G	GS	CG	SH	SV	IP	H	R	HR	HB	BB	SO	RAT	ERA	ERA+	OAV	OOB	BH	AVG	PB	PR	PR+	PD	TPI
1927 Phi-A	3	1	.750	15	2	1	0	0	27	32	18	2	0	11	7	14.3	5.67	75	.308	.374	0	.000	-1	-5	-4	1	-0.5
Total 3	3	1	.750	29	4	1	0	1	64^1	72	34	4	1	25	23	13.7	3.92	108	.299	.367	2	.111	-1	1	2	1	-0.3
● DALE WILLIS Willis, Dale Jerome b: 5/29/38, Calhoun, Ga. BR/TR, 5'11", 165 lbs. Deb: 4/14/63																											
1963 KC-A	0	2	.000	25	0	0	0	1	44^2	46	28	3	4	25	47	15.1	5.04	77	.266	.371	1	.167	-0	-7	-5	1	-0.2
● JIM WILLIS Willis, James Gladden b: 3/20/27, Doyline, La. BL/TR, 6'3", 175 lbs. Deb: 4/22/53																											
1953 Chi-N	2	1	.667	13	3	2	0	0	43^1	37	15	1	3	17	15	11.8	3.12	143	.228	.313	0	.000	-1	6	6	1	0.4
1954 Chi-N	0	1	.000	14	1	0	0	0	23	22	10	1	3	18	5	16.8	3.91	107	.256	.402	0	.000	-1	0	1	1	0.0
Total 2	2	2	.500	27	4	2	0	0	66^1	59	25	2	6	35	20	13.6	3.39	129	.238	.346	0	.000	-2	6	7	2	0.4
● JOE WILLIS Willis, Joseph Denk b: 4/9/1890, Coal Grove, Ohio d: 12/4/66, Ironton, Ohio BR/TL, 6'1", 185 lbs. Deb: 5/3/11																											
1911 StL-A	0	1	.000	1	1	0	0	0	7	8	5	0	0	3	0	14.1	5.14	66	.308	.379	0	.000	0	-1	-1	-1	-0.2
StL-N	0	1	.000	2	2	1	0	0	15	13	9	0	0	4	5	10.2	4.20	80	.232	.283	0	.000	-1	-1	-1	0	-0.1
1912 StL-N	4	9	.308	31	17	4	0	2	129^2	143	83	3	5	62	55	14.6	4.44	77	.288	.372	6	.158	-2	-15	-15	-1	-1.5
1913 StL-N	0	0	—	7	0	0	0	1	9^2	9	9	0	0	11	6	18.6	7.45	43	.257	.435	0	.000	-0	-5	-4	-0	-0.3
Total 3	4	11	.267	41	20	5	0	3	161^1	173	106	3	5	80	66	14.4	4.63	74	.282	.369	6	.125	-2	-22	-22	-1	-2.1
● LES WILLIS Willis, Lester Evans "Wimpy" or "Lefty" b: 1/17/08, Nacogdoches, Tex. d: 1/22/82, Jasper, Tex. BL/TL, 5'9.5", 195 lbs. Deb: 4/28/47																											
1947 Cle-A	0	2	.000	22	2	0	0	1	44	58	26	3	0	24	10	16.8	3.48	100	.324	.404	1	.091	-1	1	0	-1	-0.2
● MIKE WILLIS Willis, Michael Henry b: 12/26/50, Oklahoma City, Okla BL/TL, 6'2", 210 lbs. Deb: 4/13/77																											
1977 Tor-A	2	6	.250	43	3	0	0	5	107^1	105	48	15	0	38	59	12.0	3.94	107	.260	.324	0	—	0	2	3	1	0.3
1978 Tor-A	3	7	.300	44	2	1	0	7	100^2	104	55	11	0	39	52	12.8	4.56	86	.271	.338	0	—	0	-9	-7	0	-0.7
1979 Tor-A	0	3	.000	17	1	0	0	0	26^2	35	27	1	1	16	8	17.6	8.44	52	.333	.426	0	—	0	-12	-12	0	-1.1
1980 Tor-A	2	1	.667	20	0	0	0	3	26^1	25	6	3	1	11	14	12.6	1.71	252	.248	.327	0	—	0	7	7	0	0.9
1981 Tor-A	0	4	.000	20	0	0	0	0	35	43	25	6	1	20	16	16.5	5.91	67	.301	.390	0	—	0	-9	-7	0	-0.7
Total 5	7	21	.250	144	6	1	0	15	296	312	161	36	3	124	149	13.3	4.59	90	.274	.347	0	—	0	-22	-15	1	-1.3
● RON WILLIS Willis, Ronald Earl b: 7/12/43, Willisville, Tenn. d: 11/21/77, Memphis, Tenn. BR/TR, 6'2", 195 lbs. Deb: 9/20/66																											
1966 StL-N	0	0	—	4	0	0	0	1	3	1	0	0	0	1	2	6.0	0.00	—	.100	.182	0	—	0	1	1	-0	0.1
1967 *StL-N	6	5	.545	65	0	0	0	10	81	76	27	3	3	43	42	13.6	2.67	123	.257	.357	3	.375	1	6	6	2	1.3
1968 *StL-N	2	3	.400	48	0	0	0	4	63^2	50	25	4	1	28	39	11.2	3.39	85	.213	.299	0	.000	-1	-3	-4	1	-0.4
1969 StL-N	1	2	.333	26	0	0	0	0	32^1	26	16	4	1	19	23	12.8	4.18	86	.224	.338	1	1.000	0	-2	-2	1	0.0
Hou-N	0	0	—	3	0	0	0	0	2^1	3	0	0	0	0	2	11.6	0.00	—	.300	.300	0	—	0	1	1	-0	0.0
Yr	1	2	.333	29	0	0	0	0	34^2	29	16	4	1	19	25	12.7	3.89	92	.230	.336	1	1.000	0	-1	-1	1	0.0
1970 SD-N	2	2	.500	42	0	0	0	4	56	53	33	4	4	28	20	13.7	4.02	99	.247	.344	0	.000	-1	0	-0	1	0.1
Total 5	11	12	.478	188	0	0	0	19	238^1	209	101	15	9	119	128	12.7	3.32	102	.237	.334	4	.160	0	4	2	5	1.1
● VIC WILLIS Willis, Victor Gazaway b: 4/12/1876, Cecil Co., Md. d: 8/3/47, Elkton, Md. BR/TR, 6'2", 185 lbs. Deb: 4/20/1898 H																											
1898 Bos-N	25	13	.658	41	38	29	1	0	311	264	143	5	29	148	160	12.8	2.84	130	.228	.331	17	.145	-6	27	29	-0	2.5
1899 Bos-N	27	8	.771	41	38	35	**5**	2	342^2	277	126	6	30	117	120	11.1	2.50	**167**	**.221**	.303	29	.216	-4	52	**59**	0	4.9
1900 Bos-N	10	17	.370	32	29	22	2	0	236	258	157	11	12	106	53	14.3	4.19	98	.277	.359	12	.136	-6	-13	-2	-2	-0.8
1901 Bos-N	20	17	.541	38	35	33	**6**	0	305^1	262	111	6	11	78	133	10.3	2.36	**153**	.230	.286	20	.187	-1	33	**39**	-1	4.2
1902 Bos-N	27	20	.574	**51**	46	**45**	4	**3**	**410**	372	142	6	14	101	**225**	10.7	2.20	129	.242	.295	23	.153	-6	27	28	4	3.1
1903 Bos-N	12	18	.400	33	32	29	2	0	278	256	121	3	10	88	125	11.5	2.98	108	.251	.317	24	.188	-1	9	7	3	0.8
1904 Bos-N	18	25	.419	43	43	**39**	2	0	350	357	174	7	14	109	196	12.3	2.85	97	.266	.327	27	.182	1	-4	-4	7	0.4
1905 Bos-N	12	29	.293	41	41	36	4	0	342	340	174	7	13	107	149	12.1	3.21	97	.265	.328	20	.153	-3	-8	-4	6	-0.1
1906 Pit-N	23	13	.639	41	36	32	6	1	322	295	84	0	5	76	124	10.5	1.73	154	.250	.298	20	.174	-1	32	33	5	4.5
1907 Pit-N	21	11	.656	39	37	27	6	1	292^2	234	96	4	7	69	107	9.5	2.34	104	.219	.271	14	.136	-2	4	3	2	0.3
1908 Pit-N	23	11	.676	41	38	25	7	0	304^2	239	95	2	6	69	97	9.3	2.07	111	.213	.262	17	.165	-1	10	8	-1	0.7
1909 *Pit-N	22	11	.667	39	35	24	4	1	289^2	243	84	3	4	83	95	10.3	2.24	122	.231	.289	14	.136	-2	12	15	1	1.5
1910 StL-N	9	12	.429	33	23	12	1	1	212	224	113	6	1	61	67	12.1	3.35	89	.275	.326	11	.167	-2	-8	-9	2	-0.8
Total 13	249	205	.548	513	471	388	50	11	3996	3621	1620	66	156	1212	1651	11.2	2.63	118	.243	.307	248	.166	-33	172	202	27	21.2
● CLAUDE WILLOUGHBY Willoughby, Claude William "Flunky" or "Weeping Willie" b: 11/14/1898, Buffalo, Kan. d: 8/14/73, McPherson, Kan. BR/TR, 5'9.5", 165 lbs. Deb: 9/18/25																											
1925 Phi-N	2	1	.667	3	3	1	0	0	23	26	7	0	1	11	6	14.9	1.96	244	.295	.380	0	.000	-1	6	6	-1	0.6
1926 Phi-N	8	12	.400	47	19	6	0	1	168	218	125	7	5	71	37	15.8	5.95	70	.327	.396	11	.212	-1	-40	-31	3	-3.0
1927 Phi-N	3	7	.300	35	6	1	1	2	97^2	126	83	7	2	53	14	16.7	6.54	63	.321	.404	2	.077	-2	-28	-25	-1	-2.5
1928 Phi-N	6	5	.545	35	13	5	1	1	130^2	180	92	6	3	83	26	18.3	5.30	81	.340	.432	6	.150	-1	-19	-14	-1	-1.2
1929 Phi-N	15	14	.517	49	35	14	1	4	243^1	288	156	15	5	108	50	14.8	4.99	104	.296	.370	13	.143	-5	-7	5	4	0.5
1930 Phi-N	4	17	.190	41	24	5	1	1	153	241	147	17	2	68	38	18.3	7.59	72	.369	.430	5	.104	-4	-44	-33	2	-3.6
1931 Pit-N	0	2	.000	9	2	1	0	0	25^2	32	21	4	0	12	4	15.4	6.31	61	.305	.376	2	.286	0	-7	-7	0	-0.4
Total 7	38	58	.396	219	102	33	4	9	841^1	1111	631	56	18	406	175	16.4	5.84	81	.326	.401	39	.143	-14	-140	-98	8	-9.6
● JIM WILLOUGHBY Willoughby, James Arthur b: 1/31/49, Salinas, Cal. BR/TR, 6'2", 185 lbs. Deb: 9/5/71																											
1971 SF-N	0	1	.000	2	1	0	0	0	4	8	4	0	0	1	3	20.3	9.00	38	.400	.429	0	.000	-0	-2	-3	0	-0.5
1972 SF-N	6	4	.600	11	11	7	0	0	87^2	72	25	8	2	14	40	9.0	2.36	148	.222	.259	5	.185	0	11	11	0	1.3
1973 SF-N	4	5	.444	39	12	1	1	0	123	138	74	21	3	37	60	13.0	4.68	82	.295	.350	4	.143	1	-14	-11	-1	-0.8
1974 SF-N	1	4	.200	18	4	0	0	0	40^2	51	27	7	0	9	12	13.3	4.65	82	.304	.339	1	.100	-0	-5	-4	1	-0.3
1975 *Bos-A	5	2	.714	24	0	0	0	8	48^1	46	25	6	2	16	29	11.9	3.54	115	.247	.314	0	—	0	1	3	0	0.5
1976 Bos-A	3	12	.200	54	0	0	0	10	99	94	38	4	8	31	37	12.1	2.82	139	.256	.328	0	.000	-0	8	11	1	2.0
1977 Bos-A	6	2	.750	31	0	0	0	2	54^2	54	32	5	2	18	33	12.2	4.94	91	.258	.323	0	—	0	-5	-2	1	-0.2
1978 Chi-A	1	6	.143	59	0	0	0	13	93^1	95	41	6	4	19	36	11.4	3.86	99	.275	.320	0	—	0	-1	-0	2	0.1
Total 8	26	36	.419	238	28	8	1	34	550^2	558	266	57	21	145	250	11.8	3.79	102	.267	.321	10	.149	1	-7	5	5	2.1
● FRANK WILLS Wills, Frank Lee b: 10/26/58, New Orleans, La. BR/TR, 6'2", 202 lbs. Deb: 7/31/83																											
1983 KC-A	2	1	.667	6	4	0	0	0	34^2	35	17	2	0	15	23	13.0	4.15	98	.259	.333	0	—	0	-0	-0	-0	-0.1
1984 KC-A	2	3	.400	10	5	0	0	0	37	39	21	3	0	13	21	12.6	5.11	79	.271	.331	0	—	0	-5	-4	-1	-0.6
1985 Sea-A	5	11	.313	24	18	1	0	1	123	122	85	18	3	68	67	14.1	6.00	70	.266	.365	0	—	0	-25	-24	0	-2.6
1986 Cle-A	4	4	.500	26	0	0	0	4	40^1	43	23	6	0	16	32	13.2	4.91	85	.272	.339	0	—	0	-3	-3	0	-0.6
1987 Cle-A	0	1	.000	6	0	0	0	0	5^1	3	3	0	1	7	4	16.9	5.06	90	.176	.417	0	—	0	-0	-0	0	0.0
1988 Tor-A	0	0	—	10	0	0	0	0	20^2	22	12	2	0	6	19	12.2	5.23	75	.272	.322	0	—	0	-3	-3	1	-0.1
1989 Tor-A	3	1	.750	24	4	0	0	0	71^1	65	31	4	1	30	41	12.1	3.66	103	.242	.320	0	—	0	2	1	-0	0.0
1990 Tor-A	6	4	.600	44	4	0	0	0	99	101	54	13	1	38	72	12.7	4.73	84	.266	.334	0	—	0	-9	-8	0	-0.8
1991 Tor-A	0	1	.000	4	0	0	0	0	4^1	8	8	2	1	5	2	29.1	16.62	25	.421	.560	0	—	0	-6	-6	0	-1.0
Total 9	22	26	.458	154	35	1	0	6	435^2	438	254	50	6	198	281	13.3	5.06	80	.264	.344	0	—	0	-50	-49	0	-5.8
● TED WILLS Wills, Theodore Carl b: 2/9/34, Fresno, Cal. BL/TL, 6'2", 200 lbs. Deb: 5/24/59																											
1959 Bos-A	2	6	.250	9	8	2	0	0	56^1	68	35	9	1	24	24	14.9	5.27	77	.302	.372	4	.250	1	-9	-7	-0	-0.8
1960 Bos-A	1	1	.500	15	0	0	0	1	30^1	38	26	4	3	16	28	16.9	7.42	55	.317	.410	2	.250	1	-12	-11	1	-0.6
1961 Bos-A	3	2	.600	17	0	0	0	0	19^2	24	17	2	0	19	11	19.7	5.95	70	.304	.439	0	.000	-0	-4	-4	0	-0.7
1962 Bos-A	0	0	—	1	0	0	0	0	0	2	0	0	1	—	—	∞	—	1.000	1.000	104	—	0	-1	-1	0	-0.1	
Cin-N	0	2	.000	26	5	0	0	3	61	61	36	12	5	23	58	13.1	5.31	76	.266	.346	5	.313	1	-9	-9	-0	-0.3
1965 Chi-A	2	0	1.000	15	0	0	0	1	19	17	8	2	1	14	12	15.2	2.84	112	.258	.395	0	.000	0	1	1	0	0.1
Total 5	8	11	.421	83	13	2	0	5	186^1	210	123	29	10	97	133	15.3	5.51	72	.291	.383	11	.250	3	-34	-31	1	-2.4
● PAUL WILMET Wilmet, Paul Richard b: 11/8/58, Green Bay, Wis. BR/TR, 5'11", 170 lbs. Deb: 7/25/89																											
1989 Tex-A	0	0	—	3	0	0	0	0	2^1	5	4	0	0	2	1	27.0	15.43	26	.417	.500	0	—	0	-3	-3	0	-0.1

YEAR	TM/L	W	L	PCT	G	GS	CG	SH	SV	IP	H	R	HR	HB	BB	SO	RAT	ERA	ERA+	OAV	OOB	BH	AVG	PB	PR	PR+	PD	TPI
● WHITEY WILSHERE	Wilshere, Vernon Sprague b: 8/3/12, Poplar Ridge, N.Y. d: 5/23/85, Cooperstown, N.Y. BL/TL, 6', 180 lbs. Deb: 6/24/34																											
1934	Phi-A	0	1	.000	9	2	0	0	0	21^2	39	30	0	1	15	19	22.8	12.05	36	.394	.478	0	.000	-0	-18	-19	-1	-0.9
1935	Phi-A	9	9	.500	27	18	7	3	1	142^1	136	69	8	10	78	80	14.2	4.05	112	.253	.358	4	.093	-4	6	8	-0	0.5
1936	Phi-A	1	2	.333	5	3	0	0	0	18^1	21	17	1	0	19	4	19.6	6.87	74	.288	.435	0	.000	-0	-4	-4	-0	-0.5
Total	3	10	12	.455	41	23	7	3	1	182^1	196	116	9	11	112	103	15.7	5.28	87	.276	.383	4	.080	-4	-15	-14	-1	-0.9
● TERRY WILSHUSEN	Wilshusen, Terry Wayne b: 3/22/49, Atascadero, Cal. BR/TR, 6'2", 210 lbs. Deb: 4/7/73																											
1973	Cal-A	0	0	—	1	0	0	0	0	0^1	0	3	0	1	2	0	81.0	81.00	4	.000	.750	0	—	0	-3	-3	0	-0.1
● DON WILSON	Wilson, Donald Edward b: 2/12/45, Monroe, La. d: 1/5/75, Houston, Tex. BR/TR, 6'3", 205 lbs. Deb: 9/29/66																											
1966	Hou-N	1	0	1.000	1	0	0	0	0	6	5	2	1	0	1	7	9.0	3.00	114	.238	.273	1	.500	1	0	0	0	0.1
1967	Hou-N	10	9	.526	31	28	7	3	0	184	141	67	10	7	69	159	10.6	2.79	119	.209	.289	6	.091	-2	12	11	-2	0.7
1968	Hou-N	13	16	.448	33	30	9	3	0	208^2	187	85	9	4	70	175	11.3	3.28	90	.236	.302	15	.214	4	-7	-8	-2	-0.8
1969	Hou-N	16	12	.571	34	34	13	1	0	225	210	119	16	9	97	235	12.6	4.00	89	.245	.328	8	.099	-1	-10	-12	-0	-1.5
1970	Hou-N	11	6	.647	29	27	3	0	0	184^1	188	92	15	7	66	94	12.7	3.91	99	.259	.327	8	.116	-2	3	-0	-3	-0.5
1971	Hou-N★	16	10	.615	35	34	18	3	0	268	195	80	15	7	79	180	9.4	2.45	137	**.202**	.268	14	.154	-1	30	28	-3	2.3
1972	Hou-N	15	10	.600	33	33	13	3	0	228^1	196	79	16	2	66	172	10.4	2.68	126	.233	.290	8	.105	-2	20	18	1	1.8
1973	Hou-N	11	16	.407	37	32	10	3	2	239^1	187	94	21	7	92	149	10.8	3.20	114	.213	.293	14	.177	1	13	12	-2	1.2
1974	Hou-N	11	13	.458	33	27	5	4	0	204^2	170	80	16	4	100	112	12.0	3.08	113	.227	.321	13	.206	2	13	9	-3	1.0
Total	9	104	92	.531	266	245	78	20	2	1748^1	1479	698	119	47	640	1283	11.2	3.15	109	.228	.301	87	.146	-1	74	59	-14	4.3
● DUANE WILSON	Wilson, Duane Lewis b: 6/29/34, Wichita, Kan. BL/TL, 6'1", 185 lbs. Deb: 7/3/58																											
1958	Bos-A	0	0	—	2	2	0	0	0	6^1	10	5	0	0	7	3	24.2	5.68	70	.400	.531	0	.000	-0	-1	-1	0	-0.1
● FIN WILSON	Wilson, Finis Elbert b: 12/9/1889, East Fork, Ky. d: 3/9/59, Coral Gables, Fla. BL/TL, 6'1", 194 lbs. Deb: 9/26/14																											
1914	Bro-F	0	1	.000	2	1	1	0	0	7	7	7	0	0	11	4	23.1	7.71	37	.269	.486	1	.500	1	-4	-4	-0	-0.4
1915	Bro-F	1	8	.111	18	11	5	0	0	102^1	85	56	2	4	53	47	12.5	3.78	72	.249	.356	11	.314	2	-12	-12	0	-0.8
Total	2	1	9	.100	20	12	6	0	0	109^1	92	63	2	4	64	51	13.2	4.03	68	.250	.367	12	.324	3	-16	-16	-0	-1.2
● ZEKE WILSON	Wilson, Frank Ealton b: 12/24/1869, Benton, Ala. d: 4/26/28, Montgomery, Ala. BR/TR, 5'10", 165 lbs. Deb: 4/23/1895																											
1895	Bos-N	2	4	.333	6	6	4	0	0	45	54	48	1	0	27	5	16.2	5.20	98	.293	.384	6	.316	1	-2	-0	1	0.1
	Cle-N	3	1	.750	9	8	4	0	0	52^2	75	38	4	4	24	20	17.6	4.27	117	.329	.402	3	.136	-2	3	4	-0	0.0
	Yr	5	5	.500	15	14	8	0	0	97^2	129	86	5	4	51	25	17.0	4.70	107	.313	.394	9	.220	-2	1	3	1	0.1
1896	Cle-N	17	9	.654	33	29	20	1	1	240	265	150	9	8	81	56	13.3	4.01	113	.278	.339	27	.270	2	9	14	6	1.8
1897	Cle-N	16	11	.593	34	30	26	1	0	263^2	323	171	9	9	83	69	14.2	4.16	108	.299	.354	26	.224	-3	4	9	1	0.5
1898	Cle-N	13	18	.419	33	31	28	1	0	254^2	307	141	4	7	51	45	12.9	3.60	100	.296	.333	21	.178	-3	0	0	4	0.1
1899	StL-N	1	1	.500	5	2	2	0	0	26	30	18	0	2	4	3	12.5	4.50	88	.288	.327	0	.000	-1	-2	-1	1	-0.1
Total	5	52	44	.542	120	106	84	3	1	882	1054	566	27	30	270	198	13.8	4.03	106	.294	.348	83	.216	-8	13	25	14	2.4
● GARY WILSON	Wilson, Gary Morris b: 1/1/70, Arcata, Cal. BR/TR, 6'3", 190 lbs. Deb: 4/28/95																											
1995	Pit-N	0	1	.000	10	0	0	0	0	14^1	13	8	2	2	5	8	12.6	5.02	86	.241	.328	0	—	0	-1	-1	-0	-0.1
● GARY WILSON	Wilson, Gary Steven b: 11/21/54, Camden, Ark. BR/TR, 6'2", 185 lbs. Deb: 4/13/79																											
1979	Hou-N	0	0	—	6	0	0	0	0	7^1	15	11	2	0	6	6	25.8	12.27	29	.441	.525	0	—	0	-7	-8	-0	-0.4
● GLENN WILSON	Wilson, Glenn Dwight b: 12/22/58, Baytown, Tex. BR/TR, 6'1", 190 lbs. Deb: 4/15/82 ◆																											
1987	Phi-N	0	0	—	1	0	0	0	0	1	0	0	0	0	0	1	0.0	0.00	—	.000	.000	150	.264	0	0	0	0	0.0
● TEX WILSON	Wilson, Gomer Russell b: 7/8/01, Trenton, Tex. d: 9/15/46, Sulphur Springs, Tex. BR/TL, 5'10", 170 lbs. Deb: 9/2/24																											
1924	Bro-N	0	0	—	2	0	0	0	0	3^2	7	6	0	0	1	1	19.6	14.73	25	.412	.444	0	.000	-0	-4	-5	0	-0.2
● HIGHBALL WILSON	Wilson, Howard Paul b: 8/9/1878, Philadelphia, Pa. d: 10/16/34, Havre De Grace, Md TR, 5'9", 164 lbs. Deb: 9/13/1899																											
1899	Cle-N	0	1	.000	1	1	1	0	0	8	12	8	0	0	5	1	19.1	9.00	41	.343	.425	1	.333	0	-5	-5	-0	-0.4
1902	Phi-A	7	4	.636	13	10	8	0	0	96^1	103	44	1	9	19	18	12.2	2.43	151	.274	.324	6	.171	-1	12	13	-1	1.1
1903	Was-A	7	18	.280	30	28	25	1	0	242^1	269	123	7	10	43	56	12.0	3.31	95	.280	.318	17	.200	2	-9	-4	-4	-0.6
1904	Was-A	0	3	.000	3	3	3	0	0	25	33	17	0	2	4	11	14.0	4.68	57	.317	.355	2	.222	1	-6	-5	0	-0.5
Total	4	14	26	.350	47	42	37	1	0	371^2	417	192	8	21	71	86	12.3	3.29	99	.283	.325	26	.197	2	-7	-1	-5	-0.4
● JIM WILSON	Wilson, James Alger b: 2/20/22, San Diego, Cal. d: 9/2/86, Newport Beach, Cal BR/TR, 6'1.5", 200 lbs. Deb: 4/18/45																											
1945	Bos-A	6	8	.429	23	21	8	2	0	144^1	121	61	7	1	88	50	13.1	3.30	103	.228	.339	13	.245	2	1	2	-2	0.1
1946	Bos-A	0	0	—	1	0	0	0	0	0^2	2	2	1	0	0	0	27.0	27.00	14	.500	.500	0	—	0	-2	-2	-0	-0.1
1948	StL-A	0	0	—	4	0	0	0	0	2^2	5	4	0	0	5	1	33.8	13.50	34	.417	.588	0	—	0	-3	-2	0	-0.1
1949	Phi-A	0	0	—	2	0	0	0	0	5	7	8	2	0	5	2	21.6	14.40	29	.350	.480	0	.000	-0	-6	-6	-0	-0.3
1951	Bos-N	7	7	.500	20	15	5	0	1	110	131	67	14	4	40	33	14.3	5.40	68	.294	.357	7	.179	0	-18	-23	-1	-2.6
1952	Bos-N	12	14	.462	33	33	14	0	0	234	234	114	19	4	90	104	12.6	4.23	85	.262	.333	14	.163	-0	-13	-17	-1	-1.8
1953	Mil-N	4	9	.308	20	18	5	0	0	114	107	59	16	3	43	71	12.1	4.34	90	.243	.315	6	.167	1	-1	-6	1	-0.4
1954	Mil-N☆	8	2	.800	27	19	6	4	0	127^2	129	55	12	5	36	52	12.0	3.52	106	.266	.323	7	.159	0	8	3	1	0.3
1955	Bal-A☆	12	18	.400	34	31	14	4	0	235^1	200	104	17	4	87	96	11.1	3.44	111	.228	.300	15	.169	-2	14	10	-0	1.0
1956	Bal-A	4	2	.667	7	7	1	0	0	48^1	49	27	5	2	16	31	12.5	5.03	78	.268	.333	4	.267	2	-5	-6	0	-0.4
	Chi-A★	9	12	.429	28	21	6	3	0	159^2	149	82	15	2	70	82	12.5	4.06	101	.248	.329	19	.306	4	2	1	-0	0.5
	Yr	13	14	.481	35	28	7	3	0	208	198	109	20	4	86	113	12.5	4.28	95	.253	.330	23	.299	6	-3	-5	0	0.1
1957	Chi-A	15	8	.652	30	29	12	**5**	0	201^2	189	85	22	3	65	100	11.5	3.48	107	.249	.310	10	.147	-0	7	6	-2	0.4
1958	Chi-A	9	9	.500	28	23	4	1	1	155^2	156	75	21	1	63	70	12.7	4.10	89	.268	.341	4	.078	-3	-6	-8	-1	-1.3
Total	12	86	89	.491	257	217	75	19	2	1539	1479	743	151	29	608	692	12.4	4.01	93	.254	.327	99	.181	4	-21	-47	-5	-4.7
● JACK WILSON	Wilson, John Francis "Black Jack" b: 4/12/12, Portland, Ore. d: 4/19/95, Edmonds, Wash. BR/TR, 5'11", 210 lbs. Deb: 9/9/34																											
1934	Phi-A	0	1	.000	2	2	1	0	0	9	15	12	1	0	9	2	24.0	12.00	37	.405	.522	0	.000	-0	-8	-8	-0	-0.7
1935	Bos-A	3	4	.429	23	6	2	0	1	64	72	35	0	2	36	19	15.5	4.22	112	.290	.385	5	.313	2	2	4	1	0.6
1936	Bos-A	6	8	.429	43	9	2	0	3	136^1	152	83	4	1	86	74	15.8	4.42	120	.284	.384	11	.220	-0	9	13	0	1.1
1937	Bos-A	16	10	.615	51	21	14	1	7	221^1	209	111	13	3	119	137	13.5	3.70	128	.248	.343	14	.165	-3	23	25	1	2.4
1938	Bos-A	15	15	.500	37	27	11	3	1	194^2	200	108	16	2	91	96	13.5	4.30	115	.262	.342	15	.221	0	11	13	-1	1.6
1939	Bos-A	11	11	.500	36	22	6	0	2	177^1	198	109	10	1	75	80	13.9	4.67	101	.281	.351	10	.159	-4	-1	1	-0	-0.2
1940	Bos-A	12	6	.667	41	16	9	0	5	157^2	170	104	17	3	87	102	14.8	5.08	89	.270	.362	18	.273	4	-12	-10	-2	-0.8
1941	Bos-A	4	13	.235	27	12	4	1	1	116^1	140	82	7	5	70	55	16.6	5.03	83	.300	.397	7	.159	-1	-11	-11	2	-1.3
1942	Was-A	1	4	.200	12	6	1	0	0	42	57	34	2	1	23	18	17.4	6.64	55	.322	.403	2	.118	-1	-14	-14	-1	-1.6
	Det-A	0	0	—	9	0	0	0	0	13	20	8	3	0	5	7	17.3	4.85	81	.351	.403	0	.000	-0	-2	-1	0	0.0
	Yr	1	4	.200	21	6	1	0	0	55	77	42	5	1	28	25	17.3	6.22	60	.329	.403	2	.111	-1	-16	-15	-0	-1.6
Total	9	68	72	.486	281	121	50	5	20	1131^2	1233	686	73	18	601	590	14.7	4.59	102	.276	.364	82	.199	-3	-4	13	1	1.1
● JOHN WILSON	Wilson, John Nicodemus b: 6/15/1890, Boonsboro, Md. d: 9/23/54, Annapolis, Md. BR/TL, 6'1", 185 lbs. Deb: 6/11/13																											
1913	Was-A	0	0	—	3	0	0	0	0	4	4	2	0	0	3	1	15.8	4.50	66	.267	.389	0	—	0	-1	-1	0	0.0
● JOHN WILSON	Wilson, John Samuel b: 4/25/03, Coal City, Ala. d: 8/27/80, Chattanooga, Tenn. BR/TR, 6'2", 164 lbs. Deb: 5/9/27																											
1927	Bos-A	0	2	.000	5	2	2	0	0	25^1	31	19	1	0	13	8	15.6	3.55	119	.326	.407	1	.111	-1	2	2	-0	0.0
1928	Bos-A	0	0	—	2	0	0	0	0	5	6	5	0	0	6	1	21.6	9.00	46	.333	.500	0	.000	-0	-3	-3	0	-0.1
Total	2	0	2	.000	7	2	2	0	0	30^1	37	24	1	0	19	9	16.6	4.45	94	.327	.424	1	.100	-1	-1	-1	-0	-0.1
● KRIS WILSON	Wilson, Kristopher Kyle b: 8/6/76, Washington, D.C. BR/TR, 6'4", 225 lbs. Deb: 7/28/2000																											
2000	KC-A	0	1	.000	20	0	0	0	0	34^1	38	16	3	0	11	17	12.8	4.19	119	.288	.343	0	—	0	3	3	1	0.2
● MAX WILSON	Wilson, Max b: 6/3/16, Haw River, N.C. d: 1/2/77, Greensboro, N.C. BL/TL, 5'7", 160 lbs. Deb: 9/10/40																											
1940	Phi-N	0	0	—	3	0	0	0	0	7	16	13	1	0	2	3	23.1	12.86	30	.444	.474	0	.000	-0	-7	-7	0	-0.3

YEAR	TM/L	W	L	PCT	G	GS	CG	SH	SV	IP	H	R	HR	HB	BB	SO	RAT	ERA	ERA+	OAV	OOB	BH	AVG	PB	PR	PR+	PD	TPI
1946	Was-A	0	1	.000	9	0	0	0	0	12^2	16	12	1	0	9	8	17.8	7.11	47	.320	.424	0	.000	0	-5	-6	-0	-0.4
Total	2	0	1	.000	12	0	0	0	0	19^2	32	25	2	0	11	11	19.7	9.15	39	.372	.443	0	.000	-0	-12	-13	-0	-0.7
● **PAUL WILSON**	Wilson, Paul Anthony b: 3/28/73, Orlando, Fla. BR/TR, 6'5", 235 lbs. Deb: 4/4/96																											
1996	NY-N	5	12	.294	26	26	1	0	0	149	157	102	15	10	71	109	14.4	5.38	75	.268	.357	4	.080	-2	-19	-24	-2	-2.5
2000	TB-A	1	4	.200	11	7	0	0	0	51	38	20	1	4	16	40	10.2	3.35	148	.209	.287	0	—	0	9	9	-0	0.7
Total	2	6	16	.273	37	33	1	0	0	200	195	122	16	14	87	149	13.3	4.86	87	.254	.341	4	.080	-2	-10	-14	-2	-1.8
● **PETE WILSON**	Wilson, Peter Alex b: 10/9/1885, Springfield, Mass. d: 6/5/57, St.Petersburg, Fla TL, Deb: 9/15/08																											
1908	NY-A	3	3	.500	6	6	4	1	0	39	27	16	0	1	33	28	14.1	3.46	72	.191	.349	1	.071	-1	-5	-4	-0	-0.7
1909	NY-A	6	5	.545	14	13	7	1	0	93^2	82	55	2	4	43	44	12.4	3.17	80	.230	.320	4	.118	-1	-7	-7	-1	-0.9
Total	2	9	8	.529	20	19	11	2	0	132^2	109	71	2	5	76	72	12.9	3.26	77	.219	.329	5	.104	-2	-12	-11	-1	-1.6
● **EARL WILSON**	Wilson, Robert Earl (Name Changed From Wilson, Earl Lawrence) b: 10/2/34, Ponchatoula, La. BR/TR, 6'3", 216 lbs. Deb: 7/28/59																											
1959	Bos-A	1	1	.500	9	4	0	0	0	23^2	21	17	2	0	31	17	19.8	6.08	67	.241	.441	4	.500	2	-6	-5	0	-0.2
1960	Bos-A	3	2	.600	13	9	2	0	0	65	61	36	4	0	48	40	15.1	4.71	86	.247	.369	4	.174	-0	-6	-5	0	-0.3
1962	Bos-A	12	8	.600	31	28	4	1	0	191^1	163	86	21	6	111	137	13.2	3.90	106	.231	.340	12	.174	3	0	5	1	0.7
1963	Bos-A	11	16	.407	37	34	6	3	0	210^2	184	99	18	1	105	123	12.4	3.76	101	.234	.325	15	.208	5	-3	1	1	0.7
1964	Bos-A	11	12	.478	33	31	5	0	0	202^1	213	121	37	2	73	166	12.8	4.49	86	.269	.332	15	.205	8	-20	-13	0	-0.6
1965	Bos-A	13	14	.481	36	36	8	1	0	230^2	221	119	27	4	77	164	11.8	3.98	94	.250	.313	14	.177	8	-13	-6	1	0.1
1966	Bos-A	5	5	.500	15	14	5	1	0	100^2	88	45	14	2	36	67	11.3	3.84	99	.235	.306	8	.250	3	-5	-0	-0	0.3
	Det-A	13	6	.684	23	23	8	2	0	163^1	126	49	16	4	38	133	9.3	2.59	134	.213	.265	15	.234	9	15	16	2	3.2
	Yr	18	11	.621	38	37	13	3	0	264	214	94	30	6	74	200	10.0	3.07	117	.222	.281	23	.240	12	11	15	2	3.5
1967	Det-A	**22**	11	.667	39	38	12	0	0	264	216	103	34	3	92	184	10.6	3.27	100	.224	.294	20	.185	7	-1	-0	2	0.9
1968	*Det-A	13	12	.520	34	33	10	3	0	224^1	192	77	20	0	65	168	10.3	2.85	106	.231	.287	20	.227	10	3	4	1	1.7
1969	Det-A	12	10	.545	35	35	5	1	0	214^2	209	93	23	4	69	150	11.8	3.31	113	.256	.317	10	.132	-0	8	10	1	1.0
1970	Det-A	4	6	.400	18	16	4	1	0	96	87	53	15	2	32	74	11.3	4.41	85	.238	.303	6	.194	2	-7	-7	-0	-0.5
	SD-N	1	6	.143	15	9	0	0	0	65	82	36	5	2	19	29	14.3	4.85	82	.309	.360	1	.059	0	-6	-6	-1	-0.7
Total	11	121	109	.526	338	310	69	13	0	2051^2	1863	934	236	30	796	1452	11.8	3.69	99	.242	.315	144	.195	57	-39	-10	2	6.3
● **ROY WILSON**	Wilson, Roy Edward "Lefty" b: 9/13/1896, Foster, Iowa d: 12/3/69, Clarion, Iowa BL/TL, 6', 175 lbs. Deb: 4/18/28																											
1928	Chi-A	0	0	—	1	0	0	0	0	3^1	2	0	0	0	3	2	13.5	0.00	—	.167	.333	0	.000	-0	1	1	0	0.1
● **STEVE WILSON**	Wilson, Stephen Douglas b: 12/13/64, Victoria, B.C., Can. BL/TL, 6'4", 195 lbs. Deb: 9/16/88																											
1988	Tex-A	0	0	—	3	0	0	0	0	7^2	7	5	1	0	4	1	12.9	5.87	70	.259	.355	0	—	0	-2	-1	-0	-0.1
1989	*Chi-N	6	4	.600	53	8	0	0	2	85^2	83	43	6	1	31	65	12.1	4.20	90	.257	.324	1	.063	-1	-7	-4	0	-0.5
1990	Chi-N	4	9	.308	45	15	1	0	1	139	140	77	17	2	43	95	12.0	4.79	85	.259	.316	6	.162	0	-15	-10	-1	-1.0
1991	Chi-N	0	0	—	8	0	0	0	0	12^1	13	7	1	0	5	9	13.1	4.38	89	.277	.346	0	.000	-0	-1	-1	-0	-0.1
	LA-N	0	0	—	11	0	0	0	2	8^1	1	0	0	0	4	5	5.4	0.00	—	.042	.179	0	.000	-0	3	3	-0	0.1
	Yr	0	0	—	19	0	0	0	2	20^2	14	7	1	0	9	14	10.0	2.61	144	.197	.287	0	.000	-0	2	3	-1	0.0
1992	LA-N	2	5	.286	60	0	0	0	0	66^2	74	37	6	1	29	54	14.0	4.18	82	.282	.356	1	.333	0	-5	-6	-0	-0.6
1993	LA-N	1	0	1.000	25	0	0	0	1	25^2	30	13	2	1	14	23	15.8	4.56	84	.288	.378	0	.000	-0	-1	-2	0	-0.1
Total	6	13	18	.419	205	23	1	0	6	345^1	348	182	33	5	130	252	12.6	4.40	87	.262	.330	8	.133	-1	-28	-21	-2	-2.3
● **TREVOR WILSON**	Wilson, Trevor Kirk b: 6/7/66, Torrance, Cal. BL/TL, 6', 195 lbs. Deb: 9/5/88																											
1988	SF-N	0	2	.000	4	4	0	0	0	22	25	14	1	0	8	15	13.5	4.09	80	.298	.359	2	.286	1	-2	-2	-1	-0.2
1989	SF-N	2	3	.400	14	4	0	0	0	39^1	28	20	2	4	24	22	12.8	4.35	78	.207	.344	2	.250	1	-4	-4	-0	-0.4
1990	SF-N	8	7	.533	27	17	3	2	0	110^1	87	52	11	1	49	66	11.2	4.00	91	.218	.305	4	.138	0	-2	-4	2	-0.4
1991	SF-N	13	11	.542	44	29	2	1	0	202	173	87	13	5	77	139	11.4	3.56	101	.234	.310	12	.235	5	3	0	3	0.8
1992	SF-N	8	14	.364	26	26	1	1	0	154	152	82	18	6	64	88	13.0	4.21	79	.265	.345	3	.077	-1	-12	-16	1	-2.1
1993	SF-N	7	5	.583	22	18	1	0	0	110	110	45	8	6	40	57	12.8	3.60	109	.275	.350	4	.138	1	5	4	-1	0.4
1995	SF-N	3	4	.429	17	17	0	0	0	82^2	82	42	8	4	38	38	13.5	3.92	104	.269	.357	7	.233	1	2	2	1	0.3
1998	Ana-A	0	0	—	15	0	0	0	0	7^2	8	4	0	1	5	6	16.4	3.52	133	.267	.389	0	—	0	1	1	0	0.1
Total	8	41	46	.471	169	115	7	4	0	728	665	346	61	27	305	431	12.3	3.87	94	.249	.332	34	.176	7	-8	-20	5	-1.5
● **WALTER WILSON**	Wilson, Walter Wood b: 11/24/13, Glenn, Ga. d: 4/17/94, Bremen, Ga. BL/TR, 6'4", 190 lbs. Deb: 4/17/45																											
1945	Det-A	1	3	.250	25	4	1	0	0	70^1	76	40	4	3	35	28	14.6	4.61	76	.284	.373	1	.053	-2	-10	-8	1	-0.5
● **WILLY WILSON**	Wilson, William b: 1/7/1884, Columbus, Ohio d: 10/28/25, Seattle, Wash. BR/TR, Deb: 10/3/06																											
1906	Was-A	0	1	.000	1	1	1	0	0	7	3	2	0	1	2	1	7.7	2.57	102	.130	.231	0	.000	-0	0	0	0	0.0
● **MUTT WILSON**	Wilson, William Clarence "Lank" b: 7/20/1896, Kiser, N.C. d: 8/31/62, Leesburg, Fla. BR/TR, 6'3", 167 lbs. Deb: 9/11/20																											
1920	Det-A	1	1	.500	3	2	1	0	0	13	12	10	0	0	5	4	11.8	3.46	108	.240	.309	1	.250	-0	0	0	-1	0.0
● **BILL WILSON**	Wilson, William Donald b: 11/6/28, Central City, Neb. BR/TR, 6'2", 200 lbs. Deb: 9/24/50 ◆																											
1955	KC-A	0	0	—	1	0	0	0	0	1	1	0	0	0	1	1	18.0	0.00	—	.250	.400	61	.223	0	0	0	0	0.0
● **BILL WILSON**	Wilson, William Harlan b: 9/21/42, Pomeroy, Ohio d: 8/11/93, Broken Arrow, Okla. BR/TR, 6'2", 200 lbs. Deb: 4/8/69																											
1969	Phi-N	2	5	.286	37	0	0	0	6	62^1	53	26	6	1	36	48	13.0	3.32	107	.231	.338	0	.000	-0	2	2	-1	0.1
1970	Phi-N	1	0	1.000	37	0	0	0	0	58^1	57	35	5	0	33	41	13.9	4.78	84	.263	.360	1	.250	0	-5	-5	-0	-0.2
1971	Phi-N	4	6	.400	38	0	0	0	7	58^2	39	20	4	1	22	40	9.5	3.07	115	.188	.268	1	.100	-1	3	3	2	0.7
1972	Phi-N	1	1	.500	23	0	0	0	0	30	26	13	1	0	11	18	11.1	3.30	109	.234	.303	0	—	0	1	1	0	0.1
1973	Phi-N	1	3	.250	44	0	0	0	4	48^2	54	39	7	0	29	24	15.3	6.66	57	.293	.390	0	.000	-0	-16	-15	-0	-1.5
Total	5	9	15	.375	179	0	0	0	17	258	229	133	23	2	131	171	12.6	4.22	88	.241	.335	2	.083	-1	-16	-15	0	-0.8
● **HOOKS WILTSE**	Wiltse, George Leroy b: 9/7/1880, Hamilton, N.Y. d: 1/21/59, Long Beach, N.Y. BR/TL, 6', 185 lbs. Deb: 4/21/04 FC																											
1904	NY-N	13	3	.813	24	16	14	2	3	164^2	150	66	8	5	61	105	11.8	2.84	96	.240	.313	15	.224	3	-2	-2	3	0.4
1905	NY-N	15	6	.714	32	19	18	1	3	197	158	71	5	4	61	120	10.2	2.47	119	.219	.284	20	.278	7	12	10	5	2.4
1906	NY-N	16	11	.593	38	26	21	4	6	249^1	227	92	3	3	58	125	10.4	2.27	115	.241	.288	18	.191	2	10	9	-1	1.2
1907	NY-N	13	12	.520	33	21	14	3	2	190^1	171	63	3	5	48	79	10.6	2.18	114	.241	.294	9	.134	0	6	6	2	1.1
1908	NY-N	23	14	.622	44	38	30	7	2	330	266	95	4	9	73	118	9.5	2.24	108	.224	.274	26	.236	6	5	6	-0	1.4
1909	NY-N	20	11	.645	37	30	22	4	3	269^1	228	91	9	6	51	119	9.5	2.00	128	.233	.275	19	.200	2	18	17	2	2.0
1910	NY-N	14	12	.538	36	30	18	2	2	235^1	232	96	4	2	52	88	10.9	2.72	109	.261	.303	13	.176	0	8	7	-3	0.4
1911	*NY-N	12	9	.571	30	24	11	4	2	187^1	177	83	7	2	39	92	10.5	3.27	103	.251	.292	13	.188	-1	3	2	0	0.1
1912	NY-N	9	6	.600	28	17	5	0	3	134	140	63	7	1	28	58	11.4	3.16	107	.273	.312	15	.326	4	4	3	2	0.8
1913	*NY-N	0	0	—	17	2	0	0	3	57^2	53	24	1	1	8	25	9.7	1.56	200	.237	.266	5	.208	0	11	10	0	0.6
1914	NY-N	1	1	.500	20	0	0	0	1	38	41	21	2	0	12	19	12.6	2.84	93	.289	.344	2	.667	2	-0	-1	0	0.1
1915	Bro-F	3	5	.375	18	3	1	0	5	59^1	49	22	1	2	7	17	8.8	2.28	120	.226	.257	1	.045	-3	3	3	-1	0.1
Total	12	139	90	.607	357	226	154	27	33	2112^1	1892	787	54	40	498	965	10.4	2.47	112	.241	.290	156	.210	22	77	72	5	10.6
● **HAL WILTSE**	Wiltse, Harold James "Whitey" b: 8/6/03, Clay City, Ill. d: 11/2/83, Bunkie, La. BL/TL, 5'9", 168 lbs. Deb: 4/13/26																											
1926	Bos-A	8	15	.348	37	29	9	1	0	196^1	201	112	6	6	99	59	14.0	4.22	97	.273	.363	5	.085	-5	-4	-3	-0	-0.7
1927	Bos-A	10	18	.357	36	29	13	1	1	219	276	146	5	4	76	47	14.6	5.10	83	.321	.379	16	.208	-2	-23	-21	1	-2.2
1928	Bos-A	0	2	.000	2	2	1	0	0	12	16	12	1	3	1	5	15.0	9.00	46	.314	.364	0	.000	-1	-7	-6	-0	-0.8
	StL-A	2	5	.286	26	5	0	0	0	72	93	49	4	3	35	23	16.4	5.25	80	.316	.395	5	.227	0	-10	-8	0	-0.6
	Yr	2	7	.222	28	7	1	0	0	84	109	61	5	6	36	28	16.2	5.79	72	.316	.390	5	.192	-1	-16	-14	-0	-1.4
1931	Phi-N	0	0	—	1	0	0	0	0	1	3	1	0	0	0	0	27.0	9.00	47	.600	.600	0	—	0	-1	-0	0	0.0
Total	4	20	40	.333	102	65	23	2	1	500^1	589	320	16	16	211	134	14.7	4.87	85	.303	.375	26	.160	-7	-44	-39	2	-4.3
● **SNAKE WILTSE**	Wiltse, Lewis De Witt b: 12/5/1871, Bouckville, N.Y. d: 8/25/28, Harrisburg, Pa. BR/TL, Deb: 5/5/01 F																											
1901	Pit-N	1	4	.200	7	5	3	0	0	44^1	57	28	2	5	13	10	15.2	4.26	77	.310	.371	3	.158	-1	-5	-5	1	-0.5
	Phi-A	13	5	.722	19	19	18	2	0	166	185	91	1	7	35	40	12.3	3.58	105	.279	.322	25	.373	8	2	3	1	1.2

YEAR TM/L	W	L	PCT	G	GS	CG	SH	SV	IP	H	R	HR	HB	BB	SO	RAT	ERA	ERA+	OAV	OOB	BH	AVG	PB	PR	PR+	PD	TPI
1902 Phi-A	8	8	.500	19	17	13	0	1	138	182	99	7	5	41	28	14.9	5.15	71	.318	.368	10	.175	-0	-24	-22	-1	-2.2
Bal-A	7	11	.389	19	18	18	0	0	164	215	127	4	8	51	37	15.0	5.10	74	.316	.371	39	.295	6	-28	-23	-0	-1.6
Yr	15	19	.441	38	35	31	0	1	302	397	226	11	13	92	65	15.0	5.13	73	.317	.370	49	.259	5	-52	-45	-1	-3.8
1903 NY-A	0	3	.000	4	3	2	0	1	25	35	17	1	1	6	6	15.1	5.40	58	.330	.372	2	.222	0	-7	-6	-0	-0.7
Total 3	29	31	.483	68	62	54	2	2	537^1	674	362	15	26	146	121	14.2	4.59	80	.305	.356	79	.278	13	-62	-53	0	-3.8
● **FRED WINCHELL** Winchell, Frederick Russell (b: Frederick Cook) b: 1/23/1882, Arlington, Mass. d: 8/8/58, Toronto, Ont., Can. TR, 5'8", Deb: 9/16/09																											
1909 Cle-A	0	3	.000	4	3	0	0	1	14^1	16	11	0	0	2	7	11.3	6.28	41	.296	.321	1	.200	0	-6	-6	-0	-1.1
● **SCOTT WINCHESTER** Winchester, Scott Joseph b: 4/20/73, Midland, Mich. BR/TR, 6'2", 210 lbs. Deb: 9/8/97																											
1997 Cin-N	0	0	—	5	0	0	0	0	6	9	5	1	1	2	3	18.0	6.00	71	.360	.429	0	—	0	-1	-1	-0	-0.1
1998 Cin-N	3	6	.333	16	16	1	0	0	79	101	56	12	4	27	40	15.0	5.81	74	.312	.372	3	.130	-1	-14	-13	-0	-1.4
2000 Cin-N	0	0	—	5	0	0	0	0	7^1	10	4	1	0	2	3	14.7	3.68	130	.313	.353	0	—	0	1	1	0	0.0
Total 3	3	6	.333	26	16	1	0	0	92^1	120	65	14	5	31	46	15.2	5.65	76	.315	.374	3	.130	-1	-14	-14	-0	-1.5
● **ED WINEAPPLE** Wineapple, Edward "Lefty" b: 8/10/05, Boston, Mass. d: 7/23/96, Delray Beach, Fla. BL/TL, 6', 210 lbs. Deb: 9/15/29																											
1929 Was-A	0	0	—	1	0	0	0	0	4	7	4	0	0	3	1	22.5	4.50	94	.467	.556	0	.000	-0	-0	-0	-0	-0.1
● **RALPH WINEGARNER** Winegarner, Ralph Lee b: 10/29/09, Benton, Kan. d: 4/14/88, Wichita, Kan. BR/TR, 6', 182 lbs. Deb: 9/20/30 C◆																											
1932 Cle-A	1	0	1.000	5	1	1	0	0	17^1	7	4	0	0	13	5	10.4	1.04	457	.123	.286	1	.143	-0	7	7	-0	0.3
1934 Cle-A	5	4	.556	22	6	4	0	0	78^1	91	55	1	2	39	32	15.2	5.51	82	.289	.371	10	.196	1	-9	-8	0	-0.7
1935 Cle-A	2	2	.500	25	4	2	0	0	67^1	89	51	10	1	29	41	15.9	5.75	78	.313	.379	26	.310	4	-10	-9	0	0.0
1936 Cle-A	0	0	—	9	0	0	0	0	14^2	18	9	0	0	6	3	14.7	4.91	103	.295	.358	2	.125	-1	0	0	-0	-0.1
1949 StL-A	0	0	—	9	0	0	0	0	16^2	24	16	2	0	2	8	14.0	7.56	60	.329	.347	2	.400	2	-6	-5	-0	-0.1
Total 5	8	6	.571	70	11	7	0	0	194^1	229	135	13	3	89	89	14.9	5.33	86	.290	.364	51	.276	5	-18	-16	-1	-0.6
● **JIM WINFORD** Winford, James Head "Cowboy" b: 10/9/09, Shelbyville, Tenn. d: 12/16/70, Miami, Okla. BR/TR, 6'1", 180 lbs. Deb: 9/10/32																											
1932 StL-N	1	1	.500	4	1	0	0	0	8^1	9	7	0	0	5	4	15.1	6.48	61	.273	.368	2	.667	1	-2	-2	0	-0.3
1934 StL-N	0	2	.000	5	1	0	0	0	12^2	17	13	0	2	6	3	17.8	7.82	54	.327	.417	0	.000	0	-5	-5	0	-0.6
1935 StL-N	0	0	—	2	1	0	0	0	11^1	13	5	1	0	5	7	14.3	3.97	103	.283	.353	0	.000	-0	0	0	-1	-0.1
1936 StL-N	11	10	.524	39	23	10	1	3	192	203	90	10	5	68	72	12.9	3.80	104	.269	.333	5	.085	-4	5	3	-4	-0.5
1937 StL-N	2	4	.333	16	4	0	0	0	46^1	56	31	2	0	27	17	16.1	5.83	68	.311	.401	1	.125	-1	-10	-9	-0	-1.1
1938 Bro-N	0	1	.000	2	1	0	0	0	5^2	9	10	1	0	4	4	20.6	11.12	35	.346	.433	0	.000	0	-5	-4	-0	-0.6
Total 6	14	18	.438	68	31	10	1	3	276^1	307	156	14	7	115	107	14.0	4.56	87	.281	.353	8	.108	-3	-17	-18	-5	-3.2
● **ERNIE WINGARD** Wingard, Ernest James "Jim" b: 10/17/1900, Prattville, Ala. d: 1/17/77, Prattville, Ala. BL/TL, 6'2", 176 lbs. Deb: 5/1/24																											
1924 StL-A	13	12	.520	36	26	14	0	1	218	215	103	6	3	85	23	12.5	3.51	129	.262	.334	18	.234	2	17	23	-3	2.2
1925 StL-A	9	10	.474	32	18	8	0	0	145	183	111	10	3	77	20	16.3	5.52	85	.319	.403	15	.288	3	-18	-13	2	-0.9
1926 StL-A	5	8	.385	39	16	7	0	3	169	188	86	9	5	76	30	14.3	3.57	120	.290	.369	14	.230	1	8	13	3	1.3
1927 StL-A	2	13	.133	38	17	7	0	0	156^1	213	132	7	2	79	28	16.9	6.56	66	.340	.415	10	.179	2	-42	-36	2	-2.6
Total 4	29	43	.403	145	77	36	0	4	688^1	799	432	32	13	317	101	14.8	4.64	96	.299	.377	57	.232	7	-34	-13	4	0.0
● **TED WINGFIELD** Wingfield, Frederick Davis b: 8/7/1899, Bedford, Va. d: 7/18/75, Johnson City, Tenn. BR/TR, 5'11", 168 lbs. Deb: 9/23/23																											
1923 Was-A	0	0	—	1	0	0	0	0	1	0	0	0	0	0	1	0.0	0.00	—	.000	.000	0	—	0	0	0	0	0.0
1924 Was-A	0	0	—	4	0	0	0	0	7	9	2	0	0	4	2	16.7	2.57	157	.300	.382	0	.000	-0	1	1	-0	0.1
Bos-A	0	2	.000	4	3	2	0	0	25^2	23	12	0	0	8	4	10.9	2.45	178	.240	.298	3	.333	1	5	5	0	0.4
Yr	0	2	.000	8	3	2	0	0	32^2	32	14	0	0	12	6	12.1	2.48	173	.254	.319	3	.273	0	6	6	-0	0.4
1925 Bos-A	12	19	.387	41	27	18	2	2	254^1	267	149	11	8	92	30	13.0	3.96	115	.278	.346	23	.245	1	12	16	7	2.5
1926 Bos-A	11	16	.407	43	20	9	1	3	190^2	220	119	11	2	50	30	12.8	4.44	92	.298	.344	15	.217	-0	-9	-8	2	-0.8
1927 Bos-A	1	7	.125	20	8	2	0	0	74^2	105	60	2	3	27	1	16.3	5.06	83	.357	.417	4	.222	0	-8	-7	2	-0.4
Total 5	24	44	.353	113	58	31	3	5	553^1	624	342	24	13	181	68	13.3	4.18	103	.294	.353	45	.234	1	3	8	11	1.7
● **LAVE WINHAM** Winham, Lafayette Sharkey "Lefty" b: 10/23/1881, Brooklyn, N.Y. d: 9/12/51, Brooklyn, N.Y. BL/TL, 5'11", 200 lbs. Deb: 4/21/02																											
1902 Bro-N	0	0	—	1	0	0	0	0	3	4	2	0	0	2	1	18.0	0.00	—	.308	.400	0	.000	-0	1	1	0	0.1
1903 Pit-N	3	1	.750	5	4	3	1	0	36	33	20	0	0	21	22	13.5	2.25	144	.231	.329	1	.071	-1	4	4	-1	0.1
Total 2	3	1	.750	6	4	3	1	0	39	37	22	0	0	23	23	13.8	2.08	154	.237	.335	1	.063	-2	5	5	-1	0.2
● **GEORGE WINKELMAN** Winkelman, George Edward b: 2/18/1865, Washington, D.C. d: 5/19/60, Washington, D.C. BL/TL, Deb: 8/4/1883 ◆																											
1886 Was-N	0	1	.000	1	1	0	0	0	6	12	11	0		5	4	25.5	10.50	31	.400	.486	1	.200	-0	-5	-5	-0	-0.5
● **JOE WINKELSAS** Winkelsas, Joseph b: 9/14/73, Buffalo, N.Y. BR/TR, 6'3", 188 lbs. Deb: 4/10/99																											
1999 Atl-N	0	0	—	1	0	0	0	0	0^1	4	2	0	0	1	0	135.0	54.00	8	1.000	1.000	0	—	0	-2	-2	0	-0.1
● **GEORGE WINN** Winn, George Benjamin "Breezy" or "Lefty" b: 10/26/1897, Perry, Ga. d: 11/1/69, Roberta, Ga. BL/TL, 5'11", 170 lbs. Deb: 4/29/19																											
1919 Bos-A	0	0	—	3	0	0	0	0	4^2	6	4	0	0	1	0	13.5	7.71	39	.353	.389	0	.000	-0	-2	-3	-0	-0.2
1922 Cle-A	1	2	.333	8	3	1	0	0	33^2	44	20	2	0	5	7	13.1	4.54	88	.317	.340	3	.333	1	-2	-2	0	-0.1
1923 Cle-A	0	0	—	1	0	0	0	0	2	0	0	0	0	1	0	4.5	0.00	—	.000	.143	0	—	0	1	1	-0	0.0
Total 3	1	2	.333	12	3	1	0	0	40^1	50	24	2	0	7	7	12.7	4.69	83	.309	.337	3	.300	1	-3	-4	-0	-0.3
● **JIM WINN** Winn, James Francis b: 9/23/59, Stockton, Cal. BR/TR, 6'3", 210 lbs. Deb: 4/10/83																											
1983 Pit-N	0	0	—	7	0	0	0	0	11	12	9	2	0	6	3	14.7	7.36	50	.267	.353	0	—	0	-5	-4	0	-0.2
1984 Pit-N	1	0	1.000	9	0	0	0	1	18^2	19	8	2	0	9	11	13.5	3.86	93	.264	.346	0	.000	-0	-1	-1	0	0.0
1985 Pit-N	3	6	.333	30	7	0	0	0	75^2	77	45	4	2	31	22	13.1	5.23	69	.266	.341	2	.111	-1	-14	-14	2	-1.4
1986 Pit-N	3	5	.375	50	3	0	0	3	88	85	44	9	2	38	70	12.8	3.58	107	.258	.338	1	.063	-1	1	2	1	0.3
1987 Chi-A	4	6	.400	56	0	0	0	6	94	95	54	10	6	62	44	15.6	4.79	96	.271	.390	0	—	0	-3	-2	3	0.1
1988 Min-A	1	0	1.000	9	0	0	0	0	21	33	15	4	0	10	9	18.4	6.00	68	.355	.417	0	—	0	-5	-4	-0	-0.2
Total 6	12	17	.414	161	10	0	0	10	308^1	321	175	31	10	156	159	14.2	4.67	86	.272	.362	3	.086	-1	-25	-22	6	-1.4
● **TOM WINSETT** Winsett, John Thomas "Long Tom" b: 11/24/09, McKenzie, Tenn. d: 7/20/87, Memphis, Tenn. BL/TR, 6'2", 190 lbs. Deb: 4/20/30 ◆																											
1937 Bro-N	0	0	—	1	0	0	0	0	1	3	2	0	0	2	0	45.0	18.00	22	.600	.714	83	.237	0	-2	-2	-0	-0.1
● **DARRIN WINSTON** Winston, Darrin Alexander b: 7/6/66, Passaic, N.J. BR/TL, 6', 195 lbs. Deb: 9/10/97																											
1997 Phi-N	2	0	1.000	7	1	0	0	0	12	8	8	4	2	3	8	9.8	5.25	81	.178	.260	1	.500	1	-1	-1	-0	-0.2
1998 Phi-N	2	2	.500	27	0	0	0	1	25	31	18	7	2	6	11	14.0	6.12	71	.298	.348	0	.000	-0	-5	-5	-0	-0.7
Total 2	4	2	.667	34	1	0	0	1	37	39	26	11	4	9	19	12.6	5.84	74	.262	.321	1	.333	1	-7	-6	-1	-0.9
● **HANK WINSTON** Winston, Henry Rudolph b: 6/15/04, Youngsville, N.C. d: 2/4/74, Jacksonville, Fla. BL/TR, 6'3.5", 226 lbs. Deb: 9/30/33																											
1933 Phi-A	0	0	—	1	0	0	0	0	6^2	7	5	0	0	6	2	17.6	6.75	63	.280	.419	0	.000	-0	-2	-2	0	-0.1
1936 Bro-N	1	3	.250	14	0	0	0	0	32^1	40	27	2	1	16	8	15.9	6.12	67	.301	.380	1	.091	-1	-8	-7	-0	-0.8
Total 2	1	3	.250	15	0	0	0	0	39	47	32	2	1	22	10	16.2	6.23	67	.297	.387	1	.071	-1	-9	-9	0	-0.9
● **GEORGE WINTER** Winter, George Lovington "Sassafras" b: 4/27/1878, New Providence, Pa d: 5/26/51, Franklin Lakes, N.J. TR, 5'8", 155 lbs. Deb: 6/15/01																											
1901 Bos-A	16	12	.571	28	28	26	1	0	241	234	127	4	4	66	63	11.4	2.80	126	.252	.304	19	.190	-4	23	20	-1	1.6
1902 Bos-A	11	9	.550	20	20	18	0	0	168^1	149	77	2	7	53	51	11.2	2.99	119	.238	.305	10	.164	-2	11	11	-0	0.8
1903 Bos-A	9	8	.529	24	19	14	0	0	178^1	182	92	4	7	37	64	11.4	3.08	99	.263	.307	7	.106	-4	-2	-1	-1	-0.6
1904 Bos-A	8	4	.667	20	16	12	1	0	135^2	126	47	4	6	27	31	10.5	2.32	115	.247	.293	5	.116	-2	4	5	-2	0.1
1905 Bos-A	16	17	.485	35	27	24	2	0	264^1	249	118	5	5	54	119	10.5	2.96	91	.251	.293	24	.261	3	-9	-8	1	-0.5
1906 Bos-A	6	18	.250	29	22	18	1	2	207^2	215	118	8	5	38	72	11.2	4.12	67	.270	.308	17	.246	2	-33	-31	-0	-3.2
1907 Bos-A	12	15	.444	35	27	21	4	1	256^2	198	91	2	3	61	88	9.2	2.07	124	.215	.267	21	.223	1	14	14	-2	1.5
1908 Bos-A	4	14	.222	22	17	8	0	0	147^2	150	71	3	4	34	55	11.5	3.05	81	.274	.321	9	.184	-1	-11	-9	-0	-1.3
*Det-A	1	5	.167	7	6	5	0	1	56^1	49	19	0	3	7	25	9.4	1.60	151	.240	.276	2	.111	-1	5	5	1	0.6
Yr	5	19	.208	29	23	13	0	1	204	199	90	3	7	41	80	10.9	2.65	93	.265	.309	11	.164	-2	-6	-4	1	-0.7
Total 8	83	102	.449	220	182	146	9	4	1656	1552	760	32	44	377	568	10.7	2.87	101	.250	.297	114	.193	-8	2	7	-4	-1.0

YEAR	TM/L	W	L	PCT	G	GS	CG	SH	SV	IP	H	R	HR	HB	BB	SO	RAT	ERA	ERA+	OAV	OOB	BH	AVG	PB	PR	PR+	PD	TPI
● CLARENCE WINTERS	Winters, Clarence John b: 9/7/1898, Detroit, Mich. d: 6/29/45, Detroit, Mich. TR, Deb: 8/28/24																											
1924	Bos-A	0	1	.000	4	2	0	0	0	7	22	16	0	0	4	3	33.4	20.57	21	.512	.553	1	.333	0	-13	-12	-0	-1.3
● JESSE WINTERS	Winters, Jesse Franklin "Buck" or "T-Bone" b: 12/22/1893, Stephenville, Tex. d: 6/5/86, Abilene, Texas BR/TR, 6'1", 165 lbs. Deb: 5/3/19																											
1919	NY-N	1	2	.333	16	2	0	0	3	28	39	18	1	3	13	6	17.7	5.46	51	.339	.420	0	.000	-0	-8	-9	-0	-1.1
1920	NY-N	0	0	—	21	0	0	0	0	46^{1}	37	19	1	4	28	14	13.4	3.50	86	.233	.361	0	.000	-1	-2	-3	1	-0.2
1921	Phi-N	5	10	.333	18	14	10	0	0	114	142	73	4	4	28	22	13.7	3.63	116	.310	.355	5	.128	-3	2	7	2	0.7
1922	Phi-N	6	6	.500	34	9	4	0	2	138^{1}	176	100	8	4	56	29	15.4	5.33	87	.319	.386	11	.256	0	-19	-9	1	-0.6
1923	Phi-N	1	6	.143	21	6	1	0	1	78^{1}	116	76	7	4	39	23	18.3	7.35	63	.348	.423	4	.160	-1	-29	-21	-1	-1.7
Total	5	13	24	.351	110	31	15	0	6	405	510	286	21	19	164	94	15.4	5.04	83	.316	.385	20	.171	-5	-56	-35	2	-2.9
● ALAN WIRTH	Wirth, Alan Lee b: 12/8/56, Mesa, Ariz. BR/TR, 6'4", 190 lbs. Deb: 4/9/78																											
1978	Oak-A	5	6	.455	16	14	2	1	0	81^{1}	72	39	6	3	34	31	12.1	3.43	106	.252	.337	0	—	0	3	2	-1	0.2
1979	Oak-A	1	0	1.000	5	1	0	0	0	12	14	8	2	1	8	7	17.3	6.00	68	.298	.411	0	—	0	-2	-3	0	-0.2
1980	Oak-A	0	0	—	2	0	0	0	0	2	3	1	0	0	0	1	13.5	4.50	84	.333	.333	0	—	0	-0	-0	-0	0.0
Total	3	6	6	.500	23	15	2	1	0	95^{1}	89	48	8	4	42	39	12.7	3.78	98	.260	.348	0	—	0	1	-1	-1	0.0
● ARCHIE WISE	Wise, Archibald Edwin b: 7/31/12, Waxahachie, Tex. d: 2/2/78, Dallas, Tex. BR/TR, 6', 165 lbs. Deb: 7/24/32																											
1932	Chi-A	0	0	—	2	0	0	0	0	7^{1}	8	5	1	1	5	2	17.2	4.91	88	.258	.378	0	.000	-1	-0	-0	0	-0.1
● MATT WISE	Wise, Matthew John b: 11/18/75, Montclair, Cal. BR/TR, 6'4", 190 lbs. Deb: 8/2/2000																											
2000	Ana-A	3	3	.500	8	6	0	0	0	37^{1}	40	23	7	1	13	20	13.0	5.54	90	.272	.335	0	—	0	-3	-2	0	-0.3
● RICK WISE	Wise, Richard Charles b: 9/13/45, Jackson, Mich. BR/TR, 6'2", 195 lbs. Deb: 4/18/64																											
1964	Phi-N	5	3	.625	25	8	0	0	0	69	78	41	7	3	25	39	13.8	4.04	86	.277	.342	5	.294	2	-4	-4	-2	-0.5
1966	Phi-N	5	6	.455	22	13	3	0	0	99^{1}	100	50	5	3	24	58	11.5	3.71	97	.262	.311	0	.000	-4	-1	-1	-1	-0.6
1967	Phi-N	11	11	.500	36	25	6	3	0	181^{1}	177	69	8	4	45	111	11.2	3.28	104	.259	.308	11	.208	3	2	3	1	0.7
1968	Phi-N	9	15	.375	30	30	7	1	0	182	210	100	12	6	37	97	12.5	4.55	66	.292	.332	14	.241	7	-32	-31	1	-3.1
1969	Phi-N	15	13	.536	33	31	14	4	0	220	215	100	17	2	61	144	11.4	3.23	110	.257	.309	20	.270	7	9	8	1	1.9
1970	Phi-N	13	14	.481	35	34	5	1	0	220^{1}	253	115	15	3	65	113	13.1	4.17	96	.287	.338	15	.200	5	-3	-4	1	0.1
1971	Phi-N☆	17	14	.548	38	37	17	4	0	272^{1}	261	110	20	4	70	155	11.1	2.88	123	.254	.304	23	.237	10	18	19	0	3.4
1972	StL-N	16	16	.500	35	35	20	2	0	269	250	98	16	1	71	142	10.8	3.11	109	.251	.301	16	.172	1	10	9	2	1.4
1973	StL-N★	16	12	.571	35	34	14	5	0	259	259	113	18	3	59	144	11.2	3.37	108	.257	.300	17	.193	6	9	8	-1	1.5
1974	Bos-A	3	4	.429	9	9	1	0	0	49	47	23	2	1	16	25	11.8	3.86	100	.251	.314	0	—	0	-1	-0	-0	0.0
1975	*Bos-A	19	12	.613	35	35	17	1	0	255^{1}	262	126	34	4	72	141	11.9	3.95	103	.263	.315	0	—	0	-5	4	-1	0.3
1976	Bos-A	14	11	.560	34	34	11	4	0	224^{1}	218	100	18	2	48	93	10.8	3.53	111	.255	.296	0	—	0	-0	9	2	1.1
1977	Bos-A	11	5	.688	26	20	4	2	0	128^{1}	151	68	19	4	28	85	12.8	4.77	94	.291	.332	0	—	0	-10	-3	1	-0.3
1978	Cle-A	9	19	.321	33	31	9	1	0	211^{2}	226	116	22	3	59	106	12.2	4.34	86	.275	.325	0	—	0	-13	-14	-0	-1.7
1979	Cle-A	15	10	.600	34	34	9	2	0	231^{2}	229	111	24	1	68	108	11.6	3.73	114	.256	.309	0	—	0	13	14	4	1.8
1980	SD-N	6	8	.429	27	27	1	0	0	154^{1}	172	69	14	0	37	59	12.2	3.67	94	.285	.326	8	.138	-1	-5	-4	1	-0.5
1981	SD-N	4	8	.333	18	18	0	0	0	98	116	44	10	0	19	27	12.4	3.77	87	.296	.328	1	.040	-2	-3	-6	0	-0.8
1982	SD-N	0	0	—	1	0	0	0	0	2	3	2	0	0	0	0	13.5	9.00	38	.333	.333	0	—	0	-1	-1	0	-0.1
Total	18	188	181	.509	506	455	138	30	0	3127	3227	1455	261	44	804	1647	11.7	3.69	100	.267	.315	130	.195	34	-13	4	9	4.6
● ROY WISE	Wise, Roy Ogden b: 11/18/24, Springfield, Ill. BB/TR, 6'2", 170 lbs. Deb: 5/13/44																											
1944	Pit-N	0	0	—	2	0	0	0	0	3	4	3	0	0	3	1	21.0	9.00	41	.333	.467	0	—	0	-2	-2	-0	-0.1
● BILL WISE	Wise, William E. b: 3/15/1861, Washington, D.C. d: 5/5/40, Washington, D.C. Deb: 5/2/1882																											
1882	Bal-a	1	2	.333	3	3	3	0	0	26	30	14	1		4	9	11.8	2.77	99	.270	.296	2	.100	-1	-0	-0	-0	-0.1
1884	Was-U	23	18	.561	50	41	34	4	0	364^{1}	383	219	5		60	268	10.9	3.04	79	.252	.281	79	.233	-8	-24	-26	5	-2.4
1886	Was-N	0	1	.000	1	1	0	0	0	3	6	6	0		2	0	24.0	9.00	37	.400	.471	0	.000	-0	-2	-2	-0	-0.3
Total	3	24	21	.533	54	45	37	4	0	393^{1}	419	239	6		66	277	11.1	3.07	79	.255	.284	81	.224	-9	-26	-28	4	-2.8
● JACK WISNER	Wisner, John Henry b: 11/5/1899, Grand Rapids, Mich. d: 12/15/81, Jackson, Mich. BR/TR, 6'3", 195 lbs. Deb: 9/12/19																											
1919	Pit-N	1	0	1.000	4	1	1	0	0	18^{2}	12	3	0	1	7	4	9.6	0.96	313	.185	.274	0	.000	-1	4	4	-0	0.1
1920	Pit-N	1	3	.250	17	2	1	0	0	44^{2}	46	19	1	1	10	13	11.5	3.43	94	.274	.318	0	.000	-1	-1	-1	1	-0.1
1925	NY-N	0	0	—	25	0	0	0	0	40^{1}	33	19	4	2	14	13	10.9	3.79	106	.228	.304	0	.000	-1	2	1	0	0.0
1926	NY-N	2	2	.500	5	3	2	0	0	28	21	12	4	0	10	5	10.0	3.54	106	.208	.279	2	.200	-0	1	1	-0	0.0
Total	4	4	5	.444	51	6	4	0	0	131^{2}	112	53	9	4	41	35	10.7	3.21	111	.234	.300	2	.065	-3	6	5	1	0.0
● WHITEY WISTERT	Wistert, Francis Michael b: 2/20/12, Chicago, Ill. d: 4/23/85, Painesville, Ohio BR/TR, 6'4", 210 lbs. Deb: 9/11/34																											
1934	Cin-N	0	1	.000	2	1	0	0	0	8	5	1	1	0	5	1	11.3	1.13	363	.185	.313	0	.000	-0	3	3	-0	0.2
● JAY WITASICK	Witasick, Gerald Alfonse b: 8/28/72, Baltimore, Md. BR/TR, 6'4", 205 lbs. Deb: 7/7/96																											
1996	Oak-A	1	1	.500	12	0	0	0	0	13	12	9	5	0	5	12	11.8	6.23	79	.245	.315	0	—	0	-2	-2	-0	-0.3
1997	Oak-A	0	0	—	8	0	0	0	0	11	14	7	2	0	6	8	16.4	5.73	79	.304	.385	0	—	0	-1	-1	-0	-0.1
1998	Oak-A	1	3	.250	7	3	0	0	0	27	36	24	9	0	15	29	17.0	6.33	72	.310	.389	0	—	0	-5	-5	-0	-0.7
1999	KC-A	9	12	.429	32	28	1	1	0	158^{1}	191	108	23	8	83	102	16.0	5.57	90	.304	.392	0	.000	-1	-12	-9	-3	-1.3
2000	KC-A	3	8	.273	22	14	2	0	0	89^{1}	109	65	15	4	38	67	15.2	5.94	84	.301	.374	0	.000	-0	-10	-9	-1	-1.0
	SD-N	3	2	.600	11	11	0	0	0	60^{2}	69	42	9	3	35	54	15.9	5.64	78	.284	.381	3	.136	-0	-7	-9	1	-0.6
Total	5	17	26	.395	92	56	3	1	0	359^{1}	431	255	63	15	182	272	15.7	5.76	84	.298	.382	3	.097	-1	-37	-36	-4	-4.0
● SHANNON WITHEM	Withem, Shannon Bolt b: 9/21/72, Ann Arbor, Mich. BR/TR, 6'3", 185 lbs. Deb: 9/18/98																											
1998	Tor-A	0	0	—	1	0	0	0	0	3	3	1	0	0	2	2	15.0	3.00	156	.250	.357	0	—	0	1	1	0	0.0
● CHARLES WITHEROW	Witherow, Charles Samuel Deb: 7/1/1875																											
1875	Was-n	0	1	.000	1	1	0	0	0	1	4	5	0		0	0	36.0	18.00	13	.444	.444	0	.000	-0	-2	-2		-0.3
● ROY WITHERUP	Witherup, Foster Leroy b: 7/26/1886, N.Washington, Pa. d: 12/23/41, New Bethlehem, Pa. BR/TR, 6', 185 lbs. Deb: 5/14/06																											
1906	Bos-N	0	3	.000	8	3	3	0	0	46	59	37	2	1	19	14	15.5	6.26	43	.322	.389	2	.133	-1	-19	-18	-1	-1.2
1908	Was-A	2	4	.333	6	6	4	0	0	48^{1}	51	21	0	1	8	31	11.2	2.98	77	.264	.297	3	.167	-1	-3	-4	0	-0.5
1909	Was-A	1	5	.167	12	8	5	0	0	68	79	41	1	0	20	26	13.1	4.24	57	.306	.356	1	.053	-2	-13	-14	-2	-1.5
Total	3	3	12	.200	26	17	12	0	0	162^{1}	189	99	3	2	47	71	13.2	4.44	55	.298	.348	6	.115	-3	-35	-36	-2	-3.2
● GEORGE WITT	Witt, George Adrian "Red" b: 11/9/33, Long Beach, Cal. BR/TR, 6'3", 200 lbs. Deb: 9/21/57																											
1957	Pit-N	0	1	.000	1	1	0	0	0	1^{1}	4	6	1	0	5	1	60.8	40.50	9	.500	.692	0	—	0	-5	-6	0	-0.8
1958	Pit-N	9	2	.818	18	15	5	3	0	106	78	22	2	2	59	81	11.8	1.61	240	.209	.320	6	.154	-1	28	27	-0	2.6
1959	Pit-N	0	7	.000	15	11	0	0	0	50^{2}	58	43	7	1	32	30	16.2	6.93	56	.293	.394	0	.000	-1	-17	-18	-0	-2.2
1960	*Pit-N	1	2	.333	10	6	0	0	0	30	33	18	3	0	12	15	13.5	4.20	89	.300	.369	0	.000	-1	-1	-2	-0	-0.3
1961	Pit-N	0	1	.000	9	1	0	0	0	15^{2}	17	12	5	0	5	9	12.6	6.32	63	.274	.328	1	.500	1	-4	-4	-1	-0.2
1962	LA-A	1	1	.500	5	2	0	0	0	10	15	12	4	0	5	10	18.0	8.10	48	.349	.417	1	.333	0	-5	-5	-0	-0.8
	Hou-N	0	2	.000	8	2	0	0	0	15^{1}	20	14	2	1	9	10	17.6	7.04	53	.339	.435	1	.250	0	-5	-6	0	-0.6
Total	6	11	16	.407	66	38	5	3	0	229	225	127	24	4	127	156	14.0	4.32	89	.263	.361	9	.130	-2	-10	-12	-2	-2.3
● MIKE WITT	Witt, Michael Atwater b: 7/20/60, Fullerton, Cal. BR/TR, 6'7", 192 lbs. Deb: 4/11/81																											
1981	Cal-A	8	9	.471	22	21	7	1	0	129	123	60	9	11	47	75	12.6	3.28	111	.251	.330	0	—	0	6	5	-1	0.6
1982	*Cal-A	8	6	.571	33	26	5	1	0	179^{2}	177	77	8	7	47	85	11.6	3.51	116	.260	.314	0	—	0	12	11	-0	0.8
1983	Cal-A	7	14	.333	43	19	2	0	5	154	173	90	14	6	75	77	14.8	4.91	82	.293	.379	0	—	0	-14	-15	0	-1.9
1984	Cal-A	15	11	.577	34	34	9	2	0	246^{2}	227	103	17	5	84	196	11.5	3.47	115	.244	.310	0	—	0	15	14	-1	1.3
1985	Cal-A	15	9	.625	35	35	6	1	0	250	228	115	22	4	98	180	11.9	3.56	115	.243	.317	0	—	0	16	15	0	1.4
1986	*Cal-A☆	18	10	.643	34	34	14	3	0	269	218	95	22	3	73	208	9.8	2.84	145	.221	.277	0	—	0	40	39	2	4.0

YEAR	TM/L	W	L	PCT	G	GS	CG	SH	SV	IP	H	R	HR	HB	BB	SO	RAT	ERA	ERA+	OAV	OOB	BH	AVG	PB	PR	PR+	PD	TPI
1987	Cal-A☆	16	14	.533	36	36	10	0	0	247	252	128	34	4	84	192	12.4	4.01	108	.261	.323	0	—	0	13	9	-1	0.9
1988	Cal-A	13	16	.448	34	34	12	2	0	249^2	263	130	14	5	87	133	12.8	4.15	93	.272	.335	0	—	0	-5	-8	-0	-0.8
1989	Cal-A	9	15	.375	33	33	5	0	0	220	252	119	26	2	48	123	12.4	4.54	84	.292	.330	0	—	0	-16	-18	4	-1.4
1990	Cal-A	0	3	.000	10	0	0	0	1	20^1	19	9	1	1	13	14	14.6	1.77	216	.250	.367	0	—	0	5	5	1	0.8
	NY-A	5	6	.455	16	16	2	1	0	96^2	87	53	8	4	34	60	11.6	4.47	89	.240	.312	0	—	0	-6	-5	0	-0.5
	Yr	5	9	.357	26	16	2	1	1	117	106	62	9	5	47	74	12.2	4.00	99	.241	.322	0	—	0	-1	-1	1	0.3
1991	NY-A	0	1	.000	2	2	0	0	0	5^1	8	7	1	0	1	0	15.2	10.13	41	.320	.346	0	—	0	-4	-4	0	-0.5
1993	NY-A	3	2	.600	9	9	0	0	0	41	39	26	7	3	22	30	14.0	5.27	79	.248	.352	0	—	0	-4	-5	0	-0.5
Total	12	117	116	.502	341	299	72	11	6	2108^1	2066	1012	183	55	713	1373	12.1	3.83	105	.257	.322	0	—	0	57	44	4	4.2

● BOBBY WITT Witt, Robert Andrew b: 5/11/64, Arlington, Mass. BR/TR, 6'2", 205 lbs. Deb: 4/10/86

YEAR	TM/L	W	L	PCT	G	GS	CG	SH	SV	IP	H	R	HR	HB	BB	SO	RAT	ERA	ERA+	OAV	OOB	BH	AVG	PB	PR	PR+	PD	TPI
1986	Tex-A	11	9	.550	31	31	0	0	0	157^2	130	104	18	3	143	174	15.8	5.48	79	.223	.379	0	—	0	-23	-20	0	-2.1
1987	Tex-A	8	10	.444	26	25	1	0	0	143	114	82	10	3	140	160	16.2	4.91	91	.219	.388	0	.000	-0	-7	-7	0	-0.7
1988	Tex-A	8	10	.444	22	22	13	2	0	174^1	134	83	13	1	101	148	12.2	3.92	104	.216	.326	0	—	0	1	3	-1	0.2
1989	Tex-A	12	13	.480	31	31	5	1	0	194^1	182	123	14	2	114	166	13.8	5.14	77	.248	.351	0	—	0	-27	-25	-0	-2.8
1990	Tex-A	17	10	.630	33	32	7	1	0	222	197	98	12	4	110	221	12.6	3.36	117	.238	.330	0	—	0	14	14	-1	1.5
1991	Tex-A	3	7	.300	17	16	1	1	0	88^2	84	66	4	1	74	82	16.1	6.09	66	.254	.392	0	—	0	-20	-21	-1	-2.0
1992	Tex-A	9	13	.409	25	25	0	0	0	161^1	152	87	14	2	95	100	13.9	4.46	85	.254	.358	0	—	0	-9	-12	-0	-1.5
	*Oak-A	1	1	.500	6	6	0	0	0	31^2	31	12	2	0	19	25	14.2	3.41	110	.265	.368	0	—	0	2	1	0	0.1
	Yr	10	14	.417	31	31	0	0	0	193	183	99	16	2	114	125	13.9	4.29	88	.256	.360	0	—	0	-7	-11	-0	-1.4
1993	Oak-A	14	13	.519	35	33	5	1	0	220	226	112	16	3	91	131	13.1	4.21	97	.269	.343	0	—	0	3	-3	2	-0.2
1994	Oak-A	8	10	.444	24	24	5	3	0	135^2	151	88	22	5	70	111	15.0	5.04	88	.283	.371	0	—	0	-4	-10	-1	-1.2
1995	Fla-N	2	7	.222	19	19	1	0	0	110^2	104	52	8	2	47	95	12.4	3.90	108	.251	.330	2	.063	-2	3	4	0	0.1
	Tex-A	3	4	.429	10	10	1	0	0	61^1	81	35	4	1	21	46	15.1	4.55	106	.324	.379	0	—	0	1	2	-1	0.1
1996	*Tex-A	16	12	.571	33	32	2	0	0	199^2	235	129	28	2	96	157	15.0	5.41	97	.295	.372	0	—	0	-9	-4	1	-0.4
1997	Tex-A	12	12	.500	34	32	3	0	0	209	245	118	33	2	74	121	13.8	4.82	99	.294	.353	2	.333	2	-6	-1	-0	0.1
1998	Tex-A	5	4	.556	14	13	0	0	0	69^1	95	62	14	0	33	30	16.6	7.66	63	.328	.396	0	.000	-0	-23	-21	-2	-2.3
	StL-N	2	5	.286	17	5	0	0	0	47^1	55	32	7	2	20	28	14.6	4.94	85	.289	.363	2	.200	1	-4	-4	1	-0.4
1999	TB-A	7	15	.318	32	32	3	2	0	180^1	213	130	23	3	96	123	15.6	5.84	85	.304	.390	0	.000	-0	-19	-17	1	-1.6
2000	Cle-A	0	1	.000	7	2	0	0	0	15^1	28	13	4	0	6	6	20.0	7.63	65	.394	.442	0	—	0	-5	-4	0	-0.2
Total	15	138	156	.469	416	390	47	11	0	2421^2	2457	1426	246	36	1350	1924	14.3	4.84	90	.266	.361	6	.115	0	-131	-124	-2	-13.3

● JOHNNIE WITTIG Wittig, John Carl "Hans" b: 6/16/14, Baltimore, Md. d: 2/24/99, Nassawadox, Va. BR/TR, 6', 180 lbs. Deb: 8/4/38

YEAR	TM/L	W	L	PCT	G	GS	CG	SH	SV	IP	H	R	HR	HB	BB	SO	RAT	ERA	ERA+	OAV	OOB	BH	AVG	PB	PR	PR+	PD	TPI
1938	NY-N	2	3	.400	13	6	2	0	0	39^1	41	22	4	0	26	14	15.3	4.81	78	.263	.368	0	.000	-1	-4	-5	-1	-0.8
1939	NY-N	0	2	.000	5	2	1	0	0	16^2	18	15	0	1	14	4	17.8	7.56	52	.281	.418	0	.000	-1	-7	-7	0	-0.7
1941	NY-N	3	5	.375	25	9	0	0	0	85^1	111	57	5	1	45	47	16.6	5.59	66	.319	.398	5	.200	-0	-19	-18	-2	-1.6
1943	NY-N	5	15	.250	40	22	4	1	4	164	172	85	14	0	76	56	13.6	4.23	82	.273	.352	5	.098	-3	-15	-14	-3	-2.3
1949	Bos-A	0	0	—	1	0	0	0	0	2	2	2	0	0	2	0	18.0	9.00	48	.286	.444	0	—	0	-1	-1	0	0.0
Total	5	10	25	.286	84	39	7	1	4	307^1	344	181	23	2	163	121	14.9	4.89	73	.286	.372	10	.110	-6	-46	-44	-6	-5.4

● MARK WOHLERS Wohlers, Mark Edward b: 1/23/70, Holyoke, Mass. BR/TR, 6'4", 207 lbs. Deb: 8/17/91

YEAR	TM/L	W	L	PCT	G	GS	CG	SH	SV	IP	H	R	HR	HB	BB	SO	RAT	ERA	ERA+	OAV	OOB	BH	AVG	PB	PR	PR+	PD	TPI
1991	*Atl-N	3	1	.750	17	0	0	0	2	19^2	17	7	1	2	13	13	14.6	3.20	121	.239	.372	0	.000	-0	1	1	0	0.3
1992	*Atl-N	1	2	.333	32	0	0	0	4	35^1	28	11	0	1	14	17	11.0	2.55	144	.235	.321	0	.000	-0	4	4	0	0.4
1993	*Atl-N	6	2	.750	46	0	0	0	0	48	37	25	2	1	22	45	11.3	4.50	89	.218	.311	0	—	0	-2	-3	0	-0.3
1994	Atl-N	7	2	.778	51	0	0	0	1	51	51	35	1	0	33	58	14.8	4.59	93	.264	.372	1	1.000	0	-2	-2	0	-0.2
1995	*Atl-N	7	3	.700	65	0	0	0	25	64^2	51	16	2	1	24	90	10.6	2.09	204	.211	.285	0	.000	-0	15	15	-1	3.0
1996	*Atl-N★	2	4	.333	77	0	0	0	39	77^1	71	30	8	2	21	100	10.9	3.03	146	.240	.295	0	.000	-0	10	11	-1	1.6
1997	*Atl-N	5	7	.417	71	0	0	0	33	69^1	57	29	4	0	38	92	12.3	3.50	120	.224	.325	0	.000	-0	5	5	-1	1.0
1998	Atl-N	0	1	.000	27	0	0	0	8	20^1	18	23	2	1	33	22	23.0	10.18	41	.231	.464	0	—	0	-13	-14	-0	-1.5
1999	Atl-N	0	0	—	2	0	0	0	0	0^2	1	2	0	0	6	0	94.5	27.00	17	.333	.778	0	—	0	-2	-2	-0	-0.1
2000	Cin-N	1	2	.333	20	0	0	0	0	28	19	14	3	0	17	20	11.6	4.50	106	.192	.310	0	—	0	0	1	-0	0.1
Total	10	32	24	.571	408	0	0	0	112	414^1	350	192	23	8	221	457	12.6	3.78	111	.230	.330	1	.083	-1	16	20	-2	4.3

● STEVE WOJCIECHOWSKI Wojciechowski, Steven Joseph b: 7/29/70, Blue Island, Ill. BL/TL, 6'2", 185 lbs. Deb: 7/18/95

YEAR	TM/L	W	L	PCT	G	GS	CG	SH	SV	IP	H	R	HR	HB	BB	SO	RAT	ERA	ERA+	OAV	OOB	BH	AVG	PB	PR	PR+	PD	TPI
1995	Oak-A	2	3	.400	14	7	0	0	0	48^2	51	28	7	1	28	13	14.8	5.18	86	.273	.370	0	—	0	-2	-4	-0	-0.4
1996	Oak-A	5	5	.500	16	15	0	0	0	79^2	97	57	10	2	28	30	14.3	5.65	87	.300	.360	0	—	0	-6	-6	-1	-0.7
1997	Oak-A	0	2	.000	2	2	0	0	0	10^1	17	9	2	0	1	5	15.7	7.84	58	.386	.400	0	—	0	-4	-4	0	-0.5
Total	3	7	10	.412	32	24	0	0	0	138^2	165	94	19	3	57	48	14.6	5.65	84	.298	.366	0	—	0	-12	-14	-1	-1.6

● PETE WOJEY Wojey, Peter Paul b: 12/1/19, Stowe, Pa. d: 4/23/91, Mobile, Ala. BR/TR, 5'11", 185 lbs. Deb: 7/2/54

YEAR	TM/L	W	L	PCT	G	GS	CG	SH	SV	IP	H	R	HR	HB	BB	SO	RAT	ERA	ERA+	OAV	OOB	BH	AVG	PB	PR	PR+	PD	TPI
1954	Bro-N	1	1	.500	14	1	0	0	1	27^2	24	13	3	2	14	21	13.0	3.25	126	.242	.348	0	.000	-0	3	3	1	0.2
1956	Det-A	0	0	—	2	0	0	0	0	4	2	1	0	0	1	1	6.8	2.25	183	.167	.231	0	—	0	1	1	0	0.1
1957	Det-A	0	0	—	2	0	0	0	0	1^1	1	0	0	0	0	0	6.8	0.00	—	.200	.200	0	—	0	1	1	0	0.0
Total	3	1	1	.500	18	1	0	0	1	33	27	14	3	2	15	22	12.0	3.00	136	.233	.331	0	.000	-0	4	4	1	0.3

● ED WOJNA Wojna, Edward David b: 8/20/60, Bridgeport, Conn. BR/TR, 6'1", 185 lbs. Deb: 6/16/85

YEAR	TM/L	W	L	PCT	G	GS	CG	SH	SV	IP	H	R	HR	HB	BB	SO	RAT	ERA	ERA+	OAV	OOB	BH	AVG	PB	PR	PR+	PD	TPI
1985	SD-N	2	4	.333	15	7	0	0	0	42	53	35	6	3	19	18	16.1	5.79	61	.312	.391	2	.167	-0	-10	-11	0	-1.4
1986	SD-N	2	2	.500	7	7	1	0	0	39	42	19	2	1	16	19	13.6	3.23	113	.268	.339	2	.143	-0	2	2	-1	0.1
1987	SD-N	0	3	.000	5	3	0	0	0	18^1	25	12	2	1	6	13	15.7	5.89	67	.333	.390	0	.000	-1	-4	-4	1	-0.5
1989	Cle-A	0	1	.000	9	3	0	0	0	33	31	17	0	0	14	10	12.3	4.09	97	.254	.331	0	—	0	-1	-0	1	0.0
Total	4	4	10	.286	36	20	1	0	0	132^1	151	83	10	5	55	60	14.4	4.62	81	.288	.361	4	.129	-1	-12	-13	1	-1.8

● BOB WOLCOTT Wolcott, Robert William b: 9/8/73, Huntington Beach, Cal. BR/TR, 6', 190 lbs. Deb: 8/18/95

YEAR	TM/L	W	L	PCT	G	GS	CG	SH	SV	IP	H	R	HR	HB	BB	SO	RAT	ERA	ERA+	OAV	OOB	BH	AVG	PB	PR	PR+	PD	TPI
1995	*Sea-A	3	2	.600	7	6	0	0	0	36^2	43	18	6	2	14	19	14.5	4.42	107	.297	.366	0	—	0	1	1	-1	0.1
1996	Sea-A	7	10	.412	30	28	1	0	0	149^1	179	101	26	7	54	78	14.5	5.73	87	.297	.361	0	—	0	-12	-13	-0	-1.2
1997	Sea-A	5	6	.455	19	18	0	0	0	100	129	71	22	5	29	58	14.7	6.03	75	.314	.366	0	.000	-0	-16	-17	-0	-1.6
1998	Ari-N	1	3	.250	6	6	0	0	0	33	32	27	7	0	13	21	12.3	7.09	59	.252	.321	2	.222	0	-10	-11	-1	-1.1
1999	Bos-A	0	0	—	4	0	0	0	0	6^2	8	6	1	1	3	2	16.2	8.10	61	.333	.429	0	—	0	-2	-2	-0	-0.1
Total	5	16	21	.432	66	58	1	0	0	325^2	391	223	62	15	113	178	14.3	5.86	81	.298	.361	2	.200	0	-40	-42	-2	-3.9

● ERNIE WOLF Wolf, Ernest Adolph b: 2/2/1889, Newark, N.J. d: 5/23/64, Atlantic Highlands, N.J. BR/TR, 5'11", 174 lbs. Deb: 9/10/12

YEAR	TM/L	W	L	PCT	G	GS	CG	SH	SV	IP	H	R	HR	HB	BB	SO	RAT	ERA	ERA+	OAV	OOB	BH	AVG	PB	PR	PR+	PD	TPI
1912	Cle-A	0	0	—	1	0	0	0	0	5^2	8	6	0	0	4	1	19.1	6.35	54	.348	.444	0	.000	-0	-2	-2	-0	-0.1

● RANDY WOLF Wolf, Randall C. b: 8/22/76, Canoga Park, Cal. BL/TL, 6', 190 lbs. Deb: 6/11/99

YEAR	TM/L	W	L	PCT	G	GS	CG	SH	SV	IP	H	R	HR	HB	BB	SO	RAT	ERA	ERA+	OAV	OOB	BH	AVG	PB	PR	PR+	PD	TPI
1999	Phi-N	6	9	.400	22	21	0	0	0	121^2	126	78	20	5	67	116	14.6	5.55	85	.266	.363	7	.233	1	-13	-11	-1	-1.0
2000	Phi-N	11	9	.550	32	32	1	0	0	206^1	210	107	25	8	83	160	13.1	4.36	108	.269	.346	11	.193	1	6	8	-1	0.8
Total	2	17	18	.486	54	53	1	0	0	328	336	185	45	13	150	276	13.7	4.80	98	.268	.352	18	.207	3	-7	-3	-1	-0.2

● WALLY WOLF Wolf, Walter Beck b: 1/5/42, Los Angeles, Cal. BR/TR, 6'0.5", 191 lbs. Deb: 9/27/69

YEAR	TM/L	W	L	PCT	G	GS	CG	SH	SV	IP	H	R	HR	HB	BB	SO	RAT	ERA	ERA+	OAV	OOB	BH	AVG	PB	PR	PR+	PD	TPI
1969	Cal-A	0	0	—	2	0	0	0	0	2^1	3	3	1	0	3	2	23.1	11.57	30	.333	.500	0	—	0	-2	-2	-0	-0.1
1970	Cal-A	0	0	—	4	0	0	0	0	5^1	3	3	1	0	4	5	11.8	5.06	71	.176	.333	0	—	0	-1	-1	-0	-0.1
Total	2	0	0	—	6	0	0	0	0	7^2	6	6	2	0	7	7	15.3	7.04	51	.231	.394	0	—	0	-3	-3	-0	-0.2

● LEFTY WOLF Wolf, Walter Francis b: 6/10/1900, Hartford, Conn. d: 9/25/71, New Orleans, La. BR/TL, 5'10", 163 lbs. Deb: 7/4/21

YEAR	TM/L	W	L	PCT	G	GS	CG	SH	SV	IP	H	R	HR	HB	BB	SO	RAT	ERA	ERA+	OAV	OOB	BH	AVG	PB	PR	PR+	PD	TPI
1921	Phi-A	0	0	—	8	0	0	0	0	15	15	15	0	2	16	11	19.8	7.20	62	.273	.452	1	.250	-0	-5	-4	-0	-0.2

● JIMMY WOLF Wolf, William Van Winkle "Chicken" b: 5/12/1862, Louisville, Ky. d: 5/16/03, Louisville, Ky. BR/TR, 5'9", 190 lbs. Deb: 5/2/1882 M◆

YEAR	TM/L	W	L	PCT	G	GS	CG	SH	SV	IP	H	R	HR	HB	BB	SO	RAT	ERA	ERA+	OAV	OOB	BH	AVG	PB	PR	PR+	PD	TPI
1882	Lou-a	0	0	—	1	0	0	0	0	6	11	11	0		3	1	21.0	9.00	28	.367	.424	95	.299	0	-4	-5	-0	-0.2
1885	Lou-a	0	0	—	1	0	0	0	0	1	1	2	0	0	0	1	9.0	9.00	36	.200	.200	141	.292	0	-1	-1	0	0.0
1886	Lou-a	0	0	—	1	0	0	0	0	3	7	8	0	0	0	0	21.0	15.00	24	.350	.350	148	.272	0	-4	-4	0	-0.1
Total	3	0	0	—	3	0	0	0	0	10	19	21	0	0	3	2	19.8	10.80	27	.345	.379	1473	.295	1	-9	-9	-0	-0.3

YEAR	TM/L	W	L	PCT	G	GS	CG	SH	SV	IP	H	R	HR	HB	BB	SO	RAT	ERA	ERA+	OAV	OOB	BH	AVG	PB	PR	PR+	PD	TPI
● **CHUCK WOLFE**	Wolfe, Charles Hunt b: 2/15/1897, Wolfsburg, Pa. d: 11/27/57, Schellsburg, Pa. BL/TR, 5'7", 175 lbs. Deb: 8/2/23																											
1923	Phi-A	0	0	—	3	0	0	0	0	9^2	6	4	1	0	8	1	13.0	3.72	110	.194	.359	1	.333	0	0	0	-0	0.0
● **ED WOLFE**	Wolfe, Edward Anthony b: 1/2/28, Los Angeles, Cal. BR/TR, 6'3", 185 lbs. Deb: 4/19/52																											
1952	Pit-N	0	0	—	3	0	0	0	0	3^2	7	3	1	1	5	1	31.9	7.36	54	.467	.619	0	—	0	-1	-1	0	0.0
● **BARNEY WOLFE**	Wolfe, Wilbert Otto b: 1/9/1876, Independence, Pa. d: 2/27/53, N.Charleroi, Pa. BR/TR, 6'1", Deb: 4/24/03																											
1903	NY-A	6	9	.400	20	16	12	1	0	148^1	143	66	1	6	26	48	10.6	2.97	105	.253	.293	4	.075	-4	-0	2	-0	-0.3
1904	NY-A	0	3	.000	7	3	2	0	0	33^2	31	18	1	2	4	8	9.9	3.21	85	.246	.280	0	.000	-1	-2	-2	0	-0.3
	Was-A	6	10	.375	17	16	13	2	0	126^2	131	64	0	11	22	44	11.7	3.27	81	.268	.314	5	.119	-2	-9	-8	-2	-1.4
	Yr	6	13	.316	24	19	15	2	0	160^1	162	82	1	13	26	52	11.3	3.26	82	.263	.307	5	.096	-3	-12	-10	-2	-1.7
1905	Was-A	9	14	.391	28	23	17	1	1	182	162	76	1	8	37	52	10.2	2.57	103	.240	.287	8	.127	-1	2	2	-2	-0.2
1906	Was-A	0	3	.000	4	3	2	0	0	20	17	11	0	2	10	8	13.0	4.05	65	.233	.341	2	.286	0	-3	-3	0	-0.4
Total	4	21	39	.350	76	61	46	4	1	510^2	484	235	3	29	99	160	10.8	2.96	94	.251	.298	19	.109	-8	-13	-9	-4	-2.6
● **BILL WOLFE**	Wolfe, William b: Jersey City, N.J. Deb: 9/10/02																											
1902	Phi-N	0	1	.000	1	1	1	0	0	9	11	5	0	1	4	3	16.0	4.00	70	.297	.381	1	.333	0	-1	-1	0	-0.1
● **ROGER WOLFF**	Wolff, Roger Francis b: 4/10/11, Evansville, Ill. d: 3/23/94, Chester, Ill. BR/TR, 6'0.5", 208 lbs. Deb: 9/20/41																											
1941	Phi-A	0	2	.000	2	2	2	0	0	17	15	6	0	0	4	2	10.1	3.18	132	.231	.275	1	.200	-0	2	2	-0	0.2
1942	Phi-A	12	15	.444	32	25	15	2	3	214^1	206	99	16	3	69	94	11.7	3.32	114	.249	.309	6	.088	-3	8	11	0	1.0
1943	Phi-A	10	15	.400	41	26	13	2	6	221	232	97	11	4	72	91	12.5	3.54	96	.274	.334	9	.122	-4	-6	-4	-3	-1.1
1944	Was-A	4	15	.211	33	21	5	0	2	155	186	107	9	6	60	73	14.6	4.99	65	.295	.362	12	.218	1	-27	-32	2	-3.2
1945	Was-A	20	10	.667	33	29	21	4	2	250	200	68	7	1	53	108	**9.1**	2.12	146	.215	**.258**	9	.107	-5	35	30	-1	3.0
1946	Was-A	5	8	.385	21	17	6	0	0	122	115	51	8	5	30	50	11.1	2.58	130	.249	.302	4	.103	-1	12	11	-1	0.9
1947	Cle-A	0	0	—	7	2	0	0	0	16	15	7	1	2	10	5	15.2	3.94	88	.259	.386	0	.000	-0	-0	-1	-1	0.0
	Pit-N	1	4	.200	13	6	1	0	0	30	49	33	4	1	18	7	20.4	8.70	49	.368	.447	0	.000	-1	-15	-14	-1	-2.1
Total	7	52	69	.430	182	128	63	8	13	1025^1	1018	468	56	22	316	430	11.9	3.41	100	.258	.316	41	.122	-13	8	1	-3	-1.3
● **MELLIE WOLFGANG**	Wolfgang, Meldon John "Red" b: 3/20/1890, Albany, N.Y. d: 6/30/47, Albany, N.Y. BR/TR, 5'9", 160 lbs. Deb: 4/18/14																											
1914	Chi-A	9	5	.643	24	11	9	2	0	119^1	96	42	0	0	32	50	9.7	1.89	142	.219	.272	7	.175	-0	11	11	4	1.8
1915	Chi-A	2	2	.500	17	2	0	0	0	53^2	39	18	0	1	12	21	8.7	1.84	161	.211	.263	2	.118	-1	7	7	-1	0.2
1916	Chi-A	4	6	.400	27	14	6	1	0	127	103	39	2	2	42	36	10.4	1.98	139	.228	.296	9	.225	0	12	11	-1	1.1
1917	Chi-A	0	0	—	5	0	0	0	0	17^2	18	10	1	1	6	3	12.7	5.09	52	.305	.379	0	.000	-1	-5	-5	-0	-0.3
1918	Chi-A	0	1	.000	4	0	0	0	0	8^1	12	6	0	0	3	1	16.2	5.40	51	.333	.385	1	.500	0	-2	-3	0	-0.2
Total	5	15	14	.517	77	27	15	3	0	326	268	115	3	4	95	111	10.1	2.18	127	.229	.289	19	.184	-1	23	21	4	2.6
● **HARRY WOLTER**	Wolter, Harry Meigs b: 7/11/1884, Monterey, Cal. d: 7/7/70, Palo Alto, Cal. BL/TL, 5'10", 175 lbs. Deb: 5/14/07 ♦																											
1907	Pit-N	0	0	—	1	0	0	0	0	2	3	2	0	0	2	0	22.5	4.50	54	.333	.455	0	.000	-0	-0	-0	-0	-0.1
	StL-N	0	2	.000	3	3	1	0	0	23	27	13	1	2	18	8	18.4	4.30	58	.318	.448	16	.340	1	-5	-5	-1	-0.4
	Yr	0	2	.000	4	3	1	0	0	25	30	15	1	2	20	8	18.7	4.32	58	.319	.448	16	.333	1	-5	-5	-1	-0.5
1909	Bos-A	4	4	.500	11	6	0	0	0	59	66	33	0	4	30	21	15.3	3.51	71	.303	.397	29	.240	2	-7	-7	-1	-0.8
Total	2	4	6	.400	15	9	1	0	0	84	96	48	1	6	50	29	16.3	3.75	67	.308	.413	514	.270	3	-12	-12	-2	-1.3
● **RYNIE WOLTERS**	Wolters, Reinder Albertus b: 3/17/1842, Schantz, Netherlands d: 1/3/17, Newark, N.J. TR, 6', 165 lbs. Deb: 5/18/1871																											
1871	Mut-n	16	16	.500	**32**	32	**31**	**1**	0	**283**	345	283	7		39	22	12.2	3.43	110	**.263**	.285	51	.370	20	25	12		2.0
1872	Cle-n	3	6	.333	12	8	5	0	0	75^1	115	106	3		7	4	14.6	6.09	58	.304	.317	16	.232	-0	-21	-22		-1.5
1873	Res-n	0	1	.000	1	1	1	0	0	9	13	23	0		1	1	14.0	0.00	—	.220	.233	0	.000	-1	3	3		0.2
Total	3 n	19	23	.452	45	41	37	1	0	367^1	473	412	10		47	27	12.7	3.90	86	.271	.290	67	.318	19	-26	-21		0.7
● **DOOLEY WOMACK**	Womack, Horace Guy b: 8/25/39, Columbia, S.C. BL/TR, 6', 170 lbs. Deb: 4/14/66																											
1966	NY-A	7	3	.700	42	1	0	0	4	75	52	25	6	3	23	50	9.4	2.64	126	.198	.270	1	.200	0	7	6	2	1.1
1967	NY-A	5	6	.455	65	0	0	0	18	97	80	33	6	3	35	57	10.9	2.41	130	.230	.306	4	.286	1	9	8	4	1.8
1968	NY-A	3	7	.300	45	0	0	0	2	61^2	53	23	6	1	29	27	12.1	3.21	90	.244	.336	1	.200	0	-2	-2	2	-0.1
1969	Hou-N	2	1	.667	30	0	0	0	0	51^1	49	21	1	3	20	32	12.6	3.51	101	.259	.340	1	.167	-0	1	0	2	0.2
	Sea-A	2	1	.667	9	0	0	0	0	14^1	15	4	0	0	3	8	11.3	2.51	145	.273	.310	0	.000	-0	2	2	0	0.4
1970	Oak-A	0	0	—	2	0	0	0	0	3	4	5	2	0	1	3	15.0	15.00	24	.308	.357	0	—	0	-4	-4	0	-0.2
Total	5	19	18	.514	193	1	0	0	24	302^1	253	111	21	10	111	177	11.1	2.95	110	.233	.310	7	.226	1	12	10	11	3.2
● **SPADES WOOD**	Wood, Charles Asher b: 1/13/09, Spartanburg, S.C. d: 5/18/86, Wichita, Kan. BL/TL, 5'10.5", 150 lbs. Deb: 8/16/30																											
1930	Pit-N	4	3	.571	9	7	4	2	0	58	61	34	4	0	32	23	14.4	5.12	97	.270	.360	5	.250	1	-1	-1	-2	-0.2
1931	Pit-N	2	6	.250	15	10	2	0	0	64	69	45	2	1	46	33	16.3	6.05	64	.273	.387	5	.227	1	-16	-16	-0	-1.6
Total	2	6	9	.400	24	17	6	2	0	122	130	79	6	1	78	56	15.4	5.61	78	.271	.375	10	.238	1	-16	-17	-2	-1.8
● **GEORGE WOOD**	Wood, George A. "Dandy" b: 11/9/1858, Boston, Mass. d: 4/4/24, Harrisburg, Pa. BL/TR, 5'10.5", 175 lbs. Deb: 5/1/1880 MU ♦																											
1883	Det-N	0	0	—	1	0	0	0	0	5	8	9	0		3	0	19.8	7.20	43	.348	.423	133	.302	0	-2	-2	0	0.0
1885	Det-N	0	0	—	1	0	0	0	0	4	5	2	0		1	1	13.5	0.00	—	.333	.375	105	.290	0	1	1	-0	0.1
1888	Phi-N	0	0	—	2	0	0	0	**2**	2	3	3	0	0	1	0	18.0	4.50	66	.300	.364	99	.229	1	-0	-0	0	0.0
1889	Phi-N	0	0	—	1	0	0	0	0	1	2	2	0	0	0	2	18.0	18.00	24	.400	.400	106	.251	0	-2	-1	0	-0.1
Total	4	0	0	—	5	0	0	0	2	12	18	16	0	0	5	3	17.3	5.25	59	.340	.397	1507	.279	1	-3	-3	0	0.0
● **JOE WOOD**	Wood, Joe "Smokey Joe" (b: Howard Ellsworth Wood) b: 10/25/1889, Kansas City, Mo. d: 7/27/85, West Haven, Conn BR/TR, 5'11", 180 lbs. Deb: 8/24/08 F♦																											
1908	Bos-A	1	1	.500	6	2	1	1	0	22^2	14	12	0	1	16	11	12.3	2.38	103	.161	.298	0	.000	-1	0	0	-0	-0.1
1909	Bos-A	11	7	.611	24	19	13	4	0	160^2	121	51	1	6	43	88	9.5	2.18	114	.209	.270	9	.164	-0	5	6	-4	0.2
1910	Bos-A	12	13	.480	35	17	14	3	0	196^2	155	81	3	10	56	145	10.1	1.69	151	.220	.287	18	.261	5	18	19	2	3.3
1911	Bos-A	23	17	.575	44	33	25	5	3	275^2	226	113	2	11	76	231	10.2	2.02	162	.223	.284	23	.261	9	40	39	2	**6.6**
1912	*Bos-A	**34**	5	**.872**	43	38	**35**	**10**	1	344	267	104	2	12	82	258	9.4	1.91	178	.216	.272	36	.290	11	54	56	8	8.4
1913	Bos-A	11	5	.688	23	18	12	1	2	145^2	120	54	0	8	61	123	11.7	2.29	129	.229	.319	15	.268	4	10	11	4	2.1
1914	Bos-A	10	3	.769	18	14	11	1	0	113^1	94	38	1	0	34	67	10.2	2.62	103	.229	.288	6	.140	-0	2	1	1	0.1
1915	Bos-A	15	5	**.750**	25	16	10	3	2	157^1	120	32	1	1	44	63	9.4	**1.49**	187	.216	.275	14	.259	4	25	24	1	3.8
1917	Cle-A	0	1	.000	5	1	0	0	1	15^2	17	7	0	0	7	2	13.8	3.45	82	.309	.387	0	.000	-1	-1	-1	0	-0.2
1919	Cle-A	0	0	—	1	0	0	0	1	0^2	0	0	0	0	0	0	0.0	0.00	—	.000	.000	49	.255	0	0	0	0	0.1
1920	*Cle-A	0	0	—	1	0	0	0	0	2	4	5	0	0	2	1	27.0	22.50	17	.444	.545	37	.270	0	-4	-4	0	-0.2
Total	11	117	57	.672	225	158	121	28	10	1434^1	1138	497	10	49	421	989	10.1	2.03	146	.220	.285	553	.283	31	150	149	14	24.1
● **JOHN WOOD**	Wood, John B. b: 1871, 5'7", 142 lbs. Deb: 5/9/1896																											
1896	StL-N	0	0	—	1	0	0	0	0	0	1	0	1	2	—	—	∞	—	1.000	1.000	100	—	0	-1	-1		0	-0.1
● **JOE WOOD**	Wood, Joseph Frank b: 5/20/16, Shohola, Pa. BR/TR, 6', 190 lbs. Deb: 5/1/44 F																											
1944	Bos-A	0	1	.000	3	1	0	0	0	9^2	13	9	0	0	3	5	14.9	6.52	52	.317	.364	0	.000	-0	-3	-3	0	-0.3
● **KERRY WOOD**	Wood, Kerry Lee b: 6/16/77, Irving, Tex. BR/TR, 6'5", 225 lbs. Deb: 4/12/98																											
1998	*Chi-N	13	6	.684	26	26	1	1	0	166^2	117	69	14	11	85	233	11.5	3.40	129	**.196**	.307	7	.130	-0	15	18	-2	1.7
2000	Chi-N	8	7	.533	23	23	1	0	0	137	112	77	17	9	87	132	13.7	4.80	95	.226	.352	10	.250	3	-2	-4	-1	-0.1
Total	2	21	13	.618	49	49	2	1	0	303^2	229	146	31	20	172	365	12.5	4.03	111	.210	.328	17	.181	3	13	15	-3	1.6
● **PETE WOOD**	Wood, Peter Burke b: 2/1/1857, Hamilton, Ont., Can. d: 3/15/23, Chicago, Ill. TR, 5'7", 185 lbs. Deb: 7/15/1885 F																											
1885	Buf-N	8	15	.348	24	22	21	0	0	198^2	235	170	8		66	38	13.6	4.44	67	.280	.332	23	.221	-1	-36	-30	-1	-3.0
1889	Phi-N	1	1	.500	3	2	2	0	0	19	28	15	0	0	3	8	14.7	5.21	83	.333	.356	0	.000	-1	-3	-2	-0	-0.2
Total	2	9	16	.360	27	24	23	0	0	217^2	263	185	8	0	69	46	13.7	4.51	69	.285	.334	23	.205	-2	-38	-32	-1	-3.2

● **WILBUR WOOD** Wood, Wilbur Forrester b: 10/22/41, Cambridge, Mass. BR/TL, 6', 180 lbs. Deb: 6/30/61

YEAR	TM/L	W	L	PCT	G	GS	CG	SH	SV	IP	H	R	HR	HB	BB	SO	RAT	ERA	ERA+	OAV	OOB	BH	AVG	PB	PR	PR+	PD	TPI
1961	Bos-A	0	0	—	6	1	0	0	0	13	14	8	2	0	7	7	14.5	5.54	75	.269	.356	0	.000	-0	-2	-2	-0	-0.2
1962	Bos-A	0	0	—	1	1	0	0	0	7^2	6	3	0	0	3	3	10.6	3.52	117	.214	.290	0	.000	-0	0	0	0	0.0
1963	Bos-A	0	5	.000	25	6	0	0	0	64^2	67	35	10	3	13	28	11.6	3.76	101	.270	.314	0	.000	-1	-1	0	-1	-0.2
1964	Bos-A	0	0	—	4	0	0	0	0	5^2	13	11	1	0	3	5	25.4	17.47	22	.433	.485	0	.000	-0	-9	-8	0	-0.4
	Pit-N	0	2	.000	3	2	1	0	0	17^1	16	8	0	2	11	7	15.1	3.63	97	.246	.372	0	.000	-0	-0	-0	-1	-0.1
1965	Pit-N	1	1	.500	34	1	0	0	0	51^1	44	21	3	1	16	29	10.7	3.16	111	.237	.300	0	.000	-1	2	2	-1	0.0
1967	Chi-A	4	2	.667	51	8	0	0	4	95^1	95	34	2	1	28	47	11.7	2.45	126	.260	.315	1	.063	-0	8	7	-1	0.4
1968	Chi-A	13	12	.520	**88**	2	0	0	16	159	127	39	8	3	33	74	9.2	1.87	162	.222	.268	2	.091	-1	**20**	**20**	-0	3.8
1969	Chi-A	10	11	.476	**76**	0	0	0	15	119^2	113	48	13	3	40	73	11.7	3.01	128	.248	.313	0	.000	-1	8	11	1	2.0
1970	Chi-A	9	13	.409	**77**	0	0	0	21	121^2	118	50	7	2	36	85	11.5	2.81	139	.258	.315	2	.111	-1	12	14	2	3.1
1971	Chi-A☆	22	13	.629	44	42	22	7	1	334	272	95	21	7	62	210	9.2	1.91	**188**	.222	.264	5	.052	-5	**58**	**60**	2	**6.4**
1972	Chi-A★	**24**	17	.585	49	49	20	8	0	**376^2**	325	119	28	7	74	193	9.7	2.51	125	.235	.277	17	.136	-2	24	26	4	3.1
1973	Chi-A	**24**	20	.545	49	48	21	4	0	**359^1**	381	166	25	7	91	199	12.0	3.46	115	.270	.318	0	—	0	15	20	1	2.3
1974	Chi-A☆	20	19	.513	42	42	22	1	0	320^1	305	143	27	9	80	169	11.1	3.60	104	.254	.305	0	—	0	1	5	3	0.9
1975	Chi-A	16	20	.444	43	43	14	2	0	291^1	309	148	26	5	92	140	12.5	4.11	95	.272	.329	0	—	0	-10	-7	1	-0.7
1976	Chi-A	4	3	.571	7	7	5	1	0	56^1	51	24	3	0	11	31	9.9	2.24	160	.242	.279	0	—	0	8	8	1	1.1
1977	Chi-A	7	8	.467	24	18	5	1	0	122^2	139	75	10	10	50	42	14.6	4.99	82	.293	.373	0	—	0	-12	-12	2	-1.1
1978	Chi-A	10	10	.500	28	27	4	0	0	168	187	103	23	3	74	69	14.1	5.20	73	.285	.361	0	—	0	-26	-26	2	-2.5
Total	17	164	156	.512	651	297	114	24	57	2684	2582	1130	209	63	724	1411	11.3	3.24	113	.254	.308	27	.084	-14	94	119	15	17.9

● **BRAD WOODALL** Woodall, David Bradley b: 6/25/69, Atlanta, Ga. BB/TL, 6', 175 lbs. Deb: 7/22/94

YEAR	TM/L	W	L	PCT	G	GS	CG	SH	SV	IP	H	R	HR	HB	BB	SO	RAT	ERA	ERA+	OAV	OOB	BH	AVG	PB	PR	PR+	PD	TPI
1994	Atl-N	0	1	.000	1	1	0	0	0	6	5	3	2	0	2	2	10.5	4.50	94	.227	.292	1	.500	0	-0	-0	1	0.1
1995	Atl-N	1	1	.500	9	0	0	0	0	10^1	13	10	1	0	8	5	18.3	6.10	70	.310	.420	1	1.000	0	-2	-2	0	-0.3
1996	Atl-N	2	2	.500	8	3	0	0	0	19^2	28	19	4	0	4	20	14.6	7.32	60	.333	.364	1	.200	0	-7	-6	-0	-1.0
1998	Mil-N	7	9	.438	31	20	0	0	0	138	145	81	25	6	47	85	12.9	4.96	86	.273	.338	9	.237	3	-11	-11	1	-0.7
1999	Chi-N	0	1	.000	6	3	0	0	0	16	17	12	5	1	6	7	13.5	5.63	80	.270	.343	1	.500	1	-2	-2	0	0.0
Total	5	10	14	.417	55	27	0	0	0	190	208	125	37	7	67	119	13.4	5.31	81	.280	.345	13	.271	5	-22	-21	1	-1.9

● **STEVE WOODARD** Woodard, Steven Larry b: 5/15/75, Hartselle, Ala. BL/TR, 6'4", 225 lbs. Deb: 7/28/97

YEAR	TM/L	W	L	PCT	G	GS	CG	SH	SV	IP	H	R	HR	HB	BB	SO	RAT	ERA	ERA+	OAV	OOB	BH	AVG	PB	PR	PR+	PD	TPI
1997	Mil-A	3	3	.500	7	7	0	0	0	36^2	39	25	5	2	6	32	11.5	5.15	90	.269	.307	0	—	0	-2	-2	-1	-0.4
1998	Mil-N	10	12	.455	34	26	0	0	0	165^2	170	83	19	9	33	135	11.5	4.18	102	.264	.309	7	.140	-1	1	2	-2	-0.1
1999	Mil-N	11	8	.579	31	29	2	0	0	185	219	101	23	6	36	119	12.7	4.52	100	.294	.331	7	.132	0	1	0	-0	0.0
2000	Mil-N	1	7	.125	27	11	1	0	0	93^2	125	70	16	4	33	65	15.6	5.96	77	.325	.384	1	.045	-1	-14	-15	0	-1.1
	Cle-A	3	3	.500	13	11	0	0	0	54	57	35	10	2	11	35	11.7	5.67	88	.269	.311	0	—	0	-4	-4	1	-0.3
Total	4	28	33	.459	112	84	3	0	0	535	610	314	73	23	119	386	12.7	4.83	93	.286	.331	15	.120	-2	-19	-19	-1	-1.9

● **GENE WOODBURN** Woodburn, Eugene Stewart b: 8/20/1886, Bellaire, Ohio d: 1/18/61, Sandusky, Ohio BR/TR, 6', 175 lbs. Deb: 7/27/11

YEAR	TM/L	W	L	PCT	G	GS	CG	SH	SV	IP	H	R	HR	HB	BB	SO	RAT	ERA	ERA+	OAV	OOB	BH	AVG	PB	PR	PR+	PD	TPI
1911	StL-N	1	5	.167	11	6	1	0	0	38^1	22	32	0	6	40	23	16.0	5.40	63	.167	.382	1	.167	1	-9	-9	1	-1.0
1912	StL-N	1	4	.200	20	5	1	0	0	48^1	60	48	0	4	42	25	19.7	5.59	61	.306	.438	0	.000	-2	-12	-12	-1	-1.3
Total	2	2	9	.182	31	11	2	0	0	86^2	82	80	0	10	82	48	18.1	5.50	62	.250	.414	1	.053	-0	-20	-20	0	-2.3

● **FRED WOODCOCK** Woodcock, Fred Wayland b: 5/17/1868, Winchendon, Mass. d: 8/11/43, Ashburnham, Mass. BL/TL, 6'2", 190 lbs. Deb: 5/17/1892

YEAR	TM/L	W	L	PCT	G	GS	CG	SH	SV	IP	H	R	HR	HB	BB	SO	RAT	ERA	ERA+	OAV	OOB	BH	AVG	PB	PR	PR+	PD	TPI
1892	Pit-N	1	2	.333	5	4	3	0	0	33	42	28	1	2	17	8	16.6	3.55	93	.298	.381	3	.200	0	-1	-1	0	0.0

● **GEORGE WOODEND** Woodend, George Anthony b: 12/9/17, Hartford, Conn. d: 2/6/80, Hartford, Conn. BR/TR, 6', 200 lbs. Deb: 4/22/44

YEAR	TM/L	W	L	PCT	G	GS	CG	SH	SV	IP	H	R	HR	HB	BB	SO	RAT	ERA	ERA+	OAV	OOB	BH	AVG	PB	PR	PR+	PD	TPI
1944	Bos-N	0	0	—	3	0	0	0	0	2	5	4	0	0	5	0	45.0	13.50	28	.556	.714	0	—	0	-2	-2	0	-0.1

● **HAL WOODESHICK** Woodeshick, Harold Joseph b: 8/24/32, Wilkes-Barre, Pa. BR/TL, 6'3", 200 lbs. Deb: 9/14/56

YEAR	TM/L	W	L	PCT	G	GS	CG	SH	SV	IP	H	R	HR	HB	BB	SO	RAT	ERA	ERA+	OAV	OOB	BH	AVG	PB	PR	PR+	PD	TPI
1956	Det-A	0	2	.000	2	2	0	0	0	5^1	12	8	1	0	3	1	25.3	13.50	30	.444	.500	0	—	0	-6	-6	0	-0.9
1958	Cle-A	6	6	.500	14	9	3	0	0	71^2	71	32	4	6	25	27	12.8	3.64	100	.265	.341	4	.167	-1	1	0	3	0.2
1959	Was-A	2	4	.333	31	3	0	0	0	61	58	39	2	1	36	30	14.0	3.69	106	.253	.357	0	.000	-1	1	2	1	0.1
1960	Was-A	4	5	.444	41	14	1	0	4	115	131	67	7	3	60	46	15.2	4.70	83	.289	.375	2	.069	-2	-11	-10	2	-0.8
1961	Was-A	3	2	.600	7	6	1	0	0	40^1	38	19	3	3	24	24	14.5	4.02	100	.257	.371	2	.125	-1	0	-0	1	0.0
	Det-A	1	1	.500	12	2	0	0	0	18^1	25	17	3	0	17	13	20.6	7.85	52	.316	.438	0	.000	-0	-8	-8	1	-0.6
	Yr	4	3	.571	19	8	1	0	0	58^2	63	36	6	3	41	37	16.4	5.22	77	.278	.395	2	.100	-1	-8	-8	2	-0.6
1962	Hou-N	5	16	.238	31	26	2	1	0	139^1	161	84	3	3	54	82	14.1	4.39	85	.290	.356	3	.081	-1	-7	-11	0	-1.5
1963	Hou-N★	11	9	.550	55	0	0	0	10	114	75	29	3	6	42	94	9.7	1.97	160	.186	.273	3	.130	-0	17	16	3	3.4
1964	Hou-N	2	9	.182	61	0	0	0	**23**	78^1	73	32	3	7	32	58	12.9	2.76	124	.249	.337	0	.000	-0	7	6	2	1.4
1965	Hou-N	3	4	.429	27	0	0	0	3	32^1	27	13	3	0	18	22	12.5	3.06	110	.227	.328	1	.167	-0	2	1	1	0.3
	StL-N	3	2	.600	51	0	0	0	15	59^2	47	14	1	2	27	37	11.5	1.81	212	.221	.314	0	.000	-1	11	12	2	1.9
	Yr	6	6	.500	78	0	0	0	18	92	74	27	4	2	45	59	11.8	2.25	163	.223	.319	1	.071	-1	13	14	2	2.2
1966	StL-N	2	1	.667	59	0	0	0	4	70^1	57	17	5	1	23	30	10.4	1.92	187	.224	.290	1	.200	0	13	13	3	1.1
1967	*StL-N	2	1	.667	36	0	0	0	2	41^2	41	29	2	3	28	20	15.6	5.18	63	.252	.371	0	.000	-0	-8	-9	1	-0.7
Total	11	44	62	.415	427	62	7	1	61	847^1	816	400	40	35	389	484	13.2	3.56	102	.254	.342	16	.092	-7	13	7	18	3.9

● **DAN WOODMAN** Woodman, Daniel Courtenay "Cocoa" b: 7/8/1893, Danvers, Mass. d: 12/14/62, Danvers, Mass. BR/TR, 5'8", 160 lbs. Deb: 7/10/14

YEAR	TM/L	W	L	PCT	G	GS	CG	SH	SV	IP	H	R	HR	HB	BB	SO	RAT	ERA	ERA+	OAV	OOB	BH	AVG	PB	PR	PR+	PD	TPI
1914	Buf-F	0	0	—	13	0	0	0	1	33^2	30	16	0	1	11	13	11.2	2.41	123	.246	.313	1	.143	-1	2	2	-1	0.0
1915	Buf-F	0	0	—	5	1	0	0	0	15^1	14	9	0	0	9	1	13.5	4.11	68	.246	.348	1	.250	-0	-2	-2	1	0.0
Total	2	0	0	—	18	1	0	0	1	49	44	25	0	1	20	14	11.9	2.94	99	.246	.325	2	.182	-1	-1	-0	0	0.0

● **CLARENCE WOODS** Woods, Clarence Cofield b: 6/11/1892, Woods Ridge, Ohio County, Ind. d: 7/2/69, Rising Sun, Ind. BR/TR, 6'5", 230 lbs. Deb: 8/8/14

YEAR	TM/L	W	L	PCT	G	GS	CG	SH	SV	IP	H	R	HR	HB	BB	SO	RAT	ERA	ERA+	OAV	OOB	BH	AVG	PB	PR	PR+	PD	TPI
1914	Ind-F	0	0	—	2	0	0	0	1	2	1	1	0	0	2	1	13.5	4.50	69	.167	.375	0	—	0	-0	-0	0	0.0

● **PINKY WOODS** Woods, George Rowland b: 5/22/15, Waterbury, Conn. d: 10/30/82, Los Angeles, Cal. BR/TR, 6'5", 225 lbs. Deb: 6/20/43

YEAR	TM/L	W	L	PCT	G	GS	CG	SH	SV	IP	H	R	HR	HB	BB	SO	RAT	ERA	ERA+	OAV	OOB	BH	AVG	PB	PR	PR+	PD	TPI
1943	Bos-A	5	6	.455	23	12	2	0	1	100^2	109	61	6	1	55	32	14.8	4.92	67	.284	.375	8	.222	-0	-18	-18	-0	-1.9
1944	Bos-A	4	8	.333	38	20	5	1	0	170^2	171	73	4	6	88	56	14.0	3.27	104	.266	.360	7	.146	-1	3	2	2	0.2
1945	Bos-A	4	7	.364	24	12	3	0	2	107^1	108	56	3	1	63	36	14.4	4.19	81	.268	.368	9	.214	1	-10	-9	1	-0.7
Total	3	13	21	.382	85	44	10	1	3	378^2	388	190	13	8	206	124	14.3	3.97	85	.272	.366	24	.190	-1	-25	-25	3	-2.4

● **JOHN WOODS** Woods, John Fulton "Abe" b: 1/18/1898, Princeton, W.Va. d: 10/4/46, Norfolk, Va. BR/TR, 6', 175 lbs. Deb: 9/16/24

YEAR	TM/L	W	L	PCT	G	GS	CG	SH	SV	IP	H	R	HR	HB	BB	SO	RAT	ERA	ERA+	OAV	OOB	BH	AVG	PB	PR	PR+	PD	TPI
1924	Bos-A	0	0	—	1	0	0	0	0	1	0	0	0	0	3	0	27.0	0.00	—	.000	.500	0	—	0	0	0	-0	0.0

● **WALT WOODS** Woods, Walter Sydney b: 4/28/1875, Rye, N.H. d: 10/30/51, Portsmouth, N.H. BR/TR, 5'9.5", 165 lbs. Deb: 4/20/1898

YEAR	TM/L	W	L	PCT	G	GS	CG	SH	SV	IP	H	R	HR	HB	BB	SO	RAT	ERA	ERA+	OAV	OOB	BH	AVG	PB	PR	PR+	PD	TPI
1898	Chi-N	9	13	.409	27	22	18	3	0	215	224	128	7	10	59	26	12.3	3.14	114	.266	.322	27	.175	-4	11	11	1	0.6
1899	Lou-N	9	13	.409	26	21	17	0	0	186^1	216	100	9	7	37	21	12.6	3.28	117	.290	.329	19	.151	-3	12	12	5	1.3
1900	Pit-N	0	0	—	1	0	0	0	0	3	9	7	0	0	1	1	30.0	21.00	17	.500	.526	0	.000	-0	-6	-6	-0	-0.3
Total	3	18	26	.409	54	43	35	3	0	404^1	449	235	16	17	97	48	12.5	3.34	111	.280	.328	46	.164	-7	17	17	5	1.6

● **DICK WOODSON** Woodson, Richard Lee b: 3/30/45, Oelwein, Iowa BR/TR, 6'5", 207 lbs. Deb: 4/8/69

YEAR	TM/L	W	L	PCT	G	GS	CG	SH	SV	IP	H	R	HR	HB	BB	SO	RAT	ERA	ERA+	OAV	OOB	BH	AVG	PB	PR	PR+	PD	TPI
1969	*Min-A	7	5	.583	44	10	2	0	1	110^1	99	49	11	3	49	66	12.3	3.67	100	.237	.322	2	.074	-1	-1	-0	1	-0.1
1970	*Min-A	1	2	.333	21	0	0	0	1	30^2	29	18	2	0	19	22	14.1	3.82	98	.244	.348	0	.000	-0	-0	-0	0	0.0
1972	Min-A	14	14	.500	36	36	9	3	0	251^2	193	93	19	2	101	150	10.6	2.72	118	.211	.291	7	.080	-5	10	13	1	1.0
1973	Min-A	10	8	.556	23	23	4	2	0	141^1	137	68	12	2	68	53	13.2	3.95	100	.254	.339	0	—	0	-2	0	-2	-0.1
1974	Min-A	1	1	.500	5	4	0	0	0	27	30	16	5	1	4	12	11.7	4.33	86	.273	.304	0	—	0	-2	-2	1	-0.1
	NY-A	1	2	.333	8	3	0	0	0	28	34	19	6	1	12	12	15.1	5.79	61	.301	.373	0	—	0	-7	-7	-1	-0.8
	Yr	2	3	.400	13	7	0	0	0	55	64	35	11	2	16	24	13.4	5.07	72	.287	.340	0	—	0	-9	-9	-0	-0.9
Total	5	34	32	.515	137	76	15	5	2	589	522	263	55	9	253	315	12.0	3.47	102	.236	.317	9	.077	-7	-2	5	-0	-0.1

● **KERRY WOODSON** Woodson, Walter Browne b: 5/18/69, Jacksonville, Fla. BR/TR, 6'2", 190 lbs. Deb: 7/19/92

YEAR	TM/L	W	L	PCT	G	GS	CG	SH	SV	IP	H	R	HR	HB	BB	SO	RAT	ERA	ERA+	OAV	OOB	BH	AVG	PB	PR	PR+	PD	TPI
1992	Sea-A	0	1	.000	8	1	0	0	0	13^2	12	7	0	2	11	6	16.5	3.29	121	.245	.403	0	—	0	1	1	0	0.1

YEAR	TM/L	W	L	PCT	G	GS	CG	SH	SV	IP	H	R	HR	HB	BB	SO	RAT	ERA	ERA+	OAV	OOB	BH	AVG	PB	PR	PR+	PD	TPI
● **FRANK WOODWARD**	Woodward, Frank Russell b: 5/17/1894, New Haven, Conn. d: 6/11/61, New Haven, Conn. BR/TR, 5'10", 175 lbs. Deb: 4/17/18																											
1918	Phi-N	0	0	—	2	0	0	0	0	6	6	4	0	0	4	4	15.0	6.00	50	.250	.357	1	.333	0	-2	-2	-0	-0.1
1919	Phi-N	6	9	.400	17	12	6	0	0	100^2	109	63	5	5	35	27	13.3	4.74	68	.291	.359	6	.207	1	-20	-15	-2	-2.2
	StL-N	3	5	.375	17	7	2	0	1	72	65	27	1	1	28	18	11.8	2.63	106	.248	.323	1	.048	-2	2	1	-0	-0.1
	Yr	9	14	.391	34	19	8	0	1	172^2	174	90	6	6	63	45	12.7	3.86	79	.273	.344	7	.140	-1	-18	-15	-2	-2.3
1921	Was-A	0	0	—	3	1	0	0	0	10^2	11	7	0	0	3	4	11.8	5.91	70	.282	.333	1	.333	0	-2	-2	0	-0.1
1922	Was-A	0	0	—	1	0	0	0	0	2^1	3	3	0	0	3	2	23.1	11.57	33	.375	.545	0	.000	-0	-2	-2	0	-0.1
1923	Chi-A	0	1	.000	2	1	0	0	0	2	5	3	0	0	1	0	27.0	13.50	29	.500	.545	0	—	0	-2	-2	0	-0.4
Total	5	9	15	.375	42	21	8	0	1	193^2	199	107	6	6	74	55	13.0	4.23	74	.277	.350	9	.158	-1	-26	-23	-2	-3.0
● **BOB WOODWARD**	Woodward, Robert John b: 9/28/62, Hanover, N.H. BR/TR, 6'3", 185 lbs. Deb: 9/5/85																											
1985	Bos-A	1	0	1.000	5	2	0	0	0	26^2	17	8	0	2	9	16	9.5	1.69	254	.168	.250	0	—	0	7	7	-1	0.3
1986	Bos-A	2	3	.400	9	6	0	0	0	35^2	46	26	4	1	11	14	14.6	5.30	79	.313	.365	0	—	0	-4	-4	0	-0.5
1987	Bos-A	1	1	.500	9	6	0	0	0	37	53	33	6	1	15	15	16.8	7.05	65	.338	.399	0	—	0	-11	-10	-1	-0.6
1988	Bos-A	0	0	—	1	0	0	0	0	0^2	2	1	0	0	1	0	40.5	13.50	31	.500	.600	0	—	0	-1	-1	0	0.0
Total	4	4	4	.500	24	14	0	0	0	100	118	68	10	4	36	45	14.2	5.04	86	.289	.352	0	—	0	-8	-8	-1	-0.8
● **FLOYD WOOLDRIDGE**	Wooldridge, Floyd Lewis b: 8/25/28, Jerico Springs, Mo BR/TR, 6'1", 185 lbs. Deb: 5/1/55																											
1955	StL-N	2	4	.333	18	8	2	0	0	57^2	64	36	9	1	27	14	14.4	4.84	84	.281	.359	4	.222	0	-5	-5	-1	-0.6
● **JUNIOR WOOTEN**	Wooten, Earl Hazwell b: 1/16/24, Pelzer, S.C. BR/TL, 5'11", 160 lbs. Deb: 9/16/47 ◆																											
1948	Was-A	0	0	—	1	0	0	0	0	2	2	2	0	0	2	1	18.0	9.00	48	.250	.400	66	.256	0	-1	-1	0	0.0
● **FRED WORDEN**	Worden, Frederick Bamford b: 9/4/1894, St.Louis, Mo. d: 11/9/41, St.Louis, Mo. BR/TR, Deb: 9/28/14																											
1914	Phi-A	0	0	—	1	0	0	0	0	2	8	5	0	0	0	1	36.0	18.00	15	.615	.615	0	.000	-0	-3	-4	0	-0.2
● **HOGE WORKMAN**	Workman, Harry Hall b: 9/25/1899, Huntington, W.Va. d: 5/20/72, Ft.Myers, Fla. BR/TR, 5'11", 170 lbs. Deb: 6/27/24																											
1924	Bos-A	0	0	—	11	0	0	0	0	18	25	19	2	2	11	7	19.0	8.50	51	.325	.422	0	.000	-0	-9	-8	0	-0.4
● **RALPH WORKS**	Works, Ralph Talmadge "Judge" b: 3/16/1888, Payson, Ill. d: 8/8/41, Pasadena, Cal. BL/TR, 6'2.5", 185 lbs. Deb: 5/1/09																											
1909	*Det-A	4	1	.800	16	4	4	0	2	64	62	19	0	1	17	31	11.3	1.97	128	.261	.313	1	.059	-2	4	4	-1	0.1
1910	Det-A	3	6	.333	18	10	5	0	1	85^2	73	47	1	4	39	36	12.2	3.57	74	.235	.328	8	.267	1	-10	-9	-1	-0.9
1911	Det-A	11	5	.688	30	15	9	3	0	167^1	173	93	3	6	67	68	13.2	3.87	89	.268	.342	9	.148	-3	-10	-7	-4	-1.4
1912	Det-A	5	10	.333	27	16	9	1	1	157	185	101	1	7	66	64	14.8	4.24	77	.308	.383	8	.143	-3	-16	-17	0	-1.7
	Cin-N	1	1	.500	3	1	1	0	0	9^2	4	5	0	1	5	5	9.3	2.79	120	.133	.278	1	.200	-0	1	1	-0	0.1
1913	Cin-N	0	1	.000	5	2	0	0	0	15	15	14	0	3	8	4	15.6	7.80	42	.242	.356	1	.167	-0	-8	-7	-0	-0.4
Total	5	24	24	.500	99	48	28	4	4	498^2	512	279	5	22	202	208	13.3	3.79	83	.271	.348	28	.160	-8	-39	-36	-6	-4.2
● **TIM WORRELL**	Worrell, Timothy Howard b: 7/5/67, Pasadena, Cal. BR/TR, 6'4", 220 lbs. Deb: 6/25/93 F																											
1993	SD-N	2	7	.222	21	16	0	0	0	100^2	104	63	11	0	43	52	13.1	4.92	84	.269	.342	1	.032	-3	-10	-8	-1	-1.0
1994	SD-N	0	1	.000	3	3	0	0	0	14^2	9	7	0	0	5	14	8.6	3.68	112	.170	.241	1	.500	1	1	1	0	0.1
1995	SD-N	1	0	1.000	9	0	0	0	0	13^1	16	7	2	1	6	13	15.5	4.73	85	.291	.371	0	.000	-0	-1	-1	0	-0.1
1996	*SD-N	9	7	.563	50	11	0	0	1	121	109	45	9	6	39	99	11.5	3.05	130	.236	.304	3	.150	-0	16	13	-2	1.4
1997	SD-N	4	8	.333	60	10	0	0	3	106^1	116	67	14	7	50	81	14.6	5.16	75	.280	.367	3	.200	1	-11	-16	1	-1.5
1998	Det-A	2	6	.250	15	9	0	0	0	61^2	66	42	11	1	19	47	12.6	5.98	79	.270	.326	0	—	0	-9	-9	0	-0.9
	Cle-A	0	0	—	3	0	0	0	0	5^1	6	3	0	0	2	2	13.5	5.06	94	.300	.364	0	—	0	-0	-0	1	0.0
	Oak-A	0	1	.000	25	0	0	0	0	36	34	17	5	0	8	33	10.5	4.00	114	.241	.282	0	—	0	3	2	-0	0.1
	Yr	2	7	.222	43	9	0	0	0	103	106	62	16	1	29	82	11.9	5.24	89	.262	.313	0	—	0	-7	-7	1	-0.8
1999	Oak-A	2	2	.500	53	0	0	0	0	69^1	69	38	6	3	34	62	13.8	4.15	112	.256	.345	0	—	0	6	4	-1	0.1
2000	Bal-A	2	2	.500	5	0	0	0	0	7^1	12	6	3	0	5	5	20.9	7.36	65	.353	.436	0	—	0	-2	-2	-0	-0.4
	Chi-N	3	4	.429	54	0	0	0	3	62	60	20	7	1	24	52	12.3	2.47	185	.252	.323	0	.000	-0	15	15	-1	1.5
Total	8	25	38	.397	298	49	0	0	7	597^2	601	315	68	19	235	460	12.9	4.29	99	.259	.333	8	.113	-1	7	-2	-3	-0.7
● **TODD WORRELL**	Worrell, Todd Roland b: 9/28/59, Arcadia, Cal. BR/TR, 6'5", 222 lbs. Deb: 8/28/85 F																											
1985	*StL-N	3	0	1.000	17	0	0	0	5	21^2	17	7	2	0	7	17	10.0	2.91	122	.215	.279	0	.000	-0	2	2	-0	0.2
1986	StL-N	9	10	.474	74	0	0	0	**36**	103^2	86	29	9	1	41	73	11.1	2.08	175	.229	.307	1	.143	0	**19**	**18**	-2	3.8
1987	*StL-N	8	6	.571	75	0	0	0	33	94^2	86	29	8	0	34	92	11.4	2.66	156	.242	.308	1	.100	-0	15	15	0	3.1
1988	StL-N★	5	9	.357	68	0	0	0	32	90	69	32	7	1	34	78	10.4	3.00	116	.214	.291	0	.000	-0	5	5	-0	1.0
1989	StL-N	3	5	.375	47	0	0	0	20	51^2	42	21	4	0	26	41	11.8	2.96	123	.222	.316	0	.000	-0	3	4	1	0.9
1992	StL-N	5	3	.625	67	0	0	0	3	64	45	15	4	1	25	64	10.0	2.11	161	.198	.281	0	—	0	10	9	-1	1.1
1993	LA-N	1	1	.500	35	0	0	0	5	38^2	46	28	6	0	11	31	13.3	6.05	63	.313	.361	0	—	0	-9	-10	-0	-0.7
1994	LA-N	6	5	.545	38	0	0	0	11	42	37	21	4	1	12	44	10.7	4.29	92	.236	.294	0	—	0	-0	-2	-0	-0.4
1995	LA-N†	4	1	.800	59	0	0	0	32	62^1	50	15	4	1	19	61	10.1	2.02	188	.221	.285	0	.000	-0	15	14	1	2.3
1996	*LA-N★	4	6	.400	72	0	0	0	**44**	65^1	70	29	5	2	15	66	12.0	3.03	128	.265	.310	0	—	0	9	7	-1	1.2
1997	LA-N	2	6	.250	65	0	0	0	35	59^2	60	38	12	0	23	61	12.5	5.28	73	.250	.316	0	—	0	-7	-10	-1	-1.9
Total	11	50	52	.490	617	0	0	0	256	693^2	608	264	65	7	247	628	11.2	3.09	122	.235	.304	2	.074	-1	61	53	-2	10.6
● **RICH WORTHAM**	Wortham, Richard Cooper b: 10/22/53, Odessa, Tex. BR/TL, 6', 185 lbs. Deb: 5/3/78																											
1978	Chi-A	3	2	.600	8	8	2	0	0	59	59	24	1	0	23	25	12.5	3.05	125	.267	.336	0	—	0	5	5	-0	0.4
1979	Chi-A	14	14	.500	34	33	5	0	0	204	195	126	21	3	100	119	13.1	4.90	87	.255	.343	0	—	0	-15	-14	-2	-1.8
1980	Chi-A	4	7	.364	41	10	0	0	1	92	102	73	4	3	58	45	15.9	5.97	68	.285	.389	0	—	0	-20	-20	1	-2.0
1983	Oak-A	0	0	—	1	0	0	0	0	0	3	0	0	1	—	—	∞	—	1.000	1.000	95	—	0	-1	-1	0	-0.1	
Total	4	21	23	.477	84	51	7	0	1	355	359	224	26	6	182	189	13.9	4.89	84	.266	.356	0	—	0	-31	-30	-1	-3.5
● **AL WORTHINGTON**	Worthington, Allan Fulton "Red" b: 2/5/29, Birmingham, Ala. BR/TR, 6'2", 205 lbs. Deb: 7/6/53 C																											
1953	NY-N	4	8	.333	20	17	5	2	0	102	103	55	6	2	54	52	14.0	3.44	125	.258	.349	2	.065	-2	10	10	0	0.8
1954	NY-N	0	2	.000	10	1	0	0	0	18	21	7	0	0	15	8	18.0	3.50	115	.333	.462	0	.000	-1	1	1	0	0.1
1956	NY-N	7	14	.333	28	24	4	0	0	165^2	158	82	20	4	74	95	12.8	3.97	95	.254	.338	12	.235	2	-4	-3	2	0.0
1957	NY-N	8	11	.421	55	12	1	1	4	157^2	140	75	19	5	56	90	11.5	4.22	93	.237	.309	4	.100	-2	-6	-5	0	-0.8
1958	SF-N	11	7	.611	54	12	1	0	6	151^1	152	72	17	2	57	76	12.5	3.63	105	.255	.322	8	.182	0	5	3	0	0.4
1959	SF-N	2	3	.400	42	3	0	0	2	73^1	68	34	8	5	37	45	13.5	3.68	103	.253	.354	1	.077	-1	2	1	0	0.1
1960	Bos-A	0	1	.000	6	0	0	0	0	11^2	17	12	1	0	11	7	21.6	7.71	52	.340	.459	0	.000	-0	-5	-5	0	-0.4
	Chi-A	1	1	.500	4	0	0	0	0	5^1	3	2	0	0	4	1	11.8	3.38	112	.176	.333	2	1.000	1	0	0	0	0.2
	Yr	1	2	.333	10	0	0	0	0	17	20	14	1	0	15	8	18.5	6.35	62	.299	.427	2	.667	1	-5	-4	0	-0.2
1963	Cin-N	4	4	.500	50	0	0	0	10	81^1	75	34	6	3	31	55	12.1	2.99	112	.248	.324	1	.083	-0	3	3	2	0.6
1964	Cin-N	1	0	1.000	6	0	0	0	0	7	14	11	0	1	2	6	21.9	10.29	35	.400	.447	0	—	0	-5	-5	-0	-0.7
	Min-A	5	6	.455	41	0	0	0	14	72^1	47	18	4	0	28	59	9.3	1.37	261	.183	.263	1	.063	-1	18	18	1	3.4
1965	*Min-A	10	7	.588	62	0	0	0	21	80^1	57	25	4	3	41	59	11.3	2.13	167	.207	.316	1	.100	0	12	12	2	2.9
1966	Min-A	6	3	.667	65	0	0	0	16	91^1	66	26	6	1	27	93	9.3	2.46	146	.199	.261	3	.273	1	10	11	1	1.7
1967	Min-A	8	9	.471	59	0	0	0	16	92	77	36	6	1	38	80	11.3	2.84	122	.229	.309	0	.000	-1	4	6	0	1.3
1968	Min-A	4	5	.444	54	0	0	0	**18**	76^1	67	26	1	0	32	57	11.7	2.71	114	.238	.315	0	.000	-1	2	3	0	0.5
1969	*Min-A	4	1	.800	46	0	0	0	3	61	65	31	7	0	20	51	12.5	4.57	80	.278	.335	0	.000	-1	-6	-6	-1	-0.7
Total	14	75	82	.478	602	69	11	3	110	1246^2	1130	546	105	27	527	834	12.2	3.39	110	.243	.323	35	.137	-5	41	46	7	9.4
● **GENE WRIGHT**	Wright, Clarence Eugene "Big Gene" b: 12/11/1878, Cleveland, Ohio d: 10/29/30, Barberton, Ohio BR/TR, 6'2", 185 lbs. Deb: 10/5/01																											
1901	Bro-N	1	0	1.000	1	1	1	0	0	9	6	2	0	0	1	6	7.0	1.00	335	.188	.212	1	.333	0	2	2	-0	0.3
1902	Cle-A	7	10	.412	21	18	15	1	1	148	150	94	6	8	75	52	14.2	3.95	87	.263	.357	10	.143	-2	-6	-9	-2	-1.2
1903	Cle-A	3	10	.231	15	12	8	0	0	101^2	122	94	1	4	58	42	16.3	5.75	50	.296	.388	9	.209	2	-32	-34	2	-3.2
	StL-A	3	5	.375	8	8	7	1	0	61	73	29	2	4	16	37	13.7	3.69	79	.296	.348	3	.143	-1	-5	-5	1	-0.6
	Yr	6	15	.286	23	20	15	1	0	162^2	195	123	3	8	74	79	15.3	4.98	58	.296	.374	12	.188	2	-36	-39	3	-3.8

YEAR	TM/L	W	L	PCT	G	GS	CG	SH	SV	IP	H	R	HR	HB	BB	SO	RAT	ERA	ERA+	OAV	OOB	BH	AVG	PB	PR	PR+	PD	TPI
1904	StL-A	0	1	.000	1	1	0	0	0	4	10	6	0	0	2	3	27.0	13.50	18	.476	.522	0	.000	-0	-5	-5	1	-0.7
Total	4	14	26	.350	46	40	31	2	1	323^2	361	225	9	16	152	140	14.7	4.50	70	.282	.365	23	.167	-1	-45	-51	1	-5.4
● CLYDE WRIGHT Wright, Clyde b: 2/20/41, Jefferson City, Tenn. BR/TL, 6'1", 185 lbs. Deb: 6/15/66 F																												
1966	Cal-A	4	7	.364	20	13	3	1	0	91^1	92	39	11	1	25	37	11.6	3.74	90	.265	.316	3	.103	-1	-3	-4	0	-0.6
1967	Cal-A	5	5	.500	20	11	1	0	0	77^1	76	33	5	1	24	35	11.8	3.26	96	.260	.319	6	.273	2	-0	-1	0	0.1
1968	Cal-A	10	6	.625	41	13	2	1	3	125^2	123	58	13	2	44	71	12.1	3.94	74	.256	.321	8	.216	2	-13	-15	-1	-1.8
1969	Cal-A	1	8	.111	37	5	0	0	0	63^2	66	33	4	1	30	31	13.7	4.10	85	.278	.362	2	.182	0	-3	-4	0	-0.5
1970	Cal-A★	22	12	.647	39	39	7	2	0	260^2	226	97	24	7	88	110	11.1	2.83	128	.232	.300	18	.171	3	26	23	-2	3.1
1971	Cal-A	16	17	.485	37	37	10	2	0	276^2	225	105	17	3	82	135	10.1	2.99	108	.226	.287	14	.154	2	15	8	4	1.7
1972	Cal-A	18	11	.621	35	35	15	2	0	251	229	101	14	4	80	87	11.2	2.98	98	.246	.308	18	.217	7	3	-2	3	1.0
1973	Cal-A	11	19	.367	37	36	13	1	0	257	273	120	26	3	76	65	12.3	3.68	97	.273	.326	0	—	0	4	-4	4	0.0
1974	Mil-A	9	20	.310	38	32	15	0	0	232	264	122	22	0	54	64	12.3	4.42	82	.284	.323	0	—	0	-21	-21	2	-2.2
1975	Tex-A	4	6	.400	25	14	1	0	0	93^1	105	56	7	1	47	32	14.8	4.44	85	.294	.378	0	—	0	-7	-7	2	-0.5
Total	10	100	111	.474	329	235	67	9	3	1728^2	1679	764	143	23	550	667	11.7	3.50	96	.256	.316	69	.183	14	-0	-27	13	0.3
● DAVE WRIGHT Wright, David William b: 8/27/1875, Dennison, Ohio d: 1/18/46, Dennison, Ohio BR/TR, 6', 185 lbs. Deb: 7/22/1895																												
1895	Pit-N	0	0	—	1	0	0	0	0	2	6	6	0	0	1	0	31.5	27.00	17	.500	.538	0	.000	-0	-5	-5	0	-0.2
1897	Chi-N	1	0	1.000	1	1	1	0	0	7	17	14	1	2	2	4	27.0	15.43	29	.459	.512	1	.333	0	-9	-8	0	-0.6
Total	2	1	0	1.000	2	1	1	0	0	9	23	20	1	2	3	4	28.0	18.00	25	.469	.519	1	.250	0	-14	-13	0	-0.8
● GEORGE WRIGHT Wright, George b: 1/28/1847, Yonkers, N.Y. d: 8/21/37, Boston, Mass. BR/TR, 5'9.5", 150 lbs. Deb: 5/5/1871 FMH♦																												
1875	Bos-n	0	1	.000	2	0	0	0	0	4	5	3	0		0	0	11.3	6.75	32	.294	.294	136	.333	1	-2	-2		-0.3
1876	Bos-N	0	0	—	1	0	0	0	0	1	1	0	0		0	1	9.0	0.00	—	.250	.250	100	.292	0	0	0	0	0.0
● ED WRIGHT Wright, Henderson Edward b: 5/15/19, Dyersburg, Tenn. d: 11/19/95, Dyersburg, Tenn. BR/TR, 6'1", 180 lbs. Deb: 7/29/45																												
1945	Bos-N	8	3	.727	15	12	7	1	0	111^1	104	35	7	0	33	24	11.1	2.51	153	.254	.310	5	.128	-2	16	16	-1	1.2
1946	Bos-N	12	9	.571	36	21	9	2	0	176^1	164	82	8	2	71	44	12.1	3.52	97	.250	.325	18	.305	6	-2	-2	0	0.4
1947	Bos-N	3	3	.500	23	6	1	0	0	64^2	80	52	9	2	35	14	16.3	6.40	61	.305	.391	3	.130	-0	-17	-19	-0	-1.5
1948	Bos-N	0	0	—	3	0	0	0	0	4^2	9	3	0	0	2	2	21.2	1.93	199	.474	.524	0	—	0	1	1	0	0.1
1952	Phi-A	2	1	.667	24	0	0	0	1	41^1	55	36	6	3	20	9	17.0	6.53	61	.320	.400	1	.143	-0	-13	-11	-0	-0.8
Total	5	25	16	.610	101	39	17	3	1	398^1	412	208	30	7	161	93	13.1	4.00	92	.271	.344	27	.211	3	-15	-14	-2	-0.6
● JIM WRIGHT Wright, James "Jiggs" b: 9/19/1900, Hyde, England d: 4/10/63, Oakland, Cal. BR/TR, 6'2.5", 195 lbs. Deb: 9/14/27																												
1927	StL-A	1	0	1.000	2	1	1	0	0	12	8	6	0	0	4	4	9.0	4.50	97	.182	.250	0	.000	-0	-0	-0	-0	-0.1
1928	StL-A	0	0	—	2	0	0	0	0	2	3	3	0	0	2	2	22.5	13.50	31	.375	.500	0	—	0	-2	-2	0	-0.1
Total	2	1	0	1.000	4	1	1	0	0	14	11	9	0	0	6	6	10.9	5.79	75	.212	.293	0	.000	-0	-3	-2	0	-0.2
● JIM WRIGHT Wright, James Clifton b: 12/21/50, Reed City, Mich. BR/TR, 6'1", 165 lbs. Deb: 4/15/78																												
1978	Bos-A	8	4	.667	24	16	5	3	0	116	122	51	8	7	24	56	11.9	3.57	116	.276	.323	0	—	0	3	7	-2	0.5
1979	Bos-A	1	0	1.000	11	1	0	0	0	23	19	13	5	3	7	15	11.3	5.09	87	.226	.309	0	—	0	-2	-2	-0	-0.1
Total	2	9	4	.692	35	17	5	3	0	139	141	64	13	10	31	71	11.8	3.82	109	.268	.321	0	—	0	0	5	-2	0.4
● JIM WRIGHT Wright, James Leon b: 3/3/55, St.Joseph, Mo. BR/TR, 6'5", 205 lbs. Deb: 4/22/81 C																												
1981	KC-A	2	3	.400	17	4	0	0	0	52	57	21	5	2	21	27	13.8	3.46	104	.277	.349	0	—	0	1	1	-1	0.0
1982	KC-A	0	0	—	7	0	0	0	0	23^2	32	18	3	0	6	9	14.5	5.32	77	.320	.358	0	—	0	-3	-3	-1	-0.2
Total	2	2	3	.400	24	4	0	0	0	75^2	89	39	8	2	27	36	14.0	4.04	93	.291	.352	0	—	0	-2	-2	-1	-0.2
● RICKY WRIGHT Wright, James Richard b: 11/22/58, Paris, Tex. BL/TL, 6'3", 175 lbs. Deb: 7/28/82																												
1982	LA-N	2	1	.667	14	5	0	0	0	32^2	28	12	1	0	20	24	13.2	3.03	115	.233	.343	1	.125	0	2	2	0	0.2
1983	LA-N	0	0	—	6	0	0	0	0	6^1	5	2	0	0	2	5	9.9	2.84	127	.227	.292	0	—	0	1	1	-0	0.0
	Tex-A	0	0	—	1	0	0	0	0	2	0	0	0	0	1	2	4.5	0.00	—	.000	.167	0	—	0	1	1	-0	0.0
1984	Tex-A	0	2	.000	8	1	0	0	0	14^2	20	10	3	0	11	6	19.0	6.14	68	.357	.463	0	—	0	-3	-3	0	-0.3
1985	Tex-A	0	0	—	5	0	0	0	0	7^2	5	4	0	0	5	7	11.7	4.70	90	.185	.313	0	—	0	-0	-0	0	0.0
1986	Tex-A	1	0	1.000	21	1	0	0	0	39^1	44	22	1	0	21	23	14.9	5.03	86	.284	.369	0	—	0	-4	-3	1	-0.1
Total	5	3	3	.500	55	7	0	0	0	102^2	102	50	5	0	60	67	14.2	4.30	92	.265	.364	1	.125	0	-4	-4	1	-0.2
● JAMEY WRIGHT Wright, Jamey Alan b: 12/24/74, Oklahoma City, Okla. BR/TR, 6'6", 205 lbs. Deb: 7/3/96																												
1996	Col-N	4	4	.500	16	15	0	0	0	91^1	105	60	8	7	41	45	15.1	4.93	106	.298	.382	2	.077	-1	-7	2	1	0.2
1997	Col-N	8	12	.400	26	26	1	0	0	149^2	198	113	19	11	71	59	16.8	6.25	83	.327	.408	6	.125	-2	-34	-15	-0	-1.8
1998	Col-N	9	14	.391	34	34	1	0	0	206^1	235	143	24	11	95	86	14.9	5.67	91	.294	.377	10	.175	0	-33	-9	1	-0.7
1999	Col-N	4	3	.571	16	16	0	0	0	94^1	110	52	10	4	54	49	16.0	4.87	119	.307	.404	4	.125	-2	-3	8	1	0.5
2000	Mil-N	7	9	.438	26	25	0	0	0	164^2	157	81	12	18	88	96	14.4	4.10	111	.261	.371	3	.065	-3	10	9	0	0.4
Total	5	32	42	.432	118	116	2	0	0	706^1	805	449	73	51	349	335	15.4	5.22	98	.296	.387	25	.120	-8	-67	-6	4	-1.4
● JARET WRIGHT Wright, Jaret Samuel b: 12/29/75, Anaheim, Cal. BR/TR, 6'2", 220 lbs. Deb: 6/24/97 F																												
1997	*Cle-A	8	3	.727	16	16	0	0	0	90^1	81	45	9	5	35	63	12.1	4.38	107	.238	.318	0	.000	-0	2	3	-0	0.3
1998	*Cle-A	12	10	.545	32	32	1	1	0	192^2	207	109	22	11	87	140	14.2	4.72	101	.277	.361	3	.429	1	-1	1	0	0.2
1999	*Cle-A	8	10	.444	26	26	0	0	0	133^2	144	99	18	7	77	91	15.4	6.06	83	.277	.378	0	.000	-0	-18	-15	-0	-1.6
2000	Cle-A	3	4	.429	9	9	1	1	0	51^2	44	27	6	1	28	36	12.7	4.70	106	.235	.338	0	.000	-0	1	2	-0	0.1
Total	4	31	27	.534	83	83	2	2	0	468^1	476	280	55	24	227	330	14.0	5.03	97	.265	.356	3	.250	0	-16	-9	-1	-1.0
● KEN WRIGHT Wright, Kenneth Warren b: 9/4/46, Pensacola, Fla. BR/TR, 6'2", 210 lbs. Deb: 4/10/70																												
1970	KC-A	1	2	.333	47	0	0	0	3	53^1	49	33	2	7	29	30	14.3	5.23	71	.261	.379	0	.000	-0	-9	-9	-0	-0.6
1971	KC-A	3	6	.333	21	12	1	1	1	78	66	34	6	3	47	56	13.4	3.69	93	.230	.344	2	.091	-1	-2	-2	1	-0.3
1972	KC-A	1	2	.333	17	0	0	0	4	18^1	15	10	0	1	15	18	15.2	4.91	62	.231	.383	0	.000	-0	-4	-4	0	-0.9
1973	KC-A	6	5	.545	25	12	1	0	0	80^2	60	48	6	0	82	75	15.8	4.91	84	.210	.386	0	—	0	-10	-7	-1	-0.9
1974	NY-A	0	0	—	3	0	0	0	0	5^2	5	2	0	0	7	2	19.1	3.18	111	.227	.414	0	—	0	0	0	0	0.0
Total	5	11	15	.423	113	24	2	1	8	236	195	127	14	11	180	181	14.7	4.54	82	.230	.372	2	.071	-2	-24	-21	-1	-2.7
● MEL WRIGHT Wright, Melvin James b: 5/11/28, Manila, Ark. d: 5/16/83, Houston, Tex. BR/TR, 6'3", 210 lbs. Deb: 4/17/54 C																												
1954	StL-N	0	0	—	9	0	0	0	0	10^1	16	15	2	2	11	4	25.3	10.45	39	.348	.492	0	.000	-0	-7	-7	0	-0.4
1955	StL-N	2	2	.500	29	0	0	0	1	36^1	44	26	4	1	9	18	13.4	6.19	66	.308	.353	0	.000	-1	-9	-9	0	-0.9
1960	Chi-N	0	1	.000	9	0	0	0	2	16^1	17	9	1	0	3	8	11.0	4.96	76	.279	.313	0	.000	-0	-2	-2	-1	-0.3
1961	Chi-N	0	1	.000	11	0	0	0	0	21	42	26	3	0	4	6	19.7	10.71	39	.416	.438	0	.000	-0	-16	-15	1	-0.7
Total	4	2	4	.333	58	0	0	0	3	84	119	76	10	3	27	36	16.0	7.61	53	.339	.391	0	.000	-2	-34	-33	1	-2.3
● BOB WRIGHT Wright, Robert Cassius b: 12/13/1891, Decatur Co., Ind. d: 7/30/93, Carmichael, Cal. BR/TR, 6'1.5", 175 lbs. Deb: 9/21/15																												
1915	Chi-N	0	0	—	2	0	0	0	0	4	6	4	0	0	0	3	13.5	2.25	123	.353	.353	0	—	0	0	0	0	0.0
● ROY WRIGHT Wright, Roy Earl b: 9/26/33, Buchtel, Ohio BR/TR, 6'2", 170 lbs. Deb: 9/30/56																												
1956	NY-N	0	1	.000	1	1	0	0	0	2^2	8	5	1	0	2	0	33.8	16.88	22	.533	.588	0	.000	-0	-4	-4	0	-0.6
● RASTY WRIGHT Wright, Wayne Bromley b: 11/5/1895, Ceredo, W.Va. d: 6/12/48, Columbus, Ohio BR/TR, 5'11", 160 lbs. Deb: 6/22/17																												
1917	StL-A	0	1	.000	16	1	0	0	0	39^2	48	31	0	1	10	5	13.4	5.45	48	.300	.345	2	.200	0	-12	-13	0	-0.6
1918	StL-A	8	2	.800	18	13	6	1	0	111^1	99	39	1	5	18	25	9.9	2.51	109	.244	.285	10	.294	3	3	3	-1	0.5
1919	StL-A	0	5	.000	24	5	2	0	0	63^1	79	44	1	1	20	14	14.2	5.54	60	.315	.368	1	.083	-1	-16	-15	0	-1.1
1922	StL-A	9	7	.563	31	16	5	0	5	154	148	64	7	8	50	44	12.0	2.92	142	.262	.331	7	.140	-2	19	20	1	1.9
1923	StL-A	7	4	.636	20	8	4	0	0	82^2	107	64	6	5	34	26	15.9	6.42	65	.317	.387	6	.222	0	-22	-20	0	-2.1
Total	5	24	19	.558	109	43	17	1	5	451	481	242	15	20	132	114	12.6	4.05	87	.280	.338	26	.195	1	-28	-25	0	-1.4
● HARRY WRIGHT Wright, William Henry b: 1/10/1835, Sheffield, England d: 10/3/1895, Atlantic City, N.J. BR/TR, 5'9.5", 157 lbs. Deb: 5/5/1871 FMH♦																												
1871	Bos-n	1	0	1.000	9	0	0	0	**3**	18^2	34	31	0		4	0	18.3	6.27	66	.337	.362	44	.299	1	-4	-4		-0.2

YEAR	TM/L	W	L	PCT	G	GS	CG	SH	SV	IP	H	R	HR	HB	BB	SO	RAT	ERA	ERA+	OAV	OOB	BH	AVG	PB	PR	PR+	PD	TPI
1872	Bos-n	1	0	1.000	7	0	0	0	**4**	25^2	26	12	0		0	1	9.1	2.10	173	.239	.239	52	.250	-0	**4**	**4**		0.2
1873	Bos-n	2	2	.500	13	5	0	0	**4**	38^1	65	46	0		7	0	16.9	4.23	78	.330	.353	67	.252	2	-4	-4		-0.3
1874	Bos-n	0	2	.000	6	2	0	0	**3**	16^2	24	13	0		4	0	15.1	2.16	100	.324	.359	58	.315	2	0	0		0.1
Total	4 n	4	4	.500	35	7	0	0	14	99^1	149	102	0		15	1	14.9	3.71	58	.310	.331	222	.274	5	-17	-17		-0.2

● LUCKY WRIGHT Wright, William Simmons "William The Red" or "Deacon"
b: 2/21/1880, Tontogany, Ohio d: 7/6/41, Tontogany, Ohio BR/TR, 6', 178 lbs. Deb: 4/18/09

YEAR	TM/L	W	L	PCT	G	GS	CG	SH	SV	IP	H	R	HR	HB	BB	SO	RAT	ERA	ERA+	OAV	OOB	BH	AVG	PB	PR	PR+	PD	TPI
1909	Cle-A	0	4	.000	5	4	3	0	0	28	21	16	0	0	7	5	9.0	3.21	80	.223	.277	0	.000	-1	-2	-2	-0	-0.4

● KELLY WUNSCH Wunsch, Kelly Douglas b: 7/12/72, Houston, Tex. BL/TL, 6'5", 192 lbs. Deb: 4/3/2000

YEAR	TM/L	W	L	PCT	G	GS	CG	SH	SV	IP	H	R	HR	HB	BB	SO	RAT	ERA	ERA+	OAV	OOB	BH	AVG	PB	PR	PR+	PD	TPI
2000	*Chi-A	6	3	.667	**83**	0	0	0	1	61^1	50	22	4	2	29	51	11.9	2.93	169	.221	.315	0	—	0	14	14	0	1.7

● FRANK WURM Wurm, Frank James b: 4/27/24, Cambridge, N.Y. d: 9/19/93, Glens Falls, N.Y. BB/TL, 6'1", 175 lbs. Deb: 9/4/44

YEAR	TM/L	W	L	PCT	G	GS	CG	SH	SV	IP	H	R	HR	HB	BB	SO	RAT	ERA	ERA+	OAV	OOB	BH	AVG	PB	PR	PR+	PD	TPI
1944	Bro-N	0	0	—	1	1	0	0	0	0^1	1	4	0	0	5	1	162.0	108.00	3	.500	.857	0	—	0	-4	-4	0	-0.2

● JOHN WYATT Wyatt, John Thomas b: 4/19/35, Chicago, Ill. d: 4/6/98, Omaha, Neb. BR/TR, 5'11.5", 200 lbs. Deb: 9/8/61

YEAR	TM/L	W	L	PCT	G	GS	CG	SH	SV	IP	H	R	HR	HB	BB	SO	RAT	ERA	ERA+	OAV	OOB	BH	AVG	PB	PR	PR+	PD	TPI
1961	KC-A	0	0	—	5	0	0	0	1	7^1	8	3	0	1	4	6	16.0	2.45	170	.296	.406	0	—	0	1	1	0	0.1
1962	KC-A	10	7	.588	59	9	0	0	11	125	121	66	12	5	80	106	14.8	4.46	95	.253	.366	3	.103	-2	-7	-3	-1	-0.7
1963	KC-A	6	4	.600	63	0	0	0	21	92	83	37	12	0	43	81	12.3	3.13	125	.239	.323	0	.000	-1	5	7	-1	1.0
1964	KC-A★	9	8	.529	**81**	0	0	0	20	128	111	53	23	1	52	74	11.5	3.59	106	.236	.314	0	.000	-1	1	3	-1	0.3
1965	KC-A	2	6	.250	65	0	0	0	18	88^2	78	36	8	4	53	70	13.7	3.25	107	.241	.354	0	.000	-0	2	2	0	0.3
1966	KC-A	0	3	.000	19	0	0	0	2	23^2	19	14	3	2	16	25	14.1	5.32	64	.213	.346	0	—	0	-5	-5	1	-0.6
	Bos-A	3	4	.429	42	0	0	0	8	71^2	59	27	3	4	27	63	11.3	3.14	121	.229	.311	0	.000	-1	2	5	-1	0.3
	Yr	3	7	.300	61	0	0	0	10	95^1	78	41	6	6	43	88	12.0	3.68	101	.225	.321	0	.000	-1	-3	0	-1	-0.3
1967	*Bos-A	10	7	.588	60	0	0	0	20	93^1	71	30	6	2	39	68	10.8	2.60	134	.217	.304	1	.083	-0	7	8	1	2.0
1968	Bos-A	1	2	.333	8	0	0	0	0	10^2	9	7	2	1	6	11	13.5	4.22	75	.231	.348	0	—	0	-1	-1	0	-0.2
	NY-A	0	2	.000	7	0	0	0	0	8^1	7	3	1	0	9	6	17.3	2.16	134	.219	.390	0	.000	-0	1	1	-0	0.1
	Det-A	1	0	1.000	22	0	0	0	2	30^1	26	9	2	1	11	25	11.3	2.37	127	.236	.311	0	.000	-0	2	2	0	0.1
	Yr	2	4	.333	37	0	0	0	2	49^1	42	19	5	2	26	42	12.8	2.74	110	.232	.335	0	.000	-0	1	2	0	0.0
1969	Oak-A	0	1	.000	4	0	0	0	0	8^1	8	5	0	2	6	5	17.3	5.40	64	.250	.400	0	.000	-0	-2	-2	-0	-0.2
Total	9	42	44	.488	435	9	0	0	103	687^1	600	290	72	23	346	540	12.7	3.47	108	.237	.334	4	.048	-6	6	20	-2	2.5

● WHIT WYATT Wyatt, John Whitlow b: 9/27/07, Kensington, Ga. d: 7/16/99, Carrollton, Ga. BR/TR, 6'1", 185 lbs. Deb: 9/16/29 C

YEAR	TM/L	W	L	PCT	G	GS	CG	SH	SV	IP	H	R	HR	HB	BB	SO	RAT	ERA	ERA+	OAV	OOB	BH	AVG	PB	PR	PR+	PD	TPI
1929	Det-A	0	1	.000	4	4	1	0	0	25^1	30	22	1	1	18	14	17.4	6.75	64	.309	.422	1	.100	-1	-7	-7	1	-0.4
1930	Det-A	4	5	.444	21	7	2	0	2	85^2	76	41	6	3	35	68	12.0	3.57	134	.239	.320	12	.353	3	10	11	0	1.4
1931	Det-A	0	2	.000	4	1	1	0	0	20^1	30	23	2	1	12	8	19.0	8.85	52	.361	.448	2	.286	0	-10	-9	-1	-0.7
1932	Det-A	9	13	.409	43	22	10	0	1	205^2	228	136	12	3	102	82	14.6	5.03	93	.286	.369	15	.192	-0	-13	-7	-1	-0.8
1933	Det-A	0	1	.000	10	0	0	0	0	17	20	9	1	2	9	9	16.4	4.24	102	.299	.397	0	.000	-0	0	0	-0	0.0
	Chi-A	3	4	.429	26	7	2	0	1	87^2	91	51	7	2	45	31	14.2	4.62	92	.266	.355	6	.214	0	-3	-4	0	-0.2
	Yr	3	5	.375	36	7	2	0	1	104^2	111	60	8	4	54	40	14.5	4.56	93	.271	.362	6	.200	-0	-3	-4	-0	-0.2
1934	Chi-A	4	11	.267	23	6	2	0	2	67^2	83	59	10	1	37	36	16.1	7.18	66	.303	.388	6	.231	0	-20	-18	0	-3.0
1935	Chi-A	4	3	.571	30	1	0	0	5	52	65	41	6	2	25	22	15.9	6.75	68	.308	.387	3	.231	1	-13	-12	1	-1.4
1936	Chi-A	0	0	—	3	0	0	0	1	3	3	0	0	0	0	0	9.0	0.00	—	.273	.273	0	—	0	2	2	-0	0.1
1937	Cle-A	2	3	.400	29	4	2	0	0	73	67	38	3	0	40	52	13.2	4.44	104	.244	.340	7	.389	3	1	1	0	0.3
1939	Bro-N☆	8	3	.727	16	14	6	2	0	109	88	34	3	2	39	52	10.7	2.31	174	.224	.297	6	.167	-0	19	20	1	2.1
1940	Bro-N★	15	14	.517	37	34	16	**5**	0	239^1	233	105	19	5	62	124	11.3	3.46	116	.254	.304	14	.175	-0	10	14	-2	1.3
1941	*Bro-N★	**22**	10	.688	38	35	23	**7**	1	288^1	223	89	10	2	82	176	**9.6**	2.34	157	**.212**	**.270**	26	.239	7	**41**	**42**	-1	**5.3**
1942	Bro-N☆	19	7	.731	31	30	16	0	0	217^1	185	82	9	7	63	104	10.6	2.73	119	.225	.286	14	.182	1	14	13	-1	1.5
1943	Bro-N	14	5	.737	26	26	13	3	0	180^2	139	55	5	0	43	80	**9.1**	2.49	135	**.207**	**.255**	17	.283	4	18	18	-2	2.1
1944	Bro-N	2	6	.250	9	9	1	0	0	37^2	51	37	1	2	16	4	16.5	7.17	50	.311	.379	2	.154	-0	-15	-15	-0	-2.6
1945	Phi-N	0	7	.000	10	10	2	0	0	51^1	72	38	3	0	14	10	15.1	5.26	73	.330	.371	2	.125	0	-8	-8	1	-0.9
Total	16	106	95	.527	360	210	97	17	13	1761	1684	860	98	33	642	872	12.1	3.79	105	.251	.319	133	.219	18	27	39	-6	4.1

● WELDON WYCKOFF Wyckoff, John Weldon b: 2/19/1892, Williamsport, Pa. d: 5/8/61, Sheboygan Falls, Wis. BR/TR, 6'1", 175 lbs. Deb: 4/19/13

YEAR	TM/L	W	L	PCT	G	GS	CG	SH	SV	IP	H	R	HR	HB	BB	SO	RAT	ERA	ERA+	OAV	OOB	BH	AVG	PB	PR	PR+	PD	TPI
1913	Phi-A	2	4	.333	17	7	4	0	0	61^2	56	44	1	3	46	31	15.3	4.38	63	.233	.363	4	.190	-0	-10	-12	0	-1.0
1914	*Phi-A	11	7	.611	32	20	11	0	2	185	153	82	2	4	103	86	12.6	3.02	87	.228	.334	11	.147	-0	-6	-9	-5	-1.3
1915	Phi-A	10	22	.313	43	34	20	1	0	276	238	139	1	5	165	157	13.3	3.52	83	.246	.359	12	.125	-4	-18	-18	2	-2.2
1916	Phi-A	0	1	.000	7	2	1	0	0	21^1	20	16	1	1	20	4	17.3	5.48	52	.247	.402	3	.375	1	-6	-6	0	-0.2
	Bos-A	0	0	—	8	0	0	0	1	22^2	19	13	0	0	18	18	14.7	4.76	58	.232	.370	1	.167	-0	-5	-5	-1	-0.4
	Yr	0	1	.000	15	2	1	0	1	44	39	29	1	1	38	22	16.0	5.11	55	.239	.386	4	.286	1	-11	-11	-1	-0.6
1917	Bos-A	0	0	—	1	0	0	0	0	5	4	3	0	1	4	1	16.2	1.80	143	.222	.391	0	.000	-0	0	0	0	0.0
1918	Bos-A	0	0	—	1	0	0	0	0	2	4	1	0	0	1	2	22.5	0.00	—	.400	.455	0	.000	-0	1	1	-0	0.0
Total	6	23	34	.404	109	63	36	1	3	573^2	494	298	5	14	357	299	13.6	3.55	79	.239	.355	31	.149	-4	-44	-49	-3	-5.1

● FRANK WYMAN Wyman, Frank H. b: 5/10/1862, Haverhill, Mass. d: 2/4/16, Everett, Mass. Deb: 6/10/1884 ♦

YEAR	TM/L	W	L	PCT	G	GS	CG	SH	SV	IP	H	R	HR	HB	BB	SO	RAT	ERA	ERA+	OAV	OOB	BH	AVG	PB	PR	PR+	PD	TPI
1884	KC-U	0	1	.000	3	1	1	0	0	21	37	29	0		3	9	17.1	6.86	33	.363	.381	27	.218	-1	-10	-12	-1	-0.6

● EARLY WYNN Wynn, Early "Gus" b: 1/6/20, Hartford, Ala. d: 4/4/99, Venice, Fla. BB/TR, 6', 200 lbs. Deb: 9/13/39 CH♦

YEAR	TM/L	W	L	PCT	G	GS	CG	SH	SV	IP	H	R	HR	HB	BB	SO	RAT	ERA	ERA+	OAV	OOB	BH	AVG	PB	PR	PR+	PD	TPI
1939	Was-A	0	2	.000	3	3	1	0	0	20^1	26	15	0	0	10	1	15.9	5.75	76	.313	.387	1	.167	0	-3	-3	-1	-0.3
1941	Was-A	3	1	.750	5	5	4	0	0	40	35	14	1	0	10	15	10.1	1.57	257	.226	.273	2	.133	-0	11	11	0	1.1
1942	Was-A	10	16	.385	30	28	10	1	0	190	246	129	6	3	73	58	15.3	5.12	71	.314	.374	15	.217	2	-31	-31	-1	-3.6
1943	Was-A	18	12	.600	37	33	12	3	0	256^2	232	97	15	1	83	89	11.1	2.91	110	.240	.301	29	.296	7	11	9	-2	1.6
1944	Was-A	8	17	.320	33	25	19	2	2	207^2	221	97	3	2	67	65	12.6	3.38	96	.277	.334	19	.207	2	1	-3	-2	-0.4
1946	Was-A	8	5	.615	17	12	9	0	0	107	112	45	8	3	33	36	12.4	3.11	108	.267	.325	15	.319	7	5	3	-0	1.1
1947	Was-A☆	17	15	.531	33	31	22	2	0	247	251	114	13	5	90	73	12.6	3.64	102	.262	.329	33	.275	7	2	2	-1	0.9
1948	Was-A	8	19	.296	33	31	15	1	0	198	236	144	18	1	94	49	15.0	5.82	75	.295	.370	23	.217	3	-34	-32	-1	-3.4
1949	Cle-A	11	7	.611	26	23	6	0	0	164^2	186	84	8	1	57	62	13.3	4.15	96	.282	.340	10	.143	-2	1	-3	1	-0.4
1950	Cle-A	18	8	.692	32	28	14	2	0	213^2	166	88	20	4	101	143	**11.4**	**3.20**	135	**.212**	**.305**	18	.234	7	33	28	0	3.8
1951	Cle-A	20	13	.606	37	34	21	3	1	**274^1**	227	102	18	3	107	133	11.1	3.02	126	.225	.301	20	.185	2	**34**	26	-1	2.9
1952	Cle-A	23	12	.657	42	33	19	4	3	285^2	239	103	23	1	132	153	11.7	2.90	115	.231	.318	22	.222	5	25	16	-1	2.3
1953	Cle-A	17	12	.586	36	34	16	1	0	251^2	234	121	19	4	107	138	12.3	3.93	95	.245	.324	25	.275	9	2	-5	-1	0.2
1954	*Cle-A	**23**	11	.676	40	36	20	3	2	**270^2**	225	93	21	0	83	155	10.2	2.73	135	.225	.284	17	.183	1	30	29	-3	3.3
1955	Cle-A★	17	11	.607	32	31	16	6	0	230	207	86	19	3	80	122	11.3	2.82	142	.240	.307	15	.179	1	29	30	-3	3.3
1956	Cle-A★	20	9	.690	38	35	18	4	2	277^2	233	93	19	5	91	158	10.7	2.72	154	.228	.294	23	.228	3	44	45	1	5.0
1957	Cle-A★	14	17	.452	40	37	13	1	1	263	270	139	32	5	104	**184**	13.0	4.31	86	.265	.336	10	.116	-2	-15	-18	-1	-2.2
1958	Chi-A★	14	16	.467	40	34	11	4	2	239^2	214	115	27	6	104	**179**	12.2	4.13	88	.242	.325	15	.200	3	-10	-14	-2	-1.5
1959	*Chi-A★	**22**	10	.688	37	37	14	5	0	**255^2**	202	106	20	9	119	179	11.6	3.17	119	.216	.310	22	.244	9	20	17	-1	2.8
1960	Chi-A★	13	12	.520	36	35	13	**4**	1	237^1	220	105	20	4	112	158	12.7	3.49	108	.247	.334	15	.200	7	10	8	-2	1.2
1961	Chi-A	8	2	.800	17	16	5	0	0	110^1	88	43	11	1	47	64	11.1	3.51	112	.220	.304	6	.162	-0	6	5	-2	0.3
1962	Chi-A	7	15	.318	27	26	11	3	0	167^2	171	90	15	3	56	91	12.3	4.46	88	.264	.326	7	.130	0	-9	-10	-2	-1.4
1963	Cle-A	1	2	.333	20	5	1	0	1	55^1	50	14	2	0	15	29	10.6	2.28	159	.250	.302	3	.273	1	8	8	-0	0.5
Total	23	300	244	.551	691	612	290	49	15	4564	4291	2037	338	64	1775	2334	12.1	3.54	106	.248	.321	365	.214	72	170	116	-25	17.1

● BILLY WYNNE Wynne, Billy Vernon b: 7/31/43, Williamston, N.C. BL/TR, 6'5", 206 lbs. Deb: 8/6/67

YEAR	TM/L	W	L	PCT	G	GS	CG	SH	SV	IP	H	R	HR	HB	BB	SO	RAT	ERA	ERA+	OAV	OOB	BH	AVG	PB	PR	PR+	PD	TPI
1967	NY-N	0	0	—	6	1	0	0	0	8^2	12	4	0	0	2	4	14.5	3.12	109	.324	.359	0	.000	-0	0	0	-0	0.0
1968	Chi-A	0	0	—	1	0	0	0	0	2	2	2	0	0	2	1	18.0	4.50	67	.250	.400	0	—	0	-0	-0	-0	0.0
1969	Chi-A	7	7	.500	20	20	6	1	0	128^2	143	63	14	3	50	67	13.7	4.06	95	.283	.351	5	.122	-1	-6	-3	0	-0.3
1970	Chi-A	1	4	.200	12	9	0	0	0	44	54	30	8	1	22	19	15.8	5.32	73	.298	.377	1	.077	-1	-8	-7	1	-0.7
1971	Cal-A	0	0	—	3	0	0	0	0	3^2	6	2	0	0	2	6	19.6	4.91	66	.375	.444	0	—	0	-1	-1	0	0.0
Total	5	8	11	.421	42	30	6	1	0	187	217	101	22	4	78	97	14.4	4.33	88	.290	.361	6	.109	-2	-15	-10	1	-1.0

● BILL WYNNE Wynne, William Andrew b: 3/27/1869, Neuse, N.C. d: 8/7/51, Raleigh, N.C. BR/TR, 5'11.5", 161 lbs. Deb: 8/31/1894

YEAR	TM/L	W	L	PCT	G	GS	CG	SH	SV	IP	H	R	HR	HB	BB	SO	RAT	ERA	ERA+	OAV	OOB	BH	AVG	PB	PR	PR+	PD	TPI
1894	Was-N	0	1	.000	1	1	1	0	0	8	10	11	0	2	8	2	22.5	6.75	78	.303	.465	0	.000	-0	-1	-1	-0	-0.1

● HANK WYSE Wyse, Henry Washington "Hooks" b: 3/1/18, Lunsford, Ark. d: 10/22/2000, Pryor, Okla. BR/TR, 5'11.5", 185 lbs. Deb: 9/7/42

YEAR	TM/L	W	L	PCT	G	GS	CG	SH	SV	IP	H	R	HR	HB	BB	SO	RAT	ERA	ERA+	OAV	OOB	BH	AVG	PB	PR	PR+	PD	TPI
1942	Chi-N	2	1	.667	4	4	1	1	0	28	33	10	1	0	6	8	12.5	1.93	166	.287	.322	1	.125	-0	4	4	-0	0.4
1943	Chi-N	9	7	.563	38	15	8	2	5	156	159	57	4	2	34	45	11.3	2.94	113	.264	.306	4	.080	-4	8	7	3	0.7
1944	Chi-N	16	15	.516	41	34	14	3	1	257^1	277	113	9	2	57	86	11.8	3.15	112	.278	.318	16	.178	-1	13	11	0	1.2
1945	*Chi-N†	22	10	.688	38	34	23	2	0	278^1	272	95	17	5	55	77	10.7	2.68	136	.256	.296	17	.168	-2	**35**	31	2	3.4
1946	Chi-N	14	12	.538	40	27	12	2	1	201^1	206	73	7	3	52	52	11.7	2.68	124	.265	.313	18	.243	1	16	15	2	2.2
1947	Chi-N	6	9	.400	37	19	5	1	1	142	158	84	12	3	64	53	14.3	4.31	92	.286	.363	5	.111	-1	-4	-6	1	-0.6
1950	Phi-A	9	14	.391	41	23	4	0	0	170^2	192	121	16	8	87	33	15.1	5.85	78	.287	.376	9	.153	-3	-24	-25	0	-3.0
1951	Phi-A	1	2	.333	9	1	0	0	0	14^2	24	14	0	0	8	5	19.6	7.98	54	.381	.451	1	.250	-0	-6	-6	-0	-1.0
	Was-A	0	0	—	3	2	0	0	0	9^1	17	14	0	1	10	3	27.0	9.64	42	.378	.500	0	.000	-1	-6	-6	0	-0.3
	Yr	1	2	.333	12	3	0	0	0	24	41	28	0	1	18	8	22.5	8.63	49	.380	.472	1	.125	-1	-12	-12	0	-1.3
Total	8	79	70	.530	251	159	67	11	8	1257^2	1338	581	66	24	373	362	12.4	3.52	105	.274	.329	71	.163	-11	36	24	9	3.0

● BIFF WYSONG Wysong, Harlan b: 4/13/05, Clarksville, Ohio d: 8/8/51, Xenia, Ohio BL/TL, 6'3", 195 lbs. Deb: 8/10/30

YEAR	TM/L	W	L	PCT	G	GS	CG	SH	SV	IP	H	R	HR	HB	BB	SO	RAT	ERA	ERA+	OAV	OOB	BH	AVG	PB	PR	PR+	PD	TPI
1930	Cin-N	0	1	.000	1	1	0	0	0	2^1	6	5	0	0	3	1	34.7	19.29	25	.545	.643	0	—	0	-4	-4	-0	-0.5
1931	Cin-N	0	2	.000	12	2	0	0	0	21^2	25	22	2	0	23	5	19.9	7.89	47	.298	.449	1	.250	0	-10	-10	-1	-0.9
1932	Cin-N	1	0	1.000	7	0	0	0	0	12^1	13	7	0	0	8	5	15.3	3.65	106	.277	.382	0	.000	-0	0	0	0	0.0
Total	3	1	3	.250	20	3	0	0	0	36^1	44	34	2	0	34	11	19.3	7.18	54	.310	.443	1	.167	-0	-13	-14	-0	-1.4

● ESTEBAN YAN Yan, Esteban Luis b: 6/22/74, Campina, D.R. BR/TR, 6'4", 230 lbs. Deb: 5/20/96

YEAR	TM/L	W	L	PCT	G	GS	CG	SH	SV	IP	H	R	HR	HB	BB	SO	RAT	ERA	ERA+	OAV	OOB	BH	AVG	PB	PR	PR+	PD	TPI
1996	Bal-A	0	0	—	4	0	0	0	0	9^1	13	7	3	0	3	7	15.4	5.79	85	.333	.381	0	—	0	-1	-1	-0	-0.1
1997	Bal-A	0	1	.000	3	2	0	0	0	9^2	20	18	3	2	7	4	27.0	15.83	28	.417	.509	0	—	0	-12	-13	-0	-1.0
1998	TB-A	5	4	.556	64	0	0	0	1	88^2	78	41	11	5	41	77	12.6	3.86	124	.236	.329	0	—	0	8	9	0	0.8
1999	TB-A	3	4	.429	50	1	0	0	0	61	77	41	8	9	32	46	17.4	5.90	84	.326	.426	0	—	0	-7	-6	1	-0.5
2000	TB-A	7	8	.467	43	20	0	0	0	137^2	158	98	26	11	42	111	13.8	6.21	80	.285	.347	1	1.000	1	-20	-19	-1	-1.7
Total	5	15	17	.469	164	23	0	0	1	306^1	346	205	51	27	125	245	14.6	5.76	85	.286	.366	1	1.000	1	-32	-29	-1	-2.5

● ED YARNALL Yarnall, Harvey Edward b: 12/4/75, Lima, Pa. BL/TL, 6'3", 234 lbs. Deb: 7/15/99

YEAR	TM/L	W	L	PCT	G	GS	CG	SH	SV	IP	H	R	HR	HB	BB	SO	RAT	ERA	ERA+	OAV	OOB	BH	AVG	PB	PR	PR+	PD	TPI
1999	NY-A	1	0	1.000	5	2	0	0	0	17	17	8	1	0	10	13	14.3	3.71	128	.254	.351	0	—	0	2	2	0	0.1
2000	NY-A	0	0	—	2	1	0	0	0	3	5	5	1	1	3	1	27.0	15.00	32	.417	.563	0	—	0	-3	-3	-0	-0.2
Total	2	1	0	1.000	7	3	0	0	0	20	22	13	2	1	13	14	16.2	5.40	88	.278	.387	0	—	0	-1	-1	0	-0.1

● RUSTY YARNALL Yarnall, Waldo William b: 10/22/02, Chicago, Ill. d: 10/9/85, Lowell, Mass. BR/TR, 6', 175 lbs. Deb: 6/30/26

YEAR	TM/L	W	L	PCT	G	GS	CG	SH	SV	IP	H	R	HR	HB	BB	SO	RAT	ERA	ERA+	OAV	OOB	BH	AVG	PB	PR	PR+	PD	TPI
1926	Phi-N	0	1	.000	1	0	0	0	0	1	3	2	0	0	1	0	36.0	18.00	23	.500	.571	0	.000	-0	-2	-1	0	-0.2

● RUBE YARRISON Yarrison, Byron Wardsworth b: 3/9/1896, Montgomery, Pa. d: 4/22/77, Williamsport, Pa. BR/TR, 5'11", 165 lbs. Deb: 4/13/22

YEAR	TM/L	W	L	PCT	G	GS	CG	SH	SV	IP	H	R	HR	HB	BB	SO	RAT	ERA	ERA+	OAV	OOB	BH	AVG	PB	PR	PR+	PD	TPI
1922	Phi-A	1	2	.333	18	1	0	0	0	33^2	50	32	4	2	12	10	17.1	8.29	51	.362	.421	1	.167	-0	-16	-14	-0	-1.1
1924	Bro-N	0	2	.000	3	2	0	0	0	11	12	10	0	1	3	2	13.1	6.55	57	.267	.327	0	.000	-0	-3	-4	0	-0.5
Total	2	1	4	.200	21	3	0	0	0	44^2	62	42	4	3	15	12	16.1	7.86	53	.339	.398	1	.125	-0	-19	-18	0	-1.6

● EMIL YDE Yde, Emil Ogden b: 1/28/1900, Great Lakes, Ill. d: 12/4/68, Leesburg, Fla. BB/TL (BL 1925), 5'11", 165 lbs. Deb: 4/21/24

YEAR	TM/L	W	L	PCT	G	GS	CG	SH	SV	IP	H	R	HR	HB	BB	SO	RAT	ERA	ERA+	OAV	OOB	BH	AVG	PB	PR	PR+	PD	TPI
1924	Pit-N	16	3	**.842**	33	22	14	**4**	0	194	171	70	3	6	62	53	11.1	2.83	136	.244	.311	21	.239	2	22	22	1	2.3
1925	*Pit-N	17	9	.654	33	28	13	0	0	207	254	125	11	2	75	41	14.4	4.13	108	.309	.369	17	.191	-2	3	7	-0	0.5
1926	Pit-N	8	7	.533	37	22	12	1	0	187^1	181	97	3	2	81	34	12.7	3.65	108	.260	.339	17	.230	3	4	6	0	0.7
1927	*Pit-N	1	3	.250	9	2	0	0	0	29^2	45	35	1	2	15	9	18.8	9.71	42	.375	.453	3	.167	-0	-19	-18	1	-1.8
1929	Det-A	7	3	.700	29	6	4	1	0	86^2	100	60	8	0	63	23	16.9	5.30	81	.296	.406	16	.333	2	-10	-10	-1	-0.6
Total	5	49	25	.662	141	80	43	6	0	704^2	751	387	26	12	296	160	13.5	4.02	102	.281	.355	74	.233	5	-0	7	1	1.1

● JOE YEAGER Yeager, Joseph F. "Little Joe" b: 8/28/1875, Philadelphia, Pa. d: 7/2/37, Detroit, Mich. BR/TR, 5'10", 160 lbs. Deb: 4/22/1898 ♦

YEAR	TM/L	W	L	PCT	G	GS	CG	SH	SV	IP	H	R	HR	HB	BB	SO	RAT	ERA	ERA+	OAV	OOB	BH	AVG	PB	PR	PR+	PD	TPI
1898	Bro-N	12	22	.353	36	33	32	0	0	291^1	333	177	4	6	80	70	12.9	3.65	98	.285	.334	23	.172	-3	-1	-2	5	0.0
1899	Bro-N	2	2	.500	10	4	2	1	1	47^2	56	29	1	2	16	6	14.0	4.72	83	.292	.352	9	.191	1	-5	-4	1	-0.2
1900	Bro-N	1	1	.500	2	2	2	0	0	17	21	13	1	0	5	2	13.8	6.88	56	.304	.351	3	.333	0	-6	-6	-0	-0.5
1901	Det-A	12	11	.522	26	25	22	2	1	199^2	209	105	4	8	46	38	11.9	2.61	147	.266	.313	37	.296	5	23	26	2	3.4
1902	Det-A	6	12	.333	19	15	14	0	0	140	171	90	5	5	41	28	13.9	4.82	76	.301	.353	39	.242	3	-19	-18	3	-1.4
1903	Det-A	0	1	.000	1	1	1	0	0	9	15	7	0	0	0	1	15.0	4.00	73	.366	.366	103	.256	0	-1	-1	0	-0.1
Total	6	33	49	.402	94	80	73	3	2	704^2	805	421	15	21	188	145	13.0	3.74	99	.285	.334	467	.252	6	-9	-4	11	1.2

● AL YEARGIN Yeargin, James Almond b: 10/16/01, Mauldin, S.C. d: 5/8/37, Greenville, S.C. BR/TR, 5'11", 170 lbs. Deb: 10/1/22

YEAR	TM/L	W	L	PCT	G	GS	CG	SH	SV	IP	H	R	HR	HB	BB	SO	RAT	ERA	ERA+	OAV	OOB	BH	AVG	PB	PR	PR+	PD	TPI
1922	Bos-N	0	1	.000	1	1	1	0	0	7	5	3	1	0	2	1	9.0	1.29	311	.192	.250	0	.000	-0	2	2	0	0.3
1924	Bos-N	1	11	.083	32	12	6	0	0	141^1	162	90	7	3	42	34	13.2	5.09	75	.293	.346	6	.143	-2	-19	-20	4	-1.3
Total	2	1	12	.077	33	13	7	0	0	148^1	167	93	8	3	44	35	13.0	4.91	78	.288	.342	6	.133	-2	-17	-18	4	-1.0

● LARRY YELLEN Yellen, Lawrence Alan b: 1/4/43, Brooklyn, N.Y. BR/TR, 5'11", 190 lbs. Deb: 9/26/63

YEAR	TM/L	W	L	PCT	G	GS	CG	SH	SV	IP	H	R	HR	HB	BB	SO	RAT	ERA	ERA+	OAV	OOB	BH	AVG	PB	PR	PR+	PD	TPI
1963	Hou-N	0	0	—	1	1	0	0	0	5	7	4	0	0	1	3	14.4	3.60	88	.280	.308	0	.000	-0	-0	-0	0	0.0
1964	Hou-N	0	0	—	13	1	0	0	0	21	27	19	4	0	10	9	15.9	6.86	50	.297	.366	0	.000	-0	-8	-8	-0	-0.5
Total	2	0	0	—	14	2	0	0	0	26	34	23	4	0	11	12	15.6	6.23	54	.293	.354	0	.000	-0	-8	-9	0	-0.5

● CHIEF YELLOWHORSE Yellowhorse, Moses J. b: 1/28/1898, Pawnee, Okla. d: 4/10/64, Pawnee, Okla. BR/TR, 5'10", 180 lbs. Deb: 4/15/21

YEAR	TM/L	W	L	PCT	G	GS	CG	SH	SV	IP	H	R	HR	HB	BB	SO	RAT	ERA	ERA+	OAV	OOB	BH	AVG	PB	PR	PR+	PD	TPI
1921	Pit-N	5	3	.625	10	4	1	0	1	48^1	45	17	1	0	13	19	10.8	2.98	129	.254	.305	0	.000	-2	4	5	-2	0.3
1922	Pit-N	3	1	.750	28	4	2	0	0	77^2	92	48	0	2	20	24	13.2	4.52	90	.305	.352	6	.316	1	-4	-4	-1	-0.2
Total	2	8	4	.667	38	8	3	0	1	126	137	65	1	2	33	43	12.3	3.93	101	.286	.335	6	.167	-2	1	1	-3	0.1

● CARROLL YERKES Yerkes, Charles Carroll "Lefty" b: 6/13/03, McSherrystown, Pa. d: 12/20/50, Oakland, Cal. BR/TL, 5'11", 180 lbs. Deb: 5/31/27

YEAR	TM/L	W	L	PCT	G	GS	CG	SH	SV	IP	H	R	HR	HB	BB	SO	RAT	ERA	ERA+	OAV	OOB	BH	AVG	PB	PR	PR+	PD	TPI
1927	Phi-A	0	0	—	1	0	0	0	0	1	0	0	0	0	1	0	9.0	0.00	—	.000	.333	0	—	0	0	0	0	0.1
1928	Phi-A	0	1	.000	2	1	1	0	0	8^2	7	2	0	0	2	1	9.3	2.08	193	.233	.281	0	.000	-0	2	2	1	0.2
1929	Phi-A	1	0	1.000	19	2	0	0	1	37^1	47	20	0	1	13	11	14.7	4.58	92	.329	.389	0	.000	-2	-1	-1	2	0.0
1932	Chi-N	0	0	—	2	0	0	0	0	9	5	3	2	0	3	4	8.0	3.00	126	.167	.242	1	.333	0	1	1	-0	0.0
1933	Chi-N	0	0	—	1	0	0	0	0	2	2	1	0	0	1	0	13.5	4.50	73	.286	.375	0	—	0	-0	-0	0	0.0
Total	5	1	1	.500	25	3	1	0	1	58	61	26	2	1	20	16	12.7	3.88	106	.288	.352	1	.063	-2	2	1	3	0.3

● STAN YERKES Yerkes, Stanley Lewis "Yank" b: 11/28/1874, Cheltenham, Pa. d: 7/28/40, Boston, Mass. BR/TR, 5'10", 165 lbs. Deb: 5/3/01

YEAR	TM/L	W	L	PCT	G	GS	CG	SH	SV	IP	H	R	HR	HB	BB	SO	RAT	ERA	ERA+	OAV	OOB	BH	AVG	PB	PR	PR+	PD	TPI
1901	Bal-A	0	1	.000	1	1	1	0	0	8	12	9	0	0	2	4	15.8	6.75	57	.343	.378	1	.333	0	-3	-2	0	-0.2
	StL-N	3	1	.750	4	4	4	0	0	34	35	14	2	1	6	15	11.1	3.18	100	.265	.302	1	.083	-1	1	0	-0	-0.1
1902	StL-N	12	21	.364	39	37	27	1	0	272^2	341	160	1	2	79	81	13.9	3.66	75	.306	.353	12	.132	-3	-27	-28	-2	-3.6
1903	StL-N	0	1	.000	1	1	0	0	0	5	8	6	0	0	0	3	14.4	1.80	181	.333	.333	0	.000	-0	1	1	-0	0.1
Total	3	15	24	.385	45	43	32	1	0	319^2	396	189	3	3	87	103	13.7	3.66	77	.303	.348	14	.130	-4	-28	-30	-3	-3.8

● RICH YETT Yett, Richard Martin b: 10/6/62, Pomona, Cal. BR/TR, 6'2", 187 lbs. Deb: 4/13/85

YEAR	TM/L	W	L	PCT	G	GS	CG	SH	SV	IP	H	R	HR	HB	BB	SO	RAT	ERA	ERA+	OAV	OOB	BH	AVG	PB	PR	PR+	PD	TPI
1985	Min-A	0	0	—	1	1	0	0	0	0^1	1	1	0	0	2	0	81.0	27.00	16	.333	.600	0	—	0	-1	-1	0	0.0
1986	Cle-A	5	3	.625	39	3	1	1	1	78^2	84	48	10	1	37	50	14.0	5.15	81	.275	.355	0	—	0	-8	-9	-1	-0.9
1987	Cle-A	3	9	.250	37	11	2	0	1	97^2	96	63	21	3	49	59	13.6	5.25	86	.257	.347	0	—	0	-8	-8	-1	-0.9
1988	Cle-A	9	6	.600	23	22	0	0	0	134^1	146	72	11	1	55	71	13.5	4.62	89	.275	.344	0	—	0	-10	-7	-2	-0.9
1989	Cle-A	5	6	.455	32	12	1	0	0	99	111	56	10	2	47	47	14.5	5.00	79	.283	.363	0	—	0	-12	-11	-1	-1.2
1990	Min-A	0	0	—	4	0	0	0	0	4^1	6	2	1	0	1	2	14.5	2.08	201	.353	.389	0	—	0	1	1	0	0.1
Total	6	22	24	.478	136	49	4	1	2	414^1	444	242	53	7	191	229	13.9	4.95	85	.274	.353	0	—	0	-39	-34	-5	-3.8

● EARL YINGLING Yingling, Earl Hershey "Chink" b: 10/29/1888, Chillicothe, Ohio d: 10/2/62, Columbus, Ohio BL/TL, 5'11.5", 180 lbs. Deb: 4/12/11

YEAR	TM/L	W	L	PCT	G	GS	CG	SH	SV	IP	H	R	HR	HB	BB	SO	RAT	ERA	ERA+	OAV	OOB	BH	AVG	PB	PR	PR+	PD	TPI
1911	Cle-A	1	0	1.000	4	3	1	0	0	22^1	30	17	1	1	9	6	16.1	4.43	77	.326	.392	3	.273	0	-3	-2	0	-0.1
1912	Bro-N	6	11	.353	25	16	12	0	0	163	186	90	10	1	56	51	13.4	3.59	93	.293	.351	16	.250	3	-3	-4	-1	-0.2

YEAR	TM/L	W	L	PCT	G	GS	CG	SH	SV	IP	H	R	HR	HB	BB	SO	RAT	ERA	ERA+	OAV	OOB	BH	AVG	PB	PR	PR+	PD	TPI
1913	Bro-N	8	8	.500	26	13	8	2	0	146^2	158	56	2	2	10	40	10.4	2.58	128	.280	.295	23	.383	8	10	11	-1	2.0
1914	Cin-N	9	13	.409	34	27	8	3	0	198	207	102	6	6	54	80	12.1	3.45	85	.274	.328	23	.192	1	-15	-11	-2	-1.2
1918	Was-A	1	2	.333	5	2	2	0	0	38	30	15	0	0	12	15	9.9	2.13	128	.238	.304	7	.467	3	3	3	1	0.7
Total	5	25	34	.424	94	61	31	5	0	568	611	280	19	10	141	192	12.1	3.22	98	.281	.328	72	.267	16	-8	-4	-3	1.2
● **JOE YINGLING** Yingling, Joseph Granville b: 7/23/1866, Westminster, Md. d: 10/24/46, Manchester, Md. BR/TL, 5'7.5", 145 lbs. Deb: 5/28/1886 ♦																												
1886	Was-N	0	0	—	1	0	0	0	0	3	7	6	0		1	1	24.0	12.00	27	.412	.444	0	.000	-0	-3	-3	0	-0.1
● **LEN YOCHIM** Yochim, Leonard Joseph b: 10/16/28, New Orleans, La. BL/TL, 6'2", 200 lbs. Deb: 9/18/51 F																												
1951	Pit-N	1	1	.500	2	2	0	0	0	8^2	10	9	0	1	11	5	22.8	8.31	51	.278	.458	0	.000	-0	-4	-4	0	-0.6
1954	Pit-N	0	1	.000	10	1	0	0	0	19^2	30	17	2	0	8	7	17.4	7.32	57	.361	.418	1	.500	0	-7	-7	1	-0.2
Total	2	1	2	.333	12	3	0	0	0	28^1	40	26	2	1	19	12	19.1	7.62	55	.336	.432	1	.200	-0	-11	-10	1	-0.8
● **RAY YOCHIM** Yochim, Raymond Austin Aloysius b: 7/19/22, New Orleans, La. BR/TR, 6'1", 170 lbs. Deb: 5/2/48 F																												
1948	StL-N	0	0	—	1	0	0	0	0	1	0	0	0	0	3	1	27.0	0.00	—	.000	.500	0	—	0	0	0	0	0.0
1949	StL-N	0	0	—	3	0	0	0	0	2^1	3	4	1	0	4	3	27.0	15.43	27	.273	.467	0	—	0	-3	-3	-0	-0.1
Total	2	0	0	—	4	0	0	0	0	3^1	3	4	1	0	7	4	27.0	10.80	38	.214	.476	0	—	0	-3	-2	-0	-0.1
● **LEFTY YORK** York, James Edward b: 11/1/1892, West Fork, Ark. d: 4/9/61, York, Pa. BL/TL, 5'10", 185 lbs. Deb: 9/12/19																												
1919	Phi-A	0	2	.000	2	2	0	0	0	4^1	13	13	0	0	5	2	37.4	24.92	14	.500	.581	0	.000	-0	-10	-10	0	-1.4
1921	Chi-N	5	9	.357	40	11	4	1	1	139	170	82	5	5	63	57	15.4	4.73	81	.308	.384	5	.128	-2	-15	-14	-3	-1.7
Total	2	5	11	.313	42	13	4	1	1	143^1	183	95	5	5	68	59	16.1	5.34	71	.317	.393	5	.125	-2	-25	-24	-3	-3.1
● **JIM YORK** York, James Harlan b: 8/27/47, Maywood, Cal. BR/TR, 6'3", 200 lbs. Deb: 9/21/70																												
1970	KC-A	1	1	.500	4	0	0	0	0	8	5	3	2	0	2	6	7.9	3.38	111	.179	.233	0	.000	-0	0	0	-0	0.0
1971	KC-A	5	5	.500	53	0	0	0	3	93^1	70	32	7	3	44	103	11.3	2.89	119	.203	.299	2	.118	1	6	6	-0	0.7
1972	Hou-N	0	1	.000	26	0	0	0	0	36	45	21	3	1	18	25	16.0	5.25	64	.321	.403	0	.000	-0	-7	-8	0	-0.4
1973	Hou-N	3	4	.429	41	0	0	0	6	53	65	26	4	1	20	22	14.6	4.42	82	.305	.368	0	.000	-0	-4	-5	0	-0.7
1974	Hou-N	2	2	.500	28	0	0	0	1	38^1	48	20	1	1	19	15	16.0	3.29	106	.298	.376	0	.000	-1	1	1	0	0.0
1975	Hou-N	4	4	.500	19	4	0	0	0	46^2	43	22	1	5	25	17	14.1	3.86	88	.251	.363	1	.091	-0	-1	-3	-1	-0.6
1976	NY-A	1	0	1.000	3	0	0	0	0	9^2	14	7	1	1	4	6	17.7	5.59	61	.333	.404	0	—	0	-2	-2	-0	-0.2
Total	7	16	17	.485	174	4	0	0	10	285	290	131	19	12	132	194	13.7	3.79	92	.264	.349	3	.075	-1	-7	-10	-1	-1.2
● **MIKE YORK** York, Michael David b: 9/6/64, Oak Park, Ill. BR/TR, 6'1", 187 lbs. Deb: 8/17/90																												
1990	Pit-N	1	1	.500	4	1	0	0	0	12^2	13	5	0	1	5	4	13.5	2.84	127	.277	.358	1	.333	0	1	1	0	0.2
1991	Cle-A	1	4	.200	14	4	0	0	0	34^2	45	29	2	2	19	19	17.1	6.75	62	.333	.423	0	—	0	-10	-10	-0	-1.3
Total	2	2	5	.286	18	5	0	0	0	47^1	58	34	2	3	24	23	16.2	5.70	70	.319	.407	1	.333	0	-9	-9	-0	-1.1
● **MASATO YOSHII** Yoshii, Masato b: 4/20/65, Osaka, Japan BR/TR, 6'2", 210 lbs. Deb: 4/5/98																												
1998	NY-N	6	8	.429	29	29	1	0	0	171^2	166	79	22	6	53	117	11.8	3.93	105	.255	.316	3	.063	-2	6	4	-1	0.0
1999	*NY-N	12	8	.600	31	29	1	0	0	174	168	86	25	6	58	105	12.0	4.40	100	.260	.327	9	.164	-1	3	-0	-3	-0.4
2000	Col-N	6	15	.286	29	29	0	0	0	167^1	201	112	32	2	53	88	13.8	5.86	101	.306	.360	9	.180	-1	-23	1	-0	0.1
Total	3	24	31	.436	89	87	2	0	0	513	535	277	79	14	164	310	12.5	4.72	102	.274	.334	21	.137	-4	-14	4	-4	-0.3
● **GUS YOST** Yost, August 6'5", Deb: 6/12/1893																												
1893	Chi-N	0	1	.000	1	1	0	0	0	2^2	3	4	0	0	8	1	37.1	13.50	34	.273	.579	0	.000	-0	-3	-3	0	-0.4
● **FLOYD YOUMANS** Youmans, Floyd Everett b: 5/11/64, Tampa, Fla. BR/TR, 6'1", 190 lbs. Deb: 7/1/85																												
1985	Mon-N	4	3	.571	14	12	0	0	0	77	57	27	3	1	49	54	12.5	2.45	138	.206	.327	1	.053	-0	10	9	-2	0.5
1986	Mon-N	13	12	.520	33	32	6	2	0	219	145	93	14	4	118	202	11.0	3.53	105	.188	.299	12	.160	2	5	4	-3	0.3
1987	Mon-N	9	8	.529	23	23	3	3	0	116^1	112	63	13	1	47	94	12.4	4.64	91	.251	.324	6	.150	1	-7	-5	-0	-0.7
1988	Mon-N	3	6	.333	14	13	1	1	0	84	64	35	8	2	41	54	11.5	3.21	112	.213	.311	4	.154	-0	2	3	-1	0.3
1989	Phi-N	1	5	.167	10	10	0	0	0	42^2	50	31	7	2	25	20	16.2	5.70	62	.299	.397	1	.077	-1	-10	-10	0	-1.3
Total	5	30	34	.469	94	90	10	6	0	539	428	249	45	10	280	424	12.0	3.74	100	.218	.319	24	.139	1	-1	-0	-6	-0.9
● **ANTHONY YOUNG** Young, Anthony Wayne b: 1/19/66, Houston, Tex. BR/TR, 6'2", 210 lbs. Deb: 8/5/91																												
1991	NY-N	2	5	.286	10	8	0	0	0	49^1	48	20	4	1	12	20	11.1	3.10	117	.257	.305	2	.143	0	3	3	-1	0.3
1992	NY-N	2	14	.125	52	13	1	0	15	121	134	66	8	1	31	64	12.3	4.17	84	.285	.331	3	.111	-1	-9	-9	-0	-1.5
1993	NY-N	1	16	.059	39	10	1	0	3	100^1	103	62	8	1	42	62	13.1	3.77	107	.265	.339	2	.143	-0	3	3	0	0.4
1994	Chi-N	4	6	.400	20	19	0	0	0	114^2	103	57	12	0	46	65	11.7	3.92	106	.246	.320	6	.176	0	4	3	1	0.3
1995	Chi-N	3	4	.429	32	1	0	0	2	41^1	47	20	5	3	14	15	13.9	3.70	111	.288	.356	2	.667	1	2	2	-1	0.3
1996	Hou-N	3	3	.500	28	0	0	0	0	33^1	36	18	4	4	22	19	16.7	4.59	84	.279	.400	0	.000	-0	-1	-3	0	-0.5
Total	6	15	48	.238	181	51	2	0	20	460	471	243	41	10	167	245	12.7	3.89	99	.268	.335	15	.160	-0	2	-1	-1	-0.7
● **PETE YOUNG** Young, Bryan Owen b: 3/19/68, Meadville, Miss. BR/TR, 6', 225 lbs. Deb: 6/5/92																												
1992	Mon-N	0	0	—	13	0	0	0	0	20^1	18	9	0	1	9	11	12.4	3.98	87	.247	.337	0	—	0	-1	-1	-0	-0.1
1993	Mon-N	1	0	1.000	4	0	0	0	0	5^1	4	2	1	0	0	3	6.8	3.38	124	.211	.211	0	.000	-0	0	0	0	0.1
Total	2	1	0	1.000	17	0	0	0	0	25^2	22	11	1	1	9	14	11.2	3.86	94	.239	.314	0	.000	-0	-1	-1	-0	0.0
● **CHARLIE YOUNG** Young, Charles "Cy" b: 1/12/1893, Philadelphia, Pa. d: 5/12/52, Riverside, N.J. BB/TR, 5'10.5", 155 lbs. Deb: 9/5/15																												
1915	Bal-F	2	3	.400	9	5	1	0	0	35	39	32	0	4	21	13	16.5	5.91	49	.289	.400	2	.222	0	-12	-11	2	-1.3
● **CLIFF YOUNG** Young, Clifford Raphael b: 8/2/64, Willis, Tex. d: 11/4/93, Montgomery Co., Tex. BL/TL, 6'4", 200 lbs. Deb: 7/14/90																												
1990	Cal-A	1	1	.500	17	0	0	0	0	30^2	40	14	2	1	7	19	14.1	3.52	109	.325	.366	0	—	0	1	1	-0	0.1
1991	Cal-A	1	0	1.000	11	0	0	0	0	12^2	12	6	3	0	3	6	10.7	4.26	96	.261	.306	0	—	0	-0	-0	0	0.0
1993	Cle-A	3	3	.500	21	7	0	0	1	60^1	74	35	9	3	18	31	14.2	4.62	94	.298	.353	0	—	0	-2	-2	-1	-0.2
Total	3	5	4	.556	49	7	0	0	1	103^2	126	55	14	4	28	56	13.7	4.25	98	.302	.352	0	—	0	-1	-1	-1	-0.1
● **CURT YOUNG** Young, Curtis Allen b: 4/16/60, Saginaw, Mich. BR/TL, 6'1", 180 lbs. Deb: 6/24/83																												
1983	Oak-A	0	1	.000	8	2	0	0	0	9	17	17	1	1	5	5	23.0	16.00	24	.386	.460	0	—	0	-12	-13	-0	-1.2
1984	Oak-A	9	4	.692	20	17	2	1	0	108^2	118	53	9	8	31	41	13.0	4.06	92	.274	.334	0	—	0	-1	-4	-1	-0.5
1985	Oak-A	0	4	.000	19	7	0	0	0	46	57	38	15	1	22	19	15.7	7.24	53	.300	.376	0	—	0	-16	-19	-1	-1.4
1986	Oak-A	13	9	.591	29	27	5	2	0	198	176	88	19	7	57	116	10.9	3.45	112	.236	.297	0	—	0	16	10	1	1.0
1987	Oak-A	13	7	.650	31	31	6	0	0	203	194	102	38	3	44	124	10.7	4.08	102	.252	.295	0	.000	-0	9	2	0	0.1
1988	*Oak-A	11	8	.579	26	26	1	0	0	156^1	162	77	23	4	50	69	12.4	4.14	91	.275	.336	0	—	0	-3	-7	-1	-0.8
1989	Oak-A	5	9	.357	25	20	1	0	0	111	117	56	10	3	47	55	13.5	3.73	99	.264	.338	0	—	0	2	-1	-1	-0.2
1990	*Oak-A	9	6	.600	26	21	0	0	0	124^1	124	70	17	2	53	56	13.0	4.85	77	.266	.344	0	—	0	-13	-16	1	-1.6
1991	Oak-A	4	2	.667	41	1	0	0	0	68^1	74	38	8	2	34	27	14.5	5.00	77	.278	.364	0	—	0	-7	-9	1	-0.7
1992	KC-A	1	2	.333	10	2	0	0	0	24^1	29	14	1	0	7	7	13.3	5.18	78	.293	.340	0	—	0	-3	-3	-0	-0.3
	NY-A	3	0	1.000	13	5	0	0	0	43^1	51	21	1	2	10	13	13.1	3.32	118	.298	.344	0	—	0	3	3	0	0.2
	Yr	4	2	.667	23	7	0	0	0	67^2	80	35	2	2	17	20	13.2	3.99	100	.296	.343	0	—	0	-0	-0	0	-0.1
1993	Oak-A	1	1	.500	3	3	0	0	0	14^2	14	7	5	0	6	4	12.3	4.30	95	.241	.313	0	—	0	0	-0	0	0.0
Total	11	69	53	.566	251	162	15	3	0	1107	1133	581	147	33	366	536	12.5	4.31	90	.265	.328	0	.000	-0	-24	-57	-1	-5.4
● **DANNY YOUNG** Young, Daniel Bracy b: 11/3/71, Smyrna, Tenn. BR/TL, 6'4", 210 lbs. Deb: 3/30/2000																												
2000	Chi-N	0	1	.000	4	0	0	0	0	3	5	7	1	0	6	0	33.0	21.00	22	.357	.550	0	—	0	-5	-6	-0	-0.9
● **CY YOUNG** Young, Denton True b: 3/29/1867, Gilmore, Ohio d: 11/4/55, Newcomerstown, Ohio BR/TR, 6'2", 210 lbs. Deb: 8/6/1890 MH																												
1890	Cle-N	9	7	.563	17	16	16	0	0	147^2	145	87	6	8	30	39	11.2	3.47	103	.249	.295	8	.123	-6	2	2	1	-0.3
1891	Cle-N	27	22	.551	55	46	43	0	2	423^2	431	244	4	10	140	147	12.3	2.85	122	.254	.314	29	.167	-3	24	28	-1	2.3
1892	*Cle-N	**36**	12	**.750**	53	49	48	**9**	0	453	363	158	8	11	118	168	**9.8**	**1.93**	**176**	.211	**.266**	31	.158	-8	**68**	**71**	5	**6.4**
1893	Cle-N	34	16	.680	53	46	42	1	1	422^2	442	230	10	10	103	102	**11.8**	3.36	145	.261	**.307**	44	.235	-6	61	68	4	6.1
1894	Cle-N	26	21	.553	52	47	44	2	1	408^2	488	265	19	5	106	108	13.2	3.94	139	.293	.337	40	.215	-8	63	67	7	5.4

YEAR	TM/L	W	L	PCT	G	GS	CG	SH	SV	IP	H	R	HR	HB	BB	SO	RAT	ERA	ERA+	OAV	OOB	BH	AVG	PB	PR	PR+	PD	TPI
1895	*Cle-N	**35**	10	.778	47	40	36	**4**	0	369^2	363	177	10	8	75	121	**10.9**	3.26	153	.253	**.294**	30	.214	-4	62	68	8	6.7
1896	*Cle-N	28	15	.651	51	46	42	**5**	**3**	414^1	477	214	7	11	62	**140**	11.9	3.24	140	.286	.316	52	.289	7	52	58	8	6.2
1897	Cle-N	21	19	.525	46	38	35	2	0	335^2	391	189	7	9	49	88	12.0	3.78	119	.289	.318	34	.222	-4	20	25	3	2.2
1898	Cle-N	25	13	.658	46	41	40	1	0	377^2	387	167	6	9	41	101	10.4	2.53	143	.263	.287	39	.253	5	45	46	7	5.3
1899	StL-N	26	16	.619	44	42	**40**	4	1	369^1	368	173	10	6	44	111	**10.2**	2.58	154	.260	**.285**	32	.216	-1	**52**	55	6	**6.0**
1900	StL-N	19	19	.500	41	35	32	**4**	0	321^1	337	144	7	3	36	115	10.5	3.00	121	.269	.291	22	.177	-2	25	23	0	2.1
1901	Bos-A	**33**	10	.767	43	41	38	**5**	0	371^1	324	112	6	7	37	**158**	**8.9**	**1.62**	**217**	**.232**	**.256**	32	.209	0	**84**	**82**	1	**8.6**
1902	Bos-A	**32**	11	.744	**45**	43	**41**	3	0	**384**^{2}	350	136	6	13	53	160	9.7	2.15	166	.243	.276	34	.230	2	**61**	**61**	-6	**5.8**
1903	*Bos-A	**28**	9	**.757**	40	35	**34**	**7**	**2**	**341**^{2}	294	115	6	9	37	176	9.0	2.08	146	.232	.259	44	.321	12	34	**35**	-3	**4.8**
1904	Bos-A	26	16	.619	43	41	40	**10**	1	380	327	104	6	4	29	200	**8.5**	1.97	136	.233	**.251**	33	.223	2	27	29	-5	3.0
1905	Bos-A	18	19	.486	38	33	31	4	0	320^2	248	99	3	8	30	210	**8.0**	1.82	148	.215	**.241**	18	.150	-2	30	31	-2	3.2
1906	Bos-A	13	21	.382	39	34	28	0	2	287^2	288	137	3	8	25	140	10.0	3.19	86	.263	.285	16	.154	-2	-16	-14	-1	-1.9
1907	Bos-A	21	15	.583	43	37	33	6	2	343^1	286	101	3	7	51	147	**9.0**	1.99	129	.229	**.263**	27	.216	0	21	22	-6	1.7
1908	Bos-A	21	11	.656	36	33	30	3	2	299	230	68	1	1	37	150	8.1	1.26	195	.213	.240	26	.226	1	38	39	-6	4.0
1909	Cle-A	19	15	.559	35	34	30	3	0	294^1	267	110	4	8	59	109	10.2	2.26	113	.250	.294	21	.196	-0	7	9	-1	0.9
1910	Cle-A	7	10	.412	21	20	14	1	0	163^1	149	62	0	4	27	58	9.9	2.53	102	.252	.289	8	.145	-0	-0	1	1	0.2
1911	Cle-A	3	4	.429	7	7	4	0	0	46^1	54	28	2	1	13	20	13.2	3.88	88	.298	.349	1	.063	-2	-3	-2	-0	-0.5
	Bos-N	4	5	.444	11	11	8	2	0	80	83	47	4	3	15	35	11.4	3.71	103	.268	.308	2	.080	-2	-3	1	0	-0.2
Total	22	511	316	.618	906	815	749	76	17	7356	7092	3167	138	163	1217	2803	10.4	2.63	138	.252	.287	623	.210	-22	753	801	19	78.0

● **HARLEY YOUNG** Young, Harlan Edward "Cy The Third" b: 9/28/1883, Portland, Ind. d: 3/26/75, Jacksonville, Fla. BR/TR, 6'2", Deb: 4/21/08

YEAR	TM/L	W	L	PCT	G	GS	CG	SH	SV	IP	H	R	HR	HB	BB	SO	RAT	ERA	ERA+	OAV	OOB	BH	AVG	PB	PR	PR+	PD	TPI
1908	Pit-N	0	2	.000	8	3	0	0	0	48^1	40	21	0	5	10	17	10.2	2.23	103	.234	.296	1	.083	-1	1	0	1	0.0
	Bos-N	0	1	.000	6	2	1	0	0	27^1	29	19	0	3	4	12	11.9	3.29	73	.269	.313	2	.200	0	-3	-3	-0	-0.1
	Yr	0	3	.000	14	5	1	0	0	75^2	69	40	0	8	14	29	10.8	2.62	89	.247	.302	3	.136	-0	-2	-2	1	-0.1

● **IRV YOUNG** Young, Irving Melrose "Young Cy" or "Cy The Second"
b: 7/21/1877, Columbia Falls, Maine d: 1/14/35, Brewer, Maine BL/TL, 5'10", 170 lbs. Deb: 4/14/05

YEAR	TM/L	W	L	PCT	G	GS	CG	SH	SV	IP	H	R	HR	HB	BB	SO	RAT	ERA	ERA+	OAV	OOB	BH	AVG	PB	PR	PR+	PD	TPI
1905	Bos-N	20	21	.488	43	42	**41**	7	0	**378**	337	146	6	8	71	156	9.9	2.90	107	.241	.282	14	.103	-8	4	8	4	0.4
1906	Bos-N	16	25	.390	43	41	**37**	4	0	**358**^{1}	349	157	7	6	83	151	11.0	2.91	92	.263	.309	12	.096	-7	-11	-9	3	-1.5
1907	Bos-N	10	23	.303	40	32	22	3	1	245^1	287	131	5	13	58	86	13.1	3.96	64	.306	.354	13	.162	-1	-41	-37	1	-4.8
1908	Bos-N	4	9	.308	16	11	7	1	0	85	94	49	2	2	19	32	12.2	2.86	84	.289	.332	5	.156	-1	-5	-4	-1	-0.9
	Pit-N	4	3	.571	16	7	3	1	1	89^2	73	33	1	5	21	31	9.9	2.01	115	.225	.283	6	.200	1	4	3	-1	0.3
	Yr	8	12	.400	32	18	10	2	1	174^2	167	82	3	7	40	63	11.0	2.42	97	.257	.307	11	.177	0	-1	-1	-2	-0.6
1910	Chi-A	4	8	.333	27	17	7	4	0	135^2	122	52	0	3	39	64	10.9	2.72	88	.247	.306	5	.114	-2	-3	-5	-0	-0.7
1911	Chi-A	5	6	.455	24	11	3	1	2	92^2	99	61	2	0	25	40	12.0	4.37	74	.229	.271	5	.179	-0	-11	-12	1	-1.3
Total	6	63	95	.399	209	161	120	21	4	1384^2	1361	629	23	37	316	560	11.1	3.11	88	.260	.307	60	.126	-18	-62	-56	6	-8.5

● **J. B. YOUNG** Young, J. B. b: Mt.Carmel, Pa. Deb: 6/10/1892

YEAR	TM/L	W	L	PCT	G	GS	CG	SH	SV	IP	H	R	HR	HB	BB	SO	RAT	ERA	ERA+	OAV	OOB	BH	AVG	PB	PR	PR+	PD	TPI
1892	StL-N	0	0	—	1	0	0	0	0	2	9	13	0	0	2	1	49.5	22.50	14	.600	.647	0	.000	-0	-4	-4	-0	-0.2

● **KIP YOUNG** Young, Kip Lane b: 10/29/54, Georgetown, Ohio BR/TR, 5'11", 175 lbs. Deb: 7/21/78

YEAR	TM/L	W	L	PCT	G	GS	CG	SH	SV	IP	H	R	HR	HB	BB	SO	RAT	ERA	ERA+	OAV	OOB	BH	AVG	PB	PR	PR+	PD	TPI
1978	Det-A	6	7	.462	14	13	7	0	0	105^2	94	34	9	2	30	49	10.7	2.81	138	.246	.304	0	—	0	11	12	-2	1.3
1979	Det-A	2	2	.500	13	7	0	0	0	43^2	60	32	11	1	11	22	14.8	6.39	68	.323	.364	0	—	0	-10	-10	1	-0.7
Total	2	8	9	.471	27	20	7	0	0	149^1	154	66	20	3	41	71	11.9	3.86	104	.271	.324	0	—	0	1	3	-1	0.6

● **MATT YOUNG** Young, Matthew John b: 8/9/58, Pasadena, Cal. BL/TL, 6'3", 205 lbs. Deb: 4/6/83

YEAR	TM/L	W	L	PCT	G	GS	CG	SH	SV	IP	H	R	HR	HB	BB	SO	RAT	ERA	ERA+	OAV	OOB	BH	AVG	PB	PR	PR+	PD	TPI
1983	Sea-A★	11	15	.423	33	32	5	2	0	203^2	178	86	17	7	79	130	11.7	3.27	131	.236	.315	0	—	0	18	22	2	2.8
1984	Sea-A	6	8	.429	22	22	1	0	0	113^1	141	81	11	1	57	73	15.8	5.72	70	.307	.384	0	—	0	-22	-22	1	-2.2
1985	Sea-A	12	19	.387	37	35	5	2	1	218^1	242	135	23	7	76	136	13.4	4.91	86	.282	.345	0	—	0	-18	-16	-2	-2.2
1986	Sea-A	8	6	.571	65	5	1	0	13	103^2	108	50	9	8	46	82	14.1	3.82	111	.272	.359	0	—	0	4	5	-1	0.6
1987	LA-N	5	8	.385	47	0	0	0	11	54^1	62	30	3	0	17	42	13.1	4.47	89	.288	.341	0	.000	-0	-2	-3	-2	-0.8
1989	*Oak-A	1	4	.200	26	4	0	0	0	37^1	42	31	2	0	31	27	17.6	6.75	55	.286	.410	0	—	0	-12	-13	0	-1.6
1990	Sea-A	8	18	.308	34	33	7	1	0	225^1	198	106	15	6	107	176	12.4	3.51	113	.237	.328	0	—	0	10	11	-0	1.2
1991	Bos-A	3	7	.300	19	16	0	0	0	88^2	92	55	4	2	53	69	14.9	5.18	83	.266	.367	0	—	0	-11	-8	-0	-0.8
1992	Bos-A	0	4	.000	28	8	1	0	0	70^2	69	42	7	3	42	57	14.5	4.58	92	.257	.363	0	—	0	-5	-3	-1	-0.2
1993	Cle-A	1	6	.143	22	8	0	0	0	74^1	75	45	8	3	57	65	16.3	5.21	83	.266	.395	0	—	0	-7	-7	0	-0.6
Total	10	55	95	.367	333	163	20	5	25	1189^2	1207	661	99	37	565	857	13.7	4.40	94	.265	.350	0	.000	-0	-44	-33	-3	-3.8

● **TIM YOUNG** Young, Timothy R. b: 10/15/73, Gulfport, Miss. BL/TL, 5'9", 170 lbs. Deb: 9/5/98

YEAR	TM/L	W	L	PCT	G	GS	CG	SH	SV	IP	H	R	HR	HB	BB	SO	RAT	ERA	ERA+	OAV	OOB	BH	AVG	PB	PR	PR+	PD	TPI
1998	Mon-N	0	0	—	10	0	0	0	0	6	6	4	0	0	4	7	15.0	6.00	70	.250	.357	0	—	0	-1	-1	0	0.0
2000	Bos-A	0	0	—	8	0	0	0	0	7	7	5	3	1	2	6	12.9	6.43	79	.269	.345	0	—	0	-1	-1	-0	-0.1
Total	2	0	0	—	18	0	0	0	0	13	13	9	3	1	6	13	13.8	6.23	75	.260	.351	0	—	0	-2	-2	0	-0.1

● **CHIEF YOUNGBLOOD** Youngblood, Albert Clyde b: 6/13/1900, Hillsboro, Tex. d: 7/6/68, Amarillo, Tex. BL/TR, 6'3", 202 lbs. Deb: 7/16/22

YEAR	TM/L	W	L	PCT	G	GS	CG	SH	SV	IP	H	R	HR	HB	BB	SO	RAT	ERA	ERA+	OAV	OOB	BH	AVG	PB	PR	PR+	PD	TPI
1922	Was-A	0	0	—	2	0	0	0	0	4^1	9	9	0	2	7	0	37.4	14.54	27	.429	.600	0	.000	-0	-5	-5	0	-0.3

● **DUCKY YOUNT** Yount, Herbert Macon "Hub" b: 12/7/1885, Iredell Co., N.C. d: 5/9/70, Winston-Salem, N.C. BR/TR, 6'2", 178 lbs. Deb: 5/20/14

YEAR	TM/L	W	L	PCT	G	GS	CG	SH	SV	IP	H	R	HR	HB	BB	SO	RAT	ERA	ERA+	OAV	OOB	BH	AVG	PB	PR	PR+	PD	TPI
1914	Bal-F	1	1	.500	13	1	1	0	0	41^1	44	28	2	2	19	19	14.2	4.14	73	.280	.365	1	.083	-1	-6	-5	1	-0.3

● **LARRY YOUNT** Yount, Lawrence King b: 2/15/50, Houston, Tex. BR/TR, 6'2", 185 lbs. Deb: 9/15/71 F

YEAR	TM/L	W	L	PCT	G	GS	CG	SH	SV	IP	H	R	HR	HB	BB	SO	RAT	ERA	ERA+	OAV	OOB	BH	AVG	PB	PR	PR+	PD	TPI
1971	Hou-N	0	0	—	1	0	0	0	0	0	0	0	0	0	—	—	—	—	—	—	97	—	0	0	0	0	0.0	

● **CARL YOWELL** Yowell, Carl Columbus "Sundown" b: 12/20/02, Madison, Va. d: 7/27/85, Jacksonville, Tex. BL/TL, 6'4", 180 lbs. Deb: 9/5/24

YEAR	TM/L	W	L	PCT	G	GS	CG	SH	SV	IP	H	R	HR	HB	BB	SO	RAT	ERA	ERA+	OAV	OOB	BH	AVG	PB	PR	PR+	PD	TPI
1924	Cle-A	1	1	.500	4	2	2	0	0	27	37	21	1	0	13	8	16.7	6.67	64	.343	.413	2	.182	-1	-7	-7	-0	-0.5
1925	Cle-A	2	3	.400	12	4	1	0	0	36^1	40	21	1	1	17	12	14.4	4.46	99	.310	.395	1	.125	-1	-0	-0	0	-0.1
Total	2	3	4	.429	16	6	3	0	0	63^1	77	42	2	1	30	20	15.3	5.40	81	.325	.403	3	.158	-1	-8	-7	0	-0.6

● **EDDIE YUHAS** Yuhas, John Edward b: 8/5/24, Youngstown, Ohio d: 7/6/86, Winston-Salem, N.C BR/TR, 6'1", 180 lbs. Deb: 4/17/52

YEAR	TM/L	W	L	PCT	G	GS	CG	SH	SV	IP	H	R	HR	HB	BB	SO	RAT	ERA	ERA+	OAV	OOB	BH	AVG	PB	PR	PR+	PD	TPI
1952	StL-N	12	2	.857	54	2	0	0	6	99^1	90	35	5	2	35	39	11.5	2.72	137	.243	.312	4	.190	1	11	11	-1	1.6
1953	StL-N	0	0	—	2	0	0	0	0	1	3	2	0	0	0	0	27.0	18.00	24	.500	.500	0	—	0	-2	-2	-0	-0.1
Total	2	12	2	.857	56	2	0	0	6	100^1	93	37	5	2	35	39	11.7	2.87	130	.247	.315	4	.190	1	10	10	-1	1.5

● **ADRIAN ZABALA** Zabala, Adrian (Rodriguez) b: 8/26/16, San Antonio De Los Banos, Cuba BL/TL, 5'11", 165 lbs. Deb: 8/11/45

YEAR	TM/L	W	L	PCT	G	GS	CG	SH	SV	IP	H	R	HR	HB	BB	SO	RAT	ERA	ERA+	OAV	OOB	BH	AVG	PB	PR	PR+	PD	TPI
1945	NY-N	2	4	.333	11	5	1	0	0	43^1	46	25	2	0	20	14	13.7	4.78	82	.284	.363	3	.231	1	-5	-4	0	-0.4
1949	NY-N	2	3	.400	15	4	2	1	1	41	44	28	5	1	10	13	12.1	5.27	76	.278	.325	1	.077	-1	-6	-6	-1	-0.9
Total	2	4	7	.364	26	9	3	1	1	84^1	90	53	7	1	30	27	12.9	5.02	79	.281	.345	4	.154	-0	-10	-10	-1	-1.3

● **ZIP ZABEL** Zabel, George Washington b: 2/18/1891, Wetmore, Kan. d: 5/31/70, Beloit, Wis. BR/TR, 6'1.5", 185 lbs. Deb: 10/5/13

YEAR	TM/L	W	L	PCT	G	GS	CG	SH	SV	IP	H	R	HR	HB	BB	SO	RAT	ERA	ERA+	OAV	OOB	BH	AVG	PB	PR	PR+	PD	TPI
1913	Chi-N	1	0	1.000	1	1	0	0	0	5	3	0	0	0	1	0	7.2	0.00	—	.167	.211	0	.000	0	2	2	0	0.4
1914	Chi-N	4	4	.500	29	7	2	0	3	128	104	45	5	2	45	50	10.6	2.18	128	.235	.309	7	.184	-1	9	9	-1	0.4
1915	Chi-N	7	10	.412	36	17	8	3	0	163	124	80	3	4	84	60	11.7	3.20	87	.218	.323	4	.074	-4	-8	-8	3	-0.8
Total	3	12	14	.462	66	25	10	3	3	296	231	125	8	6	130	110	11.2	2.71	103	.224	.315	11	.117	-4	2	3	2	0.0

● **CHINK ZACHARY** Zachary, Albert Myron (b: Albert Myron Zarski) b: 10/19/17, Brooklyn, N.Y. BR/TR, 5'11", 182 lbs. Deb: 4/23/44

YEAR	TM/L	W	L	PCT	G	GS	CG	SH	SV	IP	H	R	HR	HB	BB	SO	RAT	ERA	ERA+	OAV	OOB	BH	AVG	PB	PR	PR+	PD	TPI
1944	Bro-N	0	2	.000	4	2	0	0	0	10^1	10	11	2	1	7	3	15.7	9.58	37	.238	.360	0	.000	-0	-7	-7	-0	-1.1

● **TOM ZACHARY** Zachary, Jonathan Thompson Walton (a.k.a. Zach Walton In 1918)
b: 5/7/1896, Graham, N.C. d: 1/24/69, Burlington, N.C. BL/TL, 6'1", 187 lbs. Deb: 7/11/18

YEAR	TM/L	W	L	PCT	G	GS	CG	SH	SV	IP	H	R	HR	HB	BB	SO	RAT	ERA	ERA+	OAV	OOB	BH	AVG	PB	PR	PR+	PD	TPI
1918	Phi-A	2	0	1.000	2	2	0	0	0	8	9	5	0	0	7	1	18.0	5.63	52	.321	.457	2	.500	1	-3	-2	-0	-0.4
1919	Was-A	1	5	.167	17	7	0	0	0	61^2	68	29	0	1	20	9	13.0	2.92	110	.292	.350	5	.333	2	2	2	-1	0.3
1920	Was-A	15	16	.484	44	31	19	3	2	262^2	289	141	7	4	78	53	12.7	3.77	99	.285	.339	29	.261	6	1	-1	0	0.4
1921	Was-A	18	16	.529	39	30	17	2	1	250	314	130	10	6	59	53	13.6	3.96	104	.319	.361	23	.256	3	9	5	-0	0.8
1922	Was-A	15	10	.600	32	25	13	1	1	184^2	190	74	6	3	43	37	11.5	3.12	124	.275	.321	21	.296	5	19	16	0	2.5

YEAR	TM/L	W	L	PCT	G	GS	CG	SH	SV	IP	H	R	HR	HB	BB	SO	RAT	ERA	ERA+	OAV	OOB	BH	AVG	PB	PR	PR+	PD	TPI
1923	Was-A	10	16	.385	35	29	10	0	0	204^1	270	117	9	4	63	40	14.8	4.49	84	.321	.372	15	.192	-0	-12	-17	-1	-2.0
1924	*Was-A	15	9	.625	33	27	13	1	2	202^2	198	74	5	3	53	45	11.3	2.75	147	.264	.315	22	.306	4	33	30	2	3.8
1925	*Was-A	12	15	.444	38	33	11	1	2	217^2	247	112	10	2	74	58	13.4	3.85	110	.296	.355	12	.174	-2	13	10	-0	0.8
1926	StL-A	14	15	.483	34	31	18	3	0	247^1	264	126	14	6	97	53	13.4	3.60	119	.288	.359	23	.267	4	11	18	3	2.6
1927	StL-A	4	6	.400	13	12	6	0	0	78^1	110	48	4	0	27	13	15.7	4.37	100	.345	.396	3	.107	-2	-2	-0	-1	-0.3
	Was-A	4	7	.364	15	14	5	1	0	102^2	116	54	2	2	30	13	13.0	3.94	103	.290	.343	5	.139	-2	2	1	-3	-0.3
	Yr	8	13	.381	28	26	11	1	0	181	226	102	6	2	57	26	14.2	4.13	102	.314	.366	8	.125	-4	0	1	-3	-0.6
1928	Was-A	6	9	.400	20	14	5	1	0	102^2	130	72	5	1	40	19	15.0	5.44	74	.322	.384	10	.303	1	-16	-16	1	-1.8
	*NY-A	3	3	.500	7	6	3	0	1	45^2	54	26	1	0	15	7	13.6	3.94	95	.320	.375	2	.133	-0	1	-1	1	-0.1
	Yr	9	12	.429	27	20	8	1	1	148^1	184	98	6	1	55	26	14.6	4.98	79	.321	.382	12	.250	1	-15	-18	2	-1.9
1929	NY-A	12	0	1.000	26	11	7	2	2	119^2	131	43	5	2	30	35	12.3	2.48	155	.277	.323	10	.238	1	23	20	-3	1.7
1930	NY-A	1	1	.500	3	3	0	0	0	16^2	18	16	0	0	9	1	14.6	6.48	66	.269	.355	2	.250	1	-3	-4	1	-0.3
	Bos-N	11	5	.688	24	22	10	0	0	151^1	192	90	9	0	50	57	14.4	4.58	108	.317	.369	13	.241	2	7	6	-1	0.6
1931	Bos-N	11	15	.423	33	28	16	3	2	229	243	87	8	1	53	64	11.7	3.10	122	.272	.314	14	.167	-1	19	18	2	2.0
1932	Bos-N	12	11	.522	32	24	12	1	0	212	231	83	5	2	55	67	12.2	3.10	121	.280	.326	21	.273	5	18	16	-2	2.0
1933	Bos-N	7	9	.438	26	20	6	2	2	125	134	64	1	0	35	22	12.2	3.53	87	.276	.325	5	.119	-2	-3	-7	-0	-1.0
1934	Bos-N	1	2	.333	5	4	2	1	0	24	27	9	1	0	8	4	13.1	3.38	113	.278	.333	0	.000	-1	2	1	-0	0.0
	Bro-N	5	6	.455	22	12	4	0	2	101^2	122	53	5	2	21	28	12.8	4.43	88	.301	.339	7	.184	1	-4	-6	-1	-0.6
	Yr	6	8	.429	27	16	6	1	2	125^2	149	62	6	2	29	32	12.9	4.15	92	.297	.338	7	.152	-0	-2	-5	-1	-0.6
1935	Bro-N	7	12	.368	25	21	9	1	4	158	193	76	10	2	35	33	13.1	3.59	111	.297	.335	7	.135	-1	8	7	0	0.7
1936	Bro-N	0	0	—	1	0	0	0	0	0^1	2	2	0	0	1	0	81.0	54.00	8	1.000	1.000	0	—	0	-2	-2	0	-0.1
	Phi-N	0	3	.000	7	2	0	0	1	20^1	28	20	2	0	11	8	17.3	7.97	57	.329	.406	3	.333	1	-9	-7	0	-0.8
	Yr	0	3	.000	8	2	0	0	1	20^2	30	22	2	0	12	8	18.3	8.71	52	.345	.424	3	.333	1	-11	-9	0	-0.9
Total	19	186	191	.493	533	408	186	24	22	3126^1	3580	1551	119	41	914	720	13.1	3.73	106	.294	.345	254	.226	25	116	84	-2	10.5

● CHRIS ZACHARY

Zachary, William Christopher b: 2/19/44, Knoxville, Tenn. BL/TR, 6'2", 200 lbs. Deb: 4/11/63

YEAR	TM/L	W	L	PCT	G	GS	CG	SH	SV	IP	H	R	HR	HB	BB	SO	RAT	ERA	ERA+	OAV	OOB	BH	AVG	PB	PR	PR+	PD	TPI
1963	Hou-N	2	2	.500	22	7	0	0	0	57	62	38	5	3	22	42	13.7	4.89	64	.272	.344	0	.000	-1	-10	-12	1	-0.8
1964	Hou-N	0	1	.000	1	1	0	0	0	4	6	5	1	0	1	2	15.8	9.00	38	.333	.368	0	.000	-0	-2	-3	0	-0.4
1965	Hou-N	0	2	.000	4	2	0	0	0	10^2	12	6	0	0	6	4	15.2	4.22	80	.273	.360	0	.000	-0	-1	-1	-0	-0.2
1966	Hou-N	3	5	.375	10	8	0	0	0	55	44	22	1	1	32	37	12.6	3.44	100	.221	.332	4	.222	1	1	-0	-1	0.0
1967	Hou-N	1	6	.143	9	7	0	0	0	36^1	42	27	5	2	12	18	13.9	5.70	58	.290	.352	1	.100	-0	-9	-10	-0	-1.7
1969	KC-A	0	1	.000	8	2	0	0	0	18^1	27	17	4	0	7	6	16.7	7.85	47	.346	.400	1	.500	0	-9	-8	-0	-0.4
1971	StL-N	3	10	.231	23	12	1	1	0	89^2	114	58	3	4	26	48	14.5	5.32	68	.316	.368	8	.242	1	-18	-16	0	-2.1
1972	*Det-A	1	1	.500	25	1	0	0	1	38^1	27	6	2	1	15	21	10.1	1.41	224	.201	.287	1	.500	1	7	7	-0	0.5
1973	Pit-N	0	1	.000	6	0	0	0	1	12	10	4	1	0	1	6	8.3	3.00	118	.222	.239	0	.000	-0	1	1	-0	0.0
Total	9	10	29	.256	108	40	1	1	2	321^1	344	183	22	11	122	184	13.4	4.57	74	.275	.344	15	.181	1	-41	-42	-1	-5.1

● PAT ZACHRY

Zachry, Patrick Paul b: 4/24/52, Richmond, Tex. BR/TR, 6'5", 180 lbs. Deb: 4/11/76

YEAR	TM/L	W	L	PCT	G	GS	CG	SH	SV	IP	H	R	HR	HB	BB	SO	RAT	ERA	ERA+	OAV	OOB	BH	AVG	PB	PR	PR+	PD	TPI
1976	*Cin-N	14	7	.667	38	28	6	1	0	204	170	70	8	2	83	143	11.3	2.74	128	.228	.307	7	.113	-2	17	18	-2	1.4
1977	Cin-N	3	7	.300	12	12	3	0	0	75	78	45	7	1	29	36	13.0	5.04	78	.273	.342	3	.136	-1	-9	-9	1	-1.0
	NY-N	7	6	.538	19	19	2	1	0	119^2	129	59	14	3	48	63	13.5	3.76	100	.278	.350	6	.143	-1	2	-0	-2	-0.3
	Yr	10	13	.435	31	31	5	1	0	194^2	207	104	21	4	77	99	13.3	4.25	90	.276	.347	9	.141	-2	-7	-10	-0	-1.3
1978	NY-N☆	10	6	.625	21	21	5	2	0	138	120	57	9	1	60	78	11.8	3.33	105	.236	.318	3	.070	-2	4	3	1	0.2
1979	NY-N	5	1	.833	7	7	1	0	0	42^2	44	19	3	2	21	17	14.1	3.59	102	.267	.356	2	.125	-1	1	0	0	0.0
1980	NY-N	6	10	.375	28	26	7	3	0	164^2	145	65	16	5	58	88	11.4	3.01	118	.240	.312	2	.043	-4	11	10	-2	0.4
1981	NY-N	7	14	.333	24	24	3	0	0	139	151	78	13	4	56	76	13.7	4.14	84	.282	.354	6	.158	0	-10	-10	1	-1.4
1982	NY-N	6	9	.400	36	16	2	0	1	137^2	149	69	10	0	57	69	13.5	4.05	90	.279	.349	3	.079	-2	-7	-6	-0	-0.9
1983	*LA-N	6	1	.857	40	1	0	0	0	61^1	63	22	4	1	21	36	12.5	2.49	144	.278	.341	2	.500	1	8	8	0	0.9
1984	LA-N	5	6	.455	58	0	0	0	2	82^2	84	38	3	2	51	55	14.9	3.81	93	.267	.372	2	.333	1	-2	-3	1	-0.2
1985	Phi-N	0	0	—	10	0	0	0	0	12^2	14	7	1	0	11	8	17.8	4.26	87	.280	.410	0	.000	-0	-1	-1	1	0.0
Total	10	69	67	.507	293	154	29	7	3	1177^1	1147	529	88	21	495	669	12.7	3.52	102	.259	.336	36	.113	-11	14	9	-1	-0.9

● GEORGE ZACKERT

Zackert, George Carl "Zeke" b: 12/24/1884, Buchanan Co., Mo. d: 2/18/77, Burlington, Iowa BL/TL, 6', 177 lbs. Deb: 9/22/11

YEAR	TM/L	W	L	PCT	G	GS	CG	SH	SV	IP	H	R	HR	HB	BB	SO	RAT	ERA	ERA+	OAV	OOB	BH	AVG	PB	PR	PR+	PD	TPI
1911	StL-N	0	2	.000	4	1	0	0	0	7^1	17	13	0	0	6	6	28.2	11.05	31	.486	.561	0	.000	-0	-6	-6	1	-1.1
1912	StL-N	0	0	—	1	0	0	0	0	1	2	2	0	1	1	0	36.0	18.00	19	.667	.800	0	—	0	-2	-2	0	-0.1
Total	2	0	2	.000	5	1	0	0	0	8^1	19	15	0	1	7	6	29.2	11.88	28	.500	.587	0	.000	-0	-8	-8	1	-1.2

● GEOFF ZAHN

Zahn, Geoffrey Clayton b: 12/19/45, Baltimore, Md. BL/TL, 6'1", 180 lbs. Deb: 9/2/73

YEAR	TM/L	W	L	PCT	G	GS	CG	SH	SV	IP	H	R	HR	HB	BB	SO	RAT	ERA	ERA+	OAV	OOB	BH	AVG	PB	PR	PR+	PD	TPI
1973	LA-N	1	0	1.000	6	1	0	0	0	13^1	5	2	2	0	2	9	4.7	1.35	255	.116	.156	0	.000	-0	3	3	0	0.2
1974	LA-N	3	5	.375	21	10	1	0	0	79^2	78	28	3	2	16	33	10.8	2.03	168	.254	.295	4	.174	-0	14	13	0	1.2
1975	LA-N	0	1	.000	2	0	0	0	0	3	5	3	0	0	5	1	21.0	9.00	38	.222	.500	0	—	0	-2	-2	-0	-0.4
	Chi-N	2	7	.222	16	10	0	0	1	62^2	67	37	2	0	26	21	13.4	4.45	87	.282	.352	2	.133	-1	-6	-4	1	-0.5
	Yr	2	8	.200	18	10	0	0	1	65^2	69	40	2	0	31	22	13.7	4.66	82	.279	.360	2	.133	-1	-7	-6	1	-0.9
1976	Chi-N	0	1	.000	3	2	0	0	0	8^1	16	10	0	1	2	4	20.5	10.80	36	.410	.452	0	.000	-0	-7	-6	0	-0.6
1977	Min-A	12	14	.462	34	32	7	1	0	198	234	116	20	5	66	88	13.9	4.68	85	.299	.358	0	—	0	-13	-15	2	-1.5
1978	Min-A	14	14	.500	35	35	12	1	0	252^1	260	101	18	4	81	106	12.3	3.03	126	.274	.334	0	—	0	21	22	-0	2.3
1979	Min-A	13	7	.650	26	24	4	0	0	169	181	74	13	0	41	58	11.8	3.57	123	.279	.322	0	—	0	12	15	2	1.8
1980	Min-A	14	18	.438	38	35	13	5	0	232^2	273	138	17	2	66	96	13.2	4.41	99	.302	.351	0	—	0	-9	-1	0	-0.1
1981	Cal-A	10	11	.476	25	25	9	0	0	161^1	181	93	18	0	43	52	12.5	4.41	83	.285	.330	0	—	0	-13	-14	0	-1.6
1982	*Cal-A	18	8	.692	34	34	12	4	0	229^1	225	100	18	4	65	81	11.5	3.73	109	.259	.314	0	—	0	9	9	-1	0.8
1983	Cal-A	9	11	.450	29	28	11	3	0	203	212	90	22	0	51	81	11.7	3.33	121	.269	.314	0	—	0	17	16	-2	1.3
1984	Cal-A	13	10	.565	28	27	9	**5**	0	199^1	200	78	11	1	48	61	11.2	3.12	128	.263	.308	0	—	0	20	19	1	2.2
1985	Cal-A	2	2	.500	7	7	1	1	0	37	44	19	5	0	14	14	14.1	4.38	94	.299	.360	0	—	0	-1	-1	1	-0.1
Total	13	111	109	.505	304	270	79	20	1	1849	1978	889	149	19	526	705	12.3	3.74	107	.278	.329	6	.140	-2	45	53	4	5.0

● PAUL ZAHNISER

Zahniser, Paul Vernon b: 9/6/1896, Sac City, Iowa d: 9/26/64, Klamath Falls, Ore. BR/TR, 5'10.5", 170 lbs. Deb: 5/18/23

YEAR	TM/L	W	L	PCT	G	GS	CG	SH	SV	IP	H	R	HR	HB	BB	SO	RAT	ERA	ERA+	OAV	OOB	BH	AVG	PB	PR	PR+	PD	TPI
1923	Was-A	9	10	.474	33	21	10	1	0	177	201	103	7	3	76	52	14.2	3.86	97	.291	.364	5	.096	-1	2	-2	-2	-0.5
1924	Was-A	5	7	.417	24	14	5	1	0	92	98	52	2	4	49	28	14.8	4.40	92	.283	.378	4	.129	-2	-2	-4	-2	-0.7
1925	Bos-A	5	12	.294	37	21	7	1	1	176^2	232	124	6	1	89	30	16.4	5.15	88	.327	.403	8	.138	-4	-15	-11	-2	-1.5
1926	Bos-A	6	18	.250	30	24	7	1	0	172	213	106	5	3	69	35	14.9	4.97	82	.321	.387	8	.163	-1	-18	-17	3	-1.8
1929	Cin-N	0	0	—	1	0	0	0	0	1	2	3	1	0	1	0	27.0	27.00	17	.400	.500	0	—	0	-2	-3	-0	-0.1
Total	5	25	47	.347	125	80	29	4	1	618^2	746	388	21	11	284	145	15.1	4.66	88	.309	.384	25	.132	-8	-35	-38	-3	-4.6

● CARL ZAMLOCH

Zamloch, Carl Eugene b: 10/6/1889, Oakland, Cal. d: 8/19/63, Santa Barbara, Cal BR/TR, 6'1", 176 lbs. Deb: 5/7/13

YEAR	TM/L	W	L	PCT	G	GS	CG	SH	SV	IP	H	R	HR	HB	BB	SO	RAT	ERA	ERA+	OAV	OOB	BH	AVG	PB	PR	PR+	PD	TPI
1913	Det-A	1	6	.143	17	5	3	0	1	69^2	66	31	1	3	23	28	11.9	2.45	119	.257	.325	4	.182	-1	4	4	-1	0.2

● OSCAR ZAMORA

Zamora, Oscar Jose (Sosa) b: 9/23/44, Camaguey, Cuba BR/TR, 5'10", 178 lbs. Deb: 6/18/74

YEAR	TM/L	W	L	PCT	G	GS	CG	SH	SV	IP	H	R	HR	HB	BB	SO	RAT	ERA	ERA+	OAV	OOB	BH	AVG	PB	PR	PR+	PD	TPI
1974	Chi-N	3	9	.250	56	0	0	0	10	83^2	82	33	6	0	19	38	10.9	3.12	123	.264	.306	2	.182	-0	5	6	-0	1.0
1975	Chi-N	5	2	.714	52	0	0	0	10	71	84	42	17	0	15	28	12.5	5.07	76	.298	.333	1	.167	-0	-11	-9	-0	-1.2
1976	Chi-N	5	3	.625	40	2	0	0	3	55	70	34	8	1	17	27	14.4	5.24	74	.317	.368	0	.000	-1	-11	-8	-1	-1.3
1978	Hou-N	0	0	—	10	0	0	0	0	15	20	12	2	0	7	6	16.2	7.20	46	.328	.397	0	.000	-0	-6	-7	0	-0.4
Total	4	13	14	.481	158	2	0	0	23	224^2	256	121	33	1	58	99	12.6	4.53	84	.293	.337	3	.107	-2	-23	-17	-1	-1.9

● DOM ZANNI

Zanni, Dominick Thomas b: 3/1/32, Bronx, N.Y. BR/TR, 5'11", 180 lbs. Deb: 9/28/58

YEAR	TM/L	W	L	PCT	G	GS	CG	SH	SV	IP	H	R	HR	HB	BB	SO	RAT	ERA	ERA+	OAV	OOB	BH	AVG	PB	PR	PR+	PD	TPI
1958	SF-N	1	0	1.000	1	0	0	0	0	4	7	1	1	0	1	3	18.0	2.25	169	.412	.444	0	.000	-0	1	1	-0	0.1
1959	SF-N	0	0	—	9	0	0	0	0	11	12	10	2	1	8	11	17.2	6.55	58	.273	.396	0	—	0	-3	-3	1	0.0
1961	SF-N	1	0	1.000	8	0	0	0	0	13^2	13	7	1	0	12	11	16.5	3.95	96	.277	.424	0	—	0	0	-0	0	0.0
1962	Chi-A	6	5	.545	44	2	0	0	5	86^1	67	42	12	1	31	66	10.3	3.75	104	.214	.287	5	.278	2	2	1	2	0.6
1963	Chi-A	0	0	—	5	0	0	0	0	4^1	5	4	1	0	4	2	18.7	8.31	42	.294	.429	0	—	0	-2	-2	0	-0.1
	Cin-N	1	1	.500	31	1	0	0	5	43	39	22	2	4	21	40	13.4	4.19	80	.247	.350	1	.333	0	-4	-4	1	-0.2
1965	Cin-N	0	0	—	8	0	0	0	0	13^1	7	2	1	0	5	10	8.1	1.35	278	.159	.245	0	.000	-0	3	3	0	0.2

YEAR TM/L	W	L	PCT	G	GS	CG	SH	SV	IP	H	R	HR	HB	BB	SO	RAT	ERA	ERA+	OAV	OOB	BH	AVG	PB	PR	PR+	PD	TPI
1966 Cin-N	0	0	—	5	0	0	0	0	7^1	5	1	0	1	3	5	11.0	0.00	—	.192	.300	1	1.000	0	3	3	-0	0.2
Total 7	9	6	.600	111	3	0	0	10	183	155	89	20	7	85	148	12.1	3.79	99	.233	.326	7	.280	2	-1	-1	4	0.8
● JEFF ZASKE Zaske, Lloyd Jeffrey b: 10/6/60, Seattle, Wash. BR/TR, 6'5", 180 lbs. Deb: 7/21/84																											
1984 Pit-N	0	0	—	3	0	0	0	0	5	4	0	0	0	1	2	9.0	0.00	—	.211	.250	0	—	0	2	2	0	0.1
● CLINT ZAVARAS Zavaras, Clinton Wayne b: 1/4/67, Denver, Colo. BR/TR, 6'1", 175 lbs. Deb: 6/3/89																											
1989 Sea-A	1	6	.143	10	10	0	0	0	52	49	33	4	2	30	31	14.0	5.19	78	.253	.358	0	—	0	-8	-6	-0	-0.8
● ZAY Zay Deb: 10/7/1886 ♦																											
1886 Bal-a	0	1	.000	1	1	0	0	0	2	4	4	0	0	4	2	36.0	9.00	38	.333	.500	0	.000	-0	-1	-1	-0	-0.2
● MATT ZEISER Zeiser, Matthew J. b: 9/25/1888, Chicago, Ill. d: 6/10/42, Chicago, Ill BR/TR, 5'10", 170 lbs. Deb: 4/27/14																											
1914 Bos-A	0	0	—	2	0	0	0	0	10	9	4	0	1	8	0	16.2	1.80	150	.281	.439	0	.000	-0	1	1	-1	0.0
● BILL ZEPP Zepp, William Clinton b: 7/22/46, Detroit, Mich. BR/TR, 6'2", 185 lbs. Deb: 8/12/69																											
1969 Min-A	0	0	—	4	0	0	0	0	5^1	6	7	1	0	4	2	16.9	6.75	54	.286	.400	0	.000	-0	-2	-2	-0	-0.1
1970 *Min-A	9	4	.692	43	20	1	1	2	151	154	63	9	9	51	64	12.8	3.22	116	.266	.335	6	.136	-1	8	8	-2	0.4
1971 Det-A	1	1	.500	16	4	0	0	2	31^2	41	20	2	3	17	15	17.3	5.12	70	.328	.421	0	.000	-0	-6	-5	0	-0.4
Total 3	10	5	.667	63	24	1	1	4	188	201	90	12	12	72	81	13.6	3.64	102	.278	.353	6	.122	-2	1	1	-2	-0.1
● CHAD ZERBE Zerbe, William Chad b: 4/27/72, Findlay, Ohio BL/TL, 6', 190 lbs. Deb: 9/18/2000																											
2000 SF-N	0	0	—	4	0	0	0	0	6	6	3	1	0	1	5	10.5	4.50	94	.273	.304	0	—	0	0	-0	0	0.0
● GEORGE ZETTLEIN Zettlein, George "Charmer" b: 7/18/1844, Brooklyn, N.Y. d: 5/23/05, Patchogue, N.Y. BR/TR, 5'9", 162 lbs. Deb: 5/8/1871																											
1871 Chi-n	18	9	.667	28	28	25	0	0	240^2	298	233	6		25	22	**12.1**	**2.73**	**168**	.267	**.283**	32	.250	-7	**40**	**46**		**2.6**
1872 Tro-n	14	8	.636	25	22	17	2	1	187^2	207	132	2		8	17	10.3	2.16	168	.250	.257	29	.257	1	31	31		2.4
Eck-n	1	8	.111	9	9	8	0	0	75^1	106	62	1		6	8	13.4	2.75	123	.300	.312	3	.088	-4	7	6		0.2
Yr	15	16	.484	34	31	25	2	1	263	313	194	3		14	25	11.2	2.33	153	.265	.274	32	.218	-4	38	37		2.6
1873 Phi-n	36	15	.706	51	51	49	0	0	460	593	368	3		41	28	12.4	2.70	122	.283	.297	50	.207	-8	28	30		1.9
1874 Chi-n	27	30	.474	57	57	57	3	0	515^2	640	439	3		43	26	11.9	2.43	92	.273	.286	47	.193	-9	-14	-11		-1.5
1875 Chi-n	17	14	.548	31	31	29	6	0	282	266	142	0		6	18	8.7	1.28	178	.230	.234	29	.218	-3	30	30		2.5
Phi-n	12	8	.600	21	21	20	1	0	181^1	209	121	0		10	13	10.9	2.08	109	.264	.273	15	.181	-4	3	4		-0.1
Yr	29	22	.569	52	52	49	**7**	0	463^1	475	263	0		16	31	9.5	1.59	143	.244	.250	44	.204	-7	33	34		2.4
1876 Phi-N	4	20	.167	28	25	23	1	2	234	358	212	2		6	10	14.0	3.88	62	.329	.334	27	.211	-5	-41	-36	-1	-3.2
Total 5 n	125	92	.576	222	219	205	12	1	1942^2	2319	1497	15		139	132	11.4	2.32	128	.267	.278	205	.210	-35	126	136		8.0
● BOB ZICK Zick, Robert George b: 4/26/27, Chicago, Ill. BL/TR, 6', 168 lbs. Deb: 5/2/54																											
1954 Chi-N	0	0	—	8	0	0	0	0	16^1	23	15	1	0	7	9	16.5	8.27	51	.343	.405	1	.250	0	-8	-7	-0	-0.4
● GEORGE ZIEGLER Ziegler, George J. b: 1872, Chicago, Ill. d: 7/22/16, Kankakee, Ill. Deb: 6/19/1890																											
1890 Pit-N	0	1	.000	1	1	0	0	0	6	12	7	0	0	0	1	18.0	10.50	31	.400	.400	0	.000	-0	-5	-5	-0	-0.6
● STEVE ZIEM Ziem, Stephen Graeling b: 10/24/61, Milwaukee, Wis. BR/TR, 6'2", 210 lbs. Deb: 4/30/87																											
1987 Atl-N	0	1	.000	2	0	0	0	0	2^1	4	3	0	0	1	0	19.3	7.71	56	.364	.417	0	—	0	-1	-1	-0	-0.2
● JEFF ZIMMERMAN Zimmerman, Jeffrey Ross b: 8/9/72, Kelowna, B.C., Can. BR/TR, 6'1", 200 lbs. Deb: 4/13/99 F																											
1999 *Tex-A★	9	3	.750	65	0	0	0	3	87^2	50	24	9	2	23	67	7.7	2.36	215	.166	.229	0	—	0	24	25	-1	3.0
2000 Tex-A	4	5	.444	65	0	0	0	1	69^2	80	45	10	2	34	74	15.0	5.30	96	.286	.367	0	—	0	-3	-1	-0	-0.2
Total 2	13	8	.619	130	0	0	0	4	157^1	130	69	19	4	57	141	10.9	3.66	139	.223	.297	0	—	0	22	24	-1	2.8
● JORDAN ZIMMERMAN Zimmerman, Jordan William b: 4/28/75, Kelowna, B.C., Can. BR/TL, 6', 200 lbs. Deb: 5/17/99 F																											
1999 Sea-A	0	0	—	12	0	0	0	0	8	14	8	0	1	4	3	21.4	7.88	60	.389	.463	0	—	0	-3	-3	-0	-0.1
● WALTER ZINK Zink, Walter Noble b: 11/21/1898, Pittsfield, Mass. d: 6/12/64, Quincy, Mass. BR/TR, 6', 165 lbs. Deb: 7/6/21																											
1921 NY-N	0	0	—	2	0	0	0	0	4	4	3	0	0	3	1	15.8	2.25	163	.235	.350	0	.000	-0	1	1	-0	0.0
● JIMMY ZINN Zinn, James Edward b: 1/21/1895, Benton, Ark. d: 2/26/91, Memphis, Tenn. BL/TR (BL 1929), 6'0.5", 195 lbs. Deb: 9/4/19																											
1919 Phi-A	1	3	.250	5	3	2	0	0	25^2	38	20	1	1	10	9	17.2	6.31	54	.365	.426	4	.308	2	-9	-8	-0	-0.9
1920 Pit-N	1	1	.500	6	3	2	0	0	31	32	14	2	1	5	18	11.0	3.48	92	.260	.295	3	.200	0	-1	-1	-0	0.0
1921 Pit-N	7	6	.538	32	9	5	1	4	127^1	159	63	3	2	30	49	13.5	3.68	104	.318	.359	11	.224	0	2	2	-2	0.0
1922 Pit-N	0	0	—	5	0	0	0	1	9^2	11	4	1	0	2	3	12.1	1.86	219	.297	.333	0	.000	-0	2	2	-0	0.1
1929 Cle-A	4	6	.400	18	11	6	1	2	105^1	150	75	8	3	33	29	15.9	5.04	88	.340	.390	16	.381	7	-9	-7	-0	0.1
Total 5	13	16	.448	66	26	15	2	7	299	390	176	15	7	80	108	14.4	4.30	92	.324	.369	34	.283	9	-15	-11	-3	-0.7
● BILL ZINSER Zinser, William Francis b: 1/6/18, Astoria, N.Y. d: 2/16/93, Englewood, Fla. BR/TR, 6'1", 185 lbs. Deb: 8/19/44																											
1944 Was-A	0	0	—	2	0	0	0	0	0^2	1	2	0	0	5	1	81.0	27.00	12	.333	.750	0	—	0	-2	-2	0	-0.1
● BARRY ZITO Zito, Barry William b: 5/13/78, Las Vegas, Nev. BL/TL, 6'4", 205 lbs. Deb: 7/22/2000																											
2000 *Oak-A	7	4	.636	14	14	1	1	0	92^2	64	30	6	2	45	78	10.8	2.72	175	.195	.296	0	—	0	23	22	-0	2.3
● ED ZMICH Zmich, Edward Albert b: 10/1/1884, Cleveland, Ohio d: 8/20/50, Cleveland, Ohio BL/TL, 6', 180 lbs. Deb: 7/23/10																											
1910 StL-N	0	5	.000	9	6	2	0	0	36	38	27	0	3	29	19	17.5	6.25	48	.304	.446	1	.077	-1	-13	-13	1	-1.6
1911 StL-N	1	0	1.000	4	0	0	0	0	12^2	8	5	0	1	8	4	12.1	2.13	158	.182	.321	0	.000	-1	2	2	-1	0.0
Total 2	1	5	.167	13	6	2	0	0	48^2	46	32	0	4	37	23	16.1	5.18	60	.272	.414	1	.059	-2	-11	-12	0	-1.6
● SAM ZOLDAK Zoldak, Samuel Walter "Sad Sam" b: 12/8/18, Brooklyn, N.Y. d: 8/25/66, New Hyde Park, N.Y BL/TL, 5'11.5", 185 lbs. Deb: 5/13/44																											
1944 StL-A	0	0	—	18	0	0	0	0	38^2	49	22	1	0	19	15	15.8	3.72	97	.310	.384	2	.333	0	-1	-1	0	0.0
1945 StL-A	3	2	.600	26	1	1	0	0	69^2	74	32	3	0	18	19	11.9	3.36	105	.267	.312	1	.050	-2	0	1	-1	-0.3
1946 StL-A	9	11	.450	35	21	9	2	2	170^1	166	71	11	1	57	51	11.8	3.43	109	.256	.317	9	.173	-0	1	5	1	0.6
1947 StL-A	9	10	.474	35	19	6	1	1	171	162	76	7	0	76	36	12.5	3.47	112	.254	.334	10	.172	-1	4	7	3	1.0
1948 StL-A	2	4	.333	11	9	0	0	0	54	64	30	4	1	19	13	14.0	4.67	98	.296	.356	6	.273	0	-2	-1	0	0.0
Cle-A	9	6	.600	23	12	4	1	0	105^2	104	37	6	0	24	17	10.9	2.81	144	.261	.303	5	.139	-2	17	15	2	2.0
Yr	11	10	.524	34	21	4	1	0	159^2	168	67	10	1	43	30	11.9	3.44	123	.274	.322	11	.190	-2	15	14	2	2.0
1949 Cle-A	1	2	.333	27	0	0	0	0	53	60	30	4	0	18	11	13.2	4.25	94	.291	.348	3	.375	1	-0	-2	3	0.3
1950 Cle-A	4	2	.667	33	3	0	0	4	63^2	64	33	6	1	21	15	12.2	3.96	109	.259	.320	3	.188	0	4	3	-0	0.3
1951 Phi-A	6	10	.375	26	18	8	1	0	128	127	51	9	0	24	18	10.6	3.16	135	.257	.292	7	.156	-3	14	15	-2	1.3
1952 Phi-A	0	6	.000	16	10	2	0	1	75^1	86	41	3	0	25	12	13.3	4.06	97	.290	.345	4	.174	-1	-3	-1	2	0.1
Total 9	43	53	.448	250	93	30	5	8	929^1	956	423	54	3	301	207	12.2	3.54	112	.267	.325	50	.175	-7	34	44	7	5.3
● BILL ZUBER Zuber, William Henry "Goober" b: 3/26/13, Middle Amana, Iowa d: 11/2/82, Cedar Rapids, Iowa BR/TR, 6'2", 195 lbs. Deb: 9/16/36																											
1936 Cle-A	1	1	.500	2	2	1	0	0	13^2	14	11	0	0	15	5	19.1	6.59	76	.269	.433	1	.200	-0	-2	-2	-0	-0.3
1938 Cle-A	0	3	.000	15	0	0	0	1	28^2	33	18	0	0	20	14	16.6	5.02	92	.295	.402	0	.000	-1	-1	-1	-0	-0.2
1939 Cle-A	2	0	1.000	16	1	0	0	0	31^2	41	24	2	1	19	16	17.3	5.97	74	.323	.415	1	.200	1	-5	-6	1	-0.2
1940 Cle-A	1	1	.500	17	0	0	0	0	24	25	17	3	0	14	12	14.6	5.63	75	.260	.355	1	.333	0	-3	-4	-0	-0.3
1941 Was-A	6	4	.600	36	7	1	0	2	96^1	110	63	5	2	61	51	16.2	5.42	75	.291	.392	0	.000	-3	-14	-15	-1	-1.8
1942 Was-A	9	9	.500	37	7	3	1	1	126^2	115	66	5	0	82	64	14.0	3.84	95	.243	.355	6	.154	0	-3	-3	-3	-0.5
1943 NY-A	8	4	.667	20	13	7	0	1	118	100	54	3	0	74	57	13.3	3.89	83	.234	.347	7	.184	2	-8	-9	-2	-0.9
1944 NY-A	5	7	.417	22	13	2	1	0	107	101	54	5	1	54	59	13.1	4.21	83	.255	.346	4	.129	-2	-9	-8	-1	-1.1
1945 NY-A	5	11	.313	21	14	7	0	1	127	121	50	2	0	56	50	12.5	3.19	109	.259	.338	7	.167	-1	2	4	-1	0.2
1946 NY-A	0	1	.000	3	0	0	0	0	5^2	10	9	2	0	3	3	20.6	12.71	27	.385	.448	0	.000	-0	-6	-6	-0	-0.9
*Bos-A	5	1	.833	15	7	2	1	0	56^2	37	20	4	0	39	29	12.1	2.54	144	.187	.321	2	.111	-1	6	7	0	0.6
Yr	5	2	.714	18	7	2	1	0	62^1	47	29	6	0	42	32	12.9	3.47	105	.210	.335	2	.100	-1	0	1	-0	-0.3

YEAR	TM/L	W	L	PCT	G	GS	CG	SH	SV	IP	H	R	HR	HB	BB	SO	RAT	ERA	ERA+	OAV	OOB	BH	AVG	PB	PR	PR+	PD	TPI
1947	Bos-A	1	0	1.000	20	1	0	0	0	50^{2}	60	32	4	0	31	23	16.2	5.33	73	.311	.406	2	.154	-0	-9	-8	-0	-0.4
Total	11	43	42	.506	224	65	23	3	6	786	767	418	35	4	468	383	14.2	4.28	87	.260	.362	31	.135	-6	-51	-50	-8	-5.8

● **GEORGE ZUVERINK** Zuverink, George b: 8/20/24, Holland, Mich. BR/TR, 6'4", 200 lbs. Deb: 4/21/51

YEAR	TM/L	W	L	PCT	G	GS	CG	SH	SV	IP	H	R	HR	HB	BB	SO	RAT	ERA	ERA+	OAV	OOB	BH	AVG	PB	PR	PR+	PD	TPI
1951	Cle-A	0	0	—	16	0	0	0	0	25^{1}	24	17	2	1	13	14	13.5	5.33	71	.253	.349	0	—	0	-3	-5	0	-0.2
1952	Cle-A	0	0	—	1	0	0	0	0	1^{1}	1	0	0	0	0	1	6.8	0.00	—	.200	.200	0	—	0	1	1	0	0.0
1954	Cin-N	0	0	—	2	0	0	0	0	6	10	6	1	0	1	2	16.5	9.00	47	.385	.407	1	.500	0	-3	-3	-0	-0.1
	Det-A	9	13	.409	35	25	9	2	4	203	201	93	22	8	62	70	12.0	3.59	103	.257	.318	8	.125	-3	3	2	3	0.2
1955	Det-A	0	5	.000	14	1	0	0	0	28^{1}	38	27	6	1	14	13	16.8	6.99	55	.309	.384	0	.000	-1	-10	-10	0	-1.6
	Bal-A	4	3	.571	28	5	0	0	4	86^{1}	80	28	5	4	17	31	10.5	2.19	174	.264	.312	5	.217	1	17	16	1	1.6
	Yr	4	8	.333	42	6	0	0	4	114^{2}	118	55	11	5	31	44	12.1	3.38	113	.277	.333	5	.185	0	7	6	1	0.0
1956	Bal-A	7	6	.538	**62**	0	0	0	**16**	97^{1}	112	52	6	3	34	33	13.8	4.16	94	.294	.356	2	.118	-1	-0	-3	1	-0.5
1957	Bal-A	10	6	.625	**56**	0	0	0	9	112^{2}	105	37	9	4	39	36	11.8	2.48	145	.257	.327	3	.130	-0	16	15	1	2.4
1958	Bal-A	2	2	.500	45	0	0	0	7	69	74	29	4	6	17	22	12.7	3.39	106	.286	.344	2	.222	1	3	2	1	0.4
1959	Bal-A	0	1	.000	6	0	0	0	0	13	15	7	1	0	6	1	14.5	4.15	91	.306	.382	0	—	1	-0	-1	0	0.0
Total	8	32	36	.471	265	31	9	2	40	642^{1}	660	296	56	27	203	223	12.5	3.54	105	.271	.334	21	.148	-2	23	14	7	2.2

The Situational Statistics Register

Baseball has been blessed over the years with a wealth of numbers. The carefully crafted statistics of the grand old game make the exploits of long-gone players almost tangible to fans that never saw them play. Perhaps as importantly, the unparalleled accuracy and scope of baseball's numbers make possible meaningful comparisons between players from different eras.

While one does not have to be a scholar of baseball statistics to understand the National Pastime, it is safe to say that one cannot understand many elements of the game without a careful examination of the statistical evidence. Part of that evidence is what has come to be called *situational statistics*. These situational statistics add depth and texture to the official batting and pitching statistics, giving everyone another tool for understanding the way the game is played.

The familiar traditional stats—batting average, runs, home runs, runs batted in, wins, losses, earned run average, and strikeouts—obviously have considerable merit, otherwise they wouldn't be universally known and discussed. In contrast to these traditional totals and averages, *situational stats* are an attempt to break baseball numbers into *how* and *when* they happened—and knowing *how* and *when* things happen often opens the doors to understanding *why* things happen.

Baseball encyclopedias have always contained numerous batting and pitching statistics, but this edition of *Total Baseball* also presents the most comprehensive register of situational statistics ever published. This Situational Statistics Register covers the careers of most active players as well as most prominent players of the past two decades. Most of the data used in compiling this register originally came from Gary Gillette and his Baseball Workshop. Data prior to 1984 came from David W. Smith and Retrosheet, a volunteer, non-profit group that is doing a terrific job of collecting and compiling play-by-play accounts of games from the 1970s, 1960s, and earlier.

Situational stats have been part of the game for decades, even when not labeled as such. Generations of fans have argued about whether DiMaggio or Williams was the greater hitter. Barrels of ink were spilled throughout the 20th century about the advantage lefthanded sluggers enjoyed at legendary Yankee Stadium with its short right field porch. Hundreds of managers have made out their lineups according to whether the opposing pitcher was righthanded or lefthanded. Millions of Cubs fans have watched in agony as their daytime heroes fell short when not playing in the sunshine in the friendly confines of Wrigley Field.

The most important situational categories are what are commonly referred to as *left/right* and *home/road* breakdowns. *Left/right* refers to how batters perform versus lefthanded and righthanded pitchers as well as to how pitchers fare against lefthanded and righthanded batters. *Home/road* (also frequently called *home/away*) refers to how players perform in games in their home park as opposed to in games on the road (i.e., away from home).

Aside from these two key categories, several other types of breakdowns have become prominent in recent years. These include month-by-month statistics, performance on grass fields as opposed to artificial turf, performance in day games as opposed to night games, and performance in several circumstances with runners on base or in scoring position. Statistics for matchups between individual pitchers and batters have also become quite popular and certainly qualify as situational stats, even though they are not commonly labeled as such.

Various players, writers, analysts, and companies have advanced measures of what is colloquially called "clutch" performance. So-called "clutch" statistics have many problems, not the least of which is that there is no consensus as to how to define a *clutch* situation. Moreover, every carefully designed, comprehensive study of "clutch" performance by players has failed to show that it is consistent over long periods of time, meaning that no one has yet shown that so-called "clutch" performance is anything more than random variation in the stats.

The biggest problem with most situational statistics is not the accuracy of the numbers. The problem has been in the gross misinterpretation of the numbers. Most baseball statistics published and quoted are literally true. That is, they are accounts of events that actually happened on the field. Assuming no mistakes were made in compiling these numbers, they must be true: the fact that a player batted .390 with runners in scoring position doesn't leave anything to argue over.

Manifestly false, however, are most of the claims made about these statistics. If one argues that batting .390 with runners in scoring position means that the player is a good "clutch" hitter, the validity of that statement depends not on the actual numbers, but the interpretation of those numbers. Misinterpretation of the numbers, combined with unsound speculation and unfounded predictions based on them, is what causes heated arguments about the value of situational stats.

In the computerized world of modern baseball, the issue is how to use the wealth of data now available to executives, managers, coaches, players, and agents. For example, when a manager chooses to start a righthanded-hitting player who otherwise would normally be platooned against a righthanded pitcher, he can justify it statistically in any number of ways. He could base his decisions on that hitter's past performance against the opposing team, by his performance in that ballpark, by his performance in day games, by his performance against groundball pitchers, or even by his performance in the last week if he's been on a hot streak.

All of these statistics (and many more) are available to teams on a daily basis. Of course, many of these numbers will be contradictory: a hitter might have fared poorly against righthanded pitchers, but have done extremely well against that particular team. He could also carry a pitiful average against that day's starting pitcher, but could likewise have excelled in day games.

With such a dense smog of conflicting numbers clouding the atmosphere of the game, many fans are confused about which statistics are reliable indicators of performance and which are just compilations of coincidental data. The first thing to remember is that almost all statistics are unreliable in small samples. Making judgments about hitters based on 50 at bats is much more dangerous than making judgments based on 500 at bats. Evaluating a pitcher based on 25 innings is sheer folly, as there is a substantial amount of chance even in a sample of 250 innings. All other things being equal, looking for meaning in statistics with larger sample sizes is much more profitable than trolling for correlations in categories with little data.

Left/right breakdowns are generally reliable so long as a player has faced both lefty and righty pitchers (or hitters) and has not made a major change in the way he pitches or bats. Home/road breakdowns are certainly valuable, but they still can change significantly from season to season—even for players who turn in consistent performance. The best use of home/road stats is to look for patterns over multiple seasons when the player has the same (or similar) home parks.

Grass/turf situational stats are often misleading, as the effect of the playing surface in a player's home park frequently pollutes the former. Day/night stats suffer from another problem, as most players who don't play half their games in Wrigley Field don't see enough action under the sun to make valid comparisons between sunlight and artificial light. Factor in domed ballparks, and day/night numbers are rarely illuminating.

Monthly performance stats are often quoted but are rarely helpful when looking at a single season for the obvious reason that the sample is so small. The best usage of monthly stats is to aggregate them into first half/second half breakdowns, which frequently show very distinct patterns even in individual seasons. Some of these patterns—hot starts, slow starts, tiring late in the season—can be strikingly important across a player's career. Other meaningful monthly patterns can emerge, especially when a player's performance is strikingly different in the cold-weather months (April, May, September, and October) than in the warm-weather months (June, July, and August).

Batting statistics with runners on base, with runners in scoring position, with a runner on third base and less than two out, in the late innings of close games, etc., are a staple of the pundits yet are highly unreliable for multiple reasons. One of the best indications that such stats generally lack any predictive value is that they are almost never quoted for pitchers, who certainly experience similar pressures in the same situations.

Batting statistics by position in the lineup and when leading off innings are also favorite fodder for the media. Like the various batting stats with runners on base, they can suffer greatly from other influences, making them only occasionally informative.

Finally, there are the oft-cited matchup stats between individual pitchers and batters. These can be very significant, for the style and strengths of each pitcher can make him unhittable to one batter while making him very vulnerable to another. There is no question about the soundness of matchup statistics; the only caution is to resist making judgments when the batter and pitcher haven't seen each other very much—20 times is a good standard to use before reading too much into them.

The Situational Statistics Register includes year-by-year statistics and career totals (1978–2000) for most regular players in the major leagues in the past 23 seasons. If a player qualified for the register, his statistics are shown for every year in which he played in the majors, whether he was a regular or not. In order to qualify for a listing in this register, a player needed to meet one of two criteria:

- Players currently active in the major leagues are included if they have played regularly for at least three seasons in their career (including 2000).

- Players not in the majors in 2000 must have played regularly for a total of six seasons between 1978 and 2000.

Regular batters are defined as having played in 100 or more games during a season. Regular pitchers are defined as having pitched at least 150 innings *or* appeared in 55 or more games in a season. Because of the six-year criterion for retired players, many stalwarts of the 1970s whose careers lasted into the 1980s (e.g., Johnny Bench) will generally not have enough seasons as a regular after 1977 to appear in this register. (All is not lost, however, as we anticipate expanding this register in subsequent editions of *Total Baseball*.)

Six separate situations are shown in the register, both for batters and pitchers:

- "Vs. Left" and "Vs. Right" categories break batters' statistics down into how they batted against lefthanded pitchers and how they batted against righthanded pitchers. For pitchers, the breakdowns represent how opposing lefthanded and righthanded batters hit when facing them.

- "At Home" and "On Road" categories break players' statistics into how they performed in games in their home ballpark and how they performed in games in all other ballparks.

- "First Half" and "Second Half" categories break players' statistics into how they performed in each season before July 1 and after July 1. While "first half" and "second half" statistics are frequently compiled using the annual All-Star Game as the dividing point, the beginning of July is almost always closer to the actual midpoint of the season than the Midsummer Classic. Therefore, for consistency's sake, July 1 is used as the dividing line for all seasons.

Five statistics are shown for each situation for batters: At Bats, Home Runs, Batting Average, On-Base Percentage, and Slugging Percentage. For pitchers, these same statistics are shown for opposing batters in the "Vs. Left" and "Vs. Right" categories. However, for pitchers' Home/Road and First Half/Second Half breakdowns, Wins, Losses, Saves, Innings Pitched, and Earned Run Average are shown. The abbreviations used in all cases are the same as those used elsewhere in *Total Baseball*.

For a key to the team and league abbreviations used in the Situational Statistics Register, go the last page of the book. For definitions of the terms found in the headings, consult the Glossary.

YEAR	TM/L	TOTAL AB	TOTAL HR	TOTAL AVG	TOTAL OBP	TOTAL SLG	HOME AB	HOME HR	HOME AVG	HOME OBP	HOME SLG	AWAY AB	AWAY HR	AWAY AVG	AWAY OBP	AWAY SLG	1ST HALF AB	1ST HALF HR	1ST HALF AVG	1ST HALF OBP	1ST HALF SLG	2ND HALF AB	2ND HALF HR	2ND HALF AVG	2ND HALF OBP	2ND HALF SLG	LEFT AB	LEFT HR	LEFT AVG	LEFT OBP	LEFT SLG	RIGHT AB	RIGHT HR	RIGHT AVG	RIGHT OBP	RIGHT SLG
■ **Bobby Abreu** BL/TR																																				
1996	Hou-N	22	0	.227	.292	.273	18	0	.278	.316	.333	4	0	.000	.200	.000	0	0	—	—	—	22	0	.227	.292	.273	0	0	—	—	—	22	0	.227	.292	.273
1997	Hou-N	188	3	.250	.329	.372	101	3	.277	.342	.416	87	0	.218	.313	.322	147	2	.245	.335	.361	41	1	.268	.302	.415	33	0	.182	.289	.333	155	3	.265	.337	.381
1998	Phi-N	497	17	.312	.409	.497	239	10	.301	.419	.531	258	7	.322	.399	.465	258	6	.318	.406	.496	239	11	.305	.411	.498	103	0	.320	.379	.408	394	17	.310	.416	.520
1999	Phi-N	546	20	.335	.446	.549	275	13	.342	.471	.582	271	7	.328	.418	.517	246	13	.329	.409	.569	300	7	.340	.473	.533	141	0	.298	.425	.369	405	20	.348	.453	.612
2000	Phi-N	576	25	.316	.416	.554	284	14	.338	.435	.588	292	11	.295	.398	.521	275	10	.326	.409	.531	301	15	.316	.422	.575	136	3	.243	.316	.353	440	22	.339	.445	.616
TOTALS		1829	65	.313	.413	.515	917	40	.322	.431	.547	912	25	.304	.395	.482	926	31	.309	.397	.504	903	34	.317	.429	.526	413	3	.276	.369	.370	1416	62	.323	.426	.557
■ **Edgardo Alfonzo** BR/TR																																				
1995	NY-N	335	4	.278	.301	.382	167	0	.281	.315	.335	168	4	.274	.287	.429	162	3	.259	.274	.383	173	1	.295	.326	.382	98	2	.286	.314	.418	237	2	.274	.296	.367
1996	NY-N	368	4	.261	.304	.345	182	2	.258	.315	.357	186	2	.263	.292	.333	111	0	.243	.292	.306	257	4	.268	.309	.362	89	1	.258	.317	.371	279	3	.262	.300	.337
1997	NY-N	518	10	.315	.391	.432	248	4	.327	.391	.448	270	6	.304	.390	.419	235	5	.315	.374	.447	283	5	.314	.404	.420	135	4	.378	.448	.541	383	6	.292	.371	.394
1998	NY-N	557	17	.278	.355	.427	263	8	.228	.334	.354	294	9	.323	.375	.493	239	4	.259	.342	.368	318	13	.292	.365	.472	141	4	.234	.321	.362	416	13	.293	.367	.450
1999	NY-N	628	27	.304	.385	.502	303	11	.281	.362	.442	325	16	.326	.406	.557	306	11	.301	.375	.474	322	16	.307	.394	.528	138	6	.268	.367	.464	490	21	.314	.390	.512
2000	NY-N	544	25	.324	.425	.542	255	13	.302	.434	.525	289	12	.343	.416	.557	270	12	.341	.439	.578	274	13	.307	.410	.507	104	5	.298	.390	.519	440	20	.330	.433	.548
TOTALS		2950	87	.296	.370	.450	1418	38	.280	.365	.418	1532	49	.311	.374	.479	1323	35	.294	.365	.446	1627	52	.298	.374	.453	705	22	.288	.364	.448	2245	65	.299	.371	.450
■ **Luis Alicea** BB/TR																																				
1988	StL-N	297	1	.212	.276	.283	144	1	.229	.302	.326	153	0	.196	.251	.242	227	1	.220	.287	.304	70	0	.186	.240	.214	92	0	.130	.190	.152	205	1	.249	.314	.341
1991	StL-N	68	0	.191	.276	.235	28	0	.179	.281	.214	40	0	.200	.273	.250	12	0	.333	.429	.500	56	0	.161	.242	.179	16	0	.250	.333	.313	52	0	.173	.259	.212
1992	StL-N	265	2	.245	.320	.385	145	2	.276	.361	.497	120	0	.208	.269	.250	107	1	.252	.320	.421	158	1	.241	.320	.361	85	0	.294	.340	.412	180	2	.222	.311	.372
1993	StL-N	362	3	.279	.362	.373	202	2	.287	.361	.371	160	1	.269	.364	.375	119	1	.319	.399	.403	243	2	.259	.344	.358	79	1	.367	.432	.468	283	2	.254	.343	.346
1994	StL-N	205	5	.278	.373	.459	79	3	.190	.270	.380	126	2	.333	.434	.508	136	3	.228	.346	.397	69	2	.377	.430	.580	39	0	.308	.391	.410	166	5	.271	.369	.470
1995	Bos-A	419	6	.270	.367	.375	208	0	.255	.332	.327	211	6	.284	.400	.422	169	2	.243	.358	.320	250	4	.288	.374	.412	99	2	.293	.388	.384	320	4	.262	.361	.372
1996	StL-N	380	5	.258	.350	.382	180	4	.250	.352	.394	200	1	.265	.348	.370	247	4	.235	.320	.344	133	1	.301	.401	.451	64	1	.266	.351	.406	316	4	.256	.350	.377
1997	Ana-A	388	5	.253	.375	.369	187	2	.235	.373	.364	201	3	.269	.377	.373	222	3	.284	.395	.414	166	2	.211	.348	.307	110	0	.245	.323	.300	278	5	.255	.394	.396
1998	Tex-A	259	6	.274	.372	.425	101	1	.356	.455	.465	158	5	.222	.315	.399	142	3	.282	.370	.415	117	3	.265	.373	.436	43	2	.302	.423	.512	216	4	.269	.361	.407
1999	Tex-A	164	3	.201	.316	.317	62	0	.161	.268	.242	102	3	.225	.344	.363	85	0	.165	.290	.212	79	3	.241	.344	.430	62	1	.290	.371	.452	102	2	.147	.285	.235
2000	Tex-A	540	6	.294	.365	.404	272	4	.301	.368	.415	268	2	.287	.362	.392	263	3	.319	.397	.441	277	3	.271	.334	.368	114	0	.316	.394	.386	426	6	.289	.357	.408
TOTALS		3347	42	.260	.350	.375	1608	19	.262	.351	.381	1739	23	.259	.350	.370	1729	21	.260	.352	.374	1618	21	.260	.349	.377	803	7	.276	.354	.371	2544	35	.255	.349	.377
■ **Bill Almon** BR/TR																																				
1978	SD-N	405	0	.252	.308	.309	198	0	.288	.352	.338	207	0	.217	.264	.280	258	0	.275	.331	.341	147	0	.211	.266	.252	135	0	.289	.338	.356	270	0	.233	.293	.285
1979	SD-N	198	1	.227	.299	.258	80	0	.188	.298	.200	118	1	.254	.299	.297	99	0	.242	.300	.273	99	1	.212	.297	.242	46	0	.261	.375	.261	152	1	.217	.273	.257
1980	Mon-N	38	0	.263	.275	.342	17	0	.294	.294	.353	21	0	.238	.261	.333	38	0	.263	.275	.342	0	0	—	—	—	15	0	.267	.267	.333	23	0	.261	.280	.348
1980	NY-N	112	0	.170	.225	.232	60	0	.183	.246	.217	52	0	.154	.200	.250	0	0	—	—	—	112	0	.170	.225	.232	43	0	.163	.234	.209	69	0	.174	.219	.246
1981	Chi-A	349	4	.301	.341	.375	152	1	.276	.333	.316	197	3	.320	.348	.421	187	1	.326	.368	.380	162	3	.272	.310	.370	86	2	.337	.380	.419	263	2	.289	.329	.361
1982	Chi-A	308	4	.256	.313	.354	136	2	.301	.349	.412	172	2	.221	.286	.308	224	4	.277	.343	.397	84	0	.202	.230	.238	98	0	.265	.314	.347	210	4	.252	.313	.357
1983	Oak-A	451	4	.266	.302	.361	216	3	.278	.319	.398	235	1	.255	.286	.328	208	1	.317	.347	.404	243	3	.222	.265	.325	217	2	.286	.323	.410	234	2	.248	.282	.316
1984	Oak-A	211	7	.223	.253	.374	121	5	.223	.258	.397	90	2	.222	.247	.344	61	0	.148	.188	.180	150	7	.253	.280	.453	131	6	.260	.295	.450	80	1	.162	.186	.250
1985	Pit-N	244	6	.270	.330	.414	113	3	.345	.408	.522	131	3	.206	.262	.321	157	4	.287	.349	.420	87	2	.241	.295	.402	137	3	.277	.336	.431	107	3	.262	.322	.393
1986	Pit-N	196	7	.219	.319	.383	108	4	.213	.336	.370	88	3	.227	.296	.398	131	7	.244	.346	.458	65	0	.169	.260	.231	121	3	.198	.317	.322	75	4	.253	.321	.480
1987	Pit-N	20	0	.200	.238	.250	9	0	.333	.400	.333	11	0	.091	.091	.182	20	0	.200	.238	.250	0	0	—	—	—	16	0	.250	.250	.313	4	0	.000	.200	.000
1987	NY-N	54	0	.241	.339	.296	21	0	.286	.400	.286	33	0	.212	.297	.303	24	0	.208	.296	.250	30	0	.267	.371	.333	28	0	.179	.281	.214	26	0	.308	.400	.385
1988	Phi-N	26	0	.115	.207	.192	17	0	.059	.059	.059	9	0	.222	.417	.444	26	0	.115	.207	.192	0	0	—	—	—	16	0	.188	.188	.313	10	0	.000	.231	.000
TOTALS		2612	33	.251	.305	.344	1248	18	.264	.327	.360	1364	15	.239	.285	.330	1433	17	.274	.330	.366	1179	16	.224	.275	.317	1089	16	.264	.320	.373	1523	17	.242	.294	.324
■ **Roberto Alomar** BB/TR																																				
1988	SD-N	545	9	.266	.328	.382	279	5	.254	.309	.355	266	4	.278	.347	.410	252	6	.234	.280	.345	293	3	.294	.367	.413	178	4	.258	.330	.382	367	5	.270	.327	.381
1989	SD-N	623	7	.295	.347	.376	286	3	.329	.394	.399	337	4	.267	.306	.356	317	2	.256	.311	.303	306	5	.337	.385	.451	195	4	.256	.316	.369	428	3	.313	.362	.379
1990	SD-N	586	6	.287	.340	.381	298	4	.285	.334	.383	288	2	.288	.346	.378	292	2	.322	.375	.425	294	4	.252	.305	.337	204	3	.260	.330	.377	382	3	.301	.345	.382
1991	Tor-A	637	9	.295	.354	.436	313	6	.297	.367	.479	324	3	.293	.341	.395	295	5	.275	.345	.441	342	4	.313	.363	.433	191	5	.246	.295	.419	446	4	.316	.379	.444
1992	Tor-A	571	8	.310	.405	.427	268	5	.354	.444	.500	303	3	.271	.369	.363	262	6	.336	.416	.469	309	2	.288	.395	.392	156	5	.308	.414	.436	415	3	.311	.401	.424
1993	Tor-A	589	17	.326	.408	.492	289	8	.325	.409	.498	300	9	.327	.407	.487	297	9	.310	.390	.455	292	8	.342	.426	.531	166	4	.241	.297	.373	423	13	.359	.449	.539
1994	Tor-A	392	8	.306	.386	.452	185	4	.292	.379	.432	207	4	.319	.393	.469	267	6	.333	.395	.483	125	2	.248	.369	.384	114	4	.254	.331	.412	278	4	.327	.408	.468
1995	Tor-A	517	13	.300	.354	.449	247	7	.296	.347	.429	270	6	.304	.360	.467	221	8	.317	.370	.529	296	5	.287	.341	.389	130	2	.231	.289	.308	387	11	.323	.375	.496
1996	Bal-A	588	22	.328	.411	.527	283	14	.357	.435	.576	305	8	.302	.389	.482	305	11	.364	.433	.554	283	11	.290	.388	.498	192	9	.313	.405	.547	396	13	.336	.414	.518
1997	Bal-A	412	14	.333	.390	.500	211	10	.379	.429	.578	201	4	.284	.348	.418	250	7	.308	.371	.444	162	7	.370	.419	.586	113	0	.248	.298	.292	299	14	.365	.423	.579
1998	Bal-A	588	14	.282	.347	.418	292	7	.288	.349	.432	296	7	.277	.345	.405	310	8	.300	.377	.439	278	6	.263	.312	.396	167	7	.311	.376	.509	421	7	.271	.335	.382
1999	Cle-A	563	24	.323	.422	.533	282	12	.333	.424	.543	281	12	.313	.421	.523	278	10	.331	.429	.518	285	14	.316	.416	.547	145	6	.338	.422	.545	418	18	.318	.422	.529
2000	Cle-A	610	19	.310	.378	.475	303	8	.314	.387	.452	307	11	.306	.368	.498	294	9	.276	.345	.435	316	10	.342	.408	.513	151	3	.318	.364	.464	459	16	.307	.382	.479
TOTALS		7221	170	.304	.375	.448	3536	93	.315	.385	.464	3685	77	.294	.365	.433	3640	89	.304	.373	.448	3581	81	.304	.376	.449	2102	56	.276	.345	.422	5119	114	.316	.387	.459
■ **Moises Alou** BR/TR																																				
1990	Pit-N	5	0	.200	.200	.200	5	0	.200	.200	.200	0	0	—	—	—	0	0	—	—	—	5	0	.200	.200	.200	5	0	.200	.200	.200	0	0	—	—	—
1990	Mon-N	15	0	.200	.200	.333	13	0	.231	.231	.385	2	0	.000	.000	.000	0	0	—	—	—	15	0	.200	.200	.333	12	0	.167	.167	.333	3	0	.333	.333	.333
1992	Mon-N	341	9	.282	.328	.455	143	6	.336	.376	.587	198	3	.242	.293	.359	139	4	.317	.364	.518	202	5	.257	.303	.411	136	2	.294	.329	.419	205	7	.273	.327	.478
1993	Mon-N	482	18	.286	.340	.483	222	10	.252	.310	.432	260	8	.315	.366	.527	263	7	.266	.323	.414	219	11	.311	.361	.566	164	5	.268	.320	.445	318	13	.296	.350	.503
1994	Mon-N	422	22	.339	.397	.592	186	9	.371	.444	.640	236	13	.314	.357	.555	282	14	.340	.412	.571	140	8	.336	.363	.636	104	5	.365	.426	.587	318	17	.330	.388	.594
1995	Mon-N	344	14	.273	.342	.459	151	4	.245	.331	.384	193	10	.295	.351	.518	204	8	.294	.347	.475	140	6	.243	.335	.436	82	5	.341	.409	.622	262	9	.252	.321	.408
1996	Mon-N	540	21	.281	.339	.457	272	14	.320	.371	.559	268	7	.243	.308	.354	297	11	.256	.318	.424	243	10	.313	.366	.498	114	4	.333	.384	.553	426	17	.268	.328	.432
1997	Fla-N	538	23	.292	.373	.493	261	12	.276	.364	.498	277	11	.307	.382	.487	282	9	.298	.380	.482	256	14	.285	.365	.504	97	5	.340	.454	.629	441	18	.281	.354	.463
1998	Hou-N	584	38	.312	.399	.582	276	19	.319	.420	.620	308	19	.305	.380	.549	291	18	.320	.392	.588	293	20	.304	.406	.577	125	6	.288	.405	.504	459	32	.318	.397	.603
2000	Hou-N	454	30	.355	.416	.623	222	17	.347	.419	.667	232	13	.362	.412	.582	172	10	.343	.405	.587	282	20	.362	.422	.645	100	8	.370	.413	.700	354	22	.350	.417	.602
TOTALS		3725	175	.303	.369	.520	1751	91	.307	.380	.551	1974	84	.298	.358	.493	1930	81	.302	.367	.504	1795	94	.304	.370	.537	939	40	.316	.383	.537	2786	135	.298	.364	.514
■ **Brady Anderson** BL/TL																																				
1988	Bos-A	148	0	.230	.315	.304	79	0	.253	.352	.316	69	0	.203	.273	.290	148	0	.230	.315	.304	0	0	—	—	—	37	0	.297	.435	.378	111	0	.207	.270	.279
1988	Bal-A	177	1	.198	.232	.271	95	1	.147	.173	.221	82	0	.256	.299	.329	0	0	—	—	—	177	1	.198	.232	.271	48	0	.125	.143	.146	129	1	.225	.265	.318
1989	Bal-A	266	4	.207	.324	.312	135	2	.222	.327	.333	131	2	.191	.321	.290	212	4	.217	.328	.349	54	0	.167	.308	.167	70	1	.129	.265	.243	196	3	.235	.345	.337
1990	Bal-A	234	3	.231	.327	.308	126	1	.175	.272	.238	108	2	.296	.391	.389	49	0	.245	.356	.245	185	3	.227	.319	.324	46	0	.152	.250	.174	188	3	.250	.347	.340
1991	Bal-A	256	2	.230	.338	.324	111	1	.225	.336	.306	145	1	.234	.339	.338	129	1	.178	.319	.264	127	1	.283	.359	.386	36	0	.139	.347	.194	220	2	.245	.336	.345
1992	Bal-A	623	21	.271	.373	.449	313	15	.262	.364	.463	310	6	.281	.383	.435	301	13	.282	.370	.512	322	8	.261	.377	.391	190	5	.226	.345	.368	433	16	.291	.386	.485
1993	Bal-A	560	13	.263	.363	.425	265	2	.242	.344	.343	295	11	.281	.381	.498	276	7	.236	.333	.406	284	6	.289	.391	.444	170	2	.259	.390	.353	390	11	.264	.350	.456
1994	Bal-A	453	12	.263	.356	.419	214	7	.257	.350	.425	239	5	.268	.362	.414	308	9	.247	.348	.399	145	3	.297	.374	.462	125	1	.248	.347	.344	328	11	.268	.360	.448
1995	Bal-A	554	16	.262	.371	.444	277	10	.260	.361	.451	277	6	.264	.380	.437	226	9	.265	.359	.473	328	7	.259	.379	.424	178	3	.213	.320	.331	376	13	.285	.394	.497
1996	Bal-A	579	50	.297	.396	.637	300	19	.280	.385	.567	279	31	.315	.409	.713	279	27	.290	.401	.659	300	23	.303	.392	.617	187	13	.251	.355	.535	392	37	.319	.416	.686
1997	Bal-A	590	18	.288	.393	.469	271	8	.251	.366	.395	319	10	.320	.417	.533	301	7	.306	.421	.449	289	11	.270	.363	.491	192	5	.281	.381	.448	398	13	.291	.399	.480
1998	Bal-A	479	18	.236	.356	.420	235	7	.226	.342	.383	244	11	.246	.370	.455	237	9	.211	.304	.405	242	9	.260	.403	.434	134	3	.179	.270	.321	345	15	.258	.388	.458
1999	Bal-A	564	24	.282	.404	.477	269	10	.249	.391	.401	295	14	.312	.416	.546	270	12	.267	.409	.470	294	12	.296	.398	.483	93	4	.237	.339	.387	471	20	.291	.416	.495
2000	Bal-A	506	19	.257	.375	.421	240	9	.267	.385	.421	266	10	.248	.366	.421	264	9	.254	.352	.413	242	10	.260	.399	.430	146	3	.260	.384	.390	360	16	.256	.372	.433
TOTALS		5989	201	.261	.366	.436	2930	92	.246	.354	.404	3059	109	.275	.378	.468	3000	107	.254	.361	.437	2989	94	.267	.372	.436	1652	40	.229	.341	.367	4337	161	.273	.376	.463
■ **Garret Anderson** BL/TL																																				
1994	Cal-A	13	0	.385	.385	.385	5	0	.600	.600	.600	8	0	.250	.250	.250	0	0	—	—	—	13	0	.385	.385	.385	1	0	.000	.000	.000	12	0	.417	.417	.417
1995	Cal-A	374	16	.321	.352	.505	184	7	.332	.367	.505	190	9	.311	.337	.505	56	2	.268	.359	.500	318	14	.330	.350	.506	115	5	.252	.285	.417	259	11	.351	.382	.544
1996	Cal-A	607	12	.285	.314	.405	306	7	.284	.322	.422	301	5	.286	.306	.389	324	9	.281	.308	.426	283	3	.290	.321	.382	212	3	.292	.296	.401	395	9	.281	.323	.408
1997	Ana-A	624	8	.303	.334	.396	327	5	.327	.353	.440	297	3	.276	.314	.374	309	2	.317	.340	.388	315	6	.289	.329	.429	184	0	.293	.296	.353	440	8	.307	.350	.432
1998	Ana-A	622	15	.294	.325	.455	315	4	.298	.319	.429	307	11	.290	.331	.482	300	10	.290	.321	.477	322	5	.298	.329	.435	168	4	.292	.312	.440	454	11	.295	.330	.460
1999	Ana-A	620	21	.303	.336	.469	299	10	.294	.321	.455	321	11	.312	.351	.483	302	12	.275	.299	.460	318	9	.330	.371	.478	161	3	.280	.302	.366	459	18	.312	.348	.505
2000	Ana-A	647	35	.286	.307	.519	322	20	.276	.296	.540	325	15	.295	.319	.498	320	22	.241	.256	.500	327	13	.330	.356	.538	189	15	.333	.348	.661	458	20	.266	.290	.461
TOTALS		3507	107	.297	.327	.458	1758	53	.301	.328	.463	1749	54	.294	.326	.452	1611	57	.280	.306	.452	1896	50	.312	.344	.463	1030	30	.293	.308	.443	2477	77	.299	.334	.464

YEAR	TM/L	TOTAL AB	HR	AVG	OBP	SLG	HOME AB	HR	AVG	OBP	SLG	AWAY AB	HR	AVG	OBP	SLG	1ST HALF AB	HR	AVG	OBP	SLG	2ND HALF AB	HR	AVG	OBP	SLG	LEFT AB	HR	AVG	OBP	SLG	RIGHT AB	HR	AVG	OBP	SLG
■ Tony Armas	BR/TR																																			
1978	Oak-A	239	2	.213	.250	.272	123	0	.203	.244	.220	116	2	.224	.256	.328	154	1	.227	.264	.286	85	1	.188	.225	.247	91	2	.176	.200	.286	148	0	.236	.280	.264
1979	Oak-A	278	11	.248	.290	.421	156	4	.263	.305	.410	122	7	.230	.269	.434	100	3	.250	.300	.380	178	8	.247	.283	.444	102	0	.225	.286	.275	176	11	.261	.292	.506
1980	Oak-A	628	35	.279	.310	.500	286	17	.269	.308	.507	342	18	.287	.312	.494	272	14	.272	.306	.460	356	21	.284	.314	.531	229	10	.301	.335	.498	399	25	.266	.296	.501
1981	Oak-A	440	22	.261	.294	.480	225	13	.240	.265	.471	215	9	.284	.325	.488	242	13	.289	.320	.525	198	9	.227	.263	.424	153	9	.294	.321	.569	287	13	.244	.281	.432
1982	Oak-A	536	28	.233	.275	.433	297	14	.199	.236	.387	239	14	.276	.323	.490	252	7	.226	.265	.365	284	21	.239	.284	.493	182	7	.231	.290	.385	354	21	.234	.267	.458
1983	Bos-A	574	36	.218	.254	.453	273	17	.253	.294	.509	301	19	.186	.218	.402	264	17	.242	.286	.489	310	19	.197	.227	.423	168	9	.238	.286	.452	406	27	.209	.241	.453
1984	Bos-A	639	43	.268	.300	.531	315	21	.289	.325	.552	324	22	.247	.276	.509	305	19	.285	.318	.541	334	24	.251	.285	.521	151	4	.245	.299	.377	488	39	.275	.301	.578
1985	Bos-A	385	23	.265	.298	.514	173	11	.289	.332	.555	212	12	.245	.268	.481	192	14	.245	.263	.516	193	9	.285	.330	.513	140	9	.336	.377	.636	245	14	.224	.251	.445
1986	Bos-A	425	11	.264	.305	.409	210	5	.271	.328	.429	215	6	.256	.281	.391	166	3	.265	.326	.380	259	8	.263	.290	.429	128	2	.289	.319	.430	297	9	.253	.299	.401
1987	Cal-A	81	3	.198	.205	.370	34	1	.176	.171	.324	47	2	.213	.229	.404	0	0	—	—	—	81	3	.198	.205	.370	51	2	.216	.216	.412	30	1	.167	.188	.300
1988	Cal-A	368	13	.272	.311	.443	199	5	.241	.282	.387	169	8	.308	.346	.509	176	3	.216	.285	.330	192	10	.323	.337	.547	165	8	.297	.345	.515	203	5	.251	.284	.384
1989	Cal-A	202	11	.257	.280	.465	104	5	.221	.257	.404	98	6	.296	.304	.531	37	4	.432	.447	.757	165	7	.218	.243	.400	102	5	.235	.264	.422	100	6	.280	.295	.510
TOTALS		4795	238	.253	.288	.458	2395	113	.251	.290	.453	2400	125	.255	.287	.463	2160	98	.258	.297	.448	2635	140	.249	.281	.466	1662	67	.265	.306	.452	3133	171	.247	.279	.462
■ Rich Aurilia	BR/TR																																			
1995	SF-N	19	2	.474	.476	.947	1	0	.000	.000	.000	18	2	.500	.500	1.000	0	0	—	—	—	19	2	.474	.476	.947	2	1	.500	.667	2.000	17	1	.471	.444	.824
1996	SF-N	318	3	.239	.295	.296	180	1	.261	.311	.300	138	2	.210	.275	.290	107	3	.224	.308	.346	211	0	.246	.288	.270	67	1	.224	.278	.313	251	2	.243	.299	.291
1997	SF-N	102	5	.275	.321	.500	49	1	.204	.245	.347	53	4	.340	.390	.642	36	3	.278	.341	.583	66	2	.273	.310	.455	50	3	.280	.345	.580	52	2	.269	.298	.423
1998	SF-N	413	9	.266	.319	.407	202	5	.252	.309	.401	211	4	.280	.329	.412	226	7	.296	.348	.482	187	2	.230	.284	.316	109	4	.275	.331	.477	304	5	.263	.315	.382
1999	SF-N	558	22	.281	.336	.444	275	9	.273	.324	.404	283	13	.290	.346	.484	272	12	.290	.346	.460	286	10	.273	.326	.430	142	5	.296	.357	.437	416	17	.276	.328	.447
2000	SF-N	509	20	.271	.339	.444	254	12	.287	.351	.492	255	8	.255	.326	.396	231	6	.247	.314	.377	278	14	.291	.359	.500	119	7	.286	.368	.521	390	13	.267	.329	.421
TOTALS		1919	61	.270	.327	.419	961	28	.266	.322	.404	958	33	.273	.332	.435	872	31	.272	.333	.435	1047	30	.268	.322	.407	489	21	.278	.344	.470	1430	40	.267	.321	.402
■ Brad Ausmus	BR/TR																																			
1993	SD-N	160	5	.256	.283	.412	80	4	.325	.341	.575	80	1	.188	.226	.250	0	0	—	—	—	160	5	.256	.283	.412	44	1	.295	.340	.477	116	4	.241	.261	.388
1994	SD-N	327	7	.251	.314	.358	159	6	.283	.352	.447	168	1	.220	.277	.274	230	4	.235	.302	.335	97	3	.289	.343	.412	86	1	.244	.309	.326	241	6	.253	.316	.369
1995	SD-N	328	5	.293	.353	.412	173	2	.266	.326	.370	155	3	.323	.383	.458	151	1	.298	.335	.397	177	4	.288	.368	.424	70	3	.314	.415	.500	258	2	.287	.336	.388
1996	SD-N	149	1	.181	.261	.228	72	0	.167	.259	.167	77	1	.195	.262	.286	149	1	.181	.261	.228	0	0	—	—	—	34	0	.118	.167	.118	115	1	.200	.287	.261
1996	Det-A	226	4	.248	.328	.354	121	2	.240	.329	.331	105	2	.257	.328	.381	23	0	.217	.333	.217	203	4	.251	.328	.369	56	2	.161	.213	.321	170	2	.276	.364	.365
1997	Hou-N	425	4	.266	.326	.358	196	1	.276	.344	.357	229	3	.258	.311	.358	211	2	.280	.328	.379	214	2	.252	.325	.336	96	1	.240	.295	.333	329	3	.274	.335	.365
1998	Hou-N	412	6	.269	.356	.357	199	2	.307	.414	.407	213	4	.235	.297	.310	208	4	.245	.351	.351	204	2	.294	.361	.363	86	1	.267	.396	.337	326	5	.270	.344	.362
1999	Det-A	458	9	.275	.365	.415	234	5	.291	.379	.436	224	4	.259	.349	.393	211	7	.284	.356	.436	247	2	.267	.372	.397	72	0	.264	.354	.333	386	9	.277	.367	.430
2000	Det-A	523	7	.266	.357	.365	254	3	.287	.377	.382	269	4	.245	.338	.349	261	5	.245	.340	.352	262	2	.286	.373	.378	137	3	.321	.422	.431	386	4	.246	.333	.342
TOTALS		3008	48	.263	.338	.370	1488	25	.278	.358	.392	1520	23	.248	.318	.348	1444	24	.253	.328	.355	1564	24	.272	.348	.383	681	12	.261	.346	.367	2327	36	.263	.336	.370
■ Carlos Baerga	BB/TR																																			
1990	Cle-A	312	7	.260	.300	.394	150	3	.300	.348	.440	162	4	.222	.254	.352	140	3	.214	.258	.336	172	4	.297	.333	.442	103	2	.243	.257	.340	209	5	.268	.320	.421
1991	Cle-A	593	11	.288	.346	.398	299	2	.291	.337	.368	294	9	.286	.355	.429	246	8	.276	.353	.415	347	3	.297	.341	.386	161	2	.329	.376	.416	432	9	.273	.335	.391
1992	Cle-A	657	20	.312	.354	.455	329	9	.353	.392	.486	328	11	.271	.318	.424	309	9	.304	.340	.434	348	11	.319	.366	.474	168	4	.375	.387	.500	489	16	.290	.343	.440
1993	Cle-A	624	21	.321	.355	.486	299	8	.331	.356	.468	325	13	.311	.353	.502	305	13	.298	.324	.508	319	8	.342	.383	.464	219	6	.315	.345	.447	405	15	.323	.360	.506
1994	Cle-A	442	19	.314	.333	.525	193	8	.290	.311	.503	249	11	.333	.350	.542	319	10	.292	.309	.458	123	9	.374	.395	.699	161	8	.261	.284	.472	281	11	.345	.360	.555
1995	Cle-A	557	15	.314	.355	.452	265	7	.336	.373	.468	292	8	.295	.339	.438	245	10	.347	.385	.547	312	5	.288	.331	.378	160	4	.331	.389	.494	397	11	.307	.340	.436
1996	Cle-A	424	10	.267	.302	.396	204	5	.275	.296	.407	220	5	.259	.306	.386	336	9	.265	.299	.408	88	1	.273	.312	.352	106	0	.245	.319	.311	318	10	.274	.295	.425
1996	NY-N	83	2	.193	.253	.301	29	0	.276	.300	.310	54	2	.148	.230	.296	0	0	—	—	—	83	2	.193	.253	.301	17	0	.059	.200	.059	66	2	.227	.268	.364
1997	NY-N	467	9	.281	.311	.396	229	4	.319	.347	.445	238	5	.244	.277	.349	245	3	.282	.305	.376	222	6	.279	.318	.419	94	1	.170	.196	.223	373	8	.308	.339	.440
1998	NY-N	511	7	.266	.303	.364	248	3	.278	.323	.391	263	4	.255	.283	.338	265	5	.283	.311	.404	246	2	.248	.294	.321	103	2	.204	.267	.282	408	5	.282	.313	.385
1999	SD-N	80	2	.250	.318	.338	40	1	.250	.302	.350	40	1	.250	.333	.325	4	0	.250	.571	.500	76	2	.250	.296	.329	10	0	.300	.364	.300	70	2	.243	.312	.343
1999	Cle-A	57	1	.228	.274	.281	26	1	.269	.345	.385	31	0	.194	.212	.194	0	0	—	—	—	57	1	.228	.274	.281	17	0	.176	.222	.176	40	1	.250	.295	.325
TOTALS		4807	124	.291	.330	.427	2311	51	.309	.345	.438	2496	73	.274	.317	.417	2414	70	.288	.323	.437	2393	54	.295	.337	.416	1319	29	.284	.324	.401	3488	95	.294	.333	.437
■ Jeff Bagwell	BR/TR																																			
1991	Hou-N	554	15	.294	.387	.437	274	6	.296	.392	.431	280	9	.293	.382	.443	252	7	.286	.369	.433	302	8	.301	.401	.440	206	7	.320	.417	.471	348	8	.279	.369	.417
1992	Hou-N	586	18	.273	.368	.444	294	8	.259	.355	.432	292	10	.288	.382	.455	280	9	.250	.354	.404	306	9	.294	.381	.480	210	10	.290	.394	.524	376	8	.263	.354	.399
1993	Hou-N	535	20	.320	.388	.516	267	9	.330	.409	.509	268	11	.310	.365	.522	284	12	.324	.391	.525	251	8	.315	.384	.506	179	10	.318	.408	.592	356	10	.320	.376	.478
1994	Hou-N	400	39	.368	.451	.750	201	23	.373	.459	.816	199	16	.362	.443	.683	281	25	.352	.426	.708	119	14	.403	.507	.849	105	18	.457	.544	1.095	295	21	.336	.418	.627
1995	Hou-N	448	21	.290	.399	.496	221	10	.285	.408	.489	227	11	.295	.390	.502	224	9	.259	.371	.446	224	12	.321	.426	.545	84	2	.298	.439	.440	364	19	.288	.389	.508
1996	Hou-N	568	31	.315	.451	.570	278	16	.331	.469	.594	290	15	.300	.433	.548	292	21	.325	.460	.644	276	10	.304	.441	.493	110	3	.364	.517	.564	458	28	.303	.434	.572
1997	Hou-N	566	43	.286	.425	.592	264	22	.258	.416	.580	302	21	.311	.434	.603	298	22	.315	.436	.631	268	21	.254	.414	.549	120	5	.242	.432	.450	446	38	.298	.423	.630
1998	Hou-N	540	34	.304	.424	.557	248	20	.347	.459	.673	292	14	.267	.394	.459	248	17	.278	.409	.548	292	17	.325	.436	.565	107	7	.402	.538	.692	433	27	.279	.391	.524
1999	Hou-N	562	42	.304	.454	.591	277	12	.271	.430	.469	285	30	.337	.477	.709	267	25	.318	.462	.663	295	17	.292	.447	.525	130	9	.354	.476	.623	432	33	.289	.448	.581
2000	Hou-N	590	47	.310	.424	.615	286	28	.353	.462	.720	304	19	.270	.389	.516	298	18	.279	.393	.530	292	29	.342	.455	.702	112	9	.366	.497	.688	478	38	.297	.406	.598
TOTALS		5349	310	.305	.417	.552	2610	154	.308	.425	.565	2739	156	.301	.410	.541	2724	165	.300	.409	.557	2625	145	.310	.425	.548	1363	80	.335	.456	.596	3986	230	.295	.404	.537
■ Harold Baines	BL/TL																																			
1980	Chi-A	491	13	.255	.281	.405	250	3	.260	.288	.384	241	10	.249	.274	.427	222	5	.275	.303	.419	269	8	.238	.262	.394	88	1	.159	.169	.239	403	12	.275	.304	.442
1981	Chi-A	280	10	.286	.318	.482	111	3	.261	.303	.405	169	7	.302	.328	.533	171	2	.257	.285	.374	109	8	.330	.368	.651	25	0	.320	.333	.480	255	10	.282	.316	.482
1982	Chi-A	608	25	.271	.321	.469	288	11	.288	.350	.483	320	14	.256	.295	.456	268	6	.246	.298	.399	340	19	.291	.340	.524	202	9	.282	.323	.485	406	16	.266	.321	.461
1983	Chi-A	596	20	.280	.333	.443	284	12	.285	.334	.486	312	8	.276	.331	.404	270	5	.270	.339	.393	326	15	.288	.328	.485	192	3	.234	.255	.344	404	17	.302	.367	.490
1984	Chi-A	569	29	.304	.361	.541	261	16	.330	.385	.582	308	13	.282	.342	.506	281	12	.270	.313	.452	288	17	.337	.407	.628	198	10	.278	.318	.515	371	19	.318	.384	.555
1985	Chi-A	640	22	.309	.348	.467	315	13	.283	.324	.463	325	9	.335	.371	.471	264	6	.273	.330	.398	376	16	.335	.361	.516	217	6	.341	.368	.465	423	16	.293	.338	.468
1986	Chi-A	570	21	.296	.338	.465	275	8	.331	.372	.491	295	13	.264	.306	.441	286	10	.308	.353	.465	284	11	.285	.322	.465	206	3	.262	.297	.354	364	18	.316	.361	.527
1987	Chi-A	505	20	.293	.352	.479	253	12	.312	.353	.538	252	8	.274	.351	.421	187	10	.283	.365	.497	318	10	.299	.344	.469	181	6	.254	.308	.409	324	14	.315	.376	.519
1988	Chi-A	599	13	.277	.347	.411	295	5	.281	.369	.424	304	8	.273	.325	.398	283	10	.258	.333	.406	316	3	.294	.360	.415	190	2	.253	.316	.358	409	11	.289	.361	.435
1989	Chi-A	333	13	.321	.423	.505	165	4	.291	.411	.455	168	9	.351	.436	.554	263	10	.316	.415	.479	70	3	.343	.453	.600	120	3	.250	.348	.367	213	10	.362	.463	.582
1989	Tex-A	172	3	.285	.333	.390	82	1	.305	.360	.427	90	2	.267	.309	.356	0	0	—	—	—	172	3	.285	.333	.390	36	1	.306	.342	.444	136	2	.279	.331	.375
1990	Tex-A	321	13	.290	.377	.449	157	6	.287	.363	.420	164	7	.293	.391	.476	212	9	.288	.384	.467	109	4	.294	.364	.413	83	3	.241	.312	.373	238	10	.307	.399	.475
1990	Oak-A	94	3	.266	.381	.415	43	3	.256	.345	.488	51	0	.275	.413	.353	0	0	—	—	—	94	3	.266	.381	.415	8	0	.375	.462	.500	86	3	.256	.371	.407
1991	Oak-A	488	20	.295	.383	.473	227	11	.264	.358	.458	261	9	.322	.406	.487	233	9	.326	.410	.515	255	11	.267	.359	.435	83	4	.301	.348	.506	405	16	.294	.390	.467
1992	Oak-A	478	16	.253	.331	.391	231	10	.277	.346	.442	247	6	.231	.318	.344	226	7	.235	.311	.363	252	9	.270	.350	.417	53	1	.245	.310	.302	425	15	.254	.334	.402
1993	Bal-A	416	20	.313	.390	.510	197	12	.345	.431	.584	219	8	.283	.352	.443	169	4	.302	.375	.438	247	16	.320	.401	.559	96	4	.260	.330	.427	320	16	.328	.408	.534
1994	Bal-A	326	16	.294	.356	.485	152	11	.316	.377	.566	174	5	.276	.337	.414	225	12	.293	.348	.493	101	4	.297	.372	.465	51	1	.176	.208	.255	275	15	.316	.382	.527
1995	Bal-A	385	24	.299	.403	.540	172	7	.291	.418	.488	213	17	.305	.390	.582	147	9	.306	.412	.537	238	15	.294	.397	.542	62	3	.290	.353	.452	323	21	.300	.412	.557
1996	Chi-A	495	22	.311	.399	.503	237	9	.283	.396	.430	258	13	.337	.401	.570	239	12	.293	.380	.494	256	10	.328	.416	.512	105	4	.333	.379	.486	390	18	.305	.404	.508
1997	Chi-A	318	12	.305	.382	.475	163	5	.270	.365	.423	155	7	.342	.401	.529	235	9	.298	.386	.485	83	3	.325	.371	.446	67	3	.299	.333	.493	251	9	.307	.394	.470
1997	Bal-A	134	4	.291	.356	.418	68	1	.221	.299	.294	66	3	.364	.417	.545	0	0	—	—	—	134	4	.291	.356	.418	25	0	.200	.200	.280	109	4	.312	.387	.450
1998	Bal-A	293	9	.300	.369	.451	151	5	.318	.391	.464	142	4	.282	.346	.437	190	5	.326	.383	.474	103	4	.252	.345	.408	49	1	.204	.291	.286	244	8	.320	.385	.484
1999	Bal-A	345	24	.322	.395	.583	168	12	.333	.405	.619	177	12	.311	.385	.548	195	15	.344	.419	.610	150	9	.293	.363	.547	48	3	.313	.340	.563	297	21	.323	.404	.586
1999	Cle-A	85	1	.271	.354	.329	43	1	.209	.292	.279	42	0	.333	.417	.381	0	0	—	—	—	85	1	.271	.354	.329	5	0	.200	.200	.200	80	1	.275	.363	.338
2000	Bal-A	222	10	.266	.349	.437	105	4	.229	.347	.362	117	6	.299	.352	.504	175	6	.240	.309	.377	47	4	.362	.483	.660	22	0	.227	.292	.227	200	10	.270	.355	.460
2000	Chi-A	61	1	.213	.294	.344	37	0	.216	.293	.324	24	1	.208	.296	.375	0	0	—	—	—	61	1	.213	.294	.344	4	0	.000	.000	.000	57	1	.228	.313	.368
TOTALS		9824	384	.291	.357	.467	4730	185	.291	.362	.471	5094	199	.290	.352	.464	4741	173	.285	.354	.452	5083	211	.296	.359	.482	2416	71	.267	.314	.409	7408	313	.298	.370	.487
■ Dusty Baker	BR/TR																																			
1978	LA-N	522	11	.262	.325	.375	246	5	.280	.351	.398	276	6	.246	.301	.355	258	5	.260	.313	.364	264	6	.265	.337	.386	130	0	.262	.347	.300	392	11	.263	.318	.401
1979	LA-N	554	23	.274	.340	.455	278	14	.277	.342	.478	276	9	.272	.339	.431	278	10	.276	.332	.451	268	13	.272	.349	.459	154	6	.331	.385	.506	400	17	.253	.324	.435
1980	LA-N	579	29	.294	.339	.503	287	14	.272	.316	.456	292	15	.315	.361	.548	257	18	.296	.329	.572	322	11	.292	.347	.447	107	4	.271	.295	.477	472	25	.299	.349	.508
1981	LA-N	400	9	.320	.363	.445	198	4	.283	.324	.389	202	5	.356	.400	.500	221	4	.303	.343	.439	179	5	.341	.388	.453	61	1	.361	.385	.492	339	8	.313	.359	.437
1982	LA-N	570	23	.300	.361	.458	290	7	.286	.346	.383	280	16	.314	.376	.536	266	15	.289	.351	.489	304	8	.309	.368	.431	96	5	.323	.387	.521	474	18	.295	.355	.445
1983	LA-N	531	15	.260	.346	.395	276	8	.257	.350	.388	255	7	.263	.342	.404	264	8	.227	.306	.367	267	7	.292	.384	.423	101	2	.248	.345	.347	430	13	.263	.347	.407
1984	SF-N	243	3	.292	.387	.374	112	2	.313	.439	.411	131	1	.275	.338	.344	78	1	.295	.408	.359	165	2	.291	.376	.382	82	0	.280	.390	.317	161	3	.298	.385	.404

YEAR	TM/L	TOTAL					HOME					AWAY					1ST HALF					2ND HALF					LEFT					RIGHT				
		AB	HR	AVG	OBP	SLG	AB	HR	AVG	OBP	SLG	AB	HR	AVG	OBP	SLG	AB	HR	AVG	OBP	SLG	AB	HR	AVG	OBP	SLG	AB	HR	AVG	OBP	SLG	AB	HR	AVG	OBP	SLG
1985	Oak-A	343	14	.268	.359	.440	161	5	.248	.339	.385	182	9	.286	.376	.489	138	9	.290	.385	.529	205	5	.254	.340	.380	144	5	.250	.355	.396	199	9	.281	.361	.472
1986	Oak-A	242	4	.240	.314	.322	112	1	.223	.313	.268	130	3	.254	.315	.369	144	2	.257	.316	.313	98	2	.214	.310	.337	110	2	.227	.306	.309	132	2	.250	.320	.333
TOTALS		3984	131	.280	.347	.429	1960	60	.272	.344	.406	2024	71	.288	.351	.451	1912	72	.275	.336	.439	2072	59	.285	.357	.419	985	25	.280	.354	.406	2999	106	.280	.345	.436
■ Steve Balboni BR/TR																																				
1981	NY-A	7	0	.286	.375	.714	4	0	.250	.400	.750	3	0	.333	.333	.667	5	0	.400	.500	1.000	2	0	.000	.000	.000	7	0	.286	.375	.714	0	0	—	—	—
1982	NY-A	107	2	.187	.228	.280	17	0	.059	.111	.059	90	2	.211	.250	.322	28	1	.214	.258	.357	79	1	.177	.217	.253	50	1	.220	.291	.340	57	1	.158	.169	.228
1983	NY-A	86	5	.233	.295	.430	33	0	.212	.270	.242	53	5	.245	.310	.547	10	0	.100	.250	.100	76	5	.250	.301	.474	64	3	.219	.296	.375	22	2	.273	.292	.591
1984	KC-A	438	28	.244	.320	.498	218	10	.216	.280	.431	220	18	.273	.357	.564	204	10	.235	.304	.436	234	18	.252	.333	.551	152	10	.270	.366	.507	286	18	.231	.294	.493
1985	KC-A	600	36	.243	.307	.477	304	17	.253	.308	.497	296	19	.233	.305	.456	277	13	.249	.302	.433	323	23	.238	.310	.514	164	8	.220	.312	.421	436	28	.252	.305	.498
1986	KC-A	512	29	.229	.286	.451	251	10	.203	.264	.386	261	19	.253	.309	.513	273	15	.212	.282	.429	239	14	.247	.292	.477	134	12	.276	.370	.590	378	17	.212	.255	.402
1987	KC-A	386	24	.207	.273	.427	190	8	.189	.255	.347	196	16	.224	.290	.505	220	11	.209	.278	.391	166	13	.205	.266	.476	103	6	.194	.265	.379	283	18	.212	.276	.445
1988	KC-A	63	2	.143	.156	.270	31	1	.194	.219	.355	32	1	.094	.094	.188	63	2	.143	.156	.270	0	0	—	—	—	44	0	.136	.156	.182	19	2	.158	.158	.474
1988	Sea-A	350	21	.251	.298	.480	184	14	.245	.296	.527	166	7	.259	.299	.428	44	2	.159	.245	.341	306	19	.265	.306	.500	120	6	.225	.273	.433	230	15	.265	.310	.504
1989	NY-A	300	17	.237	.296	.460	127	7	.236	.296	.425	173	10	.237	.297	.486	151	10	.252	.301	.503	149	7	.221	.292	.416	194	13	.247	.296	.505	106	4	.217	.298	.377
1990	NY-A	266	17	.192	.291	.406	123	8	.211	.315	.447	143	9	.175	.270	.371	115	7	.217	.319	.417	151	10	.172	.269	.397	161	14	.211	.340	.497	105	3	.162	.205	.267
1993	Tex-A	5	0	.600	.600	.600	5	0	.600	.600	.600	0	0	—	—	—	0	0	—	—	—	5	0	.600	.600	.600	0	0	—	—	—	5	0	.600	.600	.600
TOTALS		3120	181	.229	.293	.451	1487	75	.222	.284	.430	1633	106	.235	.300	.469	1390	71	.222	.287	.420	1730	110	.234	.297	.475	1193	73	.231	.313	.459	1927	108	.227	.279	.445
■ Jesse Barfield BR/TR																																				
1981	Tor-A	95	2	.232	.270	.368	46	1	.261	.320	.457	49	1	.204	.220	.286	0	0	—	—	—	95	2	.232	.270	.368	37	1	.189	.231	.270	58	1	.259	.295	.431
1982	Tor-A	394	18	.246	.323	.426	173	11	.249	.342	.451	221	7	.244	.307	.407	171	6	.251	.319	.415	223	12	.242	.325	.435	246	15	.260	.325	.492	148	3	.223	.320	.318
1983	Tor-A	388	27	.253	.296	.510	207	22	.304	.347	.696	181	5	.193	.239	.298	180	10	.211	.245	.417	208	17	.288	.338	.591	212	13	.259	.298	.500	176	14	.244	.293	.523
1984	Tor-A	320	14	.284	.357	.466	166	10	.289	.344	.536	154	4	.279	.369	.390	155	5	.271	.315	.426	165	9	.297	.393	.503	187	6	.310	.382	.460	133	8	.248	.320	.474
1985	Tor-A	539	27	.289	.369	.536	255	15	.286	.368	.565	284	12	.292	.371	.511	244	12	.258	.344	.463	295	15	.315	.390	.597	207	9	.309	.379	.541	332	18	.277	.363	.533
1986	Tor-A	589	40	.289	.368	.559	291	16	.278	.371	.526	298	24	.299	.365	.591	290	19	.286	.352	.548	299	21	.291	.383	.569	148	9	.284	.397	.527	441	31	.290	.358	.569
1987	Tor-A	590	28	.263	.331	.458	302	11	.305	.371	.487	288	17	.219	.288	.427	280	19	.286	.357	.536	310	9	.242	.307	.387	177	9	.299	.380	.525	413	19	.247	.309	.429
1988	Tor-A	468	18	.244	.302	.425	236	12	.250	.309	.483	232	6	.237	.296	.366	214	6	.215	.272	.355	254	12	.268	.327	.484	165	9	.212	.284	.406	303	9	.261	.312	.436
1989	Tor-A	80	5	.200	.256	.438	29	1	.138	.219	.276	51	4	.235	.278	.529	80	5	.200	.256	.438	0	0	—	—	—	34	3	.176	.243	.441	46	2	.217	.265	.435
1989	NY-A	441	18	.240	.360	.410	232	6	.254	.367	.392	209	12	.225	.352	.431	163	6	.239	.376	.362	278	12	.241	.350	.439	126	5	.254	.432	.413	315	13	.235	.326	.410
1990	NY-A	476	25	.246	.359	.456	239	12	.218	.314	.410	237	13	.274	.403	.502	230	12	.257	.346	.478	246	13	.236	.371	.435	162	13	.259	.394	.543	314	12	.239	.341	.411
1991	NY-A	284	17	.225	.312	.447	130	11	.231	.331	.538	154	6	.221	.294	.370	243	15	.226	.310	.457	41	2	.220	.319	.390	108	9	.315	.408	.602	176	8	.170	.250	.352
1992	NY-A	95	2	.137	.210	.221	54	2	.148	.190	.278	41	0	.122	.234	.146	95	2	.137	.210	.221	0	0	—	—	—	33	1	.152	.282	.242	62	1	.129	.167	.210
TOTALS		4759	241	.256	.335	.466	2360	130	.264	.343	.497	2399	111	.248	.328	.436	2345	117	.246	.320	.446	2414	124	.266	.350	.486	1842	102	.270	.357	.489	2917	139	.248	.321	.451
■ Kevin Bass BB/TR																																				
1982	Mil-A	9	0	.000	.100	.000	3	0	.000	.000	.000	6	0	.000	.143	.000	9	0	.000	.100	.000	0	0	—	—	—	0	0	—	—	—	9	0	.000	.100	.000
1982	Hou-N	24	0	.042	.042	.042	17	0	.059	.059	.059	7	0	.000	.000	.000	0	0	—	—	—	24	0	.042	.042	.042	13	0	.077	.077	.077	11	0	.000	.000	.000
1983	Hou-N	195	2	.236	.257	.333	118	2	.254	.276	.390	77	0	.208	.228	.247	103	1	.243	.264	.350	92	1	.228	.250	.315	118	1	.212	.231	.297	77	1	.273	.296	.390
1984	Hou-N	331	2	.260	.279	.360	161	1	.292	.321	.404	170	1	.229	.238	.318	176	1	.244	.265	.318	155	1	.277	.296	.406	158	2	.228	.261	.329	173	0	.289	.297	.387
1985	Hou-N	539	16	.269	.315	.427	264	9	.250	.307	.402	275	7	.287	.323	.451	219	7	.237	.263	.379	320	9	.291	.349	.459	219	10	.311	.359	.553	320	6	.241	.284	.341
1986	Hou-N	591	20	.311	.357	.486	296	5	.314	.361	.426	295	15	.308	.353	.546	272	11	.313	.368	.504	319	9	.310	.347	.470	248	12	.323	.345	.540	343	8	.303	.365	.446
1987	Hou-N	592	19	.284	.344	.449	302	10	.285	.348	.454	290	9	.283	.340	.445	285	8	.277	.338	.449	307	11	.290	.350	.450	227	10	.282	.315	.507	365	9	.285	.361	.414
1988	Hou-N	541	14	.255	.314	.390	249	5	.277	.347	.390	292	9	.236	.286	.390	258	6	.260	.314	.384	283	8	.251	.314	.396	193	6	.316	.354	.503	348	8	.221	.293	.328
1989	Hou-N	313	5	.300	.357	.435	168	2	.298	.346	.417	145	3	.303	.370	.455	162	1	.290	.359	.414	151	4	.311	.356	.457	83	2	.265	.315	.434	230	3	.313	.373	.435
1990	SF-N	214	7	.252	.303	.402	115	3	.226	.282	.339	99	4	.283	.327	.475	149	6	.268	.301	.450	65	1	.215	.307	.292	90	5	.256	.302	.467	124	2	.250	.304	.355
1991	SF-N	361	10	.233	.307	.366	167	5	.210	.298	.335	194	5	.253	.315	.392	204	4	.230	.299	.333	157	6	.236	.317	.408	113	6	.239	.276	.442	248	4	.230	.320	.331
1992	SF-N	265	7	.268	.310	.411	148	5	.284	.323	.453	117	2	.248	.294	.359	173	4	.266	.306	.428	92	3	.272	.316	.380	93	4	.194	.200	.376	172	3	.308	.365	.430
1992	NY-N	137	2	.270	.303	.431	68	2	.309	.342	.544	69	0	.232	.264	.319	0	0	—	—	—	137	2	.270	.303	.431	51	0	.275	.302	.471	86	2	.267	.304	.407
1993	Hou-N	229	3	.284	.359	.402	100	2	.270	.336	.400	129	1	.295	.377	.403	98	1	.245	.288	.357	131	2	.313	.408	.435	80	2	.225	.303	.412	149	1	.315	.389	.396
1994	Hou-N	203	6	.310	.393	.483	89	3	.360	.453	.584	114	3	.272	.344	.404	110	3	.300	.378	.455	93	3	.323	.411	.516	69	3	.420	.481	.652	134	3	.254	.348	.396
1995	Bal-A	295	5	.244	.303	.336	142	2	.232	.299	.310	153	3	.255	.307	.359	145	4	.317	.377	.462	150	1	.173	.230	.213	115	3	.252	.301	.365	180	2	.239	.305	.317
TOTALS		4839	118	.270	.323	.411	2407	56	.273	.330	.408	2432	62	.267	.317	.414	2363	57	.268	.319	.409	2476	61	.272	.328	.413	1870	66	.275	.313	.461	2969	52	.267	.329	.380
■ Tony Batista BR/TR																																				
1996	Oak-A	238	6	.298	.350	.433	110	1	.255	.336	.355	128	5	.336	.363	.500	32	1	.406	.406	.594	206	5	.282	.342	.408	65	2	.277	.347	.431	173	4	.306	.351	.434
1997	Oak-A	188	4	.202	.265	.330	107	0	.206	.261	.252	81	4	.198	.270	.432	84	2	.167	.239	.274	104	2	.231	.286	.375	60	0	.150	.190	.200	128	4	.227	.298	.391
1998	Ari-N	293	18	.273	.318	.519	162	9	.296	.343	.512	131	9	.244	.286	.527	85	2	.235	.298	.353	208	16	.288	.326	.587	103	6	.320	.381	.573	190	12	.247	.283	.489
1999	Ari-N	144	5	.257	.335	.396	57	1	.263	.358	.368	87	4	.253	.320	.414	144	5	.257	.335	.396	0	0	—	—	—	49	3	.347	.414	.571	95	2	.211	.292	.305
1999	Tor-A	375	26	.285	.328	.565	184	9	.283	.325	.495	191	17	.288	.330	.634	64	6	.281	.324	.594	311	20	.286	.328	.559	61	3	.230	.338	.443	314	23	.296	.325	.589
2000	Tor-A	620	41	.263	.307	.519	307	25	.270	.324	.580	313	16	.256	.290	.460	289	21	.280	.323	.557	331	20	.248	.294	.486	162	6	.235	.287	.414	458	35	.273	.314	.557
TOTALS		1858	100	.267	.316	.489	927	45	.268	.324	.474	931	55	.266	.309	.504	698	37	.262	.316	.470	1160	63	.270	.317	.500	500	20	.258	.323	.442	1358	80	.270	.314	.506
■ Don Baylor BR/TR																																				
1978	Cal-A	591	34	.255	.332	.472	300	21	.290	.344	.557	291	13	.220	.321	.385	270	18	.252	.328	.489	321	16	.259	.336	.458	139	12	.317	.392	.612	452	22	.237	.313	.429
1979	Cal-A	628	36	.296	.371	.530	305	17	.292	.381	.511	323	19	.300	.361	.548	307	14	.280	.364	.485	321	22	.312	.378	.573	166	14	.325	.408	.633	462	22	.286	.358	.494
1980	Cal-A	340	5	.250	.316	.341	176	0	.233	.286	.261	164	5	.268	.348	.427	108	0	.250	.364	.315	232	5	.250	.290	.353	102	1	.245	.282	.294	238	4	.252	.330	.361
1981	Cal-A	377	17	.239	.322	.427	175	10	.251	.330	.480	202	7	.228	.315	.381	198	9	.187	.289	.359	179	8	.296	.360	.503	110	5	.255	.336	.409	267	12	.232	.316	.434
1982	Cal-A	608	24	.263	.329	.424	305	13	.262	.333	.430	303	11	.264	.325	.419	296	11	.274	.309	.429	312	13	.253	.347	.420	238	8	.261	.322	.408	370	16	.265	.334	.435
1983	NY-A	534	21	.303	.361	.494	261	10	.303	.359	.494	273	11	.304	.364	.495	239	8	.297	.360	.464	295	13	.308	.363	.519	249	13	.357	.423	.602	285	8	.256	.305	.400
1984	NY-A	493	27	.262	.341	.489	223	10	.247	.325	.430	270	17	.274	.354	.537	236	16	.254	.335	.513	257	11	.268	.347	.467	188	9	.282	.366	.473	305	18	.249	.326	.498
1985	NY-A	477	23	.231	.330	.430	231	12	.216	.315	.433	246	11	.244	.345	.427	234	12	.226	.332	.432	243	11	.235	.329	.428	193	11	.254	.377	.492	284	12	.215	.297	.387
1986	Bos-A	585	31	.238	.344	.439	279	9	.233	.370	.376	306	22	.242	.317	.497	271	15	.251	.360	.469	314	16	.226	.329	.414	152	5	.230	.359	.388	433	26	.240	.338	.457
1987	Bos-A	339	16	.239	.355	.404	151	10	.272	.387	.483	188	6	.213	.327	.340	257	14	.249	.370	.440	82	2	.207	.306	.293	118	6	.237	.313	.390	221	10	.240	.375	.412
1987	Min-A	49	0	.286	.397	.306	32	0	.250	.314	.281	17	0	.353	.522	.353	0	0	—	—	—	49	0	.286	.397	.306	17	0	.471	.591	.529	32	0	.188	.278	.188
1988	Oak-A	264	7	.220	.332	.326	110	2	.200	.268	.273	154	5	.234	.374	.364	154	3	.208	.289	.286	110	4	.236	.386	.382	123	1	.220	.305	.285	141	6	.220	.355	.362
TOTALS		5285	241	.258	.342	.445	2548	114	.259	.342	.442	2737	127	.257	.341	.448	2570	120	.252	.338	.440	2715	121	.264	.345	.450	1795	85	.280	.363	.471	3490	156	.247	.331	.432
■ Rich Becker BL/TL																																				
1993	Min-A	7	0	.286	.583	.571	0	0	—	—	—	7	0	.286	.583	.571	0	0	—	—	—	7	0	.286	.583	.571	3	0	.333	.500	.667	4	0	.250	.625	.500
1994	Min-A	98	1	.265	.351	.327	51	1	.373	.458	.490	47	0	.149	.231	.149	66	1	.303	.410	.394	32	0	.188	.212	.188	16	0	.313	.421	.375	82	1	.256	.337	.317
1995	Min-A	392	2	.237	.303	.296	180	1	.217	.289	.267	212	1	.255	.316	.321	104	1	.221	.293	.269	288	1	.243	.307	.306	87	0	.149	.237	.161	305	2	.262	.322	.334
1996	Min-A	525	12	.291	.372	.434	267	8	.311	.375	.472	258	4	.271	.370	.395	220	5	.241	.328	.382	305	7	.328	.404	.472	105	0	.171	.228	.219	420	12	.321	.406	.488
1997	Min-A	443	10	.264	.354	.395	223	4	.278	.376	.404	220	6	.250	.332	.386	233	5	.270	.369	.386	210	5	.257	.338	.405	64	0	.156	.260	.188	379	10	.282	.370	.430
1998	NY-N	100	3	.190	.331	.360	55	3	.218	.358	.455	45	0	.156	.296	.244	100	3	.190	.331	.360	0	0	—	—	—	7	0	.286	.500	.286	93	3	.183	.315	.366
1998	Bal-A	113	3	.204	.343	.292	48	1	.250	.368	.333	65	2	.169	.325	.262	15	0	.200	.294	.200	98	3	.204	.350	.306	24	1	.083	.241	.208	89	2	.236	.370	.315
1999	Mil-A	139	5	.252	.395	.424	59	4	.322	.429	.576	80	1	.200	.373	.313	76	2	.237	.363	.368	63	3	.270	.432	.492	11	0	.091	.231	.091	128	5	.266	.409	.453
1999	Oak-A	125	1	.264	.395	.312	57	1	.246	.394	.333	68	0	.279	.395	.294	0	0	—	—	—	125	1	.264	.395	.312	8	0	.250	.250	.250	117	1	.265	.403	.316
2000	Oak-A	47	1	.234	.390	.340	36	1	.222	.349	.333	11	0	.273	.500	.364	47	1	.234	.390	.340	0	0	—	—	—	4	0	.250	.500	.250	43	1	.233	.377	.326
2000	Det-A	238	7	.244	.383	.382	121	3	.264	.387	.380	117	4	.222	.378	.385	80	3	.250	.358	.425	158	4	.241	.394	.361	28	0	.107	.219	.143	210	7	.262	.402	.414
TOTALS		2227	45	.256	.358	.372	1097	27	.273	.369	.402	1130	18	.239	.348	.343	941	21	.244	.349	.367	1286	24	.264	.365	.376	357	1	.162	.259	.204	1870	44	.274	.377	.404
■ Buddy Bell BR/TR																																				
1978	Cle-A	556	6	.282	.328	.392	260	3	.269	.319	.369	296	3	.294	.336	.412	264	3	.311	.344	.378	292	3	.257	.314	.332	142	2	.275	.329	.394	414	4	.285	.328	.391
1979	Tex-A	670	18	.299	.327	.451	327	9	.315	.347	.477	343	9	.283	.308	.426	309	4	.278	.320	.395	361	14	.316	.333	.499	209	9	.306	.362	.478	461	9	.295	.310	.438
1980	Tex-A	490	17	.329	.379	.498	253	8	.352	.399	.510	237	9	.304	.358	.485	209	9	.335	.379	.531	281	8	.324	.379	.473	163	4	.313	.391	.429	327	13	.336	.373	.532
1981	Tex-A	360	10	.294	.364	.428	174	2	.293	.382	.368	186	8	.296	.346	.484	191	9	.293	.364	.476	169	1	.296	.364	.373	112	3	.339	.432	.482	248	7	.274	.332	.403
1982	Tex-A	537	13	.296	.376	.426	264	3	.303	.381	.398	273	10	.289	.371	.454	264	8	.303	.358	.439	273	5	.289	.393	.414	114	3	.298	.418	.439	423	10	.296	.364	.423
1983	Tex-A	618	14	.277	.332	.411	306	8	.301	.359	.431	312	6	.253	.305	.391	297	9	.279	.334	.438	321	5	.274	.330	.386	197	3	.299	.359	.411	421	11	.266	.319	.411
1984	Tex-A	553	11	.315	.382	.458	271	6	.310	.375	.458	282	5	.319	.389	.457	268	4	.299	.370	.410	285	7	.330	.394	.502	152	4	.336	.412	.513	401	7	.307	.370	.436
1985	Tex-A	313	4	.236	.308	.335	155	2	.226	.311	.310	158	2	.247	.305	.361	269	4	.253	.315	.368	44	0	.136	.264	.136	76	0	.289	.356	.382	237	4	.219	.292	.321
1985	Cin-N	247	6	.219	.311	.368	118	4	.246	.323	.466	129	2	.194	.300	.279	0	0	—	—	—	247	6	.219	.311	.368	72	1	.250	.321	.361	175	5	.206	.307	.371

		TOTAL					HOME					AWAY					1ST HALF					2ND HALF					LEFT					RIGHT				
YEAR	TM/L	AB	HR	AVG	OBP	SLG	AB	HR	AVG	OBP	SLG	AB	HR	AVG	OBP	SLG	AB	HR	AVG	OBP	SLG	AB	HR	AVG	OBP	SLG	AB	HR	AVG	OBP	SLG	AB	HR	AVG	OBP	SLG
1986	Cin-N	568	20	.278	.362	.445	276	14	.308	.387	.525	292	6	.250	.339	.370	235	4	.234	.315	.345	333	16	.309	.395	.517	174	8	.270	.348	.471	394	12	.282	.368	.434
1987	Cin-N	522	17	.284	.369	.425	262	8	.298	.395	.435	260	9	.269	.342	.415	220	6	.282	.352	.436	302	11	.285	.381	.417	142	7	.261	.367	.430	380	10	.292	.370	.424
1988	Cin-N	54	0	.185	.270	.185	25	0	.200	.333	.200	29	0	.172	.212	.172	54	0	.185	.270	.185	0	0	—	—	—	8	0	.125	.222	.125	46	0	.196	.278	.196
1988	Hou-N	269	7	.253	.301	.375	124	1	.234	.269	.315	145	6	.269	.327	.428	33	0	.182	.270	.303	236	7	.263	.306	.386	83	2	.253	.323	.386	186	5	.253	.291	.371
1989	Tex-A	82	0	.183	.247	.232	49	0	.224	.309	.265	33	0	.121	.147	.182	82	0	.183	.247	.232	0	0	—	—	—	49	0	.163	.212	.224	33	0	.212	.297	.242
TOTALS		5839	143	.283	.347	.420	2864	68	.294	.360	.428	2975	75	.274	.335	.413	2695	60	.279	.338	.414	3144	83	.287	.355	.426	1693	46	.289	.366	.432	4146	97	.281	.339	.416
■ **David Bell** BR/TR																																				
1995	Cle-A	2	0	.000	.000	.000	1	0	.000	.000	.000	1	0	.000	.000	.000	2	0	.000	.000	.000	0	0	—	—	—	2	0	.000	.000	.000	0	0	—	—	—
1995	StL-N	144	2	.250	.278	.368	75	1	.213	.259	.307	69	1	.290	.300	.435	0	0	—	—	—	144	2	.250	.278	.368	34	0	.382	.417	.412	110	2	.209	.235	.355
1996	StL-N	145	1	.214	.268	.276	72	1	.250	.286	.319	73	0	.178	.250	.233	122	1	.221	.278	.287	23	0	.174	.208	.217	64	0	.250	.304	.313	81	1	.185	.239	.247
1997	StL-N	142	1	.211	.261	.310	77	1	.273	.305	.390	65	0	.138	.211	.215	22	0	.136	.174	.136	120	1	.225	.277	.342	50	0	.280	.315	.360	92	1	.174	.232	.283
1998	StL-N	9	0	.222	.222	.333	9	0	.222	.222	.333	0	0	—	—	—	9	0	.222	.222	.333	0	0	—	—	—	3	0	.000	.000	.000	6	0	.333	.333	.500
1998	Cle-A	340	10	.262	.306	.424	178	2	.253	.277	.365	162	8	.272	.337	.488	203	4	.286	.323	.429	137	6	.226	.283	.416	89	3	.247	.306	.404	251	7	.267	.306	.430
1998	Sea-A	80	0	.325	.365	.425	40	0	.350	.409	.500	40	0	.300	.317	.350	0	0	—	—	—	80	0	.325	.365	.425	22	0	.318	.375	.409	58	0	.328	.361	.431
1999	Sea-A	597	21	.268	.331	.432	293	11	.263	.332	.444	304	10	.273	.330	.421	285	15	.263	.335	.477	312	6	.272	.328	.391	118	3	.220	.311	.347	479	18	.280	.336	.453
2000	Sea-A	454	11	.247	.316	.381	225	4	.244	.325	.356	229	7	.249	.307	.406	244	5	.225	.291	.344	210	6	.271	.345	.424	108	4	.287	.331	.454	346	7	.234	.312	.358
TOTALS		1913	46	.254	.310	.392	970	20	.256	.312	.386	943	26	.252	.308	.398	887	25	.248	.307	.392	1026	21	.259	.313	.391	490	10	.263	.321	.382	1423	36	.251	.306	.395
■ **Derek Bell** BR/TR																																				
1991	Tor-A	28	0	.143	.314	.143	15	0	.067	.222	.067	13	0	.231	.412	.231	3	0	.000	.250	.000	25	0	.160	.323	.160	20	0	.150	.292	.150	8	0	.125	.364	.125
1992	Tor-A	161	2	.242	.324	.354	84	2	.167	.278	.298	77	0	.325	.376	.416	77	1	.195	.284	.273	84	1	.286	.362	.429	47	2	.255	.333	.489	114	0	.237	.320	.298
1993	SD-N	542	21	.262	.303	.417	274	12	.252	.309	.416	268	9	.272	.296	.418	277	13	.271	.318	.437	265	8	.253	.286	.396	177	11	.299	.342	.520	365	10	.244	.284	.367
1994	SD-N	434	14	.311	.354	.454	202	8	.317	.381	.480	232	6	.306	.329	.431	303	11	.297	.346	.452	131	3	.344	.374	.458	117	4	.299	.369	.427	317	10	.315	.348	.464
1995	Hou-N	452	8	.334	.385	.442	219	3	.306	.379	.374	233	5	.361	.390	.506	233	3	.343	.391	.442	219	5	.324	.379	.443	100	2	.410	.455	.510	352	6	.313	.365	.423
1996	Hou-N	627	17	.263	.311	.418	311	8	.260	.316	.431	316	9	.266	.307	.405	332	9	.289	.338	.455	295	8	.234	.281	.376	134	4	.284	.312	.470	493	13	.258	.311	.404
1997	Hou-N	493	15	.276	.344	.438	241	7	.295	.360	.473	252	8	.258	.329	.405	199	5	.251	.321	.387	294	10	.293	.359	.473	119	1	.235	.270	.311	374	14	.289	.366	.479
1998	Hou-N	630	22	.314	.364	.490	310	12	.335	.387	.526	320	10	.294	.342	.456	321	11	.330	.368	.508	309	11	.298	.360	.472	147	6	.347	.400	.571	483	16	.304	.353	.466
1999	Hou-N	509	12	.236	.306	.350	232	5	.224	.323	.319	277	7	.245	.291	.375	309	9	.243	.297	.366	200	3	.225	.320	.325	122	5	.303	.365	.475	387	7	.214	.288	.310
2000	NY-N	546	18	.266	.348	.425	257	8	.280	.395	.467	289	10	.232	.304	.388	292	9	.305	.389	.462	254	9	.220	.301	.382	109	0	.156	.258	.193	437	18	.293	.371	.483
TOTALS		4422	129	.279	.338	.425	2145	65	.280	.351	.431	2277	64	.278	.325	.420	2346	71	.288	.344	.435	2076	58	.269	.331	.414	1092	35	.288	.344	.441	3330	94	.276	.335	.420
■ **George Bell** BR/TR																																				
1981	Tor-A	163	5	.233	.256	.350	81	3	.247	.274	.370	82	2	.220	.238	.329	84	4	.238	.264	.393	79	1	.228	.247	.304	107	4	.280	.287	.421	56	1	.143	.200	.214
1983	Tor-A	112	2	.268	.305	.438	55	1	.327	.339	.545	57	1	.211	.274	.333	0	0	—	—	—	112	2	.268	.305	.438	96	2	.292	.333	.469	16	0	.125	.125	.250
1984	Tor-A	606	26	.292	.326	.498	294	12	.320	.353	.534	312	14	.266	.301	.465	280	9	.314	.350	.486	326	17	.273	.305	.509	210	11	.310	.348	.557	396	15	.283	.314	.467
1985	Tor-A	607	28	.275	.327	.479	286	10	.255	.321	.430	321	18	.293	.333	.523	290	14	.283	.323	.497	317	14	.268	.331	.464	214	11	.252	.314	.463	393	17	.288	.335	.489
1986	Tor-A	641	31	.309	.349	.532	300	15	.327	.375	.567	341	16	.293	.326	.501	302	14	.318	.355	.536	339	17	.301	.344	.528	179	10	.330	.363	.553	462	21	.301	.344	.524
1987	Tor-A	610	47	.308	.352	.605	302	19	.291	.346	.543	308	28	.325	.357	.666	294	27	.296	.328	.633	316	20	.320	.373	.579	175	16	.343	.385	.686	435	31	.294	.339	.572
1988	Tor-A	614	24	.269	.304	.446	304	9	.296	.329	.461	310	15	.242	.280	.432	297	9	.279	.312	.444	317	15	.259	.297	.448	196	10	.270	.296	.485	418	14	.268	.308	.428
1989	Tor-A	613	18	.297	.330	.458	281	8	.306	.350	.466	332	10	.289	.312	.452	290	9	.269	.310	.421	323	9	.322	.348	.492	178	9	.287	.323	.517	435	9	.301	.333	.434
1990	Tor-A	562	21	.265	.303	.422	274	11	.255	.299	.420	288	10	.274	.306	.424	306	17	.284	.324	.497	256	4	.242	.277	.332	149	5	.248	.315	.389	413	16	.271	.298	.433
1991	Chi-N	558	25	.285	.323	.468	288	9	.267	.294	.413	270	16	.304	.354	.526	279	15	.290	.329	.487	279	10	.280	.318	.448	208	15	.288	.341	.543	350	10	.283	.313	.423
1992	Chi-A	627	25	.255	.294	.418	326	16	.261	.293	.442	301	9	.249	.295	.392	287	10	.258	.294	.404	340	15	.253	.294	.429	142	7	.310	.355	.514	485	18	.239	.276	.390
1993	Chi-A	410	13	.217	.243	.363	201	7	.224	.249	.388	209	6	.211	.238	.340	294	6	.228	.255	.350	116	7	.190	.213	.397	109	3	.193	.217	.312	301	10	.226	.252	.382
TOTALS		6123	265	.278	.316	.469	2992	120	.282	.323	.468	3131	145	.274	.310	.470	3003	134	.281	.317	.474	3120	131	.275	.316	.465	1963	103	.286	.328	.504	4160	162	.274	.311	.453
■ **Jay Bell** BR/TR																																				
1986	Cle-A	14	1	.357	.438	.714	4	0	.250	.400	.500	10	1	.400	.455	.800	0	0	—	—	—	14	1	.357	.438	.714	9	0	.444	.545	.667	5	1	.200	.200	.800
1987	Cle-A	125	2	.216	.269	.352	63	1	.222	.300	.381	62	1	.210	.234	.323	0	0	—	—	—	125	2	.216	.269	.352	38	1	.289	.357	.500	87	1	.184	.228	.287
1988	Cle-A	211	2	.218	.289	.280	117	2	.197	.267	.291	94	0	.245	.317	.266	153	1	.196	.287	.242	58	1	.276	.295	.379	40	0	.350	.386	.425	171	2	.187	.267	.246
1989	Pit-N	271	2	.258	.307	.351	141	1	.255	.303	.340	130	1	.262	.312	.362	20	0	.050	.095	.050	251	2	.275	.324	.375	107	1	.271	.331	.355	164	1	.250	.291	.348
1990	Pit-N	583	7	.254	.329	.362	287	1	.261	.336	.348	296	6	.247	.321	.375	260	2	.269	.333	.392	323	5	.241	.325	.337	251	2	.275	.359	.382	332	5	.238	.305	.346
1991	Pit-N	608	16	.270	.330	.428	303	7	.281	.332	.446	305	9	.259	.327	.410	264	8	.269	.323	.439	344	8	.270	.335	.419	194	6	.289	.368	.500	414	10	.261	.311	.394
1992	Pit-N	632	9	.264	.326	.383	302	5	.278	.352	.411	330	4	.252	.301	.358	287	3	.251	.340	.341	345	6	.275	.313	.417	238	1	.324	.396	.450	394	8	.228	.282	.343
1993	Pit-N	604	9	.310	.392	.437	286	3	.322	.424	.441	318	6	.299	.362	.434	291	4	.316	.390	.450	313	5	.304	.394	.425	190	3	.342	.449	.484	414	6	.295	.364	.415
1994	Pit-N	424	9	.276	.353	.441	224	3	.277	.351	.415	200	6	.275	.355	.470	277	7	.249	.334	.419	147	2	.327	.389	.483	106	4	.377	.432	.660	318	5	.242	.327	.368
1995	Pit-N	530	13	.262	.336	.404	260	8	.227	.303	.377	270	5	.296	.367	.430	208	3	.221	.319	.298	322	10	.289	.347	.472	144	7	.306	.387	.535	386	6	.246	.316	.355
1996	Pit-N	527	13	.250	.323	.391	256	7	.258	.347	.410	271	6	.244	.299	.373	270	5	.230	.311	.367	257	8	.272	.334	.416	103	3	.233	.339	.340	424	10	.255	.318	.403
1997	KC-A	573	21	.291	.368	.461	275	10	.287	.368	.469	298	11	.295	.368	.453	280	13	.279	.366	.471	293	8	.304	.371	.451	173	4	.260	.330	.370	400	17	.305	.384	.500
1998	Ari-N	549	20	.251	.353	.432	277	11	.271	.372	.473	272	9	.232	.334	.390	298	11	.235	.332	.413	251	9	.271	.378	.454	145	4	.255	.370	.379	404	16	.250	.347	.450
1999	Ari-N	589	38	.289	.374	.557	293	21	.304	.383	.621	296	17	.274	.366	.493	297	22	.283	.370	.569	292	16	.295	.379	.545	168	12	.339	.479	.661	421	26	.268	.327	.515
2000	Ari-N	565	18	.267	.348	.437	286	9	.276	.354	.441	279	9	.258	.343	.434	291	9	.275	.372	.436	274	9	.259	.322	.438	147	6	.347	.430	.571	418	12	.239	.318	.390
TOTALS		6805	180	.269	.344	.421	3374	89	.272	.351	.432	3431	91	.265	.337	.411	3196	88	.258	.342	.411	3609	92	.278	.346	.431	2053	54	.303	.391	.472	4752	126	.254	.323	.400
■ **Albert Belle** BR/TR																																				
1989	Cle-A	218	7	.225	.269	.394	115	3	.243	.276	.391	103	4	.204	.261	.398	0	0	—	—	—	218	7	.225	.269	.394	58	3	.259	.308	.448	160	4	.213	.254	.375
1990	Cle-A	23	1	.174	.208	.304	13	1	.231	.286	.462	10	0	.100	.100	.100	23	1	.174	.208	.304	0	0	—	—	—	9	1	.222	.222	.556	14	0	.143	.200	.143
1991	Cle-A	461	28	.282	.323	.540	236	8	.254	.294	.419	225	20	.311	.352	.667	186	10	.258	.310	.495	275	18	.298	.331	.571	132	8	.288	.312	.568	329	20	.280	.327	.529
1992	Cle-A	585	34	.260	.320	.477	285	15	.267	.331	.481	300	19	.253	.310	.473	277	17	.264	.328	.491	308	17	.256	.314	.464	138	8	.254	.307	.500	447	26	.262	.325	.470
1993	Cle-A	594	38	.290	.370	.552	271	20	.306	.399	.583	323	18	.276	.344	.526	275	20	.291	.374	.593	319	18	.288	.366	.517	162	12	.327	.412	.617	432	26	.275	.353	.528
1994	Cle-A	412	36	.357	.438	.714	179	21	.413	.509	.894	233	15	.313	.381	.575	283	23	.371	.464	.721	129	13	.326	.376	.698	120	9	.367	.480	.675	292	27	.353	.419	.729
1995	Cle-A	546	50	.317	.401	.690	268	25	.328	.415	.720	278	25	.306	.387	.662	227	12	.308	.379	.581	319	38	.323	.416	.768	133	8	.293	.399	.571	413	42	.324	.401	.729
1996	Cle-A	602	48	.311	.410	.623	299	22	.291	.378	.599	303	26	.330	.440	.647	294	25	.306	.410	.626	308	23	.315	.410	.620	151	15	.318	.439	.675	451	33	.308	.400	.605
1997	Chi-A	634	30	.274	.332	.491	313	14	.294	.333	.495	321	16	.255	.331	.486	318	18	.289	.347	.525	316	12	.259	.317	.456	122	7	.295	.399	.525	512	23	.270	.315	.482
1998	Chi-A	609	49	.328	.399	.655	296	29	.348	.412	.733	313	20	.310	.388	.581	309	17	.275	.352	.511	300	32	.383	.448	.803	134	12	.313	.380	.679	475	37	.333	.405	.648
1999	Bal-A	610	37	.297	.400	.541	299	19	.304	.411	.559	311	18	.289	.390	.524	280	16	.279	.402	.479	330	21	.312	.398	.594	98	11	.367	.508	.776	512	26	.283	.377	.496
2000	Bal-A	559	23	.281	.342	.474	278	14	.273	.334	.493	281	9	.288	.350	.456	297	18	.310	.381	.566	262	5	.248	.297	.370	137	10	.343	.424	.650	422	13	.261	.315	.417
TOTALS		5853	381	.295	.369	.564	2852	191	.302	.375	.580	3001	190	.288	.364	.549	2769	177	.295	.377	.558	3084	204	.295	.363	.569	1394	104	.312	.401	.613	4459	277	.290	.359	.549
■ **Adrian Beltre** BR/TR																																				
1998	LA-N	195	7	.215	.278	.369	113	5	.186	.264	.354	82	2	.256	.299	.390	23	1	.174	.208	.348	172	6	.221	.287	.372	40	0	.175	.267	.225	155	7	.226	.281	.406
1999	LA-N	538	15	.275	.352	.428	266	6	.256	.332	.387	272	9	.294	.372	.467	251	7	.295	.375	.458	287	8	.258	.332	.401	135	1	.230	.329	.319	403	14	.290	.361	.464
2000	LA-N	510	20	.290	.360	.475	228	7	.281	.358	.430	282	13	.298	.362	.511	228	7	.259	.310	.430	282	13	.316	.398	.511	119	4	.277	.415	.412	391	16	.294	.341	.494
TOTALS		1243	42	.272	.344	.438	607	18	.252	.329	.397	636	24	.291	.359	.476	502	15	.273	.339	.440	741	27	.271	.348	.436	294	5	.241	.357	.344	949	37	.281	.340	.467
■ **Marvin Benard** BL/TL																																				
1995	SF-N	34	1	.382	.400	.529	10	0	.300	.300	.300	24	1	.417	.440	.625	0	0	—	—	—	34	1	.382	.400	.529	6	1	.167	.167	.667	28	0	.429	.448	.500
1996	SF-N	488	5	.248	.333	.330	257	2	.249	.342	.315	231	3	.247	.323	.346	207	0	.261	.328	.304	281	5	.238	.337	.349	69	0	.261	.338	.275	419	5	.246	.333	.339
1997	SF-N	114	1	.228	.315	.289	55	0	.200	.286	.218	59	1	.254	.343	.356	62	0	.258	.343	.274	52	1	.192	.283	.308	14	0	.214	.313	.214	100	1	.230	.316	.300
1998	SF-N	286	3	.322	.396	.434	143	2	.308	.379	.441	143	1	.336	.414	.427	87	1	.218	.313	.287	199	2	.367	.433	.497	38	0	.237	.348	.263	248	3	.335	.404	.460
1999	SF-N	562	16	.290	.359	.457	272	9	.294	.366	.471	290	7	.286	.352	.445	264	4	.288	.354	.424	298	12	.292	.363	.487	114	3	.263	.320	.386	448	13	.297	.369	.475
2000	SF-N	560	12	.262	.342	.396	275	6	.269	.362	.415	285	6	.256	.323	.379	265	5	.272	.349	.392	295	7	.254	.336	.400	102	1	.216	.283	.275	458	11	.273	.355	.424
TOTALS		2044	38	.275	.352	.399	1012	19	.273	.356	.396	1032	19	.277	.348	.401	885	10	.268	.341	.363	1159	28	.280	.359	.426	343	5	.242	.313	.315	1701	33	.282	.359	.416
■ **Todd Benzinger** BB/TR																																				
1987	Bos-A	223	8	.278	.344	.444	106	5	.311	.390	.528	117	3	.248	.299	.368	29	0	.310	.459	.345	194	8	.273	.324	.459	80	2	.325	.371	.450	143	6	.252	.329	.441
1988	Bos-A	405	13	.254	.293	.425	204	6	.270	.315	.446	201	7	.239	.270	.403	105	2	.238	.283	.371	300	11	.260	.297	.443	104	1	.212	.259	.308	301	12	.269	.305	.465
1989	Cin-N	628	17	.245	.293	.381	306	6	.278	.327	.418	322	11	.214	.261	.345	293	8	.246	.302	.379	335	9	.245	.286	.382	231	7	.242	.283	.377	397	10	.247	.299	.383
1990	Cin-N	376	5	.253	.291	.340	190	4	.258	.296	.374	186	1	.247	.285	.306	256	4	.285	.324	.383	120	1	.183	.216	.250	172	2	.285	.306	.360	204	3	.225	.279	.324
1991	Cin-N	123	1	.187	.244	.268	78	1	.167	.195	.256	45	0	.222	.321	.289	119	1	.185	.244	.269	4	0	.250	.250	.250	49	1	.224	.264	.327	74	0	.162	.232	.230
1991	KC-A	293	2	.294	.338	.386	138	1	.326	.367	.457	155	1	.265	.311	.323	0	0	—	—	—	293	2	.294	.338	.386	94	0	.266	.289	.309	199	2	.307	.359	.422

		TOTAL					HOME					AWAY					1ST HALF					2ND HALF					LEFT					RIGHT				
YEAR	TM/L	AB	HR	AVG	OBP	SLG	AB	HR	AVG	OBP	SLG	AB	HR	AVG	OBP	SLG	AB	HR	AVG	OBP	SLG	AB	HR	AVG	OBP	SLG	AB	HR	AVG	OBP	SLG	AB	HR	AVG	OBP	SLG
1992	LA-N	293	4	.239	.272	.348	143	1	.238	.275	.336	150	3	.240	.269	.360	177	2	.237	.266	.350	116	2	.241	.280	.345	126	1	.270	.282	.349	167	3	.216	.264	.347
1993	SF-N	177	6	.288	.332	.452	72	0	.194	.218	.222	105	6	.352	.409	.610	65	0	.246	.275	.292	112	6	.313	.363	.545	37	2	.486	.512	.730	140	4	.236	.280	.379
1994	SF-N	328	9	.265	.304	.399	155	5	.290	.343	.452	173	4	.243	.267	.353	253	7	.249	.286	.372	75	2	.320	.363	.493	98	1	.245	.292	.337	230	8	.274	.309	.426
1995	SF-N	10	1	.200	.308	.500	6	1	.333	.375	.833	4	0	.000	.200	.000	10	1	.200	.308	.500	0	0	—	—	—	4	1	.500	.400	1.250	6	0	.000	.250	.000
TOTALS		2856	66	.257	.301	.386	1398	30	.268	.314	.406	1458	36	.246	.288	.366	1307	25	.248	.295	.360	1549	41	.264	.306	.408	995	18	.268	.302	.373	1861	48	.250	.300	.393
■ **Dave Bergman** BL/TL																																				
1978	Hou-N	186	0	.231	.361	.269	87	0	.241	.370	.299	99	0	.222	.353	.242	39	0	.154	.320	.154	147	0	.252	.373	.299	24	0	.167	.286	.167	162	0	.241	.372	.284
1979	Hou-N	15	1	.400	.400	.600	5	0	.400	.400	.400	10	1	.400	.400	.700	0	0	—	—	—	15	1	.400	.400	.600	0	0	—	—	—	15	1	.400	.400	.600
1980	Hou-N	78	0	.256	.341	.359	38	0	.289	.357	.368	40	0	.225	.326	.350	36	0	.111	.200	.139	42	0	.381	.458	.548	10	0	.200	.200	.300	68	0	.265	.359	.368
1981	Hou-N	6	1	.167	.167	.667	4	0	.000	.000	.000	2	1	.500	.500	2.000	6	1	.167	.167	.667	0	0	—	—	—	0	0	—	—	—	6	1	.167	.167	.667
1981	SF-N	145	3	.255	.339	.379	77	1	.208	.326	.299	68	2	.309	.356	.471	67	1	.239	.333	.373	78	2	.269	.345	.385	7	0	.143	.143	.143	138	3	.261	.348	.391
1982	SF-N	121	4	.273	.364	.413	67	2	.269	.380	.373	54	2	.278	.344	.463	67	1	.269	.367	.358	54	3	.278	.361	.481	19	1	.211	.250	.474	102	3	.284	.383	.402
1983	SF-N	140	6	.286	.394	.457	59	3	.305	.414	.492	81	3	.272	.379	.432	54	1	.185	.333	.259	86	5	.349	.434	.581	12	1	.250	.357	.500	128	5	.289	.397	.453
1984	Det-A	271	7	.273	.351	.417	133	4	.248	.342	.414	138	3	.297	.361	.420	121	2	.289	.370	.405	150	5	.260	.337	.427	23	0	.217	.250	.217	248	7	.278	.360	.435
1985	Det-A	140	3	.179	.250	.257	78	2	.167	.221	.256	62	1	.194	.286	.258	35	1	.200	.326	.286	105	2	.171	.221	.248	5	0	.200	.333	.200	135	3	.178	.247	.259
1986	Det-A	130	1	.231	.338	.315	61	0	.213	.360	.295	69	1	.246	.316	.333	69	1	.275	.383	.391	61	0	.180	.286	.230	8	0	.250	.500	.625	122	1	.230	.324	.295
1987	Det-A	172	6	.273	.379	.453	85	4	.306	.394	.482	87	2	.241	.364	.425	68	4	.309	.448	.544	104	2	.250	.328	.394	19	0	.263	.263	.263	153	6	.275	.390	.477
1988	Det-A	289	5	.294	.372	.394	127	4	.283	.394	.425	162	1	.302	.352	.370	77	1	.299	.385	.403	212	4	.292	.367	.392	17	0	.235	.278	.294	272	5	.298	.377	.401
1989	Det-A	385	7	.268	.345	.361	173	6	.249	.325	.382	212	1	.283	.361	.344	160	2	.269	.355	.331	225	5	.267	.337	.382	60	0	.200	.250	.233	325	7	.280	.361	.385
1990	Det-A	205	2	.278	.375	.366	109	1	.248	.354	.367	96	1	.313	.398	.365	79	1	.228	.315	.304	126	1	.310	.412	.405	13	0	.231	.286	.385	192	2	.281	.381	.365
1991	Det-A	194	7	.237	.351	.407	87	2	.218	.346	.322	107	5	.252	.355	.477	67	1	.209	.325	.299	127	6	.252	.364	.465	19	0	.053	.182	.105	175	7	.257	.368	.440
1992	Det-A	181	1	.232	.305	.265	93	1	.204	.262	.247	88	0	.261	.350	.284	92	0	.228	.301	.250	89	1	.236	.310	.281	14	0	.143	.250	.214	167	1	.240	.310	.269
TOTALS		2658	54	.259	.350	.370	1283	30	.246	.344	.362	1375	24	.272	.355	.377	1037	17	.247	.348	.339	1621	37	.267	.352	.389	250	2	.196	.266	.272	2408	52	.266	.358	.380
■ **Tony Bernazard** BB/TR																																				
1979	Mon-N	40	1	.300	.500	.425	14	0	.143	.478	.214	26	1	.385	.515	.538	0	0	—	—	—	40	1	.300	.500	.425	10	0	.200	.500	.300	30	1	.333	.500	.467
1980	Mon-N	183	5	.224	.289	.355	84	2	.250	.323	.357	99	3	.202	.259	.354	118	2	.229	.295	.322	65	3	.215	.278	.415	40	0	.275	.370	.350	143	5	.210	.265	.357
1981	Chi-A	384	6	.276	.367	.380	172	3	.297	.393	.413	212	3	.259	.346	.354	200	3	.270	.326	.385	184	3	.283	.408	.375	87	1	.299	.351	.448	297	5	.269	.372	.360
1982	Chi-A	540	11	.256	.337	.396	241	1	.232	.322	.336	299	10	.274	.349	.445	287	4	.272	.342	.387	253	7	.237	.332	.407	173	2	.260	.343	.353	367	9	.253	.334	.417
1983	Chi-A	233	2	.262	.306	.373	104	2	.269	.322	.413	129	0	.256	.293	.341	233	2	.262	.306	.373	0	0	—	—	—	81	1	.296	.341	.420	152	1	.243	.287	.349
1983	Sea-A	300	6	.267	.351	.393	143	4	.301	.404	.462	157	2	.236	.298	.331	44	1	.295	.426	.386	256	5	.262	.337	.395	97	0	.278	.377	.299	203	6	.261	.338	.438
1984	Cle-A	439	2	.221	.290	.287	207	1	.246	.325	.343	232	1	.198	.257	.237	260	1	.227	.313	.273	179	1	.212	.254	.307	135	2	.237	.321	.341	304	0	.214	.275	.263
1985	Cle-A	500	11	.274	.361	.404	246	4	.301	.383	.431	254	7	.248	.339	.378	199	6	.281	.358	.447	301	5	.269	.362	.375	128	0	.258	.364	.313	372	11	.280	.359	.435
1986	Cle-A	562	17	.301	.362	.456	286	9	.329	.384	.486	276	8	.272	.341	.424	247	5	.312	.372	.441	315	12	.292	.355	.467	151	5	.338	.419	.510	411	12	.287	.341	.436
1987	Cle-A	293	11	.239	.300	.399	153	3	.229	.276	.346	140	8	.250	.325	.457	249	11	.229	.285	.406	44	0	.295	.380	.364	68	3	.250	.292	.441	225	8	.236	.302	.387
1987	Oak-A	214	3	.266	.354	.383	74	0	.257	.382	.324	140	3	.271	.338	.414	0	0	—	—	—	214	3	.266	.354	.383	71	1	.211	.349	.324	143	2	.294	.356	.413
1991	Det-A	12	0	.167	.167	.167	5	0	.200	.200	.200	7	0	.143	.143	.143	12	0	.167	.167	.167	0	0	—	—	—	1	0	1.000	1.000	1.000	11	0	.091	.091	.091
TOTALS		3700	75	.262	.339	.387	1729	29	.275	.356	.398	1971	46	.251	.323	.377	1849	35	.262	.328	.380	1851	40	.263	.349	.394	1042	15	.273	.358	.381	2658	60	.258	.331	.389
■ **Sean Berry** BR/TR																																				
1990	KC-A	23	0	.217	.280	.348	0	0	—	—	—	23	0	.217	.280	.348	0	0	—	—	—	23	0	.217	.280	.348	13	0	.231	.286	.385	10	0	.200	.273	.300
1991	KC-A	60	0	.133	.212	.183	22	0	.136	.240	.227	38	0	.132	.195	.158	14	0	.071	.133	.143	46	0	.152	.235	.196	30	0	.167	.219	.200	30	0	.100	.206	.167
1992	Mon-N	57	1	.333	.345	.404	22	0	.409	.435	.455	35	1	.286	.286	.371	0	0	—	—	—	57	1	.333	.345	.404	3	0	.667	.667	.667	54	1	.315	.327	.389
1993	Mon-N	299	14	.261	.348	.465	134	5	.261	.362	.410	165	9	.261	.335	.509	85	5	.247	.365	.447	214	9	.266	.340	.472	95	3	.232	.348	.379	204	11	.275	.347	.505
1994	Mon-N	320	11	.278	.347	.453	138	4	.283	.344	.457	182	7	.275	.350	.451	191	5	.262	.333	.408	129	6	.302	.368	.519	76	6	.316	.409	.579	244	5	.266	.327	.414
1995	Mon-N	314	14	.318	.367	.529	157	5	.268	.322	.414	157	9	.369	.411	.643	111	2	.234	.294	.333	203	12	.365	.409	.635	74	1	.284	.372	.405	240	13	.329	.365	.567
1996	Hou-N	431	17	.281	.328	.492	183	4	.262	.320	.404	248	13	.294	.333	.556	252	10	.282	.321	.480	179	7	.279	.337	.508	106	3	.264	.304	.453	325	14	.286	.335	.505
1997	Hou-N	301	8	.256	.318	.422	156	4	.256	.322	.429	145	4	.255	.313	.414	183	4	.224	.276	.344	118	4	.305	.377	.542	75	2	.240	.272	.387	226	6	.261	.332	.434
1998	Hou-N	299	13	.314	.387	.508	154	7	.331	.418	.552	145	6	.297	.352	.462	144	5	.243	.343	.396	155	8	.381	.430	.613	107	5	.383	.429	.598	192	8	.276	.365	.458
1999	Mil-A	259	2	.228	.281	.301	118	0	.229	.289	.271	141	2	.227	.275	.326	192	2	.245	.298	.333	67	0	.179	.233	.209	80	0	.175	.212	.250	179	2	.251	.311	.324
2000	Mil-A	46	1	.152	.220	.261	24	1	.208	.296	.375	22	0	.091	.130	.136	46	1	.152	.220	.261	0	0	—	—	—	21	1	.190	.190	.381	25	0	.120	.241	.160
2000	Bos-A	4	0	.000	.000	.000	4	0	.000	.000	.000	0	0	—	—	—	0	0	—	—	—	4	0	.000	.000	.000	4	0	.000	.000	.000	0	0	—	—	—
TOTALS		2413	81	.272	.334	.445	1112	30	.269	.339	.418	1301	51	.275	.330	.467	1218	34	.245	.311	.388	1195	47	.300	.358	.503	684	21	.266	.329	.427	1729	60	.275	.336	.452
■ **Dante Bichette** BR/TR																																				
1988	Cal-A	46	0	.261	.240	.304	21	0	.238	.227	.333	25	0	.280	.250	.280	0	0	—	—	—	46	0	.261	.240	.304	27	0	.296	.276	.370	19	0	.211	.190	.211
1989	Cal-A	138	3	.210	.240	.326	68	2	.206	.203	.338	70	1	.214	.273	.314	113	2	.195	.218	.310	25	1	.280	.333	.400	86	3	.221	.253	.395	52	0	.192	.218	.212
1990	Cal-A	349	15	.255	.292	.433	159	8	.258	.296	.447	190	7	.253	.289	.421	221	8	.244	.276	.407	128	7	.273	.319	.477	146	5	.274	.312	.445	203	10	.241	.278	.424
1991	Mil-A	445	15	.238	.272	.393	213	6	.249	.296	.399	232	9	.228	.249	.388	231	11	.225	.271	.411	214	4	.252	.274	.374	154	6	.253	.299	.429	291	9	.230	.257	.375
1992	Mil-A	387	5	.287	.318	.406	170	3	.241	.280	.371	217	2	.323	.348	.433	205	4	.322	.353	.478	182	1	.247	.277	.324	119	2	.286	.336	.437	268	3	.287	.309	.392
1993	Col-N	538	21	.310	.348	.526	260	11	.373	.408	.650	278	10	.252	.291	.410	265	8	.309	.352	.498	273	13	.311	.344	.553	119	4	.286	.346	.496	419	17	.317	.348	.535
1994	Col-N	484	27	.304	.334	.548	241	15	.353	.387	.614	243	12	.255	.281	.481	324	20	.315	.341	.568	160	7	.281	.320	.506	105	10	.400	.413	.848	379	17	.277	.313	.464
1995	Col-N	579	40	.340	.364	.620	302	31	.377	.397	.755	277	9	.300	.329	.473	239	9	.335	.360	.536	340	31	.344	.368	.679	149	14	.336	.377	.691	430	26	.342	.360	.595
1996	Col-N	633	31	.313	.359	.531	336	22	.366	.413	.646	297	9	.253	.296	.401	328	17	.348	.392	.585	305	14	.275	.323	.472	139	8	.353	.377	.612	494	23	.302	.354	.508
1997	Col-N	561	26	.308	.343	.510	301	20	.362	.393	.635	260	6	.246	.284	.365	295	12	.312	.343	.488	266	14	.305	.343	.534	133	8	.263	.303	.496	428	18	.322	.355	.514
1998	Col-N	662	22	.331	.357	.509	336	17	.381	.413	.619	326	5	.279	.297	.396	348	11	.336	.351	.511	314	11	.325	.363	.506	185	4	.292	.320	.400	477	18	.346	.371	.551
1999	Col-N	593	34	.298	.354	.541	318	20	.308	.363	.575	275	14	.287	.342	.502	287	16	.282	.328	.537	306	18	.314	.377	.546	166	8	.313	.380	.530	427	26	.293	.343	.546
2000	Cin-N	461	16	.295	.353	.466	226	11	.319	.381	.527	235	5	.272	.326	.409	276	12	.293	.350	.475	185	4	.297	.357	.454	99	4	.283	.385	.455	362	12	.298	.343	.470
2000	Bos-A	114	7	.289	.336	.518	72	4	.278	.316	.486	42	3	.310	.370	.571	0	0	—	—	—	114	7	.289	.336	.518	28	4	.321	.367	.786	86	3	.279	.326	.430
TOTALS		5990	262	.299	.337	.501	3023	170	.331	.369	.578	2967	92	.268	.303	.423	3132	130	.301	.336	.498	2858	132	.298	.337	.505	1655	80	.298	.342	.518	4335	182	.300	.335	.495
■ **Craig Biggio** BR/TR																																				
1988	Hou-N	123	3	.211	.254	.350	55	1	.164	.207	.291	68	2	.250	.292	.397	14	0	.071	.133	.071	109	3	.229	.270	.385	39	2	.231	.268	.385	84	1	.202	.247	.333
1989	Hou-N	443	13	.257	.336	.402	219	6	.233	.323	.379	224	7	.281	.349	.424	189	5	.265	.327	.402	254	8	.252	.342	.402	122	1	.270	.352	.336	321	12	.252	.330	.427
1990	Hou-N	555	4	.276	.342	.348	277	2	.274	.338	.343	278	2	.277	.345	.353	272	3	.279	.355	.346	283	1	.272	.328	.350	218	2	.229	.316	.294	337	2	.306	.359	.383
1991	Hou-N	546	4	.295	.358	.374	277	0	.343	.401	.437	269	4	.245	.313	.309	251	3	.323	.384	.402	295	1	.271	.335	.349	186	1	.274	.346	.366	360	3	.306	.364	.378
1992	Hou-N	613	6	.277	.378	.369	303	3	.281	.384	.386	310	3	.274	.373	.352	292	5	.284	.379	.404	321	1	.271	.378	.336	218	3	.275	.410	.372	395	3	.278	.359	.367
1993	Hou-N	610	21	.287	.373	.474	295	8	.285	.389	.444	315	13	.289	.358	.502	289	12	.263	.352	.474	321	9	.308	.392	.474	183	8	.295	.408	.508	427	13	.283	.357	.459
1994	Hou-N	437	6	.318	.411	.483	220	4	.332	.422	.514	217	2	.304	.398	.452	292	3	.301	.389	.445	145	3	.352	.453	.559	109	0	.294	.439	.422	328	6	.326	.400	.503
1995	Hou-N	553	22	.302	.406	.483	265	6	.275	.402	.411	288	16	.326	.411	.549	220	7	.273	.395	.441	333	15	.321	.414	.511	107	7	.383	.493	.626	446	15	.283	.384	.448
1996	Hou-N	605	15	.288	.386	.415	289	7	.277	.390	.401	316	8	.297	.383	.427	306	10	.288	.395	.444	299	5	.288	.376	.385	125	5	.328	.423	.520	480	10	.277	.376	.387
1997	Hou-N	619	22	.309	.415	.501	301	7	.306	.406	.488	318	15	.311	.424	.513	326	13	.310	.396	.509	293	9	.307	.435	.491	138	6	.326	.444	.543	481	16	.304	.407	.489
1998	Hou-N	646	20	.325	.403	.503	316	10	.326	.414	.484	330	10	.324	.392	.521	321	11	.330	.401	.523	325	9	.320	.405	.483	137	4	.343	.438	.518	509	16	.320	.393	.499
1999	Hou-N	639	16	.294	.386	.457	324	10	.284	.367	.460	315	6	.305	.404	.454	308	5	.279	.365	.429	331	11	.308	.405	.483	150	4	.307	.410	.513	489	12	.290	.378	.440
2000	Hou-N	377	8	.268	.388	.393	170	2	.259	.374	.371	207	6	.275	.399	.411	280	4	.257	.400	.361	97	4	.299	.349	.485	68	0	.235	.430	.294	309	8	.275	.377	.414
TOTALS		6766	160	.291	.381	.434	3311	66	.289	.383	.427	3455	94	.293	.379	.441	3360	81	.288	.379	.434	3406	79	.294	.382	.435	1800	43	.292	.400	.435	4966	117	.291	.374	.434
■ **Jeff Blauser** BR/TR																																				
1987	Atl-N	165	2	.242	.328	.352	78	1	.295	.382	.462	87	1	.195	.278	.253	0	0	—	—	—	165	2	.242	.328	.352	47	2	.277	.346	.511	118	0	.229	.321	.288
1988	Atl-N	67	2	.239	.268	.403	28	2	.286	.286	.571	39	0	.205	.256	.282	0	0	—	—	—	67	2	.239	.268	.403	26	1	.308	.321	.462	41	1	.195	.233	.366
1989	Atl-N	456	12	.270	.325	.410	229	5	.249	.308	.376	227	7	.291	.341	.445	172	3	.250	.284	.395	284	9	.282	.348	.419	197	4	.279	.342	.416	259	8	.263	.311	.405
1990	Atl-N	386	8	.269	.338	.409	172	3	.297	.373	.442	214	5	.248	.309	.383	165	4	.291	.357	.442	221	4	.253	.324	.385	136	3	.294	.373	.463	250	5	.256	.319	.380
1991	Atl-N	352	11	.259	.358	.409	174	7	.270	.382	.425	178	4	.247	.333	.393	166	5	.265	.367	.446	186	6	.253	.349	.376	128	4	.305	.416	.484	224	7	.232	.323	.366
1992	Atl-N	343	14	.262	.354	.458	162	5	.284	.380	.457	181	9	.243	.330	.459	146	3	.212	.273	.349	197	11	.299	.409	.558	142	9	.303	.402	.585	201	5	.234	.317	.368
1993	Atl-N	597	15	.305	.401	.436	282	4	.277	.396	.369	315	11	.330	.407	.495	274	5	.318	.423	.438	323	10	.294	.382	.433	145	5	.283	.374	.469	452	10	.312	.410	.425
1994	Atl-N	380	6	.258	.329	.382	187	3	.246	.316	.374	193	3	.269	.341	.389	251	4	.267	.330	.386	129	2	.240	.327	.372	116	1	.267	.326	.371	264	5	.254	.330	.386
1995	Atl-N	431	12	.211	.319	.341	203	7	.217	.324	.369	228	5	.206	.314	.316	224	8	.232	.344	.393	207	4	.188	.292	.285	84	1	.226	.383	.286	347	11	.207	.301	.354
1996	Atl-N	265	10	.245	.356	.419	152	4	.217	.333	.362	113	6	.283	.386	.496	214	10	.248	.344	.435	51	0	.235	.400	.353	67	3	.209	.354	.358	198	7	.258	.357	.439
1997	Atl-N	519	17	.308	.405	.482	255	9	.325	.425	.510	264	8	.292	.385	.455	259	11	.347	.442	.575	260	6	.269	.367	.388	125	7	.312	.417	.568	394	10	.307	.400	.454
1998	Chi-N	361	4	.219	.340	.299	187	0	.251	.360	.310	174	4	.184	.319	.287	245	1	.233	.344	.298	116	3	.190	.333	.302	100	2	.270	.387	.380	261	2	.199	.323	.268

YEAR	TM/L	TOTAL AB	HR	AVG	OBP	SLG	HOME AB	HR	AVG	OBP	SLG	AWAY AB	HR	AVG	OBP	SLG	1ST HALF AB	HR	AVG	OBP	SLG	2ND HALF AB	HR	AVG	OBP	SLG	LEFT AB	HR	AVG	OBP	SLG	RIGHT AB	HR	AVG	OBP	SLG
1999	Chi-N	200	9	.240	.347	.420	117	7	.222	.311	.436	83	2	.265	.396	.398	102	5	.265	.367	.471	98	4	.214	.328	.367	94	4	.266	.384	.436	106	5	.217	.315	.406
TOTALS		4522	122	.262	.354	.406	2226	57	.265	.360	.407	2296	65	.260	.347	.405	2218	59	.270	.359	.421	2304	63	.255	.348	.391	1407	46	.280	.376	.451	3115	76	.255	.343	.386
■ **Bruce Bochte** BL/TL																																				
1978	Sea-A	486	11	.263	.342	.395	250	8	.284	.368	.448	236	3	.242	.313	.339	285	5	.263	.331	.389	201	6	.264	.356	.403	130	1	.246	.327	.338	356	10	.270	.347	.416
1979	Sea-A	554	16	.316	.385	.493	281	11	.320	.386	.523	273	5	.311	.385	.462	276	9	.341	.404	.511	278	7	.291	.368	.475	166	4	.259	.321	.422	388	12	.340	.412	.523
1980	Sea-A	520	13	.300	.381	.456	251	10	.315	.405	.526	269	3	.286	.356	.390	246	6	.276	.354	.423	274	7	.321	.404	.485	164	5	.293	.352	.445	356	8	.303	.393	.461
1981	Sea-A	335	6	.260	.354	.361	174	4	.259	.374	.385	161	2	.261	.331	.335	172	2	.262	.342	.355	163	4	.258	.366	.368	79	3	.228	.291	.380	256	3	.270	.372	.355
1982	Sea-A	509	12	.297	.380	.409	242	7	.347	.438	.492	267	5	.251	.324	.333	249	5	.289	.386	.386	260	7	.304	.373	.431	182	3	.313	.377	.407	327	9	.287	.381	.410
1984	Oak-A	469	5	.264	.333	.345	223	1	.269	.356	.327	246	4	.260	.310	.362	232	3	.246	.326	.328	237	2	.283	.340	.363	112	0	.241	.277	.259	357	5	.272	.349	.373
1985	Oak-A	424	14	.295	.367	.439	204	6	.314	.378	.466	220	8	.277	.357	.414	172	3	.326	.396	.430	252	11	.274	.348	.444	54	4	.333	.438	.611	370	10	.289	.356	.414
1986	Oak-A	407	6	.256	.357	.337	198	3	.247	.362	.328	209	3	.263	.353	.344	204	5	.245	.349	.353	203	1	.266	.366	.320	49	0	.204	.278	.204	358	6	.263	.368	.355
TOTALS		3704	83	.283	.364	.409	1823	50	.297	.385	.444	1881	33	.270	.342	.375	1836	38	.282	.361	.400	1868	45	.285	.366	.418	936	20	.270	.336	.388	2768	63	.288	.373	.417
■ **Wade Boggs** BL/TR																																				
1982	Bos-A	338	5	.349	.406	.441	180	4	.356	.415	.500	158	1	.342	.395	.373	57	1	.316	.365	.421	281	4	.356	.414	.445	105	0	.333	.366	.371	233	5	.356	.423	.472
1983	Bos-A	582	5	.361	.444	.486	302	2	.397	.487	.550	280	3	.321	.398	.418	268	0	.362	.452	.463	314	5	.360	.438	.506	185	1	.281	.368	.351	397	4	.398	.479	.549
1984	Bos-A	625	6	.325	.407	.416	318	5	.352	.436	.472	307	1	.296	.376	.358	281	1	.292	.390	.363	344	5	.352	.421	.459	167	2	.240	.335	.293	458	4	.356	.433	.461
1985	Bos-A	653	8	.368	.450	.478	311	6	.418	.503	.566	342	2	.322	.401	.398	285	2	.333	.429	.428	368	6	.394	.468	.516	213	2	.347	.418	.441	440	6	.377	.465	.495
1986	Bos-A	580	8	.357	.453	.486	277	3	.357	.456	.495	303	5	.356	.450	.479	251	5	.382	.485	.526	329	3	.337	.427	.456	182	3	.352	.420	.489	398	5	.359	.467	.485
1987	Bos-A	551	24	.363	.461	.588	282	10	.411	.500	.638	269	14	.312	.421	.535	279	13	.391	.487	.624	272	11	.335	.435	.551	169	7	.331	.403	.544	382	17	.377	.484	.607
1988	Bos-A	584	5	.366	.476	.490	285	4	.382	.512	.547	299	1	.351	.438	.435	264	1	.348	.465	.451	320	4	.381	.485	.522	172	2	.331	.458	.453	412	3	.381	.483	.505
1989	Bos-A	621	3	.330	.430	.449	300	2	.377	.475	.547	321	1	.287	.386	.358	283	2	.325	.417	.466	338	1	.334	.441	.435	210	0	.295	.377	.352	411	3	.348	.455	.499
1990	Bos-A	619	6	.302	.386	.418	309	3	.359	.449	.492	310	3	.245	.320	.345	271	5	.295	.408	.439	348	1	.307	.367	.402	230	1	.274	.332	.365	389	5	.319	.415	.450
1991	Bos-A	546	8	.332	.421	.460	252	6	.389	.482	.587	294	2	.282	.368	.350	264	5	.311	.412	.447	282	3	.351	.430	.472	166	2	.265	.333	.361	380	6	.361	.456	.503
1992	Bos-A	514	7	.259	.353	.358	251	4	.243	.366	.367	263	3	.274	.339	.350	256	6	.262	.368	.395	258	1	.256	.338	.322	158	1	.272	.326	.367	356	6	.253	.364	.354
1993	NY-A	560	2	.302	.378	.363	271	1	.314	.383	.373	289	1	.291	.373	.353	277	1	.307	.376	.375	283	1	.297	.380	.350	168	1	.262	.323	.339	392	1	.319	.401	.372
1994	NY-A	366	11	.342	.433	.489	181	6	.359	.441	.514	185	5	.324	.425	.465	241	9	.332	.434	.494	125	2	.360	.431	.480	108	1	.315	.409	.380	258	10	.353	.443	.535
1995	NY-A	460	5	.324	.412	.422	253	4	.379	.459	.502	207	1	.256	.355	.324	180	2	.306	.397	.389	280	3	.336	.422	.443	132	1	.311	.397	.364	328	4	.329	.418	.445
1996	NY-A	501	2	.311	.389	.389	273	2	.330	.402	.414	228	0	.289	.374	.360	271	2	.339	.406	.421	230	0	.278	.370	.352	138	0	.268	.350	.319	363	2	.328	.404	.416
1997	NY-A	353	4	.292	.373	.397	157	0	.287	.367	.350	196	4	.296	.377	.434	191	2	.251	.360	.330	162	2	.340	.390	.475	72	1	.361	.418	.444	281	3	.274	.362	.384
1998	TB-A	435	7	.280	.348	.400	234	7	.252	.328	.389	201	0	.313	.371	.413	203	5	.281	.347	.424	232	2	.280	.349	.379	118	3	.254	.294	.373	317	4	.290	.367	.410
1999	TB-A	292	2	.301	.377	.377	154	1	.325	.383	.403	138	1	.275	.371	.348	162	1	.290	.350	.352	130	1	.315	.409	.408	47	1	.277	.320	.383	245	1	.306	.387	.376
TOTALS		9180	118	.328	.415	.443	4590	70	.354	.443	.491	4590	48	.302	.387	.395	4284	63	.321	.414	.439	4896	55	.334	.416	.446	2740	29	.297	.372	.389	6440	89	.341	.433	.466
■ **Barry Bonds** BL/TL																																				
1986	Pit-N	413	16	.223	.330	.416	211	9	.242	.355	.469	202	7	.203	.303	.361	120	6	.242	.364	.492	293	10	.215	.316	.386	151	3	.219	.348	.371	262	13	.225	.319	.443
1987	Pit-N	551	25	.261	.329	.492	268	12	.265	.324	.500	283	13	.258	.333	.484	279	12	.254	.329	.480	272	13	.268	.329	.504	206	8	.228	.303	.456	345	17	.281	.345	.513
1988	Pit-N	538	24	.283	.368	.491	256	14	.285	.374	.516	282	10	.280	.363	.468	289	14	.287	.361	.522	249	10	.277	.376	.454	162	9	.302	.383	.556	376	15	.274	.362	.463
1989	Pit-N	580	19	.248	.351	.426	280	7	.204	.309	.343	300	12	.290	.390	.503	292	10	.240	.348	.432	288	9	.257	.354	.420	178	4	.264	.371	.421	402	15	.241	.342	.428
1990	Pit-N	519	33	.301	.406	.565	239	14	.276	.401	.515	280	19	.321	.410	.607	232	13	.332	.416	.612	287	20	.275	.398	.526	240	17	.304	.386	.592	279	16	.297	.422	.541
1991	Pit-N	510	25	.292	.410	.514	261	12	.272	.384	.448	249	13	.313	.436	.582	224	10	.268	.386	.464	286	15	.311	.428	.552	201	7	.284	.385	.473	309	18	.298	.425	.540
1992	Pit-N	473	34	.311	.456	.624	210	15	.338	.498	.671	263	19	.289	.418	.586	205	15	.293	.434	.580	268	19	.325	.472	.657	222	13	.311	.445	.599	251	21	.311	.465	.645
1993	SF-N	539	46	.336	.458	.677	266	21	.312	.403	.613	273	25	.359	.507	.740	263	21	.354	.469	.696	276	25	.319	.448	.659	218	15	.326	.423	.619	321	31	.343	.481	.717
1994	SF-N	391	37	.312	.426	.647	195	15	.282	.410	.569	196	22	.342	.443	.724	255	21	.286	.416	.580	136	16	.360	.447	.772	117	11	.291	.400	.607	274	26	.321	.437	.664
1995	SF-N	506	33	.294	.431	.577	238	16	.307	.475	.605	268	17	.284	.389	.552	220	13	.309	.419	.577	286	20	.283	.441	.577	138	5	.268	.388	.478	368	28	.304	.447	.614
1996	SF-N	517	42	.308	.461	.615	242	23	.326	.489	.661	275	19	.291	.434	.575	294	21	.299	.420	.575	223	21	.318	.506	.668	150	12	.307	.398	.593	367	30	.308	.483	.624
1997	SF-N	532	40	.291	.446	.585	264	24	.326	.466	.678	268	16	.257	.428	.493	266	19	.278	.425	.549	266	21	.305	.467	.620	166	11	.295	.427	.584	366	29	.290	.455	.585
1998	SF-N	552	37	.303	.438	.609	246	21	.325	.473	.667	306	16	.284	.409	.562	287	17	.286	.431	.547	265	20	.321	.447	.675	168	9	.280	.418	.494	384	28	.313	.447	.659
1999	SF-N	355	34	.262	.389	.617	174	16	.247	.365	.586	181	18	.276	.413	.646	96	6	.281	.430	.531	259	28	.255	.374	.649	128	12	.266	.394	.594	227	22	.260	.387	.630
2000	SF-N	480	49	.306	.440	.688	243	25	.321	.449	.741	237	24	.291	.431	.633	241	28	.315	.444	.743	239	21	.297	.436	.632	148	12	.230	.320	.527	332	37	.340	.487	.759
TOTALS		7456	494	.289	.412	.567	3593	244	.289	.414	.569	3863	250	.290	.409	.565	3563	226	.289	.406	.560	3893	268	.289	.416	.574	2593	148	.280	.388	.532	4863	346	.294	.424	.586
■ **Bobby Bonilla** BB/TR																																				
1986	Chi-A	234	2	.269	.361	.355	108	2	.287	.381	.417	126	0	.254	.343	.302	200	2	.265	.365	.360	34	0	.294	.333	.324	93	0	.269	.330	.323	141	2	.270	.380	.376
1986	Pit-N	192	1	.240	.342	.307	92	0	.250	.349	.304	100	1	.230	.336	.310	1	0	.000	.500	.000	191	1	.241	.341	.309	89	0	.270	.375	.337	103	1	.214	.314	.282
1987	Pit-N	466	15	.300	.351	.481	223	7	.265	.327	.430	243	8	.333	.374	.527	184	3	.288	.327	.418	282	12	.309	.367	.521	234	7	.308	.345	.474	232	8	.293	.357	.487
1988	Pit-N	584	24	.274	.366	.476	286	9	.217	.320	.353	298	15	.329	.411	.594	288	17	.313	.394	.563	296	7	.236	.338	.392	212	6	.278	.366	.420	372	18	.272	.366	.508
1989	Pit-N	616	24	.281	.358	.490	296	13	.311	.393	.551	320	11	.253	.325	.434	288	9	.281	.353	.476	328	15	.280	.363	.503	221	8	.226	.310	.389	395	16	.311	.386	.547
1990	Pit-N	625	32	.280	.322	.518	310	13	.261	.295	.461	315	19	.298	.347	.575	284	17	.271	.303	.539	341	15	.287	.338	.501	280	14	.261	.303	.493	345	18	.296	.338	.539
1991	Pit-N	577	18	.302	.391	.492	285	9	.309	.408	.512	292	9	.295	.374	.473	249	7	.281	.371	.458	328	11	.317	.406	.518	232	14	.284	.349	.530	345	4	.313	.418	.467
1992	NY-N	438	19	.249	.348	.432	196	5	.214	.325	.347	242	14	.277	.367	.500	261	8	.264	.379	.421	177	11	.226	.297	.446	175	4	.240	.307	.349	263	15	.255	.373	.487
1993	NY-N	502	34	.265	.352	.522	240	18	.275	.341	.550	262	16	.256	.362	.496	286	18	.255	.329	.500	216	16	.278	.381	.551	155	10	.277	.325	.516	347	24	.259	.363	.524
1994	NY-N	403	20	.290	.374	.504	181	8	.293	.357	.481	222	12	.288	.387	.523	258	12	.302	.401	.516	145	8	.269	.321	.483	119	9	.261	.338	.538	284	11	.303	.388	.489
1995	NY-N	317	18	.325	.385	.599	153	7	.327	.366	.556	164	11	.323	.401	.640	227	12	.313	.373	.564	90	6	.356	.414	.689	87	4	.391	.455	.667	230	14	.300	.357	.574
1995	Bal-A	237	10	.333	.392	.544	125	7	.344	.397	.552	112	3	.321	.386	.536	0	0	—	—	—	237	10	.333	.392	.544	77	4	.338	.378	.545	160	6	.331	.398	.544
1996	Bal-A	595	28	.287	.363	.491	293	9	.276	.354	.444	302	19	.298	.372	.536	283	8	.283	.353	.420	312	20	.292	.372	.554	195	10	.303	.362	.528	400	18	.280	.363	.473
1997	Fla-N	562	17	.297	.378	.468	282	8	.312	.401	.479	280	9	.282	.354	.457	281	7	.313	.384	.488	281	10	.281	.373	.448	113	6	.372	.419	.602	449	11	.278	.368	.434
1998	Fla-N	97	4	.278	.355	.454	54	3	.241	.323	.444	43	1	.326	.396	.465	97	4	.278	.355	.454	0	0	—	—	—	17	2	.412	.444	.765	80	2	.250	.337	.387
1998	LA-N	236	7	.237	.315	.360	131	5	.267	.336	.412	105	2	.200	.289	.295	98	1	.173	.224	.235	138	6	.283	.374	.449	41	2	.220	.298	.366	195	5	.241	.318	.359
1999	NY-N	119	4	.160	.277	.303	48	2	.208	.264	.354	71	2	.127	.284	.268	105	4	.162	.268	.305	14	0	.143	.333	.286	31	2	.129	.270	.323	88	2	.170	.279	.295
2000	Atl-N	239	5	.255	.356	.397	120	4	.258	.360	.425	119	1	.252	.353	.370	143	3	.273	.373	.427	96	2	.229	.330	.354	43	1	.372	.438	.651	196	4	.230	.339	.342
TOTALS		7039	282	.280	.359	.475	3423	129	.277	.354	.460	3616	153	.283	.363	.489	3533	132	.278	.356	.466	3506	150	.282	.362	.484	2414	103	.283	.346	.476	4625	179	.279	.365	.474
■ **Barry Bonnell** BR/TR																																				
1978	Atl-N	304	1	.240	.287	.306	143	1	.238	.283	.315	161	0	.242	.291	.298	171	0	.222	.281	.275	133	1	.263	.295	.346	166	0	.241	.300	.301	138	1	.239	.271	.312
1979	Atl-N	375	12	.259	.311	.424	203	9	.291	.336	.473	172	3	.221	.282	.366	206	8	.257	.309	.437	169	4	.260	.313	.408	159	2	.226	.279	.340	216	10	.282	.335	.486
1980	Tor-A	463	13	.268	.322	.417	217	4	.295	.358	.401	246	9	.244	.289	.431	203	4	.251	.305	.384	260	9	.281	.336	.442	171	5	.304	.366	.450	292	8	.247	.295	.397
1981	Tor-A	227	4	.220	.262	.339	119	2	.202	.228	.336	108	2	.241	.299	.343	181	4	.238	.285	.381	46	0	.152	.170	.174	84	3	.345	.382	.583	143	1	.147	.192	.196
1982	Tor-A	437	6	.293	.342	.407	222	4	.252	.301	.383	215	2	.335	.384	.433	202	4	.337	.383	.475	235	2	.255	.307	.349	250	5	.320	.363	.480	187	1	.257	.316	.310
1983	Tor-A	377	10	.318	.369	.469	174	6	.339	.384	.529	203	4	.300	.356	.419	178	4	.309	.357	.444	199	6	.327	.379	.492	185	6	.357	.407	.541	192	4	.281	.332	.401
1984	Sea-A	363	8	.264	.315	.394	161	4	.261	.324	.391	202	4	.267	.308	.396	231	5	.273	.328	.407	132	3	.250	.293	.371	137	4	.314	.369	.482	226	4	.235	.282	.341
1985	Sea-A	111	1	.243	.282	.342	60	1	.217	.277	.383	51	0	.275	.288	.294	77	0	.234	.272	.286	34	1	.265	.306	.471	36	0	.278	.333	.389	75	1	.227	.256	.320
1986	Sea-A	51	0	.196	.208	.235	17	0	.176	.167	.235	34	0	.206	.229	.235	46	0	.152	.149	.196	5	0	.600	.667	.600	13	0	.154	.214	.154	38	0	.211	.205	.263
TOTALS		2708	55	.268	.317	.395	1316	31	.269	.319	.407	1392	24	.267	.315	.384	1495	29	.265	.315	.391	1213	26	.271	.320	.401	1201	25	.298	.350	.443	1507	30	.244	.290	.357
■ **Bret Boone** BR/TR																																				
1992	Sea-A	129	4	.194	.224	.318	56	2	.250	.276	.429	73	2	.151	.184	.233	0	0	—	—	—	129	4	.194	.224	.318	40	0	.150	.190	.175	89	4	.213	.239	.382
1993	Sea-A	271	12	.251	.301	.443	135	7	.259	.301	.489	136	5	.243	.300	.397	51	2	.235	.310	.392	220	10	.255	.298	.455	79	4	.266	.337	.494	192	8	.245	.285	.422
1994	Cin-N	381	12	.320	.368	.491	195	5	.323	.369	.477	186	7	.317	.366	.505	249	5	.321	.366	.454	132	7	.318	.371	.561	89	2	.270	.316	.416	292	10	.336	.383	.514
1995	Cin-N	513	15	.267	.326	.429	244	6	.225	.306	.369	269	9	.305	.345	.483	223	4	.274	.328	.381	290	11	.262	.324	.466	123	4	.252	.293	.439	390	11	.272	.336	.426
1996	Cin-N	520	12	.233	.275	.354	242	7	.244	.301	.405	278	5	.223	.253	.309	210	8	.233	.277	.405	310	4	.232	.274	.319	117	6	.231	.303	.444	403	6	.233	.267	.328
1997	Cin-N	443	7	.223	.298	.332	223	4	.247	.317	.354	220	3	.200	.278	.309	202	2	.198	.286	.277	241	5	.245	.308	.378	100	0	.210	.328	.290	343	7	.227	.288	.344
1998	Cin-N	583	24	.266	.324	.458	293	13	.263	.323	.471	290	11	.269	.325	.445	317	10	.287	.331	.467	266	14	.241	.315	.447	135	4	.230	.291	.370	448	20	.277	.334	.484
1999	Atl-N	608	20	.252	.310	.416	292	9	.271	.329	.425	316	11	.234	.292	.408	306	8	.252	.318	.389	302	12	.252	.302	.444	164	5	.280	.339	.445	444	15	.241	.299	.405
2000	SD-N	463	19	.251	.326	.421	223	8	.238	.312	.395	240	11	.262	.338	.446	286	13	.259	.323	.444	177	6	.237	.330	.384	132	5	.235	.318	.394	331	14	.257	.329	.432
TOTALS		3911	125	.255	.312	.413	1903	61	.257	.319	.420	2008	64	.252	.306	.405	1844	52	.262	.320	.408	2067	73	.248	.305	.417	979	30	.243	.310	.401	2932	95	.259	.313	.416
■ **Bob Boone** BR/TR																																				
1978	Phi-N	435	12	.283	.347	.425	227	8	.286	.352	.454	208	4	.279	.342	.394	190	6	.253	.327	.405	245	6	.306	.363	.441	112	3	.295	.357	.482	323	9	.279	.343	.406
1979	Phi-N	398	9	.286	.367	.422	187	4	.289	.387	.433	211	5	.284	.348	.412	200	5	.270	.355	.425	198	4	.303	.378	.419	114	2	.342	.419	.491	284	7	.264	.346	.394
1980	Phi-N	480	9	.229	.299	.338	234	5	.244	.331	.380	246	4	.215	.268	.297	233	5	.223	.283	.348	247	4	.235	.314	.328	96	0	.219	.306	.313	384	9	.232	.298	.344

YEAR	TM/L	TOTAL AB	HR	AVG	OBP	SLG	HOME AB	HR	AVG	OBP	SLG	AWAY AB	HR	AVG	OBP	SLG	1ST HALF AB	HR	AVG	OBP	SLG	2ND HALF AB	HR	AVG	OBP	SLG	LEFT AB	HR	AVG	OBP	SLG	RIGHT AB	HR	AVG	OBP	SLG
1981	Phi-N	227	4	.211	.279	.295	112	2	.188	.273	.268	115	2	.235	.285	.322	153	3	.235	.300	.333	74	1	.162	.235	.216	36	0	.139	.311	.167	191	4	.225	.272	.319
1982	Cal-A	472	7	.256	.310	.337	224	5	.263	.335	.362	248	2	.250	.287	.315	212	1	.292	.348	.349	260	6	.227	.279	.327	148	3	.284	.348	.372	324	4	.244	.293	.321
1983	Cal-A	468	9	.256	.289	.353	227	6	.264	.302	.388	241	3	.249	.276	.320	230	3	.257	.286	.339	238	6	.256	.291	.366	171	4	.199	.243	.287	297	5	.290	.315	.391
1984	Cal-A	450	3	.202	.242	.262	220	1	.200	.250	.250	230	2	.204	.234	.274	220	0	.191	.225	.259	230	3	.213	.258	.265	159	0	.176	.222	.214	291	3	.216	.252	.289
1985	Cal-A	460	5	.248	.306	.317	221	0	.235	.305	.258	239	5	.259	.306	.372	201	3	.269	.333	.338	259	2	.232	.284	.301	135	1	.259	.331	.326	325	4	.243	.295	.314
1986	Cal-A	442	7	.222	.287	.305	212	1	.189	.264	.250	230	6	.252	.310	.357	216	3	.204	.266	.269	226	4	.239	.307	.341	152	2	.217	.292	.276	290	5	.224	.284	.321
1987	Cal-A	389	3	.242	.304	.311	186	1	.242	.316	.296	203	2	.241	.292	.325	144	1	.264	.346	.326	245	2	.229	.278	.302	134	0	.284	.333	.321	255	3	.220	.288	.306
1988	Cal-A	352	5	.295	.352	.386	177	3	.282	.339	.390	175	2	.309	.366	.383	163	2	.264	.310	.344	189	3	.323	.388	.423	140	1	.264	.318	.336	212	4	.316	.375	.420
1989	KC-A	405	1	.274	.351	.323	199	1	.317	.392	.372	206	0	.233	.312	.277	200	1	.295	.360	.370	205	0	.254	.343	.278	97	0	.289	.408	.330	308	1	.269	.331	.321
1990	KC-A	117	0	.239	.336	.265	69	0	.290	.380	.333	48	0	.167	.273	.167	66	0	.242	.333	.288	51	0	.235	.339	.235	40	0	.250	.348	.275	77	0	.234	.330	.260
TOTALS		5095	74	.250	.312	.338	2495	37	.253	.323	.344	2600	37	.248	.300	.333	2428	33	.250	.311	.340	2667	41	.251	.313	.337	1534	16	.250	.320	.328	3561	58	.251	.308	.343
■ **Mike Bordick** BR/TR																																				
1990	Oak-A	14	0	.071	.133	.071	5	0	.000	.000	.000	9	0	.111	.200	.111	6	0	.000	.000	.000	8	0	.125	.222	.125	6	0	.000	.000	.000	8	0	.125	.222	.125
1991	Oak-A	235	0	.238	.289	.268	106	0	.226	.287	.264	129	0	.248	.290	.271	10	0	.200	.200	.300	225	0	.240	.292	.267	58	0	.224	.274	.241	177	0	.243	.293	.277
1992	Oak-A	504	3	.300	.358	.371	240	3	.296	.360	.396	264	0	.303	.357	.348	242	2	.314	.364	.384	262	1	.286	.354	.359	131	1	.336	.393	.427	373	2	.287	.346	.351
1993	Oak-A	546	3	.249	.332	.311	280	2	.250	.324	.314	266	1	.248	.341	.308	238	2	.256	.349	.332	308	1	.244	.319	.295	162	1	.265	.351	.346	384	2	.242	.324	.297
1994	Oak-A	391	2	.253	.320	.335	191	1	.230	.309	.335	200	1	.275	.332	.335	263	1	.266	.340	.357	128	1	.227	.279	.289	135	1	.252	.333	.348	256	1	.254	.313	.328
1995	Oak-A	428	8	.264	.325	.350	204	2	.270	.329	.324	224	6	.259	.321	.375	149	2	.275	.349	.342	279	6	.258	.311	.355	109	2	.239	.298	.303	319	6	.273	.334	.367
1996	Oak-A	525	5	.240	.307	.318	260	2	.262	.333	.335	265	3	.219	.281	.302	256	2	.223	.297	.297	269	3	.257	.317	.338	137	1	.226	.287	.292	388	4	.245	.314	.327
1997	Bal-A	509	7	.236	.283	.318	231	5	.229	.274	.333	278	2	.241	.290	.306	270	3	.219	.269	.289	239	4	.255	.298	.351	154	1	.195	.233	.234	355	6	.254	.304	.355
1998	Bal-A	465	13	.260	.328	.411	225	10	.267	.328	.458	240	3	.254	.328	.367	230	5	.261	.321	.383	235	8	.260	.335	.438	114	4	.184	.256	.360	351	9	.285	.352	.427
1999	Bal-A	631	10	.277	.334	.403	302	3	.248	.304	.361	329	7	.304	.363	.441	301	6	.282	.328	.399	330	4	.273	.340	.406	107	3	.402	.472	.570	524	7	.252	.304	.368
2000	Bal-A	391	16	.297	.350	.481	174	6	.282	.350	.425	217	10	.309	.350	.525	298	13	.292	.341	.483	93	3	.312	.379	.473	117	4	.299	.344	.479	274	12	.296	.353	.482
2000	NY-N	192	4	.260	.321	.365	96	3	.281	.310	.417	96	1	.240	.330	.313	0	0	—	—	—	192	4	.260	.321	.365	36	1	.333	.429	.556	156	3	.244	.293	.321
TOTALS		4831	71	.262	.324	.359	2314	37	.258	.320	.359	2517	34	.265	.327	.359	2263	36	.264	.326	.365	2568	35	.259	.322	.354	1266	19	.262	.327	.363	3565	52	.261	.322	.357
■ **Daryl Boston** BL/TL																																				
1984	Chi-A	83	0	.169	.207	.229	43	0	.163	.217	.256	40	0	.175	.195	.200	24	0	.250	.280	.375	59	0	.136	.177	.169	17	0	.059	.111	.059	66	0	.197	.232	.273
1985	Chi-A	232	3	.228	.271	.332	97	1	.175	.214	.237	135	2	.267	.313	.400	163	3	.215	.264	.331	69	0	.261	.288	.333	17	0	.118	.211	.118	215	3	.237	.276	.349
1986	Chi-A	199	5	.266	.335	.427	97	1	.309	.393	.454	102	4	.225	.275	.402	0	0	—	—	—	199	5	.266	.335	.427	48	1	.250	.333	.417	151	4	.272	.335	.430
1987	Chi-A	337	10	.258	.307	.421	168	5	.321	.365	.488	169	5	.195	.250	.355	221	8	.235	.298	.403	116	2	.302	.325	.457	59	0	.305	.311	.373	278	10	.248	.306	.432
1988	Chi-A	281	15	.217	.271	.434	138	6	.181	.231	.362	143	9	.252	.308	.503	110	7	.200	.241	.464	171	8	.228	.289	.415	28	0	.250	.241	.393	253	15	.213	.274	.439
1989	Chi-A	218	5	.252	.325	.372	114	3	.289	.339	.447	104	2	.212	.311	.288	83	2	.229	.286	.349	135	3	.267	.349	.385	27	0	.111	.107	.185	191	5	.272	.353	.398
1990	Chi-A	1	0	.000	.000	.000	1	0	.000	.000	.000	0	0	—	—	—	1	0	.000	.000	.000	0	0	—	—	—	0	0	—	—	—	1	0	.000	.000	.000
1990	NY-N	366	12	.273	.328	.440	185	4	.270	.328	.411	181	8	.276	.328	.470	132	5	.280	.354	.492	234	7	.269	.313	.410	60	0	.250	.328	.283	306	12	.278	.328	.471
1991	NY-N	255	4	.275	.350	.416	135	2	.244	.338	.400	120	2	.308	.364	.433	97	0	.227	.286	.340	158	4	.304	.387	.462	31	1	.194	.194	.387	224	3	.286	.369	.420
1992	NY-N	289	11	.249	.338	.426	140	5	.229	.311	.386	149	6	.268	.364	.463	138	5	.246	.323	.420	151	6	.252	.352	.430	47	1	.319	.407	.447	242	10	.236	.325	.421
1993	Col-N	291	14	.261	.325	.464	136	3	.279	.359	.412	155	11	.245	.293	.510	140	5	.236	.327	.386	151	9	.285	.323	.536	13	1	.231	.286	.462	278	13	.263	.327	.464
1994	NY-A	77	4	.182	.250	.364	43	2	.116	.208	.256	34	2	.265	.306	.500	60	4	.217	.277	.450	17	0	.059	.158	.059	1	0	.000	.000	.000	76	4	.184	.253	.368
TOTALS		2629	83	.249	.312	.410	1297	32	.250	.315	.395	1332	51	.248	.308	.426	1169	39	.234	.298	.401	1460	44	.262	.323	.418	348	4	.236	.285	.336	2281	79	.251	.316	.422
■ **Larry Bowa** BB/TR																																				
1978	Phi-N	654	3	.294	.319	.370	326	1	.328	.359	.417	328	2	.259	.278	.323	293	1	.317	.340	.379	361	2	.274	.301	.363	186	2	.280	.293	.366	468	1	.299	.329	.372
1979	Phi-N	539	0	.241	.316	.314	266	0	.233	.322	.301	273	0	.249	.310	.326	243	0	.280	.338	.354	296	0	.209	.299	.280	142	0	.239	.302	.352	397	0	.242	.321	.300
1980	Phi-N	540	2	.267	.300	.322	271	1	.244	.279	.314	269	1	.290	.322	.331	229	1	.262	.280	.336	311	1	.270	.314	.312	115	0	.296	.317	.374	425	2	.259	.296	.308
1981	Phi-N	360	0	.283	.331	.339	186	0	.317	.363	.376	174	0	.247	.296	.299	198	0	.268	.301	.293	162	0	.302	.365	.395	64	0	.250	.279	.359	296	0	.291	.342	.334
1982	Chi-N	499	0	.246	.302	.305	247	0	.263	.317	.324	252	0	.230	.287	.286	260	0	.250	.300	.315	239	0	.243	.304	.293	115	0	.287	.333	.365	384	0	.234	.293	.286
1983	Chi-N	499	2	.267	.312	.339	240	1	.262	.317	.346	259	1	.270	.308	.332	251	2	.251	.300	.335	248	0	.282	.325	.343	128	2	.320	.348	.477	371	0	.248	.300	.291
1984	Chi-N	391	0	.223	.274	.269	196	0	.224	.271	.265	195	0	.221	.276	.272	212	0	.236	.288	.297	179	0	.207	.257	.235	122	0	.287	.315	.361	269	0	.193	.256	.227
1985	Chi-N	195	0	.246	.285	.318	99	0	.293	.340	.394	96	0	.198	.228	.240	99	0	.192	.229	.222	96	0	.302	.343	.417	68	0	.250	.278	.338	127	0	.244	.289	.307
1985	NY-N	19	0	.105	.190	.158	8	0	.125	.125	.125	11	0	.091	.231	.182	0	0	—	—	—	19	0	.105	.190	.158	12	0	.167	.231	.250	7	0	.000	.125	.000
TOTALS		3696	7	.260	.306	.324	1839	3	.270	.320	.340	1857	4	.250	.293	.308	1785	4	.264	.304	.327	1911	3	.256	.309	.322	952	4	.277	.310	.375	2744	3	.254	.305	.306
■ **Phil Bradley** BR/TR																																				
1983	Sea-A	67	0	.269	.342	.299	29	0	.207	.303	.207	38	0	.316	.372	.368	0	0	—	—	—	67	0	.269	.342	.299	36	0	.222	.275	.250	31	0	.323	.417	.355
1984	Sea-A	322	0	.301	.373	.363	163	0	.331	.404	.417	159	0	.270	.341	.308	147	0	.245	.331	.286	175	0	.349	.409	.429	112	0	.205	.270	.277	210	0	.352	.426	.410
1985	Sea-A	641	26	.300	.365	.498	321	15	.305	.376	.526	320	11	.294	.353	.469	294	11	.320	.380	.527	347	15	.282	.352	.473	176	9	.267	.337	.483	465	17	.312	.375	.503
1986	Sea-A	526	12	.310	.405	.445	287	5	.324	.417	.467	239	7	.293	.390	.418	228	6	.259	.357	.404	298	6	.349	.440	.477	126	2	.325	.418	.421	400	10	.305	.400	.452
1987	Sea-A	603	14	.297	.387	.463	304	12	.309	.398	.520	299	2	.284	.376	.405	279	5	.265	.377	.437	324	9	.324	.396	.485	176	11	.347	.426	.642	427	3	.276	.371	.389
1988	Phi-N	569	11	.264	.341	.392	284	8	.268	.339	.423	285	3	.260	.344	.361	270	2	.226	.321	.307	299	9	.298	.360	.468	169	4	.272	.342	.420	400	7	.260	.341	.380
1989	Bal-A	545	11	.277	.364	.417	255	3	.286	.378	.400	290	8	.269	.352	.431	258	4	.279	.370	.415	287	7	.275	.359	.418	192	8	.297	.379	.531	353	3	.266	.356	.354
1990	Bal-A	289	4	.270	.352	.349	142	4	.268	.348	.394	147	0	.272	.355	.306	223	1	.274	.358	.332	66	3	.258	.329	.409	95	2	.242	.314	.368	194	2	.284	.369	.340
1990	Chi-A	133	0	.226	.344	.278	48	0	.146	.305	.188	85	0	.271	.367	.329	0	0	—	—	—	133	0	.226	.344	.278	66	0	.227	.370	.303	67	0	.224	.316	.254
TOTALS		3695	78	.286	.369	.421	1833	47	.294	.378	.448	1862	31	.279	.360	.395	1699	29	.269	.358	.397	1996	49	.301	.378	.442	1148	36	.280	.360	.452	2547	42	.289	.373	.408
■ **Sid Bream** BL/TL																																				
1983	LA-N	11	0	.182	.308	.182	7	0	.286	.375	.286	4	0	.000	.200	.000	0	0	—	—	—	11	0	.182	.308	.182	0	0	—	—	—	11	0	.182	.308	.182
1984	LA-N	49	0	.184	.263	.245	25	0	.160	.214	.200	24	0	.208	.310	.292	0	0	—	—	—	49	0	.184	.263	.245	2	0	.000	.000	.000	47	0	.191	.273	.255
1985	LA-N	53	3	.132	.230	.302	24	2	.167	.250	.417	29	1	.103	.212	.207	52	3	.135	.233	.308	1	0	.000	.000	.000	18	1	.056	.150	.222	35	2	.171	.268	.343
1985	Pit-N	95	3	.284	.355	.453	32	0	.250	.342	.313	63	3	.302	.362	.524	0	0	—	—	—	95	3	.284	.355	.453	23	0	.261	.320	.261	72	3	.292	.366	.514
1986	Pit-N	522	16	.268	.341	.450	262	5	.282	.348	.450	260	11	.254	.333	.450	235	10	.264	.362	.489	287	6	.272	.322	.418	152	2	.224	.268	.349	370	14	.286	.370	.492
1987	Pit-N	516	13	.275	.336	.411	259	10	.282	.347	.467	257	3	.268	.324	.354	243	9	.288	.356	.469	273	4	.264	.318	.359	193	8	.275	.314	.456	323	5	.276	.348	.384
1988	Pit-N	462	10	.264	.328	.409	226	6	.235	.292	.425	236	4	.292	.362	.394	214	7	.304	.343	.509	248	3	.230	.316	.323	116	3	.190	.220	.319	346	7	.289	.362	.439
1989	Pit-N	36	0	.222	.417	.306	8	0	.375	.615	.375	28	0	.179	.343	.286	36	0	.222	.417	.306	0	0	—	—	—	10	0	.300	.500	.500	26	0	.192	.382	.231
1990	Pit-N	389	15	.270	.349	.455	181	8	.276	.356	.481	208	7	.264	.343	.433	169	5	.278	.344	.432	220	10	.264	.353	.473	96	2	.260	.308	.427	293	13	.273	.362	.464
1991	Atl-N	265	11	.253	.313	.423	115	3	.270	.310	.391	150	8	.240	.315	.447	178	9	.287	.333	.500	87	2	.184	.273	.264	40	1	.150	.150	.225	225	10	.271	.339	.458
1992	Atl-N	372	10	.261	.340	.414	178	4	.264	.353	.393	194	6	.258	.329	.433	165	2	.242	.344	.358	207	8	.275	.338	.459	33	1	.242	.265	.455	339	9	.263	.347	.410
1993	Atl-N	277	9	.260	.332	.415	125	5	.232	.309	.392	152	4	.283	.351	.434	211	6	.251	.321	.398	66	3	.288	.368	.470	29	0	.276	.290	.379	248	9	.258	.337	.419
1994	Hou-N	61	0	.344	.429	.426	33	0	.485	.541	.606	28	0	.179	.303	.214	33	0	.394	.500	.545	28	0	.286	.333	.286	6	0	.167	.375	.167	55	0	.364	.435	.455
TOTALS		3108	90	.264	.336	.420	1475	43	.267	.337	.431	1633	47	.260	.335	.409	1536	51	.271	.346	.448	1572	39	.256	.326	.392	718	18	.233	.276	.376	2390	72	.273	.353	.433
■ **George Brett** BL/TR																																				
1978	KC-A	510	9	.294	.342	.467	261	4	.352	.395	.563	249	5	.233	.286	.365	235	4	.311	.357	.506	275	5	.280	.330	.433	149	1	.255	.305	.356	361	8	.310	.358	.512
1979	KC-A	645	23	.329	.376	.563	324	11	.373	.423	.633	321	12	.283	.327	.492	328	9	.329	.386	.543	317	14	.328	.365	.584	191	4	.272	.327	.435	454	19	.352	.396	.617
1980	KC-A	449	24	.390	.454	.664	235	13	.391	.450	.685	214	11	.388	.459	.640	169	8	.337	.407	.609	280	16	.421	.482	.696	179	8	.318	.359	.531	270	16	.437	.512	.752
1981	KC-A	347	6	.314	.361	.484	159	2	.333	.374	.516	188	4	.298	.351	.457	155	1	.323	.365	.452	192	5	.307	.358	.510	136	1	.309	.342	.441	211	5	.318	.373	.512
1982	KC-A	552	21	.301	.378	.505	275	9	.273	.359	.451	277	12	.329	.398	.560	265	10	.317	.397	.528	287	11	.286	.361	.484	203	5	.271	.324	.409	349	16	.318	.408	.562
1983	KC-A	464	25	.310	.385	.563	200	7	.315	.400	.535	264	18	.307	.373	.583	168	12	.363	.449	.685	296	13	.280	.347	.493	156	6	.237	.298	.397	308	19	.347	.427	.646
1984	KC-A	377	13	.284	.344	.459	172	6	.314	.385	.506	205	7	.259	.308	.420	144	6	.285	.362	.486	233	7	.283	.332	.442	137	8	.270	.325	.496	240	5	.292	.354	.438
1985	KC-A	550	30	.335	.436	.585	285	15	.368	.469	.628	265	15	.298	.400	.540	236	8	.322	.428	.517	314	22	.344	.442	.637	191	10	.330	.395	.550	359	20	.337	.456	.604
1986	KC-A	441	16	.290	.401	.481	205	8	.322	.418	.556	236	8	.263	.386	.415	264	8	.288	.422	.447	177	8	.294	.365	.531	148	5	.243	.329	.385	293	11	.314	.435	.529
1987	KC-A	427	22	.290	.388	.496	231	14	.268	.364	.494	196	8	.316	.415	.500	101	5	.317	.421	.545	326	17	.282	.377	.482	149	7	.268	.317	.430	278	15	.302	.422	.532
1988	KC-A	589	24	.306	.389	.509	290	13	.293	.377	.500	299	11	.318	.401	.518	288	13	.330	.408	.566	301	11	.282	.371	.455	198	10	.313	.379	.530	391	14	.302	.394	.499
1989	KC-A	457	12	.282	.362	.431	229	3	.275	.363	.389	228	9	.289	.360	.474	156	3	.231	.311	.340	301	9	.309	.388	.478	167	2	.222	.296	.323	290	10	.317	.398	.493
1990	KC-A	544	14	.329	.387	.515	288	3	.319	.373	.448	256	11	.340	.403	.590	234	1	.256	.331	.325	310	13	.384	.431	.658	187	5	.316	.366	.487	357	9	.336	.398	.529
1991	KC-A	505	10	.255	.327	.402	243	3	.247	.326	.379	262	7	.263	.329	.424	181	2	.249	.320	.359	324	8	.259	.332	.426	167	2	.234	.309	.353	338	8	.266	.337	.426
1992	KC-A	592	7	.285	.330	.397	312	1	.288	.328	.378	280	6	.282	.331	.418	251	3	.259	.319	.386	341	4	.305	.338	.405	184	0	.277	.320	.348	408	7	.289	.334	.419
1993	KC-A	560	19	.266	.312	.434	275	7	.269	.313	.429	285	12	.263	.311	.439	273	7	.256	.300	.396	287	12	.275	.324	.470	187	2	.209	.246	.299	373	17	.295	.344	.501
TOTALS		8009	275	.304	.374	.497	3984	119	.313	.383	.505	4025	156	.295	.365	.490	3448	100	.298	.374	.479	4561	175	.308	.373	.511	2729	76	.273	.329	.425	5280	199	.320	.396	.535

		TOTAL					HOME					AWAY					1ST HALF					2ND HALF					LEFT					RIGHT				
YEAR	TM/L	AB	HR	AVG	OBP	SLG	AB	HR	AVG	OBP	SLG	AB	HR	AVG	OBP	SLG	AB	HR	AVG	OBP	SLG	AB	HR	AVG	OBP	SLG	AB	HR	AVG	OBP	SLG	AB	HR	AVG	OBP	SLG
■ Greg Brock	BL/TR																																			
1982	LA-N	17	0	.118	.167	.176	8	0	.125	.222	.125	9	0	.111	.111	.222	0	0	—	—	—	17	0	.118	.167	.176	2	0	.500	.500	.500	15	0	.067	.125	.133
1983	LA-N	455	20	.224	.343	.396	215	14	.228	.328	.447	240	6	.221	.355	.350	234	11	.222	.343	.410	221	9	.226	.342	.380	73	2	.219	.284	.329	382	18	.225	.353	.408
1984	LA-N	271	14	.225	.319	.402	145	8	.248	.319	.455	126	6	.198	.320	.341	127	9	.213	.309	.441	144	5	.236	.329	.368	77	6	.208	.244	.468	194	8	.232	.346	.376
1985	LA-N	438	21	.251	.332	.438	219	7	.251	.331	.388	219	14	.251	.333	.489	182	11	.242	.324	.456	256	10	.258	.338	.426	102	2	.176	.222	.255	336	19	.274	.363	.494
1986	LA-N	325	16	.234	.309	.422	140	5	.236	.306	.343	185	11	.232	.311	.481	174	8	.213	.303	.374	151	8	.258	.315	.477	59	0	.102	.221	.153	266	16	.263	.329	.481
1987	Mil-A	532	13	.299	.371	.438	270	5	.300	.370	.426	262	8	.298	.372	.450	200	8	.270	.348	.435	332	5	.316	.385	.440	157	3	.287	.351	.395	375	10	.304	.380	.456
1988	Mil-A	364	6	.212	.329	.310	195	4	.231	.335	.344	169	2	.189	.324	.272	166	3	.247	.371	.367	198	3	.182	.293	.263	103	1	.233	.316	.320	261	5	.203	.334	.307
1989	Mil-A	373	12	.265	.345	.405	176	7	.261	.350	.403	197	5	.269	.341	.406	94	3	.266	.355	.394	279	9	.265	.342	.409	90	2	.333	.388	.444	283	10	.244	.332	.392
1990	Mil-A	367	7	.248	.324	.368	176	3	.239	.319	.341	191	4	.257	.329	.393	212	2	.250	.321	.358	155	5	.245	.328	.381	86	2	.209	.283	.337	281	5	.260	.336	.377
1991	Mil-A	60	1	.283	.419	.400	18	0	.278	.480	.389	42	1	.286	.388	.405	60	1	.283	.419	.400	0	0	—	—	—	15	1	.400	.471	.667	45	0	.244	.404	.311
TOTALS		3202	110	.248	.338	.399	1562	53	.252	.337	.394	1640	57	.245	.339	.403	1449	56	.242	.338	.404	1753	54	.253	.338	.395	764	19	.236	.301	.353	2438	91	.252	.349	.413
■ Tom Brookens	BR/TR																																			
1979	Det-A	190	4	.263	.309	.374	92	3	.337	.378	.457	98	1	.194	.245	.296	0	0	—	—	—	190	4	.263	.309	.374	91	1	.286	.323	.352	99	3	.242	.296	.394
1980	Det-A	509	10	.275	.315	.418	251	7	.275	.326	.438	258	3	.275	.304	.399	172	1	.273	.326	.372	337	9	.276	.309	.442	236	6	.322	.359	.508	273	4	.234	.276	.341
1981	Det-A	239	4	.243	.284	.343	114	3	.254	.287	.377	125	1	.232	.281	.312	114	2	.281	.301	.377	125	2	.208	.268	.312	98	1	.255	.294	.347	141	3	.234	.276	.340
1982	Det-A	398	9	.231	.277	.352	203	4	.222	.274	.335	195	5	.241	.280	.369	132	4	.250	.324	.379	266	5	.222	.252	.338	149	2	.262	.319	.362	249	7	.213	.250	.345
1983	Det-A	332	6	.214	.276	.325	164	5	.238	.298	.390	168	1	.190	.257	.262	196	3	.224	.294	.321	136	3	.199	.250	.331	145	4	.241	.315	.366	187	2	.193	.245	.294
1984	Det-A	224	5	.246	.306	.397	110	4	.245	.333	.427	114	1	.246	.277	.368	118	1	.229	.287	.339	106	4	.264	.328	.462	138	3	.261	.313	.413	86	2	.221	.295	.372
1985	Det-A	485	7	.237	.277	.375	232	3	.233	.270	.379	253	4	.241	.283	.372	190	3	.263	.309	.432	295	4	.220	.256	.339	162	4	.290	.350	.481	323	3	.211	.238	.322
1986	Det-A	281	3	.270	.319	.356	144	2	.257	.299	.354	137	1	.285	.340	.358	125	1	.312	.362	.408	156	2	.237	.283	.314	171	2	.298	.337	.409	110	1	.227	.292	.273
1987	Det-A	444	13	.241	.295	.376	212	6	.226	.291	.325	232	7	.254	.300	.422	211	7	.246	.312	.422	233	6	.236	.280	.335	154	7	.240	.310	.422	290	6	.241	.287	.352
1988	Det-A	441	5	.243	.313	.351	221	4	.258	.331	.394	220	1	.227	.295	.309	206	4	.272	.341	.403	235	1	.217	.288	.306	177	2	.220	.310	.311	264	3	.258	.315	.379
1989	NY-A	168	4	.226	.272	.333	69	0	.246	.293	.290	99	4	.212	.257	.364	116	3	.224	.280	.353	52	1	.231	.255	.288	116	4	.267	.312	.422	52	0	.135	.182	.135
1990	Cle-A	154	1	.266	.322	.357	71	0	.225	.284	.282	83	1	.301	.356	.422	50	0	.260	.315	.340	104	1	.269	.325	.365	93	1	.258	.340	.376	61	0	.279	.292	.328
TOTALS		3865	71	.246	.296	.367	1883	41	.249	.304	.377	1982	30	.243	.290	.358	1630	29	.257	.315	.382	2235	42	.238	.283	.356	1730	37	.269	.326	.406	2135	34	.227	.272	.335
■ Hubie Brooks	BR/TR																																			
1980	NY-N	81	1	.309	.364	.395	43	0	.279	.367	.326	38	1	.342	.359	.474	0	0	—	—	—	81	1	.309	.364	.395	26	0	.231	.310	.269	55	1	.345	.390	.455
1981	NY-N	358	4	.307	.345	.411	183	2	.322	.345	.426	175	2	.291	.345	.394	169	0	.302	.330	.355	189	4	.312	.359	.460	78	2	.410	.435	.577	280	2	.279	.320	.364
1982	NY-N	457	2	.249	.297	.317	228	1	.246	.296	.320	229	1	.253	.298	.314	210	0	.262	.319	.329	247	2	.239	.278	.308	85	0	.259	.308	.306	372	2	.247	.295	.320
1983	NY-N	586	5	.251	.284	.321	299	4	.254	.295	.344	287	1	.247	.272	.296	288	5	.288	.317	.392	298	0	.215	.252	.252	147	1	.272	.308	.347	439	4	.244	.275	.312
1984	NY-N	561	16	.283	.341	.417	277	12	.321	.382	.516	284	4	.246	.301	.320	235	9	.315	.382	.481	326	7	.261	.311	.371	183	7	.290	.361	.459	378	9	.280	.331	.397
1985	Mon-N	605	13	.269	.310	.413	278	4	.281	.313	.428	327	9	.260	.307	.401	271	5	.269	.312	.391	334	8	.269	.308	.431	187	4	.310	.361	.476	418	9	.251	.287	.385
1986	Mon-N	306	14	.340	.388	.569	137	3	.350	.409	.504	169	11	.331	.370	.621	241	14	.336	.394	.610	65	0	.354	.362	.415	85	5	.365	.450	.682	221	9	.330	.361	.525
1987	Mon-N	430	14	.263	.301	.426	228	9	.289	.333	.478	202	5	.233	.263	.366	112	5	.295	.339	.491	318	9	.252	.287	.403	121	5	.331	.354	.554	309	9	.236	.280	.375
1988	Mon-N	588	20	.279	.318	.447	292	9	.260	.300	.411	296	11	.297	.337	.483	311	9	.273	.310	.415	277	11	.285	.328	.484	156	7	.314	.366	.538	432	13	.266	.300	.414
1989	Mon-N	542	14	.268	.317	.404	260	7	.288	.339	.438	282	7	.248	.297	.372	278	5	.277	.319	.399	264	9	.258	.315	.409	162	6	.284	.352	.463	380	8	.261	.302	.379
1990	LA-N	568	20	.266	.307	.424	275	9	.251	.303	.385	293	11	.280	.312	.461	257	10	.245	.279	.409	311	10	.283	.330	.437	217	9	.240	.294	.419	351	11	.282	.316	.427
1991	NY-N	357	16	.238	.324	.409	172	4	.238	.340	.355	185	12	.238	.309	.459	220	13	.273	.363	.495	137	3	.182	.258	.270	121	5	.248	.343	.413	236	11	.233	.315	.407
1992	Cal-A	306	8	.216	.247	.337	150	2	.247	.280	.333	156	6	.186	.215	.340	230	7	.213	.245	.348	76	1	.224	.253	.303	82	1	.220	.256	.280	224	7	.214	.244	.357
1993	KC-A	168	1	.286	.331	.375	84	0	.286	.330	.381	84	1	.286	.333	.369	84	0	.274	.315	.310	84	1	.298	.348	.440	110	1	.327	.368	.445	58	0	.207	.266	.241
1994	KC-A	61	1	.230	.239	.311	23	1	.304	.308	.478	38	0	.184	.195	.211	57	1	.211	.226	.298	4	0	.500	.400	.500	33	1	.273	.270	.394	28	0	.179	.200	.214
TOTALS		5974	149	.269	.315	.403	2929	67	.278	.326	.410	3045	82	.261	.303	.396	2963	83	.276	.323	.418	3011	66	.262	.307	.388	1793	54	.291	.345	.453	4181	95	.260	.301	.381
■ Scott Brosius	BR/TR																																			
1991	Oak-A	68	2	.235	.268	.397	37	1	.189	.211	.324	31	1	.290	.333	.484	0	0	—	—	—	68	2	.235	.268	.397	24	0	.208	.296	.250	44	2	.250	.250	.477
1992	Oak-A	87	4	.218	.258	.379	31	1	.194	.235	.355	56	3	.232	.271	.393	34	0	.176	.176	.206	53	4	.245	.305	.491	24	3	.292	.346	.667	63	1	.190	.224	.270
1993	Oak-A	213	6	.249	.296	.390	106	3	.208	.274	.321	107	3	.290	.319	.458	70	2	.171	.227	.286	143	4	.287	.329	.441	81	3	.210	.261	.370	132	3	.273	.317	.402
1994	Oak-A	324	14	.238	.289	.417	167	9	.257	.330	.467	157	5	.217	.246	.363	202	6	.233	.290	.381	122	8	.246	.288	.475	118	7	.229	.282	.432	206	7	.243	.293	.408
1995	Oak-A	388	17	.263	.342	.454	177	12	.271	.337	.514	211	5	.256	.347	.403	177	5	.249	.348	.401	211	12	.275	.338	.498	124	3	.234	.324	.371	264	14	.277	.351	.492
1996	Oak-A	428	22	.304	.393	.516	221	15	.312	.389	.579	207	7	.295	.397	.449	114	10	.333	.462	.640	314	12	.293	.365	.471	90	4	.356	.482	.622	338	18	.290	.367	.488
1997	Oak-A	479	11	.203	.259	.317	219	7	.247	.306	.393	260	4	.165	.219	.254	294	4	.194	.253	.282	185	7	.216	.269	.373	125	2	.160	.215	.232	354	9	.218	.275	.347
1998	NY-A	530	19	.300	.371	.472	248	8	.286	.353	.456	282	11	.312	.388	.486	260	8	.308	.380	.469	270	11	.293	.363	.474	119	7	.370	.436	.681	411	12	.280	.353	.411
1999	NY-A	473	17	.247	.307	.414	215	4	.237	.307	.344	258	13	.256	.308	.473	224	7	.246	.293	.402	249	10	.249	.320	.426	108	10	.194	.270	.500	365	7	.263	.319	.389
2000	NY-A	470	16	.230	.299	.374	243	7	.214	.289	.342	227	9	.247	.309	.410	196	6	.260	.324	.398	274	10	.208	.281	.358	104	6	.260	.325	.471	366	10	.221	.291	.347
TOTALS		3460	128	.254	.320	.419	1664	67	.254	.322	.427	1796	61	.253	.319	.411	1571	48	.248	.319	.395	1889	80	.258	.322	.438	917	45	.250	.324	.456	2543	83	.255	.319	.405
■ Jerry Browne	BB/TR																																			
1986	Tex-A	24	0	.417	.440	.500	22	0	.409	.435	.500	2	0	.500	.500	.500	0	0	—	—	—	24	0	.417	.440	.500	5	0	.600	.600	.800	19	0	.368	.400	.421
1987	Tex-A	454	1	.271	.358	.339	245	1	.306	.390	.380	209	0	.230	.321	.292	218	0	.243	.348	.321	236	1	.297	.369	.356	119	1	.311	.403	.420	335	0	.257	.342	.310
1988	Tex-A	214	1	.229	.308	.304	121	1	.256	.341	.355	93	0	.194	.265	.237	132	0	.197	.287	.227	82	1	.280	.344	.427	70	0	.243	.289	.300	144	1	.222	.317	.306
1989	Cle-A	598	5	.299	.370	.390	316	1	.332	.399	.424	282	4	.262	.336	.351	280	2	.300	.350	.393	318	3	.299	.386	.387	175	2	.309	.349	.417	423	3	.296	.378	.378
1990	Cle-A	513	6	.267	.353	.372	250	2	.272	.369	.376	263	4	.262	.337	.369	259	3	.247	.309	.317	254	3	.287	.393	.429	139	0	.281	.392	.388	374	6	.262	.337	.366
1991	Cle-A	290	1	.228	.292	.269	135	1	.259	.313	.304	155	0	.200	.274	.239	161	0	.205	.263	.242	129	1	.256	.329	.302	78	0	.231	.310	.244	212	1	.226	.285	.278
1992	Oak-A	324	3	.287	.366	.364	146	1	.281	.369	.336	178	2	.292	.364	.388	143	0	.266	.342	.287	181	3	.304	.385	.425	49	0	.184	.226	.204	275	3	.305	.389	.393
1993	Oak-A	260	2	.250	.306	.323	112	1	.321	.372	.393	148	1	.196	.258	.270	32	0	.313	.389	.313	228	2	.241	.294	.325	60	1	.267	.302	.350	200	1	.245	.308	.315
1994	Fla-N	329	3	.295	.392	.398	162	0	.315	.395	.401	167	3	.275	.390	.395	212	0	.292	.391	.368	117	3	.299	.394	.453	104	2	.327	.413	.462	225	1	.280	.383	.369
1995	Fla-N	184	1	.255	.346	.293	111	0	.270	.354	.288	73	1	.233	.333	.301	71	1	.197	.296	.254	113	0	.292	.377	.319	46	0	.174	.283	.174	138	1	.283	.367	.333
TOTALS		3190	23	.271	.351	.351	1620	8	.297	.374	.374	1570	15	.245	.326	.327	1508	6	.255	.331	.317	1682	17	.287	.367	.382	845	6	.278	.352	.364	2345	17	.269	.350	.346
■ Tom Brunansky	BR/TR																																			
1981	Cal-A	33	3	.152	.317	.424	20	1	.100	.280	.250	13	2	.231	.375	.692	33	3	.152	.317	.424	0	0	—	—	—	9	2	.222	.300	.889	24	1	.125	.323	.250
1982	Min-A	463	20	.272	.377	.471	233	10	.270	.363	.489	230	10	.274	.390	.452	151	10	.291	.397	.550	312	10	.263	.367	.433	149	9	.302	.422	.564	314	11	.258	.354	.427
1983	Min-A	542	28	.227	.308	.445	261	8	.234	.330	.410	281	20	.221	.287	.477	274	11	.204	.288	.383	268	17	.250	.329	.507	169	10	.302	.370	.556	373	18	.193	.280	.394
1984	Min-A	567	32	.254	.320	.460	273	14	.234	.310	.425	294	18	.272	.329	.493	264	12	.239	.312	.405	303	20	.267	.327	.508	163	15	.239	.342	.546	404	17	.260	.310	.426
1985	Min-A	567	27	.242	.320	.448	287	12	.254	.326	.439	280	15	.229	.313	.457	261	17	.284	.385	.540	306	10	.206	.258	.369	182	5	.214	.302	.379	385	22	.255	.328	.481
1986	Min-A	593	23	.256	.315	.423	296	15	.267	.324	.480	297	8	.246	.306	.367	302	17	.291	.337	.520	291	6	.220	.292	.323	167	11	.311	.354	.575	426	12	.235	.300	.364
1987	Min-A	532	32	.259	.352	.489	277	19	.300	.384	.574	255	13	.216	.318	.396	248	16	.266	.363	.500	284	16	.254	.342	.479	158	10	.228	.321	.481	374	22	.273	.365	.492
1988	Min-A	49	1	.184	.286	.265	26	0	.154	.214	.154	23	1	.217	.357	.391	49	1	.184	.286	.265	0	0	—	—	—	21	0	.190	.227	.238	28	1	.179	.324	.286
1988	StL-N	523	22	.245	.345	.428	253	7	.225	.336	.364	270	15	.263	.354	.489	237	9	.287	.396	.451	286	13	.210	.301	.409	171	4	.281	.376	.421	352	18	.227	.329	.432
1989	StL-N	556	20	.239	.312	.410	263	4	.232	.300	.354	293	16	.246	.322	.461	262	9	.244	.318	.416	294	11	.235	.307	.405	220	11	.236	.320	.423	336	9	.241	.306	.402
1990	StL-N	57	1	.158	.310	.263	17	0	.235	.381	.294	40	1	.125	.280	.250	57	1	.158	.310	.263	0	0	—	—	—	29	0	.172	.265	.241	28	1	.143	.351	.286
1990	Bos-A	461	15	.267	.342	.438	235	13	.340	.395	.626	226	2	.190	.289	.243	174	5	.293	.373	.477	287	10	.251	.323	.415	150	6	.307	.347	.527	311	9	.248	.340	.395
1991	Bos-A	459	16	.229	.303	.390	234	10	.256	.335	.453	225	6	.200	.269	.324	242	11	.211	.292	.397	217	5	.249	.314	.382	142	5	.254	.321	.423	317	11	.218	.294	.375
1992	Bos-A	458	15	.266	.354	.445	217	10	.323	.405	.576	241	5	.216	.308	.328	164	2	.274	.351	.409	294	13	.262	.356	.466	132	6	.227	.354	.439	326	9	.282	.354	.448
1993	Mil-A	224	6	.183	.265	.321	100	2	.180	.261	.310	124	4	.185	.268	.331	169	3	.189	.275	.320	55	3	.164	.233	.327	101	3	.178	.284	.347	123	3	.187	.248	.301
1994	Mil-A	28	0	.214	.241	.286	22	0	.227	.227	.318	6	0	.167	.286	.167	28	0	.214	.241	.286	0	0	—	—	—	18	0	.167	.167	.278	10	0	.300	.364	.300
1994	Bos-A	177	10	.237	.319	.475	87	4	.184	.291	.402	90	6	.289	.347	.544	49	3	.286	.357	.510	128	7	.219	.304	.461	40	1	.200	.377	.350	137	9	.248	.298	.511
TOTALS		6289	271	.245	.327	.434	3101	129	.258	.338	.456	3188	142	.233	.316	.412	2964	130	.251	.337	.441	3325	141	.240	.318	.427	2021	98	.254	.341	.467	4268	173	.241	.321	.418
■ Bill Buckner	BL/TL																																			
1978	Chi-N	446	5	.323	.345	.419	217	3	.346	.371	.465	229	2	.301	.321	.376	154	1	.299	.323	.370	292	4	.336	.357	.445	162	2	.389	.389	.512	284	3	.285	.321	.366
1979	Chi-N	591	14	.284	.319	.437	307	8	.313	.355	.502	284	6	.254	.279	.366	297	8	.290	.322	.471	294	6	.279	.316	.401	195	5	.262	.295	.426	396	9	.295	.331	.442
1980	Chi-N	578	10	.324	.353	.457	292	3	.305	.334	.418	286	7	.343	.373	.497	217	4	.300	.343	.429	361	6	.338	.360	.474	156	1	.295	.299	.378	422	9	.334	.372	.486
1981	Chi-N	421	10	.311	.349	.480	229	7	.319	.354	.511	192	3	.302	.343	.443	208	4	.313	.350	.471	213	6	.310	.348	.488	112	3	.313	.333	.482	309	7	.311	.354	.479
1982	Chi-N	657	15	.306	.342	.441	329	9	.307	.340	.453	328	6	.305	.344	.430	304	4	.293	.338	.395	353	11	.317	.345	.482	186	2	.258	.305	.349	471	13	.325	.356	.478
1983	Chi-N	626	16	.280	.310	.436	314	6	.277	.313	.420	312	10	.282	.308	.452	302	9	.258	.291	.424	324	7	.299	.328	.448	186	2	.280	.304	.376	440	14	.280	.313	.461
1984	Chi-N	43	0	.209	.239	.209	22	0	.091	.125	.091	21	0	.333	.364	.333	43	0	.209	.239	.209	0	0	—	—	—	12	0	.250	.286	.250	31	0	.194	.219	.194
1984	Bos-A	439	11	.278	.321	.410	230	6	.274	.327	.422	209	5	.282	.314	.397	103	2	.291	.348	.447	336	9	.274	.312	.399	137	5	.277	.338	.416	302	6	.278	.313	.407

		TOTAL					HOME					AWAY					1ST HALF					2ND HALF					LEFT					RIGHT				
YEAR	TM/L	AB	HR	AVG	OBP	SLG	AB	HR	AVG	OBP	SLG	AB	HR	AVG	OBP	SLG	AB	HR	AVG	OBP	SLG	AB	HR	AVG	OBP	SLG	AB	HR	AVG	OBP	SLG	AB	HR	AVG	OBP	SLG
1985	Bos-A	673	16	.299	.325	.447	328	6	.299	.322	.433	345	10	.299	.329	.461	291	7	.289	.322	.426	382	9	.306	.328	.463	230	4	.291	.311	.404	443	12	.302	.333	.470
1986	Bos-A	629	18	.267	.311	.421	299	8	.258	.303	.411	330	10	.276	.318	.430	302	8	.238	.282	.387	327	10	.294	.338	.453	202	4	.218	.257	.322	427	14	.290	.336	.468
1987	Bos-A	286	2	.273	.299	.322	148	0	.297	.329	.331	138	2	.246	.266	.312	226	2	.270	.289	.323	60	0	.283	.338	.317	76	0	.250	.259	.250	210	2	.281	.314	.348
1987	Cal-A	183	3	.306	.337	.432	90	2	.311	.340	.456	93	1	.301	.333	.409	0	0	—	—	—	183	3	.306	.337	.432	43	0	.279	.295	.349	140	3	.314	.349	.457
1988	Cal-A	43	0	.209	.271	.209	21	0	.190	.217	.190	22	0	.227	.320	.227	43	0	.209	.271	.209	0	0	—	—	—	1	0	.000	.000	.000	42	0	.214	.277	.214
1988	KC-A	242	3	.256	.290	.351	116	0	.284	.323	.336	126	3	.230	.259	.365	117	3	.248	.272	.376	125	0	.264	.306	.328	31	0	.290	.324	.387	211	3	.251	.284	.346
1989	KC-A	176	1	.216	.240	.267	84	0	.190	.225	.214	92	1	.239	.255	.315	117	1	.231	.248	.282	59	0	.186	.226	.237	23	0	.348	.375	.391	153	1	.196	.220	.248
1990	Bos-A	43	1	.186	.234	.256	26	1	.269	.333	.385	17	0	.059	.059	.059	43	1	.186	.234	.256	0	0	—	—	—	1	0	.000	.000	.000	42	1	.190	.239	.262
TOTALS		6076	125	.289	.323	.420	3052	59	.293	.328	.426	3024	66	.286	.317	.414	2767	54	.274	.309	.398	3309	71	.302	.334	.438	1753	28	.282	.309	.392	4323	97	.292	.328	.431
■ **Steve Buechele** BR/TR																																				
1985	Tex-A	219	6	.219	.271	.356	110	5	.218	.256	.409	109	1	.220	.286	.303	0	0	—	—	—	219	6	.219	.271	.356	75	3	.267	.304	.427	144	3	.194	.255	.319
1986	Tex-A	461	18	.243	.302	.410	224	6	.237	.292	.353	237	12	.249	.310	.464	226	12	.265	.317	.469	235	6	.221	.287	.353	139	5	.273	.346	.446	322	13	.230	.282	.394
1987	Tex-A	363	13	.237	.290	.399	188	6	.250	.316	.404	175	7	.223	.262	.394	203	7	.212	.262	.384	160	6	.269	.326	.419	177	8	.288	.333	.497	186	5	.188	.250	.306
1988	Tex-A	503	16	.250	.342	.404	246	8	.260	.352	.415	257	8	.241	.332	.393	238	10	.261	.358	.433	265	6	.242	.328	.377	153	5	.235	.335	.392	350	11	.257	.345	.409
1989	Tex-A	486	16	.235	.294	.387	227	7	.225	.296	.339	259	9	.243	.291	.429	254	4	.240	.297	.343	232	12	.228	.290	.435	148	6	.257	.323	.439	338	10	.225	.280	.364
1990	Tex-A	251	7	.215	.294	.339	136	5	.243	.316	.397	115	2	.183	.269	.270	98	3	.194	.282	.337	153	4	.229	.302	.340	80	4	.275	.372	.488	171	3	.187	.255	.269
1991	Tex-A	416	18	.267	.335	.447	190	7	.300	.368	.474	226	11	.239	.308	.425	228	11	.268	.344	.465	188	7	.266	.325	.426	97	6	.289	.391	.546	319	12	.260	.317	.417
1991	Pit-N	114	4	.246	.315	.412	61	2	.197	.265	.361	53	2	.302	.373	.472	0	0	—	—	—	114	4	.246	.315	.412	34	3	.324	.439	.647	80	1	.213	.256	.313
1992	Pit-N	285	8	.249	.331	.389	149	3	.235	.318	.322	136	5	.265	.346	.463	256	8	.246	.337	.398	29	0	.276	.276	.310	113	4	.292	.375	.478	172	4	.221	.303	.331
1992	Chi-N	239	1	.276	.338	.351	127	1	.260	.314	.370	112	0	.295	.365	.330	0	0	—	—	—	239	1	.276	.338	.351	94	1	.319	.369	.457	145	0	.248	.319	.283
1993	Chi-N	460	15	.272	.345	.437	224	8	.281	.359	.451	236	7	.263	.332	.424	210	6	.233	.279	.405	250	9	.304	.397	.464	128	5	.281	.378	.469	332	10	.268	.332	.425
1994	Chi-N	339	14	.242	.325	.404	173	7	.260	.342	.416	166	7	.223	.307	.392	223	9	.229	.316	.381	116	5	.267	.341	.448	85	2	.235	.330	.376	254	12	.244	.323	.413
1995	Chi-N	106	1	.189	.265	.236	50	0	.160	.250	.180	56	1	.214	.279	.286	106	1	.189	.265	.236	0	0	—	—	—	24	1	.208	.296	.417	82	0	.183	.256	.183
1995	Tex-A	24	0	.125	.250	.125	12	0	.167	.286	.167	12	0	.083	.214	.083	0	0	—	—	—	24	0	.125	.250	.125	9	0	.111	.333	.111	15	0	.133	.188	.133
TOTALS		4266	137	.245	.316	.394	2117	65	.249	.321	.389	2149	72	.242	.311	.399	2042	71	.239	.311	.397	2224	66	.250	.320	.392	1356	53	.272	.351	.458	2910	84	.233	.299	.365
■ **Damon Buford** BR/TR																																				
1993	Bal-A	79	2	.228	.315	.367	32	0	.125	.243	.156	47	2	.298	.365	.511	59	2	.237	.338	.390	20	0	.200	.238	.300	23	0	.217	.250	.348	56	2	.232	.338	.375
1994	Bal-A	2	0	.500	.500	.500	0	0	—	—	—	2	0	.500	.500	.500	2	0	.500	.500	.500	0	0	—	—	—	0	0	—	—	—	2	0	.500	.500	.500
1995	Bal-A	32	0	.063	.205	.063	16	0	.063	.200	.063	16	0	.063	.211	.063	32	0	.063	.205	.063	0	0	—	—	—	13	0	.000	.133	.000	19	0	.105	.250	.105
1995	NY-N	136	4	.235	.346	.360	72	2	.208	.287	.333	64	2	.266	.402	.391	0	0	—	—	—	136	4	.235	.346	.360	43	2	.349	.462	.512	93	2	.183	.291	.290
1996	Tex-A	145	6	.283	.348	.469	81	3	.309	.380	.481	64	3	.250	.304	.453	80	3	.275	.330	.438	65	3	.292	.370	.508	90	5	.289	.356	.500	55	1	.273	.333	.418
1997	Tex-A	366	8	.224	.287	.339	178	4	.247	.320	.365	188	4	.202	.254	.314	242	5	.211	.281	.318	124	3	.250	.299	.379	139	4	.252	.289	.374	227	4	.207	.286	.317
1998	Bos-A	216	10	.282	.349	.523	99	4	.293	.355	.535	117	6	.274	.344	.513	112	5	.277	.344	.509	104	5	.288	.353	.538	132	8	.333	.390	.621	84	2	.202	.284	.369
1999	Bos-A	297	6	.242	.294	.367	155	3	.226	.267	.355	142	3	.261	.323	.380	163	2	.258	.303	.374	134	4	.224	.284	.358	110	1	.245	.325	.327	187	5	.241	.275	.390
2000	Chi-N	495	15	.251	.324	.390	242	9	.269	.353	.426	253	6	.233	.296	.356	262	11	.267	.338	.435	233	4	.232	.309	.339	135	4	.326	.397	.504	360	11	.222	.297	.347
TOTALS		1768	51	.245	.316	.389	875	25	.249	.322	.394	893	26	.241	.310	.384	952	28	.245	.313	.389	816	23	.245	.319	.390	685	24	.286	.352	.457	1083	27	.219	.293	.346
■ **Jay Buhner** BR/TR																																				
1987	NY-A	22	0	.227	.261	.318	15	0	.200	.250	.333	7	0	.286	.286	.286	0	0	—	—	—	22	0	.227	.261	.318	20	0	.200	.200	.250	2	0	.500	.667	1.000
1988	NY-A	69	3	.188	.250	.319	29	1	.241	.281	.345	40	2	.150	.227	.300	66	3	.182	.236	.318	3	0	.333	.500	.333	28	1	.179	.200	.286	41	2	.195	.283	.341
1988	Sea-A	192	10	.224	.320	.458	97	7	.206	.284	.485	95	3	.242	.354	.432	0	0	—	—	—	192	10	.224	.320	.458	61	3	.164	.212	.344	131	7	.252	.365	.511
1989	Sea-A	204	9	.275	.341	.490	104	7	.279	.342	.529	100	2	.270	.339	.450	79	5	.291	.360	.570	125	4	.264	.328	.440	60	2	.233	.299	.400	144	7	.292	.358	.528
1990	Sea-A	163	7	.276	.357	.479	68	2	.250	.378	.412	95	5	.295	.340	.526	55	5	.255	.354	.582	108	2	.287	.358	.426	56	4	.357	.438	.714	107	3	.234	.314	.355
1991	Sea-A	406	27	.244	.337	.498	212	14	.212	.321	.472	194	13	.278	.355	.526	144	9	.222	.337	.472	262	18	.256	.337	.511	146	9	.240	.371	.486	260	18	.246	.316	.504
1992	Sea-A	543	25	.243	.333	.422	263	9	.259	.353	.430	280	16	.229	.313	.414	255	9	.216	.300	.345	288	16	.267	.361	.490	148	10	.230	.327	.459	395	15	.248	.335	.408
1993	Sea-A	563	27	.272	.379	.476	275	13	.273	.402	.491	288	14	.271	.355	.462	271	15	.295	.386	.517	292	12	.250	.373	.438	172	9	.320	.435	.535	391	18	.251	.353	.450
1994	Sea-A	358	21	.279	.394	.542	159	8	.270	.390	.535	199	13	.286	.397	.548	261	15	.276	.391	.548	97	6	.289	.402	.526	110	8	.336	.439	.655	248	13	.254	.374	.492
1995	Sea-A	470	40	.262	.343	.566	236	21	.284	.376	.597	234	19	.239	.308	.534	161	9	.273	.318	.528	309	31	.256	.354	.586	118	8	.254	.341	.500	352	32	.264	.343	.588
1996	Sea-A	564	44	.271	.369	.557	267	21	.270	.379	.562	297	23	.273	.359	.552	259	21	.301	.400	.598	305	23	.246	.342	.521	125	11	.304	.407	.640	439	33	.262	.358	.533
1997	Sea-A	540	40	.243	.383	.506	243	13	.235	.416	.465	297	27	.249	.354	.539	280	21	.239	.387	.496	260	19	.246	.380	.515	126	11	.317	.449	.627	414	29	.220	.363	.469
1998	Sea-A	244	15	.242	.344	.463	132	8	.235	.357	.462	112	7	.250	.328	.464	77	4	.234	.326	.416	167	11	.246	.352	.485	52	4	.173	.241	.423	192	11	.260	.370	.474
1999	Sea-A	266	14	.222	.388	.421	158	5	.190	.377	.329	108	9	.269	.404	.556	82	6	.268	.415	.549	184	8	.201	.376	.364	64	8	.266	.453	.656	202	6	.208	.366	.347
2000	Sea-A	364	26	.253	.361	.522	194	15	.227	.323	.500	170	11	.282	.403	.547	198	14	.237	.366	.490	166	12	.271	.356	.560	90	6	.278	.405	.567	274	20	.245	.346	.507
TOTALS		4968	308	.254	.359	.494	2452	144	.248	.366	.486	2516	164	.260	.351	.502	2188	136	.258	.362	.498	2780	172	.251	.356	.491	1376	94	.271	.378	.533	3592	214	.248	.351	.479
■ **Al Bumbry** BL/TR																																				
1978	Bal-A	114	2	.237	.346	.368	59	0	.220	.324	.288	55	2	.255	.369	.455	109	2	.239	.352	.376	5	0	.200	.200	.200	43	0	.163	.280	.233	71	2	.282	.386	.451
1979	Bal-A	569	7	.285	.336	.376	241	2	.278	.349	.369	328	5	.290	.326	.381	273	2	.282	.338	.359	296	5	.287	.334	.392	133	1	.286	.336	.368	436	6	.284	.336	.378
1980	Bal-A	645	9	.318	.392	.433	307	6	.326	.416	.440	338	3	.311	.370	.426	282	4	.326	.405	.457	363	5	.311	.382	.413	206	2	.272	.349	.340	439	7	.339	.412	.476
1981	Bal-A	392	1	.273	.358	.337	208	1	.293	.370	.361	184	0	.250	.344	.310	188	1	.255	.357	.324	204	0	.289	.358	.348	98	0	.286	.413	.337	294	1	.269	.337	.337
1982	Bal-A	562	5	.262	.314	.338	270	4	.252	.319	.337	292	1	.271	.310	.339	277	1	.253	.301	.310	285	4	.270	.327	.365	120	1	.225	.277	.275	442	4	.271	.324	.355
1983	Bal-A	378	3	.275	.328	.357	197	2	.315	.363	.401	181	1	.232	.289	.309	171	3	.269	.321	.363	207	0	.280	.333	.353	13	0	.154	.267	.154	365	3	.279	.330	.364
1984	Bal-A	344	3	.270	.317	.337	171	0	.263	.294	.310	173	3	.277	.339	.364	159	0	.264	.298	.296	185	3	.276	.333	.373	3	0	.000	.000	.000	341	3	.273	.320	.340
1985	SD-N	95	1	.200	.255	.263	35	0	.057	.108	.057	60	1	.283	.338	.383	53	0	.245	.286	.264	42	1	.143	.217	.262	8	0	.000	.111	.000	87	1	.218	.269	.287
TOTALS		3099	31	.279	.342	.366	1488	15	.281	.350	.364	1611	16	.277	.334	.367	1512	13	.274	.340	.356	1587	18	.284	.344	.375	624	4	.253	.333	.316	2475	27	.285	.344	.378
■ **Ellis Burks** BR/TR																																				
1987	Bos-A	558	20	.272	.324	.441	256	11	.289	.365	.480	302	9	.258	.287	.407	197	12	.244	.294	.487	361	8	.288	.340	.416	151	4	.325	.380	.483	407	16	.253	.303	.425
1988	Bos-A	540	18	.294	.367	.481	246	8	.325	.402	.524	294	10	.269	.335	.446	227	8	.326	.386	.524	313	10	.272	.353	.450	142	5	.324	.410	.486	398	13	.284	.351	.480
1989	Bos-A	399	12	.303	.365	.471	204	6	.319	.376	.480	195	6	.287	.353	.462	236	7	.280	.351	.475	163	5	.337	.386	.466	104	2	.279	.361	.413	295	10	.312	.366	.492
1990	Bos-A	588	21	.296	.349	.486	297	10	.306	.357	.502	291	11	.285	.341	.471	278	10	.295	.349	.507	310	11	.297	.349	.468	188	5	.298	.365	.452	400	16	.295	.341	.503
1991	Bos-A	474	14	.251	.314	.422	232	8	.267	.328	.466	242	6	.236	.301	.380	253	9	.241	.308	.411	221	5	.262	.321	.434	135	5	.259	.313	.489	339	9	.248	.315	.395
1992	Bos-A	235	8	.255	.327	.417	108	4	.231	.309	.426	127	4	.276	.343	.409	235	8	.255	.327	.417	0	0	—	—	—	66	3	.197	.299	.394	169	5	.278	.339	.426
1993	Chi-A	499	17	.275	.352	.441	238	7	.298	.383	.475	261	10	.253	.323	.410	232	9	.280	.351	.466	267	8	.270	.353	.419	153	8	.281	.380	.477	346	9	.272	.339	.425
1994	Col-N	149	13	.322	.388	.678	65	7	.369	.423	.815	84	6	.286	.362	.571	130	12	.354	.421	.738	19	1	.105	.150	.263	35	4	.343	.395	.771	114	9	.316	.386	.649
1995	Col-N	278	14	.266	.359	.496	141	8	.291	.387	.567	137	6	.241	.331	.423	113	5	.239	.333	.442	165	9	.285	.377	.533	104	5	.327	.397	.567	174	9	.230	.338	.454
1996	Col-N	613	40	.344	.408	.639	331	23	.390	.443	.728	282	17	.291	.367	.535	306	21	.350	.422	.647	307	19	.339	.393	.632	143	8	.427	.488	.741	470	32	.319	.383	.609
1997	Col-N	424	32	.290	.363	.571	205	17	.337	.407	.649	219	15	.247	.322	.498	245	17	.253	.332	.514	179	15	.341	.407	.648	100	5	.280	.345	.450	324	27	.293	.369	.608
1998	Col-N	357	16	.286	.355	.510	181	8	.271	.350	.481	176	8	.301	.360	.540	276	13	.275	.348	.511	81	3	.321	.378	.506	107	6	.336	.416	.598	250	10	.264	.327	.472
1998	SF-N	147	5	.306	.387	.463	82	2	.280	.330	.402	65	3	.338	.456	.538	0	0	—	—	—	147	5	.306	.387	.463	32	1	.281	.410	.375	115	4	.313	.381	.487
1999	SF-N	390	31	.282	.394	.569	192	16	.250	.350	.542	198	15	.313	.435	.596	187	11	.267	.379	.508	203	20	.296	.409	.626	116	9	.345	.465	.612	274	22	.255	.363	.551
2000	SF-N	393	24	.344	.419	.606	185	15	.362	.446	.697	208	9	.327	.394	.524	169	9	.337	.415	.562	224	15	.348	.422	.638	100	4	.360	.441	.550	293	20	.338	.412	.625
TOTALS		6044	285	.293	.364	.510	2963	150	.310	.381	.549	3081	135	.277	.347	.472	3084	151	.286	.358	.512	2960	134	.300	.370	.507	1676	74	.314	.393	.521	4368	211	.285	.352	.505
■ **Jeromy Burnitz** BL/TR																																				
1993	NY-N	263	13	.243	.339	.475	141	6	.255	.325	.475	122	7	.230	.354	.475	17	1	.235	.316	.529	246	12	.244	.340	.472	33	1	.242	.324	.485	230	12	.243	.341	.474
1994	NY-N	143	3	.238	.347	.329	63	2	.238	.385	.365	80	1	.237	.315	.300	78	3	.192	.300	.321	65	0	.292	.403	.338	36	0	.111	.220	.139	107	3	.280	.389	.393
1995	Cle-A	7	0	.571	.571	.714	2	0	.500	.500	1.000	5	0	.600	.600	.600	0	0	—	—	—	7	0	.571	.571	.714	1	0	1.000	1.000	1.000	6	0	.500	.500	.667
1996	Cle-A	128	7	.281	.406	.523	55	4	.291	.418	.600	73	3	.274	.398	.466	48	3	.292	.443	.563	80	4	.275	.383	.500	16	1	.250	.429	.438	112	6	.286	.403	.536
1996	Mil-A	72	2	.236	.321	.375	39	1	.256	.341	.385	33	1	.212	.300	.364	0	0	—	—	—	72	2	.236	.321	.375	10	0	.300	.364	.400	62	2	.226	.315	.371
1997	Mil-A	494	27	.281	.382	.553	245	18	.302	.402	.657	249	9	.261	.361	.450	228	11	.285	.407	.553	266	16	.278	.358	.553	121	3	.273	.343	.430	373	24	.284	.393	.592
1998	Mil-A	609	38	.263	.339	.499	293	17	.273	.353	.485	316	21	.253	.326	.513	297	18	.273	.365	.512	312	20	.253	.313	.487	199	8	.271	.321	.447	410	30	.259	.347	.524
1999	Mil-A	467	33	.270	.402	.561	210	12	.281	.423	.500	257	21	.261	.384	.611	277	22	.289	.399	.610	190	11	.242	.405	.489	162	11	.247	.399	.537	305	22	.282	.403	.574
2000	Mil-A	564	31	.232	.356	.456	285	12	.232	.351	.439	279	19	.233	.360	.473	286	16	.213	.341	.423	278	15	.252	.371	.489	160	7	.237	.347	.438	404	24	.230	.359	.463
TOTALS		2747	154	.259	.365	.498	1333	72	.268	.375	.505	1414	82	.250	.356	.491	1231	74	.260	.374	.511	1516	80	.258	.358	.487	738	31	.251	.348	.449	2009	123	.262	.371	.516
■ **Randy Bush** BL/TL																																				
1982	Min-A	119	4	.244	.305	.412	61	2	.230	.304	.377	58	2	.259	.306	.448	23	0	.217	.280	.261	96	4	.250	.311	.448	4	0	.000	.333	.000	115	4	.252	.304	.426
1983	Min-A	373	11	.249	.323	.418	192	4	.281	.368	.458	181	7	.215	.272	.376	189	6	.302	.365	.508	184	5	.196	.280	.326	14	0	.143	.188	.143	359	11	.253	.328	.429
1984	Min-A	311	11	.222	.292	.389	154	8	.227	.313	.455	157	3	.217	.272	.325	150	5	.227	.301	.407	161	6	.217	.283	.373	3	0	.000	.000	.000	308	11	.224	.295	.393

		TOTAL					HOME					AWAY					1ST HALF					2ND HALF					LEFT					RIGHT				
YEAR	TM/L	AB	HR	AVG	OBP	SLG	AB	HR	AVG	OBP	SLG	AB	HR	AVG	OBP	SLG	AB	HR	AVG	OBP	SLG	AB	HR	AVG	OBP	SLG	AB	HR	AVG	OBP	SLG	AB	HR	AVG	OBP	SLG
1985	Min-A	234	10	.239	.321	.449	136	5	.250	.335	.456	98	5	.224	.300	.439	94	6	.202	.255	.457	140	4	.264	.362	.443	12	0	.083	.214	.167	222	10	.248	.327	.464
1986	Min-A	357	7	.269	.347	.420	181	6	.304	.376	.525	176	1	.233	.317	.313	163	6	.252	.339	.479	194	1	.284	.353	.371	12	0	.167	.286	.250	345	7	.272	.349	.426
1987	Min-A	293	11	.253	.349	.413	128	3	.258	.380	.367	165	8	.248	.323	.448	129	5	.248	.342	.419	164	6	.256	.354	.409	9	0	.222	.417	.222	284	11	.254	.346	.419
1988	Min-A	394	14	.261	.365	.434	185	10	.243	.372	.492	209	4	.278	.358	.383	178	7	.264	.384	.461	216	7	.259	.348	.412	11	0	.182	.333	.364	383	14	.264	.366	.436
1989	Min-A	391	14	.263	.347	.435	181	6	.265	.368	.436	210	8	.262	.328	.433	170	9	.271	.357	.512	221	5	.258	.339	.376	20	0	.250	.250	.400	371	14	.264	.351	.437
1990	Min-A	181	6	.243	.338	.387	98	4	.296	.375	.490	83	2	.181	.296	.265	68	2	.206	.273	.353	113	4	.265	.376	.407	4	0	.250	.333	.500	177	6	.243	.338	.384
1991	Min-A	165	6	.303	.401	.485	64	2	.250	.377	.391	101	4	.337	.417	.545	67	2	.194	.289	.328	98	4	.378	.474	.592	2	0	.000	.000	.000	163	6	.307	.405	.491
1992	Min-A	182	2	.214	.263	.302	83	0	.217	.286	.253	99	2	.212	.243	.343	80	1	.213	.270	.287	102	1	.216	.257	.314	8	0	.000	.000	.000	174	2	.224	.274	.316
1993	Min-A	45	0	.156	.269	.200	20	0	.200	.333	.250	25	0	.120	.214	.160	45	0	.156	.269	.200	0	0	—	—	—	1	0	.000	.000	.000	44	0	.159	.275	.205
TOTALS		3045	96	.251	.334	.413	1483	50	.260	.355	.441	1562	46	.242	.313	.386	1356	49	.245	.329	.431	1689	47	.255	.338	.398	100	0	.150	.248	.230	2945	96	.254	.337	.419
■ **Brett Butler**	BL/TL																																			
1981	Atl-N	126	0	.254	.352	.317	60	0	.233	.343	.283	66	0	.273	.360	.348	0	0	—	—	—	126	0	.254	.352	.317	6	0	.333	.500	.333	120	0	.250	.343	.317
1982	Atl-N	240	0	.217	.291	.225	111	0	.207	.273	.225	129	0	.225	.306	.225	202	0	.228	.310	.238	38	0	.158	.179	.158	25	0	.240	.296	.240	215	0	.214	.290	.223
1983	Atl-N	549	5	.281	.344	.393	265	4	.332	.395	.453	284	1	.232	.297	.338	232	2	.263	.323	.379	317	3	.293	.360	.404	101	0	.277	.345	.347	448	5	.281	.344	.404
1984	Cle-A	602	3	.269	.361	.355	297	1	.279	.360	.360	305	2	.259	.362	.351	286	1	.266	.370	.325	316	2	.272	.353	.383	190	0	.295	.400	.363	412	3	.257	.342	.352
1985	Cle-A	591	5	.311	.377	.431	289	1	.329	.382	.429	302	4	.295	.372	.434	288	2	.302	.354	.434	303	3	.320	.398	.429	193	1	.332	.378	.430	398	4	.302	.376	.432
1986	Cle-A	587	4	.278	.356	.375	276	0	.272	.360	.351	311	4	.283	.352	.395	270	1	.237	.327	.326	317	3	.312	.381	.416	160	1	.306	.390	.412	427	3	.267	.342	.361
1987	Cle-A	522	9	.295	.399	.425	246	4	.337	.443	.492	276	5	.257	.359	.366	208	1	.288	.410	.409	314	8	.299	.392	.436	146	2	.267	.397	.342	376	7	.306	.400	.457
1988	SF-N	568	6	.287	.393	.398	276	1	.290	.401	.366	292	5	.284	.387	.428	280	3	.282	.378	.386	288	3	.292	.408	.410	190	1	.253	.380	.332	378	5	.304	.400	.431
1989	SF-N	594	4	.283	.349	.354	296	2	.304	.370	.382	298	2	.262	.328	.326	274	2	.299	.373	.372	320	2	.269	.328	.338	200	1	.280	.353	.350	394	3	.284	.347	.355
1990	SF-N	622	3	.309	.397	.384	312	3	.337	.427	.410	310	0	.281	.367	.358	291	1	.271	.378	.320	331	2	.341	.414	.441	245	1	.302	.389	.355	377	2	.313	.403	.403
1991	LA-N	615	2	.296	.401	.343	295	2	.312	.425	.369	320	0	.281	.377	.319	288	1	.288	.389	.330	327	1	.303	.411	.355	256	0	.281	.397	.313	359	2	.306	.404	.365
1992	LA-N	553	3	.309	.413	.391	267	1	.303	.411	.375	286	2	.315	.414	.406	268	1	.269	.371	.354	285	2	.347	.451	.425	223	1	.296	.402	.345	330	2	.318	.420	.421
1993	LA-N	607	1	.298	.387	.371	291	0	.347	.441	.409	316	1	.253	.336	.335	297	0	.316	.385	.374	310	1	.281	.390	.368	206	0	.330	.407	.374	401	1	.282	.378	.369
1994	LA-N	417	8	.314	.411	.446	190	2	.274	.400	.379	227	6	.348	.421	.502	284	5	.317	.425	.447	133	3	.308	.380	.444	128	1	.281	.388	.367	289	7	.329	.421	.481
1995	NY-N	367	1	.311	.381	.392	186	0	.280	.351	.333	181	1	.343	.412	.453	215	0	.256	.333	.307	152	1	.388	.450	.513	99	1	.283	.333	.384	268	0	.321	.398	.396
1995	LA-N	146	0	.274	.368	.336	67	0	.343	.439	.373	79	0	.215	.304	.304	0	0	—	—	—	146	0	.274	.368	.336	31	0	.258	.425	.323	115	0	.278	.351	.339
1996	LA-N	131	0	.267	.313	.290	72	0	.250	.291	.250	59	0	.288	.338	.339	117	0	.265	.294	.291	14	0	.286	.444	.286	32	0	.313	.333	.375	99	0	.253	.306	.263
1997	LA-N	343	0	.283	.363	.324	163	0	.288	.386	.325	180	0	.278	.340	.322	167	0	.311	.413	.347	176	0	.256	.311	.301	93	0	.333	.367	.387	250	0	.264	.361	.300
TOTALS		8180	54	.290	.377	.376	3959	21	.304	.393	.382	4221	33	.278	.362	.371	3967	20	.280	.368	.357	4213	34	.300	.385	.394	2524	10	.294	.384	.360	5656	44	.289	.374	.383
■ **Enos Cabell**	BR/TR																																			
1978	Hou-N	660	7	.295	.321	.398	328	2	.314	.329	.405	332	5	.277	.313	.392	304	4	.289	.314	.372	356	3	.301	.327	.421	208	1	.284	.317	.380	452	6	.301	.323	.407
1979	Hou-N	603	6	.272	.299	.368	292	1	.236	.262	.315	311	5	.305	.334	.418	293	5	.263	.292	.362	310	1	.281	.307	.374	212	3	.264	.291	.382	391	3	.276	.304	.361
1980	Hou-N	604	2	.276	.305	.351	285	0	.256	.288	.326	319	2	.295	.320	.373	253	1	.261	.299	.332	351	1	.288	.310	.365	234	1	.291	.317	.376	370	1	.268	.297	.335
1981	SF-N	396	2	.255	.274	.326	174	0	.264	.281	.333	222	2	.248	.268	.320	233	2	.262	.275	.335	163	0	.245	.272	.313	86	1	.244	.267	.349	310	1	.258	.276	.319
1982	Det-A	464	2	.261	.284	.323	229	2	.249	.281	.310	235	0	.272	.287	.336	276	2	.279	.295	.362	188	0	.234	.269	.266	183	2	.268	.295	.350	281	0	.256	.277	.306
1983	Det-A	392	5	.311	.335	.434	198	1	.323	.357	.439	194	4	.299	.312	.428	153	3	.320	.342	.444	239	2	.305	.331	.427	171	3	.333	.360	.450	221	2	.294	.316	.421
1984	Hou-N	436	8	.310	.341	.417	212	2	.269	.299	.373	224	6	.348	.380	.460	202	3	.337	.360	.441	234	5	.286	.324	.397	184	4	.332	.371	.435	252	4	.294	.318	.405
1985	Hou-N	143	2	.245	.321	.357	80	1	.250	.326	.363	63	1	.238	.314	.349	131	2	.252	.329	.374	12	0	.167	.231	.167	100	1	.270	.348	.400	43	1	.186	.255	.256
1985	LA-N	192	0	.292	.340	.349	102	0	.284	.342	.343	90	0	.300	.337	.356	0	0	—	—	—	192	0	.292	.340	.349	81	0	.333	.400	.395	111	0	.261	.293	.315
1986	LA-N	277	2	.256	.294	.318	144	2	.271	.308	.361	133	0	.241	.279	.271	130	0	.238	.281	.269	147	2	.272	.306	.361	197	2	.284	.321	.371	80	0	.188	.230	.188
TOTALS		4167	36	.280	.310	.368	2044	11	.273	.303	.357	2123	25	.287	.316	.379	1975	22	.278	.307	.366	2192	14	.281	.312	.370	1656	18	.290	.326	.389	2511	18	.273	.299	.354
■ **Orlando Cabrera**	BR/TR																																			
1997	Mon-N	18	0	.222	.263	.222	12	0	.083	.154	.083	6	0	.500	.500	.500	0	0	—	—	—	18	0	.222	.263	.222	7	0	.143	.250	.143	11	0	.273	.273	.273
1998	Mon-N	261	3	.280	.325	.414	102	2	.225	.273	.392	159	1	.314	.359	.428	5	0	.600	.600	.800	256	3	.273	.320	.406	52	0	.308	.357	.327	209	3	.273	.317	.435
1999	Mon-N	382	8	.254	.293	.403	206	6	.252	.287	.422	176	2	.256	.299	.381	279	4	.269	.306	.412	103	4	.214	.257	.379	93	1	.333	.367	.473	289	7	.228	.269	.381
2000	Mon-N	422	13	.237	.279	.393	225	7	.231	.255	.409	197	6	.244	.306	.376	234	6	.231	.266	.363	188	7	.245	.296	.431	105	2	.286	.342	.429	317	11	.221	.257	.382
TOTALS		1083	24	.253	.295	.399	545	15	.235	.268	.404	538	9	.271	.321	.394	518	10	.255	.291	.394	565	14	.251	.299	.404	257	3	.304	.351	.416	826	21	.237	.277	.393
■ **Miguel Cairo**	BR/TR																																			
1996	Tor-A	27	0	.222	.300	.296	3	0	.000	.000	.000	24	0	.250	.333	.333	8	0	.250	.250	.500	19	0	.211	.318	.211	18	0	.167	.286	.278	9	0	.333	.333	.333
1997	Chi-N	29	0	.241	.313	.276	7	0	.714	.778	.714	22	0	.091	.130	.136	2	0	.000	.333	.000	27	0	.259	.310	.296	13	0	.154	.154	.154	16	0	.313	.421	.375
1998	TB-A	515	5	.268	.307	.367	253	3	.265	.305	.372	262	2	.271	.309	.363	243	3	.276	.314	.379	272	2	.261	.301	.357	125	2	.328	.375	.456	390	3	.249	.285	.338
1999	TB-A	465	3	.295	.335	.368	213	1	.272	.320	.333	252	2	.313	.348	.397	192	1	.323	.361	.406	273	2	.275	.317	.341	86	0	.384	.424	.430	379	3	.274	.315	.354
2000	TB-A	375	1	.261	.314	.328	167	0	.204	.286	.275	208	1	.308	.338	.370	215	0	.270	.320	.335	160	1	.250	.306	.319	74	0	.270	.300	.338	301	1	.259	.317	.326
TOTALS		1411	9	.274	.318	.354	643	4	.255	.309	.336	768	5	.289	.326	.368	660	4	.286	.329	.373	751	5	.262	.309	.337	316	2	.313	.357	.399	1095	7	.262	.307	.341
■ **Mike Cameron**	BR/TR																																			
1995	Chi-A	38	1	.184	.244	.316	15	0	.267	.353	.400	23	1	.130	.167	.261	0	0	—	—	—	38	1	.184	.244	.316	21	1	.238	.273	.476	17	0	.118	.211	.118
1996	Chi-A	11	0	.091	.167	.091	4	0	.000	.000	.000	7	0	.143	.250	.143	0	0	—	—	—	11	0	.091	.167	.091	7	0	.143	.250	.143	4	0	.000	.000	.000
1997	Chi-A	379	14	.259	.356	.433	176	10	.273	.376	.494	203	4	.246	.338	.379	120	5	.258	.343	.433	259	9	.259	.362	.432	114	4	.228	.336	.412	265	10	.272	.365	.442
1998	Chi-A	396	8	.210	.285	.336	221	5	.258	.329	.394	175	3	.149	.230	.263	234	4	.209	.285	.316	162	4	.210	.285	.364	87	2	.218	.324	.333	309	6	.207	.273	.337
1999	Cin-N	542	21	.256	.357	.469	275	12	.287	.384	.524	267	9	.225	.328	.412	262	6	.252	.351	.420	280	15	.261	.362	.514	120	7	.292	.418	.575	422	14	.246	.338	.438
2000	Sea-A	543	19	.267	.365	.438	255	5	.220	.340	.337	288	14	.309	.388	.528	259	10	.274	.366	.463	284	9	.261	.364	.415	110	3	.273	.352	.427	433	16	.266	.368	.441
TOTALS		1909	63	.248	.341	.420	946	32	.258	.356	.433	963	31	.238	.326	.407	875	25	.248	.337	.407	1034	38	.248	.345	.431	459	17	.253	.356	.442	1450	46	.246	.337	.413
■ **Ken Caminiti**	BB/TR																																			
1987	Hou-N	203	3	.246	.287	.335	90	2	.267	.313	.389	113	1	.230	.267	.292	0	0	—	—	—	203	3	.246	.287	.335	100	2	.310	.349	.430	103	1	.184	.227	.243
1988	Hou-N	83	1	.181	.225	.241	40	0	.200	.233	.225	43	1	.163	.217	.256	0	0	—	—	—	83	1	.181	.225	.241	24	1	.125	.222	.250	59	0	.203	.226	.237
1989	Hou-N	585	10	.255	.316	.369	293	3	.256	.313	.362	292	7	.253	.319	.377	291	5	.251	.303	.368	294	5	.259	.328	.371	165	4	.315	.363	.473	420	6	.231	.297	.329
1990	Hou-N	541	4	.242	.302	.309	285	2	.288	.348	.361	256	2	.191	.250	.250	257	2	.257	.308	.311	284	2	.229	.296	.306	240	2	.246	.280	.317	301	2	.239	.318	.302
1991	Hou-N	574	13	.253	.312	.383	289	9	.253	.307	.422	285	4	.253	.316	.344	267	6	.232	.290	.341	307	7	.270	.330	.420	232	9	.310	.347	.504	342	4	.213	.289	.301
1992	Hou-N	506	13	.294	.350	.441	246	7	.329	.389	.496	260	6	.262	.311	.388	185	5	.319	.385	.476	321	8	.280	.329	.421	208	7	.303	.357	.476	298	6	.289	.345	.416
1993	Hou-N	543	13	.262	.321	.390	288	5	.257	.308	.375	255	8	.267	.336	.408	286	9	.252	.289	.416	257	4	.272	.354	.362	187	5	.246	.319	.401	356	8	.270	.322	.385
1994	Hou-N	406	18	.283	.352	.495	204	6	.289	.350	.466	202	12	.277	.355	.525	260	14	.296	.361	.542	146	4	.260	.337	.411	128	5	.266	.331	.484	278	13	.291	.362	.500
1995	SD-N	526	26	.302	.380	.513	261	16	.303	.364	.525	265	10	.302	.395	.502	219	11	.279	.344	.475	307	15	.319	.405	.541	169	10	.331	.374	.574	357	16	.289	.383	.485
1996	SD-N	546	40	.326	.408	.621	260	20	.338	.407	.646	286	20	.315	.408	.598	256	11	.289	.353	.480	290	29	.359	.451	.745	165	15	.358	.415	.721	381	25	.312	.404	.577
1997	SD-N	486	26	.290	.389	.508	230	15	.309	.406	.565	256	11	.273	.374	.457	228	6	.250	.332	.382	258	20	.326	.435	.620	144	6	.306	.404	.479	342	20	.284	.383	.520
1998	SD-N	452	29	.252	.353	.509	235	14	.238	.349	.472	217	15	.267	.358	.548	210	11	.267	.360	.490	242	18	.240	.347	.525	161	9	.230	.317	.453	291	20	.265	.372	.540
1999	Hou-N	273	13	.286	.386	.476	146	4	.295	.389	.425	127	9	.276	.383	.535	130	2	.292	.373	.377	143	11	.280	.397	.566	68	1	.338	.420	.485	205	12	.268	.375	.473
2000	Hou-N	208	15	.303	.419	.582	91	9	.242	.377	.571	117	6	.350	.453	.590	208	15	.303	.419	.582	0	0	—	—	—	40	1	.300	.429	.425	168	14	.304	.417	.619
TOTALS		5932	224	.275	.349	.449	2958	112	.282	.353	.460	2974	112	.267	.345	.438	2797	97	.271	.339	.434	3135	127	.278	.357	.463	2031	77	.291	.351	.475	3901	147	.266	.348	.436
■ **John Cangelosi**	BB/TL																																			
1985	Chi-A	2	0	.000	.333	.000	2	0	.000	.000	.000	0	0	—	1.000	—	2	0	.000	.000	.000	0	0	—	1.000	—	0	0	—	1.000	—	2	0	.000	.000	.000
1986	Chi-A	438	2	.235	.349	.299	202	1	.238	.384	.317	236	1	.233	.316	.284	230	1	.248	.392	.304	208	1	.221	.294	.293	134	2	.216	.350	.343	304	0	.243	.348	.280
1987	Pit-N	182	4	.275	.427	.418	102	2	.294	.411	.431	80	2	.250	.444	.400	67	0	.254	.510	.284	115	4	.287	.362	.496	103	4	.282	.400	.485	79	0	.266	.458	.329
1988	Pit-N	118	0	.254	.353	.305	61	0	.246	.352	.328	57	0	.263	.354	.281	49	0	.163	.305	.204	69	0	.319	.390	.377	60	0	.267	.353	.317	58	0	.241	.353	.293
1989	Pit-N	160	0	.219	.365	.269	78	0	.269	.430	.333	82	0	.171	.300	.207	69	0	.246	.388	.304	91	0	.198	.348	.242	82	0	.207	.327	.268	78	0	.231	.402	.269
1990	Pit-N	76	0	.197	.307	.224	43	0	.186	.286	.233	33	0	.212	.333	.212	40	0	.175	.313	.175	36	0	.222	.300	.278	42	0	.214	.283	.238	34	0	.176	.333	.206
1992	Tex-A	85	1	.188	.330	.247	37	0	.189	.318	.216	48	1	.188	.339	.271	75	1	.187	.337	.253	10	0	.200	.273	.200	19	1	.158	.385	.368	66	0	.197	.312	.212
1994	NY-N	111	0	.252	.371	.288	46	0	.217	.379	.239	65	0	.277	.365	.323	104	0	.240	.368	.269	7	0	.429	.429	.571	48	0	.229	.339	.292	63	0	.270	.395	.286
1995	Hou-N	201	2	.318	.457	.393	114	2	.333	.453	.421	87	0	.299	.461	.356	42	2	.262	.415	.405	159	0	.333	.468	.390	33	2	.303	.410	.545	168	0	.321	.465	.363
1996	Hou-N	262	1	.263	.378	.347	155	1	.284	.395	.400	107	0	.234	.354	.271	119	1	.294	.433	.395	143	0	.238	.327	.308	32	1	.156	.289	.313	230	0	.278	.391	.352
1997	Fla-N	192	1	.245	.321	.302	91	1	.275	.371	.341	101	0	.218	.273	.267	86	1	.279	.364	.360	106	0	.217	.284	.255	51	0	.235	.310	.294	141	1	.248	.325	.305
1998	Fla-N	171	1	.251	.365	.316	84	0	.274	.380	.298	87	1	.230	.350	.333	79	1	.228	.358	.291	92	0	.272	.370	.337	86	1	.221	.320	.326	85	0	.282	.408	.306
1999	Col-N	6	0	.167	.167	.333	6	0	.167	.167	.333	0	0	—	—	—	0	0	—	—	—	6	0	.167	.167	.333	1	0	.000	.000	.000	5	0	.200	.200	.400
TOTALS		2004	12	.250	.370	.319	1021	7	.264	.388	.344	983	5	.235	.351	.294	962	7	.242	.388	.304	1042	5	.257	.353	.334	691	11	.232	.346	.346	1313	1	.260	.383	.305

		TOTAL					HOME					AWAY					1ST HALF					2ND HALF					LEFT					RIGHT				
YEAR	**TM/L**	AB	HR	AVG	OBP	SLG	AB	HR	AVG	OBP	SLG	AB	HR	AVG	OBP	SLG	AB	HR	AVG	OBP	SLG	AB	HR	AVG	OBP	SLG	AB	HR	AVG	OBP	SLG	AB	HR	AVG	OBP	SLG
■ Jose Canseco BR/TR																																				
1985	Oak-A	96	5	.302	.330	.490	45	4	.333	.375	.622	51	1	.275	.288	.373	0	0	—	—	—	96	5	.302	.330	.490	28	1	.250	.276	.393	68	4	.324	.352	.529
1986	Oak-A	600	33	.240	.318	.457	301	14	.213	.296	.385	299	19	.268	.340	.528	292	19	.260	.357	.514	308	14	.221	.279	.403	185	8	.281	.323	.470	415	25	.222	.316	.451
1987	Oak-A	630	31	.257	.310	.470	298	16	.275	.332	.507	332	15	.241	.289	.437	289	14	.266	.310	.460	341	17	.249	.310	.478	204	15	.309	.356	.618	426	16	.232	.288	.399
1988	Oak-A	610	42	.307	.391	.569	288	16	.313	.407	.538	322	26	.301	.375	.596	297	20	.290	.384	.522	313	22	.323	.397	.613	150	10	.340	.412	.620	460	32	.296	.384	.552
1989	Oak-A	227	17	.269	.333	.542	104	8	.269	.328	.538	123	9	.268	.338	.545	0	0	—	—	—	227	17	.269	.333	.542	50	7	.260	.381	.700	177	10	.271	.318	.497
1990	Oak-A	481	37	.274	.371	.543	217	18	.258	.386	.539	264	19	.288	.358	.545	203	20	.305	.410	.616	278	17	.252	.342	.489	123	12	.276	.357	.610	358	25	.274	.376	.520
1991	Oak-A	572	44	.266	.359	.556	267	16	.270	.371	.506	305	28	.262	.349	.600	255	18	.243	.359	.525	317	26	.284	.359	.580	136	8	.250	.370	.493	436	36	.271	.356	.576
1992	Oak-A	366	22	.246	.335	.456	170	12	.253	.340	.482	196	10	.240	.330	.434	249	18	.253	.323	.490	117	4	.231	.359	.385	81	7	.284	.392	.580	285	15	.235	.318	.421
1992	Tex-A	73	4	.233	.385	.452	34	3	.265	.405	.559	39	1	.205	.367	.359	0	0	—	—	—	73	4	.233	.385	.452	13	0	.077	.250	.077	60	4	.267	.413	.533
1993	Tex-A	231	10	.255	.308	.455	110	6	.291	.331	.536	121	4	.223	.289	.380	231	10	.255	.308	.455	0	0	—	—	—	38	3	.237	.302	.474	193	7	.259	.310	.451
1994	Tex-A	429	31	.282	.386	.552	223	17	.260	.370	.538	206	14	.306	.404	.568	281	22	.295	.411	.577	148	9	.257	.355	.507	92	7	.293	.426	.565	337	24	.279	.374	.549
1995	Bos-A	396	24	.306	.378	.556	199	10	.337	.401	.553	197	14	.274	.354	.558	81	3	.235	.351	.407	315	21	.324	.385	.594	93	12	.280	.409	.699	303	12	.314	.367	.512
1996	Bos-A	360	28	.289	.400	.589	170	17	.312	.422	.671	190	11	.268	.382	.516	255	24	.302	.405	.647	105	4	.257	.391	.448	95	6	.326	.444	.611	265	22	.275	.384	.581
1997	Oak-A	388	23	.235	.325	.461	187	10	.251	.350	.460	201	13	.219	.301	.463	296	17	.240	.321	.463	92	6	.217	.336	.457	79	2	.241	.318	.380	309	21	.233	.327	.482
1998	Tor-A	583	46	.237	.318	.518	277	25	.235	.324	.552	306	21	.239	.312	.487	284	24	.236	.336	.528	299	22	.237	.299	.508	141	15	.213	.327	.553	442	31	.244	.314	.507
1999	TB-A	430	34	.279	.369	.563	204	12	.250	.333	.466	226	22	.305	.399	.650	281	28	.285	.366	.637	149	6	.268	.373	.423	89	8	.292	.369	.640	341	26	.276	.368	.543
2000	TB-A	218	9	.257	.383	.450	81	4	.198	.309	.407	137	5	.292	.424	.474	157	7	.261	.363	.452	61	2	.246	.427	.443	42	3	.214	.313	.476	176	6	.267	.398	.443
2000	NY-A	111	6	.243	.365	.432	43	2	.209	.345	.372	68	4	.265	.378	.471	0	0	—	—	—	111	6	.243	.365	.432	35	3	.371	.489	.657	76	3	.184	.304	.329
TOTALS		6801	446	.266	.352	.516	3218	210	.266	.356	.511	3583	236	.266	.349	.520	3451	244	.267	.358	.528	3350	202	.265	.346	.504	1674	127	.280	.369	.563	5127	319	.262	.347	.500
■ Rod Carew BL/TR																																				
1978	Min-A	564	5	.333	.411	.441	293	1	.331	.407	.440	271	4	.336	.416	.443	247	5	.344	.418	.478	317	0	.325	.406	.413	211	1	.322	.405	.393	353	4	.340	.415	.470
1979	Cal-A	409	3	.318	.419	.391	182	1	.313	.430	.363	227	2	.322	.409	.414	186	1	.355	.457	.446	223	2	.287	.385	.345	110	1	.291	.419	.336	299	2	.328	.418	.411
1980	Cal-A	540	3	.331	.396	.437	278	2	.317	.385	.424	262	1	.347	.409	.450	266	1	.346	.419	.459	274	2	.318	.373	.416	159	1	.321	.374	.453	381	2	.336	.406	.430
1981	Cal-A	364	2	.305	.380	.374	178	0	.303	.387	.354	186	2	.306	.372	.392	236	2	.305	.374	.381	128	0	.305	.390	.359	102	0	.255	.306	.304	262	2	.324	.407	.401
1982	Cal-A	523	3	.319	.396	.403	226	1	.345	.426	.429	297	2	.300	.372	.384	246	1	.313	.408	.386	277	2	.325	.384	.419	162	1	.241	.321	.315	361	2	.355	.430	.443
1983	Cal-A	472	2	.339	.409	.411	239	1	.310	.381	.389	233	1	.369	.437	.433	228	2	.404	.458	.500	244	0	.279	.364	.328	162	1	.302	.374	.364	310	1	.358	.427	.435
1984	Cal-A	329	3	.295	.367	.353	146	3	.349	.416	.432	183	0	.251	.329	.290	217	3	.295	.366	.359	112	0	.295	.370	.339	58	0	.259	.353	.276	271	3	.303	.370	.369
1985	Cal-A	443	2	.280	.371	.345	219	1	.279	.374	.338	224	1	.281	.369	.353	152	1	.250	.370	.322	291	1	.296	.372	.357	106	0	.264	.371	.283	337	2	.285	.371	.365
TOTALS		3644	23	.317	.396	.399	1761	10	.318	.400	.399	1883	13	.317	.392	.399	1778	16	.330	.410	.421	1866	7	.305	.382	.378	1070	5	.288	.369	.354	2574	18	.329	.406	.418
■ Gary Carter BR/TR																																				
1978	Mon-N	533	20	.255	.336	.422	264	7	.235	.322	.356	269	13	.275	.349	.487	252	6	.234	.321	.345	281	14	.274	.349	.491	128	6	.234	.324	.430	405	14	.262	.339	.420
1979	Mon-N	505	22	.283	.338	.485	253	12	.304	.355	.538	252	10	.262	.320	.433	235	12	.294	.352	.511	270	10	.274	.324	.463	82	4	.256	.319	.476	423	18	.288	.341	.487
1980	Mon-N	549	29	.264	.331	.486	249	12	.253	.351	.470	300	17	.273	.314	.500	246	13	.236	.309	.443	303	16	.287	.349	.521	119	9	.311	.376	.622	430	20	.251	.319	.449
1981	Mon-N	374	16	.251	.313	.444	191	7	.246	.329	.424	183	9	.257	.294	.464	188	7	.245	.316	.404	186	9	.258	.309	.484	67	3	.179	.321	.358	307	13	.267	.310	.463
1982	Mon-N	557	29	.293	.381	.510	259	16	.290	.408	.556	298	13	.295	.355	.470	236	15	.288	.375	.534	321	14	.296	.385	.492	151	11	.311	.413	.603	406	18	.286	.368	.475
1983	Mon-N	541	17	.270	.336	.444	237	6	.278	.367	.451	304	11	.263	.310	.438	247	8	.263	.324	.429	294	9	.276	.346	.456	149	3	.289	.341	.423	392	14	.263	.334	.452
1984	Mon-N	596	27	.294	.366	.487	286	14	.301	.396	.493	310	13	.287	.337	.481	276	14	.297	.365	.511	320	13	.291	.367	.466	156	7	.340	.406	.551	440	20	.277	.352	.464
1985	NY-N	555	32	.281	.365	.488	263	12	.266	.355	.437	292	20	.295	.373	.534	247	11	.271	.368	.449	308	21	.289	.362	.519	219	13	.329	.429	.566	336	19	.250	.320	.438
1986	NY-N	490	24	.255	.337	.439	228	13	.268	.352	.478	262	11	.244	.323	.405	235	13	.251	.340	.447	255	11	.259	.333	.431	171	10	.275	.397	.480	319	14	.245	.301	.417
1987	NY-N	523	20	.235	.290	.392	255	9	.231	.294	.376	268	11	.239	.286	.407	244	9	.242	.305	.398	279	11	.229	.277	.387	183	7	.240	.322	.404	340	13	.232	.271	.385
1988	NY-N	455	11	.242	.301	.358	228	5	.211	.258	.298	227	6	.273	.343	.419	238	8	.252	.320	.403	217	3	.230	.279	.309	164	5	.256	.295	.396	291	6	.234	.304	.337
1989	NY-N	153	2	.183	.241	.275	77	1	.143	.173	.234	76	1	.224	.306	.316	79	1	.114	.186	.177	74	1	.257	.300	.378	66	2	.167	.225	.273	87	0	.195	.253	.276
1990	SF-N	244	9	.254	.324	.406	127	6	.307	.350	.504	117	3	.197	.296	.299	124	4	.266	.366	.435	120	5	.242	.276	.375	127	3	.236	.322	.362	117	6	.274	.325	.453
1991	LA-N	248	6	.246	.323	.375	125	3	.216	.298	.304	123	3	.276	.348	.447	97	3	.227	.309	.361	151	3	.258	.331	.384	151	3	.252	.343	.371	97	3	.237	.288	.381
1992	Mon-N	285	5	.218	.299	.340	153	2	.242	.335	.353	132	3	.189	.257	.326	159	3	.239	.315	.365	126	2	.190	.281	.310	139	2	.230	.301	.367	146	3	.205	.298	.315
TOTALS		6608	269	.262	.333	.439	3195	125	.259	.341	.433	3413	144	.264	.325	.445	3103	127	.256	.332	.430	3505	142	.267	.334	.447	2072	88	.270	.353	.458	4536	181	.258	.323	.431
■ Joe Carter BR/TR																																				
1983	Chi-N	51	0	.176	.176	.235	24	0	.208	.208	.292	27	0	.148	.148	.185	0	0	—	—	—	51	0	.176	.176	.235	15	0	.200	.200	.267	36	0	.167	.167	.222
1984	Cle-A	244	13	.275	.307	.467	125	9	.312	.344	.568	119	4	.235	.270	.361	9	1	.222	.222	.556	235	12	.277	.310	.464	85	8	.329	.352	.659	159	5	.245	.284	.365
1985	Cle-A	489	15	.262	.298	.409	247	5	.267	.320	.389	242	10	.256	.276	.430	208	6	.240	.286	.375	281	9	.278	.307	.434	161	5	.248	.303	.391	328	10	.268	.296	.418
1986	Cle-A	663	29	.302	.335	.514	324	14	.312	.350	.522	339	15	.292	.320	.507	283	12	.304	.340	.491	380	17	.300	.331	.532	181	7	.315	.354	.530	482	22	.297	.327	.508
1987	Cle-A	588	32	.264	.304	.480	279	9	.251	.298	.409	309	23	.275	.310	.544	280	16	.243	.290	.471	308	16	.282	.317	.487	153	7	.248	.287	.431	435	25	.269	.310	.497
1988	Cle-A	621	27	.271	.314	.478	299	16	.281	.336	.498	322	11	.261	.292	.460	294	15	.269	.317	.490	327	12	.272	.311	.468	132	7	.311	.348	.553	489	20	.260	.305	.458
1989	Cle-A	651	35	.243	.292	.465	329	16	.243	.294	.456	322	19	.242	.289	.475	311	12	.254	.299	.441	340	23	.232	.285	.488	186	8	.215	.267	.387	465	27	.254	.301	.497
1990	SD-N	634	24	.232	.290	.391	322	12	.220	.263	.366	312	12	.244	.316	.417	287	13	.223	.273	.408	347	11	.239	.303	.378	203	7	.197	.258	.335	431	17	.248	.305	.418
1991	Tor-A	638	33	.273	.330	.503	321	23	.290	.348	.583	317	10	.256	.311	.423	295	17	.308	.368	.569	343	16	.242	.297	.446	188	10	.335	.366	.569	450	23	.247	.315	.476
1992	Tor-A	622	34	.264	.309	.498	301	21	.259	.303	.538	321	13	.268	.315	.461	301	17	.282	.324	.518	321	17	.246	.296	.480	157	7	.312	.355	.535	465	27	.247	.294	.486
1993	Tor-A	603	33	.254	.312	.489	312	21	.250	.304	.529	291	12	.258	.321	.447	285	18	.277	.331	.568	318	15	.233	.295	.418	162	10	.296	.341	.531	441	23	.238	.302	.474
1994	Tor-A	435	27	.271	.317	.524	207	18	.300	.335	.628	228	9	.246	.300	.430	281	16	.270	.313	.512	154	11	.273	.323	.545	114	9	.298	.346	.596	321	18	.262	.306	.498
1995	Tor-A	558	25	.253	.300	.428	275	13	.258	.307	.455	283	12	.247	.293	.403	218	10	.284	.328	.463	340	15	.232	.283	.406	136	8	.294	.331	.529	422	17	.239	.290	.396
1996	Tor-A	625	30	.253	.306	.475	321	14	.240	.287	.442	304	16	.266	.326	.510	317	19	.281	.346	.555	308	11	.224	.264	.393	166	6	.247	.304	.452	459	24	.255	.307	.484
1997	Tor-A	612	21	.234	.284	.399	299	11	.217	.279	.378	313	10	.249	.290	.419	292	9	.240	.291	.384	320	12	.228	.278	.412	180	6	.289	.328	.472	432	15	.211	.266	.368
1998	Bal-A	283	11	.247	.297	.424	147	6	.259	.319	.429	136	5	.235	.273	.419	238	9	.252	.288	.433	45	2	.222	.340	.378	106	7	.302	.351	.557	177	4	.215	.265	.345
1998	SF-N	105	7	.295	.322	.562	51	5	.353	.357	.725	54	2	.241	.288	.407	0	0	—	—	—	105	7	.295	.322	.562	42	3	.286	.311	.571	63	4	.302	.329	.556
TOTALS		8422	396	.259	.306	.464	4183	213	.262	.310	.478	4239	183	.257	.302	.451	3899	190	.267	.315	.481	4523	206	.253	.299	.450	2367	115	.278	.322	.489	6055	281	.252	.300	.455
■ Sean Casey BL/TR																																				
1997	Cle-A	10	0	.200	.333	.200	8	0	.125	.300	.125	2	0	.500	.500	.500	0	0	—	—	—	10	0	.200	.333	.200	2	0	.000	.500	.000	8	0	.250	.250	.250
1998	Cin-N	302	7	.272	.365	.417	144	3	.264	.355	.375	158	4	.278	.373	.456	72	0	.181	.259	.194	230	7	.300	.396	.487	45	1	.222	.308	.333	257	6	.280	.375	.432
1999	Cin-N	594	25	.332	.399	.539	298	11	.322	.399	.503	296	14	.341	.399	.574	275	16	.382	.430	.655	319	9	.288	.373	.439	170	8	.271	.361	.465	424	17	.356	.415	.568
2000	Cin-N	480	20	.315	.385	.517	244	9	.316	.394	.512	236	11	.314	.375	.521	215	4	.251	.339	.353	265	16	.366	.423	.649	104	1	.250	.328	.356	376	19	.332	.401	.561
TOTALS		1386	52	.312	.386	.502	694	23	.305	.387	.476	692	29	.318	.385	.529	562	20	.306	.373	.480	824	32	.316	.395	.517	321	10	.255	.344	.408	1065	42	.329	.399	.531
■ Vinny Castilla BR/TR																																				
1991	Atl-N	5	0	.200	.200	.200	4	0	.250	.250	.250	1	0	.000	.000	.000	0	0	—	—	—	5	0	.200	.200	.200	0	0	—	—	—	5	0	.200	.200	.200
1992	Atl-N	16	0	.250	.333	.313	16	0	.250	.333	.313	0	0	—	—	—	0	0	—	—	—	16	0	.250	.333	.313	6	0	.167	.167	.167	10	0	.300	.417	.400
1993	Col-N	337	9	.255	.283	.404	167	5	.305	.346	.497	170	4	.206	.217	.312	166	5	.313	.339	.500	171	4	.199	.230	.310	87	3	.333	.370	.529	250	6	.228	.253	.360
1994	Col-N	130	3	.331	.357	.500	61	1	.344	.354	.525	69	2	.319	.360	.478	72	3	.333	.351	.569	58	0	.328	.365	.414	36	0	.222	.250	.278	94	3	.372	.400	.585
1995	Col-N	527	32	.309	.347	.564	274	23	.383	.413	.730	253	9	.229	.277	.383	226	12	.314	.342	.558	301	20	.306	.352	.568	134	12	.388	.417	.769	393	20	.282	.324	.494
1996	Col-N	629	40	.304	.343	.548	328	27	.345	.389	.659	301	13	.259	.291	.429	310	17	.313	.354	.548	319	23	.295	.332	.549	137	5	.255	.315	.423	492	35	.317	.351	.583
1997	Col-N	612	40	.304	.356	.547	316	21	.320	.361	.560	296	19	.287	.352	.534	304	20	.289	.348	.536	308	20	.318	.364	.558	129	11	.380	.434	.698	483	29	.284	.335	.507
1998	Col-N	645	46	.319	.362	.589	326	26	.368	.410	.687	319	20	.270	.311	.489	335	23	.301	.349	.561	310	23	.339	.375	.619	172	11	.320	.362	.576	473	35	.319	.361	.594
1999	Col-N	615	33	.275	.331	.478	307	20	.280	.340	.511	308	13	.269	.321	.445	287	17	.282	.338	.509	328	16	.268	.325	.451	169	8	.225	.307	.385	446	25	.294	.340	.513
2000	TB-A	331	6	.221	.254	.308	150	2	.207	.242	.293	181	4	.232	.264	.320	219	6	.219	.263	.329	112	0	.223	.237	.268	69	1	.203	.240	.275	262	5	.225	.258	.317
TOTALS		3847	209	.292	.334	.509	1949	125	.325	.367	.584	1898	84	.258	.301	.433	1919	103	.293	.337	.515	1928	106	.290	.332	.504	939	51	.299	.349	.523	2908	158	.289	.330	.505
■ Luis Castillo BB/TR																																				
1996	Fla-N	164	1	.262	.320	.305	93	0	.247	.300	.280	71	1	.282	.346	.338	0	0	—	—	—	164	1	.262	.320	.305	38	1	.269	.308	.447	126	0	.254	.324	.262
1997	Fla-N	263	0	.240	.310	.270	138	0	.217	.312	.254	125	0	.264	.308	.288	217	0	.258	.321	.286	46	0	.152	.264	.196	45	0	.222	.271	.267	218	0	.243	.318	.271
1998	Fla-N	153	1	.203	.307	.268	57	0	.140	.269	.175	96	1	.240	.330	.323	0	0	—	—	—	153	1	.203	.307	.268	45	1	.200	.368	.333	108	0	.204	.277	.241
1999	Fla-N	487	0	.302	.384	.366	262	0	.294	.382	.355	225	0	.311	.387	.378	263	0	.270	.345	.335	224	0	.339	.429	.402	100	0	.310	.397	.410	387	0	.300	.381	.354
2000	Fla-N	539	2	.334	.418	.388	258	1	.372	.471	.434	281	1	.299	.367	.345	232	1	.362	.462	.435	307	1	.313	.383	.352	148	2	.291	.367	.392	391	0	.350	.437	.386
TOTALS		1606	4	.289	.370	.342	808	1	.290	.382	.342	798	3	.288	.357	.342	712	1	.296	.377	.353	894	3	.283	.364	.333	376	4	.277	.359	.380	1230	0	.293	.374	.330
■ Ron Cey BR/TR																																				
1978	LA-N	555	23	.270	.380	.452	279	10	.305	.415	.480	276	13	.236	.345	.424	271	11	.269	.375	.454	284	12	.271	.385	.451	125	10	.288	.434	.584	430	13	.265	.364	.414
1979	LA-N	487	28	.281	.389	.499	255	17	.306	.410	.529	232	11	.254	.364	.466	224	16	.281	.392	.536	263	12	.281	.386	.468	123	12	.309	.394	.634	364	16	.272	.387	.453
1980	LA-N	551	28	.254	.342	.452	267	16	.258	.356	.472	284	12	.250	.328	.433	258	11	.256	.337	.419	293	17	.253	.346	.481	85	6	.294	.400	.565	466	22	.247	.331	.431

		TOTAL					HOME					AWAY					1ST HALF					2ND HALF					LEFT					RIGHT				
YEAR	TM/L	AB	HR	AVG	OBP	SLG	AB	HR	AVG	OBP	SLG	AB	HR	AVG	OBP	SLG	AB	HR	AVG	OBP	SLG	AB	HR	AVG	OBP	SLG	AB	HR	AVG	OBP	SLG	AB	HR	AVG	OBP	SLG
1981	LA-N	312	13	.288	.372	.474	165	9	.315	.404	.552	147	4	.259	.333	.388	201	9	.274	.359	.468	111	4	.315	.394	.486	44	1	.159	.240	.295	268	12	.310	.393	.504
1982	LA-N	556	24	.254	.323	.428	281	10	.238	.283	.363	275	14	.269	.362	.495	273	9	.267	.337	.425	283	15	.240	.310	.431	96	9	.281	.333	.635	460	15	.248	.321	.385
1983	Chi-N	581	24	.275	.346	.460	286	11	.259	.334	.437	295	13	.292	.357	.481	269	8	.257	.320	.394	312	16	.292	.367	.516	151	10	.238	.328	.483	430	14	.288	.352	.451
1984	Chi-N	505	25	.240	.324	.442	249	12	.237	.329	.450	256	13	.242	.319	.434	236	10	.229	.309	.411	269	15	.249	.338	.468	132	10	.250	.366	.515	373	15	.236	.308	.416
1985	Chi-N	500	22	.232	.316	.408	238	15	.261	.354	.483	262	7	.206	.279	.340	237	12	.215	.316	.401	263	10	.247	.315	.414	122	7	.221	.312	.443	378	15	.235	.317	.397
1986	Chi-N	256	13	.273	.384	.508	137	4	.241	.354	.401	119	9	.311	.418	.630	129	6	.279	.372	.504	127	7	.268	.395	.512	80	5	.325	.460	.637	176	8	.250	.346	.449
1987	Oak-A	104	4	.221	.359	.394	69	3	.203	.345	.362	35	1	.257	.386	.457	93	4	.215	.362	.409	11	0	.273	.333	.273	76	3	.237	.372	.421	28	1	.179	.324	.321
TOTALS		4407	204	.260	.351	.452	2226	107	.266	.359	.458	2181	97	.254	.342	.447	2191	96	.256	.346	.439	2216	108	.265	.355	.466	1034	73	.264	.369	.533	3373	131	.259	.344	.428
■ Chris Chambliss BL/TR																																				
1978	NY-A	625	12	.274	.321	.382	299	6	.251	.313	.371	326	6	.294	.328	.393	295	6	.305	.353	.410	330	6	.245	.292	.358	322	4	.289	.332	.376	303	8	.257	.309	.389
1979	NY-A	554	18	.280	.324	.437	268	10	.280	.324	.444	286	8	.280	.325	.430	268	9	.257	.301	.429	286	9	.301	.346	.444	243	6	.239	.266	.358	311	12	.312	.368	.498
1980	Atl-N	602	18	.282	.338	.440	304	12	.299	.352	.487	298	6	.265	.324	.393	281	8	.295	.333	.459	321	10	.271	.343	.424	157	3	.223	.230	.318	445	15	.303	.373	.483
1981	Atl-N	404	8	.272	.343	.403	189	2	.270	.341	.381	215	6	.274	.344	.423	210	2	.271	.346	.376	194	6	.273	.339	.433	95	1	.242	.301	.326	309	7	.282	.355	.427
1982	Atl-N	534	20	.270	.337	.436	256	11	.285	.352	.465	278	9	.255	.323	.410	250	10	.264	.335	.436	284	10	.275	.339	.437	100	1	.280	.301	.370	434	19	.267	.344	.452
1983	Atl-N	447	20	.280	.366	.481	212	9	.307	.397	.524	235	11	.255	.338	.443	227	8	.278	.360	.449	220	12	.282	.373	.514	79	2	.203	.276	.342	368	18	.296	.385	.511
1984	Atl-N	389	9	.257	.350	.362	190	6	.284	.355	.432	199	3	.231	.346	.296	232	6	.267	.354	.379	157	3	.242	.344	.338	79	0	.177	.230	.203	310	9	.277	.379	.403
1985	Atl-N	170	3	.235	.307	.329	84	1	.226	.290	.286	86	2	.244	.323	.372	112	0	.196	.266	.241	58	3	.310	.385	.500	36	0	.194	.286	.250	134	3	.246	.313	.351
1986	Atl-N	122	2	.311	.384	.426	59	2	.288	.358	.475	63	0	.333	.408	.381	51	1	.373	.439	.471	71	1	.268	.346	.394	15	0	.267	.313	.333	107	2	.318	.393	.439
1988	NY-A	1	0	.000	.000	.000	0	0	—	—	—	1	0	.000	.000	.000	1	0	.000	.000	.000	0	0	—	—	—	0	0	—	—	—	1	0	.000	.000	.000
TOTALS		3848	110	.274	.339	.417	1861	59	.279	.344	.437	1987	51	.268	.333	.399	1927	50	.276	.338	.412	1921	60	.272	.339	.423	1126	17	.247	.286	.340	2722	93	.285	.359	.449
■ Ryan Christenson BR/TR																																				
1998	Oak-A	370	5	.257	.321	.368	162	2	.222	.291	.309	208	3	.284	.345	.413	140	2	.250	.333	.357	230	3	.261	.313	.374	108	1	.241	.349	.324	262	4	.263	.309	.385
1999	Oak-A	268	4	.209	.305	.306	120	2	.242	.345	.358	148	2	.182	.272	.264	104	2	.183	.264	.260	164	2	.226	.332	.335	93	3	.301	.405	.495	175	1	.160	.250	.206
2000	Oak-A	129	4	.248	.349	.388	53	3	.170	.290	.377	76	1	.303	.391	.395	64	1	.250	.377	.313	65	3	.246	.319	.462	54	2	.167	.286	.278	75	2	.307	.395	.467
TOTALS		767	13	.239	.320	.349	335	7	.221	.311	.337	432	6	.252	.328	.359	308	5	.227	.319	.315	459	8	.246	.321	.373	255	6	.247	.357	.376	512	7	.234	.301	.336
■ Jeff Cirillo BR/TR																																				
1994	Mil-A	126	3	.238	.309	.381	74	1	.216	.284	.311	52	2	.269	.345	.481	22	0	.136	.240	.182	104	3	.260	.325	.423	39	0	.256	.310	.410	87	3	.230	.309	.368
1995	Mil-A	328	9	.277	.371	.442	153	6	.320	.412	.516	175	3	.240	.333	.377	98	3	.316	.380	.500	230	6	.261	.367	.417	119	2	.294	.384	.429	209	7	.268	.363	.450
1996	Mil-A	566	15	.325	.391	.504	272	6	.298	.378	.456	294	9	.350	.404	.548	253	6	.336	.398	.506	313	9	.316	.385	.502	161	6	.311	.387	.528	405	9	.331	.393	.494
1997	Mil-A	580	10	.288	.367	.426	300	6	.287	.363	.417	280	4	.289	.371	.436	283	6	.304	.383	.470	297	4	.273	.351	.384	165	3	.261	.354	.370	415	7	.299	.372	.448
1998	Mil-A	604	14	.321	.402	.445	297	6	.313	.395	.421	307	8	.329	.409	.469	295	6	.312	.410	.431	309	8	.330	.394	.460	167	3	.299	.400	.389	437	11	.330	.403	.467
1999	Mil-A	607	15	.326	.401	.461	294	6	.354	.428	.469	313	9	.300	.375	.454	294	6	.313	.389	.429	313	9	.339	.411	.492	158	9	.323	.422	.557	449	6	.327	.393	.428
2000	Col-N	598	11	.326	.392	.477	318	9	.403	.472	.607	280	2	.239	.299	.329	267	8	.348	.424	.554	331	3	.308	.365	.414	132	2	.379	.445	.530	466	9	.311	.377	.461
TOTALS		3409	77	.311	.386	.457	1708	40	.326	.404	.472	1701	37	.295	.368	.442	1512	35	.319	.397	.473	1897	42	.304	.377	.445	941	25	.307	.395	.463	2468	52	.312	.382	.455
■ Jack Clark BR/TR																																				
1978	SF-N	592	25	.306	.358	.537	272	10	.301	.373	.544	320	15	.309	.344	.531	270	12	.304	.365	.548	322	13	.307	.351	.528	191	12	.330	.405	.607	401	13	.294	.335	.504
1979	SF-N	527	26	.273	.348	.476	242	10	.260	.350	.438	285	16	.284	.347	.509	295	13	.281	.358	.478	232	13	.263	.336	.474	118	8	.280	.393	.508	409	18	.271	.334	.467
1980	SF-N	437	22	.284	.382	.517	203	8	.330	.426	.547	234	14	.244	.344	.491	243	14	.292	.378	.568	194	8	.273	.387	.454	108	4	.380	.507	.648	329	18	.252	.337	.474
1981	SF-N	385	17	.268	.341	.460	194	7	.273	.333	.438	191	10	.262	.348	.482	201	6	.224	.296	.378	184	11	.315	.388	.549	78	3	.269	.412	.436	307	14	.267	.321	.466
1982	SF-N	563	27	.274	.372	.481	277	9	.267	.370	.422	286	18	.280	.373	.538	247	13	.243	.340	.433	316	14	.297	.396	.519	161	7	.298	.413	.522	402	20	.264	.354	.465
1983	SF-N	492	20	.268	.361	.441	250	11	.260	.358	.452	242	9	.277	.363	.430	267	13	.255	.349	.453	225	7	.284	.374	.427	140	8	.271	.382	.493	352	12	.267	.352	.420
1984	SF-N	203	11	.320	.434	.537	97	4	.278	.410	.443	106	7	.358	.457	.623	203	11	.320	.434	.537	0	0	—	—	—	53	4	.283	.479	.528	150	7	.333	.415	.540
1985	StL-N	442	22	.281	.393	.502	225	8	.231	.335	.409	217	14	.332	.450	.599	263	15	.289	.391	.536	179	7	.268	.395	.453	139	9	.324	.467	.597	303	13	.261	.355	.459
1986	StL-N	232	9	.237	.362	.422	117	4	.274	.393	.453	115	5	.200	.331	.391	232	9	.237	.362	.422	0	0	—	—	—	89	6	.303	.415	.596	143	3	.196	.329	.315
1987	StL-N	419	35	.286	.459	.597	202	17	.292	.457	.604	217	18	.281	.460	.590	257	23	.307	.441	.650	162	12	.253	.483	.512	138	10	.261	.480	.543	281	25	.299	.447	.623
1988	NY-A	496	27	.242	.381	.433	232	13	.233	.384	.422	264	14	.250	.380	.443	225	16	.249	.408	.489	271	11	.236	.358	.387	149	10	.248	.435	.483	347	17	.239	.356	.412
1989	SD-N	455	26	.242	.410	.459	211	11	.232	.406	.436	244	15	.250	.413	.480	237	9	.219	.388	.363	218	17	.266	.434	.564	125	4	.272	.474	.440	330	22	.230	.383	.467
1990	SD-N	334	25	.266	.441	.533	176	16	.256	.419	.568	158	9	.278	.465	.494	130	9	.223	.396	.469	204	16	.294	.469	.574	114	9	.377	.541	.667	220	16	.209	.386	.464
1991	Bos-A	481	28	.249	.374	.466	253	18	.281	.377	.542	228	10	.215	.372	.382	215	10	.214	.358	.372	266	18	.278	.387	.541	117	6	.325	.465	.530	364	22	.225	.342	.445
1992	Bos-A	257	5	.210	.350	.311	116	0	.259	.390	.310	141	5	.170	.316	.312	173	3	.220	.355	.312	84	2	.190	.340	.310	95	2	.295	.460	.421	162	3	.160	.278	.247
TOTALS		6315	325	.268	.383	.482	3067	146	.268	.384	.474	3248	179	.268	.383	.490	3458	176	.262	.375	.473	2857	149	.277	.393	.493	1815	102	.301	.448	.538	4500	223	.255	.355	.460
■ Will Clark BL/TL																																				
1986	SF-N	408	11	.287	.343	.444	220	7	.336	.388	.509	188	4	.229	.290	.367	192	6	.260	.322	.432	216	5	.310	.361	.454	130	2	.308	.348	.415	278	9	.277	.341	.457
1987	SF-N	529	35	.308	.371	.580	274	22	.339	.393	.657	255	13	.275	.347	.498	248	14	.323	.365	.573	281	21	.295	.376	.587	173	7	.318	.341	.555	356	28	.303	.385	.593
1988	SF-N	575	29	.282	.386	.508	283	14	.269	.364	.484	292	15	.295	.407	.531	272	19	.272	.380	.570	303	10	.290	.391	.452	221	7	.262	.331	.434	354	22	.294	.417	.554
1989	SF-N	588	23	.333	.407	.546	277	9	.325	.394	.516	311	14	.341	.420	.572	284	13	.342	.432	.577	304	10	.326	.382	.516	215	8	.321	.371	.512	373	15	.340	.428	.566
1990	SF-N	600	19	.295	.357	.448	296	8	.318	.384	.459	304	11	.273	.329	.438	304	14	.286	.343	.477	296	5	.304	.370	.419	249	9	.317	.372	.486	351	10	.279	.347	.422
1991	SF-N	565	29	.301	.359	.536	283	17	.283	.344	.558	282	12	.319	.373	.514	258	12	.291	.345	.488	307	17	.309	.370	.577	197	9	.239	.291	.452	368	20	.334	.394	.582
1992	SF-N	513	16	.300	.384	.476	270	11	.337	.422	.563	243	5	.259	.342	.379	246	8	.317	.413	.492	267	8	.285	.357	.461	205	2	.307	.366	.395	308	14	.295	.396	.529
1993	SF-N	491	14	.283	.367	.432	257	5	.249	.349	.362	234	9	.321	.389	.509	273	5	.256	.352	.377	218	9	.317	.387	.500	182	1	.269	.335	.330	309	13	.291	.386	.492
1994	Tex-A	389	13	.329	.431	.501	210	9	.338	.443	.533	179	4	.318	.417	.464	273	12	.352	.446	.575	116	1	.276	.396	.328	118	1	.314	.370	.449	271	12	.336	.455	.524
1995	Tex-A	454	16	.302	.389	.480	218	10	.303	.409	.518	236	6	.301	.370	.445	186	8	.290	.389	.478	268	8	.310	.389	.481	148	4	.291	.384	.453	306	12	.307	.392	.493
1996	Tex-A	436	13	.284	.377	.436	220	9	.295	.370	.477	216	4	.273	.384	.394	241	6	.299	.388	.436	195	7	.267	.364	.436	134	4	.246	.318	.388	302	9	.301	.402	.457
1997	Tex-A	393	12	.326	.400	.496	202	6	.351	.422	.530	191	6	.298	.377	.461	246	7	.333	.421	.496	147	5	.313	.364	.497	129	3	.302	.366	.442	264	9	.337	.416	.523
1998	Tex-A	554	23	.305	.384	.507	285	11	.295	.375	.498	269	12	.316	.393	.517	282	12	.305	.397	.504	272	11	.305	.369	.511	147	5	.327	.386	.517	407	18	.297	.383	.504
1999	Bal-A	251	10	.303	.395	.482	115	5	.304	.397	.461	136	5	.301	.392	.500	151	6	.298	.363	.477	100	4	.310	.439	.490	52	0	.192	.250	.212	199	10	.332	.429	.553
2000	Bal-A	256	9	.301	.413	.473	130	6	.331	.457	.569	126	3	.270	.365	.373	169	3	.284	.421	.414	87	6	.333	.396	.586	74	0	.230	.341	.297	182	9	.330	.441	.544
2000	StL-N	171	12	.345	.426	.655	82	6	.293	.396	.549	89	6	.393	.455	.753	0	0	—	—	—	171	12	.345	.426	.655	39	2	.282	.349	.513	132	10	.364	.448	.697
TOTALS		7173	284	.303	.384	.497	3622	155	.309	.391	.514	3551	129	.297	.376	.479	3625	145	.302	.387	.495	3548	139	.305	.380	.498	2413	64	.289	.349	.441	4760	220	.311	.400	.525
■ Royce Clayton BR/TR																																				
1991	SF-N	26	0	.115	.148	.154	13	0	.154	.154	.154	13	0	.077	.143	.154	0	0	—	—	—	26	0	.115	.148	.154	5	0	.200	.200	.200	21	0	.095	.136	.143
1992	SF-N	321	4	.224	.281	.308	172	3	.250	.309	.343	149	1	.195	.248	.268	179	3	.207	.273	.324	142	1	.246	.291	.289	96	0	.250	.327	.333	225	4	.213	.260	.298
1993	SF-N	549	6	.282	.331	.372	266	5	.305	.346	.421	283	1	.261	.316	.325	277	2	.282	.315	.350	272	4	.283	.345	.393	170	2	.247	.286	.341	379	4	.298	.350	.385
1994	SF-N	385	3	.236	.295	.327	208	1	.240	.301	.341	177	2	.232	.288	.311	261	2	.253	.304	.352	124	1	.202	.277	.274	85	2	.176	.255	.341	300	1	.253	.307	.323
1995	SF-N	509	5	.244	.298	.342	251	2	.215	.272	.291	258	3	.271	.324	.391	212	2	.241	.320	.349	297	3	.246	.282	.337	104	4	.260	.304	.423	405	1	.240	.297	.321
1996	StL-N	491	6	.277	.321	.371	237	6	.253	.301	.380	254	0	.299	.341	.362	257	3	.280	.331	.389	234	3	.274	.310	.350	135	1	.281	.315	.356	356	5	.275	.324	.376
1997	StL-N	576	9	.266	.306	.398	262	5	.298	.351	.427	314	4	.239	.267	.373	298	6	.258	.310	.409	278	3	.273	.303	.385	139	2	.252	.295	.396	437	7	.270	.310	.398
1998	StL-N	355	4	.234	.313	.327	181	1	.221	.319	.287	174	3	.247	.307	.368	267	2	.240	.323	.318	88	2	.216	.281	.352	102	1	.265	.364	.382	253	3	.221	.292	.304
1998	Tex-A	186	5	.285	.330	.441	97	1	.247	.286	.351	89	4	.326	.378	.539	0	0	—	—	—	186	5	.285	.330	.441	40	4	.400	.458	.800	146	1	.253	.290	.342
1999	Tex-A	465	14	.288	.346	.445	210	6	.310	.375	.476	255	8	.271	.323	.420	177	3	.243	.282	.339	288	11	.316	.384	.510	98	5	.306	.370	.531	367	9	.283	.340	.422
2000	Tex-A	513	14	.242	.301	.384	240	9	.258	.323	.425	273	5	.227	.281	.348	275	13	.240	.297	.436	238	1	.244	.307	.324	107	4	.196	.263	.336	406	10	.254	.312	.397
TOTALS		4376	70	.258	.312	.370	2137	39	.262	.320	.378	2239	31	.254	.304	.363	2203	36	.251	.308	.367	2173	34	.264	.315	.374	1081	25	.255	.313	.394	3295	45	.259	.311	.362
■ Vince Coleman BB/TR																																				
1985	StL-N	636	1	.267	.320	.335	315	1	.305	.356	.387	321	0	.231	.285	.283	264	1	.261	.328	.333	372	0	.272	.315	.336	211	0	.237	.284	.341	425	1	.282	.338	.332
1986	StL-N	600	0	.232	.301	.280	320	0	.269	.345	.316	280	0	.189	.250	.239	269	0	.257	.330	.327	331	0	.211	.277	.242	227	0	.238	.327	.278	373	0	.228	.285	.282
1987	StL-N	623	3	.289	.363	.358	287	3	.275	.348	.376	336	0	.301	.376	.342	290	0	.293	.377	.345	333	3	.285	.351	.369	209	3	.268	.361	.416	414	0	.300	.364	.329
1988	StL-N	616	3	.260	.313	.339	326	2	.276	.330	.374	290	1	.241	.294	.300	324	2	.284	.333	.392	292	1	.233	.291	.281	220	2	.273	.324	.395	396	1	.253	.307	.308
1989	StL-N	563	2	.254	.316	.334	277	1	.260	.316	.361	286	1	.248	.316	.308	284	0	.264	.319	.356	279	2	.244	.313	.312	264	2	.235	.285	.326	299	0	.271	.342	.341
1990	StL-N	497	6	.292	.340	.400	259	5	.297	.352	.440	238	1	.286	.327	.357	299	3	.301	.343	.401	198	3	.278	.336	.399	191	5	.262	.297	.450	306	1	.310	.366	.369
1991	NY-N	278	1	.255	.347	.327	107	0	.234	.364	.262	171	1	.269	.335	.368	216	1	.259	.360	.343	62	0	.242	.299	.274	105	1	.248	.307	.305	173	0	.260	.369	.341
1992	NY-N	229	2	.275	.355	.358	119	2	.277	.370	.353	110	0	.273	.339	.364	114	2	.316	.395	.421	115	0	.235	.315	.296	60	1	.283	.358	.433	169	1	.272	.354	.331
1993	NY-N	373	2	.279	.316	.375	190	2	.284	.328	.389	183	0	.273	.302	.361	292	2	.264	.305	.363	81	0	.333	.353	.420	100	1	.290	.333	.430	273	1	.275	.309	.355
1994	KC-A	438	2	.240	.285	.340	217	1	.300	.347	.438	221	1	.181	.224	.244	321	2	.237	.285	.343	117	0	.248	.286	.333	126	2	.262	.293	.389	312	0	.231	.282	.321
1995	KC-A	293	4	.287	.348	.399	158	2	.291	.337	.405	135	2	.281	.359	.393	168	2	.286	.349	.417	125	2	.288	.346	.376	99	3	.232	.309	.384	194	1	.314	.368	.407
1995	Sea-A	162	1	.290	.335	.395	82	1	.293	.341	.427	80	0	.287	.329	.363	0	0	—	—	—	162	1	.290	.335	.395	39	0	.308	.308	.385	123	1	.285	.343	.398

YEAR	TM/L	TOTAL					HOME					AWAY					1ST HALF					2ND HALF					LEFT					RIGHT				
		AB	HR	AVG	OBP	SLG	AB	HR	AVG	OBP	SLG	AB	HR	AVG	OBP	SLG	AB	HR	AVG	OBP	SLG	AB	HR	AVG	OBP	SLG	AB	HR	AVG	OBP	SLG	AB	HR	AVG	OBP	SLG
1996	Cin-N	84	1	.155	.237	.226	35	1	.229	.325	.371	49	0	.102	.170	.122	84	1	.155	.237	.226	0	0	—	—	—	27	0	.111	.143	.185	57	1	.175	.277	.246
1997	Det-A	14	0	.071	.133	.071	10	0	.100	.182	.100	4	0	.000	.000	.000	14	0	.071	.133	.071	0	0	—	—	—	1	0	.000	.500	.000	13	0	.077	.077	.077
TOTALS		5406	28	.264	.324	.345	2702	21	.280	.342	.377	2704	7	.247	.305	.312	2939	16	.268	.330	.358	2467	12	.259	.316	.329	1879	20	.253	.312	.367	3527	8	.269	.330	.333
■ Dave Collins BB/TL																																				
1978	Cin-N	102	0	.216	.311	.225	54	0	.259	.388	.278	48	0	.167	.212	.167	59	0	.220	.304	.220	43	0	.209	.320	.233	51	0	.235	.273	.255	51	0	.196	.344	.196
1979	Cin-N	396	3	.318	.364	.402	168	0	.345	.397	.387	228	3	.298	.339	.412	98	1	.347	.379	.439	298	2	.309	.359	.389	161	1	.317	.339	.391	235	2	.319	.380	.409
1980	Cin-N	551	3	.303	.366	.370	269	3	.327	.392	.435	282	0	.280	.340	.309	251	2	.275	.343	.351	300	1	.327	.384	.387	164	0	.268	.309	.354	387	3	.318	.389	.377
1981	Cin-N	360	3	.272	.355	.381	189	1	.296	.368	.413	171	2	.246	.340	.345	215	2	.312	.387	.442	145	1	.214	.307	.290	104	0	.231	.322	.308	256	3	.289	.368	.410
1982	NY-A	348	3	.253	.315	.330	185	2	.281	.348	.389	163	1	.221	.277	.264	188	1	.255	.307	.324	160	2	.250	.324	.338	152	0	.230	.285	.276	196	3	.270	.338	.372
1983	Tor-A	402	1	.271	.343	.328	199	0	.221	.320	.281	203	1	.320	.367	.374	167	0	.216	.284	.251	235	1	.311	.383	.383	79	0	.316	.407	.342	323	1	.260	.327	.325
1984	Tor-A	441	2	.308	.366	.444	210	2	.310	.366	.514	231	0	.307	.366	.381	212	2	.311	.351	.476	229	0	.306	.379	.415	63	0	.349	.391	.476	378	2	.302	.362	.439
1985	Oak-A	379	4	.251	.303	.346	190	1	.232	.300	.284	189	3	.270	.305	.407	257	2	.253	.296	.339	122	2	.246	.316	.361	87	1	.218	.260	.287	292	3	.260	.315	.363
1986	Det-A	419	1	.270	.340	.329	196	0	.250	.326	.311	223	1	.287	.354	.345	211	0	.280	.359	.351	208	1	.260	.322	.308	108	1	.231	.261	.343	311	0	.283	.366	.325
1987	Cin-N	85	0	.294	.388	.353	46	0	.239	.300	.283	39	0	.359	.479	.436	0	0	—	—	—	85	0	.294	.388	.353	28	0	.321	.424	.393	57	0	.281	.369	.333
1988	Cin-N	174	0	.236	.286	.293	90	0	.200	.232	.256	84	0	.274	.340	.333	103	0	.233	.277	.282	71	0	.239	.299	.310	60	0	.233	.277	.317	114	0	.237	.290	.281
1989	Cin-N	106	0	.236	.302	.274	49	0	.184	.216	.204	57	0	.281	.369	.333	30	0	.233	.303	.233	76	0	.237	.301	.289	62	0	.258	.313	.323	44	0	.205	.286	.205
1990	StL-N	58	0	.224	.366	.241	28	0	.179	.361	.179	30	0	.267	.371	.300	29	0	.172	.314	.172	29	0	.276	.417	.310	36	0	.194	.293	.222	22	0	.273	.467	.273
TOTALS		3821	20	.277	.342	.356	1873	9	.274	.344	.361	1948	11	.280	.340	.350	1820	10	.271	.331	.354	2001	10	.282	.352	.357	1155	3	.262	.314	.333	2666	17	.283	.354	.365
■ Dave Concepcion BR/TR																																				
1978	Cin-N	565	6	.301	.357	.405	270	3	.304	.348	.441	295	3	.298	.366	.373	280	2	.300	.347	.400	285	4	.302	.368	.411	227	5	.357	.426	.502	338	1	.263	.310	.340
1979	Cin-N	590	16	.281	.348	.415	253	10	.269	.355	.451	337	6	.291	.343	.389	317	8	.287	.342	.423	273	8	.275	.356	.407	216	6	.296	.373	.435	374	10	.273	.334	.404
1980	Cin-N	622	5	.260	.300	.360	300	4	.267	.309	.397	322	1	.255	.292	.326	284	3	.239	.291	.345	338	2	.278	.308	.373	180	3	.272	.318	.411	442	2	.256	.293	.339
1981	Cin-N	421	5	.306	.358	.409	204	4	.314	.374	.431	217	1	.300	.343	.387	219	4	.306	.360	.447	202	1	.307	.357	.366	99	2	.364	.416	.475	322	3	.289	.340	.388
1982	Cin-N	572	5	.287	.337	.371	272	3	.327	.378	.426	300	2	.250	.298	.320	282	1	.301	.344	.379	290	4	.272	.329	.362	165	3	.267	.337	.388	407	2	.295	.336	.364
1983	Cin-N	528	1	.233	.303	.280	270	0	.244	.316	.289	258	1	.221	.289	.271	263	1	.224	.289	.281	265	0	.242	.317	.279	134	0	.246	.325	.313	394	1	.228	.295	.269
1984	Cin-N	531	4	.245	.307	.320	283	3	.219	.289	.307	248	1	.274	.328	.335	275	3	.240	.291	.324	256	1	.250	.324	.316	191	3	.288	.352	.398	340	1	.221	.282	.276
1985	Cin-N	560	7	.252	.314	.330	273	1	.271	.342	.333	287	6	.233	.288	.328	257	5	.272	.326	.393	303	2	.234	.305	.277	156	4	.244	.322	.359	404	3	.255	.312	.319
1986	Cin-N	311	3	.260	.314	.344	135	0	.274	.331	.348	176	3	.250	.301	.341	237	2	.249	.308	.329	74	1	.297	.333	.392	101	1	.337	.384	.455	210	2	.224	.279	.290
1987	Cin-N	279	1	.319	.377	.384	133	1	.316	.361	.406	146	0	.322	.392	.363	139	0	.309	.369	.360	140	1	.329	.386	.407	150	1	.340	.392	.420	129	0	.295	.361	.341
1988	Cin-N	197	0	.198	.265	.244	104	0	.240	.313	.298	93	0	.151	.210	.183	134	0	.216	.281	.261	63	0	.159	.232	.206	114	0	.202	.278	.237	83	0	.193	.247	.253
TOTALS		5176	53	.269	.327	.357	2497	29	.276	.337	.378	2679	24	.263	.318	.337	2687	29	.268	.322	.363	2489	24	.270	.332	.350	1733	28	.293	.359	.406	3443	25	.257	.311	.332
■ Jeff Conine BR/TR																																				
1990	KC-A	20	0	.250	.318	.350	1	0	.000	.500	.000	19	0	.263	.300	.368	0	0	—	—	—	20	0	.250	.318	.350	11	0	.364	.462	.455	9	0	.111	.111	.222
1992	KC-A	91	0	.253	.313	.352	31	0	.258	.343	.355	60	0	.250	.297	.350	0	0	—	—	—	91	0	.253	.313	.352	23	0	.304	.429	.348	68	0	.235	.268	.353
1993	Fla-N	595	12	.292	.351	.403	307	5	.296	.340	.381	288	7	.288	.362	.427	263	5	.289	.379	.403	332	7	.295	.327	.404	167	5	.299	.366	.455	428	7	.290	.345	.383
1994	Fla-N	451	18	.319	.373	.525	230	8	.283	.345	.457	221	10	.357	.402	.597	300	12	.313	.372	.520	151	6	.331	.376	.536	136	6	.316	.375	.566	315	12	.321	.372	.508
1995	Fla-N	483	25	.302	.379	.520	243	13	.350	.414	.564	240	12	.254	.345	.475	189	13	.328	.429	.598	294	12	.286	.346	.469	120	9	.317	.407	.592	363	16	.298	.369	.496
1996	Fla-N	597	26	.293	.360	.484	292	15	.312	.372	.541	305	11	.275	.348	.430	292	14	.298	.370	.493	305	12	.289	.350	.475	122	9	.393	.449	.656	475	17	.267	.337	.440
1997	Fla-N	405	17	.242	.337	.405	190	7	.247	.360	.379	215	10	.237	.315	.428	242	7	.240	.344	.376	163	10	.245	.326	.448	105	4	.248	.325	.390	300	13	.240	.341	.410
1998	KC-A	309	8	.256	.312	.417	138	4	.254	.300	.399	171	4	.257	.321	.433	152	6	.250	.306	.447	157	2	.261	.318	.389	79	0	.241	.311	.304	230	8	.261	.312	.457
1999	Bal-A	444	13	.291	.335	.453	218	7	.317	.365	.505	226	6	.265	.305	.403	193	7	.290	.346	.482	251	6	.291	.326	.430	93	5	.280	.333	.516	351	8	.293	.335	.436
2000	Bal-A	409	13	.284	.341	.438	179	6	.285	.357	.436	230	7	.283	.329	.439	201	10	.308	.347	.522	208	3	.260	.336	.356	120	7	.333	.403	.567	289	6	.263	.315	.384
TOTALS		3804	132	.286	.350	.455	1829	65	.296	.360	.461	1975	67	.277	.341	.449	1832	74	.291	.364	.478	1972	58	.282	.337	.433	976	45	.308	.378	.510	2828	87	.279	.340	.435
■ Ron Coomer BR/TR																																				
1995	Min-A	101	5	.257	.324	.455	44	2	.250	.353	.455	57	3	.263	.300	.456	0	0	—	—	—	101	5	.257	.324	.455	47	3	.319	.407	.553	54	2	.204	.246	.370
1996	Min-A	233	12	.296	.340	.511	126	5	.286	.306	.476	107	7	.308	.378	.551	124	7	.306	.360	.516	109	5	.284	.316	.505	146	10	.308	.356	.582	87	2	.276	.312	.391
1997	Min-A	523	13	.298	.324	.438	258	4	.310	.337	.442	265	9	.287	.311	.434	209	8	.316	.342	.493	314	5	.287	.311	.401	123	3	.415	.459	.593	400	10	.262	.281	.390
1998	Min-A	529	15	.276	.295	.406	246	6	.276	.300	.398	283	9	.276	.291	.413	267	11	.255	.288	.431	262	4	.298	.303	.382	135	8	.281	.285	.459	394	10	.274	.299	.388
1999	Min-A	467	16	.263	.307	.424	229	6	.266	.309	.415	238	10	.261	.306	.433	255	10	.286	.315	.463	212	6	.236	.299	.377	115	5	.278	.336	.470	352	11	.259	.298	.409
2000	Min-A	544	16	.270	.317	.415	287	3	.261	.302	.359	257	13	.280	.335	.479	288	10	.288	.343	.451	256	6	.250	.288	.375	125	5	.256	.321	.456	419	11	.274	.316	.403
TOTALS		2397	77	.278	.315	.431	1190	26	.278	.313	.412	1207	51	.278	.316	.450	1143	46	.287	.326	.464	1254	31	.270	.304	.401	691	31	.308	.355	.517	1706	46	.266	.298	.396
■ Cecil Cooper BL/TL																																				
1978	Mil-A	407	13	.312	.359	.474	192	5	.349	.398	.505	215	8	.279	.323	.447	195	7	.313	.372	.487	212	6	.311	.347	.462	69	2	.333	.373	.464	338	11	.308	.356	.476
1979	Mil-A	590	24	.308	.364	.508	297	13	.313	.367	.529	293	11	.304	.360	.488	301	11	.306	.383	.482	289	13	.311	.343	.536	136	1	.235	.279	.301	454	23	.330	.389	.570
1980	Mil-A	622	25	.352	.387	.539	311	12	.318	.345	.498	311	13	.386	.428	.579	262	9	.336	.374	.515	360	16	.364	.397	.556	195	5	.323	.330	.446	427	20	.365	.412	.581
1981	Mil-A	416	12	.320	.363	.495	187	5	.364	.385	.545	229	7	.284	.345	.454	204	4	.270	.326	.387	212	8	.368	.399	.599	123	4	.276	.326	.447	293	8	.338	.379	.515
1982	Mil-A	654	32	.313	.342	.528	317	12	.303	.337	.479	337	20	.323	.347	.573	278	16	.331	.368	.579	376	16	.301	.323	.489	234	8	.282	.312	.449	420	24	.331	.360	.571
1983	Mil-A	661	30	.307	.341	.508	322	14	.307	.335	.497	339	16	.307	.346	.519	289	14	.277	.318	.502	372	16	.331	.359	.513	258	7	.283	.315	.407	403	23	.323	.357	.573
1984	Mil-A	603	11	.275	.307	.386	272	3	.279	.315	.364	331	8	.272	.301	.405	272	4	.272	.305	.375	331	7	.278	.309	.396	215	1	.298	.336	.386	388	10	.263	.291	.387
1985	Mil-A	631	16	.293	.322	.456	309	6	.285	.315	.430	322	10	.301	.329	.481	267	4	.315	.336	.483	364	12	.277	.313	.437	209	6	.321	.360	.498	422	10	.280	.303	.436
1986	Mil-A	542	12	.258	.310	.373	255	6	.235	.294	.349	287	6	.279	.324	.394	243	7	.255	.308	.391	299	5	.261	.311	.358	137	3	.285	.342	.358	405	9	.249	.298	.378
1987	Mil-A	250	6	.248	.293	.372	108	4	.296	.342	.463	142	2	.211	.255	.303	222	6	.252	.293	.387	28	0	.214	.290	.250	81	1	.259	.308	.358	169	5	.243	.285	.379
TOTALS		5376	181	.302	.341	.471	2570	80	.303	.341	.465	2806	101	.301	.341	.476	2533	82	.294	.340	.463	2843	99	.309	.342	.478	1657	38	.291	.327	.416	3719	143	.307	.347	.495
■ Joey Cora BB/TR																																				
1987	SD-N	241	0	.237	.317	.282	111	0	.207	.310	.225	130	0	.262	.324	.331	184	0	.234	.330	.293	57	0	.246	.271	.246	98	0	.245	.308	.286	143	0	.231	.323	.280
1989	SD-N	19	0	.316	.350	.368	19	0	.316	.350	.368	0	0	—	—	—	0	0	—	—	—	19	0	.316	.350	.368	2	0	1.000	1.000	1.000	17	0	.235	.278	.294
1990	SD-N	100	0	.270	.311	.300	40	0	.275	.341	.325	60	0	.267	.290	.283	34	0	.206	.289	.265	66	0	.303	.324	.318	28	0	.250	.300	.250	72	0	.278	.316	.319
1991	Chi-A	228	0	.241	.313	.276	113	0	.319	.394	.372	115	0	.165	.233	.183	78	0	.321	.365	.372	150	0	.200	.287	.227	57	0	.298	.365	.298	171	0	.222	.295	.269
1992	Chi-A	122	0	.246	.371	.320	46	0	.174	.316	.217	76	0	.289	.404	.382	58	0	.190	.300	.241	64	0	.297	.432	.391	27	0	.222	.353	.296	95	0	.253	.376	.326
1993	Chi-A	579	2	.268	.351	.349	279	0	.262	.350	.333	300	2	.273	.351	.363	269	1	.279	.375	.357	310	1	.258	.329	.342	161	0	.255	.337	.292	418	2	.273	.356	.371
1994	Chi-A	312	2	.276	.353	.362	139	2	.324	.389	.446	173	0	.237	.323	.295	230	1	.287	.365	.374	82	1	.244	.319	.329	67	0	.269	.319	.313	245	2	.278	.361	.376
1995	Sea-A	427	3	.297	.359	.372	198	1	.293	.370	.354	229	2	.301	.348	.389	174	1	.276	.326	.333	253	2	.312	.380	.399	40	0	.325	.391	.375	387	3	.295	.355	.372
1996	Sea-A	530	6	.291	.340	.417	267	2	.288	.336	.412	263	4	.293	.344	.422	264	3	.277	.316	.409	266	3	.305	.363	.425	55	0	.218	.254	.255	475	6	.299	.349	.436
1997	Sea-A	574	11	.300	.359	.441	277	4	.300	.367	.422	297	7	.300	.352	.458	284	7	.331	.401	.507	290	4	.269	.317	.376	107	5	.364	.403	.617	467	6	.285	.349	.400
1998	Sea-A	519	6	.283	.362	.385	261	2	.299	.375	.406	258	4	.267	.349	.364	315	2	.260	.352	.349	204	4	.319	.379	.441	91	0	.231	.336	.286	428	6	.294	.368	.407
1998	Cle-A	83	0	.229	.326	.277	45	0	.311	.392	.400	38	0	.132	.250	.132	0	0	—	—	—	83	0	.229	.326	.277	22	0	.273	.385	.364	61	0	.213	.304	.246
TOTALS		3734	30	.277	.348	.369	1795	11	.285	.360	.375	1939	19	.270	.337	.364	1890	15	.277	.353	.375	1844	15	.277	.343	.363	755	5	.273	.343	.343	2979	25	.278	.349	.376
■ Henry Cotto BR/TR																																				
1984	Chi-N	146	0	.274	.325	.308	73	0	.329	.355	.356	73	0	.219	.296	.260	52	0	.288	.339	.308	94	0	.266	.317	.309	59	0	.271	.317	.322	87	0	.276	.330	.299
1985	NY-A	56	1	.304	.339	.375	37	0	.297	.333	.297	19	1	.316	.350	.526	28	0	.286	.310	.321	28	1	.321	.367	.429	52	0	.308	.333	.327	4	1	.250	.400	1.000
1986	NY-A	80	1	.213	.229	.287	41	0	.220	.214	.268	39	1	.205	.244	.308	42	0	.167	.182	.190	38	1	.263	.282	.395	57	0	.193	.203	.228	23	1	.261	.292	.435
1987	NY-A	149	5	.235	.269	.403	87	5	.253	.286	.506	62	0	.210	.246	.258	74	4	.257	.295	.500	75	1	.213	.244	.307	80	2	.200	.229	.325	69	3	.275	.315	.493
1988	Sea-A	386	8	.259	.302	.373	188	5	.255	.307	.383	198	3	.263	.297	.364	229	3	.266	.305	.354	157	5	.248	.298	.401	148	4	.277	.306	.412	238	4	.248	.300	.349
1989	Sea-A	295	9	.264	.300	.407	149	5	.248	.282	.376	146	4	.281	.318	.438	147	4	.272	.310	.395	148	5	.257	.290	.419	160	5	.262	.306	.412	135	4	.267	.293	.400
1990	Sea-A	355	4	.259	.307	.349	173	2	.260	.321	.358	182	2	.258	.294	.341	175	2	.314	.351	.400	180	2	.206	.265	.300	192	2	.260	.308	.349	163	2	.258	.307	.350
1991	Sea-A	177	6	.305	.347	.463	73	2	.301	.366	.438	104	4	.308	.333	.481	123	4	.309	.356	.439	54	2	.296	.328	.519	96	4	.323	.359	.490	81	2	.284	.333	.432
1992	Sea-A	294	5	.259	.294	.354	117	2	.248	.315	.350	177	3	.266	.278	.356	109	4	.275	.325	.431	185	1	.249	.275	.308	168	4	.321	.375	.446	126	1	.175	.175	.230
1993	Sea-A	105	2	.190	.213	.257	51	0	.235	.235	.255	54	2	.148	.193	.259	105	2	.190	.213	.257	0	0	—	—	—	81	1	.210	.229	.259	24	1	.125	.160	.250
1993	Fla-N	135	3	.296	.312	.415	65	1	.277	.310	.400	70	2	.314	.314	.429	3	0	.000	.000	.000	132	3	.303	.319	.424	68	1	.368	.384	.471	67	2	.224	.235	.358
TOTALS		2178	44	.261	.299	.370	1054	22	.263	.307	.374	1124	22	.260	.292	.367	1087	23	.270	.308	.374	1091	21	.253	.291	.366	1161	23	.275	.312	.382	1017	21	.246	.285	.356
■ Al Cowens BR/TR																																				
1978	KC-A	485	5	.274	.319	.388	232	1	.293	.335	.422	253	4	.257	.305	.356	245	2	.249	.314	.376	240	3	.300	.324	.400	165	4	.297	.344	.436	320	1	.262	.306	.363
1979	KC-A	516	9	.295	.345	.409	262	3	.290	.339	.397	254	6	.299	.350	.421	215	5	.321	.366	.465	301	4	.276	.329	.369	164	3	.311	.359	.433	352	6	.287	.338	.398
1980	Cal-A	119	1	.227	.303	.294	64	0	.203	.301	.219	55	1	.255	.305	.382	119	1	.227	.303	.294	0	0	—	—	—	32	1	.219	.286	.375	87	0	.230	.309	.264

		TOTAL					HOME					AWAY					1ST HALF					2ND HALF					LEFT					RIGHT				
YEAR	TM/L	AB	HR	AVG	OBP	SLG	AB	HR	AVG	OBP	SLG	AB	HR	AVG	OBP	SLG	AB	HR	AVG	OBP	SLG	AB	HR	AVG	OBP	SLG	AB	HR	AVG	OBP	SLG	AB	HR	AVG	OBP	SLG
1980	Det-A	403	5	.280	.339	.370	247	2	.283	.331	.364	156	3	.276	.352	.378	79	1	.304	.353	.405	324	4	.275	.336	.361	171	2	.298	.351	.398	232	3	.267	.331	.349
1981	Det-A	253	1	.261	.319	.348	132	1	.258	.315	.348	121	0	.264	.323	.347	167	0	.269	.326	.365	86	1	.244	.306	.314	161	1	.273	.331	.391	92	0	.239	.297	.272
1982	Sea-A	560	20	.270	.325	.475	291	13	.296	.343	.526	269	7	.242	.305	.420	291	11	.296	.350	.515	269	9	.242	.297	.431	197	4	.294	.356	.467	363	16	.256	.307	.479
1983	Sea-A	356	7	.205	.255	.329	164	2	.189	.246	.268	192	5	.219	.263	.380	220	2	.182	.241	.268	136	5	.243	.280	.426	169	4	.219	.264	.349	187	3	.193	.248	.310
1984	Sea-A	524	15	.277	.312	.435	247	7	.263	.301	.413	277	8	.289	.322	.455	247	8	.275	.310	.457	277	7	.278	.313	.415	173	6	.260	.307	.439	351	9	.285	.314	.433
1985	Sea-A	452	14	.265	.310	.451	211	8	.284	.341	.464	241	6	.249	.282	.440	183	7	.246	.284	.437	269	7	.279	.328	.461	140	5	.264	.331	.486	312	9	.266	.300	.436
1986	Sea-A	82	0	.183	.209	.232	34	0	.206	.206	.294	48	0	.167	.212	.188	82	0	.183	.209	.232	0	0	—	—	—	14	0	.286	.286	.429	68	0	.162	.194	.191
TOTALS		3750	77	.265	.315	.401	1884	37	.271	.320	.403	1866	40	.260	.310	.400	1848	37	.260	.311	.401	1902	40	.271	.318	.402	1386	30	.276	.330	.424	2364	47	.259	.306	.388
■ Deivi Cruz BR/TR																																				
1997	Det-A	436	2	.241	.263	.314	207	0	.227	.260	.290	229	2	.253	.265	.336	207	1	.208	.227	.290	229	1	.271	.295	.336	112	0	.214	.258	.259	324	2	.250	.264	.333
1998	Det-A	454	5	.260	.284	.355	233	5	.262	.288	.378	221	0	.258	.279	.330	191	2	.257	.290	.325	263	3	.262	.279	.376	103	2	.340	.370	.505	351	3	.236	.258	.311
1999	Det-A	518	13	.284	.302	.427	241	9	.278	.306	.444	277	4	.289	.299	.412	220	2	.259	.278	.341	298	11	.302	.321	.490	93	1	.290	.320	.376	425	12	.282	.298	.438
2000	Det-A	583	10	.302	.318	.449	287	1	.307	.319	.422	296	9	.297	.317	.476	257	4	.284	.302	.420	326	6	.316	.330	.472	139	5	.345	.364	.540	444	5	.288	.304	.421
TOTALS		1991	30	.274	.294	.392	968	15	.272	.296	.388	1023	15	.277	.293	.396	875	9	.254	.276	.349	1116	21	.290	.309	.427	447	8	.300	.329	.427	1544	22	.267	.284	.382
■ Jose Cruz BL/TL																																				
1978	Hou-N	565	10	.315	.376	.460	275	7	.353	.411	.538	290	3	.279	.343	.386	259	3	.266	.333	.382	306	7	.356	.412	.526	177	3	.260	.290	.373	388	7	.340	.412	.500
1979	Hou-N	558	9	.289	.367	.421	261	2	.287	.398	.414	297	7	.290	.336	.428	284	4	.278	.360	.408	274	5	.299	.374	.434	215	4	.233	.281	.335	343	5	.324	.417	.475
1980	Hou-N	612	11	.302	.360	.426	297	4	.333	.390	.444	315	7	.273	.332	.410	266	5	.320	.369	.444	346	6	.289	.353	.413	257	7	.265	.297	.393	355	4	.330	.403	.451
1981	Hou-N	409	13	.267	.319	.425	186	3	.247	.290	.355	223	10	.283	.343	.484	230	11	.278	.323	.474	179	2	.251	.315	.363	157	2	.236	.282	.299	252	11	.286	.342	.504
1982	Hou-N	570	9	.275	.342	.377	282	3	.277	.362	.358	288	6	.274	.322	.396	272	4	.265	.338	.379	298	5	.285	.347	.376	184	4	.283	.337	.397	386	5	.272	.345	.368
1983	Hou-N	594	14	.318	.385	.463	288	3	.313	.389	.431	306	11	.324	.381	.493	274	3	.292	.375	.409	320	11	.341	.393	.509	179	2	.307	.352	.402	415	12	.323	.398	.489
1984	Hou-N	600	12	.312	.381	.462	286	0	.276	.367	.371	314	12	.344	.394	.545	290	3	.266	.332	.383	310	9	.355	.425	.535	223	4	.296	.357	.426	377	8	.321	.394	.483
1985	Hou-N	544	9	.300	.349	.426	255	1	.310	.355	.396	289	8	.291	.344	.453	238	5	.307	.340	.433	306	4	.294	.356	.422	220	5	.277	.306	.405	324	4	.315	.377	.441
1986	Hou-N	479	10	.278	.351	.403	245	5	.298	.378	.416	234	5	.256	.322	.389	209	0	.263	.332	.321	270	10	.289	.365	.467	194	2	.284	.325	.392	285	8	.274	.367	.411
1987	Hou-N	365	11	.241	.307	.400	180	6	.267	.320	.444	185	5	.216	.295	.357	227	7	.256	.323	.414	138	4	.217	.281	.377	128	4	.227	.270	.359	237	7	.249	.326	.422
1988	NY-A	80	1	.200	.273	.262	44	1	.182	.250	.273	36	0	.222	.300	.250	68	0	.206	.289	.235	12	1	.167	.167	.417	5	0	.600	.600	.800	75	1	.173	.253	.227
TOTALS		5376	109	.291	.356	.426	2599	35	.297	.369	.416	2777	74	.286	.343	.435	2617	45	.277	.342	.400	2759	64	.304	.369	.450	1939	37	.269	.312	.382	3437	72	.304	.379	.450
■ Jose Cruz BB/TR																																				
1997	Sea-A	183	12	.268	.315	.541	90	7	.267	.309	.578	93	5	.269	.320	.505	97	6	.237	.295	.485	86	6	.302	.337	.605	43	1	.233	.292	.395	140	11	.279	.322	.586
1997	Tor-A	212	14	.231	.316	.462	85	4	.259	.353	.447	127	10	.213	.289	.472	0	0	—	—	—	212	14	.231	.316	.462	54	4	.278	.365	.537	158	10	.215	.298	.437
1998	Tor-A	352	11	.253	.354	.403	188	4	.239	.351	.372	164	7	.268	.356	.439	159	3	.214	.312	.283	193	8	.285	.388	.503	90	2	.289	.420	.422	262	9	.240	.329	.397
1999	Tor-A	349	14	.241	.358	.433	187	8	.267	.386	.476	162	6	.210	.326	.383	240	9	.225	.352	.421	109	5	.275	.373	.459	80	2	.275	.348	.438	269	12	.230	.361	.431
2000	Tor-A	603	31	.242	.323	.466	288	15	.250	.341	.479	315	16	.235	.305	.454	314	18	.242	.322	.471	289	13	.242	.323	.460	162	5	.290	.339	.481	441	26	.224	.317	.460
TOTALS		1699	82	.245	.335	.454	838	38	.254	.352	.462	861	44	.237	.318	.446	810	36	.231	.326	.421	889	46	.259	.343	.484	429	14	.280	.358	.459	1270	68	.234	.327	.452
■ Julio Cruz BB/TR																																				
1978	Sea-A	550	1	.235	.319	.269	276	1	.225	.322	.279	274	0	.245	.316	.259	267	1	.266	.362	.322	283	0	.205	.276	.219	195	0	.190	.256	.231	355	1	.259	.352	.290
1979	Sea-A	414	1	.271	.363	.326	222	1	.270	.389	.324	192	0	.271	.332	.328	204	1	.230	.331	.279	210	0	.310	.395	.371	131	0	.336	.403	.397	283	1	.240	.345	.293
1980	Sea-A	422	2	.209	.306	.258	225	1	.191	.302	.253	197	1	.228	.311	.264	191	1	.220	.317	.283	231	1	.199	.297	.238	123	2	.195	.277	.285	299	0	.214	.317	.247
1981	Sea-A	352	2	.256	.332	.324	177	1	.249	.353	.322	175	1	.263	.311	.326	170	1	.224	.313	.288	182	1	.286	.351	.357	111	2	.270	.346	.378	241	0	.249	.326	.299
1982	Sea-A	549	8	.242	.316	.344	263	8	.255	.342	.411	286	0	.231	.290	.283	269	5	.238	.320	.323	280	3	.246	.312	.364	200	7	.300	.365	.500	349	1	.209	.288	.255
1983	Sea-A	181	2	.254	.332	.354	93	1	.269	.361	.387	88	1	.239	.299	.318	181	2	.254	.332	.354	0	0	—	—	—	73	2	.301	.366	.466	108	0	.222	.309	.278
1983	Chi-A	334	1	.251	.311	.311	168	0	.250	.311	.310	166	1	.253	.311	.313	43	0	.163	.229	.209	291	1	.265	.323	.326	111	1	.279	.297	.360	223	0	.238	.317	.287
1984	Chi-A	415	5	.222	.295	.311	215	1	.228	.313	.288	200	4	.215	.274	.335	208	3	.197	.266	.279	207	2	.246	.322	.343	156	2	.250	.318	.353	259	3	.205	.280	.286
1985	Chi-A	234	0	.197	.297	.231	86	0	.140	.267	.186	148	0	.230	.315	.257	134	0	.187	.313	.194	100	0	.210	.275	.280	116	0	.250	.360	.319	118	0	.144	.233	.144
1986	Chi-A	209	0	.215	.343	.225	98	0	.265	.408	.265	111	0	.171	.279	.189	106	0	.264	.388	.274	103	0	.165	.296	.175	73	0	.219	.310	.233	136	0	.213	.359	.221
TOTALS		3660	22	.236	.321	.299	1823	14	.236	.336	.309	1837	8	.237	.305	.289	1773	14	.231	.323	.293	1887	8	.242	.318	.304	1289	16	.258	.328	.355	2371	6	.225	.317	.268
■ Chad Curtis BR/TR																																				
1992	Cal-A	441	10	.259	.341	.372	201	5	.264	.349	.378	240	5	.254	.333	.367	169	4	.266	.346	.396	272	6	.254	.338	.357	122	6	.270	.393	.484	319	4	.254	.318	.329
1993	Cal-A	583	6	.285	.361	.369	303	3	.310	.374	.403	280	3	.257	.349	.332	255	2	.298	.404	.380	328	4	.274	.325	.360	148	2	.324	.405	.446	435	4	.271	.347	.343
1994	Cal-A	453	11	.256	.317	.397	237	8	.253	.332	.418	216	3	.259	.299	.375	309	5	.239	.296	.362	144	6	.292	.360	.472	132	2	.280	.367	.432	321	9	.246	.295	.383
1995	Det-A	586	21	.268	.349	.435	281	11	.278	.372	.448	305	10	.259	.327	.423	251	10	.283	.358	.462	335	11	.257	.343	.415	135	5	.348	.419	.556	451	16	.244	.328	.399
1996	Det-A	400	10	.262	.346	.393	167	2	.228	.325	.317	233	8	.288	.361	.446	310	5	.265	.346	.374	90	5	.256	.343	.456	103	2	.320	.385	.427	297	8	.242	.332	.380
1996	LA-N	104	2	.212	.322	.317	51	1	.157	.259	.235	53	1	.264	.381	.396	0	0	—	—	—	104	2	.212	.322	.317	40	1	.250	.348	.375	64	1	.188	.307	.281
1997	Cle-A	29	3	.207	.361	.552	13	1	.077	.200	.308	16	2	.313	.476	.750	29	3	.207	.361	.552	0	0	—	—	—	16	2	.313	.450	.750	13	1	.077	.250	.308
1997	NY-A	320	12	.291	.362	.475	136	3	.301	.388	.426	184	9	.283	.341	.511	53	2	.264	.317	.453	267	10	.296	.371	.479	89	2	.315	.394	.483	231	10	.281	.350	.472
1998	NY-A	456	10	.243	.355	.360	214	6	.257	.390	.388	242	4	.231	.321	.335	237	7	.270	.385	.405	219	3	.215	.322	.311	137	8	.241	.358	.482	319	2	.245	.354	.307
1999	NY-A	195	5	.262	.398	.369	80	0	.225	.380	.300	115	5	.287	.410	.417	114	4	.219	.355	.342	81	1	.321	.456	.407	74	1	.297	.447	.378	121	4	.240	.367	.364
2000	Tex-A	335	8	.272	.343	.424	157	5	.312	.380	.497	178	3	.236	.310	.360	206	7	.248	.325	.437	129	1	.310	.373	.403	116	2	.328	.395	.474	219	6	.242	.316	.397
TOTALS		3902	98	.264	.349	.397	1840	45	.269	.361	.399	2062	53	.260	.339	.395	1933	49	.263	.351	.400	1969	49	.266	.348	.395	1112	33	.300	.393	.468	2790	65	.250	.332	.369
■ Johnny Damon BL/TL																																				
1995	KC-A	188	3	.282	.324	.441	100	1	.290	.330	.450	88	2	.273	.316	.432	0	0	—	—	—	188	3	.282	.324	.441	39	0	.231	.268	.308	149	3	.295	.337	.477
1996	KC-A	517	6	.271	.313	.368	252	3	.258	.297	.353	265	3	.283	.328	.381	278	4	.284	.328	.403	239	2	.255	.296	.326	133	1	.226	.298	.293	384	5	.286	.319	.393
1997	KC-A	472	8	.275	.338	.386	231	3	.290	.349	.407	241	5	.261	.327	.365	197	4	.320	.363	.457	275	4	.244	.320	.335	117	2	.248	.313	.316	355	6	.285	.346	.408
1998	KC-A	642	18	.277	.339	.439	312	11	.263	.345	.442	330	7	.291	.334	.436	338	8	.278	.332	.420	304	10	.276	.347	.461	192	3	.245	.301	.349	450	15	.291	.355	.478
1999	KC-A	583	14	.307	.379	.477	294	5	.299	.381	.456	289	9	.315	.377	.498	307	7	.309	.381	.489	276	7	.304	.377	.464	140	1	.329	.370	.407	443	13	.300	.382	.499
2000	KC-A	655	16	.327	.382	.495	330	10	.361	.413	.570	325	6	.292	.349	.418	293	7	.263	.345	.403	362	9	.378	.414	.569	171	4	.357	.418	.520	484	12	.316	.369	.486
TOTALS		3057	65	.292	.351	.438	1519	33	.296	.359	.453	1538	32	.289	.342	.423	1413	30	.289	.349	.433	1644	35	.296	.352	.442	792	11	.280	.339	.380	2265	54	.297	.355	.458
■ Rich Dauer BR/TR																																				
1978	Bal-A	459	6	.264	.301	.353	242	3	.244	.268	.339	217	3	.286	.338	.369	150	4	.287	.339	.413	309	2	.252	.282	.324	166	3	.235	.291	.343	293	3	.280	.307	.358
1979	Bal-A	479	9	.257	.305	.355	220	1	.250	.310	.314	259	8	.263	.301	.390	246	6	.264	.322	.382	233	3	.249	.287	.326	155	4	.297	.329	.400	324	5	.238	.294	.333
1980	Bal-A	557	2	.284	.338	.352	269	1	.301	.355	.368	288	1	.267	.323	.337	223	0	.278	.344	.327	334	2	.287	.334	.368	185	0	.254	.300	.292	372	2	.298	.357	.382
1981	Bal-A	369	4	.263	.317	.369	203	0	.241	.313	.320	166	4	.289	.322	.428	180	1	.283	.335	.356	189	3	.243	.299	.381	111	1	.261	.325	.369	258	3	.264	.313	.368
1982	Bal-A	558	8	.280	.337	.373	274	4	.255	.306	.350	284	4	.303	.366	.394	268	5	.291	.337	.403	290	3	.269	.336	.345	174	4	.305	.356	.448	384	4	.268	.328	.339
1983	Bal-A	459	5	.235	.306	.309	226	2	.252	.332	.336	233	3	.219	.280	.283	210	2	.205	.276	.267	249	3	.261	.331	.345	163	2	.258	.333	.331	296	3	.223	.291	.297
1984	Bal-A	397	2	.254	.296	.335	185	1	.249	.302	.335	212	1	.259	.290	.335	218	1	.257	.283	.335	179	1	.251	.310	.335	110	0	.245	.291	.327	287	2	.258	.297	.338
1985	Bal-A	208	2	.202	.275	.264	101	1	.178	.259	.238	107	1	.224	.291	.290	151	1	.205	.290	.258	57	1	.193	.233	.281	81	2	.247	.322	.358	127	0	.173	.245	.205
TOTALS		3486	38	.260	.314	.345	1720	13	.253	.310	.333	1766	25	.267	.317	.356	1646	20	.261	.317	.346	1840	18	.259	.311	.344	1145	16	.265	.319	.359	2341	22	.258	.311	.338
■ Alvin Davis BL/TR																																				
1984	Sea-A	567	27	.284	.391	.497	277	15	.296	.409	.556	290	12	.272	.374	.441	255	17	.294	.403	.553	312	10	.276	.381	.452	206	5	.286	.389	.417	361	22	.283	.392	.543
1985	Sea-A	578	18	.287	.381	.441	297	11	.293	.393	.461	281	7	.281	.369	.420	250	6	.260	.361	.376	328	12	.308	.396	.491	176	4	.239	.340	.358	402	14	.308	.399	.478
1986	Sea-A	479	18	.271	.373	.426	249	14	.281	.385	.494	230	4	.261	.361	.352	237	11	.283	.402	.485	242	7	.260	.343	.368	122	0	.246	.376	.270	357	18	.280	.372	.479
1987	Sea-A	580	29	.295	.370	.516	277	18	.307	.402	.570	303	11	.284	.339	.465	264	6	.303	.381	.447	316	23	.288	.361	.573	208	5	.240	.301	.380	372	24	.325	.406	.591
1988	Sea-A	478	18	.295	.412	.462	228	12	.294	.423	.509	250	6	.296	.403	.420	240	12	.287	.392	.508	238	6	.303	.432	.416	137	3	.321	.428	.496	341	15	.284	.406	.449
1989	Sea-A	498	21	.305	.424	.496	249	13	.365	.453	.614	249	8	.245	.396	.378	214	7	.322	.426	.472	284	14	.292	.422	.514	154	6	.318	.416	.526	344	15	.299	.427	.483
1990	Sea-A	494	17	.283	.387	.429	252	12	.278	.392	.464	242	5	.289	.381	.393	244	5	.287	.387	.381	250	12	.280	.387	.476	168	6	.256	.360	.405	326	11	.298	.401	.442
1991	Sea-A	462	12	.221	.299	.335	226	6	.230	.313	.354	236	6	.212	.286	.318	233	8	.227	.313	.365	229	4	.214	.285	.306	101	4	.238	.339	.376	361	8	.216	.288	.324
1992	Cal-A	104	0	.250	.331	.327	46	0	.304	.418	.413	58	0	.207	.254	.259	104	0	.250	.331	.327	0	0	—	—	—	12	0	.167	.231	.167	92	0	.261	.343	.348
TOTALS		4240	160	.280	.380	.450	2101	101	.294	.398	.503	2139	59	.267	.362	.398	2041	72	.281	.381	.442	2199	88	.280	.379	.457	1284	33	.267	.366	.403	2956	127	.286	.386	.471
■ Chili Davis BB/TR																																				
1981	SF-N	15	0	.133	.188	.133	8	0	.000	.111	.000	7	0	.286	.286	.286	15	0	.133	.188	.133	0	0	—	—	—	3	0	.000	.000	.000	12	0	.167	.231	.167
1982	SF-N	641	19	.261	.308	.410	306	6	.278	.328	.389	335	13	.245	.290	.430	303	8	.264	.327	.399	338	11	.257	.291	.420	198	3	.288	.321	.389	443	16	.248	.303	.420
1983	SF-N	486	11	.233	.305	.352	256	7	.234	.312	.363	230	4	.230	.298	.339	243	9	.222	.306	.383	243	2	.243	.305	.321	157	7	.210	.269	.420	329	4	.243	.323	.319
1984	SF-N	499	21	.315	.368	.507	229	7	.306	.351	.467	270	14	.322	.381	.541	273	11	.286	.326	.480	226	10	.350	.415	.540	112	2	.259	.300	.384	387	19	.331	.387	.543
1985	SF-N	481	13	.270	.349	.412	234	7	.265	.335	.406	247	6	.275	.363	.417	243	7	.267	.331	.420	238	6	.273	.367	.403	105	1	.248	.296	.314	376	12	.277	.363	.439

YEAR	TM/L	TOTAL					HOME					AWAY					1ST HALF					2ND HALF					LEFT					RIGHT				
		AB	HR	AVG	OBP	SLG	AB	HR	AVG	OBP	SLG	AB	HR	AVG	OBP	SLG	AB	HR	AVG	OBP	SLG	AB	HR	AVG	OBP	SLG	AB	HR	AVG	OBP	SLG	AB	HR	AVG	OBP	SLG
1986	SF-N	526	13	.278	.375	.416	258	7	.291	.389	.426	268	6	.265	.361	.407	249	7	.293	.377	.466	277	6	.264	.373	.372	168	5	.226	.267	.345	358	8	.302	.420	.450
1987	SF-N	500	24	.250	.344	.442	223	9	.242	.352	.404	277	15	.256	.338	.473	277	11	.242	.321	.404	223	13	.260	.372	.489	183	14	.262	.337	.536	317	10	.243	.349	.388
1988	Cal-A	600	21	.268	.326	.432	291	11	.251	.302	.405	309	10	.285	.348	.456	295	9	.254	.287	.403	305	12	.282	.361	.459	219	8	.256	.307	.429	381	13	.276	.336	.433
1989	Cal-A	560	22	.271	.340	.436	274	6	.248	.337	.354	286	16	.294	.343	.514	255	9	.255	.314	.400	305	13	.285	.360	.466	200	8	.245	.300	.415	360	14	.286	.361	.447
1990	Cal-A	412	12	.265	.357	.398	216	10	.306	.389	.495	196	2	.219	.323	.291	270	10	.278	.369	.444	142	2	.239	.335	.310	126	4	.254	.345	.389	286	8	.269	.363	.402
1991	Min-A	534	29	.277	.385	.507	267	14	.303	.420	.539	267	15	.251	.348	.476	270	19	.281	.374	.552	264	10	.273	.396	.462	174	11	.270	.358	.511	360	18	.281	.397	.506
1992	Min-A	444	12	.288	.386	.439	245	6	.273	.364	.437	199	6	.307	.412	.442	216	5	.282	.387	.421	228	7	.294	.384	.456	121	4	.256	.321	.397	323	8	.300	.408	.455
1993	Cal-A	573	27	.243	.327	.440	283	13	.269	.353	.466	290	14	.217	.302	.414	261	10	.230	.307	.410	312	17	.253	.344	.465	131	8	.260	.326	.496	442	19	.238	.327	.423
1994	Cal-A	392	26	.311	.410	.561	215	14	.270	.387	.502	177	12	.362	.440	.633	259	13	.332	.434	.537	133	13	.271	.363	.609	116	8	.319	.414	.578	276	18	.308	.409	.554
1995	Cal-A	424	20	.318	.429	.514	212	11	.358	.470	.585	212	9	.278	.388	.443	181	9	.359	.464	.569	243	11	.288	.403	.473	129	6	.349	.427	.543	295	14	.305	.430	.502
1996	Cal-A	530	28	.292	.387	.496	267	15	.296	.389	.513	263	13	.289	.386	.479	254	15	.283	.380	.508	276	13	.301	.394	.486	176	9	.290	.371	.483	354	19	.294	.396	.503
1997	KC-A	477	30	.279	.386	.509	264	21	.265	.371	.538	213	9	.296	.406	.474	215	13	.288	.408	.502	262	17	.271	.367	.515	147	9	.327	.395	.585	330	21	.258	.382	.476
1998	NY-A	103	3	.291	.373	.447	45	1	.244	.300	.400	58	2	.328	.426	.483	4	0	.250	.571	.250	99	3	.293	.360	.455	42	3	.357	.426	.690	61	0	.246	.338	.279
1999	NY-A	476	19	.269	.366	.445	266	12	.293	.384	.481	210	7	.238	.344	.400	249	11	.293	.395	.482	227	8	.242	.333	.405	146	6	.267	.353	.425	330	13	.270	.372	.455
TOTALS		8673	350	.274	.360	.451	4359	177	.277	.365	.453	4314	173	.271	.355	.449	4332	176	.275	.357	.454	4341	174	.274	.362	.449	2653	116	.270	.336	.453	6020	234	.277	.370	.450
■ Eric Davis BR/TR																																				
1984	Cin-N	174	10	.224	.320	.466	78	3	.256	.389	.462	96	7	.198	.257	.469	30	0	.267	.290	.467	144	10	.215	.325	.465	81	5	.185	.283	.420	93	5	.258	.352	.505
1985	Cin-N	122	8	.246	.287	.516	48	1	.271	.314	.479	74	7	.230	.269	.541	90	5	.189	.215	.422	32	3	.406	.472	.781	53	5	.264	.316	.604	69	3	.232	.264	.449
1986	Cin-N	415	27	.277	.378	.523	197	12	.264	.368	.497	218	15	.289	.387	.546	151	9	.265	.364	.483	264	18	.284	.386	.545	144	11	.319	.422	.590	271	16	.255	.354	.487
1987	Cin-N	474	37	.293	.399	.593	232	17	.280	.394	.560	242	20	.306	.403	.624	235	23	.315	.411	.685	239	14	.272	.387	.502	147	17	.340	.440	.741	327	20	.272	.380	.526
1988	Cin-N	472	26	.273	.363	.489	212	14	.259	.377	.491	260	12	.285	.350	.488	232	13	.241	.326	.440	240	13	.304	.398	.538	120	7	.292	.390	.517	352	19	.267	.353	.480
1989	Cin-N	462	34	.281	.367	.541	204	15	.289	.380	.544	258	19	.275	.357	.539	191	14	.293	.359	.560	271	20	.273	.373	.528	156	10	.250	.369	.481	306	24	.297	.366	.572
1990	Cin-N	453	24	.260	.347	.486	193	13	.223	.344	.487	260	11	.281	.351	.485	167	11	.246	.359	.509	286	13	.269	.341	.472	150	8	.287	.365	.520	303	16	.248	.339	.469
1991	Cin-N	285	11	.235	.353	.386	140	5	.243	.376	.393	145	6	.228	.329	.379	161	8	.248	.386	.435	124	3	.218	.308	.323	105	3	.229	.359	.362	180	8	.239	.349	.400
1992	LA-N	267	5	.228	.325	.322	133	1	.233	.316	.301	134	4	.224	.333	.343	156	4	.244	.331	.365	111	1	.207	.315	.261	89	4	.236	.393	.416	178	1	.225	.286	.275
1993	LA-N	376	14	.234	.308	.391	191	7	.236	.326	.372	185	7	.232	.289	.411	208	7	.221	.313	.356	168	7	.250	.302	.435	106	3	.226	.328	.368	270	11	.237	.300	.400
1993	Det-A	75	6	.253	.371	.533	41	3	.317	.417	.561	34	3	.176	.317	.500	0	0	—	—	—	75	6	.253	.371	.533	31	1	.194	.306	.290	44	5	.295	.415	.705
1994	Det-A	120	3	.183	.290	.292	67	3	.224	.342	.418	53	0	.132	.220	.132	118	3	.186	.289	.297	2	0	.000	.333	.000	24	0	.125	.323	.125	96	3	.198	.280	.333
1996	Cin-N	415	26	.287	.394	.523	186	8	.285	.409	.468	229	18	.288	.381	.568	180	14	.289	.409	.578	235	12	.285	.382	.481	93	4	.247	.340	.409	322	22	.298	.409	.556
1997	Bal-A	158	8	.304	.358	.525	88	7	.375	.418	.705	70	1	.214	.282	.300	129	7	.302	.363	.543	29	1	.310	.333	.448	55	3	.382	.443	.636	103	5	.262	.313	.466
1998	Bal-A	452	28	.327	.388	.582	242	16	.335	.384	.612	210	12	.319	.392	.548	175	11	.297	.387	.571	277	17	.347	.388	.588	162	10	.296	.368	.556	290	18	.345	.399	.597
1999	StL-N	191	5	.257	.359	.403	87	2	.230	.309	.368	104	3	.279	.397	.433	191	5	.257	.359	.403	0	0	—	—	—	49	2	.286	.375	.469	142	3	.246	.353	.380
2000	StL-N	254	6	.303	.389	.429	133	2	.271	.370	.383	121	4	.339	.410	.479	141	6	.305	.396	.511	113	0	.301	.380	.327	105	3	.390	.463	.543	149	3	.242	.337	.349
TOTALS		5165	278	.271	.361	.486	2472	129	.271	.369	.483	2693	149	.270	.353	.489	2555	140	.263	.357	.485	2610	138	.278	.365	.487	1670	96	.280	.378	.505	3495	182	.266	.353	.477
■ Glenn Davis BR/TR																																				
1984	Hou-N	61	2	.213	.258	.393	40	1	.225	.256	.375	21	1	.190	.261	.429	0	0	—	—	—	61	2	.213	.258	.393	33	0	.242	.286	.394	28	2	.179	.226	.393
1985	Hou-N	350	20	.271	.332	.474	164	8	.317	.367	.494	186	12	.231	.303	.457	47	1	.234	.265	.298	303	19	.277	.342	.502	144	12	.278	.346	.563	206	8	.267	.323	.413
1986	Hou-N	574	31	.265	.344	.493	285	17	.298	.372	.547	289	14	.232	.316	.439	276	16	.272	.332	.514	298	15	.258	.354	.473	211	12	.270	.359	.512	363	19	.262	.335	.482
1987	Hou-N	578	27	.251	.310	.458	285	12	.249	.312	.439	293	15	.253	.308	.478	277	13	.285	.340	.502	301	14	.219	.283	.419	193	10	.244	.323	.477	385	17	.255	.304	.449
1988	Hou-N	561	30	.271	.341	.478	290	15	.297	.363	.510	271	15	.244	.317	.443	284	17	.243	.309	.451	277	13	.300	.372	.505	167	7	.228	.322	.395	394	23	.289	.349	.513
1989	Hou-N	581	34	.269	.350	.492	287	15	.317	.402	.551	294	19	.221	.297	.435	301	16	.256	.328	.462	280	18	.282	.373	.525	146	14	.288	.392	.616	435	20	.262	.335	.451
1990	Hou-N	327	22	.251	.357	.523	175	4	.217	.315	.349	152	18	.289	.403	.724	234	19	.252	.335	.556	93	3	.247	.407	.441	123	11	.252	.378	.569	204	11	.250	.343	.495
1991	Bal-A	176	10	.227	.307	.460	73	3	.247	.304	.438	103	7	.214	.308	.476	41	4	.244	.367	.585	135	6	.222	.287	.422	47	5	.255	.314	.638	129	5	.217	.304	.395
1992	Bal-A	398	13	.276	.338	.422	200	5	.290	.330	.415	198	8	.263	.345	.429	113	5	.248	.298	.416	285	8	.288	.353	.425	107	4	.252	.287	.411	291	9	.285	.356	.426
1993	Bal-A	113	1	.177	.230	.230	51	1	.157	.214	.235	62	0	.194	.242	.226	113	1	.177	.230	.230	0	0	—	—	—	36	0	.222	.282	.222	77	1	.156	.205	.234
TOTALS		3719	190	.259	.332	.467	1850	81	.279	.347	.471	1869	109	.240	.318	.464	1686	92	.254	.319	.468	2033	98	.264	.343	.467	1207	75	.257	.341	.499	2512	115	.261	.328	.452
■ Jody Davis BR/TR																																				
1981	Chi-N	180	4	.256	.333	.361	92	4	.261	.346	.424	88	0	.250	.320	.295	43	1	.256	.313	.349	137	3	.255	.340	.365	58	2	.328	.400	.483	122	2	.221	.302	.303
1982	Chi-N	418	12	.261	.316	.404	228	6	.246	.298	.382	190	6	.279	.336	.432	184	4	.239	.289	.364	234	8	.278	.337	.436	105	2	.314	.387	.390	313	10	.243	.292	.409
1983	Chi-N	510	24	.271	.315	.480	239	15	.285	.333	.565	271	9	.258	.298	.406	212	12	.250	.299	.481	298	12	.285	.326	.480	126	5	.286	.328	.468	384	19	.266	.310	.484
1984	Chi-N	523	19	.256	.315	.421	248	13	.282	.356	.496	275	6	.233	.276	.353	247	13	.296	.374	.514	276	6	.221	.259	.337	144	6	.271	.354	.493	379	13	.251	.300	.393
1985	Chi-N	482	17	.232	.300	.400	259	10	.255	.325	.429	223	7	.206	.269	.368	203	6	.256	.316	.419	279	11	.215	.288	.387	115	5	.235	.291	.470	367	12	.232	.302	.379
1986	Chi-N	528	21	.250	.300	.428	262	14	.267	.315	.481	266	7	.233	.285	.376	258	10	.256	.302	.438	270	11	.244	.298	.419	133	3	.233	.286	.353	395	18	.256	.305	.453
1987	Chi-N	428	19	.248	.331	.418	207	7	.256	.347	.411	221	12	.240	.315	.425	239	10	.247	.314	.414	189	9	.249	.350	.423	107	5	.252	.325	.430	321	14	.246	.332	.414
1988	Chi-N	249	6	.229	.309	.337	105	3	.181	.263	.295	144	3	.264	.341	.368	168	6	.262	.335	.411	81	0	.160	.253	.185	95	1	.179	.269	.221	154	5	.260	.333	.409
1988	Atl-N	8	1	.250	.250	.625	0	0	—	—	—	8	1	.250	.250	.625	0	0	—	—	—	8	1	.250	.250	.625	7	1	.286	.286	.714	1	0	.000	.000	.000
1989	Atl-N	231	4	.169	.246	.242	105	1	.143	.224	.200	126	3	.190	.264	.278	168	2	.167	.239	.226	63	2	.175	.264	.286	93	1	.204	.286	.280	138	3	.145	.219	.217
1990	Atl-N	28	0	.071	.161	.071	15	0	.067	.125	.067	13	0	.077	.200	.077	28	0	.071	.161	.071	0	0	—	—	—	19	0	.105	.227	.105	9	0	.000	.000	.000
TOTALS		3585	127	.245	.307	.403	1760	73	.251	.318	.431	1825	54	.238	.297	.375	1750	64	.247	.309	.410	1835	63	.243	.306	.396	1002	31	.251	.320	.399	2583	96	.242	.302	.404
■ Mike Davis BL/TL																																				
1980	Oak-A	95	1	.211	.262	.284	69	1	.203	.253	.290	26	0	.231	.286	.269	43	1	.209	.227	.279	52	0	.212	.288	.288	12	0	.333	.333	.333	83	1	.193	.253	.277
1981	Oak-A	20	0	.050	.136	.100	2	0	.000	.333	.000	18	0	.056	.105	.111	0	0	—	—	—	20	0	.050	.136	.100	1	0	.000	.000	.000	19	0	.053	.143	.105
1982	Oak-A	75	1	.400	.416	.493	36	1	.389	.405	.556	39	0	.410	.425	.436	0	0	—	—	—	75	1	.400	.416	.493	11	0	.455	.455	.545	64	1	.391	.409	.484
1983	Oak-A	443	8	.275	.322	.402	203	3	.251	.314	.374	240	5	.296	.328	.425	261	2	.276	.309	.368	182	6	.275	.338	.451	135	2	.237	.297	.356	308	6	.292	.332	.422
1984	Oak-A	382	9	.230	.285	.364	177	4	.237	.291	.373	205	5	.224	.280	.356	204	3	.196	.246	.324	178	6	.270	.330	.410	73	1	.205	.262	.356	309	8	.236	.291	.366
1985	Oak-A	547	24	.287	.348	.484	246	12	.276	.349	.492	301	12	.296	.347	.478	256	14	.313	.384	.547	291	10	.265	.314	.430	155	8	.271	.335	.484	392	16	.293	.353	.485
1986	Oak-A	489	19	.268	.314	.454	244	11	.266	.338	.475	245	8	.269	.287	.433	227	9	.251	.304	.445	262	10	.282	.323	.462	117	4	.299	.339	.479	372	15	.258	.306	.446
1987	Oak-A	494	22	.265	.320	.468	234	9	.261	.318	.449	260	13	.269	.323	.485	253	17	.292	.357	.569	241	5	.237	.281	.361	126	6	.278	.326	.500	368	16	.261	.319	.457
1988	LA-N	281	2	.196	.260	.270	133	1	.150	.210	.203	148	1	.236	.303	.331	183	1	.202	.270	.257	98	1	.184	.241	.296	64	0	.172	.229	.297	217	2	.203	.269	.263
1989	LA-N	173	5	.249	.309	.387	88	2	.273	.333	.386	85	3	.224	.283	.388	155	5	.252	.310	.406	18	0	.222	.300	.222	17	0	.118	.118	.118	156	5	.263	.328	.417
TOTALS		2999	91	.259	.313	.415	1432	44	.251	.313	.409	1567	47	.267	.312	.421	1582	52	.258	.314	.423	1417	39	.261	.311	.406	711	21	.255	.306	.421	2288	70	.261	.315	.413
■ Andre Dawson BR/TR																																				
1978	Mon-N	609	25	.253	.299	.442	309	12	.259	.313	.447	300	13	.247	.284	.437	265	10	.249	.308	.404	344	15	.256	.291	.471	142	6	.261	.289	.458	467	19	.251	.302	.437
1979	Mon-N	639	25	.275	.309	.468	315	13	.263	.301	.483	324	12	.287	.317	.454	281	14	.267	.299	.484	358	11	.282	.317	.455	122	4	.303	.317	.467	517	21	.269	.307	.468
1980	Mon-N	577	17	.308	.358	.492	264	7	.303	.366	.508	313	10	.313	.351	.479	222	9	.284	.365	.486	355	8	.324	.353	.496	118	8	.339	.412	.636	459	9	.301	.343	.455
1981	Mon-N	394	24	.302	.365	.553	200	9	.255	.339	.460	194	15	.351	.393	.649	194	13	.325	.380	.598	200	11	.280	.351	.510	75	6	.320	.363	.613	319	18	.298	.366	.539
1982	Mon-N	608	23	.301	.343	.498	297	9	.290	.337	.458	311	14	.312	.348	.537	281	10	.313	.353	.495	327	13	.291	.334	.502	164	4	.250	.305	.384	444	19	.320	.357	.541
1983	Mon-N	633	32	.299	.338	.539	298	10	.272	.324	.453	335	22	.322	.351	.615	288	15	.316	.332	.576	345	17	.284	.343	.507	153	6	.327	.403	.556	480	26	.290	.316	.533
1984	Mon-N	533	17	.248	.301	.409	252	6	.210	.268	.345	281	11	.281	.330	.466	238	3	.214	.283	.319	295	14	.275	.315	.481	146	7	.281	.354	.479	387	10	.235	.280	.382
1985	Mon-N	529	23	.255	.295	.444	253	11	.249	.297	.419	276	12	.261	.294	.467	229	9	.258	.295	.437	300	14	.253	.295	.450	167	10	.275	.303	.515	362	13	.246	.292	.412
1986	Mon-N	496	20	.284	.338	.478	243	11	.296	.356	.477	253	9	.273	.320	.478	175	12	.291	.347	.571	321	8	.280	.332	.427	160	11	.331	.384	.625	336	9	.262	.315	.408
1987	Chi-N	621	49	.287	.328	.568	292	27	.332	.373	.668	329	22	.246	.288	.480	303	20	.287	.319	.535	318	29	.286	.336	.601	141	9	.298	.348	.525	480	40	.283	.321	.581
1988	Chi-N	591	24	.303	.344	.504	293	12	.314	.360	.515	298	12	.292	.329	.493	297	14	.310	.353	.532	294	10	.296	.335	.476	159	4	.296	.339	.453	432	20	.306	.346	.523
1989	Chi-N	416	21	.252	.307	.476	218	6	.239	.293	.385	198	15	.268	.323	.576	156	7	.256	.302	.487	260	14	.250	.310	.469	114	8	.298	.364	.579	302	13	.235	.284	.437
1990	Chi-N	529	27	.310	.358	.535	266	14	.316	.374	.534	263	13	.304	.342	.536	258	18	.322	.378	.612	271	9	.299	.338	.461	181	8	.298	.343	.508	348	19	.316	.366	.549
1991	Chi-N	563	31	.272	.302	.488	280	22	.293	.328	.575	283	9	.251	.277	.403	258	11	.283	.315	.473	305	20	.262	.291	.502	223	16	.296	.319	.556	340	15	.256	.291	.444
1992	Chi-N	542	22	.277	.316	.456	252	13	.306	.357	.540	290	9	.252	.279	.383	244	10	.287	.314	.463	298	12	.268	.318	.450	195	7	.287	.321	.467	347	15	.271	.314	.450
1993	Bos-A	461	13	.273	.313	.425	247	8	.304	.340	.486	214	5	.238	.283	.355	206	3	.233	.265	.330	255	10	.306	.351	.502	125	7	.320	.356	.576	336	6	.256	.298	.369
1994	Bos-A	292	16	.240	.271	.466	146	7	.267	.291	.500	146	9	.212	.252	.432	213	14	.263	.298	.531	79	2	.177	.198	.291	80	6	.287	.329	.587	212	10	.222	.249	.420
1995	Fla-N	226	8	.257	.305	.434	110	1	.218	.250	.309	116	7	.293	.354	.552	100	4	.230	.278	.430	126	4	.278	.326	.437	80	4	.313	.333	.563	146	4	.226	.290	.363
1996	Fla-N	58	2	.276	.311	.414	26	2	.462	.500	.731	32	0	.125	.152	.156	28	1	.250	.250	.393	30	1	.300	.364	.433	17	0	.294	.294	.353	41	2	.268	.318	.439
TOTALS		9317	419	.280	.324	.484	4561	200	.281	.331	.485	4756	219	.278	.316	.484	4236	197	.280	.323	.489	5081	222	.279	.324	.480	2562	131	.297	.342	.521	6755	288	.273	.317	.470
■ Doug DeCinces BR/TR																																				
1978	Bal-A	511	28	.286	.346	.526	250	14	.308	.366	.564	261	14	.264	.326	.490	190	7	.226	.316	.389	321	21	.321	.364	.607	150	8	.300	.373	.560	361	20	.280	.334	.512
1979	Bal-A	422	16	.230	.318	.412	221	10	.231	.315	.439	201	6	.229	.322	.383	145	7	.221	.320	.414	277	9	.235	.317	.412	131	3	.183	.268	.313	291	13	.251	.340	.457

		TOTAL					HOME					AWAY					1ST HALF					2ND HALF					LEFT					RIGHT				
YEAR	TM/L	AB	HR	AVG	OBP	SLG	AB	HR	AVG	OBP	SLG	AB	HR	AVG	OBP	SLG	AB	HR	AVG	OBP	SLG	AB	HR	AVG	OBP	SLG	AB	HR	AVG	OBP	SLG	AB	HR	AVG	OBP	SLG
1980	Bal-A	489	16	.249	.319	.403	227	7	.225	.287	.370	262	9	.271	.347	.431	228	6	.237	.307	.368	261	10	.261	.330	.433	158	11	.310	.393	.589	331	5	.221	.282	.314
1981	Bal-A	346	13	.263	.341	.454	185	10	.270	.351	.481	161	3	.255	.330	.422	166	7	.223	.312	.434	180	6	.300	.368	.472	98	2	.255	.342	.388	248	11	.266	.341	.480
1982	Cal-A	575	30	.301	.369	.548	266	17	.308	.381	.575	309	13	.294	.358	.524	273	9	.256	.316	.440	302	21	.341	.416	.646	212	13	.344	.431	.627	363	17	.275	.330	.501
1983	Cal-A	370	18	.281	.332	.495	171	10	.287	.339	.538	199	8	.276	.326	.457	240	15	.313	.363	.587	130	3	.223	.273	.323	158	6	.278	.346	.462	212	12	.283	.320	.519
1984	Cal-A	547	20	.269	.327	.431	266	10	.256	.327	.406	281	10	.281	.327	.456	269	10	.257	.309	.428	278	10	.281	.344	.435	175	9	.309	.383	.514	372	11	.250	.299	.392
1985	Cal-A	427	20	.244	.317	.440	208	12	.264	.345	.505	219	8	.224	.290	.379	198	7	.242	.328	.399	229	13	.245	.307	.476	127	6	.244	.345	.449	300	14	.243	.304	.437
1986	Cal-A	512	26	.256	.325	.459	259	14	.263	.328	.456	253	12	.249	.322	.462	248	10	.242	.317	.411	264	16	.269	.332	.504	173	9	.272	.345	.486	339	17	.248	.314	.445
1987	Cal-A	453	16	.234	.337	.391	226	10	.274	.385	.451	227	6	.194	.287	.330	234	9	.222	.337	.385	219	7	.247	.337	.397	159	7	.283	.413	.459	294	9	.207	.292	.354
1987	StL-N	9	0	.222	.222	.444	9	0	.222	.222	.444	0	0	—	—	—	0	0	—	—	—	9	0	.222	.222	.444	4	0	.250	.250	.500	5	0	.200	.200	.400
TOTALS		4661	203	.262	.334	.458	2288	114	.269	.343	.478	2373	89	.256	.325	.439	2191	87	.246	.323	.428	2470	116	.277	.343	.485	1545	74	.283	.370	.497	3116	129	.252	.315	.439

■ Rob Deer BR/TR

YEAR	TM/L	AB	HR	AVG	OBP	SLG	AB	HR	AVG	OBP	SLG	AB	HR	AVG	OBP	SLG	AB	HR	AVG	OBP	SLG	AB	HR	AVG	OBP	SLG	AB	HR	AVG	OBP	SLG	AB	HR	AVG	OBP	SLG
1984	SF-N	24	3	.167	.375	.542	14	2	.143	.429	.571	10	1	.200	.273	.500	0	0	—	—	—	24	3	.167	.375	.542	3	1	.333	.333	1.333	21	2	.143	.379	.429
1985	SF-N	162	8	.185	.283	.377	82	5	.159	.271	.378	80	3	.213	.297	.375	61	3	.213	.279	.377	101	5	.168	.286	.376	67	6	.209	.289	.522	95	2	.168	.279	.274
1986	Mil-A	466	33	.232	.336	.494	238	19	.227	.329	.504	228	14	.237	.345	.482	195	13	.221	.319	.462	271	20	.240	.349	.517	129	11	.279	.416	.605	337	22	.214	.303	.451
1987	Mil-A	474	28	.238	.360	.456	232	11	.228	.332	.409	242	17	.248	.386	.500	230	16	.270	.367	.539	244	12	.209	.355	.377	152	8	.257	.394	.467	322	20	.230	.344	.450
1988	Mil-A	492	23	.252	.328	.441	246	12	.256	.344	.455	246	11	.248	.311	.427	259	12	.212	.295	.394	233	11	.296	.365	.494	137	8	.255	.366	.482	355	15	.251	.312	.425
1989	Mil-A	466	26	.210	.305	.425	234	15	.201	.310	.436	232	11	.220	.299	.414	286	21	.227	.322	.490	180	5	.183	.276	.322	134	8	.254	.340	.470	332	18	.193	.290	.407
1990	Mil-A	440	27	.209	.313	.432	214	11	.187	.310	.374	226	16	.230	.317	.487	179	13	.212	.341	.469	261	14	.207	.293	.406	140	16	.293	.399	.671	300	11	.170	.271	.320
1991	Det-A	448	25	.179	.314	.386	218	12	.193	.332	.399	230	13	.165	.296	.374	244	15	.189	.316	.410	204	10	.167	.310	.358	138	9	.196	.327	.449	310	16	.171	.307	.358
1992	Det-A	393	32	.247	.337	.547	173	13	.254	.352	.549	220	19	.241	.325	.545	231	21	.208	.300	.528	162	11	.302	.389	.574	99	14	.293	.369	.747	294	18	.231	.326	.480
1993	Det-A	323	14	.217	.302	.381	126	9	.238	.340	.492	197	5	.203	.276	.310	203	11	.217	.310	.424	120	3	.217	.289	.308	90	6	.267	.385	.511	233	8	.197	.267	.330
1993	Bos-A	143	7	.196	.303	.399	66	3	.167	.313	.333	77	4	.221	.294	.455	0	0	—	—	—	143	7	.196	.303	.399	31	3	.323	.432	.774	112	4	.161	.266	.295
1996	SD-N	50	4	.180	.359	.480	20	3	.300	.417	.800	30	1	.100	.325	.267	0	0	—	—	—	50	4	.180	.359	.480	13	0	.231	.444	.385	37	4	.162	.326	.514
TOTALS		3881	230	.220	.324	.442	1863	115	.217	.329	.446	2018	115	.222	.319	.440	1888	125	.219	.319	.461	1993	105	.220	.328	.424	1133	90	.259	.373	.549	2748	140	.204	.303	.398

■ Ivan DeJesus BR/TR

YEAR	TM/L	AB	HR	AVG	OBP	SLG	AB	HR	AVG	OBP	SLG	AB	HR	AVG	OBP	SLG	AB	HR	AVG	OBP	SLG	AB	HR	AVG	OBP	SLG	AB	HR	AVG	OBP	SLG	AB	HR	AVG	OBP	SLG
1978	Chi-N	619	3	.278	.356	.354	314	1	.287	.366	.354	305	2	.269	.345	.354	288	3	.260	.345	.372	331	0	.293	.366	.338	233	1	.292	.373	.382	386	2	.269	.346	.337
1979	Chi-N	636	5	.283	.345	.379	314	4	.299	.361	.411	322	1	.267	.329	.348	277	2	.271	.334	.347	359	3	.292	.353	.404	187	0	.273	.333	.369	449	5	.287	.350	.383
1980	Chi-N	618	3	.259	.327	.325	293	3	.297	.359	.396	325	0	.225	.299	.262	264	3	.273	.338	.383	354	0	.249	.320	.282	156	2	.269	.341	.372	462	1	.255	.323	.310
1981	Chi-N	403	0	.194	.276	.233	223	0	.197	.271	.247	180	0	.189	.281	.217	200	0	.160	.263	.185	203	0	.227	.288	.281	83	0	.229	.354	.253	320	0	.184	.254	.228
1982	Phi-N	536	3	.239	.309	.313	266	1	.214	.273	.271	270	2	.263	.343	.356	262	1	.244	.301	.290	274	2	.234	.317	.336	105	1	.200	.282	.276	431	2	.248	.316	.323
1983	Phi-N	497	4	.254	.323	.336	236	2	.254	.319	.360	261	2	.253	.327	.314	211	1	.237	.296	.303	286	3	.266	.343	.360	120	0	.308	.390	.392	377	4	.236	.300	.318
1984	Phi-N	435	0	.257	.325	.306	192	0	.240	.305	.307	243	0	.272	.341	.305	252	0	.266	.315	.306	183	0	.246	.338	.306	121	0	.240	.311	.281	314	0	.264	.330	.315
1985	StL-N	72	0	.222	.260	.292	30	0	.367	.394	.500	42	0	.119	.159	.143	34	0	.294	.333	.412	38	0	.158	.195	.184	41	0	.171	.209	.220	31	0	.290	.324	.387
1986	NY-A	4	0	.000	.200	.000	2	0	.000	.000	.000	2	0	.000	.333	.000	4	0	.000	.200	.000	0	0	—	—	—	0	0	—	—	—	4	0	.000	.200	.000
1987	SF-N	10	0	.200	.200	.200	4	0	.000	.000	.000	6	0	.333	.333	.333	10	0	.200	.200	.200	0	0	—	—	—	2	0	.000	.000	.000	8	0	.250	.250	.250
1988	Det-A	17	0	.176	.222	.176	13	0	.154	.214	.154	4	0	.250	.250	.250	0	0	—	—	—	17	0	.176	.222	.176	5	0	.000	.000	.000	12	0	.250	.308	.250
TOTALS		3847	18	.254	.324	.325	1887	11	.260	.326	.341	1960	7	.248	.322	.309	1802	10	.248	.315	.319	2045	8	.259	.331	.330	1053	4	.260	.338	.338	2794	14	.252	.319	.320

■ Carlos Delgado BL/TR

YEAR	TM/L	AB	HR	AVG	OBP	SLG	AB	HR	AVG	OBP	SLG	AB	HR	AVG	OBP	SLG	AB	HR	AVG	OBP	SLG	AB	HR	AVG	OBP	SLG	AB	HR	AVG	OBP	SLG	AB	HR	AVG	OBP	SLG
1993	Tor-A	1	0	.000	.500	.000	0	0	—	—	—	1	0	.000	.500	.000	0	0	—	—	—	1	0	.000	.500	.000	0	0	—	—	—	1	0	.000	.500	.000
1994	Tor-A	130	9	.215	.352	.438	72	5	.236	.398	.458	58	4	.190	.288	.414	130	9	.215	.352	.438	0	0	—	—	—	34	3	.176	.194	.441	96	6	.229	.398	.438
1995	Tor-A	91	3	.165	.212	.297	53	2	.208	.271	.377	38	1	.105	.125	.184	26	1	.154	.207	.308	65	2	.169	.214	.292	11	1	.273	.273	.727	80	2	.150	.205	.237
1996	Tor-A	488	25	.270	.353	.490	241	12	.282	.368	.502	247	13	.259	.339	.478	265	12	.291	.375	.498	223	13	.247	.327	.480	92	2	.152	.240	.283	396	23	.298	.379	.538
1997	Tor-A	519	30	.262	.350	.528	258	17	.271	.368	.570	261	13	.253	.331	.487	228	15	.268	.358	.553	291	15	.258	.343	.509	134	2	.254	.325	.433	385	28	.265	.358	.561
1998	Tor-A	530	38	.292	.385	.592	257	20	.304	.390	.646	273	18	.282	.381	.542	243	14	.305	.387	.588	287	24	.282	.384	.596	155	5	.303	.387	.484	375	33	.288	.385	.637
1999	Tor-A	573	44	.272	.377	.571	284	17	.271	.383	.542	289	27	.273	.371	.599	305	17	.246	.353	.485	268	27	.302	.406	.668	152	12	.309	.416	.605	421	32	.259	.363	.558
2000	Tor-A	569	41	.344	.470	.664	283	30	.360	.477	.777	286	11	.329	.463	.552	292	27	.356	.462	.705	277	14	.332	.478	.621	188	6	.319	.422	.537	381	35	.357	.492	.727
TOTALS		2901	190	.282	.383	.557	1448	103	.292	.395	.595	1453	87	.272	.371	.520	1489	95	.284	.382	.551	1412	95	.280	.384	.564	766	31	.275	.365	.490	2135	159	.284	.390	.581

■ Rick Dempsey BR/TR

YEAR	TM/L	AB	HR	AVG	OBP	SLG	AB	HR	AVG	OBP	SLG	AB	HR	AVG	OBP	SLG	AB	HR	AVG	OBP	SLG	AB	HR	AVG	OBP	SLG	AB	HR	AVG	OBP	SLG	AB	HR	AVG	OBP	SLG
1978	Bal-A	441	6	.259	.327	.356	218	4	.275	.348	.390	223	2	.242	.306	.323	196	4	.235	.295	.342	245	2	.278	.353	.367	136	3	.272	.331	.397	305	3	.252	.326	.338
1979	Bal-A	368	6	.239	.307	.351	173	1	.191	.276	.266	195	5	.282	.336	.426	185	3	.254	.338	.368	183	3	.224	.275	.333	109	1	.248	.349	.349	259	5	.236	.288	.351
1980	Bal-A	362	9	.262	.333	.425	181	5	.260	.332	.409	181	4	.265	.335	.442	170	4	.229	.296	.400	192	5	.292	.366	.448	178	6	.303	.356	.483	184	3	.223	.313	.370
1981	Bal-A	251	6	.215	.306	.335	125	4	.192	.268	.312	126	2	.238	.342	.357	117	3	.197	.338	.333	134	3	.231	.275	.336	86	4	.291	.390	.500	165	2	.176	.261	.248
1982	Bal-A	344	5	.256	.339	.349	168	2	.274	.359	.357	176	3	.239	.320	.341	159	4	.220	.315	.327	185	1	.286	.360	.368	135	2	.252	.350	.356	209	3	.258	.332	.344
1983	Bal-A	347	4	.231	.311	.323	163	3	.221	.316	.350	184	1	.239	.307	.299	165	2	.242	.321	.321	182	2	.220	.303	.324	162	2	.222	.302	.321	185	2	.238	.319	.324
1984	Bal-A	330	11	.230	.312	.364	145	6	.228	.315	.379	185	5	.232	.310	.351	144	2	.208	.297	.285	186	9	.247	.324	.425	85	5	.282	.392	.518	245	6	.212	.282	.310
1985	Bal-A	362	12	.254	.345	.406	179	4	.235	.346	.358	183	8	.273	.343	.454	180	5	.233	.332	.356	182	7	.275	.357	.456	157	7	.325	.403	.529	205	5	.200	.299	.312
1986	Bal-A	327	13	.208	.309	.379	158	7	.215	.326	.380	169	6	.201	.293	.379	170	8	.206	.301	.388	157	5	.210	.319	.369	138	6	.254	.356	.457	189	7	.175	.274	.323
1987	Cle-A	141	1	.177	.295	.270	71	1	.169	.250	.282	70	0	.186	.337	.257	111	1	.180	.319	.279	30	0	.167	.194	.233	42	1	.167	.286	.333	99	0	.182	.299	.242
1988	LA-N	167	7	.251	.338	.455	65	3	.277	.354	.492	102	4	.235	.328	.431	65	4	.277	.355	.554	102	3	.235	.328	.392	122	5	.246	.324	.434	45	2	.267	.375	.511
1989	LA-N	151	4	.179	.319	.305	72	2	.181	.306	.278	79	2	.177	.330	.329	70	1	.157	.289	.229	81	3	.198	.343	.370	117	1	.171	.307	.239	34	3	.206	.357	.529
1990	LA-N	128	2	.195	.318	.281	64	2	.234	.329	.391	64	0	.156	.308	.172	45	2	.200	.345	.356	83	0	.193	.302	.241	94	2	.170	.310	.266	34	0	.265	.342	.324
1991	Mil-A	147	4	.231	.329	.347	73	2	.260	.364	.384	74	2	.203	.294	.311	70	2	.200	.263	.343	77	2	.260	.381	.351	97	3	.237	.330	.371	50	1	.220	.328	.300
1992	Bal-A	9	0	.111	.273	.111	6	0	.167	.375	.167	3	0	.000	.000	.000	0	0	—	—	—	9	0	.111	.273	.111	3	0	.000	.250	.000	6	0	.167	.286	.167
TOTALS		3875	90	.235	.322	.360	1861	46	.233	.323	.358	2014	44	.236	.320	.362	1847	45	.221	.314	.347	2028	45	.247	.329	.372	1661	48	.252	.344	.402	2214	42	.221	.305	.329

■ Bob Dernier BR/TR

YEAR	TM/L	AB	HR	AVG	OBP	SLG	AB	HR	AVG	OBP	SLG	AB	HR	AVG	OBP	SLG	AB	HR	AVG	OBP	SLG	AB	HR	AVG	OBP	SLG	AB	HR	AVG	OBP	SLG	AB	HR	AVG	OBP	SLG
1980	Phi-N	7	0	.571	.625	.571	2	0	1.000	1.000	1.000	5	0	.400	.400	.400	0	0	—	—	—	7	0	.571	.625	.571	2	0	1.000	1.000	1.000	5	0	.400	.400	.400
1981	Phi-N	4	0	.750	.750	.750	1	0	1.000	1.000	1.000	3	0	.667	.667	.667	0	0	—	—	—	4	0	.750	.750	.750	0	0	—	—	—	4	0	.750	.750	.750
1982	Phi-N	370	4	.249	.315	.319	175	3	.269	.342	.349	195	1	.231	.291	.292	242	2	.277	.355	.347	128	2	.195	.235	.266	98	4	.337	.411	.510	272	0	.217	.279	.250
1983	Phi-N	221	1	.231	.287	.290	100	0	.250	.290	.310	121	1	.215	.286	.273	80	1	.237	.299	.325	141	0	.227	.281	.270	84	0	.202	.256	.238	137	1	.248	.307	.321
1984	Chi-N	536	3	.278	.356	.362	254	2	.303	.377	.402	282	1	.255	.338	.326	253	2	.320	.407	.391	283	1	.240	.309	.336	123	0	.260	.355	.317	413	3	.283	.357	.375
1985	Chi-N	469	1	.254	.315	.316	230	1	.278	.328	.352	239	0	.230	.303	.280	194	0	.263	.324	.320	275	1	.247	.309	.313	118	0	.288	.351	.373	351	1	.242	.303	.296
1986	Chi-N	324	4	.225	.275	.312	157	2	.255	.299	.350	167	2	.198	.251	.275	170	1	.176	.239	.235	154	3	.279	.315	.396	105	2	.305	.360	.429	219	2	.187	.233	.256
1987	Chi-N	199	8	.317	.379	.497	99	4	.313	.364	.475	100	4	.320	.393	.520	87	3	.368	.415	.529	112	5	.277	.352	.473	141	7	.340	.408	.553	58	1	.259	.306	.362
1988	Phi-N	166	1	.289	.330	.337	72	0	.208	.240	.250	94	1	.351	.396	.404	64	0	.344	.400	.359	102	1	.255	.283	.324	137	1	.314	.361	.372	29	0	.172	.172	.172
1989	Phi-N	187	1	.171	.225	.214	97	1	.165	.210	.206	90	0	.178	.242	.222	122	1	.172	.239	.221	65	0	.169	.200	.200	132	1	.197	.253	.250	55	0	.109	.155	.127
TOTALS		2483	23	.255	.318	.333	1187	13	.268	.324	.352	1296	10	.244	.311	.316	1212	10	.267	.337	.336	1271	13	.245	.299	.330	940	15	.284	.349	.385	1543	8	.238	.298	.301

■ Delino DeShields BL/TR

YEAR	TM/L	AB	HR	AVG	OBP	SLG	AB	HR	AVG	OBP	SLG	AB	HR	AVG	OBP	SLG	AB	HR	AVG	OBP	SLG	AB	HR	AVG	OBP	SLG	AB	HR	AVG	OBP	SLG	AB	HR	AVG	OBP	SLG
1990	Mon-N	499	4	.289	.375	.393	226	3	.314	.402	.438	273	1	.267	.352	.355	224	2	.304	.398	.424	275	2	.276	.356	.367	193	2	.264	.356	.373	306	2	.304	.387	.405
1991	Mon-N	563	10	.238	.347	.332	238	3	.265	.379	.349	325	7	.218	.324	.320	269	7	.245	.374	.364	294	3	.231	.322	.303	189	3	.217	.338	.275	374	7	.249	.352	.361
1992	Mon-N	530	7	.292	.359	.398	271	1	.277	.338	.351	259	6	.309	.381	.448	277	2	.285	.360	.379	253	5	.300	.359	.419	185	2	.314	.389	.400	345	5	.281	.343	.397
1993	Mon-N	481	2	.295	.389	.372	234	2	.333	.435	.432	247	0	.259	.343	.316	267	2	.262	.371	.330	214	0	.336	.412	.425	161	2	.311	.407	.435	320	0	.287	.379	.341
1994	LA-N	320	2	.250	.357	.322	151	1	.285	.366	.351	169	1	.219	.350	.296	188	0	.271	.378	.324	132	2	.220	.327	.318	98	0	.276	.398	.337	222	2	.239	.339	.315
1995	LA-N	425	8	.256	.353	.369	205	2	.210	.332	.283	220	6	.300	.374	.450	231	4	.251	.345	.351	194	4	.263	.363	.392	121	2	.207	.273	.314	304	6	.276	.383	.391
1996	LA-N	581	5	.224	.287	.298	261	3	.222	.295	.303	320	2	.225	.281	.294	315	4	.251	.295	.346	266	1	.192	.279	.241	133	1	.211	.257	.316	448	4	.228	.296	.292
1997	StL-N	572	11	.295	.357	.448	277	6	.285	.353	.422	295	5	.305	.361	.471	279	5	.287	.342	.455	293	6	.304	.371	.440	118	1	.280	.358	.398	454	10	.300	.357	.460
1998	StL-N	420	7	.290	.371	.429	204	3	.294	.383	.417	216	4	.287	.359	.440	276	3	.319	.402	.457	144	4	.236	.308	.375	101	0	.267	.333	.386	319	7	.298	.382	.442
1999	Bal-A	330	6	.264	.339	.364	145	4	.262	.323	.372	185	2	.265	.351	.357	190	4	.274	.355	.374	140	2	.250	.316	.350	41	1	.171	.227	.244	289	5	.277	.354	.381
2000	Bal-A	561	10	.296	.369	.444	265	4	.283	.379	.411	296	6	.307	.359	.473	272	3	.298	.372	.434	289	7	.294	.366	.453	154	2	.344	.415	.481	407	8	.278	.351	.430
TOTALS		5282	72	.272	.354	.381	2477	32	.276	.363	.377	2805	40	.269	.346	.384	2788	36	.277	.362	.387	2494	36	.267	.346	.374	1494	16	.268	.353	.369	3788	56	.274	.355	.385

■ Mike Devereaux BR/TR

YEAR	TM/L	AB	HR	AVG	OBP	SLG	AB	HR	AVG	OBP	SLG	AB	HR	AVG	OBP	SLG	AB	HR	AVG	OBP	SLG	AB	HR	AVG	OBP	SLG	AB	HR	AVG	OBP	SLG	AB	HR	AVG	OBP	SLG
1987	LA-N	54	0	.222	.263	.278	27	0	.296	.345	.296	27	0	.148	.179	.259	0	0	—	—	—	54	0	.222	.263	.278	39	0	.205	.244	.256	15	0	.267	.313	.333
1988	LA-N	43	0	.116	.156	.140	22	0	.136	.136	.136	21	0	.095	.174	.143	26	0	.115	.148	.115	17	0	.118	.167	.176	24	0	.125	.192	.125	19	0	.105	.105	.158
1989	Bal-A	391	8	.266	.329	.379	191	4	.246	.327	.366	200	4	.285	.330	.390	146	3	.288	.348	.418	245	5	.253	.317	.355	189	3	.280	.351	.402	202	5	.252	.308	.356
1990	Bal-A	367	12	.240	.291	.392	150	6	.233	.304	.400	217	6	.244	.281	.387	116	2	.207	.252	.302	251	10	.255	.309	.434	160	7	.231	.273	.406	207	5	.246	.304	.382
1991	Bal-A	608	19	.260	.313	.431	305	10	.252	.302	.420	303	9	.267	.324	.442	268	9	.254	.318	.440	340	10	.265	.310	.424	167	6	.293	.350	.515	441	13	.247	.299	.399

		TOTAL					HOME					AWAY					1ST HALF					2ND HALF					LEFT					RIGHT				
YEAR	TM/L	AB	HR	AVG	OBP	SLG	AB	HR	AVG	OBP	SLG	AB	HR	AVG	OBP	SLG	AB	HR	AVG	OBP	SLG	AB	HR	AVG	OBP	SLG	AB	HR	AVG	OBP	SLG	AB	HR	AVG	OBP	SLG
1992	Bal-A	653	24	.276	.321	.464	334	14	.257	.301	.461	319	10	.295	.342	.467	303	12	.284	.333	.488	350	12	.269	.311	.443	168	9	.351	.383	.589	485	15	.249	.300	.421
1993	Bal-A	527	14	.250	.306	.400	247	8	.263	.331	.457	280	6	.239	.283	.350	227	4	.251	.303	.401	300	10	.250	.308	.400	156	5	.276	.352	.442	371	9	.240	.286	.383
1994	Bal-A	301	9	.203	.256	.332	124	5	.210	.286	.363	177	4	.198	.234	.311	223	8	.220	.276	.363	78	1	.154	.195	.244	81	2	.235	.267	.358	220	7	.191	.252	.323
1995	Chi-A	333	10	.306	.352	.465	159	4	.277	.322	.396	174	6	.333	.380	.529	170	4	.294	.339	.429	163	6	.319	.365	.503	112	5	.313	.364	.500	221	5	.303	.346	.448
1995	Atl-N	55	1	.255	.281	.364	20	1	.300	.364	.550	35	0	.229	.229	.257	1	0	.000	.000	.000	54	1	.259	.286	.370	18	0	.278	.278	.333	37	1	.243	.282	.378
1996	Bal-A	323	8	.229	.305	.350	145	5	.214	.290	.345	178	3	.242	.317	.354	193	3	.238	.316	.326	130	5	.215	.288	.385	135	5	.244	.333	.422	188	3	.218	.283	.298
1997	Tex-A	72	0	.208	.275	.250	38	0	.158	.238	.211	34	0	.265	.316	.294	72	0	.208	.275	.250	0	0	—	—	—	44	0	.227	.292	.273	28	0	.179	.250	.214
1998	LA-N	13	0	.308	.438	.385	9	0	.222	.222	.222	4	0	.500	.714	.750	13	0	.308	.438	.385	0	0	—	—	—	9	0	.333	.500	.444	4	0	.250	.250	.250
TOTALS		3740	105	.254	.308	.401	1771	57	.246	.306	.404	1969	48	.261	.310	.399	1758	45	.253	.310	.396	1982	60	.255	.306	.406	1302	42	.274	.332	.439	2438	63	.243	.295	.381
■ **Gary DiSarcina** BR/TR																																				
1989	Cal-A	0	0	—	—	—	0	0	—	—	—	0	0	—	—	—	0	0	—	—	—	0	0	—	—	—	0	0	—	—	—	0	0	—	—	—
1990	Cal-A	57	0	.140	.183	.193	26	0	.038	.107	.038	31	0	.226	.250	.323	50	0	.120	.154	.180	7	0	.286	.375	.286	12	0	.000	.077	.000	45	0	.178	.213	.244
1991	Cal-A	57	0	.211	.274	.246	27	0	.148	.258	.185	30	0	.267	.290	.300	0	0	—	—	—	57	0	.211	.274	.246	18	0	.222	.222	.278	39	0	.205	.295	.231
1992	Cal-A	518	3	.247	.283	.301	251	2	.235	.269	.295	267	1	.258	.296	.307	227	2	.260	.309	.326	291	1	.237	.262	.282	114	0	.228	.264	.263	404	3	.252	.288	.312
1993	Cal-A	416	3	.238	.273	.313	216	2	.250	.279	.324	200	1	.225	.265	.300	246	3	.248	.277	.346	170	0	.224	.267	.265	119	0	.210	.234	.244	297	3	.249	.288	.340
1994	Cal-A	389	3	.260	.294	.329	207	2	.261	.294	.329	182	1	.258	.295	.330	262	3	.271	.303	.359	127	0	.236	.276	.268	117	2	.274	.303	.376	272	1	.254	.291	.309
1995	Cal-A	362	5	.307	.344	.459	182	1	.302	.332	.423	180	4	.311	.355	.494	216	3	.329	.372	.495	146	2	.274	.301	.404	97	2	.289	.314	.495	265	3	.313	.354	.445
1996	Cal-A	536	5	.256	.286	.347	286	2	.231	.256	.311	250	3	.284	.319	.388	253	1	.245	.271	.308	283	4	.265	.299	.382	164	2	.293	.304	.409	372	3	.239	.278	.320
1997	Ana-A	549	4	.246	.271	.326	288	2	.278	.298	.358	261	2	.211	.242	.291	272	3	.254	.280	.360	277	1	.238	.263	.292	158	1	.209	.246	.247	391	3	.261	.282	.358
1998	Ana-A	551	3	.287	.321	.385	266	0	.267	.297	.338	285	3	.305	.342	.428	267	3	.307	.337	.431	284	0	.268	.306	.342	135	1	.311	.345	.415	416	2	.279	.313	.375
1999	Ana-A	271	1	.229	.273	.273	149	1	.215	.259	.262	122	0	.246	.290	.287	22	0	.182	.217	.182	249	1	.233	.278	.281	60	0	.200	.226	.267	211	1	.237	.286	.275
2000	Ana-A	38	1	.395	.425	.526	36	1	.361	.395	.500	2	0	1.000	1.000	1.000	38	1	.395	.425	.526	0	0	—	—	—	4	0	.250	.250	.250	34	1	.412	.444	.559
TOTALS		3744	28	.258	.292	.341	1934	13	.253	.284	.328	1810	15	.264	.301	.355	1853	19	.270	.303	.369	1891	9	.246	.281	.313	998	8	.252	.279	.336	2746	20	.260	.297	.343
■ **Bill Doran** BB/TR																																				
1982	Hou-N	97	0	.278	.304	.309	47	0	.319	.347	.362	50	0	.240	.264	.260	0	0	—	—	—	97	0	.278	.304	.309	40	0	.200	.256	.225	57	0	.333	.339	.368
1983	Hou-N	535	8	.271	.371	.364	264	1	.250	.347	.314	271	7	.292	.395	.413	235	3	.230	.343	.319	300	5	.303	.394	.400	179	3	.212	.299	.285	356	5	.301	.406	.404
1984	Hou-N	548	4	.261	.341	.356	267	2	.232	.311	.333	281	2	.288	.369	.377	232	1	.250	.336	.341	316	3	.269	.345	.367	176	2	.295	.375	.364	372	2	.245	.325	.352
1985	Hou-N	578	14	.287	.362	.434	269	5	.283	.372	.450	309	9	.291	.354	.421	271	7	.277	.355	.406	307	7	.296	.369	.459	217	5	.300	.383	.461	361	9	.280	.350	.418
1986	Hou-N	550	6	.276	.368	.373	270	3	.274	.379	.374	280	3	.279	.358	.371	270	5	.274	.371	.381	280	1	.279	.365	.364	214	3	.304	.371	.407	336	3	.259	.366	.351
1987	Hou-N	625	16	.283	.365	.406	292	7	.305	.412	.414	333	9	.264	.320	.399	298	10	.268	.343	.406	327	6	.297	.385	.407	223	7	.291	.395	.417	402	9	.279	.348	.400
1988	Hou-N	480	7	.248	.338	.333	229	2	.249	.351	.323	251	5	.247	.325	.343	215	3	.265	.350	.344	265	4	.234	.328	.325	156	2	.263	.372	.346	324	5	.241	.321	.327
1989	Hou-N	507	8	.219	.301	.323	250	3	.252	.332	.360	257	5	.187	.271	.288	302	8	.272	.340	.417	205	0	.141	.246	.185	140	4	.229	.312	.357	367	4	.215	.297	.311
1990	Hou-N	344	6	.288	.405	.413	169	3	.314	.420	.456	175	3	.263	.390	.371	209	1	.268	.377	.335	135	5	.319	.446	.533	135	2	.267	.409	.415	209	4	.301	.402	.411
1990	Cin-N	59	1	.373	.448	.559	30	1	.433	.500	.633	29	0	.310	.394	.483	0	0	—	—	—	59	1	.373	.448	.559	7	0	.286	.375	.286	52	1	.385	.458	.596
1991	Cin-N	361	6	.280	.359	.374	169	3	.296	.390	.408	192	3	.266	.330	.344	134	2	.328	.418	.433	227	4	.251	.321	.339	80	2	.262	.362	.412	281	4	.285	.358	.363
1992	Cin-N	387	8	.235	.342	.349	197	6	.223	.338	.345	190	2	.247	.347	.353	194	5	.242	.332	.381	193	3	.228	.352	.316	125	2	.200	.353	.288	262	6	.252	.337	.378
1993	Mil-A	60	0	.217	.284	.283	27	0	.185	.267	.222	33	0	.242	.297	.333	47	0	.191	.278	.277	13	0	.308	.308	.308	40	0	.200	.267	.275	20	0	.250	.318	.300
TOTALS		5131	84	.266	.354	.373	2480	36	.269	.365	.377	2651	48	.264	.344	.370	2407	45	.264	.352	.375	2724	39	.268	.356	.372	1732	32	.264	.361	.373	3399	52	.267	.351	.374
■ **Brian Downing** BR/TR																																				
1978	Cal-A	412	7	.255	.345	.342	186	2	.237	.351	.301	226	5	.270	.340	.376	134	3	.216	.346	.313	278	4	.273	.345	.356	120	3	.283	.338	.383	292	4	.243	.348	.325
1979	Cal-A	509	12	.326	.418	.462	242	3	.289	.396	.376	267	9	.360	.439	.539	259	7	.351	.411	.521	250	5	.300	.425	.400	127	2	.386	.473	.496	382	10	.306	.400	.450
1980	Cal-A	93	2	.290	.364	.419	41	2	.293	.375	.488	52	0	.288	.356	.365	26	1	.077	.172	.192	67	1	.373	.436	.507	35	2	.371	.465	.629	58	0	.241	.297	.293
1981	Cal-A	317	9	.249	.351	.379	158	6	.285	.402	.449	159	3	.214	.298	.308	164	6	.268	.385	.415	153	3	.229	.314	.340	98	2	.245	.378	.347	219	7	.251	.339	.393
1982	Cal-A	623	28	.281	.368	.482	315	15	.295	.365	.505	308	13	.266	.371	.458	293	11	.290	.342	.471	330	17	.273	.390	.491	220	9	.318	.398	.509	403	19	.261	.352	.467
1983	Cal-A	403	19	.246	.352	.429	229	10	.218	.323	.384	174	9	.282	.388	.489	124	5	.234	.395	.403	279	14	.251	.330	.441	153	10	.294	.411	.510	250	9	.216	.314	.380
1984	Cal-A	539	23	.275	.360	.462	263	9	.255	.345	.403	276	14	.293	.374	.518	256	9	.227	.339	.379	283	14	.318	.381	.537	174	7	.293	.394	.471	365	16	.266	.344	.458
1985	Cal-A	520	20	.263	.371	.427	249	10	.241	.362	.406	271	10	.284	.379	.446	215	4	.219	.342	.321	305	16	.295	.392	.502	172	8	.262	.343	.483	348	12	.264	.384	.399
1986	Cal-A	513	20	.267	.389	.452	260	13	.277	.392	.488	253	7	.257	.385	.415	250	9	.300	.416	.500	263	11	.236	.363	.407	183	7	.240	.385	.443	330	13	.282	.390	.458
1987	Cal-A	567	29	.272	.400	.487	280	11	.279	.412	.475	287	18	.265	.388	.498	279	17	.280	.405	.534	288	12	.264	.394	.441	177	11	.299	.432	.554	390	18	.259	.384	.456
1988	Cal-A	484	25	.242	.362	.442	239	11	.238	.365	.423	245	14	.245	.360	.461	215	9	.251	.374	.433	269	16	.234	.353	.450	175	8	.223	.385	.383	309	17	.252	.349	.476
1989	Cal-A	544	14	.283	.354	.414	250	10	.296	.370	.464	294	4	.272	.340	.371	284	8	.310	.382	.465	260	6	.254	.324	.358	187	8	.299	.388	.476	357	6	.275	.336	.381
1990	Cal-A	330	14	.273	.374	.467	162	11	.302	.403	.562	168	3	.244	.347	.375	105	4	.229	.314	.390	225	10	.293	.401	.502	119	5	.345	.466	.555	211	9	.232	.318	.417
1991	Tex-A	407	17	.278	.377	.455	204	8	.255	.365	.431	203	9	.300	.389	.478	189	7	.270	.379	.429	218	10	.284	.375	.477	139	9	.281	.401	.511	268	8	.276	.364	.425
1992	Tex-A	320	10	.278	.407	.428	163	4	.307	.430	.454	157	6	.248	.382	.401	144	5	.257	.422	.403	176	5	.295	.393	.449	121	3	.281	.429	.421	199	7	.276	.392	.432
TOTALS		6581	249	.272	.374	.441	3241	125	.269	.376	.439	3340	124	.275	.372	.443	2937	105	.270	.375	.437	3644	144	.274	.373	.444	2200	94	.290	.402	.474	4381	155	.263	.360	.424
■ **Dan Driessen** BL/TR																																				
1978	Cin-N	524	16	.250	.345	.397	252	10	.262	.354	.437	272	6	.239	.337	.360	251	9	.295	.383	.474	273	7	.209	.310	.326	204	2	.230	.298	.304	320	14	.262	.373	.456
1979	Cin-N	515	18	.250	.330	.414	242	12	.277	.345	.471	273	6	.227	.317	.363	255	12	.259	.336	.451	260	6	.242	.326	.377	184	7	.245	.307	.402	331	11	.254	.343	.420
1980	Cin-N	524	14	.265	.377	.418	251	11	.263	.364	.482	273	3	.267	.388	.359	232	8	.284	.389	.453	292	6	.250	.366	.390	166	3	.271	.353	.398	358	11	.263	.387	.427
1981	Cin-N	233	7	.236	.349	.386	94	2	.223	.330	.383	139	5	.245	.361	.388	122	5	.205	.355	.393	111	2	.270	.341	.378	51	1	.294	.448	.490	182	6	.220	.318	.357
1982	Cin-N	516	17	.269	.368	.421	253	7	.292	.389	.431	263	10	.247	.347	.411	265	8	.302	.391	.449	251	9	.235	.344	.390	143	2	.210	.305	.287	373	15	.292	.392	.472
1983	Cin-N	386	12	.277	.390	.420	184	3	.277	.409	.380	202	9	.277	.370	.455	146	5	.267	.374	.384	240	7	.283	.399	.442	78	2	.218	.340	.346	308	10	.292	.403	.438
1984	Cin-N	218	7	.280	.378	.436	91	3	.242	.386	.407	127	4	.307	.372	.457	166	3	.277	.379	.386	52	4	.288	.377	.596	38	1	.211	.348	.316	180	6	.294	.385	.461
1984	Mon-N	169	9	.254	.321	.479	92	8	.304	.390	.641	77	1	.195	.232	.286	0	0	—	—	—	169	9	.254	.321	.479	32	0	.063	.091	.063	137	9	.299	.370	.577
1985	Mon-N	312	6	.250	.324	.365	158	2	.228	.324	.323	154	4	.273	.323	.409	228	6	.254	.323	.390	84	0	.238	.326	.298	78	1	.295	.317	.410	234	5	.235	.326	.350
1985	SF-N	181	3	.232	.297	.326	104	2	.240	.283	.346	77	1	.221	.315	.299	0	0	—	—	—	181	3	.232	.297	.326	17	0	.235	.316	.235	164	3	.232	.295	.335
1986	SF-N	16	0	.188	.350	.313	11	0	.273	.429	.455	5	0	.000	.167	.000	16	0	.188	.350	.313	0	0	—	—	—	8	0	.250	.455	.500	8	0	.125	.222	.125
1986	Hou-N	24	1	.292	.414	.458	4	1	.500	.600	1.250	20	0	.250	.375	.300	0	0	—	—	—	24	1	.292	.414	.458	7	0	.286	.286	.286	17	1	.294	.455	.529
1987	StL-N	60	1	.233	.309	.317	35	0	.286	.316	.314	25	1	.160	.300	.320	0	0	—	—	—	60	1	.233	.309	.317	8	0	.250	.222	.250	52	1	.231	.322	.327
TOTALS		3678	111	.258	.353	.406	1771	61	.266	.362	.431	1907	50	.250	.345	.382	1681	56	.272	.367	.428	1997	55	.246	.341	.387	1014	19	.239	.320	.348	2664	92	.265	.365	.428
■ **Rob Ducey** BL/TR																																				
1987	Tor-A	48	1	.188	.298	.271	18	1	.222	.318	.389	30	0	.167	.286	.200	27	0	.148	.333	.148	21	1	.238	.238	.429	17	1	.176	.300	.353	31	0	.194	.297	.226
1988	Tor-A	54	0	.315	.361	.426	28	0	.214	.281	.321	26	0	.423	.448	.538	0	0	—	—	—	54	0	.315	.361	.426	28	0	.357	.379	.393	26	0	.269	.344	.462
1989	Tor-A	76	0	.211	.294	.263	43	0	.233	.340	.302	33	0	.182	.229	.212	70	0	.214	.304	.257	6	0	.167	.167	.333	18	0	.222	.300	.222	58	0	.207	.292	.276
1990	Tor-A	53	0	.302	.387	.396	29	0	.241	.389	.310	24	0	.375	.385	.500	0	0	—	—	—	53	0	.302	.387	.396	6	0	.333	.429	.500	47	0	.298	.382	.383
1991	Tor-A	68	1	.235	.297	.368	33	0	.242	.265	.303	35	1	.229	.325	.429	8	0	.375	.375	.625	60	1	.217	.288	.333	12	1	.333	.385	.750	56	0	.214	.279	.286
1992	Tor-A	21	0	.048	.048	.095	11	0	.000	.000	.000	10	0	.100	.100	.200	16	0	.063	.063	.125	5	0	.000	.000	.000	5	0	.200	.200	.400	16	0	.000	.000	.000
1992	Cal-A	59	0	.237	.292	.288	43	0	.279	.347	.326	16	0	.125	.125	.188	0	0	—	—	—	59	0	.237	.292	.288	4	0	.000	.200	.000	55	0	.255	.300	.309
1993	Tex-A	85	2	.282	.351	.494	46	2	.348	.400	.609	39	0	.205	.298	.359	0	0	—	—	—	85	2	.282	.351	.494	11	0	.182	.167	.364	74	2	.297	.376	.514
1994	Tex-A	29	0	.172	.226	.207	22	0	.182	.250	.227	7	0	.143	.143	.143	29	0	.172	.226	.207	0	0	—	—	—	0	0	—	—	—	29	0	.172	.226	.207
1997	Sea-A	143	5	.287	.311	.524	72	0	.264	.280	.403	71	5	.310	.342	.648	69	1	.246	.289	.406	74	4	.324	.333	.635	9	0	.111	.111	.111	134	5	.299	.324	.552
1998	Sea-A	217	5	.240	.336	.410	110	2	.245	.346	.391	107	3	.234	.325	.430	153	2	.242	.326	.399	64	3	.234	.359	.438	17	0	.118	.167	.176	200	5	.250	.349	.430
1999	Phi-N	188	8	.261	.383	.463	97	3	.278	.393	.464	91	5	.242	.373	.462	68	4	.279	.417	.544	120	4	.250	.364	.417	7	0	.143	.250	.143	181	8	.265	.388	.475
2000	Phi-N	152	6	.197	.322	.355	80	4	.275	.355	.475	72	2	.111	.289	.222	78	4	.205	.347	.423	74	2	.189	.295	.284	10	0	.000	.167	.000	142	6	.211	.333	.380
2000	Tor-A	13	0	.154	.267	.231	1	0	.000	.000	.000	12	0	.167	.286	.250	0	0	—	—	—	13	0	.154	.267	.231	2	0	.500	.500	1.000	11	0	.091	.231	.091
TOTALS		1206	28	.242	.328	.396	633	12	.256	.337	.395	573	16	.227	.318	.396	518	11	.226	.323	.375	688	17	.254	.331	.411	146	2	.212	.275	.315	1060	26	.246	.335	.407
■ **Mariano Duncan** BR/TR																																				
1985	LA-N	562	6	.244	.293	.340	275	1	.240	.286	.313	287	5	.247	.300	.366	219	2	.242	.291	.320	343	4	.245	.295	.353	182	4	.286	.332	.429	380	2	.224	.275	.297
1986	LA-N	407	8	.229	.284	.305	205	2	.220	.275	.259	202	6	.238	.294	.351	256	6	.223	.282	.309	151	2	.238	.288	.298	173	4	.260	.295	.347	234	4	.205	.276	.274
1987	LA-N	261	6	.215	.267	.322	110	3	.227	.277	.336	151	3	.205	.259	.311	194	3	.222	.269	.299	67	3	.194	.260	.388	91	4	.275	.305	.451	170	2	.182	.247	.253
1989	LA-N	84	0	.250	.267	.333	62	0	.210	.222	.306	22	0	.364	.391	.409	83	0	.253	.271	.337	1	0	.000	.000	.000	45	0	.356	.356	.489	39	0	.128	.171	.154
1989	Cin-N	174	3	.247	.292	.368	68	2	.250	.311	.397	106	1	.245	.279	.349	0	0	—	—	—	174	3	.247	.292	.368	54	2	.222	.300	.444	120	1	.258	.288	.333
1990	Cin-N	435	10	.306	.345	.476	230	5	.309	.346	.470	205	5	.302	.344	.483	190	6	.305	.354	.489	245	4	.306	.337	.465	188	4	.410	.437	.606	247	6	.227	.276	.377
1991	Cin-N	333	12	.258	.288	.411	167	10	.311	.333	.539	166	2	.205	.243	.283	167	2	.210	.253	.305	166	10	.307	.324	.518	140	5	.314	.347	.493	193	7	.218	.244	.352
1992	Phi-N	574	8	.267	.292	.389	276	3	.243	.277	.351	298	5	.289	.305	.423	314	4	.283	.306	.408	260	4	.246	.275	.365	231	4	.286	.308	.407	343	4	.254	.281	.376

YEAR	TM/L	TOTAL AB	HR	AVG	OBP	SLG	HOME AB	HR	AVG	OBP	SLG	AWAY AB	HR	AVG	OBP	SLG	1ST HALF AB	HR	AVG	OBP	SLG	2ND HALF AB	HR	AVG	OBP	SLG	LEFT AB	HR	AVG	OBP	SLG	RIGHT AB	HR	AVG	OBP	SLG
1993	Phi-N	496	11	.282	.304	.417	211	5	.289	.315	.427	285	6	.277	.295	.411	241	6	.253	.283	.390	255	5	.310	.323	.443	198	6	.273	.291	.429	298	5	.289	.312	.409
1994	Phi-N	347	8	.268	.306	.406	190	6	.247	.285	.389	157	2	.293	.331	.427	271	6	.273	.320	.413	76	2	.250	.256	.382	111	4	.297	.345	.495	236	4	.254	.289	.364
1995	Phi-N	196	3	.286	.285	.403	88	1	.284	.289	.398	108	2	.287	.282	.407	135	2	.281	.283	.385	61	1	.295	.290	.443	82	1	.293	.289	.415	114	2	.281	.282	.395
1995	Cin-N	69	3	.290	.329	.478	30	2	.400	.429	.667	39	1	.205	.244	.333	0	0	—	—	—	69	3	.290	.329	.478	32	1	.313	.395	.469	37	2	.270	.263	.486
1996	NY-A	400	8	.340	.352	.500	160	5	.406	.423	.613	240	3	.296	.304	.425	186	3	.296	.316	.419	214	5	.379	.383	.570	123	2	.317	.338	.472	277	6	.350	.358	.513
1997	NY-A	172	1	.244	.270	.308	74	1	.230	.260	.284	98	0	.255	.277	.327	158	1	.247	.270	.310	14	0	.214	.267	.286	59	0	.220	.258	.288	113	1	.257	.276	.319
1997	Tor-A	167	0	.228	.267	.263	69	0	.217	.270	.261	98	0	.235	.265	.265	0	0	—	—	—	167	0	.228	.267	.263	43	0	.233	.250	.233	124	0	.226	.273	.274
TOTALS		4677	87	.267	.300	.388	2215	46	.270	.305	.394	2462	41	.264	.295	.383	2414	41	.258	.295	.370	2263	46	.276	.306	.408	1752	41	.297	.328	.443	2925	46	.249	.284	.355
■ Shawon Dunston BR/TR																																				
1985	Chi-N	250	4	.260	.310	.388	147	3	.299	.362	.449	103	1	.204	.231	.301	72	1	.194	.266	.319	178	3	.287	.328	.416	45	1	.222	.255	.356	205	3	.268	.321	.395
1986	Chi-N	581	17	.250	.278	.411	305	10	.262	.287	.443	276	7	.236	.269	.377	286	8	.276	.315	.441	295	9	.224	.243	.383	156	6	.231	.247	.423	425	11	.256	.290	.407
1987	Chi-N	346	5	.246	.267	.358	181	3	.221	.239	.337	165	2	.273	.298	.382	240	5	.258	.275	.400	106	0	.217	.250	.264	78	1	.231	.237	.321	268	4	.250	.276	.369
1988	Chi-N	575	9	.249	.271	.357	263	5	.278	.300	.407	312	4	.224	.245	.314	286	8	.297	.315	.444	289	1	.201	.227	.270	167	4	.234	.247	.371	408	5	.255	.280	.350
1989	Chi-N	471	9	.278	.320	.403	225	3	.307	.347	.404	246	6	.252	.295	.402	187	4	.225	.295	.385	284	5	.313	.338	.415	139	2	.338	.382	.489	332	7	.253	.294	.367
1990	Chi-N	545	17	.262	.283	.426	268	7	.250	.275	.403	277	10	.274	.291	.448	269	10	.283	.297	.446	276	7	.243	.269	.406	188	9	.287	.295	.505	357	8	.249	.277	.384
1991	Chi-N	492	12	.260	.292	.407	237	7	.295	.329	.451	255	5	.227	.258	.365	254	8	.236	.270	.390	238	4	.286	.316	.424	194	5	.232	.269	.366	298	7	.279	.308	.433
1992	Chi-N	73	0	.315	.342	.384	28	0	.321	.367	.429	45	0	.311	.326	.356	73	0	.315	.342	.384	0	0	—	—	—	24	0	.417	.417	.417	49	0	.265	.308	.367
1993	Chi-N	10	0	.400	.400	.600	3	0	.667	.667	1.000	7	0	.286	.286	.429	0	0	—	—	—	10	0	.400	.400	.600	7	0	.429	.429	.714	3	0	.333	.333	.333
1994	Chi-N	331	11	.278	.313	.435	159	2	.220	.256	.308	172	9	.331	.366	.552	233	8	.270	.310	.421	98	3	.296	.320	.469	90	6	.267	.302	.556	241	5	.282	.318	.390
1995	Chi-N	477	14	.296	.317	.472	232	8	.306	.321	.474	245	6	.286	.313	.469	192	6	.333	.345	.521	285	8	.270	.298	.439	138	5	.348	.372	.543	339	9	.274	.293	.442
1996	SF-N	287	5	.300	.331	.408	131	3	.359	.391	.504	156	2	.250	.280	.327	188	4	.309	.332	.436	99	1	.283	.330	.354	55	0	.255	.281	.327	232	5	.310	.343	.427
1997	Chi-N	419	9	.284	.300	.411	215	7	.312	.321	.470	204	2	.255	.277	.348	221	2	.285	.310	.398	198	7	.283	.287	.424	81	2	.247	.271	.370	338	7	.293	.307	.420
1997	Pit-N	71	5	.394	.389	.690	42	3	.357	.357	.619	29	2	.448	.433	.793	0	0	—	—	—	71	5	.394	.389	.690	13	1	.462	.429	.769	58	4	.379	.379	.672
1998	Cle-A	156	3	.237	.265	.404	70	1	.300	.316	.486	86	2	.186	.222	.337	134	2	.231	.264	.396	22	1	.273	.273	.455	71	3	.225	.253	.423	85	0	.247	.275	.388
1998	SF-N	51	3	.176	.222	.392	21	1	.190	.227	.333	30	2	.167	.219	.433	0	0	—	—	—	51	3	.176	.222	.392	15	0	.133	.235	.200	36	3	.194	.216	.472
1999	StL-N	150	5	.307	.327	.467	77	4	.364	.375	.558	73	1	.247	.276	.370	122	5	.361	.378	.557	28	0	.071	.103	.071	50	1	.280	.308	.380	100	4	.320	.337	.510
1999	NY-N	93	0	.344	.354	.430	45	0	.311	.304	.378	48	0	.375	.400	.479	0	0	—	—	—	93	0	.344	.354	.430	44	0	.409	.409	.523	49	0	.286	.308	.347
2000	StL-N	216	12	.250	.278	.486	101	6	.248	.283	.485	115	6	.252	.273	.487	101	7	.238	.267	.495	115	5	.261	.287	.478	106	6	.226	.245	.443	110	6	.273	.308	.527
TOTALS		5594	140	.270	.297	.416	2750	73	.284	.311	.433	2844	67	.257	.284	.399	2858	78	.276	.305	.430	2736	62	.264	.289	.401	1661	52	.270	.293	.435	3933	88	.270	.299	.408
■ Leon Durham BL/TL																																				
1980	StL-N	303	8	.271	.309	.426	135	3	.274	.313	.437	168	5	.268	.306	.417	58	1	.224	.288	.345	245	7	.282	.314	.445	49	0	.224	.264	.327	254	8	.280	.318	.445
1981	Chi-N	328	10	.290	.344	.460	179	8	.335	.383	.553	149	2	.235	.296	.349	157	4	.312	.353	.484	171	6	.269	.335	.439	81	1	.210	.264	.296	247	9	.316	.369	.514
1982	Chi-N	539	22	.312	.388	.521	281	9	.288	.368	.484	258	13	.337	.409	.562	261	10	.287	.367	.479	278	12	.335	.406	.561	126	5	.286	.389	.460	413	17	.320	.387	.540
1983	Chi-N	337	12	.258	.381	.466	181	9	.271	.395	.514	156	3	.244	.366	.410	166	9	.301	.431	.554	171	3	.216	.332	.380	85	2	.329	.458	.506	252	10	.234	.354	.452
1984	Chi-N	473	23	.279	.369	.505	245	19	.327	.417	.645	228	4	.228	.315	.355	237	12	.308	.394	.527	236	11	.250	.343	.483	109	2	.257	.362	.385	364	21	.286	.371	.541
1985	Chi-N	542	21	.282	.357	.465	257	15	.331	.414	.595	285	6	.239	.304	.347	244	8	.279	.347	.443	298	13	.285	.366	.483	127	4	.268	.340	.425	415	17	.287	.363	.477
1986	Chi-N	484	20	.262	.350	.452	279	13	.283	.360	.505	205	7	.234	.338	.380	240	8	.242	.330	.387	244	12	.283	.370	.516	128	3	.227	.275	.367	356	17	.275	.375	.483
1987	Chi-N	439	27	.273	.348	.513	236	16	.297	.375	.551	203	11	.246	.316	.468	243	15	.300	.369	.535	196	12	.240	.321	.485	74	2	.257	.286	.378	365	25	.277	.359	.540
1988	Chi-N	73	3	.219	.305	.452	22	0	.091	.167	.227	51	3	.275	.362	.549	73	3	.219	.305	.452	0	0	—	—	—	4	0	.250	.400	.250	69	3	.217	.299	.464
1988	Cin-N	51	1	.216	.286	.333	42	1	.190	.244	.333	9	0	.333	.455	.333	43	1	.233	.298	.372	8	0	.125	.222	.125	3	0	.333	.333	.333	48	1	.208	.283	.333
1989	StL-N	18	0	.056	.182	.111	7	0	.143	.364	.286	11	0	.000	.000	.000	5	0	.000	.286	.000	13	0	.077	.133	.154	5	0	.200	.333	.400	13	0	.000	.125	.000
TOTALS		3587	147	.277	.356	.475	1864	93	.296	.376	.531	1723	54	.255	.333	.415	1727	71	.281	.361	.474	1860	76	.273	.350	.477	791	19	.259	.339	.399	2796	128	.281	.360	.497
■ Ray Durham BB/TR																																				
1995	Chi-A	471	7	.257	.309	.384	230	1	.235	.291	.330	241	6	.278	.326	.436	202	2	.287	.344	.396	269	5	.234	.281	.375	149	3	.315	.373	.490	322	4	.230	.277	.335
1996	Chi-A	557	10	.275	.350	.406	275	3	.258	.333	.356	282	7	.291	.366	.454	257	5	.280	.380	.432	300	5	.270	.322	.383	168	3	.262	.308	.423	389	7	.280	.367	.398
1997	Chi-A	634	11	.271	.337	.382	295	3	.258	.328	.353	339	8	.283	.345	.407	319	5	.254	.327	.357	315	6	.289	.348	.406	177	3	.237	.285	.305	457	8	.284	.357	.411
1998	Chi-A	635	19	.285	.363	.455	299	10	.288	.378	.465	336	9	.283	.349	.446	316	7	.288	.372	.449	319	12	.282	.353	.461	171	6	.281	.322	.444	464	13	.287	.376	.459
1999	Chi-A	612	13	.296	.373	.435	297	7	.290	.369	.418	315	6	.302	.377	.451	303	9	.300	.372	.485	309	4	.291	.374	.385	136	3	.301	.396	.449	476	10	.294	.367	.431
2000	Chi-A	614	17	.280	.361	.450	288	5	.299	.395	.444	326	12	.264	.329	.454	316	12	.278	.345	.484	298	5	.282	.378	.413	129	4	.248	.305	.419	485	13	.289	.375	.458
TOTALS		3523	77	.278	.351	.420	1684	29	.273	.352	.397	1839	48	.283	.349	.441	1713	40	.281	.357	.436	1810	37	.276	.345	.405	930	22	.273	.330	.418	2593	55	.280	.358	.421
■ Jermaine Dye BR/TR																																				
1996	Atl-N	292	12	.281	.304	.459	126	4	.310	.326	.468	166	8	.259	.288	.452	73	4	.315	.315	.534	219	8	.269	.300	.434	93	5	.323	.340	.538	199	7	.261	.287	.422
1997	KC-A	263	7	.236	.284	.369	127	3	.228	.274	.354	136	4	.243	.293	.382	110	2	.218	.246	.327	153	5	.248	.310	.399	84	4	.286	.315	.488	179	3	.212	.269	.313
1998	KC-A	214	5	.234	.270	.336	103	3	.272	.315	.427	111	2	.198	.227	.252	136	2	.213	.260	.287	78	3	.269	.287	.423	43	1	.256	.304	.372	171	4	.228	.261	.327
1999	KC-A	608	27	.294	.354	.526	299	15	.308	.381	.565	309	12	.282	.326	.489	283	11	.293	.356	.488	325	16	.295	.352	.560	101	5	.267	.333	.505	507	22	.300	.358	.531
2000	KC-A	601	33	.321	.390	.561	305	15	.341	.399	.570	296	18	.301	.381	.551	273	20	.319	.399	.630	328	13	.323	.383	.503	133	7	.323	.379	.579	468	26	.321	.393	.556
TOTALS		1978	84	.286	.340	.485	960	40	.304	.359	.511	1018	44	.269	.322	.461	875	39	.281	.339	.485	1103	45	.290	.341	.486	454	22	.297	.342	.518	1524	62	.283	.339	.476
■ Lenny Dykstra BL/TL																																				
1985	NY-N	236	1	.254	.338	.331	109	0	.239	.323	.294	127	1	.268	.352	.362	30	1	.267	.290	.433	206	0	.252	.345	.316	56	0	.268	.349	.321	180	1	.250	.335	.333
1986	NY-N	431	8	.295	.377	.445	211	4	.322	.397	.493	220	4	.268	.357	.400	181	2	.309	.387	.442	250	6	.284	.369	.448	103	0	.233	.336	.291	328	8	.314	.390	.494
1987	NY-N	431	10	.285	.352	.455	212	7	.292	.359	.481	219	3	.279	.344	.429	200	6	.285	.344	.465	231	4	.286	.358	.446	74	1	.203	.289	.324	357	9	.303	.365	.482
1988	NY-N	429	8	.270	.321	.385	201	3	.254	.306	.343	228	5	.285	.335	.421	227	3	.308	.349	.414	202	5	.228	.291	.351	74	1	.270	.321	.365	355	7	.270	.321	.389
1989	NY-N	159	3	.270	.362	.415	69	2	.275	.373	.449	90	1	.267	.352	.389	159	3	.270	.362	.415	0	0	—	—	—	34	0	.294	.316	.412	125	3	.264	.373	.416
1989	Phi-N	352	4	.222	.297	.330	165	3	.242	.332	.376	187	1	.203	.265	.289	37	1	.324	.419	.595	315	3	.210	.282	.298	119	0	.202	.296	.261	233	4	.232	.297	.365
1990	Phi-N	590	9	.325	.418	.441	280	6	.339	.445	.464	310	3	.313	.392	.419	269	4	.372	.459	.491	321	5	.287	.384	.399	200	1	.290	.385	.345	390	8	.344	.434	.490
1991	Phi-N	246	3	.297	.391	.427	118	3	.322	.424	.492	128	0	.273	.359	.367	96	2	.302	.422	.479	150	1	.293	.369	.393	94	2	.309	.414	.500	152	1	.289	.376	.382
1992	Phi-N	345	6	.301	.375	.406	196	5	.306	.385	.423	149	1	.295	.361	.383	232	3	.280	.356	.375	113	3	.345	.414	.469	146	4	.322	.389	.452	199	2	.286	.364	.372
1993	Phi-N	637	19	.305	.420	.482	307	12	.300	.425	.518	330	7	.309	.416	.448	307	7	.287	.406	.436	330	12	.321	.434	.524	217	2	.281	.414	.392	420	17	.317	.424	.529
1994	Phi-N	315	5	.273	.404	.435	165	3	.291	.426	.497	150	2	.253	.379	.367	250	5	.296	.414	.480	65	0	.185	.369	.262	91	1	.231	.388	.330	224	4	.290	.411	.478
1995	Phi-N	254	2	.264	.353	.354	131	2	.237	.306	.344	123	0	.293	.400	.366	154	0	.260	.341	.299	100	2	.270	.371	.440	88	1	.307	.380	.398	166	1	.241	.339	.331
1996	Phi-N	134	3	.261	.387	.418	63	1	.238	.360	.349	71	2	.282	.409	.479	134	3	.261	.387	.418	0	0	—	—	—	38	2	.421	.551	.658	96	1	.198	.316	.323
TOTALS		4559	81	.285	.375	.419	2227	51	.290	.384	.440	2332	30	.280	.366	.398	2276	40	.297	.387	.435	2283	41	.272	.362	.403	1334	15	.275	.375	.376	3225	66	.289	.375	.436
■ Mike Easler BL/TR																																				
1979	Pit-N	54	2	.278	.371	.444	25	1	.240	.387	.440	29	1	.310	.355	.448	22	2	.318	.500	.636	32	0	.250	.250	.313	3	0	.667	.833	.667	51	2	.255	.321	.431
1980	Pit-N	393	21	.338	.396	.583	190	9	.353	.422	.579	203	12	.325	.369	.586	124	11	.355	.417	.694	269	10	.331	.386	.532	68	1	.250	.289	.338	325	20	.357	.417	.634
1981	Pit-N	339	7	.286	.328	.431	165	4	.273	.318	.436	174	3	.299	.337	.425	167	6	.317	.351	.515	172	1	.256	.304	.349	80	0	.175	.209	.225	259	7	.320	.364	.494
1982	Pit-N	475	15	.276	.337	.436	238	9	.282	.320	.471	237	6	.270	.353	.401	196	5	.276	.362	.403	279	10	.276	.319	.459	64	2	.328	.357	.516	411	13	.268	.334	.423
1983	Pit-N	381	10	.307	.349	.441	176	2	.341	.393	.420	205	8	.278	.310	.459	180	4	.339	.378	.450	201	6	.279	.322	.433	43	0	.302	.333	.349	338	10	.308	.351	.453
1984	Bos-A	601	27	.313	.376	.516	299	16	.375	.434	.612	302	11	.252	.317	.421	284	13	.299	.374	.511	317	14	.325	.378	.521	179	7	.240	.290	.425	422	20	.344	.411	.555
1985	Bos-A	568	16	.262	.325	.412	273	4	.249	.311	.377	295	12	.275	.337	.444	269	8	.264	.322	.413	299	8	.261	.327	.411	173	2	.277	.345	.364	395	14	.256	.316	.433
1986	NY-A	490	14	.302	.362	.449	233	6	.288	.349	.442	257	8	.315	.375	.455	245	6	.335	.383	.482	245	8	.269	.342	.416	106	1	.226	.252	.302	384	13	.323	.390	.490
1987	Phi-N	110	1	.282	.316	.345	69	1	.261	.288	.333	41	0	.317	.364	.366	110	1	.282	.316	.345	0	0	—	—	—	15	0	.133	.188	.133	95	1	.305	.337	.379
1987	NY-A	167	4	.281	.337	.389	90	2	.356	.416	.478	77	2	.195	.241	.286	52	0	.269	.328	.327	115	4	.287	.341	.417	21	0	.190	.333	.190	146	4	.295	.338	.418
TOTALS		3578	117	.295	.352	.459	1758	54	.308	.365	.474	1820	63	.282	.339	.443	1649	56	.304	.364	.470	1929	61	.287	.342	.449	752	13	.250	.301	.356	2826	104	.307	.365	.486
■ Damion Easley BR/TR																																				
1992	Cal-A	151	1	.258	.307	.311	67	1	.269	.329	.343	84	0	.250	.289	.286	0	0	—	—	—	151	1	.258	.307	.311	36	0	.278	.316	.306	115	1	.252	.304	.313
1993	Cal-A	230	2	.313	.392	.413	129	0	.302	.381	.388	101	2	.327	.405	.446	175	2	.309	.374	.423	55	0	.327	.441	.382	72	1	.361	.418	.500	158	1	.291	.380	.373
1994	Cal-A	316	6	.215	.288	.329	153	4	.209	.291	.340	163	2	.221	.285	.319	211	4	.227	.295	.332	105	2	.190	.274	.324	106	3	.189	.263	.330	210	3	.229	.300	.329
1995	Cal-A	357	4	.216	.288	.300	170	1	.206	.283	.288	187	3	.225	.293	.310	168	3	.196	.279	.292	189	1	.233	.297	.307	118	2	.246	.302	.381	239	2	.201	.281	.259
1996	Cal-A	45	2	.156	.255	.311	13	1	.154	.267	.385	32	1	.156	.250	.281	38	2	.184	.279	.368	7	0	.000	.125	.000	19	1	.211	.286	.368	26	1	.115	.233	.269
1996	Det-A	67	2	.343	.384	.448	27	0	.333	.419	.333	40	2	.350	.357	.525	0	0	—	—	—	67	2	.343	.384	.448	29	2	.414	.452	.655	38	0	.289	.333	.289
1997	Det-A	527	22	.264	.362	.471	256	12	.250	.346	.453	271	10	.277	.377	.487	244	11	.262	.360	.467	283	11	.265	.364	.473	143	7	.231	.299	.441	384	15	.276	.383	.482
1998	Det-A	594	27	.271	.332	.478	300	19	.283	.334	.520	294	8	.259	.329	.435	302	19	.291	.349	.543	292	8	.250	.313	.411	138	4	.290	.355	.442	456	23	.265	.325	.489
1999	Det-A	549	20	.266	.346	.434	265	12	.268	.359	.460	284	8	.264	.333	.408	274	10	.252	.343	.431	275	10	.280	.349	.436	86	4	.291	.394	.500	463	16	.261	.336	.421

YEAR	TM/L	TOTAL					HOME					AWAY					1ST HALF					2ND HALF					LEFT					RIGHT				
		AB	HR	AVG	OBP	SLG	AB	HR	AVG	OBP	SLG	AB	HR	AVG	OBP	SLG	AB	HR	AVG	OBP	SLG	AB	HR	AVG	OBP	SLG	AB	HR	AVG	OBP	SLG	AB	HR	AVG	OBP	SLG
2000	Det-A	464	14	.259	.350	.416	213	5	.305	.384	.474	251	9	.219	.322	.367	160	3	.244	.346	.356	304	11	.266	.353	.447	125	3	.280	.357	.424	339	11	.251	.348	.413
TOTALS		3300	100	.258	.336	.412	1593	55	.264	.342	.429	1707	45	.253	.331	.397	1572	54	.256	.336	.420	1728	46	.260	.336	.405	872	27	.268	.337	.428	2428	73	.255	.336	.407
■ Jim Edmonds	BL/TL																																			
1993	Cal-A	61	0	.246	.270	.344	35	0	.257	.278	.343	26	0	.231	.259	.346	0	0	—	—	—	61	0	.246	.270	.344	9	0	.222	.300	.222	52	0	.250	.264	.365
1994	Cal-A	289	5	.273	.343	.377	162	3	.296	.365	.401	127	2	.244	.314	.346	168	4	.310	.380	.423	121	1	.223	.291	.314	76	2	.289	.325	.421	213	3	.268	.349	.362
1995	Cal-A	558	33	.290	.352	.536	270	16	.300	.375	.552	288	17	.281	.329	.521	227	11	.304	.361	.502	331	22	.281	.346	.559	164	7	.293	.359	.482	394	26	.289	.349	.558
1996	Cal-A	431	27	.304	.375	.571	230	17	.317	.378	.609	201	10	.289	.371	.527	187	13	.305	.373	.583	244	14	.303	.376	.561	122	2	.189	.293	.311	309	25	.350	.408	.673
1997	Ana-A	502	26	.291	.368	.500	237	14	.295	.377	.515	265	12	.287	.359	.487	286	13	.308	.361	.503	216	13	.269	.376	.495	143	6	.273	.342	.420	359	20	.298	.378	.532
1998	Ana-A	599	25	.307	.368	.506	290	9	.303	.371	.472	309	16	.311	.365	.537	296	14	.307	.371	.534	303	11	.307	.364	.479	195	4	.272	.324	.385	404	21	.324	.388	.564
1999	Ana-A	204	5	.250	.339	.426	117	3	.256	.362	.436	87	2	.241	.305	.414	0	0	—	—	—	204	5	.250	.339	.426	63	0	.190	.311	.254	141	5	.277	.352	.504
2000	StL-N	525	42	.295	.411	.583	250	22	.296	.423	.612	275	20	.295	.400	.556	267	22	.341	.453	.640	258	20	.248	.367	.523	152	11	.270	.376	.513	373	31	.306	.425	.611
TOTALS		3169	163	.291	.368	.512	1591	84	.297	.379	.521	1578	79	.285	.356	.503	1431	77	.313	.385	.536	1738	86	.273	.354	.492	924	32	.260	.337	.411	2245	131	.304	.381	.553
■ Jim Eisenreich	BL/TL																																			
1982	Min-A	99	2	.303	.378	.424	59	1	.288	.333	.373	40	1	.325	.438	.500	99	2	.303	.378	.424	0	0	—	—	—	16	0	.313	.389	.313	83	2	.301	.376	.446
1983	Min-A	7	0	.286	.375	.429	7	0	.286	.375	.429	0	0	—	—	—	7	0	.286	.375	.429	0	0	—	—	—	0	0	—	—	—	7	0	.286	.375	.429
1984	Min-A	32	0	.219	.250	.250	27	0	.222	.258	.259	5	0	.200	.200	.200	32	0	.219	.250	.250	0	0	—	—	—	0	0	—	.000	—	32	0	.219	.257	.250
1987	KC-A	105	4	.238	.278	.467	53	3	.302	.350	.660	52	1	.173	.200	.269	12	0	.083	.077	.167	93	4	.258	.304	.505	3	0	.000	.000	.000	102	4	.245	.286	.480
1988	KC-A	202	1	.218	.236	.282	99	0	.222	.238	.283	103	1	.214	.234	.282	142	0	.197	.213	.254	60	1	.267	.290	.350	38	0	.368	.385	.421	164	1	.183	.202	.250
1989	KC-A	475	9	.293	.341	.448	228	4	.307	.359	.482	247	5	.279	.325	.417	222	3	.297	.355	.423	253	6	.289	.328	.470	107	2	.336	.360	.430	368	7	.280	.336	.454
1990	KC-A	496	5	.280	.335	.397	236	2	.258	.327	.377	260	3	.300	.343	.415	235	2	.285	.342	.387	261	3	.276	.329	.406	156	1	.224	.268	.327	340	4	.306	.365	.429
1991	KC-A	375	2	.301	.333	.392	193	2	.311	.337	.409	182	0	.291	.330	.374	211	1	.303	.336	.393	164	1	.299	.330	.390	87	1	.322	.351	.402	288	1	.295	.328	.389
1992	KC-A	353	2	.269	.313	.340	160	1	.244	.301	.313	193	1	.290	.324	.363	169	2	.266	.321	.355	184	0	.272	.306	.326	75	0	.240	.284	.320	278	2	.277	.321	.345
1993	Phi-N	362	7	.318	.363	.445	156	3	.327	.371	.455	206	4	.311	.357	.437	137	2	.350	.399	.518	225	5	.298	.342	.400	58	1	.293	.354	.414	304	6	.322	.365	.451
1994	Phi-N	290	4	.300	.371	.421	148	3	.372	.430	.534	142	1	.225	.311	.303	189	2	.312	.372	.413	101	2	.277	.370	.436	53	0	.264	.316	.321	237	4	.308	.383	.443
1995	Phi-N	377	10	.316	.375	.464	183	5	.333	.392	.508	194	5	.299	.359	.423	161	3	.360	.420	.503	216	7	.282	.342	.435	75	0	.213	.287	.253	302	10	.341	.398	.517
1996	Phi-N	338	3	.361	.413	.476	163	1	.356	.418	.460	175	2	.366	.408	.491	178	2	.326	.381	.427	160	1	.400	.449	.531	40	0	.375	.405	.400	298	3	.359	.414	.487
1997	Fla-N	293	2	.280	.345	.372	134	2	.276	.353	.381	159	0	.283	.337	.365	163	1	.270	.333	.362	130	1	.292	.359	.385	29	0	.241	.361	.276	264	2	.284	.342	.383
1998	Fla-N	64	1	.250	.294	.313	41	1	.293	.341	.390	23	0	.174	.208	.174	64	1	.250	.294	.313	0	0	—	—	—	9	0	.111	.111	.111	55	1	.273	.322	.345
1998	LA-N	127	0	.197	.266	.244	63	0	.206	.265	.254	64	0	.188	.268	.234	54	0	.204	.246	.222	73	0	.192	.280	.260	6	0	.333	.333	.333	121	0	.190	.263	.240
TOTALS		3995	52	.290	.341	.404	1950	28	.297	.351	.423	2045	24	.284	.333	.387	2075	21	.291	.343	.393	1920	31	.290	.340	.416	752	5	.277	.321	.351	3243	47	.294	.346	.417
■ Juan Encarnacion	BR/TR																																			
1997	Det-A	33	1	.212	.316	.394	9	1	.333	.571	.889	24	0	.167	.167	.208	0	0	—	—	—	33	1	.212	.316	.394	12	1	.167	.231	.500	21	0	.238	.360	.333
1998	Det-A	164	7	.329	.354	.561	72	4	.292	.321	.542	92	3	.359	.381	.576	0	0	—	—	—	164	7	.329	.354	.561	28	0	.250	.344	.321	136	7	.346	.357	.610
1999	Det-A	509	19	.255	.287	.450	250	6	.216	.242	.376	259	13	.293	.328	.521	255	8	.275	.305	.459	254	11	.236	.268	.441	95	5	.263	.314	.505	414	14	.254	.280	.437
2000	Det-A	547	14	.289	.330	.433	256	4	.266	.313	.383	291	10	.309	.346	.478	249	7	.305	.348	.430	298	7	.275	.316	.436	140	7	.314	.349	.529	407	7	.280	.324	.400
TOTALS		1253	41	.279	.316	.456	587	15	.249	.290	.407	666	26	.305	.338	.498	504	15	.290	.326	.444	749	26	.271	.308	.463	275	13	.284	.331	.498	978	28	.277	.311	.444
■ Darin Erstad	BL/TL																																			
1996	Cal-A	208	4	.284	.333	.375	95	1	.263	.327	.337	113	3	.301	.339	.407	64	2	.266	.360	.375	144	2	.292	.320	.375	65	1	.308	.333	.400	143	3	.273	.333	.364
1997	Ana-A	539	16	.299	.360	.466	276	8	.308	.361	.486	263	8	.289	.359	.445	275	7	.298	.355	.447	264	9	.299	.365	.485	159	8	.302	.354	.497	380	8	.297	.362	.453
1998	Ana-A	537	19	.296	.353	.486	280	9	.314	.363	.500	257	10	.276	.343	.471	345	17	.316	.366	.557	192	2	.260	.330	.359	167	7	.263	.335	.467	370	12	.311	.361	.495
1999	Ana-A	585	13	.253	.308	.374	282	7	.262	.320	.401	303	6	.244	.297	.350	309	7	.252	.314	.385	276	6	.254	.302	.362	157	5	.274	.310	.420	428	8	.245	.308	.357
2000	Ana-A	676	25	.355	.409	.541	348	11	.388	.432	.549	328	14	.320	.386	.534	342	16	.374	.429	.573	334	9	.335	.389	.509	210	9	.338	.377	.538	466	16	.363	.423	.543
TOTALS		2545	77	.301	.358	.462	1281	36	.318	.369	.476	1264	41	.285	.346	.447	1335	49	.310	.368	.490	1210	28	.292	.347	.431	758	30	.298	.345	.478	1787	47	.303	.363	.455
■ Nick Esasky	BR/TR																																			
1983	Cin-N	302	12	.265	.328	.450	137	5	.241	.331	.409	165	7	.285	.326	.485	42	0	.214	.283	.238	260	12	.273	.336	.485	72	2	.389	.459	.597	230	10	.226	.284	.404
1984	Cin-N	322	10	.193	.301	.348	168	5	.208	.323	.375	154	5	.175	.275	.318	142	5	.183	.285	.366	180	5	.200	.313	.333	143	6	.224	.339	.441	179	4	.168	.269	.274
1985	Cin-N	413	21	.262	.332	.465	196	7	.230	.276	.403	217	14	.290	.378	.521	167	5	.251	.355	.401	246	16	.268	.314	.508	141	7	.298	.375	.518	272	14	.243	.309	.438
1986	Cin-N	330	12	.230	.325	.403	159	9	.226	.306	.459	171	3	.234	.342	.351	143	6	.224	.337	.420	187	6	.235	.315	.390	118	5	.237	.331	.458	212	7	.226	.321	.373
1987	Cin-N	346	22	.272	.327	.529	191	10	.246	.313	.461	155	12	.303	.345	.613	88	8	.239	.299	.580	258	14	.283	.337	.512	91	6	.253	.370	.505	255	16	.278	.310	.537
1988	Cin-N	391	15	.243	.327	.412	213	7	.254	.321	.408	178	8	.230	.333	.416	168	5	.244	.342	.393	223	10	.242	.315	.426	116	3	.250	.357	.388	275	12	.240	.313	.422
1989	Bos-A	564	30	.277	.355	.500	283	15	.300	.379	.541	281	15	.253	.331	.459	256	12	.258	.319	.453	308	18	.292	.384	.539	172	11	.250	.345	.488	392	19	.288	.360	.505
1990	Atl-N	35	0	.171	.256	.171	23	0	.217	.308	.217	12	0	.083	.154	.083	35	0	.171	.256	.171	0	0	—	—	—	10	0	.400	.455	.400	25	0	.080	.179	.080
TOTALS		2703	122	.250	.329	.446	1370	58	.248	.325	.441	1333	64	.253	.334	.451	1041	41	.233	.322	.411	1662	81	.261	.334	.468	863	40	.265	.362	.477	1840	82	.243	.313	.431
■ Darrell Evans	BL/TR																																			
1978	SF-N	547	20	.243	.360	.404	252	7	.238	.371	.377	295	13	.247	.350	.427	261	7	.253	.373	.395	286	13	.234	.347	.413	194	8	.258	.350	.423	353	12	.235	.365	.394
1979	SF-N	562	17	.253	.356	.391	269	8	.253	.351	.398	293	9	.253	.360	.386	272	6	.254	.338	.360	290	11	.252	.372	.421	152	8	.237	.299	.421	410	9	.259	.375	.380
1980	SF-N	556	20	.264	.359	.414	259	8	.255	.352	.390	297	12	.273	.364	.434	266	8	.252	.337	.368	290	12	.276	.378	.455	146	5	.260	.343	.404	410	15	.266	.364	.417
1981	SF-N	357	12	.258	.356	.417	170	6	.265	.374	.429	187	6	.251	.338	.406	197	9	.223	.314	.406	160	3	.300	.405	.431	78	2	.269	.337	.410	279	10	.254	.361	.419
1982	SF-N	465	16	.256	.360	.419	224	8	.223	.346	.357	241	8	.286	.374	.477	231	10	.247	.352	.424	234	6	.265	.368	.415	162	3	.235	.335	.352	303	13	.267	.373	.455
1983	SF-N	523	30	.277	.378	.516	254	16	.256	.361	.504	269	14	.297	.394	.528	263	19	.297	.400	.574	260	11	.258	.355	.458	164	5	.226	.294	.366	359	25	.301	.413	.585
1984	Det-A	401	16	.232	.353	.384	188	6	.239	.351	.356	213	10	.225	.354	.408	200	5	.245	.369	.350	201	11	.219	.336	.418	90	1	.267	.400	.344	311	15	.222	.339	.395
1985	Det-A	505	40	.248	.356	.519	242	21	.244	.362	.533	263	19	.251	.350	.506	208	14	.264	.369	.510	297	26	.236	.347	.525	120	9	.208	.275	.467	385	31	.260	.379	.535
1986	Det-A	507	29	.241	.356	.442	246	15	.236	.351	.451	261	14	.245	.361	.433	220	12	.245	.348	.445	287	17	.237	.362	.439	147	9	.272	.374	.483	360	20	.228	.349	.425
1987	Det-A	499	34	.257	.379	.501	246	19	.248	.359	.512	253	15	.265	.397	.490	218	14	.252	.383	.505	281	20	.260	.376	.498	148	5	.209	.312	.338	351	29	.276	.406	.570
1988	Det-A	437	22	.208	.337	.380	215	14	.223	.365	.442	222	8	.194	.309	.320	195	8	.195	.335	.338	242	14	.219	.339	.413	64	0	.156	.270	.188	373	22	.217	.348	.413
1989	Atl-N	276	11	.207	.303	.355	144	5	.229	.309	.382	132	6	.182	.298	.326	104	4	.173	.285	.308	172	7	.227	.315	.384	73	2	.247	.298	.384	203	9	.192	.305	.345
TOTALS		5635	267	.247	.357	.433	2709	133	.243	.356	.431	2926	134	.252	.358	.435	2635	116	.247	.354	.421	3000	151	.248	.359	.443	1538	57	.239	.327	.391	4097	210	.250	.367	.448
■ Dwight Evans	BR/TR																																			
1978	Bos-A	497	24	.247	.336	.449	218	13	.284	.373	.560	279	11	.219	.306	.362	241	16	.286	.375	.544	256	8	.211	.298	.359	147	6	.286	.348	.463	350	18	.231	.331	.443
1979	Bos-A	489	21	.274	.364	.456	230	12	.304	.405	.539	259	9	.247	.326	.382	237	9	.270	.356	.435	252	12	.278	.372	.476	135	7	.333	.400	.556	354	14	.251	.351	.418
1980	Bos-A	463	18	.266	.358	.484	239	11	.268	.365	.506	224	7	.263	.351	.460	171	5	.199	.291	.357	292	13	.305	.397	.558	158	5	.297	.358	.538	305	13	.249	.358	.456
1981	Bos-A	412	22	.296	.415	.522	198	15	.313	.430	.636	214	7	.280	.402	.416	211	13	.341	.453	.578	201	9	.249	.376	.463	93	7	.312	.444	.581	319	15	.292	.406	.505
1982	Bos-A	609	32	.292	.402	.534	304	19	.289	.400	.572	305	13	.295	.404	.495	275	7	.262	.387	.433	334	25	.317	.415	.617	174	7	.333	.424	.592	435	25	.276	.393	.510
1983	Bos-A	470	22	.238	.338	.436	237	12	.232	.328	.426	233	10	.245	.348	.446	289	14	.228	.328	.443	181	8	.254	.354	.425	152	7	.263	.347	.474	318	15	.226	.334	.418
1984	Bos-A	630	32	.295	.388	.532	315	15	.330	.415	.587	315	17	.260	.361	.476	291	13	.278	.388	.485	339	19	.310	.388	.572	142	7	.331	.462	.585	488	25	.285	.364	.516
1985	Bos-A	617	29	.263	.378	.454	292	14	.277	.382	.483	325	15	.249	.375	.428	254	9	.228	.382	.382	363	20	.287	.375	.504	170	12	.271	.416	.518	447	17	.260	.363	.430
1986	Bos-A	529	26	.259	.376	.476	241	8	.253	.384	.436	288	18	.264	.370	.510	260	9	.242	.357	.427	269	17	.275	.394	.524	136	6	.228	.363	.397	393	20	.270	.381	.504
1987	Bos-A	541	34	.305	.417	.569	263	14	.304	.399	.567	278	20	.306	.433	.572	246	13	.305	.408	.549	295	21	.305	.425	.586	144	12	.368	.465	.688	397	22	.282	.400	.526
1988	Bos-A	559	21	.293	.375	.487	277	11	.318	.398	.542	282	10	.270	.352	.433	291	5	.306	.365	.430	268	16	.280	.385	.549	144	6	.333	.439	.521	415	15	.280	.351	.475
1989	Bos-A	520	20	.285	.397	.463	242	8	.273	.403	.430	278	12	.295	.392	.493	258	10	.291	.417	.473	262	10	.279	.377	.454	155	4	.303	.401	.452	365	16	.277	.396	.468
1990	Bos-A	445	13	.249	.349	.391	218	7	.252	.348	.413	227	6	.247	.349	.370	258	9	.240	.352	.395	187	4	.262	.344	.385	147	3	.265	.375	.422	298	10	.242	.335	.376
1991	Bal-A	270	6	.270	.393	.378	135	4	.259	.373	.370	135	2	.281	.413	.385	139	3	.273	.391	.388	131	3	.267	.396	.366	107	1	.308	.468	.364	163	5	.245	.339	.387
TOTALS		7051	320	.275	.378	.479	3409	163	.285	.387	.511	3642	157	.266	.370	.449	3421	135	.268	.376	.453	3630	185	.281	.381	.504	2004	90	.302	.407	.512	5047	230	.264	.367	.466
■ Carl Everett	BB/TR																																			
1993	Fla-N	19	0	.105	.150	.105	4	0	.000	.200	.000	15	0	.133	.133	.133	0	0	—	—	—	19	0	.105	.150	.105	5	0	.000	.000	.000	14	0	.143	.200	.143
1994	Fla-N	51	2	.216	.259	.353	23	2	.174	.269	.478	28	0	.250	.250	.250	43	2	.209	.261	.372	8	0	.250	.250	.250	19	1	.158	.238	.368	32	1	.250	.273	.344
1995	NY-N	289	12	.260	.352	.436	138	9	.312	.410	.551	151	3	.212	.296	.331	57	3	.193	.233	.386	232	9	.276	.378	.448	100	4	.210	.269	.400	189	8	.286	.392	.455
1996	NY-N	192	1	.240	.326	.307	84	1	.298	.381	.381	108	0	.194	.281	.250	73	0	.164	.291	.233	119	1	.286	.348	.353	36	0	.250	.378	.333	156	1	.237	.312	.301
1997	NY-N	443	14	.248	.308	.420	219	11	.292	.363	.553	224	3	.205	.251	.290	224	9	.263	.322	.460	219	5	.233	.293	.379	101	2	.208	.270	.327	342	12	.260	.319	.447
1998	Hou-N	467	15	.296	.359	.482	214	5	.285	.353	.458	253	10	.304	.363	.502	219	8	.338	.411	.543	248	7	.258	.310	.427	82	3	.268	.294	.427	385	12	.301	.371	.494
1999	Hou-N	464	25	.325	.398	.571	226	11	.319	.387	.562	238	14	.332	.408	.580	273	8	.308	.372	.473	191	17	.351	.433	.712	117	4	.325	.394	.462	347	21	.326	.399	.608
2000	Bos-A	496	34	.300	.373	.587	252	17	.282	.362	.556	244	17	.320	.383	.619	255	23	.329	.400	.663	241	11	.270	.343	.506	132	4	.348	.411	.515	364	30	.283	.359	.613
TOTALS		2421	103	.282	.353	.484	1160	56	.293	.370	.522	1261	47	.271	.337	.450	1144	53	.291	.361	.503	1277	50	.273	.346	.468	592	18	.270	.334	.421	1829	85	.285	.359	.505

YEAR	TM/L	TOTAL AB	HR	AVG	OBP	SLG	HOME AB	HR	AVG	OBP	SLG	AWAY AB	HR	AVG	OBP	SLG	1ST HALF AB	HR	AVG	OBP	SLG	2ND HALF AB	HR	AVG	OBP	SLG	LEFT AB	HR	AVG	OBP	SLG	RIGHT AB	HR	AVG	OBP	SLG
■ Mike Felder	BB/TR																																			
1985	Mil-A	56	0	.196	.262	.214	34	0	.235	.297	.265	22	0	.136	.208	.136	0	0	—	—	—	56	0	.196	.262	.214	22	0	.091	.130	.091	34	0	.265	.342	.294
1986	Mil-A	155	1	.239	.289	.323	86	1	.267	.340	.384	69	0	.203	.224	.246	116	1	.259	.321	.371	39	0	.179	.179	.179	44	0	.409	.426	.500	111	1	.171	.238	.252
1987	Mil-A	289	2	.266	.329	.353	126	1	.302	.399	.421	163	1	.239	.269	.301	84	0	.262	.297	.345	205	2	.268	.342	.356	94	0	.309	.380	.372	195	2	.246	.303	.344
1988	Mil-A	81	0	.173	.183	.185	35	0	.086	.086	.086	46	0	.239	.255	.261	45	0	.200	.217	.222	36	0	.139	.139	.139	23	0	.043	.043	.043	58	0	.224	.237	.241
1989	Mil-A	315	3	.241	.293	.324	139	1	.180	.250	.230	176	2	.290	.328	.398	110	0	.236	.282	.273	205	3	.244	.299	.351	101	0	.277	.336	.297	214	3	.224	.272	.336
1990	Mil-A	237	3	.274	.330	.359	110	1	.264	.311	.336	127	2	.283	.345	.378	106	0	.255	.331	.292	131	3	.290	.329	.412	80	3	.275	.315	.463	157	0	.274	.337	.306
1991	SF-N	348	0	.264	.325	.328	168	0	.286	.337	.351	180	0	.244	.313	.306	219	0	.292	.346	.370	129	0	.217	.289	.256	107	0	.271	.316	.336	241	0	.261	.328	.324
1992	SF-N	322	4	.286	.330	.382	164	1	.262	.299	.335	158	3	.310	.362	.430	141	1	.270	.314	.362	181	3	.298	.344	.398	88	1	.307	.340	.398	234	3	.278	.327	.376
1993	Sea-A	342	1	.211	.262	.269	167	0	.234	.287	.293	175	1	.189	.237	.246	233	1	.223	.278	.292	109	0	.183	.226	.220	63	0	.190	.271	.238	279	1	.215	.259	.276
1994	Hou-N	117	0	.239	.264	.291	64	0	.234	.269	.328	53	0	.245	.259	.245	85	0	.224	.241	.271	32	0	.281	.324	.344	35	0	.257	.257	.371	82	0	.232	.267	.256
TOTALS		2262	14	.249	.301	.322	1093	5	.248	.306	.321	1169	9	.251	.297	.323	1139	3	.252	.302	.321	1123	11	.247	.300	.323	657	4	.269	.317	.344	1605	10	.241	.294	.313
■ Tony Fernandez	BB/TR																																			
1983	Tor-A	34	0	.265	.324	.353	22	0	.273	.304	.409	12	0	.250	.357	.250	0	0	—	—	—	34	0	.265	.324	.353	9	0	.222	.300	.333	25	0	.280	.333	.360
1984	Tor-A	233	3	.270	.317	.356	96	1	.229	.283	.313	137	2	.299	.342	.387	36	0	.139	.158	.167	197	3	.294	.346	.391	76	0	.250	.313	.303	157	3	.280	.320	.382
1985	Tor-A	564	2	.289	.340	.390	265	1	.306	.366	.445	299	1	.274	.318	.341	252	2	.302	.352	.421	312	0	.279	.331	.365	194	0	.294	.366	.412	370	2	.286	.327	.378
1986	Tor-A	687	10	.310	.338	.428	337	4	.320	.345	.427	350	6	.300	.332	.429	314	4	.315	.352	.430	373	6	.306	.326	.426	205	5	.317	.347	.468	482	5	.307	.334	.411
1987	Tor-A	578	5	.322	.379	.426	299	1	.301	.363	.395	279	4	.344	.397	.459	292	4	.315	.392	.452	286	1	.329	.365	.399	192	2	.297	.367	.380	386	3	.334	.385	.448
1988	Tor-A	648	5	.287	.335	.386	316	3	.285	.337	.399	332	2	.289	.333	.373	309	2	.275	.322	.362	339	3	.298	.347	.407	219	3	.279	.318	.374	429	2	.291	.344	.392
1989	Tor-A	573	11	.257	.291	.389	276	2	.239	.286	.341	297	9	.273	.296	.434	248	5	.262	.297	.371	325	6	.252	.287	.403	184	2	.272	.307	.380	389	9	.249	.284	.393
1990	Tor-A	635	4	.276	.352	.391	321	2	.308	.376	.455	314	2	.242	.328	.325	304	2	.257	.347	.365	331	2	.293	.357	.414	202	1	.238	.340	.302	433	3	.293	.358	.432
1991	SD-N	558	4	.272	.337	.360	271	1	.292	.362	.365	287	3	.254	.313	.355	294	2	.289	.359	.384	264	2	.254	.313	.333	184	2	.261	.323	.342	374	2	.278	.344	.369
1992	SD-N	622	4	.275	.337	.359	301	3	.282	.355	.372	321	1	.268	.320	.346	294	2	.306	.372	.395	328	2	.247	.305	.326	207	1	.280	.349	.338	415	3	.272	.331	.369
1993	NY-N	173	1	.225	.323	.295	91	0	.209	.311	.275	82	1	.244	.337	.317	173	1	.225	.323	.295	0	0	—	—	—	43	0	.233	.382	.256	130	1	.223	.301	.308
1993	Tor-A	353	4	.306	.361	.442	164	1	.305	.374	.433	189	3	.307	.350	.450	70	2	.329	.390	.614	283	2	.300	.354	.399	122	0	.254	.321	.344	231	4	.333	.382	.494
1994	Cin-N	366	8	.279	.361	.426	184	3	.245	.332	.337	182	5	.313	.391	.516	234	6	.274	.379	.419	132	2	.288	.326	.439	100	3	.290	.348	.460	266	5	.274	.366	.414
1995	NY-A	384	5	.245	.322	.346	189	3	.249	.332	.370	195	2	.241	.312	.323	152	2	.224	.314	.309	232	3	.259	.327	.371	128	2	.195	.241	.266	256	3	.270	.359	.387
1997	Cle-A	409	11	.286	.323	.423	192	7	.297	.327	.464	217	4	.276	.320	.387	186	3	.253	.294	.360	223	8	.314	.347	.475	123	5	.407	.435	.593	286	6	.234	.275	.350
1998	Tor-A	486	9	.321	.387	.459	231	4	.333	.398	.472	255	5	.310	.376	.447	225	6	.284	.363	.440	261	3	.352	.408	.475	122	2	.361	.389	.549	364	7	.308	.386	.429
1999	Tor-A	485	6	.328	.427	.449	239	5	.351	.443	.510	246	1	.305	.412	.390	262	5	.393	.482	.542	223	1	.251	.363	.341	143	1	.322	.374	.434	342	5	.330	.447	.456
TOTALS		7788	92	.288	.347	.399	3794	41	.291	.354	.407	3994	51	.284	.341	.392	3645	48	.288	.356	.403	4143	44	.287	.339	.396	2453	29	.285	.343	.390	5335	63	.289	.349	.404
■ Cecil Fielder	BR/TR																																			
1985	Tor-A	74	4	.311	.358	.527	40	2	.300	.349	.525	34	2	.324	.368	.529	0	0	—	—	—	74	4	.311	.358	.527	69	4	.319	.360	.551	5	0	.200	.333	.200
1986	Tor-A	83	4	.157	.222	.325	24	0	.083	.120	.083	59	4	.186	.262	.424	45	3	.156	.224	.378	38	1	.158	.220	.263	40	0	.150	.227	.175	43	4	.163	.217	.465
1987	Tor-A	175	14	.269	.345	.560	90	10	.344	.422	.756	85	4	.188	.263	.353	86	7	.291	.386	.628	89	7	.247	.302	.494	153	13	.268	.343	.582	22	1	.273	.360	.409
1988	Tor-A	174	9	.230	.289	.431	79	6	.190	.220	.430	95	3	.263	.343	.432	84	6	.250	.297	.512	90	3	.211	.283	.356	145	9	.228	.294	.462	29	0	.241	.267	.276
1990	Det-A	573	51	.277	.377	.592	271	25	.280	.396	.605	302	26	.275	.359	.579	272	26	.298	.388	.629	301	25	.259	.368	.558	178	25	.371	.479	.854	395	26	.235	.330	.473
1991	Det-A	624	44	.261	.347	.513	305	27	.256	.348	.561	319	17	.266	.345	.467	279	18	.272	.368	.513	345	26	.252	.329	.513	159	13	.296	.399	.597	465	31	.249	.328	.484
1992	Det-A	594	35	.244	.325	.458	296	18	.257	.339	.490	298	17	.232	.312	.426	266	16	.241	.320	.474	328	19	.247	.330	.445	134	9	.231	.352	.470	460	26	.248	.317	.454
1993	Det-A	573	30	.267	.368	.464	283	20	.283	.381	.537	290	10	.252	.354	.393	275	19	.269	.385	.509	298	11	.265	.351	.423	142	8	.324	.462	.570	431	22	.248	.333	.429
1994	Det-A	425	28	.259	.337	.504	204	12	.284	.369	.520	221	16	.235	.306	.489	278	17	.255	.333	.486	147	11	.265	.343	.537	77	6	.260	.387	.584	348	22	.259	.325	.486
1995	Det-A	494	31	.243	.346	.472	247	16	.231	.354	.445	247	15	.255	.338	.498	214	17	.257	.374	.533	280	14	.232	.324	.425	102	6	.265	.330	.471	392	25	.237	.350	.472
1996	Det-A	391	26	.248	.354	.478	169	9	.243	.348	.432	222	17	.252	.359	.514	298	18	.255	.350	.470	93	8	.226	.368	.505	83	7	.241	.394	.554	308	19	.250	.343	.458
1996	NY-A	200	13	.260	.342	.495	104	9	.288	.345	.606	96	4	.229	.339	.375	0	0	—	—	—	200	13	.260	.342	.495	55	4	.327	.465	.582	145	9	.234	.287	.462
1997	NY-A	361	13	.260	.358	.410	191	6	.277	.350	.414	170	7	.241	.365	.406	285	9	.263	.364	.404	76	4	.250	.333	.434	90	1	.211	.379	.256	271	12	.277	.350	.461
1998	Ana-A	381	17	.241	.335	.423	201	7	.214	.298	.363	180	10	.272	.374	.489	283	14	.251	.352	.449	98	3	.214	.284	.347	107	7	.280	.389	.514	274	10	.226	.313	.387
1998	Cle-A	35	0	.143	.189	.171	25	0	.160	.222	.200	10	0	.100	.100	.100	0	0	—	—	—	35	0	.143	.189	.171	23	0	.130	.200	.130	12	0	.167	.167	.250
TOTALS		5157	319	.255	.345	.482	2529	167	.259	.351	.501	2628	152	.250	.340	.463	2665	170	.261	.356	.497	2492	149	.248	.333	.465	1557	112	.276	.383	.542	3600	207	.246	.328	.456
■ Steve Finley	BL/TL																																			
1989	Bal-A	217	2	.249	.298	.318	114	0	.219	.280	.254	103	2	.282	.318	.388	113	2	.221	.274	.327	104	0	.279	.324	.308	38	1	.158	.220	.263	179	1	.268	.314	.330
1990	Bal-A	464	3	.256	.304	.328	247	1	.231	.274	.304	217	2	.286	.338	.355	214	0	.238	.300	.313	250	3	.272	.307	.340	114	1	.193	.202	.237	350	2	.277	.336	.357
1991	Hou-N	596	8	.285	.331	.406	300	0	.273	.309	.377	296	8	.297	.353	.436	264	5	.284	.342	.413	332	3	.286	.322	.401	184	1	.250	.290	.310	412	7	.301	.350	.449
1992	Hou-N	607	5	.292	.355	.407	294	5	.303	.381	.439	313	0	.281	.329	.377	308	2	.282	.332	.422	299	3	.301	.378	.391	226	1	.279	.336	.372	381	4	.299	.366	.428
1993	Hou-N	545	8	.266	.304	.385	252	1	.246	.280	.333	293	7	.283	.325	.430	212	1	.236	.296	.311	333	7	.285	.309	.432	164	2	.268	.297	.378	381	6	.265	.307	.388
1994	Hou-N	373	11	.276	.329	.434	185	4	.270	.318	.400	188	7	.282	.340	.468	228	8	.254	.317	.417	145	3	.310	.348	.462	108	1	.204	.283	.250	265	10	.306	.349	.509
1995	SD-N	562	10	.297	.366	.420	255	4	.275	.350	.384	307	6	.316	.379	.450	236	4	.267	.343	.369	326	6	.319	.382	.457	187	3	.326	.388	.433	375	7	.283	.355	.413
1996	SD-N	655	30	.298	.354	.531	312	15	.333	.391	.590	343	15	.265	.321	.478	337	15	.273	.332	.499	318	15	.324	.377	.566	180	4	.267	.318	.428	475	26	.309	.368	.571
1997	SD-N	560	28	.261	.313	.475	273	5	.216	.278	.315	287	23	.303	.347	.627	265	14	.283	.337	.528	295	14	.241	.292	.427	152	5	.263	.309	.408	408	23	.260	.315	.500
1998	SD-N	619	14	.249	.301	.401	291	8	.210	.277	.361	328	6	.284	.323	.436	332	5	.241	.286	.389	287	9	.258	.318	.415	197	2	.188	.244	.289	422	12	.277	.328	.453
1999	Ari-N	590	34	.264	.336	.525	282	17	.262	.330	.500	308	17	.266	.341	.549	288	15	.271	.330	.500	302	19	.258	.341	.550	189	10	.259	.322	.481	401	24	.267	.342	.546
2000	Ari-N	539	35	.280	.361	.544	260	17	.335	.424	.631	279	18	.229	.298	.462	283	22	.297	.377	.587	256	13	.262	.342	.496	157	11	.274	.350	.535	382	24	.283	.365	.547
TOTALS		6327	188	.275	.332	.440	3065	77	.268	.329	.418	3262	111	.281	.335	.460	3080	93	.266	.326	.434	3247	95	.283	.338	.445	1896	42	.254	.307	.379	4431	146	.283	.343	.466
■ Carlton Fisk	BR/TR																																			
1978	Bos-A	571	20	.284	.366	.475	268	8	.313	.417	.511	303	12	.257	.317	.442	257	9	.280	.370	.498	314	11	.287	.363	.455	142	5	.275	.373	.430	429	15	.287	.364	.490
1979	Bos-A	320	10	.272	.304	.450	158	5	.329	.369	.557	162	5	.216	.240	.346	105	2	.295	.339	.476	215	8	.260	.286	.437	103	2	.291	.305	.456	217	8	.263	.303	.447
1980	Bos-A	478	18	.289	.353	.467	244	12	.275	.338	.488	234	6	.303	.368	.444	179	9	.302	.376	.531	299	9	.281	.338	.428	136	9	.316	.367	.588	342	9	.278	.347	.418
1981	Chi-A	338	7	.263	.354	.361	162	4	.235	.347	.333	176	3	.290	.360	.386	158	5	.291	.395	.430	180	2	.239	.315	.300	74	2	.284	.372	.392	264	5	.258	.349	.352
1982	Chi-A	476	14	.267	.336	.403	237	7	.274	.331	.418	239	7	.259	.342	.389	209	7	.268	.342	.397	267	7	.266	.332	.408	152	5	.283	.355	.461	324	9	.259	.328	.377
1983	Chi-A	488	26	.289	.355	.518	245	17	.298	.381	.571	243	9	.280	.328	.465	192	9	.245	.322	.453	296	17	.318	.377	.561	165	8	.291	.366	.539	323	18	.288	.350	.508
1984	Chi-A	359	21	.231	.289	.468	195	11	.231	.288	.477	164	10	.232	.291	.457	147	6	.197	.273	.381	212	15	.255	.301	.528	141	9	.241	.292	.475	218	12	.225	.287	.463
1985	Chi-A	543	37	.238	.320	.488	271	20	.203	.294	.465	272	17	.272	.346	.511	222	18	.239	.315	.514	321	19	.237	.324	.470	183	9	.251	.329	.464	360	28	.231	.316	.500
1986	Chi-A	457	14	.221	.263	.337	232	5	.207	.236	.289	225	9	.236	.290	.387	268	7	.228	.292	.336	189	7	.212	.216	.339	157	5	.223	.253	.350	300	9	.220	.268	.330
1987	Chi-A	454	23	.256	.321	.460	218	5	.266	.328	.394	236	18	.246	.316	.521	210	7	.205	.283	.348	244	16	.299	.356	.557	182	9	.236	.305	.451	272	14	.268	.332	.467
1988	Chi-A	253	19	.277	.377	.542	121	9	.273	.371	.537	132	10	.280	.382	.545	84	8	.286	.368	.619	169	11	.272	.381	.503	93	10	.290	.427	.667	160	9	.269	.344	.469
1989	Chi-A	375	13	.293	.356	.475	172	4	.343	.417	.500	203	9	.251	.300	.453	114	4	.307	.357	.465	261	9	.287	.355	.479	120	4	.325	.371	.508	255	9	.278	.348	.459
1990	Chi-A	452	18	.285	.378	.451	219	5	.288	.387	.416	233	13	.283	.370	.485	193	6	.275	.372	.399	259	12	.293	.383	.490	165	9	.315	.397	.539	287	9	.268	.367	.401
1991	Chi-A	460	18	.241	.299	.413	233	9	.236	.295	.408	227	9	.247	.304	.419	224	5	.259	.327	.388	236	13	.225	.273	.436	157	5	.229	.274	.376	303	13	.248	.312	.432
1992	Chi-A	188	3	.229	.313	.309	79	2	.228	.340	.329	109	1	.229	.292	.294	44	0	.205	.271	.205	144	3	.236	.325	.340	49	0	.204	.328	.204	139	3	.237	.308	.345
1993	Chi-A	53	1	.189	.228	.245	30	0	.133	.212	.133	23	1	.261	.250	.391	53	1	.189	.228	.245	0	0	—	—	—	31	1	.290	.290	.387	22	0	.045	.154	.045
TOTALS		6265	262	.263	.333	.444	3084	123	.265	.341	.446	3181	139	.261	.325	.442	2659	103	.256	.332	.427	3606	159	.268	.333	.456	2050	92	.271	.338	.467	4215	170	.259	.330	.433
■ John Flaherty	BR/TR																																			
1992	Bos-A	66	0	.197	.229	.227	36	0	.222	.237	.250	30	0	.167	.219	.200	35	0	.143	.162	.171	31	0	.258	.303	.290	20	0	.200	.238	.250	46	0	.196	.224	.217
1993	Bos-A	25	0	.120	.214	.200	21	0	.095	.208	.143	4	0	.250	.250	.500	0	0	—	—	—	25	0	.120	.214	.200	7	0	.286	.375	.571	18	0	.056	.150	.056
1994	Det-A	40	0	.150	.167	.175	16	0	.063	.059	.063	24	0	.208	.240	.250	30	0	.167	.194	.200	10	0	.100	.091	.100	27	0	.111	.143	.111	13	0	.231	.214	.308
1995	Det-A	354	11	.243	.284	.404	171	6	.269	.330	.474	183	5	.219	.238	.339	144	8	.292	.335	.528	210	3	.210	.248	.319	86	0	.209	.261	.291	268	11	.254	.291	.440
1996	Det-A	152	4	.250	.290	.408	60	2	.200	.250	.383	92	2	.283	.316	.424	152	4	.250	.290	.408	0	0	—	—	—	46	1	.283	.333	.435	106	3	.236	.270	.396
1996	SD-N	264	9	.303	.327	.451	129	6	.341	.351	.535	135	3	.267	.306	.370	39	4	.308	.325	.641	225	5	.302	.328	.418	47	0	.340	.396	.404	217	9	.295	.311	.461
1997	SD-N	439	9	.273	.323	.387	214	4	.243	.293	.360	225	5	.302	.351	.413	249	4	.245	.281	.345	190	5	.311	.374	.442	68	1	.265	.367	.382	371	8	.275	.314	.388
1998	TB-A	304	3	.207	.261	.273	147	1	.197	.232	.265	157	2	.217	.286	.280	129	2	.186	.277	.271	175	1	.223	.247	.274	64	1	.234	.282	.344	240	2	.200	.255	.254
1999	TB-A	446	14	.278	.310	.415	217	3	.286	.304	.378	229	11	.271	.315	.450	227	8	.273	.313	.414	219	6	.283	.306	.416	80	1	.175	.212	.237	366	13	.301	.331	.454
2000	TB-A	394	10	.261	.296	.376	191	7	.272	.307	.435	203	3	.251	.285	.320	202	4	.277	.313	.381	192	6	.245	.277	.370	89	2	.270	.309	.404	305	8	.259	.292	.367
TOTALS		2484	60	.256	.295	.377	1202	29	.256	.293	.386	1282	31	.256	.298	.367	1207	34	.253	.296	.387	1277	26	.259	.295	.368	534	6	.238	.292	.335	1950	54	.261	.296	.389
■ Darrin Fletcher	BL/TR																																			
1989	LA-N	8	1	.500	.556	.875	4	1	.500	.500	1.250	4	0	.500	.600	.500	0	0	—	—	—	8	1	.500	.556	.875	0	0	—	—	—	8	1	.500	.556	.875
1990	LA-N	1	0	.000	.000	.000	1	0	.000	.000	.000	0	0	—	—	—	0	0	—	—	—	1	0	.000	.000	.000	0	0	—	—	—	1	0	.000	.000	.000

		TOTAL					HOME					AWAY					1ST HALF					2ND HALF					LEFT					RIGHT				
YEAR	TM/L	AB	HR	AVG	OBP	SLG	AB	HR	AVG	OBP	SLG	AB	HR	AVG	OBP	SLG	AB	HR	AVG	OBP	SLG	AB	HR	AVG	OBP	SLG	AB	HR	AVG	OBP	SLG	AB	HR	AVG	OBP	SLG
1990	Phi-N	22	0	.136	.174	.182	10	0	.000	.091	.000	12	0	.250	.250	.333	0	0	—	—	—	22	0	.136	.174	.182	4	0	.250	.250	.250	18	0	.111	.158	.167
1991	Phi-N	136	1	.228	.255	.309	59	1	.237	.262	.339	77	0	.221	.250	.286	80	1	.225	.253	.338	56	0	.232	.259	.268	22	0	.273	.273	.364	114	1	.219	.252	.298
1992	Mon-N	222	2	.243	.289	.333	85	0	.224	.258	.294	137	2	.255	.309	.358	74	1	.189	.228	.243	148	1	.270	.319	.378	14	0	.286	.412	.357	208	2	.240	.280	.332
1993	Mon-N	396	9	.255	.320	.379	183	5	.257	.322	.404	213	4	.254	.319	.357	146	2	.240	.311	.322	250	7	.264	.326	.412	77	2	.260	.356	.377	319	7	.254	.311	.379
1994	Mon-N	285	10	.260	.314	.435	123	4	.293	.338	.480	162	6	.235	.296	.401	203	7	.291	.345	.453	82	3	.183	.240	.390	36	2	.139	.162	.361	249	8	.277	.333	.446
1995	Mon-N	350	11	.286	.351	.446	163	3	.282	.350	.429	187	8	.289	.351	.460	134	5	.284	.358	.448	216	6	.287	.346	.444	44	1	.227	.333	.341	306	10	.294	.353	.461
1996	Mon-N	394	12	.266	.321	.414	199	7	.276	.326	.447	195	5	.256	.316	.379	207	7	.271	.323	.449	187	5	.262	.319	.374	61	1	.295	.338	.410	333	11	.261	.318	.414
1997	Mon-N	310	17	.277	.323	.513	150	10	.307	.373	.567	160	7	.250	.274	.463	157	10	.287	.323	.535	153	7	.268	.323	.490	75	4	.253	.291	.467	235	13	.285	.333	.528
1998	Tor-A	407	9	.283	.328	.410	195	3	.251	.291	.349	212	6	.311	.362	.467	180	5	.294	.355	.461	227	4	.273	.306	.370	59	1	.203	.279	.288	348	8	.296	.337	.431
1999	Tor-A	412	18	.291	.339	.485	194	10	.299	.366	.515	218	8	.284	.315	.459	160	9	.306	.345	.556	252	9	.282	.336	.440	79	7	.228	.344	.557	333	11	.306	.338	.468
2000	Tor-A	416	20	.320	.355	.514	220	10	.332	.365	.518	196	10	.306	.344	.510	167	9	.335	.364	.563	249	11	.309	.349	.482	79	1	.342	.391	.468	337	19	.315	.346	.525
TOTALS		3359	110	.276	.326	.435	1586	54	.281	.332	.447	1773	56	.271	.320	.424	1508	56	.281	.331	.456	1851	54	.272	.322	.418	550	19	.255	.325	.416	2809	91	.280	.326	.438
■ **Scott Fletcher** BR/TR																																				
1981	Chi-N	46	0	.217	.250	.304	35	0	.171	.194	.200	11	0	.364	.417	.636	35	0	.171	.194	.200	11	0	.364	.417	.636	10	0	.500	.500	.800	36	0	.139	.184	.167
1982	Chi-N	24	0	.167	.286	.167	14	0	.286	.333	.286	10	0	.000	.231	.000	0	0	—	—	—	24	0	.167	.286	.167	8	0	.250	.333	.250	16	0	.125	.263	.125
1983	Chi-A	262	3	.237	.315	.370	119	1	.277	.374	.429	143	2	.203	.263	.322	68	1	.235	.349	.426	194	2	.237	.302	.351	86	2	.221	.287	.372	176	1	.244	.328	.369
1984	Chi-A	456	3	.250	.328	.311	227	2	.282	.362	.361	229	1	.218	.294	.262	209	1	.244	.352	.301	247	2	.255	.306	.320	165	1	.230	.335	.267	291	2	.261	.324	.337
1985	Chi-A	301	2	.256	.332	.309	142	0	.225	.327	.246	159	2	.283	.337	.365	147	0	.238	.317	.265	154	2	.273	.347	.351	168	2	.298	.374	.381	133	0	.203	.279	.218
1986	Tex-A	530	3	.300	.360	.400	253	2	.308	.360	.415	277	1	.292	.359	.386	220	0	.291	.359	.386	310	3	.306	.360	.410	175	2	.291	.347	.423	355	1	.304	.365	.389
1987	Tex-A	588	5	.287	.358	.374	287	4	.341	.413	.463	301	1	.236	.305	.289	288	4	.313	.368	.431	300	1	.263	.349	.320	220	3	.318	.388	.409	368	2	.269	.341	.353
1988	Tex-A	515	0	.276	.364	.328	252	0	.286	.368	.341	263	0	.266	.359	.316	279	0	.276	.356	.323	236	0	.275	.372	.335	163	0	.337	.407	.399	352	0	.247	.345	.295
1989	Tex-A	314	0	.239	.323	.290	159	0	.233	.318	.289	155	0	.245	.328	.290	271	0	.255	.344	.310	43	0	.140	.178	.163	99	0	.293	.369	.384	215	0	.214	.302	.247
1989	Chi-A	232	1	.272	.344	.341	111	0	.288	.341	.324	121	1	.256	.345	.355	0	0	—	—	—	232	1	.272	.344	.341	65	0	.262	.342	.354	167	1	.275	.344	.335
1990	Chi-A	509	4	.242	.304	.312	265	1	.242	.291	.294	244	3	.242	.319	.332	230	2	.235	.314	.326	279	2	.247	.296	.301	173	1	.283	.365	.324	336	3	.220	.271	.307
1991	Chi-A	248	1	.206	.262	.266	115	0	.200	.285	.252	133	1	.211	.241	.278	166	1	.199	.280	.271	82	0	.220	.224	.256	101	0	.188	.248	.218	147	1	.218	.272	.299
1992	Mil-A	386	3	.275	.335	.360	175	2	.314	.379	.423	211	1	.242	.297	.308	154	1	.312	.374	.396	232	2	.250	.309	.336	104	0	.308	.360	.375	282	3	.262	.326	.355
1993	Bos-A	480	5	.285	.341	.402	250	2	.284	.348	.380	230	3	.287	.333	.426	175	4	.274	.350	.429	305	1	.292	.335	.387	123	3	.268	.292	.423	357	2	.291	.357	.395
1994	Bos-A	185	3	.227	.296	.335	111	2	.216	.293	.324	74	1	.243	.300	.351	114	2	.246	.312	.351	71	1	.197	.269	.310	68	1	.206	.250	.353	117	2	.239	.321	.325
1995	Det-A	182	1	.231	.312	.313	79	1	.253	.359	.329	103	0	.214	.274	.301	60	0	.217	.304	.283	122	1	.238	.316	.328	56	1	.161	.226	.268	126	0	.262	.350	.333
TOTALS		5258	34	.262	.332	.342	2594	17	.275	.347	.356	2664	17	.249	.317	.328	2416	16	.262	.340	.345	2842	18	.262	.325	.339	1784	16	.276	.344	.363	3474	18	.254	.326	.331
■ **Doug Flynn** BR/TR																																				
1978	NY-N	532	0	.237	.277	.289	253	0	.213	.259	.249	279	0	.258	.294	.326	277	0	.238	.269	.264	255	0	.235	.286	.318	181	0	.243	.286	.315	351	0	.234	.273	.276
1979	NY-N	555	4	.243	.265	.317	257	3	.210	.232	.288	298	1	.272	.293	.342	250	3	.220	.247	.312	305	1	.262	.279	.321	170	2	.259	.297	.359	385	2	.236	.250	.299
1980	NY-N	443	0	.255	.288	.312	217	0	.258	.288	.290	226	0	.252	.289	.332	246	0	.232	.272	.260	197	0	.284	.309	.376	124	0	.210	.256	.274	319	0	.273	.301	.326
1981	NY-N	325	1	.222	.247	.292	159	1	.239	.262	.321	166	0	.205	.233	.265	176	1	.239	.272	.341	149	0	.201	.217	.235	63	0	.270	.303	.333	262	1	.210	.233	.282
1982	Tex-A	270	0	.211	.221	.248	130	0	.200	.203	.215	140	0	.221	.238	.279	191	0	.225	.235	.257	79	0	.177	.188	.228	49	0	.224	.220	.245	221	0	.208	.221	.249
1982	Mon-N	193	0	.244	.256	.295	94	0	.170	.177	.245	99	0	.313	.330	.343	0	0	—	—	—	193	0	.244	.256	.295	37	0	.162	.184	.162	156	0	.263	.273	.327
1983	Mon-N	452	0	.237	.267	.294	233	0	.249	.283	.318	219	0	.224	.250	.269	202	0	.208	.238	.262	250	0	.260	.290	.320	134	0	.231	.248	.321	318	0	.239	.275	.283
1984	Mon-N	366	0	.243	.267	.281	181	0	.243	.267	.298	185	0	.243	.267	.265	157	0	.274	.296	.318	209	0	.220	.245	.254	122	0	.279	.313	.311	244	0	.225	.244	.266
1985	Mon-N	6	0	.167	.167	.167	1	0	.000	.000	.000	5	0	.200	.200	.200	6	0	.167	.167	.167	0	0	—	—	—	4	0	.000	.000	.000	2	0	.500	.500	.500
1985	Det-A	51	0	.255	.250	.333	28	0	.214	.214	.321	23	0	.304	.292	.348	9	0	.111	.111	.111	42	0	.286	.279	.381	26	0	.308	.296	.423	25	0	.200	.200	.240
TOTALS		3193	5	.238	.265	.295	1553	4	.227	.253	.283	1640	1	.249	.275	.306	1514	4	.231	.259	.283	1679	1	.244	.269	.305	910	2	.243	.275	.311	2283	3	.236	.260	.288
■ **George Foster** BR/TR																																				
1978	Cin-N	604	40	.281	.360	.546	296	25	.291	.375	.611	308	15	.273	.344	.484	301	16	.302	.369	.535	303	24	.261	.350	.558	244	16	.328	.395	.623	360	24	.250	.336	.494
1979	Cin-N	440	30	.302	.386	.561	226	20	.314	.391	.633	214	10	.290	.382	.486	260	19	.335	.403	.615	180	11	.256	.362	.483	161	11	.311	.391	.565	279	19	.297	.383	.559
1980	Cin-N	528	25	.273	.362	.473	240	14	.229	.332	.463	288	11	.309	.387	.483	216	9	.231	.328	.398	312	16	.301	.385	.526	153	9	.288	.380	.549	375	16	.267	.354	.443
1981	Cin-N	414	22	.295	.373	.519	205	8	.298	.374	.493	209	14	.292	.371	.545	222	14	.297	.361	.563	192	8	.292	.386	.469	94	3	.298	.402	.457	320	19	.294	.364	.538
1982	NY-N	550	13	.247	.309	.367	280	7	.254	.304	.375	270	6	.241	.315	.359	267	8	.273	.350	.401	283	5	.223	.269	.336	111	4	.288	.355	.477	439	9	.237	.298	.339
1983	NY-N	601	28	.241	.289	.419	295	17	.247	.299	.468	306	11	.235	.279	.373	267	13	.255	.309	.434	334	15	.231	.272	.407	161	12	.261	.310	.516	440	16	.234	.281	.384
1984	NY-N	553	24	.269	.311	.443	250	11	.256	.301	.416	303	13	.281	.319	.465	255	10	.224	.269	.388	298	14	.309	.347	.490	195	10	.287	.325	.487	358	14	.260	.303	.419
1985	NY-N	452	21	.263	.331	.460	225	9	.262	.341	.444	227	12	.264	.321	.476	198	11	.237	.305	.455	254	10	.283	.352	.465	188	9	.271	.358	.468	264	12	.258	.311	.455
1986	NY-N	233	13	.227	.289	.429	120	9	.208	.284	.458	113	4	.248	.295	.398	181	13	.254	.322	.497	52	0	.135	.167	.192	104	7	.221	.261	.442	129	6	.233	.310	.419
1986	Chi-A	51	1	.216	.259	.353	25	1	.200	.259	.400	26	0	.231	.259	.308	0	0	—	—	—	51	1	.216	.259	.353	21	0	.143	.182	.238	30	1	.267	.313	.433
TOTALS		4426	217	.267	.335	.467	2162	121	.264	.335	.485	2264	96	.270	.335	.450	2167	113	.270	.337	.477	2259	104	.264	.332	.457	1432	81	.286	.355	.517	2994	136	.258	.325	.443
■ **Andy Fox** BL/TR																																				
1996	NY-A	189	3	.196	.276	.265	90	1	.178	.253	.222	99	2	.212	.297	.303	111	2	.198	.276	.288	78	1	.192	.276	.231	29	1	.172	.226	.276	160	2	.200	.285	.262
1997	NY-A	31	0	.226	.368	.258	18	0	.278	.381	.333	13	0	.154	.353	.154	1	0	.000	.000	.000	30	0	.233	.378	.267	3	0	.333	.333	.333	28	0	.214	.371	.250
1998	Ari-N	502	9	.277	.355	.396	252	5	.278	.355	.401	250	4	.276	.355	.392	220	6	.268	.335	.395	282	3	.284	.370	.397	96	0	.333	.413	.427	406	9	.264	.341	.389
1999	Ari-N	274	6	.255	.351	.380	128	4	.258	.362	.391	146	2	.253	.341	.370	124	3	.282	.379	.427	150	3	.233	.328	.340	46	0	.152	.273	.152	228	6	.276	.367	.425
2000	Ari-N	86	1	.209	.244	.291	41	1	.317	.349	.439	45	0	.111	.149	.156	86	1	.209	.244	.291	0	0	—	—	—	14	0	.286	.333	.429	72	1	.194	.227	.264
2000	Fla-N	164	3	.244	.330	.348	78	1	.295	.389	.385	86	2	.198	.274	.314	30	1	.167	.242	.267	134	2	.261	.349	.366	10	0	.200	.273	.200	154	3	.247	.333	.357
TOTALS		1246	22	.250	.332	.356	607	12	.264	.346	.371	639	10	.236	.318	.341	572	13	.243	.315	.358	674	9	.255	.346	.353	198	1	.258	.339	.328	1048	21	.248	.331	.361
■ **Julio Franco** BR/TR																																				
1982	Phi-N	29	0	.276	.323	.310	15	0	.267	.353	.267	14	0	.286	.286	.357	23	0	.261	.320	.304	6	0	.333	.333	.333	4	0	.000	.200	.000	25	0	.320	.346	.360
1983	Cle-A	560	8	.273	.306	.387	286	6	.315	.347	.451	274	2	.230	.261	.321	265	5	.279	.309	.419	295	3	.268	.303	.359	187	2	.321	.369	.465	373	6	.249	.273	.349
1984	Cle-A	658	3	.286	.331	.348	318	1	.302	.357	.362	340	2	.271	.305	.335	291	1	.261	.320	.316	367	2	.305	.339	.373	188	3	.330	.381	.447	470	0	.268	.310	.309
1985	Cle-A	636	6	.288	.343	.381	307	3	.306	.354	.394	329	3	.271	.332	.368	268	2	.280	.342	.373	368	4	.293	.343	.386	196	4	.286	.340	.408	440	2	.289	.344	.368
1986	Cle-A	599	10	.306	.338	.422	302	4	.291	.318	.401	297	6	.320	.358	.444	282	4	.270	.314	.372	317	6	.338	.360	.467	164	6	.341	.370	.537	435	4	.292	.326	.379
1987	Cle-A	495	8	.319	.389	.428	242	5	.310	.383	.421	253	3	.328	.395	.435	291	4	.313	.383	.423	204	4	.328	.398	.436	130	4	.308	.389	.492	365	4	.323	.389	.405
1988	Cle-A	613	10	.303	.361	.409	286	3	.364	.416	.462	327	7	.251	.314	.364	305	8	.289	.342	.423	308	2	.318	.380	.396	133	5	.383	.461	.624	480	5	.281	.333	.350
1989	Tex-A	548	13	.316	.386	.462	267	9	.356	.430	.554	281	4	.278	.343	.374	286	10	.339	.407	.517	262	3	.290	.364	.401	161	5	.286	.361	.453	387	8	.328	.397	.465
1990	Tex-A	582	11	.296	.383	.402	303	4	.317	.399	.409	279	7	.272	.366	.394	292	6	.295	.366	.411	290	5	.297	.399	.393	179	3	.296	.398	.397	403	8	.295	.376	.404
1991	Tex-A	589	15	.341	.408	.474	294	7	.344	.409	.480	295	8	.339	.407	.468	285	9	.323	.388	.474	304	6	.359	.427	.474	155	8	.368	.424	.626	434	7	.332	.402	.419
1992	Tex-A	107	2	.234	.328	.355	64	2	.313	.397	.500	43	0	.116	.224	.140	84	1	.238	.347	.345	23	1	.217	.250	.391	39	1	.333	.409	.487	68	1	.176	.282	.279
1993	Tex-A	532	14	.289	.360	.438	264	6	.330	.400	.500	268	8	.250	.321	.377	217	6	.258	.309	.424	315	8	.311	.393	.448	102	3	.265	.330	.422	430	11	.295	.368	.442
1994	Chi-A	433	20	.319	.406	.510	198	10	.359	.427	.571	235	10	.285	.389	.460	286	12	.318	.402	.493	147	8	.320	.414	.544	99	7	.364	.496	.677	334	13	.305	.376	.461
1996	Cle-A	432	14	.322	.407	.470	217	7	.364	.467	.512	215	7	.279	.340	.428	296	10	.324	.422	.486	136	4	.316	.372	.434	128	2	.336	.397	.445	304	12	.316	.411	.480
1997	Cle-A	289	3	.284	.367	.367	145	2	.276	.393	.359	144	1	.292	.338	.375	254	2	.295	.381	.370	35	1	.200	.263	.343	71	0	.254	.391	.296	218	3	.294	.358	.390
1997	Mil-A	141	4	.241	.373	.348	76	3	.237	.371	.368	65	1	.246	.375	.323	0	0	—	—	—	141	4	.241	.373	.348	40	0	.250	.385	.250	101	4	.238	.368	.386
1999	TB-A	1	0	.000	.000	.000	0	0	—	—	—	1	0	.000	.000	.000	0	0	—	—	—	1	0	.000	.000	.000	1	0	.000	.000	.000	0	0	—	—	—
TOTALS		7244	141	.301	.366	.418	3584	72	.323	.390	.448	3660	69	.278	.342	.389	3725	80	.295	.362	.421	3519	61	.306	.370	.415	1977	53	.318	.390	.477	5267	88	.294	.357	.396
■ **Matt Franco** BL/TR																																				
1995	Chi-N	17	0	.294	.294	.353	14	0	.286	.286	.286	3	0	.333	.333	.667	0	0	—	—	—	17	0	.294	.294	.353	1	0	.000	.000	.000	16	0	.313	.313	.375
1996	NY-N	31	1	.194	.235	.323	13	0	.385	.400	.462	18	1	.056	.105	.222	0	0	—	—	—	31	1	.194	.235	.323	2	0	.000	.000	.000	29	1	.207	.250	.345
1997	NY-N	163	5	.276	.330	.399	92	3	.250	.310	.380	71	2	.310	.355	.423	84	3	.321	.374	.464	79	2	.228	.282	.329	22	0	.227	.261	.227	141	5	.284	.340	.426
1998	NY-N	161	1	.273	.366	.360	70	1	.314	.410	.486	91	0	.242	.330	.264	95	0	.263	.375	.347	66	1	.288	.351	.379	12	0	.333	.385	.333	149	1	.268	.364	.362
1999	NY-N	132	4	.235	.366	.364	58	0	.276	.442	.310	74	4	.203	.298	.405	70	3	.271	.346	.429	62	1	.194	.386	.290	7	0	.000	.000	.000	125	4	.248	.383	.384
2000	NY-N	134	2	.239	.340	.313	62	1	.242	.338	.339	72	1	.236	.341	.292	70	0	.243	.346	.271	64	2	.234	.333	.359	10	0	.200	.385	.200	124	2	.242	.336	.323
TOTALS		638	13	.255	.344	.359	309	5	.275	.369	.382	329	8	.237	.319	.337	319	6	.276	.362	.379	319	7	.235	.326	.339	54	0	.204	.271	.204	584	13	.260	.350	.373
■ **Travis Fryman** BR/TR																																				
1990	Det-A	232	9	.297	.348	.470	108	5	.259	.350	.426	124	4	.331	.346	.508	0	0	—	—	—	232	9	.297	.348	.470	88	5	.318	.375	.568	144	4	.285	.331	.410
1991	Det-A	557	21	.259	.309	.447	261	8	.249	.303	.421	296	13	.267	.313	.470	250	8	.232	.286	.384	307	13	.280	.327	.498	152	5	.296	.349	.480	405	16	.244	.293	.435
1992	Det-A	659	20	.266	.316	.416	319	9	.232	.289	.357	340	11	.297	.341	.471	313	12	.291	.330	.470	346	8	.243	.303	.367	158	7	.285	.333	.475	501	13	.259	.310	.397
1993	Det-A	607	22	.300	.379	.486	285	13	.316	.402	.537	322	9	.286	.358	.441	291	10	.271	.337	.436	316	12	.326	.416	.532	166	9	.265	.349	.482	441	13	.313	.390	.488
1994	Det-A	464	18	.263	.326	.474	229	10	.262	.314	.502	235	8	.264	.338	.447	307	11	.296	.353	.505	157	7	.197	.276	.414	94	7	.255	.311	.574	370	11	.265	.330	.449

YEAR	TM/L	TOTAL					HOME					AWAY					1ST HALF					2ND HALF					LEFT					RIGHT				
		AB	HR	AVG	OBP	SLG	AB	HR	AVG	OBP	SLG	AB	HR	AVG	OBP	SLG	AB	HR	AVG	OBP	SLG	AB	HR	AVG	OBP	SLG	AB	HR	AVG	OBP	SLG	AB	HR	AVG	OBP	SLG
1995	Det-A	567	15	.275	.347	.409	267	9	.292	.394	.419	300	6	.260	.302	.400	234	4	.252	.341	.333	333	11	.291	.351	.462	128	1	.211	.275	.281	439	14	.294	.367	.446
1996	Det-A	616	22	.268	.329	.437	288	10	.271	.340	.434	328	12	.265	.320	.439	300	12	.273	.322	.460	316	10	.263	.335	.415	125	3	.248	.349	.376	491	19	.273	.323	.452
1997	Det-A	595	22	.274	.326	.440	282	13	.277	.335	.472	313	9	.272	.317	.412	272	10	.298	.359	.474	323	12	.254	.296	.412	151	5	.298	.359	.457	444	17	.266	.314	.435
1998	Cle-A	557	28	.287	.340	.504	291	16	.302	.355	.522	266	12	.271	.324	.485	300	13	.270	.319	.467	257	15	.307	.365	.549	136	4	.309	.375	.471	421	24	.280	.329	.515
1999	Cle-A	322	10	.255	.309	.410	148	6	.230	.275	.399	174	4	.276	.337	.420	228	8	.254	.317	.425	94	2	.255	.286	.372	66	2	.273	.367	.455	256	8	.250	.292	.398
2000	Cle-A	574	22	.321	.392	.516	293	9	.311	.378	.491	281	13	.331	.407	.541	271	14	.317	.406	.546	303	8	.323	.380	.488	118	4	.297	.422	.432	456	18	.327	.384	.537
TOTALS		5750	209	.279	.339	.455	2771	108	.276	.343	.456	2979	101	.281	.336	.455	2766	102	.277	.338	.454	2984	107	.280	.341	.457	1382	52	.278	.351	.455	4368	157	.279	.336	.456
■ Brad Fullmer BL/TR																																				
1997	Mon-N	40	3	.300	.349	.575	24	1	.292	.346	.500	16	2	.313	.353	.688	0	0	—	—	—	40	3	.300	.349	.575	11	0	.182	.250	.273	29	3	.345	.387	.690
1998	Mon-N	505	13	.273	.327	.446	256	3	.242	.292	.367	249	10	.305	.363	.526	281	6	.292	.338	.484	224	7	.250	.314	.397	90	2	.244	.320	.400	415	11	.280	.329	.455
1999	Mon-N	347	9	.277	.321	.464	177	4	.282	.317	.492	170	5	.271	.324	.435	105	3	.219	.274	.419	242	6	.302	.341	.483	50	2	.240	.264	.480	297	7	.283	.330	.461
2000	Tor-A	482	32	.295	.340	.558	254	16	.291	.337	.543	228	16	.298	.343	.575	240	14	.313	.373	.575	242	18	.277	.305	.541	93	5	.226	.279	.430	389	27	.311	.355	.589
TOTALS		1374	57	.282	.331	.493	711	24	.271	.316	.466	663	33	.294	.346	.523	626	23	.288	.341	.508	748	34	.278	.322	.481	244	9	.234	.290	.422	1130	48	.293	.340	.509
■ Gary Gaetti BR/TR																																				
1981	Min-A	26	2	.192	.192	.423	8	1	.250	.250	.625	18	1	.167	.167	.333	0	0	—	—	—	26	2	.192	.192	.423	12	0	.083	.083	.083	14	2	.286	.286	.714
1982	Min-A	508	25	.230	.280	.443	268	15	.235	.285	.474	240	10	.225	.274	.408	206	9	.209	.270	.413	302	16	.245	.287	.464	171	15	.269	.326	.620	337	10	.211	.255	.353
1983	Min-A	584	21	.245	.309	.414	291	7	.241	.305	.395	293	14	.249	.314	.433	297	9	.242	.308	.384	287	12	.247	.311	.446	169	6	.284	.348	.438	415	15	.229	.294	.405
1984	Min-A	588	5	.262	.315	.350	294	2	.282	.331	.388	294	3	.241	.299	.313	274	2	.255	.321	.350	314	3	.268	.310	.350	179	2	.240	.294	.335	409	3	.271	.324	.357
1985	Min-A	560	20	.246	.301	.409	280	10	.261	.309	.425	280	10	.232	.293	.393	246	9	.256	.333	.447	314	11	.239	.274	.379	175	6	.206	.272	.349	385	14	.265	.314	.436
1986	Min-A	596	34	.287	.347	.518	296	16	.250	.311	.473	300	18	.323	.383	.563	277	17	.267	.334	.516	319	17	.304	.358	.520	151	11	.344	.409	.603	445	23	.267	.325	.490
1987	Min-A	584	31	.257	.303	.485	301	18	.306	.352	.575	283	13	.205	.250	.389	268	15	.265	.318	.489	316	16	.250	.290	.481	166	7	.235	.287	.422	418	24	.266	.309	.510
1988	Min-A	468	28	.301	.353	.551	219	9	.297	.363	.489	249	19	.305	.344	.606	290	16	.303	.357	.538	178	12	.298	.347	.573	130	8	.338	.400	.592	338	20	.287	.334	.536
1989	Min-A	498	19	.251	.286	.404	249	10	.249	.278	.398	249	9	.253	.294	.410	304	15	.266	.297	.457	194	4	.227	.268	.320	152	5	.230	.274	.368	346	14	.260	.291	.419
1990	Min-A	577	16	.229	.274	.376	286	7	.238	.279	.385	291	9	.220	.269	.368	256	9	.246	.292	.422	321	7	.215	.259	.340	166	5	.223	.283	.361	411	11	.231	.270	.382
1991	Cal-A	586	18	.246	.293	.379	280	12	.275	.331	.429	306	6	.219	.257	.333	267	8	.255	.289	.382	319	10	.238	.296	.376	159	6	.239	.303	.396	427	12	.248	.289	.372
1992	Cal-A	456	12	.226	.267	.342	231	8	.260	.289	.403	225	4	.191	.246	.280	240	5	.229	.276	.329	216	7	.222	.258	.356	124	5	.250	.299	.419	332	7	.217	.256	.313
1993	Cal-A	50	0	.180	.250	.220	26	0	.231	.286	.308	24	0	.125	.214	.125	50	0	.180	.250	.220	0	0	—	—	—	26	0	.154	.281	.154	24	0	.208	.208	.292
1993	KC-A	281	14	.256	.309	.477	142	6	.296	.352	.528	139	8	.216	.263	.424	24	1	.250	.308	.458	257	13	.257	.309	.479	71	7	.324	.398	.718	210	7	.233	.276	.395
1994	KC-A	327	12	.287	.328	.462	154	5	.292	.325	.487	173	7	.283	.330	.439	259	10	.286	.322	.463	68	2	.294	.347	.456	95	5	.263	.317	.537	232	7	.297	.332	.431
1995	KC-A	514	35	.261	.329	.518	257	16	.272	.336	.514	257	19	.249	.322	.521	208	16	.264	.330	.538	306	19	.258	.328	.503	132	9	.212	.316	.432	382	26	.277	.333	.547
1996	StL-N	522	23	.274	.326	.473	244	13	.303	.357	.566	278	10	.248	.299	.392	234	8	.244	.304	.389	288	15	.299	.345	.542	105	3	.248	.283	.410	417	20	.281	.337	.489
1997	StL-N	502	17	.251	.305	.404	256	7	.250	.295	.402	246	10	.252	.316	.407	235	6	.264	.320	.413	267	11	.240	.293	.397	112	5	.277	.359	.464	390	12	.244	.289	.387
1998	StL-N	306	11	.265	.339	.454	125	1	.224	.329	.304	181	10	.293	.347	.558	226	7	.265	.355	.434	80	4	.262	.289	.512	101	6	.257	.342	.505	205	5	.268	.338	.429
1998	Chi-N	128	8	.320	.397	.594	54	4	.278	.361	.537	74	4	.351	.424	.635	0	0	—	—	—	128	8	.320	.397	.594	40	4	.375	.458	.800	88	4	.295	.367	.500
1999	Chi-N	280	9	.204	.260	.339	141	6	.206	.252	.383	139	3	.201	.268	.295	155	6	.181	.256	.335	125	3	.232	.265	.344	118	3	.220	.298	.347	162	6	.191	.232	.333
2000	Bos-A	10	0	.000	.000	.000	4	0	.000	.000	.000	6	0	.000	.000	.000	10	0	.000	.000	.000	0	0	—	—	—	7	0	.000	.000	.000	3	0	.000	.000	.000
TOTALS		8951	360	.255	.308	.434	4406	173	.264	.316	.448	4545	187	.246	.300	.420	4326	168	.254	.311	.429	4625	192	.255	.304	.438	2561	118	.255	.320	.450	6390	242	.254	.303	.427
■ Greg Gagne BR/TR																																				
1983	Min-A	27	0	.111	.103	.148	19	0	.158	.150	.211	8	0	.000	.000	.000	19	0	.053	.048	.105	8	0	.250	.250	.250	12	0	.083	.077	.083	15	0	.133	.125	.200
1984	Min-A	1	0	.000	.000	.000	0	0	—	—	—	1	0	.000	.000	.000	0	0	—	—	—	1	0	.000	.000	.000	0	0	—	—	—	1	0	.000	.000	.000
1985	Min-A	293	2	.225	.279	.317	142	0	.232	.297	.331	151	2	.219	.261	.305	155	2	.265	.327	.394	138	0	.181	.223	.232	127	1	.244	.265	.354	166	1	.211	.289	.289
1986	Min-A	472	12	.250	.301	.398	238	10	.239	.295	.441	234	2	.261	.308	.355	236	3	.246	.291	.347	236	9	.254	.311	.449	126	6	.230	.277	.452	346	6	.257	.310	.379
1987	Min-A	437	10	.265	.310	.430	212	7	.241	.303	.434	225	3	.289	.316	.427	181	5	.249	.301	.431	256	5	.277	.316	.430	128	0	.266	.294	.367	309	10	.265	.316	.456
1988	Min-A	461	14	.236	.288	.397	225	5	.222	.279	.360	236	9	.250	.298	.432	223	8	.247	.300	.439	238	6	.227	.277	.357	111	2	.297	.352	.477	350	12	.217	.267	.371
1989	Min-A	460	9	.272	.298	.424	218	5	.298	.326	.477	242	4	.248	.272	.376	241	4	.257	.297	.390	219	5	.288	.298	.461	171	5	.292	.320	.515	289	4	.260	.284	.370
1990	Min-A	388	7	.235	.280	.361	182	3	.247	.298	.390	206	4	.223	.263	.335	210	4	.233	.283	.381	178	3	.236	.275	.337	124	3	.298	.353	.484	264	4	.205	.244	.303
1991	Min-A	408	8	.265	.310	.395	194	3	.263	.321	.376	214	5	.266	.300	.411	207	5	.256	.308	.406	201	3	.274	.312	.383	118	2	.280	.348	.432	290	6	.259	.294	.379
1992	Min-A	439	7	.246	.280	.346	219	1	.228	.265	.297	220	6	.264	.294	.395	224	5	.259	.300	.375	215	2	.233	.259	.316	105	1	.181	.225	.248	334	6	.266	.297	.377
1993	KC-A	540	10	.280	.319	.406	269	3	.305	.340	.420	271	7	.255	.298	.391	245	3	.265	.314	.351	295	7	.292	.323	.451	137	2	.314	.364	.445	403	8	.268	.303	.392
1994	KC-A	375	7	.259	.314	.392	176	2	.313	.395	.438	199	5	.211	.237	.352	243	6	.263	.326	.407	132	1	.250	.293	.364	90	1	.233	.289	.311	285	6	.267	.323	.418
1995	KC-A	430	6	.256	.316	.374	202	2	.272	.327	.376	228	4	.241	.306	.373	167	2	.269	.339	.407	263	4	.247	.301	.354	117	1	.248	.308	.350	313	5	.259	.319	.383
1996	LA-N	428	10	.255	.333	.364	198	3	.212	.293	.288	230	7	.291	.368	.430	155	5	.258	.354	.387	273	5	.253	.321	.352	93	3	.247	.346	.398	335	7	.257	.330	.355
1997	LA-N	514	9	.251	.298	.354	260	2	.235	.284	.288	254	7	.268	.313	.421	285	5	.267	.301	.379	229	4	.231	.295	.323	133	3	.256	.303	.391	381	6	.249	.297	.341
TOTALS		5673	111	.254	.302	.382	2754	46	.254	.308	.378	2919	65	.254	.296	.387	2791	57	.255	.307	.388	2882	54	.253	.296	.376	1592	30	.262	.311	.406	4081	81	.251	.298	.373
■ Andres Galarraga BR/TR																																				
1985	Mon-N	75	2	.187	.228	.280	36	0	.167	.211	.194	39	2	.205	.244	.359	0	0	—	—	—	75	2	.187	.228	.280	42	0	.190	.244	.214	33	2	.182	.206	.364
1986	Mon-N	321	10	.271	.338	.405	161	4	.286	.348	.410	160	6	.256	.328	.400	203	8	.261	.332	.414	118	2	.288	.349	.390	120	4	.333	.398	.475	201	6	.234	.302	.363
1987	Mon-N	551	13	.305	.361	.459	264	7	.314	.385	.492	287	6	.296	.339	.429	255	7	.345	.411	.537	296	6	.270	.317	.392	164	7	.323	.385	.543	387	6	.297	.351	.424
1988	Mon-N	609	29	.302	.352	.540	296	14	.314	.369	.588	313	15	.291	.336	.495	307	18	.319	.361	.593	302	11	.285	.344	.487	173	10	.283	.332	.543	436	19	.310	.361	.539
1989	Mon-N	572	23	.257	.327	.434	286	13	.241	.324	.448	286	10	.273	.330	.420	271	12	.258	.334	.443	301	11	.256	.320	.425	174	11	.385	.449	.672	398	12	.201	.273	.329
1990	Mon-N	579	20	.256	.306	.409	286	6	.266	.317	.399	293	14	.246	.294	.420	268	6	.257	.315	.377	311	14	.254	.297	.437	217	9	.226	.260	.392	362	11	.273	.332	.420
1991	Mon-N	375	9	.219	.268	.336	152	3	.224	.258	.336	223	6	.215	.274	.336	141	3	.255	.305	.376	234	6	.197	.245	.312	128	6	.180	.222	.359	247	3	.239	.291	.324
1992	StL-N	325	10	.243	.282	.391	159	4	.264	.298	.390	166	6	.223	.268	.392	119	0	.185	.230	.235	206	10	.277	.312	.481	125	6	.320	.348	.536	200	4	.195	.242	.300
1993	Col-N	470	22	.370	.403	.602	266	13	.402	.430	.647	204	9	.328	.368	.544	235	11	.404	.434	.647	235	11	.336	.373	.557	117	6	.350	.383	.573	353	16	.377	.410	.612
1994	Col-N	417	31	.319	.356	.592	204	16	.348	.390	.627	213	15	.291	.323	.559	315	22	.330	.363	.600	102	9	.284	.336	.569	88	12	.386	.406	.886	329	19	.301	.343	.514
1995	Col-N	554	31	.280	.331	.511	273	18	.297	.355	.571	281	13	.263	.307	.452	223	12	.274	.337	.489	331	19	.284	.327	.526	137	10	.270	.327	.562	417	21	.283	.333	.494
1996	Col-N	626	47	.304	.357	.601	320	32	.359	.419	.738	306	15	.245	.290	.458	295	22	.292	.353	.590	331	25	.314	.361	.610	141	12	.326	.371	.660	485	35	.297	.353	.584
1997	Col-N	600	41	.318	.389	.585	298	21	.342	.406	.611	302	20	.295	.372	.560	308	22	.334	.410	.607	292	19	.301	.365	.562	126	10	.333	.426	.643	474	31	.314	.378	.570
1998	Atl-N	555	44	.305	.397	.595	251	16	.315	.422	.570	304	28	.296	.375	.615	294	27	.310	.390	.636	261	17	.299	.404	.548	134	12	.328	.414	.642	421	32	.297	.391	.580
2000	Atl-N	494	28	.302	.369	.526	224	14	.317	.379	.571	270	14	.289	.360	.489	266	19	.305	.375	.575	228	9	.298	.361	.469	118	3	.347	.400	.483	376	25	.287	.359	.540
TOTALS		7123	360	.291	.348	.506	3476	181	.309	.369	.540	3647	179	.273	.328	.473	3500	189	.302	.362	.530	3623	171	.280	.335	.482	2004	118	.306	.360	.550	5119	242	.284	.343	.488
■ Ron Gant BR/TR																																				
1987	Atl-N	83	2	.265	.271	.386	38	1	.289	.308	.395	45	1	.244	.239	.378	0	0	—	—	—	83	2	.265	.271	.386	24	0	.208	.240	.208	59	2	.288	.283	.458
1988	Atl-N	563	19	.259	.317	.439	267	7	.247	.316	.423	296	12	.270	.317	.453	231	8	.242	.276	.429	332	11	.271	.343	.446	193	9	.280	.355	.513	370	10	.249	.296	.400
1989	Atl-N	260	9	.177	.237	.335	135	5	.178	.240	.341	125	4	.176	.234	.328	204	6	.172	.233	.309	56	3	.196	.250	.429	79	1	.114	.205	.203	181	8	.204	.251	.392
1990	Atl-N	575	32	.303	.357	.539	288	18	.313	.362	.559	287	14	.293	.352	.519	226	15	.314	.364	.588	349	17	.295	.352	.507	204	10	.299	.361	.520	371	22	.305	.355	.550
1991	Atl-N	561	32	.251	.338	.496	258	18	.279	.370	.558	303	14	.228	.310	.442	249	13	.225	.292	.454	312	19	.272	.372	.529	164	10	.287	.383	.567	397	22	.237	.318	.466
1992	Atl-N	544	17	.259	.321	.415	257	10	.276	.336	.463	287	7	.244	.307	.373	280	10	.279	.354	.464	264	7	.239	.283	.364	177	5	.254	.322	.412	367	12	.262	.320	.417
1993	Atl-N	606	36	.274	.345	.510	301	17	.279	.352	.505	305	19	.269	.337	.515	280	17	.268	.341	.532	326	19	.279	.348	.491	149	8	.295	.385	.510	457	28	.267	.331	.510
1995	Cin-N	410	29	.276	.386	.554	189	12	.275	.390	.524	221	17	.276	.383	.579	194	17	.299	.409	.629	216	12	.255	.365	.486	84	7	.250	.413	.536	326	22	.282	.379	.558
1996	StL-N	419	30	.246	.359	.504	221	17	.226	.342	.502	198	13	.268	.377	.505	153	11	.242	.365	.529	266	19	.248	.355	.489	94	5	.202	.333	.383	325	25	.258	.366	.538
1997	StL-N	502	17	.229	.310	.388	244	11	.234	.307	.430	258	6	.225	.312	.349	270	12	.230	.314	.426	232	5	.228	.305	.345	122	5	.197	.295	.385	380	12	.239	.314	.389
1998	StL-N	383	26	.240	.331	.493	201	14	.229	.326	.483	182	12	.253	.337	.505	188	12	.213	.304	.463	195	14	.267	.357	.523	105	8	.286	.392	.571	278	18	.223	.307	.464
1999	Phi-N	516	17	.260	.364	.430	235	6	.255	.373	.421	281	11	.263	.356	.438	251	9	.259	.355	.434	265	8	.260	.371	.426	130	5	.300	.421	.469	386	12	.246	.343	.417
2000	Phi-N	343	20	.254	.324	.487	152	9	.257	.350	.493	191	11	.251	.301	.482	268	14	.246	.310	.459	75	6	.280	.371	.587	85	6	.365	.427	.694	258	14	.217	.289	.419
2000	Ana-A	82	6	.232	.379	.512	36	5	.278	.422	.694	46	1	.196	.345	.370	0	0	—	—	—	82	6	.232	.379	.512	39	1	.205	.385	.282	43	5	.256	.373	.721
TOTALS		5847	292	.256	.336	.469	2822	150	.259	.343	.482	3025	142	.254	.329	.457	2794	144	.250	.327	.474	3053	148	.262	.345	.464	1649	80	.265	.359	.477	4198	212	.253	.327	.466
■ Jim Gantner BL/TR																																				
1978	Mil-A	97	1	.216	.269	.258	52	0	.250	.316	.250	45	1	.178	.213	.267	58	1	.224	.274	.293	39	0	.205	.262	.205	8	0	.000	.000	.000	89	1	.236	.292	.281
1979	Mil-A	208	2	.284	.336	.389	123	0	.236	.299	.333	85	2	.353	.389	.471	91	0	.264	.333	.319	117	2	.299	.339	.444	22	0	.227	.320	.273	186	2	.290	.338	.403
1980	Mil-A	415	4	.282	.330	.376	201	1	.264	.310	.323	214	3	.299	.348	.425	157	2	.274	.315	.350	258	2	.287	.338	.391	84	0	.262	.300	.321	331	4	.287	.337	.390
1981	Mil-A	352	2	.267	.325	.330	162	0	.253	.295	.290	190	2	.279	.349	.363	194	1	.273	.327	.340	158	1	.259	.322	.316	80	0	.213	.270	.225	272	2	.283	.341	.360
1982	Mil-A	447	4	.295	.335	.369	215	2	.302	.338	.391	232	2	.289	.332	.349	194	3	.309	.369	.407	253	1	.285	.307	.340	128	0	.289	.336	.313	319	4	.298	.334	.392
1983	Mil-A	603	11	.282	.328	.401	281	5	.260	.328	.356	322	6	.301	.329	.441	259	6	.278	.324	.409	344	5	.285	.332	.395	211	2	.232	.296	.336	392	9	.309	.347	.436
1984	Mil-A	613	3	.282	.314	.344	296	0	.291	.325	.331	317	3	.274	.304	.356	291	2	.285	.311	.347	322	1	.280	.316	.342	204	0	.270	.315	.299	409	3	.289	.313	.367

YEAR	TM/L	TOTAL AB	HR	AVG	OBP	SLG	HOME AB	HR	AVG	OBP	SLG	AWAY AB	HR	AVG	OBP	SLG	1ST HALF AB	HR	AVG	OBP	SLG	2ND HALF AB	HR	AVG	OBP	SLG	LEFT AB	HR	AVG	OBP	SLG	RIGHT AB	HR	AVG	OBP	SLG
1985	Mil-A	523	5	.254	.300	.327	261	4	.238	.274	.322	262	1	.271	.325	.332	238	3	.269	.311	.357	285	2	.242	.291	.302	164	0	.329	.368	.372	359	5	.220	.270	.306
1986	Mil-A	497	7	.274	.313	.370	247	4	.259	.301	.372	250	3	.288	.326	.368	235	3	.264	.320	.362	262	4	.282	.307	.378	128	0	.219	.268	.250	369	7	.293	.329	.412
1987	Mil-A	265	4	.272	.331	.370	121	0	.298	.370	.347	144	4	.250	.297	.389	232	4	.276	.340	.379	33	0	.242	.265	.303	86	0	.233	.280	.279	179	4	.291	.355	.413
1988	Mil-A	539	0	.276	.322	.336	275	0	.273	.311	.342	264	0	.280	.333	.330	250	0	.280	.322	.324	289	0	.273	.322	.346	146	0	.274	.318	.329	393	0	.277	.323	.338
1989	Mil-A	409	0	.274	.321	.333	189	0	.254	.321	.302	220	0	.291	.322	.359	249	0	.237	.289	.289	160	0	.331	.372	.400	113	0	.274	.320	.336	296	0	.274	.322	.331
1990	Mil-A	323	0	.263	.328	.319	158	0	.278	.356	.310	165	0	.248	.299	.327	33	0	.273	.385	.303	290	0	.262	.321	.321	88	0	.307	.390	.330	235	0	.247	.303	.315
1991	Mil-A	526	2	.283	.320	.361	254	1	.287	.328	.362	272	1	.279	.311	.360	230	0	.274	.313	.339	296	2	.291	.325	.378	139	0	.266	.304	.288	387	2	.289	.325	.388
1992	Mil-A	256	1	.246	.278	.313	136	1	.243	.278	.309	120	0	.250	.278	.317	153	0	.229	.268	.288	103	1	.272	.292	.350	34	0	.206	.300	.235	222	1	.252	.274	.324
TOTALS		6073	46	.274	.319	.352	2971	18	.268	.316	.337	3102	28	.280	.322	.367	2864	25	.270	.319	.348	3209	21	.278	.320	.356	1635	2	.262	.313	.308	4438	44	.279	.321	.369
■ Damaso Garcia BR/TR																																				
1978	NY-A	41	0	.195	.227	.195	20	0	.200	.261	.200	21	0	.190	.190	.190	20	0	.200	.227	.200	21	0	.190	.227	.190	25	0	.160	.160	.160	16	0	.250	.316	.250
1979	NY-A	38	0	.263	.263	.289	23	0	.261	.261	.261	15	0	.267	.267	.333	0	0	—	—	—	38	0	.263	.263	.289	9	0	.000	.000	.000	29	0	.345	.345	.379
1980	Tor-A	543	4	.278	.296	.381	290	2	.300	.321	.428	253	2	.253	.266	.328	241	3	.274	.289	.402	302	1	.281	.301	.364	202	1	.267	.290	.347	341	3	.284	.299	.402
1981	Tor-A	250	1	.252	.277	.304	123	1	.268	.297	.350	127	0	.236	.258	.260	210	1	.229	.257	.271	40	0	.375	.381	.475	86	0	.267	.308	.326	164	1	.244	.260	.293
1982	Tor-A	597	5	.310	.338	.399	289	3	.332	.359	.436	308	2	.289	.319	.364	299	4	.314	.351	.418	298	1	.305	.325	.379	266	0	.323	.345	.380	331	5	.299	.332	.414
1983	Tor-A	525	3	.307	.336	.390	261	1	.326	.359	.433	264	2	.288	.313	.348	250	2	.288	.308	.364	275	1	.324	.361	.415	224	1	.295	.310	.388	301	2	.316	.355	.392
1984	Tor-A	633	5	.284	.310	.374	313	2	.268	.303	.351	320	3	.300	.316	.397	328	0	.305	.333	.384	305	5	.262	.284	.364	202	3	.347	.377	.460	431	2	.255	.277	.334
1985	Tor-A	600	8	.282	.302	.377	300	4	.303	.334	.423	300	4	.260	.269	.330	314	2	.280	.303	.363	286	6	.283	.302	.392	219	2	.251	.276	.333	381	6	.299	.317	.402
1986	Tor-A	424	6	.281	.306	.375	174	3	.282	.300	.391	250	3	.280	.311	.364	229	2	.284	.317	.376	195	4	.277	.294	.374	139	2	.324	.336	.432	285	4	.260	.292	.347
1988	Atl-N	60	1	.117	.159	.183	37	0	.162	.184	.189	23	1	.043	.120	.174	60	1	.117	.159	.183	0	0	—	—	—	19	0	.158	.200	.158	41	1	.098	.140	.195
1989	Mon-N	203	3	.271	.317	.369	109	3	.284	.322	.413	94	0	.255	.311	.319	105	0	.229	.281	.276	98	3	.316	.355	.469	131	3	.298	.343	.427	72	0	.222	.269	.264
TOTALS		3914	36	.283	.309	.371	1939	19	.295	.324	.399	1975	17	.271	.294	.344	2056	15	.276	.305	.360	1858	21	.291	.314	.384	1522	12	.292	.317	.378	2392	24	.277	.304	.367
■ Nomar Garciaparra BR/TR																																				
1996	Bos-A	87	4	.241	.272	.471	43	3	.209	.205	.535	44	1	.273	.333	.409	0	0	—	—	—	87	4	.241	.272	.471	31	1	.161	.212	.323	56	3	.286	.305	.554
1997	Bos-A	684	30	.306	.342	.534	356	11	.298	.327	.492	328	19	.314	.357	.579	330	12	.291	.337	.488	354	18	.319	.346	.576	184	9	.266	.303	.511	500	21	.320	.356	.542
1998	Bos-A	604	35	.323	.362	.584	287	17	.324	.366	.610	317	18	.322	.358	.562	277	11	.314	.354	.534	327	24	.330	.369	.627	153	7	.320	.374	.556	451	28	.324	.358	.594
1999	Bos-A	532	27	.357	.418	.603	296	14	.378	.436	.625	236	13	.331	.397	.576	270	14	.359	.413	.633	262	13	.355	.424	.573	110	9	.400	.476	.764	422	18	.346	.403	.562
2000	Bos-A	529	21	.372	.434	.599	259	7	.375	.449	.571	270	14	.370	.419	.626	222	8	.396	.454	.608	307	13	.355	.420	.593	141	6	.383	.457	.596	388	15	.369	.425	.601
TOTALS		2436	117	.333	.382	.573	1241	52	.336	.385	.569	1195	65	.331	.379	.578	1099	45	.335	.384	.560	1337	72	.332	.380	.585	619	32	.325	.385	.577	1817	85	.336	.381	.572
■ Phil Garner BR/TR																																				
1978	Pit-N	528	10	.261	.345	.400	267	4	.251	.339	.367	261	6	.272	.351	.433	259	2	.255	.325	.355	269	8	.268	.363	.442	190	4	.247	.356	.389	338	6	.269	.339	.405
1979	Pit-N	549	11	.293	.359	.441	270	6	.304	.380	.444	279	5	.283	.338	.437	247	3	.296	.368	.437	302	8	.291	.351	.444	205	5	.273	.341	.429	344	6	.305	.370	.448
1980	Pit-N	548	5	.259	.315	.358	268	3	.265	.330	.369	280	2	.254	.300	.346	247	5	.267	.327	.389	301	0	.252	.305	.332	181	3	.254	.312	.398	367	2	.262	.317	.338
1981	Pit-N	181	1	.254	.327	.326	79	0	.228	.312	.266	102	1	.275	.339	.373	102	1	.284	.362	.392	79	0	.215	.281	.241	43	0	.302	.326	.395	138	1	.239	.327	.304
1981	Hou-N	113	0	.239	.326	.283	51	0	.255	.377	.314	62	0	.226	.279	.258	0	0	—	—	—	113	0	.239	.326	.283	35	0	.257	.395	.257	78	0	.231	.291	.295
1982	Hou-N	588	13	.274	.320	.423	290	6	.266	.323	.417	298	7	.282	.317	.430	293	4	.263	.309	.410	295	9	.285	.330	.437	179	2	.229	.278	.346	409	11	.293	.338	.457
1983	Hou-N	567	14	.238	.317	.362	283	4	.247	.327	.353	284	10	.229	.307	.370	278	9	.248	.339	.388	289	5	.228	.295	.336	174	5	.236	.323	.362	393	9	.239	.314	.361
1984	Hou-N	374	4	.278	.355	.388	195	1	.328	.394	.436	179	3	.223	.316	.335	167	1	.216	.304	.275	207	3	.329	.397	.478	177	2	.328	.396	.480	197	2	.234	.318	.305
1985	Hou-N	463	6	.268	.317	.400	232	2	.272	.325	.371	231	4	.264	.309	.429	245	4	.237	.291	.371	218	2	.303	.347	.431	220	1	.268	.318	.368	243	5	.267	.317	.428
1986	Hou-N	313	9	.265	.329	.415	151	2	.265	.335	.364	162	7	.265	.322	.463	185	6	.281	.343	.454	128	3	.242	.308	.359	192	6	.292	.356	.469	121	3	.223	.282	.331
1987	Hou-N	112	3	.223	.268	.348	52	0	.192	.246	.212	60	3	.250	.288	.467	112	3	.223	.268	.348	0	0	—	—	—	72	2	.222	.275	.347	40	1	.225	.256	.350
1987	LA-N	126	2	.190	.299	.270	59	0	.203	.329	.237	67	2	.179	.273	.299	12	0	.083	.267	.083	114	2	.202	.303	.289	71	2	.239	.345	.366	55	0	.127	.238	.145
1988	SF-N	13	0	.154	.214	.154	10	0	.200	.200	.200	3	0	.000	.250	.000	2	0	.000	.000	.000	11	0	.182	.250	.182	8	0	.125	.125	.125	5	0	.200	.333	.200
TOTALS		4475	78	.262	.328	.386	2207	28	.267	.339	.375	2268	50	.257	.317	.397	2149	38	.257	.324	.384	2326	40	.267	.332	.389	1747	32	.263	.334	.397	2728	46	.261	.325	.380
■ Steve Garvey BR/TR																																				
1978	LA-N	639	21	.316	.353	.499	328	15	.317	.338	.530	311	6	.315	.368	.466	307	10	.296	.336	.459	332	11	.334	.369	.536	157	7	.287	.319	.497	482	14	.326	.364	.500
1979	LA-N	648	28	.315	.351	.497	324	20	.333	.361	.549	324	8	.296	.341	.444	320	12	.316	.349	.481	328	16	.314	.352	.512	166	7	.331	.362	.530	482	21	.309	.347	.485
1980	LA-N	658	26	.304	.341	.467	323	16	.337	.374	.529	335	10	.272	.309	.406	302	17	.281	.318	.477	356	9	.323	.361	.458	109	5	.275	.295	.468	549	21	.310	.350	.466
1981	LA-N	431	10	.283	.322	.411	215	5	.293	.332	.419	216	5	.273	.312	.403	233	6	.279	.323	.425	198	4	.288	.321	.394	63	4	.302	.366	.571	368	6	.280	.314	.383
1982	LA-N	625	16	.282	.301	.418	302	5	.285	.311	.381	323	11	.279	.291	.452	306	10	.258	.274	.415	319	6	.304	.325	.420	99	2	.273	.298	.384	526	14	.283	.301	.424
1983	SD-N	388	14	.294	.344	.459	192	8	.292	.344	.474	196	6	.296	.343	.444	297	12	.293	.346	.478	91	2	.297	.337	.396	105	7	.333	.402	.590	283	7	.279	.320	.410
1984	SD-N	617	8	.284	.307	.373	302	5	.278	.303	.381	315	3	.289	.310	.365	302	4	.281	.303	.368	315	4	.286	.310	.378	195	3	.292	.327	.390	422	5	.280	.297	.365
1985	SD-N	654	17	.281	.318	.430	313	10	.288	.331	.454	341	7	.279	.306	.408	307	12	.267	.292	.440	347	5	.294	.340	.421	209	9	.297	.345	.502	445	8	.274	.305	.396
1986	SD-N	557	21	.255	.284	.408	279	11	.244	.282	.398	278	10	.266	.287	.417	283	13	.240	.263	.413	274	8	.270	.306	.401	184	12	.283	.311	.527	373	9	.241	.271	.349
1987	SD-N	76	1	.211	.231	.276	33	0	.242	.265	.273	43	1	.186	.205	.279	76	1	.211	.231	.276	0	0	—	—	—	31	1	.258	.258	.387	45	0	.178	.213	.200
TOTALS		5293	162	.290	.323	.439	2611	95	.297	.330	.458	2682	67	.283	.317	.420	2733	97	.278	.310	.436	2560	65	.303	.338	.442	1318	57	.296	.333	.488	3975	105	.288	.320	.423
■ Jason Giambi BL/TR																																				
1995	Oak-A	176	6	.256	.364	.398	97	3	.227	.333	.361	79	3	.291	.400	.443	11	0	.182	.308	.182	165	6	.261	.367	.412	18	1	.222	.333	.389	158	5	.259	.367	.399
1996	Oak-A	536	20	.291	.355	.481	234	6	.312	.404	.504	302	14	.275	.314	.464	293	16	.307	.370	.536	243	4	.272	.337	.416	126	2	.238	.307	.349	410	18	.307	.370	.522
1997	Oak-A	519	20	.293	.362	.495	261	14	.314	.392	.559	258	6	.271	.332	.430	247	8	.316	.370	.510	272	12	.272	.356	.482	126	6	.302	.397	.492	393	14	.290	.350	.496
1998	Oak-A	562	27	.295	.384	.489	275	12	.280	.374	.469	287	15	.310	.393	.509	277	10	.278	.372	.448	285	17	.312	.395	.530	206	8	.257	.351	.413	356	19	.317	.402	.534
1999	Oak-A	575	33	.315	.422	.553	278	17	.353	.446	.604	297	16	.279	.398	.505	273	15	.267	.378	.484	302	18	.358	.459	.616	181	8	.282	.381	.481	394	25	.330	.440	.586
2000	Oak-A	510	43	.333	.476	.647	252	23	.349	.499	.675	258	20	.318	.452	.620	261	22	.345	.482	.667	249	21	.321	.469	.627	176	7	.324	.427	.511	334	36	.338	.499	.719
TOTALS		2878	149	.302	.399	.524	1397	75	.315	.419	.548	1481	74	.290	.381	.501	1362	71	.301	.395	.525	1516	78	.303	.403	.523	833	32	.280	.375	.450	2045	117	.311	.409	.554
■ Kirk Gibson BL/TL																																				
1979	Det-A	38	1	.237	.256	.395	24	0	.292	.292	.417	14	1	.143	.200	.357	0	0	—	—	—	38	1	.237	.256	.395	5	0	.400	.400	.600	33	1	.212	.235	.364
1980	Det-A	175	9	.263	.303	.440	72	3	.236	.287	.375	103	6	.282	.315	.485	175	9	.263	.303	.440	0	0	—	—	—	59	2	.153	.206	.254	116	7	.319	.352	.534
1981	Det-A	290	9	.328	.369	.479	127	4	.339	.380	.504	163	5	.319	.360	.460	98	3	.235	.276	.347	192	6	.375	.415	.547	123	4	.366	.395	.512	167	5	.299	.350	.455
1982	Det-A	266	8	.278	.341	.444	129	4	.271	.326	.411	137	4	.285	.355	.474	258	8	.275	.342	.442	8	0	.375	.333	.500	95	2	.221	.288	.316	171	6	.310	.370	.515
1983	Det-A	401	15	.227	.320	.414	193	5	.218	.311	.394	208	10	.236	.329	.433	191	6	.225	.301	.408	210	9	.229	.337	.419	40	1	.150	.205	.275	361	14	.235	.333	.429
1984	Det-A	531	27	.282	.363	.516	262	11	.275	.349	.508	269	16	.290	.377	.524	244	11	.279	.341	.496	287	16	.286	.382	.533	168	9	.256	.333	.464	363	18	.295	.377	.540
1985	Det-A	581	29	.287	.364	.518	286	18	.311	.384	.580	295	11	.264	.345	.458	264	16	.288	.358	.553	317	13	.287	.370	.489	170	7	.224	.297	.424	411	22	.314	.392	.557
1986	Det-A	441	28	.268	.371	.492	216	15	.278	.378	.505	225	13	.258	.365	.480	140	10	.286	.422	.550	301	18	.259	.346	.465	164	7	.262	.360	.421	277	21	.271	.378	.534
1987	Det-A	487	24	.277	.372	.489	240	14	.242	.350	.471	247	10	.312	.394	.506	198	9	.298	.389	.520	289	15	.263	.361	.467	179	4	.268	.374	.385	308	20	.282	.371	.549
1988	LA-N	542	25	.290	.377	.483	256	14	.316	.389	.527	286	11	.266	.366	.444	267	14	.288	.374	.513	275	11	.291	.379	.455	204	11	.294	.344	.520	338	14	.287	.396	.462
1989	LA-N	253	9	.213	.312	.368	135	4	.222	.318	.378	118	5	.203	.304	.356	193	8	.238	.336	.415	60	1	.133	.232	.217	95	4	.126	.227	.263	158	5	.266	.363	.430
1990	LA-N	315	8	.260	.345	.400	157	2	.248	.339	.338	158	6	.272	.352	.462	60	3	.200	.279	.383	255	5	.275	.361	.404	102	3	.255	.347	.412	213	5	.263	.344	.394
1991	KC-A	462	16	.236	.341	.403	239	4	.222	.327	.343	223	12	.251	.356	.466	251	12	.235	.325	.434	211	4	.237	.360	.365	132	2	.197	.307	.303	330	14	.252	.355	.442
1992	Pit-N	56	2	.196	.237	.304	16	0	.188	.278	.188	40	2	.200	.220	.350	56	2	.196	.237	.304	0	0	—	—	—	7	0	.000	.000	.000	49	2	.224	.269	.347
1993	Det-A	403	13	.261	.337	.442	197	5	.254	.326	.421	206	8	.267	.348	.442	211	7	.251	.342	.427	192	6	.271	.332	.438	40	0	.275	.326	.325	363	13	.259	.338	.444
1994	Det-A	330	23	.276	.358	.548	164	9	.305	.380	.530	166	14	.247	.337	.566	211	13	.265	.354	.507	119	10	.294	.365	.622	33	3	.273	.350	.576	297	20	.276	.359	.545
1995	Det-A	227	9	.260	.358	.449	109	7	.257	.359	.541	118	2	.263	.358	.364	148	9	.264	.370	.493	79	0	.253	.337	.367	34	2	.265	.316	.500	193	7	.259	.366	.440
TOTALS		5798	255	.268	.352	.463	2822	119	.268	.351	.462	2976	136	.267	.353	.464	2965	140	.263	.344	.467	2833	115	.273	.359	.459	1650	61	.247	.324	.407	4148	194	.276	.362	.486
■ Brian Giles BL/TL																																				
1995	Cle-A	9	1	.556	.556	.889	7	0	.429	.429	.429	2	1	1.000	1.000	2.500	0	0	—	—	—	9	1	.556	.556	.889	3	0	.667	.667	.667	6	1	.500	.500	1.000
1996	Cle-A	121	5	.355	.434	.612	54	2	.315	.406	.519	67	3	.388	.456	.687	0	0	—	—	—	121	5	.355	.434	.612	22	0	.364	.440	.500	99	5	.354	.432	.636
1997	Cle-A	377	17	.268	.368	.459	197	7	.239	.346	.406	180	10	.300	.393	.517	130	8	.254	.368	.492	247	9	.275	.369	.441	61	1	.295	.429	.443	316	16	.263	.356	.462
1998	Cle-A	350	16	.269	.396	.460	170	10	.306	.441	.547	180	6	.233	.352	.378	144	10	.243	.390	.479	206	6	.286	.401	.447	48	0	.229	.383	.250	302	16	.275	.398	.493
1999	Pit-N	521	39	.315	.418	.614	265	24	.336	.443	.683	256	15	.293	.390	.543	265	16	.302	.395	.558	256	23	.328	.440	.672	177	9	.299	.393	.520	344	30	.323	.430	.663
2000	Pit-N	559	35	.315	.432	.594	269	16	.323	.446	.606	290	19	.307	.418	.583	289	21	.322	.428	.637	270	14	.307	.435	.548	150	5	.293	.393	.447	409	30	.323	.446	.648
TOTALS		1937	113	.301	.410	.551	962	59	.307	.423	.570	975	54	.295	.397	.533	828	55	.291	.402	.562	1109	58	.308	.416	.544	461	15	.295	.401	.458	1476	98	.303	.413	.581
■ Bernard Gilkey BR/TR																																				
1990	StL-N	64	1	.297	.375	.484	33	0	.152	.243	.242	31	1	.452	.514	.742	0	0	—	—	—	64	1	.297	.375	.484	29	0	.276	.364	.483	35	1	.314	.385	.486
1991	StL-N	268	5	.216	.316	.313	149	2	.215	.316	.295	119	3	.218	.317	.336	185	3	.232	.336	.324	83	2	.181	.271	.289	137	2	.190	.297	.270	131	3	.244	.336	.359

		TOTAL					HOME					AWAY					1ST HALF					2ND HALF					LEFT					RIGHT				
YEAR	TM/L	AB	HR	AVG	OBP	SLG	AB	HR	AVG	OBP	SLG	AB	HR	AVG	OBP	SLG	AB	HR	AVG	OBP	SLG	AB	HR	AVG	OBP	SLG	AB	HR	AVG	OBP	SLG	AB	HR	AVG	OBP	SLG
1992	StL-N	384	7	.302	.364	.427	196	3	.296	.338	.418	188	4	.309	.391	.436	128	0	.328	.379	.414	256	7	.289	.358	.434	176	2	.352	.402	.449	208	5	.260	.333	.409
1993	StL-N	557	16	.305	.370	.481	265	7	.325	.380	.506	292	9	.288	.361	.459	231	5	.320	.381	.502	326	11	.294	.362	.466	137	4	.343	.396	.518	420	12	.293	.362	.469
1994	StL-N	380	6	.253	.336	.363	180	0	.189	.279	.233	200	6	.310	.388	.480	243	4	.259	.344	.379	137	2	.241	.323	.336	104	2	.279	.395	.385	276	4	.243	.313	.355
1995	StL-N	480	17	.298	.358	.490	238	5	.277	.342	.445	242	12	.318	.375	.533	222	8	.311	.352	.464	258	9	.287	.364	.512	106	2	.311	.378	.472	374	15	.294	.353	.495
1996	NY-N	571	30	.317	.393	.562	279	14	.330	.401	.566	292	16	.305	.386	.558	300	15	.310	.368	.523	271	15	.325	.420	.605	134	7	.343	.399	.604	437	23	.309	.392	.549
1997	NY-N	518	18	.249	.338	.417	235	7	.226	.333	.366	283	11	.269	.343	.459	257	7	.206	.310	.342	261	11	.291	.366	.490	139	9	.288	.386	.561	379	9	.235	.320	.364
1998	NY-N	264	4	.227	.317	.330	138	1	.239	.331	.312	126	3	.214	.301	.349	198	3	.242	.332	.354	66	1	.182	.273	.258	67	1	.224	.333	.328	197	3	.228	.311	.330
1998	Ari-N	101	1	.248	.327	.277	54	1	.259	.310	.315	47	0	.234	.345	.234	0	0	—	—	—	101	1	.248	.327	.277	34	0	.176	.222	.176	67	1	.284	.377	.328
1999	Ari-N	204	8	.294	.379	.500	78	4	.333	.417	.590	126	4	.270	.354	.444	104	4	.298	.390	.481	100	4	.290	.368	.520	104	4	.337	.438	.587	100	4	.250	.313	.410
2000	Ari-N	73	2	.110	.185	.205	40	1	.100	.140	.175	33	1	.121	.237	.242	73	2	.110	.185	.205	0	0	—	—	—	46	2	.109	.212	.261	27	0	.111	.138	.111
2000	Bos-A	91	1	.231	.327	.341	41	0	.220	.289	.317	50	1	.240	.356	.360	0	0	—	—	—	91	1	.231	.327	.341	58	0	.224	.308	.310	33	1	.242	.359	.394
TOTALS		3955	116	.275	.352	.435	1926	45	.266	.341	.408	2029	71	.283	.362	.460	1941	51	.270	.345	.414	2014	65	.279	.358	.455	1271	35	.287	.368	.448	2684	81	.269	.344	.429
■ Dan Gladden BR/TR																																				
1983	SF-N	63	1	.222	.275	.302	28	1	.214	.324	.321	35	0	.229	.229	.286	0	0	—	—	—	63	1	.222	.275	.302	15	0	.267	.313	.333	48	1	.208	.264	.292
1984	SF-N	342	4	.351	.410	.447	170	4	.371	.432	.482	172	0	.331	.388	.413	18	2	.444	.545	.833	324	2	.346	.402	.426	80	2	.375	.451	.525	262	2	.344	.397	.424
1985	SF-N	502	7	.243	.307	.347	254	6	.232	.306	.362	248	1	.254	.307	.331	265	2	.219	.274	.306	237	5	.270	.342	.392	147	1	.259	.335	.320	355	6	.237	.295	.358
1986	SF-N	351	4	.276	.357	.362	162	1	.272	.376	.321	189	3	.280	.340	.397	185	2	.281	.348	.362	166	2	.271	.366	.361	123	0	.276	.373	.325	228	4	.276	.348	.382
1987	Min-A	438	8	.249	.312	.361	203	4	.271	.342	.404	235	4	.230	.285	.323	219	4	.265	.329	.370	219	4	.233	.294	.352	163	2	.258	.307	.362	275	6	.244	.315	.360
1988	Min-A	576	11	.269	.325	.403	300	8	.317	.365	.473	276	3	.217	.282	.326	289	6	.270	.319	.433	287	5	.268	.330	.373	159	6	.321	.388	.509	417	5	.249	.300	.362
1989	Min-A	461	8	.295	.331	.410	222	1	.284	.331	.351	239	7	.305	.331	.464	263	4	.293	.337	.395	198	4	.298	.322	.429	157	3	.306	.345	.427	304	5	.289	.323	.401
1990	Min-A	534	5	.275	.314	.376	263	2	.300	.339	.418	271	3	.251	.290	.336	283	4	.293	.327	.403	251	1	.255	.300	.347	163	2	.270	.297	.356	371	3	.278	.322	.385
1991	Min-A	461	6	.247	.306	.356	244	3	.266	.333	.381	217	3	.226	.275	.327	239	4	.259	.328	.377	222	2	.234	.282	.333	118	1	.254	.341	.390	343	5	.245	.293	.344
1992	Det-A	417	7	.254	.304	.357	177	3	.226	.291	.339	240	4	.275	.314	.371	170	3	.288	.341	.406	247	4	.231	.279	.324	124	4	.282	.341	.460	293	3	.242	.288	.314
1993	Det-A	356	13	.267	.312	.433	167	11	.251	.302	.497	189	2	.280	.320	.376	94	3	.266	.304	.436	262	10	.267	.314	.431	138	8	.261	.304	.478	218	5	.271	.316	.404
TOTALS		4501	74	.270	.324	.382	2190	44	.279	.341	.403	2311	30	.261	.309	.362	2025	34	.272	.325	.389	2476	40	.269	.324	.377	1387	29	.283	.343	.410	3114	45	.264	.316	.370
■ Doug Glanville BR/TR																																				
1996	Chi-N	83	1	.241	.264	.361	39	1	.179	.195	.308	44	0	.295	.326	.409	28	0	.214	.207	.321	55	1	.255	.293	.382	48	1	.292	.327	.438	35	0	.171	.171	.257
1997	Chi-N	474	4	.300	.333	.392	254	2	.327	.366	.425	220	2	.268	.294	.355	178	1	.298	.339	.410	296	3	.301	.330	.382	156	3	.276	.317	.372	318	1	.311	.341	.403
1998	Phi-N	678	8	.279	.325	.376	325	3	.305	.368	.403	353	5	.255	.282	.351	347	6	.311	.347	.438	331	2	.245	.302	.311	162	2	.259	.298	.346	516	6	.285	.333	.386
1999	Phi-N	628	11	.325	.376	.457	304	5	.286	.345	.428	324	6	.361	.404	.485	301	5	.312	.375	.432	327	6	.336	.376	.480	140	2	.250	.340	.336	488	9	.346	.386	.492
2000	Phi-N	637	8	.275	.307	.374	315	3	.276	.312	.368	322	5	.273	.302	.379	305	5	.259	.300	.361	332	3	.289	.314	.386	139	1	.237	.285	.302	498	7	.285	.314	.394
TOTALS		2500	32	.292	.333	.398	1237	14	.293	.343	.402	1263	18	.291	.323	.395	1159	17	.293	.338	.409	1341	15	.291	.329	.389	645	9	.259	.311	.347	1855	23	.304	.341	.416
■ Troy Glaus BR/TR																																				
1998	Ana-A	165	1	.218	.280	.291	68	0	.221	.257	.294	97	1	.216	.296	.289	0	0	—	—	—	165	1	.218	.280	.291	32	0	.281	.378	.406	133	1	.203	.255	.263
1999	Ana-A	551	29	.240	.331	.450	263	12	.243	.345	.445	288	17	.236	.318	.455	262	11	.229	.299	.424	289	18	.249	.359	.474	116	5	.216	.321	.431	435	24	.246	.334	.455
2000	Ana-A	563	47	.284	.404	.604	271	24	.266	.381	.587	292	23	.301	.425	.620	272	23	.305	.417	.636	291	24	.265	.393	.574	130	17	.369	.500	.854	433	30	.259	.373	.529
TOTALS		1279	77	.256	.358	.497	602	36	.251	.352	.492	677	41	.261	.363	.502	534	34	.268	.361	.532	745	43	.248	.356	.472	278	22	.295	.415	.626	1001	55	.246	.341	.462
■ Juan Gonzalez BR/TR																																				
1989	Tex-A	60	1	.150	.227	.250	37	1	.135	.179	.216	23	0	.174	.296	.304	0	0	—	—	—	60	1	.150	.227	.250	24	0	.125	.160	.125	36	1	.167	.268	.333
1990	Tex-A	90	4	.289	.316	.522	47	3	.340	.373	.660	43	1	.233	.250	.372	0	0	—	—	—	90	4	.289	.316	.522	24	1	.292	.333	.542	66	3	.288	.309	.515
1991	Tex-A	545	27	.264	.321	.479	262	7	.267	.328	.408	283	20	.261	.315	.544	220	10	.300	.376	.509	325	17	.240	.281	.458	147	9	.299	.366	.531	398	18	.251	.304	.460
1992	Tex-A	584	43	.260	.304	.529	294	19	.265	.305	.534	290	24	.255	.303	.524	289	18	.270	.312	.505	295	25	.251	.296	.553	158	8	.253	.302	.443	426	35	.263	.304	.561
1993	Tex-A	536	46	.310	.368	.632	273	24	.330	.386	.656	263	22	.289	.349	.608	240	20	.325	.389	.646	296	26	.297	.351	.622	108	9	.333	.374	.657	428	37	.304	.367	.626
1994	Tex-A	422	19	.275	.330	.472	228	6	.272	.346	.425	194	13	.278	.311	.526	280	11	.257	.319	.454	142	8	.310	.353	.507	94	5	.298	.382	.521	328	14	.268	.314	.457
1995	Tex-A	352	27	.295	.324	.594	161	15	.317	.349	.689	191	12	.277	.302	.513	98	8	.296	.294	.633	254	19	.295	.335	.579	101	9	.327	.352	.653	251	18	.283	.312	.570
1996	Tex-A	541	47	.314	.368	.643	237	23	.333	.408	.713	304	24	.299	.335	.589	217	17	.304	.366	.594	324	30	.321	.370	.676	141	20	.376	.436	.887	400	27	.292	.344	.558
1997	Tex-A	533	42	.296	.335	.589	246	18	.289	.336	.577	287	24	.303	.334	.599	222	17	.270	.317	.554	311	25	.315	.348	.614	148	15	.297	.355	.649	385	27	.296	.327	.566
1998	Tex-A	606	45	.318	.366	.630	293	21	.345	.405	.648	313	24	.294	.328	.613	334	24	.296	.335	.590	272	21	.346	.403	.680	155	11	.355	.429	.652	451	34	.306	.344	.623
1999	Tex-A	562	39	.326	.378	.601	271	14	.321	.371	.550	291	25	.330	.385	.649	280	23	.318	.362	.614	282	16	.333	.394	.589	114	9	.342	.409	.632	448	30	.321	.371	.594
2000	Det-A	461	22	.289	.337	.505	217	8	.267	.331	.461	244	14	.307	.342	.545	254	13	.264	.313	.512	207	9	.319	.366	.498	114	6	.360	.403	.579	347	16	.265	.315	.481
TOTALS		5292	362	.294	.343	.566	2566	159	.299	.355	.561	2726	203	.288	.331	.570	2434	161	.289	.340	.556	2858	201	.297	.345	.574	1328	102	.319	.376	.610	3964	260	.285	.331	.551
■ Luis Gonzalez BL/TR																																				
1990	Hou-N	21	0	.190	.261	.286	7	0	.286	.444	.429	14	0	.143	.143	.214	0	0	—	—	—	21	0	.190	.261	.286	1	0	.000	.000	.000	20	0	.200	.273	.300
1991	Hou-N	473	13	.254	.320	.433	227	4	.273	.339	.445	246	9	.236	.303	.423	240	7	.229	.294	.433	233	6	.279	.346	.433	122	1	.172	.257	.270	351	12	.282	.342	.490
1992	Hou-N	387	10	.243	.289	.385	204	4	.206	.255	.324	183	6	.284	.328	.454	164	6	.226	.273	.384	223	4	.256	.301	.386	80	1	.350	.404	.512	307	9	.215	.258	.352
1993	Hou-N	540	15	.300	.361	.457	265	8	.291	.341	.445	275	7	.309	.379	.469	233	8	.262	.336	.416	307	7	.329	.380	.489	172	3	.302	.369	.413	368	12	.299	.357	.478
1994	Hou-N	392	8	.273	.353	.429	204	3	.294	.365	.436	188	5	.250	.341	.420	262	5	.248	.315	.385	130	3	.323	.426	.515	101	1	.267	.347	.366	291	7	.275	.355	.450
1995	Hou-N	209	6	.258	.322	.431	97	1	.268	.327	.392	112	5	.250	.317	.464	209	6	.258	.322	.431	0	0	—	—	—	49	2	.265	.333	.551	160	4	.256	.318	.394
1995	Chi-N	262	7	.290	.384	.473	133	5	.278	.390	.459	129	2	.302	.378	.488	8	0	.125	.125	.125	254	7	.295	.391	.484	63	2	.270	.356	.460	199	5	.296	.393	.477
1996	Chi-N	483	15	.271	.354	.443	229	6	.310	.392	.493	254	9	.236	.318	.398	235	6	.272	.359	.430	248	9	.270	.349	.456	80	2	.188	.244	.287	403	13	.288	.374	.474
1997	Hou-N	550	10	.258	.345	.376	253	4	.261	.348	.375	297	6	.256	.343	.377	282	3	.284	.370	.387	268	7	.231	.320	.366	132	3	.250	.338	.356	418	7	.261	.348	.383
1998	Det-A	547	23	.267	.340	.475	274	15	.230	.312	.449	273	8	.304	.369	.502	274	8	.303	.376	.493	273	15	.231	.304	.458	151	1	.278	.359	.377	396	22	.263	.333	.513
1999	Ari-N	614	26	.336	.403	.549	299	10	.318	.377	.528	315	16	.352	.428	.568	286	13	.364	.427	.594	328	13	.311	.382	.509	165	3	.327	.421	.479	449	23	.339	.396	.575
2000	Ari-N	618	31	.311	.392	.544	305	14	.341	.423	.570	313	17	.281	.361	.518	299	17	.298	.393	.538	319	14	.323	.391	.549	177	8	.254	.335	.446	441	23	.333	.415	.583
TOTALS		5096	164	.281	.355	.460	2497	74	.282	.355	.456	2599	90	.280	.355	.463	2492	79	.278	.352	.454	2604	85	.285	.358	.465	1293	27	.268	.347	.404	3803	137	.286	.358	.479
■ Tom Goodwin BL/TR																																				
1991	LA-N	7	0	.143	.143	.143	1	0	1.000	1.000	1.000	6	0	.000	.000	.000	0	0	—	—	—	7	0	.143	.143	.143	2	0	.000	.000	.000	5	0	.200	.200	.200
1992	LA-N	73	0	.233	.291	.274	39	0	.231	.250	.231	34	0	.235	.333	.324	2	0	.500	.500	.500	71	0	.225	.286	.268	8	0	.250	.250	.250	65	0	.231	.296	.277
1993	LA-N	17	0	.294	.333	.353	7	0	.286	.286	.286	10	0	.300	.364	.400	2	0	.000	.000	.000	15	0	.333	.375	.400	1	0	.000	.000	.000	16	0	.313	.353	.375
1994	KC-A	2	0	.000	.000	.000	2	0	.000	.000	.000	0	0	—	—	—	2	0	.000	.000	.000	0	0	—	—	—	0	0	—	—	—	2	0	.000	.000	.000
1995	KC-A	480	4	.287	.346	.358	239	2	.305	.354	.397	241	2	.270	.338	.320	183	1	.290	.366	.339	297	3	.286	.333	.370	115	0	.252	.312	.296	365	4	.299	.357	.378
1996	KC-A	524	1	.282	.334	.330	259	0	.228	.281	.263	265	1	.336	.385	.396	287	1	.268	.324	.307	237	0	.300	.346	.359	162	0	.315	.380	.389	362	1	.268	.313	.304
1997	KC-A	367	2	.272	.311	.346	174	0	.270	.312	.305	193	2	.275	.310	.383	288	1	.292	.329	.365	79	1	.203	.247	.278	113	0	.292	.328	.354	254	2	.264	.304	.343
1997	Tex-A	207	0	.237	.319	.319	79	0	.304	.404	.367	128	0	.195	.262	.289	0	0	—	—	—	207	0	.237	.319	.319	47	0	.234	.294	.277	160	0	.237	.326	.331
1998	Tex-A	520	2	.290	.378	.338	260	2	.277	.341	.338	260	0	.304	.412	.338	286	1	.280	.373	.308	234	1	.303	.384	.376	80	0	.300	.364	.325	440	2	.289	.380	.341
1999	Tex-A	405	3	.259	.324	.341	200	1	.260	.338	.330	205	2	.259	.309	.351	212	1	.241	.319	.311	193	2	.280	.329	.373	61	0	.262	.313	.295	344	3	.259	.325	.349
2000	Col-N	317	5	.271	.368	.394	149	4	.342	.429	.517	168	1	.208	.313	.286	244	4	.316	.408	.455	73	1	.123	.235	.192	51	2	.373	.433	.588	266	3	.252	.356	.357
2000	LA-N	211	1	.251	.310	.289	119	0	.252	.282	.277	92	1	.250	.343	.304	0	0	—	—	—	211	1	.251	.310	.289	55	0	.309	.333	.345	156	1	.231	.302	.269
TOTALS		3130	18	.273	.339	.340	1528	9	.275	.336	.341	1602	9	.270	.342	.340	1506	9	.281	.353	.346	1624	9	.265	.326	.335	695	2	.291	.345	.353	2435	16	.267	.337	.337
■ Mark Grace BL/TL																																				
1988	Chi-N	486	7	.296	.371	.403	250	0	.296	.378	.340	236	7	.297	.364	.470	188	4	.298	.371	.426	298	3	.295	.371	.389	147	3	.286	.373	.429	339	4	.301	.370	.392
1989	Chi-N	510	13	.314	.405	.457	258	8	.337	.440	.504	252	5	.290	.367	.409	212	2	.316	.399	.392	298	11	.312	.409	.503	159	4	.264	.343	.421	351	9	.336	.431	.473
1990	Chi-N	589	9	.309	.372	.413	308	4	.331	.391	.429	281	5	.285	.352	.395	281	2	.281	.348	.359	308	7	.334	.395	.461	185	3	.308	.378	.422	404	6	.309	.369	.408
1991	Chi-N	619	8	.273	.346	.373	322	5	.289	.364	.398	297	3	.256	.327	.347	281	4	.278	.349	.388	338	4	.269	.344	.361	252	2	.270	.333	.345	367	6	.275	.355	.392
1992	Chi-N	603	9	.307	.380	.430	285	5	.281	.373	.393	318	4	.330	.387	.462	266	4	.327	.419	.466	337	5	.291	.347	.401	225	3	.280	.332	.378	378	6	.323	.407	.460
1993	Chi-N	594	14	.325	.393	.475	300	5	.353	.421	.480	294	9	.296	.364	.469	288	8	.330	.388	.507	306	6	.320	.397	.444	193	6	.352	.412	.528	401	8	.312	.383	.449
1994	Chi-N	403	6	.298	.370	.414	222	5	.270	.349	.369	181	1	.331	.396	.470	268	1	.287	.366	.369	135	5	.319	.378	.504	122	1	.295	.343	.393	281	5	.299	.381	.423
1995	Chi-N	552	16	.326	.395	.516	280	4	.375	.421	.550	272	12	.276	.369	.482	229	9	.336	.395	.594	323	7	.319	.395	.461	186	3	.290	.330	.430	366	13	.344	.425	.560
1996	Chi-N	547	9	.331	.396	.455	290	4	.341	.401	.455	257	5	.319	.391	.455	246	3	.333	.398	.451	301	6	.329	.395	.458	153	1	.301	.352	.366	394	8	.343	.412	.490
1997	Chi-N	555	13	.319	.409	.465	276	6	.355	.455	.489	279	7	.283	.361	.441	264	8	.318	.424	.466	291	5	.320	.395	.464	143	3	.336	.412	.469	412	10	.313	.408	.464
1998	Chi-N	595	17	.309	.401	.471	284	7	.327	.428	.482	311	10	.293	.375	.460	312	8	.333	.416	.497	283	9	.283	.385	.442	203	4	.271	.351	.374	392	13	.329	.426	.520
1999	Chi-N	593	16	.309	.390	.481	297	8	.330	.408	.522	296	8	.287	.371	.439	268	10	.306	.404	.496	325	6	.311	.377	.468	199	4	.307	.364	.457	394	12	.310	.402	.492
2000	Chi-N	510	11	.280	.394	.429	260	3	.296	.414	.423	250	8	.264	.373	.436	220	7	.291	.404	.455	290	4	.272	.386	.410	131	6	.305	.419	.511	379	5	.272	.386	.401
TOTALS		7156	148	.308	.386	.445	3632	64	.323	.404	.450	3524	84	.292	.368	.440	3323	70	.311	.391	.451	3833	78	.305	.382	.440	2298	43	.296	.363	.421	4858	105	.313	.397	.457

YEAR	TM/L	TOTAL AB	HR	AVG	OBP	SLG	HOME AB	HR	AVG	OBP	SLG	AWAY AB	HR	AVG	OBP	SLG	1ST HALF AB	HR	AVG	OBP	SLG	2ND HALF AB	HR	AVG	OBP	SLG	LEFT AB	HR	AVG	OBP	SLG	RIGHT AB	HR	AVG	OBP	SLG
■ Shawn Green BL/TL																																				
1993	Tor-A	6	0	.000	.000	.000	0	0	—	—	—	6	0	.000	.000	.000	0	0	—	—	—	6	0	.000	.000	.000	1	0	.000	.000	.000	5	0	.000	.000	.000
1994	Tor-A	33	0	.091	.118	.121	13	0	.077	.077	.077	20	0	.100	.143	.150	31	0	.097	.125	.129	2	0	.000	.000	.000	0	0	—	—	—	33	0	.091	.118	.121
1995	Tor-A	379	15	.288	.326	.509	182	5	.247	.292	.418	197	10	.325	.357	.594	139	6	.252	.318	.482	240	9	.308	.331	.525	45	0	.222	.234	.333	334	15	.296	.338	.533
1996	Tor-A	422	11	.280	.342	.448	202	7	.272	.338	.465	220	4	.286	.346	.432	215	6	.233	.297	.391	207	5	.329	.389	.507	59	1	.254	.343	.356	363	10	.284	.342	.463
1997	Tor-A	429	16	.287	.340	.469	210	10	.276	.338	.490	219	6	.297	.343	.447	140	6	.271	.331	.471	289	10	.294	.345	.467	101	0	.287	.339	.337	328	16	.287	.341	.509
1998	Tor-A	630	35	.278	.334	.510	304	21	.280	.350	.576	326	14	.276	.319	.448	315	15	.283	.334	.473	315	20	.273	.334	.546	172	8	.221	.265	.413	458	27	.299	.360	.546
1999	Tor-A	614	42	.309	.384	.588	289	20	.284	.354	.547	325	22	.332	.410	.625	280	20	.318	.399	.614	334	22	.302	.371	.566	164	8	.280	.376	.506	450	34	.320	.386	.618
2000	LA-N	610	24	.269	.367	.472	297	15	.300	.390	.539	313	9	.240	.346	.409	291	12	.309	.423	.533	319	12	.232	.312	.417	185	4	.259	.333	.389	425	20	.273	.381	.508
TOTALS		3123	143	.282	.349	.499	1497	78	.277	.347	.512	1626	65	.287	.351	.486	1411	65	.279	.355	.494	1712	78	.285	.344	.502	727	21	.256	.323	.407	2396	122	.290	.357	.526
■ Mike Greenwell BL/TR																																				
1985	Bos-A	31	4	.323	.382	.742	10	1	.400	.455	.800	21	3	.286	.348	.714	0	0	—	—	—	31	4	.323	.382	.742	6	2	.667	.714	1.833	25	2	.240	.296	.480
1986	Bos-A	35	0	.314	.400	.371	12	0	.417	.462	.417	23	0	.261	.370	.348	0	0	—	—	—	35	0	.314	.400	.371	3	0	.333	.333	.667	32	0	.313	.405	.344
1987	Bos-A	412	19	.328	.386	.570	217	8	.327	.387	.571	195	11	.328	.385	.569	136	9	.301	.351	.588	276	10	.341	.403	.562	74	1	.378	.420	.514	338	18	.317	.379	.583
1988	Bos-A	590	22	.325	.416	.531	305	12	.331	.417	.564	285	10	.319	.414	.495	264	14	.341	.439	.587	326	8	.313	.396	.485	197	4	.289	.332	.416	393	18	.344	.453	.588
1989	Bos-A	578	14	.308	.370	.443	286	6	.325	.387	.465	292	8	.291	.352	.421	303	8	.300	.373	.429	275	6	.316	.366	.458	202	2	.272	.295	.332	376	12	.327	.406	.503
1990	Bos-A	610	14	.297	.367	.434	306	6	.310	.379	.451	304	8	.283	.354	.418	276	2	.268	.354	.326	334	12	.320	.378	.524	202	3	.257	.326	.361	408	11	.316	.386	.471
1991	Bos-A	544	9	.300	.350	.419	255	5	.302	.365	.451	289	4	.298	.337	.391	272	5	.316	.366	.434	272	4	.283	.334	.404	168	4	.327	.357	.476	376	5	.287	.347	.394
1992	Bos-A	180	2	.233	.307	.278	83	0	.229	.313	.229	97	2	.237	.302	.320	180	2	.233	.307	.278	0	0	—	—	—	58	0	.224	.308	.241	122	2	.238	.307	.295
1993	Bos-A	540	13	.315	.379	.480	247	6	.332	.401	.522	293	7	.300	.361	.444	239	6	.301	.365	.473	301	7	.326	.391	.485	161	5	.304	.362	.466	379	8	.319	.387	.485
1994	Bos-A	327	11	.269	.348	.453	180	10	.272	.350	.511	147	1	.265	.345	.381	251	9	.283	.370	.478	76	2	.224	.268	.368	104	5	.288	.313	.500	223	6	.260	.363	.430
1995	Bos-A	481	15	.297	.349	.459	235	6	.319	.373	.489	246	9	.276	.325	.431	226	6	.301	.360	.451	255	9	.294	.338	.467	142	5	.268	.329	.423	339	10	.310	.357	.475
1996	Bos-A	295	7	.295	.336	.441	143	4	.287	.327	.462	152	3	.303	.345	.421	90	1	.222	.258	.311	205	6	.327	.371	.498	81	0	.346	.372	.432	214	7	.276	.323	.444
TOTALS		4623	130	.303	.368	.463	2279	64	.312	.379	.490	2344	66	.294	.357	.437	2237	62	.293	.364	.441	2386	68	.312	.371	.484	1398	31	.293	.338	.421	3225	99	.307	.380	.481
■ Rusty Greer BL/TL																																				
1994	Tex-A	277	10	.314	.410	.487	143	3	.287	.393	.378	134	7	.343	.429	.604	150	5	.307	.390	.487	127	5	.323	.433	.488	72	3	.264	.313	.458	205	7	.332	.442	.498
1995	Tex-A	417	13	.271	.355	.424	190	7	.232	.332	.379	227	6	.304	.375	.463	176	6	.273	.377	.432	241	7	.270	.338	.419	78	2	.244	.314	.346	339	11	.277	.364	.442
1996	Tex-A	542	18	.332	.397	.530	271	9	.358	.425	.561	271	9	.306	.368	.498	273	7	.315	.380	.491	269	11	.349	.414	.569	174	6	.322	.381	.517	368	12	.337	.405	.535
1997	Tex-A	601	26	.321	.405	.531	300	18	.370	.446	.637	301	8	.272	.363	.425	293	11	.334	.430	.539	308	15	.308	.380	.523	178	7	.309	.406	.511	423	19	.326	.405	.539
1998	Tex-A	598	16	.306	.386	.455	285	8	.323	.414	.488	313	8	.291	.361	.425	311	7	.280	.374	.412	287	9	.334	.401	.502	175	4	.337	.401	.451	423	12	.293	.380	.456
1999	Tex-A	556	20	.300	.405	.493	258	10	.318	.434	.535	298	10	.285	.379	.456	287	7	.275	.373	.439	269	13	.327	.438	.550	124	3	.282	.411	.435	432	17	.306	.403	.509
2000	Tex-A	394	8	.297	.377	.459	199	3	.322	.409	.472	195	5	.272	.345	.446	145	2	.283	.348	.428	249	6	.305	.394	.478	98	1	.245	.330	.388	296	7	.314	.393	.483
TOTALS		3385	111	.307	.392	.486	1646	58	.323	.413	.510	1739	53	.293	.371	.463	1635	45	.297	.384	.463	1750	66	.317	.399	.507	899	26	.297	.378	.458	2486	85	.311	.397	.496
■ Bobby Grich BR/TR																																				
1978	Cal-A	487	6	.251	.357	.329	257	4	.284	.375	.362	230	2	.213	.337	.291	270	4	.237	.343	.315	217	2	.267	.374	.346	138	3	.275	.390	.406	349	3	.241	.343	.298
1979	Cal-A	534	30	.294	.365	.537	267	15	.307	.384	.554	267	15	.281	.346	.521	266	17	.323	.399	.602	268	13	.265	.331	.474	142	7	.289	.380	.528	392	23	.296	.359	.541
1980	Cal-A	498	14	.271	.377	.408	248	5	.258	.366	.363	250	9	.284	.389	.452	210	5	.257	.365	.362	288	9	.281	.386	.441	140	2	.164	.312	.236	358	12	.313	.404	.475
1981	Cal-A	352	22	.304	.378	.543	155	7	.265	.328	.445	197	15	.335	.418	.619	160	6	.275	.385	.469	192	16	.328	.372	.604	92	5	.326	.410	.511	260	17	.296	.367	.554
1982	Cal-A	506	19	.261	.371	.449	252	8	.258	.378	.437	254	11	.264	.363	.461	243	8	.276	.375	.457	263	11	.247	.366	.441	195	7	.272	.370	.467	311	12	.254	.371	.437
1983	Cal-A	387	16	.292	.414	.460	174	8	.345	.470	.523	213	8	.249	.366	.408	216	8	.269	.401	.407	171	8	.322	.432	.526	155	7	.310	.450	.490	232	9	.280	.388	.440
1984	Cal-A	363	18	.256	.357	.452	197	9	.254	.352	.426	166	9	.259	.362	.482	141	5	.248	.329	.404	222	13	.261	.373	.482	141	7	.248	.355	.433	222	11	.261	.358	.464
1985	Cal-A	479	13	.242	.355	.372	248	7	.250	.356	.371	231	6	.234	.354	.372	210	4	.238	.355	.333	269	9	.245	.356	.401	147	5	.265	.372	.442	332	8	.232	.348	.340
1986	Cal-A	313	9	.268	.354	.412	135	5	.311	.372	.496	178	4	.236	.341	.348	123	3	.244	.301	.350	190	6	.284	.386	.453	166	6	.295	.369	.458	147	3	.238	.337	.361
TOTALS		3919	147	.270	.370	.438	1933	68	.279	.376	.437	1986	79	.262	.364	.440	1839	60	.265	.366	.416	2080	87	.275	.373	.458	1316	49	.271	.378	.441	2603	98	.270	.365	.437
■ Ben Grieve BL/TR																																				
1997	Oak-A	93	3	.312	.402	.473	50	3	.240	.321	.480	43	0	.395	.490	.465	0	0	—	—	—	93	3	.312	.402	.473	38	1	.316	.409	.447	55	2	.309	.397	.491
1998	Oak-A	583	18	.288	.386	.458	286	5	.252	.328	.367	297	13	.323	.439	.545	311	12	.318	.415	.524	272	6	.254	.354	.382	217	8	.253	.345	.433	366	10	.309	.410	.473
1999	Oak-A	486	28	.265	.358	.481	243	13	.255	.343	.457	243	15	.276	.374	.506	219	9	.247	.343	.416	267	19	.281	.371	.536	109	3	.156	.240	.266	377	25	.297	.391	.544
2000	Oak-A	594	27	.279	.359	.487	293	13	.256	.329	.444	301	14	.302	.386	.528	302	15	.301	.357	.523	292	12	.257	.360	.449	190	8	.268	.338	.463	404	19	.285	.368	.498
TOTALS		1756	76	.280	.370	.475	872	34	.253	.332	.424	884	42	.307	.406	.525	832	36	.293	.375	.495	924	40	.268	.366	.457	554	20	.244	.327	.412	1202	56	.297	.390	.504
■ Ken Griffey BL/TL																																				
1989	Sea-A	455	16	.264	.329	.420	218	10	.261	.335	.459	237	6	.266	.323	.384	250	11	.284	.347	.468	205	5	.239	.307	.361	118	3	.212	.271	.339	337	13	.282	.348	.448
1990	Sea-A	597	22	.300	.366	.481	305	8	.292	.364	.452	292	14	.308	.369	.510	295	12	.332	.400	.519	302	10	.268	.333	.444	219	5	.306	.357	.447	378	17	.296	.371	.500
1991	Sea-A	548	22	.327	.399	.527	282	16	.365	.432	.617	266	6	.286	.364	.432	249	7	.273	.356	.426	299	15	.371	.435	.612	159	5	.314	.386	.472	389	17	.332	.404	.550
1992	Sea-A	565	27	.308	.361	.535	277	16	.314	.369	.581	288	11	.302	.354	.490	226	14	.292	.347	.549	339	13	.319	.371	.525	173	12	.358	.413	.624	392	15	.286	.339	.495
1993	Sea-A	582	45	.309	.408	.617	274	21	.332	.455	.646	308	24	.289	.363	.591	288	20	.309	.396	.594	294	25	.310	.420	.639	211	13	.318	.394	.569	371	32	.305	.416	.644
1994	Sea-A	433	40	.323	.402	.674	166	18	.343	.441	.771	267	22	.311	.376	.614	298	32	.319	.401	.715	135	8	.333	.403	.585	162	16	.296	.343	.654	271	24	.339	.434	.686
1995	Sea-A	260	17	.258	.379	.481	133	13	.308	.419	.639	127	4	.205	.338	.315	99	7	.263	.387	.505	161	10	.255	.374	.466	86	3	.279	.370	.419	174	14	.247	.383	.511
1996	Sea-A	545	49	.303	.392	.628	270	26	.293	.377	.633	275	23	.313	.407	.622	261	23	.299	.388	.628	284	26	.306	.396	.627	158	21	.297	.382	.741	387	28	.305	.397	.581
1997	Sea-A	608	56	.304	.382	.646	289	27	.322	.396	.675	319	29	.288	.369	.621	301	29	.309	.388	.661	307	27	.300	.376	.632	196	14	.270	.332	.536	412	42	.320	.405	.699
1998	Sea-A	633	56	.284	.365	.611	315	30	.279	.366	.632	318	26	.289	.365	.591	327	33	.281	.366	.648	306	23	.288	.364	.572	177	21	.299	.360	.701	456	35	.279	.367	.577
1999	Sea-A	606	48	.285	.384	.576	295	27	.288	.385	.617	311	21	.283	.383	.537	291	27	.306	.406	.636	315	21	.267	.363	.521	170	8	.229	.318	.412	436	40	.307	.409	.640
2000	Cin-N	520	40	.271	.387	.556	256	22	.289	.399	.602	264	18	.254	.375	.511	271	26	.244	.398	.565	249	14	.301	.373	.546	152	11	.263	.341	.513	368	29	.274	.404	.573
TOTALS		6352	438	.296	.380	.568	3080	234	.306	.393	.605	3272	204	.287	.368	.532	3156	241	.295	.383	.585	3196	197	.298	.377	.550	1981	132	.290	.358	.544	4371	306	.299	.390	.578
■ Ken Griffey BL/TL																																				
1978	Cin-N	614	10	.288	.344	.417	289	7	.284	.353	.457	325	3	.292	.336	.382	312	3	.311	.353	.436	302	7	.265	.335	.397	251	3	.267	.330	.382	363	7	.303	.354	.441
1979	Cin-N	380	8	.316	.374	.471	177	3	.299	.367	.452	203	5	.330	.380	.488	289	6	.298	.354	.446	91	2	.374	.436	.549	138	1	.297	.349	.428	242	7	.326	.388	.496
1980	Cin-N	544	13	.294	.364	.454	244	9	.299	.392	.512	300	4	.290	.340	.407	260	7	.312	.383	.477	284	6	.278	.348	.433	153	2	.268	.313	.392	391	11	.304	.383	.478
1981	Cin-N	396	2	.311	.370	.409	187	0	.299	.360	.390	209	2	.321	.380	.426	223	1	.300	.344	.404	173	1	.324	.402	.416	107	0	.327	.393	.393	289	2	.304	.362	.415
1982	NY-A	484	12	.277	.329	.407	243	8	.267	.308	.432	241	4	.286	.350	.382	209	4	.282	.323	.392	275	8	.273	.333	.418	178	3	.264	.311	.365	306	9	.284	.339	.431
1983	NY-A	458	11	.306	.355	.437	223	8	.305	.358	.462	235	3	.306	.352	.413	238	5	.336	.384	.462	220	6	.273	.324	.409	178	5	.287	.321	.410	280	6	.318	.376	.454
1984	NY-A	399	7	.273	.321	.381	208	5	.279	.327	.409	191	2	.267	.314	.351	184	0	.261	.313	.310	215	7	.284	.328	.442	124	1	.274	.300	.387	275	6	.273	.330	.378
1985	NY-A	438	10	.274	.331	.425	195	6	.292	.359	.477	243	4	.259	.307	.383	179	3	.257	.315	.408	259	7	.286	.342	.436	107	2	.243	.278	.346	331	8	.284	.347	.450
1986	NY-A	198	9	.303	.349	.475	90	5	.244	.306	.444	108	4	.352	.383	.500	198	9	.303	.349	.475	0	0	—	—	—	34	0	.235	.257	.294	164	9	.317	.366	.512
1986	Atl-N	292	12	.308	.351	.503	155	9	.342	.387	.587	137	3	.270	.310	.409	5	0	.200	.200	.200	287	12	.310	.354	.509	85	3	.259	.300	.447	207	9	.329	.372	.527
1987	Atl-N	399	14	.286	.358	.456	223	8	.291	.355	.475	176	6	.278	.362	.432	205	10	.317	.376	.541	194	4	.253	.339	.366	87	2	.253	.298	.345	312	12	.295	.374	.487
1988	Atl-N	193	2	.249	.307	.306	102	2	.255	.300	.343	91	0	.242	.314	.264	155	2	.245	.296	.316	38	0	.263	.349	.263	21	1	.190	.190	.381	172	1	.256	.319	.297
1988	Cin-N	50	2	.280	.308	.420	21	1	.333	.391	.524	29	1	.241	.241	.345	0	0	—	—	—	50	2	.280	.308	.420	3	0	.667	.667	.667	47	2	.255	.286	.404
1989	Cin-N	236	8	.263	.346	.424	120	2	.267	.353	.375	116	6	.259	.338	.474	108	4	.269	.342	.407	128	4	.258	.349	.438	16	0	.313	.500	.500	220	8	.259	.332	.418
1990	Cin-N	63	1	.206	.235	.286	20	1	.200	.273	.350	43	0	.209	.217	.256	45	1	.267	.271	.356	18	0	.056	.150	.111	4	0	.250	.250	.250	59	1	.203	.234	.288
1990	Sea-A	77	3	.377	.443	.519	30	1	.300	.400	.400	47	2	.426	.472	.596	0	0	—	—	—	77	3	.377	.443	.519	11	0	.273	.385	.273	66	3	.394	.453	.561
1991	Sea-A	85	1	.282	.380	.400	44	1	.318	.404	.500	41	0	.244	.354	.293	85	1	.282	.380	.400	0	0	—	—	—	3	0	.333	.333	.667	82	1	.280	.381	.390
TOTALS		5306	125	.290	.348	.429	2571	76	.289	.353	.453	2735	49	.290	.343	.405	2695	56	.294	.348	.427	2611	69	.285	.348	.430	1500	23	.273	.322	.388	3806	102	.296	.358	.445
■ Alfredo Griffin BB/TR																																				
1978	Cle-A	4	0	.500	.667	.750	0	0	—	—	—	4	0	.500	.667	.750	0	0	—	—	—	4	0	.500	.667	.750	0	0	—	—	—	4	0	.500	.667	.750
1979	Tor-A	624	2	.287	.333	.364	305	2	.308	.359	.393	319	0	.266	.308	.335	304	0	.263	.329	.332	320	2	.309	.336	.394	198	0	.293	.333	.359	426	2	.284	.333	.366
1980	Tor-A	653	2	.254	.283	.349	307	1	.270	.311	.391	346	1	.240	.258	.312	291	1	.244	.275	.354	362	1	.262	.289	.345	223	1	.260	.268	.336	430	1	.251	.290	.356
1981	Tor-A	388	0	.209	.243	.289	195	0	.221	.261	.328	193	0	.197	.224	.249	215	0	.200	.247	.302	173	0	.220	.237	.272	155	0	.168	.196	.226	233	0	.236	.273	.330
1982	Tor-A	539	1	.241	.269	.314	266	0	.259	.295	.361	273	1	.223	.243	.267	248	0	.226	.252	.290	291	1	.254	.283	.333	237	0	.215	.232	.291	302	1	.262	.298	.331
1983	Tor-A	528	4	.250	.289	.348	258	2	.271	.312	.384	270	2	.230	.267	.315	242	2	.244	.270	.355	286	2	.255	.304	.343	198	1	.293	.314	.364	330	3	.224	.275	.339
1984	Tor-A	419	4	.241	.248	.298	203	1	.207	.210	.256	216	3	.273	.283	.338	233	3	.249	.258	.318	186	1	.231	.234	.274	131	1	.229	.235	.275	288	3	.247	.253	.309
1985	Oak-A	614	2	.270	.290	.332	292	0	.257	.277	.298	322	2	.283	.302	.363	258	2	.295	.325	.368	356	0	.253	.264	.306	187	1	.326	.337	.401	427	1	.246	.270	.302
1986	Oak-A	594	4	.285	.323	.364	302	1	.281	.319	.331	292	3	.288	.328	.397	271	1	.292	.339	.365	323	3	.279	.310	.362	205	0	.254	.282	.298	389	4	.301	.344	.398
1987	Oak-A	494	3	.263	.306	.348	233	2	.236	.278	.318	261	1	.287	.331	.375	245	1	.265	.313	.343	249	2	.261	.300	.353	188	1	.245	.292	.309	306	2	.275	.315	.373
1988	LA-N	316	1	.199	.259	.253	158	0	.184	.254	.209	158	1	.215	.265	.297	144	0	.167	.214	.243	172	1	.227	.296	.262	90	0	.167	.269	.222	226	1	.212	.255	.265

		TOTAL					HOME					AWAY					1ST HALF					2ND HALF					LEFT					RIGHT				
YEAR	TM/L	AB	HR	AVG	OBP	SLG	AB	HR	AVG	OBP	SLG	AB	HR	AVG	OBP	SLG	AB	HR	AVG	OBP	SLG	AB	HR	AVG	OBP	SLG	AB	HR	AVG	OBP	SLG	AB	HR	AVG	OBP	SLG
1989	LA-N	506	0	.247	.287	.308	250	0	.252	.289	.312	256	0	.242	.286	.305	206	0	.277	.310	.359	300	0	.227	.272	.273	177	0	.282	.323	.339	329	0	.228	.268	.292
1990	LA-N	461	1	.210	.258	.254	218	0	.220	.268	.248	243	1	.202	.249	.259	255	1	.247	.297	.306	206	0	.165	.207	.189	169	1	.207	.257	.237	292	0	.212	.259	.264
1991	LA-N	350	0	.243	.286	.271	158	0	.203	.247	.215	192	0	.276	.319	.318	187	0	.235	.270	.257	163	0	.252	.303	.288	148	0	.270	.319	.291	202	0	.223	.261	.257
1992	Tor-A	150	0	.233	.273	.280	70	0	.214	.269	.271	80	0	.250	.277	.287	32	0	.156	.176	.156	118	0	.254	.299	.314	29	0	.310	.394	.345	121	0	.215	.242	.264
1993	Tor-A	95	0	.211	.235	.242	46	0	.261	.292	.304	49	0	.163	.180	.184	51	0	.255	.283	.294	44	0	.159	.178	.182	27	0	.148	.148	.148	68	0	.235	.268	.279
TOTALS		6735	24	.250	.286	.320	3261	9	.250	.289	.320	3474	15	.249	.283	.319	3182	11	.249	.288	.325	3553	13	.250	.284	.315	2362	6	.251	.283	.309	4373	18	.249	.287	.326
■ Marquis Grissom BR/TR																																				
1989	Mon-N	74	1	.257	.360	.324	37	0	.324	.432	.378	37	1	.189	.286	.270	0	0	—	—	—	74	1	.257	.360	.324	34	0	.265	.324	.294	40	1	.250	.388	.350
1990	Mon-N	288	3	.257	.320	.351	146	2	.247	.321	.349	142	1	.268	.318	.352	154	0	.253	.311	.325	134	3	.261	.329	.381	181	2	.243	.317	.359	107	1	.280	.325	.336
1991	Mon-N	558	6	.267	.310	.373	233	3	.279	.323	.373	325	3	.258	.301	.372	265	5	.279	.330	.389	293	1	.256	.292	.358	211	3	.284	.341	.389	347	3	.256	.291	.363
1992	Mon-N	653	14	.276	.322	.418	316	8	.266	.309	.430	337	6	.285	.335	.407	289	5	.284	.346	.419	364	9	.269	.303	.418	212	6	.269	.325	.458	441	8	.279	.321	.399
1993	Mon-N	630	19	.298	.351	.438	307	9	.319	.366	.450	323	10	.279	.336	.427	282	10	.298	.357	.472	348	9	.299	.346	.411	192	7	.307	.362	.495	438	12	.295	.346	.413
1994	Mon-N	475	11	.288	.344	.427	210	4	.295	.336	.429	265	7	.283	.349	.426	320	6	.300	.359	.434	155	5	.265	.311	.413	112	4	.250	.323	.420	363	7	.300	.350	.430
1995	Atl-N	551	12	.258	.317	.376	257	5	.230	.293	.335	294	7	.282	.339	.412	242	7	.298	.337	.438	309	5	.227	.303	.327	132	4	.273	.338	.432	419	8	.253	.311	.358
1996	Atl-N	671	23	.308	.349	.489	337	11	.312	.360	.499	334	12	.305	.338	.479	338	10	.290	.336	.453	333	13	.327	.362	.526	168	9	.310	.333	.565	503	14	.308	.354	.463
1997	Cle-A	558	12	.262	.317	.396	255	5	.255	.313	.380	303	7	.267	.319	.409	250	2	.256	.318	.328	308	10	.266	.315	.451	138	5	.261	.315	.442	420	7	.262	.317	.381
1998	Mil-A	542	10	.271	.304	.382	249	2	.285	.322	.369	293	8	.259	.288	.392	248	5	.306	.329	.431	294	5	.241	.282	.340	150	3	.253	.289	.367	392	7	.278	.309	.388
1999	Mil-A	603	20	.267	.320	.415	295	9	.244	.306	.386	308	11	.289	.333	.442	272	7	.283	.338	.412	331	13	.254	.305	.417	171	4	.322	.384	.468	432	16	.245	.293	.394
2000	Mil-A	595	14	.244	.288	.351	307	4	.251	.302	.329	288	10	.236	.274	.375	317	8	.256	.294	.385	278	6	.230	.282	.313	125	2	.304	.343	.408	470	12	.228	.273	.336
TOTALS		6198	145	.273	.323	.404	2949	62	.273	.325	.398	3249	83	.274	.321	.410	2977	65	.283	.333	.412	3221	80	.265	.313	.397	1826	49	.280	.335	.435	4372	96	.271	.318	.392
■ Greg Gross BL/TL																																				
1978	Chi-N	347	1	.265	.323	.349	167	0	.269	.332	.383	180	1	.261	.315	.317	174	1	.276	.330	.385	173	0	.254	.316	.312	38	0	.158	.200	.211	309	1	.278	.337	.366
1979	Phi-N	174	0	.333	.422	.402	112	0	.277	.379	.330	62	0	.435	.500	.532	45	0	.311	.333	.444	129	0	.341	.449	.388	17	0	.118	.333	.118	157	0	.357	.434	.433
1980	Phi-N	154	0	.240	.346	.312	73	0	.233	.333	.342	81	0	.247	.358	.284	63	0	.175	.278	.270	91	0	.286	.393	.341	22	0	.091	.259	.136	132	0	.265	.362	.341
1981	Phi-N	102	0	.225	.319	.304	60	0	.233	.319	.300	42	0	.214	.320	.310	62	0	.290	.361	.387	40	0	.125	.255	.175	8	0	.375	.444	.500	94	0	.213	.309	.287
1982	Phi-N	134	0	.299	.386	.328	46	0	.304	.475	.326	88	0	.295	.326	.330	71	0	.282	.346	.324	63	0	.317	.427	.333	4	0	.250	.400	.250	130	0	.300	.385	.331
1983	Phi-N	245	0	.302	.385	.376	116	0	.353	.431	.457	129	0	.256	.342	.302	66	0	.258	.367	.333	179	0	.318	.392	.391	21	0	.190	.217	.238	224	0	.313	.400	.388
1984	Phi-N	202	0	.322	.393	.376	77	0	.364	.451	.468	125	0	.296	.355	.320	61	0	.361	.438	.377	141	0	.305	.372	.376	20	0	.250	.348	.300	182	0	.330	.398	.385
1985	Phi-N	169	0	.260	.374	.314	76	0	.263	.389	.355	93	0	.258	.361	.280	84	0	.250	.369	.310	85	0	.271	.380	.318	6	0	.333	.500	.333	163	0	.258	.368	.313
1986	Phi-N	101	0	.248	.379	.297	43	0	.302	.426	.395	58	0	.207	.343	.224	49	0	.306	.443	.367	52	0	.192	.317	.231	18	0	.167	.286	.167	83	0	.265	.398	.325
1987	Phi-N	133	1	.286	.395	.353	57	0	.316	.420	.386	76	1	.263	.376	.329	63	1	.317	.413	.413	70	0	.257	.379	.300	10	0	.300	.364	.300	123	1	.285	.397	.358
1988	Phi-N	133	0	.203	.291	.211	71	0	.197	.278	.211	62	0	.210	.306	.210	64	0	.203	.297	.219	69	0	.203	.286	.203	8	0	.125	.125	.125	125	0	.208	.301	.216
1989	Hou-N	75	0	.200	.310	.200	37	0	.162	.295	.162	38	0	.237	.326	.237	47	0	.170	.316	.170	28	0	.250	.300	.250	3	0	.333	.333	.333	72	0	.194	.310	.194
TOTALS		1969	2	.273	.363	.333	935	0	.279	.377	.358	1034	2	.268	.350	.309	849	2	.267	.355	.339	1120	0	.278	.368	.328	175	0	.189	.289	.223	1794	2	.281	.370	.343
■ Wayne Gross BL/TR																																				
1978	Oak-A	285	7	.200	.308	.323	143	4	.217	.351	.357	142	3	.183	.261	.289	191	5	.209	.333	.335	94	2	.181	.252	.298	99	1	.192	.310	.242	186	6	.204	.307	.366
1979	Oak-A	442	14	.224	.332	.367	211	3	.213	.329	.294	231	11	.234	.335	.433	240	9	.242	.360	.417	202	5	.203	.297	.307	118	2	.212	.319	.314	324	12	.228	.337	.386
1980	Oak-A	366	14	.281	.355	.467	169	3	.296	.378	.414	197	11	.269	.335	.513	171	5	.269	.353	.427	195	9	.292	.356	.503	55	0	.218	.232	.291	311	14	.293	.374	.498
1981	Oak-A	243	10	.206	.304	.366	117	3	.205	.296	.316	126	7	.206	.311	.413	130	5	.192	.294	.338	113	5	.221	.315	.398	26	0	.154	.233	.154	217	10	.212	.312	.392
1982	Oak-A	386	9	.251	.342	.358	206	3	.252	.342	.345	180	6	.250	.343	.372	176	2	.256	.356	.324	210	7	.248	.331	.386	40	0	.150	.209	.175	346	9	.263	.357	.379
1983	Oak-A	339	12	.233	.311	.392	157	4	.217	.299	.344	182	8	.247	.320	.434	192	9	.255	.345	.453	147	3	.204	.262	.313	86	1	.186	.263	.256	253	11	.249	.326	.439
1984	Bal-A	342	22	.216	.346	.442	164	12	.213	.372	.457	178	10	.219	.320	.427	149	9	.215	.378	.436	193	13	.218	.320	.446	5	0	.000	.167	.000	337	22	.220	.349	.448
1985	Bal-A	217	11	.235	.369	.424	102	9	.225	.392	.510	115	2	.243	.346	.348	141	8	.262	.406	.489	76	3	.184	.295	.303	4	1	.250	.400	1.000	213	10	.235	.368	.413
1986	Oak-A	2	0	.000	.333	.000	1	0	.000	.000	.000	1	0	.000	.500	.000	0	0	—	—	—	2	0	.000	.333	.000	0	0	—	—	—	2	0	.000	.333	.000
TOTALS		2622	99	.233	.334	.392	1270	41	.231	.345	.372	1352	58	.234	.323	.411	1390	52	.239	.354	.402	1232	47	.226	.310	.381	433	5	.192	.280	.263	2189	94	.241	.344	.418
■ Kelly Gruber BR/TR																																				
1984	Tor-A	16	1	.063	.063	.250	5	0	.000	.000	.000	11	1	.091	.091	.364	3	0	.000	.000	.000	13	1	.077	.077	.308	10	0	.000	.000	.000	6	1	.167	.167	.667
1985	Tor-A	13	0	.231	.231	.231	10	0	.200	.200	.200	3	0	.333	.333	.333	0	0	—	—	—	13	0	.231	.231	.231	4	0	.250	.250	.250	9	0	.222	.222	.222
1986	Tor-A	143	5	.196	.220	.343	71	4	.183	.231	.394	72	1	.208	.208	.292	65	3	.154	.191	.338	78	2	.231	.244	.346	60	2	.217	.226	.350	83	3	.181	.216	.337
1987	Tor-A	341	12	.235	.283	.399	144	5	.222	.283	.396	197	7	.244	.284	.401	181	6	.282	.326	.442	160	6	.181	.236	.350	152	4	.230	.289	.395	189	8	.238	.279	.402
1988	Tor-A	569	16	.278	.328	.438	294	5	.269	.316	.384	275	11	.287	.341	.495	280	11	.307	.359	.518	289	5	.249	.299	.360	187	1	.251	.288	.364	382	15	.291	.348	.474
1989	Tor-A	545	18	.290	.328	.448	278	8	.295	.324	.453	267	10	.285	.331	.442	284	9	.317	.366	.468	261	9	.261	.285	.425	166	7	.325	.356	.500	379	11	.274	.315	.425
1990	Tor-A	592	31	.274	.330	.512	305	23	.292	.331	.587	287	8	.254	.328	.432	299	20	.308	.363	.592	293	11	.239	.296	.430	166	8	.295	.349	.554	426	23	.265	.322	.495
1991	Tor-A	429	20	.252	.308	.443	221	8	.262	.327	.398	208	12	.240	.288	.490	130	6	.231	.320	.408	299	14	.261	.302	.458	112	8	.277	.323	.527	317	12	.243	.303	.413
1992	Tor-A	446	11	.229	.275	.352	211	7	.242	.284	.408	235	4	.217	.267	.302	238	8	.231	.269	.395	208	3	.226	.282	.303	107	3	.243	.291	.393	339	8	.224	.270	.339
1993	Cal-A	65	3	.277	.309	.462	19	1	.158	.273	.316	46	2	.326	.326	.522	65	3	.277	.309	.462	0	0	—	—	—	23	1	.304	.304	.478	42	2	.262	.311	.452
TOTALS		3159	117	.259	.307	.432	1558	61	.263	.309	.440	1601	56	.255	.305	.425	1545	66	.280	.331	.475	1614	51	.239	.284	.391	987	34	.266	.308	.443	2172	83	.256	.306	.427
■ Mark Grudzielanek BR/TR																																				
1995	Mon-N	269	1	.245	.300	.316	112	1	.330	.375	.455	157	0	.185	.247	.217	152	1	.250	.305	.329	117	0	.239	.294	.299	70	0	.343	.387	.400	199	1	.211	.270	.286
1996	Mon-N	657	6	.306	.340	.397	304	5	.326	.368	.457	353	1	.289	.314	.346	324	5	.324	.358	.441	333	1	.288	.322	.354	133	1	.308	.331	.406	524	5	.305	.342	.395
1997	Mon-N	649	4	.273	.307	.384	330	1	.285	.308	.397	319	3	.260	.305	.370	320	2	.287	.337	.403	329	2	.258	.276	.365	147	1	.224	.252	.313	502	3	.287	.323	.404
1998	Mon-N	396	8	.275	.323	.379	205	3	.288	.344	.361	191	5	.262	.301	.398	313	5	.249	.299	.323	83	3	.373	.413	.590	80	1	.287	.348	.375	316	7	.272	.317	.380
1998	LA-N	193	2	.264	.286	.326	107	2	.262	.289	.374	86	0	.267	.281	.267	0	0	—	—	—	193	2	.264	.286	.326	49	2	.224	.220	.367	144	0	.278	.307	.313
1999	LA-N	488	7	.326	.376	.436	219	4	.361	.417	.475	269	3	.297	.341	.405	169	2	.284	.339	.355	319	5	.348	.395	.480	144	2	.389	.451	.521	344	5	.299	.343	.401
2000	LA-N	617	7	.279	.335	.389	287	4	.282	.337	.383	330	3	.276	.334	.394	332	4	.298	.346	.410	285	3	.256	.323	.365	168	2	.250	.317	.357	449	5	.290	.342	.401
TOTALS		3269	35	.286	.329	.386	1564	20	.305	.349	.415	1705	15	.269	.311	.359	1610	19	.286	.333	.384	1659	16	.286	.326	.387	791	9	.291	.336	.393	2478	26	.285	.327	.383
■ Pedro Guerrero BR/TR																																				
1978	LA-N	8	0	.625	.625	.875	1	0	1.000	1.000	1.000	7	0	.571	.571	.857	0	0	—	—	—	8	0	.625	.625	.875	4	0	.750	.750	1.250	4	0	.500	.500	.500
1979	LA-N	62	2	.242	.250	.371	41	0	.244	.238	.293	21	2	.238	.273	.524	10	0	.200	.200	.200	52	2	.250	.259	.404	27	2	.259	.250	.519	35	0	.229	.250	.257
1980	LA-N	183	7	.322	.359	.497	86	3	.337	.366	.477	97	4	.309	.352	.515	39	1	.410	.465	.615	144	6	.299	.329	.465	52	4	.385	.439	.731	131	3	.298	.326	.405
1981	LA-N	347	12	.300	.365	.464	172	5	.302	.368	.453	175	7	.297	.361	.474	191	10	.325	.375	.550	156	2	.269	.352	.359	51	3	.255	.316	.490	296	9	.307	.373	.459
1982	LA-N	575	32	.304	.378	.536	286	15	.290	.375	.524	289	17	.318	.381	.547	284	13	.292	.345	.507	291	19	.316	.408	.564	86	5	.256	.347	.465	489	27	.313	.384	.548
1983	LA-N	584	32	.298	.373	.531	283	13	.290	.361	.481	301	19	.306	.386	.578	271	17	.306	.387	.542	313	15	.291	.362	.521	114	7	.272	.341	.518	470	25	.304	.381	.534
1984	LA-N	535	16	.303	.358	.462	286	7	.322	.368	.462	249	9	.281	.346	.462	291	6	.278	.340	.412	244	10	.332	.378	.520	168	3	.298	.374	.387	367	13	.305	.349	.496
1985	LA-N	487	33	.320	.422	.577	257	13	.311	.416	.498	230	20	.330	.429	.665	261	19	.295	.390	.559	226	14	.350	.458	.597	135	9	.304	.412	.556	352	24	.327	.425	.585
1986	LA-N	61	5	.246	.281	.541	23	1	.217	.250	.348	38	4	.263	.300	.658	0	0	—	—	—	61	5	.246	.281	.541	29	2	.345	.345	.621	32	3	.156	.229	.469
1987	LA-N	545	27	.338	.416	.539	275	12	.324	.397	.495	270	15	.352	.434	.585	270	16	.315	.383	.544	275	11	.360	.447	.535	167	8	.365	.451	.575	378	19	.325	.400	.524
1988	LA-N	215	5	.298	.374	.409	118	3	.364	.412	.508	97	2	.216	.330	.289	158	3	.316	.393	.411	57	2	.246	.317	.404	71	2	.268	.354	.352	144	3	.313	.384	.438
1988	StL-N	149	5	.268	.358	.430	74	2	.230	.314	.365	75	3	.307	.400	.493	0	0	—	—	—	149	5	.268	.358	.430	54	1	.296	.424	.444	95	4	.253	.318	.421
1989	StL-N	570	17	.311	.391	.477	281	3	.288	.372	.409	289	14	.332	.410	.543	262	6	.302	.378	.462	308	11	.318	.402	.490	218	8	.317	.402	.505	352	9	.307	.384	.460
1990	StL-N	498	13	.281	.334	.426	261	8	.276	.333	.437	237	5	.287	.335	.414	274	8	.292	.347	.456	224	5	.268	.317	.388	168	4	.274	.319	.446	330	9	.285	.341	.415
1991	StL-N	427	8	.272	.326	.361	216	4	.282	.340	.370	211	4	.261	.311	.351	259	4	.274	.337	.355	168	4	.268	.309	.369	160	0	.256	.326	.300	267	8	.281	.327	.397
1992	StL-N	146	1	.219	.270	.295	71	1	.254	.325	.338	75	0	.187	.215	.253	145	1	.221	.272	.297	1	0	.000	.000	.000	38	1	.211	.286	.316	108	0	.222	.265	.287
TOTALS		5392	215	.300	.370	.480	2731	90	.298	.367	.455	2661	125	.302	.373	.506	2715	104	.295	.362	.472	2677	111	.305	.378	.488	1542	59	.296	.373	.473	3850	156	.302	.369	.483
■ Vladimir Guerrero BR/TR																																				
1996	Mon-N	27	1	.185	.185	.296	7	0	.143	.143	.143	20	1	.200	.200	.350	0	0	—	—	—	27	1	.185	.185	.296	15	0	.200	.200	.200	12	1	.167	.167	.417
1997	Mon-N	325	11	.302	.350	.483	166	5	.265	.315	.434	159	6	.340	.387	.535	145	4	.317	.369	.476	180	7	.289	.335	.489	93	4	.301	.350	.505	232	7	.302	.350	.474
1998	Mon-N	623	38	.324	.371	.589	319	19	.345	.379	.599	304	19	.303	.362	.579	312	14	.308	.343	.522	311	24	.341	.397	.656	127	5	.339	.391	.528	496	33	.321	.365	.605
1999	Mon-N	610	42	.316	.378	.600	314	23	.331	.378	.643	296	19	.301	.378	.554	279	16	.290	.371	.541	331	26	.338	.385	.650	129	12	.287	.363	.612	481	30	.324	.383	.597
2000	Mon-N	571	44	.345	.410	.664	293	25	.338	.407	.679	278	19	.353	.414	.647	282	22	.365	.430	.713	289	22	.325	.391	.616	133	12	.376	.447	.744	438	32	.336	.399	.639
TOTALS		2156	136	.322	.378	.592	1099	72	.326	.375	.605	1057	64	.319	.381	.579	1018	56	.320	.379	.574	1138	80	.324	.378	.609	497	33	.324	.386	.594	1659	103	.322	.376	.592
■ Wilton Guerrero BB/TR																																				
1996	LA-N	2	0	.000	.000	.000	1	0	.000	.000	.000	1	0	.000	.000	.000	0	0	—	—	—	2	0	.000	.000	.000	1	0	.000	.000	.000	1	0	.000	.000	.000
1997	LA-N	357	4	.291	.305	.403	176	2	.273	.297	.403	181	2	.309	.314	.403	245	2	.294	.308	.420	112	2	.286	.298	.366	90	3	.222	.237	.356	267	1	.315	.328	.419

YEAR	TM/L	TOTAL					HOME					AWAY					1ST HALF					2ND HALF					LEFT					RIGHT				
		AB	HR	AVG	OBP	SLG	AB	HR	AVG	OBP	SLG	AB	HR	AVG	OBP	SLG	AB	HR	AVG	OBP	SLG	AB	HR	AVG	OBP	SLG	AB	HR	AVG	OBP	SLG	AB	HR	AVG	OBP	SLG
1998	LA-N	180	0	.283	.299	.339	79	0	.367	.386	.456	101	0	.218	.231	.248	82	0	.244	.264	.305	98	0	.316	.330	.367	29	0	.483	.483	.517	151	0	.245	.266	.305
1998	Mon-N	222	2	.284	.313	.410	89	0	.270	.301	.360	133	2	.293	.321	.444	0	0	—	—	—	222	2	.284	.313	.410	54	1	.241	.241	.407	168	1	.298	.335	.411
1999	Mon-N	315	2	.292	.324	.403	144	0	.257	.282	.333	171	2	.322	.359	.462	138	0	.275	.315	.370	177	2	.305	.332	.429	97	1	.330	.356	.495	218	1	.275	.310	.362
2000	Mon-N	288	2	.267	.312	.326	124	2	.258	.290	.347	164	0	.274	.328	.311	92	1	.250	.293	.293	196	1	.276	.321	.342	106	2	.292	.321	.387	182	0	.253	.306	.291
TOTALS		1364	10	.284	.311	.379	613	4	.277	.304	.375	751	6	.289	.317	.382	557	3	.275	.301	.370	807	7	.290	.318	.385	377	7	.292	.310	.419	987	3	.281	.311	.364
■ Ozzie Guillen BL/TR																																				
1985	Chi-A	491	1	.273	.291	.358	244	1	.279	.298	.377	247	0	.267	.285	.340	212	0	.226	.250	.255	279	1	.308	.323	.437	90	0	.211	.228	.244	401	1	.287	.305	.384
1986	Chi-A	547	2	.250	.265	.311	272	1	.254	.264	.305	275	1	.247	.267	.316	230	2	.243	.262	.330	317	0	.256	.268	.297	167	1	.257	.283	.299	380	1	.247	.258	.316
1987	Chi-A	560	2	.279	.303	.354	269	2	.316	.352	.409	291	0	.244	.256	.302	250	1	.284	.323	.364	310	1	.274	.286	.345	164	0	.201	.227	.238	396	2	.311	.334	.402
1988	Chi-A	566	0	.261	.294	.314	280	0	.261	.303	.311	286	0	.262	.284	.318	293	0	.266	.291	.307	273	0	.256	.297	.322	171	0	.263	.285	.287	395	0	.261	.297	.327
1989	Chi-A	597	1	.253	.270	.318	292	0	.240	.246	.298	305	1	.266	.292	.338	335	0	.239	.258	.290	262	1	.271	.285	.355	209	0	.254	.264	.292	388	1	.253	.273	.332
1990	Chi-A	516	1	.279	.312	.341	247	1	.279	.318	.356	269	0	.279	.306	.327	230	0	.322	.340	.391	286	1	.245	.290	.301	206	0	.267	.288	.316	310	1	.287	.327	.358
1991	Chi-A	524	3	.273	.284	.340	247	1	.287	.291	.364	277	2	.260	.278	.318	253	0	.273	.285	.324	271	3	.273	.283	.354	161	1	.211	.213	.248	363	2	.300	.315	.380
1992	Chi-A	40	0	.200	.214	.300	17	0	.176	.222	.294	23	0	.217	.208	.304	40	0	.200	.214	.300	0	0	—	—	—	19	0	.158	.158	.316	21	0	.238	.261	.286
1993	Chi-A	457	4	.280	.292	.374	212	3	.297	.309	.396	245	1	.265	.277	.355	211	1	.265	.284	.336	246	3	.293	.299	.407	130	0	.231	.241	.292	327	4	.300	.312	.407
1994	Chi-A	365	1	.288	.311	.348	164	0	.250	.277	.311	201	1	.318	.338	.378	240	1	.275	.302	.338	125	0	.312	.328	.368	115	1	.261	.298	.313	250	0	.300	.317	.364
1995	Chi-A	415	1	.248	.270	.318	216	1	.287	.313	.366	199	0	.206	.224	.266	163	0	.294	.322	.368	252	1	.218	.236	.286	101	0	.198	.204	.248	314	1	.264	.291	.341
1996	Chi-A	499	4	.263	.273	.367	239	0	.251	.263	.339	260	4	.273	.283	.392	272	2	.276	.287	.382	227	2	.247	.256	.348	117	1	.239	.246	.308	382	3	.270	.281	.385
1997	Chi-A	490	4	.245	.275	.337	236	1	.263	.307	.369	254	3	.228	.245	.307	251	1	.275	.321	.359	239	3	.213	.226	.314	108	1	.278	.322	.380	382	3	.236	.262	.325
1998	Bal-A	16	0	.063	.118	.063	8	0	.125	.125	.125	8	0	.000	.111	.000	16	0	.063	.118	.063	0	0	—	—	—	1	0	.000	.000	.000	15	0	.067	.125	.067
1998	Atl-N	264	1	.277	.337	.352	91	1	.275	.347	.363	173	0	.277	.332	.347	91	1	.264	.343	.385	173	0	.283	.333	.335	65	0	.262	.310	.323	199	1	.281	.345	.362
1999	Atl-N	232	1	.241	.284	.323	133	0	.218	.261	.286	99	1	.273	.315	.374	165	0	.242	.290	.303	67	1	.239	.270	.373	50	0	.280	.327	.340	182	1	.231	.272	.319
2000	TB-A	107	2	.243	.283	.336	42	1	.190	.244	.333	65	1	.277	.309	.338	58	1	.276	.323	.362	49	1	.204	.235	.306	7	0	.143	.143	.143	100	2	.250	.292	.350
TOTALS		6686	28	.264	.287	.338	3209	13	.268	.294	.346	3477	15	.260	.282	.331	3310	10	.266	.293	.334	3376	18	.262	.282	.342	1881	5	.242	.263	.291	4805	23	.272	.297	.357
■ Ricky Gutierrez BR/TR																																				
1993	SD-N	438	5	.251	.334	.331	230	5	.257	.335	.339	208	0	.245	.333	.322	156	1	.288	.351	.333	282	4	.230	.325	.330	159	3	.277	.365	.365	279	2	.237	.316	.312
1994	SD-N	275	1	.240	.321	.305	129	1	.248	.353	.302	146	0	.233	.289	.308	202	1	.252	.336	.332	73	0	.205	.277	.233	93	1	.258	.311	.376	182	0	.231	.325	.269
1995	Hou-N	156	0	.276	.321	.314	70	0	.257	.297	.271	86	0	.291	.340	.349	10	0	.100	.100	.100	146	0	.288	.335	.329	40	0	.250	.250	.275	116	0	.284	.344	.328
1996	Hou-N	218	1	.284	.359	.344	112	1	.348	.416	.438	106	0	.217	.300	.245	128	0	.313	.373	.375	90	1	.244	.340	.300	68	0	.324	.403	.412	150	1	.267	.339	.313
1997	Hou-N	303	3	.261	.315	.363	129	0	.202	.264	.264	174	3	.305	.353	.437	113	1	.257	.323	.319	190	2	.263	.310	.389	78	1	.256	.301	.346	225	2	.262	.320	.369
1998	Hou-N	491	2	.261	.337	.334	239	1	.251	.335	.322	252	1	.270	.339	.345	227	0	.295	.385	.357	264	2	.231	.294	.314	122	0	.287	.366	.361	369	2	.252	.327	.325
1999	Hou-N	268	1	.261	.354	.336	142	1	.303	.389	.415	126	0	.214	.315	.246	105	1	.295	.375	.429	163	0	.239	.340	.276	66	0	.379	.468	.500	202	1	.223	.316	.282
2000	Chi-N	449	11	.276	.375	.401	216	7	.287	.383	.421	233	4	.266	.366	.382	190	7	.284	.378	.442	259	4	.270	.372	.371	90	1	.356	.416	.478	359	10	.256	.365	.382
TOTALS		2598	24	.263	.342	.345	1267	16	.268	.350	.352	1331	8	.258	.334	.339	1131	11	.281	.360	.366	1467	13	.248	.327	.329	716	6	.296	.366	.390	1882	18	.250	.333	.328
■ Tony Gwynn BL/TL																																				
1982	SD-N	190	1	.289	.337	.389	87	0	.241	.272	.322	103	1	.330	.389	.447	0	0	—	—	—	190	1	.289	.337	.389	41	0	.317	.333	.366	149	1	.282	.337	.396
1983	SD-N	304	1	.309	.355	.372	158	0	.310	.343	.386	146	1	.308	.366	.356	31	0	.290	.313	.323	273	1	.311	.359	.377	63	0	.238	.290	.286	241	1	.328	.372	.394
1984	SD-N	606	5	.351	.410	.444	303	3	.376	.422	.492	303	2	.327	.398	.396	290	3	.352	.432	.479	316	2	.351	.387	.411	202	1	.312	.368	.356	404	4	.371	.430	.488
1985	SD-N	622	6	.317	.364	.408	316	3	.326	.368	.424	306	3	.307	.360	.392	298	4	.309	.346	.436	324	2	.324	.380	.383	205	2	.288	.354	.351	417	4	.331	.369	.436
1986	SD-N	642	14	.329	.381	.467	317	8	.341	.392	.486	325	6	.317	.369	.449	293	7	.345	.407	.495	349	7	.315	.358	.444	235	7	.328	.384	.523	407	7	.329	.379	.435
1987	SD-N	589	7	.370	.447	.511	282	5	.390	.473	.574	307	2	.352	.423	.453	278	4	.381	.453	.540	311	3	.360	.442	.486	249	3	.361	.433	.470	340	4	.376	.457	.541
1988	SD-N	521	7	.313	.373	.415	242	3	.310	.393	.393	279	4	.315	.355	.434	221	3	.249	.325	.330	300	4	.360	.409	.477	204	0	.314	.358	.358	317	7	.312	.382	.451
1989	SD-N	604	4	.336	.389	.424	288	3	.326	.384	.427	316	1	.345	.394	.421	316	4	.361	.409	.481	288	0	.309	.368	.361	200	0	.305	.355	.345	404	4	.351	.406	.463
1990	SD-N	573	4	.309	.357	.415	306	2	.310	.356	.422	267	2	.307	.358	.408	288	2	.316	.371	.431	285	2	.302	.342	.400	228	3	.281	.307	.373	345	1	.328	.388	.443
1991	SD-N	530	4	.317	.355	.432	244	1	.307	.348	.406	286	3	.325	.361	.455	308	2	.357	.386	.490	222	2	.261	.313	.351	211	2	.294	.332	.393	319	2	.332	.370	.458
1992	SD-N	520	6	.317	.371	.415	229	4	.306	.371	.393	291	2	.326	.371	.433	295	6	.325	.390	.451	225	0	.307	.345	.369	205	3	.327	.368	.420	315	3	.311	.372	.413
1993	SD-N	489	7	.358	.398	.497	254	4	.382	.421	.524	235	3	.332	.373	.468	262	2	.313	.357	.424	227	5	.410	.445	.581	192	3	.359	.393	.490	297	4	.357	.401	.502
1994	SD-N	419	12	.394	.454	.568	181	4	.403	.486	.558	238	8	.387	.427	.576	279	9	.391	.449	.573	140	3	.400	.463	.557	139	2	.374	.429	.504	280	10	.404	.466	.600
1995	SD-N	535	9	.368	.404	.484	266	5	.387	.420	.511	269	4	.349	.388	.457	224	5	.344	.393	.478	311	4	.386	.412	.489	188	2	.330	.365	.404	347	7	.389	.424	.527
1996	SD-N	451	3	.353	.400	.441	245	2	.351	.398	.449	206	1	.354	.404	.432	265	3	.336	.384	.438	186	0	.376	.424	.446	136	1	.353	.392	.434	315	2	.352	.404	.444
1997	SD-N	592	17	.372	.409	.547	296	8	.378	.408	.557	296	9	.365	.411	.537	306	13	.392	.430	.598	286	4	.350	.387	.493	163	6	.356	.391	.583	429	11	.378	.416	.534
1998	SD-N	461	16	.321	.364	.501	199	5	.312	.347	.467	262	11	.328	.377	.527	270	7	.333	.378	.489	191	9	.304	.345	.518	161	8	.323	.358	.534	300	8	.320	.367	.483
1999	SD-N	411	10	.338	.381	.477	203	5	.340	.389	.463	208	5	.337	.373	.490	160	3	.338	.397	.456	251	7	.339	.371	.490	139	6	.324	.360	.489	272	4	.346	.392	.471
2000	SD-N	127	1	.323	.364	.441	56	1	.321	.345	.500	71	0	.324	.378	.394	127	1	.323	.364	.441	0	0	—	—	—	36	1	.417	.462	.556	91	0	.286	.327	.396
TOTALS		9186	134	.338	.388	.459	4472	66	.343	.394	.466	4714	68	.334	.383	.451	4511	78	.341	.394	.476	4675	56	.336	.382	.442	3197	50	.324	.370	.432	5989	84	.346	.398	.473
■ Mel Hall BL/TL																																				
1981	Chi-N	11	1	.091	.167	.364	5	1	.200	.200	.800	6	0	.000	.143	.000	0	0	—	—	—	11	1	.091	.167	.364	0	0	—	—	—	11	1	.091	.167	.364
1982	Chi-N	80	0	.262	.318	.350	36	0	.278	.308	.333	44	0	.250	.327	.364	0	0	—	—	—	80	0	.262	.318	.350	14	0	.071	.133	.143	66	0	.303	.356	.394
1983	Chi-N	410	17	.283	.352	.488	206	6	.277	.364	.447	204	11	.289	.339	.529	120	2	.308	.368	.425	290	15	.272	.346	.514	68	0	.118	.208	.118	342	17	.316	.382	.561
1984	Chi-N	150	4	.280	.329	.473	67	3	.313	.365	.567	83	1	.253	.300	.398	150	4	.280	.329	.473	0	0	—	—	—	9	0	.000	.100	.000	141	4	.298	.344	.504
1984	Cle-A	257	7	.257	.344	.397	139	4	.266	.344	.388	118	3	.246	.345	.407	38	2	.316	.447	.526	219	5	.247	.325	.374	26	0	.192	.371	.231	231	7	.264	.341	.416
1985	Cle-A	66	0	.318	.387	.409	30	0	.367	.394	.467	36	0	.278	.381	.361	66	0	.318	.387	.409	0	0	—	—	—	4	0	.000	.200	.000	62	0	.339	.400	.435
1986	Cle-A	442	18	.296	.346	.493	206	8	.277	.318	.466	236	10	.314	.369	.517	194	12	.304	.362	.577	248	6	.290	.333	.427	26	0	.154	.241	.231	416	18	.305	.353	.510
1987	Cle-A	485	18	.280	.309	.439	222	8	.288	.319	.441	263	10	.274	.301	.437	226	8	.239	.268	.376	259	10	.317	.344	.494	33	1	.364	.417	.515	452	17	.274	.301	.434
1988	Cle-A	515	6	.280	.312	.392	249	3	.289	.322	.418	266	3	.271	.302	.368	245	1	.294	.328	.376	270	5	.267	.297	.407	46	1	.109	.163	.196	469	5	.296	.327	.412
1989	NY-A	361	17	.260	.295	.427	202	11	.282	.317	.465	159	6	.233	.267	.377	113	5	.274	.320	.434	248	12	.254	.283	.423	69	1	.159	.224	.217	292	16	.284	.312	.476
1990	NY-A	360	12	.258	.272	.433	187	3	.273	.287	.412	173	9	.243	.256	.457	216	9	.259	.271	.468	144	3	.257	.273	.382	58	1	.207	.203	.310	302	11	.268	.285	.457
1991	NY-A	492	19	.285	.321	.455	245	13	.273	.317	.478	247	6	.296	.324	.433	192	11	.292	.327	.521	300	8	.280	.317	.413	162	5	.309	.353	.444	330	14	.273	.305	.461
1992	NY-A	583	15	.280	.310	.429	285	7	.246	.292	.361	298	8	.312	.328	.493	300	11	.260	.280	.460	283	4	.300	.342	.396	179	2	.257	.284	.346	404	13	.290	.322	.465
1996	SF-N	25	0	.120	.148	.120	11	0	.091	.083	.091	14	0	.143	.200	.143	25	0	.120	.148	.120	0	0	—	—	—	3	0	.333	.250	.333	22	0	.091	.130	.091
TOTALS		4237	134	.276	.318	.437	2090	67	.276	.320	.433	2147	67	.277	.316	.442	1885	65	.276	.316	.450	2352	69	.276	.320	.426	697	11	.222	.274	.310	3540	123	.287	.327	.462
■ Darryl Hamilton BL/TR																																				
1988	Mil-A	103	1	.184	.274	.252	34	1	.176	.293	.324	69	0	.188	.263	.217	25	0	.280	.333	.320	78	1	.154	.256	.231	30	0	.067	.152	.133	73	1	.233	.321	.301
1990	Mil-A	156	1	.295	.333	.346	72	1	.250	.280	.306	84	0	.333	.378	.381	41	0	.220	.273	.268	115	1	.322	.355	.374	9	0	.111	.273	.222	147	1	.306	.338	.354
1991	Mil-A	405	1	.311	.361	.385	195	0	.344	.406	.436	210	1	.281	.317	.338	105	0	.295	.339	.343	300	1	.317	.368	.400	87	0	.276	.308	.322	318	1	.321	.374	.403
1992	Mil-A	470	5	.298	.356	.400	233	1	.288	.356	.382	237	4	.308	.355	.418	186	2	.296	.357	.392	284	3	.299	.354	.405	89	0	.247	.323	.303	381	5	.310	.363	.423
1993	Mil-A	520	9	.310	.367	.406	262	5	.317	.388	.416	258	4	.302	.345	.395	239	2	.322	.375	.385	281	7	.299	.360	.423	182	1	.264	.316	.308	338	8	.334	.394	.459
1994	Mil-A	141	1	.262	.331	.369	72	0	.306	.378	.403	69	1	.217	.280	.333	141	1	.262	.331	.369	0	0	—	—	—	31	0	.258	.324	.387	110	1	.264	.333	.364
1995	Mil-A	398	5	.271	.350	.389	209	3	.273	.368	.383	189	2	.270	.330	.397	177	2	.271	.348	.367	221	3	.271	.352	.407	114	0	.237	.346	.289	284	5	.285	.352	.430
1996	Tex-A	627	6	.293	.348	.381	306	2	.324	.386	.402	321	4	.265	.311	.361	316	2	.313	.371	.392	311	4	.273	.324	.370	182	1	.264	.328	.330	445	5	.306	.357	.402
1997	SF-N	460	5	.270	.354	.365	203	1	.251	.349	.330	257	4	.284	.358	.393	194	2	.278	.344	.381	266	3	.263	.360	.353	104	1	.250	.316	.327	356	4	.275	.365	.376
1998	SF-N	367	1	.294	.393	.365	169	1	.278	.397	.337	198	0	.308	.389	.389	276	1	.290	.389	.362	91	0	.308	.406	.374	99	0	.283	.360	.354	268	1	.299	.404	.369
1998	Col-N	194	5	.335	.406	.469	101	2	.327	.424	.426	93	3	.344	.386	.516	0	0	—	—	—	194	5	.335	.406	.469	65	2	.369	.423	.523	129	3	.318	.399	.442
1999	Col-N	337	4	.303	.374	.389	155	2	.335	.405	.426	182	2	.275	.348	.357	265	3	.306	.362	.389	72	1	.292	.414	.389	108	2	.306	.375	.380	229	2	.301	.374	.393
1999	NY-N	168	5	.339	.410	.488	80	3	.412	.460	.600	88	2	.273	.366	.386	0	0	—	—	—	168	5	.339	.410	.488	39	0	.231	.268	.256	129	5	.372	.449	.558
2000	NY-N	105	1	.276	.358	.362	57	0	.228	.308	.281	48	1	.333	.418	.458	15	0	.133	.125	.133	90	1	.300	.394	.400	1	0	.000	.000	.000	104	1	.279	.361	.365
TOTALS		4451	50	.293	.361	.388	2148	22	.302	.379	.393	2303	28	.286	.344	.382	1980	15	.293	.358	.374	2471	35	.294	.363	.399	1140	7	.263	.330	.330	3311	43	.304	.372	.407
■ Jeffrey Hammonds BR/TR																																				
1993	Bal-A	105	3	.305	.312	.467	65	2	.277	.284	.415	40	1	.350	.357	.550	23	1	.391	.417	.565	82	2	.280	.282	.439	43	2	.279	.273	.488	62	1	.323	.338	.452
1994	Bal-A	250	8	.296	.339	.480	122	6	.287	.323	.500	128	2	.305	.355	.461	129	5	.295	.331	.504	121	3	.298	.348	.455	63	2	.238	.301	.381	187	6	.316	.353	.513
1995	Bal-A	178	4	.242	.279	.371	86	2	.279	.323	.407	92	2	.207	.237	.337	135	4	.267	.291	.422	43	0	.163	.245	.209	53	0	.208	.254	.245	125	4	.256	.290	.424
1996	Bal-A	248	9	.226	.301	.383	110	3	.264	.341	.418	138	6	.196	.268	.355	194	6	.237	.312	.376	54	3	.185	.262	.407	81	2	.247	.326	.407	167	7	.216	.288	.371
1997	Bal-A	397	21	.264	.323	.486	194	9	.258	.316	.438	203	12	.271	.329	.532	203	10	.276	.321	.473	194	11	.253	.324	.500	148	8	.277	.337	.514	249	13	.257	.314	.470
1998	Bal-A	171	6	.269	.369	.456	77	1	.208	.330	.299	94	5	.319	.402	.585	141	5	.262	.367	.440	30	1	.300	.382	.533	78	3	.282	.356	.500	93	3	.258	.379	.419
1998	Cin-N	86	0	.302	.390	.372	38	0	.368	.479	.526	48	0	.250	.308	.250	0	0	—	—	—	86	0	.302	.390	.372	18	0	.222	.286	.278	68	0	.324	.418	.397

		TOTAL					HOME					AWAY					1ST HALF					2ND HALF					LEFT					RIGHT				
YEAR	TM/L	AB	HR	AVG	OBP	SLG	AB	HR	AVG	OBP	SLG	AB	HR	AVG	OBP	SLG	AB	HR	AVG	OBP	SLG	AB	HR	AVG	OBP	SLG	AB	HR	AVG	OBP	SLG	AB	HR	AVG	OBP	SLG
1999	Cin-N	262	17	.279	.347	.523	105	5	.248	.328	.400	157	12	.299	.360	.605	113	7	.248	.328	.478	149	10	.302	.362	.557	140	8	.300	.359	.529	122	9	.254	.333	.516
2000	Col-N	454	20	.335	.395	.529	218	14	.399	.465	.651	236	6	.275	.325	.415	186	13	.382	.454	.672	268	7	.302	.352	.429	98	6	.378	.439	.633	356	14	.323	.382	.500
TOTALS		2151	88	.282	.343	.470	1015	42	.295	.361	.474	1136	46	.271	.327	.466	1124	51	.286	.349	.485	1027	37	.278	.337	.453	722	31	.283	.342	.481	1429	57	.282	.344	.464
■ **Mike Hargrove** BL/TL																																				
1978	Tex-A	494	7	.251	.388	.346	246	4	.248	.377	.341	248	3	.254	.398	.351	259	4	.263	.391	.375	235	3	.238	.384	.315	140	3	.236	.361	.357	354	4	.257	.398	.342
1979	SD-N	125	0	.192	.325	.232	56	0	.214	.343	.232	69	0	.174	.310	.232	125	0	.192	.325	.232	0	0	—	—	—	34	0	.265	.381	.324	91	0	.165	.303	.198
1979	Cle-A	338	10	.325	.433	.500	168	5	.357	.460	.536	170	5	.294	.407	.465	47	1	.191	.291	.319	291	9	.347	.455	.529	83	2	.181	.310	.301	255	8	.373	.473	.565
1980	Cle-A	589	11	.304	.415	.404	280	6	.296	.431	.400	309	5	.311	.399	.408	258	8	.295	.416	.430	331	3	.311	.415	.384	234	4	.303	.401	.402	355	7	.304	.424	.406
1981	Cle-A	322	2	.317	.424	.401	176	2	.313	.416	.409	146	0	.322	.432	.390	174	0	.299	.364	.356	148	2	.338	.482	.453	130	0	.262	.370	.315	192	2	.354	.458	.458
1982	Cle-A	591	4	.271	.377	.338	276	0	.261	.375	.312	315	4	.279	.378	.362	275	2	.273	.396	.335	316	2	.269	.359	.342	212	1	.241	.337	.292	379	3	.288	.398	.364
1983	Cle-A	469	3	.286	.388	.367	212	0	.302	.405	.354	257	3	.272	.374	.377	243	3	.288	.395	.391	226	0	.283	.381	.341	141	0	.277	.388	.383	328	3	.290	.388	.360
1984	Cle-A	352	2	.267	.361	.335	173	1	.283	.376	.335	179	1	.251	.346	.335	178	2	.298	.397	.399	174	0	.236	.323	.270	81	0	.185	.305	.210	271	2	.292	.378	.373
1985	Cle-A	284	1	.285	.370	.352	139	0	.302	.384	.367	145	1	.269	.358	.338	89	0	.247	.352	.303	195	1	.303	.379	.374	22	0	.091	.300	.091	262	1	.302	.378	.374
TOTALS		3564	40	.283	.392	.372	1726	18	.289	.401	.371	1838	22	.277	.384	.373	1648	20	.272	.385	.363	1916	20	.292	.399	.379	1077	10	.250	.361	.331	2487	30	.297	.405	.390
■ **Toby Harrah** BR/TR																																				
1978	Tex-A	450	12	.229	.349	.360	217	6	.221	.347	.341	233	6	.236	.351	.378	227	2	.207	.331	.291	223	10	.251	.368	.430	121	4	.231	.373	.388	329	8	.228	.340	.350
1979	Cle-A	527	20	.279	.389	.444	274	15	.292	.413	.504	253	5	.265	.361	.379	269	9	.275	.389	.416	258	11	.283	.388	.473	125	6	.288	.426	.512	402	14	.276	.376	.423
1980	Cle-A	561	11	.267	.379	.380	266	7	.289	.400	.436	295	4	.247	.360	.329	255	6	.275	.377	.392	306	5	.261	.380	.369	182	3	.275	.417	.385	379	8	.264	.359	.377
1981	Cle-A	361	5	.291	.382	.388	186	3	.280	.362	.387	175	2	.303	.402	.389	176	4	.250	.343	.364	185	1	.330	.417	.411	124	3	.347	.487	.476	237	2	.262	.320	.342
1982	Cle-A	602	25	.304	.398	.490	298	17	.336	.419	.570	304	8	.273	.378	.411	277	14	.354	.455	.560	325	11	.262	.348	.431	196	8	.337	.435	.536	406	17	.288	.380	.468
1983	Cle-A	526	9	.266	.363	.365	258	7	.267	.380	.395	268	2	.265	.347	.336	178	4	.258	.377	.365	348	5	.270	.356	.365	167	4	.257	.367	.371	359	5	.270	.362	.362
1984	NY-A	253	1	.217	.331	.296	121	0	.223	.340	.298	132	1	.212	.323	.295	164	1	.171	.294	.262	89	0	.303	.400	.360	140	0	.236	.361	.300	113	1	.195	.292	.292
1985	Tex-A	396	9	.270	.432	.389	187	5	.289	.458	.417	209	4	.254	.407	.364	206	6	.296	.473	.422	190	3	.242	.382	.353	142	5	.310	.448	.465	254	4	.248	.423	.346
1986	Tex-A	289	7	.218	.322	.367	140	3	.207	.305	.321	149	4	.228	.339	.409	153	2	.203	.301	.314	136	5	.235	.346	.426	103	2	.233	.385	.417	186	5	.210	.284	.339
TOTALS		3965	99	.266	.377	.396	1947	63	.275	.388	.427	2018	36	.256	.365	.367	1905	48	.262	.380	.388	2060	51	.269	.373	.403	1300	35	.282	.412	.429	2665	64	.257	.358	.380
■ **Lenny Harris** BL/TR																																				
1988	Cin-N	43	0	.372	.420	.395	22	0	.409	.462	.455	21	0	.333	.375	.333	0	0	—	—	—	43	0	.372	.420	.395	3	0	.667	.667	.667	40	0	.350	.404	.375
1989	Cin-N	188	2	.223	.263	.277	91	0	.275	.298	.308	97	2	.175	.231	.247	142	1	.239	.285	.289	46	1	.174	.191	.239	55	0	.200	.254	.218	133	2	.233	.266	.301
1989	LA-N	147	1	.252	.308	.327	70	1	.229	.280	.329	77	0	.273	.333	.325	0	0	—	—	—	147	1	.252	.308	.327	13	0	.154	.267	.231	134	1	.261	.313	.336
1990	LA-N	431	2	.304	.348	.374	217	0	.276	.322	.332	214	2	.332	.376	.416	191	1	.304	.337	.387	240	1	.304	.358	.363	42	0	.238	.304	.286	389	2	.311	.353	.383
1991	LA-N	429	3	.287	.349	.350	211	1	.275	.341	.318	218	2	.298	.357	.381	192	1	.302	.368	.349	237	2	.274	.333	.350	87	1	.241	.309	.276	342	2	.298	.359	.368
1992	LA-N	347	0	.271	.318	.303	177	0	.266	.307	.294	170	0	.276	.330	.312	171	0	.292	.339	.327	176	0	.250	.298	.278	36	0	.139	.205	.139	311	0	.286	.331	.322
1993	LA-N	160	2	.237	.303	.325	67	0	.284	.314	.343	93	2	.204	.295	.312	76	0	.250	.313	.316	84	2	.226	.293	.333	15	0	.333	.333	.400	145	2	.228	.300	.317
1994	Cin-N	100	0	.310	.340	.360	50	0	.300	.308	.320	50	0	.320	.370	.400	70	0	.357	.384	.429	30	0	.200	.242	.200	11	0	.545	.583	.545	89	0	.281	.309	.337
1995	Cin-N	197	2	.208	.259	.310	90	0	.178	.242	.211	107	2	.234	.274	.393	117	0	.222	.264	.308	80	2	.188	.253	.313	17	1	.235	.278	.471	180	1	.206	.258	.294
1996	Cin-N	302	5	.285	.330	.404	137	2	.263	.331	.380	165	3	.303	.329	.424	83	2	.265	.319	.458	219	3	.292	.335	.384	45	1	.311	.380	.444	257	4	.280	.321	.397
1997	Cin-N	238	3	.273	.327	.374	123	2	.293	.328	.407	115	1	.252	.326	.339	150	3	.267	.288	.400	88	0	.284	.385	.330	24	0	.250	.250	.292	214	3	.276	.335	.383
1998	Cin-N	122	0	.295	.338	.361	48	0	.167	.241	.229	74	0	.378	.405	.446	120	0	.292	.336	.350	2	0	.500	.500	1.000	7	0	.714	.750	.714	115	0	.270	.312	.339
1998	NY-N	168	6	.232	.272	.381	78	2	.256	.301	.397	90	4	.211	.247	.367	0	0	—	—	—	168	6	.232	.272	.381	12	0	.000	.077	.000	156	6	.250	.287	.410
1999	Col-N	158	0	.297	.323	.373	84	0	.345	.345	.464	74	0	.243	.300	.270	91	0	.242	.281	.275	67	0	.373	.382	.507	13	0	.385	.429	.385	145	0	.290	.313	.372
1999	Ari-N	29	1	.379	.367	.517	22	1	.318	.304	.455	7	0	.571	.571	.714	0	0	—	—	—	29	1	.379	.367	.517	4	1	.500	.500	1.250	25	0	.360	.346	.400
2000	Ari-N	85	1	.188	.209	.259	35	1	.200	.211	.314	50	0	.180	.208	.220	85	1	.188	.209	.259	0	0	—	—	—	13	0	.154	.154	.154	72	1	.194	.218	.278
2000	NY-N	138	3	.304	.381	.457	55	1	.327	.403	.473	83	2	.289	.366	.446	16	0	.125	.125	.188	122	3	.328	.410	.492	6	0	.167	.167	.167	132	3	.311	.389	.470
TOTALS		3282	31	.273	.321	.353	1577	11	.270	.315	.342	1705	20	.275	.326	.364	1504	9	.271	.313	.344	1778	22	.274	.328	.361	403	4	.251	.305	.305	2879	27	.276	.323	.360
■ **Billy Hatcher** BR/TR																																				
1984	Chi-N	9	0	.111	.200	.111	4	0	.000	.200	.000	5	0	.200	.200	.200	0	0	—	—	—	9	0	.111	.200	.111	1	0	.000	.500	.000	8	0	.125	.125	.125
1985	Chi-N	163	2	.245	.290	.368	109	2	.229	.259	.339	54	0	.278	.350	.426	29	1	.310	.355	.552	134	1	.231	.276	.328	40	0	.225	.244	.250	123	2	.252	.304	.407
1986	Hou-N	419	6	.258	.302	.356	218	2	.257	.300	.339	201	4	.259	.304	.373	161	1	.255	.277	.323	258	5	.260	.317	.376	210	3	.286	.326	.390	209	3	.230	.278	.321
1987	Hou-N	564	11	.296	.352	.415	259	3	.305	.358	.382	305	8	.289	.346	.443	303	7	.317	.374	.452	261	4	.272	.325	.372	202	4	.277	.335	.406	362	7	.307	.361	.420
1988	Hou-N	530	7	.268	.321	.370	263	3	.243	.308	.342	267	4	.292	.333	.397	287	3	.289	.335	.383	243	4	.243	.303	.354	183	4	.284	.333	.415	347	3	.259	.314	.346
1989	Hou-N	395	3	.228	.281	.304	197	0	.234	.301	.299	198	3	.222	.261	.308	273	3	.231	.273	.330	122	0	.221	.299	.246	139	2	.281	.315	.374	256	1	.199	.263	.266
1989	Pit-N	86	1	.244	.253	.326	34	0	.235	.235	.294	52	1	.250	.264	.346	0	0	—	—	—	86	1	.244	.253	.326	54	0	.241	.241	.278	32	1	.250	.273	.406
1990	Cin-N	504	5	.276	.327	.381	246	2	.264	.314	.378	258	3	.287	.339	.384	265	1	.309	.359	.404	239	4	.238	.292	.356	207	1	.246	.299	.319	297	4	.296	.347	.424
1991	Cin-N	442	4	.262	.312	.360	216	2	.269	.323	.380	226	2	.257	.300	.341	205	3	.263	.311	.390	237	1	.262	.313	.333	130	1	.277	.324	.369	312	3	.256	.307	.356
1992	Cin-N	94	2	.287	.314	.383	34	0	.294	.333	.353	60	2	.283	.303	.400	88	2	.295	.326	.398	6	0	.167	.143	.167	60	2	.283	.313	.417	34	0	.294	.316	.324
1992	Bos-A	315	1	.238	.283	.311	157	1	.268	.326	.350	158	0	.209	.238	.272	0	0	—	—	—	315	1	.238	.283	.311	81	0	.210	.247	.284	234	1	.248	.295	.321
1993	Bos-A	508	9	.287	.336	.400	261	5	.295	.344	.418	247	4	.279	.327	.381	262	5	.302	.353	.416	246	4	.272	.317	.382	138	1	.232	.269	.304	370	8	.308	.360	.435
1994	Bos-A	164	1	.244	.292	.329	80	0	.338	.391	.450	84	1	.155	.198	.214	164	1	.244	.292	.329	0	0	—	—	—	53	0	.189	.214	.208	111	1	.270	.328	.387
1994	Phi-N	134	2	.246	.271	.343	63	0	.238	.261	.286	71	2	.254	.280	.394	57	2	.281	.311	.439	77	0	.221	.241	.273	53	1	.208	.250	.302	81	1	.272	.286	.370
1995	Tex-A	12	0	.083	.154	.167	6	0	.000	.143	.000	6	0	.167	.167	.333	12	0	.083	.154	.167	0	0	—	—	—	10	0	.100	.182	.200	2	0	.000	.000	.000
TOTALS		4339	54	.264	.312	.364	2147	20	.266	.318	.361	2192	34	.262	.306	.367	2106	29	.280	.326	.388	2233	25	.249	.299	.341	1561	19	.259	.302	.352	2778	35	.267	.318	.370
■ **Charlie Hayes** BR/TR																																				
1988	SF-N	11	0	.091	.091	.091	5	0	.000	.000	.000	6	0	.167	.167	.167	0	0	—	—	—	11	0	.091	.091	.091	11	0	.091	.091	.091	0	0	—	—	—
1989	SF-N	5	0	.200	.200	.200	4	0	.250	.250	.250	1	0	.000	.000	.000	5	0	.200	.200	.200	0	0	—	—	—	4	0	.000	.000	.000	1	0	1.000	1.000	1.000
1989	Phi-N	299	8	.258	.281	.395	152	3	.230	.262	.362	147	5	.286	.301	.429	7	0	.286	.375	.429	292	8	.257	.279	.394	101	1	.277	.306	.376	198	7	.247	.268	.404
1990	Phi-N	561	10	.258	.293	.348	282	3	.245	.272	.309	279	7	.272	.314	.387	260	5	.288	.324	.385	301	5	.233	.267	.316	193	5	.295	.324	.425	368	5	.239	.277	.307
1991	Phi-N	460	12	.230	.257	.363	248	6	.262	.292	.407	212	6	.193	.216	.311	236	6	.203	.232	.326	224	6	.259	.284	.402	190	4	.258	.283	.395	270	8	.211	.239	.341
1992	NY-A	509	18	.257	.297	.409	245	7	.220	.267	.351	264	11	.292	.325	.462	264	9	.269	.305	.417	245	9	.245	.288	.400	150	6	.213	.262	.353	359	12	.276	.312	.432
1993	Col-N	573	25	.305	.355	.522	296	17	.338	.387	.601	277	8	.271	.319	.437	270	12	.307	.366	.511	303	13	.304	.344	.531	142	5	.338	.367	.542	431	20	.295	.351	.515
1994	Col-N	423	10	.288	.348	.433	208	4	.317	.364	.481	215	6	.260	.332	.386	284	7	.285	.336	.430	139	3	.295	.372	.439	89	4	.270	.323	.494	334	6	.293	.354	.416
1995	Phi-N	529	11	.276	.340	.406	257	6	.288	.354	.432	272	5	.265	.326	.382	210	6	.295	.381	.443	319	5	.263	.310	.382	147	3	.313	.388	.476	382	8	.262	.321	.380
1996	Pit-N	459	10	.248	.301	.368	220	5	.268	.339	.432	239	5	.230	.265	.310	277	9	.242	.304	.397	182	1	.258	.297	.324	95	4	.274	.337	.421	364	6	.242	.292	.354
1996	NY-A	67	2	.284	.294	.418	14	0	.214	.214	.286	53	2	.302	.315	.453	0	0	—	—	—	67	2	.284	.294	.418	17	0	.294	.294	.412	50	2	.280	.294	.420
1997	NY-A	353	11	.258	.332	.397	182	5	.269	.348	.423	171	6	.246	.314	.368	130	6	.292	.396	.485	223	5	.238	.291	.345	135	8	.311	.394	.541	218	3	.225	.292	.307
1998	SF-N	329	12	.286	.351	.419	165	7	.309	.372	.467	164	5	.262	.330	.372	170	4	.306	.365	.412	159	8	.264	.335	.428	130	5	.338	.407	.492	199	7	.251	.314	.372
1999	SF-N	264	6	.205	.292	.314	119	2	.202	.284	.311	145	4	.207	.299	.317	174	2	.184	.276	.259	90	4	.244	.324	.422	117	4	.197	.264	.333	147	2	.211	.314	.299
2000	Mil-A	370	9	.251	.348	.370	171	2	.216	.318	.292	199	7	.281	.373	.437	198	6	.258	.375	.414	172	3	.244	.314	.320	117	4	.256	.373	.436	253	5	.249	.336	.340
TOTALS		5212	144	.263	.317	.399	2568	67	.268	.323	.412	2644	77	.258	.310	.387	2485	72	.267	.330	.408	2727	72	.259	.304	.392	1638	53	.278	.333	.436	3574	91	.256	.309	.383
■ **Von Hayes** BL/TR																																				
1981	Cle-A	109	1	.257	.346	.394	56	0	.232	.295	.357	53	1	.283	.394	.434	0	0	—	—	—	109	1	.257	.346	.394	20	0	.250	.385	.400	89	1	.258	.337	.393
1982	Cle-A	527	14	.250	.310	.389	257	3	.265	.324	.389	270	11	.237	.296	.389	240	5	.254	.300	.392	287	9	.247	.318	.387	168	3	.244	.302	.363	359	11	.253	.313	.401
1983	Phi-N	351	6	.265	.337	.370	198	3	.217	.288	.308	153	3	.327	.399	.451	162	3	.272	.357	.407	189	3	.259	.319	.339	44	0	.318	.423	.386	307	6	.257	.324	.368
1984	Phi-N	561	16	.292	.359	.447	264	10	.292	.362	.473	297	6	.293	.356	.424	220	5	.295	.370	.432	341	11	.290	.351	.457	111	2	.234	.267	.333	450	14	.307	.379	.476
1985	Phi-N	570	13	.263	.332	.398	278	12	.288	.360	.493	292	1	.240	.306	.308	229	6	.271	.363	.406	341	7	.258	.310	.393	157	4	.229	.291	.338	413	9	.276	.348	.421
1986	Phi-N	610	19	.305	.379	.480	296	11	.314	.393	.503	314	8	.296	.365	.459	266	4	.301	.386	.436	344	15	.308	.373	.515	195	3	.231	.301	.328	415	16	.340	.414	.552
1987	Phi-N	556	21	.277	.404	.473	278	14	.252	.401	.475	278	7	.302	.407	.471	227	8	.278	.424	.476	329	13	.277	.389	.471	168	3	.232	.361	.345	388	18	.296	.422	.528
1988	Phi-N	367	6	.272	.355	.409	175	2	.229	.310	.354	192	4	.313	.396	.458	272	4	.272	.356	.419	95	2	.274	.355	.379	101	2	.129	.196	.238	266	4	.327	.413	.474
1989	Phi-N	540	26	.259	.376	.461	257	15	.249	.377	.479	283	11	.269	.375	.445	259	13	.270	.399	.490	281	13	.249	.353	.434	208	8	.245	.356	.404	332	18	.268	.388	.497
1990	Phi-N	467	17	.261	.375	.413	203	10	.276	.392	.478	264	7	.250	.362	.364	209	9	.268	.399	.450	258	8	.256	.354	.384	179	6	.274	.365	.419	288	11	.253	.381	.410
1991	Phi-N	284	0	.225	.303	.285	99	0	.202	.319	.242	185	0	.238	.294	.308	217	0	.226	.308	.290	67	0	.224	.288	.269	90	0	.267	.355	.333	194	0	.206	.278	.263
1992	Cal-A	307	4	.225	.305	.326	162	2	.241	.315	.346	145	2	.207	.294	.303	187	3	.257	.347	.380	120	1	.175	.237	.242	42	0	.119	.208	.143	265	4	.242	.321	.355
TOTALS		5249	143	.267	.354	.416	2523	82	.263	.355	.430	2726	61	.271	.353	.403	2488	60	.270	.367	.418	2761	83	.264	.342	.414	1483	31	.235	.320	.349	3766	112	.280	.367	.443
■ **Todd Helton** BL/TL																																				
1997	Col-N	93	5	.280	.337	.484	48	3	.292	.333	.542	45	2	.267	.340	.422	0	0	—	—	—	93	5	.280	.337	.484	10	0	.200	.200	.200	83	5	.289	.352	.518
1998	Col-N	530	25	.315	.380	.530	277	13	.354	.417	.585	253	12	.273	.340	.470	256	11	.277	.347	.477	274	14	.350	.411	.580	112	5	.304	.394	.482	418	20	.318	.377	.543

YEAR	TM/L	TOTAL AB	HR	AVG	OBP	SLG	HOME AB	HR	AVG	OBP	SLG	AWAY AB	HR	AVG	OBP	SLG	1ST HALF AB	HR	AVG	OBP	SLG	2ND HALF AB	HR	AVG	OBP	SLG	LEFT AB	HR	AVG	OBP	SLG	RIGHT AB	HR	AVG	OBP	SLG
1999	Col-N	578	35	.320	.395	.587	296	23	.385	.459	.720	282	12	.252	.324	.447	256	15	.297	.380	.551	322	20	.339	.407	.615	163	4	.245	.319	.374	415	31	.349	.424	.670
2000	Col-N	580	42	.372	.463	.698	302	27	.391	.484	.758	278	15	.353	.441	.633	263	21	.384	.481	.734	317	21	.363	.448	.669	143	7	.329	.451	.594	437	35	.387	.467	.732
TOTALS		1781	107	.334	.411	.601	923	66	.373	.449	.683	858	41	.291	.369	.513	775	47	.320	.406	.588	1006	60	.344	.415	.610	428	16	.287	.383	.472	1353	91	.348	.420	.642
■ **Dave Henderson** BR/TR																																				
1981	Sea-A	126	6	.167	.264	.333	54	5	.185	.254	.500	72	1	.153	.271	.208	109	6	.156	.244	.349	17	0	.235	.381	.235	56	4	.232	.317	.500	70	2	.114	.222	.200
1982	Sea-A	324	14	.253	.327	.441	158	8	.228	.318	.443	166	6	.277	.335	.440	122	9	.287	.365	.582	202	5	.233	.304	.356	163	8	.258	.326	.485	161	6	.248	.328	.398
1983	Sea-A	484	17	.269	.306	.444	239	9	.280	.319	.481	245	8	.257	.294	.408	262	6	.263	.306	.385	222	11	.275	.306	.514	207	6	.271	.314	.411	277	11	.267	.301	.469
1984	Sea-A	350	14	.280	.320	.466	188	8	.314	.355	.521	162	6	.241	.279	.401	163	6	.233	.288	.387	187	8	.321	.349	.535	134	5	.291	.324	.478	216	9	.273	.317	.458
1985	Sea-A	502	14	.241	.310	.388	253	8	.249	.330	.403	249	6	.233	.289	.373	235	6	.260	.322	.396	267	8	.225	.300	.382	132	3	.280	.345	.439	370	11	.227	.298	.370
1986	Sea-A	337	14	.276	.350	.481	168	10	.304	.369	.565	169	4	.249	.332	.396	236	11	.250	.326	.453	101	3	.337	.407	.545	86	6	.291	.361	.547	251	8	.271	.346	.458
1986	Bos-A	51	1	.196	.226	.314	38	0	.211	.231	.289	13	1	.154	.214	.385	0	0	—	—	—	51	1	.196	.226	.314	15	0	.133	.188	.200	36	1	.222	.243	.361
1987	Bos-A	184	8	.234	.313	.418	107	4	.234	.320	.411	77	4	.234	.302	.429	136	6	.206	.297	.397	48	2	.313	.358	.479	66	4	.258	.319	.515	118	4	.220	.309	.364
1987	SF-N	21	0	.238	.448	.333	14	0	.214	.389	.357	7	0	.286	.545	.286	0	0	—	—	—	21	0	.238	.448	.333	15	0	.333	.524	.467	6	0	.000	.250	.000
1988	Oak-A	507	24	.304	.363	.525	246	12	.293	.354	.512	261	12	.314	.371	.536	201	10	.303	.366	.552	306	14	.304	.361	.507	147	6	.306	.372	.524	360	18	.303	.359	.525
1989	Oak-A	579	15	.250	.315	.380	289	10	.280	.333	.433	290	5	.221	.297	.328	288	7	.250	.323	.375	291	8	.251	.306	.385	171	5	.287	.347	.427	408	10	.235	.301	.360
1990	Oak-A	450	20	.271	.331	.467	222	11	.302	.353	.514	228	9	.241	.310	.421	252	14	.254	.311	.488	198	6	.293	.355	.439	133	11	.353	.404	.654	317	9	.237	.300	.388
1991	Oak-A	572	25	.276	.346	.465	282	15	.259	.329	.450	290	10	.293	.362	.479	270	18	.311	.387	.574	302	7	.245	.308	.368	144	8	.354	.416	.618	428	17	.250	.322	.414
1992	Oak-A	63	0	.143	.169	.159	39	0	.128	.171	.128	24	0	.167	.167	.208	12	0	.167	.167	.167	51	0	.137	.170	.157	24	0	.208	.208	.250	39	0	.103	.146	.103
1993	Oak-A	382	20	.220	.275	.427	211	7	.194	.239	.336	171	13	.251	.318	.538	139	8	.194	.255	.396	243	12	.235	.286	.444	142	11	.225	.291	.500	240	9	.217	.265	.383
1994	KC-A	198	5	.247	.304	.404	97	2	.278	.330	.464	101	3	.218	.279	.347	152	5	.243	.293	.401	46	0	.261	.340	.413	84	3	.298	.362	.488	114	2	.211	.260	.342
TOTALS		5130	197	.258	.320	.436	2605	109	.264	.324	.453	2525	88	.252	.316	.418	2577	112	.254	.320	.443	2553	85	.262	.321	.428	1719	80	.285	.345	.494	3411	117	.245	.307	.406
■ **Rickey Henderson** BR/TL																																				
1979	Oak-A	351	1	.274	.338	.336	166	1	.289	.346	.380	185	0	.259	.332	.297	27	0	.222	.344	.259	324	1	.278	.338	.343	119	0	.345	.396	.429	232	1	.237	.309	.289
1980	Oak-A	591	9	.303	.420	.399	281	3	.299	.427	.374	310	6	.306	.415	.423	276	3	.304	.418	.406	315	6	.302	.422	.394	214	5	.350	.451	.481	377	4	.276	.403	.353
1981	Oak-A	423	6	.319	.408	.437	218	5	.339	.402	.472	205	1	.298	.413	.400	225	3	.320	.419	.444	198	3	.318	.395	.429	147	4	.320	.392	.476	276	2	.319	.416	.417
1982	Oak-A	536	10	.267	.398	.382	281	5	.278	.412	.388	255	5	.255	.383	.376	288	6	.271	.418	.399	248	4	.262	.373	.363	204	3	.265	.359	.377	332	7	.268	.420	.386
1983	Oak-A	513	9	.292	.414	.421	252	5	.262	.387	.377	261	4	.322	.440	.464	238	4	.256	.388	.382	275	5	.324	.436	.455	194	4	.304	.418	.459	319	5	.285	.411	.398
1984	Oak-A	502	16	.293	.399	.458	228	7	.285	.408	.447	274	9	.299	.392	.467	283	9	.304	.399	.466	219	7	.279	.400	.447	185	7	.286	.379	.465	317	9	.297	.411	.454
1985	NY-A	547	24	.314	.419	.516	246	8	.305	.416	.459	301	16	.322	.422	.561	229	9	.354	.438	.550	318	15	.286	.406	.491	180	12	.361	.487	.656	367	12	.292	.383	.447
1986	NY-A	608	28	.263	.358	.469	298	13	.235	.332	.440	310	15	.290	.383	.497	312	15	.288	.375	.510	296	13	.236	.341	.426	192	8	.234	.370	.443	416	20	.276	.352	.481
1987	NY-A	358	17	.291	.423	.497	161	10	.317	.453	.590	197	7	.269	.397	.421	179	10	.318	.440	.564	179	7	.263	.405	.430	118	7	.314	.445	.585	240	10	.279	.412	.454
1988	NY-A	554	6	.305	.394	.399	256	2	.297	.389	.391	298	4	.312	.398	.406	225	5	.316	.406	.440	329	1	.298	.385	.371	163	4	.368	.470	.521	391	2	.279	.360	.348
1989	NY-A	235	3	.247	.392	.349	109	1	.257	.401	.349	126	2	.238	.385	.349	235	3	.247	.392	.349	0	0	—	—	—	89	0	.292	.427	.326	146	3	.219	.372	.363
1989	Oak-A	306	9	.294	.425	.438	144	6	.313	.466	.507	162	3	.278	.384	.377	32	1	.375	.487	.500	274	8	.285	.418	.431	84	1	.262	.398	.393	222	8	.306	.435	.455
1990	Oak-A	489	28	.325	.439	.577	220	8	.305	.425	.486	269	20	.342	.451	.651	244	13	.336	.448	.590	245	15	.314	.431	.563	134	9	.313	.421	.604	355	19	.330	.446	.566
1991	Oak-A	470	18	.268	.400	.423	248	8	.278	.401	.415	222	10	.257	.399	.432	198	4	.283	.435	.384	272	14	.257	.372	.452	114	8	.289	.401	.526	356	10	.261	.399	.390
1992	Oak-A	396	15	.283	.426	.457	200	10	.295	.441	.495	196	5	.270	.410	.418	195	7	.277	.422	.436	201	8	.289	.430	.478	105	5	.267	.398	.476	291	10	.289	.435	.450
1993	Oak-A	318	17	.327	.469	.553	168	8	.327	.475	.524	150	9	.327	.463	.587	227	9	.304	.466	.480	91	8	.385	.477	.736	74	10	.378	.535	.811	244	7	.311	.448	.475
1993	Tor-A	163	4	.215	.356	.319	83	2	.193	.306	.325	80	2	.237	.404	.313	0	0	—	—	—	163	4	.215	.356	.319	56	2	.232	.348	.375	107	2	.206	.360	.290
1994	Oak-A	296	6	.260	.411	.365	132	4	.250	.415	.379	164	2	.268	.407	.354	185	4	.259	.410	.384	111	2	.261	.411	.333	105	3	.248	.407	.371	191	3	.267	.412	.361
1995	Oak-A	407	9	.300	.407	.447	208	3	.298	.403	.404	199	6	.302	.412	.492	177	4	.266	.383	.401	230	5	.326	.426	.483	120	2	.233	.374	.325	287	7	.328	.422	.498
1996	SD-N	465	9	.241	.410	.344	233	6	.275	.436	.391	232	3	.207	.385	.297	243	6	.226	.406	.337	222	3	.257	.415	.351	114	4	.263	.433	.404	351	5	.234	.403	.325
1997	SD-N	288	6	.274	.422	.375	144	5	.264	.409	.410	144	1	.285	.435	.340	153	3	.288	.453	.379	135	3	.259	.384	.370	49	3	.286	.478	.510	239	3	.272	.409	.347
1997	Ana-A	115	2	.183	.343	.261	65	1	.154	.313	.231	50	1	.220	.381	.300	0	0	—	—	—	115	2	.183	.343	.261	28	1	.250	.488	.393	87	1	.161	.284	.218
1998	Oak-A	542	14	.236	.376	.347	260	6	.223	.367	.315	282	8	.248	.384	.376	295	7	.241	.368	.356	247	7	.231	.385	.336	156	5	.256	.396	.410	386	9	.228	.368	.321
1999	NY-N	438	12	.315	.423	.466	200	1	.270	.376	.320	238	11	.353	.462	.588	164	6	.280	.434	.463	274	6	.336	.415	.467	105	6	.343	.481	.581	333	6	.306	.403	.429
2000	NY-N	96	0	.219	.387	.229	46	0	.196	.327	.196	50	0	.240	.435	.260	96	0	.219	.387	.229	0	0	—	—	—	20	0	.100	.379	.100	76	0	.250	.389	.263
2000	Sea-A	324	4	.238	.362	.327	153	2	.248	.400	.333	171	2	.228	.325	.322	119	4	.235	.338	.345	205	0	.239	.375	.317	70	0	.229	.379	.286	254	4	.240	.357	.339
TOTALS		10331	282	.282	.404	.423	5000	130	.278	.403	.411	5331	152	.285	.405	.434	4845	135	.284	.412	.429	5486	147	.280	.396	.417	3139	113	.295	.418	.470	7192	169	.276	.397	.403
■ **George Hendrick** BR/TR																																				
1978	SD-N	111	3	.243	.317	.360	56	2	.232	.338	.357	55	1	.255	.293	.364	111	3	.243	.317	.360	0	0	—	—	—	31	0	.194	.342	.258	80	3	.262	.306	.400
1978	StL-N	382	17	.288	.337	.497	187	7	.316	.351	.497	195	10	.262	.322	.497	104	3	.212	.284	.385	278	14	.317	.357	.540	158	8	.297	.339	.519	224	9	.281	.335	.482
1979	StL-N	493	16	.300	.359	.456	235	7	.340	.405	.506	258	9	.264	.315	.411	249	7	.345	.397	.518	244	9	.254	.321	.393	218	7	.326	.383	.486	275	9	.280	.341	.433
1980	StL-N	572	25	.302	.342	.498	277	13	.264	.319	.484	295	12	.339	.364	.512	273	16	.311	.354	.549	299	9	.294	.330	.452	184	10	.283	.327	.495	388	15	.312	.349	.500
1981	StL-N	394	18	.284	.356	.485	192	6	.245	.338	.391	202	12	.322	.374	.574	191	10	.277	.353	.492	203	8	.291	.358	.478	127	7	.331	.410	.559	267	11	.262	.330	.449
1982	StL-N	515	19	.282	.323	.450	271	10	.292	.325	.483	244	9	.270	.320	.414	239	12	.255	.293	.448	276	7	.304	.347	.453	166	4	.307	.348	.446	349	15	.269	.311	.453
1983	StL-N	529	18	.318	.373	.493	259	10	.305	.358	.498	270	8	.330	.387	.489	248	11	.331	.384	.532	281	7	.306	.363	.459	157	7	.350	.420	.561	372	11	.304	.353	.465
1984	StL-N	441	9	.277	.324	.406	220	2	.259	.308	.373	221	7	.294	.339	.439	248	5	.262	.319	.379	193	4	.295	.330	.440	146	3	.288	.342	.438	295	6	.271	.314	.390
1985	Pit-N	256	2	.230	.278	.313	149	0	.242	.301	.282	107	2	.215	.246	.355	199	2	.236	.289	.327	57	0	.211	.237	.263	99	0	.202	.252	.273	157	2	.248	.294	.338
1985	Cal-A	41	2	.122	.196	.293	20	0	.050	.136	.100	21	2	.190	.250	.476	0	0	—	—	—	41	2	.122	.196	.293	31	1	.129	.222	.258	10	1	.100	.100	.400
1986	Cal-A	283	14	.272	.332	.473	135	8	.289	.344	.511	148	6	.257	.321	.439	149	7	.255	.317	.443	134	7	.291	.349	.507	174	9	.299	.352	.506	109	5	.229	.300	.422
1987	Cal-A	162	5	.241	.301	.395	69	1	.174	.240	.290	93	4	.290	.347	.473	38	2	.184	.184	.342	124	3	.258	.333	.411	125	4	.232	.294	.384	37	1	.270	.325	.432
1988	Cal-A	127	3	.244	.283	.323	70	2	.257	.280	.343	57	1	.228	.286	.298	66	1	.197	.225	.258	61	2	.295	.343	.393	76	2	.276	.296	.368	51	1	.196	.263	.255
TOTALS		4306	151	.282	.335	.449	2140	68	.277	.333	.439	2166	83	.288	.336	.459	2115	79	.277	.331	.448	2191	72	.288	.338	.450	1692	62	.291	.347	.463	2614	89	.277	.327	.440
■ **Jose Hernandez** BR/TR																																				
1991	Tex-A	98	0	.184	.208	.224	40	0	.225	.279	.300	58	0	.155	.155	.172	0	0	—	—	—	98	0	.184	.208	.224	29	0	.241	.241	.345	69	0	.159	.194	.174
1992	Cle-A	4	0	.000	.000	.000	2	0	.000	.000	.000	2	0	.000	.000	.000	0	0	—	—	—	4	0	.000	.000	.000	0	0	—	—	—	4	0	.000	.000	.000
1994	Chi-N	132	1	.242	.291	.326	67	0	.239	.311	.284	65	1	.246	.269	.369	40	1	.275	.310	.400	92	0	.228	.283	.293	31	1	.290	.313	.452	101	0	.228	.284	.287
1995	Chi-N	245	13	.245	.281	.482	119	6	.193	.224	.395	126	7	.294	.333	.563	75	3	.253	.282	.427	170	10	.241	.280	.506	72	4	.264	.293	.514	173	9	.237	.276	.468
1996	Chi-N	331	10	.242	.293	.381	163	4	.252	.311	.362	168	6	.232	.275	.399	163	3	.221	.274	.319	168	7	.262	.311	.440	81	1	.173	.209	.247	250	9	.264	.320	.424
1997	Chi-N	183	7	.273	.323	.486	84	4	.274	.337	.536	99	3	.273	.311	.444	91	3	.286	.327	.462	92	4	.261	.320	.511	84	3	.250	.319	.452	99	4	.293	.327	.515
1998	Chi-N	488	23	.254	.311	.471	240	11	.287	.348	.508	248	12	.222	.273	.435	201	11	.279	.333	.547	287	12	.237	.295	.418	157	9	.255	.314	.522	331	14	.254	.309	.447
1999	Chi-N	342	15	.272	.357	.450	144	5	.292	.386	.424	198	10	.258	.335	.470	252	9	.254	.338	.413	90	6	.322	.408	.556	109	7	.257	.331	.495	233	8	.279	.368	.429
1999	Atl-N	166	4	.253	.302	.373	77	1	.247	.314	.351	89	3	.258	.290	.393	0	0	—	—	—	166	4	.253	.302	.373	59	1	.356	.424	.508	107	3	.196	.230	.299
2000	Mil-A	446	11	.244	.315	.372	210	8	.238	.309	.405	236	3	.250	.319	.343	271	9	.232	.307	.391	175	2	.263	.327	.343	113	2	.212	.310	.327	333	9	.255	.316	.387
TOTALS		2435	84	.250	.308	.415	1146	39	.255	.320	.416	1289	45	.245	.296	.413	1093	39	.252	.314	.423	1342	45	.248	.302	.408	735	28	.249	.310	.438	1700	56	.250	.307	.405
■ **Keith Hernandez** BL/TL																																				
1978	StL-N	542	11	.255	.351	.389	248	4	.270	.363	.415	294	7	.241	.341	.367	272	9	.268	.368	.438	270	2	.241	.334	.341	192	6	.266	.366	.432	350	5	.249	.343	.366
1979	StL-N	610	11	.344	.417	.513	299	5	.338	.416	.538	311	6	.350	.418	.489	285	7	.326	.389	.516	325	4	.360	.440	.511	247	6	.332	.394	.514	363	5	.353	.432	.512
1980	StL-N	595	16	.321	.408	.494	302	8	.341	.416	.526	293	8	.300	.399	.461	266	7	.335	.419	.508	329	9	.310	.399	.483	213	4	.357	.456	.540	382	12	.301	.380	.469
1981	StL-N	376	8	.306	.401	.463	189	4	.280	.380	.444	187	4	.332	.422	.481	191	4	.272	.375	.440	185	4	.341	.427	.486	135	1	.274	.365	.348	241	7	.324	.421	.527
1982	StL-N	579	7	.299	.397	.413	287	4	.286	.383	.415	292	3	.312	.410	.411	286	3	.297	.384	.388	293	4	.300	.409	.437	198	2	.283	.351	.384	381	5	.307	.419	.428
1983	StL-N	218	3	.284	.352	.431	106	2	.340	.405	.519	112	1	.232	.301	.348	218	3	.284	.352	.431	0	0	—	—	—	73	2	.274	.346	.493	145	1	.290	.356	.400
1983	NY-N	320	9	.306	.424	.434	173	8	.301	.402	.457	147	1	.313	.448	.408	65	2	.415	.486	.569	255	7	.278	.409	.400	94	1	.245	.349	.330	226	8	.332	.453	.478
1984	NY-N	550	15	.311	.409	.449	268	10	.366	.461	.537	282	5	.259	.360	.365	254	6	.319	.396	.445	296	9	.304	.420	.453	196	3	.291	.371	.362	354	12	.322	.430	.497
1985	NY-N	593	10	.309	.384	.430	285	4	.284	.365	.375	308	6	.331	.402	.481	255	4	.251	.348	.349	338	6	.352	.413	.491	260	3	.315	.358	.415	333	7	.303	.403	.441
1986	NY-N	551	13	.310	.413	.446	239	6	.310	.422	.431	312	7	.311	.405	.458	265	5	.298	.385	.411	286	8	.322	.437	.479	218	4	.312	.409	.422	333	9	.309	.415	.462
1987	NY-N	587	18	.290	.377	.436	281	6	.288	.386	.406	306	12	.291	.369	.464	273	10	.297	.371	.462	314	8	.283	.382	.414	252	6	.254	.343	.373	335	12	.316	.403	.484
1988	NY-N	348	11	.276	.333	.417	146	2	.274	.348	.349	202	9	.277	.323	.465	198	5	.298	.366	.434	150	6	.247	.287	.393	135	6	.274	.333	.452	213	5	.277	.333	.394
1989	NY-N	215	4	.233	.324	.326	95	2	.263	.358	.358	120	2	.208	.296	.300	117	3	.282	.364	.410	98	1	.173	.277	.224	79	1	.291	.364	.354	136	3	.199	.301	.309
1990	Cle-A	130	1	.200	.283	.238	42	0	.167	.286	.190	88	1	.216	.281	.261	106	1	.208	.294	.255	24	0	.167	.231	.167	27	0	.148	.233	.148	103	1	.214	.296	.262
TOTALS		6214	137	.298	.387	.437	2960	65	.304	.395	.446	3254	72	.293	.381	.428	3051	69	.295	.377	.434	3163	68	.302	.397	.439	2319	45	.293	.372	.420	3895	92	.301	.396	.447
■ **Larry Herndon** BR/TR																																				
1978	SF-N	471	1	.259	.311	.335	236	0	.258	.324	.347	235	1	.260	.297	.323	265	0	.291	.356	.377	206	1	.218	.250	.282	172	0	.273	.340	.355	299	1	.251	.293	.324
1979	SF-N	354	7	.257	.313	.384	155	2	.232	.294	.329	199	5	.276	.329	.427	124	4	.315	.363	.524	230	3	.226	.287	.309	110	3	.255	.308	.464	244	4	.258	.316	.348

		TOTAL					HOME					AWAY					1ST HALF					2ND HALF					LEFT					RIGHT				
YEAR	TM/L	AB	HR	AVG	OBP	SLG	AB	HR	AVG	OBP	SLG	AB	HR	AVG	OBP	SLG	AB	HR	AVG	OBP	SLG	AB	HR	AVG	OBP	SLG	AB	HR	AVG	OBP	SLG	AB	HR	AVG	OBP	SLG
1980	SF-N	493	8	.258	.284	.385	250	3	.248	.277	.364	243	5	.267	.292	.407	193	3	.233	.268	.342	300	5	.273	.295	.413	162	5	.259	.277	.407	331	3	.257	.288	.375
1981	SF-N	364	5	.288	.325	.415	164	4	.317	.349	.470	200	1	.265	.305	.370	203	2	.300	.325	.424	161	3	.273	.324	.404	93	1	.355	.365	.548	271	4	.266	.312	.369
1982	Det-A	614	23	.292	.332	.480	287	9	.300	.353	.449	327	14	.284	.313	.508	270	14	.319	.363	.567	344	9	.270	.307	.413	185	6	.335	.380	.551	429	17	.273	.311	.450
1983	Det-A	603	20	.302	.351	.478	288	7	.281	.356	.448	315	13	.321	.346	.505	270	6	.263	.303	.426	333	14	.333	.389	.520	201	11	.353	.387	.597	402	9	.276	.333	.418
1984	Det-A	407	7	.280	.333	.400	204	3	.314	.365	.441	203	4	.246	.302	.360	228	1	.254	.312	.333	179	6	.313	.361	.486	223	4	.314	.360	.448	184	3	.239	.302	.342
1985	Det-A	442	12	.244	.298	.385	211	7	.256	.308	.417	231	5	.234	.288	.355	237	5	.236	.293	.367	205	7	.254	.303	.405	155	7	.265	.347	.484	287	5	.233	.269	.331
1986	Det-A	283	8	.247	.310	.385	137	4	.234	.289	.358	146	4	.260	.329	.411	166	4	.235	.285	.373	117	4	.265	.343	.402	189	6	.233	.302	.365	94	2	.277	.327	.426
1987	Det-A	225	9	.324	.378	.520	115	7	.313	.372	.583	110	2	.336	.384	.455	110	4	.327	.383	.509	115	5	.322	.373	.530	177	8	.373	.426	.593	48	1	.146	.192	.250
1988	Det-A	174	4	.224	.313	.322	91	2	.198	.302	.297	83	2	.253	.326	.349	96	2	.240	.306	.323	78	2	.205	.323	.321	157	4	.236	.328	.344	17	0	.118	.167	.118
TOTALS		4430	104	.273	.322	.414	2138	48	.272	.328	.412	2292	56	.274	.316	.416	2162	45	.273	.323	.415	2268	59	.273	.322	.413	1824	55	.297	.350	.468	2606	49	.257	.302	.376
■ Tom Herr BB/TR																																				
1979	StL-N	10	0	.200	.333	.200	4	0	.250	.250	.250	6	0	.167	.375	.167	0	0	—	—	—	10	0	.200	.333	.200	3	0	.333	.333	.333	7	0	.143	.333	.143
1980	StL-N	222	0	.248	.299	.347	105	0	.219	.272	.324	117	0	.274	.323	.368	104	0	.163	.194	.269	118	0	.322	.383	.415	95	0	.221	.253	.253	127	0	.268	.331	.417
1981	StL-N	411	0	.268	.329	.345	205	0	.273	.330	.376	206	0	.262	.328	.316	184	0	.277	.348	.386	227	0	.260	.313	.313	145	0	.221	.285	.283	266	0	.293	.352	.380
1982	StL-N	493	0	.266	.341	.320	236	0	.271	.352	.322	257	0	.261	.331	.319	168	0	.250	.342	.327	325	0	.274	.341	.317	142	0	.190	.239	.225	351	0	.296	.381	.359
1983	StL-N	313	2	.323	.403	.412	133	1	.383	.465	.474	180	1	.278	.356	.367	193	2	.280	.372	.373	120	0	.392	.453	.475	86	0	.302	.375	.326	227	2	.330	.413	.445
1984	StL-N	558	4	.276	.335	.346	266	1	.271	.321	.323	292	3	.281	.348	.366	291	3	.278	.343	.354	267	1	.273	.326	.337	178	2	.287	.335	.388	380	2	.271	.335	.326
1985	StL-N	596	8	.302	.379	.416	287	4	.303	.375	.432	309	4	.301	.383	.401	268	3	.347	.410	.463	328	5	.265	.354	.378	212	3	.283	.333	.368	384	5	.313	.402	.443
1986	StL-N	559	2	.252	.342	.331	273	1	.260	.367	.322	286	1	.245	.315	.339	252	2	.222	.316	.290	307	0	.277	.363	.365	219	1	.315	.407	.402	340	1	.212	.299	.285
1987	StL-N	510	2	.263	.346	.331	246	1	.280	.368	.341	264	1	.246	.325	.322	214	1	.299	.390	.374	296	1	.236	.314	.301	191	2	.298	.386	.398	319	0	.241	.322	.292
1988	StL-N	50	1	.260	.393	.320	26	1	.231	.355	.346	24	0	.292	.433	.292	50	1	.260	.393	.320	0	0	—	—	—	17	1	.412	.500	.588	33	0	.182	.341	.182
1988	Min-A	304	1	.263	.349	.326	167	0	.228	.314	.263	137	1	.307	.391	.401	160	1	.275	.341	.350	144	0	.250	.357	.299	76	1	.289	.349	.395	228	0	.254	.349	.303
1989	Phi-N	561	2	.287	.352	.364	270	0	.285	.360	.367	291	2	.289	.344	.361	275	1	.284	.350	.367	286	1	.290	.353	.360	229	1	.288	.353	.349	332	1	.286	.351	.373
1990	Phi-N	447	4	.264	.320	.351	211	3	.265	.328	.384	236	1	.263	.314	.322	255	3	.259	.314	.353	192	1	.271	.329	.349	157	1	.268	.327	.331	290	3	.262	.316	.362
1990	NY-N	100	1	.250	.342	.330	54	1	.296	.377	.407	46	0	.196	.302	.239	0	0	—	—	—	100	1	.250	.342	.330	51	0	.255	.333	.314	49	1	.245	.351	.347
1991	NY-N	155	1	.194	.328	.258	70	0	.157	.286	.200	85	1	.224	.362	.306	127	1	.197	.338	.268	28	0	.179	.281	.214	63	0	.190	.346	.238	92	1	.196	.315	.272
1991	SF-N	60	0	.250	.384	.300	30	0	.267	.405	.267	30	0	.233	.361	.333	0	0	—	—	—	60	0	.250	.384	.300	20	0	.300	.391	.400	40	0	.225	.380	.250
TOTALS		5349	28	.271	.347	.350	2583	13	.273	.351	.352	2766	15	.269	.343	.347	2541	18	.269	.347	.355	2808	10	.273	.347	.344	1884	12	.272	.341	.344	3465	16	.271	.350	.353
■ Richard Hidalgo BR/TR																																				
1997	Hou-N	62	2	.306	.358	.484	33	0	.303	.343	.394	29	2	.310	.375	.586	0	0	—	—	—	62	2	.306	.358	.484	22	1	.455	.478	.682	40	1	.225	.295	.375
1998	Hou-N	211	7	.303	.355	.474	114	3	.272	.353	.404	97	4	.340	.356	.557	122	2	.279	.310	.385	89	5	.337	.410	.596	80	1	.313	.378	.438	131	6	.298	.340	.496
1999	Hou-N	383	15	.227	.328	.420	183	5	.213	.342	.410	200	10	.240	.314	.430	269	13	.249	.328	.483	114	2	.175	.329	.272	98	3	.224	.313	.378	285	12	.228	.333	.435
2000	Hou-N	558	44	.314	.391	.636	269	16	.316	.391	.617	289	28	.311	.392	.654	251	20	.287	.388	.598	307	24	.336	.394	.668	117	5	.333	.410	.598	441	39	.308	.386	.646
TOTALS		1214	68	.284	.363	.532	599	24	.275	.366	.501	615	44	.293	.360	.563	642	35	.269	.349	.509	572	33	.301	.379	.558	317	10	.303	.376	.495	897	58	.278	.359	.545
■ Bobby Higginson BL/TR																																				
1995	Det-A	410	14	.224	.329	.393	206	10	.214	.318	.432	204	4	.235	.339	.353	178	9	.253	.355	.472	232	5	.203	.308	.332	66	2	.212	.307	.333	344	12	.227	.333	.404
1996	Det-A	440	26	.320	.404	.577	232	15	.336	.408	.603	208	11	.303	.401	.548	178	11	.309	.395	.573	262	15	.328	.410	.580	61	1	.230	.358	.295	379	25	.335	.413	.623
1997	Det-A	546	27	.299	.379	.520	236	16	.322	.423	.597	310	11	.281	.342	.461	234	12	.265	.357	.474	312	15	.324	.395	.554	156	7	.301	.375	.526	390	20	.297	.380	.518
1998	Det-A	612	25	.284	.355	.480	302	10	.291	.364	.467	310	15	.277	.345	.494	304	16	.326	.405	.563	308	9	.244	.304	.399	188	6	.277	.343	.436	424	19	.288	.360	.500
1999	Det-A	377	12	.239	.351	.382	193	8	.254	.374	.415	184	4	.223	.326	.348	265	8	.234	.344	.374	112	4	.250	.366	.402	83	2	.265	.396	.349	294	10	.231	.337	.391
2000	Det-A	597	30	.300	.377	.538	288	12	.333	.416	.563	309	18	.269	.340	.515	259	15	.286	.382	.560	338	15	.311	.373	.521	182	4	.264	.338	.396	415	26	.316	.394	.600
TOTALS		2982	134	.281	.367	.489	1457	71	.296	.386	.517	1525	63	.268	.348	.462	1418	71	.280	.374	.502	1564	63	.283	.360	.477	736	22	.268	.353	.414	2246	112	.286	.371	.513
■ Glenallen Hill BR/TR																																				
1989	Tor-A	52	1	.288	.327	.346	20	1	.250	.286	.400	32	0	.313	.353	.313	0	0	—	—	—	52	1	.288	.327	.346	31	1	.258	.303	.355	21	0	.333	.364	.333
1990	Tor-A	260	12	.231	.281	.435	140	7	.236	.291	.443	120	5	.225	.268	.425	134	6	.224	.278	.403	126	6	.238	.284	.468	143	5	.224	.275	.406	117	7	.239	.288	.470
1991	Tor-A	99	3	.253	.296	.434	50	2	.300	.352	.540	49	1	.204	.241	.327	99	3	.253	.296	.434	0	0	—	—	—	57	2	.298	.355	.526	42	1	.190	.217	.310
1991	Cle-A	122	5	.262	.345	.410	58	1	.293	.328	.379	64	4	.234	.359	.438	5	0	.400	.625	.400	117	5	.256	.328	.410	39	2	.256	.370	.462	83	3	.265	.333	.386
1992	Cle-A	369	18	.241	.287	.436	179	7	.257	.311	.425	190	11	.226	.264	.447	149	6	.248	.282	.430	220	12	.236	.290	.441	105	7	.267	.319	.533	264	11	.231	.274	.398
1993	Cle-A	174	5	.224	.268	.374	68	0	.162	.205	.250	106	5	.264	.308	.453	110	3	.236	.265	.409	64	2	.203	.274	.313	105	5	.219	.254	.410	69	0	.232	.289	.319
1993	Chi-N	87	10	.345	.387	.770	28	5	.393	.452	.964	59	5	.322	.355	.678	0	0	—	—	—	87	10	.345	.387	.770	48	7	.396	.453	.896	39	3	.282	.300	.615
1994	Chi-N	269	10	.297	.365	.461	142	3	.261	.340	.387	127	7	.339	.393	.543	136	6	.294	.349	.463	133	4	.301	.380	.459	114	3	.281	.333	.395	155	7	.310	.386	.510
1995	SF-N	497	24	.264	.317	.483	234	13	.261	.316	.496	263	11	.266	.318	.471	225	8	.253	.316	.427	272	16	.272	.318	.529	91	8	.308	.357	.615	406	16	.254	.308	.453
1996	SF-N	379	19	.280	.344	.499	193	9	.285	.336	.497	186	10	.274	.352	.500	170	10	.271	.332	.506	209	9	.287	.355	.493	71	7	.366	.425	.732	308	12	.260	.326	.445
1997	SF-N	398	11	.261	.297	.435	193	3	.228	.276	.342	205	8	.293	.317	.522	268	8	.246	.273	.433	130	3	.292	.345	.438	111	4	.270	.311	.450	287	7	.258	.291	.429
1998	Sea-A	259	12	.290	.332	.521	107	5	.308	.364	.523	152	7	.276	.308	.520	240	12	.292	.337	.533	19	0	.263	.263	.368	54	1	.241	.281	.315	205	11	.302	.345	.576
1998	Chi-N	131	8	.351	.414	.573	37	6	.459	.524	.973	94	2	.309	.369	.415	0	0	—	—	—	131	8	.351	.414	.573	76	5	.368	.435	.605	55	3	.327	.383	.527
1999	Chi-N	253	20	.300	.353	.581	105	11	.286	.347	.619	148	9	.311	.356	.554	114	12	.395	.427	.772	139	8	.223	.292	.424	106	4	.358	.409	.538	147	16	.259	.313	.612
2000	Chi-N	168	11	.262	.303	.494	84	6	.286	.348	.548	84	5	.238	.256	.440	126	9	.246	.291	.492	42	2	.310	.341	.500	81	5	.272	.314	.494	87	6	.253	.293	.494
2000	NY-A	132	16	.333	.378	.735	73	11	.397	.444	.890	59	5	.254	.290	.542	0	0	—	—	—	132	16	.333	.378	.735	59	8	.356	.381	.797	73	8	.315	.375	.685
TOTALS		3649	185	.273	.324	.488	1711	90	.274	.329	.491	1938	95	.272	.320	.485	1776	83	.267	.313	.477	1873	102	.278	.335	.498	1291	74	.290	.341	.518	2358	111	.263	.315	.471
■ Denny Hocking BB/TR																																				
1993	Min-A	36	0	.139	.262	.167	22	0	.091	.200	.091	14	0	.214	.353	.286	0	0	—	—	—	36	0	.139	.262	.167	6	0	.167	.286	.167	30	0	.133	.257	.167
1994	Min-A	31	0	.323	.323	.419	22	0	.455	.455	.591	9	0	.000	.000	.000	9	0	.556	.556	.778	22	0	.227	.227	.273	10	0	.300	.300	.300	21	0	.333	.333	.476
1995	Min-A	25	0	.200	.259	.360	14	0	.286	.333	.571	11	0	.091	.167	.091	0	0	—	—	—	25	0	.200	.259	.360	7	0	.286	.286	.857	18	0	.167	.250	.167
1996	Min-A	127	1	.197	.243	.268	56	0	.250	.300	.321	71	1	.155	.197	.225	63	1	.127	.188	.222	64	0	.266	.299	.313	30	0	.167	.219	.233	97	1	.206	.250	.278
1997	Min-A	253	2	.257	.308	.360	95	0	.284	.327	.358	158	2	.241	.297	.361	108	1	.278	.316	.370	145	1	.241	.302	.352	84	1	.310	.363	.452	169	1	.231	.280	.314
1998	Min-A	198	3	.202	.259	.288	80	1	.188	.287	.262	118	2	.212	.238	.305	82	0	.183	.266	.207	116	3	.216	.254	.345	57	0	.158	.254	.158	141	3	.220	.262	.340
1999	Min-A	386	7	.267	.307	.378	199	2	.221	.252	.281	187	5	.316	.365	.481	171	2	.281	.333	.380	215	5	.256	.286	.377	128	3	.242	.285	.375	258	4	.279	.318	.380
2000	Min-A	373	4	.298	.373	.416	174	1	.316	.379	.420	199	3	.281	.368	.412	164	2	.280	.368	.427	209	2	.311	.377	.407	111	2	.279	.373	.378	262	2	.305	.373	.431
TOTALS		1429	17	.255	.311	.358	662	4	.258	.311	.340	767	13	.252	.311	.373	597	6	.255	.319	.357	832	11	.255	.306	.358	433	6	.249	.315	.356	996	11	.257	.309	.358
■ Bob Horner BR/TR																																				
1978	Atl-N	323	23	.266	.313	.539	167	19	.323	.370	.743	156	4	.205	.247	.321	52	2	.173	.214	.365	271	21	.284	.331	.572	86	3	.244	.263	.430	237	20	.274	.331	.578
1979	Atl-N	487	33	.314	.346	.552	240	21	.317	.352	.608	247	12	.312	.340	.498	167	11	.317	.359	.569	320	22	.313	.338	.544	143	11	.266	.309	.524	344	22	.334	.361	.564
1980	Atl-N	463	35	.268	.307	.529	225	23	.307	.350	.644	238	12	.231	.266	.420	130	7	.200	.215	.392	333	28	.294	.342	.583	93	6	.258	.311	.495	370	29	.270	.306	.538
1981	Atl-N	300	15	.277	.345	.460	132	9	.295	.354	.500	168	6	.262	.339	.429	115	4	.287	.341	.435	185	11	.270	.348	.476	56	3	.268	.349	.464	244	12	.279	.344	.459
1982	Atl-N	499	32	.261	.350	.501	262	25	.244	.347	.565	237	7	.278	.352	.430	245	13	.302	.391	.527	254	19	.220	.309	.476	95	7	.274	.384	.526	404	25	.257	.341	.495
1983	Atl-N	386	20	.303	.383	.528	213	12	.333	.409	.587	173	8	.266	.350	.457	228	13	.294	.384	.531	158	7	.316	.381	.525	104	6	.327	.369	.596	282	14	.294	.387	.504
1984	Atl-N	113	3	.274	.349	.425	67	0	.239	.321	.299	46	3	.326	.392	.609	113	3	.274	.349	.425	0	0	—	—	—	27	0	.185	.313	.222	86	3	.302	.361	.488
1985	Atl-N	483	27	.267	.333	.499	219	13	.269	.333	.553	264	14	.265	.333	.455	218	11	.261	.317	.486	265	16	.272	.347	.509	161	10	.298	.358	.553	322	17	.252	.321	.472
1986	Atl-N	517	27	.273	.336	.472	268	20	.306	.360	.571	249	7	.237	.309	.365	262	13	.279	.348	.473	255	14	.267	.323	.471	166	7	.313	.385	.500	351	20	.254	.312	.459
1988	StL-N	206	3	.257	.348	.354	108	0	.278	.379	.333	98	3	.235	.313	.378	206	3	.257	.348	.354	0	0	—	—	—	68	2	.309	.402	.485	138	1	.232	.321	.290
TOTALS		3777	218	.277	.340	.499	1901	142	.295	.359	.570	1876	76	.260	.321	.428	1736	80	.274	.343	.470	2041	138	.280	.337	.524	999	55	.284	.349	.508	2778	163	.275	.337	.496
■ Tyler Houston BL/TR																																				
1996	Atl-N	27	1	.222	.250	.481	17	1	.294	.333	.647	10	0	.100	.100	.200	27	1	.222	.250	.481	0	0	—	—	—	1	0	.000	.000	.000	26	1	.231	.259	.500
1996	Chi-N	115	2	.339	.382	.452	40	0	.300	.349	.350	75	2	.360	.400	.507	1	0	.000	.000	.000	114	2	.342	.385	.456	4	0	.250	.400	.250	111	2	.342	.381	.459
1997	Chi-N	196	2	.260	.290	.342	96	0	.250	.282	.313	100	2	.270	.298	.370	90	1	.222	.234	.322	106	1	.292	.336	.358	13	0	.154	.154	.231	183	2	.268	.299	.350
1998	Chi-N	255	9	.255	.290	.396	121	4	.223	.269	.347	134	5	.284	.309	.440	76	3	.250	.269	.382	179	6	.257	.298	.402	19	0	.263	.391	.263	236	9	.254	.280	.407
1999	Chi-N	249	9	.233	.309	.386	107	2	.196	.263	.308	142	7	.261	.344	.444	128	8	.297	.366	.539	121	1	.165	.250	.223	26	1	.192	.250	.385	223	8	.238	.316	.386
1999	Cle-A	27	1	.148	.233	.296	17	0	.176	.263	.235	10	1	.100	.182	.400	0	0	—	—	—	27	1	.148	.233	.296	3	0	.333	.333	.333	24	1	.125	.222	.292
2000	Mil-A	284	18	.250	.292	.493	129	6	.240	.300	.419	155	12	.258	.286	.555	106	5	.245	.310	.434	178	13	.253	.281	.528	22	2	.182	.217	.500	262	16	.256	.299	.492
TOTALS		1153	42	.255	.302	.414	527	13	.233	.285	.357	626	29	.273	.316	.462	428	18	.255	.301	.435	725	24	.255	.302	.401	88	3	.205	.271	.352	1065	39	.259	.304	.419
■ Thomas Howard BB/TR																																				
1990	SD-N	44	0	.273	.273	.318	22	0	.318	.318	.318	22	0	.227	.227	.318	0	0	—	—	—	44	0	.273	.273	.318	16	0	.188	.188	.188	28	0	.321	.321	.393
1991	SD-N	281	4	.249	.309	.356	140	4	.257	.316	.386	141	0	.241	.303	.326	121	1	.264	.323	.355	160	3	.237	.299	.356	28	1	.286	.394	.464	253	3	.245	.299	.344

		TOTAL					HOME					AWAY					1ST HALF					2ND HALF					LEFT					RIGHT				
YEAR	TM/L	AB	HR	AVG	OBP	SLG	AB	HR	AVG	OBP	SLG	AB	HR	AVG	OBP	SLG	AB	HR	AVG	OBP	SLG	AB	HR	AVG	OBP	SLG	AB	HR	AVG	OBP	SLG	AB	HR	AVG	OBP	SLG
1992	SD-N	3	0	.333	.333	.333	2	0	.500	.500	.500	1	0	.000	.000	.000	3	0	.333	.333	.333	0	0	—	—	—	0	0	—	—	—	3	0	.333	.333	.333
1992	Cle-A	358	2	.277	.308	.346	179	1	.268	.302	.335	179	1	.285	.314	.358	186	0	.285	.308	.339	172	2	.267	.308	.355	104	2	.288	.321	.375	254	0	.272	.302	.335
1993	Cle-A	178	3	.236	.278	.326	82	3	.220	.280	.354	96	0	.250	.277	.302	131	2	.237	.270	.321	47	1	.234	.302	.340	75	1	.160	.224	.213	103	2	.291	.321	.408
1993	Cin-N	141	4	.277	.331	.461	61	2	.295	.377	.492	80	2	.262	.294	.438	0	0	—	—	—	141	4	.277	.331	.461	34	0	.147	.189	.147	107	4	.318	.376	.561
1994	Cin-N	178	5	.264	.302	.410	88	4	.318	.365	.500	90	1	.211	.237	.322	138	4	.268	.301	.406	40	1	.250	.302	.425	28	0	.214	.267	.250	150	5	.273	.308	.440
1995	Cin-N	281	3	.302	.350	.402	127	1	.307	.369	.402	154	2	.299	.333	.403	71	0	.282	.354	.366	210	3	.310	.348	.414	19	0	.158	.273	.263	262	3	.313	.356	.412
1996	Cin-N	360	6	.272	.307	.431	188	1	.261	.284	.410	172	5	.285	.332	.453	129	1	.233	.279	.310	231	5	.294	.324	.498	67	0	.224	.278	.269	293	6	.283	.314	.468
1997	Hou-N	255	3	.247	.323	.353	120	0	.192	.274	.258	135	3	.296	.367	.437	151	2	.252	.325	.364	104	1	.240	.319	.337	18	0	.333	.400	.444	237	3	.241	.317	.346
1998	LA-N	76	2	.184	.215	.316	39	1	.179	.200	.333	37	1	.189	.231	.297	76	2	.184	.215	.316	0	0	—	—	—	7	0	.000	.125	.000	69	2	.203	.225	.348
1999	StL-N	195	6	.292	.353	.436	101	3	.297	.351	.416	94	3	.287	.356	.457	58	2	.293	.379	.414	137	4	.292	.342	.445	37	1	.351	.444	.486	158	5	.278	.329	.424
2000	StL-N	133	6	.211	.255	.391	57	1	.158	.200	.228	76	5	.250	.296	.513	75	5	.187	.237	.427	58	1	.241	.279	.345	11	0	.000	.083	.000	122	6	.230	.271	.426
TOTALS		2483	44	.264	.311	.384	1206	21	.260	.309	.375	1277	23	.268	.312	.393	1139	19	.252	.300	.356	1344	25	.274	.320	.408	444	5	.227	.288	.297	2039	39	.272	.316	.403
■ Kent Hrbek	BL/TR																																			
1981	Min-A	67	1	.239	.301	.358	27	0	.222	.276	.333	40	1	.250	.318	.375	0	0	—	—	—	67	1	.239	.301	.358	12	0	.083	.214	.083	55	1	.273	.322	.418
1982	Min-A	532	23	.301	.363	.485	272	11	.316	.393	.507	260	12	.285	.330	.462	244	16	.328	.392	.607	288	7	.278	.338	.382	185	4	.314	.361	.443	347	19	.294	.363	.507
1983	Min-A	515	16	.297	.366	.489	278	7	.320	.381	.511	237	9	.270	.348	.464	225	6	.320	.388	.524	290	10	.279	.349	.462	146	6	.281	.365	.473	369	10	.304	.367	.496
1984	Min-A	559	27	.311	.383	.522	285	15	.358	.428	.596	274	12	.263	.337	.445	245	7	.318	.391	.465	314	20	.306	.377	.567	186	10	.296	.368	.495	373	17	.319	.391	.536
1985	Min-A	593	21	.278	.351	.444	314	10	.312	.378	.487	279	11	.240	.322	.394	276	9	.257	.332	.420	317	12	.297	.368	.464	199	6	.256	.324	.402	394	15	.289	.365	.464
1986	Min-A	550	29	.267	.353	.478	278	18	.273	.359	.529	272	11	.261	.347	.426	263	17	.327	.421	.589	287	12	.213	.289	.376	152	4	.270	.333	.382	398	25	.266	.361	.515
1987	Min-A	477	34	.285	.389	.545	234	20	.295	.413	.594	243	14	.276	.364	.498	246	20	.272	.362	.537	231	14	.299	.415	.554	138	6	.225	.290	.370	339	28	.310	.426	.617
1988	Min-A	510	25	.312	.387	.520	253	13	.304	.386	.526	257	12	.319	.388	.514	246	12	.301	.385	.500	264	13	.322	.389	.538	132	2	.250	.336	.379	378	23	.333	.405	.569
1989	Min-A	375	25	.272	.360	.517	191	17	.283	.371	.597	184	8	.261	.349	.435	114	7	.289	.388	.535	261	18	.264	.348	.510	109	6	.266	.374	.468	266	19	.274	.354	.538
1990	Min-A	492	22	.287	.377	.474	247	8	.279	.362	.437	245	14	.294	.391	.510	237	10	.257	.363	.451	255	12	.314	.390	.494	129	2	.287	.377	.357	363	20	.287	.376	.515
1991	Min-A	462	20	.284	.373	.461	236	11	.318	.407	.504	226	9	.248	.336	.416	216	7	.282	.366	.435	246	13	.285	.379	.484	128	6	.281	.357	.445	334	14	.284	.379	.467
1992	Min-A	394	15	.244	.357	.409	193	10	.259	.358	.466	201	5	.229	.355	.353	193	10	.301	.417	.528	201	5	.189	.296	.294	83	1	.265	.319	.361	311	14	.238	.366	.421
1993	Min-A	392	25	.242	.357	.467	193	12	.249	.364	.482	199	13	.236	.350	.452	161	9	.236	.349	.447	231	16	.247	.362	.481	58	3	.224	.352	.397	334	22	.246	.358	.479
1994	Min-A	274	10	.270	.353	.420	135	4	.274	.374	.422	139	6	.266	.331	.417	156	5	.250	.348	.391	118	5	.297	.361	.458	39	2	.282	.378	.462	235	8	.268	.349	.413
TOTALS		6192	293	.282	.367	.481	3136	156	.298	.383	.514	3056	137	.266	.350	.446	2822	135	.290	.378	.497	3370	158	.276	.358	.467	1696	58	.271	.347	.417	4496	235	.287	.374	.504
■ Glenn Hubbard	BR/TR																																			
1978	Atl-N	163	2	.258	.309	.319	84	1	.262	.340	.321	79	1	.253	.272	.316	0	0	—	—	—	163	2	.258	.309	.319	44	0	.273	.304	.295	119	2	.252	.310	.328
1979	Atl-N	325	3	.231	.290	.295	176	0	.233	.303	.261	149	3	.228	.275	.336	261	2	.226	.282	.284	64	1	.250	.324	.344	98	1	.255	.291	.316	227	2	.220	.290	.286
1980	Atl-N	431	9	.248	.322	.374	214	6	.248	.324	.379	217	3	.249	.320	.369	113	3	.310	.363	.531	318	6	.226	.307	.318	86	3	.209	.303	.360	345	6	.258	.326	.377
1981	Atl-N	361	6	.235	.302	.349	174	4	.230	.301	.379	187	2	.241	.304	.321	174	3	.236	.314	.356	187	3	.235	.291	.342	71	0	.239	.289	.366	290	6	.234	.305	.345
1982	Atl-N	532	9	.248	.324	.350	253	7	.253	.336	.368	279	2	.244	.314	.333	239	4	.264	.344	.360	293	5	.235	.308	.341	128	3	.281	.348	.391	404	6	.238	.317	.337
1983	Atl-N	517	12	.263	.334	.402	261	6	.261	.325	.387	256	6	.266	.344	.418	246	5	.293	.358	.431	271	7	.236	.314	.376	135	5	.267	.336	.474	382	7	.262	.334	.377
1984	Atl-N	397	9	.234	.331	.380	189	3	.254	.364	.397	208	6	.216	.299	.365	246	6	.248	.351	.390	151	3	.212	.298	.364	120	2	.225	.304	.367	277	7	.238	.343	.386
1985	Atl-N	439	5	.232	.321	.314	232	3	.250	.323	.328	207	2	.213	.318	.300	188	3	.229	.332	.324	251	2	.235	.312	.307	144	1	.229	.335	.278	295	4	.234	.313	.332
1986	Atl-N	408	4	.230	.340	.304	203	4	.246	.370	.355	205	0	.215	.309	.254	195	3	.241	.360	.344	213	1	.221	.321	.268	127	1	.220	.365	.291	281	3	.235	.328	.310
1987	Atl-N	443	5	.264	.378	.381	222	3	.252	.383	.365	221	2	.276	.373	.398	222	4	.306	.444	.459	221	1	.222	.304	.303	104	2	.288	.419	.433	339	3	.257	.365	.366
1988	Oak-A	294	3	.255	.334	.340	131	3	.267	.351	.374	163	0	.245	.321	.313	137	0	.226	.325	.277	157	3	.280	.343	.395	79	1	.278	.329	.342	215	2	.247	.336	.340
1989	Oak-A	131	3	.198	.296	.313	70	2	.171	.247	.314	61	1	.230	.347	.311	97	3	.227	.319	.361	34	0	.118	.231	.176	57	1	.228	.323	.316	74	2	.176	.276	.311
TOTALS		4441	70	.244	.328	.349	2209	42	.248	.336	.357	2232	28	.241	.319	.342	2118	36	.256	.347	.372	2323	34	.233	.310	.329	1193	20	.249	.335	.357	3248	50	.242	.325	.347
■ Brian Hunter	BR/TR																																			
1994	Hou-N	24	0	.250	.280	.292	24	0	.250	.280	.292	0	0	—	—	—	15	0	.200	.250	.267	9	0	.333	.333	.333	3	0	.333	.333	.333	21	0	.238	.273	.286
1995	Hou-N	321	2	.302	.346	.396	153	0	.275	.313	.333	168	2	.327	.375	.452	82	1	.378	.433	.488	239	1	.276	.315	.364	80	0	.287	.344	.375	241	2	.307	.346	.402
1996	Hou-N	526	5	.276	.297	.363	252	1	.302	.325	.377	274	4	.252	.272	.350	314	2	.271	.292	.347	212	3	.283	.305	.387	131	0	.260	.267	.344	395	5	.281	.307	.370
1997	Det-A	658	4	.269	.334	.353	313	2	.272	.355	.367	345	2	.267	.315	.339	320	3	.237	.308	.328	338	1	.299	.359	.376	159	1	.264	.337	.371	499	3	.271	.333	.347
1998	Det-A	595	4	.254	.298	.333	272	1	.265	.324	.327	323	3	.245	.275	.337	311	3	.257	.308	.350	284	1	.250	.287	.313	148	1	.264	.306	.338	447	3	.251	.296	.331
1999	Det-A	55	0	.236	.311	.309	35	0	.286	.324	.400	20	0	.150	.292	.150	55	0	.236	.311	.309	0	0	—	—	—	12	0	.250	.308	.250	43	0	.233	.313	.326
1999	Sea-A	484	4	.231	.277	.300	207	0	.193	.245	.242	277	4	.260	.302	.343	219	2	.283	.324	.365	265	2	.189	.238	.245	90	0	.178	.219	.200	394	4	.244	.290	.322
2000	Col-N	200	1	.275	.347	.320	113	1	.336	.405	.407	87	0	.195	.271	.207	111	0	.288	.373	.324	89	1	.258	.313	.315	75	0	.240	.329	.253	125	1	.296	.358	.360
2000	Cin-N	40	0	.225	.319	.250	17	0	.118	.250	.118	23	0	.304	.370	.348	0	0	—	—	—	40	0	.225	.319	.250	19	0	.158	.273	.211	21	0	.286	.360	.286
TOTALS		2903	20	.264	.312	.341	1386	5	.268	.323	.338	1517	15	.260	.301	.344	1427	11	.268	.319	.350	1476	9	.259	.305	.333	717	2	.250	.302	.319	2186	18	.268	.315	.349
■ Butch Huskey	BR/TR																																			
1993	NY-N	41	0	.146	.159	.171	22	0	.136	.160	.136	19	0	.158	.158	.211	0	0	—	—	—	41	0	.146	.159	.171	15	0	.067	.067	.067	26	0	.192	.207	.231
1995	NY-N	90	3	.189	.267	.300	30	2	.267	.324	.500	60	1	.150	.239	.200	0	0	—	—	—	90	3	.189	.267	.300	22	0	.182	.280	.227	68	3	.191	.263	.324
1996	NY-N	414	15	.278	.319	.435	243	9	.288	.316	.440	171	6	.263	.323	.427	220	5	.250	.288	.359	194	10	.309	.354	.521	111	6	.279	.336	.468	303	9	.277	.313	.422
1997	NY-N	471	24	.287	.319	.503	235	7	.306	.328	.472	236	17	.267	.310	.534	210	10	.290	.319	.495	261	14	.284	.319	.510	139	7	.338	.373	.547	332	17	.265	.296	.485
1998	NY-N	369	13	.252	.300	.407	189	4	.243	.291	.360	180	9	.261	.310	.456	257	10	.237	.284	.397	112	3	.286	.336	.429	117	5	.299	.363	.470	252	8	.230	.268	.377
1999	Sea-A	262	15	.290	.353	.496	129	7	.326	.376	.543	133	8	.256	.331	.451	217	14	.309	.370	.539	45	1	.200	.265	.289	60	6	.383	.465	.683	202	9	.262	.317	.441
1999	Bos-A	124	7	.266	.305	.484	55	2	.273	.298	.418	69	5	.261	.311	.536	0	0	—	—	—	124	7	.266	.305	.484	50	3	.260	.315	.500	74	4	.270	.299	.473
2000	Min-A	215	5	.223	.306	.353	92	4	.239	.349	.424	123	1	.211	.272	.301	198	5	.232	.320	.369	17	0	.118	.118	.176	80	2	.275	.348	.400	135	3	.193	.282	.326
2000	Col-N	92	4	.348	.432	.565	57	2	.333	.420	.544	35	2	.371	.452	.600	0	0	—	—	—	92	4	.348	.432	.565	40	1	.375	.447	.550	52	3	.327	.422	.577
TOTALS		2078	86	.267	.318	.442	1052	37	.282	.327	.444	1026	49	.251	.309	.441	1102	44	.263	.315	.431	976	42	.272	.321	.455	634	30	.301	.362	.487	1444	56	.252	.298	.422
■ Pete Incaviglia	BR/TR																																			
1986	Tex-A	540	30	.250	.320	.463	275	17	.287	.353	.527	265	13	.211	.286	.396	244	13	.266	.332	.492	296	17	.236	.310	.439	160	12	.306	.374	.600	380	18	.226	.297	.405
1987	Tex-A	509	27	.271	.332	.497	255	11	.259	.336	.451	254	16	.283	.328	.543	273	16	.271	.332	.516	236	11	.271	.332	.475	182	13	.341	.407	.632	327	14	.232	.290	.422
1988	Tex-A	418	22	.249	.321	.467	193	12	.249	.316	.492	225	10	.249	.325	.444	244	14	.258	.339	.496	174	8	.236	.295	.425	126	9	.254	.319	.524	292	13	.247	.322	.442
1989	Tex-A	453	21	.236	.293	.453	223	13	.251	.327	.480	230	8	.222	.257	.426	220	6	.214	.254	.373	233	15	.258	.328	.528	148	6	.209	.264	.412	305	15	.249	.307	.472
1990	Tex-A	529	24	.233	.302	.420	247	15	.247	.333	.482	282	9	.220	.272	.365	252	12	.246	.313	.444	277	12	.220	.291	.397	169	8	.249	.347	.444	360	16	.225	.279	.408
1991	Det-A	337	11	.214	.290	.353	171	6	.205	.283	.357	166	5	.223	.297	.349	167	5	.210	.272	.347	170	6	.218	.307	.359	97	0	.206	.264	.258	240	11	.217	.300	.392
1992	Hou-N	349	11	.266	.319	.430	189	6	.296	.338	.471	160	5	.231	.298	.381	211	6	.265	.310	.408	138	5	.268	.333	.464	170	7	.282	.344	.494	179	4	.251	.295	.369
1993	Phi-N	368	24	.274	.318	.530	205	15	.278	.324	.551	163	9	.270	.311	.503	191	13	.277	.309	.550	177	11	.271	.328	.508	162	13	.278	.318	.586	206	11	.272	.319	.485
1994	Phi-N	244	13	.230	.278	.439	115	6	.209	.276	.409	129	7	.248	.279	.465	163	11	.239	.298	.472	81	2	.210	.235	.370	103	4	.252	.319	.417	141	9	.213	.247	.454
1996	Phi-N	269	16	.234	.318	.454	107	6	.252	.333	.495	162	10	.222	.308	.426	196	14	.265	.336	.505	73	2	.151	.271	.315	52	6	.365	.459	.769	217	10	.203	.282	.378
1996	Bal-A	33	2	.303	.314	.545	15	0	.267	.267	.267	18	2	.333	.350	.778	0	0	—	—	—	33	2	.303	.314	.545	22	2	.318	.304	.636	11	0	.273	.333	.364
1997	Bal-A	138	5	.246	.314	.384	70	2	.214	.276	.343	68	3	.279	.351	.426	129	5	.240	.298	.372	9	0	.333	.500	.556	60	3	.317	.406	.517	78	2	.192	.238	.282
1997	NY-A	16	0	.250	.250	.250	4	0	.750	.750	.750	12	0	.083	.083	.083	0	0	—	—	—	16	0	.250	.250	.250	12	0	.250	.250	.250	4	0	.250	.250	.250
1998	Det-A	14	0	.071	.133	.071	8	0	.125	.125	.125	6	0	.000	.143	.000	14	0	.071	.133	.071	0	0	—	—	—	7	0	.000	.125	.000	7	0	.143	.143	.143
1998	Hou-N	16	0	.125	.176	.188	12	0	.167	.231	.250	4	0	.000	.000	.000	0	0	—	—	—	16	0	.125	.176	.188	8	0	.125	.222	.125	8	0	.125	.125	.250
TOTALS		4233	206	.246	.310	.448	2089	109	.256	.323	.469	2144	97	.237	.296	.428	2304	115	.251	.310	.456	1929	91	.241	.309	.439	1478	83	.273	.340	.507	2755	123	.232	.293	.417
■ Garth Iorg	BR/TR																																			
1978	Tor-A	49	0	.163	.218	.163	18	0	.167	.200	.167	31	0	.161	.229	.161	49	0	.163	.218	.163	0	0	—	—	—	25	0	.160	.192	.160	24	0	.167	.241	.167
1980	Tor-A	222	2	.248	.286	.329	112	1	.259	.303	.348	110	1	.236	.270	.309	41	1	.268	.318	.439	181	1	.243	.279	.304	84	2	.321	.360	.464	138	0	.203	.241	.246
1981	Tor-A	215	0	.242	.269	.293	104	0	.212	.248	.279	111	0	.270	.289	.306	81	0	.247	.265	.296	134	0	.239	.271	.291	92	0	.196	.229	.228	123	0	.276	.299	.341
1982	Tor-A	417	1	.285	.307	.365	198	1	.293	.322	.399	219	0	.279	.293	.333	159	0	.308	.319	.396	258	1	.271	.299	.345	278	1	.281	.308	.363	139	0	.295	.304	.367
1983	Tor-A	375	2	.275	.298	.376	184	1	.299	.333	.424	191	1	.251	.264	.330	163	0	.264	.301	.319	212	2	.283	.297	.420	235	2	.289	.316	.421	140	0	.250	.269	.300
1984	Tor-A	247	1	.227	.244	.304	134	1	.269	.288	.351	113	0	.177	.191	.248	126	0	.246	.269	.302	121	1	.207	.218	.306	180	1	.250	.269	.344	67	0	.164	.176	.194
1985	Tor-A	288	7	.313	.358	.469	119	5	.378	.417	.588	169	2	.266	.317	.385	110	2	.318	.370	.445	178	5	.309	.351	.483	200	5	.310	.361	.480	88	2	.318	.351	.443
1986	Tor-A	327	3	.260	.303	.352	167	1	.216	.251	.305	160	2	.306	.354	.400	126	2	.262	.296	.325	201	1	.259	.307	.368	166	3	.289	.335	.410	161	0	.230	.269	.292
1987	Tor-A	310	4	.210	.262	.284	148	1	.209	.267	.264	162	3	.210	.257	.302	136	0	.213	.262	.221	174	4	.207	.262	.333	138	1	.181	.238	.225	172	3	.233	.281	.331
TOTALS		2450	20	.258	.292	.347	1184	11	.266	.302	.367	1266	9	.251	.283	.328	991	5	.261	.295	.326	1459	15	.256	.290	.361	1398	15	.268	.304	.373	1052	5	.245	.276	.313
■ Reggie Jackson	BL/TL																																			
1978	NY-A	511	27	.274	.356	.477	257	17	.288	.376	.541	254	10	.260	.336	.413	255	13	.271	.344	.471	256	14	.277	.369	.484	263	9	.243	.312	.395	248	18	.306	.401	.565
1979	NY-A	465	29	.297	.382	.544	235	15	.302	.384	.536	230	14	.291	.380	.552	179	10	.268	.361	.497	286	19	.315	.395	.573	185	10	.303	.376	.508	280	19	.293	.385	.568

YEAR	TM/L	TOTAL AB	HR	AVG	OBP	SLG	HOME AB	HR	AVG	OBP	SLG	AWAY AB	HR	AVG	OBP	SLG	1ST HALF AB	HR	AVG	OBP	SLG	2ND HALF AB	HR	AVG	OBP	SLG	LEFT AB	HR	AVG	OBP	SLG	RIGHT AB	HR	AVG	OBP	SLG
1980	NY-A	514	41	.300	.398	.597	256	16	.273	.361	.504	258	25	.326	.433	.690	213	18	.282	.358	.573	301	23	.312	.424	.615	227	19	.291	.362	.581	287	22	.307	.424	.610
1981	NY-A	334	15	.237	.330	.428	145	7	.207	.311	.372	189	8	.259	.344	.471	161	6	.199	.330	.379	173	9	.272	.330	.474	144	4	.201	.261	.340	190	11	.263	.378	.495
1982	Cal-A	530	39	.275	.375	.532	267	21	.285	.377	.554	263	18	.266	.374	.510	235	15	.247	.346	.443	295	24	.298	.398	.603	204	14	.260	.321	.500	326	25	.285	.406	.552
1983	Cal-A	397	14	.194	.290	.340	192	7	.193	.293	.344	205	7	.195	.288	.337	201	12	.214	.344	.428	196	2	.173	.229	.250	149	4	.215	.292	.356	248	10	.181	.290	.331
1984	Cal-A	525	25	.223	.300	.406	246	15	.211	.287	.415	279	10	.233	.312	.398	251	12	.243	.317	.442	274	13	.204	.285	.372	146	10	.219	.265	.432	379	15	.224	.313	.396
1985	Cal-A	460	27	.252	.360	.487	225	15	.218	.328	.462	235	12	.285	.391	.511	196	11	.250	.366	.480	264	16	.254	.356	.492	113	4	.221	.355	.398	347	23	.262	.362	.516
1986	Cal-A	419	18	.241	.379	.408	195	11	.277	.426	.497	224	7	.210	.336	.330	191	7	.304	.435	.445	228	11	.189	.331	.377	71	0	.239	.349	.282	348	18	.241	.385	.434
1987	Oak-A	336	15	.220	.297	.402	165	7	.218	.303	.394	171	8	.222	.291	.409	207	10	.208	.292	.396	129	5	.240	.305	.411	48	2	.292	.333	.521	288	13	.208	.291	.382
TOTALS		4491	250	.254	.350	.469	2183	131	.251	.348	.472	2308	119	.257	.352	.467	2089	114	.249	.349	.457	2402	136	.259	.352	.480	1550	76	.250	.323	.443	2941	174	.256	.364	.483
■ Brook Jacoby BR/TR																																				
1981	Atl-N	10	0	.200	.200	.200	4	0	.250	.250	.250	6	0	.167	.167	.167	0	0	—	—	—	10	0	.200	.200	.200	8	0	.250	.250	.250	2	0	.000	.000	.000
1983	Atl-N	8	0	.000	.000	.000	8	0	.000	.000	.000	0	0	—	—	—	0	0	—	—	—	8	0	.000	.000	.000	3	0	.000	.000	.000	5	0	.000	.000	.000
1984	Cle-A	439	7	.264	.314	.369	222	2	.261	.320	.342	217	5	.267	.308	.396	270	5	.241	.295	.333	169	2	.302	.344	.426	139	3	.317	.378	.446	300	4	.240	.283	.333
1985	Cle-A	606	20	.274	.324	.426	303	9	.271	.323	.426	303	11	.277	.324	.426	269	10	.290	.342	.446	337	10	.261	.309	.409	185	9	.276	.335	.459	421	11	.273	.319	.411
1986	Cle-A	583	17	.288	.350	.441	274	10	.266	.338	.431	309	7	.307	.361	.450	275	9	.269	.330	.429	308	8	.305	.368	.451	161	5	.261	.339	.404	422	12	.299	.354	.455
1987	Cle-A	540	32	.300	.387	.541	280	21	.279	.366	.564	260	11	.323	.410	.515	262	13	.248	.339	.454	278	19	.349	.432	.622	142	5	.261	.382	.444	398	27	.314	.389	.575
1988	Cle-A	552	9	.241	.300	.335	264	3	.239	.307	.333	288	6	.243	.294	.337	296	6	.267	.321	.389	256	3	.211	.277	.273	129	3	.233	.277	.357	423	6	.243	.307	.329
1989	Cle-A	519	13	.272	.348	.416	248	7	.266	.353	.423	271	6	.277	.343	.410	256	9	.262	.346	.418	263	4	.281	.350	.414	152	6	.296	.363	.493	367	7	.262	.342	.384
1990	Cle-A	553	14	.293	.365	.427	261	10	.287	.374	.464	292	4	.298	.356	.394	251	10	.319	.378	.506	302	4	.272	.355	.361	158	3	.316	.383	.411	395	11	.284	.358	.433
1991	Cle-A	231	4	.234	.289	.333	102	2	.216	.279	.314	129	2	.248	.297	.349	200	4	.220	.271	.325	31	0	.323	.400	.387	62	1	.242	.347	.339	169	3	.231	.266	.331
1991	Oak-A	188	0	.213	.255	.277	88	0	.216	.273	.284	100	0	.210	.238	.270	0	0	—	—	—	188	0	.213	.255	.277	54	0	.259	.300	.315	134	0	.194	.236	.261
1992	Cle-A	291	4	.261	.324	.326	126	3	.310	.362	.421	165	1	.224	.295	.255	176	3	.267	.333	.347	115	1	.252	.310	.296	97	2	.258	.311	.351	194	2	.263	.330	.314
TOTALS		4520	120	.270	.334	.405	2180	67	.264	.335	.416	2340	53	.275	.333	.396	2255	69	.266	.330	.409	2265	51	.274	.338	.402	1290	37	.275	.346	.415	3230	83	.268	.329	.402
■ Chris James BR/TR																																				
1986	Phi-N	46	1	.283	.298	.413	22	0	.318	.318	.409	24	1	.250	.280	.417	11	1	.273	.333	.545	35	0	.286	.286	.371	22	1	.227	.261	.409	24	0	.333	.333	.417
1987	Phi-N	358	17	.293	.344	.525	172	9	.302	.366	.552	186	8	.285	.322	.500	99	6	.303	.352	.556	259	11	.290	.340	.514	149	9	.282	.327	.570	209	8	.301	.355	.493
1988	Phi-N	566	19	.242	.283	.389	298	10	.262	.300	.419	268	9	.220	.264	.354	266	11	.256	.298	.436	300	8	.230	.269	.347	157	7	.229	.265	.408	409	12	.247	.289	.381
1989	Phi-N	179	2	.207	.223	.263	80	1	.225	.253	.287	99	1	.192	.198	.242	179	2	.207	.223	.263	0	0	—	—	—	73	2	.219	.247	.301	106	0	.198	.206	.236
1989	SD-N	303	11	.264	.314	.429	130	6	.292	.343	.485	173	5	.243	.292	.387	55	0	.182	.237	.218	248	11	.282	.331	.476	95	5	.347	.400	.579	208	6	.226	.274	.361
1990	Cle-A	528	12	.299	.341	.443	234	6	.286	.333	.427	294	6	.310	.347	.456	226	4	.283	.321	.403	302	8	.311	.356	.474	162	4	.302	.361	.432	366	8	.298	.332	.448
1991	Cle-A	437	5	.238	.273	.318	221	1	.290	.328	.357	216	4	.185	.217	.278	269	4	.264	.309	.357	168	1	.196	.214	.256	131	2	.198	.239	.298	306	3	.255	.288	.327
1992	SF-N	248	5	.242	.285	.375	127	3	.213	.239	.370	121	2	.273	.331	.380	78	1	.167	.264	.295	170	3	.276	.295	.412	116	2	.302	.333	.431	132	3	.189	.243	.326
1993	Hou-N	129	6	.256	.333	.488	65	6	.277	.333	.662	64	0	.234	.333	.313	77	4	.260	.333	.506	52	2	.250	.333	.462	103	6	.243	.310	.524	26	0	.308	.419	.346
1993	Tex-A	31	3	.355	.412	.677	0	0	—	—	—	31	3	.355	.412	.677	0	0	—	—	—	31	3	.355	.412	.677	15	2	.267	.313	.733	16	1	.438	.500	.625
1994	Tex-A	133	7	.256	.361	.534	60	4	.233	.351	.533	73	3	.274	.369	.534	94	2	.234	.362	.436	39	5	.308	.357	.769	63	5	.349	.434	.762	70	2	.171	.293	.329
1995	KC-A	58	2	.310	.373	.466	28	0	.250	.313	.286	30	2	.367	.429	.633	4	0	.250	.250	.250	54	2	.315	.381	.481	43	1	.349	.412	.488	15	1	.200	.250	.400
1995	Bos-A	24	0	.167	.200	.208	11	0	.273	.333	.273	13	0	.077	.077	.154	0	0	—	—	—	24	0	.167	.200	.208	19	0	.158	.200	.211	5	0	.200	.200	.200
TOTALS		3040	90	.261	.307	.413	1448	46	.271	.318	.433	1592	44	.252	.297	.396	1358	36	.250	.301	.388	1682	54	.271	.312	.434	1148	46	.271	.321	.463	1892	44	.255	.299	.383
■ Stan Javier BB/TR																																				
1984	NY-A	7	0	.143	.143	.143	6	0	.000	.000	.000	1	0	1.000	1.000	1.000	7	0	.143	.143	.143	0	0	—	—	—	5	0	.000	.000	.000	2	0	.500	.500	.500
1986	Oak-A	114	0	.202	.305	.272	56	0	.214	.371	.268	58	0	.190	.230	.276	74	0	.189	.318	.257	40	0	.225	.279	.300	50	0	.160	.250	.240	64	0	.234	.347	.297
1987	Oak-A	151	2	.185	.276	.258	87	1	.264	.354	.345	64	1	.078	.169	.141	110	2	.227	.320	.327	41	0	.073	.156	.073	85	1	.165	.253	.212	66	1	.212	.307	.318
1988	Oak-A	397	2	.257	.313	.320	176	0	.261	.323	.307	221	2	.253	.305	.330	219	1	.274	.319	.338	178	1	.236	.306	.298	91	1	.253	.277	.308	306	1	.258	.324	.324
1989	Oak-A	310	1	.248	.317	.316	138	1	.225	.319	.290	172	0	.267	.315	.337	211	1	.261	.332	.346	99	0	.222	.284	.253	74	1	.230	.278	.311	236	0	.254	.328	.318
1990	Oak-A	33	0	.242	.306	.364	23	0	.261	.346	.348	10	0	.200	.200	.400	33	0	.242	.306	.364	0	0	—	—	—	5	0	.400	.400	.800	28	0	.214	.290	.286
1990	LA-N	276	3	.304	.384	.399	138	1	.290	.369	.348	138	2	.319	.399	.449	109	1	.339	.407	.468	167	2	.281	.370	.353	119	1	.311	.401	.387	157	2	.299	.371	.408
1991	LA-N	176	1	.205	.268	.284	83	0	.205	.292	.229	93	1	.204	.245	.333	117	1	.231	.287	.350	59	0	.153	.231	.153	97	0	.247	.315	.320	79	1	.152	.209	.241
1992	LA-N	58	1	.190	.277	.293	25	1	.160	.250	.320	33	0	.212	.297	.273	57	1	.175	.266	.281	1	0	1.000	1.000	1.000	22	0	.227	.320	.273	36	1	.167	.250	.306
1992	Phi-N	276	0	.261	.338	.319	125	0	.296	.355	.376	151	0	.232	.324	.272	0	0	—	—	—	276	0	.261	.338	.319	124	0	.218	.276	.290	152	0	.296	.384	.342
1993	Cal-A	237	3	.291	.362	.405	88	0	.318	.396	.375	149	3	.275	.341	.423	90	0	.222	.297	.300	147	3	.333	.401	.469	85	1	.271	.357	.376	152	2	.303	.365	.421
1994	Oak-A	419	10	.272	.349	.399	191	1	.267	.363	.330	228	9	.276	.336	.456	294	10	.293	.368	.446	125	0	.224	.302	.288	154	3	.318	.386	.461	265	7	.245	.328	.362
1995	Oak-A	442	8	.278	.353	.387	202	3	.257	.342	.376	240	5	.296	.362	.396	184	3	.261	.317	.332	258	5	.291	.377	.426	119	3	.303	.359	.471	323	5	.269	.351	.356
1996	SF-N	274	2	.270	.336	.383	115	1	.261	.325	.391	159	1	.277	.343	.377	222	2	.252	.322	.369	52	0	.346	.393	.442	78	1	.282	.349	.410	196	1	.265	.330	.372
1997	SF-N	440	8	.286	.368	.395	220	6	.305	.391	.427	220	2	.268	.345	.364	191	5	.304	.388	.461	249	3	.273	.353	.345	135	2	.252	.336	.341	305	6	.302	.382	.420
1998	SF-N	417	4	.290	.385	.374	197	1	.330	.430	.396	220	3	.255	.343	.355	261	1	.268	.350	.349	156	3	.327	.439	.417	103	0	.291	.342	.311	314	4	.290	.397	.395
1999	SF-N	333	3	.276	.335	.354	162	2	.265	.324	.333	171	1	.287	.346	.374	230	3	.287	.343	.383	103	0	.252	.319	.291	94	3	.340	.374	.500	239	0	.251	.321	.297
1999	Hou-N	64	0	.328	.405	.422	20	0	.300	.348	.500	44	0	.341	.431	.386	0	0	—	—	—	64	0	.328	.405	.422	15	0	.200	.294	.200	49	0	.367	.439	.490
2000	Sea-A	342	5	.275	.351	.401	165	5	.248	.326	.424	177	0	.299	.373	.379	167	3	.275	.365	.419	175	2	.274	.337	.383	55	0	.291	.409	.327	287	5	.272	.339	.415
TOTALS		4766	53	.268	.343	.362	2217	23	.270	.353	.357	2549	30	.266	.334	.366	2576	34	.267	.339	.373	2190	19	.269	.347	.348	1510	17	.266	.334	.358	3256	36	.268	.347	.363
■ Gregg Jefferies BB/TR																																				
1987	NY-N	6	0	.500	.500	.667	4	0	.750	.750	1.000	2	0	.000	.000	.000	0	0	—	—	—	6	0	.500	.500	.667	2	0	.500	.500	.500	4	0	.500	.500	.750
1988	NY-N	109	6	.321	.364	.596	67	3	.328	.352	.567	42	3	.310	.383	.643	0	0	—	—	—	109	6	.321	.364	.596	36	4	.306	.342	.722	73	2	.329	.375	.534
1989	NY-N	508	12	.258	.314	.392	237	7	.287	.357	.464	271	5	.232	.274	.328	231	1	.221	.277	.316	277	11	.289	.344	.455	174	5	.253	.294	.402	334	7	.260	.324	.386
1990	NY-N	604	15	.283	.337	.434	311	9	.318	.380	.495	293	6	.246	.290	.369	275	10	.313	.360	.495	329	5	.258	.318	.383	222	5	.266	.308	.419	382	10	.293	.353	.442
1991	NY-N	486	9	.272	.336	.374	244	5	.295	.371	.406	242	4	.248	.300	.343	206	5	.272	.341	.398	280	4	.271	.333	.357	174	1	.293	.353	.379	312	8	.260	.328	.372
1992	KC-A	604	10	.285	.329	.404	280	3	.289	.346	.396	324	7	.281	.313	.410	274	4	.274	.310	.394	330	6	.294	.344	.412	179	3	.257	.282	.363	425	7	.296	.348	.421
1993	StL-N	544	16	.342	.408	.485	249	10	.341	.417	.518	295	6	.342	.401	.458	284	10	.331	.379	.500	260	6	.354	.439	.469	148	8	.351	.394	.568	396	8	.338	.414	.455
1994	StL-N	397	12	.325	.391	.489	201	7	.343	.414	.537	196	5	.306	.368	.439	252	7	.333	.413	.504	145	5	.310	.351	.462	123	2	.301	.350	.423	274	10	.336	.410	.518
1995	Phi-N	480	11	.306	.349	.448	211	4	.327	.383	.464	269	7	.290	.322	.435	168	4	.262	.317	.405	312	7	.330	.367	.471	151	4	.351	.390	.510	329	7	.286	.331	.419
1996	Phi-N	404	7	.292	.348	.401	217	4	.300	.350	.424	187	3	.283	.345	.374	97	2	.227	.283	.340	307	5	.313	.368	.420	87	1	.287	.330	.379	317	6	.293	.352	.407
1997	Phi-N	476	11	.256	.333	.391	202	2	.292	.364	.411	274	9	.230	.310	.376	280	4	.254	.330	.364	196	7	.260	.338	.429	114	5	.325	.389	.518	362	6	.235	.316	.351
1998	Phi-N	483	8	.294	.331	.402	255	3	.306	.343	.416	228	5	.281	.318	.386	296	6	.318	.360	.449	187	2	.257	.284	.326	109	2	.284	.314	.404	374	6	.297	.337	.401
1998	Ana-A	72	1	.347	.347	.472	28	0	.321	.321	.321	44	1	.364	.364	.568	0	0	—	—	—	72	1	.347	.347	.472	10	0	.300	.300	.300	62	1	.355	.355	.500
1999	Det-A	205	6	.200	.258	.327	106	5	.189	.239	.377	99	1	.212	.278	.273	171	5	.211	.275	.333	34	1	.147	.167	.294	47	1	.149	.160	.255	158	5	.215	.286	.348
2000	Det-A	142	2	.275	.344	.373	80	0	.250	.341	.313	62	2	.306	.348	.452	142	2	.275	.344	.373	0	0	—	—	—	40	0	.225	.326	.275	102	2	.294	.351	.412
TOTALS		5520	126	.289	.344	.421	2692	62	.304	.365	.448	2828	64	.274	.324	.396	2676	60	.281	.339	.416	2844	66	.296	.349	.426	1616	41	.288	.332	.431	3904	85	.289	.349	.417
■ Geoff Jenkins BL/TR																																				
1998	Mil-A	262	9	.229	.288	.385	118	4	.229	.283	.398	144	5	.229	.291	.375	138	6	.239	.279	.420	124	3	.218	.297	.347	45	0	.200	.229	.289	217	9	.235	.300	.406
1999	Mil-A	447	21	.313	.371	.564	220	10	.323	.394	.573	227	11	.304	.348	.555	199	12	.307	.387	.578	248	9	.319	.358	.552	85	2	.259	.330	.400	362	19	.326	.381	.602
2000	Mil-A	512	34	.303	.360	.588	248	15	.278	.348	.528	264	19	.326	.372	.644	201	13	.303	.338	.577	311	21	.302	.373	.595	120	5	.283	.351	.500	392	29	.309	.363	.615
TOTALS		1221	64	.291	.349	.536	586	29	.285	.353	.519	635	35	.296	.345	.551	538	31	.288	.342	.537	683	33	.293	.354	.534	250	7	.260	.322	.428	971	57	.299	.356	.563
■ Derek Jeter BR/TR																																				
1995	NY-A	48	0	.250	.294	.375	36	0	.222	.243	.361	12	0	.333	.429	.417	47	0	.234	.280	.340	1	0	1.000	1.000	2.000	14	0	.357	.357	.571	34	0	.206	.270	.294
1996	NY-A	582	10	.314	.370	.430	285	3	.302	.371	.393	297	7	.327	.370	.465	263	3	.270	.352	.365	319	7	.351	.387	.483	162	2	.340	.409	.420	420	8	.305	.355	.433
1997	NY-A	654	10	.291	.370	.405	313	5	.284	.367	.390	341	5	.296	.373	.419	322	4	.286	.368	.398	332	6	.295	.373	.413	169	5	.290	.366	.420	485	5	.291	.372	.400
1998	NY-A	626	19	.324	.384	.481	312	9	.333	.384	.484	314	10	.315	.383	.478	277	9	.310	.366	.477	349	10	.335	.397	.484	148	6	.345	.409	.574	478	13	.318	.376	.452
1999	NY-A	627	24	.349	.438	.552	313	15	.329	.419	.559	314	9	.369	.456	.545	289	13	.374	.459	.623	338	11	.328	.418	.491	124	5	.282	.366	.452	503	19	.366	.455	.577
2000	NY-A	593	15	.339	.416	.481	299	8	.338	.420	.475	294	7	.340	.411	.486	262	7	.332	.380	.481	331	8	.344	.441	.480	147	4	.395	.461	.585	446	11	.321	.401	.446
TOTALS		3130	78	.322	.394	.468	1558	40	.315	.390	.459	1572	38	.329	.399	.477	1460	36	.312	.383	.464	1670	42	.331	.404	.471	764	22	.331	.402	.490	2366	56	.319	.392	.461
■ Charles Johnson BR/TR																																				
1994	Fla-N	11	1	.455	.462	.818	11	1	.455	.462	.818	0	0	—	—	—	11	1	.455	.462	.818	0	0	—	—	—	2	0	.500	.500	.500	9	1	.444	.455	.889
1995	Fla-N	315	11	.251	.351	.410	157	3	.229	.313	.318	158	8	.272	.388	.500	165	5	.188	.289	.315	150	6	.320	.418	.513	83	3	.289	.417	.470	232	8	.237	.326	.388
1996	Fla-N	386	13	.218	.292	.358	208	9	.221	.294	.389	178	4	.213	.289	.320	257	9	.210	.273	.354	129	4	.233	.327	.364	87	1	.207	.278	.299	299	12	.221	.296	.375
1997	Fla-N	416	19	.250	.347	.454	206	7	.243	.359	.398	210	12	.257	.335	.510	198	6	.227	.328	.389	218	13	.271	.365	.514	90	5	.300	.376	.544	326	14	.236	.339	.429
1998	Fla-N	113	7	.221	.315	.451	71	5	.211	.325	.451	42	2	.238	.298	.452	113	7	.221	.315	.451	0	0	—	—	—	13	1	.154	.267	.385	100	6	.230	.322	.460

YEAR	TM/L	TOTAL					HOME					AWAY					1ST HALF					2ND HALF					LEFT					RIGHT				
		AB	HR	AVG	OBP	SLG	AB	HR	AVG	OBP	SLG	AB	HR	AVG	OBP	SLG	AB	HR	AVG	OBP	SLG	AB	HR	AVG	OBP	SLG	AB	HR	AVG	OBP	SLG	AB	HR	AVG	OBP	SLG
1998	LA-N	346	12	.217	.279	.358	176	9	.250	.320	.438	170	3	.182	.236	.276	132	3	.197	.237	.303	214	9	.229	.304	.393	70	2	.286	.359	.414	276	10	.199	.258	.344
1999	Bal-A	426	16	.251	.340	.413	196	8	.265	.357	.439	230	8	.239	.326	.391	206	13	.262	.347	.495	220	3	.241	.333	.336	62	3	.355	.423	.548	364	13	.234	.326	.390
2000	Bal-A	286	21	.294	.364	.570	135	12	.304	.373	.615	151	9	.285	.355	.530	221	17	.299	.355	.584	65	4	.277	.390	.523	84	4	.238	.309	.417	202	17	.317	.387	.634
2000	Chi-A	135	10	.326	.411	.607	66	7	.348	.438	.727	69	3	.304	.385	.493	0	0	—	—	—	135	10	.326	.411	.607	31	2	.290	.389	.581	104	8	.337	.418	.615
TOTALS		2434	110	.249	.333	.436	1226	61	.254	.342	.447	1208	49	.244	.325	.425	1303	61	.235	.311	.423	1131	49	.266	.358	.451	522	21	.274	.358	.452	1912	89	.243	.326	.431
■ Cliff Johnson	BR/TR																																			
1978	NY-A	174	6	.184	.307	.351	75	2	.187	.330	.333	99	4	.182	.289	.364	104	3	.192	.323	.346	70	3	.171	.284	.357	131	6	.206	.342	.412	43	0	.116	.191	.163
1979	NY-A	64	2	.266	.360	.453	34	1	.176	.275	.324	30	1	.367	.457	.600	64	2	.266	.360	.453	0	0	—	—	—	51	2	.275	.387	.490	13	0	.231	.231	.308
1979	Cle-A	240	18	.271	.343	.538	108	10	.287	.336	.593	132	8	.258	.348	.492	23	0	.217	.333	.261	217	18	.276	.344	.567	77	8	.390	.473	.753	163	10	.215	.279	.436
1980	Cle-A	174	6	.230	.320	.362	100	4	.210	.317	.370	74	2	.257	.325	.351	174	6	.230	.320	.362	0	0	—	—	—	51	1	.255	.418	.353	123	5	.220	.272	.366
1980	Chi-N	196	10	.235	.335	.429	115	6	.235	.315	.417	81	4	.235	.361	.444	21	1	.286	.304	.429	175	9	.229	.338	.429	50	3	.360	.484	.620	146	7	.192	.276	.363
1981	Oak-A	273	17	.260	.329	.476	127	11	.276	.369	.535	146	6	.247	.292	.425	135	9	.237	.329	.452	138	8	.283	.329	.500	129	10	.279	.368	.543	144	7	.243	.291	.417
1982	Oak-A	214	7	.238	.324	.383	100	4	.210	.304	.350	114	3	.263	.341	.412	170	7	.218	.304	.376	44	0	.318	.400	.409	131	6	.260	.355	.443	83	1	.205	.272	.289
1983	Tor-A	407	22	.265	.373	.489	193	10	.249	.379	.482	214	12	.280	.367	.495	186	14	.285	.405	.586	221	8	.249	.344	.407	211	14	.265	.381	.531	196	8	.265	.364	.444
1984	Tor-A	359	16	.304	.390	.507	164	3	.311	.399	.433	195	13	.297	.383	.569	168	6	.280	.380	.464	191	10	.325	.400	.545	180	6	.317	.422	.511	179	10	.291	.355	.503
1985	Tex-A	296	12	.257	.330	.443	130	8	.254	.344	.492	166	4	.259	.319	.404	192	9	.255	.339	.464	104	3	.260	.313	.404	70	1	.329	.412	.457	226	11	.235	.304	.438
1985	Tor-A	73	1	.274	.349	.315	42	1	.238	.340	.310	31	0	.323	.364	.323	0	0	—	—	—	73	1	.274	.349	.315	42	1	.333	.429	.405	31	0	.194	.235	.194
1986	Tor-A	336	15	.250	.355	.426	174	11	.270	.365	.494	162	4	.228	.346	.352	206	10	.291	.373	.495	130	5	.185	.329	.315	107	8	.290	.408	.579	229	7	.231	.330	.354
TOTALS		2806	132	.256	.347	.448	1362	71	.253	.350	.452	1444	61	.260	.344	.444	1443	67	.254	.350	.448	1363	65	.259	.345	.448	1230	66	.287	.397	.511	1576	66	.232	.306	.398
■ Howard Johnson	BB/TR																																			
1982	Det-A	155	4	.316	.384	.426	77	1	.390	.472	.429	78	3	.244	.289	.423	33	1	.182	.206	.273	122	3	.352	.428	.467	23	0	.217	.357	.217	132	4	.333	.389	.462
1983	Det-A	66	3	.212	.297	.348	36	2	.167	.286	.333	30	1	.267	.313	.367	66	3	.212	.297	.348	0	0	—	—	—	1	0	.000	.000	.000	65	3	.215	.301	.354
1984	Det-A	355	12	.248	.324	.394	180	4	.222	.316	.322	175	8	.274	.333	.469	140	6	.293	.379	.464	215	6	.219	.287	.349	97	2	.227	.269	.351	258	10	.256	.344	.411
1985	NY-N	389	11	.242	.300	.393	188	5	.229	.297	.367	201	6	.254	.303	.418	161	2	.186	.254	.255	228	9	.281	.332	.491	77	3	.156	.241	.299	312	8	.263	.315	.417
1986	NY-N	220	10	.245	.341	.445	92	5	.217	.345	.457	128	5	.266	.338	.438	91	3	.264	.368	.440	129	7	.233	.322	.450	47	2	.213	.339	.404	173	8	.254	.342	.457
1987	NY-N	554	36	.265	.364	.504	271	13	.262	.364	.450	283	23	.269	.365	.555	247	15	.267	.351	.486	307	21	.264	.375	.518	194	15	.289	.376	.552	360	21	.253	.358	.478
1988	NY-N	495	24	.230	.343	.422	221	9	.213	.339	.389	274	15	.245	.346	.449	264	14	.246	.346	.455	231	10	.212	.339	.385	142	6	.183	.304	.338	353	18	.249	.359	.456
1989	NY-N	571	36	.287	.369	.559	276	19	.290	.371	.572	295	17	.285	.368	.546	262	21	.290	.364	.607	309	15	.285	.374	.518	194	7	.278	.383	.464	377	29	.292	.362	.607
1990	NY-N	590	23	.244	.319	.434	291	13	.234	.297	.416	299	10	.254	.339	.452	271	12	.236	.292	.446	319	11	.251	.341	.423	221	6	.208	.296	.344	369	17	.266	.333	.488
1991	NY-N	564	38	.259	.342	.535	280	21	.268	.347	.557	284	17	.250	.337	.514	242	17	.244	.339	.525	322	21	.270	.344	.543	217	14	.253	.320	.498	347	24	.262	.355	.559
1992	NY-N	350	7	.223	.329	.337	164	2	.189	.293	.274	186	5	.253	.361	.392	256	7	.223	.336	.367	94	0	.223	.311	.255	132	4	.227	.340	.379	218	3	.220	.323	.312
1993	NY-N	235	7	.238	.354	.379	116	3	.207	.313	.319	119	4	.269	.390	.437	181	5	.243	.353	.387	54	2	.222	.354	.352	68	0	.162	.269	.206	167	7	.269	.386	.449
1994	Col-N	227	10	.211	.323	.405	90	3	.278	.391	.489	137	7	.168	.277	.350	160	8	.219	.342	.431	67	2	.194	.276	.343	34	1	.176	.300	.353	193	9	.218	.328	.415
1995	Chi-N	169	7	.195	.330	.355	108	6	.250	.376	.463	61	1	.098	.247	.164	82	5	.122	.277	.317	87	2	.264	.381	.391	22	0	.182	.357	.182	147	7	.197	.326	.381
TOTALS		4940	228	.249	.340	.446	2390	106	.246	.340	.432	2550	122	.252	.339	.459	2456	119	.241	.333	.441	2484	109	.257	.346	.451	1469	60	.229	.324	.402	3471	168	.257	.346	.465
■ Lance Johnson	BL/TL																																			
1987	StL-N	59	0	.220	.270	.288	42	0	.262	.295	.333	17	0	.118	.211	.176	0	0	—	—	—	59	0	.220	.270	.288	6	0	.167	.167	.167	53	0	.226	.281	.302
1988	Chi-A	124	0	.185	.223	.234	63	0	.143	.194	.175	61	0	.230	.254	.295	84	0	.190	.236	.250	40	0	.175	.195	.200	22	0	.091	.130	.091	102	0	.206	.243	.265
1989	Chi-A	180	0	.300	.360	.367	84	0	.274	.330	.369	96	0	.323	.387	.365	0	0	—	—	—	180	0	.300	.360	.367	58	0	.259	.306	.328	122	0	.320	.385	.385
1990	Chi-A	541	1	.285	.325	.357	265	0	.302	.336	.381	276	1	.268	.314	.333	242	0	.281	.326	.339	299	1	.288	.324	.371	156	0	.321	.353	.378	385	1	.270	.313	.348
1991	Chi-A	588	0	.274	.304	.342	286	0	.266	.298	.325	302	0	.281	.310	.358	278	0	.259	.281	.284	310	0	.287	.324	.394	164	0	.244	.291	.274	424	0	.285	.309	.368
1992	Chi-A	567	3	.279	.318	.363	274	2	.263	.312	.339	293	1	.294	.324	.386	250	1	.268	.298	.332	317	2	.287	.333	.388	158	0	.266	.302	.310	409	3	.284	.324	.384
1993	Chi-A	540	0	.311	.354	.396	259	0	.320	.369	.386	281	0	.302	.340	.406	273	0	.304	.347	.370	267	0	.318	.361	.423	147	0	.272	.318	.333	393	0	.326	.368	.420
1994	Chi-A	412	3	.277	.321	.393	201	1	.254	.301	.353	211	2	.299	.339	.431	283	1	.269	.321	.385	129	2	.295	.319	.411	131	1	.298	.338	.382	281	2	.267	.312	.399
1995	Chi-A	607	10	.306	.341	.425	311	2	.289	.324	.379	296	8	.324	.358	.473	224	0	.250	.293	.290	383	10	.339	.369	.504	171	1	.287	.328	.351	436	9	.314	.346	.454
1996	NY-N	682	9	.333	.362	.479	335	1	.296	.316	.412	347	8	.369	.405	.545	342	4	.313	.339	.453	340	5	.353	.385	.506	182	0	.330	.346	.434	500	9	.334	.368	.496
1997	NY-N	265	1	.309	.385	.404	118	1	.356	.430	.500	147	0	.272	.348	.327	149	1	.289	.374	.383	116	0	.336	.398	.431	94	0	.330	.366	.436	171	1	.298	.394	.386
1997	Chi-N	145	4	.303	.342	.455	61	3	.328	.369	.541	84	1	.286	.322	.393	0	0	—	—	—	145	4	.303	.342	.455	37	1	.216	.310	.297	108	3	.333	.354	.509
1998	Chi-N	304	2	.280	.335	.352	124	1	.290	.353	.355	180	1	.272	.323	.350	52	0	.115	.164	.192	252	2	.313	.370	.385	109	2	.257	.331	.349	195	0	.292	.338	.354
1999	Chi-N	335	1	.260	.332	.337	166	1	.259	.349	.373	169	0	.260	.315	.302	200	1	.260	.332	.365	135	0	.259	.333	.296	69	0	.188	.300	.246	266	1	.278	.341	.361
2000	NY-A	30	0	.300	.300	.333	12	0	.083	.083	.083	18	0	.444	.444	.500	30	0	.300	.300	.333	0	0	—	—	—	3	0	.333	.333	.333	27	0	.296	.296	.333
TOTALS		5379	34	.291	.334	.386	2601	12	.283	.328	.373	2778	22	.298	.339	.398	2407	8	.272	.316	.351	2972	26	.306	.349	.414	1507	5	.278	.322	.346	3872	29	.296	.338	.402
■ Andruw Jones	BR/TR																																			
1996	Atl-N	106	5	.217	.265	.443	52	3	.269	.296	.577	54	2	.167	.237	.315	0	0	—	—	—	106	5	.217	.265	.443	29	5	.379	.455	1.103	77	0	.156	.188	.195
1997	Atl-N	399	18	.231	.329	.416	187	5	.203	.336	.342	212	13	.255	.322	.481	169	6	.272	.375	.438	230	12	.200	.294	.400	139	7	.281	.383	.496	260	11	.204	.300	.373
1998	Atl-N	582	31	.271	.321	.515	284	16	.278	.331	.521	298	15	.265	.310	.510	292	12	.271	.320	.497	290	19	.272	.322	.534	141	12	.312	.370	.681	441	19	.259	.305	.463
1999	Atl-N	592	26	.275	.365	.483	285	10	.260	.343	.446	307	16	.290	.386	.518	287	14	.275	.358	.495	305	12	.275	.372	.472	140	6	.271	.376	.486	452	20	.277	.362	.482
2000	Atl-N	656	36	.303	.366	.541	318	15	.296	.363	.497	338	21	.311	.370	.583	309	21	.320	.406	.579	347	15	.288	.329	.507	134	4	.313	.403	.448	522	32	.301	.357	.565
TOTALS		2335	116	.272	.344	.494	1126	49	.266	.342	.468	1209	67	.278	.346	.519	1057	53	.287	.365	.511	1278	63	.260	.327	.480	583	34	.298	.386	.557	1752	82	.263	.330	.473
■ Chipper Jones	BB/TR																																			
1993	Atl-N	3	0	.667	.750	1.000	2	0	.500	.500	.500	1	0	1.000	1.000	2.000	0	0	—	—	—	3	0	.667	.750	1.000	1	0	1.000	1.000	1.000	2	0	.500	.500	1.000
1995	Atl-N	524	23	.265	.353	.450	268	15	.272	.356	.493	256	8	.258	.349	.406	231	11	.242	.340	.446	293	12	.283	.363	.454	127	3	.283	.393	.417	397	20	.259	.339	.461
1996	Atl-N	598	30	.309	.393	.530	292	18	.339	.414	.613	306	12	.281	.374	.451	301	15	.309	.372	.528	297	15	.310	.414	.532	173	6	.295	.366	.445	425	24	.315	.404	.565
1997	Atl-N	597	21	.295	.371	.479	304	7	.316	.402	.470	293	14	.273	.338	.488	297	13	.303	.381	.505	300	8	.287	.361	.453	196	1	.250	.324	.342	401	20	.317	.393	.546
1998	Atl-N	601	34	.313	.404	.547	293	17	.321	.406	.556	308	17	.305	.401	.539	317	18	.300	.389	.527	284	16	.327	.420	.570	181	2	.298	.380	.403	420	32	.319	.413	.610
1999	Atl-N	567	45	.319	.441	.633	276	25	.366	.467	.732	291	20	.275	.416	.540	292	14	.291	.395	.517	275	31	.349	.485	.756	142	15	.352	.450	.739	425	30	.308	.438	.598
2000	Atl-N	579	36	.311	.404	.566	288	18	.323	.424	.580	291	18	.299	.383	.553	272	19	.324	.420	.603	307	17	.300	.389	.534	130	12	.415	.480	.777	449	24	.281	.382	.506
TOTALS		3469	189	.303	.396	.536	1723	100	.323	.412	.573	1746	89	.283	.379	.499	1710	90	.296	.384	.523	1759	99	.309	.406	.548	950	39	.311	.394	.502	2519	150	.300	.396	.548
■ Ruppert Jones	BL/TL																																			
1978	Sea-A	472	6	.235	.312	.337	230	4	.243	.316	.357	242	2	.227	.308	.318	234	3	.256	.337	.346	238	3	.214	.287	.328	171	0	.216	.265	.275	301	6	.246	.337	.372
1979	Sea-A	622	21	.267	.356	.444	300	17	.293	.382	.537	322	4	.242	.332	.357	291	15	.244	.345	.481	331	6	.287	.365	.411	210	7	.267	.325	.433	412	14	.267	.370	.449
1980	NY-A	328	9	.223	.299	.357	149	5	.248	.292	.409	179	4	.201	.304	.313	162	5	.222	.312	.383	166	4	.223	.286	.331	180	3	.178	.250	.261	148	6	.277	.357	.473
1981	SD-N	397	4	.249	.318	.370	201	2	.284	.344	.423	196	2	.214	.291	.316	194	2	.242	.323	.351	203	2	.256	.313	.389	114	0	.228	.307	.298	283	4	.258	.322	.399
1982	SD-N	424	12	.283	.373	.425	201	6	.328	.415	.468	223	6	.242	.336	.386	248	9	.298	.405	.460	176	3	.261	.327	.375	130	2	.231	.313	.315	294	10	.306	.400	.473
1983	SD-N	335	12	.233	.305	.394	149	5	.188	.288	.329	186	7	.269	.320	.446	148	4	.203	.272	.318	187	8	.257	.332	.455	67	1	.119	.192	.179	268	11	.261	.333	.448
1984	Det-A	215	12	.284	.346	.516	105	6	.276	.342	.533	110	6	.291	.350	.500	42	4	.262	.273	.595	173	8	.289	.363	.497	10	0	.200	.200	.300	205	12	.288	.352	.527
1985	Cal-A	389	21	.231	.328	.447	180	10	.256	.364	.478	209	11	.211	.295	.421	163	11	.245	.365	.497	226	10	.221	.299	.412	46	2	.174	.255	.370	343	19	.239	.338	.458
1986	Cal-A	393	17	.229	.339	.427	182	10	.247	.380	.478	211	7	.213	.302	.384	182	8	.253	.370	.495	211	9	.209	.311	.370	45	2	.178	.296	.378	348	15	.236	.345	.434
1987	Cal-A	192	8	.245	.316	.432	85	3	.259	.323	.400	107	5	.234	.311	.458	68	6	.221	.329	.529	124	2	.258	.308	.379	14	1	.357	.400	.643	178	7	.236	.310	.416
TOTALS		3767	122	.248	.332	.411	1782	68	.266	.351	.446	1985	54	.232	.314	.379	1732	67	.248	.344	.430	2035	55	.248	.321	.395	987	18	.215	.284	.322	2780	104	.260	.348	.442
■ Brian Jordan	BR/TR																																			
1992	StL-N	193	5	.207	.250	.373	80	3	.237	.291	.475	113	2	.186	.220	.301	161	5	.211	.253	.404	32	0	.188	.235	.219	64	4	.219	.286	.438	129	1	.202	.231	.341
1993	StL-N	223	10	.309	.351	.543	137	4	.299	.342	.504	86	6	.326	.366	.605	55	0	.218	.271	.309	168	10	.339	.377	.619	63	7	.365	.412	.825	160	3	.287	.328	.431
1994	StL-N	178	5	.258	.320	.410	104	4	.269	.310	.442	74	1	.243	.333	.365	162	4	.259	.326	.407	16	1	.250	.250	.438	61	2	.262	.313	.426	117	3	.256	.323	.402
1995	StL-N	490	22	.296	.339	.488	259	14	.313	.357	.541	231	8	.277	.319	.429	221	9	.281	.322	.480	269	13	.309	.353	.494	121	5	.273	.328	.455	369	17	.304	.343	.499
1996	StL-N	513	17	.310	.349	.483	267	3	.341	.379	.483	246	14	.276	.317	.484	241	7	.290	.320	.440	272	10	.327	.374	.522	108	3	.343	.395	.528	405	14	.301	.337	.472
1997	StL-N	145	0	.234	.311	.269	72	0	.250	.316	.278	73	0	.219	.305	.260	114	0	.254	.341	.289	31	0	.161	.188	.194	35	0	.286	.359	.371	110	0	.218	.295	.236
1998	StL-N	564	25	.316	.368	.534	291	9	.333	.375	.546	273	16	.297	.361	.520	277	14	.347	.389	.585	287	11	.286	.349	.484	151	6	.351	.393	.609	413	19	.303	.359	.506
1999	Atl-N	576	23	.283	.346	.465	270	11	.274	.337	.444	306	12	.291	.354	.484	294	15	.293	.358	.510	282	8	.273	.333	.418	124	6	.331	.380	.565	452	17	.270	.337	.438
2000	Atl-N	489	17	.264	.320	.421	232	7	.280	.331	.418	257	10	.249	.311	.424	241	13	.299	.348	.510	248	4	.230	.293	.335	112	5	.402	.444	.643	377	12	.223	.283	.355
TOTALS		3371	124	.286	.337	.465	1712	55	.300	.348	.478	1659	69	.271	.327	.451	1766	67	.285	.336	.469	1605	57	.287	.339	.460	839	38	.324	.375	.554	2532	86	.273	.325	.435
■ Kevin Jordan	BR/TR																																			
1995	Phi-N	54	2	.185	.228	.315	33	1	.152	.200	.242	21	1	.238	.273	.429	0	0	—	—	—	54	2	.185	.228	.315	33	2	.273	.314	.485	21	0	.048	.091	.048
1996	Phi-N	131	3	.282	.309	.427	54	2	.278	.298	.481	77	1	.286	.317	.390	131	3	.282	.309	.427	0	0	—	—	—	23	1	.130	.130	.261	108	2	.315	.345	.463

		TOTAL					HOME					AWAY					1ST HALF					2ND HALF					LEFT					RIGHT				
YEAR	TM/L	AB	HR	AVG	OBP	SLG	AB	HR	AVG	OBP	SLG	AB	HR	AVG	OBP	SLG	AB	HR	AVG	OBP	SLG	AB	HR	AVG	OBP	SLG	AB	HR	AVG	OBP	SLG	AB	HR	AVG	OBP	SLG
1997	Phi-N	177	6	.266	.273	.412	118	4	.246	.258	.381	59	2	.305	.305	.475	56	3	.214	.217	.411	121	3	.289	.301	.413	75	4	.240	.259	.453	102	2	.284	.284	.382
1998	Phi-N	250	2	.276	.303	.352	120	1	.258	.288	.350	130	1	.292	.316	.354	122	1	.303	.341	.402	128	1	.250	.265	.305	81	0	.210	.229	.272	169	2	.308	.337	.391
1999	Phi-N	347	4	.285	.339	.386	174	2	.293	.353	.402	173	2	.277	.326	.370	103	1	.301	.351	.427	244	3	.279	.335	.369	123	2	.301	.341	.415	224	2	.277	.339	.371
2000	Phi-N	337	5	.220	.257	.323	171	2	.222	.265	.327	166	3	.217	.249	.319	181	2	.243	.278	.337	156	3	.192	.232	.308	113	1	.212	.244	.336	224	4	.223	.264	.317
TOTALS		1296	22	.259	.295	.368	670	12	.252	.291	.369	626	10	.267	.299	.367	593	10	.272	.305	.393	703	12	.249	.286	.347	448	10	.241	.271	.373	848	12	.269	.307	.366
■ Wally Joyner BL/TL																																				
1986	Cal-A	593	22	.290	.348	.457	294	11	.279	.347	.432	299	11	.301	.348	.482	298	19	.302	.345	.537	295	3	.278	.351	.376	192	6	.234	.289	.354	401	16	.317	.375	.506
1987	Cal-A	564	34	.285	.366	.528	307	19	.261	.336	.505	257	15	.315	.399	.556	273	18	.286	.371	.538	291	16	.285	.361	.519	201	8	.284	.347	.478	363	26	.287	.376	.556
1988	Cal-A	597	13	.295	.356	.419	290	6	.279	.339	.403	307	7	.309	.372	.433	289	4	.280	.344	.381	308	9	.308	.367	.455	212	1	.264	.309	.321	385	12	.312	.381	.473
1989	Cal-A	593	16	.282	.335	.420	286	8	.273	.332	.406	307	8	.290	.338	.433	262	2	.286	.338	.374	331	14	.278	.333	.456	206	6	.262	.305	.379	387	10	.292	.351	.442
1990	Cal-A	310	8	.268	.350	.394	135	5	.274	.367	.422	175	3	.263	.337	.371	269	8	.275	.363	.405	41	0	.220	.256	.317	106	2	.226	.291	.302	204	6	.289	.379	.441
1991	Cal-A	551	21	.301	.360	.488	268	10	.276	.343	.448	283	11	.325	.375	.527	279	10	.326	.387	.509	272	11	.276	.331	.467	189	5	.275	.308	.444	362	16	.315	.384	.511
1992	KC-A	572	9	.269	.336	.386	282	1	.266	.324	.358	290	8	.272	.349	.414	253	5	.285	.332	.427	319	4	.257	.340	.354	192	2	.240	.307	.339	380	7	.284	.352	.411
1993	KC-A	497	15	.292	.375	.467	256	4	.320	.389	.488	241	11	.261	.360	.444	269	7	.290	.383	.435	228	8	.294	.364	.504	166	2	.259	.340	.367	331	13	.308	.392	.517
1994	KC-A	363	8	.311	.386	.449	192	2	.359	.418	.484	171	6	.257	.349	.409	252	6	.302	.384	.448	111	2	.333	.390	.450	124	1	.306	.367	.379	239	7	.314	.395	.485
1995	KC-A	465	12	.310	.394	.447	220	6	.336	.404	.473	245	6	.286	.386	.424	188	4	.293	.405	.436	277	8	.321	.387	.455	146	0	.274	.327	.295	319	12	.326	.422	.517
1996	SD-N	433	8	.277	.377	.404	194	5	.242	.361	.366	239	3	.305	.391	.435	184	5	.321	.435	.500	249	3	.245	.332	.333	117	2	.214	.290	.316	316	6	.301	.407	.437
1997	SD-N	455	13	.327	.390	.486	216	6	.324	.377	.472	239	7	.331	.401	.498	228	8	.338	.407	.509	227	5	.317	.373	.463	80	3	.262	.307	.425	375	10	.341	.407	.499
1998	SD-N	439	12	.298	.370	.453	205	4	.273	.339	.395	234	8	.321	.398	.504	233	6	.318	.397	.468	206	6	.277	.339	.437	114	3	.307	.365	.447	325	9	.295	.372	.455
1999	SD-N	323	5	.248	.363	.350	169	2	.296	.394	.396	154	3	.195	.330	.299	128	1	.227	.357	.328	195	4	.262	.367	.364	81	3	.247	.340	.432	242	2	.248	.370	.322
2000	Atl-N	224	5	.281	.365	.402	108	2	.278	.372	.389	116	3	.284	.359	.414	82	1	.183	.292	.268	142	4	.338	.409	.479	15	0	.267	.353	.267	209	5	.282	.366	.411
TOTALS		6979	201	.290	.364	.441	3422	91	.288	.359	.432	3557	110	.292	.368	.451	3487	104	.294	.371	.449	3492	97	.286	.356	.434	2141	44	.262	.320	.375	4838	157	.303	.382	.471
■ David Justice BL/TL																																				
1989	Atl-N	51	1	.235	.291	.353	37	1	.243	.282	.405	14	0	.214	.313	.214	20	0	.050	.174	.050	31	1	.355	.375	.548	10	0	.100	.100	.100	41	1	.268	.333	.415
1990	Atl-N	439	28	.282	.373	.535	225	19	.320	.405	.662	214	9	.243	.340	.402	145	4	.269	.354	.428	294	24	.289	.382	.588	131	10	.366	.443	.656	308	18	.247	.344	.484
1991	Atl-N	396	21	.275	.377	.503	175	11	.269	.371	.537	221	10	.281	.382	.475	236	11	.297	.380	.517	160	10	.244	.374	.481	155	7	.277	.333	.465	241	14	.274	.403	.527
1992	Atl-N	484	21	.256	.359	.446	245	10	.229	.346	.420	239	11	.285	.373	.473	212	8	.231	.344	.387	272	13	.276	.371	.493	159	5	.283	.352	.447	325	16	.243	.362	.446
1993	Atl-N	585	40	.270	.357	.515	290	18	.272	.348	.486	295	22	.268	.365	.542	281	16	.228	.307	.438	304	24	.309	.401	.586	177	11	.294	.362	.508	408	29	.260	.354	.517
1994	Atl-N	352	19	.313	.427	.531	173	9	.335	.436	.549	179	10	.291	.418	.514	224	12	.330	.447	.554	128	7	.281	.391	.492	122	4	.287	.416	.451	230	15	.326	.433	.574
1995	Atl-N	411	24	.253	.365	.479	189	15	.302	.390	.614	222	9	.212	.344	.365	131	7	.267	.405	.504	280	17	.246	.345	.468	141	7	.241	.366	.433	270	17	.259	.364	.504
1996	Atl-N	140	6	.321	.409	.514	79	5	.342	.419	.608	61	1	.295	.394	.393	140	6	.321	.409	.514	0	0	—	—	—	53	3	.321	.413	.585	87	3	.322	.406	.471
1997	Cle-A	495	33	.329	.418	.596	238	17	.353	.440	.630	257	16	.307	.396	.564	218	17	.335	.430	.642	277	16	.325	.408	.560	146	11	.322	.377	.616	349	22	.332	.433	.587
1998	Cle-A	540	21	.280	.363	.476	265	7	.268	.352	.415	275	14	.291	.374	.535	303	12	.290	.367	.492	237	9	.266	.359	.456	155	3	.232	.275	.381	385	18	.299	.395	.514
1999	Cle-A	429	21	.287	.413	.476	223	11	.305	.423	.475	206	10	.267	.403	.476	236	15	.292	.383	.513	193	6	.280	.445	.430	101	5	.248	.353	.406	328	16	.299	.431	.497
2000	Cle-A	249	21	.265	.361	.582	120	10	.267	.353	.567	129	11	.264	.368	.597	249	21	.265	.361	.582	0	0	—	—	—	53	6	.283	.367	.679	196	15	.260	.360	.556
2000	NY-A	275	20	.305	.391	.585	148	14	.311	.405	.642	127	6	.299	.375	.520	3	0	.000	.000	.000	272	20	.309	.395	.592	81	9	.321	.368	.741	194	11	.299	.400	.521
TOTALS		4846	276	.283	.381	.513	2407	147	.293	.386	.536	2439	129	.273	.376	.491	2398	129	.281	.376	.503	2448	147	.286	.386	.523	1484	81	.286	.363	.507	3362	195	.282	.389	.516
■ Eric Karros BR/TR																																				
1991	LA-N	14	0	.071	.133	.143	6	0	.167	.286	.333	8	0	.000	.000	.000	0	0	—	—	—	14	0	.071	.133	.143	10	0	.000	.091	.000	4	0	.250	.250	.500
1992	LA-N	545	20	.257	.304	.426	251	6	.259	.320	.394	294	14	.255	.289	.452	199	9	.271	.304	.457	346	11	.249	.304	.408	213	8	.277	.325	.437	332	12	.244	.291	.419
1993	LA-N	619	23	.247	.287	.409	303	13	.231	.279	.403	316	10	.263	.295	.415	287	8	.282	.324	.422	332	15	.217	.256	.398	170	5	.312	.343	.494	449	18	.223	.267	.376
1994	LA-N	406	14	.266	.310	.426	191	5	.267	.313	.377	215	9	.265	.308	.470	279	8	.276	.323	.419	127	6	.244	.283	.441	102	4	.265	.331	.412	304	10	.266	.303	.431
1995	LA-N	551	32	.298	.369	.535	263	19	.293	.370	.548	288	13	.302	.369	.524	237	14	.312	.379	.544	314	18	.287	.362	.529	124	4	.315	.384	.484	427	28	.293	.365	.550
1996	LA-N	608	34	.260	.316	.479	287	16	.275	.319	.495	321	18	.246	.314	.464	287	18	.247	.305	.470	321	16	.271	.327	.486	101	6	.327	.417	.574	507	28	.247	.295	.460
1997	LA-N	628	31	.266	.329	.459	296	13	.267	.343	.446	332	18	.265	.315	.470	304	16	.266	.346	.470	324	15	.265	.312	.448	153	6	.229	.306	.379	475	25	.278	.336	.484
1998	LA-N	507	23	.296	.355	.475	256	9	.301	.358	.441	251	14	.291	.351	.510	209	8	.282	.350	.440	298	15	.305	.358	.500	101	4	.297	.377	.455	406	19	.296	.349	.480
1999	LA-N	578	34	.304	.362	.550	269	17	.297	.363	.558	309	17	.311	.360	.544	271	13	.295	.354	.524	307	21	.313	.368	.573	146	11	.308	.391	.582	432	23	.303	.351	.539
2000	LA-N	584	31	.250	.321	.459	289	16	.235	.296	.443	295	15	.264	.345	.475	287	23	.254	.336	.547	297	8	.246	.306	.374	140	5	.286	.383	.471	444	26	.239	.301	.455
TOTALS		5040	242	.270	.328	.468	2411	114	.268	.329	.458	2629	128	.272	.327	.478	2360	117	.275	.335	.478	2680	125	.266	.321	.460	1260	53	.287	.356	.470	3780	189	.265	.318	.468
■ Roberto Kelly BR/TR																																				
1987	NY-A	52	1	.269	.328	.385	29	0	.207	.303	.241	23	1	.348	.360	.565	0	0	—	—	—	52	1	.269	.328	.385	33	1	.242	.333	.424	19	0	.316	.316	.316
1988	NY-A	77	1	.247	.272	.364	49	1	.245	.275	.388	28	0	.250	.267	.321	77	1	.247	.272	.364	0	0	—	—	—	54	0	.241	.268	.296	23	1	.261	.280	.522
1989	NY-A	441	9	.302	.369	.417	205	2	.317	.397	.405	236	7	.288	.344	.428	189	4	.307	.361	.429	252	5	.298	.375	.409	145	3	.372	.424	.497	296	6	.267	.342	.378
1990	NY-A	641	15	.285	.323	.418	315	5	.305	.334	.435	326	10	.267	.311	.402	277	4	.289	.327	.390	364	11	.283	.320	.440	181	5	.304	.352	.442	460	10	.278	.311	.409
1991	NY-A	486	20	.267	.333	.444	232	11	.310	.369	.500	254	9	.228	.301	.394	279	9	.251	.309	.394	207	11	.290	.363	.512	159	9	.296	.372	.503	327	11	.254	.313	.416
1992	NY-A	580	10	.272	.322	.384	296	6	.257	.309	.378	284	4	.289	.336	.391	284	7	.289	.327	.433	296	3	.257	.317	.338	184	4	.277	.344	.391	396	6	.270	.310	.381
1993	Cin-N	320	9	.319	.354	.475	152	4	.296	.337	.421	168	5	.339	.369	.524	312	8	.317	.353	.465	8	1	.375	.375	.875	96	3	.250	.280	.427	224	6	.348	.384	.496
1994	Cin-N	179	3	.302	.351	.397	77	1	.234	.294	.325	102	2	.353	.394	.451	179	3	.302	.351	.397	0	0	—	—	—	41	0	.293	.341	.317	138	3	.304	.353	.420
1994	Atl-N	255	6	.286	.345	.439	128	3	.281	.340	.414	127	3	.291	.350	.465	121	3	.339	.403	.529	134	3	.239	.293	.358	67	2	.299	.373	.448	188	4	.282	.335	.436
1995	Mon-N	95	1	.274	.337	.347	43	0	.395	.422	.442	52	1	.173	.271	.269	95	1	.274	.337	.347	0	0	—	—	—	15	0	.333	.375	.467	80	1	.262	.330	.325
1995	LA-N	409	6	.279	.306	.379	193	2	.254	.284	.342	216	4	.301	.325	.412	142	1	.268	.289	.331	267	5	.285	.315	.404	102	2	.294	.324	.431	307	4	.274	.300	.362
1996	Min-A	322	6	.323	.375	.457	158	3	.316	.389	.456	164	3	.329	.362	.457	173	1	.312	.369	.428	149	5	.336	.383	.490	128	4	.406	.462	.594	194	2	.268	.318	.366
1997	Min-A	247	5	.287	.336	.441	123	5	.260	.295	.455	124	0	.315	.374	.427	158	1	.272	.343	.399	89	4	.315	.322	.517	94	2	.287	.352	.436	153	3	.288	.325	.444
1997	Sea-A	121	7	.298	.328	.529	65	3	.277	.309	.492	56	4	.321	.350	.571	0	0	—	—	—	121	7	.298	.328	.529	30	3	.333	.364	.700	91	4	.286	.316	.473
1998	Tex-A	257	16	.323	.349	.560	137	6	.314	.333	.511	120	10	.333	.367	.617	78	6	.321	.346	.628	179	10	.324	.351	.531	146	9	.349	.367	.589	111	7	.288	.328	.523
1999	Tex-A	290	8	.300	.355	.448	145	4	.324	.400	.462	145	4	.276	.307	.434	135	3	.311	.367	.437	155	5	.290	.345	.458	95	2	.358	.421	.505	195	6	.272	.322	.421
2000	NY-A	25	1	.120	.185	.280	9	1	.222	.300	.556	16	0	.063	.118	.125	25	1	.120	.185	.280	0	0	—	—	—	21	1	.143	.217	.333	4	0	.000	.000	.000
TOTALS		4797	124	.290	.337	.430	2356	57	.290	.340	.426	2441	67	.289	.334	.434	2524	53	.291	.338	.421	2273	71	.289	.337	.440	1591	50	.312	.365	.470	3206	74	.279	.324	.410
■ Steve Kemp BL/TL																																				
1978	Det-A	582	15	.277	.379	.399	292	9	.295	.397	.435	290	6	.259	.361	.362	258	4	.267	.409	.360	324	11	.284	.353	.429	290	3	.245	.349	.317	292	12	.308	.409	.479
1979	Det-A	490	26	.318	.398	.543	263	17	.319	.403	.567	227	9	.317	.391	.515	250	10	.340	.432	.536	240	16	.296	.360	.550	186	8	.323	.388	.500	304	18	.316	.404	.569
1980	Det-A	508	21	.293	.376	.474	268	15	.310	.399	.541	240	6	.275	.349	.400	202	6	.297	.395	.446	306	15	.291	.363	.493	209	6	.258	.342	.402	299	15	.318	.401	.525
1981	Det-A	372	9	.277	.389	.419	183	6	.301	.387	.475	189	3	.254	.391	.365	205	6	.293	.382	.463	167	3	.257	.398	.365	185	4	.238	.335	.378	187	5	.316	.440	.460
1982	Chi-A	580	19	.286	.381	.428	274	4	.259	.359	.336	306	15	.310	.400	.510	265	8	.283	.376	.415	315	11	.289	.385	.438	205	4	.278	.359	.376	375	15	.291	.392	.456
1983	NY-A	373	12	.241	.318	.399	178	3	.208	.276	.303	195	9	.272	.356	.487	230	9	.270	.340	.457	143	3	.196	.284	.308	124	1	.242	.312	.306	249	11	.241	.321	.446
1984	NY-A	313	7	.291	.369	.403	156	2	.314	.383	.385	157	5	.268	.355	.420	192	4	.297	.376	.406	121	3	.281	.357	.397	63	1	.254	.324	.317	250	6	.300	.380	.424
1985	Pit-N	236	2	.250	.317	.347	102	1	.275	.358	.363	134	1	.231	.283	.336	139	0	.209	.298	.266	97	2	.309	.346	.464	28	0	.214	.250	.250	208	2	.255	.326	.361
1986	Pit-N	16	1	.188	.350	.375	8	0	.000	.200	.000	8	1	.375	.500	.750	16	1	.188	.350	.375	0	0	—	—	—	0	0	—	—	—	16	1	.188	.350	.375
1988	Tex-A	36	0	.222	.256	.222	23	0	.261	.280	.261	13	0	.154	.214	.154	36	0	.222	.256	.222	0	0	—	—	—	0	0	—	—	—	36	0	.222	.256	.222
TOTALS		3506	112	.281	.370	.432	1747	57	.286	.374	.433	1759	55	.277	.367	.430	1793	48	.283	.379	.422	1713	64	.279	.361	.442	1290	27	.262	.346	.373	2216	85	.292	.384	.466
■ Jason Kendall BR/TR																																				
1996	Pit-N	414	3	.300	.372	.401	216	2	.306	.350	.417	198	1	.293	.393	.384	211	1	.299	.352	.384	203	2	.300	.391	.419	78	0	.295	.371	.410	336	3	.301	.372	.399
1997	Pit-N	486	8	.294	.391	.434	234	5	.308	.409	.457	252	3	.282	.373	.413	244	2	.275	.382	.406	242	6	.314	.399	.463	101	3	.297	.374	.465	385	5	.294	.395	.426
1998	Pit-N	535	12	.327	.411	.473	268	6	.306	.387	.451	267	6	.348	.435	.494	278	5	.335	.413	.453	257	7	.319	.409	.494	129	5	.372	.443	.612	406	7	.313	.401	.429
1999	Pit-N	280	8	.332	.428	.511	136	5	.360	.454	.610	144	3	.306	.404	.417	268	8	.340	.434	.522	12	0	.167	.286	.250	59	4	.271	.392	.508	221	4	.348	.438	.511
2000	Pit-N	579	14	.320	.412	.470	289	7	.304	.389	.467	290	7	.334	.435	.472	274	6	.328	.435	.464	305	8	.311	.390	.475	127	2	.331	.411	.496	452	12	.316	.412	.462
TOTALS		2294	45	.314	.402	.456	1143	25	.312	.394	.469	1151	20	.315	.410	.442	1275	22	.317	.407	.449	1019	23	.310	.396	.463	494	14	.322	.403	.508	1800	31	.312	.402	.441
■ Terry Kennedy BL/TR																																				
1978	StL-N	29	0	.172	.273	.172	14	0	.143	.200	.143	15	0	.200	.333	.200	0	0	—	—	—	29	0	.172	.273	.172	0	0	—	—	—	29	0	.172	.273	.172
1979	StL-N	109	2	.284	.319	.404	58	2	.293	.311	.448	51	0	.275	.327	.353	13	0	.154	.154	.308	96	2	.302	.340	.417	14	1	.286	.333	.571	95	1	.284	.317	.379
1980	StL-N	248	4	.254	.325	.375	111	1	.243	.301	.387	137	3	.263	.344	.365	105	3	.295	.367	.476	143	1	.224	.294	.301	25	0	.160	.233	.160	223	4	.265	.336	.399
1981	SD-N	382	2	.301	.341	.385	194	1	.289	.324	.376	188	1	.314	.358	.394	195	0	.308	.345	.369	187	2	.294	.337	.401	96	0	.292	.333	.365	286	2	.304	.343	.392
1982	SD-N	562	21	.295	.328	.486	287	10	.289	.317	.467	275	11	.302	.339	.505	257	8	.261	.289	.455	305	13	.325	.360	.511	156	4	.314	.357	.487	406	17	.288	.316	.485
1983	SD-N	549	17	.284	.342	.434	271	7	.288	.357	.421	278	10	.281	.327	.446	268	6	.302	.351	.425	281	11	.267	.333	.441	148	5	.284	.317	.446	401	12	.284	.351	.429
1984	SD-N	530	14	.240	.284	.353	272	8	.235	.275	.371	258	6	.244	.294	.333	267	7	.258	.309	.386	263	7	.221	.258	.319	160	4	.188	.206	.287	370	10	.262	.316	.381

YEAR	TM/L	TOTAL AB	HR	AVG	OBP	SLG	HOME AB	HR	AVG	OBP	SLG	AWAY AB	HR	AVG	OBP	SLG	1ST HALF AB	HR	AVG	OBP	SLG	2ND HALF AB	HR	AVG	OBP	SLG	LEFT AB	HR	AVG	OBP	SLG	RIGHT AB	HR	AVG	OBP	SLG
1985	SD-N	532	10	.261	.301	.372	279	7	.233	.274	.358	253	3	.292	.331	.387	251	7	.255	.297	.398	281	3	.267	.304	.349	147	3	.259	.283	.374	385	7	.262	.308	.371
1986	SD-N	432	12	.264	.324	.403	214	7	.280	.346	.421	218	5	.248	.302	.385	225	6	.262	.332	.396	207	6	.266	.315	.411	96	3	.229	.288	.396	336	9	.274	.334	.405
1987	Bal-A	512	18	.250	.299	.385	240	11	.213	.279	.383	272	7	.283	.318	.386	273	13	.267	.313	.443	239	5	.230	.284	.318	183	6	.219	.255	.339	329	12	.267	.323	.410
1988	Bal-A	265	3	.226	.269	.298	136	2	.176	.211	.243	129	1	.279	.326	.357	142	0	.197	.237	.239	123	3	.260	.305	.366	39	1	.231	.268	.308	226	2	.226	.269	.296
1989	SF-N	355	5	.239	.306	.324	172	1	.267	.332	.326	183	4	.213	.282	.322	167	4	.251	.339	.377	188	1	.229	.275	.277	39	0	.154	.233	.205	316	5	.250	.315	.339
1990	SF-N	303	2	.277	.342	.370	148	2	.291	.369	.399	155	0	.265	.315	.342	150	1	.280	.355	.373	153	1	.275	.329	.366	32	0	.188	.257	.219	271	2	.288	.352	.387
1991	SF-N	171	3	.234	.283	.339	75	2	.240	.287	.413	96	1	.229	.279	.281	103	2	.204	.259	.340	68	1	.279	.319	.338	10	1	.300	.273	.800	161	2	.230	.283	.311
TOTALS		4979	113	.264	.314	.386	2471	61	.257	.308	.386	2508	52	.271	.320	.385	2416	57	.264	.317	.397	2563	56	.263	.311	.375	1145	28	.245	.284	.371	3834	85	.269	.322	.390
■ Jeff Kent BR/TR																																				
1992	Tor-A	192	8	.240	.324	.443	99	2	.232	.328	.394	93	6	.247	.321	.495	90	3	.267	.380	.489	102	5	.216	.272	.402	48	2	.250	.327	.438	144	6	.236	.323	.444
1992	NY-N	113	3	.239	.289	.407	68	2	.250	.301	.426	45	1	.222	.271	.378	0	0	—	—	—	113	3	.239	.289	.407	44	1	.182	.250	.295	69	2	.275	.315	.478
1993	NY-N	496	21	.270	.320	.446	247	9	.275	.319	.437	249	12	.265	.320	.454	209	6	.234	.282	.373	287	15	.296	.347	.498	148	0	.230	.277	.291	348	21	.287	.338	.511
1994	NY-N	415	14	.292	.341	.475	188	10	.319	.360	.580	227	4	.269	.327	.388	275	12	.298	.359	.509	140	2	.279	.306	.407	110	4	.373	.434	.582	305	10	.262	.307	.436
1995	NY-N	472	20	.278	.327	.464	243	11	.284	.336	.494	229	9	.271	.319	.432	212	9	.274	.330	.453	260	11	.281	.325	.473	133	3	.248	.306	.376	339	17	.289	.336	.499
1996	NY-N	335	9	.290	.331	.436	148	2	.270	.310	.378	187	7	.305	.347	.481	284	9	.282	.319	.444	51	0	.333	.393	.392	81	0	.358	.416	.469	254	9	.268	.303	.425
1996	Cle-A	102	3	.265	.328	.422	60	2	.283	.333	.467	42	1	.238	.319	.357	0	0	—	—	—	102	3	.265	.328	.422	42	0	.262	.358	.333	60	3	.267	.302	.483
1997	SF-N	580	29	.250	.316	.472	281	13	.246	.321	.452	299	16	.254	.312	.492	276	16	.254	.319	.500	304	13	.247	.314	.447	148	6	.230	.307	.412	432	23	.257	.320	.493
1998	SF-N	526	31	.297	.359	.555	237	17	.287	.337	.578	289	14	.304	.377	.536	256	7	.301	.355	.492	270	24	.293	.363	.615	126	4	.254	.342	.452	400	27	.310	.365	.587
1999	SF-N	511	23	.290	.366	.511	252	11	.246	.329	.448	259	12	.332	.402	.571	289	11	.298	.377	.505	222	12	.279	.352	.518	132	7	.273	.344	.538	379	16	.296	.373	.501
2000	SF-N	587	33	.334	.424	.596	284	14	.335	.419	.567	303	19	.333	.429	.624	293	21	.355	.438	.679	294	12	.313	.410	.514	145	5	.324	.459	.524	442	28	.337	.412	.620
TOTALS		4329	194	.284	.348	.493	2107	93	.279	.342	.487	2222	101	.288	.354	.498	2184	94	.288	.353	.500	2145	100	.279	.343	.485	1157	32	.274	.353	.439	3172	162	.287	.346	.513
■ Jeff King BR/TR																																				
1989	Pit-N	215	5	.195	.266	.353	119	3	.185	.252	.345	96	2	.208	.282	.365	26	0	.192	.300	.423	189	5	.196	.261	.344	112	0	.196	.279	.321	103	5	.194	.250	.388
1990	Pit-N	371	14	.245	.283	.410	179	9	.274	.304	.475	192	5	.219	.263	.349	140	2	.214	.265	.300	231	12	.264	.293	.476	231	9	.264	.303	.446	140	5	.214	.248	.350
1991	Pit-N	109	4	.239	.328	.376	63	3	.222	.310	.413	46	1	.261	.352	.326	109	4	.239	.328	.376	0	0	—	—	—	31	1	.323	.500	.419	78	3	.205	.241	.359
1992	Pit-N	480	14	.231	.272	.371	247	6	.239	.280	.360	233	8	.223	.264	.382	213	6	.188	.230	.315	267	8	.266	.306	.416	216	6	.236	.277	.394	264	8	.227	.269	.352
1993	Pit-N	611	9	.295	.356	.406	297	4	.306	.366	.428	314	5	.283	.347	.385	295	5	.281	.343	.386	316	4	.307	.369	.424	188	4	.324	.383	.463	423	5	.281	.345	.381
1994	Pit-N	339	5	.263	.316	.375	184	2	.288	.338	.408	155	3	.232	.291	.335	212	3	.264	.324	.387	127	2	.260	.304	.354	86	2	.244	.323	.384	253	3	.269	.314	.372
1995	Pit-N	445	18	.265	.342	.456	222	7	.239	.306	.410	223	11	.291	.377	.502	150	6	.287	.377	.493	295	12	.254	.323	.437	112	7	.241	.348	.509	333	11	.273	.340	.438
1996	Pit-N	591	30	.271	.346	.497	298	14	.265	.344	.480	293	16	.276	.347	.515	307	18	.270	.331	.505	284	12	.271	.360	.489	137	7	.285	.387	.555	454	23	.267	.333	.480
1997	KC-A	543	28	.238	.341	.451	272	11	.250	.347	.441	271	17	.225	.334	.461	263	15	.274	.397	.521	280	13	.204	.283	.386	149	9	.268	.391	.523	394	19	.226	.320	.424
1998	KC-A	486	24	.263	.319	.451	248	13	.254	.317	.448	238	11	.273	.321	.454	293	16	.266	.336	.474	193	8	.259	.290	.415	133	6	.308	.376	.504	353	18	.246	.297	.431
1999	KC-A	72	3	.236	.385	.389	32	2	.281	.489	.500	40	1	.200	.283	.300	72	3	.236	.385	.389	0	0	—	—	—	13	1	.231	.353	.462	59	2	.237	.392	.373
TOTALS		4262	154	.256	.324	.425	2161	74	.259	.326	.428	2101	80	.253	.321	.422	2080	78	.256	.333	.428	2182	76	.256	.315	.422	1408	52	.267	.344	.455	2854	102	.251	.314	.410
■ Dave Kingman BR/TR																																				
1978	Chi-N	395	28	.266	.336	.542	232	18	.289	.341	.591	163	10	.233	.330	.472	212	16	.245	.321	.528	183	12	.290	.355	.557	158	12	.285	.385	.582	237	16	.253	.301	.515
1979	Chi-N	532	48	.288	.343	.613	276	25	.315	.379	.649	256	23	.258	.302	.574	251	27	.299	.379	.669	281	21	.278	.309	.562	167	16	.317	.366	.689	365	32	.274	.333	.578
1980	Chi-N	255	18	.278	.329	.522	91	6	.319	.375	.571	164	12	.256	.301	.494	147	10	.293	.342	.531	108	8	.259	.311	.509	62	1	.194	.292	.274	193	17	.306	.341	.601
1981	NY-N	353	22	.221	.326	.456	162	11	.210	.338	.444	191	11	.230	.315	.466	173	14	.220	.346	.497	180	8	.222	.305	.417	64	5	.234	.387	.516	289	17	.218	.311	.443
1982	NY-N	535	37	.204	.285	.432	270	19	.215	.291	.444	265	18	.192	.278	.419	241	17	.216	.297	.452	294	20	.194	.275	.415	96	11	.229	.359	.583	439	26	.198	.267	.399
1983	NY-N	248	13	.198	.265	.383	113	8	.204	.254	.442	135	5	.193	.273	.333	204	12	.211	.274	.422	44	1	.136	.224	.205	96	3	.219	.286	.354	152	10	.184	.251	.401
1984	Oak-A	549	35	.268	.321	.505	279	19	.272	.328	.509	270	16	.263	.315	.500	240	20	.262	.313	.546	309	15	.272	.328	.472	178	9	.270	.345	.472	371	26	.267	.310	.520
1985	Oak-A	592	30	.238	.309	.417	278	14	.223	.312	.410	314	16	.252	.305	.424	278	19	.245	.323	.475	314	11	.232	.296	.366	176	13	.244	.325	.483	416	17	.236	.302	.389
1986	Oak-A	561	35	.210	.255	.431	297	15	.212	.244	.391	264	20	.208	.266	.477	268	17	.201	.248	.414	293	18	.218	.261	.447	173	14	.220	.277	.509	388	21	.206	.245	.397
TOTALS		4020	266	.242	.307	.479	1998	135	.250	.317	.491	2022	131	.233	.298	.467	2014	152	.242	.314	.503	2006	114	.241	.300	.455	1170	84	.254	.337	.516	2850	182	.236	.295	.464
■ Ryan Klesko BL/TL																																				
1992	Atl-N	14	0	.000	.067	.000	10	0	.000	.091	.000	4	0	.000	.000	.000	0	0	—	—	—	14	0	.000	.067	.000	1	0	.000	.000	.000	13	0	.000	.071	.000
1993	Atl-N	17	2	.353	.450	.765	10	2	.500	.500	1.200	7	0	.143	.400	.143	11	1	.273	.385	.545	6	1	.500	.571	1.167	1	0	.000	.500	.000	16	2	.375	.444	.813
1994	Atl-N	245	17	.278	.344	.563	117	7	.248	.270	.487	128	10	.305	.403	.633	178	15	.326	.374	.674	67	2	.149	.272	.269	22	0	.227	.320	.364	223	17	.283	.347	.583
1995	Atl-N	329	23	.310	.396	.608	172	15	.302	.374	.605	157	8	.318	.419	.611	111	7	.342	.417	.622	218	16	.294	.386	.601	78	3	.244	.348	.449	251	20	.331	.412	.657
1996	Atl-N	528	34	.282	.364	.530	266	20	.323	.405	.605	262	14	.240	.321	.454	273	22	.289	.368	.590	255	12	.275	.360	.467	139	3	.230	.285	.324	389	31	.301	.390	.604
1997	Atl-N	467	24	.261	.334	.490	230	10	.270	.346	.470	237	14	.253	.322	.511	251	12	.243	.319	.470	216	12	.282	.351	.514	106	3	.198	.283	.340	361	21	.280	.349	.535
1998	Atl-N	427	18	.274	.359	.473	220	8	.309	.375	.482	207	10	.237	.343	.464	253	13	.285	.348	.514	174	5	.259	.375	.414	61	0	.213	.342	.262	366	18	.284	.362	.508
1999	Atl-N	404	21	.297	.376	.532	214	12	.266	.340	.500	190	9	.332	.414	.568	198	9	.288	.351	.480	206	12	.306	.398	.583	49	1	.102	.179	.163	355	20	.324	.402	.583
2000	SD-N	494	26	.283	.393	.516	250	9	.280	.397	.476	244	17	.287	.390	.557	220	17	.318	.410	.636	274	9	.255	.380	.420	121	2	.256	.343	.380	373	24	.292	.408	.560
TOTALS		2925	165	.282	.367	.524	1489	83	.288	.366	.520	1436	82	.275	.367	.528	1495	96	.293	.365	.561	1430	69	.270	.368	.485	578	12	.218	.304	.336	2347	153	.297	.382	.570
■ Ray Knight BR/TR																																				
1978	Cin-N	65	1	.200	.235	.292	33	1	.182	.229	.273	32	0	.219	.242	.313	40	1	.150	.190	.300	25	0	.280	.308	.280	41	0	.171	.227	.195	24	1	.250	.250	.458
1979	Cin-N	551	10	.318	.360	.454	269	4	.309	.349	.454	282	6	.326	.370	.454	259	2	.309	.372	.394	292	8	.325	.349	.507	182	5	.363	.415	.511	369	5	.295	.332	.425
1980	Cin-N	618	14	.264	.307	.417	294	6	.238	.285	.381	324	8	.287	.327	.451	277	8	.292	.332	.491	341	6	.240	.286	.358	165	4	.339	.385	.509	453	10	.236	.277	.384
1981	Cin-N	386	6	.259	.322	.370	193	1	.254	.324	.358	193	5	.264	.319	.383	204	5	.250	.325	.373	182	1	.269	.318	.368	95	0	.305	.358	.400	291	6	.244	.309	.361
1982	Hou-N	609	6	.294	.344	.402	301	0	.269	.322	.369	308	6	.318	.365	.435	288	4	.316	.359	.441	321	2	.274	.330	.368	183	2	.268	.332	.383	426	4	.305	.349	.411
1983	Hou-N	507	9	.304	.355	.444	241	3	.261	.321	.402	266	6	.342	.385	.481	240	5	.342	.387	.492	267	4	.270	.325	.401	164	3	.293	.339	.427	343	6	.309	.362	.452
1984	Hou-N	278	2	.223	.259	.281	134	1	.239	.278	.321	144	1	.208	.242	.243	225	2	.236	.271	.307	53	0	.170	.211	.170	101	1	.248	.274	.317	177	1	.209	.251	.260
1984	NY-N	93	1	.280	.337	.355	55	1	.236	.300	.327	38	0	.342	.390	.395	0	0	—	—	—	93	1	.280	.337	.355	35	1	.257	.278	.400	58	0	.293	.369	.328
1985	NY-N	271	6	.218	.252	.328	127	4	.197	.234	.339	144	2	.236	.268	.319	123	3	.171	.216	.293	148	3	.257	.282	.358	170	6	.259	.285	.418	101	0	.149	.198	.178
1986	NY-N	486	11	.298	.351	.424	228	7	.289	.353	.452	258	4	.306	.350	.399	236	8	.314	.362	.479	250	3	.284	.342	.372	197	9	.381	.410	.604	289	2	.242	.314	.301
1987	Bal-A	563	14	.256	.310	.373	270	8	.274	.319	.411	293	6	.239	.302	.338	277	8	.274	.331	.412	286	6	.238	.290	.336	206	8	.218	.293	.354	357	6	.277	.321	.384
1988	Det-A	299	3	.217	.271	.301	154	3	.188	.242	.286	145	0	.248	.300	.317	177	1	.232	.297	.299	122	2	.197	.231	.303	169	3	.219	.256	.325	130	0	.215	.290	.269
TOTALS		4726	83	.272	.321	.391	2299	39	.257	.309	.384	2427	44	.286	.332	.397	2346	47	.280	.331	.408	2380	36	.264	.311	.374	1708	42	.287	.334	.426	3018	41	.263	.314	.371
■ Chuck Knoblauch BR/TR																																				
1991	Min-A	565	1	.281	.351	.350	287	1	.328	.391	.415	278	0	.234	.310	.284	255	0	.282	.353	.345	310	1	.281	.349	.355	148	0	.257	.325	.324	417	1	.290	.360	.360
1992	Min-A	600	2	.297	.384	.358	289	0	.287	.388	.318	311	2	.305	.381	.395	274	1	.303	.400	.369	326	1	.291	.371	.350	124	1	.315	.405	.419	476	1	.292	.379	.342
1993	Min-A	602	2	.277	.354	.346	312	2	.298	.369	.362	290	0	.255	.337	.328	274	0	.263	.354	.318	328	2	.290	.354	.369	156	0	.269	.321	.327	446	2	.280	.365	.352
1994	Min-A	445	5	.312	.381	.461	227	1	.344	.411	.485	218	4	.280	.349	.436	297	4	.323	.380	.495	148	1	.291	.382	.392	105	2	.286	.348	.438	340	3	.321	.391	.468
1995	Min-A	538	11	.333	.424	.487	282	4	.330	.413	.465	256	7	.336	.437	.512	216	1	.315	.402	.398	322	10	.345	.439	.547	141	4	.355	.397	.553	397	7	.325	.433	.463
1996	Min-A	578	13	.341	.448	.517	300	7	.347	.454	.527	278	6	.335	.442	.507	280	5	.354	.438	.518	298	8	.329	.457	.517	147	4	.388	.480	.578	431	9	.325	.438	.497
1997	Min-A	611	9	.291	.390	.411	305	2	.289	.384	.380	306	7	.294	.395	.441	298	4	.292	.414	.399	313	5	.291	.365	.422	132	3	.295	.404	.394	479	6	.290	.386	.415
1998	NY-A	603	17	.265	.361	.405	285	5	.295	.391	.421	318	12	.239	.333	.390	288	4	.260	.385	.358	315	13	.270	.337	.448	139	3	.252	.369	.388	464	14	.269	.358	.409
1999	NY-A	603	18	.292	.393	.454	300	11	.293	.389	.470	303	7	.290	.398	.439	270	4	.267	.376	.374	333	14	.312	.408	.520	114	4	.272	.375	.491	489	14	.297	.398	.446
2000	NY-A	400	5	.283	.366	.385	181	5	.320	.429	.481	219	0	.251	.310	.306	237	3	.287	.342	.397	163	2	.276	.397	.368	100	2	.210	.266	.360	300	3	.307	.398	.393
TOTALS		5545	83	.297	.386	.417	2768	38	.312	.401	.429	2777	45	.282	.371	.404	2689	26	.295	.386	.398	2856	57	.299	.386	.434	1306	23	.292	.373	.427	4239	60	.298	.390	.413
■ Paul Konerko BR/TR																																				
1997	LA-N	7	0	.143	.250	.143	2	0	.500	.500	.500	5	0	.000	.167	.000	0	0	—	—	—	7	0	.143	.250	.143	4	0	.250	.250	.250	3	0	.000	.250	.000
1998	LA-N	144	4	.215	.272	.306	48	2	.271	.321	.396	96	2	.188	.248	.260	137	4	.219	.280	.314	7	0	.143	.125	.143	39	1	.231	.273	.333	105	3	.210	.272	.295
1998	Cin-N	73	3	.219	.284	.384	31	0	.194	.278	.290	42	3	.238	.289	.452	0	0	—	—	—	73	3	.219	.284	.384	27	1	.370	.379	.593	46	2	.130	.231	.261
1999	Chi-A	513	24	.294	.352	.511	259	16	.324	.380	.591	254	8	.264	.323	.429	207	8	.256	.295	.430	306	16	.320	.388	.565	116	5	.319	.363	.509	397	19	.287	.349	.511
2000	Chi-A	524	21	.298	.363	.481	258	10	.291	.360	.461	266	11	.305	.367	.500	271	11	.295	.364	.498	253	10	.300	.363	.462	96	2	.302	.356	.438	428	19	.297	.365	.491
TOTALS		1261	52	.282	.343	.466	598	28	.299	.361	.503	663	24	.265	.326	.431	615	23	.265	.323	.434	646	29	.297	.362	.495	282	9	.305	.348	.465	979	43	.275	.342	.466
■ Mark Kotsay BL/TL																																				
1997	Fla-N	52	0	.192	.250	.250	36	0	.222	.282	.306	16	0	.125	.176	.125	0	0	—	—	—	52	0	.192	.250	.250	1	0	.000	.000	.000	51	0	.196	.255	.255
1998	Fla-N	578	11	.279	.318	.403	278	5	.252	.310	.367	300	6	.303	.326	.437	292	5	.291	.337	.414	286	6	.266	.299	.392	138	3	.261	.277	.413	440	8	.284	.331	.400
1999	Fla-N	495	8	.271	.306	.402	245	5	.282	.330	.433	250	3	.260	.282	.372	244	5	.246	.299	.381	251	3	.295	.313	.422	81	1	.272	.314	.420	414	7	.271	.304	.399

YEAR	TM/L	TOTAL AB	HR	AVG	OBP	SLG	HOME AB	HR	AVG	OBP	SLG	AWAY AB	HR	AVG	OBP	SLG	1ST HALF AB	HR	AVG	OBP	SLG	2ND HALF AB	HR	AVG	OBP	SLG	LEFT AB	HR	AVG	OBP	SLG	RIGHT AB	HR	AVG	OBP	SLG
2000	Fla-N	530	12	.298	.347	.443	261	5	.291	.348	.414	269	7	.305	.346	.472	261	6	.310	.352	.475	269	6	.286	.342	.413	104	1	.308	.348	.413	426	11	.296	.347	.451
TOTALS		1655	31	.280	.322	.411	820	15	.272	.327	.399	835	16	.287	.316	.423	797	16	.284	.330	.424	858	15	.276	.314	.399	324	5	.278	.309	.414	1331	26	.280	.325	.410
■ John Kruk BL/TL																																				
1986	SD-N	278	4	.309	.403	.424	103	1	.311	.408	.447	175	3	.309	.400	.411	71	1	.296	.383	.394	207	3	.314	.410	.435	79	0	.304	.402	.342	199	4	.312	.403	.457
1987	SD-N	447	20	.313	.406	.488	215	8	.298	.416	.437	232	12	.328	.397	.534	189	6	.339	.454	.476	258	14	.295	.369	.496	137	4	.255	.329	.380	310	16	.339	.439	.535
1988	SD-N	378	9	.241	.369	.362	182	8	.253	.414	.429	196	1	.230	.321	.301	195	6	.262	.383	.410	183	3	.219	.354	.311	98	3	.194	.270	.337	280	6	.257	.401	.371
1989	SD-N	76	3	.184	.333	.303	44	2	.182	.308	.318	32	1	.188	.366	.281	76	3	.184	.333	.303	0	0	—	—	—	10	0	.100	.250	.100	66	3	.197	.346	.333
1989	Phi-N	281	5	.331	.386	.473	148	4	.351	.409	.554	133	1	.308	.361	.383	86	0	.314	.355	.407	195	5	.338	.399	.503	91	0	.286	.323	.352	190	5	.353	.414	.532
1990	Phi-N	443	7	.291	.386	.431	220	2	.318	.401	.450	223	5	.265	.372	.413	212	2	.269	.362	.387	231	5	.312	.407	.472	117	2	.222	.303	.325	326	5	.316	.415	.469
1991	Phi-N	538	21	.294	.367	.483	276	8	.286	.363	.442	262	13	.302	.372	.527	260	10	.288	.350	.477	278	11	.299	.383	.489	202	4	.297	.350	.436	336	17	.292	.378	.512
1992	Phi-N	507	10	.323	.423	.458	248	7	.306	.409	.444	259	3	.340	.437	.471	253	5	.368	.453	.502	254	5	.280	.395	.413	210	1	.314	.414	.381	297	9	.330	.430	.512
1993	Phi-N	535	14	.316	.430	.475	257	8	.327	.441	.506	278	6	.306	.420	.446	253	7	.344	.473	.514	282	7	.291	.389	.440	185	5	.292	.377	.416	350	9	.329	.456	.506
1994	Phi-N	255	5	.302	.395	.427	124	3	.290	.399	.435	131	2	.313	.392	.420	153	3	.307	.410	.431	102	2	.294	.373	.422	73	1	.219	.321	.274	182	4	.335	.424	.489
1995	Chi-A	159	2	.308	.399	.390	78	2	.333	.419	.449	81	0	.284	.379	.333	82	0	.317	.408	.390	77	2	.299	.389	.390	51	0	.255	.394	.275	108	2	.333	.402	.444
TOTALS		3897	100	.300	.397	.446	1895	53	.302	.405	.456	2002	47	.298	.389	.436	1830	43	.307	.407	.446	2067	57	.294	.388	.445	1253	20	.271	.353	.369	2644	80	.314	.416	.482
■ Lee Lacy BR/TR																																				
1978	LA-N	245	13	.261	.335	.518	146	10	.240	.309	.507	99	3	.293	.372	.535	134	7	.284	.358	.560	111	6	.234	.306	.468	81	5	.247	.351	.580	164	8	.268	.326	.488
1979	Pit-N	182	5	.247	.327	.412	85	3	.176	.253	.353	97	2	.309	.389	.464	91	3	.275	.355	.505	91	2	.220	.297	.319	119	5	.277	.338	.487	63	0	.190	.307	.270
1980	Pit-N	278	7	.335	.394	.511	145	4	.359	.423	.545	133	3	.308	.361	.474	119	3	.387	.425	.563	159	4	.296	.373	.472	177	7	.379	.418	.633	101	0	.257	.356	.297
1981	Pit-N	213	2	.268	.307	.385	87	1	.264	.312	.356	126	1	.270	.303	.405	95	0	.284	.306	.379	118	2	.254	.307	.390	102	1	.235	.278	.324	111	1	.297	.333	.441
1982	Pit-N	359	5	.312	.369	.415	192	2	.333	.383	.417	167	3	.287	.353	.413	160	2	.306	.380	.394	199	3	.317	.360	.432	148	4	.304	.358	.473	211	1	.318	.377	.374
1983	Pit-N	288	4	.302	.352	.406	139	1	.353	.396	.460	149	3	.255	.311	.356	174	3	.282	.313	.391	114	1	.333	.406	.430	144	3	.354	.400	.486	144	1	.250	.303	.326
1984	Pit-N	474	12	.321	.362	.464	238	6	.332	.377	.492	236	6	.309	.347	.436	176	6	.301	.351	.455	298	6	.332	.369	.470	168	7	.345	.396	.548	306	5	.307	.344	.418
1985	Bal-A	492	9	.293	.343	.409	250	3	.308	.358	.396	242	6	.277	.328	.421	188	3	.298	.325	.394	304	6	.289	.354	.418	166	5	.313	.375	.470	326	4	.282	.327	.377
1986	Bal-A	491	11	.287	.334	.391	230	5	.304	.353	.404	261	6	.272	.317	.379	257	6	.276	.309	.389	234	5	.299	.360	.393	157	5	.280	.333	.408	334	6	.290	.334	.383
1987	Bal-A	258	7	.244	.326	.399	130	2	.231	.318	.346	128	5	.258	.336	.453	138	4	.232	.333	.384	120	3	.258	.318	.417	156	4	.237	.306	.404	102	3	.255	.356	.392
TOTALS		3280	75	.292	.347	.429	1642	37	.301	.356	.434	1638	38	.283	.338	.425	1532	37	.291	.342	.432	1748	38	.293	.352	.427	1418	46	.304	.360	.484	1862	29	.283	.338	.387
■ Ken Landreaux BL/TR																																				
1978	Cal-A	260	5	.223	.284	.346	140	4	.279	.340	.450	120	1	.158	.217	.225	126	1	.238	.278	.325	134	4	.209	.289	.366	43	0	.093	.170	.116	217	5	.249	.306	.392
1979	Min-A	564	15	.305	.347	.450	272	8	.327	.362	.482	292	7	.284	.333	.421	270	6	.270	.328	.389	294	9	.337	.366	.507	153	4	.248	.299	.373	411	11	.326	.365	.479
1980	Min-A	484	7	.281	.334	.417	232	4	.319	.371	.478	252	3	.246	.299	.361	271	3	.292	.347	.384	213	4	.268	.318	.460	206	3	.272	.320	.388	278	4	.288	.344	.439
1981	LA-N	390	7	.251	.297	.367	178	3	.253	.291	.365	212	4	.250	.303	.368	211	4	.270	.319	.403	179	3	.229	.272	.324	64	2	.281	.352	.391	326	5	.245	.286	.362
1982	LA-N	461	7	.284	.341	.410	209	1	.249	.328	.306	252	6	.313	.353	.496	220	2	.314	.379	.418	241	5	.257	.304	.402	62	1	.210	.246	.323	399	6	.296	.355	.424
1983	LA-N	481	17	.281	.328	.451	213	10	.296	.346	.479	268	7	.269	.313	.429	231	7	.268	.320	.424	250	10	.292	.335	.476	45	0	.133	.208	.133	436	17	.296	.341	.484
1984	LA-N	438	11	.251	.295	.374	231	5	.251	.310	.359	207	6	.251	.279	.391	214	5	.276	.339	.379	224	6	.228	.251	.371	57	1	.281	.373	.368	381	10	.247	.283	.375
1985	LA-N	482	12	.268	.311	.405	223	2	.247	.294	.318	259	10	.286	.326	.479	208	4	.240	.273	.365	274	8	.288	.339	.434	59	2	.186	.246	.339	423	10	.279	.320	.414
1986	LA-N	283	4	.261	.313	.364	127	1	.236	.308	.291	156	3	.282	.317	.423	189	3	.254	.306	.370	94	1	.277	.327	.351	45	0	.267	.313	.333	238	4	.261	.313	.370
1987	LA-N	182	6	.203	.269	.324	91	4	.297	.343	.462	91	2	.110	.196	.187	90	2	.211	.301	.300	92	4	.196	.235	.348	20	0	.200	.238	.250	162	6	.204	.272	.333
TOTALS		4025	91	.268	.318	.401	1916	42	.278	.331	.401	2109	49	.260	.306	.402	2030	37	.269	.324	.384	1995	54	.268	.312	.420	754	13	.236	.293	.337	3271	78	.276	.324	.416
■ Ray Lankford BL/TL																																				
1990	StL-N	126	3	.286	.353	.452	43	2	.256	.360	.512	83	1	.301	.348	.422	0	0	—	—	—	126	3	.286	.353	.452	45	0	.311	.367	.422	81	3	.272	.344	.469
1991	StL-N	566	9	.251	.301	.392	283	4	.237	.294	.385	283	5	.265	.308	.399	242	0	.248	.296	.335	324	9	.253	.305	.435	220	0	.236	.290	.350	346	9	.260	.308	.419
1992	StL-N	598	20	.293	.371	.480	314	13	.309	.375	.510	284	7	.275	.366	.447	295	8	.285	.369	.444	303	12	.300	.372	.515	216	4	.255	.345	.380	382	16	.314	.385	.537
1993	StL-N	407	7	.238	.366	.346	197	6	.249	.375	.396	210	1	.229	.358	.300	234	3	.269	.392	.355	173	4	.197	.332	.335	116	0	.207	.357	.233	291	7	.251	.370	.392
1994	StL-N	416	19	.267	.359	.488	195	8	.318	.390	.559	221	11	.222	.332	.425	275	15	.276	.385	.520	141	4	.248	.303	.426	105	3	.190	.317	.324	311	16	.293	.374	.543
1995	StL-N	483	25	.277	.360	.513	237	16	.308	.387	.612	246	9	.248	.333	.419	233	8	.270	.341	.459	250	17	.284	.377	.564	142	3	.275	.354	.444	341	22	.279	.362	.543
1996	StL-N	545	21	.275	.366	.486	257	8	.304	.394	.502	288	13	.250	.340	.472	278	14	.281	.362	.522	267	7	.270	.370	.449	122	0	.246	.278	.361	423	21	.284	.389	.522
1997	StL-N	465	31	.295	.411	.585	259	10	.290	.392	.521	206	21	.301	.432	.665	220	16	.327	.422	.641	245	15	.265	.401	.535	136	12	.301	.368	.662	329	19	.292	.426	.553
1998	StL-N	533	31	.293	.391	.540	282	20	.312	.404	.599	251	11	.271	.378	.474	248	11	.266	.388	.464	285	20	.316	.394	.607	140	6	.264	.376	.457	393	25	.303	.397	.570
1999	StL-N	422	15	.306	.380	.493	210	8	.305	.371	.490	212	7	.307	.389	.495	199	12	.317	.369	.573	223	3	.296	.390	.422	114	2	.237	.298	.316	308	13	.331	.409	.558
2000	StL-N	392	26	.253	.367	.508	190	18	.300	.395	.663	202	8	.208	.340	.361	192	11	.234	.342	.448	200	15	.270	.389	.565	74	2	.135	.286	.284	318	24	.280	.386	.560
TOTALS		4953	207	.276	.367	.483	2467	113	.292	.377	.521	2486	94	.259	.357	.444	2416	98	.277	.368	.474	2537	109	.274	.365	.490	1430	32	.244	.331	.390	3523	175	.289	.381	.520
■ Carney Lansford BR/TR																																				
1978	Cal-A	453	8	.294	.339	.406	221	4	.321	.372	.452	232	4	.267	.306	.362	139	3	.281	.340	.439	314	5	.299	.339	.392	125	3	.344	.399	.472	328	5	.274	.317	.381
1979	Cal-A	654	19	.287	.329	.436	312	5	.285	.324	.385	342	14	.289	.332	.482	322	10	.314	.355	.475	332	9	.262	.302	.398	182	3	.308	.340	.440	472	16	.280	.324	.434
1980	Cal-A	602	15	.261	.312	.390	295	8	.261	.316	.407	307	7	.261	.309	.375	259	8	.286	.326	.432	343	7	.242	.302	.359	177	5	.316	.361	.480	425	10	.238	.292	.353
1981	Bos-A	399	4	.336	.389	.439	179	1	.363	.428	.458	220	3	.314	.356	.423	228	3	.329	.361	.447	171	1	.345	.423	.427	91	2	.363	.427	.505	308	2	.328	.377	.419
1982	Bos-A	482	11	.301	.359	.444	231	4	.329	.387	.472	251	7	.275	.333	.418	243	3	.288	.344	.387	239	8	.314	.373	.502	116	3	.276	.338	.371	366	8	.309	.365	.467
1983	Oak-A	299	10	.308	.357	.475	133	4	.316	.370	.459	166	6	.301	.346	.488	108	3	.287	.322	.407	191	7	.319	.376	.513	100	4	.240	.316	.390	199	6	.342	.379	.518
1984	Oak-A	597	14	.300	.342	.439	280	7	.329	.360	.482	317	7	.274	.327	.401	281	6	.270	.332	.395	316	8	.326	.351	.478	202	4	.342	.373	.465	395	10	.278	.326	.425
1985	Oak-A	401	13	.277	.311	.429	205	7	.302	.321	.463	196	6	.250	.300	.393	295	12	.268	.306	.431	106	1	.302	.324	.425	131	3	.237	.266	.359	270	10	.296	.332	.463
1986	Oak-A	591	19	.284	.332	.421	298	10	.319	.368	.477	293	9	.249	.294	.365	278	7	.284	.332	.392	313	12	.284	.331	.447	187	6	.305	.363	.460	404	13	.275	.317	.403
1987	Oak-A	554	19	.289	.366	.455	271	9	.288	.371	.469	283	10	.290	.361	.442	247	7	.275	.375	.429	307	12	.300	.358	.476	175	8	.280	.352	.440	379	11	.293	.372	.462
1988	Oak-A	556	7	.279	.327	.360	277	1	.245	.299	.307	279	6	.312	.355	.412	312	5	.321	.371	.426	244	2	.225	.272	.275	153	0	.203	.244	.222	403	7	.308	.358	.412
1989	Oak-A	551	2	.336	.398	.405	259	1	.309	.372	.363	292	1	.360	.422	.442	253	1	.340	.411	.431	298	1	.332	.388	.383	149	1	.389	.465	.503	402	1	.316	.372	.368
1990	Oak-A	507	3	.268	.333	.320	215	1	.298	.376	.335	292	2	.247	.300	.308	273	2	.278	.330	.337	234	1	.256	.336	.299	119	1	.345	.443	.429	388	2	.245	.296	.286
1991	Oak-A	16	0	.063	.063	.063	11	0	.091	.091	.091	5	0	.000	.000	.000	0	0	—	—	—	16	0	.063	.063	.063	9	0	.000	.000	.000	7	0	.143	.143	.143
1992	Oak-A	496	7	.262	.325	.369	218	4	.234	.301	.358	278	3	.284	.344	.378	257	1	.268	.322	.350	239	6	.255	.328	.389	132	1	.280	.342	.394	364	6	.255	.319	.360
TOTALS		7158	151	.290	.343	.411	3405	66	.297	.351	.417	3753	85	.283	.335	.404	3495	71	.293	.346	.413	3663	80	.287	.340	.408	2048	44	.301	.358	.424	5110	107	.285	.337	.405
■ Mike Lansing BR/TR																																				
1993	Mon-N	491	3	.287	.352	.369	261	1	.261	.331	.337	230	2	.317	.376	.404	245	3	.273	.339	.380	246	0	.301	.365	.358	150	1	.247	.315	.307	341	2	.305	.369	.396
1994	Mon-N	394	5	.266	.328	.368	179	3	.313	.371	.453	215	2	.228	.292	.298	272	3	.250	.312	.342	122	2	.303	.363	.426	91	3	.308	.337	.495	303	2	.254	.325	.330
1995	Mon-N	467	10	.255	.299	.392	243	4	.259	.295	.366	224	6	.250	.305	.420	166	4	.229	.283	.355	301	6	.269	.308	.412	107	4	.271	.322	.421	360	6	.250	.292	.383
1996	Mon-N	641	11	.285	.341	.406	310	3	.258	.330	.358	331	8	.311	.350	.450	315	5	.314	.376	.454	326	6	.258	.306	.359	135	1	.296	.358	.363	506	10	.283	.336	.417
1997	Mon-N	572	20	.281	.338	.472	259	11	.297	.361	.517	313	9	.268	.318	.435	305	12	.275	.337	.469	267	8	.288	.338	.476	117	4	.299	.364	.487	455	16	.277	.331	.468
1998	Col-N	584	12	.276	.325	.411	291	7	.326	.369	.485	293	5	.225	.281	.338	310	4	.261	.307	.352	274	8	.292	.344	.478	161	5	.248	.309	.398	423	7	.286	.331	.416
1999	Col-N	145	4	.310	.344	.455	58	2	.310	.349	.466	87	2	.310	.341	.448	145	4	.310	.344	.455	0	0	—	—	—	53	1	.340	.386	.491	92	3	.293	.320	.435
2000	Col-N	365	11	.258	.315	.419	171	9	.316	.376	.579	194	2	.206	.260	.278	286	11	.273	.339	.469	79	0	.203	.222	.241	85	1	.247	.301	.341	280	10	.261	.319	.443
2000	Bos-A	139	0	.194	.230	.223	56	0	.161	.190	.214	83	0	.217	.256	.229	0	0	—	—	—	139	0	.194	.230	.223	30	0	.167	.219	.200	109	0	.202	.233	.229
TOTALS		3798	76	.273	.327	.403	1828	40	.284	.341	.428	1970	36	.262	.313	.379	2044	46	.274	.332	.411	1754	30	.271	.320	.393	929	20	.272	.329	.395	2869	56	.273	.326	.405
■ Barry Larkin BR/TR																																				
1986	Cin-N	159	3	.283	.320	.403	82	3	.280	.310	.463	77	0	.286	.329	.338	0	0	—	—	—	159	3	.283	.320	.403	50	2	.340	.382	.480	109	1	.257	.289	.367
1987	Cin-N	439	12	.244	.306	.371	241	6	.237	.306	.349	198	6	.253	.307	.399	148	6	.203	.276	.378	291	6	.265	.322	.368	131	5	.275	.349	.450	308	7	.231	.288	.338
1988	Cin-N	588	12	.296	.347	.429	303	9	.307	.353	.469	285	3	.284	.342	.386	292	9	.301	.352	.449	296	3	.291	.343	.409	145	5	.352	.421	.559	443	7	.278	.322	.386
1989	Cin-N	325	4	.342	.375	.446	156	1	.353	.376	.455	169	3	.331	.373	.438	283	3	.357	.384	.463	42	1	.238	.313	.333	121	2	.372	.421	.488	204	2	.324	.347	.422
1990	Cin-N	614	7	.301	.358	.396	286	4	.273	.349	.357	328	3	.326	.365	.430	281	2	.317	.370	.381	333	5	.288	.347	.408	203	4	.266	.344	.404	411	3	.319	.365	.392
1991	Cin-N	464	20	.302	.378	.506	242	16	.326	.404	.612	222	4	.275	.349	.392	190	14	.316	.408	.605	274	6	.292	.355	.438	135	8	.326	.433	.585	329	12	.292	.353	.474
1992	Cin-N	533	12	.304	.377	.454	254	8	.307	.389	.472	279	4	.301	.366	.437	228	4	.254	.321	.364	305	8	.341	.417	.521	200	6	.355	.443	.585	333	6	.273	.336	.375
1993	Cin-N	384	8	.315	.394	.445	195	4	.292	.379	.400	189	4	.339	.409	.492	294	5	.313	.391	.422	90	3	.322	.404	.522	95	4	.358	.448	.579	289	4	.301	.375	.401
1994	Cin-N	427	9	.279	.369	.419	219	3	.260	.365	.365	208	6	.298	.373	.476	288	5	.281	.377	.399	139	4	.273	.352	.460	102	3	.284	.382	.441	325	6	.277	.365	.412
1995	Cin-N	496	15	.319	.394	.492	253	8	.328	.424	.498	243	7	.309	.360	.486	188	6	.282	.391	.468	308	9	.341	.395	.506	111	8	.288	.370	.577	385	7	.327	.400	.468
1996	Cin-N	517	33	.298	.410	.567	269	14	.297	.423	.543	248	19	.298	.394	.593	237	9	.300	.408	.481	280	24	.296	.411	.639	121	9	.298	.435	.603	396	24	.298	.402	.556
1997	Cin-N	224	4	.317	.440	.473	110	0	.391	.518	.545	114	4	.246	.358	.404	186	4	.317	.446	.489	38	0	.316	.409	.395	47	2	.447	.559	.745	177	2	.282	.407	.401
1998	Cin-N	538	17	.309	.397	.504	244	8	.328	.423	.545	294	9	.293	.375	.469	277	6	.282	.369	.451	261	11	.337	.426	.559	123	4	.285	.411	.496	415	13	.316	.393	.506
1999	Cin-N	583	12	.293	.390	.420	281	7	.320	.434	.484	302	5	.268	.347	.361	276	9	.319	.389	.464	307	3	.270	.391	.381	147	5	.259	.349	.408	436	7	.305	.404	.424

YEAR	TM/L	TOTAL					HOME					AWAY					1ST HALF					2ND HALF					LEFT					RIGHT				
		AB	HR	AVG	OBP	SLG	AB	HR	AVG	OBP	SLG	AB	HR	AVG	OBP	SLG	AB	HR	AVG	OBP	SLG	AB	HR	AVG	OBP	SLG	AB	HR	AVG	OBP	SLG	AB	HR	AVG	OBP	SLG
2000	Cin-N	396	11	.313	.389	.487	187	6	.305	.412	.497	209	5	.321	.366	.478	226	8	.314	.382	.504	170	3	.312	.397	.465	75	3	.307	.409	.560	321	8	.315	.384	.470
TOTALS		6687	179	.300	.377	.456	3322	97	.304	.392	.469	3365	82	.297	.362	.442	3394	90	.300	.378	.448	3293	89	.300	.376	.463	1806	70	.313	.404	.518	4881	109	.295	.367	.432
■ **Vance Law** BR/TR																																				
1980	Pit-N	74	0	.230	.260	.311	28	0	.286	.310	.500	46	0	.196	.229	.196	40	0	.225	.262	.300	34	0	.235	.257	.324	23	0	.217	.217	.435	51	0	.235	.278	.255
1981	Pit-N	67	0	.134	.157	.164	27	0	.111	.172	.111	40	0	.150	.146	.200	45	0	.156	.170	.200	22	0	.091	.130	.091	26	0	.154	.214	.154	41	0	.122	.119	.171
1982	Chi-A	359	5	.281	.327	.384	172	2	.314	.362	.424	187	3	.251	.296	.348	56	1	.357	.419	.446	303	4	.267	.310	.373	122	4	.279	.331	.467	237	1	.283	.325	.342
1983	Chi-A	408	4	.243	.325	.348	202	1	.243	.342	.347	206	3	.243	.307	.350	155	3	.239	.305	.374	253	1	.245	.337	.332	137	1	.299	.396	.416	271	3	.214	.288	.314
1984	Chi-A	481	17	.252	.309	.403	238	11	.269	.318	.458	243	6	.235	.301	.350	245	11	.237	.286	.412	236	6	.267	.333	.394	187	9	.241	.309	.422	294	8	.259	.309	.391
1985	Mon-N	519	10	.266	.369	.405	247	5	.263	.393	.409	272	5	.268	.344	.401	225	4	.240	.345	.364	294	6	.286	.387	.435	159	4	.245	.353	.384	360	6	.275	.376	.414
1986	Mon-N	360	5	.225	.298	.325	177	3	.260	.333	.384	183	2	.191	.262	.268	224	3	.219	.297	.313	136	2	.235	.298	.346	127	4	.252	.307	.417	233	1	.210	.292	.275
1987	Mon-N	436	12	.273	.347	.422	209	3	.268	.339	.397	227	9	.278	.354	.445	230	6	.283	.365	.426	206	6	.262	.326	.417	153	3	.288	.384	.412	283	9	.265	.326	.428
1988	Chi-N	556	11	.293	.358	.412	285	5	.302	.362	.411	271	6	.284	.354	.413	279	5	.308	.363	.427	277	6	.278	.354	.397	151	5	.291	.371	.464	405	6	.294	.353	.393
1989	Chi-N	408	7	.235	.296	.355	187	4	.235	.303	.364	221	3	.235	.289	.348	231	3	.234	.280	.329	177	4	.237	.315	.390	111	3	.297	.363	.441	297	4	.212	.271	.323
1991	Oak-A	134	0	.209	.303	.276	63	0	.206	.286	.286	71	0	.211	.317	.268	96	0	.229	.302	.302	38	0	.158	.304	.211	54	0	.259	.365	.352	80	0	.175	.258	.225
TOTALS		3802	71	.256	.326	.376	1835	34	.266	.342	.395	1967	37	.246	.312	.359	1826	36	.252	.319	.372	1976	35	.259	.333	.380	1250	33	.268	.347	.418	2552	38	.250	.316	.356
■ **Matt Lawton** BL/TR																																				
1995	Min-A	60	1	.317	.414	.467	23	1	.391	.481	.739	37	0	.270	.372	.297	0	0	—	—	—	60	1	.317	.414	.467	17	0	.176	.222	.176	43	1	.372	.481	.581
1996	Min-A	252	6	.258	.339	.365	110	1	.227	.328	.309	142	5	.282	.348	.408	111	2	.243	.339	.324	141	4	.270	.340	.397	49	0	.245	.339	.265	203	6	.261	.339	.389
1997	Min-A	460	14	.248	.366	.415	218	8	.248	.389	.440	242	6	.248	.343	.393	245	6	.265	.367	.429	215	8	.228	.364	.400	84	1	.274	.386	.357	376	13	.242	.361	.428
1998	Min-A	557	21	.278	.387	.478	270	11	.285	.386	.507	287	10	.272	.387	.449	272	9	.257	.363	.441	285	12	.298	.409	.512	131	6	.275	.392	.504	426	15	.279	.385	.469
1999	Min-A	406	7	.259	.353	.355	206	2	.272	.388	.354	200	5	.245	.314	.355	202	5	.262	.345	.406	204	2	.255	.361	.304	100	2	.290	.357	.390	306	5	.248	.352	.343
2000	Min-A	561	13	.305	.405	.460	290	8	.324	.433	.517	271	5	.284	.374	.399	294	6	.340	.443	.500	267	7	.266	.362	.416	163	2	.294	.355	.387	398	11	.309	.424	.490
TOTALS		2296	62	.274	.377	.426	1117	31	.282	.396	.454	1179	31	.266	.358	.400	1124	28	.280	.380	.436	1172	34	.268	.374	.417	544	11	.278	.365	.393	1752	51	.273	.380	.437
■ **Derrek Lee** BR/TR																																				
1997	SD-N	54	1	.259	.365	.370	30	0	.167	.286	.200	24	1	.375	.464	.583	30	0	.200	.351	.200	24	1	.333	.385	.583	16	0	.250	.400	.375	38	1	.263	.349	.368
1998	Fla-N	454	17	.233	.318	.414	200	4	.215	.301	.355	254	13	.248	.331	.461	204	8	.206	.305	.377	250	9	.256	.329	.444	129	5	.217	.311	.411	325	12	.240	.321	.415
1999	Fla-N	218	5	.206	.263	.326	115	0	.217	.260	.287	103	5	.194	.265	.369	158	3	.190	.256	.310	60	2	.250	.281	.367	47	1	.234	.294	.383	171	4	.199	.254	.310
2000	Fla-N	477	28	.281	.368	.507	209	9	.292	.388	.459	268	19	.272	.352	.545	202	16	.272	.370	.535	275	12	.287	.367	.487	101	6	.228	.328	.436	376	22	.295	.379	.527
TOTALS		1203	51	.249	.331	.433	554	13	.242	.326	.372	649	38	.254	.335	.485	594	27	.224	.318	.404	609	24	.273	.344	.461	293	12	.225	.319	.413	910	39	.256	.334	.440
■ **Travis Lee** BL/TL																																				
1998	Ari-N	562	22	.269	.346	.429	286	12	.283	.358	.462	276	10	.254	.333	.395	317	17	.284	.354	.492	245	5	.249	.336	.347	180	4	.239	.286	.350	382	18	.283	.372	.466
1999	Ari-N	375	9	.237	.337	.363	176	7	.301	.402	.483	199	2	.181	.278	.256	268	9	.265	.359	.429	107	0	.168	.282	.196	102	3	.216	.293	.343	273	6	.245	.353	.370
2000	Ari-N	224	8	.232	.308	.397	113	1	.230	.296	.301	111	7	.234	.320	.495	185	7	.249	.324	.422	39	1	.154	.233	.282	48	0	.229	.275	.292	176	8	.233	.317	.426
2000	Phi-N	180	1	.239	.381	.328	92	1	.207	.392	.293	88	0	.273	.369	.364	0	0	—	—	—	180	1	.239	.381	.328	25	0	.160	.300	.200	155	1	.252	.394	.348
TOTALS		1341	40	.250	.342	.391	667	21	.268	.365	.417	674	19	.231	.319	.366	770	33	.269	.349	.453	571	7	.224	.334	.308	355	7	.225	.288	.330	986	33	.259	.361	.414
■ **Johnnie LeMaster** BR/TR																																				
1978	SF-N	272	1	.235	.293	.335	128	0	.164	.213	.227	144	1	.299	.361	.431	178	0	.213	.271	.292	94	1	.277	.333	.415	131	0	.282	.333	.405	141	1	.191	.255	.270
1979	SF-N	343	3	.254	.304	.324	162	2	.247	.305	.302	181	1	.260	.302	.343	114	1	.263	.320	.316	229	2	.249	.295	.328	121	2	.298	.338	.421	222	1	.230	.285	.270
1980	SF-N	405	3	.215	.257	.306	181	0	.160	.207	.199	224	3	.259	.298	.393	236	2	.220	.242	.335	169	1	.207	.278	.266	115	2	.235	.299	.348	290	1	.207	.240	.290
1981	SF-N	324	0	.253	.306	.287	155	0	.271	.327	.310	169	0	.237	.286	.266	163	0	.252	.305	.294	161	0	.255	.306	.280	73	0	.274	.354	.315	251	0	.247	.291	.279
1982	SF-N	436	2	.216	.267	.266	206	1	.233	.295	.296	230	1	.200	.240	.239	250	2	.220	.259	.280	186	0	.210	.276	.247	140	2	.243	.307	.314	296	0	.203	.247	.243
1983	SF-N	534	6	.240	.317	.307	264	4	.250	.338	.326	270	2	.230	.295	.289	263	4	.262	.367	.354	271	2	.218	.264	.262	162	2	.253	.348	.333	372	4	.234	.303	.296
1984	SF-N	451	4	.217	.265	.282	200	1	.230	.280	.295	251	3	.207	.254	.271	249	4	.217	.272	.293	202	0	.218	.257	.267	138	3	.217	.265	.304	313	1	.217	.265	.272
1985	SF-N	16	0	.000	.059	.000	5	0	.000	.000	.000	11	0	.000	.083	.000	16	0	.000	.059	.000	0	0	—	—	—	8	0	.000	.111	.000	8	0	.000	.000	.000
1985	Cle-A	20	0	.150	.150	.150	6	0	.167	.167	.167	14	0	.143	.143	.143	20	0	.150	.150	.150	0	0	—	—	—	13	0	.077	.077	.077	7	0	.286	.286	.286
1985	Pit-N	58	1	.155	.222	.207	26	0	.192	.250	.192	32	1	.125	.200	.219	53	1	.151	.224	.208	5	0	.200	.200	.200	19	0	.211	.250	.211	39	1	.128	.209	.205
1987	Oak-A	24	0	.083	.120	.083	16	0	.063	.118	.063	8	0	.125	.125	.125	6	0	.167	.286	.167	18	0	.056	.056	.056	11	0	.091	.091	.091	13	0	.077	.143	.077
TOTALS		2883	20	.227	.282	.292	1349	8	.222	.283	.278	1534	12	.231	.281	.305	1548	14	.227	.285	.301	1335	6	.227	.279	.282	931	11	.248	.311	.336	1952	9	.217	.268	.272
■ **Mark Lemke** BB/TR																																				
1988	Atl-N	58	0	.224	.274	.293	41	0	.220	.273	.268	17	0	.235	.278	.353	0	0	—	—	—	58	0	.224	.274	.293	38	0	.158	.200	.211	20	0	.350	.409	.450
1989	Atl-N	55	2	.182	.250	.364	29	1	.241	.290	.483	26	1	.115	.207	.231	0	0	—	—	—	55	2	.182	.250	.364	17	2	.412	.444	.941	38	0	.079	.167	.105
1990	Atl-N	239	0	.226	.286	.280	109	0	.211	.265	.275	130	0	.238	.303	.285	76	0	.171	.286	.224	163	0	.252	.287	.307	97	0	.268	.330	.351	142	0	.197	.256	.232
1991	Atl-N	269	2	.234	.305	.312	132	2	.280	.345	.386	137	0	.190	.266	.241	73	0	.247	.337	.342	196	2	.230	.292	.301	114	0	.254	.313	.333	155	2	.219	.299	.297
1992	Atl-N	427	6	.227	.307	.304	222	4	.225	.302	.302	205	2	.229	.312	.307	214	2	.229	.279	.294	213	4	.225	.332	.315	145	5	.228	.289	.352	282	1	.227	.316	.280
1993	Atl-N	493	7	.252	.335	.341	246	3	.256	.338	.341	247	4	.247	.332	.340	243	6	.263	.351	.395	250	1	.240	.319	.288	139	5	.309	.382	.482	354	2	.229	.317	.285
1994	Atl-N	350	3	.294	.363	.363	177	2	.316	.373	.384	173	1	.272	.354	.341	247	3	.300	.369	.381	103	0	.282	.351	.320	102	3	.294	.357	.431	248	0	.294	.366	.335
1995	Atl-N	399	5	.253	.325	.356	191	3	.251	.308	.361	208	2	.255	.340	.351	166	2	.241	.326	.355	233	3	.262	.324	.356	93	2	.290	.362	.441	306	3	.242	.314	.330
1996	Atl-N	498	5	.255	.323	.319	269	3	.297	.363	.368	229	2	.205	.276	.262	227	4	.291	.378	.379	271	1	.225	.275	.269	128	3	.219	.325	.320	370	2	.268	.323	.319
1997	Atl-N	351	2	.245	.306	.316	178	2	.258	.302	.331	173	0	.231	.310	.301	226	2	.230	.279	.301	125	0	.272	.352	.344	69	1	.261	.329	.362	282	1	.241	.300	.305
1998	Bos-A	91	0	.187	.232	.231	50	0	.140	.211	.180	41	0	.244	.262	.293	91	0	.187	.232	.231	0	0	—	—	—	32	0	.063	.118	.063	59	0	.254	.292	.322
TOTALS		3230	32	.246	.317	.324	1644	20	.259	.323	.341	1586	12	.233	.310	.306	1563	19	.251	.325	.338	1667	13	.241	.309	.310	974	21	.256	.325	.377	2256	11	.242	.313	.301
■ **Chet Lemon** BR/TR																																				
1978	Chi-A	357	13	.300	.377	.510	185	8	.292	.387	.519	172	5	.308	.366	.500	220	9	.286	.373	.495	137	4	.321	.385	.533	136	7	.279	.363	.507	221	6	.312	.386	.511
1979	Chi-A	556	17	.318	.391	.496	259	7	.336	.415	.525	297	10	.303	.370	.471	274	8	.303	.390	.478	282	9	.333	.392	.514	211	9	.327	.391	.545	345	8	.313	.391	.467
1980	Chi-A	514	11	.292	.388	.442	250	5	.260	.354	.400	264	6	.322	.420	.481	244	6	.262	.349	.426	270	5	.319	.422	.456	150	2	.247	.377	.400	364	9	.310	.393	.459
1981	Chi-A	328	9	.302	.384	.491	128	4	.289	.397	.469	200	5	.310	.374	.505	164	3	.299	.384	.470	164	6	.305	.383	.512	65	1	.292	.395	.446	263	8	.304	.381	.502
1982	Det-A	436	19	.266	.368	.447	219	12	.297	.405	.502	217	7	.235	.329	.392	201	4	.229	.354	.323	235	15	.298	.381	.553	136	6	.279	.368	.471	300	13	.260	.368	.437
1983	Det-A	491	24	.255	.350	.464	234	14	.239	.328	.474	257	10	.268	.369	.455	223	11	.260	.377	.457	268	13	.250	.326	.470	149	6	.235	.356	.409	342	18	.263	.347	.488
1984	Det-A	509	20	.287	.357	.495	256	12	.273	.350	.465	253	8	.300	.365	.526	262	12	.309	.380	.553	247	8	.263	.332	.433	198	9	.384	.441	.636	311	11	.225	.304	.405
1985	Det-A	517	18	.265	.334	.439	243	9	.288	.348	.473	274	9	.245	.321	.409	214	4	.271	.329	.411	303	14	.261	.337	.459	149	8	.322	.378	.564	368	10	.242	.316	.389
1986	Det-A	403	12	.251	.326	.407	190	7	.237	.318	.416	213	5	.263	.333	.399	176	3	.250	.311	.375	227	9	.251	.337	.432	162	7	.284	.346	.500	241	5	.228	.313	.344
1987	Det-A	470	20	.277	.376	.481	223	10	.260	.379	.471	247	10	.291	.373	.490	191	9	.251	.371	.471	279	11	.294	.380	.487	180	8	.272	.382	.494	290	12	.279	.372	.472
1988	Det-A	512	17	.264	.346	.436	245	12	.278	.349	.498	267	5	.251	.343	.378	229	4	.275	.354	.432	283	13	.254	.340	.438	165	9	.297	.370	.539	347	8	.248	.335	.386
1989	Det-A	414	7	.237	.323	.343	189	4	.228	.332	.365	225	3	.244	.316	.324	201	2	.239	.345	.328	213	5	.235	.302	.357	153	5	.275	.376	.438	261	2	.215	.291	.287
1990	Det-A	322	5	.258	.359	.379	133	2	.256	.380	.361	189	3	.259	.343	.392	114	4	.263	.346	.439	208	1	.255	.366	.346	138	3	.283	.375	.420	184	2	.239	.347	.348
TOTALS		5829	192	.275	.360	.450	2754	106	.273	.364	.461	3075	86	.277	.357	.441	2713	79	.271	.361	.439	3116	113	.279	.360	.460	1992	80	.294	.379	.498	3837	112	.266	.350	.426
■ **Jeffrey Leonard** BR/TR																																				
1978	Hou-N	26	0	.385	.407	.462	9	0	.444	.500	.556	17	0	.353	.353	.412	0	0	—	—	—	26	0	.385	.407	.462	12	0	.333	.385	.417	14	0	.429	.429	.500
1979	Hou-N	411	0	.290	.360	.350	206	0	.296	.387	.364	205	0	.283	.332	.337	161	0	.292	.359	.354	250	0	.288	.361	.348	200	0	.280	.329	.325	211	0	.299	.388	.374
1980	Hou-N	216	3	.213	.274	.333	119	3	.235	.283	.395	97	0	.186	.264	.258	115	1	.209	.272	.287	101	2	.218	.277	.386	117	3	.222	.281	.359	99	0	.202	.266	.303
1981	Hou-N	18	0	.167	.158	.333	13	0	.154	.154	.308	5	0	.200	.167	.400	18	0	.167	.158	.333	0	0	—	—	—	8	0	.125	.111	.375	10	0	.200	.200	.300
1981	SF-N	127	4	.307	.371	.535	50	0	.320	.414	.500	77	4	.299	.341	.558	0	0	—	—	—	127	4	.307	.371	.535	29	2	.448	.500	.966	98	2	.265	.333	.408
1982	SF-N	278	9	.259	.306	.421	146	4	.253	.319	.411	132	5	.265	.291	.432	61	2	.295	.302	.426	217	7	.249	.307	.419	90	2	.278	.343	.389	188	7	.250	.287	.436
1983	SF-N	516	21	.279	.323	.461	261	9	.264	.315	.429	255	12	.294	.331	.494	219	6	.269	.314	.411	297	15	.286	.329	.498	161	11	.323	.373	.559	355	10	.259	.299	.417
1984	SF-N	514	21	.302	.357	.484	260	13	.300	.364	.504	254	8	.303	.350	.465	255	10	.282	.354	.455	259	11	.320	.360	.514	166	13	.380	.419	.681	348	8	.264	.328	.391
1985	SF-N	507	17	.241	.272	.393	238	8	.239	.263	.370	269	9	.242	.279	.413	281	9	.235	.273	.388	226	8	.248	.270	.398	141	7	.255	.266	.489	366	10	.235	.274	.355
1986	SF-N	341	6	.279	.322	.381	168	2	.315	.350	.417	173	4	.243	.294	.347	274	6	.288	.329	.409	67	0	.239	.292	.269	119	3	.328	.350	.437	222	3	.252	.307	.351
1987	SF-N	503	19	.280	.309	.467	225	9	.280	.311	.471	278	10	.281	.307	.464	292	14	.312	.340	.562	211	5	.237	.266	.336	145	5	.283	.306	.462	358	14	.279	.310	.469
1988	SF-N	160	2	.256	.292	.356	79	0	.215	.247	.278	81	2	.296	.337	.432	160	2	.256	.292	.356	0	0	—	—	—	55	1	.236	.295	.382	105	1	.267	.291	.343
1988	Mil-A	374	8	.235	.270	.350	188	5	.239	.286	.372	186	3	.231	.253	.328	75	2	.253	.277	.347	299	6	.231	.268	.351	111	3	.270	.317	.441	263	5	.221	.249	.312
1989	Sea-A	566	24	.254	.301	.420	258	9	.260	.307	.407	308	15	.250	.296	.432	282	15	.270	.323	.457	284	9	.239	.279	.384	157	8	.280	.326	.497	409	16	.244	.292	.391
1990	Sea-A	478	10	.251	.305	.356	234	7	.222	.285	.363	244	3	.279	.325	.348	302	9	.242	.274	.368	176	1	.267	.355	.335	175	6	.309	.361	.463	303	4	.218	.272	.294
TOTALS		5035	144	.266	.312	.410	2454	69	.264	.316	.410	2581	75	.267	.308	.411	2495	76	.268	.312	.415	2540	68	.264	.312	.406	1686	64	.295	.337	.473	3349	80	.251	.299	.379

YEAR	TM/L	TOTAL AB	HR	AVG	OBP	SLG	HOME AB	HR	AVG	OBP	SLG	AWAY AB	HR	AVG	OBP	SLG	1ST HALF AB	HR	AVG	OBP	SLG	2ND HALF AB	HR	AVG	OBP	SLG	LEFT AB	HR	AVG	OBP	SLG	RIGHT AB	HR	AVG	OBP	SLG
■ **Darren Lewis** BR/TR																																				
1990	Oak-A	35	0	.229	.372	.229	18	0	.167	.250	.167	17	0	.294	.478	.294	0	0	—	—	—	35	0	.229	.372	.229	8	0	.375	.500	.375	27	0	.185	.333	.185
1991	SF-N	222	1	.248	.358	.311	121	0	.231	.354	.248	101	1	.267	.362	.386	0	0	—	—	—	222	1	.248	.358	.311	75	1	.280	.386	.400	147	0	.231	.343	.265
1992	SF-N	320	1	.231	.295	.272	142	1	.176	.248	.211	178	0	.275	.333	.320	229	1	.231	.302	.271	91	0	.231	.278	.275	125	1	.216	.285	.264	195	0	.241	.302	.277
1993	SF-N	522	2	.253	.302	.324	250	2	.256	.302	.344	272	0	.250	.301	.305	273	1	.253	.312	.352	249	1	.253	.290	.293	172	0	.267	.321	.343	350	2	.246	.292	.314
1994	SF-N	451	4	.257	.340	.357	228	4	.259	.339	.364	223	0	.256	.341	.350	294	1	.255	.353	.327	157	3	.261	.314	.414	115	1	.217	.297	.287	336	3	.271	.354	.381
1995	SF-N	309	1	.252	.303	.314	146	1	.212	.263	.267	163	0	.288	.339	.356	250	0	.256	.303	.304	59	1	.237	.303	.356	59	0	.237	.258	.339	250	1	.256	.314	.308
1995	Cin-N	163	0	.245	.324	.264	74	0	.284	.384	.311	89	0	.213	.271	.225	0	0	—	—	—	163	0	.245	.324	.264	45	0	.222	.286	.222	118	0	.254	.338	.280
1996	Chi-A	337	4	.228	.321	.312	172	0	.209	.296	.244	165	4	.248	.346	.382	201	3	.249	.352	.343	136	1	.199	.273	.265	112	1	.188	.268	.241	225	3	.249	.346	.347
1997	Chi-A	77	0	.234	.330	.247	42	0	.214	.313	.238	35	0	.257	.350	.257	52	0	.212	.328	.231	25	0	.280	.333	.280	41	0	.244	.311	.244	36	0	.222	.349	.250
1997	LA-N	77	1	.299	.349	.403	38	0	.316	.395	.421	39	1	.282	.300	.385	0	0	—	—	—	77	1	.299	.349	.403	23	0	.304	.333	.435	54	1	.296	.356	.389
1998	Bos-A	585	8	.268	.352	.362	272	5	.294	.378	.408	313	3	.246	.329	.323	278	3	.277	.369	.360	307	5	.261	.336	.365	163	3	.313	.414	.423	422	5	.251	.327	.339
1999	Bos-A	470	2	.240	.311	.309	210	1	.233	.305	.295	260	1	.246	.316	.319	221	2	.267	.344	.348	249	0	.217	.281	.273	140	1	.229	.270	.279	330	1	.245	.327	.321
2000	Bos-A	270	2	.241	.305	.307	143	0	.231	.308	.273	127	2	.252	.301	.346	122	1	.254	.316	.336	148	1	.230	.296	.284	112	1	.277	.352	.357	158	1	.215	.271	.272
TOTALS		3838	26	.249	.323	.320	1856	14	.242	.320	.309	1982	12	.255	.327	.330	1920	12	.255	.333	.328	1918	14	.243	.313	.313	1190	9	.250	.322	.322	2648	17	.248	.324	.319
■ **Sixto Lezcano** BR/TR																																				
1978	Mil-A	442	15	.292	.377	.459	248	10	.323	.386	.520	194	5	.253	.367	.381	204	10	.314	.393	.539	238	5	.273	.364	.391	105	3	.295	.409	.457	337	12	.291	.367	.460
1979	Mil-A	473	28	.321	.414	.573	240	14	.304	.397	.538	233	14	.339	.432	.609	226	9	.323	.426	.509	247	19	.320	.403	.632	112	9	.411	.535	.777	361	19	.294	.373	.510
1980	Mil-A	411	18	.229	.298	.421	210	8	.229	.289	.395	201	10	.229	.307	.448	237	12	.232	.316	.451	174	6	.224	.270	.379	117	7	.248	.333	.504	294	11	.221	.283	.388
1981	StL-N	214	5	.266	.376	.393	117	2	.274	.390	.393	97	3	.258	.359	.392	123	2	.268	.395	.382	91	3	.264	.349	.407	82	1	.207	.333	.268	132	4	.303	.404	.470
1982	SD-N	470	16	.289	.388	.472	223	5	.269	.394	.413	247	11	.308	.382	.526	254	7	.287	.372	.461	216	9	.292	.405	.486	136	6	.331	.442	.574	334	10	.272	.365	.431
1983	SD-N	317	8	.233	.331	.356	157	6	.229	.313	.376	160	2	.237	.347	.338	206	5	.238	.339	.350	111	3	.225	.315	.369	109	3	.239	.351	.404	208	5	.231	.319	.332
1983	Phi-N	39	0	.282	.364	.308	20	0	.200	.304	.250	19	0	.368	.429	.368	0	0	—	—	—	39	0	.282	.364	.308	19	0	.474	.545	.474	20	0	.100	.182	.150
1984	Phi-N	256	14	.277	.371	.480	144	9	.257	.355	.486	112	5	.304	.391	.473	143	11	.280	.372	.552	113	3	.274	.369	.389	115	5	.278	.399	.461	141	9	.277	.346	.496
1985	Pit-N	116	3	.207	.392	.302	66	2	.227	.420	.333	50	1	.180	.354	.260	72	2	.194	.385	.306	44	1	.227	.404	.295	79	3	.215	.376	.342	37	0	.189	.423	.216
TOTALS		2738	107	.273	.369	.451	1425	56	.270	.366	.446	1313	51	.276	.372	.458	1465	58	.274	.373	.457	1273	49	.273	.364	.445	874	37	.288	.406	.489	1864	70	.266	.350	.434
■ **Mike Lieberthal** BR/TR																																				
1994	Phi-N	79	1	.266	.301	.367	54	1	.204	.218	.259	25	0	.400	.464	.600	3	0	.333	.333	.333	76	1	.263	.300	.368	15	0	.267	.313	.333	64	1	.266	.299	.375
1995	Phi-N	47	0	.255	.327	.298	21	0	.333	.333	.429	26	0	.192	.323	.192	1	0	.000	.000	.000	46	0	.261	.333	.304	10	0	.300	.417	.300	37	0	.243	.300	.297
1996	Phi-N	166	7	.253	.297	.428	82	4	.244	.284	.451	84	3	.262	.309	.405	113	7	.283	.325	.504	53	0	.189	.237	.264	29	1	.241	.267	.448	137	6	.255	.303	.423
1997	Phi-N	455	20	.246	.314	.442	219	11	.228	.319	.438	236	9	.263	.309	.445	213	10	.202	.261	.404	242	10	.285	.357	.475	109	5	.248	.320	.468	346	15	.246	.312	.434
1998	Phi-N	313	8	.256	.304	.399	144	5	.257	.301	.444	169	3	.254	.306	.361	253	7	.257	.296	.407	60	1	.250	.338	.367	65	2	.308	.392	.462	248	6	.242	.280	.383
1999	Phi-N	510	31	.300	.363	.551	245	10	.273	.358	.449	265	21	.325	.368	.645	242	17	.318	.384	.599	268	14	.284	.343	.507	122	10	.377	.443	.697	388	21	.276	.337	.505
2000	Phi-N	389	15	.278	.352	.470	199	8	.261	.327	.472	190	7	.295	.376	.468	255	12	.290	.365	.514	134	3	.254	.327	.388	80	4	.350	.447	.575	309	11	.259	.326	.443
TOTALS		1959	82	.270	.331	.461	964	39	.253	.321	.440	995	43	.285	.341	.482	1080	53	.270	.329	.484	879	29	.268	.334	.433	430	22	.314	.389	.542	1529	60	.257	.314	.439
■ **Jose Lind** BR/TR																																				
1987	Pit-N	143	0	.322	.358	.434	80	0	.313	.353	.425	63	0	.333	.364	.444	0	0	—	—	—	143	0	.322	.358	.434	73	0	.342	.368	.507	70	0	.300	.347	.357
1988	Pit-N	611	2	.262	.308	.324	313	1	.300	.342	.377	298	1	.221	.272	.268	328	1	.244	.297	.299	283	1	.283	.321	.353	214	0	.248	.305	.304	397	2	.270	.310	.335
1989	Pit-N	578	2	.232	.280	.289	296	2	.220	.273	.277	282	0	.245	.288	.301	289	2	.239	.288	.308	289	0	.225	.273	.270	195	1	.256	.315	.318	383	1	.219	.262	.274
1990	Pit-N	514	1	.261	.305	.340	245	1	.261	.293	.347	269	0	.260	.316	.335	248	0	.306	.344	.395	266	1	.218	.268	.289	216	1	.231	.285	.329	298	0	.282	.321	.349
1991	Pit-N	502	3	.265	.306	.339	262	2	.244	.290	.332	240	1	.287	.323	.346	205	3	.254	.292	.332	297	0	.273	.315	.343	167	2	.269	.326	.329	335	1	.263	.295	.343
1992	Pit-N	468	0	.235	.275	.269	229	0	.253	.298	.293	239	0	.218	.251	.247	223	0	.251	.283	.291	245	0	.220	.267	.249	177	0	.237	.277	.282	291	0	.234	.273	.261
1993	KC-A	431	0	.248	.271	.288	207	0	.246	.267	.295	224	0	.250	.274	.281	200	0	.260	.282	.310	231	0	.238	.261	.268	105	0	.257	.270	.333	326	0	.245	.271	.273
1994	KC-A	290	1	.269	.306	.348	163	0	.313	.351	.399	127	1	.213	.248	.283	184	0	.250	.284	.310	106	1	.302	.345	.415	74	1	.257	.321	.432	216	0	.273	.301	.319
1995	KC-A	97	0	.268	.290	.299	52	0	.269	.283	.308	45	0	.267	.298	.289	97	0	.268	.290	.299	0	0	—	—	—	29	0	.310	.333	.345	68	0	.250	.271	.279
1995	Cal-A	43	0	.163	.217	.209	18	0	.167	.167	.222	25	0	.160	.250	.200	0	0	—	—	—	43	0	.163	.217	.209	8	0	.125	.364	.125	35	0	.171	.171	.229
TOTALS		3677	9	.254	.295	.316	1865	6	.262	.302	.332	1812	3	.246	.287	.299	1774	6	.258	.296	.319	1903	3	.251	.293	.313	1258	5	.255	.305	.332	2419	4	.254	.289	.307
■ **Keith Lockhart** BL/TR																																				
1994	SD-N	43	2	.209	.286	.349	31	2	.258	.294	.452	12	0	.083	.267	.083	43	2	.209	.286	.349	0	0	—	—	—	3	0	.000	.400	.000	40	2	.225	.273	.375
1995	KC-A	274	6	.321	.355	.478	131	3	.336	.378	.473	143	3	.308	.333	.483	52	1	.404	.459	.596	222	5	.302	.328	.450	16	0	.188	.188	.250	258	6	.329	.364	.492
1996	KC-A	433	7	.273	.319	.411	190	4	.279	.338	.416	243	3	.267	.304	.407	219	3	.311	.369	.452	214	4	.234	.265	.369	62	0	.210	.222	.323	371	7	.283	.334	.426
1997	Atl-N	147	6	.279	.337	.476	55	3	.309	.381	.545	92	3	.261	.311	.435	71	3	.239	.293	.423	76	3	.316	.381	.526	9	1	.667	.700	1.444	138	5	.254	.314	.413
1998	Atl-N	366	9	.257	.311	.388	198	4	.273	.321	.399	168	5	.238	.299	.375	230	4	.278	.331	.404	136	5	.221	.277	.360	37	0	.189	.250	.243	329	9	.264	.318	.404
1999	Atl-N	161	1	.261	.337	.311	62	0	.210	.271	.210	99	1	.293	.377	.374	67	1	.224	.288	.284	94	0	.287	.369	.330	12	0	.083	.313	.083	149	1	.275	.339	.329
2000	Atl-N	275	2	.265	.331	.353	137	1	.277	.325	.380	138	1	.254	.338	.326	84	2	.238	.312	.429	191	0	.277	.340	.319	32	0	.375	.429	.500	243	2	.251	.319	.333
TOTALS		1699	33	.274	.327	.402	804	17	.282	.334	.409	895	16	.266	.322	.396	766	16	.279	.339	.422	933	17	.269	.318	.386	171	1	.246	.303	.368	1528	32	.277	.330	.406
■ **Kenny Lofton** BL/TL																																				
1991	Hou-N	74	0	.203	.253	.216	34	0	.176	.222	.176	40	0	.225	.279	.250	0	0	—	—	—	74	0	.203	.253	.216	20	0	.250	.318	.250	54	0	.185	.228	.204
1992	Cle-A	576	5	.285	.362	.365	277	3	.292	.375	.379	299	2	.278	.349	.351	271	1	.262	.331	.314	305	4	.305	.388	.410	122	0	.369	.466	.434	454	5	.262	.331	.346
1993	Cle-A	569	1	.325	.408	.408	278	1	.313	.414	.410	291	0	.337	.401	.405	284	1	.320	.401	.423	285	0	.330	.414	.393	195	0	.292	.388	.349	374	1	.342	.418	.439
1994	Cle-A	459	12	.349	.412	.536	200	10	.365	.433	.625	259	2	.336	.395	.467	303	8	.363	.430	.554	156	4	.321	.379	.500	169	3	.331	.409	.503	290	9	.359	.414	.555
1995	Cle-A	481	7	.310	.362	.453	273	5	.319	.365	.469	208	2	.298	.358	.433	220	5	.327	.366	.491	261	2	.295	.359	.421	146	0	.274	.342	.342	335	7	.325	.371	.501
1996	Cle-A	662	14	.317	.372	.446	321	7	.343	.399	.480	341	7	.293	.345	.413	332	5	.316	.382	.428	330	9	.318	.361	.464	235	2	.302	.357	.391	427	12	.326	.380	.475
1997	Atl-N	493	5	.333	.409	.428	258	3	.322	.399	.407	235	2	.345	.420	.451	285	3	.344	.400	.435	208	2	.317	.421	.418	152	2	.336	.382	.454	341	3	.331	.421	.416
1998	Cle-A	600	12	.282	.371	.413	304	6	.286	.374	.418	296	6	.277	.368	.409	311	7	.280	.370	.412	289	5	.284	.372	.415	188	4	.293	.377	.404	412	8	.277	.369	.417
1999	Cle-A	465	7	.301	.405	.432	235	1	.272	.384	.340	230	6	.330	.428	.526	291	6	.320	.431	.457	174	1	.270	.361	.391	116	0	.224	.364	.259	349	7	.327	.420	.490
2000	Cle-A	543	15	.278	.369	.422	265	10	.317	.422	.494	278	5	.241	.315	.353	219	6	.237	.328	.379	324	9	.306	.396	.451	123	2	.260	.391	.374	420	13	.283	.362	.436
TOTALS		4922	78	.306	.383	.428	2445	46	.312	.393	.440	2477	32	.301	.372	.416	2516	42	.310	.385	.434	2406	36	.303	.380	.422	1466	13	.299	.383	.392	3456	65	.309	.382	.443
■ **Greg Luzinski** BR/TR																																				
1978	Phi-N	540	35	.265	.388	.526	263	20	.304	.432	.616	277	15	.227	.344	.440	245	18	.245	.361	.510	295	17	.281	.409	.539	134	5	.246	.414	.418	406	30	.271	.378	.562
1979	Phi-N	452	18	.252	.343	.427	198	7	.187	.299	.338	254	11	.303	.378	.496	233	8	.270	.372	.433	219	10	.233	.311	.420	93	5	.226	.348	.419	359	13	.259	.341	.429
1980	Phi-N	368	19	.228	.342	.440	189	15	.291	.403	.582	179	4	.162	.278	.291	230	15	.252	.384	.517	138	4	.188	.266	.312	77	5	.247	.333	.468	291	14	.223	.345	.433
1981	Chi-A	378	21	.265	.365	.476	164	9	.244	.364	.463	214	12	.280	.366	.486	187	9	.267	.384	.449	191	12	.262	.346	.503	72	5	.222	.391	.444	306	16	.275	.358	.484
1982	Chi-A	583	18	.292	.386	.451	274	13	.325	.419	.547	309	5	.262	.357	.366	285	10	.305	.377	.484	298	8	.279	.395	.419	187	6	.321	.431	.508	396	12	.278	.363	.424
1983	Chi-A	502	32	.255	.352	.502	273	18	.289	.370	.560	229	14	.214	.332	.432	224	11	.228	.331	.429	278	21	.277	.370	.561	175	13	.263	.362	.554	327	19	.251	.347	.474
1984	Chi-A	412	13	.238	.329	.364	201	9	.234	.318	.408	211	4	.242	.340	.322	214	3	.220	.327	.294	198	10	.258	.332	.439	164	5	.220	.337	.354	248	8	.250	.324	.371
TOTALS		3235	156	.259	.361	.459	1562	91	.273	.377	.512	1673	65	.245	.345	.409	1618	74	.257	.363	.449	1617	82	.260	.359	.469	902	44	.256	.379	.458	2333	112	.260	.353	.459
■ **Fred Lynn** BL/TL																																				
1978	Bos-A	541	22	.298	.380	.492	276	11	.312	.389	.514	265	11	.283	.371	.468	250	10	.324	.396	.520	291	12	.275	.367	.467	154	4	.201	.272	.318	387	18	.336	.421	.561
1979	Bos-A	531	39	.333	.423	.637	277	28	.386	.470	.798	254	11	.276	.371	.461	276	19	.308	.381	.598	255	20	.361	.465	.678	133	5	.241	.342	.421	398	34	.364	.450	.709
1980	Bos-A	415	12	.301	.383	.480	174	6	.345	.453	.586	241	6	.270	.326	.402	241	8	.307	.376	.498	174	4	.293	.391	.454	125	1	.272	.331	.360	290	11	.314	.404	.531
1981	Cal-A	256	5	.219	.322	.316	125	3	.272	.376	.384	131	2	.168	.270	.252	157	5	.274	.345	.427	99	0	.131	.290	.141	71	3	.211	.296	.408	185	2	.222	.332	.281
1982	Cal-A	472	21	.299	.374	.517	251	13	.291	.359	.526	221	8	.308	.390	.507	242	5	.281	.359	.442	230	16	.317	.390	.596	156	7	.250	.299	.442	316	14	.323	.410	.554
1983	Cal-A	437	22	.272	.352	.483	212	14	.274	.371	.519	225	8	.271	.333	.449	222	14	.261	.375	.514	215	8	.284	.326	.451	158	6	.272	.348	.437	279	16	.272	.354	.509
1984	Cal-A	517	23	.271	.366	.474	242	16	.240	.341	.492	275	7	.298	.389	.458	238	9	.252	.337	.424	279	14	.287	.390	.516	135	6	.222	.348	.430	382	17	.288	.373	.490
1985	Bal-A	448	23	.263	.339	.449	217	14	.272	.343	.502	231	9	.255	.335	.398	257	13	.265	.333	.440	191	10	.262	.345	.461	153	4	.242	.312	.379	295	19	.275	.352	.485
1986	Bal-A	397	23	.287	.371	.499	197	13	.284	.371	.513	200	10	.290	.370	.485	180	8	.311	.386	.478	217	15	.267	.357	.516	96	7	.271	.333	.521	301	16	.292	.382	.492
1987	Bal-A	396	23	.253	.320	.487	191	11	.241	.290	.461	205	12	.263	.346	.512	235	12	.251	.336	.447	161	11	.255	.294	.547	125	5	.224	.297	.400	271	18	.266	.330	.528
1988	Bal-A	301	18	.252	.312	.482	142	11	.275	.344	.563	159	7	.233	.282	.409	230	13	.261	.320	.487	71	5	.225	.287	.465	83	1	.157	.200	.277	218	17	.289	.354	.560
1988	Det-A	90	7	.222	.265	.467	52	2	.212	.241	.327	38	5	.237	.295	.658	0	0	—	—	—	90	7	.222	.265	.467	26	3	.231	.222	.577	64	4	.219	.282	.422
1989	Det-A	353	11	.241	.328	.371	173	9	.214	.324	.405	180	2	.267	.332	.339	181	4	.238	.314	.348	172	7	.244	.342	.395	63	0	.175	.257	.190	290	11	.255	.342	.410
1990	SD-N	196	6	.240	.315	.357	112	2	.241	.315	.321	84	4	.238	.316	.405	115	5	.278	.356	.452	81	1	.185	.256	.222	20	0	.250	.348	.250	176	6	.239	.312	.369
TOTALS		5350	255	.276	.358	.479	2641	153	.284	.369	.521	2709	102	.269	.347	.439	2824	125	.279	.356	.473	2526	130	.274	.360	.487	1498	52	.234	.308	.393	3852	203	.293	.377	.513

YEAR	TM/L	TOTAL AB	HR	AVG	OBP	SLG	HOME AB	HR	AVG	OBP	SLG	AWAY AB	HR	AVG	OBP	SLG	1ST HALF AB	HR	AVG	OBP	SLG	2ND HALF AB	HR	AVG	OBP	SLG	LEFT AB	HR	AVG	OBP	SLG	RIGHT AB	HR	AVG	OBP	SLG
■ Bill Madlock BR/TR																																				
1978	SF-N	447	15	.309	.378	.481	220	5	.291	.362	.436	227	10	.326	.394	.524	206	8	.325	.404	.505	241	7	.295	.355	.461	136	5	.309	.397	.500	311	10	.309	.369	.473
1979	SF-N	249	7	.261	.309	.398	118	1	.220	.266	.288	131	6	.298	.348	.496	249	7	.261	.309	.398	0	0	—	—	—	68	2	.309	.373	.456	181	5	.243	.284	.376
1979	Pit-N	311	7	.328	.390	.469	124	2	.290	.397	.411	187	5	.353	.385	.508	0	0	—	—	—	311	7	.328	.390	.469	102	2	.314	.377	.431	209	5	.335	.397	.488
1980	Pit-N	494	10	.277	.341	.399	251	7	.279	.348	.454	243	3	.276	.333	.342	211	4	.251	.306	.365	283	6	.297	.366	.424	177	3	.271	.340	.390	317	7	.281	.341	.404
1981	Pit-N	279	6	.341	.412	.495	140	2	.343	.424	.500	139	4	.338	.400	.489	138	3	.326	.426	.471	141	3	.355	.399	.518	87	2	.391	.481	.563	192	4	.318	.380	.464
1982	Pit-N	568	19	.319	.368	.488	274	13	.339	.356	.555	294	6	.299	.379	.425	260	6	.288	.353	.419	308	13	.344	.382	.545	144	6	.264	.352	.465	424	13	.337	.374	.495
1983	Pit-N	473	12	.323	.386	.444	248	8	.351	.388	.488	225	4	.293	.383	.396	235	5	.311	.362	.421	238	7	.336	.408	.466	120	6	.367	.430	.558	353	6	.309	.371	.405
1984	Pit-N	403	4	.253	.297	.323	196	1	.270	.318	.332	207	3	.237	.277	.314	285	3	.267	.312	.337	118	1	.220	.262	.288	115	2	.270	.320	.391	288	2	.247	.288	.295
1985	Pit-N	399	10	.251	.323	.388	198	6	.273	.348	.429	201	4	.229	.297	.348	233	3	.236	.305	.352	166	7	.271	.347	.440	123	3	.252	.345	.382	276	7	.250	.313	.391
1985	LA-N	114	2	.360	.422	.447	52	0	.365	.460	.385	62	2	.355	.385	.500	0	0	—	—	—	114	2	.360	.422	.447	35	1	.371	.439	.486	79	1	.354	.414	.430
1986	LA-N	379	10	.280	.336	.404	186	4	.263	.336	.360	193	6	.295	.335	.446	174	4	.230	.278	.328	205	6	.322	.382	.468	141	6	.312	.364	.482	238	4	.261	.320	.357
1987	LA-N	61	3	.180	.265	.344	28	1	.214	.313	.357	33	2	.152	.222	.333	61	3	.180	.265	.344	0	0	—	—	—	21	1	.190	.320	.381	40	2	.175	.233	.325
1987	Det-A	326	14	.279	.351	.460	152	7	.270	.323	.447	174	7	.287	.373	.471	83	6	.301	.344	.542	243	8	.272	.353	.432	151	7	.278	.323	.477	175	7	.280	.373	.446
TOTALS		4503	119	.294	.355	.431	2187	57	.295	.356	.436	2316	62	.292	.354	.427	2135	52	.274	.335	.400	2368	67	.311	.373	.459	1420	46	.299	.369	.459	3083	73	.291	.348	.418
■ Dave Magadan BL/TR																																				
1986	NY-N	18	0	.444	.524	.444	17	0	.471	.550	.471	1	0	.000	.000	.000	0	0	—	—	—	18	0	.444	.524	.444	3	0	.000	.000	.000	15	0	.533	.611	.533
1987	NY-N	192	3	.318	.386	.443	89	2	.382	.451	.539	103	1	.262	.327	.359	93	2	.280	.358	.430	99	1	.354	.413	.455	48	2	.438	.481	.625	144	1	.278	.354	.382
1988	NY-N	314	1	.277	.393	.334	166	1	.301	.407	.361	148	0	.250	.378	.304	130	1	.308	.424	.369	184	0	.255	.371	.310	86	0	.279	.394	.314	228	1	.276	.393	.342
1989	NY-N	374	4	.286	.367	.393	183	3	.306	.378	.415	191	1	.267	.356	.372	181	4	.309	.379	.448	193	0	.264	.356	.342	92	0	.261	.327	.304	282	4	.294	.379	.422
1990	NY-N	451	6	.328	.417	.457	212	2	.278	.391	.373	239	4	.372	.442	.531	147	2	.361	.443	.483	304	4	.313	.405	.444	168	2	.256	.335	.351	283	4	.371	.462	.519
1991	NY-N	418	4	.258	.378	.342	202	2	.243	.358	.322	216	2	.273	.398	.361	230	3	.243	.373	.343	188	1	.277	.385	.340	151	0	.245	.347	.272	267	4	.266	.395	.382
1992	NY-N	321	3	.283	.390	.346	153	2	.314	.426	.399	168	1	.256	.356	.298	212	1	.288	.396	.344	109	2	.275	.378	.349	120	0	.308	.390	.333	201	3	.269	.390	.353
1993	Fla-N	227	4	.286	.400	.392	104	3	.317	.455	.471	123	1	.260	.348	.325	227	4	.286	.400	.392	0	0	—	—	—	74	0	.243	.344	.311	153	4	.307	.427	.431
1993	Sea-A	228	1	.259	.356	.320	102	0	.255	.391	.333	126	1	.262	.324	.310	13	0	.385	.429	.385	215	1	.251	.352	.316	44	0	.227	.314	.273	184	1	.266	.366	.332
1994	Fla-N	211	1	.275	.386	.322	121	1	.306	.407	.372	90	0	.233	.358	.256	168	1	.256	.363	.292	43	0	.349	.472	.442	67	0	.269	.315	.313	144	1	.278	.414	.326
1995	Hou-N	348	2	.313	.428	.399	157	0	.344	.447	.414	191	2	.288	.412	.387	106	1	.292	.445	.406	242	1	.322	.419	.397	35	0	.171	.237	.200	313	2	.329	.446	.422
1996	Chi-N	169	3	.254	.360	.367	72	2	.250	.365	.389	97	1	.258	.357	.351	33	0	.121	.341	.121	136	3	.287	.365	.426	8	0	.375	.545	.500	161	3	.248	.349	.360
1997	Oak-A	271	4	.303	.414	.391	129	2	.302	.409	.372	142	2	.303	.418	.408	108	2	.259	.375	.333	163	2	.331	.439	.429	41	0	.220	.313	.220	230	4	.317	.431	.422
1998	Oak-A	109	1	.321	.390	.422	57	0	.316	.409	.386	52	1	.327	.368	.462	109	1	.321	.390	.422	0	0	—	—	—	16	0	.125	.222	.188	93	1	.355	.419	.462
1999	SD-N	248	2	.274	.377	.355	117	1	.316	.425	.436	131	1	.237	.331	.282	161	2	.292	.369	.398	87	0	.241	.389	.276	38	0	.211	.388	.237	210	2	.286	.375	.376
2000	SD-N	132	2	.273	.410	.371	63	1	.238	.395	.302	69	1	.304	.424	.435	56	0	.161	.277	.214	76	2	.355	.495	.487	20	0	.250	.464	.250	112	2	.277	.399	.393
TOTALS		4031	41	.289	.392	.378	1944	22	.299	.406	.390	2087	19	.280	.379	.368	1974	24	.283	.388	.375	2057	17	.295	.396	.382	1011	4	.262	.354	.315	3020	37	.298	.405	.400
■ Candy Maldonado BR/TR																																				
1981	LA-N	12	0	.083	.083	.083	5	0	.000	.000	.000	7	0	.143	.143	.143	0	0	—	—	—	12	0	.083	.083	.083	4	0	.000	.000	.000	8	0	.125	.125	.125
1982	LA-N	4	0	.000	.200	.000	4	0	.000	.200	.000	0	0	—	—	—	0	0	—	—	—	4	0	.000	.200	.000	1	0	.000	.500	.000	3	0	.000	.000	.000
1983	LA-N	62	1	.194	.254	.290	33	1	.212	.235	.303	29	0	.172	.273	.276	20	0	.150	.150	.150	42	1	.214	.298	.357	51	0	.157	.218	.176	11	1	.364	.417	.818
1984	LA-N	254	5	.268	.318	.382	117	1	.265	.301	.342	137	4	.270	.331	.416	132	3	.295	.349	.417	122	2	.238	.282	.344	198	4	.303	.343	.429	56	1	.143	.234	.214
1985	LA-N	213	5	.225	.288	.338	103	2	.194	.270	.272	110	3	.255	.305	.400	89	2	.180	.237	.270	124	3	.258	.324	.387	168	5	.232	.301	.363	45	0	.200	.234	.244
1986	SF-N	405	18	.252	.289	.477	197	6	.228	.258	.411	208	12	.274	.318	.538	156	5	.250	.282	.462	249	13	.253	.294	.486	132	6	.235	.252	.477	273	12	.260	.307	.476
1987	SF-N	442	20	.292	.346	.509	228	14	.241	.288	.474	214	6	.346	.406	.547	277	12	.332	.382	.556	165	8	.224	.287	.430	132	6	.295	.371	.515	310	14	.290	.334	.506
1988	SF-N	499	12	.255	.311	.377	246	5	.236	.283	.346	253	7	.273	.338	.407	272	7	.268	.320	.393	227	5	.238	.302	.357	183	1	.251	.303	.311	316	11	.256	.316	.415
1989	SF-N	345	9	.217	.296	.362	156	1	.199	.256	.269	189	8	.233	.329	.439	203	5	.212	.305	.345	142	4	.225	.284	.387	147	2	.211	.310	.313	198	7	.222	.286	.399
1990	Cle-A	590	22	.273	.330	.446	298	12	.268	.307	.426	292	10	.277	.353	.466	257	13	.268	.336	.486	333	9	.276	.326	.414	175	10	.331	.387	.543	415	12	.248	.306	.405
1991	Mil-A	111	5	.207	.288	.396	50	3	.200	.317	.460	61	2	.213	.262	.344	15	2	.267	.421	.733	96	3	.198	.264	.344	27	0	.148	.351	.185	84	5	.226	.261	.464
1991	Tor-A	177	7	.277	.375	.446	77	4	.247	.355	.416	100	3	.300	.391	.470	0	0	—	—	—	177	7	.277	.375	.446	49	3	.347	.429	.612	128	4	.250	.355	.383
1992	Tor-A	489	20	.272	.357	.462	219	8	.251	.343	.434	270	12	.289	.368	.485	202	5	.248	.316	.406	287	15	.289	.384	.502	117	4	.291	.400	.444	372	16	.266	.342	.468
1993	Chi-N	140	3	.186	.260	.286	69	1	.203	.236	.290	71	2	.169	.280	.282	101	3	.178	.278	.287	39	0	.205	.205	.282	70	2	.243	.312	.371	70	1	.129	.208	.200
1993	Cle-A	81	5	.247	.333	.457	36	4	.306	.381	.667	45	1	.200	.294	.289	0	0	—	—	—	81	5	.247	.333	.457	35	3	.286	.375	.600	46	2	.217	.302	.348
1994	Cle-A	92	5	.196	.333	.435	35	4	.286	.444	.743	57	1	.140	.258	.246	61	5	.197	.338	.525	31	0	.194	.324	.258	76	5	.211	.362	.500	16	0	.125	.176	.125
1995	Tor-A	160	7	.269	.368	.481	77	5	.273	.372	.558	83	2	.265	.365	.410	90	5	.311	.409	.567	70	2	.214	.313	.371	81	4	.284	.370	.506	79	3	.253	.367	.456
1995	Tex-A	30	2	.233	.378	.533	19	2	.158	.333	.526	11	0	.364	.462	.545	0	0	—	—	—	30	2	.233	.378	.533	22	1	.182	.357	.409	8	1	.375	.444	.875
TOTALS		4106	146	.254	.322	.424	1969	73	.239	.300	.403	2137	73	.268	.342	.443	1875	67	.259	.326	.435	2231	79	.249	.318	.415	1668	56	.262	.336	.423	2438	90	.248	.312	.425
■ Rick Manning BL/TR																																				
1978	Cle-A	566	3	.263	.309	.337	281	1	.299	.341	.370	285	2	.228	.278	.305	248	2	.262	.325	.351	318	1	.264	.297	.327	133	1	.233	.259	.286	433	2	.273	.324	.353
1979	Cle-A	560	3	.259	.323	.304	269	1	.257	.320	.301	291	2	.261	.325	.306	276	1	.261	.332	.308	284	2	.257	.313	.299	162	2	.210	.263	.259	398	1	.279	.347	.322
1980	Cle-A	471	3	.234	.321	.306	228	3	.268	.354	.377	243	0	.202	.289	.239	189	0	.217	.342	.254	282	3	.245	.306	.340	168	0	.167	.230	.196	303	3	.271	.369	.366
1981	Cle-A	360	4	.244	.318	.336	181	2	.260	.337	.365	179	2	.229	.300	.307	164	2	.226	.306	.317	196	2	.260	.329	.352	126	1	.206	.257	.270	234	3	.265	.350	.372
1982	Cle-A	562	8	.270	.334	.352	275	1	.258	.315	.298	287	7	.282	.351	.404	252	4	.270	.336	.365	310	4	.271	.332	.342	215	2	.270	.340	.326	347	6	.271	.330	.369
1983	Cle-A	194	1	.278	.319	.325	86	0	.302	.348	.314	108	1	.259	.296	.333	194	1	.278	.319	.325	0	0	—	—	—	81	0	.235	.279	.235	113	1	.310	.347	.389
1983	Mil-A	375	3	.229	.279	.312	187	2	.262	.303	.337	188	1	.197	.255	.287	81	1	.222	.261	.296	294	2	.231	.284	.316	143	1	.217	.240	.280	232	2	.237	.302	.332
1984	Mil-A	341	7	.249	.318	.370	149	1	.255	.319	.349	192	6	.245	.318	.385	183	3	.246	.313	.361	158	4	.253	.324	.380	80	2	.225	.271	.338	261	5	.257	.332	.379
1985	Mil-A	216	2	.218	.265	.296	101	1	.218	.255	.297	115	1	.217	.274	.296	102	0	.235	.264	.304	114	2	.202	.266	.289	34	1	.235	.297	.353	182	1	.214	.259	.286
1986	Mil-A	205	8	.254	.310	.434	88	4	.216	.286	.409	117	4	.282	.328	.453	71	1	.239	.276	.338	134	7	.261	.327	.485	35	1	.143	.200	.257	170	7	.276	.333	.471
1987	Mil-A	114	0	.228	.299	.307	42	0	.238	.333	.310	72	0	.222	.278	.306	48	0	.271	.368	.375	66	0	.197	.243	.258	21	0	.333	.348	.429	93	0	.204	.288	.280
TOTALS		3964	42	.251	.313	.332	1887	16	.263	.323	.339	2077	26	.240	.303	.326	1808	15	.251	.319	.326	2156	27	.250	.307	.338	1198	11	.221	.271	.278	2766	31	.264	.331	.356
■ Mike Marshall BR/TR																																				
1981	LA-N	25	0	.200	.259	.320	14	0	.286	.375	.500	11	0	.091	.091	.091	0	0	—	—	—	25	0	.200	.259	.320	8	0	.250	.333	.375	17	0	.176	.222	.294
1982	LA-N	95	5	.242	.336	.432	56	2	.250	.344	.375	39	3	.231	.326	.513	13	1	.385	.385	.692	82	4	.220	.330	.390	37	2	.216	.318	.405	58	3	.259	.348	.448
1983	LA-N	465	17	.284	.347	.434	225	9	.307	.372	.467	240	8	.262	.325	.404	170	7	.253	.310	.424	295	10	.302	.369	.441	105	2	.238	.319	.324	360	15	.297	.356	.467
1984	LA-N	495	21	.257	.315	.438	254	11	.260	.303	.437	241	10	.253	.327	.440	225	13	.284	.357	.507	270	8	.233	.278	.381	158	8	.278	.378	.500	337	13	.246	.282	.409
1985	LA-N	518	28	.293	.342	.515	261	15	.303	.345	.536	257	13	.284	.338	.494	218	10	.261	.324	.440	300	18	.317	.355	.570	157	8	.287	.349	.490	361	20	.296	.339	.526
1986	LA-N	330	19	.233	.298	.439	179	13	.240	.305	.497	151	6	.225	.291	.371	267	17	.266	.332	.498	63	2	.095	.149	.190	129	9	.248	.329	.512	201	10	.224	.278	.393
1987	LA-N	402	16	.294	.327	.460	183	5	.284	.327	.404	219	11	.301	.328	.507	194	8	.304	.341	.479	208	8	.284	.314	.442	125	5	.280	.313	.464	277	11	.300	.333	.458
1988	LA-N	542	20	.277	.314	.445	264	9	.261	.299	.432	278	11	.291	.328	.457	289	9	.273	.313	.419	253	11	.281	.315	.474	186	4	.231	.277	.366	356	16	.301	.333	.486
1989	LA-N	377	11	.260	.325	.408	177	6	.294	.352	.480	200	5	.230	.300	.345	149	4	.242	.318	.356	228	7	.272	.329	.443	130	7	.246	.340	.469	247	4	.267	.316	.377
1990	NY-N	163	6	.239	.278	.411	85	4	.235	.280	.435	78	2	.244	.277	.385	157	6	.248	.290	.427	6	0	.000	.000	.000	67	3	.224	.257	.418	96	3	.250	.292	.406
1990	Bos-A	112	4	.286	.316	.464	61	3	.279	.313	.475	51	1	.294	.321	.451	0	0	—	—	—	112	4	.286	.316	.464	29	1	.207	.258	.379	83	3	.313	.337	.494
1991	Bos-A	62	1	.290	.290	.403	31	1	.290	.290	.452	31	0	.290	.290	.355	61	1	.279	.279	.393	1	0	1.000	1.000	1.000	13	0	.385	.385	.462	49	1	.265	.265	.388
1991	Cal-A	7	0	.000	.000	.000	7	0	.000	.000	.000	0	0	—	—	—	0	0	—	—	—	7	0	.000	.000	.000	3	0	.000	.000	.000	4	0	.000	.000	.000
TOTALS		3593	148	.270	.321	.446	1797	78	.275	.325	.460	1796	70	.266	.318	.433	1743	76	.270	.324	.449	1850	72	.271	.319	.444	1147	49	.255	.323	.441	2446	99	.278	.321	.449
■ Al Martin BL/TL																																				
1992	Pit-N	12	0	.167	.154	.333	5	0	.200	.200	.200	7	0	.143	.125	.429	0	0	—	—	—	12	0	.167	.154	.333	2	0	.000	.000	.000	10	0	.200	.182	.400
1993	Pit-N	480	18	.281	.338	.481	253	15	.273	.337	.538	227	3	.291	.340	.419	212	6	.255	.298	.443	268	12	.302	.369	.511	89	1	.191	.277	.303	391	17	.302	.353	.522
1994	Pit-N	276	9	.286	.367	.457	135	6	.319	.399	.556	141	3	.255	.338	.362	262	9	.294	.376	.473	14	0	.143	.200	.143	52	1	.288	.339	.423	224	8	.286	.374	.464
1995	Pit-N	439	13	.282	.351	.442	224	8	.308	.362	.482	215	5	.256	.339	.400	191	6	.215	.302	.346	248	7	.335	.389	.516	68	1	.132	.145	.176	371	12	.310	.385	.491
1996	Pit-N	630	18	.300	.354	.452	315	8	.298	.349	.444	315	10	.302	.358	.460	326	10	.276	.327	.417	304	8	.326	.382	.490	135	4	.200	.290	.326	495	14	.327	.372	.487
1997	Pit-N	423	13	.291	.359	.473	202	8	.302	.361	.545	221	5	.281	.357	.407	155	7	.316	.404	.529	268	6	.276	.332	.440	92	1	.326	.417	.446	331	12	.281	.342	.480
1998	Pit-N	440	12	.239	.296	.364	212	5	.250	.333	.373	228	7	.228	.259	.355	278	7	.230	.286	.353	162	5	.253	.315	.383	88	1	.216	.258	.295	352	11	.244	.306	.381
1999	Pit-N	541	24	.277	.337	.506	275	12	.295	.352	.516	266	12	.259	.322	.496	245	8	.290	.348	.531	296	16	.267	.328	.486	120	2	.242	.305	.358	421	22	.287	.346	.549
2000	SD-N	346	11	.306	.360	.474	161	8	.317	.374	.553	185	3	.297	.347	.405	270	10	.307	.353	.489	76	1	.303	.384	.421	76	0	.158	.200	.171	270	11	.348	.403	.559
2000	Sea-A	134	4	.231	.283	.396	57	2	.193	.277	.368	77	2	.260	.287	.416	0	0	—	—	—	134	4	.231	.283	.396	1	0	.000	.000	.000	133	4	.233	.285	.398
TOTALS		3721	122	.281	.341	.454	1839	72	.290	.352	.490	1882	50	.272	.331	.420	1939	63	.273	.335	.445	1782	59	.289	.348	.465	723	11	.219	.285	.315	2998	111	.296	.355	.488
■ Carmelo Martinez BR/TR																																				
1983	Chi-N	89	6	.258	.287	.494	39	2	.154	.195	.359	50	4	.340	.358	.600	0	0	—	—	—	89	6	.258	.287	.494	13	1	.308	.357	.615	76	5	.250	.275	.474

		TOTAL					HOME					AWAY					1ST HALF					2ND HALF					LEFT					RIGHT				
YEAR	TM/L	AB	HR	AVG	OBP	SLG	AB	HR	AVG	OBP	SLG	AB	HR	AVG	OBP	SLG	AB	HR	AVG	OBP	SLG	AB	HR	AVG	OBP	SLG	AB	HR	AVG	OBP	SLG	AB	HR	AVG	OBP	SLG
1984	SD-N	488	13	.250	.340	.395	230	6	.252	.360	.391	258	7	.248	.322	.399	232	9	.267	.356	.435	256	4	.234	.327	.359	161	2	.267	.372	.410	327	11	.242	.325	.388
1985	SD-N	514	21	.253	.362	.434	256	15	.273	.390	.496	258	6	.233	.333	.372	232	10	.263	.347	.466	282	11	.245	.373	.408	166	8	.247	.379	.452	348	13	.256	.353	.425
1986	SD-N	244	9	.238	.333	.389	123	6	.179	.297	.358	121	3	.298	.372	.421	167	5	.257	.361	.395	77	4	.195	.273	.377	110	7	.282	.407	.518	134	2	.201	.265	.284
1987	SD-N	447	15	.273	.372	.430	216	10	.282	.390	.468	231	5	.264	.355	.394	204	9	.270	.380	.456	243	6	.276	.365	.407	184	9	.272	.395	.478	263	6	.274	.355	.395
1988	SD-N	365	18	.236	.301	.416	178	11	.258	.337	.489	187	7	.214	.266	.348	136	3	.206	.253	.316	229	15	.253	.328	.476	154	7	.234	.318	.390	211	11	.237	.288	.436
1989	SD-N	267	6	.221	.302	.348	121	2	.165	.257	.248	146	4	.267	.339	.432	173	3	.220	.306	.335	94	3	.223	.295	.372	118	2	.271	.348	.390	149	4	.181	.266	.315
1990	Phi-N	198	8	.242	.339	.404	107	4	.224	.297	.374	91	4	.264	.385	.440	87	5	.264	.340	.483	111	3	.225	.338	.342	79	3	.215	.333	.380	119	5	.261	.343	.420
1990	Pit-N	19	2	.211	.250	.579	15	2	.267	.313	.733	4	0	.000	.000	.000	0	0	—	—	—	19	2	.211	.250	.579	11	2	.364	.417	1.000	8	0	.000	.000	.000
1991	Pit-N	16	0	.250	.294	.250	7	0	.286	.286	.286	9	0	.222	.300	.222	16	0	.250	.294	.250	0	0	—	—	—	7	0	.143	.250	.143	9	0	.333	.333	.333
1991	KC-A	121	4	.207	.351	.355	57	3	.228	.371	.439	64	1	.188	.333	.281	115	4	.209	.350	.357	6	0	.167	.375	.333	51	2	.216	.375	.392	70	2	.200	.333	.329
1991	Cin-N	138	6	.232	.301	.399	66	2	.197	.247	.303	72	4	.264	.349	.486	0	0	—	—	—	138	6	.232	.301	.399	73	0	.233	.313	.288	65	6	.231	.288	.523
TOTALS		2906	108	.245	.337	.408	1415	63	.240	.339	.418	1491	45	.251	.334	.398	1362	48	.248	.341	.408	1544	60	.243	.333	.407	1127	43	.255	.364	.429	1779	65	.239	.319	.395
■ **Tino Martinez** BL/TR																																				
1990	Sea-A	68	0	.221	.308	.279	17	0	.118	.250	.118	51	0	.255	.328	.333	0	0	—	—	—	68	0	.221	.308	.279	15	0	.267	.368	.333	53	0	.208	.288	.264
1991	Sea-A	112	4	.205	.272	.330	57	3	.228	.290	.404	55	1	.182	.254	.255	0	0	—	—	—	112	4	.205	.272	.330	35	1	.257	.333	.400	77	3	.182	.244	.299
1992	Sea-A	460	16	.257	.316	.411	232	10	.267	.326	.448	228	6	.246	.307	.373	228	7	.268	.315	.425	232	9	.246	.318	.397	101	3	.228	.261	.356	359	13	.265	.332	.426
1993	Sea-A	408	17	.265	.343	.456	193	9	.238	.330	.430	215	8	.288	.354	.479	279	13	.262	.357	.470	129	4	.271	.309	.426	132	5	.250	.322	.439	276	12	.272	.352	.464
1994	Sea-A	329	20	.261	.320	.508	121	8	.264	.350	.537	208	12	.260	.302	.490	214	9	.215	.293	.402	115	11	.348	.375	.704	77	4	.273	.345	.481	252	16	.258	.313	.516
1995	Sea-A	519	31	.293	.369	.551	256	14	.273	.371	.508	263	17	.312	.366	.593	205	13	.288	.371	.561	314	18	.296	.367	.545	152	10	.322	.389	.605	367	21	.281	.361	.529
1996	NY-A	595	25	.292	.364	.466	286	9	.283	.357	.420	309	16	.301	.371	.508	313	13	.284	.340	.460	282	12	.301	.390	.472	219	6	.279	.336	.429	376	19	.301	.380	.487
1997	NY-A	594	44	.296	.371	.577	280	18	.282	.361	.532	314	26	.309	.380	.618	309	28	.307	.377	.638	285	16	.284	.364	.512	231	12	.268	.330	.485	363	32	.314	.396	.636
1998	NY-A	531	28	.281	.355	.505	259	12	.290	.367	.498	272	16	.272	.344	.511	245	11	.265	.355	.473	286	17	.294	.355	.531	168	9	.268	.330	.488	363	19	.287	.366	.512
1999	NY-A	589	28	.263	.341	.458	286	7	.227	.308	.343	303	21	.297	.374	.568	283	13	.272	.363	.481	306	15	.255	.321	.438	180	7	.261	.315	.428	409	21	.264	.353	.472
2000	NY-A	569	16	.258	.328	.422	282	12	.248	.321	.447	287	4	.268	.334	.397	278	7	.259	.327	.428	291	9	.258	.328	.416	171	3	.281	.339	.421	398	13	.249	.323	.422
TOTALS		4774	229	.273	.345	.478	2269	102	.262	.341	.454	2505	127	.283	.349	.500	2354	114	.271	.346	.485	2420	115	.275	.344	.471	1481	60	.271	.332	.458	3293	169	.274	.351	.487
■ **Dave Martinez** BL/TL																																				
1986	Chi-N	108	1	.139	.190	.194	66	1	.136	.186	.212	42	0	.143	.196	.167	33	0	.182	.250	.212	75	1	.120	.162	.187	10	0	.200	.200	.200	98	1	.133	.189	.194
1987	Chi-N	459	8	.292	.372	.418	231	5	.281	.366	.433	228	3	.303	.377	.404	206	2	.301	.401	.408	253	6	.285	.347	.427	23	1	.261	.320	.391	436	7	.294	.374	.420
1988	Chi-N	256	4	.254	.311	.348	105	2	.295	.367	.390	151	2	.225	.270	.318	225	3	.244	.301	.329	31	1	.323	.382	.484	34	2	.206	.282	.412	222	2	.261	.316	.338
1988	Mon-N	191	2	.257	.316	.356	95	0	.221	.286	.316	96	2	.292	.346	.396	0	0	—	—	—	191	2	.257	.316	.356	12	0	.167	.333	.167	179	2	.263	.314	.369
1989	Mon-N	361	3	.274	.324	.382	178	1	.208	.258	.264	183	2	.339	.387	.497	165	3	.273	.326	.412	196	0	.276	.322	.357	30	0	.133	.161	.133	331	3	.287	.338	.405
1990	Mon-N	391	11	.279	.321	.422	204	5	.275	.309	.382	187	6	.283	.333	.465	166	5	.289	.333	.452	225	6	.271	.311	.400	78	1	.244	.333	.308	313	10	.288	.317	.450
1991	Mon-N	396	7	.295	.332	.419	173	3	.283	.315	.410	223	4	.305	.345	.426	187	2	.246	.278	.353	209	5	.340	.379	.478	93	0	.237	.287	.323	303	7	.314	.346	.449
1992	Cin-N	393	3	.254	.323	.354	196	3	.291	.355	.423	197	0	.218	.292	.284	182	0	.258	.325	.335	211	3	.251	.322	.370	59	0	.271	.348	.356	334	3	.251	.319	.353
1993	SF-N	241	5	.241	.317	.361	117	1	.197	.254	.274	124	4	.282	.373	.444	85	3	.224	.298	.376	156	2	.250	.328	.353	27	0	.259	.394	.407	214	5	.238	.306	.355
1994	SF-N	235	4	.247	.314	.362	125	1	.200	.270	.256	110	3	.300	.364	.482	144	2	.250	.329	.375	91	2	.242	.289	.341	28	0	.250	.300	.321	207	4	.246	.316	.367
1995	Chi-A	303	5	.307	.371	.436	136	2	.279	.365	.419	167	3	.329	.375	.449	82	3	.244	.311	.439	221	2	.330	.392	.434	33	0	.212	.297	.212	270	5	.319	.380	.463
1996	Chi-A	440	10	.318	.393	.468	206	3	.282	.368	.413	234	7	.350	.416	.517	179	5	.330	.397	.480	261	5	.310	.391	.460	74	1	.311	.402	.486	366	9	.320	.391	.464
1997	Chi-A	504	12	.286	.356	.413	241	5	.307	.375	.432	263	7	.266	.338	.395	245	10	.286	.365	.461	259	2	.286	.346	.367	85	3	.259	.333	.400	419	9	.291	.360	.415
1998	TB-A	309	3	.256	.334	.320	147	2	.259	.347	.333	162	1	.253	.322	.309	265	2	.245	.330	.306	44	1	.318	.362	.409	84	0	.250	.319	.274	225	3	.258	.340	.338
1999	TB-A	514	6	.284	.361	.387	243	2	.251	.338	.337	271	4	.314	.382	.432	258	5	.295	.384	.434	256	1	.273	.337	.340	88	1	.239	.310	.295	426	5	.293	.372	.406
2000	TB-A	104	1	.260	.319	.365	36	1	.250	.341	.444	68	0	.265	.307	.324	104	1	.260	.319	.365	0	0	—	—	—	8	0	.250	.250	.375	96	1	.260	.324	.365
2000	Chi-N	54	0	.185	.214	.241	35	0	.229	.270	.314	19	0	.105	.105	.105	54	0	.185	.214	.241	0	0	—	—	—	5	0	.000	.000	.000	49	0	.204	.235	.265
2000	Tex-A	119	2	.269	.351	.370	54	1	.278	.381	.426	65	1	.262	.324	.323	51	2	.235	.316	.392	68	0	.294	.377	.353	9	1	.111	.333	.444	110	1	.282	.352	.364
2000	Tor-A	180	2	.311	.393	.411	87	1	.310	.400	.460	93	1	.312	.387	.366	0	0	—	—	—	180	2	.311	.393	.411	50	0	.360	.429	.440	130	2	.292	.380	.400
TOTALS		5558	89	.275	.341	.389	2675	39	.262	.332	.372	2883	50	.288	.350	.405	2631	48	.267	.337	.388	2927	41	.283	.345	.391	830	10	.249	.325	.339	4728	79	.280	.344	.398
■ **Edgar Martinez** BR/TR																																				
1987	Sea-A	43	0	.372	.413	.581	13	0	.308	.400	.615	30	0	.400	.419	.567	0	0	—	—	—	43	0	.372	.413	.581	14	0	.214	.313	.286	29	0	.448	.467	.724
1988	Sea-A	32	0	.281	.351	.406	10	0	.400	.400	.600	22	0	.227	.333	.318	14	0	.143	.294	.214	18	0	.389	.400	.556	8	0	.375	.500	.625	24	0	.250	.296	.333
1989	Sea-A	171	2	.240	.314	.304	77	0	.221	.291	.260	94	2	.255	.333	.340	115	2	.270	.333	.357	56	0	.179	.277	.196	69	1	.261	.288	.348	102	1	.225	.331	.275
1990	Sea-A	487	11	.302	.397	.433	244	3	.299	.401	.414	243	8	.305	.393	.453	246	7	.313	.413	.463	241	4	.290	.381	.402	156	6	.308	.412	.487	331	5	.299	.390	.408
1991	Sea-A	544	14	.307	.405	.452	250	8	.320	.427	.480	294	6	.296	.385	.429	241	5	.311	.412	.415	303	9	.304	.399	.482	156	2	.359	.442	.481	388	12	.286	.390	.441
1992	Sea-A	528	18	.343	.404	.544	268	11	.313	.377	.545	260	7	.373	.432	.542	278	12	.317	.384	.554	250	6	.372	.427	.532	141	4	.376	.444	.574	387	14	.331	.390	.532
1993	Sea-A	135	4	.237	.366	.378	57	1	.228	.371	.316	78	3	.244	.362	.423	61	1	.213	.329	.311	74	3	.257	.396	.432	36	0	.111	.298	.139	99	4	.283	.393	.465
1994	Sea-A	326	13	.285	.387	.482	119	4	.319	.427	.504	207	9	.266	.364	.469	192	8	.302	.405	.505	134	5	.261	.361	.448	82	4	.329	.471	.573	244	9	.270	.356	.451
1995	Sea-A	511	29	.356	.479	.628	252	16	.377	.498	.694	259	13	.336	.460	.564	209	13	.373	.480	.665	302	16	.344	.478	.603	127	8	.433	.562	.709	384	21	.331	.449	.602
1996	Sea-A	499	26	.327	.464	.595	238	14	.345	.482	.647	261	12	.310	.446	.548	291	18	.333	.451	.667	208	8	.317	.480	.495	115	8	.339	.473	.635	384	18	.323	.461	.583
1997	Sea-A	542	28	.330	.456	.554	268	12	.321	.450	.541	274	16	.339	.462	.566	295	13	.342	.446	.542	247	15	.316	.467	.567	131	4	.282	.412	.420	411	24	.345	.469	.596
1998	Sea-A	556	29	.322	.429	.565	280	17	.321	.449	.589	276	12	.322	.406	.540	279	12	.290	.401	.516	277	17	.354	.456	.614	106	2	.311	.468	.481	450	27	.324	.418	.584
1999	Sea-A	502	24	.337	.447	.554	278	12	.360	.464	.565	224	12	.308	.426	.540	229	11	.310	.442	.520	273	13	.359	.452	.582	109	10	.358	.478	.725	393	14	.331	.438	.506
2000	Sea-A	556	37	.324	.423	.579	263	19	.304	.423	.563	293	18	.341	.422	.594	250	22	.352	.445	.680	306	15	.301	.404	.497	92	9	.359	.451	.707	464	28	.317	.417	.554
TOTALS		5432	235	.320	.426	.529	2617	117	.323	.436	.544	2815	118	.317	.416	.515	2700	124	.319	.421	.539	2732	111	.321	.430	.520	1342	58	.334	.447	.544	4090	177	.315	.419	.524
■ **Gary Matthews** BR/TR																																				
1978	Atl-N	474	18	.285	.366	.462	239	10	.293	.384	.485	235	8	.277	.347	.438	168	9	.286	.379	.518	306	9	.284	.359	.431	133	6	.368	.445	.617	341	12	.252	.334	.402
1979	Atl-N	631	27	.304	.363	.502	313	18	.329	.394	.588	318	9	.280	.332	.418	312	16	.308	.374	.548	319	11	.301	.353	.458	167	5	.305	.354	.491	464	22	.304	.366	.506
1980	Atl-N	571	19	.278	.325	.419	275	9	.262	.319	.393	296	10	.294	.331	.443	222	6	.261	.308	.392	349	13	.289	.336	.436	108	2	.333	.397	.444	463	17	.266	.308	.413
1981	Phi-N	359	9	.301	.398	.451	198	5	.333	.416	.520	161	4	.261	.376	.366	186	2	.317	.395	.446	173	7	.283	.401	.457	72	3	.292	.358	.472	287	6	.303	.408	.446
1982	Phi-N	616	19	.281	.349	.427	289	10	.298	.373	.457	327	9	.266	.328	.401	277	11	.285	.350	.455	339	8	.277	.348	.404	119	5	.294	.359	.471	497	14	.278	.347	.416
1983	Phi-N	446	10	.258	.352	.374	206	3	.257	.359	.354	240	7	.258	.347	.392	251	8	.243	.328	.386	195	2	.277	.384	.359	126	2	.294	.372	.413	320	8	.244	.345	.359
1984	Chi-N	491	14	.291	.410	.428	240	8	.271	.392	.421	251	6	.311	.427	.434	238	4	.273	.395	.378	253	10	.308	.424	.474	144	5	.326	.393	.465	347	9	.277	.417	.412
1985	Chi-N	298	13	.235	.362	.406	125	8	.264	.396	.504	173	5	.214	.337	.335	106	4	.236	.381	.377	192	9	.234	.351	.422	82	4	.232	.340	.402	216	9	.236	.370	.407
1986	Chi-N	370	21	.259	.361	.478	185	11	.286	.382	.514	185	10	.232	.340	.443	151	5	.219	.362	.377	219	16	.288	.360	.548	105	6	.352	.465	.600	265	15	.223	.317	.430
1987	Chi-N	42	0	.262	.326	.333	28	0	.286	.355	.393	14	0	.214	.267	.214	35	0	.229	.289	.257	7	0	.429	.500	.714	11	0	.273	.273	.364	31	0	.258	.343	.323
1987	Sea-A	119	3	.235	.319	.319	36	2	.222	.310	.389	83	1	.241	.323	.289	0	0	—	—	—	119	3	.235	.319	.319	71	1	.239	.341	.296	48	2	.229	.283	.354
TOTALS		4417	153	.278	.363	.436	2134	84	.289	.376	.469	2283	69	.269	.349	.406	1946	65	.273	.361	.435	2471	88	.282	.364	.437	1138	39	.309	.385	.476	3279	114	.268	.355	.422
■ **Don Mattingly** BL/TL																																				
1982	NY-A	12	0	.167	.154	.167	12	0	.167	.167	.167	0	0	—	.000	—	0	0	—	—	—	12	0	.167	.154	.167	2	0	.000	.000	.000	10	0	.200	.182	.200
1983	NY-A	279	4	.283	.333	.409	134	0	.306	.377	.403	145	4	.262	.289	.414	36	1	.306	.333	.444	243	3	.280	.333	.403	87	2	.264	.320	.379	192	2	.292	.340	.422
1984	NY-A	603	23	.343	.381	.537	282	12	.319	.357	.514	321	11	.364	.401	.558	279	12	.344	.383	.548	324	11	.343	.379	.528	184	5	.326	.373	.500	419	18	.351	.384	.554
1985	NY-A	652	35	.324	.371	.567	318	22	.336	.374	.616	334	13	.311	.368	.521	279	6	.294	.341	.444	373	29	.346	.394	.660	264	18	.288	.328	.568	388	17	.348	.400	.567
1986	NY-A	677	31	.352	.394	.573	320	17	.334	.383	.566	357	14	.367	.404	.580	322	13	.339	.381	.531	355	18	.363	.406	.611	243	5	.358	.398	.523	434	26	.348	.392	.601
1987	NY-A	569	30	.327	.378	.559	283	17	.336	.384	.572	286	13	.318	.373	.545	231	8	.316	.392	.502	338	22	.334	.368	.598	199	11	.302	.355	.523	370	19	.341	.391	.578
1988	NY-A	599	18	.311	.353	.462	296	11	.294	.334	.453	303	7	.327	.372	.472	239	5	.305	.369	.448	360	13	.314	.342	.472	221	3	.290	.316	.389	378	15	.323	.374	.505
1989	NY-A	631	23	.303	.351	.477	317	19	.334	.378	.577	314	4	.271	.323	.376	297	10	.306	.363	.468	334	13	.299	.340	.485	237	8	.338	.382	.532	394	15	.282	.332	.444
1990	NY-A	394	5	.256	.308	.335	183	4	.246	.308	.333	211	1	.265	.308	.336	288	5	.257	.303	.351	106	0	.255	.322	.292	126	0	.262	.301	.310	268	5	.254	.312	.347
1991	NY-A	587	9	.288	.339	.394	266	7	.305	.356	.462	321	2	.274	.325	.336	262	6	.309	.360	.416	325	3	.271	.322	.375	227	5	.264	.321	.383	360	4	.303	.350	.400
1992	NY-A	640	14	.287	.327	.416	303	6	.317	.371	.449	337	8	.261	.284	.386	305	9	.272	.322	.433	335	5	.301	.331	.400	204	2	.284	.318	.397	436	12	.289	.330	.424
1993	NY-A	530	17	.291	.364	.445	241	8	.303	.386	.481	289	9	.280	.345	.415	219	5	.288	.347	.402	311	12	.293	.375	.476	201	5	.264	.344	.388	329	12	.307	.377	.480
1994	NY-A	372	6	.304	.397	.411	173	3	.295	.377	.382	199	3	.312	.414	.437	268	5	.306	.396	.425	104	1	.298	.398	.375	134	1	.299	.382	.373	238	5	.307	.405	.433
1995	NY-A	458	7	.288	.341	.413	238	5	.303	.337	.445	220	2	.273	.345	.377	160	1	.269	.326	.375	298	6	.299	.350	.433	151	2	.265	.313	.384	307	5	.300	.355	.427
TOTALS		7003	222	.307	.358	.471	3366	131	.313	.364	.495	3637	91	.302	.353	.450	3185	86	.302	.358	.449	3818	136	.312	.359	.490	2480	67	.296	.345	.448	4523	155	.314	.366	.484
■ **Brent Mayne** BL/TR																																				
1990	KC-A	13	0	.231	.375	.231	2	0	.500	.500	.500	11	0	.182	.357	.182	0	0	—	—	—	13	0	.231	.375	.231	0	0	—	—	—	13	0	.231	.375	.231
1991	KC-A	231	3	.251	.315	.325	130	2	.269	.333	.346	101	1	.228	.292	.297	57	0	.281	.349	.298	174	3	.241	.304	.333	22	0	.091	.179	.091	209	3	.268	.332	.349
1992	KC-A	213	0	.225	.260	.272	117	0	.231	.264	.291	96	0	.219	.255	.250	71	0	.254	.286	.310	142	0	.211	.247	.254	22	0	.136	.208	.136	191	0	.236	.266	.288

		TOTAL					HOME					AWAY					1ST HALF					2ND HALF					LEFT					RIGHT				
YEAR	TM/L	AB	HR	AVG	OBP	SLG	AB	HR	AVG	OBP	SLG	AB	HR	AVG	OBP	SLG	AB	HR	AVG	OBP	SLG	AB	HR	AVG	OBP	SLG	AB	HR	AVG	OBP	SLG	AB	HR	AVG	OBP	SLG
1993	KC-A	205	2	.254	.317	.337	97	0	.320	.371	.371	108	2	.194	.269	.306	116	1	.284	.331	.379	89	1	.213	.300	.281	19	0	.211	.250	.211	186	2	.258	.324	.349
1994	KC-A	144	2	.257	.323	.347	78	1	.282	.364	.385	66	1	.227	.271	.303	80	1	.225	.279	.300	64	1	.297	.375	.406	16	0	.250	.294	.250	128	2	.258	.326	.359
1995	KC-A	307	1	.251	.313	.326	137	1	.292	.362	.409	170	0	.218	.272	.259	137	1	.204	.253	.277	170	0	.288	.358	.365	45	0	.178	.229	.222	262	1	.263	.326	.344
1996	NY-N	99	1	.263	.342	.354	55	0	.236	.311	.255	44	1	.295	.380	.477	52	1	.269	.367	.365	47	0	.255	.314	.340	10	0	.300	.300	.400	89	1	.258	.347	.348
1997	Oak-A	256	6	.289	.343	.406	130	4	.315	.381	.454	126	2	.262	.301	.357	83	2	.205	.267	.301	173	4	.329	.379	.457	43	0	.279	.326	.326	213	6	.291	.346	.423
1998	SF-N	275	3	.273	.359	.360	126	0	.286	.401	.341	149	3	.262	.319	.376	132	2	.288	.397	.364	143	1	.259	.321	.357	36	0	.306	.324	.417	239	3	.268	.363	.351
1999	SF-N	322	2	.301	.389	.419	163	1	.319	.406	.466	159	1	.283	.371	.371	169	1	.314	.385	.438	153	1	.288	.392	.399	56	0	.286	.388	.393	266	2	.305	.389	.425
2000	Col-N	335	6	.301	.381	.418	156	3	.314	.377	.455	179	3	.291	.385	.385	160	4	.313	.404	.469	175	2	.291	.359	.371	46	1	.196	.255	.304	289	5	.318	.402	.436
TOTALS		2400	26	.270	.340	.362	1191	12	.291	.363	.390	1209	14	.249	.317	.333	1057	13	.270	.342	.365	1343	13	.270	.338	.359	315	1	.229	.287	.292	2085	25	.276	.348	.372
■ Lee Mazzilli BB/TR																																				
1978	NY-N	542	16	.273	.353	.432	263	8	.247	.345	.426	279	8	.297	.361	.437	302	6	.278	.348	.414	240	10	.267	.360	.454	175	5	.286	.324	.446	367	11	.267	.366	.425
1979	NY-N	597	15	.303	.395	.449	293	6	.294	.387	.427	304	9	.313	.403	.470	265	8	.340	.435	.517	332	7	.274	.363	.395	196	5	.306	.391	.474	401	10	.302	.397	.436
1980	NY-N	578	16	.280	.370	.431	301	10	.272	.361	.445	277	6	.289	.379	.415	252	2	.266	.373	.365	326	14	.291	.367	.482	163	10	.258	.326	.528	415	6	.289	.386	.393
1981	NY-N	324	6	.228	.324	.358	144	1	.243	.345	.368	180	5	.217	.308	.350	163	3	.215	.328	.325	161	3	.242	.320	.391	72	1	.208	.266	.306	252	5	.234	.340	.373
1982	Tex-A	195	4	.241	.339	.344	79	2	.241	.341	.329	116	2	.241	.338	.353	111	2	.243	.344	.342	84	2	.238	.333	.345	42	2	.286	.362	.429	153	2	.229	.333	.320
1982	NY-A	128	6	.266	.347	.422	69	3	.232	.293	.362	59	3	.305	.406	.492	0	0	—	—	—	128	6	.266	.347	.422	57	5	.246	.338	.509	71	1	.282	.354	.352
1983	Pit-N	246	5	.240	.365	.337	110	1	.191	.285	.282	136	4	.279	.427	.382	184	5	.272	.408	.397	62	0	.145	.221	.161	58	0	.155	.286	.172	188	5	.266	.390	.388
1984	Pit-N	266	4	.237	.338	.331	128	3	.234	.353	.352	138	1	.239	.323	.312	140	3	.221	.337	.307	126	1	.254	.338	.357	25	0	.280	.357	.280	241	4	.232	.336	.336
1985	Pit-N	117	1	.282	.425	.376	49	0	.327	.459	.388	68	1	.250	.400	.368	72	1	.292	.457	.417	45	0	.267	.365	.311	17	0	.294	.455	.294	100	1	.280	.419	.390
1986	Pit-N	93	1	.226	.392	.301	44	0	.250	.414	.295	49	1	.204	.371	.306	78	0	.205	.382	.256	15	1	.333	.444	.533	24	0	.125	.276	.125	69	1	.261	.429	.362
1986	NY-N	58	2	.276	.417	.431	36	1	.333	.400	.500	22	1	.182	.438	.318	0	0	—	—	—	58	2	.276	.417	.431	28	1	.214	.241	.393	30	1	.333	.535	.467
1987	NY-N	124	3	.306	.399	.460	56	3	.429	.514	.679	68	0	.206	.289	.279	72	2	.333	.419	.528	52	1	.269	.371	.365	44	2	.341	.420	.477	80	1	.287	.388	.450
1988	NY-N	116	0	.147	.227	.164	46	0	.217	.308	.261	70	0	.100	.175	.100	64	0	.188	.243	.219	52	0	.096	.210	.096	35	0	.086	.083	.114	81	0	.173	.281	.185
1989	NY-N	60	2	.183	.364	.317	34	1	.206	.400	.324	26	1	.154	.313	.308	49	2	.184	.385	.347	11	0	.182	.250	.182	7	0	.286	.500	.429	53	2	.170	.343	.302
1989	Tor-A	66	4	.227	.395	.455	41	2	.195	.389	.366	25	2	.280	.406	.600	0	0	—	—	—	66	4	.227	.395	.455	15	0	.067	.263	.067	51	4	.275	.433	.569
TOTALS		3510	85	.262	.363	.393	1693	41	.261	.364	.400	1817	44	.263	.361	.387	1752	34	.266	.375	.388	1758	51	.258	.349	.399	958	31	.255	.331	.408	2552	54	.264	.374	.388
■ Oddibe McDowell BL/TL																																				
1985	Tex-A	406	18	.239	.304	.431	203	10	.266	.323	.463	203	8	.212	.286	.399	153	3	.222	.262	.353	253	15	.249	.329	.478	123	3	.244	.311	.431	283	15	.237	.301	.431
1986	Tex-A	572	18	.266	.341	.427	290	8	.279	.340	.441	282	10	.252	.342	.411	273	11	.275	.353	.473	299	7	.258	.329	.385	128	3	.219	.296	.336	444	15	.279	.353	.453
1987	Tex-A	407	14	.241	.324	.428	196	5	.250	.315	.413	211	9	.232	.332	.441	195	8	.267	.374	.477	212	6	.217	.274	.382	71	2	.225	.371	.352	336	12	.244	.313	.443
1988	Tex-A	437	6	.247	.311	.355	211	4	.246	.321	.374	226	2	.248	.302	.336	171	3	.205	.285	.310	266	3	.274	.329	.383	96	2	.229	.288	.354	341	4	.252	.318	.355
1989	Cle-A	239	3	.222	.296	.297	96	1	.250	.348	.344	143	2	.203	.258	.266	236	3	.216	.292	.292	3	0	.667	.667	.667	70	0	.214	.304	.229	169	3	.225	.293	.325
1989	Atl-N	280	7	.304	.365	.471	136	2	.316	.380	.449	144	5	.292	.350	.493	0	0	—	—	—	280	7	.304	.365	.471	100	0	.230	.280	.280	180	7	.344	.410	.578
1990	Atl-N	305	7	.243	.295	.357	150	4	.273	.321	.400	155	3	.213	.269	.316	189	5	.265	.307	.392	116	2	.207	.276	.302	39	0	.103	.222	.103	266	7	.263	.306	.395
1994	Tex-A	183	1	.262	.355	.317	104	1	.231	.344	.288	79	0	.304	.371	.354	121	0	.306	.399	.339	62	1	.177	.268	.274	26	0	.308	.444	.308	157	1	.255	.337	.318
TOTALS		2829	74	.253	.323	.395	1386	35	.266	.334	.408	1443	39	.240	.313	.383	1338	33	.250	.325	.383	1491	41	.256	.322	.406	653	10	.224	.308	.323	2176	64	.261	.328	.417
■ Willie McGee BB/TR																																				
1982	StL-N	422	4	.296	.318	.391	220	2	.327	.346	.414	202	2	.262	.287	.366	141	0	.340	.365	.447	281	4	.274	.294	.363	113	2	.265	.306	.381	309	2	.307	.323	.395
1983	StL-N	601	5	.286	.314	.374	275	4	.240	.280	.360	326	1	.325	.344	.387	241	3	.311	.345	.394	360	2	.269	.293	.361	158	2	.272	.288	.373	443	3	.291	.323	.375
1984	StL-N	571	6	.291	.325	.394	263	2	.304	.338	.392	308	4	.279	.313	.396	273	2	.267	.309	.359	298	4	.312	.339	.426	164	5	.268	.297	.433	407	1	.300	.336	.378
1985	StL-N	612	10	.353	.384	.503	283	3	.353	.370	.473	329	7	.353	.395	.529	253	2	.340	.375	.478	359	8	.362	.391	.521	210	7	.348	.372	.571	402	3	.356	.390	.468
1986	StL-N	497	7	.256	.306	.370	264	7	.280	.325	.462	233	0	.227	.285	.266	303	3	.241	.289	.327	194	4	.278	.333	.438	199	5	.246	.301	.387	298	2	.262	.310	.359
1987	StL-N	620	11	.285	.312	.434	300	6	.297	.316	.457	320	5	.275	.308	.412	271	5	.292	.318	.432	349	6	.281	.307	.436	208	6	.288	.309	.500	412	5	.284	.313	.400
1988	StL-N	562	3	.292	.329	.372	283	1	.283	.322	.353	279	2	.301	.337	.391	325	1	.320	.356	.397	237	2	.253	.292	.338	197	0	.294	.322	.355	365	3	.290	.333	.381
1989	StL-N	199	3	.236	.275	.352	106	1	.255	.292	.349	93	2	.215	.255	.355	100	2	.220	.271	.350	99	1	.253	.279	.354	77	2	.156	.195	.273	122	1	.287	.326	.402
1990	StL-N	501	3	.335	.382	.437	273	1	.348	.388	.447	228	2	.320	.375	.425	302	1	.315	.370	.407	199	2	.367	.401	.482	197	2	.335	.362	.442	304	1	.336	.394	.434
1990	Oak-A	113	0	.274	.333	.336	55	0	.273	.333	.309	58	0	.276	.333	.362	0	0	—	—	—	113	0	.274	.333	.336	28	0	.250	.276	.321	85	0	.282	.351	.341
1991	SF-N	497	4	.312	.357	.408	222	2	.270	.306	.351	275	2	.345	.397	.455	259	4	.324	.372	.448	238	0	.298	.340	.366	154	2	.338	.380	.448	343	2	.300	.347	.391
1992	SF-N	474	1	.297	.339	.354	224	0	.317	.361	.384	250	1	.280	.318	.328	249	0	.305	.343	.349	225	1	.289	.333	.360	159	1	.283	.305	.365	315	0	.305	.355	.349
1993	SF-N	475	4	.301	.353	.389	217	0	.318	.374	.382	258	4	.287	.335	.395	251	1	.327	.374	.418	224	3	.272	.329	.357	144	1	.319	.349	.403	331	3	.293	.354	.384
1994	SF-N	156	5	.282	.337	.397	97	2	.299	.349	.381	59	3	.254	.318	.424	156	5	.282	.337	.397	0	0	—	—	—	43	2	.279	.326	.442	113	3	.283	.341	.381
1995	Bos-A	200	2	.285	.311	.400	105	1	.286	.315	.400	95	1	.284	.307	.400	0	0	—	—	—	200	2	.285	.311	.400	85	2	.341	.352	.529	115	0	.243	.281	.304
1996	StL-N	309	5	.307	.348	.417	151	2	.358	.394	.470	158	3	.259	.306	.367	180	3	.317	.356	.422	129	2	.295	.338	.411	88	3	.295	.311	.477	221	2	.312	.363	.394
1997	StL-N	300	3	.300	.347	.420	128	2	.336	.380	.477	172	1	.273	.323	.378	140	2	.300	.368	.421	160	1	.300	.327	.419	95	1	.274	.324	.389	205	2	.312	.357	.434
1998	StL-N	269	3	.253	.287	.331	113	0	.274	.323	.327	156	3	.237	.259	.333	181	1	.271	.306	.326	88	2	.216	.247	.341	76	0	.224	.241	.237	193	3	.264	.304	.368
1999	StL-N	271	0	.251	.293	.277	133	0	.241	.270	.271	138	0	.261	.315	.283	137	0	.263	.313	.299	134	0	.239	.271	.254	46	0	.174	.235	.196	225	0	.267	.305	.293
TOTALS		7649	79	.295	.333	.396	3712	36	.301	.337	.402	3937	43	.289	.329	.390	3762	35	.299	.341	.395	3887	44	.290	.325	.397	2441	43	.288	.318	.416	5208	36	.298	.340	.387
■ Fred McGriff BL/TL																																				
1986	Tor-A	5	0	.200	.200	.200	1	0	1.000	1.000	1.000	4	0	.000	.000	.000	5	0	.200	.200	.200	0	0	—	—	—	0	0	—	—	—	5	0	.200	.200	.200
1987	Tor-A	295	20	.247	.376	.505	139	7	.223	.368	.453	156	13	.269	.384	.551	127	7	.252	.383	.465	168	13	.244	.371	.536	26	1	.154	.241	.346	269	19	.257	.388	.520
1988	Tor-A	536	34	.282	.376	.552	250	18	.256	.363	.536	286	16	.304	.387	.566	248	15	.294	.397	.569	288	19	.271	.357	.538	171	5	.234	.307	.368	365	29	.304	.406	.638
1989	Tor-A	551	36	.269	.399	.525	273	18	.282	.406	.549	278	18	.255	.393	.500	275	17	.280	.381	.535	276	19	.257	.416	.514	189	5	.254	.360	.376	362	31	.276	.419	.602
1990	Tor-A	557	35	.300	.400	.530	264	14	.277	.399	.473	293	21	.321	.401	.580	235	16	.268	.399	.498	322	19	.323	.401	.553	202	8	.257	.324	.411	355	27	.324	.440	.597
1991	SD-N	528	31	.278	.396	.494	239	18	.280	.426	.536	289	13	.277	.369	.460	254	15	.272	.401	.488	274	16	.285	.391	.500	213	14	.272	.380	.512	315	17	.283	.406	.483
1992	SD-N	531	35	.286	.394	.556	273	21	.304	.406	.612	258	14	.267	.381	.496	240	14	.321	.431	.579	291	21	.258	.363	.536	205	13	.283	.369	.551	326	22	.288	.409	.558
1993	SD-N	302	18	.275	.361	.497	138	7	.225	.335	.391	164	11	.317	.384	.585	267	16	.258	.355	.476	35	2	.400	.410	.657	119	4	.252	.346	.378	183	14	.290	.371	.574
1993	Atl-N	255	19	.310	.392	.612	117	8	.350	.449	.624	138	11	.275	.340	.601	0	0	—	—	—	255	19	.310	.392	.612	82	4	.305	.367	.549	173	15	.312	.403	.642
1994	Atl-N	424	34	.318	.389	.623	201	13	.284	.365	.547	223	21	.350	.411	.691	287	19	.303	.386	.575	137	15	.350	.396	.723	157	10	.293	.351	.522	267	24	.333	.411	.682
1995	Atl-N	528	27	.280	.361	.489	261	15	.291	.368	.510	267	12	.270	.354	.468	215	10	.274	.376	.484	313	17	.284	.350	.492	188	6	.255	.332	.410	340	21	.294	.377	.532
1996	Atl-N	617	28	.295	.365	.494	312	17	.282	.344	.510	305	11	.308	.386	.479	313	19	.300	.361	.543	304	9	.289	.368	.444	200	11	.325	.369	.555	417	17	.281	.363	.465
1997	Atl-N	564	22	.277	.356	.441	294	8	.265	.338	.401	270	14	.289	.375	.485	296	10	.280	.362	.419	268	12	.272	.349	.466	183	6	.268	.362	.404	381	16	.281	.353	.459
1998	TB-A	564	19	.284	.371	.443	292	14	.305	.388	.493	272	5	.261	.354	.390	295	8	.264	.350	.397	269	11	.305	.394	.494	179	3	.274	.365	.369	385	16	.288	.374	.478
1999	TB-A	529	32	.310	.405	.552	241	18	.344	.433	.643	288	14	.281	.382	.476	267	19	.303	.407	.592	262	13	.317	.403	.511	148	8	.236	.319	.446	381	24	.339	.436	.593
2000	TB-A	566	27	.277	.373	.452	268	10	.243	.356	.381	298	17	.309	.390	.517	285	15	.281	.364	.477	281	12	.274	.383	.427	161	10	.273	.355	.484	405	17	.279	.380	.440
TOTALS		7352	417	.286	.381	.512	3563	206	.282	.382	.510	3789	211	.290	.380	.515	3609	200	.283	.381	.507	3743	217	.289	.381	.517	2423	108	.269	.350	.451	4929	309	.295	.396	.543
■ Mark McGwire BR/TR																																				
1986	Oak-A	53	3	.189	.259	.377	21	1	.143	.250	.286	32	2	.219	.265	.438	0	0	—	—	—	53	3	.189	.259	.377	36	2	.250	.325	.444	17	1	.059	.111	.235
1987	Oak-A	557	49	.289	.370	.618	278	21	.277	.366	.572	279	28	.301	.373	.663	245	28	.282	.373	.682	312	21	.295	.367	.567	171	16	.287	.400	.626	386	33	.290	.355	.614
1988	Oak-A	550	32	.260	.352	.478	256	12	.246	.347	.430	294	20	.272	.356	.520	275	13	.236	.335	.429	275	19	.284	.368	.527	150	11	.247	.358	.533	400	21	.265	.349	.458
1989	Oak-A	490	33	.231	.339	.467	246	12	.232	.321	.427	244	21	.230	.357	.508	229	15	.245	.331	.480	261	18	.218	.346	.456	132	6	.235	.344	.439	358	27	.229	.337	.478
1990	Oak-A	523	39	.235	.370	.489	245	14	.224	.369	.429	278	25	.245	.370	.543	232	20	.228	.366	.509	291	19	.241	.373	.474	132	11	.258	.387	.530	391	28	.228	.364	.476
1991	Oak-A	483	22	.201	.330	.383	243	15	.185	.329	.412	240	7	.217	.332	.354	231	13	.203	.361	.416	252	9	.198	.300	.353	130	5	.200	.316	.354	353	17	.201	.336	.394
1992	Oak-A	467	42	.268	.385	.585	218	24	.252	.398	.619	249	18	.281	.373	.554	262	26	.279	.406	.618	205	16	.254	.358	.541	97	14	.330	.447	.804	370	28	.251	.368	.527
1993	Oak-A	84	9	.333	.467	.726	41	5	.341	.491	.756	43	4	.326	.442	.698	83	9	.337	.467	.735	1	0	.000	.500	.000	22	3	.455	.556	1.000	62	6	.290	.438	.629
1994	Oak-A	135	9	.252	.413	.474	62	6	.210	.395	.516	73	3	.288	.429	.438	77	5	.273	.462	.506	58	4	.224	.338	.431	62	4	.194	.405	.403	73	5	.301	.420	.534
1995	Oak-A	317	39	.274	.441	.685	145	15	.248	.425	.586	172	24	.297	.454	.767	191	22	.288	.444	.681	126	17	.254	.436	.690	79	14	.278	.478	.835	238	25	.273	.427	.634
1996	Oak-A	423	52	.312	.467	.730	213	24	.310	.464	.704	210	28	.314	.471	.757	186	25	.328	.490	.796	237	27	.300	.449	.679	102	12	.373	.511	.784	321	40	.293	.453	.713
1997	Oak-A	366	34	.284	.383	.628	164	17	.329	.433	.744	202	17	.248	.343	.535	280	29	.279	.380	.650	86	5	.302	.394	.558	76	7	.303	.448	.671	290	27	.279	.365	.617
1997	StL-N	174	24	.253	.411	.684	84	13	.286	.445	.762	90	11	.222	.377	.611	0	0	—	—	—	174	24	.253	.411	.684	41	5	.244	.415	.634	133	19	.256	.409	.699
1998	StL-N	509	70	.299	.470	.752	263	38	.316	.497	.787	246	32	.280	.438	.715	257	37	.319	.481	.798	252	33	.278	.459	.706	130	15	.254	.459	.631	379	55	.314	.474	.794
1999	StL-N	521	65	.278	.424	.697	260	37	.285	.436	.765	261	28	.272	.411	.628	252	23	.258	.411	.583	269	42	.297	.435	.803	122	16	.254	.425	.705	399	49	.286	.423	.694
2000	StL-N	236	32	.305	.483	.746	120	18	.342	.530	.817	116	14	.267	.431	.672	207	29	.300	.479	.754	29	3	.345	.513	.690	53	8	.321	.507	.830	183	24	.301	.476	.721
TOTALS		5888	554	.267	.398	.593	2859	272	.266	.406	.597	3029	282	.267	.390	.589	3007	294	.271	.407	.612	2881	260	.262	.388	.574	1535	149	.270	.414	.610	4353	405	.266	.392	.587
■ Mark McLemore BB/TR																																				
1986	Cal-A	4	0	.000	.200	.000	1	0	.000	.500	.000	3	0	.000	.000	.000	0	0	—	—	—	4	0	.000	.200	.000	0	0	—	—	—	4	0	.000	.200	.000

		TOTAL					HOME					AWAY					1ST HALF					2ND HALF					LEFT					RIGHT				
YEAR	TM/L	AB	HR	AVG	OBP	SLG	AB	HR	AVG	OBP	SLG	AB	HR	AVG	OBP	SLG	AB	HR	AVG	OBP	SLG	AB	HR	AVG	OBP	SLG	AB	HR	AVG	OBP	SLG	AB	HR	AVG	OBP	SLG
1987	Cal-A	433	3	.236	.310	.300	213	3	.235	.315	.319	220	0	.236	.305	.282	252	0	.226	.309	.278	181	3	.249	.312	.331	126	1	.222	.293	.294	307	2	.241	.317	.303
1988	Cal-A	233	2	.240	.312	.330	102	1	.216	.298	.294	131	1	.260	.322	.359	167	1	.251	.333	.341	66	1	.212	.254	.303	65	0	.200	.268	.246	168	2	.256	.328	.363
1989	Cal-A	103	0	.243	.295	.291	43	0	.302	.362	.372	60	0	.200	.246	.233	62	0	.242	.277	.290	41	0	.244	.319	.293	35	0	.314	.351	.400	68	0	.206	.267	.235
1990	Cal-A	48	0	.146	.212	.188	26	0	.154	.267	.192	22	0	.136	.136	.182	48	0	.146	.212	.188	0	0	—	—	—	17	0	.235	.235	.294	31	0	.097	.200	.129
1990	Cle-A	12	0	.167	.167	.167	6	0	.333	.333	.333	6	0	.000	.000	.000	0	0	—	—	—	12	0	.167	.167	.167	5	0	.200	.200	.200	7	0	.143	.143	.143
1991	Hou-N	61	0	.148	.221	.164	34	0	.088	.158	.088	27	0	.222	.300	.259	61	0	.148	.221	.164	0	0	—	—	—	28	0	.179	.233	.214	33	0	.121	.211	.121
1992	Bal-A	228	0	.246	.308	.294	111	0	.198	.250	.252	117	0	.291	.362	.333	126	0	.230	.315	.262	102	0	.265	.299	.333	58	0	.276	.333	.310	170	0	.235	.299	.288
1993	Bal-A	581	4	.284	.353	.368	293	2	.314	.377	.399	288	2	.253	.328	.337	263	2	.297	.358	.384	318	2	.274	.348	.355	162	0	.216	.270	.253	419	4	.310	.383	.413
1994	Bal-A	343	3	.257	.354	.321	162	2	.272	.355	.340	181	1	.243	.352	.304	236	2	.267	.366	.326	107	1	.234	.325	.308	54	0	.167	.318	.185	289	3	.273	.361	.346
1995	Tex-A	467	5	.261	.346	.358	240	3	.292	.375	.400	227	2	.229	.315	.313	206	3	.296	.395	.388	261	2	.234	.304	.333	131	1	.267	.358	.359	336	4	.259	.341	.357
1996	Tex-A	517	5	.290	.389	.379	252	3	.294	.407	.393	265	2	.287	.372	.366	239	2	.326	.425	.414	278	3	.259	.357	.349	160	1	.250	.354	.294	357	4	.308	.405	.417
1997	Tex-A	349	1	.261	.338	.330	188	0	.234	.313	.298	161	1	.292	.368	.366	188	0	.234	.329	.287	161	1	.292	.350	.379	90	0	.267	.330	.333	259	1	.259	.341	.328
1998	Tex-A	461	5	.247	.369	.317	239	4	.259	.395	.360	222	1	.234	.341	.270	230	4	.296	.419	.387	231	1	.199	.319	.247	135	0	.259	.394	.319	326	5	.242	.359	.316
1999	Tex-A	566	6	.274	.363	.366	279	2	.305	.393	.391	287	4	.244	.334	.341	262	3	.279	.366	.374	304	3	.270	.361	.359	104	1	.163	.252	.221	462	5	.299	.388	.398
2000	Sea-A	481	3	.245	.353	.316	227	2	.220	.342	.282	254	1	.268	.363	.346	246	1	.232	.355	.285	235	2	.260	.351	.349	75	1	.293	.393	.373	406	2	.236	.345	.305
TOTALS		4887	37	.258	.346	.334	2416	22	.264	.356	.345	2471	15	.252	.336	.323	2586	18	.263	.357	.334	2301	19	.252	.333	.333	1245	5	.237	.323	.294	3642	32	.265	.353	.348
■ **Brian McRae**	BB/TR																																			
1990	KC-A	168	2	.286	.318	.405	81	1	.309	.348	.469	87	1	.264	.289	.345	0	0	—	—	—	168	2	.286	.318	.405	72	1	.361	.382	.458	96	1	.229	.272	.365
1991	KC-A	629	8	.261	.288	.372	318	3	.267	.305	.384	311	5	.254	.270	.360	272	4	.254	.287	.360	357	4	.266	.288	.381	204	2	.294	.326	.407	425	6	.245	.270	.355
1992	KC-A	533	4	.223	.285	.308	257	2	.245	.301	.346	276	2	.203	.271	.272	272	2	.221	.282	.313	261	2	.226	.289	.303	163	3	.233	.282	.362	370	1	.219	.287	.284
1993	KC-A	627	12	.282	.325	.413	321	5	.287	.322	.408	306	7	.278	.328	.418	308	3	.308	.350	.422	319	9	.257	.300	.404	199	5	.322	.340	.477	428	7	.264	.318	.383
1994	KC-A	436	4	.273	.359	.378	221	2	.285	.377	.389	215	2	.260	.339	.367	295	3	.288	.376	.414	141	1	.241	.321	.305	127	1	.307	.380	.425	309	3	.259	.350	.359
1995	Chi-N	580	12	.288	.348	.440	283	6	.286	.350	.428	297	6	.290	.346	.451	243	5	.272	.331	.436	337	7	.300	.360	.442	163	2	.313	.333	.429	417	10	.278	.353	.444
1996	Chi-N	624	17	.276	.360	.425	304	9	.289	.380	.454	320	8	.262	.340	.397	327	3	.272	.353	.364	297	14	.279	.367	.492	142	2	.296	.346	.401	482	15	.270	.364	.432
1997	Chi-N	417	6	.240	.329	.372	217	4	.267	.350	.424	200	2	.210	.307	.315	308	4	.231	.296	.354	109	2	.266	.412	.422	107	3	.290	.339	.486	310	3	.223	.326	.332
1997	NY-N	145	5	.248	.317	.414	80	2	.300	.345	.450	65	3	.185	.284	.369	0	0	—	—	—	145	5	.248	.317	.414	37	1	.243	.317	.324	108	4	.250	.317	.444
1998	NY-N	552	21	.264	.360	.462	266	12	.271	.371	.481	286	9	.259	.349	.444	247	10	.235	.358	.437	305	11	.289	.362	.482	151	2	.252	.341	.364	401	19	.269	.367	.499
1999	NY-N	298	8	.221	.320	.349	139	5	.194	.307	.338	159	3	.245	.331	.358	233	7	.240	.333	.378	65	1	.154	.273	.246	61	0	.230	.288	.279	237	8	.219	.327	.367
1999	Col-N	23	1	.261	.370	.478	0	0	—	—	—	23	1	.261	.370	.478	0	0	—	—	—	23	1	.261	.370	.478	1	0	.000	.500	.000	22	1	.273	.360	.500
1999	Tor-A	82	3	.195	.340	.366	35	1	.171	.310	.286	47	2	.213	.362	.426	0	0	—	—	—	82	3	.195	.340	.366	29	1	.310	.429	.586	53	2	.132	.292	.245
TOTALS		5114	103	.261	.331	.396	2522	52	.271	.342	.412	2592	51	.252	.320	.381	2505	41	.259	.331	.385	2609	62	.263	.330	.406	1456	23	.289	.337	.415	3658	80	.250	.328	.388
■ **Hal McRae**	BR/TR																																			
1978	KC-A	623	16	.273	.329	.429	304	8	.303	.352	.467	319	8	.245	.306	.392	301	9	.266	.318	.439	322	7	.280	.338	.419	192	8	.286	.340	.495	431	8	.267	.324	.399
1979	KC-A	393	10	.288	.351	.466	201	5	.323	.381	.537	192	5	.250	.320	.391	199	4	.241	.302	.412	194	6	.335	.401	.521	124	5	.250	.305	.444	269	5	.305	.372	.476
1980	KC-A	489	14	.297	.342	.483	233	6	.313	.344	.498	256	8	.281	.340	.469	180	5	.250	.313	.417	309	9	.324	.359	.521	197	5	.320	.364	.497	292	9	.281	.327	.473
1981	KC-A	389	7	.272	.330	.396	176	2	.227	.267	.335	213	5	.310	.379	.446	194	4	.242	.281	.351	195	3	.303	.377	.441	127	1	.252	.329	.331	262	6	.282	.331	.427
1982	KC-A	613	27	.308	.369	.542	304	12	.299	.358	.526	309	15	.317	.379	.557	279	12	.323	.394	.552	334	15	.296	.347	.533	208	14	.313	.371	.596	405	13	.306	.368	.514
1983	KC-A	589	12	.311	.372	.462	290	5	.341	.404	.510	299	7	.281	.340	.415	259	4	.332	.397	.486	330	8	.294	.352	.442	190	5	.342	.416	.547	399	7	.296	.350	.421
1984	KC-A	317	3	.303	.363	.397	173	2	.312	.371	.428	144	1	.292	.354	.361	199	1	.266	.330	.342	118	2	.364	.418	.492	157	3	.331	.388	.459	160	0	.275	.337	.338
1985	KC-A	320	14	.259	.349	.450	165	7	.267	.349	.461	155	7	.252	.348	.439	83	5	.229	.356	.470	237	9	.270	.346	.443	150	8	.233	.345	.467	170	6	.282	.353	.435
1986	KC-A	278	7	.252	.298	.378	125	1	.272	.331	.360	153	6	.235	.270	.392	140	3	.243	.285	.393	138	4	.261	.311	.362	153	5	.268	.325	.431	125	2	.232	.263	.312
1987	KC-A	32	1	.313	.405	.500	22	1	.227	.320	.455	10	0	.500	.583	.600	30	1	.333	.412	.533	2	0	.000	.333	.000	16	1	.438	.571	.750	16	0	.188	.188	.250
TOTALS		4043	111	.288	.348	.454	1993	49	.300	.355	.471	2050	62	.277	.341	.438	1864	48	.275	.337	.437	2179	63	.300	.357	.468	1514	55	.295	.360	.487	2529	56	.284	.340	.434
■ **Kevin McReynolds**	BR/TR																																			
1983	SD-N	140	4	.221	.277	.343	76	3	.237	.314	.408	64	1	.203	.232	.266	73	2	.178	.235	.301	67	2	.269	.324	.388	35	1	.171	.286	.314	105	3	.238	.274	.352
1984	SD-N	525	20	.278	.317	.465	264	10	.299	.347	.496	261	10	.257	.286	.433	253	11	.277	.303	.482	272	9	.279	.329	.449	161	9	.267	.331	.509	364	11	.283	.310	.445
1985	SD-N	564	15	.234	.290	.371	264	6	.235	.282	.360	300	9	.233	.297	.380	276	8	.261	.319	.406	288	7	.208	.261	.337	173	3	.260	.340	.370	391	12	.223	.266	.371
1986	SD-N	560	26	.287	.358	.504	276	14	.293	.368	.514	284	12	.282	.349	.493	269	12	.275	.345	.491	291	14	.299	.370	.515	192	10	.339	.395	.589	368	16	.261	.339	.459
1987	NY-N	590	29	.276	.318	.495	298	18	.275	.324	.503	292	11	.277	.312	.486	262	14	.282	.332	.508	328	15	.271	.307	.485	221	12	.290	.325	.534	369	17	.268	.314	.472
1988	NY-N	552	27	.288	.336	.496	279	13	.276	.320	.470	273	14	.300	.351	.524	267	9	.273	.326	.423	285	18	.302	.344	.565	185	12	.270	.308	.546	367	15	.297	.349	.471
1989	NY-N	545	22	.272	.326	.450	274	12	.266	.330	.445	271	10	.277	.321	.454	254	7	.283	.349	.409	291	15	.261	.305	.485	189	10	.296	.377	.508	356	12	.258	.297	.419
1990	NY-N	521	24	.269	.353	.455	244	11	.258	.336	.426	277	13	.278	.368	.480	226	12	.252	.361	.460	295	12	.281	.346	.451	194	4	.232	.358	.351	327	20	.291	.350	.517
1991	NY-N	522	16	.259	.322	.416	236	7	.237	.289	.386	286	9	.276	.349	.441	232	7	.293	.354	.470	290	9	.231	.297	.372	189	6	.259	.311	.418	333	10	.258	.329	.414
1992	KC-A	373	13	.247	.357	.418	186	4	.253	.363	.398	187	9	.241	.351	.439	250	8	.244	.349	.404	123	5	.252	.373	.447	113	5	.345	.461	.575	260	8	.204	.309	.350
1993	KC-A	351	11	.245	.316	.425	194	8	.284	.340	.515	157	3	.197	.289	.312	114	3	.228	.307	.404	237	8	.253	.321	.435	126	2	.222	.333	.349	225	9	.258	.306	.467
1994	NY-N	180	4	.256	.328	.406	86	3	.291	.351	.477	94	1	.223	.308	.340	149	4	.248	.319	.416	31	0	.290	.371	.355	43	1	.279	.404	.488	137	3	.248	.302	.380
TOTALS		5423	211	.265	.328	.447	2677	109	.268	.330	.453	2746	102	.263	.326	.442	2625	97	.266	.332	.442	2798	114	.265	.324	.452	1821	75	.276	.352	.473	3602	136	.260	.315	.434
■ **Pat Meares**	BR/TR																																			
1993	Min-A	346	0	.251	.266	.309	157	0	.287	.313	.338	189	0	.222	.225	.286	133	0	.316	.333	.398	213	0	.211	.224	.254	95	0	.242	.267	.253	251	0	.255	.266	.331
1994	Min-A	229	2	.266	.310	.354	108	0	.259	.289	.306	121	2	.273	.328	.397	159	2	.289	.337	.403	70	0	.214	.247	.243	62	0	.242	.294	.274	167	2	.275	.317	.383
1995	Min-A	390	12	.269	.311	.431	194	3	.268	.310	.397	196	9	.270	.313	.464	163	7	.294	.318	.497	227	5	.251	.307	.383	121	5	.231	.254	.413	269	7	.286	.336	.439
1996	Min-A	517	8	.267	.298	.391	272	3	.254	.267	.371	245	5	.282	.332	.412	256	5	.266	.294	.398	261	3	.268	.302	.383	138	4	.297	.333	.486	379	4	.256	.285	.356
1997	Min-A	439	10	.276	.323	.410	246	5	.244	.288	.370	193	5	.316	.366	.461	241	7	.286	.337	.461	198	3	.263	.305	.348	99	1	.182	.243	.263	340	9	.303	.347	.453
1998	Min-A	543	9	.260	.296	.368	261	2	.291	.339	.406	282	7	.230	.254	.333	279	5	.258	.298	.380	264	4	.261	.294	.356	133	3	.248	.284	.346	410	6	.263	.300	.376
1999	Pit-N	91	0	.308	.382	.352	33	0	.152	.282	.212	58	0	.397	.444	.431	74	0	.297	.373	.338	17	0	.353	.421	.412	44	0	.341	.396	.364	47	0	.277	.370	.340
2000	Pit-N	462	13	.240	.305	.381	222	7	.248	.303	.405	240	6	.233	.306	.358	255	5	.247	.298	.373	207	8	.232	.312	.391	121	3	.231	.306	.347	341	10	.243	.304	.393
TOTALS		3017	54	.263	.304	.380	1493	20	.261	.301	.374	1524	34	.264	.307	.386	1560	31	.276	.316	.408	1457	23	.248	.291	.349	813	16	.247	.291	.354	2204	38	.268	.309	.389
■ **Orlando Merced**	BB/TR																																			
1990	Pit-N	24	0	.208	.240	.250	12	0	.250	.308	.333	12	0	.167	.167	.167	4	0	.250	.250	.500	20	0	.200	.238	.200	8	0	.125	.125	.125	16	0	.250	.294	.313
1991	Pit-N	411	10	.275	.373	.399	192	5	.255	.370	.391	219	5	.292	.376	.406	157	4	.268	.366	.401	254	6	.280	.378	.398	53	0	.208	.263	.302	358	10	.285	.388	.413
1992	Pit-N	405	6	.247	.332	.385	199	4	.251	.345	.407	206	2	.243	.319	.364	189	3	.243	.335	.402	216	3	.250	.329	.370	84	0	.190	.306	.226	321	6	.262	.339	.427
1993	Pit-N	447	8	.313	.414	.443	205	3	.298	.401	.415	242	5	.326	.425	.467	220	5	.350	.450	.464	227	3	.278	.377	.423	111	0	.297	.386	.405	336	8	.318	.423	.455
1994	Pit-N	386	9	.272	.343	.412	201	4	.249	.338	.383	185	5	.297	.350	.443	251	5	.299	.364	.442	135	4	.222	.305	.356	96	3	.281	.361	.427	290	6	.269	.337	.407
1995	Pit-N	487	15	.300	.365	.468	242	8	.306	.376	.479	245	7	.294	.354	.457	180	4	.272	.323	.417	307	11	.316	.389	.498	120	5	.225	.301	.408	367	10	.324	.386	.488
1996	Pit-N	453	17	.287	.357	.457	205	9	.322	.390	.527	248	8	.258	.330	.399	242	11	.277	.368	.463	211	6	.299	.343	.450	114	2	.263	.341	.412	339	15	.295	.362	.472
1997	Tor-A	368	9	.266	.352	.413	192	3	.307	.409	.453	176	6	.222	.287	.369	284	7	.282	.354	.444	84	2	.214	.347	.310	121	4	.223	.312	.364	247	5	.287	.372	.437
1998	Min-A	204	5	.289	.345	.422	108	3	.333	.365	.463	96	2	.240	.324	.375	180	5	.300	.344	.444	24	0	.208	.355	.250	13	1	.154	.267	.385	191	4	.298	.351	.424
1998	Bos-A	9	0	.000	.167	.000	3	0	.000	.000	.000	6	0	.000	.250	.000	0	0	—	—	—	9	0	.000	.167	.000	-2	0	.000	.000	.000	7	0	.000	.200	.000
1998	Chi-N	10	1	.300	.333	.600	6	1	.333	.333	.833	4	0	.250	.333	.250	0	0	—	—	—	10	1	.300	.333	.600	0	0	—	—	—	10	1	.300	.333	.600
1999	Mon-N	194	8	.268	.353	.464	96	3	.313	.412	.521	98	5	.224	.290	.408	122	7	.279	.369	.516	72	1	.250	.325	.375	10	0	.300	.417	.400	184	8	.266	.349	.467
TOTALS		3398	88	.280	.361	.427	1661	43	.289	.376	.444	1737	45	.271	.346	.411	1829	51	.287	.366	.443	1569	37	.272	.355	.409	732	15	.242	.327	.370	2666	73	.290	.370	.443
■ **Eddie Milner**	BL/TL																																			
1980	Cin-N	3	0	.000	.000	.000	1	0	.000	.000	.000	2	0	.000	.000	.000	0	0	—	—	—	3	0	.000	.000	.000	0	0	—	—	—	3	0	.000	.000	.000
1981	Cin-N	5	0	.200	.333	.400	1	0	.000	.000	.000	4	0	.250	.400	.500	0	0	—	—	—	5	0	.200	.333	.400	0	0	—	1.000	—	5	0	.200	.200	.400
1982	Cin-N	407	4	.268	.338	.378	194	1	.289	.367	.412	213	3	.249	.310	.347	253	3	.269	.342	.391	154	1	.266	.331	.357	119	0	.286	.351	.361	288	4	.260	.332	.385
1983	Cin-N	502	9	.261	.350	.384	254	3	.268	.353	.390	248	6	.254	.346	.379	262	3	.237	.336	.332	240	6	.287	.365	.442	91	1	.143	.235	.242	411	8	.287	.374	.416
1984	Cin-N	336	7	.232	.333	.342	148	5	.264	.373	.399	188	2	.207	.301	.298	252	6	.258	.362	.389	84	1	.155	.242	.202	77	1	.221	.330	.312	259	6	.236	.334	.351
1985	Cin-N	453	3	.254	.342	.347	223	1	.247	.336	.350	230	2	.261	.347	.343	193	0	.233	.323	.275	260	3	.269	.356	.400	47	0	.213	.327	.234	406	3	.259	.343	.360
1986	Cin-N	424	15	.259	.317	.446	208	8	.288	.346	.486	216	7	.231	.288	.407	196	4	.240	.304	.378	228	11	.276	.328	.504	58	0	.224	.262	.276	366	15	.265	.325	.473
1987	SF-N	214	4	.252	.328	.374	110	4	.236	.317	.400	104	0	.269	.339	.346	49	1	.204	.235	.286	165	3	.267	.353	.400	32	0	.156	.229	.156	182	4	.269	.345	.412
1988	Cin-N	51	0	.176	.236	.196	18	0	.111	.158	.167	33	0	.212	.278	.212	21	0	.190	.261	.238	30	0	.167	.219	.167	14	0	.214	.267	.214	37	0	.162	.225	.189
TOTALS		2395	42	.253	.333	.376	1157	22	.264	.347	.401	1238	20	.243	.321	.352	1226	17	.246	.331	.351	1169	25	.262	.336	.402	438	2	.217	.299	.283	1957	40	.262	.341	.397
■ **Kevin Mitchell**	BR/TR																																			
1984	NY-N	14	0	.214	.214	.214	6	0	.167	.167	.167	8	0	.250	.250	.250	0	0	—	—	—	14	0	.214	.214	.214	7	0	.286	.286	.286	7	0	.143	.143	.143
1986	NY-N	328	12	.277	.344	.466	162	4	.302	.370	.481	166	8	.253	.319	.452	125	4	.368	.423	.584	203	8	.222	.296	.394	199	7	.307	.358	.503	129	5	.233	.324	.411

		TOTAL					HOME					AWAY					1ST HALF					2ND HALF					LEFT					RIGHT				
YEAR	TM/L	AB	HR	AVG	OBP	SLG	AB	HR	AVG	OBP	SLG	AB	HR	AVG	OBP	SLG	AB	HR	AVG	OBP	SLG	AB	HR	AVG	OBP	SLG	AB	HR	AVG	OBP	SLG	AB	HR	AVG	OBP	SLG
1987	SD-N	196	7	.245	.313	.398	83	2	.241	.312	.398	113	5	.248	.315	.398	185	5	.243	.316	.373	11	2	.273	.273	.818	66	4	.258	.338	.515	130	3	.238	.301	.338
1987	SF-N	268	15	.306	.376	.530	144	7	.319	.387	.521	124	8	.290	.362	.540	0	0	—	—	—	268	15	.306	.376	.530	73	6	.411	.488	.767	195	9	.267	.332	.441
1988	SF-N	505	19	.251	.319	.442	253	10	.265	.319	.470	252	9	.238	.318	.413	252	8	.246	.322	.433	253	11	.257	.315	.451	160	5	.200	.280	.338	345	14	.275	.337	.490
1989	SF-N	543	47	.291	.387	.635	255	22	.298	.403	.663	288	25	.285	.373	.611	283	25	.290	.373	.654	260	22	.292	.403	.615	171	19	.304	.426	.725	372	28	.285	.369	.594
1990	SF-N	524	35	.290	.360	.544	241	15	.278	.360	.515	283	20	.300	.360	.569	258	19	.310	.378	.589	266	16	.271	.342	.500	170	10	.306	.395	.547	354	25	.282	.342	.542
1991	SF-N	371	27	.256	.338	.515	190	9	.242	.307	.432	181	18	.271	.370	.602	132	13	.280	.386	.614	239	14	.243	.309	.460	114	7	.272	.370	.491	257	20	.249	.323	.525
1992	Sea-A	360	9	.286	.351	.428	207	5	.319	.368	.473	153	4	.242	.328	.366	252	5	.262	.320	.385	108	4	.343	.419	.528	92	5	.380	.438	.598	268	4	.254	.320	.369
1993	Cin-N	323	19	.341	.385	.601	186	10	.349	.386	.613	137	9	.328	.384	.584	211	11	.370	.406	.611	112	8	.286	.347	.580	94	8	.394	.424	.745	229	11	.319	.370	.541
1994	Cin-N	310	30	.326	.429	.681	170	18	.347	.462	.724	140	12	.300	.387	.629	206	19	.325	.413	.665	104	11	.327	.459	.712	78	9	.346	.441	.769	232	21	.319	.425	.651
1996	Bos-A	92	2	.304	.385	.413	48	1	.333	.418	.458	44	1	.273	.347	.364	58	1	.293	.349	.379	34	1	.324	.439	.471	25	0	.360	.448	.400	67	2	.284	.360	.418
1996	Cin-N	114	6	.325	.447	.579	62	5	.371	.500	.710	52	1	.269	.377	.423	0	0	—	—	—	114	6	.325	.447	.579	25	3	.440	.548	.880	89	3	.292	.418	.494
1997	Cle-A	59	4	.153	.275	.373	24	1	.167	.310	.292	35	3	.143	.250	.429	59	4	.153	.275	.373	0	0	—	—	—	18	1	.111	.200	.278	41	3	.171	.306	.415
1998	Oak-A	127	2	.228	.279	.346	76	1	.211	.250	.316	51	1	.255	.321	.392	79	0	.241	.302	.329	48	2	.208	.240	.375	78	2	.218	.265	.372	49	0	.245	.302	.306
TOTALS		4134	234	.284	.360	.520	2107	110	.295	.370	.528	2027	124	.272	.350	.511	2100	114	.290	.361	.525	2034	120	.278	.359	.515	1370	86	.303	.383	.562	2764	148	.274	.349	.499
■ **Paul Molitor** BR/TR																																				
1978	Mil-A	521	6	.273	.301	.372	260	4	.315	.328	.419	261	2	.230	.274	.326	268	5	.310	.336	.437	253	1	.233	.263	.304	136	1	.265	.288	.353	385	5	.275	.305	.379
1979	Mil-A	584	9	.322	.372	.469	283	3	.311	.356	.459	301	6	.332	.388	.478	288	5	.323	.375	.462	296	4	.321	.370	.476	142	4	.387	.446	.585	442	5	.301	.349	.432
1980	Mil-A	450	9	.304	.372	.438	218	2	.303	.385	.408	232	7	.306	.358	.466	190	4	.358	.439	.484	260	5	.265	.319	.404	165	5	.364	.412	.576	285	4	.270	.349	.358
1981	Mil-A	251	2	.267	.341	.335	113	1	.274	.349	.319	138	1	.261	.333	.348	77	1	.273	.333	.351	174	1	.264	.344	.328	73	0	.288	.358	.329	178	2	.258	.333	.337
1982	Mil-A	666	19	.302	.366	.450	318	9	.318	.381	.500	348	10	.287	.351	.405	285	7	.291	.367	.428	381	12	.310	.365	.467	225	4	.307	.359	.413	441	15	.299	.369	.469
1983	Mil-A	608	15	.270	.333	.410	299	9	.258	.327	.398	309	6	.282	.339	.421	253	5	.261	.323	.391	355	10	.276	.341	.423	217	9	.286	.368	.475	391	6	.261	.313	.373
1984	Mil-A	46	0	.217	.245	.239	21	0	.238	.273	.286	25	0	.200	.222	.200	46	0	.217	.245	.239	0	0	—	—	—	24	0	.250	.280	.250	22	0	.182	.208	.227
1985	Mil-A	576	10	.297	.356	.408	257	6	.323	.382	.467	319	4	.276	.334	.361	268	7	.317	.388	.466	308	3	.279	.326	.357	179	5	.324	.384	.464	397	5	.285	.343	.383
1986	Mil-A	437	9	.281	.340	.426	213	5	.300	.345	.451	224	4	.263	.335	.402	120	3	.283	.379	.458	317	6	.281	.324	.413	100	1	.270	.318	.400	337	8	.285	.346	.433
1987	Mil-A	465	16	.353	.438	.566	231	7	.394	.470	.610	234	9	.312	.406	.521	155	4	.323	.397	.503	310	12	.368	.457	.597	145	3	.331	.426	.476	320	13	.363	.443	.606
1988	Mil-A	609	13	.312	.384	.452	316	9	.316	.382	.468	293	4	.307	.386	.433	277	3	.318	.392	.408	332	10	.307	.377	.488	196	4	.276	.353	.393	413	9	.329	.399	.479
1989	Mil-A	615	11	.315	.379	.439	296	6	.328	.399	.453	319	5	.304	.359	.426	287	5	.307	.375	.436	328	6	.323	.382	.442	157	4	.325	.413	.484	458	7	.312	.366	.424
1990	Mil-A	418	12	.285	.343	.464	185	6	.286	.343	.470	233	6	.283	.343	.459	189	7	.291	.346	.476	229	5	.279	.340	.454	112	5	.313	.364	.563	306	7	.275	.335	.428
1991	Mil-A	665	17	.325	.399	.489	315	7	.292	.374	.454	350	10	.354	.422	.520	290	8	.334	.404	.524	375	9	.317	.395	.461	174	5	.322	.405	.489	491	12	.326	.397	.489
1992	Mil-A	609	12	.320	.389	.461	286	4	.304	.390	.420	323	8	.334	.389	.498	273	10	.322	.390	.505	336	2	.318	.388	.426	132	6	.424	.464	.659	477	6	.291	.369	.407
1993	Tor-A	636	22	.332	.402	.509	316	13	.364	.431	.573	320	9	.300	.374	.447	313	9	.319	.399	.463	323	13	.344	.405	.554	171	7	.363	.446	.585	465	15	.320	.385	.482
1994	Tor-A	454	14	.341	.410	.518	230	8	.378	.430	.570	224	6	.304	.390	.464	298	8	.329	.401	.493	156	6	.365	.426	.564	110	5	.391	.481	.627	344	9	.326	.385	.483
1995	Tor-A	525	15	.270	.350	.423	252	6	.270	.361	.417	273	9	.271	.339	.429	189	4	.233	.327	.339	336	11	.292	.362	.470	111	4	.279	.371	.468	414	11	.268	.343	.411
1996	Min-A	660	9	.341	.390	.468	334	6	.359	.399	.500	326	3	.322	.381	.436	325	6	.320	.371	.434	335	3	.361	.409	.501	148	2	.345	.426	.466	512	7	.340	.379	.469
1997	Min-A	538	10	.305	.351	.435	289	5	.322	.365	.450	249	5	.285	.336	.418	244	3	.324	.374	.447	294	7	.289	.332	.425	113	0	.336	.395	.407	425	10	.296	.339	.442
1998	Min-A	502	4	.281	.335	.382	260	0	.292	.337	.369	242	4	.269	.333	.397	262	1	.279	.336	.359	240	3	.283	.335	.408	121	1	.264	.328	.380	381	3	.286	.337	.383
TOTALS		10835	234	.306	.369	.448	5292	116	.317	.378	.462	5543	118	.296	.360	.434	4897	105	.308	.373	.445	5938	129	.305	.365	.451	2951	75	.322	.391	.479	7884	159	.300	.361	.436
■ **Raul Mondesi** BR/TR																																				
1993	LA-N	86	4	.291	.322	.488	43	2	.302	.318	.488	43	2	.279	.326	.488	0	0	—	—	—	86	4	.291	.322	.488	54	2	.315	.339	.519	32	2	.250	.294	.438
1994	LA-N	434	16	.306	.333	.516	210	10	.281	.306	.486	224	6	.330	.357	.545	299	13	.321	.339	.548	135	3	.274	.319	.444	122	4	.262	.278	.434	312	12	.324	.354	.548
1995	LA-N	536	26	.285	.328	.496	257	13	.288	.330	.502	279	13	.283	.326	.491	241	13	.320	.368	.568	295	13	.258	.295	.437	112	5	.250	.315	.473	424	21	.295	.331	.502
1996	LA-N	634	24	.297	.334	.495	298	11	.309	.343	.500	336	13	.286	.327	.491	314	16	.261	.291	.478	320	8	.331	.376	.512	113	4	.274	.322	.442	521	20	.301	.337	.507
1997	LA-N	616	30	.310	.360	.541	304	16	.316	.360	.556	312	14	.304	.360	.526	299	16	.288	.340	.525	317	14	.331	.379	.555	148	7	.284	.355	.500	468	23	.318	.362	.553
1998	LA-N	580	30	.279	.316	.497	281	13	.253	.287	.438	299	17	.304	.344	.552	313	17	.278	.315	.508	267	13	.281	.317	.483	116	6	.241	.285	.422	464	24	.289	.324	.515
1999	LA-N	601	33	.253	.332	.483	286	18	.266	.349	.510	315	15	.241	.317	.457	287	19	.261	.343	.523	314	14	.245	.323	.446	139	6	.273	.389	.468	462	27	.247	.314	.487
2000	Tor-A	388	24	.271	.329	.523	202	10	.252	.301	.485	186	14	.290	.357	.565	312	18	.276	.328	.519	76	6	.250	.329	.539	74	4	.311	.386	.541	314	20	.261	.315	.519
TOTALS		3875	187	.286	.333	.506	1881	93	.283	.327	.498	1994	94	.289	.339	.513	2065	112	.285	.331	.523	1810	75	.287	.337	.487	878	38	.272	.334	.469	2997	149	.290	.333	.517
■ **Mickey Morandini** BL/TR																																				
1990	Phi-N	79	1	.241	.294	.329	47	1	.298	.340	.383	32	0	.156	.229	.250	0	0	—	—	—	79	1	.241	.294	.329	15	0	.133	.188	.200	64	1	.266	.319	.359
1991	Phi-N	325	1	.249	.313	.317	166	1	.235	.295	.313	159	0	.264	.331	.321	152	1	.257	.321	.303	173	0	.243	.305	.329	65	0	.185	.221	.185	260	1	.265	.334	.350
1992	Phi-N	422	3	.265	.305	.344	202	2	.272	.313	.366	220	1	.259	.298	.323	178	2	.247	.311	.354	244	1	.279	.300	.336	121	1	.198	.240	.248	301	2	.292	.331	.382
1993	Phi-N	425	3	.247	.309	.355	225	2	.262	.311	.360	200	1	.230	.306	.350	256	1	.242	.292	.352	169	2	.254	.333	.361	99	1	.212	.284	.303	326	2	.258	.317	.371
1994	Phi-N	274	2	.292	.378	.409	142	1	.261	.352	.380	132	1	.326	.407	.439	161	1	.280	.383	.404	113	1	.310	.371	.416	51	0	.235	.361	.353	223	2	.305	.382	.422
1995	Phi-N	494	6	.283	.350	.417	242	3	.302	.370	.426	252	3	.266	.330	.409	195	4	.287	.347	.436	299	2	.281	.351	.405	105	1	.229	.287	.343	389	5	.298	.367	.437
1996	Phi-N	539	3	.250	.321	.334	262	2	.240	.313	.336	277	1	.260	.329	.332	256	1	.262	.340	.359	283	2	.240	.304	.311	104	0	.240	.322	.308	435	3	.253	.321	.340
1997	Phi-N	553	1	.295	.371	.380	267	1	.288	.371	.375	286	0	.301	.371	.385	287	1	.310	.388	.418	266	0	.278	.353	.338	128	0	.305	.416	.367	425	1	.292	.357	.384
1998	Chi-N	582	8	.296	.380	.385	275	4	.320	.423	.425	307	4	.274	.340	.349	287	4	.317	.403	.436	295	4	.275	.358	.336	156	0	.224	.337	.250	426	8	.322	.397	.434
1999	Chi-N	456	4	.241	.319	.329	219	3	.269	.348	.384	237	1	.215	.292	.278	243	1	.263	.326	.350	213	3	.216	.311	.305	97	0	.155	.255	.237	359	4	.265	.337	.354
2000	Phi-N	302	0	.252	.324	.315	152	0	.243	.327	.322	150	0	.260	.321	.307	217	0	.244	.318	.304	85	0	.271	.340	.341	50	0	.200	.245	.220	252	0	.262	.339	.333
2000	Tor-A	107	0	.271	.316	.308	54	0	.278	.328	.352	53	0	.264	.304	.264	0	0	—	—	—	107	0	.271	.316	.308	6	0	.167	.167	.167	101	0	.277	.324	.317
TOTALS		4558	32	.268	.338	.359	2253	20	.273	.347	.372	2305	12	.263	.329	.345	2232	16	.273	.346	.375	2326	16	.263	.330	.343	997	3	.221	.304	.283	3561	29	.281	.348	.380
■ **Keith Moreland** BR/TR																																				
1978	Phi-N	2	0	.000	.000	.000	0	0	—	—	—	2	0	.000	.000	.000	0	0	—	—	—	2	0	.000	.000	.000	0	0	—	—	—	2	0	.000	.000	.000
1979	Phi-N	48	0	.375	.412	.521	35	0	.400	.417	.600	13	0	.308	.400	.308	0	0	—	—	—	48	0	.375	.412	.521	16	0	.438	.438	.500	32	0	.344	.400	.531
1980	Phi-N	159	4	.314	.341	.440	88	1	.307	.326	.386	71	3	.324	.359	.507	46	2	.239	.250	.435	113	2	.345	.377	.442	53	0	.302	.321	.396	106	4	.321	.351	.462
1981	Phi-N	196	6	.255	.307	.383	108	4	.269	.339	.417	88	2	.239	.264	.341	60	2	.233	.262	.383	136	4	.265	.327	.382	40	0	.250	.348	.275	156	6	.256	.296	.410
1982	Chi-N	476	15	.261	.326	.399	239	8	.247	.327	.406	237	7	.274	.324	.392	273	10	.275	.336	.425	203	5	.241	.313	.365	124	5	.298	.409	.460	352	10	.247	.293	.378
1983	Chi-N	533	16	.302	.378	.460	263	8	.312	.385	.475	270	8	.293	.371	.444	253	11	.300	.360	.490	280	5	.304	.393	.432	134	7	.388	.472	.627	399	9	.273	.345	.404
1984	Chi-N	495	16	.279	.326	.422	244	13	.262	.321	.463	251	3	.295	.331	.382	180	6	.267	.338	.417	315	10	.286	.318	.425	161	7	.298	.361	.497	334	9	.269	.308	.386
1985	Chi-N	587	14	.307	.374	.440	300	11	.340	.411	.517	287	3	.272	.336	.359	255	6	.302	.382	.427	332	8	.310	.369	.449	124	3	.315	.415	.460	463	11	.305	.363	.434
1986	Chi-N	586	12	.271	.326	.384	297	8	.293	.339	.438	289	4	.249	.314	.329	278	7	.277	.335	.396	308	5	.266	.318	.373	147	5	.306	.395	.449	439	7	.260	.301	.362
1987	Chi-N	563	27	.266	.309	.465	272	19	.290	.338	.548	291	8	.244	.282	.388	285	13	.232	.267	.407	278	14	.302	.352	.525	122	3	.295	.362	.451	441	24	.259	.294	.469
1988	SD-N	511	5	.256	.305	.331	235	3	.268	.327	.336	276	2	.246	.286	.326	251	3	.275	.324	.367	260	2	.238	.288	.296	179	2	.240	.303	.307	332	3	.265	.307	.343
1989	Det-A	318	5	.299	.357	.396	158	2	.278	.333	.361	160	3	.319	.381	.431	224	5	.304	.368	.424	94	0	.287	.330	.330	119	2	.328	.385	.437	199	3	.281	.341	.372
1989	Bal-A	107	1	.215	.243	.280	56	0	.214	.214	.250	51	1	.216	.273	.314	0	0	—	—	—	107	1	.215	.243	.280	58	0	.207	.220	.241	49	1	.224	.269	.327
TOTALS		4581	121	.279	.335	.411	2295	77	.288	.347	.444	2286	44	.270	.323	.378	2105	65	.276	.334	.418	2476	56	.282	.336	.405	1277	34	.301	.375	.439	3304	87	.271	.319	.401
■ **Omar Moreno** BL/TL																																				
1978	Pit-N	515	2	.235	.339	.303	263	1	.266	.373	.331	252	1	.202	.304	.274	239	1	.209	.314	.264	276	1	.257	.361	.337	174	1	.144	.261	.190	341	1	.282	.379	.361
1979	Pit-N	695	8	.282	.333	.381	334	1	.293	.351	.359	361	7	.271	.316	.402	300	4	.300	.353	.400	395	4	.268	.318	.367	247	2	.287	.347	.368	448	6	.279	.325	.388
1980	Pit-N	676	2	.249	.306	.325	330	1	.261	.320	.352	346	1	.237	.293	.301	307	2	.274	.331	.375	369	0	.228	.285	.285	231	0	.238	.275	.320	445	2	.254	.321	.328
1981	Pit-N	434	1	.276	.319	.362	202	0	.257	.301	.342	232	1	.293	.335	.379	211	0	.261	.295	.332	223	1	.291	.342	.390	139	0	.288	.338	.388	295	1	.271	.310	.349
1982	Pit-N	645	3	.245	.292	.315	317	1	.278	.313	.372	328	2	.213	.271	.259	304	1	.237	.282	.289	341	2	.252	.301	.337	174	1	.195	.238	.253	471	2	.263	.311	.338
1983	Hou-N	405	0	.242	.282	.326	202	0	.257	.294	.356	203	0	.227	.270	.296	303	0	.241	.280	.320	102	0	.245	.287	.343	100	0	.200	.245	.270	305	0	.256	.294	.344
1983	NY-A	152	1	.250	.287	.342	70	1	.357	.375	.543	82	0	.159	.216	.171	0	0	—	—	—	152	1	.250	.287	.342	65	1	.262	.284	.385	87	0	.241	.290	.310
1984	NY-A	355	4	.259	.294	.361	175	2	.234	.270	.337	180	2	.283	.317	.383	132	1	.227	.266	.311	223	3	.278	.310	.390	67	0	.209	.267	.269	288	4	.271	.300	.382
1985	NY-A	66	1	.197	.209	.333	26	1	.269	.296	.538	40	0	.150	.150	.200	52	1	.192	.208	.308	14	0	.214	.214	.429	7	0	.286	.286	.571	59	1	.186	.200	.305
1985	KC-A	70	2	.243	.280	.429	39	2	.333	.372	.667	31	0	.129	.156	.129	0	0	—	—	—	70	2	.243	.280	.429	9	0	.222	.222	.222	61	2	.246	.288	.459
1986	Atl-N	359	4	.234	.276	.351	181	3	.282	.323	.420	178	1	.185	.229	.281	159	1	.245	.302	.390	200	3	.225	.255	.320	41	0	.146	.205	.220	318	4	.245	.286	.368
TOTALS		4372	28	.253	.306	.341	2139	13	.273	.325	.372	2233	15	.234	.287	.312	2007	11	.251	.304	.335	2365	17	.255	.307	.346	1254	5	.228	.284	.304	3118	23	.263	.314	.356
■ **Joe Morgan** BL/TR																																				
1978	Cin-N	441	13	.236	.347	.385	203	6	.251	.354	.409	238	7	.223	.341	.366	225	8	.258	.379	.444	216	5	.213	.311	.324	179	4	.223	.339	.330	262	9	.244	.352	.424
1979	Cin-N	436	9	.250	.379	.376	210	4	.257	.388	.390	226	5	.243	.371	.363	188	4	.271	.390	.420	248	5	.234	.371	.343	164	4	.244	.370	.354	272	5	.254	.385	.390
1980	Hou-N	461	11	.243	.367	.373	217	2	.286	.425	.401	244	9	.205	.311	.348	200	5	.240	.358	.385	261	6	.245	.373	.364	169	3	.237	.345	.337	292	8	.247	.379	.394
1981	SF-N	308	8	.240	.371	.377	142	4	.275	.406	.430	166	4	.211	.342	.331	157	5	.242	.346	.389	151	3	.238	.396	.364	61	1	.279	.400	.426	247	7	.231	.364	.364
1982	SF-N	463	14	.289	.400	.438	223	6	.265	.381	.377	240	8	.313	.418	.496	204	4	.275	.392	.377	259	10	.301	.406	.486	153	6	.301	.409	.497	310	8	.284	.395	.410

YEAR	TM/L	TOTAL					HOME					AWAY					1ST HALF					2ND HALF					LEFT					RIGHT				
		AB	HR	AVG	OBP	SLG	AB	HR	AVG	OBP	SLG	AB	HR	AVG	OBP	SLG	AB	HR	AVG	OBP	SLG	AB	HR	AVG	OBP	SLG	AB	HR	AVG	OBP	SLG	AB	HR	AVG	OBP	SLG
1983	Phi-N	404	16	.230	.370	.403	160	9	.256	.426	.475	244	7	.213	.330	.357	193	6	.218	.366	.358	211	10	.242	.373	.445	64	1	.203	.341	.297	340	15	.235	.375	.424
1984	Oak-A	365	6	.244	.356	.351	180	2	.278	.377	.361	185	4	.211	.336	.341	212	5	.264	.380	.406	153	1	.216	.322	.275	116	2	.293	.366	.431	249	4	.221	.352	.313
TOTALS		2878	77	.248	.370	.388	1335	33	.267	.393	.403	1543	44	.233	.350	.375	1379	37	.253	.374	.398	1499	40	.244	.367	.378	906	21	.254	.365	.381	1972	56	.246	.373	.391
■ Hal Morris BL/TL																																				
1988	NY-A	20	0	.100	.100	.100	9	0	.111	.111	.111	11	0	.091	.091	.091	0	0	—	—	—	20	0	.100	.100	.100	7	0	.000	.000	.000	13	0	.154	.154	.154
1989	NY-A	18	0	.278	.316	.278	11	0	.182	.250	.182	7	0	.429	.429	.429	6	0	.333	.333	.333	12	0	.250	.308	.250	1	0	.000	.500	.000	17	0	.294	.294	.294
1990	Cin-N	309	7	.340	.381	.498	148	3	.338	.383	.493	161	4	.342	.380	.503	45	0	.311	.367	.378	264	7	.345	.384	.519	76	0	.224	.280	.224	233	7	.378	.414	.588
1991	Cin-N	478	14	.318	.374	.479	238	9	.319	.370	.525	240	5	.317	.378	.433	227	5	.308	.340	.463	251	9	.327	.403	.494	103	1	.252	.288	.379	375	13	.336	.397	.507
1992	Cin-N	395	6	.271	.347	.385	198	3	.273	.333	.389	197	3	.269	.360	.381	158	2	.323	.407	.456	237	4	.236	.305	.338	139	1	.252	.325	.309	256	5	.281	.359	.426
1993	Cin-N	379	7	.317	.371	.420	184	2	.321	.376	.418	195	5	.313	.366	.421	81	0	.284	.307	.296	298	7	.326	.387	.453	86	0	.244	.305	.291	293	7	.338	.390	.457
1994	Cin-N	436	10	.335	.385	.491	232	5	.328	.375	.496	204	5	.343	.396	.485	297	5	.350	.393	.502	139	5	.302	.368	.468	110	0	.255	.325	.327	326	10	.362	.405	.546
1995	Cin-N	359	11	.279	.333	.451	161	6	.335	.378	.559	198	5	.232	.298	.364	110	3	.209	.241	.327	249	8	.309	.372	.506	68	0	.221	.284	.294	291	11	.292	.345	.488
1996	Cin-N	528	16	.313	.374	.479	250	7	.340	.401	.540	278	9	.288	.348	.424	272	7	.290	.356	.438	256	9	.336	.392	.523	132	1	.273	.322	.341	396	15	.326	.390	.525
1997	Cin-N	333	1	.276	.328	.351	167	1	.299	.343	.395	166	0	.253	.313	.307	258	1	.256	.306	.329	75	0	.347	.402	.427	72	0	.250	.286	.292	261	1	.284	.339	.368
1998	KC-A	472	1	.309	.350	.381	228	0	.320	.354	.390	244	1	.299	.346	.373	250	1	.352	.387	.448	222	0	.261	.309	.306	102	0	.294	.363	.333	370	1	.314	.346	.395
1999	Cin-N	102	0	.284	.348	.373	40	0	.225	.279	.350	62	0	.323	.391	.387	58	0	.259	.348	.328	44	0	.318	.348	.432	21	0	.286	.318	.429	81	0	.284	.356	.358
2000	Cin-N	63	2	.222	.351	.381	21	1	.381	.462	.619	42	1	.143	.294	.262	51	1	.216	.359	.353	12	1	.250	.308	.500	5	0	.200	.200	.200	58	2	.224	.361	.397
2000	Det-A	106	1	.311	.416	.406	49	0	.327	.468	.388	57	1	.298	.365	.421	0	0	—	—	—	106	1	.311	.416	.406	21	0	.238	.360	.286	85	1	.329	.430	.435
TOTALS		3998	76	.304	.361	.433	1936	37	.317	.369	.463	2062	39	.292	.353	.405	1813	25	.301	.353	.418	2185	51	.307	.368	.446	943	3	.252	.312	.314	3055	73	.320	.376	.470
■ Lloyd Moseby BL/TR																																				
1980	Tor-A	389	9	.229	.281	.365	198	4	.253	.300	.399	191	5	.204	.261	.330	101	3	.267	.299	.416	288	6	.215	.275	.347	111	2	.234	.265	.378	278	7	.227	.287	.360
1981	Tor-A	378	9	.233	.278	.357	179	3	.235	.294	.341	199	6	.231	.262	.372	196	6	.235	.290	.393	182	3	.231	.264	.319	144	3	.194	.235	.299	234	6	.256	.303	.393
1982	Tor-A	487	9	.236	.294	.370	221	4	.253	.328	.389	266	5	.222	.265	.353	225	3	.218	.283	.342	262	6	.252	.304	.393	171	6	.222	.276	.433	316	3	.244	.304	.335
1983	Tor-A	539	18	.315	.376	.499	267	13	.330	.401	.573	272	5	.301	.350	.426	229	9	.297	.359	.498	310	9	.329	.388	.500	186	4	.296	.342	.452	353	14	.326	.393	.524
1984	Tor-A	592	18	.280	.368	.470	277	10	.296	.389	.534	315	8	.267	.349	.413	295	12	.281	.362	.515	297	6	.279	.373	.424	210	2	.252	.332	.371	382	16	.296	.387	.524
1985	Tor-A	584	18	.259	.345	.426	283	11	.258	.344	.466	301	7	.259	.347	.389	279	5	.251	.348	.398	305	13	.266	.343	.452	234	7	.256	.330	.393	350	11	.260	.355	.449
1986	Tor-A	589	21	.253	.329	.418	290	11	.248	.337	.410	299	10	.258	.320	.425	298	12	.295	.380	.480	291	9	.210	.275	.354	188	6	.229	.277	.378	401	15	.264	.352	.436
1987	Tor-A	592	26	.282	.358	.473	298	15	.292	.371	.503	294	11	.272	.345	.442	282	13	.266	.334	.457	310	13	.297	.379	.487	198	5	.278	.362	.419	394	21	.284	.357	.500
1988	Tor-A	472	10	.239	.343	.369	211	2	.232	.345	.336	261	8	.245	.341	.395	266	7	.237	.356	.376	206	3	.243	.325	.359	170	2	.253	.344	.359	302	8	.232	.343	.374
1989	Tor-A	502	11	.221	.306	.349	222	4	.180	.293	.293	280	7	.254	.317	.393	233	6	.202	.294	.313	269	5	.238	.317	.379	138	2	.196	.297	.268	364	9	.231	.310	.379
1990	Det-A	431	14	.248	.329	.406	221	8	.240	.341	.394	210	6	.257	.316	.419	229	7	.253	.329	.393	202	7	.243	.329	.421	132	2	.182	.264	.242	299	12	.278	.358	.478
1991	Det-A	260	6	.262	.321	.396	151	4	.272	.335	.417	109	2	.248	.299	.367	81	0	.247	.287	.296	179	6	.268	.335	.441	46	1	.239	.340	.391	214	5	.266	.316	.397
TOTALS		5815	169	.257	.332	.414	2818	89	.260	.344	.431	2997	80	.254	.320	.398	2714	83	.256	.335	.417	3101	86	.258	.329	.411	1928	42	.240	.309	.371	3887	127	.265	.343	.435
■ Bill Mueller BB/TR																																				
1996	SF-N	200	0	.330	.401	.415	107	0	.308	.377	.374	93	0	.355	.429	.462	2	0	.500	.500	.500	198	0	.328	.400	.414	28	0	.321	.367	.393	172	0	.331	.406	.419
1997	SF-N	390	7	.292	.369	.428	189	5	.291	.385	.423	201	2	.294	.354	.433	185	2	.270	.343	.373	205	5	.312	.393	.478	85	2	.282	.365	.435	305	5	.295	.370	.426
1998	SF-N	534	9	.294	.383	.395	257	1	.257	.348	.331	277	8	.329	.415	.455	302	5	.301	.384	.411	232	4	.284	.381	.375	121	3	.298	.407	.446	413	6	.293	.376	.380
1999	SF-N	414	2	.290	.388	.362	196	1	.291	.395	.362	218	1	.289	.382	.362	142	1	.296	.409	.373	272	1	.287	.377	.357	113	2	.248	.338	.336	301	0	.306	.407	.372
2000	SF-N	560	10	.268	.333	.387	276	3	.243	.291	.337	284	7	.292	.373	.437	280	6	.289	.349	.407	280	4	.246	.317	.368	108	3	.306	.390	.435	452	7	.259	.319	.376
TOTALS		2098	28	.289	.370	.395	1025	10	.271	.353	.360	1073	18	.307	.387	.428	911	14	.291	.370	.396	1187	14	.288	.371	.393	455	10	.286	.376	.411	1643	18	.290	.369	.390
■ Rance Mulliniks BL/TR																																				
1978	Cal-A	119	1	.185	.238	.252	73	1	.164	.203	.233	46	0	.217	.294	.283	119	1	.185	.238	.252	0	0	—	—	—	15	0	.067	.067	.067	104	1	.202	.261	.279
1979	Cal-A	68	1	.147	.192	.191	29	0	.138	.242	.138	39	1	.154	.156	.231	61	1	.148	.197	.197	7	0	.143	.143	.143	18	1	.167	.200	.333	50	0	.140	.190	.140
1980	KC-A	54	0	.259	.339	.315	22	0	.273	.407	.409	32	0	.250	.286	.250	9	0	.111	.250	.111	45	0	.289	.360	.356	4	0	.250	.250	.250	50	0	.260	.345	.320
1981	KC-A	44	0	.227	.261	.295	19	0	.158	.200	.158	25	0	.280	.308	.400	20	0	.200	.200	.250	24	0	.250	.308	.333	7	0	.429	.429	.714	37	0	.189	.231	.216
1982	Tor-A	311	4	.244	.326	.363	174	2	.241	.314	.356	137	2	.248	.340	.372	159	1	.226	.309	.327	152	3	.263	.343	.401	32	0	.250	.294	.281	279	4	.244	.329	.373
1983	Tor-A	364	10	.275	.373	.467	182	4	.313	.392	.533	182	6	.236	.353	.401	157	3	.293	.390	.490	207	7	.261	.360	.449	25	1	.200	.300	.400	339	9	.280	.378	.472
1984	Tor-A	343	3	.324	.383	.440	159	1	.296	.362	.415	184	2	.348	.401	.462	162	0	.284	.364	.358	181	3	.359	.400	.514	7	0	.429	.500	.429	336	3	.321	.380	.440
1985	Tor-A	366	10	.295	.383	.454	174	4	.316	.407	.483	192	6	.276	.360	.427	165	4	.297	.402	.442	201	6	.294	.366	.463	22	0	.227	.393	.318	344	10	.299	.382	.462
1986	Tor-A	348	11	.259	.340	.417	176	5	.284	.373	.449	172	6	.233	.306	.384	211	8	.270	.355	.436	137	3	.241	.316	.387	20	0	.200	.238	.250	328	11	.262	.346	.427
1987	Tor-A	332	11	.310	.371	.500	162	6	.315	.364	.531	170	5	.306	.378	.471	136	3	.272	.338	.404	196	8	.337	.394	.566	18	1	.389	.450	.667	314	10	.306	.367	.490
1988	Tor-A	337	12	.300	.395	.475	165	7	.303	.382	.521	172	5	.297	.408	.430	156	6	.327	.401	.513	181	6	.276	.391	.442	15	1	.267	.389	.533	322	11	.301	.396	.472
1989	Tor-A	273	3	.238	.320	.326	117	1	.231	.316	.308	156	2	.244	.324	.340	186	1	.237	.308	.301	87	2	.241	.347	.379	16	0	.188	.316	.250	257	3	.241	.321	.331
1990	Tor-A	97	2	.289	.417	.392	44	1	.318	.444	.477	53	1	.264	.394	.321	41	1	.244	.380	.415	56	1	.321	.443	.375	7	0	.429	.636	.571	90	2	.278	.394	.378
1991	Tor-A	240	2	.250	.364	.333	120	1	.250	.355	.333	120	1	.250	.372	.333	92	1	.283	.432	.391	148	1	.230	.315	.297	12	0	.083	.083	.083	228	2	.259	.376	.346
1992	Tor-A	2	0	.500	.667	.500	2	0	.500	.667	.500	0	0	—	—	—	0	0	—	—	—	2	0	.500	.667	.500	1	0	1.000	1.000	1.000	1	0	.000	.500	.000
TOTALS		3298	70	.273	.356	.410	1618	33	.278	.358	.427	1680	37	.268	.354	.393	1674	30	.262	.347	.385	1624	40	.284	.365	.436	219	4	.237	.319	.352	3079	66	.275	.358	.414
■ Jerry Mumphrey BB/TR																																				
1978	StL-N	367	2	.262	.317	.335	188	1	.261	.305	.330	179	1	.263	.328	.341	132	0	.197	.265	.235	235	2	.298	.346	.391	116	0	.250	.321	.336	251	2	.267	.315	.335
1979	StL-N	339	3	.295	.341	.369	179	2	.279	.328	.363	160	1	.313	.356	.375	94	0	.266	.317	.340	245	3	.306	.351	.380	174	0	.247	.304	.299	165	3	.345	.382	.442
1980	SD-N	564	4	.298	.352	.372	274	1	.274	.338	.336	290	3	.321	.365	.407	237	0	.262	.320	.321	327	4	.324	.374	.410	135	0	.267	.317	.281	429	4	.308	.362	.401
1981	NY-A	319	6	.307	.354	.429	140	3	.357	.381	.479	179	3	.268	.333	.391	174	4	.322	.382	.448	145	2	.290	.318	.407	117	1	.299	.346	.359	202	5	.312	.358	.470
1982	NY-A	477	9	.300	.364	.449	243	6	.321	.382	.498	234	3	.278	.345	.397	136	0	.294	.374	.368	341	9	.302	.360	.481	165	1	.230	.317	.315	312	8	.337	.390	.519
1983	NY-A	267	7	.262	.327	.412	123	1	.309	.370	.439	144	6	.222	.290	.389	159	5	.226	.288	.390	108	2	.315	.382	.444	98	2	.245	.321	.367	169	5	.272	.330	.438
1983	Hou-N	143	1	.336	.425	.455	62	1	.339	.446	.468	81	0	.333	.409	.444	0	0	—	—	—	143	1	.336	.425	.455	42	0	.333	.404	.357	101	1	.337	.433	.495
1984	Hou-N	524	9	.290	.355	.391	258	1	.302	.372	.376	266	8	.278	.339	.406	273	4	.289	.351	.381	251	5	.291	.359	.402	175	0	.246	.309	.280	349	9	.312	.378	.447
1985	Hou-N	444	8	.277	.329	.396	200	4	.305	.369	.445	244	4	.254	.294	.357	194	4	.263	.313	.387	250	4	.288	.341	.404	133	0	.241	.323	.293	311	8	.293	.331	.441
1986	Chi-N	309	5	.304	.355	.401	147	4	.361	.417	.517	162	1	.253	.297	.296	154	1	.273	.354	.331	155	4	.335	.356	.471	61	0	.197	.279	.213	248	5	.331	.374	.448
1987	Chi-N	309	13	.333	.400	.534	156	7	.288	.366	.487	153	6	.379	.435	.582	146	5	.329	.396	.486	163	8	.337	.403	.577	7	0	.143	.250	.286	302	13	.338	.404	.540
1988	Chi-N	66	0	.136	.219	.167	35	0	.143	.231	.143	31	0	.129	.206	.194	41	0	.122	.182	.146	25	0	.160	.276	.200	0	0	—	—	—	66	0	.136	.219	.167
TOTALS		4128	67	.292	.350	.403	2005	31	.301	.362	.415	2123	36	.283	.339	.392	1740	23	.270	.334	.366	2388	44	.307	.362	.431	1223	4	.251	.319	.308	2905	63	.309	.363	.443
■ Dale Murphy BR/TR																																				
1978	Atl-N	530	23	.226	.284	.394	261	17	.264	.337	.494	269	6	.190	.232	.297	244	8	.209	.280	.332	286	15	.241	.288	.448	167	6	.251	.304	.389	363	17	.215	.276	.397
1979	Atl-N	384	21	.276	.340	.469	182	12	.297	.378	.522	202	9	.257	.305	.421	142	13	.352	.424	.662	242	8	.231	.288	.355	86	5	.360	.417	.547	298	16	.252	.318	.446
1980	Atl-N	569	33	.281	.349	.510	292	17	.267	.322	.493	277	16	.296	.376	.527	247	13	.291	.362	.502	322	20	.273	.338	.516	137	8	.277	.349	.526	432	25	.282	.349	.505
1981	Atl-N	369	13	.247	.325	.390	175	8	.251	.327	.400	194	5	.242	.324	.381	208	6	.250	.305	.370	161	7	.242	.349	.416	77	4	.260	.345	.455	292	9	.243	.320	.373
1982	Atl-N	598	36	.281	.378	.507	297	24	.310	.392	.596	301	12	.252	.365	.419	277	22	.285	.380	.567	321	14	.277	.377	.455	134	11	.351	.453	.649	464	25	.261	.356	.466
1983	Atl-N	589	36	.302	.393	.540	285	17	.340	.432	.579	304	19	.266	.356	.503	278	19	.320	.407	.594	311	17	.286	.380	.492	159	5	.252	.330	.396	430	31	.321	.416	.593
1984	Atl-N	607	36	.290	.372	.547	300	18	.297	.376	.543	307	18	.283	.368	.550	297	17	.273	.364	.512	310	19	.306	.379	.581	169	15	.314	.415	.651	438	21	.281	.354	.507
1985	Atl-N	616	37	.300	.388	.539	308	19	.299	.401	.539	308	18	.302	.374	.539	276	18	.290	.377	.540	340	19	.309	.396	.538	183	10	.333	.440	.552	433	27	.286	.364	.533
1986	Atl-N	614	29	.265	.347	.477	298	17	.268	.366	.503	316	12	.263	.328	.453	279	13	.283	.378	.484	335	16	.251	.320	.472	193	9	.280	.382	.508	421	20	.259	.330	.463
1987	Atl-N	566	44	.295	.417	.580	269	25	.346	.493	.673	297	19	.249	.338	.495	277	24	.318	.446	.639	289	20	.273	.389	.522	150	14	.320	.512	.653	416	30	.286	.376	.553
1988	Atl-N	592	24	.226	.313	.421	283	14	.261	.358	.505	309	10	.194	.270	.343	279	12	.222	.328	.434	313	12	.230	.299	.409	180	9	.256	.379	.478	412	15	.214	.281	.396
1989	Atl-N	574	20	.228	.306	.361	276	9	.257	.329	.380	298	11	.201	.285	.342	301	6	.249	.305	.352	273	14	.205	.307	.370	172	5	.244	.373	.355	402	15	.221	.274	.363
1990	Atl-N	349	17	.232	.312	.418	174	8	.218	.290	.385	175	9	.246	.333	.451	257	11	.230	.308	.401	92	6	.239	.324	.467	110	10	.309	.438	.645	239	7	.197	.245	.314
1990	Phi-N	214	7	.266	.328	.416	105	1	.248	.333	.333	109	6	.284	.322	.495	0	0	—	—	—	214	7	.266	.328	.416	70	4	.314	.360	.571	144	3	.243	.313	.340
1991	Phi-N	544	18	.252	.309	.415	279	9	.280	.343	.452	265	9	.223	.272	.377	248	11	.262	.313	.448	296	7	.243	.306	.389	192	5	.297	.351	.443	352	13	.227	.286	.401
1992	Phi-N	62	2	.161	.175	.274	47	2	.149	.167	.277	15	0	.200	.200	.267	61	2	.164	.177	.279	1	0	.000	.000	.000	31	1	.194	.219	.323	31	1	.129	.129	.226
1993	Col-N	42	0	.143	.224	.167	23	0	.130	.259	.174	19	0	.158	.182	.158	42	0	.143	.224	.167	0	0	—	—	—	28	0	.143	.235	.179	14	0	.143	.200	.143
TOTALS		7819	396	.265	.346	.469	3854	217	.282	.369	.502	3965	179	.248	.324	.438	3713	195	.269	.352	.478	4106	201	.261	.341	.461	2238	121	.288	.388	.507	5581	275	.255	.329	.454
■ Dwayne Murphy BL/TR																																				
1978	Oak-A	52	0	.192	.279	.231	26	0	.192	.323	.231	26	0	.192	.233	.231	33	0	.121	.244	.121	19	0	.316	.350	.421	15	0	.133	.263	.133	37	0	.216	.286	.270
1979	Oak-A	388	11	.255	.387	.387	185	4	.254	.399	.346	203	7	.256	.374	.424	194	5	.273	.427	.381	194	6	.237	.343	.392	112	1	.223	.425	.313	276	10	.268	.368	.417
1980	Oak-A	573	13	.274	.384	.380	275	5	.255	.365	.327	298	8	.292	.401	.430	257	7	.304	.405	.412	316	6	.250	.367	.354	219	4	.251	.362	.324	354	9	.288	.398	.415
1981	Oak-A	390	15	.251	.369	.408	193	7	.202	.336	.342	197	8	.299	.402	.472	212	9	.250	.366	.420	178	6	.253	.372	.393	150	4	.213	.324	.313	240	11	.275	.396	.467

YEAR	TM/L	TOTAL					HOME					AWAY					1ST HALF					2ND HALF					LEFT					RIGHT				
		AB	HR	AVG	OBP	SLG	AB	HR	AVG	OBP	SLG	AB	HR	AVG	OBP	SLG	AB	HR	AVG	OBP	SLG	AB	HR	AVG	OBP	SLG	AB	HR	AVG	OBP	SLG	AB	HR	AVG	OBP	SLG
1982	Oak-A	543	27	.238	.349	.418	276	15	.236	.354	.424	267	12	.240	.343	.412	256	14	.207	.338	.398	287	13	.265	.359	.436	202	9	.233	.325	.396	341	18	.240	.362	.431
1983	Oak-A	471	17	.227	.314	.380	232	12	.230	.323	.422	239	5	.222	.304	.339	223	5	.224	.328	.323	248	12	.230	.300	.431	203	3	.182	.246	.251	268	14	.261	.362	.478
1984	Oak-A	559	33	.256	.342	.472	271	12	.232	.344	.399	288	21	.278	.341	.542	253	15	.257	.341	.474	306	18	.255	.343	.471	212	8	.241	.298	.401	347	25	.265	.368	.516
1985	Oak-A	523	20	.233	.340	.400	242	5	.215	.326	.335	281	15	.249	.353	.456	238	12	.223	.351	.416	285	8	.242	.331	.386	147	7	.197	.297	.374	376	13	.247	.357	.410
1986	Oak-A	329	9	.252	.364	.386	168	5	.256	.379	.387	161	4	.248	.347	.385	91	2	.242	.377	.363	238	7	.256	.358	.395	92	1	.228	.330	.293	237	8	.262	.377	.422
1987	Oak-A	219	8	.233	.388	.374	101	2	.178	.339	.297	118	6	.280	.429	.441	51	2	.235	.381	.392	168	6	.232	.390	.369	66	2	.182	.304	.288	153	6	.255	.421	.412
1988	Det-A	144	4	.250	.361	.368	70	2	.271	.386	.386	74	2	.230	.337	.351	0	0	—	—	—	144	4	.250	.361	.368	31	1	.161	.257	.290	113	3	.274	.388	.389
1989	Phi-N	156	9	.218	.341	.423	74	4	.270	.393	.500	82	5	.171	.292	.354	64	3	.203	.301	.375	92	6	.228	.366	.457	17	1	.235	.350	.471	139	8	.216	.339	.417
TOTALS		4347	166	.246	.356	.402	2113	73	.234	.354	.373	2234	93	.257	.358	.428	1872	74	.244	.361	.397	2475	92	.248	.352	.405	1466	41	.218	.320	.334	2881	125	.260	.374	.436

■ Eddie Murray BB/TR

YEAR	TM/L	AB	HR	AVG	OBP	SLG	AB	HR	AVG	OBP	SLG	AB	HR	AVG	OBP	SLG	AB	HR	AVG	OBP	SLG	AB	HR	AVG	OBP	SLG	AB	HR	AVG	OBP	SLG	AB	HR	AVG	OBP	SLG
1978	Bal-A	610	27	.285	.356	.480	297	10	.276	.333	.444	313	17	.294	.376	.514	293	17	.270	.333	.498	317	10	.300	.376	.464	198	6	.293	.335	.449	412	21	.282	.365	.495
1979	Bal-A	606	25	.295	.369	.475	292	10	.315	.379	.476	314	15	.277	.359	.475	291	8	.271	.352	.402	315	17	.317	.384	.543	179	9	.318	.394	.520	427	16	.286	.358	.457
1980	Bal-A	621	32	.300	.354	.519	297	10	.273	.342	.428	324	22	.324	.366	.602	287	12	.293	.349	.488	334	20	.305	.359	.545	210	9	.286	.330	.495	411	23	.307	.366	.530
1981	Bal-A	378	22	.294	.360	.534	190	12	.279	.370	.521	188	10	.309	.350	.548	197	8	.259	.303	.442	181	14	.331	.417	.635	103	6	.369	.421	.612	275	16	.265	.338	.505
1982	Bal-A	550	32	.316	.391	.549	287	18	.338	.417	.575	263	14	.293	.362	.521	198	10	.323	.404	.561	352	22	.313	.383	.543	184	11	.370	.416	.614	366	21	.290	.379	.516
1983	Bal-A	582	33	.306	.393	.538	272	16	.305	.383	.529	310	17	.306	.401	.545	274	11	.299	.384	.464	308	22	.312	.400	.604	204	12	.289	.381	.505	378	21	.315	.399	.556
1984	Bal-A	588	29	.306	.410	.509	283	18	.329	.437	.572	305	11	.285	.385	.449	276	14	.312	.417	.504	312	15	.301	.404	.513	150	5	.267	.392	.413	438	24	.320	.416	.541
1985	Bal-A	583	31	.297	.383	.523	291	15	.296	.396	.515	292	16	.298	.369	.531	249	11	.289	.364	.498	334	20	.302	.396	.542	203	10	.286	.384	.502	380	21	.303	.382	.534
1986	Bal-A	495	17	.305	.396	.463	242	9	.310	.387	.471	253	8	.300	.405	.455	266	11	.289	.384	.455	229	6	.323	.411	.472	136	6	.301	.360	.493	359	11	.306	.409	.451
1987	Bal-A	618	30	.277	.352	.477	300	14	.263	.347	.433	318	16	.289	.356	.519	300	14	.267	.330	.477	318	16	.286	.371	.478	221	11	.271	.336	.475	397	19	.280	.360	.479
1988	Bal-A	603	28	.284	.361	.474	297	14	.283	.368	.461	306	14	.284	.355	.487	291	11	.251	.335	.409	312	17	.314	.385	.535	213	7	.230	.288	.371	390	21	.313	.400	.531
1989	LA-N	594	20	.247	.342	.401	292	4	.253	.342	.346	302	16	.242	.342	.454	287	7	.237	.348	.380	307	13	.257	.336	.420	210	4	.210	.317	.329	384	16	.268	.356	.440
1990	LA-N	558	26	.330	.414	.520	271	12	.343	.444	.524	287	14	.317	.384	.516	231	9	.290	.378	.463	327	17	.358	.439	.560	206	8	.316	.385	.466	352	18	.338	.431	.551
1991	LA-N	576	19	.260	.321	.403	282	11	.270	.347	.426	294	8	.252	.295	.381	255	8	.271	.333	.420	321	11	.252	.311	.389	254	6	.217	.269	.327	322	13	.295	.361	.463
1992	NY-N	551	16	.261	.336	.423	266	7	.226	.303	.380	285	9	.295	.366	.463	266	8	.252	.331	.410	285	8	.270	.341	.435	202	3	.238	.286	.371	349	13	.275	.364	.453
1993	NY-N	610	27	.285	.325	.467	314	15	.290	.320	.475	296	12	.280	.329	.459	271	9	.266	.305	.410	339	18	.301	.341	.513	183	8	.311	.355	.497	427	19	.274	.312	.454
1994	Cle-A	433	17	.254	.302	.425	199	7	.266	.313	.437	234	10	.244	.292	.415	279	11	.283	.331	.470	154	6	.201	.248	.344	153	5	.216	.242	.366	280	12	.275	.333	.457
1995	Cle-A	436	21	.323	.375	.516	210	11	.348	.404	.552	226	10	.301	.347	.482	226	11	.310	.360	.496	210	10	.338	.391	.538	104	3	.269	.304	.404	332	18	.340	.397	.551
1996	Cle-A	336	12	.262	.326	.402	160	7	.244	.313	.419	176	5	.278	.338	.386	296	11	.260	.324	.402	40	1	.275	.341	.400	91	3	.286	.398	.407	245	9	.253	.297	.400
1996	Bal-A	230	10	.257	.327	.439	102	6	.206	.282	.402	128	4	.297	.363	.469	0	0	—	—	—	230	10	.257	.327	.439	65	3	.246	.297	.400	165	7	.261	.339	.455
1997	Ana-A	160	3	.219	.273	.319	82	2	.220	.272	.354	78	1	.218	.274	.282	146	3	.219	.270	.322	14	0	.214	.294	.286	63	0	.270	.299	.302	97	3	.186	.257	.330
1997	LA-N	7	0	.286	.444	.286	4	0	.500	.600	.500	3	0	.000	.250	.000	0	0	—	—	—	7	0	.286	.444	.286	1	0	1.000	1.000	1.000	6	0	.167	.375	.167
TOTALS		10725	477	.287	.361	.476	5230	228	.288	.364	.469	5495	249	.287	.357	.483	5179	204	.276	.349	.449	5546	273	.298	.372	.502	3533	135	.277	.342	.446	7192	342	.293	.370	.492

■ Graig Nettles BL/TR

YEAR	TM/L	AB	HR	AVG	OBP	SLG	AB	HR	AVG	OBP	SLG	AB	HR	AVG	OBP	SLG	AB	HR	AVG	OBP	SLG	AB	HR	AVG	OBP	SLG	AB	HR	AVG	OBP	SLG	AB	HR	AVG	OBP	SLG
1978	NY-A	587	27	.276	.343	.460	289	16	.284	.364	.498	298	11	.268	.323	.423	268	13	.243	.330	.422	319	14	.304	.355	.492	302	9	.235	.305	.361	285	18	.319	.384	.565
1979	NY-A	521	20	.253	.325	.401	258	11	.260	.318	.422	263	9	.247	.331	.380	282	13	.273	.345	.433	239	7	.230	.301	.364	225	7	.253	.302	.387	296	13	.253	.341	.412
1980	NY-A	324	16	.244	.331	.435	161	11	.273	.355	.522	163	5	.215	.306	.350	241	13	.253	.343	.452	83	3	.217	.293	.386	140	4	.229	.303	.336	184	12	.255	.350	.511
1981	NY-A	349	15	.244	.333	.398	162	11	.278	.369	.500	187	4	.214	.300	.310	189	7	.249	.333	.386	160	8	.237	.332	.412	137	5	.234	.341	.372	212	10	.250	.326	.415
1982	NY-A	405	18	.232	.317	.402	222	10	.212	.283	.392	183	8	.257	.355	.415	167	5	.204	.300	.341	238	13	.252	.328	.445	156	3	.224	.291	.321	249	15	.237	.332	.454
1983	NY-A	462	20	.266	.341	.446	209	11	.311	.373	.531	253	9	.229	.315	.375	213	11	.263	.355	.455	249	9	.269	.328	.438	161	4	.280	.352	.404	301	16	.259	.335	.468
1984	SD-N	395	20	.228	.329	.413	195	11	.210	.313	.405	200	9	.245	.345	.420	216	11	.222	.329	.398	179	9	.235	.329	.430	77	1	.130	.216	.182	318	19	.252	.355	.469
1985	SD-N	440	15	.261	.363	.420	217	6	.258	.358	.387	223	9	.265	.368	.453	187	8	.219	.366	.380	253	7	.292	.360	.451	97	4	.216	.300	.433	343	11	.274	.380	.417
1986	SD-N	354	16	.218	.300	.379	166	13	.265	.374	.530	188	3	.176	.229	.245	169	12	.231	.314	.444	185	4	.205	.287	.319	53	3	.170	.224	.358	301	13	.226	.313	.382
1987	Atl-N	177	5	.209	.294	.350	82	2	.232	.330	.378	95	3	.189	.260	.326	94	4	.191	.300	.340	83	1	.229	.286	.361	48	0	.229	.291	.313	129	5	.202	.295	.364
1988	Mon-N	93	1	.172	.240	.247	42	1	.214	.267	.357	51	0	.137	.220	.157	45	1	.156	.220	.244	48	0	.188	.259	.250	5	0	.200	.333	.400	88	1	.170	.235	.239
TOTALS		4107	173	.246	.329	.413	2003	103	.259	.342	.456	2104	70	.233	.316	.372	2071	98	.238	.332	.408	2036	75	.254	.325	.417	1401	40	.231	.303	.358	2706	133	.254	.342	.441

■ Phil Nevin BR/TR

YEAR	TM/L	AB	HR	AVG	OBP	SLG	AB	HR	AVG	OBP	SLG	AB	HR	AVG	OBP	SLG	AB	HR	AVG	OBP	SLG	AB	HR	AVG	OBP	SLG	AB	HR	AVG	OBP	SLG	AB	HR	AVG	OBP	SLG
1995	Hou-N	60	0	.117	.221	.133	29	0	.034	.152	.034	31	0	.194	.286	.226	50	0	.080	.164	.100	10	0	.300	.462	.300	18	0	.222	.300	.278	42	0	.071	.188	.071
1995	Det-A	96	2	.219	.318	.333	45	2	.222	.340	.444	51	0	.216	.298	.235	0	0	—	—	—	96	2	.219	.318	.333	17	0	.294	.294	.294	79	2	.203	.323	.342
1996	Det-A	120	8	.292	.338	.533	70	3	.286	.333	.471	50	5	.300	.345	.620	0	0	—	—	—	120	8	.292	.338	.533	36	2	.306	.375	.500	84	6	.286	.322	.548
1997	Det-A	251	9	.235	.306	.414	112	4	.214	.315	.384	139	5	.252	.297	.439	94	3	.277	.378	.479	157	6	.210	.257	.376	114	6	.307	.368	.570	137	3	.175	.255	.285
1998	Ana-A	237	8	.228	.291	.371	113	3	.212	.286	.327	124	5	.242	.296	.411	120	5	.258	.353	.450	117	3	.197	.221	.291	91	4	.242	.310	.429	146	4	.219	.280	.336
1999	SD-N	383	24	.269	.352	.527	184	12	.293	.367	.543	199	12	.246	.339	.513	121	8	.231	.307	.496	262	16	.286	.373	.542	137	11	.270	.383	.569	246	13	.268	.333	.504
2000	SD-N	538	31	.303	.374	.543	262	13	.256	.331	.447	276	18	.348	.414	.634	292	16	.281	.341	.514	246	15	.329	.411	.577	146	13	.342	.439	.685	392	18	.288	.347	.490
TOTALS		1685	82	.262	.336	.469	815	37	.245	.325	.431	870	45	.278	.347	.505	677	32	.253	.329	.464	1008	50	.269	.341	.472	559	36	.293	.379	.555	1126	46	.247	.314	.426

■ Al Newman BB/TR

YEAR	TM/L	AB	HR	AVG	OBP	SLG	AB	HR	AVG	OBP	SLG	AB	HR	AVG	OBP	SLG	AB	HR	AVG	OBP	SLG	AB	HR	AVG	OBP	SLG	AB	HR	AVG	OBP	SLG	AB	HR	AVG	OBP	SLG
1985	Mon-N	29	0	.172	.250	.207	16	0	.125	.222	.125	13	0	.231	.286	.308	8	0	.125	.125	.125	21	0	.190	.292	.238	9	0	.222	.300	.333	20	0	.150	.227	.150
1986	Mon-N	185	1	.200	.279	.232	84	0	.190	.278	.202	101	1	.208	.279	.257	99	0	.242	.321	.263	86	1	.151	.229	.198	41	1	.220	.327	.317	144	0	.194	.264	.208
1987	Min-A	307	0	.221	.298	.303	153	0	.235	.339	.327	154	0	.208	.255	.279	184	0	.201	.278	.293	123	0	.252	.328	.317	94	0	.319	.407	.489	213	0	.178	.248	.221
1988	Min-A	260	0	.223	.301	.250	128	0	.234	.319	.266	132	0	.212	.283	.235	57	0	.211	.274	.211	203	0	.227	.308	.261	69	0	.174	.260	.188	191	0	.241	.316	.272
1989	Min-A	446	0	.253	.341	.303	224	0	.259	.351	.295	222	0	.248	.329	.311	191	0	.251	.350	.298	255	0	.255	.333	.306	163	0	.252	.328	.319	283	0	.254	.348	.293
1990	Min-A	388	0	.242	.304	.278	199	0	.261	.338	.302	189	0	.222	.265	.254	165	0	.236	.281	.279	223	0	.247	.320	.278	123	0	.252	.333	.301	265	0	.238	.289	.268
1991	Min-A	246	0	.191	.260	.211	117	0	.179	.263	.205	129	0	.202	.257	.217	111	0	.198	.280	.216	135	0	.185	.243	.207	66	0	.242	.265	.303	180	0	.172	.259	.178
1992	Tex-A	246	0	.220	.317	.240	114	0	.202	.300	.228	132	0	.235	.331	.250	142	0	.225	.304	.254	104	0	.212	.333	.221	56	0	.268	.423	.286	190	0	.205	.281	.226
TOTALS		2107	1	.226	.304	.266	1035	0	.230	.320	.270	1072	1	.222	.289	.263	957	0	.225	.301	.268	1150	1	.227	.307	.265	621	1	.251	.337	.322	1486	0	.215	.290	.243

■ Dave Nilsson BL/TR

YEAR	TM/L	AB	HR	AVG	OBP	SLG	AB	HR	AVG	OBP	SLG	AB	HR	AVG	OBP	SLG	AB	HR	AVG	OBP	SLG	AB	HR	AVG	OBP	SLG	AB	HR	AVG	OBP	SLG	AB	HR	AVG	OBP	SLG
1992	Mil-A	164	4	.232	.304	.354	55	1	.236	.373	.309	109	3	.229	.263	.376	92	3	.217	.250	.348	72	1	.250	.365	.361	27	0	.222	.276	.296	137	4	.234	.309	.365
1993	Mil-A	296	7	.257	.336	.375	164	5	.274	.344	.433	132	2	.235	.327	.303	75	1	.160	.203	.213	221	6	.290	.377	.430	81	2	.272	.358	.457	215	5	.251	.328	.344
1994	Mil-A	397	12	.275	.326	.451	195	4	.292	.335	.451	202	8	.257	.317	.450	266	9	.293	.331	.485	131	3	.237	.316	.382	92	2	.228	.232	.348	305	10	.289	.352	.482
1995	Mil-A	263	12	.278	.337	.468	139	7	.317	.353	.518	124	5	.234	.319	.411	22	2	.273	.360	.545	241	10	.278	.335	.461	55	2	.273	.328	.436	208	10	.279	.339	.476
1996	Mil-A	453	17	.331	.407	.525	228	3	.325	.403	.461	225	14	.338	.411	.591	157	9	.331	.409	.611	296	8	.331	.406	.480	105	1	.238	.293	.295	348	16	.359	.440	.595
1997	Mil-A	554	20	.278	.352	.446	257	5	.300	.389	.436	297	15	.259	.318	.455	284	7	.271	.346	.401	270	13	.285	.359	.493	199	4	.236	.282	.322	355	16	.301	.388	.515
1998	Mil-A	309	12	.269	.339	.437	154	6	.279	.341	.442	155	6	.258	.337	.432	118	1	.280	.336	.356	191	11	.262	.341	.487	55	0	.127	.222	.164	254	12	.299	.365	.496
1999	Mil-A	343	21	.309	.400	.554	157	9	.274	.354	.497	186	12	.339	.438	.602	220	17	.314	.385	.614	123	4	.301	.427	.447	91	5	.253	.352	.440	252	16	.329	.418	.595
TOTALS		2779	105	.284	.356	.461	1349	40	.294	.365	.453	1430	65	.275	.348	.469	1234	49	.281	.343	.467	1545	56	.286	.367	.456	705	16	.235	.295	.348	2074	89	.300	.377	.500

■ Otis Nixon BB/TR

YEAR	TM/L	AB	HR	AVG	OBP	SLG	AB	HR	AVG	OBP	SLG	AB	HR	AVG	OBP	SLG	AB	HR	AVG	OBP	SLG	AB	HR	AVG	OBP	SLG	AB	HR	AVG	OBP	SLG	AB	HR	AVG	OBP	SLG
1983	NY-A	14	0	.143	.200	.143	1	0	1.000	1.000	1.000	13	0	.077	.143	.077	0	0	—	—	—	14	0	.143	.200	.143	3	0	.000	.000	.000	11	0	.182	.250	.182
1984	Cle-A	91	0	.154	.220	.154	40	0	.175	.267	.175	51	0	.137	.182	.137	91	0	.154	.220	.154	0	0	—	—	—	27	0	.148	.226	.148	64	0	.156	.217	.156
1985	Cle-A	162	3	.235	.271	.315	69	1	.275	.315	.348	93	2	.204	.237	.290	51	0	.196	.196	.216	111	3	.252	.303	.360	50	1	.220	.235	.300	112	2	.241	.286	.321
1986	Cle-A	95	0	.263	.352	.326	45	0	.156	.255	.178	50	0	.360	.439	.460	45	0	.200	.234	.200	50	0	.320	.443	.440	37	0	.270	.357	.324	58	0	.259	.348	.328
1987	Cle-A	17	0	.059	.200	.059	6	0	.000	.250	.000	11	0	.091	.167	.091	17	0	.059	.200	.059	0	0	—	—	—	2	0	.000	.333	.000	15	0	.067	.176	.067
1988	Mon-N	271	0	.244	.312	.288	145	0	.234	.321	.276	126	0	.254	.301	.302	44	0	.227	.292	.273	227	0	.247	.316	.291	93	0	.226	.308	.280	178	0	.253	.315	.292
1989	Mon-N	258	0	.217	.306	.260	132	0	.212	.302	.273	126	0	.222	.310	.246	161	0	.230	.330	.280	97	0	.196	.264	.227	150	0	.233	.299	.273	108	0	.194	.315	.241
1990	Mon-N	231	1	.251	.331	.307	108	0	.241	.322	.306	123	1	.260	.338	.309	63	0	.238	.347	.302	168	1	.256	.324	.310	151	1	.238	.307	.305	80	0	.275	.372	.313
1991	Atl-N	401	0	.297	.371	.327	207	0	.329	.404	.367	194	0	.263	.335	.284	186	0	.323	.392	.355	215	0	.274	.352	.302	95	0	.305	.405	.358	306	0	.294	.360	.317
1992	Atl-N	456	2	.294	.348	.346	221	1	.299	.366	.335	235	1	.289	.331	.357	152	2	.342	.392	.408	304	0	.270	.326	.316	178	2	.343	.379	.433	278	0	.263	.329	.291
1993	Atl-N	461	1	.269	.351	.315	216	1	.287	.379	.361	245	0	.253	.325	.273	207	0	.242	.333	.271	254	1	.291	.366	.350	152	1	.263	.335	.316	309	0	.272	.359	.314
1994	Bos-A	398	0	.274	.360	.317	216	0	.301	.386	.347	182	0	.242	.330	.280	279	0	.276	.362	.330	119	0	.269	.358	.286	108	0	.231	.303	.269	290	0	.290	.381	.334
1995	Tex-A	589	0	.295	.357	.338	299	0	.274	.338	.314	290	0	.317	.376	.362	251	0	.287	.337	.311	338	0	.302	.371	.358	177	0	.333	.376	.379	412	0	.279	.349	.320
1996	Tor-A	496	1	.286	.377	.327	258	1	.264	.371	.298	238	0	.311	.383	.357	222	1	.279	.385	.338	274	0	.292	.370	.318	151	0	.298	.369	.344	345	1	.281	.380	.319
1997	Tor-A	401	1	.262	.343	.304	214	0	.257	.336	.285	187	1	.267	.350	.326	267	0	.273	.365	.307	134	1	.239	.295	.299	118	0	.169	.238	.212	283	1	.300	.384	.343
1997	LA-N	175	1	.274	.323	.349	84	0	.274	.299	.321	91	1	.275	.343	.374	0	0	—	—	—	175	1	.274	.323	.349	50	1	.320	.358	.480	125	0	.256	.309	.296
1998	Min-A	448	1	.297	.361	.344	221	1	.312	.380	.376	227	0	.282	.343	.313	201	1	.269	.341	.303	247	0	.320	.377	.377	102	1	.216	.283	.265	346	0	.321	.384	.367
1999	Atl-N	151	0	.205	.309	.232	70	0	.186	.269	.200	81	0	.222	.340	.259	117	0	.171	.285	.188	34	0	.324	.395	.382	27	0	.259	.333	.259	124	0	.194	.303	.226
TOTALS		5115	11	.270	.343	.314	2552	5	.272	.351	.317	2563	6	.268	.336	.312	2354	4	.262	.342	.299	2761	7	.276	.345	.327	1671	7	.264	.328	.320	3444	4	.272	.351	.312

		TOTAL					HOME					AWAY					1ST HALF					2ND HALF					LEFT					RIGHT				
YEAR	TM/L	AB	HR	AVG	OBP	SLG	AB	HR	AVG	OBP	SLG	AB	HR	AVG	OBP	SLG	AB	HR	AVG	OBP	SLG	AB	HR	AVG	OBP	SLG	AB	HR	AVG	OBP	SLG	AB	HR	AVG	OBP	SLG
■ Ken Oberkfell BL/TR																																				
1978	StL-N	50	0	.120	.170	.140	24	0	.125	.192	.125	26	0	.115	.148	.154	0	0	—	—	—	50	0	.120	.170	.140	0	0	—	—	—	50	0	.120	.170	.140
1979	StL-N	369	1	.301	.396	.388	173	1	.295	.404	.410	196	0	.306	.389	.367	100	1	.300	.369	.450	269	0	.301	.406	.364	94	0	.287	.417	.362	275	1	.305	.389	.396
1980	StL-N	422	3	.303	.377	.417	204	0	.333	.420	.431	218	3	.275	.335	.404	112	1	.268	.388	.366	310	2	.316	.373	.435	120	0	.233	.316	.342	302	3	.331	.402	.447
1981	StL-N	376	2	.293	.353	.372	190	0	.316	.374	.400	186	2	.269	.330	.344	180	0	.283	.353	.350	196	2	.301	.352	.393	127	1	.291	.328	.394	249	1	.293	.364	.361
1982	StL-N	470	2	.289	.345	.370	235	1	.264	.333	.349	235	1	.315	.357	.391	214	0	.285	.326	.341	256	2	.293	.360	.395	123	0	.236	.293	.276	347	2	.308	.363	.403
1983	StL-N	488	3	.293	.371	.385	225	0	.307	.396	.382	263	3	.281	.348	.388	258	0	.283	.352	.357	230	3	.304	.391	.417	91	0	.198	.263	.242	397	3	.315	.394	.418
1984	StL-N	152	0	.309	.379	.395	72	0	.222	.273	.306	80	0	.387	.467	.475	152	0	.309	.379	.395	0	0	—	—	—	22	0	.273	.273	.318	130	0	.315	.395	.408
1984	Atl-N	172	1	.233	.289	.308	90	1	.244	.290	.356	82	0	.220	.289	.256	53	0	.283	.321	.358	119	1	.210	.276	.286	38	0	.237	.268	.342	134	1	.231	.295	.299
1985	Atl-N	412	3	.272	.359	.359	209	2	.301	.402	.392	203	1	.241	.311	.325	178	1	.287	.335	.376	234	2	.261	.375	.346	115	0	.243	.323	.287	297	3	.283	.372	.387
1986	Atl-N	503	5	.270	.373	.360	268	2	.284	.382	.362	235	3	.255	.363	.357	227	5	.304	.390	.414	276	0	.243	.360	.315	129	2	.233	.333	.310	374	3	.283	.387	.377
1987	Atl-N	508	3	.280	.342	.362	259	2	.293	.363	.382	249	1	.265	.320	.341	250	0	.308	.371	.404	258	3	.252	.313	.322	142	0	.310	.349	.415	366	3	.268	.340	.342
1988	Atl-N	422	3	.277	.325	.365	201	1	.279	.323	.358	221	2	.276	.328	.371	256	2	.258	.311	.340	166	1	.307	.348	.404	88	0	.273	.296	.364	334	3	.278	.333	.365
1988	Pit-N	54	0	.222	.288	.259	23	0	.391	.440	.391	31	0	.097	.176	.161	0	0	—	—	—	54	0	.222	.288	.259	12	0	.167	.231	.250	42	0	.238	.304	.262
1989	Pit-N	40	0	.125	.163	.150	18	0	.222	.286	.278	22	0	.045	.045	.045	40	0	.125	.163	.150	0	0	—	—	—	4	0	.000	.000	.000	36	0	.139	.179	.167
1989	SF-N	116	2	.319	.367	.431	49	1	.306	.364	.388	67	1	.328	.370	.463	39	2	.231	.262	.436	77	0	.364	.419	.429	17	0	.118	.167	.118	99	2	.354	.400	.485
1990	Hou-N	150	1	.207	.281	.280	59	0	.136	.188	.186	91	1	.253	.340	.341	66	1	.212	.293	.318	84	0	.202	.272	.250	17	0	.059	.158	.059	133	1	.226	.297	.308
1991	Hou-N	70	0	.229	.357	.286	24	0	.250	.486	.292	46	0	.217	.265	.283	57	0	.228	.362	.281	13	0	.231	.333	.308	3	0	.333	.333	.333	67	0	.224	.358	.284
1992	Cal-A	91	0	.264	.317	.275	51	0	.235	.293	.235	40	0	.300	.349	.325	0	0	—	—	—	91	0	.264	.317	.275	12	0	.083	.083	.083	79	0	.291	.348	.304
TOTALS		4865	29	.278	.351	.363	2374	11	.285	.364	.368	2491	18	.272	.338	.358	2182	13	.280	.347	.368	2683	16	.277	.354	.359	1154	3	.249	.314	.323	3711	26	.287	.362	.375
■ Pete O'Brien BL/TL																																				
1982	Tex-A	67	4	.239	.297	.507	25	2	.240	.345	.520	42	2	.238	.267	.500	0	0	—	—	—	67	4	.239	.297	.507	9	1	.444	.615	1.000	58	3	.207	.230	.431
1983	Tex-A	524	8	.237	.313	.347	264	4	.261	.347	.394	260	4	.212	.277	.300	253	3	.241	.319	.348	271	5	.232	.307	.347	141	0	.262	.340	.326	383	8	.227	.303	.355
1984	Tex-A	520	18	.287	.348	.448	262	7	.317	.378	.462	258	11	.256	.318	.434	256	8	.309	.365	.477	264	10	.265	.332	.420	150	2	.213	.294	.293	370	16	.316	.371	.511
1985	Tex-A	573	22	.267	.342	.452	277	12	.292	.367	.487	296	10	.243	.318	.419	261	8	.234	.316	.387	312	14	.295	.363	.506	169	2	.225	.289	.296	404	20	.285	.364	.517
1986	Tex-A	551	23	.290	.385	.468	265	11	.268	.356	.442	286	12	.311	.411	.493	248	8	.294	.377	.464	303	15	.287	.392	.472	165	4	.309	.380	.448	386	19	.282	.387	.477
1987	Tex-A	569	23	.286	.348	.457	265	9	.272	.341	.426	304	14	.299	.354	.484	269	17	.283	.343	.509	300	6	.290	.352	.410	186	3	.247	.294	.339	383	20	.305	.373	.514
1988	Tex-A	547	16	.272	.352	.408	266	6	.286	.370	.402	281	10	.260	.335	.413	265	8	.287	.366	.423	282	8	.259	.340	.394	163	3	.252	.305	.350	384	13	.281	.371	.432
1989	Cle-A	554	12	.260	.356	.372	261	5	.287	.386	.398	293	7	.235	.327	.348	274	10	.285	.385	.453	280	2	.236	.325	.293	167	4	.293	.362	.425	387	8	.245	.353	.349
1990	Sea-A	366	5	.224	.308	.314	172	3	.262	.361	.372	194	2	.191	.257	.263	123	2	.187	.268	.268	243	3	.243	.327	.337	130	1	.200	.291	.238	236	4	.237	.317	.356
1991	Sea-A	560	17	.248	.300	.402	290	12	.238	.279	.441	270	5	.259	.321	.359	271	7	.240	.299	.380	289	10	.256	.301	.422	179	4	.235	.280	.363	381	13	.255	.309	.420
1992	Sea-A	396	14	.222	.289	.371	188	6	.218	.286	.372	208	8	.226	.292	.370	238	12	.223	.284	.420	158	2	.222	.297	.297	56	1	.214	.288	.339	340	13	.224	.289	.376
1993	Sea-A	210	7	.257	.335	.390	99	1	.222	.310	.283	111	6	.288	.357	.486	185	7	.265	.338	.416	25	0	.200	.310	.200	25	0	.200	.286	.200	185	7	.265	.341	.416
TOTALS		5437	169	.261	.336	.409	2634	78	.270	.347	.419	2803	91	.254	.326	.400	2643	90	.263	.337	.421	2794	79	.260	.336	.398	1540	25	.249	.316	.347	3897	144	.266	.344	.434
■ Alex Ochoa BR/TR																																				
1995	NY-N	37	0	.297	.333	.324	24	0	.250	.250	.292	13	0	.385	.467	.385	0	0	—	—	—	37	0	.297	.333	.324	18	0	.333	.400	.389	19	0	.263	.263	.263
1996	NY-N	282	4	.294	.336	.426	145	1	.276	.327	.352	137	3	.314	.345	.504	28	0	.357	.387	.500	254	4	.287	.330	.417	91	2	.330	.367	.538	191	2	.277	.320	.372
1997	NY-N	238	3	.244	.300	.349	119	1	.261	.323	.370	119	2	.227	.276	.328	149	1	.221	.272	.309	89	2	.281	.347	.416	107	1	.224	.250	.290	131	2	.260	.338	.397
1998	Min-A	249	2	.257	.288	.353	127	1	.252	.291	.362	122	1	.262	.286	.344	142	2	.239	.275	.345	107	0	.280	.306	.364	106	1	.245	.286	.311	143	1	.266	.291	.385
1999	Mil-A	277	8	.300	.404	.466	148	8	.297	.392	.493	129	0	.302	.418	.434	96	3	.313	.417	.531	181	5	.293	.397	.431	138	5	.319	.418	.522	139	3	.281	.390	.410
2000	Cin-N	244	13	.316	.378	.586	130	9	.285	.371	.592	114	4	.351	.387	.579	63	3	.286	.370	.492	181	10	.326	.381	.619	90	5	.300	.398	.578	154	8	.325	.365	.591
TOTALS		1327	30	.283	.344	.433	693	20	.274	.341	.430	634	10	.293	.348	.437	478	9	.262	.325	.400	849	21	.296	.355	.452	550	14	.285	.351	.444	777	16	.282	.339	.426
■ Ron Oester BB/TR																																				
1978	Cin-N	8	0	.375	.375	.375	8	0	.375	.375	.375	0	0	—	—	—	0	0	—	—	—	8	0	.375	.375	.375	1	0	.000	.000	.000	7	0	.429	.429	.429
1979	Cin-N	3	0	.000	.000	.000	2	0	.000	.000	.000	1	0	.000	.000	.000	0	0	—	—	—	3	0	.000	.000	.000	0	0	—	—	—	3	0	.000	.000	.000
1980	Cin-N	303	2	.277	.336	.363	123	0	.211	.265	.309	180	2	.322	.384	.400	57	0	.281	.305	.351	246	2	.276	.343	.366	79	2	.304	.345	.443	224	0	.268	.333	.335
1981	Cin-N	354	5	.271	.342	.398	180	3	.317	.390	.467	174	2	.224	.293	.328	185	1	.292	.362	.427	169	4	.249	.321	.367	99	0	.253	.286	.283	255	5	.278	.362	.443
1982	Cin-N	549	9	.260	.303	.359	274	4	.281	.334	.391	275	5	.240	.271	.327	302	2	.272	.313	.344	247	7	.247	.292	.377	142	0	.239	.280	.289	407	9	.268	.311	.383
1983	Cin-N	549	11	.264	.322	.384	274	6	.292	.348	.449	275	5	.236	.297	.320	278	6	.295	.332	.432	271	5	.232	.313	.336	142	1	.239	.281	.303	407	10	.273	.336	.413
1984	Cin-N	553	3	.242	.295	.316	288	2	.247	.308	.326	265	1	.238	.281	.306	260	0	.212	.270	.269	293	3	.270	.318	.358	164	1	.232	.272	.287	389	2	.247	.305	.329
1985	Cin-N	526	1	.295	.354	.361	270	0	.304	.354	.378	256	1	.285	.354	.344	214	0	.290	.343	.379	312	1	.298	.361	.349	148	0	.277	.312	.338	378	1	.302	.369	.370
1986	Cin-N	523	8	.258	.325	.356	261	6	.280	.349	.410	262	2	.237	.300	.302	239	5	.234	.297	.339	284	3	.278	.348	.370	136	1	.184	.263	.243	387	7	.284	.347	.395
1987	Cin-N	237	2	.253	.317	.367	125	0	.232	.304	.296	112	2	.277	.331	.446	219	2	.247	.313	.365	18	0	.333	.368	.389	60	0	.200	.262	.217	177	2	.271	.335	.418
1988	Cin-N	150	0	.280	.319	.327	83	0	.253	.315	.277	67	0	.313	.324	.388	0	0	—	—	—	150	0	.280	.319	.327	26	0	.231	.300	.308	124	0	.290	.323	.331
1989	Cin-N	305	1	.246	.318	.305	148	1	.270	.345	.358	157	0	.223	.291	.255	142	1	.190	.253	.246	163	0	.294	.372	.356	63	0	.175	.288	.175	242	1	.264	.326	.339
1990	Cin-N	154	0	.299	.339	.377	53	0	.321	.390	.396	101	0	.287	.311	.366	85	0	.329	.352	.388	69	0	.261	.325	.362	40	0	.300	.349	.375	114	0	.298	.336	.377
TOTALS		4214	42	.265	.323	.356	2089	22	.276	.337	.379	2125	20	.255	.309	.333	1981	17	.260	.313	.355	2233	25	.270	.332	.357	1100	5	.238	.288	.295	3114	37	.275	.335	.378
■ Jose Offerman BB/TR																																				
1990	LA-N	58	1	.155	.210	.207	35	1	.143	.167	.229	23	0	.174	.269	.174	0	0	—	—	—	58	1	.155	.210	.207	26	0	.192	.192	.192	32	1	.125	.222	.219
1991	LA-N	113	0	.195	.345	.212	61	0	.230	.390	.262	52	0	.154	.290	.154	41	0	.195	.327	.220	72	0	.194	.356	.208	50	0	.300	.386	.320	63	0	.111	.317	.127
1992	LA-N	534	1	.260	.331	.333	283	1	.272	.348	.367	251	0	.247	.310	.295	229	0	.262	.335	.336	305	1	.259	.327	.331	201	1	.269	.332	.333	333	0	.255	.330	.333
1993	LA-N	590	1	.269	.346	.331	288	1	.326	.409	.382	302	0	.215	.284	.281	273	0	.271	.350	.330	317	1	.268	.343	.331	184	1	.250	.327	.326	406	0	.278	.354	.333
1994	LA-N	243	1	.210	.314	.288	114	0	.184	.285	.219	129	1	.233	.340	.349	243	1	.210	.314	.288	0	0	—	—	—	68	0	.162	.250	.221	175	1	.229	.338	.314
1995	LA-N	429	4	.287	.389	.375	207	2	.280	.389	.372	222	2	.293	.389	.378	218	1	.321	.429	.422	211	3	.251	.347	.327	123	1	.301	.403	.390	306	3	.281	.384	.369
1996	KC-A	561	5	.303	.384	.417	275	1	.305	.371	.411	286	4	.301	.396	.423	247	1	.279	.370	.344	314	4	.322	.395	.475	193	4	.249	.318	.378	368	1	.332	.417	.438
1997	KC-A	424	2	.297	.359	.394	206	2	.301	.379	.413	218	0	.294	.339	.376	250	2	.312	.377	.428	174	0	.276	.333	.345	129	0	.380	.433	.519	295	2	.261	.327	.339
1998	KC-A	607	7	.315	.403	.438	293	4	.331	.422	.485	314	3	.299	.385	.395	314	4	.280	.372	.424	293	3	.352	.436	.454	195	1	.338	.422	.436	412	6	.303	.394	.439
1999	Bos-A	586	8	.294	.391	.435	283	5	.325	.442	.484	303	3	.264	.338	.389	297	3	.300	.378	.448	289	5	.287	.403	.422	138	3	.268	.377	.399	448	5	.301	.395	.446
2000	Bos-A	451	9	.255	.354	.359	234	3	.282	.378	.380	217	6	.226	.328	.336	228	3	.246	.337	.320	223	6	.265	.372	.399	134	4	.291	.358	.425	317	5	.240	.353	.331
TOTALS		4596	39	.278	.365	.375	2279	20	.294	.386	.398	2317	19	.262	.344	.353	2340	15	.275	.362	.371	2256	24	.281	.368	.379	1441	15	.282	.360	.380	3155	24	.276	.368	.373
■ Ben Oglivie BL/TL																																				
1978	Mil-A	469	18	.303	.370	.497	212	6	.311	.373	.486	257	12	.296	.368	.506	205	12	.273	.359	.512	264	6	.326	.379	.485	36	1	.222	.310	.444	433	17	.309	.376	.501
1979	Mil-A	514	29	.282	.343	.525	267	16	.296	.364	.547	247	13	.267	.321	.502	244	15	.246	.325	.492	270	14	.315	.361	.556	85	6	.341	.392	.588	429	23	.270	.333	.513
1980	Mil-A	592	41	.304	.362	.563	292	15	.253	.311	.445	300	26	.353	.409	.677	253	21	.336	.401	.644	339	20	.280	.332	.501	201	12	.308	.344	.547	391	29	.302	.371	.570
1981	Mil-A	400	14	.243	.310	.395	169	3	.231	.323	.337	231	11	.251	.301	.437	207	5	.237	.315	.362	193	9	.249	.305	.430	119	3	.218	.291	.336	281	11	.253	.319	.420
1982	Mil-A	602	34	.244	.326	.453	284	16	.264	.362	.504	318	18	.226	.293	.409	283	19	.261	.337	.502	319	15	.229	.318	.411	221	9	.222	.283	.389	381	25	.257	.350	.491
1983	Mil-A	411	13	.280	.371	.436	188	8	.309	.385	.495	223	5	.256	.358	.386	219	6	.292	.392	.466	192	7	.266	.345	.401	165	6	.255	.308	.424	246	7	.297	.409	.443
1984	Mil-A	461	12	.262	.327	.384	216	7	.264	.325	.412	245	5	.261	.328	.359	242	4	.269	.331	.364	219	8	.256	.322	.406	153	2	.235	.304	.307	308	10	.276	.338	.422
1985	Mil-A	341	10	.290	.354	.440	160	4	.319	.363	.488	181	6	.265	.346	.398	172	3	.238	.309	.331	169	7	.343	.398	.550	75	2	.213	.237	.387	266	8	.312	.384	.455
1986	Mil-A	346	5	.283	.334	.390	169	2	.290	.340	.402	177	3	.277	.328	.379	198	3	.318	.358	.429	148	2	.236	.304	.338	63	0	.254	.294	.349	283	5	.290	.343	.399
TOTALS		4136	176	.277	.345	.461	1957	77	.280	.349	.463	2179	99	.274	.340	.459	2023	88	.275	.349	.463	2113	88	.278	.340	.460	1118	41	.254	.308	.420	3018	135	.285	.358	.476
■ Troy O'Leary BL/TL																																				
1993	Mil-A	41	0	.293	.370	.366	23	0	.217	.280	.217	18	0	.389	.476	.556	2	0	.500	.500	.500	39	0	.282	.364	.359	9	0	.111	.273	.111	32	0	.344	.400	.438
1994	Mil-A	66	2	.273	.329	.409	20	0	.300	.417	.350	46	2	.261	.286	.435	13	1	.385	.429	.769	53	1	.245	.305	.321	1	0	.000	.000	.000	65	2	.277	.333	.415
1995	Bos-A	399	10	.308	.355	.491	209	5	.349	.390	.555	190	5	.263	.317	.421	167	4	.347	.384	.527	232	6	.280	.335	.466	52	0	.231	.310	.250	347	10	.320	.362	.527
1996	Bos-A	497	15	.260	.327	.427	263	10	.300	.369	.525	234	5	.214	.277	.316	272	8	.261	.332	.412	225	7	.258	.320	.444	106	0	.198	.286	.264	391	15	.276	.338	.471
1997	Bos-A	499	15	.309	.358	.479	246	5	.317	.375	.488	253	10	.300	.342	.470	227	8	.286	.347	.467	272	7	.327	.369	.489	101	2	.277	.327	.426	398	13	.317	.366	.492
1998	Bos-A	611	23	.270	.314	.468	303	12	.323	.364	.558	308	11	.218	.264	.380	311	14	.293	.327	.521	300	9	.247	.300	.413	197	4	.284	.329	.431	414	19	.263	.306	.486
1999	Bos-A	596	28	.280	.343	.495	304	13	.289	.349	.493	292	15	.271	.337	.497	288	16	.309	.364	.545	308	12	.253	.325	.448	156	4	.346	.415	.506	440	24	.257	.318	.491
2000	Bos-A	513	13	.261	.320	.411	261	7	.280	.321	.448	252	6	.242	.318	.373	209	5	.211	.285	.335	304	8	.296	.345	.464	147	3	.252	.291	.367	366	10	.265	.331	.429
TOTALS		3222	106	.280	.335	.460	1629	52	.307	.360	.505	1593	54	.252	.310	.414	1489	56	.285	.339	.474	1733	50	.276	.332	.447	769	13	.272	.331	.394	2453	93	.283	.337	.480
■ John Olerud BL/TL																																				
1989	Tor-A	8	0	.375	.375	.375	7	0	.429	.429	.429	1	0	.000	.000	.000	0	0	—	—	—	8	0	.375	.375	.375	1	0	.000	.000	.000	7	0	.429	.429	.429
1990	Tor-A	358	14	.265	.364	.430	187	11	.273	.372	.497	171	3	.257	.356	.357	194	8	.278	.377	.454	164	6	.250	.349	.402	73	3	.342	.444	.534	285	11	.246	.342	.404
1991	Tor-A	454	17	.256	.353	.438	226	7	.270	.374	.447	228	10	.241	.332	.430	208	8	.226	.322	.394	246	9	.280	.378	.476	83	3	.217	.358	.386	371	14	.264	.352	.450

		TOTAL					HOME					AWAY					1ST HALF					2ND HALF					LEFT					RIGHT				
YEAR	TM/L	AB	HR	AVG	OBP	SLG	AB	HR	AVG	OBP	SLG	AB	HR	AVG	OBP	SLG	AB	HR	AVG	OBP	SLG	AB	HR	AVG	OBP	SLG	AB	HR	AVG	OBP	SLG	AB	HR	AVG	OBP	SLG
1992	Tor-A	458	16	.284	.375	.450	231	4	.264	.368	.385	227	12	.304	.383	.515	223	8	.265	.361	.430	235	8	.302	.388	.468	97	3	.258	.393	.392	361	13	.291	.370	.465
1993	Tor-A	551	24	.363	.473	.599	269	9	.346	.464	.550	282	15	.379	.481	.645	268	14	.407	.506	.690	283	10	.322	.441	.512	172	4	.291	.413	.424	379	20	.396	.500	.678
1994	Tor-A	384	12	.297	.393	.477	190	6	.305	.412	.479	194	6	.289	.373	.474	267	6	.288	.380	.446	117	6	.316	.421	.547	121	3	.264	.353	.380	263	9	.312	.411	.521
1995	Tor-A	492	8	.291	.398	.404	237	1	.270	.384	.359	255	7	.310	.410	.447	210	3	.238	.331	.333	282	5	.330	.444	.457	143	1	.259	.333	.350	349	7	.304	.422	.427
1996	Tor-A	398	18	.274	.382	.472	201	9	.303	.392	.512	197	9	.244	.371	.431	217	11	.253	.378	.452	181	7	.298	.386	.497	64	1	.219	.301	.281	334	17	.284	.396	.509
1997	NY-N	524	22	.294	.400	.489	247	13	.304	.417	.543	277	9	.285	.385	.440	283	13	.322	.413	.541	241	9	.261	.385	.427	145	6	.276	.414	.476	379	16	.301	.394	.493
1998	NY-N	557	22	.354	.447	.551	278	13	.335	.443	.532	279	9	.373	.452	.570	257	6	.319	.430	.459	300	16	.383	.463	.630	152	5	.375	.467	.513	405	17	.346	.440	.565
1999	NY-N	581	19	.298	.427	.463	283	11	.297	.425	.470	298	8	.299	.430	.456	272	12	.309	.444	.522	309	7	.288	.412	.411	166	2	.247	.380	.325	415	17	.318	.447	.518
2000	Sea-A	565	14	.285	.392	.439	284	8	.250	.348	.405	281	6	.320	.435	.473	276	7	.308	.418	.482	289	7	.263	.366	.398	124	0	.242	.354	.315	441	14	.297	.403	.474
TOTALS		5330	186	.299	.404	.477	2640	92	.294	.402	.471	2690	94	.305	.407	.483	2675	96	.296	.402	.480	2655	90	.302	.406	.474	1341	31	.275	.388	.400	3989	155	.307	.410	.503
■ Al Oliver BL/TL																																				
1978	Tex-A	525	14	.324	.358	.490	255	6	.298	.336	.427	270	8	.348	.379	.548	222	8	.288	.318	.486	303	6	.350	.387	.492	162	4	.296	.317	.451	363	10	.336	.375	.507
1979	Tex-A	492	12	.323	.367	.470	227	8	.352	.392	.529	265	4	.298	.346	.419	243	9	.305	.340	.486	249	3	.341	.393	.454	144	1	.250	.314	.319	348	11	.353	.389	.532
1980	Tex-A	656	19	.319	.357	.480	314	8	.385	.415	.548	342	11	.257	.305	.418	286	8	.308	.362	.455	370	11	.327	.354	.500	260	4	.269	.302	.381	396	15	.351	.393	.545
1981	Tex-A	421	4	.309	.348	.411	216	3	.352	.391	.505	205	1	.263	.303	.312	233	3	.322	.351	.451	188	1	.293	.345	.362	158	2	.297	.323	.386	263	2	.316	.363	.426
1982	Mon-N	617	22	.331	.392	.514	296	12	.334	.408	.534	321	10	.327	.377	.495	264	13	.318	.389	.545	353	9	.340	.394	.490	179	7	.330	.389	.531	438	15	.331	.393	.507
1983	Mon-N	614	8	.300	.347	.410	312	5	.311	.358	.439	302	3	.288	.335	.381	288	5	.306	.352	.434	326	3	.294	.343	.390	174	1	.207	.240	.282	440	7	.336	.387	.461
1984	SF-N	339	0	.298	.339	.366	181	0	.320	.353	.409	158	0	.272	.324	.316	262	0	.294	.337	.363	77	0	.312	.346	.377	88	0	.307	.330	.341	251	0	.295	.342	.375
1984	Phi-N	93	0	.312	.360	.387	53	0	.245	.286	.302	40	0	.400	.455	.500	0	0	—	—	—	93	0	.312	.360	.387	20	0	.150	.190	.150	73	0	.356	.405	.452
1985	LA-N	79	0	.253	.294	.316	38	0	.289	.341	.316	41	0	.220	.250	.317	77	0	.260	.301	.325	2	0	.000	.000	.000	18	0	.222	.222	.222	61	0	.262	.313	.344
1985	Tor-A	187	5	.251	.282	.374	86	1	.244	.293	.326	101	4	.257	.272	.416	0	0	—	—	—	187	5	.251	.282	.374	17	1	.235	.235	.529	170	4	.253	.287	.359
TOTALS		4023	84	.311	.355	.447	1978	43	.330	.374	.473	2045	41	.294	.338	.423	1875	46	.304	.349	.453	2148	38	.318	.361	.442	1220	20	.274	.311	.384	2803	64	.328	.374	.475
■ Paul O'Neill BL/TL																																				
1985	Cin-N	12	0	.333	.333	.417	1	0	.000	.000	.000	11	0	.364	.364	.455	0	0	—	—	—	12	0	.333	.333	.417	0	0	—	—	—	12	0	.333	.333	.417
1986	Cin-N	2	0	.000	.333	.000	2	0	.000	.000	.000	0	0	—	1.000	—	2	0	.000	.333	.000	0	0	—	—	—	0	0	—	—	—	2	0	.000	.333	.000
1987	Cin-N	160	7	.256	.331	.488	83	4	.253	.347	.494	77	3	.260	.313	.481	39	2	.154	.250	.359	121	5	.289	.358	.529	11	0	.091	.167	.182	149	7	.268	.343	.510
1988	Cin-N	485	16	.252	.306	.414	237	12	.245	.297	.435	248	4	.258	.314	.395	224	7	.263	.328	.411	261	9	.241	.286	.418	86	1	.233	.280	.349	399	15	.256	.311	.429
1989	Cin-N	428	15	.276	.346	.446	231	11	.316	.373	.545	197	4	.228	.316	.330	278	12	.281	.345	.464	150	3	.267	.347	.413	152	4	.178	.246	.303	276	11	.330	.399	.525
1990	Cin-N	503	16	.270	.339	.421	241	10	.290	.357	.456	262	6	.252	.323	.389	243	10	.284	.357	.461	260	6	.258	.323	.385	143	3	.259	.310	.406	360	13	.275	.351	.428
1991	Cin-N	532	28	.256	.346	.481	268	20	.284	.361	.586	264	8	.227	.331	.375	238	15	.265	.359	.525	294	13	.248	.335	.446	169	3	.201	.254	.308	363	25	.281	.385	.562
1992	Cin-N	496	14	.246	.346	.373	245	6	.237	.354	.359	251	8	.255	.338	.386	227	9	.260	.372	.432	269	5	.234	.324	.323	173	2	.225	.279	.295	323	12	.257	.379	.415
1993	NY-A	498	20	.311	.367	.504	249	8	.325	.377	.498	249	12	.297	.358	.510	259	11	.332	.370	.537	239	9	.289	.365	.469	135	2	.230	.279	.319	363	18	.342	.400	.573
1994	NY-A	368	21	.359	.460	.603	176	10	.409	.490	.659	192	11	.313	.435	.552	244	13	.365	.460	.598	124	8	.347	.461	.613	105	7	.305	.439	.571	263	14	.380	.469	.616
1995	NY-A	460	22	.300	.387	.526	226	12	.319	.419	.580	234	10	.282	.353	.474	148	9	.338	.429	.615	312	13	.282	.366	.484	170	9	.259	.326	.494	290	13	.324	.419	.545
1996	NY-A	546	19	.302	.411	.474	252	7	.325	.438	.460	294	12	.282	.386	.486	288	7	.319	.437	.469	258	12	.283	.380	.481	197	7	.239	.348	.391	349	12	.338	.445	.521
1997	NY-A	553	21	.324	.399	.514	263	10	.308	.393	.494	290	11	.338	.404	.531	267	11	.326	.417	.547	286	10	.322	.381	.483	189	4	.280	.343	.423	364	17	.346	.427	.560
1998	NY-A	602	24	.317	.372	.510	290	10	.324	.383	.493	312	14	.311	.361	.526	306	10	.324	.377	.507	296	14	.311	.367	.514	182	6	.286	.320	.440	420	18	.331	.394	.540
1999	NY-A	597	19	.285	.353	.459	292	9	.253	.349	.418	305	10	.315	.356	.498	270	7	.285	.363	.441	327	12	.284	.343	.474	158	3	.190	.246	.297	439	16	.319	.390	.517
2000	NY-A	566	18	.283	.336	.424	279	10	.287	.350	.448	287	8	.279	.322	.401	288	9	.295	.351	.441	278	9	.270	.320	.406	156	3	.346	.374	.462	410	15	.259	.322	.410
TOTALS		6808	260	.289	.365	.471	3335	139	.297	.377	.489	3473	121	.281	.353	.453	3321	132	.301	.380	.490	3487	128	.278	.350	.453	2026	54	.247	.311	.386	4782	206	.307	.387	.507
■ Jose Oquendo BB/TR																																				
1983	NY-N	328	1	.213	.260	.244	166	0	.217	.278	.253	162	1	.210	.241	.235	153	0	.268	.327	.307	175	1	.166	.198	.189	92	1	.261	.317	.304	236	0	.195	.237	.220
1984	NY-N	189	0	.222	.284	.249	104	0	.231	.264	.260	85	0	.212	.306	.235	176	0	.210	.273	.239	13	0	.385	.429	.385	59	0	.237	.303	.271	130	0	.215	.275	.238
1986	StL-N	138	0	.297	.359	.341	61	0	.311	.386	.377	77	0	.286	.337	.312	60	0	.367	.437	.433	78	0	.244	.294	.269	44	0	.364	.408	.432	94	0	.266	.336	.298
1987	StL-N	248	1	.286	.408	.335	111	0	.297	.424	.342	137	1	.277	.395	.328	134	0	.321	.437	.381	114	1	.246	.374	.281	112	1	.277	.375	.339	136	0	.294	.435	.331
1988	StL-N	451	7	.277	.350	.350	228	4	.289	.362	.360	223	3	.265	.337	.341	192	2	.286	.343	.349	259	5	.270	.355	.351	154	7	.299	.343	.461	297	0	.266	.353	.293
1989	StL-N	556	1	.291	.375	.372	269	0	.301	.387	.409	287	1	.282	.364	.338	258	0	.252	.330	.306	298	1	.326	.412	.430	229	0	.266	.340	.354	327	1	.309	.398	.385
1990	StL-N	469	1	.252	.350	.316	238	1	.239	.330	.294	231	0	.264	.371	.338	235	1	.247	.350	.311	234	0	.256	.351	.321	164	1	.220	.319	.287	305	0	.269	.367	.331
1991	StL-N	366	1	.240	.357	.301	184	0	.261	.372	.299	182	1	.220	.342	.302	181	1	.215	.353	.282	185	0	.265	.361	.319	150	1	.240	.365	.327	216	0	.241	.352	.282
1992	StL-N	35	0	.257	.350	.400	12	0	.250	.357	.250	23	0	.261	.346	.478	10	0	.200	.385	.300	25	0	.280	.333	.440	12	0	.167	.333	.250	23	0	.304	.360	.478
1993	StL-N	73	0	.205	.314	.205	26	0	.192	.250	.192	47	0	.213	.345	.213	47	0	.255	.375	.255	26	0	.115	.200	.115	24	0	.125	.160	.125	49	0	.245	.377	.245
1994	StL-N	129	0	.264	.364	.310	58	0	.293	.425	.397	71	0	.239	.308	.239	87	0	.264	.393	.310	42	0	.262	.295	.310	35	0	.343	.385	.371	94	0	.234	.357	.287
1995	StL-N	220	2	.209	.316	.300	100	0	.230	.369	.330	120	2	.192	.269	.275	125	1	.224	.340	.304	95	1	.189	.284	.295	54	2	.204	.317	.426	166	0	.211	.316	.259
TOTALS		3202	14	.256	.346	.317	1557	5	.265	.355	.328	1645	9	.249	.337	.306	1658	5	.256	.350	.311	1544	9	.256	.341	.323	1129	13	.259	.340	.346	2073	1	.255	.348	.301
■ Magglio Ordonez BR/TR																																				
1997	Chi-A	69	4	.319	.338	.580	46	2	.326	.354	.565	23	2	.304	.304	.609	0	0	—	—	—	69	4	.319	.338	.580	17	1	.294	.294	.588	52	3	.327	.352	.577
1998	Chi-A	535	14	.282	.326	.415	266	8	.293	.339	.451	269	6	.271	.314	.379	266	9	.271	.307	.421	269	5	.294	.345	.409	120	5	.267	.302	.433	415	9	.287	.333	.410
1999	Chi-A	624	30	.301	.349	.510	294	16	.303	.358	.514	330	14	.300	.340	.506	294	17	.333	.377	.568	330	13	.273	.323	.458	103	3	.320	.388	.476	521	27	.298	.340	.516
2000	Chi-A	588	32	.315	.371	.546	283	21	.329	.397	.625	305	11	.302	.347	.472	278	17	.331	.405	.601	310	15	.300	.339	.497	98	6	.337	.393	.602	490	26	.310	.367	.535
TOTALS		1816	80	.301	.349	.496	889	47	.309	.365	.533	927	33	.292	.334	.461	838	43	.313	.366	.532	978	37	.290	.335	.465	338	15	.305	.356	.503	1478	65	.300	.348	.495
■ Joe Orsulak BL/TL																																				
1983	Pit-N	11	0	.182	.167	.182	1	0	.000	.000	.000	10	0	.200	.182	.200	0	0	—	—	—	11	0	.182	.167	.182	2	0	1.000	1.000	1.000	9	0	.000	.000	.000
1984	Pit-N	67	0	.254	.271	.328	43	0	.233	.261	.326	24	0	.292	.292	.333	21	0	.143	.182	.143	46	0	.304	.313	.413	13	0	.308	.357	.308	54	0	.241	.250	.333
1985	Pit-N	397	0	.300	.342	.365	184	0	.370	.410	.451	213	0	.239	.282	.291	138	0	.297	.349	.370	259	0	.301	.338	.363	65	0	.215	.224	.231	332	0	.316	.364	.392
1986	Pit-N	401	2	.249	.299	.342	183	0	.224	.285	.301	218	2	.271	.312	.376	208	1	.250	.308	.332	193	1	.249	.289	.352	50	0	.260	.288	.320	351	2	.248	.301	.345
1988	Bal-A	379	8	.288	.331	.422	174	3	.287	.326	.408	205	5	.288	.335	.434	170	0	.271	.322	.318	209	8	.301	.338	.507	68	0	.235	.321	.235	311	8	.299	.333	.463
1989	Bal-A	390	7	.285	.351	.421	194	0	.273	.339	.366	196	7	.296	.362	.474	196	2	.291	.355	.423	194	5	.278	.347	.418	84	0	.202	.244	.262	306	7	.307	.378	.464
1990	Bal-A	413	11	.269	.343	.397	202	9	.272	.348	.441	211	2	.265	.338	.355	225	6	.289	.363	.436	188	5	.245	.319	.351	72	0	.250	.325	.278	341	11	.273	.346	.422
1991	Bal-A	486	5	.278	.321	.358	235	3	.277	.322	.357	251	2	.279	.320	.359	220	3	.232	.277	.300	266	2	.316	.357	.406	64	0	.234	.286	.281	422	5	.284	.326	.370
1992	Bal-A	391	4	.289	.342	.381	180	2	.278	.347	.361	211	2	.299	.338	.398	169	1	.278	.328	.349	222	3	.297	.353	.405	80	0	.250	.307	.338	311	4	.299	.351	.392
1993	NY-N	409	8	.284	.331	.399	179	5	.285	.350	.413	230	3	.283	.315	.387	178	4	.298	.340	.399	231	4	.273	.324	.398	42	0	.357	.364	.429	367	8	.275	.327	.395
1994	NY-N	292	8	.260	.299	.353	132	4	.303	.349	.402	160	4	.225	.256	.313	214	7	.262	.301	.374	78	1	.256	.293	.295	42	0	.214	.261	.238	250	8	.268	.305	.372
1995	NY-N	290	1	.283	.323	.372	126	1	.325	.353	.437	164	0	.250	.300	.323	123	0	.301	.336	.374	167	1	.269	.314	.371	25	0	.160	.185	.200	265	1	.294	.336	.389
1996	Fla-N	217	2	.221	.274	.286	115	2	.261	.301	.348	102	0	.176	.243	.216	73	1	.192	.244	.274	144	1	.236	.288	.292	22	0	.273	.304	.318	195	2	.215	.270	.282
1997	Mon-N	150	1	.227	.310	.340	81	0	.198	.293	.284	69	1	.261	.329	.406	95	1	.232	.330	.358	55	0	.218	.271	.309	14	0	.000	.067	.000	136	1	.250	.333	.375
TOTALS		4293	57	.273	.324	.374	2029	29	.281	.336	.383	2264	28	.266	.314	.365	2030	26	.268	.322	.362	2263	31	.278	.326	.384	643	0	.238	.284	.280	3650	57	.279	.331	.390
■ Jorge Orta BL/TR																																				
1978	Chi-A	420	13	.274	.340	.421	200	9	.330	.389	.530	220	4	.223	.296	.323	255	11	.286	.339	.475	165	2	.255	.342	.339	156	0	.269	.331	.321	264	13	.277	.346	.481
1979	Chi-A	325	11	.262	.348	.437	164	5	.226	.303	.372	161	6	.298	.392	.503	177	3	.220	.324	.322	148	8	.311	.377	.574	55	0	.164	.277	.182	270	11	.281	.362	.489
1980	Cle-A	481	10	.291	.379	.403	227	6	.322	.409	.454	254	4	.264	.352	.358	234	4	.338	.428	.436	247	6	.247	.332	.372	174	0	.316	.401	.368	307	10	.277	.367	.423
1981	Cle-A	338	5	.272	.312	.376	181	2	.238	.276	.309	157	3	.312	.355	.452	157	3	.268	.282	.363	181	2	.276	.337	.387	120	1	.217	.254	.283	218	4	.303	.345	.427
1982	LA-N	115	2	.217	.295	.313	57	1	.158	.250	.246	58	1	.276	.338	.379	68	2	.250	.307	.382	47	0	.170	.278	.213	1	0	.000	.000	.000	114	2	.219	.297	.316
1983	Tor-A	245	10	.237	.287	.408	118	7	.229	.277	.466	127	3	.244	.297	.354	97	4	.268	.330	.454	148	6	.216	.259	.378	3	0	.000	.000	.000	242	10	.240	.291	.413
1984	KC-A	403	9	.298	.343	.457	196	3	.265	.315	.418	207	6	.329	.371	.493	172	5	.308	.348	.494	231	4	.290	.340	.429	20	0	.350	.435	.350	383	9	.295	.338	.462
1985	KC-A	300	4	.267	.317	.383	142	1	.275	.329	.373	158	3	.259	.306	.392	198	2	.268	.310	.374	102	2	.265	.330	.402	12	0	.083	.083	.083	288	4	.274	.326	.396
1986	KC-A	336	9	.277	.321	.411	188	5	.298	.343	.452	148	4	.250	.294	.358	155	2	.316	.361	.419	181	7	.243	.286	.403	19	0	.211	.250	.211	317	9	.281	.326	.423
1987	KC-A	50	2	.180	.226	.380	9	0	.000	.000	.000	41	2	.220	.273	.463	50	2	.180	.226	.380	0	0	—	—	—	0	0	—	—	—	50	2	.180	.226	.380
TOTALS		3013	75	.271	.333	.409	1482	39	.271	.332	.415	1531	36	.271	.334	.403	1563	38	.282	.340	.416	1450	37	.260	.325	.401	560	1	.257	.326	.304	2453	74	.274	.334	.433
■ Spike Owen BB/TR																																				
1983	Sea-A	306	2	.196	.257	.271	159	1	.201	.251	.302	147	1	.190	.262	.238	21	0	.333	.417	.571	285	2	.186	.244	.249	113	1	.239	.282	.389	193	1	.171	.242	.202
1984	Sea-A	530	3	.245	.308	.326	261	2	.226	.285	.303	269	1	.264	.330	.349	258	2	.279	.353	.399	272	1	.213	.264	.257	158	1	.234	.297	.342	372	2	.250	.313	.320
1985	Sea-A	352	6	.259	.322	.372	201	3	.274	.338	.383	151	3	.238	.301	.358	192	3	.245	.321	.359	160	3	.275	.324	.387	90	1	.256	.302	.356	262	5	.260	.329	.378
1986	Sea-A	402	0	.246	.305	.331	203	0	.251	.317	.374	199	0	.241	.293	.286	256	0	.258	.310	.367	146	0	.226	.296	.267	86	0	.267	.337	.349	316	0	.241	.297	.326
1986	Bos-A	126	1	.183	.283	.238	65	0	.231	.359	.292	61	1	.131	.194	.180	0	0	—	—	—	126	1	.183	.283	.238	35	1	.286	.350	.400	91	0	.143	.257	.176
1987	Bos-A	437	2	.259	.337	.343	224	2	.263	.341	.371	213	0	.254	.333	.315	170	0	.241	.323	.353	267	2	.270	.347	.337	134	2	.321	.393	.455	303	0	.231	.313	.294

YEAR	TM/L	TOTAL AB	HR	AVG	OBP	SLG	HOME AB	HR	AVG	OBP	SLG	AWAY AB	HR	AVG	OBP	SLG	1ST HALF AB	HR	AVG	OBP	SLG	2ND HALF AB	HR	AVG	OBP	SLG	LEFT AB	HR	AVG	OBP	SLG	RIGHT AB	HR	AVG	OBP	SLG
1988	Bos-A	257	5	.249	.324	.370	104	2	.279	.348	.423	153	3	.229	.308	.333	167	5	.251	.330	.407	90	0	.244	.313	.300	98	4	.276	.324	.480	159	1	.233	.324	.302
1989	Mon-N	437	6	.233	.349	.332	201	5	.274	.383	.408	236	1	.199	.319	.267	227	4	.238	.379	.366	210	2	.229	.312	.295	131	2	.275	.371	.374	306	4	.216	.340	.314
1990	Mon-N	453	5	.234	.333	.342	215	2	.228	.332	.335	238	3	.239	.335	.349	233	4	.245	.345	.365	220	1	.223	.320	.318	201	3	.259	.330	.403	252	2	.214	.336	.294
1991	Mon-N	424	3	.255	.321	.366	161	1	.211	.291	.280	263	2	.281	.339	.418	197	1	.203	.299	.294	227	2	.300	.340	.427	200	1	.305	.350	.430	224	2	.210	.296	.308
1992	Mon-N	386	7	.269	.348	.381	173	3	.243	.323	.347	213	4	.291	.369	.408	204	6	.260	.333	.422	182	1	.280	.365	.335	161	4	.286	.346	.447	225	3	.258	.350	.333
1993	NY-A	334	2	.234	.294	.311	157	1	.210	.256	.280	177	1	.254	.327	.339	239	2	.259	.335	.343	95	0	.168	.184	.232	137	1	.248	.290	.328	197	1	.223	.297	.299
1994	Cal-A	268	3	.310	.418	.422	164	2	.311	.408	.451	104	1	.308	.433	.375	147	2	.293	.395	.422	121	1	.331	.445	.421	83	3	.289	.416	.494	185	0	.319	.419	.389
1995	Cal-A	218	1	.229	.288	.312	96	0	.229	.282	.292	122	1	.230	.293	.328	123	1	.228	.301	.325	95	0	.232	.270	.295	44	0	.205	.271	.273	174	1	.236	.293	.322
TOTALS		4930	46	.246	.324	.341	2384	24	.246	.323	.349	2546	22	.245	.324	.334	2434	30	.251	.337	.371	2496	16	.240	.310	.313	1671	24	.270	.335	.400	3259	22	.233	.318	.311
■ Eric Owens	BR/TR																																			
1995	Cin-N	2	0	1.000	1.000	1.000	2	0	1.000	1.000	1.000	0	0	—	—	—	2	0	1.000	1.000	1.000	0	0	—	—	—	1	0	1.000	1.000	1.000	1	0	1.000	1.000	1.000
1996	Cin-N	205	0	.200	.281	.229	120	0	.225	.304	.267	85	0	.165	.250	.176	134	0	.231	.309	.269	71	0	.141	.228	.155	106	0	.236	.308	.274	99	0	.162	.252	.182
1997	Cin-N	57	0	.263	.311	.263	36	0	.222	.243	.222	21	0	.333	.417	.333	16	0	.250	.333	.250	41	0	.268	.302	.268	23	0	.217	.280	.217	34	0	.294	.333	.294
1998	Mil-A	40	1	.125	.167	.250	23	0	.174	.240	.261	17	1	.059	.059	.235	40	1	.125	.167	.250	0	0	—	—	—	19	0	.158	.200	.263	21	1	.095	.136	.238
1999	SD-N	440	9	.266	.327	.391	202	2	.267	.344	.356	238	7	.265	.313	.420	204	5	.284	.326	.422	236	4	.250	.328	.364	130	4	.231	.318	.392	310	5	.281	.331	.390
2000	SD-N	583	6	.293	.346	.381	288	4	.299	.350	.389	295	2	.288	.342	.373	296	4	.338	.390	.432	287	2	.247	.300	.328	179	4	.307	.359	.436	404	2	.287	.340	.356
TOTALS		1327	16	.265	.324	.353	671	6	.270	.332	.346	656	10	.259	.315	.360	692	10	.289	.343	.384	635	6	.238	.303	.318	458	8	.260	.326	.369	869	8	.267	.322	.344
■ Tom Paciorek	BR/TR																																			
1978	Atl-N	9	0	.333	.333	.333	4	0	.500	.500	.500	5	0	.200	.200	.200	9	0	.333	.333	.333	0	0	—	—	—	7	0	.286	.286	.286	2	0	.500	.500	.500
1978	Sea-A	251	4	.299	.336	.450	107	3	.308	.359	.467	144	1	.292	.318	.438	9	0	.000	.000	.000	242	4	.310	.347	.467	102	1	.373	.398	.529	149	3	.248	.294	.396
1979	Sea-A	310	6	.287	.353	.445	156	6	.314	.386	.526	154	0	.260	.318	.364	102	2	.294	.342	.461	208	4	.284	.357	.438	156	4	.327	.391	.526	154	2	.247	.314	.364
1980	Sea-A	418	15	.273	.301	.431	209	11	.282	.307	.493	209	4	.263	.295	.368	169	8	.331	.360	.533	249	7	.233	.262	.361	169	7	.272	.313	.462	249	8	.273	.293	.410
1981	Sea-A	405	14	.326	.379	.509	202	7	.302	.364	.470	203	7	.350	.395	.547	201	5	.328	.371	.483	204	9	.324	.387	.534	123	4	.301	.362	.463	282	10	.337	.387	.528
1982	Chi-A	382	11	.312	.361	.490	178	0	.281	.330	.382	204	11	.338	.388	.583	234	4	.312	.357	.453	148	7	.311	.367	.547	122	3	.336	.396	.533	260	8	.300	.344	.469
1983	Chi-A	420	9	.307	.347	.462	192	4	.333	.377	.495	228	5	.285	.322	.434	195	4	.256	.292	.379	225	5	.351	.395	.533	197	5	.340	.373	.497	223	4	.278	.325	.430
1984	Chi-A	363	4	.256	.308	.358	190	2	.284	.335	.389	173	2	.225	.279	.324	208	2	.269	.317	.365	155	2	.239	.296	.348	192	3	.266	.302	.375	171	1	.246	.314	.339
1985	Chi-A	122	0	.246	.293	.262	46	0	.239	.308	.261	76	0	.250	.284	.263	92	0	.261	.303	.283	30	0	.200	.265	.200	85	0	.282	.326	.306	37	0	.162	.220	.162
1985	NY-N	116	1	.284	.325	.353	59	1	.356	.406	.441	57	0	.211	.237	.263	0	0	—	—	—	116	1	.284	.325	.353	92	1	.337	.378	.424	24	0	.083	.120	.083
1986	Tex-A	213	4	.286	.305	.376	90	0	.233	.250	.267	123	4	.325	.344	.455	118	2	.305	.322	.398	95	2	.263	.283	.347	125	2	.288	.310	.344	88	2	.284	.297	.420
1987	Tex-A	60	3	.283	.302	.483	41	2	.293	.286	.488	19	1	.263	.333	.474	25	0	.200	.222	.200	35	3	.343	.361	.686	41	3	.244	.256	.512	19	0	.368	.400	.421
TOTALS		3069	71	.292	.336	.434	1474	36	.296	.344	.442	1595	35	.287	.328	.428	1362	27	.293	.332	.419	1707	44	.291	.339	.446	1411	33	.308	.350	.451	1658	38	.278	.323	.420
■ Mike Pagliarulo	BL/TR																																			
1984	NY-A	201	7	.239	.288	.448	105	4	.257	.313	.457	96	3	.219	.260	.438	0	0	—	—	—	201	7	.239	.288	.448	30	0	.233	.361	.367	171	7	.240	.273	.462
1985	NY-A	380	19	.239	.324	.442	178	8	.242	.320	.416	202	11	.238	.328	.465	146	5	.212	.328	.370	234	14	.256	.322	.487	51	2	.157	.267	.275	329	17	.252	.333	.468
1986	NY-A	504	28	.238	.316	.464	243	14	.230	.325	.453	261	14	.245	.307	.475	251	16	.247	.323	.506	253	12	.229	.309	.423	163	2	.196	.254	.288	341	26	.258	.344	.548
1987	NY-A	522	32	.234	.305	.479	243	17	.214	.308	.473	279	15	.251	.302	.484	250	12	.232	.314	.436	272	20	.235	.296	.518	152	4	.230	.283	.355	370	28	.235	.314	.530
1988	NY-A	444	15	.216	.276	.367	203	8	.192	.250	.355	241	7	.237	.298	.378	277	9	.220	.279	.375	167	6	.210	.271	.353	106	5	.170	.224	.358	338	10	.231	.292	.370
1989	NY-A	223	4	.197	.266	.296	113	3	.204	.268	.319	110	1	.191	.264	.273	178	3	.202	.276	.303	45	1	.178	.229	.267	33	0	.242	.306	.303	190	4	.189	.260	.295
1989	SD-N	148	3	.196	.287	.304	69	2	.188	.291	.290	79	1	.203	.284	.316	0	0	—	—	—	148	3	.196	.287	.304	26	0	.154	.185	.192	122	3	.205	.307	.328
1990	SD-N	398	7	.254	.322	.374	169	1	.272	.354	.361	229	6	.240	.298	.384	167	3	.263	.347	.395	231	4	.247	.303	.359	101	4	.248	.353	.396	297	3	.256	.311	.367
1991	Min-A	365	6	.279	.322	.384	190	4	.284	.332	.405	175	2	.274	.312	.360	167	3	.246	.280	.359	198	3	.308	.356	.404	16	0	.188	.316	.250	349	6	.284	.323	.390
1992	Min-A	105	0	.200	.213	.238	46	0	.217	.229	.261	59	0	.186	.200	.220	17	0	.118	.118	.118	88	0	.216	.231	.261	6	0	.167	.167	.167	99	0	.202	.216	.242
1993	Min-A	253	3	.292	.350	.423	107	2	.336	.388	.533	146	1	.260	.323	.342	143	3	.294	.340	.483	110	0	.291	.363	.345	20	0	.450	.500	.500	233	3	.279	.337	.416
1993	Bal-A	117	6	.325	.373	.556	62	3	.355	.403	.581	55	3	.291	.339	.527	0	0	—	—	—	117	6	.325	.373	.556	16	0	.375	.412	.438	101	6	.317	.367	.574
1995	Tex-A	241	4	.232	.277	.349	114	1	.219	.252	.272	127	3	.244	.298	.417	104	0	.260	.304	.327	137	4	.212	.257	.365	18	0	.222	.364	.333	223	4	.233	.269	.350
TOTALS		3901	134	.241	.306	.407	1842	67	.242	.312	.407	2059	67	.241	.300	.407	1700	54	.238	.307	.399	2201	80	.244	.304	.412	738	17	.217	.289	.335	3163	117	.247	.309	.423
■ Rafael Palmeiro	BL/TL																																			
1986	Chi-N	73	3	.247	.295	.425	38	1	.211	.268	.342	35	2	.286	.324	.514	0	0	—	—	—	73	3	.247	.295	.425	8	0	.125	.125	.250	65	3	.262	.314	.446
1987	Chi-N	221	14	.276	.336	.543	88	5	.273	.333	.500	133	9	.278	.338	.571	34	2	.265	.350	.559	187	12	.278	.333	.540	26	1	.115	.226	.231	195	13	.297	.352	.585
1988	Chi-N	580	8	.307	.349	.436	290	8	.321	.362	.486	290	0	.293	.337	.386	306	6	.324	.363	.467	274	2	.288	.334	.401	171	2	.333	.364	.480	409	6	.296	.343	.418
1989	Tex-A	559	8	.275	.354	.374	263	4	.259	.348	.354	296	4	.291	.360	.392	302	5	.315	.378	.430	257	3	.230	.327	.307	165	2	.248	.302	.333	394	6	.287	.375	.391
1990	Tex-A	598	14	.319	.361	.468	295	9	.288	.354	.478	303	5	.350	.367	.459	271	7	.321	.361	.472	327	7	.318	.361	.465	189	5	.339	.361	.476	409	9	.311	.360	.465
1991	Tex-A	631	26	.322	.389	.532	298	12	.339	.408	.540	333	14	.306	.372	.526	293	9	.317	.368	.495	338	17	.325	.407	.565	186	9	.274	.333	.473	445	17	.342	.411	.557
1992	Tex-A	608	22	.268	.352	.434	297	8	.263	.354	.401	311	14	.273	.350	.466	291	8	.254	.351	.402	317	14	.281	.353	.464	178	5	.281	.365	.438	430	17	.263	.347	.433
1993	Tex-A	597	37	.295	.371	.554	294	22	.282	.360	.578	303	15	.307	.382	.531	279	13	.276	.329	.480	318	24	.311	.406	.619	149	2	.268	.323	.356	448	35	.304	.387	.621
1994	Bal-A	436	23	.319	.392	.550	209	11	.340	.401	.574	227	12	.300	.383	.529	291	13	.326	.408	.540	145	10	.303	.358	.572	145	10	.352	.424	.641	291	13	.302	.375	.505
1995	Bal-A	554	39	.310	.380	.583	265	21	.336	.417	.634	289	18	.287	.344	.536	226	13	.305	.378	.553	328	26	.314	.381	.604	202	14	.292	.347	.545	352	25	.321	.398	.605
1996	Bal-A	626	39	.289	.381	.546	299	21	.284	.396	.545	327	18	.294	.366	.547	305	20	.308	.403	.570	321	19	.271	.360	.523	244	14	.295	.367	.545	382	25	.285	.389	.547
1997	Bal-A	614	38	.254	.329	.485	299	20	.247	.326	.475	315	18	.260	.332	.495	312	13	.253	.327	.426	302	25	.255	.332	.546	225	15	.213	.275	.440	389	23	.278	.360	.512
1998	Bal-A	619	43	.296	.379	.565	298	25	.275	.365	.567	321	18	.315	.393	.564	323	24	.294	.379	.579	296	19	.297	.379	.551	230	15	.317	.387	.591	389	28	.283	.375	.550
1999	Tex-A	565	47	.324	.420	.630	271	28	.325	.438	.697	294	19	.323	.402	.568	276	20	.362	.444	.641	289	27	.287	.398	.619	146	11	.274	.345	.555	419	36	.341	.444	.656
2000	Tex-A	565	39	.288	.397	.558	288	26	.292	.417	.622	277	13	.285	.375	.491	272	21	.294	.400	.577	293	18	.283	.394	.539	144	10	.326	.415	.569	421	29	.276	.391	.553
TOTALS		7846	400	.296	.372	.516	3792	221	.294	.378	.531	4054	179	.298	.365	.502	3781	174	.303	.376	.509	4065	226	.289	.368	.522	2408	115	.289	.351	.493	5438	285	.299	.380	.526
■ Dean Palmer	BR/TR																																			
1989	Tex-A	19	0	.105	.100	.211	11	0	.091	.083	.182	8	0	.125	.125	.250	0	0	—	—	—	19	0	.105	.100	.211	11	0	.182	.182	.364	8	0	.000	.000	.000
1991	Tex-A	268	15	.187	.281	.403	114	6	.140	.279	.342	154	9	.221	.281	.448	19	2	.316	.381	.632	249	13	.177	.273	.386	81	9	.247	.337	.617	187	6	.160	.256	.310
1992	Tex-A	541	26	.229	.311	.420	264	11	.242	.337	.413	277	15	.217	.286	.426	271	12	.247	.327	.443	270	14	.211	.295	.396	143	8	.252	.333	.469	398	18	.221	.303	.402
1993	Tex-A	519	33	.245	.321	.503	252	12	.246	.329	.437	267	21	.243	.314	.566	250	16	.232	.321	.512	269	17	.257	.322	.494	101	6	.257	.367	.475	418	27	.242	.310	.510
1994	Tex-A	342	19	.246	.302	.465	187	11	.225	.271	.444	155	8	.271	.337	.490	205	13	.254	.316	.512	137	6	.234	.281	.394	76	4	.276	.337	.461	266	15	.237	.292	.466
1995	Tex-A	119	9	.336	.448	.613	71	5	.338	.448	.592	48	4	.333	.448	.646	115	9	.330	.447	.617	4	0	.500	.500	.500	37	3	.432	.500	.757	82	6	.293	.427	.549
1996	Tex-A	582	38	.280	.348	.527	275	19	.276	.350	.535	307	19	.283	.347	.521	283	18	.293	.364	.544	299	20	.268	.332	.512	152	12	.303	.382	.599	430	26	.272	.336	.502
1997	Tex-A	355	14	.245	.296	.423	177	6	.226	.275	.373	178	8	.264	.318	.472	287	7	.237	.288	.373	68	7	.279	.329	.632	98	4	.235	.276	.398	257	10	.249	.304	.432
1997	KC-A	187	9	.278	.335	.487	95	4	.263	.339	.432	92	5	.293	.330	.543	0	0	—	—	—	187	9	.278	.335	.487	48	4	.250	.302	.521	139	5	.288	.346	.475
1998	KC-A	572	34	.278	.333	.510	284	21	.264	.321	.525	288	13	.292	.346	.497	285	16	.288	.334	.523	287	18	.268	.332	.498	139	6	.317	.357	.511	433	28	.266	.326	.510
1999	Det-A	560	38	.262	.339	.518	265	24	.264	.343	.558	295	14	.261	.335	.481	271	21	.284	.353	.568	289	17	.242	.326	.471	100	10	.390	.432	.750	460	28	.235	.319	.467
2000	Det-A	524	29	.256	.338	.471	251	15	.263	.351	.494	273	14	.249	.325	.451	229	15	.266	.358	.515	295	14	.247	.322	.437	123	6	.228	.329	.415	401	23	.264	.341	.489
TOTALS		4588	264	.255	.327	.481	2246	134	.250	.328	.472	2342	130	.260	.326	.491	2215	129	.267	.340	.505	2373	135	.243	.314	.460	1109	72	.282	.353	.527	3479	192	.246	.318	.467
■ Dave Parker	BL/TR																																			
1978	Pit-N	581	30	.334	.394	.585	281	14	.367	.424	.673	300	16	.303	.366	.503	282	13	.316	.377	.535	299	17	.351	.410	.632	236	10	.322	.370	.538	345	20	.342	.410	.617
1979	Pit-N	622	25	.310	.380	.526	308	14	.341	.395	.562	314	11	.280	.367	.490	288	13	.295	.362	.514	334	12	.323	.396	.536	247	13	.300	.352	.551	375	12	.317	.399	.509
1980	Pit-N	518	17	.295	.327	.458	235	10	.294	.332	.494	283	7	.297	.323	.428	268	9	.295	.329	.451	250	8	.296	.326	.464	185	5	.276	.306	.432	333	12	.306	.339	.471
1981	Pit-N	240	9	.258	.287	.454	96	4	.219	.260	.406	144	5	.285	.307	.486	126	5	.286	.303	.476	114	4	.228	.270	.430	74	2	.257	.291	.419	166	7	.259	.286	.470
1982	Pit-N	244	6	.270	.330	.447	102	4	.284	.342	.500	142	2	.261	.321	.408	139	3	.266	.344	.432	105	3	.276	.310	.467	52	0	.231	.255	.346	192	6	.281	.349	.474
1983	Pit-N	552	12	.279	.311	.411	269	6	.294	.313	.468	283	6	.265	.308	.357	219	3	.251	.292	.361	333	9	.297	.323	.444	139	7	.245	.267	.468	413	5	.291	.325	.392
1984	Cin-N	607	16	.285	.328	.410	299	10	.308	.360	.458	308	6	.263	.296	.364	299	6	.284	.318	.395	308	10	.286	.338	.425	207	5	.285	.304	.391	400	11	.285	.340	.420
1985	Cin-N	635	34	.312	.365	.551	312	16	.308	.356	.535	323	18	.316	.373	.567	282	14	.316	.374	.539	353	20	.309	.357	.561	201	7	.279	.305	.443	434	27	.327	.390	.601
1986	Cin-N	637	31	.273	.330	.477	313	17	.268	.325	.505	324	14	.278	.335	.451	289	15	.287	.350	.495	348	16	.261	.313	.463	232	10	.302	.325	.513	405	21	.257	.333	.457
1987	Cin-N	589	26	.253	.311	.433	291	14	.282	.339	.478	298	12	.225	.284	.389	301	18	.269	.328	.492	288	8	.236	.292	.372	205	8	.239	.285	.410	384	18	.260	.324	.445
1988	Oak-A	377	12	.257	.314	.406	177	6	.271	.325	.407	200	6	.245	.305	.405	263	9	.266	.319	.430	114	3	.237	.302	.351	55	2	.182	.274	.309	322	10	.270	.321	.422
1989	Oak-A	553	22	.264	.308	.432	272	10	.279	.334	.426	281	12	.249	.282	.438	275	11	.273	.308	.447	278	11	.255	.308	.417	127	6	.228	.233	.409	426	16	.275	.329	.439
1990	Mil-A	610	21	.289	.330	.451	293	9	.273	.316	.427	317	12	.303	.344	.473	271	9	.321	.358	.506	339	12	.263	.308	.407	185	6	.259	.282	.389	425	15	.301	.350	.478
1991	Cal-A	466	11	.232	.279	.358	213	6	.202	.260	.333	253	5	.257	.296	.379	275	6	.222	.269	.342	191	5	.246	.294	.382	128	4	.234	.261	.383	338	7	.231	.286	.349
1991	Tor-A	36	0	.333	.400	.444	16	0	.375	.444	.563	20	0	.300	.364	.350	0	0	—	—	—	36	0	.333	.400	.444	5	0	.200	.200	.400	31	0	.355	.429	.452
TOTALS		7267	272	.283	.333	.462	3477	140	.291	.341	.485	3790	132	.275	.325	.440	3577	134	.283	.333	.460	3690	138	.283	.333	.463	2278	85	.271	.304	.449	4989	187	.288	.345	.468

		TOTAL					HOME					AWAY					1ST HALF					2ND HALF					LEFT					RIGHT				
YEAR	TM/L	AB	HR	AVG	OBP	SLG	AB	HR	AVG	OBP	SLG	AB	HR	AVG	OBP	SLG	AB	HR	AVG	OBP	SLG	AB	HR	AVG	OBP	SLG	AB	HR	AVG	OBP	SLG	AB	HR	AVG	OBP	SLG
■ Lance Parrish BR/TR																																				
1978	Det-A	288	14	.219	.254	.424	140	7	.200	.248	.386	148	7	.236	.260	.459	133	5	.226	.259	.398	155	9	.213	.250	.445	226	13	.235	.266	.460	62	1	.161	.212	.290
1979	Det-A	493	19	.276	.343	.456	250	8	.248	.321	.392	243	11	.305	.366	.523	240	9	.279	.354	.446	253	10	.273	.332	.466	189	11	.307	.385	.534	304	8	.257	.316	.408
1980	Det-A	553	24	.286	.325	.499	280	7	.261	.307	.418	273	17	.311	.345	.582	263	10	.278	.312	.471	290	14	.293	.338	.524	253	16	.308	.338	.605	300	8	.267	.315	.410
1981	Det-A	348	10	.244	.311	.394	168	8	.250	.333	.458	180	2	.239	.289	.333	185	6	.232	.297	.384	163	4	.258	.326	.405	176	6	.290	.349	.472	172	4	.198	.272	.314
1982	Det-A	486	32	.284	.338	.529	238	22	.269	.331	.601	248	10	.298	.346	.460	172	9	.314	.389	.529	314	23	.268	.310	.529	142	12	.345	.405	.662	344	20	.259	.310	.474
1983	Det-A	605	27	.269	.314	.483	283	12	.283	.331	.491	322	15	.258	.298	.475	268	7	.299	.329	.470	337	20	.246	.302	.493	185	9	.249	.306	.438	420	18	.279	.317	.502
1984	Det-A	578	33	.237	.287	.443	271	13	.269	.317	.461	307	20	.208	.260	.427	276	14	.275	.298	.471	302	19	.202	.278	.417	209	14	.263	.339	.502	369	19	.222	.256	.409
1985	Det-A	549	28	.273	.323	.479	268	11	.280	.341	.463	281	17	.267	.306	.495	278	11	.284	.329	.446	271	17	.262	.318	.513	151	9	.305	.372	.563	398	19	.261	.304	.447
1986	Det-A	327	22	.257	.340	.483	158	8	.247	.341	.411	169	14	.266	.340	.550	258	17	.252	.339	.481	69	5	.275	.346	.493	122	5	.262	.328	.410	205	17	.254	.347	.527
1987	Phi-N	466	17	.245	.313	.399	234	5	.252	.322	.389	232	12	.237	.305	.409	216	7	.218	.278	.347	250	10	.268	.343	.444	138	6	.304	.391	.464	328	11	.220	.278	.372
1988	Phi-N	424	15	.215	.293	.370	213	11	.225	.294	.441	211	4	.204	.292	.299	243	11	.235	.319	.424	181	4	.188	.256	.298	131	4	.252	.336	.397	293	11	.198	.274	.358
1989	Cal-A	433	17	.238	.306	.388	215	8	.251	.305	.400	218	9	.225	.306	.376	221	8	.231	.305	.385	212	9	.245	.306	.392	144	7	.236	.317	.410	289	10	.239	.300	.377
1990	Cal-A	470	24	.268	.338	.451	235	14	.277	.346	.485	235	10	.260	.331	.417	215	14	.293	.370	.526	255	10	.247	.311	.388	125	7	.304	.370	.488	345	17	.255	.327	.438
1991	Cal-A	402	19	.216	.285	.388	216	9	.227	.280	.380	186	10	.204	.292	.398	178	8	.242	.318	.421	224	11	.196	.259	.362	105	3	.219	.297	.314	297	16	.215	.281	.414
1992	Cal-A	83	4	.229	.270	.398	43	1	.209	.222	.279	40	3	.250	.318	.525	83	4	.229	.270	.398	0	0	—	—	—	17	0	.235	.263	.235	66	4	.227	.271	.439
1992	Sea-A	192	8	.234	.304	.427	92	6	.239	.301	.500	100	2	.230	.306	.360	1	0	.000	.000	.000	191	8	.236	.305	.429	78	4	.231	.326	.474	114	4	.237	.288	.395
1993	Cle-A	20	1	.200	.333	.400	5	1	.200	.429	.800	15	0	.200	.294	.267	20	1	.200	.333	.400	0	0	—	—	—	5	0	.000	.000	.000	15	1	.267	.421	.533
1994	Pit-N	126	3	.270	.363	.381	64	3	.297	.395	.516	62	0	.242	.329	.242	77	2	.273	.380	.364	49	1	.265	.333	.408	34	1	.265	.286	.412	92	2	.272	.387	.370
1995	Tor-A	178	4	.202	.265	.320	100	4	.230	.282	.400	78	0	.167	.244	.218	105	3	.190	.248	.314	73	1	.219	.289	.329	58	0	.207	.288	.276	120	4	.200	.254	.342
TOTALS		7021	321	.253	.313	.441	3473	158	.255	.317	.445	3548	163	.250	.309	.437	3432	146	.260	.321	.438	3589	175	.245	.306	.443	2488	127	.274	.338	.481	4533	194	.241	.299	.418
■ Larry Parrish BR/TR																																				
1978	Mon-N	520	15	.277	.321	.454	272	4	.272	.313	.412	248	11	.282	.330	.500	236	8	.284	.328	.475	284	7	.271	.315	.437	110	7	.327	.378	.618	410	8	.263	.305	.410
1979	Mon-N	544	30	.307	.357	.551	261	14	.299	.351	.556	283	16	.314	.363	.548	229	7	.293	.352	.472	315	23	.317	.361	.610	93	2	.355	.408	.559	451	28	.297	.346	.550
1980	Mon-N	452	15	.254	.310	.427	201	6	.249	.307	.423	251	9	.259	.313	.430	138	6	.239	.289	.442	314	9	.261	.319	.420	87	2	.184	.279	.345	365	13	.271	.318	.447
1981	Mon-N	349	8	.244	.297	.384	187	3	.230	.295	.348	162	5	.259	.301	.426	168	2	.220	.284	.327	181	6	.265	.310	.436	71	3	.225	.313	.394	278	5	.248	.293	.381
1982	Tex-A	440	17	.264	.314	.414	204	6	.270	.312	.397	236	11	.258	.315	.428	129	1	.186	.232	.233	311	16	.296	.347	.489	119	5	.227	.301	.395	321	12	.277	.319	.421
1983	Tex-A	555	26	.272	.326	.474	275	10	.295	.357	.480	280	16	.250	.295	.468	229	12	.288	.358	.515	326	14	.261	.303	.445	171	7	.263	.330	.450	384	19	.276	.325	.484
1984	Tex-A	613	22	.285	.336	.465	310	11	.310	.367	.500	303	11	.261	.303	.429	289	12	.294	.353	.488	324	10	.278	.320	.444	178	8	.309	.364	.517	435	14	.276	.324	.444
1985	Tex-A	346	17	.249	.314	.434	188	8	.218	.285	.378	158	9	.285	.349	.500	252	13	.246	.318	.429	94	4	.255	.304	.447	94	8	.245	.321	.532	252	9	.250	.312	.397
1986	Tex-A	464	28	.276	.347	.509	225	14	.289	.354	.533	239	14	.264	.341	.485	171	11	.240	.302	.480	293	17	.297	.373	.526	130	11	.254	.351	.569	334	17	.284	.346	.485
1987	Tex-A	557	32	.268	.328	.483	277	16	.264	.335	.477	280	16	.271	.320	.489	262	18	.290	.345	.550	295	14	.247	.313	.424	190	14	.268	.346	.516	367	18	.267	.318	.466
1988	Tex-A	248	7	.190	.253	.319	137	4	.212	.262	.358	111	3	.162	.242	.270	221	7	.181	.246	.317	27	0	.259	.310	.333	84	2	.167	.220	.274	164	5	.201	.269	.341
1988	Bos-A	158	7	.259	.298	.424	98	3	.296	.320	.439	60	4	.200	.262	.400	0	0	—	—	—	158	7	.259	.298	.424	42	1	.333	.378	.429	116	6	.233	.268	.422
TOTALS		5246	224	.268	.323	.456	2635	99	.271	.327	.452	2611	125	.264	.318	.461	2324	97	.257	.317	.443	2922	127	.276	.327	.467	1369	70	.265	.335	.480	3877	154	.269	.318	.448
■ Tony Pena BR/TR																																				
1980	Pit-N	21	0	.429	.429	.571	11	0	.364	.364	.636	10	0	.500	.500	.500	0	0	—	—	—	21	0	.429	.429	.571	9	0	.556	.556	.667	12	0	.333	.333	.500
1981	Pit-N	210	2	.300	.326	.381	86	1	.337	.374	.465	124	1	.274	.292	.323	70	1	.271	.316	.371	140	1	.314	.331	.386	70	2	.300	.315	.443	140	0	.300	.331	.350
1982	Pit-N	497	11	.296	.323	.435	240	5	.279	.297	.392	257	6	.311	.347	.475	234	5	.333	.361	.479	263	6	.262	.290	.395	116	3	.336	.384	.474	381	8	.283	.304	.423
1983	Pit-N	542	15	.301	.338	.435	274	8	.321	.347	.464	268	7	.280	.329	.407	215	2	.270	.304	.353	327	13	.321	.360	.489	132	3	.295	.354	.402	410	12	.302	.333	.446
1984	Pit-N	546	15	.286	.333	.425	264	7	.280	.321	.417	282	8	.291	.344	.433	263	8	.262	.307	.403	283	7	.307	.357	.445	150	7	.320	.350	.520	396	8	.273	.327	.389
1985	Pit-N	546	10	.249	.284	.361	280	2	.246	.294	.336	266	8	.252	.274	.387	255	5	.282	.313	.396	291	5	.220	.260	.330	151	2	.258	.309	.344	395	8	.246	.275	.367
1986	Pit-N	510	10	.288	.356	.406	255	5	.298	.384	.404	255	5	.278	.326	.408	238	5	.239	.317	.374	272	5	.331	.390	.434	174	4	.333	.405	.471	336	6	.265	.330	.372
1987	StL-N	384	5	.214	.281	.307	187	1	.225	.274	.310	197	4	.203	.288	.305	134	1	.276	.333	.366	250	4	.180	.254	.276	137	3	.226	.280	.321	247	2	.206	.282	.300
1988	StL-N	505	10	.263	.308	.372	255	4	.259	.301	.349	250	6	.268	.314	.396	272	7	.257	.294	.371	233	3	.270	.323	.373	166	5	.331	.380	.512	339	5	.230	.272	.304
1989	StL-N	424	4	.259	.318	.337	201	3	.229	.304	.313	223	1	.287	.332	.359	223	3	.260	.294	.363	201	1	.259	.344	.308	170	2	.294	.366	.371	254	2	.236	.284	.315
1990	Bos-A	491	7	.263	.322	.348	247	3	.275	.344	.348	244	4	.250	.298	.348	233	4	.279	.321	.378	258	3	.248	.322	.322	155	5	.290	.341	.413	336	2	.250	.313	.318
1991	Bos-A	464	5	.231	.291	.321	230	2	.222	.290	.313	234	3	.239	.293	.329	229	2	.262	.316	.367	235	3	.200	.268	.277	106	4	.283	.336	.434	358	1	.215	.278	.288
1992	Bos-A	410	1	.241	.284	.305	203	1	.276	.316	.379	207	0	.208	.252	.232	203	1	.232	.270	.291	207	0	.251	.297	.319	111	1	.252	.270	.333	299	0	.237	.289	.294
1993	Bos-A	304	4	.181	.246	.257	155	2	.155	.227	.232	149	2	.208	.265	.282	158	1	.177	.238	.234	146	3	.185	.253	.281	83	2	.253	.264	.373	221	2	.154	.239	.213
1994	Cle-A	112	2	.295	.341	.438	40	1	.300	.349	.450	72	1	.292	.338	.431	72	1	.347	.392	.514	40	1	.200	.250	.300	54	2	.352	.390	.574	58	0	.241	.297	.310
1995	Cle-A	263	5	.262	.302	.376	123	1	.236	.271	.358	140	4	.286	.329	.393	149	3	.215	.269	.322	114	2	.325	.347	.447	84	1	.298	.322	.381	179	4	.246	.293	.374
1996	Cle-A	174	1	.195	.255	.236	82	0	.159	.255	.171	92	1	.228	.255	.293	78	1	.282	.367	.346	96	0	.125	.157	.146	62	1	.226	.262	.290	112	0	.179	.252	.205
1997	Chi-A	67	0	.164	.250	.179	35	0	.171	.302	.200	32	0	.156	.182	.156	40	0	.175	.244	.175	27	0	.148	.258	.185	37	0	.243	.300	.270	30	0	.067	.194	.067
1997	Hou-N	19	0	.211	.273	.368	10	0	.100	.167	.200	9	0	.333	.400	.556	0	0	—	—	—	19	0	.211	.273	.368	4	0	.500	.667	1.000	15	0	.133	.125	.200
TOTALS		6489	107	.260	.309	.364	3178	46	.258	.311	.359	3311	61	.262	.307	.368	3066	50	.262	.308	.368	3423	57	.258	.310	.360	1971	47	.293	.341	.417	4518	60	.245	.295	.340
■ Terry Pendleton BB/TR																																				
1984	StL-N	262	1	.324	.357	.420	141	0	.355	.389	.454	121	1	.289	.317	.380	0	0	—	—	—	262	1	.324	.357	.420	88	0	.261	.280	.352	174	1	.356	.395	.454
1985	StL-N	559	5	.240	.285	.306	272	3	.228	.273	.313	287	2	.251	.297	.300	229	2	.227	.267	.288	330	3	.248	.298	.318	171	2	.228	.257	.298	388	3	.245	.298	.309
1986	StL-N	578	1	.239	.279	.306	286	0	.255	.294	.336	292	1	.223	.264	.277	265	0	.215	.273	.272	313	1	.259	.284	.335	209	0	.278	.325	.364	369	1	.217	.253	.274
1987	StL-N	583	12	.286	.360	.412	293	5	.266	.331	.375	290	7	.307	.388	.448	283	5	.307	.372	.406	300	7	.267	.349	.417	208	4	.337	.386	.447	375	8	.259	.346	.392
1988	StL-N	391	6	.253	.293	.361	207	3	.280	.326	.415	184	3	.223	.254	.299	146	2	.274	.337	.390	245	4	.241	.264	.343	119	1	.328	.349	.429	272	5	.221	.268	.331
1989	StL-N	613	13	.264	.313	.390	295	8	.271	.324	.437	318	5	.258	.302	.346	290	4	.231	.289	.310	323	9	.294	.334	.461	247	2	.279	.313	.377	366	11	.254	.313	.399
1990	StL-N	447	6	.230	.277	.324	251	6	.243	.289	.375	196	0	.214	.262	.260	237	5	.262	.314	.397	210	1	.195	.233	.243	158	4	.209	.235	.361	289	2	.242	.299	.304
1991	Atl-N	586	22	.319	.363	.517	285	13	.340	.377	.561	301	9	.299	.350	.475	226	7	.327	.382	.518	360	15	.314	.350	.517	177	4	.299	.351	.458	409	18	.328	.368	.543
1992	Atl-N	640	21	.311	.345	.473	306	13	.307	.353	.503	334	8	.314	.338	.446	308	12	.312	.332	.490	332	9	.310	.357	.458	207	8	.357	.390	.527	433	13	.289	.323	.448
1993	Atl-N	633	17	.272	.311	.408	310	9	.281	.314	.435	323	8	.263	.307	.381	307	5	.254	.287	.352	326	12	.288	.333	.460	175	4	.297	.326	.429	458	13	.262	.305	.400
1994	Atl-N	309	7	.252	.280	.398	150	3	.233	.263	.360	159	4	.270	.297	.434	246	5	.240	.267	.366	63	2	.302	.333	.524	97	1	.278	.286	.392	212	6	.241	.278	.401
1995	Fla-N	513	14	.290	.339	.439	267	8	.318	.351	.491	246	6	.260	.327	.382	208	4	.293	.332	.418	305	10	.289	.344	.452	149	3	.336	.359	.456	364	11	.272	.332	.431
1996	Fla-N	406	7	.251	.298	.357	212	4	.250	.293	.344	194	3	.253	.303	.371	283	5	.247	.296	.346	123	2	.260	.301	.382	75	1	.173	.235	.213	331	6	.269	.312	.390
1996	Atl-N	162	4	.204	.271	.315	69	2	.232	.329	.348	93	2	.183	.224	.290	0	0	—	—	—	162	4	.204	.271	.315	37	0	.189	.268	.189	125	4	.208	.272	.352
1997	Cin-N	113	1	.248	.320	.354	73	1	.274	.329	.397	40	0	.200	.304	.275	105	0	.238	.298	.324	8	1	.375	.545	.750	38	0	.316	.409	.421	75	1	.213	.272	.320
1998	KC-A	237	3	.257	.299	.338	123	2	.252	.311	.325	114	1	.263	.286	.351	90	1	.267	.320	.356	147	2	.252	.287	.327	51	1	.314	.357	.392	186	2	.242	.283	.323
TOTALS		7032	140	.270	.316	.391	3540	80	.277	.322	.414	3492	60	.263	.309	.369	3223	57	.264	.311	.376	3809	83	.274	.319	.404	2206	35	.288	.325	.400	4826	105	.262	.311	.387
■ Neifi Perez BB/TR																																				
1996	Col-N	45	0	.156	.156	.200	22	0	.227	.227	.273	23	0	.087	.087	.130	0	0	—	—	—	45	0	.156	.156	.200	4	0	.250	.250	.500	41	0	.146	.146	.171
1997	Col-N	313	5	.291	.333	.444	169	3	.343	.378	.509	144	2	.229	.283	.368	24	2	.250	.250	.625	289	3	.294	.340	.429	77	2	.312	.333	.519	236	3	.284	.333	.419
1998	Col-N	647	9	.274	.313	.382	334	6	.296	.338	.416	313	3	.249	.286	.345	329	5	.280	.331	.398	318	4	.267	.294	.365	215	6	.302	.333	.442	432	3	.259	.303	.352
1999	Col-N	690	12	.280	.307	.403	356	8	.306	.326	.447	334	4	.251	.287	.356	293	5	.294	.318	.420	397	7	.270	.299	.390	209	6	.230	.257	.368	481	6	.301	.329	.418
2000	Col-N	651	10	.287	.314	.427	341	7	.323	.333	.507	310	3	.248	.293	.339	285	4	.277	.305	.421	366	6	.295	.320	.432	154	7	.357	.366	.584	497	3	.266	.297	.378
TOTALS		2346	36	.279	.311	.405	1222	24	.312	.337	.461	1124	12	.244	.284	.345	931	16	.282	.317	.418	1415	20	.277	.308	.397	659	21	.293	.316	.461	1687	15	.274	.309	.384
■ Gerald Perry BL/TR																																				
1983	Atl-N	39	1	.359	.422	.487	17	0	.353	.389	.412	22	1	.364	.444	.545	0	0	—	—	—	39	1	.359	.422	.487	4	0	.500	.600	.500	35	1	.343	.400	.486
1984	Atl-N	347	7	.265	.372	.372	170	3	.294	.410	.394	177	4	.237	.333	.350	178	3	.275	.359	.371	169	4	.254	.385	.373	74	1	.216	.310	.284	273	6	.278	.387	.396
1985	Atl-N	238	3	.214	.282	.273	137	3	.226	.282	.321	101	0	.198	.283	.208	138	1	.210	.276	.254	100	2	.220	.291	.300	41	1	.171	.190	.244	197	2	.223	.300	.279
1986	Atl-N	70	2	.271	.342	.386	32	2	.250	.306	.438	38	0	.289	.372	.342	50	1	.280	.373	.380	20	1	.250	.250	.400	3	1	1.000	1.000	2.000	67	1	.239	.307	.313
1987	Atl-N	533	12	.270	.329	.411	255	2	.259	.331	.369	278	10	.281	.327	.450	230	4	.243	.307	.352	303	8	.290	.345	.455	125	5	.256	.321	.480	408	7	.275	.331	.390
1988	Atl-N	547	8	.300	.338	.400	280	4	.314	.351	.429	267	4	.285	.325	.371	241	5	.332	.372	.440	306	3	.275	.312	.369	211	3	.270	.279	.346	336	5	.318	.373	.435
1989	Atl-N	266	4	.252	.337	.338	142	2	.289	.368	.380	124	2	.210	.300	.290	240	3	.246	.338	.325	26	1	.308	.321	.462	104	3	.337	.386	.471	162	1	.198	.307	.253
1990	KC-A	465	8	.254	.313	.361	238	3	.286	.333	.395	227	5	.220	.291	.326	251	4	.251	.303	.355	214	4	.257	.324	.369	134	1	.209	.252	.269	331	7	.272	.336	.399
1991	StL-N	242	6	.240	.300	.380	130	1	.185	.246	.277	112	5	.304	.360	.500	62	3	.258	.319	.516	180	3	.233	.292	.333	104	2	.240	.286	.365	138	4	.239	.310	.391
1992	StL-N	143	1	.238	.311	.315	73	1	.260	.329	.356	70	0	.214	.291	.271	93	0	.258	.333	.333	50	1	.200	.268	.280	25	0	.200	.310	.200	118	1	.246	.311	.339
1993	StL-N	98	4	.337	.440	.510	32	3	.281	.452	.594	66	1	.364	.432	.470	33	2	.333	.436	.545	65	2	.338	.442	.492	8	0	.250	.400	.250	90	4	.344	.443	.533
1994	StL-N	77	3	.325	.435	.532	27	1	.333	.471	.444	50	2	.320	.414	.580	54	2	.315	.439	.500	23	1	.348	.423	.609	4	0	.000	.333	.000	73	3	.342	.442	.562
1995	StL-N	79	0	.165	.224	.215	45	0	.178	.229	.267	34	0	.147	.216	.147	50	0	.140	.204	.180	29	0	.207	.258	.276	5	0	.000	.000	.000	74	0	.176	.237	.230
TOTALS		3144	59	.265	.333	.376	1578	25	.271	.339	.380	1566	34	.259	.326	.372	1620	28	.262	.332	.365	1524	31	.267	.333	.387	842	17	.252	.300	.359	2302	42	.269	.344	.382

■ Gary Pettis BB/TR

YEAR	TM/L	TOTAL AB	HR	AVG	OBP	SLG	HOME AB	HR	AVG	OBP	SLG	AWAY AB	HR	AVG	OBP	SLG	1ST HALF AB	HR	AVG	OBP	SLG	2ND HALF AB	HR	AVG	OBP	SLG	LEFT AB	HR	AVG	OBP	SLG	RIGHT AB	HR	AVG	OBP	SLG
1982	Cal-A	5	1	.200	.200	.800	4	1	.250	.250	1.000	1	0	.000	.000	.000	0	0	—	—	—	5	1	.200	.200	.800	2	0	.000	.000	.000	3	1	.333	.333	1.333
1983	Cal-A	85	3	.294	.348	.494	42	3	.310	.326	.571	43	0	.279	.367	.419	0	0	—	—	—	85	3	.294	.348	.494	30	0	.233	.303	.267	55	3	.327	.373	.618
1984	Cal-A	397	2	.227	.332	.300	182	1	.242	.325	.308	215	1	.214	.337	.293	239	2	.226	.324	.305	158	0	.228	.344	.291	134	0	.246	.325	.299	263	2	.217	.335	.300
1985	Cal-A	443	1	.257	.347	.323	182	0	.231	.340	.302	261	1	.276	.353	.337	227	1	.256	.356	.326	216	0	.259	.337	.319	139	0	.281	.370	.331	304	1	.247	.336	.319
1986	Cal-A	539	5	.258	.339	.343	251	1	.235	.320	.283	288	4	.278	.356	.396	251	2	.247	.312	.315	288	3	.267	.362	.368	176	2	.278	.328	.369	363	3	.248	.344	.331
1987	Cal-A	394	1	.208	.302	.259	204	1	.221	.300	.284	190	0	.195	.305	.232	264	1	.223	.317	.288	130	0	.177	.272	.200	128	1	.172	.248	.250	266	0	.226	.327	.263
1988	Det-A	458	3	.210	.285	.277	210	0	.200	.282	.248	248	3	.218	.287	.302	286	2	.227	.316	.297	172	1	.180	.230	.244	168	0	.214	.258	.250	290	3	.207	.299	.293
1989	Det-A	444	1	.257	.375	.309	234	1	.265	.392	.342	210	0	.248	.355	.271	151	1	.238	.372	.325	293	0	.266	.377	.300	152	0	.263	.374	.316	292	1	.253	.375	.305
1990	Tex-A	424	3	.238	.332	.335	222	3	.252	.346	.360	202	0	.223	.316	.307	214	3	.238	.331	.350	210	0	.238	.333	.319	153	0	.216	.318	.294	271	3	.251	.340	.358
1991	Tex-A	282	0	.216	.341	.277	137	0	.212	.343	.299	145	0	.221	.339	.255	151	0	.219	.335	.252	131	0	.214	.348	.305	77	0	.195	.315	.234	205	0	.224	.351	.293
1992	SD-N	30	0	.200	.250	.233	12	0	.167	.286	.167	18	0	.222	.222	.278	30	0	.200	.250	.233	0	0	—	—	—	5	0	.200	.429	.200	25	0	.200	.200	.240
1992	Det-A	129	1	.202	.338	.302	48	1	.271	.426	.375	81	0	.160	.281	.259	0	0	—	—	—	129	1	.202	.338	.302	38	0	.316	.435	.553	91	1	.154	.297	.198
TOTALS		3630	21	.236	.332	.310	1728	12	.236	.335	.313	1902	9	.235	.330	.307	1813	12	.234	.329	.307	1817	9	.237	.335	.313	1202	3	.239	.322	.304	2428	18	.234	.337	.313

■ Tony Phillips BB/TR

YEAR	TM/L	TOTAL AB	HR	AVG	OBP	SLG	HOME AB	HR	AVG	OBP	SLG	AWAY AB	HR	AVG	OBP	SLG	1ST HALF AB	HR	AVG	OBP	SLG	2ND HALF AB	HR	AVG	OBP	SLG	LEFT AB	HR	AVG	OBP	SLG	RIGHT AB	HR	AVG	OBP	SLG
1982	Oak-A	81	0	.210	.326	.284	46	0	.174	.309	.174	35	0	.257	.350	.429	79	0	.215	.326	.291	2	0	.000	.333	.000	15	0	.267	.450	.267	66	0	.197	.293	.288
1983	Oak-A	412	4	.248	.327	.320	217	1	.258	.340	.309	195	3	.236	.312	.333	216	2	.218	.302	.269	196	2	.281	.355	.378	152	1	.197	.248	.224	260	3	.277	.370	.377
1984	Oak-A	451	4	.266	.325	.359	226	2	.226	.279	.301	225	2	.307	.371	.418	184	1	.255	.303	.310	267	3	.273	.340	.393	153	1	.307	.349	.405	298	3	.245	.313	.336
1985	Oak-A	161	4	.280	.331	.453	73	2	.288	.342	.507	88	2	.273	.323	.409	0	0	—	—	—	161	4	.280	.331	.453	58	2	.362	.383	.517	103	2	.233	.304	.417
1986	Oak-A	441	5	.256	.367	.345	214	3	.234	.362	.322	227	2	.278	.373	.366	303	2	.257	.363	.330	138	3	.254	.376	.377	134	3	.321	.443	.455	307	2	.228	.331	.296
1987	Oak-A	379	10	.240	.337	.372	175	5	.251	.351	.383	204	5	.230	.325	.363	261	8	.249	.355	.395	118	2	.220	.296	.322	128	3	.289	.403	.383	251	7	.215	.302	.367
1988	Oak-A	212	2	.203	.320	.307	106	2	.217	.297	.377	106	0	.189	.341	.236	86	0	.198	.320	.256	126	2	.206	.320	.341	71	0	.282	.427	.423	141	2	.163	.261	.248
1989	Oak-A	451	4	.262	.345	.348	214	2	.271	.363	.327	237	2	.253	.328	.367	210	2	.281	.377	.390	241	2	.245	.316	.311	139	0	.259	.364	.360	312	4	.263	.336	.343
1990	Det-A	573	8	.251	.364	.351	286	4	.241	.360	.322	287	4	.261	.369	.380	284	5	.225	.331	.342	289	3	.277	.395	.360	202	2	.248	.343	.351	371	6	.253	.375	.350
1991	Det-A	564	17	.284	.371	.438	292	9	.295	.398	.438	272	8	.272	.341	.438	264	7	.288	.387	.420	300	10	.280	.356	.453	154	11	.357	.466	.617	410	6	.256	.333	.371
1992	Det-A	606	10	.276	.387	.388	289	3	.273	.398	.353	317	7	.278	.377	.420	262	7	.240	.389	.382	344	3	.302	.386	.392	174	5	.270	.401	.420	432	5	.278	.382	.375
1993	Det-A	566	7	.313	.443	.398	256	3	.309	.452	.391	310	4	.316	.436	.403	278	4	.302	.434	.396	288	3	.323	.453	.399	171	1	.316	.444	.380	395	6	.311	.443	.405
1994	Det-A	438	19	.281	.409	.468	218	12	.252	.399	.468	220	7	.309	.419	.468	287	11	.275	.408	.443	151	8	.291	.410	.517	108	4	.269	.429	.444	330	15	.285	.402	.476
1995	Cal-A	525	27	.261	.394	.459	267	13	.255	.378	.446	258	14	.267	.410	.473	219	10	.274	.410	.466	306	17	.252	.383	.454	132	7	.280	.441	.500	393	20	.254	.377	.445
1996	Chi-A	581	12	.277	.404	.399	284	6	.292	.421	.408	297	6	.263	.387	.391	301	7	.306	.428	.435	280	5	.246	.378	.361	149	3	.302	.456	.430	432	9	.269	.384	.389
1997	Chi-A	129	2	.310	.440	.403	70	1	.271	.363	.357	59	1	.356	.519	.458	129	2	.310	.440	.403	0	0	—	—	—	31	0	.323	.475	.355	98	2	.306	.429	.418
1997	Ana-A	405	6	.264	.376	.388	202	4	.238	.366	.342	203	2	.291	.387	.433	155	1	.284	.406	.368	250	5	.252	.357	.400	108	1	.222	.373	.333	297	5	.279	.377	.407
1998	Tor-A	48	1	.354	.467	.521	30	0	.267	.405	.400	18	1	.500	.565	.722	0	0	—	—	—	48	1	.354	.467	.521	13	0	.308	.471	.462	35	1	.371	.465	.543
1998	NY-N	188	3	.223	.351	.330	85	3	.282	.364	.471	103	0	.175	.341	.214	0	0	—	—	—	188	3	.223	.351	.330	46	2	.261	.469	.478	142	1	.211	.305	.282
1999	Oak-A	406	15	.244	.362	.433	196	5	.230	.352	.372	210	10	.257	.371	.490	296	13	.240	.350	.463	110	2	.255	.393	.355	92	0	.196	.333	.293	314	15	.258	.370	.475
TOTALS		7617	160	.266	.374	.389	3746	80	.260	.373	.375	3871	80	.271	.375	.403	3814	82	.263	.377	.385	3803	78	.268	.371	.393	2230	46	.279	.400	.405	5387	114	.260	.363	.382

■ Mike Piazza BR/TR

YEAR	TM/L	TOTAL AB	HR	AVG	OBP	SLG	HOME AB	HR	AVG	OBP	SLG	AWAY AB	HR	AVG	OBP	SLG	1ST HALF AB	HR	AVG	OBP	SLG	2ND HALF AB	HR	AVG	OBP	SLG	LEFT AB	HR	AVG	OBP	SLG	RIGHT AB	HR	AVG	OBP	SLG
1992	LA-N	69	1	.232	.284	.319	18	1	.278	.316	.444	51	0	.216	.273	.275	0	0	—	—	—	69	1	.232	.284	.319	30	0	.267	.313	.333	39	1	.205	.262	.308
1993	LA-N	547	35	.318	.370	.561	281	21	.313	.370	.584	266	14	.323	.371	.538	267	15	.318	.358	.536	280	20	.318	.382	.586	142	13	.324	.377	.655	405	22	.316	.368	.528
1994	LA-N	405	24	.319	.370	.541	193	13	.275	.307	.508	212	11	.358	.424	.571	287	19	.338	.377	.582	118	5	.271	.353	.441	94	7	.351	.413	.638	311	17	.309	.356	.511
1995	LA-N	434	32	.346	.400	.606	205	9	.302	.364	.463	229	23	.384	.432	.734	136	13	.390	.439	.728	298	19	.326	.382	.550	89	8	.326	.362	.607	345	24	.351	.409	.606
1996	LA-N	547	36	.336	.422	.563	278	14	.320	.394	.493	269	22	.353	.448	.636	275	22	.356	.431	.618	272	14	.316	.412	.507	93	6	.409	.477	.634	454	30	.322	.410	.548
1997	LA-N	556	40	.362	.431	.638	279	22	.355	.432	.634	277	18	.368	.431	.643	274	16	.365	.435	.602	282	24	.358	.428	.674	124	7	.363	.450	.621	432	33	.361	.426	.644
1998	LA-N	149	9	.282	.329	.497	55	5	.309	.356	.582	94	4	.266	.314	.447	149	9	.282	.329	.497	0	0	—	—	—	30	2	.267	.313	.467	119	7	.286	.333	.504
1998	Fla-N	18	0	.278	.263	.389	8	0	.250	.250	.250	10	0	.300	.273	.500	18	0	.278	.263	.389	0	0	—	—	—	6	0	.333	.333	.333	12	0	.250	.231	.417
1998	NY-N	394	23	.348	.417	.607	180	10	.306	.389	.556	214	13	.383	.441	.650	119	4	.345	.388	.504	275	19	.349	.429	.651	94	6	.340	.423	.628	300	17	.350	.415	.600
1999	NY-N	534	40	.303	.361	.575	252	18	.282	.336	.536	282	22	.323	.383	.610	238	16	.311	.367	.571	296	24	.297	.356	.578	131	11	.298	.392	.580	403	29	.305	.350	.573
2000	NY-N	482	38	.324	.398	.614	238	17	.269	.333	.525	244	21	.377	.459	.701	239	22	.364	.429	.715	243	16	.284	.368	.514	79	11	.354	.427	.848	403	27	.318	.393	.568
TOTALS		4135	278	.328	.392	.580	1987	130	.304	.368	.540	2148	148	.350	.414	.616	2002	136	.341	.396	.595	2133	142	.316	.389	.565	912	71	.338	.407	.626	3223	207	.325	.388	.567

■ Luis Polonia BL/TL

YEAR	TM/L	TOTAL AB	HR	AVG	OBP	SLG	HOME AB	HR	AVG	OBP	SLG	AWAY AB	HR	AVG	OBP	SLG	1ST HALF AB	HR	AVG	OBP	SLG	2ND HALF AB	HR	AVG	OBP	SLG	LEFT AB	HR	AVG	OBP	SLG	RIGHT AB	HR	AVG	OBP	SLG
1987	Oak-A	435	4	.287	.335	.398	217	1	.258	.312	.364	218	3	.317	.359	.431	173	3	.318	.376	.445	262	1	.267	.308	.366	89	0	.236	.292	.326	346	4	.301	.347	.416
1988	Oak-A	288	2	.292	.338	.378	152	1	.322	.387	.401	136	1	.257	.280	.353	36	0	.306	.390	.361	252	2	.290	.330	.381	18	0	.167	.158	.278	270	2	.300	.349	.385
1989	Oak-A	206	1	.286	.315	.369	90	0	.367	.400	.433	116	1	.224	.248	.319	206	1	.286	.315	.369	0	0	—	—	—	26	0	.308	.333	.308	180	1	.283	.312	.378
1989	NY-A	227	2	.313	.359	.405	109	1	.376	.417	.477	118	1	.254	.305	.339	23	0	.304	.360	.348	204	2	.314	.359	.412	45	0	.311	.354	.356	182	2	.313	.360	.418
1990	NY-A	22	0	.318	.304	.318	12	0	.417	.417	.417	10	0	.200	.182	.200	22	0	.318	.304	.318	0	0	—	—	—	0	0	—	—	—	22	0	.318	.304	.318
1990	Cal-A	381	2	.336	.376	.417	195	2	.349	.376	.431	186	0	.323	.376	.403	126	1	.302	.348	.373	255	1	.353	.390	.439	51	0	.294	.345	.373	330	2	.342	.380	.424
1991	Cal-A	604	2	.296	.352	.379	303	1	.261	.329	.333	301	1	.332	.374	.425	294	0	.299	.345	.374	310	2	.294	.358	.384	168	0	.238	.283	.298	436	2	.319	.377	.411
1992	Cal-A	577	0	.286	.337	.329	266	0	.286	.340	.350	311	0	.286	.333	.312	281	0	.292	.346	.335	296	0	.280	.327	.324	132	0	.227	.280	.250	445	0	.303	.353	.353
1993	Cal-A	576	1	.271	.328	.326	288	0	.229	.282	.271	288	1	.313	.372	.382	268	1	.254	.309	.317	308	0	.286	.343	.334	112	0	.232	.248	.241	464	1	.280	.346	.347
1994	NY-A	350	1	.311	.383	.414	173	0	.295	.379	.393	177	1	.328	.387	.435	253	1	.304	.372	.387	97	0	.330	.409	.485	54	0	.185	.290	.222	296	1	.334	.400	.449
1995	NY-A	238	2	.261	.326	.349	112	2	.277	.346	.384	126	0	.246	.307	.317	154	1	.260	.326	.351	84	1	.262	.326	.345	27	1	.222	.300	.370	211	1	.265	.329	.346
1995	Atl-N	53	0	.264	.304	.396	32	0	.188	.235	.313	21	0	.381	.409	.524	1	0	1.000	1.000	1.000	52	0	.250	.291	.385	2	0	.500	.500	1.000	51	0	.255	.296	.373
1996	Bal-A	175	2	.240	.285	.309	107	2	.271	.310	.355	68	0	.191	.247	.235	108	1	.222	.276	.296	67	1	.269	.300	.328	16	1	.500	.529	.750	159	1	.214	.260	.264
1996	Atl-N	31	0	.419	.424	.419	8	0	.125	.200	.125	23	0	.522	.522	.522	0	0	—	—	—	31	0	.419	.424	.419	3	0	.667	.667	.667	28	0	.393	.400	.393
1999	Det-A	333	10	.324	.357	.526	182	8	.346	.379	.615	151	2	.298	.329	.417	101	2	.396	.411	.574	232	8	.293	.333	.504	23	1	.217	.280	.348	310	9	.332	.363	.539
2000	Det-A	267	6	.273	.325	.416	157	3	.280	.337	.414	110	3	.264	.308	.418	202	4	.252	.309	.371	65	2	.338	.375	.554	31	1	.226	.286	.419	236	5	.280	.331	.415
2000	NY-A	77	1	.286	.341	.377	41	1	.317	.378	.463	36	0	.250	.300	.278	0	0	—	—	—	77	1	.286	.341	.377	2	0	.000	.000	.000	75	1	.293	.349	.387
TOTALS		4840	36	.293	.342	.383	2444	22	.291	.344	.388	2396	14	.295	.340	.378	2248	15	.288	.340	.371	2592	21	.297	.345	.393	799	4	.245	.293	.308	4041	32	.302	.352	.398

■ Darrell Porter BL/TR

YEAR	TM/L	TOTAL AB	HR	AVG	OBP	SLG	HOME AB	HR	AVG	OBP	SLG	AWAY AB	HR	AVG	OBP	SLG	1ST HALF AB	HR	AVG	OBP	SLG	2ND HALF AB	HR	AVG	OBP	SLG	LEFT AB	HR	AVG	OBP	SLG	RIGHT AB	HR	AVG	OBP	SLG
1978	KC-A	520	18	.265	.358	.444	260	7	.269	.362	.458	260	11	.262	.353	.431	237	6	.287	.378	.430	283	12	.247	.340	.456	145	5	.221	.302	.379	375	13	.283	.378	.469
1979	KC-A	533	20	.291	.421	.484	271	8	.321	.429	.509	262	12	.260	.412	.458	261	10	.307	.433	.498	272	10	.276	.409	.471	161	6	.280	.414	.447	372	14	.296	.424	.500
1980	KC-A	418	7	.249	.354	.342	201	1	.264	.389	.328	217	6	.235	.319	.355	182	3	.297	.379	.396	236	4	.212	.335	.301	148	5	.243	.367	.385	270	2	.252	.346	.319
1981	StL-N	174	6	.224	.364	.408	85	2	.235	.347	.353	89	4	.213	.379	.461	52	2	.173	.394	.385	122	4	.246	.349	.418	58	1	.224	.338	.345	116	5	.224	.377	.440
1982	StL-N	373	12	.231	.347	.402	186	3	.199	.332	.323	187	9	.262	.362	.481	170	5	.241	.325	.406	203	7	.222	.364	.399	68	1	.206	.325	.294	305	11	.236	.352	.426
1983	StL-N	443	15	.262	.363	.431	211	5	.256	.354	.398	232	10	.267	.371	.461	212	8	.231	.340	.406	231	7	.290	.384	.455	101	1	.228	.333	.337	342	14	.272	.372	.459
1984	StL-N	422	11	.232	.331	.363	203	4	.232	.326	.350	219	7	.233	.335	.374	199	6	.256	.374	.402	223	5	.211	.288	.327	89	5	.292	.368	.551	333	6	.216	.320	.312
1985	StL-N	240	10	.221	.335	.412	102	4	.255	.364	.471	138	6	.196	.313	.370	64	2	.125	.250	.266	176	8	.256	.365	.466	38	1	.184	.295	.289	202	9	.228	.342	.436
1986	Tex-A	155	12	.265	.360	.535	67	6	.299	.397	.597	88	6	.239	.330	.489	67	5	.269	.355	.522	88	7	.261	.363	.545	7	0	.000	.222	.000	148	12	.277	.367	.561
1987	Tex-A	130	7	.238	.387	.423	62	4	.242	.415	.435	68	3	.235	.358	.412	58	3	.190	.329	.362	72	4	.278	.430	.472	8	0	.250	.250	.250	122	7	.238	.394	.434
TOTALS		3408	118	.253	.364	.421	1648	44	.260	.371	.414	1760	74	.245	.357	.427	1502	50	.259	.369	.421	1906	68	.248	.360	.421	823	25	.241	.351	.389	2585	93	.256	.368	.431

■ Jorge Posada BB/TR

YEAR	TM/L	TOTAL AB	HR	AVG	OBP	SLG	HOME AB	HR	AVG	OBP	SLG	AWAY AB	HR	AVG	OBP	SLG	1ST HALF AB	HR	AVG	OBP	SLG	2ND HALF AB	HR	AVG	OBP	SLG	LEFT AB	HR	AVG	OBP	SLG	RIGHT AB	HR	AVG	OBP	SLG
1995	NY-A	0	0	—	—	—	0	0	—	—	—	0	0	—	—	—	0	0	—	—	—	0	0	—	—	—	0	0	—	—	—	0	0	—	—	—
1996	NY-A	14	0	.071	.133	.071	8	0	.125	.125	.125	6	0	.000	.143	.000	2	0	.000	.000	.000	12	0	.083	.154	.083	5	0	.200	.200	.200	9	0	.000	.100	.000
1997	NY-A	188	6	.250	.359	.410	78	2	.282	.364	.449	110	4	.227	.356	.382	90	1	.256	.340	.333	98	5	.245	.375	.480	42	1	.310	.310	.476	146	5	.233	.370	.390
1998	NY-A	358	17	.268	.350	.475	167	6	.281	.370	.479	191	11	.257	.332	.471	157	8	.268	.363	.478	201	9	.269	.339	.473	112	5	.357	.402	.580	246	12	.228	.328	.427
1999	NY-A	379	12	.245	.341	.401	168	4	.220	.347	.333	211	8	.265	.336	.455	167	7	.210	.304	.377	212	5	.274	.370	.420	99	4	.303	.349	.505	280	8	.225	.338	.364
2000	NY-A	505	28	.287	.417	.527	250	18	.316	.443	.612	255	10	.259	.390	.443	233	13	.313	.443	.549	272	15	.265	.394	.507	159	6	.321	.405	.535	346	22	.272	.421	.523
TOTALS		1444	63	.265	.371	.461	671	30	.277	.389	.484	773	33	.254	.355	.441	649	29	.267	.374	.456	795	34	.263	.369	.465	417	16	.324	.380	.530	1027	47	.241	.368	.433

■ Jim Presley BR/TR

YEAR	TM/L	TOTAL AB	HR	AVG	OBP	SLG	HOME AB	HR	AVG	OBP	SLG	AWAY AB	HR	AVG	OBP	SLG	1ST HALF AB	HR	AVG	OBP	SLG	2ND HALF AB	HR	AVG	OBP	SLG	LEFT AB	HR	AVG	OBP	SLG	RIGHT AB	HR	AVG	OBP	SLG
1984	Sea-A	251	10	.227	.247	.402	126	5	.214	.237	.381	125	5	.240	.258	.424	26	1	.269	.269	.577	225	9	.222	.245	.382	84	4	.167	.176	.333	167	6	.257	.282	.437
1985	Sea-A	570	28	.275	.324	.484	296	12	.264	.320	.449	274	16	.288	.328	.522	262	16	.282	.338	.527	308	12	.269	.312	.448	157	8	.344	.398	.573	413	20	.249	.295	.450
1986	Sea-A	616	27	.265	.303	.463	319	16	.307	.348	.549	297	11	.219	.254	.370	293	16	.283	.327	.519	323	11	.248	.281	.412	158	6	.323	.367	.506	458	21	.245	.281	.448
1987	Sea-A	575	24	.247	.296	.433	288	11	.257	.295	.455	287	13	.237	.297	.411	293	14	.259	.302	.464	282	10	.234	.291	.401	190	5	.268	.310	.426	385	19	.236	.289	.436
1988	Sea-A	544	14	.230	.280	.355	269	7	.245	.290	.394	275	7	.215	.271	.316	272	8	.217	.264	.342	272	6	.243	.296	.368	164	2	.232	.278	.323	380	12	.229	.281	.368
1989	Sea-A	390	12	.236	.275	.385	213	7	.258	.295	.423	177	5	.209	.253	.339	211	5	.275	.313	.403	179	7	.190	.232	.363	116	4	.328	.352	.491	274	8	.197	.243	.339

		TOTAL					HOME					AWAY					1ST HALF					2ND HALF					LEFT					RIGHT				
YEAR	TM/L	AB	HR	AVG	OBP	SLG	AB	HR	AVG	OBP	SLG	AB	HR	AVG	OBP	SLG	AB	HR	AVG	OBP	SLG	AB	HR	AVG	OBP	SLG	AB	HR	AVG	OBP	SLG	AB	HR	AVG	OBP	SLG
1990	Atl-N	541	19	.242	.282	.414	288	10	.260	.304	.427	253	9	.221	.257	.399	263	8	.274	.311	.445	278	11	.212	.256	.385	180	6	.267	.333	.450	361	13	.230	.255	.396
1991	SD-N	59	1	.136	.200	.186	39	0	.128	.209	.128	20	1	.150	.182	.300	59	1	.136	.200	.186	0	0	—	—	—	23	1	.130	.167	.261	36	0	.139	.220	.139
TOTALS		3546	135	.247	.290	.420	1838	68	.260	.303	.441	1708	67	.232	.276	.397	1679	69	.260	.304	.445	1867	66	.235	.277	.397	1072	36	.277	.323	.444	2474	99	.234	.276	.409
■ Kirby Puckett BR/TR																																				
1984	Min-A	557	0	.296	.320	.336	276	0	.326	.347	.373	281	0	.267	.293	.299	191	0	.335	.345	.366	366	0	.276	.306	.320	179	0	.313	.335	.358	378	0	.288	.312	.325
1985	Min-A	691	4	.288	.330	.385	352	2	.324	.374	.429	339	2	.251	.283	.339	317	2	.284	.320	.388	374	2	.291	.338	.382	219	4	.356	.383	.525	472	0	.256	.306	.320
1986	Min-A	680	31	.328	.366	.537	346	14	.367	.405	.584	334	17	.287	.326	.488	330	15	.342	.382	.542	350	16	.314	.351	.531	166	6	.325	.364	.524	514	25	.329	.367	.541
1987	Min-A	624	28	.332	.367	.534	309	18	.301	.343	.537	315	10	.362	.390	.530	299	14	.351	.389	.562	325	14	.314	.346	.508	177	11	.339	.377	.627	447	17	.329	.363	.497
1988	Min-A	657	24	.356	.375	.545	323	13	.406	.436	.638	334	11	.308	.314	.455	309	10	.346	.361	.518	348	14	.365	.387	.569	166	8	.398	.425	.614	491	16	.342	.358	.521
1989	Min-A	635	9	.339	.379	.465	328	7	.390	.412	.552	307	2	.283	.344	.371	315	5	.333	.380	.476	320	4	.344	.377	.453	191	1	.304	.341	.403	444	8	.354	.395	.491
1990	Min-A	551	12	.298	.365	.446	273	6	.344	.403	.505	278	6	.252	.328	.388	275	10	.302	.375	.513	276	2	.293	.354	.380	164	4	.299	.382	.451	387	8	.297	.357	.444
1991	Min-A	611	15	.319	.352	.460	328	7	.326	.356	.463	283	8	.311	.348	.456	293	10	.324	.361	.498	318	5	.314	.344	.425	155	7	.406	.436	.658	456	8	.289	.324	.393
1992	Min-A	639	19	.329	.374	.490	325	9	.348	.392	.508	314	10	.309	.356	.471	314	14	.341	.366	.564	325	5	.317	.382	.418	125	3	.328	.381	.456	514	16	.329	.372	.498
1993	Min-A	622	22	.296	.349	.474	320	12	.322	.392	.522	302	10	.268	.302	.424	280	10	.289	.347	.457	342	12	.301	.351	.488	139	7	.295	.371	.518	483	15	.296	.343	.462
1994	Min-A	439	20	.317	.362	.540	232	12	.366	.419	.638	207	8	.261	.296	.430	305	12	.325	.356	.521	134	8	.299	.374	.582	103	8	.359	.389	.738	336	12	.304	.353	.479
1995	Min-A	538	23	.314	.379	.515	277	13	.303	.373	.520	261	10	.326	.385	.510	227	10	.282	.348	.454	311	13	.338	.401	.559	128	6	.320	.404	.523	410	17	.312	.371	.512
TOTALS		7244	207	.318	.360	.477	3689	113	.344	.388	.521	3555	94	.291	.331	.430	3455	112	.322	.362	.493	3789	95	.314	.358	.462	1912	65	.337	.381	.525	5332	142	.311	.352	.459
■ Terry Puhl BL/TR																																				
1978	Hou-N	585	3	.289	.343	.368	278	1	.273	.322	.342	307	2	.303	.362	.391	268	2	.328	.368	.414	317	1	.256	.323	.328	176	2	.244	.313	.307	409	1	.308	.356	.394
1979	Hou-N	600	8	.287	.352	.377	288	2	.285	.361	.375	312	6	.288	.344	.378	306	6	.278	.351	.379	294	2	.296	.354	.374	219	2	.237	.318	.329	381	6	.315	.372	.404
1980	Hou-N	535	13	.282	.357	.419	251	4	.287	.354	.402	284	9	.278	.360	.433	239	7	.289	.361	.448	296	6	.277	.354	.395	183	3	.262	.337	.361	352	10	.293	.368	.449
1981	Hou-N	350	3	.251	.315	.354	162	1	.216	.284	.327	188	2	.282	.343	.378	212	2	.269	.338	.373	138	1	.225	.280	.326	100	0	.220	.241	.320	250	3	.264	.344	.368
1982	Hou-N	507	8	.262	.331	.379	271	5	.277	.329	.421	236	3	.246	.333	.331	258	7	.248	.326	.380	249	1	.277	.336	.378	134	2	.224	.268	.336	373	6	.276	.352	.394
1983	Hou-N	465	8	.292	.343	.428	225	1	.284	.326	.364	240	7	.300	.358	.488	164	1	.274	.333	.360	301	7	.302	.349	.465	97	0	.165	.241	.196	368	8	.326	.371	.489
1984	Hou-N	449	9	.301	.380	.434	221	2	.299	.387	.403	228	7	.303	.374	.465	171	2	.310	.376	.421	278	7	.295	.382	.442	139	1	.259	.321	.331	310	8	.319	.406	.481
1985	Hou-N	194	2	.284	.343	.418	123	1	.325	.375	.455	71	1	.211	.287	.352	158	2	.291	.350	.424	36	0	.250	.308	.389	68	0	.294	.342	.382	126	2	.278	.343	.437
1986	Hou-N	172	3	.244	.302	.355	70	1	.214	.257	.271	102	2	.265	.330	.412	126	2	.238	.285	.333	46	1	.261	.346	.413	23	0	.304	.333	.348	149	3	.235	.297	.356
1987	Hou-N	122	2	.230	.293	.320	71	1	.197	.250	.268	51	1	.275	.351	.392	74	0	.216	.275	.270	48	2	.250	.321	.396	9	0	.111	.200	.111	113	2	.239	.301	.336
1988	Hou-N	234	3	.303	.395	.389	106	2	.377	.464	.509	128	1	.242	.336	.289	86	0	.337	.436	.360	148	3	.284	.371	.405	19	0	.211	.250	.211	215	3	.312	.406	.405
1989	Hou-N	354	0	.271	.353	.364	189	0	.254	.330	.339	165	0	.291	.379	.394	183	0	.290	.359	.399	171	0	.251	.347	.327	57	0	.246	.338	.333	297	0	.276	.356	.370
1990	Hou-N	41	0	.293	.375	.317	19	0	.211	.375	.211	22	0	.364	.375	.409	28	0	.214	.267	.214	13	0	.462	.556	.538	3	0	.667	.667	.667	38	0	.263	.356	.289
1991	KC-A	18	0	.222	.333	.222	9	0	.111	.333	.111	9	0	.333	.333	.333	18	0	.222	.333	.222	0	0	—	—	—	2	0	.000	.000	.000	16	0	.250	.368	.250
TOTALS		4626	62	.279	.347	.388	2283	21	.277	.343	.376	2343	41	.282	.352	.399	2291	31	.282	.347	.386	2335	31	.277	.347	.389	1229	10	.240	.304	.321	3397	52	.293	.363	.412
■ Tim Raines BB/TR																																				
1979	Mon-N	0	0	—	—	—	0	0	—	—	—	0	0	—	—	—	0	0	—	—	—	0	0	—	—	—	0	0	—	—	—	0	0	—	—	—
1980	Mon-N	20	0	.050	.269	.050	17	0	.059	.200	.059	3	0	.000	.500	.000	1	0	.000	.500	.000	19	0	.053	.250	.053	4	0	.000	.333	.000	16	0	.063	.250	.063
1981	Mon-N	313	5	.304	.391	.438	147	3	.347	.424	.497	166	2	.265	.361	.386	202	3	.322	.419	.470	111	2	.270	.336	.378	65	1	.246	.351	.323	248	4	.319	.402	.468
1982	Mon-N	647	4	.277	.353	.369	308	1	.273	.353	.357	339	3	.280	.354	.381	284	2	.289	.362	.387	363	2	.267	.346	.355	183	2	.306	.373	.393	464	2	.265	.345	.360
1983	Mon-N	615	11	.298	.393	.429	311	5	.305	.418	.453	304	6	.289	.365	.405	279	4	.283	.377	.405	336	7	.310	.406	.449	162	7	.296	.416	.506	453	4	.298	.384	.402
1984	Mon-N	622	8	.309	.393	.437	303	2	.281	.365	.376	319	6	.335	.420	.495	279	6	.297	.393	.423	343	2	.318	.393	.449	193	3	.306	.363	.446	429	5	.310	.406	.434
1985	Mon-N	575	11	.320	.405	.475	280	4	.346	.446	.529	295	7	.295	.364	.424	263	4	.297	.362	.430	312	7	.340	.439	.513	178	6	.275	.351	.438	397	5	.340	.428	.491
1986	Mon-N	580	9	.334	.413	.476	282	4	.326	.409	.450	298	5	.342	.417	.500	267	6	.330	.412	.509	313	3	.339	.415	.447	181	4	.315	.382	.453	399	5	.343	.427	.486
1987	Mon-N	530	18	.330	.429	.526	276	9	.337	.437	.525	254	9	.323	.420	.528	209	7	.368	.452	.560	321	11	.305	.415	.505	164	5	.396	.471	.616	366	13	.301	.411	.486
1988	Mon-N	429	12	.270	.350	.431	202	5	.282	.350	.436	227	7	.260	.351	.427	277	7	.274	.372	.433	152	5	.263	.309	.428	125	4	.264	.321	.408	304	8	.273	.362	.441
1989	Mon-N	517	9	.286	.395	.418	258	6	.271	.375	.419	259	3	.301	.415	.417	253	4	.292	.417	.462	264	5	.280	.372	.375	133	3	.286	.389	.406	384	6	.286	.397	.422
1990	Mon-N	457	9	.287	.379	.392	202	6	.307	.391	.446	255	3	.271	.370	.349	211	2	.284	.382	.355	246	7	.289	.376	.423	180	3	.289	.357	.361	277	6	.285	.393	.412
1991	Chi-A	609	5	.268	.359	.345	284	1	.254	.348	.303	325	4	.280	.368	.382	269	2	.286	.377	.379	340	3	.253	.344	.318	208	2	.279	.343	.346	401	3	.262	.366	.344
1992	Chi-A	551	7	.294	.380	.405	263	4	.319	.405	.445	288	3	.271	.356	.368	260	2	.250	.345	.342	291	5	.333	.411	.460	135	0	.252	.369	.304	416	7	.308	.383	.438
1993	Chi-A	415	16	.306	.401	.480	196	7	.291	.378	.434	219	9	.320	.421	.521	112	7	.304	.440	.536	303	9	.307	.385	.459	112	3	.348	.439	.473	303	13	.290	.386	.482
1994	Chi-A	384	10	.266	.365	.409	168	5	.262	.367	.405	216	5	.269	.364	.412	254	8	.260	.369	.409	130	2	.277	.358	.408	96	1	.208	.303	.260	288	9	.285	.385	.458
1995	Chi-A	502	12	.285	.374	.422	239	6	.297	.399	.448	263	6	.274	.350	.399	213	8	.305	.366	.484	289	4	.270	.379	.377	140	3	.279	.395	.414	362	9	.287	.365	.425
1996	NY-A	201	9	.284	.383	.468	112	7	.313	.424	.536	89	2	.247	.327	.382	84	2	.286	.390	.405	117	7	.282	.379	.513	39	0	.256	.412	.282	162	9	.290	.376	.512
1997	NY-A	271	4	.321	.403	.454	149	3	.349	.416	.517	122	1	.287	.386	.377	151	1	.305	.400	.404	120	3	.342	.406	.517	59	1	.339	.412	.441	212	3	.316	.400	.458
1998	NY-A	321	5	.290	.395	.383	146	2	.301	.412	.384	175	3	.280	.380	.383	167	3	.287	.361	.401	154	2	.292	.429	.364	127	0	.307	.428	.331	194	5	.278	.372	.418
1999	Oak-A	135	4	.215	.337	.341	58	2	.224	.384	.362	77	2	.208	.300	.325	110	3	.218	.353	.345	25	1	.200	.259	.320	64	3	.234	.351	.422	71	1	.197	.326	.268
TOTALS		8694	168	.295	.385	.427	4201	82	.300	.393	.434	4493	86	.290	.378	.420	4145	81	.292	.385	.428	4549	87	.297	.386	.426	2548	51	.293	.380	.411	6146	117	.295	.388	.433
■ Manny Ramirez BR/TR																																				
1993	Cle-A	53	2	.170	.200	.302	31	0	.194	.242	.194	22	2	.136	.136	.455	0	0	—	—	—	53	2	.170	.200	.302	26	1	.115	.115	.231	27	1	.222	.276	.370
1994	Cle-A	290	17	.269	.357	.521	138	9	.203	.291	.486	152	8	.329	.416	.553	204	13	.255	.353	.520	86	4	.302	.367	.523	119	8	.361	.447	.647	171	9	.205	.292	.433
1995	Cle-A	484	31	.308	.402	.558	225	12	.289	.408	.511	259	19	.324	.397	.598	200	14	.325	.411	.600	284	17	.296	.396	.528	123	7	.407	.507	.659	361	24	.274	.365	.524
1996	Cle-A	550	33	.309	.399	.582	275	19	.316	.404	.622	275	14	.302	.393	.542	267	20	.273	.378	.573	283	13	.343	.420	.590	149	7	.322	.411	.577	401	26	.304	.394	.584
1997	Cle-A	561	26	.328	.415	.538	279	14	.333	.420	.552	282	12	.323	.410	.525	242	10	.335	.420	.533	319	16	.323	.411	.542	137	6	.350	.433	.577	424	20	.321	.409	.526
1998	Cle-A	571	45	.294	.377	.599	273	25	.308	.375	.648	298	20	.282	.379	.554	278	15	.302	.370	.540	293	30	.287	.383	.655	150	18	.340	.402	.767	421	27	.278	.368	.539
1999	Cle-A	522	44	.333	.442	.663	254	21	.311	.427	.634	268	23	.354	.456	.690	262	20	.340	.423	.626	260	24	.327	.459	.700	115	8	.383	.493	.687	407	36	.319	.427	.656
2000	Cle-A	439	38	.351	.457	.697	213	22	.357	.452	.742	226	16	.345	.461	.655	183	13	.322	.419	.623	256	25	.371	.483	.750	91	7	.396	.525	.747	348	31	.339	.437	.684
TOTALS		3470	236	.313	.407	.592	1688	122	.307	.401	.598	1782	114	.319	.412	.586	1636	105	.307	.396	.572	1834	131	.318	.416	.609	910	62	.355	.447	.649	2560	174	.298	.392	.571
■ Rafael Ramirez BR/TR																																				
1980	Atl-N	165	2	.267	.292	.352	70	2	.329	.347	.471	95	0	.221	.253	.263	0	0	—	—	—	165	2	.267	.292	.352	22	0	.364	.364	.364	143	2	.252	.282	.350
1981	Atl-N	307	2	.218	.276	.303	133	1	.218	.278	.331	174	1	.218	.275	.282	168	1	.214	.298	.292	139	1	.223	.248	.317	61	0	.230	.294	.262	246	2	.215	.272	.313
1982	Atl-N	609	10	.278	.319	.379	295	7	.268	.296	.410	314	3	.287	.339	.350	280	2	.254	.287	.336	329	8	.298	.345	.416	145	4	.338	.381	.469	464	6	.259	.299	.351
1983	Atl-N	622	7	.297	.337	.368	294	2	.286	.323	.340	328	5	.308	.350	.393	297	2	.293	.340	.347	325	5	.302	.334	.388	160	3	.350	.388	.475	462	4	.279	.319	.331
1984	Atl-N	591	2	.266	.295	.327	267	1	.255	.295	.311	324	1	.275	.295	.340	300	0	.313	.341	.370	291	2	.216	.248	.282	167	1	.263	.287	.329	424	1	.267	.298	.325
1985	Atl-N	568	5	.248	.272	.333	272	4	.294	.321	.401	296	1	.206	.225	.270	277	3	.260	.282	.357	291	2	.237	.261	.309	192	0	.240	.271	.323	376	5	.253	.272	.338
1986	Atl-N	496	8	.240	.273	.335	238	1	.235	.287	.311	258	7	.244	.260	.357	278	4	.245	.261	.349	218	4	.234	.288	.317	179	2	.207	.247	.263	317	6	.259	.288	.375
1987	Atl-N	179	1	.263	.300	.346	83	0	.253	.300	.325	96	1	.271	.300	.365	175	1	.263	.301	.349	4	0	.250	.250	.250	65	0	.323	.353	.400	114	1	.228	.270	.316
1988	Hou-N	566	6	.276	.298	.378	274	2	.255	.274	.336	292	4	.295	.321	.418	248	2	.258	.290	.359	318	4	.289	.305	.393	193	2	.306	.322	.440	373	4	.260	.287	.346
1989	Hou-N	537	6	.246	.283	.324	268	3	.246	.291	.328	269	3	.245	.275	.320	279	2	.258	.285	.312	258	4	.233	.281	.337	156	2	.269	.311	.353	381	4	.236	.271	.312
1990	Hou-N	445	2	.261	.299	.330	206	1	.267	.320	.350	239	1	.255	.281	.314	234	1	.265	.301	.329	211	1	.256	.298	.332	192	1	.260	.306	.333	253	1	.261	.294	.328
1991	Hou-N	233	1	.236	.274	.292	91	0	.242	.300	.308	142	1	.232	.257	.282	121	1	.223	.266	.289	112	0	.250	.283	.295	110	1	.245	.294	.309	123	0	.228	.256	.276
1992	Hou-N	176	1	.250	.283	.301	89	0	.225	.266	.258	87	1	.276	.300	.345	136	1	.243	.280	.309	40	0	.275	.293	.275	82	1	.329	.353	.427	94	0	.181	.222	.191
TOTALS		5494	53	.261	.295	.342	2580	24	.261	.299	.347	2914	29	.260	.292	.337	2793	20	.262	.297	.338	2701	33	.259	.294	.345	1724	17	.278	.314	.366	3770	36	.253	.287	.331
■ Joe Randa BR/TR																																				
1995	KC-A	70	1	.171	.237	.243	40	1	.225	.311	.325	30	0	.100	.129	.133	45	1	.156	.208	.222	25	0	.200	.286	.280	42	1	.190	.244	.310	28	0	.143	.226	.143
1996	KC-A	337	6	.303	.351	.433	163	2	.331	.388	.472	174	4	.276	.316	.397	131	1	.321	.381	.427	206	5	.291	.330	.437	147	1	.340	.385	.463	190	5	.274	.324	.411
1997	Pit-N	443	7	.302	.366	.451	227	5	.304	.375	.515	216	2	.301	.356	.384	249	5	.297	.359	.478	194	2	.309	.374	.418	99	2	.232	.303	.354	344	5	.323	.383	.480
1998	Det-A	460	9	.254	.323	.367	214	3	.238	.306	.322	246	6	.268	.337	.407	274	4	.237	.317	.332	186	5	.280	.332	.419	130	2	.254	.345	.377	330	7	.255	.314	.364
1999	KC-A	628	16	.314	.363	.473	316	7	.320	.356	.475	312	9	.308	.370	.471	292	7	.288	.346	.442	336	9	.336	.379	.500	101	1	.356	.393	.554	527	15	.306	.358	.457
2000	KC-A	612	15	.304	.343	.438	303	9	.330	.369	.472	309	6	.278	.318	.405	285	8	.316	.371	.467	327	7	.294	.318	.413	126	0	.310	.350	.405	486	15	.302	.342	.447
TOTALS		2550	54	.293	.347	.430	1263	27	.304	.357	.451	1287	27	.283	.337	.410	1276	26	.284	.347	.422	1274	28	.303	.346	.439	645	7	.293	.350	.422	1905	47	.293	.345	.433
■ Willie Randolph BR/TR																																				
1978	NY-A	499	3	.279	.381	.357	239	2	.280	.376	.381	260	1	.277	.386	.335	235	2	.247	.359	.319	264	1	.307	.401	.390	243	2	.305	.423	.399	256	1	.254	.338	.316
1979	NY-A	574	5	.270	.374	.368	277	2	.282	.400	.383	297	3	.259	.348	.354	287	1	.258	.357	.328	287	4	.282	.391	.408	250	3	.284	.392	.404	324	2	.259	.360	.340
1980	NY-A	513	7	.294	.427	.407	269	2	.309	.438	.409	244	5	.279	.415	.406	265	4	.291	.429	.415	248	3	.298	.425	.399	207	6	.333	.447	.488	306	1	.268	.414	.353
1981	NY-A	357	2	.232	.336	.305	166	1	.235	.350	.319	191	1	.230	.323	.293	204	2	.235	.342	.319	153	0	.229	.328	.288	138	1	.217	.329	.261	219	1	.242	.340	.333
1982	NY-A	553	3	.280	.368	.349	270	1	.300	.401	.378	283	2	.261	.334	.322	234	2	.274	.371	.368	319	1	.285	.366	.335	220	2	.268	.348	.368	333	1	.288	.381	.336

YEAR	TM/L	TOTAL AB	HR	AVG	OBP	SLG	HOME AB	HR	AVG	OBP	SLG	AWAY AB	HR	AVG	OBP	SLG	1ST HALF AB	HR	AVG	OBP	SLG	2ND HALF AB	HR	AVG	OBP	SLG	LEFT AB	HR	AVG	OBP	SLG	RIGHT AB	HR	AVG	OBP	SLG
1983	NY-A	420	2	.279	.361	.348	221	1	.290	.369	.339	199	1	.266	.351	.357	191	1	.257	.340	.314	229	1	.297	.378	.376	167	0	.269	.361	.335	253	2	.285	.360	.356
1984	NY-A	564	2	.287	.377	.348	278	1	.273	.371	.324	286	1	.301	.384	.371	284	2	.292	.382	.359	280	0	.282	.373	.336	189	1	.333	.423	.429	375	1	.264	.354	.307
1985	NY-A	497	5	.276	.382	.356	221	3	.262	.387	.367	276	2	.286	.377	.348	247	1	.267	.374	.328	250	4	.284	.389	.384	181	2	.315	.418	.414	316	3	.253	.361	.323
1986	NY-A	492	5	.276	.393	.346	241	2	.311	.451	.390	251	3	.243	.332	.303	267	1	.273	.402	.333	225	4	.280	.381	.360	183	4	.311	.392	.426	309	1	.256	.393	.298
1987	NY-A	449	7	.305	.411	.414	253	3	.292	.395	.399	196	4	.321	.430	.434	279	4	.319	.427	.441	170	3	.282	.383	.371	133	3	.331	.467	.459	316	4	.294	.385	.396
1988	NY-A	404	2	.230	.322	.300	206	1	.218	.318	.267	198	1	.242	.326	.333	205	1	.205	.295	.278	199	1	.256	.349	.322	125	1	.208	.318	.288	279	1	.240	.324	.305
1989	LA-N	549	2	.282	.366	.326	266	0	.305	.393	.338	283	2	.261	.340	.314	283	0	.297	.388	.325	266	2	.267	.341	.327	191	1	.298	.385	.356	358	1	.274	.355	.310
1990	LA-N	96	1	.271	.364	.344	37	0	.270	.341	.351	59	1	.271	.377	.339	96	1	.271	.364	.344	0	0	—	—	—	34	0	.353	.450	.441	62	1	.226	.314	.290
1990	Oak-A	292	1	.257	.331	.318	127	1	.244	.322	.299	165	0	.267	.339	.333	115	1	.217	.283	.278	177	0	.282	.362	.345	82	0	.354	.376	.439	210	1	.219	.315	.271
1991	Mil-A	431	0	.327	.424	.374	220	0	.336	.410	.400	211	0	.318	.438	.346	145	0	.345	.435	.372	286	0	.318	.419	.374	148	0	.358	.457	.405	283	0	.311	.407	.357
1992	NY-N	286	2	.252	.352	.318	153	2	.255	.349	.359	133	0	.248	.355	.271	229	2	.245	.337	.323	57	0	.281	.406	.298	105	2	.276	.397	.371	181	0	.238	.324	.287
TOTALS		6976	49	.277	.377	.352	3444	22	.283	.387	.361	3532	27	.272	.367	.343	3566	25	.270	.373	.344	3410	24	.284	.381	.360	2596	28	.299	.399	.393	4380	21	.265	.363	.327
■ Johnny Ray	BB/TR																																			
1981	Pit-N	102	0	.245	.284	.353	45	0	.267	.313	.378	57	0	.228	.262	.333	0	0	—	—	—	102	0	.245	.284	.353	35	0	.257	.333	.343	67	0	.239	.257	.358
1982	Pit-N	647	7	.281	.318	.382	307	6	.306	.352	.453	340	1	.259	.285	.318	290	5	.307	.341	.424	357	2	.261	.299	.347	170	0	.224	.267	.282	477	7	.302	.336	.417
1983	Pit-N	576	5	.283	.323	.399	276	3	.293	.328	.428	300	2	.273	.319	.373	262	1	.286	.329	.378	314	4	.280	.318	.417	90	0	.222	.263	.267	486	5	.294	.334	.424
1984	Pit-N	555	6	.312	.354	.434	274	3	.252	.301	.347	281	3	.370	.407	.520	259	0	.297	.350	.386	296	6	.324	.358	.476	101	0	.317	.357	.406	454	6	.311	.354	.441
1985	Pit-N	594	7	.274	.325	.375	278	3	.291	.353	.406	316	4	.259	.299	.348	283	3	.265	.292	.360	311	4	.283	.352	.389	170	1	.253	.291	.335	424	6	.283	.338	.392
1986	Pit-N	579	7	.301	.363	.394	298	2	.285	.356	.366	281	5	.317	.371	.423	256	2	.301	.368	.398	323	5	.300	.359	.390	222	1	.261	.318	.311	357	6	.325	.390	.445
1987	Pit-N	472	5	.273	.328	.358	228	5	.303	.361	.412	244	0	.246	.297	.307	294	4	.262	.309	.354	178	1	.292	.359	.365	191	2	.257	.322	.319	281	3	.285	.332	.384
1987	Cal-A	127	0	.346	.359	.433	47	0	.298	.313	.362	80	0	.375	.386	.475	0	0	—	—	—	127	0	.346	.359	.433	47	0	.298	.298	.362	80	0	.375	.393	.475
1988	Cal-A	602	6	.306	.345	.429	287	4	.296	.348	.418	315	2	.314	.341	.438	272	2	.301	.345	.412	330	4	.309	.345	.442	210	2	.281	.327	.395	392	4	.319	.354	.446
1989	Cal-A	530	5	.289	.327	.358	268	3	.265	.296	.340	262	2	.313	.357	.378	242	2	.281	.306	.364	288	3	.295	.344	.354	195	1	.262	.299	.318	335	4	.304	.343	.382
1990	Cal-A	404	5	.277	.308	.371	210	5	.271	.302	.386	194	0	.284	.314	.356	158	2	.234	.285	.323	246	3	.305	.323	.402	120	0	.300	.317	.342	284	5	.268	.304	.384
TOTALS		5188	53	.290	.333	.391	2518	34	.285	.334	.395	2670	19	.294	.332	.387	2316	21	.284	.327	.380	2872	32	.294	.338	.399	1551	7	.264	.308	.332	3637	46	.301	.343	.416
■ Jody Reed	BR/TR																																			
1987	Bos-A	30	0	.300	.382	.400	4	0	.000	.000	.000	26	0	.346	.433	.462	0	0	—	—	—	30	0	.300	.382	.400	10	0	.500	.615	.600	20	0	.200	.238	.300
1988	Bos-A	338	1	.293	.380	.376	188	1	.309	.399	.399	150	0	.273	.357	.347	70	1	.214	.341	.314	268	0	.313	.391	.392	84	0	.226	.301	.262	254	1	.315	.405	.413
1989	Bos-A	524	3	.288	.376	.393	270	2	.300	.384	.415	254	1	.276	.368	.370	257	0	.268	.353	.346	267	3	.307	.398	.438	140	1	.321	.401	.450	384	2	.276	.367	.372
1990	Bos-A	598	5	.289	.371	.390	311	3	.293	.365	.405	287	2	.286	.377	.373	267	3	.292	.360	.412	331	2	.287	.379	.372	184	0	.299	.376	.386	414	5	.285	.368	.391
1991	Bos-A	618	5	.283	.349	.382	312	3	.263	.336	.385	306	2	.304	.362	.379	264	1	.246	.308	.330	354	4	.311	.379	.421	165	0	.267	.328	.321	453	5	.289	.356	.404
1992	Bos-A	550	3	.247	.321	.316	279	2	.276	.364	.358	271	1	.218	.276	.273	295	1	.261	.328	.339	255	2	.231	.314	.290	154	1	.260	.345	.370	396	2	.242	.312	.295
1993	LA-N	445	2	.276	.333	.346	233	0	.292	.357	.348	212	2	.259	.306	.344	209	2	.287	.345	.368	236	0	.267	.322	.326	123	0	.325	.381	.390	322	2	.258	.314	.329
1994	Mil-A	399	2	.271	.362	.341	199	1	.246	.333	.296	200	1	.295	.391	.385	261	1	.276	.375	.337	138	1	.261	.338	.348	78	0	.218	.390	.269	321	2	.283	.355	.358
1995	SD-N	445	4	.256	.348	.328	212	4	.278	.384	.382	233	0	.236	.313	.279	133	1	.248	.371	.301	312	3	.260	.337	.340	131	0	.290	.400	.366	314	4	.242	.325	.312
1996	SD-N	495	2	.244	.325	.297	222	1	.239	.319	.288	273	1	.249	.330	.304	297	1	.239	.313	.293	198	1	.253	.342	.303	118	0	.212	.319	.237	377	2	.255	.327	.316
1997	Det-A	112	0	.196	.278	.214	57	0	.246	.353	.281	55	0	.145	.190	.145	91	0	.209	.291	.231	21	0	.143	.217	.143	30	0	.233	.333	.233	82	0	.183	.256	.207
TOTALS		4554	27	.270	.349	.350	2287	17	.276	.359	.365	2267	10	.264	.340	.336	2144	11	.261	.340	.336	2410	16	.279	.358	.363	1217	2	.275	.363	.348	3337	25	.269	.344	.351
■ Pokey Reese	BR/TR																																			
1997	Cin-N	397	4	.219	.284	.287	178	3	.270	.350	.365	219	1	.178	.227	.224	117	2	.239	.305	.316	280	2	.211	.275	.275	87	1	.172	.273	.241	310	3	.232	.287	.300
1998	Cin-N	133	1	.256	.322	.323	59	0	.271	.338	.322	74	1	.243	.309	.324	71	1	.197	.256	.268	62	0	.323	.394	.387	30	0	.133	.212	.167	103	1	.291	.353	.369
1999	Cin-N	585	10	.285	.330	.417	273	5	.264	.302	.363	312	5	.304	.353	.465	287	5	.300	.331	.443	298	5	.272	.328	.393	146	3	.295	.350	.445	439	7	.282	.323	.408
2000	Cin-N	518	12	.255	.319	.386	258	3	.260	.313	.353	260	9	.250	.324	.419	296	5	.267	.333	.392	222	7	.239	.299	.378	109	1	.257	.347	.358	409	11	.254	.311	.394
TOTALS		1633	27	.257	.314	.368	768	11	.264	.320	.357	865	16	.251	.309	.378	771	13	.268	.321	.388	862	14	.247	.309	.350	372	5	.242	.320	.349	1261	22	.262	.313	.374
■ Edgar Renteria	BR/TR																																			
1996	Fla-N	431	5	.309	.358	.399	188	2	.309	.385	.415	243	3	.309	.336	.387	129	1	.248	.293	.349	302	4	.334	.386	.421	90	2	.244	.300	.400	341	3	.326	.374	.399
1997	Fla-N	617	4	.277	.327	.340	306	3	.265	.324	.333	311	1	.289	.330	.347	308	1	.256	.310	.318	309	3	.298	.344	.362	108	0	.259	.336	.296	509	4	.281	.325	.350
1998	Fla-N	517	3	.282	.347	.342	265	2	.302	.366	.358	252	1	.262	.326	.325	320	1	.306	.371	.366	197	2	.244	.307	.305	110	1	.227	.312	.300	407	2	.297	.357	.354
1999	StL-N	585	11	.275	.334	.400	297	6	.266	.319	.377	288	5	.285	.349	.424	269	5	.286	.343	.420	316	6	.266	.326	.383	140	2	.250	.354	.386	445	9	.283	.327	.404
2000	StL-N	562	16	.278	.346	.423	279	4	.254	.333	.362	283	12	.300	.360	.484	294	10	.282	.328	.432	268	6	.272	.365	.414	139	5	.259	.381	.453	423	11	.284	.334	.414
TOTALS		2712	39	.283	.341	.380	1335	17	.276	.342	.366	1377	22	.289	.341	.394	1320	18	.280	.334	.379	1392	21	.286	.348	.381	587	10	.249	.342	.371	2125	29	.292	.341	.383
■ Craig Reynolds	BL/TR																																			
1978	Sea-A	548	5	.292	.336	.374	263	2	.304	.354	.369	285	3	.281	.318	.379	248	3	.323	.361	.399	300	2	.267	.315	.353	177	1	.299	.351	.362	371	4	.288	.328	.380
1979	Hou-N	555	0	.265	.292	.333	276	0	.239	.270	.315	279	0	.290	.315	.351	300	0	.287	.304	.353	255	0	.239	.278	.310	176	0	.278	.316	.341	379	0	.259	.281	.330
1980	Hou-N	381	3	.226	.262	.304	185	2	.249	.286	.351	196	1	.204	.238	.260	173	2	.191	.228	.289	208	1	.255	.290	.317	91	0	.187	.219	.231	290	3	.238	.275	.328
1981	Hou-N	323	4	.260	.286	.402	153	0	.242	.255	.359	170	4	.276	.313	.441	195	3	.256	.279	.426	128	1	.266	.296	.367	65	0	.246	.279	.385	258	4	.264	.287	.407
1982	Hou-N	118	1	.254	.321	.347	59	0	.220	.281	.288	59	1	.288	.358	.407	95	1	.232	.308	.316	23	0	.348	.375	.478	14	0	.143	.250	.143	104	1	.269	.330	.375
1983	Hou-N	98	1	.214	.260	.276	47	1	.255	.300	.340	51	0	.176	.222	.216	44	0	.250	.267	.295	54	1	.185	.254	.259	18	0	.111	.158	.167	80	1	.237	.282	.300
1984	Hou-N	527	6	.260	.286	.364	251	0	.263	.291	.355	276	6	.257	.282	.373	256	4	.273	.292	.395	271	2	.247	.281	.336	157	2	.223	.252	.293	370	4	.276	.301	.395
1985	Hou-N	379	4	.272	.293	.393	191	1	.230	.264	.319	188	3	.314	.323	.468	175	3	.286	.317	.423	204	1	.260	.271	.368	54	0	.315	.339	.407	325	4	.265	.285	.391
1986	Hou-N	313	6	.249	.274	.348	144	4	.319	.340	.438	169	2	.189	.219	.272	127	3	.283	.306	.402	186	3	.226	.253	.312	35	0	.143	.143	.171	278	6	.263	.290	.371
1987	Hou-N	374	4	.254	.303	.348	189	0	.259	.316	.323	185	4	.249	.291	.373	159	2	.296	.335	.403	215	2	.223	.280	.307	43	0	.140	.196	.140	331	4	.269	.317	.375
1988	Hou-N	161	1	.255	.290	.317	78	0	.231	.268	.256	83	1	.277	.310	.373	86	1	.267	.308	.337	75	0	.240	.269	.293	12	0	.333	.333	.333	149	1	.248	.287	.315
1989	Hou-N	189	2	.201	.274	.254	102	0	.196	.281	.206	87	2	.207	.266	.310	86	1	.198	.274	.244	103	1	.204	.274	.262	8	0	.125	.300	.125	181	2	.204	.273	.260
TOTALS		3966	37	.257	.293	.349	1938	10	.256	.295	.336	2028	27	.258	.291	.360	1944	23	.270	.303	.371	2022	14	.245	.284	.327	850	3	.244	.283	.306	3116	34	.261	.296	.360
■ Harold Reynolds	BB/TR																																			
1983	Sea-A	59	0	.203	.226	.305	28	0	.107	.133	.179	31	0	.290	.313	.419	0	0	—	—	—	59	0	.203	.226	.305	20	0	.200	.190	.350	39	0	.205	.244	.282
1984	Sea-A	10	0	.300	.364	.300	6	0	.500	.571	.500	4	0	.000	.000	.000	0	0	—	—	—	10	0	.300	.364	.300	8	0	.375	.444	.375	2	0	.000	.000	.000
1985	Sea-A	104	0	.144	.264	.192	59	0	.136	.261	.203	45	0	.156	.269	.178	27	0	.037	.212	.074	77	0	.182	.284	.234	31	0	.129	.289	.161	73	0	.151	.253	.205
1986	Sea-A	445	1	.222	.275	.290	220	1	.227	.283	.332	225	0	.218	.267	.249	174	0	.224	.274	.282	271	1	.221	.275	.295	117	1	.205	.250	.274	328	0	.229	.283	.296
1987	Sea-A	530	1	.275	.325	.370	257	1	.233	.296	.319	273	0	.315	.353	.418	244	0	.270	.321	.352	286	1	.280	.328	.385	162	1	.278	.320	.370	368	0	.274	.327	.370
1988	Sea-A	598	4	.283	.340	.383	290	4	.286	.344	.407	308	0	.279	.336	.360	275	2	.287	.322	.389	323	2	.279	.355	.378	185	2	.314	.344	.411	413	2	.269	.338	.370
1989	Sea-A	613	0	.300	.359	.369	307	0	.300	.351	.375	306	0	.301	.367	.363	290	0	.290	.344	.369	323	0	.310	.373	.368	170	0	.324	.378	.388	443	0	.291	.352	.361
1990	Sea-A	642	5	.252	.336	.347	297	0	.253	.350	.310	345	5	.252	.324	.380	298	1	.238	.329	.329	344	4	.265	.342	.363	207	1	.285	.335	.391	435	4	.237	.337	.326
1991	Sea-A	631	3	.254	.332	.341	314	1	.299	.387	.404	317	2	.208	.276	.278	293	1	.276	.354	.355	338	2	.234	.312	.328	174	1	.264	.326	.322	457	2	.249	.334	.348
1992	Sea-A	458	3	.247	.316	.330	237	2	.262	.326	.376	221	1	.231	.305	.281	270	2	.244	.317	.333	188	1	.250	.314	.324	116	0	.250	.348	.302	342	3	.246	.304	.339
1993	Bal-A	485	4	.252	.343	.334	261	2	.249	.331	.345	224	2	.254	.356	.321	247	0	.263	.343	.320	238	4	.239	.343	.349	134	0	.179	.213	.209	351	4	.279	.387	.382
1994	Cal-A	207	0	.232	.310	.290	117	0	.205	.277	.291	90	0	.267	.353	.289	183	0	.235	.322	.295	24	0	.208	.208	.250	17	0	.235	.381	.235	190	0	.232	.303	.295
TOTALS		4782	21	.258	.327	.341	2393	11	.259	.330	.351	2389	10	.257	.323	.332	2301	6	.259	.327	.337	2481	15	.257	.327	.345	1341	6	.265	.319	.338	3441	15	.255	.330	.343
■ Jim Rice	BR/TR																																			
1978	Bos-A	677	46	.315	.370	.600	335	28	.361	.416	.690	342	18	.269	.325	.512	311	23	.325	.384	.630	366	23	.306	.358	.574	173	10	.301	.365	.566	504	36	.319	.373	.611
1979	Bos-A	619	39	.325	.381	.596	301	27	.369	.425	.728	318	12	.283	.337	.472	294	18	.323	.387	.582	325	21	.326	.375	.609	154	14	.331	.409	.682	465	25	.323	.371	.568
1980	Bos-A	504	24	.294	.336	.504	239	11	.305	.351	.523	265	13	.283	.323	.487	264	13	.261	.307	.462	240	11	.329	.368	.550	126	11	.310	.365	.603	378	13	.288	.327	.471
1981	Bos-A	451	17	.284	.333	.441	215	10	.307	.360	.493	236	7	.263	.309	.394	232	9	.267	.299	.427	219	8	.301	.369	.457	98	4	.306	.355	.480	353	13	.278	.327	.431
1982	Bos-A	573	24	.309	.375	.494	306	9	.330	.396	.480	267	15	.285	.350	.509	252	11	.310	.390	.496	321	13	.308	.362	.492	155	2	.297	.408	.426	418	22	.313	.361	.519
1983	Bos-A	626	39	.305	.361	.550	329	16	.325	.383	.535	297	23	.283	.337	.566	294	18	.293	.358	.534	332	21	.316	.365	.563	169	10	.331	.400	.568	457	29	.295	.347	.543
1984	Bos-A	657	28	.280	.323	.467	330	17	.288	.334	.506	327	11	.272	.313	.428	300	14	.280	.320	.493	357	14	.280	.326	.445	153	8	.327	.394	.529	504	20	.266	.301	.448
1985	Bos-A	546	27	.291	.349	.487	274	11	.350	.391	.540	272	16	.232	.309	.434	293	14	.294	.348	.478	253	13	.289	.350	.498	151	7	.258	.363	.470	395	20	.304	.343	.494
1986	Bos-A	618	20	.324	.384	.490	312	10	.337	.387	.526	306	10	.310	.381	.454	297	7	.330	.384	.481	321	13	.318	.384	.498	168	7	.351	.413	.560	450	13	.313	.373	.464
1987	Bos-A	404	13	.277	.357	.408	190	7	.305	.391	.447	214	6	.252	.326	.374	231	5	.268	.354	.385	173	8	.289	.362	.439	123	4	.285	.371	.398	281	9	.274	.351	.413
1988	Bos-A	485	15	.264	.330	.406	225	9	.276	.362	.453	260	6	.254	.301	.365	241	4	.274	.344	.365	244	11	.254	.316	.447	155	6	.290	.349	.477	330	9	.252	.322	.373
1989	Bos-A	209	3	.234	.276	.344	110	1	.245	.283	.327	99	2	.222	.269	.364	160	3	.237	.278	.356	49	0	.224	.269	.306	63	1	.254	.294	.397	146	2	.226	.269	.322
TOTALS		6369	295	.297	.353	.497	3166	156	.323	.379	.539	3203	139	.271	.327	.456	3169	139	.292	.350	.484	3200	156	.302	.356	.509	1688	84	.307	.380	.523	4681	211	.293	.344	.488

YEAR	TM/L	TOTAL AB	HR	AVG	OBP	SLG	HOME AB	HR	AVG	OBP	SLG	AWAY AB	HR	AVG	OBP	SLG	1ST HALF AB	HR	AVG	OBP	SLG	2ND HALF AB	HR	AVG	OBP	SLG	LEFT AB	HR	AVG	OBP	SLG	RIGHT AB	HR	AVG	OBP	SLG
■ Cal Ripken BR/TR																																				
1981	Bal-A	39	0	.128	.150	.128	14	0	.143	.143	.143	25	0	.120	.154	.120	0	0	—	—	—	39	0	.128	.150	.128	10	0	.100	.182	.100	29	0	.138	.138	.138
1982	Bal-A	598	28	.264	.317	.475	289	11	.246	.303	.415	309	17	.282	.330	.531	255	8	.267	.300	.455	343	20	.262	.329	.490	169	12	.284	.333	.556	429	16	.256	.311	.443
1983	Bal-A	663	27	.318	.371	.517	321	12	.315	.368	.505	342	15	.322	.373	.529	290	12	.283	.358	.476	373	15	.346	.381	.550	218	8	.312	.370	.500	445	19	.321	.371	.526
1984	Bal-A	641	27	.304	.374	.510	307	16	.287	.367	.508	334	11	.320	.381	.512	301	13	.289	.364	.498	340	14	.318	.384	.521	159	7	.308	.385	.547	482	20	.303	.371	.498
1985	Bal-A	642	26	.282	.347	.469	311	15	.289	.371	.482	331	11	.275	.323	.456	282	11	.277	.342	.457	360	15	.286	.351	.478	202	6	.272	.346	.436	440	20	.286	.347	.484
1986	Bal-A	627	25	.282	.355	.461	291	10	.265	.344	.430	336	15	.298	.365	.488	274	9	.274	.362	.445	353	16	.289	.349	.473	164	12	.360	.428	.683	463	13	.255	.329	.382
1987	Bal-A	624	27	.252	.333	.436	310	17	.248	.313	.465	314	10	.255	.352	.408	309	17	.282	.355	.511	315	10	.222	.313	.362	211	7	.242	.311	.431	413	20	.257	.344	.438
1988	Bal-A	575	23	.264	.372	.431	285	11	.263	.370	.414	290	12	.266	.373	.448	271	12	.262	.390	.450	304	11	.266	.354	.414	190	9	.316	.430	.500	385	14	.239	.342	.397
1989	Bal-A	646	21	.257	.317	.401	312	13	.247	.317	.413	334	8	.266	.318	.389	308	8	.282	.348	.409	338	13	.234	.289	.393	196	5	.235	.287	.372	450	16	.267	.331	.413
1990	Bal-A	600	21	.250	.341	.415	300	8	.213	.295	.350	300	13	.287	.386	.480	283	8	.251	.353	.396	317	13	.249	.331	.432	182	9	.264	.363	.473	418	12	.244	.332	.390
1991	Bal-A	650	34	.323	.374	.566	315	16	.286	.343	.505	335	18	.358	.403	.624	290	17	.355	.413	.614	360	17	.297	.342	.528	164	12	.348	.411	.677	486	22	.315	.361	.529
1992	Bal-A	637	14	.251	.323	.366	312	5	.237	.310	.346	325	9	.265	.335	.385	295	10	.285	.365	.441	342	4	.222	.286	.301	165	2	.230	.297	.315	472	12	.258	.332	.383
1993	Bal-A	641	24	.257	.329	.420	311	14	.273	.360	.437	330	10	.242	.297	.403	307	9	.228	.318	.381	334	15	.284	.339	.455	177	7	.282	.355	.441	464	17	.248	.318	.412
1994	Bal-A	444	13	.315	.364	.459	203	5	.305	.368	.433	241	8	.324	.359	.481	303	10	.307	.348	.465	141	3	.333	.397	.447	110	2	.345	.381	.427	334	11	.305	.358	.470
1995	Bal-A	550	17	.262	.324	.422	271	10	.288	.342	.465	279	7	.237	.305	.380	232	7	.284	.332	.466	318	10	.245	.318	.390	154	7	.286	.354	.487	396	10	.253	.311	.396
1996	Bal-A	640	26	.278	.341	.466	311	10	.228	.301	.379	329	16	.325	.380	.547	304	15	.296	.365	.500	336	11	.262	.318	.435	191	7	.288	.351	.461	449	19	.274	.337	.468
1997	Bal-A	615	17	.270	.331	.402	290	10	.272	.337	.421	325	7	.268	.325	.385	309	11	.288	.339	.443	306	6	.252	.323	.359	181	5	.260	.335	.392	434	12	.274	.329	.406
1998	Bal-A	601	14	.271	.331	.389	296	8	.264	.321	.385	305	6	.279	.341	.393	310	7	.261	.327	.371	291	7	.282	.337	.409	163	5	.258	.331	.399	438	9	.276	.331	.386
1999	Bal-A	332	18	.340	.368	.584	150	12	.353	.393	.640	182	6	.330	.346	.538	194	10	.304	.328	.531	138	8	.391	.420	.659	49	2	.327	.365	.551	283	16	.343	.368	.590
2000	Bal-A	309	15	.256	.310	.453	123	8	.285	.357	.537	186	7	.237	.276	.398	234	13	.239	.289	.444	75	2	.307	.373	.480	95	2	.263	.330	.379	214	13	.252	.300	.486
TOTALS		11074	417	.277	.343	.451	5322	211	.268	.338	.440	5752	206	.286	.347	.461	5351	207	.280	.349	.459	5723	210	.275	.337	.443	3150	126	.285	.355	.472	7924	291	.274	.338	.443
■ Ruben Rivera BR/TR																																				
1995	NY-A	1	0	.000	.000	.000	1	0	.000	.000	.000	0	0	—	—	—	0	0	—	—	—	1	0	.000	.000	.000	0	0	—	—	—	1	0	.000	.000	.000
1996	NY-A	88	2	.284	.381	.443	24	0	.292	.333	.375	64	2	.281	.397	.469	47	1	.277	.410	.426	41	1	.293	.341	.463	25	2	.280	.424	.600	63	0	.286	.361	.381
1997	SD-N	20	0	.250	.318	.300	4	0	.000	.200	.000	16	0	.313	.353	.375	0	0	—	—	—	20	0	.250	.318	.300	12	0	.250	.250	.333	8	0	.250	.400	.250
1998	SD-N	172	6	.209	.325	.378	85	2	.200	.320	.329	87	4	.218	.330	.425	58	2	.276	.411	.500	114	4	.175	.277	.316	97	5	.268	.343	.505	75	1	.133	.305	.213
1999	SD-N	411	23	.195	.295	.406	197	10	.178	.261	.360	214	13	.210	.324	.449	196	12	.199	.264	.439	215	11	.191	.320	.377	140	8	.200	.280	.436	271	15	.192	.302	.391
2000	SD-N	423	17	.208	.296	.400	190	8	.232	.319	.447	233	9	.189	.278	.361	167	10	.251	.347	.509	256	7	.180	.262	.328	149	5	.188	.284	.369	274	12	.219	.303	.416
TOTALS		1115	48	.210	.307	.400	501	20	.206	.296	.385	614	28	.213	.317	.412	468	25	.235	.330	.470	647	23	.192	.291	.349	423	20	.217	.305	.435	692	28	.205	.309	.379
■ Bip Roberts BB/TR																																				
1986	SD-N	241	1	.253	.293	.303	118	0	.237	.283	.271	123	1	.268	.302	.333	131	0	.221	.255	.282	110	1	.291	.336	.327	138	1	.203	.247	.268	103	0	.320	.355	.350
1988	SD-N	9	0	.333	.400	.333	7	0	.429	.500	.429	2	0	.000	.000	.000	0	0	—	—	—	9	0	.333	.400	.333	1	0	.000	.000	.000	8	0	.375	.444	.375
1989	SD-N	329	3	.301	.391	.422	159	2	.302	.385	.434	170	1	.300	.397	.412	93	0	.301	.393	.452	236	3	.301	.391	.411	117	3	.325	.397	.513	212	0	.288	.388	.373
1990	SD-N	556	9	.309	.375	.433	287	4	.282	.334	.387	269	5	.338	.416	.483	263	5	.297	.367	.445	293	4	.321	.382	.423	221	4	.294	.350	.425	335	5	.319	.391	.439
1991	SD-N	424	3	.281	.342	.347	223	3	.287	.331	.354	201	0	.274	.354	.338	253	0	.265	.337	.320	171	3	.304	.349	.386	118	0	.254	.302	.297	306	3	.291	.357	.366
1992	Cin-N	532	4	.323	.393	.432	252	3	.353	.432	.500	280	1	.296	.357	.371	277	0	.303	.374	.379	255	4	.345	.415	.490	185	3	.292	.350	.378	347	1	.340	.416	.461
1993	Cin-N	292	1	.240	.330	.295	140	0	.221	.313	.250	152	1	.257	.347	.336	260	1	.250	.336	.308	32	0	.156	.289	.188	84	0	.179	.258	.238	208	1	.264	.358	.317
1994	SD-N	403	2	.320	.383	.397	198	1	.308	.367	.409	205	1	.332	.397	.385	263	1	.319	.392	.392	140	1	.321	.364	.407	126	2	.302	.385	.405	277	0	.329	.382	.394
1995	SD-N	296	2	.304	.346	.372	172	2	.308	.335	.390	124	0	.298	.360	.347	208	1	.317	.372	.389	88	1	.273	.281	.330	79	0	.253	.306	.278	217	2	.323	.361	.406
1996	KC-A	339	0	.283	.331	.357	155	0	.284	.331	.368	184	0	.283	.330	.348	222	0	.302	.346	.392	117	0	.248	.303	.291	112	0	.277	.297	.339	227	0	.286	.346	.366
1997	KC-A	346	1	.309	.348	.379	158	0	.316	.366	.392	188	1	.303	.332	.367	196	1	.321	.351	.393	150	0	.293	.344	.360	110	1	.345	.354	.409	236	0	.292	.345	.364
1997	Cle-A	85	3	.271	.333	.412	30	1	.267	.371	.400	55	2	.273	.311	.418	0	0	—	—	—	85	3	.271	.333	.412	35	1	.257	.297	.371	50	2	.280	.356	.440
1998	Det-A	113	0	.248	.351	.301	44	0	.182	.345	.182	69	0	.290	.355	.377	113	0	.248	.351	.301	0	0	—	—	—	35	0	.171	.216	.200	78	0	.282	.404	.346
1998	Oak-A	182	1	.280	.340	.357	80	0	.262	.348	.300	102	1	.294	.333	.402	18	1	.333	.368	.500	164	0	.274	.337	.341	44	0	.227	.320	.318	138	1	.297	.347	.370
TOTALS		4147	30	.294	.358	.380	2023	16	.291	.354	.379	2124	14	.297	.361	.381	2297	10	.290	.355	.371	1850	20	.300	.360	.390	1405	15	.272	.326	.360	2742	15	.306	.373	.390
■ Alex Rodriguez BR/TR																																				
1994	Sea-A	54	0	.204	.241	.204	17	0	.235	.350	.235	37	0	.189	.184	.189	0	0	—	—	—	54	0	.204	.241	.204	17	0	.176	.222	.176	37	0	.216	.250	.216
1995	Sea-A	142	5	.232	.264	.408	57	1	.298	.333	.456	85	4	.188	.216	.376	74	2	.257	.267	.378	68	3	.206	.260	.441	53	2	.245	.298	.491	89	3	.225	.242	.360
1996	Sea-A	601	36	.358	.414	.631	294	18	.364	.424	.643	307	18	.352	.405	.619	255	15	.341	.394	.612	346	21	.370	.429	.645	143	9	.371	.449	.664	458	27	.354	.403	.620
1997	Sea-A	587	23	.300	.350	.496	289	16	.311	.351	.571	298	7	.289	.350	.423	285	11	.319	.367	.530	302	12	.281	.334	.464	157	8	.299	.337	.548	430	15	.300	.355	.477
1998	Sea-A	686	42	.310	.360	.560	343	18	.286	.332	.484	343	24	.335	.387	.636	355	27	.310	.363	.594	331	15	.311	.357	.523	144	12	.313	.353	.618	542	30	.310	.362	.544
1999	Sea-A	502	42	.285	.357	.586	250	20	.284	.350	.568	252	22	.286	.365	.603	178	12	.298	.385	.579	324	30	.278	.342	.590	112	7	.277	.352	.500	390	35	.287	.359	.610
2000	Sea-A	554	41	.316	.420	.606	265	13	.272	.406	.502	289	28	.356	.433	.702	288	21	.344	.443	.635	266	20	.286	.395	.575	93	11	.366	.447	.774	461	30	.306	.414	.573
TOTALS		3126	189	.309	.374	.561	1515	86	.303	.371	.545	1611	103	.315	.376	.576	1435	88	.320	.385	.580	1691	101	.300	.364	.545	719	49	.314	.376	.594	2407	140	.307	.373	.551
■ Henry Rodriguez BL/TL																																				
1992	LA-N	146	3	.219	.258	.329	83	2	.253	.292	.361	63	1	.175	.212	.286	0	0	—	—	—	146	3	.219	.258	.329	15	0	.400	.438	.400	131	3	.198	.237	.321
1993	LA-N	176	8	.222	.266	.415	97	5	.237	.288	.443	79	3	.203	.238	.380	20	1	.200	.238	.350	156	7	.224	.269	.423	6	0	.000	.000	.000	170	8	.229	.275	.429
1994	LA-N	306	8	.268	.307	.405	141	5	.298	.340	.447	165	3	.242	.278	.370	221	5	.299	.347	.439	85	3	.188	.195	.318	14	2	.357	.400	.857	292	6	.264	.303	.384
1995	LA-N	80	1	.262	.306	.375	33	0	.152	.176	.212	47	1	.340	.392	.489	80	1	.262	.306	.375	0	0	—	—	—	21	0	.190	.190	.238	59	1	.288	.344	.424
1995	Mon-N	58	1	.207	.277	.259	49	1	.224	.291	.286	9	0	.111	.200	.111	28	1	.250	.333	.357	30	0	.167	.219	.167	11	0	.273	.357	.273	47	1	.191	.255	.255
1996	Mon-N	532	36	.276	.325	.562	262	20	.271	.324	.584	270	16	.281	.325	.541	290	25	.297	.338	.638	242	11	.252	.309	.471	110	7	.218	.263	.491	422	29	.291	.341	.581
1997	Mon-N	476	26	.244	.306	.479	248	14	.266	.328	.540	228	12	.219	.281	.412	293	16	.280	.333	.529	183	10	.186	.262	.399	133	5	.218	.305	.376	343	21	.254	.306	.519
1998	Chi-N	415	31	.251	.334	.530	210	16	.267	.363	.562	205	15	.234	.303	.498	252	18	.230	.326	.508	163	13	.282	.346	.564	96	3	.250	.321	.396	319	28	.251	.338	.571
1999	Chi-N	447	26	.304	.381	.544	234	14	.303	.383	.547	213	12	.305	.379	.540	213	14	.352	.439	.620	234	12	.261	.326	.474	139	8	.237	.316	.446	308	18	.334	.410	.588
2000	Chi-N	259	18	.251	.314	.525	122	6	.238	.293	.443	137	12	.263	.331	.599	198	13	.242	.304	.500	61	5	.279	.343	.607	39	2	.282	.378	.513	220	16	.245	.302	.527
2000	Fla-N	108	2	.269	.358	.380	44	1	.273	.360	.432	64	1	.266	.356	.344	0	0	—	—	—	108	2	.269	.358	.380	14	0	.143	.200	.143	94	2	.287	.380	.415
TOTALS		3003	160	.261	.322	.485	1523	84	.267	.332	.501	1480	76	.254	.312	.469	1595	94	.280	.344	.529	1408	66	.239	.298	.436	598	27	.236	.305	.421	2405	133	.267	.327	.501
■ Ivan Rodriguez BR/TR																																				
1991	Tex-A	280	3	.264	.276	.354	135	3	.237	.248	.370	145	0	.290	.302	.338	37	0	.378	.368	.432	243	3	.247	.262	.342	71	1	.239	.260	.366	209	2	.273	.282	.349
1992	Tex-A	420	8	.260	.300	.360	211	4	.237	.270	.327	209	4	.282	.329	.392	172	7	.279	.323	.436	248	1	.246	.284	.306	105	2	.276	.319	.371	315	6	.254	.293	.356
1993	Tex-A	473	10	.273	.315	.412	242	7	.244	.286	.417	231	3	.303	.345	.407	236	4	.288	.327	.424	237	6	.257	.304	.401	108	2	.278	.325	.389	365	8	.271	.312	.419
1994	Tex-A	363	16	.298	.360	.488	207	7	.309	.360	.464	156	9	.282	.361	.519	219	8	.292	.372	.475	144	8	.306	.342	.507	70	4	.300	.387	.514	293	12	.297	.354	.481
1995	Tex-A	492	12	.303	.327	.449	232	5	.297	.333	.431	260	7	.308	.321	.465	177	4	.311	.340	.475	315	8	.298	.319	.435	146	4	.301	.340	.452	346	8	.303	.321	.448
1996	Tex-A	639	19	.300	.342	.473	295	10	.325	.379	.519	344	9	.279	.309	.433	312	10	.311	.351	.497	327	9	.291	.332	.450	190	10	.311	.364	.547	449	9	.296	.332	.441
1997	Tex-A	597	20	.313	.360	.484	311	12	.347	.376	.534	286	8	.276	.344	.430	318	10	.346	.379	.535	279	10	.276	.340	.427	162	5	.321	.360	.488	435	15	.310	.360	.483
1998	Tex-A	579	21	.321	.358	.513	286	12	.325	.359	.517	293	9	.317	.357	.509	288	10	.354	.397	.566	291	11	.289	.318	.460	139	5	.317	.368	.482	440	16	.323	.355	.523
1999	Tex-A	600	35	.332	.356	.558	305	12	.357	.372	.525	295	23	.305	.339	.593	263	13	.308	.341	.498	337	22	.350	.368	.605	114	6	.325	.366	.509	486	29	.333	.353	.570
2000	Tex-A	363	27	.347	.375	.667	177	16	.333	.366	.667	186	11	.360	.385	.667	298	23	.362	.392	.691	65	4	.277	.301	.554	79	8	.342	.404	.684	284	19	.349	.367	.662
TOTALS		4806	171	.304	.340	.480	2401	88	.308	.342	.484	2405	83	.299	.338	.477	2320	89	.322	.362	.519	2486	82	.286	.320	.444	1184	47	.304	.352	.482	3622	124	.303	.336	.480
■ Gary Roenicke BR/TR																																				
1978	Bal-A	58	3	.259	.348	.466	29	1	.276	.371	.448	29	2	.241	.324	.483	36	0	.194	.279	.194	22	3	.364	.462	.909	50	3	.280	.367	.520	8	0	.125	.222	.125
1979	Bal-A	376	25	.261	.378	.508	191	9	.262	.372	.461	185	16	.259	.385	.557	192	13	.286	.429	.536	184	12	.234	.319	.478	128	8	.281	.403	.508	248	17	.250	.366	.508
1980	Bal-A	297	10	.239	.340	.384	134	4	.216	.352	.366	163	6	.258	.330	.399	130	2	.246	.338	.346	167	8	.234	.342	.413	151	3	.278	.373	.384	146	7	.199	.306	.384
1981	Bal-A	219	3	.269	.340	.384	106	0	.255	.336	.321	113	3	.283	.344	.442	125	0	.328	.399	.424	94	3	.191	.260	.330	90	2	.211	.287	.322	129	1	.310	.377	.426
1982	Bal-A	393	21	.270	.392	.499	183	6	.240	.379	.404	210	15	.295	.403	.581	179	15	.263	.392	.559	214	6	.276	.392	.449	153	8	.281	.424	.523	240	13	.262	.370	.483
1983	Bal-A	323	19	.260	.326	.477	169	10	.254	.314	.473	154	9	.266	.339	.481	147	9	.279	.333	.517	176	10	.244	.320	.443	207	18	.285	.349	.589	116	1	.216	.285	.276
1984	Bal-A	326	10	.224	.346	.380	155	7	.232	.365	.426	171	3	.216	.328	.339	134	3	.239	.354	.381	192	7	.214	.341	.380	143	5	.259	.398	.448	183	5	.197	.304	.328
1985	Bal-A	225	15	.218	.342	.458	116	9	.250	.353	.509	109	6	.183	.331	.404	98	6	.255	.359	.500	127	9	.189	.329	.425	172	12	.209	.350	.453	53	3	.245	.310	.472
1986	NY-A	136	3	.265	.388	.368	64	3	.281	.440	.422	72	0	.250	.333	.319	76	3	.276	.423	.434	60	0	.250	.338	.283	117	3	.256	.376	.368	19	0	.316	.458	.368
1987	Atl-N	151	9	.219	.353	.450	73	8	.288	.409	.671	78	1	.154	.303	.244	58	1	.190	.310	.259	93	8	.237	.379	.570	117	8	.205	.329	.453	34	1	.265	.432	.441
1988	Atl-N	114	1	.228	.279	.298	52	0	.212	.255	.269	62	1	.242	.299	.323	77	1	.260	.313	.364	37	0	.162	.205	.162	88	1	.216	.309	.352	26	0	.115	.179	.115
TOTALS		2618	119	.248	.354	.437	1272	57	.248	.360	.435	1346	62	.248	.348	.440	1252	53	.265	.371	.447	1366	66	.233	.339	.428	1416	71	.256	.365	.458	1202	48	.239	.340	.413
■ Scott Rolen BR/TR																																				
1996	Phi-N	130	4	.254	.322	.400	87	2	.253	.340	.379	43	2	.256	.283	.442	0	0	—	—	—	130	4	.254	.322	.400	24	0	.333	.448	.458	106	4	.236	.291	.387

		TOTAL					HOME					AWAY					1ST HALF					2ND HALF					LEFT					RIGHT				
YEAR	TM/L	AB	HR	AVG	OBP	SLG	AB	HR	AVG	OBP	SLG	AB	HR	AVG	OBP	SLG	AB	HR	AVG	OBP	SLG	AB	HR	AVG	OBP	SLG	AB	HR	AVG	OBP	SLG	AB	HR	AVG	OBP	SLG
1997	Phi-N	561	21	.283	.377	.469	265	11	.279	.392	.487	296	10	.287	.364	.453	283	8	.272	.358	.438	278	13	.295	.397	.500	133	3	.286	.384	.436	428	18	.283	.376	.479
1998	Phi-N	601	31	.290	.391	.532	286	19	.322	.431	.615	315	12	.260	.353	.457	314	15	.306	.382	.522	287	16	.272	.400	.544	132	11	.280	.422	.606	469	20	.292	.382	.512
1999	Phi-N	421	26	.268	.368	.525	203	9	.266	.349	.478	218	17	.271	.385	.569	275	14	.251	.346	.469	146	12	.301	.409	.630	91	9	.330	.452	.714	330	17	.252	.343	.473
2000	Phi-N	483	26	.298	.370	.551	220	12	.327	.396	.614	263	14	.274	.348	.498	227	16	.273	.339	.555	256	10	.320	.397	.547	106	8	.283	.387	.575	377	18	.302	.365	.544
TOTALS		2196	108	.284	.375	.511	1061	53	.296	.391	.537	1135	55	.272	.359	.486	1099	53	.277	.358	.494	1097	55	.291	.391	.528	486	31	.294	.411	.566	1710	77	.281	.363	.495
■ Pete Rose	BB/TR																																			
1978	Cin-N	655	7	.302	.362	.421	317	2	.319	.371	.429	338	5	.287	.353	.414	321	4	.293	.349	.414	334	3	.311	.373	.428	257	1	.300	.366	.420	398	6	.304	.359	.422
1979	Phi-N	628	4	.331	.418	.430	293	1	.338	.447	.433	335	3	.325	.390	.427	295	3	.325	.408	.444	333	1	.336	.427	.417	168	1	.327	.397	.423	460	3	.333	.425	.433
1980	Phi-N	655	1	.282	.352	.354	313	0	.284	.375	.377	342	1	.281	.329	.333	271	1	.280	.371	.380	384	0	.284	.337	.336	129	0	.256	.329	.318	526	1	.289	.357	.363
1981	Phi-N	431	0	.325	.391	.390	218	0	.349	.423	.445	213	0	.300	.359	.333	221	0	.330	.389	.421	210	0	.319	.393	.357	87	0	.299	.351	.345	344	0	.331	.402	.401
1982	Phi-N	634	3	.271	.345	.338	307	2	.257	.320	.322	327	1	.284	.368	.352	298	1	.292	.355	.376	336	2	.253	.337	.304	133	0	.271	.329	.331	501	3	.271	.349	.339
1983	Phi-N	493	0	.245	.316	.286	241	0	.261	.327	.320	252	0	.230	.305	.254	235	0	.247	.322	.311	258	0	.244	.310	.264	105	0	.286	.345	.305	388	0	.235	.308	.281
1984	Mon-N	278	0	.259	.334	.295	107	0	.206	.271	.224	171	0	.292	.373	.339	180	0	.278	.353	.322	98	0	.224	.300	.245	78	0	.205	.287	.231	200	0	.280	.353	.320
1984	Cin-N	96	0	.365	.430	.458	69	0	.362	.443	.449	27	0	.370	.393	.481	0	0	—	—	—	96	0	.365	.430	.458	12	0	.250	.357	.333	84	0	.381	.441	.476
1985	Cin-N	405	2	.264	.395	.319	196	0	.255	.404	.301	209	2	.273	.386	.335	196	1	.286	.408	.352	209	1	.244	.383	.287	49	0	.347	.467	.408	356	2	.253	.385	.306
1986	Cin-N	237	0	.219	.316	.270	121	0	.256	.341	.322	116	0	.181	.291	.216	153	0	.216	.320	.268	84	0	.226	.309	.274	22	0	.273	.304	.364	215	0	.214	.317	.260
TOTALS		4512	17	.286	.364	.359	2182	5	.291	.375	.370	2330	12	.281	.354	.349	2170	10	.287	.366	.375	2342	7	.285	.363	.345	1040	2	.287	.356	.362	3472	15	.285	.367	.358
■ Bill Russell	BR/TR																																			
1978	LA-N	625	3	.286	.320	.365	316	0	.278	.323	.332	309	3	.294	.316	.398	321	2	.271	.300	.349	304	1	.303	.341	.382	156	0	.321	.369	.391	469	3	.275	.303	.356
1979	LA-N	627	7	.271	.297	.359	317	4	.274	.298	.347	310	3	.268	.297	.371	331	4	.290	.307	.381	296	3	.250	.287	.334	163	3	.313	.351	.405	464	4	.256	.278	.343
1980	LA-N	466	3	.264	.295	.341	224	2	.241	.275	.313	242	1	.285	.313	.368	265	3	.287	.314	.389	201	0	.234	.270	.279	86	2	.314	.337	.453	380	1	.253	.286	.316
1981	LA-N	262	0	.233	.284	.282	120	0	.275	.308	.350	142	0	.197	.265	.225	158	0	.196	.249	.228	104	0	.288	.336	.365	45	0	.178	.213	.178	217	0	.244	.298	.304
1982	LA-N	497	3	.274	.357	.340	243	2	.305	.369	.391	254	1	.244	.347	.291	216	2	.255	.358	.319	281	1	.288	.357	.356	90	0	.300	.376	.344	407	3	.268	.353	.339
1983	LA-N	451	1	.246	.302	.286	216	0	.245	.296	.278	235	1	.247	.307	.294	174	1	.259	.333	.305	277	0	.238	.281	.274	110	0	.218	.265	.236	341	1	.255	.314	.302
1984	LA-N	262	0	.267	.329	.321	118	0	.220	.301	.229	144	0	.306	.353	.396	144	0	.299	.360	.361	118	0	.229	.289	.271	118	0	.254	.328	.322	144	0	.278	.329	.319
1985	LA-N	169	0	.260	.333	.308	86	0	.326	.385	.384	83	0	.193	.280	.229	110	0	.264	.333	.309	59	0	.254	.333	.305	85	0	.318	.402	.365	84	0	.202	.261	.250
1986	LA-N	216	0	.250	.302	.301	110	0	.236	.309	.273	106	0	.264	.295	.330	81	0	.235	.284	.284	135	0	.259	.313	.311	114	0	.325	.386	.368	102	0	.167	.204	.225
TOTALS		3575	17	.265	.314	.331	1750	8	.268	.316	.327	1825	9	.262	.312	.336	1800	12	.267	.316	.338	1775	5	.263	.311	.325	967	5	.291	.345	.354	2608	12	.256	.302	.323
■ Luis Salazar	BR/TR																																			
1980	SD-N	169	1	.337	.372	.462	89	0	.348	.370	.461	80	1	.325	.375	.463	0	0	—	—	—	169	1	.337	.372	.462	34	0	.324	.395	.471	135	1	.341	.366	.459
1981	SD-N	400	3	.303	.329	.403	198	2	.283	.314	.389	202	1	.322	.344	.416	201	1	.294	.304	.388	199	2	.312	.354	.417	124	0	.274	.328	.387	276	3	.315	.330	.409
1982	SD-N	524	8	.242	.274	.336	283	6	.272	.303	.378	241	2	.207	.240	.286	242	4	.227	.255	.339	282	4	.255	.291	.333	170	3	.265	.304	.406	354	5	.232	.260	.302
1983	SD-N	481	14	.258	.285	.387	237	10	.257	.273	.409	244	4	.258	.296	.365	213	3	.305	.326	.385	268	11	.220	.253	.388	156	8	.301	.345	.494	325	6	.237	.254	.335
1984	SD-N	228	3	.241	.261	.329	99	1	.202	.218	.253	129	2	.271	.293	.388	75	0	.293	.303	.320	153	3	.216	.241	.333	143	3	.252	.272	.357	85	0	.224	.241	.282
1985	Chi-A	327	10	.245	.267	.404	150	4	.260	.298	.413	177	6	.232	.240	.395	124	5	.169	.211	.306	203	5	.291	.303	.463	171	4	.246	.268	.398	156	6	.244	.267	.410
1986	Chi-A	7	0	.143	.250	.143	1	0	.000	.000	.000	6	0	.167	.286	.167	0	0	—	—	—	7	0	.143	.250	.143	7	0	.143	.250	.143	0	0	—	—	—
1987	SD-N	189	3	.254	.302	.328	95	1	.284	.310	.326	94	2	.223	.295	.330	102	2	.284	.333	.363	87	1	.218	.266	.287	97	2	.258	.287	.361	92	1	.250	.317	.293
1988	Det-A	452	12	.270	.305	.385	213	5	.254	.292	.357	239	7	.285	.316	.410	220	8	.323	.346	.459	232	4	.220	.266	.315	200	8	.320	.351	.500	252	4	.230	.269	.294
1989	SD-N	246	8	.268	.302	.411	138	5	.232	.274	.384	108	3	.315	.339	.444	187	4	.251	.282	.358	59	4	.322	.365	.576	92	4	.283	.320	.489	154	4	.260	.292	.364
1989	Chi-N	80	1	.325	.357	.425	36	1	.361	.395	.556	44	0	.295	.326	.318	0	0	—	—	—	80	1	.325	.357	.425	33	1	.333	.389	.485	47	0	.319	.333	.383
1990	Chi-N	410	12	.254	.293	.388	218	7	.294	.333	.440	192	5	.208	.246	.328	146	4	.281	.333	.418	264	8	.239	.269	.371	157	6	.293	.319	.465	253	6	.229	.277	.340
1991	Chi-N	333	14	.258	.292	.432	165	8	.261	.278	.473	168	6	.256	.306	.393	125	6	.264	.328	.432	208	8	.255	.269	.433	166	10	.271	.309	.500	167	4	.246	.276	.365
1992	Chi-N	255	5	.208	.237	.310	119	3	.235	.271	.378	136	2	.184	.206	.250	142	2	.211	.255	.289	113	3	.204	.214	.336	156	4	.250	.273	.391	99	1	.141	.181	.182
TOTALS		4101	94	.261	.293	.381	2041	53	.267	.297	.396	2060	41	.255	.288	.366	1777	39	.266	.298	.374	2324	55	.257	.288	.386	1706	53	.277	.311	.436	2395	41	.250	.279	.342
■ Tim Salmon	BR/TR																																			
1992	Cal-A	79	2	.177	.283	.266	32	1	.219	.359	.344	47	1	.149	.226	.213	0	0	—	—	—	79	2	.177	.283	.266	13	1	.231	.375	.462	66	1	.167	.263	.227
1993	Cal-A	515	31	.283	.382	.536	258	23	.314	.406	.636	257	8	.253	.358	.436	249	14	.277	.386	.510	266	17	.289	.378	.560	122	7	.230	.368	.434	393	24	.300	.386	.567
1994	Cal-A	373	23	.287	.382	.531	196	12	.270	.364	.505	177	11	.305	.401	.559	294	16	.282	.380	.507	79	7	.304	.389	.620	85	5	.259	.387	.494	288	18	.295	.380	.542
1995	Cal-A	537	34	.330	.429	.594	258	15	.291	.405	.531	279	19	.366	.453	.652	219	15	.301	.432	.571	318	19	.349	.428	.610	139	11	.338	.456	.647	398	23	.327	.420	.575
1996	Cal-A	581	30	.286	.386	.501	293	18	.266	.356	.509	288	12	.306	.416	.493	302	20	.281	.378	.536	279	10	.290	.395	.462	164	10	.268	.418	.512	417	20	.293	.372	.496
1997	Ana-A	582	33	.296	.394	.517	297	17	.283	.384	.495	285	16	.309	.405	.540	282	12	.277	.382	.461	300	21	.313	.406	.570	139	9	.288	.423	.525	443	24	.298	.385	.515
1998	Ana-A	463	26	.300	.410	.533	231	13	.281	.415	.511	232	13	.319	.404	.556	181	15	.276	.414	.558	282	11	.316	.407	.518	128	4	.273	.395	.414	335	22	.310	.416	.579
1999	Ana-A	353	17	.266	.372	.490	192	7	.245	.345	.417	161	10	.292	.403	.578	95	7	.347	.443	.642	258	10	.236	.345	.434	73	2	.301	.430	.438	280	15	.257	.356	.504
2000	Ana-A	568	34	.290	.404	.540	268	17	.272	.404	.526	300	17	.307	.405	.553	282	17	.270	.394	.507	286	17	.311	.415	.573	155	12	.226	.360	.497	413	22	.315	.422	.557
TOTALS		4051	230	.291	.394	.527	2025	123	.278	.386	.517	2026	107	.305	.403	.537	1904	116	.284	.395	.524	2147	114	.298	.393	.529	1018	61	.271	.404	.501	3033	169	.298	.391	.535
■ Juan Samuel	BR/TR																																			
1983	Phi-N	65	2	.277	.324	.446	51	1	.275	.321	.392	14	1	.286	.333	.643	0	0	—	—	—	65	2	.277	.324	.446	36	1	.250	.317	.389	29	1	.310	.333	.517
1984	Phi-N	701	15	.272	.307	.442	331	8	.251	.287	.423	370	7	.292	.325	.459	330	6	.312	.356	.479	371	9	.237	.261	.410	192	1	.276	.287	.380	509	14	.271	.314	.466
1985	Phi-N	663	19	.264	.303	.436	327	8	.248	.298	.394	336	11	.280	.307	.476	309	6	.262	.293	.408	354	13	.266	.311	.460	197	5	.239	.266	.386	466	14	.275	.318	.457
1986	Phi-N	591	16	.266	.302	.448	286	10	.266	.313	.486	305	6	.266	.292	.413	237	6	.253	.294	.414	354	10	.274	.308	.472	180	5	.256	.283	.456	411	11	.270	.310	.445
1987	Phi-N	655	28	.272	.335	.502	320	15	.287	.367	.559	335	13	.257	.302	.448	293	12	.266	.328	.485	362	16	.276	.340	.517	181	9	.249	.344	.492	474	19	.281	.331	.506
1988	Phi-N	629	12	.243	.298	.380	320	7	.272	.339	.459	309	5	.214	.253	.298	315	6	.238	.296	.371	314	6	.248	.300	.389	168	2	.244	.319	.381	461	10	.243	.290	.380
1989	Phi-N	199	8	.246	.311	.392	96	3	.260	.324	.396	103	5	.233	.298	.388	199	8	.246	.311	.392	0	0	—	—	—	80	4	.237	.299	.425	119	4	.252	.318	.370
1989	NY-N	333	3	.228	.299	.300	173	2	.214	.280	.277	160	1	.244	.318	.325	26	0	.231	.355	.308	307	3	.228	.294	.300	110	2	.273	.367	.355	223	1	.206	.262	.274
1990	LA-N	492	13	.242	.316	.382	224	6	.246	.329	.388	268	7	.239	.305	.377	260	5	.212	.282	.327	232	8	.276	.353	.444	187	10	.289	.350	.524	305	3	.213	.297	.295
1991	LA-N	594	12	.271	.328	.389	295	4	.254	.315	.342	299	8	.288	.342	.435	287	8	.321	.369	.453	307	4	.225	.290	.329	250	7	.252	.294	.396	344	5	.285	.352	.384
1992	LA-N	122	0	.262	.303	.303	57	0	.298	.344	.368	65	0	.231	.268	.246	84	0	.262	.312	.274	38	0	.263	.282	.368	76	0	.303	.354	.368	46	0	.196	.220	.196
1992	KC-A	102	0	.284	.336	.392	48	0	.292	.333	.354	54	0	.278	.339	.426	0	0	—	—	—	102	0	.284	.336	.392	28	0	.250	.323	.393	74	0	.297	.342	.392
1993	Cin-N	261	4	.230	.298	.345	98	1	.224	.310	.316	163	3	.233	.290	.362	74	2	.189	.221	.311	187	2	.246	.325	.358	98	1	.265	.339	.418	163	3	.209	.272	.301
1994	Det-A	136	5	.309	.364	.559	55	4	.364	.379	.764	81	1	.272	.355	.420	74	2	.284	.360	.514	62	3	.339	.369	.613	52	1	.269	.322	.442	84	4	.333	.391	.631
1995	Det-A	171	10	.281	.376	.526	85	6	.365	.455	.682	86	4	.198	.296	.372	80	8	.338	.442	.725	91	2	.231	.314	.352	94	6	.277	.376	.489	77	4	.286	.375	.571
1995	KC-A	34	2	.176	.282	.353	19	0	.105	.261	.105	15	2	.267	.313	.667	0	0	—	—	—	34	2	.176	.282	.353	25	2	.200	.310	.440	9	0	.111	.200	.111
1996	Tor-A	188	8	.255	.319	.457	87	4	.299	.365	.552	101	4	.218	.279	.376	97	4	.247	.277	.464	91	4	.264	.358	.451	137	7	.277	.338	.504	51	1	.196	.268	.333
1997	Tor-A	95	3	.284	.364	.516	47	2	.255	.386	.574	48	1	.313	.340	.458	46	0	.217	.294	.283	49	3	.347	.429	.735	67	1	.284	.342	.433	28	2	.286	.412	.714
1998	Tor-A	50	1	.180	.293	.280	22	1	.182	.333	.318	28	0	.179	.258	.250	45	1	.178	.275	.289	5	0	.200	.429	.200	23	1	.217	.333	.435	27	0	.148	.258	.148
TOTALS		6081	161	.259	.315	.420	2941	82	.263	.326	.436	3140	79	.256	.304	.405	2756	74	.263	.318	.419	3325	87	.257	.313	.420	2181	65	.261	.320	.429	3900	96	.258	.313	.414
■ Rey Sanchez	BR/TR																																			
1991	Chi-N	23	0	.261	.370	.261	18	0	.111	.158	.111	5	0	.800	.875	.800	0	0	—	—	—	23	0	.261	.370	.261	5	0	.000	.286	.000	18	0	.333	.400	.333
1992	Chi-N	255	1	.251	.285	.341	130	1	.300	.328	.408	125	0	.200	.241	.272	64	0	.234	.242	.375	191	1	.257	.299	.330	106	0	.283	.327	.396	149	1	.228	.255	.302
1993	Chi-N	344	0	.282	.316	.326	159	0	.308	.345	.365	185	0	.259	.291	.292	204	0	.328	.350	.382	140	0	.214	.267	.243	118	0	.297	.314	.305	226	0	.274	.317	.336
1994	Chi-N	291	0	.285	.345	.337	149	0	.228	.281	.268	142	0	.345	.409	.408	168	0	.280	.348	.321	123	0	.293	.341	.358	71	0	.254	.338	.268	220	0	.295	.347	.359
1995	Chi-N	428	3	.278	.301	.360	197	0	.294	.322	.345	231	3	.264	.283	.372	249	0	.293	.307	.361	179	3	.257	.293	.358	114	1	.263	.276	.360	314	2	.283	.310	.360
1996	Chi-N	289	1	.211	.272	.253	136	1	.176	.226	.221	153	0	.242	.312	.281	161	1	.211	.287	.261	128	0	.211	.254	.242	51	0	.196	.241	.255	238	1	.214	.279	.252
1997	Chi-N	205	1	.249	.287	.307	88	1	.273	.289	.341	117	0	.231	.286	.282	151	1	.265	.306	.331	54	0	.204	.232	.241	36	0	.222	.263	.250	169	1	.254	.292	.320
1997	NY-A	138	1	.312	.338	.420	49	0	.306	.333	.388	89	1	.315	.340	.438	0	0	—	—	—	138	1	.312	.338	.420	29	1	.414	.419	.655	109	0	.284	.316	.358
1998	SF-N	316	2	.285	.325	.361	156	0	.295	.345	.365	160	2	.275	.306	.356	183	2	.295	.335	.350	133	0	.271	.312	.376	69	2	.377	.429	.536	247	0	.259	.295	.312
1999	KC-A	479	2	.294	.329	.370	240	1	.267	.304	.346	239	1	.322	.355	.393	247	2	.255	.294	.344	232	0	.336	.366	.397	95	0	.326	.354	.400	384	2	.286	.323	.362
2000	KC-A	509	1	.273	.314	.322	251	1	.291	.331	.347	258	0	.256	.298	.298	230	1	.230	.267	.296	279	0	.308	.354	.344	131	0	.290	.329	.321	378	1	.267	.309	.323
TOTALS		3277	12	.273	.312	.338	1573	5	.272	.310	.335	1704	7	.273	.314	.340	1657	7	.269	.307	.335	1620	5	.277	.318	.340	825	4	.288	.326	.359	2452	8	.268	.308	.330
■ Ryne Sandberg	BR/TR																																			
1981	Phi-N	6	0	.167	.167	.167	2	0	.000	.000	.000	4	0	.250	.250	.250	0	0	—	—	—	6	0	.167	.167	.167	1	0	.000	.000	.000	5	0	.200	.200	.200
1982	Chi-N	635	7	.271	.312	.372	306	5	.320	.369	.467	329	2	.225	.256	.283	281	3	.260	.291	.335	354	4	.280	.328	.401	155	0	.303	.353	.400	480	7	.260	.298	.363
1983	Chi-N	633	8	.261	.316	.351	308	4	.289	.357	.393	325	4	.234	.277	.311	278	5	.266	.326	.396	355	3	.256	.309	.315	173	2	.249	.311	.353	460	6	.265	.319	.350
1984	Chi-N	636	19	.314	.367	.520	313	11	.332	.397	.575	323	8	.297	.336	.467	316	11	.345	.392	.582	320	8	.284	.342	.459	162	3	.358	.399	.562	474	16	.300	.356	.506
1985	Chi-N	609	26	.305	.364	.504	293	17	.304	.371	.560	316	9	.307	.357	.453	265	9	.275	.326	.438	344	17	.328	.391	.555	152	5	.276	.339	.434	457	21	.315	.372	.527

YEAR	TM/L	TOTAL AB	HR	AVG	OBP	SLG	HOME AB	HR	AVG	OBP	SLG	AWAY AB	HR	AVG	OBP	SLG	1ST HALF AB	HR	AVG	OBP	SLG	2ND HALF AB	HR	AVG	OBP	SLG	LEFT AB	HR	AVG	OBP	SLG	RIGHT AB	HR	AVG	OBP	SLG
1986	Chi-N	627	14	.284	.330	.411	321	8	.302	.344	.445	306	6	.265	.315	.376	301	8	.282	.327	.432	326	6	.285	.332	.393	159	4	.264	.314	.377	468	10	.291	.335	.423
1987	Chi-N	523	16	.294	.367	.442	257	8	.300	.357	.463	266	8	.289	.376	.421	234	11	.286	.375	.509	289	5	.301	.361	.388	114	2	.307	.412	.439	409	14	.291	.353	.443
1988	Chi-N	618	19	.264	.322	.419	312	10	.279	.342	.452	306	9	.248	.300	.386	295	10	.261	.320	.437	323	9	.266	.323	.402	164	7	.293	.363	.482	454	12	.253	.306	.396
1989	Chi-N	606	30	.290	.356	.497	303	16	.297	.351	.505	303	14	.284	.362	.488	280	10	.268	.333	.425	326	20	.310	.376	.558	172	7	.314	.414	.517	434	23	.281	.331	.488
1990	Chi-N	615	40	.306	.354	.559	305	25	.357	.405	.679	310	15	.255	.303	.442	308	24	.344	.393	.636	307	16	.267	.315	.482	214	10	.252	.316	.453	401	30	.334	.374	.616
1991	Chi-N	585	26	.291	.379	.485	291	15	.309	.394	.526	294	11	.272	.364	.446	290	12	.293	.365	.483	295	14	.288	.392	.488	209	8	.359	.456	.565	376	18	.253	.335	.441
1992	Chi-N	612	26	.304	.371	.510	300	16	.307	.386	.570	312	10	.301	.357	.452	282	10	.280	.348	.465	330	16	.324	.391	.548	206	4	.340	.403	.500	406	22	.286	.355	.515
1993	Chi-N	456	9	.309	.359	.412	243	5	.296	.352	.399	213	4	.324	.368	.427	189	4	.302	.351	.397	267	5	.315	.366	.423	109	1	.385	.427	.459	347	8	.285	.339	.398
1994	Chi-N	223	5	.238	.312	.390	111	3	.252	.325	.396	112	2	.223	.298	.384	223	5	.238	.312	.390	0	0	—	—	—	65	2	.154	.267	.292	158	3	.272	.331	.430
1996	Chi-N	554	25	.244	.316	.444	287	12	.240	.321	.418	267	13	.247	.311	.472	264	14	.227	.304	.458	290	11	.259	.327	.431	117	12	.239	.338	.615	437	13	.245	.310	.398
1997	Chi-N	447	12	.264	.308	.403	246	9	.272	.316	.435	201	3	.254	.299	.363	237	3	.245	.300	.338	210	9	.286	.318	.476	116	5	.293	.354	.491	331	7	.254	.291	.372
TOTALS		8385	282	.285	.344	.452	4198	164	.300	.361	.491	4187	118	.269	.326	.412	4043	139	.280	.339	.453	4342	143	.289	.349	.450	2288	72	.298	.369	.469	6097	210	.279	.334	.445
■ **Reggie Sanders** BR/TR																																				
1991	Cin-N	40	1	.200	.200	.275	11	0	.000	.000	.000	29	1	.276	.276	.379	0	0	—	—	—	40	1	.200	.200	.275	16	0	.125	.125	.125	24	1	.250	.250	.375
1992	Cin-N	385	12	.270	.356	.462	205	6	.244	.353	.429	180	6	.300	.360	.500	192	4	.281	.344	.443	193	8	.259	.367	.482	175	7	.314	.391	.566	210	5	.233	.328	.376
1993	Cin-N	496	20	.274	.343	.444	237	8	.287	.357	.447	259	12	.263	.330	.440	258	11	.264	.340	.426	238	9	.286	.346	.462	129	6	.310	.366	.496	367	14	.262	.335	.425
1994	Cin-N	400	17	.262	.332	.480	210	10	.281	.363	.500	190	7	.242	.297	.458	273	13	.271	.330	.520	127	4	.244	.336	.394	91	6	.330	.386	.659	309	11	.243	.316	.427
1995	Cin-N	484	28	.306	.397	.579	240	9	.296	.378	.517	244	19	.316	.415	.639	216	13	.315	.398	.602	268	15	.299	.396	.560	104	8	.365	.447	.692	380	20	.289	.383	.547
1996	Cin-N	287	14	.251	.353	.463	128	7	.242	.380	.500	159	7	.258	.330	.434	113	7	.301	.402	.558	174	7	.218	.322	.402	62	2	.258	.395	.435	225	12	.249	.341	.471
1997	Cin-N	312	19	.253	.347	.510	152	11	.263	.349	.566	160	8	.244	.346	.456	109	6	.229	.317	.468	203	13	.266	.363	.532	68	4	.309	.420	.588	244	15	.238	.326	.488
1998	Cin-N	481	14	.268	.346	.418	226	7	.265	.379	.429	255	7	.271	.313	.408	238	8	.248	.325	.408	243	6	.288	.366	.428	113	4	.248	.325	.407	368	10	.274	.352	.421
1999	SD-N	478	26	.285	.376	.527	217	11	.295	.398	.530	261	15	.276	.357	.525	189	12	.275	.381	.519	289	14	.291	.373	.533	142	8	.303	.396	.549	336	18	.277	.368	.518
2000	Atl-N	340	11	.232	.302	.403	157	4	.261	.341	.414	183	7	.208	.268	.393	181	3	.171	.235	.254	159	8	.302	.376	.572	72	2	.264	.361	.417	268	9	.224	.285	.399
TOTALS		3703	162	.269	.351	.476	1783	73	.271	.366	.477	1920	89	.267	.337	.476	1769	77	.263	.341	.465	1934	85	.275	.361	.487	972	47	.300	.383	.533	2731	115	.258	.340	.456
■ **Benito Santiago** BR/TR																																				
1986	SD-N	62	3	.290	.308	.468	27	2	.259	.300	.556	35	1	.314	.314	.400	0	0	—	—	—	62	3	.290	.308	.468	22	2	.364	.375	.636	40	1	.250	.268	.375
1987	SD-N	546	18	.300	.324	.467	274	11	.281	.307	.471	272	7	.320	.342	.463	244	6	.270	.297	.389	302	12	.325	.346	.530	182	8	.341	.363	.577	364	10	.280	.304	.412
1988	SD-N	492	10	.248	.282	.362	261	3	.230	.253	.326	231	7	.268	.313	.403	244	3	.230	.255	.307	248	7	.266	.307	.415	140	5	.257	.291	.407	352	5	.244	.278	.344
1989	SD-N	462	16	.236	.277	.387	212	8	.264	.302	.434	250	8	.212	.256	.348	239	5	.247	.271	.364	223	11	.224	.283	.413	117	2	.222	.289	.316	345	14	.241	.273	.412
1990	SD-N	344	11	.270	.323	.419	189	5	.286	.350	.429	155	6	.252	.287	.406	186	9	.317	.369	.511	158	2	.215	.269	.310	116	1	.276	.323	.328	228	10	.268	.323	.465
1991	SD-N	580	17	.267	.296	.403	287	6	.244	.267	.334	293	11	.290	.325	.471	282	7	.252	.271	.365	298	10	.282	.320	.440	204	8	.284	.318	.480	376	9	.258	.284	.362
1992	SD-N	386	10	.251	.287	.383	195	8	.308	.328	.482	191	2	.194	.246	.283	183	4	.257	.289	.377	203	6	.246	.286	.389	130	7	.292	.326	.508	256	3	.230	.267	.320
1993	Fla-N	469	13	.230	.291	.380	233	6	.227	.291	.386	236	7	.233	.292	.373	258	6	.240	.310	.388	211	7	.218	.268	.370	123	4	.276	.355	.488	346	9	.214	.268	.341
1994	Fla-N	337	11	.273	.322	.424	169	4	.284	.344	.420	168	7	.262	.298	.429	224	6	.272	.328	.411	113	5	.274	.309	.451	100	3	.340	.391	.490	237	8	.245	.292	.397
1995	Cin-N	266	11	.286	.351	.485	144	7	.333	.398	.576	122	4	.230	.296	.377	34	1	.324	.361	.500	232	10	.280	.350	.483	62	3	.355	.444	.597	204	8	.265	.321	.451
1996	Phi-N	481	30	.264	.332	.503	240	8	.258	.318	.396	241	22	.270	.346	.610	241	13	.245	.323	.469	240	17	.283	.341	.538	72	6	.333	.400	.625	409	24	.252	.320	.482
1997	Tor-A	341	13	.243	.279	.387	184	7	.261	.284	.408	157	6	.223	.275	.363	174	3	.195	.230	.276	167	10	.293	.330	.503	93	6	.301	.333	.495	248	7	.222	.259	.347
1998	Tor-A	29	0	.310	.333	.483	7	0	.429	.500	.714	22	0	.273	.273	.409	0	0	—	—	—	29	0	.310	.333	.483	14	0	.429	.429	.714	15	0	.200	.250	.267
1999	Chi-N	350	7	.249	.313	.377	168	2	.250	.328	.375	182	5	.247	.299	.379	231	5	.216	.282	.346	119	2	.311	.374	.437	132	5	.250	.313	.409	218	2	.248	.314	.358
2000	Cin-N	252	8	.262	.310	.409	154	7	.286	.335	.487	98	1	.224	.269	.286	110	3	.264	.311	.409	142	5	.261	.310	.408	82	2	.268	.315	.402	170	6	.259	.309	.412
TOTALS		5397	178	.261	.305	.415	2744	84	.267	.311	.419	2653	94	.254	.300	.411	2650	71	.251	.295	.385	2747	107	.270	.315	.444	1589	62	.291	.338	.471	3808	116	.248	.292	.392
■ **Steve Sax** BR/TR																																				
1981	LA-N	119	2	.277	.317	.345	64	0	.234	.290	.266	55	2	.327	.351	.436	0	0	—	—	—	119	2	.277	.317	.345	20	1	.300	.417	.450	99	1	.273	.294	.323
1982	LA-N	638	4	.282	.335	.359	311	2	.289	.332	.344	327	2	.275	.338	.373	318	0	.296	.356	.358	320	4	.269	.314	.359	113	0	.283	.341	.319	525	4	.282	.334	.368
1983	LA-N	623	5	.281	.342	.350	304	3	.296	.359	.365	319	2	.266	.326	.335	270	4	.274	.342	.385	353	1	.286	.342	.323	126	1	.286	.328	.365	497	4	.280	.345	.346
1984	LA-N	569	1	.243	.300	.304	269	1	.249	.297	.309	300	0	.237	.303	.300	268	1	.250	.310	.321	301	0	.236	.291	.289	207	0	.275	.324	.348	362	1	.224	.286	.279
1985	LA-N	488	1	.279	.352	.318	239	1	.226	.317	.255	249	0	.329	.386	.378	179	0	.229	.313	.251	309	1	.307	.375	.356	144	1	.215	.324	.278	344	0	.305	.365	.334
1986	LA-N	633	6	.332	.390	.441	306	1	.310	.377	.389	327	5	.352	.402	.489	287	4	.321	.381	.439	346	2	.341	.397	.442	225	3	.329	.374	.467	408	3	.333	.398	.426
1987	LA-N	610	6	.280	.331	.369	289	2	.260	.310	.325	321	4	.299	.351	.408	306	3	.265	.320	.350	304	3	.296	.343	.388	205	2	.278	.330	.376	405	4	.281	.332	.365
1988	LA-N	632	5	.277	.325	.343	311	2	.302	.348	.354	321	3	.252	.303	.333	293	5	.287	.348	.379	339	0	.268	.304	.313	200	3	.290	.352	.375	432	2	.271	.312	.329
1989	NY-A	651	5	.315	.364	.387	324	2	.324	.363	.401	327	3	.306	.365	.373	314	2	.331	.386	.401	337	3	.300	.343	.374	202	2	.381	.427	.470	449	3	.285	.335	.350
1990	NY-A	615	4	.260	.316	.325	294	3	.259	.327	.347	321	1	.262	.305	.305	278	1	.281	.336	.335	337	3	.243	.300	.318	177	0	.249	.325	.299	438	4	.265	.312	.336
1991	NY-A	652	10	.304	.345	.414	327	6	.291	.340	.413	325	4	.317	.350	.415	297	3	.283	.329	.360	355	7	.321	.358	.459	215	5	.344	.390	.507	437	5	.284	.322	.368
1992	Chi-A	567	4	.236	.290	.317	292	1	.226	.287	.312	275	3	.247	.293	.324	250	1	.224	.290	.280	317	3	.246	.289	.347	157	1	.229	.278	.299	410	3	.239	.294	.324
1993	Chi-A	119	1	.235	.283	.303	60	1	.250	.286	.333	59	0	.220	.281	.271	48	1	.229	.288	.354	71	0	.239	.280	.268	67	0	.239	.282	.299	52	1	.231	.286	.308
1994	Oak-A	24	0	.250	.250	.333	17	0	.294	.294	.412	7	0	.143	.143	.143	24	0	.250	.250	.333	0	0	—	—	—	11	0	.455	.455	.455	13	0	.077	.077	.231
TOTALS		6940	54	.281	.335	.358	3407	25	.276	.332	.348	3533	29	.285	.337	.367	3132	25	.278	.338	.356	3808	29	.283	.332	.360	2069	19	.291	.348	.381	4871	35	.276	.329	.348
■ **Mike Schmidt** BR/TR																																				
1978	Phi-N	513	21	.251	.364	.435	269	13	.245	.353	.461	244	8	.258	.375	.406	245	11	.249	.350	.441	268	10	.254	.376	.429	138	8	.210	.317	.435	375	13	.267	.380	.435
1979	Phi-N	541	45	.253	.386	.564	252	16	.262	.410	.516	289	29	.246	.365	.606	259	23	.251	.388	.575	282	22	.255	.385	.553	123	9	.341	.475	.667	418	36	.227	.359	.533
1980	Phi-N	548	48	.286	.380	.624	282	25	.277	.378	.635	266	23	.297	.383	.613	242	21	.281	.367	.620	306	27	.291	.390	.627	107	10	.327	.393	.701	441	38	.277	.377	.605
1981	Phi-N	354	31	.316	.435	.644	170	17	.335	.450	.724	184	14	.299	.422	.571	194	14	.284	.381	.582	160	17	.356	.495	.719	64	8	.328	.456	.813	290	23	.314	.431	.607
1982	Phi-N	514	35	.280	.403	.547	257	17	.249	.386	.514	257	18	.311	.420	.580	204	7	.299	.438	.490	310	28	.268	.378	.584	101	10	.297	.411	.693	413	25	.276	.400	.511
1983	Phi-N	534	40	.255	.399	.524	254	19	.252	.399	.531	280	21	.257	.399	.518	237	14	.241	.377	.456	297	26	.266	.416	.579	113	7	.257	.444	.504	421	33	.254	.386	.530
1984	Phi-N	528	36	.277	.383	.536	235	16	.268	.375	.523	293	20	.283	.389	.546	261	16	.295	.406	.533	267	20	.258	.360	.539	130	8	.246	.379	.462	398	28	.286	.384	.560
1985	Phi-N	549	33	.277	.375	.532	265	14	.279	.379	.513	284	19	.275	.372	.549	245	9	.237	.325	.412	304	24	.309	.414	.628	155	6	.284	.391	.484	394	27	.274	.369	.551
1986	Phi-N	552	37	.290	.390	.547	258	20	.298	.406	.597	294	17	.282	.374	.503	258	14	.302	.376	.531	294	23	.279	.401	.561	157	15	.357	.474	.707	395	22	.263	.354	.484
1987	Phi-N	522	35	.293	.388	.548	260	15	.342	.433	.585	262	20	.244	.343	.511	207	17	.290	.377	.575	315	18	.295	.396	.530	133	7	.331	.442	.556	389	28	.280	.368	.545
1988	Phi-N	390	12	.249	.337	.405	186	6	.290	.401	.468	204	6	.211	.272	.348	276	6	.236	.320	.355	114	6	.281	.378	.526	91	3	.330	.435	.516	299	9	.224	.306	.371
1989	Phi-N	148	6	.203	.297	.372	63	2	.222	.306	.365	85	4	.188	.290	.376	148	6	.203	.297	.372	0	0	—	—	—	57	2	.263	.328	.404	91	4	.165	.278	.352
TOTALS		5693	379	.273	.383	.533	2751	180	.278	.393	.545	2942	199	.268	.373	.522	2776	158	.265	.368	.496	2917	221	.280	.397	.568	1369	93	.297	.415	.574	4324	286	.265	.373	.520
■ **Dick Schofield** BR/TR																																				
1983	Cal-A	54	3	.204	.295	.407	29	2	.207	.303	.483	25	1	.200	.286	.320	0	0	—	—	—	54	3	.204	.295	.407	20	0	.100	.250	.150	34	3	.265	.324	.559
1984	Cal-A	400	4	.192	.264	.262	181	0	.149	.234	.193	219	4	.228	.290	.320	226	3	.199	.264	.301	174	1	.184	.264	.213	141	1	.191	.260	.270	259	3	.193	.267	.259
1985	Cal-A	438	8	.219	.287	.331	219	5	.219	.269	.333	219	3	.219	.305	.329	207	5	.193	.265	.309	231	3	.242	.307	.351	147	2	.259	.323	.354	291	6	.199	.269	.320
1986	Cal-A	458	13	.249	.321	.397	226	7	.230	.322	.363	232	6	.267	.321	.431	198	6	.232	.313	.379	260	7	.262	.328	.412	163	4	.294	.397	.454	295	9	.224	.276	.366
1987	Cal-A	479	9	.251	.305	.355	257	4	.257	.310	.335	222	5	.243	.300	.378	281	7	.217	.271	.327	198	2	.298	.353	.394	161	2	.267	.324	.379	318	7	.242	.296	.343
1988	Cal-A	527	6	.239	.303	.317	274	3	.230	.271	.303	253	3	.249	.336	.332	267	3	.243	.301	.326	260	3	.235	.304	.308	180	4	.228	.302	.344	347	2	.245	.303	.303
1989	Cal-A	302	4	.228	.299	.318	143	1	.203	.280	.273	159	3	.252	.316	.358	156	0	.218	.257	.269	146	4	.240	.339	.370	127	1	.260	.304	.346	175	3	.206	.295	.297
1990	Cal-A	310	1	.255	.363	.297	158	1	.272	.384	.329	152	0	.237	.341	.263	66	1	.197	.338	.242	244	0	.270	.371	.311	89	1	.281	.404	.337	221	0	.244	.346	.281
1991	Cal-A	427	0	.225	.310	.260	211	0	.209	.286	.237	216	0	.241	.333	.282	186	0	.263	.363	.306	241	0	.195	.268	.224	115	0	.183	.314	.191	312	0	.240	.309	.285
1992	Cal-A	3	0	.333	.500	.333	3	0	.333	.500	.333	0	0	—	—	—	3	0	.333	.500	.333	0	0	—	—	—	0	0	—	—	—	3	0	.333	.500	.333
1992	NY-N	420	4	.205	.309	.286	201	3	.214	.323	.303	219	1	.196	.296	.269	227	2	.207	.316	.278	193	2	.202	.302	.295	145	2	.200	.316	.310	275	2	.207	.306	.273
1993	Tor-A	110	0	.191	.294	.236	55	0	.255	.388	.345	55	0	.127	.186	.127	90	0	.211	.317	.267	20	0	.100	.182	.100	35	0	.171	.293	.171	75	0	.200	.294	.267
1994	Tor-A	325	4	.255	.332	.342	141	2	.241	.318	.333	184	2	.266	.341	.348	190	1	.263	.325	.337	135	3	.244	.340	.348	87	1	.253	.320	.368	238	3	.256	.336	.332
1995	LA-N	10	0	.100	.182	.100	2	0	.500	.500	.500	8	0	.000	.111	.000	10	0	.100	.182	.100	0	0	—	—	—	8	0	.125	.125	.125	2	0	.000	.333	.000
1995	Cal-A	20	0	.250	.375	.250	18	0	.222	.364	.222	2	0	.500	.500	.500	0	0	—	—	—	20	0	.250	.375	.250	5	0	.400	.667	.400	15	0	.200	.200	.200
1996	Cal-A	16	0	.250	.294	.250	4	0	.250	.250	.250	12	0	.250	.308	.250	0	0	—	—	—	16	0	.250	.294	.250	4	0	.250	.400	.250	12	0	.250	.250	.250
TOTALS		4299	56	.230	.308	.316	2122	28	.224	.302	.305	2177	28	.236	.313	.326	2107	28	.224	.299	.310	2192	28	.236	.316	.321	1427	18	.238	.325	.331	2872	38	.226	.299	.308
■ **Mike Scioscia** BL/TR																																				
1980	LA-N	134	1	.254	.313	.328	82	1	.341	.389	.402	52	0	.115	.193	.212	65	0	.292	.356	.400	69	1	.217	.270	.261	11	0	.455	.500	.455	123	1	.236	.296	.317
1981	LA-N	290	2	.276	.353	.331	143	0	.252	.339	.266	147	2	.299	.367	.395	154	1	.299	.375	.351	136	1	.250	.329	.309	15	0	.333	.333	.333	275	2	.273	.354	.331
1982	LA-N	365	5	.219	.302	.296	197	2	.239	.320	.305	168	3	.196	.281	.286	184	2	.212	.302	.288	181	3	.227	.302	.304	26	1	.115	.148	.231	339	4	.227	.313	.301
1983	LA-N	35	1	.314	.400	.486	17	0	.353	.389	.529	18	1	.278	.409	.444	35	1	.314	.400	.486	0	0	—	—	—	3	0	.667	.750	1.000	32	1	.281	.361	.438
1984	LA-N	341	5	.273	.367	.370	145	0	.283	.397	.324	196	5	.265	.342	.403	142	1	.282	.371	.338	199	4	.266	.364	.392	39	0	.128	.227	.154	302	5	.291	.384	.397

YEAR	TM/L	TOTAL AB	HR	AVG	OBP	SLG	HOME AB	HR	AVG	OBP	SLG	AWAY AB	HR	AVG	OBP	SLG	1ST HALF AB	HR	AVG	OBP	SLG	2ND HALF AB	HR	AVG	OBP	SLG	LEFT AB	HR	AVG	OBP	SLG	RIGHT AB	HR	AVG	OBP	SLG
1985	LA-N	429	7	.296	.407	.420	202	1	.297	.415	.366	227	6	.295	.399	.467	192	3	.266	.376	.375	237	4	.321	.432	.456	87	1	.253	.337	.345	342	6	.307	.424	.439
1986	LA-N	374	5	.251	.359	.345	169	2	.249	.350	.325	205	3	.254	.366	.361	158	2	.272	.407	.367	216	3	.236	.321	.329	107	2	.234	.341	.308	267	3	.258	.366	.360
1987	LA-N	461	6	.265	.343	.364	219	2	.260	.345	.315	242	4	.269	.341	.409	203	3	.261	.351	.350	258	3	.267	.337	.376	132	0	.273	.356	.348	329	6	.261	.338	.371
1988	LA-N	408	3	.257	.318	.324	208	1	.264	.313	.313	200	2	.250	.324	.335	209	2	.278	.341	.344	199	1	.236	.295	.302	78	0	.244	.289	.244	330	3	.261	.325	.342
1989	LA-N	408	10	.250	.338	.363	200	4	.235	.329	.335	208	6	.264	.347	.389	221	3	.244	.332	.326	187	7	.257	.346	.406	100	3	.230	.300	.330	308	7	.256	.350	.373
1990	LA-N	435	12	.264	.348	.405	208	5	.279	.363	.409	227	7	.251	.335	.401	221	8	.258	.314	.403	214	4	.271	.380	.407	119	2	.235	.295	.328	316	10	.275	.367	.434
1991	LA-N	345	8	.264	.353	.391	163	3	.288	.380	.399	182	5	.242	.329	.385	178	3	.275	.376	.404	167	5	.251	.328	.377	106	3	.189	.276	.292	239	5	.297	.388	.435
1992	LA-N	348	3	.221	.286	.282	178	1	.247	.297	.315	170	2	.194	.275	.247	172	2	.198	.275	.267	176	1	.244	.298	.295	81	1	.235	.297	.333	267	2	.217	.283	.266
TOTALS		4373	68	.259	.344	.356	2131	22	.267	.352	.339	2242	46	.251	.337	.372	2134	31	.260	.347	.351	2239	37	.258	.341	.360	904	13	.235	.310	.313	3469	55	.265	.353	.367
■ **David Segui** BB/TL																																				
1990	Bal-A	123	2	.244	.311	.350	69	1	.246	.316	.333	54	1	.241	.305	.370	42	0	.167	.222	.238	81	2	.284	.356	.407	40	1	.250	.268	.425	83	1	.241	.330	.313
1991	Bal-A	212	2	.278	.316	.340	116	1	.250	.279	.302	96	1	.313	.359	.385	99	1	.263	.302	.343	113	1	.292	.328	.336	98	1	.337	.363	.408	114	1	.228	.276	.281
1992	Bal-A	189	1	.233	.306	.296	75	1	.213	.289	.280	114	0	.246	.317	.307	120	1	.242	.316	.317	69	0	.217	.289	.261	78	0	.205	.271	.244	111	1	.252	.331	.333
1993	Bal-A	450	10	.273	.351	.400	236	6	.280	.357	.436	214	4	.266	.344	.360	175	4	.331	.408	.480	275	6	.236	.313	.349	144	5	.292	.364	.444	306	5	.265	.345	.379
1994	NY-N	336	10	.241	.308	.387	162	5	.241	.319	.401	174	5	.241	.298	.374	235	10	.260	.335	.447	101	0	.198	.243	.248	100	5	.190	.250	.380	236	5	.263	.332	.390
1995	NY-N	73	2	.329	.420	.479	43	2	.349	.420	.512	30	0	.300	.421	.433	73	2	.329	.420	.479	0	0	—	—	—	19	1	.211	.346	.474	54	1	.370	.452	.481
1995	Mon-N	383	10	.305	.355	.457	191	4	.283	.337	.414	192	6	.328	.374	.500	75	1	.333	.383	.480	308	9	.299	.348	.451	93	1	.355	.417	.462	290	9	.290	.334	.455
1996	Mon-N	416	11	.286	.375	.442	212	6	.311	.390	.491	204	5	.260	.360	.392	260	5	.281	.345	.419	156	6	.295	.421	.481	110	4	.300	.369	.473	306	7	.281	.377	.431
1997	Mon-N	459	21	.307	.380	.505	206	10	.345	.424	.549	253	11	.277	.343	.470	199	6	.327	.412	.508	260	15	.292	.355	.504	122	5	.295	.396	.467	337	16	.312	.375	.519
1998	Sea-A	522	19	.305	.359	.487	261	10	.337	.399	.544	261	9	.272	.318	.429	290	12	.328	.386	.531	232	7	.276	.324	.431	118	6	.297	.356	.483	404	13	.307	.359	.488
1999	Sea-A	345	9	.293	.352	.452	158	4	.266	.337	.437	187	5	.316	.365	.465	258	8	.295	.370	.473	87	1	.287	.293	.391	62	1	.226	.300	.290	283	8	.307	.363	.488
1999	Tor-A	95	5	.316	.365	.526	35	1	.314	.368	.457	60	4	.317	.364	.567	0	0	—	—	—	95	5	.316	.365	.526	8	0	.625	.625	.625	87	5	.287	.344	.517
2000	Tex-A	351	11	.336	.391	.519	199	4	.332	.386	.472	152	7	.342	.396	.579	272	8	.342	.399	.515	79	3	.316	.360	.532	93	2	.301	.363	.430	258	9	.349	.401	.550
2000	Cle-A	223	8	.332	.384	.498	115	4	.348	.398	.522	108	4	.315	.368	.472	0	0	—	—	—	223	8	.332	.384	.498	62	2	.323	.373	.484	161	6	.335	.388	.503
TOTALS		4177	121	.292	.357	.445	2078	59	.298	.365	.455	2099	62	.286	.348	.435	2098	58	.301	.370	.461	2079	63	.283	.343	.429	1147	34	.286	.351	.426	3030	87	.294	.359	.452
■ **Kevin Seitzer** BR/TR																																				
1986	KC-A	96	2	.323	.440	.448	48	1	.458	.552	.646	48	1	.188	.328	.250	0	0	—	—	—	96	2	.323	.440	.448	18	1	.278	.480	.444	78	1	.333	.429	.449
1987	KC-A	641	15	.323	.399	.470	319	7	.335	.413	.511	322	8	.311	.386	.429	291	4	.302	.385	.412	350	11	.340	.411	.517	175	2	.309	.386	.434	466	13	.328	.404	.483
1988	KC-A	559	5	.304	.387	.406	272	4	.320	.401	.441	287	1	.289	.374	.373	277	4	.310	.387	.426	282	1	.298	.388	.387	153	1	.353	.432	.477	406	4	.286	.371	.379
1989	KC-A	597	4	.281	.387	.337	299	2	.311	.405	.368	298	2	.252	.370	.305	289	3	.287	.386	.349	308	1	.276	.388	.325	175	3	.257	.387	.343	422	1	.291	.387	.334
1990	KC-A	622	6	.275	.346	.370	308	5	.312	.384	.451	314	1	.239	.308	.290	295	3	.302	.357	.403	327	3	.251	.337	.339	209	4	.278	.345	.455	413	2	.274	.347	.327
1991	KC-A	234	1	.265	.350	.350	117	0	.274	.344	.368	117	1	.256	.356	.333	151	1	.245	.339	.325	83	0	.301	.370	.398	66	1	.333	.429	.424	168	0	.238	.317	.321
1992	Mil-A	540	5	.270	.337	.367	259	2	.236	.315	.305	281	3	.302	.358	.423	268	2	.302	.355	.403	272	3	.239	.320	.331	128	2	.313	.404	.453	412	3	.257	.315	.340
1993	Oak-A	255	4	.255	.324	.357	121	2	.231	.331	.314	134	2	.276	.318	.396	225	4	.244	.312	.351	30	0	.333	.412	.400	65	0	.262	.359	.308	190	4	.253	.311	.374
1993	Mil-A	162	7	.290	.359	.457	86	4	.314	.406	.488	76	3	.263	.300	.421	0	0	—	—	—	162	7	.290	.359	.457	78	4	.295	.353	.474	84	3	.286	.365	.440
1994	Mil-A	309	5	.314	.375	.453	143	4	.280	.358	.427	166	1	.343	.390	.476	166	4	.325	.375	.494	143	1	.301	.375	.406	60	1	.267	.413	.417	249	4	.325	.364	.462
1995	Mil-A	492	5	.311	.395	.421	237	1	.304	.381	.401	255	4	.318	.407	.439	200	2	.345	.424	.485	292	3	.288	.375	.377	139	0	.252	.342	.317	353	5	.334	.416	.462
1996	Mil-A	490	12	.316	.406	.453	241	5	.290	.399	.402	249	7	.341	.412	.502	286	9	.353	.446	.517	204	3	.265	.346	.363	138	3	.341	.414	.486	352	9	.307	.402	.440
1996	Cle-A	83	1	.386	.480	.542	48	0	.333	.439	.438	35	1	.457	.537	.686	0	0	—	—	—	83	1	.386	.480	.542	36	0	.472	.537	.611	47	1	.319	.439	.489
1997	Cle-A	198	2	.268	.326	.369	103	1	.282	.362	.388	95	1	.253	.284	.347	89	2	.270	.337	.404	109	0	.266	.316	.339	97	2	.268	.345	.392	101	0	.267	.306	.347
TOTALS		5278	74	.295	.375	.404	2601	38	.300	.385	.415	2677	36	.290	.366	.394	2537	38	.302	.378	.417	2741	36	.288	.373	.393	1537	24	.299	.388	.424	3741	50	.294	.370	.396
■ **Richie Sexson** BR/TR																																				
1997	Cle-A	11	0	.273	.273	.273	6	0	.000	.000	.000	5	0	.600	.600	.600	0	0	—	—	—	11	0	.273	.273	.273	10	0	.300	.300	.300	1	0	.000	.000	.000
1998	Cle-A	174	11	.310	.344	.592	108	9	.352	.391	.694	66	2	.242	.265	.424	4	0	.500	.500	.750	170	11	.306	.341	.588	58	3	.241	.254	.466	116	8	.345	.387	.655
1999	Cle-A	479	31	.255	.305	.514	244	18	.262	.311	.537	235	13	.247	.298	.489	213	15	.254	.312	.526	266	16	.256	.299	.504	137	11	.277	.336	.584	342	20	.246	.292	.485
2000	Cle-A	324	16	.256	.315	.460	145	8	.262	.318	.483	179	8	.251	.312	.441	278	14	.255	.313	.457	46	2	.261	.327	.478	75	4	.267	.333	.480	249	12	.253	.309	.454
2000	Mil-A	213	14	.296	.398	.559	110	7	.309	.412	.582	103	7	.282	.383	.534	0	0	—	—	—	213	14	.296	.398	.559	43	1	.140	.302	.256	170	13	.335	.424	.635
TOTALS		1201	72	.271	.330	.516	613	42	.284	.343	.555	588	30	.257	.317	.476	495	29	.257	.314	.489	706	43	.280	.342	.535	323	19	.251	.316	.486	878	53	.278	.336	.527
■ **Larry Sheets** BL/TR																																				
1984	Bal-A	16	1	.438	.471	.688	6	0	.500	.571	.667	10	1	.400	.400	.700	0	0	—	—	—	16	1	.438	.471	.688	1	0	.000	.000	.000	15	1	.467	.500	.733
1985	Bal-A	328	17	.262	.323	.442	170	5	.276	.344	.394	158	12	.247	.300	.494	173	9	.277	.337	.462	155	8	.245	.308	.419	17	0	.118	.273	.176	311	17	.270	.326	.457
1986	Bal-A	338	18	.272	.317	.488	181	10	.276	.302	.497	157	8	.268	.333	.478	164	9	.311	.362	.543	174	9	.236	.274	.437	26	1	.154	.207	.308	312	17	.282	.326	.503
1987	Bal-A	469	31	.316	.358	.563	241	21	.324	.371	.627	228	10	.307	.344	.496	187	14	.316	.366	.588	282	17	.316	.353	.546	145	10	.303	.348	.538	324	21	.321	.363	.574
1988	Bal-A	452	10	.230	.302	.343	218	6	.206	.275	.339	234	4	.252	.327	.346	256	4	.207	.296	.305	196	6	.260	.310	.393	114	1	.202	.305	.237	338	9	.240	.300	.379
1989	Bal-A	304	7	.243	.305	.359	133	1	.233	.302	.301	171	6	.251	.307	.404	176	6	.239	.303	.386	128	1	.250	.307	.320	39	0	.154	.209	.179	265	7	.257	.319	.385
1990	Det-A	360	10	.261	.308	.403	179	7	.246	.288	.419	181	3	.276	.327	.387	161	4	.280	.328	.422	199	6	.246	.291	.387	17	0	.235	.278	.235	343	10	.262	.309	.411
1993	Sea-A	17	0	.118	.250	.176	7	0	.000	.300	.000	10	0	.200	.200	.300	0	0	—	—	—	17	0	.118	.250	.176	0	0	—	—	—	17	0	.118	.250	.176
TOTALS		2284	94	.266	.321	.437	1135	50	.263	.317	.441	1149	44	.269	.324	.432	1117	46	.267	.329	.441	1167	48	.265	.312	.432	359	12	.231	.301	.354	1925	82	.272	.324	.452
■ **Gary Sheffield** BR/TR																																				
1988	Mil-A	80	4	.237	.295	.400	32	1	.188	.289	.313	48	3	.271	.300	.458	0	0	—	—	—	80	4	.237	.295	.400	23	1	.217	.280	.348	57	3	.246	.302	.421
1989	Mil-A	368	5	.247	.303	.337	198	2	.258	.307	.343	170	3	.235	.299	.329	276	4	.261	.319	.355	92	1	.207	.255	.283	113	3	.292	.336	.442	255	2	.227	.289	.290
1990	Mil-A	487	10	.294	.350	.421	239	3	.272	.338	.381	248	7	.315	.361	.460	227	4	.300	.350	.441	260	6	.288	.349	.404	135	3	.274	.338	.444	352	7	.301	.355	.412
1991	Mil-A	175	2	.194	.277	.320	74	2	.257	.368	.459	101	0	.149	.209	.218	121	2	.215	.286	.364	54	0	.148	.258	.222	43	0	.140	.264	.233	132	2	.212	.282	.348
1992	SD-N	557	33	.330	.385	.580	288	23	.365	.426	.684	269	10	.294	.340	.468	283	15	.318	.382	.534	274	18	.343	.389	.628	189	13	.365	.420	.640	368	20	.313	.367	.549
1993	SD-N	258	10	.295	.344	.473	117	6	.350	.397	.590	141	4	.248	.298	.376	258	10	.295	.344	.473	0	0	—	—	—	78	2	.321	.360	.436	180	8	.283	.337	.489
1993	Fla-N	236	10	.292	.378	.479	124	4	.282	.369	.427	112	6	.304	.388	.536	20	1	.300	.364	.450	216	9	.292	.379	.481	57	2	.333	.449	.456	179	8	.279	.354	.486
1994	Fla-N	322	27	.276	.380	.584	167	15	.269	.382	.593	155	12	.284	.378	.574	183	15	.284	.395	.596	139	12	.266	.360	.568	104	8	.212	.299	.452	218	19	.307	.416	.647
1995	Fla-N	213	16	.324	.467	.587	102	4	.333	.481	.490	111	12	.315	.455	.676	143	6	.315	.459	.483	70	10	.343	.484	.800	61	3	.328	.488	.525	152	13	.322	.459	.612
1996	Fla-N	519	42	.314	.465	.624	233	19	.326	.503	.652	286	23	.304	.431	.601	262	23	.294	.444	.615	257	19	.335	.487	.634	99	9	.313	.460	.636	420	33	.314	.466	.621
1997	Fla-N	444	21	.250	.424	.446	214	13	.276	.460	.509	230	8	.226	.390	.387	211	8	.232	.446	.408	233	13	.266	.403	.481	67	5	.343	.536	.627	377	16	.233	.402	.414
1998	Fla-N	136	6	.272	.392	.500	82	6	.329	.462	.671	54	0	.185	.274	.241	136	6	.272	.392	.500	0	0	—	—	—	18	2	.389	.421	.778	118	4	.254	.388	.458
1998	LA-N	301	16	.316	.444	.535	145	5	.276	.431	.421	156	11	.353	.456	.641	131	7	.336	.468	.565	170	9	.300	.425	.512	59	4	.288	.416	.492	242	12	.322	.451	.545
1999	LA-N	549	34	.301	.407	.523	265	15	.294	.393	.494	284	19	.306	.420	.549	265	16	.298	.401	.521	284	18	.303	.413	.525	146	8	.336	.434	.548	403	26	.288	.398	.514
2000	LA-N	501	43	.325	.438	.643	237	23	.308	.424	.637	264	20	.341	.450	.648	273	27	.337	.443	.689	228	16	.311	.432	.588	123	7	.285	.425	.512	378	36	.339	.442	.685
TOTALS		5146	279	.293	.397	.515	2517	141	.300	.411	.528	2629	138	.287	.383	.501	2789	144	.292	.396	.508	2357	135	.295	.398	.522	1315	70	.303	.403	.516	3831	209	.290	.395	.514
■ **John Shelby** BB/TR																																				
1981	Bal-A	2	0	.000	.000	.000	2	0	.000	.000	.000	0	0	—	—	—	0	0	—	—	—	2	0	.000	.000	.000	0	0	—	—	—	2	0	.000	.000	.000
1982	Bal-A	35	1	.314	.314	.486	24	1	.458	.458	.708	11	0	.000	.000	.000	0	0	—	—	—	35	1	.314	.314	.486	25	1	.320	.320	.520	10	0	.300	.300	.400
1983	Bal-A	325	5	.258	.297	.363	134	0	.224	.257	.284	191	5	.283	.325	.419	163	3	.270	.308	.399	162	2	.247	.287	.327	203	4	.256	.284	.384	122	1	.262	.318	.328
1984	Bal-A	383	6	.209	.248	.313	184	2	.190	.232	.261	199	4	.226	.263	.362	189	3	.196	.236	.291	194	3	.222	.260	.335	158	4	.215	.257	.329	225	2	.204	.242	.302
1985	Bal-A	205	7	.283	.307	.434	102	4	.245	.267	.402	103	3	.320	.346	.466	29	2	.379	.400	.655	176	5	.267	.291	.398	82	2	.244	.262	.378	123	5	.309	.336	.472
1986	Bal-A	404	11	.228	.263	.364	186	5	.199	.226	.312	218	6	.252	.294	.408	192	5	.224	.255	.344	212	6	.231	.270	.382	134	5	.231	.264	.388	270	6	.226	.262	.352
1987	Bal-A	32	1	.188	.212	.281	21	0	.143	.182	.143	11	1	.273	.273	.545	32	1	.188	.212	.281	0	0	—	—	—	17	1	.176	.222	.353	15	0	.200	.200	.200
1987	LA-N	476	21	.277	.317	.464	239	8	.243	.284	.377	237	13	.312	.352	.553	150	8	.240	.284	.460	326	13	.294	.332	.466	158	10	.335	.366	.595	318	11	.248	.293	.399
1988	LA-N	494	10	.263	.320	.395	236	5	.309	.351	.445	258	5	.221	.291	.349	206	4	.301	.380	.447	288	6	.236	.274	.358	189	2	.238	.286	.323	305	8	.279	.340	.439
1989	LA-N	345	1	.183	.237	.229	186	0	.183	.221	.215	159	1	.182	.256	.245	238	1	.160	.231	.197	107	0	.234	.252	.299	125	0	.168	.206	.208	220	1	.191	.254	.241
1990	LA-N	24	0	.250	.250	.292	11	0	.182	.182	.273	13	0	.308	.308	.308	24	0	.250	.250	.292	0	0	—	—	—	12	0	.167	.167	.167	12	0	.333	.333	.417
1990	Det-A	222	4	.248	.280	.369	103	3	.262	.303	.417	119	1	.235	.260	.328	47	1	.277	.277	.383	175	3	.240	.281	.366	66	2	.182	.217	.333	156	2	.276	.307	.385
1991	Det-A	143	3	.154	.204	.287	63	2	.159	.221	.317	80	1	.150	.190	.262	102	3	.196	.255	.373	41	0	.049	.071	.073	63	2	.175	.212	.349	80	1	.138	.198	.237
TOTALS		3090	70	.239	.281	.364	1491	30	.231	.269	.339	1599	40	.246	.292	.387	1372	31	.230	.280	.353	1718	39	.246	.281	.373	1232	33	.237	.272	.373	1858	37	.241	.287	.358
■ **Ruben Sierra** BB/TR																																				
1986	Tex-A	382	16	.264	.302	.476	172	8	.238	.256	.459	210	8	.286	.339	.490	109	4	.193	.228	.358	273	12	.293	.331	.524	99	4	.253	.269	.434	283	12	.269	.315	.491
1987	Tex-A	643	30	.263	.302	.470	315	15	.276	.323	.502	328	15	.250	.282	.439	294	10	.265	.321	.435	349	20	.261	.285	.499	237	12	.249	.267	.456	406	18	.271	.321	.478
1988	Tex-A	615	23	.254	.301	.424	299	15	.281	.336	.505	316	8	.228	.266	.348	280	11	.254	.305	.443	335	12	.254	.298	.409	193	8	.285	.305	.487	422	15	.239	.299	.396
1989	Tex-A	634	29	.306	.347	.543	309	21	.317	.356	.621	325	8	.295	.338	.468	310	12	.335	.375	.590	324	17	.278	.320	.497	205	10	.341	.378	.600	429	19	.289	.332	.515

YEAR	TM/L	TOTAL AB	HR	AVG	OBP	SLG	HOME AB	HR	AVG	OBP	SLG	AWAY AB	HR	AVG	OBP	SLG	1ST HALF AB	HR	AVG	OBP	SLG	2ND HALF AB	HR	AVG	OBP	SLG	LEFT AB	HR	AVG	OBP	SLG	RIGHT AB	HR	AVG	OBP	SLG
1990	Tex-A	608	16	.280	.330	.426	301	10	.266	.317	.429	307	6	.293	.343	.423	282	8	.273	.332	.418	326	8	.285	.329	.433	216	3	.324	.361	.440	392	13	.255	.314	.418
1991	Tex-A	661	25	.307	.357	.502	328	12	.320	.353	.521	333	13	.294	.360	.483	294	12	.337	.401	.548	367	13	.283	.321	.466	188	7	.335	.393	.548	473	18	.296	.342	.484
1992	Tex-A	500	14	.278	.315	.446	239	8	.230	.267	.397	261	6	.322	.359	.490	296	10	.307	.342	.500	204	4	.235	.277	.368	145	3	.338	.376	.510	355	11	.254	.291	.420
1992	Oak-A	101	3	.277	.359	.426	55	2	.291	.361	.455	46	1	.261	.357	.391	0	0	—	—	—	101	3	.277	.359	.426	26	2	.346	.433	.577	75	1	.253	.333	.373
1993	Oak-A	630	22	.233	.288	.390	306	9	.222	.280	.353	324	13	.244	.295	.426	297	11	.242	.291	.411	333	11	.225	.285	.372	199	8	.231	.297	.392	431	14	.234	.283	.390
1994	Oak-A	426	23	.268	.298	.484	208	11	.255	.303	.466	218	12	.280	.293	.500	294	17	.259	.288	.480	132	6	.288	.319	.492	156	10	.327	.374	.603	270	13	.233	.252	.415
1995	Oak-A	264	12	.265	.323	.466	114	3	.211	.272	.325	150	9	.307	.361	.573	230	12	.270	.327	.496	34	0	.235	.297	.265	81	2	.296	.363	.420	183	10	.251	.305	.486
1995	NY-A	215	7	.260	.322	.428	105	5	.295	.356	.514	110	2	.227	.290	.345	0	0	—	—	—	215	7	.260	.322	.428	80	3	.250	.287	.438	135	4	.267	.342	.422
1996	NY-A	360	11	.258	.327	.403	180	4	.261	.328	.389	180	7	.256	.325	.417	278	9	.255	.334	.410	82	2	.268	.300	.378	121	1	.298	.336	.397	239	10	.238	.322	.406
1996	Det-A	158	1	.222	.306	.310	81	0	.235	.308	.321	77	1	.208	.303	.299	0	0	—	—	—	158	1	.222	.306	.310	37	1	.378	.457	.568	121	0	.174	.254	.231
1997	Cin-N	90	2	.244	.292	.389	36	2	.222	.263	.472	54	0	.259	.310	.333	90	2	.244	.292	.389	0	0	—	—	—	20	1	.200	.238	.350	70	1	.257	.307	.400
1997	Tor-A	48	1	.208	.250	.354	35	1	.257	.316	.457	13	0	.077	.071	.077	48	1	.208	.250	.354	0	0	—	—	—	18	0	.167	.167	.167	30	1	.233	.294	.467
1998	Chi-A	74	4	.216	.247	.459	33	0	.152	.176	.152	41	4	.268	.302	.707	74	4	.216	.247	.459	0	0	—	—	—	12	0	.333	.385	.333	62	4	.194	.219	.484
2000	Tex-A	60	1	.233	.281	.283	22	0	.136	.174	.136	38	1	.289	.341	.368	0	0	—	—	—	60	1	.233	.281	.283	15	0	.400	.438	.400	45	1	.178	.229	.244
TOTALS		6469	240	.269	.317	.450	3138	126	.265	.313	.457	3331	114	.271	.320	.443	3176	123	.274	.324	.465	3293	117	.263	.309	.435	2048	75	.297	.338	.481	4421	165	.255	.307	.435
■ Ted Simmons	BB/TR																																			
1978	StL-N	516	22	.287	.377	.512	243	9	.276	.356	.506	273	13	.297	.397	.516	262	8	.305	.389	.511	254	14	.268	.366	.512	185	5	.292	.381	.465	331	17	.284	.375	.538
1979	StL-N	448	26	.283	.369	.507	200	17	.315	.385	.625	248	9	.258	.355	.411	221	18	.321	.412	.633	227	8	.247	.324	.383	191	15	.277	.340	.545	257	11	.288	.389	.479
1980	StL-N	495	21	.303	.375	.505	241	8	.303	.369	.494	254	13	.303	.381	.516	226	11	.305	.395	.527	269	10	.301	.358	.487	201	7	.313	.374	.473	294	14	.296	.376	.527
1981	Mil-A	380	14	.216	.262	.376	157	8	.204	.251	.414	223	6	.224	.270	.350	193	9	.207	.275	.404	187	5	.225	.247	.348	113	4	.221	.258	.372	267	10	.213	.264	.378
1982	Mil-A	539	23	.269	.309	.451	265	7	.253	.290	.385	274	16	.285	.327	.515	235	9	.238	.280	.404	304	14	.293	.330	.487	185	10	.270	.308	.476	354	13	.268	.309	.438
1983	Mil-A	600	13	.308	.351	.448	295	8	.288	.324	.454	305	5	.328	.377	.443	265	6	.306	.344	.442	335	7	.310	.356	.454	234	3	.325	.364	.440	366	10	.298	.343	.454
1984	Mil-A	497	4	.221	.269	.300	253	0	.206	.244	.249	244	4	.238	.294	.352	287	2	.226	.269	.296	210	2	.214	.270	.305	196	1	.214	.256	.306	301	3	.226	.278	.296
1985	Mil-A	528	12	.273	.342	.402	251	8	.283	.344	.438	277	4	.264	.340	.368	234	3	.248	.315	.346	294	9	.293	.363	.446	166	7	.307	.380	.500	362	5	.257	.324	.356
1986	Atl-N	127	4	.252	.313	.386	55	3	.164	.262	.327	72	1	.319	.354	.431	58	1	.276	.348	.379	69	3	.232	.282	.391	39	2	.256	.295	.487	88	2	.250	.320	.341
1987	Atl-N	177	4	.277	.350	.390	79	1	.278	.337	.367	98	3	.276	.360	.408	92	3	.261	.330	.424	85	1	.294	.371	.353	91	3	.264	.306	.440	86	1	.291	.392	.337
1988	Atl-N	107	2	.196	.293	.308	56	0	.196	.250	.250	51	2	.196	.333	.373	47	1	.234	.321	.383	60	1	.167	.271	.250	41	1	.171	.244	.293	66	1	.212	.321	.318
TOTALS		4414	145	.270	.334	.432	2095	69	.263	.320	.431	2319	76	.276	.347	.434	2120	71	.269	.336	.438	2294	74	.271	.332	.427	1642	58	.277	.333	.446	2772	87	.266	.335	.424
■ Ken Singleton	BB/TR																																			
1978	Bal-A	502	20	.293	.409	.462	235	12	.289	.418	.502	267	8	.296	.401	.427	209	7	.287	.413	.426	293	13	.297	.406	.488	144	4	.229	.331	.333	358	16	.318	.438	.514
1979	Bal-A	570	35	.295	.405	.533	274	13	.299	.401	.504	296	22	.291	.408	.561	271	17	.317	.429	.554	299	18	.274	.381	.515	164	10	.250	.370	.518	406	25	.313	.419	.539
1980	Bal-A	583	24	.304	.397	.485	265	12	.325	.438	.517	318	12	.286	.360	.459	255	11	.282	.369	.459	328	13	.320	.418	.506	201	8	.299	.369	.483	382	16	.306	.411	.487
1981	Bal-A	363	13	.278	.380	.435	185	5	.249	.368	.389	178	8	.309	.393	.483	191	9	.340	.433	.545	172	4	.209	.322	.314	105	2	.238	.304	.314	258	11	.295	.408	.484
1982	Bal-A	561	14	.251	.349	.381	272	9	.235	.339	.386	289	5	.266	.359	.377	259	5	.251	.365	.344	302	9	.252	.335	.414	147	0	.177	.305	.224	414	14	.278	.365	.437
1983	Bal-A	507	18	.276	.393	.436	236	8	.220	.358	.360	271	10	.325	.425	.502	207	9	.285	.404	.502	300	9	.270	.386	.390	173	5	.260	.369	.405	334	13	.284	.405	.452
1984	Bal-A	363	6	.215	.286	.289	168	2	.220	.286	.268	195	4	.210	.286	.308	219	2	.233	.302	.292	144	4	.188	.262	.285	76	1	.211	.277	.276	287	5	.216	.288	.293
TOTALS		3449	130	.276	.379	.440	1635	61	.266	.378	.428	1814	69	.285	.380	.450	1611	60	.284	.388	.445	1838	70	.269	.371	.435	1010	30	.244	.341	.383	2439	100	.289	.394	.463
■ Roy Smalley	BB/TR																																			
1978	Min-A	586	19	.273	.362	.433	288	8	.243	.339	.375	298	11	.302	.384	.490	274	7	.270	.349	.401	312	12	.276	.373	.462	224	7	.263	.353	.411	362	12	.279	.368	.448
1979	Min-A	621	24	.271	.353	.441	308	19	.331	.407	.578	313	5	.211	.299	.307	279	14	.373	.450	.591	342	10	.187	.270	.319	229	13	.275	.328	.489	392	11	.268	.367	.413
1980	Min-A	486	12	.278	.359	.405	246	5	.309	.385	.431	240	7	.246	.332	.379	229	8	.262	.363	.419	257	4	.292	.356	.393	209	3	.258	.326	.364	277	9	.292	.383	.437
1981	Min-A	167	7	.263	.375	.443	92	2	.250	.358	.359	75	5	.280	.396	.547	128	7	.258	.389	.477	39	0	.282	.326	.333	58	4	.310	.406	.552	109	3	.239	.359	.385
1982	Min-A	13	0	.154	.313	.231	13	0	.154	.313	.231	0	0	—	—	—	13	0	.154	.313	.231	0	0	—	—	—	8	0	.250	.250	.375	5	0	.000	.375	.000
1982	NY-A	486	20	.257	.346	.418	236	8	.280	.369	.428	250	12	.236	.324	.408	199	8	.251	.358	.412	287	12	.261	.337	.422	188	4	.234	.308	.340	298	16	.272	.369	.466
1983	NY-A	451	18	.275	.357	.452	209	7	.273	.378	.426	242	11	.277	.338	.475	233	9	.270	.363	.429	218	9	.280	.351	.477	196	6	.281	.341	.444	255	12	.271	.369	.459
1984	NY-A	209	7	.239	.286	.388	105	4	.238	.296	.371	104	3	.240	.277	.404	185	6	.243	.289	.395	24	1	.208	.269	.333	53	2	.170	.254	.302	156	5	.263	.298	.417
1984	Chi-A	135	4	.170	.285	.289	68	4	.191	.309	.397	67	0	.149	.260	.179	0	0	—	—	—	135	4	.170	.285	.289	31	0	.097	.152	.097	104	4	.192	.320	.346
1985	Min-A	388	12	.258	.357	.402	201	7	.249	.348	.408	187	5	.267	.367	.396	199	5	.291	.393	.427	189	7	.222	.318	.376	72	0	.236	.349	.333	316	12	.263	.359	.418
1986	Min-A	459	20	.246	.342	.438	222	9	.266	.368	.464	237	11	.228	.317	.414	221	14	.262	.340	.534	238	6	.231	.344	.349	58	2	.138	.250	.310	401	18	.262	.356	.456
1987	Min-A	309	8	.275	.352	.411	140	5	.271	.342	.436	169	3	.278	.359	.391	185	5	.324	.382	.497	124	3	.202	.308	.282	24	1	.250	.280	.375	285	7	.277	.357	.414
TOTALS		4310	151	.262	.349	.421	2128	78	.273	.363	.437	2182	73	.251	.335	.405	2145	83	.283	.370	.459	2165	68	.241	.329	.382	1350	42	.250	.324	.397	2960	109	.267	.360	.431
■ Dwight Smith	BL/TR																																			
1989	Chi-N	343	9	.324	.382	.493	157	5	.363	.423	.541	186	4	.290	.347	.452	142	2	.331	.399	.486	201	7	.318	.370	.498	29	1	.241	.324	.414	314	8	.331	.388	.500
1990	Chi-N	290	6	.262	.329	.376	131	3	.252	.317	.382	159	3	.270	.339	.371	186	5	.274	.341	.414	104	1	.240	.307	.308	36	1	.222	.263	.361	254	5	.268	.338	.378
1991	Chi-N	167	3	.228	.279	.347	95	2	.253	.297	.379	72	1	.194	.256	.306	66	2	.242	.286	.409	101	1	.218	.275	.307	5	0	.000	.167	.000	162	3	.235	.283	.358
1992	Chi-N	217	3	.276	.318	.392	100	3	.290	.339	.430	117	0	.265	.298	.359	92	1	.250	.281	.348	125	2	.296	.343	.424	20	1	.200	.200	.350	197	2	.284	.329	.396
1993	Chi-N	310	11	.300	.355	.494	146	6	.377	.440	.637	164	5	.232	.274	.366	202	8	.292	.332	.490	108	3	.315	.395	.500	11	0	.364	.462	.636	299	11	.298	.351	.488
1994	Cal-A	122	5	.262	.300	.443	66	2	.182	.229	.303	56	3	.357	.383	.607	122	5	.262	.300	.443	0	0	—	—	—	5	0	.200	.375	.200	117	5	.265	.295	.453
1994	Bal-A	74	3	.311	.363	.486	32	0	.344	.400	.438	42	3	.286	.333	.524	17	1	.176	.176	.353	57	2	.351	.413	.526	3	0	.667	.750	.667	71	3	.296	.342	.479
1995	Atl-N	131	3	.252	.327	.412	73	1	.205	.289	.301	58	2	.310	.375	.552	61	2	.279	.323	.475	70	1	.229	.329	.357	8	0	.125	.364	.125	123	3	.260	.324	.431
1996	Atl-N	153	3	.203	.285	.294	68	2	.162	.284	.265	85	1	.235	.286	.318	100	3	.220	.288	.330	53	0	.170	.279	.226	7	0	.000	.125	.000	146	3	.212	.293	.308
TOTALS		1807	46	.275	.333	.422	868	24	.285	.349	.439	939	22	.266	.318	.407	988	29	.273	.325	.431	819	17	.277	.343	.411	124	3	.218	.303	.347	1683	43	.279	.336	.428
■ Lonnie Smith	BR/TR																																			
1978	Phi-N	4	0	.000	.500	.000	1	0	.000	.000	.000	3	0	.000	.571	.000	0	0	—	—	—	4	0	.000	.500	.000	2	0	.000	.333	.000	2	0	.000	.600	.000
1979	Phi-N	30	0	.167	.194	.233	19	0	.211	.211	.316	11	0	.091	.167	.091	5	0	.000	.167	.000	25	0	.200	.200	.280	23	0	.087	.087	.130	7	0	.429	.500	.571
1980	Phi-N	298	3	.339	.397	.443	159	2	.365	.410	.478	139	1	.309	.382	.403	51	0	.373	.418	.490	247	3	.332	.393	.433	93	1	.301	.359	.387	205	2	.356	.414	.468
1981	Phi-N	176	2	.324	.402	.472	68	1	.426	.500	.676	108	1	.259	.339	.343	82	0	.256	.330	.329	94	2	.383	.463	.596	47	0	.255	.364	.319	129	2	.349	.417	.527
1982	StL-N	592	8	.307	.381	.434	287	3	.314	.381	.463	305	5	.302	.382	.407	285	5	.309	.388	.449	307	3	.306	.374	.420	187	2	.316	.396	.439	405	6	.304	.374	.432
1983	StL-N	492	8	.321	.381	.453	243	4	.342	.401	.510	249	4	.301	.361	.398	196	3	.311	.370	.429	296	5	.328	.388	.470	144	2	.326	.366	.472	348	6	.319	.387	.445
1984	StL-N	504	6	.250	.349	.341	232	3	.241	.364	.345	272	3	.257	.336	.338	272	5	.265	.365	.379	232	1	.233	.331	.297	159	2	.245	.342	.352	345	4	.252	.352	.336
1985	StL-N	96	0	.260	.377	.323	49	0	.306	.414	.408	47	0	.213	.339	.234	96	0	.260	.377	.323	0	0	—	—	—	34	0	.265	.405	.324	62	0	.258	.361	.323
1985	KC-A	448	6	.257	.321	.366	225	2	.231	.307	.338	223	4	.283	.336	.395	136	1	.206	.299	.324	312	5	.279	.331	.385	140	2	.293	.350	.414	308	4	.240	.308	.344
1986	KC-A	508	8	.287	.357	.411	243	2	.317	.390	.432	265	6	.260	.327	.392	183	3	.251	.350	.377	325	5	.308	.361	.431	149	2	.309	.360	.443	359	6	.279	.356	.398
1987	KC-A	167	3	.251	.355	.359	81	1	.259	.365	.346	86	2	.244	.347	.372	0	0	—	—	—	167	3	.251	.355	.359	50	0	.280	.400	.380	117	3	.239	.336	.350
1988	Atl-N	114	3	.237	.296	.342	59	2	.237	.292	.373	55	1	.236	.300	.309	0	0	—	—	—	114	3	.237	.296	.342	79	3	.253	.306	.405	35	0	.200	.275	.200
1989	Atl-N	482	21	.315	.415	.533	226	10	.358	.442	.597	256	11	.277	.392	.477	203	10	.325	.437	.571	279	11	.308	.398	.505	165	7	.321	.429	.564	317	14	.312	.408	.517
1990	Atl-N	466	9	.305	.384	.459	231	2	.312	.390	.442	235	7	.298	.379	.477	188	5	.271	.347	.447	278	4	.327	.409	.468	197	6	.294	.365	.487	269	3	.312	.397	.439
1991	Atl-N	353	7	.275	.377	.394	193	6	.290	.374	.435	160	1	.256	.380	.344	140	3	.257	.364	.379	213	4	.286	.386	.404	115	0	.339	.435	.435	238	7	.244	.348	.374
1992	Atl-N	158	6	.247	.324	.437	71	3	.239	.333	.437	87	3	.253	.316	.437	46	0	.196	.278	.217	112	6	.268	.344	.527	65	3	.277	.347	.508	93	3	.226	.308	.387
1993	Pit-N	199	6	.286	.422	.442	90	4	.300	.432	.467	109	2	.275	.413	.422	110	2	.264	.393	.373	89	4	.315	.456	.528	120	3	.300	.414	.417	79	3	.266	.433	.481
1993	Bal-A	24	2	.208	.406	.500	9	2	.444	.583	1.111	15	0	.067	.300	.133	0	0	—	—	—	24	2	.208	.406	.500	12	2	.333	.529	.833	12	0	.083	.267	.167
1994	Bal-A	59	0	.203	.333	.254	39	0	.256	.408	.333	20	0	.100	.174	.100	48	0	.229	.345	.292	11	0	.091	.286	.091	42	0	.286	.404	.357	17	0	.000	.150	.000
TOTALS		5170	98	.288	.371	.420	2525	47	.303	.385	.449	2645	51	.273	.358	.392	2041	37	.275	.368	.406	3129	61	.296	.374	.429	1823	35	.295	.377	.435	3347	63	.284	.369	.412
■ Ozzie Smith	BB/TR																																			
1978	SD-N	590	1	.258	.311	.312	275	0	.236	.298	.276	315	1	.276	.322	.343	265	0	.268	.312	.321	325	1	.249	.310	.305	200	1	.195	.249	.255	390	0	.290	.343	.341
1979	SD-N	587	0	.211	.260	.262	286	0	.220	.280	.269	301	0	.203	.241	.256	273	0	.176	.236	.212	314	0	.242	.281	.306	171	0	.228	.286	.298	416	0	.204	.249	.248
1980	SD-N	609	0	.230	.313	.276	280	0	.189	.286	.218	329	0	.264	.338	.325	279	0	.237	.335	.283	330	0	.224	.294	.270	143	0	.224	.333	.273	466	0	.232	.307	.277
1981	SD-N	450	0	.222	.294	.256	218	0	.206	.278	.252	232	0	.237	.309	.259	232	0	.259	.328	.276	218	0	.183	.257	.234	140	0	.171	.240	.186	310	0	.245	.318	.287
1982	StL-N	488	2	.248	.339	.314	246	0	.236	.338	.293	242	2	.260	.341	.335	272	2	.265	.338	.364	216	0	.227	.341	.250	162	2	.259	.335	.364	326	0	.242	.341	.288
1983	StL-N	552	3	.243	.321	.335	256	1	.227	.325	.320	296	2	.257	.318	.348	255	0	.188	.251	.247	297	3	.290	.379	.411	155	3	.213	.305	.374	397	0	.254	.328	.320
1984	StL-N	412	1	.257	.347	.337	176	1	.244	.304	.313	236	0	.267	.376	.356	253	1	.249	.341	.320	159	0	.270	.355	.365	118	1	.305	.424	.415	294	0	.238	.313	.306
1985	StL-N	537	6	.276	.355	.361	258	2	.298	.389	.388	279	4	.254	.321	.337	247	3	.259	.325	.340	290	3	.290	.379	.379	161	6	.298	.407	.484	376	0	.266	.330	.309
1986	StL-N	514	0	.280	.376	.333	254	0	.287	.400	.346	260	0	.273	.352	.319	237	0	.300	.399	.363	277	0	.264	.357	.307	203	0	.276	.370	.315	311	0	.283	.380	.344
1987	StL-N	600	0	.303	.392	.383	286	0	.287	.375	.371	314	0	.318	.408	.395	271	0	.292	.387	.365	329	0	.313	.396	.398	220	0	.250	.346	.318	380	0	.334	.419	.421
1988	StL-N	575	3	.270	.350	.336	288	2	.278	.366	.344	287	1	.261	.334	.328	305	2	.275	.345	.331	270	1	.263	.356	.341	201	2	.259	.355	.343	374	1	.275	.348	.332

YEAR	TM/L	TOTAL					HOME					AWAY					1ST HALF					2ND HALF					LEFT					RIGHT				
		AB	HR	AVG	OBP	SLG	AB	HR	AVG	OBP	SLG	AB	HR	AVG	OBP	SLG	AB	HR	AVG	OBP	SLG	AB	HR	AVG	OBP	SLG	AB	HR	AVG	OBP	SLG	AB	HR	AVG	OBP	SLG
1989	StL-N	593	2	.273	.335	.361	297	1	.253	.323	.330	296	1	.294	.348	.392	262	1	.290	.365	.385	331	1	.260	.311	.341	248	1	.286	.346	.383	345	1	.264	.328	.345
1990	StL-N	512	1	.254	.330	.305	256	0	.266	.347	.332	256	1	.242	.313	.277	242	0	.219	.317	.256	270	1	.285	.342	.348	201	1	.289	.347	.373	311	0	.232	.319	.260
1991	StL-N	550	3	.285	.380	.367	291	2	.323	.416	.416	259	1	.243	.338	.313	247	0	.316	.414	.381	303	3	.261	.351	.356	248	3	.262	.356	.387	302	0	.305	.399	.351
1992	StL-N	518	0	.295	.367	.342	278	0	.335	.396	.378	240	0	.250	.333	.300	221	0	.290	.357	.326	297	0	.300	.374	.354	202	0	.272	.339	.332	316	0	.310	.384	.348
1993	StL-N	545	1	.288	.337	.356	288	1	.299	.357	.375	257	0	.276	.314	.335	276	1	.279	.329	.359	269	0	.297	.346	.353	150	1	.320	.354	.413	395	0	.276	.331	.334
1994	StL-N	381	3	.262	.326	.349	183	1	.284	.343	.377	198	2	.242	.311	.323	248	3	.230	.308	.310	133	0	.323	.361	.421	126	2	.262	.309	.389	255	1	.263	.335	.329
1995	StL-N	156	0	.199	.282	.244	97	0	.175	.283	.216	59	0	.237	.281	.288	68	0	.250	.320	.294	88	0	.159	.255	.205	35	0	.143	.205	.200	121	0	.215	.304	.256
1996	StL-N	227	2	.282	.358	.370	114	2	.351	.444	.491	113	0	.212	.264	.248	88	0	.261	.309	.307	139	2	.295	.387	.410	25	0	.240	.345	.320	202	2	.287	.360	.376
TOTALS		9396	28	.262	.337	.328	4627	13	.264	.346	.332	4769	15	.260	.329	.325	4541	13	.258	.334	.320	4855	15	.265	.341	.336	3109	23	.256	.336	.345	6287	5	.265	.338	.320
■ J. T. Snow BB/TL																																				
1992	NY-A	14	0	.143	.368	.214	6	0	.167	.545	.333	8	0	.125	.125	.125	0	0	—	—	—	14	0	.143	.368	.214	3	0	.000	.000	.000	11	0	.182	.438	.273
1993	Cal-A	419	16	.241	.328	.408	196	10	.286	.359	.480	223	6	.202	.301	.345	228	10	.241	.331	.421	191	6	.241	.324	.393	87	2	.218	.306	.345	332	14	.247	.333	.425
1994	Cal-A	223	8	.220	.289	.345	143	7	.252	.296	.427	80	1	.162	.277	.200	94	2	.202	.242	.277	129	6	.233	.320	.395	84	2	.226	.301	.333	139	6	.216	.281	.353
1995	Cal-A	544	24	.289	.353	.465	270	14	.304	.374	.496	274	10	.274	.331	.434	228	10	.294	.355	.474	316	14	.285	.351	.459	161	5	.267	.351	.404	383	19	.298	.353	.491
1996	Cal-A	575	17	.257	.327	.384	290	8	.266	.342	.376	285	9	.249	.312	.393	289	9	.256	.337	.381	286	8	.259	.316	.388	186	3	.199	.249	.274	389	14	.285	.363	.437
1997	SF-N	531	28	.281	.387	.510	257	14	.272	.391	.510	274	14	.288	.384	.511	266	9	.301	.411	.489	265	19	.260	.364	.532	133	1	.188	.304	.256	398	27	.312	.415	.595
1998	SF-N	435	15	.248	.332	.423	195	9	.282	.382	.503	240	6	.221	.288	.358	221	7	.213	.307	.357	214	8	.285	.358	.491	73	1	.164	.259	.247	362	14	.265	.347	.459
1999	SF-N	570	24	.274	.370	.451	273	7	.242	.350	.341	297	17	.303	.390	.552	275	9	.302	.403	.465	295	15	.247	.339	.437	169	3	.231	.313	.331	401	21	.292	.394	.501
2000	SF-N	536	19	.284	.365	.459	262	10	.313	.373	.508	274	9	.255	.358	.412	265	7	.309	.374	.453	271	12	.258	.357	.465	129	4	.256	.351	.395	407	15	.292	.370	.479
TOTALS		3847	151	.266	.350	.437	1892	79	.277	.363	.452	1955	72	.254	.337	.424	1866	63	.272	.357	.427	1981	88	.260	.343	.447	1025	21	.221	.305	.325	2822	130	.282	.366	.478
■ Cory Snyder BR/TR																																				
1986	Cle-A	416	24	.272	.299	.500	186	12	.280	.309	.532	230	12	.265	.290	.474	62	5	.274	.286	.629	354	19	.271	.301	.477	118	8	.322	.333	.585	298	16	.252	.285	.466
1987	Cle-A	577	33	.236	.273	.456	276	17	.214	.255	.442	301	16	.256	.290	.468	265	13	.230	.266	.419	312	20	.240	.279	.487	163	5	.221	.271	.399	414	28	.242	.274	.478
1988	Cle-A	511	26	.272	.326	.483	270	11	.233	.283	.396	241	15	.315	.374	.581	265	17	.260	.320	.506	246	9	.285	.333	.459	111	9	.342	.400	.667	400	17	.253	.305	.433
1989	Cle-A	489	18	.215	.251	.360	246	6	.207	.244	.329	243	12	.222	.258	.391	285	11	.232	.263	.386	204	7	.191	.234	.324	164	10	.250	.309	.463	325	8	.197	.220	.308
1990	Cle-A	438	14	.233	.268	.404	196	3	.235	.287	.357	242	11	.231	.251	.442	258	11	.264	.292	.484	180	3	.189	.233	.289	135	4	.222	.291	.370	303	10	.238	.256	.419
1991	Chi-A	117	3	.188	.228	.299	56	2	.196	.237	.357	61	1	.180	.219	.246	112	3	.179	.220	.286	5	0	.400	.400	.600	93	3	.183	.208	.323	24	0	.208	.296	.208
1991	Tor-A	49	0	.143	.189	.184	15	0	.133	.188	.133	34	0	.147	.189	.206	0	0	—	—	—	49	0	.143	.189	.184	23	0	.087	.125	.087	26	0	.192	.241	.269
1992	SF-N	390	14	.269	.311	.444	184	8	.299	.342	.505	206	6	.243	.283	.388	165	8	.303	.333	.533	225	6	.244	.295	.378	170	6	.294	.331	.471	220	8	.250	.295	.423
1993	LA-N	516	11	.266	.331	.397	256	5	.266	.335	.379	260	6	.265	.327	.415	193	6	.311	.395	.472	323	5	.238	.290	.353	151	3	.265	.333	.397	365	8	.266	.330	.397
1994	LA-N	153	6	.235	.300	.392	64	1	.250	.351	.328	89	5	.225	.258	.438	105	6	.257	.325	.476	48	0	.188	.245	.208	100	5	.250	.300	.440	53	1	.208	.300	.302
TOTALS		3656	149	.247	.291	.425	1749	65	.242	.291	.407	1907	84	.251	.291	.441	1710	80	.256	.301	.456	1946	69	.238	.282	.397	1228	53	.258	.308	.448	2428	96	.241	.282	.413
■ Paul Sorrento BL/TR																																				
1989	Min-A	21	0	.238	.370	.238	14	0	.286	.375	.286	7	0	.143	.364	.143	0	0	—	—	—	21	0	.238	.370	.238	2	0	.000	.000	.000	19	0	.263	.400	.263
1990	Min-A	121	5	.207	.281	.380	69	2	.232	.280	.377	52	3	.173	.283	.385	23	1	.261	.346	.435	98	4	.194	.266	.367	3	0	.000	.400	.000	118	5	.212	.277	.390
1991	Min-A	47	4	.255	.314	.553	18	2	.333	.400	.722	29	2	.207	.258	.448	0	0	—	—	—	47	4	.255	.314	.553	5	1	.600	.600	1.400	42	3	.214	.283	.452
1992	Cle-A	458	18	.269	.341	.443	226	11	.288	.362	.500	232	7	.250	.320	.388	213	8	.258	.329	.394	245	10	.278	.351	.486	45	0	.156	.250	.178	413	18	.281	.351	.472
1993	Cle-A	463	18	.257	.340	.434	217	8	.281	.389	.452	246	10	.236	.293	.419	231	13	.264	.347	.494	232	5	.250	.332	.375	87	2	.241	.305	.333	376	16	.261	.347	.457
1994	Cle-A	322	14	.280	.345	.453	157	8	.312	.359	.503	165	6	.248	.333	.406	204	6	.255	.326	.377	118	8	.322	.380	.585	74	3	.270	.329	.459	248	11	.282	.350	.452
1995	Cle-A	323	25	.235	.336	.511	161	12	.230	.342	.503	162	13	.241	.330	.519	140	13	.264	.356	.593	183	12	.213	.321	.448	43	2	.163	.269	.326	280	23	.246	.347	.539
1996	Sea-A	471	23	.289	.370	.507	230	13	.313	.401	.574	241	10	.266	.339	.444	225	14	.320	.407	.587	246	9	.260	.336	.435	60	2	.167	.242	.367	411	21	.307	.388	.528
1997	Sea-A	457	31	.269	.345	.514	221	18	.299	.380	.588	236	13	.242	.312	.445	239	15	.285	.352	.515	218	16	.252	.337	.514	39	4	.205	.279	.513	418	27	.275	.351	.514
1998	TB-A	435	17	.225	.313	.405	227	10	.220	.294	.414	208	7	.231	.333	.394	239	12	.243	.315	.473	196	5	.204	.311	.321	74	1	.203	.322	.338	361	16	.230	.311	.418
1999	TB-A	294	11	.235	.351	.401	152	6	.224	.377	.375	142	5	.246	.318	.430	123	4	.236	.331	.382	171	7	.234	.364	.415	38	2	.289	.400	.500	256	9	.227	.343	.387
TOTALS		3412	166	.257	.340	.457	1692	90	.272	.361	.489	1720	76	.242	.320	.426	1637	86	.268	.346	.478	1775	80	.247	.335	.438	470	17	.217	.304	.379	2942	149	.263	.346	.470
■ Sammy Sosa BR/TR																																				
1989	Tex-A	84	1	.238	.238	.310	24	0	.375	.375	.375	60	1	.183	.183	.283	52	1	.269	.269	.346	32	0	.188	.188	.250	44	0	.318	.318	.364	40	1	.150	.150	.250
1989	Chi-A	99	3	.273	.351	.414	43	1	.233	.327	.349	56	2	.304	.371	.464	0	0	—	—	—	99	3	.273	.351	.414	34	2	.382	.465	.647	65	1	.215	.282	.292
1990	Chi-A	532	15	.233	.282	.404	266	10	.256	.314	.477	266	5	.211	.251	.331	247	7	.271	.308	.462	285	8	.200	.260	.354	233	12	.262	.316	.502	299	3	.211	.255	.328
1991	Chi-A	316	10	.203	.240	.335	145	3	.186	.222	.297	171	7	.216	.256	.368	230	9	.204	.243	.352	86	1	.198	.233	.291	128	5	.227	.277	.383	188	5	.186	.214	.303
1992	Chi-N	262	8	.260	.317	.393	116	4	.267	.344	.440	146	4	.253	.295	.356	223	5	.238	.301	.350	39	3	.385	.415	.641	75	0	.280	.353	.320	187	8	.251	.302	.422
1993	Chi-N	598	33	.261	.309	.485	298	23	.272	.323	.557	300	10	.250	.295	.413	279	16	.265	.307	.498	319	17	.257	.310	.473	150	10	.287	.344	.567	448	23	.252	.297	.458
1994	Chi-N	426	25	.300	.339	.545	228	11	.285	.331	.518	198	14	.318	.349	.576	268	16	.287	.333	.537	158	9	.323	.349	.557	113	9	.336	.395	.619	313	16	.288	.318	.518
1995	Chi-N	564	36	.268	.340	.500	276	19	.272	.342	.514	288	17	.264	.339	.486	245	14	.286	.335	.502	319	22	.254	.344	.498	148	9	.257	.345	.493	416	27	.272	.338	.502
1996	Chi-N	498	40	.273	.323	.564	266	26	.282	.325	.620	232	14	.263	.322	.500	323	26	.257	.303	.545	175	14	.303	.361	.600	113	8	.248	.312	.522	385	32	.281	.327	.577
1997	Chi-N	642	36	.251	.300	.480	312	25	.269	.335	.554	330	11	.233	.264	.409	322	16	.258	.303	.481	320	20	.244	.297	.478	141	12	.270	.340	.574	501	24	.246	.288	.453
1998	Chi-N	643	66	.308	.377	.647	310	35	.300	.366	.674	333	31	.315	.387	.622	318	33	.327	.386	.676	325	33	.289	.368	.618	164	12	.287	.418	.537	479	54	.315	.361	.685
1999	Chi-N	625	63	.288	.367	.635	308	33	.325	.406	.701	317	30	.252	.328	.571	292	30	.291	.364	.647	333	33	.285	.369	.625	163	18	.313	.396	.712	462	45	.279	.356	.608
2000	Chi-N	604	50	.320	.406	.634	291	22	.306	.400	.591	313	28	.332	.411	.674	306	21	.314	.398	.588	298	29	.326	.413	.681	124	8	.347	.461	.597	480	42	.313	.390	.644
TOTALS		5893	386	.273	.333	.523	2883	212	.280	.345	.557	3010	174	.265	.322	.490	3105	194	.275	.328	.519	2788	192	.270	.338	.527	1630	105	.285	.362	.536	4263	281	.268	.322	.517
■ Chris Speier BR/TR																																				
1978	Mon-N	501	5	.251	.329	.329	250	2	.264	.348	.352	251	3	.239	.310	.307	224	3	.250	.337	.330	277	2	.253	.323	.329	111	3	.279	.386	.468	390	2	.244	.312	.290
1979	Mon-N	344	7	.227	.317	.331	167	1	.228	.347	.287	177	6	.226	.286	.373	212	2	.241	.325	.335	132	5	.205	.305	.326	60	0	.250	.392	.300	284	7	.222	.300	.338
1980	Mon-N	388	1	.265	.351	.330	177	0	.288	.377	.345	211	1	.246	.329	.318	137	1	.255	.352	.343	251	0	.271	.351	.323	92	0	.250	.352	.304	296	1	.270	.351	.338
1981	Mon-N	307	2	.225	.310	.290	169	1	.213	.293	.278	138	1	.239	.331	.304	172	2	.256	.340	.349	135	0	.185	.272	.215	63	1	.238	.324	.333	244	1	.221	.307	.279
1982	Mon-N	530	7	.257	.316	.360	267	2	.236	.305	.326	263	5	.278	.328	.395	229	2	.240	.282	.336	301	5	.269	.341	.379	146	1	.240	.297	.315	384	6	.263	.323	.378
1983	Mon-N	261	2	.257	.332	.341	141	1	.291	.380	.404	120	1	.217	.273	.267	146	0	.247	.349	.322	115	2	.270	.310	.365	93	1	.215	.312	.269	168	1	.280	.344	.381
1984	Mon-N	40	0	.150	.171	.150	14	0	.143	.200	.143	26	0	.154	.154	.154	40	0	.150	.171	.150	0	0	—	—	—	15	0	.133	.133	.133	25	0	.160	.192	.160
1984	StL-N	118	3	.178	.242	.331	79	2	.177	.244	.329	39	1	.179	.238	.333	0	0	—	—	—	118	3	.178	.242	.331	48	1	.167	.245	.292	70	2	.186	.240	.357
1984	Min-A	33	0	.212	.278	.212	24	0	.167	.231	.167	9	0	.333	.400	.333	0	0	—	—	—	33	0	.212	.278	.212	14	0	.214	.267	.214	19	0	.211	.286	.211
1985	Chi-N	218	4	.243	.295	.349	112	1	.223	.273	.295	106	3	.264	.319	.406	117	3	.239	.295	.376	101	1	.248	.296	.317	66	3	.333	.378	.515	152	1	.204	.258	.276
1986	Chi-N	155	6	.284	.349	.452	68	2	.309	.390	.441	87	4	.264	.316	.460	55	3	.218	.323	.382	100	3	.320	.364	.490	45	2	.244	.306	.444	110	4	.300	.366	.455
1987	SF-N	317	11	.249	.342	.394	159	6	.226	.332	.365	158	5	.272	.352	.424	176	7	.261	.348	.426	141	4	.234	.333	.355	92	4	.272	.337	.424	225	7	.240	.344	.382
1988	SF-N	171	3	.216	.311	.333	90	3	.278	.363	.489	81	0	.148	.255	.160	91	1	.198	.302	.275	80	2	.237	.322	.400	66	0	.258	.419	.379	105	3	.190	.227	.305
1989	SF-N	37	0	.243	.333	.351	19	0	.211	.348	.316	18	0	.278	.316	.389	26	0	.115	.233	.154	11	0	.545	.583	.818	20	0	.150	.227	.200	17	0	.353	.450	.529
TOTALS		3420	51	.244	.321	.342	1736	21	.245	.331	.340	1684	30	.243	.311	.343	1625	24	.240	.321	.339	1795	27	.248	.321	.344	931	16	.247	.336	.356	2489	35	.243	.315	.337
■ Bill Spiers BL/TR																																				
1989	Mil-A	345	4	.255	.298	.333	172	1	.273	.298	.343	173	3	.237	.298	.324	105	1	.229	.311	.286	240	3	.267	.292	.354	70	1	.271	.282	.371	275	3	.251	.302	.324
1990	Mil-A	363	2	.242	.274	.317	176	2	.267	.305	.375	187	0	.219	.245	.262	128	1	.258	.296	.367	235	1	.234	.262	.289	81	0	.235	.279	.296	282	2	.245	.273	.323
1991	Mil-A	414	8	.283	.337	.401	187	1	.299	.370	.369	227	7	.269	.309	.427	173	3	.243	.307	.341	241	5	.311	.358	.444	117	2	.222	.305	.282	297	6	.306	.350	.448
1992	Mil-A	16	0	.313	.353	.438	6	0	.667	.667	1.000	10	0	.100	.182	.100	0	0	—	—	—	16	0	.313	.353	.438	3	0	.000	.000	.000	13	0	.385	.429	.538
1993	Mil-A	340	2	.238	.302	.303	166	2	.277	.344	.367	174	0	.201	.262	.241	212	0	.226	.298	.274	128	2	.258	.309	.352	68	0	.176	.273	.235	272	2	.254	.310	.320
1994	Mil-A	214	0	.252	.316	.308	86	0	.291	.344	.326	128	0	.227	.298	.297	158	0	.259	.331	.310	56	0	.232	.271	.304	35	0	.114	.184	.114	179	0	.279	.342	.346
1995	NY-N	72	0	.208	.314	.264	31	0	.355	.475	.419	41	0	.098	.174	.146	24	0	.167	.276	.292	48	0	.229	.333	.250	3	0	.667	.750	1.000	69	0	.188	.293	.232
1996	Hou-N	218	6	.252	.320	.390	122	3	.287	.353	.434	96	3	.208	.276	.333	85	3	.235	.270	.388	133	3	.263	.349	.391	17	0	.059	.200	.059	201	6	.269	.330	.418
1997	Hou-N	291	4	.320	.438	.481	142	0	.310	.410	.437	149	4	.329	.463	.523	140	1	.307	.446	.429	151	3	.331	.429	.530	41	0	.317	.451	.463	250	4	.320	.436	.484
1998	Hou-N	384	4	.273	.356	.396	191	1	.262	.341	.377	193	3	.285	.369	.415	204	2	.289	.394	.422	180	2	.256	.308	.367	35	0	.143	.220	.200	349	4	.287	.370	.415
1999	Hou-N	393	4	.288	.363	.389	196	1	.260	.341	.342	197	3	.315	.385	.437	173	3	.272	.344	.405	220	1	.300	.378	.377	40	0	.375	.432	.450	353	4	.278	.355	.382
2000	Hou-N	355	3	.301	.386	.392	169	2	.337	.420	.450	186	1	.269	.355	.339	165	1	.309	.390	.388	190	2	.295	.382	.395	32	0	.250	.400	.281	323	3	.307	.384	.402
TOTALS		3405	37	.270	.340	.370	1644	13	.288	.356	.384	1761	24	.254	.326	.357	1567	15	.263	.344	.359	1838	22	.277	.337	.379	542	3	.229	.307	.295	2863	34	.278	.347	.384
■ Scott Spiezio BB/TR																																				
1996	Oak-A	29	2	.310	.394	.586	14	1	.357	.400	.643	15	1	.267	.389	.533	0	0	—	—	—	29	2	.310	.394	.586	14	0	.143	.143	.143	15	2	.467	.579	1.000
1997	Oak-A	538	14	.243	.300	.388	280	6	.243	.300	.393	258	8	.244	.300	.384	252	7	.246	.303	.397	286	7	.241	.297	.381	149	7	.235	.311	.423	389	7	.247	.295	.375
1998	Oak-A	406	9	.258	.333	.377	199	6	.296	.362	.437	207	3	.222	.305	.319	241	7	.270	.335	.407	165	2	.242	.330	.333	121	1	.264	.343	.339	285	8	.256	.328	.393
1999	Oak-A	247	8	.243	.324	.437	122	3	.230	.287	.402	125	5	.256	.359	.472	127	2	.189	.279	.331	120	6	.300	.373	.550	70	1	.229	.316	.357	177	7	.249	.327	.469

YEAR	TM/L	TOTAL AB	HR	AVG	OBP	SLG	HOME AB	HR	AVG	OBP	SLG	AWAY AB	HR	AVG	OBP	SLG	1ST HALF AB	HR	AVG	OBP	SLG	2ND HALF AB	HR	AVG	OBP	SLG	LEFT AB	HR	AVG	OBP	SLG	RIGHT AB	HR	AVG	OBP	SLG
2000	Ana-A	297	17	.242	.334	.465	155	10	.245	.367	.471	142	7	.239	.295	.458	178	8	.247	.349	.438	119	9	.235	.311	.504	56	2	.250	.288	.411	241	15	.241	.344	.477
TOTALS		1517	50	.249	.321	.412	770	26	.257	.330	.426	747	24	.240	.313	.398	798	24	.244	.319	.398	719	26	.253	.324	.427	410	11	.241	.314	.376	1107	39	.251	.324	.425
■ Ed Sprague BR/TR																																				
1991	Tor-A	160	4	.275	.361	.394	77	3	.286	.329	.429	83	1	.265	.386	.361	108	2	.296	.364	.398	52	2	.231	.355	.385	90	3	.267	.347	.400	70	1	.286	.378	.386
1992	Tor-A	47	1	.234	.280	.340	24	1	.167	.231	.292	23	0	.304	.333	.391	0	0	—	—	—	47	1	.234	.280	.340	10	0	.400	.455	.500	37	1	.189	.231	.297
1993	Tor-A	546	12	.260	.310	.386	268	8	.291	.328	.463	278	4	.230	.293	.313	271	9	.262	.310	.417	275	3	.258	.310	.356	146	2	.247	.304	.363	400	10	.265	.312	.395
1994	Tor-A	405	11	.240	.296	.373	210	6	.243	.306	.367	195	5	.236	.285	.379	281	6	.235	.291	.349	124	5	.250	.307	.427	118	3	.288	.356	.441	287	8	.220	.270	.345
1995	Tor-A	521	18	.244	.333	.407	252	12	.242	.355	.437	269	6	.245	.311	.379	201	9	.284	.361	.468	320	9	.219	.315	.369	135	5	.222	.282	.341	386	13	.251	.350	.430
1996	Tor-A	591	36	.247	.325	.496	295	17	.234	.309	.461	296	19	.260	.341	.530	282	21	.273	.365	.571	309	15	.223	.287	.427	155	14	.310	.385	.645	436	22	.225	.303	.443
1997	Tor-A	504	14	.228	.306	.385	254	5	.217	.287	.350	250	9	.240	.325	.420	284	10	.250	.325	.465	220	4	.200	.282	.282	148	7	.250	.327	.486	356	7	.219	.297	.343
1998	Tor-A	382	17	.238	.301	.424	171	6	.257	.345	.433	211	11	.223	.262	.417	282	9	.238	.309	.390	100	8	.240	.276	.520	91	3	.198	.245	.352	291	14	.251	.318	.447
1998	Oak-A	87	3	.149	.187	.310	33	3	.212	.257	.576	54	0	.111	.143	.148	0	0	—	—	—	87	3	.149	.187	.310	15	0	.133	.188	.200	72	3	.153	.187	.333
1999	Pit-N	490	22	.267	.352	.465	252	10	.262	.333	.425	238	12	.273	.370	.508	253	14	.304	.401	.561	237	8	.228	.295	.363	137	6	.212	.311	.372	353	16	.289	.368	.501
2000	SD-N	157	10	.261	.326	.529	67	4	.209	.284	.448	90	6	.300	.356	.589	117	10	.274	.336	.615	40	0	.225	.295	.275	100	8	.340	.402	.690	57	2	.123	.190	.246
2000	Bos-A	111	2	.216	.293	.306	39	1	.179	.238	.282	72	1	.236	.321	.319	0	0	—	—	—	111	2	.216	.293	.306	37	1	.162	.279	.270	74	1	.243	.300	.324
TOTALS		4001	150	.245	.317	.418	1942	76	.246	.318	.421	2059	74	.245	.317	.416	2079	90	.265	.338	.464	1922	60	.225	.294	.369	1182	52	.255	.328	.448	2819	98	.241	.313	.406
■ Matt Stairs BL/TR																																				
1992	Mon-N	30	0	.167	.316	.233	9	0	.111	.333	.111	21	0	.190	.308	.286	30	0	.167	.316	.233	0	0	—	—	—	2	0	.000	.500	.000	28	0	.179	.294	.250
1993	Mon-N	8	0	.375	.375	.500	2	0	.500	.500	1.000	6	0	.333	.333	.333	8	0	.375	.375	.500	0	0	—	—	—	2	0	.500	.500	1.000	6	0	.333	.333	.333
1995	Bos-A	88	1	.261	.298	.398	45	0	.289	.333	.444	43	1	.233	.261	.349	9	0	.333	.333	.444	79	1	.253	.294	.392	3	0	.333	.333	.333	85	1	.259	.297	.400
1996	Oak-A	137	10	.277	.367	.547	79	5	.278	.348	.506	58	5	.276	.391	.603	15	1	.200	.250	.400	122	9	.287	.380	.566	9	0	.222	.417	.222	128	10	.281	.363	.570
1997	Oak-A	352	27	.298	.386	.582	197	20	.305	.393	.655	155	7	.290	.378	.490	123	12	.382	.458	.756	229	15	.253	.347	.489	85	8	.259	.347	.565	267	19	.311	.399	.588
1998	Oak-A	523	26	.294	.370	.511	261	16	.314	.385	.571	262	10	.275	.355	.450	242	11	.331	.409	.562	281	15	.263	.335	.466	164	8	.280	.352	.488	359	18	.301	.378	.521
1999	Oak-A	531	38	.258	.366	.533	256	15	.250	.360	.492	275	23	.265	.372	.571	251	16	.255	.344	.514	280	22	.261	.385	.550	165	8	.236	.342	.436	366	30	.268	.377	.577
2000	Oak-A	476	21	.227	.333	.414	243	9	.230	.334	.407	233	12	.223	.332	.421	255	12	.216	.333	.400	221	9	.240	.333	.430	114	5	.202	.295	.368	362	16	.235	.345	.428
TOTALS		2145	123	.267	.360	.500	1092	65	.274	.364	.518	1053	58	.260	.355	.481	933	52	.279	.371	.516	1212	71	.258	.351	.488	544	29	.246	.339	.454	1601	94	.274	.367	.516
■ Mike Stanley BR/TR																																				
1986	Tex-A	30	1	.333	.394	.533	11	0	.182	.250	.182	19	1	.421	.476	.737	13	0	.231	.231	.308	17	1	.412	.500	.706	17	1	.471	.500	.765	13	0	.154	.267	.231
1987	Tex-A	216	6	.273	.361	.403	109	3	.321	.402	.459	107	3	.224	.320	.346	71	2	.324	.385	.408	145	4	.248	.351	.400	99	2	.283	.354	.404	117	4	.265	.367	.402
1988	Tex-A	249	3	.229	.323	.297	143	1	.259	.337	.322	106	2	.189	.305	.264	146	2	.219	.318	.288	103	1	.243	.331	.311	122	2	.238	.354	.320	127	1	.220	.293	.276
1989	Tex-A	122	1	.246	.324	.311	57	1	.298	.355	.368	65	0	.200	.297	.262	46	0	.152	.250	.152	76	1	.303	.369	.408	78	1	.256	.310	.333	44	0	.227	.346	.273
1990	Tex-A	189	2	.249	.350	.333	85	1	.282	.384	.388	104	1	.221	.322	.288	96	2	.198	.278	.281	93	0	.301	.420	.387	137	2	.277	.385	.380	52	0	.173	.254	.212
1991	Tex-A	181	3	.249	.372	.381	96	1	.281	.389	.406	85	2	.212	.352	.353	109	2	.229	.356	.376	72	1	.278	.395	.389	94	3	.277	.405	.479	87	0	.218	.333	.276
1992	NY-A	173	8	.249	.372	.428	91	5	.264	.391	.484	82	3	.232	.351	.366	60	2	.200	.333	.317	113	6	.274	.393	.487	112	5	.241	.366	.411	61	3	.262	.384	.459
1993	NY-A	423	26	.305	.389	.534	199	17	.312	.408	.608	224	9	.299	.372	.469	193	10	.311	.389	.518	230	16	.300	.389	.548	166	14	.307	.415	.596	257	12	.304	.371	.494
1994	NY-A	290	17	.300	.384	.545	140	8	.300	.384	.521	150	9	.300	.385	.567	171	9	.251	.347	.456	119	8	.370	.440	.672	114	9	.316	.400	.605	176	8	.290	.374	.506
1995	NY-A	399	18	.268	.360	.481	195	13	.313	.396	.590	204	5	.225	.325	.377	160	6	.275	.364	.456	239	12	.264	.357	.498	139	8	.281	.380	.511	260	10	.262	.349	.465
1996	Bos-A	397	24	.270	.383	.506	195	10	.287	.426	.497	202	14	.252	.336	.515	223	11	.265	.387	.480	174	13	.276	.377	.540	106	10	.302	.431	.632	291	14	.258	.364	.460
1997	Bos-A	260	13	.300	.394	.515	142	5	.310	.399	.479	118	8	.288	.389	.559	165	8	.315	.408	.533	95	5	.274	.369	.484	112	5	.286	.397	.500	148	8	.311	.392	.527
1997	NY-A	87	3	.287	.388	.483	41	1	.244	.304	.415	46	2	.326	.456	.543	0	0	—	—	—	87	3	.287	.388	.483	32	1	.375	.512	.594	55	2	.236	.306	.418
1998	Tor-A	341	22	.240	.353	.472	176	11	.244	.341	.466	165	11	.236	.365	.479	260	18	.262	.362	.515	81	4	.173	.327	.333	84	8	.298	.438	.619	257	14	.222	.323	.424
1998	Bos-A	156	7	.288	.388	.500	81	1	.259	.378	.395	75	6	.320	.400	.613	0	0	—	—	—	156	7	.288	.388	.500	33	2	.303	.400	.576	123	5	.285	.385	.480
1999	Bos-A	427	19	.281	.393	.466	216	8	.259	.389	.426	211	11	.303	.397	.507	227	9	.282	.399	.476	200	10	.280	.386	.455	126	8	.302	.413	.548	301	11	.272	.384	.432
2000	Bos-A	185	10	.222	.327	.411	96	5	.198	.287	.375	89	5	.247	.367	.449	184	10	.217	.324	.408	1	0	1.000	1.000	1.000	43	2	.256	.360	.419	142	8	.211	.317	.408
2000	Oak-A	97	4	.268	.363	.464	47	3	.234	.362	.468	50	1	.300	.364	.460	0	0	—	—	—	97	4	.268	.363	.464	40	4	.350	.435	.725	57	0	.211	.313	.281
TOTALS		4222	187	.270	.370	.458	2120	94	.279	.380	.467	2102	93	.260	.359	.449	2124	91	.259	.360	.439	2098	96	.280	.379	.477	1654	87	.288	.395	.501	2568	100	.258	.353	.430
■ Terry Steinbach BR/TR																																				
1986	Oak-A	15	2	.333	.375	.733	4	0	.250	.400	.250	11	2	.364	.364	.909	0	0	—	—	—	15	2	.333	.375	.733	6	2	.500	.500	1.500	9	0	.222	.300	.222
1987	Oak-A	391	16	.284	.349	.463	175	6	.234	.308	.360	216	10	.324	.384	.546	157	6	.280	.360	.459	234	10	.286	.342	.466	137	5	.292	.359	.504	254	11	.280	.344	.441
1988	Oak-A	351	9	.265	.334	.402	171	6	.287	.347	.439	180	3	.244	.322	.367	124	3	.218	.295	.347	227	6	.291	.355	.432	114	2	.342	.400	.421	237	7	.228	.302	.392
1989	Oak-A	454	7	.273	.319	.352	216	5	.292	.328	.384	238	2	.256	.312	.324	240	4	.313	.357	.404	214	3	.229	.277	.294	159	3	.258	.298	.352	295	4	.281	.330	.353
1990	Oak-A	379	9	.251	.291	.372	185	3	.249	.302	.324	194	6	.253	.281	.418	219	5	.242	.277	.370	160	4	.262	.310	.375	109	3	.284	.336	.440	270	6	.237	.273	.344
1991	Oak-A	456	6	.274	.312	.386	220	1	.277	.314	.377	236	5	.271	.310	.394	205	5	.293	.332	.439	251	1	.259	.296	.343	139	3	.266	.302	.410	317	3	.278	.316	.375
1992	Oak-A	438	12	.279	.345	.411	214	3	.229	.301	.313	224	9	.326	.386	.504	183	7	.273	.350	.426	255	5	.282	.342	.400	110	5	.300	.361	.482	328	7	.271	.340	.387
1993	Oak-A	389	10	.285	.333	.416	184	5	.326	.377	.489	205	5	.249	.292	.351	255	5	.294	.342	.424	134	5	.269	.315	.403	108	6	.296	.350	.500	281	4	.281	.326	.384
1994	Oak-A	369	11	.285	.327	.442	172	5	.302	.340	.471	197	6	.269	.315	.416	243	9	.280	.330	.453	126	2	.294	.321	.421	140	6	.343	.394	.564	229	5	.249	.285	.367
1995	Oak-A	406	15	.278	.322	.458	189	9	.270	.298	.476	217	6	.286	.342	.442	197	8	.254	.310	.452	209	7	.301	.333	.464	123	6	.301	.365	.504	283	9	.269	.302	.438
1996	Oak-A	514	35	.272	.342	.529	254	16	.276	.344	.512	260	19	.269	.339	.546	255	15	.275	.349	.518	259	20	.270	.334	.541	120	9	.292	.366	.558	394	26	.266	.334	.520
1997	Min-A	447	12	.248	.302	.394	224	6	.281	.345	.433	223	6	.215	.256	.354	226	8	.265	.329	.425	221	4	.231	.272	.362	117	4	.308	.374	.470	330	8	.227	.275	.367
1998	Min-A	422	14	.242	.310	.410	205	6	.259	.315	.410	217	8	.226	.305	.410	202	4	.243	.322	.386	220	10	.241	.298	.432	99	1	.222	.300	.364	323	13	.248	.313	.424
1999	Min-A	338	4	.284	.358	.391	163	3	.301	.376	.472	175	1	.269	.340	.314	121	3	.298	.370	.413	217	1	.276	.351	.378	55	0	.255	.379	.345	283	4	.290	.354	.399
TOTALS		5369	162	.271	.326	.420	2576	74	.275	.330	.420	2793	88	.267	.323	.420	2627	82	.273	.332	.428	2742	80	.268	.320	.412	1536	55	.292	.352	.464	3833	107	.262	.316	.402
■ Lee Stevens BL/TL																																				
1990	Cal-A	248	7	.214	.275	.339	133	4	.256	.313	.391	115	3	.165	.230	.278	0	0	—	—	—	248	7	.214	.275	.339	54	1	.204	.267	.278	194	6	.216	.277	.356
1991	Cal-A	58	0	.293	.354	.414	33	0	.333	.378	.424	25	0	.240	.321	.400	0	0	—	—	—	58	0	.293	.354	.414	17	0	.294	.294	.353	41	0	.293	.375	.439
1992	Cal-A	312	7	.221	.288	.349	169	2	.183	.223	.284	143	5	.266	.358	.427	170	5	.200	.269	.341	142	2	.246	.310	.359	44	0	.159	.245	.205	268	7	.231	.295	.373
1996	Tex-A	78	3	.231	.291	.449	39	2	.308	.386	.590	39	1	.154	.190	.308	0	0	—	—	—	78	3	.231	.291	.449	22	0	.136	.240	.136	56	3	.268	.311	.571
1997	Tex-A	426	21	.300	.336	.514	218	12	.321	.345	.550	208	9	.279	.326	.476	175	9	.280	.328	.503	251	12	.315	.341	.522	67	4	.284	.333	.522	359	17	.304	.336	.513
1998	Tex-A	344	20	.265	.324	.512	168	13	.339	.390	.667	176	7	.193	.263	.364	214	13	.238	.296	.467	130	7	.308	.371	.585	30	1	.167	.161	.267	314	19	.274	.339	.535
1999	Tex-A	517	24	.282	.344	.485	269	10	.275	.343	.450	248	14	.290	.344	.524	248	14	.294	.380	.536	269	10	.271	.308	.439	102	4	.304	.398	.461	415	20	.277	.330	.492
2000	Mon-N	449	22	.265	.337	.481	236	14	.258	.338	.496	213	8	.272	.336	.465	258	17	.260	.347	.527	191	5	.272	.324	.419	114	7	.281	.352	.544	335	15	.260	.332	.460
TOTALS		2432	104	.264	.323	.458	1265	57	.277	.332	.480	1167	47	.249	.312	.434	1065	58	.257	.330	.484	1367	46	.268	.317	.438	450	17	.251	.320	.411	1982	87	.266	.323	.469
■ Shannon Stewart BR/TR																																				
1995	Tor-A	38	0	.211	.318	.211	21	0	.238	.333	.238	17	0	.176	.300	.176	0	0	—	—	—	38	0	.211	.318	.211	13	0	.154	.267	.154	25	0	.240	.345	.240
1996	Tor-A	17	0	.176	.222	.235	3	0	.000	.000	.000	14	0	.214	.267	.286	0	0	—	—	—	17	0	.176	.222	.235	6	0	.333	.429	.500	11	0	.091	.091	.091
1997	Tor-A	168	0	.286	.368	.446	78	0	.269	.352	.385	90	0	.300	.381	.500	1	0	.000	.500	.000	167	0	.287	.366	.449	35	0	.343	.452	.543	133	0	.271	.344	.421
1998	Tor-A	516	12	.279	.377	.417	242	6	.289	.410	.430	274	6	.270	.346	.405	230	2	.252	.341	.330	286	10	.301	.405	.486	135	2	.296	.418	.393	381	10	.273	.362	.425
1999	Tor-A	608	11	.304	.371	.411	298	4	.289	.367	.379	310	7	.319	.375	.442	321	6	.308	.380	.411	287	5	.300	.361	.411	103	1	.369	.445	.456	505	10	.291	.355	.402
2000	Tor-A	583	21	.319	.363	.518	276	12	.286	.332	.518	307	9	.349	.391	.518	234	10	.338	.377	.568	349	11	.307	.354	.484	139	3	.309	.340	.468	444	18	.322	.371	.534
TOTALS		1930	44	.297	.368	.442	918	22	.284	.366	.430	1012	22	.309	.370	.454	786	18	.300	.368	.434	1144	26	.295	.368	.448	431	6	.318	.400	.439	1499	38	.292	.359	.444
■ Kurt Stillwell BB/TR																																				
1986	Cin-N	279	0	.229	.309	.258	151	0	.219	.298	.245	128	0	.242	.322	.273	102	0	.176	.282	.206	177	0	.260	.325	.288	86	0	.244	.363	.279	193	0	.223	.282	.249
1987	Cin-N	395	4	.258	.316	.375	150	3	.260	.323	.433	245	1	.257	.311	.339	212	3	.269	.323	.373	183	1	.246	.307	.377	97	0	.227	.286	.289	298	4	.268	.325	.403
1988	KC-A	459	10	.251	.322	.399	249	4	.257	.320	.398	210	6	.243	.325	.400	269	7	.264	.339	.435	190	3	.232	.298	.347	124	2	.226	.299	.323	335	8	.260	.331	.427
1989	KC-A	463	7	.261	.325	.380	217	2	.226	.293	.309	246	5	.293	.353	.443	245	3	.257	.320	.347	218	4	.266	.331	.417	121	1	.264	.336	.364	342	6	.260	.321	.386
1990	KC-A	506	3	.249	.304	.352	254	3	.268	.319	.413	252	0	.230	.289	.290	243	1	.296	.366	.420	263	2	.205	.244	.289	128	0	.211	.302	.313	378	3	.262	.305	.365
1991	KC-A	385	6	.265	.322	.361	183	1	.257	.324	.339	202	5	.272	.320	.381	243	4	.259	.312	.354	142	2	.275	.338	.373	109	1	.266	.304	.367	276	5	.264	.328	.359
1992	SD-N	379	2	.227	.274	.298	191	1	.220	.274	.277	188	1	.234	.275	.319	199	0	.241	.286	.302	180	2	.211	.262	.294	112	1	.250	.289	.321	267	1	.217	.268	.288
1993	SD-N	121	1	.215	.286	.273	56	1	.232	.328	.321	65	0	.200	.246	.231	107	1	.234	.299	.299	14	0	.071	.188	.071	21	0	.143	.280	.143	100	1	.230	.287	.300
1993	Cal-A	61	0	.262	.299	.361	28	0	.286	.323	.357	33	0	.242	.278	.364	0	0	—	—	—	61	0	.262	.299	.361	4	0	.250	.250	.250	57	0	.263	.302	.368
1996	Tex-A	77	1	.273	.364	.364	46	1	.261	.320	.391	31	0	.290	.421	.323	47	0	.298	.365	.362	30	1	.233	.361	.367	10	0	.200	.333	.400	67	1	.284	.368	.358
TOTALS		3125	34	.249	.311	.349	1525	16	.246	.309	.350	1600	18	.253	.313	.349	1667	19	.259	.323	.359	1458	15	.239	.297	.338	812	5	.238	.310	.320	2313	29	.253	.311	.360
■ Darryl Strawberry BL/TL																																				
1983	NY-N	420	26	.257	.336	.512	222	10	.248	.329	.455	198	16	.268	.344	.576	156	7	.212	.272	.404	264	19	.284	.372	.576	99	4	.232	.300	.414	321	22	.265	.347	.542

YEAR	TM/L	TOTAL					HOME					AWAY					1ST HALF					2ND HALF					LEFT					RIGHT				
		AB	HR	AVG	OBP	SLG	AB	HR	AVG	OBP	SLG	AB	HR	AVG	OBP	SLG	AB	HR	AVG	OBP	SLG	AB	HR	AVG	OBP	SLG	AB	HR	AVG	OBP	SLG	AB	HR	AVG	OBP	SLG
1984	NY-N	522	26	.251	.343	.467	242	8	.215	.309	.393	280	18	.282	.372	.532	234	9	.265	.359	.436	288	17	.240	.329	.493	167	6	.222	.278	.359	355	20	.265	.371	.518
1985	NY-N	393	29	.277	.389	.557	188	14	.298	.399	.585	205	15	.259	.381	.532	101	6	.208	.292	.426	292	23	.301	.420	.603	156	11	.256	.348	.506	237	18	.291	.414	.591
1986	NY-N	475	27	.259	.358	.507	211	11	.227	.324	.445	264	16	.284	.385	.557	212	10	.288	.393	.528	263	17	.236	.328	.490	187	5	.209	.296	.353	288	22	.292	.396	.608
1987	NY-N	532	39	.284	.398	.583	264	20	.322	.418	.629	268	19	.246	.380	.537	239	20	.268	.385	.598	293	19	.297	.409	.570	230	16	.248	.330	.517	302	23	.311	.446	.632
1988	NY-N	543	39	.269	.366	.545	253	21	.265	.375	.581	290	18	.272	.357	.514	257	19	.292	.399	.595	286	20	.248	.333	.500	216	20	.250	.318	.560	327	19	.281	.395	.535
1989	NY-N	476	29	.225	.312	.466	224	15	.272	.355	.549	252	14	.183	.274	.393	223	16	.224	.312	.493	253	13	.225	.313	.443	178	9	.219	.279	.438	298	20	.228	.331	.483
1990	NY-N	542	37	.277	.361	.518	268	24	.254	.332	.549	274	13	.299	.388	.489	243	17	.296	.397	.535	299	20	.261	.329	.505	217	9	.244	.300	.406	325	28	.298	.398	.594
1991	LA-N	505	28	.265	.361	.491	257	14	.284	.374	.510	248	14	.246	.347	.472	183	7	.224	.345	.399	322	21	.289	.370	.543	228	11	.276	.370	.478	277	17	.256	.353	.502
1992	LA-N	156	5	.237	.322	.385	72	3	.278	.366	.458	84	2	.202	.284	.321	100	5	.250	.336	.450	56	0	.214	.297	.268	66	2	.242	.324	.348	90	3	.233	.320	.411
1993	LA-N	100	5	.140	.267	.310	38	3	.158	.227	.421	62	2	.129	.289	.242	100	5	.140	.267	.310	0	0	—	—	—	21	0	.143	.367	.190	79	5	.139	.233	.342
1994	SF-N	92	4	.239	.363	.424	44	2	.182	.327	.341	48	2	.292	.397	.500	0	0	—	—	—	92	4	.239	.363	.424	29	1	.207	.324	.310	63	3	.254	.380	.476
1995	NY-A	87	3	.276	.364	.448	42	3	.286	.388	.571	45	0	.267	.340	.333	0	0	—	—	—	87	3	.276	.364	.448	12	0	.167	.167	.167	75	3	.293	.391	.493
1996	NY-A	202	11	.262	.359	.490	100	8	.330	.395	.630	102	3	.196	.325	.353	0	0	—	—	—	202	11	.262	.359	.490	53	4	.208	.323	.491	149	7	.282	.371	.490
1997	NY-A	29	0	.103	.188	.138	3	0	.000	.250	.000	26	0	.115	.179	.154	14	0	.000	.125	.000	15	0	.200	.250	.267	7	0	.000	.125	.000	22	0	.136	.208	.182
1998	NY-A	295	24	.247	.354	.542	141	14	.298	.405	.652	154	10	.201	.305	.442	158	11	.278	.390	.570	137	13	.212	.310	.511	36	2	.250	.357	.444	259	22	.247	.353	.556
1999	NY-A	49	3	.327	.500	.612	18	1	.333	.455	.611	31	2	.323	.523	.613	0	0	—	—	—	49	3	.327	.500	.612	6	1	.500	.750	1.167	43	2	.302	.444	.535
TOTALS		5418	335	.259	.357	.505	2587	171	.267	.361	.529	2831	164	.250	.353	.484	2220	132	.253	.356	.493	3198	203	.262	.357	.514	1908	101	.238	.319	.444	3510	234	.270	.376	.538
■ Jim Sundberg BR/TR																																				
1978	Tex-A	518	6	.278	.358	.380	263	0	.274	.351	.350	255	6	.282	.365	.412	238	2	.324	.389	.412	280	4	.239	.332	.354	144	1	.306	.375	.410	374	5	.267	.352	.369
1979	Tex-A	495	5	.275	.345	.368	249	3	.297	.371	.410	246	2	.252	.319	.325	238	2	.218	.285	.307	257	3	.327	.401	.424	155	2	.245	.304	.348	340	3	.288	.364	.376
1980	Tex-A	505	10	.273	.353	.384	248	5	.262	.347	.379	257	5	.284	.359	.389	230	5	.243	.320	.361	275	5	.298	.380	.404	155	4	.316	.402	.477	350	6	.254	.331	.343
1981	Tex-A	339	3	.277	.369	.366	168	1	.232	.330	.298	171	2	.322	.408	.433	176	3	.244	.335	.352	163	0	.313	.405	.380	110	2	.264	.377	.364	229	1	.284	.365	.367
1982	Tex-A	470	10	.251	.322	.383	217	3	.230	.324	.350	253	7	.269	.321	.411	217	4	.267	.343	.369	253	6	.237	.305	.395	105	2	.295	.383	.448	365	8	.238	.304	.364
1983	Tex-A	378	2	.201	.272	.254	195	0	.231	.298	.287	183	2	.169	.244	.219	207	1	.208	.260	.261	171	1	.193	.285	.246	124	0	.218	.300	.274	254	2	.193	.257	.244
1984	Mil-A	348	7	.261	.332	.399	174	4	.236	.302	.362	174	3	.287	.360	.437	204	3	.289	.345	.417	144	4	.222	.313	.375	121	2	.298	.386	.455	227	5	.242	.301	.370
1985	KC-A	367	10	.245	.308	.381	188	2	.250	.294	.340	179	8	.240	.322	.425	217	8	.249	.296	.429	150	2	.240	.324	.313	115	7	.217	.268	.452	252	3	.258	.325	.349
1986	KC-A	429	12	.212	.303	.322	209	5	.196	.278	.287	220	7	.227	.325	.355	213	2	.216	.287	.277	216	10	.208	.317	.366	141	6	.191	.272	.348	288	6	.222	.317	.309
1987	Chi-N	139	4	.201	.306	.302	68	2	.206	.316	.309	71	2	.197	.296	.296	56	3	.232	.338	.393	83	1	.181	.284	.241	23	1	.261	.414	.435	116	3	.190	.282	.276
1988	Chi-N	54	2	.241	.333	.370	20	1	.150	.250	.300	34	1	.294	.385	.412	37	1	.270	.378	.378	17	1	.176	.222	.353	4	1	.250	.500	1.000	50	1	.240	.316	.320
1988	Tex-A	91	4	.286	.323	.462	43	1	.209	.244	.302	48	3	.354	.392	.604	0	0	—	—	—	91	4	.286	.323	.462	35	2	.314	.351	.514	56	2	.268	.305	.429
1989	Tex-A	147	2	.197	.304	.299	65	2	.108	.244	.231	82	0	.268	.355	.354	93	2	.237	.336	.376	54	0	.130	.250	.167	80	1	.262	.366	.412	67	1	.119	.231	.164
TOTALS		4280	77	.251	.329	.359	2107	29	.241	.320	.338	2173	48	.261	.338	.380	2126	36	.251	.321	.357	2154	41	.251	.337	.362	1312	31	.263	.345	.403	2968	46	.246	.322	.340
■ B.J. Surhoff BL/TR																																				
1987	Mil-A	395	7	.299	.350	.423	194	5	.314	.355	.464	201	2	.284	.345	.383	165	5	.297	.339	.461	230	2	.300	.358	.396	85	2	.318	.379	.424	310	5	.294	.342	.423
1988	Mil-A	493	5	.245	.292	.318	244	2	.225	.294	.291	249	3	.265	.291	.345	228	2	.259	.303	.333	265	3	.234	.283	.306	115	2	.191	.256	.270	378	3	.262	.304	.333
1989	Mil-A	436	5	.248	.287	.339	213	3	.239	.302	.333	223	2	.256	.272	.345	232	4	.237	.274	.328	204	1	.260	.301	.353	84	2	.310	.314	.452	352	3	.233	.281	.313
1990	Mil-A	474	6	.276	.331	.376	235	4	.306	.364	.417	239	2	.247	.298	.335	222	5	.284	.325	.428	252	1	.270	.336	.329	104	2	.317	.353	.433	370	4	.265	.324	.359
1991	Mil-A	505	5	.289	.319	.372	236	3	.267	.303	.364	269	2	.309	.332	.379	206	0	.228	.270	.252	299	5	.331	.354	.455	102	0	.255	.291	.294	403	5	.298	.326	.392
1992	Mil-A	480	4	.252	.314	.321	243	3	.280	.349	.350	237	1	.224	.278	.291	226	3	.239	.278	.314	254	1	.264	.345	.327	126	2	.270	.329	.357	354	2	.246	.309	.308
1993	Mil-A	552	7	.274	.318	.391	263	4	.289	.325	.422	289	3	.260	.311	.363	241	0	.220	.276	.270	311	7	.315	.350	.486	186	3	.274	.328	.403	366	4	.273	.312	.385
1994	Mil-A	134	5	.261	.336	.485	79	2	.253	.344	.443	55	3	.273	.322	.545	122	5	.270	.350	.508	12	0	.167	.167	.250	34	2	.324	.400	.618	100	3	.240	.313	.440
1995	Mil-A	415	13	.320	.378	.492	205	7	.341	.409	.541	210	6	.300	.347	.443	112	0	.348	.403	.446	303	13	.310	.369	.508	128	3	.367	.409	.531	287	10	.300	.365	.474
1996	Bal-A	537	21	.292	.352	.482	257	12	.288	.344	.498	280	9	.296	.359	.468	250	12	.276	.341	.496	287	9	.307	.362	.470	162	3	.290	.348	.420	375	18	.293	.354	.509
1997	Bal-A	528	18	.284	.345	.458	238	10	.269	.345	.454	290	8	.297	.345	.462	250	11	.304	.379	.516	278	7	.266	.313	.406	160	3	.287	.335	.400	368	15	.283	.348	.484
1998	Bal-A	573	22	.279	.332	.457	278	9	.273	.331	.432	295	13	.285	.332	.481	298	12	.282	.327	.477	275	10	.276	.337	.436	177	7	.254	.302	.418	396	15	.290	.345	.475
1999	Bal-A	673	28	.308	.347	.492	322	9	.317	.363	.457	351	19	.299	.332	.524	324	18	.340	.364	.568	349	10	.278	.332	.421	159	7	.327	.341	.516	514	21	.302	.349	.484
2000	Bal-A	411	13	.292	.341	.453	189	6	.280	.337	.423	222	7	.302	.345	.477	304	11	.276	.334	.447	107	2	.336	.360	.467	139	6	.295	.344	.468	272	7	.290	.339	.445
2000	Atl-N	128	1	.289	.352	.414	60	1	.300	.364	.417	68	0	.279	.342	.412	0	0	—	—	—	128	1	.289	.352	.414	10	0	.300	.417	.400	118	1	.288	.346	.415
TOTALS		6734	160	.281	.332	.417	3256	80	.283	.341	.420	3478	80	.279	.323	.415	3180	88	.275	.324	.421	3554	72	.287	.338	.414	1771	44	.289	.335	.421	4963	116	.279	.331	.416
■ Mike Sweeney BR/TR																																				
1995	KC-A	4	0	.250	.250	.250	2	0	.000	.000	.000	2	0	.500	.500	.500	0	0	—	—	—	4	0	.250	.250	.250	3	0	.333	.333	.333	1	0	.000	.000	.000
1996	KC-A	165	4	.279	.358	.412	68	1	.265	.338	.353	97	3	.289	.372	.454	0	0	—	—	—	165	4	.279	.358	.412	49	1	.245	.362	.347	116	3	.293	.356	.440
1997	KC-A	240	7	.242	.306	.363	116	5	.241	.313	.405	124	2	.242	.299	.323	70	4	.243	.329	.443	170	3	.241	.296	.329	74	1	.189	.228	.257	166	6	.265	.339	.410
1998	KC-A	282	8	.259	.320	.408	146	6	.260	.314	.445	136	2	.257	.327	.368	143	4	.245	.299	.336	139	4	.273	.342	.482	63	3	.302	.397	.540	219	5	.247	.297	.370
1999	KC-A	575	22	.322	.387	.520	289	10	.336	.413	.529	286	12	.308	.360	.510	253	9	.324	.391	.506	322	13	.320	.384	.531	100	4	.350	.440	.560	475	18	.316	.376	.512
2000	KC-A	618	29	.333	.407	.523	309	17	.307	.386	.515	309	12	.359	.429	.531	301	14	.352	.412	.571	317	15	.315	.403	.476	131	6	.374	.443	.580	487	23	.322	.398	.507
TOTALS		1884	70	.302	.371	.474	930	39	.297	.371	.482	954	31	.307	.372	.466	767	31	.313	.377	.494	1117	39	.295	.367	.460	420	15	.310	.389	.483	1464	55	.300	.366	.471
■ Pat Tabler BR/TR																																				
1981	Chi-N	101	1	.188	.281	.267	43	1	.233	.327	.395	58	0	.155	.246	.172	0	0	—	—	—	101	1	.188	.281	.267	26	0	.154	.313	.192	75	1	.200	.268	.293
1982	Chi-N	85	1	.235	.287	.365	40	0	.275	.302	.425	45	1	.200	.275	.311	0	0	—	—	—	85	1	.235	.287	.365	30	0	.233	.250	.267	55	1	.236	.306	.418
1983	Cle-A	430	6	.291	.370	.409	217	3	.281	.373	.392	213	3	.300	.367	.427	134	2	.321	.403	.455	296	4	.277	.355	.389	144	3	.299	.387	.444	286	3	.287	.361	.392
1984	Cle-A	473	10	.290	.354	.410	223	5	.336	.405	.466	250	5	.248	.308	.360	199	1	.296	.376	.357	274	9	.285	.338	.449	159	3	.283	.370	.403	314	7	.293	.346	.414
1985	Cle-A	404	5	.275	.321	.371	218	5	.326	.366	.445	186	0	.215	.269	.285	243	2	.280	.323	.358	161	3	.267	.318	.391	154	3	.312	.353	.416	250	2	.252	.301	.344
1986	Cle-A	473	6	.326	.368	.433	227	5	.348	.389	.467	246	1	.305	.347	.402	198	3	.288	.333	.419	275	3	.353	.392	.444	150	2	.333	.387	.447	323	4	.322	.359	.427
1987	Cle-A	553	11	.307	.369	.439	285	5	.333	.394	.481	268	6	.280	.342	.396	285	7	.309	.361	.463	268	4	.306	.377	.414	172	6	.366	.412	.564	381	5	.281	.350	.383
1988	Cle-A	143	1	.224	.333	.294	67	0	.239	.354	.284	76	1	.211	.315	.303	143	1	.224	.333	.294	0	0	—	—	—	41	1	.220	.319	.341	102	0	.225	.339	.275
1988	KC-A	301	1	.309	.358	.389	147	0	.299	.360	.401	154	1	.318	.355	.377	79	0	.241	.271	.304	222	1	.333	.388	.419	98	0	.337	.402	.429	203	1	.296	.335	.369
1989	KC-A	390	2	.259	.325	.308	181	2	.271	.327	.343	209	0	.249	.323	.278	208	0	.269	.329	.293	182	2	.247	.320	.324	160	2	.350	.403	.412	230	0	.196	.271	.235
1990	KC-A	195	1	.272	.338	.359	98	0	.245	.327	.327	97	1	.299	.349	.392	91	0	.231	.314	.297	104	1	.308	.359	.413	81	1	.333	.396	.457	114	0	.228	.297	.289
1990	NY-N	43	1	.279	.340	.419	16	1	.250	.333	.438	27	0	.296	.345	.407	0	0	—	—	—	43	1	.279	.340	.419	24	0	.333	.385	.417	19	1	.211	.286	.421
1991	Tor-A	185	1	.216	.318	.270	93	1	.215	.286	.290	92	0	.217	.348	.250	103	1	.214	.336	.272	82	0	.220	.295	.268	147	0	.190	.275	.238	38	1	.316	.469	.395
1992	Tor-A	135	0	.252	.306	.289	51	0	.196	.293	.235	84	0	.286	.315	.321	64	0	.219	.271	.219	71	0	.282	.338	.352	67	0	.284	.355	.313	68	0	.221	.254	.265
TOTALS		3911	47	.282	.345	.379	1906	28	.299	.363	.410	2005	19	.265	.328	.350	1747	17	.274	.341	.361	2164	30	.287	.349	.394	1453	21	.303	.368	.409	2458	26	.269	.331	.361
■ Danny Tartabull BR/TR																																				
1984	Sea-A	20	2	.300	.375	.650	7	1	.286	.444	.714	13	1	.308	.333	.615	0	0	—	—	—	20	2	.300	.375	.650	7	0	.000	.000	.000	13	2	.462	.529	1.000
1985	Sea-A	61	1	.328	.406	.525	23	0	.348	.444	.478	38	1	.316	.381	.553	0	0	—	—	—	61	1	.328	.406	.525	21	1	.476	.577	.810	40	0	.250	.302	.375
1986	Sea-A	511	25	.270	.347	.489	268	13	.272	.338	.500	243	12	.267	.357	.477	214	11	.276	.357	.509	297	14	.266	.340	.475	125	3	.304	.385	.464	386	22	.259	.335	.497
1987	KC-A	582	34	.309	.390	.541	282	15	.291	.381	.511	300	19	.327	.398	.570	258	11	.318	.383	.481	324	23	.302	.395	.590	149	7	.289	.389	.503	433	27	.316	.390	.554
1988	KC-A	507	26	.274	.369	.515	249	15	.289	.397	.562	258	11	.260	.341	.469	239	13	.285	.391	.536	268	13	.265	.350	.496	149	8	.289	.404	.537	358	18	.268	.354	.506
1989	KC-A	441	18	.268	.369	.440	214	9	.280	.388	.463	227	9	.256	.350	.419	214	9	.262	.363	.430	227	9	.273	.375	.449	125	8	.312	.420	.568	316	10	.250	.348	.389
1990	KC-A	313	15	.268	.341	.473	142	5	.232	.291	.366	171	10	.298	.381	.561	136	8	.250	.309	.471	177	7	.282	.365	.475	106	5	.321	.426	.509	207	10	.242	.291	.454
1991	KC-A	484	31	.316	.397	.593	226	13	.314	.395	.571	258	18	.318	.398	.612	248	14	.319	.362	.560	236	17	.314	.429	.627	142	8	.296	.408	.542	342	23	.325	.392	.614
1992	NY-A	421	25	.266	.409	.489	204	11	.289	.428	.500	217	14	.244	.390	.479	186	6	.253	.412	.392	235	19	.277	.406	.566	119	11	.286	.494	.613	302	14	.258	.368	.440
1993	NY-A	513	31	.250	.363	.503	229	11	.210	.343	.410	284	20	.282	.381	.577	205	11	.224	.339	.463	308	20	.266	.380	.529	175	7	.200	.341	.394	338	24	.275	.375	.559
1994	NY-A	399	19	.256	.360	.464	199	10	.246	.326	.472	200	9	.265	.391	.455	273	14	.245	.346	.469	126	5	.278	.389	.452	121	9	.339	.490	.645	278	10	.219	.294	.385
1995	NY-A	192	6	.224	.335	.380	70	2	.243	.313	.400	122	4	.213	.347	.369	156	4	.244	.348	.391	36	2	.139	.279	.333	75	4	.240	.398	.467	117	2	.214	.288	.325
1995	Oak-A	88	2	.261	.337	.375	43	1	.326	.383	.465	45	1	.200	.294	.289	0	0	—	—	—	88	2	.261	.337	.375	24	2	.292	.370	.583	64	0	.250	.324	.297
1996	Chi-A	472	27	.254	.340	.487	225	11	.244	.309	.436	247	16	.263	.366	.534	233	9	.227	.320	.416	239	18	.280	.360	.556	133	4	.271	.398	.429	339	23	.248	.316	.510
1997	Phi-N	7	0	.000	.364	.000	0	0	—	—	—	7	0	.000	.364	.000	7	0	.000	.364	.000	0	0	—	—	—	5	0	.000	.286	.000	2	0	.000	.500	.000
TOTALS		5011	262	.273	.368	.496	2381	117	.270	.363	.483	2630	145	.275	.373	.508	2369	110	.266	.359	.469	2642	152	.279	.377	.520	1476	77	.285	.412	.514	3535	185	.268	.349	.489
■ Miguel Tejada BR/TR																																				
1997	Oak-A	99	2	.202	.240	.333	50	1	.120	.154	.240	49	1	.286	.327	.429	0	0	—	—	—	99	2	.202	.240	.333	28	1	.250	.276	.393	71	1	.183	.227	.310
1998	Oak-A	365	11	.233	.298	.384	181	5	.204	.263	.331	184	6	.261	.332	.435	108	1	.250	.317	.343	257	10	.226	.290	.401	100	5	.210	.282	.400	265	6	.242	.304	.377
1999	Oak-A	593	21	.251	.325	.427	290	12	.272	.335	.466	303	9	.231	.315	.389	282	8	.266	.331	.433	311	13	.238	.319	.421	140	4	.271	.364	.443	453	17	.245	.312	.422

YEAR	TM/L	TOTAL					HOME					AWAY					1ST HALF					2ND HALF					LEFT					RIGHT				
		AB	HR	AVG	OBP	SLG	AB	HR	AVG	OBP	SLG	AB	HR	AVG	OBP	SLG	AB	HR	AVG	OBP	SLG	AB	HR	AVG	OBP	SLG	AB	HR	AVG	OBP	SLG	AB	HR	AVG	OBP	SLG
2000	Oak-A	607	30	.275	.349	.479	297	16	.269	.342	.468	310	14	.281	.355	.490	301	12	.256	.317	.432	306	18	.294	.379	.526	168	10	.220	.313	.446	439	20	.296	.363	.492
TOTALS		1664	64	.253	.323	.431	818	34	.247	.312	.423	846	30	.259	.334	.439	691	21	.259	.323	.418	973	43	.249	.323	.440	436	20	.236	.320	.431	1228	44	.259	.324	.431
■ **Garry Templeton**	BB/TR																																			
1978	StL-N	647	2	.280	.303	.377	309	1	.288	.305	.405	338	1	.272	.301	.352	317	1	.240	.262	.315	330	1	.318	.342	.436	260	2	.288	.307	.404	387	0	.274	.300	.359
1979	StL-N	672	9	.314	.331	.458	310	2	.329	.348	.468	362	7	.301	.317	.450	289	1	.325	.349	.426	383	8	.305	.318	.483	272	4	.346	.355	.511	400	5	.292	.316	.423
1980	StL-N	504	4	.319	.342	.417	251	1	.355	.380	.462	253	3	.285	.304	.372	317	2	.322	.351	.407	187	2	.316	.326	.433	184	2	.321	.347	.418	320	2	.319	.339	.416
1981	StL-N	333	1	.288	.315	.393	162	1	.290	.310	.414	171	0	.287	.320	.374	200	1	.265	.302	.395	133	0	.323	.336	.391	106	1	.264	.295	.368	227	0	.300	.325	.405
1982	SD-N	563	6	.247	.279	.352	280	2	.211	.245	.275	283	4	.283	.312	.428	294	3	.262	.290	.381	269	3	.230	.267	.320	178	1	.253	.272	.343	385	5	.244	.282	.356
1983	SD-N	460	3	.263	.294	.335	202	1	.248	.292	.302	258	2	.275	.296	.360	151	2	.252	.283	.351	309	1	.269	.299	.327	118	1	.288	.328	.390	342	2	.254	.282	.316
1984	SD-N	493	2	.258	.312	.320	254	2	.240	.297	.307	239	0	.276	.328	.335	259	1	.270	.314	.336	234	1	.244	.310	.303	144	0	.250	.285	.313	349	2	.261	.323	.324
1985	SD-N	546	6	.282	.332	.377	267	4	.281	.319	.393	279	2	.283	.343	.362	256	3	.293	.332	.398	290	3	.272	.331	.359	177	1	.254	.291	.316	369	5	.295	.351	.407
1986	SD-N	510	2	.247	.296	.308	269	1	.230	.284	.294	241	1	.266	.309	.324	255	2	.231	.285	.278	255	0	.263	.307	.337	175	2	.257	.323	.343	335	0	.242	.281	.290
1987	SD-N	510	5	.222	.281	.296	250	2	.204	.267	.288	260	3	.238	.293	.304	232	1	.203	.272	.263	278	4	.237	.288	.324	189	2	.233	.284	.307	321	3	.215	.278	.290
1988	SD-N	362	3	.249	.286	.354	186	3	.253	.307	.398	176	0	.244	.262	.307	166	0	.205	.254	.283	196	3	.286	.314	.413	76	0	.237	.256	.289	286	3	.252	.293	.371
1989	SD-N	506	6	.255	.286	.354	255	5	.259	.292	.384	251	1	.251	.279	.323	248	2	.254	.284	.347	258	4	.256	.288	.360	145	1	.317	.353	.421	361	5	.230	.259	.327
1990	SD-N	505	9	.248	.280	.362	255	6	.247	.278	.380	250	3	.248	.281	.344	226	5	.261	.290	.376	279	4	.237	.271	.351	189	4	.254	.286	.370	316	5	.244	.275	.358
1991	SD-N	57	1	.193	.203	.298	31	1	.194	.219	.323	26	0	.192	.185	.269	57	1	.193	.203	.298	0	0	—	—	—	13	1	.385	.385	.769	44	0	.136	.152	.159
1991	NY-N	219	2	.228	.257	.306	107	1	.271	.322	.374	112	1	.188	.191	.241	65	1	.277	.299	.369	154	1	.208	.239	.279	83	0	.337	.378	.410	136	2	.162	.179	.243
TOTALS		6887	61	.266	.301	.362	3388	33	.264	.302	.367	3499	28	.268	.301	.356	3332	26	.263	.298	.353	3555	35	.269	.304	.370	2309	22	.282	.313	.382	4578	39	.259	.295	.351
■ **Mickey Tettleton**	BB/TR																																			
1984	Oak-A	76	1	.263	.352	.355	47	1	.298	.404	.447	29	0	.207	.258	.207	0	0	—	—	—	76	1	.263	.352	.355	34	1	.206	.300	.324	42	0	.310	.396	.381
1985	Oak-A	211	3	.251	.344	.351	110	1	.245	.336	.309	101	2	.257	.353	.396	62	1	.274	.375	.387	149	2	.242	.331	.336	61	1	.213	.304	.344	150	2	.267	.360	.353
1986	Oak-A	211	10	.204	.325	.389	106	4	.198	.326	.349	105	6	.210	.325	.429	83	2	.205	.292	.325	128	8	.203	.346	.430	84	6	.262	.370	.524	127	4	.165	.297	.299
1987	Oak-A	211	8	.194	.292	.322	105	5	.219	.311	.381	106	3	.170	.273	.264	111	2	.171	.258	.252	100	6	.220	.328	.400	84	2	.214	.323	.310	127	6	.181	.271	.331
1988	Bal-A	283	11	.261	.330	.424	133	7	.278	.358	.474	150	4	.247	.305	.380	103	5	.243	.292	.427	180	6	.272	.351	.422	147	9	.252	.313	.463	136	2	.272	.349	.382
1989	Bal-A	411	26	.258	.369	.509	203	15	.310	.401	.611	208	11	.207	.339	.409	252	18	.254	.359	.532	159	8	.264	.384	.472	139	10	.245	.342	.532	272	16	.265	.382	.496
1990	Bal-A	444	15	.223	.376	.381	215	8	.237	.394	.419	229	7	.210	.358	.345	222	11	.252	.411	.464	222	4	.194	.338	.297	128	5	.234	.351	.414	316	10	.218	.385	.367
1991	Det-A	501	31	.263	.387	.491	239	15	.264	.402	.498	262	16	.263	.371	.485	217	14	.272	.397	.507	284	17	.257	.378	.479	109	9	.248	.349	.532	392	22	.268	.397	.480
1992	Det-A	525	32	.238	.379	.469	255	18	.271	.408	.545	270	14	.207	.352	.396	268	18	.250	.359	.500	257	14	.226	.398	.436	135	8	.274	.377	.511	390	24	.226	.380	.454
1993	Det-A	522	32	.245	.372	.492	256	16	.230	.360	.480	266	16	.259	.384	.504	254	20	.244	.350	.535	268	12	.246	.392	.451	123	7	.260	.408	.520	399	25	.241	.360	.484
1994	Det-A	339	17	.248	.419	.463	167	9	.263	.431	.491	172	8	.233	.407	.436	223	14	.269	.435	.525	116	3	.207	.388	.345	81	3	.235	.376	.407	258	14	.252	.431	.481
1995	Tex-A	429	32	.238	.396	.510	228	22	.263	.414	.610	201	10	.209	.374	.398	199	12	.216	.363	.427	230	20	.257	.423	.583	142	8	.225	.358	.444	287	24	.244	.413	.544
1996	Tex-A	491	24	.246	.366	.450	243	14	.255	.391	.477	248	10	.238	.340	.423	259	13	.255	.380	.467	232	11	.237	.351	.431	155	6	.245	.370	.452	336	18	.247	.365	.449
1997	Tex-A	44	3	.091	.167	.318	26	2	.115	.207	.385	18	1	.056	.105	.222	40	3	.100	.163	.350	4	0	.000	.200	.000	15	1	.067	.067	.267	29	2	.103	.212	.345
TOTALS		4698	245	.241	.369	.449	2333	137	.255	.385	.487	2365	108	.227	.352	.411	2293	133	.244	.366	.470	2405	112	.238	.372	.429	1437	76	.241	.352	.458	3261	169	.241	.376	.445
■ **Frank Thomas**	BR/TR																																			
1990	Chi-A	191	7	.330	.454	.529	73	2	.342	.510	.534	118	5	.322	.413	.525	0	0	—	—	—	191	7	.330	.454	.529	71	5	.408	.538	.732	120	2	.283	.401	.408
1991	Chi-A	559	32	.318	.453	.553	267	24	.371	.509	.708	292	8	.271	.399	.411	258	13	.302	.441	.516	301	19	.332	.463	.585	170	11	.376	.500	.624	389	21	.293	.432	.522
1992	Chi-A	573	24	.323	.439	.536	292	10	.305	.430	.500	281	14	.342	.448	.573	257	11	.296	.435	.506	316	13	.345	.442	.560	140	8	.357	.456	.650	433	16	.312	.433	.499
1993	Chi-A	549	41	.317	.426	.607	279	26	.326	.432	.681	270	15	.307	.420	.530	274	16	.307	.408	.551	275	25	.327	.443	.662	151	14	.311	.419	.649	398	27	.319	.429	.590
1994	Chi-A	399	38	.353	.487	.729	179	22	.385	.519	.832	220	16	.327	.461	.645	267	29	.371	.503	.779	132	9	.318	.457	.629	104	12	.385	.504	.798	295	26	.342	.482	.705
1995	Chi-A	493	40	.308	.454	.606	247	15	.296	.444	.530	246	25	.321	.465	.683	199	18	.312	.481	.643	294	22	.306	.436	.582	126	16	.389	.521	.849	367	24	.281	.431	.523
1996	Chi-A	527	40	.349	.459	.626	251	16	.335	.449	.570	276	24	.362	.468	.678	305	22	.344	.455	.620	222	18	.356	.465	.635	119	13	.403	.544	.798	408	27	.333	.432	.576
1997	Chi-A	530	35	.347	.456	.611	251	16	.319	.434	.558	279	19	.373	.476	.659	236	16	.377	.495	.648	294	19	.323	.422	.582	106	12	.358	.435	.792	424	23	.344	.461	.566
1998	Chi-A	585	29	.265	.381	.480	284	15	.289	.410	.521	301	14	.243	.353	.442	301	14	.269	.377	.462	284	15	.261	.384	.500	137	5	.226	.327	.365	448	24	.277	.396	.516
1999	Chi-A	486	15	.305	.414	.471	252	9	.310	.410	.504	234	6	.299	.417	.436	278	11	.327	.425	.525	208	4	.274	.398	.399	75	3	.253	.387	.453	411	12	.314	.419	.474
2000	Chi-A	582	43	.328	.436	.625	291	30	.347	.446	.753	291	13	.309	.425	.498	281	22	.331	.436	.630	301	21	.326	.435	.621	91	10	.407	.549	.824	491	33	.314	.412	.589
TOTALS		5474	344	.321	.440	.579	2666	185	.327	.448	.608	2808	159	.315	.431	.551	2656	172	.323	.444	.585	2818	172	.318	.435	.573	1290	109	.350	.470	.678	4184	235	.311	.430	.548
■ **Gorman Thomas**	BR/TR																																			
1978	Mil-A	452	32	.246	.351	.515	239	19	.268	.348	.577	213	13	.221	.354	.446	211	17	.242	.357	.536	241	15	.249	.345	.498	108	10	.296	.397	.648	344	22	.230	.337	.474
1979	Mil-A	557	45	.244	.356	.539	275	22	.251	.346	.549	282	23	.238	.365	.528	254	19	.252	.383	.539	303	26	.238	.332	.538	132	12	.265	.405	.598	425	33	.238	.340	.520
1980	Mil-A	628	38	.239	.303	.471	308	18	.247	.315	.468	320	20	.231	.291	.475	273	15	.216	.289	.440	355	23	.256	.313	.496	183	14	.251	.324	.530	445	24	.234	.294	.447
1981	Mil-A	363	21	.259	.348	.493	154	8	.208	.313	.409	209	13	.297	.373	.555	168	15	.262	.364	.571	195	6	.256	.333	.426	100	3	.240	.394	.440	263	18	.266	.328	.513
1982	Mil-A	567	39	.245	.343	.506	287	19	.233	.333	.488	280	20	.257	.354	.525	247	19	.259	.349	.538	320	20	.234	.340	.481	198	15	.258	.366	.540	369	24	.238	.331	.488
1983	Mil-A	164	5	.183	.284	.323	74	2	.216	.318	.338	90	3	.156	.255	.311	164	5	.183	.284	.323	0	0	—	—	—	60	1	.233	.314	.333	104	4	.154	.267	.317
1983	Cle-A	371	17	.221	.322	.404	190	8	.216	.320	.384	181	9	.227	.324	.425	81	3	.210	.290	.370	290	14	.224	.330	.414	108	3	.194	.302	.333	263	14	.232	.330	.433
1984	Sea-A	108	1	.157	.322	.213	44	0	.227	.315	.273	64	1	.109	.326	.172	108	1	.157	.322	.213	0	0	—	—	—	27	0	.074	.375	.111	81	1	.185	.301	.247
1985	Sea-A	484	32	.215	.330	.450	251	16	.207	.337	.434	233	16	.223	.323	.468	164	12	.238	.373	.482	320	20	.203	.307	.434	152	13	.211	.326	.493	332	19	.217	.332	.431
1986	Sea-A	170	10	.194	.308	.394	76	5	.132	.214	.342	94	5	.245	.377	.436	170	10	.194	.308	.394	0	0	—	—	—	43	2	.163	.333	.326	127	8	.205	.299	.417
1986	Mil-A	145	6	.179	.324	.345	62	2	.145	.329	.274	83	4	.205	.320	.398	0	0	—	—	—	145	6	.179	.324	.345	54	3	.185	.353	.389	91	3	.176	.306	.319
TOTALS		4009	246	.230	.331	.463	1960	119	.228	.326	.458	2049	127	.232	.337	.468	1840	116	.227	.336	.463	2169	130	.232	.327	.463	1165	76	.235	.354	.486	2844	170	.228	.322	.454
■ **Jim Thome**	BL/TR																																			
1991	Cle-A	98	1	.255	.298	.367	53	0	.245	.310	.358	45	1	.267	.283	.378	0	0	—	—	—	98	1	.255	.298	.367	20	0	.050	.050	.050	78	1	.308	.357	.449
1992	Cle-A	117	2	.205	.275	.299	81	1	.222	.297	.309	36	1	.167	.225	.278	21	1	.190	.227	.381	96	1	.208	.284	.281	14	0	.214	.214	.214	103	2	.204	.282	.311
1993	Cle-A	154	7	.266	.385	.474	81	5	.247	.350	.494	73	2	.288	.424	.452	0	0	—	—	—	154	7	.266	.385	.474	43	2	.302	.456	.558	111	5	.252	.356	.441
1994	Cle-A	321	20	.268	.359	.523	149	10	.295	.384	.584	172	10	.244	.337	.471	209	10	.258	.351	.483	112	10	.286	.372	.598	84	2	.167	.247	.298	237	18	.304	.396	.603
1995	Cle-A	452	25	.314	.438	.558	226	13	.305	.431	.566	226	12	.323	.445	.549	185	16	.324	.439	.638	267	9	.307	.437	.502	109	3	.275	.380	.422	343	22	.327	.456	.601
1996	Cle-A	505	38	.311	.450	.612	246	18	.293	.451	.581	259	20	.328	.448	.641	236	15	.305	.457	.602	269	23	.316	.443	.621	160	7	.250	.355	.431	345	31	.339	.489	.696
1997	Cle-A	496	40	.286	.423	.579	238	17	.286	.429	.550	258	23	.287	.416	.605	246	22	.293	.435	.610	250	18	.280	.411	.548	131	4	.275	.355	.412	365	36	.290	.445	.638
1998	Cle-A	440	30	.293	.413	.584	200	18	.335	.456	.705	240	12	.258	.377	.483	286	21	.332	.436	.661	154	9	.221	.372	.442	142	7	.289	.386	.500	298	23	.295	.426	.624
1999	Cle-A	494	33	.277	.426	.540	238	19	.282	.434	.588	256	14	.273	.418	.496	219	11	.265	.425	.493	275	22	.287	.427	.578	134	6	.239	.363	.425	360	27	.292	.448	.583
2000	Cle-A	557	37	.269	.398	.531	275	21	.309	.434	.600	282	16	.230	.362	.465	272	23	.265	.368	.585	285	14	.274	.424	.481	152	6	.250	.352	.408	405	31	.277	.413	.578
TOTALS		3634	233	.284	.410	.545	1787	122	.293	.421	.570	1847	111	.276	.398	.520	1674	119	.291	.415	.582	1960	114	.279	.406	.513	989	37	.251	.352	.417	2645	196	.297	.430	.593
■ **Jason Thompson**	BL/TL																																			
1978	Det-A	589	26	.287	.364	.472	286	13	.322	.407	.517	303	13	.254	.321	.429	298	17	.302	.360	.527	291	9	.271	.368	.416	300	10	.277	.337	.420	289	16	.298	.389	.526
1979	Det-A	492	20	.246	.338	.404	241	13	.253	.332	.461	251	7	.239	.344	.351	237	8	.270	.379	.405	255	12	.224	.297	.404	152	3	.224	.320	.309	340	17	.256	.346	.447
1980	Det-A	126	4	.214	.289	.349	51	2	.216	.263	.353	75	2	.213	.306	.347	126	4	.214	.289	.349	0	0	—	—	—	44	0	.159	.213	.205	82	4	.244	.326	.427
1980	Cal-A	312	17	.317	.439	.526	151	9	.344	.455	.596	161	8	.292	.424	.460	86	2	.302	.430	.430	226	15	.323	.442	.562	55	2	.218	.286	.382	257	15	.339	.469	.556
1981	Pit-N	223	15	.242	.396	.502	107	8	.290	.450	.598	116	7	.198	.345	.414	117	7	.171	.327	.376	106	8	.321	.471	.642	42	2	.262	.365	.500	181	13	.238	.403	.503
1982	Pit-N	550	31	.284	.391	.511	261	17	.310	.416	.582	289	14	.260	.368	.446	254	15	.319	.435	.567	296	16	.253	.353	.463	150	1	.233	.360	.300	400	30	.303	.403	.590
1983	Pit-N	517	18	.259	.376	.406	255	10	.263	.385	.412	262	8	.256	.366	.401	242	9	.269	.392	.434	275	9	.251	.361	.382	121	2	.240	.352	.314	396	16	.265	.383	.434
1984	Pit-N	543	17	.254	.357	.389	270	6	.256	.370	.367	273	11	.253	.343	.410	248	8	.258	.351	.415	295	9	.251	.362	.366	130	1	.238	.329	.292	413	16	.259	.366	.419
1985	Pit-N	402	12	.241	.369	.378	215	9	.200	.338	.367	187	3	.289	.406	.390	204	9	.245	.342	.431	198	3	.237	.396	.323	123	3	.260	.374	.350	279	9	.233	.367	.391
1986	Mon-N	51	0	.196	.406	.275	24	0	.125	.382	.208	27	0	.259	.429	.333	51	0	.196	.406	.275	0	0	—	—	—	4	0	.000	.333	.000	47	0	.213	.413	.298
TOTALS		3805	160	.264	.373	.438	1861	87	.274	.385	.468	1944	73	.255	.360	.408	1863	79	.267	.372	.447	1942	81	.262	.373	.429	1121	24	.244	.337	.346	2684	136	.272	.387	.476
■ **Milt Thompson**	BL/TR																																			
1984	Atl-N	99	2	.303	.373	.374	43	0	.302	.375	.326	56	2	.304	.371	.411	0	0	—	—	—	99	2	.303	.373	.374	17	0	.059	.059	.059	82	2	.354	.430	.439
1985	Atl-N	182	0	.302	.339	.363	95	0	.326	.354	.421	87	0	.276	.323	.299	0	0	—	—	—	182	0	.302	.339	.363	14	0	.143	.143	.143	168	0	.315	.354	.381
1986	Phi-N	299	6	.251	.311	.341	154	4	.273	.331	.390	145	2	.228	.289	.290	164	3	.207	.260	.280	135	3	.304	.371	.415	50	0	.220	.264	.240	249	6	.257	.320	.361
1987	Phi-N	527	7	.302	.351	.425	270	3	.330	.382	.474	257	4	.272	.319	.374	254	2	.256	.313	.362	273	5	.344	.387	.484	84	0	.214	.283	.250	443	7	.318	.365	.458
1988	Phi-N	378	2	.288	.354	.357	173	1	.295	.377	.370	205	1	.283	.333	.346	208	1	.264	.340	.327	170	1	.318	.371	.394	20	0	.350	.462	.400	358	2	.285	.347	.355
1989	StL-N	545	4	.290	.340	.393	271	2	.303	.336	.432	274	2	.277	.344	.354	221	2	.294	.367	.407	324	2	.287	.321	.383	210	1	.267	.297	.381	335	3	.304	.366	.400
1990	StL-N	418	6	.218	.292	.328	221	3	.213	.290	.312	197	3	.223	.295	.345	206	4	.214	.293	.345	212	2	.222	.292	.311	120	0	.175	.227	.233	298	6	.235	.317	.366
1991	StL-N	326	6	.307	.368	.442	159	4	.283	.347	.447	167	2	.329	.388	.437	135	2	.363	.428	.533	191	4	.267	.324	.377	74	1	.216	.247	.297	252	5	.333	.401	.484
1992	StL-N	208	4	.293	.350	.404	105	1	.276	.327	.362	103	3	.311	.372	.447	120	3	.317	.354	.450	88	1	.261	.343	.341	22	0	.318	.375	.455	186	4	.290	.347	.398

		TOTAL					HOME					AWAY					1ST HALF					2ND HALF					LEFT					RIGHT				
YEAR	TM/L	AB	HR	AVG	OBP	SLG	AB	HR	AVG	OBP	SLG	AB	HR	AVG	OBP	SLG	AB	HR	AVG	OBP	SLG	AB	HR	AVG	OBP	SLG	AB	HR	AVG	OBP	SLG	AB	HR	AVG	OBP	SLG
1993	Phi-N	340	4	.262	.341	.350	159	2	.252	.341	.346	181	2	.271	.342	.354	152	1	.243	.333	.289	188	3	.277	.348	.399	57	0	.175	.250	.175	283	4	.279	.359	.385
1994	Phi-N	220	3	.273	.348	.345	103	3	.311	.379	.456	117	0	.239	.321	.248	159	3	.277	.322	.377	61	0	.262	.408	.262	33	0	.182	.250	.182	187	3	.289	.365	.374
1994	Hou-N	21	1	.286	.318	.429	21	1	.286	.318	.429	0	0	—	—	—	0	0	—	—	—	21	1	.286	.318	.429	3	0	.333	.333	.333	18	1	.278	.316	.444
1995	Hou-N	132	2	.220	.297	.333	62	0	.226	.329	.339	70	2	.214	.267	.329	53	0	.226	.293	.321	79	2	.215	.300	.342	5	0	.000	.000	.000	127	2	.228	.308	.346
1996	LA-N	51	0	.118	.211	.137	32	0	.156	.250	.188	19	0	.053	.143	.053	51	0	.118	.211	.137	0	0	—	—	—	0	0	—	—	—	51	0	.118	.211	.137
1996	Col-N	15	0	.067	.125	.133	11	0	.091	.167	.182	4	0	.000	.000	.000	3	0	.000	.000	.000	12	0	.083	.154	.167	0	0	—	—	—	15	0	.067	.125	.133
TOTALS		3761	47	.274	.335	.372	1879	24	.280	.343	.394	1882	23	.267	.328	.350	1726	21	.260	.326	.360	2035	26	.285	.343	.383	709	2	.220	.268	.283	3052	45	.286	.351	.393
■ **Robby Thompson**	BR/TR																																			
1986	SF-N	549	7	.271	.328	.370	255	4	.294	.364	.424	294	3	.252	.296	.323	258	3	.264	.325	.349	291	4	.278	.331	.388	168	3	.286	.344	.411	381	4	.265	.321	.352
1987	SF-N	420	10	.262	.338	.419	205	7	.263	.346	.449	215	3	.260	.329	.391	183	7	.257	.327	.432	237	3	.266	.346	.409	129	3	.310	.382	.465	291	7	.241	.318	.399
1988	SF-N	477	7	.264	.323	.384	214	3	.257	.326	.374	263	4	.270	.321	.392	227	1	.304	.380	.410	250	6	.228	.269	.360	154	1	.325	.385	.487	323	6	.235	.293	.334
1989	SF-N	547	13	.241	.321	.400	286	7	.266	.333	.434	261	6	.215	.307	.364	284	9	.275	.354	.482	263	4	.205	.284	.312	194	5	.304	.378	.505	353	8	.207	.289	.343
1990	SF-N	498	15	.245	.299	.392	248	8	.266	.335	.435	250	7	.224	.262	.348	264	8	.239	.292	.371	234	7	.252	.307	.415	183	8	.273	.325	.475	315	7	.229	.284	.343
1991	SF-N	492	19	.262	.352	.447	241	11	.295	.399	.519	251	8	.231	.305	.378	225	9	.253	.347	.449	267	10	.270	.356	.446	135	7	.281	.378	.511	357	12	.255	.342	.423
1992	SF-N	443	14	.260	.333	.415	236	8	.271	.342	.441	207	6	.246	.323	.386	171	4	.246	.345	.374	272	10	.268	.326	.441	164	1	.280	.357	.396	279	13	.247	.319	.427
1993	SF-N	494	19	.312	.375	.496	223	13	.309	.389	.561	271	6	.314	.362	.443	265	9	.332	.378	.498	229	10	.288	.371	.493	145	5	.352	.409	.538	349	14	.295	.361	.479
1994	SF-N	129	2	.209	.290	.349	68	1	.206	.286	.309	61	1	.213	.294	.393	122	1	.197	.277	.320	7	1	.429	.500	.857	42	2	.286	.348	.524	87	0	.172	.263	.264
1995	SF-N	336	8	.223	.317	.339	170	4	.212	.306	.324	166	4	.235	.328	.355	135	2	.215	.293	.319	201	6	.229	.332	.353	77	1	.247	.363	.338	259	7	.216	.302	.340
1996	SF-N	227	5	.211	.301	.335	112	2	.188	.305	.304	115	3	.235	.296	.365	171	4	.234	.296	.380	56	1	.143	.314	.196	54	2	.259	.310	.481	173	3	.197	.298	.289
TOTALS		4612	119	.257	.329	.403	2258	68	.266	.346	.432	2354	51	.249	.313	.376	2305	57	.262	.334	.408	2307	62	.252	.325	.398	1445	38	.296	.365	.467	3167	81	.240	.313	.374
■ **Dickie Thon**	BR/TR																																			
1979	Cal-A	56	0	.339	.393	.393	13	0	.231	.286	.308	43	0	.372	.426	.419	18	0	.333	.368	.389	38	0	.342	.405	.395	12	0	.417	.417	.417	44	0	.318	.388	.386
1980	Cal-A	267	0	.255	.282	.315	153	0	.288	.299	.346	114	0	.211	.260	.272	84	0	.286	.307	.345	183	0	.240	.271	.301	118	0	.254	.294	.305	149	0	.255	.273	.322
1981	Hou-N	95	0	.274	.337	.337	39	0	.308	.400	.333	56	0	.250	.288	.339	51	0	.157	.271	.176	44	0	.409	.422	.523	46	0	.370	.383	.457	49	0	.184	.298	.224
1982	Hou-N	496	3	.276	.327	.397	254	1	.315	.382	.457	242	2	.236	.266	.335	156	1	.250	.310	.353	340	2	.288	.335	.418	166	0	.271	.316	.355	330	3	.279	.332	.418
1983	Hou-N	619	20	.286	.341	.457	305	4	.292	.352	.420	314	16	.280	.330	.494	307	10	.303	.346	.469	312	10	.269	.336	.446	186	3	.323	.389	.468	433	17	.270	.320	.453
1984	Hou-N	17	0	.353	.389	.471	17	0	.353	.389	.471	0	0	—	—	—	17	0	.353	.389	.471	0	0	—	—	—	1	0	1.000	1.000	1.000	16	0	.313	.353	.438
1985	Hou-N	251	6	.251	.299	.355	121	3	.190	.246	.298	130	3	.308	.348	.408	101	0	.188	.226	.208	150	6	.293	.345	.453	162	4	.272	.324	.383	89	2	.213	.253	.303
1986	Hou-N	278	3	.248	.318	.335	148	0	.250	.321	.324	130	3	.246	.315	.346	135	1	.230	.300	.333	143	2	.266	.335	.336	177	1	.243	.318	.305	101	2	.257	.318	.386
1987	Hou-N	66	1	.212	.366	.273	34	0	.176	.300	.206	32	1	.250	.429	.344	64	1	.203	.354	.266	2	0	.500	.667	.500	56	1	.196	.348	.250	10	0	.300	.462	.400
1988	SD-N	258	1	.264	.347	.337	112	0	.223	.331	.268	146	1	.295	.360	.390	125	0	.240	.342	.288	133	1	.286	.351	.383	139	1	.302	.391	.403	119	0	.218	.293	.261
1989	Phi-N	435	15	.271	.321	.434	208	8	.264	.292	.428	227	7	.278	.345	.441	194	6	.227	.290	.356	241	9	.307	.346	.498	176	6	.273	.328	.443	259	9	.270	.315	.429
1990	Phi-N	552	8	.255	.305	.350	254	3	.248	.316	.311	298	5	.262	.295	.383	248	2	.254	.307	.327	304	6	.257	.302	.368	202	5	.262	.310	.391	350	3	.251	.302	.326
1991	Phi-N	539	9	.252	.283	.351	270	4	.270	.299	.359	269	5	.234	.268	.342	246	4	.248	.291	.346	293	5	.256	.277	.355	205	2	.259	.306	.341	334	7	.249	.269	.356
1992	Tex-A	275	4	.247	.293	.367	142	2	.261	.306	.408	133	2	.233	.280	.323	213	4	.239	.295	.357	62	0	.274	.288	.403	99	3	.293	.360	.495	176	1	.222	.254	.295
1993	Mil-A	245	1	.269	.324	.331	118	0	.280	.333	.322	127	1	.260	.315	.339	156	0	.301	.345	.365	89	1	.213	.286	.270	122	1	.270	.336	.320	123	0	.268	.311	.341
TOTALS		4449	71	.264	.317	.374	2188	25	.268	.323	.367	2261	46	.261	.311	.381	2115	29	.253	.311	.349	2334	42	.275	.322	.397	1867	27	.275	.336	.380	2582	44	.256	.303	.370
■ **Andy Thornton**	BR/TR																																			
1978	Cle-A	508	33	.262	.377	.516	255	16	.259	.382	.510	253	17	.265	.373	.522	223	12	.265	.385	.502	285	21	.260	.371	.526	136	12	.309	.421	.654	372	21	.245	.361	.465
1979	Cle-A	515	26	.233	.347	.449	252	17	.250	.355	.508	263	9	.217	.341	.392	242	11	.244	.359	.450	273	15	.223	.337	.447	129	5	.271	.395	.504	386	21	.220	.331	.430
1981	Cle-A	226	6	.239	.303	.372	105	2	.267	.317	.362	121	4	.215	.291	.380	155	3	.219	.293	.316	71	3	.282	.325	.493	108	4	.324	.382	.519	118	2	.161	.229	.237
1982	Cle-A	589	32	.273	.386	.484	289	16	.256	.366	.467	300	16	.290	.404	.500	266	19	.308	.429	.575	323	13	.245	.349	.409	192	11	.333	.471	.578	397	21	.244	.341	.438
1983	Cle-A	508	17	.281	.383	.439	269	6	.257	.346	.375	239	11	.310	.423	.510	230	10	.317	.436	.509	278	7	.252	.336	.381	185	4	.314	.410	.470	323	13	.263	.368	.421
1984	Cle-A	587	33	.271	.366	.484	284	19	.320	.414	.577	303	14	.224	.319	.396	280	18	.279	.360	.511	307	15	.264	.371	.459	157	10	.274	.403	.510	430	23	.270	.351	.474
1985	Cle-A	461	22	.236	.304	.408	221	12	.231	.302	.421	240	10	.242	.305	.396	162	3	.142	.208	.198	299	19	.288	.354	.522	153	8	.268	.358	.451	308	14	.221	.275	.386
1986	Cle-A	401	17	.229	.333	.392	222	12	.279	.357	.477	179	5	.168	.305	.285	242	11	.215	.328	.388	159	6	.252	.340	.396	123	6	.236	.356	.407	278	11	.227	.322	.385
1987	Cle-A	85	0	.118	.206	.141	43	0	.163	.245	.186	42	0	.071	.167	.095	66	0	.136	.227	.167	19	0	.053	.136	.053	53	0	.075	.150	.094	32	0	.188	.297	.219
TOTALS		3880	186	.253	.353	.445	1940	100	.263	.358	.465	1940	86	.242	.348	.424	1866	87	.251	.357	.439	2014	99	.254	.350	.450	1236	60	.284	.394	.495	2644	126	.238	.333	.421
■ **Alan Trammell**	BR/TR																																			
1978	Det-A	448	2	.268	.335	.339	236	0	.242	.308	.292	212	2	.297	.366	.392	181	2	.265	.302	.337	267	0	.270	.356	.341	191	0	.251	.321	.325	257	2	.280	.346	.350
1979	Det-A	460	6	.276	.335	.357	223	4	.283	.358	.381	237	2	.270	.311	.333	210	2	.276	.314	.324	250	4	.276	.351	.384	169	2	.284	.339	.385	291	4	.271	.332	.340
1980	Det-A	560	9	.300	.376	.404	265	5	.332	.416	.460	295	4	.271	.338	.353	245	3	.327	.401	.433	315	6	.279	.356	.381	241	3	.286	.382	.386	319	6	.310	.370	.417
1981	Det-A	392	2	.258	.342	.327	192	2	.286	.374	.365	200	0	.230	.311	.290	194	1	.273	.344	.356	198	1	.242	.341	.298	176	2	.273	.366	.358	216	0	.245	.322	.301
1982	Det-A	489	9	.258	.325	.395	239	5	.301	.371	.469	250	4	.216	.280	.324	205	2	.210	.290	.302	284	7	.292	.351	.461	143	3	.259	.344	.427	346	6	.257	.318	.382
1983	Det-A	505	14	.319	.385	.471	238	8	.303	.365	.437	267	6	.333	.403	.502	194	3	.278	.353	.402	311	11	.344	.405	.514	169	3	.343	.405	.462	336	11	.307	.375	.476
1984	Det-A	555	14	.314	.382	.468	260	7	.304	.391	.454	295	7	.322	.374	.481	307	8	.309	.380	.472	248	6	.319	.385	.464	198	9	.318	.416	.540	357	5	.311	.362	.429
1985	Det-A	605	13	.258	.312	.380	296	7	.287	.347	.405	309	6	.230	.278	.356	292	7	.281	.325	.421	313	6	.236	.301	.342	184	4	.250	.324	.364	421	9	.261	.307	.387
1986	Det-A	574	21	.277	.347	.469	282	8	.262	.335	.415	292	13	.291	.359	.521	261	5	.245	.293	.372	313	16	.304	.390	.550	204	8	.279	.344	.505	370	13	.276	.349	.449
1987	Det-A	597	28	.343	.402	.551	296	13	.348	.404	.534	301	15	.339	.401	.568	263	13	.350	.399	.559	334	15	.338	.405	.545	214	11	.360	.419	.575	383	17	.334	.393	.538
1988	Det-A	466	15	.311	.373	.464	215	7	.312	.364	.465	251	8	.311	.380	.462	267	10	.330	.384	.498	199	5	.286	.358	.417	138	5	.348	.417	.522	328	10	.296	.354	.439
1989	Det-A	449	5	.243	.314	.334	236	2	.250	.326	.339	213	3	.235	.301	.329	204	2	.265	.352	.328	245	3	.224	.281	.339	161	1	.286	.341	.373	288	4	.219	.300	.313
1990	Det-A	559	14	.304	.377	.449	271	9	.339	.413	.513	288	5	.271	.342	.389	288	6	.302	.378	.417	271	8	.306	.376	.483	173	7	.289	.370	.486	386	7	.311	.380	.433
1991	Det-A	375	9	.248	.320	.373	218	6	.243	.318	.376	157	3	.255	.322	.369	247	6	.235	.313	.368	128	3	.273	.333	.383	113	4	.212	.268	.372	262	5	.263	.341	.374
1992	Det-A	102	1	.275	.370	.392	48	0	.229	.339	.333	54	1	.315	.397	.444	102	1	.275	.370	.392	0	0	—	—	—	28	0	.357	.406	.500	74	1	.243	.356	.351
1993	Det-A	401	12	.329	.388	.496	203	6	.330	.396	.498	198	6	.328	.380	.495	160	3	.300	.367	.431	241	9	.349	.402	.539	135	7	.289	.386	.504	266	5	.350	.389	.492
1994	Det-A	292	8	.267	.307	.414	154	6	.299	.345	.481	138	2	.232	.264	.341	201	6	.318	.357	.488	91	2	.154	.198	.253	91	3	.297	.340	.462	201	5	.254	.292	.393
1995	Det-A	223	2	.269	.345	.350	121	1	.281	.348	.347	102	1	.255	.342	.353	116	2	.302	.400	.422	107	0	.234	.282	.271	90	1	.311	.386	.433	133	1	.241	.318	.293
1996	Det-A	193	1	.233	.267	.259	96	1	.219	.252	.271	97	0	.247	.282	.247	155	1	.258	.301	.290	38	0	.132	.125	.132	49	0	.327	.327	.347	144	1	.201	.248	.229
TOTALS		8245	185	.286	.352	.416	4089	97	.293	.363	.424	4156	88	.279	.341	.409	4092	83	.286	.349	.408	4153	102	.286	.354	.425	2867	73	.293	.366	.439	5378	112	.282	.345	.404
■ **Manny Trillo**	BR/TR																																			
1978	Chi-N	552	4	.261	.320	.332	258	4	.295	.358	.380	294	0	.231	.287	.289	246	2	.272	.339	.374	306	2	.252	.305	.297	217	2	.323	.373	.401	335	2	.221	.287	.287
1979	Phi-N	431	6	.260	.296	.357	229	5	.253	.289	.384	202	1	.267	.304	.327	128	0	.305	.348	.359	303	6	.241	.274	.356	113	2	.257	.288	.389	318	4	.261	.299	.346
1980	Phi-N	531	7	.292	.334	.412	261	4	.299	.348	.437	270	3	.285	.321	.389	188	0	.309	.367	.394	343	7	.283	.315	.423	105	1	.314	.376	.457	426	6	.286	.323	.401
1981	Phi-N	349	6	.287	.338	.395	161	5	.311	.367	.478	188	1	.266	.312	.324	161	3	.292	.352	.398	188	3	.282	.325	.394	65	1	.262	.347	.385	284	5	.292	.336	.398
1982	Phi-N	549	0	.271	.316	.319	257	0	.307	.358	.366	292	0	.240	.277	.277	233	0	.262	.313	.305	316	0	.278	.317	.329	97	0	.247	.267	.278	452	0	.277	.326	.327
1983	Cle-A	320	1	.272	.315	.328	176	1	.290	.333	.364	144	0	.250	.292	.285	242	0	.256	.312	.293	78	1	.321	.325	.436	130	1	.308	.353	.385	190	0	.247	.289	.289
1983	Mon-N	121	2	.264	.331	.380	79	2	.266	.318	.430	42	0	.262	.354	.286	0	0	—	—	—	121	2	.264	.331	.380	45	0	.311	.340	.400	76	2	.237	.326	.368
1984	SF-N	401	4	.254	.300	.342	173	3	.243	.285	.358	228	1	.263	.312	.329	125	4	.296	.378	.464	276	0	.236	.262	.286	100	1	.230	.260	.280	301	3	.262	.313	.362
1985	SF-N	451	3	.224	.287	.288	230	1	.200	.266	.252	221	2	.249	.310	.326	256	0	.223	.288	.270	195	3	.226	.286	.313	131	1	.229	.294	.282	320	2	.222	.285	.291
1986	Chi-N	152	1	.296	.359	.382	65	1	.308	.352	.431	87	0	.287	.364	.345	40	0	.275	.370	.350	112	1	.304	.355	.393	58	0	.328	.400	.431	94	1	.277	.333	.351
1987	Chi-N	214	8	.294	.367	.444	112	6	.348	.416	.554	102	2	.235	.313	.324	96	4	.260	.336	.427	118	4	.322	.391	.458	94	4	.298	.362	.447	120	4	.292	.370	.442
1988	Chi-N	164	1	.250	.283	.299	65	0	.231	.254	.246	99	1	.263	.302	.333	72	0	.236	.282	.278	92	1	.261	.284	.315	67	1	.269	.338	.343	97	0	.237	.242	.268
1989	Cin-N	39	0	.205	.262	.205	26	0	.154	.214	.154	13	0	.308	.357	.308	39	0	.205	.262	.205	0	0	—	—	—	29	0	.172	.226	.172	10	0	.300	.364	.300
TOTALS		4274	43	.266	.317	.350	2092	32	.277	.328	.382	2182	11	.257	.306	.320	1826	13	.268	.329	.344	2448	30	.266	.307	.355	1251	14	.280	.331	.367	3023	29	.261	.311	.343
■ **Michael Tucker**	BL/TR																																			
1995	KC-A	177	4	.260	.332	.384	88	1	.227	.320	.318	89	3	.292	.344	.449	82	0	.207	.261	.244	95	4	.305	.389	.505	19	0	.211	.211	.211	158	4	.266	.345	.405
1996	KC-A	339	12	.260	.346	.442	166	2	.265	.347	.410	173	10	.254	.345	.474	187	6	.219	.313	.390	152	6	.309	.387	.507	72	5	.236	.313	.500	267	7	.266	.355	.427
1997	Atl-N	499	14	.283	.347	.445	239	5	.280	.342	.418	260	9	.285	.352	.469	288	8	.302	.368	.476	211	6	.256	.319	.403	113	0	.283	.352	.327	386	14	.282	.346	.479
1998	Atl-N	414	13	.244	.327	.418	204	10	.270	.353	.505	210	3	.219	.301	.333	245	11	.278	.347	.494	169	2	.195	.299	.308	38	1	.263	.364	.500	376	12	.242	.323	.410
1999	Cin-N	296	11	.253	.338	.426	131	5	.237	.329	.405	165	6	.267	.346	.442	158	6	.285	.343	.462	138	5	.217	.333	.384	39	2	.154	.244	.385	257	9	.268	.353	.432
2000	Cin-N	270	15	.267	.381	.511	125	7	.320	.435	.552	145	8	.221	.331	.476	119	9	.286	.390	.563	151	6	.252	.374	.470	24	2	.167	.375	.500	246	13	.276	.381	.512
TOTALS		1995	69	.262	.345	.440	953	30	.270	.355	.442	1042	39	.255	.336	.438	1079	40	.271	.345	.455	916	29	.252	.345	.421	305	10	.239	.325	.403	1690	59	.266	.349	.446
■ **Willie Upshaw**	BL/TL																																			
1978	Tor-A	224	1	.237	.298	.304	98	0	.214	.262	.235	126	1	.254	.326	.357	157	1	.274	.322	.369	67	0	.149	.247	.149	42	0	.167	.280	.214	182	1	.253	.303	.324
1980	Tor-A	61	1	.213	.284	.344	34	0	.147	.216	.176	27	1	.296	.367	.556	33	0	.152	.200	.242	28	1	.286	.375	.464	7	0	.286	.375	.429	54	1	.204	.271	.333

YEAR	TM/L	TOTAL					HOME					AWAY					1ST HALF					2ND HALF					LEFT					RIGHT				
		AB	HR	AVG	OBP	SLG	AB	HR	AVG	OBP	SLG	AB	HR	AVG	OBP	SLG	AB	HR	AVG	OBP	SLG	AB	HR	AVG	OBP	SLG	AB	HR	AVG	OBP	SLG	AB	HR	AVG	OBP	SLG
1981	Tor-A	111	4	.171	.252	.324	38	1	.184	.262	.316	73	3	.164	.247	.329	79	3	.165	.241	.329	32	1	.188	.278	.313	13	0	.154	.313	.154	98	4	.173	.243	.347
1982	Tor-A	580	21	.267	.327	.443	290	11	.307	.347	.514	290	10	.228	.308	.372	253	10	.300	.357	.514	327	11	.242	.304	.388	264	6	.273	.302	.402	316	15	.263	.346	.478
1983	Tor-A	579	27	.306	.373	.515	286	16	.339	.403	.584	293	11	.273	.343	.447	258	15	.298	.371	.535	321	12	.312	.374	.498	207	7	.309	.371	.478	372	20	.304	.374	.535
1984	Tor-A	569	19	.278	.345	.464	271	6	.284	.348	.472	298	13	.272	.342	.456	273	13	.308	.384	.546	296	6	.250	.307	.389	199	4	.266	.313	.432	370	15	.284	.361	.481
1985	Tor-A	501	15	.275	.342	.447	236	6	.297	.366	.479	265	9	.257	.320	.419	272	8	.232	.312	.390	229	7	.328	.379	.515	171	5	.275	.309	.462	330	10	.276	.357	.439
1986	Tor-A	573	9	.251	.341	.368	267	3	.247	.350	.363	306	6	.255	.332	.373	260	2	.265	.373	.362	313	7	.240	.313	.374	179	4	.223	.291	.341	394	5	.264	.362	.381
1987	Tor-A	512	15	.244	.324	.391	236	7	.225	.319	.369	276	8	.261	.329	.409	263	10	.266	.330	.464	249	5	.221	.318	.313	144	2	.208	.305	.319	368	13	.258	.332	.418
1988	Cle-A	493	11	.245	.330	.369	244	3	.238	.325	.336	249	8	.253	.335	.402	257	8	.226	.316	.381	236	3	.267	.344	.356	74	0	.203	.280	.216	419	11	.253	.338	.396
TOTALS		4203	123	.262	.335	.419	2000	53	.271	.344	.432	2203	70	.254	.327	.407	2105	70	.265	.341	.441	2098	53	.260	.330	.397	1300	28	.255	.313	.390	2903	95	.266	.345	.432
■ John Valentin BR/TR																																				
1992	Bos-A	185	5	.276	.351	.427	89	1	.247	.327	.348	96	4	.302	.374	.500	0	0	—	—	—	185	5	.276	.351	.427	33	1	.212	.381	.394	152	4	.289	.343	.434
1993	Bos-A	468	11	.278	.346	.447	242	7	.293	.376	.483	226	4	.261	.313	.407	199	5	.241	.306	.372	269	6	.305	.375	.502	129	3	.248	.319	.419	339	8	.289	.356	.457
1994	Bos-A	301	9	.316	.400	.505	170	6	.347	.425	.547	131	3	.275	.367	.450	168	4	.310	.387	.488	133	5	.323	.415	.526	68	3	.324	.448	.603	233	6	.313	.384	.476
1995	Bos-A	520	27	.298	.399	.533	251	11	.319	.431	.554	269	16	.279	.367	.513	224	12	.290	.392	.531	296	15	.304	.404	.534	132	6	.356	.465	.568	388	21	.278	.376	.521
1996	Bos-A	527	13	.296	.374	.436	246	9	.313	.410	.500	281	4	.281	.341	.381	323	10	.282	.369	.455	204	3	.319	.382	.407	129	1	.380	.481	.519	398	12	.269	.337	.410
1997	Bos-A	575	18	.306	.372	.499	287	11	.328	.402	.544	288	7	.285	.340	.455	278	6	.288	.353	.439	297	12	.323	.390	.556	154	5	.221	.322	.409	421	13	.337	.391	.532
1998	Bos-A	588	23	.247	.340	.442	288	11	.229	.319	.444	300	12	.263	.360	.440	290	10	.255	.339	.434	298	13	.238	.341	.450	160	9	.250	.354	.494	428	14	.245	.335	.423
1999	Bos-A	450	12	.253	.315	.398	238	5	.252	.313	.391	212	7	.255	.316	.406	271	7	.251	.306	.395	179	5	.257	.327	.402	94	0	.277	.346	.298	356	12	.247	.307	.424
2000	Bos-A	35	2	.257	.297	.457	16	0	.188	.278	.188	19	2	.316	.316	.684	35	2	.257	.297	.457	0	0	—	—	—	5	0	.400	.400	.600	30	2	.233	.281	.433
TOTALS		3649	120	.283	.362	.463	1827	61	.291	.377	.483	1822	59	.274	.345	.442	1788	56	.272	.349	.444	1861	64	.292	.373	.481	904	28	.287	.387	.468	2745	92	.281	.353	.461
■ Jose Valentin BB/TR																																				
1992	Mil-A	3	0	.000	.000	.000	0	0	—	—	—	3	0	.000	.000	.000	0	0	—	—	—	3	0	.000	.000	.000	0	0	—	—	—	3	0	.000	.000	.000
1993	Mil-A	53	1	.245	.344	.396	21	1	.333	.391	.667	32	0	.188	.316	.219	0	0	—	—	—	53	1	.245	.344	.396	19	0	.263	.333	.368	34	1	.235	.350	.412
1994	Mil-A	285	11	.239	.330	.421	145	8	.283	.356	.531	140	3	.193	.305	.307	174	5	.253	.313	.414	111	6	.216	.356	.432	52	0	.135	.246	.173	233	11	.262	.350	.476
1995	Mil-A	338	11	.219	.293	.402	172	3	.180	.263	.314	166	8	.259	.324	.494	172	5	.227	.278	.419	166	6	.211	.307	.386	83	0	.133	.232	.157	255	11	.247	.313	.482
1996	Mil-A	552	24	.259	.336	.475	283	10	.265	.348	.466	269	14	.253	.323	.483	284	11	.278	.339	.493	268	13	.239	.333	.455	121	2	.248	.324	.355	431	22	.262	.340	.508
1997	Mil-A	494	17	.253	.310	.407	231	4	.208	.298	.320	263	13	.293	.321	.483	188	6	.271	.325	.410	306	11	.242	.301	.405	158	2	.259	.299	.316	336	15	.250	.315	.449
1998	Mil-A	428	16	.224	.323	.393	196	7	.235	.327	.413	232	9	.216	.320	.375	251	12	.223	.324	.418	177	4	.226	.322	.356	105	0	.229	.308	.276	323	16	.223	.328	.430
1999	Mil-A	256	10	.227	.347	.418	119	3	.218	.347	.387	137	7	.234	.347	.445	53	3	.321	.429	.660	203	7	.202	.327	.355	75	1	.253	.341	.333	181	9	.215	.350	.453
2000	Chi-A	568	25	.273	.343	.491	262	16	.302	.395	.576	306	9	.248	.295	.418	293	12	.266	.328	.485	275	13	.280	.359	.498	79	1	.215	.319	.354	489	24	.282	.348	.513
TOTALS		2977	115	.246	.327	.435	1429	52	.247	.337	.440	1548	63	.245	.317	.430	1415	54	.257	.325	.454	1562	61	.236	.328	.417	692	6	.223	.301	.295	2285	109	.253	.335	.477
■ John Vander Wal BL/TL																																				
1991	Mon-N	61	1	.213	.222	.361	4	0	.500	.500	1.000	57	1	.193	.203	.316	0	0	—	—	—	61	1	.213	.222	.361	16	0	.063	.059	.063	45	1	.267	.283	.467
1992	Mon-N	213	4	.239	.316	.352	99	2	.242	.324	.354	114	2	.237	.310	.351	88	2	.239	.337	.364	125	2	.240	.301	.344	29	0	.241	.290	.241	184	4	.239	.320	.370
1993	Mon-N	215	5	.233	.320	.372	79	1	.241	.355	.329	136	4	.228	.298	.397	112	3	.268	.331	.420	103	2	.194	.308	.320	17	0	.118	.286	.176	198	5	.242	.323	.389
1994	Col-N	110	5	.245	.339	.427	48	1	.250	.345	.354	62	4	.242	.333	.484	66	4	.258	.319	.515	44	1	.227	.364	.295	4	0	.500	.500	.500	106	5	.236	.333	.425
1995	Col-N	101	5	.347	.432	.594	45	2	.400	.500	.711	56	3	.304	.371	.500	42	2	.429	.529	.690	59	3	.288	.358	.525	5	0	.400	.400	.600	96	5	.344	.434	.594
1996	Col-N	151	5	.252	.335	.417	72	5	.306	.378	.583	79	0	.203	.297	.266	91	4	.264	.340	.451	60	1	.233	.329	.367	10	0	.200	.273	.200	141	5	.255	.340	.433
1997	Col-N	92	1	.174	.255	.228	44	0	.250	.298	.273	48	1	.104	.218	.188	56	0	.196	.286	.232	36	1	.139	.205	.222	7	0	.000	.125	.000	85	1	.188	.266	.247
1998	Col-N	104	5	.288	.380	.548	41	3	.317	.442	.707	63	2	.270	.333	.444	48	3	.229	.387	.500	56	2	.339	.373	.589	5	0	.200	.429	.200	99	5	.293	.377	.566
1998	SD-N	25	0	.240	.387	.360	18	0	.222	.417	.278	7	0	.286	.286	.571	0	0	—	—	—	25	0	.240	.387	.360	1	0	.000	.000	.000	24	0	.250	.400	.375
1999	SD-N	246	6	.272	.368	.419	139	2	.302	.414	.460	107	4	.234	.303	.364	131	4	.321	.406	.489	115	2	.217	.323	.339	18	0	.111	.200	.167	228	6	.285	.381	.439
2000	Pit-N	384	24	.299	.410	.563	175	13	.309	.423	.629	209	11	.292	.399	.507	166	9	.283	.385	.530	218	15	.312	.429	.587	50	2	.200	.310	.320	334	22	.314	.424	.599
TOTALS		1702	61	.263	.355	.442	764	29	.289	.393	.492	938	32	.242	.323	.402	800	31	.276	.367	.465	902	30	.252	.345	.422	162	2	.179	.268	.235	1540	59	.272	.364	.464
■ Andy Van Slyke BL/TR																																				
1983	StL-N	309	8	.262	.357	.421	145	3	.248	.339	.421	164	5	.274	.372	.421	58	4	.190	.304	.466	251	4	.279	.369	.410	48	2	.250	.345	.438	261	6	.264	.359	.418
1984	StL-N	361	7	.244	.354	.368	177	3	.232	.344	.345	184	4	.255	.364	.391	181	2	.243	.358	.337	180	5	.244	.351	.400	42	0	.262	.340	.405	319	7	.241	.356	.364
1985	StL-N	424	13	.259	.335	.439	193	5	.301	.386	.497	231	8	.225	.291	.390	183	6	.295	.383	.514	241	7	.232	.298	.382	54	0	.111	.158	.148	370	13	.281	.360	.481
1986	StL-N	418	13	.270	.343	.452	211	6	.280	.365	.474	207	7	.261	.320	.430	181	4	.227	.310	.354	237	9	.304	.368	.527	116	1	.207	.290	.353	302	12	.295	.364	.490
1987	Pit-N	564	21	.293	.359	.507	278	11	.273	.353	.475	286	10	.311	.365	.538	234	11	.286	.355	.517	330	10	.297	.362	.500	229	3	.231	.292	.358	335	18	.334	.403	.609
1988	Pit-N	587	25	.288	.345	.506	280	16	.293	.364	.575	307	9	.283	.327	.443	297	12	.286	.341	.515	290	13	.290	.349	.497	204	3	.191	.239	.319	383	22	.339	.399	.606
1989	Pit-N	476	9	.237	.308	.370	216	4	.213	.304	.347	260	5	.258	.311	.388	192	2	.276	.347	.406	284	7	.211	.280	.345	162	1	.247	.339	.358	314	8	.232	.291	.376
1990	Pit-N	493	17	.284	.367	.465	219	6	.288	.373	.447	274	11	.281	.362	.478	235	7	.302	.383	.460	258	10	.267	.353	.469	188	5	.261	.349	.378	305	12	.298	.378	.518
1991	Pit-N	491	17	.265	.355	.446	265	9	.226	.319	.392	226	8	.310	.397	.509	233	6	.223	.320	.356	258	11	.302	.387	.527	185	4	.195	.287	.330	306	13	.307	.396	.516
1992	Pit-N	614	14	.324	.381	.505	315	6	.321	.360	.492	299	8	.328	.402	.518	264	3	.337	.416	.485	350	11	.314	.353	.520	269	4	.297	.341	.454	345	10	.345	.411	.545
1993	Pit-N	323	8	.310	.357	.449	153	5	.255	.297	.412	170	3	.359	.410	.482	242	6	.322	.373	.475	81	2	.272	.306	.370	117	1	.308	.347	.376	206	7	.311	.362	.490
1994	Pit-N	374	6	.246	.340	.358	200	4	.265	.338	.390	174	2	.224	.341	.322	246	4	.248	.359	.358	128	2	.242	.300	.359	106	1	.255	.333	.377	268	5	.243	.342	.351
1995	Bal-A	63	3	.159	.221	.317	21	1	.190	.292	.333	42	2	.143	.182	.310	63	3	.159	.221	.317	0	0	—	—	—	14	0	.071	.133	.071	49	3	.184	.245	.388
1995	Phi-N	214	3	.243	.333	.350	122	0	.205	.281	.270	92	3	.293	.396	.457	6	1	.333	.556	.833	208	2	.240	.325	.337	45	0	.200	.315	.333	169	3	.254	.339	.355
TOTALS		5711	164	.274	.349	.443	2795	79	.266	.344	.438	2916	85	.281	.354	.448	2615	71	.275	.356	.438	3096	93	.273	.343	.447	1779	25	.238	.307	.363	3932	139	.290	.367	.479
■ Jason Varitek BB/TR																																				
1997	Bos-A	1	0	1.000	1.000	1.000	0	0	—	—	—	1	0	1.000	1.000	1.000	0	0	—	—	—	1	0	1.000	1.000	1.000	0	0	—	—	—	1	0	1.000	1.000	1.000
1998	Bos-A	221	7	.253	.309	.407	103	1	.282	.333	.388	118	6	.229	.287	.424	125	3	.240	.307	.360	96	4	.271	.311	.469	133	3	.278	.345	.421	88	4	.216	.253	.386
1999	Bos-A	483	20	.269	.330	.482	248	12	.315	.363	.565	235	8	.221	.297	.396	224	9	.250	.304	.469	259	11	.286	.353	.494	103	3	.282	.325	.447	380	17	.266	.332	.492
2000	Bos-A	448	10	.248	.342	.388	218	2	.289	.378	.427	230	8	.209	.307	.352	203	4	.276	.389	.419	245	6	.224	.299	.363	130	3	.254	.329	.392	318	7	.245	.347	.387
TOTALS		1153	37	.258	.331	.432	569	15	.299	.363	.480	584	22	.219	.300	.385	552	16	.257	.338	.426	601	21	.260	.325	.438	366	9	.270	.333	.418	787	28	.253	.330	.438
■ Greg Vaughn BR/TR																																				
1989	Mil-A	113	5	.265	.336	.425	50	1	.200	.286	.260	63	4	.317	.375	.556	0	0	—	—	—	113	5	.265	.336	.425	22	0	.227	.367	.227	91	5	.275	.327	.473
1990	Mil-A	382	17	.220	.280	.432	193	9	.218	.277	.435	189	8	.222	.282	.429	159	5	.245	.317	.440	223	12	.202	.252	.426	127	4	.197	.254	.386	255	13	.231	.292	.455
1991	Mil-A	542	27	.244	.319	.456	256	16	.246	.332	.504	286	11	.241	.306	.413	237	15	.249	.331	.511	305	12	.239	.309	.413	154	5	.227	.307	.377	388	22	.250	.323	.487
1992	Mil-A	501	23	.228	.313	.409	244	11	.234	.330	.410	257	12	.222	.297	.409	214	10	.187	.282	.369	287	13	.258	.337	.439	105	6	.248	.370	.476	396	17	.222	.297	.391
1993	Mil-A	569	30	.267	.369	.482	271	12	.284	.389	.469	298	18	.252	.350	.493	276	17	.286	.373	.529	293	13	.249	.365	.437	166	7	.319	.443	.518	403	23	.246	.336	.467
1994	Mil-A	370	19	.254	.345	.478	178	9	.292	.377	.539	192	10	.219	.315	.422	219	18	.256	.369	.580	151	1	.252	.307	.331	64	7	.266	.390	.656	306	12	.252	.335	.441
1995	Mil-A	392	17	.224	.317	.408	189	8	.265	.359	.466	203	9	.187	.277	.355	201	7	.194	.288	.343	191	10	.257	.347	.476	118	5	.246	.362	.432	274	12	.215	.297	.398
1996	Mil-A	375	31	.280	.378	.571	173	16	.289	.396	.613	202	15	.272	.361	.535	278	24	.302	.403	.604	97	7	.216	.304	.474	103	8	.243	.352	.495	272	23	.294	.387	.599
1996	SD-N	141	10	.206	.329	.454	70	6	.214	.295	.514	71	4	.197	.360	.394	0	0	—	—	—	141	10	.206	.329	.454	36	2	.194	.370	.444	105	8	.210	.314	.457
1997	SD-N	361	18	.216	.322	.393	163	11	.202	.294	.429	198	7	.227	.345	.364	191	9	.215	.304	.372	170	9	.218	.341	.418	76	8	.237	.385	.566	285	10	.211	.304	.347
1998	SD-N	573	50	.272	.363	.597	281	23	.253	.356	.548	292	27	.291	.370	.644	301	27	.296	.382	.645	272	23	.246	.343	.544	191	14	.267	.371	.545	382	36	.275	.359	.623
1999	Cin-N	550	45	.245	.347	.535	270	20	.226	.345	.485	280	25	.264	.349	.582	244	17	.213	.321	.467	306	28	.271	.368	.588	141	11	.262	.410	.532	409	34	.240	.323	.535
2000	TB-A	461	28	.254	.365	.499	201	13	.308	.424	.597	260	15	.212	.317	.423	204	13	.289	.389	.549	257	15	.226	.346	.459	87	4	.264	.440	.471	374	24	.251	.345	.505
TOTALS		5330	320	.247	.340	.481	2539	155	.253	.351	.494	2791	165	.240	.329	.469	2524	162	.252	.346	.504	2806	158	.241	.333	.460	1390	81	.253	.372	.483	3940	239	.244	.328	.480
■ Mo Vaughn BL/TR																																				
1991	Bos-A	219	4	.260	.339	.370	100	1	.320	.421	.430	119	3	.210	.262	.319	11	1	.273	.308	.545	208	3	.260	.340	.361	33	0	.212	.257	.273	186	4	.269	.352	.387
1992	Bos-A	355	13	.234	.326	.400	202	8	.262	.343	.455	153	5	.196	.303	.327	93	3	.226	.381	.355	262	10	.237	.303	.416	79	5	.190	.281	.418	276	8	.246	.339	.395
1993	Bos-A	539	29	.297	.390	.525	277	13	.332	.418	.563	262	16	.260	.361	.485	260	10	.308	.407	.508	279	19	.287	.374	.541	164	12	.268	.351	.543	375	17	.309	.407	.517
1994	Bos-A	394	26	.310	.408	.576	215	15	.302	.411	.567	179	11	.318	.405	.587	275	19	.313	.403	.582	119	7	.303	.420	.563	126	11	.310	.386	.635	268	15	.310	.418	.549
1995	Bos-A	550	39	.300	.388	.575	266	15	.301	.395	.549	284	24	.299	.382	.599	227	19	.282	.390	.564	323	20	.313	.387	.582	174	6	.253	.330	.402	376	33	.322	.414	.654
1996	Bos-A	635	44	.326	.420	.583	318	27	.381	.472	.695	317	17	.271	.368	.470	317	24	.350	.439	.634	318	20	.302	.402	.531	200	10	.315	.414	.510	435	34	.331	.423	.616
1997	Bos-A	527	35	.315	.420	.560	260	20	.338	.453	.615	267	15	.292	.387	.506	239	20	.335	.441	.628	288	15	.299	.403	.503	196	15	.337	.440	.607	331	20	.302	.409	.532
1998	Bos-A	609	40	.337	.402	.591	290	19	.345	.416	.600	319	21	.329	.390	.583	309	21	.327	.385	.583	300	19	.347	.419	.600	198	14	.333	.400	.586	411	26	.338	.403	.594
1999	Ana-A	524	33	.281	.358	.508	252	16	.266	.361	.500	272	17	.294	.355	.515	232	16	.276	.344	.509	292	17	.284	.369	.507	152	11	.336	.433	.599	372	22	.258	.325	.470
2000	Ana-A	614	36	.272	.365	.498	300	18	.280	.380	.510	314	18	.264	.351	.487	308	21	.292	.373	.545	306	15	.252	.357	.451	191	6	.204	.323	.361	423	30	.303	.385	.560
TOTALS		4966	299	.298	.387	.533	2480	152	.315	.409	.562	2486	147	.280	.364	.504	2271	154	.308	.398	.562	2695	145	.289	.378	.508	1513	90	.287	.377	.514	3453	209	.303	.391	.541

YEAR	TM/L	TOTAL					HOME					AWAY					1ST HALF					2ND HALF					LEFT					RIGHT				
		AB	HR	AVG	OBP	SLG	AB	HR	AVG	OBP	SLG	AB	HR	AVG	OBP	SLG	AB	HR	AVG	OBP	SLG	AB	HR	AVG	OBP	SLG	AB	HR	AVG	OBP	SLG	AB	HR	AVG	OBP	SLG
■ **Randy Velarde** BR/TR																																				
1987	NY-A	22	0	.182	.182	.182	1	0	.000	.000	.000	21	0	.190	.190	.190	0	0	—	—	—	22	0	.182	.182	.182	5	0	.000	.000	.000	17	0	.235	.235	.235
1988	NY-A	115	5	.174	.240	.357	65	2	.215	.250	.385	50	3	.120	.228	.320	12	1	.167	.231	.417	103	4	.175	.241	.350	31	1	.194	.265	.355	84	4	.167	.231	.357
1989	NY-A	100	2	.340	.389	.480	59	1	.322	.365	.475	41	1	.366	.422	.488	0	0	—	—	—	100	2	.340	.389	.480	29	0	.276	.323	.379	71	2	.366	.416	.521
1990	NY-A	229	5	.210	.275	.319	105	1	.210	.306	.276	124	4	.210	.246	.355	112	1	.196	.262	.277	117	4	.222	.287	.359	65	1	.277	.314	.385	164	4	.183	.260	.293
1991	NY-A	184	1	.245	.322	.332	74	0	.297	.381	.378	110	1	.209	.281	.300	66	1	.227	.320	.318	118	0	.254	.323	.339	75	0	.253	.349	.307	109	1	.239	.303	.349
1992	NY-A	412	7	.272	.333	.386	198	2	.278	.345	.348	214	5	.266	.321	.421	146	2	.233	.276	.322	266	5	.293	.362	.421	140	4	.307	.376	.464	272	3	.254	.310	.346
1993	NY-A	226	7	.301	.360	.469	115	4	.313	.365	.487	111	3	.288	.355	.450	92	3	.261	.370	.424	134	4	.328	.352	.500	116	6	.345	.402	.595	110	1	.255	.317	.336
1994	NY-A	280	9	.279	.338	.439	126	3	.230	.298	.341	154	6	.318	.371	.519	181	6	.282	.347	.431	99	3	.273	.321	.455	126	5	.278	.331	.452	154	4	.279	.343	.429
1995	NY-A	367	7	.278	.375	.392	162	2	.302	.407	.407	205	5	.259	.349	.380	150	3	.260	.321	.367	217	4	.290	.409	.410	136	1	.279	.377	.375	231	6	.277	.374	.403
1996	Cal-A	530	14	.285	.372	.426	275	8	.324	.398	.469	255	6	.243	.346	.380	257	6	.296	.384	.432	273	8	.275	.361	.421	152	3	.283	.393	.428	378	11	.286	.363	.426
1997	Ana-A	0	0	—	—	—	0	0	—	—	—	0	0	—	—	—	0	0	—	—	—	0	0	—	—	—	0	0	—	—	—	0	0	—	—	—
1998	Ana-A	188	4	.261	.375	.404	76	1	.276	.391	.421	112	3	.250	.364	.393	5	2	.600	.667	1.800	183	2	.251	.367	.366	33	1	.303	.500	.455	155	3	.252	.343	.394
1999	Ana-A	376	9	.306	.383	.439	166	4	.313	.397	.428	210	5	.300	.372	.448	277	7	.296	.377	.422	99	2	.333	.400	.485	92	3	.348	.444	.489	284	6	.292	.362	.423
1999	Oak-A	255	7	.333	.401	.478	134	4	.306	.392	.455	121	3	.364	.412	.504	0	0	—	—	—	255	7	.333	.401	.478	49	1	.347	.448	.490	206	6	.330	.389	.476
2000	Oak-A	485	12	.278	.354	.400	260	11	.281	.360	.462	225	1	.276	.347	.329	174	6	.287	.392	.437	311	6	.273	.330	.379	145	3	.262	.329	.393	340	9	.285	.364	.403
TOTALS		3769	89	.278	.353	.409	1816	43	.287	.366	.417	1953	46	.268	.341	.402	1472	38	.270	.350	.400	2297	51	.282	.355	.415	1194	29	.291	.373	.434	2575	60	.271	.344	.398
■ **Robin Ventura** BL/TR																																				
1989	Chi-A	45	0	.178	.298	.244	23	0	.174	.300	.217	22	0	.182	.296	.273	0	0	—	—	—	45	0	.178	.298	.244	7	0	.286	.500	.286	38	0	.158	.255	.237
1990	Chi-A	493	5	.249	.324	.318	238	2	.273	.348	.324	255	3	.227	.302	.314	208	3	.231	.328	.317	285	2	.263	.322	.319	154	0	.221	.318	.247	339	5	.263	.327	.351
1991	Chi-A	606	23	.284	.367	.442	304	16	.289	.368	.490	302	7	.278	.367	.394	269	4	.275	.353	.353	337	19	.291	.378	.513	192	5	.260	.364	.370	414	18	.295	.369	.476
1992	Chi-A	592	16	.282	.375	.431	285	7	.295	.392	.442	307	9	.270	.359	.420	269	7	.309	.409	.465	323	9	.260	.346	.402	182	2	.258	.348	.368	410	14	.293	.387	.459
1993	Chi-A	554	22	.262	.379	.433	254	12	.248	.386	.437	300	10	.273	.372	.430	263	13	.247	.370	.433	291	9	.275	.387	.433	176	5	.267	.361	.420	378	17	.259	.387	.439
1994	Chi-A	401	18	.282	.373	.459	182	8	.275	.372	.429	219	10	.288	.374	.484	258	13	.275	.375	.469	143	5	.294	.368	.441	122	4	.270	.311	.418	279	14	.287	.398	.477
1995	Chi-A	492	26	.295	.384	.498	222	8	.284	.371	.428	270	18	.304	.394	.556	213	13	.305	.383	.540	279	13	.287	.384	.466	132	5	.265	.335	.409	360	21	.306	.401	.531
1996	Chi-A	586	34	.287	.368	.520	285	13	.333	.399	.530	301	21	.243	.340	.512	287	17	.275	.371	.502	299	17	.298	.365	.538	185	14	.265	.332	.557	401	20	.297	.384	.504
1997	Chi-A	183	6	.262	.373	.426	93	2	.290	.398	.430	90	4	.233	.346	.422	0	0	—	—	—	183	6	.262	.373	.426	39	0	.256	.375	.282	144	6	.264	.372	.465
1998	Chi-A	590	21	.263	.349	.436	287	15	.272	.355	.502	303	6	.254	.344	.373	297	10	.273	.365	.448	293	11	.253	.332	.423	155	7	.277	.360	.477	435	14	.257	.345	.421
1999	NY-N	588	32	.301	.379	.529	282	13	.309	.368	.507	306	19	.294	.389	.549	286	15	.287	.359	.510	302	17	.315	.398	.546	181	9	.271	.351	.486	407	23	.314	.391	.548
2000	NY-N	469	24	.232	.338	.439	224	12	.232	.336	.446	245	12	.233	.340	.433	254	16	.240	.361	.496	215	8	.223	.310	.372	102	5	.225	.328	.412	367	19	.234	.341	.447
TOTALS		5599	227	.273	.364	.450	2679	108	.282	.371	.455	2920	119	.265	.358	.445	2604	111	.272	.368	.455	2995	116	.274	.360	.445	1627	56	.259	.345	.415	3972	171	.279	.372	.464
■ **Jose Vidro** BB/TR																																				
1997	Mon-N	169	2	.249	.297	.367	62	0	.226	.300	.355	107	2	.262	.296	.374	23	0	.130	.160	.217	146	2	.267	.319	.390	47	0	.213	.288	.277	122	2	.262	.301	.402
1998	Mon-N	205	0	.220	.318	.278	113	0	.212	.328	.274	92	0	.228	.305	.283	175	0	.234	.335	.297	30	0	.133	.212	.167	32	0	.125	.237	.188	173	0	.237	.333	.295
1999	Mon-N	494	12	.304	.346	.476	247	5	.320	.361	.482	247	7	.287	.331	.470	223	8	.327	.363	.543	271	4	.284	.332	.421	100	1	.260	.292	.400	394	11	.315	.359	.495
2000	Mon-N	606	24	.330	.379	.540	307	11	.368	.404	.580	299	13	.291	.353	.498	286	13	.367	.406	.605	320	11	.297	.354	.481	161	7	.373	.423	.602	445	17	.315	.363	.517
TOTALS		1474	38	.296	.350	.462	729	16	.316	.368	.480	745	22	.278	.332	.444	707	21	.314	.366	.496	767	17	.280	.334	.430	340	8	.294	.348	.459	1134	30	.297	.350	.463
■ **Jose Vizcaino** BB/TR																																				
1989	LA-N	10	0	.200	.200	.200	3	0	.333	.333	.333	7	0	.143	.143	.143	0	0	—	—	—	10	0	.200	.200	.200	1	0	.000	.000	.000	9	0	.222	.222	.222
1990	LA-N	51	0	.275	.327	.333	32	0	.281	.324	.375	19	0	.263	.333	.263	2	0	.000	.333	.000	49	0	.286	.327	.347	19	0	.368	.478	.368	32	0	.219	.219	.313
1991	Chi-N	145	0	.262	.283	.297	81	0	.235	.256	.284	64	0	.297	.318	.313	62	0	.258	.294	.274	83	0	.265	.274	.313	37	0	.216	.231	.216	108	0	.278	.301	.324
1992	Chi-N	285	1	.225	.260	.298	126	0	.230	.269	.278	159	1	.220	.253	.314	191	0	.209	.244	.267	94	1	.255	.293	.362	88	0	.216	.242	.318	197	1	.228	.268	.289
1993	Chi-N	551	4	.287	.340	.358	278	1	.338	.384	.399	273	3	.234	.296	.315	268	1	.321	.359	.388	283	3	.254	.323	.329	128	0	.297	.364	.328	423	4	.284	.333	.366
1994	NY-N	410	3	.256	.310	.324	184	1	.223	.291	.266	226	2	.283	.327	.372	286	3	.269	.324	.339	124	0	.226	.279	.290	107	0	.280	.325	.299	303	3	.248	.305	.333
1995	NY-N	509	3	.287	.332	.365	263	2	.289	.339	.369	246	1	.285	.324	.362	206	1	.262	.311	.325	303	2	.304	.347	.393	130	0	.346	.388	.385	379	3	.266	.313	.359
1996	NY-N	363	1	.303	.356	.377	174	1	.270	.328	.316	189	0	.333	.382	.434	268	1	.313	.369	.399	95	0	.274	.320	.316	86	0	.302	.318	.314	277	1	.303	.367	.397
1996	Cle-A	179	0	.285	.310	.335	97	0	.299	.324	.320	82	0	.268	.294	.354	0	0	—	—	—	179	0	.285	.310	.335	67	0	.284	.314	.313	112	0	.286	.308	.348
1997	SF-N	568	5	.266	.323	.350	279	1	.237	.307	.305	289	4	.294	.338	.394	283	2	.258	.336	.318	285	3	.274	.308	.382	125	0	.240	.324	.288	443	5	.273	.322	.368
1998	LA-N	237	3	.262	.311	.338	91	0	.253	.286	.286	146	3	.267	.327	.370	237	3	.262	.311	.338	0	0	—	—	—	50	1	.380	.418	.480	187	2	.230	.282	.299
1999	LA-N	266	1	.252	.304	.297	140	1	.236	.273	.293	126	0	.270	.338	.302	163	1	.239	.287	.276	103	0	.272	.330	.330	70	0	.329	.412	.400	196	1	.224	.263	.260
2000	LA-N	93	0	.204	.288	.247	43	0	.140	.229	.209	50	0	.260	.339	.280	93	0	.204	.288	.247	0	0	—	—	—	40	0	.225	.311	.275	53	0	.189	.271	.226
2000	NY-A	174	0	.276	.319	.333	81	0	.259	.302	.309	93	0	.290	.333	.355	25	0	.280	.269	.280	149	0	.275	.327	.342	33	0	.242	.257	.333	141	0	.284	.333	.333
TOTALS		3841	21	.269	.319	.338	1872	7	.264	.314	.321	1969	14	.275	.323	.355	2084	12	.267	.320	.330	1757	9	.272	.317	.348	981	1	.286	.338	.331	2860	20	.264	.312	.341
■ **Omar Vizquel** BB/TR																																				
1989	Sea-A	387	1	.220	.273	.261	189	1	.228	.254	.296	198	0	.212	.290	.227	188	0	.234	.293	.271	199	1	.206	.254	.251	102	1	.196	.212	.265	285	0	.228	.293	.260
1990	Sea-A	255	2	.247	.295	.298	114	0	.237	.299	.254	141	2	.255	.291	.333	0	0	—	—	—	255	2	.247	.295	.298	81	1	.235	.279	.296	174	1	.253	.302	.299
1991	Sea-A	426	1	.230	.302	.293	206	1	.252	.319	.359	220	0	.209	.286	.232	200	0	.215	.287	.280	226	1	.243	.315	.305	87	0	.230	.284	.276	339	1	.230	.306	.298
1992	Sea-A	483	0	.294	.340	.352	241	0	.286	.337	.357	242	0	.302	.342	.347	151	0	.298	.348	.358	332	0	.292	.336	.349	105	0	.229	.283	.267	378	0	.312	.356	.376
1993	Sea-A	560	2	.255	.319	.298	274	1	.266	.333	.303	286	1	.245	.306	.294	289	1	.294	.367	.329	271	1	.214	.266	.266	132	0	.197	.264	.242	428	2	.273	.336	.315
1994	Cle-A	286	1	.273	.325	.325	134	0	.284	.333	.313	152	1	.263	.317	.336	123	1	.325	.382	.407	163	0	.233	.280	.264	115	1	.226	.274	.287	171	0	.304	.358	.351
1995	Cle-A	542	6	.266	.333	.351	258	3	.267	.336	.345	284	3	.264	.331	.356	237	4	.257	.322	.333	305	2	.272	.342	.364	168	2	.262	.330	.375	374	4	.267	.335	.340
1996	Cle-A	542	9	.297	.362	.417	281	2	.306	.369	.427	261	7	.287	.354	.406	280	4	.293	.357	.407	262	5	.302	.367	.427	168	4	.274	.342	.417	374	5	.307	.371	.417
1997	Cle-A	565	5	.280	.347	.368	290	3	.300	.354	.407	275	2	.258	.339	.327	275	2	.265	.337	.364	290	3	.293	.356	.372	151	2	.265	.306	.351	414	3	.285	.361	.374
1998	Cle-A	576	2	.288	.358	.372	284	0	.289	.370	.338	292	2	.288	.346	.404	303	0	.300	.366	.380	273	2	.275	.350	.363	168	1	.274	.363	.375	408	1	.294	.356	.370
1999	Cle-A	574	5	.333	.397	.436	273	3	.359	.419	.447	301	2	.309	.378	.425	258	2	.337	.394	.430	316	3	.329	.400	.440	147	1	.333	.390	.449	427	4	.333	.400	.431
2000	Cle-A	613	7	.287	.377	.375	303	1	.254	.335	.323	310	6	.319	.418	.426	290	2	.259	.344	.348	323	5	.313	.406	.399	156	1	.218	.313	.282	457	6	.311	.400	.407
TOTALS		5809	41	.276	.342	.353	2847	15	.281	.344	.356	2962	26	.271	.339	.350	2594	16	.280	.347	.357	3215	25	.273	.338	.350	1580	14	.249	.312	.334	4229	27	.286	.353	.360
■ **Larry Walker** BL/TR																																				
1989	Mon-N	47	0	.170	.264	.170	37	0	.189	.286	.189	10	0	.100	.182	.100	0	0	—	—	—	47	0	.170	.264	.170	4	0	.000	.000	.000	43	0	.186	.286	.186
1990	Mon-N	419	19	.241	.326	.434	196	9	.255	.338	.454	223	10	.229	.316	.417	191	8	.262	.344	.471	228	11	.224	.311	.404	116	6	.207	.264	.414	303	13	.254	.349	.442
1991	Mon-N	487	16	.290	.349	.458	187	5	.273	.330	.428	300	11	.300	.361	.477	224	6	.232	.318	.362	263	10	.338	.378	.540	160	4	.287	.352	.419	327	12	.291	.348	.477
1992	Mon-N	528	23	.301	.353	.506	257	13	.284	.349	.506	271	10	.317	.357	.506	224	14	.281	.343	.527	304	9	.316	.361	.490	209	10	.316	.354	.517	319	13	.292	.353	.498
1993	Mon-N	490	22	.265	.371	.469	241	13	.307	.410	.560	249	9	.225	.333	.382	204	10	.279	.379	.500	286	12	.255	.365	.448	185	7	.238	.336	.400	305	15	.282	.391	.511
1994	Mon-N	395	19	.322	.394	.587	169	7	.331	.401	.604	226	12	.314	.388	.575	275	12	.305	.380	.564	120	7	.358	.426	.642	115	4	.330	.410	.574	280	15	.318	.387	.593
1995	Col-N	494	36	.306	.381	.607	248	24	.343	.401	.730	246	12	.268	.361	.484	199	17	.322	.396	.653	295	19	.295	.371	.576	141	7	.319	.389	.532	353	29	.300	.378	.637
1996	Col-N	272	18	.276	.342	.570	145	12	.393	.448	.800	127	6	.142	.216	.307	198	14	.283	.354	.586	74	4	.257	.309	.527	75	5	.280	.349	.600	197	13	.274	.339	.558
1997	Col-N	568	49	.366	.452	.720	302	20	.384	.460	.709	266	29	.346	.443	.733	292	25	.408	.507	.771	276	24	.322	.390	.667	144	6	.299	.400	.521	424	43	.389	.470	.788
1998	Col-N	454	23	.363	.445	.630	239	17	.418	.483	.757	215	6	.302	.403	.488	235	9	.336	.420	.583	219	14	.393	.471	.680	131	3	.321	.412	.511	323	20	.381	.458	.678
1999	Col-N	438	37	.379	.458	.710	232	26	.461	.531	.879	206	11	.286	.375	.519	239	20	.381	.445	.724	199	17	.377	.473	.693	142	9	.345	.424	.620	296	28	.395	.474	.753
2000	Col-N	314	9	.309	.409	.506	156	7	.359	.446	.615	158	2	.259	.371	.399	181	4	.354	.436	.552	133	5	.248	.373	.444	85	2	.341	.440	.506	229	7	.297	.397	.507
TOTALS		4906	271	.311	.390	.563	2409	153	.345	.419	.637	2497	118	.279	.363	.491	2462	139	.316	.397	.580	2444	132	.306	.383	.546	1507	63	.297	.373	.502	3399	208	.318	.398	.590
■ **Tim Wallach** BR/TR																																				
1980	Mon-N	11	1	.182	.250	.455	6	0	.167	.167	.167	5	1	.200	.333	.800	0	0	—	—	—	11	1	.182	.250	.455	10	1	.200	.273	.500	1	0	.000	.000	.000
1981	Mon-N	212	4	.236	.299	.344	101	1	.297	.360	.426	111	3	.180	.242	.270	98	3	.224	.309	.357	114	1	.246	.289	.333	69	0	.145	.253	.188	143	4	.280	.322	.420
1982	Mon-N	596	28	.268	.313	.471	291	11	.289	.336	.488	305	17	.249	.289	.456	248	11	.278	.335	.460	348	17	.261	.296	.480	161	13	.329	.368	.652	435	15	.246	.292	.405
1983	Mon-N	581	19	.269	.335	.434	289	9	.260	.330	.433	292	10	.277	.340	.435	276	8	.275	.341	.438	305	11	.262	.330	.430	141	5	.270	.354	.454	440	14	.268	.329	.427
1984	Mon-N	582	18	.246	.311	.395	279	4	.251	.319	.355	303	14	.241	.303	.432	275	12	.276	.341	.462	307	6	.218	.284	.336	155	7	.265	.341	.471	427	11	.239	.300	.368
1985	Mon-N	569	22	.260	.310	.450	272	9	.257	.322	.430	297	13	.263	.297	.468	252	4	.282	.328	.437	317	18	.243	.294	.461	168	5	.256	.287	.423	401	17	.262	.319	.461
1986	Mon-N	480	18	.233	.308	.396	230	6	.226	.309	.348	250	12	.240	.307	.440	254	12	.276	.353	.488	226	6	.186	.255	.292	135	3	.215	.305	.356	345	15	.241	.309	.412
1987	Mon-N	593	26	.298	.343	.514	290	13	.300	.349	.552	303	13	.297	.337	.479	279	11	.297	.345	.505	314	15	.299	.341	.522	160	1	.306	.353	.444	433	25	.296	.340	.540
1988	Mon-N	592	12	.257	.302	.389	292	3	.253	.302	.346	300	9	.260	.301	.430	293	6	.263	.310	.413	299	6	.251	.293	.365	172	4	.262	.310	.413	420	8	.255	.298	.379
1989	Mon-N	573	13	.277	.341	.419	286	6	.318	.386	.479	287	7	.237	.297	.359	281	3	.263	.327	.377	292	10	.291	.355	.459	160	8	.287	.358	.500	413	5	.274	.335	.387
1990	Mon-N	626	21	.296	.339	.471	301	9	.276	.328	.452	325	12	.314	.350	.489	287	12	.303	.358	.526	339	9	.289	.323	.425	204	6	.289	.355	.456	422	15	.299	.331	.479
1991	Mon-N	577	13	.225	.292	.334	230	5	.213	.303	.317	347	8	.233	.285	.346	293	8	.242	.317	.355	284	5	.208	.266	.313	185	5	.222	.293	.346	392	8	.227	.292	.329
1992	Mon-N	537	9	.223	.296	.331	262	5	.263	.333	.393	275	4	.185	.259	.273	262	3	.248	.320	.351	275	6	.200	.273	.313	198	7	.263	.329	.434	339	2	.201	.276	.271

YEAR	TM/L	TOTAL					HOME					AWAY					1ST HALF					2ND HALF					LEFT					RIGHT				
		AB	HR	AVG	OBP	SLG	AB	HR	AVG	OBP	SLG	AB	HR	AVG	OBP	SLG	AB	HR	AVG	OBP	SLG	AB	HR	AVG	OBP	SLG	AB	HR	AVG	OBP	SLG	AB	HR	AVG	OBP	SLG
1993	LA-N	477	12	.222	.271	.342	217	4	.253	.297	.346	260	8	.196	.249	.338	261	8	.211	.254	.356	216	4	.236	.291	.324	139	5	.194	.223	.338	338	7	.234	.290	.343
1994	LA-N	414	23	.280	.356	.502	187	7	.235	.326	.401	227	16	.317	.382	.586	288	18	.257	.342	.497	126	5	.333	.390	.516	111	8	.279	.341	.577	303	15	.281	.362	.475
1995	LA-N	327	9	.266	.326	.428	168	4	.232	.284	.357	159	5	.302	.369	.503	129	3	.264	.331	.403	198	6	.268	.323	.444	85	4	.259	.315	.459	242	5	.269	.330	.417
1996	Cal-A	190	8	.237	.306	.400	89	5	.258	.320	.461	101	3	.218	.295	.347	168	8	.244	.310	.429	22	0	.182	.280	.182	93	3	.204	.275	.366	97	5	.268	.336	.433
1996	LA-N	162	4	.228	.286	.333	88	2	.250	.283	.352	74	2	.203	.289	.311	0	0	—	—	—	162	4	.228	.286	.333	28	1	.357	.357	.500	134	3	.201	.272	.299
TOTALS		8099	260	.257	.316	.416	3878	103	.263	.325	.412	4221	157	.253	.307	.419	3944	130	.265	.328	.433	4155	130	.250	.304	.400	2374	86	.260	.321	.439	5725	174	.256	.314	.406
■ **Denny Walling**	BL/TR																																			
1978	Hou-N	247	3	.251	.332	.356	141	2	.248	.342	.362	106	1	.255	.319	.349	98	1	.245	.318	.337	149	2	.255	.341	.369	31	0	.065	.194	.129	216	3	.278	.352	.389
1979	Hou-N	147	3	.327	.394	.497	73	3	.370	.420	.658	74	0	.284	.369	.338	54	3	.352	.470	.630	93	0	.312	.343	.419	14	0	.429	.438	.857	133	3	.316	.389	.459
1980	Hou-N	284	3	.299	.374	.387	127	1	.339	.414	.417	157	2	.268	.341	.363	152	2	.336	.417	.441	132	1	.258	.322	.326	53	0	.302	.327	.377	231	3	.299	.383	.390
1981	Hou-N	158	5	.234	.346	.367	91	2	.165	.284	.242	67	3	.328	.430	.537	87	3	.207	.349	.333	71	2	.268	.342	.408	24	0	.292	.387	.375	134	5	.224	.338	.366
1982	Hou-N	146	1	.205	.312	.267	96	1	.177	.292	.260	50	0	.260	.351	.280	89	1	.180	.282	.281	57	0	.246	.358	.246	19	1	.211	.348	.368	127	0	.205	.306	.252
1983	Hou-N	135	3	.296	.364	.444	71	1	.282	.333	.394	64	2	.313	.397	.500	45	0	.200	.250	.244	90	3	.344	.417	.544	18	2	.444	.524	.944	117	1	.274	.338	.368
1984	Hou-N	249	3	.281	.325	.402	122	0	.344	.364	.467	127	3	.220	.288	.339	58	1	.241	.318	.397	191	2	.293	.327	.403	32	0	.250	.273	.281	217	3	.286	.332	.419
1985	Hou-N	345	7	.270	.316	.394	181	2	.260	.306	.370	164	5	.280	.326	.421	197	3	.269	.301	.381	148	4	.270	.333	.412	45	0	.267	.298	.289	300	7	.270	.318	.410
1986	Hou-N	382	13	.312	.367	.479	190	5	.295	.349	.426	192	8	.328	.385	.531	147	2	.293	.358	.388	235	11	.323	.374	.536	58	0	.190	.266	.207	324	13	.333	.385	.528
1987	Hou-N	325	5	.283	.356	.418	156	2	.288	.364	.372	169	3	.278	.349	.462	154	3	.286	.345	.416	171	2	.281	.365	.421	35	1	.200	.222	.314	290	4	.293	.370	.431
1988	Hou-N	176	1	.244	.304	.341	85	0	.282	.322	.353	91	1	.209	.287	.330	146	1	.247	.308	.349	30	0	.233	.281	.300	12	0	.250	.357	.333	164	1	.244	.299	.341
1988	StL-N	58	0	.224	.250	.276	28	0	.107	.138	.179	30	0	.333	.355	.367	0	0	—	—	—	58	0	.224	.250	.276	2	0	.000	.000	.000	56	0	.232	.259	.286
1989	StL-N	79	1	.304	.409	.430	30	0	.367	.486	.500	49	1	.265	.357	.388	26	0	.231	.375	.346	53	1	.340	.426	.472	9	0	.333	.455	.444	70	1	.300	.402	.429
1990	StL-N	127	1	.220	.265	.283	63	1	.254	.319	.381	64	0	.188	.209	.188	76	0	.237	.272	.263	51	1	.196	.255	.314	7	0	.000	.000	.000	120	1	.233	.279	.300
1991	Tex-A	44	0	.091	.184	.114	19	0	.000	.208	.000	25	0	.160	.160	.200	44	0	.091	.184	.114	0	0	—	—	—	6	0	.000	.000	.000	38	0	.105	.209	.132
1992	Hou-N	3	0	.333	.333	.333	3	0	.333	.333	.333	0	0	—	—	—	3	0	.333	.333	.333	0	0	—	—	—	0	0	—	—	—	3	0	.333	.333	.333
TOTALS		2905	49	.272	.339	.391	1476	20	.272	.341	.383	1429	29	.271	.338	.399	1376	20	.259	.332	.366	1529	29	.283	.346	.413	365	4	.238	.301	.334	2540	45	.276	.345	.399
■ **Gary Ward**	BR/TR																																			
1979	Min-A	14	0	.286	.412	.286	9	0	.333	.400	.333	5	0	.200	.429	.200	0	0	—	—	—	14	0	.286	.412	.286	12	0	.333	.467	.333	2	0	.000	.000	.000
1980	Min-A	41	1	.463	.489	.780	17	0	.412	.474	.529	24	1	.500	.500	.958	0	0	—	—	—	41	1	.463	.489	.780	30	1	.533	.559	.867	11	0	.273	.273	.545
1981	Min-A	295	3	.264	.325	.359	165	2	.242	.308	.339	130	1	.292	.347	.385	134	3	.231	.297	.321	161	0	.292	.348	.391	127	1	.315	.355	.386	168	2	.226	.303	.339
1982	Min-A	570	28	.289	.330	.519	290	16	.310	.354	.586	280	12	.268	.306	.450	247	9	.239	.281	.393	323	19	.328	.368	.616	196	10	.291	.340	.546	374	18	.289	.325	.505
1983	Min-A	623	19	.278	.326	.440	314	7	.277	.321	.420	309	12	.278	.331	.460	319	14	.288	.329	.489	304	5	.266	.322	.388	175	11	.303	.340	.571	448	8	.268	.320	.388
1984	Tex-A	602	21	.284	.343	.447	288	7	.285	.357	.424	314	14	.283	.330	.468	287	6	.223	.288	.307	315	15	.340	.394	.575	185	5	.270	.332	.427	417	16	.290	.349	.456
1985	Tex-A	593	15	.287	.329	.433	282	10	.344	.375	.539	311	5	.235	.288	.338	290	5	.286	.331	.417	303	10	.287	.327	.449	176	7	.301	.354	.511	417	8	.281	.318	.400
1986	Tex-A	380	5	.316	.372	.405	193	3	.321	.370	.420	187	2	.310	.373	.390	225	3	.293	.360	.400	155	2	.348	.389	.413	120	3	.317	.388	.467	260	2	.315	.364	.377
1987	NY-A	529	16	.248	.291	.384	259	7	.282	.320	.402	270	9	.215	.263	.367	288	10	.267	.308	.420	241	6	.224	.270	.340	197	4	.279	.321	.376	332	12	.229	.274	.389
1988	NY-A	231	4	.225	.302	.312	100	3	.230	.306	.360	131	1	.221	.299	.275	122	2	.221	.307	.287	109	2	.229	.298	.339	128	4	.227	.308	.375	103	0	.223	.296	.233
1989	NY-A	17	0	.294	.400	.353	10	0	.300	.417	.300	7	0	.286	.375	.429	17	0	.294	.400	.353	0	0	—	—	—	17	0	.294	.400	.353	0	0	—	—	—
1989	Det-A	275	9	.251	.300	.400	129	6	.256	.305	.465	146	3	.247	.296	.342	104	3	.260	.313	.375	171	6	.246	.293	.415	170	9	.276	.330	.500	105	0	.210	.252	.238
1990	Det-A	309	9	.256	.322	.392	131	2	.260	.331	.389	178	7	.253	.314	.393	173	4	.237	.300	.335	136	5	.279	.349	.463	152	5	.257	.315	.421	157	4	.255	.328	.363
TOTALS		4479	130	.276	.328	.425	2187	63	.290	.341	.448	2292	67	.263	.315	.404	2206	59	.259	.313	.387	2273	71	.292	.342	.462	1685	60	.288	.343	.468	2794	70	.268	.319	.399
■ **Claudell Washington**	BL/TL																																			
1978	Tex-A	42	0	.167	.186	.167	21	0	.190	.227	.190	21	0	.143	.143	.143	42	0	.167	.186	.167	0	0	—	—	—	3	0	.000	.000	.000	39	0	.179	.200	.179
1978	Chi-A	314	6	.264	.290	.404	146	3	.267	.288	.418	168	3	.262	.292	.393	57	2	.351	.362	.561	257	4	.245	.275	.370	100	2	.220	.252	.320	214	4	.285	.308	.444
1979	Chi-A	471	13	.280	.322	.454	218	10	.266	.318	.482	253	3	.292	.326	.431	277	6	.271	.312	.430	194	7	.294	.337	.490	142	1	.254	.310	.338	329	12	.292	.328	.505
1980	Chi-A	90	1	.289	.333	.411	37	0	.297	.366	.405	53	1	.283	.309	.415	90	1	.289	.333	.411	0	0	—	—	—	13	0	.385	.385	.462	77	1	.273	.325	.403
1980	NY-N	284	10	.275	.324	.465	134	5	.328	.377	.530	150	5	.227	.275	.407	52	4	.192	.259	.462	232	6	.293	.339	.466	49	0	.184	.231	.286	235	10	.294	.343	.502
1981	Atl-N	320	5	.291	.328	.425	137	3	.299	.342	.460	183	2	.284	.318	.399	160	1	.294	.327	.419	160	4	.287	.329	.431	62	0	.210	.279	.226	258	5	.310	.341	.473
1982	Atl-N	563	16	.266	.330	.416	304	8	.293	.335	.441	259	8	.236	.323	.386	267	6	.285	.353	.416	296	10	.250	.308	.416	113	3	.265	.349	.363	450	13	.267	.325	.429
1983	Atl-N	496	9	.278	.322	.413	246	4	.329	.372	.476	250	5	.228	.272	.352	259	3	.286	.322	.417	237	6	.270	.322	.409	75	0	.200	.228	.240	421	9	.292	.338	.444
1984	Atl-N	416	17	.286	.374	.469	239	12	.293	.367	.515	177	5	.277	.383	.407	190	9	.326	.432	.553	226	8	.252	.321	.398	115	3	.304	.389	.443	301	14	.279	.368	.478
1985	Atl-N	398	15	.276	.342	.455	191	4	.277	.337	.398	207	11	.275	.348	.507	217	9	.276	.325	.456	181	6	.276	.362	.453	63	1	.206	.261	.365	335	14	.290	.358	.472
1986	Atl-N	137	5	.270	.336	.460	71	3	.239	.321	.408	66	2	.303	.352	.515	137	5	.270	.336	.460	0	0	—	—	—	34	0	.265	.278	.353	103	5	.272	.353	.495
1986	NY-A	135	6	.237	.285	.407	55	4	.236	.263	.491	80	2	.237	.299	.350	4	0	.250	.250	.250	131	6	.237	.286	.412	14	0	.214	.267	.286	121	6	.240	.287	.421
1987	NY-A	312	9	.279	.336	.420	144	5	.299	.361	.451	168	4	.262	.315	.393	126	4	.294	.355	.444	186	5	.269	.323	.403	61	1	.361	.435	.475	251	8	.259	.311	.406
1988	NY-A	455	11	.308	.342	.442	218	6	.358	.397	.509	237	5	.262	.290	.380	216	4	.319	.345	.454	239	7	.297	.340	.431	48	1	.313	.333	.458	407	10	.307	.343	.440
1989	Cal-A	418	13	.273	.319	.428	210	9	.295	.344	.495	208	4	.250	.294	.361	201	9	.284	.330	.468	217	4	.263	.309	.392	102	0	.294	.333	.382	316	13	.266	.315	.443
1990	Cal-A	34	1	.176	.222	.294	13	0	.077	.200	.077	21	1	.238	.238	.429	34	1	.176	.222	.294	0	0	—	—	—	3	0	.333	.333	.333	31	1	.161	.212	.290
1990	NY-A	80	0	.162	.181	.200	41	0	.171	.209	.171	39	0	.154	.150	.231	80	0	.162	.181	.200	0	0	—	—	—	9	0	.333	.300	.333	71	0	.141	.164	.183
TOTALS		4965	137	.275	.326	.428	2425	76	.293	.343	.459	2540	61	.257	.309	.398	2409	64	.281	.332	.435	2556	73	.269	.320	.421	1006	12	.259	.313	.355	3959	125	.279	.329	.446
■ **Mitch Webster**	BB/TL																																			
1983	Tor-A	11	0	.182	.250	.182	5	0	.200	.200	.200	6	0	.167	.286	.167	0	0	—	—	—	11	0	.182	.250	.182	3	0	.333	.333	.333	8	0	.125	.222	.125
1984	Tor-A	22	0	.227	.261	.409	13	0	.231	.231	.308	9	0	.222	.300	.556	9	0	.333	.333	.556	13	0	.154	.214	.308	16	0	.188	.188	.375	6	0	.333	.429	.500
1985	Tor-A	1	0	.000	.000	.000	1	0	.000	.000	.000	0	0	—	—	—	1	0	.000	.000	.000	0	0	—	—	—	0	0	—	—	—	1	0	.000	.000	.000
1985	Mon-N	212	11	.274	.335	.486	81	3	.247	.287	.444	131	8	.290	.363	.511	20	1	.300	.333	.650	192	10	.271	.335	.469	90	6	.322	.361	.578	122	5	.238	.316	.418
1986	Mon-N	576	8	.290	.355	.431	283	2	.265	.329	.396	293	6	.314	.380	.464	253	4	.261	.350	.387	323	4	.313	.359	.464	199	5	.337	.376	.513	377	3	.265	.345	.387
1987	Mon-N	588	15	.281	.361	.435	285	9	.267	.353	.439	303	6	.294	.368	.432	281	4	.295	.371	.423	307	11	.267	.351	.446	200	7	.285	.344	.455	388	8	.278	.369	.425
1988	Mon-N	259	2	.255	.354	.313	122	0	.303	.415	.369	137	2	.212	.297	.263	233	1	.249	.348	.300	26	1	.308	.406	.423	95	0	.253	.318	.274	164	2	.256	.374	.335
1988	Chi-N	264	4	.265	.319	.398	151	3	.265	.329	.391	113	1	.265	.306	.407	0	0	—	—	—	264	4	.265	.319	.398	73	0	.219	.250	.260	191	4	.283	.344	.450
1989	Chi-N	272	3	.257	.331	.364	132	1	.250	.315	.341	140	2	.264	.346	.386	193	3	.259	.330	.363	79	0	.253	.333	.367	61	1	.311	.364	.443	211	2	.242	.322	.341
1990	Cle-A	437	12	.252	.285	.407	231	6	.247	.284	.372	206	6	.257	.287	.447	231	5	.251	.280	.394	206	7	.252	.291	.422	192	8	.292	.320	.495	245	4	.220	.259	.339
1991	Cle-A	32	0	.125	.200	.125	12	0	.250	.308	.250	20	0	.050	.136	.050	32	0	.125	.200	.125	0	0	—	—	—	20	0	.200	.304	.200	12	0	.000	.000	.000
1991	Pit-N	97	1	.175	.245	.320	32	1	.156	.308	.313	65	0	.185	.209	.323	91	1	.176	.250	.308	6	0	.167	.167	.500	35	1	.200	.282	.400	62	0	.161	.224	.274
1991	LA-N	74	1	.284	.361	.419	22	1	.227	.346	.500	52	0	.308	.368	.385	0	0	—	—	—	74	1	.284	.361	.419	49	1	.286	.340	.429	25	0	.280	.400	.400
1992	LA-N	262	6	.267	.334	.420	125	1	.216	.308	.296	137	5	.314	.360	.533	101	3	.248	.342	.416	161	3	.280	.330	.422	130	3	.292	.361	.438	132	3	.242	.309	.402
1993	LA-N	172	2	.244	.293	.337	77	1	.221	.279	.299	95	1	.263	.304	.368	108	1	.269	.317	.343	64	1	.203	.250	.328	69	0	.275	.292	.391	103	2	.223	.293	.301
1994	LA-N	84	4	.274	.344	.464	38	1	.316	.350	.395	46	3	.239	.340	.522	57	2	.281	.339	.421	27	2	.259	.355	.556	61	3	.295	.348	.508	23	1	.217	.333	.348
1995	LA-N	56	1	.179	.246	.286	26	0	.269	.345	.346	30	1	.100	.156	.233	31	1	.161	.188	.290	25	0	.200	.310	.280	37	1	.189	.231	.351	19	0	.158	.273	.158
TOTALS		3419	70	.263	.330	.401	1636	29	.256	.326	.380	1783	41	.270	.333	.420	1641	26	.255	.327	.372	1778	44	.271	.332	.427	1330	36	.285	.332	.441	2089	34	.249	.328	.375
■ **Walt Weiss**	BB/TR																																			
1987	Oak-A	26	0	.462	.500	.615	14	0	.500	.563	.643	12	0	.417	.417	.583	0	0	—	—	—	26	0	.462	.500	.615	10	0	.300	.300	.400	16	0	.563	.611	.750
1988	Oak-A	452	3	.250	.312	.321	211	0	.237	.292	.289	241	3	.261	.330	.349	211	2	.246	.305	.303	241	1	.253	.318	.336	101	0	.208	.250	.257	351	3	.262	.329	.339
1989	Oak-A	236	3	.233	.298	.318	120	2	.200	.273	.283	116	1	.267	.325	.353	108	2	.213	.292	.315	128	1	.250	.304	.320	57	0	.228	.254	.281	179	3	.235	.312	.330
1990	Oak-A	445	2	.265	.337	.321	235	1	.247	.316	.281	210	1	.286	.360	.367	237	2	.283	.344	.367	208	0	.245	.329	.269	115	0	.261	.306	.304	330	2	.267	.347	.327
1991	Oak-A	133	0	.226	.286	.286	78	0	.167	.233	.192	55	0	.309	.361	.418	133	0	.226	.286	.286	0	0	—	—	—	31	0	.194	.219	.258	102	0	.235	.304	.294
1992	Oak-A	316	0	.212	.305	.241	144	0	.174	.280	.208	172	0	.244	.327	.267	82	0	.232	.304	.244	234	0	.205	.305	.239	74	0	.135	.190	.162	242	0	.236	.337	.264
1993	Fla-N	500	1	.266	.367	.308	244	0	.250	.362	.283	256	1	.281	.372	.332	241	1	.290	.379	.344	259	0	.243	.356	.274	128	0	.234	.353	.281	372	1	.277	.372	.317
1994	Col-N	423	1	.251	.336	.303	214	1	.262	.331	.318	209	0	.239	.342	.287	309	1	.269	.342	.324	114	0	.202	.321	.246	96	1	.323	.400	.385	327	0	.229	.317	.278
1995	Col-N	427	1	.260	.403	.321	217	0	.281	.429	.323	210	1	.238	.375	.319	199	0	.251	.375	.312	228	1	.268	.426	.329	114	0	.263	.387	.298	313	1	.259	.409	.329
1996	Col-N	517	8	.282	.381	.375	261	5	.337	.436	.444	256	3	.227	.322	.305	271	2	.299	.408	.358	246	6	.264	.350	.394	141	0	.277	.381	.319	376	8	.285	.381	.396
1997	Col-N	393	4	.270	.377	.384	206	2	.301	.411	.432	187	2	.235	.338	.332	232	2	.263	.362	.353	161	2	.280	.397	.429	99	1	.192	.304	.273	294	3	.296	.401	.422
1998	Atl-N	347	0	.280	.386	.343	209	0	.254	.371	.335	138	0	.319	.410	.355	195	0	.323	.439	.385	152	0	.224	.314	.289	96	0	.250	.348	.323	251	0	.291	.400	.351
1999	Atl-N	279	2	.226	.315	.323	114	0	.246	.353	.325	165	2	.212	.286	.321	150	1	.267	.352	.360	129	1	.178	.269	.279	75	2	.200	.295	.320	204	0	.235	.322	.324
2000	Atl-N	192	0	.260	.353	.313	96	0	.323	.416	.396	96	0	.198	.288	.229	90	0	.300	.407	.367	102	0	.225	.302	.265	67	0	.299	.342	.328	125	0	.240	.358	.304
TOTALS		4686	25	.258	.351	.326	2363	11	.261	.359	.327	2323	14	.254	.343	.325	2458	13	.271	.360	.337	2228	12	.243	.341	.313	1204	4	.242	.325	.297	3482	21	.263	.360	.336
■ **Lou Whitaker**	BL/TR																																			
1978	Det-A	484	3	.285	.361	.357	273	2	.315	.387	.399	211	1	.246	.326	.303	200	0	.300	.346	.350	284	3	.275	.371	.363	187	2	.257	.358	.326	297	1	.303	.363	.377

YEAR	TM/L	TOTAL AB	HR	AVG	OBP	SLG	HOME AB	HR	AVG	OBP	SLG	AWAY AB	HR	AVG	OBP	SLG	1ST HALF AB	HR	AVG	OBP	SLG	2ND HALF AB	HR	AVG	OBP	SLG	LEFT AB	HR	AVG	OBP	SLG	RIGHT AB	HR	AVG	OBP	SLG
1979	Det-A	423	3	.286	.395	.378	211	3	.327	.435	.450	212	0	.245	.356	.307	179	2	.302	.390	.425	244	1	.275	.399	.344	143	1	.273	.371	.336	280	2	.293	.407	.400
1980	Det-A	477	1	.233	.331	.283	238	1	.206	.307	.256	239	0	.259	.355	.310	197	0	.218	.357	.259	280	1	.243	.311	.300	165	0	.188	.284	.212	312	1	.256	.355	.321
1981	Det-A	335	5	.263	.340	.373	172	4	.250	.312	.413	163	1	.276	.368	.331	175	2	.269	.343	.371	160	3	.256	.337	.375	146	2	.240	.304	.336	189	3	.280	.367	.402
1982	Det-A	560	15	.286	.341	.434	276	9	.290	.340	.467	284	6	.282	.342	.401	224	4	.246	.305	.348	336	11	.313	.365	.491	147	3	.299	.342	.415	413	12	.281	.341	.441
1983	Det-A	643	12	.320	.380	.457	315	7	.314	.368	.457	328	5	.326	.391	.457	300	5	.313	.368	.460	343	7	.327	.391	.455	205	4	.307	.370	.420	438	8	.326	.385	.475
1984	Det-A	558	13	.289	.357	.407	273	8	.300	.362	.436	285	5	.277	.352	.379	282	5	.309	.379	.401	276	8	.268	.333	.413	174	2	.230	.292	.305	384	11	.315	.386	.453
1985	Det-A	609	21	.279	.362	.456	303	11	.267	.352	.439	306	10	.291	.372	.474	271	12	.306	.390	.494	338	9	.257	.339	.426	145	2	.228	.323	.324	464	19	.295	.374	.498
1986	Det-A	584	20	.269	.338	.437	286	8	.248	.334	.406	298	12	.289	.341	.466	286	9	.269	.326	.448	298	11	.268	.349	.426	163	3	.221	.283	.325	421	17	.287	.359	.480
1987	Det-A	604	16	.265	.341	.427	283	10	.261	.341	.435	321	6	.268	.342	.421	272	9	.265	.337	.423	332	7	.265	.345	.431	226	4	.217	.279	.327	378	12	.294	.376	.487
1988	Det-A	403	12	.275	.376	.419	175	8	.269	.388	.457	228	4	.281	.366	.390	233	5	.279	.386	.403	170	7	.271	.361	.441	92	0	.228	.330	.272	311	12	.289	.390	.463
1989	Det-A	509	28	.251	.361	.462	235	17	.264	.377	.519	274	11	.241	.347	.412	261	16	.264	.370	.494	248	12	.238	.351	.427	149	5	.188	.305	.349	360	23	.278	.383	.508
1990	Det-A	472	18	.237	.338	.407	219	8	.215	.316	.370	253	10	.257	.356	.439	243	10	.206	.303	.362	229	8	.271	.375	.454	99	2	.162	.278	.253	373	16	.257	.353	.448
1991	Det-A	470	23	.279	.391	.489	237	15	.304	.442	.557	233	8	.253	.335	.421	206	10	.243	.382	.442	264	13	.307	.399	.527	97	2	.247	.354	.340	373	21	.287	.400	.528
1992	Det-A	453	19	.278	.386	.461	228	11	.320	.442	.548	225	8	.236	.326	.373	210	9	.281	.402	.481	243	10	.276	.372	.444	62	2	.355	.481	.548	391	17	.266	.370	.448
1993	Det-A	383	9	.290	.412	.449	193	5	.269	.388	.440	190	4	.311	.435	.458	207	7	.324	.431	.527	176	2	.250	.389	.358	49	0	.122	.254	.143	334	9	.314	.434	.494
1994	Det-A	322	12	.301	.377	.491	154	8	.318	.403	.545	168	4	.286	.352	.440	204	10	.265	.360	.490	118	2	.364	.408	.492	36	1	.278	.349	.417	286	11	.304	.380	.500
1995	Det-A	249	14	.293	.372	.518	123	11	.276	.377	.585	126	3	.310	.367	.452	119	5	.319	.390	.521	130	9	.269	.356	.515	26	1	.308	.357	.538	223	13	.291	.374	.516
TOTALS		8538	244	.277	.363	.427	4194	146	.279	.370	.448	4344	98	.274	.357	.405	4069	120	.276	.364	.428	4469	124	.277	.362	.425	2311	36	.239	.323	.334	6227	208	.290	.378	.461
■ **Devon White** BB/TR																																				
1985	Cal-A	7	0	.143	.333	.143	2	0	.000	.500	.000	5	0	.200	.200	.200	0	0	—	—	—	7	0	.143	.333	.143	0	0	—	1.000	—	7	0	.143	.250	.143
1986	Cal-A	51	1	.235	.316	.353	21	0	.190	.261	.286	30	1	.267	.353	.400	0	0	—	—	—	51	1	.235	.316	.353	17	0	.294	.333	.294	34	1	.206	.308	.382
1987	Cal-A	639	24	.263	.306	.443	314	11	.248	.293	.417	325	13	.277	.320	.468	309	15	.291	.333	.518	330	9	.236	.281	.373	199	11	.246	.296	.477	440	13	.270	.311	.427
1988	Cal-A	455	11	.259	.297	.389	211	3	.237	.283	.341	244	8	.279	.310	.430	168	3	.238	.291	.351	287	8	.272	.301	.411	150	6	.247	.289	.420	305	5	.266	.301	.374
1989	Cal-A	636	12	.245	.282	.371	317	9	.243	.283	.394	319	3	.248	.281	.348	310	9	.268	.298	.448	326	3	.224	.267	.298	214	2	.248	.291	.355	422	10	.244	.277	.379
1990	Cal-A	443	11	.217	.290	.343	219	5	.215	.278	.352	224	6	.219	.302	.335	243	7	.214	.288	.362	200	4	.220	.293	.320	130	3	.246	.315	.354	313	8	.204	.280	.339
1991	Tor-A	642	17	.282	.342	.455	326	9	.298	.355	.497	316	8	.266	.330	.411	288	2	.292	.359	.424	354	15	.274	.328	.480	199	8	.302	.350	.518	443	9	.273	.339	.427
1992	Tor-A	641	17	.248	.303	.390	306	7	.265	.321	.415	335	10	.233	.286	.367	312	9	.244	.307	.388	329	8	.252	.299	.392	179	5	.212	.272	.324	462	12	.262	.315	.416
1993	Tor-A	598	15	.273	.341	.438	307	10	.290	.361	.498	291	5	.254	.321	.375	293	10	.297	.352	.502	305	5	.249	.331	.377	185	3	.254	.324	.395	413	12	.281	.349	.458
1994	Tor-A	403	13	.270	.313	.457	193	5	.275	.311	.440	210	8	.267	.316	.471	297	10	.279	.321	.458	106	3	.245	.292	.453	124	4	.306	.328	.508	279	9	.254	.307	.434
1995	Tor-A	427	10	.283	.334	.431	210	4	.300	.354	.471	217	6	.267	.315	.392	197	5	.289	.341	.462	230	5	.278	.328	.404	100	1	.230	.287	.330	327	9	.300	.348	.462
1996	Fla-N	552	17	.274	.325	.455	282	5	.255	.297	.394	270	12	.293	.352	.519	277	7	.271	.323	.444	275	10	.276	.326	.465	119	6	.345	.389	.597	433	11	.254	.307	.416
1997	Fla-N	265	6	.245	.338	.370	152	4	.250	.335	.382	113	2	.239	.341	.354	70	0	.271	.407	.386	195	6	.236	.311	.364	48	1	.188	.286	.271	217	5	.258	.349	.392
1998	Ari-N	563	22	.279	.335	.456	267	11	.270	.330	.446	296	11	.287	.341	.466	320	12	.287	.333	.469	243	10	.267	.338	.440	165	5	.291	.337	.430	398	17	.274	.335	.467
1999	LA-N	474	14	.268	.337	.407	227	8	.304	.375	.454	247	6	.235	.300	.364	213	7	.258	.321	.408	261	7	.276	.349	.406	139	5	.288	.367	.468	335	9	.260	.323	.382
2000	LA-N	158	4	.266	.310	.386	61	2	.344	.385	.492	97	2	.216	.262	.320	83	3	.289	.322	.422	75	1	.240	.296	.347	65	2	.308	.348	.477	93	2	.237	.283	.323
TOTALS		6954	194	.263	.318	.417	3415	93	.267	.322	.427	3539	101	.259	.314	.407	3380	99	.271	.325	.439	3574	95	.254	.311	.396	2033	62	.266	.319	.426	4921	132	.261	.318	.413
■ **Frank White** BR/TR																																				
1978	KC-A	461	7	.275	.317	.399	238	3	.290	.333	.416	223	4	.260	.300	.381	229	3	.275	.327	.393	232	4	.276	.307	.405	156	2	.276	.331	.417	305	5	.275	.310	.390
1979	KC-A	467	10	.266	.300	.403	229	5	.236	.282	.376	238	5	.294	.317	.429	173	4	.295	.335	.457	294	6	.248	.279	.371	155	4	.252	.287	.394	312	6	.272	.306	.407
1980	KC-A	560	7	.264	.289	.357	262	1	.244	.278	.317	298	6	.282	.299	.393	284	4	.257	.276	.335	276	3	.272	.302	.380	217	6	.286	.300	.438	343	1	.251	.282	.306
1981	KC-A	364	9	.250	.285	.376	159	4	.245	.287	.403	205	5	.254	.284	.356	140	3	.271	.307	.407	224	6	.237	.271	.357	122	7	.230	.266	.467	242	2	.260	.295	.331
1982	KC-A	524	11	.298	.318	.469	269	7	.320	.342	.543	255	4	.275	.293	.392	227	2	.317	.331	.463	297	9	.283	.309	.475	178	5	.326	.332	.551	346	6	.283	.311	.428
1983	KC-A	549	11	.260	.283	.406	275	8	.273	.300	.458	274	3	.248	.266	.354	258	6	.264	.292	.430	291	5	.258	.276	.385	181	5	.326	.353	.525	368	6	.228	.249	.348
1984	KC-A	479	17	.271	.311	.445	240	6	.258	.306	.412	239	11	.285	.316	.477	227	7	.269	.314	.419	252	10	.274	.309	.468	127	7	.299	.336	.520	352	10	.261	.302	.418
1985	KC-A	563	22	.249	.284	.414	297	9	.242	.277	.377	266	13	.256	.292	.455	247	9	.227	.264	.381	316	13	.266	.299	.440	166	9	.247	.277	.446	397	13	.249	.287	.401
1986	KC-A	566	22	.272	.322	.465	277	12	.282	.329	.491	289	10	.263	.315	.439	282	8	.280	.316	.443	284	14	.264	.328	.486	149	1	.268	.337	.349	417	21	.273	.316	.506
1987	KC-A	563	17	.245	.308	.400	256	6	.273	.355	.418	307	11	.221	.267	.384	260	6	.238	.306	.365	303	11	.251	.310	.429	148	5	.284	.352	.453	415	12	.231	.292	.381
1988	KC-A	537	8	.235	.266	.330	269	3	.242	.274	.338	268	5	.228	.257	.321	245	6	.241	.279	.371	292	2	.229	.255	.295	155	2	.265	.296	.368	382	6	.223	.254	.314
1989	KC-A	418	2	.256	.307	.328	210	1	.238	.277	.314	208	1	.274	.336	.341	196	0	.245	.301	.301	222	2	.266	.312	.351	125	0	.240	.307	.296	293	2	.263	.307	.341
1990	KC-A	241	2	.216	.253	.307	145	2	.248	.281	.366	96	0	.167	.212	.219	113	1	.204	.233	.292	128	1	.227	.270	.320	93	1	.194	.240	.280	148	1	.230	.261	.324
TOTALS		6292	145	.260	.297	.397	3126	67	.262	.303	.406	3166	78	.258	.292	.389	2881	59	.261	.300	.392	3411	86	.259	.296	.402	1972	54	.273	.312	.431	4320	91	.254	.291	.382
■ **Ernie Whitt** BL/TR																																				
1978	Tor-A	4	0	.000	.200	.000	1	0	.000	.000	.000	3	0	.000	.250	.000	0	0	—	—	—	4	0	.000	.200	.000	0	0	—	—	—	4	0	.000	.200	.000
1980	Tor-A	295	6	.237	.287	.353	137	2	.190	.253	.292	158	4	.278	.318	.405	90	1	.200	.277	.244	205	5	.254	.292	.400	60	0	.283	.328	.350	235	6	.226	.277	.353
1981	Tor-A	195	1	.236	.307	.297	80	0	.225	.333	.287	115	1	.243	.287	.304	138	0	.232	.284	.268	57	1	.246	.358	.368	47	0	.234	.280	.255	148	1	.236	.315	.311
1982	Tor-A	284	11	.261	.317	.440	150	8	.273	.349	.527	134	3	.246	.280	.343	163	6	.258	.326	.411	121	5	.264	.306	.479	35	1	.143	.250	.286	249	10	.277	.327	.462
1983	Tor-A	344	17	.256	.346	.459	168	11	.304	.383	.589	176	6	.210	.311	.335	163	8	.264	.353	.460	181	9	.249	.340	.459	35	0	.114	.289	.114	309	17	.272	.353	.498
1984	Tor-A	315	15	.238	.327	.425	144	5	.236	.343	.403	171	10	.240	.313	.444	130	4	.246	.344	.408	185	11	.232	.314	.438	25	0	.160	.222	.320	290	15	.245	.335	.434
1985	Tor-A	412	19	.245	.323	.444	197	7	.223	.319	.406	215	12	.265	.326	.479	176	9	.290	.342	.523	236	10	.212	.309	.386	75	2	.213	.318	.320	337	17	.252	.324	.472
1986	Tor-A	395	16	.268	.326	.448	189	7	.265	.341	.460	206	9	.272	.311	.437	162	8	.228	.304	.420	233	8	.296	.341	.468	46	3	.370	.396	.565	349	13	.255	.317	.433
1987	Tor-A	446	19	.269	.334	.455	214	11	.262	.339	.481	232	8	.276	.329	.431	198	5	.247	.317	.394	248	14	.286	.348	.504	63	0	.238	.314	.286	383	19	.274	.337	.483
1988	Tor-A	398	16	.251	.348	.410	194	9	.242	.359	.418	204	7	.260	.336	.402	184	3	.223	.315	.310	214	13	.276	.375	.495	39	2	.282	.408	.462	359	14	.248	.341	.404
1989	Tor-A	385	11	.262	.349	.416	184	8	.234	.346	.418	201	3	.289	.351	.413	188	5	.319	.406	.479	197	6	.208	.293	.355	44	1	.159	.240	.227	341	10	.276	.362	.440
1990	Atl-N	180	2	.172	.265	.250	86	2	.163	.284	.279	94	0	.181	.245	.223	71	2	.169	.298	.324	109	0	.174	.242	.202	17	0	.118	.167	.118	163	2	.178	.274	.264
1991	Bal-A	62	0	.242	.329	.274	29	0	.276	.344	.310	33	0	.212	.316	.242	60	0	.250	.338	.283	2	0	.000	.000	.000	5	0	.200	.200	.200	57	0	.246	.338	.281
TOTALS		3715	133	.250	.326	.411	1773	70	.244	.336	.429	1942	63	.255	.316	.395	1723	51	.251	.330	.394	1992	82	.248	.322	.426	491	9	.224	.305	.314	3224	124	.253	.329	.426
■ **Bernie Williams** BB/TR																																				
1991	NY-A	320	3	.237	.336	.350	159	1	.264	.355	.371	161	2	.211	.317	.329	0	0	—	—	—	320	3	.237	.336	.350	104	2	.202	.309	.317	216	1	.255	.349	.366
1992	NY-A	261	5	.280	.354	.406	134	3	.291	.375	.433	127	2	.268	.331	.378	5	0	.200	.200	.200	256	5	.281	.357	.410	84	1	.298	.379	.429	177	4	.271	.342	.395
1993	NY-A	567	12	.268	.333	.400	256	5	.266	.339	.395	311	7	.270	.328	.405	239	7	.251	.322	.418	328	5	.280	.342	.387	191	7	.325	.402	.503	376	5	.239	.297	.348
1994	NY-A	408	12	.289	.384	.453	184	4	.261	.358	.391	224	8	.313	.405	.504	246	10	.264	.381	.459	162	2	.327	.389	.444	145	6	.366	.426	.600	263	6	.247	.362	.373
1995	NY-A	563	18	.307	.392	.487	280	7	.329	.413	.479	283	11	.286	.370	.495	216	9	.259	.339	.458	347	9	.337	.424	.504	195	13	.303	.378	.590	368	5	.310	.399	.432
1996	NY-A	551	29	.305	.391	.535	259	12	.328	.419	.548	292	17	.284	.364	.524	247	15	.328	.406	.579	304	14	.286	.378	.500	173	16	.376	.447	.694	378	13	.272	.365	.463
1997	NY-A	509	21	.328	.408	.544	240	13	.300	.366	.554	269	8	.353	.443	.535	262	10	.317	.422	.511	247	11	.340	.391	.579	141	9	.326	.443	.596	368	12	.329	.393	.524
1998	NY-A	499	26	.339	.422	.575	256	14	.355	.442	.590	243	12	.321	.401	.560	224	10	.353	.455	.603	275	16	.327	.394	.553	163	9	.350	.443	.583	336	17	.333	.411	.571
1999	NY-A	591	25	.342	.435	.536	285	11	.337	.440	.502	306	14	.346	.430	.569	294	13	.344	.418	.531	297	12	.340	.450	.542	165	5	.297	.393	.467	426	20	.359	.451	.563
2000	NY-A	537	30	.307	.391	.566	239	15	.310	.424	.598	298	15	.305	.363	.540	296	18	.321	.390	.601	241	12	.290	.392	.523	166	9	.289	.381	.494	371	21	.315	.396	.598
TOTALS		4806	181	.304	.389	.496	2292	85	.308	.398	.496	2514	96	.301	.380	.496	2029	92	.306	.393	.522	2777	89	.303	.386	.477	1527	77	.318	.404	.540	3279	104	.298	.382	.475
■ **Gerald Williams** BR/TR																																				
1992	NY-A	27	3	.296	.296	.704	12	2	.333	.333	.917	15	1	.267	.267	.533	0	0	—	—	—	27	3	.296	.296	.704	14	2	.357	.357	.857	13	1	.231	.231	.538
1993	NY-A	67	0	.149	.183	.269	37	0	.108	.132	.216	30	0	.200	.242	.333	39	0	.205	.225	.410	28	0	.071	.129	.071	36	0	.139	.179	.194	31	0	.161	.188	.355
1994	NY-A	86	4	.291	.319	.523	44	2	.318	.354	.568	42	2	.262	.279	.476	51	2	.294	.294	.490	35	2	.286	.350	.571	65	3	.277	.314	.523	21	1	.333	.333	.524
1995	NY-A	182	6	.247	.327	.467	95	4	.242	.315	.484	87	2	.253	.340	.448	64	4	.281	.356	.609	118	2	.229	.311	.390	126	4	.278	.378	.508	56	2	.179	.200	.375
1996	NY-A	233	5	.270	.319	.433	117	3	.282	.326	.444	116	2	.259	.313	.422	176	5	.318	.374	.506	57	0	.123	.145	.211	98	4	.276	.327	.480	135	1	.267	.313	.400
1996	Mil-A	92	0	.207	.247	.250	30	0	.233	.233	.267	62	0	.194	.254	.242	0	0	—	—	—	92	0	.207	.247	.250	26	0	.346	.370	.462	66	0	.152	.200	.167
1997	Mil-A	566	10	.253	.282	.369	267	3	.262	.299	.356	299	7	.244	.266	.381	286	7	.269	.310	.395	280	3	.236	.252	.343	157	6	.274	.303	.459	409	4	.244	.274	.335
1998	Atl-N	266	10	.305	.352	.504	125	5	.336	.368	.560	141	5	.277	.338	.454	107	2	.299	.342	.430	159	8	.308	.358	.553	146	7	.363	.408	.616	120	3	.233	.285	.367
1999	Atl-N	422	17	.275	.335	.457	213	7	.291	.345	.460	209	10	.258	.325	.455	156	5	.256	.328	.397	266	12	.286	.339	.492	182	9	.286	.333	.511	240	8	.267	.336	.417
2000	TB-A	632	21	.274	.312	.427	297	6	.269	.308	.387	335	15	.278	.316	.463	299	8	.281	.317	.425	333	13	.267	.308	.429	123	5	.260	.303	.431	509	16	.277	.314	.426
TOTALS		2573	76	.265	.310	.426	1237	32	.274	.316	.427	1336	44	.257	.304	.426	1178	33	.280	.326	.439	1395	43	.253	.296	.416	973	40	.287	.336	.497	1600	36	.253	.294	.383
■ **Matt Williams** BR/TR																																				
1987	SF-N	245	8	.188	.240	.339	112	5	.179	.227	.357	133	3	.195	.250	.323	219	8	.196	.247	.361	26	0	.115	.179	.154	78	4	.192	.241	.385	167	4	.186	.239	.317
1988	SF-N	156	8	.205	.251	.410	97	7	.227	.257	.474	59	1	.169	.242	.305	34	3	.206	.250	.500	122	5	.205	.252	.385	54	5	.167	.237	.463	102	3	.225	.259	.382
1989	SF-N	292	18	.202	.242	.455	144	10	.215	.248	.514	148	8	.189	.236	.399	54	2	.130	.175	.259	238	16	.218	.257	.500	87	9	.264	.330	.644	205	9	.176	.202	.376
1990	SF-N	617	33	.277	.319	.488	303	20	.271	.312	.521	314	13	.283	.325	.455	292	16	.301	.332	.510	325	17	.255	.307	.468	208	12	.284	.332	.500	409	21	.274	.312	.482

		TOTAL					HOME					AWAY					1ST HALF					2ND HALF					LEFT					RIGHT				
YEAR	TM/L	AB	HR	AVG	OBP	SLG	AB	HR	AVG	OBP	SLG	AB	HR	AVG	OBP	SLG	AB	HR	AVG	OBP	SLG	AB	HR	AVG	OBP	SLG	AB	HR	AVG	OBP	SLG	AB	HR	AVG	OBP	SLG
1991	SF-N	589	34	.268	.310	.499	289	17	.287	.327	.526	300	17	.250	.294	.473	280	10	.229	.266	.396	309	24	.304	.349	.592	165	7	.279	.315	.455	424	27	.264	.309	.517
1992	SF-N	529	20	.227	.286	.384	269	9	.230	.283	.387	260	11	.223	.290	.381	256	11	.211	.270	.383	273	9	.242	.302	.385	164	10	.226	.279	.445	365	10	.227	.290	.356
1993	SF-N	579	38	.294	.325	.561	287	19	.293	.330	.571	292	19	.295	.319	.551	290	21	.290	.322	.572	289	17	.298	.328	.550	186	17	.328	.363	.683	393	21	.277	.306	.504
1994	SF-N	445	43	.267	.319	.607	219	20	.265	.326	.584	226	23	.270	.311	.628	303	29	.241	.302	.571	142	14	.324	.356	.683	104	16	.298	.373	.788	341	27	.258	.301	.551
1995	SF-N	283	23	.336	.399	.647	120	9	.325	.394	.617	163	14	.344	.403	.669	134	13	.381	.436	.754	149	10	.295	.367	.550	53	6	.377	.468	.811	230	17	.326	.383	.609
1996	SF-N	404	22	.302	.367	.510	201	13	.313	.401	.547	203	9	.291	.332	.473	299	17	.308	.375	.528	105	5	.286	.345	.457	90	7	.233	.333	.500	314	15	.322	.377	.513
1997	Cle-A	596	32	.263	.307	.488	272	7	.265	.313	.404	324	25	.262	.301	.559	289	19	.235	.287	.488	307	13	.290	.325	.489	139	13	.281	.327	.647	457	19	.258	.300	.440
1998	Ari-N	510	20	.267	.327	.439	262	11	.279	.339	.447	248	9	.254	.314	.431	305	14	.272	.326	.472	205	6	.259	.327	.390	130	5	.300	.372	.454	380	15	.255	.311	.434
1999	Ari-N	627	35	.303	.344	.536	308	17	.279	.325	.510	319	18	.326	.361	.561	318	21	.324	.358	.594	309	14	.282	.329	.476	177	12	.333	.396	.610	450	23	.291	.322	.507
2000	Ari-N	371	12	.275	.315	.431	180	5	.250	.303	.394	191	7	.298	.327	.466	93	2	.269	.313	.387	278	10	.277	.315	.446	106	5	.311	.362	.472	265	7	.260	.295	.415
TOTALS		6243	346	.269	.316	.492	3063	169	.268	.319	.491	3180	177	.269	.314	.493	3166	186	.266	.314	.498	3077	160	.271	.318	.487	1741	128	.283	.340	.555	4502	218	.263	.307	.468
■ Glenn Wilson BR/TR																																				
1982	Det-A	322	12	.292	.322	.457	169	9	.314	.348	.544	153	3	.268	.291	.359	38	1	.342	.405	.526	284	11	.285	.310	.447	98	0	.316	.340	.378	224	12	.281	.314	.491
1983	Det-A	503	11	.268	.306	.408	251	9	.283	.326	.458	252	2	.254	.286	.357	248	8	.278	.307	.464	255	3	.259	.305	.353	182	2	.297	.335	.418	321	9	.252	.289	.402
1984	Phi-N	341	6	.240	.276	.372	160	5	.244	.282	.394	181	1	.238	.271	.354	201	5	.254	.286	.418	140	1	.221	.262	.307	125	3	.264	.295	.408	216	3	.227	.265	.352
1985	Phi-N	608	14	.275	.311	.424	301	7	.292	.329	.452	307	7	.257	.292	.397	261	7	.264	.297	.448	347	7	.282	.321	.406	171	6	.287	.330	.485	437	8	.270	.303	.400
1986	Phi-N	584	15	.271	.319	.413	285	7	.302	.357	.467	299	8	.241	.283	.361	272	6	.235	.293	.353	312	9	.301	.342	.465	185	4	.222	.271	.335	399	11	.293	.341	.449
1987	Phi-N	569	14	.264	.308	.381	278	5	.252	.315	.342	291	9	.275	.300	.419	266	10	.289	.325	.455	303	4	.241	.293	.317	155	2	.271	.307	.355	414	12	.261	.308	.391
1988	Sea-A	284	3	.250	.286	.324	132	2	.273	.297	.371	152	1	.230	.276	.283	237	3	.257	.300	.342	47	0	.213	.208	.234	101	1	.317	.340	.396	183	2	.213	.256	.284
1988	Pit-N	126	2	.270	.288	.381	54	0	.259	.293	.370	72	2	.278	.284	.389	0	0	—	—	—	126	2	.270	.288	.381	63	2	.254	.277	.429	63	0	.286	.299	.333
1989	Pit-N	330	9	.282	.342	.448	147	2	.259	.341	.367	183	7	.301	.343	.514	195	7	.277	.336	.456	135	2	.289	.351	.437	119	3	.319	.371	.513	211	6	.261	.326	.412
1989	Hou-N	102	2	.216	.250	.333	51	2	.275	.302	.490	51	0	.157	.200	.176	0	0	—	—	—	102	2	.216	.250	.333	24	1	.333	.385	.542	78	1	.179	.207	.269
1990	Hou-N	368	10	.245	.293	.364	174	5	.259	.307	.402	194	5	.232	.281	.330	214	7	.243	.283	.364	154	3	.247	.308	.364	164	2	.262	.311	.360	204	8	.230	.279	.368
1993	Pit-N	14	0	.143	.143	.143	5	0	.000	.000	.000	9	0	.222	.222	.222	14	0	.143	.143	.143	0	0	—	—	—	12	0	.167	.167	.167	2	0	.000	.000	.000
TOTALS		4151	98	.265	.306	.398	2007	53	.276	.323	.425	2144	45	.254	.289	.374	1946	54	.263	.304	.413	2205	44	.266	.307	.385	1399	26	.278	.317	.405	2752	72	.258	.300	.395
■ Preston Wilson BR/TR																																				
1998	NY-N	20	0	.300	.364	.400	8	0	.750	.778	1.000	12	0	.000	.077	.000	20	0	.300	.364	.400	0	0	—	—	—	8	0	.250	.250	.250	12	0	.333	.429	.500
1998	Fla-N	31	1	.065	.194	.161	15	1	.133	.350	.333	16	0	.000	.000	.000	0	0	—	—	—	31	1	.065	.194	.161	17	0	.000	.105	.000	14	1	.143	.294	.357
1999	Fla-N	482	26	.280	.350	.502	233	8	.253	.339	.425	249	18	.305	.360	.574	222	15	.252	.313	.509	260	11	.304	.380	.496	123	9	.285	.366	.585	359	17	.279	.344	.474
2000	Fla-N	605	31	.264	.331	.486	297	12	.266	.336	.461	308	19	.263	.326	.510	308	17	.250	.322	.490	297	14	.279	.340	.481	144	9	.250	.314	.493	461	22	.269	.336	.484
TOTALS		1138	58	.266	.336	.482	553	21	.264	.344	.450	585	37	.268	.327	.513	550	32	.253	.320	.495	588	26	.279	.350	.471	292	18	.250	.323	.497	846	40	.272	.340	.478
■ Mookie Wilson BB/TR																																				
1980	NY-N	105	0	.248	.325	.352	41	0	.317	.378	.439	64	0	.203	.292	.297	0	0	—	—	—	105	0	.248	.325	.352	21	0	.143	.280	.286	84	0	.274	.337	.369
1981	NY-N	328	3	.271	.317	.372	168	2	.286	.330	.387	160	1	.256	.304	.356	139	1	.288	.340	.388	189	2	.259	.300	.360	60	1	.250	.286	.367	268	2	.276	.324	.373
1982	NY-N	639	5	.279	.314	.369	307	2	.277	.323	.349	332	3	.280	.304	.389	302	2	.281	.314	.351	337	3	.276	.313	.386	132	1	.288	.326	.364	507	4	.276	.310	.371
1983	NY-N	638	7	.276	.300	.367	335	4	.299	.330	.379	303	3	.251	.265	.353	311	2	.251	.282	.334	327	5	.300	.316	.398	175	3	.257	.268	.343	463	4	.283	.311	.376
1984	NY-N	587	10	.276	.308	.409	309	7	.278	.308	.440	278	3	.273	.308	.374	281	5	.281	.299	.370	306	5	.271	.316	.444	199	4	.276	.306	.437	388	6	.276	.309	.394
1985	NY-N	337	6	.276	.331	.424	152	2	.329	.396	.441	185	4	.232	.274	.411	222	3	.261	.305	.387	115	3	.304	.377	.496	149	4	.295	.361	.490	188	2	.261	.305	.372
1986	NY-N	381	9	.289	.345	.430	173	4	.289	.351	.422	208	5	.288	.339	.438	139	4	.288	.340	.460	242	5	.289	.347	.413	196	3	.291	.341	.418	185	6	.286	.348	.443
1987	NY-N	385	9	.299	.359	.455	176	5	.267	.337	.415	209	4	.325	.379	.488	187	6	.316	.373	.535	198	3	.283	.347	.379	225	3	.271	.329	.404	160	6	.338	.401	.525
1988	NY-N	378	8	.296	.345	.431	185	1	.259	.292	.335	193	7	.332	.393	.523	169	2	.254	.306	.367	209	6	.330	.376	.483	195	4	.282	.335	.421	183	4	.311	.355	.443
1989	NY-N	249	3	.205	.237	.289	120	1	.192	.218	.267	129	2	.217	.254	.310	204	3	.206	.238	.299	45	0	.200	.229	.244	122	1	.164	.203	.221	127	2	.244	.269	.354
1989	Tor-A	238	2	.298	.311	.370	127	1	.252	.267	.323	111	1	.351	.363	.423	0	0	—	—	—	238	2	.298	.311	.370	78	0	.346	.346	.397	160	2	.275	.295	.356
1990	Tor-A	588	3	.265	.300	.355	271	0	.247	.279	.321	317	3	.281	.318	.385	265	1	.238	.294	.309	323	2	.288	.305	.393	188	2	.245	.294	.351	400	1	.275	.303	.357
1991	Tor-A	241	2	.241	.277	.349	115	1	.270	.298	.383	126	1	.214	.259	.317	146	2	.253	.275	.390	95	0	.221	.282	.284	43	0	.209	.209	.256	198	2	.247	.291	.369
TOTALS		5094	67	.274	.314	.386	2479	30	.274	.315	.376	2615	37	.274	.313	.396	2365	31	.264	.303	.372	2729	36	.283	.323	.398	1783	26	.266	.309	.385	3311	41	.278	.317	.387
■ Willie Wilson BB/TR																																				
1978	KC-A	198	0	.217	.280	.278	111	0	.189	.242	.252	87	0	.253	.327	.310	141	0	.241	.312	.326	57	0	.158	.197	.158	81	0	.235	.319	.284	117	0	.205	.250	.274
1979	KC-A	588	6	.315	.351	.420	307	3	.329	.366	.430	281	3	.299	.334	.409	224	4	.321	.363	.460	364	2	.310	.343	.396	193	2	.290	.322	.404	395	4	.327	.365	.428
1980	KC-A	705	3	.326	.357	.421	339	2	.324	.360	.425	366	1	.328	.353	.418	329	2	.307	.339	.404	376	1	.343	.372	.436	275	2	.360	.385	.487	430	1	.305	.339	.379
1981	KC-A	439	1	.303	.335	.364	198	0	.283	.317	.354	241	1	.320	.350	.373	210	0	.271	.303	.329	229	1	.332	.365	.397	158	1	.297	.315	.380	281	0	.306	.347	.356
1982	KC-A	585	3	.332	.365	.431	288	2	.347	.381	.441	297	1	.316	.349	.421	212	1	.330	.362	.443	373	2	.332	.367	.424	221	0	.285	.315	.344	364	3	.360	.395	.484
1983	KC-A	576	2	.276	.316	.352	275	2	.302	.349	.415	301	0	.252	.286	.296	299	1	.288	.330	.368	277	1	.264	.301	.336	186	1	.274	.311	.382	390	1	.277	.319	.338
1984	KC-A	541	2	.301	.350	.390	260	1	.304	.360	.381	281	1	.299	.340	.399	169	1	.284	.341	.373	372	1	.309	.354	.398	167	1	.341	.387	.449	374	1	.283	.333	.364
1985	KC-A	605	4	.278	.316	.408	302	1	.275	.313	.417	303	3	.281	.319	.399	305	2	.279	.324	.416	300	2	.277	.307	.400	164	1	.293	.316	.409	441	3	.272	.316	.408
1986	KC-A	631	9	.269	.313	.366	309	5	.265	.322	.379	322	4	.273	.303	.354	307	4	.261	.315	.349	324	5	.278	.310	.383	175	4	.309	.328	.429	456	5	.254	.307	.342
1987	KC-A	610	4	.279	.320	.377	321	0	.296	.334	.399	289	4	.260	.305	.353	275	3	.284	.316	.378	335	1	.275	.324	.376	170	1	.241	.270	.312	440	3	.293	.340	.402
1988	KC-A	591	1	.262	.289	.333	297	0	.283	.303	.364	294	1	.241	.274	.303	306	1	.281	.300	.366	285	0	.242	.277	.298	186	0	.258	.275	.366	405	1	.264	.295	.319
1989	KC-A	383	3	.253	.300	.358	197	1	.269	.318	.345	186	2	.237	.281	.371	143	1	.196	.272	.245	240	2	.287	.318	.425	123	1	.276	.306	.398	260	2	.242	.297	.338
1990	KC-A	307	2	.290	.354	.371	166	1	.331	.381	.422	141	1	.241	.323	.312	165	1	.285	.344	.364	142	1	.296	.365	.380	103	0	.272	.306	.350	204	2	.299	.377	.382
1991	Oak-A	294	0	.238	.290	.313	132	0	.250	.303	.341	162	0	.228	.280	.290	160	0	.225	.273	.319	134	0	.254	.310	.306	99	0	.253	.302	.293	195	0	.231	.284	.323
1992	Oak-A	396	0	.270	.329	.333	199	0	.271	.339	.322	197	0	.269	.318	.345	208	0	.264	.346	.337	188	0	.277	.308	.330	121	0	.248	.316	.306	275	0	.280	.334	.345
1993	Chi-N	221	1	.258	.301	.348	114	0	.289	.331	.395	107	1	.224	.270	.299	130	0	.246	.274	.315	91	1	.275	.337	.396	102	0	.235	.257	.275	119	1	.277	.336	.412
1994	Chi-N	21	0	.238	.273	.429	10	0	.100	.182	.100	11	0	.364	.364	.727	21	0	.238	.273	.429	0	0	—	—	—	14	0	.214	.214	.500	7	0	.286	.375	.286
TOTALS		7691	41	.285	.326	.376	3825	18	.294	.337	.388	3866	23	.277	.316	.363	3604	21	.277	.322	.370	4087	20	.292	.330	.381	2538	14	.286	.319	.381	5153	27	.285	.330	.374
■ Dave Winfield BR/TR																																				
1978	SD-N	587	24	.308	.367	.499	299	11	.311	.372	.482	288	13	.306	.361	.517	278	14	.295	.341	.493	309	10	.320	.389	.505	171	10	.316	.420	.573	416	14	.305	.342	.469
1979	SD-N	597	34	.308	.395	.558	290	16	.286	.389	.534	307	18	.329	.401	.580	296	16	.328	.407	.608	301	18	.289	.384	.508	154	12	.331	.453	.649	443	22	.300	.373	.526
1980	SD-N	558	20	.276	.365	.450	275	7	.273	.353	.440	283	13	.279	.378	.459	252	7	.286	.382	.433	306	13	.268	.352	.464	132	8	.273	.385	.508	426	12	.277	.359	.432
1981	NY-A	388	13	.294	.360	.464	176	4	.261	.337	.398	212	9	.321	.380	.519	210	7	.324	.395	.495	178	6	.258	.316	.427	161	7	.298	.358	.522	227	6	.291	.362	.423
1982	NY-A	539	37	.280	.331	.560	272	14	.287	.322	.504	267	23	.273	.340	.618	208	9	.288	.346	.495	331	28	.275	.321	.601	208	19	.274	.351	.577	331	18	.284	.317	.550
1983	NY-A	598	32	.283	.345	.513	284	13	.261	.323	.493	314	19	.303	.365	.532	268	12	.246	.312	.448	330	20	.312	.372	.567	249	14	.297	.354	.558	349	18	.272	.338	.481
1984	NY-A	567	19	.340	.393	.515	260	9	.331	.401	.504	307	10	.349	.386	.524	250	8	.368	.395	.556	317	11	.319	.391	.483	170	5	.324	.395	.476	397	14	.348	.392	.531
1985	NY-A	633	26	.275	.328	.471	298	15	.285	.343	.507	335	11	.266	.315	.439	280	9	.289	.329	.439	353	17	.263	.327	.496	215	10	.251	.343	.470	418	16	.287	.320	.471
1986	NY-A	565	24	.262	.349	.462	279	12	.272	.362	.477	286	12	.252	.336	.448	267	12	.228	.345	.438	298	12	.292	.354	.483	197	12	.259	.373	.523	368	12	.264	.336	.429
1987	NY-A	575	27	.275	.358	.457	269	11	.283	.374	.450	306	16	.268	.343	.464	279	18	.297	.393	.541	296	9	.253	.323	.378	177	13	.345	.449	.621	398	14	.244	.314	.384
1988	NY-A	559	25	.322	.398	.530	274	12	.332	.405	.518	285	13	.312	.391	.540	272	15	.346	.428	.592	287	10	.300	.368	.470	175	11	.331	.426	.594	384	14	.318	.384	.500
1990	NY-A	61	2	.213	.269	.361	33	0	.091	.118	.152	28	2	.357	.424	.607	61	2	.213	.269	.361	0	0	—	—	—	30	0	.200	.250	.300	31	2	.226	.286	.419
1990	Cal-A	414	19	.275	.348	.466	205	13	.288	.364	.537	209	6	.263	.330	.397	129	7	.240	.308	.457	285	12	.291	.365	.470	126	5	.310	.390	.508	288	14	.260	.328	.448
1991	Cal-A	568	28	.262	.326	.472	271	13	.244	.305	.432	297	15	.279	.345	.508	265	16	.287	.332	.558	303	12	.241	.322	.396	160	11	.300	.381	.575	408	17	.248	.304	.431
1992	Tor-A	583	26	.290	.377	.491	268	13	.302	.403	.500	315	13	.279	.353	.483	280	13	.304	.390	.511	303	13	.277	.364	.472	146	8	.301	.395	.527	437	18	.286	.370	.478
1993	Min-A	547	21	.271	.325	.442	278	12	.255	.313	.439	269	9	.286	.338	.446	243	8	.243	.290	.383	304	13	.293	.352	.490	137	4	.292	.345	.460	410	17	.263	.318	.437
1994	Min-A	294	10	.252	.321	.425	139	5	.281	.369	.460	155	5	.226	.275	.394	244	8	.250	.325	.418	50	2	.260	.302	.460	67	5	.343	.470	.657	227	5	.225	.270	.357
1995	Cle-A	115	2	.191	.285	.287	39	1	.077	.217	.179	76	1	.250	.321	.342	53	1	.189	.283	.302	62	1	.194	.286	.274	65	1	.154	.257	.246	50	1	.240	.321	.340
TOTALS		8748	389	.285	.355	.485	4209	181	.282	.356	.476	4539	208	.289	.355	.494	4135	182	.288	.358	.490	4613	207	.283	.353	.481	2740	155	.295	.384	.537	6008	234	.281	.341	.462
■ Tony Womack BL/TR																																				
1993	Pit-N	24	0	.083	.185	.083	18	0	.111	.238	.111	6	0	.000	.000	.000	0	0	—	—	—	24	0	.083	.185	.083	5	0	.000	.000	.000	19	0	.105	.227	.105
1994	Pit-N	12	0	.333	.429	.333	4	0	.250	.400	.250	8	0	.375	.444	.375	6	0	.167	.286	.167	6	0	.500	.571	.500	3	0	.333	.333	.333	9	0	.333	.455	.333
1996	Pit-N	30	0	.333	.459	.500	6	0	.500	.571	.833	24	0	.292	.433	.417	0	0	—	—	—	30	0	.333	.459	.500	0	0	—	—	—	30	0	.333	.459	.500
1997	Pit-N	641	6	.278	.326	.374	314	5	.277	.330	.389	327	1	.278	.322	.361	317	3	.265	.309	.347	324	3	.290	.343	.401	129	0	.310	.360	.357	512	6	.270	.318	.379
1998	Pit-N	655	3	.282	.319	.357	313	2	.288	.325	.380	342	1	.277	.314	.336	344	1	.247	.293	.311	311	2	.322	.350	.408	164	0	.244	.302	.268	491	3	.295	.326	.387
1999	Ari-N	614	4	.277	.332	.370	320	1	.262	.330	.353	294	3	.293	.334	.388	286	2	.266	.316	.357	328	2	.287	.345	.381	169	2	.290	.348	.373	445	2	.272	.326	.369
2000	Ari-N	617	7	.271	.307	.384	316	4	.269	.299	.392	301	3	.272	.317	.375	318	5	.283	.304	.409	299	2	.258	.311	.358	123	1	.276	.331	.366	494	6	.269	.301	.389
TOTALS		2593	20	.276	.322	.370	1291	12	.273	.321	.376	1302	8	.280	.323	.363	1271	11	.264	.305	.354	1322	9	.287	.339	.385	593	3	.277	.331	.336	2000	17	.276	.320	.380

YEAR	TM/L	TOTAL					HOME					AWAY					1ST HALF					2ND HALF					LEFT					RIGHT				
		AB	HR	AVG	OBP	SLG	AB	HR	AVG	OBP	SLG	AB	HR	AVG	OBP	SLG	AB	HR	AVG	OBP	SLG	AB	HR	AVG	OBP	SLG	AB	HR	AVG	OBP	SLG	AB	HR	AVG	OBP	SLG
■ **Marvell Wynne** BL/TL																																				
1983	Pit-N	366	7	.243	.319	.355	189	3	.249	.329	.354	177	4	.237	.308	.356	64	2	.313	.397	.500	302	5	.228	.301	.325	56	0	.286	.375	.339	310	7	.235	.308	.358
1984	Pit-N	653	0	.266	.310	.337	310	0	.271	.313	.348	343	0	.262	.307	.327	324	0	.290	.337	.358	329	0	.243	.283	.316	166	0	.259	.328	.337	487	0	.269	.304	.337
1985	Pit-N	337	2	.205	.247	.258	158	1	.234	.297	.297	179	1	.179	.201	.223	163	1	.233	.273	.301	174	1	.178	.223	.218	111	1	.252	.278	.306	226	1	.181	.232	.235
1986	SD-N	288	7	.264	.300	.417	177	5	.311	.328	.492	111	2	.189	.258	.297	115	3	.296	.320	.417	173	4	.243	.286	.416	70	2	.186	.230	.329	218	5	.289	.322	.445
1987	SD-N	188	2	.250	.321	.346	80	2	.162	.230	.300	108	0	.315	.385	.380	107	1	.271	.352	.346	81	1	.222	.276	.346	39	0	.231	.318	.256	149	2	.255	.321	.369
1988	SD-N	333	11	.264	.325	.426	164	6	.280	.343	.463	169	5	.249	.308	.391	162	9	.296	.361	.543	171	2	.234	.290	.316	55	1	.327	.413	.491	278	10	.252	.307	.414
1989	SD-N	294	6	.252	.282	.357	131	3	.244	.286	.351	163	3	.258	.280	.362	170	3	.259	.288	.371	124	3	.242	.275	.339	33	1	.424	.441	.606	261	5	.230	.263	.326
1989	Chi-N	48	1	.188	.220	.333	19	0	.316	.316	.421	29	1	.103	.161	.276	0	0	—	—	—	48	1	.188	.220	.333	12	0	.167	.167	.250	36	1	.194	.237	.361
1990	Chi-N	186	4	.204	.264	.333	103	2	.233	.275	.369	83	2	.169	.250	.289	109	3	.174	.244	.321	77	1	.247	.293	.351	17	1	.176	.263	.353	169	3	.207	.264	.331
TOTALS		2693	40	.247	.297	.352	1331	22	.258	.308	.376	1362	18	.235	.287	.327	1214	22	.269	.320	.386	1479	18	.229	.279	.324	559	6	.261	.321	.354	2134	34	.243	.291	.351
■ **Dmitri Young** BB/TR																																				
1996	StL-N	29	0	.241	.353	.241	15	0	.267	.313	.267	14	0	.214	.389	.214	0	0	—	—	—	29	0	.241	.353	.241	10	0	.200	.273	.200	19	0	.263	.391	.263
1997	StL-N	333	5	.258	.335	.363	175	2	.240	.330	.326	158	3	.278	.341	.405	190	3	.289	.352	.421	143	2	.217	.313	.287	83	1	.265	.330	.337	250	4	.256	.337	.372
1998	Cin-N	536	14	.310	.364	.481	246	3	.276	.337	.411	290	11	.338	.388	.541	300	8	.317	.362	.500	236	6	.301	.367	.458	147	1	.320	.387	.422	389	13	.306	.356	.504
1999	Cin-N	373	14	.300	.352	.504	191	9	.304	.353	.539	182	5	.297	.351	.467	128	2	.219	.266	.344	245	12	.343	.396	.588	109	3	.266	.308	.431	264	11	.314	.370	.534
2000	Cin-N	548	18	.303	.346	.491	267	6	.326	.370	.479	281	12	.281	.323	.502	276	9	.279	.322	.442	272	9	.327	.370	.540	141	5	.333	.364	.546	407	13	.292	.340	.472
TOTALS		1819	51	.295	.351	.463	894	20	.290	.348	.440	925	31	.301	.353	.486	894	22	.285	.334	.443	925	29	.305	.367	.483	490	10	.300	.351	.441	1329	41	.293	.351	.472
■ **Eric Young** BR/TR																																				
1992	LA-N	132	1	.258	.300	.288	56	0	.250	.288	.250	76	1	.263	.309	.316	0	0	—	—	—	132	1	.258	.300	.288	66	1	.273	.304	.318	66	0	.242	.296	.258
1993	Col-N	490	3	.269	.355	.353	238	3	.303	.401	.420	252	0	.238	.307	.290	255	1	.259	.340	.333	235	2	.281	.370	.374	128	0	.289	.372	.375	362	3	.262	.349	.345
1994	Col-N	228	7	.272	.378	.430	136	6	.309	.404	.515	92	1	.217	.339	.304	140	5	.279	.389	.457	88	2	.261	.359	.386	65	1	.215	.329	.292	163	6	.294	.397	.485
1995	Col-N	366	6	.317	.404	.473	169	5	.331	.430	.533	197	1	.305	.380	.421	67	0	.149	.275	.194	299	6	.355	.434	.535	125	4	.400	.449	.648	241	2	.274	.382	.382
1996	Col-N	568	8	.324	.393	.421	308	7	.412	.473	.549	260	1	.219	.298	.269	247	4	.352	.436	.466	321	4	.302	.358	.386	140	3	.286	.375	.421	428	5	.336	.399	.421
1997	Col-N	468	6	.282	.363	.408	220	2	.327	.419	.432	248	4	.242	.309	.387	323	4	.300	.379	.427	145	2	.241	.325	.366	115	2	.296	.376	.452	353	4	.278	.358	.394
1997	LA-N	154	2	.273	.347	.364	57	0	.158	.284	.228	97	2	.340	.387	.443	0	0	—	—	—	154	2	.273	.347	.364	42	1	.238	.304	.333	112	1	.286	.362	.375
1998	LA-N	452	8	.285	.355	.396	229	7	.314	.391	.459	223	1	.256	.317	.332	269	2	.283	.359	.375	183	6	.290	.350	.426	93	2	.258	.349	.376	359	6	.292	.357	.401
1999	LA-N	456	2	.281	.371	.355	217	2	.272	.380	.350	239	0	.289	.363	.360	252	2	.274	.355	.345	204	0	.289	.390	.368	132	1	.295	.419	.386	324	1	.275	.351	.343
2000	Chi-N	607	6	.297	.367	.399	316	5	.294	.351	.402	291	1	.299	.384	.395	311	5	.322	.397	.460	296	1	.270	.335	.334	138	2	.341	.404	.478	469	4	.284	.357	.375
TOTALS		3921	49	.290	.369	.396	1946	37	.317	.399	.441	1975	12	.265	.338	.350	1864	23	.292	.375	.400	2057	26	.289	.363	.391	1044	17	.300	.381	.427	2877	32	.287	.365	.384
■ **Kevin Young** BR/TR																																				
1992	Pit-N	7	0	.571	.667	.571	2	0	.500	.500	.500	5	0	.600	.714	.600	0	0	—	—	—	7	0	.571	.667	.571	1	0	.000	.500	.000	6	0	.667	.714	.667
1993	Pit-N	449	6	.236	.300	.343	229	6	.240	.317	.384	220	0	.232	.282	.300	217	4	.226	.305	.336	232	2	.246	.295	.349	169	3	.237	.303	.355	280	3	.236	.298	.336
1994	Pit-N	122	1	.205	.258	.320	56	1	.179	.230	.304	66	0	.227	.282	.333	113	1	.221	.276	.345	9	0	.000	.000	.000	34	0	.118	.189	.147	88	1	.239	.284	.386
1995	Pit-N	181	6	.232	.268	.381	97	5	.258	.311	.495	84	1	.202	.216	.250	32	1	.250	.273	.375	149	5	.228	.267	.383	64	3	.156	.191	.313	117	3	.274	.310	.419
1996	KC-A	132	8	.242	.301	.470	72	4	.236	.304	.458	60	4	.250	.297	.483	36	2	.250	.308	.444	96	6	.240	.298	.479	87	7	.322	.392	.632	45	1	.089	.109	.156
1997	Pit-N	333	18	.300	.332	.535	173	11	.277	.311	.543	160	7	.325	.357	.525	181	8	.304	.335	.541	152	10	.296	.329	.526	86	5	.360	.376	.605	247	13	.279	.317	.510
1998	Pit-N	592	27	.270	.328	.481	283	15	.283	.346	.534	309	12	.259	.310	.434	307	16	.267	.330	.489	285	11	.274	.325	.474	137	5	.248	.302	.467	455	22	.277	.335	.486
1999	Pit-N	584	26	.298	.387	.522	287	16	.324	.414	.610	297	10	.273	.360	.438	284	9	.317	.421	.511	300	17	.280	.352	.533	159	5	.308	.378	.535	425	21	.294	.390	.518
2000	Pit-N	496	20	.258	.311	.433	228	11	.259	.317	.461	268	9	.257	.304	.410	290	11	.255	.306	.431	206	9	.262	.317	.437	129	7	.264	.321	.488	367	13	.256	.307	.414
TOTALS		2896	112	.266	.327	.453	1427	69	.272	.338	.499	1469	43	.261	.315	.408	1460	52	.268	.335	.451	1436	60	.264	.318	.455	866	35	.266	.324	.467	2030	77	.267	.328	.447
■ **Joel Youngblood** BR/TR																																				
1978	NY-N	266	7	.252	.294	.436	141	3	.248	.284	.440	125	4	.256	.304	.432	84	1	.250	.289	.381	182	6	.253	.296	.462	121	2	.190	.242	.355	145	5	.303	.338	.503
1979	NY-N	590	16	.275	.346	.436	309	8	.265	.316	.421	281	8	.285	.377	.452	249	11	.285	.357	.478	341	5	.267	.339	.405	184	7	.277	.356	.462	406	9	.273	.342	.424
1980	NY-N	514	8	.276	.340	.381	268	6	.254	.320	.369	246	2	.301	.361	.394	226	4	.274	.344	.412	288	4	.278	.336	.358	155	5	.310	.379	.465	359	3	.262	.323	.345
1981	NY-N	143	4	.350	.398	.531	64	2	.453	.493	.641	79	2	.266	.322	.443	128	4	.359	.406	.555	15	0	.267	.333	.333	43	2	.349	.415	.512	100	2	.350	.389	.540
1982	NY-N	202	3	.257	.302	.361	111	2	.297	.345	.414	91	1	.209	.250	.297	151	3	.238	.272	.351	51	0	.314	.386	.392	68	1	.294	.333	.426	134	2	.239	.287	.328
1982	Mon-N	90	0	.200	.291	.222	43	0	.233	.320	.279	47	0	.170	.264	.170	0	0	—	—	—	90	0	.200	.291	.222	31	0	.290	.361	.323	59	0	.153	.254	.169
1983	SF-N	373	17	.292	.356	.499	177	6	.305	.388	.475	196	11	.281	.325	.520	118	6	.254	.302	.449	255	11	.310	.380	.522	142	8	.338	.416	.585	231	9	.264	.317	.446
1984	SF-N	469	10	.254	.328	.358	243	6	.235	.324	.329	226	4	.274	.333	.389	271	6	.280	.354	.387	198	4	.217	.292	.318	131	3	.275	.349	.374	338	7	.246	.320	.352
1985	SF-N	230	4	.270	.355	.348	107	1	.271	.345	.336	123	3	.268	.364	.358	92	0	.196	.267	.207	138	4	.319	.410	.442	78	1	.308	.379	.385	152	3	.250	.343	.329
1986	SF-N	184	5	.255	.320	.402	77	0	.234	.295	.338	107	5	.271	.339	.449	61	3	.279	.375	.475	123	2	.244	.291	.366	76	0	.211	.265	.276	108	5	.287	.358	.491
1987	SF-N	91	3	.253	.296	.385	42	2	.286	.318	.500	49	1	.224	.278	.286	40	1	.250	.279	.375	51	2	.255	.309	.392	59	2	.169	.231	.288	32	1	.406	.424	.563
1988	SF-N	123	0	.252	.307	.285	58	0	.259	.297	.276	65	0	.246	.315	.292	57	0	.298	.359	.351	66	0	.212	.260	.227	65	0	.262	.329	.277	58	0	.241	.279	.293
1989	Cin-N	118	3	.212	.299	.331	60	1	.250	.313	.350	58	2	.172	.284	.310	62	2	.242	.314	.387	56	1	.179	.281	.268	85	2	.247	.337	.376	33	1	.121	.194	.212
TOTALS		3393	80	.267	.333	.399	1700	37	.269	.332	.396	1693	43	.266	.334	.402	1539	41	.272	.335	.411	1854	39	.263	.331	.389	1238	33	.273	.343	.413	2155	47	.264	.327	.392
■ **Robin Yount** BR/TR																																				
1978	Mil-A	502	9	.293	.323	.428	247	5	.320	.351	.490	255	4	.267	.296	.369	171	1	.269	.301	.333	331	8	.305	.335	.477	101	2	.327	.370	.515	401	7	.284	.311	.406
1979	Mil-A	577	8	.267	.308	.371	272	4	.316	.353	.445	305	4	.223	.269	.305	283	5	.251	.305	.367	294	3	.282	.312	.374	144	1	.222	.248	.292	433	7	.282	.328	.397
1980	Mil-A	611	23	.293	.321	.519	323	13	.300	.324	.526	288	10	.285	.318	.510	254	11	.327	.356	.575	357	12	.269	.297	.479	188	7	.277	.307	.484	423	16	.300	.328	.534
1981	Mil-A	377	10	.273	.312	.419	149	1	.262	.313	.336	228	9	.281	.311	.474	174	5	.259	.300	.408	203	5	.286	.323	.429	114	4	.333	.369	.509	263	6	.247	.288	.380
1982	Mil-A	635	29	.331	.379	.578	304	9	.313	.360	.516	331	20	.347	.396	.634	275	11	.305	.348	.549	360	18	.350	.401	.600	199	7	.357	.424	.618	436	22	.319	.357	.560
1983	Mil-A	578	17	.308	.383	.503	280	6	.318	.395	.493	298	11	.299	.371	.513	276	10	.319	.397	.525	302	7	.298	.369	.483	202	4	.287	.397	.475	376	13	.319	.375	.519
1984	Mil-A	624	16	.298	.362	.441	303	8	.310	.360	.469	321	8	.287	.364	.414	296	6	.301	.371	.426	328	10	.296	.354	.454	207	5	.304	.387	.459	417	11	.295	.349	.432
1985	Mil-A	466	15	.277	.342	.442	243	11	.309	.382	.523	223	4	.242	.297	.354	255	6	.282	.337	.416	211	9	.270	.349	.474	150	4	.300	.357	.453	316	11	.266	.335	.437
1986	Mil-A	522	9	.312	.388	.450	259	4	.297	.370	.436	263	5	.327	.406	.464	225	3	.351	.426	.484	297	6	.283	.359	.424	121	3	.248	.343	.355	401	6	.332	.402	.479
1987	Mil-A	635	21	.312	.384	.479	311	12	.354	.422	.550	324	9	.272	.347	.410	275	9	.298	.373	.462	360	12	.322	.392	.492	195	2	.272	.336	.369	440	19	.330	.404	.527
1988	Mil-A	621	13	.306	.369	.465	300	7	.307	.374	.450	321	6	.305	.364	.480	295	8	.295	.365	.478	326	5	.316	.372	.454	183	7	.284	.381	.448	438	6	.315	.363	.473
1989	Mil-A	614	21	.318	.384	.511	300	14	.307	.383	.533	314	7	.328	.386	.490	299	8	.301	.371	.462	315	13	.333	.397	.559	167	6	.341	.398	.587	447	15	.309	.379	.483
1990	Mil-A	587	17	.247	.337	.380	293	8	.222	.310	.365	294	9	.272	.364	.395	273	7	.249	.338	.363	314	10	.245	.337	.395	156	5	.269	.359	.410	431	12	.239	.329	.369
1991	Mil-A	503	10	.260	.332	.376	250	8	.236	.311	.396	253	2	.285	.352	.356	283	9	.258	.328	.410	220	1	.264	.336	.332	129	2	.256	.377	.341	374	8	.262	.314	.388
1992	Mil-A	557	8	.264	.325	.390	269	3	.268	.327	.379	288	5	.260	.323	.399	257	5	.280	.348	.416	300	3	.250	.304	.367	125	2	.280	.359	.424	432	6	.259	.315	.380
1993	Mil-A	454	8	.258	.326	.379	234	1	.256	.344	.333	220	7	.259	.305	.427	183	5	.262	.329	.393	271	3	.255	.325	.369	122	2	.262	.362	.369	332	6	.256	.313	.383
TOTALS		8863	234	.290	.351	.450	4337	114	.295	.357	.459	4526	120	.285	.345	.441	4074	109	.289	.352	.446	4789	125	.291	.350	.453	2503	63	.290	.364	.450	6360	171	.290	.346	.450
■ **Todd Zeile** BR/TR																																				
1989	StL-N	82	1	.256	.326	.354	39	0	.231	.279	.282	43	1	.279	.367	.419	0	0	—	—	—	82	1	.256	.326	.354	39	0	.282	.364	.308	43	1	.233	.292	.395
1990	StL-N	495	15	.244	.333	.398	233	8	.262	.358	.429	262	7	.229	.311	.370	233	8	.227	.321	.391	262	7	.260	.344	.405	173	6	.266	.347	.451	322	9	.233	.326	.370
1991	StL-N	565	11	.280	.353	.412	279	7	.297	.374	.459	286	4	.262	.331	.367	258	3	.287	.354	.403	307	8	.274	.351	.420	237	5	.304	.375	.439	328	6	.262	.337	.393
1992	StL-N	439	7	.257	.352	.364	226	4	.230	.337	.332	213	3	.286	.368	.399	248	4	.242	.336	.363	191	3	.277	.374	.366	133	1	.278	.394	.353	306	6	.248	.333	.369
1993	StL-N	571	17	.277	.352	.433	280	8	.304	.376	.454	291	9	.251	.329	.412	267	2	.247	.312	.337	304	15	.303	.386	.516	133	4	.271	.355	.429	438	13	.279	.352	.434
1994	StL-N	415	19	.267	.348	.470	199	9	.307	.372	.518	216	10	.231	.327	.426	278	10	.241	.321	.399	137	9	.321	.403	.613	107	7	.299	.389	.579	308	12	.256	.333	.432
1995	StL-N	127	5	.291	.378	.457	49	2	.224	.298	.367	78	3	.333	.429	.513	127	5	.291	.378	.457	0	0	—	—	—	29	0	.138	.219	.207	98	5	.337	.422	.531
1995	Chi-N	299	9	.227	.271	.371	131	6	.244	.277	.427	168	3	.214	.266	.327	60	2	.283	.302	.467	239	7	.213	.264	.347	77	3	.182	.229	.364	222	6	.243	.286	.374
1996	Phi-N	500	20	.268	.353	.436	235	9	.272	.353	.426	265	11	.264	.353	.445	299	12	.254	.333	.428	201	8	.289	.381	.448	83	5	.277	.357	.518	417	15	.266	.352	.420
1996	Bal-A	117	5	.239	.326	.436	45	1	.200	.280	.333	72	4	.264	.354	.500	0	0	—	—	—	117	5	.239	.326	.436	35	1	.286	.419	.429	82	4	.220	.281	.439
1997	LA-N	575	31	.268	.365	.459	284	17	.271	.357	.475	291	14	.265	.372	.443	292	16	.226	.315	.414	283	15	.311	.413	.505	140	5	.257	.361	.407	435	26	.271	.366	.476
1998	LA-N	158	7	.253	.300	.437	63	1	.317	.358	.444	95	6	.211	.262	.432	158	7	.253	.300	.437	0	0	—	—	—	30	2	.267	.313	.633	128	5	.250	.297	.391
1998	Fla-N	234	6	.291	.374	.427	111	2	.315	.391	.432	123	4	.268	.359	.423	141	3	.262	.350	.390	93	3	.333	.411	.484	56	1	.286	.385	.411	178	5	.292	.371	.433
1998	Tex-A	180	6	.261	.358	.450	88	4	.261	.362	.489	92	2	.261	.355	.413	0	0	—	—	—	180	6	.261	.358	.450	43	3	.279	.354	.605	137	3	.255	.360	.401
1999	Tex-A	588	24	.293	.354	.488	297	13	.283	.348	.505	291	11	.302	.360	.471	286	11	.280	.348	.479	302	13	.305	.360	.497	117	3	.291	.378	.427	471	21	.293	.348	.503
2000	NY-N	544	22	.268	.356	.467	257	8	.280	.368	.440	287	14	.258	.346	.491	267	11	.303	.378	.513	277	11	.235	.335	.422	117	10	.248	.364	.564	427	12	.274	.354	.440
TOTALS		5889	205	.268	.348	.434	2816	99	.276	.355	.444	3073	106	.260	.342	.424	2914	94	.259	.335	.418	2975	111	.276	.360	.449	1549	56	.271	.360	.447	4340	149	.266	.343	.429

YEAR	TM/L	TOTAL AB	HR	AVG	OBP	SLG	HOME W	L	SV	IP	ERA	AWAY W	L	SV	IP	ERA	1ST HALF W	L	SV	IP	ERA	2ND HALF W	L	SV	IP	ERA	LEFT AB	HR	AVG	OBP	SLG	RIGHT AB	HR	AVG	OBP	SLG
● Jim Abbott BL/TL																																				
1989	Cal-A	694	13	.274	.345	.379	5	5	0	87	4.84	7	7	0	94	3.06	6	5	0	79	3.86	6	7	0	102	3.97	123	2	.325	.388	.463	571	11	.263	.335	.361
1990	Cal-A	833	16	.295	.353	.401	4	7	0	110	4.75	6	7	0	102	4.25	5	6	0	97	4.92	5	8	0	115	4.16	110	3	.318	.398	.436	723	13	.292	.345	.396
1991	Cal-A	909	14	.244	.302	.336	8	7	0	129	2.57	10	4	0	114	3.25	6	5	0	103	3.51	12	6	0	140	2.44	142	3	.303	.348	.430	767	11	.233	.293	.318
1992	Cal-A	790	12	.263	.323	.349	2	8	0	95	3.32	5	7	0	116	2.33	4	9	0	114	3.00	3	6	0	97	2.51	128	0	.273	.343	.359	662	12	.261	.320	.347
1993	NY-A	814	22	.271	.332	.400	8	6	0	112	3.12	3	8	0	102	5.75	5	7	0	101	4.28	6	7	0	113	4.46	102	0	.294	.376	.363	712	22	.268	.326	.406
1994	NY-A	612	24	.273	.341	.456	5	5	0	93	3.86	4	3	0	67	5.51	7	5	0	108	3.85	2	3	0	53	5.98	102	3	.275	.308	.431	510	21	.273	.347	.461
1995	Chi-A	432	10	.269	.324	.382	3	3	0	49	3.12	3	1	0	63	3.55	4	3	0	76	3.33	2	1	0	37	3.44	85	2	.318	.356	.424	347	8	.256	.317	.372
1995	Cal-A	332	4	.280	.337	.364	0	3	0	37	7.54	5	1	0	48	1.51	0	0	0	0	—	5	4	0	85	4.15	62	0	.226	.304	.274	270	4	.293	.345	.385
1996	Cal-A	558	23	.306	.389	.505	0	8	0	56	8.52	2	10	0	86	6.80	1	11	0	82	7.82	1	7	0	60	7.01	125	12	.352	.404	.736	433	11	.293	.385	.439
1998	Chi-A	120	2	.292	.358	.392	2	0	0	13	5.40	3	0	0	18	3.93	0	0	0	0	—	5	0	0	32	4.55	28	1	.393	.452	.571	92	1	.261	.330	.337
1999	Mil-A	347	14	.317	.393	.496	1	4	0	38	5.73	1	4	0	44	7.92	1	7	0	69	7.14	1	1	0	13	5.68	87	3	.299	.380	.494	260	11	.323	.397	.496
TOTALS		6441	154	.276	.340	.399	38	56	0	820	4.27	49	52	0	854	4.24	39	58	0	828	4.49	48	50	0	846	4.02	1094	29	.304	.366	.454	5347	125	.270	.335	.388
● Terry Adams BR/TR																																				
1995	Chi-N	76	0	.289	.372	.434	1	1	0	12	5.40	0	0	1	6	8.53	0	0	0	0	—	1	1	1	18	6.50	27	0	.259	.412	.370	49	0	.306	.346	.469
1996	Chi-N	363	6	.231	.322	.328	2	4	2	53	3.57	1	2	2	48	2.25	2	2	1	52	2.26	1	4	3	49	3.65	146	3	.240	.304	.342	217	3	.226	.333	.318
1997	Chi-N	297	3	.306	.388	.394	2	5	6	35	5.66	0	4	12	39	3.69	1	4	8	38	3.29	1	5	10	36	6.06	137	1	.299	.404	.409	160	2	.313	.374	.381
1998	Chi-N	282	7	.255	.349	.369	5	3	0	41	4.20	2	4	1	32	4.50	6	5	0	47	3.06	1	2	1	26	6.66	121	2	.223	.312	.306	161	5	.280	.376	.416
1999	Chi-N	245	9	.245	.319	.408	2	0	5	31	4.02	4	3	8	34	4.01	2	1	4	20	3.15	4	2	9	45	4.40	103	3	.184	.270	.320	142	6	.289	.354	.472
2000	LA-N	328	6	.244	.324	.335	4	4	0	41	2.85	2	5	2	44	4.12	3	3	2	44	3.05	3	6	0	40	4.02	160	1	.225	.322	.281	168	5	.262	.326	.387
TOTALS		1591	31	.257	.342	.366	16	17	13	213	4.06	9	18	26	203	3.77	14	15	15	201	2.91	11	20	24	214	4.88	694	10	.238	.330	.333	897	21	.272	.351	.392
● Rick Aguilera BR/TR																																				
1985	NY-N	457	8	.258	.314	.372	3	2	0	46	2.14	7	5	0	76	3.91	1	2	0	13	4.72	9	5	0	109	3.06	224	3	.241	.310	.335	233	5	.275	.317	.408
1986	NY-N	551	15	.263	.314	.425	5	2	0	68	3.72	5	5	0	74	4.01	1	3	0	43	5.91	9	4	0	99	3.00	269	4	.290	.341	.442	282	11	.238	.288	.408
1987	NY-N	449	12	.276	.329	.421	6	2	0	68	3.82	5	1	0	47	3.28	4	2	0	58	4.03	7	1	0	57	3.16	219	6	.301	.361	.447	230	6	.252	.297	.396
1988	NY-N	98	2	.296	.367	.408	0	1	0	13	4.72	0	3	0	11	9.53	0	3	0	12	9.26	0	1	0	13	4.85	45	0	.222	.286	.267	53	2	.358	.433	.528
1989	NY-N	255	3	.231	.294	.298	5	3	3	37	1.72	1	3	4	33	3.03	3	3	6	49	1.48	3	3	1	21	4.35	133	1	.241	.301	.293	122	2	.221	.286	.303
1989	Min-A	290	5	.245	.289	.390	1	2	0	36	3.53	2	3	0	40	2.93	0	0	0	0	—	3	5	0	76	3.21	142	2	.275	.318	.437	148	3	.216	.261	.345
1990	Min-A	245	5	.224	.291	.322	3	2	16	34	3.44	2	1	16	31	2.01	1	1	18	34	1.85	4	2	14	31	3.73	114	0	.219	.299	.237	131	5	.229	.284	.397
1991	Min-A	240	3	.183	.274	.275	2	0	23	36	1.00	2	5	19	33	3.82	2	3	20	36	2.78	2	2	22	33	1.89	136	2	.184	.285	.272	104	1	.183	.259	.279
1992	Min-A	252	7	.238	.287	.353	1	3	17	30	4.25	1	3	24	37	1.70	1	4	22	36	3.25	1	2	19	31	2.35	129	3	.248	.310	.326	123	4	.228	.262	.382
1993	Min-A	269	9	.223	.263	.379	2	1	15	36	2.97	2	2	19	36	3.25	1	0	22	35	2.04	3	3	12	37	4.14	145	3	.200	.247	.324	124	6	.250	.282	.444
1994	Min-A	186	7	.306	.340	.446	0	2	13	25	3.65	1	2	10	20	3.60	0	2	17	29	4.40	1	2	6	16	2.25	95	3	.242	.301	.358	91	4	.374	.383	.538
1995	Min-A	90	2	.222	.273	.322	0	0	6	12	0.00	1	1	6	13	4.97	1	1	11	23	1.96	0	0	1	2	9.00	50	1	.200	.255	.260	40	1	.250	.295	.400
1995	Bos-A	114	4	.228	.268	.377	2	2	8	15	2.35	0	0	12	15	3.00	0	0	0	0	—	2	2	20	30	2.67	67	1	.209	.236	.299	47	3	.255	.314	.489
1996	Min-A	450	20	.276	.319	.493	3	4	0	53	7.13	5	2	0	58	3.86	1	2	0	28	5.40	7	4	0	83	5.42	243	10	.288	.319	.498	207	10	.261	.319	.488
1997	Min-A	253	9	.257	.318	.419	3	2	12	36	2.75	2	2	14	32	5.01	3	1	15	35	4.15	2	3	11	34	3.48	114	5	.237	.302	.439	139	4	.273	.331	.403
1998	Min-A	286	8	.262	.299	.416	2	3	16	33	3.55	2	6	22	41	4.79	3	4	16	41	3.54	1	5	22	34	5.08	136	3	.243	.286	.375	150	5	.280	.312	.453
1999	Min-A	74	2	.135	.158	.284	0	1	3	9	2.08	3	0	3	13	0.71	3	1	6	21	1.27	0	0	0	0	—	28	2	.179	.207	.429	46	0	.109	.128	.196
1999	Chi-A	173	6	.254	.299	.405	4	2	4	24	4.81	2	1	4	22	2.45	3	3	3	16	8.04	3	0	5	31	1.47	68	2	.338	.395	.485	105	4	.200	.234	.352
2000	Chi-N	187	11	.251	.330	.465	1	1	13	22	6.23	0	1	16	26	3.81	1	1	17	28	5.08	0	1	12	19	4.66	74	3	.257	.345	.419	113	8	.248	.320	.496
TOTALS		4919	138	.251	.303	.394	43	35	149	633	3.54	43	46	169	658	3.60	29	36	173	536	3.71	57	45	145	755	3.47	2431	54	.253	.310	.380	2488	84	.249	.297	.408
● Doyle Alexander BR/TR																																				
1978	Tex-A	732	18	.270	.333	.423	4	7	0	92	3.72	5	3	0	99	4.00	6	4	0	107	3.61	3	6	0	84	4.20	387	10	.258	.333	.406	345	8	.284	.332	.443
1979	Tex-A	426	3	.268	.366	.362	3	4	0	60	4.18	2	3	0	53	4.75	3	5	0	72	3.73	2	2	0	41	5.71	211	1	.246	.337	.336	215	2	.288	.393	.386
1980	Atl-N	887	20	.256	.315	.387	9	4	0	130	3.33	5	7	0	102	5.29	5	3	0	100	3.52	9	8	0	132	4.70	424	6	.262	.333	.370	463	14	.251	.297	.402
1981	SF-N	593	11	.263	.315	.368	6	0	0	65	2.07	5	7	0	87	3.52	5	4	0	77	2.70	6	3	0	76	3.09	301	4	.246	.301	.339	292	7	.281	.330	.397
1982	NY-A	272	14	.298	.329	.559	0	3	0	38	5.73	1	4	0	29	6.52	0	2	0	16	3.94	1	5	0	51	6.75	117	7	.342	.378	.581	155	7	.265	.290	.542
1983	NY-A	112	6	.277	.317	.509	0	1	0	16	8.04	0	1	0	13	4.26	0	2	0	28	6.35	0	0	0	0	—	54	2	.204	.241	.370	58	4	.345	.387	.638
1983	Tor-A	452	14	.279	.317	.454	4	3	0	57	4.42	3	3	0	60	3.47	0	0	0	0	—	7	6	0	117	3.93	200	8	.285	.327	.505	252	6	.274	.310	.413
1984	Tor-A	983	21	.242	.284	.383	12	3	0	164	2.58	5	3	0	98	4.04	6	4	0	115	3.14	11	2	0	147	3.12	509	17	.261	.306	.420	474	4	.222	.259	.342
1985	Tor-A	1008	28	.266	.315	.396	11	5	0	162	2.83	6	5	0	98	4.48	7	4	0	107	4.54	10	6	0	154	2.69	515	16	.264	.330	.416	493	12	.268	.297	.375
1986	Tor-A	440	18	.273	.308	.468	2	2	0	62	3.65	3	2	0	49	5.47	5	3	0	108	3.99	0	1	0	3	23.63	228	7	.268	.303	.417	212	11	.278	.314	.524
1986	Atl-N	470	9	.287	.311	.409	4	2	0	62	4.09	2	4	0	56	3.56	0	0	0	0	—	6	6	0	117	3.84	217	4	.295	.339	.424	253	5	.281	.286	.395
1987	Atl-N	448	21	.257	.300	.442	3	5	0	69	4.30	2	5	0	49	3.88	4	3	0	60	3.32	1	7	0	58	4.97	207	15	.300	.345	.560	241	6	.220	.261	.340
1987	Det-A	313	3	.201	.263	.262	5	0	0	39	1.14	4	0	0	49	1.84	0	0	0	0	—	9	0	0	88	1.53	151	1	.199	.288	.258	162	2	.204	.237	.265
1988	Det-A	922	30	.282	.317	.456	9	5	0	128	3.09	5	6	0	101	5.88	7	4	0	122	3.25	7	7	0	107	5.55	458	12	.293	.337	.476	464	18	.272	.297	.435
1989	Det-A	876	28	.280	.337	.434	3	9	0	120	4.44	3	9	0	103	4.44	4	7	0	121	3.42	2	11	0	102	5.65	490	14	.284	.330	.437	386	14	.275	.345	.430
TOTALS		8934	244	.266	.315	.413	75	53	0	1263	3.47	51	62	0	1046	4.38	52	45	0	1033	3.62	74	70	0	1276	4.09	4469	124	.269	.325	.420	4465	120	.263	.305	.406
● Antonio Alfonseca BR/TR																																				
1997	Fla-N	111	3	.324	.385	.523	0	1	0	18	3.00	1	2	0	8	9.39	1	0	0	1	0.00	0	3	0	25	5.04	31	1	.323	.382	.516	80	2	.325	.386	.525
1998	Fla-N	267	10	.281	.359	.446	2	2	3	37	4.62	2	4	5	34	3.48	1	2	3	34	3.97	3	4	5	37	4.17	100	4	.330	.444	.500	167	6	.251	.303	.413
1999	Fla-N	288	4	.274	.348	.368	3	1	10	50	1.98	1	4	11	28	5.53	4	4	0	40	3.79	0	1	21	37	2.65	126	1	.270	.333	.349	162	3	.278	.359	.383
2000	Fla-N	282	7	.291	.347	.426	2	4	23	38	4.70	3	2	22	32	3.69	3	4	23	38	4.78	2	2	22	32	3.62	130	2	.277	.347	.392	152	5	.303	.348	.454
TOTALS		948	24	.287	.355	.425	7	8	36	143	3.52	7	12	38	101	4.56	9	10	26	113	4.15	5	10	48	131	3.77	387	8	.292	.373	.416	561	16	.283	.343	.431
● Wilson Alvarez BL/TL																																				
1989	Tex-A	3	2	1.000	1.000	3.000	0	1	0	0		0	0	0	0	—	0	0	0	0	—	0	1	0	0		0	0	—	1.000	—	3	2	1.000	1.000	3.000
1991	Chi-A	204	9	.230	.325	.407	1	1	0	19	2.79	2	1	0	37	3.89	0	0	0	0	—	3	2	0	56	3.51	18	0	.222	.263	.222	186	9	.231	.330	.425
1992	Chi-A	379	12	.272	.381	.401	2	1	0	45	5.56	3	2	1	55	4.91	0	2	1	32	4.50	5	1	0	68	5.53	91	0	.220	.348	.286	288	12	.288	.391	.438
1993	Chi-A	729	14	.230	.344	.329	7	5	0	107	3.38	8	3	0	101	2.50	7	4	0	104	3.19	8	4	0	103	2.70	89	1	.258	.432	.315	640	13	.227	.330	.331
1994	Chi-A	611	16	.241	.309	.354	6	4	0	84	3.11	6	4	0	78	3.82	9	3	0	109	3.15	3	5	0	53	4.08	95	1	.232	.288	.305	516	15	.242	.313	.362
1995	Chi-A	663	21	.258	.349	.415	7	2	0	84	4.80	1	9	0	91	3.87	1	5	0	69	5.32	7	6	0	106	3.66	109	2	.294	.376	.422	554	19	.251	.343	.413
1996	Chi-A	838	21	.258	.337	.408	7	6	0	93	3.79	8	4	0	125	4.55	9	4	0	109	3.96	6	6	0	108	4.49	145	1	.303	.350	.407	693	20	.248	.334	.408
1997	Chi-A	544	9	.232	.303	.336	3	5	0	79	3.40	6	3	0	66	2.58	7	6	0	112	2.57	2	2	0	34	4.54	98	4	.255	.318	.418	446	5	.226	.300	.318
1997	SF-N	241	9	.224	.326	.353	2	1	0	29	4.60	2	2	0	37	4.38	0	0	0	0	—	4	3	0	66	4.48	58	1	.241	.333	.293	183	8	.219	.324	.372
1998	TB-A	544	18	.239	.332	.392	2	8	0	69	6.13	4	6	0	74	3.42	4	5	0	55	4.39	2	9	0	87	4.95	116	3	.250	.371	.371	428	15	.236	.321	.397
1999	TB-A	611	22	.260	.349	.429	4	2	0	76	3.32	5	7	0	84	5.04	3	5	0	71	5.07	6	4	0	89	3.54	116	7	.276	.341	.500	495	15	.257	.351	.412
TOTALS		5367	153	.247	.337	.384	41	36	0	686	4.07	45	41	1	747	3.87	40	34	1	662	3.79	46	43	0	771	4.11	935	20	.262	.352	.375	4432	133	.243	.333	.386
● Larry Andersen BR/TR																																				
1979	Cle-A	70	3	.357	.382	.600	0	0	0	13	9.00	0	0	0	4	2.45	0	0	0	0	—	0	0	0	17	7.56	30	1	.300	.371	.467	40	2	.400	.390	.700
1981	Sea-A	250	4	.228	.282	.304	1	2	1	30	3.86	2	1	4	37	1.69	1	3	1	29	2.48	2	0	4	39	2.79	96	2	.260	.351	.354	154	2	.208	.235	.273
1982	Sea-A	322	16	.311	.361	.543	0	0	0	45	8.06	0	0	1	35	3.34	0	0	1	41	6.15	0	0	0	39	5.82	124	3	.355	.421	.532	198	13	.283	.321	.551
1983	Phi-N	95	0	.200	.267	.253	0	0	0	15	0.59	1	0	0	11	4.91	0	0	0	0	—	1	0	0	26	2.39	41	0	.317	.391	.415	54	0	.111	.169	.130
1984	Phi-N	343	5	.248	.296	.338	1	2	2	37	2.17	2	5	2	53	2.53	1	1	2	39	2.31	2	6	2	52	2.44	163	3	.264	.330	.374	180	2	.233	.263	.306
1985	Phi-N	285	5	.274	.340	.393	3	0	2	42	3.21	0	3	1	31	5.81	2	2	2	45	3.60	1	1	1	28	5.46	123	2	.309	.403	.415	162	3	.247	.287	.377
1986	Phi-N	49	0	.388	.415	.531	0	0	0	8	1.17	0	0	0	5	9.00	0	0	0	13	4.26	0	0	0	0	—	20	0	.450	.500	.600	29	0	.345	.355	.483
1986	Hou-N	232	2	.276	.338	.353	2	0	0	29	3.07	0	1	1	35	2.55	1	0	0	25	3.28	1	1	1	40	2.48	108	1	.278	.350	.343	124	1	.274	.329	.363
1987	Hou-N	385	7	.247	.319	.366	4	4	1	53	2.56	5	1	4	49	4.41	5	4	1	46	3.35	4	1	4	56	3.54	191	3	.230	.323	.340	194	4	.263	.316	.392
1988	Hou-N	323	3	.254	.297	.334	1	2	0	40	2.03	1	2	5	43	3.80	2	3	3	36	3.25	0	1	2	47	2.70	150	1	.293	.359	.360	173	2	.220	.239	.312
1989	Hou-N	318	2	.198	.251	.245	2	3	2	52	1.22	2	1	1	36	2.00	1	1	1	45	0.40	3	3	2	42	2.76	160	2	.250	.305	.306	158	0	.146	.194	.184
1990	Hou-N	266	2	.229	.291	.282	4	0	3	39	0.23	1	2	3	34	3.93	4	1	2	43	1.47	1	1	4	31	2.64	124	2	.282	.361	.371	142	0	.183	.224	.204
1990	Bos-A	82	0	.220	.256	.244	0	0	0	14	1.93	0	0	1	8	0.00	0	0	0	0	—	0	0	1	22	1.23	42	0	.262	.295	.286	40	0	.175	.214	.200
1991	SD-N	168	0	.232	.284	.268	3	0	8	25	2.19	0	4	5	22	2.42	2	1	3	23	2.70	1	3	10	24	1.90	89	0	.281	.340	.337	79	0	.177	.217	.190
1992	SD-N	129	2	.202	.252	.264	1	0	2	19	3.26	0	1	0	16	3.45	0	0	0	11	3.97	1	1	2	24	3.04	69	1	.203	.295	.275	60	1	.200	.197	.250
1993	Phi-N	232	4	.233	.299	.332	1	0	0	32	1.14	2	2	0	30	4.80	3	1	0	23	1.93	0	1	0	38	3.52	86	2	.291	.330	.395	146	2	.199	.282	.295

		TOTAL					HOME					AWAY					1ST HALF					2ND HALF					LEFT					RIGHT				
YEAR	TM/L	AB	HR	AVG	OBP	SLG	W	L	SV	IP	ERA	W	L	SV	IP	ERA	W	L	SV	IP	ERA	W	L	SV	IP	ERA	AB	HR	AVG	OBP	SLG	AB	HR	AVG	OBP	SLG
1994	Phi-N	129	2	.256	.333	.372	0	1	0	14	5.02	1	1	0	18	3.93	1	1	0	18	4.00	0	1	0	15	4.91	71	2	.310	.364	.451	58	0	.190	.299	.276
TOTALS		3678	57	.250	.306	.348	23	14	21	507	2.87	17	24	28	468	3.42	23	18	16	437	2.94	17	20	33	538	3.30	1687	25	.279	.350	.375	1991	32	.225	.267	.324
● Brian Anderson BL/TL																																				
1993	Cal-A	43	1	.256	.289	.442	0	0	0	3	2.70	0	0	0	8	4.50	0	0	0	0	—	0	0	0	11	3.97	6	0	.167	.167	.167	37	1	.270	.308	.486
1994	Cal-A	400	13	.300	.347	.488	2	3	0	52	6.40	5	2	0	50	3.99	5	3	0	60	5.70	2	2	0	42	4.54	84	4	.333	.360	.548	316	9	.291	.344	.472
1995	Cal-A	390	24	.282	.334	.526	4	3	0	58	3.24	2	5	0	41	9.58	1	1	0	20	4.87	5	7	0	79	6.13	79	6	.342	.354	.633	311	18	.267	.329	.498
1996	Cle-A	196	9	.296	.338	.520	2	1	0	33	5.45	1	0	0	18	3.93	0	1	0	29	5.90	3	0	0	22	3.63	39	3	.231	.302	.487	157	6	.312	.347	.529
1997	Cle-A	183	7	.301	.332	.443	3	2	0	33	4.32	1	0	0	15	5.52	2	1	0	24	3.70	2	1	0	24	5.70	35	1	.314	.333	.429	148	6	.297	.331	.446
1998	Ari-N	806	39	.274	.297	.473	3	8	0	106	4.49	9	5	0	102	4.16	5	7	0	104	4.14	7	6	0	104	4.51	139	7	.295	.305	.518	667	32	.270	.296	.463
1999	Ari-N	516	18	.279	.317	.438	7	0	1	88	2.97	1	2	0	42	7.93	1	1	1	49	6.57	7	1	0	81	3.35	105	1	.295	.333	.362	411	17	.275	.313	.457
2000	Ari-N	822	38	.275	.308	.481	6	3	0	110	3.51	5	4	0	103	4.63	8	2	0	104	4.50	3	5	0	109	3.62	188	7	.266	.310	.447	634	31	.278	.307	.491
TOTALS		3356	149	.282	.318	.478	27	20	1	485	4.09	24	18	0	379	5.32	22	16	1	391	4.92	29	22	0	472	4.39	675	29	.293	.323	.481	2681	120	.279	.316	.477
● Joaquin Andujar BB/TR																																				
1978	Hou-N	392	3	.224	.327	.306	3	2	1	51	3.38	2	5	0	60	3.45	3	4	0	82	3.07	2	3	1	29	4.40	202	1	.262	.359	.361	190	2	.184	.293	.247
1979	Hou-N	720	7	.233	.316	.317	8	5	2	110	2.13	4	7	2	84	5.14	9	4	3	96	2.63	3	8	1	98	4.21	303	4	.281	.353	.380	417	3	.199	.290	.271
1980	Hou-N	476	8	.277	.335	.366	2	3	0	60	3.92	1	5	2	62	3.90	0	3	2	35	4.08	3	5	0	87	3.84	203	4	.315	.364	.419	273	4	.249	.315	.326
1981	Hou-N	98	2	.296	.366	.408	0	2	0	8	6.48	2	1	0	15	4.11	2	3	0	24	4.94	0	0	0	0	—	31	1	.387	.432	.581	67	1	.254	.333	.328
1981	StL-N	211	4	.265	.302	.374	3	1	0	26	3.81	3	0	0	29	3.68	0	0	0	0	—	6	1	0	55	3.74	96	1	.240	.270	.323	115	3	.287	.328	.417
1982	StL-N	987	11	.240	.281	.328	8	5	0	140	2.44	7	5	0	126	2.51	7	5	0	134	2.29	8	5	0	132	2.66	444	3	.255	.300	.329	543	8	.228	.264	.328
1983	StL-N	850	23	.253	.315	.405	2	7	0	98	4.42	4	9	1	127	3.96	3	11	1	121	4.01	3	5	0	104	4.34	425	12	.280	.353	.440	425	11	.226	.275	.369
1984	StL-N	954	20	.229	.284	.345	8	11	0	139	3.70	12	3	0	123	2.93	13	6	0	142	2.98	7	8	0	119	3.77	463	10	.233	.300	.341	491	10	.224	.268	.348
1985	StL-N	1019	15	.260	.321	.362	9	9	0	144	3.06	12	3	0	125	3.81	13	3	0	126	2.50	8	9	0	144	4.20	494	6	.300	.357	.405	525	9	.223	.286	.322
1986	Oak-A	582	23	.239	.308	.399	8	4	1	88	3.87	4	3	0	67	3.76	4	2	0	45	3.83	8	5	1	111	3.82	307	15	.254	.318	.453	275	8	.222	.297	.338
1987	Oak-A	234	11	.269	.348	.449	1	4	0	40	6.02	2	1	0	20	6.20	2	1	0	23	4.76	1	4	0	38	6.87	116	3	.267	.356	.397	118	8	.271	.341	.500
1988	Hou-N	317	9	.297	.346	.454	1	2	0	48	3.78	1	3	0	31	4.35	0	3	0	24	3.80	2	2	0	55	4.09	148	4	.284	.345	.439	169	5	.308	.346	.467
TOTALS		6840	136	.249	.311	.364	53	55	4	952	3.45	54	45	5	870	3.70	56	45	6	851	3.13	51	55	3	971	3.96	3232	64	.271	.335	.391	3608	72	.229	.290	.340
● Kevin Appier BR/TR																																				
1989	KC-A	91	3	.374	.434	.527	1	1	0	6	12.71	0	3	0	16	7.87	1	3	0	19	7.71	0	1	0	3	18.00	44	3	.386	.434	.614	47	0	.362	.434	.447
1990	KC-A	709	13	.252	.307	.334	7	4	0	84	2.77	5	4	0	101	2.75	2	3	0	62	3.18	10	5	0	123	2.55	311	7	.260	.331	.363	398	6	.246	.287	.312
1991	KC-A	803	13	.255	.307	.357	5	5	0	97	2.79	8	5	0	111	3.97	4	7	0	95	3.80	9	3	0	113	3.11	403	8	.268	.327	.395	400	5	.243	.287	.320
1992	KC-A	771	10	.217	.281	.319	8	5	0	104	2.60	7	3	0	104	2.33	8	3	0	115	2.35	7	5	0	94	2.59	370	7	.205	.283	.324	401	3	.227	.278	.314
1993	KC-A	863	8	.212	.279	.292	8	5	0	117	2.39	10	3	0	122	2.73	9	4	0	121	3.04	9	4	0	117	2.07	439	5	.239	.311	.321	424	3	.184	.245	.262
1994	KC-A	570	11	.240	.317	.358	4	2	0	76	4.01	3	4	0	79	3.66	5	6	0	90	4.58	2	0	0	65	2.78	290	3	.279	.370	.390	280	8	.200	.259	.325
1995	KC-A	738	14	.221	.303	.351	7	6	0	109	4.38	8	4	0	92	3.31	11	3	0	110	2.30	4	7	0	92	5.79	430	11	.251	.335	.419	308	3	.179	.256	.256
1996	KC-A	783	17	.245	.314	.370	6	5	0	97	3.43	8	6	0	114	3.78	7	7	0	110	3.45	7	4	0	102	3.81	427	11	.260	.348	.400	356	6	.228	.269	.334
1997	KC-A	886	24	.243	.303	.378	3	7	0	121	3.50	6	6	0	115	3.30	6	5	0	125	2.59	3	8	0	111	4.31	465	14	.258	.333	.411	421	10	.226	.267	.342
1998	KC-A	62	3	.339	.391	.548	1	1	0	10	8.10	0	1	0	5	7.20	0	0	0	0	—	1	2	0	15	7.80	39	1	.333	.381	.487	23	2	.348	.407	.652
1999	KC-A	548	18	.279	.345	.438	5	3	0	80	4.29	4	6	0	61	5.64	7	6	0	104	5.00	2	3	0	36	4.50	276	7	.319	.402	.475	272	11	.239	.284	.401
1999	Oak-A	275	9	.280	.357	.469	5	2	0	43	2.91	2	3	0	25	10.66	0	0	0	0	—	7	5	0	69	5.77	135	4	.252	.350	.430	140	5	.307	.364	.507
2000	Oak-A	762	23	.262	.354	.421	6	6	0	105	3.84	9	5	0	90	5.30	8	4	0	87	4.24	7	7	0	108	4.74	405	13	.296	.393	.467	357	10	.224	.308	.370
TOTALS		7861	166	.245	.313	.367	66	52	0	1049	3.45	70	53	0	1036	3.81	68	51	0	1038	3.47	68	54	0	1047	3.79	4034	94	.263	.343	.400	3827	72	.226	.280	.332
● Rolando Arrojo BR/TR																																				
1998	TB-A	761	21	.256	.329	.398	5	5	0	100	4.24	9	7	0	102	2.90	10	4	0	113	3.02	4	8	0	89	4.26	413	12	.300	.378	.477	348	9	.204	.270	.305
1999	TB-A	548	23	.296	.378	.504	2	9	0	85	5.95	5	3	0	56	4.02	2	5	0	48	7.31	5	7	0	93	4.08	302	16	.315	.399	.570	246	7	.272	.350	.423
2000	Col-N	402	14	.299	.381	.493	3	4	0	47	7.33	2	5	0	55	4.94	5	5	0	71	6.31	0	4	0	30	5.40	186	10	.317	.397	.581	216	4	.282	.367	.417
2000	Bos-A	274	10	.245	.310	.420	2	1	0	33	6.48	3	1	0	38	3.79	0	0	0	0	—	5	2	0	71	5.05	146	7	.274	.333	.500	128	3	.211	.284	.328
TOTALS		1985	68	.274	.351	.449	12	19	0	264	5.62	19	16	0	251	3.73	17	14	0	233	4.91	14	21	0	283	4.52	1047	45	.304	.382	.525	938	23	.241	.316	.365
● Andy Ashby BR/TR																																				
1991	Phi-N	160	5	.256	.341	.431	0	3	0	26	6.49	1	2	0	16	5.17	0	2	0	9	8.00	1	3	0	33	5.45	93	3	.247	.317	.409	67	2	.269	.370	.463
1992	Phi-N	145	6	.290	.379	.490	1	1	0	21	6.00	0	2	0	16	9.56	1	0	0	16	4.02	0	3	0	21	10.13	85	4	.318	.406	.506	60	2	.250	.338	.467
1993	Col-N	236	5	.377	.453	.525	0	2	0	28	8.58	0	2	1	26	8.42	0	4	1	54	8.50	0	0	0	0	—	128	1	.352	.439	.422	108	4	.407	.468	.648
1993	SD-N	268	14	.295	.350	.507	2	1	0	38	4.06	1	5	0	31	7.18	0	0	0	0	—	3	6	0	69	5.48	146	6	.267	.325	.425	122	8	.328	.380	.607
1994	SD-N	622	16	.233	.285	.370	3	4	0	71	2.52	3	7	0	93	4.06	3	6	0	113	2.96	3	5	0	52	4.35	316	8	.247	.305	.389	306	8	.219	.263	.350
1995	SD-N	712	17	.253	.321	.369	7	3	0	94	2.21	5	7	0	99	3.64	5	4	0	79	3.32	7	6	0	114	2.68	325	5	.274	.336	.378	387	12	.235	.308	.362
1996	SD-N	567	17	.259	.304	.392	3	3	0	64	3.36	6	2	0	86	3.13	8	2	0	101	2.93	1	3	0	49	3.83	248	6	.270	.326	.399	319	11	.251	.286	.386
1997	SD-N	778	17	.266	.311	.382	5	4	0	109	3.29	4	7	0	91	5.12	4	4	0	89	3.43	5	7	0	111	4.69	406	14	.286	.332	.443	372	3	.245	.289	.315
1998	SD-N	861	23	.259	.309	.402	10	4	0	120	2.85	7	5	0	107	3.88	10	5	0	133	2.57	7	4	0	94	4.42	455	10	.251	.300	.393	406	13	.268	.320	.411
1999	SD-N	790	26	.258	.311	.406	5	6	0	101	4.20	9	4	0	105	3.42	7	4	0	88	3.39	7	6	0	118	4.11	356	9	.281	.327	.419	434	17	.240	.298	.396
2000	Phi-N	392	17	.288	.351	.480	1	3	0	49	5.51	3	4	0	52	5.85	2	7	0	86	6.36	2	0	0	15	1.80	181	8	.282	.370	.470	211	9	.294	.335	.488
2000	Atl-N	380	12	.271	.314	.429	5	3	0	60	2.85	3	3	0	38	6.16	0	0	0	0	—	8	6	0	98	4.13	188	8	.340	.377	.532	192	4	.203	.252	.328
TOTALS		5911	175	.266	.322	.411	42	37	0	782	3.66	42	50	1	761	4.56	40	38	1	768	3.88	44	49	0	775	4.32	2927	82	.278	.335	.422	2984	93	.255	.309	.400
● Paul Assenmacher BL/TL																																				
1986	Atl-N	253	5	.241	.311	.332	4	1	5	39	1.15	3	2	2	29	4.30	3	2	7	37	2.17	4	1	0	31	2.90	82	1	.268	.348	.354	171	4	.228	.293	.322
1987	Atl-N	223	8	.260	.333	.448	0	0	2	26	5.47	1	1	0	28	4.76	1	1	0	23	5.09	0	0	2	32	5.12	79	1	.177	.261	.253	144	7	.306	.373	.556
1988	Atl-N	287	4	.251	.327	.341	7	5	3	41	4.87	1	2	2	39	1.16	2	4	2	43	4.19	6	3	3	36	1.73	91	2	.275	.320	.385	196	2	.240	.330	.321
1989	Atl-N	221	2	.249	.300	.330	1	3	0	32	3.69	0	0	0	26	3.46	0	2	0	32	5.01	1	1	0	25	1.78	64	0	.234	.258	.250	157	2	.255	.316	.363
1989	Chi-N	69	1	.275	.378	.362	2	0	0	10	4.35	0	1	0	9	6.23	0	0	0	0	—	2	1	0	19	5.21	21	0	.286	.423	.333	48	1	.271	.357	.375
1990	Chi-N	376	10	.239	.305	.351	6	1	3	52	3.46	1	1	7	51	2.12	2	1	3	53	3.23	5	1	7	50	2.34	122	1	.221	.265	.279	254	9	.248	.324	.386
1991	Chi-N	381	10	.223	.284	.357	4	2	8	61	2.07	3	6	7	42	4.97	3	4	6	48	3.78	4	4	9	55	2.78	134	1	.179	.247	.261	247	9	.247	.304	.409
1992	Chi-N	266	6	.271	.340	.414	2	3	5	39	4.15	2	1	3	29	4.03	1	1	5	31	1.76	3	3	3	37	6.03	91	3	.220	.294	.374	175	3	.297	.364	.434
1993	Chi-N	153	5	.288	.343	.431	1	0	0	23	3.09	1	1	0	15	4.11	2	1	0	30	3.86	0	0	0	8	2.16	65	4	.277	.309	.477	88	1	.295	.367	.398
1993	NY-A	57	0	.175	.299	.211	1	1	0	9	4.00	1	1	0	8	2.16	0	0	0	0	—	2	2	0	17	3.12	26	0	.154	.333	.154	31	0	.194	.265	.258
1994	Chi-A	116	2	.224	.301	.319	1	2	0	14	4.40	0	0	1	19	2.89	1	2	1	22	4.98	0	0	0	11	0.79	50	1	.200	.246	.280	66	1	.242	.342	.348
1995	Cle-A	142	3	.225	.296	.324	3	1	0	21	3.48	3	1	0	18	2.04	2	1	0	11	0.79	4	1	0	27	3.67	62	1	.177	.227	.226	80	2	.262	.344	.400
1996	Cle-A	177	1	.260	.325	.345	3	1	1	28	2.28	1	1	0	19	4.26	0	1	0	22	2.49	4	1	1	25	3.60	86	0	.256	.293	.314	91	1	.264	.352	.374
1997	Cle-A	186	5	.231	.289	.344	4	0	2	26	4.15	1	0	2	23	1.57	2	0	0	18	6.38	3	0	4	31	0.88	90	3	.233	.286	.356	96	2	.229	.292	.333
1998	Cle-A	189	5	.286	.351	.418	2	3	2	18	4.42	0	2	1	29	2.51	2	4	0	26	3.51	0	1	3	21	2.95	99	3	.313	.358	.475	90	2	.256	.343	.356
1999	Cle-A	144	6	.347	.415	.542	1	1	0	18	6.00	1	0	0	15	10.80	1	1	0	16	4.50	1	0	0	17	11.65	66	3	.227	.297	.379	78	3	.449	.511	.679
TOTALS		3240	73	.252	.320	.371	42	24	31	457	3.54	19	20	25	398	3.52	22	25	24	412	3.67	39	19	32	444	3.41	1228	24	.232	.291	.329	2012	49	.264	.337	.396
● Pedro Astacio BR/TR																																				
1992	LA-N	314	1	.255	.302	.303	3	3	0	48	1.68	2	2	0	34	2.41	0	0	0	0	—	5	5	0	82	1.98	180	1	.244	.315	.300	134	0	.269	.283	.306
1993	LA-N	689	14	.239	.309	.353	6	3	0	97	3.34	8	6	0	89	3.83	6	4	0	86	4.08	8	5	0	100	3.14	392	9	.240	.304	.355	297	5	.239	.315	.350
1994	LA-N	563	18	.252	.312	.416	4	3	0	82	2.63	2	5	0	67	6.31	6	5	0	109	4.05	0	3	0	40	4.95	269	10	.268	.330	.465	294	8	.238	.295	.371
1995	LA-N	395	12	.261	.316	.410	4	3	0	49	4.04	3	5	0	55	4.42	1	6	0	67	4.59	6	2	0	37	3.62	192	8	.260	.322	.458	203	4	.261	.309	.365
1996	LA-N	793	18	.261	.324	.385	5	4	0	110	2.86	4	4	0	102	4.07	3	6	0	93	4.08	6	2	0	119	2.95	336	8	.274	.330	.420	457	10	.252	.320	.359
1997	LA-N	589	15	.256	.313	.404	3	4	0	64	3.96	4	5	0	90	4.20	4	7	0	106	4.15	3	2	0	47	3.99	281	9	.288	.354	.463	308	6	.227	.274	.351
1997	Col-N	187	9	.262	.327	.455	2	1	0	20	6.75	3	0	0	29	2.51	0	0	0	0	—	5	1	0	49	4.25	56	2	.179	.262	.357	131	7	.298	.357	.496
1998	Col-N	832	39	.294	.363	.496	7	7	0	112	7.39	6	7	0	97	4.90	6	8	0	113	6.07	7	6	0	97	6.42	412	20	.257	.343	.451	420	19	.331	.383	.540
1999	Col-N	906	38	.285	.338	.482	5	5	0	94	7.16	12	6	0	138	3.60	7	6	0	106	5.03	10	5	0	126	5.06	409	13	.306	.379	.506	497	25	.268	.312	.457
2000	Col-N	772	32	.281	.356	.474	7	4	0	96	6.54	5	5	0	100	4.05	7	5	0	116	5.04	5	4	0	80	5.60	359	17	.290	.367	.499	413	15	.274	.346	.453
TOTALS		6040	196	.268	.331	.426	46	37	0	773	4.73	49	45	0	800	4.16	40	47	0	795	4.68	55	35	0	778	4.20	2886	97	.270	.340	.440	3154	99	.266	.323	.414
● James Baldwin BR/TR																																				
1995	Chi-A	72	6	.444	.506	.792	0	1	0	8	10.80	0	0	0	6	15.63	0	1	0	15	12.89	0	0	0	0	—	38	2	.447	.533	.711	34	4	.441	.472	.882
1996	Chi-A	654	24	.257	.319	.422	6	3	0	98	3.75	5	3	0	71	5.35	7	1	0	66	3.68	4	5	0	103	4.89	355	11	.265	.330	.406	299	13	.247	.307	.441

YEAR	TM/L	TOTAL					HOME					AWAY					1ST HALF					2ND HALF					LEFT					RIGHT				
		AB	HR	AVG	OBP	SLG	W	L	SV	IP	ERA	W	L	SV	IP	ERA	W	L	SV	IP	ERA	W	L	SV	IP	ERA	AB	HR	AVG	OBP	SLG	AB	HR	AVG	OBP	SLG
1997	Chi-A	782	19	.262	.334	.421	5	7	0	94	5.17	7	8	0	106	5.35	5	8	0	104	4.60	7	7	0	96	5.98	384	8	.276	.363	.422	398	11	.249	.305	.420
1998	Chi-A	634	18	.278	.347	.445	4	4	0	81	5.69	9	2	0	78	4.94	2	3	0	68	7.41	11	3	0	91	3.76	344	8	.291	.358	.445	290	10	.262	.334	.445
1999	Chi-A	787	34	.278	.348	.468	5	8	0	97	5.73	7	5	0	102	4.50	3	8	0	84	6.51	9	5	0	115	4.07	419	16	.272	.353	.444	368	18	.285	.342	.495
2000	Chi-A	680	34	.272	.335	.471	5	5	0	80	6.07	9	2	0	98	3.49	10	3	0	100	3.88	4	4	0	78	5.63	361	17	.277	.332	.476	319	17	.266	.339	.464
TOTALS		3609	135	.273	.341	.452	25	28	0	459	5.34	37	20	0	461	4.84	27	24	0	436	5.38	35	24	0	484	4.82	1901	62	.279	.352	.444	1708	73	.266	.328	.461
● Floyd Bannister	BL/TL																																			
1978	Hou-N	428	13	.280	.372	.465	3	3	0	58	2.34	0	6	0	53	7.52	3	3	0	69	2.61	0	6	0	41	8.49	87	3	.253	.365	.437	341	10	.287	.373	.472
1979	Sea-A	711	25	.260	.327	.442	8	7	0	119	3.03	2	8	0	63	5.97	3	6	0	69	4.15	7	9	0	113	3.98	162	6	.216	.287	.383	549	19	.273	.339	.459
1980	Sea-A	837	24	.239	.295	.391	5	6	0	119	3.56	4	7	0	99	3.36	5	6	0	100	3.25	4	7	0	118	3.66	175	4	.211	.291	.320	662	20	.246	.296	.409
1981	Sea-A	478	14	.268	.327	.425	5	5	0	66	3.82	4	4	0	55	5.20	6	5	0	75	4.54	3	4	0	46	4.30	98	4	.316	.356	.469	380	10	.255	.320	.413
1982	Sea-A	927	32	.243	.301	.401	5	8	0	120	3.75	7	5	0	127	3.12	7	4	0	124	2.91	5	9	0	123	3.94	135	6	.252	.315	.422	792	26	.241	.299	.398
1983	Chi-A	821	19	.233	.294	.361	9	3	0	119	3.09	7	7	0	98	3.67	3	9	0	94	4.42	13	1	0	124	2.55	115	1	.191	.254	.252	706	18	.239	.301	.378
1984	Chi-A	835	30	.253	.319	.422	6	4	0	105	4.47	8	7	0	113	5.16	4	6	0	95	5.10	10	5	0	123	4.62	150	6	.260	.335	.413	685	24	.251	.315	.423
1985	Chi-A	806	30	.262	.343	.445	5	6	0	95	3.61	5	8	0	116	5.90	5	6	0	90	4.70	5	8	0	121	5.00	146	6	.301	.360	.548	660	24	.253	.339	.423
1986	Chi-A	626	17	.259	.311	.398	5	6	0	98	2.84	5	8	0	67	4.57	3	4	0	49	2.96	7	10	0	117	3.78	98	2	.204	.255	.316	528	15	.269	.322	.413
1987	Chi-A	878	38	.246	.285	.426	6	5	0	92	3.93	10	6	0	137	3.35	3	7	0	92	4.97	13	4	0	136	2.64	125	3	.240	.314	.376	753	35	.247	.280	.434
1988	KC-A	733	22	.248	.316	.405	4	6	0	96	4.22	8	7	0	93	4.44	8	6	0	99	4.45	4	7	0	90	4.18	145	0	.214	.253	.276	588	22	.257	.330	.437
1989	KC-A	300	8	.290	.330	.430	2	1	0	45	4.60	2	0	0	30	4.75	4	1	0	75	4.66	0	0	0	0	—	48	1	.354	.404	.500	252	7	.278	.316	.417
1991	Cal-A	94	5	.266	.337	.500	0	0	0	12	2.25	0	0	0	13	5.54	0	0	0	18	3.50	0	0	0	7	5.14	31	2	.258	.343	.484	63	3	.270	.333	.508
1992	Tex-A	139	3	.281	.371	.424	1	0	0	24	5.70	0	1	0	13	7.43	1	1	0	25	7.46	0	0	0	12	3.86	46	2	.174	.288	.391	93	1	.333	.414	.441
TOTALS		8613	280	.253	.316	.415	64	60	0	1167	3.61	62	74	0	1079	4.56	55	64	0	1075	4.15	71	70	0	1171	3.98	1561	46	.242	.310	.388	7052	234	.256	.317	.421
● Rod Beck	BR/TR																																			
1991	SF-N	194	4	.273	.319	.412	0	1	1	26	3.86	1	0	0	27	3.71	0	1	0	7	9.00	1	0	1	45	2.98	89	4	.292	.337	.517	105	0	.257	.304	.324
1992	SF-N	327	4	.190	.228	.257	2	3	9	44	2.06	1	0	8	48	1.49	0	2	4	46	2.33	3	1	13	46	1.18	180	2	.178	.212	.256	147	2	.204	.248	.259
1993	SF-N	284	11	.201	.241	.335	3	0	21	39	1.62	0	1	27	40	2.68	2	1	23	37	1.46	1	0	25	42	2.76	161	6	.180	.231	.304	123	5	.228	.254	.374
1994	SF-N	188	10	.261	.304	.463	1	3	13	28	3.25	1	1	15	21	2.14	2	3	14	26	4.15	0	1	14	23	1.19	87	2	.253	.330	.356	101	8	.267	.279	.554
1995	SF-N	225	7	.267	.331	.391	5	3	16	36	4.54	0	3	17	23	4.30	4	2	12	29	2.79	1	4	21	30	6.07	109	3	.275	.333	.404	116	4	.259	.328	.379
1996	SF-N	235	9	.238	.270	.413	0	4	20	35	3.31	0	5	15	27	3.38	0	4	16	31	2.32	0	5	19	31	4.35	105	4	.219	.236	.410	130	5	.254	.297	.415
1997	SF-N	269	7	.249	.276	.361	4	1	21	40	2.72	3	3	16	30	4.45	4	2	26	35	2.60	3	2	11	35	4.33	137	2	.234	.271	.285	132	5	.265	.281	.439
1998	Chi-N	320	11	.269	.311	.434	2	1	29	42	2.59	1	3	22	39	3.49	1	2	18	39	3.92	2	2	33	41	2.18	148	6	.270	.323	.453	172	5	.267	.301	.419
1999	Chi-N	124	5	.331	.388	.581	1	1	4	17	7.94	1	3	3	13	7.62	2	4	7	14	10.54	0	0	0	16	5.51	51	1	.373	.441	.549	73	4	.301	.350	.603
1999	Bos-A	49	0	.184	.273	.224	0	1	1	3	9.00	0	0	2	11	0.00	0	0	0	0	—	0	1	3	14	1.93	26	0	.115	.179	.115	23	0	.261	.370	.348
2000	Bos-A	153	2	.222	.287	.307	1	0	0	25	2.92	2	0	0	16	3.38	0	0	0	6	1.50	3	0	0	35	3.38	69	1	.246	.288	.362	84	1	.202	.287	.262
TOTALS		2368	70	.242	.288	.379	19	18	135	333	3.22	10	19	125	295	3.17	15	21	120	270	3.27	14	16	140	358	3.14	1162	31	.235	.283	.362	1206	39	.250	.292	.395
● Steve Bedrosian	BR/TR																																			
1981	Atl-N	89	2	.169	.292	.281	0	1	0	15	5.28	1	1	0	9	3.00	0	0	0	0	—	1	2	0	24	4.44	39	1	.205	.354	.359	50	1	.140	.241	.220
1982	Atl-N	495	7	.206	.292	.273	7	3	6	74	2.92	1	3	5	64	1.84	4	1	3	62	1.88	4	5	8	75	2.87	243	4	.189	.282	.255	252	3	.222	.302	.290
1983	Atl-N	437	11	.229	.313	.355	4	6	10	59	4.25	5	4	9	61	2.97	5	2	9	53	2.87	4	8	10	67	4.18	225	4	.227	.313	.347	212	7	.231	.312	.363
1984	Atl-N	309	5	.210	.288	.324	3	3	4	46	2.93	6	3	7	38	1.67	5	5	8	49	2.20	4	1	3	35	2.60	171	4	.240	.338	.386	138	1	.174	.219	.246
1985	Atl-N	779	17	.254	.348	.372	4	5	0	96	3.46	3	10	0	110	4.16	5	6	0	104	2.78	2	9	0	103	4.89	386	13	.282	.386	.443	393	4	.226	.309	.303
1986	Phi-N	341	12	.232	.299	.364	2	3	14	39	3.00	6	3	15	51	3.68	5	3	9	38	3.76	3	3	20	52	3.12	178	10	.213	.300	.410	163	2	.252	.297	.313
1987	Phi-N	334	11	.237	.297	.362	2	2	17	43	3.38	3	1	23	46	2.33	3	1	20	41	2.66	2	2	20	48	2.98	193	8	.249	.315	.394	141	3	.220	.272	.319
1988	Phi-N	292	6	.257	.317	.384	5	3	13	37	4.42	1	3	15	38	3.11	1	3	13	30	4.20	5	3	15	44	3.45	154	4	.292	.366	.461	138	2	.217	.259	.297
1989	Phi-N	115	7	.183	.289	.409	2	1	4	20	3.66	0	2	2	14	2.57	2	3	6	34	3.21	0	0	0	0	—	66	5	.197	.313	.485	49	2	.163	.255	.306
1989	SF-N	182	5	.192	.277	.280	0	1	10	26	0.68	1	3	7	25	4.74	0	1	5	7	2.70	1	3	12	44	2.64	98	3	.204	.316	.296	84	2	.179	.228	.262
1990	SF-N	299	6	.241	.341	.341	8	4	11	48	3.54	1	5	6	31	5.23	3	5	7	39	4.38	6	4	10	40	4.02	165	4	.267	.373	.388	134	2	.209	.301	.284
1991	Min-A	288	11	.243	.327	.420	2	3	2	44	5.52	3	0	4	33	2.97	2	2	3	39	3.69	3	1	3	38	5.17	123	4	.260	.365	.439	165	7	.230	.297	.406
1993	Atl-N	175	4	.194	.256	.303	2	1	0	27	1.32	3	1	0	22	2.01	0	2	0	17	2.12	5	0	0	33	1.38	74	2	.203	.256	.311	101	2	.188	.257	.297
1994	Atl-N	169	4	.243	.319	.373	0	0	0	21	1.71	0	2	0	25	4.68	0	1	0	30	3.90	0	1	0	16	2.25	69	2	.304	.364	.507	100	2	.200	.289	.280
1995	Atl-N	113	6	.354	.414	.566	1	2	0	11	10.64	0	0	0	17	3.18	1	2	0	18	4.91	0	0	0	10	8.38	38	3	.342	.409	.579	75	3	.360	.417	.560
TOTALS		4417	114	.232	.314	.354	42	38	91	607	3.51	34	41	93	584	3.24	36	37	83	561	3.08	40	42	101	630	3.64	2222	71	.245	.337	.392	2195	43	.220	.290	.316
● Tim Belcher	BR/TR																																			
1987	LA-N	125	2	.240	.278	.320	4	1	0	29	2.17	0	1	0	5	3.60	0	0	0	0	—	4	2	0	34	2.38	63	1	.286	.343	.349	62	1	.194	.206	.290
1988	LA-N	659	8	.217	.275	.296	6	3	2	78	2.90	6	3	2	102	2.91	5	4	2	73	3.93	7	2	2	106	2.20	340	5	.212	.271	.306	319	3	.223	.279	.285
1989	LA-N	838	20	.217	.289	.322	10	4	0	124	2.10	5	8	1	106	3.66	4	8	1	110	3.28	11	4	0	120	2.39	473	7	.218	.298	.292	365	13	.216	.278	.362
1990	LA-N	566	17	.240	.299	.382	6	3	0	75	2.77	3	6	0	78	5.17	5	6	0	97	4.28	4	3	0	56	3.51	298	8	.228	.295	.359	268	9	.254	.303	.407
1991	LA-N	789	10	.240	.306	.318	7	4	0	121	2.67	3	5	0	88	2.56	7	4	0	101	2.22	3	5	0	108	3.00	445	4	.274	.343	.342	344	6	.195	.258	.288
1992	Cin-N	843	17	.238	.303	.368	11	7	0	126	3.43	4	7	0	102	4.51	7	6	0	111	3.48	8	8	0	116	4.33	512	9	.277	.350	.410	331	8	.178	.228	.302
1993	Cin-N	527	11	.254	.322	.383	6	2	0	73	5.52	3	4	0	64	3.25	6	5	0	106	3.49	3	1	0	31	7.76	279	5	.262	.352	.387	248	6	.246	.285	.379
1993	Chi-A	265	8	.242	.313	.377	2	2	0	41	3.32	1	3	0	31	5.81	0	0	0	0	—	3	5	0	72	4.40	117	3	.248	.313	.359	148	5	.236	.313	.392
1994	Det-A	662	21	.290	.367	.467	3	6	0	73	5.79	4	9	0	89	5.97	6	8	0	108	5.58	1	7	0	54	6.50	347	8	.294	.366	.427	315	13	.286	.368	.511
1995	Sea-A	700	19	.269	.352	.430	5	7	0	99	4.36	5	5	0	80	4.71	3	3	0	54	4.80	7	9	0	125	4.39	425	9	.268	.350	.405	275	10	.269	.356	.469
1996	KC-A	931	28	.281	.331	.436	7	4	0	118	3.97	8	7	0	121	3.88	6	3	0	105	4.47	9	8	0	134	3.49	510	12	.288	.343	.418	421	16	.273	.316	.458
1997	KC-A	841	31	.288	.345	.471	7	8	0	112	5.87	6	4	0	101	4.09	8	7	0	124	3.63	5	5	0	89	6.95	403	17	.278	.345	.474	438	14	.297	.345	.468
1998	KC-A	909	37	.272	.328	.449	4	9	0	101	5.51	10	5	0	133	3.32	6	7	0	114	3.86	8	7	0	120	4.66	449	22	.256	.331	.445	460	15	.287	.324	.452
1999	Ana-A	534	27	.315	.369	.545	3	3	0	65	6.06	3	5	0	67	7.39	5	6	0	91	6.53	1	2	0	41	7.19	276	13	.312	.383	.522	258	14	.318	.353	.570
2000	Ana-A	160	8	.281	.373	.519	2	2	0	16	9.00	2	3	0	25	5.47	2	1	0	13	4.97	2	4	0	28	7.71	74	2	.311	.409	.527	86	6	.256	.340	.512
TOTALS		9349	264	.259	.323	.404	83	65	2	1252	4.10	63	75	3	1191	4.23	70	68	3	1207	4.08	76	72	2	1236	4.25	5011	125	.265	.336	.397	4338	139	.253	.308	.412
● Stan Belinda	BR/TR																																			
1989	Pit-N	44	0	.295	.326	.295	0	1	0	7	9.00	0	0	0	3	0.00	0	0	0	0	—	0	1	0	10	6.10	19	0	.368	.429	.368	25	0	.240	.240	.240
1990	Pit-N	211	4	.227	.321	.346	1	2	2	25	4.97	2	2	6	33	2.45	2	2	3	19	2.89	1	2	5	40	3.86	88	1	.182	.282	.273	123	3	.260	.350	.398
1991	Pit-N	272	10	.184	.283	.327	2	1	13	42	1.94	5	4	3	37	5.15	3	1	6	33	3.58	4	4	10	46	3.35	123	4	.203	.298	.325	149	6	.168	.272	.329
1992	Pit-N	260	8	.223	.295	.381	2	1	8	33	1.89	4	3	10	38	4.26	3	2	11	32	2.81	3	2	7	39	3.43	135	4	.193	.277	.326	125	4	.256	.314	.440
1993	Pit-N	156	4	.224	.276	.359	3	1	8	22	5.40	0	0	11	21	1.74	3	0	14	34	2.62	0	1	5	8	7.87	75	3	.253	.325	.427	81	1	.198	.230	.296
1993	KC-A	107	2	.280	.325	.393	1	0	0	13	3.46	0	1	0	14	5.02	0	0	0	0	—	1	1	0	27	4.28	44	2	.386	.426	.636	63	0	.206	.254	.222
1994	KC-A	188	6	.250	.345	.441	0	0	1	23	3.47	2	2	0	26	6.66	2	2	0	30	4.80	0	0	1	19	5.68	62	1	.242	.367	.387	126	5	.254	.333	.468
1995	Bos-A	249	5	.205	.291	.313	5	0	3	43	2.91	3	1	7	26	3.42	5	0	5	35	2.06	3	1	5	35	4.15	111	3	.207	.308	.333	138	2	.203	.277	.297
1996	Bos-A	114	3	.272	.399	.412	1	0	0	17	4.76	1	1	2	12	9.26	1	1	0	18	8.66	1	0	2	11	3.27	58	1	.276	.391	.397	56	2	.268	.406	.429
1997	Cin-N	367	11	.229	.304	.395	0	4	0	54	4.50	1	1	1	45	2.78	0	2	0	51	3.68	1	3	1	48	3.75	159	6	.264	.344	.478	208	5	.202	.274	.332
1998	Cin-N	217	7	.212	.304	.359	1	3	0	26	3.08	3	5	1	35	3.34	3	6	1	41	3.32	1	2	0	21	3.05	91	2	.220	.345	.341	126	5	.206	.270	.373
1999	Cin-N	163	11	.258	.333	.509	1	1	0	20	9.30	2	0	2	22	1.61	0	0	0	1	0.00	3	1	2	42	5.40	66	5	.258	.333	.561	97	6	.258	.333	.474
2000	Col-N	141	10	.277	.358	.603	1	1	1	21	5.66	0	2	0	15	9.00	1	1	1	27	5.06	0	2	0	9	13.00	48	2	.229	.350	.500	93	8	.301	.363	.656
2000	Atl-N	46	4	.348	.407	.761	0	0	0	5	9.00	0	0	0	6	10.50	0	0	0	0	—	0	0	0	11	9.82	19	2	.316	.400	.789	27	2	.370	.414	.741
TOTALS		2535	85	.233	.315	.397	18	15	36	352	4.14	23	22	43	333	4.16	23	17	41	320	3.68	18	20	38	365	4.56	1098	36	.237	.330	.403	1437	49	.230	.303	.392
● Andy Benes	BR/TR																																			
1989	SD-N	240	7	.213	.303	.350	3	2	0	39	4.38	3	1	0	28	2.28	0	0	0	0	—	6	3	0	67	3.51	131	4	.214	.333	.359	109	3	.211	.263	.339
1990	SD-N	730	18	.242	.306	.374	6	4	0	89	3.93	4	7	0	103	3.32	6	6	0	99	3.64	4	5	0	93	3.57	436	9	.243	.306	.369	294	9	.241	.308	.381
1991	SD-N	836	23	.232	.285	.358	6	5	0	111	3.73	9	6	0	112	2.33	4	8	0	102	4.22	11	3	0	121	2.01	466	13	.230	.281	.354	370	10	.235	.289	.362
1992	SD-N	870	14	.264	.314	.371	7	6	0	117	3.55	6	8	0	115	3.14	6	5	0	112	3.55	7	9	0	120	3.16	533	10	.276	.333	.394	337	4	.246	.283	.335
1993	SD-N	862	23	.232	.303	.371	6	7	0	104	3.47	9	8	0	127	4.04	8	6	0	121	2.60	7	9	0	109	5.10	433	10	.242	.327	.374	429	13	.221	.278	.368
1994	SD-N	653	20	.237	.293	.401	5	7	0	94	4.60	1	7	0	78	2.99	5	9	0	119	3.87	1	5	0	54	3.86	324	5	.225	.293	.346	329	15	.249	.293	.456
1995	SD-N	462	10	.262	.330	.381	1	5	0	65	3.90	3	2	0	54	4.50	2	5	0	81	3.87	2	2	0	37	4.82	217	2	.249	.328	.323	245	8	.273	.332	.433
1995	Sea-A	251	8	.287	.369	.478	3	1	0	35	5.19	4	1	0	28	6.67	0	0	0	0	—	7	2	0	63	5.86	164	5	.329	.426	.530	87	3	.207	.253	.379
1996	StL-N	872	28	.247	.310	.393	8	4	1	112	3.93	10	6	0	118	3.74	5	8	1	111	4.53	13	2	0	119	3.18	365	11	.268	.346	.414	507	17	.231	.283	.379
1997	StL-N	648	9	.230	.298	.330	7	2	0	89	2.82	3	5	0	88	3.39	6	3	0	87	3.10	4	4	0	90	3.10	334	6	.246	.305	.371	314	3	.213	.291	.287

		TOTAL					HOME					AWAY					1ST HALF					2ND HALF					LEFT					RIGHT				
YEAR	TM/L	AB	HR	AVG	OBP	SLG	W	L	SV	IP	ERA	W	L	SV	IP	ERA	W	L	SV	IP	ERA	W	L	SV	IP	ERA	AB	HR	AVG	OBP	SLG	AB	HR	AVG	OBP	SLG
1998	Ari-N	880	25	.251	.311	.410	6	7	0	115	3.83	8	6	0	116	4.10	6	8	0	124	4.56	8	5	0	107	3.28	456	11	.259	.313	.419	424	14	.243	.309	.401
1999	Ari-N	791	34	.273	.343	.460	6	8	0	94	5.53	7	4	0	104	4.15	4	8	0	99	5.62	9	4	0	99	4.00	366	14	.273	.338	.434	425	20	.273	.347	.482
2000	StL-N	633	30	.275	.342	.499	5	3	0	68	5.03	7	6	0	98	4.78	8	3	0	100	4.40	4	6	0	66	5.62	265	15	.268	.341	.502	368	15	.280	.343	.497
TOTALS		8728	249	.249	.313	.396	69	61	1	1132	4.04	74	67	0	1169	3.70	60	69	1	1157	3.99	83	59	0	1144	3.74	4490	115	.255	.323	.395	4238	134	.244	.302	.397
● **Armando Benitez**	BR/TR																																			
1994	Bal-A	37	0	.216	.310	.243	0	0	0	6	0.00	0	0	0	4	2.45	0	0	0	0	—	0	0	0	10	0.90	17	0	.294	.368	.353	20	0	.150	.261	.150
1995	Bal-A	174	8	.213	.361	.397	0	1	1	25	6.57	1	4	1	23	4.70	0	3	1	25	4.74	1	2	1	23	6.65	67	2	.239	.420	.403	107	6	.196	.321	.393
1996	Bal-A	49	2	.143	.232	.286	1	0	1	8	1.13	0	0	3	6	7.11	1	0	0	4	6.75	0	0	4	10	2.61	15	0	.133	.316	.200	34	2	.147	.189	.324
1997	Bal-A	257	7	.191	.305	.300	2	4	3	35	3.89	2	1	6	39	1.16	0	3	6	34	3.44	4	2	3	39	1.60	102	3	.196	.333	.324	155	4	.187	.286	.284
1998	Bal-A	241	10	.199	.318	.361	3	2	11	38	3.32	2	4	11	30	4.45	2	2	8	38	4.50	3	4	14	30	2.97	94	4	.181	.366	.340	147	6	.211	.282	.374
1999	NY-N	271	4	.148	.260	.236	3	1	12	41	1.54	1	2	10	37	2.19	0	2	3	42	1.50	4	1	19	36	2.25	113	2	.177	.331	.292	158	2	.127	.202	.196
2000	NY-N	263	10	.148	.255	.304	3	3	25	42	2.38	1	1	16	34	2.88	2	3	18	40	3.63	2	1	23	36	1.49	119	1	.134	.273	.210	144	9	.160	.239	.382
TOTALS		1292	41	.176	.294	.310	12	11	53	194	3.06	7	12	47	173	3.01	5	13	36	182	3.50	14	10	64	185	2.57	527	12	.182	.338	.302	765	29	.173	.260	.315
● **Bud Black**	BL/TL																																			
1981	Sea-A	4	0	.500	.714	.750	0	0	0	0	—	0	0	0	1	0.00	0	0	0	0	—	0	0	0	1	0.00	1	0	1.000	1.000	1.000	3	0	.333	.600	.667
1982	KC-A	342	10	.269	.338	.421	2	1	0	46	3.94	2	5	0	43	5.27	2	2	0	30	5.40	2	4	0	58	4.17	63	1	.270	.299	.413	279	9	.269	.346	.423
1983	KC-A	618	19	.257	.305	.396	4	2	0	69	3.93	6	5	0	93	3.69	3	2	0	44	3.05	7	5	0	117	4.08	81	2	.235	.287	.333	537	17	.261	.308	.406
1984	KC-A	969	22	.233	.283	.347	10	7	0	146	2.66	7	5	0	111	3.72	9	5	0	127	3.05	8	7	0	130	3.18	205	4	.205	.265	.298	764	18	.241	.288	.360
1985	KC-A	805	17	.268	.323	.398	6	7	0	109	4.38	4	8	0	97	4.28	5	8	0	106	3.55	5	7	0	99	5.16	176	2	.267	.303	.364	629	15	.269	.328	.407
1986	KC-A	445	14	.225	.301	.373	3	2	5	62	2.63	2	8	4	59	3.79	4	4	2	53	4.27	1	6	7	68	2.37	137	3	.219	.285	.336	308	11	.227	.307	.390
1987	KC-A	475	16	.265	.320	.432	5	1	1	63	3.14	3	5	0	59	4.10	3	2	1	43	2.53	5	4	0	80	4.18	117	4	.231	.278	.393	358	12	.277	.334	.444
1988	KC-A	86	2	.267	.351	.360	1	1	0	12	4.63	1	0	0	10	5.23	2	1	0	22	4.91	0	0	0	0	—	17	0	.176	.364	.176	69	2	.290	.347	.406
1988	Cle-A	225	6	.262	.337	.378	0	1	1	30	6.37	2	2	0	29	3.68	1	1	0	18	6.00	1	2	1	41	4.61	52	1	.173	.274	.231	173	5	.289	.358	.422
1989	Cle-A	844	14	.252	.295	.363	5	9	0	115	4.06	7	2	0	107	2.61	6	7	0	105	3.61	6	4	0	118	3.14	120	2	.158	.215	.233	724	12	.268	.308	.384
1990	Cle-A	725	17	.236	.294	.350	7	5	0	102	3.10	4	5	0	89	4.03	6	4	0	108	3.49	5	6	0	83	3.59	131	6	.275	.329	.443	594	11	.227	.287	.330
1990	Tor-A	53	2	.189	.237	.340	1	0	0	2	4.50	1	1	0	14	3.95	0	0	0	0	—	2	1	0	16	4.02	14	1	.214	.188	.429	39	1	.179	.256	.308
1991	SF-N	800	25	.251	.313	.396	8	7	0	112	2.81	4	9	0	102	5.28	6	6	0	117	3.46	6	10	0	97	4.62	175	6	.274	.326	.406	625	19	.245	.309	.394
1992	SF-N	677	23	.263	.321	.422	8	5	0	111	2.91	2	7	0	66	5.76	4	2	0	63	3.88	6	10	0	114	4.01	140	4	.229	.281	.364	537	19	.272	.332	.438
1993	SF-N	347	13	.256	.321	.409	4	2	0	39	3.96	4	0	0	55	3.27	7	1	0	72	3.13	1	1	0	22	4.98	51	1	.294	.333	.392	296	12	.250	.319	.412
1994	SF-N	204	9	.245	.307	.456	2	1	0	18	7.50	2	1	0	36	2.97	1	0	0	13	2.08	3	2	0	41	5.23	32	0	.313	.389	.375	172	9	.233	.291	.471
1995	Cle-A	199	8	.317	.362	.533	2	1	0	25	7.11	2	1	0	22	6.55	4	2	0	42	6.05	0	0	0	6	12.71	35	3	.371	.368	.771	164	5	.305	.361	.482
TOTALS		7818	217	.253	.310	.391	68	52	7	1059	3.60	53	64	4	994	4.09	63	47	3	962	3.66	58	69	8	1091	4.00	1547	40	.240	.293	.361	6271	177	.256	.314	.398
● **Bert Blyleven**	BR/TR																																			
1978	Pit-N	923	17	.235	.290	.345	5	3	0	120	3.38	9	7	0	124	2.69	7	5	0	118	3.50	7	5	0	125	2.59	426	8	.254	.313	.373	497	9	.219	.270	.320
1979	Pit-N	897	21	.265	.335	.395	5	4	0	125	4.16	7	1	0	112	2.97	5	3	0	113	3.89	7	2	0	124	3.34	392	6	.242	.321	.355	505	15	.283	.346	.426
1980	Pit-N	836	20	.262	.310	.392	4	2	0	110	3.03	4	11	0	107	4.64	2	7	0	97	4.27	6	6	0	120	3.46	385	9	.249	.303	.361	451	11	.273	.316	.419
1981	Cle-A	593	9	.245	.296	.332	4	5	0	82	3.06	7	2	0	77	2.69	7	4	0	92	2.83	4	3	0	67	2.96	315	5	.241	.293	.327	278	4	.248	.300	.338
1982	Cle-A	76	2	.211	.303	.368	1	1	0	8	5.40	1	1	0	12	4.50	2	2	0	20	4.87	0	0	0	0	—	28	1	.179	.314	.357	48	1	.229	.296	.375
1983	Cle-A	599	8	.267	.325	.374	2	4	0	67	4.54	5	6	0	89	3.44	5	7	0	106	3.92	2	3	0	51	3.91	279	5	.287	.342	.423	320	3	.250	.311	.331
1984	Cle-A	910	19	.224	.285	.330	10	2	0	123	3.23	9	5	0	122	2.50	6	3	0	92	3.44	13	4	0	153	2.52	475	7	.200	.269	.282	435	12	.251	.302	.382
1985	Cle-A	679	14	.240	.296	.359	5	8	0	109	3.48	4	3	0	71	2.92	7	7	0	127	3.05	2	4	0	53	3.76	384	7	.263	.322	.380	295	7	.210	.262	.332
1985	Min-A	427	9	.237	.281	.342	6	1	0	61	1.91	2	4	0	53	4.27	0	0	0	0	—	8	5	0	114	3.00	260	4	.250	.295	.335	167	5	.216	.258	.353
1986	Min-A	1049	50	.250	.294	.448	12	5	0	155	4.12	5	9	0	117	3.86	6	7	0	119	5.43	11	7	0	152	2.89	638	26	.238	.279	.415	411	24	.268	.318	.499
1987	Min-A	1002	46	.249	.321	.433	9	6	0	165	3.83	6	6	0	102	4.31	7	6	0	127	4.11	8	6	0	140	3.92	555	32	.234	.313	.447	447	14	.266	.331	.416
1988	Min-A	816	21	.294	.345	.434	6	9	0	108	5.83	4	8	0	99	4.98	7	6	0	118	4.51	3	11	0	90	6.62	438	10	.304	.356	.441	378	11	.283	.333	.426
1989	Cal-A	907	14	.248	.287	.336	8	1	0	119	2.64	9	4	0	122	2.81	7	2	0	110	2.30	10	3	0	131	3.08	485	4	.252	.290	.318	422	10	.244	.283	.358
1990	Cal-A	538	15	.303	.339	.463	4	2	0	71	3.82	4	5	0	63	6.82	7	4	0	100	4.52	1	3	0	34	7.34	270	8	.311	.346	.470	268	7	.295	.331	.455
1992	Cal-A	526	17	.285	.326	.439	4	6	0	65	4.31	4	6	0	68	5.14	3	2	0	38	3.79	5	10	0	95	5.12	253	6	.261	.305	.387	273	11	.308	.345	.487
TOTALS		10778	282	.255	.309	.388	85	59	0	1488	3.71	80	78	0	1338	3.72	78	65	0	1377	3.84	87	72	0	1449	3.59	5583	138	.252	.308	.380	5195	144	.259	.310	.397
● **Mike Boddicker**	BR/TR																																			
1980	Bal-A	29	1	.207	.324	.414	0	1	0	7	6.14	0	0	0	0	—	0	0	0	0	—	0	1	0	7	6.14	13	1	.154	.313	.462	16	0	.250	.333	.375
1981	Bal-A	23	1	.261	.320	.391	0	0	0	4	4.15	0	0	0	1	6.75	0	0	0	0	—	0	0	0	6	4.76	12	1	.167	.286	.417	11	0	.364	.364	.364
1982	Bal-A	97	2	.258	.339	.371	1	0	0	13	2.84	0	0	0	13	4.15	0	0	0	0	—	1	0	0	26	3.51	37	1	.324	.432	.486	60	1	.217	.277	.300
1983	Bal-A	652	13	.216	.273	.328	11	3	0	115	2.11	5	5	0	64	3.94	4	3	0	51	3.35	12	5	0	128	2.53	330	4	.230	.293	.336	322	9	.202	.252	.320
1984	Bal-A	956	23	.228	.290	.344	8	6	0	120	2.17	12	5	0	141	3.32	9	6	0	120	2.69	11	5	0	141	2.87	529	11	.238	.299	.340	427	12	.215	.278	.349
1985	Bal-A	794	13	.286	.361	.385	5	9	0	103	3.40	7	8	0	100	4.77	8	7	0	111	4.15	4	10	0	93	3.98	452	8	.294	.375	.405	342	5	.275	.342	.360
1986	Bal-A	840	30	.255	.321	.410	7	4	0	102	4.66	7	8	0	116	4.73	10	3	0	103	4.18	4	9	0	115	5.17	428	12	.266	.329	.404	412	18	.243	.313	.415
1987	Bal-A	854	29	.248	.315	.413	5	6	0	117	4.24	5	6	0	109	4.12	5	4	0	122	2.88	5	8	0	104	5.69	485	18	.239	.303	.416	369	11	.260	.330	.409
1988	Bal-A	563	14	.265	.333	.387	2	5	0	67	3.11	4	7	0	80	4.48	3	10	0	107	4.13	3	2	0	40	3.12	292	7	.288	.367	.397	271	7	.240	.295	.376
1988	Bos-A	331	3	.257	.313	.332	5	1	0	40	3.38	2	2	0	49	2.02	0	0	0	0	—	7	3	0	89	2.63	167	1	.246	.283	.323	164	2	.268	.342	.341
1989	Bos-A	813	19	.267	.330	.400	7	8	0	103	4.89	8	3	0	109	3.15	5	7	0	101	5.26	10	4	0	111	2.85	444	12	.279	.333	.421	369	7	.252	.325	.374
1990	Bos-A	873	16	.258	.319	.368	11	5	0	136	2.97	6	3	0	92	3.93	10	3	0	111	3.25	7	5	0	117	3.45	464	7	.261	.317	.366	409	9	.254	.321	.369
1991	KC-A	692	13	.272	.340	.408	7	8	0	111	4.07	5	4	0	70	4.11	6	6	0	90	3.10	6	6	0	91	5.06	355	7	.301	.365	.470	337	6	.240	.314	.341
1992	KC-A	341	5	.270	.352	.390	1	2	0	36	5.70	0	2	3	50	4.47	0	4	2	57	5.21	1	0	1	30	4.55	168	2	.292	.355	.387	173	3	.249	.350	.393
1993	Mil-A	228	6	.338	.387	.478	3	2	0	35	5.09	0	3	0	19	6.75	3	5	0	54	5.67	0	0	0	0	—	130	6	.392	.429	.592	98	0	.265	.333	.327
TOTALS		8086	188	.257	.323	.384	73	60	0	1110	3.62	61	56	3	1013	4.01	63	58	2	1026	3.85	71	58	1	1097	3.76	4306	98	.269	.332	.398	3780	90	.244	.313	.367
● **Joe Boever**	BR/TR																																			
1985	StL-N	63	3	.270	.309	.460	0	0	0	7	2.57	0	0	0	9	5.79	0	0	0	0	—	0	0	0	16	4.41	21	0	.238	.273	.286	42	3	.286	.326	.548
1986	StL-N	82	2	.232	.323	.317	0	1	0	14	1.88	0	0	0	7	1.23	0	0	0	1	0.00	0	1	0	21	1.74	27	1	.296	.441	.407	55	1	.200	.254	.273
1987	Atl-N	79	4	.367	.446	.608	0	0	0	10	7.20	1	0	0	8	7.56	0	0	0	0	—	1	0	0	18	7.36	43	1	.349	.431	.512	36	3	.389	.463	.722
1988	Atl-N	66	1	.182	.206	.242	0	1	1	15	0.60	0	1	0	5	5.06	0	0	0	0	—	0	2	1	20	1.77	35	0	.143	.167	.171	31	1	.226	.250	.323
1989	Atl-N	309	6	.252	.328	.356	4	6	9	51	3.53	0	5	12	31	4.60	2	2	13	40	3.63	2	9	8	43	4.22	179	1	.251	.333	.307	130	5	.254	.322	.423
1990	Atl-N	159	6	.252	.383	.434	1	1	2	22	6.45	0	2	6	20	2.70	1	3	6	36	4.50	0	0	2	6	5.68	85	1	.188	.343	.282	74	5	.324	.429	.608
1990	Phi-N	172	0	.215	.282	.267	1	2	3	30	2.37	1	1	3	16	1.72	0	0	0	0	—	2	3	6	46	2.15	89	0	.180	.291	.202	83	0	.253	.271	.337
1991	Phi-N	368	10	.245	.336	.383	2	1	0	54	3.17	1	4	0	44	4.67	3	5	0	59	4.14	0	0	0	40	3.40	171	4	.257	.361	.380	197	6	.234	.314	.386
1992	Hou-N	416	3	.248	.324	.310	1	2	1	61	1.32	2	4	1	50	3.96	2	3	1	57	2.83	1	3	1	54	2.17	186	1	.242	.346	.317	230	2	.252	.306	.304
1993	Oak-A	311	8	.280	.353	.431	4	2	0	37	3.89	0	0	0	42	3.83	2	2	0	53	3.04	2	0	0	26	5.54	141	3	.305	.379	.461	170	5	.259	.332	.406
1993	Det-A	78	1	.179	.269	.282	1	0	1	11	0.84	1	1	2	12	4.38	0	0	0	0	—	2	1	3	23	2.74	31	1	.226	.306	.355	47	0	.149	.246	.234
1994	Det-A	304	12	.263	.345	.421	7	0	1	46	3.15	2	2	2	36	5.05	6	1	1	58	3.86	3	1	2	23	4.30	140	3	.214	.296	.307	164	9	.305	.387	.518
1995	Det-A	401	17	.319	.384	.521	3	4	2	53	6.28	2	3	1	46	6.50	4	3	3	45	4.17	1	4	0	53	8.27	221	10	.299	.368	.489	180	7	.344	.404	.561
1996	Pit-N	59	2	.288	.364	.390	0	0	0	7	8.10	0	2	2	8	3.24	0	0	0	6	9.53	0	2	2	9	2.89	25	1	.400	.483	.520	34	1	.206	.270	.294
TOTALS		2867	75	.262	.341	.394	24	20	20	418	3.49	10	25	29	336	4.47	20	19	24	355	3.77	14	26	25	399	4.06	1394	27	.255	.346	.363	1473	48	.269	.336	.424
● **Brian Bohanon**	BL/TL																																			
1990	Tex-A	134	6	.299	.382	.493	0	2	0	17	7.27	0	1	0	17	5.94	0	3	0	34	6.62	0	0	0	0	—	25	0	.200	.276	.280	109	6	.321	.406	.541
1991	Tex-A	241	4	.274	.336	.378	1	2	0	21	5.91	3	1	0	40	4.28	0	0	0	0	—	4	3	0	61	4.84	34	0	.265	.286	.324	207	4	.275	.343	.386
1992	Tex-A	192	7	.297	.377	.464	1	1	0	27	4.94	0	0	0	18	8.35	0	0	0	12	8.76	1	1	0	33	5.40	34	1	.235	.325	.324	158	6	.310	.389	.494
1993	Tex-A	361	8	.296	.377	.429	4	2	0	52	4.35	0	2	0	41	5.27	3	1	0	36	3.47	1	3	0	56	5.59	89	2	.326	.434	.427	272	6	.287	.358	.430
1994	Tex-A	159	7	.321	.357	.509	2	2	0	23	8.10	0	0	0	14	5.79	0	0	0	6	4.50	2	2	0	31	7.76	36	3	.444	.459	.778	123	4	.285	.328	.431
1995	Det-A	424	10	.285	.350	.443	1	0	0	44	6.60	0	1	1	62	4.79	0	1	0	43	5.82	1	0	1	62	5.34	128	3	.250	.310	.359	296	7	.301	.367	.480
1996	Tor-A	89	4	.303	.429	.506	0	1	0	13	9.24	0	0	1	9	5.79	0	1	1	22	7.77	0	0	0	0	—	27	0	.296	.406	.333	62	4	.306	.438	.581
1997	NY-N	368	9	.258	.328	.399	2	2	0	40	3.38	4	2	0	54	4.14	1	1	0	13	6.75	5	3	0	81	3.33	76	1	.263	.325	.355	292	8	.257	.328	.411
1998	NY-N	201	4	.234	.325	.378	1	1	0	23	2.35	1	3	0	31	3.73	2	3	0	50	2.86	0	1	0	4	6.75	70	2	.271	.329	.471	131	2	.214	.322	.328
1998	LA-N	348	9	.213	.294	.348	4	3	0	57	2.83	1	4	0	40	1.80	0	0	0	0	—	5	7	0	97	2.40	65	1	.262	.319	.415	283	8	.201	.288	.332
1999	Col-N	775	30	.305	.387	.498	6	5	0	97	7.42	6	7	0	100	5.02	9	5	0	98	6.08	3	7	0	100	6.32	147	7	.320	.422	.537	628	23	.301	.378	.489

		TOTAL					HOME					AWAY					1ST HALF					2ND HALF					LEFT					RIGHT				
YEAR	TM/L	AB	HR	AVG	OBP	SLG	W	L	SV	IP	ERA	W	L	SV	IP	ERA	W	L	SV	IP	ERA	W	L	SV	IP	ERA	AB	HR	AVG	OBP	SLG	AB	HR	AVG	OBP	SLG
2000	Col-N	680	24	.266	.346	.429	6	5	0	87	6.65	6	5	0	90	2.79	3	5	0	66	6.82	9	5	0	111	3.41	165	5	.200	.273	.339	515	19	.287	.369	.458
TOTALS		3972	122	.277	.355	.437	28	26	0	501	5.69	21	26	2	518	4.33	18	20	1	381	5.74	31	32	1	638	4.56	896	25	.271	.346	.415	3076	97	.279	.357	.444
● Ricky Bones BR/TR																																				
1991	SD-N	212	3	.269	.321	.354	3	3	0	33	5.40	1	3	0	21	3.92	0	0	0	0	—	4	6	0	54	4.83	116	2	.267	.323	.345	96	1	.271	.317	.365
1992	Mil-A	641	27	.264	.321	.448	6	4	0	100	3.25	3	6	0	64	6.64	4	4	0	81	4.69	5	6	0	83	4.46	302	9	.268	.321	.421	339	18	.260	.322	.472
1993	Mil-A	800	28	.278	.334	.461	4	6	0	72	4.75	7	5	0	132	4.92	4	5	0	80	4.82	7	6	0	123	4.89	390	12	.256	.303	.433	410	16	.296	.363	.488
1994	Mil-A	651	17	.255	.304	.406	4	5	0	82	3.51	6	4	0	89	3.35	7	5	0	117	2.99	3	4	0	53	4.39	321	8	.255	.309	.386	330	9	.255	.299	.424
1995	Mil-A	776	26	.281	.349	.450	5	6	0	95	5.80	5	6	0	106	3.58	4	6	0	85	4.15	6	6	0	116	4.98	449	10	.281	.339	.405	327	16	.281	.362	.511
1996	Mil-A	579	28	.294	.369	.504	4	6	0	77	5.03	3	8	0	68	6.75	6	9	0	106	5.62	1	5	0	39	6.41	316	20	.329	.401	.579	263	8	.251	.330	.414
1996	NY-A	32	2	.438	.525	.781	0	0	0	0	54.00	0	0	0	7	12.15	0	0	0	0	—	0	0	0	7	14.14	14	0	.357	.412	.500	18	2	.500	.609	1.000
1997	Cin-N	82	2	.378	.454	.537	0	0	0	4	12.27	0	1	0	14	9.64	0	1	0	18	10.19	0	0	0	0	—	34	1	.412	.474	.559	48	1	.354	.441	.521
1997	KC-A	314	10	.325	.377	.475	2	2	0	43	5.48	2	5	0	36	6.56	0	1	0	4	6.23	4	6	0	74	5.96	154	7	.331	.373	.526	160	3	.319	.381	.425
1998	KC-A	201	4	.244	.327	.363	1	2	0	28	3.25	1	0	1	26	2.81	0	0	1	11	1.64	2	2	0	42	3.40	76	1	.197	.307	.276	125	3	.272	.341	.416
1999	Bal-A	183	7	.322	.390	.508	0	1	0	22	6.55	0	2	0	22	5.40	0	2	0	33	5.23	0	1	0	11	8.18	85	3	.353	.421	.588	98	4	.296	.364	.439
2000	Fla-N	310	6	.303	.358	.413	1	2	0	38	2.63	1	1	0	40	6.35	2	2	0	46	1.76	0	1	0	31	8.62	110	3	.364	.415	.482	200	3	.270	.327	.375
TOTALS		4781	160	.283	.344	.449	30	37	0	593	4.56	29	41	1	622	5.11	27	35	1	580	4.37	32	43	0	634	5.27	2367	76	.287	.345	.446	2414	84	.278	.344	.452
● Chris Bosio BR/TR																																				
1986	Mil-A	140	9	.293	.353	.571	0	2	0	19	6.05	0	2	0	15	8.22	0	0	0	0	—	0	4	0	35	7.01	68	5	.324	.378	.662	72	4	.264	.329	.486
1987	Mil-A	677	18	.276	.326	.415	4	4	0	74	6.23	7	4	2	96	4.48	3	2	2	50	5.94	8	6	0	120	4.95	356	11	.264	.322	.424	321	7	.290	.329	.405
1988	Mil-A	710	13	.268	.303	.370	5	6	3	92	2.73	2	9	3	90	4.01	6	8	0	125	3.09	1	7	6	57	3.97	405	7	.259	.294	.356	305	6	.279	.315	.390
1989	Mil-A	905	16	.249	.289	.336	9	3	0	127	2.06	6	7	0	108	4.01	7	5	0	122	2.87	8	5	0	112	3.04	458	8	.247	.294	.325	447	8	.251	.285	.347
1990	Mil-A	508	15	.258	.311	.411	2	7	0	81	5.11	2	2	0	52	2.26	4	6	0	109	3.95	0	3	0	23	4.24	273	10	.286	.336	.465	235	5	.226	.282	.349
1991	Mil-A	766	15	.244	.302	.350	5	6	0	96	3.83	9	4	0	108	2.74	6	7	0	103	3.24	8	3	0	102	3.26	418	6	.251	.303	.347	348	9	.236	.300	.353
1992	Mil-A	878	21	.254	.291	.376	9	3	0	128	3.03	7	3	0	104	4.34	6	4	0	103	4.47	10	2	0	129	2.94	421	10	.273	.310	.399	457	11	.236	.273	.354
1993	Sea-A	602	14	.229	.303	.352	6	6	1	95	2.95	3	3	0	70	4.13	2	3	0	48	3.19	7	6	1	116	3.56	296	8	.260	.339	.402	306	6	.199	.266	.304
1994	Sea-A	495	15	.277	.330	.438	3	2	0	67	2.83	1	8	0	58	6.02	3	9	0	113	4.22	1	1	0	12	5.25	279	5	.301	.344	.430	216	10	.245	.311	.449
1995	Sea-A	675	18	.313	.375	.476	8	4	0	88	5.52	2	4	0	82	4.28	6	1	0	68	4.24	4	7	0	102	5.38	377	5	.313	.379	.443	298	13	.312	.369	.517
1996	Sea-A	241	8	.299	.364	.465	1	3	0	31	6.46	3	1	0	30	5.40	3	2	0	38	6.16	1	2	0	23	5.56	118	3	.297	.383	.466	123	5	.301	.343	.463
TOTALS		6597	162	.264	.315	.394	52	46	4	897	3.80	42	47	5	813	4.14	46	47	2	879	3.88	48	46	7	831	4.05	3469	78	.273	.326	.401	3128	84	.254	.304	.386
● Ricky Bottalico BL/TR																																				
1994	Phi-N	12	0	.250	.308	.250	0	0	0	1	0.00	0	0	0	2	0.00	0	0	0	0	—	0	0	0	3	0.00	6	0	.333	.333	.333	6	0	.167	.286	.167
1995	Phi-N	300	7	.167	.277	.267	3	2	0	48	1.88	2	1	1	40	3.18	3	1	1	30	1.19	2	2	0	57	3.14	111	3	.180	.324	.288	189	4	.159	.246	.254
1996	Phi-N	238	6	.197	.272	.336	3	3	15	36	4.04	1	2	19	32	2.25	2	4	16	38	4.06	2	1	18	30	2.10	92	3	.217	.318	.380	146	3	.185	.241	.308
1997	Phi-N	277	7	.245	.347	.375	2	3	17	42	3.21	0	2	17	32	4.22	1	3	14	34	3.67	1	2	20	40	3.63	138	2	.254	.354	.355	139	5	.237	.340	.396
1998	Phi-N	177	7	.305	.390	.503	1	2	3	22	6.55	0	3	3	21	6.33	1	1	3	10	4.66	0	4	3	34	6.95	72	3	.375	.460	.556	105	4	.257	.339	.467
1999	StL-N	292	8	.284	.392	.449	2	1	10	35	2.29	1	6	10	38	7.34	1	5	10	43	4.01	2	2	10	31	6.16	113	3	.310	.422	.513	179	5	.268	.373	.408
2000	KC-A	272	12	.239	.342	.441	8	3	8	40	3.18	1	3	8	33	6.82	7	1	5	36	4.95	2	5	11	36	4.71	133	6	.241	.348	.474	139	6	.237	.335	.410
TOTALS		1568	47	.236	.335	.387	19	14	53	224	3.22	5	17	58	198	4.91	15	15	49	191	3.72	9	16	62	231	4.25	665	20	.257	.366	.420	903	27	.220	.311	.363
● Kent Bottenfield BB/TR																																				
1992	Mon-N	120	1	.217	.284	.300	0	1	0	15	3.68	1	1	1	18	1.02	0	0	0	0	—	1	2	1	32	2.23	62	1	.194	.271	.306	58	0	.241	.297	.293
1993	Mon-N	323	11	.288	.362	.464	1	1	0	46	3.74	1	4	0	37	4.58	2	4	0	72	3.61	0	1	0	11	7.59	163	5	.325	.399	.509	160	6	.250	.324	.419
1993	Col-N	285	13	.302	.382	.498	1	2	0	31	7.55	2	3	0	46	5.12	0	0	0	0	—	3	5	0	77	6.10	123	6	.325	.414	.520	162	7	.284	.357	.481
1994	Col-N	99	1	.283	.360	.434	2	1	0	16	8.04	1	0	1	9	2.00	3	1	1	25	5.84	0	0	0	0	—	49	0	.286	.364	.388	50	1	.280	.357	.480
1994	SF-N	9	1	.556	.556	1.111	0	0	0	0	—	0	0	0	2	10.80	0	0	0	0	—	0	0	0	2	10.80	4	1	.750	.750	1.750	5	0	.400	.400	.600
1996	Chi-N	231	3	.255	.320	.364	1	1	0	35	2.06	2	4	1	27	3.38	0	0	0	9	2.08	3	5	1	53	2.72	89	0	.292	.337	.371	142	3	.232	.310	.359
1997	Chi-N	316	13	.259	.333	.434	1	1	1	38	4.93	1	2	1	46	2.96	1	1	1	50	2.68	1	2	1	34	5.61	123	1	.252	.343	.341	193	12	.264	.327	.492
1998	StL-N	503	13	.254	.333	.378	1	3	2	74	3.67	3	3	2	60	5.40	2	5	4	61	5.31	2	1	0	73	3.72	247	3	.235	.323	.300	256	10	.273	.344	.453
1999	StL-N	729	21	.270	.350	.432	9	3	0	92	4.21	9	4	0	98	3.75	11	3	0	95	3.51	7	4	0	95	4.44	322	7	.245	.319	.366	407	14	.290	.374	.484
2000	Ana-A	505	25	.285	.357	.493	4	6	0	87	5.87	3	2	0	40	5.36	4	7	0	88	5.60	3	1	0	39	5.95	256	11	.320	.397	.520	249	14	.249	.314	.466
2000	Phi-N	171	5	.240	.320	.392	0	1	0	23	5.09	1	1	0	21	3.86	0	0	0	0	—	1	2	0	44	4.50	96	2	.260	.357	.417	75	3	.213	.268	.360
TOTALS		3291	107	.270	.346	.432	20	20	3	456	4.67	24	24	6	403	4.15	23	21	6	400	4.27	21	23	3	459	4.57	1534	37	.276	.355	.412	1757	70	.265	.338	.450
● Jeff Brantley BR/TR																																				
1988	SF-N	80	2	.275	.333	.425	0	1	0	7	5.14	0	0	1	14	5.93	0	0	0	0	—	0	1	1	21	5.66	26	0	.192	.323	.192	54	2	.315	.339	.537
1989	SF-N	373	10	.271	.337	.394	4	1	0	45	3.60	3	0	0	52	4.47	1	0	0	44	4.06	6	1	0	53	4.08	192	4	.302	.364	.422	181	6	.238	.308	.365
1990	SF-N	321	3	.240	.315	.293	4	1	9	41	1.77	1	2	10	46	1.37	2	1	10	60	1.50	3	2	9	27	1.69	186	1	.274	.341	.328	135	2	.193	.278	.244
1991	SF-N	346	8	.225	.332	.338	2	0	7	42	2.14	3	2	8	53	2.70	3	1	5	42	2.14	2	1	10	53	2.70	185	3	.205	.338	.286	161	5	.248	.324	.398
1992	SF-N	323	8	.207	.307	.319	4	3	3	47	2.30	3	4	4	45	3.63	3	4	6	34	2.88	4	3	1	57	2.98	193	4	.181	.300	.280	130	4	.246	.320	.377
1993	SF-N	433	19	.259	.336	.439	3	2	0	60	3.58	2	4	0	53	5.06	4	5	0	68	4.48	1	1	0	45	3.97	221	11	.285	.374	.511	212	8	.231	.295	.363
1994	Cin-N	228	6	.202	.288	.316	4	4	6	38	3.29	2	2	9	27	1.33	5	4	8	43	2.74	1	2	7	23	1.99	96	1	.208	.303	.292	132	5	.197	.277	.333
1995	Cin-N	257	11	.206	.263	.366	1	2	12	37	3.86	2	0	16	33	1.64	3	0	12	34	2.62	0	2	16	36	3.00	118	7	.229	.316	.449	139	4	.187	.214	.295
1996	Cin-N	251	7	.215	.289	.327	0	0	21	33	2.45	1	2	23	38	2.37	1	1	19	38	3.32	0	1	25	33	1.36	121	2	.248	.345	.322	130	5	.185	.232	.331
1997	Cin-N	44	2	.205	.340	.364	0	0	0	5	1.80	1	1	1	7	5.40	1	1	1	12	3.86	0	0	0	0	—	18	0	.056	.320	.056	26	2	.308	.357	.577
1998	StL-N	182	12	.220	.289	.445	0	1	7	24	6.38	0	4	7	27	2.70	0	4	11	22	5.24	0	1	3	28	3.81	72	6	.236	.325	.514	110	6	.209	.264	.400
1999	Phi-N	31	0	.161	.325	.194	1	1	1	3	6.00	0	1	4	6	4.76	1	2	5	9	5.19	0	0	0	0	—	12	0	.083	.267	.083	19	0	.211	.360	.263
2000	Phi-N	222	12	.288	.373	.491	2	3	14	35	3.82	0	4	9	20	9.45	1	1	10	22	4.91	1	6	13	33	6.48	103	2	.291	.403	.379	119	10	.286	.344	.588
TOTALS		3091	100	.236	.317	.370	25	19	80	418	3.23	18	26	92	420	3.47	25	24	87	429	3.30	18	21	85	410	3.41	1543	41	.244	.341	.366	1548	59	.227	.292	.375
● Kevin Brown BR/TR																																				
1986	Tex-A	19	0	.316	.316	.421	1	0	0	5	3.60	0	0	0	0	—	0	0	0	0	—	1	0	0	5	3.60	13	0	.308	.308	.385	6	0	.333	.333	.500
1988	Tex-A	100	2	.330	.385	.450	0	1	0	12	5.11	1	0	0	11	3.27	0	0	0	0	—	1	1	0	23	4.24	42	1	.405	.444	.595	58	1	.276	.344	.345
1989	Tex-A	715	10	.234	.303	.312	6	3	0	80	3.25	6	6	0	111	3.42	7	4	0	108	2.82	5	5	0	83	4.03	351	5	.225	.294	.291	364	5	.242	.312	.332
1990	Tex-A	685	13	.255	.315	.365	6	4	0	87	2.58	6	6	0	93	4.56	9	5	0	112	3.06	3	5	0	68	4.48	337	6	.249	.309	.362	348	7	.261	.321	.368
1991	Tex-A	821	17	.284	.362	.404	4	5	0	111	4.14	5	7	0	100	4.70	6	5	0	89	4.63	3	7	0	121	4.23	410	8	.273	.349	.395	411	9	.294	.375	.414
1992	Tex-A	1007	11	.260	.316	.335	11	4	0	123	2.71	10	7	0	143	3.85	12	4	0	129	3.27	9	7	0	136	3.37	488	7	.268	.339	.365	519	4	.252	.294	.306
1993	Tex-A	903	14	.252	.319	.353	9	5	0	124	2.46	6	7	0	109	4.89	6	6	0	111	2.91	9	6	0	122	4.22	509	9	.253	.324	.358	394	5	.251	.312	.348
1994	Tex-A	695	18	.314	.361	.455	5	5	0	97	4.07	2	4	0	73	5.82	5	8	0	118	5.43	2	1	0	52	3.44	379	9	.335	.379	.485	316	9	.291	.341	.418
1995	Bal-A	642	10	.241	.302	.341	6	5	0	94	3.56	4	4	0	79	3.66	5	6	0	76	3.91	5	3	0	96	3.36	364	5	.247	.311	.343	278	5	.234	.291	.338
1996	Fla-N	849	8	.220	.262	.289	12	4	0	138	1.69	5	7	0	95	2.19	7	5	0	105	1.89	10	6	0	128	1.90	414	3	.220	.259	.280	435	5	.221	.264	.297
1997	Fla-N	890	10	.240	.303	.319	8	4	0	125	2.51	8	4	0	112	2.89	7	5	0	121	2.67	9	3	0	116	2.72	430	4	.247	.330	.326	460	6	.235	.276	.313
1998	SD-N	957	8	.235	.279	.294	8	5	0	136	2.05	10	2	0	121	2.75	9	3	0	127	2.77	9	4	0	130	2.00	490	3	.245	.292	.296	467	5	.225	.265	.291
1999	LA-N	944	19	.222	.273	.336	9	3	0	120	1.95	9	6	0	132	3.94	9	5	0	118	3.43	9	4	0	134	2.61	478	7	.255	.305	.368	466	12	.189	.239	.303
2000	LA-N	848	21	.213	.261	.337	7	1	0	116	1.79	6	5	0	114	3.38	7	2	0	117	2.31	6	4	0	113	2.87	414	5	.225	.284	.329	434	16	.203	.238	.346
TOTALS		10075	161	.248	.305	.344	92	49	0	1370	2.67	78	65	0	1291	3.77	89	58	0	1332	3.22	81	56	0	1329	3.19	5119	72	.255	.316	.351	4956	89	.240	.292	.336
● Tom Browning BL/TL																																				
1984	Cin-N	89	0	.303	.340	.348	0	0	0	8	2.25	1	0	0	15	1.17	0	0	0	0	—	1	0	0	23	1.54	10	0	.600	.636	.600	79	0	.266	.301	.316
1985	Cin-N	987	29	.245	.297	.384	10	6	0	131	4.11	10	3	0	130	2.98	7	5	0	100	3.59	13	4	0	161	3.52	148	1	.223	.282	.277	839	28	.249	.300	.403
1986	Cin-N	918	26	.245	.296	.375	7	6	0	107	3.80	7	7	0	137	3.82	5	7	0	104	4.43	9	6	0	140	3.35	133	4	.241	.325	.353	785	22	.246	.291	.378
1987	Cin-N	708	27	.284	.342	.472	6	6	0	101	4.92	4	7	0	82	5.14	4	6	0	63	7.76	6	7	0	120	3.59	116	4	.267	.351	.431	592	23	.287	.340	.480
1988	Cin-N	916	36	.224	.277	.397	5	3	0	117	4.40	13	2	0	134	2.55	6	3	0	101	3.48	12	2	0	150	3.37	151	8	.285	.347	.536	765	28	.212	.263	.370
1989	Cin-N	946	31	.255	.302	.408	7	8	0	126	4.14	8	4	0	124	2.62	6	6	0	122	3.25	9	6	0	128	3.52	132	6	.265	.327	.424	814	25	.253	.298	.405
1990	Cin-N	882	24	.266	.309	.412	8	8	0	128	4.64	7	1	0	100	2.71	7	5	0	116	2.94	8	4	0	111	4.69	162	5	.253	.309	.395	720	19	.269	.309	.415
1991	Cin-N	906	32	.266	.309	.427	10	4	0	121	3.50	4	10	0	109	4.94	10	4	0	113	3.49	4	10	0	117	4.85	212	4	.203	.269	.344	694	28	.285	.321	.452
1992	Cin-N	347	6	.311	.362	.484	5	1	0	34	5.03	1	4	0	53	5.09	6	5	0	82	5.16	0	0	0	5	3.60	83	1	.325	.385	.470	264	5	.307	.355	.489
1993	Cin-N	478	15	.333	.359	.506	4	2	0	51	2.84	3	5	0	63	6.25	5	3	0	73	5.28	2	4	0	41	3.76	78	2	.244	.302	.372	400	13	.350	.371	.533
1994	Cin-N	153	8	.222	.284	.392	1	0	0	12	5.84	2	1	0	28	3.49	3	1	0	41	4.20	0	0	0	0	—	24	1	.083	.233	.208	129	7	.248	.295	.426

YEAR	TM/L	TOTAL					HOME					AWAY					1ST HALF					2ND HALF					LEFT					RIGHT				
		AB	HR	AVG	OBP	SLG	W	L	SV	IP	ERA	W	L	SV	IP	ERA	W	L	SV	IP	ERA	W	L	SV	IP	ERA	AB	HR	AVG	OBP	SLG	AB	HR	AVG	OBP	SLG
1995	KC-A	43	2	.302	.375	.535	0	2	0	10	8.10	0	0	0	0	—	0	2	0	10	8.10	0	0	0	0	—	3	0	.000	.000	.000	40	2	.325	.400	.575
TOTALS		7373	236	.262	.310	.418	63	46	0	945	4.21	60	44	0	976	3.68	59	47	0	925	4.16	64	43	0	996	3.73	1252	36	.249	.316	.392	6121	200	.264	.309	.423
● Dave Burba BR/TR																																				
1990	Sea-A	30	0	.267	.333	.267	0	0	0	5	0.00	0	0	0	3	13.50	0	0	0	0	—	0	0	0	8	4.50	9	0	.111	.273	.111	21	0	.333	.364	.333
1991	Sea-A	139	6	.245	.314	.453	1	1	1	15	5.28	1	1	0	21	2.53	0	1	1	21	3.80	2	1	0	15	3.52	59	2	.288	.373	.441	80	4	.213	.267	.463
1992	SF-N	279	4	.287	.358	.398	1	2	0	34	2.94	1	5	0	37	6.81	2	6	0	52	5.40	0	1	0	19	3.79	151	1	.318	.370	.424	128	3	.250	.344	.367
1993	SF-N	359	14	.265	.336	.421	5	1	0	58	3.39	5	2	0	37	5.59	5	2	0	45	4.37	5	1	0	50	4.14	151	6	.318	.379	.464	208	8	.226	.305	.389
1994	SF-N	267	5	.221	.345	.352	2	4	0	35	4.11	1	2	0	39	4.62	0	4	0	53	4.27	3	2	0	21	4.64	100	1	.180	.328	.270	167	4	.246	.355	.401
1995	SF-N	162	5	.235	.335	.377	1	0	0	23	3.86	3	2	0	20	6.30	3	2	0	36	4.50	1	0	0	7	7.36	61	2	.295	.413	.426	101	3	.198	.283	.347
1995	Cin-N	233	4	.223	.301	.330	3	1	0	36	1.49	3	1	0	27	5.67	0	0	0	0	—	6	2	0	63	3.27	96	3	.260	.330	.438	137	1	.197	.281	.255
1996	Cin-N	733	18	.244	.329	.381	6	9	0	118	3.75	5	4	0	77	3.96	2	9	0	95	4.44	9	4	0	100	3.25	314	8	.255	.350	.411	419	10	.236	.314	.358
1997	Cin-N	615	22	.255	.341	.429	7	8	0	96	4.67	4	2	0	64	4.81	4	8	0	89	5.84	7	2	0	71	3.31	292	10	.298	.391	.479	323	12	.217	.294	.384
1998	Cle-A	781	30	.269	.330	.440	8	4	0	111	4.07	7	6	0	93	4.16	9	5	0	105	3.67	6	5	0	98	4.58	411	13	.253	.320	.414	370	17	.286	.341	.470
1999	Cle-A	831	30	.254	.336	.421	6	5	0	127	4.10	9	4	0	93	4.47	7	3	0	103	4.44	8	6	0	117	4.09	379	13	.224	.316	.369	452	17	.279	.353	.465
2000	Cle-A	745	19	.267	.346	.415	9	3	0	111	5.04	7	3	0	81	3.68	8	3	0	90	5.72	8	3	0	102	3.36	351	8	.259	.348	.396	394	11	.274	.345	.431
TOTALS		5174	157	.256	.336	.408	49	38	1	770	4.01	46	32	0	591	4.60	40	43	1	690	4.71	55	27	0	671	3.81	2374	67	.262	.348	.410	2800	90	.250	.326	.406
● Tim Burke BR/TR																																				
1985	Mon-N	421	9	.204	.288	.309	4	3	2	50	2.88	5	1	6	70	2.05	4	0	2	45	1.79	5	4	6	75	2.76	186	3	.253	.355	.360	235	6	.166	.233	.268
1986	Mon-N	393	7	.262	.344	.369	4	2	2	47	1.74	5	5	2	55	3.95	5	2	4	60	1.94	4	5	0	41	4.39	205	5	.302	.391	.415	188	2	.218	.290	.319
1987	Mon-N	327	3	.196	.234	.254	5	0	7	46	0.97	2	0	11	45	1.41	0	0	7	41	1.96	7	0	11	50	0.54	174	2	.213	.258	.282	153	1	.176	.206	.222
1988	Mon-N	309	7	.272	.327	.395	3	2	5	48	4.50	0	3	13	34	1.85	2	2	6	41	3.70	1	3	12	41	3.10	147	5	.306	.385	.449	162	2	.241	.272	.346
1989	Mon-N	302	6	.225	.274	.325	7	0	13	46	2.35	2	3	15	39	2.79	5	1	16	46	2.53	4	2	12	38	2.58	159	5	.239	.287	.371	143	1	.210	.258	.273
1990	Mon-N	287	6	.247	.300	.345	2	2	8	31	2.87	1	1	12	44	2.27	0	1	11	23	4.30	3	2	9	52	1.73	144	3	.285	.331	.403	143	3	.210	.270	.287
1991	Mon-N	169	3	.243	.314	.361	0	2	3	21	3.43	3	2	2	25	4.68	3	3	4	42	4.29	0	1	1	4	2.25	74	1	.351	.395	.514	95	2	.158	.252	.242
1991	NY-N	216	5	.255	.291	.375	2	0	1	29	1.24	1	3	0	27	4.39	0	0	0	0	—	3	3	1	56	2.75	118	1	.263	.315	.356	98	4	.245	.262	.398
1992	NY-N	70	1	.371	.392	.486	0	0	0	9	1.04	1	2	0	7	11.57	1	2	0	16	5.74	0	0	0	0	—	38	0	.289	.308	.368	32	1	.469	.486	.625
1992	NY-A	104	2	.250	.350	.413	1	1	0	15	4.80	1	1	0	13	1.42	1	1	0	9	1.04	1	1	0	19	4.26	40	0	.150	.244	.200	64	2	.313	.413	.547
TOTALS		2598	49	.240	.302	.345	28	12	41	342	2.55	21	21	61	357	2.87	21	12	50	324	2.86	28	21	52	375	2.59	1285	25	.268	.335	.378	1313	24	.213	.269	.312
● John Burkett BR/TR																																				
1987	SF-N	23	2	.304	.407	.652	0	0	0	4	6.75	0	0	0	2	0.00	0	0	0	0	—	0	0	0	6	4.50	11	0	.182	.182	.182	12	2	.417	.563	1.083
1990	SF-N	781	18	.257	.313	.374	6	2	0	104	3.98	8	5	1	100	3.60	7	2	0	84	3.54	7	5	1	120	3.97	454	11	.258	.312	.377	327	7	.257	.314	.370
1991	SF-N	804	19	.277	.332	.392	6	6	0	109	3.54	6	5	0	97	4.90	4	4	0	105	3.16	8	7	0	101	5.24	467	14	.293	.347	.441	337	5	.255	.312	.323
1992	SF-N	735	13	.264	.308	.382	10	2	0	102	3.09	3	7	0	88	4.72	5	5	0	86	4.41	8	4	0	104	3.38	466	11	.296	.334	.448	269	2	.208	.265	.268
1993	SF-N	879	18	.255	.294	.366	9	3	0	122	2.66	13	4	0	110	4.75	12	2	0	119	3.10	10	5	0	113	4.23	464	8	.282	.318	.386	415	10	.224	.269	.345
1994	SF-N	616	14	.286	.330	.417	2	6	0	92	4.87	4	2	0	67	1.88	5	6	0	112	3.36	1	2	0	47	4.21	321	4	.274	.325	.355	295	10	.298	.335	.485
1995	Fla-N	737	22	.282	.339	.455	7	7	0	96	4.42	7	7	0	93	4.18	5	7	0	70	5.50	9	7	0	118	3.58	361	6	.274	.338	.418	376	16	.290	.339	.489
1996	Fla-N	585	15	.263	.314	.400	3	5	0	77	4.42	3	5	0	77	4.23	5	8	0	115	3.92	1	2	0	39	5.49	249	6	.257	.316	.394	336	9	.268	.312	.405
1996	Tex-A	268	4	.280	.323	.403	2	1	0	20	6.30	3	1	0	49	3.14	0	0	0	0	—	5	2	0	69	4.06	157	1	.248	.302	.350	111	3	.324	.353	.477
1997	Tex-A	783	20	.307	.333	.439	3	5	0	84	5.59	6	7	0	106	3.75	5	7	0	108	4.92	4	5	0	81	4.09	396	10	.298	.328	.429	387	10	.315	.337	.450
1998	Tex-A	788	19	.292	.335	.439	5	8	0	112	5.61	4	5	0	83	5.77	4	8	0	109	5.71	5	5	0	86	5.63	391	11	.279	.331	.435	397	8	.305	.340	.443
1999	Tex-A	599	18	.307	.358	.474	6	4	0	68	7.64	3	4	0	79	3.87	2	3	0	52	6.23	7	5	0	95	5.29	307	7	.280	.331	.401	292	11	.336	.386	.551
2000	Atl-N	535	13	.303	.365	.445	3	3	0	62	5.52	7	3	0	72	4.35	6	3	0	66	4.88	4	3	0	68	4.90	218	4	.294	.363	.436	317	9	.309	.366	.451
TOTALS		8133	195	.280	.328	.414	62	52	0	1053	4.53	67	55	1	1022	4.17	60	55	0	1026	4.28	69	52	1	1048	4.42	4262	93	.280	.329	.409	3871	102	.281	.326	.421
● John Candelaria BL/TL																																				
1978	Pit-N	732	15	.261	.311	.391	6	6	1	107	3.21	6	5	0	82	3.28	7	7	1	120	3.08	5	4	0	69	3.50	109	1	.174	.224	.266	623	14	.276	.326	.413
1979	Pit-N	795	25	.253	.290	.416	5	3	0	90	2.99	9	6	0	117	3.39	6	6	0	91	3.66	8	3	0	116	2.87	108	3	.259	.310	.426	687	22	.252	.286	.415
1980	Pit-N	890	14	.276	.313	.397	6	6	1	113	4.47	5	8	0	121	3.58	4	7	0	117	3.76	7	7	1	116	4.27	146	2	.226	.276	.329	744	12	.286	.320	.410
1981	Pit-N	155	3	.271	.317	.413	0	1	0	7	3.86	2	1	0	34	3.48	2	2	0	41	3.54	0	0	0	0	—	24	0	.250	.280	.333	131	3	.275	.324	.427
1982	Pit-N	652	13	.255	.296	.379	6	5	0	97	3.61	6	2	1	77	2.09	3	4	1	79	3.20	9	3	0	96	2.72	119	3	.235	.290	.387	533	10	.259	.298	.377
1983	Pit-N	742	15	.257	.300	.379	8	5	0	112	2.66	7	3	0	86	3.98	6	6	0	86	4.29	9	2	0	112	2.42	109	2	.174	.189	.257	633	13	.272	.318	.400
1984	Pit-N	700	19	.256	.289	.403	5	6	1	95	3.30	7	5	1	90	2.10	5	6	0	81	2.88	7	5	2	104	2.60	87	0	.195	.231	.230	613	19	.264	.297	.427
1985	Pit-N	207	7	.275	.319	.464	2	2	6	28	2.57	0	2	3	26	4.78	1	3	7	37	3.68	1	1	2	18	3.57	49	0	.204	.200	.265	158	7	.297	.352	.525
1985	Cal-A	267	7	.262	.327	.423	2	2	0	33	7.02	5	1	0	38	0.96	0	0	0	0	—	7	3	0	71	3.80	45	1	.156	.152	.244	222	6	.284	.359	.459
1986	Cal-A	330	4	.206	.268	.306	5	1	0	47	2.66	5	1	0	44	2.44	0	0	0	2	18.00	10	2	0	90	2.21	59	0	.186	.254	.271	271	4	.210	.271	.314
1987	Cal-A	455	17	.279	.308	.444	6	3	0	74	4.72	2	3	0	42	4.68	5	3	0	70	4.78	3	3	0	47	4.60	71	2	.338	.377	.465	384	15	.268	.295	.440
1987	NY-N	51	1	.333	.364	.569	1	0	0	6	4.50	1	0	0	6	7.11	0	0	0	0	—	2	0	0	12	5.84	3	0	.000	.000	.000	48	1	.354	.385	.604
1988	NY-A	605	18	.248	.275	.398	7	5	0	99	3.28	6	2	1	58	3.55	8	4	1	99	2.99	5	3	0	58	4.06	97	4	.144	.189	.268	508	14	.268	.292	.423
1989	NY-A	190	8	.258	.299	.432	2	2	0	26	5.54	1	1	0	23	4.70	3	2	0	40	4.46	0	1	0	9	8.31	34	0	.147	.194	.147	156	8	.282	.321	.494
1989	Mon-N	60	3	.283	.313	.583	0	1	0	7	3.86	0	1	0	9	2.89	0	0	0	0	—	0	2	0	16	3.31	16	0	.188	.211	.375	44	3	.318	.354	.659
1990	Min-A	225	9	.244	.270	.418	2	2	4	33	3.86	5	1	0	26	2.81	7	3	3	50	3.60	0	0	1	8	2.16	51	0	.196	.222	.255	174	9	.259	.284	.466
1990	Tor-A	90	2	.356	.425	.544	0	0	1	7	2.70	0	3	0	15	6.75	0	0	0	0	—	0	3	1	21	5.48	28	0	.357	.367	.464	62	2	.355	.447	.581
1991	LA-N	123	3	.252	.307	.415	1	0	1	15	3.60	0	1	1	19	3.86	0	0	2	18	2.04	1	1	0	16	5.63	58	1	.138	.206	.207	65	2	.354	.392	.600
1992	LA-N	91	1	.220	.311	.297	1	3	2	12	2.92	1	2	3	13	2.77	1	1	3	14	1.26	1	4	2	11	4.91	52	1	.269	.328	.385	39	0	.154	.292	.179
1993	Pit-N	80	2	.313	.385	.500	0	3	1	11	8.74	0	0	0	8	7.56	0	3	1	19	8.53	0	0	0	1	0.00	31	0	.290	.333	.355	49	2	.327	.414	.592
TOTALS		7440	186	.260	.302	.404	65	56	18	1020	3.67	68	48	10	935	3.32	58	57	19	964	3.65	75	47	9	991	3.36	1296	20	.212	.254	.312	6144	166	.270	.312	.423
● Tom Candiotti BR/TR																																				
1983	Mil-A	213	4	.291	.343	.366	3	2	0	37	2.19	1	2	0	19	5.30	0	0	0	0	—	4	4	0	56	3.23	115	1	.304	.362	.339	98	3	.276	.321	.398
1984	Mil-A	137	5	.277	.327	.438	2	0	0	17	2.16	0	2	0	16	8.62	0	0	0	0	—	2	2	0	32	5.29	90	4	.344	.379	.533	47	1	.149	.231	.255
1986	Cle-A	952	18	.246	.324	.357	10	6	0	137	3.35	6	6	0	115	3.82	6	6	0	105	4.02	10	6	0	147	3.24	497	7	.237	.311	.334	455	11	.255	.337	.382
1987	Cle-A	773	28	.250	.330	.406	5	11	0	135	4.39	2	7	0	66	5.56	2	9	0	83	5.40	5	9	0	118	4.34	389	12	.237	.318	.365	384	16	.263	.341	.448
1988	Cle-A	827	15	.272	.319	.372	10	2	0	123	2.63	4	6	0	93	4.15	7	7	0	123	3.51	7	1	0	94	2.98	457	7	.280	.333	.383	370	8	.262	.301	.359
1989	Cle-A	778	10	.242	.294	.319	7	3	0	101	2.95	6	7	0	105	3.25	7	6	0	103	3.66	6	4	0	103	2.54	395	5	.246	.306	.327	383	5	.238	.280	.311
1990	Cle-A	788	23	.263	.315	.388	7	6	0	112	4.10	8	5	0	90	3.10	9	3	0	87	3.52	6	8	0	115	3.76	403	9	.256	.311	.355	385	14	.270	.318	.423
1991	Cle-A	404	6	.218	.268	.317	3	3	0	45	3.20	4	3	0	63	1.56	7	6	0	108	2.24	0	0	0	0	—	198	4	.237	.289	.354	206	2	.199	.247	.282
1991	Tor-A	483	6	.236	.304	.354	3	3	0	65	3.05	3	4	0	65	2.92	0	1	0	6	4.50	6	6	0	124	2.91	251	2	.247	.300	.355	232	4	.224	.308	.353
1992	LA-N	746	13	.237	.297	.347	6	6	0	89	2.33	5	9	0	115	3.53	6	6	0	105	3.00	5	9	0	99	3.01	408	6	.245	.321	.343	338	7	.228	.267	.352
1993	LA-N	797	12	.241	.305	.338	5	3	0	116	1.95	3	7	0	98	4.50	3	5	0	98	3.20	5	5	0	115	3.04	410	5	.232	.304	.312	387	7	.251	.305	.364
1994	LA-N	576	9	.259	.323	.377	3	4	0	64	5.46	4	3	0	89	3.15	5	3	0	102	4.13	2	4	0	51	4.09	282	4	.248	.316	.362	294	5	.269	.330	.391
1995	LA-N	732	18	.255	.316	.384	3	9	0	102	3.35	4	5	0	88	3.67	4	6	0	88	3.08	3	8	0	103	3.86	320	7	.266	.340	.387	412	11	.248	.297	.381
1996	LA-N	598	18	.288	.336	.430	5	5	0	71	5.58	4	6	0	81	3.54	5	7	0	87	4.24	4	4	0	65	4.82	275	10	.265	.317	.407	323	8	.307	.352	.449
1997	LA-N	517	21	.248	.314	.424	7	3	0	74	3.16	3	4	0	61	4.13	4	2	0	42	2.76	6	5	0	93	3.98	241	10	.266	.328	.444	276	11	.232	.302	.406
1998	Oak-A	791	30	.281	.338	.460	7	10	0	121	3.64	4	6	0	80	6.64	4	10	0	105	5.07	7	6	0	96	4.58	432	15	.292	.340	.454	359	15	.267	.335	.468
1999	Oak-A	225	11	.298	.362	.511	2	2	0	36	5.94	1	3	0	20	7.08	3	5	0	57	6.35	0	0	0	0	—	101	2	.228	.319	.386	124	9	.355	.399	.613
1999	Cle-A	62	3	.306	.386	.548	1	0	0	8	7.56	0	1	0	6	15.63	0	0	0	0	—	1	1	0	15	11.05	24	2	.333	.385	.625	38	1	.289	.386	.500
TOTALS		10399	250	.256	.317	.382	89	78	0	1454	3.49	62	86	0	1271	4.01	72	82	0	1300	3.81	79	82	0	1425	3.66	5288	112	.257	.320	.371	5111	138	.255	.313	.392
● Steve Carlton BL/TL																																				
1978	Phi-N	924	30	.247	.295	.409	10	5	0	126	2.57	6	8	0	121	3.12	8	7	0	122	2.51	8	6	0	125	3.16	194	7	.216	.257	.392	730	23	.255	.305	.414
1979	Phi-N	921	25	.219	.290	.368	8	4	0	115	3.44	10	7	0	136	3.77	8	8	0	126	3.80	10	3	0	125	3.45	194	6	.186	.255	.335	727	19	.228	.300	.377
1980	Phi-N	1114	15	.218	.276	.327	11	5	0	162	2.23	13	4	0	142	2.47	13	3	0	140	1.93	11	6	0	164	2.69	164	1	.183	.220	.262	950	14	.224	.285	.338
1981	Phi-N	684	9	.222	.286	.310	8	1	0	91	2.97	5	3	0	99	1.91	9	1	0	106	2.80	4	3	0	84	1.93	109	3	.202	.269	.339	575	6	.226	.290	.304
1982	Phi-N	1090	17	.232	.288	.337	13	4	0	148	2.49	10	7	0	148	3.72	10	7	0	133	3.58	13	4	0	162	2.72	174	2	.247	.305	.345	916	15	.229	.284	.335
1983	Phi-N	1072	20	.258	.313	.359	9	9	0	139	3.68	6	7	0	144	2.56	8	9	0	140	3.29	7	7	0	144	2.94	129	1	.240	.310	.271	943	19	.261	.313	.371
1984	Phi-N	870	14	.246	.306	.361	5	5	0	113	3.98	8	2	0	116	3.18	6	4	0	119	3.09	7	3	0	110	4.10	125	1	.224	.271	.320	745	13	.250	.312	.368
1985	Phi-N	338	6	.249	.349	.358	1	3	0	44	1.22	0	5	0	48	5.29	1	7	0	78	2.43	0	1	0	14	8.16	43	0	.233	.298	.256	295	6	.251	.357	.373
1986	Phi-N	343	15	.297	.376	.478	2	2	0	34	5.77	2	6	0	49	6.47	4	8	0	83	6.18	0	0	0	0	—	50	2	.280	.368	.460	293	13	.300	.377	.481

		TOTAL					HOME					AWAY					1ST HALF					2ND HALF					LEFT					RIGHT				
YEAR	TM/L	AB	HR	AVG	OBP	SLG	W	L	SV	IP	ERA	W	L	SV	IP	ERA	W	L	SV	IP	ERA	W	L	SV	IP	ERA	AB	HR	AVG	OBP	SLG	AB	HR	AVG	OBP	SLG
1986	SF-N	119	4	.303	.390	.462	0	2	0	17	7.41	1	1	0	13	2.08	0	0	0	0	—	1	3	0	30	5.10	15	0	.333	.375	.467	104	4	.298	.392	.462
1986	Chi-A	230	6	.252	.323	.400	2	0	0	33	3.51	2	3	0	30	3.90	0	0	0	0	—	4	3	0	63	3.69	16	0	.188	.235	.188	214	6	.257	.329	.416
1987	Cle-A	418	17	.266	.361	.447	2	5	0	56	5.59	3	4	1	53	5.13	5	5	1	75	4.34	0	4	0	34	7.60	82	2	.244	.315	.390	336	15	.271	.372	.461
1987	Min-A	174	7	.310	.397	.494	1	2	0	28	3.86	0	3	0	15	12.00	0	0	0	0	—	1	5	0	43	6.70	31	0	.290	.389	.387	143	7	.315	.399	.517
1988	Min-A	49	5	.408	.463	.898	0	1	0	9	18.69	0	0	0	1	0.00	0	1	0	10	16.76	0	0	0	0	—	12	0	.500	.500	.833	37	5	.378	.452	.919
TOTALS		8346	190	.244	.308	.372	72	48	0	1116	3.37	66	60	1	1115	3.48	72	60	1	1131	3.40	66	48	0	1100	3.45	1338	25	.223	.282	.339	7008	165	.248	.313	.379
● Chris Carpenter BR/TR																																				
1997	Tor-A	332	7	.325	.394	.443	2	4	0	43	4.22	1	3	0	39	6.05	0	2	0	11	12.71	3	5	0	70	3.86	172	4	.314	.368	.436	160	3	.338	.421	.450
1998	Tor-A	667	18	.265	.329	.415	7	4	0	96	3.66	5	3	0	79	5.24	4	3	0	72	5.25	8	4	0	103	3.76	345	8	.267	.341	.394	322	10	.264	.316	.438
1999	Tor-A	602	16	.294	.346	.450	4	4	0	77	4.54	5	4	0	73	4.21	5	5	0	79	3.63	4	3	0	71	5.22	278	11	.299	.349	.500	324	5	.290	.344	.407
2000	Tor-A	703	30	.290	.369	.496	3	6	0	78	7.53	7	6	0	98	5.25	6	6	0	98	5.49	4	6	0	77	7.25	327	12	.294	.384	.502	376	18	.287	.355	.492
TOTALS		2304	71	.289	.355	.453	16	18	0	294	5.00	18	16	0	288	5.09	15	16	0	261	5.17	19	18	0	321	4.94	1122	35	.290	.360	.458	1182	36	.288	.351	.448
● Norm Charlton BB/TL																																				
1988	Cin-N	234	6	.256	.318	.385	3	1	0	35	3.34	1	4	0	26	4.78	0	0	0	0	—	4	5	0	61	3.96	38	1	.184	.279	.289	196	5	.270	.326	.403
1989	Cin-N	340	5	.197	.284	.288	2	1	0	46	2.93	6	2	0	49	2.92	3	0	0	41	3.29	5	3	0	54	2.65	81	0	.148	.258	.173	259	5	.212	.292	.324
1990	Cin-N	567	10	.231	.319	.326	6	4	1	76	3.09	6	5	1	79	2.40	6	1	2	44	3.05	6	8	0	110	2.62	116	4	.224	.338	.379	451	6	.233	.314	.313
1991	Cin-N	390	6	.236	.306	.336	0	4	1	43	4.01	3	1	0	66	2.19	3	5	0	66	4.25	0	0	1	43	0.84	87	0	.253	.359	.299	303	6	.231	.290	.347
1992	Cin-N	302	7	.262	.323	.397	2	1	13	40	2.27	2	1	13	42	3.67	3	0	17	44	2.27	1	2	9	38	3.82	71	2	.296	.359	.465	231	5	.251	.313	.377
1993	Sea-A	123	4	.179	.277	.301	1	1	10	20	0.90	0	2	8	15	4.30	1	1	16	29	2.48	0	2	2	6	1.59	21	0	.095	.269	.095	102	4	.196	.278	.343
1995	Phi-N	82	2	.280	.406	.390	2	1	0	11	7.15	0	4	0	11	7.59	2	4	0	19	6.75	0	1	0	3	10.80	32	0	.219	.297	.250	50	2	.320	.469	.480
1995	Sea-A	161	2	.143	.223	.199	2	0	5	25	1.42	0	1	9	22	1.61	0	0	0	0	—	2	1	14	48	1.51	45	1	.178	.315	.244	116	1	.129	.184	.181
1996	Sea-A	279	7	.244	.334	.380	3	2	9	43	3.98	1	5	11	33	4.13	2	2	13	37	3.19	2	5	7	39	4.85	75	0	.187	.284	.240	204	7	.265	.353	.431
1997	Sea-A	285	7	.312	.417	.453	2	6	7	36	8.17	1	2	7	33	6.27	2	5	12	38	7.17	1	3	2	32	7.39	93	1	.312	.407	.398	192	6	.313	.421	.479
1998	Bal-A	151	5	.305	.401	.470	2	0	0	19	7.58	0	1	0	16	6.19	2	1	0	33	7.09	0	0	0	2	4.50	50	2	.340	.443	.540	101	3	.287	.379	.436
1998	Atl-N	42	0	.167	.308	.190	0	0	1	7	1.35	0	0	0	6	1.42	0	0	0	0	—	0	0	1	13	1.38	11	0	.000	.083	.000	31	0	.226	.375	.258
1999	TB-A	191	4	.257	.372	.403	2	1	0	27	4.00	0	2	0	24	4.94	0	1	0	15	2.93	2	2	0	35	5.09	61	1	.295	.421	.426	130	3	.238	.348	.392
2000	Cin-N	14	1	.429	.600	.786	0	0	0	3	27.00	0	0	0	0	—	0	0	0	3	27.00	0	0	0	0	—	6	0	.167	.167	.167	8	1	.625	.786	1.250
TOTALS		3161	66	.241	.329	.357	27	22	47	431	3.93	20	30	49	421	3.57	24	20	60	368	4.33	23	32	36	484	3.31	787	12	.234	.339	.328	2374	54	.243	.326	.366
● Jim Clancy BR/TR																																				
1978	Tor-A	736	10	.270	.347	.370	7	5	0	115	2.73	3	7	0	78	6.09	5	7	0	86	4.80	5	5	0	107	3.52	374	3	.278	.355	.361	362	7	.262	.339	.378
1979	Tor-A	239	8	.272	.349	.435	1	5	0	35	5.40	1	2	0	29	5.65	2	5	0	45	4.40	0	2	0	19	8.20	113	3	.248	.336	.372	126	5	.294	.361	.492
1980	Tor-A	932	19	.233	.326	.332	9	8	0	151	3.58	4	8	0	100	2.89	6	4	0	97	2.59	7	12	0	153	3.76	502	12	.277	.376	.375	430	7	.181	.264	.281
1981	Tor-A	481	12	.262	.352	.397	4	8	0	71	6.08	2	4	0	54	3.33	3	5	0	49	6.10	3	7	0	76	4.13	230	7	.261	.363	.426	251	5	.263	.342	.371
1982	Tor-A	1012	26	.248	.301	.381	7	8	0	118	4.79	9	6	0	148	2.85	7	4	0	133	3.39	9	10	0	134	4.03	483	6	.257	.310	.364	529	20	.240	.294	.397
1983	Tor-A	877	23	.271	.315	.433	9	4	0	115	4.08	6	7	0	108	3.74	7	5	0	102	3.63	8	6	0	121	4.15	414	11	.297	.343	.471	463	12	.248	.291	.400
1984	Tor-A	867	25	.287	.353	.426	6	9	0	86	5.86	7	6	0	134	4.65	6	8	0	99	5.07	7	7	0	120	5.16	432	9	.310	.386	.433	435	16	.264	.320	.418
1985	Tor-A	485	15	.241	.292	.414	4	1	0	46	2.53	5	5	0	82	4.48	4	4	0	69	4.80	5	2	0	59	2.58	255	5	.251	.316	.396	230	10	.230	.265	.435
1986	Tor-A	832	24	.243	.296	.373	5	6	0	87	5.26	9	8	0	132	3.07	7	5	0	96	4.33	7	9	0	124	3.64	441	9	.229	.287	.333	391	15	.258	.307	.417
1987	Tor-A	918	24	.255	.314	.401	7	5	0	120	3.00	8	6	0	121	4.08	8	5	0	119	2.72	7	6	0	122	4.35	508	12	.281	.335	.433	410	12	.222	.288	.361
1988	Tor-A	760	26	.272	.321	.424	6	6	0	91	5.26	5	7	1	106	3.83	4	10	0	102	5.19	7	3	1	94	3.73	404	10	.280	.324	.411	356	16	.264	.317	.438
1989	Hou-N	576	13	.269	.342	.422	4	5	0	62	5.66	3	9	0	85	4.66	5	5	0	83	3.59	2	9	0	64	6.99	313	10	.291	.377	.460	263	3	.243	.298	.376
1990	Hou-N	311	4	.322	.387	.463	1	2	1	30	6.67	1	6	0	46	6.41	2	8	0	56	5.34	0	0	1	20	9.74	164	1	.366	.436	.488	147	3	.272	.331	.435
1991	Hou-N	192	5	.193	.266	.318	0	3	1	25	4.01	0	0	4	30	1.78	0	2	4	42	1.91	0	1	1	13	5.68	95	1	.179	.269	.284	97	4	.206	.264	.351
1991	Atl-N	135	3	.267	.336	.452	2	0	2	15	4.70	1	2	1	19	6.52	0	0	0	0	—	3	2	3	35	5.71	52	1	.308	.373	.519	83	2	.241	.312	.410
TOTALS		9353	237	.260	.325	.398	72	75	4	1167	4.41	64	83	6	1273	4.01	66	77	4	1178	4.04	70	81	6	1262	4.35	4780	100	.276	.345	.404	4573	137	.244	.304	.391
● Roger Clemens BR/TR																																				
1984	Bos-A	538	13	.271	.309	.400	5	2	0	78	4.27	4	2	0	55	4.39	3	2	0	56	5.17	6	2	0	78	3.71	291	3	.261	.305	.357	247	10	.283	.314	.449
1985	Bos-A	364	5	.228	.303	.299	4	2	0	51	3.73	3	3	0	48	2.83	6	4	0	83	3.46	1	1	0	15	2.40	202	1	.248	.308	.297	162	4	.204	.297	.302
1986	Bos-A	916	21	.195	.252	.306	11	3	0	119	2.56	13	1	0	135	2.41	14	0	0	124	2.18	10	4	0	130	2.76	523	8	.210	.274	.317	393	13	.176	.221	.290
1987	Bos-A	1055	19	.235	.295	.348	11	6	0	160	2.75	9	3	0	121	3.26	6	6	0	120	3.66	14	3	0	161	2.45	603	6	.235	.299	.332	452	13	.235	.290	.369
1988	Bos-A	986	17	.220	.270	.320	6	8	0	122	3.91	12	4	0	142	2.09	11	5	0	144	2.44	7	7	0	120	3.52	504	8	.256	.308	.363	482	9	.183	.229	.276
1989	Bos-A	929	20	.231	.305	.338	9	3	0	106	2.90	8	8	0	148	3.29	8	6	0	124	3.06	9	5	0	130	3.19	503	7	.243	.320	.332	426	13	.218	.287	.345
1990	Bos-A	847	7	.228	.278	.306	11	2	0	112	1.53	10	4	0	117	2.31	12	3	0	123	2.64	9	3	0	106	1.11	443	7	.242	.288	.343	404	0	.213	.267	.265
1991	Bos-A	993	15	.221	.270	.328	8	5	0	143	2.59	10	5	0	129	2.66	9	5	0	119	2.20	9	5	0	153	2.95	563	3	.218	.279	.302	430	12	.223	.258	.363
1992	Bos-A	907	11	.224	.279	.308	8	6	0	128	2.88	10	5	0	118	1.90	9	5	0	127	1.84	9	6	0	120	3.01	447	6	.226	.277	.304	460	5	.222	.280	.311
1993	Bos-A	718	17	.244	.315	.372	6	8	0	105	5.14	5	6	0	87	3.63	7	6	0	104	3.63	4	8	0	88	5.44	404	8	.260	.346	.381	314	9	.223	.273	.360
1994	Bos-A	609	15	.204	.289	.325	5	3	0	79	2.75	4	4	0	92	2.93	6	4	0	119	3.03	3	3	0	52	2.44	319	7	.219	.315	.339	290	8	.186	.259	.310
1995	Bos-A	544	15	.259	.346	.393	6	3	0	71	4.56	4	2	0	69	3.78	2	1	0	36	3.53	8	4	0	104	4.40	303	7	.257	.349	.380	241	8	.261	.343	.411
1996	Bos-A	911	19	.237	.317	.358	5	4	0	107	3.45	5	9	0	136	3.78	3	6	0	118	4.18	7	7	0	124	3.11	510	10	.235	.333	.359	401	9	.239	.296	.357
1997	Tor-A	957	9	.213	.273	.290	10	4	0	148	1.52	11	3	0	116	2.71	12	2	0	121	1.79	9	5	0	143	2.27	498	3	.205	.265	.277	459	6	.222	.283	.305
1998	Tor-A	855	11	.198	.277	.296	12	4	0	150	2.77	8	2	0	85	2.44	9	6	0	112	3.71	11	0	0	123	1.68	452	9	.197	.290	.312	403	2	.199	.263	.278
1999	NY-A	708	20	.261	.350	.394	9	5	0	114	3.56	5	5	0	74	6.20	8	2	0	76	4.52	6	8	0	112	4.66	365	6	.263	.377	.351	343	14	.259	.318	.440
2000	NY-A	781	26	.236	.317	.384	8	4	0	126	3.86	5	4	0	78	3.45	4	6	0	81	4.76	9	2	0	123	3.00	405	11	.207	.311	.328	376	15	.266	.324	.444
TOTALS		13618	260	.228	.294	.336	134	72	0	1917	3.10	126	70	0	1749	3.05	129	69	0	1785	3.11	131	73	0	1881	3.04	7335	110	.232	.306	.332	6283	150	.222	.279	.341
● Bartolo Colon BR/TR																																				
1997	Cle-A	374	12	.286	.366	.447	2	3	0	44	4.53	2	4	0	50	6.62	1	2	0	27	6.75	3	5	0	67	5.21	200	5	.280	.353	.420	174	7	.293	.382	.477
1998	Cle-A	789	15	.260	.329	.379	9	4	0	113	3.98	5	5	0	91	3.36	8	4	0	118	2.51	6	5	0	86	5.36	407	10	.273	.348	.428	382	5	.246	.308	.327
1999	Cle-A	766	24	.242	.314	.398	9	2	0	103	4.12	9	3	0	102	3.78	6	3	0	90	5.30	12	2	0	115	2.90	364	14	.255	.325	.456	402	10	.229	.304	.346
2000	Cle-A	700	21	.233	.329	.371	6	2	0	87	4.34	9	6	0	101	3.48	7	5	0	75	4.42	8	3	0	113	3.51	335	12	.242	.344	.403	365	9	.225	.316	.342
TOTALS		2629	72	.251	.330	.392	26	11	0	346	4.18	25	18	0	345	4.00	22	14	0	310	4.15	29	15	0	381	4.04	1306	41	.261	.341	.428	1323	31	.241	.319	.357
● David Cone BL/TR																																				
1986	KC-A	94	2	.309	.398	.479	0	0	0	10	6.97	0	0	0	12	4.38	0	0	0	7	7.71	0	0	0	16	4.60	46	2	.413	.500	.674	48	0	.208	.296	.292
1987	NY-N	364	11	.239	.327	.387	3	3	0	46	3.94	2	3	1	54	3.52	2	2	0	47	4.60	3	4	1	52	2.92	192	5	.229	.333	.370	172	6	.250	.319	.407
1988	NY-N	836	10	.213	.283	.293	10	1	0	118	1.29	10	2	0	113	3.19	9	1	0	100	2.15	11	2	0	131	2.27	436	5	.257	.335	.351	400	5	.165	.225	.230
1989	NY-N	822	20	.223	.289	.359	8	2	0	114	2.61	6	6	0	106	4.50	4	5	0	92	4.32	10	3	0	128	2.95	449	9	.234	.309	.379	373	11	.209	.263	.335
1990	NY-N	784	21	.226	.284	.364	7	6	0	108	3.85	7	4	0	104	2.60	4	4	0	79	4.46	10	6	0	133	2.50	467	14	.214	.274	.377	317	7	.243	.299	.344
1991	NY-N	868	13	.235	.296	.329	6	7	0	115	3.91	8	7	0	118	2.68	7	5	0	105	3.01	7	9	0	128	3.52	545	7	.248	.311	.345	323	6	.214	.270	.303
1992	NY-N	728	12	.223	.307	.324	6	3	0	85	3.40	7	4	0	112	2.49	7	4	0	118	2.52	6	3	0	79	3.42	410	9	.232	.328	.346	318	3	.211	.277	.296
1992	Tor-A	188	3	.207	.318	.309	2	3	0	38	3.35	2	0	0	15	0.59	0	0	0	0	—	4	3	0	53	2.55	95	1	.221	.342	.305	93	2	.194	.294	.312
1993	KC-A	920	20	.223	.312	.343	4	6	0	127	4.05	7	8	0	127	2.62	5	8	0	118	3.44	6	6	0	136	3.23	498	14	.227	.319	.355	422	6	.218	.304	.329
1994	KC-A	623	15	.209	.277	.332	8	3	0	85	3.06	8	2	0	86	2.81	11	4	0	121	2.76	5	1	0	51	3.35	340	9	.238	.319	.376	283	6	.173	.224	.279
1995	Tor-A	487	12	.232	.297	.368	3	3	0	43	3.14	6	3	0	87	3.50	6	4	0	90	3.40	3	2	0	40	3.35	284	8	.239	.306	.384	203	4	.222	.285	.345
1995	NY-A	368	12	.223	.312	.375	7	0	0	62	3.36	2	2	0	37	4.58	0	0	0	0	—	9	2	0	99	3.82	216	5	.227	.318	.338	152	7	.217	.302	.428
1996	NY-A	253	3	.198	.293	.281	3	1	0	34	2.91	4	1	0	38	2.84	4	1	0	40	2.03	3	1	0	32	3.94	147	1	.197	.318	.272	106	2	.198	.252	.292
1997	NY-A	710	17	.218	.305	.332	5	2	0	90	3.20	7	4	0	105	2.49	8	3	0	127	2.62	4	3	0	68	3.18	370	11	.214	.316	.341	340	6	.224	.293	.324
1998	NY-A	784	20	.237	.302	.371	12	2	0	117	3.16	8	5	0	91	4.05	11	2	0	96	4.39	9	5	0	111	2.83	427	12	.253	.331	.405	357	8	.218	.266	.331
1999	NY-A	715	21	.229	.322	.375	6	5	0	104	1.90	6	4	0	89	5.24	8	3	0	100	2.60	4	6	0	93	4.35	363	15	.245	.353	.416	352	6	.213	.289	.332
2000	NY-A	628	25	.306	.389	.502	2	6	0	78	5.33	2	8	0	77	8.50	1	6	0	84	6.40	3	8	0	71	7.51	318	11	.302	.396	.487	310	14	.310	.382	.516
TOTALS		10172	237	.230	.307	.355	92	53	0	1372	3.25	92	63	1	1373	3.55	87	52	0	1323	3.42	97	64	1	1422	3.38	5603	138	.240	.325	.373	4569	99	.217	.283	.333
● Dennis Cook BL/TL																																				
1988	SF-N	72	1	.125	.233	.181	1	0	0	9	0.00	1	1	0	13	4.85	0	0	0	0	—	2	1	0	22	2.86	7	0	.429	.375	.429	65	1	.092	.218	.154
1989	SF-N	53	1	.245	.310	.377	1	0	0	9	1.00	0	0	0	6	3.00	1	0	0	15	1.80	0	0	0	0	—	9	1	.222	.300	.556	44	0	.250	.313	.341
1989	Phi-N	399	17	.243	.303	.431	4	3	0	62	2.76	2	5	0	44	5.73	2	0	0	15	1.80	4	8	0	91	4.35	54	3	.204	.313	.407	345	14	.249	.301	.435
1990	Phi-N	528	13	.250	.319	.367	4	2	1	87	3.50	4	1	0	54	3.64	5	2	0	89	3.44	3	1	1	53	3.76	117	3	.299	.388	.444	411	10	.236	.299	.345
1990	LA-N	63	7	.365	.373	.794	1	1	0	11	4.76	0	0	0	3	18.00	0	0	0	0	—	1	1	0	14	7.53	18	1	.278	.263	.667	45	6	.400	.417	.844

		TOTAL					HOME					AWAY					1ST HALF					2ND HALF					LEFT					RIGHT				
YEAR	TM/L	AB	HR	AVG	OBP	SLG	W	L	SV	IP	ERA	W	L	SV	IP	ERA	W	L	SV	IP	ERA	W	L	SV	IP	ERA	AB	HR	AVG	OBP	SLG	AB	HR	AVG	OBP	SLG
1991	LA-N	59	0	.203	.279	.254	0	0	0	3	2.70	1	0	0	14	0.00	0	0	0	0	—	1	0	0	18	0.51	25	0	.160	.214	.200	34	0	.235	.325	.294
1992	Cle-A	611	29	.255	.312	.463	4	3	0	91	4.04	1	4	0	67	3.51	1	5	0	59	4.73	4	2	0	99	3.27	98	4	.235	.257	.408	513	25	.259	.322	.474
1993	Cle-A	210	9	.295	.348	.543	3	3	0	26	4.56	2	2	0	28	6.67	5	4	0	49	5.88	0	1	0	5	3.60	54	2	.259	.276	.444	156	7	.308	.372	.577
1994	Chi-A	126	4	.230	.307	.357	1	0	0	16	2.76	2	1	0	17	4.32	3	1	0	23	4.70	0	0	0	10	0.90	49	2	.245	.315	.367	77	2	.221	.302	.351
1995	Cle-A	50	3	.320	.443	.560	0	0	0	4	4.50	0	0	0	9	7.27	0	0	0	13	6.39	0	0	0	0	—	20	1	.300	.391	.500	30	2	.333	.474	.600
1995	Tex-A	168	6	.280	.337	.476	0	1	1	23	4.76	0	1	1	22	3.22	0	0	1	8	3.38	0	2	1	37	4.14	68	2	.279	.342	.426	100	4	.280	.333	.510
1996	Tex-A	248	2	.214	.322	.310	4	1	0	35	3.60	1	1	0	35	4.58	4	1	0	44	2.68	1	1	0	27	6.41	107	1	.206	.290	.336	141	1	.220	.345	.291
1997	Fla-N	240	4	.267	.347	.400	1	1	0	34	2.62	0	1	0	28	5.46	1	1	0	28	1.93	0	1	0	34	5.50	91	1	.264	.337	.396	149	3	.268	.353	.403
1998	NY-N	250	5	.240	.318	.348	4	3	1	31	2.93	4	1	0	37	1.93	4	2	0	30	2.10	4	2	1	38	2.61	97	2	.299	.320	.412	153	3	.203	.317	.307
1999	NY-N	231	11	.216	.299	.424	6	3	1	33	4.41	4	2	2	30	3.26	6	1	1	36	2.27	4	4	2	27	5.93	70	0	.200	.273	.257	161	11	.224	.310	.497
2000	NY-N	233	8	.270	.368	.421	3	1	1	30	5.46	3	2	1	29	5.22	5	2	1	30	6.30	1	1	1	29	4.34	89	3	.315	.384	.461	144	5	.243	.359	.396
TOTALS		3541	120	.250	.322	.415	37	22	5	504	3.60	25	22	4	438	4.24	37	19	3	438	3.76	25	25	6	504	4.02	973	26	.258	.320	.402	2568	94	.247	.323	.420
● Tim Crabtree BR/TR																																				
1995	Tor-A	125	1	.240	.319	.312	0	2	0	17	3.18	0	0	0	15	3.00	0	0	0	1	0.00	0	2	0	31	3.23	71	1	.296	.346	.408	54	0	.167	.286	.185
1996	Tor-A	255	4	.231	.298	.333	4	2	1	33	1.36	1	1	0	34	3.67	3	2	1	42	2.16	2	1	0	26	3.16	119	1	.227	.298	.311	136	3	.235	.298	.353
1997	Tor-A	174	7	.374	.431	.563	2	1	1	15	9.00	1	2	1	26	5.96	2	2	2	22	8.46	1	1	0	18	5.40	78	4	.346	.384	.577	96	3	.396	.468	.552
1998	Tex-A	326	3	.264	.335	.347	4	0	0	44	4.06	2	1	0	41	3.07	3	0	0	39	3.66	3	1	0	46	3.52	114	2	.228	.303	.342	212	1	.283	.353	.349
1999	Tex-A	254	4	.280	.328	.386	3	1	0	40	3.40	2	0	0	25	3.55	4	0	0	27	3.29	1	1	0	38	3.58	98	1	.224	.290	.276	156	3	.314	.353	.455
2000	Tex-A	314	7	.274	.339	.395	1	4	2	41	6.97	1	3	0	39	3.23	1	5	0	40	6.13	1	2	2	41	4.20	127	1	.323	.401	.425	187	6	.241	.294	.374
TOTALS		1448	26	.274	.338	.385	14	10	4	190	4.40	7	7	1	180	3.69	13	9	3	172	4.40	8	8	2	199	3.75	607	10	.270	.336	.381	841	16	.277	.340	.388
● Omar Daal BL/TL																																				
1993	LA-N	130	5	.277	.373	.438	0	3	0	16	5.74	2	0	0	20	4.58	1	1	0	13	2.84	1	2	0	23	6.35	74	2	.230	.326	.338	56	3	.339	.433	.571
1994	LA-N	49	1	.245	.315	.367	0	0	0	7	2.57	0	0	0	7	4.05	0	0	0	7	2.57	0	0	0	7	4.05	27	1	.185	.241	.370	22	0	.318	.400	.364
1995	LA-N	82	1	.354	.455	.451	1	0	0	9	5.00	3	0	0	11	9.00	3	0	0	15	6.14	1	0	0	5	10.13	45	0	.267	.346	.311	37	1	.459	.574	.622
1996	Mon-N	324	10	.228	.308	.373	2	2	0	49	2.76	2	3	0	38	5.63	1	2	0	41	3.07	3	3	0	46	4.86	98	1	.255	.308	.357	226	9	.217	.307	.381
1997	Mon-N	127	4	.378	.448	.535	0	1	0	19	10.42	1	1	1	11	8.74	1	1	1	26	9.82	0	1	0	5	9.64	52	2	.404	.456	.577	75	2	.360	.443	.507
1997	Tor-A	112	3	.304	.339	.482	0	1	0	9	2.89	1	0	0	18	4.58	0	0	0	0	—	1	1	0	27	4.00	24	0	.292	.320	.458	88	3	.307	.344	.489
1998	Ari-N	595	12	.245	.305	.348	3	6	0	73	2.84	5	6	0	90	2.91	3	4	0	66	2.74	5	8	0	97	2.97	113	1	.283	.341	.363	482	11	.237	.297	.344
1999	Ari-N	798	21	.236	.308	.378	8	5	0	111	3.32	8	4	0	104	3.99	7	4	0	102	3.54	9	5	0	113	3.74	140	2	.207	.270	.307	658	19	.242	.315	.394
2000	Ari-N	403	17	.315	.385	.519	2	6	0	52	8.13	0	4	0	44	6.14	2	8	0	88	6.83	0	2	0	8	11.74	89	5	.315	.365	.539	314	12	.315	.391	.513
2000	Phi-N	279	9	.290	.362	.448	1	4	0	34	5.03	1	5	0	37	4.38	0	0	0	0	—	2	9	0	71	4.69	32	1	.250	.324	.375	247	8	.296	.367	.457
TOTALS		2899	83	.267	.338	.413	17	28	0	379	4.44	23	23	1	379	4.54	18	20	1	357	4.67	22	31	0	401	4.33	694	15	.265	.327	.388	2205	68	.268	.342	.421
● Vic Darensbourg BL/TL																																				
1998	Fla-N	251	5	.207	.289	.311	0	4	1	42	3.24	0	3	0	29	4.30	0	6	0	38	5.02	0	1	1	33	2.16	107	0	.168	.264	.206	144	5	.236	.307	.389
1999	Fla-N	147	3	.340	.434	.497	0	1	0	18	6.00	0	0	0	17	11.88	0	1	0	22	9.00	0	0	0	13	8.53	72	2	.264	.341	.444	75	1	.413	.516	.547
2000	Fla-N	235	7	.260	.336	.421	3	1	0	39	5.03	2	2	0	23	2.38	3	0	0	35	3.89	2	3	0	27	4.28	79	2	.190	.297	.316	156	5	.295	.356	.474
TOTALS		633	15	.258	.341	.395	3	6	1	99	4.45	2	5	0	69	5.50	3	7	0	94	5.53	2	4	1	73	4.05	258	4	.202	.296	.306	375	11	.296	.372	.456
● Ron Darling BR/TR																																				
1983	NY-N	124	0	.250	.354	.298	0	1	0	12	2.92	1	2	0	23	2.74	0	0	0	0	—	1	3	0	35	2.80	69	0	.261	.363	.290	55	0	.236	.344	.309
1984	NY-N	761	17	.235	.329	.357	7	2	0	102	3.01	5	7	0	104	4.59	8	3	0	92	3.93	4	6	0	114	3.71	365	4	.247	.337	.348	396	13	.225	.321	.366
1985	NY-N	909	21	.235	.321	.360	9	5	0	148	3.09	7	1	0	100	2.62	6	2	0	116	2.32	10	4	0	132	3.42	461	8	.241	.323	.354	448	13	.230	.320	.366
1986	NY-N	867	21	.234	.300	.354	10	2	0	118	2.36	5	4	0	119	3.26	8	2	0	99	3.19	7	4	0	138	2.54	503	12	.227	.288	.344	364	9	.245	.316	.368
1987	NY-N	784	24	.233	.318	.380	4	6	0	89	3.86	8	2	0	119	4.61	2	5	0	104	4.86	10	3	0	104	3.72	447	10	.221	.297	.353	337	14	.249	.345	.415
1988	NY-N	888	24	.245	.294	.383	14	1	0	149	2.29	3	8	0	91	4.83	8	5	0	119	2.56	9	4	0	121	3.93	452	12	.254	.304	.387	436	12	.236	.285	.378
1989	NY-N	829	19	.258	.314	.385	8	6	0	121	3.04	6	8	0	96	4.13	6	5	0	98	4.13	8	9	0	119	3.02	481	9	.283	.338	.407	348	10	.224	.281	.353
1990	NY-N	495	20	.273	.336	.451	4	2	0	54	3.52	3	7	0	72	5.23	2	4	0	50	4.89	5	5	0	76	4.24	283	10	.258	.333	.403	212	10	.292	.341	.514
1991	NY-N	382	9	.251	.310	.395	1	4	0	40	6.30	4	2	0	62	2.31	4	5	0	87	4.43	1	1	0	15	0.60	213	3	.254	.302	.366	169	6	.249	.319	.432
1991	Mon-N	75	6	.333	.383	.653	0	1	0	6	6.00	0	1	0	11	8.18	0	0	0	0	—	0	2	0	17	7.41	33	2	.273	.273	.485	42	4	.381	.458	.786
1991	Oak-A	270	7	.237	.331	.374	2	4	0	44	4.50	1	3	0	31	3.48	0	0	0	0	—	3	7	0	75	4.08	145	3	.207	.310	.317	125	4	.272	.357	.440
1992	Oak-A	783	15	.253	.318	.379	8	6	0	106	3.57	7	4	0	100	3.77	7	5	0	89	4.45	8	5	0	117	3.07	371	6	.270	.348	.402	412	9	.238	.290	.359
1993	Oak-A	705	22	.281	.349	.441	3	6	0	95	4.75	2	3	0	83	5.62	1	4	0	74	6.11	4	5	0	104	4.49	346	12	.275	.350	.442	359	10	.287	.348	.440
1994	Oak-A	606	18	.267	.337	.413	4	7	0	83	4.25	6	4	0	77	4.77	5	9	0	100	4.93	5	2	0	60	3.77	298	12	.255	.330	.409	308	6	.279	.343	.416
1995	Oak-A	419	16	.296	.365	.477	1	3	0	50	5.80	3	4	0	54	6.63	2	3	0	62	5.98	2	4	0	42	6.59	245	10	.310	.364	.498	174	6	.276	.365	.448
TOTALS		8897	239	.252	.323	.391	75	56	0	1217	3.51	61	60	0	1144	4.26	59	52	0	1089	4.13	77	64	0	1271	3.65	4712	113	.254	.324	.385	4185	126	.250	.322	.399
● Danny Darwin BR/TR																																				
1978	Tex-A	34	0	.324	.333	.382	1	0	0	7	4.05	0	0	0	2	4.50	0	0	0	0	—	1	0	0	9	4.15	22	0	.273	.273	.273	12	0	.417	.429	.583
1979	Tex-A	269	5	.186	.274	.286	2	3	0	43	5.27	2	1	0	35	2.55	1	0	0	15	2.93	3	4	0	63	4.31	94	2	.181	.313	.319	175	3	.189	.251	.269
1980	Tex-A	404	4	.243	.324	.322	8	3	5	66	2.05	5	1	3	44	3.50	4	1	1	48	1.86	9	3	7	61	3.23	174	2	.241	.360	.339	230	2	.243	.294	.309
1981	Tex-A	527	12	.218	.300	.357	5	4	0	88	2.34	4	5	0	58	5.62	7	4	0	75	3.46	2	5	0	71	3.82	266	9	.244	.336	.414	261	3	.192	.262	.299
1982	Tex-A	340	6	.279	.349	.379	7	2	6	46	2.93	3	6	1	43	3.98	4	2	3	38	3.05	6	6	4	51	3.73	143	3	.266	.355	.385	197	3	.289	.344	.376
1983	Tex-A	701	9	.250	.310	.359	5	6	0	99	2.73	3	7	0	84	4.39	6	6	0	101	2.67	2	7	0	82	4.50	354	7	.251	.322	.393	347	2	.248	.299	.326
1984	Tex-A	891	19	.279	.322	.402	4	6	0	104	3.89	4	6	0	120	3.99	5	4	0	113	4.21	3	8	0	110	3.67	470	14	.317	.367	.481	421	5	.238	.270	.314
1985	Mil-A	834	34	.254	.308	.432	2	10	1	95	2.85	6	8	1	123	4.54	6	7	0	115	3.82	2	11	2	102	3.78	418	17	.270	.343	.459	416	17	.238	.270	.404
1986	Mil-A	488	13	.246	.297	.375	2	6	0	74	3.75	4	2	0	56	3.21	4	4	0	73	2.97	2	4	0	58	4.21	243	8	.259	.332	.412	245	5	.233	.260	.339
1986	Hou-N	209	3	.239	.267	.335	0	2	0	17	4.86	5	0	0	38	1.19	0	0	0	0	—	5	2	0	54	2.32	102	3	.304	.343	.471	107	0	.178	.195	.206
1987	Hou-N	748	17	.246	.313	.374	5	4	0	99	3.09	4	6	0	97	4.10	4	4	0	97	3.33	5	6	0	98	3.84	372	11	.266	.342	.433	376	6	.226	.283	.316
1988	Hou-N	730	20	.259	.307	.392	2	5	1	92	3.33	6	8	2	100	4.32	3	7	0	99	4.53	5	6	3	93	3.11	387	10	.264	.313	.401	343	10	.254	.301	.382
1989	Hou-N	434	8	.212	.268	.302	7	0	4	73	1.98	4	4	3	49	2.92	7	2	3	64	2.39	4	2	4	58	2.33	240	3	.246	.295	.329	194	5	.170	.236	.268
1990	Hou-N	605	11	.225	.266	.331	6	2	1	78	2.42	5	2	1	85	2.02	2	1	2	45	2.40	9	3	0	118	2.14	364	7	.264	.311	.382	241	4	.166	.198	.253
1991	Bos-A	270	15	.263	.309	.500	2	4	0	45	4.84	1	2	0	23	5.79	3	5	0	63	4.86	0	1	0	5	9.00	139	3	.245	.301	.396	131	12	.282	.319	.611
1992	Bos-A	618	11	.257	.319	.380	6	4	1	76	4.26	3	5	2	85	3.69	4	4	3	48	5.10	5	5	0	114	3.48	274	1	.281	.345	.387	344	10	.238	.297	.375
1993	Bos-A	852	31	.230	.272	.399	8	3	0	101	3.38	7	8	0	128	3.16	7	7	0	100	3.24	8	4	0	129	3.27	467	19	.255	.300	.450	385	12	.200	.237	.338
1994	Bos-A	319	13	.317	.361	.520	4	4	0	51	6.66	3	1	0	24	5.55	7	5	0	76	6.30	0	0	0	0	—	157	7	.369	.414	.592	162	6	.265	.309	.451
1995	Tor-A	268	13	.340	.393	.578	0	4	0	31	6.75	1	4	0	34	8.39	1	8	0	62	7.44	0	0	0	3	10.80	176	6	.358	.417	.568	92	7	.304	.347	.598
1995	Tex-A	137	12	.292	.331	.599	2	1	0	20	7.65	0	1	0	14	6.43	0	0	0	0	—	2	2	0	34	7.15	77	5	.312	.354	.545	60	7	.267	.302	.667
1996	Pit-N	462	9	.253	.285	.374	2	5	0	58	3.72	5	4	0	64	2.38	6	7	0	102	2.64	1	2	0	20	4.95	212	4	.311	.335	.429	250	5	.204	.243	.328
1996	Hou-N	161	7	.267	.331	.497	3	0	0	33	4.09	0	2	0	9	12.54	0	0	0	0	—	3	2	0	42	5.95	64	5	.391	.458	.734	97	2	.186	.248	.340
1997	Chi-A	455	21	.286	.329	.477	1	4	0	51	3.33	3	4	0	62	4.79	2	6	0	87	3.40	2	2	0	26	6.58	222	14	.324	.373	.581	233	7	.249	.286	.378
1997	SF-N	177	5	.288	.342	.429	0	0	0	13	4.72	1	3	0	31	4.99	0	0	0	0	—	1	3	0	44	4.91	89	2	.270	.333	.427	88	3	.307	.351	.432
1998	SF-N	593	23	.297	.352	.482	4	5	0	78	5.33	4	5	0	71	5.70	6	5	0	89	4.74	2	5	0	59	6.67	300	10	.283	.328	.457	293	13	.311	.375	.509
TOTALS		11526	321	.256	.310	.399	88	87	19	1537	3.62	83	95	13	1479	4.06	89	89	12	1512	3.80	82	93	20	1504	3.87	5826	172	.277	.338	.437	5700	149	.234	.281	.361
● Storm Davis BR/TR																																				
1982	Bal-A	374	8	.257	.304	.361	5	2	0	55	2.93	3	2	0	45	4.17	0	1	0	21	1.27	8	3	0	79	4.08	181	6	.249	.305	.370	193	2	.264	.303	.352
1983	Bal-A	756	14	.238	.298	.344	2	5	0	92	3.34	11	2	0	109	3.81	5	3	0	94	3.06	8	4	0	106	4.06	362	6	.221	.294	.315	394	8	.254	.301	.371
1984	Bal-A	831	7	.247	.307	.320	8	6	1	119	3.17	6	3	0	106	3.07	6	4	1	119	2.64	8	5	0	106	3.66	409	3	.254	.330	.330	422	4	.239	.282	.310
1985	Bal-A	673	11	.256	.325	.376	5	5	0	89	4.53	5	3	0	86	4.52	4	4	0	95	4.93	6	4	0	80	4.05	360	6	.258	.346	.394	313	5	.252	.300	.355
1986	Bal-A	603	16	.275	.329	.400	5	7	0	83	3.35	4	5	0	71	3.95	6	8	0	100	3.33	3	4	0	54	4.17	300	11	.293	.358	.453	303	5	.257	.298	.347
1987	SD-N	250	5	.280	.372	.432	2	3	0	31	4.06	0	4	0	32	8.24	2	7	0	58	5.93	0	0	0	5	9.00	128	2	.313	.417	.461	122	3	.246	.324	.402
1987	Oak-A	116	3	.241	.305	.362	0	1	0	17	4.67	1	0	0	13	1.38	0	0	0	0	—	1	1	0	30	3.26	73	1	.274	.316	.342	43	2	.186	.286	.395
1988	Oak-A	769	16	.274	.349	.394	7	3	0	97	3.71	9	4	0	105	3.70	5	4	0	100	3.59	11	3	0	101	3.82	396	4	.263	.336	.348	373	12	.287	.362	.442
1989	Oak-A	649	19	.288	.355	.435	9	3	0	82	4.70	10	4	0	87	4.03	6	3	0	57	5.53	13	4	0	112	3.77	314	10	.264	.353	.414	335	9	.310	.356	.454
1990	KC-A	459	9	.281	.330	.407	5	7	0	80	4.50	2	3	0	32	5.34	2	6	0	56	5.30	5	4	0	56	4.18	235	4	.294	.353	.421	224	5	.268	.305	.393
1991	KC-A	458	11	.306	.367	.437	2	3	0	55	4.12	1	6	2	60	5.73	2	7	1	72	4.14	1	2	1	43	6.33	227	6	.335	.402	.498	231	5	.277	.333	.377
1992	Bal-A	324	5	.244	.320	.321	5	1	1	47	2.85	2	2	3	42	4.07	3	2	2	50	3.22	4	1	2	39	3.69	137	2	.241	.338	.299	187	3	.246	.306	.337
1993	Oak-A	246	5	.276	.364	.394	1	2	0	43	4.98	1	4	0	19	8.84	2	6	0	56	6.63	0	0	0	7	2.57	120	1	.267	.373	.342	126	4	.286	.355	.444

YEAR	TM/L	TOTAL AB	HR	AVG	OBP	SLG	HOME W	L	SV	IP	ERA	AWAY W	L	SV	IP	ERA	1ST HALF W	L	SV	IP	ERA	2ND HALF W	L	SV	IP	ERA	LEFT AB	HR	AVG	OBP	SLG	RIGHT AB	HR	AVG	OBP	SLG
1993	Det-A	126	4	.198	.287	.373	0	2	3	20	3.54	0	0	1	15	2.40	0	0	0	0	—	0	2	4	35	3.06	56	2	.161	.294	.304	70	2	.229	.280	.429
1994	Det-A	174	3	.207	.335	.322	1	1	0	25	4.01	1	3	0	23	3.09	0	2	0	35	3.60	2	2	0	13	3.46	69	1	.116	.291	.217	105	2	.267	.366	.390
TOTALS		6808	136	.263	.330	.379	57	51	5	937	3.83	56	45	6	844	4.24	43	57	4	913	4.05	70	39	7	867	4.00	3367	65	.263	.342	.378	3441	71	.264	.318	.380
● **Mark Davis** BL/TL																																				
1980	Phi-N	25	0	.160	.300	.200	0	0	0	2	0.00	0	0	0	5	3.60	0	0	0	0	—	0	0	0	7	2.57	4	0	.250	.500	.250	21	0	.143	.250	.190
1981	Phi-N	164	7	.299	.380	.482	0	3	0	25	9.24	1	1	0	18	5.60	0	0	0	0	—	1	4	0	43	7.74	30	1	.300	.417	.433	134	6	.299	.372	.493
1983	SF-N	410	14	.227	.313	.378	2	3	0	58	3.75	4	1	0	53	3.21	0	1	0	10	3.60	6	3	0	101	3.48	67	1	.209	.308	.284	343	13	.230	.314	.397
1984	SF-N	686	25	.293	.344	.472	3	12	0	92	4.97	2	5	0	82	5.79	3	6	0	90	4.50	2	11	0	85	6.27	142	3	.211	.253	.310	544	22	.314	.368	.515
1985	SF-N	407	13	.219	.294	.346	4	5	5	53	3.71	1	7	2	61	3.39	3	5	4	56	2.25	2	7	3	58	4.78	114	3	.184	.231	.316	293	10	.232	.317	.358
1986	SF-N	297	6	.212	.291	.310	3	2	0	40	2.50	2	5	4	45	3.43	2	4	3	41	2.43	3	3	1	44	3.50	84	1	.131	.213	.190	213	5	.244	.321	.357
1987	SF-N	264	9	.273	.349	.432	1	4	0	31	5.17	3	1	0	39	4.35	4	5	0	70	4.78	0	0	0	1	0.00	52	3	.308	.368	.500	212	6	.264	.344	.415
1987	SD-N	228	5	.224	.322	.342	3	0	1	32	0.85	2	3	1	31	5.58	0	0	0	0	—	5	3	2	62	3.18	61	0	.148	.246	.213	167	5	.251	.349	.389
1988	SD-N	352	2	.199	.284	.244	4	2	14	48	0.94	1	8	14	50	3.04	2	6	14	51	2.82	3	4	14	47	1.14	86	1	.209	.277	.302	266	1	.195	.286	.226
1989	SD-N	330	6	.200	.270	.294	2	0	21	46	1.17	2	3	23	47	2.51	2	3	21	42	2.79	2	0	23	51	1.07	46	2	.239	.321	.457	284	4	.194	.261	.268
1990	KC-A	274	9	.259	.383	.423	2	1	5	38	4.46	0	6	1	30	5.93	1	5	5	31	5.52	1	2	1	38	4.78	55	0	.182	.348	.236	219	9	.279	.392	.470
1991	KC-A	229	6	.240	.347	.376	4	1	0	29	4.66	2	2	1	34	4.28	3	1	1	16	7.31	3	2	0	47	3.47	56	0	.304	.394	.339	173	6	.220	.332	.387
1992	KC-A	143	6	.294	.400	.503	0	2	0	15	9.82	1	1	0	22	5.40	1	2	0	33	5.40	0	1	0	3	27.00	37	1	.243	.310	.378	106	5	.311	.429	.547
1992	Atl-N	70	3	.314	.424	.514	1	0	0	11	7.36	0	0	0	6	6.35	0	0	0	0	—	1	0	0	17	7.02	22	0	.409	.462	.455	48	3	.271	.407	.542
1993	Phi-N	128	4	.273	.392	.438	1	1	0	14	3.29	0	1	0	18	6.62	1	2	0	31	4.65	0	0	0	1	54.00	31	0	.258	.410	.355	97	4	.278	.386	.464
1993	SD-N	149	6	.295	.376	.477	0	2	2	23	4.63	0	1	2	15	1.80	0	0	0	0	—	0	3	4	38	3.52	64	5	.250	.304	.516	85	1	.329	.426	.447
1994	SD-N	67	4	.299	.412	.507	0	0	0	8	10.80	0	1	0	8	6.75	0	1	0	16	8.82	0	0	0	0	—	23	0	.217	.379	.261	44	4	.341	.431	.636
1997	Mil-A	65	4	.323	.380	.523	0	0	0	11	7.15	0	0	0	5	1.80	0	0	0	0	—	0	0	0	16	5.51	36	1	.278	.350	.361	29	3	.379	.419	.724
TOTALS		4288	129	.249	.333	.391	30	38	48	577	4.07	21	46	48	568	4.26	22	41	48	487	4.14	29	43	48	658	4.19	1010	22	.222	.304	.331	3278	107	.257	.342	.409
● **Jose DeLeon** BR/TR																																				
1983	Pit-N	383	5	.196	.283	.300	6	2	0	70	2.44	1	1	0	38	3.55	0	0	0	0	—	7	3	0	108	2.83	184	2	.196	.302	.315	199	3	.196	.266	.286
1984	Pit-N	686	10	.214	.307	.312	5	8	0	113	3.12	2	5	0	80	4.63	5	4	0	87	2.91	2	9	0	106	4.43	355	6	.256	.361	.377	331	4	.169	.245	.242
1985	Pit-N	597	15	.231	.332	.357	2	9	1	93	3.97	0	10	2	70	5.68	2	10	0	98	4.61	0	9	3	65	4.85	285	7	.277	.389	.414	312	8	.189	.278	.304
1986	Pit-N	64	2	.266	.427	.469	1	3	1	15	7.80	0	0	0	1	13.50	1	3	1	16	8.27	0	0	0	0	—	32	1	.375	.545	.625	32	1	.156	.289	.313
1986	Chi-A	274	7	.179	.296	.285	2	3	0	32	3.94	2	2	0	47	2.30	0	0	0	0	—	4	5	0	79	2.96	136	4	.184	.306	.309	138	3	.174	.286	.261
1987	Chi-A	770	24	.230	.322	.370	3	7	0	95	5.12	8	5	0	111	3.08	5	7	0	96	3.95	6	5	0	110	4.08	397	13	.254	.351	.393	373	11	.204	.290	.346
1988	StL-N	835	13	.237	.308	.345	7	6	0	112	3.79	6	4	0	114	3.56	5	5	0	100	4.13	8	5	0	125	3.31	431	5	.260	.349	.355	404	8	.213	.259	.334
1989	StL-N	878	16	.197	.268	.309	8	6	0	134	2.55	8	6	0	110	3.67	8	7	0	121	3.41	8	5	0	123	2.70	509	10	.234	.312	.360	369	6	.146	.204	.238
1990	StL-N	683	15	.246	.331	.370	3	9	0	84	5.55	4	10	0	98	3.48	6	6	0	93	3.77	1	13	0	90	5.12	404	8	.285	.373	.423	279	7	.190	.268	.294
1991	StL-N	603	15	.239	.313	.378	3	4	0	89	2.42	2	5	0	73	3.07	3	6	0	94	3.16	2	3	0	69	2.10	326	9	.252	.339	.408	277	6	.224	.281	.343
1992	StL-N	387	7	.245	.320	.385	2	3	0	62	3.50	0	4	0	41	6.20	2	6	0	74	4.38	0	1	0	28	5.08	216	5	.278	.348	.435	171	2	.205	.284	.322
1992	Phi-N	57	0	.281	.339	.298	0	0	0	6	1.50	0	1	0	9	4.00	0	0	0	0	—	0	1	0	15	3.00	29	0	.310	.375	.345	28	0	.250	.300	.250
1993	Phi-N	169	5	.231	.350	.373	1	0	0	28	3.18	2	0	0	19	3.38	3	0	0	28	3.90	0	0	0	19	2.33	85	3	.271	.382	.471	84	2	.190	.317	.274
1993	Chi-A	33	2	.152	.243	.333	0	0	0	6	0.00	0	0	0	4	4.15	0	0	0	0	—	0	0	0	10	1.74	7	0	.143	.333	.143	26	2	.154	.214	.385
1994	Chi-A	240	5	.200	.301	.313	0	2	0	29	4.40	3	0	2	38	2.58	2	2	1	43	3.12	1	0	1	24	3.80	92	2	.228	.339	.370	148	3	.182	.277	.277
1995	Chi-A	252	10	.238	.323	.417	3	0	0	36	4.75	2	3	0	32	5.68	3	3	0	37	5.54	2	0	0	30	4.75	110	2	.273	.354	.409	142	8	.211	.298	.423
1995	Mon-N	30	2	.233	.375	.433	0	0	0	4	4.50	0	1	0	4	10.38	0	0	0	0	—	0	1	0	8	7.56	13	0	.308	.375	.308	17	2	.176	.375	.529
TOTALS		6941	153	.224	.311	.347	46	62	2	1008	3.67	40	57	4	889	3.87	45	59	2	887	3.90	41	60	4	1010	3.64	3611	77	.255	.349	.387	3330	76	.191	.268	.304
● **John Denny** BR/TR																																				
1978	StL-N	840	13	.238	.302	.333	10	4	0	125	2.09	4	7	0	109	3.96	6	6	0	121	2.97	8	5	0	113	2.96	358	6	.265	.327	.363	482	7	.218	.284	.311
1979	StL-N	778	24	.265	.350	.407	4	3	0	98	4.12	4	8	0	108	5.52	3	6	0	101	4.80	5	5	0	105	4.90	324	8	.275	.365	.414	454	16	.258	.339	.403
1980	Cle-A	408	4	.284	.363	.365	3	2	0	45	2.78	5	4	0	63	5.54	7	5	0	91	3.57	1	1	0	18	8.50	209	3	.297	.381	.383	199	1	.271	.344	.347
1981	Cle-A	547	9	.254	.335	.347	6	5	0	85	3.07	4	1	0	61	3.26	3	2	0	60	3.17	7	4	0	86	3.14	292	5	.264	.337	.353	255	4	.243	.332	.341
1982	Cle-A	524	11	.240	.338	.357	4	5	0	74	4.50	2	6	0	64	5.60	5	8	0	104	4.76	1	3	0	34	5.77	259	7	.266	.351	.405	265	4	.215	.326	.309
1982	Phi-N	83	1	.217	.301	.289	0	1	0	12	2.25	0	1	0	10	6.10	0	0	0	0	—	0	2	0	22	4.03	40	0	.100	.234	.125	43	1	.326	.370	.442
1983	Phi-N	915	9	.250	.293	.332	11	2	0	136	2.05	8	4	0	107	2.78	5	4	0	101	2.24	14	2	0	142	2.47	476	4	.288	.327	.370	439	5	.210	.257	.292
1984	Phi-N	570	11	.214	.256	.326	3	5	0	88	2.45	4	2	0	66	2.44	4	3	0	64	1.55	3	4	0	90	3.09	323	6	.223	.265	.331	247	5	.202	.244	.320
1985	Phi-N	893	15	.282	.342	.392	4	10	0	123	4.02	7	4	0	108	3.59	5	5	0	108	4.00	6	9	0	123	3.67	456	6	.285	.356	.388	437	9	.279	.328	.396
1986	Cin-N	658	15	.272	.331	.410	6	5	0	89	4.43	5	5	0	82	3.95	5	7	0	103	4.38	6	3	0	69	3.93	327	8	.318	.381	.486	331	7	.227	.281	.335
TOTALS		6216	112	.255	.322	.363	51	42	0	876	3.20	43	42	0	778	4.07	43	46	0	852	3.59	51	38	0	802	3.63	3064	53	.274	.340	.384	3152	59	.237	.304	.343
● **Jim Deshaies** BL/TL																																				
1984	NY-A	32	1	.438	.525	.656	0	1	0	4	9.00	0	0	0	3	15.00	0	0	0	0	—	0	1	0	7	11.57	8	1	.500	.500	1.375	24	0	.417	.531	.417
1985	Hou-N	10	0	.100	.100	.100	0	0	0	1	0.00	0	0	0	2	0.00	0	0	0	0	—	0	0	0	3	0.00	4	0	.250	.250	.250	6	0	.000	.000	.000
1986	Hou-N	531	16	.234	.311	.379	6	3	0	85	3.39	6	2	0	59	3.05	5	2	0	60	3.75	7	3	0	84	2.89	87	3	.241	.333	.402	444	13	.232	.306	.374
1987	Hou-N	579	22	.257	.322	.427	6	0	0	75	2.75	5	6	0	77	6.46	8	2	0	85	3.48	3	4	0	67	6.07	99	2	.263	.345	.404	480	20	.256	.317	.431
1988	Hou-N	752	20	.218	.284	.366	7	8	0	111	2.91	4	6	0	96	3.10	5	5	0	92	2.54	6	9	0	115	3.37	129	6	.248	.310	.465	623	14	.212	.278	.345
1989	Hou-N	829	15	.217	.287	.331	8	4	0	118	3.13	7	6	0	108	2.67	8	3	0	114	3.16	7	7	0	112	2.66	120	0	.258	.361	.317	709	15	.210	.273	.333
1990	Hou-N	760	21	.245	.322	.386	4	3	0	98	2.75	3	9	0	111	4.70	4	5	0	91	4.27	3	7	0	119	3.41	115	1	.304	.429	.426	645	20	.234	.301	.378
1991	Hou-N	602	19	.259	.336	.430	2	3	0	65	3.72	3	9	0	96	5.83	2	7	0	93	5.50	3	5	0	68	4.26	104	4	.279	.386	.471	498	15	.255	.324	.422
1992	SD-N	356	6	.258	.321	.360	2	4	0	50	4.11	2	3	0	46	2.36	0	0	0	0	—	4	7	0	96	3.28	59	1	.356	.451	.458	297	5	.239	.293	.340
1993	Min-A	625	24	.254	.313	.434	8	4	0	84	3.42	3	9	0	83	5.42	9	5	0	97	3.88	2	8	0	70	5.14	109	3	.229	.317	.349	516	21	.260	.313	.452
1993	SF-N	69	2	.348	.408	.536	0	2	0	5	10.13	2	0	0	12	1.54	0	0	0	0	—	2	2	0	17	4.24	13	0	.231	.231	.385	56	2	.375	.444	.571
1994	Min-A	530	30	.321	.382	.583	4	5	0	71	6.85	2	7	0	59	8.04	4	7	0	92	6.55	2	5	0	38	9.39	68	4	.338	.422	.574	462	26	.318	.376	.584
1995	Phi-N	31	3	.484	.500	.871	0	0	0	4	13.50	0	1	0	1	40.50	0	0	0	0	—	0	1	0	5	20.25	4	0	.750	.750	.750	27	3	.444	.464	.889
TOTALS		5706	179	.251	.320	.411	47	37	0	774	3.65	37	58	0	751	4.65	45	36	0	725	4.14	39	59	0	800	4.15	919	25	.276	.368	.430	4787	154	.247	.310	.407
● **Frank DiPino** BL/TL																																				
1981	Mil-A	7	0	.000	.300	.000	0	0	0	1	0.00	0	0	0	1	0.00	0	0	0	0	—	0	0	0	2	0.00	2	0	.000	.333	.000	5	0	.000	.286	.000
1982	Hou-N	106	1	.302	.361	.377	2	1	0	20	4.95	0	1	0	8	8.64	0	0	0	0	—	2	2	0	28	6.04	22	0	.227	.227	.318	84	1	.321	.392	.393
1983	Hou-N	254	2	.205	.263	.287	2	1	10	34	2.12	1	3	10	37	3.13	3	3	6	34	2.88	0	1	14	37	2.43	73	1	.151	.198	.233	181	1	.227	.289	.309
1984	Hou-N	285	3	.260	.343	.323	3	7	7	40	4.54	1	2	7	36	2.02	1	5	8	36	4.04	3	4	6	40	2.72	71	0	.211	.253	.225	214	3	.276	.369	.355
1985	Hou-N	278	7	.248	.350	.381	2	3	1	32	4.26	1	4	5	44	3.86	1	4	5	35	3.89	2	3	1	41	4.14	64	2	.344	.442	.500	214	5	.220	.321	.346
1986	Hou-N	143	5	.189	.278	.329	1	0	1	23	1.96	0	3	2	17	5.71	1	2	3	32	2.84	0	1	0	9	6.23	42	1	.167	.239	.262	101	4	.198	.293	.356
1986	Chi-N	158	6	.297	.351	.481	1	2	0	18	5.50	1	2	0	22	4.91	0	1	0	1	6.75	2	3	0	39	5.12	51	2	.176	.232	.314	107	4	.355	.407	.561
1987	Chi-N	297	7	.253	.327	.367	3	2	3	44	2.68	0	1	1	36	3.72	1	1	1	33	2.73	2	2	3	47	3.45	94	2	.245	.284	.340	203	5	.256	.346	.379
1988	Chi-N	358	6	.285	.338	.394	2	1	2	48	3.72	0	2	4	42	6.43	0	3	3	47	4.21	2	0	3	43	5.82	125	0	.192	.228	.248	233	6	.335	.396	.472
1989	StL-N	321	6	.227	.269	.349	4	0	0	46	1.58	5	0	0	43	3.38	4	0	0	42	2.98	5	0	0	46	1.96	129	0	.209	.241	.248	192	6	.240	.287	.417
1990	StL-N	313	8	.294	.352	.447	3	2	3	41	3.92	2	0	0	40	5.22	3	1	0	33	5.45	2	1	3	48	3.94	133	2	.293	.349	.391	180	6	.294	.354	.489
1992	StL-N	41	0	.220	.273	.268	0	0	0	5	3.60	0	0	0	6	0.00	0	0	0	0	—	0	0	0	11	1.64	16	0	.188	.235	.250	25	0	.240	.296	.280
1993	KC-A	64	2	.328	.392	.578	0	0	0	10	4.35	1	1	0	5	11.81	1	1	0	7	4.91	0	0	0	8	8.64	12	0	.333	.467	.583	52	2	.327	.373	.577
TOTALS		2625	53	.256	.324	.375	23	19	27	362	3.38	12	19	29	338	4.31	15	21	26	300	3.69	20	17	30	400	3.94	834	10	.227	.278	.308	1791	43	.270	.344	.406
● **Richard Dotson** BR/TR																																				
1979	Chi-A	98	0	.286	.321	.357	1	0	0	7	0.00	1	0	0	17	5.19	0	0	0	0	—	2	0	0	24	3.70	49	0	.286	.321	.367	49	0	.286	.321	.347
1980	Chi-A	748	20	.247	.328	.380	6	3	0	97	3.79	6	7	0	101	4.74	7	3	0	83	3.69	5	7	0	115	4.70	424	13	.257	.338	.406	324	7	.235	.314	.346
1981	Chi-A	537	13	.270	.333	.397	6	5	0	82	3.20	3	3	0	59	4.55	7	3	0	89	2.82	2	5	0	52	5.40	288	9	.292	.342	.444	249	4	.245	.323	.341
1982	Chi-A	776	19	.280	.345	.419	3	9	0	98	3.50	8	6	0	99	4.18	3	8	0	79	4.81	8	7	0	118	3.20	372	8	.285	.337	.409	404	11	.280	.352	.428
1983	Chi-A	872	19	.240	.325	.351	10	4	0	117	3.30	12	3	0	123	3.15	7	5	0	96	4.67	15	2	0	144	2.26	463	11	.253	.337	.371	409	8	.225	.312	.328
1984	Chi-A	907	24	.238	.317	.380	6	9	0	133	3.92	8	6	0	112	3.20	10	4	0	128	2.74	4	11	0	117	4.53	477	17	.237	.327	.394	430	7	.240	.306	.365
1985	Chi-A	203	5	.261	.324	.384	3	1	0	39	2.75	0	3	0	13	9.69	3	4	0	52	4.47	0	0	0	0	—	107	4	.290	.372	.477	96	1	.229	.269	.281
1986	Chi-A	782	24	.289	.347	.435	7	9	0	106	4.84	3	8	0	91	6.23	6	7	0	97	5.38	4	10	0	100	5.58	408	14	.265	.324	.407	374	10	.316	.371	.465
1987	Chi-A	807	24	.249	.320	.399	6	8	0	108	4.35	5	4	0	104	3.99	5	5	0	112	4.19	6	7	0	100	4.15	430	15	.251	.326	.419	377	9	.247	.314	.377
1988	NY-A	669	27	.266	.338	.454	6	3	0	79	3.99	6	6	0	92	5.87	7	3	0	92	4.32	5	6	0	79	5.79	347	11	.239	.306	.392	322	16	.295	.372	.522

		TOTAL					HOME					AWAY					1ST HALF					2ND HALF					LEFT					RIGHT				
YEAR	TM/L	AB	HR	AVG	OBP	SLG	W	L	SV	IP	ERA	W	L	SV	IP	ERA	W	L	SV	IP	ERA	W	L	SV	IP	ERA	AB	HR	AVG	OBP	SLG	AB	HR	AVG	OBP	SLG
1989	NY-A	218	8	.317	.366	.523	1	3	0	16	10.91	1	2	0	36	3.25	2	5	0	52	5.57	0	0	0	0	—	105	4	.314	.357	.571	113	4	.319	.374	.478
1989	Chi-A	397	8	.282	.348	.421	2	4	0	58	2.81	1	3	0	42	5.36	0	0	0	0	—	3	7	0	100	3.88	208	5	.279	.335	.433	189	3	.286	.362	.407
1990	KC-A	121	3	.355	.410	.579	0	2	0	18	7.00	0	2	0	11	10.97	0	4	0	29	8.48	0	0	0	0	—	56	3	.357	.393	.643	65	0	.354	.423	.523
TOTALS		7135	194	.264	.334	.407	57	60	0	958	3.91	54	53	0	900	4.56	57	51	0	909	4.28	54	62	0	949	4.17	3734	114	.264	.333	.415	3401	80	.265	.335	.398
● **Doug Drabek** BR/TR																																				
1986	NY-A	501	13	.251	.322	.397	2	3	0	62	3.75	5	5	0	69	4.41	0	1	0	23	6.75	7	7	0	109	3.55	259	9	.278	.356	.456	242	4	.223	.284	.335
1987	Pit-N	668	22	.247	.294	.415	6	5	0	79	3.66	5	7	0	98	4.05	1	7	0	69	4.72	10	5	0	108	3.34	345	15	.275	.332	.481	323	7	.217	.251	.344
1988	Pit-N	812	21	.239	.286	.366	7	3	0	103	3.22	8	4	0	116	2.95	5	5	0	104	4.23	10	2	0	115	2.03	375	6	.237	.290	.325	437	15	.240	.283	.400
1989	Pit-N	902	21	.238	.293	.350	8	5	0	136	1.85	6	7	0	108	3.99	5	5	0	113	2.24	9	7	0	132	3.28	492	7	.250	.311	.339	410	14	.224	.270	.363
1990	Pit-N	846	15	.225	.274	.331	11	3	0	120	3.00	11	3	0	111	2.51	8	4	0	97	3.26	14	2	0	135	2.41	532	10	.244	.290	.370	314	5	.191	.248	.264
1991	Pit-N	894	16	.274	.321	.385	9	8	0	131	2.40	6	6	0	104	3.91	6	8	0	106	2.96	9	6	0	128	3.16	530	8	.287	.337	.391	364	8	.255	.298	.376
1992	Pit-N	945	17	.231	.274	.330	8	3	0	111	2.44	7	8	0	146	3.02	6	6	0	123	3.00	9	5	0	134	2.56	548	11	.261	.314	.370	397	6	.189	.217	.275
1993	Hou-N	906	18	.267	.312	.381	5	8	0	142	3.04	4	10	0	95	4.91	6	8	0	126	3.29	3	10	0	112	4.34	459	11	.288	.337	.427	447	7	.246	.287	.333
1994	Hou-N	599	14	.220	.275	.331	6	5	0	87	3.50	6	1	0	77	2.09	10	4	0	119	2.80	2	2	0	46	2.96	305	6	.220	.283	.318	294	8	.221	.266	.344
1995	Hou-N	728	18	.282	.337	.427	4	6	0	100	3.95	6	3	0	85	5.74	4	5	0	76	4.62	6	4	0	109	4.87	378	10	.291	.345	.442	350	8	.271	.327	.411
1996	Hou-N	699	21	.298	.355	.455	5	4	0	94	3.64	2	5	0	81	5.64	3	6	0	89	5.06	4	3	0	86	4.07	314	10	.277	.349	.449	385	11	.314	.360	.460
1997	Chi-A	652	30	.261	.334	.474	9	4	0	95	5.66	3	7	0	74	5.84	6	5	0	82	6.83	6	6	0	88	4.72	308	12	.260	.360	.442	344	18	.262	.309	.503
1998	Bal-A	443	20	.312	.355	.506	4	5	0	61	7.27	2	6	0	48	7.31	5	8	0	73	7.12	1	3	0	35	7.64	239	5	.318	.355	.452	204	15	.304	.356	.569
TOTALS		9595	246	.255	.308	.389	84	62	0	1322	3.41	71	72	0	1213	4.09	65	72	0	1199	4.00	90	62	0	1336	3.50	5084	120	.267	.325	.398	4511	126	.242	.288	.378
● **Darren Dreifort** BR/TR																																				
1994	LA-N	126	0	.357	.441	.421	0	0	2	11	0.79	0	5	4	18	9.68	0	5	6	29	6.21	0	0	0	0	—	57	0	.316	.418	.421	69	0	.391	.462	.420
1996	LA-N	90	2	.256	.340	.367	0	3	0	11	9.00	1	1	0	13	1.42	0	0	0	0	—	1	4	0	24	4.94	42	1	.310	.348	.429	48	1	.208	.333	.313
1997	LA-N	223	3	.202	.308	.296	4	0	2	34	2.38	1	2	2	29	3.41	2	0	1	19	2.84	3	2	3	44	2.86	103	0	.184	.306	.223	120	3	.217	.309	.358
1998	LA-N	668	12	.256	.321	.377	4	7	0	100	5.13	4	5	0	80	2.59	5	6	0	106	3.55	3	6	0	74	4.64	353	5	.280	.354	.414	315	7	.229	.283	.337
1999	LA-N	680	20	.260	.340	.403	7	6	0	98	4.79	6	7	0	81	4.78	6	6	0	81	5.67	7	7	0	98	4.05	308	11	.273	.351	.451	372	9	.250	.331	.363
2000	LA-N	734	31	.238	.329	.424	6	5	0	97	4.44	6	4	0	95	3.87	4	7	0	93	4.94	8	2	0	100	3.43	356	19	.264	.350	.492	378	12	.214	.309	.360
TOTALS		2521	68	.252	.334	.392	21	21	4	351	4.56	18	24	6	316	3.96	17	24	7	328	4.66	22	21	3	339	3.91	1219	36	.268	.351	.431	1302	32	.237	.318	.356
● **Dennis Eckersley** BR/TR																																				
1978	Bos-A	1028	30	.251	.302	.383	11	1	0	134	2.75	9	7	0	134	3.28	8	2	0	121	3.12	12	6	0	147	2.93	582	19	.280	.333	.431	446	11	.213	.260	.321
1979	Bos-A	936	29	.250	.297	.393	12	5	0	138	2.54	5	5	0	108	3.57	8	3	0	116	3.02	9	7	0	130	2.97	477	19	.289	.333	.455	459	10	.209	.260	.329
1980	Bos-A	757	25	.248	.289	.399	4	8	0	83	5.86	8	6	0	115	3.14	4	5	0	63	4.31	8	9	0	135	4.27	409	16	.286	.325	.465	348	9	.204	.245	.322
1981	Bos-A	600	9	.267	.308	.367	4	6	0	78	4.87	5	2	0	76	3.66	5	4	0	82	4.39	4	4	0	72	4.13	331	4	.290	.331	.384	269	5	.238	.278	.346
1982	Bos-A	873	31	.261	.296	.435	8	7	0	129	4.06	5	6	0	96	3.29	8	6	0	114	3.32	5	7	0	110	4.16	475	19	.259	.300	.434	398	12	.264	.291	.437
1983	Bos-A	736	27	.303	.341	.497	6	7	0	104	5.52	3	6	0	72	5.75	5	5	0	79	4.88	4	8	0	97	6.22	368	15	.315	.350	.527	368	12	.291	.332	.467
1984	Bos-A	250	10	.284	.318	.480	2	2	0	27	6.00	2	2	0	38	4.30	4	4	0	65	5.01	0	0	0	0	—	132	6	.288	.324	.515	118	4	.280	.312	.441
1984	Chi-N	608	11	.250	.294	.362	7	5	0	84	3.23	3	3	0	77	2.82	1	5	0	42	5.57	9	3	0	118	2.13	319	5	.270	.318	.392	289	6	.228	.266	.329
1985	Chi-N	634	15	.229	.254	.352	5	2	0	70	3.45	6	5	0	99	2.82	7	5	0	113	2.95	4	2	0	56	3.36	324	11	.256	.282	.414	310	4	.200	.224	.287
1986	Chi-N	793	21	.285	.320	.455	4	5	0	83	5.18	2	6	0	118	4.13	2	4	0	95	5.66	4	7	0	106	3.58	425	9	.301	.347	.471	368	12	.266	.289	.438
1987	Oak-A	434	11	.228	.260	.362	6	3	8	62	1.31	0	5	8	54	5.03	5	4	3	67	2.81	1	4	13	48	3.35	184	5	.272	.313	.429	250	6	.196	.220	.312
1988	Oak-A	263	5	.198	.230	.270	3	1	22	39	2.33	1	1	23	34	2.38	2	1	23	37	1.70	2	1	22	36	3.03	126	3	.198	.229	.286	137	2	.197	.231	.255
1989	Oak-A	198	5	.162	.175	.258	2	0	19	31	2.01	2	0	14	26	1.03	1	0	14	19	1.45	3	0	19	39	1.62	97	1	.206	.218	.258	101	4	.119	.133	.257
1990	Oak-A	257	2	.160	.172	.226	3	2	22	35	1.02	1	0	26	38	0.24	2	1	24	33	0.54	2	1	24	40	0.68	119	1	.168	.180	.244	138	1	.152	.164	.210
1991	Oak-A	288	11	.208	.235	.365	5	1	18	39	1.83	0	3	25	37	4.17	1	1	22	35	2.08	4	3	21	41	3.70	150	5	.227	.261	.353	138	6	.188	.206	.377
1992	Oak-A	294	5	.211	.242	.306	7	0	21	42	2.76	0	1	30	38	0.96	2	0	27	39	1.86	5	1	24	41	1.96	149	3	.262	.299	.369	145	2	.159	.181	.241
1993	Oak-A	257	7	.261	.299	.405	1	3	19	38	3.08	1	1	17	29	5.59	2	1	16	31	4.31	0	3	20	36	4.04	129	5	.326	.367	.543	128	2	.195	.230	.266
1994	Oak-A	178	5	.275	.328	.455	4	3	7	23	3.57	1	1	12	22	4.98	2	3	11	29	4.97	3	1	8	15	2.93	87	2	.322	.398	.483	91	3	.231	.255	.429
1995	Oak-A	197	5	.269	.308	.406	3	3	19	25	5.68	1	3	10	25	3.96	1	2	16	26	3.12	3	4	13	24	6.66	122	3	.344	.383	.500	75	2	.147	.179	.253
1996	StL-N	237	8	.274	.300	.426	0	1	14	33	2.70	0	5	16	27	4.05	0	5	11	27	3.71	0	1	19	33	2.97	99	4	.293	.304	.485	138	4	.261	.297	.384
1997	StL-N	206	9	.238	.273	.427	0	5	20	29	5.02	1	0	16	24	2.59	0	2	17	24	3.70	1	3	19	29	4.08	105	2	.210	.245	.333	101	7	.267	.302	.525
1998	Bos-A	158	6	.291	.331	.462	3	1	1	22	7.48	1	0	0	18	1.50	2	1	1	20	6.75	2	0	0	20	2.75	46	4	.304	.407	.630	112	2	.286	.296	.393
TOTALS		10182	287	.251	.289	.394	100	71	190	1349	3.70	57	68	197	1303	3.44	72	64	185	1277	3.66	85	75	202	1375	3.48	5255	161	.276	.318	.433	4927	126	.225	.258	.353
● **Alan Embree** BL/TL																																				
1992	Cle-A	70	3	.271	.346	.471	0	1	0	10	7.20	0	1	0	8	6.75	0	0	0	0	—	0	2	0	18	7.00	10	0	.100	.308	.100	60	3	.300	.353	.533
1995	Cle-A	91	2	.253	.358	.385	3	1	0	13	4.05	0	1	1	11	6.35	0	0	0	0	—	3	2	1	25	5.11	23	1	.217	.357	.435	68	1	.265	.358	.368
1996	Cle-A	116	10	.259	.364	.595	1	0	0	13	4.26	0	1	0	18	7.85	1	1	0	22	5.82	0	0	0	9	7.71	43	0	.186	.294	.233	73	10	.301	.404	.808
1997	Atl-N	163	1	.221	.312	.264	3	0	0	27	2.96	0	1	0	19	1.93	1	1	0	23	2.78	2	0	0	23	2.31	73	1	.247	.333	.288	90	0	.200	.294	.244
1998	Atl-N	75	2	.307	.384	.440	1	0	0	9	7.00	0	0	0	10	1.86	1	0	0	19	4.34	0	0	0	0	—	27	1	.259	.310	.407	48	1	.333	.421	.458
1998	Ari-N	133	5	.248	.320	.421	2	2	1	25	2.92	1	0	0	10	6.97	1	0	0	6	4.50	2	2	1	29	4.03	50	2	.260	.302	.420	83	3	.241	.330	.422
1999	SF-N	210	6	.200	.295	.314	2	0	0	32	2.27	1	2	0	27	4.67	3	0	0	29	3.07	0	2	0	29	3.68	90	4	.200	.318	.356	120	2	.200	.276	.283
2000	SF-N	226	4	.274	.347	.389	0	2	2	29	3.14	3	3	0	31	6.61	0	2	1	33	6.21	3	3	1	27	3.38	91	2	.286	.349	.407	135	2	.267	.346	.378
TOTALS		1084	33	.247	.334	.390	12	6	3	157	3.55	5	9	1	135	5.41	7	4	1	132	4.51	10	11	3	160	4.32	407	11	.236	.325	.351	677	22	.254	.339	.414
● **Scott Erickson** BR/TR																																				
1990	Min-A	422	9	.256	.342	.367	7	2	0	78	3.45	1	2	0	35	1.56	1	1	0	12	2.92	7	3	0	101	2.86	224	4	.246	.329	.348	198	5	.268	.356	.389
1991	Min-A	762	13	.248	.314	.364	10	3	0	97	3.53	10	5	0	107	2.86	12	3	0	123	1.83	8	5	0	81	5.20	417	8	.295	.363	.424	345	5	.191	.255	.290
1992	Min-A	781	18	.252	.328	.371	8	6	0	123	3.43	5	6	0	89	3.35	6	5	0	89	4.47	7	7	0	123	2.63	410	7	.241	.311	.337	371	11	.264	.345	.410
1993	Min-A	872	17	.305	.359	.431	4	11	0	127	5.30	4	8	0	91	5.03	4	9	0	99	5.80	4	10	0	119	4.68	474	7	.342	.392	.481	398	10	.261	.320	.372
1994	Min-A	579	15	.299	.370	.449	6	3	0	70	4.13	2	8	0	74	6.66	7	5	0	92	5.07	1	6	0	52	6.10	308	10	.338	.415	.513	271	5	.255	.318	.376
1995	Min-A	351	11	.291	.356	.464	1	4	0	30	7.89	3	2	0	58	4.97	3	6	0	80	6.44	1	0	0	8	1.13	220	7	.286	.339	.441	131	4	.298	.383	.504
1995	Bal-A	407	7	.273	.330	.388	5	1	0	56	3.70	4	3	0	53	4.10	0	0	0	0	—	9	4	0	109	3.89	254	3	.291	.354	.394	153	4	.242	.291	.379
1996	Bal-A	881	21	.297	.352	.445	6	5	0	108	4.76	7	7	0	115	5.26	4	6	0	98	4.88	9	6	0	125	5.13	475	10	.322	.370	.467	406	11	.268	.332	.419
1997	Bal-A	849	16	.257	.309	.362	8	4	0	109	3.29	8	3	0	112	4.09	10	3	0	104	3.29	6	4	0	118	4.05	452	10	.248	.302	.369	397	6	.267	.317	.353
1998	Bal-A	1011	23	.281	.334	.401	9	6	0	130	3.73	7	7	0	121	4.31	8	6	0	132	4.43	8	7	0	119	3.54	566	12	.309	.368	.443	445	11	.245	.290	.346
1999	Bal-A	872	27	.280	.358	.432	7	4	0	106	4.49	8	8	0	124	5.08	3	8	0	96	6.66	12	4	0	134	3.48	440	14	.270	.370	.420	432	13	.289	.345	.444
2000	Bal-A	384	14	.331	.407	.505	3	3	0	34	8.47	2	5	0	59	7.52	3	6	0	64	7.77	2	2	0	29	8.07	191	8	.387	.463	.571	193	6	.275	.349	.440
TOTALS		8171	191	.279	.344	.410	74	52	0	1069	4.27	61	64	0	1037	4.60	61	58	0	988	4.81	74	58	0	1118	4.10	4431	100	.296	.362	.431	3740	91	.259	.321	.386
● **Shawn Estes** BR/TL																																				
1995	SF-N	70	2	.229	.289	.343	0	2	0	12	6.00	0	1	0	5	8.44	0	0	0	0	—	0	3	0	17	6.75	8	0	.250	.455	.250	62	2	.226	.262	.355
1996	SF-N	259	3	.243	.347	.336	1	2	0	31	4.02	2	3	0	39	3.26	0	0	0	0	—	3	5	0	70	3.60	31	0	.258	.378	.258	228	3	.241	.342	.346
1997	SF-N	726	12	.223	.323	.311	11	1	0	104	2.33	8	4	0	97	4.10	11	2	0	103	2.72	8	3	0	98	3.66	162	1	.241	.363	.309	564	11	.218	.311	.312
1998	SF-N	557	14	.269	.364	.397	6	3	0	74	2.66	1	9	0	75	7.44	6	7	0	116	4.28	1	5	0	34	7.75	93	2	.247	.369	.366	464	12	.274	.363	.403
1999	SF-N	780	21	.268	.362	.403	7	5	0	111	3.72	4	6	0	92	6.38	4	5	0	89	4.77	7	6	0	114	5.04	122	4	.270	.359	.418	658	17	.267	.363	.400
2000	SF-N	705	11	.275	.371	.377	9	4	0	93	3.21	6	2	0	98	5.25	7	3	0	85	3.81	8	3	0	105	4.61	102	1	.216	.328	.314	603	10	.285	.379	.388
TOTALS		3097	63	.256	.353	.367	34	17	0	426	3.17	21	25	0	405	5.49	28	17	0	392	3.88	27	25	0	439	4.67	518	8	.245	.359	.342	2579	55	.259	.351	.373
● **Jeff Fassero** BL/TL																																				
1991	Mon-N	199	1	.196	.263	.266	2	2	3	29	2.17	0	3	5	26	2.73	1	1	2	17	1.59	1	4	6	38	2.82	70	0	.243	.293	.329	129	1	.171	.246	.233
1992	Mon-N	325	1	.249	.322	.326	6	3	0	40	4.05	2	4	1	46	1.77	3	4	1	48	2.79	5	3	0	37	2.89	93	1	.269	.320	.344	232	0	.241	.323	.319
1993	Mon-N	551	7	.216	.284	.290	7	1	1	68	2.00	5	4	0	82	2.52	5	1	1	49	2.37	7	4	0	100	2.24	114	1	.184	.275	.246	437	6	.224	.287	.302
1994	Mon-N	519	13	.229	.285	.349	4	3	0	70	3.99	4	3	0	69	1.97	6	5	0	112	3.20	2	1	0	26	2.05	93	2	.204	.272	.312	426	11	.235	.288	.357
1995	Mon-N	731	15	.283	.348	.420	6	10	0	110	4.65	7	4	0	79	3.89	7	5	0	77	3.51	6	9	0	112	4.90	108	0	.185	.229	.231	623	15	.300	.368	.453
1996	Mon-N	888	20	.244	.289	.361	8	5	0	117	2.77	7	6	0	115	3.85	8	5	0	116	3.18	7	6	0	116	3.42	111	0	.234	.271	.270	777	20	.246	.292	.375
1997	Sea-A	906	21	.249	.312	.385	6	5	0	108	3.85	10	4	0	127	3.41	8	3	0	116	3.65	8	6	0	118	3.57	175	2	.263	.323	.354	731	19	.246	.309	.393
1998	Sea-A	862	33	.259	.316	.436	6	5	0	100	4.24	7	7	0	125	3.74	6	5	0	97	4.25	7	7	0	127	3.75	170	2	.288	.351	.394	692	31	.251	.307	.447
1999	Sea-A	585	34	.321	.397	.573	2	6	0	67	7.35	2	8	0	72	7.41	3	8	0	99	7.21	1	6	0	40	7.81	127	3	.252	.336	.362	458	31	.341	.414	.631
1999	Tex-A	70	1	.286	.370	.400	1	0	0	9	2.89	0	0	0	8	9.00	0	0	0	0	—	1	0	0	17	5.71	13	0	.462	.467	.538	57	1	.246	.348	.368

		TOTAL					HOME					AWAY					1ST HALF					2ND HALF					LEFT					RIGHT				
YEAR	TM/L	AB	HR	AVG	OBP	SLG	W	L	SV	IP	ERA	W	L	SV	IP	ERA	W	L	SV	IP	ERA	W	L	SV	IP	ERA	AB	HR	AVG	OBP	SLG	AB	HR	AVG	OBP	SLG
2000	Bos-A	517	16	.296	.358	.451	6	4	0	78	4.06	2	4	0	52	5.85	6	3	0	68	4.35	2	5	0	62	5.25	106	2	.255	.307	.377	411	14	.307	.371	.470
TOTALS		6153	162	.259	.321	.398	54	44	4	796	3.96	46	47	6	800	3.82	53	40	4	800	3.90	47	51	6	795	3.87	1180	13	.244	.305	.330	4973	149	.262	.325	.414
● **Alex Fernandez** BR/TR																																				
1990	Chi-A	336	6	.265	.338	.360	2	1	0	27	3.67	3	4	0	61	3.86	0	0	0	0	—	5	5	0	88	3.80	176	3	.273	.340	.369	160	3	.256	.335	.350
1991	Chi-A	719	16	.259	.337	.388	5	7	0	96	4.48	4	6	0	95	4.53	4	7	0	86	5.63	5	6	0	105	3.59	330	4	.252	.331	.355	389	12	.265	.342	.416
1992	Chi-A	736	21	.270	.322	.405	4	7	0	111	4.39	4	4	0	77	4.09	3	7	0	94	4.23	5	4	0	94	4.31	351	9	.251	.295	.385	385	12	.288	.346	.423
1993	Chi-A	919	27	.240	.295	.381	9	4	0	119	2.79	9	5	0	128	3.45	8	4	0	118	2.90	10	5	0	129	3.34	437	15	.261	.313	.430	482	12	.222	.280	.336
1994	Chi-A	651	25	.250	.302	.415	8	1	0	89	2.23	3	6	0	82	5.62	6	7	0	111	4.14	5	0	0	59	3.34	325	14	.240	.309	.418	326	11	.261	.295	.411
1995	Chi-A	783	19	.255	.310	.391	8	3	0	114	3.39	4	5	0	90	4.32	4	4	0	75	5.14	8	4	0	128	3.02	414	11	.278	.338	.437	369	8	.230	.279	.339
1996	Chi-A	980	34	.253	.307	.397	7	7	0	130	3.74	9	3	0	128	3.16	7	4	0	116	3.97	9	6	0	142	3.04	535	18	.258	.306	.396	445	16	.247	.308	.398
1997	Fla-N	812	25	.238	.299	.401	7	6	0	92	4.39	10	6	0	128	3.02	9	6	0	109	3.48	8	6	0	112	3.70	386	13	.293	.351	.487	426	12	.188	.251	.324
1999	Fla-N	536	10	.252	.307	.382	5	4	0	96	2.92	2	4	0	45	4.37	2	5	0	65	3.44	5	3	0	76	3.33	283	7	.276	.331	.431	253	3	.225	.279	.328
2000	Fla-N	202	7	.292	.342	.455	3	3	0	39	3.43	1	1	0	13	6.23	4	4	0	52	4.13	0	0	0	0	—	84	3	.250	.289	.452	118	4	.322	.380	.458
TOTALS		6674	190	.254	.312	.395	58	43	0	913	3.55	49	44	0	847	3.94	47	48	0	826	4.05	60	39	0	934	3.46	3321	97	.264	.321	.416	3353	93	.244	.302	.374
● **Sid Fernandez** BL/TL																																				
1983	LA-N	25	0	.280	.455	.400	0	1	0	6	6.00	0	0	0	0	—	0	0	0	0	—	0	1	0	6	6.00	4	0	.250	.500	.500	21	0	.286	.444	.381
1984	NY-N	327	8	.226	.295	.370	3	3	0	40	3.57	3	3	0	50	3.44	0	0	0	0	—	6	6	0	90	3.50	65	1	.200	.246	.262	262	7	.233	.306	.397
1985	NY-N	596	14	.181	.279	.302	5	4	0	71	2.67	4	5	0	100	2.89	2	4	0	56	2.75	7	5	0	115	2.83	92	2	.163	.222	.326	504	12	.185	.289	.298
1986	NY-N	746	13	.216	.300	.324	8	3	1	108	2.17	8	3	0	97	5.03	9	2	0	95	3.12	7	4	1	109	3.88	97	1	.227	.350	.289	649	12	.214	.292	.330
1987	NY-N	581	16	.224	.310	.363	9	3	0	94	2.98	3	5	0	62	5.05	9	4	0	97	3.17	3	4	0	59	4.85	71	2	.225	.291	.408	510	14	.224	.312	.357
1988	NY-N	666	15	.191	.271	.305	8	4	0	98	1.83	4	6	0	89	4.36	4	6	0	85	3.71	8	4	0	102	2.47	72	1	.236	.325	.347	594	14	.185	.264	.300
1989	NY-N	794	21	.198	.271	.334	7	2	0	130	2.78	7	3	0	90	2.91	5	2	0	85	3.16	9	3	0	134	2.62	117	2	.197	.258	.299	677	19	.198	.273	.340
1990	NY-N	650	18	.200	.277	.340	8	5	0	105	2.41	1	9	0	75	4.94	5	5	0	76	3.57	4	9	0	104	3.39	124	3	.226	.322	.363	526	15	.194	.267	.335
1991	NY-N	162	4	.222	.262	.327	1	1	0	19	1.42	0	2	0	25	3.96	0	0	0	0	—	1	3	0	44	2.86	35	1	.371	.389	.457	127	3	.181	.228	.291
1992	NY-N	771	12	.210	.273	.328	7	4	0	99	2.17	7	7	0	115	3.20	6	7	0	101	3.03	8	4	0	114	2.45	152	0	.184	.267	.289	619	12	.216	.275	.338
1993	NY-N	426	17	.192	.260	.338	2	2	0	58	3.24	3	4	0	61	2.64	1	0	0	28	4.13	4	6	0	91	2.56	81	2	.185	.298	.284	345	15	.194	.250	.351
1994	Bal-A	439	27	.248	.320	.508	3	4	0	63	4.69	3	2	0	52	5.71	4	4	0	81	4.44	2	2	0	34	6.82	55	1	.255	.305	.382	384	26	.247	.323	.526
1995	Bal-A	118	9	.305	.390	.619	0	1	0	11	4.22	0	3	0	17	9.35	0	4	0	27	7.67	0	0	0	1	0.00	12	1	.250	.308	.500	106	8	.311	.398	.632
1995	Phi-N	240	11	.200	.267	.371	4	0	0	36	3.79	2	1	0	29	2.79	0	0	0	0	—	6	1	0	65	3.34	39	0	.103	.167	.103	201	11	.219	.286	.423
1996	Phi-N	233	5	.215	.294	.339	1	3	0	37	1.95	2	3	0	26	5.54	3	6	0	63	3.43	0	0	0	0	—	32	1	.313	.361	.406	201	4	.199	.283	.328
1997	Hou-N	19	1	.211	.286	.421	1	0	0	5	3.60	0	0	0	0	—	1	0	0	5	3.60	0	0	0	0	—	4	1	.250	.250	1.000	15	0	.200	.294	.267
TOTALS		6793	191	.209	.286	.350	67	40	1	979	2.73	47	56	0	887	4.05	49	44	0	799	3.55	65	52	1	1068	3.21	1052	19	.212	.291	.325	5741	172	.209	.285	.354
● **Chuck Finley** BL/TL																																				
1986	Cal-A	170	2	.235	.330	.306	1	0	0	26	4.50	2	1	0	20	1.77	1	0	0	10	5.23	2	1	0	36	2.75	78	0	.269	.360	.308	92	2	.207	.305	.304
1987	Cal-A	355	7	.287	.367	.411	2	4	0	41	5.23	0	3	0	49	4.20	0	3	0	33	4.91	2	4	0	58	4.53	135	1	.259	.299	.356	220	6	.305	.405	.445
1988	Cal-A	726	15	.263	.339	.384	5	8	0	95	4.44	4	7	0	99	3.91	5	8	0	105	3.77	4	7	0	89	4.63	135	1	.289	.374	.370	591	14	.257	.330	.387
1989	Cal-A	733	13	.233	.311	.334	8	7	0	113	2.23	8	2	0	87	3.01	9	6	0	116	2.33	7	3	0	84	2.89	99	0	.172	.252	.192	634	13	.243	.320	.356
1990	Cal-A	864	17	.243	.308	.351	11	4	0	132	1.63	7	5	0	104	3.39	10	4	0	100	2.62	8	5	0	136	2.24	121	0	.256	.333	.273	743	17	.241	.304	.363
1991	Cal-A	839	23	.244	.330	.385	9	3	0	125	3.03	9	6	0	103	4.73	11	3	0	106	3.72	7	6	0	121	3.87	109	4	.257	.336	.422	730	19	.242	.329	.379
1992	Cal-A	762	24	.278	.359	.425	3	5	0	105	3.93	4	7	0	99	4.00	2	8	0	78	5.63	5	4	0	126	2.93	87	1	.402	.441	.517	675	23	.262	.349	.413
1993	Cal-A	959	22	.253	.314	.364	8	5	0	123	2.79	8	9	0	129	3.50	9	5	0	114	2.69	7	9	0	138	3.53	128	2	.313	.381	.414	831	20	.244	.303	.356
1994	Cal-A	685	21	.260	.329	.413	4	6	0	106	4.50	6	4	0	77	4.07	5	8	0	126	4.13	5	2	0	57	4.74	111	5	.288	.392	.477	574	16	.254	.317	.401
1995	Cal-A	771	20	.249	.333	.387	9	5	0	106	3.55	6	7	0	97	4.93	6	6	0	89	3.15	9	6	0	114	5.04	113	1	.248	.312	.292	658	19	.249	.337	.403
1996	Cal-A	916	27	.263	.336	.404	12	6	0	140	3.29	3	10	0	98	5.40	9	6	0	118	4.73	6	10	0	120	3.60	124	5	.234	.309	.403	792	22	.268	.340	.404
1997	Ana-A	613	20	.248	.323	.387	8	1	0	83	3.36	5	5	0	81	5.11	3	6	0	87	5.71	10	0	0	77	2.56	61	0	.164	.338	.197	552	20	.257	.321	.408
1998	Ana-A	853	20	.246	.334	.374	5	5	0	123	2.56	6	4	0	100	4.40	8	4	0	124	3.05	3	5	0	99	3.81	174	5	.253	.362	.379	679	15	.244	.326	.373
1999	Ana-A	801	23	.246	.330	.386	4	4	0	99	4.56	8	7	0	115	4.32	4	8	0	101	5.17	8	3	0	112	3.77	158	3	.234	.324	.335	643	20	.249	.331	.398
2000	Cle-A	824	23	.256	.337	.392	10	3	0	107	3.20	6	8	0	111	5.11	6	5	0	108	3.99	10	6	0	110	4.35	172	4	.238	.302	.355	652	19	.261	.346	.402
TOTALS		10871	277	.253	.331	.383	99	66	0	1524	3.32	82	85	0	1369	4.25	88	80	0	1415	3.87	93	71	0	1478	3.65	1805	32	.259	.339	.358	9066	245	.252	.329	.388
● **Mike Flanagan** BL/TL																																				
1978	Bal-A	1053	22	.257	.314	.377	12	6	0	162	2.94	7	9	0	119	5.52	11	5	0	139	3.30	8	10	0	142	4.74	289	6	.242	.303	.339	764	16	.263	.319	.391
1979	Bal-A	998	23	.245	.296	.364	14	2	0	137	2.50	9	7	0	129	3.71	10	5	0	124	3.64	13	4	0	142	2.60	181	6	.243	.302	.387	817	17	.246	.295	.359
1980	Bal-A	970	27	.287	.333	.429	6	6	0	106	4.50	10	7	0	145	3.84	7	6	0	129	3.71	9	7	0	123	4.55	172	6	.262	.310	.413	798	21	.292	.338	.432
1981	Bal-A	443	11	.244	.305	.386	6	2	0	63	3.59	3	4	0	53	4.89	7	4	0	87	3.61	2	2	0	29	5.97	94	3	.181	.287	.287	349	8	.261	.310	.413
1982	Bal-A	900	24	.259	.317	.386	9	4	0	120	3.75	6	7	0	116	4.19	6	6	0	105	3.25	9	5	0	131	4.55	174	1	.167	.225	.213	726	23	.281	.339	.427
1983	Bal-A	485	10	.278	.321	.390	8	3	0	75	3.50	4	1	0	51	3.02	6	0	0	53	2.72	6	4	0	72	3.73	87	1	.230	.295	.310	398	9	.289	.326	.407
1984	Bal-A	851	24	.250	.314	.375	8	4	0	109	2.90	5	9	0	118	4.12	8	5	0	111	3.56	5	8	0	115	3.51	164	3	.207	.258	.293	687	21	.261	.327	.394
1985	Bal-A	340	14	.297	.352	.485	2	2	0	32	6.40	2	3	0	54	4.36	0	0	0	0	—	4	5	0	86	5.13	49	0	.306	.346	.388	291	14	.296	.353	.502
1986	Bal-A	664	15	.270	.334	.410	5	2	0	72	3.73	2	9	0	100	4.61	1	5	0	69	4.33	6	6	0	103	4.18	129	1	.248	.312	.349	535	14	.275	.339	.424
1987	Bal-A	367	9	.278	.342	.441	2	2	0	49	4.01	1	4	0	45	5.96	0	5	0	41	6.53	3	1	0	53	3.71	50	0	.280	.357	.320	317	9	.278	.339	.461
1987	Tor-A	194	3	.237	.292	.345	3	1	0	32	2.25	0	1	0	17	2.60	0	0	0	0	—	3	2	0	49	2.37	50	0	.220	.264	.220	144	3	.243	.301	.389
1988	Tor-A	812	23	.271	.339	.424	6	6	0	108	3.76	7	7	0	103	4.62	7	5	0	104	4.25	6	8	0	107	4.11	115	3	.270	.320	.426	697	20	.271	.342	.423
1989	Tor-A	658	10	.283	.331	.406	5	4	0	85	3.51	3	6	0	87	4.34	4	6	0	83	3.67	4	4	0	88	4.18	97	0	.206	.279	.237	561	10	.296	.341	.435
1990	Tor-A	85	3	.329	.387	.471	2	1	0	16	5.06	0	1	0	4	6.23	2	2	0	20	5.31	0	0	0	0	—	10	1	.300	.364	.600	75	2	.333	.390	.453
1991	Bal-A	356	6	.236	.289	.323	0	5	0	45	3.18	2	2	3	53	1.70	1	3	1	53	2.55	1	4	2	45	2.18	127	2	.181	.221	.236	229	4	.266	.327	.371
1992	Bal-A	148	3	.338	.438	.453	0	0	0	14	7.71	0	0	0	21	8.27	0	0	0	17	10.38	0	0	0	17	5.71	62	0	.274	.378	.274	86	3	.384	.481	.581
TOTALS		9324	227	.266	.323	.397	88	50	0	1225	3.53	61	77	3	1215	4.30	70	57	1	1136	3.80	79	70	2	1304	4.02	1850	33	.230	.291	.321	7474	194	.275	.331	.416
● **Bob Forsch** BR/TR																																				
1978	StL-N	862	15	.238	.316	.353	5	11	0	143	3.21	6	6	0	91	4.47	9	6	0	127	3.18	2	11	0	106	4.32	375	4	.264	.333	.357	487	11	.218	.303	.349
1979	StL-N	819	16	.263	.304	.389	4	4	0	110	4.10	7	7	0	109	3.55	3	8	0	104	4.85	8	3	0	115	2.90	351	7	.271	.313	.396	468	9	.256	.298	.385
1980	StL-N	822	12	.274	.302	.393	8	5	0	116	3.33	3	5	0	98	4.30	5	5	0	104	4.43	6	5	0	111	3.16	338	4	.272	.301	.370	484	8	.275	.303	.409
1981	StL-N	457	7	.232	.281	.348	6	3	0	64	3.25	4	2	0	61	3.12	6	2	0	60	3.17	4	3	0	65	3.20	220	2	.241	.285	.327	237	5	.224	.278	.367
1982	StL-N	889	16	.268	.310	.393	11	2	0	134	3.16	4	7	1	99	3.90	8	4	1	113	4.29	7	5	0	120	2.71	413	8	.283	.335	.416	476	8	.254	.289	.372
1983	StL-N	714	23	.266	.317	.429	6	5	0	103	3.51	4	7	0	84	5.23	5	7	0	98	4.68	5	5	0	89	3.84	334	10	.249	.294	.416	380	13	.282	.337	.439
1984	StL-N	211	6	.303	.358	.474	1	3	0	21	6.97	1	2	0	32	5.40	1	4	0	42	5.62	1	1	0	11	7.59	99	2	.293	.383	.465	112	4	.313	.333	.482
1985	StL-N	512	11	.258	.322	.377	5	3	0	74	3.54	4	3	2	62	4.33	4	4	1	56	4.31	5	2	1	80	3.62	203	0	.241	.299	.296	309	11	.269	.337	.430
1986	StL-N	855	19	.247	.301	.374	8	4	0	125	2.66	6	6	0	105	3.94	6	4	0	108	2.42	8	6	0	122	3.97	423	10	.262	.330	.392	432	9	.231	.271	.356
1987	StL-N	693	15	.273	.318	.410	3	4	0	69	4.54	8	3	0	110	4.19	6	3	0	80	5.29	5	4	0	99	3.55	375	4	.264	.313	.363	318	11	.283	.324	.465
1988	StL-N	411	8	.270	.330	.389	6	2	0	69	2.47	3	2	0	39	5.95	4	3	0	51	4.09	5	1	0	58	3.41	170	1	.212	.275	.282	241	7	.311	.370	.465
1988	Hou-N	117	2	.359	.385	.487	1	2	0	15	4.30	0	2	0	13	9.00	0	0	0	0	—	1	4	0	28	6.51	68	0	.294	.329	.338	49	2	.449	.471	.694
1989	Hou-N	439	10	.303	.367	.435	2	1	0	57	4.92	2	4	0	52	5.75	1	2	0	59	4.10	3	3	0	49	6.80	253	6	.304	.379	.447	186	4	.301	.350	.419
TOTALS		7801	160	.264	.316	.393	66	49	0	1098	3.51	52	56	3	955	4.39	58	52	2	1002	4.11	60	53	1	1052	3.74	3622	58	.265	.320	.379	4179	102	.263	.312	.405
● **Tony Fossas** BL/TL																																				
1988	Tex-A	26	0	.423	.464	.615	0	0	0	4	7.36	0	0	0	2	0.00	0	0	0	6	4.76	0	0	0	0	—	6	0	.167	.375	.167	20	0	.500	.500	.750
1989	Mil-A	223	3	.256	.321	.341	2	0	1	39	2.79	0	2	0	22	4.84	1	0	0	17	2.65	1	2	1	44	3.89	82	1	.183	.253	.220	141	2	.298	.361	.411
1990	Mil-A	133	5	.331	.375	.504	0	0	0	16	4.50	2	3	0	13	8.77	2	3	0	25	5.84	0	0	0	5	9.64	40	1	.300	.349	.375	93	4	.344	.386	.559
1991	Bos-A	208	3	.236	.335	.327	1	0	1	22	2.45	2	2	0	35	4.11	0	1	0	24	2.66	3	1	1	33	4.05	84	2	.190	.277	.298	124	1	.266	.372	.347
1992	Bos-A	111	1	.279	.365	.414	1	2	1	19	1.40	0	0	1	10	4.35	0	1	1	12	4.63	1	1	1	18	1.00	56	0	.214	.254	.321	55	1	.345	.463	.509
1993	Bos-A	157	4	.242	.314	.363	1	1	0	22	3.68	0	0	0	18	7.00	0	0	0	15	4.20	1	1	0	25	5.76	68	0	.132	.211	.162	89	4	.326	.394	.517
1994	Bos-A	133	6	.263	.342	.474	1	0	0	17	3.12	1	0	1	17	6.48	2	0	1	18	5.50	0	0	0	16	3.94	55	1	.182	.286	.273	78	5	.321	.384	.615
1995	StL-N	131	1	.214	.273	.290	2	0	0	20	0.44	1	0	0	16	2.76	1	0	0	18	1.02	2	0	0	19	1.89	72	0	.181	.203	.250	59	1	.254	.348	.339
1996	StL-N	186	7	.231	.308	.376	0	2	1	25	2.19	0	2	1	22	3.22	0	4	1	25	3.24	0	0	1	22	2.05	91	4	.231	.290	.385	95	3	.232	.324	.368
1997	StL-N	208	7	.298	.377	.438	2	4	0	23	3.18	0	3	0	29	4.34	1	1	0	26	1.37	1	6	0	25	6.39	94	0	.266	.337	.309	114	7	.325	.409	.544
1998	Sea-A	47	1	.404	.463	.553	0	2	0	5	8.44	0	1	0	6	9.00	0	3	0	11	8.74	0	0	0	0	—	29	1	.379	.424	.586	18	0	.444	.524	.500
1998	Chi-N	19	0	.421	.560	.526	0	0	0	1	13.50	0	0	0	3	6.75	0	0	0	0	—	0	0	0	4	9.00	9	0	.333	.538	.556	10	0	.500	.583	.500

		TOTAL					HOME					AWAY					1ST HALF					2ND HALF					LEFT					RIGHT				
YEAR	TM/L	AB	HR	AVG	OBP	SLG	W	L	SV	IP	ERA	W	L	SV	IP	ERA	W	L	SV	IP	ERA	W	L	SV	IP	ERA	AB	HR	AVG	OBP	SLG	AB	HR	AVG	OBP	SLG
1998	Tex-A	25	0	.120	.241	.120	0	0	0	2	0.00	1	0	0	5	0.00	0	0	0	0	—	1	0	0	7	0.00	16	0	.063	.167	.063	9	0	.222	.364	.222
1999	NY-A	9	1	.667	.700	1.000	0	0	0	0	0.00	0	0	0	1	54.00	0	0	0	1	36.00	0	0	0	0	—	5	1	.600	.600	1.200	4	0	.750	.800	.750
TOTALS		1616	39	.269	.344	.396	10	11	4	216	2.88	7	13	3	200	4.99	7	13	3	197	3.88	10	11	4	219	3.91	707	11	.215	.284	.303	909	28	.310	.389	.469
● **Keith Foulke** BR/TR																																				
1997	SF-N	185	9	.324	.396	.541	1	0	0	19	4.74	0	5	0	26	10.87	1	2	0	29	7.36	0	3	0	15	9.98	84	2	.345	.396	.500	101	7	.307	.397	.574
1997	Chi-A	110	4	.255	.284	.418	2	0	2	23	2.78	1	0	1	6	6.00	0	0	0	0	—	3	0	3	29	3.45	48	3	.333	.327	.563	62	1	.194	.254	.306
1998	Chi-A	239	9	.213	.283	.389	3	1	1	37	3.13	0	1	0	28	5.46	1	1	1	41	4.79	2	1	0	24	3.00	100	4	.270	.351	.460	139	5	.173	.232	.338
1999	Chi-A	384	11	.188	.235	.320	2	2	5	53	2.19	1	1	4	52	2.25	0	1	3	47	2.85	3	2	6	58	1.71	187	6	.182	.231	.310	197	5	.193	.239	.330
2000	Chi-A	319	9	.207	.261	.339	1	1	12	43	4.85	2	0	22	45	1.19	1	0	16	47	3.45	2	1	18	41	2.41	163	7	.221	.271	.417	156	2	.192	.250	.256
TOTALS		1237	42	.224	.280	.380	9	4	20	175	3.39	4	7	27	157	4.07	3	4	20	165	4.31	10	7	27	167	3.13	582	22	.244	.295	.414	655	20	.206	.267	.350
● **John Franco** BL/TL																																				
1984	Cin-N	289	3	.256	.338	.329	4	2	3	48	2.25	2	0	1	31	3.16	3	0	3	37	3.44	3	2	1	43	1.90	76	1	.237	.318	.289	213	2	.263	.346	.343
1985	Cin-N	354	5	.234	.313	.322	7	0	5	58	1.25	5	3	7	41	3.48	4	1	3	33	2.43	8	2	9	66	2.06	85	1	.176	.222	.224	269	4	.253	.340	.353
1986	Cin-N	371	7	.243	.324	.332	2	2	16	54	3.02	4	4	13	47	2.85	1	4	12	55	2.44	5	2	17	46	3.55	76	0	.211	.250	.250	295	7	.251	.341	.353
1987	Cin-N	310	6	.245	.304	.345	4	2	16	37	4.14	4	3	16	45	1.20	5	2	15	37	0.74	3	3	17	45	3.97	46	0	.239	.280	.283	264	6	.246	.308	.356
1988	Cin-N	303	3	.198	.263	.241	4	2	20	46	0.99	2	4	19	40	2.23	2	5	9	41	1.98	4	1	30	45	1.20	51	1	.137	.167	.235	252	2	.210	.282	.242
1989	Cin-N	299	3	.258	.334	.311	4	4	17	41	3.92	0	4	15	39	2.29	2	1	20	37	1.46	2	7	12	44	4.53	50	0	.200	.245	.240	249	3	.269	.351	.325
1990	NY-N	262	4	.252	.306	.347	4	2	17	38	2.82	1	1	16	29	2.15	3	0	14	32	1.71	2	3	19	36	3.25	57	0	.228	.323	.298	205	4	.259	.301	.361
1991	NY-N	225	2	.271	.328	.360	1	4	18	27	3.00	4	5	12	28	2.86	1	6	15	24	3.38	4	3	15	31	2.59	53	0	.340	.397	.415	172	2	.250	.306	.343
1992	NY-N	115	1	.209	.273	.304	4	1	8	20	0.92	2	1	7	13	2.70	6	1	11	25	1.44	0	1	4	8	2.25	28	0	.250	.389	.286	87	1	.195	.228	.310
1993	NY-N	147	6	.313	.393	.463	1	0	6	16	3.31	3	3	4	20	6.75	2	0	2	16	1.69	2	3	8	20	7.97	41	2	.317	.378	.488	106	4	.311	.398	.453
1994	NY-N	193	2	.244	.313	.321	1	2	15	25	2.55	0	2	15	25	2.84	1	4	17	32	2.78	0	0	13	18	2.55	49	0	.306	.340	.347	144	2	.222	.304	.313
1995	NY-N	191	4	.251	.311	.372	4	1	18	32	2.51	1	2	11	19	2.33	2	1	8	23	3.18	3	2	21	29	1.86	32	0	.281	.314	.344	159	4	.245	.310	.377
1996	NY-N	208	2	.260	.328	.308	4	1	16	35	2.31	0	2	12	19	0.95	2	2	18	28	1.95	2	1	10	26	1.71	49	0	.143	.236	.163	159	2	.296	.356	.352
1997	NY-N	217	3	.226	.293	.318	4	0	17	32	1.95	1	3	19	28	3.25	1	1	19	31	2.93	4	2	17	29	2.15	46	0	.304	.373	.370	171	3	.205	.271	.304
1998	NY-N	247	4	.267	.347	.364	0	5	14	32	5.06	0	3	24	33	2.20	0	1	18	29	2.45	0	7	20	35	4.58	53	0	.340	.386	.358	194	4	.247	.338	.366
1999	NY-N	157	1	.255	.341	.344	0	2	10	21	3.05	0	0	9	20	2.70	0	2	19	31	2.64	0	0	0	10	3.60	30	0	.300	.405	.333	127	1	.244	.324	.346
2000	NY-N	208	6	.221	.314	.327	2	1	3	26	3.81	3	3	1	30	3.03	3	3	3	33	3.86	2	1	1	23	2.74	67	0	.209	.264	.209	141	6	.227	.335	.383
TOTALS		4096	62	.246	.318	.332	50	31	219	588	2.68	32	43	201	509	2.69	38	34	206	543	2.37	44	40	214	554	2.99	889	5	.241	.302	.292	3207	57	.247	.322	.342
● **John Frascatore** BR/TR																																				
1994	StL-N	16	2	.438	.500	.938	0	1	0	3	16.20	0	0	0	0	—	0	0	0	0	—	0	1	0	3	16.20	6	1	.333	.500	1.000	10	1	.500	.500	.900
1995	StL-N	131	3	.298	.380	.458	0	1	0	12	8.03	1	0	0	20	2.21	1	1	0	21	5.91	0	0	0	11	1.59	51	1	.275	.403	.412	80	2	.313	.364	.488
1997	StL-N	299	5	.247	.329	.334	3	0	0	38	2.82	2	2	0	42	2.16	3	2	0	39	2.31	2	0	0	41	2.63	117	1	.214	.321	.274	182	4	.269	.335	.374
1998	StL-N	371	11	.256	.326	.415	2	2	0	50	4.53	1	2	0	46	3.72	1	2	0	51	4.38	2	2	0	44	3.86	163	3	.245	.328	.387	208	8	.264	.325	.438
1999	Ari-N	121	6	.256	.326	.488	0	0	0	14	0.64	1	4	0	19	6.63	1	4	0	33	4.09	0	0	0	0	—	44	2	.159	.224	.318	77	4	.312	.384	.584
1999	Tor-A	144	5	.292	.333	.465	4	0	0	17	4.67	3	1	1	20	2.29	2	0	0	7	4.05	5	1	1	30	3.26	58	1	.310	.375	.466	86	4	.279	.304	.465
2000	Tor-A	289	14	.301	.381	.491	1	1	0	34	6.09	1	3	0	39	4.85	1	2	0	37	7.23	1	2	0	36	3.53	102	4	.324	.413	.500	187	10	.289	.363	.487
TOTALS		1371	46	.274	.347	.435	10	5	0	169	4.63	9	12	1	186	3.59	9	11	0	189	4.63	10	6	1	166	3.47	541	13	.257	.349	.396	830	33	.284	.345	.461
● **Gene Garber** BR/TR																																				
1978	Phi-N	136	1	.191	.267	.257	1	0	2	19	0.47	1	1	1	19	2.33	2	1	3	39	1.40	0	0	0	0	—	48	0	.146	.268	.167	88	1	.216	.266	.307
1978	Atl-N	284	11	.204	.244	.342	1	2	13	42	2.34	3	2	9	36	2.75	1	0	3	9	3.00	3	4	19	69	2.47	139	2	.165	.200	.216	145	9	.241	.286	.462
1979	Atl-N	428	10	.283	.326	.411	2	7	13	53	4.89	4	9	12	53	3.76	4	10	15	67	3.61	2	6	10	39	5.59	206	8	.316	.363	.490	222	2	.252	.291	.338
1980	Atl-N	330	6	.288	.335	.388	2	2	3	40	3.60	3	3	4	42	4.04	2	4	6	29	4.30	3	1	1	53	3.57	136	1	.353	.399	.449	194	5	.242	.290	.345
1981	Atl-N	229	2	.214	.277	.288	2	3	0	21	2.53	2	3	2	37	2.65	1	1	0	12	3.65	3	5	2	46	2.33	113	0	.204	.268	.274	116	2	.224	.286	.302
1982	Atl-N	432	4	.231	.285	.299	3	5	12	56	3.67	5	5	18	63	1.14	6	3	12	51	1.59	2	7	18	68	2.90	218	2	.234	.289	.307	214	2	.229	.280	.290
1983	Atl-N	240	8	.300	.358	.425	1	2	5	35	4.93	3	3	4	26	4.15	2	3	5	33	5.13	2	2	4	27	3.95	116	5	.345	.412	.517	124	3	.258	.304	.339
1984	Atl-N	406	7	.254	.294	.352	2	3	4	58	4.50	1	3	7	48	1.31	1	1	3	40	4.28	2	5	8	66	2.32	193	5	.254	.293	.368	213	2	.254	.294	.338
1985	Atl-N	371	8	.264	.313	.375	4	4	0	55	3.42	2	2	1	42	3.86	1	3	0	33	5.45	5	3	1	64	2.66	195	3	.246	.293	.349	176	5	.284	.335	.403
1986	Atl-N	292	3	.260	.309	.332	3	3	9	35	2.55	2	2	15	43	2.53	4	1	8	41	1.32	1	4	16	37	3.89	138	0	.246	.316	.297	154	3	.273	.302	.364
1987	Atl-N	280	7	.311	.372	.450	7	3	5	42	3.83	1	7	5	27	5.33	8	6	8	43	3.95	0	4	2	26	5.19	129	2	.279	.350	.380	151	5	.338	.391	.510
1987	KC-A	53	1	.245	.273	.377	0	0	2	7	5.14	0	0	6	7	0.00	0	0	0	0	—	0	0	8	14	2.51	24	1	.250	.280	.417	29	0	.241	.267	.345
1988	KC-A	122	4	.238	.321	.352	0	3	1	20	4.58	0	1	5	13	2.08	0	4	6	32	3.69	0	0	0	1	0.00	60	3	.233	.292	.417	62	1	.242	.347	.290
TOTALS		3603	72	.257	.309	.361	28	37	69	485	3.66	27	41	89	457	2.84	32	37	69	430	3.35	23	41	89	512	3.18	1715	32	.259	.314	.363	1888	40	.256	.304	.360
● **Mark Gardner** BR/TR																																				
1989	Mon-N	104	2	.250	.333	.375	0	1	0	10	2.70	0	2	0	16	6.61	0	1	0	6	4.76	0	2	0	21	5.23	66	0	.197	.293	.258	38	2	.342	.405	.579
1990	Mon-N	561	13	.230	.312	.351	5	3	0	80	1.91	2	6	0	73	5.08	4	4	0	87	2.80	3	5	0	66	4.23	318	8	.230	.327	.362	243	5	.230	.291	.337
1991	Mon-N	604	17	.230	.318	.356	4	4	0	65	2.51	5	7	0	104	4.69	3	4	0	53	4.25	6	7	0	115	3.67	381	10	.228	.321	.352	223	7	.233	.313	.363
1992	Mon-N	690	15	.259	.324	.386	6	5	0	105	4.80	6	5	0	75	3.74	6	6	0	90	3.81	6	4	0	90	4.90	397	7	.272	.330	.398	293	8	.242	.316	.369
1993	KC-A	338	17	.272	.343	.512	3	2	0	40	6.30	1	4	0	52	6.10	4	5	0	86	5.88	0	1	0	6	10.50	164	7	.311	.376	.512	174	10	.236	.312	.511
1994	Fla-N	351	14	.276	.331	.479	0	3	0	48	5.63	4	1	0	44	4.06	2	2	0	46	4.47	2	2	0	46	5.28	161	4	.329	.382	.509	190	10	.232	.287	.453
1995	Fla-N	401	14	.272	.350	.451	3	3	0	56	4.82	2	2	1	46	4.08	1	4	0	39	5.82	4	1	1	64	3.68	168	6	.274	.378	.440	233	8	.270	.328	.459
1996	SF-N	706	28	.283	.341	.456	7	2	0	105	4.13	5	5	0	75	4.82	7	3	0	91	3.96	5	4	0	88	4.89	332	12	.277	.333	.449	374	16	.289	.349	.463
1997	SF-N	690	28	.272	.326	.449	6	4	0	97	4.19	6	5	0	84	4.41	8	4	0	105	3.94	4	5	0	75	4.78	332	13	.304	.366	.485	358	15	.243	.289	.416
1998	SF-N	802	29	.253	.311	.436	7	3	0	104	4.33	6	3	0	108	4.33	7	3	0	104	4.95	6	3	0	108	3.74	372	9	.274	.337	.433	430	20	.235	.289	.440
1999	SF-N	532	27	.267	.341	.472	2	4	0	60	5.55	3	7	0	79	7.18	2	6	0	74	7.02	3	5	0	65	5.85	226	11	.279	.358	.456	306	16	.258	.329	.484
2000	SF-N	575	16	.270	.322	.421	6	3	0	73	4.56	5	4	0	76	3.55	4	4	0	53	5.98	7	3	0	96	2.99	240	7	.304	.365	.463	335	9	.245	.290	.391
TOTALS		6354	220	.261	.327	.427	49	37	0	842	4.26	45	51	1	831	4.77	48	46	0	832	4.68	46	42	1	841	4.35	3157	94	.273	.345	.427	3197	126	.249	.310	.427
● **Scott Garrelts** BR/TR																																				
1982	SF-N	9	0	.333	.455	.444	0	0	0	2	13.50	0	0	0	0	—	0	0	0	0	—	0	0	0	2	13.50	5	0	.000	.000	.000	4	0	.750	.833	1.000
1983	SF-N	130	4	.254	.358	.346	1	1	0	14	1.93	1	1	0	22	2.91	0	0	0	0	—	2	2	0	36	2.52	64	2	.266	.382	.359	66	2	.242	.333	.333
1984	SF-N	164	6	.274	.398	.390	2	1	0	24	4.18	0	2	0	19	7.45	1	1	0	28	6.67	1	2	0	15	3.68	75	1	.320	.485	.360	89	5	.236	.314	.416
1985	SF-N	384	2	.198	.306	.253	7	4	4	56	2.26	2	2	9	50	2.34	2	3	5	56	1.13	7	3	8	50	3.62	169	1	.231	.314	.302	215	1	.172	.300	.214
1986	SF-N	624	17	.231	.311	.351	8	4	7	97	2.23	5	5	3	77	4.23	6	6	0	112	3.05	7	3	10	62	3.21	337	6	.237	.322	.320	287	11	.223	.298	.387
1987	SF-N	364	10	.192	.297	.310	5	3	4	42	3.86	6	4	8	64	2.80	6	5	9	60	3.13	5	2	3	46	3.33	197	4	.183	.286	.284	167	6	.204	.309	.341
1988	SF-N	354	3	.226	.317	.294	1	7	9	45	4.20	4	2	4	53	3.06	1	4	5	49	4.99	4	5	8	49	2.19	157	1	.217	.313	.287	197	2	.234	.320	.299
1989	SF-N	704	11	.212	.258	.313	10	2	0	109	1.57	4	3	0	85	3.19	6	3	0	108	2.75	8	2	0	85	1.69	377	6	.236	.296	.353	327	5	.183	.211	.266
1990	SF-N	698	16	.272	.339	.404	6	7	0	103	3.83	6	4	0	79	4.58	5	6	0	91	4.65	7	5	0	91	3.66	389	8	.296	.365	.427	309	8	.243	.306	.375
1991	SF-N	80	5	.313	.378	.563	0	1	0	6	12.00	1	0	0	14	3.95	1	1	0	20	6.41	0	0	0	0	—	42	2	.405	.458	.643	38	3	.211	.286	.474
TOTALS		3511	74	.232	.313	.340	40	30	24	497	2.99	29	23	24	462	3.62	28	29	19	524	3.57	41	24	29	435	2.96	1812	31	.249	.333	.351	1699	43	.214	.292	.328
● **Tom Glavine** BL/TL																																				
1987	Atl-N	197	5	.279	.386	.421	2	2	0	24	5.55	0	2	0	26	5.54	0	0	0	0	—	2	4	0	50	5.54	27	0	.259	.375	.333	170	5	.282	.387	.435
1988	Atl-N	745	12	.270	.329	.372	2	7	0	86	5.00	5	10	0	109	4.21	3	9	0	88	5.60	4	8	0	107	3.70	123	3	.244	.343	.350	622	9	.275	.326	.376
1989	Atl-N	709	20	.243	.283	.371	6	4	0	94	3.72	8	4	0	92	3.63	8	4	0	97	3.44	6	4	0	89	3.93	108	0	.204	.252	.269	601	20	.250	.289	.389
1990	Atl-N	827	18	.281	.343	.410	5	8	0	104	4.86	5	4	0	111	3.74	4	5	0	100	3.95	6	7	0	114	4.58	154	2	.221	.310	.279	673	16	.294	.350	.440
1991	Atl-N	905	17	.222	.277	.330	10	4	0	106	2.71	10	7	0	140	2.44	11	4	0	118	2.06	9	7	0	129	3.01	171	4	.292	.354	.433	734	13	.206	.259	.307
1992	Atl-N	839	6	.235	.293	.310	13	4	0	140	2.31	7	4	0	85	3.49	11	3	0	124	2.82	9	5	0	101	2.68	176	1	.273	.353	.341	663	5	.225	.277	.302
1993	Atl-N	910	16	.259	.327	.376	13	3	0	136	3.18	9	3	0	104	3.21	9	3	0	111	2.91	13	3	0	128	3.45	166	1	.271	.349	.349	744	15	.257	.322	.382
1994	Atl-N	645	10	.268	.338	.377	5	5	0	74	3.89	8	4	0	91	4.04	8	7	0	110	4.02	5	2	0	56	3.88	125	1	.320	.393	.424	520	9	.256	.325	.365
1995	Atl-N	739	9	.246	.310	.334	6	4	0	92	3.63	10	3	0	107	2.61	6	4	0	80	3.59	10	3	0	118	2.74	136	2	.316	.392	.419	603	7	.231	.292	.315
1996	Atl-N	892	14	.249	.314	.353	8	3	0	114	2.45	7	7	0	121	3.49	8	5	0	117	2.62	7	5	0	119	3.34	160	1	.225	.273	.281	732	13	.254	.322	.369
1997	Atl-N	870	20	.226	.292	.333	5	2	0	97	2.13	9	5	0	143	3.53	8	4	0	126	2.57	6	3	0	114	3.39	178	4	.236	.294	.354	692	16	.224	.292	.328
1998	Atl-N	850	13	.238	.300	.325	8	4	0	103	3.32	12	2	0	126	1.78	11	3	0	116	2.71	9	3	0	113	2.23	209	6	.244	.293	.354	641	7	.236	.302	.315
1999	Atl-N	904	18	.287	.346	.390	8	4	0	124	3.55	6	7	0	110	4.76	6	7	0	105	4.53	8	4	0	129	3.78	197	2	.274	.313	.340	707	16	.290	.354	.405
2000	Atl-N	909	24	.244	.296	.376	12	3	0	130	3.05	9	6	0	111	3.81	7	5	0	117	3.68	14	4	0	124	3.13	196	4	.240	.292	.357	713	20	.245	.297	.381
TOTALS		10941	202	.251	.313	.359	103	57	0	1425	3.33	105	68	0	1476	3.43	100	63	0	1411	3.35	108	62	0	1490	3.42	2126	31	.258	.324	.350	8815	171	.250	.310	.361

		TOTAL					HOME					AWAY					1ST HALF					2ND HALF					LEFT					RIGHT				
YEAR	TM/L	AB	HR	AVG	OBP	SLG	W	L	SV	IP	ERA	W	L	SV	IP	ERA	W	L	SV	IP	ERA	W	L	SV	IP	ERA	AB	HR	AVG	OBP	SLG	AB	HR	AVG	OBP	SLG
● **Wayne Gomes** BR/TR																																				
1997	Phi-N	164	4	.274	.370	.402	3	0	0	25	4.32	2	1	0	18	6.62	1	0	0	11	4.91	4	1	0	32	5.40	63	1	.254	.382	.365	101	3	.287	.363	.426
1998	Phi-N	364	9	.258	.328	.374	4	3	1	46	4.47	5	3	0	47	4.02	6	3	0	49	3.65	3	3	1	44	4.91	149	3	.295	.373	.409	215	6	.233	.295	.349
1999	Phi-N	275	5	.255	.381	.349	4	3	10	40	3.86	1	2	9	34	4.72	1	1	11	37	3.68	4	4	8	37	4.82	114	0	.254	.401	.272	161	5	.255	.366	.404
2000	Phi-N	275	6	.262	.347	.396	2	4	2	39	4.89	2	2	5	35	3.86	4	4	6	46	3.35	0	2	1	28	6.11	108	2	.306	.379	.444	167	4	.234	.326	.365
TOTALS		1078	24	.261	.353	.378	13	10	13	150	4.39	10	8	14	134	4.50	12	8	17	143	3.66	11	10	10	141	5.23	434	6	.281	.384	.376	644	18	.247	.332	.379
● **Dwight Gooden** BR/TR																																				
1984	NY-N	799	7	.202	.269	.275	12	2	0	118	1.90	5	7	0	100	3.43	6	5	0	97	2.89	11	4	0	121	2.37	425	4	.228	.290	.311	374	3	.171	.246	.235
1985	NY-N	986	13	.201	.254	.270	13	2	0	144	1.50	11	2	0	133	1.56	11	3	0	136	1.65	13	1	0	140	1.41	567	3	.203	.260	.249	419	10	.198	.246	.298
1986	NY-N	917	17	.215	.278	.321	9	3	0	123	2.20	8	3	0	127	3.47	9	3	0	123	2.70	8	3	0	127	2.98	527	7	.211	.283	.306	390	10	.221	.273	.341
1987	NY-N	665	11	.244	.299	.344	8	5	0	95	3.41	7	2	0	85	2.98	5	1	0	47	2.12	10	6	0	133	3.59	365	5	.241	.304	.321	300	6	.247	.293	.373
1988	NY-N	944	8	.256	.301	.333	8	4	0	117	2.46	10	5	0	131	3.84	10	4	0	127	3.11	8	5	0	121	3.27	491	4	.236	.290	.308	453	4	.278	.313	.360
1989	NY-N	441	9	.211	.288	.313	6	1	0	66	2.33	3	3	1	53	3.59	9	3	0	109	2.88	0	1	1	9	3.00	232	3	.181	.270	.259	209	6	.244	.309	.373
1990	NY-N	888	10	.258	.315	.345	9	3	0	126	3.56	10	4	0	106	4.15	7	5	0	107	4.19	12	2	0	125	3.52	522	6	.259	.316	.354	366	4	.257	.313	.331
1991	NY-N	721	12	.257	.311	.369	9	3	0	106	3.55	4	4	0	84	3.66	7	6	0	119	4.39	6	1	0	71	2.28	412	4	.252	.321	.345	309	8	.262	.298	.401
1992	NY-N	773	11	.255	.317	.371	7	5	0	97	4.25	3	8	0	109	3.15	5	7	0	104	3.81	5	6	0	102	3.53	450	9	.267	.337	.380	323	2	.238	.288	.359
1993	NY-N	778	16	.242	.302	.357	8	10	0	139	2.78	4	5	0	70	4.78	7	7	0	122	3.03	5	8	0	87	4.03	396	9	.247	.307	.366	382	7	.236	.296	.348
1994	NY-N	163	9	.282	.346	.503	1	3	0	22	6.45	2	1	0	19	6.16	3	4	0	41	6.31	0	0	0	0	—	78	6	.256	.333	.526	85	3	.306	.359	.482
1996	NY-A	653	19	.259	.352	.415	8	1	0	101	3.56	3	6	0	70	7.11	7	4	0	89	4.33	4	3	0	81	5.75	382	10	.254	.345	.398	271	9	.266	.363	.439
1997	NY-A	410	14	.283	.373	.437	4	3	0	55	3.74	5	2	0	51	6.18	3	0	0	24	3.04	6	5	0	83	5.44	211	8	.299	.393	.464	199	6	.266	.351	.407
1998	Cle-A	515	13	.262	.337	.394	3	4	0	66	4.50	5	2	0	68	3.04	2	3	0	38	4.03	6	3	0	96	3.66	268	10	.272	.340	.440	247	3	.251	.333	.344
1999	Cle-A	451	18	.282	.382	.463	1	3	0	68	6.22	2	1	0	47	6.32	2	3	0	67	5.91	1	1	0	48	6.75	213	10	.286	.413	.493	238	8	.277	.353	.437
2000	Hou-N	17	1	.353	.450	.706	0	0	0	4	9.00	0	0	0	0	—	0	0	0	4	9.00	0	0	0	0	—	6	0	.667	.750	1.000	11	1	.182	.250	.545
2000	TB-A	149	14	.315	.407	.638	0	2	0	16	8.82	2	1	0	20	4.87	2	3	0	37	6.63	0	0	0	0	—	74	6	.284	.418	.541	75	8	.347	.395	.733
2000	NY-A	248	8	.266	.321	.431	1	2	0	26	4.21	3	0	2	39	2.79	0	0	0	0	—	4	2	2	64	3.36	105	4	.248	.314	.429	143	4	.280	.327	.434
TOTALS		10518	210	.244	.310	.357	107	56	0	1491	3.24	87	56	3	1310	3.81	95	61	0	1392	3.54	99	51	3	1409	3.47	5724	108	.243	.314	.351	4794	102	.245	.304	.364
● **Tom Gordon** BR/TR																																				
1988	KC-A	60	1	.267	.343	.367	0	1	0	6	8.53	0	1	0	9	2.89	0	0	0	0	—	0	2	0	16	5.17	30	0	.233	.303	.300	30	1	.300	.382	.433
1989	KC-A	582	10	.210	.311	.306	11	5	0	99	3.38	6	4	1	64	4.06	9	2	1	57	2.84	8	7	0	106	4.08	307	4	.218	.322	.306	275	6	.200	.297	.305
1990	KC-A	745	17	.258	.346	.387	7	5	0	93	3.10	5	6	0	102	4.31	5	4	0	82	3.18	7	7	0	113	4.13	365	6	.252	.352	.345	380	11	.263	.340	.426
1991	KC-A	585	16	.221	.324	.357	2	8	1	92	4.00	7	6	0	66	3.70	4	6	0	88	3.38	5	8	1	70	4.50	302	4	.248	.340	.344	283	12	.191	.307	.371
1992	KC-A	449	9	.258	.340	.379	5	4	0	59	3.36	1	6	0	59	5.83	1	7	0	60	5.97	5	3	0	57	3.14	202	3	.287	.352	.391	247	6	.235	.331	.368
1993	KC-A	561	11	.223	.315	.340	6	1	1	72	2.38	6	5	0	84	4.63	4	2	1	51	4.26	8	4	0	105	3.26	293	6	.229	.320	.341	268	5	.216	.309	.340
1994	KC-A	574	15	.237	.336	.371	4	4	0	79	4.33	7	3	0	76	4.36	8	4	0	105	3.93	3	3	0	50	5.22	282	6	.248	.346	.372	292	9	.226	.328	.370
1995	KC-A	731	12	.279	.356	.372	4	7	0	91	3.46	8	5	0	98	5.33	5	3	0	69	4.02	7	9	0	120	4.66	398	5	.314	.389	.394	333	7	.237	.315	.345
1996	Bos-A	876	28	.284	.359	.455	6	4	0	131	5.36	6	5	0	85	5.95	6	4	0	100	6.32	6	5	0	116	4.97	478	15	.301	.391	.454	398	13	.264	.319	.457
1997	Bos-A	686	10	.226	.306	.319	2	6	3	112	4.34	4	4	8	71	2.80	5	6	0	106	3.30	1	4	11	76	4.36	363	3	.231	.320	.320	323	7	.220	.290	.319
1998	Bos-A	288	2	.191	.254	.247	7	2	26	45	2.00	0	2	20	34	3.67	4	2	24	44	2.68	3	2	22	36	2.78	167	0	.186	.239	.198	121	2	.198	.274	.314
1999	Bos-A	69	2	.246	.366	.391	0	1	4	6	3.18	0	1	7	12	6.75	0	1	11	14	4.50	0	1	0	4	9.82	31	0	.290	.436	.355	38	2	.211	.302	.421
TOTALS		6206	133	.244	.331	.364	54	48	35	885	3.80	50	48	36	760	4.56	51	41	37	776	4.06	53	55	34	869	4.24	3218	52	.258	.346	.358	2988	81	.230	.315	.371
● **Jim Gott** BR/TR																																				
1982	Tor-A	526	15	.255	.340	.384	3	5	0	73	4.09	2	5	0	63	4.83	1	4	0	47	4.40	4	6	0	89	4.45	238	6	.269	.367	.382	288	9	.243	.317	.385
1983	Tor-A	696	15	.280	.347	.408	7	6	0	91	5.04	2	8	0	86	4.41	5	6	0	91	4.14	4	8	0	85	5.38	301	6	.312	.381	.445	395	9	.256	.321	.380
1984	Tor-A	399	7	.233	.317	.371	5	3	2	71	3.69	2	3	0	39	4.62	4	2	0	57	4.11	3	4	2	53	3.93	183	2	.219	.315	.333	216	5	.245	.320	.403
1985	SF-N	567	10	.254	.315	.377	4	4	0	78	2.32	3	6	0	71	5.60	3	5	0	74	3.41	4	5	0	74	4.36	294	4	.245	.321	.357	273	6	.264	.307	.399
1986	SF-N	51	0	.314	.446	.353	0	0	0	7	6.43	0	0	1	6	9.00	0	0	1	13	7.62	0	0	0	0	—	29	0	.345	.457	.414	22	0	.273	.433	.273
1987	SF-N	217	4	.244	.345	.346	0	0	0	19	4.66	1	0	0	37	4.42	1	0	0	43	4.81	0	0	0	13	3.46	98	4	.306	.444	.500	119	0	.193	.250	.218
1987	Pit-N	120	0	.233	.281	.258	0	1	8	21	1.74	0	1	5	10	0.87	0	0	0	0	—	0	2	13	31	1.45	63	0	.254	.309	.286	57	0	.211	.250	.228
1988	Pit-N	280	9	.243	.300	.386	4	2	17	41	1.99	2	4	17	37	5.15	4	2	9	38	2.84	2	4	25	39	4.12	132	6	.220	.293	.394	148	3	.264	.306	.378
1989	Pit-N	3	0	.333	.500	.333	0	0	0	0	—	0	0	0	1	0.00	0	0	0	1	0.00	0	0	0	0	—	0	0	—	—	—	3	0	.333	.500	.333
1990	LA-N	230	5	.257	.347	.370	2	3	1	34	2.88	1	2	2	28	2.93	0	2	0	14	6.28	3	3	3	48	1.89	132	1	.288	.379	.379	98	4	.214	.304	.357
1991	LA-N	282	5	.223	.304	.312	1	0	1	37	2.68	3	3	1	39	3.23	1	2	1	28	3.18	3	1	1	48	2.83	142	2	.190	.277	.268	140	3	.257	.331	.357
1992	LA-N	320	4	.225	.314	.287	1	1	2	40	1.79	2	2	4	48	3.02	1	2	2	44	1.85	2	1	4	44	3.05	148	3	.264	.382	.365	172	1	.192	.249	.221
1993	LA-N	286	6	.248	.291	.339	2	4	12	42	3.19	2	4	13	35	1.27	2	5	13	43	2.51	2	3	12	35	2.08	153	5	.222	.264	.346	133	1	.278	.322	.331
1994	LA-N	143	3	.322	.413	.434	4	1	0	11	6.35	1	2	2	25	5.76	5	2	1	26	5.13	0	1	1	10	8.10	65	1	.338	.429	.446	78	2	.308	.400	.423
1995	Pit-N	132	2	.288	.349	.439	1	3	0	19	5.12	1	1	3	12	7.50	0	2	3	19	7.45	2	2	0	12	3.75	54	0	.296	.387	.444	78	2	.282	.321	.436
TOTALS		4252	85	.254	.329	.368	34	33	43	584	3.47	22	41	48	536	4.30	27	34	30	539	3.96	29	40	61	581	3.78	2032	40	.261	.348	.379	2220	45	.248	.311	.357
● **Danny Graves** BR/TR																																				
1996	Cle-A	118	2	.246	.302	.381	2	0	0	17	4.15	0	0	0	12	5.11	0	0	0	0	—	2	0	0	30	4.55	56	2	.268	.328	.464	62	0	.226	.279	.306
1997	Cle-A	46	2	.326	.429	.500	0	0	0	3	5.40	0	0	0	8	4.50	0	0	0	11	4.76	0	0	0	0	—	26	0	.192	.300	.231	20	2	.500	.577	.850
1997	Cin-N	63	0	.413	.493	.540	0	0	0	9	5.19	0	0	0	6	7.50	0	0	0	0	—	0	0	0	15	6.14	23	0	.348	.444	.478	40	0	.450	.521	.575
1998	Cin-N	302	6	.252	.315	.354	1	0	5	42	4.25	1	1	3	39	2.31	1	0	0	38	3.08	1	1	8	43	3.53	129	4	.256	.319	.388	173	2	.249	.311	.329
1999	Cin-N	396	10	.227	.314	.359	4	6	15	55	3.93	4	1	12	56	2.25	5	3	10	54	3.67	3	4	17	57	2.53	173	4	.220	.294	.347	223	6	.233	.329	.368
2000	Cin-N	332	8	.244	.331	.361	7	3	12	50	2.68	3	2	18	41	2.41	9	1	12	51	1.75	1	4	18	40	3.60	166	4	.265	.333	.386	166	4	.223	.328	.337
TOTALS		1257	28	.252	.331	.375	14	9	32	177	3.76	8	4	33	162	2.83	15	4	22	155	2.97	7	9	43	185	3.61	573	14	.250	.321	.379	684	14	.254	.340	.371
● **Buddy Groom** BL/TL																																				
1992	Det-A	150	4	.320	.402	.493	0	3	0	19	6.63	0	2	1	20	5.03	0	2	0	17	4.15	0	3	1	21	7.17	31	0	.355	.432	.419	119	4	.311	.394	.513
1993	Det-A	149	4	.322	.375	.483	0	0	0	16	5.51	0	2	0	20	6.64	0	0	0	18	4.08	0	2	0	19	8.05	44	2	.273	.313	.477	105	2	.343	.400	.486
1994	Det-A	121	4	.256	.331	.397	0	0	0	12	6.57	0	1	1	20	2.29	0	1	0	19	4.74	0	0	1	13	2.77	42	1	.286	.319	.405	79	3	.241	.337	.392
1995	Det-A	171	6	.322	.413	.474	0	2	0	23	9.53	1	1	1	18	5.00	1	2	1	31	6.75	0	1	0	10	9.90	45	2	.333	.446	.533	126	4	.317	.400	.452
1995	Fla-N	65	2	.400	.451	.585	1	0	0	8	4.32	0	2	0	7	10.80	0	0	0	1	0.00	1	2	0	14	7.71	21	0	.381	.480	.429	44	2	.409	.435	.659
1996	Oak-A	302	8	.281	.360	.397	0	0	0	38	5.50	5	0	2	40	2.27	3	0	2	44	3.09	2	0	0	34	4.81	123	2	.268	.323	.341	179	6	.291	.383	.436
1997	Oak-A	257	9	.292	.347	.455	0	0	1	36	6.31	2	2	2	29	3.72	1	1	2	27	5.06	1	1	1	38	5.21	121	3	.231	.296	.347	136	6	.346	.393	.551
1998	Oak-A	226	4	.274	.332	.385	1	1	0	27	5.67	2	0	0	30	2.97	3	1	0	33	5.67	0	0	0	24	2.25	111	2	.243	.309	.360	115	2	.304	.354	.409
1999	Oak-A	175	1	.274	.345	.331	1	1	0	24	3.38	2	1	0	22	6.95	2	1	0	20	7.78	1	1	0	26	3.08	102	0	.245	.294	.275	73	1	.315	.412	.411
2000	Bal-A	229	5	.275	.329	.393	3	0	1	28	3.18	3	3	3	31	6.39	3	3	4	32	4.78	3	0	0	27	4.94	88	2	.193	.229	.273	141	3	.326	.390	.468
TOTALS		1845	47	.293	.361	.425	6	7	2	231	5.64	15	14	10	236	4.57	13	11	9	241	5.00	8	10	3	227	5.20	728	14	.258	.319	.357	1117	33	.316	.388	.470
● **Kevin Gross** BR/TR																																				
1983	Phi-N	377	13	.265	.332	.424	3	3	0	58	3.09	1	3	0	38	4.30	2	0	0	14	1.93	2	6	0	82	3.84	197	7	.284	.347	.447	180	6	.244	.315	.400
1984	Phi-N	504	8	.278	.340	.385	5	4	0	71	4.29	3	1	1	58	3.90	4	2	0	62	2.61	4	3	1	67	5.51	251	6	.275	.351	.398	253	2	.281	.328	.372
1985	Phi-N	773	11	.251	.326	.361	8	4	0	96	2.99	7	9	0	109	3.79	6	7	0	84	3.20	9	6	0	121	3.56	426	4	.242	.329	.354	347	7	.262	.322	.369
1986	Phi-N	923	28	.260	.332	.417	7	7	0	134	3.56	5	5	0	108	4.60	6	5	0	112	4.34	6	7	0	130	3.75	530	16	.272	.360	.445	393	12	.244	.291	.379
1987	Phi-N	767	26	.267	.347	.429	5	11	0	119	3.85	4	5	0	81	5.09	6	7	0	94	4.23	3	9	0	107	4.46	428	12	.280	.370	.432	339	14	.251	.316	.425
1988	Phi-N	876	18	.239	.315	.357	6	6	0	114	3.64	6	8	0	118	3.74	8	3	0	120	2.78	4	11	0	112	4.67	491	10	.255	.349	.383	385	8	.218	.270	.325
1989	Mon-N	760	20	.247	.329	.388	6	4	0	94	4.29	5	8	0	107	4.46	7	7	0	114	4.57	4	5	0	87	4.14	415	10	.241	.337	.378	345	10	.255	.319	.400
1990	Mon-N	628	9	.272	.340	.368	3	5	0	69	4.43	6	7	0	94	4.67	8	5	0	104	3.62	1	7	0	59	6.25	369	7	.295	.373	.415	259	2	.239	.291	.301
1991	LA-N	447	10	.275	.348	.380	7	3	1	61	2.79	3	8	2	54	4.47	4	5	2	47	4.60	6	6	1	69	2.88	233	6	.313	.398	.446	214	4	.234	.291	.308
1992	LA-N	756	11	.241	.311	.337	5	9	0	113	3.35	3	4	0	92	2.95	3	8	0	87	3.72	5	5	0	118	2.75	409	5	.276	.356	.389	347	6	.199	.255	.277
1993	LA-N	795	15	.282	.344	.379	8	5	0	109	3.29	5	8	0	93	5.13	6	6	0	95	3.88	7	7	0	107	4.36	394	7	.277	.363	.360	401	8	.287	.325	.397
1994	LA-N	615	11	.263	.313	.371	4	3	1	76	3.07	5	4	0	81	4.11	7	4	0	103	3.84	2	3	1	54	3.15	321	8	.271	.342	.411	294	3	.255	.280	.327
1995	Tex-A	715	27	.280	.363	.455	4	7	0	79	6.35	5	8	0	104	4.92	3	7	0	64	8.11	6	8	0	119	4.15	378	11	.280	.347	.439	337	16	.279	.379	.472
1996	Tex-A	515	19	.293	.355	.485	6	2	0	59	4.85	5	6	0	70	5.53	8	5	0	87	4.97	3	3	0	42	5.74	263	11	.297	.362	.487	252	8	.290	.348	.484
1997	Ana-A	96	4	.313	.429	.490	2	0	0	13	2.84	0	1	0	13	10.66	1	1	0	11	8.44	1	0	0	15	5.52	41	2	.268	.436	.488	55	2	.345	.422	.491
TOTALS		9547	230	.264	.336	.394	79	73	2	1268	3.79	63	85	3	1220	4.45	79	72	2	1199	4.11	63	86	3	1289	4.12	5146	122	.273	.356	.410	4401	108	.254	.311	.376

YEAR	TM/L	TOTAL AB	HR	AVG	OBP	SLG	HOME W	L	SV	IP	ERA	AWAY W	L	SV	IP	ERA	1ST HALF W	L	SV	IP	ERA	2ND HALF W	L	SV	IP	ERA	LEFT AB	HR	AVG	OBP	SLG	RIGHT AB	HR	AVG	OBP	SLG
● **Eddie Guardado** BR/TL																																				
1993	Min-A	385	13	.319	.376	.535	1	3	0	44	6.39	2	5	0	51	6.00	0	2	0	21	6.53	3	6	0	74	6.08	88	2	.318	.348	.523	297	11	.320	.384	.539
1994	Min-A	74	3	.351	.375	.622	0	0	0	8	3.52	0	2	0	9	12.54	0	0	0	0	—	0	2	0	17	8.47	5	0	.400	.400	.400	69	3	.348	.373	.638
1995	Min-A	354	13	.280	.356	.438	3	4	2	40	3.60	1	5	0	51	6.31	0	6	0	43	6.44	4	3	2	48	3.94	121	2	.223	.254	.298	233	11	.309	.405	.511
1996	Min-A	267	12	.228	.316	.423	3	4	2	35	6.88	3	1	2	38	3.76	3	3	2	43	4.64	3	2	2	31	6.10	111	2	.198	.254	.288	156	10	.250	.357	.519
1997	Min-A	179	7	.251	.322	.419	0	1	0	24	3.00	0	3	1	22	4.91	0	2	0	19	4.19	0	2	1	27	3.71	76	4	.250	.305	.487	103	3	.252	.333	.369
1998	Min-A	249	10	.265	.332	.458	1	1	0	36	5.25	2	0	0	30	3.64	2	1	0	32	2.84	1	0	0	34	6.09	126	5	.206	.273	.373	123	5	.325	.393	.545
1999	Min-A	167	6	.222	.328	.443	2	1	2	28	4.23	0	4	0	20	4.87	1	2	0	15	5.28	1	3	2	33	4.13	74	2	.176	.265	.365	93	4	.258	.375	.505
2000	Min-A	231	14	.238	.313	.459	4	2	3	25	5.40	3	2	6	37	2.95	3	2	4	30	3.26	4	2	5	31	4.60	86	5	.291	.344	.535	145	9	.207	.294	.414
TOTALS		1906	78	.269	.341	.466	14	16	9	239	5.04	11	22	9	259	5.08	9	18	6	203	4.74	16	20	12	295	5.28	687	22	.236	.288	.397	1219	56	.287	.370	.505
● **Mark Gubicza** BR/TR																																				
1984	KC-A	707	13	.243	.317	.358	8	8	0	134	3.01	2	6	0	55	6.59	5	7	0	95	3.12	5	7	0	94	5.00	364	9	.239	.323	.376	343	4	.248	.310	.338
1985	KC-A	671	14	.238	.319	.368	7	5	0	86	3.47	7	5	0	92	4.61	6	4	0	74	3.91	8	6	0	104	4.17	379	9	.253	.329	.391	292	5	.219	.305	.339
1986	KC-A	664	8	.233	.321	.325	8	4	0	118	2.91	4	2	0	63	5.00	3	4	0	68	4.66	9	2	0	113	3.03	352	4	.247	.345	.332	312	4	.218	.292	.317
1987	KC-A	893	18	.259	.347	.384	7	10	0	122	3.75	6	8	0	119	4.22	6	8	0	106	4.25	7	10	0	136	3.78	512	10	.260	.350	.385	381	8	.257	.342	.383
1988	KC-A	1012	11	.234	.294	.320	8	5	0	141	2.99	12	3	0	128	2.38	11	5	0	123	2.77	9	3	0	146	2.64	523	7	.252	.318	.340	489	4	.215	.269	.299
1989	KC-A	973	10	.259	.305	.343	8	6	0	142	3.17	7	5	0	113	2.87	8	5	0	145	2.61	7	6	0	110	3.60	513	4	.246	.299	.320	460	6	.274	.312	.370
1990	KC-A	357	5	.283	.355	.389	3	2	0	38	5.45	1	5	0	56	3.86	4	7	0	94	4.50	0	0	0	0	—	158	3	.266	.371	.367	199	2	.296	.341	.407
1991	KC-A	545	10	.308	.361	.424	4	6	0	66	5.21	5	6	0	67	6.15	3	4	0	41	5.09	6	8	0	92	5.95	258	3	.326	.394	.438	287	7	.293	.330	.411
1992	KC-A	425	8	.259	.316	.374	5	2	0	69	2.88	2	4	0	43	5.06	7	6	0	105	3.84	0	0	0	6	1.50	215	5	.228	.285	.363	210	3	.290	.348	.386
1993	KC-A	417	2	.307	.370	.393	4	4	2	61	5.02	1	4	0	43	4.15	0	6	0	63	5.12	5	2	2	41	3.95	190	1	.311	.382	.411	227	1	.304	.359	.379
1994	KC-A	525	11	.301	.331	.434	5	3	0	75	4.34	2	6	0	55	4.72	5	7	0	90	4.20	2	2	0	40	5.17	261	4	.291	.326	.418	264	7	.311	.336	.451
1995	KC-A	815	21	.272	.326	.410	6	8	0	124	3.69	6	6	0	89	3.84	5	6	0	88	3.38	7	8	0	125	4.02	457	9	.274	.323	.389	358	12	.271	.330	.436
1996	KC-A	464	22	.284	.339	.476	2	8	0	72	4.50	2	4	0	47	6.08	4	12	0	118	5.17	0	0	0	1	0.00	265	9	.306	.363	.460	199	13	.256	.307	.497
1997	Ana-A	27	2	.481	.533	.815	0	0	0	4	17.18	0	1	0	1	54.00	0	1	0	5	25.07	0	0	0	0	—	12	1	.417	.500	.750	15	1	.533	.563	.867
TOTALS		8495	155	.264	.327	.378	75	71	2	1251	3.68	57	65	0	972	4.32	67	82	0	1215	3.98	65	54	2	1008	3.94	4459	78	.265	.335	.378	4036	77	.262	.319	.379
● **Ron Guidry** BL/TL																																				
1978	NY-A	969	13	.193	.249	.279	12	1	0	141	1.79	13	2	0	133	1.69	12	0	0	126	1.71	13	3	0	148	1.77	212	2	.156	.215	.193	757	11	.203	.259	.303
1979	NY-A	861	20	.236	.292	.369	13	2	1	134	2.22	5	6	1	103	3.51	6	4	2	106	2.04	12	4	0	131	3.38	160	3	.237	.268	.369	701	17	.235	.298	.369
1980	NY-A	827	19	.260	.322	.394	9	7	1	118	3.67	8	3	0	102	3.44	8	4	0	117	3.38	9	6	1	102	3.78	181	6	.243	.294	.392	646	13	.265	.329	.395
1981	NY-A	468	12	.214	.256	.329	6	2	0	65	2.49	5	3	0	62	3.05	5	3	0	65	3.74	6	2	0	62	1.74	100	0	.190	.221	.210	368	12	.220	.265	.361
1982	NY-A	850	22	.254	.309	.395	6	5	0	113	3.57	8	3	0	109	4.06	8	3	0	111	3.57	6	5	0	111	4.05	167	5	.287	.348	.437	683	17	.246	.299	.385
1983	NY-A	949	26	.244	.288	.395	14	2	0	138	2.34	7	7	0	112	4.74	10	4	0	113	2.96	11	5	0	138	3.79	142	2	.225	.270	.317	807	24	.248	.291	.409
1984	NY-A	777	24	.287	.323	.454	8	2	0	101	2.93	2	9	0	94	6.20	6	6	0	129	4.24	4	5	0	66	5.02	131	2	.305	.313	.420	646	22	.283	.324	.461
1985	NY-A	980	28	.248	.277	.392	13	2	0	137	2.82	9	4	0	122	3.77	9	3	0	120	2.78	13	3	0	139	3.68	184	8	.212	.241	.348	796	20	.256	.285	.402
1986	NY-A	761	28	.265	.300	.424	6	8	0	121	4.39	3	4	0	71	3.28	4	7	0	100	4.06	5	5	0	93	3.88	137	4	.248	.290	.394	624	24	.269	.302	.431
1987	NY-A	448	14	.248	.307	.417	2	4	0	59	2.58	3	4	0	58	4.78	1	3	0	36	3.00	4	5	0	82	3.97	86	3	.302	.362	.453	362	11	.235	.294	.409
1988	NY-A	220	7	.259	.311	.455	1	1	0	17	2.65	1	2	0	39	4.85	0	0	0	0	—	2	3	0	56	4.18	49	2	.265	.294	.449	171	5	.257	.316	.456
TOTALS		8110	213	.245	.293	.385	90	36	2	1145	2.87	64	47	1	1005	3.82	69	37	2	1022	3.13	85	46	1	1127	3.49	1549	37	.236	.278	.351	6561	176	.247	.296	.394
● **Bill Gullickson** BR/TR																																				
1979	Mon-N	4	0	.500	.500	.500	0	0	0	0	—	0	0	0	1	0.00	0	0	0	0	—	0	0	0	1	0.00	2	0	.000	.000	.000	2	0	1.000	1.000	1.000
1980	Mon-N	534	6	.238	.303	.333	6	2	0	69	2.61	4	3	0	72	3.38	0	2	0	37	4.34	10	3	0	104	2.52	293	3	.266	.326	.369	241	3	.203	.276	.290
1981	Mon-N	595	3	.239	.283	.304	5	5	0	100	2.70	2	4	0	57	2.98	3	6	0	84	3.43	4	3	0	73	2.09	291	0	.268	.313	.337	304	3	.211	.255	.273
1982	Mon-N	910	25	.254	.302	.379	5	5	0	100	4.15	7	9	0	137	3.15	5	7	0	107	3.79	7	7	0	130	3.40	487	12	.273	.323	.394	423	13	.232	.278	.362
1983	Mon-N	916	19	.251	.297	.392	12	4	0	139	3.83	5	8	0	104	3.65	7	8	0	109	4.03	10	4	0	133	3.52	487	8	.265	.312	.400	429	11	.235	.280	.382
1984	Mon-N	869	27	.265	.294	.436	7	3	0	123	3.15	5	6	0	104	4.17	4	5	0	95	3.71	8	4	0	132	3.55	445	13	.261	.291	.429	424	14	.269	.298	.443
1985	Mon-N	691	8	.271	.315	.363	10	2	0	98	1.65	4	10	0	83	5.75	7	5	0	71	3.31	7	7	0	111	3.66	362	3	.282	.338	.362	329	5	.258	.288	.365
1986	Cin-N	927	24	.264	.306	.392	9	6	0	124	3.70	6	6	0	121	3.06	5	6	0	102	4.15	10	6	0	143	2.84	484	10	.275	.329	.399	443	14	.253	.281	.384
1987	Cin-N	645	33	.267	.308	.487	5	5	0	77	5.63	5	6	0	88	4.18	7	5	0	102	4.75	3	6	0	63	5.03	336	17	.262	.305	.479	309	16	.272	.311	.495
1987	NY-A	182	7	.253	.296	.423	4	1	0	39	4.66	0	1	0	9	5.79	0	0	0	0	—	4	2	0	48	4.88	106	7	.283	.336	.528	76	0	.211	.237	.276
1990	Hou-N	769	21	.287	.338	.441	8	7	0	114	3.94	2	7	0	79	3.65	5	6	0	92	3.23	5	8	0	101	4.35	468	11	.314	.372	.453	301	10	.246	.285	.422
1991	Det-A	890	22	.288	.321	.435	10	4	0	104	4.95	10	5	0	123	3.01	9	4	0	105	3.94	11	5	0	121	3.86	487	15	.275	.312	.444	403	7	.303	.333	.424
1992	Det-A	853	35	.267	.305	.447	6	9	0	130	4.28	8	4	0	91	4.43	9	4	0	103	3.14	5	9	0	118	5.40	414	18	.280	.322	.473	439	17	.255	.288	.421
1993	Det-A	639	28	.291	.336	.496	7	7	0	95	5.02	6	2	0	64	5.88	4	4	0	58	5.43	9	5	0	101	5.33	316	13	.329	.373	.554	323	15	.254	.300	.440
1994	Det-A	484	24	.322	.360	.552	3	2	0	67	4.01	1	3	0	48	8.63	4	4	0	77	6.19	0	1	0	38	5.40	245	10	.335	.379	.543	239	14	.310	.340	.561
TOTALS		9908	282	.268	.311	.418	97	62	0	1379	3.83	65	74	0	1181	4.05	69	66	0	1143	4.04	93	70	0	1417	3.84	5223	140	.281	.328	.432	4685	142	.254	.292	.402
● **Larry Gura** BB/TL																																				
1978	KC-A	798	13	.229	.283	.341	7	1	0	102	2.37	9	3	0	119	3.02	5	2	0	74	3.18	11	2	0	148	2.49	226	2	.164	.209	.226	572	11	.255	.312	.386
1979	KC-A	892	29	.253	.312	.416	6	4	0	109	4.56	7	8	0	125	4.39	5	6	0	113	5.40	8	6	0	120	3.59	237	4	.215	.284	.325	655	25	.267	.322	.449
1980	KC-A	1068	20	.255	.304	.371	8	4	0	140	2.64	10	6	0	144	3.26	10	3	0	138	2.09	8	7	0	145	3.78	235	1	.213	.249	.285	833	19	.267	.319	.395
1981	KC-A	623	11	.223	.265	.335	3	6	0	88	2.56	8	2	0	84	2.88	4	5	0	86	4.20	7	3	0	87	1.25	127	1	.228	.261	.276	496	10	.222	.266	.351
1982	KC-A	961	31	.261	.309	.414	11	6	0	152	3.79	7	6	0	96	4.41	8	4	0	111	4.20	10	8	0	137	3.89	174	6	.224	.269	.368	787	25	.269	.318	.424
1983	KC-A	775	23	.284	.347	.455	7	5	0	85	4.34	4	13	0	115	5.31	6	9	0	113	4.45	5	9	0	87	5.48	127	2	.157	.207	.291	648	21	.309	.374	.488
1984	KC-A	651	26	.269	.338	.459	4	3	0	57	6.19	8	6	0	112	4.66	8	4	0	99	4.91	4	5	0	70	5.56	131	3	.282	.356	.389	520	23	.265	.333	.477
1985	KC-A	19	1	.368	.478	.684	0	0	0	0	—	0	0	1	4	12.46	0	0	1	4	12.46	0	0	0	0	—	6	0	.333	.500	.500	13	1	.385	.467	.769
1985	Chi-N	92	4	.370	.414	.576	0	1	0	3	18.90	0	2	0	17	6.35	0	1	0	7	10.29	0	2	0	13	7.43	16	0	.250	.294	.313	76	4	.395	.439	.632
TOTALS		5879	158	.256	.311	.402	46	30	0	736	3.66	53	46	1	817	4.09	46	34	1	746	4.13	53	42	0	807	3.66	1279	19	.210	.262	.305	4600	139	.269	.325	.429
● **Mark Guthrie** BR/TL																																				
1989	Min-A	226	7	.292	.348	.442	2	1	0	33	3.03	0	3	0	25	6.57	0	0	0	0	—	2	4	0	57	4.55	44	2	.295	.333	.477	182	5	.291	.351	.434
1990	Min-A	557	8	.276	.325	.370	2	4	0	69	3.93	5	5	0	76	3.67	2	2	0	35	5.45	5	7	0	110	3.27	99	1	.343	.363	.414	458	7	.262	.317	.360
1991	Min-A	383	11	.303	.369	.465	1	4	1	45	6.25	6	1	1	53	2.70	5	4	0	56	5.66	2	1	2	42	2.55	86	4	.337	.383	.500	297	7	.293	.365	.455
1992	Min-A	274	7	.215	.274	.321	2	0	3	36	2.02	0	3	2	39	3.66	1	2	1	38	4.23	1	1	4	37	1.47	88	0	.205	.242	.261	186	7	.220	.289	.349
1993	Min-A	75	2	.267	.387	.400	2	1	0	12	5.11	1	0	0	9	4.15	2	1	0	21	4.71	0	0	0	0	—	27	0	.148	.233	.185	48	2	.333	.460	.521
1994	Min-A	206	8	.316	.366	.573	3	0	1	22	3.68	1	2	0	29	7.98	4	1	1	38	7.17	0	1	0	14	3.29	67	1	.284	.363	.433	139	7	.331	.368	.640
1995	Min-A	162	5	.290	.358	.432	2	1	0	20	5.03	3	2	0	23	3.97	3	3	0	30	5.10	2	0	0	12	2.92	65	2	.262	.294	.369	97	3	.309	.396	.474
1995	LA-N	79	1	.241	.326	.329	0	1	0	11	3.97	0	1	0	8	3.24	0	0	0	0	—	0	2	0	20	3.66	29	0	.207	.303	.207	50	1	.260	.339	.400
1996	LA-N	271	3	.240	.295	.310	1	2	1	32	1.39	1	1	0	41	2.88	1	0	0	37	1.22	1	3	1	36	3.25	85	1	.247	.301	.318	186	2	.237	.293	.306
1997	LA-N	261	12	.272	.344	.460	1	3	0	30	3.94	0	1	1	40	6.35	1	2	0	38	3.58	0	2	1	32	7.39	85	3	.282	.351	.424	176	9	.267	.340	.477
1998	LA-N	210	3	.267	.347	.367	1	0	0	26	1.73	1	1	0	28	5.14	1	1	0	31	2.03	1	0	0	23	5.48	86	1	.256	.289	.349	124	2	.274	.384	.379
1999	Bos-A	182	9	.275	.348	.511	0	0	2	28	2.93	1	1	0	19	10.13	0	1	2	30	5.40	1	0	0	16	6.61	69	2	.333	.385	.536	113	7	.239	.326	.496
1999	Chi-N	41	1	.171	.244	.293	0	2	0	8	5.63	0	0	0	4	0.00	0	0	0	0	—	0	2	0	12	3.65	11	0	.182	.250	.182	30	1	.167	.242	.333
2000	Chi-N	66	1	.258	.350	.348	2	2	0	11	4.76	0	1	0	7	4.91	2	3	0	19	4.82	0	0	0	0	—	15	0	.333	.389	.333	51	1	.235	.339	.353
2000	TB-A	126	4	.262	.354	.389	0	0	0	13	7.11	1	1	0	19	2.79	1	1	0	22	2.86	0	0	0	10	8.10	47	2	.234	.308	.383	79	2	.278	.380	.392
2000	Tor-A	76	3	.263	.345	.395	0	1	0	10	5.23	0	1	0	10	4.35	0	0	0	0	—	0	2	0	21	4.79	36	0	.306	.405	.306	40	3	.225	.289	.475
TOTALS		3195	85	.271	.337	.408	18	22	8	405	3.80	20	24	4	431	4.53	23	21	4	394	4.44	15	25	8	442	3.95	939	19	.276	.328	.381	2256	66	.269	.340	.419
● **Jose Guzman** BR/TR																																				
1985	Tex-A	126	3	.214	.293	.325	3	0	0	23	0.79	0	2	0	10	7.20	0	0	0	0	—	3	2	0	33	2.76	70	2	.229	.270	.357	56	1	.196	.318	.286
1986	Tex-A	680	23	.293	.353	.446	6	7	0	103	3.92	3	8	0	69	5.48	7	8	0	103	4.03	2	7	0	70	5.30	375	13	.309	.367	.480	305	10	.272	.336	.403
1987	Tex-A	781	30	.251	.322	.420	9	9	0	108	4.98	5	5	0	100	4.32	6	6	0	81	5.13	8	8	0	128	4.37	408	11	.240	.300	.363	373	19	.263	.344	.483
1988	Tex-A	779	20	.231	.306	.359	6	7	0	115	3.14	5	6	0	92	4.40	7	6	0	122	3.54	4	7	0	85	3.93	375	8	.205	.286	.312	404	12	.255	.325	.403
1991	Tex-A	636	10	.239	.330	.341	5	3	0	61	3.86	8	4	0	109	2.64	3	3	0	55	3.13	10	4	0	115	3.05	283	6	.244	.353	.367	353	4	.235	.311	.320
1992	Tex-A	853	17	.268	.327	.399	6	7	0	103	4.28	10	4	0	121	3.12	7	5	0	105	3.94	9	6	0	119	3.40	399	6	.278	.323	.409	454	11	.260	.330	.390
1993	Chi-N	729	25	.258	.327	.428	8	5	0	115	4.32	4	5	0	76	4.36	7	6	0	103	4.38	5	4	0	88	4.28	396	16	.273	.345	.475	333	9	.240	.305	.372
1994	Chi-N	76	1	.289	.396	.408	1	1	0	8	9.72	1	1	0	11	8.74	2	2	0	20	9.15	0	0	0	0	—	32	0	.344	.523	.406	44	1	.250	.277	.409
TOTALS		4660	129	.256	.327	.397	44	39	0	636	4.05	36	35	0	589	4.05	39	36	0	587	4.21	41	38	0	637	3.90	2338	62	.259	.329	.401	2322	67	.253	.325	.394

		TOTAL					HOME					AWAY					1ST HALF					2ND HALF					LEFT					RIGHT				
YEAR	TM/L	AB	HR	AVG	OBP	SLG	W	L	SV	IP	ERA	W	L	SV	IP	ERA	W	L	SV	IP	ERA	W	L	SV	IP	ERA	AB	HR	AVG	OBP	SLG	AB	HR	AVG	OBP	SLG
● Moose Haas BR/TR																																				
1978	Mil-A	121	6	.273	.315	.479	2	1	0	21	5.23	0	2	1	10	8.10	2	3	0	28	6.83	0	0	1	3	0.00	75	4	.293	.338	.547	46	2	.239	.280	.370
1979	Mil-A	719	26	.275	.327	.437	5	5	0	88	4.30	6	6	0	97	5.21	5	5	0	92	5.48	6	6	0	93	4.08	366	17	.303	.346	.505	353	9	.246	.308	.365
1980	Mil-A	954	25	.258	.297	.390	8	11	0	155	3.30	8	4	0	97	2.78	8	6	0	107	3.11	8	9	0	145	3.10	548	14	.285	.321	.425	406	11	.222	.265	.342
1981	Mil-A	531	10	.275	.324	.394	5	4	0	61	4.40	6	3	0	76	4.50	5	4	0	71	4.56	6	3	0	66	4.34	274	4	.310	.362	.416	257	6	.237	.282	.370
1982	Mil-A	767	15	.302	.334	.434	5	4	0	82	4.08	6	4	1	112	4.76	4	4	0	94	4.69	7	4	1	99	4.26	355	6	.335	.380	.465	412	9	.274	.293	.408
1983	Mil-A	676	12	.251	.294	.357	8	2	0	97	2.51	5	1	0	82	4.15	5	2	0	89	4.06	8	1	0	90	2.49	318	4	.258	.313	.336	358	8	.246	.276	.374
1984	Mil-A	736	15	.279	.316	.408	7	3	0	101	2.93	2	8	0	88	5.22	5	6	0	92	4.32	4	5	0	98	3.69	407	5	.265	.318	.364	329	10	.295	.312	.462
1985	Mil-A	634	21	.260	.287	.410	6	3	0	103	3.42	2	5	0	59	4.58	7	3	0	95	2.38	1	5	0	67	5.91	334	10	.260	.291	.389	300	11	.260	.283	.433
1986	Oak-A	266	4	.218	.271	.316	2	1	0	25	2.49	5	1	0	47	2.87	7	2	0	63	2.98	0	0	0	9	1.00	120	3	.283	.351	.392	146	1	.164	.201	.253
1987	Oak-A	170	7	.335	.367	.541	1	2	0	20	5.85	1	0	0	21	5.66	2	2	0	41	5.75	0	0	0	0	—	101	3	.307	.336	.446	69	4	.377	.411	.681
TOTALS		5574	141	.271	.311	.406	49	36	0	753	3.55	41	34	2	688	4.43	50	37	0	771	4.15	40	33	2	671	3.77	2898	70	.288	.333	.419	2676	71	.252	.286	.392
● Mike Hampton BR/TL																																				
1993	Sea-A	76	3	.368	.479	.592	1	2	0	10	12.60	0	1	1	7	5.14	1	2	0	10	8.38	0	1	1	7	11.05	29	2	.345	.367	.655	47	1	.383	.531	.553
1994	Hou-N	163	4	.282	.354	.417	2	1	0	20	3.98	0	0	0	21	3.43	1	1	0	28	3.54	1	0	0	13	4.05	70	2	.329	.397	.486	93	2	.247	.320	.366
1995	Hou-N	572	13	.247	.308	.364	4	4	0	80	2.48	5	4	0	71	4.33	2	3	0	43	2.08	7	5	0	107	3.86	114	3	.272	.341	.412	458	10	.240	.300	.352
1996	Hou-N	625	12	.280	.334	.402	6	4	0	86	3.45	4	6	0	74	3.75	5	4	0	82	3.17	5	6	0	78	4.04	128	2	.281	.319	.398	497	10	.280	.338	.402
1997	Hou-N	844	16	.257	.318	.372	10	2	0	114	3.09	5	8	0	109	4.61	3	8	0	95	5.29	12	3	0	128	2.75	155	3	.303	.353	.426	689	13	.247	.311	.360
1998	Hou-N	817	18	.278	.334	.398	3	3	0	91	2.98	8	4	0	121	3.64	8	3	0	103	2.80	3	4	0	109	3.89	166	2	.277	.358	.380	651	16	.278	.340	.402
1999	Hou-N	854	12	.241	.322	.324	13	2	0	141	2.49	9	2	0	98	3.49	10	3	0	118	3.04	12	1	0	121	2.76	141	2	.149	.218	.199	713	10	.259	.342	.349
2000	NY-N	806	10	.241	.328	.325	11	4	0	132	2.05	4	6	0	86	4.83	7	5	0	108	3.68	8	5	0	110	2.62	152	3	.257	.317	.388	654	7	.237	.330	.310
TOTALS		4757	88	.259	.330	.368	50	22	0	674	2.89	35	31	1	587	4.08	37	28	0	588	3.54	48	25	1	673	3.36	955	19	.265	.326	.384	3802	69	.258	.331	.364
● Erik Hanson BR/TR																																				
1988	Sea-A	152	4	.230	.291	.388	0	2	0	21	5.14	2	1	0	21	1.31	0	0	0	0	—	2	3	0	42	3.24	70	1	.271	.338	.357	82	3	.195	.250	.415
1989	Sea-A	423	7	.243	.304	.336	5	2	0	58	3.57	4	3	0	55	2.77	4	4	0	60	3.75	5	1	0	53	2.53	226	2	.212	.267	.283	197	5	.279	.344	.396
1990	Sea-A	883	15	.232	.287	.332	7	6	0	111	3.56	11	3	0	125	2.96	8	6	0	103	4.19	10	3	0	133	2.50	465	5	.222	.283	.308	418	10	.244	.291	.359
1991	Sea-A	676	16	.269	.323	.414	4	5	0	89	4.25	4	3	0	86	3.36	4	3	0	64	3.66	4	5	0	111	3.90	355	10	.239	.275	.411	321	6	.302	.374	.417
1992	Sea-A	728	14	.287	.341	.402	6	6	0	90	4.78	2	11	0	96	4.86	5	10	0	113	4.05	3	7	0	73	6.01	365	5	.241	.291	.329	363	9	.333	.390	.477
1993	Sea-A	819	17	.263	.315	.402	6	5	0	119	2.79	5	7	0	96	4.33	5	6	0	115	3.14	6	6	0	100	3.86	425	4	.231	.285	.327	394	13	.297	.348	.482
1994	Cin-N	484	10	.283	.317	.407	1	1	0	50	3.58	4	4	0	72	4.48	4	5	0	85	4.87	1	0	0	38	2.39	222	6	.275	.317	.419	262	4	.290	.318	.397
1995	Bos-A	726	17	.258	.311	.386	5	3	0	93	4.37	10	2	0	94	4.12	7	1	0	77	2.91	8	4	0	109	5.19	409	7	.215	.266	.303	317	10	.312	.369	.492
1996	Tor-A	842	26	.289	.365	.445	5	7	0	97	5.31	8	10	0	118	5.49	8	9	0	107	6.12	5	8	0	107	4.70	425	13	.268	.350	.414	417	13	.309	.380	.477
1997	Tor-A	59	3	.254	.323	.458	0	0	0	5	7.20	0	0	0	10	8.10	0	0	0	12	7.50	0	0	0	3	9.00	29	1	.241	.333	.379	30	2	.267	.313	.533
1998	Tor-A	210	10	.348	.429	.567	0	0	0	24	4.50	0	3	0	25	7.92	0	3	0	49	6.24	0	0	0	0	—	118	4	.381	.443	.585	92	6	.304	.413	.543
TOTALS		6002	139	.267	.325	.399	39	37	0	758	4.09	50	47	0	798	4.21	45	47	0	786	4.33	44	37	0	770	3.96	3109	58	.243	.300	.357	2893	81	.293	.351	.444
● Pete Harnisch BB/TR																																				
1988	Bal-A	50	1	.260	.373	.400	0	0	0	0	—	0	2	0	13	5.54	0	0	0	0	—	0	2	0	13	5.54	16	0	.188	.350	.313	34	1	.294	.385	.441
1989	Bal-A	390	10	.249	.358	.385	3	1	0	34	3.41	2	8	0	69	5.22	0	1	0	11	3.27	5	8	0	92	4.78	183	3	.257	.390	.377	207	7	.242	.328	.391
1990	Bal-A	723	17	.261	.339	.394	7	6	0	89	4.63	4	5	0	99	4.08	7	4	0	93	3.87	4	7	0	96	4.80	435	10	.287	.358	.439	288	7	.222	.310	.326
1991	Hou-N	796	14	.212	.288	.313	7	4	0	119	2.41	5	5	0	97	3.05	5	6	0	109	2.32	7	3	0	108	3.08	457	10	.234	.319	.352	339	4	.183	.247	.260
1992	Hou-N	779	18	.234	.294	.371	7	4	0	138	2.75	2	6	0	69	5.61	3	7	0	105	4.02	6	3	0	101	3.38	466	10	.234	.300	.365	313	8	.233	.285	.380
1993	Hou-N	798	20	.214	.289	.340	9	5	0	129	2.52	7	4	0	89	3.64	6	5	0	97	3.79	10	4	0	120	2.32	429	13	.238	.327	.375	369	7	.187	.241	.298
1994	Hou-N	372	13	.269	.341	.441	5	3	0	59	5.49	3	2	0	36	5.25	3	4	0	51	6.66	5	1	0	44	3.92	168	4	.274	.349	.440	204	9	.265	.335	.441
1995	NY-N	425	13	.261	.301	.431	1	4	0	66	2.73	1	4	0	44	5.11	1	5	0	72	4.13	1	3	0	38	2.84	195	6	.308	.357	.503	230	7	.222	.253	.370
1996	NY-N	749	30	.260	.318	.434	5	6	0	113	3.83	3	6	0	82	4.72	4	4	0	81	4.87	4	8	0	113	3.73	350	11	.271	.336	.431	399	19	.251	.303	.436
1997	NY-N	107	5	.327	.388	.570	0	1	0	16	9.77	0	0	0	10	5.40	0	0	0	5	5.40	0	1	0	21	8.71	48	1	.417	.491	.604	59	4	.254	.297	.542
1997	Mil-A	53	1	.245	.385	.415	1	0	0	6	1.50	0	1	0	8	7.87	0	0	0	0	—	1	1	0	14	5.14	22	1	.318	.483	.591	31	0	.194	.306	.290
1998	Cin-N	771	24	.228	.291	.388	6	5	0	101	3.46	8	2	0	108	2.84	7	3	0	113	2.95	7	4	0	96	3.38	380	13	.216	.278	.382	391	11	.240	.304	.394
1999	Cin-N	754	25	.252	.307	.420	5	5	0	79	3.29	11	5	0	119	3.93	7	6	0	96	3.46	9	4	0	102	3.88	336	14	.256	.315	.455	418	11	.249	.300	.392
2000	Cin-N	510	23	.261	.321	.475	4	3	0	66	6.30	4	3	0	65	3.17	1	4	0	31	8.62	7	2	0	100	3.52	226	6	.265	.341	.420	284	17	.257	.304	.518
TOTALS		7277	214	.244	.312	.395	60	47	0	1015	3.59	50	53	0	909	4.12	44	49	0	866	3.97	66	51	0	1058	3.73	3711	102	.256	.331	.408	3566	112	.231	.291	.382
● Greg Harris BB/TR																																				
1981	NY-N	264	8	.246	.322	.405	2	2	0	39	4.38	1	3	1	30	4.55	2	1	0	28	4.18	1	4	1	41	4.65	109	2	.248	.333	.376	155	6	.245	.314	.426
1982	Cin-N	351	12	.274	.344	.427	1	2	0	41	5.71	1	4	1	50	4.11	2	2	0	34	4.19	0	4	1	57	5.21	124	2	.298	.362	.403	227	10	.260	.333	.441
1983	Cin-N	4	0	.500	.750	.500	0	0	0	1	27.00	0	0	0	0	—	0	0	0	1	27.00	0	0	0	0	—	2	0	.500	.833	.500	2	0	.500	.500	.500
1984	Mon-N	58	0	.172	.284	.207	0	1	0	5	1.69	0	0	2	12	2.19	0	1	2	18	2.04	0	0	0	0	—	26	0	.192	.344	.231	32	0	.156	.229	.188
1984	SD-N	134	3	.209	.306	.343	0	0	0	11	3.27	2	1	1	26	2.45	0	0	0	0	—	2	1	1	37	2.70	59	2	.237	.313	.390	75	1	.187	.300	.307
1985	Tex-A	397	7	.186	.273	.290	4	2	3	57	2.68	1	2	8	56	2.25	2	1	6	56	2.24	3	3	5	57	2.70	206	4	.175	.257	.286	191	3	.199	.290	.293
1986	Tex-A	410	12	.251	.318	.402	9	4	13	65	2.64	1	4	7	47	3.09	3	7	14	54	3.17	7	1	6	57	2.51	179	5	.251	.335	.397	231	7	.251	.304	.407
1987	Tex-A	559	18	.281	.349	.440	3	2	0	81	4.65	2	8	0	59	5.16	2	7	0	60	5.58	3	3	0	81	4.33	270	4	.256	.319	.363	289	14	.304	.377	.512
1988	Phi-N	382	7	.209	.309	.301	1	6	1	58	2.18	3	0	0	49	2.55	3	2	1	42	3.00	1	4	0	65	1.94	182	3	.209	.316	.302	200	4	.210	.303	.300
1989	Phi-N	274	7	.234	.340	.369	1	1	1	41	5.01	1	1	0	34	1.85	1	1	0	55	3.29	1	1	1	21	4.35	121	1	.190	.329	.281	153	6	.268	.349	.438
1989	Bos-A	101	1	.208	.308	.287	1	0	0	9	1.00	1	2	0	19	3.32	0	0	0	0	—	2	2	0	28	2.57	56	1	.196	.297	.304	45	0	.222	.321	.267
1990	Bos-A	703	13	.265	.338	.381	8	5	0	89	4.45	5	4	0	95	3.59	7	3	0	82	3.09	6	6	0	103	4.73	352	5	.239	.312	.338	351	8	.291	.364	.425
1991	Bos-A	645	13	.243	.318	.363	4	6	2	71	3.80	7	6	0	102	3.88	4	7	1	84	4.39	7	5	1	89	3.34	303	5	.244	.322	.353	342	8	.243	.314	.371
1992	Bos-A	382	6	.215	.324	.312	3	1	3	58	2.79	1	8	1	50	2.17	2	3	0	50	1.45	2	6	4	58	3.41	142	2	.211	.335	.303	240	4	.217	.317	.317
1993	Bos-A	410	7	.232	.341	.329	3	5	5	55	4.77	3	2	3	58	2.81	3	3	2	54	2.85	3	4	6	59	4.60	198	2	.253	.353	.348	212	5	.212	.329	.311
1994	Bos-A	187	8	.321	.396	.513	1	1	1	29	7.53	2	3	1	17	9.53	3	4	2	46	8.28	0	0	0	0	—	85	1	.282	.390	.388	102	7	.353	.402	.618
1994	NY-A	18	1	.222	.375	.444	0	1	0	5	5.40	0	0	0	0	—	0	0	0	0	—	0	1	0	5	5.40	9	0	.333	.455	.444	9	1	.111	.308	.444
1995	Mon-N	184	6	.245	.308	.402	0	1	0	24	3.00	2	2	0	24	2.22	0	0	0	15	3.00	2	3	0	33	2.43	83	3	.289	.344	.422	101	3	.208	.279	.386
TOTALS		5463	129	.243	.327	.370	41	40	29	739	3.96	33	50	25	728	3.41	34	42	28	677	3.73	40	48	26	790	3.65	2506	42	.237	.326	.345	2957	87	.248	.328	.391
● Shigetoshi Hasegawa BR/TR																																				
1997	Ana-A	438	14	.269	.339	.438	0	4	0	66	4.23	3	3	0	51	3.55	1	4	0	61	4.40	2	3	0	55	3.42	176	5	.278	.350	.438	262	9	.263	.332	.439
1998	Ana-A	357	14	.241	.302	.431	4	1	2	51	3.71	4	2	3	46	2.53	3	1	1	52	3.48	5	2	4	46	2.76	146	4	.212	.259	.377	211	10	.261	.331	.469
1999	Ana-A	290	14	.276	.352	.462	2	3	0	40	5.63	2	3	2	37	4.14	1	2	0	39	3.69	3	4	2	38	6.16	113	3	.274	.368	.398	177	11	.277	.340	.503
2000	Ana-A	370	11	.270	.339	.411	6	2	5	48	2.83	4	4	4	48	4.31	6	2	2	46	5.52	4	4	7	50	1.80	171	5	.246	.326	.368	199	6	.291	.350	.447
TOTALS		1455	53	.264	.333	.434	12	10	7	205	4.05	13	12	9	182	3.61	11	9	3	198	4.28	14	13	13	189	3.38	606	17	.252	.326	.396	849	36	.272	.338	.462
● Jimmy Haynes BR/TR																																				
1995	Bal-A	81	2	.136	.247	.235	0	1	0	9	1.00	2	0	0	15	3.00	0	0	0	0	—	2	1	0	24	2.25	34	1	.147	.256	.294	47	1	.128	.241	.191
1996	Bal-A	366	14	.333	.422	.519	3	3	0	51	6.84	0	3	1	38	10.27	2	5	1	68	7.05	1	1	0	21	12.23	159	5	.302	.414	.472	207	9	.357	.429	.556
1997	Oak-A	282	7	.262	.354	.383	1	5	0	44	4.91	2	1	0	29	3.68	0	0	0	0	—	3	6	0	73	4.42	141	4	.248	.339	.376	141	3	.277	.368	.390
1998	Oak-A	768	25	.298	.370	.478	4	6	0	94	6.01	7	3	0	100	4.23	6	3	0	105	4.04	5	6	0	90	6.32	389	8	.308	.400	.455	379	17	.288	.337	.501
1999	Oak-A	561	21	.282	.370	.467	5	5	0	73	5.92	2	7	0	69	6.78	5	6	0	88	5.03	2	6	0	54	8.45	307	6	.283	.373	.420	254	15	.280	.367	.524
2000	Mil-A	774	21	.295	.378	.428	4	6	0	101	5.45	8	7	0	99	5.20	7	7	0	101	4.63	5	6	0	98	6.04	329	11	.319	.405	.462	445	10	.276	.357	.402
TOTALS		2832	90	.290	.374	.451	17	26	0	372	5.70	21	21	1	350	5.56	20	21	1	361	5.01	18	26	0	361	6.26	1359	35	.294	.387	.439	1473	55	.286	.361	.462
● Rick Helling BR/TR																																				
1994	Tex-A	210	14	.295	.351	.557	3	1	0	24	4.94	0	1	0	28	6.67	3	2	0	52	5.88	0	0	0	0	—	98	11	.398	.478	.847	112	3	.205	.226	.304
1995	Tex-A	50	2	.340	.435	.500	0	1	0	7	8.59	0	1	0	5	3.60	0	2	0	12	6.57	0	0	0	0	—	25	1	.320	.457	.440	25	1	.360	.407	.560
1996	Tex-A	82	7	.280	.348	.683	0	1	0	10	13.03	1	1	0	11	2.53	1	1	0	16	4.96	0	1	0	4	18.00	50	4	.220	.298	.600	32	3	.375	.429	.813
1996	Fla-N	98	2	.143	.200	.245	2	0	0	16	1.13	0	1	0	12	3.09	0	0	0	0	—	2	1	0	28	1.95	31	1	.258	.361	.484	67	1	.090	.116	.134
1997	Fla-N	263	12	.232	.351	.445	1	2	0	34	2.62	1	4	0	42	5.83	2	5	0	60	4.50	0	1	0	16	3.94	109	6	.239	.386	.505	154	6	.227	.324	.403
1997	Tex-A	200	5	.235	.311	.355	1	2	0	24	5.55	2	1	0	31	3.82	0	0	0	0	—	3	3	0	55	4.58	113	3	.204	.291	.319	87	2	.276	.337	.402
1998	Tex-A	827	27	.253	.314	.416	9	3	0	89	5.18	11	4	0	128	3.88	11	4	0	114	4.25	9	3	0	102	4.59	417	16	.252	.330	.441	410	11	.254	.298	.390
1999	Tex-A	837	41	.272	.340	.497	6	4	0	104	4.76	7	7	0	115	4.92	6	7	0	106	4.34	7	4	0	114	5.30	401	20	.262	.343	.479	436	21	.282	.338	.514

YEAR	TM/L	TOTAL AB	HR	AVG	OBP	SLG	HOME W	L	SV	IP	ERA	AWAY W	L	SV	IP	ERA	1ST HALF W	L	SV	IP	ERA	2ND HALF W	L	SV	IP	ERA	LEFT AB	HR	AVG	OBP	SLG	RIGHT AB	HR	AVG	OBP	SLG
2000	Tex-A	842	29	.252	.334	.445	9	6	0	103	4.91	7	7	0	114	4.09	8	7	0	109	4.14	8	6	0	108	4.82	453	16	.238	.329	.435	389	13	.267	.339	.458
TOTALS		3409	139	.256	.330	.453	31	20	0	411	4.89	29	27	0	485	4.45	31	28	0	469	4.54	29	19	0	427	4.77	1697	78	.255	.345	.473	1712	61	.257	.315	.433
● Tom Henke BR/TR																																				
1982	Tex-A	57	0	.246	.348	.316	1	0	0	8	1.13	0	0	0	8	1.17	0	0	0	0	—	1	0	0	16	1.15	20	0	.400	.520	.450	37	0	.162	.244	.243
1983	Tex-A	61	1	.262	.308	.328	1	0	1	11	0.82	0	0	0	5	9.00	0	0	0	0	—	1	0	1	16	3.38	28	1	.250	.276	.357	33	0	.273	.333	.303
1984	Tex-A	115	0	.313	.407	.400	1	0	0	14	5.02	0	1	2	14	7.71	0	0	0	8	7.87	1	1	2	20	5.75	58	0	.310	.438	.362	57	0	.316	.373	.439
1985	Tor-A	141	4	.206	.245	.312	0	2	7	21	2.61	3	1	6	19	1.40	0	0	0	0	—	3	3	13	40	2.03	80	4	.225	.262	.387	61	0	.180	.224	.213
1986	Tor-A	329	6	.191	.261	.286	5	2	12	43	3.16	4	3	15	49	3.51	6	3	10	40	4.28	3	2	17	51	2.63	177	4	.220	.299	.322	152	2	.158	.216	.243
1987	Tor-A	330	10	.188	.242	.330	0	2	17	50	1.62	0	4	17	44	3.48	0	3	13	42	3.02	0	3	21	52	2.06	163	3	.172	.225	.288	167	7	.204	.258	.371
1988	Tor-A	253	6	.237	.306	.364	2	1	11	33	2.48	2	3	14	35	3.31	0	1	16	33	2.18	4	3	9	35	3.60	134	2	.261	.322	.321	119	4	.210	.289	.412
1989	Tor-A	322	5	.205	.264	.314	6	0	7	36	2.48	2	3	13	53	1.54	6	3	3	34	3.48	2	0	17	55	0.98	149	3	.195	.272	.315	173	2	.214	.257	.312
1990	Tor-A	272	8	.213	.266	.342	2	0	16	38	2.39	0	4	16	37	1.95	0	1	12	37	1.70	2	3	20	38	2.63	138	4	.210	.267	.355	134	4	.216	.266	.328
1991	Tor-A	179	4	.184	.232	.307	0	1	14	23	2.31	0	1	18	27	2.33	0	0	14	19	1.45	0	2	18	32	2.84	95	3	.179	.243	.347	84	1	.190	.218	.262
1992	Tor-A	203	5	.197	.272	.315	2	0	19	29	2.48	1	2	15	27	2.03	2	1	13	23	1.96	1	1	21	33	2.48	105	2	.190	.279	.286	98	3	.204	.264	.347
1993	Tex-A	268	7	.205	.278	.306	5	1	27	44	1.62	0	4	13	30	4.80	4	2	15	35	2.57	1	3	25	39	3.20	132	3	.205	.289	.303	136	4	.206	.267	.309
1994	Tex-A	142	6	.232	.290	.444	1	2	9	20	2.21	2	4	6	18	5.60	2	3	6	20	4.43	1	3	9	18	3.06	72	4	.208	.293	.486	70	2	.257	.288	.400
1995	StL-N	201	2	.209	.274	.274	1	1	20	31	1.72	0	0	16	23	1.96	0	0	16	25	1.78	1	1	20	29	1.86	97	2	.196	.243	.309	104	0	.221	.302	.240
TOTALS		2873	64	.211	.275	.326	27	12	160	402	2.29	14	30	151	388	3.06	20	17	118	316	2.88	21	25	193	474	2.53	1448	35	.213	.284	.333	1425	29	.209	.265	.319
● Mike Henneman BR/TR																																				
1987	Det-A	362	8	.238	.300	.351	7	0	4	49	1.65	4	3	3	48	4.34	3	0	1	31	2.61	8	3	6	66	3.15	170	6	.241	.328	.412	192	2	.234	.273	.297
1988	Det-A	331	7	.218	.273	.308	7	3	9	43	2.28	2	3	13	48	1.50	2	2	14	35	2.04	7	4	8	56	1.77	142	2	.218	.293	.303	189	5	.217	.257	.312
1989	Det-A	335	4	.251	.355	.337	8	0	5	49	3.65	3	4	3	41	3.76	5	1	1	39	3.46	6	3	7	51	3.88	155	1	.265	.377	.361	180	3	.239	.336	.317
1990	Det-A	356	4	.253	.320	.334	5	3	8	48	3.72	3	3	14	46	2.35	4	4	17	46	2.53	4	2	5	48	3.56	144	0	.278	.364	.326	212	4	.236	.288	.340
1991	Det-A	314	2	.258	.326	.344	7	0	15	51	1.95	3	2	6	34	4.28	5	2	11	49	2.96	5	0	10	36	2.78	127	0	.268	.373	.339	187	2	.251	.290	.348
1992	Det-A	293	6	.256	.299	.369	1	4	14	42	3.19	1	2	10	35	4.89	0	3	12	39	3.72	2	3	12	39	4.19	144	2	.278	.314	.389	149	4	.235	.284	.349
1993	Det-A	275	4	.251	.331	.356	3	1	7	32	3.41	2	2	17	40	2.03	1	1	12	35	1.78	4	2	12	36	3.47	129	3	.287	.376	.442	146	1	.219	.290	.281
1994	Det-A	145	5	.297	.376	.462	1	1	4	18	8.15	0	2	4	17	2.12	1	1	8	28	4.82	0	2	0	7	6.75	64	2	.281	.397	.438	81	3	.309	.356	.481
1995	Det-A	108	0	.222	.282	.278	0	0	11	14	0.63	0	1	7	15	2.40	0	1	14	21	2.11	0	0	4	8	0.00	61	0	.279	.323	.344	47	0	.149	.231	.191
1995	Hou-N	79	1	.266	.310	.354	0	0	4	10	1.86	0	1	4	11	3.97	0	0	0	0	—	0	1	8	21	3.00	37	1	.297	.341	.459	42	0	.238	.283	.262
1996	Tex-A	159	6	.258	.326	.409	0	2	15	21	4.22	0	5	16	21	7.40	0	5	20	26	6.92	0	2	11	16	3.94	78	3	.295	.367	.449	81	3	.222	.284	.370
TOTALS		2757	47	.249	.318	.350	39	14	96	378	3.03	18	28	97	355	3.40	21	20	110	350	3.19	36	22	83	383	3.22	1251	20	.266	.349	.378	1506	27	.234	.290	.327
● Pat Hentgen BR/TR																																				
1991	Tor-A	24	1	.208	.345	.417	0	0	0	2	3.86	0	0	0	5	1.80	0	0	0	0	—	0	0	0	7	2.45	6	1	.333	.500	.833	18	0	.167	.286	.278
1992	Tor-A	193	7	.254	.357	.430	3	1	0	29	4.91	2	1	0	21	6.00	5	0	0	30	4.25	0	2	0	21	6.97	87	1	.253	.383	.368	106	6	.255	.333	.481
1993	Tor-A	834	27	.258	.322	.414	7	6	0	111	4.77	12	3	0	105	2.91	11	2	0	101	3.02	8	7	0	115	4.62	421	11	.285	.339	.430	413	16	.230	.305	.397
1994	Tor-A	657	21	.240	.305	.379	7	4	0	92	2.05	6	4	0	82	4.92	9	5	0	116	3.10	4	3	0	59	3.99	346	11	.266	.321	.408	311	10	.212	.287	.347
1995	Tor-A	815	24	.290	.363	.444	4	8	0	112	5.69	6	6	0	88	4.38	4	6	0	77	6.22	6	8	0	124	4.43	453	11	.298	.379	.442	362	13	.279	.343	.448
1996	Tor-A	988	20	.241	.308	.355	9	7	0	152	3.19	11	3	0	113	3.26	7	5	0	118	3.89	13	5	0	148	2.68	507	14	.249	.313	.381	481	6	.233	.303	.328
1997	Tor-A	995	31	.254	.308	.404	8	5	0	135	3.33	7	5	0	129	4.05	8	5	0	145	3.11	7	5	0	119	4.37	511	14	.241	.308	.380	484	17	.269	.307	.430
1998	Tor-A	709	28	.293	.357	.481	4	6	0	84	4.39	8	5	0	94	5.86	9	4	0	107	4.30	3	7	0	71	6.46	364	13	.288	.361	.464	345	15	.299	.352	.499
1999	Tor-A	787	32	.286	.338	.474	5	6	0	90	6.83	6	6	0	109	3.13	5	6	0	91	5.64	6	6	0	108	4.08	395	18	.306	.362	.524	392	14	.265	.315	.423
2000	StL-N	733	24	.276	.353	.439	6	6	0	94	4.71	9	6	0	101	4.74	6	6	0	93	5.54	9	6	0	102	3.98	337	7	.252	.342	.392	396	17	.295	.363	.480
TOTALS		6735	215	.266	.331	.421	53	49	0	902	4.29	67	39	0	848	4.12	64	39	0	877	4.18	56	49	0	873	4.24	3427	101	.272	.341	.424	3308	114	.259	.321	.418
● Felix Heredia BL/TL																																				
1996	Fla-N	67	1	.313	.397	.448	1	0	0	6	3.18	0	1	0	11	4.91	0	0	0	0	—	1	1	0	17	4.32	26	0	.154	.185	.192	41	1	.415	.510	.610
1997	Fla-N	218	3	.243	.345	.358	2	0	0	32	3.06	3	3	0	24	5.92	4	0	0	32	1.97	1	3	0	25	7.30	69	0	.188	.325	.246	149	3	.268	.355	.409
1998	Fla-N	158	1	.241	.368	.361	0	2	2	25	6.39	0	1	0	16	4.02	0	3	1	35	6.23	0	0	1	6	1.42	74	0	.189	.274	.284	84	1	.286	.440	.429
1998	Chi-N	68	1	.279	.338	.382	2	0	0	9	3.12	1	0	0	9	5.00	0	0	0	0	—	3	0	0	18	4.08	34	0	.235	.278	.294	34	1	.324	.395	.471
1999	Chi-N	206	7	.272	.347	.442	1	0	1	24	5.70	2	1	0	28	4.13	3	0	1	29	4.91	0	1	0	23	4.76	93	3	.247	.324	.409	113	4	.292	.366	.469
2000	Chi-N	209	6	.220	.329	.349	6	1	2	33	3.51	1	2	0	25	6.39	3	3	1	31	5.23	4	0	1	28	4.23	82	2	.195	.283	.341	127	4	.236	.357	.354
TOTALS		926	19	.252	.349	.383	12	3	5	129	4.33	7	8	0	114	5.15	10	6	3	127	4.61	9	5	2	116	4.82	378	5	.206	.293	.315	548	14	.283	.386	.431
● Dustin Hermanson BR/TR																																				
1995	SD-N	125	8	.280	.392	.512	2	0	0	18	7.13	1	1	0	14	6.43	3	1	0	12	8.25	0	0	0	20	5.95	54	3	.278	.381	.481	71	5	.282	.400	.535
1996	SD-N	53	3	.340	.367	.604	1	0	0	9	8.31	0	0	0	5	9.00	0	0	0	0	—	1	0	0	14	8.56	22	1	.273	.320	.455	31	2	.387	.400	.710
1997	Mon-N	572	15	.234	.312	.372	3	4	0	68	4.12	5	4	0	91	3.38	3	4	0	72	3.38	5	4	0	86	3.96	271	8	.232	.322	.369	301	7	.236	.302	.375
1998	Mon-N	697	21	.234	.292	.366	9	5	0	108	2.66	5	6	0	79	3.78	6	6	0	78	3.24	8	5	0	109	3.05	344	10	.235	.310	.366	353	11	.232	.275	.365
1999	Mon-N	829	20	.271	.330	.419	2	9	0	100	5.49	7	5	0	116	3.09	3	7	0	95	5.57	6	7	0	121	3.12	378	10	.272	.339	.418	451	10	.271	.323	.419
2000	Mon-N	778	26	.290	.352	.467	8	7	3	103	4.91	4	7	1	95	4.63	6	5	4	82	4.94	6	9	0	116	4.66	318	17	.321	.393	.572	460	9	.270	.322	.393
TOTALS		3054	93	.262	.327	.417	25	25	3	405	4.49	22	23	1	400	3.85	21	23	4	339	4.51	26	25	0	466	3.92	1387	49	.267	.343	.434	1667	44	.259	.314	.403
● Livan Hernandez BR/TR																																				
1996	Fla-N	11	0	.273	.385	.273	0	0	0	3	0.00	0	0	0	0	—	0	0	0	0	—	0	0	0	3	0.00	4	0	.250	.500	.250	7	0	.286	.286	.286
1997	Fla-N	353	5	.229	.304	.343	5	3	0	57	3.45	4	0	0	39	2.77	1	0	0	10	4.50	8	3	0	86	3.02	157	3	.248	.344	.395	196	2	.214	.271	.301
1998	Fla-N	917	37	.289	.363	.472	5	7	0	128	4.30	5	5	0	107	5.23	6	4	0	121	4.24	4	8	0	113	5.24	419	18	.277	.352	.470	498	19	.299	.373	.474
1999	Fla-N	548	17	.294	.358	.443	4	5	0	70	4.76	1	4	0	66	4.77	3	8	0	108	4.82	2	1	0	28	4.55	269	9	.297	.371	.446	279	8	.290	.345	.441
1999	SF-N	247	6	.267	.322	.409	1	2	0	28	5.40	2	1	0	35	3.57	0	0	0	0	—	3	3	0	64	4.38	115	3	.278	.362	.435	132	3	.258	.286	.386
2000	SF-N	932	22	.273	.325	.407	12	3	0	127	2.98	5	8	0	113	4.61	6	6	0	112	4.41	11	5	0	128	3.17	414	9	.271	.336	.408	518	13	.274	.316	.405
TOTALS		3008	87	.276	.340	.426	27	20	0	413	3.90	17	18	0	360	4.52	16	18	0	352	4.48	28	20	0	422	3.95	1378	42	.276	.352	.435	1630	45	.276	.331	.418
● Willie Hernandez BL/TL																																				
1978	Chi-N	217	6	.263	.363	.401	5	1	2	38	3.76	3	1	1	21	3.80	5	2	1	33	3.82	3	0	2	27	3.71	79	2	.190	.293	.291	138	4	.304	.402	.464
1979	Chi-N	303	8	.281	.364	.429	2	1	0	42	4.75	2	3	0	37	5.30	1	0	0	35	4.89	3	4	0	44	5.11	105	1	.219	.281	.324	198	7	.313	.407	.485
1980	Chi-N	417	8	.276	.347	.391	0	6	0	57	5.34	1	3	0	51	3.35	1	7	0	54	5.20	0	2	0	55	3.62	120	1	.225	.285	.283	297	7	.296	.371	.434
1981	Chi-N	50	0	.280	.367	.380	0	0	2	6	8.53	0	0	0	7	0.00	0	0	0	0	—	0	0	2	14	3.95	23	0	.217	.310	.304	27	0	.333	.419	.444
1982	Chi-N	276	3	.268	.326	.337	2	1	2	33	3.27	2	5	8	42	2.79	2	5	5	42	4.07	2	1	5	33	1.64	110	0	.227	.252	.282	166	3	.295	.370	.373
1983	Chi-N	72	0	.222	.282	.278	0	0	1	9	3.00	1	0	0	11	3.38	1	0	1	20	3.20	0	0	0	0	—	23	0	.217	.308	.261	49	0	.224	.269	.286
1983	Phi-N	366	9	.254	.305	.399	5	2	3	48	2.81	3	2	4	48	3.78	1	0	4	31	0.29	7	4	3	65	4.71	107	1	.252	.310	.346	259	8	.255	.303	.421
1984	Det-A	496	6	.194	.252	.254	3	2	18	66	2.19	6	1	14	75	1.69	4	0	14	71	2.15	5	3	18	69	1.69	139	0	.173	.212	.194	357	6	.202	.267	.277
1985	Det-A	391	13	.210	.236	.353	6	4	13	59	2.15	2	6	18	48	3.38	4	3	16	55	1.80	4	7	15	52	3.66	105	1	.171	.193	.229	286	12	.224	.252	.399
1986	Det-A	346	13	.251	.301	.413	6	3	9	43	3.77	2	4	15	46	3.35	3	3	15	49	3.28	5	4	9	39	3.89	97	1	.206	.238	.268	249	12	.269	.325	.470
1987	Det-A	192	8	.276	.340	.469	2	2	1	17	4.76	1	2	7	32	3.09	1	1	4	22	3.74	2	3	4	27	3.62	70	2	.243	.286	.386	122	6	.295	.370	.516
1988	Det-A	240	8	.208	.306	.350	4	3	6	38	2.11	2	2	4	29	4.30	5	2	3	36	2.23	1	3	7	31	4.02	85	3	.224	.296	.365	155	5	.200	.311	.342
1989	Det-A	123	4	.293	.379	.455	2	2	8	18	8.00	0	0	7	13	2.70	2	1	12	24	5.63	0	1	3	7	6.14	40	1	.200	.289	.275	83	3	.337	.421	.542
TOTALS		3489	86	.246	.311	.371	37	27	65	474	3.61	25	29	78	460	3.23	30	24	75	471	3.25	32	32	68	463	3.59	1103	13	.211	.266	.288	2386	73	.262	.332	.409
● Orlando Hernandez BR/TR																																				
1998	NY-A	508	11	.222	.299	.341	8	1	0	62	1.74	4	3	0	79	4.22	2	1	0	35	2.04	10	3	0	106	3.49	276	8	.275	.359	.431	232	3	.159	.228	.233
1999	NY-A	801	24	.233	.311	.392	7	4	0	98	3.96	10	5	0	117	4.24	9	6	0	104	3.91	8	3	0	111	4.31	432	15	.273	.352	.442	369	9	.187	.261	.333
2000	NY-A	754	34	.247	.298	.442	4	8	0	82	5.57	8	5	0	113	3.73	6	6	0	93	4.65	6	7	0	103	4.38	394	20	.282	.342	.500	360	14	.208	.248	.378
TOTALS		2063	69	.236	.303	.397	19	13	0	242	3.94	22	13	0	309	4.05	17	13	0	232	3.92	24	13	0	319	4.06	1102	43	.277	.350	.460	961	26	.188	.248	.326
● Roberto Hernandez BR/TR																																				
1991	Chi-A	62	1	.290	.362	.403	1	0	0	9	3.00	0	0	0	6	15.00	0	0	0	0	—	1	0	0	15	7.80	33	1	.212	.297	.333	29	0	.379	.438	.483
1992	Chi-A	250	4	.180	.249	.272	5	1	6	41	0.44	2	2	6	30	3.26	2	0	0	15	2.35	5	3	12	56	1.46	107	1	.187	.264	.280	143	3	.175	.237	.266
1993	Chi-A	290	6	.228	.276	.324	2	3	18	39	2.77	1	1	20	40	1.82	1	3	14	36	2.75	2	1	24	43	1.90	117	2	.231	.311	.308	173	4	.225	.250	.335
1994	Chi-A	185	5	.238	.311	.357	2	2	7	21	4.79	2	2	7	27	5.00	2	3	8	29	6.91	2	1	6	19	1.89	92	2	.217	.291	.293	93	3	.258	.330	.419
1995	Chi-A	237	9	.266	.351	.426	2	1	21	31	2.90	1	6	11	29	5.02	2	3	12	25	4.62	1	4	20	34	3.41	129	5	.279	.384	.450	108	4	.250	.308	.398
1996	Chi-A	313	2	.208	.292	.262	2	2	20	43	1.66	4	3	18	41	2.18	1	0	23	41	1.31	5	5	15	43	2.49	162	1	.191	.271	.228	151	1	.225	.314	.298

		TOTAL					HOME					AWAY					1ST HALF					2ND HALF					LEFT					RIGHT				
YEAR	TM/L	AB	HR	AVG	OBP	SLG	W	L	SV	IP	ERA	W	L	SV	IP	ERA	W	L	SV	IP	ERA	W	L	SV	IP	ERA	AB	HR	AVG	OBP	SLG	AB	HR	AVG	OBP	SLG
1997	Chi-A	176	5	.216	.312	.324	3	0	14	26	2.77	2	1	13	22	2.05	4	1	19	35	2.29	1	0	8	13	2.84	96	2	.188	.297	.250	80	3	.250	.330	.412
1997	SF-N	122	2	.238	.316	.303	1	0	3	13	0.68	4	2	1	19	3.72	0	0	0	0	—	5	2	4	33	2.48	64	0	.203	.271	.219	58	2	.276	.364	.397
1998	TB-A	260	5	.212	.330	.296	2	3	12	36	4.95	0	3	14	35	3.09	0	2	17	39	2.97	2	4	9	32	5.34	132	2	.182	.312	.250	128	3	.242	.349	.344
1999	TB-A	278	1	.245	.330	.295	1	3	22	37	3.68	1	0	21	37	2.45	1	3	21	41	3.95	1	0	22	32	1.95	141	0	.241	.319	.298	137	1	.248	.342	.292
2000	TB-A	279	9	.272	.331	.423	2	6	16	44	4.06	2	1	16	29	1.86	2	2	11	38	4.30	2	5	21	36	2.02	131	4	.328	.399	.496	148	5	.223	.269	.358
TOTALS		2452	49	.231	.310	.329	23	21	139	340	2.91	19	21	127	315	3.17	15	17	125	300	3.42	27	25	141	355	2.71	1204	20	.227	.315	.313	1248	29	.236	.306	.345
● Orel Hershiser	BR/TR																																			
1983	LA-N	29	1	.241	.371	.414	0	0	1	4	2.45	0	0	0	4	4.15	0	0	0	0	—	0	0	1	8	3.38	10	1	.300	.500	.700	19	0	.211	.286	.263
1984	LA-N	712	9	.225	.278	.296	5	5	0	101	3.40	6	3	2	89	1.82	3	3	2	61	4.15	8	5	0	129	1.95	343	2	.245	.296	.300	369	7	.206	.262	.293
1985	LA-N	870	8	.206	.267	.272	11	0	0	133	1.08	8	3	0	106	3.22	7	2	0	100	2.51	12	1	0	139	1.68	477	3	.222	.281	.289	393	5	.186	.249	.252
1986	LA-N	877	13	.243	.312	.339	10	5	0	129	3.07	4	9	0	102	4.84	7	5	0	118	3.35	7	9	0	113	4.38	469	7	.252	.320	.354	408	6	.233	.303	.321
1987	LA-N	1000	17	.247	.304	.352	9	6	0	134	2.42	7	10	1	131	3.71	9	7	1	132	2.39	7	9	0	133	3.73	589	10	.272	.330	.385	411	7	.212	.266	.304
1988	LA-N	975	18	.213	.269	.310	11	5	0	125	2.31	12	3	1	142	2.21	12	3	1	128	2.38	11	5	0	139	2.14	533	13	.220	.294	.343	442	5	.206	.238	.269
1989	LA-N	942	9	.240	.298	.316	9	8	0	126	2.71	6	7	0	131	1.93	9	7	0	127	2.42	6	8	0	130	2.22	519	5	.258	.323	.339	423	4	.217	.265	.288
1990	LA-N	100	1	.260	.295	.330	1	1	0	19	4.19	0	0	0	6	4.50	1	1	0	25	4.26	0	0	0	0	—	53	1	.189	.218	.264	47	0	.340	.380	.404
1991	LA-N	433	3	.259	.316	.330	3	2	0	63	3.27	4	0	0	49	3.70	2	2	0	39	3.46	5	0	0	73	3.45	208	2	.284	.345	.375	225	1	.236	.289	.289
1992	LA-N	812	15	.257	.320	.372	7	5	0	118	2.75	3	10	0	93	4.86	6	5	0	96	3.27	4	10	0	114	4.01	455	11	.286	.366	.418	357	4	.221	.257	.314
1993	LA-N	817	17	.246	.311	.375	4	8	0	99	3.17	8	6	0	116	3.95	6	7	0	105	3.78	6	7	0	111	3.41	436	5	.241	.319	.351	381	12	.252	.302	.402
1994	LA-N	524	15	.279	.333	.439	3	4	0	80	3.59	3	2	0	55	4.09	4	4	0	104	4.05	2	2	0	31	2.90	273	9	.297	.368	.484	251	6	.259	.292	.390
1995	Cle-A	620	21	.244	.304	.410	9	2	0	81	2.67	7	4	0	86	5.00	5	3	0	72	3.77	11	3	0	96	3.95	349	12	.281	.336	.461	271	9	.196	.264	.343
1996	Cle-A	828	21	.287	.341	.428	6	2	0	85	4.04	9	7	0	121	4.38	9	4	0	98	4.42	6	5	0	108	4.07	459	7	.314	.374	.436	369	14	.255	.301	.417
1997	Cle-A	732	26	.272	.340	.443	6	1	0	100	3.87	8	5	0	95	5.10	7	4	0	112	4.26	7	2	0	83	4.75	340	12	.282	.365	.468	392	14	.263	.318	.421
1998	SF-N	772	22	.259	.341	.400	5	6	0	107	4.22	6	4	0	95	4.63	6	6	0	103	3.84	5	4	0	99	5.00	377	6	.247	.335	.340	395	16	.271	.346	.458
1999	NY-N	674	14	.260	.342	.401	6	6	0	83	4.88	7	6	0	96	4.31	8	5	0	84	4.48	5	7	0	95	4.66	294	9	.279	.389	.486	380	5	.245	.301	.334
2000	LA-N	108	5	.389	.493	.602	1	3	0	17	12.71	0	2	0	8	14.09	1	5	0	25	13.14	0	0	0	0	—	48	1	.417	.464	.563	60	4	.367	.512	.633
TOTALS		11825	235	.249	.312	.364	106	69	1	1604	3.17	98	81	4	1527	3.81	102	73	4	1529	3.58	102	77	1	1601	3.38	6232	116	.263	.334	.383	5593	119	.232	.287	.342
● Ken Hill	BR/TR																																			
1988	StL-N	56	0	.286	.355	.411	0	0	0	0	—	0	1	0	14	5.14	0	0	0	0	—	0	1	0	14	5.14	24	0	.250	.333	.333	32	0	.313	.371	.469
1989	StL-N	739	9	.252	.342	.346	2	5	0	97	3.80	5	10	0	100	3.79	4	4	0	96	2.91	3	11	0	101	4.65	395	3	.271	.372	.359	344	6	.230	.306	.331
1990	StL-N	299	7	.264	.334	.411	2	2	0	28	6.75	3	4	0	51	4.80	0	0	0	4	17.18	5	6	0	75	4.92	184	4	.261	.344	.397	115	3	.270	.317	.435
1991	StL-N	656	15	.224	.299	.346	6	4	0	88	3.18	5	6	0	94	3.94	7	5	0	92	3.34	4	5	0	90	3.81	367	8	.237	.307	.341	289	7	.208	.288	.353
1992	Mon-N	812	13	.230	.297	.335	6	6	0	94	3.15	10	3	0	124	2.33	8	4	0	103	2.61	8	5	0	115	2.75	469	6	.222	.298	.318	343	7	.242	.295	.359
1993	Mon-N	684	7	.238	.315	.336	4	4	0	101	3.12	5	3	0	83	3.38	6	2	0	100	2.62	3	5	0	84	3.96	376	4	.234	.322	.343	308	3	.244	.307	.328
1994	Mon-N	585	12	.248	.304	.376	7	2	0	63	2.59	9	3	0	92	3.82	11	3	0	106	3.23	5	2	0	49	3.51	296	5	.270	.330	.409	289	7	.225	.277	.343
1995	StL-N	437	16	.286	.351	.465	4	5	0	69	4.93	2	2	0	41	5.27	5	4	0	88	4.21	1	3	0	23	8.34	214	9	.285	.365	.467	223	7	.287	.337	.462
1995	Cle-A	287	5	.268	.343	.411	1	1	0	36	3.75	3	0	0	39	4.19	0	0	0	0	—	4	1	0	75	3.98	154	2	.266	.337	.416	133	3	.271	.349	.406
1996	Tex-A	949	19	.263	.332	.378	9	7	0	121	4.45	7	3	0	129	2.85	8	5	0	118	4.27	8	5	0	133	3.05	501	5	.263	.343	.347	448	14	.263	.320	.413
1997	Tex-A	433	11	.298	.376	.464	2	3	0	58	4.78	3	5	0	53	5.64	4	5	0	84	4.07	1	3	0	27	8.67	228	7	.298	.386	.461	205	4	.298	.365	.468
1997	Ana-A	292	8	.223	.315	.346	0	3	0	28	5.79	4	1	0	51	2.47	0	0	0	0	—	4	4	0	79	3.65	161	5	.211	.317	.348	131	3	.237	.313	.344
1998	Ana-A	396	6	.311	.384	.439	5	2	0	64	3.50	4	4	0	39	7.45	8	5	0	79	5.15	1	1	0	24	4.44	216	3	.319	.395	.472	180	3	.300	.369	.400
1999	Ana-A	478	14	.270	.369	.418	3	7	0	78	3.92	1	4	0	50	6.08	3	8	0	90	5.58	1	3	0	38	2.84	246	7	.240	.359	.378	232	7	.302	.381	.461
2000	Ana-A	316	16	.323	.415	.513	3	4	0	44	5.89	2	3	0	34	7.34	4	4	0	44	6.60	1	3	0	35	6.43	135	6	.311	.412	.481	181	10	.331	.418	.536
2000	Chi-A	11	0	.455	.611	.818	0	1	0	2	23.14	0	0	0	1	27.00	0	0	0	0	—	0	1	0	3	24.00	2	0	.500	.800	1.000	9	0	.444	.538	.778
TOTALS		7430	158	.259	.336	.387	54	56	0	973	4.03	63	52	0	993	4.04	68	49	0	1003	3.92	49	59	0	963	4.15	3968	74	.259	.344	.380	3462	84	.260	.327	.396
● Trevor Hoffman	BR/TR																																			
1993	Fla-N	130	5	.185	.287	.346	1	0	0	14	1.26	1	2	2	21	4.64	2	2	2	36	3.28	0	0	0	0	—	59	4	.169	.319	.373	71	1	.197	.256	.324
1993	SD-N	212	5	.264	.325	.420	1	3	1	31	4.40	1	1	2	24	4.18	0	0	0	3	18.00	2	4	3	51	3.51	100	2	.250	.336	.400	112	3	.277	.314	.438
1994	SD-N	202	4	.193	.263	.337	3	2	11	27	2.63	1	2	9	29	2.51	3	3	13	38	2.37	1	1	7	18	3.00	104	0	.212	.293	.308	98	4	.173	.231	.367
1995	SD-N	204	10	.235	.284	.426	6	1	15	27	3.00	1	3	16	26	4.78	4	2	10	20	4.58	3	2	21	34	3.48	99	3	.202	.282	.313	105	7	.267	.287	.533
1996	SD-N	311	6	.161	.240	.257	5	1	19	40	1.35	4	4	23	48	3.00	5	2	16	41	1.10	4	3	26	47	3.26	134	2	.149	.255	.216	177	4	.169	.228	.288
1997	SD-N	295	9	.200	.259	.342	6	0	16	41	2.85	0	4	21	40	2.45	3	3	15	35	3.89	3	1	22	47	1.74	157	3	.185	.229	.299	138	6	.217	.292	.391
1998	SD-N	249	2	.165	.232	.229	2	2	27	37	1.23	2	0	26	36	1.73	3	0	24	37	1.96	1	2	29	36	0.99	123	0	.171	.244	.211	126	2	.159	.221	.246
1999	SD-N	244	5	.197	.240	.307	1	1	24	38	1.67	1	2	16	30	2.73	0	3	19	33	3.24	2	0	21	34	1.06	107	1	.215	.289	.271	137	4	.182	.199	.336
2000	SD-N	272	7	.224	.250	.360	2	5	26	47	2.51	2	2	17	26	3.86	1	2	20	33	3.24	3	5	23	39	2.77	130	2	.200	.239	.323	142	5	.246	.260	.394
TOTALS		2119	53	.201	.261	.330	27	15	139	301	2.33	13	20	132	280	3.15	21	17	119	275	2.97	19	18	152	306	2.50	1013	17	.193	.271	.294	1106	36	.208	.252	.363
● Rick Honeycutt	BL/TL																																			
1978	Sea-A	526	12	.285	.345	.418	4	6	0	70	5.12	1	5	0	64	4.64	2	4	0	51	3.71	3	7	0	83	5.62	129	2	.271	.340	.357	397	10	.290	.347	.438
1979	Sea-A	749	22	.268	.331	.421	5	6	0	98	4.78	6	6	0	96	3.28	4	5	0	79	4.22	7	7	0	115	3.91	143	3	.224	.313	.336	606	19	.279	.335	.441
1980	Sea-A	790	22	.280	.330	.441	6	10	0	114	3.70	4	7	0	89	4.25	7	5	0	109	2.82	3	12	0	95	5.23	170	11	.265	.314	.506	620	11	.284	.335	.423
1981	Tex-A	487	12	.246	.272	.366	5	2	0	65	2.23	6	4	0	63	4.43	6	1	0	64	3.23	5	5	0	64	3.39	75	5	.240	.260	.440	412	7	.248	.274	.352
1982	Tex-A	659	20	.305	.356	.466	3	10	0	90	5.32	2	7	0	74	5.21	4	7	0	92	4.03	1	10	0	72	6.84	146	4	.308	.346	.445	513	16	.304	.359	.472
1983	Tex-A	641	9	.262	.306	.346	8	2	0	79	0.91	6	6	0	96	3.67	10	4	0	123	1.61	4	4	0	52	4.33	111	2	.207	.250	.297	530	7	.274	.318	.357
1983	LA-N	155	6	.297	.359	.484	1	1	0	17	5.82	1	2	0	22	5.73	0	0	0	0	—	2	3	0	39	5.77	20	1	.250	.348	.450	135	5	.304	.361	.489
1984	LA-N	698	11	.258	.308	.341	6	2	0	96	2.24	4	7	0	87	3.50	7	3	0	113	2.87	3	6	0	71	2.80	135	3	.185	.206	.252	563	8	.275	.332	.362
1985	LA-N	541	9	.261	.321	.388	5	6	0	80	2.70	3	6	1	62	4.35	5	7	0	80	2.71	3	5	1	62	4.33	73	0	.219	.272	.329	468	9	.267	.329	.397
1986	LA-N	658	9	.249	.300	.368	6	4	0	97	2.69	5	5	0	74	4.14	4	4	0	79	1.93	7	5	0	92	4.52	105	0	.238	.266	.343	553	9	.251	.306	.373
1987	LA-N	478	10	.278	.343	.416	2	7	0	64	3.92	0	5	0	51	5.44	2	7	0	80	2.91	0	5	0	35	8.41	87	2	.218	.253	.333	391	8	.292	.362	.435
1987	Oak-A	91	3	.275	.343	.473	0	2	0	13	6.07	1	2	0	10	4.35	0	0	0	0	—	1	4	0	24	5.32	25	0	.120	.233	.240	66	3	.333	.387	.561
1988	Oak-A	293	6	.253	.312	.375	2	1	2	33	2.18	1	1	5	47	4.44	2	1	4	41	3.95	1	1	3	39	3.03	97	3	.227	.282	.371	196	3	.265	.327	.378
1989	Oak-A	271	5	.207	.277	.277	0	2	6	41	2.85	2	0	6	36	1.77	1	0	9	41	1.98	1	2	3	36	2.78	90	1	.156	.248	.200	181	4	.232	.291	.315
1990	Oak-A	225	2	.204	.272	.276	2	0	6	30	1.80	0	2	1	33	3.51	1	1	2	32	1.99	1	1	5	32	3.41	86	1	.163	.204	.221	139	1	.230	.311	.309
1991	Oak-A	142	3	.261	.358	.394	0	2	0	21	2.14	2	2	0	17	5.40	0	1	0	6	4.26	2	3	0	31	3.45	54	1	.204	.306	.315	88	2	.295	.388	.443
1992	Oak-A	151	2	.272	.327	.371	1	2	2	18	3.06	0	2	1	21	4.22	1	2	1	21	2.61	0	2	2	18	4.91	62	1	.258	.313	.339	89	1	.281	.337	.393
1993	Oak-A	142	2	.211	.305	.296	0	2	1	21	2.14	1	2	0	21	3.48	0	2	1	22	3.32	1	2	0	20	2.25	54	1	.241	.317	.352	88	1	.193	.298	.261
1994	Tex-A	106	4	.349	.410	.557	0	1	0	12	8.25	1	1	1	13	6.23	1	2	1	19	7.11	0	0	0	6	7.50	51	1	.412	.423	.608	55	3	.291	.400	.509
1995	Oak-A	160	5	.231	.275	.338	5	0	1	19	3.32	0	1	1	26	1.75	3	1	1	19	3.79	2	0	1	26	1.40	82	0	.183	.218	.207	78	5	.282	.333	.474
1995	NY-A	5	1	.400	.500	1.200	0	0	0	0	—	0	0	0	1	27.00	0	0	0	0	—	0	0	0	1	27.00	3	0	.000	.250	.000	2	1	1.000	1.000	3.000
1996	StL-N	175	3	.240	.265	.320	2	1	2	27	2.00	0	0	2	20	3.98	1	0	2	25	2.84	1	1	2	22	2.86	67	3	.239	.257	.403	108	0	.241	.270	.269
1997	StL-N	10	0	.500	.545	.500	0	0	0	1	9.00	0	0	0	1	18.00	0	0	0	2	13.50	0	0	0	0	—	1	0	.000	.000	.000	9	0	.556	.600	.556
TOTALS		8153	178	.265	.320	.390	63	69	20	1107	3.33	46	73	18	1024	4.13	61	57	21	1097	3.00	48	85	17	1034	4.47	1866	45	.232	.283	.350	6287	133	.274	.330	.401
● Charlie Hough	BR/TR																																			
1978	LA-N	337	6	.205	.313	.288	3	3	3	34	3.41	2	2	4	59	3.20	2	1	3	48	2.42	3	4	4	45	4.20	134	2	.239	.342	.321	203	4	.182	.294	.266
1979	LA-N	575	16	.264	.346	.397	3	3	0	73	3.96	4	2	0	79	5.49	0	2	0	52	5.85	7	3	0	99	4.18	235	5	.311	.390	.413	340	11	.232	.316	.385
1980	LA-N	127	4	.291	.392	.409	1	1	1	18	4.58	0	2	0	15	6.75	1	3	1	31	5.46	0	0	0	1	9.00	54	2	.407	.507	.537	73	2	.205	.302	.315
1980	Tex-A	225	2	.240	.353	.338	0	2	0	33	3.31	2	0	0	29	4.71	0	0	0	0	—	2	2	0	61	3.96	105	1	.248	.350	.371	120	1	.233	.357	.308
1981	Tex-A	294	4	.207	.289	.293	2	0	1	38	2.61	2	1	0	44	3.27	0	0	1	26	4.44	4	1	0	56	2.26	130	1	.200	.273	.277	164	3	.213	.301	.305
1982	Tex-A	864	21	.251	.313	.384	9	6	0	130	3.80	7	7	0	98	4.15	6	5	0	104	3.36	10	8	0	124	4.44	432	10	.269	.336	.394	432	11	.234	.288	.375
1983	Tex-A	922	22	.238	.309	.366	10	7	0	149	2.97	5	6	0	103	3.48	7	6	0	114	3.31	8	7	0	138	3.07	452	8	.241	.316	.361	470	14	.234	.303	.370
1984	Tex-A	1016	26	.256	.322	.402	8	5	0	129	2.94	8	9	0	137	4.52	8	6	0	128	3.38	8	8	0	138	4.10	541	14	.274	.342	.420	475	12	.236	.300	.381
1985	Tex-A	920	23	.215	.283	.338	8	6	0	115	3.52	6	10	0	135	3.13	5	10	0	136	3.58	9	6	0	115	2.98	495	11	.226	.290	.343	425	12	.202	.275	.332
1986	Tex-A	850	32	.221	.301	.379	8	5	0	106	3.99	9	5	0	124	3.62	7	3	0	85	2.87	10	7	0	146	4.32	436	13	.204	.282	.335	414	19	.239	.322	.425
1987	Tex-A	1069	36	.223	.311	.372	11	8	0	153	4.40	7	5	0	132	3.07	8	3	0	125	3.74	10	10	0	160	3.82	509	17	.240	.336	.375	560	19	.207	.288	.370
1988	Tex-A	913	20	.221	.321	.326	9	8	0	126	3.63	6	8	0	126	3.01	8	7	0	133	2.97	7	9	0	119	3.72	451	9	.220	.321	.317	462	11	.223	.321	.335
1989	Tex-A	685	28	.245	.340	.415	5	6	0	79	4.88	5	7	0	103	3.94	5	8	0	94	4.88	5	5	0	88	3.78	336	9	.238	.327	.366	349	19	.252	.351	.461
1990	Tex-A	807	24	.235	.338	.369	5	8	0	97	4.47	7	4	0	122	3.76	7	5	0	107	4.21	5	7	0	112	3.95	349	7	.241	.345	.347	458	17	.231	.332	.386
1991	Chi-A	729	21	.229	.320	.381	5	5	0	107	3.38	4	5	0	93	4.76	5	3	0	85	3.80	4	7	0	114	4.18	355	8	.237	.323	.375	374	13	.222	.317	.388

		TOTAL					HOME					AWAY					1ST HALF					2ND HALF					LEFT					RIGHT				
YEAR	TM/L	AB	HR	AVG	OBP	SLG	W	L	SV	IP	ERA	W	L	SV	IP	ERA	W	L	SV	IP	ERA	W	L	SV	IP	ERA	AB	HR	AVG	OBP	SLG	AB	HR	AVG	OBP	SLG
1992	Chi-A	670	19	.239	.311	.373	6	4	0	101	3.49	1	8	0	76	4.52	4	4	0	80	3.39	3	8	0	97	4.38	267	7	.236	.304	.352	403	12	.241	.316	.387
1993	Fla-N	779	20	.259	.325	.395	5	6	0	114	4.18	4	10	0	90	4.38	3	8	0	98	4.30	6	8	0	106	4.25	382	11	.251	.311	.387	397	9	.267	.338	.403
1994	Fla-N	430	17	.274	.359	.470	1	5	0	45	7.94	4	4	0	68	3.29	5	7	0	99	4.27	0	2	0	15	11.05	188	3	.245	.318	.346	242	14	.298	.390	.566
TOTALS		12212	341	.237	.319	.374	99	88	5	1646	3.85	83	95	4	1632	3.87	81	81	5	1547	3.76	101	102	4	1732	3.94	5851	138	.244	.325	.365	6361	203	.232	.315	.382
● **Bobby Howry** BL/TR																																				
1998	Chi-A	191	7	.194	.270	.356	0	1	3	31	2.03	0	2	6	23	4.63	0	0	0	7	2.70	0	3	9	48	3.21	87	4	.149	.260	.322	104	3	.231	.279	.385
1999	Chi-A	253	8	.229	.336	.364	3	2	16	34	4.98	2	1	12	33	2.16	1	1	13	31	4.02	4	2	15	36	3.22	133	3	.226	.342	.346	120	5	.233	.328	.383
2000	Chi-A	250	6	.216	.303	.328	0	2	3	28	4.45	2	2	4	43	2.32	1	1	4	34	3.67	1	3	3	37	2.70	121	2	.174	.239	.231	129	4	.256	.359	.419
TOTALS		694	21	.215	.306	.349	3	5	22	94	3.84	4	5	22	99	2.81	2	2	17	72	3.73	5	8	27	121	3.06	341	9	.188	.285	.299	353	12	.241	.327	.397
● **Bruce Hurst** BL/TL																																				
1980	Bos-A	127	4	.307	.388	.520	0	0	0	7	17.18	2	2	0	23	6.56	2	1	0	23	10.57	0	1	0	8	4.70	31	0	.355	.474	.452	96	4	.292	.358	.542
1981	Bos-A	89	1	.258	.346	.427	2	0	0	21	3.43	0	0	0	2	13.50	0	0	0	0	—	2	0	0	23	4.30	18	0	.111	.100	.167	71	1	.296	.405	.493
1982	Bos-A	483	16	.333	.383	.513	3	3	0	55	5.89	0	4	0	62	5.66	2	3	0	62	4.65	1	4	0	55	7.04	116	3	.310	.352	.422	367	13	.341	.392	.542
1983	Bos-A	831	22	.290	.340	.432	6	7	0	112	3.93	6	5	0	99	4.27	5	7	0	93	4.56	7	5	0	119	3.72	174	3	.276	.300	.379	657	19	.294	.350	.446
1984	Bos-A	857	25	.271	.341	.431	6	6	0	108	4.67	6	6	0	110	3.19	8	5	0	118	2.59	4	7	0	100	5.49	153	1	.248	.303	.346	704	24	.276	.349	.449
1985	Bos-A	890	31	.273	.327	.439	6	8	0	106	4.66	5	5	0	123	4.39	3	7	0	80	6.19	8	6	0	149	3.62	153	5	.281	.337	.425	737	26	.271	.325	.442
1986	Bos-A	660	18	.256	.310	.392	8	3	0	102	2.37	5	5	0	72	3.88	5	3	0	77	2.79	8	5	0	97	3.15	86	4	.256	.312	.442	574	14	.256	.310	.385
1987	Bos-A	911	35	.262	.317	.432	12	4	0	136	4.30	3	9	0	103	4.56	9	5	0	128	3.30	6	8	0	110	5.71	129	4	.248	.333	.419	782	31	.265	.314	.435
1988	Bos-A	842	21	.264	.316	.388	13	2	0	130	3.33	5	4	0	87	4.14	9	3	0	114	4.09	9	3	0	102	3.17	147	2	.279	.327	.374	695	19	.260	.314	.391
1989	SD-N	903	16	.237	.288	.339	9	6	0	140	2.58	6	5	0	105	2.83	6	5	0	119	2.95	9	6	0	126	2.44	144	2	.299	.357	.424	759	14	.225	.275	.323
1990	SD-N	823	21	.228	.284	.357	7	3	0	122	2.66	4	6	0	102	3.72	4	7	0	96	4.67	7	2	0	127	1.98	165	7	.230	.302	.400	658	14	.228	.279	.347
1991	SD-N	835	17	.241	.292	.340	7	5	0	127	3.34	8	3	0	95	3.22	9	4	0	119	2.94	6	4	0	102	3.69	136	1	.176	.247	.221	699	16	.253	.301	.363
1992	SD-N	835	22	.267	.308	.390	5	4	0	101	4.38	9	5	0	117	3.39	8	5	0	123	3.01	6	4	0	95	4.94	157	8	.293	.335	.478	678	14	.261	.302	.370
1993	SD-N	22	0	.409	.480	.455	0	1	0	1	6.75	0	0	0	3	15.00	0	1	0	4	12.46	0	0	0	0	—	3	0	.333	.500	.333	19	0	.421	.476	.474
1993	Col-N	31	1	.194	.265	.290	0	1	0	9	5.19	0	0	0	0	—	0	0	0	0	—	0	1	0	9	5.19	2	0	.000	.000	.000	29	1	.207	.281	.310
1994	Tex-A	155	8	.342	.394	.594	1	0	0	23	6.17	1	1	0	15	8.59	2	1	0	38	7.11	0	0	0	0	—	25	3	.280	.333	.720	130	5	.354	.405	.569
TOTALS		9294	258	.265	.319	.406	85	53	0	1300	3.82	60	60	0	1117	4.03	72	57	0	1195	3.94	73	56	0	1222	3.90	1639	43	.264	.319	.395	7655	215	.265	.319	.408
● **Danny Jackson** BR/TL																																				
1983	KC-A	80	1	.325	.372	.412	0	1	0	11	7.36	1	0	0	8	2.25	0	0	0	0	—	1	1	0	19	5.21	12	0	.333	.333	.333	68	1	.324	.378	.426
1984	KC-A	295	4	.285	.370	.380	2	2	0	37	4.14	0	4	0	39	4.38	1	5	0	47	4.63	1	1	0	29	3.68	60	1	.217	.319	.350	235	3	.302	.383	.387
1985	KC-A	801	7	.261	.328	.361	6	5	0	99	3.38	8	7	0	109	3.46	6	4	0	91	3.25	8	8	0	117	3.55	158	1	.272	.350	.367	643	6	.258	.322	.359
1986	KC-A	692	13	.256	.334	.364	6	4	1	80	2.15	5	8	0	106	3.99	4	5	0	68	3.86	7	7	1	118	2.82	137	2	.292	.362	.409	555	11	.247	.327	.353
1987	KC-A	849	11	.258	.345	.364	6	9	0	121	4.30	3	9	0	103	3.68	4	10	0	106	4.23	5	8	0	118	3.82	159	1	.277	.328	.346	690	10	.254	.348	.368
1988	Cin-N	943	13	.218	.273	.312	12	3	0	134	2.63	11	5	0	127	2.83	8	4	0	103	3.42	15	4	0	158	2.28	134	1	.261	.299	.336	809	12	.211	.269	.308
1989	Cin-N	451	10	.271	.351	.395	3	5	0	60	5.10	3	6	0	56	6.14	5	9	0	91	6.03	1	2	0	25	4.01	67	1	.269	.333	.373	384	9	.271	.354	.398
1990	Cin-N	448	11	.266	.325	.386	2	3	0	54	3.83	4	3	0	63	3.41	2	2	0	51	3.71	4	4	0	66	3.53	85	2	.235	.330	.365	363	9	.273	.324	.391
1991	Chi-N	288	8	.309	.407	.451	0	2	0	40	7.20	1	3	0	31	6.16	1	2	0	33	5.67	0	3	0	37	7.71	60	0	.300	.417	.383	228	8	.311	.404	.469
1992	Chi-N	434	5	.270	.343	.371	2	2	0	53	2.21	2	7	0	60	6.00	4	8	0	101	4.37	0	1	0	12	3.00	68	1	.279	.370	.353	366	4	.268	.337	.374
1992	Pit-N	341	1	.276	.330	.349	4	2	0	64	3.39	0	2	0	25	3.28	0	0	0	0	—	4	4	0	88	3.36	51	1	.196	.276	.255	290	0	.290	.340	.366
1993	Phi-N	813	12	.263	.329	.370	8	5	0	110	3.86	4	6	0	101	3.67	7	4	0	111	3.42	5	7	0	100	4.15	142	4	.296	.379	.415	671	8	.256	.319	.361
1994	Phi-N	687	13	.266	.312	.381	8	4	0	110	3.10	6	2	0	69	3.52	10	2	0	123	3.28	4	4	0	56	3.21	96	0	.240	.260	.260	591	13	.271	.320	.401
1995	StL-N	396	10	.303	.381	.475	1	5	0	46	6.26	1	7	0	55	5.60	0	8	0	49	8.08	2	4	0	52	3.83	58	1	.259	.348	.362	338	9	.311	.386	.494
1996	StL-N	136	3	.243	.325	.360	1	0	0	20	3.10	0	1	0	16	6.19	0	0	0	0	—	1	1	0	36	4.46	33	1	.364	.400	.576	103	2	.204	.303	.291
1997	StL-N	75	3	.347	.414	.600	1	1	0	11	4.76	0	1	0	7	12.27	1	2	0	19	7.71	0	0	0	0	—	7	0	.286	.545	.429	68	3	.353	.395	.618
1997	SD-N	204	8	.353	.413	.564	1	2	0	24	5.55	0	5	0	25	9.49	0	4	0	22	7.48	1	3	0	27	7.57	28	1	.286	.429	.464	176	7	.364	.410	.580
TOTALS		7933	133	.266	.336	.379	63	55	1	1074	3.77	49	76	0	999	4.26	53	69	0	1014	4.37	59	62	1	1058	3.67	1355	18	.270	.343	.365	6578	115	.265	.334	.382
● **Mike Jackson** BR/TR																																				
1986	Phi-N	48	2	.250	.333	.417	0	0	0	8	4.50	0	0	0	5	1.69	0	0	0	0	—	0	0	0	13	3.38	25	0	.320	.414	.360	23	2	.174	.240	.478
1987	Phi-N	402	16	.219	.316	.378	2	3	1	55	2.13	1	7	0	54	6.29	2	6	0	60	4.77	1	4	1	49	3.49	189	6	.265	.397	.407	213	10	.178	.236	.352
1988	Sea-A	354	10	.209	.291	.339	5	3	0	45	3.00	1	2	4	54	2.32	3	2	1	51	2.31	3	3	3	49	2.96	159	5	.258	.340	.421	195	5	.169	.249	.272
1989	Sea-A	363	8	.223	.332	.339	2	2	4	54	3.50	2	4	3	45	2.78	2	2	4	52	4.18	2	4	3	48	2.08	158	5	.222	.344	.367	205	3	.224	.322	.317
1990	Sea-A	279	8	.229	.333	.348	3	4	0	40	4.95	2	3	3	37	4.10	3	3	2	42	3.24	2	4	1	36	6.06	105	5	.257	.375	.438	174	3	.213	.307	.293
1991	Sea-A	319	5	.201	.290	.298	3	2	6	48	2.64	4	5	8	41	3.95	4	2	13	43	2.70	3	5	1	45	3.77	119	2	.252	.355	.387	200	3	.170	.249	.245
1992	SF-N	302	7	.252	.331	.387	3	0	1	40	3.15	3	6	1	42	4.29	3	2	2	43	2.74	3	4	0	39	4.81	162	3	.265	.363	.401	140	4	.236	.291	.371
1993	SF-N	284	7	.204	.272	.313	3	4	1	33	4.32	3	2	0	44	2.05	4	2	1	42	2.36	2	4	0	35	3.82	126	3	.246	.317	.365	158	4	.171	.236	.272
1994	SF-N	140	4	.164	.234	.264	2	1	2	25	1.44	1	1	2	17	1.56	3	2	4	40	1.13	0	0	0	3	6.75	67	2	.194	.267	.299	73	2	.137	.203	.233
1995	Cin-N	178	5	.213	.291	.371	4	0	2	25	1.78	2	1	0	24	3.04	1	0	0	7	7.36	5	1	2	42	1.51	63	2	.206	.333	.349	115	3	.217	.266	.383
1996	Sea-A	271	11	.225	.301	.387	1	0	4	37	2.65	0	1	2	35	4.67	1	1	3	36	5.50	0	0	3	36	1.75	97	4	.268	.336	.423	174	7	.201	.282	.368
1997	Cle-A	274	3	.215	.297	.292	1	3	8	35	4.33	1	2	7	40	2.27	0	1	9	40	2.45	2	4	6	35	4.15	116	0	.302	.394	.379	158	3	.152	.220	.228
1998	Cle-A	221	4	.195	.252	.290	1	0	20	34	1.31	0	1	20	30	1.82	0	1	17	31	2.03	1	0	23	33	1.09	99	1	.202	.275	.313	122	3	.189	.233	.270
1999	Cle-A	259	11	.232	.304	.386	3	3	16	35	4.33	0	1	23	33	3.78	2	2	15	34	4.76	1	2	24	35	3.38	129	2	.240	.322	.318	130	9	.223	.287	.454
TOTALS		3694	101	.217	.301	.342	33	25	65	516	3.11	20	36	73	502	3.42	28	26	71	521	3.28	25	35	67	497	3.24	1614	40	.250	.348	.380	2080	61	.191	.263	.313
● **Tommy John** BR/TL																																				
1978	LA-N	848	11	.271	.317	.349	11	4	1	125	2.81	6	6	0	88	3.99	9	6	0	113	3.89	8	4	1	100	2.62	172	0	.209	.271	.238	676	11	.287	.329	.377
1979	NY-A	1031	9	.260	.305	.337	12	5	0	140	3.08	9	4	0	136	2.85	11	3	0	140	2.45	10	6	0	137	3.49	204	2	.260	.301	.333	827	7	.260	.306	.337
1980	NY-A	1007	13	.268	.309	.380	11	4	0	135	2.41	11	5	0	131	4.48	11	3	0	124	3.13	11	6	0	142	3.68	234	7	.226	.279	.380	773	6	.281	.318	.380
1981	NY-A	528	10	.256	.309	.352	5	3	0	69	2.47	4	5	0	71	2.79	5	4	0	68	3.19	4	4	0	73	2.11	137	1	.241	.297	.270	391	9	.261	.314	.381
1982	NY-A	715	11	.266	.299	.380	6	6	0	110	3.43	4	4	0	76	4.01	5	6	0	113	3.36	5	4	0	74	4.14	165	3	.297	.324	.436	550	8	.256	.292	.364
1982	Cal-A	146	4	.336	.358	.507	2	1	0	16	5.74	2	1	0	19	2.33	0	0	0	0	—	4	2	0	35	3.86	32	0	.375	.375	.438	114	4	.325	.353	.526
1983	Cal-A	944	20	.304	.337	.431	8	6	0	146	2.64	3	7	0	88	7.13	6	4	0	108	4.08	5	9	0	127	4.55	166	4	.271	.299	.404	778	16	.311	.345	.437
1984	Cal-A	728	15	.306	.356	.434	1	4	0	55	6.02	6	9	0	126	3.86	4	6	0	105	3.69	3	7	0	76	5.66	150	1	.287	.352	.367	578	14	.311	.358	.452
1985	Cal-A	155	3	.329	.387	.465	0	3	0	14	4.50	2	1	0	24	4.81	2	4	0	38	4.70	0	0	0	0	—	43	0	.302	.375	.349	112	3	.339	.392	.509
1985	Oak-A	199	6	.332	.372	.503	1	2	0	24	3.75	1	4	0	24	8.63	0	0	0	0	—	2	6	0	48	6.19	41	1	.317	.326	.439	158	5	.335	.384	.519
1986	NY-A	265	8	.275	.316	.392	2	2	0	41	3.76	3	1	0	30	1.80	3	1	0	37	3.62	2	2	0	33	2.16	42	2	.286	.354	.500	223	6	.274	.308	.372
1987	NY-A	736	12	.288	.335	.387	6	3	0	90	4.38	7	3	0	97	3.70	7	3	0	76	4.64	6	3	0	112	3.62	123	1	.203	.258	.260	613	11	.305	.351	.413
1988	NY-A	717	11	.308	.354	.423	3	5	0	86	4.19	6	3	0	90	4.78	6	2	0	89	3.32	3	6	0	87	5.69	146	3	.281	.335	.418	571	8	.315	.359	.424
1989	NY-A	259	6	.336	.392	.444	0	3	0	26	7.01	2	4	0	38	4.97	2	7	0	64	5.80	0	0	0	0	—	36	2	.444	.487	.611	223	4	.318	.377	.417
TOTALS		8278	139	.285	.329	.394	68	51	1	1078	3.44	66	57	0	1040	4.18	71	49	0	1074	3.65	63	59	1	1043	3.96	1691	27	.263	.310	.362	6587	112	.291	.334	.402
● **Randy Johnson** BR/TL																																				
1988	Mon-N	102	3	.225	.275	.363	2	0	0	17	3.18	1	0	0	9	1.00	0	0	0	0	—	3	0	0	26	2.42	8	0	.125	.125	.125	94	3	.234	.287	.383
1989	Mon-N	110	2	.264	.393	.364	0	1	0	15	1.80	0	3	0	15	11.66	0	4	0	30	6.67	0	0	0	0	—	29	1	.276	.323	.483	81	1	.259	.413	.321
1989	Sea-A	483	11	.244	.338	.373	2	5	0	55	5.56	5	4	0	76	3.55	3	0	0	26	3.86	4	9	0	105	4.53	59	1	.169	.254	.271	424	10	.255	.349	.387
1990	Sea-A	806	26	.216	.319	.355	8	4	0	102	2.90	6	7	0	117	4.30	8	3	0	104	3.72	6	8	0	116	3.58	82	0	.195	.256	.232	724	26	.218	.326	.369
1991	Sea-A	708	15	.213	.358	.325	6	5	0	106	3.92	7	5	0	96	4.05	6	6	0	91	4.25	7	4	0	110	3.75	85	2	.212	.337	.306	623	13	.213	.361	.327
1992	Sea-A	749	13	.206	.344	.307	8	6	0	117	2.76	4	8	0	93	5.03	5	7	0	80	4.03	7	7	0	130	3.60	75	1	.187	.303	.240	674	12	.208	.348	.315
1993	Sea-A	913	22	.203	.290	.322	11	3	1	151	2.86	8	5	0	104	3.80	10	4	0	130	2.85	9	4	1	126	3.65	71	0	.183	.256	.239	842	22	.204	.293	.329
1994	Sea-A	612	14	.216	.304	.338	5	3	0	69	3.39	8	3	0	103	3.06	9	4	0	119	3.19	4	2	0	53	3.21	51	0	.235	.316	.333	561	14	.214	.303	.339
1995	Sea-A	792	12	.201	.266	.303	11	1	0	122	2.57	7	1	0	92	2.35	8	1	0	94	3.05	10	1	0	120	2.03	85	0	.129	.196	.188	707	12	.209	.275	.317
1996	Sea-A	228	8	.211	.294	.364	4	0	1	41	2.43	1	0	0	21	6.10	5	0	0	45	3.83	0	0	1	17	3.24	39	1	.205	.225	.282	189	7	.212	.307	.381
1997	Sea-A	758	20	.194	.277	.318	9	1	0	114	1.89	11	3	0	99	2.73	11	2	0	124	2.18	9	2	0	89	2.43	77	4	.260	.337	.468	681	16	.186	.270	.301
1998	Sea-A	608	19	.240	.319	.387	6	4	0	87	4.26	3	6	0	73	4.42	7	7	0	118	4.81	2	3	0	42	3.00	65	0	.169	.289	.200	543	19	.249	.323	.409
1998	Hou-N	299	4	.191	.261	.258	5	0	0	43	0.42	5	1	0	41	2.18	0	0	0	0	—	10	1	0	84	1.28	18	0	.222	.263	.222	281	4	.189	.261	.260
1999	Ari-N	993	30	.208	.266	.335	9	6	0	128	2.96	8	3	0	144	2.06	9	5	0	138	3.14	8	4	0	134	1.81	87	0	.103	.204	.126	906	30	.219	.272	.355
2000	Ari-N	900	23	.224	.288	.356	11	3	0	133	2.51	8	4	0	116	2.79	12	2	0	132	1.57	7	5	0	117	3.85	83	0	.229	.319	.253	817	23	.224	.284	.366
TOTALS		9061	222	.213	.303	.335	97	42	2	1299	2.94	82	53	0	1199	3.47	93	45	0	1229	3.32	86	50	2	1269	3.08	914	10	.190	.276	.263	8147	212	.216	.306	.343

YEAR	TM/L	TOTAL AB	HR	AVG	OBP	SLG	HOME W	L	SV	IP	ERA	AWAY W	L	SV	IP	ERA	1ST HALF W	L	SV	IP	ERA	2ND HALF W	L	SV	IP	ERA	LEFT AB	HR	AVG	OBP	SLG	RIGHT AB	HR	AVG	OBP	SLG
● Doug Jones BR/TR																																				
1982	Mil-A	13	1	.385	.429	.615	0	0	0	0	54.00	0	0	0	2	3.86	0	0	0	3	10.13	0	0	0	0	—	4	1	.250	.250	1.000	9	0	.444	.500	.444
1986	Cle-A	70	0	.257	.321	.286	0	0	1	7	2.45	1	0	0	11	2.53	0	0	0	0	—	1	0	1	18	2.50	33	0	.273	.314	.303	37	0	.243	.326	.270
1987	Cle-A	360	4	.281	.332	.353	5	1	0	53	3.76	1	4	8	39	2.33	0	1	0	15	7.98	6	4	8	77	2.23	186	1	.269	.310	.317	174	3	.293	.354	.391
1988	Cle-A	317	1	.218	.260	.268	1	4	19	38	3.99	2	0	18	45	0.80	1	1	18	36	1.75	2	3	19	47	2.66	177	1	.203	.254	.266	140	0	.236	.267	.271
1989	Cle-A	303	4	.251	.279	.337	6	4	15	46	2.15	1	6	17	35	2.60	2	3	18	33	1.89	5	7	14	47	2.66	160	4	.244	.281	.369	143	0	.259	.276	.301
1990	Cle-A	303	5	.218	.274	.323	4	4	23	46	3.11	1	1	20	38	1.89	4	2	22	42	1.50	1	3	21	42	3.61	165	3	.200	.249	.315	138	2	.239	.303	.333
1991	Cle-A	272	7	.320	.357	.496	1	4	1	27	6.41	3	4	6	37	4.91	1	6	6	25	7.46	3	2	1	38	4.26	132	4	.341	.380	.530	140	3	.300	.336	.464
1992	Hou-N	409	5	.235	.274	.320	6	5	17	63	2.42	5	3	19	48	1.12	4	5	17	52	2.09	7	3	19	60	1.65	217	3	.253	.296	.355	192	2	.214	.249	.281
1993	Hou-N	342	7	.298	.344	.392	3	4	8	36	5.00	1	6	18	49	4.20	3	6	13	46	5.09	1	4	13	39	3.89	165	2	.273	.335	.339	177	5	.322	.353	.441
1994	Phi-N	216	2	.255	.275	.301	2	2	19	32	1.14	0	2	8	22	3.63	2	2	20	39	2.33	0	2	7	15	1.76	110	2	.327	.345	.409	106	0	.179	.202	.189
1995	Bal-A	192	6	.286	.348	.443	0	4	10	22	7.77	0	0	12	25	2.55	0	2	11	24	4.13	0	2	11	23	5.96	106	1	.226	.299	.302	86	5	.360	.409	.616
1996	Chi-N	134	4	.306	.345	.470	2	0	0	18	3.93	0	2	2	14	6.43	2	2	2	32	5.01	0	0	0	0	—	53	3	.321	.357	.566	81	1	.296	.337	.407
1996	Mil-A	122	3	.254	.331	.402	2	0	0	17	3.18	3	0	1	15	3.68	0	0	0	0	—	5	0	1	32	3.41	59	2	.220	.309	.407	63	1	.286	.352	.397
1997	Mil-A	289	4	.215	.242	.301	6	2	19	46	1.55	0	4	17	34	2.65	3	3	19	40	2.68	3	3	17	40	1.35	149	3	.228	.258	.336	140	1	.200	.224	.264
1998	Mil-A	218	15	.298	.339	.550	2	1	7	32	4.22	1	3	5	22	6.55	3	4	12	47	4.21	0	0	0	7	11.57	90	6	.267	.316	.489	128	9	.320	.355	.594
1998	Cle-A	121	2	.281	.308	.380	0	1	1	18	2.55	1	1	0	14	4.61	0	0	0	0	—	1	2	1	31	3.45	48	1	.292	.352	.458	73	1	.274	.276	.329
1999	Oak-A	397	10	.267	.311	.406	4	1	5	57	3.00	1	4	5	47	4.21	1	2	3	56	3.20	4	3	7	48	3.97	204	5	.255	.284	.392	193	5	.280	.340	.420
2000	Oak-A	295	6	.292	.334	.427	3	1	1	43	3.35	1	1	1	30	4.75	2	1	2	38	4.54	2	1	0	36	3.28	139	4	.281	.340	.417	156	2	.301	.329	.436
TOTALS		4373	86	.264	.307	.375	47	38	146	602	3.38	22	41	157	526	3.21	28	40	163	528	3.55	41	39	140	600	3.09	2197	46	.258	.303	.373	2176	40	.271	.311	.378
● Bobby Jones BR/TR																																				
1993	NY-N	233	6	.262	.327	.425	0	3	0	28	3.54	2	1	0	34	3.74	0	0	0	0	—	2	4	0	62	3.65	125	1	.224	.317	.320	108	5	.306	.339	.546
1994	NY-N	610	10	.257	.322	.351	4	6	0	89	4.25	8	1	0	71	1.77	7	7	0	104	3.46	5	0	0	56	2.57	330	5	.267	.332	.364	280	5	.246	.309	.336
1995	NY-N	762	20	.274	.325	.427	5	3	0	96	3.28	5	7	0	100	5.06	4	5	0	96	3.01	6	5	0	100	5.31	347	9	.248	.299	.406	415	11	.296	.346	.443
1996	NY-N	760	26	.288	.329	.446	5	4	0	94	3.91	7	4	0	101	4.88	7	4	0	96	4.31	5	4	0	100	4.52	341	10	.287	.333	.443	419	16	.289	.326	.449
1997	NY-N	730	24	.242	.303	.395	5	4	0	90	3.59	10	5	0	103	3.67	12	4	0	115	2.67	3	5	0	79	5.03	352	13	.239	.311	.406	378	11	.246	.295	.384
1998	NY-N	732	23	.262	.316	.419	4	6	0	109	4.14	5	3	0	87	3.95	6	5	0	96	3.94	3	4	0	99	4.17	353	9	.232	.284	.368	379	14	.290	.346	.467
1999	NY-N	234	3	.295	.328	.449	2	2	0	38	5.92	1	1	0	21	5.06	3	3	0	53	5.81	0	0	0	7	4.05	98	3	.327	.362	.541	136	0	.272	.303	.382
2000	NY-N	609	25	.281	.336	.489	7	3	0	75	3.60	4	3	0	80	6.44	3	3	0	47	8.10	8	3	0	108	3.75	303	15	.264	.324	.495	306	10	.297	.348	.484
TOTALS		4670	137	.269	.322	.423	32	31	0	619	3.92	42	25	0	596	4.35	42	31	0	606	4.01	32	25	0	610	4.25	2249	65	.257	.316	.413	2421	72	.280	.328	.432
● Todd Jones BL/TR																																				
1993	Hou-N	131	4	.214	.297	.336	1	1	1	19	1.42	0	1	1	18	4.91	0	0	0	0	—	1	2	2	37	3.13	62	0	.194	.282	.226	69	4	.232	.312	.435
1994	Hou-N	257	3	.202	.277	.304	3	1	4	40	1.79	2	1	1	32	3.90	2	2	2	44	2.89	3	0	3	29	2.48	113	1	.265	.344	.398	144	2	.153	.223	.229
1995	Hou-N	375	8	.237	.336	.360	3	4	5	50	2.86	3	1	10	49	3.28	4	1	4	46	1.76	2	4	11	54	4.19	164	3	.268	.376	.396	211	5	.213	.304	.332
1996	Hou-N	223	5	.274	.375	.381	4	2	7	23	4.24	2	1	10	34	4.50	6	1	15	41	3.32	0	2	2	17	7.02	95	3	.316	.409	.442	128	2	.242	.351	.336
1997	Det-A	260	3	.231	.320	.296	1	2	16	32	3.66	4	2	15	38	2.61	1	3	9	32	3.62	4	1	22	38	2.63	133	3	.248	.325	.361	127	0	.213	.315	.228
1998	Det-A	233	7	.249	.347	.382	1	4	14	35	6.17	0	0	14	28	3.49	0	3	12	28	5.53	1	1	16	36	4.54	120	4	.242	.338	.367	113	3	.257	.356	.398
1999	Det-A	247	7	.259	.352	.401	3	2	14	33	3.86	1	2	16	34	3.74	1	2	12	32	5.12	3	2	18	35	2.60	131	4	.290	.376	.450	116	3	.224	.326	.345
2000	Det-A	243	6	.276	.344	.383	2	1	21	33	3.00	0	3	21	31	4.06	0	1	21	27	2.96	2	3	21	37	3.93	126	3	.294	.375	.413	117	3	.256	.310	.350
TOTALS		1969	43	.243	.333	.356	18	17	82	266	3.39	12	11	88	265	3.70	14	13	75	249	3.43	16	15	95	281	3.65	944	21	.268	.357	.391	1025	22	.220	.310	.323
● Jimmy Key BR/TL																																				
1984	Tor-A	245	8	.286	.369	.445	1	2	3	26	5.13	3	3	7	36	4.29	2	4	4	28	4.23	2	1	6	34	4.98	95	2	.316	.394	.442	150	6	.267	.353	.447
1985	Tor-A	794	22	.237	.282	.384	10	3	0	129	2.66	4	3	0	84	3.54	6	2	0	96	2.45	8	4	0	117	3.46	157	4	.178	.233	.306	637	18	.251	.295	.403
1986	Tor-A	866	24	.256	.315	.403	7	9	0	114	4.50	7	2	0	118	2.67	6	5	0	96	4.61	8	6	0	136	2.84	190	1	.268	.319	.321	676	23	.253	.314	.426
1987	Tor-A	951	24	.221	.272	.344	10	4	0	157	2.36	7	4	0	104	3.36	8	5	0	124	2.90	9	3	0	137	2.63	157	4	.248	.290	.382	794	20	.215	.268	.336
1988	Tor-A	509	13	.250	.296	.385	4	3	0	55	4.45	8	2	0	77	2.47	3	1	0	23	2.74	9	4	0	108	3.41	75	1	.147	.200	.253	434	12	.267	.313	.408
1989	Tor-A	838	18	.270	.292	.415	7	8	0	120	3.81	6	6	0	96	3.95	7	7	0	128	3.52	6	7	0	88	4.38	150	2	.227	.245	.327	688	16	.279	.302	.435
1990	Tor-A	602	20	.281	.304	.439	7	3	0	89	4.47	6	4	0	66	3.95	4	3	0	46	6.85	9	4	0	109	3.15	88	0	.182	.213	.193	514	20	.298	.320	.481
1991	Tor-A	815	12	.254	.293	.347	7	8	0	110	3.43	9	4	0	99	2.64	10	3	0	106	2.30	6	9	0	104	3.82	112	2	.286	.325	.357	703	10	.249	.288	.346
1992	Tor-A	828	24	.248	.298	.391	7	5	0	105	3.35	6	8	0	112	3.70	4	6	0	104	3.19	9	7	0	112	3.85	131	2	.176	.216	.252	697	22	.261	.314	.418
1993	NY-A	889	26	.246	.279	.382	8	2	0	105	2.75	10	4	0	132	3.20	10	2	0	121	2.30	8	4	0	115	3.75	131	6	.260	.292	.420	758	20	.244	.277	.376
1994	NY-A	649	10	.273	.329	.374	7	4	0	91	3.86	10	0	0	77	2.57	12	1	0	117	3.01	5	3	0	51	3.86	126	1	.238	.273	.341	523	9	.281	.341	.382
1995	NY-A	124	3	.323	.351	.500	1	2	0	24	5.18	0	0	0	6	7.50	1	2	0	30	5.64	0	0	0	0	—	18	0	.333	.333	.389	106	3	.321	.354	.519
1996	NY-A	643	21	.266	.326	.429	4	5	0	77	5.05	8	6	0	93	4.37	3	6	0	64	6.08	9	5	0	106	3.83	95	1	.168	.248	.242	548	20	.283	.340	.462
1997	Bal-A	804	24	.261	.331	.398	6	8	0	101	3.93	10	2	0	112	2.98	11	4	0	108	2.66	5	6	0	104	4.24	140	5	.271	.362	.421	664	19	.259	.324	.393
1998	Bal-A	299	5	.258	.316	.398	3	1	0	35	1.78	3	2	0	44	6.14	4	3	0	62	4.06	2	0	0	17	4.67	73	2	.233	.282	.384	226	3	.265	.327	.403
TOTALS		9856	254	.255	.303	.392	89	67	3	1337	3.59	97	50	7	1255	3.42	91	54	4	1252	3.42	95	63	6	1340	3.59	1738	33	.233	.282	.336	8118	221	.260	.308	.404
● Darryl Kile BR/TR																																				
1991	Hou-N	585	16	.246	.344	.393	4	5	0	78	3.36	3	6	0	76	4.03	2	2	0	61	3.54	5	9	0	93	3.79	343	7	.262	.365	.399	242	9	.223	.314	.384
1992	Hou-N	476	8	.261	.348	.391	3	5	0	64	3.53	2	5	0	62	4.38	2	6	0	65	4.13	3	4	0	60	3.75	271	5	.255	.361	.391	205	3	.268	.329	.390
1993	Hou-N	637	12	.239	.324	.341	9	4	0	92	2.35	6	4	0	80	4.86	8	1	0	63	2.27	7	7	0	108	4.24	330	8	.236	.326	.345	307	4	.241	.322	.336
1994	Hou-N	557	13	.275	.375	.413	4	3	0	82	4.37	5	3	0	65	4.82	5	3	0	99	4.83	4	3	0	49	4.04	283	7	.269	.372	.403	274	6	.281	.379	.423
1995	Hou-N	475	5	.240	.353	.328	1	8	0	60	5.82	3	4	0	67	4.18	3	7	0	72	5.00	1	5	0	55	4.91	216	3	.250	.386	.319	259	2	.232	.324	.336
1996	Hou-N	843	16	.276	.359	.395	4	6	0	109	3.79	8	5	0	110	4.60	7	5	0	114	3.87	5	6	0	105	4.54	404	9	.314	.392	.460	439	7	.241	.328	.335
1997	Hou-N	924	19	.225	.301	.337	10	3	0	132	2.59	9	4	0	124	2.55	9	3	0	133	2.23	10	4	0	122	2.94	483	11	.232	.305	.346	441	8	.218	.296	.327
1998	Col-N	894	28	.287	.358	.450	5	9	0	110	6.22	8	8	0	120	4.26	5	10	0	125	4.40	8	7	0	106	6.13	471	7	.312	.379	.437	423	21	.260	.335	.463
1999	Col-N	754	33	.298	.387	.504	5	3	0	88	7.44	3	10	0	102	5.89	4	5	0	95	5.66	4	8	0	95	7.55	359	16	.318	.400	.540	395	17	.281	.376	.471
2000	StL-N	870	33	.247	.301	.428	11	5	0	125	3.67	9	4	0	107	4.19	11	4	0	108	4.51	9	5	0	125	3.39	404	15	.230	.295	.406	466	18	.262	.307	.446
TOTALS		7015	183	.260	.343	.402	56	51	0	941	4.22	56	53	0	913	4.32	56	46	0	935	4.04	56	58	0	918	4.50	3564	88	.269	.356	.409	3451	95	.251	.330	.394
● Steve Kline BB/TL																																				
1997	Cle-A	115	6	.365	.434	.583	0	1	0	9	2.08	3	0	0	18	7.64	3	1	0	26	5.81	0	0	0	0	—	45	3	.400	.438	.667	70	3	.343	.432	.529
1997	Mon-N	101	4	.307	.368	.485	1	1	0	14	3.95	0	2	0	13	8.53	0	0	0	0	—	1	3	0	26	6.15	38	1	.289	.310	.447	63	3	.317	.403	.508
1998	Mon-N	272	4	.228	.333	.335	3	1	1	34	2.88	0	5	0	37	2.65	1	3	0	32	2.53	2	3	1	40	2.95	90	1	.178	.292	.267	182	3	.253	.354	.368
1999	Mon-N	257	8	.218	.313	.358	5	3	0	41	3.51	2	1	0	29	4.08	2	2	0	29	4.60	5	2	0	40	3.12	93	1	.194	.306	.258	164	7	.232	.317	.415
2000	Mon-N	316	8	.278	.340	.421	1	2	8	42	3.89	0	3	6	41	3.10	1	2	9	45	1.80	0	3	5	37	5.54	107	1	.243	.314	.318	209	7	.297	.354	.474
TOTALS		1061	30	.263	.344	.407	10	8	9	139	3.42	5	11	6	137	4.27	7	8	9	133	3.39	8	11	6	144	4.26	373	7	.239	.320	.346	688	23	.276	.358	.440
● Bob Knepper BL/TL																																				
1978	SF-N	953	10	.229	.292	.306	10	6	0	129	2.51	7	5	0	131	2.76	8	5	0	127	2.54	9	6	0	133	2.71	170	0	.241	.298	.300	783	10	.226	.291	.308
1979	SF-N	833	30	.289	.350	.468	5	4	0	103	3.75	4	8	0	104	5.54	6	2	0	119	4.30	3	10	0	88	5.11	151	3	.291	.344	.430	682	27	.289	.352	.477
1980	SF-N	860	15	.281	.333	.398	7	4	0	105	2.57	2	12	0	110	5.55	6	9	0	131	4.19	3	7	0	84	3.95	179	0	.263	.290	.313	681	15	.286	.344	.420
1981	Hou-N	566	5	.226	.278	.292	8	2	0	110	1.22	1	3	0	46	4.47	5	1	0	86	1.15	4	4	0	70	3.45	128	1	.164	.230	.219	438	4	.244	.292	.313
1982	Hou-N	694	14	.278	.336	.392	3	5	1	95	4.37	2	10	0	85	4.54	2	9	0	89	5.28	3	6	1	91	3.65	133	0	.271	.333	.323	561	14	.280	.336	.408
1983	Hou-N	773	12	.261	.324	.352	3	4	0	92	2.26	3	9	0	111	3.96	2	9	0	109	2.98	4	4	0	94	3.43	129	0	.194	.261	.240	644	12	.275	.336	.374
1984	Hou-N	887	26	.251	.295	.384	10	4	0	139	2.60	5	6	0	95	4.07	7	8	0	124	2.98	8	2	0	110	3.45	104	2	.269	.290	.375	783	24	.249	.295	.386
1985	Hou-N	935	21	.271	.310	.412	5	8	0	123	3.51	10	5	0	118	3.58	8	4	0	101	3.46	7	9	0	140	3.61	115	3	.261	.287	.409	820	18	.272	.313	.412
1986	Hou-N	960	19	.242	.289	.367	9	6	0	132	3.62	8	6	0	126	2.64	10	6	0	135	2.74	7	6	0	123	3.58	154	4	.227	.255	.383	806	15	.244	.295	.364
1987	Hou-N	723	26	.313	.362	.502	5	7	0	98	4.30	3	10	0	79	6.47	3	8	0	75	6.57	5	9	0	102	4.31	117	3	.282	.317	.419	606	23	.318	.370	.518
1988	Hou-N	642	13	.243	.314	.361	9	3	0	103	2.36	5	2	0	72	4.25	8	1	0	97	2.13	6	4	0	78	4.38	92	1	.239	.273	.348	550	12	.244	.321	.364
1989	Hou-N	445	12	.303	.386	.445	0	5	0	47	6.89	4	5	0	66	5.18	3	9	0	97	5.03	1	1	0	16	11.02	66	3	.318	.384	.530	379	9	.301	.387	.430
1989	SF-N	204	4	.270	.318	.407	0	2	0	24	5.92	3	0	0	28	1.30	0	0	0	0	—	3	2	0	52	3.46	34	0	.265	.324	.353	170	4	.271	.317	.418
1990	SF-N	180	7	.311	.376	.539	1	2	0	21	5.66	2	1	0	24	5.70	3	3	0	44	5.68	0	0	0	0	—	25	0	.200	.231	.240	155	7	.329	.398	.587
TOTALS		9655	214	.265	.321	.392	75	62	1	1321	3.22	59	82	0	1196	4.23	71	74	0	1335	3.60	63	70	1	1182	3.81	1597	20	.249	.294	.346	8058	194	.268	.326	.401
● Jerry Koosman BR/TL																																				
1978	NY-N	866	17	.255	.323	.357	1	7	0	116	3.33	2	8	2	119	4.16	2	8	0	116	3.96	1	7	2	119	3.54	156	1	.199	.288	.231	710	16	.268	.331	.385
1979	Min-A	999	19	.268	.325	.393	10	7	0	144	3.30	10	6	0	119	3.47	9	6	0	125	3.68	11	7	0	139	3.11	249	2	.253	.307	.321	750	17	.273	.331	.417

		TOTAL					HOME					AWAY					1ST HALF					2ND HALF					LEFT					RIGHT				
YEAR	TM/L	AB	HR	AVG	OBP	SLG	W	L	SV	IP	ERA	W	L	SV	IP	ERA	W	L	SV	IP	ERA	W	L	SV	IP	ERA	AB	HR	AVG	OBP	SLG	AB	HR	AVG	OBP	SLG
1980	Min-A	925	24	.272	.324	.415	9	2	1	103	3.32	7	11	1	140	4.55	6	7	1	107	4.46	10	6	1	136	3.70	204	4	.275	.327	.387	721	20	.272	.324	.423
1981	Min-A	360	8	.272	.331	.394	0	5	3	42	5.40	3	4	2	53	3.25	3	8	0	78	4.27	0	1	5	16	3.86	61	0	.311	.328	.361	299	8	.264	.331	.401
1981	Chi-A	104	2	.260	.306	.346	0	3	0	11	4.09	1	1	0	16	2.81	0	0	0	0	—	1	4	0	27	3.33	13	1	.231	.333	.462	91	1	.264	.302	.330
1982	Chi-A	675	9	.287	.325	.382	6	4	1	79	3.86	5	3	2	94	3.83	1	3	3	56	4.53	10	4	0	118	3.52	151	0	.318	.333	.371	524	9	.279	.322	.385
1983	Chi-A	661	19	.266	.324	.411	8	3	0	94	4.67	3	4	2	75	4.90	6	1	1	72	4.11	5	6	1	97	5.27	122	1	.254	.313	.344	539	18	.269	.327	.427
1984	Phi-N	868	8	.267	.315	.356	7	5	0	103	2.70	7	10	0	121	3.73	8	6	0	100	2.80	6	9	0	124	3.62	153	0	.229	.280	.255	715	8	.276	.322	.378
1985	Phi-N	387	14	.276	.336	.455	4	3	0	57	4.61	2	1	0	43	4.64	3	1	0	56	2.73	3	3	0	43	7.06	47	0	.319	.333	.426	340	14	.271	.337	.459
TOTALS		5845	120	.269	.324	.390	45	39	5	750	3.68	40	48	9	780	4.03	38	40	5	709	3.82	47	47	9	821	3.89	1156	9	.260	.311	.329	4689	111	.272	.327	.405
● **Mike Krukow** BR/TR																																				
1978	Chi-N	514	11	.243	.318	.368	5	1	0	72	5.23	4	2	0	66	2.45	1	0	0	19	4.26	8	3	0	119	3.85	212	4	.278	.372	.415	302	7	.219	.277	.334
1979	Chi-N	625	13	.275	.359	.410	5	4	0	88	4.58	4	5	0	76	3.77	5	5	0	88	4.11	4	4	0	77	4.32	277	7	.314	.388	.458	348	6	.244	.337	.371
1980	Chi-N	774	13	.258	.329	.391	6	8	0	115	4.62	4	7	0	90	4.20	6	8	0	112	3.62	4	7	0	93	5.42	326	5	.258	.344	.393	448	8	.259	.318	.391
1981	Chi-N	552	11	.264	.330	.364	5	4	0	77	3.52	4	5	0	68	3.86	3	6	0	61	5.28	6	3	0	83	2.49	270	6	.252	.336	.352	282	5	.277	.325	.376
1982	Phi-N	787	8	.268	.336	.367	6	7	0	92	3.31	7	4	0	116	2.96	7	5	0	105	2.65	6	6	0	103	3.59	410	6	.261	.342	.373	377	2	.276	.329	.361
1983	SF-N	725	17	.261	.332	.386	7	3	0	91	3.45	4	8	0	93	4.45	5	4	0	77	3.17	6	7	0	108	4.51	356	8	.272	.344	.404	369	9	.249	.320	.369
1984	SF-N	808	22	.290	.353	.439	6	4	0	103	3.66	5	8	1	96	5.53	3	7	0	79	5.83	8	5	1	121	3.73	408	16	.309	.376	.490	400	6	.270	.329	.387
1985	SF-N	739	19	.238	.287	.373	6	5	0	116	2.24	2	6	0	78	5.06	5	5	0	105	2.99	3	6	0	89	3.83	387	10	.282	.331	.439	352	9	.190	.239	.301
1986	SF-N	913	24	.223	.269	.355	12	4	0	127	2.47	8	5	0	118	3.67	9	4	0	119	3.41	11	5	0	126	2.71	518	11	.226	.283	.349	395	13	.220	.250	.362
1987	SF-N	633	24	.288	.334	.463	1	3	0	87	4.26	4	3	0	76	5.42	1	6	0	75	6.45	4	0	0	88	3.39	353	13	.309	.366	.479	280	11	.261	.292	.443
1988	SF-N	470	13	.236	.289	.379	4	2	0	69	3.54	3	2	0	56	3.54	6	4	0	104	3.91	1	0	0	21	1.71	245	6	.261	.314	.412	225	7	.209	.262	.342
1989	SF-N	157	5	.236	.320	.369	2	1	0	18	3.44	2	2	0	25	4.38	4	3	0	43	3.98	0	0	0	0	—	86	3	.233	.316	.360	71	2	.239	.325	.380
TOTALS		7697	180	.258	.321	.390	65	46	0	1057	3.63	51	57	1	958	4.10	55	57	0	987	3.99	61	46	1	1028	3.72	3848	95	.272	.342	.412	3849	85	.244	.301	.368
● **Mark Langston** BR/TL																																				
1984	Sea-A	819	16	.230	.330	.353	10	3	0	122	2.52	7	7	0	103	4.44	5	6	0	97	3.88	12	4	0	128	3.03	140	2	.186	.301	.300	679	14	.239	.336	.364
1985	Sea-A	479	22	.255	.375	.451	4	5	0	56	5.43	3	9	0	70	5.50	5	6	0	64	3.94	2	8	0	63	7.04	79	3	.228	.344	.392	400	19	.260	.380	.463
1986	Sea-A	917	30	.255	.343	.425	5	7	0	120	5.39	7	7	0	119	4.31	9	5	0	110	4.50	3	9	0	129	5.15	163	4	.184	.260	.294	754	26	.271	.361	.454
1987	Sea-A	1015	30	.238	.317	.383	7	8	0	126	4.29	12	5	0	146	3.45	10	6	0	139	4.00	9	7	0	133	3.66	147	4	.197	.265	.293	868	26	.245	.325	.399
1988	Sea-A	954	32	.233	.313	.389	8	6	0	137	3.48	7	5	0	124	3.18	5	8	0	122	3.98	10	3	0	139	2.78	154	2	.201	.271	.286	800	30	.239	.320	.409
1989	Sea-A	271	3	.221	.279	.325	2	2	0	34	5.82	2	3	0	39	1.60	4	5	0	73	3.56	0	0	0	0	—	32	0	.031	.114	.094	239	3	.247	.302	.356
1989	Mon-N	634	13	.218	.316	.320	6	3	0	79	2.62	6	6	0	98	2.21	4	2	0	54	2.52	8	7	0	123	2.34	81	1	.185	.283	.247	553	12	.222	.321	.331
1990	Cal-A	829	13	.259	.343	.374	3	11	0	119	4.55	7	6	0	104	4.23	4	8	0	106	3.13	6	9	0	117	5.55	138	1	.246	.318	.348	691	12	.262	.348	.379
1991	Cal-A	884	30	.215	.291	.360	9	3	0	127	3.33	10	5	0	119	2.64	11	2	0	108	3.51	8	6	0	139	2.60	129	1	.217	.294	.295	755	29	.215	.291	.371
1992	Cal-A	852	14	.242	.305	.343	9	7	0	132	3.61	4	7	0	97	3.71	8	5	0	108	3.51	5	9	0	121	3.78	110	2	.173	.252	.282	742	12	.252	.313	.352
1993	Cal-A	942	22	.234	.295	.347	9	5	0	135	3.66	7	6	0	121	2.68	9	2	0	124	2.62	7	9	0	133	3.73	135	2	.178	.235	.244	807	20	.243	.306	.364
1994	Cal-A	452	19	.268	.340	.454	3	5	0	65	4.96	4	3	0	54	4.33	4	4	0	60	5.28	3	4	0	60	4.07	70	3	.214	.247	.357	382	16	.277	.357	.471
1995	Cal-A	778	21	.272	.329	.415	9	2	0	102	3.81	6	5	0	99	5.47	6	1	0	82	4.72	9	6	0	118	4.56	127	3	.291	.343	.409	651	18	.269	.326	.416
1996	Cal-A	469	18	.247	.315	.416	3	2	0	50	4.17	3	3	0	74	5.25	5	3	0	84	4.41	1	2	0	40	5.67	48	0	.188	.235	.188	421	18	.254	.323	.442
1997	Ana-A	193	8	.316	.402	.497	1	3	0	32	5.97	1	1	0	16	5.63	2	3	0	47	5.01	0	1	0	1	45.00	27	1	.185	.267	.296	166	7	.337	.423	.530
1998	SD-N	329	11	.325	.397	.508	3	2	0	41	2.88	1	4	0	41	8.85	2	1	0	42	4.32	2	5	0	40	7.49	50	2	.360	.421	.560	279	9	.319	.393	.498
1999	Cle-A	240	9	.287	.362	.479	1	1	0	26	6.84	0	1	0	35	4.08	0	0	0	28	4.23	1	2	0	34	6.09	71	4	.254	.289	.451	169	5	.302	.390	.491
TOTALS		11057	311	.246	.325	.388	92	75	0	1503	4.01	87	83	0	1460	3.93	93	67	0	1446	3.86	86	91	0	1516	4.07	1701	35	.210	.283	.315	9356	276	.253	.333	.402
● **Dave LaPoint** BL/TL																																				
1980	Mil-A	58	2	.293	.411	.466	1	0	0	8	3.38	0	0	1	7	9.00	0	0	0	0	—	1	0	1	15	6.00	11	0	.182	.438	.273	47	2	.319	.404	.511
1981	StL-N	41	1	.293	.341	.415	1	0	0	7	3.68	0	0	0	3	5.40	0	0	0	0	—	1	0	0	11	4.22	12	1	.167	.286	.417	29	0	.345	.367	.414
1982	StL-N	587	8	.290	.348	.397	3	3	0	67	3.92	6	0	0	86	3.03	4	1	0	65	3.60	5	2	0	88	3.29	149	2	.329	.369	.436	438	6	.276	.341	.384
1983	StL-N	716	12	.267	.342	.383	6	6	0	102	3.25	6	3	0	89	4.75	5	5	0	107	3.28	7	4	0	84	4.80	136	0	.257	.370	.331	580	12	.269	.335	.395
1984	StL-N	738	9	.278	.346	.378	8	2	0	95	3.79	4	8	0	98	4.13	6	7	0	91	3.96	6	3	0	102	3.97	131	1	.305	.350	.374	607	8	.272	.345	.379
1985	SF-N	800	18	.269	.329	.398	2	10	0	111	3.09	5	7	0	96	4.13	3	7	0	106	2.64	4	10	0	101	4.54	106	4	.264	.284	.406	694	14	.269	.335	.396
1986	Det-A	277	11	.307	.377	.473	1	1	0	31	4.06	2	5	0	37	7.12	2	6	0	60	5.88	1	0	0	8	4.50	61	0	.279	.343	.328	216	11	.315	.387	.514
1986	SD-N	243	8	.276	.342	.440	0	0	0	30	3.00	1	4	0	31	5.46	0	0	0	0	—	1	4	0	61	4.26	57	2	.193	.258	.333	186	6	.301	.367	.473
1987	StL-N	74	4	.351	.392	.581	1	0	0	9	6.75	0	1	0	7	6.75	1	1	0	5	6.75	0	0	0	11	6.75	8	0	.375	.375	.500	66	4	.348	.394	.591
1987	Chi-A	308	7	.224	.297	.334	4	1	0	50	3.24	2	2	0	33	2.48	0	0	0	0	—	6	3	0	83	2.94	38	0	.211	.302	.237	270	7	.226	.296	.348
1988	Chi-A	617	10	.245	.299	.342	5	6	0	84	3.32	5	5	0	77	3.49	6	8	0	116	2.86	4	3	0	45	4.80	85	1	.259	.293	.376	532	9	.242	.300	.336
1988	Pit-N	199	4	.271	.305	.397	3	1	0	34	2.14	1	1	0	18	3.93	0	0	0	0	—	4	2	0	52	2.77	28	2	.321	.387	.571	171	2	.263	.291	.368
1989	NY-A	470	12	.311	.370	.481	3	3	0	47	4.60	3	6	0	67	6.34	6	6	0	95	5.48	0	3	0	18	6.38	86	4	.326	.389	.535	384	8	.307	.366	.469
1990	NY-A	617	11	.292	.347	.417	6	3	0	95	3.13	1	7	0	63	5.60	4	6	0	82	4.50	3	4	0	76	3.69	95	2	.284	.340	.400	522	9	.293	.348	.420
1991	Phi-N	23	0	.435	.548	.565	0	1	0	1	40.50	0	0	0	4	7.36	0	1	0	5	16.20	0	0	0	0	—	0	0	—	—	—	23	0	.435	.548	.565
TOTALS		5768	117	.277	.340	.402	44	37	0	771	3.51	36	49	1	715	4.57	37	48	0	732	3.98	43	38	1	754	4.06	1003	19	.280	.341	.393	4765	98	.276	.340	.404
● **Gary Lavelle** BB/TL																																				
1978	SF-N	365	3	.263	.341	.326	6	5	2	49	3.88	7	5	12	49	2.76	5	7	9	46	4.11	8	3	5	52	2.61	101	0	.287	.324	.297	264	3	.254	.347	.337
1979	SF-N	348	5	.247	.327	.339	5	3	11	49	2.19	2	6	9	47	2.85	6	4	10	56	2.40	1	5	10	40	2.68	101	0	.218	.269	.238	247	5	.259	.348	.381
1980	SF-N	386	4	.275	.333	.373	3	3	4	49	4.04	3	5	5	51	2.82	1	5	3	38	2.87	5	3	6	62	3.75	109	0	.248	.284	.294	277	4	.285	.352	.404
1981	SF-N	238	3	.244	.316	.324	1	2	2	34	3.93	1	4	2	31	3.73	0	3	4	35	3.57	2	3	0	30	4.15	84	1	.238	.281	.298	154	2	.247	.333	.338
1982	SF-N	392	6	.247	.299	.324	6	3	6	62	1.45	4	4	2	43	4.43	4	3	4	47	2.85	6	4	4	57	2.51	127	2	.197	.243	.252	265	4	.272	.325	.358
1983	SF-N	318	4	.230	.271	.327	5	2	8	45	3.18	2	2	12	42	1.94	5	2	11	55	2.13	2	2	9	32	3.38	93	0	.237	.250	.280	225	4	.227	.279	.347
1984	SF-N	374	5	.246	.321	.337	4	3	7	56	2.41	1	1	5	45	3.20	3	3	8	52	3.31	2	1	4	49	2.19	114	0	.158	.230	.175	260	5	.285	.361	.408
1985	Tor-A	252	5	.214	.310	.302	2	1	4	32	1.13	3	6	4	41	4.65	3	2	3	35	2.29	2	5	5	37	3.86	91	3	.220	.330	.330	161	2	.211	.298	.286
1987	Tor-A	115	2	.313	.407	.478	1	1	1	15	1.80	1	2	0	13	9.95	1	0	0	12	3.86	1	3	1	16	6.75	37	1	.216	.326	.378	78	1	.359	.446	.526
1987	Oak-A	15	0	.267	.368	.267	0	0	0	2	0.00	0	0	0	2	18.00	0	0	0	0	—	0	0	0	4	8.31	9	0	.333	.364	.333	6	0	.167	.375	.167
TOTALS		2803	37	.250	.320	.339	33	23	45	394	2.70	24	35	51	363	3.57	28	29	52	376	2.94	29	29	44	381	3.28	866	7	.224	.278	.273	1937	30	.262	.338	.369
● **Craig Lefferts** BL/TL																																				
1983	Chi-N	329	13	.243	.308	.426	3	2	0	44	3.50	0	2	1	45	2.78	2	3	1	48	3.40	1	1	0	41	2.83	107	3	.224	.303	.346	222	10	.252	.311	.464
1984	SD-N	385	4	.229	.272	.304	3	2	4	52	0.87	0	2	6	54	3.35	1	3	3	49	2.02	2	1	7	57	2.22	85	0	.200	.263	.212	300	4	.237	.274	.330
1985	SD-N	307	7	.244	.311	.375	4	1	1	44	3.86	3	5	1	39	2.77	4	2	1	37	3.41	3	4	1	46	3.30	89	1	.191	.255	.270	218	6	.266	.333	.417
1986	SD-N	387	7	.253	.327	.370	7	5	2	58	2.48	2	3	2	50	3.81	5	2	1	54	2.17	4	6	3	54	4.02	90	1	.222	.271	.289	297	6	.263	.343	.394
1987	SD-N	206	9	.272	.327	.471	1	1	1	25	2.84	1	1	1	26	5.88	2	2	2	51	4.38	0	0	0	0	—	64	4	.313	.353	.594	142	5	.254	.316	.415
1987	SF-N	167	4	.216	.289	.335	3	0	2	21	3.05	0	3	2	27	3.38	0	0	0	0	—	3	3	4	47	3.23	50	1	.120	.151	.180	117	3	.256	.343	.402
1988	SF-N	329	7	.225	.275	.337	2	3	4	38	2.84	1	5	7	54	2.98	2	5	6	48	2.83	1	3	5	45	3.02	95	2	.242	.280	.368	234	5	.218	.273	.325
1989	SF-N	399	11	.233	.272	.376	0	2	10	55	2.28	2	2	10	52	3.14	2	3	14	55	2.30	0	1	6	52	3.10	85	2	.200	.227	.282	314	9	.242	.284	.401
1990	SD-N	298	10	.228	.283	.352	4	2	11	38	2.39	3	3	12	41	2.63	5	2	11	46	2.36	2	3	12	33	2.73	87	1	.207	.281	.241	211	9	.237	.283	.398
1991	SD-N	260	5	.285	.318	.408	0	5	10	42	3.46	1	1	13	27	4.61	0	4	14	39	4.66	1	2	9	30	2.97	64	1	.281	.309	.422	196	4	.286	.321	.403
1992	SD-N	632	16	.285	.320	.419	6	5	0	82	3.83	7	4	0	81	3.56	9	5	0	90	3.49	4	4	0	73	3.95	112	2	.250	.267	.366	520	14	.292	.331	.431
1992	Bal-A	127	3	.268	.299	.370	1	1	0	13	2.70	0	2	0	20	5.03	0	0	0	0	—	1	3	0	33	4.09	11	0	.182	.231	.182	116	3	.276	.306	.388
1993	Tex-A	335	17	.304	.357	.499	1	3	0	33	5.51	2	6	0	51	6.39	1	6	0	53	7.47	2	3	0	30	3.56	86	2	.256	.312	.360	249	15	.321	.372	.546
1994	Cal-A	143	7	.350	.392	.573	1	0	1	14	3.29	0	1	0	21	5.57	1	1	1	32	3.98	0	0	0	3	12.00	44	2	.341	.380	.523	99	5	.354	.398	.596
TOTALS		4304	120	.257	.308	.395	36	32	46	559	3.03	22	40	55	587	3.80	34	38	54	601	3.52	24	34	47	545	3.32	1069	22	.231	.279	.333	3235	98	.266	.318	.416
● **Charlie Leibrandt** BR/TL																																				
1979	Cin-N	13	0	.154	.250	.154	0	0	0	2	0.00	0	0	0	2	0.00	0	0	0	0	—	0	0	0	4	0.00	2	0	.000	.000	.000	11	0	.182	.286	.182
1980	Cin-N	684	15	.292	.345	.431	7	6	0	97	3.79	3	3	0	76	4.83	7	4	0	102	3.69	3	5	0	71	5.05	159	2	.283	.320	.390	525	13	.295	.353	.444
1981	Cin-N	107	0	.262	.347	.336	0	0	0	14	3.77	1	1	0	16	3.45	0	0	0	0	—	1	1	0	30	3.60	29	0	.276	.364	.345	78	0	.256	.341	.333
1982	Cin-N	422	4	.308	.380	.419	2	3	0	54	4.80	3	4	2	53	5.40	3	3	1	61	3.82	2	4	1	46	6.80	122	3	.279	.348	.410	300	1	.320	.392	.423
1984	KC-A	569	11	.278	.323	.388	3	3	0	62	3.50	8	4	0	82	3.73	2	3	0	40	3.63	9	4	0	104	3.63	108	2	.296	.336	.370	461	9	.273	.319	.393
1985	KC-A	900	17	.248	.301	.356	9	2	0	105	2.56	8	7	0	132	2.79	6	5	0	110	2.86	11	4	0	128	2.54	204	4	.250	.294	.348	696	13	.247	.303	.358
1986	KC-A	889	18	.268	.317	.398	7	7	0	108	4.25	7	4	0	123	3.94	8	5	0	108	3.83	6	6	0	123	4.31	178	3	.281	.342	.388	711	15	.264	.311	.401
1987	KC-A	929	23	.253	.307	.392	8	4	0	113	3.28	8	7	0	128	3.52	8	6	0	120	2.70	8	5	0	120	4.11	155	2	.232	.273	.310	774	21	.257	.314	.408

YEAR	TM/L	TOTAL AB	HR	AVG	OBP	SLG	HOME W	L	SV	IP	ERA	AWAY W	L	SV	IP	ERA	1ST HALF W	L	SV	IP	ERA	2ND HALF W	L	SV	IP	ERA	LEFT AB	HR	AVG	OBP	SLG	RIGHT AB	HR	AVG	OBP	SLG
1988	KC-A	924	20	.264	.311	.381	8	3	0	110	2.94	5	9	0	133	3.39	3	10	0	109	4.05	10	2	0	134	2.49	150	2	.253	.290	.360	774	18	.266	.315	.385
1989	KC-A	644	13	.304	.358	.439	3	3	0	68	3.71	2	8	0	93	6.19	5	8	0	122	3.61	0	3	0	39	9.92	130	0	.338	.365	.431	514	13	.296	.356	.442
1990	Atl-N	628	9	.261	.302	.374	6	5	0	87	2.59	3	6	0	75	3.82	3	1	0	46	2.72	6	10	0	116	3.34	105	3	.210	.263	.314	523	6	.272	.309	.386
1991	Atl-N	864	18	.245	.292	.363	6	8	0	101	4.35	9	5	0	128	2.81	7	5	0	108	2.76	8	8	0	122	4.13	190	2	.274	.319	.389	674	16	.237	.285	.356
1992	Atl-N	741	9	.258	.301	.351	9	4	0	110	3.76	6	3	0	83	2.82	6	3	0	79	4.08	9	4	0	114	2.85	173	1	.225	.273	.266	568	8	.268	.309	.377
1993	Tex-A	595	15	.284	.336	.440	1	6	0	68	4.74	8	4	0	82	4.39	7	4	0	102	3.61	2	6	0	48	6.56	86	2	.384	.418	.581	509	13	.267	.323	.417
TOTALS		8909	172	.268	.319	.390	69	54	0	1101	3.61	71	65	2	1207	3.80	65	57	1	1108	3.44	75	62	1	1200	3.97	1791	26	.270	.316	.370	7118	146	.268	.320	.395
● **Al Leiter** BL/TL																																				
1987	NY-A	88	2	.273	.379	.375	1	2	0	16	6.75	1	0	0	7	5.40	0	0	0	0	—	2	2	0	23	6.35	20	0	.200	.238	.200	68	2	.294	.415	.426
1988	NY-A	212	7	.231	.348	.382	1	2	0	29	3.45	3	2	0	29	4.40	4	3	0	47	3.99	0	1	0	10	3.60	33	0	.152	.333	.152	179	7	.246	.351	.425
1989	NY-A	98	1	.235	.377	.316	1	1	0	13	6.07	0	1	0	13	6.07	1	2	0	27	6.07	0	0	0	0	—	14	0	.286	.412	.286	84	1	.226	.371	.321
1989	Tor-A	29	1	.310	.355	.448	0	0	0	7	4.05	0	0	0	0	—	0	0	0	7	4.05	0	0	0	0	—	0	0	—	—	—	29	1	.310	.355	.448
1990	Tor-A	20	0	.050	.136	.050	0	0	0	5	0.00	0	0	0	1	0.00	0	0	0	0	—	0	0	0	6	0.00	5	0	.000	.000	.000	15	0	.067	.176	.067
1991	Tor-A	7	0	.429	.667	.714	0	0	0	2	5.40	0	0	0	0		0	0	0	2	27.00	0	0	0	0	—	6	0	.333	.429	.500	1	0	1.000	1.000	2.000
1992	Tor-A	5	0	.200	.429	.200	0	0	0	1	9.00	0	0	0	0	—	0	0	0	0	—	0	0	0	1	9.00	0	0	—	1.000	—	5	0	.200	.333	.200
1993	Tor-A	388	8	.240	.339	.314	5	2	0	59	4.30	4	4	2	46	3.88	4	5	1	61	4.90	5	1	1	44	3.05	103	3	.233	.316	.320	285	5	.242	.347	.312
1994	Tor-A	438	6	.285	.374	.406	5	2	0	56	4.37	1	5	0	56	5.79	3	5	0	73	4.81	3	2	0	39	5.59	67	1	.269	.316	.418	371	5	.288	.384	.404
1995	Tor-A	681	15	.238	.345	.363	6	4	0	97	3.05	5	7	0	86	4.31	5	2	0	67	2.97	6	9	0	116	4.02	126	4	.254	.319	.421	555	11	.234	.351	.350
1996	Fla-N	756	14	.202	.318	.316	11	3	0	117	2.08	5	9	0	99	3.92	9	6	0	113	2.23	7	6	0	102	3.69	134	1	.246	.306	.343	622	13	.193	.321	.310
1997	Fla-N	552	13	.241	.359	.384	6	2	0	75	2.28	5	7	0	76	6.37	7	5	0	76	4.72	4	4	0	75	3.96	103	0	.194	.303	.311	449	13	.252	.371	.401
1998	NY-N	699	8	.216	.298	.306	8	3	0	98	2.30	9	3	0	95	2.64	9	4	0	102	1.86	8	2	0	91	3.15	134	2	.261	.313	.388	565	6	.205	.294	.287
1999	NY-N	798	19	.262	.342	.401	8	5	0	112	4.18	5	7	0	101	4.28	7	5	0	96	5.04	6	7	0	117	3.55	123	2	.260	.370	.374	675	17	.262	.336	.406
2000	NY-N	771	19	.228	.304	.357	9	3	0	101	2.67	7	5	0	107	3.70	9	1	0	105	3.16	7	7	0	103	3.24	119	3	.118	.189	.235	652	16	.248	.325	.379
TOTALS		5542	113	.237	.334	.356	61	29	0	786	3.18	45	50	2	716	4.33	58	38	1	775	3.73	48	41	1	727	3.74	987	16	.226	.306	.338	4555	97	.239	.340	.360
● **Curtis Leskanic** BR/TR																																				
1993	Col-N	222	7	.266	.345	.401	1	1	0	30	4.20	0	4	0	27	6.67	0	1	0	7	5.14	1	4	0	50	5.40	118	4	.305	.381	.458	104	3	.221	.306	.337
1994	Col-N	86	2	.314	.385	.430	0	1	0	7	9.00	1	0	0	15	4.11	0	0	0	5	9.00	1	1	0	17	4.67	33	1	.242	.405	.333	53	1	.358	.370	.491
1995	Col-N	368	7	.226	.288	.348	4	1	7	51	3.33	2	2	3	47	3.47	2	1	3	46	3.74	4	2	7	52	3.10	154	4	.247	.330	.403	214	3	.210	.256	.308
1996	Col-N	288	12	.285	.369	.483	4	0	2	38	5.87	3	5	4	35	6.62	4	3	6	30	6.07	3	2	0	44	6.34	128	7	.234	.313	.484	160	5	.325	.412	.481
1997	Col-N	218	8	.271	.337	.459	3	0	2	30	5.70	1	0	0	28	5.40	1	0	1	19	4.34	3	0	1	40	6.13	93	4	.312	.394	.538	125	4	.240	.292	.400
1998	Col-N	290	9	.259	.350	.414	4	3	2	42	5.62	2	1	0	34	2.91	4	3	1	39	4.85	2	1	1	37	3.93	119	5	.328	.420	.521	171	4	.211	.301	.339
1999	Col-N	320	7	.272	.374	.422	2	1	0	51	5.61	4	1	0	34	4.28	3	1	0	44	4.95	3	1	0	41	5.23	110	3	.300	.392	.482	210	4	.257	.364	.390
2000	Mil-A	274	7	.212	.337	.336	6	1	5	41	1.96	3	2	7	36	3.25	0	2	1	37	3.38	9	1	11	40	1.80	103	2	.214	.378	.330	171	5	.211	.310	.339
TOTALS		2066	59	.257	.344	.407	24	8	18	291	4.67	16	15	14	256	4.49	14	11	12	226	4.62	26	12	20	321	4.57	858	30	.274	.371	.452	1208	29	.244	.324	.374
● **Jon Lieber** BL/TR																																				
1994	Pit-N	428	12	.271	.311	.435	3	3	0	63	3.30	3	4	0	46	4.30	4	2	0	58	2.78	2	5	0	50	4.83	234	8	.308	.356	.509	194	4	.227	.255	.345
1995	Pit-N	298	7	.346	.376	.493	2	6	0	41	7.90	2	1	0	32	4.26	2	7	0	55	7.48	2	0	0	17	2.60	134	6	.396	.415	.619	164	1	.305	.344	.390
1996	Pit-N	559	19	.279	.316	.435	6	1	0	80	4.15	3	4	1	62	3.79	1	2	1	40	4.31	8	3	0	102	3.87	256	5	.273	.315	.402	303	14	.284	.317	.462
1997	Pit-N	734	23	.263	.309	.429	6	5	0	95	4.25	5	9	0	93	4.74	5	8	0	100	4.14	6	6	0	88	4.89	378	15	.304	.360	.513	356	8	.219	.253	.340
1998	Pit-N	677	23	.269	.311	.445	3	6	0	69	4.02	5	8	1	102	4.16	5	10	0	112	3.86	3	4	1	59	4.58	317	17	.309	.352	.565	360	6	.233	.274	.339
1999	Chi-N	810	28	.279	.315	.432	4	8	0	114	4.20	6	3	0	90	3.91	6	3	0	92	3.44	4	8	0	112	4.59	360	18	.333	.388	.544	450	10	.236	.252	.342
2000	Chi-N	966	36	.257	.301	.424	6	5	0	129	3.71	6	6	0	122	5.15	6	5	0	126	4.01	6	6	0	125	4.81	436	18	.284	.338	.479	530	18	.234	.269	.379
TOTALS		4472	148	.274	.314	.436	30	34	0	591	4.23	30	35	2	546	4.42	29	37	1	583	4.14	31	32	1	554	4.51	2115	87	.308	.357	.512	2357	61	.243	.275	.369
● **Jose Lima** BR/TR																																				
1994	Det-A	31	2	.355	.412	.581	0	1	0	6	10.50	0	0	0	1	40.50	0	1	0	7	13.50	0	0	0	0	—	15	0	.267	.313	.267	16	2	.438	.500	.875
1995	Det-A	295	10	.288	.336	.458	1	5	0	38	5.45	2	4	0	36	6.81	0	0	0	0	—	3	9	0	74	6.11	177	6	.305	.344	.452	118	4	.263	.326	.466
1996	Det-A	294	13	.296	.352	.514	2	2	1	34	6.35	3	4	2	39	5.12	0	4	0	25	7.82	5	2	3	47	4.56	147	7	.293	.361	.544	147	6	.299	.342	.483
1997	Hou-N	291	9	.271	.317	.436	0	3	1	35	3.89	1	3	1	40	6.47	1	3	1	51	4.62	0	3	1	24	6.66	122	3	.230	.275	.369	169	6	.302	.348	.485
1998	Hou-N	895	34	.256	.285	.423	9	3	0	125	3.16	7	5	0	108	4.33	7	4	0	115	3.69	9	4	0	119	3.72	449	11	.267	.299	.405	446	23	.244	.271	.442
1999	Hou-N	966	30	.265	.296	.427	9	5	0	113	2.31	12	5	0	133	4.66	11	4	0	118	3.13	10	6	0	128	4.00	421	14	.287	.319	.461	545	16	.248	.279	.400
2000	Hou-N	801	48	.313	.364	.578	5	8	0	108	6.92	2	8	0	88	6.32	1	12	0	96	7.10	6	4	0	100	6.21	360	25	.364	.426	.689	441	23	.272	.311	.488
TOTALS		3573	146	.279	.320	.472	26	27	2	459	4.41	27	29	3	445	5.34	20	28	1	412	4.85	33	28	4	492	4.88	1691	66	.296	.341	.493	1882	80	.264	.301	.453
● **Esteban Loaiza** BR/TR																																				
1995	Pit-N	683	21	.300	.352	.464	3	6	0	88	5.01	5	3	0	85	5.31	5	3	0	69	6.03	3	6	0	104	4.59	298	6	.279	.359	.409	385	15	.317	.347	.506
1996	Pit-N	211	11	.308	.369	.531	0	3	0	19	9.95	2	0	0	34	2.14	0	0	0	7	11.57	2	3	0	46	3.94	91	3	.297	.373	.462	120	8	.317	.366	.583
1997	Pit-N	766	17	.279	.335	.411	4	6	0	86	4.69	7	5	0	110	3.68	5	5	0	101	4.10	6	6	0	95	4.15	405	7	.289	.348	.393	361	10	.269	.322	.432
1998	Pit-N	349	13	.275	.332	.450	4	2	0	52	4.30	2	3	0	39	4.81	5	4	0	79	4.69	1	1	0	13	3.46	161	4	.280	.350	.422	188	9	.271	.316	.473
1998	Tex-A	326	15	.316	.358	.506	1	2	0	37	5.30	2	4	0	42	6.43	0	0	0	0	—	3	6	0	79	5.90	177	9	.299	.359	.508	149	6	.336	.357	.503
1999	Tex-A	466	10	.275	.329	.406	6	2	0	71	4.54	3	3	0	49	4.59	0	0	0	26	7.18	9	5	0	94	3.83	214	1	.257	.335	.322	252	9	.290	.325	.476
2000	Tex-A	440	21	.302	.349	.523	3	2	1	47	5.13	2	4	0	60	5.55	5	5	1	94	5.19	0	1	0	14	6.59	227	11	.300	.374	.537	213	10	.305	.321	.507
2000	Tor-A	352	8	.270	.337	.389	3	3	0	46	3.69	2	4	0	46	3.55	0	0	0	0	—	5	7	0	92	3.62	188	5	.271	.341	.410	164	3	.268	.331	.366
TOTALS		3593	116	.289	.343	.451	24	26	1	448	4.90	25	26	0	464	4.54	20	17	1	375	5.20	29	35	0	537	4.37	1761	46	.283	.353	.425	1832	70	.295	.333	.477
● **Derek Lowe** BR/TR																																				
1997	Sea-A	209	11	.282	.349	.507	1	2	0	28	7.62	1	2	0	25	6.20	2	3	0	43	5.86	0	1	0	10	11.70	109	8	.349	.429	.661	100	3	.210	.255	.340
1997	Bos-A	56	0	.268	.323	.304	0	2	0	7	5.40	0	0	0	9	1.93	0	0	0	0	—	0	2	0	16	3.38	26	0	.346	.379	.423	30	0	.200	.273	.200
1998	Bos-A	472	5	.267	.329	.352	3	4	1	58	3.43	0	5	3	65	4.55	0	7	0	72	4.23	3	2	4	51	3.73	219	2	.292	.360	.384	253	3	.245	.301	.324
1999	Bos-A	404	7	.208	.260	.312	5	0	8	54	2.01	1	3	7	56	3.23	0	2	4	50	3.40	6	1	11	59	1.98	182	4	.231	.281	.379	222	3	.189	.243	.257
2000	Bos-A	350	6	.257	.304	.380	4	3	16	41	3.48	0	1	26	50	1.80	2	3	17	46	2.74	2	1	25	45	2.38	164	3	.268	.339	.396	186	3	.247	.271	.366
TOTALS		1491	29	.251	.307	.368	13	11	25	188	3.74	2	11	36	205	3.60	4	15	21	212	4.04	11	7	40	181	3.23	700	17	.281	.347	.430	791	12	.224	.271	.312
● **Greg Maddux** BR/TR																																				
1986	Chi-N	131	3	.336	.392	.481	0	2	0	4	14.54	2	2	0	27	4.05	0	0	0	0	—	2	4	0	31	5.52	53	1	.321	.400	.434	78	2	.346	.386	.513
1987	Chi-N	615	17	.294	.373	.452	1	6	0	79	4.65	5	8	0	76	6.60	4	7	0	92	4.87	2	7	0	63	6.68	341	8	.323	.403	.487	274	9	.259	.336	.409
1988	Chi-N	943	13	.244	.309	.328	8	6	0	133	3.66	10	2	0	116	2.63	13	3	0	138	2.16	5	5	0	111	4.45	498	7	.237	.322	.321	445	6	.252	.294	.335
1989	Chi-N	890	13	.249	.315	.343	10	5	0	113	3.03	9	7	0	125	2.87	6	7	0	106	2.89	13	5	0	132	2.99	495	4	.279	.355	.366	395	9	.213	.263	.314
1990	Chi-N	913	11	.265	.319	.354	8	6	0	116	3.58	7	9	0	121	3.34	4	8	0	93	4.15	11	7	0	144	3.01	562	6	.292	.352	.377	351	5	.222	.266	.316
1991	Chi-N	979	18	.237	.288	.345	7	5	0	128	3.45	8	6	0	135	3.26	6	6	0	117	3.54	9	5	0	146	3.21	587	14	.252	.306	.378	392	4	.214	.262	.296
1992	Chi-N	959	7	.210	.272	.279	12	4	0	137	1.91	8	7	0	131	2.47	9	7	0	127	2.54	11	4	0	141	1.86	566	6	.233	.304	.320	393	1	.176	.226	.221
1993	Atl-N	984	14	.232	.273	.317	8	4	0	123	2.19	12	6	0	144	2.51	7	6	0	126	2.71	13	4	0	141	2.05	520	5	.235	.280	.304	464	9	.228	.264	.332
1994	Atl-N	726	4	.207	.243	.259	6	4	0	97	1.76	10	2	0	105	1.37	10	4	0	134	1.88	6	2	0	68	0.93	376	3	.199	.248	.247	350	1	.214	.239	.271
1995	Atl-N	748	8	.197	.224	.258	6	2	0	97	2.23	13	0	0	113	1.12	7	1	0	87	1.85	12	1	0	122	1.47	354	2	.195	.219	.234	394	6	.198	.229	.279
1996	Atl-N	934	11	.241	.264	.337	12	3	0	140	2.44	3	8	0	105	3.09	8	5	0	130	2.83	7	6	0	115	2.59	426	4	.228	.251	.317	508	7	.252	.275	.354
1997	Atl-N	849	9	.236	.256	.311	8	3	0	132	2.18	11	1	0	101	2.24	10	3	0	117	2.55	9	1	0	116	1.86	394	6	.213	.239	.305	455	3	.255	.271	.316
1998	Atl-N	915	13	.220	.260	.299	12	5	0	147	2.02	6	4	0	104	2.51	11	2	0	137	1.64	7	7	0	114	2.93	416	5	.219	.268	.296	499	8	.220	.254	.303
1999	Atl-N	879	16	.294	.323	.403	12	4	0	135	2.86	7	5	0	84	4.71	7	5	0	107	3.87	12	4	0	112	3.28	410	8	.300	.332	.415	469	8	.288	.316	.392
2000	Atl-N	947	19	.238	.276	.338	10	4	0	119	2.96	9	5	0	131	3.03	9	2	0	124	2.91	10	7	0	126	3.08	401	10	.269	.316	.382	546	9	.214	.246	.306
TOTALS		12412	176	.241	.286	.331	120	63	0	1700	2.76	120	72	0	1618	2.89	111	66	0	1636	2.81	129	69	0	1682	2.84	6399	89	.249	.304	.341	6013	87	.231	.268	.320
● **Rick Mahler** BR/TR																																				
1979	Atl-N	90	4	.311	.386	.522	0	0	0	14	5.79	0	0	0	8	6.75	0	0	0	20	6.30	0	0	0	2	4.50	35	3	.400	.512	.771	55	1	.255	.293	.364
1980	Atl-N	13	0	.154	.154	.231	0	0	0	0	—	0	0	0	4	2.45	0	0	0	0	—	0	0	0	4	2.45	7	0	.143	.143	.286	6	0	.167	.167	.167
1981	Atl-N	423	5	.258	.326	.345	5	2	2	57	1.59	3	4	0	56	4.04	3	2	2	43	3.38	5	4	0	70	2.45	211	1	.242	.326	.299	212	4	.274	.325	.392
1982	Atl-N	782	18	.272	.324	.385	7	5	0	132	3.27	2	5	0	73	5.89	7	6	0	116	4.11	2	4	0	89	4.33	383	8	.277	.322	.384	399	10	.268	.326	.386
1983	Atl-N	54	0	.296	.385	.407	0	0	0	6	3.00	0	0	0	8	6.48	0	0	0	14	5.02	0	0	0	0	—	27	0	.259	.364	.481	27	0	.333	.406	.333
1984	Atl-N	832	13	.251	.303	.341	5	6	0	93	4.06	8	4	0	129	2.44	6	2	0	77	2.34	7	8	0	145	3.54	454	12	.273	.327	.396	378	1	.225	.274	.275
1985	Atl-N	1014	24	.268	.321	.401	8	5	0	135	3.27	9	10	0	132	3.69	11	7	0	141	3.19	6	8	0	126	3.80	543	7	.262	.308	.372	471	17	.276	.335	.435

YEAR	TM/L	TOTAL AB	HR	AVG	OBP	SLG	HOME W	L	SV	IP	ERA	AWAY W	L	SV	IP	ERA	1ST HALF W	L	SV	IP	ERA	2ND HALF W	L	SV	IP	ERA	LEFT AB	HR	AVG	OBP	SLG	RIGHT AB	HR	AVG	OBP	SLG
1986	Atl-N	940	25	.301	.364	.439	8	6	0	118	4.56	6	12	0	119	5.20	10	5	0	127	4.17	4	13	0	110	5.71	520	14	.335	.398	.498	420	11	.260	.321	.367
1987	Atl-N	750	24	.283	.356	.437	6	6	0	114	4.18	2	7	0	83	6.07	4	8	0	118	5.25	4	5	0	79	4.58	401	11	.314	.391	.469	349	13	.246	.314	.401
1988	Atl-N	989	17	.282	.315	.390	4	6	0	114	3.96	5	10	0	135	3.46	8	7	0	116	3.58	1	9	0	133	3.78	560	7	.268	.301	.352	429	10	.301	.334	.441
1989	Cin-N	859	15	.282	.328	.407	6	6	0	120	4.42	3	7	0	101	3.13	8	8	0	130	3.39	1	5	0	91	4.47	488	8	.305	.344	.451	371	7	.251	.307	.350
1990	Cin-N	514	16	.261	.314	.403	3	1	1	57	4.45	4	5	3	78	4.15	2	3	1	49	4.78	5	3	3	86	3.99	299	9	.274	.325	.418	215	7	.242	.299	.381
1991	Mon-N	138	2	.268	.338	.384	1	0	0	13	2.03	0	3	0	24	4.50	1	3	0	37	3.62	0	0	0	0	—	70	1	.257	.329	.400	68	1	.279	.347	.368
1991	Atl-N	117	2	.282	.364	.410	1	1	0	18	5.89	0	0	0	10	5.23	0	1	0	11	5.73	1	0	0	18	5.60	62	0	.242	.309	.339	55	2	.327	.422	.491
TOTALS		7515	165	.275	.330	.399	54	44	3	991	3.86	42	67	3	960	4.13	60	52	3	1000	3.89	36	59	3	952	4.10	4060	81	.285	.340	.412	3455	84	.263	.319	.383
● Dennis Martinez	BR/TR																																			
1978	Bal-A	1029	20	.250	.312	.352	8	6	0	159	2.84	8	5	0	118	4.44	6	6	0	129	4.53	10	5	0	147	2.63	529	10	.267	.335	.365	500	10	.232	.287	.338
1979	Bal-A	1102	28	.253	.300	.383	8	9	0	147	3.31	7	7	0	145	4.03	10	4	0	141	3.64	5	12	0	151	3.69	568	16	.269	.319	.407	534	12	.236	.280	.358
1980	Bal-A	378	12	.272	.349	.426	1	1	0	40	3.18	5	3	1	60	4.50	1	1	0	16	8.44	5	3	1	84	3.12	186	6	.312	.417	.473	192	6	.234	.275	.380
1981	Bal-A	682	10	.254	.316	.342	8	0	0	91	2.27	6	5	0	88	4.40	7	3	0	74	3.42	7	2	0	105	3.25	331	2	.218	.304	.269	351	8	.288	.327	.410
1982	Bal-A	981	30	.267	.329	.412	10	4	0	135	4.79	6	8	0	117	3.55	8	4	0	116	3.73	8	8	0	136	4.62	479	15	.248	.307	.392	502	15	.285	.350	.430
1983	Bal-A	633	21	.330	.374	.499	4	8	0	81	5.56	3	8	0	72	5.50	4	11	0	97	5.55	3	5	0	56	5.50	303	7	.307	.350	.462	330	14	.352	.396	.533
1984	Bal-A	551	26	.263	.313	.466	3	6	0	75	5.04	3	3	0	67	4.99	1	4	0	49	4.99	5	5	0	93	5.03	291	13	.234	.288	.416	260	13	.296	.340	.523
1985	Bal-A	706	29	.288	.349	.472	5	6	0	74	6.11	8	5	0	106	4.49	6	5	0	80	4.39	7	6	0	100	5.76	388	14	.273	.344	.459	318	15	.305	.354	.487
1986	Bal-A	30	0	.367	.394	.567	0	0	0	1	40.50	0	0	0	6	3.00	0	0	0	7	6.75	0	0	0	0	—	8	0	.250	.250	.500	22	0	.409	.440	.591
1986	Mon-N	376	11	.274	.328	.415	1	4	0	51	5.29	2	2	0	47	3.83	0	0	0	8	9.39	3	6	0	90	4.18	209	5	.244	.300	.359	167	6	.311	.365	.485
1987	Mon-N	546	9	.244	.301	.355	6	1	0	81	2.44	5	3	0	64	4.38	3	0	0	35	2.86	8	4	0	110	3.44	342	5	.237	.293	.342	204	4	.255	.314	.377
1988	Mon-N	899	21	.239	.286	.377	6	4	0	97	2.50	9	9	0	138	2.87	7	7	0	118	2.67	8	6	0	117	2.76	473	8	.233	.291	.347	426	13	.246	.280	.411
1989	Mon-N	884	21	.257	.300	.390	7	4	0	116	2.79	9	3	0	116	3.58	8	1	0	125	2.59	8	6	0	107	3.88	492	12	.285	.330	.429	392	9	.222	.263	.342
1990	Mon-N	839	16	.228	.274	.335	6	10	0	135	3.41	4	1	0	91	2.27	5	6	0	115	2.66	5	5	0	111	3.24	506	9	.223	.263	.322	333	7	.234	.291	.354
1991	Mon-N	829	9	.226	.282	.311	7	4	0	96	2.16	7	7	0	126	2.57	9	5	0	124	2.03	5	6	0	98	2.85	489	4	.233	.304	.301	340	5	.215	.247	.326
1992	Mon-N	814	12	.211	.271	.287	8	4	0	116	2.09	8	7	0	110	2.85	8	6	0	109	2.72	8	5	0	117	2.23	503	8	.211	.261	.288	311	4	.212	.288	.286
1993	Mon-N	856	27	.246	.306	.407	9	2	1	110	3.51	6	7	0	114	4.17	8	5	0	111	3.31	7	4	1	113	4.37	434	13	.249	.312	.403	422	14	.244	.300	.410
1994	Cle-A	671	14	.247	.298	.376	3	3	0	80	3.26	8	3	0	97	3.72	6	4	0	119	4.17	5	2	0	58	2.17	359	9	.273	.311	.398	312	5	.218	.285	.349
1995	Cle-A	705	17	.247	.302	.367	4	3	0	90	3.49	8	2	0	97	2.70	7	0	0	89	2.53	5	5	0	98	3.58	424	11	.229	.274	.337	281	6	.274	.344	.413
1996	Cle-A	439	12	.278	.335	.426	4	4	0	65	4.68	5	2	0	47	4.24	8	5	0	101	4.62	1	1	0	11	3.38	221	4	.276	.351	.398	218	8	.280	.317	.454
1997	Sea-A	199	8	.327	.424	.503	0	2	0	18	7.50	1	3	0	31	7.84	1	5	0	49	7.71	0	0	0	0	—	93	5	.333	.447	.570	106	3	.321	.403	.443
1998	Atl-N	369	8	.295	.332	.417	2	1	1	49	2.59	2	5	1	42	6.59	2	4	2	57	4.11	2	2	0	34	5.03	154	3	.299	.351	.396	215	5	.293	.319	.433
TOTALS		14518	361	.256	.311	.387	110	86	2	1907	3.51	120	98	2	1898	3.86	115	86	2	1868	3.71	115	98	2	1937	3.67	7782	179	.253	.312	.375	6736	182	.260	.310	.400
● Pedro Martinez	BR/TR																																			
1992	LA-N	30	0	.200	.226	.300	0	0	0	2	0.00	0	1	0	6	3.00	0	0	0	0	—	0	1	0	8	2.25	15	0	.200	.250	.333	15	0	.200	.200	.267
1993	LA-N	378	5	.201	.309	.283	7	3	2	51	1.93	3	2	0	56	3.23	5	2	1	48	2.63	5	3	1	59	2.59	220	3	.227	.305	.309	158	2	.165	.313	.247
1994	Mon-N	523	11	.220	.294	.354	4	3	0	57	3.63	7	2	1	88	3.29	6	4	1	97	2.89	5	1	0	48	4.50	292	9	.250	.316	.418	231	2	.182	.266	.273
1995	Mon-N	697	21	.227	.302	.386	6	7	0	105	3.59	8	3	0	89	3.43	5	4	0	81	3.22	9	6	0	114	3.72	363	8	.220	.307	.364	334	13	.234	.297	.410
1996	Mon-N	813	19	.232	.294	.357	8	3	0	97	3.06	5	7	0	120	4.21	7	3	0	114	3.54	6	7	0	102	3.87	393	6	.254	.312	.369	420	13	.212	.277	.345
1997	Mon-N	860	16	.184	.250	.277	9	5	0	140	1.99	8	3	0	101	1.78	10	3	0	117	1.54	7	5	0	124	2.24	464	8	.183	.252	.274	396	8	.184	.247	.280
1998	Bos-A	865	26	.217	.278	.347	9	3	0	108	2.99	10	4	0	125	2.80	10	2	0	119	3.02	9	5	0	114	2.76	472	12	.225	.289	.343	393	14	.209	.264	.351
1999	Bos-A	780	9	.205	.248	.288	13	2	0	118	2.22	10	2	0	96	1.88	14	2	0	117	2.08	9	2	0	97	2.05	417	4	.221	.264	.307	363	5	.187	.229	.267
2000	Bos-A	768	17	.167	.213	.259	6	5	0	98	1.84	12	1	0	119	1.66	9	3	0	106	1.44	9	3	0	111	2.03	399	5	.150	.190	.216	369	12	.184	.238	.306
TOTALS		5714	124	.206	.270	.319	62	31	2	777	2.61	63	25	1	799	2.76	66	23	2	799	2.51	59	33	1	777	2.86	3035	55	.214	.276	.321	2679	69	.197	.263	.316
● Ramon Martinez	BR/TR																																			
1988	LA-N	125	0	.216	.333	.264	0	3	0	26	5.26	1	0	0	10	0.00	0	0	0	0	—	1	3	0	36	3.79	58	0	.259	.403	.293	67	0	.179	.267	.239
1989	LA-N	360	11	.219	.308	.347	3	3	0	50	2.17	3	1	0	49	4.22	1	0	0	9	0.00	5	4	0	90	3.51	203	6	.246	.343	.369	157	5	.185	.260	.318
1990	LA-N	866	22	.221	.278	.357	12	2	0	130	2.71	8	4	0	105	3.18	9	3	0	108	2.83	11	3	0	126	2.99	508	13	.246	.319	.390	358	9	.184	.216	.310
1991	LA-N	828	18	.229	.293	.337	9	4	0	105	2.91	8	9	0	115	3.59	10	3	0	108	2.67	7	10	0	112	3.85	453	7	.225	.302	.318	375	11	.235	.282	.360
1992	LA-N	575	11	.245	.331	.362	4	7	0	92	4.29	4	4	0	58	3.55	4	5	0	92	3.62	4	6	0	59	4.60	316	9	.256	.367	.415	259	2	.232	.282	.297
1993	LA-N	793	15	.255	.342	.366	5	8	0	111	4.14	5	4	0	101	2.68	6	4	0	101	3.12	4	8	0	111	3.74	414	9	.246	.362	.372	379	6	.264	.319	.359
1994	LA-N	642	18	.249	.312	.383	5	3	0	85	3.59	7	4	0	85	4.36	7	4	0	115	4.23	5	3	0	55	3.44	309	10	.236	.302	.375	333	8	.261	.321	.390
1995	LA-N	761	19	.231	.308	.359	8	5	0	118	3.57	9	2	0	88	3.78	7	5	0	84	4.39	10	2	0	122	3.16	315	8	.254	.363	.381	446	11	.215	.265	.343
1996	LA-N	625	12	.245	.341	.341	8	3	0	84	3.09	7	3	0	84	3.74	6	2	0	55	3.62	9	4	0	114	3.32	267	6	.247	.379	.356	358	6	.243	.309	.330
1997	LA-N	507	14	.243	.337	.394	7	3	0	80	3.70	3	2	0	53	3.54	6	3	0	95	3.42	4	2	0	39	4.15	243	7	.272	.386	.432	264	7	.216	.286	.360
1998	LA-N	369	8	.206	.288	.320	3	1	0	52	2.44	4	2	0	50	3.24	7	3	0	102	2.83	0	0	0	0	—	161	6	.211	.316	.373	208	2	.202	.266	.279
1999	Bos-A	73	2	.192	.286	.329	1	1	0	10	3.60	1	0	0	11	2.53	0	0	0	0	—	2	1	0	21	3.05	33	1	.182	.300	.333	40	1	.200	.273	.325
2000	Bos-A	505	16	.283	.372	.459	6	5	0	79	5.11	4	3	0	48	7.82	6	4	0	73	5.52	4	4	0	54	6.96	255	8	.275	.366	.435	250	8	.292	.379	.484
TOTALS		7029	166	.238	.318	.363	71	48	0	1023	3.53	64	38	0	857	3.74	69	36	0	941	3.52	66	50	0	939	3.73	3535	90	.246	.345	.378	3494	76	.230	.289	.347
● Kirk McCaskill	BR/TR																																			
1985	Cal-A	732	23	.258	.319	.408	7	4	0	96	4.58	5	8	0	93	4.82	2	5	0	65	4.85	10	7	0	125	4.62	407	11	.278	.339	.420	325	12	.234	.295	.394
1986	Cal-A	905	19	.229	.302	.341	6	5	0	114	2.93	11	5	0	133	3.73	8	5	0	115	3.69	9	5	0	132	3.08	504	11	.234	.311	.355	401	8	.222	.291	.324
1987	Cal-A	294	14	.286	.363	.463	1	1	0	29	5.02	3	5	0	46	6.07	2	0	0	21	2.57	2	6	0	54	6.88	156	9	.314	.382	.532	138	5	.254	.342	.384
1988	Cal-A	566	9	.274	.342	.383	5	5	0	83	3.90	3	1	0	63	4.83	4	5	0	97	3.91	4	1	0	50	5.07	288	3	.267	.336	.351	278	6	.281	.348	.417
1989	Cal-A	795	16	.254	.307	.357	10	4	0	112	3.12	5	6	0	100	2.71	8	4	0	96	3.00	7	6	0	116	2.87	401	10	.252	.297	.369	394	6	.256	.316	.345
1990	Cal-A	660	9	.244	.320	.332	7	3	0	81	2.77	5	8	0	93	3.68	6	4	0	75	2.39	6	7	0	99	3.91	334	6	.251	.322	.368	326	3	.236	.318	.294
1991	Cal-A	681	19	.283	.347	.435	4	10	0	93	4.08	6	9	0	85	4.45	7	9	0	97	3.63	3	10	0	81	5.00	351	11	.313	.355	.467	330	8	.252	.338	.400
1992	Chi-A	796	11	.242	.325	.343	6	7	0	109	3.54	6	6	0	100	4.88	5	6	0	99	3.64	7	7	0	110	4.66	379	6	.280	.358	.391	417	5	.209	.295	.300
1993	Chi-A	460	12	.313	.362	.457	2	2	1	66	3.80	2	6	1	47	7.23	2	7	0	61	5.93	2	1	2	53	4.42	200	7	.350	.410	.545	260	5	.285	.324	.388
1994	Chi-A	202	6	.252	.322	.406	1	1	1	22	2.01	0	3	2	30	4.45	0	2	2	35	3.06	1	2	1	17	4.15	77	3	.221	.330	.390	125	3	.272	.316	.416
1995	Chi-A	321	10	.302	.373	.433	5	4	1	47	4.44	1	0	1	34	5.50	4	2	0	34	4.81	2	2	2	47	4.94	141	5	.319	.409	.461	180	5	.289	.343	.411
1996	Chi-A	209	6	.344	.432	.545	4	0	0	24	4.56	1	5	0	28	9.00	5	4	0	47	5.98	0	1	0	5	16.20	93	1	.344	.421	.495	116	5	.345	.441	.586
TOTALS		6621	154	.264	.332	.389	58	46	3	876	3.65	48	62	4	853	4.60	53	53	2	841	3.88	53	55	5	888	4.35	3331	83	.277	.343	.410	3290	71	.251	.321	.368
● Jack McDowell	BR/TR																																			
1987	Chi-A	95	1	.168	.233	.232	3	0	0	21	2.57	0	0	0	7	0.00	0	0	0	0	—	3	0	0	28	1.93	51	1	.157	.218	.216	44	0	.182	.250	.250
1988	Chi-A	599	12	.245	.326	.359	2	3	0	87	3.01	3	7	0	72	5.13	3	6	0	85	4.54	2	4	0	73	3.31	306	6	.275	.357	.386	293	6	.215	.293	.331
1990	Chi-A	776	20	.244	.316	.380	9	4	0	128	3.30	5	5	0	77	4.70	5	4	0	83	3.69	9	5	0	122	3.91	408	11	.243	.302	.380	368	9	.245	.330	.380
1991	Chi-A	930	19	.228	.292	.347	10	6	0	139	3.89	7	4	0	115	2.82	9	4	0	125	3.25	8	6	0	129	3.56	485	7	.225	.289	.324	445	12	.231	.295	.373
1992	Chi-A	983	21	.251	.307	.379	9	5	0	120	2.77	11	5	0	140	3.53	11	3	0	116	3.66	9	7	0	145	2.79	486	13	.263	.328	.409	497	8	.239	.287	.350
1993	Chi-A	981	20	.266	.314	.379	9	7	0	131	4.19	13	3	0	126	2.51	12	4	0	119	3.85	10	6	0	137	2.95	491	8	.259	.302	.354	490	12	.273	.326	.404
1994	Chi-A	700	12	.266	.310	.380	5	4	0	88	3.38	5	5	0	93	4.06	4	7	0	105	5.04	6	2	0	76	1.90	343	6	.268	.317	.388	357	6	.263	.303	.373
1995	NY-A	830	25	.254	.320	.406	7	6	0	117	4.24	8	4	0	101	3.56	4	5	0	89	4.84	11	5	0	128	3.30	475	15	.255	.326	.411	355	10	.254	.312	.400
1996	Cle-A	760	22	.282	.341	.442	7	5	0	90	6.28	6	4	0	102	4.07	6	6	0	117	4.23	7	3	0	75	6.48	424	12	.283	.348	.441	336	10	.280	.332	.443
1997	Cle-A	156	6	.282	.356	.462	3	2	0	28	4.55	0	1	0	13	6.23	3	3	0	41	5.09	0	0	0	0	—	79	5	.342	.411	.582	77	1	.221	.279	.338
1998	Ana-A	309	11	.311	.350	.508	4	2	0	53	3.23	1	1	0	23	9.39	1	2	0	40	4.76	4	1	0	36	5.45	172	4	.279	.330	.430	137	7	.350	.377	.606
1999	Ana-A	84	4	.369	.413	.560	0	2	0	7	18.00	0	2	0	12	2.25	0	0	0	0	—	0	4	0	19	8.05	45	2	.378	.451	.533	39	2	.359	.366	.590
TOTALS		7203	173	.257	.317	.391	68	46	0	1009	3.91	59	41	0	880	3.79	58	44	0	920	4.17	69	43	0	969	3.56	3765	90	.260	.322	.391	3438	83	.254	.312	.390
● Roger McDowell	BR/TR																																			
1985	NY-N	470	9	.230	.286	.332	5	3	9	68	2.11	1	2	8	59	3.66	5	3	4	54	3.19	1	2	13	74	2.57	225	2	.236	.288	.320	245	7	.224	.285	.343
1986	NY-N	469	4	.228	.294	.296	7	3	10	62	1.73	7	6	12	66	4.25	7	0	6	64	2.10	7	9	16	64	3.96	227	4	.247	.341	.366	242	0	.211	.246	.231
1987	NY-N	344	7	.276	.330	.366	5	3	13	52	4.53	2	2	12	37	3.65	4	3	9	36	4.95	3	2	16	52	3.61	171	3	.246	.316	.322	173	4	.306	.344	.410
1988	NY-N	336	1	.238	.304	.283	2	1	4	35	1.53	3	4	12	54	3.35	4	1	8	46	2.33	1	4	8	43	2.95	154	0	.260	.337	.325	182	1	.220	.275	.247
1989	NY-N	134	1	.254	.340	.328	1	3	2	14	3.14	0	2	2	21	3.43	1	5	4	35	3.31	0	0	0	0	—	68	1	.324	.418	.426	66	0	.182	.257	.227
1989	Phi-N	205	2	.220	.298	.288	3	2	8	25	0.36	0	1	11	32	1.69	0	0	2	4	0.00	3	3	17	52	1.20	117	2	.231	.323	.308	88	0	.205	.263	.261
1990	Phi-N	322	2	.286	.355	.363	3	4	10	37	5.40	3	4	12	50	2.72	2	3	13	37	6.14	4	5	9	50	2.17	183	2	.328	.414	.415	139	0	.230	.270	.295
1991	Phi-N	229	1	.266	.360	.341	1	3	1	28	3.18	2	3	2	31	3.23	3	5	3	54	3.00	0	1	0	5	5.40	128	0	.289	.399	.352	101	1	.238	.306	.327

		TOTAL					HOME					AWAY					1ST HALF					2ND HALF					LEFT					RIGHT				
YEAR	TM/L	AB	HR	AVG	OBP	SLG	W	L	SV	IP	ERA	W	L	SV	IP	ERA	W	L	SV	IP	ERA	W	L	SV	IP	ERA	AB	HR	AVG	OBP	SLG	AB	HR	AVG	OBP	SLG
1991	LA-N	152	3	.257	.324	.382	4	2	3	23	3.86	2	1	4	19	0.95	0	0	0	0	—	6	3	7	42	2.55	69	2	.232	.349	.406	83	1	.277	.299	.361
1992	LA-N	337	3	.306	.381	.374	2	2	8	37	2.92	4	8	6	47	5.01	4	6	10	36	3.00	2	4	4	48	4.91	154	3	.318	.428	.422	183	0	.295	.337	.333
1993	LA-N	264	2	.288	.364	.360	2	1	0	33	2.45	3	2	2	35	2.06	4	0	1	36	1.50	1	3	1	32	3.09	125	1	.312	.399	.400	139	1	.266	.331	.324
1994	LA-N	165	3	.303	.388	.430	0	1	0	18	3.57	0	2	0	24	6.46	0	3	0	29	4.97	0	0	0	12	5.84	72	1	.333	.448	.444	93	2	.280	.337	.419
1995	Tex-A	311	5	.277	.354	.373	4	1	1	42	3.43	3	3	3	43	4.60	3	0	1	37	3.62	4	4	3	48	4.34	134	2	.269	.367	.373	177	3	.282	.343	.373
1996	Bal-A	233	7	.296	.363	.425	1	1	2	31	3.48	0	0	2	28	5.08	1	1	3	51	2.84	0	0	1	9	12.46	92	1	.304	.379	.402	141	6	.291	.353	.440
TOTALS		3971	50	.263	.334	.347	40	30	71	506	2.92	30	40	88	544	3.65	38	30	64	520	3.24	32	40	95	530	3.36	1919	24	.276	.365	.369	2052	26	.251	.303	.327
● Scott McGregor BB/TL																																				
1978	Bal-A	874	19	.248	.286	.365	5	5	0	96	3.09	10	8	1	137	3.48	8	6	0	96	3.39	7	7	1	137	3.28	228	3	.281	.307	.395	646	16	.237	.279	.354
1979	Bal-A	665	19	.248	.273	.392	7	2	0	82	3.97	6	4	0	93	2.81	2	2	0	56	4.53	11	4	0	119	2.80	139	6	.288	.333	.475	526	13	.238	.256	.371
1980	Bal-A	958	16	.265	.306	.377	11	4	0	130	2.64	9	4	0	122	4.05	8	3	0	101	3.40	12	5	0	151	3.27	216	6	.241	.260	.375	742	10	.272	.319	.377
1981	Bal-A	611	13	.273	.315	.398	7	2	0	87	3.50	6	3	0	73	2.97	6	2	0	74	3.15	7	3	0	86	3.36	125	1	.272	.306	.352	486	12	.274	.317	.409
1982	Bal-A	892	31	.267	.306	.422	7	6	0	120	4.50	7	6	0	106	4.74	8	6	0	128	3.86	6	6	0	98	5.60	162	8	.259	.297	.438	730	23	.268	.308	.418
1983	Bal-A	1008	24	.269	.298	.409	4	6	0	98	4.21	14	1	0	162	2.56	8	4	0	115	3.61	10	3	0	145	2.85	181	3	.210	.241	.326	827	21	.282	.310	.427
1984	Bal-A	772	18	.280	.329	.398	11	4	0	124	2.90	4	8	0	72	5.72	9	6	0	118	3.89	6	6	0	78	4.02	159	5	.245	.299	.384	613	13	.289	.337	.401
1985	Bal-A	800	34	.283	.334	.470	8	6	0	100	4.14	6	8	0	104	5.45	6	6	0	91	4.17	8	8	0	113	5.32	177	12	.260	.286	.520	623	22	.289	.347	.456
1986	Bal-A	799	35	.270	.319	.457	5	8	0	87	4.53	6	7	0	116	4.51	6	7	0	107	4.22	5	8	0	96	4.86	166	10	.223	.260	.452	633	25	.283	.334	.458
1987	Bal-A	344	15	.326	.388	.509	0	5	0	42	6.43	2	2	0	43	6.85	2	7	0	71	6.69	0	0	0	14	6.43	62	2	.242	.324	.339	282	13	.344	.403	.546
1988	Bal-A	73	3	.370	.415	.603	0	1	0	7	3.68	0	2	0	10	12.60	0	3	0	17	8.83	0	0	0	0	—	7	0	.429	.429	.714	66	3	.364	.413	.591
TOTALS		7796	227	.271	.312	.415	65	49	0	974	3.79	70	53	1	1038	4.13	63	52	0	973	4.09	72	50	1	1039	3.86	1622	56	.253	.288	.410	6174	171	.275	.318	.417
● Brian Meadows BR/TR																																				
1998	Fla-N	705	20	.315	.358	.465	7	6	0	95	4.47	4	7	0	80	6.10	6	6	0	98	4.58	5	7	0	76	6.04	345	12	.351	.396	.533	360	8	.281	.319	.400
1999	Fla-N	709	31	.302	.354	.505	5	7	0	87	4.26	6	8	0	92	6.87	5	9	0	92	5.89	6	6	0	87	5.30	351	18	.313	.356	.541	358	13	.291	.352	.469
2000	SD-N	498	24	.301	.373	.532	5	5	0	74	3.91	2	3	0	51	7.41	6	5	0	87	5.17	1	3	0	38	5.73	231	15	.316	.410	.593	267	9	.288	.338	.479
2000	KC-A	287	8	.293	.322	.453	1	1	0	28	6.75	5	1	0	44	3.50	0	0	0	0	—	6	2	0	72	4.77	164	4	.299	.333	.470	123	4	.285	.308	.431
TOTALS		2199	83	.305	.356	.492	18	19	0	283	4.48	17	19	0	266	6.19	17	20	0	277	5.20	18	18	0	272	5.43	1091	49	.324	.378	.539	1108	34	.286	.334	.445
● Jose Mesa BR/TR																																				
1987	Bal-A	128	7	.297	.371	.539	0	2	0	10	10.24	1	1	0	22	4.15	0	0	0	0	—	1	3	0	31	6.03	71	5	.324	.385	.606	57	2	.263	.354	.456
1990	Bal-A	170	2	.218	.325	.306	2	1	0	27	4.33	1	1	0	20	3.20	0	0	0	0	—	3	2	0	47	3.86	91	0	.220	.339	.253	79	2	.215	.308	.367
1991	Bal-A	492	11	.307	.385	.449	2	8	0	59	5.68	4	3	0	65	6.23	4	8	0	88	5.75	2	3	0	36	6.50	258	4	.302	.380	.407	234	7	.312	.390	.496
1992	Bal-A	268	9	.287	.353	.459	0	4	0	26	5.81	3	4	0	41	4.79	3	8	0	65	5.23	0	0	0	2	3.86	148	5	.331	.377	.507	120	4	.233	.326	.400
1992	Cle-A	351	5	.262	.344	.350	2	1	0	51	3.68	2	3	0	42	4.75	0	0	0	0	—	4	4	0	93	4.16	180	3	.283	.352	.378	171	2	.240	.337	.322
1993	Cle-A	810	21	.286	.339	.414	7	5	0	101	4.63	3	7	0	108	5.18	7	5	0	105	3.61	3	7	0	104	6.23	372	7	.304	.363	.392	438	14	.272	.318	.432
1994	Cle-A	279	3	.254	.321	.330	5	3	1	44	2.45	2	2	1	29	5.90	7	4	2	47	3.64	0	1	0	26	4.15	119	1	.269	.346	.328	160	2	.244	.301	.331
1995	Cle-A	227	3	.216	.268	.273	1	0	21	32	0.28	2	0	25	32	1.95	1	0	20	28	1.91	2	0	26	36	0.50	126	0	.230	.290	.246	101	3	.198	.241	.307
1996	Cle-A	269	6	.257	.331	.349	0	6	19	39	3.66	2	1	20	33	3.82	0	2	24	35	4.63	2	5	15	37	2.89	133	2	.226	.325	.308	136	4	.287	.338	.390
1997	Cle-A	321	7	.259	.322	.368	2	1	7	47	2.09	2	3	9	35	2.83	1	4	3	29	5.22	3	0	13	53	0.85	149	1	.309	.364	.369	172	6	.215	.286	.366
1998	Cle-A	216	7	.282	.351	.421	2	3	0	33	7.02	1	1	1	21	2.18	3	4	1	45	4.63	0	0	0	9	7.71	87	4	.345	.383	.506	129	3	.240	.331	.364
1998	SF-N	117	1	.256	.356	.333	4	1	0	14	1.93	1	2	0	17	4.86	0	0	0	0	—	5	3	0	31	3.52	55	0	.327	.422	.382	62	1	.194	.296	.290
1999	Sea-A	275	11	.305	.396	.440	3	3	16	32	8.44	0	3	17	37	1.96	0	3	17	33	7.29	3	3	16	35	2.80	157	8	.331	.419	.503	118	3	.271	.365	.356
2000	Sea-A	318	11	.280	.365	.450	3	2	0	47	4.21	1	4	1	34	6.95	2	4	1	39	5.82	2	2	0	42	4.93	148	5	.257	.323	.426	170	6	.300	.399	.471
TOTALS		4241	104	.274	.346	.397	33	40	64	563	4.35	25	35	74	534	4.50	28	42	68	514	4.75	30	33	70	583	4.14	2094	45	.291	.361	.398	2147	59	.258	.332	.396
● Kevin Millwood BR/TR																																				
1997	Atl-N	195	1	.282	.350	.354	3	1	0	21	2.53	2	2	0	30	5.10	0	0	0	0	—	5	3	0	51	4.03	108	1	.306	.384	.389	87	0	.253	.306	.310
1998	Atl-N	678	18	.258	.316	.398	9	4	0	93	2.72	8	4	0	82	5.62	9	4	0	87	4.78	8	4	0	88	3.39	303	8	.277	.358	.422	375	10	.243	.281	.379
1999	Atl-N	831	24	.202	.258	.337	11	3	0	100	2.70	7	4	0	128	2.67	9	4	0	101	3.56	9	3	0	127	1.98	413	15	.230	.292	.397	418	9	.175	.223	.278
2000	Atl-N	825	26	.258	.311	.421	6	7	0	110	4.81	4	6	0	102	4.49	5	6	0	104	4.85	5	7	0	109	4.47	357	11	.289	.356	.459	468	15	.235	.274	.391
TOTALS		2529	69	.242	.298	.382	29	15	0	324	3.41	21	16	0	342	4.13	23	14	0	292	4.38	27	17	0	375	3.31	1181	35	.267	.337	.422	1348	34	.220	.262	.347
● Eric Milton BL/TL																																				
1998	Min-A	692	25	.282	.347	.471	2	9	0	80	6.39	6	5	0	92	4.99	4	7	0	93	5.13	4	7	0	79	6.24	155	9	.361	.412	.606	537	16	.259	.328	.432
1999	Min-A	783	28	.243	.299	.406	4	5	0	105	3.61	3	6	0	102	5.40	3	7	0	99	5.20	4	4	0	108	3.85	154	7	.253	.305	.435	629	21	.240	.298	.399
2000	Min-A	787	35	.260	.303	.455	4	6	0	97	5.64	9	4	0	103	4.12	8	2	0	103	4.81	5	8	0	97	4.92	149	7	.242	.286	.416	638	28	.265	.307	.464
TOTALS		2262	88	.261	.316	.443	10	20	0	282	5.10	18	15	0	296	4.83	15	16	0	295	5.04	13	19	0	284	4.88	458	23	.286	.335	.487	1804	65	.254	.311	.432
● Greg Minton BB/TR																																				
1978	SF-N	65	3	.338	.413	.554	0	1	0	6	4.76	0	0	0	10	9.90	0	0	0	6	3.00	0	1	0	10	11.17	18	0	.389	.522	.556	47	3	.319	.365	.553
1979	SF-N	275	0	.215	.289	.255	2	1	4	40	0.45	2	2	0	40	3.18	1	0	0	17	2.12	3	3	4	63	1.72	115	0	.243	.331	.296	160	0	.194	.257	.225
1980	SF-N	333	0	.243	.313	.276	4	2	9	47	1.15	0	4	10	44	3.86	2	3	5	33	3.24	2	3	14	58	2.02	131	0	.267	.364	.305	202	0	.228	.276	.257
1981	SF-N	313	0	.268	.342	.300	1	2	10	45	2.40	3	3	11	39	3.43	2	3	9	45	3.80	2	2	12	39	1.83	146	0	.260	.359	.295	167	0	.275	.326	.305
1982	SF-N	442	5	.244	.310	.314	3	1	10	55	1.98	7	3	20	68	1.71	4	4	12	60	2.25	6	0	18	63	1.43	219	1	.274	.352	.342	223	4	.215	.267	.287
1983	SF-N	414	6	.283	.352	.374	3	6	9	50	3.75	4	5	13	56	3.36	2	5	8	44	4.50	5	6	14	63	2.87	195	3	.303	.385	.400	219	3	.265	.321	.352
1984	SF-N	486	6	.267	.341	.342	2	3	7	57	5.05	2	6	12	67	2.67	1	5	6	57	3.92	3	4	13	67	3.63	218	2	.248	.319	.312	268	4	.284	.359	.366
1985	SF-N	360	6	.272	.364	.372	3	2	3	40	1.80	2	2	1	57	4.76	1	1	1	45	2.82	4	3	3	52	4.15	139	1	.353	.462	.432	221	5	.222	.294	.335
1986	SF-N	251	4	.251	.339	.371	1	2	3	31	3.16	3	2	2	37	4.58	3	4	4	46	4.70	1	0	1	23	2.38	126	3	.302	.396	.468	125	1	.200	.279	.272
1987	SF-N	93	2	.323	.394	.473	0	0	0	5	5.06	1	0	1	18	3.00	1	0	1	23	3.47	0	0	0	0	—	44	0	.341	.408	.386	49	2	.306	.382	.551
1987	Cal-A	276	4	.257	.328	.333	3	1	4	41	2.85	2	3	6	35	3.34	1	0	4	17	1.56	4	4	6	59	3.53	127	3	.268	.338	.378	149	1	.248	.319	.295
1988	Cal-A	287	1	.233	.318	.282	1	3	2	39	3.03	3	2	5	40	2.68	2	1	1	20	5.75	2	4	6	59	1.84	133	1	.241	.325	.308	154	0	.227	.313	.260
1989	Cal-A	331	4	.230	.310	.299	4	2	3	50	1.97	0	1	5	40	2.50	1	2	5	44	1.84	3	1	3	46	2.54	147	0	.211	.282	.272	184	4	.245	.332	.321
1990	Cal-A	52	1	.212	.317	.269	0	0	0	9	0.00	1	1	0	6	6.00	0	0	0	7	0.00	1	1	0	9	4.15	18	0	.222	.333	.222	34	1	.206	.308	.294
TOTALS		3978	42	.256	.332	.329	27	26	64	516	2.57	30	34	86	558	3.35	21	28	56	465	3.31	36	32	94	609	2.72	1776	14	.273	.359	.347	2202	28	.242	.309	.314
● Brian Moehler BR/TR																																				
1996	Det-A	42	1	.262	.380	.524	0	1	0	5	9.00	0	0	0	5	0.00	0	0	0	0	—	0	1	0	10	4.35	21	0	.190	.370	.381	21	1	.333	.391	.667
1997	Det-A	695	22	.285	.345	.445	5	6	0	83	4.90	6	6	0	93	4.47	5	6	0	88	4.41	6	6	0	88	4.93	372	12	.323	.376	.508	323	10	.241	.306	.372
1998	Det-A	847	30	.260	.306	.427	9	3	0	121	2.83	5	10	0	100	5.20	8	5	0	113	3.58	6	8	0	108	4.24	431	16	.267	.323	.452	416	14	.252	.288	.401
1999	Det-A	780	22	.294	.347	.441	6	10	0	115	5.46	4	6	0	81	4.44	7	8	0	99	4.47	3	8	0	98	5.62	392	15	.293	.362	.482	388	7	.294	.331	.399
2000	Det-A	727	20	.305	.352	.464	9	3	0	101	4.17	3	6	0	77	4.93	5	4	0	69	3.50	7	5	0	109	5.13	351	13	.285	.326	.487	376	7	.324	.356	.441
TOTALS		3091	95	.285	.334	.445	29	23	0	425	4.34	18	28	0	356	4.70	25	23	0	369	4.00	22	28	0	413	4.95	1567	56	.290	.347	.480	1524	39	.280	.321	.408
● Jeff Montgomery BR/TR																																				
1987	Cin-N	80	2	.313	.382	.438	2	1	0	8	4.50	0	1	0	11	7.94	0	0	0	0	—	2	2	0	19	6.52	42	1	.381	.469	.524	38	1	.237	.275	.342
1988	KC-A	234	6	.231	.321	.372	6	0	1	32	2.78	1	2	0	30	4.15	0	1	1	15	5.40	7	1	0	48	2.83	101	2	.218	.316	.347	133	4	.241	.325	.391
1989	KC-A	334	3	.198	.257	.251	6	3	9	48	1.32	1	0	9	44	1.42	6	1	2	47	1.53	1	2	16	45	1.20	152	2	.211	.264	.270	182	1	.187	.251	.236
1990	KC-A	356	6	.228	.302	.331	3	1	14	53	1.20	3	4	10	42	3.89	4	2	7	48	2.27	2	3	17	47	2.51	176	4	.278	.357	.415	180	2	.178	.247	.250
1991	KC-A	338	6	.246	.305	.355	3	3	15	50	3.44	1	1	18	40	2.23	1	4	14	44	4.74	3	0	19	46	1.17	168	4	.262	.323	.399	170	2	.229	.288	.312
1992	KC-A	297	5	.205	.277	.279	1	4	24	49	1.85	0	2	15	34	2.65	0	4	19	38	1.66	1	2	20	45	2.62	146	2	.205	.293	.274	151	3	.205	.261	.285
1993	KC-A	316	3	.206	.263	.291	5	4	16	43	2.49	2	1	29	44	2.05	2	2	23	44	2.03	5	3	22	43	2.51	158	1	.234	.297	.329	158	2	.177	.229	.253
1994	KC-A	174	5	.276	.335	.431	2	2	12	23	5.09	0	1	15	22	2.91	1	3	13	27	6.26	1	0	14	17	0.52	96	3	.302	.364	.469	78	2	.244	.298	.385
1995	KC-A	238	7	.252	.322	.378	2	0	9	32	3.09	0	3	22	34	3.34	1	1	13	26	3.51	2	2	18	40	3.38	138	4	.290	.357	.428	100	3	.200	.274	.310
1996	KC-A	235	14	.251	.314	.485	3	1	9	33	2.97	1	5	15	30	5.70	1	5	16	43	3.80	3	1	8	21	5.23	134	5	.239	.304	.403	101	9	.267	.327	.594
1997	KC-A	221	9	.240	.295	.394	0	1	5	33	4.13	1	3	9	27	2.70	0	3	3	25	7.11	1	1	11	34	0.79	101	6	.267	.327	.475	120	3	.217	.267	.325
1998	KC-A	220	8	.264	.335	.418	1	1	11	26	3.51	1	4	25	30	6.23	1	3	16	28	6.67	1	2	20	28	3.25	116	5	.293	.352	.457	104	3	.231	.316	.375
1999	KC-A	210	7	.343	.404	.514	1	4	6	31	5.74	0	0	6	20	8.55	1	3	5	33	7.16	0	1	7	19	6.27	95	2	.379	.439	.526	115	5	.313	.375	.504
TOTALS		3253	81	.241	.308	.364	35	25	131	460	2.91	11	27	173	408	3.68	17	32	132	418	3.94	29	20	172	451	2.65	1623	41	.264	.333	.394	1630	40	.219	.283	.335
● Mike Moore BR/TR																																				
1982	Sea-A	558	21	.285	.373	.450	5	6	0	73	5.15	2	8	0	71	5.58	3	6	0	57	6.51	4	8	0	88	4.62	278	9	.284	.385	.428	280	12	.286	.362	.471
1983	Sea-A	486	10	.267	.348	.409	3	3	0	65	4.98	3	5	0	63	4.43	0	3	0	22	7.25	6	5	0	106	4.17	211	3	.299	.398	.427	275	7	.244	.307	.396

		TOTAL					HOME					AWAY					1ST HALF					2ND HALF					LEFT					RIGHT				
YEAR	TM/L	AB	HR	AVG	OBP	SLG	W	L	SV	IP	ERA	W	L	SV	IP	ERA	W	L	SV	IP	ERA	W	L	SV	IP	ERA	AB	HR	AVG	OBP	SLG	AB	HR	AVG	OBP	SLG
1984	Sea-A	836	16	.282	.350	.413	6	8	0	121	4.55	1	9	0	91	5.52	3	5	0	95	4.25	4	12	0	117	5.55	481	9	.297	.375	.414	355	7	.262	.314	.411
1985	Sea-A	933	18	.247	.300	.360	8	5	0	133	3.18	9	5	0	114	3.79	6	4	0	84	3.98	11	6	0	163	3.20	514	9	.226	.285	.337	419	9	.272	.319	.389
1986	Sea-A	1023	28	.273	.339	.408	7	4	1	127	4.18	4	9	0	139	4.40	4	7	0	125	4.69	7	6	1	141	3.95	529	11	.282	.362	.405	494	17	.263	.314	.411
1987	Sea-A	919	29	.292	.348	.460	4	8	0	109	4.12	5	11	0	122	5.25	3	9	0	94	5.27	6	10	0	137	4.34	547	15	.298	.353	.463	372	14	.282	.341	.457
1988	Sea-A	846	24	.232	.286	.363	6	4	1	103	3.31	3	11	0	125	4.16	4	8	1	103	4.19	5	7	0	126	3.44	493	12	.233	.292	.357	353	12	.229	.279	.371
1989	Oak-A	880	14	.219	.286	.307	10	4	0	125	2.02	9	7	0	117	3.23	9	5	0	117	2.23	10	6	0	125	2.96	426	3	.218	.296	.277	454	11	.220	.277	.335
1990	Oak-A	764	14	.267	.339	.397	7	10	0	120	4.66	6	5	0	80	4.63	5	7	0	99	4.45	8	8	0	100	4.84	404	5	.260	.333	.374	360	9	.275	.346	.422
1991	Oak-A	768	11	.229	.324	.318	11	3	0	118	2.14	6	5	0	92	4.00	9	6	0	104	3.88	8	2	0	106	2.04	394	4	.228	.322	.307	374	7	.230	.327	.329
1992	Oak-A	852	20	.269	.349	.399	7	4	0	104	3.46	10	8	0	119	4.69	7	7	0	103	4.79	10	5	0	120	3.53	445	8	.261	.326	.364	407	12	.278	.373	.437
1993	Det-A	838	35	.271	.340	.453	6	4	0	91	5.12	7	5	0	122	5.30	5	5	0	94	6.22	8	4	0	120	4.44	428	15	.271	.345	.439	410	20	.271	.335	.468
1994	Det-A	579	27	.263	.361	.472	6	4	0	87	4.74	5	6	0	67	6.31	7	7	0	97	6.47	4	3	0	57	3.63	300	12	.260	.375	.440	279	15	.265	.347	.505
1995	Det-A	554	24	.323	.396	.534	2	7	0	68	7.51	3	8	0	64	7.55	5	6	0	82	5.95	0	9	0	51	10.06	319	12	.332	.407	.524	235	12	.311	.382	.549
TOTALS		10836	291	.264	.335	.405	88	74	2	1445	4.02	73	102	0	1387	4.77	70	85	1	1276	4.77	91	91	1	1555	4.08	5769	127	.266	.342	.392	5067	164	.262	.328	.419
● Mike Morgan	BR/TR																																			
1978	Oak-A	51	1	.373	.458	.549	0	1	0	9	2.00	0	2	0	3	21.60	0	3	0	12	7.30	0	0	0	0	—	25	0	.400	.464	.520	26	1	.346	.452	.577
1979	Oak-A	307	7	.332	.426	.459	1	3	0	25	4.62	1	7	0	52	6.58	0	1	0	4	7.36	2	9	0	74	5.86	177	5	.299	.398	.452	130	2	.377	.464	.469
1982	NY-A	586	15	.285	.358	.428	2	6	0	67	4.54	5	5	0	83	4.23	4	4	0	61	4.28	3	7	0	89	4.43	295	7	.312	.376	.458	291	8	.258	.340	.399
1983	Tor-A	176	6	.273	.348	.477	0	2	0	29	4.66	0	1	0	16	6.06	0	3	0	36	4.71	0	0	0	9	7.00	80	0	.200	.297	.287	96	6	.333	.393	.635
1985	Sea-A	28	2	.393	.485	.643	1	0	0	5	10.80	0	1	0	1	18.00	1	1	0	6	12.00	0	0	0	0	—	18	1	.444	.524	.667	10	1	.300	.417	.600
1986	Sea-A	851	24	.286	.353	.427	4	10	0	100	5.11	7	7	1	116	4.03	5	7	0	93	4.08	6	10	0	124	4.88	441	10	.274	.347	.390	410	14	.298	.359	.466
1987	Sea-A	827	25	.296	.340	.455	7	10	0	128	4.79	5	7	0	79	4.42	6	8	0	112	4.02	6	9	0	95	5.40	447	13	.302	.345	.468	380	12	.289	.335	.439
1988	Bal-A	274	6	.255	.315	.387	0	2	1	43	2.30	1	4	0	28	10.16	0	5	1	53	5.30	1	1	0	19	5.79	126	4	.317	.372	.492	148	2	.203	.267	.297
1989	LA-N	555	6	.234	.277	.319	4	6	0	87	2.27	4	5	0	65	2.89	5	7	0	101	1.69	3	4	0	52	4.18	299	5	.254	.310	.355	256	1	.211	.236	.277
1990	LA-N	811	19	.266	.319	.392	5	6	0	105	3.77	6	9	0	106	3.74	7	6	0	106	3.24	4	9	0	105	4.27	455	9	.290	.341	.418	356	10	.236	.292	.360
1991	LA-N	871	12	.226	.278	.307	6	5	1	119	3.32	8	5	0	117	2.23	9	5	0	114	2.38	5	5	1	123	3.15	495	9	.228	.290	.321	376	3	.223	.262	.287
1992	Chi-N	868	14	.234	.298	.334	9	2	0	130	1.38	7	6	0	110	3.94	7	2	0	104	2.94	9	6	0	136	2.25	491	8	.248	.328	.354	377	6	.215	.257	.308
1993	Chi-N	786	15	.262	.329	.372	5	6	0	104	3.12	5	9	0	104	4.95	5	8	0	93	3.97	5	7	0	115	4.08	424	7	.245	.330	.351	362	8	.282	.328	.395
1994	Chi-N	328	12	.338	.402	.515	0	5	0	38	6.69	2	5	0	43	6.70	1	8	0	51	7.24	1	2	0	30	5.76	146	6	.384	.448	.568	182	6	.302	.363	.473
1995	Chi-N	88	2	.216	.296	.341	2	1	0	19	0.47	0	0	0	5	8.44	2	1	0	25	2.19	0	0	0	0	—	51	1	.216	.322	.373	37	1	.216	.256	.297
1995	StL-N	403	10	.283	.329	.409	2	3	0	54	3.48	3	3	0	52	4.30	1	2	0	19	4.19	4	4	0	87	3.81	174	4	.287	.349	.408	229	6	.279	.313	.410
1996	StL-N	401	14	.294	.353	.471	0	4	0	43	4.98	4	4	0	60	5.43	2	2	0	51	4.09	2	6	0	52	6.36	156	3	.282	.366	.436	245	11	.302	.345	.494
1996	Cin-N	105	2	.267	.316	.381	1	1	0	11	1.59	1	2	0	16	2.81	0	0	0	0	—	2	3	0	27	2.30	47	1	.255	.314	.383	58	1	.276	.317	.379
1997	Cin-N	620	13	.266	.327	.427	5	5	0	76	4.76	4	7	0	86	4.80	2	5	0	67	5.78	7	7	0	95	4.07	288	7	.274	.333	.441	332	6	.259	.321	.416
1998	Min-A	378	13	.286	.337	.452	2	1	0	54	3.15	2	1	0	44	3.92	4	2	0	93	3.59	0	0	0	5	1.69	203	7	.286	.344	.463	175	6	.286	.330	.440
1998	Chi-N	93	8	.323	.422	.710	0	0	0	8	10.57	0	1	0	15	5.40	0	0	0	0	—	0	1	0	23	7.15	42	2	.286	.388	.619	51	6	.353	.450	.784
1999	Tex-A	569	25	.323	.380	.541	6	6	0	66	6.68	7	4	0	74	5.84	9	5	0	83	5.18	4	5	0	57	7.78	274	14	.318	.395	.547	295	11	.329	.365	.536
2000	Ari-N	396	10	.311	.372	.442	3	1	1	45	4.37	2	4	4	56	5.27	3	2	5	60	3.62	2	3	0	42	6.64	139	3	.273	.333	.396	257	7	.331	.392	.467
TOTALS		10372	261	.275	.336	.414	65	86	3	1368	3.86	74	99	5	1333	4.58	73	87	7	1342	3.92	66	98	1	1358	4.51	5293	126	.278	.345	.415	5079	135	.273	.326	.412
● Jack Morris	BR/TR																																			
1978	Det-A	400	8	.268	.345	.373	2	3	0	62	4.62	1	2	0	44	3.92	1	3	0	50	4.50	2	2	0	56	4.18	162	1	.265	.354	.340	238	7	.269	.338	.395
1979	Det-A	734	19	.244	.301	.364	9	3	0	101	2.32	8	4	0	97	4.28	5	4	0	76	3.81	12	3	0	122	2.95	357	12	.277	.333	.434	377	7	.212	.271	.297
1980	Det-A	960	20	.262	.322	.379	9	7	0	125	4.62	7	8	0	125	3.73	9	6	0	130	3.96	7	9	0	120	4.41	504	14	.272	.327	.421	456	6	.252	.317	.333
1981	Det-A	701	14	.218	.295	.334	6	4	0	97	3.25	8	3	0	101	2.85	9	3	0	112	2.56	5	4	0	86	3.68	364	7	.250	.333	.376	337	7	.184	.253	.288
1982	Det-A	1002	37	.247	.311	.407	9	6	0	138	3.45	8	10	0	128	4.71	8	9	0	118	4.34	9	7	0	148	3.83	531	22	.232	.305	.401	471	15	.263	.318	.414
1983	Det-A	1101	30	.233	.287	.363	10	4	0	131	3.44	10	9	0	163	3.26	8	7	0	134	4.23	12	6	0	160	2.59	524	14	.219	.269	.342	577	16	.246	.303	.383
1984	Det-A	918	20	.241	.307	.353	11	7	0	139	3.81	8	4	0	101	3.30	12	4	0	130	2.63	7	7	0	110	4.73	491	13	.244	.310	.379	427	7	.237	.304	.323
1985	Det-A	944	21	.225	.307	.340	5	5	0	106	4.49	11	6	0	151	2.51	9	5	0	134	3.22	7	6	0	123	3.44	533	11	.223	.310	.341	411	10	.226	.302	.338
1986	Det-A	1000	40	.229	.287	.403	10	3	0	111	2.76	11	5	0	156	3.63	7	5	0	115	4.37	14	3	0	152	2.43	529	13	.223	.281	.344	471	27	.236	.293	.469
1987	Det-A	996	39	.228	.293	.391	8	7	0	157	3.15	10	4	0	109	3.73	11	3	0	123	3.58	7	8	0	143	3.22	533	28	.236	.313	.441	463	11	.218	.269	.333
1988	Det-A	895	20	.251	.317	.375	6	6	0	106	4.82	9	7	0	129	3.22	7	8	0	109	4.87	8	5	0	126	3.14	487	9	.234	.306	.337	408	11	.272	.330	.422
1989	Det-A	669	23	.283	.339	.450	4	6	0	85	4.75	2	8	0	85	4.98	2	7	0	62	4.94	4	7	0	108	4.82	307	11	.296	.358	.479	362	12	.271	.322	.425
1990	Det-A	953	26	.242	.313	.375	8	8	0	113	4.06	7	10	0	137	4.87	6	9	0	111	5.45	9	9	0	139	3.76	466	13	.268	.350	.397	487	13	.218	.277	.353
1991	Min-A	922	18	.245	.315	.347	13	3	0	133	3.31	5	9	0	113	3.57	11	5	0	123	3.60	7	7	0	124	3.27	456	9	.281	.359	.393	466	9	.210	.269	.303
1992	Tor-A	902	18	.246	.312	.358	11	2	0	128	3.09	10	4	0	113	5.11	9	3	0	114	4.28	12	3	0	127	3.83	460	10	.263	.322	.389	442	8	.229	.302	.326
1993	Tor-A	625	18	.302	.368	.458	3	6	0	76	7.34	4	6	0	77	5.05	5	7	0	75	7.68	2	5	0	78	4.75	321	9	.318	.385	.480	304	9	.286	.350	.434
1994	Cle-A	559	14	.292	.369	.444	6	2	0	72	5.97	4	4	0	69	5.22	6	5	0	99	5.26	4	1	0	42	6.43	301	8	.302	.365	.468	258	6	.279	.373	.415
TOTALS		14281	385	.247	.313	.380	130	82	0	1883	3.91	123	103	0	1896	3.90	125	93	0	1815	4.18	128	92	0	1963	3.65	7326	204	.254	.323	.394	6955	181	.240	.302	.366
● Jamie Moyer	BL/TL																																			
1986	Chi-N	344	10	.311	.388	.451	4	1	0	59	4.88	3	3	0	28	5.40	1	1	0	9	10.00	6	3	0	78	4.48	40	2	.300	.417	.575	304	8	.313	.384	.434
1987	Chi-N	776	28	.271	.353	.428	5	7	0	108	4.82	7	8	0	93	5.44	8	5	0	101	4.11	4	10	0	100	6.10	108	5	.222	.336	.398	668	23	.278	.355	.433
1988	Chi-N	778	20	.272	.322	.405	3	8	0	101	3.65	6	7	0	101	3.30	4	7	0	98	3.29	5	8	0	104	3.65	127	3	.228	.267	.331	651	17	.281	.333	.419
1989	Tex-A	297	10	.283	.354	.438	3	4	0	48	4.34	1	5	0	28	5.72	3	5	0	53	4.39	1	4	0	23	5.96	42	1	.214	.377	.310	255	9	.294	.350	.459
1990	Tex-A	396	6	.290	.354	.434	2	2	0	60	3.77	0	4	0	43	5.91	0	3	0	43	4.22	2	3	0	60	4.98	81	1	.222	.267	.333	315	5	.308	.376	.460
1991	StL-N	119	5	.319	.399	.529	0	1	0	13	6.07	0	4	0	18	5.50	0	5	0	31	5.74	0	0	0	0	—	25	3	.520	.556	1.000	94	2	.266	.360	.404
1993	Bal-A	582	11	.265	.316	.376	3	5	0	67	4.68	9	4	0	85	2.44	3	3	0	43	4.36	9	6	0	109	3.06	102	3	.304	.377	.471	480	8	.256	.302	.356
1994	Bal-A	584	23	.271	.316	.459	2	3	0	71	4.71	3	4	0	78	4.83	2	6	0	100	5.42	3	1	0	49	3.47	84	5	.286	.347	.512	500	18	.268	.311	.450
1995	Bal-A	442	18	.265	.314	.439	3	5	0	61	6.08	5	1	0	55	4.25	2	3	0	39	4.58	6	3	0	76	5.54	108	2	.306	.367	.407	334	16	.251	.296	.449
1996	Bos-A	370	14	.300	.347	.459	4	1	0	50	4.17	3	0	0	40	4.91	4	1	0	64	5.32	3	0	0	26	2.45	86	4	.314	.362	.477	284	10	.296	.342	.454
1996	Sea-A	272	9	.243	.292	.386	3	1	0	36	3.47	3	1	0	34	3.15	0	0	0	0	—	6	2	0	71	3.31	66	3	.303	.352	.485	206	6	.223	.272	.354
1997	Sea-A	730	21	.256	.303	.382	12	2	0	102	3.63	5	3	0	87	4.14	7	2	0	72	4.63	10	3	0	117	3.39	183	6	.322	.380	.464	547	15	.234	.277	.355
1998	Sea-A	915	23	.256	.295	.408	7	6	0	115	3.43	8	3	0	119	3.63	5	6	0	125	3.53	10	3	0	109	3.54	271	10	.258	.301	.446	644	13	.255	.292	.391
1999	Sea-A	880	23	.267	.311	.394	7	6	0	127	4.17	7	2	0	101	3.49	8	4	0	120	4.59	6	4	0	108	3.07	211	7	.232	.286	.360	669	16	.278	.319	.405
2000	Sea-A	616	22	.281	.339	.464	6	5	0	81	4.76	7	5	0	73	6.32	6	3	0	56	4.20	7	7	0	98	6.22	162	5	.290	.329	.463	454	17	.278	.343	.465
TOTALS		8101	243	.272	.326	.421	64	57	0	1099	4.30	67	54	0	983	4.30	53	54	0	954	4.43	78	57	0	1128	4.19	1696	60	.274	.334	.435	6405	183	.271	.324	.417
● Terry Mulholland	BR/TL																																			
1986	SF-N	203	3	.251	.363	.360	1	3	0	32	3.13	0	4	0	23	7.43	0	3	0	21	4.29	1	4	0	34	5.35	44	1	.273	.407	.432	159	2	.245	.349	.340
1988	SF-N	178	3	.281	.312	.404	2	1	0	31	1.72	0	0	0	15	7.98	0	0	0	5	15.43	2	1	0	41	2.40	22	0	.227	.261	.273	156	3	.288	.319	.423
1989	SF-N	47	0	.319	.373	.426	0	0	0	6	3.00	0	0	0	5	5.40	0	0	0	11	4.09	0	0	0	0	—	12	0	.417	.500	.583	35	0	.286	.324	.371
1989	Phi-N	418	8	.292	.347	.407	2	3	0	53	4.05	2	4	0	51	6.00	1	2	0	18	6.62	3	5	0	87	4.67	73	0	.178	.208	.233	345	8	.316	.376	.443
1990	Phi-N	683	15	.252	.292	.388	3	4	0	71	2.66	6	6	0	110	3.78	3	3	0	55	4.75	6	7	0	126	2.72	101	2	.277	.299	.366	582	13	.247	.291	.392
1991	Phi-N	887	15	.260	.299	.374	11	2	0	131	2.96	5	11	0	101	4.44	6	8	0	102	4.15	10	5	0	130	3.18	157	6	.255	.280	.414	730	9	.262	.303	.366
1992	Phi-N	871	14	.261	.298	.365	9	6	0	146	3.63	4	5	0	83	4.14	8	4	0	118	3.65	5	7	0	111	3.98	161	4	.211	.263	.342	710	10	.272	.306	.370
1993	Phi-N	734	20	.241	.282	.380	6	4	0	92	3.62	6	5	0	99	2.91	9	5	0	110	2.61	3	4	0	81	4.13	137	3	.212	.265	.343	597	17	.248	.285	.389
1994	NY-A	495	24	.303	.353	.539	4	2	0	52	6.27	2	5	0	69	6.65	6	6	0	106	6.20	0	1	0	15	8.59	68	4	.338	.390	.588	427	20	.297	.346	.532
1995	SF-N	607	25	.313	.354	.494	2	5	0	66	4.66	3	8	0	83	6.70	2	6	0	47	7.04	3	7	0	102	5.22	108	3	.278	.317	.407	499	22	.321	.363	.513
1996	Phi-N	536	17	.293	.320	.465	2	5	0	52	8.01	6	2	0	82	2.53	6	6	0	97	5.12	2	1	0	37	3.44	96	1	.229	.235	.323	440	16	.307	.338	.495
1996	Sea-A	262	5	.286	.356	.424	4	2	0	35	3.86	1	2	0	34	5.50	0	0	0	0	—	5	4	0	69	4.67	51	1	.275	.377	.412	211	4	.289	.350	.427
1997	Chi-N	598	20	.271	.330	.443	2	4	0	73	3.80	4	8	0	84	4.30	5	9	0	114	3.64	1	3	0	43	5.19	111	1	.261	.322	.360	487	19	.273	.331	.462
1997	SF-N	113	4	.248	.295	.407	0	1	0	21	2.14	0	0	0	9	12.46	0	0	0	0	—	0	1	0	30	5.16	29	1	.310	.344	.483	84	3	.226	.278	.381
1998	Chi-N	425	7	.235	.304	.327	2	3	2	45	4.43	4	2	1	67	1.87	2	2	2	48	3.35	4	3	1	64	2.54	125	3	.256	.299	.376	300	4	.227	.305	.307
1999	Chi-N	443	16	.309	.355	.488	4	2	0	47	5.55	2	4	0	63	4.86	4	3	0	81	4.69	2	3	0	29	6.44	107	3	.327	.390	.505	336	13	.304	.343	.482
1999	Atl-N	234	5	.274	.310	.380	1	0	0	24	2.22	3	2	1	36	3.50	0	0	0	0	—	4	2	1	60	2.98	37	1	.189	.231	.270	197	4	.289	.325	.401
2000	Atl-N	642	24	.308	.351	.474	4	5	1	73	5.55	5	4	0	84	4.73	8	7	1	103	5.70	1	2	0	54	4.00	119	2	.294	.341	.387	523	22	.312	.353	.493
TOTALS		8376	225	.275	.322	.420	59	52	3	1050	4.05	53	72	2	1097	4.51	60	64	3	1035	4.59	52	60	2	1111	4.00	1558	36	.258	.306	.385	6818	189	.279	.325	.428
● Rob Murphy	BL/TL																																			
1985	Cin-N	10	1	.200	.333	.600	0	0	0	1	18.00	0	0	0	2	0.00	0	0	0	0	—	0	0	0	3	6.00	2	0	.000	.333	.000	8	1	.250	.333	.750

		TOTAL					HOME					AWAY					1ST HALF					2ND HALF					LEFT					RIGHT				
YEAR	TM/L	AB	HR	AVG	OBP	SLG	W	L	SV	IP	ERA	W	L	SV	IP	ERA	W	L	SV	IP	ERA	W	L	SV	IP	ERA	AB	HR	AVG	OBP	SLG	AB	HR	AVG	OBP	SLG
1986	Cin-N	168	0	.155	.245	.179	2	0	1	28	0.65	4	0	0	23	0.79	0	0	0	0	—	6	0	1	50	0.72	45	0	.133	.184	.156	123	0	.163	.266	.187
1987	Cin-N	380	7	.239	.297	.355	5	3	1	55	3.93	3	2	2	46	1.97	4	3	0	49	2.96	4	2	3	52	3.12	121	1	.240	.292	.314	259	6	.239	.299	.375
1988	Cin-N	301	3	.229	.317	.306	0	3	1	47	2.30	0	3	2	38	4.06	0	3	1	43	2.08	0	3	2	41	4.14	82	0	.207	.270	.220	219	3	.237	.333	.338
1989	Bos-A	386	7	.251	.323	.363	2	2	2	47	3.26	3	5	7	58	2.33	0	3	3	46	2.54	5	4	6	59	2.90	114	2	.254	.280	.386	272	5	.250	.339	.353
1990	Bos-A	244	10	.348	.420	.545	0	2	2	30	5.10	0	4	5	27	7.67	0	4	4	38	5.45	0	2	3	19	8.05	83	0	.241	.340	.289	161	10	.404	.462	.677
1991	Sea-A	188	4	.250	.322	.410	0	0	3	26	1.40	0	1	1	22	4.84	0	0	1	30	2.67	0	1	3	18	3.57	74	2	.203	.224	.351	114	2	.281	.379	.447
1992	Hou-N	215	2	.260	.322	.353	1	1	0	32	3.69	2	0	0	24	4.50	1	1	0	25	3.24	2	0	0	31	4.70	86	0	.256	.337	.279	129	2	.264	.312	.403
1993	StL-N	252	8	.290	.342	.429	2	2	1	32	4.22	3	5	0	33	5.51	1	4	0	31	3.16	4	3	1	33	6.48	82	2	.293	.326	.402	170	6	.288	.349	.441
1994	StL-N	152	7	.230	.291	.408	3	2	0	22	4.43	1	1	2	18	3.00	4	3	2	29	3.99	0	0	0	11	3.27	58	3	.241	.267	.448	94	4	.223	.305	.383
1994	NY-A	8	2	.375	.375	1.250	0	0	0	0		0	0	0	2	10.80	0	0	0	0	—	0	0	0	2	16.20	3	0	.333	.333	.667	5	2	.400	.400	1.600
1995	LA-N	20	2	.300	.391	.650	0	1	0	1	6.75	0	0	0	4	14.73	0	1	0	5	12.60	0	0	0	0	—	10	1	.300	.364	.600	10	1	.300	.417	.700
1995	Fla-N	28	1	.286	.394	.393	0	1	0	4	6.75	1	0	0	3	13.50	0	1	0	2	7.71	1	0	0	5	10.80	13	0	.308	.471	.308	15	1	.267	.313	.467
TOTALS		2352	54	.254	.324	.380	15	17	11	325	3.38	17	21	19	299	3.92	10	23	11	299	3.40	22	15	19	324	3.86	773	11	.238	.293	.326	1579	43	.262	.339	.406
● **Mike Mussina**	BR/TR																																			
1991	Bal-A	322	7	.239	.286	.354	3	1	0	43	2.74	1	4	0	45	3.00	0	0	0	0	—	4	5	0	88	2.87	182	3	.214	.273	.302	140	4	.271	.304	.421
1992	Bal-A	888	16	.239	.278	.348	7	3	0	116	2.65	11	2	0	125	2.44	8	3	0	105	2.41	10	2	0	136	2.64	422	1	.220	.269	.280	466	15	.255	.286	.410
1993	Bal-A	636	20	.256	.306	.410	5	2	0	74	4.72	9	4	0	93	4.24	9	3	0	106	3.83	5	3	0	62	5.52	281	4	.256	.308	.352	355	16	.256	.304	.456
1994	Bal-A	657	19	.248	.291	.388	8	4	0	93	3.98	8	1	0	84	2.04	11	4	0	128	2.67	5	1	0	48	4.10	361	7	.241	.284	.335	296	12	.257	.299	.453
1995	Bal-A	827	24	.226	.270	.385	11	3	0	117	3.38	8	6	0	105	3.18	7	5	0	81	4.65	12	4	0	140	2.50	483	9	.209	.261	.331	344	15	.250	.285	.459
1996	Bal-A	959	31	.275	.325	.440	9	8	0	132	5.39	10	3	0	111	4.12	10	5	0	121	5.04	9	6	0	122	4.57	495	8	.251	.311	.366	464	23	.302	.340	.519
1997	Bal-A	843	27	.234	.282	.388	8	4	0	118	2.68	7	4	0	107	3.79	10	2	0	117	3.14	5	6	0	107	3.27	426	14	.223	.278	.385	417	13	.245	.286	.391
1998	Bal-A	780	22	.242	.283	.382	7	5	0	115	3.59	6	5	0	91	3.36	6	5	0	82	3.73	7	5	0	124	3.33	399	9	.246	.287	.378	381	13	.239	.278	.386
1999	Bal-A	773	16	.268	.312	.411	10	3	0	89	3.22	8	4	0	114	3.71	9	4	0	117	3.70	9	3	0	87	3.22	362	7	.268	.324	.409	411	9	.268	.301	.414
2000	Bal-A	924	28	.255	.291	.404	7	7	0	134	2.90	4	8	0	104	4.93	5	7	0	120	3.99	6	8	0	118	3.58	404	9	.223	.266	.332	520	19	.281	.311	.460
TOTALS		7609	210	.249	.293	.394	75	40	0	1030	3.55	72	41	0	979	3.52	75	38	0	977	3.66	72	43	0	1033	3.42	3815	71	.235	.286	.349	3794	139	.263	.300	.439
● **Mike Myers**	BL/TL																																			
1995	Fla-N	6	0	.167	.444	.167	0	0	0	2	0.00	0	0	0	0	—	0	0	0	2	0.00	0	0	0	0	—	2	0	.000	.333	.000	4	0	.250	.500	.250
1995	Det-A	26	1	.385	.485	.615	1	0	0	2	19.29	0	0	0	4	4.50	0	0	0	0	—	1	0	0	6	9.95	13	0	.231	.389	.308	13	1	.538	.600	.923
1996	Det-A	257	6	.272	.365	.405	0	2	2	34	5.03	1	3	4	31	4.99	0	4	2	37	6.32	1	1	4	28	3.25	118	1	.229	.295	.314	139	5	.309	.419	.482
1997	Det-A	212	12	.274	.351	.495	0	2	1	26	5.54	0	2	1	28	5.86	0	4	2	23	5.56	0	0	0	31	5.81	108	5	.250	.333	.417	104	7	.298	.370	.577
1998	Mil-A	177	5	.249	.348	.379	1	1	0	28	3.21	1	1	1	22	2.05	2	1	1	29	0.62	0	1	0	21	5.57	68	2	.162	.305	.250	109	3	.303	.376	.459
1999	Mil-A	158	7	.291	.356	.475	1	1	0	24	3.38	1	0	0	17	7.79	1	1	0	21	6.75	1	0	0	20	3.60	80	2	.188	.293	.313	78	5	.397	.427	.641
2000	Col-N	150	2	.160	.284	.267	0	0	0	26	2.05	0	1	1	19	1.89	0	0	1	18	0.00	0	1	0	28	3.25	92	1	.120	.198	.207	58	1	.224	.400	.362
TOTALS		986	33	.257	.349	.414	3	6	3	143	4.10	3	7	7	121	4.55	3	10	6	130	4.03	3	3	4	134	4.58	481	11	.195	.290	.306	505	22	.315	.404	.517
● **Randy Myers**	BL/TL																																			
1985	NY-N	6	0	.000	.143	.000	0	0	0	2	0.00	0	0	0	0	—	0	0	0	0	—	0	0	0	2	0.00	0	0	—	—	—	6	0	.000	.143	.000
1986	NY-N	43	1	.256	.396	.372	0	0	0	5	5.40	0	0	0	6	3.18	0	0	0	0	—	0	0	0	11	4.22	9	0	.111	.385	.111	34	1	.294	.400	.441
1987	NY-N	271	6	.225	.296	.343	1	0	3	35	4.37	2	6	3	40	3.60	0	3	0	21	6.33	3	3	6	54	3.02	79	1	.177	.247	.304	192	5	.245	.317	.359
1988	NY-N	237	5	.190	.248	.278	6	1	14	38	1.64	1	2	12	30	1.82	5	0	11	30	1.48	2	3	15	38	1.91	50	0	.180	.250	.220	187	5	.193	.248	.294
1989	NY-N	301	4	.206	.297	.309	4	0	17	49	2.02	3	4	7	35	2.80	6	3	11	48	1.50	1	1	13	36	3.47	73	2	.164	.244	.315	228	2	.219	.314	.307
1990	Cin-N	306	6	.193	.287	.281	2	2	15	43	0.62	2	4	16	43	3.53	3	2	15	43	2.30	1	4	16	44	1.85	72	2	.181	.294	.264	234	4	.197	.284	.286
1991	Cin-N	480	8	.242	.347	.342	3	5	5	72	3.75	3	8	1	60	3.30	4	5	6	45	2.58	2	8	0	87	4.05	122	3	.287	.407	.426	358	5	.226	.326	.313
1992	SD-N	301	7	.279	.349	.402	2	3	20	39	4.58	1	3	18	40	4.02	2	3	13	36	6.00	1	4	25	44	2.89	63	0	.270	.390	.365	238	7	.282	.337	.412
1993	Chi-N	283	7	.230	.295	.364	1	2	25	37	3.16	1	2	28	38	3.05	1	1	24	35	1.82	1	3	29	41	4.20	45	1	.178	.302	.289	238	6	.239	.293	.378
1994	Chi-N	154	3	.260	.327	.357	0	3	11	22	4.43	1	2	10	18	3.00	1	3	16	26	1.71	0	2	5	14	7.71	30	0	.133	.206	.167	124	3	.290	.358	.403
1995	Chi-N	207	7	.237	.324	.396	0	0	17	26	4.50	1	2	21	30	3.34	0	1	16	23	2.70	1	1	22	32	4.73	46	0	.130	.196	.196	161	7	.267	.358	.453
1996	Bal-A	226	7	.265	.347	.403	1	1	16	28	1.61	3	3	15	31	5.28	0	1	15	27	2.70	4	3	16	32	4.22	48	3	.208	.367	.396	178	4	.281	.342	.404
1997	Bal-A	217	2	.217	.289	.286	1	2	22	30	2.40	1	1	23	30	0.61	1	3	25	31	1.44	1	0	20	28	1.59	48	1	.188	.316	.313	169	1	.225	.280	.278
1998	Tor-A	166	4	.265	.346	.410	3	1	11	19	4.82	0	3	17	24	4.18	2	2	22	33	4.32	1	2	6	9	5.00	44	1	.250	.327	.386	122	3	.270	.353	.418
1998	SD-N	55	2	.273	.355	.418	1	2	0	10	4.66	0	1	0	5	9.64	0	0	0	0	—	1	3	0	14	6.28	27	1	.333	.357	.519	28	1	.214	.353	.321
TOTALS		3253	69	.233	.316	.345	25	22	176	456	3.08	19	41	171	429	3.31	25	26	174	400	2.79	19	37	173	485	3.53	756	15	.209	.312	.324	2497	54	.240	.317	.352
● **Charles Nagy**	BL/TR																																			
1990	Cle-A	184	7	.315	.386	.478	2	3	0	38	5.21	0	1	0	8	9.39	0	1	0	4	8.31	2	3	0	41	5.66	106	3	.321	.392	.434	78	4	.308	.379	.538
1991	Cle-A	828	15	.275	.330	.403	6	5	0	94	3.56	4	10	0	118	4.59	3	9	0	99	3.90	7	6	0	112	4.34	460	7	.289	.341	.417	368	8	.258	.316	.386
1992	Cle-A	944	11	.260	.300	.346	8	4	0	134	2.34	9	6	0	118	3.67	9	4	0	125	2.38	8	6	0	127	3.53	424	5	.250	.292	.330	520	6	.267	.308	.360
1993	Cle-A	205	6	.322	.367	.463	2	2	0	23	4.37	0	4	0	26	7.96	2	5	0	46	6.31	0	1	0	3	6.00	104	2	.288	.324	.385	101	4	.356	.409	.545
1994	Cle-A	660	15	.265	.319	.370	5	2	0	73	3.22	5	6	0	97	3.63	6	4	0	108	3.33	4	4	0	61	3.67	330	5	.224	.285	.312	330	10	.306	.353	.427
1995	Cle-A	697	20	.278	.339	.433	10	3	0	109	3.48	6	3	0	69	6.23	5	4	0	71	4.04	11	2	0	107	4.89	377	6	.313	.375	.435	320	14	.237	.296	.431
1996	Cle-A	851	21	.255	.306	.388	8	3	0	126	3.37	9	2	0	96	3.46	11	1	0	107	3.52	6	4	0	115	3.30	436	10	.261	.317	.390	415	11	.248	.294	.386
1997	Cle-A	895	27	.283	.342	.434	9	6	0	130	4.37	6	5	0	97	4.16	8	4	0	115	3.85	7	7	0	112	4.73	418	13	.280	.349	.433	477	14	.285	.336	.434
1998	Cle-A	840	34	.298	.353	.493	6	5	0	87	6.08	9	5	0	123	4.61	7	4	0	108	5.48	8	6	0	102	4.94	404	17	.275	.339	.478	436	17	.319	.366	.507
1999	Cle-A	813	26	.293	.344	.458	8	6	0	102	4.94	9	5	0	100	4.95	10	4	0	95	3.99	7	7	0	107	5.79	402	11	.323	.378	.478	411	15	.263	.309	.438
2000	Cle-A	237	15	.300	.359	.574	1	3	0	23	5.79	1	4	0	34	9.89	2	4	0	46	7.19	0	3	0	11	12.66	132	7	.303	.361	.530	105	8	.295	.356	.629
TOTALS		7154	197	.279	.332	.424	65	42	0	938	3.96	58	51	0	885	4.71	63	44	0	925	4.09	60	49	0	899	4.57	3593	86	.280	.338	.415	3561	111	.277	.327	.432
● **Jaime Navarro**	BR/TR																																			
1989	Mil-A	430	6	.277	.327	.370	6	4	0	67	2.82	1	4	0	43	3.59	1	0	0	20	2.21	6	8	0	89	3.32	194	2	.273	.327	.356	236	4	.280	.327	.381
1990	Mil-A	600	11	.293	.340	.403	4	4	1	73	4.09	4	3	0	77	4.81	2	2	0	45	6.65	6	5	1	105	3.53	321	4	.299	.348	.374	279	7	.287	.330	.437
1991	Mil-A	908	18	.261	.318	.370	9	3	0	113	3.58	6	9	0	121	4.24	7	4	0	103	3.83	8	8	0	131	3.99	480	13	.271	.328	.392	428	5	.250	.305	.346
1992	Mil-A	912	14	.246	.295	.351	9	4	0	109	3.29	8	7	0	137	3.36	8	6	0	117	4.01	9	5	0	129	2.71	435	6	.257	.304	.370	477	8	.235	.288	.333
1993	Mil-A	848	21	.300	.356	.440	5	5	0	98	5.03	6	7	0	116	5.59	5	4	0	109	4.39	6	8	0	106	6.30	448	11	.317	.367	.475	400	10	.280	.344	.400
1994	Mil-A	366	10	.314	.377	.478	1	5	0	42	7.87	3	4	0	47	5.51	3	6	0	65	7.20	1	3	0	25	5.11	183	7	.344	.387	.546	183	3	.284	.367	.410
1995	Chi-N	773	19	.251	.303	.362	5	4	0	97	3.24	9	2	0	103	3.32	5	2	0	77	3.14	9	4	0	123	3.37	336	7	.250	.314	.351	437	12	.252	.295	.371
1996	Chi-N	906	25	.269	.328	.421	5	7	0	115	4.24	10	5	0	122	3.61	6	7	0	124	3.71	9	5	0	113	4.14	374	10	.270	.331	.436	532	15	.269	.325	.410
1997	Chi-A	865	22	.309	.359	.455	6	6	0	102	4.57	3	8	0	107	6.96	6	6	0	114	4.91	3	8	0	96	6.84	396	9	.321	.392	.475	469	13	.299	.329	.439
1998	Chi-A	708	30	.315	.384	.499	5	7	0	91	6.01	3	9	1	81	6.75	6	10	0	105	5.83	2	6	1	68	7.18	376	15	.327	.392	.519	332	15	.301	.375	.476
1999	Chi-A	659	29	.313	.387	.492	4	6	0	83	5.31	4	7	0	77	6.93	6	6	0	84	5.16	2	7	0	76	7.11	330	17	.361	.430	.576	329	12	.264	.342	.407
2000	Mil-A	83	6	.410	.505	.747	0	2	0	7	7.71	0	3	0	12	15.43	0	5	0	19	12.54	0	0	0	0	—	34	3	.294	.419	.647	49	3	.490	.567	.816
2000	Cle-A	61	3	.328	.377	.590	0	1	0	7	10.80	0	0	0	8	5.63	0	1	0	8	10.13	0	0	0	7	5.40	23	3	.391	.423	.870	38	0	.289	.349	.421
TOTALS		8119	214	.285	.342	.423	59	58	1	1005	4.44	57	68	1	1050	4.99	55	59	0	989	4.82	61	67	2	1067	4.62	3930	107	.297	.356	.445	4189	107	.273	.329	.403
● **Denny Neagle**	BL/TL																																			
1991	Min-A	85	3	.329	.380	.553	0	1	0	18	4.50	0	0	0	2	0.00	0	0	0	0	—	0	1	0	20	4.05	21	0	.238	.238	.429	64	3	.359	.423	.594
1992	Pit-N	328	9	.247	.335	.387	1	5	0	39	6.05	3	1	2	48	3.21	3	4	1	49	5.36	1	2	1	38	3.35	92	2	.228	.343	.348	236	7	.254	.332	.403
1993	Pit-N	318	10	.258	.340	.421	1	1	0	37	4.86	2	4	1	44	5.68	2	3	0	50	5.54	1	2	1	31	4.94	94	3	.223	.305	.383	224	7	.272	.354	.438
1994	Pit-N	522	18	.259	.322	.439	5	4	0	69	4.70	4	6	0	68	5.56	7	8	0	97	4.47	2	2	0	40	6.69	96	2	.271	.327	.417	426	16	.256	.321	.444
1995	Pit-N	809	20	.273	.312	.405	6	0	0	81	3.56	7	8	0	129	3.36	9	3	0	96	2.90	4	5	0	113	3.89	126	5	.270	.348	.484	683	15	.274	.305	.391
1996	Pit-N	696	21	.267	.303	.420	8	2	0	94	2.79	6	4	0	89	3.34	8	4	0	106	3.07	6	2	0	77	3.04	92	2	.293	.330	.413	604	19	.263	.299	.421
1996	Atl-N	149	5	.268	.329	.423	1	0	0	13	5.40	1	3	0	25	5.68	0	0	0	0	—	2	3	0	39	5.59	19	0	.263	.263	.368	130	5	.269	.338	.431
1997	Atl-N	874	18	.233	.277	.362	10	1	0	121	3.06	10	4	0	113	2.88	11	1	0	116	3.27	9	4	0	118	2.68	174	5	.236	.272	.397	700	13	.233	.278	.353
1998	Atl-N	785	25	.250	.307	.400	9	3	0	99	4.47	7	8	0	112	2.74	9	6	0	125	3.46	7	5	0	85	3.69	148	3	.257	.317	.392	637	22	.248	.304	.402
1999	Cin-N	415	23	.229	.300	.470	6	3	0	67	4.41	3	2	0	44	4.06	0	3	0	25	8.17	9	2	0	86	3.13	81	4	.198	.287	.395	334	19	.237	.303	.488
2000	Cin-N	450	15	.247	.325	.402	5	0	0	68	3.56	3	2	0	49	3.47	6	2	0	103	3.86	2	0	0	15	1.20	100	6	.280	.314	.510	350	9	.237	.328	.371
2000	NY-A	356	16	.278	.335	.475	5	5	0	64	5.20	2	2	0	27	7.24	0	0	0	0	—	7	7	0	91	5.81	100	3	.310	.378	.470	256	13	.266	.318	.477
TOTALS		5787	183	.255	.312	.414	57	25	0	770	4.06	48	44	3	750	3.78	55	34	1	766	3.90	50	35	2	754	3.94	1143	35	.256	.318	.420	4644	148	.255	.311	.412
● **Jeff Nelson**	BR/TR																																			
1992	Sea-A	290	7	.245	.353	.372	1	2	5	42	3.46	0	5	1	39	3.43	0	3	0	35	4.11	1	4	6	46	2.93	108	2	.287	.418	.398	182	5	.220	.311	.357

		TOTAL					HOME					AWAY					1ST HALF					2ND HALF					LEFT					RIGHT				
YEAR	TM/L	AB	HR	AVG	OBP	SLG	W	L	SV	IP	ERA	W	L	SV	IP	ERA	W	L	SV	IP	ERA	W	L	SV	IP	ERA	AB	HR	AVG	OBP	SLG	AB	HR	AVG	OBP	SLG
1993	Sea-A	221	5	.258	.371	.362	3	0	1	35	3.57	2	3	0	25	5.47	2	1	0	28	3.18	3	2	1	32	5.40	48	3	.354	.484	.625	173	2	.231	.337	.289
1994	Sea-A	155	3	.226	.342	.342	0	0	0	17	2.12	0	0	0	25	3.20	0	0	0	24	2.25	0	0	0	18	3.44	48	1	.354	.500	.458	107	2	.168	.262	.290
1995	Sea-A	277	4	.209	.291	.296	5	2	1	44	1.24	2	1	1	35	3.34	3	1	1	34	1.60	4	2	1	45	2.60	120	2	.233	.343	.317	157	2	.191	.249	.280
1996	NY-A	286	6	.262	.348	.388	1	3	1	34	6.03	3	1	1	40	2.93	2	2	2	37	4.82	2	2	0	37	3.89	127	5	.283	.348	.504	159	1	.245	.348	.296
1997	NY-A	277	7	.191	.294	.325	2	2	0	41	2.88	1	5	2	38	2.84	2	5	1	43	3.16	1	2	1	36	2.50	98	3	.235	.364	.439	179	4	.168	.252	.263
1998	NY-A	158	1	.278	.387	.392	2	0	2	16	1.65	3	3	1	24	5.25	5	3	2	34	4.54	0	0	1	7	0.00	61	0	.295	.411	.426	97	1	.268	.373	.371
1999	NY-A	110	2	.245	.380	.364	2	0	0	18	2.55	0	1	1	13	6.39	1	1	0	16	5.74	1	0	1	15	2.45	35	1	.229	.426	.400	75	1	.253	.356	.347
2000	NY-A	241	2	.183	.314	.253	7	1	0	39	2.54	1	3	0	31	2.35	6	2	0	42	1.91	2	2	0	27	3.29	82	1	.232	.351	.354	159	1	.157	.295	.201
TOTALS		2015	37	.230	.337	.341	23	10	10	286	2.99	12	22	7	270	3.60	21	18	6	293	3.35	14	14	11	263	3.22	727	18	.271	.390	.425	1288	19	.207	.305	.293
● **Robb Nen** BR/TR																																				
1993	Tex-A	86	1	.326	.478	.465	1	0	0	15	3.68	0	1	0	8	11.25	1	1	0	23	6.35	0	0	0	0	—	38	0	.263	.417	.316	48	1	.375	.523	.583
1993	Fla-N	137	5	.255	.348	.453	1	0	0	24	7.87	0	0	0	9	4.82	0	0	0	0	—	1	0	0	33	7.02	59	0	.186	.284	.271	78	5	.308	.396	.590
1994	Fla-N	207	6	.222	.280	.382	2	2	6	32	2.51	3	3	9	26	3.51	2	4	7	39	3.00	3	1	8	19	2.84	93	1	.161	.257	.247	114	5	.272	.300	.491
1995	Fla-N	254	6	.244	.308	.406	0	5	11	38	4.30	0	2	12	28	1.93	0	5	4	29	4.30	0	2	19	36	2.48	121	3	.273	.336	.471	133	3	.218	.283	.346
1996	Fla-N	298	2	.225	.277	.299	4	0	19	44	0.82	1	1	16	39	3.23	3	1	16	43	2.51	2	0	19	40	1.35	141	0	.241	.299	.298	157	2	.210	.257	.299
1997	Fla-N	288	7	.250	.338	.372	7	1	16	39	3.89	2	2	19	35	3.89	5	2	23	38	4.23	4	1	12	36	3.53	145	4	.221	.311	.331	143	3	.280	.366	.413
1998	SF-N	327	4	.180	.239	.251	4	2	23	42	0.43	3	5	17	47	2.49	5	1	23	51	1.05	2	6	17	37	2.17	167	1	.234	.285	.293	160	3	.125	.193	.206
1999	SF-N	287	8	.275	.337	.411	1	4	23	42	3.21	2	4	14	30	5.04	3	2	20	42	3.67	0	6	17	31	4.40	130	5	.354	.421	.538	157	3	.210	.265	.306
2000	SF-N	228	4	.162	.230	.241	3	1	21	34	1.07	1	2	20	32	1.95	1	3	12	27	2.63	3	0	29	39	0.70	119	3	.193	.267	.303	109	1	.128	.190	.174
TOTALS		2112	43	.230	.301	.348	23	15	119	309	2.79	12	20	107	254	3.43	20	19	105	293	3.20	15	16	121	271	2.96	1013	17	.240	.315	.348	1099	26	.220	.289	.348
● **Joe Niekro** BR/TR																																				
1978	Hou-N	765	13	.248	.318	.358	8	6	0	109	3.72	6	8	0	94	4.04	5	4	0	65	5.98	9	10	0	138	2.87	326	5	.252	.321	.362	439	8	.246	.316	.355
1979	Hou-N	970	17	.228	.308	.322	8	4	0	125	2.66	13	7	0	138	3.32	11	3	0	128	3.02	10	8	0	135	2.99	405	3	.217	.300	.289	565	14	.235	.313	.345
1980	Hou-N	993	12	.270	.323	.355	11	4	0	130	3.05	9	8	0	126	4.06	8	6	0	113	3.34	12	6	0	143	3.72	450	5	.267	.324	.338	543	7	.273	.322	.370
1981	Hou-N	617	8	.243	.294	.329	4	3	0	69	2.08	5	6	0	97	3.35	6	5	0	95	2.83	3	4	0	71	2.80	287	3	.261	.331	.355	330	5	.227	.260	.306
1982	Hou-N	980	12	.229	.278	.303	10	5	0	143	2.39	7	7	0	127	2.55	6	6	0	124	2.61	11	6	0	146	2.34	478	6	.211	.275	.289	502	6	.245	.281	.317
1983	Hou-N	987	15	.241	.311	.336	10	6	0	150	2.40	5	8	0	114	4.91	4	7	0	117	3.84	11	7	0	146	3.20	476	8	.252	.316	.359	511	7	.231	.306	.315
1984	Hou-N	925	16	.241	.308	.343	6	8	0	136	2.71	10	4	0	112	3.45	7	7	0	112	2.98	9	5	0	137	3.10	450	9	.262	.338	.373	475	7	.221	.279	.314
1985	Hou-N	799	21	.247	.329	.357	2	5	0	89	4.15	7	7	0	124	3.41	6	7	0	113	3.18	3	5	0	100	4.33	382	9	.270	.368	.377	417	12	.225	.291	.338
1985	NY-A	50	3	.280	.379	.480	2	0	0	11	1.69	0	1	0	2	32.40	0	0	0	0	—	2	1	0	12	5.84	35	3	.257	.350	.543	15	0	.333	.444	.333
1986	NY-A	505	15	.275	.357	.432	4	5	0	60	5.97	5	5	0	65	3.86	7	6	0	91	4.34	2	4	0	34	6.29	238	5	.273	.378	.395	267	10	.277	.337	.464
1987	NY-A	186	4	.215	.300	.323	1	1	0	19	2.89	2	3	0	32	3.94	3	4	0	51	3.55	0	0	0	0	—	92	1	.228	.339	.304	94	3	.202	.257	.340
1987	Min-A	388	11	.296	.375	.466	3	3	0	35	5.35	1	6	0	61	6.79	2	1	0	16	5.06	2	9	0	80	6.50	214	10	.313	.379	.561	174	1	.276	.369	.351
1988	Min-A	50	2	.320	.424	.480	0	1	0	7	10.80	1	0	0	5	9.00	1	1	0	12	10.03	0	0	0	0	—	14	1	.357	.526	.643	36	1	.306	.375	.417
TOTALS		8215	149	.248	.316	.351	69	51	0	1083	3.15	71	70	0	1097	3.88	66	56	0	1038	3.53	74	65	0	1142	3.51	3847	68	.253	.329	.359	4368	81	.243	.304	.343
● **Phil Niekro** BR/TR																																				
1978	Atl-N	1254	16	.235	.298	.323	10	8	1	163	3.20	9	10	0	171	2.57	8	9	0	149	3.09	11	9	1	186	2.71	540	5	.231	.299	.309	714	11	.238	.298	.333
1979	Atl-N	1290	41	.241	.306	.384	12	9	0	183	3.60	9	11	0	159	3.16	9	10	0	151	3.99	12	10	0	191	2.92	568	14	.266	.322	.387	722	27	.222	.294	.382
1980	Atl-N	1030	30	.249	.306	.383	10	8	1	153	3.59	5	10	0	122	3.69	5	10	0	128	4.14	10	8	1	147	3.19	455	16	.248	.309	.396	575	14	.249	.304	.372
1981	Atl-N	514	6	.233	.309	.321	3	3	0	48	3.54	4	4	0	91	2.87	4	4	0	73	3.58	3	3	0	66	2.58	257	3	.253	.334	.354	257	3	.214	.283	.288
1982	Atl-N	883	23	.255	.313	.368	3	3	0	91	5.04	14	1	0	143	2.70	6	2	0	102	3.00	11	2	0	132	4.08	418	8	.227	.290	.316	465	15	.280	.333	.415
1983	Atl-N	769	18	.276	.362	.391	4	5	0	95	4.53	7	5	0	106	3.47	3	6	0	89	4.63	8	4	0	112	3.45	378	7	.272	.346	.386	391	11	.279	.377	.396
1984	NY-A	821	15	.267	.327	.376	7	4	0	106	3.49	9	4	0	110	2.70	10	4	0	124	1.96	6	4	0	92	4.61	449	11	.261	.329	.388	372	4	.274	.325	.363
1985	NY-A	829	29	.245	.341	.409	9	5	0	110	3.85	7	7	0	110	4.34	7	7	0	94	4.98	9	5	0	126	3.43	440	17	.261	.366	.432	389	12	.226	.311	.383
1986	Cle-A	841	24	.287	.362	.429	6	5	0	96	4.05	5	6	0	115	4.55	4	6	0	94	4.60	7	5	0	116	4.10	455	9	.284	.360	.404	386	15	.290	.365	.459
1987	Tor-A	49	4	.306	.393	.673	0	1	0	6	11.37	0	1	0	6	4.76	0	0	0	0	—	0	2	0	12	8.25	31	2	.387	.472	.710	18	2	.167	.250	.611
1987	Cle-A	497	18	.286	.356	.469	2	5	0	46	7.29	5	6	0	78	5.08	6	7	0	91	4.93	1	4	0	32	8.63	273	9	.311	.382	.491	224	9	.254	.324	.442
1987	Atl-N	14	0	.429	.600	.571	0	0	0	3	15.00	0	0	0	0	—	0	0	0	0	—	0	0	0	3	15.00	8	0	.500	.667	.500	6	0	.333	.500	.667
TOTALS		8791	224	.255	.326	.383	66	56	2	1100	4.02	74	65	0	1212	3.41	62	65	0	1096	3.80	78	56	2	1216	3.61	4272	101	.261	.333	.385	4519	123	.250	.319	.382
● **C. J. Nitkowski** BL/TL																																				
1995	Cin-N	134	4	.306	.382	.478	0	2	0	15	9.00	1	1	0	17	3.63	1	1	0	23	2.74	0	2	0	9	14.46	26	0	.231	.300	.231	108	4	.324	.402	.537
1995	Det-A	158	7	.335	.413	.582	0	3	0	12	8.03	1	1	0	27	6.67	0	0	0	0	—	1	4	0	39	7.09	31	0	.290	.281	.419	127	7	.346	.441	.622
1996	Det-A	187	7	.332	.457	.519	2	2	0	31	6.61	0	1	0	14	11.30	0	0	0	0	—	2	3	0	46	8.08	40	1	.350	.458	.475	147	6	.327	.457	.531
1998	Hou-N	215	4	.228	.317	.340	2	2	0	27	4.05	1	1	3	33	3.55	3	2	3	47	3.06	0	1	0	13	6.39	59	0	.186	.310	.254	156	4	.244	.320	.372
1999	Det-A	296	11	.213	.319	.358	1	3	0	41	4.35	3	2	0	40	4.24	1	2	0	26	5.88	3	3	0	56	3.56	104	5	.212	.306	.375	192	6	.214	.326	.349
2000	Det-A	433	13	.286	.358	.443	2	1	0	45	3.77	2	8	0	64	6.30	4	7	0	69	6.00	0	2	0	41	3.98	147	5	.218	.292	.361	286	8	.322	.393	.486
TOTALS		1423	46	.275	.366	.439	7	13	0	172	5.23	8	14	3	196	5.59	9	12	3	165	4.69	6	15	0	203	6.02	407	11	.231	.315	.356	1016	35	.293	.386	.471
● **Hideo Nomo** BR/TR																																				
1995	LA-N	681	14	.182	.270	.286	8	2	0	99	1.73	5	4	0	92	3.41	6	1	0	83	2.05	7	5	0	108	2.92	310	8	.200	.287	.326	371	6	.167	.255	.253
1996	LA-N	827	23	.218	.290	.343	9	6	0	134	2.75	7	5	0	94	3.82	8	7	0	113	3.67	8	4	0	116	2.72	355	8	.217	.286	.324	472	15	.218	.293	.358
1997	LA-N	795	23	.243	.328	.400	6	7	0	110	3.60	8	5	0	97	4.99	7	7	0	110	4.02	7	5	0	98	4.52	412	9	.252	.330	.388	383	14	.232	.326	.413
1998	LA-N	250	8	.228	.334	.376	2	3	0	33	4.13	0	4	0	35	5.91	2	7	0	68	5.05	0	0	0	0	—	117	6	.222	.338	.419	133	2	.233	.331	.338
1998	NY-N	326	11	.224	.337	.368	2	2	0	45	4.17	2	3	0	44	5.48	0	1	0	23	3.91	4	4	0	67	5.13	154	5	.201	.313	.344	172	6	.244	.358	.390
1999	Mil-A	676	27	.256	.333	.441	5	6	0	90	4.20	7	2	0	86	4.90	6	1	0	65	3.72	6	7	0	111	5.03	319	11	.279	.354	.464	357	16	.235	.315	.420
2000	Det-A	727	31	.263	.344	.451	3	5	0	91	4.37	5	7	0	99	5.07	2	7	0	105	5.16	6	5	0	85	4.22	357	16	.241	.340	.420	370	15	.284	.349	.481
TOTALS		4282	137	.231	.316	.382	35	31	0	602	3.38	34	30	0	549	4.62	31	31	0	566	3.96	38	30	0	584	3.99	2024	63	.235	.320	.383	2258	74	.229	.312	.381
● **Bob Ojeda** BL/TL																																				
1980	Bos-A	108	2	.361	.434	.481	0	1	0	15	6.14	1	0	0	11	7.94	0	0	0	0	—	1	1	0	26	6.92	29	0	.345	.367	.448	79	2	.367	.457	.494
1981	Bos-A	236	6	.212	.292	.322	4	0	0	36	3.47	2	2	0	30	2.70	0	0	0	0	—	6	2	0	66	3.12	48	2	.188	.220	.354	188	4	.218	.308	.314
1982	Bos-A	321	13	.296	.355	.483	2	1	0	29	4.97	2	5	0	49	6.02	3	4	0	58	5.43	1	2	0	20	6.20	59	2	.271	.317	.390	262	11	.302	.363	.504
1983	Bos-A	653	15	.265	.336	.395	6	3	0	86	4.59	6	4	0	87	3.50	4	3	0	58	5.43	8	4	0	116	3.35	112	1	.259	.325	.366	541	14	.266	.339	.401
1984	Bos-A	816	17	.259	.336	.377	4	5	0	92	4.89	8	7	0	125	3.32	6	6	0	107	4.71	6	6	0	110	3.28	157	2	.248	.310	.318	659	15	.261	.342	.392
1985	Bos-A	608	11	.273	.327	.396	4	7	0	98	3.50	5	4	1	60	4.80	4	3	1	66	3.00	5	8	0	92	4.71	127	2	.315	.346	.449	481	9	.262	.322	.383
1986	NY-N	804	15	.230	.278	.330	9	2	0	107	2.86	9	3	0	110	2.28	9	2	0	99	2.54	9	3	0	118	2.59	107	1	.150	.207	.206	697	14	.242	.289	.349
1987	NY-N	178	5	.253	.291	.416	2	2	0	27	2.70	1	3	0	20	5.49	2	4	0	31	4.31	1	1	0	15	3.00	45	1	.244	.277	.444	133	4	.256	.296	.406
1988	NY-N	703	6	.225	.261	.317	6	9	0	109	3.15	4	4	0	82	2.53	6	6	0	101	3.48	4	7	0	89	2.22	127	2	.165	.195	.283	576	4	.238	.276	.325
1989	NY-N	731	16	.245	.317	.360	6	4	0	85	2.95	7	7	0	107	3.88	5	7	0	96	3.29	8	4	0	96	3.64	161	5	.236	.324	.379	570	11	.247	.314	.354
1990	NY-N	452	10	.272	.332	.414	4	2	0	64	3.50	3	4	0	54	3.86	4	3	0	72	3.38	3	3	0	46	4.11	113	1	.168	.230	.257	339	9	.307	.365	.466
1991	LA-N	705	15	.257	.323	.376	6	4	0	99	3.01	6	5	0	91	3.38	6	5	0	91	3.05	6	4	0	98	3.31	136	1	.257	.301	.324	569	14	.257	.328	.388
1992	LA-N	631	8	.268	.349	.371	4	2	0	83	2.40	2	7	0	84	4.84	4	4	0	80	3.60	2	5	0	86	3.65	116	1	.216	.290	.276	515	7	.280	.362	.392
1993	Cle-A	166	5	.289	.363	.470	1	1	0	21	4.22	1	0	0	22	4.57	0	0	0	0	—	2	1	0	43	4.40	36	1	.278	.341	.472	130	4	.292	.369	.469
1994	NY-A	18	1	.611	.680	.833	0	0	0	2	15.43	0	0	0	1	54.00	0	0	0	3	24.00	0	0	0	0	—	2	0	.500	.500	.500	16	1	.625	.696	.875
TOTALS		7130	145	.257	.321	.378	58	43	0	953	3.53	57	55	1	931	3.77	53	47	1	863	3.79	62	51	0	1022	3.53	1375	22	.232	.287	.337	5755	123	.263	.329	.388
● **Omar Olivares** BR/TR																																				
1990	StL-N	181	2	.249	.320	.331	0	0	0	13	2.13	1	1	0	37	3.19	0	0	0	0	—	1	1	0	49	2.92	88	0	.193	.304	.216	93	2	.301	.337	.441
1991	StL-N	609	13	.243	.316	.356	7	5	1	97	3.33	4	2	0	70	4.24	1	1	1	48	5.48	10	6	0	120	3.01	345	5	.235	.321	.322	264	8	.254	.309	.402
1992	StL-N	736	20	.257	.316	.394	5	6	0	120	3.96	4	3	0	77	3.64	4	3	0	85	3.93	5	6	0	112	3.77	428	13	.285	.345	.451	308	7	.218	.275	.315
1993	StL-N	466	10	.288	.370	.423	2	3	1	63	4.71	3	0	0	56	3.56	2	2	1	61	4.40	3	1	0	57	3.92	232	6	.276	.361	.448	234	4	.299	.378	.397
1994	StL-N	286	10	.294	.379	.469	1	2	1	35	6.17	2	2	0	39	5.35	1	1	1	27	3.95	2	4	0	46	6.80	139	5	.338	.426	.554	147	5	.252	.333	.388
1995	Col-N	126	4	.349	.447	.516	0	2	0	13	9.00	1	1	0	19	6.27	1	2	0	31	6.32	0	1	0	0	108.00	43	0	.279	.418	.326	83	4	.386	.463	.614
1995	Phi-N	39	1	.282	.326	.462	0	0	0	5	9.00	0	0	0	5	1.80	0	0	0	0	—	0	1	0	10	5.40	18	1	.389	.450	.667	21	0	.190	.217	.286
1996	Det-A	615	16	.275	.359	.429	4	4	0	70	4.35	3	7	0	90	5.32	4	3	0	62	4.62	3	8	0	98	5.07	309	8	.291	.386	.476	306	8	.258	.329	.382
1997	Det-A	434	8	.253	.344	.373	4	2	0	59	3.84	1	4	0	56	5.59	5	5	0	104	4.07	0	1	0	11	10.64	224	6	.281	.380	.438	210	2	.224	.304	.305
1997	Sea-A	257	10	.315	.387	.510	0	1	0	31	4.88	1	3	0	31	6.10	0	0	0	0	—	1	4	0	62	5.49	146	8	.342	.426	.582	111	2	.279	.333	.414
1998	Ana-A	699	19	.270	.357	.409	6	3	0	100	3.42	3	6	0	83	4.77	5	3	0	95	2.95	4	6	0	88	5.20	337	10	.279	.383	.421	362	9	.262	.331	.398

YEAR	TM/L	TOTAL					HOME					AWAY					1ST HALF					2ND HALF					LEFT					RIGHT				
		AB	HR	AVG	OBP	SLG	W	L	SV	IP	ERA	W	L	SV	IP	ERA	W	L	SV	IP	ERA	W	L	SV	IP	ERA	AB	HR	AVG	OBP	SLG	AB	HR	AVG	OBP	SLG
1999	Ana-A	495	11	.273	.342	.394	3	3	0	59	3.07	5	6	0	72	4.85	6	6	0	98	3.39	2	3	0	33	6.06	252	8	.246	.336	.397	243	3	.300	.350	.391
1999	Oak-A	290	8	.283	.358	.462	4	1	0	38	4.70	3	1	0	36	3.96	0	0	0	0	—	7	2	0	75	4.34	140	4	.293	.371	.500	150	4	.273	.345	.427
2000	Oak-A	434	10	.309	.396	.445	1	5	0	52	6.45	3	3	0	56	7.03	3	8	0	80	6.64	1	0	0	28	7.07	196	6	.301	.410	.444	238	4	.315	.383	.445
TOTALS		5667	142	.274	.353	.414	37	38	3	755	4.27	34	39	0	726	4.81	32	33	3	692	4.37	39	44	0	790	4.67	2897	80	.279	.369	.435	2770	62	.269	.335	.392
● **Gregg Olson** BR/TR																																				
1988	Bal-A	41	1	.244	.392	.341	0	0	0	4	2.08	1	1	0	7	4.05	0	0	0	0	—	1	1	0	11	3.27	18	0	.111	.333	.111	23	1	.348	.444	.522
1989	Bal-A	304	1	.188	.295	.247	3	0	12	47	0.77	2	2	15	38	2.82	3	0	12	44	1.85	2	2	15	41	1.52	141	0	.135	.247	.149	163	1	.233	.337	.331
1990	Bal-A	268	3	.213	.299	.276	5	0	13	31	2.93	1	5	24	44	2.06	4	2	15	40	1.13	2	3	22	34	3.93	145	1	.200	.298	.248	123	2	.228	.301	.309
1991	Bal-A	282	1	.262	.332	.305	3	1	13	34	3.15	1	5	18	39	3.20	1	3	15	33	3.55	3	3	16	41	2.88	139	1	.230	.316	.266	143	0	.294	.348	.343
1992	Bal-A	218	3	.211	.287	.280	1	1	17	33	1.38	0	4	19	29	2.83	1	2	20	33	1.64	0	3	16	28	2.54	113	0	.195	.252	.230	105	3	.229	.322	.333
1993	Bal-A	166	1	.223	.296	.295	0	2	16	23	1.96	0	0	13	22	1.23	0	1	21	32	1.39	0	1	8	13	2.13	85	1	.212	.281	.294	81	0	.235	.311	.296
1994	Atl-N	60	1	.317	.440	.517	0	0	0	7	8.59	0	2	1	7	9.82	0	0	0	8	9.72	0	2	1	6	8.53	23	1	.174	.321	.435	37	0	.405	.511	.568
1995	Cle-A	12	1	.417	.500	.750	0	0	0	1	9.00	0	0	0	2	16.20	0	0	0	2	21.60	0	0	0	1	0.00	6	1	.500	.571	1.000	6	0	.333	.429	.500
1995	KC-A	107	3	.215	.317	.355	1	1	2	14	3.77	2	2	1	16	2.81	0	0	0	0	—	3	3	3	30	3.26	49	1	.204	.298	.327	58	2	.224	.333	.379
1996	Det-A	166	6	.259	.369	.404	2	0	2	20	5.03	1	0	6	23	5.01	1	0	3	30	4.55	2	0	5	13	6.07	89	3	.247	.323	.382	77	3	.273	.417	.429
1996	Hou-N	39	1	.308	.404	.410	1	0	0	6	0.00	0	0	0	3	13.50	0	0	0	0	—	1	0	0	9	4.82	15	0	.333	.444	.400	24	1	.292	.379	.417
1997	Min-A	44	0	.432	.545	.523	0	0	0	4	22.85	0	0	0	4	13.50	0	0	0	8	18.36	0	0	0	0	—	16	0	.500	.529	.688	28	0	.393	.553	.429
1997	KC-A	150	3	.260	.337	.360	2	1	0	19	2.33	2	2	1	22	3.63	0	0	0	0	—	4	3	1	42	3.02	59	2	.186	.246	.356	91	1	.308	.394	.363
1998	Ari-N	251	4	.223	.295	.335	2	2	12	35	2.55	1	2	18	33	3.51	1	3	11	34	3.71	2	1	19	35	2.34	135	0	.163	.257	.215	116	4	.293	.341	.474
1999	Ari-N	227	9	.238	.316	.392	5	1	6	31	3.19	4	3	8	30	4.25	3	4	11	27	4.67	6	0	3	34	2.94	90	3	.300	.360	.456	137	6	.197	.288	.350
2000	LA-N	70	4	.300	.367	.529	0	0	0	8	3.38	0	1	0	10	6.52	0	0	0	2	9.00	0	1	0	16	4.60	26	2	.115	.233	.346	44	2	.409	.449	.636
TOTALS		2405	42	.238	.326	.336	25	9	93	318	2.89	15	29	124	329	3.66	14	15	108	293	3.47	26	23	109	354	3.12	1149	16	.206	.294	.287	1256	26	.267	.355	.380
● **Jesse Orosco** BR/TL																																				
1979	NY-N	127	4	.260	.377	.386	0	0	0	10	5.40	1	2	0	25	4.68	1	2	0	35	4.89	0	0	0	0	—	29	1	.276	.417	.379	98	3	.255	.365	.388
1981	NY-N	61	2	.213	.284	.311	0	0	1	11	0.00	0	1	0	6	4.50	0	0	0	0	—	0	1	1	17	1.56	17	0	.000	.150	.000	44	2	.295	.340	.432
1982	NY-N	400	7	.230	.300	.322	3	7	1	64	3.50	1	3	3	45	1.60	1	5	0	51	2.66	3	5	4	59	2.76	124	3	.177	.262	.266	276	4	.254	.318	.348
1983	NY-N	386	3	.197	.269	.254	8	1	8	63	1.14	5	6	9	47	1.91	4	3	7	54	1.33	9	4	10	56	1.61	105	0	.171	.243	.210	281	3	.206	.278	.270
1984	NY-N	313	7	.185	.267	.297	5	4	15	43	3.53	5	2	16	44	1.65	5	2	13	37	1.95	5	4	18	50	3.06	67	0	.179	.230	.179	246	7	.187	.277	.329
1985	NY-N	295	6	.224	.303	.315	3	3	7	37	2.45	5	3	10	42	2.98	1	4	6	38	2.87	7	2	11	41	2.61	60	0	.200	.238	.200	235	6	.230	.318	.345
1986	NY-N	295	6	.217	.304	.305	4	4	7	35	4.15	4	2	14	46	0.97	3	4	11	35	2.86	5	2	10	46	1.94	75	1	.187	.235	.253	220	5	.227	.325	.323
1987	NY-N	293	5	.266	.336	.358	2	4	8	41	2.83	1	5	8	36	6.31	1	6	11	33	5.45	2	3	5	44	3.68	74	0	.230	.275	.243	219	5	.279	.356	.397
1988	LA-N	191	4	.215	.323	.319	1	0	2	20	2.75	2	2	7	33	2.70	2	1	5	29	3.07	1	1	4	24	2.28	62	1	.226	.338	.306	129	3	.209	.316	.326
1989	Cle-A	273	7	.198	.270	.333	2	2	1	43	1.69	1	2	2	35	2.55	0	1	1	27	2.30	3	3	2	51	1.95	87	0	.138	.211	.184	186	7	.226	.297	.403
1990	Cle-A	243	9	.239	.338	.407	3	3	2	39	3.00	2	1	0	26	5.26	3	3	2	30	4.85	2	1	0	35	3.09	67	2	.224	.338	.358	176	7	.244	.338	.426
1991	Cle-A	182	4	.286	.338	.396	1	0	0	24	1.90	1	0	0	22	5.73	0	0	0	23	2.74	2	0	0	23	4.76	63	1	.286	.313	.381	119	3	.286	.351	.403
1992	Mil-A	142	5	.232	.297	.366	3	1	0	23	3.52	0	0	1	16	2.81	2	1	1	19	3.86	1	0	0	20	2.66	55	2	.273	.328	.418	87	3	.207	.278	.333
1993	Mil-A	210	2	.224	.289	.305	0	5	5	29	4.60	3	0	3	27	1.65	0	2	1	23	4.63	3	3	7	33	2.16	64	1	.313	.353	.438	146	1	.185	.262	.247
1994	Mil-A	144	4	.222	.345	.340	1	0	0	22	4.50	2	1	0	17	5.82	1	1	0	32	5.40	2	0	0	7	3.68	57	1	.263	.344	.351	87	3	.195	.345	.333
1995	Bal-A	166	4	.169	.283	.301	1	3	3	30	3.60	1	1	0	20	2.75	1	1	0	18	3.00	1	3	3	32	3.41	77	1	.143	.212	.234	89	3	.191	.336	.360
1996	Bal-A	203	5	.207	.308	.310	1	0	0	32	2.27	2	1	0	24	4.88	2	1	0	24	6.08	1	0	0	32	1.41	74	2	.216	.326	.338	129	3	.202	.297	.295
1997	Bal-A	172	6	.169	.289	.302	2	1	0	24	2.66	4	2	0	27	2.03	2	0	0	23	1.54	4	3	0	27	3.00	79	1	.101	.215	.177	93	5	.226	.351	.409
1998	Bal-A	208	6	.221	.314	.341	2	0	5	33	2.48	2	1	2	24	4.13	1	0	5	28	3.18	3	1	2	28	3.18	83	2	.205	.280	.301	125	4	.232	.336	.368
1999	Bal-A	117	5	.239	.352	.436	0	1	0	17	4.32	0	1	1	15	6.46	0	2	0	18	8.15	0	0	1	14	1.88	63	3	.270	.355	.476	54	2	.204	.348	.389
2000	StL-N	11	1	.273	.500	.545	0	0	0	2	4.50	0	0	0	0	0.00	0	0	0	2	3.86	0	0	0	0	—	6	1	.500	.625	1.000	5	0	.000	.375	.000
TOTALS		4432	102	.220	.306	.329	42	39	65	641	2.91	42	36	76	578	3.16	30	39	63	578	3.50	54	36	78	640	2.60	1388	23	.205	.281	.287	3044	79	.226	.317	.348
● **Russ Ortiz** BR/TR																																				
1998	SF-N	335	11	.269	.360	.445	3	3	0	61	4.57	1	1	0	27	5.93	0	0	0	11	0.82	4	4	0	77	5.59	180	8	.283	.355	.489	155	3	.252	.366	.394
1999	SF-N	774	24	.244	.351	.388	11	3	0	112	3.04	7	6	0	95	4.72	9	5	0	102	3.63	9	4	0	106	3.99	363	10	.251	.355	.375	411	14	.238	.348	.399
2000	SF-N	736	28	.261	.361	.431	6	5	0	92	4.21	8	7	0	104	5.73	4	8	0	90	6.93	10	4	0	106	3.40	360	8	.267	.378	.408	376	20	.255	.345	.452
TOTALS		1845	63	.255	.357	.415	20	11	0	265	3.80	16	14	0	226	5.33	13	13	0	202	4.94	23	12	0	289	4.20	903	26	.264	.364	.411	942	37	.247	.350	.419
● **Chan Ho Park** BR/TR																																				
1994	LA-N	17	1	.294	.478	.529	0	0	0	1	18.00	0	0	0	3	9.00	0	0	0	4	11.25	0	0	0	0	—	9	0	.222	.533	.333	8	1	.375	.375	.750
1995	LA-N	14	1	.143	.250	.429	0	0	0	0	—	0	0	0	4	4.50	0	0	0	0	—	0	0	0	4	4.50	5	0	.000	.286	.000	9	1	.222	.222	.667
1996	LA-N	393	7	.209	.335	.298	2	3	0	56	2.10	3	2	0	53	5.26	5	2	0	65	3.03	0	3	0	43	4.57	160	3	.262	.401	.356	233	4	.172	.287	.258
1997	LA-N	700	24	.213	.290	.354	8	3	0	105	2.92	6	5	0	87	3.92	5	5	0	93	3.40	9	3	0	99	3.35	363	13	.237	.330	.386	337	11	.187	.245	.320
1998	LA-N	817	16	.244	.328	.362	9	4	0	134	2.75	6	5	0	86	5.21	6	5	0	96	5.17	9	4	0	125	2.59	409	9	.252	.329	.394	408	7	.235	.328	.331
1999	LA-N	754	31	.276	.369	.472	3	6	0	91	5.46	10	5	0	104	5.04	4	6	0	88	5.54	9	5	0	107	4.98	344	18	.358	.454	.602	410	13	.207	.295	.363
2000	LA-N	809	21	.214	.325	.344	10	4	0	119	2.34	8	6	0	107	4.29	9	4	0	108	4.17	9	6	0	118	2.44	402	12	.229	.348	.358	407	9	.199	.302	.329
TOTALS		3504	101	.233	.330	.374	32	20	0	505	3.13	33	23	0	444	4.72	29	22	0	453	4.39	36	21	0	496	3.41	1692	55	.265	.368	.421	1812	46	.204	.294	.330
● **Jim Parque** BL/TL																																				
1998	Chi-A	451	14	.299	.375	.475	5	2	0	59	5.31	2	3	0	54	4.86	2	1	0	29	5.83	5	4	0	84	4.84	100	3	.300	.364	.470	351	11	.299	.379	.476
1999	Chi-A	702	23	.299	.374	.442	6	7	0	95	4.47	3	8	0	79	5.92	8	5	0	90	3.81	1	10	0	84	6.54	157	5	.325	.406	.459	545	18	.292	.365	.437
2000	Chi-A	736	21	.283	.352	.418	7	3	0	93	3.66	6	3	0	94	4.90	8	2	0	96	3.86	5	4	0	91	4.73	187	5	.316	.373	.455	549	16	.271	.346	.406
TOTALS		1889	58	.293	.366	.440	18	12	0	247	4.37	11	14	0	226	5.25	18	8	0	215	4.11	11	18	0	259	5.35	444	13	.315	.383	.459	1445	45	.286	.361	.435
● **Danny Patterson** BR/TR																																				
1996	Tex-A	35	0	.286	.342	.286	0	0	0	4	0.00	0	0	0	5	0.00	0	0	0	0	—	0	0	0	9	0.00	15	0	.400	.400	.400	20	0	.200	.304	.200
1997	Tex-A	266	3	.263	.318	.357	5	5	1	37	4.58	5	1	0	34	2.14	5	3	1	33	2.43	5	3	0	38	4.30	110	0	.236	.323	.291	156	3	.282	.315	.404
1998	Tex-A	234	11	.274	.332	.491	1	2	1	30	5.10	1	3	1	31	3.82	1	3	1	25	3.91	1	2	1	35	4.84	91	4	.330	.390	.549	143	7	.238	.295	.455
1999	Tex-A	253	5	.304	.353	.478	1	0	0	28	5.14	1	0	0	32	6.12	1	0	0	32	4.18	1	0	0	28	7.39	86	0	.349	.420	.488	167	5	.281	.314	.473
2000	Det-A	223	4	.309	.353	.417	2	1	0	28	5.08	3	0	0	28	2.86	2	1	0	30	3.03	3	0	0	27	5.00	95	2	.295	.323	.453	128	2	.320	.373	.391
TOTALS		1011	23	.287	.338	.429	9	8	2	127	4.81	10	4	1	130	3.60	9	7	2	121	3.36	10	5	1	137	4.94	397	6	.302	.363	.436	614	17	.277	.322	.425
● **Melido Perez** BR/TR																																				
1987	KC-A	48	2	.375	.434	.604	1	1	0	10	7.84	0	0	0	0	—	0	0	0	0	—	1	1	0	10	7.84	32	0	.375	.429	.500	16	2	.375	.444	.813
1988	Chi-A	749	26	.248	.313	.409	6	2	0	92	3.52	6	8	0	105	4.03	6	5	0	90	4.01	6	5	0	107	3.61	397	12	.232	.299	.385	352	14	.267	.329	.435
1989	Chi-A	708	23	.264	.348	.432	4	6	0	78	5.06	7	8	0	105	4.97	5	9	0	85	6.01	6	5	0	98	4.13	371	12	.264	.352	.445	337	11	.264	.344	.418
1990	Chi-A	735	14	.241	.320	.367	5	6	0	81	5.11	8	8	0	116	4.27	6	7	0	95	4.07	7	7	0	102	5.12	380	6	.250	.322	.374	355	8	.231	.318	.361
1991	Chi-A	495	15	.224	.299	.352	2	3	0	62	3.61	6	4	1	73	2.70	3	4	0	71	3.79	5	3	1	64	2.38	223	6	.202	.279	.332	272	9	.243	.315	.368
1992	NY-A	901	16	.235	.308	.332	5	6	0	99	3.01	8	10	0	149	2.78	7	6	0	112	2.96	6	10	0	135	2.79	430	8	.247	.324	.344	471	8	.225	.293	.321
1993	NY-A	647	22	.267	.333	.431	3	9	0	83	6.26	3	5	0	80	4.07	5	6	0	103	4.19	1	8	0	60	6.90	339	9	.277	.352	.407	308	13	.256	.312	.458
1994	NY-A	563	16	.238	.311	.394	4	1	0	83	3.59	5	3	0	69	4.72	6	3	0	93	3.76	3	1	0	58	4.66	263	10	.247	.337	.418	300	6	.230	.287	.373
1995	NY-A	268	10	.261	.337	.451	3	1	0	30	3.94	2	4	0	40	6.81	5	5	0	68	5.66	0	0	0	1	0.00	146	6	.260	.341	.459	122	4	.262	.331	.443
TOTALS		5114	144	.248	.321	.392	33	35	0	618	4.32	45	50	1	736	4.03	43	45	0	718	4.22	35	40	1	636	4.10	2581	69	.250	.327	.392	2533	75	.246	.315	.392
● **Gaylord Perry** BR/TR																																				
1978	SD-N	970	9	.248	.295	.338	11	2	0	139	1.75	10	4	0	122	3.85	8	3	0	116	2.80	13	3	0	145	2.67	461	2	.258	.319	.334	509	7	.240	.272	.342
1979	SD-N	876	12	.257	.312	.349	8	5	0	133	2.37	4	6	0	100	3.97	7	6	0	138	2.48	5	5	0	95	3.90	416	4	.269	.325	.341	460	8	.246	.300	.357
1980	Tex-A	593	12	.268	.327	.374	3	5	0	79	3.65	3	4	0	76	3.20	4	6	0	102	3.28	2	3	0	53	3.71	328	7	.287	.336	.396	265	5	.245	.315	.347
1980	NY-A	203	2	.320	.372	.433	2	2	0	22	4.91	2	2	0	29	4.08	0	0	0	0	—	4	4	0	51	4.44	93	2	.344	.406	.484	110	0	.300	.342	.391
1981	Atl-N	598	9	.304	.332	.393	2	5	0	66	4.91	6	4	0	85	3.19	5	4	0	83	3.48	3	5	0	68	4.50	300	3	.283	.323	.357	298	6	.326	.342	.430
1982	Sea-A	854	27	.287	.331	.433	5	5	0	109	4.89	5	7	0	108	3.92	5	7	0	118	4.41	5	5	0	98	4.39	402	12	.284	.339	.430	452	15	.290	.323	.436
1983	Sea-A	405	18	.286	.327	.467	2	5	0	46	5.87	1	5	0	56	4.18	3	10	0	102	4.94	0	0	0	0	—	191	10	.346	.379	.571	214	8	.234	.281	.374
1983	KC-A	336	6	.292	.342	.396	2	2	0	40	3.40	2	2	0	45	5.04	0	0	0	0	—	4	4	0	84	4.27	178	3	.337	.381	.455	158	3	.241	.297	.329
TOTALS		4835	95	.275	.322	.387	35	31	0	633	3.50	33	34	0	619	3.84	32	36	0	658	3.51	36	29	0	594	3.83	2369	43	.288	.339	.397	2466	52	.263	.305	.377
● **Mark Petkovsek** BR/TR																																				
1991	Tex-A	48	4	.438	.472	.750	0	0	0	5	15.43	0	1	0	5	13.50	0	1	0	9	14.46	0	0	0	0	—	21	2	.476	.542	.905	27	2	.407	.414	.630

		TOTAL					HOME					AWAY					1ST HALF					2ND HALF					LEFT					RIGHT				
YEAR	TM/L	AB	HR	AVG	OBP	SLG	W	L	SV	IP	ERA	W	L	SV	IP	ERA	W	L	SV	IP	ERA	W	L	SV	IP	ERA	AB	HR	AVG	OBP	SLG	AB	HR	AVG	OBP	SLG
1993	Pit-N	131	7	.328	.369	.603	1	0	0	18	4.50	2	0	0	14	10.05	1	0	0	12	3.75	2	0	0	20	8.85	44	2	.409	.447	.705	87	5	.287	.330	.552
1995	StL-N	520	11	.262	.313	.390	4	1	0	77	2.92	2	5	0	60	5.37	3	2	0	40	3.79	3	4	0	97	4.08	231	4	.290	.327	.424	289	7	.239	.303	.363
1996	StL-N	331	9	.251	.331	.375	9	2	0	49	3.31	2	0	0	40	3.86	5	0	0	40	4.50	6	2	0	49	2.77	142	4	.254	.327	.394	189	5	.249	.333	.360
1997	StL-N	373	14	.292	.354	.477	2	1	0	45	3.77	2	6	2	51	6.22	3	4	1	51	3.16	1	3	1	45	7.25	165	3	.267	.322	.376	208	11	.313	.379	.558
1998	StL-N	420	9	.312	.375	.445	3	0	0	53	2.21	4	4	0	53	7.35	5	4	0	64	5.51	2	0	0	42	3.64	206	0	.311	.368	.393	214	9	.313	.381	.495
1999	Ana-A	316	6	.269	.314	.377	6	3	0	43	3.59	4	1	1	40	3.35	6	2	1	40	1.80	4	2	0	43	5.02	124	1	.242	.288	.306	192	5	.286	.330	.422
2000	Ana-A	310	8	.277	.332	.419	3	2	1	49	3.31	1	0	1	32	5.63	2	2	1	34	5.61	2	0	1	47	3.23	128	3	.258	.321	.367	182	5	.291	.340	.456
TOTALS		2449	68	.283	.341	.431	28	9	1	339	3.38	17	17	4	295	5.77	25	15	3	290	4.43	20	11	2	343	4.54	1061	19	.285	.339	.407	1388	49	.282	.343	.450
● Dan Petry BR/TR																																				
1979	Det-A	354	11	.254	.321	.410	3	2	0	47	4.24	3	3	0	51	3.68	0	0	0	0	—	6	5	0	98	3.95	144	6	.271	.333	.465	210	5	.243	.312	.371
1980	Det-A	617	9	.253	.340	.342	6	3	0	69	2.86	4	6	0	95	4.72	4	4	0	74	3.05	6	5	0	91	4.65	283	3	.272	.372	.353	334	6	.237	.311	.332
1981	Det-A	514	10	.224	.301	.317	6	3	0	60	2.69	4	6	0	81	3.24	4	5	0	54	4.31	6	4	0	87	2.18	280	6	.221	.311	.321	234	4	.226	.289	.312
1982	Det-A	911	15	.241	.317	.341	9	2	0	123	2.42	6	7	0	123	4.01	7	5	0	120	3.53	8	4	0	126	2.93	471	9	.268	.342	.384	440	6	.214	.289	.295
1983	Det-A	1000	37	.256	.325	.429	6	6	0	114	4.41	13	5	0	152	3.55	7	5	0	118	3.82	12	6	0	149	4.00	491	21	.273	.353	.473	509	16	.240	.297	.387
1984	Det-A	891	21	.259	.312	.386	10	4	0	121	2.74	8	4	0	112	3.78	11	3	0	115	3.06	7	5	0	119	3.41	494	12	.249	.305	.370	397	9	.272	.321	.406
1985	Det-A	875	24	.217	.285	.346	7	9	0	132	3.60	8	4	0	106	3.05	9	6	0	124	3.05	6	7	0	115	3.69	487	13	.222	.306	.347	388	11	.211	.258	.345
1986	Det-A	456	15	.268	.348	.439	1	7	0	62	4.65	4	3	0	54	4.67	4	5	0	65	4.96	1	5	0	51	4.26	242	12	.231	.311	.442	214	3	.308	.389	.435
1987	Det-A	531	22	.279	.375	.463	4	4	0	62	5.95	5	3	0	73	5.33	5	4	0	71	5.43	4	3	0	63	5.83	254	8	.272	.367	.433	277	14	.285	.383	.491
1988	Cal-A	528	18	.263	.341	.424	3	6	0	87	3.92	0	3	0	52	5.16	3	5	0	97	3.98	0	4	0	42	5.31	264	7	.288	.377	.417	264	11	.239	.303	.432
1989	Cal-A	193	8	.275	.347	.430	3	1	0	33	4.09	0	1	0	18	8.00	2	0	0	26	4.56	1	2	0	25	6.39	88	6	.352	.404	.602	105	2	.210	.301	.286
1990	Det-A	563	14	.263	.349	.403	4	5	0	62	5.49	6	4	0	87	3.71	5	5	0	89	3.53	5	4	0	60	5.82	245	3	.249	.345	.351	318	11	.274	.353	.443
1991	Det-A	220	9	.300	.356	.495	1	1	0	29	3.41	1	2	0	26	6.66	2	3	0	55	4.94	0	0	0	0	—	93	5	.312	.373	.538	127	4	.291	.343	.465
1991	Atl-N	98	2	.296	.389	.429	0	0	0	18	7.64	0	0	0	7	0.00	0	0	0	4	13.50	0	0	0	20	3.98	48	2	.313	.377	.500	50	0	.280	.400	.360
1991	Bos-A	84	3	.250	.347	.417	0	0	0	15	4.80	0	0	1	7	3.68	0	0	0	0	—	0	0	1	22	4.43	27	0	.185	.303	.259	57	3	.281	.369	.491
TOTALS		7835	218	.253	.328	.392	63	53	0	1035	3.82	62	51	1	1045	4.07	63	50	0	1012	3.87	62	54	1	1068	4.02	3911	113	.259	.339	.401	3924	105	.248	.317	.383
● Andy Pettitte BL/TL																																				
1995	NY-A	672	15	.272	.333	.411	8	2	0	100	2.61	4	7	0	75	6.24	3	4	0	51	3.51	9	5	0	124	4.44	117	1	.256	.307	.342	555	14	.276	.339	.425
1996	NY-A	844	23	.271	.330	.404	10	4	0	120	3.22	11	4	0	101	4.65	12	4	0	109	3.98	9	4	0	112	3.77	152	1	.329	.368	.395	692	22	.259	.321	.406
1997	NY-A	910	7	.256	.307	.335	9	4	0	119	2.65	9	3	0	122	3.11	8	5	0	125	3.32	10	2	0	116	2.41	192	1	.318	.343	.406	718	6	.240	.298	.316
1998	NY-A	826	20	.274	.344	.395	9	4	0	104	4.34	7	7	0	113	4.15	9	5	0	111	4.05	7	6	0	105	4.44	184	8	.283	.347	.451	642	12	.271	.344	.379
1999	NY-A	747	20	.289	.364	.446	8	5	0	102	4.22	6	6	0	89	5.24	5	6	0	81	5.53	9	5	0	110	4.08	149	8	.275	.365	.483	598	12	.293	.364	.436
2000	NY-A	808	17	.271	.338	.402	9	2	0	94	3.93	10	7	0	111	4.72	8	4	0	88	4.40	11	5	0	117	4.32	176	1	.256	.309	.330	632	16	.275	.346	.422
TOTALS		4807	102	.272	.336	.397	53	21	0	639	3.46	47	34	0	610	4.54	45	28	0	565	4.09	55	27	0	684	3.91	970	20	.288	.341	.403	3837	82	.268	.334	.395
● Dan Plesac BL/TL																																				
1986	Mil-A	337	5	.240	.296	.341	6	3	6	50	3.58	4	4	8	41	2.21	4	5	7	39	3.23	6	2	7	52	2.77	79	1	.266	.333	.367	258	4	.233	.285	.333
1987	Mil-A	296	8	.213	.275	.318	2	2	9	35	3.31	3	4	14	44	2.05	4	0	16	42	1.29	1	6	7	37	4.10	57	2	.140	.219	.281	239	6	.230	.288	.326
1988	Mil-A	197	2	.234	.278	.320	0	0	16	27	1.69	1	2	14	26	3.16	1	1	16	33	2.16	0	1	14	19	2.84	40	0	.225	.262	.375	157	2	.236	.281	.306
1989	Mil-A	221	6	.213	.264	.326	2	1	15	33	1.89	1	3	18	28	2.89	2	3	19	35	2.31	1	1	14	26	2.39	49	1	.224	.231	.306	172	5	.209	.274	.331
1990	Mil-A	261	5	.257	.340	.372	2	3	11	31	6.03	1	4	13	38	3.11	0	3	13	30	6.00	3	4	11	39	3.23	62	0	.161	.254	.226	199	5	.286	.367	.417
1991	Mil-A	350	12	.263	.336	.434	0	4	5	48	5.63	2	3	3	44	2.84	0	2	5	26	3.16	2	5	3	67	4.72	64	4	.297	.361	.516	286	8	.255	.330	.416
1992	Mil-A	280	5	.229	.317	.343	2	2	0	29	2.48	3	2	1	50	3.24	3	2	0	42	4.46	2	2	1	37	1.23	67	2	.254	.342	.403	213	3	.221	.309	.324
1993	Chi-N	248	10	.298	.349	.472	1	1	0	32	5.85	1	0	0	30	3.56	0	0	0	37	4.62	2	1	0	26	4.91	89	2	.258	.305	.393	159	8	.321	.373	.516
1994	Chi-N	219	9	.279	.321	.461	0	1	0	28	4.23	2	2	1	27	5.00	2	2	0	39	3.89	0	1	1	15	6.46	69	1	.188	.243	.275	150	8	.320	.356	.547
1995	Pit-N	224	3	.237	.318	.344	2	2	1	29	3.77	2	2	2	32	3.41	2	0	2	25	2.49	2	4	1	35	4.37	81	2	.222	.298	.383	143	1	.245	.329	.322
1996	Pit-N	271	4	.247	.305	.343	2	2	8	36	3.50	4	3	3	34	4.72	3	1	3	36	4.29	3	4	8	35	3.89	84	1	.250	.289	.369	187	3	.246	.313	.332
1997	Tor-A	193	8	.244	.310	.404	2	3	0	21	5.14	0	1	1	29	2.45	0	3	1	23	4.70	2	1	0	27	2.63	95	4	.200	.252	.347	98	4	.286	.364	.459
1998	Tor-A	183	4	.224	.286	.372	3	1	3	25	3.60	1	2	1	25	3.96	2	2	0	28	3.21	2	1	4	22	4.50	111	2	.198	.244	.324	72	2	.264	.345	.444
1999	Tor-A	91	4	.308	.366	.505	0	1	0	11	5.73	0	2	0	12	10.80	0	3	0	23	8.34	0	0	0	0	—	44	0	.205	.239	.205	47	4	.404	.473	.787
1999	Ari-N	85	3	.259	.323	.424	0	0	0	12	3.86	2	1	1	10	2.70	0	0	0	5	3.38	2	1	1	16	3.31	52	1	.192	.250	.269	33	2	.364	.432	.667
2000	Ari-N	149	4	.228	.341	.329	2	0	0	18	2.50	3	1	0	22	3.68	1	0	0	19	2.79	4	1	0	21	3.48	77	3	.260	.333	.403	72	1	.194	.348	.250
TOTALS		3605	92	.246	.312	.376	26	26	74	465	3.93	30	36	80	492	3.39	24	27	82	483	3.69	32	35	72	474	3.61	1120	26	.223	.282	.346	2485	66	.256	.325	.389
● Eric Plunk BR/TR																																				
1986	Oak-A	425	14	.214	.370	.341	3	3	0	63	5.68	1	4	0	57	4.89	2	3	0	57	5.18	2	4	0	63	5.43	239	7	.226	.377	.339	186	7	.199	.362	.344
1987	Oak-A	359	8	.253	.362	.368	2	3	2	46	4.86	2	3	0	49	4.62	1	4	0	62	5.84	3	2	2	33	2.70	192	2	.276	.371	.365	167	6	.228	.353	.371
1988	Oak-A	286	6	.217	.311	.318	4	1	3	35	4.93	3	1	2	43	1.45	5	1	2	37	2.70	2	1	3	41	3.27	122	1	.205	.305	.279	164	5	.226	.316	.348
1989	Oak-A	99	1	.172	.268	.273	0	0	0	14	1.29	1	1	1	15	3.07	1	1	1	29	2.20	0	0	0	0	—	39	1	.179	.304	.359	60	0	.167	.242	.217
1989	NY-A	274	9	.237	.355	.372	4	2	0	36	2.72	3	3	0	39	4.58	1	0	0	6	0.00	6	5	0	69	4.02	127	5	.236	.367	.386	147	4	.238	.343	.361
1990	NY-A	258	6	.225	.340	.341	4	0	0	27	3.71	2	3	0	46	2.15	2	2	0	31	2.90	4	1	0	42	2.59	91	1	.286	.404	.385	167	5	.192	.304	.317
1991	NY-A	448	18	.286	.371	.478	2	2	0	62	4.35	0	3	0	50	5.26	0	2	0	42	5.57	2	3	0	70	4.26	223	10	.291	.385	.502	225	8	.280	.357	.453
1992	Cle-A	266	5	.229	.324	.320	6	3	2	37	4.10	3	3	2	34	3.15	1	0	1	19	3.38	8	6	3	53	3.74	118	1	.237	.297	.314	148	4	.223	.343	.324
1993	Cle-A	270	5	.226	.301	.352	3	1	7	36	2.25	1	4	8	35	3.34	3	2	7	34	2.67	1	3	8	37	2.89	104	2	.240	.336	.394	166	3	.217	.279	.325
1994	Cle-A	264	3	.231	.329	.333	6	1	0	25	4.01	1	1	3	46	1.75	6	2	1	49	2.55	1	0	2	22	2.49	124	2	.298	.408	.427	140	1	.171	.255	.250
1995	Cle-A	228	5	.211	.303	.325	4	0	2	30	2.67	2	2	0	34	2.67	4	1	1	30	2.12	2	1	1	34	3.15	109	0	.229	.317	.312	119	5	.193	.289	.336
1996	Cle-A	276	6	.203	.293	.290	2	1	1	37	2.92	1	1	1	41	1.99	2	0	1	41	2.66	1	2	1	37	2.19	135	3	.237	.325	.333	141	3	.170	.264	.248
1997	Cle-A	253	12	.245	.339	.466	2	0	0	29	4.08	2	5	0	37	5.11	2	2	0	34	6.09	2	3	0	32	3.13	94	5	.277	.382	.511	159	7	.226	.313	.440
1998	Cle-A	156	6	.282	.349	.468	2	0	0	25	5.33	1	1	0	16	4.02	3	1	0	32	3.90	0	0	0	9	8.31	52	1	.269	.333	.423	104	5	.288	.356	.490
1998	Mil-A	122	3	.270	.359	.377	0	0	0	17	3.78	1	2	1	15	3.60	0	0	0	0	—	1	2	1	32	3.69	41	1	.293	.333	.415	81	2	.259	.371	.358
1999	Mil-A	283	15	.251	.357	.491	3	2	0	40	5.45	1	2	0	36	4.54	0	1	0	36	3.53	4	3	0	40	6.35	91	4	.264	.402	.516	192	11	.245	.335	.479
TOTALS		4267	122	.236	.339	.374	47	19	17	559	4.11	25	39	18	592	3.54	33	22	14	538	3.82	39	36	21	613	3.82	1901	46	.254	.360	.389	2366	76	.222	.322	.363
● Sidney Ponson BR/TR																																				
1998	Bal-A	536	19	.293	.345	.457	4	4	0	68	3.33	4	5	1	67	7.22	1	6	1	54	6.67	7	3	0	81	4.33	267	8	.262	.321	.416	269	11	.323	.370	.498
1999	Bal-A	805	35	.282	.345	.468	7	6	0	127	4.68	5	6	0	83	4.77	7	5	0	100	3.69	5	7	0	110	5.65	390	18	.287	.364	.477	415	17	.277	.326	.460
2000	Bal-A	863	30	.258	.323	.417	4	7	0	107	4.95	5	6	0	115	4.71	4	4	0	108	4.75	5	9	0	114	4.89	417	12	.259	.342	.396	446	18	.258	.305	.437
TOTALS		2204	84	.275	.336	.446	15	17	0	302	4.47	14	17	1	265	5.37	12	15	1	262	4.74	17	19	0	305	5.02	1074	38	.270	.345	.430	1130	46	.281	.328	.460
● Mark Portugal BR/TR																																				
1985	Min-A	89	3	.270	.362	.438	1	1	0	15	5.40	0	2	0	9	5.79	0	0	0	0	—	1	3	0	24	5.55	50	2	.340	.441	.540	39	1	.179	.261	.308
1986	Min-A	422	10	.265	.342	.391	3	3	1	44	4.09	3	7	0	69	4.46	2	7	0	49	5.84	4	3	1	63	3.13	206	3	.218	.314	.325	216	7	.310	.371	.454
1987	Min-A	178	13	.326	.407	.607	0	2	0	18	11.29	1	1	0	26	5.26	1	3	0	44	7.77	0	0	0	0	—	106	6	.255	.339	.481	72	7	.431	.506	.792
1988	Min-A	219	11	.274	.325	.484	2	2	1	30	5.40	1	1	2	28	3.58	0	1	1	32	5.01	3	2	2	25	3.91	118	8	.288	.339	.542	101	3	.257	.310	.416
1989	Hou-N	392	7	.232	.301	.329	4	1	0	52	3.12	3	0	0	56	2.41	0	1	0	6	8.53	7	0	0	102	2.39	209	3	.220	.297	.321	183	4	.246	.305	.339
1990	Hou-N	747	21	.250	.313	.375	8	2	0	101	1.78	3	8	0	95	5.57	2	7	0	90	3.99	9	3	0	106	3.30	427	10	.227	.301	.330	320	11	.281	.329	.434
1991	Hou-N	637	19	.256	.318	.400	4	5	1	79	3.06	6	7	0	89	5.76	6	4	0	91	3.97	4	8	1	78	5.10	366	10	.243	.313	.380	271	9	.273	.326	.428
1992	Hou-N	357	7	.213	.295	.331	4	0	0	58	1.86	2	3	0	43	3.74	5	3	0	84	2.77	1	0	0	17	2.12	205	5	.244	.328	.395	152	2	.171	.250	.243
1993	Hou-N	781	10	.248	.318	.323	10	1	0	95	2.37	8	3	0	113	3.11	5	3	0	89	3.44	13	1	0	119	2.27	411	4	.234	.305	.294	370	6	.265	.332	.354
1994	SF-N	519	17	.260	.324	.403	5	4	0	78	3.45	5	4	0	59	4.58	5	6	0	94	3.65	5	2	0	44	4.53	259	11	.243	.321	.398	260	6	.277	.327	.408
1995	SF-N	404	10	.262	.323	.401	1	3	0	49	3.47	4	2	0	55	4.77	5	2	0	84	3.66	0	3	0	20	6.20	208	4	.260	.322	.389	196	6	.265	.324	.413
1995	Cin-N	301	7	.262	.316	.385	3	3	0	50	3.58	3	2	0	27	4.28	0	0	0	0	—	6	5	0	78	3.82	132	1	.250	.320	.303	169	6	.272	.313	.450
1996	Cin-N	589	20	.248	.297	.416	5	6	0	88	3.48	3	3	0	68	4.63	4	5	0	95	4.09	4	4	0	61	3.82	234	7	.239	.294	.385	355	13	.254	.299	.437
1997	Phi-N	53	0	.321	.373	.547	0	1	0	11	4.22	0	1	0	3	6.00	0	2	0	14	4.61	0	0	0	0	—	22	0	.364	.391	.682	31	0	.290	.361	.452
1998	Phi-N	658	26	.283	.319	.471	2	3	0	66	6.51	8	2	0	100	3.06	3	2	0	64	5.32	7	3	0	102	3.88	341	16	.267	.299	.460	317	10	.300	.340	.483
1999	Bos-A	613	28	.292	.337	.491	3	6	0	63	5.31	4	6	0	88	5.65	4	6	0	80	5.51	3	6	0	70	5.50	293	11	.280	.343	.468	320	17	.303	.332	.512
TOTALS		6959	209	.261	.321	.406	55	43	3	899	3.66	54	52	2	928	4.39	42	52	1	916	4.35	67	43	4	910	3.70	3587	101	.248	.316	.385	3372	108	.274	.327	.428
● Ted Power BR/TR																																				
1981	LA-N	56	0	.286	.364	.375	0	1	0	8	3.38	1	2	0	6	2.84	0	0	0	0	—	1	3	0	14	3.14	34	0	.382	.450	.529	22	0	.136	.231	.136
1982	LA-N	132	4	.288	.391	.424	1	0	0	17	6.23	0	1	0	16	7.16	1	1	0	34	6.68	0	0	0	0	—	58	1	.328	.429	.431	74	3	.257	.360	.419

		TOTAL					HOME					AWAY					1ST HALF					2ND HALF					LEFT					RIGHT				
YEAR	TM/L	AB	HR	AVG	OBP	SLG	W	L	SV	IP	ERA	W	L	SV	IP	ERA	W	L	SV	IP	ERA	W	L	SV	IP	ERA	AB	HR	AVG	OBP	SLG	AB	HR	AVG	OBP	SLG
1983	Cin-N	420	10	.286	.357	.436	2	3	1	63	4.88	3	3	1	48	4.10	4	4	2	60	4.68	1	2	0	51	4.38	201	7	.323	.397	.557	219	3	.251	.320	.324
1984	Cin-N	393	4	.237	.311	.316	4	5	4	56	3.67	5	2	7	52	1.89	4	4	3	64	3.22	5	3	8	44	2.23	177	3	.271	.367	.384	216	1	.208	.262	.259
1985	Cin-N	286	2	.227	.330	.297	4	3	16	46	2.15	4	3	11	34	3.44	1	2	13	32	1.95	7	4	14	48	3.21	125	1	.224	.346	.320	161	1	.230	.317	.280
1986	Cin-N	469	13	.245	.318	.371	6	2	0	69	3.38	4	4	1	60	4.07	3	5	1	34	5.61	7	1	0	95	3.02	229	6	.262	.342	.402	240	7	.229	.294	.342
1987	Cin-N	798	28	.267	.327	.439	3	5	0	85	5.72	7	8	0	119	3.63	6	3	0	104	3.81	4	10	0	100	5.22	425	11	.285	.347	.440	373	17	.247	.302	.437
1988	KC-A	321	7	.305	.366	.464	3	3	0	49	4.81	2	3	0	32	7.67	4	1	0	53	4.25	1	5	0	27	9.22	144	3	.292	.354	.424	177	4	.316	.375	.497
1988	Det-A	75	1	.307	.373	.373	0	0	0	7	3.86	1	1	0	12	6.94	0	0	0	0	—	1	1	0	19	5.79	32	1	.313	.421	.469	43	0	.302	.333	.302
1989	StL-N	377	7	.255	.294	.385	3	2	0	40	2.95	4	5	0	57	4.24	0	2	0	17	5.94	7	5	0	80	3.25	207	3	.280	.324	.396	170	4	.224	.256	.371
1990	Pit-N	196	5	.255	.312	.378	1	1	5	28	4.88	0	2	2	24	2.25	0	2	4	24	2.59	1	1	3	27	4.61	78	2	.256	.366	.372	118	3	.254	.270	.381
1991	Cin-N	328	6	.265	.329	.387	5	0	2	50	3.04	0	3	1	37	4.42	3	1	0	38	3.52	2	2	3	49	3.70	171	4	.292	.378	.456	157	2	.236	.272	.312
1992	Cle-A	355	7	.248	.316	.346	2	1	3	55	1.64	1	2	3	44	3.65	1	2	3	37	2.41	2	1	3	62	2.61	133	1	.226	.302	.301	222	6	.261	.324	.374
1993	Cle-A	90	2	.333	.384	.500	0	0	0	7	7.36	0	2	0	13	7.11	0	2	0	20	7.20	0	0	0	0	—	31	1	.387	.441	.613	59	1	.305	.354	.441
1993	Sea-A	94	1	.287	.346	.362	0	1	8	12	6.75	2	1	5	13	1.35	0	0	0	0	—	2	2	13	25	3.91	39	1	.256	.356	.359	55	0	.309	.339	.364
TOTALS		4390	97	.264	.331	.391	34	27	39	592	3.98	34	42	31	568	4.01	27	29	26	517	4.09	41	40	44	643	3.92	2084	45	.281	.359	.422	2306	52	.248	.305	.363
● **Dan Quisenberry** BR/TR																																				
1979	KC-A	151	5	.278	.306	.424	2	0	2	25	3.28	1	2	3	15	2.93	0	0	0	0	—	3	2	5	40	3.15	44	2	.364	.440	.568	107	3	.243	.245	.364
1980	KC-A	487	5	.265	.302	.351	8	5	12	60	4.33	4	2	21	68	2.12	4	4	14	55	3.58	8	3	19	73	2.84	243	3	.296	.336	.399	244	2	.234	.267	.303
1981	KC-A	229	1	.258	.301	.328	1	2	4	27	1.98	0	2	14	35	1.54	0	3	9	28	2.86	1	1	9	34	0.79	114	1	.298	.362	.351	115	0	.217	.235	.304
1982	KC-A	500	12	.252	.266	.354	6	1	20	72	1.38	3	6	15	65	3.88	4	3	20	69	2.35	5	4	15	68	2.79	238	7	.261	.277	.382	262	5	.244	.256	.328
1983	KC-A	515	6	.229	.243	.315	2	2	26	79	1.72	3	1	19	60	2.24	3	1	19	64	1.70	2	2	26	75	2.15	262	3	.260	.275	.340	253	3	.198	.210	.289
1984	KC-A	489	10	.247	.264	.344	3	1	24	59	2.43	3	2	20	70	2.83	3	2	20	60	2.09	3	1	24	69	3.13	276	5	.264	.284	.359	213	5	.225	.237	.324
1985	KC-A	508	8	.280	.301	.376	6	3	20	74	2.30	2	6	17	55	2.47	4	4	14	57	2.67	4	5	23	72	2.13	271	4	.317	.350	.435	237	4	.236	.244	.308
1986	KC-A	316	2	.291	.342	.348	2	3	2	37	2.45	1	4	10	45	3.02	0	1	8	37	1.95	3	6	4	44	3.45	145	1	.310	.380	.379	171	1	.275	.308	.322
1987	KC-A	202	3	.287	.322	.421	4	0	3	27	0.99	0	1	5	22	4.98	2	0	7	28	2.28	2	1	1	21	3.38	103	2	.320	.364	.466	99	1	.253	.279	.374
1988	KC-A	105	0	.305	.336	.362	0	1	0	9	7.00	0	0	1	16	1.65	0	1	1	25	3.55	0	0	0	0	—	40	0	.400	.429	.475	65	0	.246	.279	.292
1988	StL-N	157	4	.344	.364	.529	1	0	0	19	5.12	1	0	0	19	7.23	0	0	0	0	—	2	0	0	38	6.16	54	2	.278	.322	.426	103	2	.379	.387	.583
1989	StL-N	299	2	.261	.293	.351	3	0	4	38	4.30	0	1	2	41	1.11	2	1	3	40	2.23	1	0	3	38	3.08	143	2	.238	.297	.336	156	0	.282	.289	.365
1990	SF-N	31	1	.419	.432	.645	0	1	0	3	21.00	0	0	0	4	7.36	0	1	0	7	13.50	0	0	0	0	—	11	0	.727	.600	1.091	20	1	.250	.318	.400
TOTALS		3989	59	.267	.294	.363	38	19	117	529	2.74	18	27	127	514	2.80	22	21	115	471	2.62	34	25	129	572	2.89	1944	32	.289	.325	.393	2045	27	.245	.263	.335
● **Scott Radinsky** BL/TL																																				
1990	Chi-A	195	1	.241	.362	.297	2	1	3	26	4.50	4	0	1	26	5.13	5	0	3	29	2.15	1	1	1	23	8.22	62	0	.177	.268	.226	133	1	.271	.402	.331
1991	Chi-A	257	4	.206	.270	.288	1	2	6	42	1.51	4	3	2	30	2.73	2	2	3	32	1.97	3	3	5	39	2.06	78	3	.205	.220	.346	179	1	.207	.291	.263
1992	Chi-A	222	3	.243	.347	.351	3	2	9	31	1.17	0	5	6	29	4.40	2	5	3	29	2.76	1	2	12	30	2.70	66	2	.182	.280	.318	156	1	.269	.375	.365
1993	Chi-A	228	3	.268	.327	.333	3	2	2	30	5.70	5	0	2	25	2.55	2	0	1	28	4.88	6	2	3	27	3.67	88	0	.239	.287	.261	140	3	.286	.351	.379
1995	Chi-A	149	7	.309	.371	.523	1	1	1	21	6.86	1	0	0	17	3.71	2	0	1	18	5.89	0	1	0	20	5.03	58	2	.328	.371	.569	91	5	.297	.370	.495
1996	LA-N	197	2	.264	.318	.371	4	1	0	27	1.35	1	0	1	26	3.51	0	1	1	24	2.28	5	0	0	29	2.51	67	0	.239	.257	.284	130	2	.277	.347	.415
1997	LA-N	229	4	.236	.298	.345	2	0	1	28	0.65	3	1	2	35	4.67	2	1	0	32	3.06	3	0	3	30	2.70	87	2	.218	.278	.379	142	2	.246	.310	.324
1998	LA-N	232	5	.272	.337	.375	3	4	5	31	2.93	3	2	8	31	2.32	2	4	11	31	3.48	4	2	2	31	1.76	64	2	.281	.324	.422	168	3	.268	.342	.357
1999	StL-N	100	2	.270	.371	.400	2	0	2	16	2.20	0	1	1	11	8.74	2	1	3	23	5.56	0	0	0	5	1.80	44	2	.273	.400	.432	56	0	.268	.348	.375
2000	StL-N	0	0	—	1.000	—	0	0	0	0	—	0	0	0	0	—	0	0	0	0	—	0	0	0	0	—	0	0	—	—	—	0	0	—	1.000	—
TOTALS		1809	31	.253	.329	.355	21	13	29	251	2.84	21	12	23	229	3.89	19	14	26	246	3.40	23	11	26	233	3.28	614	13	.235	.292	.352	1195	18	.262	.347	.357
● **Brad Radke** BR/TR																																				
1995	Min-A	709	32	.275	.320	.487	6	8	0	105	4.64	5	6	0	76	6.25	3	7	0	67	5.91	8	7	0	114	4.97	400	14	.268	.313	.450	309	18	.285	.329	.534
1996	Min-A	901	40	.256	.302	.464	6	7	0	124	3.63	5	9	0	108	5.42	4	10	0	117	4.77	7	6	0	115	4.15	514	24	.259	.304	.481	387	16	.253	.298	.442
1997	Min-A	927	28	.257	.293	.412	11	5	0	135	4.00	9	5	0	105	3.70	9	5	0	119	4.22	11	5	0	120	3.52	468	15	.288	.331	.444	459	13	.224	.253	.379
1998	Min-A	840	23	.283	.324	.427	6	8	0	109	3.88	6	6	0	105	4.73	8	6	0	114	2.83	4	8	0	99	5.98	457	15	.322	.359	.490	383	8	.238	.283	.352
1999	Min-A	855	28	.280	.314	.443	5	7	0	95	4.36	7	7	0	124	3.27	5	7	0	111	3.73	7	7	0	108	3.76	458	14	.282	.329	.432	397	14	.277	.295	.456
2000	Min-A	911	27	.286	.326	.459	7	7	0	123	3.94	5	9	0	103	5.05	5	9	0	117	4.07	7	7	0	109	4.86	499	16	.297	.331	.483	412	11	.274	.321	.430
TOTALS		5143	178	.273	.313	.447	41	42	0	691	4.05	37	42	0	621	4.63	34	44	0	646	4.14	44	40	0	666	4.50	2796	98	.286	.328	.464	2347	80	.257	.295	.427
● **Pat Rapp** BR/TR																																				
1992	SF-N	34	0	.235	.366	.382	0	0	0	2	0.00	0	2	0	8	9.00	0	0	0	0	—	0	2	0	10	7.20	19	0	.316	.435	.474	15	0	.133	.278	.267
1993	Fla-N	359	7	.281	.351	.421	4	1	0	43	4.64	0	5	0	51	3.51	0	0	0	0	—	4	6	0	94	4.02	175	3	.269	.363	.406	184	4	.293	.340	.435
1994	Fla-N	496	13	.266	.361	.415	4	5	0	70	4.65	3	3	0	64	2.97	4	4	0	83	4.25	3	4	0	51	3.20	255	6	.318	.406	.467	241	7	.212	.313	.361
1995	Fla-N	625	10	.253	.340	.350	6	4	0	79	3.55	8	3	0	89	3.35	3	4	0	62	4.48	11	3	0	105	2.83	293	4	.242	.347	.355	332	6	.262	.334	.346
1996	Fla-N	611	12	.301	.390	.422	6	7	0	94	3.82	2	9	0	68	6.88	4	10	0	99	3.91	4	6	0	63	6.96	289	5	.311	.404	.408	322	7	.292	.377	.435
1997	Fla-N	422	11	.287	.365	.422	1	1	0	49	4.38	3	5	0	59	4.55	4	5	0	93	4.35	0	1	0	16	5.17	196	5	.286	.353	.393	226	6	.288	.375	.447
1997	SF-N	126	5	.294	.395	.500	0	2	0	15	6.75	1	0	0	18	5.40	0	0	0	0	—	1	2	0	33	6.00	53	2	.302	.424	.509	73	3	.288	.372	.493
1998	KC-A	729	24	.285	.381	.443	5	8	0	105	5.66	7	5	0	83	4.86	7	7	0	105	4.89	5	6	0	83	5.83	405	8	.289	.397	.402	324	16	.281	.362	.494
1999	Bos-A	559	13	.263	.351	.383	2	4	0	67	6.15	4	3	0	79	2.39	2	5	0	66	5.35	4	2	0	81	3.12	288	6	.260	.330	.389	271	7	.266	.372	.376
2000	Bal-A	701	18	.290	.366	.466	4	6	0	86	5.88	5	6	0	88	5.91	5	5	0	89	5.18	4	7	0	85	6.64	331	4	.281	.372	.429	370	14	.297	.360	.500
TOTALS		4662	113	.279	.366	.419	32	38	0	609	4.90	33	41	0	608	4.43	29	40	0	596	4.60	36	39	0	621	4.72	2304	43	.283	.376	.409	2358	70	.274	.356	.428
● **Shane Rawley** BR/TL																																				
1978	Sea-A	414	7	.275	.356	.399	3	4	1	55	3.29	1	5	3	57	4.92	3	5	4	60	3.73	1	4	0	51	4.59	132	1	.288	.386	.371	282	6	.270	.341	.411
1979	Sea-A	316	2	.278	.357	.354	2	6	6	41	3.92	3	3	5	43	3.77	5	6	10	61	4.01	0	3	1	24	3.42	106	0	.170	.198	.217	210	2	.333	.428	.424
1980	Sea-A	400	3	.257	.360	.345	3	4	7	55	4.28	4	3	6	59	2.44	3	2	5	57	3.00	4	5	8	57	3.65	140	1	.336	.433	.414	260	2	.215	.321	.308
1981	Sea-A	249	1	.257	.354	.305	1	3	3	39	4.15	3	3	5	29	3.68	0	3	4	33	4.41	4	3	4	36	3.53	81	0	.235	.315	.272	168	1	.268	.372	.321
1982	NY-A	618	10	.267	.324	.379	5	5	0	83	3.35	6	5	3	81	4.80	4	4	3	46	3.74	7	6	0	118	4.18	131	2	.260	.296	.351	487	8	.269	.331	.386
1983	NY-A	915	19	.269	.327	.403	5	8	0	118	4.11	9	6	1	120	3.45	7	6	1	111	3.98	7	8	0	128	3.60	141	0	.248	.303	.312	774	19	.273	.331	.420
1984	NY-A	169	0	.272	.372	.361	1	2	0	33	5.73	1	1	0	9	8.00	2	3	0	42	6.21	0	0	0	0	—	31	0	.226	.333	.323	138	0	.283	.381	.370
1984	Phi-N	456	13	.257	.298	.386	5	4	0	69	3.13	5	2	0	51	4.73	0	0	0	0	—	10	6	0	120	3.81	60	2	.267	.333	.400	396	11	.255	.293	.384
1985	Phi-N	755	16	.249	.321	.359	6	6	0	99	3.44	7	2	0	99	3.17	5	6	0	71	3.69	8	2	0	128	3.09	91	2	.231	.320	.319	664	14	.252	.322	.364
1986	Phi-N	615	13	.270	.325	.405	7	3	0	69	3.91	4	4	0	89	3.25	10	4	0	128	2.67	1	3	0	30	7.28	80	1	.287	.313	.425	535	12	.267	.326	.402
1987	Phi-N	895	23	.279	.343	.428	8	4	0	111	4.38	9	7	0	119	4.40	8	5	0	103	4.01	9	6	0	126	4.70	102	3	.294	.357	.471	793	20	.277	.341	.422
1988	Phi-N	768	27	.286	.351	.447	4	7	0	94	4.90	4	9	0	104	3.54	5	8	0	122	3.53	3	8	0	76	5.23	136	3	.265	.299	.368	632	24	.291	.362	.464
1989	Min-A	569	19	.293	.359	.467	2	7	0	79	6.18	3	5	0	66	4.07	4	6	0	86	4.07	1	6	0	59	6.90	116	4	.362	.393	.543	453	15	.276	.350	.448
TOTALS		7139	153	.271	.338	.398	52	63	17	945	4.18	59	55	23	926	3.86	56	58	27	920	3.76	55	60	13	952	4.27	1347	19	.272	.333	.371	5792	134	.271	.340	.405
● **Jeff Reardon** BR/TR																																				
1979	NY-N	69	2	.174	.266	.290	1	2	0	12	3.00	0	0	2	9	0.00	1	0	0	1	0.00	0	2	2	20	1.83	28	1	.107	.306	.214	41	1	.220	.233	.341
1980	NY-N	415	10	.231	.306	.349	5	5	1	58	2.16	3	2	5	52	3.12	4	3	2	40	3.15	4	4	4	70	2.30	198	4	.258	.336	.364	217	6	.207	.278	.336
1981	NY-N	110	2	.245	.323	.400	0	0	2	17	2.08	1	0	0	11	5.56	1	0	2	29	3.45	0	0	0	0	—	46	1	.261	.393	.435	64	1	.234	.265	.375
1981	Mon-N	142	3	.148	.204	.246	2	0	0	19	0.96	0	0	6	23	1.57	0	0	0	3	0.00	2	0	6	39	1.40	73	2	.151	.195	.247	69	1	.145	.213	.246
1982	Mon-N	394	6	.221	.287	.330	4	2	16	66	2.44	3	2	10	43	1.48	3	0	13	45	1.60	4	4	13	64	2.39	191	5	.230	.323	.382	203	1	.212	.251	.281
1983	Mon-N	348	7	.250	.334	.374	6	1	13	46	1.76	1	8	8	46	4.30	3	4	12	41	3.27	4	5	9	51	2.84	193	4	.249	.332	.368	155	3	.252	.337	.381
1984	Mon-N	318	5	.220	.306	.305	4	5	10	40	3.79	3	2	13	47	2.12	3	2	11	42	1.29	4	5	12	45	4.40	157	4	.280	.375	.395	161	1	.161	.233	.217
1985	Mon-N	325	7	.209	.269	.295	2	5	21	41	3.27	0	3	20	46	3.11	2	3	22	48	2.23	0	5	19	39	4.35	181	4	.210	.274	.287	144	3	.208	.263	.306
1986	Mon-N	331	12	.251	.306	.417	5	6	14	46	4.73	2	3	21	43	3.12	6	4	18	55	2.93	1	5	17	34	5.61	172	5	.250	.330	.390	159	7	.252	.279	.447
1987	Min-A	302	14	.232	.301	.417	5	2	19	44	3.48	3	6	12	36	5.70	4	4	16	38	6.10	4	4	15	42	3.00	156	9	.301	.364	.532	146	5	.158	.231	.295
1988	Min-A	277	6	.245	.288	.357	1	4	23	38	2.58	1	0	19	35	2.34	0	2	20	35	2.08	2	2	22	38	2.82	148	2	.264	.313	.338	129	4	.225	.259	.380
1989	Min-A	276	8	.246	.280	.384	4	2	19	39	4.12	1	2	12	34	4.01	2	2	14	36	4.21	3	2	17	37	3.93	129	5	.248	.286	.434	147	3	.245	.276	.340
1990	Bos-A	189	5	.206	.282	.344	5	1	12	27	2.03	0	2	9	25	4.38	3	2	13	35	3.06	2	1	8	16	3.38	91	1	.143	.243	.209	98	4	.265	.321	.469
1991	Bos-A	229	9	.236	.286	.419	1	2	19	32	3.62	0	2	21	27	2.33	0	2	19	28	2.89	1	2	21	31	3.16	127	7	.299	.348	.528	102	2	.157	.209	.284
1992	Bos-A	172	6	.308	.335	.488	1	1	18	27	3.95	1	1	9	15	4.80	1	0	15	23	3.52	1	2	12	19	5.12	80	5	.300	.333	.575	92	1	.315	.337	.413
1992	Atl-N	58	0	.241	.279	.241	2	0	1	8	2.35	1	0	2	8	0.00	0	0	0	0	—	3	0	3	16	1.15	28	0	.321	.367	.321	30	0	.167	.194	.167
1993	Cin-N	244	4	.270	.308	.398	4	3	5	30	3.34	0	3	3	32	4.78	2	1	6	28	2.54	2	5	2	33	5.40	118	0	.297	.351	.390	126	4	.246	.265	.405

		TOTAL					HOME					AWAY					1ST HALF					2ND HALF					LEFT					RIGHT				
YEAR	TM/L	AB	HR	AVG	OBP	SLG	W	L	SV	IP	ERA	W	L	SV	IP	ERA	W	L	SV	IP	ERA	W	L	SV	IP	ERA	AB	HR	AVG	OBP	SLG	AB	HR	AVG	OBP	SLG
1994	NY-A	44	3	.386	.426	.682	1	0	0	5	5.06	0	0	2	4	12.46	1	0	2	10	8.38	0	0	0	0	—	17	2	.412	.412	.824	27	1	.370	.433	.593
TOTALS		4243	109	.236	.297	.366	53	41	193	597	3.02	20	36	174	536	3.31	36	29	185	538	3.04	37	48	182	594	3.26	2133	61	.252	.324	.390	2110	48	.219	.269	.342
● Rick Reed BR/TR																																				
1988	Pit-N	43	1	.233	.267	.326	1	0	0	8	0.00	0	0	0	4	9.00	0	0	0	0	—	1	0	0	12	3.00	22	0	.182	.250	.182	21	1	.286	.286	.476
1989	Pit-N	214	5	.290	.326	.430	0	2	0	31	3.77	1	2	0	24	7.99	0	0	0	0	—	1	4	0	55	5.60	101	1	.307	.363	.436	113	4	.274	.291	.425
1990	Pit-N	222	6	.279	.318	.419	1	2	0	24	3.42	1	1	1	30	5.10	1	0	1	25	2.19	1	3	0	29	6.21	146	3	.226	.276	.342	76	3	.382	.400	.566
1991	Pit-N	20	1	.400	.429	.700	0	0	0	0	—	0	0	0	4	10.38	0	0	0	0	—	0	0	0	4	10.38	12	1	.417	.417	.750	8	0	.375	.444	.625
1992	KC-A	387	10	.271	.312	.413	1	2	0	44	4.53	2	5	0	57	3.02	1	3	0	21	3.80	2	4	0	79	3.65	169	5	.201	.236	.367	218	5	.326	.370	.450
1993	KC-A	16	0	.375	.444	.563	0	0	0	4	9.82	0	0	0	0	—	0	0	0	0	—	0	0	0	4	9.82	5	0	.200	.429	.400	11	0	.455	.455	.636
1993	Tex-A	16	1	.375	.444	.563	1	0	0	2	0.00	0	0	0	2	3.86	0	0	0	0	—	1	0	0	4	2.25	4	0	.250	.250	.250	12	1	.417	.500	.667
1994	Tex-A	67	3	.254	.333	.463	1	0	0	5	3.60	0	1	0	12	6.94	1	1	0	17	5.94	0	0	0	0	—	36	2	.278	.366	.528	31	1	.226	.294	.387
1995	Cin-N	66	5	.273	.304	.530	0	0	0	7	1.29	0	0	0	10	9.00	0	0	0	0	—	0	0	0	17	5.82	28	2	.250	.300	.464	38	3	.289	.308	.579
1997	NY-N	778	19	.239	.272	.368	8	5	0	100	3.05	5	4	0	108	2.75	5	4	0	105	2.92	8	5	0	104	2.86	385	9	.231	.277	.358	393	10	.247	.267	.377
1998	NY-N	797	30	.261	.290	.434	10	4	0	129	2.24	6	7	0	84	5.38	9	5	0	113	2.71	7	6	0	99	4.35	358	14	.249	.280	.419	439	16	.271	.299	.446
1999	NY-N	580	23	.281	.334	.474	3	2	0	65	3.86	8	3	0	84	5.14	6	3	0	80	4.95	5	2	0	69	4.15	253	13	.296	.368	.534	327	10	.269	.306	.428
2000	NY-N	721	28	.266	.302	.440	5	3	0	82	4.08	6	2	0	102	4.13	4	2	0	91	4.76	7	3	0	93	3.47	344	13	.273	.324	.442	377	15	.260	.281	.438
TOTALS		3927	132	.266	.304	.428	31	20	0	500	3.28	29	25	1	521	4.56	27	18	1	451	3.71	33	27	0	569	4.11	1863	63	.254	.303	.418	2064	69	.276	.305	.437
● Steve Reed BR/TR																																				
1992	SF-N	59	2	.220	.270	.390	0	0	0	8	2.35	1	0	0	8	2.25	0	0	0	0	—	1	0	0	16	2.30	22	0	.273	.304	.409	37	2	.189	.250	.378
1993	Col-N	309	13	.259	.328	.440	7	3	1	51	6.39	2	2	2	34	1.60	3	2	0	24	6.00	6	3	3	60	3.88	122	7	.336	.410	.607	187	6	.209	.272	.332
1994	Col-N	258	9	.306	.374	.512	1	2	1	33	5.94	2	0	2	31	1.76	2	1	1	46	3.72	1	1	2	18	4.50	94	5	.383	.455	.606	164	4	.262	.324	.457
1995	Col-N	301	8	.203	.256	.306	5	1	2	41	3.07	0	1	1	43	1.26	1	1	3	33	2.48	4	1	0	51	1.93	99	1	.202	.295	.263	202	7	.203	.236	.327
1996	Col-N	276	11	.239	.298	.406	1	1	0	42	3.02	3	2	0	33	5.13	1	2	0	43	4.19	3	1	0	32	3.66	102	5	.284	.351	.490	174	6	.213	.267	.356
1997	Col-N	224	10	.219	.315	.384	1	3	4	31	3.45	3	3	2	31	4.65	1	3	6	34	4.81	3	3	0	29	3.14	100	5	.210	.319	.380	124	5	.226	.312	.387
1998	SF-N	188	4	.160	.251	.261	1	0	0	23	1.17	1	1	1	32	1.71	2	1	1	42	1.93	0	0	0	13	0.00	59	3	.220	.343	.424	129	1	.132	.206	.186
1998	Cle-A	100	4	.260	.321	.420	2	2	0	10	10.80	0	0	0	16	4.02	0	0	0	0	—	2	2	0	26	6.66	43	3	.233	.340	.465	57	1	.281	.305	.386
1999	Cle-A	242	10	.285	.341	.463	2	0	0	30	3.86	1	2	0	31	4.60	3	0	0	32	2.81	0	2	0	30	5.76	86	7	.267	.354	.570	156	3	.295	.333	.404
2000	Cle-A	216	7	.269	.335	.403	2	0	0	31	4.99	0	0	0	25	3.55	1	0	0	26	5.96	1	0	0	30	2.97	59	3	.271	.386	.475	157	4	.268	.314	.376
TOTALS		2173	78	.244	.312	.401	22	12	8	300	4.35	13	11	8	284	2.98	14	10	11	279	3.81	21	13	5	304	3.58	786	39	.274	.362	.478	1387	39	.228	.283	.357
● Mike Remlinger BL/TL																																				
1991	SF-N	133	5	.271	.364	.451	1	1	0	22	2.49	1	0	0	13	7.43	2	0	0	23	3.91	0	1	0	12	5.25	20	1	.250	.375	.400	113	4	.274	.362	.460
1994	NY-N	211	9	.261	.364	.450	1	2	0	26	3.86	0	3	0	29	5.28	0	2	0	18	4.42	1	3	0	36	4.71	50	1	.220	.286	.300	161	8	.273	.387	.497
1995	NY-N	24	1	.292	.346	.542	0	0	0	2	5.40	0	1	0	4	6.75	0	1	0	6	6.35	0	0	0	0	—	7	0	.286	.286	.286	17	1	.294	.368	.647
1995	Cin-N	4	0	.500	.714	.750	0	0	0	0	0.00	0	0	0	1	13.50	0	0	0	1	9.00	0	0	0	0	—	3	0	.667	.667	1.000	1	0	.000	.750	.000
1996	Cin-N	98	4	.245	.380	.418	0	1	0	12	6.94	0	0	0	16	4.60	0	0	0	1	0.00	0	1	0	26	5.81	24	0	.292	.433	.333	74	4	.230	.363	.446
1997	Cin-N	448	11	.223	.322	.366	3	3	1	68	3.95	5	5	1	56	4.37	3	3	2	42	2.81	5	5	0	82	4.81	112	5	.241	.338	.411	336	6	.217	.316	.351
1998	Cin-N	616	23	.266	.358	.440	5	11	0	98	4.85	3	4	0	66	4.77	4	9	0	91	4.57	4	6	0	74	5.13	120	1	.267	.355	.350	496	22	.266	.359	.462
1999	Atl-N	307	9	.215	.297	.342	5	1	0	39	0.92	5	0	1	45	3.63	2	1	0	37	1.47	8	0	1	47	3.06	83	3	.205	.256	.325	224	6	.219	.311	.348
2000	Atl-N	266	6	.207	.308	.320	4	1	4	37	3.19	1	2	8	36	3.75	2	2	7	41	3.54	3	1	5	32	3.38	79	1	.203	.308	.266	187	5	.209	.309	.342
TOTALS		2107	68	.242	.338	.397	19	20	5	303	3.77	15	15	10	265	4.58	13	18	9	259	3.65	21	17	6	310	4.56	498	12	.239	.327	.345	1609	56	.242	.342	.413
● Rick Reuschel BR/TR																																				
1978	Chi-N	924	16	.254	.297	.365	7	6	0	125	3.46	7	9	0	118	3.37	8	5	0	115	2.26	6	10	0	127	4.45	395	7	.281	.342	.403	529	9	.234	.261	.336
1979	Chi-N	916	16	.274	.334	.381	11	4	0	120	3.76	7	8	0	119	3.47	6	5	0	100	4.04	12	7	0	139	3.31	400	9	.300	.359	.423	516	7	.254	.314	.349
1980	Chi-N	981	13	.286	.336	.390	6	3	0	118	3.27	5	10	0	139	3.44	5	7	0	111	3.97	6	6	0	146	2.90	454	7	.324	.378	.423	527	6	.254	.298	.362
1981	Chi-N	326	4	.267	.323	.365	3	4	0	56	3.67	1	3	0	29	3.07	4	7	0	86	3.47	0	0	0	0	—	141	2	.291	.351	.404	185	2	.249	.302	.335
1981	NY-A	268	4	.280	.306	.381	2	2	0	36	2.02	2	2	0	35	3.34	0	0	0	0	—	4	4	0	71	2.67	134	1	.291	.326	.366	134	3	.269	.286	.396
1983	Chi-N	77	1	.234	.318	.325	0	1	0	13	3.46	1	0	0	8	4.70	0	0	0	0	—	1	1	0	21	3.92	50	1	.280	.373	.400	27	0	.148	.207	.185
1984	Chi-N	363	7	.339	.374	.485	4	1	0	54	5.67	1	4	0	38	4.46	4	3	0	66	5.86	1	2	0	26	3.42	178	1	.326	.362	.421	185	6	.351	.387	.546
1985	Pit-N	710	7	.215	.271	.293	13	3	0	113	2.14	1	5	1	81	2.45	5	1	0	56	2.26	9	7	1	138	2.28	323	3	.226	.284	.310	387	4	.207	.260	.279
1986	Pit-N	845	20	.275	.323	.408	5	8	0	104	3.28	4	8	0	111	4.61	4	8	0	101	3.56	5	8	0	115	4.32	465	9	.305	.359	.441	380	11	.237	.277	.368
1987	Pit-N	663	12	.246	.287	.354	4	3	0	81	3.22	4	3	0	96	2.34	6	4	0	116	2.33	2	2	0	61	3.52	386	7	.262	.299	.396	277	5	.224	.271	.296
1987	SF-N	191	1	.230	.264	.335	3	1	0	27	4.00	2	2	0	23	4.70	0	0	0	0	—	5	3	0	50	4.32	103	0	.233	.266	.359	88	1	.227	.261	.307
1988	SF-N	928	11	.261	.293	.350	8	5	0	113	2.63	11	6	0	132	3.55	10	4	0	99	3.18	9	7	0	146	3.08	510	4	.284	.313	.369	418	7	.232	.268	.328
1989	SF-N	790	18	.247	.294	.380	8	5	0	110	2.79	9	3	0	99	3.10	12	2	0	124	2.10	5	6	0	84	4.16	445	5	.261	.309	.364	345	13	.229	.275	.400
1990	SF-N	343	8	.297	.353	.440	2	1	0	43	3.14	1	5	1	44	4.70	2	6	0	72	4.50	1	0	1	15	1.20	206	6	.325	.384	.505	137	2	.255	.304	.343
1991	SF-N	46	0	.370	.453	.478	0	1	0	5	3.86	0	1	0	6	4.50	0	2	0	11	4.22	0	0	0	0	—	24	0	.417	.517	.583	22	0	.318	.375	.364
TOTALS		8371	138	.265	.312	.375	76	48	0	1118	3.23	56	69	2	1078	3.48	66	54	0	1056	3.31	66	63	2	1139	3.40	4214	62	.287	.337	.400	4157	76	.243	.286	.350
● Jerry Reuss BL/TL																																				
1978	Pit-N	327	5	.297	.346	.404	3	1	0	53	4.39	0	1	0	29	5.83	0	1	0	35	7.01	3	1	0	48	3.38	69	0	.275	.324	.362	258	5	.302	.351	.415
1979	LA-N	632	4	.282	.347	.356	5	5	2	82	3.97	2	9	1	78	3.10	2	7	3	50	5.36	5	7	0	110	2.71	127	1	.307	.389	.409	505	3	.275	.336	.343
1980	LA-N	852	12	.227	.260	.309	11	5	0	124	2.68	7	1	3	105	2.31	9	1	3	91	1.87	9	5	0	138	2.93	140	1	.221	.275	.300	712	11	.228	.257	.310
1981	LA-N	568	6	.243	.282	.322	5	1	0	66	2.60	5	3	0	87	2.07	5	2	0	81	1.90	5	2	0	72	2.75	99	1	.283	.297	.404	469	5	.235	.279	.305
1982	LA-N	968	11	.240	.277	.317	9	5	0	127	2.63	9	6	0	128	3.59	9	5	0	126	3.22	9	6	0	129	3.00	195	0	.262	.314	.303	773	11	.234	.268	.321
1983	LA-N	859	12	.271	.311	.364	5	5	0	112	2.73	7	6	0	111	3.15	6	6	0	118	2.51	6	5	0	105	3.43	154	1	.188	.251	.247	705	11	.289	.324	.390
1984	LA-N	383	4	.266	.319	.337	3	4	0	59	3.49	2	3	1	40	4.31	2	3	0	35	4.89	3	4	1	64	3.23	68	1	.250	.311	.353	315	3	.270	.321	.333
1985	LA-N	808	13	.260	.310	.365	6	4	0	93	2.41	8	6	0	119	3.32	6	6	0	101	3.13	8	4	0	112	2.73	103	2	.282	.308	.369	705	11	.257	.310	.365
1986	LA-N	307	13	.313	.353	.498	2	2	0	45	4.96	0	4	1	29	7.22	2	6	1	66	5.86	0	0	0	8	5.63	50	1	.220	.278	.320	257	12	.331	.368	.533
1987	LA-N	6	0	.333	.286	.500	0	0	0	2	4.50	0	0	0	0	—	0	0	0	2	4.50	0	0	0	0	—	1	0	.000	.000	.000	5	0	.400	.400	.600
1987	Cin-N	147	2	.354	.406	.483	0	4	0	30	6.90	0	1	0	5	13.50	0	5	0	35	7.79	0	0	0	0	—	17	0	.294	.333	.412	130	2	.362	.415	.492
1987	Cal-A	343	16	.327	.361	.525	2	2	0	45	3.83	2	3	0	38	6.93	2	0	0	17	0.52	2	5	0	65	6.51	66	3	.364	.391	.530	277	13	.318	.354	.523
1988	Chi-A	696	15	.263	.307	.375	7	4	0	102	3.72	6	5	0	81	3.10	6	4	0	77	3.04	7	5	0	106	3.74	94	3	.266	.314	.415	602	12	.262	.306	.369
1989	Chi-A	438	12	.308	.340	.443	4	2	0	54	3.67	4	3	0	53	6.49	7	4	0	81	5.58	1	1	0	26	3.46	80	4	.325	.349	.525	358	8	.304	.338	.425
1989	Mil-A	132	7	.273	.342	.455	0	3	0	22	6.14	1	1	0	12	3.86	0	0	0	0	—	1	4	0	34	5.35	21	2	.286	.348	.571	111	5	.270	.341	.432
1990	Pit-N	30	1	.267	.333	.467	0	0	0	7	4.05	0	0	0	1	0.00	0	0	0	0	—	0	0	0	8	3.52	8	0	.125	.300	.250	22	1	.318	.348	.545
TOTALS		7496	133	.268	.311	.371	62	47	2	1023	3.41	53	52	6	916	3.70	56	50	7	914	3.70	59	49	1	1024	3.40	1292	20	.264	.313	.365	6204	113	.269	.311	.373
● Rick Rhoden BR/TR																																				
1978	LA-N	628	13	.255	.311	.361	6	2	0	86	3.03	4	6	0	79	4.46	6	4	0	97	4.35	4	4	0	67	2.81	284	3	.264	.322	.345	344	10	.247	.301	.375
1979	Pit-N	19	0	.263	.333	.368	0	0	0	0	—	0	1	0	5	7.20	0	1	0	5	7.20	0	0	0	0	—	2	0	.500	.750	1.000	17	0	.235	.235	.294
1980	Pit-N	486	9	.274	.331	.374	5	3	0	71	3.95	2	2	0	56	3.70	0	1	0	12	4.50	7	4	0	115	3.77	235	1	.311	.348	.391	251	8	.239	.316	.359
1981	Pit-N	519	6	.283	.348	.389	4	3	0	59	5.16	5	1	0	77	2.92	6	1	0	74	3.30	3	3	0	63	4.60	235	4	.285	.368	.417	284	2	.282	.330	.366
1982	Pit-N	895	14	.267	.321	.385	7	6	0	119	3.79	4	8	0	112	4.51	5	6	0	108	5.08	6	8	0	122	3.31	437	5	.270	.331	.359	458	9	.264	.311	.410
1983	Pit-N	928	13	.276	.325	.390	8	7	1	123	2.99	5	6	0	121	3.20	5	7	1	124	3.41	8	6	0	120	2.77	504	5	.282	.328	.387	424	8	.269	.320	.394
1984	Pit-N	888	13	.243	.292	.332	8	3	0	129	1.88	6	6	0	109	3.72	6	5	0	113	2.72	8	4	0	126	2.72	475	4	.251	.301	.318	413	9	.235	.282	.349
1985	Pit-N	859	18	.296	.352	.433	7	9	0	118	4.42	3	6	0	95	4.53	5	7	0	97	4.44	5	8	0	116	4.50	431	6	.306	.360	.425	428	12	.285	.345	.442
1986	Pit-N	926	17	.228	.286	.347	9	6	0	140	2.76	6	6	0	114	2.93	8	4	0	110	2.46	7	8	0	144	3.13	509	4	.230	.294	.303	417	13	.225	.277	.400
1987	NY-A	687	22	.268	.327	.419	10	3	0	93	3.29	6	7	0	89	4.47	9	5	0	102	3.79	7	5	0	80	3.95	363	14	.275	.342	.455	324	8	.259	.311	.380
1988	NY-A	767	20	.269	.322	.405	8	8	0	125	3.90	4	4	0	72	4.98	3	6	0	70	4.78	9	6	0	127	4.03	411	10	.280	.340	.409	356	10	.256	.300	.402
1989	Hou-N	374	7	.289	.361	.414	1	6	0	57	4.42	1	0	0	40	4.08	0	2	0	35	4.08	2	4	0	61	4.40	221	4	.271	.344	.430	153	3	.314	.385	.431
TOTALS		7976	152	.266	.322	.385	73	56	1	1120	3.45	46	53	0	968	3.92	53	49	1	947	3.80	66	60	0	1141	3.56	4107	60	.272	.331	.378	3869	92	.258	.312	.392
● Dave Righetti BL/TL																																				
1979	NY-A	55	2	.182	.303	.345	0	0	0	10	3.48	0	1	0	7	3.86	0	0	0	0	—	0	1	0	17	3.63	9	0	.111	.111	.111	46	2	.196	.333	.391
1981	NY-A	382	1	.196	.268	.259	3	3	0	53	2.70	5	1	0	52	1.38	3	0	0	30	1.50	5	4	0	75	2.27	68	0	.132	.224	.162	314	1	.210	.277	.280
1982	NY-A	677	11	.229	.338	.321	7	4	1	103	3.23	4	6	0	80	4.50	5	5	0	87	4.23	6	5	1	96	3.39	113	2	.212	.328	.301	564	9	.232	.340	.324
1983	NY-A	817	12	.237	.296	.341	9	3	0	115	3.04	5	5	0	102	3.90	9	3	0	110	3.53	5	5	0	107	3.35	158	3	.247	.306	.386	659	9	.235	.293	.331
1984	NY-A	355	5	.223	.293	.293	3	1	16	50	1.80	2	5	15	46	2.91	2	1	9	41	1.54	3	5	22	55	2.93	75	1	.173	.295	.240	280	4	.236	.292	.307

		TOTAL					HOME					AWAY					1ST HALF					2ND HALF					LEFT					RIGHT				
YEAR	TM/L	AB	HR	AVG	OBP	SLG	W	L	SV	IP	ERA	W	L	SV	IP	ERA	W	L	SV	IP	ERA	W	L	SV	IP	ERA	AB	HR	AVG	OBP	SLG	AB	HR	AVG	OBP	SLG
1985	NY-A	398	5	.241	.316	.327	9	1	17	56	2.24	3	6	12	51	3.38	5	6	13	52	3.48	7	1	16	55	2.11	112	1	.196	.308	.277	286	4	.259	.320	.346
1986	NY-A	389	4	.226	.291	.296	5	5	18	50	1.99	3	3	28	57	2.84	5	4	17	43	3.98	3	4	29	64	1.41	69	1	.304	.387	.391	320	3	.209	.269	.275
1987	NY-A	362	9	.262	.341	.362	5	2	17	48	2.79	3	4	14	47	4.24	5	3	15	50	4.35	3	3	16	45	2.58	96	3	.271	.324	.396	266	6	.259	.348	.350
1988	NY-A	335	5	.257	.332	.358	4	1	11	47	2.66	1	3	14	40	4.54	3	0	11	38	3.79	2	4	14	49	3.31	86	2	.279	.347	.442	249	3	.249	.327	.329
1989	NY-A	264	3	.277	.341	.364	0	1	10	31	3.16	2	5	15	38	2.87	2	2	15	38	2.37	0	4	10	31	3.77	62	1	.274	.343	.355	202	2	.277	.341	.366
1990	NY-A	205	8	.234	.325	.400	1	1	21	28	2.60	0	0	15	25	4.62	1	0	16	23	4.30	0	1	20	30	3.00	41	2	.244	.295	.415	164	6	.232	.332	.396
1991	SF-N	267	4	.240	.317	.330	1	4	14	37	4.14	1	3	10	35	2.60	2	3	10	39	4.19	0	4	14	33	2.45	72	0	.167	.197	.167	195	4	.267	.357	.390
1992	SF-N	294	4	.269	.344	.374	1	3	3	45	2.82	1	4	0	34	8.02	1	5	3	41	6.37	1	2	0	37	3.62	89	0	.236	.330	.337	205	4	.283	.351	.390
1993	SF-N	190	11	.305	.365	.532	0	1	1	23	3.57	1	0	0	25	7.66	1	1	0	27	3.33	0	0	1	20	8.85	59	4	.288	.311	.576	131	7	.313	.388	.511
1994	Oak-A	31	3	.419	.548	.742	0	0	0	1	13.50	0	0	0	6	17.47	0	0	0	7	16.71	0	0	0	0	—	16	3	.438	.550	1.063	15	0	.400	.545	.400
1994	Tor-A	48	2	.188	.322	.396	0	1	0	8	5.87	0	0	0	6	7.94	0	1	0	6	9.53	0	0	0	8	4.70	12	0	.167	.286	.250	36	2	.194	.333	.444
1995	Chi-A	200	6	.325	.377	.475	1	1	0	24	3.00	2	1	0	25	5.33	0	0	0	0	—	3	2	0	49	4.20	29	1	.276	.344	.414	171	5	.333	.383	.485
TOTALS		5269	95	.244	.321	.347	49	32	129	730	2.88	33	47	123	674	4.09	44	34	109	631	3.88	38	45	143	773	3.12	1166	24	.234	.313	.348	4103	71	.247	.323	.347
● **Jose Rijo**	BR/TR																																			
1984	NY-A	248	5	.298	.382	.407	1	2	0	19	4.82	1	6	2	44	4.74	2	7	2	56	4.63	0	1	0	6	6.00	102	4	.353	.450	.510	146	1	.260	.331	.336
1985	Oak-A	238	6	.239	.322	.382	2	1	0	25	3.65	4	3	0	39	3.46	0	0	0	0	—	6	4	0	64	3.53	125	5	.280	.379	.488	113	1	.195	.254	.265
1986	Oak-A	725	24	.237	.336	.406	3	4	1	90	3.90	6	7	0	104	5.30	2	7	1	86	4.94	7	4	0	108	4.42	395	11	.241	.354	.403	330	13	.233	.312	.409
1987	Oak-A	347	10	.305	.379	.455	2	3	0	41	4.35	0	4	0	41	7.46	0	4	0	36	5.94	2	3	0	46	5.87	175	6	.303	.387	.491	172	4	.308	.370	.419
1988	Cin-N	574	7	.209	.288	.300	6	7	0	92	3.12	7	1	0	70	1.42	8	3	0	78	3.00	5	5	0	84	1.82	308	6	.231	.327	.347	266	1	.184	.241	.244
1989	Cin-N	405	6	.249	.328	.338	2	2	0	43	3.16	5	4	0	68	2.63	7	5	0	104	2.94	0	1	0	7	1.29	242	5	.273	.372	.384	163	1	.215	.256	.270
1990	Cin-N	712	10	.212	.291	.313	8	4	0	108	2.24	6	4	0	89	3.25	5	3	0	86	3.56	9	5	0	111	2.03	409	7	.218	.316	.318	303	3	.205	.255	.307
1991	Cin-N	755	8	.219	.272	.305	9	0	0	99	2.99	6	6	0	105	2.06	6	2	0	102	2.66	9	4	0	103	2.37	437	5	.252	.311	.352	318	3	.173	.215	.239
1992	Cin-N	776	15	.238	.281	.340	6	4	0	89	2.74	9	6	0	122	2.43	4	6	0	83	3.47	11	4	0	128	1.97	429	6	.266	.317	.368	347	9	.205	.234	.305
1993	Cin-N	949	19	.230	.278	.342	8	6	0	135	2.60	6	3	0	122	2.35	6	3	0	118	3.19	8	6	0	139	1.88	523	10	.241	.296	.359	426	9	.216	.254	.322
1994	Cin-N	667	16	.265	.321	.396	6	3	0	103	3.58	3	3	0	69	2.34	6	4	0	117	3.14	3	2	0	55	2.95	315	7	.273	.348	.400	352	9	.259	.296	.392
1995	Cin-N	267	6	.285	.336	.423	2	3	0	32	5.06	3	1	0	37	3.41	3	4	0	57	4.58	2	0	0	12	2.25	128	4	.328	.387	.500	139	2	.245	.287	.353
TOTALS		6663	132	.240	.307	.356	55	39	1	876	3.20	56	48	2	910	3.14	49	48	3	924	3.59	62	39	0	862	2.71	3588	76	.257	.337	.384	3075	56	.221	.270	.323
● **Mariano Rivera**	BR/TR																																			
1995	NY-A	267	11	.266	.342	.442	3	2	0	32	7.11	2	1	0	35	4.08	1	2	0	15	10.20	4	1	0	52	4.15	142	6	.246	.337	.415	125	5	.288	.348	.472
1996	NY-A	386	1	.189	.258	.228	6	2	4	50	1.80	2	1	1	58	2.34	3	1	2	55	1.96	5	2	3	53	2.22	214	1	.215	.288	.248	172	0	.157	.219	.203
1997	NY-A	274	5	.237	.285	.339	4	3	23	40	2.25	2	1	20	32	1.42	2	2	26	40	2.01	4	2	17	31	1.72	153	1	.242	.282	.288	121	4	.231	.289	.405
1998	NY-A	223	3	.215	.270	.309	3	0	20	36	1.24	0	0	16	25	2.88	1	0	19	28	1.29	2	0	17	33	2.43	115	0	.235	.294	.287	108	3	.194	.246	.333
1999	NY-A	245	2	.176	.239	.237	2	2	20	33	2.48	2	1	25	36	1.24	1	1	20	30	1.50	3	2	25	39	2.08	140	1	.143	.188	.171	105	1	.219	.303	.324
2000	NY-A	279	4	.208	.271	.294	4	2	14	34	3.41	3	2	22	41	2.40	2	3	17	33	3.51	5	1	19	42	2.34	145	1	.207	.286	.276	134	3	.209	.255	.313
TOTALS		1674	26	.214	.277	.303	22	11	81	225	2.88	11	6	84	227	2.38	10	9	84	202	2.68	23	8	81	251	2.59	909	10	.215	.281	.278	765	16	.213	.273	.333
● **Don Robinson**	BR/TR																																			
1978	Pit-N	861	20	.236	.283	.355	7	1	1	90	3.79	7	5	0	138	3.26	4	2	1	103	3.33	10	4	0	126	3.58	391	9	.220	.270	.322	470	11	.249	.294	.383
1979	Pit-N	617	12	.277	.335	.400	3	5	0	86	3.34	5	3	0	74	4.48	5	4	0	85	3.16	3	4	0	75	4.66	304	5	.286	.343	.411	313	7	.268	.327	.390
1980	Pit-N	609	14	.258	.313	.389	3	7	0	87	4.47	4	3	1	74	3.42	2	3	1	60	4.62	5	7	0	100	3.60	293	6	.300	.352	.447	316	8	.218	.276	.335
1981	Pit-N	148	4	.318	.405	.500	0	0	0	14	6.59	0	3	2	25	5.47	0	1	0	11	7.59	0	2	2	28	5.20	65	1	.338	.429	.508	83	3	.301	.385	.494
1982	Pit-N	851	26	.250	.331	.410	5	8	0	112	5.96	10	5	0	115	2.65	8	3	0	108	3.99	7	10	0	119	4.55	397	8	.239	.351	.360	454	18	.260	.311	.454
1983	Pit-N	145	5	.297	.386	.490	1	2	0	15	7.36	1	0	0	22	2.49	1	0	0	11	2.53	1	2	0	26	5.26	77	4	.325	.422	.571	68	1	.265	.342	.397
1984	Pit-N	438	6	.226	.298	.324	3	2	3	56	3.21	2	4	7	66	2.86	0	3	4	58	4.21	5	3	6	64	1.96	178	3	.213	.319	.326	260	3	.235	.283	.323
1985	Pit-N	372	6	.255	.334	.363	3	2	2	44	3.07	2	9	1	51	4.56	2	3	2	50	3.58	3	8	1	45	4.20	166	0	.241	.333	.289	206	6	.267	.335	.422
1986	Pit-N	257	5	.237	.310	.342	3	3	6	37	3.19	0	1	8	33	3.58	2	0	1	18	4.91	1	4	13	51	2.82	113	0	.186	.282	.212	144	5	.278	.333	.444
1987	Pit-N	247	6	.267	.326	.393	4	1	8	34	2.94	2	5	4	32	4.83	5	5	10	49	3.86	1	1	2	16	3.86	126	1	.270	.333	.357	121	5	.264	.318	.430
1987	SF-N	163	1	.239	.311	.356	2	1	4	15	5.52	3	0	3	28	1.29	0	0	0	0	—	5	1	7	43	2.74	97	1	.206	.304	.299	66	0	.288	.324	.439
1988	SF-N	658	11	.231	.284	.343	4	0	3	66	2.47	6	5	3	111	2.43	3	1	6	48	2.42	7	4	0	128	2.45	324	6	.216	.272	.324	334	5	.246	.296	.362
1989	SF-N	743	22	.248	.283	.396	9	4	0	120	2.10	3	7	0	77	5.49	7	5	0	109	2.89	5	6	0	88	4.09	434	13	.260	.301	.412	309	9	.230	.258	.372
1990	SF-N	618	18	.280	.324	.432	4	1	0	61	5.04	6	6	0	97	4.27	3	1	0	43	3.95	7	6	0	114	4.80	365	12	.285	.343	.455	253	6	.273	.295	.399
1991	SF-N	465	12	.265	.334	.417	3	2	0	62	2.77	2	7	1	60	6.03	3	6	0	67	4.54	2	3	1	54	4.17	251	5	.279	.371	.422	214	7	.248	.286	.411
1992	Cal-A	65	1	.292	.324	.385	1	0	0	6	0.00	0	0	0	10	3.60	1	0	0	16	2.20	0	0	0	0	—	33	0	.273	.273	.303	32	1	.313	.371	.469
1992	Phi-N	169	6	.290	.300	.467	1	0	0	12	3.75	0	4	0	32	7.11	1	1	0	28	5.40	0	3	0	15	7.63	95	2	.326	.323	.463	74	4	.243	.272	.473
TOTALS		7426	175	.255	.314	.389	56	39	27	915	3.75	53	67	30	1044	3.82	47	38	25	866	3.73	62	68	32	1092	3.83	3709	76	.257	.326	.382	3717	99	.253	.302	.396
● **John Rocker**	BR/TL																																			
1998	Atl-N	128	4	.172	.307	.297	0	0	2	21	0.44	1	3	0	17	4.15	1	1	0	14	2.51	0	2	2	24	1.90	55	2	.164	.258	.273	73	2	.178	.341	.315
1999	Atl-N	261	5	.180	.284	.268	2	1	19	38	0.71	2	4	19	34	4.46	2	3	16	36	2.97	2	2	22	36	2.00	57	2	.140	.183	.246	204	3	.191	.310	.275
2000	Atl-N	200	5	.210	.368	.310	1	1	15	31	3.19	0	1	9	22	2.45	1	0	12	23	5.01	0	2	12	30	1.21	37	2	.243	.462	.405	163	3	.202	.343	.288
TOTALS		589	14	.188	.319	.289	3	2	36	90	1.51	3	8	28	74	3.79	4	4	28	74	3.53	2	6	36	89	1.71	149	6	.174	.293	.295	440	8	.193	.328	.286
● **Felix Rodriguez**	BR/TR																																			
1995	LA-N	40	2	.275	.356	.500	1	1	0	7	1.35	0	0	0	4	4.50	1	1	0	11	2.53	0	0	0	0	—	27	0	.259	.333	.370	13	2	.308	.400	.769
1997	Cin-N	177	2	.271	.387	.367	0	0	0	24	4.88	0	0	0	22	3.68	0	0	0	8	4.50	0	0	0	38	4.26	82	2	.268	.358	.390	95	0	.274	.410	.347
1998	Ari-N	170	5	.259	.365	.400	0	1	3	23	4.24	0	1	2	21	8.27	0	2	5	27	6.26	0	0	0	17	5.94	71	4	.268	.391	.535	99	1	.253	.345	.303
1999	SF-N	256	6	.262	.338	.387	2	1	0	27	4.33	0	2	0	39	3.43	0	2	0	32	4.26	2	1	0	35	3.38	104	1	.221	.317	.308	152	5	.289	.353	.441
2000	SF-N	296	5	.220	.320	.314	3	0	2	39	2.75	1	2	1	42	2.55	3	0	1	44	3.09	1	2	2	38	2.13	133	0	.158	.263	.203	163	5	.270	.365	.405
TOTALS		939	20	.250	.347	.367	6	3	5	120	3.74	1	5	3	128	4.00	4	5	6	121	4.15	3	3	2	127	3.60	417	7	.221	.322	.333	522	13	.274	.367	.395
● **Rich Rodriguez**	BL/TL																																			
1990	SD-N	181	2	.287	.347	.376	1	0	0	28	2.57	0	1	1	20	3.20	0	0	0	0		1	1	1	48	2.64	66	0	.242	.306	.258	115	2	.313	.370	.443
1991	SD-N	282	8	.234	.335	.365	1	1	0	37	4.58	2	0	0	43	2.11	2	1	0	44	3.50	1	0	0	36	2.97	96	3	.219	.336	.354	186	5	.242	.335	.371
1992	SD-N	336	4	.229	.289	.313	4	1	0	51	1.93	2	2	0	40	2.95	3	2	0	49	2.19	3	1	0	42	2.59	104	2	.231	.302	.327	232	2	.228	.283	.306
1993	SD-N	121	2	.281	.336	.372	2	1	1	13	2.13	0	2	1	17	4.15	2	3	2	30	3.30	0	0	0	0	—	36	1	.389	.436	.556	85	1	.235	.293	.294
1993	Fla-N	170	8	.229	.328	.412	0	0	1	23	4.24	0	1	0	23	3.97	0	0	0	2	10.80	0	1	1	44	3.86	63	2	.190	.301	.317	107	6	.252	.344	.467
1994	StL-N	230	6	.270	.345	.426	1	2	0	29	5.90	2	3	0	31	2.30	2	2	0	43	2.74	1	3	0	18	7.13	60	1	.183	.269	.250	170	5	.300	.372	.488
1995	StL-N	4	0	.000	.000	.000	0	0	0	2	0.00	0	0	0	0	—	0	0	0	2	0.00	0	0	0	0	—	1	0	.000	.000	.000	3	0	.000	.000	.000
1997	SF-N	246	7	.264	.325	.411	3	2	0	33	2.73	1	1	1	32	3.62	3	3	1	39	1.85	1	0	0	26	5.13	103	3	.311	.372	.495	143	4	.231	.290	.350
1998	SF-N	254	7	.272	.322	.394	1	0	1	30	1.80	3	0	1	36	5.30	1	0	1	30	3.34	3	0	1	36	4.00	108	2	.185	.246	.259	146	5	.336	.380	.493
1999	SF-N	219	8	.274	.356	.447	2	0	0	27	4.05	1	0	0	30	6.30	0	0	0	30	5.16	3	0	0	27	5.33	96	5	.271	.349	.490	123	3	.276	.362	.415
2000	NY-N	162	7	.364	.416	.617	0	0	0	20	7.52	0	1	0	17	8.10	0	1	0	29	7.67	0	0	0	8	8.22	45	3	.289	.358	.556	117	4	.393	.439	.641
TOTALS		2205	59	.264	.335	.403	15	7	3	293	3.56	11	11	4	288	3.94	13	12	4	297	3.55	13	6	3	285	3.95	778	22	.243	.320	.374	1427	37	.276	.343	.418
● **Kenny Rogers**	BL/TL																																			
1989	Tex-A	259	2	.232	.344	.301	3	3	1	46	3.33	0	1	1	28	2.28	2	0	0	35	2.55	1	4	2	38	3.29	83	0	.169	.303	.217	176	2	.261	.364	.341
1990	Tex-A	374	6	.249	.323	.372	9	1	8	54	2.01	1	5	7	44	4.50	2	3	5	48	4.31	8	3	10	50	1.99	96	1	.219	.272	.333	278	5	.259	.340	.385
1991	Tex-A	430	14	.281	.375	.444	6	5	3	47	5.59	4	5	2	63	5.29	4	7	1	61	7.38	6	3	4	49	2.96	98	3	.224	.342	.357	332	11	.298	.385	.470
1992	Tex-A	306	7	.261	.318	.392	1	4	2	43	3.53	2	2	4	35	2.55	1	3	5	40	2.90	2	3	1	38	3.29	92	1	.261	.284	.348	214	6	.262	.332	.411
1993	Tex-A	798	18	.263	.325	.406	9	4	0	94	5.00	7	6	0	115	3.38	5	6	0	86	5.55	11	4	0	122	3.09	90	0	.222	.271	.333	708	18	.268	.331	.415
1994	Tex-A	650	24	.260	.315	.442	6	5	0	102	3.72	5	3	0	66	5.62	9	4	0	119	4.61	2	4	0	48	4.10	90	8	.311	.344	.644	560	16	.252	.311	.409
1995	Tex-A	791	26	.243	.309	.382	9	1	0	109	2.96	8	6	0	99	3.83	8	3	0	83	2.59	9	4	0	125	3.90	115	2	.157	.248	.226	676	24	.257	.319	.408
1996	NY-A	686	16	.261	.346	.378	9	5	0	110	4.27	3	3	0	69	5.32	6	3	0	86	4.10	6	5	0	93	5.21	110	3	.209	.326	.318	576	13	.271	.350	.389
1997	NY-A	576	18	.280	.354	.429	3	4	0	73	5.57	3	3	0	72	5.72	4	4	0	87	5.90	2	3	0	58	5.28	104	3	.240	.344	.365	472	15	.288	.357	.443
1998	Oak-A	887	19	.242	.299	.366	11	0	0	124	1.96	5	8	0	115	4.46	7	3	0	113	3.28	9	5	0	126	3.07	199	4	.226	.322	.327	688	15	.247	.292	.378
1999	Oak-A	468	8	.288	.353	.387	4	0	0	59	4.60	1	3	0	61	4.01	4	3	0	96	3.86	1	0	0	24	6.08	104	2	.308	.376	.452	364	6	.283	.346	.368
1999	NY-N	281	8	.253	.328	.395	2	0	0	44	3.05	3	1	0	32	5.40	0	0	0	0	—	5	1	0	76	4.03	51	4	.196	.255	.451	230	4	.265	.344	.383
2000	Tex-A	902	20	.285	.348	.431	9	6	0	121	4.46	4	7	0	106	4.66	8	5	0	114	4.11	5	8	0	113	5.00	220	6	.314	.368	.518	682	14	.276	.341	.403
TOTALS		7408	186	.262	.332	.399	81	38	14	1024	3.81	46	53	14	904	4.45	60	44	11	968	4.31	67	47	17	961	3.91	1452	37	.242	.320	.381	5956	149	.267	.335	.403

YEAR	TM/L	TOTAL AB	HR	AVG	OBP	SLG	HOME W	L	SV	IP	ERA	AWAY W	L	SV	IP	ERA	1ST HALF W	L	SV	IP	ERA	2ND HALF W	L	SV	IP	ERA	LEFT AB	HR	AVG	OBP	SLG	RIGHT AB	HR	AVG	OBP	SLG
● Steve Rogers BR/TR																																				
1978	Mon-N	791	12	.235	.293	.322	8	3	0	117	2.23	5	7	1	102	2.74	9	7	0	137	2.16	4	3	1	82	2.98	385	5	.229	.289	.304	406	7	.241	.297	.340
1979	Mon-N	923	14	.251	.311	.342	11	5	0	138	2.61	2	7	0	111	3.50	7	5	0	125	2.66	6	7	0	123	3.36	474	4	.262	.321	.329	449	10	.241	.299	.356
1980	Mon-N	1037	16	.238	.296	.336	9	6	0	156	2.65	7	5	0	125	3.39	9	6	0	126	3.08	7	5	0	155	2.90	505	8	.240	.309	.337	532	8	.237	.283	.335
1981	Mon-N	601	7	.248	.296	.356	8	3	0	91	3.28	4	5	0	70	3.60	7	4	0	96	4.39	5	4	0	64	1.96	281	2	.249	.306	.349	320	5	.247	.287	.363
1982	Mon-N	1032	12	.237	.285	.324	6	7	0	147	3.01	13	1	0	130	1.73	9	3	0	130	1.87	10	5	0	147	2.87	542	6	.227	.286	.325	490	6	.249	.284	.322
1983	Mon-N	1023	14	.252	.306	.360	9	5	0	127	3.20	8	7	0	146	3.26	11	3	0	136	2.77	6	9	0	137	3.69	541	8	.248	.312	.355	482	6	.257	.300	.365
1984	Mon-N	641	12	.267	.346	.381	4	7	0	101	3.04	2	8	0	69	6.16	3	6	0	63	5.71	3	9	0	106	3.47	351	7	.268	.359	.385	290	5	.266	.329	.376
1985	Mon-N	155	1	.329	.401	.419	1	1	0	16	6.89	1	3	0	22	4.84	2	4	0	38	5.68	0	0	0	0	—	86	1	.314	.429	.407	69	0	.348	.361	.435
TOTALS		6203	88	.248	.306	.346	56	37	0	892	2.91	42	43	1	775	3.32	57	38	0	852	3.10	41	42	1	815	3.10	3165	41	.247	.314	.341	3038	47	.250	.297	.351
● Mel Rojas BR/TR																																				
1990	Mon-N	145	5	.234	.351	.386	0	0	1	14	6.59	3	1	0	26	2.05	0	0	0	0	—	3	1	1	40	3.60	92	3	.207	.342	.348	53	2	.283	.367	.453
1991	Mon-N	184	4	.228	.280	.375	1	2	2	17	3.12	2	1	4	31	4.11	0	0	0	7	6.43	3	3	6	41	3.29	89	2	.247	.310	.449	95	2	.211	.250	.305
1992	Mon-N	357	2	.199	.271	.269	5	0	3	52	1.72	2	1	7	48	1.12	1	1	3	43	1.27	6	0	7	58	1.55	199	1	.196	.268	.246	158	1	.203	.274	.297
1993	Mon-N	330	6	.242	.308	.382	4	3	4	44	3.07	1	5	6	44	2.84	3	6	6	44	3.86	2	2	4	44	2.05	185	4	.270	.338	.427	145	2	.207	.269	.324
1994	Mon-N	313	11	.227	.283	.355	2	1	6	33	3.78	1	1	10	51	3.02	3	2	12	60	3.15	0	0	4	24	3.75	169	7	.225	.294	.373	144	4	.229	.270	.333
1995	Mon-N	263	2	.262	.350	.346	1	1	13	34	4.19	0	3	17	33	4.05	1	2	12	31	4.11	0	2	18	37	4.14	127	1	.268	.367	.362	136	1	.257	.333	.331
1996	Mon-N	290	5	.193	.265	.290	4	2	19	43	4.15	3	2	17	38	2.15	5	3	11	40	4.46	2	1	25	41	1.99	129	2	.147	.224	.240	161	3	.230	.298	.329
1997	Chi-N	221	11	.244	.346	.434	0	3	9	35	3.60	0	1	4	24	5.63	0	2	6	37	4.86	0	2	7	22	3.68	106	7	.292	.387	.528	115	4	.200	.308	.348
1997	NY-N	102	4	.235	.288	.431	0	2	1	17	4.86	0	0	1	10	5.59	0	0	0	0	—	0	2	2	26	5.13	51	1	.196	.241	.333	51	3	.275	.333	.529
1998	NY-N	223	9	.305	.391	.507	3	0	1	30	5.40	2	2	1	28	6.75	3	1	2	33	3.86	2	1	0	25	8.88	100	2	.220	.342	.360	123	7	.374	.435	.626
1999	LA-N	20	3	.250	.348	.700	0	0	0	3	6.00	0	0	0	2	22.50	0	0	0	5	12.60	0	0	0	0	—	7	1	.143	.400	.571	13	2	.308	.308	.769
1999	Det-A	31	3	.387	.487	.839	0	0	0	1	0.00	0	0	0	5	28.80	0	0	0	6	22.74	0	0	0	0	—	14	2	.357	.444	.857	17	1	.412	.524	.824
1999	Mon-N	12	0	.417	.529	.583	0	0	0	3	16.88	0	0	0	0	—	0	0	0	2	19.29	0	0	0	0	0.00	4	0	.500	.600	.750	8	0	.375	.500	.500
TOTALS		2491	65	.237	.315	.375	20	14	59	327	3.83	14	17	67	340	3.81	16	17	52	308	4.29	18	14	74	359	3.41	1272	33	.230	.315	.368	1219	32	.245	.314	.381
● Kirk Rueter BL/TL																																				
1993	Mon-N	322	5	.264	.303	.373	4	0	0	38	2.82	4	0	0	47	2.66	0	0	0	0	—	8	0	0	86	2.73	48	0	.250	.280	.271	274	5	.266	.307	.391
1994	Mon-N	360	11	.294	.335	.442	3	1	0	42	6.05	4	2	0	51	4.44	3	1	0	54	6.04	4	2	0	39	3.96	75	1	.213	.286	.280	285	10	.316	.349	.484
1995	Mon-N	170	3	.224	.267	.300	2	2	0	27	3.71	3	1	0	21	2.61	0	2	0	8	10.57	5	1	0	40	1.82	21	0	.143	.182	.143	149	3	.235	.278	.322
1996	Mon-N	309	12	.294	.344	.460	2	4	0	41	6.15	3	2	0	38	2.87	5	4	0	66	3.80	0	2	0	12	8.76	57	2	.316	.350	.439	252	10	.290	.343	.464
1996	SF-N	87	0	.207	.250	.264	1	2	0	21	1.71	0	0	0	2	3.86	0	0	0	0	—	1	2	0	23	1.93	17	0	.353	.421	.412	70	0	.171	.205	.229
1997	SF-N	734	17	.264	.311	.395	7	4	0	102	3.00	6	2	0	89	3.96	5	2	0	93	3.50	8	4	0	98	3.40	141	4	.277	.318	.411	593	13	.261	.309	.391
1998	SF-N	729	27	.265	.321	.432	7	5	0	77	3.99	9	4	0	111	4.62	9	3	0	95	4.34	7	6	0	92	4.39	143	5	.238	.273	.364	586	22	.271	.332	.449
1999	SF-N	737	28	.297	.346	.480	7	5	0	93	4.56	8	5	0	92	6.26	7	3	0	89	4.94	8	7	0	95	5.85	148	1	.236	.265	.324	589	27	.312	.365	.520
2000	SF-N	707	23	.290	.345	.458	6	5	0	106	3.15	5	4	0	78	5.06	5	4	0	83	4.23	6	5	0	101	3.74	135	4	.244	.309	.400	572	19	.301	.353	.472
TOTALS		4155	126	.277	.326	.428	39	28	0	546	3.88	42	20	0	529	4.46	34	19	0	488	4.48	47	29	0	586	3.90	785	17	.250	.294	.358	3370	109	.283	.333	.444
● Jeff Russell BR/TR																																				
1983	Cin-N	249	7	.233	.290	.365	1	3	0	26	4.15	3	2	0	42	2.34	0	0	0	0	—	4	5	0	68	3.03	147	4	.231	.288	.367	102	3	.235	.292	.363
1984	Cin-N	707	15	.263	.327	.388	5	3	0	84	3.76	1	15	0	98	4.68	3	8	0	93	3.86	3	10	0	88	4.69	316	6	.282	.351	.411	391	9	.248	.308	.368
1985	Tex-A	262	10	.324	.388	.527	1	4	0	36	8.33	2	2	0	26	6.49	0	0	0	0	—	3	6	0	62	7.55	146	5	.322	.390	.534	116	5	.328	.385	.517
1986	Tex-A	303	11	.244	.315	.396	2	0	1	30	3.30	3	2	1	52	3.46	1	1	0	16	5.17	4	1	2	66	2.98	124	5	.290	.376	.452	179	6	.212	.270	.358
1987	Tex-A	383	9	.285	.369	.418	1	2	2	41	5.71	4	2	1	56	3.51	1	1	2	37	2.95	4	3	1	61	5.34	182	7	.291	.362	.467	201	2	.279	.374	.373
1988	Tex-A	713	15	.257	.324	.356	6	6	0	110	3.75	4	3	0	78	3.91	7	1	0	78	2.99	3	8	0	110	4.40	370	10	.292	.370	.411	343	5	.219	.273	.297
1989	Tex-A	247	4	.182	.260	.279	2	1	24	38	1.64	4	3	14	34	2.36	3	2	18	32	1.95	3	2	20	40	2.01	112	0	.205	.289	.241	135	4	.163	.235	.311
1990	Tex-A	91	1	.253	.361	.363	0	4	6	13	5.54	1	1	4	12	2.92	1	5	8	21	4.71	0	0	2	4	2.08	39	1	.128	.209	.231	52	0	.346	.462	.462
1991	Tex-A	301	11	.236	.295	.365	2	1	18	39	3.00	4	3	12	40	3.57	2	1	15	41	3.27	4	3	15	38	3.32	145	2	.241	.317	.297	156	9	.231	.273	.429
1992	Tex-A	214	3	.238	.313	.332	0	1	14	30	1.21	2	2	14	27	2.67	2	2	19	38	1.66	0	1	9	19	2.41	99	1	.253	.353	.364	115	2	.226	.274	.304
1992	Oak-A	32	0	.125	.200	.156	2	0	2	9	0.00	0	0	0	1	0.00	0	0	0	0	—	2	0	2	10	0.00	11	0	.182	.182	.273	21	0	.095	.208	.095
1993	Bos-A	169	1	.231	.287	.314	0	1	15	23	1.99	1	3	18	24	3.38	0	1	16	24	1.88	1	3	17	23	3.57	92	0	.261	.293	.359	77	1	.195	.281	.260
1994	Bos-A	111	3	.270	.346	.405	0	2	7	13	4.05	0	3	5	15	6.14	0	5	12	27	5.00	0	0	0	1	9.00	48	1	.292	.393	.417	63	2	.254	.310	.397
1994	Cle-A	49	2	.265	.308	.408	0	1	2	5	10.80	1	0	3	8	1.17	0	0	0	0	—	1	1	5	13	4.97	21	1	.333	.364	.524	28	1	.214	.267	.321
1995	Tex-A	130	3	.277	.324	.362	0	0	8	14	4.40	1	0	12	18	1.96	1	0	12	18	3.06	0	0	8	15	3.00	73	2	.274	.312	.356	57	1	.281	.339	.368
1996	Tex-A	216	5	.269	.341	.375	1	2	2	28	3.49	2	1	1	28	3.25	1	1	1	25	4.26	2	2	2	31	2.64	85	2	.329	.400	.459	131	3	.229	.301	.321
TOTALS		4177	100	.255	.324	.376	23	31	101	539	3.84	33	42	85	561	3.66	22	28	103	451	3.30	34	45	83	649	4.06	2010	47	.274	.346	.399	2167	53	.238	.303	.355
● Nolan Ryan BR/TR																																				
1978	Cal-A	832	12	.220	.335	.315	6	7	0	159	3.23	4	6	0	76	4.76	3	6	0	100	4.04	7	7	0	134	3.48	489	4	.231	.340	.313	343	8	.204	.329	.318
1979	Cal-A	799	15	.212	.311	.318	12	4	0	136	2.45	4	10	0	87	5.38	9	5	0	109	2.96	7	9	0	113	4.21	410	7	.229	.332	.334	389	8	.193	.289	.301
1980	Hou-N	867	10	.236	.314	.317	8	2	0	145	2.54	3	8	0	89	4.67	5	5	0	109	2.88	6	5	0	124	3.76	399	3	.221	.307	.281	468	7	.250	.320	.348
1981	Hou-N	528	2	.188	.280	.216	6	2	0	65	1.11	5	3	0	84	2.14	5	3	0	79	1.37	6	2	0	70	2.06	245	0	.155	.273	.171	283	2	.216	.287	.254
1982	Hou-N	920	20	.213	.301	.325	5	6	0	111	3.40	11	6	0	139	2.98	7	8	0	109	4.64	9	4	0	142	2.03	478	9	.209	.294	.308	442	11	.217	.308	.344
1983	Hou-N	686	9	.195	.300	.277	6	6	0	103	2.87	8	3	0	93	3.10	6	1	0	65	2.07	8	8	0	131	3.44	360	4	.200	.324	.267	326	5	.190	.272	.288
1984	Hou-N	676	12	.212	.286	.305	5	5	0	79	2.16	7	6	0	105	3.70	7	2	0	88	1.83	5	9	0	95	4.15	324	4	.188	.272	.256	352	8	.233	.299	.349
1985	Hou-N	856	12	.239	.318	.339	7	3	0	135	3.14	3	9	0	97	4.72	8	5	0	121	3.19	2	7	0	111	4.47	415	5	.246	.317	.337	441	7	.234	.319	.340
1986	Hou-N	635	14	.187	.283	.313	9	4	0	109	2.56	3	4	0	69	4.57	4	6	0	77	4.70	8	2	0	101	2.31	311	4	.186	.298	.283	324	10	.188	.267	.343
1987	Hou-N	771	14	.200	.284	.292	5	7	0	114	2.21	3	9	0	98	3.41	4	8	0	97	3.35	4	8	0	115	2.27	408	6	.213	.301	.289	363	8	.185	.265	.295
1988	Hou-N	818	18	.227	.304	.347	7	4	0	105	2.91	5	7	0	115	4.08	5	6	0	110	4.40	7	5	0	110	2.63	438	8	.215	.301	.315	380	10	.242	.308	.384
1989	Tex-A	867	17	.187	.275	.283	9	6	0	139	3.68	7	4	0	100	2.52	9	4	0	118	3.14	7	6	0	122	3.25	446	8	.177	.261	.262	421	9	.197	.289	.304
1990	Tex-A	729	18	.188	.267	.322	8	5	0	130	3.32	5	4	0	74	3.65	7	4	0	78	3.94	6	5	0	126	3.13	362	8	.218	.305	.356	367	10	.158	.230	.289
1991	Tex-A	594	12	.172	.263	.285	10	4	0	132	3.08	2	2	0	41	2.40	4	4	0	83	2.71	8	2	0	90	3.10	345	5	.183	.257	.281	249	7	.157	.271	.289
1992	Tex-A	580	9	.238	.328	.341	3	6	0	93	3.40	2	3	0	65	4.18	1	3	0	61	4.15	4	6	0	97	3.44	294	5	.245	.339	.364	286	4	.231	.316	.318
1993	Tex-A	246	5	.220	.329	.341	4	2	0	39	4.12	1	3	0	27	6.00	1	2	0	14	4.50	4	3	0	52	4.99	133	2	.188	.339	.278	113	3	.257	.315	.416
TOTALS		11404	199	.209	.299	.309	110	73	0	1794	2.91	73	87	0	1358	3.79	85	72	0	1418	3.33	98	88	0	1734	3.25	5857	82	.209	.304	.297	5547	117	.209	.293	.322
● Bret Saberhagen BR/TR																																				
1984	KC-A	583	13	.237	.281	.364	4	5	1	78	2.20	6	6	0	80	4.72	2	7	0	82	3.31	8	4	1	76	3.67	289	10	.256	.304	.429	294	3	.218	.259	.299
1985	KC-A	876	19	.241	.271	.357	10	3	0	129	2.80	10	3	0	107	2.95	7	4	0	100	3.23	13	2	0	135	2.60	501	14	.242	.280	.363	375	5	.240	.260	.349
1986	KC-A	615	15	.268	.302	.402	2	5	0	76	3.67	5	7	0	80	4.61	4	9	0	102	4.13	3	3	0	54	4.19	368	8	.253	.288	.394	247	7	.291	.323	.413
1987	KC-A	975	27	.252	.294	.400	11	4	0	138	3.58	7	6	0	119	3.11	13	2	0	125	2.17	5	8	0	132	4.49	512	14	.242	.290	.391	463	13	.263	.298	.410
1988	KC-A	1008	18	.269	.309	.400	6	9	0	130	4.36	8	7	0	131	3.24	10	6	0	132	3.34	4	10	0	129	4.27	530	6	.245	.299	.343	478	12	.295	.320	.462
1989	KC-A	961	13	.217	.251	.317	11	1	0	131	1.71	12	5	0	131	2.61	7	4	0	114	2.68	16	2	0	148	1.76	524	8	.195	.236	.290	437	5	.245	.270	.350
1990	KC-A	524	9	.279	.314	.387	3	5	0	74	3.42	2	4	0	61	3.08	5	7	0	116	2.96	0	2	0	19	5.12	222	5	.275	.318	.405	302	4	.281	.311	.374
1991	KC-A	724	12	.228	.280	.327	7	3	0	95	2.76	6	5	0	102	3.36	6	3	0	91	2.96	7	5	0	105	3.17	354	9	.215	.270	.333	370	3	.241	.290	.322
1992	NY-N	360	6	.233	.292	.344	1	2	0	60	2.41	2	3	0	38	5.21	3	2	0	52	3.81	0	3	0	46	3.15	212	3	.226	.292	.344	148	3	.243	.291	.345
1993	NY-N	524	11	.250	.275	.366	3	3	0	60	2.41	4	4	0	80	3.95	4	7	0	109	3.22	3	0	0	30	3.56	250	7	.264	.298	.412	274	4	.237	.253	.325
1994	NY-N	665	13	.254	.271	.389	4	2	0	61	2.93	10	2	0	116	2.64	8	4	0	113	3.43	6	0	0	65	1.53	366	6	.238	.256	.377	299	7	.274	.289	.405
1995	NY-N	419	13	.251	.291	.403	3	2	0	61	3.39	2	3	0	49	3.31	5	2	0	86	3.24	0	3	0	24	3.75	190	4	.205	.250	.332	229	9	.288	.325	.463
1995	Col-N	186	8	.323	.382	.527	1	1	0	23	8.74	1	0	0	20	3.54	0	0	0	0	—	2	1	0	43	6.28	87	4	.299	.344	.529	99	4	.343	.414	.525
1997	Bos-A	104	5	.288	.353	.548	0	0	0	10	2.70	0	1	0	16	9.00	0	0	0	0	—	0	1	0	26	6.58	61	4	.328	.397	.656	43	1	.233	.283	.395
1998	Bos-A	685	22	.264	.299	.422	7	3	0	83	3.89	8	5	0	92	4.03	9	5	0	78	5.10	6	3	0	97	3.05	364	12	.299	.337	.467	321	10	.224	.255	.371
1999	Bos-A	461	11	.265	.284	.414	4	5	0	65	2.49	6	1	0	54	3.50	4	2	0	49	2.02	6	4	0	70	3.60	210	3	.276	.285	.405	251	8	.255	.282	.422
TOTALS		9670	215	.252	.288	.381	77	53	1	1273	3.14	89	62	0	1275	3.52	87	64	0	1349	3.23	79	51	1	1199	3.44	5040	117	.245	.287	.379	4630	98	.259	.290	.384
● Scott Sanderson BR/TR																																				
1978	Mon-N	224	3	.232	.298	.304	2	1	0	30	1.50	2	1	0	31	3.48	0	0	0	0	—	4	2	0	61	2.51	128	1	.242	.305	.297	96	2	.219	.290	.313
1979	Mon-N	627	16	.236	.297	.372	6	2	0	84	3.21	3	6	1	84	3.64	5	4	0	91	3.25	4	4	1	77	3.64	307	10	.251	.321	.401	320	6	.222	.273	.344
1980	Mon-N	800	18	.257	.307	.384	7	4	0	114	1.97	9	7	0	97	4.45	7	4	0	83	2.82	9	7	0	128	3.30	370	7	.268	.331	.414	430	11	.249	.285	.358
1981	Mon-N	517	10	.236	.278	.348	8	3	0	98	1.74	1	4	0	39	5.95	6	2	0	71	2.17	3	5	0	67	3.78	260	6	.250	.285	.381	257	4	.222	.272	.315

		TOTAL					HOME					AWAY					1ST HALF					2ND HALF					LEFT					RIGHT				
YEAR	TM/L	AB	HR	AVG	OBP	SLG	W	L	SV	IP	ERA	W	L	SV	IP	ERA	W	L	SV	IP	ERA	W	L	SV	IP	ERA	AB	HR	AVG	OBP	SLG	AB	HR	AVG	OBP	SLG
1982	Mon-N	846	24	.251	.299	.405	6	9	0	136	3.85	6	3	0	88	2.85	6	5	0	103	2.88	6	7	0	121	3.94	438	13	.244	.295	.393	408	11	.257	.303	.419
1983	Mon-N	323	12	.303	.343	.477	2	4	1	35	5.35	4	3	0	46	4.11	4	6	0	58	4.97	2	1	1	23	3.86	157	6	.293	.339	.478	166	6	.313	.347	.476
1984	Chi-N	531	5	.264	.294	.354	3	2	0	54	3.17	5	3	0	87	3.12	4	1	0	53	2.72	4	4	0	88	3.39	282	2	.227	.266	.309	249	3	.305	.326	.406
1985	Chi-N	439	13	.228	.268	.405	3	3	0	69	3.25	2	3	0	52	2.96	4	3	0	94	2.19	1	3	0	27	6.41	251	10	.243	.296	.470	188	3	.207	.231	.319
1986	Chi-N	647	21	.255	.295	.420	7	5	0	94	3.54	2	6	1	76	5.00	3	5	0	81	4.44	6	6	1	89	3.96	358	13	.260	.296	.439	289	8	.249	.295	.398
1987	Chi-N	569	23	.274	.333	.469	3	4	1	58	4.99	5	5	1	87	3.83	3	4	0	62	4.96	5	5	2	83	3.80	325	11	.292	.364	.471	244	12	.250	.290	.467
1988	Chi-N	56	1	.232	.258	.375	0	2	0	8	7.87	1	0	0	7	2.45	0	0	0	0	—	1	2	0	15	5.28	27	0	.259	.267	.333	29	1	.207	.250	.414
1989	Chi-N	566	16	.274	.312	.413	6	3	0	70	3.75	5	6	0	77	4.11	7	6	0	87	3.61	4	3	0	59	4.42	341	8	.293	.335	.422	225	8	.244	.277	.400
1990	Oak-A	803	27	.255	.312	.422	6	7	0	97	3.17	11	4	0	110	4.51	9	4	0	90	3.51	8	7	0	117	4.17	402	13	.234	.300	.391	401	14	.277	.325	.454
1991	NY-A	795	22	.252	.279	.405	7	6	0	93	4.66	9	4	0	115	3.12	8	3	0	93	3.69	8	7	0	115	3.90	437	15	.261	.290	.437	358	7	.240	.265	.366
1992	NY-A	769	28	.286	.340	.464	5	6	0	97	5.47	7	5	0	96	4.39	7	5	0	102	4.49	5	6	0	91	5.44	367	13	.300	.362	.466	402	15	.274	.319	.463
1993	Cal-A	530	15	.289	.325	.442	3	3	0	55	5.43	4	8	0	81	3.79	7	8	0	106	3.91	0	3	0	29	6.44	259	8	.270	.318	.417	271	7	.306	.331	.465
1993	SF-N	188	12	.255	.283	.468	2	2	0	31	3.82	2	0	0	18	3.00	0	0	0	0	—	4	2	0	49	3.51	97	9	.278	.317	.577	91	3	.231	.245	.352
1994	Chi-A	371	20	.296	.321	.534	4	1	0	35	3.34	4	3	0	57	6.16	7	2	0	72	3.48	1	2	0	20	10.98	173	10	.324	.361	.578	198	10	.273	.286	.495
1995	Cal-A	161	6	.298	.320	.497	1	1	0	24	3.04	0	2	0	16	5.74	1	3	0	39	4.12	0	0	0	0	—	89	3	.258	.272	.449	72	3	.347	.377	.556
1996	Cal-A	90	5	.433	.464	.667	0	1	0	8	5.87	0	1	0	10	8.71	0	2	0	18	7.50	0	0	0	0	—	34	3	.441	.472	.735	56	2	.429	.459	.625
TOTALS		9852	297	.263	.307	.418	81	69	2	1288	3.63	82	74	3	1274	4.05	88	67	0	1304	3.59	75	76	5	1258	4.10	5102	161	.265	.315	.426	4750	136	.260	.298	.410
● Curt Schilling	BR/TR																																			
1988	Bal-A	62	3	.355	.434	.645	0	1	0	11	6.55	0	2	0	4	19.64	0	0	0	0	—	0	3	0	15	9.82	30	2	.367	.400	.767	32	1	.344	.463	.531
1989	Bal-A	35	2	.286	.342	.486	0	1	0	6	9.53	0	0	0	3	0.00	0	0	0	0	—	0	1	0	9	6.23	15	1	.267	.267	.533	20	1	.300	.391	.450
1990	Bal-A	166	1	.229	.302	.301	1	1	2	28	3.25	0	1	1	18	1.47	0	0	1	2	0.00	1	2	2	44	2.68	65	0	.308	.378	.369	101	1	.178	.252	.257
1991	Hou-N	291	2	.271	.356	.364	3	3	3	47	3.64	0	2	5	29	4.08	3	5	5	33	4.86	0	0	3	42	2.98	149	1	.255	.367	.342	142	1	.289	.344	.387
1992	Phi-N	819	11	.201	.254	.288	8	6	0	130	2.21	6	5	2	96	2.53	6	5	2	92	2.55	8	6	0	135	2.21	456	7	.197	.259	.289	363	4	.207	.247	.287
1993	Phi-N	905	23	.259	.303	.392	9	4	0	113	3.90	7	3	0	122	4.12	8	3	0	116	3.48	8	4	0	119	4.54	495	13	.257	.307	.398	410	10	.261	.298	.385
1994	Phi-N	322	10	.270	.333	.410	1	4	0	42	3.67	1	4	0	41	5.31	0	7	0	55	5.40	2	1	0	27	2.63	160	3	.250	.301	.363	162	7	.290	.365	.457
1995	Phi-N	437	12	.220	.267	.343	1	4	0	48	3.94	6	1	0	68	3.31	5	3	0	91	3.26	2	2	0	25	4.68	172	8	.238	.303	.413	265	4	.208	.243	.298
1996	Phi-N	669	16	.223	.278	.359	4	5	0	80	3.05	5	5	0	104	3.30	2	3	0	64	3.11	7	7	0	120	3.23	296	7	.213	.271	.351	373	9	.231	.284	.365
1997	Phi-N	930	25	.224	.271	.372	7	6	0	145	2.80	10	5	0	110	3.20	9	7	0	125	3.46	8	4	0	129	2.51	455	16	.235	.290	.413	475	9	.213	.252	.333
1998	Phi-N	1000	23	.236	.282	.373	8	7	0	122	2.88	7	7	0	147	3.56	7	8	0	138	3.07	8	6	0	131	3.44	497	12	.249	.304	.400	503	11	.223	.260	.346
1999	Phi-N	672	25	.237	.287	.396	7	4	0	99	4.10	8	2	0	82	2.87	11	4	0	134	3.23	4	2	0	47	4.44	337	12	.246	.289	.404	335	13	.227	.286	.388
2000	Phi-N	435	17	.253	.305	.432	3	3	0	56	3.36	3	3	0	56	4.47	3	4	0	73	4.83	3	2	0	40	2.25	213	7	.254	.304	.427	222	10	.252	.305	.437
2000	Ari-N	366	10	.257	.280	.399	3	3	0	54	3.50	2	3	0	44	3.92	0	0	0	0	—	5	6	0	98	3.69	215	3	.233	.252	.330	151	7	.291	.319	.497
TOTALS		7109	180	.237	.288	.372	55	52	5	980	3.31	55	43	8	922	3.55	54	49	8	923	3.50	56	46	5	979	3.35	3555	92	.240	.295	.381	3554	88	.235	.282	.364
● Mike Scott	BR/TR																																			
1979	NY-N	204	4	.289	.351	.387	1	1	0	35	3.09	0	2	0	17	9.87	1	1	0	41	4.39	0	2	0	11	8.74	96	3	.333	.414	.448	108	1	.250	.289	.333
1980	NY-N	121	1	.331	.369	.421	1	0	0	17	2.65	0	1	0	12	6.57	0	0	0	0	—	1	1	0	29	4.30	73	1	.356	.397	.493	48	0	.292	.327	.313
1981	NY-N	499	11	.261	.306	.405	3	6	0	54	4.50	2	4	0	82	3.51	3	4	0	70	4.24	2	6	0	66	3.55	258	7	.302	.339	.473	241	4	.216	.271	.332
1982	NY-N	576	13	.321	.381	.460	4	3	1	71	3.91	3	10	2	76	6.30	5	5	3	85	4.66	2	8	0	62	5.81	291	10	.340	.402	.522	285	3	.302	.359	.396
1983	Hou-N	555	8	.258	.318	.357	5	5	0	81	3.56	5	1	0	64	3.94	4	3	0	63	3.16	6	3	0	82	4.15	288	4	.247	.313	.365	267	4	.270	.322	.348
1984	Hou-N	609	7	.294	.338	.392	4	5	0	79	3.89	1	6	0	75	5.50	4	5	0	80	4.82	1	6	0	74	4.52	291	2	.289	.339	.395	318	5	.299	.337	.390
1985	Hou-N	827	20	.235	.302	.363	11	2	0	120	2.18	7	6	0	102	4.60	6	4	0	104	3.04	12	4	0	118	3.51	429	3	.217	.289	.289	398	17	.254	.317	.442
1986	Hou-N	976	17	.186	.242	.291	10	8	0	151	2.20	8	2	0	124	2.25	7	5	0	138	2.35	11	5	0	137	2.10	508	6	.215	.282	.307	468	11	.156	.198	.274
1987	Hou-N	916	21	.217	.281	.331	10	3	0	123	2.20	6	10	0	125	4.26	9	4	0	125	2.44	7	9	0	122	4.05	513	9	.234	.299	.333	403	12	.196	.259	.328
1988	Hou-N	793	19	.204	.260	.325	7	3	0	99	2.09	7	5	0	120	3.61	8	2	0	109	2.96	6	6	0	109	2.88	405	10	.185	.260	.311	388	9	.224	.260	.340
1989	Hou-N	848	23	.212	.267	.344	12	6	0	134	3.03	8	4	0	95	3.21	13	4	0	129	2.45	7	6	0	100	3.95	482	14	.247	.298	.392	366	9	.167	.227	.281
1990	Hou-N	789	27	.246	.302	.403	5	4	0	130	2.42	4	9	0	76	6.19	6	7	0	103	4.28	3	6	0	103	3.33	445	10	.238	.302	.366	344	17	.256	.302	.451
1991	Hou-N	30	2	.367	.457	.667	0	1	0	3	15.00	0	1	0	4	11.25	0	2	0	7	12.86	0	0	0	0	—	12	0	.417	.500	.583	18	2	.333	.429	.722
TOTALS		7743	173	.240	.297	.363	73	47	1	1097	2.83	51	61	2	972	4.33	66	46	3	1054	3.39	58	62	0	1015	3.69	4091	79	.249	.311	.369	3652	94	.230	.282	.356
● Tom Seaver	BR/TR																																			
1978	Cin-N	961	26	.227	.289	.366	6	8	0	119	3.34	10	6	0	141	2.49	9	5	0	116	3.27	7	9	0	144	2.56	415	9	.224	.304	.354	546	17	.229	.277	.375
1979	Cin-N	791	16	.236	.289	.350	8	2	0	107	2.95	8	4	0	108	3.32	6	5	0	93	3.77	10	1	0	122	2.66	359	5	.237	.290	.334	432	11	.236	.288	.363
1980	Cin-N	621	24	.225	.290	.391	6	3	0	73	4.09	4	5	0	95	3.30	3	5	0	81	4.76	7	3	0	87	2.60	301	8	.206	.279	.342	320	16	.244	.301	.438
1981	Cin-N	585	10	.205	.285	.320	7	1	0	97	2.50	7	1	0	69	2.61	7	1	0	87	2.06	7	1	0	79	3.08	306	4	.232	.310	.346	279	6	.176	.258	.290
1982	Cin-N	450	14	.302	.367	.500	3	6	0	44	5.93	2	7	0	67	5.21	4	8	0	79	5.13	1	5	0	32	6.40	219	5	.269	.346	.447	231	9	.333	.387	.550
1983	NY-N	856	18	.235	.305	.342	6	7	0	132	3.28	3	7	0	99	3.90	5	7	0	112	3.22	4	7	0	119	3.85	424	5	.226	.302	.307	432	13	.243	.308	.377
1984	Chi-A	900	27	.240	.288	.384	9	4	0	126	3.64	6	7	0	111	4.31	6	6	0	103	4.12	9	5	0	134	3.83	473	15	.220	.275	.368	427	12	.262	.302	.403
1985	Chi-A	901	22	.248	.304	.374	5	6	0	103	4.35	11	5	0	135	2.26	7	6	0	113	3.28	9	5	0	126	3.07	466	10	.249	.314	.363	435	12	.246	.293	.386
1986	Chi-A	273	9	.242	.319	.410	1	4	0	42	5.10	1	2	0	30	3.34	2	6	0	72	4.38	0	0	0	0	—	129	4	.264	.345	.473	144	5	.222	.296	.354
1986	Bos-A	410	8	.278	.326	.395	2	3	0	39	4.15	3	4	0	65	3.58	0	0	0	0	—	5	7	0	104	3.80	219	4	.288	.336	.416	191	4	.267	.314	.372
TOTALS		6748	174	.240	.301	.376	53	44	0	882	3.66	55	48	0	921	3.32	49	49	0	855	3.70	59	43	0	948	3.30	3311	69	.236	.304	.362	3437	105	.244	.298	.388
● Aaron Sele	BR/TR																																			
1993	Bos-A	422	5	.237	.322	.334	4	2	0	58	2.81	3	0	0	54	2.67	1	0	0	13	1.42	6	2	0	99	2.91	216	2	.227	.327	.310	206	3	.248	.316	.359
1994	Bos-A	536	13	.261	.343	.381	5	5	0	88	4.11	3	2	0	56	3.40	6	4	0	100	3.78	2	3	0	43	3.95	270	8	.293	.383	.452	266	5	.229	.300	.308
1995	Bos-A	127	3	.252	.338	.378	1	1	0	12	2.25	2	0	0	20	3.54	3	1	0	32	3.06	0	0	0	0	—	60	2	.317	.408	.517	67	1	.194	.270	.254
1996	Bos-A	634	14	.303	.373	.431	3	5	0	65	6.37	4	6	0	92	4.58	2	5	0	81	6.22	5	6	0	76	4.36	339	9	.322	.394	.481	295	5	.281	.348	.373
1997	Bos-A	703	25	.279	.361	.461	8	6	0	102	4.49	5	6	0	75	6.60	9	6	0	91	5.54	4	6	0	86	5.21	378	15	.325	.403	.534	325	10	.225	.313	.375
1998	Tex-A	845	14	.283	.354	.402	13	5	0	116	3.64	6	6	0	96	4.95	11	5	0	112	4.26	8	6	0	101	4.20	430	8	.293	.372	.430	415	6	.272	.335	.373
1999	Tex-A	834	21	.293	.355	.447	11	5	0	125	4.69	7	4	0	80	4.93	7	6	0	90	5.42	11	3	0	115	4.29	399	11	.286	.343	.444	435	10	.299	.365	.451
2000	Sea-A	816	17	.271	.332	.397	9	5	0	109	4.03	8	5	0	102	5.01	9	3	0	100	4.32	8	7	0	112	4.67	442	10	.276	.346	.410	374	7	.265	.315	.382
TOTALS		4917	112	.277	.350	.412	54	34	0	675	4.25	38	29	0	576	4.70	48	30	0	619	4.68	44	33	0	633	4.24	2534	65	.292	.369	.445	2383	47	.261	.328	.377
● Jeff Shaw	BR/TR																																			
1990	Cle-A	205	11	.356	.408	.605	2	3	0	34	7.34	1	1	0	14	5.02	1	1	0	24	5.92	2	3	0	24	7.40	118	4	.356	.408	.534	87	7	.356	.408	.701
1991	Cle-A	275	6	.262	.332	.371	0	3	1	41	2.61	0	2	0	31	4.35	0	1	1	12	5.11	0	4	0	60	3.00	105	2	.286	.347	.381	170	4	.247	.323	.365
1992	Cle-A	27	2	.259	.355	.481	0	1	0	8	8.22	0	0	0	0	—	0	1	0	8	8.22	0	0	0	0	—	11	1	.364	.462	.636	16	1	.188	.278	.375
1993	Mon-N	358	12	.254	.326	.422	1	3	0	56	3.07	1	4	0	40	5.63	1	4	0	53	3.93	1	3	0	43	4.40	173	7	.312	.383	.497	185	5	.200	.271	.351
1994	Mon-N	264	8	.254	.295	.402	1	0	0	33	4.64	4	2	1	34	3.15	4	2	0	49	3.88	1	0	1	19	3.86	101	4	.267	.327	.436	163	4	.245	.273	.380
1995	Mon-N	232	4	.250	.332	.384	1	4	2	28	5.08	0	2	1	34	4.24	1	4	2	36	4.95	0	2	1	26	4.15	108	1	.287	.361	.370	124	3	.218	.307	.395
1995	Chi-A	38	2	.316	.350	.553	0	0	0	7	8.10	0	0	0	3	3.00	0	0	0	0	—	0	0	0	10	6.52	11	1	.364	.364	.636	27	1	.296	.345	.519
1996	Cin-N	393	8	.252	.303	.372	6	2	3	48	2.08	2	4	1	57	2.84	2	3	2	42	3.24	6	3	2	63	2.00	158	2	.190	.275	.272	235	6	.294	.324	.438
1997	Cin-N	348	7	.227	.253	.336	2	1	24	52	1.90	2	1	18	43	2.95	2	0	16	54	1.49	2	2	26	40	3.57	177	2	.243	.272	.339	171	5	.211	.233	.333
1998	Cin-N	173	2	.231	.282	.295	1	1	11	22	2.08	1	3	12	28	1.61	1	4	22	48	1.89	1	0	1	2	0.00	83	1	.193	.272	.265	90	1	.267	.292	.322
1998	LA-N	139	6	.252	.288	.403	1	2	17	24	1.88	0	2	8	11	3.97	0	0	0	0	—	1	4	25	35	2.55	66	2	.273	.333	.394	73	4	.233	.243	.411
1999	LA-N	265	6	.242	.283	.343	2	3	15	35	3.57	0	1	19	33	1.93	1	2	18	35	2.31	1	2	16	33	3.27	134	3	.201	.245	.291	131	3	.282	.321	.397
2000	LA-N	230	7	.265	.316	.435	3	2	12	34	3.93	0	2	15	23	4.70	2	4	12	27	8.00	1	0	15	30	0.89	113	3	.301	.352	.478	117	4	.231	.280	.393
TOTALS		2947	81	.257	.310	.396	20	25	85	422	3.54	11	24	75	351	3.54	15	26	73	388	3.74	16	23	87	386	3.34	1358	33	.265	.325	.391	1589	48	.250	.298	.400
● Eric Show	BR/TR																																			
1981	SD-N	80	2	.213	.300	.325	1	1	1	14	1.29	0	2	2	9	6.00	0	0	0	0	—	1	3	3	23	3.13	25	1	.240	.367	.360	55	1	.200	.267	.309
1982	SD-N	539	10	.217	.284	.317	4	3	0	67	1.88	6	3	3	83	3.25	7	3	2	52	2.26	3	3	1	98	2.84	254	5	.264	.336	.366	285	5	.175	.237	.274
1983	SD-N	763	25	.263	.332	.402	10	3	0	119	3.72	5	9	0	82	4.83	8	5	0	104	3.04	7	7	0	97	5.38	397	10	.272	.339	.388	366	15	.254	.324	.418
1984	SD-N	748	18	.234	.316	.349	6	5	0	91	3.77	9	4	0	116	3.10	8	5	0	109	3.70	7	4	0	97	3.05	373	8	.273	.368	.386	375	10	.195	.262	.312
1985	SD-N	871	27	.243	.314	.387	6	5	0	107	3.52	6	6	0	126	2.72	6	5	0	102	3.34	6	6	0	131	2.89	464	16	.287	.362	.453	407	11	.194	.259	.312
1986	SD-N	484	11	.225	.326	.329	5	3	0	78	2.78	4	2	0	59	3.22	6	4	0	106	2.72	3	1	0	30	3.86	272	4	.250	.357	.342	212	7	.193	.285	.311
1987	SD-N	778	26	.242	.322	.404	5	6	0	112	2.73	3	10	0	94	5.15	3	9	0	103	3.93	5	7	0	103	3.75	430	13	.247	.327	.405	348	13	.236	.315	.402
1988	SD-N	869	22	.231	.279	.360	8	5	0	126	2.85	8	6	0	108	3.74	6	8	0	106	3.83	10	3	0	129	2.79	462	10	.253	.316	.392	407	12	.206	.234	.324
1989	SD-N	412	9	.274	.336	.434	4	3	0	56	4.37	4	3	0	51	4.09	8	6	0	106	4.23	0	0	0	0	—	234	4	.269	.345	.427	178	5	.281	.325	.444

YEAR	TM/L	TOTAL AB	HR	AVG	OBP	SLG	HOME W	L	SV	IP	ERA	AWAY W	L	SV	IP	ERA	1ST HALF W	L	SV	IP	ERA	2ND HALF W	L	SV	IP	ERA	LEFT AB	HR	AVG	OBP	SLG	RIGHT AB	HR	AVG	OBP	SLG
1990	SD-N	428	16	.306	.369	.472	3	5	0	51	6.22	3	3	1	56	5.34	0	6	0	41	7.84	6	2	1	65	4.43	232	8	.310	.389	.474	196	8	.301	.344	.469
1991	Oak-A	207	5	.300	.346	.464	0	2	0	26	6.84	1	0	0	25	4.97	0	0	0	9	16.39	1	2	0	42	3.61	95	4	.358	.436	.621	112	1	.250	.263	.330
TOTALS		6179	171	.247	.317	.383	52	41	1	846	3.46	49	48	6	809	3.87	52	51	2	839	3.82	49	38	5	816	3.49	3238	83	.271	.349	.410	2941	88	.221	.281	.353
● Paul Shuey BR/TR																																				
1994	Cle-A	50	1	.280	.419	.440	0	0	3	7	6.43	0	1	2	5	11.57	0	1	5	12	8.49	0	0	0	0	—	24	0	.292	.485	.417	26	1	.269	.345	.462
1995	Cle-A	21	0	.238	.385	.333	0	1	0	1	6.75	0	1	0	5	3.60	0	1	0	3	2.70	0	1	0	3	6.00	11	0	.273	.429	.455	10	0	.200	.333	.200
1996	Cle-A	195	6	.231	.317	.359	4	1	2	29	2.20	1	1	2	25	3.60	2	1	1	16	4.96	3	1	3	37	1.93	93	1	.237	.336	.301	102	5	.225	.298	.412
1997	Cle-A	177	5	.294	.389	.429	3	1	0	28	6.18	1	1	2	17	6.23	2	1	2	23	5.16	2	1	0	22	7.25	68	1	.235	.369	.294	109	4	.330	.403	.514
1998	Cle-A	192	6	.229	.327	.370	1	2	1	27	3.29	4	2	1	24	2.66	0	0	0	10	0.87	5	4	2	41	3.54	86	2	.233	.333	.360	106	4	.226	.322	.377
1999	Cle-A	305	8	.223	.314	.364	5	3	5	45	4.43	3	2	1	37	2.43	5	2	4	39	2.79	3	3	2	43	4.19	139	3	.223	.321	.353	166	5	.223	.309	.373
2000	Cle-A	233	4	.219	.312	.313	2	1	0	36	3.03	2	1	0	28	3.86	3	1	0	22	2.82	1	1	0	41	3.70	118	2	.203	.319	.288	115	2	.235	.305	.339
TOTALS		1173	30	.238	.334	.367	15	9	11	172	3.97	11	9	8	141	3.77	12	7	12	125	3.88	14	11	7	188	3.88	539	9	.228	.342	.328	634	21	.246	.327	.399
● Bill Simas BL/TR																																				
1995	Chi-A	55	1	.273	.394	.364	1	0	0	8	2.35	0	1	0	6	2.84	0	0	0	0	—	1	1	0	14	2.57	15	0	.200	.368	.333	40	1	.300	.404	.375
1996	Chi-A	283	5	.265	.358	.406	1	3	0	39	5.03	1	5	2	33	4.05	0	4	1	42	3.64	2	4	1	31	5.87	118	1	.271	.383	.381	165	4	.261	.339	.424
1997	Chi-A	165	6	.279	.375	.436	1	0	0	21	4.64	2	1	1	20	3.60	3	0	1	33	4.59	0	1	0	8	2.25	54	3	.296	.397	.519	111	3	.270	.364	.396
1998	Chi-A	262	12	.206	.270	.389	4	2	11	40	3.83	0	1	7	31	3.23	3	3	3	34	2.91	1	0	15	37	4.17	123	8	.220	.314	.472	139	4	.194	.228	.317
1999	Chi-A	278	6	.263	.347	.410	0	2	1	33	4.05	6	1	1	39	3.49	2	2	2	34	4.46	4	1	0	38	3.11	124	1	.258	.359	.347	154	5	.266	.337	.461
2000	Chi-A	250	9	.276	.332	.452	0	1	0	34	3.18	2	2	0	34	3.74	1	1	0	40	2.90	1	2	0	27	4.28	94	5	.287	.364	.511	156	4	.269	.312	.417
TOTALS		1293	39	.257	.337	.415	7	8	12	176	4.05	11	11	11	163	3.60	9	10	7	184	3.67	9	9	16	154	4.02	528	18	.259	.359	.430	765	21	.255	.322	.404
● Mike Sirotka BL/TL																																				
1995	Chi-A	131	2	.298	.371	.405	0	1	0	12	3.09	1	1	0	23	4.76	0	0	0	0	—	1	2	0	34	4.19	21	0	.333	.364	.429	110	2	.291	.372	.400
1996	Chi-A	108	3	.315	.377	.537	1	2	0	18	5.50	0	0	0	8	10.80	0	1	0	8	8.64	1	1	0	18	6.50	32	0	.219	.235	.313	76	3	.355	.432	.632
1997	Chi-A	124	4	.290	.323	.435	3	0	0	20	2.75	0	0	0	12	1.46	0	0	0	0	—	3	0	0	32	2.25	26	0	.269	.321	.308	98	4	.296	.324	.469
1998	Chi-A	850	30	.300	.336	.469	7	6	0	103	5.05	7	9	0	108	5.07	8	7	0	113	4.92	6	8	0	98	5.22	188	7	.330	.360	.527	662	23	.292	.329	.453
1999	Chi-A	835	24	.283	.327	.418	7	7	0	110	3.60	4	6	0	99	4.45	6	8	0	98	3.32	5	5	0	111	4.61	188	7	.266	.298	.426	647	17	.287	.336	.416
2000	Chi-A	755	23	.269	.330	.405	8	5	0	109	3.56	7	5	0	88	4.08	7	6	0	90	4.01	8	4	0	107	3.61	177	7	.311	.382	.475	578	16	.256	.313	.384
TOTALS		2803	86	.286	.334	.435	26	21	0	371	4.02	19	21	0	339	4.62	21	22	0	309	4.25	24	20	0	401	4.35	632	21	.297	.341	.459	2171	65	.283	.333	.428
● Heathcliff Slocumb BR/TR																																				
1991	Chi-N	229	3	.231	.321	.323	2	0	1	33	3.00	0	1	0	30	3.94	1	1	1	40	2.25	1	0	0	23	5.56	107	3	.290	.361	.439	122	0	.180	.288	.221
1992	Chi-N	148	3	.351	.430	.432	0	2	1	20	4.58	0	1	0	16	8.82	0	1	1	11	5.91	0	2	0	25	6.75	75	3	.413	.506	.533	73	0	.288	.349	.329
1993	Chi-N	37	0	.189	.262	.216	0	0	0	4	9.00	1	0	0	7	0.00	1	0	0	11	3.38	0	0	0	0	—	16	0	.188	.235	.188	21	0	.190	.280	.238
1993	Cle-A	103	3	.272	.364	.379	1	0	0	18	1.02	2	1	0	10	10.24	2	1	0	20	2.66	1	0	0	7	9.00	29	1	.276	.436	.379	74	2	.270	.329	.378
1994	Phi-N	286	0	.262	.328	.315	1	0	0	35	3.12	4	1	0	38	2.63	4	1	0	53	2.73	1	0	0	20	3.20	126	0	.238	.324	.262	160	0	.281	.331	.356
1995	Phi-N	249	2	.257	.351	.313	4	1	13	31	3.19	1	5	19	34	2.62	1	0	20	30	0.91	4	6	12	36	4.54	107	0	.224	.331	.243	142	2	.282	.366	.366
1996	Bos-A	306	2	.222	.343	.258	2	3	15	38	4.78	3	2	16	46	1.58	2	5	10	40	3.60	3	0	21	43	2.49	165	1	.285	.405	.303	141	1	.149	.269	.206
1997	Bos-A	186	4	.312	.422	.446	0	1	6	23	5.87	0	4	11	24	5.70	0	3	11	36	6.44	0	2	6	10	3.48	84	0	.274	.413	.321	102	4	.343	.430	.549
1997	Sea-A	108	2	.241	.339	.352	0	3	6	16	4.41	0	1	4	12	3.75	0	0	0	0	—	0	4	10	28	4.13	59	2	.254	.333	.441	49	0	.224	.345	.245
1998	Sea-A	262	5	.275	.379	.401	1	1	1	33	3.58	1	4	2	35	6.94	1	4	3	34	7.94	1	1	0	34	2.67	125	3	.328	.444	.488	137	2	.226	.314	.321
1999	Bal-A	38	2	.395	.531	.684	0	0	0	6	9.95	0	0	0	2	19.29	0	0	0	9	12.46	0	0	0	0	—	17	0	.412	.583	.588	21	2	.381	.480	.762
1999	StL-N	202	3	.243	.342	.337	2	1	0	30	0.00	1	1	2	24	5.32	2	0	0	16	2.81	1	2	2	37	2.17	84	0	.274	.384	.333	118	3	.220	.311	.339
2000	StL-N	188	9	.266	.349	.447	2	1	1	22	6.14	0	2	0	28	4.88	2	3	1	38	4.46	0	0	0	11	8.74	68	6	.324	.407	.618	120	3	.233	.313	.350
2000	SD-N	72	0	.264	.378	.389	0	0	0	9	3.86	0	1	0	10	3.72	0	0	0	0	—	0	1	0	19	3.79	39	0	.256	.333	.308	33	0	.273	.422	.485
TOTALS		2414	38	.263	.360	.358	15	13	44	317	3.75	13	24	54	314	4.41	16	19	47	337	4.11	12	18	51	294	4.05	1101	19	.286	.392	.378	1313	19	.244	.332	.341
● John Smiley BL/TL																																				
1986	Pit-N	38	2	.105	.190	.263	0	0	0	6	1.42	1	0	0	5	6.75	0	0	0	0	—	1	0	0	12	3.86	13	0	.154	.214	.154	25	2	.080	.179	.320
1987	Pit-N	283	7	.244	.354	.389	5	3	2	49	2.77	0	2	2	26	11.28	3	1	2	44	5.98	2	4	2	31	5.46	87	1	.195	.287	.299	196	6	.265	.383	.429
1988	Pit-N	767	15	.241	.284	.355	5	6	0	87	3.61	8	5	0	118	2.98	8	4	0	103	2.87	5	7	0	102	3.63	107	2	.159	.252	.243	660	13	.255	.290	.373
1989	Pit-N	770	22	.226	.273	.349	8	4	0	109	2.64	4	4	0	96	2.99	7	2	0	108	3.09	5	6	0	98	2.49	103	1	.243	.291	.320	667	21	.223	.271	.354
1990	Pit-N	585	15	.275	.317	.426	3	4	0	64	3.80	6	6	0	85	5.27	3	3	0	46	3.35	6	7	0	104	5.21	93	3	.301	.350	.484	492	12	.270	.311	.415
1991	Pit-N	774	17	.251	.292	.381	10	5	0	100	2.98	10	3	0	108	3.17	9	5	0	92	3.24	11	3	0	116	2.95	153	3	.196	.220	.320	621	14	.264	.309	.396
1992	Min-A	886	17	.231	.286	.356	10	4	0	137	2.83	6	5	0	104	3.71	8	3	0	108	3.43	8	6	0	133	3.04	139	1	.259	.316	.367	747	16	.226	.280	.353
1993	Cin-N	409	15	.286	.337	.452	1	5	0	49	4.81	2	4	0	57	6.32	3	9	0	101	5.35	0	0	0	5	11.57	51	1	.275	.383	.412	358	14	.288	.330	.458
1994	Cin-N	615	18	.275	.320	.421	7	4	0	86	3.77	4	6	0	73	3.96	7	8	0	107	3.36	4	2	0	52	4.88	108	3	.250	.325	.361	507	15	.280	.319	.434
1995	Cin-N	659	11	.263	.306	.379	4	4	0	72	4.00	8	1	0	105	3.10	7	1	0	79	3.32	5	4	0	98	3.58	102	4	.225	.298	.392	557	7	.269	.307	.377
1996	Cin-N	808	20	.256	.304	.408	7	7	0	107	3.87	6	7	0	110	3.43	8	6	0	100	4.31	5	8	0	117	3.08	127	4	.276	.329	.528	681	16	.253	.299	.386
1997	Cin-N	470	17	.296	.346	.460	4	4	0	44	7.16	5	6	0	73	4.07	5	10	0	83	6.07	4	0	0	34	3.18	77	2	.364	.395	.506	393	15	.282	.337	.450
1997	Cle-A	148	9	.304	.350	.547	0	2	0	11	9.28	2	2	0	27	4.05	0	0	0	0	—	2	4	0	37	5.54	30	3	.433	.500	.800	118	6	.271	.310	.483
TOTALS		7212	185	.255	.305	.394	64	52	2	920	3.64	62	51	2	988	3.95	68	52	2	970	3.93	58	51	2	938	3.67	1190	28	.248	.309	.388	6022	157	.257	.304	.395
● Bryn Smith BR/TR																																				
1981	Mon-N	50	1	.280	.321	.400	1	0	0	4	0.00	0	0	0	9	4.00	0	0	0	0	—	1	0	0	13	2.77	21	0	.190	.227	.286	29	1	.345	.387	.483
1982	Mon-N	307	5	.264	.311	.381	1	1	1	38	4.93	1	3	2	41	3.51	0	1	1	21	3.92	2	3	2	59	4.30	126	2	.270	.333	.389	181	3	.260	.296	.376
1983	Mon-N	572	13	.248	.305	.372	3	6	1	86	1.78	3	5	2	69	3.38	1	3	3	49	2.22	5	8	0	107	2.62	281	5	.278	.326	.413	291	8	.220	.286	.333
1984	Mon-N	688	15	.259	.312	.385	4	8	0	94	3.06	8	5	0	85	3.60	6	6	0	98	3.02	6	7	0	81	3.68	348	8	.273	.334	.402	340	7	.244	.288	.368
1985	Mon-N	831	12	.232	.268	.330	11	2	0	112	2.32	7	3	0	110	3.52	9	3	0	101	3.11	9	2	0	121	2.75	417	1	.240	.267	.312	414	11	.225	.269	.348
1986	Mon-N	723	15	.252	.316	.380	5	3	0	86	3.75	5	5	0	101	4.10	5	5	0	101	3.91	5	3	0	86	3.98	409	8	.286	.354	.421	314	7	.207	.265	.328
1987	Mon-N	598	16	.274	.310	.410	6	3	0	82	4.50	4	6	0	68	4.21	5	3	0	60	5.73	5	6	0	91	3.47	347	8	.259	.293	.372	251	8	.295	.333	.462
1988	Mon-N	736	15	.243	.282	.356	7	2	0	87	2.37	5	8	0	111	3.50	5	5	0	92	4.12	7	5	0	106	2.03	378	6	.259	.300	.360	358	9	.226	.263	.352
1989	Mon-N	794	16	.223	.274	.335	5	5	0	125	2.73	5	6	0	90	2.99	7	3	0	107	2.19	3	8	0	109	3.47	446	6	.215	.265	.305	348	10	.233	.286	.374
1990	StL-N	559	11	.286	.324	.401	6	4	0	84	3.84	3	4	0	57	4.89	6	6	0	89	4.26	3	2	0	53	4.27	339	3	.301	.339	.392	220	8	.264	.302	.414
1991	StL-N	749	16	.251	.297	.381	5	4	0	107	3.52	7	5	0	91	4.24	6	4	0	99	3.81	6	5	0	99	3.90	441	7	.272	.319	.401	308	9	.221	.266	.351
1992	StL-N	81	3	.247	.315	.383	2	0	0	12	5.11	2	2	0	9	4.00	0	0	0	3	6.75	4	2	0	19	4.34	37	0	.270	.341	.324	44	3	.227	.292	.432
1993	Col-N	130	2	.362	.412	.454	1	3	0	23	4.63	1	1	0	6	22.74	2	4	0	30	8.49	0	0	0	0	—	70	1	.371	.392	.471	60	1	.350	.435	.433
TOTALS		6818	140	.253	.300	.372	57	41	2	943	3.19	51	53	4	848	3.90	52	43	4	849	3.74	56	51	2	943	3.33	3660	55	.265	.312	.374	3158	85	.239	.287	.370
● Lee Smith BR/TR																																				
1980	Chi-N	81	0	.259	.365	.346	1	0	0	13	3.46	1	0	0	9	2.08	0	0	0	0	—	2	0	0	22	2.91	33	0	.273	.375	.394	48	0	.250	.357	.313
1981	Chi-N	239	2	.238	.326	.297	3	4	0	36	3.53	0	2	1	31	3.48	1	3	0	32	3.94	2	3	1	35	3.12	115	1	.243	.338	.304	124	1	.234	.314	.290
1982	Chi-N	429	5	.245	.306	.312	2	2	7	59	2.30	0	3	10	58	3.09	1	4	2	69	3.28	1	1	15	48	1.86	206	2	.233	.300	.296	223	3	.256	.312	.327
1983	Chi-N	360	5	.194	.277	.258	3	6	15	54	1.99	1	4	14	49	1.29	3	4	9	47	1.34	1	6	20	56	1.92	182	2	.192	.294	.253	178	3	.197	.259	.264
1984	Chi-N	384	6	.255	.314	.359	5	3	14	53	4.05	4	4	19	48	3.21	4	4	15	48	4.10	5	3	18	53	3.25	218	1	.271	.345	.344	166	5	.235	.269	.380
1985	Chi-N	360	9	.242	.305	.381	3	3	17	55	4.09	4	1	16	43	1.69	3	2	16	49	2.57	4	2	17	49	3.51	192	4	.266	.324	.401	168	5	.214	.283	.357
1986	Chi-N	321	7	.215	.303	.318	6	3	20	56	2.75	3	6	11	35	3.63	4	6	11	42	3.00	5	3	20	48	3.17	172	5	.221	.343	.349	149	2	.208	.252	.282
1987	Chi-N	324	4	.259	.326	.358	3	5	16	38	3.79	1	5	20	46	2.56	2	5	20	46	2.93	2	5	16	38	3.35	179	3	.268	.358	.397	145	1	.248	.283	.310
1988	Bos-A	320	7	.225	.306	.338	3	2	19	47	2.66	1	3	10	36	2.97	2	2	11	37	2.70	2	3	18	47	2.87	164	3	.232	.321	.317	156	4	.218	.289	.359
1989	Bos-A	253	6	.209	.299	.304	6	0	12	38	4.06	0	1	13	33	3.00	4	1	9	27	5.93	2	0	16	43	2.08	121	5	.223	.317	.364	132	1	.197	.282	.250
1990	Bos-A	55	0	.236	.344	.291	1	0	3	10	1.86	1	1	1	5	1.93	2	1	4	14	1.88	0	0	0	0	—	26	0	.192	.382	.269	29	0	.276	.300	.310
1990	StL-N	255	3	.227	.281	.322	2	3	9	37	2.65	1	1	18	31	1.44	1	2	9	32	2.53	2	2	18	37	1.72	152	3	.237	.306	.349	103	0	.214	.241	.282
1991	StL-N	281	5	.249	.281	.352	6	1	26	46	1.38	0	2	21	27	3.95	3	2	20	36	2.50	3	1	27	37	2.19	165	3	.255	.301	.364	116	2	.241	.252	.336
1992	StL-N	281	4	.221	.286	.320	3	8	18	44	3.25	1	1	25	31	2.93	2	3	17	33	3.55	2	6	26	42	2.79	164	2	.220	.303	.335	117	2	.222	.260	.299
1993	StL-N	195	11	.251	.282	.492	1	3	21	24	4.81	1	1	22	26	4.21	2	1	29	32	3.62	0	3	14	18	6.11	108	6	.250	.278	.463	87	5	.253	.286	.529
1993	NY-A	27	0	.148	.273	.185	0	0	2	4	0.00	0	0	1	4	0.00	0	0	0	0	—	0	0	3	8	0.00	11	0	.000	.267	.000	16	0	.250	.278	.313
1994	Bal-A	142	6	.239	.290	.408	0	2	15	18	3.00	1	2	18	20	3.54	1	1	27	29	1.55	0	3	6	9	8.68	72	4	.306	.366	.542	70	2	.171	.205	.271
1995	Cal-A	177	3	.237	.330	.356	0	2	17	23	1.99	0	3	20	27	4.72	0	2	19	20	3.10	0	3	18	29	3.72	102	1	.235	.328	.333	75	2	.240	.333	.387
1996	Cal-A	39	0	.205	.250	.231	0	0	0	5	3.60	0	0	0	6	1.50	0	0	0	11	2.45	0	0	0	0	—	19	0	.158	.150	.158	20	0	.250	.333	.300
1996	Cin-N	177	4	.277	.363	.407	1	0	2	26	3.51	2	4	0	19	4.82	1	1	2	14	1.98	2	3	0	31	4.99	80	1	.237	.330	.338	97	3	.309	.391	.464

		TOTAL					HOME					AWAY					1ST HALF					2ND HALF					LEFT					RIGHT				
YEAR	TM/L	AB	HR	AVG	OBP	SLG	W	L	SV	IP	ERA	W	L	SV	IP	ERA	W	L	SV	IP	ERA	W	L	SV	IP	ERA	AB	HR	AVG	OBP	SLG	AB	HR	AVG	OBP	SLG
1997	Mon-N	91	2	.308	.370	.440	0	1	5	12	10.03	0	0	0	10	0.90	0	1	5	20	6.41	0	0	0	2	0.00	47	1	.255	.352	.362	44	1	.364	.391	.523
TOTALS		4791	89	.236	.306	.341	49	48	238	697	3.15	22	44	240	593	2.89	36	45	225	638	3.10	35	47	253	651	2.96	2528	47	.240	.322	.348	2263	42	.232	.287	.334
● John Smoltz BR/TR																																				
1988	Atl-N	260	10	.285	.369	.473	1	4	0	35	6.11	1	3	0	29	4.71	0	0	0	0	—	2	7	0	64	5.48	156	4	.314	.409	.487	104	6	.240	.307	.452
1989	Atl-N	756	15	.212	.280	.319	6	4	0	99	2.63	6	7	0	109	3.23	9	6	0	116	2.26	3	5	0	92	3.80	454	6	.214	.289	.317	302	9	.209	.266	.321
1990	Atl-N	858	20	.240	.310	.358	9	4	0	124	2.76	5	7	0	107	5.11	5	6	0	93	4.92	9	5	0	138	3.13	506	10	.269	.347	.383	352	10	.199	.255	.321
1991	Atl-N	849	16	.243	.305	.360	9	7	0	136	4.10	5	6	0	94	3.36	2	10	0	105	4.82	12	3	0	125	2.95	486	10	.288	.363	.422	363	6	.182	.221	.278
1992	Atl-N	921	17	.224	.287	.332	5	6	0	103	2.87	10	6	0	143	2.83	9	5	0	125	3.17	6	7	0	122	2.52	544	9	.246	.309	.338	377	8	.191	.254	.324
1993	Atl-N	905	23	.230	.309	.369	4	5	0	101	3.92	11	6	0	143	3.41	7	7	0	119	3.25	8	4	0	125	3.97	459	10	.261	.346	.412	446	13	.197	.271	.325
1994	Atl-N	503	15	.239	.307	.378	2	7	0	79	5.01	4	3	0	56	2.91	6	7	0	99	3.47	0	3	0	36	6.00	240	6	.271	.357	.408	263	9	.209	.256	.350
1995	Atl-N	714	15	.232	.304	.346	6	4	0	103	3.59	6	3	0	90	2.70	7	4	0	84	3.00	5	3	0	109	3.31	345	7	.261	.345	.380	369	8	.206	.264	.314
1996	Atl-N	922	19	.216	.260	.331	13	3	0	132	2.94	11	5	0	122	2.95	14	3	0	130	2.98	10	5	0	124	2.91	394	5	.221	.288	.310	528	14	.212	.239	.347
1997	Atl-N	966	21	.242	.288	.359	6	7	0	138	3.32	9	5	0	118	2.68	7	7	0	131	3.03	8	5	0	125	3.02	524	10	.246	.301	.351	442	11	.238	.273	.369
1998	Atl-N	627	10	.231	.285	.337	8	2	0	75	3.12	9	1	0	93	2.72	5	2	0	60	3.77	12	1	0	108	2.42	331	7	.245	.306	.366	296	3	.216	.262	.304
1999	Atl-N	687	14	.245	.288	.374	7	3	0	86	3.14	4	5	0	100	3.23	8	2	0	89	3.03	3	6	0	97	3.33	311	7	.264	.315	.402	376	7	.229	.266	.351
TOTALS		8968	195	.233	.295	.354	76	56	0	1212	3.45	81	57	0	1203	3.24	79	59	0	1150	3.37	78	54	0	1265	3.32	4750	91	.255	.327	.373	4218	104	.209	.258	.332
● Lary Sorensen BR/TR																																				
1978	Mil-A	1071	14	.259	.291	.338	10	5	0	129	3.06	8	7	1	151	3.33	10	4	0	138	3.39	8	8	1	143	3.03	602	9	.277	.309	.367	469	5	.235	.269	.301
1979	Mil-A	910	30	.275	.309	.411	9	4	0	113	3.10	6	10	0	122	4.80	9	8	0	131	3.38	6	6	0	105	4.73	485	18	.258	.297	.400	425	12	.294	.322	.424
1980	Mil-A	777	13	.311	.347	.422	6	4	0	92	2.84	6	6	1	104	4.43	7	4	0	102	3.62	5	6	1	94	3.75	444	6	.324	.363	.421	333	7	.294	.326	.423
1981	StL-N	549	3	.271	.306	.344	4	4	0	75	3.24	3	3	0	65	3.31	5	5	0	81	3.46	2	2	0	60	3.02	269	1	.253	.302	.323	280	2	.289	.309	.364
1982	Cle-A	779	19	.322	.365	.462	5	6	0	95	5.76	5	9	0	94	5.46	7	6	0	99	4.56	3	9	0	91	6.75	381	7	.312	.354	.425	398	12	.332	.376	.497
1983	Cle-A	862	21	.276	.326	.410	6	4	0	127	4.12	6	7	0	96	4.41	4	7	0	100	4.68	8	4	0	123	3.89	457	12	.269	.317	.427	405	9	.284	.336	.390
1984	Oak-A	757	21	.317	.356	.444	2	6	0	92	4.29	4	7	1	91	5.54	2	8	0	104	4.76	4	5	1	79	5.11	382	14	.317	.361	.476	375	7	.317	.352	.411
1985	Chi-N	314	8	.274	.331	.427	1	5	0	38	5.17	2	2	0	44	3.48	1	1	0	24	4.44	2	6	0	58	4.19	143	4	.329	.390	.517	171	4	.228	.281	.351
1987	Mon-N	196	7	.286	.333	.459	1	4	0	19	10.24	2	0	1	28	0.95	3	4	1	48	4.72	0	0	0	0	—	93	4	.301	.362	.495	103	3	.272	.306	.427
1988	SF-N	73	1	.329	.346	.425	0	0	2	12	2.19	0	0	0	4	12.46	0	0	0	0	—	0	0	2	17	4.86	24	0	.333	.385	.333	49	1	.327	.327	.469
TOTALS		6288	137	.288	.328	.407	44	42	2	794	3.96	42	51	4	800	4.30	48	47	1	826	4.00	38	46	5	768	4.27	3280	75	.290	.332	.413	3008	62	.287	.323	.399
● Mario Soto BR/TR																																				
1978	Cin-N	66	1	.197	.329	.288	0	0	0	11	3.27	1	0	0	7	1.29	0	0	0	0	—	1	0	0	18	2.50	14	0	.143	.294	.214	52	1	.212	.339	.308
1979	Cin-N	136	2	.243	.381	.353	0	0	0	11	4.91	3	2	0	26	5.47	0	0	0	1	40.50	3	2	0	37	4.66	56	1	.357	.507	.500	80	1	.162	.284	.250
1980	Cin-N	673	11	.187	.276	.288	5	4	1	104	2.69	5	4	3	87	3.53	0	3	0	61	4.99	10	5	4	129	2.16	284	5	.243	.349	.363	389	6	.147	.221	.234
1981	Cin-N	646	13	.220	.289	.330	7	2	0	95	2.19	5	7	0	80	4.59	6	6	0	94	3.15	6	3	0	81	3.46	299	6	.221	.301	.331	347	7	.219	.278	.329
1982	Cin-N	938	19	.215	.271	.333	9	5	0	137	2.69	5	8	0	121	2.91	7	4	0	127	2.27	7	9	0	131	3.31	420	12	.240	.296	.393	518	7	.195	.251	.284
1983	Cin-N	997	28	.208	.278	.325	9	6	0	138	2.67	8	7	0	136	2.72	9	6	0	129	2.16	8	7	0	145	3.17	534	17	.199	.278	.331	463	11	.218	.277	.317
1984	Cin-N	863	26	.210	.284	.344	11	2	0	132	3.74	7	5	0	105	3.26	9	1	0	123	2.48	9	6	0	114	4.66	426	16	.200	.296	.347	437	10	.220	.272	.341
1985	Cin-N	927	30	.211	.290	.361	6	8	0	126	4.23	6	7	0	131	2.95	8	7	0	132	3.20	4	8	0	124	3.98	454	17	.209	.304	.370	473	13	.214	.276	.353
1986	Cin-N	404	15	.280	.352	.480	2	7	0	49	6.02	3	3	0	56	3.56	3	7	0	77	3.97	2	3	0	28	6.75	224	7	.299	.391	.504	180	8	.256	.299	.450
1987	Cin-N	122	7	.279	.343	.500	1	0	0	6	3.18	2	2	0	26	5.54	3	2	0	32	5.12	0	0	0	0	—	84	3	.274	.337	.452	38	4	.289	.357	.605
1988	Cin-N	330	8	.267	.326	.397	1	1	0	31	4.99	2	6	0	56	4.47	3	7	0	87	4.66	0	0	0	0	—	173	2	.289	.342	.399	157	6	.242	.308	.395
TOTALS		6102	160	.219	.292	.349	51	35	1	839	3.35	47	51	3	831	3.46	48	43	0	864	3.24	50	43	4	806	3.57	2968	86	.230	.315	.374	3134	74	.208	.270	.325
● Jerry Spradlin BB/TR																																				
1993	Cin-N	177	4	.249	.279	.401	1	0	2	24	3.75	1	1	0	25	3.24	0	0	0	0	—	2	1	2	49	3.49	69	4	.261	.297	.551	108	0	.241	.267	.306
1994	Cin-N	34	2	.353	.368	.618	0	0	0	3	3.00	0	0	0	5	14.40	0	0	0	8	10.13	0	0	0	0	—	15	1	.533	.563	.933	19	1	.211	.227	.368
1996	Cin-N	1	0	.000	.000	.000	0	0	0	0	—	0	0	0	0	0.00	0	0	0	0	—	0	0	0	0	0.00	0	0	—	—	—	1	0	.000	.000	.000
1997	Phi-N	314	9	.274	.331	.424	3	2	0	45	3.57	1	6	1	36	6.19	1	3	0	39	3.69	3	5	1	43	5.70	125	4	.272	.331	.432	189	5	.275	.332	.418
1998	Phi-N	291	9	.216	.270	.344	2	2	0	42	4.54	2	2	1	40	2.48	3	3	1	42	3.86	1	1	0	40	3.18	104	2	.231	.289	.327	187	7	.209	.259	.353
1999	Cle-A	15	1	.400	.500	.733	0	0	0	1	45.00	0	0	0	2	4.50	0	0	0	3	18.00	0	0	0	0	—	6	1	.500	.625	1.333	9	0	.333	.400	.333
1999	SF-N	228	4	.259	.367	.360	2	0	0	25	3.60	1	1	0	33	4.64	2	1	0	24	4.13	1	0	0	34	4.24	67	1	.269	.430	.343	161	3	.255	.337	.366
2000	KC-A	286	9	.283	.350	.455	3	2	1	43	5.65	1	2	6	32	5.34	2	2	6	46	3.69	2	2	1	29	8.48	151	4	.258	.321	.417	135	5	.311	.382	.496
2000	Chi-N	61	2	.328	.377	.492	0	0	0	7	12.15	0	1	0	8	5.40	0	0	0	0	—	0	1	0	15	8.40	20	1	.350	.458	.550	41	1	.317	.333	.463
TOTALS		1407	40	.264	.327	.411	11	6	3	190	4.79	6	13	8	182	4.70	8	9	7	162	4.38	9	10	4	209	5.03	557	18	.271	.345	.440	850	22	.259	.315	.392
● Bob Stanley BR/TR																																				
1978	Bos-A	533	5	.266	.308	.343	13	2	5	86	2.93	2	0	5	56	2.10	5	1	3	48	3.21	10	1	7	94	2.30	232	3	.276	.333	.379	301	2	.259	.288	.316
1979	Bos-A	849	14	.294	.330	.400	6	6	0	89	4.23	10	6	1	127	3.82	9	5	1	113	3.35	7	7	0	104	4.69	452	9	.310	.352	.427	397	5	.277	.305	.370
1980	Bos-A	668	11	.278	.335	.382	2	5	7	89	4.55	8	3	7	86	2.20	6	6	0	104	4.43	4	2	14	71	1.89	352	6	.301	.371	.420	316	5	.253	.292	.339
1981	Bos-A	374	3	.294	.365	.382	5	5	0	55	3.93	5	3	0	44	3.71	4	3	0	47	4.56	6	5	0	51	3.16	164	0	.311	.394	.402	210	3	.281	.341	.367
1982	Bos-A	632	11	.255	.312	.351	8	1	9	91	2.27	4	6	5	77	4.09	6	1	5	82	3.09	6	6	9	87	3.12	274	4	.241	.315	.336	358	7	.265	.309	.363
1983	Bos-A	545	7	.266	.315	.347	4	6	14	75	3.74	4	4	19	71	1.91	5	4	16	80	2.35	3	6	17	65	3.46	258	3	.271	.339	.364	287	4	.261	.293	.331
1984	Bos-A	423	9	.267	.307	.383	5	8	8	57	4.55	4	2	14	49	2.37	3	6	13	59	4.25	6	4	9	47	2.66	221	5	.253	.320	.389	202	4	.282	.293	.376
1985	Bos-A	321	7	.237	.303	.355	3	2	5	42	3.21	3	4	5	46	2.56	3	3	8	56	2.40	3	3	2	31	3.73	161	4	.248	.324	.354	160	3	.225	.279	.356
1986	Bos-A	338	9	.322	.360	.462	3	1	9	39	6.00	3	5	7	43	2.91	5	2	13	40	3.79	1	4	3	42	4.93	154	3	.338	.392	.442	184	6	.310	.332	.478
1987	Bos-A	616	17	.321	.363	.468	3	5	0	74	4.28	1	10	0	79	5.70	3	8	0	99	4.83	1	7	0	54	5.33	299	8	.358	.413	.522	317	9	.287	.314	.416
1988	Bos-A	372	6	.242	.304	.336	3	2	3	55	2.28	3	2	2	46	4.27	3	0	0	32	3.94	3	4	5	70	2.84	171	1	.263	.332	.339	201	5	.224	.281	.333
1989	Bos-A	318	4	.321	.366	.425	3	0	3	42	4.32	2	2	1	38	5.50	2	2	4	52	5.02	3	0	0	27	4.61	141	2	.348	.415	.489	177	2	.299	.326	.373
TOTALS		5989	103	.281	.330	.386	58	43	63	794	3.76	49	47	66	762	3.44	54	41	63	812	3.76	53	49	66	744	3.44	2879	48	.294	.357	.408	3110	55	.269	.304	.366
● Mike Stanton BL/TL																																				
1989	Atl-N	82	0	.207	.278	.268	0	1	3	14	2.63	0	0	4	10	0.00	0	0	0	0	—	0	1	7	24	1.50	14	0	.214	.313	.357	68	0	.206	.270	.250
1990	Atl-N	36	1	.444	.512	.556	0	1	1	5	19.29	0	2	1	2	15.43	0	3	2	7	18.00	0	0	0	0	—	8	0	.250	.400	.250	28	1	.500	.548	.643
1991	Atl-N	286	6	.217	.273	.325	1	1	4	41	2.21	4	4	3	37	3.62	3	1	1	30	3.30	2	4	6	48	2.63	103	1	.194	.252	.233	183	5	.230	.284	.377
1992	Atl-N	239	6	.247	.308	.368	2	1	3	30	3.00	3	3	5	34	5.08	1	4	5	25	7.20	4	0	3	39	2.09	76	4	.237	.344	.434	163	2	.252	.289	.337
1993	Atl-N	200	4	.255	.346	.370	4	3	14	28	2.25	0	3	13	24	7.50	3	2	21	28	3.21	1	4	6	24	6.38	55	1	.218	.357	.309	145	3	.269	.342	.393
1994	Atl-N	165	2	.248	.359	.321	3	1	1	31	2.93	0	0	2	15	4.80	3	1	2	34	3.97	0	0	1	12	2.31	60	1	.200	.300	.267	105	1	.276	.392	.352
1995	Atl-N	84	3	.369	.413	.548	1	0	0	14	4.61	0	1	1	6	7.94	1	1	0	17	5.40	0	0	1	3	6.75	27	0	.259	.276	.296	57	3	.421	.476	.667
1995	Bos-A	76	3	.224	.298	.368	0	0	0	8	2.35	1	0	0	13	3.38	0	0	0	0	—	1	0	0	21	3.00	25	0	.160	.222	.160	51	3	.255	.333	.471
1996	Bos-A	211	9	.275	.343	.460	3	2	1	23	3.86	1	1	0	33	3.82	4	2	1	44	3.89	0	1	0	12	3.65	81	0	.272	.322	.346	130	9	.277	.356	.531
1996	Tex-A	83	2	.241	.276	.361	0	0	0	10	4.35	0	1	0	12	2.25	0	0	0	0	—	0	1	0	22	3.22	33	1	.242	.265	.364	50	1	.240	.283	.360
1997	NY-A	244	3	.205	.310	.262	3	0	0	28	1.91	3	1	3	38	3.05	5	0	0	29	3.07	1	1	3	37	2.17	89	0	.157	.257	.157	155	3	.232	.339	.323
1998	NY-A	297	13	.239	.307	.414	1	1	3	40	5.67	3	0	3	39	5.26	3	0	5	37	5.35	1	1	1	42	5.57	99	6	.253	.295	.485	198	7	.232	.313	.379
1999	NY-A	246	5	.289	.337	.423	1	0	0	33	2.20	1	2	0	30	6.67	1	2	0	28	4.55	1	0	0	35	4.15	90	2	.256	.317	.400	156	3	.308	.349	.436
2000	NY-A	259	5	.263	.325	.375	2	2	0	38	3.58	0	1	0	30	4.75	1	1	0	38	3.29	1	2	0	30	5.16	118	3	.339	.362	.508	141	2	.199	.296	.262
TOTALS		2508	62	.252	.323	.374	21	13	30	341	3.40	16	19	35	324	4.63	25	17	37	317	4.51	12	15	28	348	3.54	878	19	.239	.307	.350	1630	43	.259	.331	.388
● Dave Stewart BR/TR																																				
1978	LA-N	6	0	.167	.167	.167	0	0	0	2	0.00	0	0	0	0	—	0	0	0	0	—	0	0	0	2	0.00	1	0	.000	.000	.000	5	0	.200	.200	.200
1981	LA-N	160	3	.250	.305	.338	1	3	3	25	2.52	3	0	3	18	2.45	3	1	0	17	0.54	1	2	6	27	3.71	68	1	.279	.354	.353	92	2	.228	.265	.326
1982	LA-N	550	14	.249	.310	.369	2	4	0	74	3.67	7	4	1	73	3.96	3	4	0	73	3.95	6	4	1	73	3.68	246	6	.256	.325	.382	304	8	.243	.298	.359
1983	LA-N	283	4	.237	.318	.322	2	2	3	39	3.46	3	0	5	37	2.43	5	2	8	50	2.15	0	0	0	26	4.56	136	1	.279	.355	.353	147	3	.197	.283	.293
1983	Tex-A	215	2	.233	.294	.312	3	0	0	24	1.52	2	2	0	35	2.55	0	0	0	0	—	5	2	0	59	2.14	101	0	.208	.277	.277	114	2	.254	.309	.342
1984	Tex-A	747	26	.258	.337	.422	3	9	0	122	4.51	4	5	0	71	5.09	4	8	0	103	5.17	3	6	0	90	4.22	394	13	.269	.355	.421	353	13	.246	.316	.422
1985	Tex-A	315	13	.273	.351	.476	0	2	1	36	7.43	0	4	3	45	3.80	0	4	4	35	4.89	0	2	0	46	5.83	164	6	.323	.408	.524	151	7	.219	.285	.424
1985	Phi-N	18	0	.278	.409	.278	0	0	0	3	8.10	0	0	0	1	0.00	0	0	0	0	—	0	0	0	4	6.23	9	0	.444	.583	.444	9	0	.111	.200	.111
1986	Phi-N	49	1	.306	.339	.510	0	0	0	7	7.36	0	0	0	5	5.40	0	0	0	12	6.57	0	0	0	0	—	10	1	.300	.429	.900	39	0	.308	.310	.410
1986	Oak-A	567	15	.242	.321	.374	5	3	0	85	2.86	4	2	0	64	4.90	0	0	0	26	4.91	9	5	0	124	3.49	284	7	.236	.318	.366	283	8	.247	.324	.382
1987	Oak-A	980	24	.229	.306	.357	11	6	0	133	2.84	9	7	0	128	4.56	9	7	0	108	3.92	11	6	0	153	3.52	554	13	.233	.314	.357	426	11	.223	.294	.357
1988	Oak-A	1027	14	.234	.307	.333	9	5	0	127	3.25	12	7	0	148	3.22	10	6	0	135	3.67	11	6	0	141	2.82	563	9	.224	.305	.323	464	5	.246	.310	.345

		TOTAL					HOME					AWAY					1ST HALF					2ND HALF					LEFT					RIGHT				
YEAR	TM/L	AB	HR	AVG	OBP	SLG	W	L	SV	IP	ERA	W	L	SV	IP	ERA	W	L	SV	IP	ERA	W	L	SV	IP	ERA	AB	HR	AVG	OBP	SLG	AB	HR	AVG	OBP	SLG
1989	Oak-A	986	23	.264	.313	.395	11	4	0	133	2.77	10	5	0	124	3.91	12	4	0	123	3.51	9	5	0	135	3.14	522	12	.264	.315	.387	464	11	.263	.310	.403
1990	Oak-A	980	16	.231	.291	.326	11	4	0	145	1.68	11	7	0	122	3.61	10	6	0	124	2.47	12	5	0	143	2.65	478	8	.207	.280	.305	502	8	.253	.303	.345
1991	Oak-A	880	24	.278	.356	.428	8	3	0	115	4.21	3	8	0	111	6.18	5	4	0	96	5.74	6	7	0	130	4.76	444	8	.302	.361	.428	436	16	.255	.350	.429
1992	Oak-A	737	25	.237	.315	.393	4	5	0	101	3.73	8	5	0	98	3.58	7	5	0	111	3.96	5	5	0	88	3.27	340	11	.262	.351	.415	397	14	.217	.282	.375
1993	Tor-A	604	23	.242	.325	.419	6	4	0	85	4.01	6	4	0	77	4.93	3	3	0	59	4.88	9	5	0	103	4.19	264	8	.246	.334	.413	340	15	.238	.317	.424
1994	Tor-A	530	26	.285	.362	.492	4	3	0	78	4.38	3	5	0	55	7.97	5	7	0	92	5.77	2	1	0	41	6.10	250	12	.284	.378	.484	280	14	.286	.346	.500
1995	Oak-A	331	11	.305	.379	.462	1	1	0	42	3.64	2	6	0	39	10.38	3	6	0	66	6.85	0	1	0	15	7.04	198	4	.313	.394	.434	133	7	.293	.356	.504
TOTALS		9965	264	.251	.322	.387	81	58	7	1378	3.45	87	71	12	1252	4.50	79	67	12	1229	4.25	89	62	7	1401	3.68	5026	120	.256	.333	.386	4939	144	.245	.311	.389
● Dave Stieb	BR/TR																																			
1979	Tor-A	503	11	.276	.342	.402	5	3	0	60	3.62	3	5	0	70	4.91	0	1	0	6	7.50	8	7	0	123	4.16	237	5	.300	.371	.439	266	6	.256	.315	.368
1980	Tor-A	894	12	.260	.324	.356	4	10	0	122	5.02	8	5	0	121	2.39	7	5	0	117	3.01	5	10	0	126	4.36	492	9	.289	.352	.417	402	3	.224	.289	.281
1981	Tor-A	664	10	.223	.296	.322	4	5	0	86	3.44	7	5	0	97	2.96	4	7	0	98	3.31	7	3	0	86	3.05	358	3	.235	.301	.307	306	7	.209	.291	.340
1982	Tor-A	1094	27	.248	.298	.360	8	6	0	129	3.20	9	8	0	159	3.28	6	9	0	123	4.09	11	5	0	165	2.62	545	9	.244	.299	.336	549	18	.251	.298	.384
1983	Tor-A	1019	21	.219	.291	.342	11	7	0	157	2.97	6	5	0	121	3.13	10	6	0	140	2.51	7	6	0	138	3.58	506	11	.206	.288	.318	513	10	.232	.293	.365
1984	Tor-A	972	19	.221	.292	.331	9	4	0	116	2.71	7	4	0	151	2.93	8	3	0	131	2.41	8	5	0	136	3.23	511	11	.225	.290	.335	461	8	.217	.294	.328
1985	Tor-A	966	22	.213	.290	.320	8	6	0	112	2.96	6	7	0	153	2.12	8	5	0	121	1.93	6	8	0	144	2.94	560	10	.198	.281	.286	406	12	.234	.302	.367
1986	Tor-A	805	29	.297	.373	.476	5	5	0	131	3.93	2	7	1	74	6.17	2	8	0	105	5.57	5	4	1	100	3.87	416	17	.329	.410	.546	389	12	.262	.333	.401
1987	Tor-A	685	16	.239	.329	.377	5	4	0	78	4.98	8	5	0	107	3.44	6	5	0	79	4.67	7	4	0	106	3.65	364	10	.242	.338	.390	321	6	.237	.319	.361
1988	Tor-A	748	15	.210	.295	.316	12	5	0	127	2.70	4	3	0	81	3.57	10	4	0	102	3.01	6	4	0	106	3.07	400	8	.218	.293	.315	348	7	.201	.298	.316
1989	Tor-A	748	12	.219	.301	.316	7	4	0	94	3.34	10	4	0	112	3.36	7	4	0	94	4.58	10	4	0	112	2.32	387	7	.248	.319	.346	361	5	.188	.283	.283
1990	Tor-A	778	11	.230	.296	.320	9	5	0	103	3.15	9	1	0	106	2.73	10	3	0	93	3.39	8	3	0	116	2.57	403	8	.253	.326	.357	375	3	.205	.263	.280
1991	Tor-A	214	4	.243	.321	.346	1	2	0	18	5.50	3	1	0	42	2.16	4	3	0	60	3.17	0	0	0	0	—	117	2	.239	.318	.333	97	2	.247	.324	.361
1992	Tor-A	357	9	.275	.355	.420	2	4	0	57	5.53	2	2	0	39	4.35	3	6	0	70	5.79	1	0	0	26	3.08	172	4	.279	.354	.419	185	5	.270	.355	.422
1993	Chi-A	90	1	.300	.390	.367	1	2	0	16	6.06	0	1	0	6	6.00	1	3	0	22	6.04	0	0	0	0	—	45	0	.222	.357	.244	45	1	.378	.429	.489
1998	Tor-A	204	6	.284	.351	.422	1	0	1	21	4.64	0	2	1	29	4.97	0	0	0	6	3.18	1	2	2	45	5.04	102	3	.304	.365	.441	102	3	.265	.336	.402
TOTALS		10741	225	.239	.312	.355	92	72	1	1428	3.60	84	65	2	1467	3.28	86	72	0	1366	3.57	90	65	3	1529	3.32	5615	117	.247	.321	.362	5126	108	.231	.302	.347
● Todd Stottlemyre	BL/TR																																			
1988	Tor-A	385	15	.283	.363	.455	1	4	0	39	7.22	3	4	0	59	4.70	3	7	0	78	4.25	1	1	0	20	11.44	198	7	.369	.442	.551	187	8	.193	.280	.353
1989	Tor-A	486	11	.282	.343	.424	4	3	0	79	3.53	3	4	0	49	4.44	0	3	0	26	5.81	7	4	0	101	3.38	223	7	.314	.362	.480	263	4	.255	.328	.376
1990	Tor-A	781	18	.274	.337	.410	7	8	0	103	4.28	6	9	0	100	4.41	8	7	0	103	4.09	5	10	0	100	4.61	393	8	.300	.365	.443	388	10	.247	.309	.376
1991	Tor-A	826	21	.235	.305	.356	9	3	0	116	3.96	6	5	0	103	3.58	9	3	0	109	3.13	6	5	0	110	4.43	422	11	.242	.310	.355	404	10	.228	.300	.356
1992	Tor-A	669	20	.262	.329	.398	7	5	0	83	4.79	5	6	0	91	4.24	5	6	0	88	5.32	7	5	0	86	3.66	284	6	.282	.355	.394	385	14	.247	.310	.400
1993	Tor-A	698	11	.292	.353	.424	6	5	0	93	4.18	5	7	0	84	5.57	5	5	0	69	4.41	6	7	0	107	5.11	374	7	.305	.375	.452	324	4	.278	.328	.392
1994	Tor-A	540	19	.276	.340	.457	4	3	1	68	3.82	3	4	0	72	4.60	5	5	1	95	3.90	2	2	0	46	4.89	274	10	.288	.356	.464	266	9	.263	.323	.451
1995	Oak-A	826	26	.276	.343	.425	6	5	0	118	3.89	8	2	0	92	5.40	6	1	0	82	3.95	8	6	0	128	4.93	483	11	.259	.333	.385	343	15	.300	.356	.481
1996	StL-N	826	30	.231	.309	.389	6	7	0	128	4.01	8	4	0	95	3.68	7	6	0	114	4.04	7	5	0	110	3.69	371	15	.272	.367	.453	455	15	.198	.259	.336
1997	StL-N	671	16	.231	.308	.356	4	5	0	70	4.89	8	4	0	111	3.24	6	5	0	109	4.21	6	4	0	72	3.38	358	11	.268	.351	.422	313	5	.188	.257	.281
1998	StL-N	607	20	.241	.302	.389	6	2	0	83	2.60	3	7	0	78	4.48	9	5	0	134	2.81	0	4	0	27	7.00	309	11	.252	.338	.434	298	9	.228	.262	.342
1998	Tex-A	241	5	.282	.358	.456	3	2	0	34	4.81	2	2	0	27	3.71	0	0	0	0	—	5	4	0	60	4.33	132	3	.333	.407	.538	109	2	.220	.298	.358
1999	Ari-N	396	12	.268	.343	.424	4	1	0	47	4.75	2	2	0	54	3.50	4	1	0	58	3.59	2	2	0	44	4.74	170	6	.312	.394	.494	226	6	.235	.304	.372
2000	Ari-N	365	18	.268	.336	.463	3	4	0	43	6.07	6	2	0	52	3.96	8	5	0	76	4.24	1	1	0	19	7.58	143	10	.273	.370	.531	222	8	.266	.313	.419
TOTALS		8317	242	.261	.330	.409	70	57	1	1103	4.24	68	62	0	1068	4.26	75	59	1	1142	3.98	63	60	0	1029	4.55	4134	123	.284	.359	.440	4183	119	.240	.301	.378
● Scott Sullivan	BR/TR																																			
1995	Cin-N	14	0	.286	.375	.286	0	0	0	3	6.75	0	0	0	1	0.00	0	0	0	4	4.91	0	0	0	0	—	5	0	.200	.429	.200	9	0	.333	.333	.333
1996	Cin-N	28	0	.250	.382	.250	0	0	0	3	0.00	0	0	0	5	3.60	0	0	0	0	—	0	0	0	8	2.25	10	0	.300	.462	.300	18	0	.222	.333	.222
1997	Cin-N	359	12	.220	.291	.376	3	0	1	51	3.51	2	3	0	46	2.93	1	2	0	38	3.11	4	1	1	60	3.32	152	7	.243	.324	.434	207	5	.203	.265	.333
1998	Cin-N	388	14	.253	.327	.420	4	2	0	53	5.47	1	3	1	49	4.93	1	3	1	63	4.69	4	2	0	39	6.05	155	2	.290	.364	.413	233	12	.227	.303	.425
1999	Cin-N	406	10	.217	.308	.347	3	2	0	51	3.33	2	2	3	62	2.74	3	0	1	56	2.43	2	4	2	58	3.57	153	3	.242	.328	.399	253	7	.202	.295	.316
2000	Cin-N	385	14	.226	.307	.387	2	5	0	59	3.34	1	1	3	47	3.64	1	3	2	50	4.68	2	3	1	56	2.40	159	5	.214	.300	.365	226	9	.235	.311	.403
TOTALS		1580	50	.230	.310	.379	12	9	1	220	3.88	6	9	7	211	3.50	6	8	4	210	3.81	12	10	4	221	3.59	634	17	.248	.332	.399	946	33	.218	.296	.366
● Jeff Suppan	BR/TR																																			
1995	Bos-A	93	4	.312	.343	.548	0	2	0	18	7.00	1	0	0	5	1.93	0	0	0	0	—	1	2	0	23	5.96	49	1	.306	.327	.490	44	3	.318	.362	.614
1996	Bos-A	88	3	.330	.406	.523	0	1	0	8	9.72	1	0	0	14	6.28	0	0	0	2	0.00	1	1	0	21	8.14	43	1	.233	.306	.349	45	2	.422	.491	.689
1997	Bos-A	459	12	.305	.358	.444	4	2	0	57	4.87	3	1	0	55	6.55	2	0	0	38	5.21	5	3	0	74	5.93	232	8	.280	.337	.448	227	4	.330	.379	.441
1998	Ari-N	272	12	.301	.351	.507	1	3	0	28	6.18	0	4	0	38	7.04	1	6	0	60	6.86	0	1	0	6	4.76	135	3	.259	.311	.415	137	9	.343	.392	.599
1998	KC-A	45	1	.200	.217	.311	0	0	0	6	0.00	0	0	0	7	1.35	0	0	0	0	—	0	0	0	13	0.71	22	0	.091	.091	.091	23	1	.304	.333	.522
1999	KC-A	810	28	.274	.326	.437	6	7	0	109	4.69	4	5	0	99	4.35	4	4	0	105	3.53	6	8	0	104	5.54	402	17	.259	.320	.445	408	11	.289	.333	.429
2000	KC-A	846	36	.284	.351	.489	8	3	0	108	4.33	2	6	0	109	5.53	2	6	0	103	5.33	8	3	0	114	4.58	457	15	.284	.353	.466	389	21	.283	.349	.517
TOTALS		2613	96	.287	.344	.467	19	18	0	335	4.89	11	16	0	327	5.42	9	16	0	308	4.97	21	18	0	354	5.31	1340	45	.269	.330	.443	1273	51	.306	.360	.493
● Rick Sutcliffe	BL/TR																																			
1978	LA-N	7	0	.286	.444	.286	0	0	0	1	0.00	0	0	0	1	0.00	0	0	0	0	—	0	0	0	2	0.00	1	0	.000	.500	.000	6	0	.333	.429	.333
1979	LA-N	892	16	.243	.316	.333	12	3	0	147	3.36	5	7	0	95	3.61	7	6	0	107	3.95	10	4	0	135	3.07	422	6	.254	.329	.341	470	10	.234	.304	.326
1980	LA-N	427	10	.286	.366	.410	2	2	2	49	4.44	1	7	3	61	6.46	2	5	4	57	5.88	1	4	1	53	5.23	224	5	.308	.382	.424	203	5	.261	.349	.394
1981	LA-N	171	5	.240	.323	.392	2	1	0	29	4.60	0	1	0	18	3.06	2	2	0	41	3.27	0	0	0	6	9.53	92	4	.239	.333	.424	79	1	.241	.311	.354
1982	Cle-A	770	16	.226	.314	.327	7	3	0	116	3.03	7	5	1	100	2.88	6	3	1	81	3.22	8	5	0	135	2.80	387	5	.233	.321	.313	383	11	.219	.306	.342
1983	Cle-A	936	23	.268	.341	.427	8	5	0	120	4.57	9	6	0	123	4.01	9	3	0	111	4.07	8	8	0	133	4.48	509	14	.285	.360	.458	427	9	.248	.319	.391
1984	Cle-A	373	7	.298	.375	.432	2	2	0	41	4.43	2	3	0	54	5.70	4	5	0	94	5.15	0	0	0	0	—	203	4	.300	.372	.453	170	3	.294	.378	.406
1984	Chi-N	560	9	.220	.271	.339	8	0	0	68	2.77	8	1	0	82	2.63	2	1	0	21	2.57	14	0	0	129	2.71	304	3	.217	.259	.316	256	6	.223	.286	.367
1985	Chi-N	495	12	.240	.304	.364	4	2	0	55	3.44	4	6	0	75	3.00	7	6	0	105	2.06	1	2	0	25	7.92	244	5	.270	.331	.410	251	7	.211	.279	.319
1986	Chi-N	659	18	.252	.347	.393	3	6	0	99	4.35	2	8	0	77	5.00	4	10	0	116	4.18	1	4	0	60	5.52	372	8	.245	.339	.368	287	10	.261	.357	.425
1987	Chi-N	884	24	.252	.332	.402	10	5	0	124	3.49	8	5	0	114	3.88	10	4	0	114	3.55	8	6	0	123	3.79	503	13	.260	.355	.417	381	11	.241	.301	.381
1988	Chi-N	864	18	.269	.323	.388	5	5	0	102	3.19	8	9	0	124	4.42	6	5	0	94	4.52	7	9	0	132	3.40	456	7	.263	.329	.371	408	11	.275	.317	.407
1989	Chi-N	842	18	.240	.296	.354	5	7	0	99	4.80	11	4	0	130	2.78	9	5	0	111	3.50	7	6	0	118	3.80	503	11	.245	.305	.362	339	7	.233	.283	.342
1990	Chi-N	82	2	.305	.385	.439	0	1	0	10	9.58	0	1	0	11	2.45	0	0	0	0	—	0	2	0	21	5.91	47	0	.298	.414	.362	35	2	.314	.342	.543
1991	Chi-N	364	4	.264	.338	.379	3	1	0	57	3.18	3	4	0	40	5.40	2	4	0	39	6.75	4	1	0	58	2.33	218	4	.289	.366	.436	146	0	.226	.294	.295
1992	Bal-A	920	20	.273	.328	.393	9	8	0	132	4.17	7	7	0	106	4.85	10	6	0	122	4.13	6	9	0	115	4.84	431	13	.265	.320	.418	489	7	.280	.335	.372
1993	Bal-A	676	23	.314	.385	.496	6	6	0	100	4.50	4	4	0	66	7.64	8	3	0	104	4.77	2	7	0	62	7.36	338	11	.308	.387	.479	338	12	.320	.382	.512
1994	StL-N	281	11	.331	.402	.530	3	2	0	38	7.11	3	2	0	30	5.76	4	3	0	46	6.02	2	1	0	21	7.59	127	6	.354	.431	.583	154	5	.312	.378	.487
TOTALS		10203	236	.261	.332	.391	89	59	2	1387	3.98	82	80	4	1306	4.20	92	71	5	1362	4.11	79	68	1	1330	4.07	5381	119	.266	.340	.399	4822	117	.255	.322	.383
● Bruce Sutter	BR/TR																																			
1978	Chi-N	373	10	.220	.285	.343	4	9	15	58	3.70	4	1	12	40	2.45	5	3	9	48	2.05	3	7	18	50	4.29	181	7	.193	.270	.331	192	3	.245	.299	.354
1979	Chi-N	361	3	.186	.249	.244	2	2	15	44	1.24	4	4	22	58	2.97	2	2	17	44	1.43	4	4	20	57	2.83	182	0	.170	.223	.203	179	3	.201	.275	.285
1980	Chi-N	371	5	.243	.306	.326	4	3	12	46	2.72	1	5	16	56	2.57	3	4	17	44	3.27	2	4	11	58	2.16	173	3	.237	.313	.324	198	2	.247	.300	.328
1981	StL-N	293	5	.218	.277	.352	2	3	12	46	2.33	1	2	13	36	3.00	2	3	11	41	3.07	1	2	14	41	2.18	162	4	.222	.299	.395	131	1	.214	.248	.298
1982	StL-N	375	8	.235	.302	.368	6	4	18	55	2.93	3	4	18	47	2.87	6	5	17	51	4.44	3	3	19	52	1.39	196	5	.204	.262	.321	179	3	.268	.345	.419
1983	StL-N	343	8	.262	.321	.373	4	5	10	40	5.90	5	5	11	50	2.90	7	3	6	44	2.86	2	7	15	45	5.56	170	2	.300	.363	.388	173	6	.225	.278	.358
1984	StL-N	445	9	.245	.281	.344	1	4	24	63	1.71	4	3	21	59	1.37	2	3	19	55	1.48	3	4	26	68	1.59	222	5	.230	.272	.320	223	4	.260	.291	.368
1985	Atl-N	341	13	.267	.328	.437	6	5	7	46	5.91	1	2	16	43	2.95	4	3	14	51	3.51	3	4	9	37	5.84	161	5	.242	.322	.366	180	8	.289	.333	.500
1986	Atl-N	70	3	.243	.329	.429	0	0	2	10	4.50	2	0	1	9	4.15	2	0	3	19	4.34	0	0	0	0	—	40	0	.175	.267	.225	30	3	.333	.412	.700
1988	Atl-N	178	4	.275	.321	.382	0	2	7	25	4.38	1	2	7	21	5.23	1	2	11	31	2.87	0	2	3	14	9.00	99	2	.273	.301	.343	79	2	.278	.345	.430
TOTALS		3150	68	.237	.296	.351	29	37	122	433	3.30	26	28	137	418	2.76	34	28	124	428	2.84	21	37	135	423	3.23	1586	33	.226	.289	.327	1564	35	.249	.303	.375
● Don Sutton	BR/TR																																			
1978	LA-N	913	29	.250	.294	.402	10	4	0	128	3.10	5	7	0	111	4.07	8	6	0	107	4.11	7	5	0	131	3.09	407	11	.251	.298	.398	506	18	.249	.291	.405
1979	LA-N	841	21	.239	.288	.352	5	8	0	112	3.69	7	7	1	114	3.96	7	8	0	124	3.99	5	7	1	102	3.62	397	6	.194	.245	.275	444	15	.279	.327	.421
1980	LA-N	773	20	.211	.257	.330	8	2	1	120	1.88	5	3	0	93	2.62	5	2	0	86	2.51	8	3	1	126	1.99	372	8	.226	.273	.333	401	12	.197	.242	.327

YEAR	TM/L	TOTAL					HOME					AWAY					1ST HALF					2ND HALF					LEFT					RIGHT				
		AB	HR	AVG	OBP	SLG	W	L	SV	IP	ERA	W	L	SV	IP	ERA	W	L	SV	IP	ERA	W	L	SV	IP	ERA	AB	HR	AVG	OBP	SLG	AB	HR	AVG	OBP	SLG
1981	Hou-N	575	6	.230	.265	.303	5	3	0	66	1.22	6	6	0	92	3.61	4	7	0	82	3.42	7	2	0	77	1.75	287	3	.233	.271	.303	288	3	.226	.260	.302
1982	Hou-N	728	10	.232	.277	.326	7	3	0	125	2.24	6	5	0	70	4.35	7	4	0	108	3.32	6	4	0	87	2.60	355	6	.231	.272	.335	373	4	.233	.281	.316
1982	Mil-A	209	8	.263	.322	.416	3	1	0	33	2.73	1	0	0	22	4.15	0	0	0	0	—	4	1	0	55	3.29	123	6	.325	.394	.528	86	2	.174	.211	.256
1983	Mil-A	851	21	.246	.292	.375	2	6	0	109	3.96	6	7	0	111	4.20	5	4	0	115	3.28	3	9	0	105	4.97	423	10	.253	.300	.383	428	11	.238	.285	.367
1984	Mil-A	843	24	.266	.306	.399	7	9	0	126	4.00	7	3	0	87	3.43	5	7	0	105	3.67	9	5	0	107	3.86	441	12	.283	.331	.420	402	12	.246	.278	.376
1985	Oak-A	759	19	.256	.301	.375	7	2	0	101	3.20	6	6	0	93	4.65	7	5	0	105	4.39	6	3	0	90	3.31	384	11	.242	.288	.367	375	8	.269	.313	.384
1985	Cal-A	116	6	.233	.282	.448	1	1	0	13	4.15	1	1	0	19	3.38	0	0	0	0	—	2	2	0	32	3.69	58	2	.259	.328	.414	58	4	.207	.233	.483
1986	Cal-A	795	31	.242	.287	.411	10	6	0	128	3.23	5	5	0	79	4.58	6	5	0	89	4.96	9	6	0	118	2.82	407	11	.224	.282	.346	388	20	.260	.293	.479
1987	Cal-A	740	38	.269	.311	.458	3	6	0	95	4.28	8	5	0	97	5.10	5	8	0	97	4.19	6	3	0	95	5.21	369	16	.233	.286	.398	371	22	.305	.338	.518
1988	LA-N	337	7	.270	.327	.374	2	3	0	41	3.27	1	3	0	46	4.50	3	5	0	80	3.70	0	1	0	7	6.43	172	4	.291	.367	.401	165	3	.248	.282	.345
TOTALS		8480	240	.246	.291	.377	70	54	1	1197	3.13	64	58	1	1033	4.06	62	61	0	1099	3.78	72	51	2	1131	3.35	4195	106	.243	.293	.366	4285	134	.249	.289	.389
● Greg Swindell	BR/TL																																			
1986	Cle-A	235	9	.243	.290	.391	3	1	0	33	4.09	2	1	0	29	4.40	0	0	0	0	—	5	2	0	62	4.23	26	0	.154	.185	.192	209	9	.254	.302	.416
1987	Cle-A	396	18	.283	.343	.467	2	3	0	47	3.80	1	5	0	55	6.22	3	8	0	102	5.10	0	0	0	0	—	68	4	.309	.333	.574	328	14	.277	.345	.445
1988	Cle-A	928	18	.252	.286	.363	9	5	0	113	2.88	9	9	0	129	3.48	10	6	0	117	3.24	8	8	0	125	3.16	164	3	.274	.301	.372	764	15	.247	.283	.361
1989	Cle-A	690	16	.246	.297	.368	6	4	0	94	3.34	7	2	0	90	3.40	10	2	0	127	2.77	3	4	0	58	4.68	109	1	.220	.265	.284	581	15	.251	.303	.384
1990	Cle-A	850	27	.288	.324	.451	7	4	0	114	4.67	5	5	0	101	4.10	2	5	0	84	5.14	10	4	0	131	3.93	126	4	.286	.318	.421	724	23	.289	.325	.456
1991	Cle-A	916	21	.263	.287	.393	7	9	0	153	2.52	2	7	0	85	5.21	4	6	0	123	2.86	5	10	0	115	4.14	153	1	.275	.309	.373	763	20	.261	.283	.397
1992	Cin-N	808	14	.260	.295	.365	7	2	0	109	2.31	5	6	0	105	3.10	7	2	0	113	3.04	5	6	0	101	2.32	168	2	.244	.285	.345	640	12	.264	.297	.370
1993	Hou-N	761	24	.283	.318	.455	3	9	0	83	4.90	9	4	0	108	3.59	6	7	0	106	4.67	6	6	0	84	3.52	127	3	.315	.353	.520	634	21	.276	.311	.442
1994	Hou-N	580	20	.302	.329	.467	5	4	0	76	3.30	3	5	0	72	5.50	5	6	0	105	3.87	3	3	0	44	5.56	100	2	.350	.398	.470	480	18	.292	.314	.467
1995	Hou-N	606	21	.297	.337	.474	5	5	0	86	3.78	5	4	0	67	5.35	5	3	0	67	4.05	5	6	0	86	4.80	111	1	.234	.265	.324	495	20	.311	.353	.507
1996	Hou-N	103	5	.340	.405	.602	0	1	0	15	6.14	0	2	0	8	10.80	0	3	0	23	7.83	0	0	0	0	—	21	0	.381	.409	.476	82	5	.329	.404	.634
1996	Cle-A	111	8	.279	.325	.604	1	0	0	19	4.74	0	1	0	10	10.24	1	1	0	12	7.71	0	0	0	17	5.82	41	2	.244	.273	.512	70	6	.300	.355	.657
1997	Min-A	428	12	.238	.282	.402	3	2	1	57	3.79	4	2	0	59	3.38	4	2	0	55	3.95	3	2	1	61	3.25	152	1	.204	.223	.296	276	11	.257	.312	.460
1998	Min-A	255	10	.263	.317	.455	3	2	0	35	2.34	0	1	2	32	5.12	2	2	2	52	2.60	1	1	0	14	7.53	112	6	.241	.280	.446	143	4	.280	.344	.462
1998	Bos-A	90	3	.278	.369	.422	2	2	0	16	2.87	0	1	0	8	4.32	0	0	0	0	—	2	3	0	24	3.38	43	1	.326	.396	.419	47	2	.234	.345	.426
1999	Ari-N	235	8	.230	.296	.383	2	0	1	28	4.82	2	0	0	37	0.74	1	0	1	26	4.21	3	0	0	39	1.38	93	1	.215	.255	.280	142	7	.239	.321	.451
2000	Ari-N	288	7	.247	.295	.378	1	4	0	40	3.15	1	2	1	36	3.25	1	1	1	36	2.02	1	5	0	40	4.24	108	2	.157	.193	.231	180	5	.300	.354	.467
TOTALS		8280	241	.269	.309	.418	66	57	2	1117	3.48	55	57	3	1030	4.15	61	54	4	1145	3.80	60	60	1	1002	3.81	1722	34	.256	.292	.376	6558	207	.272	.313	.429
● Frank Tanana	BL/TL																																			
1978	Cal-A	927	26	.258	.306	.405	8	8	0	123	3.45	10	4	0	116	3.87	11	4	0	123	2.71	7	8	0	116	4.66	207	4	.261	.306	.377	720	22	.257	.306	.412
1979	Cal-A	352	9	.264	.315	.389	5	3	0	58	3.39	2	2	0	32	4.78	5	4	0	59	4.85	2	1	0	31	2.03	68	0	.206	.229	.250	284	9	.278	.334	.423
1980	Cal-A	805	18	.277	.320	.407	7	5	0	118	3.44	4	7	0	86	5.11	3	8	0	67	5.75	8	4	0	137	3.36	156	4	.263	.311	.423	649	14	.280	.322	.404
1981	Bos-A	536	17	.265	.322	.409	1	3	0	45	5.36	3	7	0	96	3.38	3	4	0	73	4.21	1	6	0	69	3.80	81	0	.123	.145	.136	455	17	.290	.351	.457
1982	Tex-A	753	16	.264	.319	.408	2	10	0	99	3.99	5	8	0	95	4.45	3	9	0	85	4.01	4	9	0	109	4.38	133	1	.278	.319	.406	620	15	.261	.319	.408
1983	Tex-A	601	14	.240	.303	.354	4	4	0	87	3.01	3	5	0	73	3.34	3	1	0	54	1.84	4	8	0	106	3.83	82	1	.220	.273	.293	519	13	.243	.308	.364
1984	Tex-A	956	30	.245	.306	.396	6	8	0	113	3.75	9	7	0	134	2.83	8	7	0	119	2.96	7	8	0	128	3.52	172	3	.267	.337	.401	784	27	.240	.300	.395
1985	Tex-A	310	15	.287	.334	.503	2	4	0	44	6.70	0	3	0	33	4.86	2	7	0	78	5.91	0	0	0	0	—	67	5	.313	.324	.657	243	10	.280	.337	.461
1985	Det-A	524	13	.250	.296	.387	6	4	0	65	3.58	4	3	0	72	3.13	1	0	0	7	0.00	9	7	0	130	3.52	83	2	.157	.195	.277	441	11	.268	.314	.408
1986	Det-A	731	23	.268	.328	.431	8	6	0	112	3.87	4	3	0	77	4.58	7	4	0	97	4.08	5	5	0	91	4.24	123	2	.317	.354	.447	608	21	.258	.323	.428
1987	Det-A	844	27	.256	.302	.410	10	5	0	109	3.06	5	5	0	110	4.76	7	4	0	106	3.24	8	6	0	113	4.54	140	4	.236	.296	.364	704	23	.260	.304	.419
1988	Det-A	799	25	.267	.323	.417	7	5	0	108	4.08	7	6	0	95	4.36	10	4	0	104	4.60	4	7	0	99	3.81	119	2	.210	.248	.286	680	23	.276	.336	.440
1989	Det-A	856	21	.265	.326	.380	4	6	0	119	3.48	6	8	0	105	3.70	7	7	0	121	3.72	3	7	0	103	3.42	125	2	.304	.374	.400	731	19	.259	.318	.376
1990	Det-A	678	25	.280	.349	.453	4	6	0	99	6.00	5	2	1	77	4.42	5	5	0	93	5.50	4	3	1	83	5.10	113	1	.230	.290	.292	565	24	.290	.360	.485
1991	Det-A	818	26	.265	.327	.412	7	5	0	121	4.10	6	7	0	97	3.35	5	6	0	101	3.49	8	6	0	117	4.01	159	5	.233	.282	.371	659	21	.273	.338	.422
1992	Det-A	704	22	.267	.351	.415	7	5	0	78	4.98	6	6	0	109	3.96	7	5	0	83	4.97	6	6	0	103	3.92	102	2	.225	.282	.333	602	20	.274	.362	.429
1993	NY-N	711	26	.278	.330	.450	3	7	0	86	4.71	4	8	0	97	4.27	4	7	0	87	4.64	3	8	0	96	4.33	148	4	.250	.300	.378	563	22	.286	.338	.469
1993	NY-A	81	2	.222	.284	.358	0	1	0	13	4.05	0	1	0	6	1.42	0	0	0	0	—	0	2	0	20	3.20	11	0	.182	.182	.273	70	2	.229	.299	.371
TOTALS		11986	355	.263	.321	.411	91	95	0	1597	4.03	83	92	1	1510	3.97	91	86	0	1457	4.06	83	101	1	1650	3.95	2089	42	.246	.295	.364	9897	313	.267	.326	.420
● Kevin Tapani	BR/TR																																			
1989	NY-N	26	1	.192	.290	.385	0	0	0	1	9.00	0	0	0	6	2.84	0	0	0	0	—	0	0	0	7	3.68	9	1	.333	.500	.889	17	0	.118	.158	.118
1989	Min-A	128	2	.266	.307	.367	1	2	0	17	5.71	1	0	0	15	1.76	0	0	0	0	—	2	2	0	33	3.86	81	1	.284	.326	.395	47	1	.234	.275	.319
1990	Min-A	621	12	.264	.297	.393	8	2	0	75	3.38	4	6	0	85	4.68	8	5	0	97	4.07	4	3	0	62	4.06	317	6	.284	.328	.435	304	6	.243	.263	.349
1991	Min-A	917	23	.245	.277	.382	10	5	0	132	2.79	6	4	0	112	3.22	5	7	0	109	3.06	11	2	0	135	2.93	520	8	.235	.257	.342	397	15	.259	.302	.433
1992	Min-A	839	17	.269	.309	.405	11	4	0	127	3.48	5	7	0	93	4.63	8	5	0	101	4.26	8	6	0	119	3.72	434	12	.279	.313	.452	405	5	.259	.304	.356
1993	Min-A	893	21	.272	.318	.419	3	9	0	98	4.39	9	6	0	127	4.45	3	9	0	100	5.69	9	6	0	126	3.43	525	12	.280	.320	.432	368	9	.261	.317	.399
1994	Min-A	621	13	.291	.335	.441	8	3	0	95	3.33	3	4	0	61	6.60	8	5	0	108	3.93	3	2	0	48	6.14	325	5	.271	.311	.400	296	8	.314	.361	.486
1995	Min-A	535	21	.290	.335	.482	4	5	0	76	4.74	2	6	0	58	5.15	4	8	0	93	4.56	2	3	0	41	5.71	315	12	.270	.321	.457	220	9	.318	.356	.518
1995	LA-N	235	8	.306	.345	.498	1	1	0	19	9.47	3	1	0	38	2.84	0	0	0	0	—	4	2	0	57	5.05	104	3	.327	.355	.548	131	5	.290	.338	.458
1996	Chi-A	880	34	.268	.326	.447	9	3	0	120	3.91	4	7	0	106	5.37	8	5	0	118	3.57	5	5	0	107	5.72	445	21	.276	.335	.499	435	13	.260	.318	.393
1997	Chi-N	318	7	.242	.296	.374	6	0	0	49	1.65	3	3	0	36	5.75	0	0	0	0	—	9	3	0	85	3.39	174	4	.230	.270	.362	144	3	.257	.325	.389
1998	Chi-N	858	30	.284	.333	.464	9	4	0	104	3.80	10	5	0	115	5.81	8	6	0	111	4.22	11	3	0	108	5.50	400	13	.303	.358	.498	458	17	.269	.311	.434
1999	Chi-N	539	12	.280	.322	.434	3	6	0	56	5.66	3	6	0	80	4.26	6	4	0	85	3.83	0	8	0	51	6.49	235	7	.264	.307	.447	304	5	.293	.334	.424
2000	Chi-N	767	35	.271	.319	.460	6	6	0	125	4.32	2	6	0	71	6.24	4	7	0	112	4.73	4	5	0	83	5.40	312	9	.231	.278	.359	455	26	.299	.346	.530
TOTALS		8177	236	.272	.316	.429	79	50	0	1094	3.89	55	61	0	1003	4.82	62	61	0	1034	4.18	72	50	0	1063	4.49	4196	114	.270	.313	.432	3981	122	.274	.319	.427
● Kent Tekulve	BR/TR																																			
1978	Pit-N	505	5	.228	.304	.299	6	3	19	73	2.21	2	4	12	62	2.47	4	5	8	58	2.64	4	2	23	77	2.09	183	2	.268	.384	.344	322	3	.205	.254	.273
1979	Pit-N	490	5	.222	.295	.298	5	4	15	65	3.31	5	4	16	69	2.22	3	5	10	57	3.81	7	3	21	78	1.97	166	0	.283	.398	.349	324	5	.191	.234	.272
1980	Pit-N	360	6	.267	.342	.367	6	5	10	47	3.04	2	7	11	46	3.74	5	4	9	39	3.26	3	8	12	54	3.48	120	1	.267	.376	.325	240	5	.267	.323	.387
1981	Pit-N	244	1	.250	.299	.328	2	4	3	37	1.93	3	1	0	28	3.25	2	3	1	22	4.15	3	2	2	43	1.66	90	0	.244	.313	.333	154	1	.253	.291	.325
1982	Pit-N	476	7	.237	.305	.340	8	2	9	65	3.06	4	6	11	64	2.67	5	2	8	61	1.91	7	6	12	67	3.74	191	6	.277	.398	.450	285	1	.211	.231	.267
1983	Pit-N	349	1	.223	.293	.292	4	2	7	54	1.33	3	3	11	45	2.01	3	2	6	41	1.96	4	3	12	58	1.40	138	1	.254	.375	.355	211	0	.204	.231	.251
1984	Pit-N	328	4	.262	.330	.357	1	5	6	51	3.00	2	4	7	37	2.19	2	6	6	39	3.43	1	3	7	49	2.03	113	1	.292	.400	.398	215	3	.247	.288	.335
1985	Pit-N	15	1	.467	.600	.800	0	0	0	3	18.00	0	0	0	0	0.00	0	0	0	3	16.20	0	0	0	0	—	9	0	.444	.583	.556	6	1	.500	.625	1.167
1985	Phi-N	272	4	.246	.312	.335	3	4	5	36	2.97	1	6	9	36	3.00	4	2	6	34	1.83	0	8	8	38	4.03	119	2	.286	.346	.387	153	2	.216	.287	.294
1986	Phi-N	413	2	.240	.281	.300	6	2	2	54	2.35	5	3	2	56	2.72	2	1	1	48	2.81	9	4	3	62	2.32	197	1	.254	.302	.305	216	1	.227	.261	.296
1987	Phi-N	395	8	.243	.293	.349	2	2	2	57	3.47	4	2	1	48	2.63	2	3	2	52	3.63	4	1	1	53	2.55	166	5	.307	.375	.464	229	3	.197	.230	.266
1988	Phi-N	315	3	.276	.326	.365	3	2	2	43	4.15	0	5	2	37	2.95	2	4	3	34	3.93	1	3	1	46	3.35	151	1	.225	.298	.278	164	2	.323	.353	.445
1989	Cin-N	206	5	.272	.342	.398	0	2	0	30	5.76	0	1	1	22	4.03	0	1	0	41	4.83	0	2	1	11	5.73	105	4	.362	.442	.543	101	1	.178	.234	.248
TOTALS		4368	52	.245	.309	.332	46	37	80	616	3.01	31	46	83	550	2.72	34	38	60	530	3.19	43	45	103	636	2.60	1748	24	.276	.369	.376	2620	28	.224	.265	.303
● Anthony Telford	BR/TR																																			
1990	Bal-A	146	4	.295	.375	.438	3	2	0	32	3.13	0	1	0	5	17.36	0	0	0	0	—	3	3	0	36	4.95	68	3	.309	.351	.500	78	1	.282	.394	.385
1991	Bal-A	102	3	.265	.303	.402	0	0	0	13	2.84	0	0	0	14	5.14	0	0	0	0	—	0	0	0	27	4.05	48	1	.271	.300	.354	54	2	.259	.305	.444
1993	Bal-A	32	3	.344	.382	.656	0	0	0	2	0.00	0	0	0	5	13.50	0	0	0	2	0.00	0	0	0	5	13.50	17	1	.353	.389	.529	15	2	.333	.375	.800
1997	Mon-N	326	11	.236	.315	.374	2	2	1	50	2.90	2	4	0	39	3.66	2	1	0	42	2.55	2	5	1	47	3.86	136	5	.235	.318	.390	190	6	.237	.313	.363
1998	Mon-N	344	9	.247	.322	.375	0	3	0	44	3.71	3	3	1	47	3.99	3	2	0	47	3.61	0	4	1	44	4.12	139	3	.237	.340	.338	205	6	.254	.310	.400
1999	Mon-N	380	3	.295	.359	.366	3	3	1	44	3.65	2	1	1	52	4.18	2	1	1	45	3.20	3	3	1	51	4.59	172	1	.326	.397	.407	208	2	.269	.328	.332
2000	Mon-N	296	10	.257	.317	.422	2	1	2	40	4.50	3	3	1	38	3.05	5	3	1	40	4.24	0	1	2	38	3.32	121	7	.281	.338	.521	175	3	.240	.302	.354
TOTALS		1626	43	.265	.333	.394	10	11	4	224	3.50	10	12	3	201	4.44	12	7	2	177	3.36	8	16	5	248	4.36	701	21	.278	.349	.418	925	22	.255	.321	.376
● Walt Terrell	BL/TR																																			
1982	NY-N	82	2	.268	.375	.390	0	3	0	21	3.43	0	0	0	0	—	0	0	0	0	—	0	3	0	21	3.43	46	2	.370	.453	.543	36	0	.139	.279	.194
1983	NY-N	490	7	.251	.326	.357	4	4	0	68	4.35	4	4	0	65	2.76	1	2	0	17	5.82	7	6	0	117	3.24	242	3	.264	.358	.384	248	4	.238	.293	.331
1984	NY-N	823	16	.282	.345	.388	3	7	0	102	4.15	8	5	0	113	2.95	5	7	0	100	3.23	6	5	0	115	3.77	392	4	.268	.336	.347	431	12	.295	.354	.425
1985	Det-A	865	9	.255	.330	.350	9	2	0	120	2.86	6	8	0	109	4.94	9	3	0	103	3.94	6	7	0	126	3.78	502	2	.247	.309	.323	363	7	.267	.357	.388
1986	Det-A	812	30	.245	.328	.415	10	3	0	116	3.35	5	9	0	102	5.93	7	6	0	106	4.49	8	6	0	111	4.62	422	11	.242	.324	.389	390	19	.249	.331	.444
1987	Det-A	947	30	.268	.333	.424	13	2	0	138	2.47	4	8	0	106	6.09	6	7	0	105	3.69	11	3	0	140	4.32	475	15	.257	.326	.419	472	15	.280	.340	.430
1988	Det-A	771	20	.258	.326	.383	4	5	0	84	3.76	3	11	0	123	4.11	3	5	0	76	4.76	4	11	0	131	3.51	413	8	.257	.319	.366	358	12	.260	.333	.402

YEAR	TM/L	TOTAL AB	HR	AVG	OBP	SLG	HOME W	L	SV	IP	ERA	AWAY W	L	SV	IP	ERA	1ST HALF W	L	SV	IP	ERA	2ND HALF W	L	SV	IP	ERA	LEFT AB	HR	AVG	OBP	SLG	RIGHT AB	HR	AVG	OBP	SLG
1989	SD-N	484	14	.277	.313	.430	2	6	0	52	3.78	3	7	0	71	4.18	4	11	0	106	3.81	1	2	0	17	5.29	244	5	.291	.331	.398	240	9	.262	.294	.463
1989	NY-A	332	9	.307	.356	.470	2	3	0	31	6.32	4	2	0	52	4.53	0	0	0	0	—	6	5	0	83	5.20	171	8	.333	.392	.556	161	1	.280	.316	.379
1990	Pit-N	332	13	.295	.364	.491	2	2	0	38	5.68	0	5	0	45	6.04	2	6	0	75	5.62	0	1	0	7	8.59	189	11	.328	.405	.582	143	2	.252	.308	.371
1990	Det-A	297	7	.290	.358	.421	3	2	0	41	3.54	3	2	0	35	5.71	0	0	0	0	—	6	4	0	75	4.54	153	5	.314	.369	.471	144	2	.264	.346	.368
1991	Det-A	853	16	.301	.358	.433	9	7	0	112	4.84	3	7	0	107	3.62	4	8	0	105	4.36	8	6	0	113	4.13	461	9	.306	.371	.440	392	7	.296	.343	.423
1992	Det-A	547	14	.298	.354	.431	4	3	0	62	4.76	3	7	0	74	5.57	1	8	0	72	4.98	6	2	0	64	5.46	235	3	.285	.342	.387	312	11	.308	.362	.465
TOTALS		7635	187	.274	.339	.409	65	49	0	985	3.83	46	75	0	1002	4.60	42	63	0	866	4.27	69	61	0	1120	4.18	3945	86	.275	.342	.405	3690	101	.272	.335	.412
● **Bob Tewksbury** BR/TR																																				
1986	NY-A	511	8	.282	.325	.397	4	1	0	60	2.56	5	4	0	71	3.95	5	2	0	75	3.48	4	3	0	55	3.09	266	6	.252	.286	.380	245	2	.314	.365	.416
1987	NY-A	139	5	.338	.374	.482	1	2	0	21	5.48	0	2	0	12	9.00	1	2	0	23	6.35	0	2	0	11	7.59	66	0	.348	.386	.394	73	5	.329	.364	.562
1987	Chi-N	76	1	.421	.500	.539	0	1	0	5	5.40	0	3	0	13	6.92	0	0	0	0	—	0	4	0	18	6.50	43	1	.395	.458	.581	33	0	.455	.548	.485
1988	Chi-N	15	1	.400	.444	.600	0	0	0	0	—	0	0	0	3	8.10	0	0	0	3	8.10	0	0	0	0	—	7	1	.714	.750	1.143	8	0	.125	.200	.125
1989	StL-N	111	2	.225	.298	.333	0	0	0	19	3.32	1	0	0	11	3.27	0	0	0	0	—	1	0	0	30	3.30	55	1	.255	.333	.345	56	1	.196	.262	.321
1990	StL-N	565	7	.267	.286	.379	4	5	0	66	3.66	6	4	1	79	3.30	3	0	1	36	4.00	7	9	0	109	3.29	334	4	.278	.302	.383	231	3	.251	.263	.372
1991	StL-N	733	13	.281	.317	.413	6	3	0	94	3.24	5	9	0	97	3.26	6	4	0	89	2.72	5	8	0	102	3.72	406	4	.278	.326	.392	327	9	.284	.305	.440
1992	StL-N	876	15	.248	.265	.353	10	2	0	124	1.52	6	3	0	109	2.90	9	2	0	120	1.94	7	3	0	113	2.40	517	10	.242	.250	.344	359	5	.256	.286	.365
1993	StL-N	857	15	.301	.318	.412	11	7	0	132	3.35	6	3	0	82	4.61	8	6	0	99	4.01	9	4	0	115	3.68	431	6	.313	.326	.418	426	9	.289	.311	.406
1994	StL-N	626	19	.304	.328	.481	4	4	0	66	6.00	8	6	0	90	4.82	9	7	0	111	5.45	3	3	0	45	5.00	331	8	.293	.314	.447	295	11	.315	.344	.519
1995	Tex-A	529	8	.319	.346	.446	3	3	0	65	3.72	5	4	0	64	5.46	6	3	0	75	3.70	2	4	0	54	5.80	327	5	.300	.331	.434	202	3	.351	.370	.465
1996	SD-N	814	17	.275	.310	.402	5	4	0	94	3.64	5	6	0	113	4.87	6	5	0	111	4.20	4	5	0	95	4.44	318	4	.264	.309	.365	496	13	.282	.310	.425
1997	Min-A	674	12	.297	.325	.430	3	7	0	77	4.44	5	6	0	92	4.03	4	7	0	96	3.47	4	6	0	73	5.20	351	6	.308	.345	.442	323	6	.285	.304	.418
1998	Min-A	596	19	.292	.318	.455	3	6	0	76	3.89	4	7	0	72	5.75	4	9	0	88	4.58	3	4	0	60	5.10	311	7	.260	.293	.386	285	12	.326	.347	.530
TOTALS		7122	142	.287	.316	.416	54	45	0	900	3.51	56	57	1	907	4.33	61	47	1	927	3.82	49	55	0	880	4.03	3763	63	.282	.312	.400	3359	79	.293	.320	.433
● **Mike Timlin** BR/TR																																				
1991	Tor-A	404	6	.233	.317	.297	7	2	1	61	2.35	4	4	2	47	4.21	6	4	2	59	3.22	5	2	1	50	3.08	169	3	.296	.392	.373	235	3	.187	.260	.243
1992	Tor-A	166	0	.271	.351	.307	0	2	1	25	5.84	0	0	0	19	1.89	0	1	0	9	3.12	0	1	1	35	4.37	74	0	.311	.407	.378	92	0	.239	.304	.250
1993	Tor-A	222	7	.284	.360	.405	2	1	0	30	4.15	2	1	1	25	5.33	1	1	0	33	5.94	3	1	1	22	2.82	102	4	.275	.356	.441	120	3	.292	.363	.375
1994	Tor-A	157	5	.261	.352	.401	0	0	1	22	4.03	0	1	1	18	6.62	0	0	2	26	6.66	0	1	0	14	2.51	71	1	.296	.390	.408	86	4	.233	.320	.395
1995	Tor-A	157	1	.242	.324	.318	4	3	1	28	2.25	0	0	4	14	1.93	3	1	3	22	3.63	1	2	2	20	0.46	94	1	.298	.340	.415	63	0	.159	.303	.175
1996	Tor-A	205	4	.229	.294	.341	0	0	12	22	1.66	1	6	19	35	4.89	0	1	14	26	2.77	1	5	17	31	4.40	116	1	.259	.313	.353	89	3	.191	.270	.326
1997	Tor-A	169	6	.243	.306	.373	3	0	3	26	2.45	0	2	6	21	3.38	1	0	9	34	2.65	2	2	0	13	3.46	83	2	.253	.326	.373	86	4	.233	.287	.372
1997	Sea-A	100	2	.280	.314	.380	1	1	1	13	4.05	2	1	0	12	3.65	0	0	0	0	—	3	2	1	26	3.86	35	1	.286	.342	.457	65	1	.277	.299	.338
1998	Sea-A	296	5	.264	.306	.358	1	1	13	43	3.59	2	2	6	37	2.21	1	3	1	42	3.67	2	0	18	38	2.15	137	4	.263	.290	.358	159	1	.264	.320	.358
1999	Bal-A	231	9	.221	.304	.381	3	6	13	33	4.09	0	3	14	30	3.00	3	6	9	33	4.96	0	3	18	30	2.08	106	4	.198	.280	.358	125	5	.240	.324	.400
2000	Bal-A	134	6	.276	.355	.448	2	0	4	17	4.86	0	3	7	18	4.91	2	3	7	25	5.04	0	0	4	10	4.50	60	2	.333	.397	.450	74	4	.230	.321	.446
2000	StL-N	113	2	.265	.382	.354	3	0	1	15	2.35	0	1	0	14	4.40	0	0	0	0	—	3	1	1	30	3.34	46	1	.283	.365	.370	67	1	.254	.393	.343
TOTALS		2354	53	.252	.327	.356	26	16	51	335	3.36	11	24	60	291	3.87	17	20	47	308	4.12	20	20	64	318	3.08	1093	24	.275	.347	.387	1261	29	.232	.309	.330
● **Steve Trachsel** BR/TR																																				
1993	Chi-N	73	4	.219	.247	.452	0	1	0	7	2.57	0	1	0	13	5.68	0	0	0	0	—	0	2	0	20	4.58	40	1	.150	.190	.250	33	3	.303	.314	.697
1994	Chi-N	549	19	.242	.312	.404	1	7	0	78	3.56	8	0	0	68	2.79	6	5	0	102	3.81	3	2	0	44	1.83	250	6	.216	.285	.328	299	13	.264	.334	.468
1995	Chi-N	629	25	.277	.352	.453	2	8	0	76	6.19	5	5	0	85	4.24	2	6	0	71	4.06	5	7	0	90	6.02	295	13	.254	.343	.444	334	12	.296	.360	.461
1996	Chi-N	769	30	.235	.298	.411	9	5	0	119	2.58	4	4	0	86	3.65	7	4	0	103	2.00	6	5	0	102	4.07	282	13	.241	.293	.433	487	17	.232	.301	.398
1997	Chi-N	785	32	.287	.344	.476	7	4	0	121	4.15	1	8	0	80	5.06	4	6	0	104	4.76	4	6	0	97	4.25	373	12	.260	.317	.424	412	20	.311	.367	.524
1998	Chi-N	786	27	.260	.334	.425	9	3	0	118	4.13	6	5	0	90	4.88	6	5	0	101	4.46	9	3	0	107	4.46	371	9	.240	.321	.358	415	18	.277	.346	.484
1999	Chi-N	807	32	.280	.330	.457	4	8	0	98	5.14	4	10	0	108	5.93	2	10	0	95	6.18	6	8	0	111	5.03	355	16	.285	.349	.470	452	16	.277	.314	.447
2000	TB-A	544	16	.294	.356	.471	3	5	0	50	5.80	3	5	0	88	3.89	6	7	0	102	4.49	0	3	0	35	4.84	259	4	.305	.358	.421	285	12	.284	.354	.516
2000	Tor-A	246	10	.293	.357	.480	1	3	0	47	4.21	1	2	0	16	8.44	0	0	0	0	—	2	5	0	63	5.29	126	5	.278	.345	.437	120	5	.308	.368	.525
TOTALS		5188	195	.268	.332	.445	36	44	0	713	4.28	32	40	0	634	4.57	33	43	0	678	4.23	35	41	0	669	4.60	2351	79	.257	.324	.411	2837	116	.277	.338	.472
● **Mike Trombley** BR/TR																																				
1992	Min-A	174	5	.247	.318	.402	1	0	0	18	3.50	2	2	0	28	3.18	0	0	0	0	—	3	2	0	46	3.30	79	2	.278	.360	.443	95	3	.221	.282	.368
1993	Min-A	451	15	.290	.349	.490	2	4	2	61	4.28	4	2	0	53	5.57	4	3	1	53	5.30	2	3	1	62	4.52	222	9	.320	.396	.550	229	6	.262	.298	.432
1994	Min-A	195	10	.287	.353	.508	0	0	0	27	7.09	2	0	0	22	5.40	2	0	0	27	7.67	0	0	0	21	4.64	76	4	.263	.325	.447	119	6	.303	.370	.546
1995	Min-A	392	18	.273	.346	.495	3	3	0	45	5.16	1	5	0	52	6.02	0	3	0	18	5.50	4	5	0	80	5.65	219	8	.297	.380	.511	173	10	.243	.302	.474
1996	Min-A	259	2	.236	.312	.340	3	1	3	36	4.54	2	0	3	33	1.36	2	0	1	17	1.59	3	1	5	52	3.48	111	2	.297	.395	.468	148	0	.189	.245	.243
1997	Min-A	311	7	.248	.317	.357	0	1	1	43	4.78	2	2	0	39	3.92	1	1	0	47	4.44	1	2	1	36	4.29	108	2	.213	.301	.306	203	5	.266	.326	.384
1998	Min-A	363	16	.248	.332	.433	3	1	1	51	3.86	3	4	0	45	3.38	3	2	0	49	3.10	3	3	1	47	4.18	144	9	.264	.321	.500	219	7	.237	.339	.388
1999	Min-A	342	15	.272	.328	.468	2	3	9	42	4.04	0	5	15	45	4.60	1	5	12	54	3.15	1	3	12	33	6.27	146	4	.240	.335	.377	196	11	.296	.322	.536
2000	Bal-A	271	15	.247	.346	.461	3	2	2	37	3.38	1	3	2	35	4.93	3	2	1	29	4.71	1	3	3	43	3.74	108	5	.241	.341	.426	163	10	.252	.316	.485
TOTALS		2758	103	.263	.335	.444	17	15	18	361	4.46	17	23	20	353	4.39	16	16	15	294	4.35	18	22	23	420	4.48	1213	45	.275	.357	.462	1545	58	.254	.318	.430
● **John Tudor** BL/TL																																				
1979	Bos-A	113	2	.345	.384	.469	1	0	0	23	3.47	0	2	0	5	21.21	0	0	0	0	—	1	2	0	28	6.43	22	0	.182	.269	.318	91	2	.385	.414	.505
1980	Bos-A	341	4	.238	.304	.346	5	1	0	53	2.53	3	4	0	39	3.69	0	1	0	4	6.23	8	4	0	88	2.86	73	0	.205	.277	.260	268	4	.246	.312	.369
1981	Bos-A	294	11	.252	.319	.429	3	0	0	31	3.82	1	3	1	48	5.06	2	3	0	61	4.11	2	0	1	17	6.23	75	2	.253	.287	.427	219	9	.251	.329	.429
1982	Bos-A	767	20	.280	.336	.424	7	6	0	104	4.59	6	4	0	92	2.55	6	5	0	81	3.54	7	5	0	114	3.70	120	4	.267	.296	.467	647	16	.283	.343	.416
1983	Bos-A	927	32	.255	.316	.405	7	6	0	131	4.81	6	6	0	111	3.24	5	4	0	116	3.49	8	8	0	126	4.64	147	2	.204	.259	.279	780	30	.264	.326	.428
1984	Pit-N	808	19	.248	.295	.371	6	5	0	102	2.73	6	6	0	110	3.78	4	6	0	107	3.29	8	5	0	105	3.25	111	3	.243	.287	.351	697	16	.248	.296	.374
1985	StL-N	1001	14	.209	.249	.285	14	2	0	151	1.49	7	6	0	124	2.47	7	7	0	112	2.73	14	1	0	163	1.38	148	2	.203	.244	.264	853	12	.210	.249	.288
1986	StL-N	807	22	.244	.289	.388	9	2	0	127	2.48	4	5	0	92	3.52	6	4	0	134	2.41	7	3	0	85	3.72	141	1	.191	.223	.277	666	21	.255	.302	.411
1987	StL-N	367	11	.272	.331	.455	5	1	0	50	2.88	5	1	0	46	4.89	2	1	0	16	6.06	8	1	0	80	3.39	65	2	.246	.310	.446	302	9	.278	.335	.457
1988	StL-N	531	5	.247	.287	.348	3	2	0	77	2.70	3	3	0	69	1.83	4	2	0	91	1.38	2	3	0	54	3.83	88	4	.273	.305	.500	443	1	.242	.283	.318
1988	LA-N	204	5	.284	.318	.387	2	2	0	29	3.07	2	1	0	23	1.57	0	0	0	0	—	4	3	0	52	2.41	30	1	.300	.300	.433	174	4	.282	.321	.379
1989	LA-N	55	1	.309	.377	.382	0	0	0	13	1.35	0	0	0	1	27.00	0	0	0	4	4.15	0	0	0	10	2.70	10	0	.200	.273	.200	45	1	.333	.400	.422
1990	StL-N	534	10	.225	.268	.331	4	1	0	75	2.52	8	3	0	71	2.27	6	3	0	86	2.93	6	1	0	60	1.64	128	1	.211	.241	.273	406	9	.229	.276	.350
TOTALS		6749	156	.248	.299	.374	66	28	0	967	3.01	51	44	1	830	3.25	42	36	0	814	3.01	75	36	1	983	3.21	1158	22	.226	.268	.341	5591	134	.253	.305	.381
● **Fernando Valenzuela** BL/TL																																				
1980	LA-N	59	0	.136	.200	.153	1	0	0	12	0.00	1	0	1	6	0.00	0	0	0	0	—	2	0	1	18	0.00	15	0	.267	.333	.267	44	0	.091	.149	.114
1981	LA-N	684	11	.205	.270	.279	7	2	0	97	1.57	6	5	0	95	3.41	9	4	0	110	2.45	4	3	0	82	2.51	143	1	.224	.276	.273	541	10	.200	.268	.281
1982	LA-N	1046	13	.236	.292	.328	10	7	0	151	2.98	9	6	0	134	2.75	10	6	0	133	2.92	9	7	0	152	2.84	226	3	.252	.320	.381	820	10	.232	.284	.313
1983	LA-N	960	16	.255	.325	.367	8	3	0	111	3.00	7	7	0	146	4.32	8	5	0	126	3.63	7	5	0	131	3.86	197	0	.269	.332	.340	763	16	.252	.324	.374
1984	LA-N	952	14	.229	.306	.326	6	8	0	135	2.94	6	9	0	126	3.13	8	8	0	127	2.97	4	9	0	134	3.10	209	5	.244	.306	.354	743	9	.225	.305	.318
1985	LA-N	986	14	.214	.286	.292	7	5	0	134	2.09	10	5	0	139	2.79	7	8	0	126	2.51	10	2	0	147	2.39	163	3	.233	.291	.344	823	11	.210	.285	.282
1986	LA-N	998	18	.226	.287	.325	11	3	0	131	2.27	10	8	0	139	3.96	10	5	0	135	2.86	11	6	0	134	3.43	187	0	.246	.286	.321	811	18	.222	.287	.326
1987	LA-N	968	25	.262	.348	.401	6	7	0	121	3.50	8	7	0	130	4.43	7	5	0	118	3.66	7	9	0	133	4.26	167	4	.228	.283	.377	801	21	.270	.361	.406
1988	LA-N	530	11	.268	.357	.374	1	5	1	64	5.34	4	3	0	78	3.33	5	5	0	98	3.96	0	3	1	45	4.84	96	3	.313	.391	.448	434	8	.258	.349	.357
1989	LA-N	738	11	.251	.337	.351	4	6	0	99	3.26	6	7	0	97	3.61	4	6	0	87	3.92	6	7	0	109	3.05	125	1	.256	.324	.352	613	10	.250	.340	.351
1990	LA-N	808	19	.276	.337	.412	8	5	0	118	3.75	5	8	0	86	5.73	6	6	0	104	3.73	7	7	0	100	5.47	130	4	.315	.381	.454	678	15	.268	.329	.404
1991	Cal-A	31	3	.452	.486	.839	0	2	0	7	12.15	0	0	0	0	—	0	2	0	7	12.15	0	0	0	0	—	6	1	.500	.500	1.000	25	2	.440	.483	.800
1993	Bal-A	674	18	.266	.343	.429	5	3	0	88	4.40	3	7	0	91	5.46	3	7	0	86	4.29	5	3	0	93	5.54	120	4	.283	.379	.483	554	14	.262	.335	.417
1994	Phi-N	170	8	.247	.274	.435	1	0	0	33	2.76	0	2	0	12	3.65	0	0	0	6	0.00	1	2	0	39	3.46	33	1	.212	.206	.333	137	7	.255	.290	.460
1995	SD-N	349	16	.289	.351	.504	4	2	0	43	5.23	4	1	0	47	4.75	2	2	0	35	6.49	6	1	0	56	4.04	63	1	.317	.377	.460	286	15	.283	.345	.514
1996	SD-N	659	17	.269	.334	.407	8	5	0	102	3.61	5	3	0	69	3.63	4	5	0	84	3.44	9	3	0	88	3.78	92	1	.261	.327	.326	567	16	.270	.335	.420
1997	SD-N	272	10	.309	.387	.474	1	4	0	39	4.35	1	4	0	27	5.33	2	8	0	66	4.75	0	0	0	0	—	45	1	.311	.404	.444	227	9	.308	.384	.480
1997	StL-N	87	2	.253	.363	.379	0	2	0	11	3.27	0	2	0	12	7.71	0	2	0	15	4.80	0	2	0	8	7.04	22	1	.318	.423	.500	65	1	.231	.342	.338
TOTALS		10971	226	.248	.319	.364	88	69	1	1495	3.21	85	84	1	1435	3.89	85	84	0	1462	3.48	88	69	2	1468	3.61	2039	34	.260	.324	.373	8932	192	.245	.318	.362
● **Javier Vazquez** BR/TR																																				
1998	Mon-N	672	31	.292	.364	.493	3	7	0	80	6.19	2	8	0	92	5.95	2	6	0	91	5.72	3	9	0	81	6.44	352	22	.276	.338	.509	320	9	.309	.393	.475
1999	Mon-N	605	20	.255	.316	.428	4	4	0	85	4.22	5	4	0	69	5.97	2	4	0	57	6.63	7	4	0	98	4.05	274	8	.234	.305	.383	331	12	.272	.326	.465

YEAR	TM/L	TOTAL AB	HR	AVG	OBP	SLG	HOME W	L	SV	IP	ERA	AWAY W	L	SV	IP	ERA	1ST HALF W	L	SV	IP	ERA	2ND HALF W	L	SV	IP	ERA	LEFT AB	HR	AVG	OBP	SLG	RIGHT AB	HR	AVG	OBP	SLG
2000	Mon-N	865	24	.286	.335	.434	5	4	0	104	3.82	6	5	0	114	4.26	6	4	0	102	4.05	5	5	0	115	4.06	394	7	.279	.337	.401	471	17	.291	.333	.461
TOTALS		2142	75	.279	.339	.451	12	15	0	269	4.65	13	17	0	276	5.26	10	14	0	251	5.24	15	18	0	294	4.71	1020	37	.266	.329	.433	1122	38	.291	.349	.466
● **Dave Veres** BR/TR																																				
1994	Hou-N	158	4	.247	.280	.367	3	0	1	22	2.45	0	3	0	19	2.37	3	3	0	20	2.70	0	0	1	21	2.14	62	2	.258	.309	.387	96	2	.240	.260	.354
1995	Hou-N	370	5	.241	.299	.330	2	0	0	50	2.52	3	1	1	53	2.03	3	1	0	44	2.06	2	0	1	60	2.41	139	3	.237	.333	.360	231	2	.242	.276	.312
1996	Mon-N	307	10	.277	.353	.433	4	0	2	32	4.45	2	3	2	45	3.97	4	2	4	43	5.40	2	1	0	34	2.62	122	3	.311	.397	.467	185	7	.254	.324	.411
1997	Mon-N	245	5	.278	.353	.433	1	2	0	26	4.10	1	1	1	36	3.03	2	2	1	40	3.12	0	1	0	22	4.15	105	2	.295	.408	.476	140	3	.264	.307	.400
1998	Col-N	288	6	.233	.301	.337	2	0	5	45	2.98	1	1	3	31	2.61	0	0	3	43	3.77	3	1	5	33	1.62	117	3	.239	.326	.385	171	3	.228	.283	.304
1999	Col-N	303	14	.290	.369	.469	4	6	11	41	7.40	0	2	20	36	2.52	2	2	11	37	4.34	2	6	20	40	5.90	128	6	.328	.425	.516	175	8	.263	.325	.434
2000	StL-N	272	6	.239	.315	.360	2	2	15	41	2.66	1	3	14	35	3.09	1	2	15	40	2.93	2	3	14	36	2.78	119	1	.210	.301	.277	153	5	.261	.325	.425
TOTALS		1943	50	.258	.327	.389	18	10	34	258	3.80	8	14	41	255	2.82	15	12	34	268	3.53	11	12	41	245	3.08	792	20	.269	.361	.410	1151	30	.250	.301	.374
● **Frank Viola** BL/TL																																				
1982	Min-A	503	22	.302	.351	.491	1	8	0	72	6.25	3	2	0	54	3.83	2	0	0	23	5.01	2	10	0	103	5.26	74	4	.311	.338	.527	429	18	.301	.353	.485
1983	Min-A	841	34	.288	.363	.479	5	9	0	124	5.09	2	6	0	86	6.05	3	5	0	90	5.02	4	10	0	120	5.83	143	4	.245	.303	.357	698	30	.297	.374	.504
1984	Min-A	964	28	.233	.289	.373	8	2	0	105	2.40	10	10	0	153	3.77	7	7	0	110	3.18	11	5	0	147	3.24	160	3	.262	.326	.381	804	25	.228	.281	.372
1985	Min-A	979	26	.268	.315	.410	9	6	0	125	3.68	9	8	0	126	4.50	9	6	0	115	4.14	9	8	0	135	4.06	216	7	.287	.325	.454	763	19	.262	.312	.397
1986	Min-A	958	37	.268	.327	.442	6	6	0	124	4.58	10	7	0	122	4.43	8	6	0	120	4.66	8	7	0	126	4.36	154	5	.273	.311	.409	804	32	.267	.330	.448
1987	Min-A	955	29	.241	.293	.378	11	3	0	137	2.69	6	7	0	115	3.14	6	6	0	115	3.29	11	4	0	137	2.57	163	5	.245	.305	.374	792	24	.240	.291	.379
1988	Min-A	962	20	.245	.286	.357	14	2	0	132	2.18	10	5	0	123	3.14	12	2	0	123	2.34	12	5	0	132	2.93	163	4	.233	.280	.368	799	16	.248	.287	.354
1989	Min-A	668	17	.256	.306	.398	4	6	0	96	3.09	4	6	0	80	4.63	6	8	0	131	3.72	2	4	0	45	4.00	118	3	.280	.323	.475	550	14	.251	.303	.382
1989	NY-N	318	5	.236	.296	.318	2	3	0	32	4.78	3	2	0	53	2.53	0	0	0	0	—	5	5	0	85	3.38	54	0	.241	.268	.259	264	5	.235	.301	.330
1990	NY-N	938	15	.242	.288	.333	12	5	0	126	2.44	8	7	0	124	2.90	11	3	0	106	2.45	9	9	0	143	2.83	183	1	.257	.317	.328	755	14	.238	.281	.334
1991	NY-N	905	25	.286	.325	.423	8	8	0	123	4.26	5	7	0	109	3.64	8	5	0	116	3.02	5	10	0	115	4.93	193	5	.233	.273	.363	712	20	.301	.339	.440
1992	Bos-A	886	13	.242	.313	.331	8	7	0	117	4.08	5	5	0	121	2.83	7	5	0	107	3.45	6	7	0	131	3.44	109	1	.211	.281	.294	777	12	.246	.317	.336
1993	Bos-A	694	12	.259	.331	.372	5	3	0	92	2.26	6	5	0	92	4.01	4	7	0	97	3.35	7	1	0	87	2.90	114	1	.272	.341	.404	580	11	.257	.329	.366
1994	Bos-A	115	2	.296	.381	.452	0	1	0	18	6.87	1	0	0	13	1.42	1	1	0	31	4.65	0	0	0	0	—	18	0	.222	.222	.278	97	2	.309	.405	.485
1995	Cin-N	60	3	.333	.359	.483	0	0	0	6	4.76	0	1	0	9	7.27	0	0	0	0	—	0	1	0	14	6.28	8	0	.250	.250	.250	52	3	.346	.375	.519
1996	Tor-A	123	6	.350	.443	.537	0	2	0	20	9.00	1	1	0	10	5.23	1	3	0	30	7.71	0	0	0	0	—	29	1	.207	.233	.310	94	5	.394	.496	.606
TOTALS		10869	294	.260	.316	.395	93	71	0	1447	3.67	83	79	0	1389	3.79	85	64	0	1315	3.64	91	86	0	1521	3.80	1899	44	.256	.305	.383	8970	250	.261	.318	.398
● **Duane Ward** BR/TR																																				
1986	Atl-N	63	2	.349	.423	.556	0	1	0	7	5.40	0	0	0	9	8.68	0	1	0	16	7.31	0	0	0	0	—	28	2	.357	.455	.679	35	0	.343	.395	.457
1986	Tor-A	10	0	.300	.533	.500	0	0	0	1	0.00	0	1	0	1	27.00	0	0	0	0	—	0	1	0	2	13.50	5	0	.200	.500	.400	5	0	.400	.571	.600
1987	Tor-A	43	0	.326	.464	.442	0	0	0	8	9.00	1	0	0	4	2.45	0	0	0	3	15.00	1	0	0	9	4.15	15	0	.200	.455	.333	28	0	.393	.471	.500
1988	Tor-A	413	5	.245	.344	.327	5	1	8	59	2.29	4	2	7	53	4.44	5	0	5	50	2.70	4	3	10	62	3.79	173	3	.231	.332	.312	240	2	.254	.352	.338
1989	Tor-A	408	4	.230	.326	.304	2	6	8	54	3.81	2	4	7	60	3.73	4	7	5	61	3.39	0	3	10	54	4.19	172	2	.262	.383	.360	236	2	.208	.280	.263
1990	Tor-A	457	9	.221	.287	.322	0	4	5	66	3.02	2	4	6	62	3.92	1	3	6	61	3.82	1	5	5	66	3.12	189	5	.259	.372	.386	268	4	.194	.219	.276
1991	Tor-A	386	3	.207	.271	.262	5	4	14	63	3.14	2	2	9	44	2.23	1	3	14	51	2.45	6	3	9	56	3.05	187	3	.193	.275	.278	199	0	.221	.266	.246
1992	Tor-A	367	5	.207	.282	.286	6	1	6	52	1.57	1	3	6	50	2.36	3	4	8	45	2.80	4	0	4	56	1.28	183	5	.197	.289	.322	184	0	.217	.275	.250
1993	Tor-A	254	4	.193	.266	.264	1	2	21	33	2.73	1	1	24	39	1.63	1	2	22	35	2.04	1	1	23	36	2.23	123	2	.211	.310	.285	131	2	.176	.221	.244
1995	Tor-A	19	0	.579	.680	.737	0	1	0	2	43.20	0	0	0	1	0.00	0	1	0	3	27.00	0	0	0	0	—	12	0	.750	.800	1.000	7	0	.286	.500	.286
TOTALS		2420	32	.228	.310	.311	19	20	62	344	3.17	13	17	59	323	3.40	15	21	60	326	3.48	17	16	61	341	3.09	1087	22	.235	.340	.343	1333	10	.222	.284	.284
● **Dave Weathers** BR/TR																																				
1991	Tor-A	57	1	.263	.442	.386	0	0	0	6	5.68	1	0	0	8	4.32	0	0	0	0	—	1	0	0	15	4.91	17	1	.294	.455	.588	40	0	.250	.436	.300
1992	Tor-A	13	1	.385	.467	.615	0	0	0	0	—	0	0	0	3	8.10	0	0	0	0	—	0	0	0	3	8.10	6	0	.500	.500	.500	7	1	.286	.444	.714
1993	Fla-N	186	3	.306	.355	.441	0	3	0	20	7.20	2	0	0	26	3.51	0	0	0	0	—	2	3	0	46	5.12	97	1	.309	.356	.464	89	2	.303	.354	.416
1994	Fla-N	542	13	.306	.376	.439	6	7	0	80	5.27	2	5	0	55	5.27	7	6	0	103	3.41	1	6	0	32	11.25	312	6	.314	.386	.439	230	7	.296	.363	.439
1995	Fla-N	352	8	.295	.391	.423	2	1	0	36	7.43	2	4	0	54	5.00	2	3	0	48	5.25	2	2	0	42	6.80	143	2	.315	.438	.441	209	6	.282	.356	.411
1996	Fla-N	281	7	.302	.373	.441	1	0	0	28	3.90	1	2	0	44	4.95	2	1	0	50	4.17	0	1	0	22	5.40	110	2	.345	.430	.482	171	5	.275	.333	.415
1996	NY-A	73	1	.315	.433	.425	0	0	0	9	9.35	0	2	0	9	9.35	0	0	0	0	—	0	2	0	17	9.35	46	1	.435	.509	.587	27	0	.111	.314	.148
1997	NY-A	40	1	.375	.468	.575	0	0	0	4	12.27	0	1	0	5	8.44	0	1	0	9	10.00	0	0	0	0	—	15	1	.467	.529	.867	25	0	.320	.433	.400
1997	Cle-A	67	2	.343	.416	.507	1	1	0	7	7.71	0	1	0	10	7.45	0	0	0	0	—	1	2	0	17	7.56	33	1	.303	.343	.485	34	1	.382	.476	.529
1998	Cin-N	261	3	.330	.393	.437	1	4	0	33	5.79	1	0	0	30	6.67	2	4	0	62	6.21	0	0	0	0	—	116	3	.362	.444	.534	145	0	.303	.348	.359
1998	Mil-A	179	3	.246	.306	.369	3	0	0	27	2.63	1	1	0	20	3.98	0	0	0	0	—	4	1	0	48	3.21	59	1	.254	.318	.390	120	2	.242	.300	.358
1999	Mil-A	366	14	.279	.346	.459	2	2	0	48	5.81	5	2	2	45	3.40	5	3	2	51	4.09	2	1	0	42	5.31	124	7	.290	.379	.492	242	7	.273	.328	.442
2000	Mil-A	281	7	.260	.339	.384	3	3	0	43	3.14	0	2	1	33	2.97	3	3	1	47	3.45	0	2	0	29	2.45	94	1	.223	.368	.287	187	6	.278	.322	.433
TOTALS		2698	64	.296	.372	.433	19	21	0	341	5.38	15	20	3	342	4.85	21	21	3	370	4.48	13	20	0	313	5.87	1172	27	.316	.402	.461	1526	37	.280	.348	.411
● **Bob Welch** BR/TR																																				
1978	LA-N	402	6	.229	.274	.318	4	2	2	62	1.60	3	2	1	49	2.55	2	0	1	11	0.00	5	4	2	100	2.25	214	3	.234	.273	.332	188	3	.223	.275	.303
1979	LA-N	309	7	.265	.339	.372	3	1	4	33	2.70	2	5	1	48	4.88	4	5	5	62	3.36	1	1	0	20	5.95	126	4	.286	.366	.437	183	3	.251	.320	.328
1980	LA-N	785	15	.242	.310	.329	10	4	0	126	2.71	4	5	0	87	4.12	8	3	0	111	2.34	6	6	0	102	4.31	382	8	.267	.352	.369	403	7	.218	.269	.290
1981	LA-N	544	11	.259	.313	.384	5	2	0	77	3.14	4	3	0	64	3.80	4	3	0	81	3.24	5	2	0	61	3.71	241	2	.253	.309	.357	303	9	.264	.315	.406
1982	LA-N	868	19	.229	.297	.340	7	6	0	124	2.61	9	5	0	111	4.20	8	5	0	110	3.69	8	6	0	126	3.07	442	10	.249	.322	.362	426	9	.209	.272	.317
1983	LA-N	738	13	.222	.291	.318	7	7	0	102	2.64	8	5	0	102	2.66	6	7	0	97	2.70	9	5	0	107	2.60	363	10	.253	.326	.366	375	3	.192	.257	.272
1984	LA-N	699	11	.273	.330	.389	6	6	0	88	3.67	7	7	0	90	3.89	6	8	0	99	3.83	7	5	0	80	3.71	319	2	.245	.313	.348	380	9	.297	.345	.424
1985	LA-N	626	16	.225	.272	.359	9	3	0	97	2.70	5	1	0	71	1.78	1	1	0	30	3.03	13	3	0	138	2.16	327	3	.214	.254	.291	299	13	.237	.291	.435
1986	LA-N	904	14	.251	.297	.357	5	6	0	132	2.66	2	7	0	104	4.08	3	6	0	111	4.04	4	7	0	124	2.61	483	7	.265	.308	.371	421	7	.235	.284	.342
1987	LA-N	921	21	.221	.289	.342	7	6	0	136	3.24	8	3	0	116	3.19	8	4	0	115	3.52	7	5	0	137	2.96	529	10	.236	.301	.346	392	11	.202	.273	.337
1988	Oak-A	923	22	.257	.321	.384	13	4	0	148	2.56	4	5	0	97	5.29	10	4	0	122	3.38	7	5	0	122	3.90	459	12	.248	.318	.386	464	10	.265	.324	.381
1989	Oak-A	792	13	.241	.313	.357	10	2	0	107	2.77	7	6	0	102	3.25	9	4	0	98	2.66	8	4	0	112	3.30	418	3	.211	.300	.304	374	10	.275	.327	.417
1990	Oak-A	886	26	.242	.304	.391	14	2	0	117	1.92	13	4	0	121	3.94	13	2	0	121	2.69	14	4	0	117	3.22	465	12	.258	.325	.404	421	14	.223	.281	.375
1991	Oak-A	835	25	.263	.341	.404	8	7	0	125	3.60	4	6	0	95	5.87	7	5	0	114	3.72	5	8	0	106	5.50	430	8	.272	.348	.377	405	17	.254	.334	.432
1992	Oak-A	461	13	.247	.312	.360	4	3	0	52	2.94	7	4	0	72	3.52	5	4	0	60	2.87	6	3	0	64	3.66	241	6	.266	.325	.373	220	7	.227	.299	.345
1993	Oak-A	670	25	.310	.368	.491	5	6	0	85	5.61	4	5	0	82	4.96	5	6	0	97	4.55	4	5	0	70	6.33	369	11	.309	.362	.477	301	14	.312	.375	.508
1994	Oak-A	272	10	.290	.384	.482	0	1	0	26	7.86	3	5	0	42	6.59	1	5	0	54	7.79	2	1	0	14	4.40	139	5	.331	.435	.547	133	5	.248	.329	.414
TOTALS		11635	267	.249	.312	.371	117	68	6	1639	3.01	94	78	2	1453	3.98	100	72	6	1492	3.47	111	74	2	1600	3.46	5947	116	.255	.322	.372	5688	151	.242	.302	.371
● **David Wells** BL/TL																																				
1987	Tor-A	119	0	.311	.374	.370	2	1	0	13	3.38	2	2	1	16	4.50	0	1	0	4	9.00	4	2	1	25	3.20	44	0	.318	.375	.318	75	0	.307	.373	.400
1988	Tor-A	242	12	.269	.354	.492	1	3	2	32	3.66	2	2	2	32	5.57	3	4	4	54	4.36	0	1	0	11	5.91	68	0	.265	.351	.324	174	12	.270	.355	.557
1989	Tor-A	319	5	.207	.269	.298	5	2	1	49	2.40	2	2	1	38	2.39	2	3	2	52	2.79	5	1	0	35	1.82	78	1	.231	.294	.346	241	4	.199	.261	.282
1990	Tor-A	701	14	.235	.283	.371	3	2	2	83	2.61	8	4	1	106	3.55	5	2	3	65	3.72	6	4	0	124	2.84	110	2	.264	.319	.436	591	12	.230	.276	.359
1991	Tor-A	747	24	.252	.297	.403	6	5	0	86	4.81	9	5	1	112	2.88	9	4	0	98	2.93	6	6	1	100	4.50	130	3	.208	.246	.315	617	21	.261	.308	.421
1992	Tor-A	478	16	.289	.346	.471	4	3	1	60	3.60	3	6	1	60	7.20	3	3	2	55	2.93	4	6	0	65	7.52	92	3	.293	.363	.446	386	13	.288	.342	.477
1993	Det-A	721	26	.254	.300	.416	8	3	0	108	2.74	3	6	0	79	6.18	9	3	0	113	3.28	2	6	0	74	5.57	108	2	.250	.328	.361	613	24	.254	.295	.426
1994	Det-A	434	13	.260	.302	.412	3	2	0	58	3.43	2	5	0	54	4.53	1	5	0	50	5.44	4	2	0	62	2.77	75	2	.253	.253	.347	359	11	.262	.311	.426
1995	Det-A	495	17	.242	.297	.410	8	0	0	73	2.95	2	3	0	57	3.16	6	3	0	91	3.26	4	0	0	39	2.52	91	3	.264	.313	.429	404	14	.238	.293	.406
1995	Cin-N	279	6	.265	.304	.416	4	2	0	41	3.05	2	3	0	31	4.31	0	0	0	0	—	6	5	0	73	3.59	56	1	.214	.214	.411	223	5	.278	.325	.417
1996	Bal-A	866	32	.285	.325	.458	7	6	0	130	3.53	4	8	0	94	7.35	5	7	0	110	5.17	6	7	0	115	5.10	186	4	.231	.260	.339	680	28	.300	.343	.491
1997	NY-A	861	24	.278	.317	.434	8	5	0	116	3.88	8	5	0	102	4.59	8	4	0	106	4.00	8	6	0	112	4.41	159	3	.327	.344	.465	702	21	.266	.311	.427
1998	NY-A	817	29	.239	.265	.398	11	1	0	127	3.06	7	3	0	88	4.11	10	2	0	106	3.92	8	2	0	109	3.06	184	7	.245	.272	.402	633	22	.237	.263	.397
1999	Tor-A	907	32	.271	.320	.438	8	6	0	122	4.29	9	4	0	110	5.40	8	6	0	110	5.58	9	4	0	122	4.13	156	6	.295	.349	.468	751	26	.266	.314	.431
2000	Tor-A	920	23	.289	.316	.429	9	5	0	116	4.98	11	3	0	114	3.24	13	2	0	115	3.43	7	6	0	114	4.80	198	5	.288	.324	.449	722	18	.289	.313	.424
TOTALS		8906	273	.263	.307	.419	87	46	6	1213	3.59	74	61	7	1093	4.58	82	49	11	1128	3.95	79	58	2	1179	4.16	1735	42	.264	.306	.399	7171	231	.263	.307	.424
● **Bob Wells** BR/TR																																				
1994	Phi-N	17	0	.235	.381	.294	1	0	0	5	1.93	0	0	0	0	0.00	1	0	0	5	1.80	0	0	0	0	—	8	0	.250	.250	.375	9	0	.222	.462	.222
1994	Sea-A	16	0	.250	.294	.313	0	0	0	0	—	1	0	0	4	2.25	0	0	0	0	—	1	0	0	4	2.25	4	0	.500	.600	.750	12	0	.167	.167	.167
1995	Sea-A	310	11	.284	.364	.487	1	2	0	34	6.35	3	1	0	43	5.27	2	3	0	35	7.53	2	0	0	42	4.29	139	5	.295	.379	.525	171	6	.275	.352	.456
1996	Sea-A	515	25	.274	.338	.497	4	3	0	62	5.25	8	4	0	69	5.35	9	1	0	70	3.10	3	6	0	61	7.82	257	13	.300	.372	.521	258	12	.248	.304	.473

		TOTAL					HOME					AWAY					1ST HALF					2ND HALF					LEFT					RIGHT				
YEAR	TM/L	AB	HR	AVG	OBP	SLG	W	L	SV	IP	ERA	W	L	SV	IP	ERA	W	L	SV	IP	ERA	W	L	SV	IP	ERA	AB	HR	AVG	OBP	SLG	AB	HR	AVG	OBP	SLG
1997	Sea-A	280	11	.314	.360	.507	1	0	1	33	4.68	1	0	1	35	6.75	2	0	0	28	7.62	0	0	2	39	4.38	113	3	.301	.370	.398	167	8	.323	.352	.581
1998	Sea-A	207	12	.261	.319	.507	1	2	0	25	5.76	1	0	0	27	6.41	0	1	0	29	5.52	2	1	0	22	6.85	86	6	.349	.398	.628	121	6	.198	.263	.421
1999	Min-A	323	8	.245	.312	.387	4	2	1	53	2.91	4	1	0	35	5.19	4	1	0	48	3.72	4	2	1	39	3.92	121	3	.248	.321	.388	202	5	.243	.306	.386
2000	Min-A	324	14	.247	.284	.441	0	4	5	53	2.55	0	3	5	33	5.40	0	5	5	40	3.57	0	2	5	46	3.72	120	1	.233	.285	.350	204	13	.255	.284	.495
TOTALS		1992	81	.270	.331	.468	12	13	7	264	4.30	18	9	6	245	5.58	18	11	5	256	4.65	12	11	8	253	5.19	848	31	.288	.356	.473	1144	50	.257	.311	.464
● Turk Wendell BB/TR																																				
1993	Chi-N	88	0	.273	.333	.318	0	1	0	5	8.44	1	1	0	17	3.12	0	2	0	12	7.30	1	0	0	10	0.87	43	0	.372	.426	.465	45	0	.178	.245	.178
1994	Chi-N	63	3	.349	.432	.587	0	0	0	2	13.50	0	1	0	12	11.68	0	1	0	14	11.93	0	0	0	0	—	33	1	.333	.436	.515	30	2	.367	.429	.667
1995	Chi-N	238	11	.298	.363	.487	2	0	0	41	4.87	1	1	0	20	5.03	1	0	0	19	4.82	2	1	0	42	4.97	96	4	.333	.398	.490	142	7	.275	.340	.486
1996	Chi-N	288	8	.201	.313	.316	3	3	8	45	2.00	1	2	10	34	3.93	4	2	7	42	2.38	0	3	11	38	3.35	113	2	.221	.333	.301	175	6	.189	.299	.326
1997	Chi-N	223	4	.238	.350	.395	3	3	3	30	3.86	0	2	1	30	4.55	2	3	4	43	4.01	1	2	0	17	4.67	91	1	.297	.413	.484	132	3	.197	.306	.333
1997	NY-N	60	3	.250	.400	.467	0	0	1	10	6.52	0	0	0	7	2.70	0	0	0	0	—	0	0	1	16	4.96	22	3	.364	.481	.864	38	0	.184	.354	.237
1998	NY-N	281	4	.221	.306	.349	4	0	1	39	3.00	1	1	3	38	2.87	3	0	0	25	4.26	2	1	4	51	2.28	96	4	.229	.357	.427	185	0	.216	.277	.308
1999	NY-N	327	9	.245	.324	.379	3	3	3	44	2.45	2	1	0	42	3.67	1	0	2	48	3.21	4	4	1	38	2.84	131	2	.260	.333	.344	196	7	.235	.318	.403
2000	NY-N	291	9	.206	.312	.357	5	2	1	45	1.99	3	4	0	37	5.54	4	3	0	46	3.52	4	3	1	37	3.68	102	3	.225	.358	.373	189	6	.196	.286	.349
TOTALS		1859	51	.239	.333	.384	20	12	17	261	3.27	9	13	14	237	4.45	15	11	13	249	4.20	14	14	18	249	3.47	727	20	.272	.373	.420	1132	31	.218	.306	.361
● John Wetteland BR/TR																																				
1989	LA-N	371	8	.218	.283	.329	4	3	1	47	3.45	1	5	0	56	4.04	1	0	1	26	2.08	4	8	0	77	4.34	193	3	.212	.269	.295	178	5	.225	.296	.365
1990	LA-N	167	6	.263	.344	.407	1	2	0	17	4.32	1	2	0	26	5.13	2	4	0	32	6.12	0	0	0	11	0.84	88	3	.295	.392	.432	79	3	.228	.287	.380
1991	LA-N	31	0	.161	.250	.194	1	0	0	2	0.00	0	0	0	7	0.00	0	0	0	0	—	1	0	0	9	0.00	16	0	.188	.263	.250	15	0	.133	.235	.133
1992	Mon-N	301	6	.213	.304	.306	2	3	21	45	3.83	2	1	16	39	1.86	0	2	12	32	5.12	4	2	25	52	1.57	175	3	.200	.288	.291	126	3	.230	.326	.325
1993	Mon-N	308	3	.188	.260	.276	6	1	22	44	1.44	3	2	21	42	1.30	3	0	16	38	1.41	6	3	27	47	1.34	177	3	.175	.254	.266	131	0	.206	.268	.290
1994	Mon-N	228	5	.202	.273	.316	3	3	10	29	4.30	1	3	15	34	1.57	2	5	13	39	3.20	2	1	12	24	2.22	132	4	.205	.284	.341	96	1	.198	.259	.281
1995	NY-A	216	6	.185	.233	.324	0	4	15	31	4.06	1	1	16	30	1.78	1	1	10	25	2.52	0	4	21	36	3.22	113	3	.186	.250	.301	103	3	.184	.213	.350
1996	NY-A	241	9	.224	.284	.390	2	0	18	29	1.86	0	3	25	35	3.63	0	1	25	35	3.38	2	2	18	29	2.17	144	7	.285	.340	.507	97	2	.134	.200	.216
1997	Tex-A	236	5	.182	.248	.292	5	0	15	34	1.05	2	2	16	31	2.93	4	1	17	33	2.73	3	1	14	32	1.13	126	1	.167	.254	.222	110	4	.200	.241	.373
1998	Tex-A	231	6	.203	.247	.320	3	1	22	33	2.97	0	0	20	29	0.94	2	0	22	30	1.50	1	1	20	32	2.53	131	1	.191	.217	.252	100	5	.220	.284	.410
1999	Tex-A	256	9	.262	.307	.438	3	3	23	35	4.41	1	1	20	31	2.87	1	2	25	34	4.01	3	2	18	32	3.34	136	4	.265	.325	.426	120	5	.258	.287	.450
2000	Tex-A	235	10	.285	.351	.489	5	1	15	34	3.71	1	4	19	26	4.85	3	2	20	32	3.98	3	3	14	28	4.45	123	7	.309	.377	.561	112	3	.259	.323	.411
TOTALS		2821	73	.218	.284	.347	35	21	162	380	3.13	13	24	168	385	2.73	19	18	161	356	3.29	29	27	169	409	2.62	1554	39	.222	.291	.346	1267	34	.214	.275	.349
● Gabe White BL/TL																																				
1994	Mon-N	92	4	.261	.343	.543	1	1	0	14	4.61	0	0	1	10	8.10	1	1	0	20	6.64	0	0	1	3	2.70	11	0	.273	.467	.455	81	4	.259	.322	.556
1995	Mon-N	100	7	.260	.319	.510	0	0	0	7	1.29	1	2	0	19	9.16	1	1	0	17	2.70	0	1	0	9	15.00	21	2	.286	.304	.571	79	5	.253	.322	.494
1997	Cin-N	154	6	.253	.291	.448	1	1	0	21	3.86	1	1	1	20	4.95	0	0	0	0	—	2	2	1	41	4.39	18	0	.500	.526	.722	136	6	.221	.260	.412
1998	Cin-N	372	17	.231	.284	.414	1	1	5	47	3.80	4	4	4	51	4.21	2	3	0	45	5.60	3	2	9	54	2.68	121	5	.231	.282	.388	251	12	.231	.284	.426
1999	Cin-N	242	13	.281	.324	.496	0	1	0	34	3.48	1	1	0	27	5.60	1	2	0	38	4.06	0	0	0	23	5.01	76	2	.355	.410	.526	166	11	.247	.284	.482
2000	Cin-N	5	1	.400	.500	1.000	0	0	0	1	18.00	0	0	0	0	—	0	0	0	1	18.00	0	0	0	0	—	3	1	.667	.667	1.667	2	0	.000	.333	.000
2000	Col-N	298	5	.208	.246	.312	10	2	2	45	2.80	1	0	3	38	1.42	6	0	1	40	1.34	5	2	4	43	2.95	102	3	.186	.237	.304	196	2	.219	.251	.316
TOTALS		1263	53	.243	.292	.429	13	6	7	169	3.52	8	8	9	165	4.68	11	7	1	161	4.08	10	7	15	173	4.11	352	13	.267	.320	.435	911	40	.234	.281	.427
● Rick White BR/TR																																				
1994	Pit-N	282	9	.280	.329	.443	2	3	3	36	4.25	2	2	3	39	3.43	2	4	6	39	4.66	2	1	0	37	2.95	141	4	.270	.298	.411	141	5	.291	.358	.475
1995	Pit-N	221	3	.299	.352	.403	0	2	0	28	5.86	2	1	0	27	3.62	0	1	0	24	3.80	2	2	0	31	5.46	104	1	.317	.374	.433	117	2	.282	.333	.376
1998	TB-A	261	8	.253	.315	.395	2	2	0	34	3.67	0	4	0	34	3.93	1	3	0	29	4.08	1	3	0	40	3.60	125	4	.240	.307	.384	136	4	.265	.322	.404
1999	TB-A	434	8	.304	.358	.426	4	1	0	53	3.91	1	2	0	55	4.25	4	1	0	54	4.02	1	2	0	54	4.14	188	4	.309	.348	.452	246	4	.301	.365	.407
2000	TB-A	259	7	.220	.301	.347	2	0	0	40	2.04	1	6	2	32	5.12	3	4	2	59	3.38	0	2	0	13	3.55	108	3	.287	.381	.389	151	4	.172	.241	.318
2000	NY-N	112	2	.232	.315	.348	1	1	0	13	4.97	1	2	1	16	2.87	0	0	0	0	—	2	3	1	28	3.81	45	2	.222	.321	.400	67	0	.239	.311	.313
TOTALS		1569	37	.272	.332	.402	11	9	3	203	3.90	7	17	6	203	3.98	10	13	8	203	3.94	8	13	1	203	3.94	711	18	.281	.338	.416	858	19	.263	.327	.390
● Ed Whitson BR/TR																																				
1978	Pit-N	272	5	.243	.333	.346	3	2	2	34	2.12	2	4	2	40	4.28	2	2	3	20	2.29	3	4	1	54	3.64	101	2	.257	.364	.376	171	3	.234	.314	.327
1979	Pit-N	223	6	.238	.346	.359	1	2	0	37	4.58	1	1	1	20	3.98	2	3	1	58	4.37	0	0	0	0	—	91	1	.253	.376	.319	132	5	.227	.325	.386
1979	SF-N	386	5	.254	.326	.381	2	5	0	40	4.02	3	3	0	60	3.90	0	1	0	1	18.00	5	7	0	99	3.81	174	0	.264	.347	.379	212	5	.245	.309	.382
1980	SF-N	819	7	.271	.318	.355	5	6	0	96	2.99	6	7	0	115	3.20	6	7	0	118	3.29	5	6	0	94	2.87	420	3	.302	.339	.398	399	4	.238	.295	.311
1981	SF-N	477	10	.273	.339	.396	4	2	0	57	3.18	2	7	0	66	4.75	2	5	0	62	4.38	4	4	0	61	3.67	236	2	.258	.313	.352	241	8	.286	.364	.440
1982	Cle-A	394	6	.231	.324	.317	1	0	1	43	4.57	3	2	1	64	2.38	1	1	2	45	2.98	3	1	0	62	3.47	193	4	.218	.311	.316	201	2	.244	.336	.318
1983	SD-N	559	23	.256	.316	.422	1	3	0	72	3.77	4	4	1	73	4.83	2	4	0	54	3.48	3	3	1	90	4.80	256	13	.242	.297	.465	303	10	.267	.331	.386
1984	SD-N	710	16	.255	.297	.368	9	4	0	104	2.94	5	4	0	85	3.60	8	4	0	82	3.51	6	4	0	107	3.03	356	9	.267	.318	.382	354	7	.243	.275	.353
1985	NY-A	650	19	.309	.350	.469	4	2	0	68	4.08	6	6	0	90	5.48	3	6	0	72	4.38	7	2	0	87	5.30	376	11	.311	.342	.481	274	8	.307	.362	.453
1986	NY-A	161	5	.335	.412	.540	2	2	0	20	7.52	3	0	0	17	7.56	5	2	0	37	7.61	0	0	0	0	0.00	61	3	.361	.494	.656	100	2	.320	.355	.470
1986	SD-N	296	8	.287	.364	.439	1	3	0	38	4.30	0	4	0	38	6.87	0	0	0	0	—	1	7	0	76	5.59	176	4	.244	.327	.347	120	4	.350	.419	.575
1987	SD-N	784	36	.251	.309	.443	5	7	0	107	4.96	5	6	0	99	4.47	8	7	0	103	4.56	2	6	0	103	4.89	429	14	.284	.350	.441	355	22	.211	.260	.445
1988	SD-N	779	17	.259	.298	.379	9	5	0	109	3.46	4	6	0	96	4.13	7	5	0	94	4.87	6	6	0	111	2.84	399	7	.266	.312	.383	380	10	.253	.283	.374
1989	SD-N	841	22	.235	.278	.360	9	6	0	124	2.98	7	5	0	103	2.27	10	5	0	116	2.55	6	6	0	111	2.77	497	16	.262	.305	.408	344	6	.198	.238	.291
1990	SD-N	855	13	.251	.289	.347	5	6	0	126	2.65	9	3	0	103	2.53	6	5	0	106	2.88	8	4	0	122	2.35	522	6	.270	.309	.358	333	7	.222	.259	.330
1991	SD-N	311	13	.299	.332	.479	0	3	0	33	5.18	4	3	0	46	4.93	3	6	0	72	4.85	1	0	0	6	7.11	180	5	.283	.326	.439	131	8	.321	.341	.534
TOTALS		8517	211	.262	.317	.392	61	58	3	1109	3.63	64	65	5	1115	3.96	65	63	6	1040	3.90	60	60	2	1184	3.70	4467	100	.272	.327	.401	4050	111	.251	.305	.381
● Bob Wickman BR/TR																																				
1992	NY-A	187	2	.273	.344	.385	2	1	0	23	5.09	4	0	0	27	3.29	0	0	0	0	—	6	1	0	50	4.11	89	1	.281	.347	.427	98	1	.265	.342	.347
1993	NY-A	550	13	.284	.368	.425	9	0	1	69	2.75	5	4	3	71	6.43	8	1	0	84	4.30	6	3	4	56	5.11	244	6	.279	.374	.426	306	7	.288	.363	.425
1994	NY-A	253	3	.213	.287	.304	4	1	2	37	2.45	1	3	4	33	3.78	3	3	5	45	3.00	2	1	1	25	3.24	89	1	.236	.355	.371	164	2	.201	.246	.268
1995	NY-A	304	6	.253	.335	.359	1	0	0	37	3.89	1	4	1	43	4.19	2	2	0	37	4.17	0	2	1	43	3.95	128	3	.305	.369	.430	176	3	.216	.312	.307
1996	NY-A	314	7	.299	.373	.414	2	1	0	43	6.28	2	0	0	36	2.75	3	1	0	52	3.81	1	0	0	27	6.33	146	3	.329	.402	.418	168	4	.274	.347	.411
1996	Mil-A	60	3	.200	.314	.367	1	0	0	7	1.29	2	0	0	10	4.66	0	0	0	0	—	3	0	0	17	3.24	32	2	.188	.297	.375	28	1	.214	.333	.357
1997	Mil-A	353	8	.252	.333	.363	5	2	0	46	3.69	2	4	1	49	1.82	5	3	1	41	3.48	2	3	0	54	2.15	146	1	.260	.364	.329	207	7	.246	.310	.386
1998	Mil-A	301	5	.262	.352	.346	5	5	11	42	4.25	1	4	14	40	3.15	3	4	11	49	1.64	3	5	14	33	6.82	137	1	.270	.365	.321	164	4	.256	.340	.366
1999	Mil-A	286	6	.262	.351	.374	1	2	15	29	3.68	2	6	22	45	3.20	2	3	14	35	3.34	1	5	23	39	3.43	127	2	.197	.335	.283	159	4	.314	.364	.447
2000	Mil-A	172	1	.215	.299	.273	1	1	8	22	2.86	1	1	8	24	3.00	2	1	10	36	2.00	0	1	6	10	6.30	79	0	.253	.314	.304	93	1	.183	.287	.247
2000	Cle-A	100	0	.270	.348	.340	1	1	8	16	1.13	0	2	6	11	6.75	0	0	0	0	—	1	3	14	27	3.38	53	0	.264	.371	.340	47	0	.277	.320	.340
TOTALS		2880	54	.261	.343	.369	32	14	45	371	3.66	21	28	59	390	3.86	28	18	41	379	3.32	25	24	63	382	4.19	1270	20	.269	.362	.372	1610	34	.255	.328	.367
● Milt Wilcox BR/TR																																				
1978	Det-A	816	22	.255	.317	.398	8	4	0	110	3.76	5	8	0	105	3.76	4	7	0	92	4.01	9	5	0	123	3.58	362	8	.271	.361	.409	454	14	.242	.279	.390
1979	Det-A	752	18	.267	.338	.403	6	5	0	89	3.64	6	5	0	107	4.95	6	4	0	92	5.38	6	6	0	104	3.45	370	13	.295	.369	.465	382	5	.241	.307	.343
1980	Det-A	766	24	.262	.325	.420	9	6	0	113	4.55	4	5	0	86	4.40	8	4	0	112	3.61	5	7	0	86	5.63	416	12	.269	.331	.430	350	12	.254	.317	.409
1981	Det-A	615	10	.247	.310	.340	6	5	0	96	3.38	6	4	0	70	2.56	6	5	0	76	3.57	6	4	0	91	2.58	345	6	.220	.289	.316	270	4	.281	.337	.370
1982	Det-A	729	18	.257	.338	.380	6	5	0	93	3.00	6	5	0	101	4.20	5	4	0	104	3.55	7	6	0	90	3.71	354	6	.263	.347	.364	375	12	.251	.329	.395
1983	Det-A	692	19	.237	.313	.366	6	4	0	100	3.23	5	6	0	86	4.83	7	7	0	116	3.10	4	3	0	70	5.40	366	11	.246	.319	.380	326	8	.227	.306	.350
1984	Det-A	726	13	.252	.318	.371	10	4	0	104	2.67	7	4	0	89	5.54	8	5	0	97	4.16	9	3	0	96	3.83	392	3	.245	.318	.332	334	10	.260	.317	.416
1985	Det-A	162	6	.315	.369	.506	1	2	0	23	4.63	0	1	0	16	5.17	1	3	0	39	4.85	0	0	0	0	—	81	2	.358	.395	.556	81	4	.272	.344	.457
1986	Sea-A	226	11	.327	.399	.553	0	3	0	23	5.48	0	5	0	33	5.51	0	8	0	56	5.50	0	0	0	0	—	123	8	.374	.455	.650	103	3	.272	.330	.437
TOTALS		5484	141	.259	.327	.395	52	38	0	752	3.58	39	43	0	693	4.44	45	47	0	784	4.04	46	34	0	661	3.94	2809	69	.267	.341	.403	2675	72	.251	.313	.387
● Woody Williams BR/TR																																				
1993	Tor-A	146	2	.274	.371	.363	3	0	0	19	4.34	0	1	0	18	4.42	3	0	0	20	3.54	0	1	0	17	5.40	57	0	.246	.377	.281	89	2	.292	.366	.416
1994	Tor-A	215	5	.205	.313	.335	1	0	0	28	3.81	0	3	0	31	3.48	1	2	0	35	5.35	0	1	0	24	1.13	98	0	.184	.304	.214	117	5	.222	.321	.436
1995	Tor-A	200	6	.220	.322	.370	0	1	0	30	3.94	1	1	0	24	3.38	0	2	0	40	3.86	1	0	0	14	3.21	117	4	.231	.323	.385	83	2	.205	.320	.349
1996	Tor-A	230	8	.278	.340	.426	2	4	0	36	5.00	2	1	0	23	4.30	0	0	0	2	7.71	4	5	0	57	4.61	139	4	.288	.379	.439	91	4	.264	.272	.407
1997	Tor-A	748	31	.269	.329	.465	5	8	0	111	4.14	4	6	0	84	4.63	3	7	0	94	4.60	6	7	0	101	4.11	395	15	.271	.349	.443	353	16	.266	.305	.490
1998	Tor-A	800	36	.245	.314	.460	6	2	0	94	4.04	4	7	0	116	4.81	8	3	0	109	3.30	2	6	0	101	5.72	418	19	.268	.343	.507	382	17	.220	.281	.408
1999	SD-N	794	33	.268	.328	.463	6	3	0	89	3.63	6	9	0	119	4.99	4	5	0	103	3.59	8	7	0	106	5.20	356	10	.258	.309	.419	438	23	.276	.343	.500

		TOTAL					HOME					AWAY					1ST HALF					2ND HALF					LEFT					RIGHT				
YEAR	**TM/L**	**AB**	**HR**	**AVG**	**OBP**	**SLG**	**W**	**L**	**SV**	**IP**	**ERA**	**W**	**L**	**SV**	**IP**	**ERA**	**W**	**L**	**SV**	**IP**	**ERA**	**W**	**L**	**SV**	**IP**	**ERA**	**AB**	**HR**	**AVG**	**OBP**	**SLG**	**AB**	**HR**	**AVG**	**OBP**	**SLG**
2000	SD-N	636	23	.239	.300	.401	6	5	0	107	3.71	4	3	0	61	3.82	3	2	0	38	5.21	7	6	0	130	3.32	285	4	.232	.304	.326	351	19	.245	.297	.462
TOTALS		3769	144	.253	.322	.434	29	23	0	513	3.98	21	31	0	476	4.50	22	21	0	441	4.06	28	33	0	548	4.37	1865	56	.255	.333	.414	1904	88	.251	.311	.454
● **Mike Williams** BR/TR																																				
1992	Phi-N	112	3	.259	.300	.438	0	1	0	15	7.36	1	0	0	14	3.21	0	1	0	5	7.71	1	0	0	24	4.88	73	2	.247	.291	.452	39	1	.282	.317	.410
1993	Phi-N	198	5	.253	.327	.409	1	2	0	32	4.50	0	1	0	19	6.63	0	0	0	3	12.00	1	3	0	48	4.88	94	4	.234	.333	.436	104	1	.269	.321	.385
1994	Phi-N	197	7	.310	.368	.487	2	1	0	24	5.25	0	3	0	26	4.78	2	4	0	50	5.01	0	0	0	0	—	115	3	.304	.374	.470	82	4	.317	.360	.512
1995	Phi-N	327	10	.239	.304	.398	1	1	0	45	4.03	2	2	0	43	2.51	0	1	0	31	4.70	3	2	0	57	2.53	145	6	.193	.280	.372	182	4	.275	.323	.418
1996	Phi-N	648	25	.290	.360	.477	4	4	0	87	4.86	2	10	0	80	6.07	1	6	0	79	5.56	5	8	0	88	5.34	255	9	.286	.374	.486	393	16	.293	.350	.471
1997	KC-A	60	1	.333	.414	.433	0	1	1	8	6.48	0	1	0	6	6.35	0	2	1	14	6.43	0	0	0	0	—	25	1	.280	.357	.440	35	0	.371	.452	.429
1998	Pit-N	185	1	.211	.271	.292	2	2	0	24	2.63	2	0	0	27	1.33	1	0	0	11	0.00	3	2	0	40	2.50	55	0	.182	.286	.218	130	1	.223	.264	.323
1999	Pit-N	228	9	.276	.378	.447	1	1	13	31	3.52	2	3	10	28	6.83	1	1	13	33	2.43	2	3	10	25	8.64	79	3	.253	.438	.456	149	6	.289	.340	.443
2000	Pit-N	257	8	.218	.328	.350	2	0	12	35	2.80	1	4	12	37	4.17	2	1	10	34	1.85	1	3	14	38	4.97	104	6	.231	.364	.442	153	2	.209	.301	.288
TOTALS		2212	69	.264	.339	.424	13	13	26	301	4.34	10	24	22	279	4.67	7	16	24	261	4.38	16	21	24	319	4.59	945	34	.251	.350	.435	1267	35	.274	.330	.415
● **Mitch Williams** BL/TL																																				
1986	Tex-A	341	8	.202	.366	.331	3	3	5	52	3.46	5	3	3	46	3.72	6	1	2	38	2.58	2	5	6	60	4.22	118	3	.203	.331	.322	223	5	.202	.384	.336
1987	Tex-A	361	9	.175	.353	.280	6	2	1	57	2.84	2	4	5	52	3.66	5	3	1	44	3.92	3	3	5	65	2.77	123	3	.146	.309	.244	238	6	.189	.374	.298
1988	Tex-A	236	4	.203	.345	.305	1	3	10	35	5.71	1	4	8	33	3.51	1	2	11	38	4.54	1	5	7	30	4.75	65	0	.185	.345	.231	171	4	.211	.344	.333
1989	Chi-N	298	6	.238	.361	.342	3	2	15	37	3.65	1	2	21	45	2.01	1	2	19	42	2.16	3	2	17	40	3.38	71	0	.254	.352	.296	227	6	.233	.364	.357
1990	Chi-N	251	4	.239	.364	.390	1	1	4	33	3.78	0	7	12	33	4.09	1	5	9	33	2.20	0	3	7	34	5.61	66	2	.227	.369	.424	185	2	.243	.362	.378
1991	Phi-N	308	4	.182	.330	.266	9	2	17	47	2.11	3	3	13	41	2.61	1	3	13	35	3.12	11	2	17	54	1.84	68	0	.191	.353	.279	240	4	.179	.323	.262
1992	Phi-N	287	4	.240	.386	.359	3	5	16	42	4.29	2	3	13	39	3.23	2	2	17	40	2.50	3	6	12	41	5.01	49	0	.265	.379	.286	238	4	.235	.387	.374
1993	Phi-N	229	3	.245	.368	.323	1	3	19	28	4.18	2	4	24	34	2.65	1	3	23	27	3.33	2	4	20	35	3.34	40	0	.250	.340	.250	189	3	.243	.374	.339
1994	Hou-N	78	4	.269	.442	.449	0	2	3	12	6.94	1	2	3	8	8.64	1	4	6	20	7.65	0	0	0	0	—	27	1	.148	.303	.259	51	3	.333	.507	.549
1995	Cal-A	41	1	.317	.554	.390	1	2	0	8	7.04	0	0	0	3	6.00	1	2	0	11	6.75	0	0	0	0	—	18	1	.444	.615	.611	23	0	.217	.513	.217
1997	KC-A	30	2	.367	.474	.667	0	0	0	3	12.00	0	1	0	4	9.82	0	1	0	7	10.80	0	0	0	0	—	11	1	.364	.385	.636	19	1	.368	.520	.684
TOTALS		2460	49	.218	.367	.332	28	25	90	353	3.87	17	33	102	338	3.41	20	28	101	333	3.60	25	30	91	359	3.69	656	11	.212	.350	.305	1804	38	.221	.373	.341
● **Mike Witt** BR/TR																																				
1981	Cal-A	490	9	.251	.328	.349	3	3	0	55	3.62	5	6	0	74	3.03	4	5	0	60	4.18	4	4	0	69	2.49	236	4	.225	.317	.322	254	5	.276	.338	.374
1982	Cal-A	681	8	.260	.312	.352	5	3	0	94	2.59	3	3	0	86	4.50	4	1	0	75	3.12	4	5	0	105	3.78	358	4	.260	.298	.363	323	4	.260	.327	.341
1983	Cal-A	590	14	.293	.375	.420	2	10	2	100	4.93	5	4	3	54	4.86	4	5	4	61	4.40	3	9	1	93	5.24	264	8	.307	.387	.451	326	6	.282	.364	.396
1984	Cal-A	929	17	.244	.308	.356	8	5	0	120	2.69	7	6	0	126	4.20	7	7	0	118	3.82	8	4	0	129	3.14	542	9	.258	.320	.367	387	8	.225	.291	.341
1985	Cal-A	938	22	.243	.316	.360	8	5	0	123	3.38	7	4	0	127	3.75	6	6	0	118	3.13	9	3	0	132	3.95	520	11	.263	.332	.375	418	11	.218	.296	.342
1986	Cal-A	987	22	.221	.275	.335	11	5	0	141	2.62	7	5	0	128	3.09	8	6	0	126	3.29	10	4	0	143	2.45	578	15	.215	.270	.339	409	7	.230	.282	.330
1987	Cal-A	965	34	.261	.321	.435	9	8	0	138	4.05	7	6	0	109	3.95	9	5	0	115	3.38	7	9	0	132	4.56	525	22	.272	.338	.463	440	12	.248	.300	.402
1988	Cal-A	966	14	.272	.332	.376	6	7	0	133	2.77	7	9	0	117	5.71	6	7	0	117	4.09	7	9	0	133	4.20	524	7	.261	.324	.357	442	7	.285	.343	.398
1989	Cal-A	864	26	.292	.326	.433	5	7	0	108	4.85	4	8	0	112	4.25	6	7	0	112	4.27	3	8	0	108	4.82	434	12	.295	.326	.424	430	14	.288	.325	.442
1990	Cal-A	76	1	.250	.363	.316	0	2	1	11	2.45	0	1	0	9	0.96	0	3	1	20	1.77	0	0	0	0	—	28	0	.250	.400	.250	48	1	.250	.339	.354
1990	NY-A	363	8	.240	.308	.369	2	3	0	41	3.51	3	3	0	56	5.17	0	1	0	28	3.86	5	5	0	69	4.72	189	3	.270	.329	.381	174	5	.207	.286	.356
1991	NY-A	25	1	.320	.346	.520	0	0	0	5	5.40	0	1	0	0	81.00	0	1	0	5	10.13	0	0	0	0	—	13	0	.385	.385	.538	12	1	.250	.308	.500
1993	NY-A	157	7	.248	.352	.414	2	2	0	32	4.78	1	0	0	9	7.00	3	2	0	41	5.27	0	0	0	0	—	75	2	.213	.359	.320	82	5	.280	.344	.500
TOTALS		8031	183	.257	.320	.380	61	60	3	1100	3.49	56	56	3	1008	4.20	57	56	5	996	3.76	60	60	1	1112	3.90	4286	97	.260	.323	.382	3745	86	.254	.316	.377
● **Bobby Witt** BR/TR																																				
1986	Tex-A	583	18	.223	.374	.369	6	3	0	90	4.00	5	6	0	68	7.45	4	6	0	81	6.11	7	3	0	77	4.81	314	7	.248	.409	.382	269	11	.193	.330	.353
1987	Tex-A	520	10	.219	.385	.325	4	3	0	81	3.89	4	7	0	62	6.24	3	3	0	46	4.47	5	7	0	97	5.12	292	6	.229	.387	.332	228	4	.206	.382	.316
1988	Tex-A	621	13	.216	.324	.319	4	3	0	66	3.70	4	7	0	109	4.06	0	5	0	36	7.68	8	5	0	138	2.93	345	4	.223	.331	.301	276	9	.207	.315	.341
1989	Tex-A	733	14	.248	.348	.355	5	7	0	89	4.74	7	6	0	105	5.49	5	8	0	87	6.23	7	5	0	108	4.26	349	10	.249	.364	.387	384	4	.247	.332	.326
1990	Tex-A	829	12	.238	.328	.326	7	5	0	101	3.40	10	5	0	121	3.34	4	8	0	90	4.68	13	2	0	132	2.46	396	5	.232	.323	.321	433	7	.242	.332	.330
1991	Tex-A	331	4	.254	.388	.356	0	5	0	40	6.30	3	2	0	49	5.92	3	3	0	59	4.25	0	4	0	29	9.82	151	2	.232	.381	.331	180	2	.272	.394	.378
1992	Tex-A	598	14	.254	.354	.378	6	8	0	99	4.17	3	5	0	62	4.94	8	7	0	110	3.53	1	6	0	52	6.45	249	4	.245	.374	.361	349	10	.261	.338	.390
1992	Oak-A	117	2	.265	.362	.333	1	0	0	25	2.16	0	1	0	7	8.10	0	0	0	0	—	1	1	0	32	3.41	43	0	.233	.365	.233	74	2	.284	.360	.392
1993	Oak-A	839	16	.269	.340	.392	7	6	0	125	3.30	7	7	0	95	5.42	7	5	0	101	3.91	7	8	0	119	4.47	426	7	.279	.350	.418	413	9	.259	.330	.366
1994	Oak-A	534	22	.283	.367	.463	6	3	0	76	4.04	2	7	0	60	6.30	6	7	0	104	5.09	2	3	0	31	4.88	294	12	.310	.395	.507	240	10	.250	.331	.408
1995	Fla-N	415	8	.251	.328	.383	2	3	0	54	3.98	0	4	0	56	3.83	1	5	0	62	4.35	1	2	0	49	3.33	199	6	.276	.368	.442	216	2	.227	.288	.329
1995	Tex-A	250	4	.324	.376	.444	2	1	0	32	3.34	1	3	0	29	5.90	0	0	0	0	—	3	4	0	61	4.55	149	2	.349	.401	.463	101	2	.287	.339	.416
1996	Tex-A	796	28	.295	.370	.471	10	4	0	104	5.87	6	8	0	95	4.91	7	7	0	101	5.90	9	5	0	99	4.91	436	14	.294	.366	.468	360	14	.297	.374	.475
1997	Tex-A	833	33	.294	.350	.481	5	7	0	118	5.05	7	5	0	91	4.53	9	4	0	111	3.80	3	8	0	98	5.99	410	20	.334	.398	.559	423	13	.255	.303	.407
1998	Tex-A	290	14	.328	.391	.576	3	1	0	37	6.27	2	3	0	32	9.28	5	4	0	69	7.66	0	0	0	0	—	165	7	.364	.444	.606	125	7	.280	.319	.536
1998	StL-N	190	7	.289	.362	.458	1	2	0	25	2.92	1	3	0	23	7.15	0	0	0	1	20.25	2	5	0	46	4.50	87	2	.276	.376	.379	103	5	.301	.348	.524
1999	TB-A	701	23	.304	.386	.475	4	7	0	82	5.73	3	8	0	99	5.93	4	4	0	85	5.48	3	11	0	95	6.16	363	12	.292	.404	.482	338	11	.317	.366	.467
2000	Cle-A	71	4	.394	.442	.648	0	1	0	7	3.86	0	0	0	8	10.80	0	1	0	15	7.63	0	0	0	0	—	26	2	.423	.444	.769	45	2	.378	.440	.578
TOTALS		9251	246	.266	.358	.405	73	69	0	1251	4.36	65	87	0	1170	5.34	66	77	0	1161	5.12	72	79	0	1261	4.57	4694	122	.275	.376	.421	4557	124	.256	.339	.389
● **Todd Worrell** BR/TR																																				
1985	StL-N	79	2	.215	.273	.405	2	0	3	12	4.38	1	0	2	9	0.96	0	0	0	0	—	3	0	5	22	2.91	31	1	.194	.219	.419	48	1	.229	.304	.396
1986	StL-N	375	9	.229	.303	.352	6	5	17	55	1.65	3	5	19	49	2.57	5	8	13	56	1.62	4	2	23	48	2.63	181	7	.265	.352	.425	194	2	.196	.254	.284
1987	StL-N	355	8	.242	.307	.366	5	3	12	44	3.25	3	3	21	50	2.15	3	3	16	39	3.46	5	3	17	56	2.10	147	3	.231	.331	.313	208	5	.250	.288	.404
1988	StL-N	323	7	.214	.287	.337	3	6	15	49	2.76	2	3	17	41	3.29	3	4	16	53	2.36	2	5	16	37	3.93	141	5	.213	.305	.397	182	2	.214	.271	.291
1989	StL-N	189	4	.222	.315	.365	3	4	12	26	3.08	0	1	8	25	2.84	1	2	10	28	1.29	2	3	10	24	4.94	88	3	.250	.350	.455	101	1	.198	.283	.287
1992	StL-N	227	4	.198	.281	.282	1	0	2	35	0.76	4	3	1	29	3.77	3	3	0	27	4.28	2	0	3	37	0.49	121	3	.174	.254	.264	106	1	.226	.311	.302
1993	LA-N	147	6	.313	.348	.490	0	1	0	19	7.23	1	0	5	20	4.95	0	1	1	7	10.80	1	0	4	32	5.06	80	4	.313	.359	.538	67	2	.313	.333	.433
1994	LA-N	157	4	.236	.291	.382	4	2	5	25	2.19	2	3	6	17	7.27	3	3	6	24	1.88	3	2	5	18	7.50	86	3	.233	.290	.384	71	1	.239	.291	.380
1995	LA-N	226	4	.221	.282	.301	3	1	18	34	3.21	1	0	14	29	0.63	1	0	12	26	0.00	3	1	20	37	3.44	112	1	.179	.248	.223	114	3	.263	.317	.377
1996	LA-N	264	5	.265	.307	.360	3	1	20	32	1.95	1	5	24	33	4.09	3	4	22	34	3.15	1	2	22	31	2.90	124	3	.242	.286	.355	140	2	.286	.327	.364
1997	LA-N	240	12	.250	.316	.450	0	3	19	29	5.52	2	3	16	30	5.04	1	1	16	29	5.65	1	5	19	31	4.94	138	7	.225	.287	.413	102	5	.284	.354	.500
TOTALS		2582	65	.235	.301	.364	30	26	123	361	2.92	20	26	133	333	3.27	23	29	112	323	2.76	27	23	144	371	3.37	1249	40	.230	.305	.373	1333	25	.241	.297	.355
● **Masato Yoshii** BR/TR																																				
1998	NY-N	650	22	.255	.316	.425	5	4	0	96	3.27	1	4	0	75	4.78	4	3	0	86	3.45	2	5	0	86	4.41	288	12	.274	.350	.448	362	10	.240	.287	.406
1999	NY-N	646	25	.260	.324	.466	3	4	0	84	4.82	9	4	0	90	4.00	6	6	0	86	4.50	6	2	0	88	4.30	295	11	.278	.355	.495	351	14	.245	.297	.442
2000	Col-N	656	32	.306	.357	.537	2	3	0	68	5.85	4	12	0	100	5.87	4	7	0	89	5.08	2	8	0	79	6.75	305	14	.282	.343	.498	351	18	.328	.369	.570
TOTALS		1952	79	.274	.332	.476	10	11	0	248	4.50	14	20	0	265	4.92	14	16	0	261	4.35	10	15	0	252	5.10	888	37	.278	.349	.481	1064	42	.271	.317	.472
● **Geoff Zahn** BL/TL																																				
1978	Min-A	949	18	.274	.331	.390	8	7	0	123	2.92	6	7	0	129	3.14	7	5	0	116	3.10	7	9	0	136	2.97	246	3	.256	.330	.358	703	15	.280	.331	.401
1979	Min-A	648	13	.279	.319	.389	3	6	0	82	4.52	10	1	0	87	2.68	7	1	0	51	3.16	6	6	0	118	3.75	176	3	.284	.339	.358	472	10	.278	.312	.400
1980	Min-A	903	17	.302	.347	.422	8	10	0	138	4.38	6	8	0	95	4.45	6	10	0	110	4.32	8	8	0	122	4.49	209	6	.239	.294	.364	694	11	.321	.363	.439
1981	Cal-A	636	18	.285	.329	.409	5	5	0	80	3.83	5	6	0	81	4.98	7	6	0	90	3.79	3	5	0	71	5.20	110	3	.291	.363	.400	526	15	.283	.321	.411
1982	Cal-A	868	18	.259	.313	.395	10	1	0	116	2.87	8	7	0	113	4.61	9	3	0	113	3.03	9	5	0	116	4.41	150	3	.227	.304	.360	718	15	.266	.315	.403
1983	Cal-A	787	22	.269	.311	.396	6	3	0	100	2.70	3	8	0	103	3.93	5	3	0	83	3.24	4	8	0	120	3.38	125	3	.264	.288	.360	662	19	.270	.315	.403
1984	Cal-A	760	11	.263	.306	.354	4	6	0	89	3.45	9	4	0	111	2.85	9	4	0	109	1.89	4	6	0	90	4.60	150	2	.260	.287	.320	610	9	.264	.310	.362
1985	Cal-A	147	5	.299	.358	.503	1	0	0	18	3.57	1	2	0	19	5.12	2	0	0	24	1.48	0	2	0	13	9.95	17	1	.353	.421	.647	130	4	.292	.350	.485
TOTALS		5698	122	.277	.324	.397	45	38	0	745	3.50	48	43	0	739	3.80	52	32	0	698	3.15	41	49	0	786	4.10	1183	24	.260	.316	.363	4515	98	.281	.326	.406

The Postseason Register

Major league postseason competition goes back to the dawn of professional league play, in 1871. The first such contest to determine the "champions of the world" was held in 1884, and it is from that date that we present the annual and cumulative batting and pitching records of every individual to have appeared in a World Series.

In 1969 the American and National Leagues each expanded to 12 teams and realigned into Eastern and Western divisions. This produced a new layer of competition: the League Championship Series (LCS). Through 1984 it was a best-of-five match, but in the years since, it has been expanded to the best-of-seven format that has marked the World Series since 1922.

In 1995 the first Division Series was held. The major leagues' 28 teams—which expanded to 30 in 1998—were arranged into three divisions in each league. The second-place team with the best record in each league, known as the Wild Card, reached the postseason along with the three division winners.

What follows are the annual and career records for every player and pitcher in postseason history. Records are broken down by series and postseason level. For example, each Division Series performance is listed and marked with a "D"; a total for that round is given if the player made multiple Division Series appearances. (The 1981 Divisional Playoffs caused by the strike-interrupted schedule are included in Division Series totals). All LCS performances are marked with an "L." World Series statistics, for both National League vs. American Association from 1892–89 and American League vs. National League from 1903 to present, are marked with a "W."

A "T" denotes Temple Cup competition, which was held in the National League from 1894–97. This mark also signifies postseason results between NL clubs in 1892 and 1900.

For more detail about a particular year's postseason competition, see the Postseason Play chapter. For an overview of that year's regular-season play, see the Annual Record. And for further details about a particular individual, refer to the Player and Pitcher Registers.

YEAR	TM/L	AVG	G	AB	R	H	2B	3B	HR	RBI	BB	SO	SB	POS
■ Hank Aaron														
L 1969	Atl-N	.357	3	14	3	5	2	0	3	7	0	1	0	O
W 1957	Mil-N	.393	7	28	5	11	0	1	3	7	1	6	0	O
W 1958	Mil-N	.333	7	27	3	9	2	0	0	2	4	6	0	O
W Total	2	.364	14	55	8	20	2	1	3	9	5	12	0	
■ Tommie Aaron														
L 1969	Atl-N	.000	1	1	0	0	0	0	0	0	0	0	0	H
■ Ed Abbaticchio														
W 1909	Pit-N	.000	1	1	0	0	0	0	0	0	0	0	0	H
■ Jeff Abbott														
D 2000	Chi-A	.000	1	1	0	0	0	0	0	0	0	0	0	O
■ Kurt Abbott														
D 1997	Fla-N	.250	3	8	0	2	0	0	0	0	0	0	0	2-2
D 2000	NY-N	.000	1	2	0	0	0	0	0	0	0	1	0	S
D Total	2	.200	4	10	0	2	0	0	0	0	0	1	0	
L 1997	Fla-N	.375	2	8	0	3	1	0	0	0	0	2	0	2
L 2000	NY-N	.000	2	3	0	0	0	0	0	0	0	2	0	S
L Total	2	.273	4	11	0	3	1	0	0	0	0	4	0	
W 1997	Fla-N	.000	3	3	0	0	0	0	0	0	0	1	0	D-1
W 2000	NY-N	.250	5	8	0	2	1	0	0	0	1	3	0	S
W Total	2	.182	8	11	0	2	1	0	0	0	1	4	0	
■ Bob Abreu														
D 1997	Hou-N	.333	3	3	0	1	0	0	0	0	0	2	1	H
■ Bill Abstein														
W 1909	Pit-N	.231	7	26	3	6	2	0	0	2	3	10	1	1
■ Jerry Adair														
W 1967	Bos-A	.125	5	16	0	2	0	0	0	1	0	3	1	2-4
■ Sparky Adams														
W 1930	StL-N	.143	6	21	0	3	0	0	0	1	0	4	0	3
W 1931	StL-N	.250	2	4	0	1	0	0	0	0	0	1	0	3
W Total	2	.160	8	25	0	4	0	0	0	1	0	5	0	
■ Spencer Adams														
W 1925	Was-A	.000	2	1	0	0	0	0	0	0	0	0	0	2-1
W 1926	NY-A	—	2	0	0	0	0	0	0	0	0	0	0	H
W Total	2	.000	4	1	0	0	0	0	0	0	0	0	0	
■ Joe Adcock														
W 1957	Mil-N	.200	5	15	1	3	0	0	0	2	0	2	0	1
W 1958	Mil-N	.308	4	13	1	4	0	0	0	0	1	3	0	1
W Total	2	.250	9	28	2	7	0	0	0	2	1	5	0	
■ Benny Agbayani														
D 1999	NY-N	.300	4	10	1	3	1	0	0	1	0	3	0	O
D 2000	NY-N	.333	4	15	1	5	1	0	1	1	3	3	0	O
D Total	2	.320	8	25	2	8	2	0	1	2	3	6	0	
L 1999	NY-N	.143	4	7	2	1	0	0	0	0	4	2	1	O-3
L 2000	NY-N	.353	5	17	0	6	2	0	0	3	4	0	0	O
L Total	2	.292	9	24	2	7	2	0	0	3	8	2	1	
W 2000	NY-N	.278	5	18	2	5	2	0	0	2	3	6	0	O
■ Tommie Agee														
L 1969	NY-N	.357	3	14	4	5	1	0	2	4	2	5	2	O
W 1969	NY-N	.167	5	18	1	3	0	0	1	1	2	5	1	O
■ Sam Agnew														
W 1918	Bos-A	.000	4	9	0	0	0	0	0	0	0	0	0	C
■ Luis Aguayo														
D 1981	Phi-N	—	2	0	1	0	0	0	0	0	0	0	0	R
■ Willie Aikens														
D 1981	KC-A	.333	3	9	0	3	0	0	0	0	3	2	0	1
L 1980	KC-A	.364	3	11	0	4	0	0	0	2	0	1	0	1
W 1980	KC-A	.400	6	20	5	8	0	1	4	8	6	8	0	1
■ Mike Aldrete														
L 1987	SF-N	.100	5	10	0	1	0	0	0	1	0	2	0	O-3
L 1996	NY-A	—	1	0	0	0	0	0	0	0	0	0	0	H
L Total	2	.100	6	10	0	1	0	0	0	1	0	2	0	
W 1996	NY-A	.000	2	1	0	0	0	0	0	0	0	0	0	O-1
■ Manny Alexander														
D 1996	Bal-A	—	3	0	2	0	0	0	0	0	0	0	0	D-1
D 1998	Chi-N	.000	2	5	0	0	0	0	0	0	0	1	0	S-1
D Total	2	.000	5	5	2	0	0	0	0	0	0	1	0	
■ Matt Alexander														
L 1979	Pit-N	—	1	0	1	0	0	0	0	0	0	0	0	R
W 1979	Pit-N	—	1	0	0	0	0	0	0	0	0	0	0	O
■ Edgardo Alfonzo														
D 1999	NY-N	.250	4	16	6	4	1	0	3	6	3	2	0	2
D 2000	NY-N	.278	4	18	1	5	2	0	1	5	1	2	0	2
D Total	2	.265	8	34	7	9	3	0	4	11	4	4	0	
L 1999	NY-N	.222	6	27	2	6	4	0	0	1	1	9	0	2
L 2000	NY-N	.444	5	18	5	8	1	1	0	4	4	1	0	2
L Total	2	.311	11	45	7	14	5	1	0	5	5	10	0	
W 2000	NY-N	.143	5	21	1	3	0	0	0	1	1	5	0	2
■ Luis Alicea														
D 1995	Bos-A	.600	3	10	1	6	1	0	1	1	2	2	1	2
D 1996	StL-N	.182	3	11	1	2	2	0	0	0	1	4	0	2
D 1998	Tex-A	.000	1	1	0	0	0	0	0	0	0	0	0	H
D Total	3	.364	7	22	2	8	3	0	1	1	3	6	1	
L 1996	StL-N	.000	5	8	0	0	0	0	0	0	2	1	0	2
■ Dick Allen														
L 1976	Phi-N	.222	3	9	1	2	0	0	0	0	3	2	0	1
■ Gene Alley														
L 1970	Pit-N	.000	2	7	0	0	0	0	0	0	1	2	0	S
L 1971	Pit-N	.500	1	2	1	1	0	0	0	0	0	0	0	S
L 1972	Pit-N	.000	5	16	1	0	0	0	0	0	0	3	0	S
L Total	3	.040	8	25	2	1	0	0	0	0	1	5	0	
W 1971	Pit-N	.000	2	2	0	0	0	0	0	0	1	0	0	S
■ Bob Allison														
L 1969	Min-A	.000	2	8	0	0	0	0	0	1	0	0	0	O
L 1970	Min-A	.000	3	2	0	0	0	0	0	0	1	1	0	H
L Total	2	.000	5	10	0	0	0	0	0	1	1	1	0	
W 1965	Min-A	.125	5	16	3	2	1	0	1	2	2	9	1	O
■ Roberto Alomar														
D 1996	Bal-A	.294	4	17	2	5	0	0	1	4	2	3	0	2
D 1997	Bal-A	.300	4	10	1	3	2	0	0	2	1	1	0	2
D 1999	Cle-A	.368	5	19	4	7	4	0	0	3	2	3	2	2
D Total	3	.326	13	46	7	15	6	0	1	9	5	7	2	
L 1991	Tor-A	.474	5	19	3	9	0	0	0	4	2	3	2	2
L 1992	Tor-A	.423	6	26	4	11	1	0	2	4	2	1	5	2
L 1993	Tor-A	.292	6	24	3	7	1	0	0	4	4	3	4	2
L 1996	Bal-A	.217	5	23	2	5	2	0	0	1	0	4	0	2
L 1997	Bal-A	.182	6	22	2	4	0	0	1	2	7	3	0	2
L Total	5	.316	28	114	14	36	4	0	3	15	15	14	11	
W 1992	Tor-A	.208	6	24	3	5	1	0	0	0	3	3	3	2
W 1993	Tor-A	.480	6	25	5	12	2	1	0	6	2	3	4	2
W Total	2	.347	12	49	8	17	3	1	0	6	5	6	7	
■ Sandy Alomar Jr.														
D 1995	Cle-A	.182	3	11	1	2	1	0	0	1	0	1	0	C
D 1996	Cle-A	.125	4	16	0	2	0	0	0	3	0	2	0	C
D 1997	Cle-A	.316	5	19	4	6	1	0	2	5	0	2	0	C
D 1998	Cle-A	.231	4	13	2	3	3	0	0	2	1	4	0	C
D 1999	Cle-A	.143	5	14	1	2	0	0	0	1	2	6	0	C
D Total	5	.205	21	73	8	15	5	0	2	12	3	15	0	
L 1995	Cle-A	.267	5	15	0	4	1	1	0	1	1	1	0	C
L 1997	Cle-A	.125	6	24	3	3	0	0	1	4	1	3	0	C
L 1998	Cle-A	.063	5	16	1	1	0	0	0	0	0	2	0	C
L Total	3	.145	16	55	4	8	1	1	1	5	2	6	0	
W 1995	Cle-A	.200	5	15	0	3	2	0	0	1	0	2	0	C
W 1997	Cle-A	.367	7	30	5	11	1	0	2	10	2	3	0	C
W Total	2	.311	12	45	5	14	3	0	2	11	2	5	0	
■ Sandy Alomar Sr.														
L 1976	NY-A	.000	2	1	0	0	0	0	0	0	0	0	0	D-1
■ Felipe Alou														
L 1969	Atl-N	.000	1	1	0	0	0	0	0	0	0	0	0	H
W 1962	SF-N	.269	7	26	2	7	1	1	0	1	1	4	0	O
■ Jesus Alou														
L 1973	Oak-A	.333	4	6	0	2	0	0	0	1	0	1	0	D-1
L 1974	Oak-A	1.000	1	1	0	1	0	0	0	0	0	0	0	H
L Total	2	.429	5	7	0	3	0	0	0	1	0	1	0	
W 1973	Oak-A	.158	7	19	0	3	1	0	0	3	0	0	0	O-6
W 1974	Oak-A	.000	1	1	0	0	0	0	0	0	0	1	0	H
W Total	2	.150	8	20	0	3	1	0	0	3	0	1	0	
■ Matty Alou														
L 1970	Pit-N	.250	3	12	1	3	1	0	0	0	2	1	0	O
L 1972	Oak-A	.381	5	21	2	8	4	0	0	2	0	2	1	O
L Total	2	.333	8	33	3	11	5	0	0	2	2	3	1	
W 1962	SF-N	.333	6	12	2	4	1	0	0	1	0	1	0	O-4
W 1972	Oak-A	.042	7	24	0	1	0	0	0	0	3	0	1	O
W Total	2	.139	13	36	2	5	1	0	0	1	3	1	1	
■ Moises Alou														
D 1997	Fla-N	.214	3	14	1	3	1	0	0	1	0	3	0	O
D 1998	Hou-N	.188	4	16	0	3	0	0	0	0	0	2	0	O
D Total	2	.200	7	30	1	6	1	0	0	1	0	5	0	
L 1997	Fla-N	.067	5	15	0	1	1	0	0	5	1	3	0	O-4
W 1997	Fla-N	.321	7	28	6	9	2	0	3	9	3	6	1	O
■ Brant Alyea														
L 1970	Min-A	.000	3	7	1	0	0	0	0	0	2	3	0	O-2
■ Rich Amaral														
D 1997	Sea-A	.500	2	4	2	2	0	0	0	0	0	1	0	1
L 1995	Sea-A	.000	2	2	0	0	0	0	0	0	0	1	0	H
■ Ruben Amaro Jr.														
L 1995	Cle-A	.000	3	1	1	0	0	0	0	0	0	0	0	D-1
W 1995	Cle-A	.000	2	2	0	0	0	0	0	0	0	1	0	O-1
■ Sandy Amoros														
W 1952	Bro-N	—	1	0	0	0	0	0	0	0	0	0	0	H
W 1955	Bro-N	.333	5	12	3	4	0	0	1	3	4	4	0	O
W 1956	Bro-N	.053	6	19	1	1	0	0	0	1	2	4	0	O
W Total	3	.161	12	31	4	5	0	0	1	4	6	8	0	
■ Brady Anderson														
D 1996	Bal-A	.294	4	17	3	5	0	0	2	4	2	3	0	O
D 1997	Bal-A	.353	4	17	3	6	1	0	1	4	1	4	1	O
D Total	2	.324	8	34	6	11	1	0	3	8	3	7	1	

YEAR	TM/L	AVG	G	AB	R	H	2B	3B	HR	RBI	BB	SO	SB	POS
L 1996	Bal-A	.190	5	21	5	4	1	0	1	1	3	5	0	O
L 1997	Bal-A	.360	6	25	5	9	2	0	2	3	4	4	2	O
L Total	2	.283	11	46	10	13	3	0	3	4	7	9	2	
■ Dave Anderson														
L 1985	LA-N	.000	4	5	1	0	0	0	0	0	3	1	0	S-3,3-1
W 1988	LA-N	.000	1	1	0	0	0	0	0	0	0	1	0	D
■ Jim Anderson														
L 1979	Cal-A	.091	4	11	0	1	0	0	0	0	0	1	0	S
■ Mike Andrews														
L 1973	Oak-A	.000	2	1	0	0	0	0	0	0	0	0	0	1-1,D-1
W 1967	Bos-A	.308	5	13	2	4	0	0	0	1	0	1	0	2-3
W 1973	Oak-A	.000	2	3	0	0	0	0	0	0	1	1	0	2-1
W Total	2	.250	7	16	2	4	0	0	0	1	1	2	0	
■ Cap Anson														
W 1885	Chi-N	.423	7	26	8	11	1	1	0	7	2	0	0	1
W 1886	Chi-N	.238	6	21	3	5	1	0	0	1	4	0	1	1-6,C-2
W Total	2	.340	13	47	11	16	2	1	0	8	6	0	1	
■ Eric Anthony														
L 1995	Cin-N	.000	2	1	0	0	0	0	0	0	1	1	0	H
■ Luis Aparicio														
W 1959	Chi-A	.308	6	26	1	8	1	0	0	0	2	3	1	S
W 1966	Bal-A	.250	4	16	0	4	1	0	0	2	0	0	0	S
W Total	2	.286	10	42	1	12	2	0	0	2	2	3	1	
■ Jimmy Archer														
W 1907	Det-A	.000	1	3	0	0	0	0	0	0	0	1	0	C
W 1910	Chi-N	.182	3	11	1	2	1	0	0	0	0	3	0	C-2,1-1
W Total	2	.143	4	14	1	2	1	0	0	0	0	4	0	
■ Alex Arias														
D 1997	Fla-N	1.000	1	1	0	1	0	0	0	1	0	0	0	H
L 1997	Fla-N	1.000	3	1	0	1	0	0	0	0	0	0	0	3-2
W 1997	Fla-N	.000	2	1	1	0	0	0	0	0	0	0	0	3-1,D-1
■ George Arias														
D 1998	SD-N	.000	1	1	0	0	0	0	0	0	0	1	0	H
■ Tony Armas														
D 1981	Oak-A	.545	3	11	1	6	2	0	0	3	1	1	0	O
L 1981	Oak-A	.167	3	12	0	2	0	0	0	0	0	5	0	O
L 1986	Bos-A	.125	5	16	1	2	1	0	0	0	0	2	0	O
L Total	2	.143	8	28	1	4	1	0	0	0	0	7	0	
W 1986	Bos-A	.000	1	1	0	0	0	0	0	0	0	1	0	H
■ Ed Armbrister														
L 1973	Cin-N	.167	3	6	0	1	0	0	0	0	0	5	0	O-1
L 1975	Cin-N	—	2	0	0	0	0	0	0	0	1	0	0	H
L 1976	Cin-N	—	1	0	0	0	0	0	0	0	0	0	0	H
L Total	3	.167	6	6	0	1	0	0	0	0	1	5	0	
W 1975	Cin-N	.000	4	1	1	0	0	0	0	0	2	0	0	H
■ Morrie Arnovich														
W 1940	Cin-N	.000	1	1	0	0	0	0	0	0	0	0	0	O
■ Richie Ashburn														
W 1950	Phi-N	.176	4	17	0	3	1	0	0	1	0	4	0	O
■ Alan Ashby														
D 1981	Hou-N	.111	3	9	1	1	0	0	1	2	2	0	0	C
L 1980	Hou-N	.125	2	8	0	1	0	0	0	1	0	0	0	C
L 1986	Hou-N	.130	6	23	2	3	1	0	1	2	2	1	0	C
L Total	2	.129	8	31	2	4	1	0	1	3	2	1	0	
■ Billy Ashley														
D 1995	LA-N	—	1	0	0	0	0	0	0	0	1	0	0	H
D 1996	LA-N	.000	2	2	0	0	0	0	0	0	0	2	0	H
D Total	2	.000	3	2	0	0	0	0	0	0	1	2	0	
■ Bob Aspromonte														
L 1969	Atl-N	.000	3	3	0	0	0	0	0	0	0	0	0	H
■ Rick Auerbach														
L 1974	LA-N	1.000	1	1	0	1	1	0	0	0	0	0	0	H
L 1979	Cin-N	.000	2	2	0	0	0	0	0	0	0	1	0	H
L Total	2	.333	3	3	0	1	1	0	0	0	0	1	0	
W 1974	LA-N	—	1	0	0	0	0	0	0	0	0	0	0	R
■ Rich Aurilia														
D 2000	SF-N	.133	4	15	0	2	1	0	0	0	0	3	0	S
■ Brad Ausmus														
D 1997	Hou-N	.400	2	5	1	2	1	0	0	2	0	1	0	C
D 1998	Hou-N	.222	4	9	0	2	0	0	0	0	0	4	0	C
D Total	2	.286	6	14	1	4	1	0	0	2	0	5	0	
■ Earl Averill														
W 1940	Det-A	.000	3	3	0	0	0	0	0	0	0	0	0	H
■ Bobby Avila														
W 1954	Cle-A	.133	4	15	1	2	0	0	0	0	2	1	0	2
■ Ramon Aviles														
D 1981	Phi-N	—	1	0	0	0	0	0	0	0	1	0	0	H
L 1980	Phi-N	—	1	0	1	0	0	0	0	0	0	0	0	R
■ Benny Ayala														
L 1983	Bal-A	—	1	0	0	0	0	0	0	1	0	0	0	D
W 1979	Bal-A	.333	4	6	1	2	0	0	1	2	1	0	0	O-3

YEAR	TM/L	AVG	G	AB	R	H	2B	3B	HR	RBI	BB	SO	SB	POS
W 1983	Bal-A	1.000	1	1	1	1	0	0	0	1	0	0	0	H
W Total	2	.429	5	7	2	3	0	0	1	3	1	0	0	
■ Wally Backman														
L 1986	NY-N	.238	6	21	5	5	0	0	0	2	2	4	1	2
L 1988	NY-N	.273	7	22	2	6	1	0	0	2	2	5	1	2
L 1990	Pit-N	.143	3	7	1	1	1	0	0	0	1	3	1	3-2
L Total	3	.240	16	50	8	12	2	0	0	4	5	12	3	
W 1986	NY-N	.333	6	18	4	6	0	0	0	1	3	2	1	2
■ Carlos Baerga														
D 1995	Cle-A	.286	3	14	2	4	1	0	0	1	0	1	0	2
L 1995	Cle-A	.400	6	25	3	10	0	0	1	4	2	3	0	2
W 1995	Cle-A	.192	6	26	1	5	2	0	0	4	1	1	0	2
■ Jeff Bagwell														
D 1997	Hou-N	.083	3	12	0	1	0	0	0	0	1	5	0	1
D 1998	Hou-N	.143	4	14	0	2	0	0	0	4	1	6	0	1
D 1999	Hou-N	.154	4	13	3	2	0	0	0	0	5	4	0	1
D Total	3	.128	11	39	3	5	0	0	0	4	7	15	0	
■ Ed Bailey														
W 1962	SF-N	.071	6	14	1	1	0	0	1	2	0	3	0	C-3
■ Bob Bailor														
L 1985	LA-N	.000	2	1	0	0	0	0	0	0	0	0	0	3
■ Harold Baines														
D 1997	Bal-A	.400	2	5	2	2	0	0	1	1	1	0	0	D-1
D 1999	Cle-A	.357	4	14	1	5	0	0	1	4	2	1	0	D
D 2000	Chi-A	.250	2	4	1	1	0	0	0	0	0	1	0	D-1
D Total	3	.348	8	23	4	8	1	0	2	5	3	2	0	
L 1983	Chi-A	.125	4	16	0	2	0	0	0	0	1	3	0	O
L 1990	Oak-A	.357	4	14	2	5	1	0	0	3	2	1	1	D
L 1992	Oak-A	.440	6	25	6	11	2	0	1	4	0	3	0	D
L 1997	Bal-A	.353	6	17	1	6	0	0	1	2	2	1	0	D
L Total	4	.333	20	72	9	24	3	0	2	9	5	8	1	
W 1990	Oak-A	.143	3	7	1	1	0	0	1	2	1	2	0	D-2
■ Doug Baker														
L 1984	Det-A	—	1	0	0	0	0	0	0	0	0	0	0	S
■ Gene Baker														
W 1960	Pit-N	.000	3	3	0	0	0	0	0	0	0	1	0	H
■ Floyd Baker														
W 1944	StL-A	.000	2	2	0	0	0	0	0	0	0	2	0	2
■ Frank Baker														
L 1973	Bal-A	—	2	0	0	0	0	0	0	0	0	0	0	S
L 1974	Bal-A	—	2	0	0	0	0	0	0	0	0	0	0	S
L Total	2	—	4	0	0	0	0	0	0	0	0	0	0	
■ Frank Baker														
W 1910	Phi-A	.409	5	22	6	9	3	0	0	4	2	1	0	3
W 1911	Phi-A	.375	6	24	7	9	2	0	2	5	1	5	0	3
W 1913	Phi-A	.450	5	20	2	9	0	0	1	7	0	2	1	3
W 1914	Phi-A	.250	4	16	0	4	2	0	0	2	1	3	0	3
W 1921	NY-A	.250	4	8	0	2	0	0	0	0	1	0	0	3-2
W 1922	NY-A	.000	1	1	0	0	0	0	0	0	0	0	0	H
W Total	6	.363	25	91	15	33	7	0	3	18	5	11	1	
■ Dusty Baker														
D 1981	LA-N	.167	5	18	2	3	1	0	0	1	2	0	0	O
L 1977	LA-N	.357	4	14	4	5	1	0	2	8	2	3	0	O
L 1978	LA-N	.467	4	15	1	7	2	0	0	1	3	0	0	O
L 1981	LA-N	.316	5	19	3	6	1	0	0	3	1	0	0	O
L 1983	LA-N	.357	4	14	4	5	1	0	1	1	2	0	0	O
L Total	4	.371	17	62	12	23	5	0	3	13	8	3	0	
W 1977	LA-N	.292	6	24	4	7	0	0	1	5	0	2	0	O
W 1978	LA-N	.238	6	21	2	5	0	0	1	1	1	3	0	O
W 1981	LA-N	.167	6	24	3	4	0	0	0	1	1	6	0	O
W Total	3	.232	18	69	9	16	0	0	2	7	2	11	0	
■ Bill Baker														
W 1940	Cin-N	.250	3	4	1	1	0	0	0	0	0	1	0	C
■ Paul Bako														
D 2000	Atl-N	.000	2	1	0	0	0	0	0	0	0	1	0	C
■ Steve Balboni														
L 1984	KC-A	.091	3	11	0	1	0	0	0	0	1	4	0	1
L 1985	KC-A	.120	7	25	1	3	0	0	0	1	2	8	0	1
L Total	2	.111	10	36	1	4	0	0	0	1	3	12	0	
W 1985	KC-A	.320	7	25	2	8	0	0	0	3	5	4	0	1
■ Neal Ball														
W 1912	Bos-A	.000	1	1	0	0	0	0	0	0	0	1	0	H
■ Dave Bancroft														
W 1915	Phi-N	.294	5	17	2	5	0	0	0	1	2	2	0	S
W 1921	NY-N	.152	8	33	3	5	1	0	0	3	1	5	0	S
W 1922	NY-N	.211	5	19	4	4	0	0	0	2	2	1	0	S
W 1923	NY-N	.083	6	24	1	2	0	0	0	1	1	2	1	S
W Total	4	.172	24	93	10	16	1	0	0	7	6	10	1	
■ Sal Bando														
D 1981	Mil-A	.294	5	17	1	5	3	0	0	1	2	3	0	3
L 1971	Oak-A	.364	3	11	3	4	2	0	1	1	1	0	0	3
L 1972	Oak-A	.200	5	20	0	4	0	0	0	0	0	3	0	3
L 1973	Oak-A	.167	5	18	2	3	0	0	2	3	3	6	0	3
L 1974	Oak-A	.231	4	13	4	3	0	0	2	2	4	0	0	3

YEAR	TM/L	AVG	G	AB	R	H	2B	3B	HR	RBI	BB	SO	SB	POS
L 1975	Oak-A	.500	3	12	1	6	2	0	0	2	0	3	0	3
L Total	5	.270	20	74	10	20	4	0	5	8	8	12	0	
W 1972	Oak-A	.269	7	26	2	7	1	0	0	1	2	5	0	3
W 1973	Oak-A	.231	7	26	5	6	1	1	0	1	4	7	0	3
W 1974	Oak-A	.063	5	16	3	1	0	0	0	2	2	5	0	3
W Total	3	.206	19	68	10	14	2	1	0	4	8	17	0	
■ Dan Bankhead														
W 1947	Bro-N	—	1	0	1	0	0	0	0	0	0	0	0	R
■ Turner Barber														
W 1918	Chi-N	.000	3	2	0	0	0	0	0	0	0	0	0	H
■ Jim Barbieri														
W 1966	LA-N	.000	1	1	0	0	0	0	0	0	0	1	0	H
■ Jesse Barfield														
L 1985	Tor-A	.280	7	25	3	7	1	0	1	4	3	7	1	O
■ Glen Barker														
D 1999	Hou-N	.000	2	3	1	0	0	0	0	0	0	2	1	O
■ Sam Barkley														
W 1885	StL-A	.087	7	23	3	2	0	0	0	1	2	0	0	2
■ Clyde Barnhart														
W 1925	Pit-N	.250	7	28	1	7	1	0	0	5	3	5	1	O
W 1927	Pit-N	.313	4	16	0	5	1	0	0	4	0	0	0	O
W Total	2	.273	11	44	1	12	2	0	0	9	3	5	1	
■ Marty Barrett														
L 1986	Bos-A	.367	7	30	4	11	2	0	0	5	2	2	0	2
L 1988	Bos-A	.067	4	15	2	1	0	0	0	0	1	0	0	2
L 1990	Bos-A	—	3	0	0	0	0	0	0	0	0	0	0	2
L Total	3	.267	14	45	6	12	2	0	0	5	3	2	0	
W 1986	Bos-A	.433	7	30	1	13	2	0	0	4	5	2	0	2
■ Jack Barry														
W 1910	Phi-A	.235	5	17	3	4	2	0	0	3	1	3	0	S
W 1911	Phi-A	.368	6	19	2	7	4	0	0	2	0	2	2	S
W 1913	Phi-A	.300	5	20	3	6	3	0	0	1	0	0	0	S
W 1914	Phi-A	.071	4	14	1	1	0	0	0	0	1	3	1	S
W 1915	Bos-A	.176	5	17	1	3	0	0	0	1	1	2	0	2
W Total	5	.241	25	87	10	21	9	0	0	7	3	10	3	
■ Dick Bartell														
W 1936	NY-N	.381	6	21	5	8	3	0	1	3	4	4	0	S
W 1937	NY-N	.238	5	21	3	5	1	0	0	1	0	3	0	S
W 1940	Det-A	.269	7	26	2	7	2	0	0	3	3	3	0	S
W Total	3	.294	18	68	10	20	6	0	1	7	7	10	0	
■ Kevin Bass														
L 1986	Hou-N	.292	6	24	0	7	2	0	0	0	4	4	2	O
■ Jason Bates														
D 1995	Col-N	.250	4	4	0	1	0	0	0	0	0	0	0	2-1,3-1
■ Billy Bates														
L 1990	Cin-N	—	2	0	1	0	0	0	0	0	0	0	0	R
W 1990	Cin-N	1.000	1	1	1	1	0	0	0	0	0	0	0	H
■ Bill Bathe														
L 1989	SF-N	.000	2	1	0	0	0	0	0	0	0	1	0	H
W 1989	SF-N	.500	2	2	1	1	0	0	1	3	0	0	0	H
■ Kim Batiste														
L 1993	Phi-N	1.000	4	1	0	1	0	0	0	1	0	0	0	3
W 1993	Phi-N	—	3	0	0	0	0	0	0	0	0	0	0	3
■ Earl Battey														
W 1965	Min-A	.120	7	25	1	3	0	1	0	2	0	5	0	C
■ Howard Battle														
D 1999	Atl-N	.000	1	1	0	0	0	0	0	0	0	0	0	H
L 1999	Atl-N	.000	3	2	0	0	0	0	0	0	0	2	1	1-1
W 1999	Atl-N	—	1	0	0	0	0	0	0	0	0	0	0	H
■ Hank Bauer														
W 1949	NY-A	.167	3	6	0	1	0	0	0	0	0	0	0	O
W 1950	NY-A	.133	4	15	0	2	0	0	0	1	0	0	0	O
W 1951	NY-A	.167	6	18	0	3	0	1	0	3	1	1	0	O
W 1952	NY-A	.056	7	18	2	1	0	0	0	1	4	3	0	O
W 1953	NY-A	.261	6	23	6	6	0	1	0	1	2	4	0	O
W 1955	NY-A	.429	6	14	1	6	0	0	0	1	0	1	0	O-5
W 1956	NY-A	.281	7	32	3	9	0	0	1	3	0	5	1	O
W 1957	NY-A	.258	7	31	3	8	2	1	2	6	1	6	0	O
W 1958	NY-A	.323	7	31	6	10	0	0	4	8	0	5	0	O
W Total	9	.245	53	188	21	46	2	3	7	24	8	25	1	
■ Danny Bautista														
D 1997	Atl-N	.333	3	3	0	1	0	0	0	2	0	1	0	O
D 1998	Atl-N	.500	2	2	0	1	1	0	0	0	0	0	0	O
D Total	2	.400	5	5	0	2	1	0	0	2	0	1	0	
L 1997	Atl-N	.250	2	4	0	1	0	0	0	0	0	0	0	O
L 1998	Atl-N	.000	5	5	0	0	0	0	0	0	0	1	0	O-4
L Total	2	.111	7	9	0	1	0	0	0	0	0	1	0	
■ Don Baylor														
L 1973	Bal-A	.273	4	11	3	3	0	0	0	1	3	5	0	O-3
L 1974	Bal-A	.267	4	15	0	4	0	0	0	0	0	2	0	O
L 1979	Cal-A	.188	4	16	2	3	0	0	1	2	1	2	0	D-3,O-1
L 1982	Cal-A	.294	5	17	2	5	1	1	1	10	2	0	0	D
L 1986	Bos-A	.346	7	26	6	9	3	0	1	2	4	5	0	D

YEAR	TM/L	AVG	G	AB	R	H	2B	3B	HR	RBI	BB	SO	SB	POS
L 1987	Min-A	.400	2	5	0	2	0	0	0	1	0	0	0	D
L 1988	Oak-A	.000	2	6	0	0	0	0	0	1	1	2	0	D
L Total	7	.271	28	96	13	26	4	1	3	17	11	16	0	
W 1986	Bos-A	.182	4	11	1	2	1	0	0	1	1	3	0	D-3
W 1987	Min-A	.385	5	13	3	5	0	0	1	3	1	1	0	D-3
W 1988	Oak-A	.000	1	1	0	0	0	0	0	0	0	1	0	H
W Total	3	.280	10	25	4	7	1	0	1	4	2	5	0	
■ Jim Beauchamp														
W 1973	NY-N	.000	4	4	0	0	0	0	0	0	0	1	0	H
■ Ginger Beaumont														
T 1900	Pit-N	.267	4	15	2	4	0	0	0	1	1	0	1	O
W 1903	Pit-N	.265	8	34	6	9	0	1	0	1	2	4	2	O
W 1910	Chi-N	.000	3	2	1	0	0	0	0	0	1	1	0	H
W Total	2	.250	11	36	7	9	0	1	0	1	3	5	2	
■ Beals Becker														
W 1911	NY-N	.000	3	3	0	0	0	0	0	0	0	0	0	H
W 1912	NY-N	.000	2	4	1	0	0	0	0	0	2	0	0	O-1
W 1915	Phi-N	—	2	0	0	0	0	0	0	0	0	0	0	O
W Total	3	.000	7	7	1	0	0	0	0	0	2	0	0	
■ Heinz Becker														
W 1945	Chi-N	.500	3	2	0	1	0	0	0	0	1	1	0	H
■ Mark Belanger														
L 1969	Bal-A	.267	3	15	4	4	0	1	1	1	0	0	0	S
L 1970	Bal-A	.333	3	12	5	4	0	0	0	1	1	0	0	S
L 1971	Bal-A	.250	3	8	1	2	0	0	0	1	3	2	0	S
L 1973	Bal-A	.125	5	16	0	2	0	0	0	1	1	1	0	S
L 1974	Bal-A	.000	4	9	0	0	0	0	0	0	1	3	0	S
L 1979	Bal-A	.200	3	5	0	1	0	0	0	1	0	2	0	S
L Total	6	.200	21	65	10	13	0	1	1	5	6	8	0	
W 1969	Bal-A	.200	5	15	2	3	0	0	0	1	2	1	0	S
W 1970	Bal-A	.105	5	19	0	2	0	0	0	1	1	2	0	S
W 1971	Bal-A	.238	7	21	4	5	0	1	0	0	5	2	1	S
W 1979	Bal-A	.000	5	6	1	0	0	0	0	0	1	1	0	S-4
W Total	4	.164	22	61	7	10	0	1	0	2	9	6	1	
■ Wayne Belardi														
W 1953	Bro-N	.000	2	2	0	0	0	0	0	0	0	1	0	H
■ David Bell														
D 2000	Sea-A	.364	3	11	0	4	1	0	0	1	2	2	0	3
L 2000	Sea-A	.222	5	18	0	4	0	0	0	0	0	0	0	3-4,2-1
■ Gus Bell														
W 1961	Cin-N	.000	3	3	0	0	0	0	0	0	0	0	0	H
■ Derek Bell														
D 1997	Hou-N	.000	3	13	0	0	0	0	0	0	0	3	0	O
D 1998	Hou-N	.125	4	16	1	2	0	0	1	1	0	7	0	O
D 1999	Hou-N	.333	2	3	0	1	0	0	0	0	0	0	0	O-1
D 2000	NY-N	.000	1	1	0	0	0	0	0	0	0	0	0	O
D Total	4	.091	10	33	1	3	0	0	1	1	0	10	0	
L 1992	Tor-A	—	2	0	1	0	0	0	0	0	1	0	0	O
W 1992	Tor-A	.000	2	1	1	0	0	0	0	0	1	0	0	H
■ George Bell														
L 1985	Tor-A	.321	7	28	4	9	3	0	0	1	0	4	0	O
L 1989	Tor-A	.200	5	20	2	4	0	0	1	2	0	3	0	D-3,O-2
L Total	2	.271	12	48	6	13	3	0	1	3	0	7	0	
■ Jay Bell														
D 1999	Ari-N	.286	4	14	3	4	1	0	0	3	1	0	0	2
L 1990	Pit-N	.250	6	20	3	5	1	0	1	1	4	3	0	S
L 1991	Pit-N	.414	7	29	2	12	2	0	1	1	0	10	0	S
L 1992	Pit-N	.172	7	29	3	5	2	0	1	4	3	4	0	S
L Total	3	.282	20	78	8	22	5	0	3	6	7	17	0	
■ Les Bell														
W 1926	StL-N	.259	7	27	4	7	1	0	1	6	2	5	0	3
■ Albert Belle														
D 1995	Cle-A	.273	3	11	3	3	1	0	1	3	4	3	0	O
D 1996	Cle-A	.200	4	15	2	3	0	0	2	6	3	2	1	O
D Total	2	.231	7	26	5	6	1	0	3	9	7	5	1	
L 1995	Cle-A	.222	5	18	1	4	1	0	1	1	3	5	0	O
W 1995	Cle-A	.235	6	17	4	4	0	0	2	4	7	5	0	O
■ Rafael Belliard														
D 1995	Atl-N	.000	4	5	1	0	0	0	0	0	0	1	0	S
D 1996	Atl-N	—	3	0	0	0	0	0	0	0	0	0	0	S
D Total	2	.000	7	5	1	0	0	0	0	0	0	1	0	
L 1991	Atl-N	.211	7	19	0	4	0	0	0	1	3	3	0	S
L 1992	Atl-N	.000	4	2	1	0	0	0	0	0	1	0	0	S-3,2-1
L 1993	Atl-N	.000	2	1	1	0	0	0	0	0	0	1	0	2-1,S-1
L 1995	Atl-N	.273	4	11	1	3	0	0	0	0	0	3	0	S
L 1996	Atl-N	.667	4	6	0	4	0	0	0	2	0	0	0	S
L Total	5	.282	21	39	3	11	0	0	0	3	4	7	0	
W 1991	Atl-N	.375	7	16	0	6	1	0	0	4	1	2	0	S
W 1992	Atl-N	—	4	0	0	0	0	0	0	0	0	0	0	S-3,2-1
W 1995	Atl-N	.000	6	16	0	0	0	0	0	1	0	4	0	S
W 1996	Atl-N	—	4	0	0	0	0	0	0	0	0	0	0	S-3
W Total	4	.188	21	32	0	6	1	0	0	5	1	6	0	
■ Clay Bellinger														
D 1999	NY-A	—	1	0	0	0	0	0	0	0	0	0	0	D
D 2000	NY-A	1.000	2	1	0	1	1	0	0	1	0	0	0	O

YEAR	TM/L	AVG	G	AB	R	H	2B	3B	HR	RBI	BB	SO	SB	POS
D Total	2	1.000	3	1	0	1	1	0	0	1	0	0	0	
L 1999	NY-A	.000	3	1	0	0	0	0	0	0	0	1	0	D-2,S-1
L 2000	NY-A	—	5	0	0	0	0	0	0	0	0	0	0	O
L Total	2	.000	8	1	0	0	0	0	0	0	0	1	0	
W 2000	NY-A	—	4	0	0	0	0	0	0	0	0	0	0	O
■ **Marvin Benard**														
D 1997	SF-N	.000	2	2	0	0	0	0	0	0	0	1	0	H
D 2000	SF-N	.071	4	14	0	1	0	0	0	1	1	7	0	O-3
D Total	2	.063	6	16	0	1	0	0	0	1	1	8	0	
■ **Johnny Bench**														
L 1970	Cin-N	.222	3	9	2	2	0	0	1	1	3	1	0	C
L 1972	Cin-N	.333	5	18	3	6	1	1	1	2	1	3	2	C
L 1973	Cin-N	.263	5	19	1	5	2	0	1	1	2	3	0	C
L 1975	Cin-N	.077	3	13	1	1	0	0	0	0	1	6	1	C
L 1976	Cin-N	.333	3	12	3	4	1	0	1	1	1	2	1	C
L 1979	Cin-N	.250	3	12	1	3	0	1	1	1	2	2	0	C
L Total	6	.253	22	83	11	21	4	2	5	6	10	17	4	
W 1970	Cin-N	.211	5	19	3	4	0	0	1	3	1	2	0	C
W 1972	Cin-N	.261	7	23	4	6	1	0	1	1	5	5	2	C
W 1975	Cin-N	.207	7	29	5	6	2	0	1	4	2	4	0	C
W 1976	Cin-N	.533	4	15	4	8	1	1	2	6	0	1	0	C
W Total	4	.279	23	86	16	24	4	1	5	14	8	12	2	
■ **Bruce Benedict**														
L 1982	Atl-N	.250	3	8	1	2	1	0	0	0	2	1	0	C
■ **Benny Bengough**														
W 1927	NY-A	.000	2	4	1	0	0	0	0	0	1	0	0	C
W 1928	NY-A	.231	4	13	1	3	0	0	0	1	1	1	0	C
W Total	2	.176	6	17	2	3	0	0	0	1	2	1	0	
■ **Juan Beniquez**														
L 1975	Bos-A	.250	3	12	2	3	0	0	0	1	0	1	2	O
L 1982	Cal-A	—	2	0	0	0	0	0	0	0	0	0	0	H
L Total	2	.250	5	12	2	3	0	0	0	1	0	1	2	
W 1975	Bos-A	.125	3	8	0	1	0	0	0	1	1	0	0	O-2
■ **Mike Benjamin**														
D 1998	Bos-A	.091	4	11	1	1	0	0	0	0	1	3	0	2-4,1-1
■ **Charlie Bennett**														
W 1887	Det-N	.311	11	45	6	14	2	1	0	9	3	5	5	C-10,1-3
T 1892	Bos-N	.286	2	7	2	2	0	0	1	1	0	2	1	C
■ **Todd Benzinger**														
L 1988	Bos-A	.091	4	11	0	1	0	0	0	0	1	3	0	1-3
L 1990	Cin-N	.333	5	9	0	3	0	0	0	0	2	0	0	1-2
L Total	2	.200	9	20	0	4	0	0	0	0	3	3	0	
W 1990	Cin-N	.182	4	11	1	2	0	0	0	0	0	0	0	1-3
■ **Augie Bergamo**														
W 1944	StL-N	.000	3	6	0	0	0	0	0	1	2	3	0	O-2
■ **Marty Bergen**														
T 1897	Bos-N	.500	1	4	0	2	0	0	0	1	0	1	1	C
■ **Wally Berger**														
W 1937	NY-N	.000	3	3	0	0	0	0	0	0	0	1	0	H
W 1939	Cin-N	.000	4	15	0	0	0	0	0	1	0	4	0	O
W Total	2	.000	7	18	0	0	0	0	0	1	0	5	0	
■ **Dave Bergman**														
L 1980	Hou-N	.333	4	3	0	1	0	1	0	2	0	0	0	1
L 1984	Det-A	1.000	2	1	1	1	0	0	0	0	0	0	1	1-1
L 1987	Det-A	.250	4	4	0	1	0	0	0	2	0	1	0	1-1,D-1
L Total	3	.375	10	8	1	3	0	1	0	4	0	1	1	
W 1984	Det-A	.000	5	5	0	0	0	0	0	0	0	1	0	1
■ **Yogi Berra**														
W 1947	NY-A	.158	6	19	2	3	0	0	1	2	1	2	0	C-4,O-2
W 1949	NY-A	.063	4	16	2	1	0	0	0	1	1	3	0	C
W 1950	NY-A	.200	4	15	2	3	0	0	1	2	2	1	0	C
W 1951	NY-A	.261	6	23	4	6	1	0	0	0	2	1	0	C
W 1952	NY-A	.214	7	28	2	6	1	0	2	3	2	4	0	C
W 1953	NY-A	.429	6	21	3	9	1	0	1	4	3	3	0	C
W 1955	NY-A	.417	7	24	5	10	1	0	1	2	3	1	0	C
W 1956	NY-A	.360	7	25	5	9	2	0	3	10	4	1	0	C
W 1957	NY-A	.320	7	25	5	8	1	0	1	2	4	0	0	C
W 1958	NY-A	.222	7	27	3	6	3	0	0	2	1	0	0	C
W 1960	NY-A	.318	7	22	6	7	0	0	1	8	2	0	0	O-4,C-3
W 1961	NY-A	.273	4	11	2	3	0	0	1	3	5	1	0	O
W 1962	NY-A	.000	2	2	0	0	0	0	0	0	2	0	0	C-1
W 1963	NY-A	.000	1	1	0	0	0	0	0	0	0	0	0	H
W Total	14	.274	75	259	41	71	10	0	12	39	32	17	0	
■ **Geronimo Berroa**														
D 1997	Bal-A	.385	4	13	4	5	1	0	2	2	2	2	0	D-3,O-1
L 1997	Bal-A	.286	6	21	1	6	2	0	0	3	0	3	0	O-4,D-2
■ **Sean Berry**														
D 1997	Hou-N	.000	1	1	0	0	0	0	0	0	0	0	0	H
D 1998	Hou-N	.000	1	2	0	0	0	0	0	0	0	1	0	3
D Total	2	.000	2	3	0	0	0	0	0	0	0	1	0	
■ **Damon Berryhill**														
D 1997	SF-N	.000	1	1	0	0	0	0	0	0	0	0	0	H
L 1992	Atl-N	.167	7	24	1	4	1	0	0	1	3	2	0	C
L 1993	Atl-N	.211	6	19	2	4	0	0	1	3	1	5	0	C
L Total	2	.186	13	43	3	8	1	0	1	4	4	7	0	

YEAR	TM/L	AVG	G	AB	R	H	2B	3B	HR	RBI	BB	SO	SB	POS
W 1992	Atl-N	.091	6	22	1	2	0	0	1	3	1	11	0	C
■ **Kurt Bevacqua**														
L 1984	SD-N	.000	2	2	0	0	0	0	0	0	0	0	0	H
W 1984	SD-N	.412	5	17	4	7	2	0	2	4	1	2	0	D
■ **Buddy Biancalana**														
L 1984	KC-A	.000	2	1	0	0	0	0	0	0	0	1	0	S
L 1985	KC-A	.222	7	18	2	4	1	0	0	1	1	6	0	S
L Total	2	.211	9	19	2	4	1	0	0	1	1	7	0	
W 1985	KC-A	.278	7	18	2	5	0	0	0	2	5	4	0	S
■ **Dante Bichette**														
D 1995	Col-N	.588	4	17	6	10	3	0	1	3	1	3	0	O
■ **Carson Bigbee**														
W 1925	Pit-N	.333	4	3	1	1	1	0	0	1	0	0	1	O-1
■ **Craig Biggio**														
D 1997	Hou-N	.083	3	12	0	1	0	0	0	0	1	0	0	2
D 1998	Hou-N	.182	4	11	3	2	1	0	0	1	4	4	0	2
D 1999	Hou-N	.105	4	19	1	2	0	0	0	0	1	5	0	2
D Total	3	.119	11	42	4	5	1	0	0	1	6	9	0	
■ **Max Bishop**														
W 1929	Phi-A	.190	5	21	2	4	0	0	0	1	2	3	0	2
W 1930	Phi-A	.222	6	18	5	4	0	0	0	0	7	3	0	2
W 1931	Phi-A	.148	7	27	4	4	0	0	0	0	3	5	0	2
W Total	3	.182	18	66	11	12	0	0	0	1	12	11	0	
■ **Ray Blades**														
W 1928	StL-N	.000	1	1	0	0	0	0	0	0	0	1	0	H
W 1930	StL-N	.111	5	9	2	1	0	0	0	0	2	2	0	O-3
W 1931	StL-N	.000	2	2	0	0	0	0	0	0	0	2	0	H
W Total	3	.083	8	12	2	1	0	0	0	0	2	5	0	
■ **Footsie Blair**														
W 1929	Chi-N	.000	1	1	0	0	0	0	0	0	0	0	0	H
■ **Paul Blair**														
L 1969	Bal-A	.400	3	15	1	6	2	0	1	6	2	2	0	O
L 1970	Bal-A	.077	3	13	0	1	0	0	0	0	1	4	0	O
L 1971	Bal-A	.333	3	9	1	3	1	0	0	2	0	3	0	O
L 1973	Bal-A	.167	5	18	2	3	0	0	0	1	1	5	0	O
L 1974	Bal-A	.286	4	14	3	4	0	0	1	2	2	2	0	O
L 1977	NY-A	.400	3	5	1	2	0	0	0	0	0	0	0	O
L 1978	NY-A	.000	4	6	1	0	0	0	0	0	0	1	0	O-3,2-1
L Total	7	.237	25	80	9	19	3	0	2	10	6	17	0	
W 1966	Bal-A	.167	4	6	2	1	0	0	1	1	1	0	0	O
W 1969	Bal-A	.100	5	20	1	2	0	0	0	0	2	5	1	O
W 1970	Bal-A	.474	5	19	5	9	1	0	0	3	2	4	0	O
W 1971	Bal-A	.333	4	9	2	3	1	0	0	0	0	1	0	O-3
W 1977	NY-A	.250	4	4	0	1	0	0	0	1	0	0	0	O-3
W 1978	NY-A	.375	6	8	2	3	1	0	0	0	1	4	0	O
W Total	6	.288	28	66	12	19	3	0	1	5	6	14	1	
■ **Harry Blake**														
T 1895	Cle-N	.250	5	20	1	5	3	0	0	2	0	2	0	O
T 1896	Cle-N	.071	4	14	1	1	0	0	0	0	1	1	1	O
T Total	2	.176	9	34	2	6	3	0	0	2	1	3	1	
■ **Johnny Blanchard**														
W 1960	NY-A	.455	5	11	2	5	2	0	0	2	0	0	0	C-2
W 1961	NY-A	.400	4	10	4	4	1	0	2	3	2	0	0	O-2
W 1962	NY-A	.000	1	1	0	0	0	0	0	0	0	0	0	H
W 1963	NY-A	.000	1	3	0	0	0	0	0	0	0	0	0	O-1
W 1964	NY-A	.250	4	4	0	1	1	0	0	0	0	1	0	H
W Total	5	.345	15	29	6	10	4	0	2	5	2	2	0	
■ **Lance Blankenship**														
L 1989	Oak-A	—	1	0	0	0	0	0	0	0	0	0	0	2
L 1990	Oak-A	—	3	0	1	0	0	0	0	0	0	0	1	D
L 1992	Oak-A	.231	5	13	2	3	0	0	0	0	3	4	1	2
L Total	3	.231	9	13	3	3	0	0	0	0	3	4	2	
W 1989	Oak-A	.500	1	2	1	1	0	0	0	0	0	0	0	2
W 1990	Oak-A	.000	1	1	0	0	0	0	0	0	0	1	0	H
W Total	2	.333	2	3	1	1	0	0	0	0	0	1	0	
■ **Don Blasingame**														
W 1961	Cin-N	.143	3	7	1	1	0	0	0	0	0	3	0	2
■ **Jeff Blauser**														
D 1995	Atl-N	.000	3	6	0	0	0	0	0	0	1	3	0	S
D 1996	Atl-N	.111	3	9	0	1	0	0	0	0	1	3	0	S
D 1997	Atl-N	.300	3	10	2	3	0	0	1	4	2	2	0	S
D 1998	Chi-N	.000	2	2	0	0	0	0	0	0	0	1	0	H
D Total	4	.148	11	27	2	4	0	0	1	4	4	9	0	
L 1991	Atl-N	.000	2	2	0	0	0	0	0	0	0	0	0	S
L 1992	Atl-N	.208	7	24	3	5	0	1	1	4	3	2	0	S
L 1993	Atl-N	.280	6	25	5	7	1	0	2	4	4	7	0	S
L 1995	Atl-N	.000	1	4	0	0	0	0	0	0	0	1	0	S
L 1996	Atl-N	.176	7	17	5	3	0	1	0	2	4	6	0	S
L 1997	Atl-N	.300	6	20	5	6	0	0	1	1	3	6	0	S
L Total	6	.228	29	92	18	21	1	2	4	11	15	23	0	
W 1991	Atl-N	.167	5	6	0	1	0	0	0	0	1	1	0	S
W 1992	Atl-N	.250	6	24	2	6	0	0	0	0	1	9	2	S
W 1996	Atl-N	.167	6	18	2	3	1	0	0	1	1	4	0	S
W Total	3	.208	17	48	4	10	1	0	0	1	3	14	2	

YEAR	TM/L	AVG	G	AB	R	H	2B	3B	HR	RBI	BB	SO	SB	POS
■ Curt Blefary														
L 1971	Oak-A	.000	1	1	0	0	0	0	0	0	0	1	0	H
W 1966	Bal-A	.077	4	13	0	1	0	0	0	0	2	3	0	O
■ Ned Bligh														
W 1890	Lou-A	.000	2	3	0	0	0	0	0	0	0	1	0	C
■ Cy Block														
W 1945	Chi-N	—	1	0	0	0	0	0	0	0	0	0	0	R
■ Jimmy Bloodworth														
W 1950	Phi-N	—	1	0	0	0	0	0	0	0	0	0	0	2
■ Mike Blowers														
D 1995	Sea-A	.167	5	18	0	3	0	0	0	1	3	7	0	3-5,1-1
D 1997	Sea-A	.200	3	5	0	1	0	0	0	0	0	3	0	3
D Total	2	.174	8	23	0	4	0	0	0	1	3	10	0	
L 1995	Sea-A	.222	6	18	1	4	0	0	1	2	0	4	0	3
■ Ossie Bluege														
W 1924	Was-A	.192	7	26	2	5	0	0	0	3	3	4	1	S-5,3-4
W 1925	Was-A	.278	5	18	2	5	1	0	0	2	0	4	0	3
W 1933	Was-A	.125	5	16	1	2	1	0	0	0	1	6	0	3
W Total	3	.200	17	60	5	12	2	0	0	5	4	14	1	
■ Bruce Bochy														
L 1980	Hou-N	.000	1	1	0	0	0	0	0	0	0	0	0	C
W 1984	SD-N	1.000	1	1	0	1	0	0	0	0	0	0	0	H
■ Tim Bogar														
D 1999	Hou-N	.750	2	4	0	3	1	0	0	1	1	0	0	S-1
■ Wade Boggs														
D 1995	NY-A	.263	4	19	4	5	2	0	1	3	3	5	0	3
D 1996	NY-A	.083	3	12	0	1	1	0	0	0	0	2	0	3
D 1997	NY-A	.429	3	7	1	3	0	0	0	2	0	0	0	3-2
D Total	3	.237	10	38	5	9	3	0	1	5	3	7	0	
L 1986	Bos-A	.233	7	30	3	7	1	1	0	2	4	1	0	3
L 1988	Bos-A	.385	4	13	2	5	0	0	0	3	3	4	0	3
L 1990	Bos-A	.438	4	16	1	7	1	0	1	1	0	3	0	3
L 1996	NY-A	.133	3	15	1	2	0	0	0	0	1	3	0	3
L Total	4	.284	18	74	7	21	2	1	1	6	8	11	0	
W 1986	Bos-A	.290	7	31	3	9	3	0	0	3	4	2	0	3
W 1996	NY-A	.273	4	11	0	3	1	0	0	2	1	0	0	3
W Total	2	.286	11	42	3	12	4	0	0	5	5	2	0	
■ Joe Boley														
W 1929	Phi-A	.235	5	17	1	4	0	0	0	1	0	3	0	S
W 1930	Phi-A	.095	6	21	1	2	0	0	0	1	0	1	0	S
W 1931	Phi-A	.000	1	1	0	0	0	0	0	0	0	1	0	H
W Total	3	.154	12	39	2	6	0	0	0	2	0	5	0	
■ Don Bollweg														
W 1953	NY-A	.000	3	2	0	0	0	0	0	0	0	2	0	1-1
■ Cliff Bolton														
W 1933	Was-A	.000	2	2	0	0	0	0	0	0	0	0	0	H
■ Barry Bonds														
D 1997	SF-N	.250	3	12	0	3	2	0	0	2	0	3	1	O
D 2000	SF-N	.176	4	17	2	3	1	1	0	1	3	4	1	O
D Total	2	.207	7	29	2	6	3	1	0	3	3	7	2	
L 1990	Pit-N	.167	6	18	4	3	0	0	0	1	6	5	2	O
L 1991	Pit-N	.148	7	27	1	4	1	0	0	0	2	4	3	O
L 1992	Pit-N	.261	7	23	5	6	1	0	1	2	6	4	1	O
L Total	3	.191	20	68	10	13	2	0	1	3	14	13	6	
■ Bobby Bonds														
L 1971	SF-N	.250	3	8	0	2	0	0	0	0	2	4	0	O
■ Nino Bongiovanni														
W 1939	Cin-N	.000	1	1	0	0	0	0	0	0	0	0	0	H
■ Bobby Bonilla														
D 1996	Bal-A	.200	4	15	4	3	0	0	2	5	4	6	0	O
D 1997	Fla-N	.333	3	12	1	4	0	0	1	3	2	1	0	3
D 1999	NY-N	.000	2	1	1	0	0	0	0	0	1	0	0	H
D 2000	Atl-N	.000	3	2	0	0	0	0	0	0	2	0	0	O-1
D Total	4	.233	12	30	6	7	0	0	3	8	9	7	0	
L 1990	Pit-N	.190	6	21	0	4	1	0	0	1	3	1	0	O-5,3-3
L 1991	Pit-N	.304	7	23	2	7	2	0	0	1	6	2	0	O
L 1996	Bal-A	.050	5	20	1	1	0	0	1	2	1	4	0	O
L 1997	Fla-N	.261	6	23	3	6	1	0	0	4	1	6	0	3
L 1999	NY-N	.333	3	3	0	1	0	0	0	0	0	2	0	H
L Total	5	.211	27	90	6	19	4	0	1	8	11	15	0	
W 1997	Fla-N	.207	7	29	5	6	1	0	1	3	3	5	0	3
■ Frank Bonner														
T 1894	Bal-N	.000	2	5	0	0	0	0	0	0	0	2	0	S-1,O-1
■ Bret Boone														
D 1995	Cin-N	.300	3	10	4	3	1	0	1	1	1	3	1	2
D 1999	Atl-N	.474	4	19	3	9	1	0	0	1	0	4	1	2
D Total	2	.414	7	29	7	12	2	0	1	2	1	7	2	
L 1995	Cin-N	.214	4	14	1	3	0	0	0	0	1	2	0	2
L 1999	Atl-N	.182	6	22	2	4	1	0	0	1	1	7	2	2
L Total	2	.194	10	36	3	7	1	0	0	1	2	9	2	
W 1999	Atl-N	.538	4	13	1	7	4	0	0	3	1	3	0	2-3
■ Ray Boone														
W 1948	Cle-A	.000	1	1	0	0	0	0	0	0	0	1	0	H

YEAR	TM/L	AVG	G	AB	R	H	2B	3B	HR	RBI	BB	SO	SB	POS
■ Bob Boone														
D 1981	Phi-N	.000	3	5	0	0	0	0	0	0	0	0	0	C
L 1976	Phi-N	.286	3	7	0	2	0	0	0	1	1	0	0	C
L 1977	Phi-N	.400	4	10	1	4	0	0	0	0	0	0	0	C
L 1978	Phi-N	.182	3	11	0	2	0	0	0	0	0	1	0	C
L 1980	Phi-N	.222	5	18	1	4	0	0	0	2	1	2	0	C
L 1982	Cal-A	.250	5	16	3	4	0	0	1	4	0	2	0	C
L 1986	Cal-A	.455	7	22	4	10	0	0	1	2	1	3	0	C
L Total	6	.310	27	84	9	26	0	0	2	9	3	8	0	
W 1980	Phi-N	.412	6	17	3	7	2	0	0	4	4	0	0	C
■ Frenchy Bordagaray														
W 1939	Cin-N	—	2	0	0	0	0	0	0	0	0	0	0	R
W 1941	NY-A	—	1	0	0	0	0	0	0	0	0	0	0	R
W Total	2	—	3	0	0	0	0	0	0	0	0	0	0	
■ Pat Borders														
L 1989	Tor-A	1.000	1	1	0	1	0	0	0	1	0	0	0	C
L 1991	Tor-A	.263	5	19	0	5	1	0	0	2	0	0	0	C
L 1992	Tor-A	.318	6	22	3	7	0	0	1	3	1	1	0	C
L 1993	Tor-A	.250	6	24	1	6	1	0	0	3	0	6	1	C
L Total	4	.288	18	66	4	19	2	0	1	9	1	7	1	
W 1992	Tor-A	.450	6	20	2	9	3	0	1	3	2	1	0	C
W 1993	Tor-A	.304	6	23	2	7	0	0	0	1	2	1	0	C
W Total	2	.372	12	43	4	16	3	0	1	4	4	2	0	
■ Mike Bordick														
D 1997	Bal-A	.400	4	10	4	4	1	0	0	4	4	2	0	S
D 2000	NY-N	.167	4	12	3	2	0	0	0	0	3	4	0	S
D Total	2	.273	8	22	7	6	1	0	0	4	7	6	0	
L 1992	Oak-A	.053	6	19	1	1	0	0	0	0	1	2	1	S-4,2-2
L 1997	Bal-A	.158	6	19	0	3	1	0	0	2	0	6	0	S
L 2000	NY-N	.077	5	13	2	1	0	0	0	0	3	1	0	S
L Total	3	.098	17	51	3	5	1	0	0	2	4	9	1	
W 1990	Oak-A	—	3	0	0	0	0	0	0	0	0	0	0	S
W 2000	NY-N	.125	4	8	0	1	0	0	0	0	0	3	0	S
W Total	2	.125	7	8	0	1	0	0	0	0	0	3	0	
■ Red Borom														
W 1945	Det-A	.000	2	1	0	0	0	0	0	0	0	0	0	H
■ Rick Bosetti														
D 1981	Oak-A	—	1	0	0	0	0	0	0	0	0	0	0	O
L 1981	Oak-A	.250	2	4	1	1	1	0	0	0	0	1	0	O-1,D-1
■ Thad Bosley														
D 1981	Mil-A	—	1	0	0	0	0	0	0	0	0	0	0	D
L 1984	Chi-N	.000	2	2	0	0	0	0	0	0	0	2	0	H
■ Ken Boswell														
L 1969	NY-N	.333	3	12	4	4	0	0	2	5	1	2	0	2
L 1973	NY-N	.000	1	1	0	0	0	0	0	0	0	0	0	H
L Total	2	.308	4	13	4	4	0	0	2	5	1	2	0	
W 1969	NY-N	.333	1	3	1	1	0	0	0	0	0	0	0	2
W 1973	NY-N	1.000	3	3	1	3	0	0	0	0	0	0	0	H
W Total	2	.667	4	6	2	4	0	0	0	0	0	0	0	
■ Jim Bottomley														
W 1926	StL-N	.345	7	29	4	10	3	0	0	5	1	2	0	1
W 1928	StL-N	.214	4	14	1	3	0	1	1	3	2	6	0	1
W 1930	StL-N	.045	6	22	1	1	1	0	0	0	2	9	0	1
W 1931	StL-N	.160	7	25	2	4	1	0	0	2	2	5	0	1
W Total	4	.200	24	90	8	18	5	1	1	10	7	22	0	
■ Lou Boudreau														
W 1948	Cle-A	.273	6	22	1	6	4	0	0	3	1	1	0	S
■ Pat Bourque														
L 1973	Oak-A	.000	2	1	0	0	0	0	0	0	2	1	0	D
W 1973	Oak-A	.500	2	2	0	1	0	0	0	0	0	0	0	1
■ Larry Bowa														
D 1981	Phi-N	.176	5	17	0	3	1	0	0	1	0	0	0	S
L 1976	Phi-N	.125	3	8	1	1	1	0	0	1	3	0	0	S
L 1977	Phi-N	.118	4	17	2	2	0	0	0	1	1	0	0	S
L 1978	Phi-N	.333	4	18	2	6	0	0	0	0	1	2	0	S
L 1980	Phi-N	.316	5	19	2	6	0	0	0	0	3	3	1	S
L 1984	Chi-N	.200	5	15	1	3	1	0	0	1	1	0	0	S
L Total	5	.234	21	77	8	18	2	0	0	3	9	5	1	
W 1980	Phi-N	.375	6	24	3	9	1	0	0	2	0	0	3	S
■ Frank Bowerman														
T 1897	Bal-N	.500	2	8	2	4	0	1	0	4	0	0	0	C-1,1-1
■ Ernie Bowman														
W 1962	SF-N	.000	2	1	1	0	0	0	0	0	0	0	0	S-1
■ Clete Boyer														
L 1969	Atl-N	.111	3	9	0	1	0	0	0	3	2	3	0	3
W 1960	NY-A	.250	4	12	1	3	2	1	0	1	0	1	0	3-4,S-1
W 1961	NY-A	.267	5	15	0	4	2	0	0	3	4	0	0	3
W 1962	NY-A	.318	7	22	2	7	1	0	1	4	1	3	0	3
W 1963	NY-A	.077	4	13	0	1	0	0	0	0	1	6	0	3
W 1964	NY-A	.208	7	24	2	5	1	0	1	3	1	5	1	3
W Total	5	.233	27	86	5	20	6	1	2	11	7	15	1	
■ Ken Boyer														
W 1964	StL-N	.222	7	27	5	6	1	0	2	6	1	5	0	3
■ Jack Boyle														
W 1887	StL-A	.208	6	24	1	5	0	0	0	2	0	4	0	C

YEAR	TM/L	AVG	G	AB	R	H	2B	3B	HR	RBI	BB	SO	SB	POS
W 1888	StL-A	.438	4	16	4	7	0	1	0	4	2	2	3	C-4,O-1
W Total	2	.300	10	40	5	12	0	1	0	6	2	6	3	
■ Steve Brady														
W 1884	NY-A	.000	3	10	1	0	0	0	0	0	0	1	0	O
■ Bobby Bragan														
W 1947	Bro-N	1.000	1	1	0	1	1	0	0	1	0	0	0	H
■ Darren Bragg														
D 1998	Bos-A	.083	3	12	0	1	0	0	0	0	0	5	0	O
■ Glenn Braggs														
L 1990	Cin-N	.200	2	5	0	1	0	0	0	0	0	1	0	O
W 1990	Cin-N	.000	2	4	0	0	0	0	0	2	1	0	0	O-1
■ Kitty Bransfield														
W 1903	Pit-N	.207	8	29	3	6	0	2	0	1	1	6	1	1
■ Jeff Branson														
D 1995	Cin-N	.286	3	7	0	2	1	0	0	2	2	0	0	3
L 1995	Cin-N	.111	4	9	2	1	1	0	0	0	0	2	1	3
L 1997	Cle-A	.000	1	2	0	0	0	0	0	0	0	2	0	D
L 1998	Cle-A	.000	1	1	0	0	0	0	0	0	0	0	0	H
L Total	3	.083	6	12	2	1	1	0	0	0	0	4	1	
W 1997	Cle-A	.000	1	1	0	0	0	0	0	0	0	1	0	H
■ Steve Braun														
L 1978	KC-A	.000	2	5	0	0	0	0	0	0	1	1	0	O-1
L 1982	StL-N	.000	1	1	0	0	0	0	0	0	0	0	0	H
L 1985	StL-N	.000	2	2	0	0	0	0	0	0	0	0	0	H
L Total	3	.000	5	8	0	0	0	0	0	0	1	1	0	
W 1982	StL-N	.500	2	2	0	1	0	0	0	2	1	0	0	D
W 1985	StL-N	.000	1	1	0	0	0	0	0	0	0	0	0	H
W Total	2	.333	3	3	0	1	0	0	0	2	1	0	0	
■ Angel Bravo														
L 1970	Cin-N	.000	1	1	0	0	0	0	0	0	0	0	0	H
W 1970	Cin-N	.000	4	2	0	0	0	0	0	0	1	1	0	H
■ Sid Bream														
L 1990	Pit-N	.500	4	8	1	4	1	0	1	3	2	3	0	1
L 1991	Atl-N	.300	4	10	1	3	0	0	1	3	0	1	0	1
L 1992	Atl-N	.273	7	22	5	6	3	0	1	2	3	0	0	1
L 1993	Atl-N	1.000	1	1	1	1	0	0	0	0	0	0	0	1
L Total	4	.341	16	41	8	14	4	0	3	8	5	4	0	
W 1991	Atl-N	.125	7	24	0	3	2	0	0	0	3	4	0	1
W 1992	Atl-N	.200	5	15	1	3	0	0	0	0	4	0	0	1
W Total	2	.154	12	39	1	6	2	0	0	0	7	4	0	
■ Bob Brenly														
L 1987	SF-N	.235	6	17	3	4	1	0	1	2	3	7	0	C
■ Roger Bresnahan														
W 1905	NY-N	.313	5	16	3	5	2	0	0	1	4	0	1	C
■ Eddie Bressoud														
W 1967	StL-N	—	2	0	0	0	0	0	0	0	0	0	0	S
■ George Brett														
D 1981	KC-A	.167	3	12	0	2	0	0	0	0	0	0	0	3
L 1976	KC-A	.444	5	18	4	8	1	1	1	5	2	1	0	3
L 1977	KC-A	.300	5	20	2	6	0	2	0	2	1	0	0	3
L 1978	KC-A	.389	4	18	7	7	1	1	3	3	0	1	0	3
L 1980	KC-A	.273	3	11	3	3	1	0	2	4	1	0	0	3
L 1984	KC-A	.231	3	13	0	3	0	0	0	0	0	2	0	3
L 1985	KC-A	.348	7	23	6	8	2	0	3	5	7	5	0	3
L Total	6	.340	27	103	22	35	5	4	9	19	11	9	0	
W 1980	KC-A	.375	6	24	3	9	2	1	1	3	2	4	1	3
W 1985	KC-A	.370	7	27	5	10	1	0	0	1	4	7	1	3
W Total	2	.373	13	51	8	19	3	1	1	4	6	11	2	
■ Fred Brickell														
W 1927	Pit-N	.000	2	2	1	0	0	0	0	0	0	0	0	H
■ Harry Bright														
W 1963	NY-A	.000	2	2	0	0	0	0	0	0	0	2	0	H
■ Ed Brinkman														
L 1972	Det-A	.250	1	4	0	1	1	0	0	0	0	0	0	S
■ Greg Brock														
L 1983	LA-N	.000	3	9	1	0	0	0	0	0	0	3	0	1
L 1985	LA-N	.083	5	12	2	1	0	0	1	2	2	2	0	1-4
L Total	2	.048	8	21	3	1	0	0	1	2	2	5	0	
■ Lou Brock														
W 1964	StL-N	.300	7	30	2	9	2	0	1	5	0	3	0	O
W 1967	StL-N	.414	7	29	8	12	2	1	1	3	2	3	7	O
W 1968	StL-N	.464	7	28	6	13	3	1	2	5	3	4	7	O
W Total	3	.391	21	87	16	34	7	2	4	13	5	10	14	
■ Steve Brodie														
T 1894	Bal-N	.000	4	15	2	0	0	0	0	0	2	1	1	O
T 1895	Bal-N	.200	5	20	1	4	0	0	0	2	0	0	0	O
T 1896	Bal-N	.067	4	15	1	1	0	0	0	3	0	0	1	O
T Total	3	.100	13	50	4	5	0	0	0	5	2	1	2	
■ Tom Brookens														
L 1984	Det-A	.000	2	2	0	0	0	0	0	0	0	1	0	2-1,3-1
L 1987	Det-A	.000	5	13	0	0	0	0	0	0	0	3	0	3
L Total	2	.000	7	15	0	0	0	0	0	0	0	4	0	
W 1984	Det-A	.000	3	3	0	0	0	0	0	0	0	1	0	3

YEAR	TM/L	AVG	G	AB	R	H	2B	3B	HR	RBI	BB	SO	SB	POS
■ Scott Brosius														
D 1998	NY-A	.400	3	10	1	4	0	0	1	3	0	3	0	3
D 1999	NY-A	.100	3	10	0	1	1	0	0	1	0	0	0	3
D 2000	NY-A	.176	5	17	0	3	1	0	0	1	1	4	0	3
D Total	3	.216	11	37	1	8	2	0	1	5	1	7	0	
L 1998	NY-A	.300	6	20	2	6	1	0	1	6	2	4	0	3
L 1999	NY-A	.222	5	18	3	4	0	1	2	3	1	4	0	3
L 2000	NY-A	.222	6	18	2	4	0	0	0	0	2	3	0	3
L Total	3	.250	17	56	7	14	1	1	3	9	5	11	0	
W 1998	NY-A	.471	4	17	3	8	0	0	2	6	0	4	0	3
W 1999	NY-A	.375	4	16	2	6	1	0	0	1	0	5	0	3
W 2000	NY-A	.308	5	13	2	4	0	0	1	3	2	2	0	3
W Total	3	.391	13	46	7	18	1	0	3	10	2	11	0	
■ Mark Brouhard														
L 1982	Mil-A	.750	1	4	4	3	1	0	1	3	0	0	0	O
■ Dan Brouthers														
W 1887	Det-N	.667	1	3	0	2	0	0	0	0	0	0	0	1
T 1894	Bal-N	.188	4	16	2	3	0	0	0	0	1	0	3	1
■ Brant Brown														
D 1998	Chi-N	.000	1	1	0	0	0	0	0	0	0	0	0	H
■ Ike Brown														
L 1972	Det-A	.500	1	2	0	1	0	0	0	2	0	1	0	1
■ Jimmy Brown														
W 1942	StL-N	.300	5	20	2	6	0	0	0	1	3	0	0	2
■ Jarvis Brown														
L 1991	Min-A	—	1	0	1	0	0	0	0	0	0	0	0	D
W 1991	Min-A	.000	3	2	0	0	0	0	0	0	0	0	0	O-2,D-1
■ Larry Brown														
L 1973	Bal-A	—	1	0	0	0	0	0	0	0	0	0	0	3
■ Ollie Brown														
L 1976	Phi-N	.000	1	2	0	0	0	0	0	0	1	1	0	O
L 1977	Phi-N	.000	2	2	0	0	0	0	0	0	0	1	0	H
L Total	2	.000	3	4	0	0	0	0	0	0	1	2	0	
■ Bobby Brown														
W 1947	NY-A	1.000	4	3	2	3	2	0	0	3	1	0	0	H
W 1949	NY-A	.500	4	12	4	6	1	2	0	5	2	2	0	3-3
W 1950	NY-A	.333	4	12	2	4	1	1	0	1	0	0	0	3
W 1951	NY-A	.357	5	14	1	5	1	0	0	0	2	1	0	3-4
W Total	4	.439	17	41	9	18	5	3	0	9	5	3	0	
■ Bobby Brown														
D 1981	NY-A	—	1	0	0	0	0	0	0	0	0	0	0	R
L 1980	NY-A	.000	3	10	1	0	0	0	0	0	1	2	0	O
L 1981	NY-A	1.000	3	1	2	1	0	0	0	0	0	0	0	O-2
L 1984	SD-N	.000	3	4	1	0	0	0	0	0	1	2	1	O
L Total	3	.067	9	15	4	1	0	0	0	0	2	4	1	
W 1981	NY-A	.000	4	1	1	0	0	0	0	0	0	1	0	O-2
W 1984	SD-N	.067	5	15	1	1	0	0	0	2	0	4	0	O
W Total	2	.063	9	16	2	1	0	0	0	2	0	5	0	
■ Tommy Brown														
W 1949	Bro-N	.000	2	2	0	0	0	0	0	0	0	1	0	H
■ Willard Brown														
W 1888	NY-N	.375	2	8	1	3	1	0	0	0	0	0	0	C
W 1889	NY-N	.600	1	5	3	3	0	0	1	2	0	0	0	C
W Total	2	.462	3	13	4	6	1	0	1	2	0	0	0	
■ Gates Brown														
L 1972	Det-A	.000	3	2	1	0	0	0	0	0	1	0	0	H
W 1968	Det-A	.000	1	1	0	0	0	0	0	0	0	0	0	H
■ George Browne														
W 1905	NY-N	.182	5	22	2	4	0	0	0	1	0	2	2	O
■ Jerry Browne														
L 1992	Oak-A	.400	4	10	3	4	0	0	0	2	2	0	0	3-2,O-1
■ Glenn Brummer														
W 1982	StL-N	—	1	0	0	0	0	0	0	0	0	0	0	C
■ Tom Brunansky														
L 1987	Min-A	.412	5	17	5	7	4	0	2	9	4	3	0	O
L 1990	Bos-A	.083	4	12	0	1	0	0	0	1	1	3	0	O
L Total	2	.276	9	29	5	8	4	0	2	10	5	6	0	
W 1987	Min-A	.200	7	25	5	5	0	0	0	2	4	4	1	O
■ Bill Bruton														
W 1958	Mil-N	.412	7	17	2	7	0	0	1	2	5	5	0	O
■ Jerry Buchek														
W 1964	StL-N	1.000	4	1	1	1	0	0	0	0	0	0	0	2
■ Bill Buckner														
L 1974	LA-N	.167	4	18	0	3	1	0	0	0	0	2	0	O
L 1986	Bos-A	.214	7	28	3	6	1	0	0	3	0	2	0	1
L Total	2	.196	11	46	3	9	2	0	0	3	0	4	0	
W 1974	LA-N	.250	5	20	1	5	1	0	1	1	0	1	0	O
W 1986	Bos-A	.188	7	32	2	6	0	0	0	1	0	3	0	1
W Total	2	.212	12	52	3	11	1	0	1	2	0	4	0	
■ Steve Buechele														
L 1991	Pit-N	.304	7	23	2	7	2	0	0	0	4	6	0	3

YEAR	TM/L	AVG	G	AB	R	H	2B	3B	HR	RBI	BB	SO	SB	POS
■ **Damon Buford**														
D 1996	Tex-A	—	2	0	0	0	0	0	0	0	0	0	0	R
D 1998	Bos-A	.000	3	1	2	0	0	0	0	0	0	0	0	O-1,D-1
D 1999	Bos-A	.000	1	3	0	0	0	0	0	0	0	1	0	O
D Total	3	.000	6	4	2	0	0	0	0	0	0	1	0	
L 1999	Bos-A	.400	4	5	1	2	0	0	0	0	0	2	1	O
■ **Don Buford**														
L 1969	Bal-A	.286	3	14	3	4	1	0	0	1	3	0	0	O
L 1970	Bal-A	.429	2	7	2	3	1	0	1	3	2	0	0	O
L 1971	Bal-A	.429	2	7	1	3	0	1	0	0	2	1	0	O
L Total	3	.357	7	28	6	10	2	1	1	4	7	1	0	
W 1969	Bal-A	.100	5	20	1	2	1	0	1	2	2	4	0	O
W 1970	Bal-A	.267	4	15	3	4	0	0	1	1	3	2	0	O
W 1971	Bal-A	.261	6	23	3	6	1	0	2	4	3	3	0	O
W Total	3	.207	15	58	7	12	2	0	4	7	8	9	0	
■ **Jay Buhner**														
D 1995	Sea-A	.458	5	24	2	11	1	0	1	3	2	4	0	O
D 1997	Sea-A	.231	4	13	2	3	0	0	2	2	3	6	0	O
D 2000	Sea-A	.200	2	5	1	1	0	0	1	1	2	0	0	O
D Total	3	.357	11	42	5	15	1	0	4	6	7	10	0	
L 1995	Sea-A	.304	6	23	5	7	2	0	3	5	2	8	0	O
L 2000	Sea-A	.182	4	11	0	2	0	0	0	0	1	6	0	O-3
L Total	2	.265	10	34	5	9	2	0	3	5	3	14	0	
■ **Al Bumbry**														
L 1973	Bal-A	.000	2	7	1	0	0	0	0	0	2	2	1	O
L 1974	Bal-A	.000	2	1	0	0	0	0	0	0	0	1	0	H
L 1979	Bal-A	.250	4	16	5	4	0	1	0	0	4	3	2	O
L 1983	Bal-A	.125	3	8	0	1	1	0	0	1	0	2	0	O
L Total	4	.156	11	32	6	5	1	1	0	1	6	8	3	
W 1979	Bal-A	.143	7	21	3	3	0	0	0	1	2	1	0	O
W 1983	Bal-A	.091	4	11	0	1	1	0	0	1	0	1	0	O
W Total	2	.125	11	32	3	4	1	0	0	2	2	2	0	
■ **Smoky Burgess**														
W 1960	Pit-N	.333	5	18	2	6	1	0	0	0	2	1	0	C
■ **Eddie Burke**														
T 1894	NY-N	.389	4	18	3	7	1	0	0	2	1	0	1	O
■ **Glenn Burke**														
L 1977	LA-N	.000	4	7	0	0	0	0	0	0	0	3	0	O
W 1977	LA-N	.200	3	5	0	1	0	0	0	0	0	1	0	O
■ **Jesse Burkett**														
T 1892	Cle-N	.320	6	25	3	8	1	0	0	1	0	2	4	O
T 1895	Cle-N	.429	5	21	3	9	2	0	0	2	0	0	1	O
T 1896	Cle-N	.333	4	15	1	5	0	0	0	0	2	3	0	O
T Total	3	.361	15	61	7	22	3	0	0	3	2	5	5	
■ **Ellis Burks**														
D 1995	Col-N	.333	2	6	1	2	1	0	0	2	0	1	0	O
D 2000	SF-N	.231	4	13	2	3	1	0	1	4	4	2	0	O
D Total	2	.263	6	19	3	5	2	0	1	6	4	3	0	
L 1988	Bos-A	.235	4	17	2	4	1	0	0	1	0	3	0	O
L 1990	Bos-A	.267	4	15	1	4	2	0	0	0	1	1	1	O
L 1993	Chi-A	.304	6	23	4	7	1	0	1	3	3	5	0	O
L Total	3	.273	14	55	7	15	4	0	1	4	4	9	1	
■ **Rick Burleson**														
L 1975	Bos-A	.444	3	9	2	4	2	0	0	1	1	0	0	S
L 1986	Cal-A	.273	4	11	0	3	0	0	0	0	0	0	0	2-2,D-1
L Total	2	.350	7	20	2	7	2	0	0	1	1	0	0	
W 1975	Bos-A	.292	7	24	1	7	1	0	0	2	4	2	0	S
■ **Ed Burns**														
W 1915	Phi-N	.188	5	16	1	3	0	0	0	0	1	2	0	C
■ **George Burns**														
W 1920	Cle-A	.300	5	10	1	3	1	0	0	2	3	3	0	1-4
W 1929	Phi-A	.000	1	2	0	0	0	0	0	0	0	1	0	H
W Total	2	.250	6	12	1	3	1	0	0	2	3	4	0	
■ **George Burns**														
W 1913	NY-N	.158	5	19	2	3	2	0	0	2	1	5	1	O
W 1917	NY-N	.227	6	22	3	5	0	0	0	2	3	6	1	O
W 1921	NY-N	.333	8	33	2	11	4	1	0	2	3	5	1	O
W Total	3	.257	19	74	7	19	6	1	0	6	7	16	3	
■ **Tom Burns**														
W 1885	Chi-N	.080	7	25	3	2	0	1	0	0	0	0	0	S-4,3-3
W 1886	Chi-N	.286	6	21	2	6	2	1	0	1	0	2	0	3-6,O-1
W Total	2	.174	13	46	5	8	2	2	0	1	0	2	0	
■ **Oyster Burns**														
W 1889	Bro-A	.229	9	35	8	8	3	0	2	11	5	6	0	O
W 1890	Bro-N	.222	7	27	6	6	2	0	1	5	3	4	0	O-4,3-3
W Total	2	.226	16	62	14	14	5	0	3	16	8	10	0	
■ **Jeff Burroughs**														
L 1985	Tor-A	.000	1	1	0	0	0	0	0	0	0	0	0	H
■ **Homer Bush**														
D 1998	NY-A	—	1	0	0	0	0	0	0	0	0	0	1	D
L 1998	NY-A	—	2	0	1	0	0	0	0	0	0	0	1	D-1
W 1998	NY-A	—	2	0	0	0	0	0	0	0	0	0	0	D-1
■ **Donie Bush**														
W 1909	Det-A	.261	7	23	5	6	1	0	0	3	5	3	1	S
■ **Randy Bush**														
L 1987	Min-A	.250	4	12	4	3	0	1	0	2	3	2	3	D
W 1987	Min-A	.167	4	6	1	1	1	0	0	2	0	1	0	D-2
W 1991	Min-A	.250	3	4	0	1	0	0	0	0	0	1	0	O-2
W Total	2	.200	7	10	1	2	1	0	0	2	0	2	0	
■ **Doc Bushong**														
W 1885	StL-A	.154	4	13	1	2	0	0	0	2	0	0	0	C
W 1886	StL-A	.188	6	16	4	3	1	0	0	2	4	5	0	C
W 1887	StL-A	.333	9	33	3	11	0	0	0	1	4	1	0	C
W 1889	Bro-A	.000	3	8	0	0	0	0	0	0	1	0	0	C
W 1890	Bro-N	.000	2	6	0	0	0	0	0	0	0	1	0	C
W Total	5	.211	24	76	8	16	1	0	0	5	9	7	0	
■ **Sal Butera**														
L 1987	Min-A	.667	1	3	0	2	0	0	0	0	0	0	0	C
W 1987	Min-A	—	1	0	0	0	0	0	0	0	0	0	0	C
■ **Brett Butler**														
D 1995	LA-N	.267	3	15	1	4	0	0	0	1	0	3	0	O
L 1982	Atl-N	.000	2	1	0	0	0	0	0	0	0	0	0	O-1
L 1989	SF-N	.211	5	19	6	4	0	0	0	0	3	3	0	O
L Total	2	.200	7	20	6	4	0	0	0	0	3	3	0	
W 1989	SF-N	.286	4	14	1	4	1	0	0	1	2	1	2	O
■ **Rob Butler**														
W 1993	Tor-A	.500	2	2	1	1	0	0	0	0	0	0	0	H
■ **Sammy Byrd**														
W 1932	NY-A	—	1	0	0	0	0	0	0	0	0	0	0	O
■ **Bobby Byrne**														
W 1909	Pit-N	.250	7	24	5	6	1	0	0	0	1	4	1	3
W 1915	Phi-N	.000	1	1	0	0	0	0	0	0	0	0	0	H
W Total	2	.240	8	25	5	6	1	0	0	0	1	4	1	
■ **Milt Byrnes**														
W 1944	StL-A	.000	3	2	0	0	0	0	0	0	1	2	0	H
■ **Putsy Caballero**														
W 1950	Phi-N	.000	3	1	0	0	0	0	0	0	0	1	0	H
■ **Enos Cabell**														
L 1974	Bal-A	.250	3	4	0	1	0	0	0	0	0	2	0	O-1
L 1980	Hou-N	.238	5	21	1	5	1	0	0	0	1	3	0	3
L 1985	LA-N	.077	5	13	1	1	0	0	0	0	0	3	0	1-3
L Total	3	.184	13	38	2	7	1	0	0	0	1	8	0	
■ **Francisco Cabrera**														
L 1992	Atl-N	.500	2	2	0	1	0	0	0	2	0	0	0	H
L 1993	Atl-N	.667	3	3	0	2	0	0	0	1	0	1	0	C-1
L Total	2	.600	5	5	0	3	0	0	0	3	0	1	0	
W 1991	Atl-N	.000	3	1	0	0	0	0	0	0	0	0	0	C-1
W 1992	Atl-N	.000	1	1	0	0	0	0	0	0	0	0	0	H
W Total	2	.000	4	2	0	0	0	0	0	0	0	0	0	
■ **Hick Cady**														
W 1912	Bos-A	.136	7	22	1	3	0	0	0	1	0	3	0	C
W 1915	Bos-A	.333	4	6	0	2	0	0	0	0	1	2	0	C
W 1916	Bos-A	.250	2	4	1	1	0	0	0	0	3	0	0	C
W Total	3	.188	13	32	2	6	0	0	0	1	4	5	0	
■ **Mike Cameron**														
D 2000	Sea-A	.250	3	12	2	3	0	0	0	2	0	0	1	O
L 2000	Sea-A	.111	6	18	3	2	0	0	0	1	2	7	1	O
■ **Dolph Camilli**														
W 1941	Bro-N	.167	5	18	1	3	1	0	0	1	1	6	0	1
■ **Ken Caminiti**														
D 1996	SD-N	.300	3	10	3	3	0	0	3	3	2	5	0	3
D 1998	SD-N	.143	4	14	2	2	0	0	0	0	1	3	0	3
D 1999	Hou-N	.471	4	17	3	8	0	0	3	8	2	1	0	3
D Total	3	.317	11	41	8	13	0	0	6	11	5	9	0	
L 1998	SD-N	.273	6	22	3	6	0	0	2	4	5	4	0	3
W 1998	SD-N	.143	4	14	1	2	1	0	0	1	2	7	0	3
■ **Roy Campanella**														
W 1949	Bro-N	.267	5	15	2	4	1	0	1	2	3	1	0	C
W 1952	Bro-N	.214	7	28	0	6	0	0	0	1	1	6	0	C
W 1953	Bro-N	.273	6	22	6	6	0	0	1	2	2	3	0	C
W 1955	Bro-N	.259	7	27	4	7	3	0	2	4	3	3	0	C
W 1956	Bro-N	.182	7	22	2	4	1	0	0	3	3	7	0	C
W Total	5	.237	32	114	14	27	5	0	4	12	12	20	0	
■ **Bert Campaneris**														
L 1971	Oak-A	.167	3	12	0	2	1	0	0	0	0	1	0	S
L 1972	Oak-A	.429	2	7	3	3	0	0	0	0	1	0	2	S
L 1973	Oak-A	.333	5	21	3	7	1	0	2	3	2	2	3	S
L 1974	Oak-A	.176	4	17	0	3	0	0	0	3	0	3	1	S
L 1975	Oak-A	.000	3	11	1	0	0	0	0	0	1	1	0	S
L 1979	Cal-A	—	1	0	0	0	0	0	0	0	0	0	0	S
L Total	6	.221	18	68	7	15	2	0	2	6	4	7	6	
W 1972	Oak-A	.179	7	28	1	5	0	0	0	0	1	4	0	S
W 1973	Oak-A	.290	7	31	6	9	0	1	1	3	1	7	3	S
W 1974	Oak-A	.353	5	17	1	6	2	0	0	2	0	2	1	S
W Total	3	.263	19	76	8	20	2	1	1	5	2	13	4	
■ **Bruce Campbell**														
W 1940	Det-A	.360	7	25	4	9	1	0	1	5	4	4	0	O

YEAR	TM/L	AVG	G	AB	R	H	2B	3B	HR	RBI	BB	SO	SB	POS
■ **Paul Campbell**														
W 1946	Bos-A	—	1	0	0	0	0	0	0	0	0	0	0	R
■ **Willie Canate**														
W 1993	Tor-A	—	1	0	0	0	0	0	0	0	0	0	0	R
■ **Casey Candaele**														
D 1996	Cle-A	—	2	0	1	0	0	0	0	0	1	0	0	D-1
■ **John Cangelosi**														
D 1997	Fla-N	.000	1	1	0	0	0	0	0	0	0	0	0	H
L 1997	Fla-N	.200	3	5	0	1	0	0	0	0	1	0	0	O-1
W 1997	Fla-N	.333	3	3	0	1	0	0	0	0	0	2	0	H
■ **Jose Canseco**														
D 1995	Bos-A	.000	3	13	0	0	0	0	0	0	2	2	0	D-2,O-1
L 1988	Oak-A	.313	4	16	4	5	1	0	3	4	1	2	1	O
L 1989	Oak-A	.294	5	17	1	5	0	0	1	3	3	7	0	O
L 1990	Oak-A	.182	4	11	3	2	0	0	0	1	5	5	2	O
L Total	3	.273	13	44	8	12	1	0	4	8	9	14	3	
W 1988	Oak-A	.053	5	19	1	1	0	0	1	5	2	5	1	O
W 1989	Oak-A	.357	4	14	5	5	0	0	1	3	4	3	1	O
W 1990	Oak-A	.083	4	12	1	1	0	0	1	2	2	3	0	O-3,D-1
W 2000	NY-A	.000	1	1	0	0	0	0	0	0	0	1	0	H
W Total	4	.152	14	46	7	7	0	0	3	10	8	12	2	
■ **Bernie Carbo**														
L 1970	Cin-N	.000	2	6	0	0	0	0	0	0	1	2	0	O
W 1970	Cin-N	.000	4	8	0	0	0	0	0	0	2	3	0	O-2
W 1975	Bos-A	.429	4	7	3	3	1	0	2	4	1	1	0	O-2
W Total	2	.200	8	15	3	3	1	0	2	4	3	4	0	
■ **Jose Cardenal**														
L 1978	Phi-N	.167	2	6	0	1	0	0	0	0	1	1	0	1
W 1980	KC-A	.200	4	10	0	2	0	0	0	0	0	3	0	O
■ **Leo Cardenas**														
L 1969	Min-A	.154	3	13	0	2	0	1	0	0	0	7	0	S
L 1970	Min-A	.182	3	11	1	2	0	0	0	1	1	1	0	S
L Total	2	.167	6	24	1	4	0	1	0	1	1	8	0	
W 1961	Cin-N	.333	3	3	0	1	1	0	0	0	0	1	0	H
■ **Rod Carew**														
L 1969	Min-A	.071	3	14	0	1	0	0	0	0	1	4	0	2
L 1970	Min-A	.000	2	2	0	0	0	0	0	0	0	1	0	H
L 1979	Cal-A	.412	4	17	4	7	3	0	0	1	0	0	1	1
L 1982	Cal-A	.176	5	17	2	3	1	0	0	0	4	4	1	1
L Total	4	.220	14	50	6	11	4	0	0	1	5	9	2	
■ **Andy Carey**														
W 1955	NY-A	.500	2	2	0	1	0	1	0	1	0	0	0	H
W 1956	NY-A	.158	7	19	2	3	0	0	0	0	1	6	0	3
W 1957	NY-A	.286	2	7	0	2	1	0	0	1	1	0	0	3
W 1958	NY-A	.083	5	12	1	1	0	0	0	0	0	3	0	3
W Total	4	.175	16	40	3	7	1	1	0	2	2	9	0	
■ **Scoops Carey**														
T 1895	Bal-N	.263	5	19	0	5	1	0	0	1	0	0	0	1
■ **Max Carey**														
W 1925	Pit-N	.458	7	24	6	11	4	0	0	2	2	3	3	O
■ **Chuck Carr**														
D 1997	Hou-N	.250	2	4	1	1	0	0	1	1	1	3	0	O
■ **Bill Carrigan**														
W 1912	Bos-A	.000	2	7	0	0	0	0	0	0	0	0	0	C
W 1915	Bos-A	.000	1	2	0	0	0	0	0	0	1	1	0	C
W 1916	Bos-A	.667	1	3	0	2	0	0	0	1	0	1	0	C
W Total	3	.167	4	12	0	2	0	0	0	1	1	2	0	
■ **Cliff Carroll**														
W 1884	Pro-N	.100	3	10	2	1	0	0	0	1	1	1	0	O
■ **Tom Carroll**														
W 1955	NY-A	—	2	0	0	0	0	0	0	0	0	0	0	R
■ **Gary Carter**														
D 1981	Mon-N	.421	5	19	3	8	3	0	2	6	1	1	0	C
L 1981	Mon-N	.438	5	16	3	7	1	0	0	0	4	2	0	C
L 1986	NY-N	.148	6	27	1	4	1	0	0	2	2	5	0	C
L 1988	NY-N	.222	7	27	0	6	1	1	0	4	1	3	0	C
L Total	3	.243	18	70	4	17	3	1	0	6	7	10	0	
W 1986	NY-N	.276	7	29	4	8	2	0	2	9	0	4	0	C
■ **Joe Carter**														
L 1991	Tor-A	.263	5	19	3	5	2	0	1	4	1	5	0	O-3,D-2
L 1992	Tor-A	.192	6	26	2	5	0	0	1	3	2	4	2	O-6,1-2
L 1993	Tor-A	.259	6	27	2	7	0	0	0	2	1	5	0	O
L Total	3	.236	17	72	7	17	2	0	2	9	4	14	2	
W 1992	Tor-A	.273	6	22	2	6	2	0	2	3	3	2	1	O-4,1-2
W 1993	Tor-A	.280	6	25	6	7	1	0	2	8	0	4	0	O
W Total	2	.277	12	47	8	13	3	0	4	11	3	6	1	
■ **Rico Carty**														
L 1969	Atl-N	.300	3	10	4	3	2	0	0	0	3	1	0	O
■ **Bob Caruthers**														
W 1885	StL-A	.200	5	15	1	3	0	1	0	6	1	0	0	P-3,O-2
W 1886	StL-A	.250	6	24	6	6	1	2	0	5	1	4	1	P-3,O-3
W 1887	StL-A	.255	10	47	2	12	0	0	0	3	1	1	3	P-8,O-3
W 1889	Bro-A	.250	4	8	1	2	0	0	0	1	3	3	0	P
W 1890	Bro-N	.000	2	6	0	0	0	0	0	0	2	0	0	O
W Total	5	.230	27	100	10	23	1	3	0	15	8	8	4	
■ **Dave Cash**														
L 1970	Pit-N	.125	2	8	1	1	1	0	0	0	1	1	0	2
L 1971	Pit-N	.421	4	19	5	8	2	0	0	1	0	1	1	2
L 1972	Pit-N	.211	5	19	0	4	0	0	0	3	0	0	0	2
L 1976	Phi-N	.308	3	13	1	4	1	0	0	1	0	0	0	2
L Total	4	.288	14	59	7	17	4	0	0	5	1	2	1	
W 1971	Pit-N	.133	7	30	2	4	1	0	0	1	3	1	1	2
■ **Norm Cash**														
L 1972	Det-A	.267	5	15	1	4	0	0	1	2	2	3	0	1
W 1959	Chi-A	.000	4	4	0	0	0	0	0	0	0	2	0	H
W 1968	Det-A	.385	7	26	5	10	0	0	1	5	3	5	0	1
W Total	2	.333	11	30	5	10	0	0	1	5	3	7	0	
■ **Vinny Castilla**														
D 1995	Col-N	.467	4	15	3	7	1	0	3	6	0	1	0	3
■ **Marty Castillo**														
L 1984	Det-A	.250	3	8	0	2	0	0	0	2	0	3	1	3
W 1984	Det-A	.333	3	9	2	3	0	0	1	2	2	1	0	3
■ **Juan Castro**														
D 1996	LA-N	.200	2	5	0	1	1	0	0	1	1	1	0	2
■ **Ted Cather**														
W 1914	Bos-N	.000	1	5	0	0	0	0	0	0	0	1	0	O
■ **Phil Cavarretta**														
W 1935	Chi-N	.125	6	24	1	3	0	0	0	0	0	5	0	1
W 1938	Chi-N	.462	4	13	1	6	1	0	0	0	0	1	0	O-3
W 1945	Chi-N	.423	7	26	7	11	2	0	1	5	4	3	0	1
W Total	3	.317	17	63	9	20	3	0	1	5	4	9	0	
■ **Cesar Cedeno**														
D 1981	Hou-N	.231	4	13	0	3	1	0	0	0	2	2	2	1
L 1980	Hou-N	.182	3	11	1	2	0	0	0	1	1	0	0	O
L 1985	StL-N	.167	5	12	2	2	1	0	0	0	2	3	0	O-4
L Total	2	.174	8	23	3	4	1	0	0	1	3	3	0	
W 1985	StL-N	.133	5	15	1	2	1	0	0	1	2	2	0	O
■ **Roger Cedeno**														
D 1999	NY-N	.286	4	7	1	2	0	0	0	2	1	1	1	O
L 1999	NY-N	.500	5	12	2	6	1	0	0	1	0	1	2	O-4
■ **Orlando Cepeda**														
L 1969	Atl-N	.455	3	11	2	5	2	0	1	3	1	2	1	1
W 1962	SF-N	.158	5	19	1	3	1	0	0	2	0	4	0	1
W 1967	StL-N	.103	7	29	1	3	2	0	0	1	0	4	0	1
W 1968	StL-N	.250	7	28	2	7	0	0	2	6	2	3	0	1
W Total	3	.171	19	76	4	13	3	0	2	9	2	11	0	
■ **Rick Cerone**														
D 1981	NY-A	.333	5	18	1	6	2	0	1	5	0	2	0	C
L 1980	NY-A	.333	3	12	1	4	0	0	1	2	0	1	0	C
L 1981	NY-A	.100	3	10	1	1	0	0	0	0	0	0	0	C
L Total	2	.227	6	22	2	5	0	0	1	2	0	1	0	
W 1981	NY-A	.190	6	21	2	4	1	0	1	3	4	2	0	C
■ **Bob Cerv**														
W 1955	NY-A	.125	5	16	1	2	0	0	1	1	0	4	0	O-4
W 1956	NY-A	1.000	1	1	0	1	0	0	0	0	0	0	0	H
W 1960	NY-A	.357	4	14	1	5	0	0	0	0	0	3	0	O-3
W Total	3	.258	10	31	2	8	0	0	1	1	0	7	0	
■ **Ron Cey**														
L 1974	LA-N	.313	4	16	2	5	3	0	1	1	3	2	0	3
L 1977	LA-N	.308	4	13	4	4	1	0	1	4	2	4	1	3
L 1978	LA-N	.313	4	16	4	5	1	0	1	3	2	4	0	3
L 1981	LA-N	.278	5	18	1	5	1	0	0	3	3	2	0	3
L 1984	Chi-N	.158	5	19	3	3	1	0	1	3	3	3	0	3
L Total	5	.268	22	82	14	22	7	0	4	14	13	15	1	
W 1974	LA-N	.176	5	17	1	3	0	0	0	0	3	3	0	3
W 1977	LA-N	.190	6	21	2	4	1	0	1	3	3	5	0	3
W 1978	LA-N	.286	6	21	2	6	0	0	1	4	3	3	0	3
W 1981	LA-N	.350	6	20	3	7	0	0	1	6	3	3	0	3
W Total	4	.253	23	79	8	20	1	0	3	13	12	14	0	
■ **Elio Chacon**														
W 1961	Cin-N	.250	4	12	2	3	0	0	0	0	1	2	0	2-3
■ **Dave Chalk**														
W 1980	KC-A	—	1	0	1	0	0	0	0	0	1	0	1	3
■ **Wes Chamberlain**														
L 1993	Phi-N	.364	4	11	1	4	3	0	0	1	1	3	0	O-2
W 1993	Phi-N	.000	2	2	0	0	0	0	0	0	0	1	0	H
■ **Chris Chambliss**														
L 1976	NY-A	.524	5	21	5	11	1	1	2	8	0	1	2	1
L 1977	NY-A	.059	5	17	0	1	0	0	0	0	3	4	0	1
L 1978	NY-A	.400	4	15	1	6	0	0	0	2	0	4	0	1
L 1982	Atl-N	.000	3	10	0	0	0	0	0	0	1	0	0	1
L Total	4	.286	17	63	6	18	1	1	2	10	4	9	2	
W 1976	NY-A	.313	4	16	1	5	1	0	0	1	0	2	0	1
W 1977	NY-A	.292	6	24	4	7	2	0	1	4	0	2	0	1
W 1978	NY-A	.182	3	11	1	2	0	0	0	0	1	1	0	1
W Total	3	.275	13	51	6	14	3	0	1	5	1	5	0	

YEAR	TM/L	AVG	G	AB	R	H	2B	3B	HR	RBI	BB	SO	SB	POS
■ Frank Chance														
W 1906	Chi-N	.238	6	21	3	5	1	0	0	0	2	1	2	1
W 1907	Chi-N	.214	4	14	3	3	1	0	0	0	3	2	3	1
W 1908	Chi-N	.421	5	19	4	8	0	0	0	2	3	1	5	1
W 1910	Chi-N	.353	5	17	1	6	1	1	0	4	0	3	0	1
W Total	4	.310	20	71	11	22	3	1	0	6	8	7	10	
■ Darrel Chaney														
L 1972	Cin-N	.188	5	16	3	3	0	0	0	1	1	1	1	S
L 1973	Cin-N	.000	5	9	0	0	0	0	0	0	3	4	0	H
L Total	2	.120	10	25	3	3	0	0	0	1	4	5	1	
W 1970	Cin-N	.000	3	1	0	0	0	0	0	0	0	1	0	S
W 1972	Cin-N	.000	4	7	0	0	0	0	0	0	2	2	0	S-3
W 1975	Cin-N	.000	2	2	0	0	0	0	0	0	0	1	0	H
W Total	3	.000	9	10	0	0	0	0	0	0	2	4	0	
■ Ben Chapman														
W 1932	NY-A	.294	4	17	1	5	2	0	0	6	2	4	0	O
■ Ed Charles														
W 1969	NY-N	.133	4	15	1	2	1	0	0	0	0	2	0	3
■ Mike Chartak														
W 1944	StL-A	.000	2	2	0	0	0	0	0	0	0	2	0	H
■ Eric Chavez														
D 2000	Oak-A	.333	5	21	4	7	3	0	0	4	0	5	0	3
■ Cupid Childs														
T 1892	Cle-N	.409	6	22	3	9	0	2	0	0	5	1	0	2
T 1895	Cle-N	.200	5	20	4	4	1	0	0	2	1	0	1	2
T 1896	Cle-N	.231	4	13	2	3	0	0	0	0	4	0	1	2
T Total	3	.291	15	55	9	16	1	2	0	2	10	1	2	
■ Lou Chiozza														
W 1937	NY-N	.286	2	7	0	2	0	0	0	0	1	1	0	O
■ Mc Kay Christensen														
D 2000	Chi-A	—	1	0	0	0	0	0	0	0	0	0	0	O
■ Ryan Christenson														
D 2000	Oak-A	.500	2	2	0	1	0	0	0	1	0	1	0	O
■ Mark Christman														
W 1944	StL-A	.091	6	22	0	2	0	0	0	1	0	6	0	3
■ Joe Christopher														
W 1960	Pit-N	—	3	0	2	0	0	0	0	0	0	0	0	H
■ Archi Cianfrocco														
D 1996	SD-N	.333	3	3	1	1	0	0	0	0	0	1	0	1
■ Gino Cimoli														
W 1956	Bro-N	—	1	0	0	0	0	0	0	0	0	0	0	O
W 1960	Pit-N	.250	7	20	4	5	0	0	0	1	2	4	0	O-6
W Total	2	.250	8	20	4	5	0	0	0	1	2	4	0	
■ Allie Clark														
W 1947	NY-A	.500	3	2	1	1	0	0	0	1	1	0	0	O-1
W 1948	Cle-A	.000	1	3	0	0	0	0	0	0	0	1	0	O
W Total	2	.200	4	5	1	1	0	0	0	1	1	1	0	
■ Dave Clark														
D 1996	LA-N	.000	2	2	0	0	0	0	0	0	0	2	0	H
D 1998	Hou-N	—	2	0	0	0	0	0	0	0	2	0	0	H
D Total	2	.000	4	2	0	0	0	0	0	0	2	2	0	
■ Jack Clark														
L 1985	StL-N	.381	6	21	4	8	0	0	1	4	5	5	0	1
L 1987	StL-N	.000	1	1	0	0	0	0	0	0	0	1	0	H
L Total	2	.364	7	22	4	8	0	0	1	4	5	6	0	
W 1985	StL-N	.240	7	25	1	6	2	0	0	4	3	9	0	1
■ Bobby Clark														
L 1979	Cal-A	.000	1	3	0	0	0	0	0	0	0	2	0	O
L 1982	Cal-A	—	2	0	0	0	0	0	0	0	0	0	0	O
L Total	2	.000	3	3	0	0	0	0	0	0	0	2	0	
■ Bob Clark														
W 1889	Bro-A	.417	4	12	3	5	2	0	0	3	2	2	0	C
W 1890	Bro-N	.667	1	3	2	2	0	1	0	1	0	0	0	C
W Total	2	.467	5	15	5	7	2	1	0	4	2	2	0	
■ Will Clark														
D 1996	Tex-A	.125	4	16	1	2	0	0	0	0	3	2	0	1
D 1998	Tex-A	.091	3	11	0	1	0	0	0	0	1	2	0	1
D 2000	StL-N	.250	3	12	3	3	0	0	1	4	1	3	0	1
D Total	3	.154	10	39	4	6	0	0	1	4	5	7	0	
L 1987	SF-N	.360	7	25	3	9	2	0	1	3	3	6	1	1
L 1989	SF-N	.650	5	20	8	13	3	1	2	8	2	2	0	1
L 2000	StL-N	.412	5	17	3	7	2	0	1	1	2	1	0	1
L Total	3	.468	17	62	14	29	7	1	4	12	7	9	1	
W 1989	SF-N	.250	4	16	2	4	1	0	0	0	1	3	0	1
■ Fred Clarke														
W 1903	Pit-N	.265	8	34	3	9	2	1	0	2	1	5	1	O
W 1909	Pit-N	.211	7	19	7	4	0	0	2	7	5	3	3	O
W Total	2	.245	15	53	10	13	2	1	2	9	6	8	4	
■ Boileryard Clarke														
T 1895	Bal-N	.286	2	7	1	2	0	0	0	0	0	0	2	C
T 1897	Bal-N	.563	4	16	5	9	1	1	1	4	1	0	0	C
T Total	2	.478	6	23	6	11	1	1	1	4	1	0	2	

YEAR	TM/L	AVG	G	AB	R	H	2B	3B	HR	RBI	BB	SO	SB	POS
■ Ellis Clary														
W 1944	StL-A	.000	1	1	0	0	0	0	0	0	0	0	0	H
■ Royce Clayton														
D 1996	StL-N	.333	2	6	1	2	0	0	0	0	3	1	0	S
D 1998	Tex-A	.222	3	9	0	2	0	0	0	0	0	4	0	S
D 1999	Tex-A	.000	3	10	0	0	0	0	0	0	0	1	0	S
D Total	3	.160	8	25	1	4	0	0	0	0	3	6	0	
L 1996	StL-N	.350	5	20	4	7	0	0	0	1	1	4	1	S
■ Roberto Clemente														
L 1970	Pit-N	.214	3	14	1	3	0	0	0	1	0	4	0	O
L 1971	Pit-N	.333	4	18	2	6	0	0	0	4	1	6	0	O
L 1972	Pit-N	.235	5	17	1	4	1	0	1	2	3	5	0	O
L Total	3	.265	12	49	4	13	1	0	1	7	4	15	0	
W 1960	Pit-N	.310	7	29	1	9	0	0	0	3	0	4	0	O
W 1971	Pit-N	.414	7	29	3	12	2	1	2	4	2	2	0	O
W Total	2	.362	14	58	4	21	2	1	2	7	2	6	0	
■ Donn Clendenon														
W 1969	NY-N	.357	4	14	4	5	1	0	3	4	2	6	0	1
■ Flea Clifton														
W 1935	Det-A	.000	4	16	1	0	0	0	0	0	2	4	0	3
■ Ty Cline														
L 1970	Cin-N	1.000	2	1	2	1	0	1	0	0	1	0	0	O-1
W 1970	Cin-N	.333	3	3	0	1	0	0	0	0	0	0	0	H
■ Gene Clines														
L 1971	Pit-N	.333	1	3	1	1	0	0	1	1	0	1	0	O
L 1972	Pit-N	.000	3	2	1	0	0	0	0	0	0	1	0	H
L 1974	Pit-N	.000	2	1	1	0	0	0	0	0	0	0	0	O
L Total	3	.167	6	6	3	1	0	0	1	1	0	2	0	
W 1971	Pit-N	.091	3	11	2	1	0	1	0	0	1	1	1	O
■ Ty Cobb														
W 1907	Det-A	.200	5	20	1	4	0	1	0	0	0	3	0	O
W 1908	Det-A	.368	5	19	3	7	1	0	0	4	1	2	2	O
W 1909	Det-A	.231	7	26	3	6	3	0	0	5	2	2	2	O
W Total	3	.262	17	65	7	17	4	1	0	9	3	7	4	
■ Mickey Cochrane														
W 1929	Phi-A	.400	5	15	5	6	1	0	0	0	7	0	0	C
W 1930	Phi-A	.222	6	18	5	4	1	0	2	4	5	2	0	C
W 1931	Phi-A	.160	7	25	2	4	0	0	0	1	5	2	0	C
W 1934	Det-A	.214	7	28	2	6	1	0	0	1	4	3	0	C
W 1935	Det-A	.292	6	24	3	7	1	0	0	1	4	1	0	C
W Total	5	.245	31	110	17	27	4	0	2	7	25	8	0	
■ Rich Coggins														
L 1973	Bal-A	.444	2	9	1	4	1	0	0	0	0	0	0	O
L 1974	Bal-A	.000	3	11	0	0	0	0	0	0	0	3	0	O
L Total	2	.200	5	20	1	4	1	0	0	0	0	3	0	
■ Greg Colbrunn														
D 1997	Atl-N	1.000	1	1	0	1	0	0	0	2	0	0	0	H
D 1998	Atl-N	.000	2	2	0	0	0	0	0	0	0	0	0	H
D 1999	Ari-N	.400	2	5	1	2	1	0	1	2	2	2	0	1
D Total	3	.375	5	8	1	3	1	0	1	4	2	2	0	
L 1997	Atl-N	.667	3	3	0	2	0	0	0	0	0	0	0	H
L 1998	Atl-N	.333	6	6	0	2	0	0	0	0	0	2	0	H
L Total	2	.444	9	9	0	4	0	0	0	0	0	2	0	
■ Alex Cole														
L 1992	Pit-N	.200	4	10	2	2	0	0	0	1	3	2	0	O
■ Jerry Coleman														
W 1949	NY-A	.250	5	20	0	5	3	0	0	4	0	4	0	2
W 1950	NY-A	.286	4	14	2	4	1	0	0	3	2	0	0	2
W 1951	NY-A	.250	5	8	2	2	0	0	0	0	1	2	0	2
W 1955	NY-A	.000	3	3	0	0	0	0	0	0	0	1	0	S
W 1956	NY-A	.000	2	2	0	0	0	0	0	0	0	0	0	2
W 1957	NY-A	.364	7	22	2	8	2	0	0	2	3	1	0	2
W Total	6	.275	26	69	6	19	6	0	0	9	6	8	0	
■ Gordy Coleman														
W 1961	Cin-N	.250	5	20	2	5	0	0	1	2	0	1	0	1
■ Vince Coleman														
D 1995	Sea-A	.217	5	23	6	5	0	1	1	1	2	4	1	O
L 1985	StL-N	.286	3	14	2	4	0	0	0	1	0	2	1	O
L 1987	StL-N	.269	7	26	3	7	1	0	0	4	4	6	1	O
L 1995	Sea-A	.100	6	20	0	2	0	0	0	0	2	6	4	O-5
L Total	3	.217	16	60	5	13	1	0	0	5	6	14	6	
W 1987	StL-N	.143	7	28	5	4	2	0	0	2	2	10	6	O
■ Dave Collins														
L 1979	Cin-N	.357	3	14	0	5	1	0	0	1	0	2	2	O
■ Eddie Collins Sr.														
W 1910	Phi-A	.429	5	21	5	9	4	0	0	3	2	0	4	2
W 1911	Phi-A	.286	6	21	4	6	1	0	0	1	2	2	2	2
W 1913	Phi-A	.421	5	19	5	8	0	2	0	3	1	2	3	2
W 1914	Phi-A	.214	4	14	0	3	0	0	0	1	2	1	1	2
W 1917	Chi-A	.409	6	22	4	9	1	0	0	2	2	3	3	2
W 1919	Chi-A	.226	8	31	2	7	1	0	0	1	1	2	1	2
W Total	6	.328	34	128	20	42	7	2	0	11	10	10	14	
■ Hub Collins														
W 1889	Bro-A	.371	9	35	13	13	3	0	1	2	7	5	6	2

YEAR	TM/L	AVG	G	AB	R	H	2B	3B	HR	RBI	BB	SO	SB	POS
W 1890	Bro-N	.310	7	29	7	9	0	1	0	1	3	0	2	2
W Total 2		.344	16	64	20	22	3	1	1	3	10	5	8	
■ Ripper Collins														
W 1931	StL-N	.000	2	2	0	0	0	0	0	0	0	1	0	H
W 1934	StL-N	.367	7	30	4	11	1	0	0	3	1	2	0	1
W 1938	Chi-N	.133	4	15	1	2	0	0	0	0	0	3	0	1
W Total 3		.277	13	47	5	13	1	0	0	3	1	6	0	
■ Jimmy Collins														
T 1897	Bos-N	.182	5	22	2	4	0	0	0	4	1	0	0	3
W 1903	Bos-A	.250	8	36	5	9	1	2	0	1	1	1	3	3
■ Shano Collins														
W 1917	Chi-A	.286	6	21	2	6	1	0	0	0	0	2	0	O
W 1919	Chi-A	.250	4	16	2	4	1	0	0	0	0	0	0	O
W Total 2		.270	10	37	4	10	2	0	0	0	0	2	0	
■ Joe Collins														
W 1950	NY-A	—	1	0	0	0	0	0	0	0	0	0	0	1
W 1951	NY-A	.222	6	18	2	4	0	0	1	3	2	1	0	1-6,O-1
W 1952	NY-A	.000	6	12	1	0	0	0	0	0	1	3	0	1
W 1953	NY-A	.167	6	24	4	4	1	0	1	2	3	8	0	1
W 1955	NY-A	.167	5	12	6	2	0	0	2	3	6	4	1	1-5,O-1
W 1956	NY-A	.238	6	21	2	5	2	0	0	2	2	3	0	1-5
W 1957	NY-A	.000	6	5	0	0	0	0	0	0	0	3	0	1-5
W Total 7		.163	36	92	15	15	3	0	4	10	14	22	1	
■ Pat Collins														
W 1926	NY-A	.000	3	2	0	0	0	0	0	0	0	1	0	C
W 1927	NY-A	.600	2	5	0	3	1	0	0	0	3	0	0	C
W 1928	NY-A	1.000	1	1	0	1	1	0	0	0	0	0	0	C
W Total 3		.500	6	8	0	4	2	0	0	0	3	1	0	
■ Earle Combs														
W 1926	NY-A	.357	7	28	3	10	2	0	0	2	5	2	0	O
W 1927	NY-A	.313	4	16	6	5	0	0	0	2	1	2	0	O
W 1928	NY-A	—	1	0	0	0	0	0	0	1	0	0	0	H
W 1932	NY-A	.375	4	16	8	6	1	0	1	4	4	3	0	O
W Total 4		.350	16	60	17	21	3	0	1	9	10	7	0	
■ Wayne Comer														
W 1968	Det-A	1.000	1	1	0	1	0	0	0	0	0	0	0	H
■ Charlie Comiskey														
W 1885	StL-A	.292	7	24	6	7	0	0	0	1	0	0	0	1
W 1886	StL-A	.292	6	24	2	7	1	0	0	2	0	4	0	1
W 1887	StL-A	.317	15	63	8	20	2	0	0	5	1	1	4	1-14,O-1
W 1888	StL-A	.268	10	41	6	11	1	1	0	3	1	1	4	1-10,O-1
W Total 4		.296	38	152	22	45	4	1	0	11	2	6	8	
■ Clint Conatser														
W 1948	Bos-N	.000	2	4	0	0	0	0	0	1	0	0	0	O
■ Dave Concepcion														
L 1970	Cin-N	—	3	0	0	0	0	0	0	0	0	0	0	S
L 1972	Cin-N	.000	3	2	0	0	0	0	0	0	0	0	0	S-1
L 1975	Cin-N	.455	3	11	2	5	0	0	1	1	1	2	2	S
L 1976	Cin-N	.200	3	10	4	2	1	0	0	0	2	1	0	S
L 1979	Cin-N	.429	3	14	1	6	1	0	0	0	0	3	0	S
L Total 5		.351	15	37	7	13	2	0	1	1	3	6	2	
W 1970	Cin-N	.333	3	9	0	3	0	1	0	3	0	0	0	S
W 1972	Cin-N	.308	6	13	2	4	0	1	0	2	2	2	1	S-5
W 1975	Cin-N	.179	7	28	3	5	1	0	1	4	0	1	3	S
W 1976	Cin-N	.357	4	14	1	5	1	1	0	3	1	3	1	S
W Total 4		.266	20	64	6	17	2	3	1	12	3	6	5	
■ Onix Concepcion														
L 1984	KC-A	.000	3	7	0	0	0	0	0	0	0	0	0	S
L 1985	KC-A	.000	4	1	0	0	0	0	0	0	0	0	0	S
L Total 2		.000	7	8	0	0	0	0	0	0	0	0	0	
W 1980	KC-A	—	3	0	0	0	0	0	0	0	0	0	0	R
W 1985	KC-A	—	3	0	1	0	0	0	0	0	0	0	0	S-2
W Total 2		—	6	0	1	0	0	0	0	0	0	0	0	
■ Billy Conigliaro														
L 1973	Oak-A	.000	1	4	0	0	0	0	0	0	0	2	0	O
W 1973	Oak-A	.000	3	3	0	0	0	0	0	0	0	1	0	H
■ Jeff Conine														
D 1997	Fla-N	.364	3	11	3	4	1	0	0	0	1	0	0	1
L 1997	Fla-N	.111	6	18	1	2	0	0	0	1	1	4	0	1
W 1997	Fla-N	.231	6	13	1	3	0	0	0	2	0	0	0	1
■ Joe Connolly														
W 1914	Bos-N	.111	3	9	1	1	0	0	0	1	1	1	0	O
■ Roger Connor														
W 1888	NY-N	.304	7	23	7	7	1	2	0	3	4	0	4	1
W 1889	NY-N	.343	9	35	9	12	2	2	0	12	3	2	8	1
W Total 2		.328	16	58	16	19	3	4	0	15	7	2	12	
■ Cecil Cooper														
D 1981	Mil-A	.222	5	18	1	4	0	0	0	3	1	3	0	1
L 1975	Bos-A	.400	3	10	0	4	2	0	0	1	0	2	0	1
L 1982	Mil-A	.150	5	20	1	3	2	0	0	4	0	6	0	1
L Total 2		.233	8	30	1	7	4	0	0	5	0	8	0	
W 1975	Bos-A	.053	5	19	0	1	1	0	0	1	0	3	0	1
W 1982	Mil-A	.286	7	28	3	8	1	0	1	6	1	1	0	1
W Total 2		.191	12	47	3	9	2	0	1	7	1	4	0	

YEAR	TM/L	AVG	G	AB	R	H	2B	3B	HR	RBI	BB	SO	SB	POS
■ Claude Cooper														
W 1913	NY-N	—	2	0	0	0	0	0	0	0	0	0	1	R
■ Walker Cooper														
W 1942	StL-N	.286	5	21	3	6	1	0	0	4	0	1	0	C
W 1943	StL-N	.294	5	17	1	5	0	0	0	0	0	1	0	C
W 1944	StL-N	.318	6	22	1	7	2	1	0	2	3	2	0	C
W Total 3		.300	16	60	5	18	3	1	0	6	3	4	0	
■ Joey Cora														
D 1995	Sea-A	.316	5	19	7	6	1	0	1	1	3	0	1	2
D 1997	Sea-A	.176	4	17	1	3	0	0	0	0	0	4	0	2
D 1998	Cle-A	.000	4	10	2	0	0	0	0	0	3	2	0	2
D Total 3		.196	13	46	10	9	1	0	1	1	6	6	1	
L 1993	Chi-A	.136	6	22	1	3	0	0	0	1	3	6	0	2
L 1995	Sea-A	.174	6	23	3	4	1	0	0	0	1	0	2	2
L 1998	Cle-A	.143	2	7	1	1	0	0	0	0	2	1	0	2
L Total 3		.154	14	52	5	8	1	0	0	1	6	7	2	
■ Wil Cordero														
D 1999	Cle-A	.556	3	9	3	5	0	0	1	2	1	2	0	D-2,O-1
■ Pop Corkhill														
W 1889	Bro-A	.208	9	24	4	5	1	0	1	5	6	2	1	O
■ Pat Corrales														
W 1970	Cin-N	.000	1	1	0	0	0	0	0	0	0	0	0	H
■ Pete Coscarart														
W 1941	Bro-N	.000	3	7	1	0	0	0	0	0	1	2	0	2
■ Henry Cotto														
L 1984	Chi-N	1.000	3	1	1	1	0	0	0	0	0	0	0	O
■ Bill Coughlin														
W 1907	Det-A	.250	5	20	0	5	0	0	0	0	1	4	1	3
W 1908	Det-A	.125	3	8	0	1	0	0	0	1	0	1	0	3
W Total 2		.214	8	28	0	6	0	0	0	1	1	5	1	
■ Craig Counsell														
D 1997	Fla-N	.400	3	5	0	2	1	0	0	1	1	0	0	2
L 1997	Fla-N	.429	5	14	0	6	0	0	0	2	3	3	0	2-4
W 1997	Fla-N	.182	7	22	4	4	1	0	0	2	6	5	1	2
■ Wes Covington														
W 1957	Mil-N	.208	7	24	1	5	1	0	0	1	2	6	1	O
W 1958	Mil-N	.269	7	26	2	7	0	0	0	4	2	4	0	O
W 1966	LA-N	.000	1	1	0	0	0	0	0	0	0	1	0	H
W Total 3		.235	15	51	3	12	1	0	0	5	4	11	1	
■ Al Cowens														
L 1976	KC-A	.190	5	21	3	4	0	1	0	0	1	1	2	O
L 1977	KC-A	.263	5	19	2	5	0	0	1	5	1	3	0	O
L 1978	KC-A	.133	4	15	2	2	0	0	0	1	0	2	0	O
L Total 3		.200	14	55	7	11	0	1	1	6	2	6	2	
■ Billy Cox														
W 1949	Bro-N	.333	2	3	0	1	0	0	0	0	0	1	0	3-1
W 1952	Bro-N	.296	7	27	4	8	2	0	0	0	3	4	0	3
W 1953	Bro-N	.304	6	23	3	7	3	0	1	6	1	4	0	3
W Total 3		.302	15	53	7	16	5	0	1	6	4	9	0	
■ Harry Craft														
W 1939	Cin-N	.091	4	11	0	1	0	0	0	0	0	6	0	O
W 1940	Cin-N	.000	1	1	0	0	0	0	0	0	0	0	0	H
W Total 2		.083	5	12	0	1	0	0	0	0	0	6	0	
■ Doc Cramer														
W 1931	Phi-A	.500	2	2	0	1	0	0	0	2	0	0	0	H
W 1945	Det-A	.379	7	29	7	11	0	0	0	4	1	0	1	O
W Total 2		.387	9	31	7	12	0	0	0	6	1	0	1	
■ Del Crandall														
W 1957	Mil-N	.211	6	19	1	4	0	0	1	1	1	1	0	C
W 1958	Mil-N	.240	7	25	4	6	0	0	1	3	3	10	0	C
W Total 2		.227	13	44	5	10	0	0	2	4	4	11	0	
■ Gavvy Cravath														
W 1915	Phi-N	.125	5	16	2	2	1	1	0	1	2	6	0	O
■ Pat Crawford														
W 1934	StL-N	.000	2	2	0	0	0	0	0	0	0	0	0	H
■ Sam Crawford														
W 1907	Det-A	.238	5	21	1	5	1	0	0	3	0	3	0	O
W 1908	Det-A	.238	5	21	2	5	1	0	0	1	1	2	0	O
W 1909	Det-A	.250	7	28	4	7	3	0	1	4	1	1	1	O-7,1-1
W Total 3		.243	17	70	7	17	5	0	1	8	2	6	1	
■ Willie Crawford														
L 1974	LA-N	.250	2	4	1	1	0	0	0	1	1	1	0	O
W 1965	LA-N	.500	2	2	0	1	0	0	0	0	0	1	0	H
W 1974	LA-N	.333	3	6	1	2	0	0	1	1	0	0	0	O-2
W Total 2		.375	5	8	1	3	0	0	1	1	0	1	0	
■ Creepy Crespi														
W 1942	StL-N	—	1	0	1	0	0	0	0	0	0	0	0	R
■ Felipe Crespo														
D 2000	SF-N	.250	4	4	0	1	0	0	0	0	0	0	0	H
■ Lou Criger														
W 1903	Bos-A	.231	8	26	1	6	0	0	0	4	2	3	0	C

YEAR	TM/L	AVG	G	AB	R	H	2B	3B	HR	RBI	BB	SO	SB	POS
■ **Hughie Critz**														
W 1933	NY-N	.136	5	22	2	3	0	0	0	0	1	0	0	2
■ **Warren Cromartie**														
D 1981	Mon-N	.227	5	22	1	5	2	0	0	1	0	9	0	1
L 1981	Mon-N	.167	5	18	0	3	1	0	0	2	0	2	0	1
■ **Joe Cronin**														
W 1933	Was-A	.318	5	22	1	7	0	0	0	2	0	2	0	S
■ **Ed Crosby**														
L 1973	Cin-N	.500	3	2	0	1	0	0	0	0	0	1	0	S-2
■ **Frankie Crosetti**														
W 1932	NY-A	.133	4	15	2	2	1	0	0	0	2	3	0	S
W 1936	NY-A	.269	6	26	5	7	2	0	0	3	3	5	0	S
W 1937	NY-A	.048	5	21	2	1	0	0	0	0	3	2	0	S
W 1938	NY-A	.250	4	16	1	4	2	1	1	6	2	4	0	S
W 1939	NY-A	.063	4	16	2	1	0	0	0	1	2	2	0	S
W 1942	NY-A	.000	1	3	0	0	0	0	0	0	0	1	0	3
W 1943	NY-A	.278	5	18	4	5	0	0	0	1	2	3	1	S
W Total 7		.174	29	115	16	20	5	1	1	11	14	20	1	
■ **Lave Cross**														
T 1900	Bro-N	.278	4	18	2	5	0	1	0	1	0	0	1	3
W 1905	Phi-A	.105	5	19	0	2	0	0	0	0	1	1	0	3
■ **Monte Cross**														
W 1905	Phi-A	.176	5	17	0	3	0	0	0	0	0	7	0	S
■ **Frank Croucher**														
W 1940	Det-A	—	1	0	0	0	0	0	0	0	0	0	0	S
■ **Terry Crowley**														
L 1973	Bal-A	.000	2	2	0	0	0	0	0	0	0	0	0	O-1
L 1975	Cin-N	—	1	0	0	0	0	0	0	0	0	0	0	H
L 1979	Bal-A	.500	2	2	0	1	0	0	0	1	0	0	0	H
L Total 3		.250	5	4	0	1	0	0	0	1	0	0	0	
W 1970	Bal-A	.000	1	1	0	0	0	0	0	0	0	0	0	H
W 1975	Cin-N	.500	2	2	0	1	0	0	0	0	0	1	0	H
W 1979	Bal-A	.250	5	4	0	1	1	0	0	2	1	0	0	H
W Total 3		.286	8	7	0	2	1	0	0	2	1	1	0	
■ **Hector Cruz**														
L 1979	Cin-N	.200	2	5	1	1	1	0	0	0	0	1	0	O-1
■ **Jose Cruz**														
D 1981	Hou-N	.300	5	20	0	6	1	0	0	0	1	3	1	O
L 1980	Hou-N	.400	5	15	3	6	1	1	0	4	8	1	0	O
L 1986	Hou-N	.192	6	26	0	5	0	0	0	2	1	8	0	O
L Total 2		.268	11	41	3	11	1	1	0	6	9	9	0	
■ **Julio Cruz**														
L 1983	Chi-A	.333	4	12	0	4	0	0	0	0	3	4	2	2
■ **Todd Cruz**														
L 1983	Bal-A	.133	4	15	0	2	0	0	0	1	0	5	0	3
W 1983	Bal-A	.125	5	16	1	2	0	0	0	0	1	3	0	3
■ **Leon Culberson**														
W 1946	Bos-A	.222	5	9	1	2	0	0	1	1	1	2	1	O-3
■ **Tim Cullen**														
L 1972	Oak-A	.000	2	1	0	0	0	0	0	0	0	0	0	S
■ **Roy Cullenbine**														
W 1942	NY-A	.263	5	19	3	5	1	0	0	2	1	2	1	O
W 1945	Det-A	.227	7	22	5	5	2	0	0	4	8	2	1	O
W Total 2		.244	12	41	8	10	3	0	0	6	9	4	2	
■ **Midre Cummings**														
D 1998	Bos-A	.000	3	3	0	0	0	0	0	0	0	0	0	H
■ **Bill Cunningham**														
W 1922	NY-N	.200	4	10	0	2	0	0	0	2	2	1	0	O
W 1923	NY-N	.143	4	7	0	1	0	0	0	1	0	1	0	O-3
W Total 2		.176	8	17	0	3	0	0	0	3	2	2	0	
■ **Chad Curtis**														
D 1996	LA-N	.000	1	2	0	0	0	0	0	0	1	1	0	O
D 1997	NY-A	.167	4	6	0	1	0	0	0	0	3	1	0	O
D 1998	NY-A	.667	3	3	1	2	1	0	0	0	1	1	1	O
D 1999	NY-A	.000	3	3	1	0	0	0	0	0	0	0	0	O
D Total 4		.214	11	14	2	3	1	0	0	0	5	3	1	
L 1998	NY-A	.000	2	4	0	0	0	0	0	0	1	2	0	O
L 1999	NY-A	.000	3	6	1	0	0	0	0	0	0	2	1	O-2,D-1
L Total 2		.000	5	10	1	0	0	0	0	0	1	4	1	
W 1999	NY-A	.333	3	6	3	2	0	0	2	2	0	0	0	O
■ **George Cutshaw**														
W 1916	Bro-N	.105	5	19	2	2	1	0	0	2	1	1	0	2
■ **Kiki Cuyler**														
W 1925	Pit-N	.269	7	26	3	7	3	0	1	6	1	4	0	O
W 1929	Chi-N	.300	5	20	4	6	1	0	0	4	1	7	0	O
W 1932	Chi-N	.278	4	18	2	5	1	1	1	2	0	3	1	O
W Total 3		.281	16	64	9	18	5	1	2	12	2	14	1	
■ **Bill Dahlen**														
T 1900	Bro-N	.176	4	17	3	3	0	1	0	2	0	3	1	S
W 1905	NY-N	.000	5	15	1	0	0	0	0	1	3	2	3	S
■ **Babe Dahlgren**														
W 1939	NY-A	.214	4	14	2	3	2	0	1	2	0	4	0	1

YEAR	TM/L	AVG	G	AB	R	H	2B	3B	HR	RBI	BB	SO	SB	POS
■ **Ed Daily**														
W 1890	Lou-A	.136	6	22	1	3	1	1	0	3	1	2	2	O-4,P-2
■ **Abner Dalrymple**														
W 1885	Chi-N	.269	7	26	4	7	2	0	1	3	2	0	0	O
W 1886	Chi-N	.190	6	21	2	4	1	1	0	2	0	5	1	O
W Total 2		.234	13	47	6	11	3	1	1	5	2	5	1	
■ **Clay Dalrymple**														
W 1969	Bal-A	1.000	2	2	0	2	0	0	0	0	0	0	0	H
■ **Tom Daly**														
W 1890	Bro-N	.182	6	22	1	4	2	0	0	3	0	4	2	C-6,1-1
T 1900	Bro-N	.154	4	13	2	2	1	0	0	1	3	1	0	2
■ **Harry Danning**														
W 1936	NY-N	.000	2	2	0	0	0	0	0	0	0	1	0	C-1
W 1937	NY-N	.250	3	12	0	3	1	0	0	2	0	2	0	C
W Total 2		.214	5	14	0	3	1	0	0	2	0	3	0	
■ **Alvin Dark**														
W 1948	Bos-N	.167	6	24	2	4	1	0	0	0	0	2	0	S
W 1951	NY-N	.417	6	24	5	10	3	0	1	4	2	3	0	S
W 1954	NY-N	.412	4	17	2	7	0	0	0	0	1	1	0	S
W Total 3		.323	16	65	9	21	4	0	1	4	3	6	0	
■ **Brian Daubach**														
D 1999	Bos-A	.250	4	16	3	4	2	0	1	3	0	7	0	D-4,1-1
L 1999	Bos-A	.176	5	17	2	3	1	0	1	3	1	4	0	D-5,1-1
■ **Jake Daubert**														
W 1916	Bro-N	.176	4	17	1	3	0	1	0	0	2	3	0	1
W 1919	Cin-N	.241	8	29	4	7	0	1	0	1	1	2	1	1
W Total 2		.217	12	46	5	10	0	2	0	1	3	5	1	
■ **Rich Dauer**														
L 1979	Bal-A	.182	4	11	0	2	0	0	0	0	0	1	0	2
L 1983	Bal-A	.000	4	14	0	0	0	0	0	1	0	0	0	2
L Total 2		.080	8	25	0	2	0	0	0	1	0	1	0	
W 1979	Bal-A	.294	6	17	2	5	1	0	1	1	0	1	0	2-5
W 1983	Bal-A	.211	5	19	2	4	1	0	0	3	0	3	0	2
W Total 2		.250	11	36	4	9	2	0	1	4	0	4	0	
■ **Darren Daulton**														
L 1993	Phi-N	.263	6	19	2	5	1	0	1	3	6	3	0	C
L 1997	Fla-N	.250	3	4	1	1	1	0	0	1	1	2	0	1-2
L Total 2		.261	9	23	3	6	2	0	1	4	7	5	0	
W 1993	Phi-N	.217	6	23	4	5	2	0	1	4	4	5	0	C
W 1997	Fla-N	.389	7	18	7	7	2	0	1	2	3	0	1	1-5,D-1
W Total 2		.293	13	41	11	12	4	0	2	6	7	5	1	
■ **Vic Davalillo**														
L 1971	Pit-N	.000	2	2	0	0	0	0	0	0	0	1	0	H
L 1972	Pit-N	—	1	0	0	0	0	0	0	0	1	0	0	H
L 1973	Oak-A	.625	4	8	2	5	1	1	0	1	1	0	0	1-2,O-2
L 1977	LA-N	1.000	1	1	1	1	0	0	0	0	0	0	0	H
L Total 4		.545	8	11	3	6	1	1	0	1	2	1	0	
W 1971	Pit-N	.333	3	3	1	1	0	0	0	0	0	0	0	O-2
W 1973	Oak-A	.091	6	11	0	1	0	0	0	0	2	1	0	O-4,1-1
W 1977	LA-N	.333	3	3	0	1	0	0	0	1	0	0	0	H
W 1978	LA-N	.333	2	3	0	1	0	0	0	0	0	0	0	D-1
W Total 4		.200	14	20	1	4	0	0	0	1	2	1	0	
■ **Jim Davenport**														
W 1962	SF-N	.136	7	22	1	3	1	0	0	1	4	7	0	3
■ **Mark Davidson**														
L 1987	Min-A	—	1	0	0	0	0	0	0	0	0	0	0	R
W 1987	Min-A	.000	2	1	0	0	0	0	0	0	0	0	0	O-1
■ **Chili Davis**														
D 1998	NY-A	.167	2	6	0	1	0	0	0	0	0	2	0	D
D 1999	NY-A	.333	1	3	0	1	0	0	0	0	0	2	0	D
D Total 2		.222	3	9	0	2	0	0	0	0	0	4	0	
L 1987	SF-N	.150	6	20	2	3	1	0	0	0	1	4	0	O
L 1991	Min-A	.294	5	17	3	5	2	0	0	2	5	8	1	D
L 1998	NY-A	.286	5	14	2	4	1	0	1	5	2	3	0	D
L 1999	NY-A	.091	5	11	0	1	0	0	0	1	3	4	0	D
L Total 4		.210	21	62	7	13	4	0	1	8	11	19	1	
W 1991	Min-A	.222	6	18	4	4	0	0	2	4	2	3	0	D-4,O-1
W 1998	NY-A	.286	3	7	3	2	0	0	0	2	3	2	0	D-2
W 1999	NY-A	.000	1	4	0	0	0	0	0	0	0	2	0	D
W Total 3		.207	10	29	7	6	0	0	2	6	5	7	0	
■ **Eric Davis**														
D 1997	Bal-A	.222	3	9	0	2	0	0	0	2	0	5	0	O
D 2000	StL-N	.000	2	4	0	0	0	0	0	0	0	2	0	O-1
D Total 2		.154	5	13	0	2	0	0	0	2	0	7	0	
L 1990	Cin-N	.174	6	23	2	4	1	0	0	2	1	9	0	O
L 1997	Bal-A	.154	6	13	1	2	0	0	1	1	1	3	0	O-3,D-3
L 2000	StL-N	.200	4	10	1	2	1	0	0	1	0	2	0	O-3
L Total 3		.174	16	46	4	8	2	0	1	4	2	14	0	
W 1990	Cin-N	.286	4	14	3	4	0	0	1	5	0	0	0	O
■ **George Davis**														
T 1892	Cle-N	.167	3	6	0	1	0	0	0	0	0	1	0	3-2
T 1894	NY-N	.313	4	16	5	5	2	2	0	5	2	0	2	3
T Total 2		.273	7	22	5	6	2	2	0	5	2	1	2	
W 1906	Chi-A	.308	3	13	4	4	3	0	0	6	0	1	1	S

YEAR	TM/L	AVG	G	AB	R	H	2B	3B	HR	RBI	BB	SO	SB	POS
■ Kiddo Davis														
W 1933	NY-N	.368	5	19	1	7	1	0	0	0	0	3	0	O
W 1936	NY-N	.500	4	2	2	1	0	0	0	0	0	0	0	H
W Total	2	.381	9	21	3	8	1	0	0	0	0	3	0	
■ Glenn Davis														
L 1986	Hou-N	.269	6	26	3	7	1	0	1	3	1	3	0	1
■ Harry Davis														
W 1905	Phi-A	.200	5	20	0	4	1	0	0	0	0	1	0	1
W 1910	Phi-A	.353	5	17	5	6	3	0	0	2	3	4	0	1
W 1911	Phi-A	.208	6	24	3	5	1	0	0	5	0	3	0	1
W Total	3	.246	16	61	8	15	5	0	0	7	3	8	0	
■ Tommy Davis														
L 1971	Oak-A	.375	3	8	1	3	1	0	0	0	0	0	0	1-2
L 1973	Bal-A	.286	5	21	1	6	1	0	0	2	1	0	0	D
L 1974	Bal-A	.267	4	15	0	4	0	0	0	1	0	1	0	D
L Total	3	.295	12	44	2	13	2	0	0	3	1	1	0	
W 1963	LA-N	.400	4	15	0	6	0	2	0	2	0	2	1	O
W 1966	LA-N	.250	4	8	0	2	0	0	0	0	1	1	0	O-3
W Total	2	.348	8	23	0	8	0	2	0	2	1	3	1	
■ Jumbo Davis														
W 1889	Bro-A	.000	1	4	0	0	0	0	0	0	0	0	0	S
■ Jody Davis														
L 1984	Chi-N	.389	5	18	3	7	2	0	2	6	0	3	0	C
■ Mike Davis														
L 1981	Oak-A	1.000	1	1	0	1	0	0	0	0	0	0	0	H
L 1988	LA-N	.000	4	2	0	0	0	0	0	0	1	0	0	H
L Total	2	.333	5	3	0	1	0	0	0	0	1	0	0	
W 1988	LA-N	.143	4	7	3	1	0	0	1	2	4	0	2	D-2,O-1
■ Dick Davis														
D 1981	Phi-N	.000	1	2	0	0	0	0	0	0	0	1	0	O
■ Ron Davis														
W 1968	StL-N	.000	2	7	0	0	0	0	0	0	0	2	0	O
■ Russ Davis														
D 1995	NY-A	.200	2	5	0	1	0	0	0	0	0	2	0	3
D 2000	SF-N	.000	2	2	0	0	0	0	0	0	0	1	0	H
D Total	2	.143	4	7	0	1	0	0	0	0	0	3	0	
■ Spud Davis														
W 1934	StL-N	1.000	2	2	0	2	0	0	0	1	0	0	0	H
■ Willie Davis														
L 1979	Cal-A	.500	2	2	1	1	1	0	0	0	0	0	0	H
W 1963	LA-N	.167	4	12	2	2	2	0	0	3	0	6	0	O
W 1965	LA-N	.231	7	26	3	6	0	0	0	0	0	2	3	O
W 1966	LA-N	.063	4	16	0	1	0	0	0	0	0	4	0	O
W Total	3	.167	15	54	5	9	2	0	0	3	0	12	3	
■ Andre Dawson														
D 1981	Mon-N	.300	5	20	1	6	0	1	0	0	1	6	2	O
L 1981	Mon-N	.150	5	20	2	3	0	0	0	0	0	4	0	O
L 1989	Chi-N	.105	5	19	0	2	1	0	0	3	2	6	0	O
L Total	2	.128	10	39	2	5	1	0	0	3	2	10	0	
■ Charlie Deal														
W 1914	Bos-N	.125	4	16	1	2	2	0	0	0	0	0	2	3
W 1918	Chi-N	.176	6	17	0	3	0	0	0	0	0	1	0	3
W Total	2	.152	10	33	1	5	2	0	0	0	0	1	2	
■ Doug DeCinces														
L 1979	Bal-A	.308	4	13	4	4	1	0	0	3	1	1	0	3
L 1982	Cal-A	.316	5	19	5	6	2	0	0	0	1	5	0	3
L 1986	Cal-A	.281	7	32	2	9	3	0	1	3	0	2	0	3
L Total	3	.297	16	64	11	19	6	0	1	6	2	8	0	
W 1979	Bal-A	.200	7	25	2	5	0	0	1	3	5	5	1	3
■ Ivan DeJesus														
L 1983	Phi-N	.250	4	12	0	3	0	0	0	1	3	3	0	S
W 1983	Phi-N	.125	5	16	0	2	0	0	0	0	1	2	0	S
W 1985	StL-N	.000	1	1	0	0	0	0	0	0	0	0	0	H
W Total	2	.118	6	17	0	2	0	0	0	0	1	2	0	
■ Jim Delahanty														
W 1909	Det-A	.346	7	26	2	9	4	0	0	4	2	5	0	2
■ Bill DeLancey														
W 1934	StL-N	.172	7	29	3	5	3	0	1	4	2	8	0	C
■ Joe DeMaestri														
W 1960	NY-A	.500	4	2	1	1	0	0	0	0	0	1	0	S-3
■ Frank Demaree														
W 1932	Chi-N	.286	2	7	1	2	0	0	1	4	1	0	0	O
W 1935	Chi-N	.250	6	24	2	6	1	0	2	2	1	4	0	O
W 1938	Chi-N	.100	3	10	1	1	0	0	0	0	1	2	0	O
W 1943	StL-N	.000	1	1	0	0	0	0	0	0	0	0	0	H
W Total	4	.214	12	42	4	9	1	0	3	6	3	6	0	
■ John DeMerit														
W 1957	Mil-N	—	1	0	0	0	0	0	0	0	0	0	0	R
■ Don Demeter														
W 1959	LA-N	.250	6	12	2	3	0	0	0	0	1	3	0	O
■ Rick Dempsey														
L 1979	Bal-A	.400	3	10	3	4	2	0	0	2	1	0	1	C

YEAR	TM/L	AVG	G	AB	R	H	2B	3B	HR	RBI	BB	SO	SB	POS
L 1983	Bal-A	.167	4	12	1	2	0	0	0	0	1	1	0	C
L 1988	LA-N	.400	4	5	1	2	2	0	0	2	1	0	0	C-3
L Total	3	.296	11	27	5	8	4	0	0	4	3	1	1	
W 1979	Bal-A	.286	7	21	3	6	2	0	0	0	1	3	0	C-6
W 1983	Bal-A	.385	5	13	3	5	4	0	1	2	2	2	0	C
W 1988	LA-N	.200	2	5	0	1	1	0	0	1	1	2	0	C
W Total	3	.308	14	39	6	12	7	0	1	3	4	7	0	
■ Jerry Denny														
W 1884	Pro-N	.444	3	9	3	4	0	1	1	2	0	3	0	3
■ Bucky Dent														
L 1977	NY-A	.214	5	14	1	3	1	0	0	2	1	0	0	S
L 1978	NY-A	.200	4	15	0	3	0	0	0	4	0	0	0	S
L 1980	NY-A	.182	3	11	0	2	0	0	0	0	0	1	0	S
L Total	3	.200	12	40	1	8	1	0	0	6	1	1	0	
W 1977	NY-A	.263	6	19	0	5	0	0	0	2	2	1	0	S
W 1978	NY-A	.417	6	24	3	10	1	0	0	7	1	2	0	S
W Total	2	.349	12	43	3	15	1	0	0	9	3	3	0	
■ Sam Dente														
W 1954	Cle-A	.000	3	3	1	0	0	0	0	0	1	0	0	S
■ Bob Dernier														
L 1983	Phi-N	—	1	0	0	0	0	0	0	0	0	0	0	O
L 1984	Chi-N	.235	5	17	5	4	2	0	1	1	5	4	2	O
L Total	2	.235	6	17	5	4	2	0	1	1	5	4	2	
W 1983	Phi-N	—	1	0	1	0	0	0	0	0	0	0	0	R
■ Delino DeShields														
D 1995	LA-N	.250	3	12	1	3	0	0	0	0	1	3	0	2
D 1996	LA-N	.000	2	4	0	0	0	0	0	0	0	1	0	2
D Total	2	.188	5	16	1	3	0	0	0	0	1	4	0	
■ Mike Devereaux														
D 1995	Atl-N	.200	4	5	1	1	0	0	0	0	0	0	0	O-3
D 1996	Bal-A	.000	4	1	0	0	0	0	0	0	0	0	0	O-3
D Total	2	.167	8	6	1	1	0	0	0	0	0	0	0	
L 1995	Atl-N	.308	4	13	2	4	1	0	1	5	1	2	0	O
L 1996	Bal-A	.000	3	2	0	0	0	0	0	0	0	1	0	O
L Total	2	.267	7	15	2	4	1	0	1	5	1	3	0	
W 1995	Atl-N	.250	5	4	0	1	0	0	0	1	2	1	0	O-4,D-1
■ Art Devlin														
W 1905	NY-N	.250	5	16	0	4	1	0	0	1	1	3	3	3
■ Josh Devore														
W 1911	NY-N	.167	6	24	1	4	1	0	0	3	1	8	0	O
W 1912	NY-N	.250	7	24	4	6	0	0	0	0	7	5	4	O
W 1914	Bos-N	.000	1	1	0	0	0	0	0	0	0	1	0	H
W Total	3	.204	14	49	5	10	1	0	0	3	8	14	4	
■ Al DeVormer														
W 1921	NY-A	.000	2	1	0	0	0	0	0	0	0	0	0	C-1
■ Alex Diaz														
D 1995	Sea-A	.333	2	3	0	1	0	0	0	0	1	1	0	O-1
L 1995	Sea-A	.429	4	7	0	3	1	0	0	0	1	1	0	O-3
■ Bo Diaz														
L 1983	Phi-N	.154	4	13	0	2	1	0	0	0	2	1	0	C
W 1983	Phi-N	.333	5	15	1	5	1	0	0	0	1	2	0	C
■ Einar Diaz														
D 1999	Cle-A	.000	2	1	0	0	0	0	0	0	0	0	0	C
L 1998	Cle-A	.000	5	4	0	0	0	0	0	0	0	1	0	C
■ Bill Dickey														
W 1932	NY-A	.438	4	16	2	7	0	0	0	4	2	1	0	C
W 1936	NY-A	.120	6	25	5	3	0	0	1	5	3	4	0	C
W 1937	NY-A	.211	5	19	3	4	0	1	0	3	2	2	0	C
W 1938	NY-A	.400	4	15	2	6	0	0	1	2	1	0	0	C
W 1939	NY-A	.267	4	15	2	4	0	0	2	5	1	2	0	C
W 1941	NY-A	.167	5	18	3	3	1	0	0	1	3	1	0	C
W 1942	NY-A	.263	5	19	1	5	0	0	0	0	1	0	0	C
W 1943	NY-A	.278	5	18	1	5	0	0	1	4	2	2	0	C
W Total	8	.255	38	145	19	37	1	1	5	24	15	12	1	
■ Bob Didier														
L 1969	Atl-N	.000	3	11	0	0	0	0	0	0	0	2	0	C
■ Dick Dietz														
L 1971	SF-N	.067	4	15	0	1	0	0	0	0	2	5	0	C
■ Dom DiMaggio														
W 1946	Bos-A	.259	7	27	2	7	3	0	0	3	2	2	0	O
■ Joe DiMaggio														
W 1936	NY-A	.346	6	26	3	9	3	0	0	3	1	3	0	O
W 1937	NY-A	.273	5	22	2	6	0	0	1	4	0	3	0	O
W 1938	NY-A	.267	4	15	4	4	0	0	1	2	1	1	0	O
W 1939	NY-A	.313	4	16	3	5	0	0	1	3	1	1	0	O
W 1941	NY-A	.263	5	19	1	5	0	0	0	1	2	2	0	O
W 1942	NY-A	.333	5	21	3	7	0	0	0	3	0	1	0	O
W 1947	NY-A	.231	7	26	4	6	0	0	2	5	6	2	0	O
W 1949	NY-A	.111	5	18	2	2	0	0	1	2	3	5	0	O
W 1950	NY-A	.308	4	13	2	4	1	0	1	2	3	1	0	O
W 1951	NY-A	.261	6	23	3	6	2	0	1	5	2	4	0	O
W Total	10	.271	51	199	27	54	6	0	8	30	19	23	0	
■ Larry Doby														
W 1948	Cle-A	.318	6	22	1	7	1	0	1	2	2	4	0	O

YEAR	TM/L	AVG	G	AB	R	H	2B	3B	HR	RBI	BB	SO	SB	POS
W 1954	Cle-A	.125	4	16	0	2	0	0	0	0	2	4	0	O
W Total	2	.237	10	38	1	9	1	0	1	2	4	8	0	
■ **Bobby Doerr**														
W 1946	Bos-A	.409	6	22	1	9	1	0	1	3	2	2	0	2
■ **Frank Doljack**														
W 1934	Det-A	.000	2	2	0	0	0	0	0	0	0	0	0	O-1
■ **Jiggs Donahue**														
W 1906	Chi-A	.333	6	18	0	6	2	1	0	4	3	3	0	1
■ **Mike Donlin**														
W 1905	NY-N	.263	5	19	4	5	1	0	0	1	2	1	2	O
■ **Patsy Donovan**														
W 1890	Bro-N	.471	5	17	5	8	1	0	0	3	2	1	3	O
■ **Bill Doran**														
L 1986	Hou-N	.222	6	27	3	6	0	0	1	3	2	2	2	2
■ **Patsy Dougherty**														
W 1903	Bos-A	.235	8	34	3	8	0	2	2	5	2	6	0	O
W 1906	Chi-A	.100	6	20	1	2	0	0	0	1	3	4	2	O
W Total	2	.185	14	54	4	10	0	2	2	6	5	10	2	
■ **Taylor Douthit**														
W 1926	StL-N	.267	4	15	3	4	2	0	0	1	3	2	0	O
W 1928	StL-N	.091	3	11	1	1	0	0	0	1	1	1	0	O
W 1930	StL-N	.083	6	24	1	2	0	0	1	2	0	2	0	O
W Total	3	.140	13	50	5	7	2	0	1	4	4	5	0	
■ **Brian Downing**														
L 1979	Cal-A	.200	4	15	1	3	0	0	0	1	1	1	0	C
L 1982	Cal-A	.158	5	19	4	3	1	0	0	0	3	2	0	O
L 1986	Cal-A	.222	7	27	2	6	0	0	1	7	4	5	0	O
L Total	3	.197	16	61	7	12	1	0	1	8	8	8	0	
■ **Red Downs**														
W 1908	Det-A	.167	2	6	1	1	1	0	0	1	1	2	0	2
■ **Brian Doyle**														
L 1978	NY-A	.286	3	7	0	2	0	0	0	1	1	1	0	2
W 1978	NY-A	.438	6	16	4	7	1	0	0	2	0	0	0	2
■ **Jack Doyle**														
T 1894	NY-N	.588	4	17	4	10	1	1	0	6	1	1	6	1
T 1896	Bal-N	.294	4	17	3	5	1	0	0	4	0	0	2	1
T 1897	Bal-N	.526	5	19	7	10	2	0	0	9	0	1	2	1
T Total	3	.472	13	53	14	25	4	1	0	19	1	2	10	
■ **Larry Doyle**														
W 1911	NY-N	.304	6	23	3	7	3	1	0	1	2	1	2	2
W 1912	NY-N	.242	8	33	5	8	1	0	1	2	3	2	2	2
W 1913	NY-N	.150	5	20	1	3	0	0	0	2	0	1	0	2
W Total	3	.237	19	76	9	18	4	1	1	5	5	4	4	
■ **Denny Doyle**														
L 1975	Bos-A	.273	3	11	3	3	0	0	0	2	0	1	0	2
W 1975	Bos-A	.267	7	30	3	8	1	1	0	0	2	1	0	2
■ **J.D. Drew**														
D 2000	StL-N	.167	2	6	1	1	0	0	0	0	2	1	2	O
L 2000	StL-N	.333	5	12	2	4	1	0	0	1	0	3	0	O
■ **Dan Driessen**														
L 1973	Cin-N	.167	4	12	0	2	1	0	0	1	0	2	0	3
L 1976	Cin-N	.000	1	1	0	0	0	0	0	0	0	0	0	H
L 1979	Cin-N	.083	3	12	1	1	0	0	0	0	1	3	0	1
L 1987	StL-N	.250	5	12	1	3	2	0	0	1	1	1	0	1-4
L Total	4	.162	13	37	2	6	3	0	0	2	2	6	0	
W 1975	Cin-N	.000	2	2	0	0	0	0	0	0	0	0	0	H
W 1976	Cin-N	.357	4	14	4	5	2	0	1	1	2	0	1	D
W 1987	StL-N	.231	4	13	3	3	2	0	0	1	1	1	0	1
W Total	3	.276	10	29	7	8	4	0	1	2	3	1	1	
■ **Keith Drumright**														
D 1981	Oak-A	.250	1	4	0	1	0	0	0	0	0	0	0	D
L 1981	Oak-A	.000	3	4	0	0	0	0	0	0	1	0	0	D-1
■ **Jean Dubuc**														
W 1918	Bos-A	.000	1	1	0	0	0	0	0	0	0	1	0	H
■ **Rob Ducey**														
D 1997	Sea-A	.500	2	4	0	2	0	0	0	1	0	0	0	O-1
L 1991	Tor-A	.000	1	1	0	0	0	0	0	0	0	0	0	O
■ **Frank Duffy**														
L 1971	SF-N	.000	1	1	0	0	0	0	0	0	0	1	0	H
■ **Hugh Duffy**														
T 1892	Bos-N	.462	6	26	3	12	3	2	1	9	1	0	3	O
T 1897	Bos-N	.524	5	21	6	11	2	0	0	7	1	0	0	O
T Total	2	.489	11	47	9	23	5	2	1	16	2	0	3	
■ **Joe Dugan**														
W 1922	NY-A	.250	5	20	4	5	1	0	0	0	0	1	0	3
W 1923	NY-A	.280	6	25	5	7	2	1	1	5	3	0	0	3
W 1926	NY-A	.333	7	24	2	8	1	0	0	2	1	1	0	3
W 1927	NY-A	.200	4	15	2	3	0	0	0	0	0	0	0	3
W 1928	NY-A	.167	3	6	0	1	0	0	0	1	0	0	0	3
W Total	5	.267	25	90	13	24	4	1	1	8	4	2	0	

YEAR	TM/L	AVG	G	AB	R	H	2B	3B	HR	RBI	BB	SO	SB	POS
■ **Oscar Dugey**														
W 1915	Phi-N	—	2	0	0	0	0	0	0	0	0	0	1	R
■ **Dave Duncan**														
L 1971	Oak-A	.500	2	6	0	3	1	0	0	2	0	0	0	C
L 1972	Oak-A	.000	2	2	0	0	0	0	0	0	1	1	0	C
L Total	2	.375	4	8	0	3	1	0	0	2	1	1	0	
W 1972	Oak-A	.200	3	5	0	1	0	0	0	0	1	3	0	C-1
■ **Pat Duncan**														
W 1919	Cin-N	.269	8	26	3	7	2	0	0	8	2	2	0	O
■ **Mariano Duncan**														
D 1995	Cin-N	.667	2	3	1	2	0	0	0	1	0	0	1	2-1
D 1996	NY-A	.313	4	16	0	5	0	0	0	3	0	4	0	2
D Total	2	.368	6	19	1	7	0	0	0	4	0	4	1	
L 1985	LA-N	.222	5	18	2	4	2	1	0	1	1	3	1	S
L 1990	Cin-N	.300	6	20	1	6	0	0	1	4	0	8	0	2
L 1993	Phi-N	.267	3	15	3	4	0	2	0	0	0	5	0	2
L 1995	Cin-N	.000	3	3	0	0	0	0	0	0	1	1	0	1-1
L 1996	NY-A	.200	4	15	0	3	2	0	0	0	0	3	0	2
L Total	5	.239	21	71	6	17	4	3	1	5	2	20	1	
W 1990	Cin-N	.143	4	14	1	2	0	0	0	1	2	2	1	2
W 1993	Phi-N	.345	6	29	5	10	0	1	0	2	1	7	3	2-5,D-1
W 1996	NY-A	.053	6	19	1	1	0	0	0	0	0	4	1	2
W Total	3	.210	16	62	7	13	0	1	0	3	3	13	5	
■ **Fred Dunlap**														
W 1887	Det-N	.150	11	40	5	6	0	1	0	1	0	4	4	2
■ **Shawon Dunston**														
D 1999	NY-N	.167	4	6	0	1	0	0	0	0	0	1	0	O-2
D 2000	StL-N	1.000	1	1	0	1	0	0	0	0	0	0	0	H
D Total	2	.286	5	7	0	2	0	0	0	0	0	1	0	
L 1989	Chi-N	.316	5	19	2	6	0	0	0	0	1	1	1	S
L 1999	NY-N	.143	5	7	2	1	0	0	0	0	0	2	1	O-1
L 2000	StL-N	.333	4	6	1	2	1	0	0	0	0	0	0	O-2
L Total	3	.281	14	32	5	9	1	0	0	0	1	3	2	
■ **Erubiel Durazo**														
D 1999	Ari-N	.143	2	7	1	1	0	0	1	1	1	0	0	1
■ **Leon Durham**														
L 1984	Chi-N	.150	5	20	2	3	0	0	2	4	1	4	0	1
■ **Ray Durham**														
D 2000	Chi-A	.200	3	10	2	2	1	0	1	1	3	3	0	2
■ **Leo Durocher**														
W 1928	NY-A	.000	4	2	0	0	0	0	0	0	0	1	0	2
W 1934	StL-N	.259	7	27	4	7	1	1	0	0	0	0	0	S
W Total	2	.241	11	29	4	7	1	1	0	0	0	1	0	
■ **Cedric Durst**														
W 1927	NY-A	.000	1	1	0	0	0	0	0	0	0	0	0	H
W 1928	NY-A	.375	4	8	3	3	0	0	1	2	0	1	0	O
W Total	2	.333	5	9	3	3	0	0	1	2	0	1	0	
■ **Erv Dusak**														
W 1946	StL-N	.250	4	4	0	1	1	0	0	0	2	2	0	O
■ **Jim Dwyer**														
L 1983	Bal-A	.250	2	4	1	1	1	0	0	0	1	0	0	O-1
W 1983	Bal-A	.375	2	8	3	3	1	0	1	1	0	0	0	O
■ **Jerry Dybzinski**														
L 1983	Chi-A	.250	2	4	0	1	0	0	0	0	0	0	0	S
■ **Jermaine Dye**														
D 1996	Atl-N	.182	3	11	1	2	0	0	1	1	0	6	1	O
L 1996	Atl-N	.214	7	28	2	6	1	0	0	4	1	7	0	O
W 1996	Atl-N	.118	5	17	0	2	0	0	0	1	1	1	0	O
■ **Duffy Dyer**														
L 1975	Pit-N	—	1	0	0	0	0	0	0	1	1	0	0	H
W 1969	NY-N	.000	1	1	0	0	0	0	0	0	0	0	0	H
■ **Jimmy Dykes**														
W 1929	Phi-A	.421	5	19	2	8	1	0	0	4	1	1	0	3
W 1930	Phi-A	.222	6	18	2	4	3	0	1	5	5	3	0	3
W 1931	Phi-A	.227	7	22	2	5	0	0	0	2	5	1	0	3
W Total	3	.288	18	59	6	17	4	0	1	11	11	5	0	
■ **Lenny Dykstra**														
L 1986	NY-N	.304	6	23	3	7	1	1	1	3	2	4	1	O
L 1988	NY-N	.429	7	14	6	6	3	0	1	3	4	0	0	O
L 1993	Phi-N	.280	6	25	5	7	1	0	2	2	5	8	0	O
L Total	3	.323	19	62	14	20	5	1	4	8	11	12	1	
W 1986	NY-N	.296	7	27	4	8	0	0	2	3	2	7	0	O
W 1993	Phi-N	.348	6	23	9	8	1	0	4	8	7	4	4	O
W Total	2	.320	13	50	13	16	1	0	6	11	9	11	4	
■ **Mike Easler**														
L 1979	Pit-N	.000	1	1	0	0	0	0	0	0	0	0	0	H
W 1979	Pit-N	.000	2	1	0	0	0	0	0	0	1	0	0	H
■ **Zeb Eaton**														
W 1945	Det-A	.000	1	1	0	0	0	0	0	0	0	1	0	H
■ **Jim Edmonds**														
D 2000	StL-N	.571	3	14	5	8	4	0	2	7	1	2	1	O
L 2000	StL-N	.227	5	22	1	5	1	0	1	5	1	9	0	O

YEAR	TM/L	AVG	G	AB	R	H	2B	3B	HR	RBI	BB	SO	SB	POS
■ **Bruce Edwards**														
W 1947	Bro-N	.222	7	27	3	6	1	0	0	2	2	7	0	C
W 1949	Bro-N	.500	2	2	0	1	0	0	0	0	0	1	0	H
W Total	2	.241	9	29	3	7	1	0	0	2	2	8	0	
■ **Johnny Edwards**														
W 1961	Cin-N	.364	3	11	1	4	2	0	0	2	0	0	0	C
W 1968	StL-N	.000	1	1	0	0	0	0	0	0	0	1	0	H
W Total	2	.333	4	12	1	4	2	0	0	2	0	1	0	
■ **Marshall Edwards**														
D 1981	Mil-A	.000	2	1	0	0	0	0	0	0	0	1	0	O
L 1982	Mil-A	.000	3	1	2	0	0	0	0	0	0	0	1	D-2,O-1
W 1982	Mil-A	—	1	0	0	0	0	0	0	0	0	0	0	O
■ **Jim Eisenreich**														
D 1997	Fla-N	—	2	0	0	0	0	0	0	0	2	0	0	H
L 1993	Phi-N	.133	6	15	0	2	1	0	0	1	0	2	0	O-5
L 1997	Fla-N	.000	1	3	0	0	0	0	0	0	0	0	0	O
L Total	2	.111	7	18	0	2	1	0	0	1	0	2	0	
W 1993	Phi-N	.231	6	26	3	6	0	0	1	7	2	4	0	O
W 1997	Fla-N	.500	5	8	1	4	0	0	1	3	3	1	0	1-2,D-2
W Total	2	.294	11	34	4	10	0	0	2	10	5	5	0	
■ **Bob Elliott**														
W 1948	Bos-N	.333	6	21	4	7	0	0	2	5	2	2	0	3
■ **Kevin Elster**														
D 1996	Tex-A	.333	4	12	2	4	2	0	0	0	3	2	1	S
L 1986	NY-N	.000	4	3	0	0	0	0	0	0	0	1	0	S
L 1988	NY-N	.250	5	8	1	2	1	0	0	1	3	0	0	S
L Total	2	.182	9	11	1	2	1	0	0	1	3	1	0	
W 1986	NY-N	.000	1	1	0	0	0	0	0	0	0	0	0	S
■ **Fred Ely**														
T 1900	Pit-N	.286	4	14	1	4	1	0	0	0	1	1	2	S
■ **Clyde Engle**														
W 1912	Bos-A	.333	3	3	1	1	1	0	0	2	0	0	0	H
■ **Woody English**														
W 1929	Chi-N	.190	5	21	1	4	2	0	0	0	1	6	0	S
W 1932	Chi-N	.176	4	17	2	3	0	0	0	1	2	2	0	3
W Total	2	.184	9	38	3	7	2	0	0	1	3	8	0	
■ **Del Ennis**														
W 1950	Phi-N	.143	4	14	1	2	1	0	0	0	0	1	0	O
■ **Mike Epstein**														
L 1971	Oak-A	.200	2	5	0	1	0	0	0	0	0	3	0	1-1
L 1972	Oak-A	.188	5	16	1	3	0	0	1	1	4	5	1	1
L Total	2	.190	7	21	1	4	0	0	1	1	4	8	1	
W 1972	Oak-A	.000	6	16	1	0	0	0	0	0	5	3	0	1
■ **Alvaro Espinoza**														
D 1995	Cle-A	.000	1	1	0	0	0	0	0	0	0	0	0	3
L 1995	Cle-A	.125	4	8	1	1	0	0	0	0	0	3	0	3
W 1995	Cle-A	.500	2	2	1	1	0	0	0	0	0	0	0	3-1
■ **Sammy Esposito**														
W 1959	Chi-A	.000	2	2	0	0	0	0	0	0	0	1	0	3
■ **Cecil Espy**														
L 1991	Pit-N	.000	2	2	0	0	0	0	0	0	0	2	0	H
L 1992	Pit-N	.667	4	3	0	2	0	0	0	0	0	1	0	O-2
L Total	2	.400	6	5	0	2	0	0	0	0	0	3	0	
■ **Chuck Essegian**														
W 1959	LA-N	.667	4	3	2	2	0	0	2	2	1	1	0	H
■ **Bobby Estalella**														
D 2000	SF-N	.083	4	12	1	1	0	0	0	1	0	2	0	C
■ **Dude Esterbrook**														
W 1884	NY-A	.300	3	10	0	3	1	0	0	0	0	3	1	3
■ **Andy Etchebarren**														
L 1969	Bal-A	.000	2	4	0	0	0	0	0	0	0	0	0	C
L 1970	Bal-A	.111	2	9	1	1	0	0	0	0	0	3	0	C
L 1971	Bal-A	.000	2	5	0	0	0	0	0	0	0	0	0	C
L 1973	Bal-A	.357	4	14	1	5	1	0	1	4	0	1	0	C
L 1974	Bal-A	.333	2	6	0	2	0	0	0	0	0	0	0	C
L Total	5	.211	12	38	2	8	1	0	1	4	0	4	0	
W 1966	Bal-A	.083	4	12	2	1	0	0	0	0	2	4	0	C
W 1969	Bal-A	.000	2	6	0	0	0	0	0	0	0	1	0	C
W 1970	Bal-A	.143	2	7	1	1	0	0	0	0	2	3	0	C
W 1971	Bal-A	.000	1	2	0	0	0	0	0	0	0	0	0	C
W Total	4	.074	9	27	3	2	0	0	0	0	4	8	0	
■ **Nick Etten**														
W 1943	NY-A	.105	5	19	0	2	0	0	0	2	1	2	0	1
■ **Tony Eusebio**														
D 1997	Hou-N	.667	1	3	1	2	0	0	0	0	0	1	1	C
D 1998	Hou-N	.333	1	3	0	1	1	0	0	0	0	2	0	C
D 1999	Hou-N	.267	4	15	2	4	0	0	1	3	1	2	0	C
D Total	3	.333	6	21	3	7	1	0	1	3	1	5	1	
■ **Darrell Evans**														
L 1984	Det-A	.300	3	10	1	3	1	0	0	1	1	0	1	1-3,3-1
L 1987	Det-A	.294	5	17	0	5	0	0	0	0	4	2	0	1-5,3-1
L Total	2	.296	8	27	1	8	1	0	0	1	5	2	1	
W 1984	Det-A	.067	5	15	1	1	0	0	0	1	4	4	0	1-4,3-2

YEAR	TM/L	AVG	G	AB	R	H	2B	3B	HR	RBI	BB	SO	SB	POS
■ **Dwight Evans**														
L 1975	Bos-A	.100	3	10	1	1	1	0	0	0	1	2	0	O
L 1986	Bos-A	.214	7	28	2	6	1	0	1	4	3	3	0	O
L 1988	Bos-A	.167	4	12	1	2	1	0	0	1	3	5	0	O
L 1990	Bos-A	.231	4	13	0	3	1	0	0	0	1	3	0	D
L Total	4	.190	18	63	4	12	4	0	1	5	8	13	0	
W 1975	Bos-A	.292	7	24	3	7	1	1	1	5	3	4	0	O
W 1986	Bos-A	.308	7	26	4	8	2	0	2	9	4	3	0	O
W Total	2	.300	14	50	7	15	3	1	3	14	7	7	0	
■ **Joe Evans**														
W 1920	Cle-A	.308	4	13	0	4	0	0	0	0	1	0	0	O
■ **Carl Everett**														
D 1998	Hou-N	.154	4	13	1	2	0	0	0	0	0	4	0	O-3
D 1999	Hou-N	.133	4	15	2	2	0	0	0	1	2	8	0	O
D Total	2	.143	8	28	3	4	0	0	0	1	2	12	0	
■ **Johnny Evers**														
W 1906	Chi-N	.150	6	20	2	3	1	0	0	1	1	3	2	2
W 1907	Chi-N	.350	5	20	2	7	2	0	0	1	0	1	3	2-5,S-1
W 1908	Chi-N	.350	5	20	5	7	1	0	0	2	1	2	2	2
W 1914	Bos-N	.438	4	16	2	7	0	0	0	2	2	2	1	2
W Total	4	.316	20	76	11	24	4	0	0	6	4	8	8	
■ **Buck Ewing**														
W 1888	NY-N	.346	7	26	5	9	0	2	1	6	1	3	5	C-6,1-1
W 1889	NY-N	.250	8	36	5	9	4	0	0	7	2	5	1	C
W Total	2	.290	15	62	10	18	4	2	1	13	3	8	6	
■ **Jorge Fabregas**														
L 1999	Atl-N	.000	2	2	0	0	0	0	0	0	0	1	0	H
W 1999	Atl-N	.000	1	1	0	0	0	0	0	0	0	1	0	H
■ **Ron Fairly**														
W 1959	LA-N	.000	6	3	0	0	0	0	0	0	0	1	0	O-4
W 1963	LA-N	.000	4	1	0	0	0	0	0	0	3	0	0	O
W 1965	LA-N	.379	7	29	7	11	3	0	2	6	0	1	0	O
W 1966	LA-N	.143	3	7	0	1	0	0	0	2	4	0	0	O-2,1-1
W Total	4	.300	20	40	7	12	3	0	2	6	5	6	0	
■ **George Fallon**														
W 1944	StL-N	.000	2	2	0	0	0	0	0	0	0	1	0	2
■ **Duke Farrell**														
T 1894	NY-N	.400	4	15	5	6	0	0	0	2	1	1	1	C
T 1900	Bro-N	.375	2	8	0	3	0	0	0	1	0	0	1	C
T Total	2	.391	6	23	5	9	0	0	0	3	1	1	2	
W 1903	Bos-A	.000	2	2	0	0	0	0	0	1	0	0	0	H
■ **Jack Farrell**														
W 1884	Pro-N	.444	3	9	3	4	2	0	0	0	0	0	1	2
■ **Sal Fasano**														
D 2000	Oak-A	—	1	0	0	0	0	0	0	0	0	0	0	C
■ **Junior Felix**														
L 1989	Tor-A	.273	3	11	0	3	1	0	0	3	0	2	0	O
■ **Happy Felsch**														
W 1917	Chi-A	.273	6	22	4	6	1	0	1	3	1	5	0	O
W 1919	Chi-A	.192	8	26	2	5	1	0	0	3	1	4	0	O
W Total	2	.229	14	48	6	11	2	0	1	6	2	9	0	
■ **Joe Ferguson**														
L 1974	LA-N	.231	4	13	3	3	0	0	0	2	5	1	0	O-3,C-2
L 1978	LA-N	.000	2	2	0	0	0	0	0	0	0	1	0	H
L Total	2	.200	6	15	3	3	0	0	0	2	5	2	0	
W 1974	LA-N	.125	5	16	2	2	0	0	1	2	4	6	1	O-4,C-2
W 1978	LA-N	.500	2	4	1	2	2	0	0	0	0	1	0	C
W Total	2	.200	7	20	3	4	2	0	1	2	4	7	1	
■ **Felix Fermin**														
D 1995	Sea-A	.000	3	1	0	0	0	0	0	0	0	1	0	S-2,2-1
L 1995	Sea-A	—	2	0	0	0	0	0	0	0	0	0	0	2-1,S-1
■ **Tony Fernandez**														
D 1995	NY-A	.238	5	21	0	5	2	0	0	0	2	2	0	S
D 1997	Cle-A	.182	4	11	0	2	1	0	0	4	0	0	0	2
D Total	2	.219	9	32	0	7	3	0	0	4	2	2	0	
L 1985	Tor-A	.333	7	24	2	8	2	0	0	2	1	2	0	S
L 1989	Tor-A	.350	5	20	6	7	3	0	0	1	1	2	5	S
L 1993	Tor-A	.318	6	22	1	7	0	0	0	1	2	4	0	S
L 1997	Cle-A	.357	5	14	1	5	1	0	1	2	1	2	0	2
L Total	4	.338	23	80	10	27	6	0	1	6	5	10	5	
W 1993	Tor-A	.333	6	21	2	7	1	0	0	9	3	3	0	S
W 1997	Cle-A	.471	5	17	1	8	1	0	0	4	0	1	0	2
W Total	2	.395	11	38	3	15	2	0	0	13	3	4	0	
■ **Al Ferrara**														
W 1966	LA-N	1.000	1	1	0	1	0	0	0	0	0	0	0	H
■ **Hobe Ferris**														
W 1903	Bos-A	.290	8	31	3	9	0	1	0	5	0	6	0	2
■ **Chick Fewster**														
W 1921	NY-A	.200	4	10	3	2	0	0	1	2	3	3	0	O
■ **Cecil Fielder**														
D 1996	NY-A	.364	3	11	2	4	0	0	1	4	1	2	0	D
D 1997	NY-A	.125	2	8	0	1	0	0	0	1	0	3	0	D
D Total	2	.263	5	19	2	5	0	0	1	5	1	5	0	

YEAR	TM/L	AVG	G	AB	R	H	2B	3B	HR	RBI	BB	SO	SB	POS
L 1985	Tor-A	.333	3	3	0	1	1	0	0	0	0	1	0	H
L 1996	NY-A	.167	5	18	3	3	0	0	2	8	4	5	0	D
L Total	2	.190	8	21	3	4	1	0	2	8	4	6	0	
W 1996	NY-A	.391	6	23	1	9	2	0	0	2	2	2	0	1-3,D-3
■ **Jack Fimple**														
L 1983	LA-N	.143	3	7	0	1	0	0	0	1	0	3	0	C
■ **Steve Finley**														
D 1996	SD-N	.083	3	12	0	1	0	0	0	1	0	4	1	O
D 1998	SD-N	.100	4	10	2	1	1	0	0	1	1	4	0	O
D 1999	Ari-N	.385	4	13	0	5	1	0	0	5	3	1	0	O
D Total	3	.200	11	35	2	7	2	0	0	7	4	9	1	
L 1998	SD-N	.333	6	21	3	7	1	0	0	2	6	2	1	O
W 1998	SD-N	.083	3	12	0	1	1	0	0	0	0	2	1	O
■ **Showboat Fisher**														
W 1930	StL-N	.500	2	2	0	1	1	0	0	0	0	1	0	H
■ **Carlton Fisk**														
L 1975	Bos-A	.417	3	12	4	5	1	0	0	2	0	2	1	C
L 1983	Chi-A	.176	4	17	0	3	1	0	0	0	1	3	0	C
L Total	2	.276	7	29	4	8	2	0	0	2	1	5	1	
W 1975	Bos-A	.240	7	25	5	6	0	0	2	4	7	7	0	C
■ **Max Flack**														
W 1918	Chi-N	.263	6	19	2	5	0	0	0	0	4	1	1	O
■ **John Flaherty**														
D 1996	SD-N	.000	2	4	0	0	0	0	0	0	0	1	0	C
■ **Tim Flannery**														
L 1984	SD-N	.500	3	2	2	1	0	0	0	0	0	0	0	H
W 1984	SD-N	1.000	1	1	0	1	0	0	0	0	0	0	0	2
■ **Art Fletcher**														
W 1911	NY-N	.130	6	23	1	3	1	0	0	1	0	4	0	S
W 1912	NY-N	.179	8	28	1	5	1	0	0	3	1	4	1	S
W 1913	NY-N	.278	5	18	1	5	0	0	0	3	1	1	1	S
W 1917	NY-N	.200	6	25	2	5	1	0	0	0	0	2	0	S
W Total	4	.191	25	94	5	18	3	0	0	7	2	11	2	
■ **Scott Fletcher**														
L 1983	Chi-A	.000	3	7	0	0	0	0	0	0	1	0	0	S
■ **Silver Flint**														
W 1885	Chi-N	.143	4	14	0	2	0	0	0	0	0	0	0	C
W 1886	Chi-N	.000	1	3	0	0	0	0	0	1	0	1	0	C
W Total	2	.118	5	17	0	2	0	0	0	1	0	1	0	
■ **Curt Flood**														
W 1964	StL-N	.200	7	30	5	6	0	1	0	3	3	1	0	O
W 1967	StL-N	.179	7	28	2	5	1	0	0	3	3	3	0	O
W 1968	StL-N	.286	7	28	4	8	1	0	0	2	2	2	3	O
W Total	3	.221	21	86	11	19	2	1	0	8	8	6	3	
■ **Jake Flowers**														
W 1926	StL-N	.000	3	3	0	0	0	0	0	0	0	1	0	H
W 1931	StL-N	.091	5	11	1	1	1	0	0	0	1	0	0	3-4
W Total	2	.071	8	14	1	1	1	0	0	0	1	1	0	
■ **Cliff Floyd**														
W 1997	Fla-N	.000	4	2	1	0	0	0	0	0	1	1	0	D-1
■ **Doug Flynn**														
L 1976	Cin-N	—	1	0	0	0	0	0	0	0	0	0	0	2
■ **Tim Foli**														
L 1979	Pit-N	.333	3	12	1	4	1	0	0	3	0	0	0	S
L 1982	Cal-A	.125	5	16	0	2	0	0	0	1	0	3	0	S
L Total	2	.214	8	28	1	6	1	0	0	4	0	3	0	
W 1979	Pit-N	.333	7	30	6	10	1	1	0	3	2	0	0	S
■ **Chad Fonville**														
D 1995	LA-N	.500	3	12	1	6	0	0	0	0	0	1	0	S
■ **Barry Foote**														
D 1981	NY-A	—	1	0	0	0	0	0	0	0	0	0	0	H
L 1978	Phi-N	.000	1	1	0	0	0	0	0	0	0	1	0	H
L 1981	NY-A	1.000	2	1	0	1	0	0	0	0	0	0	0	C-1
L Total	2	.500	3	2	0	1	0	0	0	0	0	1	0	
W 1981	NY-A	.000	1	1	0	0	0	0	0	0	0	1	0	H
■ **Curt Ford**														
L 1987	StL-N	.333	4	9	2	3	0	0	0	0	1	1	0	O
W 1987	StL-N	.308	5	13	1	4	0	0	0	2	1	1	0	O-4
■ **Dan Ford**														
L 1979	Cal-A	.294	4	17	2	5	1	0	2	4	0	0	0	O
L 1983	Bal-A	.200	2	5	0	1	1	0	0	0	0	1	0	O-1
L Total	2	.273	6	22	2	6	2	0	2	4	0	1	0	
W 1983	Bal-A	.167	5	12	1	2	0	0	1	1	1	5	0	O-4
■ **Tom Forster**														
W 1884	NY-A	.000	1	3	0	0	0	0	0	0	0	1	0	2
■ **Ray Fosse**														
L 1973	Oak-A	.091	5	11	2	1	1	0	0	3	2	2	0	C
L 1974	Oak-A	.333	4	12	1	4	1	0	1	3	1	2	0	C
L 1975	Oak-A	.000	1	2	0	0	0	0	0	0	0	1	0	C
L Total	3	.200	10	25	3	5	2	0	1	6	3	5	0	
W 1973	Oak-A	.158	7	19	0	3	1	0	0	0	1	4	0	C
W 1974	Oak-A	.143	5	14	1	2	0	0	1	1	1	5	0	C

YEAR	TM/L	AVG	G	AB	R	H	2B	3B	HR	RBI	BB	SO	SB	POS
W Total	2	.152	12	33	1	5	1	0	1	1	2	9	0	
■ **George Foster**														
L 1972	Cin-N	—	1	0	1	0	0	0	0	0	0	0	0	R
L 1975	Cin-N	.364	3	11	3	4	0	0	0	0	1	2	1	O
L 1976	Cin-N	.167	3	12	2	2	0	0	2	4	0	4	0	O
L 1979	Cin-N	.200	3	10	1	2	0	0	1	2	4	3	0	O
L Total	4	.242	10	33	7	8	0	0	3	6	5	9	1	
W 1972	Cin-N	—	2	0	0	0	0	0	0	0	0	0	0	O-1
W 1975	Cin-N	.276	7	29	1	8	1	0	0	2	1	1	1	O
W 1976	Cin-N	.429	4	14	3	6	1	0	0	4	2	3	0	O
W Total	3	.326	13	43	4	14	2	0	0	6	3	4	1	
■ **Dave Foutz**														
W 1885	StL-A	.167	4	12	1	2	0	0	0	0	0	0	0	P
W 1886	StL-A	.200	4	15	2	3	1	1	0	3	0	3	0	P-2,O-2
W 1887	StL-A	.197	15	61	4	12	2	1	0	3	2	3	0	O-11,P-3,1-1
W 1889	Bro-A	.286	9	35	7	10	2	0	1	9	4	2	3	1-9,P-1
W 1890	Bro-N	.300	7	30	6	9	2	1	0	4	0	1	1	1-7,O-1
W Total	5	.235	39	153	20	36	7	3	1	19	6	9	4	
■ **Andy Fox**														
D 1996	NY-A	—	2	0	0	0	0	0	0	0	0	0	0	D-1
D 1997	NY-A	—	2	0	0	0	0	0	0	0	0	0	0	2
D 1999	Ari-N	.000	1	3	0	0	0	0	0	0	0	1	0	S
D Total	3	.000	5	3	0	0	0	0	0	0	0	1	0	
L 1996	NY-A	—	2	0	0	0	0	0	0	0	0	0	0	D
W 1996	NY-A	—	4	0	1	0	0	0	0	0	0	0	0	2-1,3-1
■ **Eric Fox**														
L 1992	Oak-A	.000	4	1	0	0	0	0	0	0	1	0	2	O-1,D-1
■ **Pete Fox**														
W 1934	Det-A	.286	7	28	1	8	6	0	0	2	1	4	0	O
W 1935	Det-A	.385	6	26	1	10	3	1	0	4	0	1	0	O
W 1940	Det-A	.000	1	1	0	0	0	0	0	0	0	0	0	H
W Total	3	.327	14	55	2	18	9	1	0	6	1	5	0	
■ **Nellie Fox**														
W 1959	Chi-A	.375	6	24	4	9	3	0	0	0	4	1	0	2
■ **Jimmie Foxx**														
W 1929	Phi-A	.350	5	20	5	7	1	0	2	5	1	1	0	1
W 1930	Phi-A	.333	6	21	3	7	2	1	1	3	2	4	0	1
W 1931	Phi-A	.348	7	23	3	8	0	0	1	3	6	5	0	1
W Total	3	.344	18	64	11	22	3	1	4	11	9	10	0	
■ **Joe Foy**														
W 1967	Bos-A	.133	6	15	2	2	1	0	0	1	1	5	0	3-3
■ **Julio Franco**														
D 1996	Cle-A	.133	4	15	1	2	0	0	0	1	1	6	0	1-3,D-1
■ **Matt Franco**														
D 1999	NY-N	—	1	0	0	0	0	0	0	0	1	0	0	H
L 1999	NY-N	.500	5	2	1	1	1	0	0	0	1	0	0	H
L 2000	NY-N	.000	2	3	0	0	0	0	0	0	0	1	0	1-1
L Total	2	.200	7	5	1	1	1	0	0	0	1	1	0	
W 2000	NY-N	.000	1	1	0	0	0	0	0	0	0	1	0	1
■ **Terry Francona**														
D 1981	Mon-N	.333	5	12	0	4	0	0	0	0	2	2	2	O
L 1981	Mon-N	.000	2	1	0	0	0	0	0	0	0	1	0	O-1
■ **Herman Franks**														
W 1941	Bro-N	.000	1	1	0	0	0	0	0	0	0	0	0	C
■ **Bill Freehan**														
L 1972	Det-A	.250	3	12	2	3	1	0	1	3	0	1	0	C
W 1968	Det-A	.083	7	24	0	2	1	0	0	2	4	8	0	C
■ **Buck Freeman**														
W 1903	Bos-A	.281	8	32	6	9	0	3	0	4	2	2	0	O
■ **Gene Freese**														
W 1961	Cin-N	.063	5	16	0	1	1	0	0	0	3	4	0	3
■ **Walter French**														
W 1929	Phi-A	.000	1	1	0	0	0	0	0	0	0	1	0	H
■ **Lonny Frey**														
W 1939	Cin-N	.000	4	17	0	0	0	0	0	0	1	4	0	2
W 1940	Cin-N	.000	3	2	0	0	0	0	0	0	0	0	0	H
W 1947	NY-A	.000	1	1	0	0	0	0	0	1	0	0	0	H
W Total	3	.000	8	20	0	0	0	0	0	1	1	4	0	
■ **Hanley Frias**														
D 1999	Ari-N	.000	4	7	0	0	0	0	0	0	0	3	0	S
■ **Frankie Frisch**														
W 1921	NY-N	.300	8	30	5	9	0	1	0	1	4	3	3	3
W 1922	NY-N	.471	5	17	3	8	1	0	0	2	1	0	1	2
W 1923	NY-N	.400	6	25	2	10	0	1	0	1	0	0	0	2
W 1924	NY-N	.333	7	30	1	10	4	1	0	0	4	1	1	2-7,3-1
W 1928	StL-N	.231	4	13	1	3	0	0	0	1	2	2	2	2
W 1930	StL-N	.208	6	24	0	5	2	0	0	0	0	0	1	2
W 1931	StL-N	.259	7	27	2	7	2	0	0	1	1	2	1	2
W 1934	StL-N	.194	7	31	2	6	1	0	0	4	0	1	0	2
W Total	8	.294	50	197	16	58	10	3	0	10	12	9	9	
■ **Travis Fryman**														
D 1998	Cle-A	.154	4	13	1	2	1	0	0	0	3	4	1	3
D 1999	Cle-A	.267	5	15	2	4	0	0	1	4	3	2	1	3

YEAR	TM/L	AVG	G	AB	R	H	2B	3B	HR	RBI	BB	SO	SB	POS
D Total	2	.214	9	28	3	6	1	0	1	4	6	6	2	
L 1998	Cle-A	.174	6	23	2	4	0	0	0	0	1	5	1	3
■ **Tito Fuentes**														
L 1971	SF-N	.313	4	16	4	5	1	0	1	2	1	3	0	2
■ **Shorty Fuller**														
T 1894	NY-N	.286	4	14	4	4	0	0	0	2	2	0	1	S
■ **Chick Fullis**														
W 1934	StL-N	.400	3	5	0	2	0	0	0	0	0	0	0	O
■ **Rafael Furcal**														
D 2000	Atl-N	.091	3	11	2	1	0	0	0	0	3	0	1	S-3
■ **Carl Furillo**														
W 1947	Bro-N	.353	6	17	2	6	2	0	0	3	3	0	0	O
W 1949	Bro-N	.125	3	8	0	1	0	0	0	0	1	0	0	O-2
W 1952	Bro-N	.174	7	23	1	4	2	0	0	0	3	3	0	O
W 1953	Bro-N	.333	6	24	4	8	2	0	1	4	1	3	0	O
W 1955	Bro-N	.296	7	27	4	8	1	0	1	3	3	5	0	O
W 1956	Bro-N	.240	7	25	2	6	2	0	0	1	2	3	0	O
W 1959	LA-N	.250	4	4	0	1	0	0	0	2	0	1	0	O-1
W Total	7	.266	40	128	13	34	9	0	2	13	13	15	0	
■ **Gary Gaetti**														
D 1996	StL-N	.091	3	11	1	1	0	0	1	3	0	3	0	3
D 1998	Chi-N	.091	3	11	0	1	0	0	0	0	0	4	0	3
D Total	2	.091	6	22	1	2	0	0	1	3	0	7	0	
L 1987	Min-A	.300	5	20	5	6	1	0	2	5	1	3	0	3
L 1996	StL-N	.292	7	24	1	7	0	0	1	4	1	5	0	3
L Total	2	.295	12	44	6	13	1	0	3	9	2	8	0	
W 1987	Min-A	.259	7	27	4	7	2	1	1	4	2	5	2	3
■ **Phil Gagliano**														
L 1973	Cin-N	.000	3	3	0	0	0	0	0	0	0	1	0	H
W 1967	StL-N	.000	1	1	0	0	0	0	0	0	0	0	0	H
W 1968	StL-N	.000	3	3	0	0	0	0	0	0	0	0	0	H
W Total	2	.000	4	4	0	0	0	0	0	0	0	0	0	
■ **Greg Gagne**														
D 1996	LA-N	.273	3	11	2	3	1	0	0	0	0	5	0	S
L 1987	Min-A	.278	5	18	5	5	3	0	2	3	3	4	0	S
L 1991	Min-A	.235	5	17	1	4	0	0	0	1	1	5	0	S
L Total	2	.257	10	35	6	9	3	0	2	4	4	9	0	
W 1987	Min-A	.200	7	30	5	6	1	0	1	3	1	6	0	S
W 1991	Min-A	.167	7	24	1	4	1	0	1	3	0	7	0	S
W Total	2	.185	14	54	6	10	2	0	2	6	1	13	0	
■ **Del Gainer**														
W 1915	Bos-A	.333	1	3	1	1	0	0	0	0	0	0	0	1
W 1916	Bos-A	1.000	1	1	0	1	0	0	0	1	0	0	0	H
W Total	2	.500	2	4	1	2	0	0	0	1	0	0	0	
■ **Augie Galan**														
W 1935	Chi-N	.160	6	25	2	4	1	0	0	2	2	2	0	O
W 1938	Chi-N	.000	2	2	0	0	0	0	0	0	0	1	0	H
W 1941	Bro-N	.000	2	2	0	0	0	0	0	0	0	1	0	H
W Total	3	.138	10	29	2	4	1	0	0	2	2	4	0	
■ **Andres Galarraga**														
D 1995	Col-N	.278	4	18	1	5	1	0	0	2	0	6	0	1
D 1998	Atl-N	.250	3	12	1	3	0	0	0	0	1	3	0	1
D 2000	Atl-N	.200	3	10	1	2	1	0	0	1	2	4	0	1
D Total	3	.250	10	40	3	10	2	0	0	3	3	13	0	
L 1998	Atl-N	.095	6	21	1	2	0	0	1	4	6	6	0	1
■ **Al Gallagher**														
L 1971	SF-N	.100	4	10	0	1	0	0	0	0	0	2	0	3
■ **Mike Gallego**														
D 1996	StL-N	.000	2	1	0	0	0	0	0	0	0	1	0	2-1,3-1
L 1988	Oak-A	.083	4	12	1	1	0	0	0	0	0	3	0	2
L 1989	Oak-A	.273	4	11	3	3	1	0	0	1	0	2	0	2-2,S-2
L 1990	Oak-A	.400	4	10	1	4	1	0	0	2	1	1	0	S-3,2-2
L 1996	StL-N	.143	7	14	1	2	0	0	0	0	1	3	0	2-5,3-2
L Total	4	.213	19	47	6	10	2	0	0	3	2	9	0	
W 1988	Oak-A	—	1	0	0	0	0	0	0	0	0	0	0	2
W 1989	Oak-A	.000	2	1	0	0	0	0	0	0	0	0	0	2-1,3-1
W 1990	Oak-A	.091	4	11	0	1	0	0	0	1	1	3	1	S
W Total	3	.083	7	12	0	1	0	0	0	1	1	3	1	
■ **Lee Gamble**														
W 1939	Cin-N	.000	1	1	0	0	0	0	0	0	0	1	0	H
■ **Oscar Gamble**														
D 1981	NY-A	.556	4	9	2	5	1	0	2	3	1	2	0	D
L 1976	NY-A	.250	3	8	1	2	1	0	0	1	1	1	0	O
L 1980	NY-A	.200	2	5	1	1	0	0	0	0	1	1	0	O-1,D-1
L 1981	NY-A	.167	3	6	2	1	0	0	0	1	5	3	0	D-2,O-1
L Total	3	.211	8	19	4	4	1	0	0	2	7	5	0	
W 1976	NY-A	.125	3	8	0	1	0	0	0	1	0	0	0	O-2
W 1981	NY-A	.333	3	6	1	2	0	0	0	1	1	0	0	O-2
W Total	2	.214	6	14	1	3	0	0	0	2	1	0	0	
■ **Chick Gandil**														
W 1917	Chi-A	.261	6	23	1	6	1	0	0	5	0	2	1	1
W 1919	Chi-A	.233	8	30	1	7	0	1	0	5	1	3	1	1
W Total	2	.245	14	53	2	13	1	1	0	10	1	5	2	

YEAR	TM/L	AVG	G	AB	R	H	2B	3B	HR	RBI	BB	SO	SB	POS
■ **Ron Gant**														
D 1995	Cin-N	.231	3	13	3	3	0	0	1	2	0	3	0	O
D 1996	StL-N	.400	3	10	3	4	1	0	1	4	2	0	2	O
D Total	2	.304	6	23	6	7	1	0	2	6	2	3	2	
L 1991	Atl-N	.259	7	27	4	7	1	0	1	3	2	4	7	O
L 1992	Atl-N	.182	7	22	5	4	0	0	2	6	4	4	1	O
L 1993	Atl-N	.185	6	27	4	5	3	0	0	3	2	9	0	O
L 1995	Cin-N	.188	4	16	1	3	0	0	0	1	0	3	0	O
L 1996	StL-N	.240	7	25	3	6	1	0	2	4	2	6	0	O
L Total	5	.214	31	117	17	25	5	0	5	17	10	26	8	
W 1991	Atl-N	.267	7	30	3	8	0	1	0	4	2	3	1	O
W 1992	Atl-N	.125	4	8	2	1	1	0	0	0	1	2	2	O-3
W Total	2	.237	11	38	5	9	1	1	0	4	3	5	3	
■ **Jim Gantner**														
D 1981	Mil-A	.143	4	14	1	2	1	0	0	0	0	2	0	2
L 1982	Mil-A	.188	5	16	1	3	0	0	0	2	1	1	0	2
W 1982	Mil-A	.333	7	24	5	8	4	1	0	4	1	1	0	2
■ **Charlie Ganzel**														
W 1887	Det-N	.237	14	59	5	14	1	0	0	3	1	2	3	1-10,C-7
T 1892	Bos-N	.500	2	8	1	4	0	0	0	2	1	0	0	C
■ **Joe Garagiola**														
W 1946	StL-N	.316	5	19	2	6	2	0	0	4	0	3	0	C
■ **Barbaro Garbey**														
L 1984	Det-A	.333	3	9	1	3	0	0	0	0	0	1	0	D-2
W 1984	Det-A	.000	4	12	0	0	0	0	0	0	0	2	0	D-3
■ **Kiko Garcia**														
D 1981	Hou-N	.000	2	4	0	0	0	0	0	0	0	1	0	S-1
L 1979	Bal-A	.273	3	11	1	3	0	0	0	2	2	4	0	S
W 1979	Bal-A	.400	6	20	4	8	2	1	0	6	1	3	0	S
■ **Carlos Garcia**														
L 1992	Pit-N	.000	1	1	0	0	0	0	0	0	0	0	0	2
■ **Damaso Garcia**														
L 1985	Tor-A	.233	7	30	4	7	4	0	0	1	3	3	0	2
■ **Nomar Garciaparra**														
D 1998	Bos-A	.333	4	15	4	5	1	0	3	11	1	0	0	S
D 1999	Bos-A	.417	5	12	6	5	2	0	2	4	3	3	0	S
D Total	2	.370	9	27	10	10	3	0	5	15	4	3	0	
L 1999	Bos-A	.400	5	20	2	8	2	0	2	5	2	2	1	S
■ **Billy Gardner**														
W 1961	NY-A	.000	1	1	0	0	0	0	0	0	0	0	0	H
■ **Larry Gardner**														
W 1912	Bos-A	.179	8	28	4	5	2	1	1	5	2	5	0	3
W 1915	Bos-A	.235	5	17	2	4	0	1	0	0	1	0	0	3
W 1916	Bos-A	.176	5	17	2	3	0	0	2	6	0	2	0	3
W 1920	Cle-A	.208	7	24	1	5	1	0	0	2	1	1	0	3
W Total	4	.198	25	86	9	17	3	2	3	13	4	8	0	
■ **Debs Garms**														
W 1943	StL-N	.000	2	5	0	0	0	0	0	0	0	2	0	O-1
W 1944	StL-N	.000	2	2	0	0	0	0	0	0	0	0	0	H
W Total	2	.000	4	7	0	0	0	0	0	0	0	2	0	
■ **Phil Garner**														
D 1981	Hou-N	.111	5	18	1	2	0	0	0	0	3	3	0	2
L 1975	Oak-A	.000	3	5	0	0	0	0	0	0	0	1	0	2
L 1979	Pit-N	.417	3	12	4	5	0	1	1	1	1	0	0	2-3,S-1
L 1986	Hou-N	.222	3	9	1	2	1	0	0	2	1	2	0	3
L Total	3	.269	9	26	5	7	1	1	1	3	2	3	0	
W 1979	Pit-N	.500	7	24	4	12	4	0	0	5	3	1	0	2
■ **Wayne Garrett**														
L 1969	NY-N	.385	3	13	3	5	2	0	1	3	2	2	1	3
L 1973	NY-N	.087	5	23	1	2	1	0	0	1	0	5	0	3
L Total	2	.194	8	36	4	7	3	0	1	4	2	7	1	
W 1969	NY-N	.000	2	1	0	0	0	0	0	0	2	1	0	3
W 1973	NY-N	.167	7	30	4	5	0	0	2	2	5	11	0	3
W Total	2	.161	9	31	4	5	0	0	2	2	7	12	0	
■ **Gil Garrido**														
L 1969	Atl-N	.200	3	10	0	2	0	0	0	0	1	1	0	S
■ **Steve Garvey**														
D 1981	LA-N	.368	5	19	4	7	0	1	2	4	0	2	0	1
L 1974	LA-N	.389	4	18	4	7	1	0	2	5	1	1	0	1
L 1977	LA-N	.308	4	13	2	4	0	0	0	0	2	1	1	1
L 1978	LA-N	.389	4	18	6	7	1	1	4	7	0	1	0	1
L 1981	LA-N	.286	5	21	2	6	0	0	1	2	0	4	0	1
L 1984	SD-N	.400	5	20	1	8	1	0	1	7	1	2	0	1
L Total	5	.356	22	90	15	32	3	1	8	21	4	9	1	
W 1974	LA-N	.381	5	21	2	8	0	0	0	1	0	3	0	1
W 1977	LA-N	.375	6	24	5	9	1	1	1	3	1	4	0	1
W 1978	LA-N	.208	6	24	1	5	1	0	0	0	1	7	1	1
W 1981	LA-N	.417	6	24	3	10	1	0	0	0	2	5	0	1
W 1984	SD-N	.200	5	20	2	4	2	0	0	2	0	2	0	1
W Total	5	.319	28	113	13	36	5	1	1	6	4	21	1	
■ **Rod Gaspar**														
L 1969	NY-N	—	3	0	0	0	0	0	0	0	0	0	0	O
W 1969	NY-N	.000	3	2	1	0	0	0	0	0	0	0	0	O-1

YEAR	TM/L	AVG	G	AB	R	H	2B	3B	HR	RBI	BB	SO	SB	POS
■ **Brent Gates**														
D 1997	Sea-A	.000	2	4	0	0	0	0	0	0	0	0	0	3
■ **Mike Gazella**														
W 1926	NY-A	—	1	0	0	0	0	0	0	0	0	0	0	3
■ **Dinty Gearin**														
W 1923	NY-N	—	1	0	0	0	0	0	0	0	0	0	0	R
■ **Rich Gedman**														
L 1986	Bos-A	.357	7	28	4	10	1	0	1	6	0	4	0	C
L 1988	Bos-A	.357	4	14	1	5	0	0	1	1	2	1	0	C
L Total	2	.357	11	42	5	15	1	0	2	7	2	5	0	
W 1986	Bos-A	.200	7	30	1	6	1	0	1	1	0	10	0	C
■ **Lou Gehrig**														
W 1926	NY-A	.348	7	23	1	8	2	0	0	4	5	4	0	1
W 1927	NY-A	.308	4	13	2	4	2	2	0	4	3	3	0	1
W 1928	NY-A	.545	4	11	5	6	1	0	4	9	6	0	0	1
W 1932	NY-A	.529	4	17	9	9	1	0	3	8	2	1	0	1
W 1936	NY-A	.292	6	24	5	7	1	0	2	7	3	2	0	1
W 1937	NY-A	.294	5	17	4	5	1	1	1	3	5	4	0	1
W 1938	NY-A	.286	4	14	4	4	0	0	0	0	2	3	0	1
W Total	7	.361	34	119	30	43	8	3	10	35	26	17	0	
■ **Charlie Gehringer**														
W 1934	Det-A	.379	7	29	5	11	1	0	1	2	3	0	1	2
W 1935	Det-A	.375	6	24	4	9	3	0	0	4	2	1	1	2
W 1940	Det-A	.214	7	28	3	6	0	0	0	1	2	0	0	2
W Total	3	.321	20	81	12	26	4	0	1	7	7	1	2	
■ **Charlie Gelbert**														
W 1930	StL-N	.353	6	17	2	6	0	1	0	2	3	3	0	S
W 1931	StL-N	.261	7	23	0	6	1	0	0	3	0	4	0	S
W Total	2	.300	13	40	2	12	1	1	0	5	3	7	0	
■ **Dick Gernert**														
W 1961	Cin-N	.000	4	4	0	0	0	0	0	0	0	1	0	H
■ **Cesar Geronimo**														
D 1981	KC-A	—	1	0	0	0	0	0	0	0	0	0	0	R
L 1972	Cin-N	.100	5	20	2	2	0	0	1	1	0	2	0	O
L 1973	Cin-N	.067	4	15	0	1	0	0	0	0	0	7	0	O
L 1975	Cin-N	.000	3	10	0	0	0	0	0	1	1	7	0	O
L 1976	Cin-N	.182	3	11	0	2	0	1	0	2	1	3	0	O
L 1979	Cin-N	.143	2	7	0	1	0	0	0	0	0	5	0	O
L Total	5	.095	17	63	2	6	0	1	1	4	2	24	0	
W 1972	Cin-N	.158	7	19	1	3	0	0	0	3	1	4	1	O
W 1975	Cin-N	.280	7	25	3	7	0	1	2	3	3	5	0	O
W 1976	Cin-N	.308	4	13	3	4	2	0	0	1	2	2	2	O
W Total	3	.246	18	57	7	14	2	1	2	7	6	11	3	
■ **Doc Gessler**														
W 1906	Chi-N	.000	2	1	0	0	0	0	0	0	1	0	0	H
■ **Gus Getz**														
W 1916	Bro-N	.000	1	1	0	0	0	0	0	0	0	0	0	H
■ **Jason Giambi**														
D 2000	Oak-A	.286	5	14	2	4	0	0	0	1	7	2	1	1
■ **Jeremy Giambi**														
D 2000	Oak-A	.333	4	9	1	3	0	0	0	1	2	2	0	O-2,D-2
■ **George Gibson**														
W 1909	Pit-N	.240	7	25	2	6	2	0	0	2	1	1	2	C
■ **Russ Gibson**														
W 1967	Bos-A	.000	2	2	0	0	0	0	0	0	0	2	0	C
■ **Kirk Gibson**														
L 1984	Det-A	.417	3	12	2	5	1	0	1	2	2	1	1	O
L 1987	Det-A	.286	5	21	4	6	1	0	1	4	3	8	3	O
L 1988	LA-N	.154	7	26	2	4	0	0	2	6	3	6	2	O
L Total	3	.254	15	59	8	15	2	0	4	12	8	15	6	
W 1984	Det-A	.333	5	18	4	6	0	0	2	7	4	4	3	O
W 1988	LA-N	1.000	1	1	1	1	0	0	1	2	0	0	0	H
W Total	2	.368	6	19	5	7	0	0	3	9	4	4	3	
■ **Larry Gilbert**														
W 1914	Bos-N	—	1	0	0	0	0	0	0	0	1	0	0	H
■ **Billy Gilbert**														
W 1905	NY-N	.235	5	17	1	4	0	0	0	2	0	2	1	2
■ **Brian Giles**														
D 1996	Cle-A	.000	1	1	0	0	0	0	0	0	0	1	0	H
D 1997	Cle-A	.143	3	7	0	1	0	0	0	0	0	1	0	O
D 1998	Cle-A	.200	3	10	1	2	1	0	0	0	1	4	0	O-2,D-1
D Total	3	.167	7	18	1	3	1	0	0	0	1	6	0	
L 1997	Cle-A	.188	6	16	1	3	3	0	0	0	2	6	0	O
L 1998	Cle-A	.083	4	12	0	1	0	0	0	0	1	3	0	O-3
L Total	2	.143	10	28	1	4	3	0	0	0	3	9	0	
W 1997	Cle-A	.500	5	4	1	2	1	0	0	2	4	1	0	O-2
■ **Bernard Gilkey**														
D 1999	Ari-N	.000	2	6	0	0	0	0	0	0	0	0	0	O
■ **Paul Gillespie**														
W 1945	Chi-N	.000	3	6	0	0	0	0	0	0	0	0	0	C-1
■ **Jim Gilliam**														
W 1953	Bro-N	.296	6	27	4	8	3	0	2	4	0	2	0	2
W 1955	Bro-N	.292	7	24	2	7	1	0	0	3	8	1	1	2-5,O-4
W 1956	Bro-N	.083	7	24	2	2	0	0	0	2	7	3	1	2-6,O-1
W 1959	LA-N	.240	6	25	2	6	0	0	0	0	2	2	2	3
W 1963	LA-N	.154	4	13	3	2	0	0	0	0	3	1	0	3
W 1965	LA-N	.214	7	28	2	6	1	0	0	2	1	0	0	3
W 1966	LA-N	.000	2	6	0	0	0	0	0	1	2	0	0	3
W Total	7	.211	39	147	15	31	5	0	2	12	23	9	4	
■ **Barney Gilligan**														
W 1884	Pro-N	.444	3	9	3	4	2	0	0	2	0	1	0	C
■ **Al Gionfriddo**														
W 1947	Bro-N	.000	4	3	2	0	0	0	0	0	1	0	1	O-1
■ **Charles Gipson**														
L 2000	Sea-A	—	2	0	0	0	0	0	0	0	0	0	0	O
■ **Joe Girardi**														
D 1995	Col-N	.125	4	16	0	2	0	0	0	0	0	2	0	C
D 1996	NY-A	.222	4	9	1	2	0	0	0	0	4	1	0	C
D 1997	NY-A	.133	5	15	2	2	0	0	0	0	1	3	0	C
D 1998	NY-A	.429	2	7	0	3	0	0	0	0	0	1	0	C
D 1999	NY-A	.000	2	6	0	0	0	0	0	0	0	1	0	C
D Total	5	.170	17	53	3	9	0	0	0	0	5	8	0	
L 1989	Chi-N	.100	4	10	1	1	0	0	0	0	1	2	0	C
L 1996	NY-A	.250	4	12	1	3	0	1	0	0	1	3	0	C
L 1998	NY-A	.250	3	8	2	2	0	0	0	0	1	0	0	C
L 1999	NY-A	.250	3	8	0	2	0	0	0	0	0	2	0	C
L Total	4	.211	14	38	4	8	0	1	0	0	3	7	0	
W 1996	NY-A	.200	4	10	1	2	0	1	0	1	1	2	0	C
W 1998	NY-A	.000	2	6	0	0	0	0	0	0	0	2	0	C
W 1999	NY-A	.286	2	7	1	2	0	0	0	0	0	1	0	C
W Total	3	.174	8	23	2	4	0	1	0	1	1	5	0	
■ **Dan Gladden**														
L 1987	Min-A	.350	5	20	5	7	2	0	0	5	2	1	0	O
L 1991	Min-A	.261	5	23	4	6	0	0	0	3	1	3	3	O
L Total	2	.302	10	43	9	13	2	0	0	8	3	4	3	
W 1987	Min-A	.290	7	31	3	9	2	1	1	7	3	4	2	O
W 1991	Min-A	.233	7	30	5	7	2	2	0	0	3	4	2	O
W Total	2	.262	14	61	8	16	4	3	1	7	6	8	4	
■ **Bill Gleason**														
W 1885	StL-A	.231	7	26	5	6	2	0	0	1	1	0	0	S
W 1886	StL-A	.208	6	24	3	5	0	0	0	5	1	3	0	S
W 1887	StL-A	.212	13	52	3	11	0	0	0	1	3	2	1	S
W Total	3	.216	26	102	11	22	2	0	0	7	5	5	1	
■ **Kid Gleason**														
T 1894	Bal-N	.200	2	5	0	1	0	1	0	1	0	1	0	P
T 1895	Bal-N	.105	5	19	0	2	0	0	0	0	0	1	0	2
T Total	2	.125	7	24	0	3	0	1	0	1	0	2	0	
■ **Bill Glynn**														
W 1954	Cle-A	.500	2	2	1	1	1	0	0	0	0	1	0	1-1
■ **Mike Goliat**														
W 1950	Phi-N	.214	4	14	1	3	0	0	0	1	1	2	0	2
■ **Chris Gomez**														
D 1996	SD-N	.167	3	12	0	2	0	0	0	1	0	4	0	S
D 1998	SD-N	.273	4	11	1	3	0	0	0	0	4	1	0	S
D Total	2	.217	7	23	1	5	0	0	0	1	4	5	0	
L 1998	SD-N	.150	6	20	2	3	0	0	0	0	2	5	0	S
W 1998	SD-N	.364	4	11	2	4	0	1	0	0	1	1	0	S
■ **Rene Gonzales**														
D 1996	Tex-A	—	1	0	0	0	0	0	0	0	0	0	0	S
L 1991	Tor-A	—	2	0	0	0	0	0	0	0	0	0	0	1-1,S-1
■ **Tony Gonzalez**														
L 1969	Atl-N	.357	3	14	4	5	1	0	1	2	1	4	0	O
■ **Jose Gonzalez**														
L 1988	LA-N	—	5	0	2	0	0	0	0	0	0	0	0	O-4
W 1988	LA-N	.000	4	2	0	0	0	0	0	0	0	2	0	O-3
■ **Juan Gonzalez**														
D 1996	Tex-A	.438	4	16	5	7	0	0	5	9	3	2	0	O
D 1998	Tex-A	.083	3	12	1	1	1	0	0	0	0	3	0	O
D 1999	Tex-A	.182	3	11	1	2	0	0	1	1	1	3	0	O
D Total	3	.256	10	39	7	10	1	0	6	10	4	8	0	
■ **Luis Gonzalez**														
D 1997	Hou-N	.333	3	12	0	4	0	0	0	0	0	1	0	O
D 1999	Ari-N	.200	4	10	3	2	1	0	1	2	5	1	0	O
D Total	2	.273	7	22	3	6	1	0	1	2	5	2	0	
■ **Mike Gonzalez**														
W 1929	Chi-N	.000	2	1	0	0	0	0	0	0	0	1	0	C-1
■ **Orlando Gonzalez**														
L 1978	Phi-N	.000	1	1	0	0	0	0	0	0	0	1	0	H
■ **Pedro Gonzalez**														
W 1964	NY-A	.000	1	1	0	0	0	0	0	0	0	0	0	3
■ **Johnny Gooch**														
W 1925	Pit-N	.000	3	3	0	0	0	0	0	0	0	0	0	C
W 1927	Pit-N	.000	3	5	0	0	0	0	0	0	1	1	0	C
W Total	2	.000	6	8	0	0	0	0	0	0	1	1	0	

YEAR	TM/L	AVG	G	AB	R	H	2B	3B	HR	RBI	BB	SO	SB	POS
■ Ival Goodman														
W 1939	Cin-N	.333	4	15	3	5	1	0	0	1	1	2	1	O
W 1940	Cin-N	.276	7	29	5	8	2	0	0	5	0	3	0	O
W Total	2	.295	11	44	8	13	3	0	0	6	1	5	1	
■ Billy Goodman														
W 1959	Chi-A	.231	5	13	1	3	0	0	0	1	0	5	0	3
■ Ed Goodson														
L 1977	LA-N	.000	1	1	0	0	0	0	0	0	0	0	0	H
W 1977	LA-N	.000	1	1	0	0	0	0	0	0	0	1	0	H
■ Tom Goodwin														
D 1998	Tex-A	.250	2	4	0	1	0	0	0	0	0	1	0	O
D 1999	Tex-A	.143	3	7	0	1	0	0	0	0	0	1	0	O
D Total	2	.182	5	11	0	2	0	0	0	0	0	2	0	
■ Joe Gordon														
W 1938	NY-A	.400	4	15	3	6	2	0	1	6	1	3	1	2
W 1939	NY-A	.143	4	14	1	2	0	0	1	1	0	2	0	2
W 1941	NY-A	.500	5	14	2	7	1	1	1	5	7	0	0	2
W 1942	NY-A	.095	5	21	1	2	1	0	0	0	0	7	0	2
W 1943	NY-A	.235	5	17	2	4	1	0	1	2	3	3	0	2
W 1948	Cle-A	.182	6	22	3	4	0	0	1	2	1	2	1	2
W Total	6	.243	29	103	12	25	5	1	4	16	12	17	2	
■ George Gore														
W 1885	Chi-N	.000	1	3	1	0	0	0	0	0	1	0	0	O
W 1886	Chi-N	.174	6	23	4	4	0	0	1	2	3	3	0	O
W 1888	NY-N	.455	3	11	5	5	1	0	0	0	2	2	2	O-2,3-1
W 1889	NY-N	.333	5	21	5	7	1	1	0	1	3	0	2	O
W Total	4	.276	15	58	15	16	2	1	1	3	9	5	4	
■ Goose Goslin														
W 1924	Was-A	.344	7	32	4	11	1	0	3	7	0	7	0	O
W 1925	Was-A	.308	7	26	6	8	1	0	3	6	3	3	0	O
W 1933	Was-A	.250	5	20	2	5	1	0	1	1	1	3	0	O
W 1934	Det-A	.241	7	29	2	7	1	0	0	2	3	1	0	O
W 1935	Det-A	.273	6	22	2	6	1	0	0	3	5	0	0	O
W Total	5	.287	32	129	16	37	5	0	7	19	12	14	0	
■ Hank Gowdy														
W 1914	Bos-N	.545	4	11	3	6	3	1	1	3	5	1	1	C
W 1923	NY-N	.000	3	4	0	0	0	0	0	0	1	0	0	C-2
W 1924	NY-N	.259	7	27	4	7	0	0	0	1	2	2	0	C
W Total	3	.310	14	42	7	13	3	1	1	4	8	3	1	
■ Johnny Grabowski														
W 1927	NY-A	.000	1	2	0	0	0	0	0	0	0	0	0	C
■ Mark Grace														
D 1998	Chi-N	.083	3	12	0	1	0	0	0	1	0	2	0	1
L 1989	Chi-N	.647	5	17	3	11	3	1	1	8	4	1	1	1
■ Tony Graffanino														
D 1997	Atl-N	.000	3	3	0	0	0	0	0	0	2	1	0	2
D 1998	Atl-N	—	1	0	0	0	0	0	0	0	0	0	0	H
D 2000	Chi-A	—	1	0	0	0	0	0	0	0	0	0	0	3
D Total	3	.000	5	3	0	0	0	0	0	0	2	1	0	
L 1997	Atl-N	.250	3	8	1	2	1	0	0	0	0	3	0	2
L 1998	Atl-N	.333	4	3	2	1	1	0	0	1	2	1	0	2-3
L Total	2	.273	7	11	3	3	2	0	0	1	2	4	0	
■ Jack Graney														
W 1920	Cle-A	.000	3	3	0	0	0	0	0	0	0	2	0	O-2
■ Eddie Grant														
W 1913	NY-N	.000	2	1	1	0	0	0	0	0	0	0	0	H
■ George Grantham														
W 1925	Pit-N	.133	5	15	0	2	0	0	0	0	0	3	1	1-4
W 1927	Pit-N	.364	3	11	0	4	1	0	0	0	1	1	0	2
W Total	2	.231	8	26	0	6	1	0	0	0	1	4	1	
■ Mickey Grasso														
W 1954	Cle-A	—	1	0	0	0	0	0	0	0	0	0	0	C
■ Eli Grba														
W 1960	NY-A	—	1	0	0	0	0	0	0	0	0	0	0	R
■ Craig Grebeck														
L 1993	Chi-A	1.000	1	1	0	1	0	0	0	0	0	0	0	3
■ David Green														
L 1982	StL-N	1.000	2	1	1	1	0	0	0	0	0	0	0	O
W 1982	StL-N	.200	7	10	3	2	1	1	0	0	1	3	0	O-4,D-3
■ Dick Green														
L 1971	Oak-A	.286	3	7	0	2	0	0	0	0	1	1	0	2
L 1972	Oak-A	.125	5	8	0	1	0	0	0	0	0	1	0	2
L 1973	Oak-A	.077	5	13	0	1	1	0	0	1	0	4	0	2
L 1974	Oak-A	.222	4	9	0	2	0	0	0	0	2	1	0	2
L Total	4	.162	17	37	0	6	2	0	0	1	3	6	0	
W 1972	Oak-A	.333	7	18	0	6	2	0	0	1	0	4	0	2
W 1973	Oak-A	.063	7	16	0	1	0	0	0	0	1	6	0	2
W 1974	Oak-A	.000	5	13	1	0	0	0	0	1	1	4	0	2
W Total	3	.149	19	47	1	7	2	0	0	2	2	14	0	
■ Hank Greenberg														
W 1934	Det-A	.321	7	28	4	9	2	1	1	7	4	9	1	1
W 1935	Det-A	.167	2	6	1	1	0	0	1	2	1	0	0	1
W 1940	Det-A	.357	7	28	5	10	2	1	1	6	2	5	0	O

YEAR	TM/L	AVG	G	AB	R	H	2B	3B	HR	RBI	BB	SO	SB	POS
W 1945	Det-A	.304	7	23	7	7	3	0	2	7	6	5	0	O
W Total	4	.318	23	85	17	27	7	2	5	22	13	19	1	
■ Mike Greenwell														
D 1995	Bos-A	.200	3	15	0	3	0	0	0	0	0	1	0	O
L 1986	Bos-A	.500	2	2	0	1	0	0	0	0	0	0	0	H
L 1988	Bos-A	.214	4	14	2	3	1	0	1	3	3	0	0	O
L 1990	Bos-A	.000	4	14	1	0	0	0	0	0	2	2	0	O
L Total	3	.133	10	30	3	4	1	0	1	3	5	2	0	
W 1986	Bos-A	.000	4	3	0	0	0	0	0	0	1	2	0	H
■ Rusty Greer														
D 1996	Tex-A	.125	4	16	2	2	0	0	0	0	3	3	0	O
D 1998	Tex-A	.091	3	11	0	1	0	0	0	0	1	2	0	O
D 1999	Tex-A	.111	3	9	0	1	0	0	0	0	3	1	0	O
D Total	3	.111	10	36	2	4	0	0	0	0	7	6	0	
■ Tommy Gregg														
L 1991	Atl-N	.250	4	4	0	1	0	0	0	0	0	2	0	H
L 1997	Atl-N	.000	4	4	0	0	0	0	0	0	0	1	0	H
L Total	2	.125	8	8	0	1	0	0	0	0	0	3	0	
W 1991	Atl-N	.000	4	3	0	0	0	0	0	0	0	2	0	H
■ Bobby Grich														
L 1973	Bal-A	.100	5	20	1	2	0	0	1	1	2	5	0	2
L 1974	Bal-A	.250	4	16	2	4	1	0	1	2	0	1	0	2
L 1979	Cal-A	.154	4	13	0	2	1	0	0	2	1	1	0	2
L 1982	Cal-A	.200	5	15	1	3	1	0	0	1	2	7	0	2
L 1986	Cal-A	.208	6	24	1	5	0	0	1	3	0	8	0	2-3,1-3
L Total	5	.182	24	88	5	16	3	0	3	9	5	22	0	
■ Ben Grieve														
D 2000	Oak-A	.118	5	17	1	2	0	0	0	2	3	7	0	O
■ Ken Griffey Jr.														
D 1995	Sea-A	.391	5	23	9	9	0	0	5	7	2	4	1	O
D 1997	Sea-A	.133	4	15	0	2	0	0	0	2	1	3	2	O
D Total	2	.289	9	38	9	11	0	0	5	9	3	7	3	
L 1995	Sea-A	.333	6	21	2	7	2	0	1	2	4	4	2	O
■ Ken Griffey Sr.														
L 1973	Cin-N	.143	3	7	0	1	1	0	0	0	0	1	0	O-2
L 1975	Cin-N	.333	3	12	3	4	1	0	0	4	0	3	3	O
L 1976	Cin-N	.385	3	13	2	5	0	1	0	2	2	1	2	O
L Total	3	.313	9	32	5	10	2	1	0	6	2	5	5	
W 1975	Cin-N	.269	7	26	4	7	3	1	0	4	4	2	2	O
W 1976	Cin-N	.059	4	17	2	1	0	0	0	1	0	1	1	O
W Total	2	.186	11	43	6	8	3	1	0	5	4	3	3	
■ Alfredo Griffin														
L 1988	LA-N	.160	7	25	1	4	1	0	0	3	0	5	0	S
L 1992	Tor-A	.000	2	2	0	0	0	0	0	0	0	0	0	S-1
L Total	2	.148	9	27	1	4	1	0	0	3	0	5	0	
W 1988	LA-N	.188	5	16	2	3	0	0	0	0	2	4	0	S
W 1992	Tor-A	—	2	0	0	0	0	0	0	0	0	0	0	S
W 1993	Tor-A	—	3	0	0	0	0	0	0	0	0	0	0	3-2
W Total	3	.188	10	16	2	3	0	0	0	0	2	4	0	
■ Doug Griffin														
W 1975	Bos-A	.000	1	1	0	0	0	0	0	0	0	0	0	H
■ Tommy Griffith														
W 1920	Bro-N	.190	7	21	1	4	2	0	0	3	0	2	0	O
■ Charlie Grimm														
W 1929	Chi-N	.389	5	18	2	7	0	0	1	4	1	2	0	1
W 1932	Chi-N	.333	4	15	2	5	2	0	0	1	2	2	0	1
W Total	2	.364	9	33	4	12	2	0	1	5	3	4	0	
■ Marquis Grissom														
D 1995	Atl-N	.524	4	21	5	11	2	0	3	4	0	3	2	O
D 1996	Atl-N	.083	3	12	2	1	0	0	0	0	1	2	1	O
D 1997	Cle-A	.235	5	17	3	4	0	1	0	0	1	2	0	O
D Total	3	.320	12	50	10	16	2	1	3	4	2	7	3	
L 1995	Atl-N	.263	4	19	2	5	0	1	0	0	1	4	0	O
L 1996	Atl-N	.286	7	35	7	10	1	0	1	3	0	8	2	O
L 1997	Cle-A	.261	6	23	2	6	0	0	1	4	1	9	3	O
L Total	3	.273	17	77	11	21	1	1	2	7	2	21	5	
W 1995	Atl-N	.360	6	25	3	9	1	0	0	1	1	3	3	O
W 1996	Atl-N	.444	6	27	4	12	2	1	0	5	1	2	1	O
W 1997	Cle-A	.360	7	25	5	9	1	0	0	2	4	4	0	O
W Total	3	.390	19	77	12	30	4	1	0	8	6	9	4	
■ Dick Groat														
W 1960	Pit-N	.214	7	28	3	6	2	0	0	2	0	1	0	S
W 1964	StL-N	.192	7	26	3	5	1	1	0	1	4	3	0	S
W Total	2	.204	14	54	6	11	3	1	0	3	4	4	0	
■ Heinie Groh														
W 1919	Cin-N	.172	8	29	6	5	2	0	0	2	6	4	0	3
W 1922	NY-N	.474	5	19	4	9	0	1	0	0	2	1	0	3
W 1923	NY-N	.182	6	22	3	4	0	1	0	2	3	1	0	3
W 1924	NY-N	1.000	1	1	0	1	0	0	0	0	0	0	0	H
W 1927	Pit-N	.000	1	1	0	0	0	0	0	0	0	0	0	H
W Total	5	.264	21	72	13	19	2	2	0	4	11	6	0	
■ Greg Gross														
D 1981	Phi-N	.000	4	4	0	0	0	0	0	0	0	0	0	O-2
L 1980	Phi-N	.750	4	4	2	3	0	0	0	1	0	0	0	O-1
L 1983	Phi-N	.000	4	5	1	0	0	0	0	0	2	2	0	O-3

YEAR	TM/L	AVG	G	AB	R	H	2B	3B	HR	RBI	BB	SO	SB	POS
L Total	2	.333	8	9	3	3	0	0	0	1	2	2	0	
W 1980	Phi-N	.000	4	2	0	0	0	0	0	0	0	0	0	O-3
W 1983	Phi-N	.000	2	6	0	0	0	0	0	0	0	0	0	O
W Total	2	.000	6	8	0	0	0	0	0	0	0	0	0	
■ Wayne Gross														
D 1981	Oak-A	.400	2	5	1	2	0	0	1	3	0	0	0	3-1
L 1981	Oak-A	.000	3	5	0	0	0	0	0	0	0	0	0	3
■ Jerry Grote														
L 1969	NY-N	.167	3	12	3	2	1	0	0	1	1	4	0	C
L 1973	NY-N	.211	5	19	2	4	0	0	0	2	1	3	0	C
L 1977	LA-N	—	2	0	0	0	0	0	0	0	1	0	0	C-1
L 1978	LA-N	—	1	0	0	0	0	0	0	0	0	0	0	C
L Total	4	.194	11	31	5	6	1	0	0	3	3	7	0	
W 1969	NY-N	.211	5	19	1	4	2	0	0	1	1	3	0	C
W 1973	NY-N	.267	7	30	2	8	0	0	0	0	0	1	0	C
W 1977	LA-N	.000	1	1	0	0	0	0	0	0	0	0	0	C
W 1978	LA-N	—	2	0	0	0	0	0	0	0	0	0	0	C
W Total	4	.240	15	50	3	12	2	0	0	1	1	4	0	
■ Johnny Grubb														
L 1984	Det-A	.250	1	4	0	1	1	0	0	2	0	0	0	D
L 1987	Det-A	.571	4	7	0	4	0	0	0	0	0	1	0	D-1
L Total	2	.455	5	11	0	5	1	0	0	2	0	1	0	
W 1984	Det-A	.333	4	3	0	1	0	0	0	0	0	0	0	D-2
■ Kelly Gruber														
L 1989	Tor-A	.294	5	17	2	5	1	0	0	1	3	2	1	3
L 1991	Tor-A	.286	5	21	1	6	1	0	0	4	0	4	1	3
L 1992	Tor-A	.091	6	22	3	2	1	0	1	2	2	3	0	3
L Total	3	.217	16	60	6	13	3	0	1	7	5	9	2	
W 1992	Tor-A	.105	6	19	2	2	0	0	1	1	2	5	1	3
■ Marv Gudat														
W 1932	Chi-N	.000	2	2	0	0	0	0	0	0	0	1	0	H
■ Pedro Guerrero														
D 1981	LA-N	.176	5	17	1	3	1	0	1	1	2	4	1	3
L 1981	LA-N	.105	5	19	1	2	0	0	1	2	1	4	0	O
L 1983	LA-N	.250	4	12	1	3	1	1	0	2	3	3	0	3
L 1985	LA-N	.250	6	20	2	5	1	0	0	4	5	2	2	O
L Total	3	.196	15	51	4	10	2	1	1	8	9	9	2	
W 1981	LA-N	.333	6	21	2	7	1	1	2	7	2	6	0	O
■ Ron Guidry														
L 1976	NY-A	—	1	0	0	0	0	0	0	0	0	0	0	R
L 1977	NY-A	—	2	0	0	0	0	0	0	0	0	0	0	P
L 1978	NY-A	—	1	0	0	0	0	0	0	0	0	0	0	P
L 1980	NY-A	—	1	0	0	0	0	0	0	0	0	0	0	P
L Total	4	—	5	0	0	0	0	0	0	0	0	0	0	
■ Carlos Guillen														
D 2000	Sea-A	1.000	1	1	0	1	0	0	0	1	0	0	0	H
L 2000	Sea-A	.200	2	5	1	1	0	0	1	2	2	2	0	3
■ Ozzie Guillen														
D 1998	Atl-N	.000	1	1	0	0	0	0	0	0	0	0	0	H
D 1999	Atl-N	.000	1	1	0	0	0	0	0	0	0	0	0	H
D Total	2	.000	2	2	0	0	0	0	0	0	0	0	0	
L 1993	Chi-A	.273	6	22	4	6	1	0	0	2	0	2	1	S
L 1998	Atl-N	.417	4	12	1	5	0	0	0	1	0	1	0	S-3
L 1999	Atl-N	.333	3	3	0	1	0	0	0	1	0	0	0	S-2
L Total	3	.324	13	37	5	12	1	0	0	4	0	3	1	
W 1999	Atl-N	.000	3	5	0	0	0	0	0	0	0	1	0	S-1,D-1
■ Ricky Gutierrez														
D 1997	Hou-N	.125	3	8	0	1	0	0	0	0	2	1	0	S
D 1998	Hou-N	.300	4	10	1	3	0	0	0	0	3	7	1	S
D 1999	Hou-N	.000	3	10	0	0	0	0	0	0	2	5	0	S
D Total	3	.143	10	28	1	4	0	0	0	0	7	13	1	
■ Don Gutteridge														
W 1944	StL-A	.143	6	21	1	3	1	0	0	0	3	5	0	2
W 1946	Bos-A	.400	3	5	1	2	0	0	0	1	0	0	0	2-2
W Total	2	.192	9	26	2	5	1	0	0	1	3	5	0	
■ Tony Gwynn														
D 1996	SD-N	.308	3	13	0	4	1	0	0	1	0	2	1	O
D 1998	SD-N	.200	4	15	1	3	2	0	0	2	0	2	0	O
D Total	2	.250	7	28	1	7	3	0	0	3	0	4	1	
L 1984	SD-N	.368	5	19	6	7	3	0	0	3	1	2	0	O
L 1998	SD-N	.231	6	26	1	6	1	0	0	2	1	2	0	O
L Total	2	.289	11	45	7	13	4	0	0	5	2	4	0	
W 1984	SD-N	.263	5	19	1	5	0	0	0	0	3	2	1	O
W 1998	SD-N	.500	4	16	2	8	0	0	1	3	1	0	0	O
W Total	2	.371	9	35	3	13	0	0	1	3	4	2	1	
■ Chris Gwynn														
D 1995	LA-N	.000	1	1	0	0	0	0	0	0	0	1	0	H
D 1996	SD-N	1.000	2	2	1	2	0	0	0	0	0	0	0	H
D Total	2	.667	3	3	1	2	0	0	0	0	0	1	0	
■ Mule Haas														
W 1929	Phi-A	.238	5	21	3	5	0	0	2	6	1	3	0	O
W 1930	Phi-A	.111	6	18	1	2	0	1	0	1	1	3	0	O
W 1931	Phi-A	.130	7	23	1	3	1	0	0	2	3	5	0	O
W Total	3	.161	18	62	5	10	1	1	2	9	5	11	0	

YEAR	TM/L	AVG	G	AB	R	H	2B	3B	HR	RBI	BB	SO	SB	POS
■ Stan Hack														
W 1932	Chi-N	—	1	0	0	0	0	0	0	0	0	0	0	H
W 1935	Chi-N	.227	6	22	2	5	1	1	0	0	2	2	1	3-6,S-1
W 1938	Chi-N	.471	4	17	3	8	1	0	0	1	1	2	0	3
W 1945	Chi-N	.367	7	30	1	11	3	0	0	4	4	2	0	3
W Total	4	.348	18	69	6	24	5	1	0	5	7	6	1	
■ Chick Hafey														
W 1926	StL-N	.185	7	27	2	5	2	0	0	0	0	7	0	O
W 1928	StL-N	.200	4	15	0	3	0	0	0	0	1	4	0	O
W 1930	StL-N	.273	6	22	2	6	5	0	0	2	1	3	0	O
W 1931	StL-N	.167	6	24	1	4	0	0	0	0	0	5	1	O
W Total	4	.205	23	88	5	18	7	0	0	2	2	19	1	
■ Joe Hague														
L 1972	Cin-N	.000	3	1	0	0	0	0	0	0	2	1	0	H
W 1972	Cin-N	.000	3	3	0	0	0	0	0	0	0	0	0	O-1
■ Don Hahn														
L 1973	NY-N	.235	5	17	2	4	0	0	0	1	2	4	0	O
W 1973	NY-N	.241	7	29	2	7	1	1	0	2	1	6	0	O
■ Ed Hahn														
W 1906	Chi-A	.273	6	22	4	6	0	0	0	0	1	1	0	O
■ Hinkey Haines														
W 1923	NY-A	.000	2	1	1	0	0	0	0	0	0	0	0	O
■ Jerry Hairston Sr.														
L 1983	Chi-A	.000	2	3	0	0	0	0	0	0	1	1	0	O
■ Jimmie Hall														
W 1965	Min-A	.143	2	7	0	1	0	0	0	0	1	5	0	O
■ Tom Haller														
L 1972	Det-A	.000	1	1	0	0	0	0	0	0	0	0	0	H
W 1962	SF-N	.286	4	14	1	4	1	0	1	3	0	2	0	C
■ Charlie Hamburg														
W 1890	Lou-A	.269	7	26	3	7	1	0	0	2	0	3	0	O
■ Darryl Hamilton														
D 1996	Tex-A	.158	4	19	0	3	0	0	0	0	0	2	0	O
D 1997	SF-N	.000	2	5	1	0	0	0	0	0	0	1	0	O
D 1999	NY-N	.125	4	8	0	1	0	0	0	2	2	0	0	O
D 2000	NY-N	.500	3	4	1	2	1	0	0	0	1	1	0	O-2
D Total	4	.167	13	36	2	6	1	0	0	2	3	4	0	
L 1999	NY-N	.353	5	17	0	6	1	0	0	2	0	4	0	O
L 2000	NY-N	.000	3	2	0	0	0	0	0	0	0	0	0	H
L Total	2	.316	8	19	0	6	1	0	0	2	0	4	0	
W 2000	NY-N	.000	4	3	0	0	0	0	0	0	0	2	0	H
■ Jeff Hamilton														
L 1988	LA-N	.217	7	23	2	5	0	0	0	1	3	4	0	3
W 1988	LA-N	.105	5	19	1	2	0	0	0	0	1	4	0	3
■ Billy Hamilton														
T 1897	Bos-N	.500	4	16	6	8	1	0	0	2	5	3	2	O
■ Jeffrey Hammonds														
D 1997	Bal-A	.100	4	10	3	1	1	0	0	2	2	2	1	O
L 1997	Bal-A	.000	5	3	0	0	0	0	0	0	1	2	1	O-4
■ Granny Hamner														
W 1950	Phi-N	.429	4	14	1	6	2	1	0	0	1	2	1	S
■ Harry Hanebrink														
W 1958	Mil-N	.000	2	2	0	0	0	0	0	0	0	0	0	H
■ Larry Haney														
W 1974	Oak-A	—	2	0	0	0	0	0	0	0	0	0	0	C
■ Ned Hanlon														
W 1887	Det-N	.291	15	55	5	16	1	1	0	4	5	1	7	O
■ Dave Hansen														
D 1995	LA-N	.667	3	3	0	2	0	0	0	0	0	0	0	H
D 1996	LA-N	.000	2	2	0	0	0	0	0	0	0	0	0	H
D Total	2	.400	5	5	0	2	0	0	0	0	0	0	0	
■ Larry Harlow														
L 1979	Cal-A	.125	3	8	0	1	1	0	0	1	1	2	0	O-2
■ Terry Harmon														
L 1976	Phi-N	—	1	0	1	0	0	0	0	0	0	0	0	R
■ Brian Harper														
L 1985	StL-N	.000	1	1	0	0	0	0	0	0	0	0	0	H
L 1991	Min-A	.278	5	18	1	5	2	0	0	1	0	2	0	C
L Total	2	.263	6	19	1	5	2	0	0	1	0	2	0	
W 1985	StL-N	.250	4	4	0	1	0	0	0	1	0	1	0	H
W 1991	Min-A	.381	7	21	2	8	2	0	0	1	2	2	0	C
W Total	2	.360	11	25	2	9	2	0	0	2	2	3	0	
■ George Harper														
W 1928	StL-N	.111	3	9	1	1	0	0	0	0	2	2	0	O
■ Terry Harper														
L 1982	Atl-N	.000	1	1	1	0	0	0	0	0	0	0	0	O
■ Tommy Harper														
L 1975	Oak-A	—	1	0	0	0	0	0	0	0	1	0	0	H
■ Bud Harrelson														
L 1969	NY-N	.182	3	11	2	2	1	1	0	3	1	2	0	S

YEAR	TM/L	AVG	G	AB	R	H	2B	3B	HR	RBI	BB	SO	SB	POS
L 1973	NY-N	.167	5	18	1	3	0	0	0	2	1	1	0	S
L Total	2	.172	8	29	3	5	1	1	0	5	2	3	0	
W 1969	NY-N	.176	5	17	1	3	0	0	0	0	3	4	0	S
W 1973	NY-N	.250	7	24	2	6	1	0	0	1	5	3	0	S
W Total	2	.220	12	41	3	9	1	0	0	1	8	7	0	
■ Ken Harrelson														
W 1967	Bos-A	.077	4	13	0	1	0	0	0	1	1	3	0	O
■ Dave Harris														
W 1933	Was-A	.000	3	2	0	0	0	0	0	0	2	0	0	O-1
■ Joe Harris														
W 1925	Was-A	.440	7	25	5	11	2	0	3	6	3	4	0	O
W 1927	Pit-N	.200	4	15	0	3	0	0	0	1	0	0	0	1
W Total	2	.350	11	40	5	14	2	0	3	7	3	4	0	
■ Lenny Harris														
D 1999	Ari-N	.000	2	2	0	0	0	0	0	0	0	0	0	3-1
D 2000	NY-N	.000	2	2	1	0	0	0	0	0	0	0	1	H
D Total	2	.000	4	4	1	0	0	0	0	0	0	0	1	
L 1995	Cin-N	1.000	3	2	0	2	0	0	0	1	0	0	1	H
L 2000	NY-N	.000	2	1	0	0	0	0	0	0	0	1	0	H
L Total	2	.667	5	3	0	2	0	0	0	1	0	1	1	
W 2000	NY-N	.000	3	4	1	0	0	0	0	0	1	1	0	D-1
■ Bucky Harris														
W 1924	Was-A	.333	7	33	5	11	0	0	2	7	1	4	0	2
W 1925	Was-A	.087	7	23	2	2	0	0	0	0	1	3	0	2
W Total	2	.232	14	56	7	13	0	0	2	7	2	7	0	
■ Jim Ray Hart														
L 1971	SF-N	.000	3	5	0	0	0	0	0	0	0	2	0	3-1
■ Gabby Hartnett														
W 1929	Chi-N	.000	3	3	0	0	0	0	0	0	0	3	0	H
W 1932	Chi-N	.313	4	16	2	5	2	0	1	1	1	3	0	C
W 1935	Chi-N	.292	6	24	1	7	0	0	1	2	0	3	0	C
W 1938	Chi-N	.091	3	11	0	1	0	1	0	0	0	2	0	C
W Total	4	.241	16	54	3	13	2	1	2	3	1	11	0	
■ Topsy Hartsel														
W 1905	Phi-A	.294	5	17	1	5	1	0	0	0	2	1	2	O
W 1910	Phi-A	.200	1	5	2	1	0	0	0	0	0	1	2	O
W Total	2	.273	6	22	3	6	1	0	0	0	2	2	4	
■ Clint Hartung														
W 1951	NY-N	.000	2	4	0	0	0	0	0	0	0	0	0	O
■ Bill Haselman														
D 1995	Bos-A	.000	1	2	0	0	0	0	0	0	0	0	0	C
■ Buddy Hassett														
W 1942	NY-A	.333	3	9	1	3	1	0	0	2	0	1	0	1
■ Ron Hassey														
L 1988	Oak-A	.500	4	8	2	4	1	0	1	3	1	1	0	C
L 1989	Oak-A	.167	2	6	0	1	0	0	0	1	1	2	0	C
L 1990	Oak-A	.333	2	3	0	1	0	0	0	0	2	0	0	C-1,D-1
L Total	3	.353	8	17	2	6	1	0	1	4	4	3	0	
W 1988	Oak-A	.250	5	8	0	2	0	0	0	1	3	3	0	C-4
W 1990	Oak-A	.333	3	6	0	2	0	0	0	1	0	0	0	C-1
W Total	2	.286	8	14	0	4	0	0	0	2	3	3	0	
■ Mickey Hatcher														
L 1988	LA-N	.238	6	21	4	5	2	0	0	3	3	0	0	1-6,O-1
W 1988	LA-N	.368	5	19	5	7	1	0	2	5	1	3	0	O
■ Billy Hatcher														
L 1986	Hou-N	.280	6	25	4	7	0	0	1	2	3	2	3	O
L 1990	Cin-N	.333	4	15	2	5	1	0	1	2	0	2	0	O
L Total	2	.300	10	40	6	12	1	0	2	4	3	4	3	
W 1990	Cin-N	.750	4	12	6	9	4	1	0	2	2	0	0	O
■ Scott Hatteberg														
D 1998	Bos-A	.111	3	9	0	1	0	0	0	0	3	1	0	C
D 1999	Bos-A	1.000	1	1	1	1	0	0	0	1	0	0	0	C
D Total	2	.200	4	10	1	2	0	0	0	1	3	1	0	
L 1999	Bos-A	.000	3	1	0	0	0	0	0	0	0	1	0	C-1
■ Charlie Hayes														
D 1996	NY-A	.200	3	5	0	1	0	0	0	1	0	0	0	3-2
D 1997	NY-A	.333	5	15	0	5	0	0	0	1	0	2	0	3-5,2-1
D Total	2	.300	8	20	0	6	0	0	0	2	0	2	0	
L 1996	NY-A	.143	4	7	0	1	0	0	0	0	2	2	0	3-2,D-1
W 1996	NY-A	.188	5	16	2	3	0	0	0	1	1	5	0	3-4,1-1
■ Von Hayes														
L 1983	Phi-N	.000	2	2	0	0	0	0	0	0	0	0	0	O-1
W 1983	Phi-N	.000	4	3	0	0	0	0	0	0	0	1	0	O-1
■ Red Hayworth														
W 1944	StL-A	.118	6	17	1	2	1	0	0	1	3	1	0	C
■ Ray Hayworth														
W 1934	Det-A	—	1	0	0	0	0	0	0	0	0	0	0	C
■ Bob Hazle														
W 1957	Mil-N	.154	4	13	2	2	0	0	0	0	1	2	0	O
■ Jeff Hearron														
L 1985	Tor-A	—	2	0	0	0	0	0	0	0	0	0	0	C

YEAR	TM/L	AVG	G	AB	R	H	2B	3B	HR	RBI	BB	SO	SB	POS
■ Mike Heath														
D 1981	Oak-A	.000	2	8	0	0	0	0	0	0	0	1	0	C
L 1981	Oak-A	.333	3	6	1	2	0	0	0	0	0	1	0	C-2,O-1
L 1987	Det-A	.286	3	7	1	2	0	0	1	2	0	0	0	C
L Total	2	.308	6	13	2	4	0	0	1	2	0	1	0	
W 1978	NY-A	—	1	0	0	0	0	0	0	0	0	0	0	C
■ Cliff Heathcote														
W 1929	Chi-N	.000	2	1	0	0	0	0	0	0	0	0	0	H
■ Richie Hebner														
L 1970	Pit-N	.667	2	6	0	4	2	0	0	0	2	1	0	3
L 1971	Pit-N	.294	4	17	3	5	1	0	2	4	0	4	0	3
L 1972	Pit-N	.188	5	16	2	3	1	0	0	1	1	3	0	3
L 1974	Pit-N	.231	4	13	1	3	0	0	1	4	1	4	0	3
L 1975	Pit-N	.333	3	12	2	4	1	0	0	2	1	1	0	3
L 1977	Phi-N	.357	4	14	2	5	2	0	0	0	0	1	0	1-3
L 1978	Phi-N	.111	3	9	0	1	0	0	0	1	0	0	0	1-2
L 1984	Chi-N	.000	2	1	0	0	0	0	0	0	0	0	0	H
L Total	8	.284	27	88	10	25	7	0	3	12	5	14	0	
W 1971	Pit-N	.167	3	12	2	2	0	0	1	3	3	3	0	3
■ Danny Heep														
L 1980	Hou-N	.000	1	1	0	0	0	0	0	0	0	0	0	H
L 1986	NY-N	.250	5	4	0	1	0	0	0	1	0	2	0	O-1
L 1988	LA-N	.000	3	1	0	0	0	0	0	0	1	1	0	H
L 1990	Bos-A	.000	2	2	0	0	0	0	0	0	0	0	0	H
L Total	4	.125	11	8	0	1	0	0	0	1	1	3	0	
W 1986	NY-N	.091	5	11	0	1	0	0	0	2	1	1	0	D-2,O-1
W 1988	LA-N	.250	3	8	0	2	1	0	0	0	0	2	0	O-1,D-1
W Total	2	.158	8	19	0	3	1	0	0	2	1	3	0	
■ Jim Hegan														
W 1948	Cle-A	.211	6	19	2	4	0	0	1	5	1	4	1	C
W 1954	Cle-A	.154	4	13	1	2	1	0	0	0	1	1	0	C
W Total	2	.188	10	32	3	6	1	0	1	5	2	5	1	
■ Mike Hegan														
L 1971	Oak-A	.000	1	1	0	0	0	0	0	0	0	1	0	H
L 1972	Oak-A	.000	3	1	1	0	0	0	0	0	0	0	0	1-1
L Total	2	.000	4	2	1	0	0	0	0	0	0	1	0	
W 1964	NY-A	.000	3	1	1	0	0	0	0	0	1	1	0	H
W 1972	Oak-A	.200	6	5	0	1	0	0	0	0	0	2	0	1-5
W Total	2	.167	9	6	1	1	0	0	0	0	1	3	0	
■ Tommy Helms														
L 1970	Cin-N	.273	3	11	0	3	0	0	0	0	0	1	0	2
W 1970	Cin-N	.222	5	18	1	4	0	0	0	0	1	1	0	2
■ Rollie Hemsley														
W 1932	Chi-N	.000	3	3	0	0	0	0	0	0	0	3	0	C-1
■ Dave Henderson														
L 1986	Bos-A	.111	5	9	3	1	0	0	1	4	2	2	0	O
L 1988	Oak-A	.375	4	16	2	6	1	0	1	4	1	7	0	O
L 1989	Oak-A	.263	5	19	4	5	3	0	1	1	2	5	0	O
L 1990	Oak-A	.167	2	6	0	1	0	0	0	1	0	2	1	O
L Total	4	.260	16	50	9	13	4	0	3	10	5	16	1	
W 1986	Bos-A	.400	7	25	6	10	1	1	2	5	2	6	0	O
W 1988	Oak-A	.300	5	20	1	6	2	0	0	1	2	7	0	O
W 1989	Oak-A	.308	4	13	6	4	2	0	2	4	4	3	0	O
W 1990	Oak-A	.231	4	13	2	3	1	0	0	0	1	3	0	O-3
W Total	4	.324	20	71	15	23	6	1	4	10	9	19	0	
■ Ken Henderson														
L 1971	SF-N	.313	4	16	3	5	1	0	0	2	2	1	1	O
■ Rickey Henderson														
D 1981	Oak-A	.182	3	11	3	2	0	0	0	0	2	0	2	O
D 1996	SD-N	.333	3	12	2	4	0	0	1	1	2	3	0	O
D 1999	NY-N	.400	4	15	5	6	0	0	0	1	3	1	6	O
D 2000	Sea-A	.400	3	5	3	2	0	0	0	0	1	0	1	O-2
D Total	4	.326	13	43	13	14	0	0	1	2	8	4	9	
L 1981	Oak-A	.364	3	11	0	4	2	1	0	1	1	2	2	O
L 1989	Oak-A	.400	5	15	8	6	1	1	2	5	7	0	8	O
L 1990	Oak-A	.294	4	17	1	5	0	0	0	3	1	2	2	O
L 1992	Oak-A	.261	6	23	5	6	0	0	0	1	4	4	2	O
L 1993	Tor-A	.120	6	25	4	3	2	0	0	0	4	5	2	O
L 1999	NY-N	.174	6	23	2	4	1	0	0	1	0	5	1	O
L 2000	Sea-A	.222	3	9	2	2	1	0	0	1	2	2	0	O
L Total	7	.244	33	123	22	30	7	2	2	12	19	20	17	
W 1989	Oak-A	.474	4	19	4	9	1	2	1	3	2	2	3	O
W 1990	Oak-A	.333	4	15	2	5	2	0	1	1	3	4	3	O
W 1993	Tor-A	.227	6	22	6	5	2	0	0	2	5	2	1	O
W Total	3	.339	14	56	12	19	5	2	2	6	10	8	7	
■ George Hendrick														
L 1972	Oak-A	.143	5	7	2	1	0	0	0	0	0	1	0	O-1
L 1982	StL-N	.308	3	13	2	4	0	0	0	2	1	2	0	O
L 1986	Cal-A	.083	3	12	0	1	0	0	0	0	0	2	0	O-2,1-1
L Total	3	.188	11	32	4	6	0	0	0	2	1	5	0	
W 1972	Oak-A	.133	5	15	3	2	0	0	0	0	1	2	0	O
W 1982	StL-N	.321	7	28	5	9	0	0	0	5	2	2	0	O
W Total	2	.256	12	43	8	11	0	0	0	5	3	4	0	
■ Harvey Hendrick														
W 1923	NY-A	.000	1	1	0	0	0	0	0	0	0	0	0	H

YEAR	TM/L	AVG	G	AB	R	H	2B	3B	HR	RBI	BB	SO	SB	POS
■ Ellie Hendricks														
L 1969	Bal-A	.250	3	8	2	2	2	0	0	3	1	2	0	C
L 1970	Bal-A	.400	1	5	2	2	0	0	0	0	0	1	0	C
L 1971	Bal-A	.500	2	4	1	2	0	0	1	2	1	1	0	C
L 1974	Bal-A	.167	3	6	1	1	0	0	0	0	1	3	0	C
L 1976	NY-A	1.000	1	1	0	1	0	0	0	0	0	0	0	H
L Total	5	.333	10	24	6	8	2	0	1	5	3	7	0	
W 1969	Bal-A	.100	3	10	1	1	0	0	0	0	1	0	0	C
W 1970	Bal-A	.364	3	11	1	4	1	0	1	4	1	2	0	C
W 1971	Bal-A	.263	6	19	3	5	1	0	0	1	3	3	0	C
W 1976	NY-A	.000	2	2	0	0	0	0	0	0	0	0	0	H
W Total	4	.238	14	42	5	10	2	0	1	5	5	5	0	
■ Tommy Henrich														
W 1938	NY-A	.250	4	16	3	4	1	0	1	1	0	1	0	O
W 1941	NY-A	.167	5	18	4	3	1	0	1	1	3	3	0	O
W 1947	NY-A	.323	7	31	2	10	2	0	1	5	2	3	0	O
W 1949	NY-A	.263	5	19	4	5	0	0	1	1	3	0	0	1
W Total	4	.262	21	84	13	22	4	0	4	8	8	7	0	
■ Olaf Henriksen														
W 1912	Bos-A	1.000	2	1	0	1	1	0	0	1	0	0	0	H
W 1915	Bos-A	.000	2	2	0	0	0	0	0	0	0	0	0	H
W 1916	Bos-A	—	1	0	1	0	0	0	0	0	1	0	0	H
W Total	3	.333	5	3	1	1	1	0	0	1	1	0	0	
■ Billy Herman														
W 1932	Chi-N	.222	4	18	5	4	1	0	0	1	1	3	0	2
W 1935	Chi-N	.333	6	24	3	8	2	1	1	6	0	2	0	2
W 1938	Chi-N	.188	4	16	1	3	0	0	0	0	1	4	0	2
W 1941	Bro-N	.125	4	8	0	1	0	0	0	0	2	0	0	2
W Total	4	.242	18	66	9	16	3	1	1	7	4	9	0	
■ Gene Hermanski														
W 1947	Bro-N	.158	7	19	4	3	0	1	0	1	3	3	0	O
W 1949	Bro-N	.308	4	13	1	4	0	1	0	2	3	3	0	O
W Total	2	.219	11	32	5	7	0	2	0	3	6	6	0	
■ Carlos Hernandez														
D 1998	SD-N	.417	4	12	0	5	0	0	0	0	0	0	0	C
D 2000	StL-N	.273	3	11	3	3	0	0	1	1	1	2	0	C
D Total	2	.348	7	23	3	8	0	0	1	1	1	2	0	
L 1998	SD-N	.333	6	18	2	6	2	0	0	0	1	5	0	C
L 2000	StL-N	.250	5	16	3	4	0	0	0	1	1	1	0	C
L Total	2	.294	11	34	5	10	2	0	0	1	2	6	0	
W 1998	SD-N	.200	4	10	0	2	0	0	0	0	0	3	0	C
■ Jackie Hernandez														
L 1971	Pit-N	.231	4	13	2	3	0	0	0	1	0	4	0	S
W 1971	Pit-N	.222	7	18	2	4	0	0	0	1	2	5	1	S
■ Jose Hernandez														
D 1998	Chi-N	.286	2	7	1	2	0	0	0	0	0	2	0	S
D 1999	Atl-N	.091	4	11	1	1	0	0	0	0	1	3	1	S
D Total	2	.167	6	18	2	3	0	0	0	0	1	5	1	
L 1999	Atl-N	.500	2	2	0	1	0	0	0	2	0	1	0	H
W 1999	Atl-N	.200	2	5	0	1	1	0	0	2	0	2	1	S-1,D-1
■ Keith Hernandez														
L 1982	StL-N	.333	3	12	3	4	0	0	0	1	2	3	0	1
L 1986	NY-N	.269	6	26	3	7	1	1	0	3	3	6	0	1
L 1988	NY-N	.269	7	26	2	7	0	0	1	5	6	7	1	1
L Total	3	.281	16	64	8	18	1	1	1	9	11	16	1	
W 1982	StL-N	.259	7	27	4	7	2	0	1	8	4	2	0	1
W 1986	NY-N	.231	7	26	1	6	0	0	0	4	5	1	0	1
W Total	2	.245	14	53	5	13	2	0	1	12	9	3	0	
■ Ramon Hernandez														
D 2000	Oak-A	.375	5	16	3	6	2	0	0	3	0	3	0	C
■ Larry Herndon														
L 1984	Det-A	.200	2	5	1	1	0	0	1	1	1	2	0	O
L 1987	Det-A	.333	3	9	1	3	1	0	0	2	1	1	0	O-2,D-1
L Total	2	.286	5	14	2	4	1	0	1	3	2	3	0	
W 1984	Det-A	.333	5	15	1	5	0	0	1	3	3	2	0	O
■ Ed Herr														
W 1888	StL-A	.091	3	11	2	1	0	0	0	0	0	5	1	O
■ Tom Herr														
L 1982	StL-N	.231	3	13	1	3	1	0	0	0	1	2	0	2
L 1985	StL-N	.333	6	21	2	7	4	0	1	6	5	2	1	2
L 1987	StL-N	.222	7	27	0	6	0	0	0	3	0	1	1	2
L Total	3	.262	16	61	3	16	5	0	1	9	6	5	2	
W 1982	StL-N	.160	7	25	2	4	2	0	0	5	3	3	0	2
W 1985	StL-N	.154	7	26	2	4	2	0	0	0	2	2	0	2
W 1987	StL-N	.250	7	28	2	7	0	0	1	1	2	2	0	2
W Total	3	.190	21	79	6	15	4	0	1	6	7	7	0	
■ Willard Hershberger														
W 1939	Cin-N	.500	3	2	0	1	0	0	0	1	0	0	0	C-2
■ Buck Herzog														
W 1911	NY-N	.190	6	21	3	4	2	0	0	0	2	3	2	3
W 1912	NY-N	.400	8	30	6	12	4	1	0	5	1	3	2	3
W 1913	NY-N	.053	5	19	1	1	0	0	0	0	0	1	0	3
W 1917	NY-N	.250	6	24	1	6	0	1	0	2	0	4	0	2
W Total	4	.245	25	94	11	23	6	2	0	7	3	11	4	

YEAR	TM/L	AVG	G	AB	R	H	2B	3B	HR	RBI	BB	SO	SB	POS
■ Johnnie Heving														
W 1931	Phi-A	.000	1	1	0	0	0	0	0	0	0	0	0	H
■ Richard Hidalgo														
D 1997	Hou-N	.000	2	5	1	0	0	0	0	0	1	2	0	O
D 1998	Hou-N	.250	1	4	0	1	0	0	0	0	0	1	0	O
D Total	2	.111	3	9	1	1	0	0	0	0	1	3	0	
■ Pinky Higgins														
W 1940	Det-A	.333	7	24	2	8	3	1	1	6	3	3	0	3
W 1946	Bos-A	.208	7	24	1	5	1	0	0	2	2	0	0	3
W Total	2	.271	14	48	3	13	4	1	1	8	5	3	0	
■ Andy High														
W 1928	StL-N	.294	4	17	1	5	2	0	0	1	1	3	0	3
W 1930	StL-N	.500	1	2	1	1	0	0	0	0	0	0	0	3
W 1931	StL-N	.267	4	15	3	4	0	0	0	0	0	2	0	3
W Total	3	.294	9	34	5	10	2	0	0	1	1	5	0	
■ Glenallen Hill														
D 1997	SF-N	.000	3	7	0	0	0	0	0	0	2	2	0	O-2
D 1998	Chi-N	.333	1	3	0	1	0	0	0	0	1	2	1	O
D 2000	NY-A	.083	4	12	1	1	0	0	0	2	1	5	0	D-3
D Total	3	.091	8	22	1	2	0	0	0	2	4	9	1	
L 2000	NY-A	.000	2	2	0	0	0	0	0	0	0	2	0	H
W 2000	NY-A	.000	3	3	0	0	0	0	0	0	0	0	0	D-1
■ Chuck Hiller														
W 1962	SF-N	.269	7	26	4	7	3	0	1	5	3	4	0	2
■ Paul Hines														
W 1884	Pro-N	.250	3	8	5	2	0	0	0	1	3	0	2	O
■ Myril Hoag														
W 1932	NY-A	—	1	0	1	0	0	0	0	0	0	0	0	R
W 1937	NY-A	.300	5	20	4	6	1	0	1	2	0	1	0	O
W 1938	NY-A	.400	2	5	3	2	1	0	0	1	0	0	0	O-1
W Total	3	.320	8	25	8	8	2	0	1	3	0	1	0	
■ Don Hoak														
W 1955	Bro-N	.333	3	3	0	1	0	0	0	0	2	0	0	3-1
W 1960	Pit-N	.217	7	23	3	5	2	0	0	3	4	1	0	3
W Total	2	.231	10	26	3	6	2	0	0	3	6	1	0	
■ Dick Hoblitzel														
W 1915	Bos-A	.313	5	16	1	5	0	0	0	1	0	1	1	1
W 1916	Bos-A	.235	5	17	3	4	1	1	0	2	6	0	0	1
W Total	2	.273	10	33	4	9	1	1	0	3	6	1	1	
■ Gil Hodges														
W 1947	Bro-N	.000	1	1	0	0	0	0	0	0	0	1	0	H
W 1949	Bro-N	.235	5	17	2	4	0	0	1	4	1	4	0	1
W 1952	Bro-N	.000	7	21	1	0	0	0	0	1	5	6	0	1
W 1953	Bro-N	.364	6	22	3	8	0	0	1	1	3	3	1	1
W 1955	Bro-N	.292	7	24	2	7	0	0	1	5	3	2	0	1
W 1956	Bro-N	.304	7	23	5	7	2	0	1	8	4	4	0	1
W 1959	LA-N	.391	6	23	2	9	0	1	1	2	1	2	0	1
W Total	7	.267	39	131	15	35	2	1	5	21	17	22	1	
■ Ron Hodges														
W 1973	NY-N	—	1	0	0	0	0	0	0	0	1	0	0	H
■ Danny Hoffman														
W 1905	Phi-A	.000	1	1	0	0	0	0	0	0	0	1	0	H
■ Solly Hofman														
W 1906	Chi-N	.304	6	23	3	7	1	0	0	2	3	5	1	O
W 1908	Chi-N	.316	5	19	2	6	0	1	0	4	1	4	2	O
W 1910	Chi-N	.267	5	15	2	4	0	0	0	2	4	3	0	O
W Total	3	.298	16	57	7	17	1	1	0	8	8	12	3	
■ Fred Hofmann														
W 1923	NY-A	.000	2	1	0	0	0	0	0	0	1	0	0	H
■ Chris Hoiles														
D 1996	Bal-A	.143	4	7	1	1	0	0	0	0	3	3	0	C
D 1997	Bal-A	.143	3	7	1	1	0	0	1	1	2	1	0	C
D Total	2	.143	7	14	2	2	0	0	1	1	5	4	0	
L 1996	Bal-A	.167	4	12	1	2	0	0	1	2	1	3	0	C
L 1997	Bal-A	.143	4	14	1	2	0	0	0	0	2	5	0	C
L Total	2	.154	8	26	2	4	0	0	1	2	3	8	0	
■ Bill Holbert														
W 1884	NY-A	.000	1	2	0	0	0	0	0	0	0	1	0	C
■ Walter Holke														
W 1917	NY-N	.286	6	21	2	6	2	0	0	1	0	6	0	1
■ Todd Hollandsworth														
D 1995	LA-N	.000	2	2	0	0	0	0	0	0	0	0	0	O
D 1996	LA-N	.333	3	12	1	4	3	0	0	1	0	3	0	O
D Total	2	.286	5	14	1	4	3	0	0	1	0	3	0	
■ Bug Holliday														
W 1885	Chi-N	.000	1	4	0	0	0	0	0	0	0	0	0	O
■ Dave Hollins														
L 1993	Phi-N	.200	6	20	2	4	1	0	2	4	5	4	1	3
W 1993	Phi-N	.261	6	23	5	6	1	0	0	2	6	5	0	3
■ Charlie Hollocher														
W 1918	Chi-N	.190	6	21	2	4	0	1	0	1	1	1	1	S

YEAR	TM/L	AVG	G	AB	R	H	2B	3B	HR	RBI	BB	SO	SB	POS
■ **Wattie Holm**														
W 1926	StL-N	.125	5	16	1	2	0	0	0	1	1	2	0	O-4
W 1928	StL-N	.167	3	6	0	1	0	0	0	1	0	1	0	O-1
W Total 2		.136	8	22	1	3	0	0	0	2	1	3	0	
■ **Tommy Holmes**														
W 1948	Bos-N	.192	6	26	3	5	0	0	0	1	0	0	0	O
W 1952	Bro-N	.000	3	1	0	0	0	0	0	0	0	0	0	O
W Total 2		.185	9	27	3	5	0	0	0	1	0	0	0	
■ **Jim Holt**														
L 1970	Min-A	.000	3	5	0	0	0	0	0	0	0	2	0	O
L 1974	Oak-A	—	2	0	0	0	0	0	0	0	1	0	0	1-1
L 1975	Oak-A	.333	3	3	0	1	1	0	0	0	0	0	0	1-1
L Total 3		.125	8	8	0	1	1	0	0	0	1	2	0	
W 1974	Oak-A	.667	4	3	0	2	0	0	0	2	0	0	0	1-1
■ **Don Hood**														
L 1973	Bal-A	—	1	0	0	0	0	0	0	0	0	0	0	R
■ **Harry Hooper**														
W 1912	Bos-A	.290	8	31	3	9	2	1	0	2	4	4	2	O
W 1915	Bos-A	.350	5	20	4	7	0	0	2	3	2	4	0	O
W 1916	Bos-A	.333	5	21	6	7	1	1	0	1	3	1	1	O
W 1918	Bos-A	.200	6	20	0	4	0	0	0	0	2	2	0	O
W Total 4		.293	24	92	13	27	3	2	2	6	11	11	3	
■ **Joe Hoover**														
W 1945	Det-A	.333	1	3	1	1	0	0	0	1	0	0	0	S
■ **Don Hopkins**														
L 1975	Oak-A	—	1	0	0	0	0	0	0	0	0	0	0	D
■ **Johnny Hopp**														
W 1942	StL-N	.176	5	17	3	3	0	0	0	0	1	1	0	1
W 1943	StL-N	.000	1	4	0	0	0	0	0	0	0	1	0	O
W 1944	StL-N	.185	6	27	2	5	0	0	0	0	0	8	0	O
W 1950	NY-A	.000	3	2	0	0	0	0	0	0	0	0	0	1
W 1951	NY-A	—	1	0	0	0	0	0	0	0	1	0	0	H
W Total 5		.160	16	50	5	8	0	0	0	0	2	10	0	
■ **Bob Horner**														
L 1982	Atl-N	.091	3	11	0	1	0	0	0	0	0	2	0	3
■ **Rogers Hornsby**														
W 1926	StL-N	.250	7	28	2	7	1	0	0	4	2	2	1	2
W 1929	Chi-N	.238	5	21	4	5	1	1	0	1	1	8	0	2
W Total 2		.245	12	49	6	12	2	1	0	5	3	10	1	
■ **Willie Horton**														
L 1972	Det-A	.100	5	10	0	1	0	0	0	0	1	3	0	O-3
W 1968	Det-A	.304	7	23	6	7	1	1	1	3	5	6	0	O
■ **Dwayne Hosey**														
D 1995	Bos-A	.000	3	12	1	0	0	0	0	0	2	3	1	O
■ **Chuck Hostetler**														
W 1945	Det-A	.000	3	3	0	0	0	0	0	0	0	0	0	H
■ **Ralph Houk**														
W 1947	NY-A	1.000	1	1	0	1	0	0	0	0	0	0	0	H
W 1952	NY-A	.000	1	1	0	0	0	0	0	0	0	0	0	H
W Total 2		.500	2	2	0	1	0	0	0	0	0	0	0	
■ **Tyler Houston**														
D 1998	Chi-N	.167	3	6	1	1	0	0	1	1	0	3	0	C
■ **Elston Howard**														
W 1955	NY-A	.192	7	26	3	5	0	0	1	3	1	8	0	O
W 1956	NY-A	.400	1	5	1	2	1	0	1	1	0	0	0	O
W 1957	NY-A	.273	6	11	2	3	0	0	1	3	1	3	0	1-3
W 1958	NY-A	.222	6	18	4	4	0	0	0	2	1	4	1	O
W 1960	NY-A	.462	5	13	4	6	1	1	1	4	1	4	0	C-4
W 1961	NY-A	.250	5	20	5	5	3	0	1	1	2	3	0	C
W 1962	NY-A	.143	6	21	1	3	1	0	0	1	1	4	0	C
W 1963	NY-A	.333	4	15	0	5	0	0	0	1	0	3	0	C
W 1964	NY-A	.292	7	24	5	7	1	0	0	2	4	6	0	C
W 1967	Bos-A	.111	7	18	0	2	0	0	0	1	1	2	0	C
W Total 10		.246	54	171	25	42	7	1	5	19	12	37	1	
■ **Frank Howard**														
W 1963	LA-N	.300	3	10	2	3	1	0	1	1	0	2	0	O
■ **Del Howard**														
W 1907	Chi-N	.200	2	5	0	1	0	0	0	0	0	2	1	1-1
W 1908	Chi-N	.000	1	1	0	0	0	0	0	0	0	0	0	H
W Total 2		.167	3	6	0	1	0	0	0	0	0	2	1	
■ **Thomas Howard**														
D 1995	Cin-N	.100	3	10	0	1	1	0	0	0	0	2	0	O
D 1997	Hou-N	.000	2	1	0	0	0	0	0	0	1	1	0	H
D Total 2		.091	5	11	0	1	1	0	0	0	1	3	0	
L 1995	Cin-N	.250	4	8	0	2	1	0	0	1	2	0	0	O-3
■ **Art Howe**														
D 1981	Hou-N	.235	5	17	1	4	0	0	1	1	2	1	0	3
L 1974	Pit-N	.000	1	1	0	0	0	0	0	0	0	0	0	H
L 1980	Hou-N	.200	5	15	0	3	1	1	0	2	2	2	0	1-4
L Total 2		.188	6	16	0	3	1	1	0	2	2	2	0	
■ **Jack Howell**														
L 1986	Cal-A	.000	2	1	0	0	0	0	0	0	1	1	0	H
■ **Roy Howell**														
D 1981	Mil-A	.400	4	5	0	2	0	0	0	0	2	2	0	D-3
L 1982	Mil-A	.000	1	3	0	0	0	0	0	0	0	1	0	D
W 1982	Mil-A	.000	4	11	1	0	0	0	0	0	0	3	0	D
■ **Kent Hrbek**														
L 1987	Min-A	.150	5	20	4	3	0	0	1	1	3	0	0	1
L 1991	Min-A	.143	5	21	0	3	0	0	0	3	1	3	0	1
L Total 2		.146	10	41	4	6	0	0	1	4	4	3	0	
W 1987	Min-A	.208	7	24	4	5	0	0	1	6	5	3	0	1
W 1991	Min-A	.115	7	26	2	3	1	0	1	2	2	6	0	1
W Total 2		.160	14	50	6	8	1	0	2	8	7	9	0	
■ **Glenn Hubbard**														
L 1982	Atl-N	.222	3	9	1	2	0	0	0	1	0	3	0	2
W 1988	Oak-A	.250	4	12	2	3	0	0	0	0	1	2	1	2
■ **Trenidad Hubbard**														
D 1995	Col-N	.000	3	2	0	0	0	0	0	0	0	0	0	H
■ **Roy Hughes**														
W 1945	Chi-N	.294	6	17	1	5	1	0	0	3	4	5	0	S
■ **Brian Hunter**														
D 1999	Atl-N	.000	3	4	0	0	0	0	0	0	1	3	0	1
L 1991	Atl-N	.333	5	18	2	6	2	0	1	4	0	2	0	1
L 1992	Atl-N	.200	3	5	1	1	0	0	0	0	0	1	0	1-2
L 1999	Atl-N	.100	6	10	1	1	0	0	0	2	5	2	1	1
L Total 3		.242	14	33	4	8	2	0	1	6	5	5	1	
W 1991	Atl-N	.190	7	21	2	4	1	0	1	3	0	2	0	1-4,O-4
W 1992	Atl-N	.200	4	5	0	1	0	0	0	2	0	1	0	1-3
W 1999	Atl-N	.250	2	4	0	1	0	0	0	0	0	1	0	1
W Total 3		.200	13	30	2	6	1	0	1	5	0	4	0	
■ **Clint Hurdle**														
D 1981	KC-A	.273	3	11	0	3	0	0	0	0	1	1	0	O
L 1978	KC-A	.375	4	8	1	3	0	1	0	1	2	3	0	O-2
L 1980	KC-A	.000	3	2	0	0	0	0	0	0	0	1	0	O
L Total 2		.300	7	10	1	3	0	1	0	1	2	4	0	
W 1980	KC-A	.417	4	12	1	5	1	0	0	0	2	1	1	O
■ **Butch Huskey**														
D 1999	Bos-A	.200	2	5	0	1	0	0	0	0	0	1	0	D
L 1999	Bos-A	.200	4	5	1	1	1	0	0	0	1	1	0	D-3
■ **Tom Hutton**														
L 1976	Phi-N	.000	1	1	0	0	0	0	0	0	0	0	0	H
L 1977	Phi-N	.000	3	3	0	0	0	0	0	0	0	0	0	1-1
L Total 2		.000	4	4	0	0	0	0	0	0	0	0	0	
■ **Ham Hyatt**														
W 1909	Pit-N	.000	2	4	1	0	0	0	0	1	1	0	0	O-1
■ **Raul Ibanez**														
D 2000	Sea-A	.375	3	8	2	3	0	0	0	0	0	0	0	O
L 2000	Sea-A	.000	6	9	0	0	0	0	0	0	0	2	0	O-3
■ **Pete Incaviglia**														
D 1996	Bal-A	.200	2	5	1	1	0	0	0	0	0	4	0	O
D 1998	Hou-N	.000	1	1	0	0	0	0	0	0	0	1	0	H
D Total 2		.167	3	6	1	1	0	0	0	0	0	5	0	
L 1993	Phi-N	.167	3	12	2	2	0	0	1	1	0	3	0	O
L 1996	Bal-A	.500	1	2	1	1	0	0	0	0	0	0	0	D
L Total 2		.214	4	14	3	3	0	0	1	1	0	3	0	
W 1993	Phi-N	.125	4	8	0	1	0	0	0	1	0	4	0	O
■ **Dane Iorg**														
L 1984	KC-A	.500	2	2	0	1	0	0	0	1	0	0	0	H
L 1985	KC-A	.500	4	2	0	1	1	0	0	0	2	0	0	H
L Total 2		.500	6	4	0	2	1	0	0	1	2	0	0	
W 1982	StL-N	.529	5	17	4	9	4	1	0	1	0	0	0	D
W 1985	KC-A	.500	2	2	0	1	0	0	0	2	0	0	0	H
W Total 2		.526	7	19	4	10	4	1	0	3	0	0	0	
■ **Garth Iorg**														
L 1985	Tor-A	.133	6	15	1	2	0	0	0	0	1	3	0	3
■ **Monte Irvin**														
W 1951	NY-N	.458	6	24	3	11	0	1	0	2	2	1	2	O
W 1954	NY-N	.222	4	9	1	2	1	0	0	2	0	3	0	O
W Total 2		.394	10	33	4	13	1	1	0	4	2	4	2	
■ **Arthur Irwin**														
W 1884	Pro-N	.222	3	9	3	2	0	1	0	2	0	2	0	S
■ **Frank Isbell**														
W 1906	Chi-A	.308	6	26	4	8	4	0	0	4	0	6	1	2
■ **Joe Jackson**														
W 1917	Chi-A	.304	6	23	4	7	0	0	0	2	1	0	1	O
W 1919	Chi-A	.375	8	32	5	12	3	0	1	6	1	2	0	O
W Total 2		.345	14	55	9	19	3	0	1	8	2	2	1	
■ **Randy Jackson**														
W 1956	Bro-N	.000	3	3	0	0	0	0	0	0	0	2	0	H
■ **Reggie Jackson**														
D 1981	NY-A	.300	5	20	4	6	0	0	2	4	1	5	0	O
L 1971	Oak-A	.333	3	12	2	4	1	0	2	2	0	1	0	O
L 1972	Oak-A	.278	5	18	1	5	1	0	0	2	1	6	2	O
L 1973	Oak-A	.143	5	21	0	3	0	0	0	0	0	6	0	O
L 1974	Oak-A	.167	4	12	0	2	1	0	0	1	5	2	0	D-3,O-1

YEAR	TM/L	AVG	G	AB	R	H	2B	3B	HR	RBI	BB	SO	SB	POS
L 1975	Oak-A	.417	3	12	1	5	0	0	1	3	0	2	0	O
L 1977	NY-A	.125	5	16	1	2	0	0	0	1	2	2	1	O-4,D-1
L 1978	NY-A	.462	4	13	5	6	1	0	2	6	3	4	0	D-3,O-1
L 1980	NY-A	.273	3	11	1	3	1	0	0	0	1	4	0	O
L 1981	NY-A	.000	2	4	1	0	0	0	0	1	1	0	1	O
L 1982	Cal-A	.111	5	18	2	2	0	0	1	2	2	7	0	O
L 1986	Cal-A	.192	6	26	2	5	2	0	0	2	2	7	0	D
L Total	11	.227	45	163	16	37	7	0	6	20	17	41	4	
W 1973	Oak-A	.310	7	29	3	9	3	1	1	6	2	7	0	O
W 1974	Oak-A	.286	5	14	3	4	1	0	1	1	5	3	1	O
W 1977	NY-A	.450	6	20	10	9	1	0	5	8	3	4	0	O
W 1978	NY-A	.391	6	23	2	9	1	0	2	8	3	7	0	D
W 1981	NY-A	.333	3	12	3	4	1	0	1	1	2	3	0	O
W Total	5	.357	27	98	21	35	7	1	10	24	15	24	1	
■ Sonny Jackson														
L 1969	Atl-N	—	1	0	0	0	0	0	0	0	0	0	0	S
■ Ron Jackson														
L 1982	Cal-A	1.000	1	1	0	1	0	0	0	0	0	0	0	H
■ Travis Jackson														
W 1923	NY-N	.000	1	1	0	0	0	0	0	0	0	0	0	H
W 1924	NY-N	.074	7	27	3	2	0	0	0	1	1	4	1	S
W 1933	NY-N	.222	5	18	3	4	1	0	0	2	1	3	0	3
W 1936	NY-N	.190	6	21	1	4	0	0	0	1	1	3	0	3
W Total	4	.149	19	67	7	10	1	0	0	4	3	10	1	
■ Bo Jackson														
L 1993	Chi-A	.000	3	10	1	0	0	0	0	0	3	6	0	D
■ Charlie James														
W 1964	StL-N	.000	3	3	0	0	0	0	0	0	0	1	0	H
■ Dion James														
D 1995	NY-A	.083	4	12	0	1	0	0	0	0	1	1	0	O
■ Charlie Jamieson														
W 1920	Cle-A	.333	6	15	2	5	1	0	0	1	1	0	1	O-5
■ Hal Janvrin														
W 1915	Bos-A	.000	1	1	0	0	0	0	0	0	0	0	0	S
W 1916	Bos-A	.217	5	23	2	5	3	0	0	1	0	6	0	2
W Total	2	.208	6	24	2	5	3	0	0	1	0	6	0	
■ Julian Javier														
W 1964	StL-N	—	1	0	1	0	0	0	0	0	0	0	0	2
W 1967	StL-N	.360	7	25	2	9	3	0	1	4	0	6	0	2
W 1968	StL-N	.333	7	27	1	9	1	0	0	3	3	4	1	2
W 1972	Cin-N	.000	4	2	0	0	0	0	0	0	0	0	0	H
W Total	4	.333	19	54	4	18	4	0	1	7	3	10	1	
■ Stan Javier														
D 1997	SF-N	.417	3	12	2	5	1	0	0	1	0	2	1	O
D 1999	Hou-N	.273	4	11	1	3	0	0	0	0	1	1	0	O
D 2000	Sea-A	.167	3	6	0	1	0	0	0	1	0	3	0	O
D Total	3	.310	10	29	3	9	1	0	0	2	1	6	1	
L 1988	Oak-A	.500	2	4	0	2	0	0	0	1	1	0	0	O
L 1989	Oak-A	.000	1	2	0	0	0	0	0	0	0	1	0	O
L 2000	Sea-A	.071	4	14	0	1	0	0	0	1	0	4	0	O
L Total	3	.150	7	20	0	3	0	0	0	2	1	5	0	
W 1988	Oak-A	.500	3	4	0	2	0	0	0	2	0	1	0	O-2
W 1989	Oak-A	—	1	0	0	0	0	0	0	0	0	0	0	O
W Total	2	.500	4	4	0	2	0	0	0	2	0	1	0	
■ Gregg Jefferies														
L 1988	NY-N	.333	7	27	2	9	2	0	0	1	4	0	0	3
■ Reggie Jefferson														
D 1995	Bos-A	.250	1	4	1	1	0	0	0	0	0	1	0	D
■ Hughie Jennings														
T 1894	Bal-N	.143	4	14	0	2	0	0	0	1	0	2	0	S
T 1895	Bal-N	.368	5	19	3	7	2	0	0	2	1	0	1	S
T 1896	Bal-N	.333	4	15	5	5	2	0	0	3	1	2	1	S
T 1897	Bal-N	.318	5	22	5	7	2	0	0	3	4	0	0	S
T 1900	Bro-N	.167	4	18	1	3	1	0	0	2	1	1	0	1
T Total	5	.273	22	88	14	24	7	0	0	11	7	5	2	
■ Doug Jennings														
L 1990	Oak-A	.000	1	1	0	0	0	0	0	0	0	0	0	O
W 1990	Oak-A	1.000	1	1	0	1	0	0	0	0	0	0	0	H
■ Jackie Jensen														
W 1950	NY-A	—	1	0	0	0	0	0	0	0	0	0	0	R
■ Derek Jeter														
D 1996	NY-A	.412	4	17	2	7	1	0	0	1	0	2	0	S
D 1997	NY-A	.333	5	21	6	7	1	0	2	2	3	5	1	S
D 1998	NY-A	.111	3	9	0	1	0	0	0	0	2	2	0	S
D 1999	NY-A	.455	3	11	3	5	1	1	0	0	2	3	0	S
D 2000	NY-A	.211	5	19	1	4	0	0	0	2	2	3	0	S
D Total	5	.312	20	77	12	24	3	1	2	5	9	15	1	
L 1996	NY-A	.417	5	24	5	10	2	0	1	1	0	5	2	S
L 1998	NY-A	.200	6	25	3	5	1	1	0	2	2	5	3	S
L 1999	NY-A	.350	5	20	3	7	1	0	1	3	2	3	0	S
L 2000	NY-A	.318	6	22	6	7	0	0	2	5	6	7	1	S
L Total	4	.319	22	91	17	29	4	1	4	11	10	20	6	
W 1996	NY-A	.250	6	20	5	5	0	0	0	1	4	6	1	S
W 1998	NY-A	.353	4	17	4	6	0	0	0	1	3	3	0	S
W 1999	NY-A	.353	4	17	4	6	1	0	0	1	1	3	3	S
W 2000	NY-A	.409	5	22	6	9	2	1	2	2	3	8	0	S
W Total	4	.342	19	76	19	26	3	1	2	5	11	20	4	
■ Johnny Jeter														
L 1970	Pit-N	.000	3	2	0	0	0	0	0	0	0	2	0	O-1
■ Brian Johnson														
D 1996	SD-N	.375	2	8	2	3	1	0	0	0	0	1	0	C
D 1997	SF-N	.100	3	10	2	1	0	0	1	1	1	4	0	C
D Total	2	.222	5	18	4	4	1	0	1	1	1	5	0	
■ Charles Johnson														
D 1997	Fla-N	.250	3	8	5	2	1	0	1	2	3	2	0	C
D 2000	Chi-A	.333	3	9	0	3	0	0	0	0	1	1	0	C
D Total	2	.294	6	17	5	5	1	0	1	2	4	3	0	
L 1997	Fla-N	.118	6	17	1	2	2	0	0	5	3	8	0	C
W 1997	Fla-N	.357	7	28	4	10	0	0	1	3	1	6	0	C
■ Cliff Johnson														
D 1981	Oak-A	.286	2	7	0	2	1	0	0	0	0	1	0	D
L 1977	NY-A	.400	5	15	2	6	2	0	1	2	1	2	0	D-4
L 1978	NY-A	.000	1	1	0	0	0	0	0	0	0	0	0	H
L 1981	Oak-A	.000	2	6	0	0	0	0	0	0	2	2	0	D
L 1985	Tor-A	.368	7	19	1	7	2	0	0	2	1	4	0	D
L Total	4	.317	15	41	3	13	4	0	1	4	4	8	0	
W 1977	NY-A	.000	2	1	0	0	0	0	0	0	0	0	0	C-1
W 1978	NY-A	.000	2	2	0	0	0	0	0	0	0	1	0	H
W Total	2	.000	4	3	0	0	0	0	0	0	0	1	0	
■ Darrell Johnson														
W 1961	Cin-N	.500	2	4	0	2	0	0	0	0	0	0	0	C
■ Davey Johnson														
L 1969	Bal-A	.231	3	13	2	3	0	0	0	0	2	1	0	2
L 1970	Bal-A	.364	3	11	4	4	0	0	2	4	1	1	0	2
L 1971	Bal-A	.300	3	10	2	3	2	0	0	0	3	1	0	2
L 1977	Phi-N	.250	1	4	0	1	0	0	0	2	0	1	0	1
L Total	4	.289	10	38	8	11	2	0	2	6	6	4	0	
W 1966	Bal-A	.286	4	14	1	4	1	0	0	1	0	1	0	2
W 1969	Bal-A	.063	5	16	1	1	0	0	0	0	2	1	0	2
W 1970	Bal-A	.313	5	16	2	5	2	0	0	2	5	2	0	2
W 1971	Bal-A	.148	7	27	1	4	0	0	0	3	0	1	0	2
W Total	4	.192	21	73	5	14	3	0	0	6	7	5	0	
■ Deron Johnson														
L 1973	Oak-A	.100	4	10	0	1	0	0	0	0	2	6	0	D
W 1973	Oak-A	.300	6	10	0	3	1	0	0	0	1	4	0	1-2
■ Don Johnson														
W 1945	Chi-N	.172	7	29	4	5	2	1	0	0	0	8	1	2
■ Ernie Johnson														
W 1923	NY-A	—	2	0	1	0	0	0	0	0	0	0	0	S-1
■ Howard Johnson														
L 1986	NY-N	.000	2	2	0	0	0	0	0	0	0	0	0	H
L 1988	NY-N	.056	6	18	3	1	0	0	0	0	1	6	1	S-5,3-1
L Total	2	.050	8	20	3	1	0	0	0	0	1	6	1	
W 1984	Det-A	.000	1	1	0	0	0	0	0	0	0	0	0	H
W 1986	NY-N	.000	2	5	0	0	0	0	0	0	0	2	0	3-1,S-1
W Total	2	.000	3	6	0	0	0	0	0	0	0	2	0	
■ Lance Johnson														
D 1998	Chi-N	.167	3	12	0	2	0	0	0	1	0	1	0	O
L 1987	StL-N	—	1	0	1	0	0	0	0	0	0	0	1	R
L 1993	Chi-A	.217	6	23	2	5	1	1	1	6	2	1	1	O
L Total	2	.217	7	23	3	5	1	1	1	6	2	1	2	
W 1987	StL-N	—	1	0	0	0	0	0	0	0	0	0	1	R
■ Ken Johnson														
W 1950	Phi-N	—	1	0	1	0	0	0	0	0	0	0	0	R
■ Lou Johnson														
W 1965	LA-N	.296	7	27	3	8	2	0	2	4	1	3	0	O
W 1966	LA-N	.267	4	15	1	4	1	0	0	0	1	1	0	O
W Total	2	.286	11	42	4	12	3	0	2	4	2	4	0	
■ Roy Johnson														
W 1936	NY-A	.000	2	1	0	0	0	0	0	0	0	1	0	H
■ Wallace Johnson														
D 1981	Mon-N	.500	2	2	0	1	0	0	0	1	0	0	0	H
■ Billy Johnson														
W 1943	NY-A	.300	5	20	3	6	1	1	0	3	0	3	0	3
W 1947	NY-A	.269	7	26	8	7	0	3	0	2	3	4	0	3
W 1949	NY-A	.143	2	7	0	1	0	0	0	0	0	2	1	3
W 1950	NY-A	.000	4	6	0	0	0	0	0	0	0	3	0	3
W Total	4	.237	18	59	11	14	1	4	0	5	3	12	1	
■ Russ Johnson														
D 1997	Hou-N	.000	1	1	0	0	0	0	0	0	0	1	0	H
D 1999	Hou-N	1.000	2	1	0	1	1	0	0	0	1	0	0	H
D Total	2	.500	3	2	0	1	1	0	0	0	1	1	0	
■ Jimmy Johnston														
W 1916	Bro-N	.300	3	10	1	3	0	1	0	0	1	0	0	O-2
W 1920	Bro-N	.214	4	14	2	3	0	0	0	0	0	2	1	3
W Total	2	.250	7	24	3	6	0	1	0	0	1	2	1	
■ Doc Johnston														
W 1920	Cle-A	.273	5	11	1	3	0	0	0	0	2	1	1	1

YEAR	TM/L	AVG	G	AB	R	H	2B	3B	HR	RBI	BB	SO	SB	POS
■ Jay Johnstone														
D 1981	LA-N	.000	1	1	0	0	0	0	0	0	0	0	0	H
L 1976	Phi-N	.778	3	9	1	7	1	1	0	2	1	0	0	O-2
L 1977	Phi-N	.200	2	5	0	1	0	0	0	0	0	1	0	O
L 1981	LA-N	.000	2	2	0	0	0	0	0	0	0	0	0	H
L 1985	LA-N	.000	1	1	0	0	0	0	0	0	0	0	0	H
L Total	4	.471	8	17	1	8	1	1	0	2	1	1	0	
W 1978	NY-A	—	2	0	0	0	0	0	0	0	0	0	0	O
W 1981	LA-N	.667	3	3	1	2	0	0	1	3	0	0	0	H
W Total	2	.667	5	3	1	2	0	0	1	3	0	0	0	
■ Andruw Jones														
D 1996	Atl-N	—	3	0	0	0	0	0	0	0	1	0	0	O
D 1997	Atl-N	.000	3	5	1	0	0	0	0	1	1	1	0	O
D 1998	Atl-N	.000	3	9	2	0	0	0	0	1	3	2	2	O
D 1999	Atl-N	.222	4	18	1	4	1	0	0	2	1	3	0	O
D 2000	Atl-N	.111	3	9	3	1	0	0	1	1	4	1	0	O
D Total	5	.122	16	41	7	5	1	0	1	5	10	7	2	
L 1996	Atl-N	.222	5	9	3	2	0	0	1	3	3	2	0	O
L 1997	Atl-N	.444	5	9	0	4	0	0	0	1	1	1	0	O
L 1998	Atl-N	.273	6	22	3	6	0	0	1	2	1	4	1	O
L 1999	Atl-N	.217	6	23	5	5	0	0	0	1	4	3	0	O
L Total	4	.270	22	63	11	17	0	0	2	7	9	10	1	
W 1996	Atl-N	.400	6	20	4	8	1	0	2	6	3	6	1	O
W 1999	Atl-N	.077	4	13	1	1	0	0	0	0	1	3	0	O
W Total	2	.273	10	33	5	9	1	0	2	6	4	9	1	
■ Cleon Jones														
L 1969	NY-N	.429	3	14	4	6	2	0	1	4	1	2	2	O
L 1973	NY-N	.300	5	20	3	6	2	0	0	3	2	4	0	O
L Total	2	.353	8	34	7	12	4	0	1	7	3	6	2	
W 1969	NY-N	.158	5	19	2	3	1	0	0	0	0	1	0	O
W 1973	NY-N	.286	7	28	5	8	2	0	1	1	4	2	0	O
W Total	2	.234	12	47	7	11	3	0	1	1	4	3	0	
■ Davy Jones														
W 1907	Det-A	.353	5	17	1	6	0	0	0	0	4	0	3	O
W 1908	Det-A	.000	3	2	1	0	0	0	0	0	1	1	0	H
W 1909	Det-A	.233	7	30	6	7	0	0	1	1	2	1	1	O
W Total	3	.265	15	49	8	13	0	0	1	1	7	2	4	
■ Fielder Jones														
T 1900	Bro-N	.278	4	18	3	5	0	0	0	4	1	1	1	O
W 1906	Chi-A	.095	6	21	4	2	0	0	0	0	3	3	0	O
■ Dalton Jones														
W 1967	Bos-A	.389	6	18	2	7	0	0	0	1	1	3	0	3-4
■ Chipper Jones														
D 1995	Atl-N	.389	4	18	4	7	2	0	2	4	2	2	0	3
D 1996	Atl-N	.222	3	9	2	2	0	0	1	2	3	4	1	3
D 1997	Atl-N	.500	3	8	3	4	0	0	1	2	3	2	1	3
D 1998	Atl-N	.200	2	10	2	2	0	0	0	1	4	3	0	3
D 1999	Atl-N	.231	4	13	2	3	0	0	0	1	5	2	0	3
D 2000	Atl-N	.333	3	12	2	4	1	0	0	1	1	4	0	3
D Total	6	.314	19	70	15	22	3	0	4	11	18	17	2	
L 1995	Atl-N	.438	4	16	3	7	0	0	1	3	3	1	1	3
L 1996	Atl-N	.440	7	25	6	11	2	0	0	4	3	1	1	3
L 1997	Atl-N	.292	6	24	5	7	1	0	2	4	2	3	0	3
L 1998	Atl-N	.208	6	24	2	5	1	0	0	1	4	5	0	3
L 1999	Atl-N	.263	6	19	3	5	2	0	0	1	9	7	3	3
L Total	5	.324	29	108	19	35	6	0	3	13	21	17	5	
W 1995	Atl-N	.286	6	21	3	6	3	0	0	1	4	3	0	3
W 1996	Atl-N	.286	6	21	3	6	3	0	0	3	4	2	1	3-6,S-1
W 1999	Atl-N	.231	4	13	2	3	0	0	1	2	4	2	0	3
W Total	3	.273	16	55	8	15	6	0	1	6	12	7	1	
■ Lynn Jones														
L 1984	KC-A	.200	3	5	1	1	0	0	0	0	0	0	0	O-2
L 1985	KC-A	—	5	0	0	0	0	0	0	0	0	0	0	O
L Total	2	.200	8	5	1	1	0	0	0	0	0	0	0	
W 1985	KC-A	.667	6	3	0	2	1	1	0	0	0	0	0	O-4
■ Ruppert Jones														
L 1984	Det-A	.000	2	5	1	0	0	0	0	0	1	1	0	O
L 1986	Cal-A	.176	6	17	4	3	1	0	0	2	5	2	0	O-5
L Total	2	.136	8	22	5	3	1	0	0	2	6	3	0	
W 1984	Det-A	.000	2	3	0	0	0	0	0	0	0	1	0	O
■ Tom Jones														
W 1909	Det-A	.250	7	24	3	6	1	0	0	2	2	0	1	1
■ Nippy Jones														
W 1946	StL-N	.000	1	1	0	0	0	0	0	0	0	1	0	H
W 1957	Mil-N	.000	3	2	0	0	0	0	0	0	0	0	0	H
W Total	2	.000	4	3	0	0	0	0	0	0	0	1	0	
■ Willie Jones														
W 1950	Phi-N	.286	4	14	1	4	1	0	0	0	0	3	0	3
■ Eddie Joost														
W 1940	Cin-N	.200	7	25	0	5	0	0	0	2	1	2	0	2
■ Brian Jordan														
D 1996	StL-N	.333	3	12	4	4	0	0	1	3	1	3	1	O
D 1999	Atl-N	.471	4	17	2	8	1	0	1	7	1	2	0	O
D 2000	Atl-N	.364	3	11	1	4	1	0	0	4	1	1	0	O
D Total	3	.400	10	40	7	16	2	0	2	14	3	6	1	
L 1996	StL-N	.240	7	25	3	6	1	1	1	2	1	3	0	O
L 1999	Atl-N	.200	6	25	3	5	0	0	2	5	3	5	0	O
L Total	2	.220	13	50	6	11	1	1	3	7	4	8	0	
W 1999	Atl-N	.077	4	13	1	1	0	0	0	1	4	2	0	O
■ Ricky Jordan														
L 1993	Phi-N	.000	2	1	0	0	0	0	0	0	1	0	0	H
W 1993	Phi-N	.200	3	10	0	2	0	0	0	0	0	2	0	D-2
■ Spider Jorgensen														
W 1947	Bro-N	.200	7	20	1	4	2	0	0	3	2	4	0	3
W 1949	Bro-N	.182	4	11	1	2	2	0	0	0	2	2	0	3-3
W Total	2	.194	11	31	2	6	4	0	0	3	4	6	0	
■ Mike Jorgensen														
L 1985	StL-N	.000	2	2	0	0	0	0	0	0	0	1	0	H
W 1985	StL-N	.000	2	3	0	0	0	0	0	0	0	0	0	O-1
■ Von Joshua														
L 1974	LA-N	—	1	0	0	0	0	0	0	0	1	0	0	H
W 1974	LA-N	.000	4	4	0	0	0	0	0	0	0	0	0	H
■ Wally Joyner														
D 1996	SD-N	.111	3	9	0	1	0	0	0	0	0	2	0	1
D 1998	SD-N	.167	4	6	1	1	0	0	1	2	1	2	0	1
D 2000	Atl-N	.333	3	3	0	1	1	0	0	0	0	0	0	H
D Total	3	.167	10	18	1	3	1	0	1	2	1	4	0	
L 1986	Cal-A	.455	3	11	3	5	2	0	1	2	2	0	0	1
L 1998	SD-N	.313	6	16	3	5	0	0	0	2	4	3	0	1
L Total	2	.370	9	27	6	10	2	0	1	4	6	3	0	
W 1998	SD-N	.000	3	8	0	0	0	0	0	0	3	1	0	1
■ Joe Judge														
W 1924	Was-A	.385	7	26	4	10	1	0	0	0	5	2	0	1
W 1925	Was-A	.174	7	23	2	4	1	0	1	4	3	2	0	1
W Total	2	.286	14	49	6	14	2	0	1	4	8	4	0	
■ Wally Judnich														
W 1948	Cle-A	.077	4	13	1	1	0	0	0	1	1	4	0	O
■ Billy Jurges														
W 1932	Chi-N	.364	3	11	1	4	1	0	0	1	0	1	2	S
W 1935	Chi-N	.250	6	16	3	4	0	0	0	1	4	4	0	S
W 1938	Chi-N	.231	4	13	0	3	1	0	0	0	1	3	0	S
W Total	3	.275	13	40	4	11	2	0	0	2	5	8	2	
■ David Justice														
D 1995	Atl-N	.231	4	13	2	3	0	0	0	0	5	2	0	O
D 1997	Cle-A	.263	5	19	3	5	2	0	1	2	2	3	0	D
D 1998	Cle-A	.313	4	16	2	5	4	0	1	6	0	1	0	O-2,D-2
D 1999	Cle-A	.000	3	8	0	0	0	0	0	1	2	2	0	O
D 2000	NY-A	.222	5	18	2	4	0	0	1	1	3	4	0	O
D Total	5	.230	21	74	9	17	6	0	3	10	12	12	0	
L 1991	Atl-N	.200	7	25	4	5	1	0	1	2	3	7	0	O
L 1992	Atl-N	.280	7	25	5	7	1	0	2	6	6	2	0	O
L 1993	Atl-N	.143	6	21	2	3	1	0	0	4	3	3	0	O
L 1995	Atl-N	.273	3	11	1	3	0	0	0	1	2	1	0	O
L 1997	Cle-A	.333	6	21	3	7	1	0	0	0	2	4	0	D
L 1998	Cle-A	.158	6	19	2	3	0	0	1	2	3	3	0	D-4,O-1
L 2000	NY-A	.231	6	26	4	6	2	0	2	8	2	7	0	O
L Total	7	.230	41	148	21	34	6	0	6	23	21	27	0	
W 1991	Atl-N	.259	7	27	5	7	0	0	2	6	5	5	2	O
W 1992	Atl-N	.158	6	19	4	3	0	0	1	3	6	5	1	O
W 1995	Atl-N	.250	6	20	3	5	1	0	1	5	5	1	0	O
W 1997	Cle-A	.185	7	27	4	5	0	0	0	4	6	8	0	O-4,D-3
W 2000	NY-A	.158	5	19	1	3	2	0	0	3	3	2	0	O
W Total	5	.205	31	112	17	23	3	0	4	21	25	21	3	
■ Al Kaline														
L 1972	Det-A	.263	5	19	3	5	0	0	1	1	2	2	0	O
W 1968	Det-A	.379	7	29	6	11	2	0	2	8	0	7	0	O
■ John Kane														
W 1910	Chi-N	—	1	0	0	0	0	0	0	0	0	0	0	R
■ Ron Karkovice														
L 1993	Chi-A	.000	6	15	0	0	0	0	0	0	1	7	0	C
■ Eric Karros														
D 1995	LA-N	.500	3	12	3	6	1	0	2	4	1	0	0	1
D 1996	LA-N	.000	3	9	0	0	0	0	0	0	2	3	0	1
D Total	2	.286	6	21	3	6	1	0	2	4	3	3	0	
■ Eddie Kasko														
W 1961	Cin-N	.318	5	22	1	7	0	0	0	1	0	2	0	S
■ Benny Kauff														
W 1917	NY-N	.160	6	25	2	4	1	0	2	5	0	2	1	O
■ Willie Keeler														
T 1894	Bal-N	.250	3	12	1	3	0	0	0	1	1	0	0	O
T 1895	Bal-N	.235	5	17	3	4	0	0	0	1	3	1	0	O
T 1896	Bal-N	.471	4	17	4	8	1	2	0	4	0	0	1	O
T 1897	Bal-N	.391	5	23	5	9	2	0	0	2	4	0	0	O
T 1900	Bro-N	.353	4	17	0	6	0	0	0	0	1	0	0	O
T Total	5	.349	21	86	13	30	3	2	0	8	9	1	1	
■ Charlie Keller														
W 1939	NY-A	.438	4	16	8	7	1	1	3	6	1	2	0	O
W 1941	NY-A	.389	5	18	5	7	2	0	0	5	3	1	0	O
W 1942	NY-A	.200	5	20	2	4	0	0	2	5	1	3	0	O
W 1943	NY-A	.222	5	18	3	4	0	1	0	2	2	5	1	O

YEAR	TM/L	AVG	G	AB	R	H	2B	3B	HR	RBI	BB	SO	SB	POS
W Total	4	.306	19	72	18	22	3	2	5	18	7	11	1	
■ **Frank Kellert**														
W 1955	Bro-N	.333	3	3	0	1	0	0	0	0	0	0	0	H
■ **Joe Kelley**														
T 1894	Bal-N	.333	4	15	2	5	1	1	0	0	3	2	1	O
T 1895	Bal-N	.368	5	19	1	7	0	0	0	5	1	1	1	O
T 1896	Bal-N	.471	4	17	3	8	1	0	0	4	0	1	2	O
T 1897	Bal-N	.313	4	16	7	5	3	0	0	5	5	0	0	O
T 1900	Bro-N	.176	4	17	2	3	0	0	0	1	2	3	0	O
T Total	5	.333	21	84	15	28	5	1	0	15	11	7	4	
■ **George Kelly**														
W 1921	NY-N	.233	8	30	3	7	1	0	0	4	3	10	0	1
W 1922	NY-N	.278	5	18	0	5	0	0	0	2	0	3	0	1
W 1923	NY-N	.182	6	22	1	4	0	0	0	1	1	2	0	1
W 1924	NY-N	.290	7	31	7	9	1	0	1	4	1	8	0	1-4,O-4,2-1
W Total	4	.248	26	101	11	25	2	0	1	11	5	23	0	
■ **Pat Kelly**														
L 1979	Bal-A	.364	3	11	3	4	0	0	1	4	1	3	2	D-2,O-1
W 1979	Bal-A	.250	5	4	0	1	0	0	0	0	1	1	0	H
■ **King Kelly**														
W 1885	Chi-N	.346	7	26	9	9	3	1	0	4	2	0	0	O-4,C-3
W 1886	Chi-N	.208	6	24	4	5	0	0	1	1	2	2	1	C-5,S-2,3,1
W Total	2	.280	13	50	13	14	3	1	1	5	4	2	1	
T 1892	Bos-N	.000	2	8	0	0	0	0	0	0	0	2	1	C
■ **Pat Kelly**														
D 1995	NY-A	.000	5	3	3	0	0	0	0	1	1	3	0	2-4
■ **Roberto Kelly**														
D 1995	LA-N	.364	3	11	0	4	0	0	0	0	1	0	0	O
D 1997	Sea-A	.308	4	13	1	4	3	0	0	1	0	3	0	O-3
D 1998	Tex-A	.143	1	7	0	1	1	0	0	0	0	2	0	O
D 1999	Tex-A	.333	1	3	0	1	0	0	0	0	0	2	0	O
D Total	4	.294	9	34	1	10	4	0	0	1	1	7	0	
■ **Ken Keltner**														
W 1948	Cle-A	.095	6	21	3	2	0	0	0	0	2	3	0	3
■ **Ed Kennedy**														
W 1884	NY-A	.000	3	7	0	0	0	0	0	0	0	2	0	O
■ **John Kennedy**														
W 1965	LA-N	.000	4	1	0	0	0	0	0	0	0	0	0	3
W 1966	LA-N	.200	2	5	0	1	0	0	0	0	0	0	0	3
W Total	2	.167	6	6	0	1	0	0	0	0	0	0	0	
■ **Bob Kennedy**														
W 1948	Cle-A	.500	3	2	0	1	0	0	0	1	0	1	0	O
■ **Terry Kennedy**														
L 1984	SD-N	.222	5	18	2	4	0	0	0	1	1	3	0	C
L 1989	SF-N	.188	5	16	0	3	1	0	0	0	1	4	0	C
L Total	2	.206	10	34	2	7	1	0	0	1	2	7	0	
W 1984	SD-N	.211	5	19	2	4	1	0	1	3	1	1	0	C
W 1989	SF-N	.167	4	12	1	2	0	0	0	2	1	3	0	C
W Total	2	.194	9	31	3	6	1	0	1	5	2	4	0	
■ **Jeff Kent**														
D 1996	Cle-A	.125	4	8	2	1	1	0	0	0	0	0	0	3-2,1-1,2-1
D 1997	SF-N	.300	3	10	2	3	0	0	2	2	2	1	0	2-3,1-1
D 2000	SF-N	.375	4	16	3	6	1	0	0	1	1	3	1	2-4,1-1
D Total	3	.294	11	34	7	10	2	0	2	3	3	4	1	
■ **John Kerr**														
W 1933	Was-A	—	1	0	0	0	0	0	0	0	0	0	0	R
■ **Pete Kilduff**														
W 1920	Bro-N	.095	7	21	0	2	0	0	0	0	1	4	0	2
■ **Harmon Killebrew**														
L 1969	Min-A	.125	3	8	2	1	1	0	0	0	6	2	0	3
L 1970	Min-A	.273	3	11	2	3	0	0	2	4	2	4	0	3-2,1-1
L Total	2	.211	6	19	4	4	1	0	2	4	8	6	0	
W 1965	Min-A	.286	7	21	2	6	0	0	1	2	6	4	0	3
■ **Bill Killefer**														
W 1915	Phi-N	.000	1	1	0	0	0	0	0	0	0	0	0	H
W 1918	Chi-N	.118	6	17	2	2	1	0	0	2	2	0	0	C
W Total	2	.111	7	18	2	2	1	0	0	2	2	0	0	
■ **Hal King**														
L 1973	Cin-N	.500	3	2	0	1	0	0	0	0	1	1	0	H
■ **Jeff King**														
L 1990	Pit-N	.100	5	10	0	1	0	0	0	0	1	5	0	3-4
L 1992	Pit-N	.241	7	29	4	7	4	0	0	2	0	1	0	3
L Total	2	.205	12	39	4	8	4	0	0	2	1	6	0	
■ **Lee King**														
W 1922	NY-N	1.000	2	1	0	1	0	0	0	1	0	0	0	O
■ **Mike Kingery**														
D 1995	Col-N	.200	4	10	1	2	0	0	0	0	0	1	0	O
■ **Dave Kingman**														
L 1971	SF-N	.111	4	9	0	1	0	0	0	0	1	3	0	O-2
■ **Wayne Kirby**														
D 1995	Cle-A	1.000	3	1	0	1	0	0	0	0	0	0	0	O-2
D 1996	LA-N	.125	3	8	1	1	0	0	0	0	2	1	0	O
D Total	2	.222	6	9	1	2	0	0	0	0	2	1	0	
L 1995	Cle-A	.200	5	5	2	1	0	0	0	0	0	0	1	O
W 1995	Cle-A	.000	3	1	0	0	0	0	0	0	0	1	0	O-2
■ **Ed Kirkpatrick**														
L 1974	Pit-N	.000	3	9	0	0	0	0	0	0	2	0	0	1
L 1975	Pit-N	.000	2	2	0	0	0	0	0	0	0	0	0	H
L Total	2	.000	5	11	0	0	0	0	0	0	2	0	0	
■ **Ron Kittle**														
L 1983	Chi-A	.286	3	7	1	2	1	0	0	0	1	2	0	O
■ **Chuck Klein**														
W 1935	Chi-N	.333	5	12	2	4	0	0	1	2	0	2	0	O-3
■ **Lou Klein**														
W 1943	StL-N	.136	5	22	0	3	0	0	0	0	1	2	0	2
■ **Ryan Klesko**														
D 1995	Atl-N	.467	4	15	5	7	1	0	0	1	0	3	0	O
D 1996	Atl-N	.125	3	8	1	1	0	0	1	1	3	4	1	O
D 1997	Atl-N	.250	3	8	2	2	1	0	1	1	0	2	0	O
D 1998	Atl-N	.273	3	11	1	3	0	0	1	4	0	3	0	O
D 1999	Atl-N	.333	4	12	3	4	0	0	0	1	1	4	0	1
D Total	5	.315	17	54	12	17	2	0	3	8	4	16	1	
L 1995	Atl-N	.000	4	7	0	0	0	0	0	0	3	4	0	O-3
L 1996	Atl-N	.250	6	16	1	4	0	0	1	3	2	6	0	O
L 1997	Atl-N	.235	5	17	2	4	0	0	2	4	2	3	0	O
L 1998	Atl-N	.083	5	12	2	1	0	0	0	1	6	3	0	O
L 1999	Atl-N	.125	4	8	1	1	0	0	1	1	2	1	0	1
L Total	5	.167	24	60	6	10	0	0	4	9	15	17	0	
W 1995	Atl-N	.313	6	16	4	5	0	0	3	4	3	4	0	O-3,D-3
W 1996	Atl-N	.100	5	10	2	1	0	0	0	1	2	4	0	O-2,1-1,D-1
W 1999	Atl-N	.167	4	12	0	2	0	0	0	0	0	1	0	1
W Total	3	.211	15	38	6	8	0	0	3	5	5	9	0	
■ **Johnny Kling**														
W 1906	Chi-N	.176	6	17	2	3	1	0	0	0	4	3	0	C
W 1907	Chi-N	.211	5	19	2	4	0	0	0	1	1	4	0	C
W 1908	Chi-N	.250	5	16	2	4	1	0	0	2	2	2	0	C
W 1910	Chi-N	.077	5	13	0	1	0	0	0	1	1	2	0	C-3
W Total	4	.185	21	65	6	12	2	0	0	4	8	11	0	
■ **Ted Kluszewski**														
W 1959	Chi-A	.391	6	23	5	9	1	0	3	10	2	0	0	1
■ **Mickey Klutts**														
D 1981	Oak-A	.143	2	7	0	1	0	0	0	0	0	1	0	3
L 1981	Oak-A	.429	3	7	1	3	0	0	0	0	0	1	0	3
■ **Ray Knight**														
L 1979	Cin-N	.286	3	14	0	4	1	0	0	0	0	2	1	3
L 1986	NY-N	.167	6	24	1	4	0	0	0	2	1	5	0	3
L Total	2	.211	9	38	1	8	1	0	0	2	1	7	1	
W 1986	NY-N	.391	6	23	4	9	1	0	1	5	2	2	0	3
■ **Chuck Knoblauch**														
D 1998	NY-A	.091	3	11	0	1	0	0	0	0	0	4	0	2
D 1999	NY-A	.167	3	12	1	2	0	0	0	0	1	3	0	2
D 2000	NY-A	.333	3	9	1	3	0	0	0	1	0	2	1	D-2
D Total	3	.188	9	32	2	6	0	0	0	1	1	9	1	
L 1991	Min-A	.350	5	20	5	7	2	0	0	3	3	3	2	2
L 1998	NY-A	.200	6	25	4	5	1	0	0	0	4	2	0	2
L 1999	NY-A	.333	5	18	3	6	1	0	0	1	3	0	1	2
L 2000	NY-A	.261	6	23	3	6	2	0	0	2	3	4	0	D
L Total	4	.279	22	86	15	24	6	0	0	6	13	9	3	
W 1991	Min-A	.308	7	26	3	8	1	0	0	2	4	2	4	2
W 1998	NY-A	.375	4	16	3	6	0	0	1	3	3	2	1	2
W 1999	NY-A	.313	4	16	5	5	1	0	1	3	1	3	1	2
W 2000	NY-A	.100	4	10	1	1	0	0	0	1	2	1	0	D-2
W Total	4	.294	19	68	12	20	2	0	2	9	10	8	6	
■ **Randy Knorr**														
W 1993	Tor-A	—	1	0	0	0	0	0	0	0	0	0	0	C
■ **John Knox**														
L 1972	Det-A	—	1	0	0	0	0	0	0	0	0	0	0	R
■ **Mark Koenig**														
W 1926	NY-A	.125	7	32	2	4	1	0	0	2	0	6	0	S
W 1927	NY-A	.500	4	18	5	9	2	0	0	2	0	2	0	S
W 1928	NY-A	.158	4	19	1	3	0	0	0	0	0	1	0	S
W 1932	Chi-N	.250	2	4	1	1	0	1	0	1	1	0	0	S-1
W 1936	NY-N	.333	3	3	0	1	0	0	0	0	0	1	0	2-1
W Total	5	.237	20	76	9	18	3	1	0	5	1	10	0	
■ **Paul Konerko**														
D 2000	Chi-A	.000	3	9	1	0	0	0	0	0	1	1	0	1-2
■ **Ed Konetchy**														
W 1920	Bro-N	.174	7	23	0	4	0	1	0	2	3	2	0	1
■ **Larry Kopf**														
W 1919	Cin-N	.222	8	27	3	6	0	2	0	2	3	2	0	S
■ **Andy Kosco**														
L 1973	Cin-N	.300	3	10	0	3	0	0	0	0	2	3	0	O
■ **Ed Kranepool**														
L 1969	NY-N	.250	3	12	2	3	1	0	0	1	1	2	0	1
L 1973	NY-N	.500	1	2	0	1	0	0	0	2	0	0	0	O

YEAR	TM/L	AVG	G	AB	R	H	2B	3B	HR	RBI	BB	SO	SB	POS
L Total	2	.286	4	14	2	4	1	0	0	3	1	2	0	
W 1969	NY-N	.250	1	4	1	1	0	0	1	1	0	0	0	1
W 1973	NY-N	.000	4	3	0	0	0	0	0	0	0	0	0	H
W Total	2	.143	5	7	1	1	0	0	1	1	0	0	0	
■ **Mike Kreevich**														
W 1944	StL-A	.231	6	26	0	6	3	0	0	0	0	5	0	O
■ **Ernie Krueger**														
W 1920	Bro-N	.167	4	6	0	1	0	0	0	0	0	0	0	C-3
■ **John Kruk**														
L 1993	Phi-N	.250	6	24	4	6	2	1	1	5	4	5	0	1
W 1993	Phi-N	.348	6	23	4	8	1	0	0	4	7	7	0	1
■ **Tony Kubek**														
W 1957	NY-A	.286	7	28	4	8	0	0	2	4	0	4	0	O-5,3-2
W 1958	NY-A	.048	7	21	0	1	0	0	0	1	1	7	0	S
W 1960	NY-A	.333	7	30	6	10	1	0	0	3	2	2	0	S-7,O-2
W 1961	NY-A	.227	5	22	3	5	0	0	0	1	1	4	0	S
W 1962	NY-A	.276	7	29	2	8	1	0	0	1	1	3	0	S
W 1963	NY-A	.188	4	16	1	3	0	0	0	0	0	3	0	S
W Total	6	.240	37	146	16	35	2	0	2	10	5	23	0	
■ **Ted Kubiak**														
L 1972	Oak-A	.500	4	4	0	2	0	0	0	1	0	0	0	2-3,S-1
L 1973	Oak-A	.000	3	2	0	0	0	0	0	0	0	1	0	2
L Total	2	.333	7	6	0	2	0	0	0	1	0	1	0	
W 1972	Oak-A	.333	4	3	0	1	0	0	0	0	0	0	0	2
W 1973	Oak-A	.000	4	3	1	0	0	0	0	0	1	1	0	2
W Total	2	.167	8	6	1	1	0	0	0	0	1	1	0	
■ **Harvey Kuenn**														
W 1962	SF-N	.083	3	12	1	1	0	0	0	0	1	1	0	O
■ **Joe Kuhel**														
W 1933	Was-A	.150	5	20	1	3	0	0	0	1	1	4	0	1
■ **Rusty Kuntz**														
L 1984	Det-A	.000	1	1	0	0	0	0	0	0	0	0	0	O
W 1984	Det-A	.000	2	1	0	0	0	0	0	1	0	1	0	H
■ **Whitey Kurowski**														
W 1942	StL-N	.267	5	15	3	4	0	1	1	5	2	3	0	3
W 1943	StL-N	.222	5	18	2	4	1	0	0	1	0	3	0	3
W 1944	StL-N	.217	6	23	2	5	1	0	0	1	1	4	0	3
W 1946	StL-N	.296	7	27	5	8	3	0	0	2	0	3	0	3
W Total	4	.253	23	83	12	21	5	1	1	9	3	13	0	
■ **Randy Kutcher**														
L 1990	Bos-A	—	2	0	0	0	0	0	0	0	0	0	0	R
■ **Chet Laabs**														
W 1944	StL-A	.200	5	15	1	3	1	1	0	0	2	6	0	O-4
■ **Candy LaChance**														
W 1903	Bos-A	.222	8	27	5	6	2	1	0	4	3	2	0	1
■ **Pete LaCock**														
L 1977	KC-A	.000	1	1	0	0	0	0	0	0	1	1	0	1
L 1978	KC-A	.364	4	11	1	4	2	1	0	1	3	1	1	1-3
L 1980	KC-A	—	1	0	0	0	0	0	0	0	0	0	0	1
L Total	3	.333	6	12	1	4	2	1	0	1	4	2	1	
W 1980	KC-A	—	1	0	0	0	0	0	0	0	0	0	0	1
■ **Lee Lacy**														
L 1974	LA-N	—	1	0	0	0	0	0	0	0	0	0	0	R
L 1977	LA-N	1.000	1	1	1	1	0	0	0	0	0	0	0	H
L 1978	LA-N	.000	2	2	0	0	0	0	0	0	0	0	0	H
L Total	3	.333	4	3	1	1	0	0	0	0	0	0	0	
W 1974	LA-N	.000	1	1	0	0	0	0	0	0	0	1	0	H
W 1977	LA-N	.429	4	7	1	3	0	0	0	2	1	1	0	O-2
W 1978	LA-N	.143	4	14	0	2	0	0	0	1	1	3	0	D
W 1979	Pit-N	.250	4	4	0	1	0	0	0	0	0	1	0	H
W Total	4	.231	13	26	1	6	0	0	0	3	2	6	0	
■ **Joe Lahoud**														
L 1977	KC-A	.000	1	1	2	0	0	0	0	0	2	0	0	D
■ **Fred Lake**														
T 1897	Bos-N	.000	1	3	0	0	0	0	0	0	0	1	0	C
■ **Steve Lake**														
L 1984	Chi-N	1.000	1	1	0	1	1	0	0	0	0	0	0	C
W 1987	StL-N	.333	3	3	0	1	0	0	0	1	0	0	0	C
■ **Bill Lamar**														
W 1920	Bro-N	.000	3	3	0	0	0	0	0	0	0	0	0	H
■ **Rafael Landestoy**														
L 1980	Hou-N	.222	5	9	3	2	0	0	0	2	1	0	1	2-3,S-1
L 1983	LA-N	.000	2	2	0	0	0	0	0	0	0	1	0	H
L Total	2	.182	7	11	3	2	0	0	0	2	1	1	1	
W 1977	LA-N	—	1	0	0	0	0	0	0	0	0	0	0	R
■ **Jim Landis**														
W 1959	Chi-A	.292	6	24	6	7	0	0	0	1	1	7	1	O
■ **Ken Landreaux**														
D 1981	LA-N	.200	5	20	1	4	1	0	0	1	0	1	0	O
L 1981	LA-N	.100	5	10	0	1	1	0	0	0	3	2	0	O-3
L 1983	LA-N	.143	4	14	0	2	0	0	0	1	1	3	0	O
L 1985	LA-N	.389	5	18	4	7	3	0	0	2	1	1	0	O

YEAR	TM/L	AVG	G	AB	R	H	2B	3B	HR	RBI	BB	SO	SB	POS
L Total	3	.238	14	42	4	10	4	0	0	3	5	6	0	
W 1981	LA-N	.167	5	6	1	1	1	0	0	0	0	2	1	O-3
■ **Tito Landrum**														
L 1983	Bal-A	.200	4	10	2	2	0	0	1	1	0	2	0	O-3
L 1985	StL-N	.429	5	14	2	6	0	0	0	4	1	1	1	O-4
L Total	2	.333	9	24	4	8	0	0	1	5	1	3	1	
W 1983	Bal-A	—	3	0	0	0	0	0	0	0	0	0	1	O
W 1985	StL-N	.360	7	25	3	9	2	0	1	1	0	2	0	O
W Total	2	.360	10	25	3	9	2	0	1	1	0	2	1	
■ **Hal Lanier**														
L 1971	SF-N	.000	1	1	0	0	0	0	0	0	0	0	0	3
■ **Ray Lankford**														
D 1996	StL-N	.500	1	2	1	1	0	0	0	0	1	0	0	O
D 2000	StL-N	.200	3	10	2	2	1	0	0	3	2	5	0	O
D Total	2	.250	4	12	3	3	1	0	0	3	3	5	0	
L 1996	StL-N	.000	5	13	1	0	0	0	0	1	1	4	0	O-3
L 2000	StL-N	.333	5	12	1	4	1	0	0	1	1	5	0	O-4
L Total	2	.160	10	25	2	4	1	0	0	2	2	9	0	
■ **Carney Lansford**														
L 1979	Cal-A	.294	4	17	2	5	0	0	0	3	1	2	1	3
L 1988	Oak-A	.294	4	17	4	5	1	0	1	2	0	2	0	3
L 1989	Oak-A	.455	3	11	2	5	0	0	0	4	2	1	2	3
L 1990	Oak-A	.438	4	16	2	7	1	0	0	2	0	1	0	3
L 1992	Oak-A	.167	5	18	0	3	0	0	0	1	1	1	0	3
L Total	5	.316	20	79	10	25	2	0	1	12	4	7	3	
W 1988	Oak-A	.167	5	18	2	3	0	0	0	1	2	2	0	3
W 1989	Oak-A	.438	4	16	5	7	1	0	1	4	3	1	0	3
W 1990	Oak-A	.267	4	15	0	4	0	0	0	1	1	0	1	3
W Total	3	.286	13	49	7	14	1	0	1	6	6	3	1	
■ **Jack Lapp**														
W 1910	Phi-A	.250	1	4	0	1	0	0	0	1	0	2	0	C
W 1911	Phi-A	.250	2	8	1	2	0	0	0	0	0	1	0	C
W 1913	Phi-A	.250	1	4	0	1	0	0	0	0	0	1	0	C
W 1914	Phi-A	.000	1	1	0	0	0	0	0	0	0	0	0	C
W Total	4	.235	5	17	1	4	0	0	0	1	0	4	0	
■ **Norm Larker**														
W 1959	LA-N	.188	6	16	2	3	0	0	0	0	2	3	0	O
■ **Barry Larkin**														
D 1995	Cin-N	.385	3	13	2	5	0	0	0	1	1	2	4	S
L 1990	Cin-N	.261	6	23	5	6	2	0	0	1	3	1	3	S
L 1995	Cin-N	.389	4	18	1	7	2	1	0	0	1	1	1	S
L Total	2	.317	10	41	6	13	4	1	0	1	4	2	4	
W 1990	Cin-N	.353	4	17	3	6	1	1	0	1	2	0	0	S
■ **Gene Larkin**														
L 1987	Min-A	1.000	1	1	0	1	1	0	0	1	0	0	0	H
L 1991	Min-A	.000	3	3	0	0	0	0	0	0	0	1	0	H
L Total	2	.250	4	4	0	1	1	0	0	1	0	1	0	
W 1987	Min-A	.000	5	3	1	0	0	0	0	0	1	0	0	1-1,D-1
W 1991	Min-A	.500	4	4	0	2	0	0	0	1	0	0	0	D-1
W Total	2	.286	9	7	1	2	0	0	0	1	1	0	0	
■ **Arlie Latham**														
W 1885	StL-A	.318	7	22	5	7	3	0	0	5	2	0	0	3
W 1886	StL-A	.174	6	23	4	4	0	1	0	3	3	4	2	3-6,C-1
W 1887	StL-A	.388	15	67	12	26	1	0	1	2	9	2	15	3
W 1888	StL-A	.250	10	40	10	10	0	0	0	3	5	6	11	3
W Total	4	.309	38	152	31	47	4	1	1	13	19	12	28	
■ **Tim Laudner**														
L 1987	Min-A	.071	5	14	1	1	1	0	0	2	2	5	0	C
W 1987	Min-A	.318	7	22	4	7	1	0	1	4	5	3	0	C
■ **Cookie Lavagetto**														
W 1941	Bro-N	.100	3	10	1	1	0	0	0	0	2	0	0	3
W 1947	Bro-N	.143	5	7	0	1	1	0	0	3	0	2	0	3-3
W Total	2	.118	8	17	1	2	1	0	0	3	2	2	0	
■ **Mike LaValliere**														
L 1990	Pit-N	.000	3	6	1	0	0	0	0	0	3	1	0	C
L 1991	Pit-N	.333	3	6	0	2	0	0	0	1	2	0	0	C
L 1992	Pit-N	.200	3	10	1	2	0	0	0	0	0	3	0	C
L 1993	Chi-A	.333	2	3	0	1	0	0	0	0	1	0	0	C
L Total	4	.200	11	25	2	5	0	0	0	1	6	4	0	
■ **Rudy Law**														
L 1983	Chi-A	.389	4	18	1	7	1	0	0	0	0	1	2	O
■ **Vance Law**														
L 1983	Chi-A	.182	4	11	0	2	0	0	0	1	1	3	0	3
L 1989	Chi-N	.000	2	3	0	0	0	0	0	0	0	3	0	3-1
L Total	2	.143	6	14	0	2	0	0	0	1	1	6	0	
■ **Tom Lawless**														
L 1987	StL-N	.333	3	6	0	2	0	0	0	0	1	1	0	3-2,O-1
W 1985	StL-N	—	1	0	0	0	0	0	0	0	0	0	0	R
W 1987	StL-N	.100	3	10	1	1	0	0	1	3	0	4	0	3
W Total	2	.100	4	10	1	1	0	0	1	3	0	4	0	
■ **Tony Lazzeri**														
W 1926	NY-A	.192	7	26	2	5	1	0	0	3	1	6	0	2
W 1927	NY-A	.267	4	15	1	4	1	0	0	2	1	4	0	2
W 1928	NY-A	.250	4	12	2	3	1	0	0	0	1	0	2	2
W 1932	NY-A	.294	4	17	4	5	0	0	2	5	2	1	0	2

YEAR	TM/L	AVG	G	AB	R	H	2B	3B	HR	RBI	BB	SO	SB	POS
W 1936	NY-A	.250	6	20	4	5	0	0	1	7	4	4	0	2
W 1937	NY-A	.400	5	15	3	6	0	1	1	2	3	3	0	2
W 1938	Chi-N	.000	2	2	0	0	0	0	0	0	0	1	0	H
W Total	7	.262	32	107	16	28	3	1	4	19	12	19	2	
■ Tommy Leach														
T 1900	Pit-N	.176	4	17	4	3	0	0	0	1	1	2	0	O
W 1903	Pit-N	.273	8	33	3	9	0	4	0	7	1	4	1	3
W 1909	Pit-N	.360	7	25	8	9	4	0	0	2	2	1	1	O-7,3-1
W Total	2	.310	15	58	11	18	4	4	0	9	3	5	2	
■ Ricky Ledee														
D 1999	NY-A	.273	3	11	1	3	2	0	0	2	1	5	0	O
L 1998	NY-A	.000	3	5	0	0	0	0	0	0	0	0	0	O-2,D-1
L 1999	NY-A	.250	3	8	2	2	0	0	1	4	1	4	0	O-2
L Total	2	.154	6	13	2	2	0	0	1	4	1	4	0	
W 1998	NY-A	.600	4	10	1	6	3	0	0	4	2	1	0	O
W 1999	NY-A	.200	3	10	0	2	1	0	0	1	1	4	0	O
W Total	2	.400	7	20	1	8	4	0	0	5	3	5	0	
■ Carlos Lee														
D 2000	Chi-A	.091	3	11	0	1	1	0	0	1	0	2	0	O
■ Manuel Lee														
L 1985	Tor-A	—	1	0	0	0	0	0	0	0	0	0	0	2
L 1989	Tor-A	.250	2	8	2	2	0	0	0	0	0	1	0	2
L 1991	Tor-A	.125	5	16	3	2	0	0	0	0	1	5	0	S
L 1992	Tor-A	.278	6	18	2	5	1	1	0	3	1	2	0	S
L Total	4	.214	14	42	7	9	1	1	0	3	2	8	0	
W 1992	Tor-A	.105	6	19	1	2	0	0	0	0	1	2	0	S
■ Jim Lefebvre														
W 1965	LA-N	.400	3	10	2	4	0	0	0	0	0	0	0	2
W 1966	LA-N	.167	4	12	1	2	0	0	1	1	3	4	0	2
W Total	2	.273	7	22	3	6	0	0	1	1	3	4	0	
■ Joe Lefebvre														
L 1980	NY-A	—	1	0	0	0	0	0	0	0	0	0	0	O
L 1983	Phi-N	.000	2	2	0	0	0	0	0	1	0	1	0	O-1
L Total	2	.000	3	2	0	0	0	0	0	1	0	1	0	
W 1983	Phi-N	.200	3	5	0	1	1	0	0	2	0	1	0	O-2
■ Hank Leiber														
W 1936	NY-N	.000	2	6	0	0	0	0	0	0	2	2	0	O
W 1937	NY-N	.364	3	11	2	4	0	0	0	2	1	1	0	O
W Total	2	.235	5	17	2	4	0	0	0	2	3	3	0	
■ Nemo Leibold														
W 1917	Chi-A	.400	2	5	1	2	0	0	0	1	1	1	0	O
W 1919	Chi-A	.056	5	18	0	1	0	0	0	0	2	3	1	O
W 1924	Was-A	.167	3	6	1	1	1	0	0	0	1	0	0	O-1
W 1925	Was-A	.500	3	2	1	1	1	0	0	0	1	0	0	H
W Total	4	.161	13	31	3	5	2	0	0	1	5	4	1	
■ Scott Leius														
L 1991	Min-A	.000	3	4	0	0	0	0	0	0	1	1	0	3
W 1991	Min-A	.357	7	14	2	5	0	0	1	2	1	2	0	3
■ Don LeJohn														
W 1965	LA-N	.000	1	1	0	0	0	0	0	0	0	1	0	H
■ Mark Lemke														
D 1995	Atl-N	.211	4	19	3	4	1	0	0	1	1	3	0	2
D 1996	Atl-N	.167	3	12	1	2	1	0	0	2	0	1	0	2
D Total	2	.194	7	31	4	6	2	0	0	3	1	4	0	
L 1991	Atl-N	.200	7	20	1	4	1	0	0	1	4	0	0	2
L 1992	Atl-N	.333	7	21	2	7	1	0	0	2	5	3	0	2-7,3-1
L 1993	Atl-N	.208	6	24	2	5	2	0	0	4	1	6	0	2
L 1995	Atl-N	.167	4	18	2	3	0	0	0	1	1	0	0	2
L 1996	Atl-N	.444	7	27	4	12	2	0	1	5	4	2	0	2
L Total	5	.282	31	110	11	31	6	0	1	13	15	11	0	
W 1991	Atl-N	.417	6	24	4	10	1	3	0	4	2	4	0	2
W 1992	Atl-N	.211	6	19	0	4	0	0	0	2	1	3	0	2
W 1995	Atl-N	.273	6	22	1	6	0	0	0	0	3	2	0	2
W 1996	Atl-N	.231	6	26	2	6	1	0	0	2	0	3	0	2
W Total	4	.286	24	91	7	26	2	3	0	8	6	12	0	
■ Chet Lemon														
L 1984	Det-A	.000	3	13	1	0	0	0	0	0	0	1	0	O
L 1987	Det-A	.278	5	18	4	5	0	0	2	4	1	4	0	O
L Total	2	.161	8	31	5	5	0	0	2	4	1	5	0	
W 1984	Det-A	.294	5	17	1	5	0	0	0	1	2	2	2	O
■ Jeffrey Leonard														
L 1980	Hou-N	.000	3	3	0	0	0	0	0	0	0	2	0	O-1
L 1987	SF-N	.417	7	24	5	10	0	0	4	5	3	4	0	O
L Total	2	.370	10	27	5	10	0	0	4	5	3	6	0	
■ Sam Leslie														
W 1936	NY-N	.667	3	3	0	2	0	0	0	0	0	0	0	H
W 1937	NY-N	.000	2	1	0	0	0	0	0	0	1	0	0	H
W Total	2	.500	5	4	0	2	0	0	0	0	1	0	0	
■ Allan Lewis														
L 1973	Oak-A	—	2	0	1	0	0	0	0	0	0	0	0	R
W 1972	Oak-A	—	6	0	2	0	0	0	0	0	0	0	0	R
W 1973	Oak-A	—	3	0	1	0	0	0	0	0	0	0	0	R
W Total	2	—	9	0	3	0	0	0	0	0	0	0	0	
■ Darren Lewis														
D 1995	Cin-N	.000	3	3	0	0	0	0	0	0	0	1	0	O

YEAR	TM/L	AVG	G	AB	R	H	2B	3B	HR	RBI	BB	SO	SB	POS
D 1998	Bos-A	.357	4	14	4	5	2	0	0	0	1	3	1	O
D 1999	Bos-A	.375	4	16	5	6	1	0	0	2	0	2	1	O
D Total	3	.333	11	33	9	11	3	0	0	2	1	6	2	
L 1995	Cin-N	.000	2	1	0	0	0	0	0	0	0	0	0	O
L 1999	Bos-A	.118	5	17	2	2	1	0	0	1	1	3	1	O
L Total	2	.111	7	18	2	2	1	0	0	1	1	3	1	
■ Duffy Lewis														
W 1912	Bos-A	.156	8	32	4	5	3	0	0	1	2	2	0	O
W 1915	Bos-A	.444	5	18	1	8	1	0	1	5	1	4	0	O
W 1916	Bos-A	.353	5	17	3	6	2	1	0	1	2	1	0	O
W Total	3	.284	18	67	8	19	6	1	1	7	5	7	0	
■ Mark Lewis														
D 1995	Cin-N	.500	2	2	2	1	0	0	1	5	1	0	0	3
D 1997	SF-N	.600	1	5	0	3	0	0	0	1	0	0	0	2
D Total	2	.571	3	7	2	4	0	0	1	6	1	0	0	
L 1995	Cin-N	.250	2	4	0	1	0	0	0	0	1	1	0	3
■ Jim Leyritz														
D 1995	NY-A	.143	2	7	1	1	0	0	1	2	0	1	0	C
D 1996	NY-A	.000	2	3	0	0	0	0	0	1	0	1	0	C-1
D 1998	SD-N	.400	4	10	3	4	0	0	3	5	0	2	0	1-3,C-1
D 1999	NY-A	.000	2	2	0	0	0	0	0	1	1	0	0	D
D Total	4	.227	10	22	4	5	0	0	4	9	1	4	0	
L 1996	NY-A	.250	3	8	1	2	0	0	1	2	1	4	0	C-2,O-1
L 1998	SD-N	.167	5	12	1	2	0	0	1	4	0	2	0	1-3,C-2
L Total	2	.200	8	20	2	4	0	0	2	6	1	6	0	
W 1996	NY-A	.375	4	8	1	3	0	0	1	3	3	2	1	C-3
W 1998	SD-N	.000	4	10	0	0	0	0	0	0	1	4	0	1-2,C-1,D-1
W 1999	NY-A	1.000	2	1	1	1	0	0	1	2	1	0	0	D-1
W Total	3	.211	10	19	2	4	0	0	2	5	5	6	1	
■ Sixto Lezcano														
L 1983	Phi-N	.308	4	13	2	4	0	0	1	2	1	1	0	O
W 1983	Phi-N	.125	4	8	0	1	0	0	0	0	0	2	0	O-3
■ Jose Lind														
L 1990	Pit-N	.238	6	21	1	5	1	1	1	2	1	4	0	2
L 1991	Pit-N	.160	7	25	0	4	0	0	0	3	0	6	0	2
L 1992	Pit-N	.222	7	27	5	6	2	1	1	5	1	4	0	2
L Total	3	.205	20	73	6	15	3	2	2	10	2	14	0	
■ Johnny Lindell														
W 1943	NY-A	.111	4	9	1	1	0	0	0	0	1	4	0	O
W 1947	NY-A	.500	6	18	3	9	3	1	0	7	5	2	0	O
W 1949	NY-A	.143	2	7	0	1	0	0	0	0	0	2	0	O
W Total	3	.324	12	34	4	11	3	1	0	7	6	8	0	
■ Jim Lindeman														
L 1987	StL-N	.308	5	13	1	4	0	0	1	3	0	3	0	1
W 1987	StL-N	.333	6	15	3	5	1	0	0	2	0	3	0	1-6,O-1
■ Freddie Lindstrom														
W 1924	NY-N	.333	7	30	1	10	2	0	0	4	3	6	0	3
W 1935	Chi-N	.200	4	15	0	3	1	0	0	0	1	1	0	O-4,3-1
W Total	2	.289	11	45	1	13	3	0	0	4	4	7	0	
■ Phil Linz														
W 1963	NY-A	.333	3	3	0	1	0	0	0	0	0	1	0	H
W 1964	NY-A	.226	7	31	5	7	1	0	2	2	2	5	0	S
W Total	2	.235	10	34	5	8	1	0	2	2	2	6	0	
■ Nelson Liriano														
L 1989	Tor-A	.429	3	7	1	3	0	0	0	1	2	0	3	2
■ Greg Litton														
L 1989	SF-N	1.000	1	1	0	1	0	0	0	0	0	0	0	3
W 1989	SF-N	.500	2	6	1	3	1	0	1	3	0	0	0	2-2,3-1
■ Danny Litwhiler														
W 1943	StL-N	.267	5	15	0	4	1	0	0	2	2	4	0	O-4
W 1944	StL-N	.200	5	20	2	4	1	0	1	1	2	7	0	O
W Total	2	.229	10	35	2	8	2	0	1	3	4	11	0	
■ Mickey Livingston														
W 1945	Chi-N	.364	6	22	3	8	3	0	0	4	1	1	0	C
■ Scott Livingstone														
D 1996	SD-N	.500	2	2	1	1	0	0	0	0	0	0	0	H
■ Keith Lockhart														
D 1997	Atl-N	.000	2	6	0	0	0	0	0	0	0	1	0	2
D 1998	Atl-N	.333	3	12	2	4	0	0	0	0	1	0	0	2
D 1999	Atl-N	.000	3	1	0	0	0	0	0	0	0	1	0	2-1
D 2000	Atl-N	.125	3	8	0	1	0	0	0	0	0	1	0	2
D Total	4	.185	11	27	2	5	0	0	0	0	1	3	0	
L 1997	Atl-N	.500	5	16	4	8	1	1	0	3	1	1	0	2
L 1998	Atl-N	.235	6	17	2	4	1	1	0	0	0	4	0	2
L 1999	Atl-N	.400	3	5	0	2	0	1	0	1	0	2	0	2-1
L Total	3	.368	14	38	6	14	2	3	0	4	1	7	0	
W 1999	Atl-N	.143	4	7	1	1	0	0	0	0	2	0	0	2-2,D-1
■ Whitey Lockman														
W 1951	NY-N	.240	6	25	1	6	2	0	1	4	1	2	0	1
W 1954	NY-N	.111	4	18	2	2	0	0	0	0	1	2	0	1
W Total	2	.186	10	43	3	8	2	0	1	4	2	4	0	
■ Kenny Lofton														
D 1995	Cle-A	.154	3	13	1	2	0	0	0	0	1	3	0	O
D 1996	Cle-A	.167	4	18	3	3	0	0	0	1	2	3	5	O

YEAR	TM/L	AVG	G	AB	R	H	2B	3B	HR	RBI	BB	SO	SB	POS
D 1997	Atl-N	.154	3	13	2	2	1	0	0	0	1	2	0	O
D 1998	Cle-A	.375	4	16	5	6	1	0	2	4	1	1	2	O
D 1999	Cle-A	.125	5	16	5	2	1	0	0	1	5	6	2	O
D Total	5	.197	19	76	16	15	3	0	2	6	10	15	9	
L 1995	Cle-A	.458	6	24	4	11	0	2	0	3	4	6	5	O
L 1997	Atl-N	.185	6	27	3	5	0	1	0	1	1	7	1	O
L 1998	Cle-A	.185	6	27	2	5	1	0	1	3	1	7	1	O
L Total	3	.269	18	78	9	21	1	3	1	7	6	20	7	
W 1995	Cle-A	.200	6	25	6	5	1	0	0	0	3	1	6	O
■ Johnny Logan														
W 1957	Mil-N	.185	7	27	5	5	1	0	1	2	3	6	0	S
W 1958	Mil-N	.120	7	25	3	3	2	0	0	2	2	4	0	S
W Total	2	.154	14	52	8	8	3	0	1	4	5	10	0	
■ Jack Lohrke														
W 1951	NY-N	.000	2	2	0	0	0	0	0	0	0	1	0	H
■ Sherm Lollar														
W 1947	NY-A	.750	2	4	3	3	2	0	0	1	0	0	0	C
W 1959	Chi-A	.227	6	22	3	5	0	0	1	5	1	3	0	C
W Total	2	.308	8	26	6	8	2	0	1	6	1	3	0	
■ Ernie Lombardi														
W 1939	Cin-N	.214	4	14	0	3	0	0	0	2	0	1	0	C
W 1940	Cin-N	.333	2	3	0	1	1	0	0	0	1	0	0	C-1
W Total	2	.235	6	17	0	4	1	0	0	2	1	1	0	
■ Steve Lombardozzi														
L 1987	Min-A	.267	5	15	2	4	0	0	0	1	2	2	0	2
W 1987	Min-A	.412	6	17	3	7	1	0	1	4	2	3	0	2
■ Herman Long														
T 1892	Bos-N	.222	6	27	4	6	0	0	0	1	0	0	2	S
T 1897	Bos-N	.286	5	21	4	6	1	1	1	5	2	2	1	S
T Total	2	.250	11	48	8	12	1	1	1	6	2	2	3	
■ Dale Long														
W 1960	NY-A	.333	3	3	0	1	0	0	0	0	0	0	0	H
W 1962	NY-A	.200	2	5	0	1	0	0	0	1	0	1	0	1
W Total	2	.250	5	8	0	2	0	0	0	1	0	1	0	
■ Terrence Long														
D 2000	Oak-A	.158	5	19	2	3	0	0	1	1	3	2	0	O
■ Tony Longmire														
L 1993	Phi-N	.000	1	1	0	0	0	0	0	0	0	1	0	H
■ Stan Lopata														
W 1950	Phi-N	.000	2	1	0	0	0	0	0	0	0	1	0	C-1
■ Davey Lopes														
D 1981	LA-N	.200	5	20	1	4	1	0	0	0	3	7	1	2
L 1974	LA-N	.267	4	15	4	4	0	1	0	3	5	1	3	2
L 1977	LA-N	.235	4	17	2	4	0	0	0	3	2	0	0	2
L 1978	LA-N	.389	4	18	3	7	1	1	2	5	0	1	1	2
L 1981	LA-N	.278	5	18	0	5	0	0	0	0	1	3	5	2
L 1984	Chi-N	.000	2	1	0	0	0	0	0	0	0	0	0	O-1
L 1986	Hou-N	.000	3	2	1	0	0	0	0	0	1	0	0	H
L Total	6	.282	22	71	10	20	1	2	2	11	9	5	9	
W 1974	LA-N	.111	5	18	2	2	0	0	0	0	3	4	2	2
W 1977	LA-N	.167	6	24	3	4	0	1	1	2	4	3	2	2
W 1978	LA-N	.308	6	26	7	8	0	0	3	7	2	1	2	2
W 1981	LA-N	.227	6	22	6	5	1	0	0	2	4	3	4	2
W Total	4	.211	23	90	18	19	1	1	4	11	13	11	10	
■ Hector Lopez														
W 1960	NY-A	.429	3	7	0	3	0	0	0	0	0	0	0	O-1
W 1961	NY-A	.333	4	9	3	3	0	1	1	7	2	3	0	O-3
W 1962	NY-A	.000	2	2	0	0	0	0	0	0	0	0	0	H
W 1963	NY-A	.250	3	8	1	2	2	0	0	0	0	1	0	O-2
W 1964	NY-A	.000	3	2	0	0	0	0	0	0	0	2	0	O-1
W Total	5	.286	15	28	4	8	2	1	1	7	2	6	0	
■ Javy Lopez														
D 1995	Atl-N	.444	3	9	0	4	0	0	0	3	0	3	0	C
D 1996	Atl-N	.286	2	7	1	2	0	0	1	1	1	0	1	C
D 1997	Atl-N	.286	2	7	3	2	2	0	0	1	2	1	0	C
D 1998	Atl-N	.286	2	7	1	2	0	0	1	1	1	1	0	C
D 2000	Atl-N	.091	3	11	0	1	0	0	0	0	0	1	0	C
D Total	5	.268	12	41	5	11	2	0	2	6	4	6	1	
L 1992	Atl-N	.000	1	1	0	0	0	0	0	0	0	0	0	C
L 1995	Atl-N	.357	3	14	2	5	1	0	1	3	0	1	0	C
L 1996	Atl-N	.542	7	24	8	13	5	0	2	6	3	1	1	C
L 1997	Atl-N	.059	5	17	0	1	1	0	0	2	1	7	0	C
L 1998	Atl-N	.300	6	20	2	6	0	0	1	1	0	7	0	C
L Total	5	.329	22	76	12	25	7	0	4	12	4	16	1	
W 1995	Atl-N	.176	6	17	1	3	2	0	1	3	1	1	0	C
W 1996	Atl-N	.190	6	21	3	4	0	0	0	1	3	4	0	C
W Total	2	.184	12	38	4	7	2	0	1	4	4	5	0	
■ Luis Lopez														
D 1996	SD-N	—	1	0	0	0	0	0	0	0	0	0	0	R
■ Bris Lord														
W 1905	Phi-A	.100	5	20	0	2	0	0	0	2	0	5	0	O
W 1910	Phi-A	.182	5	22	3	4	2	0	0	1	1	3	0	O
W 1911	Phi-A	.185	6	27	2	5	2	0	0	1	0	5	0	O
W Total	3	.159	16	69	5	11	4	0	0	4	1	13	0	
■ Bobby Lowe														
T 1892	Bos-N	.130	6	23	2	3	0	0	0	0	1	2	1	O
T 1897	Bos-N	.391	5	23	6	9	2	0	0	6	1	0	1	2
T Total	2	.261	11	46	8	12	2	0	0	6	2	2	2	
■ John Lowenstein														
L 1979	Bal-A	.167	4	6	2	1	0	0	1	3	2	2	0	O-3
L 1983	Bal-A	.167	3	6	0	1	1	0	0	2	1	2	0	O-2
L Total	2	.167	7	12	2	2	1	0	1	5	3	4	0	
W 1979	Bal-A	.231	6	13	2	3	1	0	0	3	1	3	0	O-3
W 1983	Bal-A	.385	4	13	2	5	1	0	1	1	0	3	0	O
W Total	2	.308	10	26	4	8	2	0	1	4	1	6	0	
■ Peanuts Lowrey														
W 1945	Chi-N	.310	7	29	4	9	1	0	0	0	1	2	0	O
■ Fred Luderus														
W 1915	Phi-N	.438	5	16	1	7	2	0	1	6	1	4	0	1
■ Mike Lum														
L 1969	Atl-N	1.000	2	2	0	2	1	0	0	0	0	0	0	O-1
L 1976	Cin-N	.000	1	1	0	0	0	0	0	0	0	0	0	H
L Total	2	.667	3	3	0	2	1	0	0	0	0	0	0	
■ Jerry Lumpe														
W 1957	NY-A	.286	6	14	0	4	0	0	0	2	1	1	0	3-3
W 1958	NY-A	.167	6	12	0	2	0	0	0	0	1	2	0	3-3,S-2
W Total	2	.231	12	26	0	6	0	0	0	2	2	3	0	
■ Harry Lunte														
W 1920	Cle-A	—	1	0	0	0	0	0	0	0	0	0	0	2
■ Greg Luzinski														
L 1976	Phi-N	.273	3	11	2	3	2	0	1	3	1	4	0	O
L 1977	Phi-N	.286	4	14	2	4	1	0	1	2	3	3	1	O
L 1978	Phi-N	.375	4	16	3	6	0	1	2	3	1	2	0	O
L 1980	Phi-N	.294	5	17	3	5	2	0	1	4	0	6	0	O
L 1983	Chi-A	.133	4	15	0	2	1	0	0	0	1	5	0	D
L Total	5	.274	20	73	10	20	6	1	5	12	6	20	1	
W 1980	Phi-N	.000	3	9	0	0	0	0	0	0	1	5	0	D-2,O-1
■ Jerry Lynch														
W 1961	Cin-N	.000	4	3	0	0	0	0	0	0	1	1	0	H
■ Byrd Lynn														
W 1917	Chi-A	.000	1	1	0	0	0	0	0	0	0	1	0	H
W 1919	Chi-A	.000	1	1	0	0	0	0	0	0	0	0	0	C
W Total	2	.000	2	2	0	0	0	0	0	0	0	1	0	
■ Fred Lynn														
L 1975	Bos-A	.364	3	11	1	4	1	0	0	3	0	0	0	O
L 1982	Cal-A	.611	5	18	4	11	2	0	1	5	2	3	0	O
L Total	2	.517	8	29	5	15	3	0	1	8	2	3	0	
W 1975	Bos-A	.280	7	25	3	7	1	0	1	5	3	5	0	O
■ Harry Lyons														
W 1887	StL-A	.375	2	8	3	3	0	0	0	2	1	0	0	S
W 1888	StL-A	.118	5	17	0	2	0	0	0	1	1	5	0	O
W Total	2	.200	7	25	3	5	0	0	0	3	2	5	0	
■ John Mabry														
D 1996	StL-N	.300	3	10	1	3	0	1	0	1	1	1	0	1
L 1996	StL-N	.261	7	23	1	6	0	0	0	0	0	6	0	1-6,O-2
■ Mike Macfarlane														
D 1995	Bos-A	.333	3	9	0	3	0	0	0	1	0	3	0	C
■ Shane Mack														
L 1991	Min-A	.333	5	18	4	6	1	1	0	3	2	4	2	O
W 1991	Min-A	.130	6	23	0	3	1	0	0	1	0	7	0	O
■ Elliott Maddox														
L 1976	NY-A	.222	3	9	0	2	1	0	0	1	0	1	0	O
W 1976	NY-A	.200	2	5	0	1	0	1	0	0	1	2	0	O-1,D-1
■ Garry Maddox														
D 1981	Phi-N	.333	2	3	0	1	1	0	0	0	0	0	0	O
L 1976	Phi-N	.231	3	13	2	3	1	0	0	1	1	0	0	O
L 1977	Phi-N	.429	2	7	1	3	0	0	0	2	0	1	0	O
L 1978	Phi-N	.263	4	19	1	5	0	0	0	2	0	3	0	O
L 1980	Phi-N	.300	5	20	2	6	2	0	0	3	2	2	2	O
L 1983	Phi-N	.273	3	11	0	3	1	0	0	1	0	1	0	O
L Total	5	.286	17	70	6	20	4	0	0	9	3	7	2	
W 1980	Phi-N	.227	6	22	1	5	2	0	0	1	1	3	0	O
W 1983	Phi-N	.250	4	12	1	3	1	0	1	1	0	2	0	O-3
W Total	2	.235	10	34	2	8	3	0	1	2	1	5	0	
■ Bill Madlock														
L 1979	Pit-N	.250	3	12	1	3	0	0	1	2	2	0	2	3
L 1985	LA-N	.333	6	24	5	8	1	0	3	7	0	2	1	3
L 1987	Det-A	.000	1	5	0	0	0	0	0	0	0	3	0	D
L Total	3	.268	10	41	6	11	1	0	4	9	2	5	3	
W 1979	Pit-N	.375	7	24	2	9	1	0	0	3	5	1	0	3
■ Dave Magadan														
L 1988	NY-N	.000	3	3	0	0	0	0	0	0	0	2	0	H
■ Sherry Magee														
W 1919	Cin-N	.500	2	2	0	1	0	0	0	0	0	0	0	H
■ Freddie Maguire														
W 1923	NY-N	—	2	0	1	0	0	0	0	0	0	0	0	R

YEAR	TM/L	AVG	G	AB	R	H	2B	3B	HR	RBI	BB	SO	SB	POS
■ Bob Maier														
W 1945	Det-A	1.000	1	1	0	1	0	0	0	0	0	0	0	H
■ Hank Majeski														
W 1954	Cle-A	.167	4	6	1	1	0	0	1	3	0	1	0	3-1
■ Candy Maldonado														
L 1983	LA-N	.000	2	2	0	0	0	0	0	0	0	1	0	H
L 1985	LA-N	.143	4	7	0	1	0	0	0	1	0	3	0	O-3
L 1987	SF-N	.211	5	19	2	4	1	0	0	2	0	3	0	O
L 1989	SF-N	.000	3	3	1	0	0	0	0	1	2	0	0	O
L 1991	Tor-A	.100	5	20	1	2	1	0	0	1	1	6	0	O
L 1992	Tor-A	.273	6	22	3	6	0	0	2	6	3	4	0	O
L Total	6	.178	25	73	7	13	2	0	2	11	6	17	0	
W 1989	SF-N	.091	4	11	1	1	0	1	0	0	0	4	0	O-3
W 1992	Tor-A	.158	6	19	1	3	0	0	1	2	2	5	0	O-5
W Total	2	.133	10	30	2	4	0	1	1	2	2	9	0	
■ Marty Malloy														
L 1998	Atl-N	.000	4	1	1	0	0	0	0	0	0	1	0	2-1
■ Gus Mancuso														
W 1930	StL-N	.286	2	7	1	2	0	0	0	0	1	2	0	C
W 1931	StL-N	.000	2	1	0	0	0	0	0	0	0	0	0	C-1
W 1933	NY-N	.118	5	17	2	2	1	0	0	2	3	0	0	C
W 1936	NY-N	.263	6	19	3	5	2	0	0	1	3	3	0	C
W 1937	NY-N	.000	3	8	0	0	0	0	0	1	0	1	0	C-2
W Total	5	.173	18	52	6	9	3	0	0	4	7	6	0	
■ Frank Mancuso														
W 1944	StL-A	.667	2	3	0	2	0	0	0	1	0	0	0	C-1
■ Angel Mangual														
L 1971	Oak-A	.167	3	12	1	2	1	1	0	2	0	1	0	O
L 1972	Oak-A	.000	3	3	0	0	0	0	0	0	0	1	0	H
L 1973	Oak-A	.111	3	9	1	1	0	0	0	0	0	3	0	O
L 1974	Oak-A	.250	1	4	0	1	0	0	0	0	0	0	0	D
L Total	4	.143	10	28	2	4	1	1	0	2	0	5	0	
W 1972	Oak-A	.300	4	10	1	3	0	0	0	1	0	0	0	O-2
W 1973	Oak-A	.000	5	6	0	0	0	0	0	0	0	3	0	O-1
W 1974	Oak-A	.000	1	1	0	0	0	0	0	0	0	1	0	H
W Total	3	.176	10	17	1	3	0	0	0	1	0	4	0	
■ Les Mann														
W 1914	Bos-N	.286	3	7	1	2	0	0	0	1	0	1	0	O-2
W 1918	Chi-N	.227	6	22	0	5	2	0	0	2	0	0	0	O
W Total	2	.241	9	29	1	7	2	0	0	3	0	1	0	
■ Felix Mantilla														
W 1957	Mil-N	.000	4	10	1	0	0	0	0	0	1	0	0	2-3
W 1958	Mil-N	—	4	0	1	0	0	0	0	0	0	0	0	S-1
W Total	2	.000	8	10	2	0	0	0	0	0	1	0	0	
■ Mickey Mantle														
W 1951	NY-A	.200	2	5	1	1	0	0	0	0	2	1	0	O
W 1952	NY-A	.345	7	29	5	10	1	1	2	3	3	4	0	O
W 1953	NY-A	.208	6	24	3	5	0	0	2	7	3	8	0	O
W 1955	NY-A	.200	3	10	1	2	0	0	1	1	0	2	0	O-2
W 1956	NY-A	.250	7	24	6	6	1	0	3	4	6	5	1	O
W 1957	NY-A	.263	6	19	3	5	0	0	1	2	3	1	0	O-5
W 1958	NY-A	.250	7	24	4	6	0	1	2	3	7	4	0	O
W 1960	NY-A	.400	7	25	8	10	1	0	3	11	8	9	0	O
W 1961	NY-A	.167	2	6	0	1	0	0	0	0	0	2	0	O
W 1962	NY-A	.120	7	25	2	3	1	0	0	0	4	5	2	O
W 1963	NY-A	.133	4	15	1	2	0	0	1	1	1	5	0	O
W 1964	NY-A	.333	7	24	8	8	2	0	3	8	6	8	0	O
W Total	12	.257	65	230	42	59	6	2	18	40	43	54	3	
■ Chuck Manuel														
L 1969	Min-A	—	1	0	0	0	0	0	0	0	1	0	0	H
L 1970	Min-A	.000	1	1	0	0	0	0	0	0	0	1	0	H
L Total	2	.000	2	1	0	0	0	0	0	0	1	1	0	
■ Jerry Manuel														
D 1981	Mon-N	.071	5	14	0	1	0	0	0	0	2	5	0	2
L 1981	Mon-N	—	1	0	0	0	0	0	0	0	0	0	0	R
■ Heinie Manush														
W 1933	Was-A	.111	5	18	2	2	0	0	0	0	2	1	0	O
■ Kirt Manwaring														
L 1989	SF-N	.000	3	2	0	0	0	0	0	0	0	0	0	C
W 1989	SF-N	1.000	1	1	1	1	1	0	0	0	0	0	0	C
■ Cliff Mapes														
W 1949	NY-A	.100	4	10	3	1	1	0	0	2	2	4	0	O
W 1950	NY-A	.000	1	4	0	0	0	0	0	0	0	1	0	O
W Total	2	.071	5	14	3	1	1	0	0	2	2	5	0	
■ Rabbit Maranville														
W 1914	Bos-N	.308	4	13	1	4	0	0	0	3	1	1	2	S
W 1928	StL-N	.308	4	13	2	4	1	0	0	0	1	1	1	S
W Total	2	.308	8	26	3	8	1	0	0	3	2	2	3	
■ Marty Marion														
W 1942	StL-N	.111	5	18	2	2	0	1	0	3	1	2	0	S
W 1943	StL-N	.357	5	14	1	5	2	0	1	2	3	1	1	S
W 1944	StL-N	.227	6	22	1	5	3	0	0	2	2	3	0	S
W 1946	StL-N	.250	7	24	1	6	2	0	0	4	1	1	0	S
W Total	4	.231	23	78	5	18	7	1	1	11	7	7	1	

YEAR	TM/L	AVG	G	AB	R	H	2B	3B	HR	RBI	BB	SO	SB	POS
■ Roger Maris														
W 1960	NY-A	.267	7	30	6	8	1	0	2	2	2	4	0	O
W 1961	NY-A	.105	5	19	4	2	1	0	1	2	4	6	0	O
W 1962	NY-A	.174	7	23	4	4	1	0	1	5	5	2	0	O
W 1963	NY-A	.000	2	5	0	0	0	0	0	0	0	1	0	O
W 1964	NY-A	.200	7	30	4	6	0	0	1	1	1	4	0	O
W 1967	StL-N	.385	7	26	3	10	1	0	1	7	3	1	0	O
W 1968	StL-N	.158	6	19	5	3	1	0	0	1	3	3	0	O-5
W Total	7	.217	41	152	26	33	5	0	6	18	18	21	0	
■ Gonzalo Marquez														
L 1972	Oak-A	.667	3	3	1	2	0	0	0	1	0	0	0	H
W 1972	Oak-A	.600	5	5	0	3	0	0	0	1	0	0	0	H
■ Eli Marrero														
L 2000	StL-N	.000	4	4	0	0	0	0	0	1	0	1	0	C-3
■ Mike Marshall														
D 1981	LA-N	.000	1	1	0	0	0	0	0	0	0	1	0	H
L 1983	LA-N	.133	4	15	1	2	1	0	1	2	1	6	0	1-3,O-2
L 1985	LA-N	.217	6	23	1	5	2	0	1	3	1	3	0	O
L 1988	LA-N	.233	7	30	3	7	1	1	0	5	2	9	0	O
L 1990	Bos-A	.333	3	3	0	1	0	0	0	0	0	0	0	H
L Total	4	.211	20	71	5	15	4	1	2	10	4	18	0	
W 1988	LA-N	.231	5	13	2	3	0	1	1	3	0	5	0	O
■ Al Martin														
D 2000	Sea-A	.000	1	1	0	0	0	0	0	0	0	0	0	H
L 2000	Sea-A	.182	4	11	2	2	2	0	0	0	2	3	0	O-3
■ Billy Martin														
W 1951	NY-A	—	1	0	1	0	0	0	0	0	0	0	0	R
W 1952	NY-A	.217	7	23	2	5	0	0	1	4	2	2	0	2
W 1953	NY-A	.500	6	24	5	12	1	2	2	8	1	2	1	2
W 1955	NY-A	.320	7	25	2	8	1	1	0	4	1	5	0	2
W 1956	NY-A	.296	7	27	5	8	0	0	2	3	1	6	0	2-7,3-1
W Total	5	.333	28	99	15	33	2	3	5	19	5	15	1	
■ Jerry Martin														
L 1976	Phi-N	.000	1	1	1	0	0	0	0	0	0	0	0	O
L 1977	Phi-N	.000	3	4	0	0	0	0	0	0	0	2	0	O-1
L 1978	Phi-N	.222	4	9	1	2	1	0	1	2	1	3	0	O-3
L Total	3	.143	8	14	2	2	1	0	1	2	1	5	0	
■ Pepper Martin														
W 1928	StL-N	—	1	0	1	0	0	0	0	0	0	0	0	R
W 1931	StL-N	.500	7	24	5	12	4	0	1	5	2	3	5	O
W 1934	StL-N	.355	7	31	8	11	3	1	0	4	3	3	2	3
W Total	3	.418	15	55	14	23	7	1	1	9	5	6	7	
■ J. C. Martin														
L 1969	NY-N	.500	2	2	0	1	0	0	0	2	0	0	0	H
W 1969	NY-N	—	1	0	0	0	0	0	0	0	0	0	0	H
■ Angel Martinez														
D 1998	Chi-N	1.000	1	1	1	1	0	0	0	0	0	0	0	C
■ Carmelo Martinez														
L 1984	SD-N	.176	5	17	1	3	0	0	0	0	2	4	0	O
L 1990	Pit-N	.250	2	8	0	2	2	0	0	2	0	1	0	1
L Total	2	.200	7	25	1	5	2	0	0	2	2	5	0	
W 1984	SD-N	.176	5	17	0	3	0	0	0	0	1	9	0	O
■ Tino Martinez														
D 1995	Sea-A	.409	5	22	4	9	1	0	1	5	3	4	0	1
D 1996	NY-A	.267	4	15	3	4	2	0	0	0	3	1	0	1
D 1997	NY-A	.222	5	18	1	4	1	0	1	4	2	4	0	1
D 1998	NY-A	.273	3	11	1	3	2	0	0	0	0	2	0	1
D 1999	NY-A	.182	3	11	2	2	0	0	0	0	2	2	0	1
D 2000	NY-A	.421	5	19	2	8	2	0	0	4	1	3	0	1
D Total	6	.313	25	96	13	30	8	0	2	13	11	16	0	
L 1995	Sea-A	.136	6	22	1	3	0	0	0	0	3	7	0	1
L 1996	NY-A	.182	5	22	3	4	1	0	0	0	0	2	0	1
L 1998	NY-A	.105	6	19	1	2	1	0	0	1	6	8	2	1
L 1999	NY-A	.263	5	19	3	5	1	0	1	3	2	4	0	1
L 2000	NY-A	.320	6	25	5	8	2	0	1	1	2	4	0	1
L Total	5	.206	28	107	13	22	5	0	2	5	13	25	2	
W 1996	NY-A	.091	6	11	0	1	0	0	0	0	2	5	0	1-5
W 1998	NY-A	.385	4	13	4	5	0	0	1	4	4	2	0	1
W 1999	NY-A	.267	4	15	3	4	0	0	1	5	2	4	0	1
W 2000	NY-A	.364	5	22	3	8	1	0	0	2	1	4	0	1
W Total	4	.295	19	61	10	18	1	0	2	11	9	15	0	
■ Edgar Martinez														
D 1995	Sea-A	.571	5	21	6	12	3	0	2	10	6	2	0	D
D 1997	Sea-A	.188	4	16	2	3	0	0	2	3	0	3	0	D
D 2000	Sea-A	.364	3	11	2	4	1	0	1	2	2	1	0	D
D Total	3	.396	12	48	10	19	4	0	5	15	8	6	0	
L 1995	Sea-A	.087	6	23	0	2	0	0	0	0	2	5	1	D
L 2000	Sea-A	.238	6	21	2	5	1	0	1	4	3	5	0	D
L Total	2	.159	12	44	2	7	1	0	1	4	5	10	1	
■ Buck Martinez														
L 1976	KC-A	.333	5	15	0	5	0	0	0	4	1	3	0	C
■ Ramon Martinez														
D 2000	SF-N	.333	2	6	0	2	0	0	0	0	0	2	0	2-1,S-1
■ Ted Martinez														
L 1975	Oak-A	—	3	0	0	0	0	0	0	0	0	0	0	2

YEAR	TM/L	AVG	G	AB	R	H	2B	3B	HR	RBI	BB	SO	SB	POS
W 1973	NY-N	—	2	0	0	0	0	0	0	0	0	0	0	R
■ **Joe Marty**														
W 1938	Chi-N	.500	3	12	1	6	1	0	1	5	0	2	0	O
■ **Phil Masi**														
W 1948	Bos-N	.125	5	8	1	1	1	0	0	1	0	0	0	C
■ **Jim Mason**														
L 1976	NY-A	—	2	0	0	0	0	0	0	0	0	0	0	S
W 1976	NY-A	1.000	3	1	1	1	0	0	1	1	0	0	0	S
■ **Tom Matchick**														
W 1968	Det-A	.000	3	3	0	0	0	0	0	0	0	1	0	H
■ **Eddie Mathews**														
W 1957	Mil-N	.227	7	22	4	5	3	0	1	4	8	5	0	3
W 1958	Mil-N	.160	7	25	3	4	2	0	0	3	6	11	1	3
W 1968	Det-A	.333	2	3	0	1	0	0	0	0	1	1	0	3-1
W Total	3	.200	16	50	7	10	5	0	1	7	15	17	1	
■ **Gary Matthews Sr.**														
D 1981	Phi-N	.400	5	20	3	8	0	1	1	1	0	2	0	O
L 1983	Phi-N	.429	4	14	4	6	0	0	3	8	2	1	1	O
L 1984	Chi-N	.200	5	15	4	3	0	0	2	5	6	4	1	O
L Total	2	.310	9	29	8	9	0	0	5	13	8	5	2	
W 1983	Phi-N	.250	5	16	1	4	0	0	1	1	2	2	0	O
■ **Don Mattingly**														
D 1995	NY-A	.417	5	24	3	10	4	0	1	6	1	5	0	1
■ **Len Matuszek**														
L 1985	LA-N	1.000	3	1	1	1	0	0	0	0	0	0	0	1-1,O-1
■ **Dal Maxvill**														
L 1972	Oak-A	.125	5	8	0	1	0	0	0	0	1	2	1	S-4,2-1
L 1974	Oak-A	.000	1	1	0	0	0	0	0	0	0	1	0	2
L Total	2	.111	6	9	0	1	0	0	0	0	1	3	1	
W 1964	StL-N	.200	7	20	0	4	1	0	0	1	1	4	0	2
W 1967	StL-N	.158	7	19	1	3	0	1	0	1	4	1	0	S
W 1968	StL-N	.000	7	22	1	0	0	0	0	0	3	5	0	S
W 1974	Oak-A	—	2	0	0	0	0	0	0	0	0	0	0	2
W Total	4	.115	23	61	2	7	1	1	0	2	8	10	0	
■ **Carlos May**														
L 1976	NY-A	.200	3	10	1	2	1	0	0	0	1	4	0	D
W 1976	NY-A	.000	4	9	0	0	0	0	0	0	0	1	0	D
■ **Dave May**														
L 1969	Bal-A	.000	1	1	0	0	0	0	0	0	0	0	0	H
W 1969	Bal-A	.000	2	1	0	0	0	0	0	0	1	1	0	H
■ **Lee May**														
D 1981	KC-A	—	1	0	0	0	0	0	0	0	0	0	0	1
L 1970	Cin-N	.167	3	12	0	2	1	0	0	2	0	2	0	1
L 1979	Bal-A	.143	2	7	0	1	0	0	0	1	1	3	0	D
L Total	2	.158	5	19	0	3	1	0	0	3	1	5	0	
W 1970	Cin-N	.389	5	18	6	7	2	0	2	8	2	2	0	1
W 1979	Bal-A	.000	2	1	0	0	0	0	0	0	1	1	0	H
W Total	2	.368	7	19	6	7	2	0	2	8	3	3	0	
■ **Milt May**														
L 1971	Pit-N	.000	1	1	0	0	0	0	0	0	0	0	0	H
L 1972	Pit-N	.500	1	2	0	1	0	0	0	1	0	0	0	C
L Total	2	.333	2	3	0	1	0	0	0	1	0	0	0	
W 1971	Pit-N	.500	2	2	0	1	0	0	0	1	0	0	0	H
■ **John Mayberry**														
L 1976	KC-A	.222	5	18	4	4	0	0	1	3	1	0	0	1
L 1977	KC-A	.167	4	12	1	2	1	0	1	3	1	2	0	1
L Total	2	.200	9	30	5	6	1	0	2	6	2	2	0	
■ **Eddie Mayo**														
W 1936	NY-N	.000	1	1	0	0	0	0	0	0	0	0	0	3
W 1945	Det-A	.250	7	28	4	7	1	0	0	2	3	2	0	2
W Total	2	.241	8	29	4	7	1	0	0	2	3	2	0	
■ **Jackie Mayo**														
W 1950	Phi-N	—	3	0	0	0	0	0	0	0	1	0	0	O-1
■ **Willie Mays**														
L 1971	SF-N	.267	4	15	2	4	2	0	1	3	3	3	1	O
L 1973	NY-N	.333	1	3	1	1	0	0	0	1	0	0	0	O
L Total	2	.278	5	18	3	5	2	0	1	4	3	3	1	
W 1951	NY-N	.182	6	22	1	4	0	0	0	1	2	2	0	O
W 1954	NY-N	.286	4	14	4	4	1	0	0	3	4	1	1	O
W 1962	SF-N	.250	7	28	3	7	2	0	0	1	1	5	1	O
W 1973	NY-N	.286	3	7	1	2	0	0	0	1	0	1	0	O-2
W Total	4	.239	20	71	9	17	3	0	0	6	7	9	2	
■ **Bill Mazeroski**														
L 1970	Pit-N	.000	1	2	0	0	0	0	0	0	2	0	0	2
L 1971	Pit-N	1.000	1	1	1	1	0	0	0	0	0	0	0	H
L 1972	Pit-N	.500	2	2	0	1	0	0	0	0	0	1	0	H
L Total	3	.400	4	5	1	2	0	0	0	0	2	1	0	
W 1960	Pit-N	.320	7	25	4	8	2	0	2	5	0	3	0	2
W 1971	Pit-N	.000	1	1	0	0	0	0	0	0	0	0	0	H
W Total	2	.308	8	26	4	8	2	0	2	5	0	3	0	
■ **Lee Mazzilli**														
L 1986	NY-N	.200	5	5	0	1	0	0	0	0	0	3	0	H
L 1988	NY-N	.500	3	2	0	1	0	0	0	0	0	0	1	H

YEAR	TM/L	AVG	G	AB	R	H	2B	3B	HR	RBI	BB	SO	SB	POS
L 1989	Tor-A	.000	3	8	0	0	0	0	0	0	0	2	0	D-2
L Total	3	.133	11	15	0	2	0	0	0	0	0	5	1	
W 1986	NY-N	.400	4	5	2	2	0	0	0	0	0	0	0	O-1
■ **Jimmy McAleer**														
T 1892	Cle-N	.182	6	22	0	4	0	0	0	1	2	2	1	O
T 1895	Cle-N	.286	5	21	2	6	0	0	0	2	0	0	1	O
T 1896	Cle-N	.133	4	15	0	2	0	0	0	1	1	2	1	O
T Total	3	.207	15	58	2	12	0	0	0	4	3	4	3	
■ **Jim McAnany**														
W 1959	Chi-A	.000	3	5	0	0	0	0	0	0	1	0	0	O
■ **Dick McAuliffe**														
L 1972	Det-A	.200	5	20	3	4	0	0	1	1	1	4	0	S-4,2-1
W 1968	Det-A	.222	7	27	5	6	0	0	1	3	4	6	0	2
■ **Bake McBride**														
D 1981	Phi-N	.200	4	15	1	3	1	0	0	0	0	5	0	O
L 1977	Phi-N	.222	4	18	2	4	0	0	1	2	1	2	0	O
L 1978	Phi-N	.222	3	9	2	2	0	0	1	1	0	2	0	O-2
L 1980	Phi-N	.238	5	21	0	5	0	0	0	0	1	5	2	O
L Total	3	.229	12	48	4	11	0	0	2	3	2	9	2	
W 1980	Phi-N	.304	6	23	3	7	1	0	1	5	2	1	0	O
■ **Tom McBride**														
W 1946	Bos-A	.167	5	12	0	2	0	0	0	1	0	1	0	O-2
■ **Bill McCabe**														
W 1918	Chi-N	.000	3	1	1	0	0	0	0	0	0	0	0	H
W 1920	Bro-N	—	1	0	0	0	0	0	0	0	0	0	0	R
W Total	2	.000	4	1	1	0	0	0	0	0	0	0	0	
■ **Johnny McCarthy**														
W 1937	NY-N	.211	5	19	1	4	1	0	0	1	1	2	0	1
■ **Tommy McCarthy**														
W 1888	StL-A	.244	10	41	10	10	1	0	1	9	0	0	6	O
T 1892	Bos-N	.381	6	21	8	8	2	0	0	2	6	1	3	O
■ **Lew McCarty**														
W 1917	NY-N	.400	3	5	1	2	0	1	0	1	0	0	0	C-2
■ **Tim McCarver**														
L 1976	Phi-N	.000	2	4	0	0	0	0	0	0	0	1	0	C-1
L 1977	Phi-N	.167	3	6	1	1	0	0	0	0	1	3	0	C-2
L 1978	Phi-N	.000	2	4	2	0	0	0	0	1	2	0	0	C-1
L Total	3	.071	7	14	3	1	0	0	0	1	3	4	0	
W 1964	StL-N	.478	7	23	4	11	1	1	1	5	5	1	1	C
W 1967	StL-N	.125	7	24	3	3	1	0	0	2	2	2	0	C
W 1968	StL-N	.333	7	27	3	9	0	2	1	4	3	2	0	C
W Total	3	.311	21	74	10	23	2	3	2	11	10	5	1	
■ **Lloyd McClendon**														
L 1989	Chi-N	.667	3	3	0	2	0	0	0	0	1	0	0	C-2,O-1
L 1991	Pit-N	.000	3	2	0	0	0	0	0	0	1	0	0	1-1
L 1992	Pit-N	.727	5	11	4	8	2	0	1	4	4	1	0	O
L Total	3	.625	11	16	4	10	2	0	1	4	6	1	0	
■ **Frank McCormick**														
W 1939	Cin-N	.400	4	15	1	6	1	0	0	1	0	1	0	1
W 1940	Cin-N	.214	7	28	2	6	1	0	0	0	1	1	0	1
W 1948	Bos-N	.200	3	5	0	1	0	0	0	0	0	2	0	1-1
W Total	3	.271	14	48	3	13	2	0	0	1	1	4	0	
■ **Moose McCormick**														
W 1912	NY-N	.250	5	4	0	1	0	0	0	1	0	0	0	H
W 1913	NY-N	.500	2	2	1	1	0	0	0	0	0	0	0	H
W Total	2	.333	7	6	1	2	0	0	0	1	0	0	0	
■ **Mike McCormick**														
W 1940	Cin-N	.310	7	29	1	9	3	0	0	2	1	6	0	O
W 1948	Bos-N	.261	6	23	1	6	0	0	0	2	0	4	0	O
W 1949	Bro-N	—	1	0	0	0	0	0	0	0	0	0	0	O
W Total	3	.288	14	52	2	15	3	0	0	4	1	10	0	
■ **Barney McCosky**														
W 1940	Det-A	.304	7	23	5	7	1	0	0	1	7	0	0	O
■ **Willie McCovey**														
L 1971	SF-N	.429	4	14	2	6	0	0	2	6	4	2	0	1
W 1962	SF-N	.200	4	15	2	3	0	1	1	1	1	3	0	1-2,O-2
■ **Clyde McCullough**														
W 1945	Chi-N	.000	1	1	0	0	0	0	0	0	0	1	0	H
■ **Gil McDougald**														
W 1951	NY-A	.261	6	23	2	6	1	0	1	7	2	2	0	3-5,2-4
W 1952	NY-A	.200	7	25	5	5	0	0	1	3	5	2	1	3
W 1953	NY-A	.167	6	24	2	4	0	1	2	4	1	3	0	3
W 1955	NY-A	.259	7	27	2	7	0	0	1	1	2	6	0	3
W 1956	NY-A	.143	7	21	0	3	0	0	0	1	3	6	0	S
W 1957	NY-A	.250	7	24	3	6	0	0	0	2	3	3	1	S
W 1958	NY-A	.321	7	28	5	9	2	0	2	4	2	4	0	2
W 1960	NY-A	.278	6	18	4	5	1	0	0	2	2	3	0	3
W Total	8	.237	53	190	23	45	4	1	7	24	20	29	2	
■ **Joe McEwing**														
D 2000	NY-N	1.000	4	1	0	1	0	0	0	0	0	0	0	O-3,3-1
L 2000	NY-N	—	4	0	2	0	0	0	0	0	0	0	0	O-3,3-1
W 2000	NY-N	.000	3	1	1	0	0	0	0	0	0	0	0	O-2

YEAR	TM/L	AVG	G	AB	R	H	2B	3B	HR	RBI	BB	SO	SB	POS
■ Ed McFarland														
W 1906	Chi-A	.000	1	1	0	0	0	0	0	0	0	0	0	H
■ Dan McGann														
W 1905	NY-N	.235	5	17	1	4	2	0	0	4	2	7	0	1
■ Chippy McGarr														
T 1895	Cle-N	.368	5	19	3	7	2	0	0	1	1	1	2	3
T 1896	Cle-N	.063	4	16	0	1	0	0	0	0	0	3	2	3
T Total	2	.229	9	35	3	8	2	0	0	1	1	4	4	
■ Willie McGee														
D 1995	Bos-A	.250	2	4	0	1	0	0	0	1	0	2	0	O
D 1996	StL-N	.100	3	10	1	1	0	0	0	1	1	3	0	O
D Total	2	.143	5	14	1	2	0	0	0	2	1	5	0	
L 1982	StL-N	.308	3	13	4	4	0	2	1	5	0	5	0	O
L 1985	StL-N	.269	6	26	6	7	1	0	0	3	3	6	2	O
L 1987	StL-N	.308	7	26	2	8	1	1	0	2	0	5	0	O
L 1990	Oak-A	.222	3	9	3	2	1	0	0	0	1	2	2	O-2,D-1
L 1996	StL-N	.333	6	15	0	5	0	0	0	0	0	3	0	O-5
L Total	5	.292	25	89	15	26	3	3	1	10	4	21	4	
W 1982	StL-N	.240	6	25	6	6	0	0	2	5	1	3	2	O
W 1985	StL-N	.259	7	27	2	7	2	0	1	2	1	3	1	O
W 1987	StL-N	.370	7	27	2	10	2	0	0	4	0	9	0	O
W 1990	Oak-A	.200	4	10	1	2	1	0	0	0	0	2	1	O-3
W Total	4	.281	24	89	11	25	5	0	3	11	2	17	4	
■ John McGraw														
T 1894	Bal-N	.250	4	16	2	4	0	0	0	2	0	0	1	3
T 1895	Bal-N	.400	5	20	4	8	2	0	0	1	2	0	2	3
T 1896	Bal-N	.267	4	15	4	4	0	0	0	1	0	0	4	3
T 1897	Bal-N	.300	5	20	6	6	1	1	0	6	7	0	0	3
T Total	4	.310	18	71	16	22	3	1	0	10	9	0	7	
■ Fred McGriff														
D 1995	Atl-N	.333	4	18	4	6	0	0	2	6	2	3	0	1
D 1996	Atl-N	.333	3	9	1	3	1	0	1	3	2	1	0	1
D 1997	Atl-N	.222	3	9	4	2	0	0	0	1	3	2	0	1
D Total	3	.306	10	36	9	11	1	0	3	10	7	6	0	
L 1989	Tor-A	.143	5	21	1	3	0	0	0	3	0	4	0	1
L 1993	Atl-N	.435	6	23	6	10	2	0	1	4	4	7	0	1
L 1995	Atl-N	.438	4	16	5	7	4	0	0	0	3	0	0	1
L 1996	Atl-N	.250	7	28	6	7	0	1	2	7	3	5	0	1
L 1997	Atl-N	.333	6	21	0	7	1	0	0	4	2	7	0	1
L Total	5	.312	28	109	18	34	7	1	3	18	12	23	0	
W 1995	Atl-N	.261	6	23	5	6	2	0	2	3	3	7	1	1
W 1996	Atl-N	.300	6	20	4	6	0	0	2	6	5	4	0	1
W Total	2	.279	12	43	9	12	2	0	4	9	8	11	1	
■ Deacon McGuire														
T 1900	Bro-N	.375	2	8	1	3	1	0	0	0	0	1	0	C
■ Mark McGwire														
D 2000	StL-N	.500	3	2	1	1	0	0	1	1	1	0	0	H
L 1988	Oak-A	.333	4	15	4	5	0	0	1	3	1	5	0	1
L 1989	Oak-A	.389	5	18	3	7	1	0	1	3	1	4	0	1
L 1990	Oak-A	.154	4	13	2	2	0	0	0	2	3	3	0	1
L 1992	Oak-A	.150	6	20	1	3	0	0	1	3	5	4	0	1
L 2000	StL-N	.000	3	2	0	0	0	0	0	0	1	0	0	H
L Total	5	.250	22	68	10	17	1	0	3	11	11	16	0	
W 1988	Oak-A	.059	5	17	1	1	0	0	1	1	3	4	0	1
W 1989	Oak-A	.294	4	17	0	5	1	0	0	1	1	3	0	1
W 1990	Oak-A	.214	4	14	1	3	0	0	0	0	2	4	0	1
W Total	3	.188	13	48	2	9	1	0	1	2	6	11	0	
■ John McHale														
W 1945	Det-A	.000	3	3	0	0	0	0	0	0	0	1	0	H
■ Stuffy McInnis														
W 1911	Phi-A	—	1	0	0	0	0	0	0	0	0	0	0	1
W 1913	Phi-A	.118	5	17	1	2	1	0	0	2	0	2	0	1
W 1914	Phi-A	.143	4	14	2	2	1	0	0	0	3	3	0	1
W 1918	Bos-A	.250	6	20	2	5	0	0	0	1	1	1	0	1
W 1925	Pit-N	.286	4	14	0	4	0	0	0	1	0	2	0	1-3
W Total	5	.200	20	65	5	13	2	0	0	4	4	8	0	
■ Matty McIntyre														
W 1908	Det-A	.222	5	18	2	4	1	0	0	0	3	2	1	O
W 1909	Det-A	.000	4	3	0	0	0	0	0	0	0	1	0	O-1
W Total	2	.190	9	21	2	4	1	0	0	0	3	3	1	
■ Dave McKay														
D 1981	Oak-A	.273	3	11	1	3	0	0	1	1	1	1	0	2
L 1981	Oak-A	.273	3	11	0	3	0	0	0	1	0	2	0	2
■ Ed McKean														
T 1892	Cle-N	.440	6	25	2	11	0	0	0	6	1	3	0	S
T 1895	Cle-N	.300	5	20	2	6	1	1	0	4	3	0	1	S
T 1896	Cle-N	.313	4	16	0	5	1	1	0	1	1	2	1	S
T Total	3	.361	15	61	4	22	2	2	0	11	5	5	2	
■ Larry McLean														
W 1913	NY-N	.500	5	12	0	6	0	0	0	2	0	0	0	C-4
■ Mark McLemore														
D 1996	Tex-A	.133	4	15	1	2	0	0	0	2	0	4	0	2
D 1998	Tex-A	.100	3	10	0	1	1	0	0	0	2	3	0	2
D 1999	Tex-A	.100	3	10	0	1	0	0	0	0	1	3	0	2
D 2000	Sea-A	.111	3	9	1	1	0	0	0	0	2	1	0	2
D Total	4	.114	13	44	2	5	1	0	0	2	5	11	0	

YEAR	TM/L	AVG	G	AB	R	H	2B	3B	HR	RBI	BB	SO	SB	POS
L 2000	Sea-A	.250	5	16	2	4	3	0	0	2	2	1	0	2
■ Norm McMillan														
W 1922	NY-A	.000	1	2	0	0	0	0	0	0	0	0	0	O
W 1929	Chi-N	.100	5	20	0	2	0	0	0	0	2	6	1	3
W Total	2	.091	6	22	0	2	0	0	0	0	2	6	1	
■ Ken McMullen														
L 1974	LA-N	.000	1	1	0	0	0	0	0	0	0	1	0	H
■ Fred McMullin														
W 1917	Chi-A	.125	6	24	1	3	1	0	0	2	1	6	0	3
W 1919	Chi-A	.500	2	2	0	1	0	0	0	0	0	0	0	H
W Total	2	.154	8	26	1	4	1	0	0	2	1	6	0	
■ Eric McNair														
W 1930	Phi-A	.000	1	1	0	0	0	0	0	0	0	0	0	H
W 1931	Phi-A	.000	2	2	1	0	0	0	0	0	0	1	0	2-1
W Total	2	.000	3	3	1	0	0	0	0	0	0	1	0	
■ Mike McNally														
W 1916	Bos-A	—	1	0	1	0	0	0	0	0	0	0	0	R
W 1921	NY-A	.200	7	20	3	4	1	0	0	1	1	3	2	3
W 1922	NY-A	—	1	0	0	0	0	0	0	0	0	0	0	2
W Total	3	.200	9	20	4	4	1	0	0	1	1	3	2	
■ Earl McNeely														
W 1924	Was-A	.222	7	27	4	6	3	0	0	1	4	4	1	O
W 1925	Was-A	—	4	0	2	0	0	0	0	0	0	0	1	O-2
W Total	2	.222	11	27	6	6	3	0	0	1	4	4	2	
■ George McQuinn														
W 1944	StL-A	.438	6	16	2	7	2	0	1	5	7	2	0	1
W 1947	NY-A	.130	7	23	3	3	0	0	0	1	5	8	0	1
W Total	2	.256	13	39	5	10	2	0	1	6	12	10	0	
■ Hal McRae														
D 1981	KC-A	.091	3	11	0	1	1	0	0	0	1	1	0	D
L 1970	Cin-N	.000	2	4	0	0	0	0	0	0	0	2	0	O-1
L 1972	Cin-N	—	1	0	0	0	0	0	0	0	0	0	0	H
L 1976	KC-A	.118	5	17	2	2	1	1	0	1	1	4	0	D-3,O-2
L 1977	KC-A	.444	5	18	6	8	3	0	1	2	3	1	0	D-3,O-2
L 1978	KC-A	.214	4	14	0	3	0	0	0	2	2	2	1	D
L 1980	KC-A	.200	3	10	0	2	0	0	0	0	1	3	0	D
L 1984	KC-A	1.000	2	2	0	2	1	0	0	1	0	0	0	H
L 1985	KC-A	.261	6	23	1	6	2	0	0	3	1	6	0	D
L Total	8	.261	28	88	9	23	7	1	1	9	8	18	1	
W 1970	Cin-N	.455	3	11	1	5	2	0	0	3	0	1	0	O
W 1972	Cin-N	.444	5	9	1	4	1	0	0	2	0	1	0	O-2
W 1980	KC-A	.375	6	24	3	9	3	0	0	1	2	2	0	D
W 1985	KC-A	.000	3	1	0	0	0	0	0	0	1	0	0	H
W Total	4	.400	17	45	5	18	6	0	0	6	3	4	0	
■ Kevin McReynolds														
L 1984	SD-N	.300	4	10	2	3	0	0	1	4	3	1	0	O
L 1988	NY-N	.250	7	28	4	7	2	0	2	4	3	5	2	O
L Total	2	.263	11	38	6	10	2	0	3	8	6	6	2	
■ Joe Medwick														
W 1934	StL-N	.379	7	29	4	11	0	1	1	5	1	7	0	O
W 1941	Bro-N	.235	5	17	1	4	1	0	0	0	1	2	0	O
W Total	2	.326	12	46	5	15	1	1	1	5	2	9	0	
■ Miguel Mejia														
D 1996	StL-N	—	1	0	0	0	0	0	0	0	0	0	0	R
L 1996	StL-N	.000	3	1	1	0	0	0	0	0	0	1	0	O-2
■ Bob Melvin														
L 1987	SF-N	.429	3	7	0	3	0	0	0	0	1	1	0	C-2
■ Mario Mendoza														
L 1974	Pit-N	.200	3	5	0	1	0	0	0	1	1	0	0	S
■ Frank Menechino														
D 2000	Oak-A	—	1	0	0	0	0	0	0	0	0	0	0	2
■ Denis Menke														
L 1972	Cin-N	.250	5	16	1	4	1	0	0	0	4	3	0	3
L 1973	Cin-N	.222	3	9	1	2	0	0	1	1	1	2	0	S-2,3-2
L Total	2	.240	8	25	2	6	1	0	1	1	5	5	0	
W 1972	Cin-N	.083	7	24	1	2	0	0	1	2	2	6	0	3
■ Orlando Merced														
L 1991	Pit-N	.222	3	9	1	2	0	0	1	1	0	1	0	1-2
L 1992	Pit-N	.100	4	10	0	1	1	0	0	2	2	4	0	1
L Total	2	.158	7	19	1	3	1	0	1	3	2	5	0	
■ Fred Merkle														
W 1911	NY-N	.150	6	20	1	3	1	0	0	1	2	6	0	1
W 1912	NY-N	.273	8	33	5	9	2	1	0	3	0	7	1	1
W 1913	NY-N	.231	4	13	3	3	0	0	1	3	1	2	0	1
W 1916	Bro-N	.250	3	4	0	1	0	0	0	1	2	0	0	1-1
W 1918	Chi-N	.278	6	18	1	5	0	0	0	1	4	3	0	1
W Total	5	.239	27	88	10	21	3	1	1	9	9	18	1	
■ Lou Merloni														
D 1999	Bos-A	.333	3	6	1	2	0	0	0	1	1	1	0	S
L 1999	Bos-A	—	1	0	0	0	0	0	0	0	1	0	0	H
■ Sam Mertes														
W 1905	NY-N	.176	5	17	2	3	1	0	0	2	2	5	0	O

YEAR TM/L	AVG	G	AB	R	H	2B	3B	HR	RBI	BB	SO	SB	POS
Lennie Merullo													
W 1945 Chi-N	.000	3	2	0	0	0	0	0	0	0	1	0	S
Bud Metheny													
W 1943 NY-A	.125	2	8	0	1	0	0	0	0	0	2	0	O
Catfish Metkovich													
W 1946 Bos-A	.500	2	2	1	1	1	0	0	0	0	0	0	H
Irish Meusel													
W 1921 NY-N	.345	8	29	4	10	2	1	1	7	2	3	1	O
W 1922 NY-N	.250	5	20	3	5	0	0	1	7	0	1	0	O
W 1923 NY-N	.280	6	25	3	7	1	1	1	2	0	2	0	O
W 1924 NY-N	.154	4	13	0	2	0	0	0	1	2	0	0	O
W Total 4	.276	23	87	10	24	3	2	3	17	4	6	1	
Bob Meusel													
W 1921 NY-A	.200	8	30	3	6	2	0	0	3	2	5	1	O
W 1922 NY-A	.300	5	20	2	6	1	0	0	2	1	3	0	O
W 1923 NY-A	.269	6	26	1	7	1	2	0	8	0	3	0	O
W 1926 NY-A	.238	7	21	3	5	1	1	0	0	6	1	0	O
W 1927 NY-A	.118	4	17	1	2	0	0	0	1	1	7	1	O
W 1928 NY-A	.200	4	15	5	3	1	0	1	3	2	5	2	O
W Total 6	.225	34	129	15	29	6	3	1	17	12	24	5	
Chief Meyers													
W 1911 NY-N	.300	6	20	2	6	2	0	0	2	0	3	0	C
W 1912 NY-N	.357	8	28	2	10	0	1	0	3	2	3	1	C
W 1913 NY-N	.000	1	4	0	0	0	0	0	0	0	0	0	C
W 1916 Bro-N	.200	3	10	0	2	0	1	0	0	1	0	0	C
W Total 4	.290	18	62	4	18	2	2	0	5	3	6	1	
Ed Mierkowicz													
W 1945 Det-A	—	1	0	0	0	0	0	0	0	0	0	0	O
Matt Mieske													
D 1999 Hou-N	.000	2	4	1	0	0	0	0	0	1	0	0	O-1
Eddie Miksis													
W 1947 Bro-N	.250	5	4	1	1	0	0	0	0	0	1	0	2-1,O-1
W 1949 Bro-N	.286	3	7	0	2	1	0	0	0	0	1	0	3-2
W Total 2	.273	8	11	1	3	1	0	0	0	0	2	0	
Larry Milbourne													
D 1981 NY-A	.316	5	19	4	6	1	0	0	0	0	1	0	S
L 1981 NY-A	.462	3	13	4	6	0	0	0	1	0	0	0	S
W 1981 NY-A	.250	6	20	2	5	2	0	0	3	4	0	0	S
Felix Millan													
L 1969 Atl-N	.333	3	12	2	4	1	0	0	0	3	0	0	2
L 1973 NY-N	.316	5	19	5	6	0	0	0	2	2	1	0	2
L Total 2	.323	8	31	7	10	1	0	0	2	5	1	0	2
W 1973 NY-N	.188	7	32	3	6	1	1	0	1	1	1	0	2
Bing Miller													
W 1929 Phi-A	.368	5	19	1	7	1	0	0	4	0	2	0	O
W 1930 Phi-A	.143	6	21	0	3	2	0	0	3	0	4	0	O
W 1931 Phi-A	.269	7	26	3	7	1	0	0	1	0	4	0	O
W Total 3	.258	18	66	4	17	4	0	0	8	0	10	0	
Elmer Miller													
W 1921 NY-A	.161	8	31	3	5	1	0	0	2	2	5	0	O
Dots Miller													
W 1909 Pit-N	.250	7	28	2	7	1	0	0	4	2	5	3	2
Hack Miller													
W 1918 Bos-A	.000	1	1	0	0	0	0	0	0	0	0	0	H
Otto Miller													
W 1916 Bro-N	.125	2	8	0	1	0	0	0	0	0	1	0	C
W 1920 Bro-N	.143	6	14	0	2	0	0	0	0	1	2	0	C
W Total 2	.136	8	22	0	3	0	0	0	0	1	3	0	
Ralph Miller													
W 1924 Was-A	.182	4	11	0	2	0	0	0	2	1	0	0	3
Rick Miller													
L 1979 Cal-A	.250	4	16	2	4	0	0	0	0	0	0	0	O
W 1975 Bos-A	.000	3	2	0	0	0	0	0	0	0	0	0	O-2
Jocko Milligan													
W 1888 StL-A	.400	8	25	5	10	2	1	0	4	3	3	0	C-8,1-1
Brad Mills													
D 1981 Mon-N	—	1	0	0	0	0	0	0	0	0	0	0	H
Eddie Milner													
L 1987 SF-N	.143	6	7	0	1	0	0	0	0	0	3	0	O-4
John Milner													
D 1981 Mon-N	.500	2	2	0	1	0	0	0	1	0	0	0	H
L 1973 NY-N	.176	5	17	2	3	0	0	0	1	5	3	0	1
L 1979 Pit-N	.000	3	9	0	0	0	0	0	0	2	0	0	O
L 1981 Mon-N	.000	1	1	0	0	0	0	0	0	0	0	0	H
L Total 3	.111	9	27	2	3	0	0	0	1	7	4	0	
W 1973 NY-N	.296	7	27	2	8	0	0	0	2	5	1	0	1
W 1979 Pit-N	.333	3	9	2	3	1	0	0	1	2	0	0	O
W Total 2	.306	10	36	4	11	1	0	0	3	7	1	0	
Don Mincher													
L 1972 Oak-A	.000	1	1	0	0	0	0	0	0	0	1	0	H
W 1965 Min-A	.130	7	23	3	3	0	0	1	1	2	7	0	1
W 1972 Oak-A	1.000	3	1	0	1	0	0	0	1	0	0	0	H

YEAR TM/L	AVG	G	AB	R	H	2B	3B	HR	RBI	BB	SO	SB	POS
W Total 2	.167	10	24	3	4	0	0	1	2	2	7	0	
Doug Mirabelli													
D 2000 SF-N	.000	1	2	0	0	0	0	0	0	1	1	0	C
Keith Mitchell													
L 1991 Atl-N	.000	5	4	0	0	0	0	0	0	0	1	0	O
W 1991 Atl-N	.000	3	2	0	0	0	0	0	0	0	1	0	O
Kevin Mitchell													
L 1986 NY-N	.250	2	8	1	2	0	0	0	0	0	1	0	O
L 1987 SF-N	.267	7	30	2	8	1	0	1	2	0	3	1	3
L 1989 SF-N	.353	5	17	5	6	0	0	2	7	3	3	0	O
L Total 3	.291	14	55	8	16	1	0	3	9	3	7	1	
W 1986 NY-N	.250	5	8	1	2	0	0	0	0	0	3	0	O-2,D-1
W 1989 SF-N	.294	4	17	2	5	0	0	1	2	0	3	0	O
W Total 2	.280	9	25	3	7	0	0	1	2	0	6	0	
Dale Mitchell													
W 1948 Cle-A	.174	6	23	4	4	1	0	1	1	2	0	0	O
W 1954 Cle-A	.000	3	2	0	0	0	0	0	0	1	0	0	H
W 1956 Bro-N	.000	4	4	0	0	0	0	0	0	0	1	0	H
W Total 3	.138	13	29	4	4	1	0	1	1	3	1	0	
George Mitterwald													
L 1969 Min-A	.143	2	7	0	1	0	0	0	0	1	3	0	C
L 1970 Min-A	.500	2	8	2	4	1	0	0	2	0	2	0	C
L Total 2	.333	4	15	2	5	1	0	0	2	1	5	0	
Johnny Mize													
W 1949 NY-A	1.000	2	2	0	2	0	0	0	2	0	0	0	H
W 1950 NY-A	.133	4	15	0	2	0	0	0	0	0	1	0	1
W 1951 NY-A	.286	4	7	2	2	1	0	0	1	2	0	0	1-2
W 1952 NY-A	.400	5	15	3	6	1	0	3	6	3	1	0	1-4
W 1953 NY-A	.000	3	3	0	0	0	0	0	0	0	1	0	H
W Total 5	.286	18	42	5	12	2	0	3	9	5	3	0	
Paul Molitor													
D 1981 Mil-A	.250	5	20	2	5	0	0	1	1	2	5	0	O
L 1982 Mil-A	.316	5	19	4	6	1	0	2	5	2	3	1	3
L 1993 Tor-A	.391	6	23	7	9	2	1	1	5	3	3	0	D
L Total 2	.357	11	42	11	15	3	1	3	10	5	6	1	
W 1982 Mil-A	.355	7	31	5	11	0	0	0	3	2	4	1	3
W 1993 Tor-A	.500	6	24	10	12	2	2	2	8	3	0	1	D-3,3-2,1-1
W Total 2	.418	13	55	15	23	2	2	2	11	5	4	2	
Rick Monday													
D 1981 LA-N	.214	5	14	1	3	0	0	0	1	2	4	0	O
L 1971 Oak-A	.000	1	3	0	0	0	0	0	0	1	2	0	O
L 1977 LA-N	.286	3	7	1	2	1	0	0	0	2	1	0	O
L 1978 LA-N	.200	3	10	2	2	0	1	0	0	1	5	0	O
L 1981 LA-N	.333	3	9	2	3	0	0	1	1	0	4	0	O-2
L 1983 LA-N	—	1	0	0	0	0	0	0	0	0	0	0	H
L Total 5	.241	11	29	5	7	1	1	1	1	4	12	0	
W 1977 LA-N	.167	4	12	0	2	0	0	0	0	0	3	0	O
W 1978 LA-N	.154	5	13	2	2	1	0	0	0	4	3	0	O-4,D-1
W 1981 LA-N	.231	5	13	1	3	1	0	0	0	3	6	0	O-4
W Total 3	.184	14	38	3	7	2	0	0	0	7	12	0	
Raul Mondesi													
D 1995 LA-N	.222	3	9	0	2	0	0	0	1	0	2	0	O
D 1996 LA-N	.182	3	11	0	2	2	0	0	1	0	4	0	O
D Total 2	.200	6	20	0	4	2	0	0	2	0	6	0	
Don Money													
D 1981 Mil-A	.000	2	3	0	0	0	0	0	0	0	0	0	2-1,D-1
L 1982 Mil-A	.182	4	11	2	2	0	0	0	1	3	1	0	D
W 1982 Mil-A	.231	5	13	4	3	1	0	0	1	2	3	0	D-4
Bob Montgomery													
W 1975 Bos-A	.000	1	1	0	0	0	0	0	0	0	0	0	H
Wally Moon													
W 1959 LA-N	.261	6	23	3	6	0	0	1	2	2	2	1	O
W 1965 LA-N	.000	2	2	0	0	0	0	0	0	0	0	0	H
W Total 2	.240	8	25	3	6	0	0	1	2	2	2	1	
Charlie Moore													
D 1981 Mil-A	.222	4	9	0	2	0	0	0	1	1	2	0	O-2,D-2
L 1982 Mil-A	.462	5	13	3	6	0	0	0	0	1	2	0	O
W 1982 Mil-A	.346	7	26	3	9	3	0	0	2	1	0	0	O
Gene Moore Jr.													
W 1944 StL-A	.182	6	22	4	4	0	0	0	0	3	6	0	O
Eddie Moore													
W 1925 Pit-N	.231	7	26	7	6	1	0	1	2	5	2	0	2
Jimmy Moore													
W 1930 Phi-A	.333	3	3	0	1	0	0	0	0	1	1	0	O-1
W 1931 Phi-A	.333	2	3	0	1	0	0	0	0	0	1	0	O-1
W Total 2	.333	5	6	0	2	0	0	0	0	1	2	0	
Johnny Moore													
W 1932 Chi-N	.000	2	7	1	0	0	0	0	0	2	1	0	O
Jo-Jo Moore													
W 1933 NY-N	.227	5	22	1	5	1	0	0	1	1	3	0	O
W 1936 NY-N	.214	6	28	4	6	2	0	1	1	1	4	0	O
W 1937 NY-N	.391	5	23	1	9	1	0	0	1	0	1	0	O
W Total 3	.274	16	73	6	20	4	0	1	3	2	8	0	

YEAR	TM/L	AVG	G	AB	R	H	2B	3B	HR	RBI	BB	SO	SB	POS
■ Kelvin Moore														
D 1981	Oak-A	.000	2	8	0	0	0	0	0	0	0	2	0	1
L 1981	Oak-A	.250	3	8	0	2	0	0	0	0	0	1	0	1
■ Terry Moore														
W 1942	StL-N	.294	5	17	2	5	1	0	0	2	2	3	0	O
W 1946	StL-N	.148	7	27	1	4	0	0	0	2	2	6	0	O
W Total	2	.205	12	44	3	9	1	0	0	4	4	9	0	
■ Melvin Mora														
D 1999	NY-N	.000	3	1	1	0	0	0	0	0	1	0	0	O
L 1999	NY-N	.429	6	14	3	6	0	0	1	2	2	2	2	O-5
■ Jose Morales														
L 1983	LA-N	.000	2	2	0	0	0	0	0	0	0	1	0	H
■ Herbie Moran														
W 1914	Bos-N	.077	3	13	2	1	1	0	0	0	1	1	1	O
■ Pat Moran														
W 1906	Chi-N	.000	2	2	0	0	0	0	0	0	0	0	0	H
W 1907	Chi-N	—	1	0	0	0	0	0	0	0	0	0	0	H
W Total	2	.000	3	2	0	0	0	0	0	0	0	0	0	
■ Mickey Morandini														
D 1998	Chi-N	.222	3	9	1	2	0	0	0	1	2	2	0	2
L 1993	Phi-N	.250	4	16	1	4	0	1	0	2	0	3	1	2
W 1993	Phi-N	.200	3	5	1	1	0	0	0	0	1	2	0	2-1
■ Mike Mordecai														
D 1995	Atl-N	.667	2	3	1	2	1	0	0	2	0	0	0	S-1
L 1995	Atl-N	.000	2	2	0	0	0	0	0	0	0	1	0	S-1
L 1996	Atl-N	.250	4	4	1	1	0	0	0	0	0	1	0	2-2,3-1
L Total	2	.167	6	6	1	1	0	0	0	0	0	2	0	
W 1995	Atl-N	.333	3	3	0	1	0	0	0	0	0	1	0	S-2,D-1
W 1996	Atl-N	.000	1	1	0	0	0	0	0	0	0	0	0	H
W Total	2	.250	4	4	0	1	0	0	0	0	0	1	0	
■ Keith Moreland														
D 1981	Phi-N	.462	4	13	2	6	0	0	1	3	1	1	0	C
L 1980	Phi-N	.000	2	1	0	0	0	0	0	1	0	0	0	C-1
L 1984	Chi-N	.333	5	18	3	6	2	0	0	2	1	1	0	O
L Total	2	.316	7	19	3	6	2	0	0	3	1	1	0	
W 1980	Phi-N	.333	3	12	1	4	0	0	0	1	0	1	0	D
■ Omar Moreno														
L 1979	Pit-N	.250	3	12	3	3	0	1	0	0	2	2	1	O
W 1979	Pit-N	.333	7	33	4	11	2	0	0	3	1	7	0	O
■ Joe Morgan														
L 1972	Cin-N	.263	5	19	5	5	0	0	2	3	1	2	1	2
L 1973	Cin-N	.100	5	20	1	2	1	0	0	1	2	2	0	2
L 1975	Cin-N	.273	3	11	2	3	3	0	0	1	3	2	4	2
L 1976	Cin-N	.000	3	7	2	0	0	0	0	0	6	1	2	2
L 1979	Cin-N	.000	3	11	0	0	0	0	0	0	3	1	1	2
L 1980	Hou-N	.154	4	13	1	2	1	1	0	0	6	1	0	2
L 1983	Phi-N	.067	4	15	1	1	0	0	0	0	2	1	0	2
L Total	7	.135	27	96	12	13	5	1	2	5	23	10	8	
W 1972	Cin-N	.125	7	24	4	3	2	0	0	1	6	3	2	2
W 1975	Cin-N	.259	7	27	4	7	1	0	0	3	5	1	2	2
W 1976	Cin-N	.333	4	15	3	5	1	1	1	2	2	2	2	2
W 1983	Phi-N	.263	5	19	3	5	0	1	2	2	2	3	1	2
W Total	4	.235	23	85	14	20	4	2	3	8	15	9	7	
■ Bobby Morgan														
W 1952	Bro-N	.000	2	1	0	0	0	0	0	0	0	0	0	3
W 1953	Bro-N	.000	1	1	0	0	0	0	0	0	0	0	0	H
W Total	2	.000	3	2	0	0	0	0	0	0	0	0	0	
■ George Moriarty														
W 1909	Det-A	.273	7	22	4	6	1	0	0	1	3	1	0	3
■ John Morris														
L 1987	StL-N	.000	2	3	0	0	0	0	0	0	0	0	0	O
W 1987	StL-N	.000	1	2	0	0	0	0	0	0	0	0	0	O
■ Hal Morris														
D 1995	Cin-N	.500	3	10	5	5	1	0	0	2	3	1	1	1
L 1990	Cin-N	.417	5	12	3	5	1	0	0	1	1	0	0	1-4
L 1995	Cin-N	.167	4	12	0	2	1	0	0	1	1	1	1	1
L Total	2	.292	9	24	3	7	2	0	0	2	2	1	1	
W 1990	Cin-N	.071	4	14	0	1	0	0	0	2	1	1	0	1-2,D-2
■ Jim Morrison														
L 1978	Phi-N	.000	1	1	0	0	0	0	0	0	0	1	0	H
L 1987	Det-A	.400	2	5	1	2	0	0	0	0	0	1	0	3-1,D-1
L Total	2	.333	3	6	1	2	0	0	0	0	0	2	0	
■ Lloyd Moseby														
L 1985	Tor-A	.226	7	31	5	7	1	0	0	4	2	3	1	O
L 1989	Tor-A	.313	5	16	4	5	0	0	1	2	5	2	1	O
L Total	2	.255	12	47	9	12	1	0	1	6	7	5	2	
■ Wally Moses														
W 1946	Bos-A	.417	4	12	1	5	0	0	0	0	1	2	0	O
■ Manny Mota														
L 1974	LA-N	.333	3	3	0	1	0	0	0	1	0	0	0	O-1
L 1977	LA-N	1.000	1	1	1	1	1	0	0	0	0	0	0	H
L 1978	LA-N	1.000	2	1	0	1	1	0	0	0	0	0	0	H
L Total	3	.600	6	5	1	3	2	0	0	1	0	0	0	
W 1977	LA-N	.000	3	3	0	0	0	0	0	0	0	1	0	H
W 1978	LA-N	—	1	0	0	0	0	0	0	0	1	0	0	H
W Total	2	.000	4	3	0	0	0	0	0	0	1	1	0	
■ Darryl Motley														
L 1984	KC-A	.167	3	12	0	2	0	0	0	1	1	3	0	O
L 1985	KC-A	.333	2	3	1	1	0	0	0	1	1	2	0	O
L Total	2	.200	5	15	1	3	0	0	0	2	2	5	0	
W 1985	KC-A	.364	5	11	1	4	0	0	1	3	0	1	0	O-4
■ Curt Motton														
L 1969	Bal-A	.500	2	2	0	1	0	0	0	1	0	0	0	H
L 1971	Bal-A	1.000	1	1	0	1	1	0	0	1	0	0	0	H
L 1974	Bal-A	.000	1	1	0	0	0	0	0	0	0	0	0	H
L Total	3	.500	4	4	0	2	1	0	0	2	0	0	0	
W 1969	Bal-A	.000	1	1	0	0	0	0	0	0	0	0	0	H
■ Mike Mowrey														
W 1916	Bro-N	.176	5	17	2	3	0	0	0	1	3	2	0	3
■ Don Mueller														
W 1954	NY-N	.389	4	18	4	7	0	0	0	1	0	1	0	O
■ Bill Mueller														
D 1997	SF-N	.250	3	12	1	3	0	0	1	1	0	0	0	3
D 2000	SF-N	.250	4	20	2	5	2	0	0	0	0	4	0	3
D Total	2	.250	7	32	3	8	2	0	1	1	0	4	0	
■ Rance Mulliniks														
L 1985	Tor-A	.364	5	11	1	4	1	0	1	3	2	2	0	3
L 1989	Tor-A	.000	1	1	0	0	0	0	0	0	0	1	0	H
L 1991	Tor-A	.125	5	8	1	1	0	0	0	0	3	0	0	D-3
L Total	3	.250	11	20	2	5	1	0	1	3	5	3	0	
■ Jerry Mumphrey														
D 1981	NY-A	.095	5	21	2	2	0	0	0	0	0	1	1	O
L 1981	NY-A	.500	3	12	2	6	1	0	0	0	3	2	0	O
W 1981	NY-A	.200	5	15	2	3	0	0	0	0	3	2	1	O
■ Thurman Munson														
L 1976	NY-A	.435	5	23	3	10	2	0	0	3	0	1	0	C
L 1977	NY-A	.286	5	21	3	6	1	0	1	5	0	2	0	C
L 1978	NY-A	.278	4	18	2	5	1	0	1	2	0	0	0	C
L Total	3	.339	14	62	8	21	4	0	2	10	0	3	0	
W 1976	NY-A	.529	4	17	2	9	0	0	0	2	0	1	0	C
W 1977	NY-A	.320	6	25	4	8	2	0	1	3	2	8	0	C
W 1978	NY-A	.320	6	25	5	8	3	0	0	7	3	7	1	C
W Total	3	.373	16	67	11	25	5	0	1	12	5	16	1	
■ Bobby Murcer														
D 1981	NY-A	.000	2	1	0	0	0	0	0	0	1	0	0	H
L 1980	NY-A	.000	1	4	0	0	0	0	0	0	0	2	0	D
L 1981	NY-A	.333	1	3	0	1	0	0	0	0	1	1	0	D
L Total	2	.143	2	7	0	1	0	0	0	0	1	3	0	
W 1981	NY-A	.000	4	3	0	0	0	0	0	0	0	0	0	H
■ Dale Murphy														
L 1982	Atl-N	.273	3	11	1	3	0	0	0	0	0	2	1	O
■ Danny Murphy														
W 1905	Phi-A	.188	5	16	0	3	1	0	0	0	0	2	0	2
W 1910	Phi-A	.350	5	20	6	7	3	0	1	9	1	0	1	O
W 1911	Phi-A	.304	6	23	4	7	3	0	0	3	0	3	0	O
W Total	3	.288	16	59	10	17	7	0	1	12	1	5	1	
■ Dwayne Murphy														
D 1981	Oak-A	.545	3	11	4	6	1	0	1	2	1	1	0	O
L 1981	Oak-A	.250	3	8	0	2	1	0	0	1	2	3	0	O
■ Eddie Murphy														
W 1913	Phi-A	.227	5	22	2	5	0	0	0	0	2	0	0	O
W 1914	Phi-A	.188	4	16	2	3	2	0	0	0	2	2	0	O
W 1919	Chi-A	.000	3	2	0	0	0	0	0	0	0	1	0	H
W Total	3	.200	12	40	4	8	2	0	0	0	4	3	0	
■ Pat Murphy														
W 1888	NY-N	.100	3	10	1	1	0	0	0	1	0	0	0	C
■ Yale Murphy														
T 1894	NY-N	.000	1	1	0	0	0	0	0	0	0	0	0	O
■ Calvin Murray														
D 2000	SF-N	.200	3	5	0	1	0	0	0	0	0	3	0	O
■ Eddie Murray														
D 1995	Cle-A	.385	3	13	3	5	0	1	1	3	2	1	0	D
D 1996	Bal-A	.400	4	15	1	6	1	0	0	1	3	4	1	D
D Total	2	.393	7	28	4	11	1	1	1	4	5	5	1	
L 1979	Bal-A	.417	4	12	3	5	0	0	1	5	5	2	0	1
L 1983	Bal-A	.267	4	15	5	4	0	0	1	3	3	3	1	1
L 1995	Cle-A	.250	6	24	2	6	1	0	1	3	2	3	0	D
L 1996	Bal-A	.267	5	15	1	4	0	0	1	2	2	2	0	D
L Total	4	.288	19	66	11	19	1	0	4	13	12	10	1	
W 1979	Bal-A	.154	7	26	3	4	1	0	1	2	4	4	1	1
W 1983	Bal-A	.250	5	20	2	5	0	0	2	3	1	4	0	1
W 1995	Cle-A	.105	6	19	1	2	0	0	1	3	5	4	0	1-3,D-3
W Total	3	.169	18	65	6	11	1	0	4	8	10	12	1	
■ Red Murray														
W 1911	NY-N	.000	6	21	0	0	0	0	0	0	2	5	0	O
W 1912	NY-N	.323	8	31	5	10	4	1	0	4	2	2	0	O
W 1913	NY-N	.250	5	16	2	4	0	0	0	1	2	2	2	O
W Total	3	.206	19	68	7	14	4	1	0	5	6	9	2	

YEAR	TM/L	AVG	G	AB	R	H	2B	3B	HR	RBI	BB	SO	SB	POS
■ **Stan Musial**														
W 1942	StL-N	.222	5	18	2	4	1	0	0	2	4	0	0	O
W 1943	StL-N	.278	5	18	2	5	0	0	0	0	2	2	0	O
W 1944	StL-N	.304	6	23	2	7	2	0	1	2	2	0	0	O
W 1946	StL-N	.222	7	27	3	6	4	1	0	4	4	2	1	1
W Total	4	.256	23	86	9	22	7	1	1	8	12	4	1	
■ **Buddy Myer**														
W 1925	Was-A	.250	3	8	0	2	0	0	0	0	1	2	0	3
W 1933	Was-A	.300	5	20	2	6	1	0	0	2	2	3	0	2
W Total	2	.286	8	28	2	8	1	0	0	2	3	5	0	
■ **Greg Myers**														
D 1998	SD-N	—	1	0	0	0	0	0	0	0	0	0	0	C
L 1998	SD-N	1.000	2	1	1	1	0	0	1	2	1	0	0	H
L 1999	Atl-N	.000	2	2	0	0	0	0	0	0	1	1	0	C
L Total	2	.333	4	3	1	1	0	0	1	2	2	1	0	
W 1998	SD-N	.000	2	4	0	0	0	0	0	0	0	2	0	C-1
W 1999	Atl-N	.333	4	6	0	2	0	0	0	1	1	0	0	C-3
W Total	2	.200	6	10	0	2	0	0	0	1	1	2	0	
■ **Hy Myers**														
W 1916	Bro-N	.182	5	22	2	4	0	0	1	3	0	3	0	O
W 1920	Bro-N	.231	7	26	0	6	0	0	0	1	0	1	0	O
W Total	2	.208	12	48	2	10	0	0	1	4	0	4	0	
■ **Billy Myers**														
W 1939	Cin-N	.333	4	12	2	4	0	1	0	0	2	3	0	S
W 1940	Cin-N	.130	7	23	0	3	0	0	0	2	2	5	0	S
W Total	2	.200	11	35	2	7	0	1	0	2	4	8	0	
■ **Tim Naehring**														
D 1995	Bos-A	.308	3	13	2	4	0	0	1	1	0	1	0	3
■ **Hal Naragon**														
W 1954	Cle-A	—	1	0	0	0	0	0	0	0	0	0	0	C
■ **Jerry Narron**														
L 1986	Cal-A	.500	4	2	1	1	0	0	0	0	1	1	0	C-3
■ **Sam Narron**														
W 1943	StL-N	.000	1	1	0	0	0	0	0	0	0	0	0	H
■ **Billy Nash**														
T 1892	Bos-N	.167	6	24	3	4	0	0	0	4	2	3	2	3
■ **Charlie Neal**														
W 1956	Bro-N	.000	1	4	0	0	0	0	0	0	0	1	0	2
W 1959	LA-N	.370	6	27	4	10	2	0	2	6	0	1	1	2
W Total	2	.323	7	31	4	10	2	0	2	6	0	2	1	
■ **Greasy Neale**														
W 1919	Cin-N	.357	8	28	3	10	1	1	0	4	2	5	1	O
■ **Tom Needham**														
W 1910	Chi-N	.000	1	1	0	0	0	0	0	0	0	0	0	H
■ **Bernie Neis**														
W 1920	Bro-N	.000	4	5	0	0	0	0	0	0	1	0	0	O-2
■ **Dave Nelson**														
L 1976	KC-A	.000	2	2	0	0	0	0	0	0	0	1	0	D-1
■ **Rocky Nelson**														
W 1952	Bro-N	.000	4	3	0	0	0	0	0	0	1	2	0	H
W 1960	Pit-N	.333	4	9	2	3	0	0	1	2	1	1	0	1-3
W Total	2	.250	8	12	2	3	0	0	1	2	2	3	0	
■ **Candy Nelson**														
W 1884	NY-A	.100	3	10	0	1	0	0	0	0	0	1	0	S
■ **Graig Nettles**														
D 1981	NY-A	.059	5	17	1	1	0	0	0	1	3	1	0	3
L 1969	Min-A	1.000	1	1	0	1	0	0	0	0	0	0	0	H
L 1976	NY-A	.235	5	17	2	4	1	0	2	4	3	3	0	3
L 1977	NY-A	.150	5	20	1	3	0	0	0	1	0	3	0	3
L 1978	NY-A	.333	4	15	3	5	0	1	1	2	0	1	0	3
L 1980	NY-A	.167	2	6	1	1	0	0	1	1	0	1	0	3
L 1981	NY-A	.500	3	12	2	6	2	0	1	9	1	0	0	3
L 1984	SD-N	.143	4	14	1	2	0	0	0	2	1	1	0	3
L Total	7	.259	24	85	10	22	3	1	5	19	5	9	0	
W 1976	NY-A	.250	4	12	0	3	0	0	0	2	3	1	0	3
W 1977	NY-A	.190	6	21	1	4	1	0	0	2	2	3	0	3
W 1978	NY-A	.160	6	25	2	4	0	0	0	1	0	6	0	3
W 1981	NY-A	.400	3	10	1	4	1	0	0	0	1	1	0	3
W 1984	SD-N	.250	5	12	2	3	0	0	0	2	5	0	0	3
W Total	5	.225	24	80	6	18	2	0	0	7	11	11	0	
■ **Al Newman**														
L 1987	Min-A	.000	1	2	0	0	0	0	0	0	0	0	0	2
L 1991	Min-A	—	2	0	0	0	0	0	0	0	0	0	0	2-1,3-1
L Total	2	.000	3	2	0	0	0	0	0	0	0	0	0	
W 1987	Min-A	.200	4	5	0	1	0	0	0	0	1	1	0	2-3
W 1991	Min-A	.500	4	2	0	1	0	1	0	1	0	0	0	3-2,2-1,S-1
W Total	2	.286	8	7	0	2	0	1	0	1	1	1	0	
■ **Jeff Newman**														
D 1981	Oak-A	.000	1	3	0	0	0	0	0	0	0	1	0	C
L 1981	Oak-A	.000	2	5	0	0	0	0	0	0	0	2	0	C
■ **Warren Newson**														
D 1995	Sea-A	.000	1	1	0	0	0	0	0	0	0	1	0	H
D 1996	Tex-A	.000	2	1	0	0	0	0	0	0	1	0	0	H
D Total	2	.000	3	2	0	0	0	0	0	0	1	1	0	
L 1993	Chi-A	.200	2	5	1	1	0	0	1	1	0	1	0	D-1
■ **Gus Niarhos**														
W 1949	NY-A	—	1	0	0	0	0	0	0	0	0	0	0	C
■ **Bill Nicholson**														
W 1945	Chi-N	.214	7	28	1	6	1	1	0	8	2	5	0	O
■ **Hugh Nicol**														
W 1885	StL-A	.000	1	2	0	0	0	0	0	0	0	0	0	O
■ **Steve Nicosia**														
W 1979	Pit-N	.063	4	16	1	1	0	0	0	0	0	2	0	C
■ **Bert Niehoff**														
W 1915	Phi-N	.063	5	16	1	1	0	0	0	0	1	5	0	2
■ **Joe Niekro**														
L 1972	Det-A	—	1	0	0	0	0	0	0	0	0	0	0	R
L 1980	Hou-N	.000	1	3	0	0	0	0	0	0	0	1	0	P
L Total	2	.000	2	3	0	0	0	0	0	0	0	1	0	
■ **Bob Nieman**														
W 1962	SF-N	—	1	0	0	0	0	0	0	0	1	0	0	H
■ **Tom Nieto**														
L 1985	StL-N	.000	1	3	1	0	0	0	0	0	1	2	0	C
W 1985	StL-N	.000	2	5	0	0	0	0	0	1	1	2	0	C
■ **Trot Nixon**														
D 1998	Bos-A	.333	2	3	0	1	0	0	0	0	1	0	0	O
D 1999	Bos-A	.214	5	14	5	3	3	0	0	6	4	5	0	O
D Total	2	.235	7	17	5	4	3	0	0	6	5	5	0	
L 1999	Bos-A	.286	5	14	2	4	2	0	0	0	1	5	0	O
■ **Otis Nixon**														
D 1999	Atl-N	1.000	1	1	1	1	0	0	0	0	0	0	1	O
L 1992	Atl-N	.286	7	28	5	8	2	0	0	2	4	4	3	O
L 1993	Atl-N	.348	6	23	3	8	2	0	0	4	5	6	0	O
L 1999	Atl-N	—	2	0	1	0	0	0	0	0	0	0	2	R
L Total	3	.314	15	51	9	16	4	0	0	6	9	10	5	
W 1992	Atl-N	.296	6	27	3	8	1	0	0	1	1	3	5	O
W 1999	Atl-N	.500	2	2	0	1	0	0	0	0	0	0	0	O-1
W Total	2	.310	8	29	3	9	1	0	0	1	1	3	5	
■ **Donell Nixon**														
L 1989	SF-N	.000	3	3	0	0	0	0	0	0	0	1	1	O-2
W 1989	SF-N	.200	2	5	1	1	0	0	0	0	1	1	0	O
■ **Ray Noble**														
W 1951	NY-N	.000	2	2	0	0	0	0	0	0	0	1	0	C
■ **Matt Nokes**														
L 1987	Det-A	.143	5	14	2	2	0	0	1	2	1	4	0	C-3,D-2
■ **Joe Nolan**														
L 1983	Bal-A	—	1	0	0	0	0	0	0	1	0	0	0	H
W 1983	Bal-A	.000	2	2	0	0	0	0	0	0	1	0	0	C
■ **Irv Noren**														
W 1952	NY-A	.300	4	10	0	3	0	0	0	1	1	3	0	O-3
W 1953	NY-A	.000	2	1	0	0	0	0	0	0	1	0	0	H
W 1955	NY-A	.063	5	16	0	1	0	0	0	1	1	1	0	O
W Total	3	.148	11	27	0	4	0	0	0	2	3	4	0	
■ **Billy North**														
L 1974	Oak-A	.063	4	16	3	1	1	0	0	0	2	1	1	O
L 1975	Oak-A	.000	3	10	0	0	0	0	0	1	2	0	0	O
L 1978	LA-N	.000	4	8	0	0	0	0	0	0	0	1	0	O
L Total	3	.029	11	34	3	1	1	0	0	1	4	2	1	
W 1974	Oak-A	.059	5	17	3	1	0	0	0	0	2	5	1	O
W 1978	LA-N	.125	4	8	2	1	1	0	0	2	1	0	1	O
W Total	2	.080	9	25	5	2	1	0	0	2	3	5	2	
■ **Jim Northrup**														
L 1972	Det-A	.357	5	14	0	5	0	0	0	1	2	3	0	O
W 1968	Det-A	.250	7	28	4	7	0	1	2	8	1	5	0	O
■ **Joe Nossek**														
W 1965	Min-A	.200	6	20	0	4	0	0	0	0	0	1	0	O-5
■ **Les Nunamaker**														
W 1920	Cle-A	.500	2	2	0	1	0	0	0	0	0	0	0	C-1
■ **Johnny Oates**														
L 1976	Phi-N	.000	1	1	0	0	0	0	0	0	0	0	0	C
W 1977	LA-N	.000	1	1	0	0	0	0	0	0	0	0	0	C
W 1978	LA-N	1.000	1	1	0	1	0	0	0	0	1	0	0	C
W Total	2	.500	2	2	0	1	0	0	0	0	1	0	0	
■ **Ken Oberkfell**														
L 1982	StL-N	.200	3	15	1	3	0	0	0	2	0	0	0	3
L 1989	SF-N	.000	3	4	0	0	0	0	0	0	0	0	0	3-1
L Total	2	.158	6	19	1	3	0	0	0	2	0	0	0	
W 1982	StL-N	.292	7	24	4	7	1	0	0	1	2	1	2	3
W 1989	SF-N	.333	4	6	1	2	0	0	0	0	3	0	0	3
W Total	2	.300	11	30	5	9	1	0	0	1	5	1	2	
■ **Charlie O'Brien**														
D 1995	Atl-N	.200	2	5	0	1	0	0	0	0	1	1	0	C
L 1995	Atl-N	.400	2	5	1	2	0	0	1	3	0	1	0	C-1
W 1995	Atl-N	.000	2	3	0	0	0	0	0	0	0	1	0	C

YEAR	TM/L	AVG	G	AB	R	H	2B	3B	HR	RBI	BB	SO	SB	POS
■ **Jack O'Brien**														
W 1903	Bos-A	.000	2	2	0	0	0	0	0	0	0	1	0	H
■ **Tom O'Brien**														
T 1897	Bal-N	.400	1	5	2	2	1	0	0	0	0	0	0	O
T 1900	Pit-N	.125	4	16	1	2	1	0	0	2	0	1	0	1
T Total	2	.190	5	21	3	4	2	0	0	2	0	1	0	
■ **Darby O'Brien**														
W 1889	Bro-A	.161	9	31	8	5	0	1	0	4	12	6	6	O
W 1890	Bro-N	.125	6	24	3	3	0	1	0	3	1	5	3	O
W Total	2	.145	15	55	11	8	0	2	0	7	13	11	9	
■ **Jimmy O'Connell**														
W 1923	NY-N	.000	2	1	0	0	0	0	0	0	0	1	0	H
■ **Jack O'Connor**														
T 1892	Cle-N	.136	6	22	1	3	0	0	0	0	2	3	0	O
T 1896	Cle-N	.286	4	14	1	4	0	0	0	1	1	2	0	1
T 1900	Pit-N	.250	2	4	0	1	0	0	0	1	0	0	0	C
T Total	3	.200	12	40	2	8	0	0	0	2	3	5	0	
■ **Paddy O'Connor**														
W 1909	Pit-N	.000	1	1	0	0	0	0	0	0	0	1	0	H
■ **Ken O'Dea**														
W 1935	Chi-N	1.000	1	1	0	1	0	0	0	1	0	0	0	H
W 1938	Chi-N	.200	3	5	1	1	0	0	1	2	1	0	0	C-1
W 1942	StL-N	1.000	1	1	0	1	0	0	0	1	0	0	0	H
W 1943	StL-N	.667	2	3	0	2	0	0	0	0	0	0	0	C-1
W 1944	StL-N	.333	3	3	0	1	0	0	0	2	0	0	0	H
W Total	5	.462	10	13	1	6	0	0	1	6	1	0	0	
■ **Lefty O'Doul**														
W 1933	NY-N	1.000	1	1	1	1	0	0	0	2	0	0	0	H
■ **Ron Oester**														
L 1990	Cin-N	.333	4	3	1	1	0	0	0	0	0	1	0	2-2
W 1990	Cin-N	1.000	1	1	0	1	0	0	0	1	0	0	0	H
■ **Bob O'Farrell**														
W 1918	Chi-N	.000	3	3	0	0	0	0	0	0	0	0	0	C-1
W 1926	StL-N	.304	7	23	2	7	1	0	0	2	2	2	0	C
W Total	2	.269	10	26	2	7	1	0	0	2	2	2	0	
■ **Jose Offerman**														
D 1995	LA-N	—	1	0	0	0	0	0	0	0	0	0	0	R
D 1999	Bos-A	.389	5	18	4	7	1	0	1	6	7	0	0	2
D Total	2	.389	6	18	4	7	1	0	1	6	7	0	0	
L 1999	Bos-A	.458	5	24	4	11	0	1	0	2	1	3	1	2
■ **Ben Oglivie**														
D 1981	Mil-A	.167	5	18	0	3	1	0	0	1	0	7	0	O
L 1982	Mil-A	.133	4	15	1	2	0	0	1	1	0	3	0	O
W 1982	Mil-A	.222	7	27	4	6	0	1	1	1	2	4	0	O
■ **Bob Oldis**														
W 1960	Pit-N	—	2	0	0	0	0	0	0	0	0	0	0	C
■ **Rube Oldring**														
W 1911	Phi-A	.200	6	25	2	5	2	0	1	3	0	5	0	O
W 1913	Phi-A	.273	5	22	5	6	0	1	0	0	0	1	1	O
W 1914	Phi-A	.067	4	15	0	1	0	0	0	0	0	5	0	O
W Total	3	.194	15	62	7	12	2	1	1	3	0	11	1	
■ **Charley O'Leary**														
W 1907	Det-A	.059	5	17	0	1	0	0	0	0	1	3	0	S
W 1908	Det-A	.158	5	19	2	3	0	0	0	0	0	3	0	S
W 1909	Det-A	.000	1	3	0	0	0	0	0	0	0	0	0	3
W Total	3	.103	11	39	2	4	0	0	0	0	1	6	0	
■ **Troy O'Leary**														
D 1998	Bos-A	.063	4	16	0	1	0	0	0	0	1	4	0	O
D 1999	Bos-A	.200	5	20	4	4	0	0	2	7	2	3	0	O
D Total	2	.139	9	36	4	5	0	0	2	7	3	7	0	
L 1999	Bos-A	.350	5	20	2	7	3	0	0	1	2	5	0	O
■ **John Olerud**														
D 1999	NY-N	.438	4	16	3	7	0	0	1	6	3	2	0	1
D 2000	Sea-A	.300	3	10	2	3	0	0	1	2	2	1	0	1
D Total	2	.385	7	26	5	10	0	0	2	8	5	3	0	
L 1991	Tor-A	.158	5	19	1	3	0	0	0	3	3	1	0	1
L 1992	Tor-A	.348	6	23	4	8	2	0	1	4	2	5	0	1
L 1993	Tor-A	.348	6	23	5	8	1	0	0	3	4	1	0	1
L 1999	NY-N	.296	6	27	4	8	0	0	2	6	2	3	0	1
L 2000	Sea-A	.350	6	20	2	7	3	0	1	2	2	2	1	1
L Total	5	.304	29	112	16	34	6	0	4	18	13	12	1	
W 1992	Tor-A	.308	4	13	2	4	0	0	0	0	0	4	0	1
W 1993	Tor-A	.235	5	17	5	4	1	0	1	2	4	1	0	1
W Total	2	.267	9	30	7	8	1	0	1	2	4	5	0	
■ **Tony Oliva**														
L 1969	Min-A	.385	3	13	3	5	2	0	1	2	1	3	1	O
L 1970	Min-A	.500	3	12	2	6	2	0	1	1	0	1	0	O
L Total	2	.440	6	25	5	11	4	0	2	3	1	4	1	
W 1965	Min-A	.192	7	26	2	5	1	0	1	2	1	6	0	O
■ **Al Oliver**														
L 1970	Pit-N	.250	2	8	0	2	0	0	0	1	1	0	0	1
L 1971	Pit-N	.250	4	12	2	3	0	0	1	5	1	3	0	O
L 1972	Pit-N	.250	5	20	3	5	2	1	1	3	0	4	0	O
L 1974	Pit-N	.143	4	14	1	2	0	0	0	1	2	2	0	O
L 1975	Pit-N	.182	3	11	1	2	0	0	1	2	2	0	0	O
L 1985	Tor-A	.375	5	8	0	3	1	0	0	3	0	0	0	D
L Total	6	.233	23	73	7	17	3	1	3	15	6	9	0	
W 1971	Pit-N	.211	5	19	1	4	2	0	0	2	2	5	0	O-4
■ **Joe Oliver**														
D 2000	Sea-A	.250	3	4	1	1	0	0	1	1	0	1	0	C
L 1990	Cin-N	.143	5	14	1	2	0	0	0	0	0	2	0	C
L 2000	Sea-A	.167	4	6	0	1	0	0	0	0	1	1	0	C
L Total	2	.150	9	20	1	3	0	0	0	0	1	3	0	
W 1990	Cin-N	.333	4	18	2	6	3	0	0	2	0	1	0	C
■ **Nate Oliver**														
W 1966	LA-N	—	1	0	0	0	0	0	0	0	0	0	0	R
■ **Luis Olmo**														
W 1949	Bro-N	.273	4	11	2	3	0	0	1	2	0	2	0	O
■ **Greg Olson**														
L 1991	Atl-N	.333	7	24	3	8	1	0	1	4	4	3	1	C
L 1993	Atl-N	.333	2	3	0	1	1	0	0	0	0	1	0	C
L Total	2	.333	9	27	3	9	2	0	1	4	4	4	1	
W 1991	Atl-N	.222	7	27	3	6	2	0	0	1	5	4	1	C
■ **Ivy Olson**														
W 1916	Bro-N	.250	5	16	1	4	0	1	0	2	2	2	0	S
W 1920	Bro-N	.320	7	25	2	8	1	0	0	0	3	1	0	S
W Total	2	.293	12	41	3	12	1	1	0	2	5	3	0	
■ **Ollie O'Mara**														
W 1916	Bro-N	.000	1	1	0	0	0	0	0	0	0	1	0	H
■ **Tip O'Neill**														
W 1885	StL-A	.208	7	24	4	5	0	0	0	3	0	0	0	O
W 1886	StL-A	.400	6	20	4	8	0	2	2	5	4	5	2	O
W 1887	StL-A	.200	15	65	7	13	2	1	1	9	0	2	0	O
W 1888	StL-A	.243	10	37	8	9	1	0	2	11	6	3	0	O
W Total	4	.240	38	146	23	35	3	3	5	28	10	10	2	
■ **Paul O'Neill**														
D 1995	NY-A	.333	5	18	5	6	0	0	3	6	5	5	0	O
D 1996	NY-A	.133	4	15	0	2	0	0	0	0	0	2	0	O
D 1997	NY-A	.421	5	19	5	8	2	0	2	7	3	0	0	O
D 1998	NY-A	.364	3	11	1	4	2	0	1	1	1	1	0	O
D 1999	NY-A	.250	3	8	2	2	0	0	0	0	1	1	0	O
D 2000	NY-A	.211	5	19	4	4	1	0	0	0	2	4	0	O
D Total	6	.289	25	90	17	26	5	0	6	14	12	13	0	
L 1990	Cin-N	.471	5	17	1	8	3	0	1	4	1	1	1	O
L 1996	NY-A	.273	4	11	1	3	0	0	1	2	3	2	0	O
L 1998	NY-A	.280	6	25	6	7	2	0	1	3	3	4	2	O
L 1999	NY-A	.286	5	21	2	6	0	0	0	1	1	5	0	O
L 2000	NY-A	.250	6	20	0	5	0	0	0	5	1	2	0	O
L Total	5	.309	26	94	10	29	5	0	3	15	9	14	3	
W 1990	Cin-N	.083	4	12	2	1	0	0	0	1	5	2	1	O
W 1996	NY-A	.167	5	12	1	2	2	0	0	0	3	2	0	O-4
W 1998	NY-A	.211	4	19	3	4	1	0	0	0	1	2	0	O
W 1999	NY-A	.200	4	15	0	3	0	0	0	4	2	2	0	O
W 2000	NY-A	.474	5	19	2	9	2	2	0	2	3	4	0	O
W Total	5	.247	22	77	8	19	5	2	0	7	14	12	1	
■ **Steve O'Neill**														
W 1920	Cle-A	.333	7	21	1	7	3	0	0	2	4	3	0	C
■ **Bill O'Neill**														
W 1906	Chi-A	.000	1	1	1	0	0	0	0	0	0	0	0	O
■ **Jose Oquendo**														
L 1987	StL-N	.167	5	12	3	2	0	0	1	4	3	2	0	O-5,3-1
W 1987	StL-N	.250	7	24	2	6	0	0	0	2	1	4	0	3-4,O-3
■ **Magglio Ordonez**														
D 2000	Chi-A	.182	3	11	0	2	0	1	0	1	2	2	1	O
■ **Rey Ordonez**														
D 1999	NY-N	.286	4	14	1	4	1	0	0	2	0	5	1	S
L 1999	NY-N	.042	6	24	0	1	0	0	0	0	0	2	0	S
■ **Jim O'Rourke**														
W 1888	NY-N	.222	10	36	4	8	0	0	0	1	4	2	3	O-7,1-2,S-1
W 1889	NY-N	.389	9	36	7	14	2	2	2	7	2	2	3	O
W Total	2	.306	19	72	11	22	2	2	2	8	6	4	6	
■ **Dave Orr**														
W 1884	NY-A	.111	3	9	0	1	0	0	0	0	0	0	0	1
■ **Ernie Orsatti**														
W 1928	StL-N	.286	4	7	1	2	1	0	0	0	1	3	0	O-1
W 1930	StL-N	.000	1	1	0	0	0	0	0	0	0	0	0	H
W 1931	StL-N	.000	1	3	0	0	0	0	0	0	0	3	0	O
W 1934	StL-N	.318	7	22	3	7	0	1	0	2	3	1	0	O
W Total	4	.273	13	33	4	9	1	1	0	2	4	7	0	
■ **John Orsino**														
W 1962	SF-N	.000	1	1	0	0	0	0	0	0	0	0	0	C
■ **Jorge Orta**														
L 1984	KC-A	.100	3	10	1	1	0	1	0	1	0	2	0	D
L 1985	KC-A	.000	2	5	0	0	0	0	0	0	0	1	0	D-1
L Total	2	.067	5	15	1	1	0	1	0	1	0	3	0	
W 1985	KC-A	.333	3	3	0	1	0	0	0	0	0	0	0	H

YEAR	TM/L	AVG	G	AB	R	H	2B	3B	HR	RBI	BB	SO	SB	POS
■ Junior Ortiz														
L 1991	Min-A	.000	3	3	0	0	0	0	0	0	0	0	0	C
W 1991	Min-A	.200	3	5	0	1	0	0	0	1	0	1	0	C
■ Amos Otis														
D 1981	KC-A	.000	3	12	0	0	0	0	0	1	0	4	0	O
L 1976	KC-A	.000	1	1	0	0	0	0	0	0	0	0	0	O
L 1977	KC-A	.125	5	16	1	2	1	0	0	2	2	3	2	O
L 1978	KC-A	.429	4	14	2	6	2	0	0	1	3	5	4	O
L 1980	KC-A	.333	3	12	2	4	1	0	0	0	0	3	2	O
L Total	4	.279	13	43	5	12	4	0	0	3	5	11	8	
W 1980	KC-A	.478	6	23	4	11	2	0	3	7	3	3	0	O
■ Mel Ott														
W 1933	NY-N	.389	5	18	3	7	0	0	2	4	4	4	0	O
W 1936	NY-N	.304	6	23	4	7	2	0	1	3	3	1	0	O
W 1937	NY-N	.200	5	20	1	4	0	0	1	3	1	4	0	3
W Total	3	.295	16	61	8	18	2	0	4	10	8	9	0	
■ Ed Ott														
L 1979	Pit-N	.231	3	13	0	3	0	0	0	0	0	2	0	C
W 1979	Pit-N	.333	3	12	2	4	1	0	0	3	0	2	0	C
■ Jimmy Outlaw														
W 1945	Det-A	.179	7	28	1	5	0	0	0	3	2	1	1	3
■ Mickey Owen														
W 1941	Bro-N	.167	5	12	1	2	0	1	0	2	3	0	0	C
■ Marv Owen														
W 1934	Det-A	.069	7	29	0	2	0	0	0	1	0	5	1	3
W 1935	Det-A	.050	6	20	2	1	0	0	0	1	2	3	0	1-4,3-2
W Total	2	.061	13	49	2	3	0	0	0	2	2	8	1	
■ Spike Owen														
L 1986	Bos-A	.429	7	21	5	9	0	1	0	3	2	2	1	S
L 1988	Bos-A	—	1	0	0	0	0	0	0	0	1	0	0	D
L Total	2	.429	8	21	5	9	0	1	0	3	3	2	1	
W 1986	Bos-A	.300	7	20	2	6	0	0	0	2	5	6	0	S
■ J Owens														
D 1995	Col-N	.000	1	1	0	0	0	0	0	0	0	1	0	C
■ Ray Oyler														
W 1968	Det-A	—	4	0	0	0	0	0	0	0	0	0	0	S
■ Tom Paciorek														
L 1974	LA-N	1.000	1	1	0	1	0	0	0	0	0	0	0	O
L 1983	Chi-A	.250	4	16	1	4	0	0	0	1	1	2	0	1-3,O-2
L Total	2	.294	5	17	1	5	0	0	0	1	1	2	0	
W 1974	LA-N	.500	3	2	1	1	1	0	0	0	0	0	0	H
■ Andy Pafko														
W 1945	Chi-N	.214	7	28	5	6	2	1	0	2	2	5	1	O
W 1952	Bro-N	.190	7	21	0	4	0	0	0	2	0	4	0	O-5
W 1957	Mil-N	.214	6	14	1	3	0	0	0	0	0	1	0	O-5
W 1958	Mil-N	.333	4	9	0	3	1	0	0	1	0	0	0	O
W Total	4	.222	24	72	6	16	3	1	0	5	2	10	1	
■ Jose Pagan														
L 1970	Pit-N	.333	1	3	0	1	0	0	0	0	1	1	0	3
L 1971	Pit-N	.000	1	1	0	0	0	0	0	0	0	0	0	3
L Total	2	.250	2	4	0	1	0	0	0	0	1	1	0	
W 1962	SF-N	.368	7	19	2	7	0	0	1	2	0	1	0	S
W 1971	Pit-N	.267	4	15	0	4	2	0	0	2	0	1	0	3
W Total	2	.324	11	34	2	11	2	0	1	4	0	2	0	
■ Mike Pagliarulo														
L 1991	Min-A	.333	5	15	4	5	1	0	1	3	0	2	0	3
W 1991	Min-A	.273	6	11	1	3	0	0	1	2	1	2	0	3
■ Tom Pagnozzi														
D 1996	StL-N	.273	3	11	0	3	0	0	0	2	1	3	0	C
L 1987	StL-N	.000	1	1	0	0	0	0	0	0	0	0	0	H
L 1996	StL-N	.158	7	19	1	3	1	0	0	1	1	4	0	C
L Total	2	.150	8	20	1	3	1	0	0	1	1	4	0	
W 1987	StL-N	.250	2	4	0	1	0	0	0	0	0	0	0	D-1
■ Rafael Palmeiro														
D 1996	Bal-A	.176	4	17	4	3	1	0	1	2	1	6	0	1
D 1997	Bal-A	.250	4	12	2	3	2	0	0	0	0	2	0	1
D 1999	Tex-A	.273	3	11	0	3	0	0	0	0	1	1	0	D
D Total	3	.225	11	40	6	9	3	0	1	2	2	9	0	
L 1996	Bal-A	.235	5	17	4	4	0	0	2	4	4	4	0	1
L 1997	Bal-A	.280	6	25	3	7	2	0	1	2	0	10	0	1
L Total	2	.262	11	42	7	11	2	0	3	6	4	14	0	
■ Dean Palmer														
D 1996	Tex-A	.211	4	19	3	4	1	0	1	2	0	5	0	3
■ Jim Palmer														
L 1969	Bal-A	.000	1	5	0	0	0	0	0	0	0	3	0	P
L 1970	Bal-A	.250	1	4	1	1	1	0	0	1	0	0	0	P
L 1971	Bal-A	.200	2	5	1	1	0	0	0	0	0	1	0	P-1
L 1973	Bal-A	—	3	0	0	0	0	0	0	0	0	0	0	P
L 1974	Bal-A	—	2	0	0	0	0	0	0	0	0	0	0	P-1
L 1979	Bal-A	—	1	0	0	0	0	0	0	0	0	0	0	P
L 1983	Bal-A	—	1	0	0	0	0	0	0	0	0	0	0	R
L Total	7	.143	11	14	2	2	1	0	0	1	0	4	0	
■ Jim Pankovits														
L 1986	Hou-N	.000	2	2	0	0	0	0	0	0	0	1	0	H

YEAR	TM/L	AVG	G	AB	R	H	2B	3B	HR	RBI	BB	SO	SB	POS
■ Craig Paquette														
D 2000	StL-N	.000	2	2	0	0	0	0	0	0	0	0	0	3-1,O-1
L 2000	StL-N	.167	4	6	0	1	0	0	0	0	0	2	0	O-2,3-1
■ Freddy Parent														
W 1903	Bos-A	.281	8	32	8	9	0	3	0	4	1	1	0	S
■ Mark Parent														
D 1996	Bal-A	.200	4	5	0	1	0	0	0	0	0	2	0	C
L 1996	Bal-A	.167	2	6	0	1	0	0	0	0	0	2	0	C
■ Dave Parker														
L 1974	Pit-N	.125	3	8	0	1	0	0	0	0	0	1	0	O-2
L 1975	Pit-N	.000	3	10	2	0	0	0	0	0	1	3	0	O
L 1979	Pit-N	.333	3	12	2	4	0	0	0	2	2	3	1	O
L 1988	Oak-A	.250	3	12	1	3	1	0	0	0	0	4	0	D-2,O-1
L 1989	Oak-A	.188	4	16	2	3	0	0	2	3	0	0	0	D
L Total	5	.190	16	58	7	11	1	0	2	5	3	11	1	
W 1979	Pit-N	.345	7	29	2	10	3	0	0	4	2	7	0	O
W 1988	Oak-A	.200	4	15	0	3	0	0	0	0	2	4	0	O-2,D-2
W 1989	Oak-A	.222	3	9	2	2	1	0	1	2	0	2	0	D-2
W Total	3	.283	14	53	4	15	4	0	1	6	4	13	0	
■ Wes Parker														
W 1965	LA-N	.304	7	23	3	7	0	1	1	2	3	3	2	1
W 1966	LA-N	.231	4	13	0	3	2	0	0	0	1	3	0	1
W Total	2	.278	11	36	3	10	2	1	1	2	4	6	2	
■ Lance Parrish														
L 1984	Det-A	.250	3	12	1	3	1	0	1	3	0	3	0	C
W 1984	Det-A	.278	5	18	3	5	1	0	1	2	3	2	1	C
■ Larry Parrish														
D 1981	Mon-N	.150	5	20	3	3	1	0	0	1	1	3	0	3
L 1981	Mon-N	.263	5	19	2	5	2	0	0	2	1	1	0	3
L 1988	Bos-A	.000	4	6	0	0	0	0	0	0	0	2	0	1-2
L Total	2	.200	9	25	2	5	2	0	0	2	1	3	0	
■ Roy Partee														
W 1946	Bos-A	.100	5	10	1	1	0	0	0	1	1	2	0	C
■ Ben Paschal														
W 1926	NY-A	.250	5	4	0	1	0	0	0	1	1	2	0	H
W 1928	NY-A	.200	3	10	0	2	0	0	0	1	1	0	0	O
W Total	2	.214	8	14	0	3	0	0	0	2	2	2	0	
■ Dode Paskert														
W 1915	Phi-N	.158	5	19	2	3	0	0	0	0	1	2	0	O
W 1918	Chi-N	.190	6	21	0	4	1	0	0	2	2	2	0	O
W Total	2	.175	11	40	2	7	1	0	0	2	3	4	0	
■ Dan Pasqua														
L 1993	Chi-A	.000	2	6	1	0	0	0	0	0	1	2	0	1
■ Freddie Patek														
L 1970	Pit-N	.000	1	3	0	0	0	0	0	0	1	2	0	S
L 1976	KC-A	.389	5	18	2	7	2	0	0	4	0	1	0	S
L 1977	KC-A	.389	5	18	4	7	3	1	0	5	1	2	0	S
L 1978	KC-A	.077	4	13	2	1	0	0	1	2	1	4	0	S
L Total	4	.288	15	52	8	15	5	1	1	11	3	9	0	
■ Josh Paul														
D 2000	Chi-A	—	1	0	0	0	0	0	0	0	0	0	0	C
■ Fred Payne														
W 1907	Det-A	.250	2	4	0	1	0	0	0	1	0	0	1	C-1
■ Jay Payton														
D 2000	NY-N	.176	4	17	1	3	0	0	0	2	0	4	1	O
L 2000	NY-N	.158	5	19	1	3	0	0	1	3	2	5	0	O
W 2000	NY-N	.333	5	21	3	7	0	0	1	3	0	5	0	O
■ Hal Peck														
W 1948	Cle-A	—	1	0	0	0	0	0	0	0	0	0	0	O
■ Roger Peckinpaugh														
W 1921	NY-A	.179	8	28	2	5	1	0	0	0	4	3	0	S
W 1924	Was-A	.417	4	12	1	5	2	0	0	2	1	0	1	S
W 1925	Was-A	.250	7	24	1	6	1	0	1	3	1	2	1	S
W Total	3	.250	19	64	4	16	4	0	1	5	6	5	2	
■ Bill Pecota														
L 1993	Atl-N	.333	4	3	1	1	0	0	0	0	1	1	0	H
■ Homer Peel														
W 1933	NY-N	.500	2	2	0	1	0	0	0	0	0	0	0	O-1
■ Tony Pena														
D 1995	Cle-A	.500	2	2	1	1	0	0	1	1	0	0	0	C
D 1996	Cle-A	—	1	0	0	0	0	0	0	0	0	0	0	C
D 1997	Hou-N	—	2	0	0	0	0	0	0	0	0	0	0	C
D Total	3	.500	5	2	1	1	0	0	1	1	0	0	0	
L 1987	StL-N	.381	7	21	5	8	0	1	0	0	3	4	1	C
L 1990	Bos-A	.214	4	14	0	3	0	0	0	0	0	0	0	C
L 1995	Cle-A	.333	4	6	1	2	1	0	0	0	1	0	0	C
L Total	3	.317	15	41	6	13	1	1	0	0	4	4	1	
W 1987	StL-N	.409	7	22	2	9	1	0	0	4	3	2	1	C-6,D-1
W 1995	Cle-A	.167	2	6	0	1	0	0	0	0	0	0	0	C
W Total	2	.357	9	28	2	10	1	0	0	4	3	2	1	
■ Terry Pendleton														
D 1996	Atl-N	.000	1	1	0	0	0	0	0	0	0	1	0	H
L 1985	StL-N	.208	6	24	2	5	1	0	0	4	1	3	0	3

YEAR	TM/L	AVG	G	AB	R	H	2B	3B	HR	RBI	BB	SO	SB	POS
L 1987	StL-N	.211	6	19	3	4	0	1	0	1	0	6	0	3
L 1991	Atl-N	.167	7	30	1	5	1	1	0	1	1	3	0	3
L 1992	Atl-N	.233	7	30	2	7	2	0	0	3	0	2	0	3
L 1993	Atl-N	.346	6	26	4	9	1	0	1	5	0	2	0	3
L 1996	Atl-N	.000	6	6	0	0	0	0	0	0	1	3	0	3-2
L Total	6	.222	38	135	12	30	5	2	1	14	3	19	0	
W 1985	StL-N	.261	7	23	3	6	1	1	0	3	3	2	0	3
W 1987	StL-N	.429	3	7	2	3	0	0	0	1	1	1	2	D-2
W 1991	Atl-N	.367	7	30	6	11	3	0	2	3	3	1	0	3
W 1992	Atl-N	.240	6	25	2	6	2	0	0	2	1	5	0	3
W 1996	Atl-N	.222	4	9	1	2	1	0	0	0	1	1	0	D-2,3-1
W Total	5	.298	27	94	14	28	7	1	2	9	9	10	2	
■ **Joe Pepitone**														
W 1963	NY-A	.154	4	13	0	2	0	0	0	0	1	3	0	1
W 1964	NY-A	.154	7	26	1	4	1	0	1	5	2	3	0	1
W Total	2	.154	11	39	1	6	1	0	1	5	3	6	0	
■ **Tony Perez**														
L 1970	Cin-N	.333	3	12	1	4	2	0	1	2	1	1	0	3-3,1-1
L 1972	Cin-N	.200	5	20	0	4	1	0	0	2	0	7	0	1
L 1973	Cin-N	.091	5	22	1	2	0	0	1	2	0	4	0	1
L 1975	Cin-N	.417	3	12	3	5	0	0	1	4	1	2	0	1
L 1976	Cin-N	.200	3	10	1	2	0	0	0	3	1	2	0	1
L 1983	Phi-N	1.000	1	1	0	1	0	0	0	0	0	0	0	H
L Total	6	.234	20	77	6	18	3	0	3	13	3	16	0	
W 1970	Cin-N	.056	5	18	2	1	0	0	0	0	3	4	0	3
W 1972	Cin-N	.435	7	23	3	10	2	0	0	2	4	4	0	1
W 1975	Cin-N	.179	7	28	4	5	0	0	3	7	3	9	1	1
W 1976	Cin-N	.313	4	16	1	5	1	0	0	2	1	2	0	1
W 1983	Phi-N	.200	4	10	0	2	0	0	0	0	0	2	0	1-2
W Total	5	.242	27	95	10	23	3	0	3	11	11	21	1	
■ **Eddie Perez**														
D 1996	Atl-N	.333	1	3	0	1	0	0	0	0	0	0	0	C
D 1997	Atl-N	.000	1	3	0	0	0	0	0	0	0	1	0	C
D 1998	Atl-N	.200	1	5	1	1	0	0	1	4	0	2	0	C
D 1999	Atl-N	.250	0	16	1	4	0	0	0	3	0	3	0	C
D Total	4	.222	3	27	2	6	0	0	1	7	0	6	0	
L 1996	Atl-N	.000	4	1	0	0	0	0	0	0	1	0	0	C
L 1997	Atl-N	.000	2	3	0	0	0	0	0	0	0	0	0	C
L 1998	Atl-N	.750	3	4	0	3	0	0	0	0	0	0	0	C
L 1999	Atl-N	.500	6	20	2	10	2	0	2	5	1	3	0	C
L Total	4	.464	15	28	2	13	2	0	2	5	2	3	0	
W 1996	Atl-N	.000	2	1	0	0	0	0	0	0	0	0	0	C
W 1999	Atl-N	.125	3	8	0	1	0	0	0	0	1	3	0	C
W Total	2	.111	5	9	0	1	0	0	0	0	1	3	0	
■ **Timo Perez**														
D 2000	NY-N	.294	4	17	2	5	1	0	0	3	0	2	1	O
L 2000	NY-N	.304	5	23	8	7	2	0	0	0	1	3	2	O
W 2000	NY-N	.125	5	16	1	2	0	0	0	0	1	4	0	O
■ **Herb Perry**														
D 1995	Cle-A	.000	1	1	0	0	0	0	0	0	0	0	0	H
D 2000	Chi-A	.444	3	9	0	4	1	0	0	1	2	2	0	3
D Total	2	.400	4	10	0	4	1	0	0	1	2	2	0	
L 1995	Cle-A	.000	3	8	0	0	0	0	0	0	1	3	0	1
W 1995	Cle-A	.000	3	5	0	0	0	0	0	0	0	2	0	1
■ **Johnny Pesky**														
W 1946	Bos-A	.233	7	30	2	7	0	0	0	0	1	3	1	S
■ **Rico Petrocelli**														
L 1975	Bos-A	.167	3	12	1	2	0	0	1	2	0	3	0	3
W 1967	Bos-A	.200	7	20	3	4	1	0	2	3	3	8	0	S
W 1975	Bos-A	.308	7	26	3	8	1	0	0	4	3	6	0	3
W Total	2	.261	14	46	6	12	2	0	2	7	6	14	0	
■ **Gary Pettis**														
L 1986	Cal-A	.346	7	26	4	9	1	0	1	4	3	5	0	O
■ **Fred Pfeffer**														
W 1885	Chi-N	.407	7	27	5	11	2	0	1	7	0	0	0	2
W 1886	Chi-N	.286	6	21	7	6	0	0	1	4	2	1	2	2
W Total	2	.354	13	48	12	17	2	0	2	11	2	1	2	
■ **Ed Phelps**														
W 1903	Pit-N	.231	8	26	1	6	2	0	0	1	1	6	0	C-7
■ **Ken Phelps**														
L 1989	Oak-A	1.000	1	1	0	1	1	0	0	0	0	0	0	H
W 1989	Oak-A	.000	1	1	0	0	0	0	0	0	0	0	0	H
■ **Dave Philley**														
W 1954	Cle-A	.125	4	8	0	1	0	0	0	0	1	3	0	O-2
■ **Jack Phillips**														
W 1947	NY-A	.000	2	2	0	0	0	0	0	0	0	0	0	1-1
■ **Bubba Phillips**														
W 1959	Chi-A	.300	3	10	0	3	1	0	0	0	0	0	0	3-3,O-1
■ **Tony Phillips**														
L 1988	Oak-A	.286	2	7	0	2	1	0	0	0	1	3	0	O-2,2-1
L 1989	Oak-A	.167	5	18	1	3	1	0	0	1	2	4	2	2-3,3-3
L Total	2	.200	7	25	1	5	2	0	0	1	3	7	2	
W 1988	Oak-A	.250	2	4	1	1	0	0	0	0	1	2	0	2-1,O-1
W 1989	Oak-A	.235	4	17	2	4	1	0	1	3	0	3	0	2-4,3-2,O-1
W Total	2	.238	6	21	3	5	1	0	1	3	1	5	0	

YEAR	TM/L	AVG	G	AB	R	H	2B	3B	HR	RBI	BB	SO	SB	POS
■ **Mike Phillips**														
D 1981	Mon-N	.000	1	1	0	0	0	0	0	0	0	0	0	2
■ **Adam Piatt**														
D 2000	Oak-A	.167	3	6	2	1	0	0	0	0	0	1	0	O-2
■ **Mike Piazza**														
D 1995	LA-N	.214	3	14	1	3	1	0	1	1	0	2	0	C
D 1996	LA-N	.300	3	10	1	3	0	0	0	2	1	2	0	C
D 1999	NY-N	.222	2	9	0	2	0	0	0	0	0	4	0	C
D 2000	NY-N	.214	4	14	1	3	1	0	0	0	4	3	0	C
D Total	4	.234	12	47	3	11	2	0	1	3	5	11	0	
L 1999	NY-N	.167	6	24	1	4	0	0	1	4	1	6	0	C
L 2000	NY-N	.412	5	17	7	7	3	0	2	4	5	0	0	C
L Total	2	.268	11	41	8	11	3	0	3	8	6	6	0	
W 2000	NY-N	.273	5	22	3	6	2	0	2	4	0	4	0	C-4,D-1
■ **Rob Picciolo**														
D 1981	Oak-A	.333	1	3	0	1	0	0	0	0	0	0	0	S
L 1981	Oak-A	.200	2	5	1	1	0	0	0	0	0	2	0	S
■ **Charlie Pick**														
W 1918	Chi-N	.389	6	18	2	7	1	0	0	0	1	1	1	2
■ **Joe Pignatano**														
W 1959	LA-N	—	1	0	0	0	0	0	0	0	0	0	0	C
■ **Lou Piniella**														
D 1981	NY-A	.200	4	10	1	2	1	0	1	3	0	0	0	D
L 1976	NY-A	.273	4	11	1	3	1	0	0	0	0	1	0	D-3
L 1977	NY-A	.333	5	21	1	7	3	0	0	2	0	1	0	O-4,D-1
L 1978	NY-A	.235	4	17	2	4	0	0	0	0	0	3	0	O
L 1980	NY-A	.200	2	5	1	1	0	0	1	1	2	1	0	O
L 1981	NY-A	.600	3	5	2	3	0	0	1	3	0	0	0	D-2,O-1
L Total	5	.305	18	59	7	18	4	0	2	6	2	6	0	
W 1976	NY-A	.333	4	9	1	3	1	0	0	0	0	0	0	O-2,D-2
W 1977	NY-A	.273	6	22	1	6	0	0	0	3	0	3	0	O
W 1978	NY-A	.280	6	25	3	7	0	0	0	4	0	0	1	O
W 1981	NY-A	.438	6	16	2	7	1	0	0	3	0	1	1	O-3
W Total	4	.319	22	72	7	23	2	0	0	10	0	4	2	
■ **George Pinkney**														
W 1889	Bro-A	.258	9	31	2	8	2	0	0	3	4	2	2	3
W 1890	Bro-N	.357	4	14	4	5	0	2	0	3	2	1	1	3
W Total	2	.289	13	45	6	13	2	2	0	6	6	3	3	
■ **Vada Pinson**														
W 1961	Cin-N	.091	5	22	0	2	1	0	0	0	0	1	0	O
■ **Wally Pipp**														
W 1921	NY-A	.154	8	26	1	4	1	0	0	2	2	3	1	1
W 1922	NY-A	.286	5	21	0	6	1	0	0	3	0	2	1	1
W 1923	NY-A	.250	6	20	2	5	0	0	0	2	4	1	0	1
W Total	3	.224	19	67	3	15	2	0	0	7	6	6	2	
■ **Joe Pittman**														
D 1981	Hou-N	.000	2	2	0	0	0	0	0	0	0	0	0	H
■ **Biff Pocoroba**														
L 1982	Atl-N	.000	1	1	0	0	0	0	0	0	0	0	0	H
■ **Placido Polanco**														
D 2000	StL-N	.300	3	10	1	3	0	0	0	3	1	0	1	3
L 2000	StL-N	.200	4	5	0	1	0	0	0	0	2	1	0	3-2
■ **Luis Polonia**														
D 1995	Atl-N	.333	3	3	0	1	0	0	0	2	0	1	1	H
D 1996	Atl-N	.000	2	2	0	0	0	0	0	0	0	1	0	H
D 2000	NY-A	1.000	1	1	0	1	0	0	0	0	0	0	0	H
D Total	3	.333	6	6	0	2	0	0	0	2	0	2	1	
L 1988	Oak-A	.400	3	5	0	2	0	0	0	0	1	2	0	O-1
L 1995	Atl-N	.500	3	2	0	1	0	0	0	1	0	0	0	O-1
L 1996	Atl-N	.000	3	3	0	0	0	0	0	0	0	0	0	H
L 2000	NY-A	.000	1	1	0	0	0	0	0	0	0	1	0	H
L Total	4	.273	10	11	0	3	0	0	0	1	1	3	0	
W 1988	Oak-A	.111	3	9	1	1	0	0	0	0	0	2	0	O-2
W 1995	Atl-N	.286	6	14	3	4	1	0	1	4	1	3	1	O-4
W 1996	Atl-N	.000	6	5	0	0	0	0	0	0	1	3	0	H
W 2000	NY-A	.500	2	2	0	1	0	0	0	0	0	0	0	H
W Total	4	.200	17	30	4	6	1	0	1	4	2	8	1	
■ **Dave Pope**														
W 1954	Cle-A	.000	3	3	0	0	0	0	0	0	1	1	0	O-2
■ **Paul Popovich**														
L 1974	Pit-N	.600	3	5	1	3	0	0	0	0	0	0	0	S
■ **Tom Poquette**														
L 1976	KC-A	.188	5	16	1	3	2	0	0	4	2	3	0	O
L 1977	KC-A	.167	2	6	0	1	0	0	0	0	0	0	0	O
L 1978	KC-A	.000	1	1	0	0	0	0	0	0	0	0	0	H
L Total	3	.174	8	23	1	4	2	0	0	4	2	3	0	
■ **Darrell Porter**														
L 1977	KC-A	.333	5	15	3	5	0	0	0	0	3	0	0	C
L 1978	KC-A	.357	4	14	1	5	1	0	0	3	2	0	0	C
L 1980	KC-A	.100	3	10	2	1	0	0	0	0	1	0	0	C
L 1982	StL-N	.556	3	9	3	5	3	0	0	1	5	2	0	C
L 1985	StL-N	.267	5	15	1	4	1	0	0	0	5	4	0	C
L Total	5	.317	20	63	10	20	5	0	0	4	16	6	0	
W 1980	KC-A	.143	5	14	1	2	0	0	0	0	3	4	0	C-4

YEAR	TM/L	AVG	G	AB	R	H	2B	3B	HR	RBI	BB	SO	SB	POS
W 1982	StL-N	.286	7	28	1	8	2	0	1	5	1	4	0	C
W 1985	StL-N	.133	5	15	0	2	0	0	0	0	2	5	0	C
W Total	3	.211	17	57	2	12	2	0	1	5	6	13	0	
■ Bo Porter														
D 2000	Oak-A	1.000	2	1	0	1	0	0	0	1	0	0	0	O
■ Jorge Posada														
D 1995	NY-A	—	1	0	1	0	0	0	0	0	0	0	0	R
D 1997	NY-A	.000	2	2	0	0	0	0	0	0	0	1	0	C
D 1998	NY-A	.000	1	2	1	0	0	0	0	0	1	2	0	C
D 1999	NY-A	.250	1	4	0	1	1	0	0	0	0	0	0	C
D 2000	NY-A	.235	5	17	2	4	2	0	0	1	3	5	0	C
D Total	5	.200	10	25	4	5	3	0	0	1	4	8	0	
L 1998	NY-A	.182	5	11	1	2	0	0	1	2	4	2	0	C
L 1999	NY-A	.100	3	10	1	1	0	0	1	2	1	2	0	C
L 2000	NY-A	.158	6	19	2	3	1	0	0	3	5	5	0	C
L Total	3	.150	14	40	4	6	1	0	2	7	10	9	0	
W 1998	NY-A	.333	3	9	2	3	0	0	1	2	2	2	0	C
W 1999	NY-A	.250	2	8	0	2	1	0	0	1	0	3	0	C
W 2000	NY-A	.222	5	18	2	4	1	0	0	1	5	4	0	C
W Total	3	.257	10	35	4	9	2	0	1	4	7	9	0	
■ Scott Pose														
D 1997	NY-A	—	1	0	0	0	0	0	0	0	0	0	0	R
■ Wally Post														
W 1961	Cin-N	.333	5	18	3	6	1	0	1	2	0	1	0	O
■ Jake Powell														
W 1936	NY-A	.455	6	22	8	10	1	0	1	5	4	4	1	O
W 1937	NY-A	.000	1	1	0	0	0	0	0	0	0	1	0	H
W 1938	NY-A	—	1	0	0	0	0	0	0	0	0	0	0	O
W Total	3	.435	8	23	8	10	1	0	1	5	4	5	1	
■ Boog Powell														
L 1969	Bal-A	.385	3	13	2	5	0	0	1	1	2	0	0	1
L 1970	Bal-A	.429	3	14	2	6	2	0	1	6	0	3	0	1
L 1971	Bal-A	.300	3	10	4	3	0	0	2	3	3	3	0	1
L 1973	Bal-A	.000	1	4	1	0	0	0	0	0	0	1	0	1
L 1974	Bal-A	.125	2	8	0	1	0	0	0	1	0	0	0	1
L Total	5	.306	12	49	9	15	2	0	4	11	5	7	0	
W 1966	Bal-A	.357	4	14	1	5	1	0	0	1	0	1	0	1
W 1969	Bal-A	.263	5	19	0	5	0	0	0	0	1	4	0	1
W 1970	Bal-A	.294	5	17	6	5	1	0	2	5	5	2	0	1
W 1971	Bal-A	.111	7	27	1	3	0	0	0	1	1	3	0	1
W Total	4	.234	21	77	8	18	2	0	2	7	7	10	0	
■ Dante Powell														
D 1997	SF-N	—	1	0	0	0	0	0	0	0	0	0	0	O
■ Mike Powers														
W 1905	Phi-A	.143	3	7	0	1	1	0	0	0	0	0	0	C
■ Todd Pratt														
D 1999	NY-N	.125	3	8	2	1	0	0	1	1	2	1	0	C-2
D 2000	NY-N	.000	1	1	0	0	0	0	0	0	0	0	0	C
D Total	2	.111	4	9	2	1	0	0	1	1	2	1	0	
L 1993	Phi-N	.000	1	1	0	0	0	0	0	0	0	1	0	C
L 1999	NY-N	.500	4	2	0	1	0	0	0	3	1	1	0	C-2
L Total	2	.333	5	3	0	1	0	0	0	3	1	2	0	
W 2000	NY-N	.000	1	2	1	0	0	0	0	0	1	2	0	C
■ Jim Price														
W 1968	Det-A	.000	2	2	0	0	0	0	0	0	0	1	0	H
■ Jerry Priddy														
W 1942	NY-A	.100	3	10	0	1	1	0	0	1	1	0	0	1-3,3-1
■ Greg Pryor														
L 1984	KC-A	—	1	0	0	0	0	0	0	0	0	0	0	3
W 1985	KC-A	—	1	0	0	0	0	0	0	0	0	0	0	3
■ George Puccinelli														
W 1930	StL-N	.000	1	1	0	0	0	0	0	0	0	0	0	H
■ Kirby Puckett														
L 1987	Min-A	.208	5	24	3	5	1	0	1	3	0	5	1	O
L 1991	Min-A	.429	5	21	4	9	1	0	2	6	1	4	0	O
L Total	2	.311	10	45	7	14	2	0	3	9	1	9	1	
W 1987	Min-A	.357	7	28	5	10	1	1	0	3	2	1	1	O
W 1991	Min-A	.250	7	24	4	6	0	1	2	4	5	7	1	O
W Total	2	.308	14	52	9	16	1	2	2	7	7	8	2	
■ Terry Puhl														
D 1981	Hou-N	.190	5	21	2	4	1	0	0	0	0	1	1	O
L 1980	Hou-N	.526	5	19	4	10	2	0	0	3	3	2	2	O-4
L 1986	Hou-N	.667	3	3	0	2	0	0	0	0	0	0	1	H
L Total	2	.545	8	22	4	12	2	0	0	3	3	2	3	
■ Luis Pujols														
D 1981	Hou-N	.000	2	6	0	0	0	0	0	0	0	1	0	C
L 1980	Hou-N	.100	4	10	1	1	0	1	0	0	3	0	0	C
■ Frank Quilici														
L 1970	Min-A	.000	3	2	0	0	0	0	0	0	0	1	0	2-2
W 1965	Min-A	.200	7	20	2	4	2	0	0	1	4	3	0	2
■ Joe Quinn														
T 1892	Bos-N	.286	6	21	2	6	1	1	0	4	1	2	0	2
T 1896	Bal-N	.000	1	3	1	0	0	0	0	0	0	0	0	3
T Total	2	.250	7	24	3	6	1	1	0	4	1	2	0	

YEAR	TM/L	AVG	G	AB	R	H	2B	3B	HR	RBI	BB	SO	SB	POS
■ Luis Quinones														
L 1990	Cin-N	.500	3	2	1	1	0	0	0	2	0	0	1	H
■ Carlos Quintana														
L 1990	Bos-A	.000	4	13	0	0	0	0	0	1	1	0	0	1
■ Jamie Quirk														
L 1976	KC-A	.143	4	7	1	1	0	1	0	2	0	2	0	D-2
L 1985	KC-A	.000	1	1	0	0	0	0	0	0	0	0	0	H
L 1990	Oak-A	1.000	1	1	0	1	0	0	0	0	0	0	0	H
L 1992	Oak-A	.000	1	1	0	0	0	0	0	0	0	0	0	H
L Total	4	.200	7	10	1	2	0	1	0	2	0	2	0	
W 1990	Oak-A	.000	1	3	0	0	0	0	0	0	0	2	0	C
■ Marv Rackley														
W 1949	Bro-N	.000	2	5	0	0	0	0	0	0	0	2	0	O
■ Paul Radford														
W 1884	Pro-N	.000	3	7	1	0	0	0	0	1	0	1	0	O
■ Tim Raines														
D 1996	NY-A	.250	4	16	3	4	0	0	0	0	3	1	0	O
D 1997	NY-A	.211	5	19	4	4	0	0	1	3	3	1	2	O-3,D-2
D 1998	NY-A	.250	2	4	1	1	1	0	0	0	1	1	0	D-1
D Total	3	.231	11	39	8	9	1	0	1	3	7	3	2	
L 1981	Mon-N	.238	5	21	1	5	2	0	0	1	0	3	0	O
L 1993	Chi-A	.444	6	27	5	12	3	0	0	1	2	2	1	O
L 1996	NY-A	.267	5	15	2	4	1	0	0	0	1	1	0	O
L 1998	NY-A	.100	3	10	0	1	0	0	0	1	2	5	0	D-2,O-1
L Total	4	.301	19	73	8	22	6	0	0	3	5	11	1	
W 1996	NY-A	.214	4	14	2	3	0	0	0	0	2	1	0	O
■ Manny Ramirez														
D 1995	Cle-A	.000	3	12	1	0	0	0	0	0	1	2	0	O
D 1996	Cle-A	.375	4	16	4	6	2	0	2	2	1	4	0	O
D 1997	Cle-A	.143	5	21	2	3	1	0	0	3	0	3	0	O
D 1998	Cle-A	.357	4	14	2	5	2	0	2	3	1	4	0	O
D 1999	Cle-A	.056	5	18	5	1	1	0	0	1	4	8	0	O
D Total	5	.185	21	81	14	15	6	0	4	9	7	21	0	
L 1995	Cle-A	.286	6	21	2	6	0	0	2	2	2	5	0	O
L 1997	Cle-A	.286	6	21	3	6	1	0	2	3	5	5	0	O
L 1998	Cle-A	.333	6	21	2	7	1	0	2	4	4	9	0	O
L Total	3	.302	18	63	7	19	2	0	6	9	11	19	0	
W 1995	Cle-A	.222	6	18	2	4	0	0	1	2	4	5	1	O
W 1997	Cle-A	.154	7	26	3	4	0	0	2	6	6	5	0	O
W Total	2	.182	13	44	5	8	0	0	3	8	10	10	1	
■ Mario Ramirez														
L 1984	SD-N	.000	2	2	0	0	0	0	0	0	0	0	0	H
■ Rafael Ramirez														
L 1982	Atl-N	.182	3	11	1	2	0	0	0	1	1	1	0	S
■ Domingo Ramos														
L 1989	Chi-N	.000	1	1	0	0	0	0	0	0	0	0	0	H
■ Mike Ramsey														
W 1982	StL-N	.000	3	1	1	0	0	0	0	0	0	1	0	3-2
■ Willie Randolph														
D 1981	NY-A	.200	5	20	0	4	0	0	0	1	1	4	0	2
L 1975	Pit-N	.000	2	2	1	0	0	0	0	0	0	1	0	2-1
L 1976	NY-A	.118	5	17	0	2	0	0	0	1	3	1	1	2
L 1977	NY-A	.278	5	18	4	5	1	0	0	2	1	0	0	2
L 1980	NY-A	.385	3	13	0	5	2	0	0	1	1	3	0	2
L 1981	NY-A	.333	3	12	2	4	0	0	1	2	0	1	0	2
L 1990	Oak-A	.375	4	8	1	3	0	0	0	3	1	0	0	2
L Total	6	.271	22	70	8	19	3	0	1	9	6	6	1	
W 1976	NY-A	.071	4	14	1	1	0	0	0	0	1	3	0	2
W 1977	NY-A	.160	6	25	5	4	2	0	1	1	2	2	0	2
W 1981	NY-A	.222	6	18	5	4	1	1	2	3	9	0	1	2
W 1990	Oak-A	.267	4	15	0	4	0	0	0	0	1	0	1	2
W Total	4	.181	20	72	11	13	3	1	3	4	13	5	2	
■ Bill Rariden														
W 1917	NY-N	.385	5	13	2	5	0	0	0	2	2	1	0	C
W 1919	Cin-N	.211	5	19	0	4	0	0	0	2	0	0	1	C
W Total	2	.281	10	32	2	9	0	0	0	4	2	1	1	
■ Morrie Rath														
W 1919	Cin-N	.226	8	31	5	7	1	0	0	2	4	1	2	2
■ Paul Ratliff														
L 1970	Min-A	.250	1	4	0	1	0	0	0	0	0	1	0	C
■ Johnny Rawlings														
W 1921	NY-N	.333	8	30	2	10	3	0	0	4	0	3	0	2
■ Harry Raymond														
W 1890	Lou-A	.148	7	27	5	4	1	1	0	1	2	5	1	S-5,S-3
■ Randy Ready														
L 1992	Oak-A	.000	1	1	0	0	0	0	0	0	0	1	0	H
■ Jeff Reboulet														
D 1997	Bal-A	.200	2	5	1	1	0	0	1	1	0	2	0	2
L 1997	Bal-A	.000	1	2	1	0	0	0	0	0	0	1	0	S
■ Gary Redus														
L 1990	Pit-N	.250	5	8	1	2	0	0	0	0	1	3	1	1-2
L 1991	Pit-N	.158	5	19	1	3	0	0	0	0	1	4	2	1
L 1992	Pit-N	.438	5	16	4	7	4	1	0	3	2	3	0	1

YEAR	TM/L	AVG	G	AB	R	H	2B	3B	HR	RBI	BB	SO	SB	POS
L Total	3	.279	15	43	6	12	4	1	0	3	4	10	3	
■ Jeff Reed														
L 1990	Cin-N	.000	4	7	0	0	0	0	0	0	0	2	0	C
■ Jody Reed														
D 1996	SD-N	.273	3	11	0	3	1	0	0	2	0	1	0	2
L 1988	Bos-A	.273	4	11	0	3	1	0	0	0	2	1	0	S
L 1990	Bos-A	.133	4	15	0	2	0	0	0	1	0	2	0	2-4,S-3
L Total	2	.192	8	26	0	5	1	0	0	1	2	3	0	
■ Jack Reed														
W 1961	NY-A	—	3	0	0	0	0	0	0	0	0	0	0	O
■ Pee Wee Reese														
W 1941	Bro-N	.200	5	20	1	4	0	0	0	2	0	0	0	S
W 1947	Bro-N	.304	7	23	5	7	1	0	0	4	6	3	3	S
W 1949	Bro-N	.316	5	19	2	6	1	0	1	2	1	0	1	S
W 1952	Bro-N	.345	7	29	4	10	0	0	1	4	2	2	1	S
W 1953	Bro-N	.208	6	24	0	5	0	1	0	0	4	1	0	S
W 1955	Bro-N	.296	7	27	5	8	1	0	0	2	3	5	0	S
W 1956	Bro-N	.222	7	27	3	6	0	1	0	2	2	6	0	S
W Total	7	.272	44	169	20	46	3	2	2	16	18	17	5	
■ Rich Reese														
L 1969	Min-A	.167	3	12	0	2	0	0	0	2	1	1	0	1
L 1970	Min-A	.143	2	7	0	1	0	0	0	0	1	1	0	1
L Total	2	.158	5	19	0	3	0	0	0	2	2	2	0	
■ Rudy Regalado														
W 1954	Cle-A	.333	4	3	0	1	0	0	0	1	0	0	0	3-1
■ Charlie Reipschlager														
W 1884	NY-A	.000	2	5	1	0	0	0	0	0	0	1	0	C
■ Pete Reiser														
W 1941	Bro-N	.200	5	20	1	4	1	1	1	3	1	6	0	O
W 1947	Bro-N	.250	5	8	1	2	0	0	0	0	3	1	0	O-3
W Total	2	.214	10	28	2	6	1	1	1	3	4	7	0	
■ Heinie Reitz														
T 1894	Bal-N	.333	4	15	1	5	0	0	0	4	1	3	1	2
T 1896	Bal-N	.133	4	15	1	2	0	0	0	2	1	0	0	2
T 1897	Bal-N	.250	5	20	4	5	1	0	1	4	2	0	0	2
T Total	3	.240	13	50	6	12	1	0	1	10	4	3	1	
■ Rick Renick														
L 1969	Min-A	.000	1	1	0	0	0	0	0	0	0	0	0	H
L 1970	Min-A	.200	2	5	0	1	0	0	0	0	0	1	0	3-1
L Total	2	.167	3	6	0	1	0	0	0	0	0	1	0	
■ Edgar Renteria														
D 1997	Fla-N	.154	3	13	1	2	0	0	0	1	2	4	0	S
D 2000	StL-N	.200	3	10	5	2	0	0	0	0	4	1	2	S
D Total	2	.174	6	23	6	4	0	0	0	1	6	5	2	
L 1997	Fla-N	.227	6	22	4	5	1	0	0	0	3	6	1	S
L 2000	StL-N	.300	5	20	4	6	1	0	0	4	0	2	3	S
L Total	2	.262	11	42	8	11	2	0	0	4	3	8	4	
W 1997	Fla-N	.290	7	31	3	9	2	0	0	3	3	5	0	S
■ Rip Repulski														
W 1959	LA-N	—	1	0	0	0	0	0	0	0	1	0	0	O
■ Merv Rettenmund														
L 1969	Bal-A	—	1	0	0	0	0	0	0	0	0	0	0	H
L 1970	Bal-A	.333	1	3	1	1	0	0	0	1	2	1	1	O
L 1971	Bal-A	.250	3	8	0	2	1	0	0	1	0	3	0	O
L 1973	Bal-A	.091	3	11	1	1	0	0	0	0	3	2	0	O
L 1975	Cin-N	.000	2	1	1	0	0	0	0	0	1	0	0	H
L 1979	Cal-A	.000	2	2	0	0	0	0	0	0	2	1	0	D
L Total	6	.160	12	25	3	4	1	0	0	2	8	7	1	
W 1969	Bal-A	—	1	0	0	0	0	0	0	0	0	0	0	R
W 1970	Bal-A	.400	2	5	2	2	0	0	1	2	1	0	0	O-1
W 1971	Bal-A	.185	7	27	3	5	0	0	1	4	0	4	0	O-6
W 1975	Cin-N	.000	3	3	0	0	0	0	0	0	0	1	0	H
W Total	4	.200	13	35	5	7	0	0	2	6	1	5	0	
■ Dave Revering														
D 1981	NY-A	—	2	0	0	0	0	0	0	0	0	0	0	1
L 1981	NY-A	.500	2	2	0	1	0	0	0	0	0	0	0	1
■ Carl Reynolds														
W 1938	Chi-N	.000	4	12	0	0	0	0	0	0	1	3	0	O-3
■ Craig Reynolds														
D 1981	Hou-N	.333	2	3	1	1	0	0	0	0	0	1	0	S-1
L 1975	Pit-N	.000	2	1	0	0	0	0	0	0	0	0	0	S-1
L 1980	Hou-N	.154	4	13	2	2	1	0	0	0	3	1	0	S
L 1986	Hou-N	.333	4	12	1	4	0	0	0	0	1	3	0	S
L Total	3	.231	10	26	3	6	1	0	0	0	4	4	0	
■ R. J. Reynolds														
L 1990	Pit-N	.200	6	10	0	2	0	0	0	0	2	2	1	O-3
■ Dusty Rhodes														
W 1954	NY-N	.667	3	6	2	4	0	0	2	7	1	2	0	O-2
■ Hal Rhyne														
W 1927	Pit-N	.000	1	4	0	0	0	0	0	0	0	0	0	2
■ Del Rice														
W 1946	StL-N	.500	3	6	2	3	1	0	0	0	2	0	0	C
W 1957	Mil-N	.167	2	6	0	1	0	0	0	0	1	2	0	C

YEAR	TM/L	AVG	G	AB	R	H	2B	3B	HR	RBI	BB	SO	SB	POS
W Total	2	.333	5	12	2	4	1	0	0	0	3	2	0	
■ Sam Rice														
W 1924	Was-A	.207	7	29	2	6	0	0	0	1	3	2	2	O
W 1925	Was-A	.364	7	33	5	12	0	0	0	3	0	1	0	O
W 1933	Was-A	1.000	1	1	0	1	0	0	0	0	0	0	0	H
W Total	3	.302	15	63	7	19	0	0	0	4	3	3	2	
■ Jim Rice														
L 1986	Bos-A	.161	7	31	8	5	1	0	2	6	1	8	0	O
L 1988	Bos-A	.154	4	13	0	2	0	0	0	1	2	4	0	D
L Total	2	.159	11	44	8	7	1	0	2	7	3	12	0	
W 1986	Bos-A	.333	7	27	6	9	1	1	0	0	6	9	0	O
■ Paul Richards														
W 1945	Det-A	.211	7	19	0	4	2	0	0	6	4	3	0	C
■ Hardy Richardson														
W 1887	Det-N	.209	15	67	12	14	5	2	1	4	1	9	7	O-10,2-5,3-1
■ Danny Richardson														
W 1888	NY-N	.167	9	36	6	6	2	0	0	6	3	5	3	2
W 1889	NY-N	.314	9	35	8	11	1	1	3	8	3	5	3	2
W Total	2	.239	18	71	14	17	3	1	3	14	6	10	6	
■ Bobby Richardson														
W 1957	NY-A	—	2	0	0	0	0	0	0	0	0	0	0	2-1
W 1958	NY-A	.000	4	5	0	0	0	0	0	0	0	0	0	3
W 1960	NY-A	.367	7	30	8	11	2	2	1	12	1	1	0	2
W 1961	NY-A	.391	5	23	2	9	1	0	0	0	0	0	1	2
W 1962	NY-A	.148	7	27	3	4	0	0	0	0	3	1	0	2
W 1963	NY-A	.214	4	14	0	3	1	0	0	0	1	3	0	2
W 1964	NY-A	.406	7	32	3	13	2	0	0	3	0	2	1	2
W Total	7	.305	36	131	16	40	6	2	1	15	5	7	2	
■ Marv Rickert														
W 1948	Bos-N	.211	5	19	2	4	0	0	1	2	0	4	0	O
■ Dave Ricketts														
W 1967	StL-N	.000	3	3	0	0	0	0	0	0	0	0	0	H
W 1968	StL-N	1.000	1	1	0	1	0	0	0	0	0	0	0	H
W Total	2	.250	4	4	0	1	0	0	0	0	0	0	0	
■ Lew Riggs														
W 1940	Cin-N	.000	3	3	1	0	0	0	0	0	0	2	0	H
W 1941	Bro-N	.250	3	8	0	2	0	0	0	1	1	1	0	3-2
W Total	2	.182	6	11	1	2	0	0	0	1	1	3	0	
■ Bill Rigney														
W 1951	NY-N	.250	4	4	0	1	0	0	0	1	0	1	0	H
■ Ernest Riles														
L 1989	SF-N	.000	1	1	0	0	0	0	0	0	0	0	0	H
W 1989	SF-N	.000	4	8	0	0	0	0	0	0	0	1	0	D-2
■ Armando Rios														
D 2000	SF-N	.500	2	2	0	1	0	0	0	0	0	0	0	H
■ Cal Ripken Jr.														
D 1996	Bal-A	.444	4	18	2	8	3	0	0	2	0	3	0	S
D 1997	Bal-A	.438	4	16	1	7	2	0	0	1	2	2	0	3
D Total	2	.441	8	34	3	15	5	0	0	3	2	5	0	
L 1983	Bal-A	.400	4	15	5	6	2	0	0	1	2	3	0	S
L 1996	Bal-A	.250	5	20	1	5	1	0	0	0	1	4	0	S
L 1997	Bal-A	.348	6	23	3	8	2	0	1	3	4	6	0	3
L Total	3	.328	15	58	9	19	5	0	1	4	7	13	0	
W 1983	Bal-A	.167	5	18	2	3	0	0	0	1	3	4	0	S
■ Jimmy Ripple														
W 1936	NY-N	.333	5	12	2	4	0	0	1	3	3	3	0	O
W 1937	NY-N	.294	5	17	2	5	0	0	0	0	3	1	0	O
W 1940	Cin-N	.333	7	21	3	7	2	0	1	6	4	2	0	O
W Total	3	.320	17	50	7	16	2	0	2	9	10	6	0	
■ Swede Risberg														
W 1917	Chi-A	.500	2	2	0	1	0	0	0	1	0	0	0	H
W 1919	Chi-A	.080	8	25	3	2	0	1	0	0	5	3	1	S
W Total	2	.111	10	27	3	3	0	1	0	1	5	3	1	
■ Claude Ritchey														
T 1900	Pit-N	.333	4	15	3	5	1	0	0	1	1	0	0	2
W 1903	Pit-N	.111	8	27	2	3	1	0	0	2	4	7	1	2
■ Luis Rivera														
L 1990	Bos-A	.222	4	9	1	2	1	0	0	0	0	2	0	S
■ Jim Rivera														
W 1959	Chi-A	.000	5	11	1	0	0	0	0	0	3	1	0	O
■ Ruben Rivera														
D 1996	NY-A	.000	2	1	0	0	0	0	0	0	0	1	0	O
D 1998	SD-N	.000	3	6	0	0	0	0	0	0	0	3	0	O
D Total	2	.000	5	7	0	0	0	0	0	0	0	4	0	
L 1998	SD-N	.231	6	13	1	3	2	0	0	0	0	7	1	O
W 1998	SD-N	.800	3	5	1	4	2	0	0	1	0	0	0	O
■ Mickey Rivers														
L 1976	NY-A	.348	5	23	5	8	0	1	0	0	1	1	0	O
L 1977	NY-A	.391	5	23	5	9	2	0	0	2	0	2	1	O
L 1978	NY-A	.455	4	11	0	5	0	0	0	0	2	0	0	O
L Total	3	.386	14	57	10	22	2	1	0	2	3	3	1	
W 1976	NY-A	.167	4	18	1	3	0	0	0	0	1	2	1	O
W 1977	NY-A	.222	6	27	1	6	2	0	0	1	0	2	1	O

YEAR	TM/L	AVG	G	AB	R	H	2B	3B	HR	RBI	BB	SO	SB	POS
W 1978	NY-A	.333	5	18	2	6	0	0	0	1	0	2	1	O-4
W Total	3	.238	15	63	4	15	2	0	0	2	1	6	3	
■ **Phil Rizzuto**														
W 1941	NY-A	.111	5	18	0	2	0	0	0	0	3	1	1	S
W 1942	NY-A	.381	5	21	2	8	0	0	1	1	2	1	2	S
W 1947	NY-A	.308	7	26	3	8	1	0	0	2	4	0	2	S
W 1949	NY-A	.167	5	18	2	3	0	0	0	1	3	1	1	S
W 1950	NY-A	.143	4	14	1	2	0	0	0	0	3	0	1	S
W 1951	NY-A	.320	6	25	5	8	0	0	1	3	2	3	0	S
W 1952	NY-A	.148	7	27	2	4	1	0	0	0	5	2	0	S
W 1953	NY-A	.316	6	19	4	6	1	0	0	0	3	2	1	S
W 1955	NY-A	.267	7	15	2	4	0	0	0	1	5	1	2	S
W Total	9	.246	52	183	21	45	3	0	2	8	30	11	10	
■ **Dave Roberts**														
D 1999	Cle-A	.000	2	3	0	0	0	0	0	0	0	2	0	O
■ **Dave Roberts**														
D 1981	Hou-N	.000	1	1	0	0	0	0	0	0	0	1	0	H
■ **Bip Roberts**														
D 1997	Cle-A	.316	5	19	1	6	0	0	0	1	2	2	2	O-4,2-2
L 1997	Cle-A	.150	5	20	0	3	1	0	0	0	0	8	1	2-4,O-2
W 1997	Cle-A	.273	6	22	3	6	4	0	0	4	3	5	0	2-4,O-2
■ **Andre Robertson**														
L 1981	NY-A	.000	1	1	0	0	0	0	0	0	0	0	0	S
W 1981	NY-A	—	1	0	0	0	0	0	0	0	0	0	0	R
■ **Dave Robertson**														
W 1917	NY-N	.500	6	22	3	11	1	1	0	1	0	0	2	O
■ **Gene Robertson**														
W 1928	NY-A	.125	3	8	1	1	0	0	0	2	1	0	0	3
■ **Bob Robertson**														
L 1970	Pit-N	.200	2	5	0	1	1	0	0	0	0	0	0	1-1
L 1971	Pit-N	.438	4	16	5	7	1	0	4	6	0	2	0	1
L 1972	Pit-N	—	4	0	0	0	0	0	0	0	1	0	0	1
L 1974	Pit-N	.000	1	5	1	0	0	0	0	0	0	0	0	1
L 1975	Pit-N	.500	3	2	0	1	0	0	0	1	1	0	0	1-1
L Total	5	.321	14	28	6	9	2	0	4	7	2	2	0	
W 1971	Pit-N	.240	7	25	4	6	0	0	2	5	4	8	0	1
■ **Aaron Robinson**														
W 1947	NY-A	.200	3	10	2	2	0	0	0	1	2	1	0	C
■ **Brooks Robinson**														
L 1969	Bal-A	.500	3	14	1	7	1	0	0	0	0	0	0	3
L 1970	Bal-A	.583	3	12	3	7	2	0	0	1	0	1	0	3
L 1971	Bal-A	.364	3	11	2	4	1	0	1	3	0	1	0	3
L 1973	Bal-A	.250	5	20	1	5	2	0	0	2	1	1	0	3
L 1974	Bal-A	.083	4	12	1	1	0	0	1	1	1	0	0	3
L Total	5	.348	18	69	8	24	6	0	2	7	2	3	0	
W 1966	Bal-A	.214	4	14	2	3	0	0	1	1	1	0	0	3
W 1969	Bal-A	.053	5	19	0	1	0	0	0	2	0	3	0	3
W 1970	Bal-A	.429	5	21	5	9	2	0	2	6	0	2	0	3
W 1971	Bal-A	.318	7	22	2	7	0	0	0	5	3	1	0	3
W Total	4	.263	21	76	9	20	2	0	3	14	4	6	0	
■ **Frank Robinson**														
L 1969	Bal-A	.333	3	12	1	4	2	0	1	2	3	3	0	O
L 1970	Bal-A	.200	3	10	3	2	0	0	1	2	5	2	0	O
L 1971	Bal-A	.083	3	12	2	1	1	0	0	1	1	4	0	O
L Total	3	.206	9	34	6	7	3	0	2	5	9	9	0	
W 1961	Cin-N	.200	5	15	3	3	2	0	1	4	3	4	0	O
W 1966	Bal-A	.286	4	14	4	4	0	1	2	3	2	3	0	O
W 1969	Bal-A	.188	5	16	2	3	0	0	1	1	4	3	0	O
W 1970	Bal-A	.273	5	22	5	6	0	0	2	4	0	5	0	O
W 1971	Bal-A	.280	7	25	5	7	0	0	2	2	2	8	0	O
W Total	5	.250	26	92	19	23	2	1	8	14	11	23	0	
■ **Jackie Robinson**														
W 1947	Bro-N	.259	7	27	3	7	2	0	0	3	2	4	2	1
W 1949	Bro-N	.188	5	16	2	3	1	0	0	2	4	2	0	2
W 1952	Bro-N	.174	7	23	4	4	0	0	1	2	7	5	2	2
W 1953	Bro-N	.320	6	25	3	8	2	0	0	2	1	0	1	O
W 1955	Bro-N	.182	6	22	5	4	1	1	0	1	2	1	1	3
W 1956	Bro-N	.250	7	24	5	6	1	0	1	2	5	2	0	3
W Total	6	.234	38	137	22	32	7	1	2	12	21	14	6	
■ **Wilbert Robinson**														
T 1894	Bal-N	.267	4	15	1	4	0	0	0	1	1	1	1	C
T 1895	Bal-N	.250	3	12	1	3	1	0	0	0	0	1	0	C
T 1896	Bal-N	.267	4	15	1	4	1	0	0	2	0	3	0	C
T Total	3	.262	11	42	3	11	2	0	0	3	1	5	1	
■ **Eddie Robinson**														
W 1948	Cle-A	.300	6	20	0	6	0	0	0	1	1	0	0	1
W 1955	NY-A	.667	4	3	0	2	0	0	0	1	2	1	0	1-1
W Total	2	.348	10	23	0	8	0	0	0	2	3	1	0	
■ **Bill Robinson**														
L 1975	Pit-N	.000	2	2	0	0	0	0	0	0	0	1	0	H
L 1979	Pit-N	.000	3	3	0	0	0	0	0	0	0	0	0	O
L Total	2	.000	5	5	0	0	0	0	0	0	0	1	0	
W 1979	Pit-N	.263	7	19	2	5	1	0	0	2	0	4	0	O-6
■ **Yank Robinson**														
W 1885	StL-A	.174	7	23	5	4	0	1	0	0	1	0	0	O-4,C-3

YEAR	TM/L	AVG	G	AB	R	H	2B	3B	HR	RBI	BB	SO	SB	POS
W 1886	StL-A	.316	6	19	5	6	1	1	0	3	2	3	2	2
W 1887	StL-A	.446	15	56	5	25	5	1	0	4	10	6	4	2
W 1888	StL-A	.250	10	36	7	9	2	1	0	7	6	12	2	2
W Total	4	.328	38	134	22	44	8	4	0	14	19	21	8	
■ **Alex Rodriguez**														
D 1995	Sea-A	.000	1	1	1	0	0	0	0	0	0	0	0	S
D 1997	Sea-A	.313	4	16	1	5	1	0	1	1	0	5	0	S
D 2000	Sea-A	.308	3	13	0	4	0	0	0	2	0	2	0	S
D Total	3	.300	8	30	2	9	1	0	1	3	0	7	0	
L 1995	Sea-A	.000	1	1	0	0	0	0	0	0	0	1	0	H
L 2000	Sea-A	.409	6	22	4	9	2	0	2	5	3	8	1	S
L Total	2	.391	7	23	4	9	2	0	2	5	3	9	1	
■ **Aurelio Rodriguez**														
L 1972	Det-A	.000	5	16	0	0	0	0	0	0	2	2	0	3
L 1980	NY-A	.333	2	6	0	2	1	0	0	0	0	0	0	3
L 1981	NY-A	—	1	0	0	0	0	0	0	0	0	0	0	3
L 1983	Chi-A	—	2	0	0	0	0	0	0	0	0	0	0	3
L Total	4	.091	10	22	0	2	1	0	0	0	2	2	0	
W 1981	NY-A	.417	4	12	1	5	0	0	0	0	1	2	0	3-3
■ **Henry Rodriguez**														
D 1998	Chi-N	.143	3	7	0	1	1	0	0	0	1	2	0	O-2
■ **Ivan Rodriguez**														
D 1996	Tex-A	.375	4	16	1	6	1	0	0	2	2	3	0	C
D 1998	Tex-A	.100	3	10	0	1	0	0	0	1	0	5	0	C
D 1999	Tex-A	.250	3	12	0	3	1	0	0	0	0	2	1	C
D Total	3	.263	10	38	1	10	2	0	0	3	2	10	1	
■ **Gary Roenicke**														
L 1979	Bal-A	.200	2	5	1	1	0	0	0	1	0	0	0	O
L 1983	Bal-A	.750	3	4	4	3	1	0	1	4	5	0	0	O
L Total	2	.444	5	9	5	4	1	0	1	5	5	0	0	
W 1979	Bal-A	.125	6	16	1	2	1	0	0	0	0	6	0	O-5
W 1983	Bal-A	.000	3	7	0	0	0	0	0	0	0	2	0	O-2
W Total	2	.087	9	23	1	2	1	0	0	0	0	8	0	
■ **Ron Roenicke**														
W 1984	SD-N	—	2	0	0	0	0	0	0	0	0	0	0	O-1
■ **Wally Roettger**														
W 1931	StL-N	.286	3	14	1	4	1	0	0	0	0	3	0	O
■ **Billy Rogell**														
W 1934	Det-A	.276	7	29	3	8	1	0	0	4	1	4	1	S
W 1935	Det-A	.292	6	24	1	7	2	0	0	1	2	5	0	S
W Total	2	.283	13	53	4	15	3	0	0	5	3	9	1	
■ **George Rohe**														
W 1906	Chi-A	.333	6	21	2	7	1	2	0	4	3	1	2	3
■ **Cookie Rojas**														
L 1976	KC-A	.333	4	9	2	3	0	0	0	1	0	0	1	2
L 1977	KC-A	.250	1	4	0	1	0	0	0	0	0	1	1	D
L Total	2	.308	5	13	2	4	0	0	0	1	0	1	2	
■ **Red Rolfe**														
W 1936	NY-A	.400	6	25	5	10	0	0	0	4	3	1	0	3
W 1937	NY-A	.300	5	20	3	6	2	1	0	1	3	2	0	3
W 1938	NY-A	.167	4	18	0	3	0	0	0	1	0	3	1	3
W 1939	NY-A	.125	4	16	2	2	0	0	0	0	0	0	0	3
W 1941	NY-A	.300	5	20	2	6	0	0	0	0	2	1	0	3
W 1942	NY-A	.353	4	17	5	6	2	0	0	0	1	2	0	3
W Total	6	.284	28	116	17	33	4	1	0	6	9	9	1	
■ **Rich Rollins**														
W 1965	Min-A	.000	3	2	0	0	0	0	0	0	1	0	0	H
■ **Johnny Romano**														
W 1959	Chi-A	.000	1	1	0	0	0	0	0	0	0	0	0	H
■ **Ed Romero**														
D 1981	Mil-A	.500	1	2	1	1	0	0	0	0	0	1	0	2
L 1986	Bos-A	.000	1	2	0	0	0	0	0	0	0	0	0	S
L 1988	Bos-A	—	1	0	0	0	0	0	0	0	0	0	0	R
L Total	2	.000	2	2	0	0	0	0	0	0	0	0	0	
W 1986	Bos-A	.000	3	1	0	0	0	0	0	0	0	0	0	S
■ **Kevin Romine**														
L 1988	Bos-A	—	2	0	1	0	0	0	0	0	0	0	0	R
■ **Buddy Rosar**														
W 1941	NY-A	—	1	0	0	0	0	0	0	0	0	0	0	C
W 1942	NY-A	1.000	1	1	0	1	0	0	0	0	0	0	0	H
W Total	2	1.000	2	1	0	1	0	0	0	0	0	0	0	
■ **Jimmy Rosario**														
L 1971	SF-N	—	1	0	0	0	0	0	0	0	0	0	0	R
■ **Pete Rose Sr.**														
D 1981	Phi-N	.300	5	20	1	6	1	0	0	2	2	0	0	1
L 1970	Cin-N	.231	3	13	1	3	0	0	0	1	0	0	0	O
L 1972	Cin-N	.450	5	20	1	9	4	0	0	2	1	2	0	O
L 1973	Cin-N	.381	5	21	3	8	1	0	2	2	2	2	0	O
L 1975	Cin-N	.357	3	14	3	5	0	0	1	2	0	2	0	3
L 1976	Cin-N	.429	3	14	3	6	2	1	0	2	1	0	0	3
L 1980	Phi-N	.400	5	20	3	8	0	0	0	2	5	3	0	1
L 1983	Phi-N	.375	4	16	3	6	0	0	0	0	1	1	1	1
L Total	7	.381	28	118	17	45	7	1	3	11	10	10	1	
W 1970	Cin-N	.250	5	20	2	5	1	0	1	2	2	0	0	O

YEAR	TM/L	AVG	G	AB	R	H	2B	3B	HR	RBI	BB	SO	SB	POS
W 1972	Cin-N	.214	7	28	3	6	0	0	1	2	4	4	1	O
W 1975	Cin-N	.370	7	27	3	10	1	1	0	2	5	1	0	3
W 1976	Cin-N	.188	4	16	1	3	1	0	0	1	2	2	0	3
W 1980	Phi-N	.261	6	23	2	6	1	0	0	1	2	2	0	1
W 1983	Phi-N	.313	5	16	1	5	1	0	0	1	1	3	0	1-3,O-1
W Total	6	.269	34	130	12	35	5	1	2	9	16	12	1	
■ **John Roseboro**														
L 1969	Min-A	.200	2	5	0	1	0	0	0	0	0	0	0	C
W 1959	LA-N	.095	6	21	0	2	0	0	0	1	0	2	0	C
W 1963	LA-N	.143	4	14	1	2	0	0	1	3	0	4	0	C
W 1965	LA-N	.286	7	21	1	6	1	0	0	3	5	3	1	C
W 1966	LA-N	.071	4	14	0	1	0	0	0	0	0	3	0	C
W Total	4	.157	21	70	2	11	1	0	1	7	5	12	1	
■ **Chief Roseman**														
W 1884	NY-A	.333	3	9	1	3	0	0	0	1	0	1	0	O
■ **Al Rosen**														
W 1948	Cle-A	.000	1	1	0	0	0	0	0	0	0	0	0	H
W 1954	Cle-A	.250	3	12	0	3	0	0	0	0	1	0	0	3
W Total	2	.231	4	13	0	3	0	0	0	0	1	0	0	
■ **Claude Rossman**														
W 1907	Det-A	.400	5	20	1	8	0	1	0	2	1	0	1	1
W 1908	Det-A	.211	5	19	3	4	0	0	0	3	1	4	1	1
W Total	2	.308	10	39	4	12	0	1	0	5	2	4	2	
■ **Jack Rothrock**														
W 1934	StL-N	.233	7	30	3	7	3	1	0	6	1	2	0	O
■ **Edd Roush**														
W 1919	Cin-N	.214	8	28	6	6	2	1	0	7	3	0	2	O
■ **Jack Rowe**														
W 1887	Det-N	.354	15	65	12	23	1	1	0	7	2	1	5	S
■ **Jerry Royster**														
L 1982	Atl-N	.182	3	11	0	2	0	0	0	0	0	2	0	O-3,3-1
■ **Joe Rudi**														
L 1971	Oak-A	.143	2	7	0	1	1	0	0	0	1	0	0	O
L 1972	Oak-A	.250	5	20	1	5	1	0	0	2	1	4	0	O
L 1973	Oak-A	.222	5	18	1	4	0	0	1	3	3	1	0	O
L 1974	Oak-A	.154	4	13	0	2	0	1	0	1	3	2	0	O
L 1975	Oak-A	.250	3	12	1	3	2	0	0	0	0	1	0	1-2,O-1
L Total	5	.214	19	70	3	15	4	1	1	6	8	8	0	
W 1972	Oak-A	.240	7	25	1	6	0	0	1	1	2	5	0	O
W 1973	Oak-A	.333	7	27	3	9	2	0	0	4	3	4	0	O
W 1974	Oak-A	.333	5	18	1	6	0	0	1	4	0	3	0	O-5,1-2
W Total	3	.300	19	70	5	21	2	0	2	9	5	12	0	
■ **Muddy Ruel**														
W 1924	Was-A	.095	7	21	2	2	1	0	0	0	6	1	0	C
W 1925	Was-A	.316	7	19	0	6	1	0	0	1	3	2	0	C
W Total	2	.200	14	40	2	8	2	0	0	1	9	3	0	
■ **Dutch Ruether**														
W 1919	Cin-N	.667	3	6	2	4	1	2	0	4	1	0	0	P-2
W 1925	Was-A	.000	1	1	0	0	0	0	0	0	0	1	0	H
W 1926	NY-A	.000	3	4	0	0	0	0	0	0	0	0	0	P-1
W Total	3	.364	7	11	2	4	1	2	0	4	1	1	0	
■ **Rip Russell**														
W 1946	Bos-A	1.000	2	2	1	2	0	0	0	0	0	0	0	3-1
■ **Bill Russell**														
D 1981	LA-N	.250	5	16	1	4	1	0	0	2	3	1	0	S
L 1974	LA-N	.389	4	18	1	7	0	0	0	3	1	0	0	S
L 1977	LA-N	.278	4	18	3	5	1	0	0	2	0	0	0	S
L 1978	LA-N	.412	4	17	1	7	1	0	0	2	1	1	0	S
L 1981	LA-N	.313	5	16	2	5	0	1	0	1	1	1	0	S
L 1983	LA-N	.286	4	14	1	4	0	0	0	0	2	4	1	S
L Total	5	.337	21	83	8	28	2	1	0	8	5	6	1	
W 1974	LA-N	.222	5	18	0	4	0	1	0	2	0	2	0	S
W 1977	LA-N	.154	6	26	3	4	0	1	0	2	1	3	0	S
W 1978	LA-N	.423	6	26	1	11	2	0	0	2	2	2	1	S
W 1981	LA-N	.240	6	25	1	6	0	0	0	2	0	1	1	S
W Total	4	.263	23	95	5	25	2	2	0	8	3	8	2	
■ **Babe Ruth**														
W 1915	Bos-A	.000	1	1	0	0	0	0	0	0	0	0	0	H
W 1916	Bos-A	.000	1	5	0	0	0	0	0	1	0	2	0	P
W 1918	Bos-A	.200	3	5	0	1	0	1	0	2	0	2	0	P-2,O-2
W 1921	NY-A	.313	6	16	3	5	0	0	1	4	5	8	2	O
W 1922	NY-A	.118	5	17	1	2	1	0	0	1	2	3	0	O
W 1923	NY-A	.368	6	19	8	7	1	1	3	3	8	6	0	O-6,1-1
W 1926	NY-A	.300	7	20	6	6	0	0	4	5	11	2	1	O
W 1927	NY-A	.400	4	15	4	6	0	0	2	7	2	2	1	O
W 1928	NY-A	.625	4	16	9	10	3	0	3	4	1	2	0	O
W 1932	NY-A	.333	4	15	6	5	0	0	2	6	4	3	0	O
W Total	10	.326	41	129	37	42	5	2	15	33	33	30	4	
■ **Connie Ryan**														
W 1948	Bos-N	.000	2	1	0	0	0	0	0	0	0	1	0	H
■ **Jimmy Ryan**														
W 1886	Chi-N	.250	6	20	4	5	1	0	0	2	0	1	1	O-6,P-1,S-1
■ **John Ryan**														
W 1890	Lou-A	.053	6	19	0	1	0	0	0	2	0	1	1	C
■ **Blondy Ryan**														
W 1933	NY-N	.278	5	18	0	5	0	0	0	1	1	5	0	S
W 1937	NY-N	.000	1	1	0	0	0	0	0	0	0	1	0	H
W Total	2	.263	6	19	0	5	0	0	0	1	1	6	0	
■ **Mike Ryan**														
W 1967	Bos-A	.000	1	2	0	0	0	0	0	0	0	1	0	C
■ **Chris Sabo**														
L 1990	Cin-N	.227	6	22	1	5	0	0	1	3	1	4	0	3
W 1990	Cin-N	.563	4	16	2	9	1	0	2	5	2	2	0	3
■ **Donnie Sadler**														
D 1998	Bos-A	—	3	0	0	0	0	0	0	0	0	0	0	2
D 1999	Bos-A	.500	2	2	1	1	1	0	0	0	0	1	0	3-1,D-1
D Total	2	.500	5	2	1	1	1	0	0	0	0	1	0	
L 1999	Bos-A	—	2	0	0	0	0	0	0	0	0	0	0	O-1,D-1
■ **Olmedo Saenz**														
D 2000	Oak-A	.231	4	13	1	3	0	0	1	4	0	2	0	D-3
■ **Lenn Sakata**														
W 1983	Bal-A	.000	1	1	0	0	0	0	0	0	0	0	0	2
■ **Luis Salazar**														
L 1984	SD-N	.200	3	5	0	1	0	1	0	0	0	1	0	O-2,3-1
L 1989	Chi-N	.368	5	19	2	7	0	1	1	2	0	0	0	3
L Total	2	.333	8	24	2	8	0	2	1	2	0	1	0	
W 1984	SD-N	.333	4	3	0	1	0	0	0	0	0	0	0	O-2,3-1
■ **Bill Salkeld**														
W 1948	Bos-N	.222	5	9	2	2	0	0	1	1	5	1	0	C
■ **Chico Salmon**														
L 1969	Bal-A	.000	1	1	0	0	0	0	0	0	0	0	0	H
W 1969	Bal-A	—	2	0	0	0	0	0	0	0	0	0	0	R
W 1970	Bal-A	1.000	1	1	1	1	0	0	0	0	0	0	0	H
W Total	2	1.000	3	1	1	1	0	0	0	0	0	0	0	
■ **Juan Samuel**														
L 1983	Phi-N	—	1	0	0	0	0	0	0	0	0	0	0	R
W 1983	Phi-N	.000	3	1	0	0	0	0	0	0	0	0	0	H
■ **Rey Sanchez**														
D 1997	NY-A	.200	5	15	1	3	1	0	0	1	1	2	0	2
■ **Ryne Sandberg**														
L 1984	Chi-N	.368	5	19	3	7	2	0	0	2	3	2	3	2
L 1989	Chi-N	.400	5	20	6	8	3	1	1	4	3	4	0	2
L Total	2	.385	10	39	9	15	5	1	1	6	6	6	3	
■ **Deion Sanders**														
L 1992	Atl-N	.000	4	5	0	0	0	0	0	0	0	3	0	O-3
L 1993	Atl-N	.000	5	3	0	0	0	0	0	0	0	1	0	O-1
L Total	2	.000	9	8	0	0	0	0	0	0	0	4	0	
W 1992	Atl-N	.533	4	15	4	8	2	0	0	1	2	1	5	O
■ **Ray Sanders**														
W 1942	StL-N	.000	2	1	1	0	0	0	0	0	1	0	0	H
W 1943	StL-N	.294	5	17	3	5	0	0	1	2	3	4	0	1
W 1944	StL-N	.286	6	21	5	6	0	0	1	1	5	8	0	1
W 1948	Bos-N	.000	1	1	0	0	0	0	0	0	0	0	0	H
W Total	4	.275	14	40	9	11	0	0	2	3	9	12	0	
■ **Reggie Sanders**														
D 1995	Cin-N	.154	3	13	3	2	1	0	1	2	1	9	2	O
D 2000	Atl-N	.000	3	9	0	0	0	0	0	0	2	5	0	O
D Total	2	.091	6	22	3	2	1	0	1	2	3	14	2	
L 1995	Cin-N	.125	4	16	0	2	0	0	0	0	2	10	0	O
■ **Charlie Sands**														
W 1971	Pit-N	.000	1	1	0	0	0	0	0	0	0	1	0	H
■ **Manny Sanguillen**														
L 1970	Pit-N	.167	3	12	0	2	0	0	0	0	0	1	0	C
L 1971	Pit-N	.267	4	15	1	4	0	0	0	1	1	1	1	C
L 1972	Pit-N	.313	5	16	4	5	1	0	1	2	0	0	0	C
L 1974	Pit-N	.250	4	16	0	4	1	0	0	0	0	0	0	C
L 1975	Pit-N	.167	3	12	0	2	0	0	0	0	0	0	0	C
L Total	5	.239	19	71	5	17	2	0	1	3	1	2	1	
W 1971	Pit-N	.379	7	29	3	11	1	0	0	0	0	3	2	C
W 1979	Pit-N	.333	3	3	0	1	0	0	0	1	0	0	0	H
W Total	2	.375	10	32	3	12	1	0	0	1	0	3	2	
■ **Rafael Santana**														
L 1986	NY-N	.176	6	17	0	3	0	0	0	0	0	3	0	S
W 1986	NY-N	.250	7	20	3	5	0	0	0	2	2	5	0	S
■ **Benito Santiago**														
D 1995	Cin-N	.333	3	9	2	3	0	0	1	3	3	3	0	C
L 1995	Cin-N	.231	4	13	0	3	0	0	0	0	2	3	0	C
■ **Mackey Sasser**														
L 1988	NY-N	.200	4	5	0	1	0	0	0	0	0	1	0	C-1
■ **Ed Sauer**														
W 1945	Chi-N	.000	2	2	0	0	0	0	0	0	0	2	0	H
■ **Carl Sawatski**														
W 1957	Mil-N	.000	2	2	0	0	0	0	0	0	0	2	0	H
■ **Steve Sax**														
D 1981	LA-N	—	1	0	0	0	0	0	0	0	0	0	0	2
L 1981	LA-N	—	1	0	0	0	0	0	0	0	0	0	0	2

YEAR	TM/L	AVG	G	AB	R	H	2B	3B	HR	RBI	BB	SO	SB	POS
L 1983	LA-N	.250	4	16	0	4	0	0	0	0	1	0	1	2
L 1985	LA-N	.300	6	20	1	6	3	0	0	1	1	5	0	2
L 1988	LA-N	.267	7	30	7	8	0	0	0	3	3	3	5	2
L Total	4	.273	18	66	8	18	3	0	0	4	5	8	6	
W 1981	LA-N	.000	2	1	0	0	0	0	0	0	0	0	0	2-1
W 1988	LA-N	.300	5	20	3	6	0	0	0	0	1	1	1	2
W Total	2	.286	7	21	3	6	0	0	0	0	1	1	1	
■ Germany Schaefer														
W 1907	Det-A	.143	5	21	1	3	0	0	0	0	0	3	0	2
W 1908	Det-A	.125	5	16	0	2	0	0	0	0	1	4	1	2-3,3-2
W Total	2	.135	10	37	1	5	0	0	0	0	1	7	1	
■ Ray Schalk														
W 1917	Chi-A	.263	6	19	1	5	0	0	0	0	2	1	1	C
W 1919	Chi-A	.304	8	23	1	7	0	0	0	2	4	2	1	C
W Total	2	.286	14	42	2	12	0	0	0	2	6	3	2	
■ Wally Schang														
W 1913	Phi-A	.357	4	14	2	5	0	1	1	7	2	4	0	C
W 1914	Phi-A	.167	4	12	1	2	1	0	0	0	1	4	0	C
W 1918	Bos-A	.444	5	9	1	4	0	0	0	1	2	3	1	C
W 1921	NY-A	.286	8	21	1	6	1	1	0	1	5	4	0	C
W 1922	NY-A	.188	5	16	0	3	1	0	0	0	0	3	0	C
W 1923	NY-A	.318	6	22	3	7	1	0	0	0	1	2	0	C
W Total	6	.287	32	94	8	27	4	2	1	9	11	20	1	
■ Hank Schenz														
W 1951	NY-N	—	1	0	0	0	0	0	0	0	0	0	0	R
■ Ray Schmandt														
W 1920	Bro-N	.000	1	1	0	0	0	0	0	0	0	0	0	H
■ Boss Schmidt														
W 1907	Det-A	.167	4	12	0	2	0	0	0	0	2	1	0	C-3
W 1908	Det-A	.071	4	14	0	1	0	0	0	1	0	2	0	C
W 1909	Det-A	.222	6	18	0	4	2	0	0	4	2	0	0	C
W Total	3	.159	14	44	0	7	2	0	0	5	4	3	0	
■ Butch Schmidt														
W 1914	Bos-N	.294	4	17	2	5	0	0	0	2	0	2	1	1
■ Mike Schmidt														
D 1981	Phi-N	.250	5	16	3	4	1	0	1	2	4	2	0	3
L 1976	Phi-N	.308	3	13	1	4	2	0	0	2	0	1	0	3
L 1977	Phi-N	.063	4	16	2	1	0	0	0	1	2	3	0	3
L 1978	Phi-N	.200	4	15	1	3	2	0	0	1	2	2	0	3
L 1980	Phi-N	.208	5	24	1	5	1	0	0	1	1	6	1	3
L 1983	Phi-N	.467	4	15	5	7	2	0	1	2	2	3	0	3
L Total	5	.241	20	83	10	20	7	0	1	7	7	15	1	
W 1980	Phi-N	.381	6	21	6	8	1	0	2	7	4	3	0	3
W 1983	Phi-N	.050	5	20	0	1	0	0	0	0	0	6	0	3
W Total	2	.220	11	41	6	9	1	0	2	7	4	9	0	
■ Red Schoendienst														
W 1946	StL-N	.233	7	30	3	7	1	0	0	1	0	2	1	2
W 1957	Mil-N	.278	5	18	0	5	1	0	0	2	0	1	0	2
W 1958	Mil-N	.300	7	30	5	9	3	1	0	0	2	1	0	2
W Total	3	.269	19	78	8	21	5	1	0	3	2	4	1	
■ Dick Schofield														
W 1960	Pit-N	.333	3	3	0	1	0	0	0	0	1	0	0	S-2
W 1968	StL-N	—	2	0	0	0	0	0	0	0	0	0	0	S-1
W Total	2	.333	5	3	0	1	0	0	0	0	1	0	0	
■ Dick Schofield														
L 1986	Cal-A	.300	7	30	4	9	1	0	1	2	1	5	1	S
■ Ossee Schreckengost														
W 1905	Phi-A	.222	3	9	2	2	1	0	0	0	0	0	0	C
■ Pop Schriver														
T 1900	Pit-N	.000	1	1	0	0	0	0	0	0	0	0	0	H
■ Frank Schulte														
W 1906	Chi-N	.269	6	26	1	7	3	0	0	3	1	3	0	O
W 1907	Chi-N	.250	5	20	3	5	0	0	0	2	1	2	0	O
W 1908	Chi-N	.389	5	18	4	7	0	1	0	2	2	1	2	O
W 1910	Chi-N	.353	5	17	3	6	3	0	0	2	2	3	0	O
W Total	4	.309	21	81	11	25	6	1	0	9	6	9	2	
■ Fred Schulte														
W 1933	Was-A	.333	5	21	1	7	1	0	1	4	1	1	0	O
■ Bill Schuster														
W 1945	Chi-N	.000	2	1	1	0	0	0	0	0	0	0	0	S-1
■ Mike Scioscia														
D 1981	LA-N	.154	4	13	0	2	0	0	0	1	1	2	0	C
L 1981	LA-N	.133	5	15	1	2	0	0	1	1	2	1	0	C
L 1985	LA-N	.250	6	16	2	4	0	0	0	1	4	0	0	C
L 1988	LA-N	.364	7	22	3	8	1	0	1	2	1	2	0	C
L Total	3	.264	18	53	6	14	1	0	2	4	7	3	0	
W 1981	LA-N	.250	3	4	1	1	0	0	0	0	1	0	0	C
W 1988	LA-N	.214	4	14	0	3	0	0	0	1	0	2	0	C
W Total	2	.222	7	18	1	4	0	0	0	1	1	2	0	
■ Tony Scott														
D 1981	Hou-N	.150	5	20	0	3	0	0	0	2	1	6	0	O
■ George Scott														
W 1967	Bos-A	.231	7	26	3	6	1	1	0	0	3	6	0	1

YEAR	TM/L	AVG	G	AB	R	H	2B	3B	HR	RBI	BB	SO	SB	POS
■ Everett Scott														
W 1915	Bos-A	.056	5	18	0	1	0	0	0	0	0	3	0	S
W 1916	Bos-A	.125	5	16	1	2	0	1	0	1	1	1	0	S
W 1918	Bos-A	.100	6	20	0	2	0	0	0	1	1	1	0	S
W 1922	NY-A	.143	5	14	0	2	0	0	0	1	1	0	0	S
W 1923	NY-A	.318	6	22	2	7	0	0	0	3	0	1	0	S
W Total	5	.156	27	90	3	14	0	1	0	6	3	6	0	
■ Rodney Scott														
L 1981	Mon-N	.167	5	18	0	3	0	0	0	0	1	3	1	2
■ Jimmy Sebring														
W 1903	Pit-N	.367	8	30	3	11	0	1	1	3	1	4	0	O
■ Frank Secory														
W 1945	Chi-N	.400	5	5	0	2	0	0	0	0	0	2	0	H
■ Bob Seeds														
W 1936	NY-A	—	1	0	0	0	0	0	0	0	0	0	0	R
■ Kevin Seitzer														
D 1996	Cle-A	.294	4	17	1	5	1	0	0	4	2	4	1	D-3,1-1
D 1997	Cle-A	.000	1	4	0	0	0	0	0	0	0	0	0	1
D Total	2	.238	5	21	1	5	1	0	0	4	2	4	1	
L 1997	Cle-A	.000	4	4	0	0	0	0	0	0	1	2	0	1-3
W 1997	Cle-A	.000	1	1	0	0	0	0	0	0	0	0	0	H
■ George Selkirk														
W 1936	NY-A	.333	6	24	6	8	0	1	2	3	4	4	0	O
W 1937	NY-A	.263	5	19	5	5	1	0	0	6	2	0	0	O
W 1938	NY-A	.200	3	10	0	2	0	0	0	1	2	1	0	O
W 1939	NY-A	.167	4	12	0	2	1	0	0	0	3	2	0	O
W 1941	NY-A	.500	2	2	0	1	0	0	0	0	0	0	0	H
W 1942	NY-A	.000	1	1	0	0	0	0	0	0	0	0	0	H
W Total	6	.265	21	68	11	18	2	1	2	10	11	7	0	
■ Andy Seminick														
W 1950	Phi-N	.182	4	11	0	2	0	0	0	0	1	3	0	C
■ Scott Servais														
D 1998	Chi-N	.667	1	3	0	2	0	0	0	0	0	0	0	C
■ Hank Severeid														
W 1925	Was-A	.333	1	3	0	1	0	0	0	0	0	0	0	C
W 1926	NY-A	.273	7	22	1	6	1	0	0	1	1	2	0	C
W Total	2	.280	8	25	1	7	1	0	0	1	1	2	0	
■ Luke Sewell														
W 1933	Was-A	.176	5	17	1	3	0	0	0	1	2	0	1	C
■ Joe Sewell														
W 1920	Cle-A	.174	7	23	0	4	0	0	0	0	2	1	0	S
W 1932	NY-A	.333	4	15	4	5	1	0	0	3	4	0	0	3
W Total	2	.237	11	38	4	9	1	0	0	3	6	1	0	
■ Richie Sexson														
D 1998	Cle-A	.000	3	2	0	0	0	0	0	0	2	1	0	1
D 1999	Cle-A	.167	3	6	1	1	0	0	0	1	1	3	0	1-1,O-1
D Total	2	.125	6	8	1	1	0	0	0	1	3	4	0	
L 1998	Cle-A	.000	3	6	0	0	0	0	0	0	0	3	0	1
■ Socks Seybold														
W 1905	Phi-A	.125	5	16	0	2	0	0	0	0	2	3	0	O
■ Tillie Shafer														
W 1912	NY-N	—	3	0	0	0	0	0	0	0	0	0	0	S
W 1913	NY-N	.158	5	19	2	3	1	1	0	1	2	3	0	O-5,3-1
W Total	2	.158	8	19	2	3	1	1	0	1	2	3	0	
■ Art Shamsky														
L 1969	NY-N	.538	3	13	3	7	0	0	0	1	0	3	0	O
W 1969	NY-N	.000	3	6	0	0	0	0	0	0	0	0	0	O-1
■ Mike Shannon														
W 1964	StL-N	.214	7	28	6	6	0	0	1	2	0	9	1	O
W 1967	StL-N	.208	7	24	3	5	1	0	1	2	1	4	0	3
W 1968	StL-N	.276	7	29	3	8	1	0	1	4	1	5	0	3
W Total	3	.235	21	81	12	19	2	0	3	8	2	18	1	
■ Mike Sharperson														
L 1988	LA-N	.000	2	1	0	0	0	0	0	1	1	0	0	S-1,3-1
■ Danny Sheaffer														
L 1996	StL-N	.000	2	3	0	0	0	0	0	0	0	1	0	C
■ Dave Shean														
W 1918	Bos-A	.211	6	19	2	4	1	0	0	0	4	3	1	2
■ Jimmy Sheckard														
W 1906	Chi-N	.000	6	21	0	0	0	0	0	1	2	4	1	O
W 1907	Chi-N	.238	5	21	0	5	2	0	0	2	0	4	1	O
W 1908	Chi-N	.238	5	21	2	5	2	0	0	1	2	3	1	O
W 1910	Chi-N	.286	5	14	5	4	2	0	0	1	7	2	1	O
W Total	4	.182	21	77	7	14	6	0	0	5	11	13	4	
■ Jack Sheehan														
W 1920	Bro-N	.182	3	11	0	2	0	0	0	0	0	1	0	3
■ Andy Sheets														
D 1997	Sea-A	.333	2	3	0	1	0	0	0	0	0	2	0	3
D 1998	SD-N	—	2	0	0	0	0	0	0	0	0	0	0	2-1
D Total	2	.333	4	3	0	1	0	0	0	0	0	2	0	
L 1998	SD-N	.000	3	3	0	0	0	0	0	0	0	1	0	S-2
W 1998	SD-N	.000	2	2	0	0	0	0	0	0	0	1	0	S

YEAR	TM/L	AVG	G	AB	R	H	2B	3B	HR	RBI	BB	SO	SB	POS
■ Gary Sheffield														
D 1997	Fla-N	.556	3	9	3	5	1	0	1	1	5	0	1	O
L 1997	Fla-N	.235	6	17	6	4	0	0	1	1	7	3	0	O
W 1997	Fla-N	.292	7	24	4	7	1	0	1	5	8	5	0	O
■ John Shelby														
L 1983	Bal-A	.222	3	9	1	2	0	0	0	0	1	3	1	O-2
L 1988	LA-N	.167	7	24	3	4	0	0	0	3	5	12	2	O
L Total	2	.182	10	33	4	6	0	0	0	3	6	15	3	
W 1983	Bal-A	.444	5	9	1	4	0	0	0	1	0	4	0	O
W 1988	LA-N	.222	5	18	0	4	1	0	0	1	2	7	1	O
W Total	2	.296	10	27	1	8	1	0	0	2	2	11	1	
■ Pat Sheridan														
L 1984	KC-A	.000	3	6	1	0	0	0	0	0	3	3	0	O
L 1985	KC-A	.150	7	20	4	3	0	0	2	3	2	3	0	O
L 1987	Det-A	.300	5	10	2	3	1	0	1	2	0	2	1	O-4
L 1989	SF-N	.154	5	13	1	2	0	1	0	0	0	4	0	O
L Total	4	.163	20	49	8	8	1	1	3	5	5	12	1	
W 1985	KC-A	.222	5	18	0	4	2	0	0	1	0	7	0	O-4
W 1989	SF-N	.000	1	2	0	0	0	0	0	0	0	0	0	O
W Total	2	.200	6	20	0	4	2	0	0	1	0	7	0	
■ Tim Shinnick														
W 1890	Lou-A	.292	7	24	3	7	1	1	0	3	2	2	2	2
■ Mule Shirley														
W 1924	Was-A	.500	3	2	1	1	0	0	0	1	0	0	0	H
■ Tom Shopay														
W 1971	Bal-A	.000	5	4	0	0	0	0	0	0	0	0	0	H
■ Chick Shorten														
W 1916	Bos-A	.571	2	7	0	4	0	0	0	2	0	1	0	O
■ George Shuba														
W 1952	Bro-N	.300	4	10	0	3	1	0	0	0	0	4	0	O-3
W 1953	Bro-N	1.000	2	1	1	1	0	0	1	2	0	0	0	H
W 1955	Bro-N	.000	1	1	0	0	0	0	0	0	0	0	0	H
W Total	3	.333	7	12	1	4	1	0	1	2	0	4	0	
■ Norm Siebern														
W 1956	NY-A	.000	1	1	0	0	0	0	0	0	0	0	0	H
W 1958	NY-A	.125	3	8	1	1	0	0	0	0	3	2	0	O
W 1967	Bos-A	.333	3	3	0	1	0	0	0	1	0	0	0	O-1
W Total	3	.167	7	12	1	2	0	0	0	1	3	2	0	
■ Ruben Sierra														
D 1995	NY-A	.174	5	23	2	4	2	0	2	5	2	7	0	D
L 1992	Oak-A	.333	6	24	4	8	2	1	1	7	2	1	1	O
■ Charlie Silvera														
W 1949	NY-A	.000	1	2	0	0	0	0	0	0	0	0	0	C
■ Ken Silvestri														
W 1950	Phi-N	—	1	0	0	0	0	0	0	0	0	0	0	C
■ Al Simmons														
W 1929	Phi-A	.300	5	20	6	6	1	0	2	5	1	4	0	O
W 1930	Phi-A	.364	6	22	4	8	2	0	2	4	2	2	0	O
W 1931	Phi-A	.333	7	27	4	9	2	0	2	8	3	3	0	O
W 1939	Cin-N	.250	1	4	1	1	1	0	0	0	0	0	0	O
W Total	4	.329	19	73	15	24	6	0	6	17	6	9	0	
■ Ted Simmons														
D 1981	Mil-A	.222	5	18	1	4	1	0	1	4	2	2	0	C
L 1982	Mil-A	.167	5	18	3	3	0	0	0	1	1	4	0	C
W 1982	Mil-A	.174	7	23	2	4	0	0	2	3	5	3	0	C
■ Mike Simms														
D 1998	Tex-A	.200	2	5	0	1	0	0	0	0	0	2	0	D
■ Harry Simpson														
W 1957	NY-A	.083	5	12	0	1	0	0	0	1	0	4	0	1-4
■ Duke Sims														
L 1972	Det-A	.214	4	14	0	3	2	1	0	0	1	2	0	C-2,O-2
■ Chris Singleton														
D 2000	Chi-A	.111	3	9	1	1	0	1	0	1	0	2	0	O
■ Ken Singleton														
L 1979	Bal-A	.375	4	16	4	6	2	0	0	2	1	2	0	O
L 1983	Bal-A	.250	4	12	0	3	2	0	0	1	2	2	0	D
L Total	2	.321	8	28	4	9	4	0	0	3	3	4	0	
W 1979	Bal-A	.357	7	28	1	10	1	0	0	2	2	5	0	O
W 1983	Bal-A	.000	2	1	0	0	0	0	0	1	1	1	0	H
W Total	2	.345	9	29	1	10	1	0	0	3	3	6	0	
■ Dick Sisler														
W 1946	StL-N	.000	2	2	0	0	0	0	0	0	0	0	0	H
W 1950	Phi-N	.059	4	17	0	1	0	0	0	1	0	5	0	O
W Total	2	.053	6	19	0	1	0	0	0	1	0	5	0	
■ Sibby Sisti														
W 1948	Bos-N	.000	2	1	0	0	0	0	0	0	0	0	0	2
■ Ted Sizemore														
L 1977	Phi-N	.231	4	13	1	3	0	0	0	0	2	0	0	2
L 1978	Phi-N	.385	4	13	3	5	0	1	0	1	1	0	0	2
L Total	2	.308	8	26	4	8	0	1	0	1	3	0	0	
■ Dave Skaggs														
L 1979	Bal-A	.000	1	4	0	0	0	0	0	0	0	0	0	C
W 1979	Bal-A	.333	1	3	1	1	0	0	0	0	0	0	0	C
■ Bob Skinner														
W 1960	Pit-N	.200	2	5	2	1	0	0	0	1	1	0	1	O
W 1964	StL-N	.667	4	3	0	2	1	0	0	1	1	0	0	H
W Total	2	.375	6	8	2	3	1	0	0	2	2	0	1	
■ Bill Skowron														
W 1955	NY-A	.333	5	12	2	4	2	0	1	3	0	1	0	1-3
W 1956	NY-A	.100	3	10	1	1	0	0	1	4	0	3	0	1-2
W 1957	NY-A	.000	2	4	0	0	0	0	0	0	0	0	0	1
W 1958	NY-A	.259	7	27	3	7	0	0	2	7	1	4	0	1
W 1960	NY-A	.375	7	32	7	12	2	0	2	6	0	6	0	1
W 1961	NY-A	.353	5	17	3	6	0	0	1	5	3	4	0	1
W 1962	NY-A	.222	6	18	1	4	0	1	0	1	1	5	0	1
W 1963	LA-N	.385	4	13	2	5	0	0	1	3	1	3	0	1
W Total	8	.293	39	133	19	39	4	1	8	29	6	26	0	
■ Jimmy Slagle														
W 1907	Chi-N	.273	5	22	3	6	0	0	0	4	2	3	6	O
■ Mike Slattery														
W 1888	NY-N	.205	10	39	6	8	2	0	0	5	0	5	6	O-10,2-1
W 1889	NY-N	.188	4	16	6	3	0	0	0	1	3	1	1	O
W Total	2	.200	14	55	12	11	2	0	0	6	3	6	7	
■ Don Slaught														
L 1984	KC-A	.364	3	11	0	4	0	0	0	0	0	0	0	C
L 1990	Pit-N	.091	4	11	0	1	1	0	0	1	2	3	0	C
L 1991	Pit-N	.235	6	17	0	4	0	0	0	1	1	4	0	C
L 1992	Pit-N	.333	5	12	5	4	1	0	1	5	6	3	0	C
L Total	4	.255	18	51	5	13	2	0	1	7	9	10	0	
■ Enos Slaughter														
W 1942	StL-N	.263	5	19	3	5	1	0	1	2	3	2	0	O
W 1946	StL-N	.320	7	25	5	8	1	1	1	2	4	3	1	O
W 1956	NY-A	.350	6	20	6	7	0	0	1	4	4	0	0	O
W 1957	NY-A	.250	5	12	2	3	1	0	0	0	3	2	0	O
W 1958	NY-A	.000	4	3	1	0	0	0	0	0	1	1	0	H
W Total	5	.291	27	79	17	23	3	1	3	8	15	8	1	
■ Roy Smalley														
W 1987	Min-A	.500	4	2	0	1	1	0	0	0	2	0	0	H
■ Al Smith														
W 1954	Cle-A	.214	4	14	2	3	0	0	1	2	2	2	0	O
W 1959	Chi-A	.250	6	20	1	5	3	0	0	1	4	4	0	O
W Total	2	.235	10	34	3	8	3	0	1	3	6	6	0	
■ Billy Smith														
L 1979	Bal-A	.000	1	4	0	0	0	0	0	0	0	1	0	2
W 1979	Bal-A	.286	4	7	1	2	0	0	0	0	2	0	0	2-2
■ Reggie Smith														
D 1981	LA-N	.000	2	1	0	0	0	0	0	1	0	1	0	H
L 1977	LA-N	.188	4	16	2	3	0	1	0	1	2	5	1	O
L 1978	LA-N	.188	4	16	2	3	1	0	0	1	0	2	0	O
L 1981	LA-N	1.000	1	1	0	1	0	0	0	1	0	0	0	H
L Total	3	.212	9	33	4	7	1	1	0	3	2	7	1	
W 1967	Bos-A	.250	7	24	3	6	1	0	2	3	2	2	0	O
W 1977	LA-N	.273	6	22	7	6	1	0	3	5	4	3	0	O
W 1978	LA-N	.200	6	25	3	5	0	0	1	5	2	6	0	O
W 1981	LA-N	.500	2	2	0	1	0	0	0	0	0	1	0	H
W Total	4	.247	21	73	13	18	2	0	6	13	8	12	0	
■ Earl Smith														
W 1921	NY-N	.000	3	7	0	0	0	0	0	0	1	0	0	C-2
W 1922	NY-N	.143	4	7	0	1	0	0	0	0	0	2	0	C-1
W 1925	Pit-N	.350	6	20	0	7	1	0	0	0	1	2	0	C
W 1927	Pit-N	.000	3	8	0	0	0	0	0	0	0	0	0	C-2
W 1928	StL-N	.750	1	4	0	3	0	0	0	0	0	0	0	C
W Total	5	.239	17	46	0	11	1	0	0	0	2	4	0	
■ Elmer Smith														
W 1920	Cle-A	.308	5	13	1	4	0	1	1	5	1	1	0	O
W 1922	NY-A	.000	2	2	0	0	0	0	0	0	0	2	0	H
W Total	2	.267	7	15	1	4	0	1	1	5	1	3	0	
■ Germany Smith														
W 1889	Bro-A	.172	8	29	2	5	2	1	0	2	3	2	2	S
W 1890	Bro-N	.276	7	29	3	8	0	2	0	7	0	3	1	S
W Total	2	.224	15	58	5	13	2	3	0	9	3	5	3	
■ Hal Smith														
W 1960	Pit-N	.375	3	8	1	3	0	0	1	3	0	0	0	C
■ Harry Smith														
W 1903	Pit-N	.000	1	3	0	0	0	0	0	0	0	0	0	C
■ Jimmy Smith														
W 1919	Cin-N	—	1	0	0	0	0	0	0	0	0	0	0	R
■ Dwight Smith														
D 1995	Atl-N	.667	4	3	0	2	1	0	0	1	0	0	0	H
L 1989	Chi-N	.200	4	15	2	3	1	0	0	0	2	2	1	O
L 1995	Atl-N	.000	2	2	0	0	0	0	0	0	0	0	0	H
L Total	2	.176	6	17	2	3	1	0	0	0	2	2	1	
W 1995	Atl-N	.500	3	2	0	1	0	0	0	0	1	0	0	H
■ Lonnie Smith														
D 1981	Phi-N	.263	5	19	1	5	1	0	0	0	0	4	0	O
L 1980	Phi-N	.600	3	5	2	3	0	0	0	0	0	0	1	O-2

YEAR	TM/L	AVG	G	AB	R	H	2B	3B	HR	RBI	BB	SO	SB	POS
L 1982	StL-N	.273	3	11	1	3	0	0	0	1	0	1	0	O
L 1985	KC-A	.250	7	28	2	7	2	0	0	1	3	6	1	O
L 1991	Atl-N	.250	7	24	3	6	3	0	0	0	4	5	1	O
L 1992	Atl-N	.333	6	6	1	2	0	1	0	1	0	0	0	H
L Total	5	.284	26	74	9	21	5	1	0	3	7	12	3	
W 1980	Phi-N	.263	6	19	2	5	1	0	0	1	1	1	0	O-5,D-1
W 1982	StL-N	.321	7	28	6	9	4	1	0	1	1	5	2	O-6,D-1
W 1985	KC-A	.333	7	27	4	9	3	0	0	4	3	8	2	O
W 1991	Atl-N	.231	7	26	5	6	0	0	3	3	3	4	1	D-4,O-3
W 1992	Atl-N	.167	5	12	1	2	0	0	1	5	1	4	0	D-3
W Total	5	.277	32	112	18	31	8	1	4	14	9	22	5	
■ Ozzie Smith														
D 1996	StL-N	.333	2	3	1	1	0	0	0	0	2	0	0	S-1
L 1982	StL-N	.556	3	9	0	5	0	0	0	3	3	0	1	S
L 1985	StL-N	.435	6	23	4	10	1	1	1	3	3	1	1	S
L 1987	StL-N	.200	7	25	2	5	0	1	0	1	3	4	0	S
L 1996	StL-N	.000	3	9	0	0	0	0	0	0	0	1	0	S-2
L Total	4	.303	19	66	6	20	1	2	1	7	9	6	2	
W 1982	StL-N	.208	7	24	3	5	0	0	0	1	3	0	1	S
W 1985	StL-N	.087	7	23	1	2	0	0	0	0	4	0	1	S
W 1987	StL-N	.214	7	28	3	6	0	0	0	2	2	3	2	S
W Total	3	.173	21	75	7	13	0	0	0	3	9	3	4	
■ Duke Snider														
W 1949	Bro-N	.143	5	21	2	3	1	0	0	0	0	8	0	O
W 1952	Bro-N	.345	7	29	5	10	2	0	4	8	1	5	1	O
W 1953	Bro-N	.320	6	25	3	8	3	0	1	5	2	6	0	O
W 1955	Bro-N	.320	7	25	5	8	1	0	4	7	2	6	0	O
W 1956	Bro-N	.304	7	23	5	7	1	0	1	4	6	8	0	O
W 1959	LA-N	.200	4	10	1	2	0	0	1	2	2	0	0	O-3
W Total	6	.286	36	133	21	38	8	0	11	26	13	33	1	
■ Fred Snodgrass														
W 1911	NY-N	.105	6	19	1	2	0	0	0	1	2	7	0	O
W 1912	NY-N	.212	8	33	2	7	2	0	0	2	2	5	1	O
W 1913	NY-N	.333	2	3	0	1	0	0	0	0	0	0	0	1-1,O-1
W Total	3	.182	16	55	3	10	2	0	0	3	4	12	1	
■ J. T. Snow														
D 1997	SF-N	.167	3	6	0	1	0	0	0	0	1	1	0	1
D 2000	SF-N	.400	4	10	1	4	0	0	1	3	4	1	0	1
D Total	2	.313	7	16	1	5	0	0	1	3	5	2	0	
■ Frank Snyder														
W 1921	NY-N	.364	7	22	4	8	1	0	1	3	0	2	0	C-6
W 1922	NY-N	.333	4	15	1	5	0	0	0	0	0	1	0	C
W 1923	NY-N	.118	5	17	1	2	0	0	1	2	0	2	0	C
W 1924	NY-N	.000	1	1	0	0	0	0	0	0	0	0	0	H
W Total	4	.273	17	55	6	15	1	0	2	5	0	5	0	
■ Russ Snyder														
W 1966	Bal-A	.167	3	6	1	1	0	0	0	1	2	0	0	O
■ Eric Soderholm														
L 1980	NY-A	.167	2	6	0	1	0	0	0	0	0	0	0	D
■ Luis Sojo														
D 1995	Sea-A	.250	5	20	0	5	0	0	0	3	0	3	0	S
D 1996	NY-A	—	2	0	0	0	0	0	0	0	0	0	0	2
D 2000	NY-A	.188	5	16	2	3	2	0	0	5	2	1	0	2
D Total	3	.222	12	36	2	8	2	0	0	8	2	4	0	
L 1995	Sea-A	.250	6	20	0	5	2	0	0	1	0	2	0	S
L 1996	NY-A	.200	3	5	0	1	0	0	0	0	0	1	0	2
L 1998	NY-A	—	1	0	0	0	0	0	0	0	0	0	0	1
L 1999	NY-A	.000	2	1	0	0	0	0	0	0	0	0	0	2
L 2000	NY-A	.261	6	23	1	6	1	0	0	2	2	3	0	2-6,3-2
L Total	5	.245	18	49	1	12	3	0	0	3	2	6	0	
W 1996	NY-A	.600	5	5	0	3	1	0	0	1	0	0	0	2-3
W 1999	NY-A	—	1	0	0	0	0	0	0	0	0	0	0	2
W 2000	NY-A	.286	4	7	0	2	0	0	0	2	1	0	1	2-2,3-2
W Total	3	.417	10	12	0	5	1	0	0	3	1	0	1	
■ Paul Sorrento														
D 1995	Cle-A	.300	3	10	2	3	0	0	0	1	2	3	0	1
D 1997	Sea-A	.300	4	10	2	3	1	0	1	1	2	3	0	1
D Total	2	.300	7	20	4	6	1	0	1	2	4	6	0	
L 1991	Min-A	.000	1	1	0	0	0	0	0	0	0	1	0	H
L 1995	Cle-A	.154	4	13	2	2	1	0	0	0	2	3	0	1
L Total	2	.143	5	14	2	2	1	0	0	0	2	4	0	
W 1991	Min-A	.000	3	2	0	0	0	0	0	0	1	2	0	1-1
W 1995	Cle-A	.182	6	11	0	2	1	0	0	0	0	4	0	1-3
W Total	2	.154	9	13	0	2	1	0	0	0	1	6	0	
■ Sammy Sosa														
D 1998	Chi-N	.182	3	11	0	2	1	0	0	0	1	4	0	O
■ Billy Southworth														
W 1924	NY-N	.000	5	1	1	0	0	0	0	0	0	0	0	O-2
W 1926	StL-N	.345	7	29	6	10	1	1	1	4	0	0	1	O
W Total	2	.333	12	30	7	10	1	1	1	4	0	0	1	
■ Tris Speaker														
W 1912	Bos-A	.300	8	30	4	9	1	2	0	2	4	2	1	O
W 1915	Bos-A	.294	5	17	2	5	0	1	0	0	4	1	0	O
W 1920	Cle-A	.320	7	25	6	8	2	1	0	1	3	1	0	O
W Total	3	.306	20	72	12	22	3	4	0	3	11	4	1	
■ Chris Speier														
D 1981	Mon-N	.400	5	15	4	6	2	0	0	3	4	2	0	S
L 1971	SF-N	.357	4	14	4	5	1	0	1	1	1	1	0	S
L 1981	Mon-N	.188	5	16	0	3	0	0	0	0	2	0	0	S
L 1987	SF-N	.000	3	5	0	0	0	0	0	0	0	2	0	2-1
L Total	3	.229	12	35	4	8	1	0	1	1	3	3	0	
■ Jim Spencer														
D 1981	Oak-A	.250	1	4	0	1	1	0	0	0	0	0	0	1
L 1980	NY-A	.000	1	1	0	0	0	0	0	0	0	0	0	H
L 1981	Oak-A	.000	2	3	0	0	0	0	0	0	0	0	0	1
L Total	2	.000	3	4	0	0	0	0	0	0	0	0	0	
W 1978	NY-A	.167	4	12	3	2	0	0	0	0	2	4	0	1-3
■ Shane Spencer														
D 1998	NY-A	.500	2	6	3	3	0	0	2	4	0	1	0	O
L 1998	NY-A	.100	3	10	1	1	0	0	0	0	1	3	0	O
L 1999	NY-A	.111	3	9	1	1	0	0	0	0	1	6	0	O
L Total	2	.105	6	19	2	2	0	0	0	0	2	9	0	
W 1998	NY-A	.333	1	3	1	1	1	0	0	0	0	2	0	O
■ Roy Spencer														
W 1927	Pit-N	.000	1	1	0	0	0	0	0	0	0	0	0	C
■ Bill Spiers														
D 1997	Hou-N	.000	3	11	1	0	0	0	0	0	1	2	0	3
D 1998	Hou-N	.286	4	14	2	4	3	0	0	1	1	3	0	3
D 1999	Hou-N	.273	4	11	0	3	0	0	0	1	0	1	1	O-3
D Total	3	.194	11	36	3	7	3	0	0	2	2	6	1	
■ Ed Spiezio														
W 1967	StL-N	.000	1	1	0	0	0	0	0	0	0	0	0	H
W 1968	StL-N	1.000	1	1	0	1	0	0	0	0	0	0	0	H
W Total	2	.500	2	2	0	1	0	0	0	0	0	0	0	
■ Harry Spilman														
D 1981	Hou-N	.000	1	1	0	0	0	0	0	0	0	0	0	H
L 1979	Cin-N	.000	2	2	0	0	0	0	0	0	0	0	0	H
L 1987	SF-N	.500	3	2	1	1	0	0	1	1	0	0	0	H
L Total	2	.250	5	4	1	1	0	0	1	1	0	0	0	
■ Ed Sprague Jr.														
L 1992	Tor-A	.500	2	2	0	1	0	0	0	0	0	1	0	H
L 1993	Tor-A	.286	6	21	0	6	0	1	0	4	2	4	0	3
L Total	2	.304	8	23	0	7	0	1	0	4	2	5	0	
W 1992	Tor-A	.500	3	2	1	1	0	0	1	2	1	0	0	1-1
W 1993	Tor-A	.067	5	15	0	1	0	0	0	2	1	6	0	3-4,1-1
W Total	2	.118	8	17	1	2	0	0	1	4	2	6	0	
■ Mike Squires														
L 1983	Chi-A	.000	4	4	0	0	0	0	0	0	0	0	0	1-3
■ Chick Stahl														
T 1897	Bos-N	.400	5	20	6	8	1	0	0	6	3	2	2	O
W 1903	Bos-A	.303	8	33	6	10	1	3	0	3	1	2	2	O
■ Jake Stahl														
W 1912	Bos-A	.281	8	32	3	9	2	0	0	2	0	6	2	1
■ Larry Stahl														
L 1973	Cin-N	.500	4	4	1	2	0	0	0	0	0	1	0	H
■ Tuck Stainback														
W 1942	NY-A	—	2	0	0	0	0	0	0	0	0	0	0	R
W 1943	NY-A	.176	5	17	0	3	0	0	0	0	0	2	0	O
W Total	2	.176	7	17	0	3	0	0	0	0	0	2	0	
■ Matt Stairs														
D 1995	Bos-A	.000	1	1	0	0	0	0	0	0	0	1	0	H
D 2000	Oak-A	.111	3	9	0	1	1	0	0	0	0	1	0	O-2
D Total	2	.100	4	10	0	1	1	0	0	0	0	2	0	
■ Oscar Stanage														
W 1909	Det-A	.200	2	5	0	1	0	0	0	2	0	2	0	C
■ Eddie Stanky														
W 1947	Bro-N	.240	7	25	4	6	1	0	0	2	3	2	0	2
W 1948	Bos-N	.286	6	14	0	4	1	0	0	1	7	0	0	2
W 1951	NY-N	.136	6	22	3	3	0	0	0	1	3	2	0	2
W Total	3	.213	19	61	7	13	2	0	0	4	13	4	0	
■ Fred Stanley														
D 1981	Oak-A	.000	3	6	0	0	0	0	0	0	1	1	0	S
L 1976	NY-A	.333	5	15	1	5	2	0	0	0	2	0	0	S
L 1977	NY-A	—	2	0	0	0	0	0	0	0	0	0	0	S
L 1978	NY-A	.200	2	5	0	1	0	0	0	0	0	2	0	2
L 1981	Oak-A	.333	2	3	0	1	0	0	0	1	0	1	0	S
L Total	4	.304	11	23	1	7	2	0	0	1	2	3	0	
W 1976	NY-A	.167	4	6	1	1	1	0	0	1	3	1	0	S
W 1977	NY-A	—	1	0	0	0	0	0	0	0	0	0	0	S
W 1978	NY-A	.200	3	5	0	1	1	0	0	0	1	0	0	2
W Total	3	.182	8	11	1	2	2	0	0	1	4	1	0	
■ Mickey Stanley														
L 1972	Det-A	.333	4	6	0	2	0	0	0	0	0	0	0	O-3
W 1968	Det-A	.214	7	28	4	6	0	1	0	0	2	4	0	S-7,O-4
■ Mike Stanley														
D 1995	NY-A	.313	4	16	2	5	0	0	1	3	2	1	0	C
D 1997	NY-A	.750	2	4	1	3	1	0	0	1	0	1	0	D-1
D 1998	Bos-A	.267	4	15	1	4	0	0	0	0	2	5	0	D
D 1999	Bos-A	.500	5	20	4	10	2	1	0	2	2	3	0	1

YEAR	TM/L	AVG	G	AB	R	H	2B	3B	HR	RBI	BB	SO	SB	POS
D Total	4	.400	15	55	8	22	3	1	1	6	6	10	0	
L 1999	Bos-A	.222	5	18	1	4	0	0	0	1	2	4	0	1
■ Dave Stapleton														
L 1986	Bos-A	.667	4	3	2	2	0	0	0	0	1	0	0	1
W 1986	Bos-A	.000	3	1	0	0	0	0	0	0	0	0	0	1
■ Willie Stargell														
L 1970	Pit-N	.500	3	12	0	6	1	0	0	1	1	1	0	O
L 1971	Pit-N	.000	4	14	1	0	0	0	0	0	2	6	0	O
L 1972	Pit-N	.063	5	16	1	1	1	0	0	1	2	5	0	1-5,O-1
L 1974	Pit-N	.400	4	15	3	6	0	0	2	4	1	2	0	O
L 1975	Pit-N	.182	3	11	1	2	1	0	0	0	1	3	0	1
L 1979	Pit-N	.455	3	11	2	5	2	0	2	6	3	2	0	1
L Total	6	.253	22	79	8	20	5	0	4	12	10	19	0	
W 1971	Pit-N	.208	7	24	3	5	1	0	0	1	7	9	0	O
W 1979	Pit-N	.400	7	30	7	12	4	0	3	7	0	6	0	1
W Total	2	.315	14	54	10	17	5	0	3	8	7	15	0	
■ Joe Start														
W 1884	Pro-N	.100	3	10	0	1	0	0	0	1	0	2	0	1
■ Rusty Staub														
L 1973	NY-N	.200	4	15	4	3	0	0	3	5	3	2	0	O
W 1973	NY-N	.423	7	26	1	11	2	0	1	6	2	2	0	O
■ Terry Steinbach														
L 1988	Oak-A	.250	2	4	0	1	0	0	0	0	2	0	0	C
L 1989	Oak-A	.200	4	15	0	3	0	0	0	1	1	5	0	C-3,D-1
L 1990	Oak-A	.455	3	11	2	5	0	0	0	1	1	2	0	C
L 1992	Oak-A	.292	6	24	1	7	0	0	1	5	2	7	0	C
L Total	4	.296	15	54	3	16	0	0	1	7	6	14	0	
W 1988	Oak-A	.364	3	11	0	4	1	0	0	0	0	2	0	C-2,D-1
W 1989	Oak-A	.250	4	16	3	4	0	1	1	7	2	1	0	C
W 1990	Oak-A	.125	3	8	0	1	0	0	0	0	0	1	0	C
W Total	3	.257	10	35	3	9	1	1	1	7	2	4	0	
■ Harry Steinfeldt														
W 1906	Chi-N	.250	6	20	2	5	1	0	0	2	1	0	0	3
W 1907	Chi-N	.471	5	17	2	8	1	1	0	2	1	2	1	3
W 1908	Chi-N	.250	5	16	3	4	0	0	0	3	2	5	1	3
W 1910	Chi-N	.100	5	20	0	2	1	0	0	1	0	4	0	3
W Total	4	.260	21	73	7	19	3	1	0	8	4	11	2	
■ Casey Stengel														
W 1916	Bro-N	.364	4	11	2	4	0	0	0	0	0	1	0	O-3
W 1922	NY-N	.400	2	5	0	2	0	0	0	0	0	1	0	O
W 1923	NY-N	.417	6	12	3	5	0	0	2	4	4	0	0	O
W Total	3	.393	12	28	5	11	0	0	2	4	4	2	0	
■ Rennie Stennett														
L 1972	Pit-N	.286	5	21	2	6	0	0	0	1	1	0	0	O-5,2-1
L 1974	Pit-N	.063	4	16	1	1	0	0	0	0	1	1	0	2
L 1975	Pit-N	.214	3	14	0	3	0	0	0	0	0	1	0	2-3,S-1
L 1979	Pit-N	—	1	0	0	0	0	0	0	0	0	0	0	2
L Total	4	.196	13	51	3	10	0	0	0	1	2	2	0	
W 1979	Pit-N	1.000	1	1	0	1	0	0	0	0	0	0	0	H
■ Jake Stenzel														
T 1897	Bal-N	.381	5	21	7	8	1	1	0	3	2	0	2	O
■ Vern Stephens														
W 1944	StL-A	.227	6	22	2	5	1	0	0	0	3	3	0	S
■ Riggs Stephenson														
W 1929	Chi-N	.316	5	19	3	6	1	0	0	3	2	2	0	O
W 1932	Chi-N	.444	4	18	2	8	1	0	0	4	0	0	0	O
W Total	2	.378	9	37	5	14	2	0	0	7	2	2	0	
■ Walter Stephenson														
W 1935	Chi-N	.000	1	1	0	0	0	0	0	0	0	1	0	H
■ Lee Stevens														
D 1998	Tex-A	.000	1	3	0	0	0	0	0	0	0	1	0	D
D 1999	Tex-A	.111	3	9	0	1	1	0	0	0	1	2	0	1
D Total	2	.083	4	12	0	1	1	0	0	0	1	3	0	
■ Jimmy Stewart														
L 1970	Cin-N	.000	1	2	0	0	0	0	0	0	0	0	0	O
W 1970	Cin-N	.000	2	2	0	0	0	0	0	0	0	1	0	H
■ Kelly Stinnett														
D 1999	Ari-N	.143	4	14	1	2	1	0	0	0	1	4	0	C
■ Bob Stinson														
L 1976	KC-A	.000	2	1	0	0	0	0	0	0	0	0	0	C-1
■ Snuffy Stirnweiss														
W 1943	NY-A	.000	1	1	1	0	0	0	0	0	0	0	0	H
W 1947	NY-A	.259	7	27	3	7	0	1	0	3	8	8	0	2
W 1949	NY-A	—	1	0	0	0	0	0	0	0	0	0	0	H
W Total	3	.250	9	28	4	7	0	1	0	3	8	8	0	
■ Milt Stock														
W 1915	Phi-N	.118	5	17	1	2	1	0	0	0	1	0	0	3
■ Kevin Stocker														
L 1993	Phi-N	.182	6	22	0	4	1	0	0	1	2	5	0	S
W 1993	Phi-N	.211	6	19	1	4	1	0	0	1	5	5	0	S
■ Sammy Strang														
W 1905	NY-N	.000	1	1	0	0	0	0	0	0	0	1	0	H

YEAR	TM/L	AVG	G	AB	R	H	2B	3B	HR	RBI	BB	SO	SB	POS
■ Doug Strange														
D 1995	Sea-A	.000	2	4	0	0	0	0	0	1	1	1	0	3
L 1995	Sea-A	.000	4	4	0	0	0	0	0	0	0	2	0	3-2
■ Darryl Strawberry														
D 1995	NY-A	.000	2	2	0	0	0	0	0	0	0	1	0	H
D 1996	NY-A	.000	2	5	0	0	0	0	0	0	0	2	0	D
D 1999	NY-A	.333	2	6	2	2	0	0	1	3	1	0	0	D
D Total	3	.154	6	13	2	2	0	0	1	3	1	3	0	
L 1986	NY-N	.227	6	22	4	5	1	0	2	5	3	12	1	O
L 1988	NY-N	.300	7	30	5	9	2	0	1	6	2	5	0	O
L 1996	NY-A	.417	4	12	4	5	0	0	3	5	2	2	0	O
L 1999	NY-A	.333	3	6	1	2	0	0	1	1	1	2	0	D
L Total	4	.300	20	70	14	21	3	0	7	17	8	21	1	
W 1986	NY-N	.208	7	24	4	5	1	0	1	1	4	6	3	O
W 1996	NY-A	.188	5	16	0	3	0	0	0	1	4	6	0	O
W 1999	NY-A	.333	2	3	0	1	0	0	0	0	1	2	0	D-1
W Total	3	.209	14	43	4	9	1	0	1	2	9	14	3	
■ George Strickland														
W 1954	Cle-A	.000	3	9	0	0	0	0	0	0	0	2	0	S
■ Amos Strunk														
W 1910	Phi-A	.278	4	18	2	5	1	1	0	2	2	5	0	O
W 1911	Phi-A	—	1	0	0	0	0	0	0	0	0	0	0	R
W 1913	Phi-A	.118	5	17	3	2	0	0	0	0	2	2	0	O
W 1914	Phi-A	.286	2	7	0	2	0	0	0	0	0	2	0	O
W 1918	Bos-A	.174	6	23	1	4	1	1	0	0	0	5	0	O
W Total	5	.200	18	65	6	13	2	2	0	2	4	14	0	
■ Dick Stuart														
W 1960	Pit-N	.150	5	20	0	3	0	0	0	0	0	3	0	1
W 1966	LA-N	.000	2	2	0	0	0	0	0	0	0	1	0	H
W Total	2	.136	7	22	0	3	0	0	0	0	0	4	0	
■ Franklin Stubbs														
L 1988	LA-N	.250	4	8	0	2	0	0	0	0	0	4	0	1-3
W 1988	LA-N	.294	5	17	3	5	2	0	0	2	1	3	0	1
■ Johnny Sturm														
W 1941	NY-A	.286	5	21	0	6	0	0	0	2	0	2	1	1
■ Billy Sullivan Jr.														
W 1940	Det-A	.154	5	13	3	2	0	0	0	0	5	2	0	C-4
■ Billy Sullivan Sr.														
W 1906	Chi-A	.000	6	21	0	0	0	0	0	0	0	9	0	C
■ Homer Summa														
W 1929	Phi-A	.000	1	1	0	0	0	0	0	0	0	1	0	H
■ Champ Summers														
L 1984	SD-N	.000	2	2	0	0	0	0	0	0	0	1	0	H
W 1984	SD-N	.000	1	1	0	0	0	0	0	0	0	1	0	H
■ Billy Sunday														
W 1885	Chi-N	.273	6	22	5	6	2	0	0	1	2	0	0	O
■ Jim Sundberg														
L 1985	KC-A	.167	7	24	3	4	1	1	1	6	1	7	0	C
W 1985	KC-A	.250	7	24	6	6	2	0	0	1	6	4	0	C
■ B.J. Surhoff														
D 1996	Bal-A	.385	4	13	3	5	0	0	3	5	0	1	0	O-3
D 1997	Bal-A	.273	3	11	0	3	1	0	0	2	0	2	0	O
D 2000	Atl-N	.500	2	2	0	1	0	0	0	0	0	0	0	H
D Total	3	.346	9	26	3	9	1	0	3	7	0	3	0	
L 1996	Bal-A	.267	5	15	0	4	0	0	0	2	1	2	0	O
L 1997	Bal-A	.200	6	25	1	5	2	0	0	1	2	2	0	O-6,1-1
L Total	2	.225	11	40	1	9	2	0	0	3	3	4	0	
■ Cy Sutcliffe														
W 1887	Det-N	.167	4	12	1	2	0	0	0	1	1	1	1	1-3,C-1
■ Mark Sweeney														
D 1996	StL-N	1.000	1	1	0	1	0	0	0	0	0	0	0	H
D 1998	SD-N	.000	2	1	0	0	0	0	0	0	1	0	0	H
D Total	2	.500	3	2	0	1	0	0	0	0	1	0	0	
L 1996	StL-N	.000	5	4	1	0	0	0	0	0	0	2	0	O-2
L 1998	SD-N	.000	3	2	1	0	0	0	0	0	1	1	0	H
L Total	2	.000	8	6	2	0	0	0	0	0	1	3	0	
W 1998	SD-N	.667	3	3	0	2	0	0	0	1	0	0	0	H
■ Bob Swift														
W 1945	Det-A	.250	3	4	1	1	0	0	0	0	2	0	0	C
■ Ron Swoboda														
W 1969	NY-N	.400	4	15	1	6	1	0	0	1	1	3	0	O
■ Pat Tabler														
L 1991	Tor-A	.000	2	1	0	0	0	0	0	0	1	0	0	D
W 1992	Tor-A	.000	2	2	0	0	0	0	0	0	0	0	0	H
■ Lee Tannehill														
W 1906	Chi-A	.111	3	9	1	1	0	0	0	0	0	2	0	S
■ Tony Tarasco														
L 1993	Atl-N	.000	2	1	0	0	0	0	0	0	0	1	0	O
L 1996	Bal-A	.000	2	1	0	0	0	0	0	0	0	1	0	O
L Total	2	.000	4	2	0	0	0	0	0	0	0	2	0	
■ Jose Tartabull														
W 1967	Bos-A	.154	7	13	1	2	0	0	0	0	1	2	0	O-6

YEAR	TM/L	AVG	G	AB	R	H	2B	3B	HR	RBI	BB	SO	SB	POS
■ **Bennie Tate**														
W 1924	Was-A	—	3	0	0	0	0	0	0	1	3	0	0	H
■ **Fernando Tatis**														
L 2000	StL-N	.231	5	13	1	3	2	0	0	2	1	5	0	3-4
■ **Eddie Taubensee**														
L 1995	Cin-N	.500	2	2	0	1	0	0	0	0	0	0	0	C-1
■ **Frank Taveras**														
L 1974	Pit-N	.000	2	2	0	0	0	0	0	0	0	0	1	S
L 1975	Pit-N	.143	3	7	0	1	0	0	0	1	1	2	0	S
L Total	2	.111	5	9	0	1	0	0	0	1	1	2	1	
■ **Tony Taylor**														
L 1972	Det-A	.133	4	15	0	2	2	0	0	0	0	2	0	2
■ **Harry Taylor**														
W 1890	Lou-A	.300	7	30	6	9	1	0	0	2	2	3	3	1
■ **Zack Taylor**														
W 1929	Chi-N	.176	5	17	0	3	0	0	0	3	0	3	0	C
■ **Tommy Taylor**														
W 1924	Was-A	.000	3	2	0	0	0	0	0	0	0	2	0	3
■ **Birdie Tebbetts**														
W 1940	Det-A	.000	4	11	0	0	0	0	0	0	0	0	0	C-3
■ **Patsy Tebeau**														
T 1892	Cle-N	.000	5	18	1	0	0	0	0	0	0	2	1	3
T 1895	Cle-N	.286	5	21	3	6	1	0	0	3	1	0	0	1
T 1896	Cle-N	.000	1	1	0	0	0	0	0	0	0	0	0	1
T Total	3	.150	11	40	4	6	1	0	0	3	1	2	1	
■ **Miguel Tejada**														
D 2000	Oak-A	.350	5	20	5	7	2	0	0	1	2	2	1	S
■ **Garry Templeton**														
L 1984	SD-N	.333	5	15	2	5	1	0	0	2	2	0	1	S
W 1984	SD-N	.316	5	19	1	6	1	0	0	0	0	3	0	S
■ **Gene Tenace**														
L 1971	Oak-A	.000	1	3	0	0	0	0	0	0	1	1	0	C
L 1972	Oak-A	.059	5	17	1	1	0	0	0	1	3	5	0	C-5,2-2
L 1973	Oak-A	.235	5	17	3	4	1	0	0	0	2	4	0	1-5,C-3
L 1974	Oak-A	.000	4	11	1	0	0	0	0	1	4	4	1	1
L 1975	Oak-A	.000	3	9	0	0	0	0	0	0	3	2	0	C-3,1-1
L Total	5	.088	18	57	5	5	1	0	0	2	13	16	1	
W 1972	Oak-A	.348	7	23	5	8	1	0	4	9	2	4	0	C-6,1-1
W 1973	Oak-A	.158	7	19	0	3	1	0	0	3	11	7	0	1-7,C-3
W 1974	Oak-A	.222	5	9	0	2	0	0	0	0	3	4	0	1
W 1982	StL-N	.000	5	6	0	0	0	0	0	0	1	2	0	D-1
W Total	4	.228	24	57	5	13	2	0	4	12	17	17	0	
■ **Fred Tenney**														
T 1897	Bos-N	.286	5	21	4	6	0	0	0	2	4	1	2	1
■ **Bill Terry**														
W 1924	NY-N	.429	5	14	3	6	0	1	1	1	3	1	0	1-4
W 1933	NY-N	.273	5	22	3	6	1	0	1	1	0	0	0	1
W 1936	NY-N	.240	6	25	1	6	0	0	0	5	1	4	0	1
W Total	3	.295	16	61	7	18	1	1	2	7	4	5	0	
■ **Mickey Tettleton**														
D 1996	Tex-A	.083	4	12	1	1	0	0	0	1	5	7	0	D
■ **Tim Teufel**														
L 1986	NY-N	.167	2	6	0	1	0	0	0	0	0	0	0	2
L 1988	NY-N	.000	1	3	0	0	0	0	0	0	0	1	0	2
L Total	2	.111	3	9	0	1	0	0	0	0	0	1	0	
W 1986	NY-N	.444	3	9	1	4	1	0	1	1	1	2	0	2
■ **George Theodore**														
W 1973	NY-N	.000	2	2	0	0	0	0	0	0	0	0	0	O-1
■ **Tommy Thevenow**														
W 1926	StL-N	.417	7	24	5	10	1	0	1	4	0	1	0	S
W 1928	StL-N	—	1	0	0	0	0	0	0	0	0	0	0	S
W Total	2	.417	8	24	5	10	1	0	1	4	0	1	0	
■ **Pinch Thomas**														
W 1915	Bos-A	.200	2	5	0	1	0	0	0	0	0	0	0	C
W 1916	Bos-A	.143	3	7	0	1	0	1	0	0	0	1	0	C
W 1920	Cle-A	—	1	0	0	0	0	0	0	0	0	0	0	C
W Total	3	.167	6	12	0	2	0	1	0	0	0	1	0	
■ **Derrel Thomas**														
D 1981	LA-N	.000	4	2	1	0	0	0	0	0	0	1	0	O
L 1981	LA-N	1.000	2	1	2	1	0	0	0	0	0	0	0	3-1,O-1
L 1983	LA-N	.444	4	9	0	4	1	0	0	0	0	3	1	O
L Total	2	.500	6	10	2	5	1	0	0	0	0	3	1	
W 1981	LA-N	.000	5	7	2	0	0	0	0	1	1	2	0	O-3,3-2,S-1
■ **Frank Thomas**														
D 2000	Chi-A	.000	3	9	0	0	0	0	0	0	4	0	0	D-2,1-1
L 1993	Chi-A	.353	6	17	2	6	0	0	1	3	10	5	0	1-4,D-2
■ **Fred Thomas**														
W 1918	Bos-A	.118	6	17	0	2	0	0	0	0	1	2	0	3
■ **George Thomas**														
W 1967	Bos-A	.000	2	2	0	0	0	0	0	0	0	1	0	O-1

YEAR	TM/L	AVG	G	AB	R	H	2B	3B	HR	RBI	BB	SO	SB	POS
■ **Ira Thomas**														
W 1908	Det-A	.500	2	4	0	2	1	0	0	1	1	0	0	C-1
W 1910	Phi-A	.250	4	12	2	3	0	0	0	1	4	1	0	C
W 1911	Phi-A	.083	4	12	1	1	0	0	0	1	1	2	0	C
W Total	3	.214	10	28	3	6	1	0	0	3	6	3	0	
■ **Gorman Thomas**														
D 1981	Mil-A	.111	5	18	2	2	0	0	1	1	1	9	0	O-3,D-2
L 1982	Mil-A	.067	5	15	1	1	0	0	1	3	2	7	0	O
W 1982	Mil-A	.115	7	26	0	3	0	0	0	3	2	7	0	O
■ **Gary Thomasson**														
L 1978	NY-A	.000	3	1	0	0	0	0	0	0	0	0	0	O
W 1978	NY-A	.250	3	4	0	1	0	0	0	0	0	1	0	O
■ **Jim Thome**														
D 1995	Cle-A	.154	3	13	1	2	0	0	1	3	1	6	0	3
D 1996	Cle-A	.300	4	10	1	3	0	0	0	0	1	5	0	3
D 1997	Cle-A	.200	4	15	1	3	0	0	0	1	0	5	0	1
D 1998	Cle-A	.133	4	15	2	2	0	0	2	2	2	5	0	1-3,D-1
D 1999	Cle-A	.353	5	17	7	6	0	0	4	10	4	5	0	1
D Total	5	.229	20	70	12	16	0	0	7	16	8	26	0	
L 1995	Cle-A	.267	5	15	2	4	0	0	2	5	2	3	0	3
L 1997	Cle-A	.071	6	14	3	1	0	0	0	0	5	4	0	1
L 1998	Cle-A	.304	6	23	4	7	0	0	4	8	1	8	0	1-4,D-2
L Total	3	.231	17	52	9	12	0	0	6	13	8	15	0	
W 1995	Cle-A	.211	6	19	1	4	1	0	1	2	2	5	0	3
W 1997	Cle-A	.286	7	28	8	8	0	1	2	4	5	7	0	1
W Total	2	.255	13	47	9	12	1	1	3	6	7	12	0	
■ **Danny Thompson**														
L 1970	Min-A	.125	3	8	0	1	1	0	0	0	1	0	0	2
■ **Don Thompson**														
W 1953	Bro-N	—	2	0	0	0	0	0	0	0	0	0	0	O
■ **Hank Thompson**														
W 1951	NY-N	.143	5	14	3	2	0	0	0	0	5	2	0	O
W 1954	NY-N	.364	4	11	6	4	1	0	0	2	7	1	0	3
W Total	2	.240	9	25	9	6	1	0	0	2	12	3	0	
■ **Milt Thompson**														
L 1993	Phi-N	.231	6	13	2	3	1	0	0	0	1	2	0	O-5
W 1993	Phi-N	.313	6	16	3	5	1	1	1	6	1	2	0	O
■ **Robby Thompson**														
L 1987	SF-N	.100	7	20	4	2	0	1	1	2	5	7	2	2-6
L 1989	SF-N	.278	5	18	5	5	0	0	2	3	3	2	0	2
L Total	2	.184	12	38	9	7	0	1	3	5	8	9	2	
W 1989	SF-N	.091	4	11	0	1	0	0	0	2	0	4	0	2
■ **Sam Thompson**														
W 1887	Det-N	.393	15	61	8	24	2	0	2	8	3	3	5	O
■ **Bobby Thomson**														
W 1951	NY-N	.238	6	21	1	5	1	0	0	2	5	0	0	3
■ **Dickie Thon**														
D 1981	Hou-N	.182	4	11	0	2	0	0	0	0	1	0	0	S
L 1979	Cal-A	—	1	0	1	0	0	0	0	0	0	0	0	S
L 1986	Hou-N	.250	6	12	1	3	0	0	1	1	0	1	0	S
L Total	2	.250	7	12	2	3	0	0	1	1	0	1	0	
■ **Lou Thornton**														
L 1985	Tor-A	—	2	0	1	0	0	0	0	0	0	0	0	R
■ **Jim Thorpe**														
W 1917	NY-N	—	1	0	0	0	0	0	0	0	0	0	0	O
■ **Marv Throneberry**														
W 1958	NY-A	.000	1	1	0	0	0	0	0	0	0	1	0	H
■ **Mike Tiernan**														
W 1888	NY-N	.342	10	38	8	13	0	0	1	6	8	2	5	O
W 1889	NY-N	.289	9	38	12	11	1	1	1	5	5	3	3	O
W Total	2	.316	19	76	20	24	1	1	2	11	13	5	8	
T 1894	NY-N	.294	4	17	5	5	0	1	0	3	2	2	0	O
■ **Bob Tillman**														
L 1969	Atl-N	—	1	0	0	0	0	0	0	0	0	0	0	C
■ **Joe Tinker**														
W 1906	Chi-N	.167	6	18	4	3	0	0	0	1	2	2	3	S
W 1907	Chi-N	.154	5	13	4	2	0	0	0	1	3	3	1	S
W 1908	Chi-N	.263	5	19	2	5	0	0	1	4	0	2	2	S
W 1910	Chi-N	.333	5	18	2	6	2	0	0	0	2	2	1	S
W Total	4	.235	21	68	12	16	2	0	1	6	7	9	7	
■ **Lee Tinsley**														
D 1995	Bos-A	.000	1	5	0	0	0	0	0	0	1	2	0	O
■ **Joe Tipton**														
W 1948	Cle-A	.000	1	1	0	0	0	0	0	0	0	1	0	H
■ **Phil Todt**														
W 1931	Phi-A	—	1	0	0	0	0	0	0	0	1	0	0	H
■ **Bobby Tolan**														
L 1970	Cin-N	.417	3	12	3	5	0	0	1	2	1	1	1	O
L 1972	Cin-N	.238	5	21	3	5	1	1	0	4	0	4	0	O
L 1976	Phi-N	.000	3	2	0	0	0	0	0	0	1	0	0	1-1,O-1
L Total	3	.286	11	35	6	10	1	1	1	6	2	5	1	
W 1967	StL-N	.000	3	2	1	0	0	0	0	0	1	1	0	H

YEAR	TM/L	AVG	G	AB	R	H	2B	3B	HR	RBI	BB	SO	SB	POS
W 1968	StL-N	.000	1	1	0	0	0	0	0	0	0	1	0	H
W 1970	Cin-N	.211	5	19	5	4	1	0	1	1	3	2	1	O
W 1972	Cin-N	.269	7	26	2	7	1	0	0	6	1	4	5	O
W Total	4	.229	16	48	8	11	2	0	1	7	5	8	6	
■ **Chick Tolson**														
W 1929	Chi-N	.000	1	1	0	0	0	0	0	0	0	1	0	H
■ **Phil Tomney**														
W 1890	Lou-A	.200	3	5	1	1	0	0	0	0	3	1	0	S
■ **Specs Toporcer**														
W 1926	StL-N	—	1	0	0	0	0	0	0	1	0	0	0	H
■ **Earl Torgeson**														
W 1948	Bos-N	.389	5	18	2	7	3	0	0	1	2	1	1	1
W 1959	Chi-A	.000	3	1	1	0	0	0	0	0	1	0	0	1-1
W Total	2	.368	8	19	3	7	3	0	0	1	3	1	1	
■ **Frank Torre**														
W 1957	Mil-N	.300	7	10	2	3	0	0	2	3	2	0	0	1
W 1958	Mil-N	.176	7	17	0	3	0	0	0	1	2	0	0	1
W Total	2	.222	14	27	2	6	0	0	2	4	4	0	0	
■ **Cesar Tovar**														
L 1969	Min-A	.077	3	13	0	1	0	0	0	0	1	2	1	O
L 1970	Min-A	.385	3	13	2	5	0	1	0	1	0	0	0	O-3,2-1
L 1975	Oak-A	.500	2	2	2	1	0	0	0	0	1	0	0	2-1
L Total	3	.250	8	28	4	7	0	1	0	1	2	2	1	
■ **Babe Towne**														
W 1906	Chi-A	.000	1	1	0	0	0	0	0	0	0	0	0	H
■ **Dick Tracewski**														
W 1963	LA-N	.154	4	13	1	2	0	0	0	0	1	2	0	2
W 1965	LA-N	.118	6	17	0	2	0	0	0	0	1	5	0	2
W 1968	Det-A	—	2	0	1	0	0	0	0	0	0	0	0	3-1
W Total	3	.133	12	30	2	4	0	0	0	0	2	7	0	
■ **Alan Trammell**														
L 1984	Det-A	.364	3	11	2	4	0	1	1	3	3	1	0	S
L 1987	Det-A	.200	5	20	3	4	1	0	0	2	1	2	0	S
L Total	2	.258	8	31	5	8	1	1	1	5	4	3	0	
W 1984	Det-A	.450	5	20	5	9	1	0	2	6	2	2	1	S
■ **Bubba Trammell**														
L 2000	NY-N	.000	3	3	0	0	0	0	0	0	0	2	0	H
W 2000	NY-N	.400	4	5	1	2	0	0	0	3	1	1	0	O-2
■ **Pie Traynor**														
W 1925	Pit-N	.346	7	26	2	9	0	2	1	4	3	1	1	3
W 1927	Pit-N	.200	4	15	1	3	1	0	0	0	0	1	0	3
W Total	2	.293	11	41	3	12	1	2	1	4	3	2	1	
■ **Jeff Treadway**														
L 1991	Atl-N	.333	1	3	0	1	0	0	0	0	0	0	0	2
L 1992	Atl-N	.667	3	3	1	2	0	0	0	0	0	1	0	2-1
L Total	2	.500	4	6	1	3	0	0	0	0	0	1	0	
W 1991	Atl-N	.250	3	4	1	1	0	0	0	0	1	2	0	2-1
W 1992	Atl-N	.000	1	1	0	0	0	0	0	0	0	0	0	H
W Total	2	.200	4	5	1	1	0	0	0	0	1	2	0	
■ **Tom Tresh**														
W 1962	NY-A	.321	7	28	5	9	1	0	1	4	1	4	2	O
W 1963	NY-A	.200	4	15	1	3	0	0	1	2	1	6	0	O
W 1964	NY-A	.273	7	22	4	6	2	0	2	7	6	7	0	O
W Total	3	.277	18	65	10	18	3	0	4	13	8	17	2	
■ **Manny Trillo**														
D 1981	Phi-N	.188	5	16	1	3	0	0	0	1	4	0	0	2
L 1974	Oak-A	—	1	0	1	0	0	0	0	0	0	0	0	R
L 1980	Phi-N	.381	5	21	1	8	2	1	0	4	0	2	0	2
L Total	2	.381	6	21	2	8	2	1	0	4	0	2	0	
W 1980	Phi-N	.217	6	23	4	5	2	0	0	2	0	0	0	2
■ **Dasher Troy**														
W 1884	NY-A	.200	2	5	0	1	0	0	0	1	0	1	0	2
■ **Michael Tucker**														
D 1997	Atl-N	.167	2	6	0	1	0	0	0	1	0	1	0	O
D 1998	Atl-N	.250	3	8	1	2	0	0	1	2	2	0	1	O
D Total	2	.214	5	14	1	3	0	0	1	3	2	1	1	
L 1997	Atl-N	.100	5	10	1	1	0	0	1	1	3	4	0	O-4
L 1998	Atl-N	.385	6	13	1	5	1	0	1	5	2	5	0	O-5
L Total	2	.261	11	23	2	6	1	0	2	6	5	9	0	
■ **Tommy Tucker**														
T 1892	Bos-N	.261	6	23	2	6	0	0	1	2	0	1	0	1
■ **Thurman Tucker**														
W 1948	Cle-A	.333	1	3	1	1	0	0	0	0	1	0	0	O
■ **Tom Turner**														
W 1944	StL-A	.000	1	1	0	0	0	0	0	0	0	0	0	H
■ **Larry Twitchell**														
W 1887	Det-N	.250	6	20	5	5	1	0	1	3	0	1	1	O
■ **Ted Uhlaender**														
L 1969	Min-A	.167	2	6	0	1	0	0	0	0	0	0	0	O
L 1972	Cin-N	.500	2	2	0	1	0	0	0	0	0	0	0	H
L Total	2	.250	4	8	0	2	0	0	0	0	0	0	0	
W 1972	Cin-N	.250	4	4	0	1	1	0	0	0	0	1	0	H

YEAR	TM/L	AVG	G	AB	R	H	2B	3B	HR	RBI	BB	SO	SB	POS
■ **Del Unser**														
L 1980	Phi-N	.400	5	5	2	2	1	0	0	1	0	2	0	O-2
W 1980	Phi-N	.500	3	6	2	3	2	0	0	2	0	1	0	O
■ **Willie Upshaw**														
L 1985	Tor-A	.231	7	26	2	6	2	0	0	1	1	4	0	1
■ **Jose Uribe**														
L 1987	SF-N	.269	7	26	1	7	1	0	0	2	0	4	1	S
L 1989	SF-N	.235	5	17	2	4	1	0	0	1	1	5	1	S
L Total	2	.256	12	43	3	11	2	0	0	3	1	9	2	
W 1989	SF-N	.200	3	5	1	1	0	0	0	0	0	0	0	S
■ **Sandy Valdespino**														
W 1965	Min-A	.273	5	11	1	3	1	0	0	0	0	1	0	O-2
■ **John Valentin**														
D 1995	Bos-A	.250	3	12	1	3	1	0	1	2	3	1	0	S
D 1998	Bos-A	.467	4	15	5	7	1	0	0	0	3	1	0	3
D 1999	Bos-A	.318	5	22	6	7	2	0	3	12	0	4	0	3
D Total	3	.347	12	49	12	17	4	0	4	14	6	6	0	
L 1999	Bos-A	.348	5	23	3	8	2	0	1	5	2	4	0	3
■ **Jose Valentin**														
D 2000	Chi-A	.300	3	10	2	3	2	0	0	1	2	2	3	S
■ **George Van Haltren**														
T 1894	NY-N	.500	4	14	3	7	1	1	0	0	2	2	2	O
■ **John Vander Wal**														
D 1995	Col-N	.000	4	4	0	0	0	0	0	0	0	2	0	H
D 1998	SD-N	.333	3	3	1	1	0	1	0	2	0	1	0	H
D Total	2	.143	7	7	1	1	0	1	0	2	0	3	0	
L 1998	SD-N	.429	3	7	1	3	0	0	1	2	0	2	0	O-2
W 1998	SD-N	.400	4	5	0	2	1	0	0	0	0	2	0	O-1
■ **Andy Van Slyke**														
L 1985	StL-N	.091	5	11	1	1	0	0	0	1	2	1	0	O
L 1990	Pit-N	.208	6	24	3	5	1	1	0	3	1	7	1	O
L 1991	Pit-N	.160	7	25	3	4	2	0	1	2	5	5	1	O
L 1992	Pit-N	.276	7	29	1	8	3	1	0	4	1	5	0	O
L Total	4	.202	25	89	8	18	6	2	1	10	9	18	2	
W 1985	StL-N	.091	6	11	0	1	0	0	0	0	0	5	0	O
■ **Jason Varitek**														
D 1998	Bos-A	.250	1	4	0	1	0	0	0	1	0	1	0	C
D 1999	Bos-A	.238	5	21	7	5	3	0	1	3	0	4	0	C
D Total	2	.240	6	25	7	6	3	0	1	4	0	5	0	
L 1999	Bos-A	.200	5	20	1	4	1	1	1	1	1	4	0	C
■ **Gary Varsho**														
L 1991	Pit-N	.500	2	2	0	1	0	0	0	0	0	1	0	H
L 1992	Pit-N	.500	2	2	0	1	0	0	0	0	0	0	0	O-1
L Total	2	.500	4	4	0	2	0	0	0	0	0	1	0	
■ **Arky Vaughan**														
W 1947	Bro-N	.500	3	2	0	1	1	0	0	0	1	0	0	H
■ **Greg Vaughn**														
D 1996	SD-N	.000	3	3	0	0	0	0	0	0	0	1	0	H
D 1998	SD-N	.333	4	15	2	5	1	0	1	1	0	4	0	O
D Total	2	.278	7	18	2	5	1	0	1	1	0	5	0	
L 1998	SD-N	.250	3	8	1	2	0	0	0	0	1	1	0	O-2
W 1998	SD-N	.133	4	15	3	2	0	0	2	4	1	2	0	O-3,D-1
■ **Mo Vaughn**														
D 1995	Bos-A	.000	3	14	0	0	0	0	0	0	1	7	0	1
D 1998	Bos-A	.412	4	17	3	7	2	0	2	7	1	5	0	1
D Total	2	.226	7	31	3	7	2	0	2	7	2	12	0	
■ **Bobby Veach**														
W 1925	Was-A	.000	2	1	0	0	0	0	0	1	0	0	0	H
■ **Randy Velarde**														
D 1995	NY-A	.176	5	17	3	3	0	0	0	1	6	4	0	2-4,3-2,O-2
D 2000	Oak-A	.250	5	20	2	5	1	0	0	3	2	3	1	2
D Total	2	.216	10	37	5	8	1	0	0	4	8	7	1	
■ **Otto Velez**														
L 1976	NY-A	.000	1	1	0	0	0	0	0	0	0	0	0	H
W 1976	NY-A	.000	3	3	0	0	0	0	0	0	0	3	0	H
■ **Robin Ventura**														
D 1999	NY-N	.214	4	14	1	3	2	0	0	1	4	2	0	3
D 2000	NY-N	.143	4	14	1	2	0	0	1	2	4	1	0	3
D Total	2	.179	8	28	2	5	2	0	1	3	8	3	0	
L 1993	Chi-A	.200	6	20	2	4	0	0	1	5	6	6	0	3-6,1-1
L 1999	NY-N	.120	6	25	2	3	1	0	0	1	2	5	0	3
L 2000	NY-N	.214	5	14	4	3	1	0	0	5	6	0	0	3
L Total	3	.169	17	59	8	10	2	0	1	11	14	11	0	
W 2000	NY-N	.150	5	20	1	3	1	0	1	1	1	5	0	3
■ **Quilvio Veras**														
D 1998	SD-N	.133	4	15	1	2	0	0	0	0	1	6	0	2
L 1998	SD-N	.250	6	24	2	6	1	0	0	2	5	7	0	2
W 1998	SD-N	.200	4	15	3	3	2	0	0	1	3	4	0	2
■ **Emil Verban**														
W 1944	StL-N	.412	6	17	1	7	0	0	0	2	2	0	0	2
■ **Zoilo Versalles**														
W 1965	Min-A	.286	7	28	3	8	1	1	1	4	2	7	1	S

YEAR	TM/L	AVG	G	AB	R	H	2B	3B	HR	RBI	BB	SO	SB	POS
■ Tom Veryzer														
L 1984	Chi-N	.000	3	1	0	0	0	0	0	0	0	0	0	S-2,3-1
■ Fernando Vina														
D 2000	StL-N	.308	3	13	3	4	0	0	1	3	1	1	0	2
L 2000	StL-N	.261	5	23	3	6	1	0	0	1	1	4	0	2
■ Bill Virdon														
W 1960	Pit-N	.241	7	29	2	7	3	0	0	5	1	3	1	O
■ Ozzie Virgil Jr.														
L 1983	Phi-N	.000	1	1	0	0	0	0	0	0	0	1	0	H
W 1983	Phi-N	.500	3	2	0	1	0	0	0	1	0	0	0	C-1
■ Jake Virtue														
T 1892	Cle-N	.125	6	24	1	3	0	0	0	0	2	5	1	1
■ Joe Visner														
W 1889	Bro-A	.125	5	16	2	2	1	0	0	0	2	3	0	C-3,O-2
■ Jose Vizcaino														
D 1996	Cle-A	.333	3	12	1	4	2	0	0	1	1	1	0	2
D 1997	SF-N	.182	3	11	1	2	1	0	0	0	0	5	0	S
D 2000	NY-A	—	1	0	1	0	0	0	0	0	0	0	0	2
D Total	3	.261	7	23	3	6	3	0	0	1	1	6	0	
L 2000	NY-A	1.000	4	2	3	2	1	0	0	2	0	0	2	2-3
W 2000	NY-A	.235	4	17	0	4	0	0	0	1	0	5	0	2
■ Omar Vizquel														
D 1995	Cle-A	.167	3	12	2	2	1	0	0	4	2	2	1	S
D 1996	Cle-A	.429	4	14	4	6	1	0	0	2	3	4	4	S
D 1997	Cle-A	.500	5	18	3	9	0	0	0	1	2	1	4	S
D 1998	Cle-A	.067	4	15	1	1	0	0	0	0	1	0	0	S
D 1999	Cle-A	.238	5	21	3	5	1	1	0	3	2	3	0	S
D Total	5	.287	21	80	13	23	3	1	0	10	10	10	9	
L 1995	Cle-A	.087	6	23	2	2	1	0	0	2	5	2	3	S
L 1997	Cle-A	.040	6	25	1	1	0	0	0	0	2	10	0	S
L 1998	Cle-A	.440	6	25	2	11	0	1	0	0	1	3	4	S
L Total	3	.192	18	73	5	14	1	1	0	2	8	15	7	
W 1995	Cle-A	.174	6	23	3	4	0	1	0	1	3	5	1	S
W 1997	Cle-A	.233	7	30	5	7	2	0	0	1	3	5	5	S
W Total	2	.208	13	53	8	11	2	1	0	2	6	10	6	
■ George Vukovich														
D 1981	Phi-N	.444	5	9	1	4	0	0	1	2	0	3	0	O-3
L 1980	Phi-N	.000	4	3	0	0	0	0	0	0	0	0	0	O-1
■ Heinie Wagner														
W 1912	Bos-A	.167	8	30	1	5	1	0	0	0	3	6	1	S
■ Hal Wagner														
W 1946	Bos-A	.000	5	13	0	0	0	0	0	0	0	1	0	C
■ Honus Wagner														
T 1900	Pit-N	.400	4	15	2	6	1	0	0	3	0	1	2	O
W 1903	Pit-N	.222	8	27	2	6	1	0	0	3	3	4	3	S
W 1909	Pit-N	.333	7	24	4	8	2	1	0	6	4	2	6	S
W Total	2	.275	15	51	6	14	3	1	0	9	7	6	9	
■ Eddie Waitkus														
W 1950	Phi-N	.267	4	15	0	4	1	0	0	0	2	0	0	1
■ Rube Walker														
W 1956	Bro-N	.000	2	2	0	0	0	0	0	0	0	0	0	H
■ Tilly Walker														
W 1916	Bos-A	.273	3	11	1	3	0	1	0	1	1	2	0	O
■ Dixie Walker														
W 1941	Bro-N	.222	5	18	3	4	2	0	0	0	2	1	0	O
W 1947	Bro-N	.222	7	27	1	6	1	0	1	4	3	1	1	O
W Total	2	.222	12	45	4	10	3	0	1	4	5	2	1	
■ Gee Walker														
W 1934	Det-A	.333	3	3	0	1	0	0	0	1	0	1	0	H
W 1935	Det-A	.250	3	4	1	1	0	0	0	0	1	0	0	O-1
W Total	2	.286	6	7	1	2	0	0	0	1	1	1	0	
■ Greg Walker														
L 1983	Chi-A	.333	2	3	0	1	0	0	0	0	1	2	0	1-1
■ Harry Walker														
W 1942	StL-N	.000	1	1	0	0	0	0	0	0	0	1	0	H
W 1943	StL-N	.167	5	18	0	3	1	0	0	0	0	2	0	O
W 1946	StL-N	.412	7	17	3	7	2	0	0	6	4	2	0	O
W Total	3	.278	13	36	3	10	3	0	0	6	4	5	0	
■ Hub Walker														
W 1945	Det-A	.500	2	2	1	1	1	0	0	0	0	0	0	H
■ Larry Walker														
D 1995	Col-N	.214	4	14	3	3	0	0	1	3	3	4	1	O
■ Tim Wallach														
D 1981	Mon-N	.250	4	4	1	1	1	0	0	0	4	0	0	O-3
D 1995	LA-N	.083	3	12	0	1	0	0	0	0	1	3	0	3
D 1996	LA-N	.000	3	11	0	0	0	0	0	0	0	1	0	3
D Total	3	.074	10	27	1	2	1	0	0	0	5	4	0	
L 1981	Mon-N	.000	1	1	0	0	0	0	0	0	0	0	0	H
■ Denny Walling														
D 1981	Hou-N	.333	3	6	0	2	0	0	0	1	0	1	0	1-2
L 1980	Hou-N	.111	3	9	2	1	0	0	0	2	1	0	0	O-2,1-1
L 1986	Hou-N	.158	5	19	1	3	1	0	0	2	0	4	0	3
L Total	2	.143	8	28	3	4	1	0	0	4	1	4	0	
■ Jimmy Walsh														
W 1914	Phi-A	.333	3	6	0	2	1	0	0	1	3	1	0	O-2
W 1916	Bos-A	.000	1	3	0	0	0	0	0	0	0	0	0	O
W Total	2	.222	4	9	0	2	1	0	0	1	3	1	0	
■ Jerome Walton														
D 1995	Cin-N	.000	3	3	0	0	0	0	0	0	1	1	0	O
D 1997	Bal-A	.000	2	4	0	0	0	0	0	0	0	2	0	1
D Total	2	.000	5	7	0	0	0	0	0	0	1	3	0	
L 1989	Chi-N	.364	5	22	4	8	0	0	0	2	2	2	0	O
L 1995	Cin-N	.000	2	7	0	0	0	0	0	0	0	2	0	O
L 1997	Bal-A	—	1	0	0	0	0	0	0	0	0	0	0	O
L Total	3	.276	8	29	4	8	0	0	0	2	2	4	0	
■ Bill Wambsganss														
W 1920	Cle-A	.154	7	26	3	4	0	0	0	1	2	1	0	2
■ Lloyd Waner														
W 1927	Pit-N	.400	4	15	5	6	1	1	0	0	1	0	0	O
■ Paul Waner														
W 1927	Pit-N	.333	4	15	0	5	1	0	0	3	0	1	0	O
■ Aaron Ward														
W 1921	NY-A	.231	8	26	1	6	0	0	0	4	2	6	0	2
W 1922	NY-A	.154	5	13	3	2	0	0	2	3	3	3	0	2
W 1923	NY-A	.417	6	24	4	10	0	0	1	2	1	3	1	2
W Total	3	.286	19	63	8	18	0	0	3	9	6	12	1	
■ Daryle Ward														
D 1999	Hou-N	.143	3	7	1	1	0	0	1	1	0	2	0	O-2
■ Monte Ward														
W 1888	NY-N	.379	8	29	4	11	1	0	0	6	1	0	6	S
W 1889	NY-N	.417	9	36	10	15	0	1	0	7	5	2	10	S
W Total	2	.400	17	65	14	26	1	1	0	13	6	2	16	
T 1894	NY-N	.294	4	17	1	5	0	0	0	6	0	0	0	2
■ Turner Ward														
D 1999	Ari-N	.500	3	2	2	1	0	0	1	3	1	0	0	H
■ Carl Warwick														
W 1964	StL-N	.750	5	4	2	3	0	0	0	1	1	0	0	H
■ Jimmy Wasdell														
W 1941	Bro-N	.200	3	5	0	1	1	0	0	2	0	0	0	O-1
■ Claudell Washington														
L 1974	Oak-A	.273	4	11	1	3	1	0	0	0	0	0	0	O-3
L 1975	Oak-A	.250	3	12	1	3	1	0	0	1	0	2	0	O-2,D-1
L 1982	Atl-N	.333	3	9	0	3	0	0	0	0	2	2	0	O
L Total	3	.281	10	32	2	9	2	0	0	1	2	4	0	
W 1974	Oak-A	.571	5	7	1	4	0	0	0	0	1	1	0	O
■ Herb Washington														
L 1974	Oak-A	—	2	0	0	0	0	0	0	0	0	0	0	R
W 1974	Oak-A	—	3	0	0	0	0	0	0	0	0	0	0	R
■ U L Washington														
D 1981	KC-A	.222	3	9	0	2	0	0	0	0	0	1	0	S
L 1980	KC-A	.364	3	11	1	4	1	0	0	1	2	3	0	S
L 1984	KC-A	.000	2	1	0	0	0	0	0	0	0	1	0	H
L Total	2	.333	5	12	1	4	1	0	0	1	2	4	0	
W 1980	KC-A	.273	6	22	1	6	0	0	0	2	0	6	0	S
■ John Wathan														
D 1981	KC-A	.300	3	10	1	3	0	0	0	0	1	1	0	C
L 1976	KC-A	—	1	0	0	0	0	0	0	0	0	0	0	C
L 1977	KC-A	.000	4	6	0	0	0	0	0	0	0	3	0	1-2,C-1,D-1
L 1978	KC-A	.000	1	3	0	0	0	0	0	0	0	0	0	1
L 1980	KC-A	.000	3	6	1	0	0	0	0	0	3	1	0	O
L 1984	KC-A	.000	1	1	0	0	0	0	0	0	0	0	0	D
L Total	5	.000	10	16	1	0	0	0	0	0	3	4	0	
W 1980	KC-A	.286	3	7	1	2	0	0	0	1	2	1	0	C-2,O-1
W 1985	KC-A	.000	2	1	0	0	0	0	0	0	0	1	0	H
W Total	2	.250	5	8	1	2	0	0	0	1	2	2	0	
■ George Watkins														
W 1930	StL-N	.167	4	12	2	2	0	0	1	1	1	3	0	O
W 1931	StL-N	.286	5	14	4	4	1	0	1	2	2	1	1	O
W Total	2	.231	9	26	6	6	1	0	2	3	3	4	1	
■ Bob Watson														
D 1981	NY-A	.438	5	16	2	7	0	0	0	1	1	1	0	1
L 1980	NY-A	.500	3	12	0	6	3	1	0	0	0	0	0	1
L 1981	NY-A	.250	3	12	0	3	0	0	0	1	0	1	0	1
L Total	2	.375	6	24	0	9	3	1	0	1	0	1	0	
W 1981	NY-A	.318	6	22	2	7	1	0	2	7	3	0	0	1
■ Roy Weatherly														
W 1943	NY-A	.000	1	1	0	0	0	0	0	0	0	0	0	H
■ Buck Weaver														
W 1917	Chi-A	.333	6	21	3	7	1	0	0	1	0	2	0	S
W 1919	Chi-A	.324	8	34	4	11	4	1	0	0	0	2	0	3
W Total	2	.327	14	55	7	18	5	1	0	1	0	4	0	
■ Farmer Weaver														
W 1890	Lou-A	.259	7	27	4	7	1	0	0	4	1	2	5	O

YEAR	TM/L	AVG	G	AB	R	H	2B	3B	HR	RBI	BB	SO	SB	POS
■ **Skeeter Webb**														
W 1945	Det-A	.185	7	27	4	5	0	0	0	1	2	1	0	S
■ **Lenny Webster**														
D 1997	Bal-A	.167	3	6	1	1	0	0	0	1	1	0	0	C
L 1997	Bal-A	.222	4	9	0	2	0	0	0	0	0	1	0	C-3
■ **Mitch Webster**														
D 1995	LA-N	.000	2	2	0	0	0	0	0	0	0	0	0	H
L 1989	Chi-N	.333	3	3	0	1	0	0	0	0	0	0	0	O-2
■ **Pete Weckbecker**														
W 1890	Lou-A	.000	1	4	0	0	0	0	0	0	0	1	0	C
■ **John Wehner**														
D 1997	Fla-N	—	1	0	0	0	0	0	0	0	0	0	0	O
L 1992	Pit-N	.000	2	2	0	0	0	0	0	0	0	2	0	H
■ **Al Weis**														
L 1969	NY-N	.000	3	1	0	0	0	0	0	0	0	0	0	2
W 1969	NY-N	.455	5	11	1	5	0	0	1	3	4	2	0	2
■ **Walt Weiss**														
D 1995	Col-N	.167	4	12	1	2	0	0	0	0	3	3	1	S
D 1998	Atl-N	.154	3	13	2	2	0	0	0	0	1	3	0	S
D 1999	Atl-N	.167	3	6	1	1	0	0	0	0	0	2	0	S
D 2000	Atl-N	.667	1	3	0	2	1	0	0	2	0	0	0	S
D Total	4	.206	11	34	4	7	1	0	0	2	4	8	1	
L 1988	Oak-A	.333	4	15	2	5	2	0	0	2	0	4	0	S
L 1989	Oak-A	.111	4	9	2	1	1	0	0	0	1	1	1	S
L 1990	Oak-A	.000	2	7	2	0	0	0	0	0	2	2	0	S
L 1992	Oak-A	.167	3	6	1	1	0	0	0	0	2	1	2	S
L 1998	Atl-N	.200	4	15	0	3	0	0	0	1	2	5	1	S
L 1999	Atl-N	.286	6	21	2	6	2	0	0	1	2	4	2	S
L Total	6	.219	23	73	9	16	5	0	0	4	9	17	6	
W 1988	Oak-A	.063	5	16	1	1	0	0	0	0	0	2	1	S
W 1989	Oak-A	.133	4	15	3	2	0	0	1	1	2	2	0	S
W 1999	Atl-N	.222	3	9	1	2	0	0	0	0	0	1	0	S
W Total	3	.125	12	40	5	5	0	0	1	1	2	5	1	
■ **Curt Welch**														
W 1885	StL-A	.148	7	27	5	4	1	1	0	2	0	0	0	O
W 1886	StL-A	.350	6	20	7	7	2	0	0	1	3	4	2	O
W 1887	StL-A	.207	15	58	6	12	3	1	1	8	0	2	1	O
W Total	3	.219	28	105	18	23	6	2	1	11	3	6	3	
■ **Billy Werber**														
W 1939	Cin-N	.250	4	16	1	4	0	0	0	2	2	0	0	3
W 1940	Cin-N	.370	7	27	5	10	4	0	0	2	4	2	0	3
W Total	2	.326	11	43	6	14	4	0	0	4	6	2	0	
■ **Don Wert**														
W 1968	Det-A	.118	6	17	1	2	0	0	0	2	6	5	0	3
■ **Vic Wertz**														
W 1954	Cle-A	.500	4	16	2	8	2	1	1	3	2	2	0	1
■ **Wally Westlake**														
W 1954	Cle-A	.143	2	7	0	1	0	0	0	0	1	3	0	O
■ **Wes Westrum**														
W 1951	NY-N	.235	6	17	1	4	1	0	0	0	5	3	0	C
W 1954	NY-N	.273	4	11	0	3	0	0	0	3	1	3	0	C
W Total	2	.250	10	28	1	7	1	0	0	3	6	6	0	
■ **Zack Wheat**														
W 1916	Bro-N	.211	5	19	2	4	0	1	0	1	2	2	1	O
W 1920	Bro-N	.333	7	27	2	9	2	0	0	2	1	2	0	O
W Total	2	.283	12	46	4	13	2	1	0	3	3	4	1	
■ **Larry Whisenton**														
L 1982	Atl-N	.000	2	2	0	0	0	0	0	0	0	1	0	H
■ **Lou Whitaker**														
L 1984	Det-A	.143	3	14	3	2	0	0	0	0	0	3	0	2
L 1987	Det-A	.176	5	17	4	3	0	0	1	1	7	3	1	2
L Total	2	.161	8	31	7	5	0	0	1	1	7	6	1	
W 1984	Det-A	.278	5	18	6	5	2	0	0	0	4	4	0	2
■ **Devon White**														
D 1997	Fla-N	.182	3	11	1	2	0	0	1	4	2	3	0	O
L 1986	Cal-A	.500	4	2	2	1	0	0	0	0	0	1	0	O-3
L 1991	Tor-A	.364	5	22	5	8	1	0	0	0	2	3	3	O
L 1992	Tor-A	.348	6	23	2	8	2	0	0	2	5	6	0	O
L 1993	Tor-A	.444	6	27	3	12	1	1	1	2	1	5	0	O
L 1997	Fla-N	.190	6	21	4	4	1	0	0	1	2	7	1	O
L Total	5	.347	27	95	16	33	5	1	1	5	10	22	4	
W 1992	Tor-A	.231	6	26	2	6	1	0	0	2	0	6	1	O
W 1993	Tor-A	.292	6	24	8	7	3	2	1	7	4	7	1	O
W 1997	Fla-N	.242	7	33	0	8	3	1	0	2	3	10	1	O
W Total	3	.253	19	83	10	21	7	3	1	11	7	23	3	
■ **Ernie White**														
W 1942	StL-N	.000	1	2	0	0	0	0	0	0	0	0	0	P
W 1943	StL-N	—	1	0	0	0	0	0	0	0	0	0	0	R
W Total	2	.000	2	2	0	0	0	0	0	0	0	0	0	
■ **Frank White**														
D 1981	KC-A	.182	3	11	1	2	0	0	0	0	1	1	0	2
L 1976	KC-A	.125	4	8	2	1	0	0	0	0	0	1	0	2
L 1977	KC-A	.278	5	18	1	5	1	0	0	2	0	4	1	2
L 1978	KC-A	.231	4	13	1	3	0	0	0	2	0	0	0	2
L 1980	KC-A	.545	3	11	3	6	1	0	1	3	0	1	1	2
L 1984	KC-A	.091	3	11	1	1	0	0	0	0	0	3	0	2
L 1985	KC-A	.200	7	25	1	5	0	0	0	3	1	2	0	2
L Total	6	.244	26	86	9	21	2	0	1	10	1	11	2	
W 1980	KC-A	.080	6	25	0	2	0	0	0	0	1	5	1	2
W 1985	KC-A	.250	7	28	4	7	3	0	1	6	3	4	1	2
W Total	2	.170	13	53	4	9	3	0	1	6	4	9	2	
■ **Deacon White**														
W 1887	Det-N	.233	15	60	8	14	1	1	0	5	2	0	2	3-14,1-1
■ **Jerry White**														
D 1981	Mon-N	.167	5	18	3	3	1	0	0	1	2	2	3	O
L 1981	Mon-N	.313	5	16	2	5	1	0	1	3	3	1	1	O
■ **Jo-Jo White**														
W 1934	Det-A	.130	7	23	6	3	0	0	0	0	8	4	1	O
W 1935	Det-A	.263	5	19	3	5	0	0	0	1	5	7	0	O
W Total	2	.190	12	42	9	8	0	0	0	1	13	11	1	
■ **Roy White**														
L 1976	NY-A	.294	5	17	4	5	3	0	0	3	5	1	1	O
L 1977	NY-A	.400	4	5	2	2	2	0	0	0	1	0	0	O-1,D-1
L 1978	NY-A	.313	4	16	5	5	1	0	1	1	1	2	0	O-3,D-1
L Total	3	.316	13	38	11	12	6	0	1	4	7	3	1	
W 1976	NY-A	.133	4	15	0	2	0	0	0	0	3	0	0	O
W 1977	NY-A	.000	2	2	0	0	0	0	0	0	0	0	0	H
W 1978	NY-A	.333	6	24	9	8	0	0	1	4	4	5	2	O
W Total	3	.244	12	41	9	10	0	0	1	4	7	5	2	
■ **Bill White**														
W 1888	StL-A	.143	10	35	4	5	1	0	0	4	3	6	1	S
■ **Bill White**														
W 1964	StL-N	.111	7	27	2	3	1	0	0	2	2	6	1	1
■ **Burgess Whitehead**														
W 1934	StL-N	—	1	0	0	0	0	0	0	0	0	0	0	S
W 1936	NY-N	.048	6	21	1	1	0	0	0	2	1	3	0	2
W 1937	NY-N	.250	5	16	1	4	2	0	0	0	2	0	1	2
W Total	3	.135	12	37	2	5	2	0	0	2	3	3	1	
■ **George Whiteman**														
W 1918	Bos-A	.250	6	20	2	5	0	1	0	1	2	1	1	O
■ **Mark Whiten**														
L 1998	Cle-A	.286	2	7	2	2	1	0	1	1	1	3	0	O
■ **Terry Whitfield**														
L 1985	LA-N	—	1	0	0	0	0	0	0	0	0	0	0	H
■ **Dick Whitman**														
W 1949	Bro-N	.000	1	1	0	0	0	0	0	0	0	1	0	H
W 1950	Phi-N	.000	3	2	0	0	0	0	0	0	1	0	0	H
W Total	2	.000	4	3	0	0	0	0	0	0	1	1	0	
■ **Art Whitney**														
W 1888	NY-N	.324	10	37	7	12	0	1	0	12	1	4	2	3-9,O-1
W 1889	NY-N	.229	9	35	4	8	2	1	0	3	1	0	0	3
W Total	2	.278	19	72	11	20	2	2	0	15	2	4	2	
■ **Ernie Whitt**														
L 1985	Tor-A	.190	7	21	1	4	1	0	0	2	2	4	0	C
L 1989	Tor-A	.125	5	16	1	2	0	0	1	3	2	3	0	C
L Total	2	.162	12	37	2	6	1	0	1	5	4	7	0	
■ **Possum Whitted**														
W 1914	Bos-N	.214	4	14	2	3	0	1	0	2	3	1	1	O
W 1915	Phi-N	.067	5	15	0	1	0	0	0	1	1	0	1	O-5,1-1
W Total	2	.138	9	29	2	4	0	1	0	3	4	1	2	
■ **Chris Widger**														
D 1995	Sea-A	.000	2	3	0	0	0	0	0	0	0	3	0	C
L 1995	Sea-A	.000	3	1	0	0	0	0	0	0	0	1	0	C
■ **Alan Wiggins**														
L 1984	SD-N	.316	5	19	4	6	0	0	0	1	2	2	0	2
W 1984	SD-N	.364	5	22	2	8	1	0	0	1	0	2	1	2
■ **Rob Wilfong**														
L 1982	Cal-A	.000	2	1	0	0	0	0	0	0	0	1	0	H
L 1986	Cal-A	.308	4	13	1	4	1	0	0	2	0	2	0	2
L Total	2	.286	6	14	1	4	1	0	0	2	0	3	0	
■ **Joe Wilhoit**														
W 1917	NY-N	.000	2	1	0	0	0	0	0	0	1	0	0	H
■ **Curtis Wilkerson**														
L 1989	Chi-N	.500	3	2	1	1	0	0	0	0	0	0	0	3-1
L 1991	Pit-N	.000	4	4	0	0	0	0	0	0	0	3	0	H
L Total	2	.167	7	6	1	1	0	0	0	0	0	3	0	
■ **Rick Wilkins**														
D 1997	Sea-A	—	1	0	0	0	0	0	0	0	1	0	0	C
L 2000	StL-N	.000	2	2	0	0	0	0	0	0	0	0	0	H
■ **Jerry Willard**														
L 1991	Atl-N	.000	2	2	0	0	0	0	0	0	0	1	0	H
W 1991	Atl-N	—	1	0	0	0	0	0	0	1	0	0	0	H
■ **Bernie Williams**														
D 1995	NY-A	.429	5	21	8	9	2	0	2	5	7	3	1	O
D 1996	NY-A	.467	4	15	5	7	0	0	3	5	2	1	1	O
D 1997	NY-A	.118	5	17	3	2	1	0	0	1	4	3	0	O

YEAR	TM/L	AVG	G	AB	R	H	2B	3B	HR	RBI	BB	SO	SB	POS
D 1998	NY-A	.000	3	11	0	0	0	0	0	0	1	4	0	O
D 1999	NY-A	.364	3	11	2	4	1	0	1	6	1	2	0	O
D 2000	NY-A	.250	5	20	3	5	3	0	0	1	1	4	0	O
D Total	6	.284	25	95	21	27	7	0	6	18	16	17	2	
L 1996	NY-A	.474	5	19	6	9	3	0	2	6	5	4	1	O
L 1998	NY-A	.381	6	21	4	8	1	0	0	5	7	4	1	O
L 1999	NY-A	.250	5	20	3	5	1	0	1	2	2	5	1	O
L 2000	NY-A	.435	6	23	5	10	1	0	1	3	2	3	1	O
L Total	4	.386	22	83	18	32	6	0	4	16	16	16	4	
W 1996	NY-A	.167	6	24	3	4	0	0	1	4	3	6	1	O
W 1998	NY-A	.063	4	16	2	1	0	0	1	3	2	5	0	O
W 1999	NY-A	.231	4	13	2	3	0	0	0	0	4	2	1	O
W 2000	NY-A	.111	5	18	2	2	0	0	1	1	5	5	0	O
W Total	4	.141	19	71	9	10	0	0	3	8	14	18	2	
■ Billy Williams														
L 1975	Oak-A	.000	3	8	0	0	0	0	0	0	1	1	0	D-2
■ Davey Williams														
W 1951	NY-N	.000	2	1	0	0	0	0	0	0	0	0	0	H
W 1954	NY-N	.000	4	11	0	0	0	0	0	1	2	2	0	2
W Total	2	.000	6	12	0	0	0	0	0	1	2	2	0	
■ Dewey Williams														
W 1945	Chi-N	.000	2	2	0	0	0	0	0	0	0	1	0	C-1
■ Earl Williams														
L 1973	Bal-A	.278	5	18	2	5	2	0	1	4	2	2	0	1-4,C-1
L 1974	Bal-A	.000	2	6	0	0	0	0	0	0	0	2	0	1
L Total	2	.208	7	24	2	5	2	0	1	4	2	4	0	
■ Dib Williams														
W 1931	Phi-A	.320	7	25	2	8	1	0	0	1	2	9	0	S
■ Gerald Williams														
D 1995	NY-A	.000	5	5	1	0	0	0	0	0	2	3	0	O
D 1998	Atl-N	.500	2	2	1	1	0	0	0	1	0	1	0	O
D 1999	Atl-N	.389	4	18	2	7	1	0	0	3	0	3	1	O
D Total	3	.320	11	25	4	8	1	0	0	4	2	7	1	
L 1998	Atl-N	.154	5	13	0	2	0	0	0	0	1	6	1	O
L 1999	Atl-N	.179	6	28	4	5	2	0	0	1	2	2	3	O
L Total	2	.171	11	41	4	7	2	0	0	1	3	8	4	
W 1999	Atl-N	.176	4	17	2	3	0	1	0	0	0	4	0	O
■ Jimmy Williams														
T 1900	Pit-N	.214	4	14	0	3	0	0	0	0	1	0	0	3
■ Matt Williams														
D 1997	Cle-A	.235	5	17	4	4	1	0	1	3	3	3	0	3
D 1999	Ari-N	.375	4	16	3	6	1	0	0	0	0	1	0	3
D Total	2	.303	9	33	7	10	2	0	1	3	3	4	0	
L 1989	SF-N	.300	5	20	2	6	1	0	2	9	0	2	0	3-5,S-1
L 1997	Cle-A	.217	6	23	1	5	1	0	0	2	3	7	1	3
L Total	2	.256	11	43	3	11	2	0	2	11	3	9	1	
W 1989	SF-N	.125	4	16	1	2	0	0	1	1	0	6	0	S-4,3-3
W 1997	Cle-A	.385	7	26	8	10	1	0	1	3	7	6	0	3
W Total	2	.286	11	42	9	12	1	0	2	4	7	12	0	
■ Dick Williams														
W 1953	Bro-N	.500	3	2	0	1	0	0	0	0	1	1	0	H
■ Ted Williams														
W 1946	Bos-A	.200	7	25	2	5	0	0	0	1	5	5	0	O
■ Ned Williamson														
W 1885	Chi-N	.087	7	23	1	2	0	0	0	3	4	0	0	3-4,S-3
W 1886	Chi-N	.056	6	18	2	1	0	1	0	3	4	5	1	S-6,P-2,C,O
W Total	2	.073	13	41	3	3	0	1	0	6	8	5	1	
■ Maury Wills														
W 1959	LA-N	.250	6	20	2	5	0	0	0	1	0	3	1	S
W 1963	LA-N	.133	4	15	1	2	0	0	0	0	1	3	1	S
W 1965	LA-N	.367	7	30	3	11	3	0	0	3	1	3	3	S
W 1966	LA-N	.077	4	13	0	1	0	0	0	0	3	3	1	S
W Total	4	.244	21	78	6	19	3	0	0	4	5	12	6	
■ Art Wilson														
W 1911	NY-N	.000	1	1	0	0	0	0	0	0	0	0	0	C
W 1912	NY-N	1.000	2	1	0	1	0	0	0	0	0	0	0	C
W 1913	NY-N	.000	3	3	0	0	0	0	0	0	0	2	0	C
W Total	3	.200	6	5	0	1	0	0	0	0	0	2	0	
■ Dan Wilson														
D 1995	Sea-A	.118	5	17	0	2	0	0	0	1	2	6	0	C
D 1997	Sea-A	.000	4	13	0	0	0	0	0	0	0	9	0	C
D 2000	Sea-A	.000	2	3	0	0	0	0	0	1	1	2	0	C
D Total	3	.061	11	33	0	2	0	0	0	2	3	17	0	
L 1995	Sea-A	.000	6	16	0	0	0	0	0	0	0	4	0	C
L 2000	Sea-A	.091	4	11	0	1	0	0	0	0	1	5	0	C
L Total	2	.037	10	27	0	1	0	0	0	0	1	9	0	
■ Enrique Wilson														
D 1998	Cle-A	.000	1	2	0	0	0	0	0	0	0	0	0	2
D 1999	Cle-A	.000	3	2	0	0	0	0	0	0	0	0	0	2-2
D Total	2	.000	4	4	0	0	0	0	0	0	0	0	0	
L 1998	Cle-A	.214	5	14	2	3	0	0	0	1	1	3	0	2
■ George Wilson														
W 1956	NY-A	.000	1	1	0	0	0	0	0	0	0	1	0	H

YEAR	TM/L	AVG	G	AB	R	H	2B	3B	HR	RBI	BB	SO	SB	POS
■ Jimmie Wilson														
W 1928	StL-N	.091	3	11	1	1	1	0	0	1	0	3	0	C
W 1930	StL-N	.267	4	15	0	4	1	0	0	2	0	1	0	C
W 1931	StL-N	.217	7	23	0	5	0	0	0	2	1	1	0	C
W 1940	Cin-N	.353	6	17	2	6	0	0	0	0	1	2	1	C
W Total	4	.242	20	66	3	16	2	0	0	5	2	7	1	
■ Chief Wilson														
W 1909	Pit-N	.154	7	26	2	4	1	0	0	1	0	2	1	O
■ Hack Wilson														
W 1924	NY-N	.233	7	30	1	7	1	0	0	3	1	9	0	O
W 1929	Chi-N	.471	5	17	2	8	0	1	0	0	4	3	0	O
W Total	2	.319	12	47	3	15	1	1	0	3	5	12	0	
■ Nigel Wilson														
D 1996	Cle-A	.000	1	1	0	0	0	0	0	0	0	0	0	H
■ Mookie Wilson														
L 1986	NY-N	.115	6	26	2	3	0	0	0	1	1	7	1	O
L 1988	NY-N	.154	4	13	2	2	0	0	0	1	2	2	0	O-3
L 1989	Tor-A	.263	5	19	2	5	0	0	0	2	2	2	1	O
L 1991	Tor-A	.250	3	8	1	2	0	0	0	0	1	3	1	O-2
L Total	4	.182	18	66	7	12	0	0	0	4	6	14	3	
W 1986	NY-N	.269	7	26	3	7	1	0	0	0	1	6	3	O
■ Willie Wilson														
D 1981	KC-A	.308	3	13	0	4	0	0	0	1	0	0	0	O
L 1978	KC-A	.250	3	4	0	1	0	0	0	0	0	2	0	O
L 1980	KC-A	.308	3	13	2	4	2	1	0	4	1	2	0	O
L 1984	KC-A	.154	3	13	0	2	0	0	0	0	1	2	0	O
L 1985	KC-A	.310	7	29	5	9	0	0	1	2	1	5	1	O
L 1992	Oak-A	.227	6	22	0	5	1	0	0	0	1	5	7	O
L Total	5	.259	22	81	7	21	3	1	1	6	4	16	8	
W 1980	KC-A	.154	6	26	3	4	1	0	0	0	4	12	2	O
W 1985	KC-A	.367	7	30	2	11	0	1	0	3	1	4	3	O
W Total	2	.268	13	56	5	15	1	1	0	3	5	16	5	
■ Hooks Wiltse														
W 1911	NY-N	.000	2	1	0	0	0	0	0	0	0	1	0	P
W 1913	NY-N	.000	2	2	0	0	0	0	0	0	0	1	0	1
W Total	2	.000	4	3	0	0	0	0	0	0	0	2	0	
■ Dave Winfield														
D 1981	NY-A	.350	5	20	2	7	3	0	0	0	1	5	0	O
L 1981	NY-A	.154	3	13	2	2	1	0	0	2	2	2	1	O
L 1992	Tor-A	.250	6	24	7	6	1	0	2	3	4	2	0	D
L Total	2	.216	9	37	9	8	2	0	2	5	6	4	1	
W 1981	NY-A	.045	6	22	0	1	0	0	0	1	5	4	1	O
W 1992	Tor-A	.227	6	22	0	5	1	0	0	3	2	3	0	O-3,D-3
W Total	2	.136	12	44	0	6	1	0	0	4	7	7	1	
■ Ivey Wingo														
W 1919	Cin-N	.571	3	7	1	4	0	0	0	1	3	1	0	C
■ Herm Winningham														
L 1990	Cin-N	.286	3	7	1	2	1	0	0	1	1	1	1	O-2
W 1990	Cin-N	.500	2	4	1	2	0	0	0	0	0	0	0	O-1
■ Casey Wise														
W 1958	Mil-N	.000	2	1	0	0	0	0	0	0	0	1	0	H
■ Whitey Witt														
W 1922	NY-A	.222	5	18	1	4	1	1	0	0	1	2	0	O
W 1923	NY-A	.240	6	25	1	6	2	0	0	4	1	1	0	O
W Total	2	.233	11	43	2	10	3	1	0	4	2	3	0	
■ Jim Wohlford														
L 1976	KC-A	.182	5	11	3	2	0	0	0	0	3	1	2	O
■ Jimmy Wolf														
W 1890	Lou-A	.360	7	25	4	9	3	1	0	8	3	0	2	3-5,O-3
■ Tony Womack														
D 1999	Ari-N	.111	4	18	2	2	0	1	0	0	0	6	0	O-4,S-2
■ Joe Wood														
W 1912	Bos-A	.286	4	7	1	2	0	0	0	1	1	0	0	P
W 1920	Cle-A	.200	4	10	2	2	1	0	0	0	1	2	0	O
W Total	2	.235	8	17	3	4	1	0	0	1	2	2	0	
■ Gene Woodling														
W 1949	NY-A	.400	3	10	4	4	3	0	0	0	3	0	0	O
W 1950	NY-A	.429	4	14	2	6	0	0	0	1	2	0	0	O
W 1951	NY-A	.167	6	18	6	3	1	1	1	1	5	3	0	O-5
W 1952	NY-A	.348	7	23	4	8	1	1	1	1	3	3	0	O-6
W 1953	NY-A	.300	6	20	5	6	0	0	1	3	6	2	0	O
W Total	5	.318	26	85	21	27	5	2	3	6	19	8	0	
■ Gary Woods														
D 1981	Hou-N	.000	2	2	0	0	0	0	0	0	0	1	0	H
L 1980	Hou-N	.250	4	8	0	2	0	0	0	1	1	3	1	O-3
L 1984	Chi-N	.000	1	1	0	0	0	0	0	0	0	1	0	O
L Total	2	.222	5	9	0	2	0	0	0	1	1	4	1	
■ Tracy Woodson														
L 1988	LA-N	.250	3	4	0	1	0	0	0	0	0	1	0	1
W 1988	LA-N	.000	4	4	0	0	0	0	0	1	0	0	0	1-3
■ Woody Woodward														
L 1970	Cin-N	.100	3	10	0	1	0	0	0	0	1	0	0	S-3,3-3
W 1970	Cin-N	.200	4	5	0	1	0	0	0	0	0	0	0	S-3

YEAR	TM/L	AVG	G	AB	R	H	2B	3B	HR	RBI	BB	SO	SB	POS
■ **Chuck Wortman**														
W 1918	Chi-N	.000	1	1	0	0	0	0	0	0	0	0	0	2
■ **Glenn Wright**														
W 1925	Pit-N	.185	7	27	3	5	1	0	1	3	1	4	0	S
W 1927	Pit-N	.154	4	13	1	2	0	0	0	2	0	0	0	S
W Total	2	.175	11	40	4	7	1	0	1	5	1	4	0	
■ **Rick Wrona**														
L 1989	Chi-N	.000	2	5	0	0	0	0	0	0	0	3	0	C
■ **Jimmy Wynn**														
L 1974	LA-N	.200	4	10	4	2	2	0	0	2	9	1	1	O
W 1974	LA-N	.188	5	16	1	3	1	0	1	2	4	4	0	O
■ **Marvell Wynne**														
L 1989	Chi-N	.167	4	6	0	1	0	0	0	0	0	0	0	O-2
■ **Carl Yastrzemski**														
L 1975	Bos-A	.455	3	11	4	5	1	0	1	2	1	1	0	O
W 1967	Bos-A	.400	7	25	4	10	2	0	3	5	4	1	0	O
W 1975	Bos-A	.310	7	29	7	9	0	0	0	4	4	1	0	1-4,O-4
W Total	2	.352	14	54	11	19	2	0	3	9	8	2	0	
■ **Emil Yde**														
W 1925	Pit-N	.000	2	1	1	0	0	0	0	0	0	0	0	P-1
W 1927	Pit-N	—	1	0	1	0	0	0	0	0	0	0	0	R
W Total	2	.000	3	1	2	0	0	0	0	0	0	0	0	
■ **George Yeager**														
T 1897	Bos-N	.500	3	12	2	6	1	1	0	2	2	0	0	C
■ **Steve Yeager**														
D 1981	LA-N	.400	2	5	1	2	1	0	0	0	0	1	0	C
L 1974	LA-N	.000	3	9	1	0	0	0	0	0	3	3	1	C
L 1977	LA-N	.231	4	13	1	3	0	0	0	2	1	3	0	C
L 1978	LA-N	.231	4	13	2	3	0	0	1	2	2	2	1	C
L 1981	LA-N	.500	1	2	1	1	0	0	0	0	0	0	0	C
L 1983	LA-N	.167	2	6	0	1	1	0	0	0	0	0	0	C
L 1985	LA-N	.000	1	2	0	0	0	0	0	0	1	1	0	C
L Total	6	.178	15	45	5	8	1	0	1	4	7	9	2	
W 1974	LA-N	.364	4	11	0	4	1	0	0	1	1	4	0	C
W 1977	LA-N	.316	6	19	2	6	1	0	2	5	1	1	0	C
W 1978	LA-N	.231	5	13	2	3	1	0	0	0	1	2	0	C
W 1981	LA-N	.286	6	14	2	4	1	0	2	4	0	2	0	C
W Total	4	.298	21	57	6	17	4	0	4	10	3	9	0	
■ **Steve Yerkes**														
W 1912	Bos-A	.250	8	32	3	8	0	2	0	4	2	3	0	2
■ **Rudy York**														
W 1940	Det-A	.231	7	26	3	6	0	1	1	2	4	7	0	1
W 1945	Det-A	.179	7	28	1	5	1	0	0	3	3	4	0	1
W 1946	Bos-A	.261	7	23	6	6	1	1	2	5	6	4	0	1
W Total	3	.221	21	77	10	17	2	2	3	10	13	15	0	
■ **Ned Yost**														
W 1982	Mil-A	—	1	0	0	0	0	0	0	0	1	0	0	C
■ **Dmitri Young**														
L 1996	StL-N	.286	4	7	1	2	0	1	0	2	0	2	0	1-2
■ **Eric Young**														
D 1995	Col-N	.438	4	16	3	7	1	0	1	2	2	2	1	2
■ **Ross Youngs**														
W 1921	NY-N	.280	8	25	3	7	1	1	0	4	7	2	2	O
W 1922	NY-N	.375	5	16	2	6	0	0	0	2	3	1	0	O
W 1923	NY-N	.348	6	23	2	8	0	0	1	3	2	0	0	O
W 1924	NY-N	.185	7	27	3	5	1	0	0	1	5	6	1	O
W Total	4	.286	26	91	10	26	2	1	1	10	17	9	3	
■ **Robin Yount**														
D 1981	Mil-A	.316	5	19	4	6	0	1	0	1	2	2	1	S
L 1982	Mil-A	.250	5	16	1	4	0	0	0	0	5	0	0	S
W 1982	Mil-A	.414	7	29	6	12	3	0	1	6	2	2	0	S
■ **Sal Yvars**														
W 1951	NY-N	.000	1	1	0	0	0	0	0	0	0	0	0	H
■ **Al Zarilla**														
W 1944	StL-A	.100	4	10	1	1	0	0	0	1	0	4	0	O-3
■ **Greg Zaun**														
L 1997	Fla-N	—	1	0	0	0	0	0	0	0	0	0	0	C
W 1997	Fla-N	.000	2	2	0	0	0	0	0	0	0	0	0	C-1
■ **Joe Zdeb**														
L 1977	KC-A	.000	4	9	0	0	0	0	0	0	0	2	1	O
■ **George Zeber**														
W 1977	NY-A	.000	2	2	0	0	0	0	0	0	0	2	0	H
■ **Rollie Zeider**														
W 1918	Chi-N	—	2	0	0	0	0	0	0	0	2	0	0	3
■ **Todd Zeile**														
D 1996	Bal-A	.263	4	19	2	5	1	0	0	0	2	5	0	3
D 1998	Tex-A	.333	3	9	0	3	0	0	0	0	0	2	0	3
D 1999	Tex-A	.100	3	10	0	1	0	0	0	0	2	1	0	3
D 2000	NY-N	.071	4	14	0	1	1	0	0	0	4	3	0	1
D Total	4	.192	14	52	2	10	2	0	0	0	8	11	0	
L 1996	Bal-A	.364	5	22	3	8	0	0	3	5	2	1	0	3
L 2000	NY-N	.368	5	19	1	7	3	0	1	8	2	4	0	1
L Total	2	.366	10	41	4	15	3	0	4	13	4	5	0	
W 2000	NY-N	.400	5	20	1	8	2	0	0	1	1	5	0	1
■ **Chief Zimmer**														
T 1892	Cle-N	.261	6	23	2	6	1	1	0	2	0	3	0	C
T 1895	Cle-N	.333	4	18	2	6	2	0	0	3	3	5	0	C
T 1896	Cle-N	.214	4	14	0	3	1	0	0	1	2	6	0	C
T 1900	Pit-N	.111	3	9	1	1	0	0	0	1	1	2	1	C
T Total	4	.250	17	64	5	16	4	1	0	7	6	16	1	
■ **Don Zimmer**														
W 1955	Bro-N	.222	4	9	0	2	0	0	0	2	2	5	0	2
W 1959	LA-N	.000	1	1	0	0	0	0	0	0	0	0	0	S
W Total	2	.200	5	10	0	2	0	0	0	2	2	5	0	
■ **Jerry Zimmerman**														
W 1961	Cin-N	—	2	0	0	0	0	0	0	0	0	0	0	C
W 1965	Min-A	.000	2	1	0	0	0	0	0	0	0	0	0	C
W Total	2	.000	4	1	0	0	0	0	0	0	0	0	0	

YEAR	TM/L	W	L	ERA	G	GS	CG	SV	SHO	IP	H	ER	BB	SO
● Don Aase														
L 1979	Cal-A	1	0	1.80	2	0	0	0	0	5	4	1	2	6
● Paul Abbott														
D 2000	Sea-A	1	0	1.59	1	1	0	0	0	5^2	5	1	3	1
L 2000	Sea-A	0	1	5.40	1	1	0	0	0	5	3	3	3	3
● Glenn Abbott														
L 1975	Oak-A	0	0	0.00	1	0	0	0	0	1	0	0	0	0
● Jim Acker														
L 1985	Tor-A	0	0	0.00	2	0	0	0	0	6	2	0	0	5
L 1989	Tor-A	0	0	1.42	5	0	0	0	0	6^1	4	1	1	4
L 1991	Tor-A	0	0	0.00	1	0	0	0	0	0^2	1	0	0	1
L Total	3	0	0	0.69	8	0	0	0	0	13	7	1	1	10
● Babe Adams														
W 1909	Pit-N	3	0	1.33	3	3	3	0	1	27	18	4	6	11
W 1925	Pit-N	0	0	0.00	1	0	0	0	0	1	2	0	0	0
W Total	2	3	0	1.29	4	3	3	0	1	28	20	4	6	11
● Juan Agosto														
L 1983	Chi-A	0	0	0.00	1	0	0	0	0	0^1	0	0	0	0
● Rick Aguilera														
D 1995	Bos-A	0	0	13.50	1	0	0	0	0	0^2	3	1	0	1
L 1986	NY-N	0	0	0.00	2	0	0	0	0	5	2	0	2	2
L 1988	NY-N	0	0	1.29	3	0	0	0	0	7	3	1	2	4
L 1991	Min-A	0	0	0.00	3	0	0	3	0	3^1	1	0	0	3
L Total	3	0	0	0.59	8	0	0	3	0	15^1	6	1	4	9
W 1986	NY-N	1	0	12.00	2	0	0	0	0	3	8	4	1	4
W 1991	Min-A	1	1	1.80	4	0	0	2	0	5	6	1	1	3
W Total	2	2	1	5.63	6	0	0	2	0	8	14	5	2	7
● Vic Aldridge														
W 1925	Pit-N	2	0	4.42	3	3	2	0	0	18^1	18	9	9	9
W 1927	Pit-N	0	1	7.36	1	1	0	0	0	7^1	10	6	4	4
W Total	2	2	1	5.26	4	4	2	0	0	25^2	28	15	13	13
● Doyle Alexander														
L 1973	Bal-A	0	1	4.91	1	1	0	0	0	3^2	5	2	0	1
L 1985	Tor-A	0	1	8.71	2	2	0	0	0	10^1	14	10	3	9
L 1987	Det-A	0	2	10.00	2	2	0	0	0	9	14	10	1	5
L Total	3	0	4	8.61	5	5	0	0	0	23	33	22	4	15
W 1976	NY-A	0	1	7.50	1	1	0	0	0	6	9	5	2	1
● Pete Alexander														
W 1915	Phi-N	1	1	1.53	2	2	2	0	0	17^2	14	3	4	10
W 1926	StL-N	2	0	1.33	3	2	2	1	0	20^1	12	3	4	17
W 1928	StL-N	0	1	19.80	2	1	0	0	0	5	10	11	4	2
W Total	3	3	2	3.56	7	5	4	1	0	43	36	17	12	29
● Antonio Alfonseca														
W 1997	Fla-N	0	0	0.00	3	0	0	0	0	6^1	6	0	1	5
● Johnny Allen														
W 1932	NY-A	0	0	40.50	1	1	0	0	0	0^2	5	3	0	0
W 1941	Bro-N	0	0	0.00	3	0	0	0	0	3^2	1	0	3	0
W Total	2	0	0	6.23	4	1	0	0	0	4^1	6	3	3	0
● Nick Altrock														
W 1906	Chi-A	1	1	1.00	2	2	2	0	0	18	11	2	2	5
● Wilson Alvarez														
D 1997	SF-N	0	1	6.00	1	1	0	0	0	6	6	4	4	4
L 1993	Chi-A	1	0	1.00	1	1	1	0	0	9	7	1	2	6
● Red Ames														
W 1905	NY-N	0	0	0.00	1	0	0	0	0	1	1	0	1	1
W 1911	NY-N	0	1	2.25	2	1	0	0	0	8	6	2	1	6
W 1912	NY-N	0	0	4.50	1	0	0	0	0	2	3	1	1	0
W Total	3	0	1	2.45	4	1	0	0	0	11	10	3	3	7
● Larry Andersen														
L 1986	Hou-N	0	0	0.00	2	0	0	0	0	5	1	0	2	3
L 1990	Bos-A	0	1	6.00	3	0	0	0	0	3	3	2	3	3
L 1993	Phi-N	0	0	15.43	3	0	0	1	0	2^1	4	4	1	3
L Total	3	0	1	5.23	8	0	0	1	0	10^1	8	6	6	9
W 1983	Phi-N	0	0	2.25	2	0	0	0	0	4	4	1	0	1
W 1993	Phi-N	0	0	12.27	4	0	0	0	0	3^2	5	5	3	3
W Total	2	0	0	7.04	6	0	0	0	0	7^2	9	6	3	4
● Brian Anderson														
D 1999	Ari-N	0	0	2.57	1	1	0	0	0	7	7	2	0	4
L 1997	Cle-A	1	0	1.42	3	0	0	0	0	6^1	1	1	3	7
W 1997	Cle-A	0	0	2.45	3	0	0	1	0	3^2	2	1	0	2
● Fred Anderson														
W 1917	NY-N	0	1	18.00	1	0	0	0	0	2	5	4	0	3
● Ivy Andrews														
W 1937	NY-A	0	0	3.18	1	0	0	0	0	5^2	6	2	4	1
● Joaquin Andujar														
L 1980	Hou-N	0	0	0.00	1	0	0	1	0	1	0	0	1	0
L 1982	StL-N	1	0	2.70	1	1	0	0	0	6^2	6	2	2	4
L 1985	StL-N	0	1	6.97	2	2	0	0	0	10^1	14	8	4	9
L Total	3	1	1	5.00	4	3	0	1	0	18	20	10	7	13
W 1982	StL-N	2	0	1.35	2	2	0	0	0	13^1	10	2	1	4
W 1985	StL-N	0	1	9.00	2	1	0	0	0	4	10	4	4	3
W Total	2	2	1	3.12	4	3	0	0	0	17^1	20	6	5	7
● Rick Ankiel														
D 2000	StL-N	0	0	13.50	1	1	0	0	0	2^2	4	4	6	3
L 2000	StL-N	0	0	20.25	2	1	0	0	0	1^1	1	3	5	2
● Johnny Antonelli														
W 1954	NY-N	1	0	0.84	2	1	1	1	0	10^2	8	1	7	12
● Kevin Appier														
D 2000	Oak-A	0	1	3.48	2	1	0	0	0	10^1	10	4	6	13
● Jack Armstrong														
W 1990	Cin-N	0	0	0.00	1	0	0	0	0	3	1	0	0	3
● Luis Arroyo														
W 1960	NY-A	0	0	13.50	1	0	0	0	0	0^2	2	1	0	1
W 1961	NY-A	1	0	2.25	2	0	0	0	0	4	4	1	2	3
W Total	2	1	0	3.86	3	0	0	0	0	4^2	6	2	2	4
● Andy Ashby														
D 1996	SD-N	0	0	6.75	1	1	0	0	0	5^1	7	4	1	5
D 1998	SD-N	0	0	6.75	1	1	0	0	0	4	6	3	1	4
D 2000	Atl-N	0	0	2.45	2	0	0	0	0	3^2	1	1	3	5
D Total	3	0	0	5.54	4	2	0	0	0	13	14	8	5	14
L 1998	SD-N	0	0	2.08	2	2	0	0	0	13	14	3	2	5
W 1998	SD-N	0	1	13.50	1	1	0	0	0	2^2	10	4	1	1
● Paul Assenmacher														
D 1995	Cle-A	0	0	0.00	3	0	0	0	0	1^2	0	0	0	3
D 1996	Cle-A	1	0	0.00	3	0	0	0	0	1^2	0	0	1	2
D 1997	Cle-A	0	0	5.40	4	0	0	0	0	3^1	2	2	2	2
D 1998	Cle-A	0	0	0.00	3	0	0	0	0	1	2	0	0	2
D 1999	Cle-A	0	0	27.00	1	0	0	0	0	1	5	3	0	0
D Total	5	1	0	5.19	14	0	0	0	0	8^2	9	5	3	9
L 1989	Chi-N	0	0	13.50	2	0	0	0	0	0^2	3	1	0	0
L 1995	Cle-A	0	0	0.00	3	0	0	0	0	1^1	0	0	1	2
L 1997	Cle-A	1	0	9.00	5	0	0	0	0	2	5	2	1	3
L 1998	Cle-A	0	0	0.00	3	0	0	0	0	2	0	0	0	3
L Total	4	1	0	4.50	13	0	0	0	0	6	8	3	2	8
W 1995	Cle-A	0	0	6.75	4	0	0	0	0	1^1	1	1	3	3
W 1997	Cle-A	0	0	0.00	5	0	0	0	0	4	5	0	0	6
W Total	2	0	0	1.69	9	0	0	0	0	5^1	6	1	3	9
● Pedro Astacio														
D 1995	LA-N	0	0	0.00	3	0	0	0	0	3^1	1	0	0	5
D 1996	LA-N	0	0	0.00	1	0	0	0	0	1^2	0	0	0	1
D Total	2	0	0	0.00	4	0	0	0	0	5	1	0	0	6
● Keith Atherton														
L 1987	Min-A	0	0	0.00	1	0	0	0	0	0^1	1	0	0	0
W 1987	Min-A	0	0	6.75	2	0	0	0	0	1^1	0	1	1	0
● Elden Auker														
W 1934	Det-A	1	1	5.56	2	2	1	0	0	11^1	16	7	5	2
W 1935	Det-A	0	0	3.00	1	1	0	0	0	6	6	2	2	1
W Total	2	1	1	4.67	3	3	1	0	0	17^1	22	9	7	3
● Steve Avery														
D 1995	Atl-N	0	0	13.50	1	0	0	0	0	0^2	1	1	0	1
L 1991	Atl-N	2	0	0.00	2	2	0	0	0	16^1	9	0	4	17
L 1992	Atl-N	1	1	9.00	3	2	0	0	0	8	13	8	2	3
L 1993	Atl-N	0	0	2.77	2	2	0	0	0	13	9	4	6	10
L 1995	Atl-N	1	0	0.00	2	1	0	0	0	6	2	0	4	6
L 1996	Atl-N	0	0	0.00	2	0	0	0	0	2	2	0	1	1
L Total	5	4	1	2.38	11	7	0	0	0	45^1	35	12	17	37
W 1991	Atl-N	0	0	3.46	2	2	0	0	0	13	10	5	1	8
W 1992	Atl-N	0	1	3.75	2	2	0	0	0	12	11	5	3	11
W 1995	Atl-N	1	0	1.50	1	1	0	0	0	6	3	1	5	3
W 1996	Atl-N	0	1	13.50	1	0	0	0	0	0^2	1	1	3	0
W Total	4	1	2	3.41	6	5	0	0	0	31^2	25	12	12	22
● Bobby Ayala														
D 1995	Sea-A	0	0	54.00	2	0	0	0	0	0^2	6	4	1	0
D 1997	Sea-A	0	0	40.50	1	0	0	0	0	1^1	4	6	3	2
D Total	2	0	0	45.00	3	0	0	0	0	2	10	10	4	2
L 1995	Sea-A	0	0	2.45	2	0	0	0	0	3^2	3	1	3	3
● Jim Bagby														
W 1946	Bos-A	0	0	3.00	1	0	0	0	0	3	6	1	1	1
● Jim Bagby														
W 1920	Cle-A	1	1	1.80	2	2	1	0	0	15	20	3	1	3
● Stan Bahnsen														
D 1981	Mon-N	0	0	0.00	1	0	0	0	0	1^1	1	0	1	1
● Doug Bair														
L 1979	Cin-N	0	1	9.00	1	0	0	0	0	1	2	1	1	0
L 1982	StL-N	0	0	0.00	1	0	0	0	0	1	2	0	3	0
L Total	2	0	1	4.50	2	0	0	0	0	2	4	1	4	0
W 1982	StL-N	0	1	9.00	3	0	0	0	0	2	2	2	2	3
W 1984	Det-A	0	0	0.00	1	0	0	0	0	0^2	0	0	0	1
W Total	2	0	1	6.75	4	0	0	0	0	2^2	2	2	2	4
● Lady Baldwin														
W 1887	Det-N	4	1	1.50	5	5	5	0	1	42	38	7	10	4
● Harry Baldwin														
W 1924	NY-N	0	0	0.00	1	0	0	0	0	2	1	0	0	1
● James Baldwin														
D 2000	Chi-A	0	0	1.50	1	1	0	0	0	6	3	1	3	2

YEAR	TM/L	W	L	ERA	G	GS	CG	SV	SHO	IP	H	ER	BB	SO
● Win Ballou														
W 1925	Was-A	0	0	0.00	2	0	0	0	0	1^2	0	0	1	1
● Floyd Bannister														
L 1983	Chi-A	0	1	4.50	1	1	0	0	0	6	5	3	1	5
● Jack Banta														
W 1949	Bro-N	0	0	3.18	3	0	0	0	0	5^2	5	2	1	4
● Lorenzo Barcelo														
D 2000	Chi-A	0	0	0.00	1	0	0	0	0	1^2	0	0	1	0
● Mike Barlow														
L 1979	Cal-A	0	0	0.00	1	0	0	0	0	1	0	0	0	0
● Jesse Barnes														
W 1921	NY-N	2	0	1.65	3	0	0	0	0	16^1	10	3	6	18
W 1922	NY-N	0	0	1.80	1	1	1	0	0	10	8	2	2	6
W Total	2	2	0	1.71	4	1	1	0	0	26^1	18	5	8	24
● Virgil Barnes														
W 1923	NY-N	0	0	0.00	2	0	0	0	0	4^2	4	0	0	4
W 1924	NY-N	0	1	5.68	2	2	0	0	0	12^2	15	8	1	9
W Total	2	0	1	4.15	4	2	0	0	0	17^1	19	8	1	13
● Rex Barney														
W 1947	Bro-N	0	1	2.70	3	1	0	0	0	6^2	4	2	10	3
W 1949	Bro-N	0	1	16.88	1	1	0	0	0	2^2	3	5	6	2
W Total	2	0	2	6.75	4	2	0	0	0	9^1	7	7	16	5
● Salome Barojas														
L 1983	Chi-A	0	0	18.00	2	0	0	0	0	1	4	2	0	0
● Jim Barr														
L 1971	SF-N	0	0	9.00	1	0	0	0	0	1	3	1	0	2
● Red Barrett														
W 1948	Bos-N	0	0	0.00	2	0	0	0	0	3^2	1	0	0	1
● Dave Beard														
D 1981	Oak-A	0	0	0.00	1	0	0	1	0	1^1	0	0	0	2
L 1981	Oak-A	0	0	40.50	1	0	0	0	0	0^2	5	3	0	0
● Gene Bearden														
W 1948	Cle-A	1	0	0.00	2	1	1	1	1	10^2	6	0	1	4
● Jim Beattie														
L 1978	NY-A	1	0	1.69	1	1	0	0	0	5^1	2	1	5	3
W 1978	NY-A	1	0	2.00	1	1	1	0	0	9	9	2	4	8
● Johnny Beazley														
W 1942	StL-N	2	0	2.50	2	2	2	0	0	18	17	5	3	6
W 1946	StL-N	0	0	0.00	1	0	0	0	0	1	1	0	0	1
W Total	2	2	0	2.37	3	2	2	0	0	19	18	5	3	7
● Buck Becannon														
W 1884	NY-A	0	1	10.50	1	1	1	0	0	6	9	7	2	1
● Rod Beck														
D 1997	SF-N	0	0	0.00	1	0	0	0	0	1^1	1	0	0	1
D 1998	Chi-N	0	0	16.20	1	0	0	0	0	1^2	5	3	2	1
D 1999	Bos-A	0	0	0.00	2	0	0	0	0	2	2	0	0	2
D Total	3	0	0	5.40	4	0	0	0	0	5	8	3	2	4
L 1999	Bos-A	0	1	27.00	2	0	0	0	0	0^2	2	2	0	1
● Joe Beckwith														
L 1983	LA-N	0	0	0.00	2	0	0	0	0	2^1	1	0	2	3
W 1985	KC-A	0	0	0.00	1	0	0	0	0	2	1	0	0	3
● Hugh Bedient														
W 1912	Bos-A	1	0	0.50	4	2	1	0	0	18	10	1	7	7
● Steve Bedrosian														
L 1982	Atl-N	0	0	18.00	2	0	0	0	0	1	3	2	1	2
L 1989	SF-N	0	0	2.70	4	0	0	3	0	3^1	4	1	2	2
L 1991	Min-A	0	0	0.00	2	0	0	0	0	1^1	3	0	2	2
L Total	3	0	0	4.76	8	0	0	3	0	5^2	10	3	5	6
W 1989	SF-N	0	0	0.00	2	0	0	0	0	2^2	0	0	2	2
W 1991	Min-A	0	0	5.40	3	0	0	0	0	3^1	3	2	0	2
W Total	2	0	0	3.00	5	0	0	0	0	6	3	2	2	4
● Joe Beggs														
W 1940	Cin-N	0	0	9.00	1	0	0	0	0	1	3	1	0	1
● Hank Behrman														
W 1947	Bro-N	0	0	7.11	5	0	0	0	0	6^1	9	5	5	3
● Tim Belcher														
D 1995	Sea-A	0	1	6.23	2	0	0	0	0	4^1	4	3	5	0
L 1988	LA-N	2	0	4.11	2	2	0	0	0	15^1	12	7	4	16
L 1993	Chi-A	1	0	2.45	1	0	0	0	0	3^2	3	1	3	1
L 1995	Sea-A	0	1	6.35	1	1	0	0	0	5^2	9	4	2	1
L Total	3	3	1	4.38	4	3	0	0	0	24^2	24	12	9	18
W 1988	LA-N	1	0	6.23	2	2	0	0	0	8^2	10	6	6	10
● Stan Belinda														
D 1995	Bos-A	0	0	0.00	1	0	0	0	0	0^1	0	0	0	0
L 1990	Pit-N	0	0	2.45	3	0	0	0	0	3^2	3	1	0	4
L 1991	Pit-N	1	0	0.00	3	0	0	0	0	5	0	0	3	4
L 1992	Pit-N	0	0	0.00	2	0	0	0	0	1^2	2	0	1	2
L Total	3	1	0	0.87	8	0	0	0	0	10^1	5	1	4	10
● Gary Bell														
W 1967	Bos-A	0	1	5.06	3	1	0	1	0	5^1	8	3	1	1
● Hi Bell														
W 1926	StL-N	0	0	9.00	1	0	0	0	0	2	4	2	1	1
W 1930	StL-N	0	0	0.00	1	0	0	0	0	1	0	0	0	0
W 1933	NY-N	0	0	0.00	1	0	0	0	0	1	0	0	0	0
W Total	3	0	0	4.50	3	0	0	0	0	4	4	2	1	1
● Chief Bender														
W 1905	Phi-A	1	1	1.06	2	2	2	0	1	17	9	2	6	13
W 1910	Phi-A	1	1	1.93	2	2	2	0	0	18^2	12	4	4	14
W 1911	Phi-A	2	1	1.04	3	3	3	0	0	26	16	3	8	20
W 1913	Phi-A	2	0	4.00	2	2	2	0	0	18	19	8	1	9
W 1914	Phi-A	0	1	10.13	1	1	0	0	0	5^1	8	6	2	3
W Total	5	6	4	2.44	10	10	9	0	1	85	64	23	21	59
● Alan Benes														
L 1996	StL-N	0	1	2.84	2	1	0	0	0	6^1	3	2	2	5
L 2000	StL-N	1	0	2.25	1	1	0	0	0	8	6	2	3	5
L Total	2	1	1	2.51	3	2	0	0	0	14^1	9	4	5	10
● Andy Benes														
D 1995	Sea-A	0	0	5.40	2	2	0	0	0	11^2	10	7	9	8
D 1996	StL-N	0	0	5.14	1	1	0	0	0	7	6	4	1	9
D Total	2	0	0	5.30	3	3	0	0	0	18^2	16	11	10	17
L 1995	Sea-A	0	1	23.14	1	1	0	0	0	2^1	6	6	2	3
L 1996	StL-N	0	0	5.28	3	2	0	0	0	15^1	19	9	3	9
L Total	2	0	1	7.64	4	3	0	0	0	17^2	25	15	5	12
● Armando Benitez														
D 1996	Bal-A	2	0	2.25	3	0	0	0	0	4	1	1	2	6
D 1997	Bal-A	0	0	3.00	3	0	0	0	0	3	3	1	2	4
D 1999	NY-N	0	0	0.00	2	0	0	0	0	2^1	2	0	1	2
D 2000	NY-N	1	0	6.00	2	0	0	0	0	3	4	2	1	3
D Total	4	3	0	2.92	10	0	0	0	0	12^1	10	4	6	15
L 1996	Bal-A	0	0	7.71	3	0	0	1	0	2^1	3	2	3	2
L 1997	Bal-A	0	2	12.00	4	0	0	0	0	3	3	4	4	6
L 1999	NY-N	0	0	1.35	5	0	0	1	0	6^2	3	1	2	9
L 2000	NY-N	0	0	0.00	3	0	0	1	0	3	3	0	2	2
L Total	4	0	2	4.20	15	0	0	3	0	15	12	7	11	19
W 2000	NY-N	0	0	3.00	3	0	0	1	0	3	3	1	2	2
● Jack Bentley														
W 1923	NY-N	0	1	9.45	2	1	0	0	0	6^2	10	7	4	1
W 1924	NY-N	1	2	3.18	3	2	1	0	0	17	18	6	8	10
W Total	2	1	3	4.94	5	3	1	0	0	23^2	28	13	12	11
● Al Benton														
W 1945	Det-A	0	0	1.93	3	0	0	0	0	4^2	6	1	0	5
● Rube Benton														
W 1917	NY-N	1	1	0.00	2	2	1	0	1	14	9	0	1	8
● Jason Bere														
L 1993	Chi-A	0	0	11.57	1	1	0	0	0	2^1	5	3	2	3
● Juan Berenguer														
L 1987	Min-A	0	0	1.50	4	0	0	1	0	6	1	1	3	6
W 1987	Min-A	0	1	10.38	3	0	0	0	0	4^1	10	5	0	1
● Dwight Bernard														
D 1981	Mil-A	0	0	0.00	2	0	0	0	0	2^1	0	0	0	0
L 1982	Mil-A	0	0	0.00	1	0	0	0	0	1	0	0	0	0
W 1982	Mil-A	0	0	0.00	1	0	0	0	0	1	0	0	0	1
● Don Bessent														
W 1955	Bro-N	0	0	0.00	3	0	0	0	0	3^1	3	0	1	1
W 1956	Bro-N	1	0	1.80	2	0	0	0	0	10	8	2	3	5
W Total	2	1	0	1.35	5	0	0	0	0	13^1	11	2	4	6
● Bill Bevens														
W 1947	NY-A	0	1	2.38	2	1	1	0	0	11^1	3	3	11	7
● Jim Bibby														
L 1979	Pit-N	0	0	1.29	1	1	0	0	0	7	4	1	4	5
W 1979	Pit-N	0	0	2.61	2	2	0	0	0	10^1	10	3	2	10
● Vern Bickford														
W 1948	Bos-N	0	1	2.70	1	1	0	0	0	3^1	4	1	5	1
● Mike Bielecki														
D 1996	Atl-N	0	0	0.00	1	0	0	0	0	0^2	0	0	1	1
L 1989	Chi-N	0	1	3.65	2	2	0	0	0	12^1	7	5	6	11
L 1996	Atl-N	0	0	0.00	3	0	0	0	0	3	0	0	1	5
L Total	2	0	1	2.93	5	2	0	0	0	15^1	7	5	7	16
W 1996	Atl-N	0	0	0.00	2	0	0	0	0	3	0	0	3	6
● Jack Billingham														
L 1972	Cin-N	0	0	3.86	1	1	0	0	0	4^2	5	2	2	4
L 1973	Cin-N	0	1	4.50	2	2	0	0	0	12	9	6	4	9
L Total	2	0	1	4.32	3	3	0	0	0	16^2	14	8	6	13
W 1972	Cin-N	1	0	0.00	3	2	0	1	0	13^2	6	0	4	11
W 1975	Cin-N	0	0	1.00	3	1	0	0	0	9	8	1	5	7
W 1976	Cin-N	1	0	0.00	1	0	0	0	0	2^2	0	0	0	1
W Total	3	2	0	0.36	7	3	0	1	0	25^1	14	1	9	19
● Doug Bird														
L 1976	KC-A	1	0	1.93	1	0	0	0	0	4^2	4	1	0	1
L 1977	KC-A	0	0	0.00	3	0	0	0	0	2	4	0	0	1
L 1978	KC-A	0	1	9.00	2	0	0	0	0	1	2	1	0	1
L Total	3	1	1	2.35	6	0	0	0	0	7^2	10	2	0	3
● Bud Black														
L 1984	KC-A	0	1	7.20	1	1	0	0	0	5	7	4	1	3

YEAR	TM/L	W	L	ERA	G	GS	CG	SV	SHO	IP	H	ER	BB	SO
L 1985	KC-A	0	0	1.69	3	1	0	0	0	10^2	11	2	4	8
L Total	2	0	1	3.45	4	2	0	0	0	15^2	18	6	5	11
W 1985	KC-A	0	1	5.06	2	1	0	0	0	5^1	4	3	5	4
● **Joe Black**														
W 1952	Bro-N	1	2	2.53	3	3	1	0	0	21^1	15	6	8	9
W 1953	Bro-N	0	0	9.00	1	0	0	0	0	1	1	1	0	2
W Total	2	1	2	2.82	4	3	1	0	0	22^1	16	7	8	11
● **Ewell Blackwell**														
W 1952	NY-A	0	0	7.20	1	1	0	0	0	5	4	4	3	4
● **Willie Blair**														
D 1996	SD-N	0	0	0.00	1	0	0	0	0	2	1	0	2	3
● **Sheriff Blake**														
W 1929	Chi-N	0	1	13.50	2	0	0	0	0	1^1	4	2	0	1
● **Steve Blass**														
L 1971	Pit-N	0	1	11.57	2	2	0	0	0	7	14	9	2	11
L 1972	Pit-N	1	0	1.72	2	2	0	0	0	15^2	12	3	6	5
L Total	2	1	1	4.76	4	4	0	0	0	22^2	26	12	8	16
W 1971	Pit-N	2	0	1.00	2	2	2	0	0	18	7	2	4	13
● **Vida Blue**														
L 1971	Oak-A	0	1	6.43	1	1	0	0	0	7	7	5	2	8
L 1972	Oak-A	0	0	0.00	4	0	0	1	0	5^1	4	0	1	5
L 1973	Oak-A	0	1	10.29	2	2	0	0	0	7	8	8	5	3
L 1974	Oak-A	1	0	0.00	1	1	1	0	1	9	2	0	0	7
L 1975	Oak-A	0	0	9.00	1	1	0	0	0	3	6	3	0	2
L Total	5	1	2	4.60	9	5	1	1	1	31^1	27	16	8	25
W 1972	Oak-A	0	1	4.15	4	1	0	1	0	8^2	8	4	5	5
W 1973	Oak-A	0	1	4.91	2	2	0	0	0	11	10	6	3	8
W 1974	Oak-A	0	1	3.29	2	2	0	0	0	13^2	10	5	7	9
W Total	3	0	3	4.05	8	5	0	1	0	33^1	28	15	15	22
● **Bert Blyleven**														
L 1970	Min-A	0	0	0.00	1	0	0	0	0	2	2	0	0	2
L 1979	Pit-N	1	0	1.00	1	1	1	0	0	9	8	1	0	9
L 1987	Min-A	2	0	4.05	2	2	0	0	0	13^1	12	6	3	9
L Total	3	3	0	2.59	4	3	1	0	0	24^1	22	7	3	20
W 1979	Pit-N	1	0	1.80	2	1	0	0	0	10	8	2	3	4
W 1987	Min-A	1	1	2.77	2	2	0	0	0	13	13	4	2	12
W Total	2	2	1	2.35	4	3	0	0	0	23	21	6	5	16
● **Doug Bochtler**														
D 1996	SD-N	0	1	27.00	1	0	0	0	0	0^1	0	1	2	0
● **Mike Boddicker**														
L 1983	Bal-A	1	0	0.00	1	1	1	0	1	9	5	0	3	14
L 1988	Bos-A	0	1	20.25	1	1	0	0	0	2^2	8	6	1	2
L 1990	Bos-A	0	1	2.25	1	1	1	0	0	8	6	2	3	7
L Total	3	1	2	3.66	3	3	2	0	1	19^2	19	8	7	23
W 1983	Bal-A	1	0	0.00	1	1	1	0	0	9	3	0	0	6
● **Brian Boehringer**														
D 1996	NY-A	1	0	6.75	2	0	0	0	0	1^1	3	1	2	0
D 1997	NY-A	0	0	0.00	1	0	0	0	0	1^2	1	0	1	2
D Total	2	1	0	3.00	3	0	0	0	0	3	4	1	3	2
L 1998	SD-N	0	0	0.00	3	0	0	0	0	3	3	0	1	1
W 1996	NY-A	0	0	5.40	2	0	0	0	0	5	5	3	0	5
W 1998	SD-N	0	0	9.00	2	0	0	0	0	2	4	2	2	3
W Total	2	0	0	6.43	4	0	0	0	0	7	9	5	2	8
● **Bobby Bolin**														
W 1962	SF-N	0	0	6.75	2	0	0	0	0	2^2	4	2	2	2
● **Tom Bolton**														
L 1990	Bos-A	0	0	0.00	2	0	0	0	0	3	2	0	2	3
● **Tiny Bonham**														
W 1941	NY-A	1	0	1.00	1	1	1	0	0	9	4	1	2	2
W 1942	NY-A	0	1	4.09	2	1	1	0	0	11	9	5	3	3
W 1943	NY-A	0	1	4.50	1	1	0	0	0	8	6	4	3	9
W Total	3	1	2	3.21	4	3	2	0	0	28	19	10	8	14
● **Greg Booker**														
L 1984	SD-N	0	0	0.00	1	0	0	0	0	2	2	0	1	2
W 1984	SD-N	0	0	9.00	1	0	0	0	0	1	0	1	4	0
● **Pedro Borbon**														
L 1972	Cin-N	0	0	2.08	3	0	0	0	0	4^1	2	1	0	1
L 1973	Cin-N	1	0	0.00	4	0	0	1	0	4^2	3	0	0	3
L 1975	Cin-N	0	0	0.00	1	0	0	1	0	1	0	0	0	1
L 1976	Cin-N	0	0	0.00	2	0	0	1	0	4^1	4	0	1	0
L Total	4	1	0	0.63	10	0	0	3	0	14^1	9	1	1	5
W 1972	Cin-N	0	1	3.86	6	0	0	0	0	7	7	3	2	4
W 1975	Cin-N	0	0	6.00	3	0	0	0	0	3	3	2	2	1
W 1976	Cin-N	0	0	0.00	1	0	0	0	0	1^2	0	0	0	0
W Total	3	0	1	3.86	10	0	0	0	0	11^2	10	5	4	5
● **Pedro Borbon**														
D 1995	Atl-N	0	0	0.00	1	0	0	0	0	1	1	0	0	3
W 1995	Atl-N	0	0	0.00	1	0	0	1	0	1	0	0	0	2
● **Hank Borowy**														
W 1942	NY-A	0	0	18.00	1	1	0	0	0	3	6	6	3	1
W 1943	NY-A	1	0	2.25	1	1	0	0	0	8	6	2	3	4
W 1945	Chi-N	2	2	4.00	4	3	1	0	1	18	21	8	6	8
W Total	3	3	2	4.97	6	5	1	0	1	29	33	16	12	13

YEAR	TM/L	W	L	ERA	G	GS	CG	SV	SHO	IP	H	ER	BB	SO
● **Chris Bosio**														
D 1995	Sea-A	0	0	10.57	2	2	0	0	0	7^2	10	9	4	2
L 1995	Sea-A	0	1	3.38	1	1	0	0	0	5^1	7	2	2	3
● **Dick Bosman**														
L 1975	Oak-A	0	0	0.00	1	0	0	0	0	0^1	0	0	0	0
● **Dave Boswell**														
L 1969	Min-A	0	1	0.84	1	1	0	0	0	10^2	7	1	7	4
W 1965	Min-A	0	0	3.38	1	0	0	0	0	2^2	3	1	2	3
● **Jim Bouton**														
W 1963	NY-A	0	1	1.29	1	1	0	0	0	7	4	1	5	4
W 1964	NY-A	2	0	1.56	2	2	1	0	0	17^1	15	3	5	7
W Total	2	2	1	1.48	3	3	1	0	0	24^1	19	4	10	11
● **Oil Can Boyd**														
L 1986	Bos-A	1	1	4.61	2	2	0	0	0	13^2	17	7	3	8
W 1986	Bos-A	0	1	7.71	1	1	0	0	0	7	9	6	1	3
● **Chad Bradford**														
D 2000	Chi-A	0	0	0.00	1	0	0	0	0	0^2	2	0	0	0
● **Ralph Branca**														
W 1947	Bro-N	1	1	8.64	3	1	0	0	0	8^1	12	8	5	8
W 1949	Bro-N	0	1	4.15	1	1	0	0	0	8^2	4	4	4	6
W Total	2	1	2	6.35	4	2	0	0	0	17	16	12	9	14
● **Jeff Brantley**														
D 1995	Cin-N	0	0	6.00	3	0	0	1	0	3	5	2	0	2
L 1989	SF-N	0	0	0.00	3	0	0	0	0	5	1	0	2	3
L 1995	Cin-N	0	0	0.00	2	0	0	0	0	2^2	0	0	2	1
L Total	2	0	0	0.00	5	0	0	0	0	7^2	1	0	4	4
W 1989	SF-N	0	0	4.15	3	0	0	0	0	4^1	5	2	3	1
● **Al Brazle**														
W 1943	StL-N	0	1	3.68	1	1	0	0	0	7^1	5	3	2	4
W 1946	StL-N	0	1	5.40	1	0	0	0	0	6^2	7	4	6	4
W Total	2	0	2	4.50	2	1	0	0	0	14	12	7	8	8
● **Harry Brecheen**														
W 1943	StL-N	0	1	2.45	3	0	0	0	0	3^2	5	1	3	3
W 1944	StL-N	1	0	1.00	1	1	1	0	0	9	9	1	4	4
W 1946	StL-N	3	0	0.45	3	2	2	0	1	20	14	1	5	11
W Total	3	4	1	0.83	7	3	3	0	1	32^2	28	3	12	18
● **Don Brennan**														
W 1937	NY-N	0	0	0.00	2	0	0	0	0	3	1	0	1	1
● **Ken Brett**														
L 1974	Pit-N	0	0	7.71	1	0	0	0	0	2^1	3	2	2	1
L 1975	Pit-N	0	0	0.00	2	0	0	0	0	2^1	1	0	0	1
L Total	2	0	0	3.86	3	0	0	0	0	4^2	4	2	2	2
W 1967	Bos-A	0	0	0.00	2	0	0	0	0	1^1	0	0	1	1
● **Marv Breuer**														
W 1941	NY-A	0	0	0.00	1	0	0	0	0	3	3	0	1	2
W 1942	NY-A	0	0	—	1	0	0	0	0	0	2	0	0	0
W Total	2	0	0	0.00	2	0	0	0	0	3	5	0	1	2
● **Jim Brewer**														
W 1965	LA-N	0	0	4.50	1	0	0	0	0	2	3	1	0	1
W 1966	LA-N	0	0	0.00	1	0	0	0	0	1	0	0	0	1
W 1974	LA-N	0	0	0.00	1	0	0	0	0	0^1	0	0	0	1
W Total	3	0	0	2.70	3	0	0	0	0	3^1	3	1	0	3
● **Marshall Bridges**														
W 1962	NY-A	0	0	4.91	2	0	0	0	0	3^2	4	2	2	3
● **Tommy Bridges**														
W 1934	Det-A	1	1	3.63	3	2	1	0	0	17^1	21	7	1	12
W 1935	Det-A	2	0	2.50	2	2	2	0	0	18	18	5	4	9
W 1940	Det-A	1	0	3.00	1	1	1	0	0	9	10	3	1	5
W 1945	Det-A	0	0	16.20	1	0	0	0	0	1^2	3	3	3	1
W Total	4	4	1	3.52	7	5	4	0	0	46	52	18	9	27
● **Nelson Briles**														
L 1972	Pit-N	0	0	3.00	1	1	0	0	0	6	6	2	1	3
W 1967	StL-N	1	0	1.64	2	1	1	0	0	11	7	2	1	4
W 1968	StL-N	0	1	5.56	2	2	0	0	0	11^1	13	7	4	7
W 1971	Pit-N	1	0	0.00	1	1	1	0	1	9	2	0	2	2
W Total	3	2	1	2.59	5	4	2	0	1	31^1	22	9	7	13
● **Jim Britton**														
L 1969	Atl-N	0	0	0.00	1	0	0	0	0	0^1	0	0	1	0
● **Jim Brosnan**														
W 1961	Cin-N	0	0	7.50	3	0	0	0	0	6	9	5	4	5
● **Kevin Brown**														
D 1997	Fla-N	0	0	1.29	1	1	0	0	0	7	4	1	0	5
D 1998	SD-N	1	0	0.61	2	2	0	0	0	14^2	5	1	7	21
D Total	2	1	0	0.83	3	3	0	0	0	21^2	9	2	7	26
L 1997	Fla-N	2	0	4.20	2	2	1	0	0	15	16	7	5	11
L 1998	SD-N	1	1	2.61	2	1	1	0	0	10^1	5	3	4	12
L Total	2	3	1	3.55	4	3	2	0	0	25^1	21	10	9	23
W 1997	Fla-N	0	2	8.18	2	2	0	0	0	11	15	10	5	6
W 1998	SD-N	0	1	4.40	2	2	0	0	0	14^1	14	7	6	13
W Total	2	0	3	6.04	4	4	0	0	0	25^1	29	17	11	19
● **Mace Brown**														
W 1946	Bos-A	0	0	27.00	1	0	0	0	0	1	4	3	1	0

YEAR	TM/L	W	L	ERA	G	GS	CG	SV	SHO	IP	H	ER	BB	SO
● Mordecai Brown														
W 1906	Chi-N	1	2	3.20	3	3	2	0	1	19^2	14	7	4	12
W 1907	Chi-N	1	0	0.00	1	1	1	0	1	9	7	0	1	4
W 1908	Chi-N	2	0	0.00	2	1	1	0	1	11	6	0	1	5
W 1910	Chi-N	1	2	5.50	3	2	1	0	0	18	23	11	7	14
W Total	4	5	4	2.81	9	7	5	0	3	57^2	50	18	13	35
● Tom Browning														
L 1990	Cin-N	1	1	3.27	2	2	0	0	0	11	9	4	6	5
W 1990	Cin-N	1	0	4.50	1	1	0	0	0	6	6	3	2	2
● Warren Brusstar														
D 1981	Phi-N	0	0	4.91	2	0	0	0	0	3^2	5	2	1	3
L 1977	Phi-N	0	0	3.38	2	0	0	0	0	2^2	2	1	1	2
L 1978	Phi-N	0	0	0.00	3	0	0	0	0	2^2	2	0	1	0
L 1980	Phi-N	1	0	3.38	2	0	0	0	0	2^2	1	1	1	0
L 1984	Chi-N	0	0	0.00	3	0	0	0	0	4^1	6	0	0	1
L Total	4	1	0	1.46	10	0	0	0	0	12^1	11	2	3	3
W 1980	Phi-N	0	0	0.00	1	0	0	0	0	2^1	0	0	1	0
● Clay Bryant														
W 1938	Chi-N	0	1	6.75	1	1	0	0	0	5^1	6	4	5	3
● Ron Bryant														
L 1971	SF-N	0	0	4.50	1	0	0	0	0	2	1	1	1	2
● Mark Buehrle														
D 2000	Chi-A	0	0	0.00	1	0	0	0	0	0^1	2	0	0	1
● Bob Buhl														
W 1957	Mil-N	0	1	10.80	2	2	0	0	0	3^1	6	4	6	4
● Wally Bunker														
W 1966	Bal-A	1	0	0.00	1	1	1	0	1	9	6	0	1	6
● Dave Burba														
D 1995	Cin-N	1	0	0.00	1	0	0	0	0	1	2	0	1	0
D 1998	Cle-A	1	0	5.06	1	0	0	0	0	5^1	4	3	2	4
D 1999	Cle-A	0	0	0.00	1	1	0	0	0	4	1	0	1	0
D Total	3	2	0	2.61	3	1	0	0	0	10^1	7	3	4	4
L 1995	Cin-N	0	0	0.00	2	0	0	0	0	3^2	3	0	4	0
L 1998	Cle-A	1	0	3.00	3	0	0	0	0	6	3	2	5	8
L Total	2	1	0	1.86	5	0	0	0	0	9^2	6	2	9	8
● Lew Burdette														
W 1957	Mil-N	3	0	0.67	3	3	3	0	2	27	21	2	4	13
W 1958	Mil-N	1	2	5.64	3	3	1	0	0	22^1	22	14	4	12
W Total	2	4	2	2.92	6	6	4	0	2	49^1	43	16	8	25
● John Burkett														
D 1996	Tex-A	1	0	2.00	1	1	1	0	0	9	10	2	1	7
D 2000	Atl-N	0	0	6.75	1	0	0	0	0	1^1	1	1	0	0
D Total	2	1	0	2.61	2	1	1	0	0	10^1	11	3	1	7
● Britt Burns														
L 1983	Chi-A	0	1	0.96	1	1	0	0	0	9^1	6	1	5	8
● Todd Burns														
W 1988	Oak-A	0	0	0.00	1	0	0	0	0	0^1	0	0	0	0
W 1989	Oak-A	0	0	0.00	2	0	0	0	0	1^2	1	0	1	0
W 1990	Oak-A	0	0	16.20	2	0	0	0	0	1^2	5	3	2	0
W Total	3	0	0	7.36	5	0	0	0	0	3^2	6	3	3	0
● Ray Burris														
D 1981	Mon-N	0	1	5.06	1	1	0	0	0	5^1	7	3	4	4
L 1981	Mon-N	1	0	0.53	2	2	1	0	1	17	10	1	3	4
● Jim Burton														
W 1975	Bos-A	0	1	9.00	2	0	0	0	0	1	1	1	3	0
● Guy Bush														
W 1929	Chi-N	1	0	0.82	2	1	1	0	0	11	12	1	2	4
W 1932	Chi-N	0	1	14.29	2	2	0	0	0	5^2	5	9	6	2
W Total	2	1	1	5.40	4	3	1	0	0	16^2	17	10	8	6
● Joe Bush														
W 1913	Phi-A	1	0	1.00	1	1	1	0	0	9	5	1	4	3
W 1914	Phi-A	0	1	3.27	1	1	1	0	0	11	9	4	4	4
W 1918	Bos-A	0	1	3.00	2	1	1	1	0	9	7	3	3	0
W 1922	NY-A	0	2	4.80	2	2	1	0	0	15	21	8	5	6
W 1923	NY-A	1	1	1.08	3	1	1	0	0	16^2	7	2	4	5
W Total	5	2	5	2.67	9	6	5	1	0	60^2	49	18	20	18
● Bud Byerly														
W 1944	StL-N	0	0	0.00	1	0	0	0	0	1^1	0	0	0	1
● Tommy Byrne														
W 1949	NY-A	0	0	2.70	1	1	0	0	0	3^1	2	1	2	1
W 1955	NY-A	1	1	1.88	2	2	1	0	0	14^1	8	3	8	8
W 1956	NY-A	0	0	0.00	1	0	0	0	0	0^1	1	0	0	1
W 1957	NY-A	0	0	5.40	2	0	0	0	0	3^1	1	2	2	1
W Total	4	1	1	2.53	6	3	1	0	0	21^1	12	6	12	11
● Marty Bystrom														
L 1980	Phi-N	0	0	1.69	1	1	0	0	0	5^1	7	1	2	1
W 1980	Phi-N	0	0	5.40	1	1	0	0	0	5	10	3	1	4
W 1983	Phi-N	0	0	0.00	1	0	0	0	0	1	0	0	0	1
W Total	2	0	0	4.50	2	1	0	0	0	6	10	3	1	5
● Jose Cabrera														
D 1999	Hou-N	0	0	0.00	1	0	0	0	0	2	2	0	0	6

YEAR	TM/L	W	L	ERA	G	GS	CG	SV	SHO	IP	H	ER	BB	SO
● Greg Cadaret														
L 1988	Oak-A	0	0	27.00	1	0	0	0	0	0^1	1	1	0	0
W 1988	Oak-A	0	0	0.00	3	0	0	0	0	2	2	0	0	3
● Leon Cadore														
W 1920	Bro-N	0	1	9.00	2	1	0	0	0	2	4	2	1	1
● Mike Caldwell														
D 1981	Mil-A	0	1	4.32	2	1	0	0	0	8^1	9	4	0	4
L 1982	Mil-A	0	1	15.00	1	1	0	0	0	3	7	5	1	2
W 1982	Mil-A	2	0	2.04	3	2	1	0	1	17^2	19	4	3	6
● Ray Caldwell														
W 1920	Cle-A	0	1	27.00	1	1	0	0	0	0^1	2	1	1	0
● Jeff Calhoun														
L 1986	Hou-N	0	0	9.00	1	0	0	0	0	1	1	1	1	0
● Howie Camnitz														
W 1909	Pit-N	0	1	9.82	2	1	0	0	0	3^2	8	4	2	2
● Rick Camp														
L 1982	Atl-N	0	1	36.00	1	1	0	0	0	1	4	4	1	0
● Bill Campbell														
L 1985	StL-N	0	0	0.00	3	0	0	0	0	2^1	3	0	0	2
W 1985	StL-N	0	0	2.25	3	0	0	0	0	4	4	1	2	5
● John Candelaria														
L 1975	Pit-N	0	0	3.52	1	1	0	0	0	7^2	3	3	2	14
L 1979	Pit-N	0	0	2.57	1	1	0	0	0	7	5	2	1	4
L 1986	Cal-A	1	1	0.84	2	2	0	0	0	10^2	11	1	6	7
L Total	3	1	1	2.13	4	4	0	0	0	25^1	19	6	9	25
W 1979	Pit-N	1	1	5.00	2	2	0	0	0	9	14	5	2	4
● Tom Candiotti														
D 1996	LA-N	0	0	0.00	1	0	0	0	0	2	0	0	0	1
L 1991	Tor-A	0	1	8.22	2	2	0	0	0	7^2	17	7	2	5
● Don Cardwell														
W 1969	NY-N	0	0	0.00	1	0	0	0	0	1	0	0	0	0
● Tex Carleton														
W 1934	StL-N	0	0	7.36	2	1	0	0	0	3^2	5	3	2	2
W 1935	Chi-N	0	1	1.29	1	1	0	0	0	7	6	1	7	4
W 1938	Chi-N	0	0	∞	1	0	0	0	0	0	1	2	2	0
W Total	3	0	1	5.06	4	2	0	0	0	10^2	12	6	11	6
● Hal Carlson														
W 1929	Chi-N	0	0	6.75	2	0	0	0	0	4	7	3	1	3
● Steve Carlton														
D 1981	Phi-N	0	2	3.86	2	2	0	0	0	14	14	6	8	13
L 1976	Phi-N	0	1	5.14	1	1	0	0	0	7	8	4	5	6
L 1977	Phi-N	0	1	6.94	2	2	0	0	0	11^2	13	9	8	6
L 1978	Phi-N	1	0	4.00	1	1	1	0	0	9	8	4	2	8
L 1980	Phi-N	1	0	2.19	2	2	0	0	0	12^1	11	3	8	6
L 1983	Phi-N	2	0	0.66	2	2	0	0	0	13^2	13	1	5	13
L Total	5	4	2	3.52	8	8	1	0	0	53^2	53	21	28	39
W 1967	StL-N	0	1	0.00	1	1	0	0	0	6	3	0	2	5
W 1968	StL-N	0	0	6.75	2	0	0	0	0	4	7	3	1	3
W 1980	Phi-N	2	0	2.40	2	2	0	0	0	15	14	4	9	17
W 1983	Phi-N	0	1	2.70	1	1	0	0	0	6^2	5	2	3	7
W Total	4	2	2	2.56	6	4	0	0	0	31^2	29	9	15	32
● Hector Carrasco														
L 1995	Cin-N	0	0	0.00	1	0	0	0	0	1^1	1	0	0	3
● Don Carrithers														
L 1971	SF-N	0	0	∞	1	0	0	0	0	0	3	3	0	0
● Clay Carroll														
L 1970	Cin-N	0	0	0.00	2	0	0	1	0	1^1	2	0	0	2
L 1972	Cin-N	1	1	3.38	2	0	0	0	0	2^2	2	1	3	0
L 1973	Cin-N	1	0	1.29	3	0	0	0	0	7	5	1	1	2
L 1975	Cin-N	0	0	0.00	1	0	0	0	0	1	0	0	1	1
L Total	4	2	1	1.50	8	0	0	1	0	12	9	2	5	5
W 1970	Cin-N	1	0	0.00	4	0	0	0	0	9	5	0	2	11
W 1972	Cin-N	0	1	1.59	5	0	0	1	0	5^2	6	1	4	3
W 1975	Cin-N	1	0	3.18	5	0	0	0	0	5^2	4	2	2	3
W Total	3	2	1	1.33	14	0	0	1	0	20^1	15	3	8	17
● Bob Caruthers														
W 1885	StL-A	1	1	2.42	3	3	3	0	0	26	25	7	4	16
W 1886	StL-A	2	1	2.42	3	3	3	0	1	26	18	7	6	12
W 1887	StL-A	4	4	2.13	8	8	8	0	0	71^2	76	17	12	19
W 1889	Bro-A	0	2	3.75	4	2	2	1	0	24	28	10	6	6
W Total	4	7	8	2.50	18	16	16	1	1	147^2	147	41	28	53
● Hugh Casey														
W 1941	Bro-N	0	2	3.38	3	0	0	0	0	5^1	9	2	2	1
W 1947	Bro-N	2	0	0.87	6	0	0	1	0	10^1	5	1	1	3
W Total	2	2	2	1.72	9	0	0	1	0	15^2	14	3	3	4
● George Caster														
W 1945	Det-A	0	0	0.00	1	0	0	0	0	0^2	0	0	0	1
● Tony Castillo														
L 1993	Tor-A	0	0	0.00	2	0	0	0	0	2	0	0	1	1
W 1993	Tor-A	1	0	8.10	2	0	0	0	0	3^1	6	3	3	1
● Bobby Castillo														
L 1981	LA-N	0	0	0.00	1	0	0	0	0	1	0	0	0	1

YEAR	TM/L	W	L	ERA	G	GS	CG	SV	SHO	IP	H	ER	BB	SO
L 1985	LA-N	0	0	3.38	1	0	0	0	0	5^1	4	2	2	4
L Total	2	0	0	2.84	2	0	0	0	0	6^1	4	2	2	5
W 1981	LA-N	0	0	9.00	1	0	0	0	0	1	0	1	5	0
● Slick Castleman														
W 1936	NY-N	0	0	2.08	1	0	0	0	0	4^1	3	1	2	5
● Mike Cather														
D 1997	Atl-N	0	0	0.00	1	0	0	0	0	2	0	0	1	2
L 1997	Atl-N	0	0	0.00	4	0	0	0	0	2^2	3	0	0	3
● John Cerutti														
L 1989	Tor-A	0	0	0.00	2	0	0	0	0	2^2	0	0	3	1
● George Chalmers														
W 1915	Phi-N	0	1	2.25	1	1	1	0	0	8	8	2	3	6
● Icebox Chamberlain														
W 1888	StL-A	2	3	5.32	5	5	5	0	1	44	52	26	16	13
● Dean Chance														
L 1969	Min-A	0	0	13.50	1	0	0	0	0	2	4	3	0	2
● Spud Chandler														
W 1941	NY-A	0	1	3.60	1	1	0	0	0	5	4	2	2	2
W 1942	NY-A	0	1	1.08	2	1	0	1	0	8^1	5	1	1	3
W 1943	NY-A	2	0	0.50	2	2	2	0	1	18	17	1	3	10
W 1947	NY-A	0	0	9.00	1	0	0	0	0	2	2	2	3	1
W Total	4	2	2	1.62	6	4	2	1	1	33^1	28	6	9	16
● Norm Charlton														
D 1995	Sea-A	1	0	2.45	4	0	0	1	0	7^1	4	2	3	9
D 1997	Sea-A	0	0	0.00	2	0	0	0	0	2^1	2	0	0	1
D Total	2	1	0	1.86	6	0	0	1	0	9^2	6	2	3	10
L 1990	Cin-N	1	1	1.80	4	0	0	0	0	5	4	1	3	3
L 1995	Sea-A	1	0	0.00	3	0	0	1	0	6	1	0	1	5
L Total	2	2	1	0.82	7	0	0	1	0	11	5	1	4	8
W 1990	Cin-N	0	0	0.00	1	0	0	0	0	1	1	0	0	0
● Larry Cheney														
W 1916	Bro-N	0	0	3.00	1	0	0	0	0	3	4	1	1	5
● Tom Cheney														
W 1960	Pit-N	0	0	4.50	3	0	0	0	0	4	4	2	1	6
● Bob Chipman														
W 1945	Chi-N	0	0	0.00	1	0	0	0	0	0^1	0	0	1	0
● Randy Choate														
D 2000	NY-A	0	0	6.75	1	0	0	0	0	1^1	0	1	1	0
L 2000	NY-A	0	0	0.00	1	0	0	0	0	0^1	0	0	0	1
● Bobby Chouinard														
D 1999	Ari-N	0	0	4.50	2	0	0	0	0	2	3	1	0	1
● Larry Christenson														
D 1981	Phi-N	1	0	1.50	1	1	0	0	0	6	4	1	1	8
L 1977	Phi-N	0	0	8.10	1	1	0	0	0	3^1	7	3	0	2
L 1978	Phi-N	0	1	12.46	1	1	0	0	0	4^1	7	6	1	3
L 1980	Phi-N	0	0	4.05	2	1	0	0	0	6^2	5	3	5	2
L Total	3	0	1	7.53	4	3	0	0	0	14^1	19	12	6	7
W 1980	Phi-N	0	1	108.00	1	1	0	0	0	0^1	5	4	0	0
● Jason Christiansen														
D 2000	StL-N	0	0	0.00	1	0	0	0	0	0^1	0	0	0	1
L 2000	StL-N	0	0	0.00	2	0	0	0	0	2	0	0	0	1
● Russ Christopher														
W 1948	Cle-A	0	0	∞	1	0	0	0	0	0	2	1	0	0
● Chuck Churn														
W 1959	LA-N	0	0	27.00	1	0	0	0	0	0^2	5	2	0	0
● Eddie Cicotte														
W 1917	Chi-A	1	1	1.96	3	2	2	0	0	23	23	5	2	13
W 1919	Chi-A	1	2	2.91	3	3	2	0	0	21^2	19	7	5	7
W Total	2	2	3	2.42	6	5	4	0	0	44^2	42	12	7	20
● Jim Clancy														
L 1985	Tor-A	0	1	9.00	1	0	0	0	0	1	2	1	1	0
L 1991	Atl-N	0	0	0.00	1	0	0	0	0	0^1	0	0	0	0
L Total	2	0	1	6.75	2	0	0	0	0	1^1	2	1	1	0
W 1991	Atl-N	1	0	4.15	3	0	0	0	0	4^1	3	2	4	2
● Mark Clark														
D 1998	Chi-N	0	1	3.00	1	1	0	0	0	6	7	2	1	4
● John Clarkson														
W 1885	Chi-N	1	1	0.78	3	3	3	0	0	23	19	2	3	19
W 1886	Chi-N	2	2	2.01	4	4	3	0	1	31^1	25	7	12	28
W Total	2	3	3	1.49	7	7	6	0	1	54^1	44	9	15	47
T 1892	Cle-N	0	2	5.29	2	2	2	0	0	17	24	10	5	9
● Ken Clay														
L 1978	NY-A	0	0	0.00	1	0	0	1	0	3^2	0	0	3	2
W 1977	NY-A	0	0	2.45	2	0	0	0	0	3^2	2	1	1	0
W 1978	NY-A	0	0	11.57	1	0	0	0	0	2^1	4	3	2	2
W Total	2	0	0	6.00	3	0	0	0	0	6	6	4	3	2
● Mark Clear														
L 1979	Cal-A	0	0	4.76	1	0	0	0	0	5^2	4	3	2	3
● Roger Clemens														
D 1995	Bos-A	0	0	3.86	1	1	0	0	0	7	5	3	1	5
D 1999	NY-A	1	0	0.00	1	1	0	0	0	7	3	0	2	2

YEAR	TM/L	W	L	ERA	G	GS	CG	SV	SHO	IP	H	ER	BB	SO
D 2000	NY-A	0	2	8.18	2	2	0	0	0	11	13	10	8	10
D Total	3	1	2	4.68	4	4	0	0	0	25	21	13	11	17
L 1986	Bos-A	1	1	4.37	3	3	0	0	0	22^2	22	11	7	17
L 1988	Bos-A	0	0	3.86	1	1	0	0	0	7	6	3	0	8
L 1990	Bos-A	0	1	3.52	2	2	0	0	0	7^2	7	3	5	4
L 1999	NY-A	0	1	22.50	1	1	0	0	0	2	6	5	2	2
L 2000	NY-A	1	0	0.00	1	1	1	0	0	9	1	0	2	15
L Total	5	2	3	4.10	8	8	1	0	0	48^1	42	22	16	46
W 1986	Bos-A	0	0	3.18	2	2	0	0	0	11^1	9	4	6	11
W 1999	NY-A	1	0	1.17	1	1	0	0	0	7^2	4	1	2	4
W 2000	NY-A	1	0	0.00	1	1	0	0	0	8	2	0	0	9
W Total	3	2	0	1.67	4	4	0	0	0	27	15	5	8	24
● Reggie Cleveland														
L 1975	Bos-A	0	0	5.40	1	1	0	0	0	5	7	3	1	2
W 1975	Bos-A	0	1	6.75	3	1	0	0	0	6^2	7	5	3	5
● Tony Cloninger														
L 1970	Cin-N	0	0	3.60	1	1	0	0	0	5	7	2	4	1
W 1970	Cin-N	0	1	7.36	2	1	0	0	0	7^1	10	6	5	4
● Brad Clontz														
D 1995	Atl-N	0	0	0.00	1	0	0	0	0	1^1	0	0	0	2
L 1995	Atl-N	0	0	0.00	1	0	0	0	0	0^1	1	0	0	0
L 1996	Atl-N	0	0	0.00	1	0	0	0	0	0^2	0	0	0	0
L Total	2	0	0	0.00	2	0	0	0	0	1	1	0	0	0
W 1995	Atl-N	0	0	2.70	2	0	0	0	0	3^1	2	1	0	2
W 1996	Atl-N	0	0	0.00	3	0	0	0	0	1^2	1	0	1	2
W Total	2	0	0	1.80	5	0	0	0	0	5	3	1	1	4
● Andy Coakley														
W 1905	Phi-A	0	1	2.00	1	1	1	0	0	9	8	2	5	2
● Jim Coates														
W 1960	NY-A	0	0	5.68	3	0	0	0	0	6^1	6	4	1	3
W 1961	NY-A	0	0	0.00	1	0	0	1	0	4	1	0	1	2
W 1962	NY-A	0	1	6.75	2	0	0	0	0	2^2	1	2	1	3
W Total	3	0	1	4.15	6	0	0	1	0	13	8	6	3	8
● Dick Coffman														
W 1936	NY-N	0	0	32.40	2	0	0	0	0	1^2	5	6	1	1
W 1937	NY-N	0	0	4.15	2	0	0	0	0	4^1	2	2	5	1
W Total	2	0	0	12.00	4	0	0	0	0	6	7	8	6	2
● King Cole														
W 1910	Chi-N	0	0	3.38	1	1	0	0	0	8	10	3	3	5
● Joe Coleman														
L 1972	Det-A	1	0	0.00	1	1	1	0	1	9	7	0	3	14
● Rip Coleman														
W 1955	NY-A	0	0	9.00	1	0	0	0	0	1	5	1	0	1
● Rip Collins														
W 1921	NY-A	0	0	54.00	1	0	0	0	0	0^2	4	4	1	0
● Ray Collins														
W 1912	Bos-A	0	0	1.26	2	1	0	0	0	14^1	14	2	0	6
● Bartolo Colon														
D 1998	Cle-A	0	0	1.59	1	1	0	0	0	5^2	5	1	3	3
D 1999	Cle-A	0	1	9.00	2	2	0	0	0	9	11	9	4	12
D Total	2	0	1	6.14	3	3	0	0	0	14^2	16	10	7	15
L 1998	Cle-A	1	0	1.00	1	1	1	0	0	9	4	1	4	3
● David Cone														
D 1995	NY-A	1	0	4.60	2	2	0	0	0	15^2	15	8	9	14
D 1996	NY-A	0	1	9.00	1	1	0	0	0	6	8	6	2	8
D 1997	NY-A	0	0	16.20	1	1	0	0	0	3^1	7	6	2	2
D 1998	NY-A	1	0	0.00	1	1	0	0	0	5^2	2	0	1	6
D Total	4	2	1	5.87	5	5	0	0	0	30^2	32	20	14	30
L 1988	NY-N	1	1	4.50	3	2	1	0	0	12	10	6	5	9
L 1992	Tor-A	1	1	3.00	2	2	0	0	0	12	11	4	5	9
L 1996	NY-A	0	0	3.00	1	1	0	0	0	6	5	2	5	5
L 1998	NY-A	1	0	4.15	2	2	0	0	0	13	12	6	6	13
L 1999	NY-A	1	0	2.57	1	1	0	0	0	7	7	2	3	9
L 2000	NY-A	0	0	0.00	1	0	0	0	0	1	0	0	0	0
L Total	6	4	2	3.53	10	8	1	0	0	51	45	20	24	45
W 1992	Tor-A	0	0	3.48	2	2	0	0	0	10^1	9	4	8	8
W 1996	NY-A	1	0	1.50	1	1	0	0	0	6	4	1	4	3
W 1998	NY-A	0	0	3.00	1	1	0	0	0	6	2	2	3	4
W 1999	NY-A	1	0	0.00	1	1	0	0	0	7	1	0	5	4
W 2000	NY-A	0	0	0.00	1	0	0	0	0	0^1	0	0	0	0
W Total	5	2	0	2.12	6	5	0	0	0	29^2	16	7	20	19
● Gene Conley														
W 1957	Mil-N	0	0	10.80	1	0	0	0	0	1^2	2	2	1	0
● Pete Conway														
W 1887	Det-N	2	2	3.00	4	4	4	0	0	33	37	11	6	10
● Dennis Cook														
D 1996	Tex-A	0	0	0.00	2	0	0	0	0	1^1	0	0	1	0
D 1997	Fla-N	1	0	0.00	2	0	0	0	0	3	0	0	1	3
D 1999	NY-N	0	0	0.00	1	0	0	0	0	1^2	1	0	1	1
D 2000	NY-N	0	0	0.00	2	0	0	0	0	1^1	0	0	2	1
D Total	4	1	0	0.00	7	0	0	0	0	7^1	1	0	5	5
L 1997	Fla-N	0	0	0.00	2	0	0	0	0	2^1	0	0	0	2
L 1999	NY-N	0	0	0.00	3	0	0	0	0	1^1	1	0	2	1
L 2000	NY-N	0	0	0.00	1	0	0	0	0	1	1	0	0	2
L Total	3	0	0	0.00	6	0	0	0	0	4^2	2	0	2	5

YEAR TM/L	W	L	ERA	G	GS	CG	SV	SHO	IP	H	ER	BB	SO
W 1997 Fla-N	1	0	0.00	3	0	0	0	0	3^2	1	0	1	5
W 2000 NY-N	0	0	0.00	3	0	0	0	0	0^2	1	0	3	1
W Total 2	1	0	0.00	6	0	0	0	0	4^1	2	0	4	6
● Jack Coombs													
W 1910 Phi-A	3	0	3.33	3	3	3	0	0	27	23	10	14	17
W 1911 Phi-A	1	0	1.35	2	2	1	0	0	20	11	3	6	16
W 1916 Bro-N	1	0	4.26	1	1	0	0	0	6^1	7	3	1	1
W Total 3	5	0	2.70	6	6	4	0	0	53^1	41	16	21	34
● Mort Cooper													
W 1942 StL-N	0	1	5.54	2	2	0	0	0	13	17	8	4	9
W 1943 StL-N	1	1	2.81	2	2	1	0	0	16	11	5	3	10
W 1944 StL-N	1	1	1.13	2	2	1	0	1	16	9	2	5	16
W Total 3	2	3	3.00	6	6	2	0	1	45	37	15	12	35
● Rocky Coppinger													
L 1996 Bal-A	0	1	8.44	1	1	0	0	0	5^1	6	5	1	3
● Doug Corbett													
L 1986 Cal-A	1	0	5.40	3	0	0	0	0	6^2	9	4	2	2
● Joe Corbett													
T 1896 Bal-N	2	0	0.53	2	2	2	0	1	17	11	1	7	10
T 1897 Bal-N	1	0	9.00	2	1	1	0	0	12	21	12	8	5
T Total 2	3	0	4.03	4	3	3	0	1	29	32	13	15	15
● Rheal Cormier													
D 1995 Bos-A	0	0	13.50	2	0	0	0	0	0^2	2	1	1	2
D 1999 Bos-A	0	0	0.00	2	0	0	0	0	4	2	0	1	4
D Total 2	0	0	1.93	4	0	0	0	0	4^2	4	1	2	6
L 1999 Bos-A	0	0	0.00	4	0	0	0	0	3^2	3	0	3	4
● Jim Corsi													
D 1998 Bos-A	0	0	0.00	2	0	0	0	0	3	1	0	1	2
L 1992 Oak-A	0	0	0.00	3	0	0	0	0	2	2	0	3	0
● Al Corwin													
W 1951 NY-N	0	0	0.00	1	0	0	0	0	1^2	1	0	0	1
● Stan Coveleski													
W 1920 Cle-A	3	0	0.67	3	3	3	0	1	27	15	2	2	8
W 1925 Was-A	0	2	3.77	2	2	1	0	0	14^1	16	6	5	3
W Total 2	3	2	1.74	5	5	4	0	1	41^1	31	8	7	11
● Danny Cox													
L 1985 StL-N	1	0	3.00	1	1	0	0	0	6	4	2	5	4
L 1987 StL-N	1	1	2.12	2	2	2	0	1	17	17	4	3	11
L 1992 Pit-N	0	0	0.00	2	0	0	0	0	1^1	1	0	1	1
L 1993 Tor-A	0	0	0.00	2	0	0	0	0	5	3	0	2	5
L Total 4	2	1	1.84	7	3	2	0	1	29^1	25	6	11	21
W 1985 StL-N	0	0	1.29	2	2	0	0	0	14	14	2	4	13
W 1987 StL-N	1	2	7.71	3	2	0	0	0	11^2	13	10	8	9
W 1993 Tor-A	0	0	8.10	3	0	0	0	0	3^1	6	3	5	6
W Total 3	1	2	4.66	8	4	0	0	0	29	33	15	17	28
● Tim Crabtree													
D 1998 Tex-A	0	0	0.00	2	0	0	0	0	4	1	0	0	2
D 1999 Tex-A	0	0	5.40	2	0	0	0	0	1^2	1	1	1	1
D Total 2	0	0	1.59	4	0	0	0	0	5^2	2	1	1	3
● Roger Craig													
W 1955 Bro-N	1	0	3.00	1	1	0	0	0	6	4	2	5	4
W 1956 Bro-N	0	1	12.00	2	1	0	0	0	6	10	8	3	4
W 1959 LA-N	0	1	8.68	2	2	0	0	0	9^1	15	9	5	8
W 1964 StL-N	1	0	0.00	2	0	0	0	0	5	2	0	3	9
W Total 4	2	2	6.49	7	4	0	0	0	26^1	31	19	16	25
● Doc Crandall													
W 1911 NY-N	1	0	0.00	2	0	0	0	0	4	2	0	0	2
W 1912 NY-N	0	0	0.00	1	0	0	0	0	2	1	0	0	2
W 1913 NY-N	0	0	3.86	2	0	0	0	0	4^2	4	2	0	2
W Total 3	1	0	1.69	5	0	0	0	0	10^2	7	2	0	6
● Ed Crane													
W 1888 NY-N	1	1	2.12	2	2	2	0	0	17	15	4	6	12
W 1889 NY-N	4	1	3.72	5	5	4	0	0	38^2	29	16	32	19
W Total 2	5	2	3.23	7	7	6	0	0	55^2	44	20	38	31
● Steve Crawford													
L 1986 Bos-A	1	0	0.00	1	0	0	0	0	1^2	1	0	2	1
W 1986 Bos-A	1	0	6.23	3	0	0	0	0	4^1	5	3	0	4
● General Crowder													
W 1933 Was-A	0	1	7.36	2	2	0	0	0	11	16	9	5	7
W 1934 Det-A	0	1	1.50	2	1	0	0	0	6	6	1	1	2
W 1935 Det-A	1	0	1.00	1	1	1	0	0	9	5	1	3	5
W Total 3	1	2	3.81	5	4	1	0	0	26	27	11	9	14
● Mike Cuellar													
L 1969 Bal-A	0	0	2.25	1	1	0	0	0	8	3	2	1	7
L 1970 Bal-A	0	0	12.46	1	1	0	0	0	4^1	10	6	1	2
L 1971 Bal-A	1	0	1.00	1	1	1	0	0	9	6	1	1	2
L 1973 Bal-A	0	1	1.80	1	1	0	0	0	10	4	2	3	11
L 1974 Bal-A	1	1	2.84	2	2	0	0	0	12^2	9	4	13	6
L Total 5	2	2	3.07	6	6	2	0	0	44	32	15	19	28
W 1969 Bal-A	1	0	1.13	2	2	1	0	0	16	13	2	4	13
W 1970 Bal-A	1	0	3.18	2	2	1	0	0	11^1	10	4	2	5
W 1971 Bal-A	0	2	3.86	2	2	0	0	0	14	11	6	6	10
W Total 3	2	2	2.61	6	6	2	0	0	41^1	34	12	12	28

YEAR TM/L	W	L	ERA	G	GS	CG	SV	SHO	IP	H	ER	BB	SO
● John Cumberland													
L 1971 SF-N	0	1	9.00	1	1	0	0	0	3	7	3	0	4
● John Cummings													
D 1995 LA-N	0	0	20.25	2	0	0	0	0	1^1	3	3	2	3
● Nig Cuppy													
T 1892 Cle-N	0	1	1.13	1	1	1	0	0	8	6	1	4	1
T 1895 Cle-N	1	1	3.18	2	2	2	0	0	17	14	6	4	6
T 1896 Cle-N	0	2	4.76	2	2	2	0	0	17	19	9	0	4
T Total 3	1	4	3.43	5	5	5	0	0	42	39	16	8	11
● Mike Cvengros													
W 1927 Pit-N	0	0	3.86	2	0	0	0	0	2^1	3	1	0	2
● Omar Daal													
D 1999 Ari-N	0	1	6.75	1	1	0	0	0	4	6	3	3	4
● Ed Daily													
W 1890 Lou-A	0	2	2.65	2	2	2	0	0	17	12	5	8	5
● Bud Daley													
W 1961 NY-A	1	0	0.00	2	0	0	0	0	7	5	0	0	3
W 1962 NY-A	0	0	0.00	1	0	0	0	0	1	1	0	1	0
W Total 2	1	0	0.00	3	0	0	0	0	8	6	0	1	3
● Dave Danforth													
W 1917 Chi-A	0	0	18.00	1	0	0	0	0	1	3	2	0	2
● Pat Darcy													
W 1975 Cin-N	0	1	4.50	2	0	0	0	0	4	3	2	2	1
● Ron Darling													
L 1986 NY-N	0	0	7.20	1	1	0	0	0	5	6	4	2	5
L 1988 NY-N	0	1	7.71	2	2	0	0	0	7	11	6	4	7
L 1992 Oak-A	0	1	3.00	1	1	0	0	0	6	4	2	2	3
L Total 3	0	2	6.00	4	4	0	0	0	18	21	12	8	15
W 1986 NY-N	1	1	1.53	3	3	0	0	0	17^2	13	3	10	12
● Curt Davis													
W 1941 Bro-N	0	1	5.06	1	1	0	0	0	5^1	6	3	3	1
● Storm Davis													
L 1983 Bal-A	0	0	0.00	1	1	0	0	0	6	5	0	2	2
L 1988 Oak-A	0	0	0.00	1	1	0	0	0	6^1	2	0	5	4
L 1989 Oak-A	0	1	7.11	1	1	0	0	0	6^1	5	5	2	3
L Total 3	0	1	2.41	3	3	0	0	0	18^2	12	5	9	9
W 1983 Bal-A	1	0	5.40	1	1	0	0	0	5	6	3	1	3
W 1988 Oak-A	0	2	11.25	2	2	0	0	0	8	14	10	1	7
W Total 2	1	2	9.00	3	3	0	0	0	13	20	13	2	10
● Ron Davis													
D 1981 NY-A	1	0	0.00	3	0	0	0	0	6	1	0	2	6
L 1980 NY-A	0	0	2.25	1	0	0	0	0	4	3	1	1	3
L 1981 NY-A	0	0	0.00	2	0	0	0	0	3^1	0	0	2	4
L Total 2	0	0	1.23	3	0	0	0	0	7^1	3	1	3	7
W 1981 NY-A	0	0	23.14	4	0	0	0	0	2^1	4	6	5	4
● Joe Dawson													
W 1927 Pit-N	0	0	0.00	1	0	0	0	0	1	0	0	0	0
● Ken Dayley													
L 1985 StL-N	0	0	0.00	5	0	0	2	0	6	2	0	1	3
L 1987 StL-N	0	0	0.00	3	0	0	2	0	4	1	0	2	4
L Total 2	0	0	0.00	8	0	0	4	0	10	3	0	3	7
W 1985 StL-N	1	0	0.00	4	0	0	0	0	6	1	0	3	5
W 1987 StL-N	0	0	1.93	4	0	0	1	0	4^2	2	1	0	3
W Total 2	1	0	0.84	8	0	0	1	0	10^2	3	1	3	8
● Dizzy Dean													
W 1934 StL-N	2	1	1.73	3	3	2	0	1	26	20	5	5	17
W 1938 Chi-N	0	1	6.48	2	1	0	0	0	8^1	8	6	1	2
W Total 2	2	2	2.88	5	4	2	0	1	34^1	28	11	6	19
● Paul Dean													
W 1934 StL-N	2	0	1.00	2	2	2	0	0	18	15	2	7	11
● Wayland Dean													
W 1924 NY-N	0	0	4.50	1	0	0	0	0	2	3	1	0	2
● Miguel Del Toro													
D 2000 SF-N	0	0	0.00	1	0	0	0	0	1	1	0	0	2
● Jose DeLeon													
L 1993 Chi-A	0	0	1.93	2	0	0	0	0	4^2	7	1	1	6
● Wheezer Dell													
W 1916 Bro-N	0	0	0.00	1	0	0	0	0	1	1	0	0	0
● Al Demaree													
W 1913 NY-N	0	1	4.50	1	1	0	0	0	4	7	2	1	0
● Larry Demery													
L 1974 Pit-N	0	0	36.00	2	0	0	0	0	1	3	4	2	0
L 1975 Pit-N	0	0	18.00	1	0	0	0	0	2	4	4	1	1
L Total 2	0	0	24.00	3	0	0	0	0	3	7	8	3	1
● John Denny													
L 1983 Phi-N	0	1	0.00	1	1	0	0	0	6	5	0	3	3
W 1983 Phi-N	1	1	3.46	2	2	0	0	0	13	12	5	3	9
● Sean DePaula													
D 1999 Cle-A	0	0	1.80	3	0	0	0	0	5	2	1	3	5

YEAR	TM/L	W	L	ERA	G	GS	CG	SV	SHO	IP	H	ER	BB	SO
● Paul Derringer														
W 1931	StL-N	0	2	4.26	3	2	0	0	0	12^2	14	6	7	14
W 1939	Cin-N	0	1	2.35	2	2	1	0	0	15^1	9	4	3	9
W 1940	Cin-N	2	1	2.79	3	3	2	0	0	19^1	17	6	10	6
W 1945	Chi-N	0	0	6.75	3	0	0	0	0	5^1	5	4	7	1
W Total	4	2	4	3.42	11	7	3	0	0	52^2	45	20	27	30
● Jim Devlin														
W 1888	StL-A	1	0	2.57	1	0	0	0	0	7	5	2	2	5
● Carlos Diaz														
L 1985	LA-N	0	0	3.00	2	0	0	0	0	3	5	1	1	2
● Rob Dibble														
L 1990	Cin-N	0	0	0.00	4	0	0	1	0	5	0	0	1	10
W 1990	Cin-N	1	0	0.00	3	0	0	0	0	4^2	3	0	1	4
● Murry Dickson														
W 1943	StL-N	0	0	0.00	1	0	0	0	0	0^2	0	0	1	0
W 1946	StL-N	0	1	3.86	2	2	0	0	0	14	11	6	4	7
W 1958	NY-A	0	0	4.50	2	0	0	0	0	4	4	2	0	1
W Total	3	0	1	3.86	5	2	0	0	0	18^2	15	8	5	8
● Bill Dinneen														
W 1903	Bos-A	3	1	2.06	4	4	4	0	2	35	29	8	8	28
● Art Ditmar														
W 1957	NY-A	0	0	0.00	2	0	0	0	0	6	2	0	0	2
W 1958	NY-A	0	0	0.00	1	0	0	0	0	3^2	2	0	0	2
W 1960	NY-A	0	2	21.60	2	2	0	0	0	1^2	6	4	1	0
W Total	3	0	2	3.18	5	2	0	0	0	11^1	10	4	1	4
● Joe Dobson														
W 1946	Bos-A	1	0	0.00	3	1	1	0	0	12^2	4	0	3	10
● Pat Dobson														
W 1968	Det-A	0	0	3.86	3	0	0	0	0	4^2	5	2	1	0
W 1971	Bal-A	0	0	4.05	3	1	0	0	0	6^2	13	3	4	6
W Total	2	0	0	3.97	6	1	0	0	0	11^1	18	5	5	6
● Atley Donald														
W 1941	NY-A	0	0	9.00	1	1	0	0	0	4	6	4	3	2
W 1942	NY-A	0	1	6.00	1	1	0	0	0	3	3	2	2	1
W Total	2	0	1	7.71	2	1	0	0	0	7	9	6	5	3
● Blix Donnelly														
W 1944	StL-N	1	0	0.00	2	0	0	0	0	6	2	0	1	9
● Dick Donovan														
W 1959	Chi-A	0	1	5.40	3	1	0	1	0	8^1	4	5	3	5
● Bill Donovan														
W 1907	Det-A	0	1	1.71	2	2	2	0	0	21	17	4	5	16
W 1908	Det-A	0	2	4.24	2	2	2	0	0	17	17	8	4	10
W 1909	Det-A	1	1	3.00	2	2	1	0	0	12	7	4	8	7
W Total	3	1	4	2.88	6	6	5	0	0	50	41	16	17	33
● Octavio Dotel														
D 1999	NY-N	0	0	54.00	1	0	0	0	0	0^1	1	2	2	0
L 1999	NY-N	1	0	3.00	1	0	0	0	0	3	4	1	2	5
● Richard Dotson														
L 1983	Chi-A	0	1	10.80	1	1	0	0	0	5	6	6	3	3
● Phil Douglas														
W 1918	Chi-N	0	1	0.00	1	0	0	0	0	1	1	0	0	0
W 1921	NY-N	2	1	2.08	3	3	2	0	0	26	20	6	5	17
W Total	2	2	2	2.00	4	3	2	0	0	27	21	6	5	17
● Al Downing														
L 1974	LA-N	0	0	0.00	1	0	0	0	0	4	1	0	1	0
W 1963	NY-A	0	1	5.40	1	1	0	0	0	5	7	3	1	6
W 1964	NY-A	0	1	8.22	3	1	0	0	0	7^2	9	7	2	5
W 1974	LA-N	0	1	2.45	1	1	0	0	0	3^2	4	1	4	3
W Total	3	0	3	6.06	5	3	0	0	0	16^1	20	11	7	14
● Kelly Downs														
L 1987	SF-N	0	0	0.00	1	0	0	0	0	1^1	1	0	1	0
L 1989	SF-N	0	0	3.12	2	0	0	0	0	8^2	8	3	6	6
L 1992	Oak-A	0	1	3.86	2	0	0	0	0	2^1	3	1	1	0
L Total	3	1	1	2.92	5	0	0	0	0	12^1	12	4	8	6
W 1989	SF-N	0	0	7.71	3	0	0	0	0	4^2	3	4	2	4
● Paul Doyle														
L 1969	Atl-N	0	0	0.00	1	0	0	0	0	1	2	0	1	3
● Doug Drabek														
L 1990	Pit-N	1	1	1.65	2	2	1	0	0	16^1	12	3	3	13
L 1991	Pit-N	1	1	0.60	2	2	1	0	0	15	10	1	5	10
L 1992	Pit-N	0	3	3.71	3	3	0	0	0	17	18	7	6	10
L Total	3	2	5	2.05	7	7	2	0	0	48^1	40	11	14	33
● Moe Drabowsky														
W 1966	Bal-A	1	0	0.00	1	0	0	0	0	6^2	1	0	2	11
W 1970	Bal-A	0	0	2.70	2	0	0	0	0	3^1	2	1	1	1
W Total	2	1	0	0.90	3	0	0	0	0	10	3	1	3	12
● Dick Drago														
L 1975	Bos-A	0	0	0.00	2	0	0	2	0	4^2	2	0	1	2
W 1975	Bos-A	0	1	2.25	2	0	0	0	0	4	3	1	1	1
● Dave Dravecky														
L 1984	SD-N	0	0	0.00	3	0	0	0	0	6	2	0	0	5
L 1987	SF-N	1	1	0.60	2	2	1	0	1	15	7	1	4	14
L Total	2	1	1	0.43	5	2	1	0	1	21	9	1	4	19
W 1984	SD-N	0	0	0.00	2	0	0	0	0	4^2	3	0	1	5
● Darren Dreifort														
D 1996	LA-N	0	0	0.00	1	0	0	0	0	0^2	0	0	0	0
● Clem Dreisewerd														
W 1946	Bos-A	0	0	0.00	1	0	0	0	0	0^1	0	0	0	0
● Karl Drews														
W 1947	NY-A	0	0	3.00	2	0	0	0	0	3	2	1	1	0
● Don Drysdale														
W 1956	Bro-N	0	0	9.00	1	0	0	0	0	2	2	2	1	1
W 1959	LA-N	1	0	1.29	1	1	0	0	0	7	11	1	4	5
W 1963	LA-N	1	0	0.00	1	1	1	0	1	9	3	0	1	9
W 1965	LA-N	1	1	3.86	2	2	1	0	0	11^2	12	5	3	15
W 1966	LA-N	0	2	4.50	2	2	1	0	0	10	8	5	3	6
W Total	5	3	3	2.95	7	6	3	0	1	39^2	36	13	12	36
● Tom Dukes														
W 1971	Bal-A	0	0	0.00	2	0	0	0	0	4	2	0	0	1
● Ryne Duren														
W 1958	NY-A	1	1	1.93	3	0	0	1	0	9^1	7	2	6	14
W 1960	NY-A	0	0	2.25	2	0	0	0	0	4	2	1	1	5
W Total	2	1	1	2.03	5	0	0	1	0	13^1	9	3	7	19
● George Earnshaw														
W 1929	Phi-A	1	1	2.63	2	2	1	0	0	13^2	14	4	6	17
W 1930	Phi-A	2	0	0.72	3	3	2	0	0	25	13	2	7	19
W 1931	Phi-A	1	2	1.88	3	3	2	0	1	24	12	5	4	20
W Total	3	4	3	1.58	8	8	5	0	1	62^2	39	11	17	56
● Jamie Easterly														
D 1981	Mil-A	0	0	6.75	2	0	0	0	0	1^1	2	1	0	1
● Rawly Eastwick														
L 1975	Cin-N	1	0	0.00	2	0	0	1	0	3^2	2	0	2	1
L 1976	Cin-N	1	0	12.00	2	0	0	0	0	3	7	4	2	1
L 1978	Phi-N	0	0	9.00	1	0	0	0	0	1	3	1	0	1
L Total	3	2	0	5.87	5	0	0	1	0	7^2	12	5	4	3
W 1975	Cin-N	2	0	2.25	5	0	0	1	0	8	6	2	3	4
● Dennis Eckersley														
D 1996	StL-N	0	0	0.00	3	0	0	3	0	3^2	3	0	0	2
D 1998	Bos-A	0	0	9.00	1	0	0	0	0	1	1	1	0	1
D Total	2	0	0	1.93	4	0	0	3	0	4^2	4	1	0	3
L 1984	Chi-N	0	1	8.44	1	1	0	0	0	5^1	9	5	0	0
L 1988	Oak-A	0	0	0.00	4	0	0	4	0	6	1	0	2	5
L 1989	Oak-A	0	0	1.59	4	0	0	3	0	5^2	4	1	0	2
L 1990	Oak-A	0	0	0.00	3	0	0	2	0	3^1	2	0	0	3
L 1992	Oak-A	0	0	6.00	3	0	0	1	0	3	8	2	0	2
L 1996	StL-N	1	0	0.00	3	0	0	1	0	3^1	2	0	0	4
L Total	6	1	1	2.70	18	1	0	11	0	26^2	26	8	2	16
W 1988	Oak-A	0	1	10.80	2	0	0	0	0	1^2	2	2	1	2
W 1989	Oak-A	0	0	0.00	2	0	0	1	0	1^2	0	0	0	0
W 1990	Oak-A	0	1	6.75	2	0	0	0	0	1^1	3	1	0	1
W Total	3	0	2	5.79	6	0	0	1	0	4^2	5	3	1	3
● Howard Ehmke														
W 1929	Phi-A	1	0	1.42	2	2	1	0	0	12^2	14	2	3	13
● Red Ehret														
W 1890	Lou-A	2	0	1.35	3	2	2	1	0	20	12	3	6	13
● Mark Eichhorn														
L 1992	Tor-A	0	0	0.00	1	0	0	0	0	1	0	0	0	0
L 1993	Tor-A	0	0	0.00	1	0	0	0	0	2	1	0	1	1
L Total	2	0	0	0.00	2	0	0	0	0	3	1	0	1	1
W 1992	Tor-A	0	0	0.00	1	0	0	0	0	1	0	0	0	1
W 1993	Tor-A	0	0	0.00	1	0	0	0	0	0^1	1	0	1	0
W Total	2	0	0	0.00	2	0	0	0	0	1^1	1	0	1	1
● Scott Elarton														
D 1998	Hou-N	0	1	4.50	1	0	0	0	0	2	1	1	1	3
D 1999	Hou-N	0	0	3.86	2	0	0	0	0	2^1	4	1	1	3
D Total	2	0	1	4.15	3	0	0	0	0	4^1	5	2	2	6
● Hod Eller														
W 1919	Cin-N	2	0	2.00	2	2	2	0	1	18	13	4	2	15
● Dock Ellis														
L 1970	Pit-N	0	1	2.79	1	1	0	0	0	9^2	9	3	4	1
L 1971	Pit-N	1	0	3.60	1	1	0	0	0	5	6	2	4	1
L 1972	Pit-N	0	1	0.00	1	1	0	0	0	5	5	0	1	3
L 1975	Pit-N	0	0	0.00	1	0	0	0	0	2	2	0	0	2
L 1976	NY-A	1	0	3.38	1	1	0	0	0	8	6	3	2	5
L Total	5	2	2	2.43	5	4	0	0	0	29^2	28	8	11	12
W 1971	Pit-N	0	1	15.43	1	1	0	0	0	2^1	4	4	1	1
W 1976	NY-A	0	1	10.80	1	1	0	0	0	3^1	7	4	0	1
W Total	2	0	2	12.71	2	2	0	0	0	5^2	11	8	1	2
● Alan Embree														
D 1996	Cle-A	0	0	9.00	3	0	0	0	0	1	0	1	0	1
D 2000	SF-N	0	0	0.00	2	0	0	0	0	1^2	0	0	0	0
D Total	2	0	0	3.38	5	0	0	0	0	2^2	0	1	0	1
L 1995	Cle-A	0	0	0.00	1	0	0	0	0	0^1	0	0	0	1
L 1997	Atl-N	0	0	0.00	1	0	0	0	0	1	0	0	1	1
L Total	2	0	0	0.00	2	0	0	0	0	1^1	0	0	1	2

YEAR	TM/L	W	L	ERA	G	GS	CG	SV	SHO	IP	H	ER	BB	SO
W 1995	Cle-A	0	0	2.70	4	0	0	0	0	3^1	2	1	2	2
● Paul Erickson														
W 1945	Chi-N	0	0	3.86	4	0	0	0	0	7	8	3	3	5
● Scott Erickson														
D 1996	Bal-A	0	0	4.05	1	1	0	0	0	6^2	6	3	2	6
D 1997	Bal-A	1	0	4.05	1	1	0	0	0	6^2	7	3	2	6
D Total	2	1	0	4.05	2	2	0	0	0	13^1	13	6	4	12
L 1991	Min-A	0	0	4.50	1	1	0	0	0	4	3	2	5	2
L 1996	Bal-A	0	1	2.38	2	2	0	0	0	11^1	14	3	4	8
L 1997	Bal-A	1	0	4.26	2	2	0	0	0	12^2	15	6	1	6
L Total	3	1	1	3.54	5	5	0	0	0	28	32	11	10	16
W 1991	Min-A	0	0	5.06	2	2	0	0	0	10^2	10	6	4	5
● Carl Erskine														
W 1949	Bro-N	0	0	16.20	2	0	0	0	0	1^2	3	3	1	0
W 1952	Bro-N	1	1	4.50	3	2	1	0	0	18	12	9	10	10
W 1953	Bro-N	1	0	5.79	3	3	1	0	0	14	14	9	9	16
W 1955	Bro-N	0	0	9.00	1	1	0	0	0	3	3	3	2	3
W 1956	Bro-N	0	1	5.40	2	1	0	0	0	5	4	3	2	2
W Total	5	2	2	5.83	11	7	2	0	0	41^2	36	27	24	31
● Duke Esper														
T 1894	Bal-N	0	1	4.00	1	1	1	0	0	9	13	4	1	3
T 1895	Bal-N	1	0	0.00	1	1	1	0	1	9	5	0	0	3
T Total	2	1	1	2.00	2	2	2	0	1	18	18	4	1	6
● Shawn Estes														
D 1997	SF-N	0	0	15.00	1	1	0	0	0	3	5	5	4	3
D 2000	SF-N	0	0	6.00	1	1	0	0	0	3	3	2	3	3
D Total	2	0	0	10.50	2	2	0	0	0	6	8	7	7	6
● Red Faber														
W 1917	Chi-A	3	1	2.33	4	3	2	0	0	27	21	7	3	9
● Roy Face														
W 1960	Pit-N	0	0	5.23	4	0	0	3	0	10^1	9	6	2	4
● Steve Farr														
L 1985	KC-A	1	0	1.42	2	0	0	0	0	6^1	4	1	1	3
● Jeff Fassero														
D 1997	Sea-A	1	0	1.13	1	1	0	0	0	8	3	1	4	3
D 1999	Tex-A	0	0	9.00	1	0	0	0	0	1	2	1	1	1
D Total	2	1	0	2.00	2	1	0	0	0	9	5	2	5	4
● Bob Feller														
W 1948	Cle-A	0	2	5.02	2	2	1	0	0	14^1	10	8	5	7
● Alex Ferguson														
W 1925	Was-A	1	1	3.21	2	2	0	0	0	14	13	5	6	11
● Alex Fernandez														
D 1997	Fla-N	1	0	2.57	1	1	0	0	0	7	7	2	0	5
L 1993	Chi-A	0	2	1.80	2	2	0	0	0	15	15	3	6	10
L 1997	Fla-N	0	1	16.88	1	1	0	0	0	2^2	6	5	1	3
L Total	2	0	3	4.08	3	3	0	0	0	17^2	21	8	7	13
● Sid Fernandez														
L 1986	NY-N	0	1	4.50	1	1	0	0	0	6	3	3	1	5
L 1988	NY-N	0	1	13.50	1	1	0	0	0	4	7	6	1	5
L Total	2	0	2	8.10	2	2	0	0	0	10	10	9	2	10
W 1986	NY-N	0	0	1.35	3	0	0	0	0	6^2	6	1	1	10
● Tom Ferrick														
W 1950	NY-A	1	0	0.00	1	0	0	0	0	1	1	0	1	0
● Dave Ferriss														
W 1946	Bos-A	1	0	2.03	2	2	1	0	1	13^1	13	3	2	4
● Ed Figueroa														
L 1976	NY-A	0	1	5.84	2	2	0	0	0	12^1	14	8	2	5
L 1977	NY-A	0	0	10.80	1	1	0	0	0	3^1	5	4	2	3
L 1978	NY-A	0	1	27.00	1	1	0	0	0	1	5	3	0	0
L Total	3	0	2	8.10	4	4	0	0	0	16^2	24	15	4	8
W 1976	NY-A	0	1	5.63	1	1	0	0	0	8	6	5	5	2
W 1978	NY-A	0	1	8.10	2	2	0	0	0	6^2	9	6	5	2
W Total	2	0	2	6.75	3	3	0	0	0	14^2	15	11	10	4
● Rollie Fingers														
D 1981	Mil-A	1	0	3.86	3	0	0	1	0	4^2	7	2	1	5
L 1971	Oak-A	0	0	7.71	2	0	0	0	0	2^1	2	2	1	2
L 1972	Oak-A	1	0	1.69	3	0	0	0	0	5^1	4	1	1	3
L 1973	Oak-A	0	1	1.93	3	0	0	1	0	4^2	4	1	2	4
L 1974	Oak-A	0	0	3.00	2	0	0	1	0	3	3	1	1	3
L 1975	Oak-A	0	1	6.75	1	0	0	0	0	4	5	3	1	3
L Total	5	1	2	3.72	11	0	0	2	0	19^1	18	8	6	15
W 1972	Oak-A	1	1	1.74	6	0	0	2	0	10^1	4	2	4	11
W 1973	Oak-A	0	1	0.66	6	0	0	2	0	13^2	13	1	4	8
W 1974	Oak-A	1	0	1.93	4	0	0	2	0	9^1	8	2	2	6
W Total	3	2	2	1.35	16	0	0	6	0	33^1	25	5	10	25
● Chuck Finley														
L 1986	Cal-A	0	0	0.00	3	0	0	0	0	2	1	0	0	1
● Ray Fisher														
W 1919	Cin-N	0	1	2.35	2	1	0	0	0	7^2	7	2	2	2
● Freddie Fitzsimmons														
W 1933	NY-N	0	1	5.14	1	1	0	0	0	7	9	4	0	2
W 1936	NY-N	0	2	5.40	2	2	1	0	0	11^2	13	7	2	6

YEAR	TM/L	W	L	ERA	G	GS	CG	SV	SHO	IP	H	ER	BB	SO
W 1941	Bro-N	0	0	0.00	1	1	0	0	0	7	4	0	3	1
W Total	3	0	3	3.86	4	4	1	0	0	25^2	26	11	5	9
● Mike Flanagan														
L 1979	Bal-A	1	0	5.14	1	1	0	0	0	7	6	4	1	2
L 1983	Bal-A	1	0	1.80	1	1	0	0	0	5	5	1	0	1
L 1989	Tor-A	0	1	10.38	1	1	0	0	0	4^1	7	5	1	3
L Total	3	2	1	5.51	3	3	0	0	0	16^1	18	10	2	6
W 1979	Bal-A	1	1	3.00	3	2	1	0	0	15	18	5	2	13
W 1983	Bal-A	0	0	4.50	1	1	0	0	0	4	6	2	1	1
W Total	2	1	1	3.32	4	3	1	0	0	19	24	7	3	14
● Whitey Ford														
W 1950	NY-A	1	0	0.00	1	1	0	0	0	8^2	7	0	1	7
W 1953	NY-A	0	1	4.50	2	2	0	0	0	8	9	4	2	7
W 1955	NY-A	2	0	2.12	2	2	1	0	0	17	13	4	8	10
W 1956	NY-A	1	1	5.25	2	2	1	0	0	12	14	7	2	8
W 1957	NY-A	1	1	1.13	2	2	1	0	0	16	11	2	5	7
W 1958	NY-A	0	1	4.11	3	3	0	0	0	15^1	19	7	5	16
W 1960	NY-A	2	0	0.00	2	2	2	0	2	18	11	0	2	8
W 1961	NY-A	2	0	0.00	2	2	1	0	1	14	6	0	1	7
W 1962	NY-A	1	1	4.12	3	3	1	0	0	19^2	24	9	4	12
W 1963	NY-A	0	2	4.50	2	2	0	0	0	12	10	6	3	8
W 1964	NY-A	0	1	8.44	1	1	0	0	0	5^1	8	5	1	4
W Total	11	10	8	2.71	22	22	7	0	3	146	132	44	34	94
● Ken Forsch														
L 1980	Hou-N	0	1	4.15	2	1	1	0	0	8^2	10	4	1	6
● Bob Forsch														
L 1982	StL-N	1	0	0.00	1	1	1	0	1	9	3	0	0	6
L 1985	StL-N	0	0	5.40	1	1	0	0	0	3^1	3	2	2	0
L 1987	StL-N	1	1	12.00	3	0	0	0	0	3	4	4	1	3
L Total	3	2	1	3.52	5	2	1	0	1	15^1	10	6	3	9
W 1982	StL-N	0	2	4.97	2	2	0	0	0	12^2	18	7	3	4
W 1985	StL-N	0	1	12.00	2	1	0	0	0	3	6	4	1	3
W 1987	StL-N	1	0	9.95	3	0	0	0	0	6^1	8	7	5	3
W Total	3	1	3	7.36	7	3	0	0	0	22	32	18	9	10
● Terry Forster														
D 1981	LA-N	0	0	0.00	1	0	0	0	0	0^1	0	0	0	0
L 1978	LA-N	1	0	0.00	1	0	0	0	0	1	1	0	0	2
L 1981	LA-N	0	0	0.00	1	0	0	0	0	0^1	0	0	0	1
L Total	2	1	0	0.00	2	0	0	0	0	1^1	1	0	0	3
W 1978	LA-N	0	0	0.00	3	0	0	0	0	4	5	0	1	6
W 1981	LA-N	0	0	0.00	2	0	0	0	0	2	1	0	3	0
W Total	2	0	0	0.00	5	0	0	0	0	6	6	0	4	6
● Tony Fossas														
L 1996	StL-N	0	0	2.08	5	0	0	0	0	4^1	1	1	3	1
● Rube Foster														
W 1915	Bos-A	2	0	2.00	2	2	2	0	0	18	12	4	2	13
W 1916	Bos-A	0	0	0.00	1	0	0	0	0	3	3	0	0	1
W Total	2	2	0	1.71	3	2	2	0	0	21	15	4	2	14
● Keith Foulke														
D 2000	Chi-A	0	1	11.57	2	0	0	0	0	2^1	4	3	2	2
● Dave Foutz														
W 1885	StL-A	2	2	0.61	4	4	4	0	0	29^1	30	2	9	14
W 1886	StL-A	1	1	3.60	2	2	2	0	0	15	16	6	6	7
W 1887	StL-A	0	3	3.46	3	3	3	0	0	26	45	10	9	6
W 1889	Bro-A	0	0	7.20	1	0	0	0	0	5	5	4	2	2
W Total	4	3	6	2.63	10	9	9	0	0	75^1	96	22	26	29
● John Franco														
D 1999	NY-N	1	0	0.00	3	0	0	0	0	3^2	1	0	0	2
D 2000	NY-N	0	0	0.00	2	0	0	1	0	2	1	0	0	2
D Total	2	1	0	0.00	5	0	0	1	0	5^2	2	0	0	4
L 1999	NY-N	0	0	3.38	3	0	0	0	0	2^2	3	1	1	3
L 2000	NY-N	0	0	6.75	3	0	0	0	0	2^2	3	2	2	2
L Total	2	0	0	5.06	6	0	0	0	0	5^1	6	3	3	5
W 2000	NY-N	1	0	0.00	4	0	0	0	0	3^1	3	0	0	1
● George Frazier														
L 1981	NY-A	1	0	0.00	1	0	0	0	0	5^2	5	0	1	5
L 1984	Chi-N	0	0	10.80	1	0	0	0	0	1^2	2	2	0	1
L Total	2	1	0	2.45	2	0	0	0	0	7^1	7	2	1	6
W 1981	NY-A	0	3	17.18	3	0	0	0	0	3^2	9	7	3	2
W 1987	Min-A	0	0	0.00	1	0	0	0	0	2	1	0	0	2
W Total	2	0	3	11.12	4	0	0	0	0	5^2	10	7	3	4
● Marvin Freeman														
L 1992	Atl-N	0	0	14.73	3	0	0	0	0	3^2	8	6	2	1
● Larry French														
W 1935	Chi-N	0	2	3.38	2	1	1	0	0	10^2	15	4	2	8
W 1938	Chi-N	0	0	2.70	3	0	0	0	0	3^1	1	1	1	2
W 1941	Bro-N	0	0	0.00	2	0	0	0	0	1	0	0	0	0
W Total	3	0	2	3.00	7	1	1	0	0	15	16	5	3	10
● Bob Friend														
W 1960	Pit-N	0	2	13.50	3	2	0	0	0	6	13	9	3	7
● Dave Frost														
L 1979	Cal-A	0	1	18.69	2	1	0	0	0	4^1	8	9	5	1
● Woody Fryman														
D 1981	Mon-N	0	0	6.75	1	0	0	0	0	1^1	3	1	1	0
L 1972	Det-A	0	2	3.65	2	2	0	0	0	12^1	11	5	2	8

YEAR	TM/L	W	L	ERA	G	GS	CG	SV	SHO	IP	H	ER	BB	SO
L 1981	Mon-N	0	0	36.00	1	0	0	0	0	1	3	4	1	1
L Total	2	0	2	6.07	3	2	0	0	0	13^{1}	14	9	3	9
● Aaron Fultz														
D 2000	SF-N	0	1	6.75	1	0	0	0	0	1^{1}	3	1	0	0
● Frank Gabler														
W 1936	NY-N	0	0	7.20	2	0	0	0	0	5	7	4	4	0
● Rich Gale														
W 1980	KC-A	0	1	4.26	2	2	0	0	0	6^{1}	11	3	4	4
● Denny Galehouse														
W 1944	StL-A	1	1	1.50	2	2	2	0	0	18	13	3	5	15
● Gene Garber														
L 1976	Phi-N	0	1	13.50	2	0	0	0	0	0^{2}	2	1	1	0
L 1977	Phi-N	1	1	3.38	3	0	0	0	0	5^{1}	4	2	0	3
L 1982	Atl-N	0	1	8.10	2	0	0	0	0	3^{1}	4	3	1	3
L Total	3	1	3	5.79	7	0	0	0	0	9^{1}	10	6	2	6
● Rich Garces														
D 1999	Bos-A	1	0	3.86	2	0	0	0	0	2^{1}	2	1	3	2
L 1999	Bos-A	0	0	12.00	2	0	0	0	0	3	3	4	1	2
● Mike Garcia														
W 1954	Cle-A	0	1	5.40	2	1	0	0	0	5	6	3	4	4
● Freddy Garcia														
D 2000	Sea-A	0	0	10.80	1	1	0	0	0	3^{1}	6	4	3	2
L 2000	Sea-A	2	0	1.54	2	2	0	0	0	11^{2}	10	2	4	11
● Ramon Garcia														
D 1997	Hou-N	0	0	0.00	2	0	0	0	0	1	1	0	1	1
● Mark Gardner														
D 2000	SF-N	0	1	8.31	1	1	0	0	0	4^{1}	4	4	2	5
● Wes Gardner														
L 1988	Bos-A	0	0	5.79	1	0	0	0	0	4^{2}	6	3	2	8
● Wayne Garland														
L 1974	Bal-A	0	0	0.00	1	0	0	0	0	0^{2}	1	0	1	0
● Mike Garman														
L 1977	LA-N	0	0	0.00	2	0	0	1	0	1^{1}	0	0	0	1
W 1977	LA-N	0	0	0.00	2	0	0	0	0	4	2	0	1	3
● Scott Garrelts														
L 1987	SF-N	0	0	6.75	2	0	0	0	0	2^{2}	2	2	4	4
L 1989	SF-N	1	0	5.40	2	2	0	0	0	11^{2}	16	7	2	8
L Total	2	1	0	5.65	4	2	0	0	0	14^{1}	18	9	6	12
W 1989	SF-N	0	2	9.82	2	2	0	0	0	7^{1}	13	8	1	8
● Gary Gentry														
L 1969	NY-N	0	0	9.00	1	1	0	0	0	2	5	2	1	1
W 1969	NY-N	1	0	0.00	1	1	0	0	0	6^{2}	3	0	5	4
● Bill George														
W 1888	NY-N	0	1	7.20	1	1	1	0	0	10	15	8	3	4
● Charlie Getzien														
W 1887	Det-N	4	2	2.53	6	6	6	0	1	57	76	16	15	17
● Joe Gibbon														
L 1970	Pit-N	0	0	0.00	2	0	0	0	0	0^{1}	1	0	0	1
W 1960	Pit-N	0	0	9.00	2	0	0	0	0	3	4	3	1	2
● Bob Gibson														
W 1964	StL-N	2	1	3.00	3	3	2	0	0	27	23	9	8	31
W 1967	StL-N	3	0	1.00	3	3	3	0	1	27	14	3	5	26
W 1968	StL-N	2	1	1.67	3	3	3	0	1	27	18	5	4	35
W Total	3	7	2	1.89	9	9	8	0	2	81	55	17	17	92
● Dave Giusti														
L 1970	Pit-N	0	0	3.86	2	0	0	0	0	2^{1}	3	1	1	2
L 1971	Pit-N	0	0	0.00	4	0	0	3	0	5^{1}	1	0	2	3
L 1972	Pit-N	0	1	6.75	3	0	0	1	0	2^{2}	5	2	0	3
L 1974	Pit-N	0	1	21.60	3	0	0	0	0	3^{1}	13	8	5	1
L 1975	Pit-N	0	0	0.00	1	0	0	0	0	1^{1}	0	0	0	1
L Total	5	0	2	6.60	13	0	0	4	0	15	22	11	8	9
W 1971	Pit-N	0	0	0.00	3	0	0	1	0	5^{1}	3	0	2	4
● Tom Glavine														
D 1995	Atl-N	0	0	2.57	1	1	0	0	0	7	5	2	1	3
D 1996	Atl-N	1	0	1.35	1	1	0	0	0	6^{2}	5	1	3	7
D 1997	Atl-N	1	0	4.50	1	1	0	0	0	6	5	3	5	4
D 1998	Atl-N	0	0	1.29	1	1	0	0	0	7	3	1	1	8
D 1999	Atl-N	0	0	3.00	1	1	0	0	0	6	5	2	3	6
D 2000	Atl-N	0	1	27.00	1	1	0	0	0	2^{1}	6	7	1	2
D Total	6	2	1	4.11	6	6	0	0	0	35	29	16	14	30
L 1991	Atl-N	0	2	3.21	2	2	0	0	0	14	12	5	6	11
L 1992	Atl-N	0	2	12.27	2	2	0	0	0	7^{1}	13	10	3	2
L 1993	Atl-N	1	0	2.57	1	1	0	0	0	7	6	2	0	5
L 1995	Atl-N	0	0	1.29	1	1	0	0	0	7	7	1	2	5
L 1996	Atl-N	1	1	2.08	2	2	0	0	0	13	10	3	0	9
L 1997	Atl-N	1	1	5.40	2	2	0	0	0	13^{1}	13	8	11	9
L 1998	Atl-N	0	2	2.31	2	2	0	0	0	11^{2}	13	3	9	8
L 1999	Atl-N	1	0	0.00	1	1	0	0	0	7	7	0	1	8
L Total	8	4	8	3.59	13	13	0	0	0	80^{1}	81	32	32	57
W 1991	Atl-N	1	1	2.70	2	2	1	0	0	13^{1}	8	4	7	8
W 1992	Atl-N	1	1	1.59	2	2	2	0	0	17	10	3	4	8
W 1995	Atl-N	2	0	1.29	2	2	0	0	0	14	4	2	6	11

YEAR	TM/L	W	L	ERA	G	GS	CG	SV	SHO	IP	H	ER	BB	SO
W 1996	Atl-N	0	1	1.29	1	1	0	0	0	7	4	1	3	8
W 1999	Atl-N	0	0	5.14	1	1	0	0	0	7	7	4	0	3
W Total	5	4	3	2.16	8	8	3	0	0	58^{1}	33	14	20	38
● Kid Gleason														
T 1894	Bal-N	0	1	9.69	2	1	1	0	0	13	25	14	6	3
● Dave Goltz														
L 1982	Cal-A	0	0	7.36	1	0	0	0	0	3^{2}	4	3	2	2
W 1981	LA-N	0	0	5.40	2	0	0	0	0	3^{1}	4	2	1	2
● Ruben Gomez														
W 1954	NY-N	1	0	2.45	1	1	0	0	0	7^{1}	4	2	3	2
● Lefty Gomez														
W 1932	NY-A	1	0	1.00	1	1	1	0	0	9	9	1	1	8
W 1936	NY-A	2	0	4.70	2	2	1	0	0	15^{1}	14	8	11	9
W 1937	NY-A	2	0	1.50	2	2	2	0	0	18	16	3	2	8
W 1938	NY-A	1	0	3.86	1	1	0	0	0	7	9	3	1	5
W 1939	NY-A	0	0	9.00	1	1	0	0	0	1	3	1	0	1
W Total	5	6	0	2.86	7	7	4	0	0	50^{1}	51	16	15	31
● Dwight Gooden														
D 1997	NY-A	0	0	1.59	1	1	0	0	0	5^{2}	5	1	3	5
D 1998	Cle-A	0	0	54.00	1	1	0	0	0	0^{1}	1	2	2	1
D 2000	NY-A	0	0	21.60	1	0	0	0	0	1^{2}	4	4	1	1
D Total	3	0	0	8.22	3	2	0	0	0	7^{2}	10	7	6	7
L 1986	NY-N	0	1	1.06	2	2	0	0	0	17	16	2	5	9
L 1988	NY-N	0	0	2.95	3	2	0	0	0	18^{1}	10	6	8	20
L 1998	Cle-A	0	1	5.79	1	1	0	0	0	4^{2}	3	3	3	3
L 2000	NY-A	0	0	0.00	1	0	0	0	0	2^{1}	1	0	0	1
L Total	4	0	2	2.34	7	5	0	0	0	42^{1}	30	11	16	33
W 1986	NY-N	0	2	8.00	2	2	0	0	0	9	17	8	4	9
● Tom Gordon														
D 1998	Bos-A	0	1	9.00	2	0	0	0	0	3	4	3	4	1
D 1999	Bos-A	0	0	4.50	2	0	0	0	0	2	1	1	1	3
D Total	2	0	1	7.20	4	0	0	0	0	5	5	4	5	4
L 1999	Bos-A	0	0	13.50	3	0	0	0	0	2	3	3	1	3
● Tom Gorman														
W 1952	NY-A	0	0	0.00	1	0	0	0	0	0^{2}	1	0	0	0
W 1953	NY-A	0	0	3.00	1	0	0	0	0	3	4	1	0	1
W Total	2	0	0	2.45	2	0	0	0	0	3^{2}	5	1	0	1
● Johnny Gorsica														
W 1940	Det-A	0	0	0.79	2	0	0	0	0	11^{1}	6	1	4	4
● Rich Gossage														
D 1981	NY-A	0	0	0.00	3	0	0	3	0	6^{2}	3	0	2	8
L 1978	NY-A	1	0	4.50	2	0	0	1	0	4	3	2	0	3
L 1980	NY-A	0	1	54.00	1	0	0	0	0	0^{1}	3	2	0	0
L 1981	NY-A	0	0	0.00	2	0	0	1	0	2^{2}	1	0	0	2
L 1984	SD-N	0	0	4.50	3	0	0	1	0	4	5	2	1	5
L Total	4	1	1	4.91	8	0	0	3	0	11	12	6	1	10
W 1978	NY-A	1	0	0.00	3	0	0	0	0	6	1	0	1	4
W 1981	NY-A	0	0	0.00	3	0	0	2	0	5	2	0	2	5
W 1984	SD-N	0	0	13.50	2	0	0	0	0	2^{2}	3	4	1	2
W Total	3	1	0	2.63	8	0	0	2	0	13^{2}	6	4	4	11
● Wayne Granger														
L 1970	Cin-N	0	0	0.00	1	0	0	0	0	0^{2}	1	0	0	0
W 1968	StL-N	0	0	0.00	1	0	0	0	0	2	0	0	1	1
W 1970	Cin-N	0	0	33.75	2	0	0	0	0	1^{1}	7	5	1	1
W Total	2	0	0	13.50	3	0	0	0	0	3^{1}	7	5	2	2
● Mudcat Grant														
L 1971	Oak-A	0	0	0.00	1	0	0	0	0	2	3	0	0	2
W 1965	Min-A	2	1	2.74	3	3	2	0	0	23	22	7	2	12
● Jeff Gray														
L 1990	Bos-A	0	0	2.70	2	0	0	0	0	3^{1}	4	1	1	2
● Fred Green														
W 1960	Pit-N	0	0	22.50	3	0	0	0	0	4	11	10	1	3
● Tommy Greene														
L 1993	Phi-N	1	1	9.64	2	2	0	0	0	9^{1}	12	10	7	7
W 1993	Phi-N	0	0	27.00	1	1	0	0	0	2^{1}	7	7	4	1
● Hal Gregg														
W 1947	Bro-N	0	1	3.55	3	1	0	0	0	12^{2}	9	5	8	10
● Bob Grim														
W 1955	NY-A	0	1	4.15	3	1	0	1	0	8^{2}	8	4	5	8
W 1957	NY-A	0	1	7.71	2	0	0	0	0	2^{1}	3	2	0	2
W Total	2	0	2	4.91	5	1	0	1	0	11	11	6	5	10
● Burleigh Grimes														
W 1920	Bro-N	1	2	4.19	3	3	1	0	1	19^{1}	23	9	9	4
W 1930	StL-N	0	2	3.71	2	2	2	0	0	17	10	7	6	13
W 1931	StL-N	2	0	2.04	2	2	1	0	0	17^{2}	9	4	9	11
W 1932	Chi-N	0	0	23.63	2	0	0	0	0	2^{2}	7	7	2	0
W Total	4	3	4	4.29	9	7	4	0	1	56^{2}	49	27	26	28
● Jason Grimsley														
L 2000	NY-A	0	0	0.00	2	0	0	0	0	1	2	0	3	1
W 1999	NY-A	0	0	0.00	1	0	0	0	0	2^{1}	2	0	2	0
● Ross Grimsley														
L 1972	Cin-N	1	0	1.00	1	1	1	0	0	9	2	1	0	5
L 1973	Cin-N	0	1	12.27	2	1	0	0	0	3^{2}	7	5	2	3

YEAR	TM/L	W	L	ERA	G	GS	CG	SV	SHO	IP	H	ER	BB	SO
L 1974	Bal-A	0	0	1.69	2	0	0	0	0	5^1	1	1	2	2
L Total	3	1	1	3.50	5	2	1	0	0	18	10	7	4	10
W 1972	Cin-N	2	1	2.57	4	1	0	0	0	7	7	2	3	2
● Lee Grissom														
W 1939	Cin-N	0	0	0.00	1	0	0	0	0	1^1	0	0	1	0
● Marv Grissom														
W 1954	NY-N	1	0	0.00	1	0	0	0	0	2^2	1	0	3	2
● Steve Gromek														
W 1948	Cle-A	1	0	1.00	1	1	1	0	0	9	7	1	1	2
● Lefty Grove														
W 1929	Phi-A	0	0	0.00	2	0	0	2	0	6^1	3	0	1	10
W 1930	Phi-A	2	1	1.42	3	2	2	0	0	19	15	3	3	10
W 1931	Phi-A	2	1	2.42	3	3	2	0	0	26	28	7	2	16
W Total	3	4	2	1.75	8	5	4	2	0	51^1	46	10	6	36
● Joe Grzenda														
L 1969	Min-A	0	0	0.00	1	0	0	0	0	0^2	0	0	0	0
● Mark Gubicza														
L 1985	KC-A	1	0	3.24	2	1	0	0	0	8^1	4	3	4	4
● Ron Guidry														
D 1981	NY-A	0	0	5.40	2	2	0	0	0	8^1	11	5	3	8
L 1977	NY-A	1	0	3.97	2	2	1	0	0	11^1	9	5	3	8
L 1978	NY-A	1	0	1.13	1	1	0	0	0	8	7	1	1	7
L 1980	NY-A	0	1	12.00	1	1	0	0	0	3	5	4	4	2
L Total	3	2	1	4.03	4	4	1	0	0	22^1	21	10	8	17
W 1977	NY-A	1	0	2.00	1	1	1	0	0	9	4	2	3	7
W 1978	NY-A	1	0	1.00	1	1	1	0	0	9	8	1	7	4
W 1981	NY-A	1	1	1.93	2	2	0	0	0	14	8	3	4	15
W Total	3	3	1	1.69	4	4	2	0	0	32	20	6	14	26
● Don Gullett														
L 1970	Cin-N	0	0	0.00	2	0	0	2	0	3^2	1	0	2	3
L 1972	Cin-N	0	1	8.00	2	2	0	0	0	9	12	8	0	5
L 1973	Cin-N	0	1	2.00	3	1	0	0	0	9	4	2	3	6
L 1975	Cin-N	1	0	3.00	1	1	1	0	0	9	8	3	2	5
L 1976	Cin-N	1	0	1.13	1	1	0	0	0	8	2	1	3	4
L 1977	NY-A	0	1	18.00	1	1	0	0	0	2	4	4	2	0
L Total	6	2	3	3.98	10	6	1	2	0	40^2	31	18	12	23
W 1970	Cin-N	0	0	1.35	3	0	0	0	0	6^2	5	1	4	4
W 1972	Cin-N	0	0	1.29	1	1	0	0	0	7	5	1	2	4
W 1975	Cin-N	1	1	4.34	3	3	0	0	0	18^2	19	9	10	15
W 1976	Cin-N	1	0	1.23	1	1	0	0	0	7^1	5	1	3	4
W 1977	NY-A	0	1	6.39	2	2	0	0	0	12^2	13	9	7	10
W Total	5	2	2	3.61	10	7	0	0	0	52^1	47	21	26	37
● Bill Gullickson														
D 1981	Mon-N	1	0	1.17	1	1	0	0	0	7^2	6	1	1	3
L 1981	Mon-N	0	2	2.51	2	2	0	0	0	14^1	12	4	6	12
● Harry Gumbert														
W 1936	NY-N	0	0	36.00	2	0	0	0	0	2	7	8	4	2
W 1937	NY-N	0	0	27.00	2	0	0	0	0	1^1	4	4	1	1
W 1942	StL-N	0	0	0.00	2	0	0	0	0	0^2	1	0	0	0
W Total	3	0	0	27.00	6	0	0	0	0	4	12	12	5	3
● Larry Gura														
D 1981	KC-A	0	1	7.36	1	1	0	0	0	3^2	7	3	3	3
L 1976	KC-A	0	1	4.22	2	2	0	0	0	10^2	18	5	1	4
L 1977	KC-A	0	1	18.00	2	1	0	0	0	2	7	4	1	2
L 1978	KC-A	1	0	2.84	1	1	0	0	0	6^1	8	2	2	2
L 1980	KC-A	1	0	2.00	1	1	1	0	0	9	10	2	1	4
L Total	4	2	2	4.18	6	5	1	0	0	28	43	13	5	12
W 1980	KC-A	0	0	2.19	2	2	0	0	0	12^1	8	3	3	4
● Mark Guthrie														
D 1995	LA-N	0	0	6.75	3	0	0	0	0	1^1	2	1	1	1
D 1996	LA-N	0	0	0.00	1	0	0	0	0	0^1	0	0	0	1
D Total	2	0	0	5.40	4	0	0	0	0	1^2	2	1	2	2
L 1991	Min-A	1	0	0.00	2	0	0	0	0	2^2	0	0	0	0
W 1991	Min-A	0	1	2.25	4	0	0	0	0	4	3	1	4	3
● Juan Guzman														
L 1991	Tor-A	1	0	3.18	1	1	0	0	0	5^2	4	2	4	2
L 1992	Tor-A	2	0	2.08	2	2	0	0	0	13	12	3	5	11
L 1993	Tor-A	2	0	2.08	2	2	0	0	0	13	8	3	9	9
L Total	3	5	0	2.27	5	5	0	0	0	31^2	24	8	18	22
W 1992	Tor-A	0	0	1.13	1	1	0	0	0	8	8	1	1	7
W 1993	Tor-A	0	1	3.75	2	2	0	0	0	12	10	5	8	12
W Total	2	0	1	2.70	3	3	0	0	0	20	18	6	9	19
● Moose Haas														
D 1981	Mil-A	0	2	9.45	2	2	0	0	0	6^2	13	7	1	1
L 1982	Mil-A	1	0	4.91	1	1	0	0	0	7^1	5	4	5	7
W 1982	Mil-A	0	0	7.36	2	1	0	0	0	7^1	8	6	3	4
● Harvey Haddix														
W 1960	Pit-N	2	0	2.45	2	1	0	0	0	7^1	6	2	2	6
● Bump Hadley														
W 1936	NY-A	1	0	1.13	1	1	0	0	0	8	10	1	1	2
W 1937	NY-A	0	1	33.75	1	1	0	0	0	1^1	6	5	0	0
W 1939	NY-A	1	0	2.25	1	0	0	0	0	8	7	2	3	2
W Total	3	2	1	4.15	3	2	0	0	0	17^1	23	8	4	4

YEAR	TM/L	W	L	ERA	G	GS	CG	SV	SHO	IP	H	ER	BB	SO
● Jesse Haines														
W 1926	StL-N	2	0	1.08	3	2	1	0	1	16^2	13	2	9	5
W 1928	StL-N	0	1	4.50	1	1	0	0	0	6	6	3	3	3
W 1930	StL-N	1	0	1.00	1	1	1	0	0	9	4	1	4	2
W 1934	StL-N	0	0	0.00	1	0	0	0	0	0^2	1	0	0	2
W Total	4	3	1	1.67	6	4	2	0	1	32^1	24	6	16	12
● John Halama														
L 2000	Sea-A	0	0	2.89	2	2	0	0	0	9^1	10	3	5	3
● Charley Hall														
W 1912	Bos-A	0	0	3.38	2	0	0	0	0	10^2	11	4	9	1
● Dick Hall														
L 1969	Bal-A	1	0	0.00	1	0	0	0	0	0^2	0	0	0	1
L 1970	Bal-A	1	0	0.00	1	0	0	0	0	4^2	1	0	0	3
L Total	2	2	0	0.00	2	0	0	0	0	5^1	1	0	0	4
W 1969	Bal-A	0	1	—	1	0	0	0	0	0	0	0	1	0
W 1970	Bal-A	0	0	0.00	1	0	0	1	0	2^1	0	0	0	0
W 1971	Bal-A	0	0	0.00	1	0	0	1	0	1	1	0	0	0
W Total	3	0	1	0.00	3	0	0	2	0	3^1	2	0	1	0
● Tom Hall														
L 1969	Min-A	0	0	0.00	1	0	0	0	0	0^2	0	0	0	0
L 1970	Min-A	0	1	6.75	2	1	0	0	0	5^1	6	4	4	6
L 1972	Cin-N	1	0	1.23	2	0	0	0	0	7^1	3	1	3	8
L 1973	Cin-N	0	0	67.50	3	0	0	0	0	0^2	3	5	4	1
L 1976	KC-A	0	0	0.00	1	0	0	0	0	0^1	1	0	0	0
L Total	5	1	1	6.28	9	1	0	0	0	14^1	13	10	11	15
W 1972	Cin-N	0	0	0.00	4	0	0	1	0	8^1	6	0	2	7
● Bill Hallahan														
W 1926	StL-N	0	0	4.50	1	0	0	0	0	2	2	1	3	1
W 1930	StL-N	1	1	1.64	2	2	1	0	1	11	9	2	8	8
W 1931	StL-N	2	0	0.49	3	2	2	1	1	18^1	12	1	8	12
W 1934	StL-N	0	0	2.16	1	1	0	0	0	8^1	6	2	4	6
W Total	4	3	1	1.36	7	5	3	1	2	39^2	29	6	23	27
● Dave Hamilton														
L 1972	Oak-A	0	0	—	1	0	0	0	0	0	1	0	1	0
W 1972	Oak-A	0	0	27.00	2	0	0	0	0	1^1	3	4	1	1
● Joey Hamilton														
D 1996	SD-N	0	1	4.50	1	1	0	0	0	6	5	3	0	6
D 1998	SD-N	0	0	0.00	2	0	0	0	0	3^1	1	0	2	3
D Total	2	0	1	2.89	3	1	0	0	0	9^1	6	3	2	9
L 1998	SD-N	0	1	4.91	2	1	0	0	0	7^1	7	4	3	6
W 1998	SD-N	0	0	0.00	1	0	0	0	0	1	0	0	1	1
● Steve Hamilton														
L 1971	SF-N	0	0	9.00	1	0	0	0	0	1	1	1	0	3
W 1963	NY-A	0	0	0.00	1	0	0	0	0	1	0	0	0	1
W 1964	NY-A	0	0	4.50	2	0	0	1	0	2	3	1	0	2
W Total	2	0	0	3.00	3	0	0	1	0	3	3	1	0	3
● Atlee Hammaker														
L 1987	SF-N	0	1	7.87	2	2	0	0	0	8	12	7	0	7
L 1989	SF-N	0	0	0.00	1	0	0	0	0	1	1	0	0	0
L Total	2	0	1	7.00	3	2	0	0	0	9	13	7	0	7
W 1989	SF-N	0	0	15.43	2	0	0	0	0	2^1	8	4	0	2
● Mike Hampton														
D 1997	Hou-N	0	1	11.57	1	1	0	0	0	4^2	2	6	8	2
D 1998	Hou-N	0	0	1.50	1	1	0	0	0	6	2	1	1	2
D 1999	Hou-N	0	0	3.86	1	1	0	0	0	7	6	3	1	9
D 2000	NY-N	0	1	8.44	1	1	0	0	0	5^1	6	5	3	2
D Total	4	0	2	5.87	4	4	0	0	0	23	16	15	13	15
L 2000	NY-N	2	0	0.00	2	2	1	0	1	16	9	0	4	12
W 2000	NY-N	0	1	6.00	1	1	0	0	0	6	8	4	5	4
● Erik Hanson														
D 1995	Bos-A	0	1	4.50	1	1	1	0	0	8	4	4	4	5
● Harry Harper														
W 1921	NY-A	0	0	20.25	1	1	0	0	0	1^1	3	3	2	1
● Greg Harris														
L 1984	SD-N	0	0	31.50	1	0	0	0	0	2	9	7	3	2
L 1990	Bos-A	0	1	27.00	1	0	0	0	0	0^1	3	1	0	0
L Total	2	0	1	30.86	2	0	0	0	0	2^1	12	8	3	2
W 1984	SD-N	0	0	0.00	1	0	0	0	0	5^1	3	0	3	5
● Mickey Harris														
W 1946	Bos-A	0	2	3.72	2	2	0	0	0	9^2	11	4	4	5
● Andy Hassler														
L 1976	KC-A	0	1	6.14	2	1	0	0	0	7^1	8	5	6	4
L 1977	KC-A	0	1	4.76	1	1	0	0	0	5^2	5	3	0	3
L 1982	Cal-A	0	0	0.00	2	0	0	0	0	2^2	0	0	0	2
L Total	3	0	2	4.60	5	2	0	0	0	15^2	13	8	6	9
● Gil Hatfield														
W 1888	NY-N	0	0	12.60	1	0	0	0	0	5	12	7	3	2
● Joe Hatten														
W 1947	Bro-N	0	0	7.00	4	1	0	0	0	9	12	7	7	5
W 1949	Bro-N	0	0	16.20	2	0	0	0	0	1^2	4	3	2	0
W Total	2	0	0	8.44	6	1	0	0	0	10^2	16	10	9	5
● Bill Hawke														
T 1894	Bal-N	0	1	9.00	1	1	0	0	0	4	9	4	1	0

YEAR	TM/L	W	L	ERA	G	GS	CG	SV	SHO	IP	H	ER	BB	SO
● **Andy Hawkins**														
L 1984	SD-N	0	0	0.00	3	0	0	0	0	3^2	0	0	2	1
W 1984	SD-N	1	1	0.75	3	0	0	0	0	12	4	1	6	4
● **Jim Hearn**														
W 1951	NY-N	1	0	1.04	2	1	0	0	0	8^2	5	1	8	1
● **Ken Heintzelman**														
W 1950	Phi-N	0	0	1.17	1	1	0	0	0	7^2	4	1	6	3
● **Rick Helling**														
D 1998	Tex-A	0	1	4.50	1	1	0	0	0	6	8	3	1	9
D 1999	Tex-A	0	1	2.84	1	1	0	0	0	6^1	5	2	1	8
D Total	2	0	2	3.65	2	2	0	0	0	12^1	13	5	2	17
● **George Hemming**														
T 1894	Bal-N	0	1	1.13	1	1	1	0	0	8	10	1	3	2
● **Claude Hendrix**														
W 1918	Chi-N	0	0	0.00	1	0	0	0	0	1	0	0	0	0
● **Tom Henke**														
L 1985	Tor-A	2	0	4.26	3	0	0	0	0	6^1	5	3	4	4
L 1989	Tor-A	0	0	0.00	3	0	0	0	0	2^2	0	0	0	3
L 1991	Tor-A	0	0	0.00	2	0	0	0	0	2^2	0	0	1	5
L 1992	Tor-A	0	0	0.00	4	0	0	3	0	4^2	3	0	2	2
L Total	4	2	0	1.65	12	0	0	3	0	16^1	8	3	7	14
W 1992	Tor-A	0	0	2.70	3	0	0	2	0	3^1	2	1	2	1
● **Mike Henneman**														
D 1996	Tex-A	0	0	0.00	3	0	0	0	0	1	1	0	1	1
L 1987	Det-A	1	0	10.80	3	0	0	0	0	5	6	6	6	3
● **Doug Henry**														
D 1997	SF-N	0	0	0.00	1	0	0	0	0	2	1	0	3	2
D 1998	Hou-N	0	0	5.40	2	0	0	0	0	1^2	2	1	0	1
D 1999	Hou-N	0	0	0.00	2	0	0	0	0	3^2	1	0	3	2
D 2000	SF-N	0	0	2.25	3	0	0	0	0	4	1	1	3	1
D Total	4	0	0	1.59	8	0	0	0	0	11^1	5	2	9	6
● **Bill Henry**														
W 1961	Cin-N	0	0	19.29	2	0	0	0	0	2^1	4	5	2	3
● **Roy Henshaw**														
W 1935	Chi-N	0	0	7.36	1	0	0	0	0	3^2	2	3	5	2
● **Pat Hentgen**														
L 1993	Tor-A	0	1	18.00	1	1	0	0	0	3	9	6	2	3
L 2000	StL-N	0	1	14.73	1	1	0	0	0	3^2	7	6	5	2
L Total	2	0	2	16.20	2	2	0	0	0	6^2	16	12	7	5
W 1993	Tor-A	1	0	1.50	1	1	0	0	0	6	5	1	3	6
● **Felix Heredia**														
D 1998	Chi-N	0	0	54.00	1	0	0	0	0	0^1	0	2	2	0
L 1997	Fla-N	0	0	5.40	2	0	0	0	0	3^1	3	2	2	4
W 1997	Fla-N	0	0	0.00	4	0	0	0	0	5^1	2	0	1	5
● **Gil Heredia**														
D 2000	Oak-A	1	1	12.79	2	2	0	0	0	6^1	11	9	3	3
● **Livan Hernandez**														
D 1997	Fla-N	0	0	2.25	1	0	0	0	0	4	3	1	0	3
D 2000	SF-N	1	0	1.17	1	1	0	0	0	7^2	5	1	5	5
D Total	2	1	0	1.54	2	1	0	0	0	11^2	8	2	5	8
L 1997	Fla-N	2	0	0.84	2	1	1	0	0	10^2	5	1	2	16
W 1997	Fla-N	2	0	5.27	2	2	0	0	0	13^2	15	8	10	7
● **Xavier Hernandez**														
L 1995	Cin-N	0	0	27.00	1	0	0	0	0	0^2	3	2	0	0
● **Willie Hernandez**														
L 1984	Det-A	0	0	2.25	3	0	0	1	0	4	3	1	1	3
L 1987	Det-A	0	0	0.00	1	0	0	0	0	0^1	2	0	0	0
L Total	2	0	0	2.08	4	0	0	1	0	4^1	5	1	1	3
W 1983	Phi-N	0	0	0.00	3	0	0	0	0	4	0	0	1	4
W 1984	Det-A	0	0	1.69	3	0	0	2	0	5^1	4	1	0	0
W Total	2	0	0	0.96	6	0	0	2	0	9^1	4	1	1	4
● **Orlando Hernandez**														
D 1999	NY-A	1	0	0.00	1	1	0	0	0	8	2	0	6	4
D 2000	NY-A	1	0	2.45	2	1	0	0	0	7^1	5	2	5	5
D Total	2	2	0	1.17	3	2	0	0	0	15^1	7	2	11	9
L 1998	NY-A	1	0	0.00	1	1	0	0	0	7	3	0	2	6
L 1999	NY-A	1	0	1.80	2	2	0	0	0	15	12	3	6	13
L 2000	NY-A	2	0	4.20	2	2	0	0	0	15	13	7	8	14
L Total	3	4	0	2.43	5	5	0	0	0	37	28	10	16	33
W 1998	NY-A	1	0	1.29	1	1	0	0	0	7	6	1	3	7
W 1999	NY-A	1	0	1.29	1	1	0	0	0	7	1	1	2	10
W 2000	NY-A	0	1	4.91	1	1	0	0	0	7^1	9	4	3	12
W Total	3	2	1	2.53	3	3	0	0	0	21^1	16	6	8	29
● **Ramon Hernandez**														
L 1972	Pit-N	0	0	2.70	3	0	0	1	0	3^1	1	1	0	3
L 1974	Pit-N	0	0	0.00	2	0	0	0	0	4^1	3	0	1	2
L 1975	Pit-N	0	1	27.00	1	0	0	0	0	0^2	3	2	0	0
L Total	3	0	1	3.24	6	0	0	1	0	8^1	7	3	1	5
● **Roberto Hernandez**														
D 1997	SF-N	0	1	20.25	3	0	0	0	0	1^1	5	3	3	1
L 1993	Chi-A	0	0	0.00	4	0	0	1	0	4	4	0	0	1
● **Orel Hershiser**														
D 1995	Cle-A	1	0	0.00	1	1	0	0	0	7^1	3	0	2	7

YEAR	TM/L	W	L	ERA	G	GS	CG	SV	SHO	IP	H	ER	BB	SO
D 1996	Cle-A	0	0	5.40	1	1	0	0	0	5	7	3	3	3
D 1997	Cle-A	0	0	3.97	2	2	0	0	0	11^1	14	5	2	4
D 1999	NY-N	0	0	0.00	1	0	0	0	0	1	0	0	0	1
D Total	4	1	0	2.92	5	4	0	0	0	24^2	24	8	7	15
L 1985	LA-N	1	0	3.52	2	2	1	0	0	15^1	17	6	6	5
L 1988	LA-N	1	0	1.09	4	3	1	1	1	24^2	18	3	7	15
L 1995	Cle-A	2	0	1.29	2	2	0	0	0	14	9	2	3	15
L 1997	Cle-A	0	0	0.00	1	1	0	0	0	7	4	0	1	7
L 1999	NY-N	0	0	0.00	2	0	0	0	0	4^1	1	0	3	5
L Total	5	4	0	1.52	11	8	2	1	1	65^1	49	11	20	47
W 1988	LA-N	2	0	1.00	2	2	2	0	1	18	7	2	6	17
W 1995	Cle-A	1	1	2.57	2	2	0	0	0	14	8	4	4	13
W 1997	Cle-A	0	2	11.70	2	2	0	0	0	10	15	13	6	5
W Total	3	3	3	4.07	6	6	2	0	1	42	30	19	16	35
● **Charlie Hickman**														
T 1897	Bos-N	0	1	3.60	1	1	0	0	0	5	7	2	2	0
● **Kirby Higbe**														
W 1941	Bro-N	0	0	7.36	1	1	0	0	0	3^2	6	3	2	1
● **Oral Hildebrand**														
W 1939	NY-A	0	0	0.00	1	1	0	0	0	4	2	0	0	3
● **Carmen Hill**														
W 1927	Pit-N	0	0	4.50	1	1	0	0	0	6	9	3	1	6
● **Ken Hill**														
D 1995	Cle-A	1	0	0.00	1	0	0	0	0	1^1	1	0	0	2
D 1996	Tex-A	0	0	4.50	1	1	0	0	0	6	5	3	3	1
D Total	2	1	0	3.68	2	1	0	0	0	7^1	6	3	3	3
L 1995	Cle-A	1	0	0.00	1	1	0	0	0	7	5	0	3	6
W 1995	Cle-A	0	1	4.26	2	1	0	0	0	6^1	7	3	4	1
● **John Hiller**														
L 1972	Det-A	1	0	0.00	3	0	0	0	0	3^1	1	0	1	1
W 1968	Det-A	0	0	13.50	2	0	0	0	0	2	6	3	3	1
● **Sterling Hitchcock**														
D 1995	NY-A	0	0	5.40	2	0	0	0	0	1^2	2	1	2	1
D 1998	SD-N	1	0	1.50	1	1	0	0	0	6	3	1	0	11
D Total	2	1	0	2.35	3	1	0	0	0	7^2	5	2	2	12
L 1998	SD-N	2	0	0.90	2	2	0	0	0	10	5	1	8	14
W 1998	SD-N	0	0	1.50	1	1	0	0	0	6	7	1	1	7
● **Joe Hoerner**														
W 1967	StL-N	0	0	40.50	2	0	0	0	0	0^2	4	3	1	0
W 1968	StL-N	0	1	3.86	3	0	0	1	0	4^2	5	2	5	3
W Total	2	0	1	8.44	5	0	0	1	0	5^1	9	5	6	3
● **Bill Hoffer**														
T 1895	Bal-N	0	2	4.24	2	2	2	0	0	17	21	8	6	4
T 1896	Bal-N	2	0	1.50	2	2	2	0	0	18	15	3	5	10
T 1897	Bal-N	2	0	3.38	2	2	2	0	0	16	25	6	4	2
T Total	3	4	2	3.00	6	6	6	0	0	51	61	17	15	16
● **Trevor Hoffman**														
D 1996	SD-N	0	1	10.80	2	0	0	0	0	1^2	3	2	1	2
D 1998	SD-N	0	0	0.00	4	0	0	2	0	3	3	0	1	4
D Total	2	0	1	3.86	6	0	0	2	0	4^2	6	2	2	6
L 1998	SD-N	1	0	2.08	3	0	0	1	0	4^1	2	1	2	7
W 1998	SD-N	0	1	9.00	1	0	0	0	0	2	2	2	1	0
● **Chief Hogsett**														
W 1934	Det-A	0	0	1.23	3	0	0	0	0	7^1	6	1	3	3
W 1935	Det-A	0	0	0.00	1	0	0	0	0	1	0	0	1	0
W Total	2	0	0	1.08	4	0	0	0	0	8^1	6	1	4	3
● **Bobby Hogue**														
W 1951	NY-A	0	0	0.00	2	0	0	0	0	2^2	1	0	0	0
● **Al Holland**														
L 1983	Phi-N	0	0	0.00	2	0	0	1	0	3	1	0	0	3
W 1983	Phi-N	0	0	0.00	2	0	0	1	0	3^2	1	0	0	5
● **Al Hollingsworth**														
W 1944	StL-A	0	0	2.25	1	0	0	0	0	4	5	1	2	1
● **Darren Holmes**														
D 1995	Col-N	1	0	0.00	3	0	0	0	0	1^2	6	0	0	2
D 1999	Ari-N	0	0	27.00	1	0	0	0	0	1^1	1	4	3	0
D Total	2	1	0	12.00	4	0	0	0	0	3	7	4	3	2
● **Chris Holt**														
D 1999	Hou-N	0	0	∞	1	0	0	0	0	0	3	3	0	0
● **Brian Holton**														
L 1988	LA-N	0	0	2.25	3	0	0	1	0	4	2	1	1	2
W 1988	LA-N	0	0	0.00	1	0	0	0	0	2	0	0	1	0
● **Ken Holtzman**														
L 1972	Oak-A	0	1	4.50	1	1	0	0	0	4	4	2	2	2
L 1973	Oak-A	1	0	0.82	1	1	1	0	0	11	3	1	1	7
L 1974	Oak-A	1	0	0.00	1	1	1	0	1	9	5	0	2	3
L 1975	Oak-A	0	2	4.09	2	2	0	0	0	11	12	5	1	7
L Total	4	2	3	2.06	5	5	2	0	1	35	24	8	6	19
W 1972	Oak-A	1	0	2.13	3	2	0	0	0	12^2	11	3	3	4
W 1973	Oak-A	2	1	4.22	3	3	0	0	0	10^2	13	5	5	6
W 1974	Oak-A	1	0	1.50	2	2	0	0	0	12	13	2	4	10
W Total	3	4	1	2.55	8	7	0	0	0	35^1	37	10	12	20

YEAR	TM/L	W	L	ERA	G	GS	CG	SV	SHO	IP	H	ER	BB	SO
● **Rick Honeycutt**														
D 1996	StL-N	1	0	3.38	3	0	0	0	0	2^2	3	1	1	2
L 1983	LA-N	0	0	21.60	2	0	0	0	0	1^2	4	4	0	2
L 1985	LA-N	0	0	13.50	2	0	0	0	0	1^1	4	2	2	1
L 1988	Oak-A	1	0	0.00	3	0	0	0	0	2	0	0	2	0
L 1989	Oak-A	0	0	32.40	3	0	0	0	0	1^2	6	6	5	1
L 1990	Oak-A	0	0	0.00	3	0	0	1	0	1^2	0	0	0	0
L 1992	Oak-A	0	0	0.00	2	0	0	0	0	2	0	0	0	1
L 1996	StL-N	0	0	9.00	5	0	0	0	0	4	5	4	3	3
L Total	7	1	0	10.05	20	0	0	1	0	14^1	19	16	12	8
W 1988	Oak-A	1	0	0.00	3	0	0	0	0	3^1	0	0	0	5
W 1989	Oak-A	0	0	6.75	3	0	0	0	0	2^2	4	2	0	2
W 1990	Oak-A	0	0	0.00	1	0	0	0	0	1^2	2	0	1	0
W Total	3	1	0	2.35	7	0	0	0	0	7^2	6	2	1	7
● **Burt Hooton**														
D 1981	LA-N	1	0	1.29	1	1	0	0	0	7	3	1	3	2
L 1977	LA-N	0	0	16.20	1	1	0	0	0	1^2	2	3	4	1
L 1978	LA-N	0	0	7.71	1	1	0	0	0	4^2	10	4	0	5
L 1981	LA-N	2	0	0.00	2	2	0	0	0	14^2	11	0	6	7
L Total	3	2	0	3.00	4	4	0	0	0	21	23	7	10	13
W 1977	LA-N	1	1	3.75	2	2	1	0	0	12	8	5	2	9
W 1978	LA-N	1	1	6.48	2	2	0	0	0	8^1	13	6	3	6
W 1981	LA-N	1	1	1.59	2	2	0	0	0	11^1	8	2	9	3
W Total	3	3	3	3.69	6	6	1	0	0	31^2	29	13	14	18
● **Joe Horlen**														
L 1972	Oak-A	0	1	∞	1	0	0	0	0	0	0	1	1	0
W 1972	Oak-A	0	0	6.75	1	0	0	0	0	1^1	2	1	2	1
● **Ricky Horton**														
L 1985	StL-N	0	0	9.00	3	0	0	0	0	3	4	3	2	1
L 1987	StL-N	0	0	0.00	1	0	0	0	0	3	2	0	0	2
L 1988	LA-N	0	0	0.00	4	0	0	0	0	4^1	4	0	2	3
L Total	3	0	0	2.61	8	0	0	0	0	10^1	10	3	4	6
W 1985	StL-N	0	0	6.75	3	0	0	0	0	4	4	3	5	5
W 1987	StL-N	0	0	6.00	2	0	0	0	0	3	5	2	0	1
W Total	2	0	0	6.43	5	0	0	0	0	7	9	5	5	6
● **Charlie Hough**														
L 1974	LA-N	0	0	7.71	1	0	0	0	0	2^1	4	2	0	2
L 1977	LA-N	0	0	4.50	1	0	0	0	0	2	2	1	0	3
L 1978	LA-N	0	0	4.50	1	0	0	0	0	2	1	1	0	1
L Total	3	0	0	5.68	3	0	0	0	0	6^1	7	4	0	6
W 1974	LA-N	0	0	0.00	1	0	0	0	0	2	0	0	1	4
W 1977	LA-N	0	0	1.80	2	0	0	0	0	5	3	1	0	5
W 1978	LA-N	0	0	8.44	2	0	0	0	0	5^1	10	5	2	5
W Total	3	0	0	4.38	5	0	0	0	0	12^1	13	6	3	14
● **Art Houtteman**														
W 1954	Cle-A	0	0	4.50	1	0	0	0	0	2	2	1	1	1
● **Steve Howe**														
D 1981	LA-N	0	0	0.00	2	0	0	0	0	2	1	0	0	2
D 1995	NY-A	0	0	18.00	2	0	0	0	0	1	4	2	0	0
D Total	2	0	0	6.00	4	0	0	0	0	3	5	2	0	2
L 1981	LA-N	0	0	0.00	2	0	0	0	0	2	1	0	0	2
W 1981	LA-N	1	0	3.86	3	0	0	1	0	7	7	3	1	4
● **Harry Howell**														
T 1900	Bro-N	0	1	3.38	1	1	1	0	0	8	13	3	2	3
● **Jay Howell**														
L 1988	LA-N	0	1	27.00	2	0	0	0	0	0^2	1	2	2	1
W 1988	LA-N	0	1	3.38	2	0	0	1	0	2^2	3	1	1	2
● **Ken Howell**														
L 1985	LA-N	0	0	0.00	1	0	0	0	0	2	0	0	0	2
● **Bobby Howry**														
D 2000	Chi-A	0	0	3.38	2	0	0	0	0	2^2	2	1	2	4
● **La Marr Hoyt**														
L 1983	Chi-A	1	0	1.00	1	1	1	0	0	9	5	1	0	4
● **Waite Hoyt**														
W 1921	NY-A	2	1	0.00	3	3	3	0	1	27	18	0	11	18
W 1922	NY-A	0	1	1.13	2	1	0	0	0	8	11	1	2	4
W 1923	NY-A	0	0	15.43	1	1	0	0	0	2^1	4	4	1	0
W 1926	NY-A	1	1	1.20	2	2	1	0	0	15	19	2	1	10
W 1927	NY-A	1	0	4.91	1	1	0	0	0	7^1	8	4	1	2
W 1928	NY-A	2	0	1.50	2	2	2	0	0	18	14	3	6	14
W 1931	Phi-A	0	1	4.50	1	1	0	0	0	6	7	3	0	1
W Total	7	6	4	1.83	12	11	6	0	1	83^2	81	17	22	49
● **Al Hrabosky**														
L 1978	KC-A	0	0	3.00	3	0	0	0	0	3	3	1	0	2
● **Carl Hubbell**														
W 1933	NY-N	2	0	0.00	2	2	2	0	0	20	13	0	6	15
W 1936	NY-N	1	1	2.25	2	2	1	0	0	16	15	4	2	10
W 1937	NY-N	1	1	3.77	2	2	1	0	0	14^1	12	6	4	7
W Total	3	4	2	1.79	6	6	4	0	0	50^1	40	10	12	32
● **Charles Hudson**														
L 1983	Phi-N	1	0	2.00	1	1	1	0	0	9	4	2	2	9
W 1983	Phi-N	0	2	8.64	2	2	0	0	0	8^1	9	8	1	6
● **Joe Hudson**														
D 1995	Bos-A	0	0	0.00	1	0	0	0	0	1	2	0	1	0

YEAR	TM/L	W	L	ERA	G	GS	CG	SV	SHO	IP	H	ER	BB	SO
● **Nat Hudson**														
W 1886	StL-A	1	0	2.57	1	1	1	0	0	7	3	2	3	3
● **Tim Hudson**														
D 2000	Oak-A	0	1	3.38	1	1	1	0	0	8	6	3	4	5
● **Jim Hughes**														
W 1953	Bro-N	0	0	2.25	1	0	0	0	0	4	3	1	1	3
● **Mickey Hughes**														
W 1889	Bro-A	1	0	7.71	1	1	0	0	0	7	14	6	3	3
● **Dick Hughes**														
W 1967	StL-N	0	1	5.00	2	2	0	0	0	9	9	5	3	7
W 1968	StL-N	0	0	0.00	1	0	0	0	0	0^1	2	0	0	0
W Total	2	0	1	4.82	3	2	0	0	0	9^1	11	5	3	7
● **Tom Hughes**														
W 1903	Bos-A	0	1	9.00	1	1	0	0	0	2	4	2	2	0
● **Tex Hughson**														
W 1946	Bos-A	0	1	3.14	3	2	0	0	0	14^1	14	5	3	8
● **Mark Huismann**														
L 1984	KC-A	0	0	6.75	1	0	0	0	0	2^2	6	2	1	2
● **Tom Hume**														
L 1979	Cin-N	0	1	6.75	3	0	0	0	0	4	6	3	0	2
● **Bob Humphreys**														
W 1964	StL-N	0	0	0.00	1	0	0	0	0	1	0	0	0	1
● **Ken Hunt**														
W 1961	Cin-N	0	0	0.00	1	0	0	0	0	1	0	0	1	1
● **Catfish Hunter**														
L 1971	Oak-A	0	1	5.63	1	1	1	0	0	8	7	5	2	6
L 1972	Oak-A	0	0	1.17	2	2	0	0	0	15^1	10	2	5	9
L 1973	Oak-A	2	0	1.65	2	2	1	0	1	16^1	12	3	5	6
L 1974	Oak-A	1	1	4.63	2	2	0	0	0	11^2	11	6	2	6
L 1976	NY-A	1	1	4.50	2	2	1	0	0	12	10	6	1	5
L 1978	NY-A	0	0	4.50	1	1	0	0	0	6	7	3	3	5
L Total	6	4	3	3.25	10	10	3	0	1	69^1	57	25	18	37
W 1972	Oak-A	2	0	2.81	3	2	0	0	0	16	12	5	6	11
W 1973	Oak-A	1	0	2.03	2	2	0	0	0	13^1	11	3	4	6
W 1974	Oak-A	1	0	1.17	2	1	0	1	0	7^2	5	1	2	5
W 1976	NY-A	0	1	3.12	1	1	1	0	0	8^2	10	3	4	5
W 1977	NY-A	0	1	10.38	2	1	0	0	0	4^1	6	5	0	1
W 1978	NY-A	1	1	4.15	2	2	0	0	0	13	13	6	1	5
W Total	6	5	3	3.29	12	9	1	1	0	63	57	23	17	33
● **Bruce Hurst**														
L 1986	Bos-A	1	0	2.40	2	2	1	0	0	15	18	4	1	8
L 1988	Bos-A	0	2	2.77	2	2	1	0	0	13	10	4	5	12
L Total	2	1	2	2.57	4	4	2	0	0	28	28	8	6	20
W 1986	Bos-A	2	0	1.96	3	3	1	0	0	23	18	5	6	17
● **Johnny Hutchings**														
W 1940	Cin-N	0	0	9.00	1	0	0	0	0	1	2	1	1	0
● **Fred Hutchinson**														
W 1940	Det-A	0	0	9.00	1	0	0	0	0	1	1	1	1	1
● **Hideki Irabu**														
L 1999	NY-A	0	0	13.50	1	0	0	0	0	4^2	13	7	0	3
● **Jason Isringhausen**														
D 2000	Oak-A	0	0	0.00	2	0	0	1	0	2	1	0	0	3
● **Danny Jackson**														
L 1985	KC-A	1	0	0.00	2	1	1	0	1	10	10	0	1	7
L 1990	Cin-N	1	0	2.38	2	2	0	0	0	11^1	8	3	7	8
L 1992	Pit-N	0	1	21.60	1	1	0	0	0	1^2	4	4	2	0
L 1993	Phi-N	1	0	1.17	1	1	0	0	0	7^2	9	1	2	6
L 1996	StL-N	0	0	9.00	1	0	0	0	0	3	7	3	3	3
L Total	5	3	1	2.94	7	5	1	0	1	33^2	38	11	15	24
W 1985	KC-A	1	1	1.69	2	2	0	0	0	16	9	3	5	12
W 1990	Cin-N	0	0	10.13	1	1	0	0	0	2^2	6	3	2	0
W 1993	Phi-N	0	1	7.20	1	1	0	0	0	5	6	4	1	1
W Total	3	1	2	3.80	4	4	1	0	0	23^2	21	10	8	13
● **Grant Jackson**														
L 1973	Bal-A	1	0	0.00	2	0	0	0	0	3	0	0	1	0
L 1974	Bal-A	0	0	0.00	1	0	0	0	0	0^1	1	0	0	1
L 1976	NY-A	0	0	8.10	2	0	0	0	0	3^1	4	3	1	3
L 1979	Pit-N	1	0	0.00	2	0	0	0	0	2	1	0	1	2
L Total	4	2	0	3.12	7	0	0	0	0	8^2	6	3	3	6
W 1971	Bal-A	0	0	0.00	1	0	0	0	0	0^2	0	0	1	0
W 1976	NY-A	0	0	4.91	1	0	0	0	0	3^2	4	2	0	3
W 1979	Pit-N	1	0	0.00	4	0	0	0	0	4^2	1	0	2	2
W Total	3	1	0	2.00	6	0	0	0	0	9	5	2	3	5
● **Mike Jackson**														
D 1995	Cin-N	0	0	0.00	3	0	0	0	0	3^2	4	0	0	1
D 1997	Cle-A	1	0	0.00	4	0	0	0	0	4^1	3	0	1	5
D 1998	Cle-A	0	0	4.50	3	0	0	3	0	4	3	2	1	1
D 1999	Cle-A	0	0	4.50	2	0	0	0	0	2	2	1	1	1
D Total	4	1	0	1.93	12	0	0	3	0	14	12	3	3	8
L 1995	Cin-N	0	1	23.14	3	0	0	0	0	2^1	5	6	4	1
L 1997	Cle-A	0	0	0.00	5	0	0	0	0	4^1	1	0	1	7
L 1998	Cle-A	0	0	0.00	1	0	0	1	0	1	0	0	0	2
L Total	3	0	1	7.04	9	0	0	1	0	7^2	6	6	5	10

YEAR	TM/L	W	L	ERA	G	GS	CG	SV	SHO	IP	H	ER	BB	SO
W 1997	Cle-A	0	0	1.93	4	0	0	0	0	4^2	5	1	3	4
● **Sig Jakucki**														
W 1944	StL-A	0	1	9.00	1	1	0	0	0	3	5	3	0	4
● **Mike James**														
D 2000	StL-N	1	0	0.00	2	0	0	0	0	4^1	1	0	1	1
L 2000	StL-N	0	0	15.43	4	0	0	0	0	2^1	5	4	1	0
● **Bill James**														
W 1919	Chi-A	0	0	5.79	1	0	0	0	0	4^2	8	3	3	2
● **Bill James**														
W 1914	Bos-N	2	0	0.00	2	1	1	0	1	11	2	0	6	9
● **Larry Jansen**														
W 1951	NY-N	0	2	6.30	3	2	0	0	0	10	8	7	4	6
● **Pat Jarvis**														
L 1969	Atl-N	0	1	12.46	1	1	0	0	0	4^1	10	6	0	6
● **Larry Jaster**														
W 1967	StL-N	0	0	0.00	1	0	0	0	0	0^1	2	0	0	0
W 1968	StL-N	0	0	∞	1	0	0	0	0	0	2	3	1	0
W Total	2	0	0	81.00	2	0	0	0	0	0^1	4	3	1	0
● **Joey Jay**														
W 1961	Cin-N	1	1	5.59	2	2	1	0	0	9^2	8	6	6	6
● **Tommy John**														
D 1981	NY-A	0	1	6.43	1	1	0	0	0	7	8	5	2	0
L 1977	LA-N	1	0	0.66	2	2	1	0	0	13^2	11	1	5	11
L 1978	LA-N	1	0	0.00	1	1	1	0	1	9	4	0	2	4
L 1980	NY-A	0	0	2.70	1	1	0	0	0	6^2	8	2	1	3
L 1981	NY-A	1	0	1.50	1	1	0	0	0	6	6	1	1	3
L 1982	Cal-A	1	1	5.11	2	2	1	0	0	12^1	11	7	6	6
L Total	5	4	1	2.08	7	7	3	0	1	47^2	40	11	15	27
W 1977	LA-N	0	1	6.00	1	1	0	0	0	6	9	4	3	7
W 1978	LA-N	1	0	3.07	2	2	0	0	0	14^2	14	5	4	6
W 1981	NY-A	1	0	0.69	3	2	0	0	0	13	11	1	0	8
W Total	3	2	1	2.67	6	5	0	0	0	33^2	34	10	7	21
● **Earl Johnson**														
W 1946	Bos-A	1	0	2.70	3	0	0	0	0	3^1	1	1	2	1
● **Ernie Johnson**														
W 1957	Mil-N	0	1	1.29	3	0	0	0	0	7	2	1	1	8
● **Jerry Johnson**														
L 1971	SF-N	0	0	13.50	1	0	0	0	0	1^1	1	2	1	2
● **Ken Johnson**														
W 1961	Cin-N	0	0	0.00	1	0	0	0	0	0^2	0	0	0	0
● **Randy Johnson**														
D 1995	Sea-A	2	0	2.70	2	1	0	0	0	10	5	3	6	16
D 1997	Sea-A	0	2	5.54	2	2	1	0	0	13	14	8	6	16
D 1998	Hou-N	0	2	1.93	2	2	0	0	0	14	12	3	2	17
D 1999	Ari-N	0	1	7.56	1	1	0	0	0	8^1	8	7	3	11
D Total	4	2	5	4.17	7	6	1	0	0	45^1	39	21	17	60
L 1995	Sea-A	0	1	2.35	2	2	0	0	0	15^1	12	4	2	13
● **Bob Johnson**														
L 1971	Pit-N	1	0	0.00	1	1	0	0	0	8	5	0	3	7
L 1972	Pit-N	0	0	3.00	2	0	0	0	0	6	4	2	2	7
L Total	2	1	0	1.29	3	1	0	0	0	14	9	2	5	14
W 1971	Pit-N	0	1	9.00	2	1	0	0	0	5	5	5	3	3
● **Syl Johnson**														
W 1928	StL-N	0	0	4.50	2	0	0	0	0	2	4	1	1	1
W 1930	StL-N	0	0	7.20	2	0	0	0	0	5	4	4	3	4
W 1931	StL-N	0	1	3.00	3	1	0	0	0	9	10	3	1	6
W Total	3	0	1	4.50	7	1	0	0	0	16	18	8	5	11
● **Walter Johnson**														
W 1924	Was-A	1	2	2.25	3	2	2	0	0	24	30	6	11	20
W 1925	Was-A	2	1	2.08	3	3	3	0	1	26	26	6	4	15
W Total	2	3	3	2.16	6	5	5	0	1	50	56	12	15	35
● **Doug Jones**														
D 1998	Cle-A	0	0	6.75	1	0	0	0	0	2^2	3	2	1	1
D 2000	Oak-A	0	0	0.00	2	0	0	0	0	1^1	1	0	0	1
D Total	2	0	0	4.50	3	0	0	0	0	4	4	2	1	2
● **Jeff Jones**														
L 1981	Oak-A	0	0	4.50	1	0	0	0	0	2	2	1	1	0
● **Mike Jones**														
D 1981	KC-A	0	1	2.25	1	1	0	0	0	8	9	2	0	2
L 1984	KC-A	0	0	6.75	1	0	0	0	0	1^1	1	1	0	0
● **Bobby Jones**														
D 2000	NY-N	1	0	0.00	1	1	1	0	1	9	1	0	2	5
L 2000	NY-N	0	0	13.50	1	1	0	0	0	4	6	6	0	2
W 2000	NY-N	0	1	5.40	1	1	0	0	0	5	4	3	3	3
● **Sam Jones**														
W 1918	Bos-A	0	1	3.00	1	1	1	0	0	9	7	3	5	5
W 1922	NY-A	0	0	0.00	2	0	0	0	0	2	1	0	1	0
W 1923	NY-A	0	1	0.90	2	1	0	1	0	10	5	1	2	3
W 1926	NY-A	0	0	9.00	1	0	0	0	0	1	2	1	2	1
W Total	4	0	2	2.05	6	2	1	1	0	22	15	5	10	9

YEAR	TM/L	W	L	ERA	G	GS	CG	SV	SHO	IP	H	ER	BB	SO
● **Sheldon Jones**														
W 1951	NY-N	0	0	2.08	2	0	0	1	0	4^1	5	1	1	2
● **Sherman Jones**														
W 1961	Cin-N	0	0	0.00	1	0	0	0	0	0^2	0	0	0	0
● **Claude Jonnard**														
W 1923	NY-N	0	0	0.00	2	0	0	0	0	2	1	0	1	1
W 1924	NY-N	0	0	—	1	0	0	0	0	0	0	0	1	0
W Total	2	0	0	0.00	3	0	0	0	0	2	1	0	2	1
● **Jeff Juden**														
L 1997	Cle-A	0	0	0.00	3	0	0	0	0	1	2	0	2	2
W 1997	Cle-A	0	0	4.50	2	0	0	0	0	2	2	1	2	0
● **Al Jurisich**														
W 1944	StL-N	0	0	27.00	1	0	0	0	0	0^2	2	2	1	0
● **Jim Kaat**														
L 1970	Min-A	0	1	9.00	1	1	0	0	0	2	6	2	2	1
L 1976	Phi-N	0	0	3.00	1	1	0	0	0	6	2	2	2	1
L Total	2	0	1	4.50	2	2	0	0	0	8	8	4	4	2
W 1965	Min-A	1	2	3.77	3	3	1	0	0	14^1	18	6	2	6
W 1982	StL-N	0	0	3.86	4	0	0	0	0	2^1	4	1	2	2
W Total	2	1	2	3.78	7	3	1	0	0	16^2	22	7	4	8
● **Scott Kamieniecki**														
D 1995	NY-A	0	0	7.20	1	1	0	0	0	5	9	4	4	4
L 1997	Bal-A	1	0	0.00	2	1	0	0	0	8	4	0	2	5
● **Matt Karchner**														
D 1998	Chi-N	0	0	13.50	1	0	0	0	0	0^2	1	1	0	1
● **Steve Karsay**														
D 1999	Cle-A	0	0	9.00	2	0	0	0	0	3	5	3	1	3
● **Tim Keefe**														
W 1884	NY-A	0	2	3.60	2	2	2	0	0	15	10	6	3	12
W 1888	NY-N	4	0	0.51	4	4	4	0	0	35	18	2	9	30
W 1889	NY-N	0	1	8.18	2	1	1	1	0	11	17	10	2	4
W Total	3	4	3	2.66	8	7	7	1	0	61	45	18	14	46
● **Vic Keen**														
W 1926	StL-N	0	0	0.00	1	0	0	0	0	1	0	0	0	0
● **Monte Kennedy**														
W 1951	NY-N	0	0	6.00	2	0	0	0	0	3	3	2	1	4
● **Brickyard Kennedy**														
W 1903	Pit-N	0	1	5.14	1	1	0	0	0	7	11	4	3	3
● **Matt Keough**														
L 1981	Oak-A	0	1	1.08	1	1	0	0	0	8^1	7	1	6	4
● **Charlie Kerfeld**														
L 1986	Hou-N	0	1	2.25	3	0	0	0	0	4	2	1	1	4
● **Dickie Kerr**														
W 1919	Chi-A	2	0	1.42	2	2	2	0	1	19	14	3	3	6
● **Jimmy Key**														
D 1996	NY-A	0	0	3.60	1	1	0	0	0	5	5	2	1	3
D 1997	Bal-A	0	1	3.86	1	1	0	0	0	4^2	8	2	0	4
D Total	2	0	1	3.72	2	2	0	0	0	9^2	13	4	1	7
L 1985	Tor-A	0	1	5.19	2	2	0	0	0	8^2	15	5	2	5
L 1989	Tor-A	1	0	4.50	1	1	0	0	0	6	7	3	2	2
L 1991	Tor-A	0	0	3.00	1	1	0	0	0	6	5	2	1	1
L 1992	Tor-A	0	0	0.00	1	0	0	0	0	3	2	0	2	1
L 1996	NY-A	1	0	2.25	1	1	0	0	0	8	3	2	1	5
L 1997	Bal-A	0	0	2.57	2	1	0	0	0	7	5	2	3	7
L Total	6	2	1	3.26	8	6	0	0	0	38^2	37	14	11	21
W 1992	Tor-A	2	0	1.00	2	1	0	0	0	9	6	1	0	6
W 1996	NY-A	1	1	3.97	2	2	0	0	0	11^1	15	5	5	1
W Total	2	3	1	2.66	4	3	0	0	0	20^1	21	6	5	7
● **Dana Kiecker**														
L 1990	Bos-A	0	0	1.59	1	1	0	0	0	5^2	6	1	1	2
● **Darryl Kile**														
D 1997	Hou-N	0	1	2.57	1	1	0	0	0	7	2	2	2	4
D 2000	StL-N	1	0	2.57	1	1	0	0	0	7	4	2	2	6
D Total	2	1	1	2.57	2	2	0	0	0	14	6	4	4	10
L 2000	StL-N	0	2	9.00	2	2	0	0	0	10	13	10	5	3
● **Paul Kilgus**														
L 1989	Chi-N	0	0	0.00	1	0	0	0	0	3	4	0	1	1
● **Ed Killian**														
W 1907	Det-A	0	0	2.25	1	0	0	0	0	4	3	1	1	1
W 1908	Det-A	0	0	11.57	1	1	0	0	0	2^1	5	3	3	1
W Total	2	0	0	5.68	2	1	0	0	0	6^1	8	4	4	2
● **Silver King**														
W 1887	StL-A	1	3	2.03	4	4	4	0	0	31	28	7	2	21
W 1888	StL-A	1	3	2.31	5	5	4	0	0	35	37	9	9	12
W Total	2	2	6	2.18	9	9	8	0	0	66	65	16	11	33
● **Eric King**														
L 1987	Det-A	0	0	1.69	2	0	0	0	0	5^1	3	1	2	4
● **Brian Kingman**														
L 1981	Oak-A	0	0	81.00	1	0	0	0	0	0^1	3	3	0	0
● **Bob Kipper**														
L 1991	Pit-N	0	0	4.50	1	0	0	0	0	2	2	1	0	1

YEAR	TM/L	W	L	ERA	G	GS	CG	SV	SHO	IP	H	ER	BB	SO
● Bruce Kison														
L 1971	Pit-N	1	0	0.00	1	0	0	0	0	4^2	2	0	2	3
L 1972	Pit-N	1	0	0.00	2	0	0	0	0	2^1	1	0	0	3
L 1974	Pit-N	1	0	0.00	1	1	0	0	0	6^2	2	0	6	5
L 1975	Pit-N	0	0	4.50	1	0	0	0	0	2	2	1	1	1
L 1982	Cal-A	1	0	1.93	2	2	1	0	0	14	8	3	3	12
L Total	5	4	0	1.21	7	3	1	0	0	29^2	15	4	12	24
W 1971	Pit-N	1	0	0.00	2	0	0	0	0	6^1	1	0	2	3
W 1979	Pit-N	0	1	108.00	1	1	0	0	0	0^1	3	4	2	0
W Total	2	1	1	5.40	3	1	0	0	0	6^2	4	4	4	3
● Frank Kitson														
T 1900	Bro-N	1	0	1.00	1	1	1	0	0	9	4	1	1	2
● Ed Klieman														
W 1948	Cle-A	0	0	∞	1	0	0	0	0	0	1	3	2	0
● Bob Klinger														
W 1946	Bos-A	0	1	13.50	1	0	0	0	0	0^2	2	1	1	0
● Joe Klink														
W 1990	Oak-A	0	0	—	1	0	0	0	0	0	0	0	1	0
● Johnny Klippstein														
W 1959	LA-N	0	0	0.00	1	0	0	0	0	2	1	0	0	2
W 1965	Min-A	0	0	0.00	2	0	0	0	0	2^2	2	0	2	3
W Total	2	0	0	0.00	3	0	0	0	0	4^2	3	0	2	5
● Fred Klobedanz														
T 1897	Bos-N	0	1	9.35	2	1	0	0	0	8^2	12	9	8	0
● Chris Knapp														
L 1979	Cal-A	0	1	7.71	1	1	0	0	0	2^1	5	2	1	0
● Bob Knepper														
D 1981	Hou-N	0	1	5.40	1	1	0	0	0	5	6	3	2	4
L 1986	Hou-N	0	0	3.52	2	2	0	0	0	15^1	13	6	1	9
● Darold Knowles														
L 1971	Oak-A	0	0	0.00	1	0	0	0	0	0^1	1	0	0	0
W 1973	Oak-A	0	0	0.00	7	0	0	2	0	6^1	4	0	5	5
● Alex Konikowski														
W 1951	NY-N	0	0	0.00	1	0	0	0	0	1	1	0	0	0
● Jim Konstanty														
W 1950	Phi-N	0	1	2.40	3	1	0	0	0	15	9	4	4	3
● Jerry Koosman														
L 1969	NY-N	0	0	11.57	1	1	0	0	0	4^2	7	6	4	5
L 1973	NY-N	1	0	2.00	1	1	1	0	0	9	8	2	0	9
L 1983	Chi-A	0	0	54.00	1	0	0	0	0	0^1	1	2	2	0
L Total	3	1	0	6.43	3	2	1	0	0	14	16	10	6	14
W 1969	NY-N	2	0	2.04	2	2	1	0	0	17^2	7	4	4	9
W 1973	NY-N	1	0	3.12	2	2	0	0	0	8^2	9	3	7	8
W Total	2	3	0	2.39	4	4	1	0	0	26^1	16	7	11	17
● Dave Koslo														
W 1951	NY-N	1	1	3.00	2	2	1	0	0	15	12	5	7	6
● Sandy Koufax														
W 1959	LA-N	0	1	1.00	2	1	0	0	0	9	5	1	1	7
W 1963	LA-N	2	0	1.50	2	2	2	0	0	18	12	3	3	23
W 1965	LA-N	2	1	0.38	3	3	2	0	2	24	13	1	5	29
W 1966	LA-N	0	1	1.50	1	1	0	0	0	6	6	1	2	2
W Total	4	4	3	0.95	8	7	4	0	2	57	36	6	11	61
● Fabian Kowalik														
W 1935	Chi-N	0	0	2.08	1	0	0	0	0	4^1	3	1	1	1
● Jack Kramer														
W 1944	StL-A	1	0	0.00	2	1	1	0	0	11	9	0	4	12
● Ray Kremer														
W 1925	Pit-N	2	1	3.00	3	2	2	0	0	21	17	7	4	9
W 1927	Pit-N	0	1	3.60	1	1	0	0	0	5	5	2	3	1
W Total	2	2	2	3.12	4	3	2	0	0	26	22	9	7	10
● Howie Krist														
W 1943	StL-N	0	0	—	1	0	0	0	0	0	1	0	0	0
● Mike Krukow														
L 1987	SF-N	1	0	2.00	1	1	1	0	0	9	9	2	1	3
● Johnny Kucks														
W 1955	NY-A	0	0	6.00	2	0	0	0	0	3	4	2	1	1
W 1956	NY-A	1	0	0.82	3	1	1	0	1	11	6	1	3	2
W 1957	NY-A	0	0	0.00	1	0	0	0	0	0^2	1	0	1	1
W 1958	NY-A	0	0	2.08	2	0	0	0	0	4^1	4	1	1	0
W Total	4	1	0	1.89	8	1	1	0	1	19	15	4	6	4
● Bob Kuzava														
W 1951	NY-A	0	0	0.00	1	0	0	1	0	1	0	0	0	0
W 1952	NY-A	0	0	0.00	1	0	0	1	0	2^2	0	0	0	2
W 1953	NY-A	0	0	13.50	1	0	0	0	0	0^2	2	1	0	1
W Total	3	0	0	2.08	3	0	0	2	0	4^1	2	1	0	3
● Clem Labine														
W 1953	Bro-N	0	2	3.60	3	0	0	1	0	5	10	2	1	3
W 1955	Bro-N	1	0	2.89	4	0	0	1	0	9^1	6	3	2	2
W 1956	Bro-N	1	0	0.00	2	1	1	0	1	12	8	0	3	7
W 1959	LA-N	0	0	0.00	1	0	0	0	0	1	0	0	0	1
W 1960	Pit-N	0	0	13.50	3	0	0	0	0	4	13	6	1	2
W Total	5	2	2	3.16	13	1	1	2	1	31^1	37	11	7	15

YEAR	TM/L	W	L	ERA	G	GS	CG	SV	SHO	IP	H	ER	BB	SO
● Frank LaCorte														
D 1981	Hou-N	0	0	0.00	2	0	0	0	0	3^2	2	0	1	5
L 1980	Hou-N	1	1	3.00	2	0	0	0	0	3	7	1	2	2
● Mike LaCoss														
L 1979	Cin-N	0	1	10.80	1	1	0	0	0	1^2	1	2	4	0
L 1987	SF-N	0	0	0.00	2	0	0	0	0	3^1	1	0	3	2
L 1989	SF-N	0	0	9.00	1	1	0	0	0	3	7	3	0	2
L Total	3	0	1	5.63	4	2	0	0	0	8	9	5	7	4
W 1989	SF-N	0	0	6.23	2	0	0	0	0	4^1	4	3	3	2
● Pete Ladd														
L 1982	Mil-A	0	0	0.00	3	0	0	2	0	3^1	0	0	0	5
W 1982	Mil-A	0	0	0.00	1	0	0	0	0	0^2	1	0	2	0
● Lerrin LaGrow														
L 1972	Det-A	0	0	0.00	1	0	0	0	0	1	0	0	0	1
● Jeff Lahti														
L 1985	StL-N	1	0	0.00	2	0	0	0	0	2	2	0	0	1
W 1982	StL-N	0	0	10.80	2	0	0	0	0	1^2	4	2	1	1
W 1985	StL-N	0	0	12.27	3	0	0	1	0	3^2	10	5	0	2
W Total	2	0	0	11.81	5	0	0	1	0	5^1	14	7	1	3
● Jack Lamabe														
W 1967	StL-N	0	1	6.75	3	0	0	0	0	2^2	5	2	0	4
● Dennis Lamp														
L 1983	Chi-A	0	0	0.00	3	0	0	0	0	2	0	0	2	1
L 1985	Tor-A	0	0	0.00	3	0	0	0	0	9^1	2	0	1	10
L 1990	Bos-A	0	0	108.00	1	0	0	0	0	0^1	2	4	2	0
L Total	3	0	0	3.09	7	0	0	0	0	11^2	4	4	5	11
● Les Lancaster														
L 1989	Chi-N	1	1	6.00	3	0	0	0	0	6	6	4	1	3
● Bill Landrum														
L 1990	Pit-N	0	0	0.00	2	0	0	0	0	2	0	0	0	1
L 1991	Pit-N	0	0	9.00	1	0	0	0	0	1	2	1	2	2
L Total	2	0	0	3.00	3	0	0	0	0	3	2	1	2	3
● Rick Langford														
D 1981	Oak-A	1	0	1.23	1	1	0	0	0	7^1	10	1	0	3
● Mark Langston														
L 1998	SD-N	0	0	0.00	3	0	0	0	0	1^1	1	0	0	1
W 1998	SD-N	0	0	40.50	1	0	0	0	0	0^2	1	3	2	0
● Max Lanier														
W 1942	StL-N	1	0	0.00	2	0	0	0	0	4	3	0	1	1
W 1943	StL-N	0	1	1.76	3	2	0	0	0	15^1	13	3	3	13
W 1944	StL-N	1	0	2.19	2	2	0	0	0	12^1	8	3	8	11
W Total	3	2	1	1.71	7	4	0	0	0	31^2	24	6	12	25
● Dave LaPoint														
W 1982	StL-N	0	0	3.24	2	1	0	0	0	8^1	10	3	2	3
● Dave LaRoche														
L 1979	Cal-A	0	0	6.75	1	0	0	0	0	1^1	2	1	1	1
W 1981	NY-A	0	0	0.00	1	0	0	0	0	1	0	0	0	2
● Don Larsen														
W 1955	NY-A	0	1	11.25	1	1	0	0	0	4	5	5	2	2
W 1956	NY-A	1	0	0.00	2	2	1	0	1	10^2	1	0	4	7
W 1957	NY-A	1	1	3.72	2	1	0	0	0	9^2	8	4	5	6
W 1958	NY-A	1	0	0.96	2	2	0	0	0	9^1	9	1	6	9
W 1962	SF-N	1	0	3.86	3	0	0	0	0	2^1	1	1	2	0
W Total	5	4	2	2.75	10	6	1	0	1	36	24	11	19	24
● Fred Lasher														
W 1968	Det-A	0	0	0.00	1	0	0	0	0	2	1	0	0	1
● Gary Lavelle														
L 1985	Tor-A	0	0	—	1	0	0	0	0	0	0	0	1	0
● Vern Law														
W 1960	Pit-N	2	0	3.44	3	3	0	0	0	18^1	22	7	3	8
● Terry Leach														
L 1988	NY-N	0	0	0.00	3	0	0	0	0	5	4	0	1	4
W 1991	Min-A	0	0	3.86	2	0	0	0	0	2^1	2	1	0	2
● Tim Leary														
L 1988	LA-N	0	1	6.23	2	1	0	0	0	4^1	8	3	3	3
W 1988	LA-N	0	0	1.35	2	0	0	0	0	6^2	6	1	2	4
● Bill Lee														
W 1935	Chi-N	0	0	4.35	2	1	0	1	0	10^1	11	5	5	5
W 1938	Chi-N	0	2	2.45	2	2	0	0	0	11	15	3	1	8
W Total	2	0	2	3.38	4	3	0	1	0	21^1	26	8	6	13
● Bill Lee														
D 1981	Mon-N	0	0	0.00	1	0	0	0	0	0^2	2	0	0	1
L 1981	Mon-N	0	0	0.00	1	0	0	0	0	0^1	1	0	0	0
W 1975	Bos-A	0	0	3.14	2	2	0	0	0	14^1	12	5	3	7
● Sam Leever														
T 1900	Pit-N	0	2	1.38	2	2	1	0	0	13	13	2	4	4
W 1903	Pit-N	0	2	5.40	2	2	1	0	0	10	13	6	3	2
● Craig Lefferts														
L 1984	SD-N	2	0	0.00	3	0	0	0	0	4	1	0	1	1
L 1987	SF-N	0	0	0.00	3	0	0	0	0	2	3	0	1	0

YEAR	TM/L	W	L	ERA	G	GS	CG	SV	SHO	IP	H	ER	BB	SO
L 1989	SF-N	0	0	9.00	2	0	0	0	0	1	1	1	2	1
L Total	3	2	0	1.29	8	0	0	0	0	7	5	1	4	2
W 1984	SD-N	0	0	0.00	3	0	0	1	0	6	2	0	1	7
W 1989	SF-N	0	0	3.38	3	0	0	0	0	2^{2}	2	1	2	1
W Total	2	0	0	1.04	6	0	0	1	0	8^{2}	4	1	3	8
● **Ken Lehman**														
W 1952	Bro-N	0	0	0.00	1	0	0	0	0	2	2	0	1	0
● **Charlie Leibrandt**														
L 1979	Cin-N	0	0	0.00	1	0	0	0	0	0^{1}	0	0	0	0
L 1984	KC-A	0	1	1.13	1	1	1	0	0	8	3	1	4	6
L 1985	KC-A	1	2	5.28	3	2	0	0	0	15^{1}	17	9	4	6
L 1991	Atl-N	0	0	1.35	1	1	0	0	0	6^{2}	8	1	3	6
L 1992	Atl-N	0	0	1.93	2	0	0	0	0	4^{2}	4	1	3	3
L Total	5	1	3	3.09	8	4	1	0	0	35	32	12	14	21
W 1985	KC-A	0	1	2.76	2	2	0	0	0	16^{1}	10	5	4	10
W 1991	Atl-N	0	2	11.25	2	1	0	0	0	4	8	5	1	3
W 1992	Atl-N	0	1	9.00	1	0	0	0	0	2	3	2	0	0
W Total	3	0	4	4.84	5	3	0	0	0	22^{1}	21	12	5	13
● **Lefty Leifield**														
W 1909	Pit-N	0	1	11.25	1	1	0	0	0	4	7	5	1	0
● **Al Leiter**														
D 1997	Fla-N	0	0	9.00	1	1	0	0	0	4	7	4	3	3
D 1999	NY-N	0	0	3.52	1	1	0	0	0	7^{2}	3	3	3	4
D 2000	NY-N	0	0	2.25	1	1	0	0	0	8	5	2	3	6
D Total	3	0	0	4.12	3	3	0	0	0	19^{2}	15	9	9	13
L 1993	Tor-A	0	0	3.38	2	0	0	0	0	2^{2}	4	1	2	2
L 1997	Fla-N	0	1	4.32	2	1	0	0	0	8^{1}	13	4	2	6
L 1999	NY-N	0	1	6.43	2	2	0	0	0	7	5	5	4	5
L 2000	NY-N	0	0	3.86	1	1	0	0	0	7	8	3	0	9
L Total	4	0	2	4.68	7	4	0	0	0	25	30	13	8	22
W 1993	Tor-A	1	0	7.71	3	0	0	0	0	7	12	6	2	5
W 1997	Fla-N	0	0	5.06	2	2	0	0	0	10^{2}	10	6	10	10
W 2000	NY-N	0	1	2.87	2	2	0	0	0	15^{2}	12	5	6	16
W Total	3	1	1	4.59	7	4	0	0	0	33^{1}	34	17	18	31
● **Bob Lemon**														
W 1948	Cle-A	2	0	1.65	2	2	1	0	0	16^{1}	16	3	7	6
W 1954	Cle-A	0	2	6.75	2	2	1	0	0	13^{1}	16	10	8	11
W Total	2	2	2	3.94	4	4	2	0	0	29^{2}	32	13	15	17
● **Dennis Leonard**														
D 1981	KC-A	0	1	1.13	1	1	0	0	0	8	7	1	1	3
L 1976	KC-A	0	0	19.29	2	2	0	0	0	2^{1}	9	5	2	0
L 1977	KC-A	1	1	3.00	2	1	1	0	0	9	5	3	2	4
L 1978	KC-A	0	2	3.75	2	2	1	0	0	12	13	5	2	11
L 1980	KC-A	1	0	2.25	1	1	0	0	0	8	7	2	1	8
L Total	4	2	3	4.31	7	6	2	0	0	31^{1}	34	15	7	23
W 1980	KC-A	1	1	6.75	2	2	0	0	0	10^{2}	15	8	2	5
● **Dutch Leonard**														
W 1915	Bos-A	1	0	1.00	1	1	1	0	0	9	3	1	0	6
W 1916	Bos-A	1	0	1.00	1	1	1	0	0	9	5	1	4	3
W Total	2	2	0	1.00	2	2	2	0	0	18	8	2	4	9
● **Dave Leonhard**														
W 1969	Bal-A	0	0	4.50	1	0	0	0	0	2	1	1	1	1
W 1971	Bal-A	0	0	0.00	1	0	0	0	0	1	0	0	1	0
W Total	2	0	0	3.00	2	0	0	0	0	3	1	1	2	1
● **Randy Lerch**														
D 1981	Mil-A	0	0	1.50	1	1	0	0	0	6	3	1	4	3
L 1978	Phi-N	0	0	5.06	1	1	0	0	0	5^{1}	7	3	0	0
● **Curt Leskanic**														
D 1995	Col-N	0	1	6.00	3	0	0	0	0	3	3	2	0	4
● **Ted Lewis**														
T 1897	Bos-N	1	1	6.00	3	1	0	0	0	12	18	8	9	4
● **Don Liddle**														
W 1954	NY-N	1	0	1.29	2	1	0	0	0	7	5	1	1	2
● **Kerry Ligtenberg**														
D 1998	Atl-N	0	0	0.00	3	0	0	0	0	3^{1}	1	0	4	3
D 2000	Atl-N	0	0	5.40	3	0	0	0	0	1^{2}	0	1	1	3
D Total	2	0	0	1.80	6	0	0	0	0	5	1	1	5	6
L 1997	Atl-N	0	0	0.00	2	0	0	0	0	3	1	0	0	4
L 1998	Atl-N	0	1	7.36	4	0	0	0	0	3^{2}	3	3	2	5
L Total	2	0	1	4.05	6	0	0	0	0	6^{2}	4	3	2	9
● **Jose Lima**														
D 1997	Hou-N	0	0	0.00	1	0	0	0	0	1	0	0	1	1
D 1999	Hou-N	0	1	5.40	1	1	0	0	0	6^{2}	9	4	2	4
D Total	2	0	1	4.70	2	1	0	0	0	7^{2}	9	4	3	5
● **Paul Lindblad**														
L 1975	Oak-A	0	0	0.00	2	0	0	0	0	4^{2}	5	0	1	0
W 1973	Oak-A	1	0	0.00	3	0	0	0	0	3^{1}	4	0	1	1
W 1978	NY-A	0	0	11.57	1	0	0	0	0	2^{1}	4	3	0	1
W Total	2	1	0	4.76	4	0	0	0	0	5^{2}	8	3	1	2
● **Jim Lindsey**														
W 1930	StL-N	0	0	1.93	2	0	0	0	0	4^{2}	1	1	1	2
W 1931	StL-N	0	0	5.40	2	0	0	0	0	3^{1}	4	2	3	2
W Total	2	0	0	3.38	4	0	0	0	0	8	5	3	4	4

YEAR	TM/L	W	L	ERA	G	GS	CG	SV	SHO	IP	H	ER	BB	SO
● **Mark Littell**														
L 1976	KC-A	0	1	1.93	3	0	0	0	0	4^{2}	4	1	1	3
L 1977	KC-A	0	0	3.00	2	0	0	0	0	3	5	1	3	1
L Total	2	0	1	2.35	5	0	0	0	0	7^{2}	9	2	4	4
● **Graeme Lloyd**														
D 1996	NY-A	0	0	0.00	2	0	0	0	0	1	1	0	0	0
D 1997	NY-A	0	0	0.00	2	0	0	0	0	1^{1}	0	0	0	1
D 1998	NY-A	0	0	0.00	1	0	0	0	0	0^{1}	0	0	0	0
D Total	3	0	0	0.00	5	0	0	0	0	2^{2}	1	0	0	1
L 1996	NY-A	0	0	0.00	2	0	0	0	0	1^{2}	0	0	0	1
L 1998	NY-A	0	0	0.00	1	0	0	0	0	0^{2}	1	0	0	0
L Total	2	0	0	0.00	3	0	0	0	0	2^{1}	1	0	0	1
W 1996	NY-A	1	0	0.00	4	0	0	0	0	2^{2}	0	0	0	4
W 1998	NY-A	0	0	0.00	1	0	0	0	0	0^{1}	0	0	0	0
W Total	2	1	0	0.00	5	0	0	0	0	3	0	0	0	4
● **Esteban Loaiza**														
D 1999	Tex-A	0	1	3.86	1	1	0	0	0	7	5	3	1	4
● **Bob Locker**														
L 1971	Oak-A	0	0	0.00	1	0	0	0	0	0^{2}	0	0	2	0
L 1972	Oak-A	0	0	13.50	2	0	0	0	0	2	4	3	0	1
L Total	2	0	0	10.13	3	0	0	0	0	2^{2}	4	3	2	1
W 1972	Oak-A	0	0	0.00	1	0	0	0	0	0^{1}	1	0	0	0
● **Billy Loes**														
W 1952	Bro-N	0	1	4.35	2	1	0	0	0	10^{1}	11	5	5	5
W 1953	Bro-N	1	0	3.38	1	1	0	0	0	8	8	3	2	8
W 1955	Bro-N	0	1	9.82	1	1	0	0	0	3^{2}	7	4	1	5
W Total	3	1	2	4.91	4	3	0	0	0	22	26	12	8	18
● **Mickey Lolich**														
L 1972	Det-A	0	1	1.42	2	2	0	0	0	19	14	3	5	10
W 1968	Det-A	3	0	1.67	3	3	3	0	0	27	20	5	6	21
● **Tim Lollar**														
L 1984	SD-N	0	0	6.23	1	1	0	0	0	4^{1}	3	3	4	3
W 1984	SD-N	0	1	21.60	1	1	0	0	0	1^{2}	4	4	4	0
● **Vic Lombardi**														
W 1947	Bro-N	0	1	12.15	2	2	0	0	0	6^{2}	14	9	1	5
● **Jim Lonborg**														
L 1976	Phi-N	0	1	1.69	1	1	0	0	0	5^{1}	2	1	2	2
L 1977	Phi-N	0	1	11.25	1	1	0	0	0	4	5	5	1	1
L Total	2	0	2	5.79	2	2	0	0	0	9^{1}	7	6	3	3
W 1967	Bos-A	2	1	2.63	3	3	2	0	1	24	14	7	2	11
● **Ed Lopat**														
W 1949	NY-A	1	0	6.35	1	1	0	0	0	5^{2}	9	4	1	4
W 1950	NY-A	0	0	2.25	1	1	0	0	0	8	9	2	0	5
W 1951	NY-A	2	0	0.50	2	2	2	0	0	18	10	1	3	4
W 1952	NY-A	0	1	4.76	2	2	0	0	0	11^{1}	14	6	4	3
W 1953	NY-A	1	0	2.00	1	1	1	0	0	9	9	2	4	3
W Total	5	4	1	2.60	7	7	3	0	0	52	51	15	12	19
● **Aurelio Lopez**														
L 1984	Det-A	1	0	0.00	1	0	0	0	0	3	4	0	1	2
L 1986	Hou-N	0	1	8.10	2	0	0	0	0	3^{1}	7	3	4	3
L Total	2	1	1	4.26	3	0	0	0	0	6^{1}	11	3	5	5
W 1984	Det-A	1	0	0.00	2	0	0	0	0	3	1	0	1	4
● **Marcelino Lopez**														
L 1969	Bal-A	0	0	0.00	1	0	0	0	0	0^{1}	1	0	2	0
W 1970	Bal-A	0	0	0.00	1	0	0	0	0	0^{1}	0	0	0	0
● **Tom Lovett**														
W 1889	Bro-A	0	1	24.00	1	1	0	0	0	3	8	8	2	1
W 1890	Bro-N	2	2	2.83	4	4	4	0	0	35	29	11	6	14
W Total	2	2	3	4.50	5	5	4	0	0	38	37	19	8	15
● **Grover Lowdermilk**														
W 1919	Chi-A	0	0	9.00	1	0	0	0	0	1	2	1	1	0
● **Derek Lowe**														
D 1998	Bos-A	0	0	2.08	2	0	0	0	0	4^{1}	3	1	1	2
D 1999	Bos-A	1	1	4.32	3	0	0	0	0	8^{1}	6	4	1	7
D Total	2	1	1	3.55	5	0	0	0	0	12^{2}	9	5	2	9
L 1999	Bos-A	0	0	1.42	3	0	0	0	0	6^{1}	6	1	2	7
● **Turk Lown**														
W 1959	Chi-A	0	0	0.00	3	0	0	0	0	3^{1}	2	0	1	3
● **Gary Lucas**														
L 1986	Cal-A	0	0	11.57	4	0	0	0	0	2^{1}	3	3	1	2
● **Dolf Luque**														
W 1919	Cin-N	0	0	0.00	2	0	0	0	0	5	1	0	0	6
W 1933	NY-N	1	0	0.00	1	0	0	0	0	4^{1}	2	0	2	5
W Total	2	1	0	0.00	3	0	0	0	0	9^{1}	3	0	2	11
● **Sparky Lyle**														
D 1981	Phi-N	0	0	0.00	3	0	0	0	0	2^{1}	4	0	2	1
L 1976	NY-A	0	0	0.00	1	0	0	1	0	1	0	0	1	0
L 1977	NY-A	2	0	0.96	4	0	0	0	0	9^{1}	7	1	0	3
L 1978	NY-A	0	0	13.50	1	0	0	0	0	1^{1}	3	2	0	0
L Total	3	2	0	2.31	6	0	0	1	0	11^{2}	10	3	1	3
W 1976	NY-A	0	0	0.00	2	0	0	0	0	2^{2}	1	0	0	3
W 1977	NY-A	1	0	1.93	2	0	0	0	0	4^{2}	2	1	0	2
W Total	2	1	0	1.23	4	0	0	0	0	7^{1}	3	1	0	5

YEAR	TM/L	W	L	ERA	G	GS	CG	SV	SHO	IP	H	ER	BB	SO
● **Duke Maas**														
W 1958	NY-A	0	0	81.00	1	0	0	0	0	0^1	2	3	1	0
W 1960	NY-A	0	0	4.50	1	0	0	0	0	2	2	1	0	1
W Total	2	0	0	15.43	2	0	0	0	0	2^1	4	4	1	1
● **Rob Mac Donald**														
L 1991	Tor-A	0	0	9.00	1	0	0	0	0	1	1	1	1	0
● **Nick Maddox**														
W 1909	Pit-N	1	0	1.00	1	1	1	0	0	9	10	1	2	4
● **Greg Maddux**														
D 1995	Atl-N	1	0	4.50	2	2	0	0	0	14	19	7	2	7
D 1996	Atl-N	1	0	0.00	1	1	0	0	0	7	3	0	0	7
D 1997	Atl-N	1	0	1.00	1	1	1	0	0	9	7	1	1	6
D 1998	Atl-N	1	0	2.57	1	1	0	0	0	7	7	2	0	4
D 1999	Atl-N	0	1	2.57	2	1	0	0	0	7	10	2	5	5
D 2000	Atl-N	0	1	11.25	1	1	0	0	0	4	9	5	3	2
D Total	6	4	2	3.19	8	7	1	0	0	48	55	17	11	31
L 1989	Chi-N	0	1	13.50	2	2	0	0	0	7^1	13	11	4	5
L 1993	Atl-N	1	1	4.97	2	2	0	0	0	12^2	11	7	7	11
L 1995	Atl-N	1	0	1.13	1	1	0	0	0	8	7	1	2	4
L 1996	Atl-N	1	1	2.51	2	2	0	0	0	14^1	15	4	2	10
L 1997	Atl-N	0	2	1.38	2	2	0	0	0	13	9	2	4	16
L 1998	Atl-N	0	1	3.00	2	1	0	1	0	6	5	2	3	4
L 1999	Atl-N	1	0	1.93	2	2	0	0	0	14	12	3	1	7
L Total	7	4	6	3.58	13	12	0	1	0	75^1	72	30	23	57
W 1995	Atl-N	1	1	2.25	2	2	1	0	0	16	9	4	3	8
W 1996	Atl-N	1	1	1.72	2	2	0	0	0	15^2	14	3	1	5
W 1999	Atl-N	0	1	2.57	1	1	0	0	0	7	5	2	3	5
W Total	3	2	3	2.09	5	5	1	0	0	38^2	28	9	7	18
● **Mike Maddux**														
D 1995	Bos-A	0	0	0.00	2	0	0	0	0	3	2	0	1	1
● **Sal Maglie**														
W 1951	NY-N	0	1	7.20	1	1	0	0	0	5	8	4	2	3
W 1954	NY-N	0	0	2.57	1	1	0	0	0	7	7	2	2	2
W 1956	Bro-N	1	1	2.65	2	2	2	0	0	17	14	5	6	15
W Total	3	1	2	3.41	4	4	2	0	0	29	29	11	10	20
● **Mike Magnante**														
D 1997	Hou-N	0	0	4.50	2	0	0	0	0	2	4	1	0	2
D 2000	Oak-A	0	0	0.00	2	0	0	0	0	3	1	0	0	2
D Total	2	0	0	1.80	4	0	0	0	0	5	5	1	0	4
● **Joe Magrane**														
L 1987	StL-N	0	0	9.00	1	1	0	0	0	4	4	4	2	3
W 1987	StL-N	0	1	8.59	2	2	0	0	0	7^1	9	7	5	5
● **Roy Mahaffey**														
W 1931	Phi-A	0	0	9.00	1	0	0	0	0	1	1	1	1	0
● **Rick Mahler**														
L 1982	Atl-N	0	0	0.00	1	0	0	0	0	1^2	3	0	2	0
L 1990	Cin-N	0	0	0.00	1	0	0	0	0	1^2	2	0	0	0
L Total	2	0	0	0.00	2	0	0	0	0	3^1	5	0	2	0
● **Pat Mahomes**														
D 1999	NY-N	0	0	5.40	1	0	0	0	0	1^2	3	1	0	1
L 1999	NY-N	0	0	1.42	3	0	0	0	0	6^1	4	1	3	3
● **Duster Mails**														
W 1920	Cle-A	1	0	0.00	2	1	1	0	1	15^2	6	0	6	6
● **Pat Malone**														
W 1929	Chi-N	0	2	4.15	3	2	1	0	0	13	12	6	7	11
W 1932	Chi-N	0	0	0.00	1	0	0	0	0	2^2	1	0	4	4
W 1936	NY-A	0	1	1.80	2	0	0	1	0	5	2	1	1	2
W Total	3	0	3	3.05	6	2	1	1	0	20^2	15	7	12	17
● **Jim Maloney**														
W 1961	Cin-N	0	0	27.00	1	0	0	0	0	0^2	4	2	1	1
● **Al Mamaux**														
W 1920	Bro-N	0	0	4.50	3	0	0	0	0	4	2	2	0	5
● **Matt Mantei**														
D 1999	Ari-N	0	1	4.50	1	0	0	0	0	2	1	1	3	1
● **Firpo Marberry**														
W 1924	Was-A	0	1	1.13	4	1	0	2	0	8	9	1	4	10
W 1925	Was-A	0	0	0.00	2	0	0	0	0	2^1	3	0	0	2
W 1934	Det-A	0	0	21.60	2	0	0	0	0	1^2	5	4	1	0
W Total	3	0	1	3.75	8	1	0	3	0	12	17	5	5	12
● **Juan Marichal**														
L 1971	SF-N	0	1	2.25	1	1	1	0	0	8	4	2	0	6
W 1962	SF-N	0	0	0.00	1	1	0	0	0	4	2	0	2	4
● **Rube Marquard**														
W 1911	NY-N	0	1	1.54	3	2	0	0	0	11^2	9	2	1	8
W 1912	NY-N	2	0	0.50	2	2	2	0	0	18	14	1	2	9
W 1913	NY-N	0	1	7.00	2	1	0	0	0	9	10	7	3	3
W 1916	Bro-N	0	2	5.73	2	2	0	0	0	11	12	7	6	9
W 1920	Bro-N	0	1	1.00	2	1	0	0	0	9	7	1	3	6
W Total	5	2	5	2.76	11	8	2	0	0	58^2	52	18	15	35
● **Mike Marshall**														
L 1974	LA-N	0	0	0.00	2	0	0	0	0	3	0	0	0	1
W 1974	LA-N	0	1	1.00	5	0	0	1	0	9	6	1	1	10

YEAR	TM/L	W	L	ERA	G	GS	CG	SV	SHO	IP	H	ER	BB	SO
● **Renie Martin**														
D 1981	KC-A	0	0	0.00	2	0	0	0	0	5^1	1	0	2	2
W 1980	KC-A	0	0	2.79	3	0	0	0	0	9^2	11	3	3	2
● **Tom Martin**														
D 1997	Hou-N	0	0	0.00	2	0	0	0	0	0^2	1	0	1	0
● **Joe Martina**														
W 1924	Was-A	0	0	0.00	1	0	0	0	0	1	0	0	0	1
● **Tippy Martinez**														
L 1983	Bal-A	1	0	0.00	2	0	0	0	0	6	5	0	3	5
W 1979	Bal-A	0	0	6.75	3	0	0	0	0	1^1	3	1	0	1
W 1983	Bal-A	0	0	3.00	3	0	0	2	0	3	3	1	0	0
W Total	2	0	0	4.15	6	0	0	2	0	4^1	6	2	0	1
● **Dennis Martinez**														
D 1995	Cle-A	0	0	3.00	1	1	0	0	0	6	5	2	0	2
L 1979	Bal-A	0	0	3.24	1	1	0	0	0	8^1	8	3	0	4
L 1995	Cle-A	1	1	2.03	2	2	0	0	0	13^1	10	3	3	7
L 1998	Atl-N	1	0	0.00	4	0	0	0	0	3^1	1	0	1	0
L Total	3	2	1	2.16	7	3	0	0	0	25	19	6	4	11
W 1979	Bal-A	0	0	18.00	2	1	0	0	0	2	6	4	0	0
W 1995	Cle-A	0	1	3.48	2	2	0	0	0	10^1	12	4	8	5
W Total	2	0	1	5.84	4	3	0	0	0	12^1	18	8	8	5
● **Pedro Martinez**														
D 1998	Bos-A	1	0	3.86	1	1	0	0	0	7	6	3	0	8
D 1999	Bos-A	1	0	0.00	2	1	0	0	0	10	3	0	4	11
D Total	2	2	0	1.59	3	2	0	0	0	17	9	3	4	19
L 1999	Bos-A	1	0	0.00	1	1	0	0	0	7	2	0	2	12
● **Ramon Martinez**														
D 1995	LA-N	0	1	14.54	1	1	0	0	0	4^1	10	7	2	3
D 1996	LA-N	0	0	1.13	1	1	0	0	0	8	3	1	3	6
D 1999	Bos-A	0	0	3.18	1	1	0	0	0	5^2	5	2	3	6
D Total	3	0	1	5.00	3	3	0	0	0	18	18	10	8	15
L 1999	Bos-A	0	1	4.05	1	1	0	0	0	6^2	6	3	3	5
● **Roger Mason**														
L 1991	Pit-N	0	0	0.00	3	0	0	1	0	4^1	3	0	1	2
L 1992	Pit-N	0	0	0.00	2	0	0	0	0	3^1	0	0	2	1
L 1993	Phi-N	0	0	0.00	2	0	0	0	0	3	1	0	0	2
L Total	3	0	0	0.00	7	0	0	1	0	10^2	4	0	3	5
W 1993	Phi-N	0	0	1.17	4	0	0	0	0	7^2	4	1	1	7
● **Greg Mathews**														
L 1987	StL-N	1	0	3.48	2	2	0	0	0	10^1	6	4	3	10
W 1987	StL-N	0	0	2.45	1	1	0	0	0	3^2	2	1	2	3
● **Terry Mathews**														
D 1996	Bal-A	0	0	0.00	3	0	0	0	0	2^2	3	0	1	2
D 1997	Bal-A	0	0	18.00	1	0	0	0	0	1	2	2	0	1
D Total	2	0	0	4.91	4	0	0	0	0	3^2	5	2	1	3
L 1996	Bal-A	0	0	0.00	3	0	0	0	0	2^1	0	0	2	3
● **T. J. Mathews**														
D 1996	StL-N	1	0	0.00	1	0	0	0	0	1	1	0	0	2
L 1996	StL-N	0	0	0.00	2	0	0	0	0	0^2	2	0	1	2
● **Christy Mathewson**														
W 1905	NY-N	3	0	0.00	3	3	3	0	3	27	14	0	1	18
W 1911	NY-N	1	2	2.00	3	3	2	0	0	27	25	6	2	13
W 1912	NY-N	0	2	1.26	3	3	3	0	0	28^2	23	4	5	10
W 1913	NY-N	1	1	0.95	2	2	2	0	1	19	14	2	2	7
W Total	4	5	5	1.06	11	11	10	0	4	101^2	76	12	10	48
● **Jon Matlack**														
L 1973	NY-N	1	0	0.00	1	1	1	0	1	9	2	0	3	9
W 1973	NY-N	1	2	2.16	3	3	0	0	0	16^2	10	4	5	11
● **Jakie May**														
W 1932	Chi-N	0	1	11.57	2	0	0	0	0	4^2	9	6	3	4
● **Rudy May**														
D 1981	NY-A	0	0	0.00	1	0	0	0	0	2	1	0	0	1
L 1980	NY-A	0	1	3.38	1	1	1	0	0	8	6	3	3	4
L 1981	NY-A	0	0	8.10	1	1	0	0	0	3^1	6	3	0	5
L Total	2	0	1	4.76	2	2	1	0	0	11^1	12	6	3	9
W 1981	NY-A	0	0	2.84	3	0	0	0	0	6^1	5	2	1	5
● **Erskine Mayer**														
W 1915	Phi-N	0	1	2.38	2	2	1	0	0	11^1	16	3	2	7
W 1919	Chi-A	0	0	0.00	1	0	0	0	0	1	0	0	1	0
W Total	2	0	1	2.19	3	2	1	0	0	12^1	16	3	3	7
● **Carl Mays**														
W 1916	Bos-A	0	1	5.06	2	1	0	1	0	5^1	8	3	3	2
W 1918	Bos-A	2	0	1.00	2	2	2	0	0	18	10	2	3	5
W 1921	NY-A	1	2	1.73	3	3	3	0	1	26	20	5	0	9
W 1922	NY-A	0	1	4.50	1	1	0	0	0	8	9	4	2	1
W Total	4	3	4	2.20	8	7	5	1	1	57^1	47	14	8	17
● **Kirk McCaskill**														
L 1986	Cal-A	0	2	7.71	2	2	0	0	0	9^1	16	8	5	7
L 1993	Chi-A	0	0	0.00	3	0	0	0	0	3^2	3	0	1	3
L Total	2	0	2	5.54	5	2	0	0	0	13	19	8	6	10
● **Steve McCatty**														
D 1981	Oak-A	1	0	1.00	1	1	1	0	0	9	6	1	4	3
L 1981	Oak-A	0	1	13.50	1	1	0	0	0	3^1	6	5	2	2

YEAR	TM/L	W	L	ERA	G	GS	CG	SV	SHO	IP	H	ER	BB	SO
● Bob McClure														
D 1981	Mil-A	0	0	0.00	3	0	0	0	0	3^1	4	0	0	2
L 1982	Mil-A	1	0	0.00	1	0	0	0	0	1^2	2	0	0	0
W 1982	Mil-A	0	2	4.15	5	0	0	2	0	4^1	5	2	3	5
● Alex McColl														
W 1933	Was-A	0	0	0.00	1	0	0	0	0	2	0	0	0	0
● Jim McCormick														
W 1885	Chi-N	2	2	2.48	4	4	4	0	0	29	23	8	4	15
W 1886	Chi-N	0	1	6.75	1	1	1	0	0	8	13	6	2	4
W Total	2	2	3	3.41	5	5	5	0	0	37	36	14	6	19
● Mickey McDermott														
W 1956	NY-A	0	0	3.00	1	0	0	0	0	3	2	1	3	3
● Jim McDonald														
W 1953	NY-A	1	0	5.87	1	1	0	0	0	7^2	12	5	0	3
● Jack McDowell														
D 1995	NY-A	0	2	9.00	2	1	0	0	0	7	8	7	4	6
D 1996	Cle-A	0	0	6.35	1	1	0	0	0	5^2	6	4	1	5
D Total	2	0	2	7.82	3	2	0	0	0	12^2	14	11	5	11
L 1993	Chi-A	0	2	10.00	2	2	0	0	0	9	18	10	5	5
● Roger McDowell														
L 1986	NY-N	0	0	0.00	2	0	0	0	0	7	1	0	0	3
L 1988	NY-N	0	1	4.50	4	0	0	0	0	6	6	3	2	5
L Total	2	0	1	2.08	6	0	0	0	0	13	7	3	2	8
W 1986	NY-N	1	0	4.91	5	0	0	0	0	7^1	10	4	6	2
● Will McEnaney														
L 1975	Cin-N	0	0	6.75	1	0	0	0	0	1^1	1	1	0	1
W 1975	Cin-N	0	0	2.70	5	0	0	1	0	6^2	3	2	2	5
W 1976	Cin-N	0	0	0.00	2	0	0	2	0	4^2	2	0	1	2
W Total	2	0	0	1.59	7	0	0	3	0	11^1	5	2	3	7
● Joe McGinnity														
T 1900	Bro-N	2	0	0.00	2	2	2	0	0	18	14	0	3	5
W 1905	NY-N	1	1	0.00	2	2	1	0	1	17	10	0	3	6
● Kevin McGlinchy														
D 1999	Atl-N	0	0	0.00	1	0	0	0	0	0^1	0	0	0	0
L 1999	Atl-N	0	1	18.00	1	0	0	0	0	1	2	2	4	1
W 1999	Atl-N	0	0	0.00	1	0	0	0	0	2	2	0	1	2
● Jim McGlothlin														
L 1972	Cin-N	0	0	0.00	1	0	0	0	0	1	0	0	0	0
W 1970	Cin-N	0	0	8.31	1	1	0	0	0	4^1	6	4	2	2
W 1972	Cin-N	0	0	12.00	1	1	0	0	0	3	2	4	2	3
W Total	2	0	0	9.82	2	2	0	0	0	7^1	8	8	4	5
● Tug McGraw														
D 1981	Phi-N	1	0	0.00	2	0	0	0	0	4	2	0	0	2
L 1969	NY-N	0	0	0.00	1	0	0	1	0	3	1	0	1	1
L 1973	NY-N	0	0	0.00	2	0	0	1	0	5	4	0	3	3
L 1976	Phi-N	0	0	11.57	2	0	0	0	0	2^1	4	3	1	5
L 1977	Phi-N	0	0	0.00	2	0	0	1	0	3	1	0	2	3
L 1978	Phi-N	0	1	1.59	3	0	0	0	0	5^2	3	1	5	5
L 1980	Phi-N	0	1	4.50	5	0	0	2	0	8	8	4	4	5
L Total	6	0	2	2.67	15	0	0	5	0	27	21	8	16	22
W 1973	NY-N	1	0	2.63	5	0	0	1	0	13^2	8	4	9	14
W 1980	Phi-N	1	1	1.17	4	0	0	2	0	7^2	7	1	8	10
W Total	2	2	1	2.11	9	0	0	3	0	21^1	15	5	17	24
● Scott McGregor														
L 1979	Bal-A	1	0	0.00	1	1	1	0	1	9	6	0	1	4
L 1983	Bal-A	0	1	1.35	1	1	0	0	0	6^2	6	1	3	2
L Total	2	1	1	0.57	2	2	1	0	1	15^2	12	1	4	6
W 1979	Bal-A	1	1	3.18	2	2	1	0	0	17	16	6	2	8
W 1983	Bal-A	1	1	1.06	2	2	1	0	1	17	9	2	2	12
W Total	2	2	2	2.12	4	4	2	0	1	34	25	8	4	20
● Harry McIntire														
W 1910	Chi-N	0	1	6.75	2	0	0	0	0	5^1	4	4	3	3
● Archie McKain														
W 1940	Det-A	0	0	3.00	1	0	0	0	0	3	4	1	0	0
● Denny McLain														
W 1968	Det-A	1	2	3.24	3	3	1	0	0	16^2	18	6	4	13
● Don McMahon														
L 1971	SF-N	0	0	0.00	2	0	0	0	0	3	0	0	0	3
W 1957	Mil-N	0	0	0.00	3	0	0	0	0	5	3	0	3	5
W 1958	Mil-N	0	0	5.40	3	0	0	0	0	3^1	3	2	3	5
W 1968	Det-A	0	0	13.50	2	0	0	0	0	2	4	3	0	1
W Total	3	0	0	4.35	8	0	0	0	0	10^1	10	5	6	11
● Sadie McMahon														
T 1895	Bal-N	0	2	5.94	2	2	2	0	0	16^2	27	11	3	2
● Greg McMichael														
D 1995	Atl-N	0	0	6.75	2	0	0	0	0	1^1	1	1	2	1
D 1996	Atl-N	0	0	6.75	2	0	0	0	0	1^1	1	1	1	3
D Total	2	0	0	6.75	4	0	0	0	0	2^2	2	2	3	4
L 1993	Atl-N	0	1	6.75	4	0	0	0	0	4	7	3	2	1
L 1995	Atl-N	1	0	0.00	3	0	0	1	0	2^2	0	0	1	2
L 1996	Atl-N	0	1	9.00	3	0	0	0	0	2	4	2	1	3
L Total	3	1	2	5.19	10	0	0	1	0	8^2	11	5	4	6
W 1995	Atl-N	0	0	2.70	3	0	0	0	0	3^1	3	1	2	2
W 1996	Atl-N	0	0	27.00	2	0	0	0	0	1	5	3	0	1
W Total	2	0	0	8.31	5	0	0	0	0	4^1	8	4	2	3
● Dave McNally														
L 1969	Bal-A	1	0	0.00	1	1	1	0	1	11	3	0	5	11
L 1970	Bal-A	1	0	3.00	1	1	1	0	0	9	6	3	5	5
L 1971	Bal-A	1	0	3.86	1	1	0	0	0	7	7	3	1	5
L 1973	Bal-A	0	1	5.87	1	1	0	0	0	7^2	7	5	2	7
L 1974	Bal-A	0	1	1.59	1	1	0	0	0	5^2	6	1	2	2
L Total	5	3	2	2.68	5	5	2	0	1	40^1	29	12	15	30
W 1966	Bal-A	1	0	1.59	2	2	1	0	1	11^1	6	2	7	5
W 1969	Bal-A	0	1	2.81	2	2	1	0	0	16	11	5	5	13
W 1970	Bal-A	1	0	3.00	1	1	1	0	0	9	9	3	2	5
W 1971	Bal-A	2	1	1.98	4	2	1	0	0	13^2	10	3	5	12
W Total	4	4	2	2.34	9	7	4	0	1	50	36	13	19	35
● Hugh McQuillan														
W 1922	NY-N	1	0	3.00	1	1	1	0	0	9	8	3	2	4
W 1923	NY-N	0	1	5.00	2	1	0	0	0	9	11	5	4	3
W 1924	NY-N	1	0	2.57	3	1	0	1	0	7	2	2	6	2
W Total	3	2	1	3.60	6	3	1	1	0	25	21	10	12	9
● Lee Meadows														
W 1925	Pit-N	0	1	3.38	1	1	0	0	0	8	6	3	0	4
W 1927	Pit-N	0	1	9.95	1	1	0	0	0	6^1	7	7	1	6
W Total	2	0	2	6.28	2	2	0	0	0	14^1	13	10	1	10
● George Meakim														
W 1890	Lou-A	0	0	0.00	1	0	0	0	0	4	6	0	1	1
● Jim Mecir														
D 2000	Oak-A	0	0	0.00	3	0	0	0	0	5^1	1	0	0	2
● Doc Medich														
W 1982	Mil-A	0	0	18.00	1	0	0	0	0	2	5	4	1	0
● Jouett Meekin														
T 1894	NY-N	2	0	1.59	2	2	2	0	0	17	13	3	8	6
● Cliff Melton														
W 1937	NY-N	0	2	4.91	3	2	0	0	0	11	12	6	6	7
● Ramiro Mendoza														
D 1997	NY-A	1	1	2.45	2	0	0	0	0	3^2	3	1	0	2
L 1998	NY-A	0	0	0.00	2	0	0	0	0	4^1	4	0	0	1
L 1999	NY-A	0	0	0.00	2	0	0	1	0	2^1	0	0	0	2
L Total	2	0	0	0.00	4	0	0	1	0	6^2	4	0	0	3
W 1998	NY-A	1	0	9.00	1	0	0	0	0	1	2	1	0	1
W 1999	NY-A	0	0	10.80	1	0	0	0	0	1^2	3	2	1	0
W Total	2	1	0	10.13	2	0	0	0	0	2^2	5	3	1	1
● Kent Mercker														
D 1995	Atl-N	0	0	0.00	1	0	0	0	0	0^1	0	0	0	0
D 1999	Bos-A	0	0	10.80	1	1	0	0	0	1^2	3	2	3	1
D Total	2	0	0	9.00	2	1	0	0	0	2	3	2	3	1
L 1991	Atl-N	0	1	13.50	1	0	0	0	0	0^2	0	1	2	0
L 1992	Atl-N	0	0	0.00	2	0	0	0	0	3	1	0	1	1
L 1993	Atl-N	0	0	1.80	5	0	0	0	0	5	3	1	2	4
L 1999	Bos-A	0	1	4.70	2	2	0	0	0	7^2	12	4	4	5
L Total	4	0	2	3.31	10	2	0	0	0	16^1	16	6	9	10
W 1991	Atl-N	0	0	0.00	2	0	0	0	0	1	0	0	0	1
W 1995	Atl-N	0	0	4.50	1	0	0	0	0	2	1	1	2	2
W Total	2	0	0	3.00	3	0	0	0	0	3	1	1	2	3
● Jim Merritt														
L 1970	Cin-N	1	0	1.69	1	1	0	0	0	5^1	3	1	0	2
W 1965	Min-A	0	0	2.70	2	0	0	0	0	3^1	2	1	0	1
W 1970	Cin-N	0	1	21.60	1	1	0	0	0	1^2	3	4	1	0
W Total	2	0	1	9.00	3	1	0	0	0	5	5	5	1	1
● Jose Mesa														
D 1995	Cle-A	0	0	0.00	2	0	0	0	0	2	0	0	2	0
D 1996	Cle-A	0	1	3.86	2	0	0	0	0	4^2	8	2	0	7
D 1997	Cle-A	0	0	2.70	2	0	0	1	0	3^1	5	1	1	2
D 2000	Sea-A	1	0	0.00	2	0	0	0	0	2	0	0	1	2
D Total	4	1	1	2.25	8	0	0	1	0	12	13	3	4	11
L 1995	Cle-A	0	0	2.25	4	0	0	1	0	4	3	1	1	1
L 1997	Cle-A	1	0	3.38	4	0	0	2	0	5^1	5	2	3	5
L 2000	Sea-A	0	0	12.46	3	0	0	0	0	4^1	5	5	3	3
L Total	3	1	0	5.93	11	0	0	3	0	13^2	13	9	7	9
W 1995	Cle-A	1	0	4.50	2	0	0	1	0	4	5	2	1	4
W 1997	Cle-A	0	0	5.40	5	0	0	1	0	5	10	3	1	5
W Total	2	1	0	5.00	7	0	0	2	0	9	15	5	2	9
● Andy Messersmith														
L 1974	LA-N	1	0	2.57	1	1	0	0	0	7	8	2	3	0
W 1974	LA-N	0	2	4.50	2	2	0	0	0	14	11	7	7	12
● Russ Meyer														
W 1950	Phi-N	0	1	5.40	2	0	0	0	0	1^2	4	1	0	1
W 1953	Bro-N	0	0	6.23	1	0	0	0	0	4^1	8	3	4	5
W 1955	Bro-N	0	0	0.00	1	0	0	0	0	5^2	4	0	2	4
W Total	3	0	1	3.09	4	0	0	0	0	11^2	16	4	6	10
● Dan Miceli														
D 1998	SD-N	1	1	2.70	3	0	0	0	0	3^1	2	1	0	4
L 1998	SD-N	0	0	13.50	3	0	0	0	0	0^2	4	1	0	1
W 1998	SD-N	0	0	0.00	2	0	0	0	0	1^2	2	0	2	1
● Pete Mikkelsen														
W 1964	NY-A	0	1	5.79	4	0	0	0	0	4^2	4	3	2	4

YEAR	TM/L	W	L	ERA	G	GS	CG	SV	SHO	IP	H	ER	BB	SO
● Johnny Miljus														
W 1927	Pit-N	0	1	1.35	2	0	0	0	0	6^2	4	1	4	6
● Bob Miller														
W 1950	Phi-N	0	1	27.00	1	1	0	0	0	0^1	2	1	0	0
● Bob Miller														
L 1969	Min-A	0	1	5.40	1	1	0	0	0	1^2	5	1	0	0
L 1971	Pit-N	0	0	6.00	1	0	0	0	0	3	3	2	3	3
L 1972	Pit-N	0	0	0.00	1	0	0	0	0	1	0	0	0	1
L Total	3	0	1	4.76	3	1	0	0	0	5^2	8	3	3	4
W 1965	LA-N	0	0	0.00	2	0	0	0	0	1^1	0	0	0	0
W 1966	LA-N	0	0	0.00	1	0	0	0	0	3	2	0	2	1
W 1971	Pit-N	0	1	3.86	3	0	0	0	0	4^2	7	2	1	2
W Total	3	0	1	2.00	6	0	0	0	0	9	9	2	3	3
● Stu Miller														
W 1962	SF-N	0	0	0.00	2	0	0	0	0	1^1	1	0	2	0
● Trever Miller														
D 1998	Hou-N	0	0	—	1	0	0	0	0	0	0	0	1	0
D 1999	Hou-N	0	0	0.00	2	0	0	0	0	1^1	1	0	0	2
D Total	2	0	0	0.00	3	0	0	0	0	1^1	1	0	1	2
● Bob Milliken														
W 1953	Bro-N	0	0	0.00	1	0	0	0	0	2	2	0	1	0
● Alan Mills														
D 1997	Bal-A	0	0	0.00	1	0	0	0	0	1	1	0	0	1
L 1996	Bal-A	0	0	3.86	3	0	0	0	0	2^1	3	1	1	3
L 1997	Bal-A	0	1	2.70	3	0	0	0	0	3^1	1	1	2	3
L Total	2	0	1	3.18	6	0	0	0	0	5^2	4	2	3	6
● Kevin Millwood														
D 1999	Atl-N	1	0	0.90	2	1	1	1	0	10	1	1	0	9
D 2000	Atl-N	0	1	7.71	1	1	0	0	0	4^2	4	4	3	3
D Total	2	1	1	3.07	3	2	1	1	0	14^2	5	5	3	12
L 1999	Atl-N	1	0	3.55	2	2	0	0	0	12^2	13	5	1	9
W 1999	Atl-N	0	1	18.00	1	1	0	0	0	2	8	4	2	2
● Steve Mingori														
L 1976	KC-A	0	0	2.70	3	0	0	1	0	3^1	4	1	0	1
L 1977	KC-A	0	0	0.00	3	0	0	0	0	1^1	0	0	0	1
L 1978	KC-A	0	0	7.36	1	0	0	0	0	3^2	5	3	3	0
L Total	3	0	0	4.32	7	0	0	1	0	8^1	9	4	3	2
● Paul Minner														
W 1949	Bro-N	0	0	0.00	1	0	0	0	0	1	1	0	0	0
● Clarence Mitchell														
W 1920	Bro-N	0	0	0.00	1	0	0	0	0	4^2	3	0	3	1
W 1928	StL-N	0	0	1.59	1	0	0	0	0	5^2	2	1	2	3
W Total	2	0	0	0.87	2	0	0	0	0	10^1	5	1	5	4
● Vinegar Bend Mizell														
W 1960	Pit-N	0	1	15.43	2	1	0	0	0	2^1	4	4	2	1
● Joe Moeller														
W 1966	LA-N	0	0	4.50	1	0	0	0	0	2	1	1	1	0
● George Mogridge														
W 1924	Was-A	1	0	2.25	2	1	0	0	0	12	7	3	6	5
● Zach Monroe														
W 1958	NY-A	0	0	27.00	1	0	0	0	0	1	3	3	1	1
● John Montague														
L 1979	Cal-A	0	1	9.00	2	0	0	0	0	4	4	4	2	2
● Jim Mooney														
W 1934	StL-N	0	0	0.00	1	0	0	0	0	1	1	0	0	0
● Donnie Moore														
L 1982	Atl-N	0	0	0.00	2	0	0	0	0	2^2	2	0	0	1
L 1986	Cal-A	0	1	7.20	3	0	0	1	0	5	8	4	2	0
L Total	2	0	1	4.70	5	0	0	1	0	7^2	10	4	2	1
● Whitey Moore														
W 1939	Cin-N	0	0	0.00	1	0	0	0	0	3	0	0	0	2
W 1940	Cin-N	0	0	3.24	3	0	0	0	0	8^1	8	3	6	7
W Total	2	0	0	2.38	4	0	0	0	0	11^1	8	3	6	9
● Mike Moore														
L 1989	Oak-A	1	0	0.00	1	1	0	0	0	7	3	0	2	3
L 1990	Oak-A	1	0	1.50	1	1	0	0	0	6	4	1	1	5
L 1992	Oak-A	0	2	7.45	2	2	0	0	0	9^2	11	8	5	7
L Total	3	2	2	3.57	4	4	0	0	0	22^2	18	9	8	15
W 1989	Oak-A	2	0	2.08	2	2	0	0	0	13	9	3	3	10
W 1990	Oak-A	0	1	6.75	1	1	0	0	0	2^2	8	2	0	1
W Total	2	2	1	2.87	3	3	0	0	0	15^2	17	5	3	11
● Ray Moore														
W 1959	Chi-A	0	0	9.00	1	0	0	0	0	1	1	1	0	1
● Wilcy Moore														
W 1927	NY-A	1	0	0.84	2	1	1	1	0	10^2	11	1	2	2
W 1932	NY-A	1	0	0.00	1	0	0	0	0	5^1	2	0	0	1
W Total	2	2	0	0.56	3	1	1	1	0	16	13	1	2	3
● Bob Moose														
L 1970	Pit-N	0	1	3.52	1	1	0	0	0	7^2	4	3	2	4
L 1971	Pit-N	0	0	0.00	1	0	0	0	0	2	0	0	0	0
L 1972	Pit-N	0	1	54.00	2	1	0	0	0	0^2	5	4	0	0
L Total	3	0	2	6.10	4	2	0	0	0	10^1	9	7	2	4

YEAR	TM/L	W	L	ERA	G	GS	CG	SV	SHO	IP	H	ER	BB	SO
W 1971	Pit-N	0	0	6.52	3	1	0	0	0	9^2	12	7	2	7
● Dave Morehead														
W 1967	Bos-A	0	0	0.00	2	0	0	0	0	3^1	0	0	4	3
● Roger Moret														
L 1975	Bos-A	1	0	0.00	1	0	0	0	0	1^1	1	0	1	0
W 1975	Bos-A	0	0	0.00	3	0	0	0	0	1^2	2	0	3	1
● Mike Morgan														
D 1998	Chi-N	0	0	0.00	2	0	0	0	0	1^1	0	0	0	1
● Tom Morgan														
W 1951	NY-A	0	0	0.00	1	0	0	0	0	2	2	0	1	3
W 1955	NY-A	0	0	4.91	2	0	0	0	0	3^2	3	2	3	1
W 1956	NY-A	0	1	9.00	2	0	0	0	0	4	6	4	4	3
W Total	3	0	1	5.59	5	0	0	0	0	9^2	11	6	8	7
● Alvin Morman														
D 1997	Cle-A	0	0	—	1	0	0	0	0	0	0	0	1	0
L 1997	Cle-A	0	0	0.00	2	0	0	0	0	1^1	0	0	0	1
W 1997	Cle-A	0	0	0.00	2	0	0	0	0	0^1	0	0	2	1
● Jack Morris														
L 1984	Det-A	1	0	1.29	1	1	0	0	0	7	5	1	1	4
L 1987	Det-A	0	1	6.75	1	1	1	0	0	8	6	6	3	7
L 1991	Min-A	2	0	4.05	2	2	0	0	0	13^1	17	6	1	7
L 1992	Tor-A	0	1	6.57	2	2	1	0	0	12^1	11	9	9	6
L Total	4	3	2	4.87	6	6	2	0	0	40^2	39	22	14	24
W 1984	Det-A	2	0	2.00	2	2	2	0	0	18	13	4	3	13
W 1991	Min-A	2	0	1.17	3	3	1	0	1	23	18	3	9	15
W 1992	Tor-A	0	2	8.44	2	2	0	0	0	10^2	13	10	6	12
W Total	3	4	2	2.96	7	7	3	0	1	51^2	44	17	18	40
● Matt Morris														
D 2000	StL-N	0	0	0.00	2	0	0	0	0	2	0	0	1	0
L 2000	StL-N	0	0	4.91	2	0	0	0	0	3^2	3	2	2	2
● Johnny Morrison														
W 1925	Pit-N	0	0	2.89	3	0	0	0	0	9^1	11	3	1	7
● Don Mossi														
W 1954	Cle-A	0	0	0.00	3	0	0	0	0	4	3	0	0	1
● Jamie Moyer														
D 1997	Sea-A	0	1	5.79	1	1	0	0	0	4^2	5	3	1	2
● Les Mueller														
W 1945	Det-A	0	0	0.00	1	0	0	0	0	2	0	0	1	1
● Terry Mulholland														
D 1998	Chi-N	0	1	11.57	2	0	0	0	0	2^1	2	3	2	2
D 1999	Atl-N	0	0	27.00	2	0	0	0	0	0^2	3	2	0	0
D 2000	Atl-N	0	0	5.40	3	0	0	0	0	3^1	1	2	2	1
D Total	3	0	1	9.95	7	0	0	0	0	6^1	6	7	4	3
L 1993	Phi-N	0	1	7.20	1	1	0	0	0	5	9	4	1	2
L 1999	Atl-N	0	0	0.00	2	0	0	0	0	2^2	1	0	1	2
L Total	2	0	1	4.70	3	1	0	0	0	7^2	10	4	2	4
W 1993	Phi-N	1	0	6.75	2	2	0	0	0	10^2	14	8	3	5
W 1999	Atl-N	0	0	7.36	2	0	0	0	0	3^2	5	3	1	3
W Total	2	1	0	6.91	4	2	0	0	0	14^1	19	11	4	8
● George Mullin														
W 1907	Det-A	0	2	2.12	2	2	2	0	0	17	16	4	6	8
W 1908	Det-A	1	0	0.00	1	1	1	0	0	9	7	0	1	8
W 1909	Det-A	2	1	2.25	4	3	3	0	1	32	23	8	8	20
W Total	3	3	3	1.86	7	6	6	0	1	58	46	12	15	36
● Bob Muncrief														
W 1944	StL-A	0	1	1.35	2	0	0	0	0	6^2	5	1	4	4
W 1948	Cle-A	0	0	0.00	1	0	0	0	0	2	1	0	0	0
W Total	2	0	1	1.04	3	0	0	0	0	8^2	6	1	4	4
● Red Munger														
W 1946	StL-N	1	0	1.00	1	1	1	0	0	9	9	1	3	2
● Mike Munoz														
D 1995	Col-N	0	1	13.50	4	0	0	0	0	1^1	4	2	1	1
● Johnny Murphy														
W 1936	NY-A	0	0	3.38	1	0	0	1	0	2^2	1	1	1	1
W 1937	NY-A	0	0	0.00	1	0	0	1	0	0^1	0	0	0	0
W 1938	NY-A	0	0	0.00	1	0	0	1	0	2	2	0	1	1
W 1939	NY-A	1	0	2.70	1	0	0	0	0	3^1	5	1	0	2
W 1941	NY-A	1	0	0.00	2	0	0	0	0	6	2	0	1	3
W 1943	NY-A	0	0	0.00	2	0	0	1	0	2	1	0	1	1
W Total	6	2	0	1.10	8	0	0	4	0	16^1	11	2	4	8
● Rob Murphy														
L 1990	Bos-A	0	0	13.50	1	0	0	0	0	0^2	2	1	1	0
● Mike Mussina														
D 1996	Bal-A	0	0	4.50	1	1	0	0	0	6	7	3	2	6
D 1997	Bal-A	2	0	1.93	2	2	0	0	0	14	7	3	3	16
D Total	2	2	0	2.70	3	3	0	0	0	20	14	6	5	22
L 1996	Bal-A	0	1	5.87	1	1	0	0	0	7^2	8	5	2	6
L 1997	Bal-A	0	0	0.60	2	2	0	0	0	15	4	1	4	25
L Total	2	0	1	2.38	3	3	0	0	0	22^2	12	6	6	31
● Randy Myers														
D 1996	Bal-A	0	0	0.00	3	0	0	2	0	3	0	0	0	3
D 1997	Bal-A	0	0	0.00	2	0	0	1	0	2	0	0	0	5
D Total	2	0	0	0.00	5	0	0	3	0	5	0	0	0	8

YEAR	TM/L	W	L	ERA	G	GS	CG	SV	SHO	IP	H	ER	BB	SO
L 1988	NY-N	2	0	0.00	3	0	0	0	0	4^2	1	0	2	0
L 1990	Cin-N	0	0	0.00	4	0	0	3	0	5^2	2	0	3	7
L 1996	Bal-A	0	1	2.25	3	0	0	0	0	4	4	1	3	2
L 1997	Bal-A	0	1	5.06	4	0	0	1	0	5^1	6	3	3	7
L 1998	SD-N	0	0	13.50	4	0	0	0	0	2	3	3	2	3
L Total	5	2	2	2.91	18	0	0	4	0	21^2	16	7	13	19
W 1990	Cin-N	0	0	0.00	3	0	0	1	0	3	2	0	0	3
W 1998	SD-N	0	0	9.00	3	0	0	0	0	1	0	1	1	2
W Total	2	0	0	2.25	6	0	0	1	0	4	2	1	1	5
● Charles Nagy														
D 1995	Cle-A	1	0	1.29	1	1	0	0	0	7	4	1	5	6
D 1996	Cle-A	0	1	7.15	2	2	0	0	0	11^1	15	9	5	13
D 1997	Cle-A	0	1	9.82	1	1	0	0	0	3^2	2	4	6	1
D 1998	Cle-A	1	0	1.13	1	1	0	0	0	8	4	1	0	3
D 1999	Cle-A	1	0	7.20	2	2	0	0	0	10	11	8	2	6
D Total	5	3	2	5.17	7	7	0	0	0	40	36	23	18	29
L 1995	Cle-A	0	0	1.13	1	1	0	0	0	8	5	1	0	6
L 1997	Cle-A	0	0	2.77	2	2	0	0	0	13	17	4	5	5
L 1998	Cle-A	0	1	3.72	2	2	0	0	0	9^2	13	4	1	6
L Total	3	0	1	2.64	5	5	0	0	0	30^2	35	9	6	17
W 1995	Cle-A	0	0	6.43	1	1	0	0	0	7	8	5	1	4
W 1997	Cle-A	0	1	6.43	2	1	0	0	0	7	8	5	5	5
W Total	2	0	1	6.43	3	2	0	0	0	14	16	10	6	9
● Ray Narleski														
W 1954	Cle-A	0	0	2.25	2	0	0	0	0	4	1	1	1	2
● Denny Neagle														
L 1992	Pit-N	0	0	27.00	2	0	0	0	0	1^2	4	5	3	0
L 1996	Atl-N	0	0	2.35	2	1	0	0	0	7^2	2	2	3	8
L 1997	Atl-N	1	0	0.00	2	1	1	0	1	12	5	0	1	9
L 1998	Atl-N	0	0	3.52	2	1	0	0	0	7^2	8	3	2	9
L 2000	NY-A	0	2	4.50	2	2	0	0	0	10	6	5	7	7
L Total	5	1	2	3.46	10	5	1	0	1	39	25	15	16	33
W 1996	Atl-N	0	0	3.00	2	1	0	0	0	6	5	2	4	3
W 2000	NY-A	0	0	3.86	1	1	0	0	0	4^2	4	2	2	3
W Total	2	0	0	3.38	3	2	0	0	0	10^2	9	4	6	6
● Art Nehf														
W 1921	NY-N	1	2	1.38	3	3	3	0	1	26	13	4	13	8
W 1922	NY-N	1	0	2.25	2	2	1	0	0	16	11	4	3	6
W 1923	NY-N	1	1	2.76	2	2	1	0	1	16^1	10	5	6	7
W 1924	NY-N	1	1	1.83	3	2	1	0	0	19^2	15	4	9	7
W 1929	Chi-N	0	0	18.00	2	0	0	0	0	1	1	2	1	0
W Total	5	4	4	2.16	12	9	6	0	2	79	50	19	32	28
● Gary Neibauer														
L 1969	Atl-N	0	0	0.00	1	0	0	0	0	1	0	0	0	1
● Jeff Nelson														
D 1995	Sea-A	0	1	3.18	3	0	0	0	0	5^2	7	2	3	7
D 1996	NY-A	1	0	0.00	2	0	0	0	0	3^2	2	0	2	5
D 1997	NY-A	0	0	0.00	4	0	0	0	0	4	4	0	2	0
D 1998	NY-A	0	0	0.00	2	0	0	0	0	2^2	2	0	1	2
D 1999	NY-A	0	0	0.00	3	0	0	0	0	1^2	1	0	1	3
D 2000	NY-A	0	0	0.00	2	0	0	0	0	2	0	0	0	2
D Total	6	1	1	0.92	16	0	0	0	0	19^2	16	2	9	19
L 1995	Sea-A	0	0	0.00	3	0	0	0	0	3	3	0	5	3
L 1996	NY-A	0	1	11.57	2	0	0	0	0	2^1	5	3	0	2
L 1998	NY-A	0	1	20.25	3	0	0	0	0	1^1	3	3	1	3
L 1999	NY-A	0	0	0.00	2	0	0	0	0	0^2	0	0	0	0
L 2000	NY-A	0	0	9.00	3	0	0	0	0	3	5	3	0	6
L Total	5	0	2	7.84	13	0	0	0	0	10^1	16	9	6	14
W 1996	NY-A	0	0	0.00	3	0	0	0	0	4^1	1	0	1	5
W 1998	NY-A	0	0	0.00	3	0	0	0	0	2^1	2	0	1	4
W 1999	NY-A	0	0	0.00	4	0	0	0	0	2^2	2	0	1	3
W 2000	NY-A	1	0	10.13	3	0	0	0	0	2^2	5	3	1	1
W Total	4	1	0	2.25	13	0	0	0	0	12	10	3	4	13
● Mel Nelson														
W 1968	StL-N	0	0	0.00	1	0	0	0	0	1	0	0	0	1
● Roger Nelson														
L 1973	Cin-N	0	0	0.00	1	0	0	0	0	2^1	0	0	1	0
● Gene Nelson														
L 1988	Oak-A	2	0	0.00	2	0	0	0	0	4^2	5	0	1	0
L 1989	Oak-A	0	0	0.00	1	0	0	0	0	1^1	1	0	0	2
L 1990	Oak-A	0	0	0.00	1	0	0	0	0	1^2	3	0	0	0
L Total	3	2	0	0.00	4	0	0	0	0	7^2	9	0	1	2
W 1988	Oak-A	0	0	1.42	3	0	0	0	0	6^1	4	1	3	3
W 1989	Oak-A	0	0	54.00	2	0	0	0	0	1	4	6	2	1
W 1990	Oak-A	0	0	0.00	2	0	0	0	0	5	3	0	2	0
W Total	3	0	0	5.11	7	0	0	0	0	12^1	11	7	7	4
● Robb Nen														
D 1997	Fla-N	1	0	0.00	2	0	0	0	0	2	1	0	2	2
D 2000	SF-N	0	0	0.00	2	0	0	0	0	2^1	2	0	1	3
D Total	2	1	0	0.00	4	0	0	0	0	4^1	3	0	3	5
L 1997	Fla-N	0	0	0.00	2	0	0	2	0	2	0	0	0	0
W 1997	Fla-N	0	0	7.71	4	0	0	2	0	4^2	8	4	2	7
● Don Newcombe														
W 1949	Bro-N	0	2	3.09	2	2	1	0	0	11^2	10	4	3	11
W 1955	Bro-N	0	1	9.53	1	1	0	0	0	5^2	8	6	2	4
W 1956	Bro-N	0	1	21.21	2	2	0	0	0	4^2	11	11	3	4
W Total	3	0	4	8.59	5	5	1	0	0	22	29	21	8	19

YEAR	TM/L	W	L	ERA	G	GS	CG	SV	SHO	IP	H	ER	BB	SO
● Hal Newhouser														
W 1945	Det-A	2	1	6.10	3	3	2	0	0	20^2	25	14	4	22
W 1954	Cle-A	0	0	∞	1	0	0	0	0	0	1	1	1	0
W Total	2	2	1	6.53	4	3	2	0	0	20^2	26	15	5	22
● Bobo Newsom														
W 1940	Det-A	2	1	1.38	3	3	3	0	1	26	18	4	4	17
W 1947	NY-A	0	1	19.29	2	1	0	0	0	2^1	6	5	2	0
W Total	2	2	2	2.86	5	4	3	0	1	28^1	24	9	6	17
● Kid Nichols														
T 1892	Bos-N	2	0	1.00	2	2	2	0	1	18	17	2	4	13
T 1897	Bos-N	0	0	12.00	1	1	0	0	0	6	14	8	0	3
T Total	2	2	0	3.75	3	3	2	0	1	24	31	10	4	16
● Tom Niedenfuer														
D 1981	LA-N	0	0	0.00	1	0	0	0	0	0^1	1	0	1	1
L 1981	LA-N	0	0	0.00	1	0	0	0	0	0^1	2	0	0	0
L 1983	LA-N	0	0	0.00	2	0	0	1	0	2	0	0	1	3
L 1985	LA-N	0	2	6.35	3	0	0	1	0	5^2	5	4	2	5
L Total	3	0	2	4.50	6	0	0	2	0	8	7	4	3	8
W 1981	LA-N	0	0	0.00	2	0	0	0	0	5	3	0	1	0
● Joe Niekro														
D 1981	Hou-N	0	0	0.00	1	1	0	0	0	8	7	0	3	4
L 1980	Hou-N	0	0	0.00	1	1	0	0	0	10	6	0	1	2
W 1987	Min-A	0	0	0.00	1	0	0	0	0	2	1	0	1	1
● Phil Niekro														
L 1969	Atl-N	0	1	4.50	1	1	0	0	0	8	9	4	4	4
L 1982	Atl-N	0	0	3.00	1	1	0	0	0	6	6	2	4	5
L Total	2	0	1	3.86	2	2	0	0	0	14	15	6	8	9
● Al Nipper														
W 1986	Bos-A	0	1	7.11	2	1	0	0	0	6^1	10	5	2	2
● Gary Nolan														
L 1970	Cin-N	1	0	0.00	1	1	0	0	0	9	8	0	4	6
L 1972	Cin-N	0	0	1.50	1	1	0	0	0	6	4	1	1	4
L 1975	Cin-N	0	0	3.00	1	1	0	0	0	6	5	2	0	5
L 1976	Cin-N	0	0	1.59	1	1	0	0	0	5^2	6	1	2	1
L Total	4	1	0	1.35	4	4	0	0	0	26^2	23	4	7	16
W 1970	Cin-N	0	1	7.71	2	2	0	0	0	9^1	9	8	3	9
W 1972	Cin-N	0	1	3.38	2	2	0	0	0	10^2	7	4	2	3
W 1975	Cin-N	0	0	6.00	2	2	0	0	0	6	6	4	1	2
W 1976	Cin-N	1	0	2.70	1	1	0	0	0	6^2	8	2	1	1
W Total	4	1	2	4.96	7	7	0	0	0	32^2	30	18	7	15
● Dickie Noles														
D 1981	Phi-N	0	0	4.50	1	1	0	0	0	4	4	2	2	5
L 1980	Phi-N	0	0	0.00	2	0	0	0	0	2^2	1	0	3	0
W 1980	Phi-N	0	0	1.93	1	0	0	0	0	4^2	5	1	2	6
● Hideo Nomo														
D 1995	LA-N	0	1	9.00	1	1	0	0	0	5	7	5	2	6
D 1996	LA-N	0	1	12.27	1	1	0	0	0	3^2	5	5	5	3
D Total	2	0	2	10.38	2	2	0	0	0	8^2	12	10	7	9
● Jerry Nops														
T 1897	Bal-N	1	1	12.86	2	2	1	0	0	14	23	20	9	3
● Fred Norman														
L 1973	Cin-N	0	0	1.80	1	1	0	0	0	5	1	1	3	3
L 1975	Cin-N	1	0	1.50	1	1	0	0	0	6	4	1	5	4
L 1979	Cin-N	0	0	18.00	1	0	0	0	0	2	4	4	1	1
L Total	3	1	0	4.15	3	2	0	0	0	13	9	6	9	8
W 1975	Cin-N	0	1	9.00	2	1	0	0	0	4	8	4	3	2
W 1976	Cin-N	0	0	4.26	1	1	0	0	0	6^1	9	3	2	2
W Total	2	0	1	6.10	3	2	0	0	0	10^1	17	7	5	4
● Mike Norris														
D 1981	Oak-A	1	0	0.00	1	1	1	0	1	9	4	0	3	2
L 1981	Oak-A	0	1	3.68	1	1	0	0	0	7^1	6	3	2	4
● Buck O'Brien														
W 1912	Bos-A	0	2	5.00	2	2	0	0	0	9	12	5	3	4
● Hank O'Day														
W 1889	NY-N	2	0	1.17	3	2	2	0	0	23	10	3	14	12
● Billy O'Dell														
W 1962	SF-N	0	1	4.38	3	1	0	1	0	12^1	12	6	3	9
● Blue Moon Odom														
L 1972	Oak-A	2	0	0.00	2	2	1	0	1	14	5	0	2	5
L 1973	Oak-A	0	0	1.80	1	0	0	0	0	5	6	1	2	4
L 1974	Oak-A	0	0	0.00	1	0	0	0	0	3^1	1	0	0	1
L Total	3	2	0	0.40	4	2	1	0	1	22^1	12	1	4	10
W 1972	Oak-A	0	1	1.59	2	2	0	0	0	11^1	5	2	6	13
W 1973	Oak-A	0	0	3.86	2	0	0	0	0	4^2	5	2	2	2
W 1974	Oak-A	1	0	0.00	2	0	0	0	0	1^1	0	0	1	2
W Total	3	1	1	2.08	6	2	0	0	0	17^1	10	4	9	17
● Curly Ogden														
W 1924	Was-A	0	0	0.00	1	1	0	0	0	0^1	0	0	1	1
● Chad Ogea														
D 1996	Cle-A	0	0	0.00	1	0	0	0	0	0^1	0	0	1	0
D 1997	Cle-A	0	0	1.69	1	0	0	0	0	5^1	2	1	0	1
D Total	2	0	0	1.59	2	0	0	0	0	5^2	2	1	1	1
L 1995	Cle-A	0	0	0.00	1	0	0	0	0	0^2	1	0	0	2
L 1997	Cle-A	0	2	3.21	2	2	0	0	0	14	12	5	5	7

YEAR	TM/L	W	L	ERA	G	GS	CG	SV	SHO	IP	H	ER	BB	SO
L 1998	Cle-A	0	1	8.10	2	1	0	0	0	6^{2}	9	6	5	4
L Total	3	0	3	4.64	5	3	0	0	0	21^{1}	22	11	10	13
W 1997	Cle-A	2	0	1.54	2	2	0	0	0	11^{2}	11	2	3	5
● **Bob Ojeda**														
L 1986	NY-N	1	0	2.57	2	2	1	0	0	14	15	4	4	6
W 1986	NY-N	1	0	2.08	2	2	0	0	0	13	13	3	5	9
● **Red Oldham**														
W 1925	Pit-N	0	0	0.00	1	0	0	1	0	1	0	0	0	2
● **Darren Oliver**														
D 1996	Tex-A	0	1	3.38	1	1	0	0	0	8	6	3	2	3
● **Gregg Olson**														
D 1999	Ari-N	0	0	0.00	2	0	0	0	0	0^{1}	0	0	1	0
● **Jesse Orosco**														
D 1996	Bal-A	0	1	36.00	4	0	0	0	0	1	2	4	3	2
D 1997	Bal-A	0	0	0.00	2	0	0	0	0	1^{1}	1	0	0	1
D Total	2	0	1	15.43	6	0	0	0	0	2^{1}	3	4	3	3
L 1986	NY-N	3	0	3.38	4	0	0	0	0	8	5	3	2	10
L 1988	LA-N	0	0	7.71	4	0	0	0	0	2^{1}	4	2	3	0
L 1996	Bal-A	0	0	4.50	4	0	0	0	0	2	2	1	1	2
L 1997	Bal-A	0	0	0.00	2	0	0	0	0	1^{1}	0	0	1	1
L Total	4	3	0	3.95	14	0	0	0	0	13^{2}	11	6	7	13
W 1986	NY-N	0	0	0.00	4	0	0	2	0	5^{2}	2	0	0	6
● **Russ Ortiz**														
D 2000	SF-N	0	0	1.69	1	1	0	0	0	5^{1}	2	1	4	4
● **Donovan Osborne**														
D 1996	StL-N	0	0	9.00	1	1	0	0	0	4	7	4	0	5
L 1996	StL-N	1	1	9.39	2	2	0	0	0	7^{2}	12	8	4	6
● **Dan Osinski**														
W 1967	Bos-A	0	0	6.75	2	0	0	0	0	1^{1}	2	1	0	0
● **Claude Osteen**														
W 1965	LA-N	1	1	0.64	2	2	1	0	1	14	9	1	5	4
W 1966	LA-N	0	1	1.29	1	1	0	0	0	7	3	1	1	3
W Total	2	1	2	0.86	3	3	1	0	1	21	12	2	6	7
● **Joe Ostrowski**														
W 1951	NY-A	0	0	0.00	1	0	0	0	0	2	1	0	0	1
● **Antonio Osuna**														
D 1995	LA-N	0	1	2.70	3	0	0	0	0	3^{1}	3	1	1	3
D 1996	LA-N	0	1	4.50	2	0	0	0	0	2	3	1	1	4
D Total	2	0	2	3.38	5	0	0	0	0	5^{1}	6	2	2	7
● **Jim O'Toole**														
W 1961	Cin-N	0	2	3.00	2	2	0	0	0	12	11	4	7	4
● **Orval Overall**														
W 1906	Chi-N	0	0	2.25	2	0	0	0	0	12	10	3	3	8
W 1907	Chi-N	1	0	1.00	2	2	1	0	0	18	14	2	4	11
W 1908	Chi-N	2	0	0.98	3	2	2	0	1	18^{1}	7	2	7	15
W 1910	Chi-N	0	1	9.00	1	1	0	0	0	3	6	3	1	1
W Total	4	3	1	1.75	8	5	3	0	1	51^{1}	37	10	15	35
● **Stubby Overmire**														
W 1945	Det-A	0	1	3.00	1	1	0	0	0	6	4	2	2	2
● **Bob Owchinko**														
L 1981	Oak-A	0	0	5.40	1	0	0	0	0	1^{2}	3	1	0	0
● **Frank Owen**														
W 1906	Chi-A	0	0	3.00	1	0	0	0	0	6	6	2	3	2
● **Joe Page**														
W 1947	NY-A	1	1	4.15	4	0	0	1	0	13	12	6	2	7
W 1949	NY-A	1	0	2.00	3	0	0	1	0	9	6	2	3	8
W Total	2	2	1	3.27	7	0	0	2	0	22	18	8	5	15
● **Vance Page**														
W 1938	Chi-N	0	0	13.50	1	0	0	0	0	1^{1}	2	2	0	0
● **Satchel Paige**														
W 1948	Cle-A	0	0	0.00	1	0	0	0	0	0^{2}	0	0	0	0
● **Lance Painter**														
D 1995	Col-N	0	0	5.40	1	1	0	0	0	5	5	3	2	4
● **Erv Palica**														
W 1949	Bro-N	0	0	0.00	1	0	0	0	0	2	1	0	1	1
● **Jim Palmer**														
L 1969	Bal-A	1	0	2.00	1	1	1	0	0	9	10	2	2	4
L 1970	Bal-A	1	0	1.00	1	1	1	0	0	9	7	1	3	12
L 1971	Bal-A	1	0	3.00	1	1	1	0	0	9	7	3	3	8
L 1973	Bal-A	1	0	1.84	3	2	1	0	1	14^{2}	11	3	8	15
L 1974	Bal-A	0	1	1.00	1	1	1	0	0	9	4	1	1	4
L 1979	Bal-A	0	0	3.00	1	1	0	0	0	9	7	3	2	3
L Total	6	4	1	1.96	8	7	5	0	1	59^{2}	46	13	19	46
W 1966	Bal-A	1	0	0.00	1	1	1	0	1	9	4	0	3	6
W 1969	Bal-A	0	1	6.00	1	1	0	0	0	6	5	4	4	5
W 1970	Bal-A	1	0	4.60	2	2	0	0	0	15^{2}	11	8	9	9
W 1971	Bal-A	1	0	2.65	2	2	0	0	0	17	15	5	9	15
W 1979	Bal-A	0	1	3.60	2	2	0	0	0	15	18	6	5	8
W 1983	Bal-A	1	0	0.00	1	0	0	0	0	2	2	0	1	1
W Total	6	4	2	3.20	9	8	1	0	1	64^{2}	55	23	31	44

YEAR	TM/L	W	L	ERA	G	GS	CG	SV	SHO	IP	H	ER	BB	SO
● **Jose Paniagua**														
D 2000	Sea-A	1	0	0.00	2	0	0	0	0	2^{1}	1	0	2	3
L 2000	Sea-A	0	1	4.15	5	0	0	0	0	4^{1}	4	2	1	4
● **Milt Pappas**														
L 1969	Atl-N	0	0	11.57	1	0	0	0	0	2^{1}	4	3	0	4
● **Harry Parker**														
L 1973	NY-N	0	1	9.00	1	0	0	0	0	1	1	1	0	0
W 1973	NY-N	0	1	0.00	3	0	0	0	0	3^{1}	2	0	2	2
● **Jim Parque**														
D 2000	Chi-A	0	0	4.50	1	0	0	0	0	6	6	3	1	2
● **Jeff Parrett**														
L 1992	Oak-A	0	0	11.57	3	0	0	0	0	2^{1}	6	3	0	1
● **Camilo Pascual**														
W 1965	Min-A	0	1	5.40	1	1	0	0	0	5	8	3	1	0
● **Claude Passeau**														
W 1945	Chi-N	1	0	2.70	3	2	1	0	1	16^{2}	7	5	8	3
● **Frank Pastore**														
L 1979	Cin-N	0	0	2.57	1	1	0	0	0	7	7	2	3	1
● **Danny Patterson**														
D 1996	Tex-A	0	0	0.00	1	0	0	0	0	0^{1}	1	0	0	0
D 1999	Tex-A	0	0	0.00	1	0	0	0	0	1	1	0	0	0
D Total	2	0	0	0.00	2	0	0	0	0	1^{1}	2	0	0	0
● **Daryl Patterson**														
W 1968	Det-A	0	0	0.00	2	0	0	0	0	3	1	0	1	0
● **Bob Patterson**														
L 1990	Pit-N	0	0	0.00	2	0	0	1	0	1	1	0	2	0
L 1991	Pit-N	0	0	0.00	1	0	0	0	0	2	1	0	0	3
L 1992	Pit-N	0	0	5.40	2	0	0	0	0	1^{2}	3	1	1	1
L Total	3	0	0	1.93	5	0	0	1	0	4^{2}	5	1	3	4
● **Marty Pattin**														
L 1976	KC-A	0	0	27.00	2	0	0	0	0	0^{1}	0	1	1	0
L 1977	KC-A	0	0	1.50	1	0	0	0	0	6	6	1	0	0
L 1978	KC-A	0	0	27.00	1	0	0	0	0	0^{2}	2	2	0	0
L Total	3	0	0	5.14	4	0	0	0	0	7	8	4	1	0
W 1980	KC-A	0	0	0.00	1	0	0	0	0	1	0	0	0	2
● **Roger Pavlik**														
D 1996	Tex-A	0	1	6.75	1	0	0	0	0	2^{2}	4	2	0	1
● **Monte Pearson**														
W 1936	NY-A	1	0	2.00	1	1	1	0	0	9	7	2	2	7
W 1937	NY-A	1	0	1.04	1	1	0	0	0	8^{2}	5	1	2	4
W 1938	NY-A	1	0	1.00	1	1	1	0	0	9	5	1	2	9
W 1939	NY-A	1	0	0.00	1	1	1	0	1	9	2	0	1	8
W Total	4	4	0	1.01	4	4	3	0	1	35^{2}	19	4	7	28
● **Alejandro Pena**														
D 1995	Atl-N	2	0	0.00	3	0	0	0	0	3	3	0	1	2
L 1981	LA-N	0	0	0.00	2	0	0	0	0	2^{1}	1	0	0	0
L 1983	LA-N	0	0	6.75	1	0	0	0	0	2^{2}	4	2	1	3
L 1988	LA-N	1	1	4.15	3	0	0	1	0	4^{1}	1	2	5	1
L 1991	Atl-N	0	0	0.00	4	0	0	3	0	4^{1}	1	0	0	4
L 1995	Atl-N	0	0	0.00	3	0	0	0	0	3	2	0	1	4
L Total	5	1	1	2.16	13	0	0	4	0	16^{2}	9	4	7	12
W 1988	LA-N	1	0	0.00	2	0	0	0	0	5	2	0	1	7
W 1991	Atl-N	0	1	3.38	3	0	0	0	0	5^{1}	6	2	3	7
W 1995	Atl-N	0	1	9.00	2	0	0	0	0	1	3	1	2	0
W Total	3	1	2	2.38	7	0	0	0	0	11^{1}	11	3	6	14
● **Herb Pennock**														
W 1914	Phi-A	0	0	0.00	1	0	0	0	0	3	2	0	2	3
W 1923	NY-A	2	0	3.63	3	2	1	1	0	17^{1}	19	7	1	8
W 1926	NY-A	2	0	1.23	3	2	2	0	0	22	13	3	4	8
W 1927	NY-A	1	0	1.00	1	1	1	0	0	9	3	1	0	1
W 1932	NY-A	0	0	2.25	2	0	0	2	0	4	2	1	1	4
W Total	5	5	0	1.95	10	5	4	3	0	55^{1}	39	12	8	24
● **Odalis Perez**														
D 1998	Atl-N	1	0	0.00	1	0	0	0	0	0^{2}	0	0	0	1
L 1998	Atl-N	0	0	54.00	2	0	0	0	0	0^{1}	5	2	2	0
● **Pascual Perez**														
L 1982	Atl-N	0	1	5.19	2	1	0	0	0	8^{2}	10	5	2	4
● **Ron Perranoski**														
L 1969	Min-A	0	1	5.79	3	0	0	0	0	4^{2}	8	3	0	2
L 1970	Min-A	0	0	19.29	2	0	0	0	0	2^{1}	5	5	1	3
L Total	2	0	1	10.29	5	0	0	0	0	7	13	8	1	5
W 1963	LA-N	0	0	0.00	1	0	0	1	0	0^{2}	1	0	0	1
W 1965	LA-N	0	0	7.36	2	0	0	0	0	3^{2}	3	3	4	1
W 1966	LA-N	0	0	5.40	2	0	0	0	0	3^{1}	4	2	1	2
W Total	3	0	0	5.87	5	0	0	1	0	7^{2}	8	5	5	4
● **Pol Perritt**														
W 1917	NY-N	0	0	1.08	3	0	0	0	0	8^{1}	9	1	3	3
● **Gaylord Perry**														
L 1971	SF-N	1	1	6.14	2	2	1	0	0	14^{2}	19	10	3	11
● **Jim Perry**														
L 1969	Min-A	0	0	3.38	1	1	0	0	0	8	6	3	3	3

YEAR TM/L	W	L	ERA	G	GS	CG	SV	SHO	IP	H	ER	BB	SO
L 1970 Min-A	0	1	13.50	2	1	0	0	0	5^1	10	8	1	3
L Total 2	0	1	7.43	3	2	0	0	0	13^1	16	11	4	6
W 1965 Min-A	0	0	4.50	2	0	0	0	0	4	5	2	2	4
● Mark Petkovsek													
D 1996 StL-N	0	0	0.00	1	0	0	0	0	2	0	0	0	1
L 1996 StL-N	0	1	7.36	6	0	0	0	0	7^1	11	6	3	7
● Dan Petry													
L 1984 Det-A	0	0	2.57	1	1	0	0	0	7	4	2	1	4
L 1987 Det-A	0	0	0.00	1	0	0	0	0	3^1	1	0	0	1
L Total 2	0	0	1.74	2	1	0	0	0	10^1	5	2	1	5
W 1984 Det-A	0	1	9.00	2	2	0	0	0	8	14	8	5	4
● Andy Pettitte													
D 1995 NY-A	0	0	5.14	1	1	0	0	0	7	9	4	3	0
D 1996 NY-A	0	0	5.68	1	1	0	0	0	6^1	4	4	6	3
D 1997 NY-A	0	2	8.49	2	2	0	0	0	11^2	15	11	1	5
D 1998 NY-A	1	0	1.29	1	1	0	0	0	7	3	1	0	8
D 1999 NY-A	1	0	1.23	1	1	0	0	0	7^1	7	1	0	5
D 2000 NY-A	1	0	3.97	2	2	0	0	0	11^1	15	5	3	7
D Total 6	3	2	4.62	8	8	0	0	0	50^2	53	26	13	28
L 1996 NY-A	1	0	3.60	2	2	0	0	0	15	10	6	5	7
L 1998 NY-A	0	1	11.57	1	1	0	0	0	4^2	8	6	3	1
L 1999 NY-A	1	0	2.45	1	1	0	0	0	7^1	8	2	1	5
L 2000 NY-A	1	0	2.70	1	1	0	0	0	6^2	9	2	1	2
L Total 4	3	1	4.28	5	5	0	0	0	33^2	35	16	10	15
W 1996 NY-A	1	1	5.91	2	2	0	0	0	10^2	11	7	4	5
W 1998 NY-A	1	0	0.00	1	1	0	0	0	7^1	5	0	3	4
W 1999 NY-A	0	0	12.27	1	1	0	0	0	3^2	10	5	1	1
W 2000 NY-A	0	0	1.98	2	2	0	0	0	13^2	16	3	4	9
W Total 4	2	1	3.82	6	6	0	0	0	35^1	42	15	12	19
● Jeff Pfeffer													
W 1916 Bro-N	0	1	1.69	3	1	0	1	0	10^2	7	2	4	5
W 1920 Bro-N	0	0	3.00	1	0	0	0	0	3	4	1	2	1
W Total 2	0	1	1.98	4	1	0	1	0	13^2	11	3	6	6
● Jack Pfiester													
W 1906 Chi-N	0	2	6.10	2	1	1	0	0	10^1	7	7	3	11
W 1907 Chi-N	1	0	1.00	1	1	1	0	0	9	9	1	1	3
W 1908 Chi-N	0	1	7.87	1	1	0	0	0	8	10	7	3	1
W 1910 Chi-N	0	0	0.00	1	0	0	0	0	6^2	9	0	1	1
W Total 4	1	3	3.97	5	3	2	0	0	34	35	15	8	16
● Deacon Phillippe													
T 1900 Pit-N	1	0	0.00	1	1	1	0	1	9	6	0	2	5
W 1903 Pit-N	3	2	2.86	5	5	5	0	0	44	38	14	3	22
W 1909 Pit-N	0	0	0.00	2	0	0	0	0	6	2	0	1	2
W Total 2	3	2	2.52	7	5	5	0	0	50	40	14	4	24
● Tom Phoebus													
W 1970 Bal-A	1	0	0.00	1	0	0	0	0	1^2	1	0	0	0
● Billy Pierce													
W 1959 Chi-A	0	0	0.00	3	0	0	0	0	4	2	0	2	3
W 1962 SF-N	1	1	2.40	2	2	1	0	0	15	8	4	2	5
W Total 2	1	1	1.89	5	2	1	0	0	19	10	4	4	8
● Bill Piercy													
W 1921 NY-A	0	0	0.00	1	0	0	0	0	1	2	0	0	2
● Horacio Pina													
L 1973 Oak-A	0	0	0.00	1	0	0	0	0	2	3	0	1	1
W 1973 Oak-A	0	0	0.00	2	0	0	0	0	3	6	0	2	0
● George Pipgras													
W 1927 NY-A	1	0	2.00	1	1	1	0	0	9	7	2	1	2
W 1928 NY-A	1	0	2.00	1	1	1	0	0	9	4	2	4	8
W 1932 NY-A	1	0	4.50	1	1	0	0	0	8	9	4	3	1
W Total 3	3	0	2.77	3	3	2	0	0	26	20	8	8	11
● Juan Pizarro													
L 1974 Pit-N	0	0	0.00	1	0	0	0	0	0^2	0	0	1	0
W 1957 Mil-N	0	0	10.80	1	0	0	0	0	1^2	3	2	2	1
W 1958 Mil-N	0	0	5.40	1	0	0	0	0	1^2	2	1	1	3
W Total 2	0	0	8.10	2	0	0	0	0	3^1	5	3	3	4
● Eddie Plank													
W 1905 Phi-A	0	2	1.59	2	2	2	0	0	17	14	3	4	11
W 1911 Phi-A	1	1	1.86	2	1	1	0	0	9^2	6	2	0	8
W 1913 Phi-A	1	1	0.95	2	2	2	0	0	19	9	2	3	7
W 1914 Phi-A	0	1	1.00	1	1	1	0	0	9	7	1	4	6
W Total 4	2	5	1.32	7	6	6	0	0	54^2	36	8	11	32
● Bill Pleis													
W 1965 Min-A	0	0	9.00	1	0	0	0	0	1	2	1	0	0
● Dan Plesac													
D 1999 Ari-N	0	0	54.00	1	0	0	0	0	0^1	3	2	0	0
● Eric Plunk													
D 1995 Cle-A	0	0	0.00	1	0	0	0	0	1^1	1	0	1	1
D 1996 Cle-A	0	1	6.75	3	0	0	0	0	4	1	3	2	6
D 1997 Cle-A	0	1	27.00	1	0	0	0	0	1^1	4	4	0	1
D Total 3	0	2	9.45	5	0	0	0	0	6^2	6	7	3	8
L 1988 Oak-A	0	0	0.00	1	0	0	0	0	0^1	1	0	0	1
L 1995 Cle-A	0	0	9.00	3	0	0	0	0	2	1	2	3	2
L 1997 Cle-A	1	0	0.00	1	0	0	0	0	0^2	1	0	0	0
L Total 3	1	0	6.00	5	0	0	0	0	3	3	2	3	3
W 1988 Oak-A	0	0	0.00	2	0	0	0	0	1^2	0	0	0	3
W 1997 Cle-A	0	1	9.00	3	0	0	0	0	3	3	3	4	3
W Total 2	0	1	5.79	5	0	0	0	0	4^2	3	3	4	6
● Johnny Podres													
W 1953 Bro-N	0	1	3.38	1	1	0	0	0	2^2	1	1	2	0
W 1955 Bro-N	2	0	1.00	2	2	2	0	1	18	15	2	4	10
W 1959 LA-N	1	0	4.82	2	2	0	0	0	9^1	7	5	6	4
W 1963 LA-N	1	0	1.08	1	1	0	0	0	8^1	6	1	1	4
W Total 4	4	1	2.11	6	6	2	0	1	38^1	29	9	13	18
● Dick Pole													
W 1975 Bos-A	0	0	∞	1	0	0	0	0	0	0	1	2	0
● Howie Pollet													
W 1942 StL-N	0	0	0.00	1	0	0	0	0	0^1	0	0	0	0
W 1946 StL-N	0	1	3.48	2	2	1	0	0	10^1	12	4	4	3
W Total 2	0	1	3.38	3	2	1	0	0	10^2	12	4	4	3
● Jim Poole													
D 1995 Cle-A	0	0	5.40	1	0	0	0	0	1^2	2	1	1	2
D 1998 Cle-A	0	0	0.00	2	0	0	0	0	1	1	0	1	2
D Total 2	0	0	3.38	3	0	0	0	0	2^2	3	1	2	4
L 1995 Cle-A	0	0	0.00	1	0	0	0	0	1	0	0	0	2
L 1998 Cle-A	0	0	0.00	4	0	0	0	0	1^1	0	0	1	2
L Total 2	0	0	0.00	5	0	0	0	0	2^1	0	0	1	4
W 1995 Cle-A	0	1	3.86	2	0	0	0	0	2^1	1	1	0	1
● Mark Portugal													
L 1995 Cin-N	0	1	36.00	1	0	0	0	0	1	3	4	1	0
● Nels Potter													
W 1944 StL-A	0	1	0.93	2	2	0	0	0	9^2	10	1	3	6
W 1948 Bos-N	0	0	8.44	2	1	0	0	0	5^1	6	5	2	1
W Total 2	0	1	3.60	4	3	0	0	0	15	16	6	5	7
● Jay Powell													
D 1998 Hou-N	0	0	11.57	3	0	0	0	0	2^1	2	3	3	3
D 1999 Hou-N	0	1	6.00	3	0	0	0	0	3	3	2	1	3
D Total 2	0	1	8.44	6	0	0	0	0	5^1	5	5	4	6
L 1997 Fla-N	0	0	0.00	1	0	0	0	0	0^2	0	0	0	1
W 1997 Fla-N	1	0	7.36	4	0	0	0	0	3^2	5	3	4	2
● Ted Power													
L 1990 Pit-N	0	0	3.60	3	1	0	1	0	5	6	2	2	3
● Joe Price													
L 1987 SF-N	1	0	0.00	2	0	0	0	0	5^2	3	0	1	7
● Ray Prim													
W 1945 Chi-N	0	1	9.00	2	1	0	0	0	4	4	4	1	1
● Bob Purkey													
W 1961 Cin-N	0	1	1.64	2	1	1	0	0	11	6	2	3	5
● Jack Quinn													
W 1921 NY-A	0	1	9.82	1	0	0	0	0	3^2	8	4	2	2
W 1929 Phi-A	0	0	9.00	1	1	0	0	0	5	7	5	2	2
W 1930 Phi-A	0	0	4.50	1	0	0	0	0	2	3	1	0	1
W Total 3	0	1	8.44	3	1	0	0	0	10^2	18	10	4	5
● Dan Quisenberry													
D 1981 KC-A	0	0	0.00	1	0	0	0	0	1	1	0	0	0
L 1980 KC-A	1	0	0.00	2	0	0	1	0	4^2	4	0	2	1
L 1984 KC-A	0	1	3.00	1	0	0	0	0	3	2	1	1	1
L 1985 KC-A	0	1	3.86	4	0	0	1	0	4^2	7	2	0	3
L Total 3	1	2	2.19	7	0	0	2	0	12^1	13	3	3	5
W 1980 KC-A	1	2	5.23	6	0	0	1	0	10^1	10	6	3	0
W 1985 KC-A	1	0	2.08	4	0	0	0	0	4^1	5	1	3	3
W Total 2	2	2	4.30	10	0	0	1	0	14^2	15	7	6	3
● Charlie Radbourn													
W 1884 Pro-N	3	0	0.00	3	3	3	0	1	22	11	0	0	17
● Scott Radinsky													
D 1996 LA-N	0	0	0.00	2	0	0	0	0	1^1	0	0	1	2
L 1993 Chi-A	0	0	10.80	4	0	0	0	0	1^2	3	2	1	1
● Robert Ramsay													
L 2000 Sea-A	0	0	0.00	2	0	0	0	0	1^2	2	0	0	1
● Pat Rapp													
L 1999 Bos-A	0	0	0.00	1	0	0	0	0	1	0	0	1	0
● Vic Raschi													
W 1947 NY-A	0	0	6.75	2	0	0	0	0	1^1	2	1	0	1
W 1949 NY-A	1	1	4.30	2	2	0	0	0	14^2	15	7	5	11
W 1950 NY-A	1	0	0.00	1	1	1	0	1	9	2	0	1	5
W 1951 NY-A	1	1	0.87	2	2	0	0	0	10^1	12	1	8	4
W 1952 NY-A	2	0	1.59	3	2	1	0	0	17	12	3	8	18
W 1953 NY-A	0	1	3.38	1	1	1	0	0	8	9	3	3	4
W Total 6	5	3	2.24	11	8	3	0	1	60^1	52	15	25	43
● Doug Rau													
L 1974 LA-N	0	1	40.50	1	1	0	0	0	0^2	3	3	1	0
L 1977 LA-N	0	0	0.00	1	0	0	0	0	1	0	0	0	1
L 1978 LA-N	0	0	3.60	1	1	0	0	0	5	5	2	2	1
L Total 3	0	1	6.75	3	2	0	0	0	6^2	8	5	3	2
W 1977 LA-N	0	1	11.57	2	1	0	0	0	2^1	4	3	0	1
W 1978 LA-N	0	0	0.00	1	0	0	0	0	2	1	0	0	3
W Total 2	0	1	6.23	3	1	0	0	0	4^1	5	3	0	4
● Lance Rautzhan													
L 1977 LA-N	1	0	0.00	1	0	0	0	0	0^1	0	0	0	0

YEAR	TM/L	W	L	ERA	G	GS	CG	SV	SHO	IP	H	ER	BB	SO
L 1978	LA-N	0	0	6.75	1	0	0	0	0	1^1	3	1	2	0
L Total	2	1	0	5.40	2	0	0	0	0	1^2	3	1	2	0
W 1977	LA-N	0	0	0.00	1	0	0	0	0	0^1	0	0	2	0
W 1978	LA-N	0	0	13.50	2	0	0	0	0	2	4	3	0	0
W Total	2	0	0	11.57	3	0	0	0	0	2^1	4	3	2	0
● **Britt Reames**														
D 2000	StL-N	1	0	0.00	2	0	0	0	0	3^1	0	0	3	2
L 2000	StL-N	0	0	1.42	2	0	0	0	0	6^1	5	1	4	6
● **Jeff Reardon**														
D 1981	Mon-N	0	1	2.08	3	0	0	2	0	4^1	1	1	1	2
L 1981	Mon-N	0	0	27.00	1	0	0	0	0	1	3	3	0	0
L 1987	Min-A	1	1	5.06	4	0	0	2	0	5^1	7	3	3	5
L 1990	Bos-A	0	0	9.00	1	0	0	0	0	2	3	2	1	0
L 1992	Atl-N	1	0	0.00	3	0	0	1	0	3	0	0	2	3
L Total	4	2	1	6.35	9	0	0	3	0	11^1	13	8	6	8
W 1987	Min-A	0	0	0.00	4	0	0	1	0	4^2	5	0	0	3
W 1992	Atl-N	0	1	13.50	2	0	0	0	0	1^1	2	2	1	1
W Total	2	0	1	3.00	6	0	0	1	0	6	7	2	1	4
● **Howie Reed**														
W 1965	LA-N	0	0	8.10	2	0	0	0	0	3^1	2	3	2	4
● **Rick Reed**														
D 1999	NY-N	1	0	3.00	1	1	0	0	0	6	4	2	3	2
D 2000	NY-N	0	0	3.00	1	1	0	0	0	6	7	2	2	6
D Total	2	1	0	3.00	2	2	0	0	0	12	11	4	5	8
L 1999	NY-N	0	0	2.57	1	1	0	0	0	7	3	2	0	5
L 2000	NY-N	0	1	10.80	1	1	0	0	0	3^1	8	4	1	4
L Total	2	0	1	5.23	2	2	0	0	0	10^1	11	6	1	9
W 2000	NY-N	0	0	3.00	1	1	0	0	0	6	6	2	1	8
● **Ron Reed**														
D 1981	Phi-N	0	0	3.00	4	0	0	0	0	6	5	2	3	4
L 1969	Atl-N	0	1	21.60	1	1	0	0	0	1^2	5	4	3	3
L 1976	Phi-N	0	0	7.71	2	0	0	0	0	4^2	6	4	2	2
L 1977	Phi-N	0	0	1.80	3	0	0	0	0	5	3	1	2	5
L 1978	Phi-N	0	0	2.25	2	0	0	0	0	4	6	1	0	2
L 1980	Phi-N	0	1	18.00	3	0	0	0	0	2	3	4	1	1
L 1983	Phi-N	0	0	2.70	2	0	0	0	0	3^1	4	1	1	3
L Total	6	0	2	6.53	13	1	0	0	0	20^2	27	15	9	16
W 1980	Phi-N	0	0	0.00	2	0	0	1	0	2	2	0	0	2
W 1983	Phi-N	0	0	2.70	3	0	0	0	0	3^1	4	1	2	4
W Total	2	0	0	1.69	5	0	0	1	0	5^1	6	1	2	6
● **Steve Reed**														
D 1995	Col-N	0	0	0.00	3	0	0	0	0	2^2	2	0	1	3
D 1998	Cle-A	1	0	40.50	2	0	0	0	0	0^2	1	3	1	1
D 1999	Cle-A	0	0	30.86	2	0	0	0	0	2^1	9	8	1	1
D Total	3	1	0	17.47	7	0	0	0	0	5^2	12	11	3	5
L 1998	Cle-A	0	0	0.00	3	0	0	0	0	1^2	0	0	1	0
● **Phil Regan**														
W 1966	LA-N	0	0	0.00	2	0	0	0	0	1^2	0	0	1	2
● **Art Reinhart**														
W 1926	StL-N	0	1	∞	1	0	0	0	0	0	1	4	4	0
● **Mike Remlinger**														
D 1999	Atl-N	0	0	9.82	2	0	0	0	0	3^2	4	4	3	4
D 2000	Atl-N	0	0	2.70	3	0	0	0	0	3^1	6	1	0	3
D Total	2	0	0	6.43	5	0	0	0	0	7	10	5	3	7
L 1999	Atl-N	0	1	3.18	5	0	0	0	0	5^2	3	2	3	4
W 1999	Atl-N	0	1	9.00	2	0	0	0	0	1	1	1	1	0
● **Hal Reniff**														
W 1963	NY-A	0	0	0.00	3	0	0	0	0	3	0	0	1	1
W 1964	NY-A	0	0	0.00	1	0	0	0	0	0^1	2	0	0	0
W Total	2	0	0	0.00	4	0	0	0	0	3^1	2	0	1	1
● **Ed Reulbach**														
W 1906	Chi-N	1	0	2.45	2	2	1	0	0	11	6	3	8	4
W 1907	Chi-N	1	0	0.75	2	1	1	0	0	12	6	1	3	4
W 1908	Chi-N	0	0	4.70	2	1	0	0	0	7^2	9	4	1	5
W 1910	Chi-N	0	0	9.00	1	1	0	0	0	2	3	2	2	0
W Total	4	2	0	2.76	7	5	2	0	0	32^2	24	10	14	13
● **Rick Reuschel**														
D 1981	NY-A	0	1	3.00	1	1	0	0	0	6	4	2	1	3
L 1987	SF-N	0	1	6.30	2	2	0	0	0	10	15	7	2	2
L 1989	SF-N	1	1	5.19	2	2	0	0	0	8^2	12	5	2	5
L Total	2	1	2	5.79	4	4	0	0	0	18^2	27	12	4	7
W 1981	NY-A	0	0	4.91	2	1	0	0	0	3^2	7	2	3	2
W 1989	SF-N	0	1	11.25	1	1	0	0	0	4	5	5	4	2
W Total	2	0	1	8.22	3	2	0	0	0	7^2	12	7	7	4
● **Jerry Reuss**														
D 1981	LA-N	1	0	0.00	2	2	1	0	1	18	10	0	5	7
L 1974	Pit-N	0	2	3.72	2	2	0	0	0	9^2	7	4	8	3
L 1975	Pit-N	0	1	13.50	1	1	0	0	0	2^2	4	4	4	1
L 1981	LA-N	0	1	5.14	1	1	0	0	0	7	7	4	1	2
L 1983	LA-N	0	2	4.50	2	2	0	0	0	12	14	6	3	4
L 1985	LA-N	0	1	10.80	1	1	0	0	0	1^2	5	2	1	0
L Total	5	0	7	5.45	7	7	0	0	0	33	37	20	17	10
W 1981	LA-N	1	1	3.86	2	2	1	0	0	11^2	10	5	3	8
● **Allie Reynolds**														
W 1947	NY-A	1	0	4.76	2	2	1	0	0	11^1	15	6	3	6
W 1949	NY-A	1	0	0.00	2	1	1	1	1	12^1	2	0	4	14

YEAR	TM/L	W	L	ERA	G	GS	CG	SV	SHO	IP	H	ER	BB	SO
W 1950	NY-A	1	0	0.87	2	1	1	1	0	10^1	7	1	4	7
W 1951	NY-A	1	1	4.20	2	2	1	0	0	15	16	7	11	8
W 1952	NY-A	2	1	1.77	4	2	1	1	1	20^1	12	4	6	18
W 1953	NY-A	1	0	6.75	3	1	0	1	0	8	9	6	4	9
W Total	6	7	2	2.79	15	9	5	4	2	77^1	61	24	32	62
● **Shane Reynolds**														
D 1997	Hou-N	0	1	3.00	1	1	0	0	0	6	5	2	1	5
D 1998	Hou-N	0	0	2.57	1	1	0	0	0	7	4	2	1	5
D 1999	Hou-N	1	1	4.09	2	2	0	0	0	11	16	5	3	5
D Total	3	1	2	3.38	4	4	0	0	0	24	25	9	5	15
● **Bob Reynolds**														
L 1973	Bal-A	0	0	3.18	2	0	0	0	0	5^2	5	2	3	5
L 1974	Bal-A	0	0	0.00	1	0	0	0	0	1^1	0	0	3	1
L Total	2	0	0	2.57	3	0	0	0	0	7	5	2	6	6
● **Armando Reynoso**														
D 1995	Col-N	0	0	0.00	1	0	0	0	0	1	2	0	0	0
● **Flint Rhem**														
W 1926	StL-N	0	0	6.75	1	1	0	0	0	4	7	3	2	4
W 1928	StL-N	0	0	0.00	1	0	0	0	0	2	0	0	0	1
W 1930	StL-N	0	1	10.80	1	1	0	0	0	3^1	7	4	2	3
W 1931	StL-N	0	0	0.00	1	0	0	0	0	1	1	0	0	1
W Total	4	0	1	6.10	4	2	0	0	0	10^1	15	7	4	9
● **Rick Rhoden**														
L 1977	LA-N	0	0	0.00	1	0	0	0	0	4^1	2	0	2	0
L 1978	LA-N	0	0	2.25	1	0	0	0	0	4	2	1	1	3
L Total	2	0	0	1.08	2	0	0	0	0	8^1	4	1	3	3
W 1977	LA-N	0	1	2.57	2	0	0	0	0	7	4	2	1	5
● **Arthur Lee Rhodes**														
D 1996	Bal-A	0	0	9.00	2	0	0	0	0	1	1	1	1	1
D 1997	Bal-A	0	0	0.00	1	0	0	0	0	2^1	0	0	0	4
D 2000	Sea-A	0	0	0.00	3	0	0	0	0	2^2	0	0	2	2
D Total	3	0	0	1.50	6	0	0	0	0	6	1	1	3	7
L 1996	Bal-A	0	0	0.00	3	0	0	0	0	2	2	0	0	2
L 1997	Bal-A	0	0	0.00	2	0	0	0	0	2^1	2	0	3	2
L 2000	Sea-A	0	1	31.50	4	0	0	0	0	2	8	7	4	5
L Total	3	0	1	9.95	9	0	0	0	0	6^1	12	7	7	9
● **Gordie Richardson**														
W 1964	StL-N	0	0	40.50	2	0	0	0	0	0^2	3	3	2	0
● **Pete Richert**														
L 1969	Bal-A	0	0	0.00	1	0	0	0	0	1	0	0	2	2
W 1969	Bal-A	0	0	—	1	0	0	0	0	0	0	0	0	0
W 1970	Bal-A	0	0	0.00	1	0	0	1	0	0^1	0	0	0	0
W 1971	Bal-A	0	0	0.00	1	0	0	0	0	0^2	0	0	0	1
W Total	3	0	0	0.00	3	0	0	1	0	1	0	0	0	1
● **Lew Richie**														
W 1910	Chi-N	0	0	0.00	1	0	0	0	0	1	1	0	0	0
● **Elmer Riddle**														
W 1940	Cin-N	0	0	0.00	1	0	0	0	0	1	0	0	0	2
● **Dave Righetti**														
D 1981	NY-A	2	0	1.00	2	1	0	0	0	9	8	1	3	13
L 1981	NY-A	1	0	0.00	1	1	0	0	0	6	4	0	2	4
W 1981	NY-A	0	0	13.50	1	1	0	0	0	2	5	3	2	1
● **Jose Rijo**														
L 1990	Cin-N	1	0	4.38	2	2	0	0	0	12^1	10	6	7	15
W 1990	Cin-N	2	0	0.59	2	2	0	0	0	15^1	9	1	5	14
● **Ricardo Rincon**														
D 1999	Cle-A	0	0	40.50	1	0	0	0	0	0^2	2	3	1	1
● **Jimmy Ring**														
W 1919	Cin-N	1	1	0.64	2	1	1	0	1	14	7	1	6	4
● **Bill Risley**														
D 1995	Sea-A	0	0	6.00	4	0	0	1	0	3	2	2	0	1
L 1995	Sea-A	0	0	0.00	3	0	0	0	0	2^2	2	0	1	2
● **Kevin Ritz**														
D 1995	Col-N	0	0	7.71	2	1	0	0	0	7	12	6	3	5
● **Ben Rivera**														
L 1993	Phi-N	0	0	4.50	1	0	0	0	0	2	1	1	1	2
W 1993	Phi-N	0	0	27.00	1	0	0	0	0	1^1	4	4	2	3
● **Mariano Rivera**														
D 1995	NY-A	1	0	0.00	3	0	0	0	0	5^1	3	0	1	8
D 1996	NY-A	0	0	0.00	2	0	0	0	0	4^2	0	0	1	1
D 1997	NY-A	0	0	4.50	2	0	0	1	0	2	2	1	0	1
D 1998	NY-A	0	0	0.00	3	0	0	2	0	3^1	1	0	1	2
D 1999	NY-A	0	0	0.00	2	0	0	2	0	3	1	0	0	3
D 2000	NY-A	0	0	0.00	3	0	0	3	0	5	2	0	0	2
D Total	6	1	0	0.39	15	0	0	8	0	23^1	9	1	3	17
L 1996	NY-A	1	0	0.00	2	0	0	0	0	4	6	0	1	5
L 1998	NY-A	0	0	0.00	4	0	0	1	0	5^2	0	0	1	5
L 1999	NY-A	1	0	0.00	3	0	0	2	0	4^2	5	0	0	3
L 2000	NY-A	0	0	1.93	3	0	0	1	0	4^2	4	1	0	1
L Total	4	2	0	0.47	12	0	0	4	0	19	15	1	2	14
W 1996	NY-A	0	0	1.59	4	0	0	0	0	5^2	4	1	3	4
W 1998	NY-A	0	0	0.00	3	0	0	3	0	4^1	5	0	0	4
W 1999	NY-A	1	0	0.00	3	0	0	2	0	4^2	3	0	1	3

YEAR	TM/L	W	L	ERA	G	GS	CG	SV	SHO	IP	H	ER	BB	SO
W 2000	NY-A	0	0	3.00	4	0	0	2	0	6	4	2	1	7
W Total	4	1	0	1.31	14	0	0	7	0	20^{2}	16	3	5	18
● **Eppa Rixey**														
W 1915	Phi-N	0	1	4.05	1	0	0	0	0	6^{2}	4	3	2	2
● **Dave Roberts**														
L 1979	Pit-N	0	0	—	1	0	0	0	0	0	0	0	1	0
● **Robin Roberts**														
W 1950	Phi-N	0	1	1.64	2	1	1	0	0	11	11	2	3	5
● **Don Robinson**														
L 1979	Pit-N	1	0	0.00	2	0	0	1	0	2	0	0	1	3
L 1987	SF-N	0	1	9.00	3	0	0	0	0	3	3	3	0	3
L 1989	SF-N	1	0	0.00	1	0	0	0	0	1^{2}	3	0	0	0
L Total	3	2	1	4.05	6	0	0	1	0	6^{2}	6	3	1	6
W 1979	Pit-N	1	0	5.40	4	0	0	0	0	5	4	3	6	3
W 1989	SF-N	0	1	21.60	1	1	0	0	0	1^{2}	4	4	1	0
W Total	2	1	1	9.45	5	1	0	0	0	6^{2}	8	7	7	3
● **Jeff Robinson**														
L 1987	Det-A	0	0	0.00	1	0	0	0	0	0^{1}	1	0	0	0
● **John Rocker**														
D 1998	Atl-N	0	0	0.00	2	0	0	0	0	1^{1}	1	0	0	2
D 1999	Atl-N	1	0	0.00	2	0	0	1	0	3^{1}	0	0	2	5
D 2000	Atl-N	0	0	0.00	1	0	0	0	0	0^{2}	0	0	1	0
D Total	3	1	0	0.00	5	0	0	1	0	5^{1}	1	0	3	7
L 1998	Atl-N	1	0	0.00	6	0	0	0	0	4^{2}	3	0	1	5
L 1999	Atl-N	0	0	0.00	6	0	0	1	0	6^{2}	3	0	2	9
L Total	2	1	0	0.00	12	0	0	1	0	11^{1}	6	0	3	14
W 1999	Atl-N	0	0	0.00	2	0	0	0	0	3	2	0	2	4
● **Felix Rodriguez**														
D 2000	SF-N	0	1	6.23	3	0	0	0	0	4^{1}	6	3	1	6
● **Rich Rodriguez**														
D 1997	SF-N	0	0	0.00	2	0	0	0	0	1	1	0	0	0
● **Rosario Rodriguez**														
L 1991	Pit-N	0	0	27.00	1	0	0	0	0	1	1	3	2	1
● **Preacher Roe**														
W 1949	Bro-N	1	0	0.00	1	1	1	0	1	9	6	0	0	3
W 1952	Bro-N	1	0	3.18	3	1	1	0	0	11^{1}	9	4	6	7
W 1953	Bro-N	0	1	4.50	1	1	1	0	0	8	5	4	4	4
W Total	3	2	1	2.54	5	3	3	0	1	28^{1}	20	8	10	14
● **Ed Roebuck**														
W 1955	Bro-N	0	0	0.00	1	0	0	0	0	2	1	0	0	0
W 1956	Bro-N	0	0	2.08	3	0	0	0	0	4^{1}	1	1	0	5
W Total	2	0	0	1.42	4	0	0	0	0	6^{1}	2	1	0	5
● **Kenny Rogers**														
D 1996	NY-A	0	0	9.00	2	1	0	0	0	2	5	2	2	1
D 1999	NY-N	0	1	8.31	1	1	0	0	0	4^{1}	5	4	2	6
D Total	2	0	1	8.53	3	2	0	0	0	6^{1}	10	6	4	7
L 1996	NY-A	0	0	12.00	1	1	0	0	0	3	5	4	2	3
L 1999	NY-N	0	2	5.87	3	1	0	0	0	7^{2}	11	5	7	2
L Total	2	0	2	7.59	4	2	0	0	0	10^{2}	16	9	9	5
W 1996	NY-A	0	0	22.50	1	1	0	0	0	2	5	5	2	0
● **Steve Rogers**														
D 1981	Mon-N	2	0	0.51	2	2	1	0	1	17^{2}	16	1	3	5
L 1981	Mon-N	1	1	1.80	2	1	1	0	0	10	8	2	1	6
● **Tom Rogers**														
W 1921	NY-A	0	0	6.75	1	0	0	0	0	1^{1}	3	1	0	1
● **Eddie Rommel**														
W 1929	Phi-A	1	0	9.00	1	0	0	0	0	1	2	1	1	0
W 1931	Phi-A	0	0	9.00	1	0	0	0	0	1	3	1	0	0
W Total	2	1	0	9.00	2	0	0	0	0	2	5	2	1	0
● **Enrique Romo**														
L 1979	Pit-N	0	0	0.00	2	0	0	0	0	0^{1}	3	0	1	1
W 1979	Pit-N	0	0	3.86	2	0	0	0	0	4^{2}	5	2	3	4
● **Jim Rooker**														
L 1974	Pit-N	0	0	2.57	1	1	0	0	0	7	6	2	5	4
L 1975	Pit-N	0	1	9.00	1	1	0	0	0	4	7	4	0	5
L Total	2	0	1	4.91	2	2	0	0	0	11	13	6	5	9
W 1979	Pit-N	0	0	1.04	2	1	0	0	0	8^{2}	5	1	3	4
● **Charlie Root**														
W 1929	Chi-N	0	1	4.72	2	2	0	0	0	13^{1}	12	7	2	8
W 1932	Chi-N	0	1	10.38	1	1	0	0	0	4^{1}	6	5	3	4
W 1935	Chi-N	0	1	18.00	2	1	0	0	0	2	5	4	1	2
W 1938	Chi-N	0	0	3.00	1	0	0	0	0	3	3	1	0	1
W Total	4	0	3	6.75	6	4	0	0	0	22^{2}	26	17	6	15
● **Schoolboy Rowe**														
W 1934	Det-A	1	1	2.95	3	2	2	0	0	21^{1}	19	7	0	12
W 1935	Det-A	1	2	2.57	3	2	2	0	0	21	19	6	1	14
W 1940	Det-A	0	2	17.18	2	2	0	0	0	3^{2}	12	7	1	1
W Total	3	2	5	3.91	8	6	4	0	0	46	50	20	2	27
● **Nap Rucker**														
W 1916	Bro-N	0	0	0.00	1	0	0	0	0	2	1	0	0	3
● **Dick Rudolph**														
W 1914	Bos-N	2	0	0.50	2	2	2	0	0	18	12	1	4	15

YEAR	TM/L	W	L	ERA	G	GS	CG	SV	SHO	IP	H	ER	BB	SO
● **Kirk Rueter**														
D 1997	SF-N	0	0	1.29	1	1	0	0	0	7	4	1	3	5
D 2000	SF-N	0	0	0.00	1	0	0	0	0	4^{1}	3	0	1	1
D Total	2	0	0	0.79	2	1	0	0	0	11^{1}	7	1	4	6
● **Dutch Ruether**														
W 1919	Cin-N	1	0	2.57	2	2	1	0	0	14	12	4	4	1
W 1926	NY-A	0	1	8.31	1	1	0	0	0	4^{1}	7	4	2	1
W Total	2	1	1	3.93	3	3	1	0	0	18^{1}	19	8	6	2
● **Bruce Ruffin**														
D 1995	Col-N	0	0	2.70	4	0	0	0	0	3^{1}	3	1	2	2
● **Red Ruffing**														
W 1932	NY-A	1	0	3.00	1	1	1	0	0	9	10	3	6	10
W 1936	NY-A	0	1	5.14	2	2	1	0	0	14	16	8	5	12
W 1937	NY-A	1	0	1.00	1	1	1	0	0	9	7	1	3	8
W 1938	NY-A	2	0	1.50	2	2	2	0	0	18	17	3	2	11
W 1939	NY-A	1	0	1.00	1	1	1	0	0	9	4	1	1	4
W 1941	NY-A	1	0	1.00	1	1	1	0	0	9	6	1	3	5
W 1942	NY-A	1	1	4.08	2	2	1	0	0	17^{2}	14	8	7	11
W Total	7	7	2	2.63	10	10	8	0	0	85^{2}	74	25	27	61
● **Vern Ruhle**														
D 1981	Hou-N	0	1	2.25	1	1	1	0	0	8	4	2	2	1
L 1980	Hou-N	0	0	3.86	1	1	0	0	0	7	8	3	1	3
L 1986	Cal-A	0	0	13.50	1	0	0	0	0	0^{2}	2	1	0	0
L Total	2	0	0	4.70	2	1	0	0	0	7^{2}	10	4	1	3
● **Glendon Rusch**														
D 2000	NY-N	0	0	0.00	1	0	0	0	0	0^{2}	0	0	0	2
L 2000	NY-N	1	0	0.00	2	0	0	0	0	3^{2}	3	0	0	3
W 2000	NY-N	0	0	2.25	3	0	0	0	0	4	6	1	2	2
● **Bob Rush**														
W 1958	Mil-N	0	1	3.00	1	1	0	0	0	6	3	2	5	2
● **Amos Rusie**														
T 1894	NY-N	2	0	0.50	2	2	2	0	0	18	14	1	3	9
● **Allan Russell**														
W 1924	Was-A	0	0	3.00	1	0	0	0	0	3	4	1	0	0
● **Reb Russell**														
W 1917	Chi-A	0	0	∞	1	1	0	0	0	0	2	1	1	0
● **Jack Russell**														
W 1933	Was-A	0	1	0.87	3	0	0	0	0	10^{1}	8	1	0	7
W 1938	Chi-N	0	0	0.00	2	0	0	0	0	1^{2}	1	0	1	0
W Total	2	0	1	0.75	5	0	0	0	0	12	9	1	1	7
● **Jeff Russell**														
D 1996	Tex-A	0	0	3.00	2	0	0	0	0	3	3	1	0	1
L 1992	Oak-A	1	0	9.00	3	0	0	0	0	2	2	2	4	0
● **Marius Russo**														
W 1941	NY-A	1	0	1.00	1	1	1	0	0	9	4	1	2	5
W 1943	NY-A	1	0	0.00	1	1	1	0	0	9	7	0	1	2
W Total	2	2	0	0.50	2	2	2	0	0	18	11	1	3	7
● **Babe Ruth**														
W 1916	Bos-A	1	0	0.64	1	1	1	0	0	14	6	1	3	4
W 1918	Bos-A	2	0	1.06	2	2	1	0	1	17	13	2	7	4
W Total	2	3	0	0.87	3	3	2	0	1	31	19	3	10	8
● **Johnny Rutherford**														
W 1952	Bro-N	0	0	9.00	1	0	0	0	0	1	1	1	1	1
● **Dick Ruthven**														
D 1981	Phi-N	0	1	4.50	1	1	0	0	0	4	3	2	1	0
L 1978	Phi-N	0	1	5.79	1	1	0	0	0	4^{2}	6	3	0	3
L 1980	Phi-N	1	0	2.00	2	1	0	0	0	9	3	2	5	4
L Total	2	1	1	3.29	3	2	0	0	0	13^{2}	9	5	5	7
W 1980	Phi-N	0	0	3.00	1	1	0	0	0	9	9	3	0	7
● **Jimmy Ryan**														
W 1886	Chi-N	0	0	9.00	1	0	0	0	0	5	8	5	4	4
● **Nolan Ryan**														
D 1981	Hou-N	1	1	1.80	2	2	1	0	0	15	6	3	3	14
L 1969	NY-N	1	0	2.57	1	0	0	0	0	7	3	2	2	7
L 1979	Cal-A	0	0	1.29	1	1	0	0	0	7	4	1	3	8
L 1980	Hou-N	0	0	5.40	2	2	0	0	0	13^{1}	16	8	3	14
L 1986	Hou-N	0	1	3.86	2	2	0	0	0	14	9	6	1	17
L Total	4	1	1	3.70	6	5	0	0	0	41^{1}	32	17	9	46
W 1969	NY-N	0	0	0.00	1	0	0	1	0	2^{1}	1	0	2	3
● **Rosy Ryan**														
W 1922	NY-N	1	0	0.00	1	0	0	0	0	2	1	0	0	2
W 1923	NY-N	1	0	0.96	3	0	0	0	0	9^{1}	11	1	3	3
W 1924	NY-N	0	0	3.18	2	0	0	0	0	5^{2}	7	2	4	3
W Total	3	2	0	1.59	6	0	0	0	0	17	19	3	7	8
● **Mike Ryba**														
W 1946	Bos-A	0	0	13.50	1	0	0	0	0	0^{2}	2	1	1	0
● **Bret Saberhagen**														
D 1995	Col-N	0	1	11.25	1	1	0	0	0	4	7	5	1	3
D 1998	Bos-A	0	1	3.86	1	1	0	0	0	7	4	3	1	7
D 1999	Bos-A	0	1	27.00	2	2	0	0	0	3^{2}	9	11	4	2
D Total	3	0	3	11.66	4	4	0	0	0	14^{2}	20	19	6	12
L 1984	KC-A	0	0	2.25	1	1	0	0	0	8	6	2	1	5
L 1985	KC-A	0	0	6.14	2	2	0	0	0	7^{1}	12	5	2	6

YEAR	TM/L	W	L	ERA	G	GS	CG	SV	SHO	IP	H	ER	BB	SO
L 1999	Bos-A	0	1	1.50	1	1	0	0	0	6	5	1	1	5
L Total	3	0	1	3.38	4	4	0	0	0	21^1	23	8	4	16
W 1985	KC-A	2	0	0.50	2	2	2	0	1	18	11	1	1	10
● Ray Sadecki														
W 1964	StL-N	1	0	8.53	2	2	0	0	0	6^1	12	6	5	2
W 1973	NY-N	0	0	1.93	4	0	0	1	0	4^2	5	1	1	6
W Total	2	1	0	5.73	6	2	0	1	0	11	17	7	6	8
● Johnny Sain														
W 1948	Bos-N	1	1	1.06	2	2	2	0	1	17	9	2	0	9
W 1951	NY-A	0	0	9.00	1	0	0	0	0	2	4	2	2	2
W 1952	NY-A	0	1	3.00	1	0	0	0	0	6	6	2	3	3
W 1953	NY-A	1	0	4.76	2	0	0	0	0	5^2	8	3	1	1
W Total	4	2	2	2.64	6	2	2	0	1	30^2	27	9	6	15
● Randy St.Claire														
W 1991	Atl-N	0	0	9.00	1	0	0	0	0	1	1	1	0	0
● Slim Sallee														
W 1917	NY-N	0	2	5.28	2	2	1	0	0	15^1	20	9	4	4
W 1919	Cin-N	1	1	1.35	2	2	1	0	0	13^1	19	2	1	2
W Total	2	1	3	3.45	4	4	2	0	0	28^2	39	11	5	6
● Joe Sambito														
D 1981	Hou-N	1	0	16.20	2	0	0	0	0	1^2	5	3	2	2
L 1980	Hou-N	0	1	4.91	3	0	0	0	0	3^2	4	2	2	6
L 1986	Bos-A	0	0	0.00	3	0	0	0	0	0^2	1	0	1	0
L Total	2	0	1	4.15	6	0	0	0	0	4^1	5	2	3	6
W 1986	Bos-A	0	0	27.00	2	0	0	0	0	0^1	2	1	2	0
● Luis Sanchez														
L 1982	Cal-A	0	1	6.75	2	0	0	0	0	2^2	4	2	1	1
● Scott Sanders														
D 1996	SD-N	0	0	8.31	1	1	0	0	0	4^1	3	4	4	4
● Scott Sanderson														
D 1981	Mon-N	0	0	6.75	1	1	0	0	0	2^2	4	2	2	2
L 1984	Chi-N	0	0	5.79	1	1	0	0	0	4^2	6	3	1	2
L 1989	Chi-N	0	0	0.00	1	0	0	0	0	2	2	0	0	1
L Total	2	0	0	4.05	2	1	0	0	0	6^2	8	3	1	3
W 1990	Oak-A	0	0	10.80	2	0	0	0	0	1^2	4	2	1	0
● Jack Sanford														
W 1962	SF-N	1	2	1.93	3	3	1	0	1	23^1	16	5	8	19
● Jose Santiago														
W 1967	Bos-A	0	2	5.59	3	2	0	0	0	9^2	16	6	3	6
● Manny Sarmiento														
L 1976	Cin-N	0	0	18.00	1	0	0	0	0	1	2	2	1	0
● Kazuhiro Sasaki														
D 2000	Sea-A	0	0	0.00	2	0	0	2	0	2	1	0	0	5
L 2000	Sea-A	0	0	0.00	2	0	0	1	0	2^2	3	0	1	3
● Kevin Saucier														
L 1980	Phi-N	0	0	0.00	2	0	0	0	0	0^2	1	0	2	0
W 1980	Phi-N	0	0	0.00	1	0	0	0	0	0^2	0	0	2	0
● Tony Saunders														
L 1997	Fla-N	0	0	3.38	1	1	0	0	0	5^1	4	2	3	3
W 1997	Fla-N	0	1	27.00	1	1	0	0	0	2	7	6	3	2
● Ray Scarborough														
W 1952	NY-A	0	0	9.00	1	0	0	0	0	1	1	1	0	1
● Art Schallock														
W 1953	NY-A	0	0	4.50	1	0	0	0	0	2	2	1	1	1
● Dan Schatzeder														
L 1987	Min-A	0	0	0.00	2	0	0	0	0	4^1	2	0	0	5
W 1987	Min-A	1	0	6.23	3	0	0	0	0	4^1	4	3	3	3
● Fred Scherman														
L 1972	Det-A	0	0	0.00	1	0	0	0	0	0^2	1	0	0	1
● Bill Scherrer														
W 1984	Det-A	0	0	3.00	3	0	0	0	0	3	5	1	0	0
● Curt Schilling														
L 1993	Phi-N	0	0	1.69	2	2	0	0	0	16	11	3	5	19
W 1993	Phi-N	1	1	3.52	2	2	1	0	1	15^1	13	6	5	9
● Calvin Schiraldi														
L 1986	Bos-A	0	1	1.50	4	0	0	1	0	6	5	1	3	9
W 1986	Bos-A	0	2	13.50	3	0	0	1	0	4	7	6	3	2
● Freddy Schmidt														
W 1944	StL-N	0	0	0.00	1	0	0	0	0	3^1	1	0	1	1
● Pete Schourek														
D 1995	Cin-N	1	0	2.57	1	1	0	0	0	7	5	2	3	5
D 1998	Bos-A	0	0	0.00	1	1	0	0	0	5^1	2	0	4	1
D Total	2	1	0	1.46	2	2	0	0	0	12^1	7	2	7	6
L 1995	Cin-N	0	1	1.26	2	2	0	0	0	14^1	14	2	3	13
● Barney Schultz														
W 1964	StL-N	0	1	18.00	4	0	0	1	0	4	9	8	3	1
● Hal Schumacher														
W 1933	NY-N	1	0	2.45	2	2	1	0	0	14^2	13	4	5	3
W 1936	NY-N	1	1	5.25	2	2	1	0	0	12	13	7	10	11

YEAR	TM/L	W	L	ERA	G	GS	CG	SV	SHO	IP	H	ER	BB	SO
W 1937	NY-N	0	1	6.00	1	1	0	0	0	6	9	4	4	3
W Total	3	2	2	4.13	5	5	2	0	0	32^2	35	15	19	17
● Ferdie Schupp														
W 1917	NY-N	1	0	1.74	2	2	1	0	1	10^1	11	2	2	9
● Jack Scott														
W 1922	NY-N	1	0	0.00	1	1	1	0	1	9	4	0	1	2
W 1923	NY-N	0	1	12.00	2	1	0	0	0	3	9	4	1	2
W Total	2	1	1	3.00	3	2	1	0	1	12	13	4	2	4
● Mike Scott														
L 1986	Hou-N	2	0	0.50	2	2	2	0	1	18	8	1	1	19
● Scott Scudder														
L 1990	Cin-N	0	0	0.00	1	0	0	0	0	1	1	0	0	1
W 1990	Cin-N	0	0	0.00	1	0	0	0	0	1^1	0	0	2	2
● Rudy Seanez														
D 1998	Atl-N	0	0	0.00	1	0	0	0	0	1	0	0	0	0
L 1998	Atl-N	0	0	6.00	4	0	0	0	0	3	2	2	1	4
● Tom Seaver														
L 1969	NY-N	1	0	6.43	1	1	0	0	0	7	8	5	3	2
L 1973	NY-N	1	1	1.62	2	2	1	0	0	16^2	13	3	5	17
L 1979	Cin-N	0	0	2.25	1	1	0	0	0	8	5	2	2	5
L Total	3	2	1	2.84	4	4	1	0	0	31^2	26	10	10	24
W 1969	NY-N	1	1	3.00	2	2	1	0	0	15	12	5	3	9
W 1973	NY-N	0	1	2.40	2	2	0	0	0	15	13	4	3	18
W Total	2	1	2	2.70	4	4	1	0	0	30	25	9	6	27
● Chuck Seelbach														
L 1972	Det-A	0	0	18.00	2	0	0	0	0	1	4	2	0	0
● Diego Segui														
L 1971	Oak-A	0	1	5.79	1	1	0	0	0	4^2	6	3	6	4
W 1975	Bos-A	0	0	0.00	1	0	0	0	0	1	0	0	0	0
● Aaron Sele														
D 1998	Tex-A	0	1	6.00	1	1	0	0	0	6	8	4	1	4
D 1999	Tex-A	0	1	5.40	1	1	0	0	0	5	6	3	5	3
D 2000	Sea-A	0	0	1.23	1	1	0	0	0	7^1	3	1	3	1
D Total	3	0	2	3.93	3	3	0	0	0	18^1	17	8	9	8
L 2000	Sea-A	0	1	6.00	1	1	0	0	0	6	9	4	0	4
● Bobby Shantz														
W 1957	NY-A	0	1	4.05	3	1	0	0	0	6^2	8	3	2	7
W 1960	NY-A	0	0	4.26	3	0	0	1	0	6^1	4	3	1	1
W Total	2	0	1	4.15	6	1	0	1	0	13	12	6	3	8
● Bob Shaw														
W 1959	Chi-A	1	1	2.57	2	2	0	0	0	14	17	4	2	2
● Bob Shawkey														
W 1914	Phi-A	0	1	3.60	1	1	0	0	0	5	4	2	2	0
W 1921	NY-A	0	1	7.00	2	1	0	0	0	9	13	7	6	5
W 1922	NY-A	0	0	2.70	1	1	1	0	0	10	8	3	2	4
W 1923	NY-A	1	0	3.52	1	1	0	0	0	7^2	12	3	4	2
W 1926	NY-A	0	1	5.40	3	1	0	0	0	10	8	6	2	7
W Total	5	1	3	4.54	8	5	1	0	0	41^2	45	21	16	18
● Spec Shea														
W 1947	NY-A	2	0	2.35	3	3	1	0	0	15^1	10	4	8	10
● Rollie Sheldon														
W 1964	NY-A	0	0	0.00	2	0	0	0	0	2^2	0	0	2	2
● Bill Sherdel														
W 1926	StL-N	0	2	2.12	2	2	1	0	0	17	15	4	8	3
W 1928	StL-N	0	2	4.72	2	2	0	0	0	13^1	15	7	3	3
W Total	2	0	4	3.26	4	4	1	0	0	30^1	30	11	11	6
● Larry Sherry														
W 1959	LA-N	2	0	0.71	4	0	0	2	0	12^2	8	1	2	5
● Tex Shirley														
W 1944	StL-A	0	0	0.00	1	0	0	0	0	2	2	0	1	1
● Urban Shocker														
W 1926	NY-A	0	1	5.87	2	1	0	0	0	7^2	13	5	0	3
● Ernie Shore														
W 1915	Bos-A	1	1	2.12	2	2	2	0	0	17	12	4	8	6
W 1916	Bos-A	2	0	1.53	2	2	1	0	0	17^2	12	3	4	9
W Total	2	3	1	1.82	4	4	3	0	0	34^2	24	7	12	15
● Bill Shores														
W 1930	Phi-A	0	0	13.50	1	0	0	0	0	1^1	3	2	0	0
● Eric Show														
L 1984	SD-N	0	1	13.50	2	2	0	0	0	5^1	8	8	4	2
W 1984	SD-N	0	1	10.13	1	1	0	0	0	2^2	4	3	1	2
● Paul Shuey														
D 1996	Cle-A	0	0	9.00	3	0	0	0	0	2	5	2	2	2
D 1998	Cle-A	0	0	0.00	3	0	0	0	0	3	3	0	1	4
D 1999	Cle-A	1	1	11.25	3	0	0	0	0	4	4	5	4	5
D Total	3	1	1	7.00	9	0	0	0	0	9	12	7	7	11
L 1998	Cle-A	0	0	0.00	5	0	0	0	0	6^1	4	0	7	7
● Ed Siever														
W 1907	Det-A	0	1	4.50	1	1	0	0	0	4	7	2	0	1
● Bill Simas														
D 2000	Chi-A	0	0	6.75	2	0	0	0	0	1^1	0	1	1	2

YEAR	TM/L	W	L	ERA	G	GS	CG	SV	SHO	IP	H	ER	BB	SO
● Curt Simmons														
W 1964	StL-N	0	1	2.51	2	2	0	0	0	14^1	11	4	3	8
● Mike Sirotka														
D 2000	Chi-A	0	1	4.76	1	0	0	0	0	5^2	7	3	2	0
● Doug Sisk														
L 1986	NY-N	0	0	0.00	1	0	0	0	0	1	1	0	1	0
W 1986	NY-N	0	0	0.00	1	0	0	0	0	0^2	0	0	1	1
● Jim Slaton														
D 1981	Mil-A	0	0	3.00	4	0	0	0	0	6	6	2	0	2
L 1982	Mil-A	0	0	1.93	2	0	0	1	0	4^2	3	1	1	3
W 1982	Mil-A	1	0	0.00	2	0	0	0	0	2^2	1	0	2	1
● Heathcliff Slocumb														
D 1997	Sea-A	0	0	4.50	2	0	0	0	0	2	3	1	1	0
● John Smiley														
D 1995	Cin-N	0	0	3.00	1	1	0	0	0	6	9	2	0	1
L 1990	Pit-N	0	0	0.00	1	0	0	0	0	2	2	0	0	0
L 1991	Pit-N	0	2	23.63	2	2	0	0	0	2^2	8	7	1	3
L 1995	Cin-N	0	0	3.60	1	1	0	0	0	5	5	2	0	1
L Total	3	0	2	8.38	4	3	0	0	0	9^2	15	9	1	4
● Al Smith														
W 1936	NY-N	0	0	81.00	1	0	0	0	0	0^1	2	3	1	0
W 1937	NY-N	0	0	3.00	2	0	0	0	0	3	2	1	0	1
W Total	2	0	0	10.80	3	0	0	0	0	3^1	4	4	1	1
● Billy Smith														
D 1981	Hou-N	0	0	0.00	1	0	0	0	0	0^1	0	0	0	0
● Clay Smith														
W 1940	Det-A	0	0	2.25	1	0	0	0	0	4	1	1	3	1
● Dave Smith														
D 1981	Hou-N	0	0	3.86	2	0	0	0	0	2^1	2	1	0	4
L 1980	Hou-N	1	0	3.86	3	0	0	0	0	2^1	4	1	2	4
L 1986	Hou-N	0	1	9.00	2	0	0	0	0	2	2	2	3	2
L Total	2	1	1	6.23	5	0	0	0	0	4^1	6	3	5	6
● Lee Smith														
L 1984	Chi-N	0	1	9.00	2	0	0	1	0	2	3	2	0	3
L 1988	Bos-A	0	1	8.10	2	0	0	0	0	3^1	6	3	1	4
L Total	2	0	2	8.44	4	0	0	1	0	5^1	9	5	1	7
● Pete Smith														
L 1992	Atl-N	0	0	2.45	2	0	0	0	0	3^2	2	1	3	3
W 1992	Atl-N	0	0	0.00	1	0	0	0	0	3	3	0	0	0
● Bob Smith														
W 1932	Chi-N	0	0	9.00	1	0	0	0	0	1	2	1	0	1
● Sherry Smith														
W 1916	Bro-N	0	1	1.35	1	1	1	0	0	13^1	7	2	6	2
W 1920	Bro-N	1	1	0.53	2	2	2	0	0	17	10	1	3	3
W Total	2	1	2	0.89	3	3	3	0	0	30^1	17	3	9	5
● Zane Smith														
D 1995	Bos-A	0	1	6.75	1	0	0	0	0	1^1	1	1	0	0
L 1990	Pit-N	0	2	6.00	2	1	0	0	0	9	14	6	1	8
L 1991	Pit-N	1	1	0.61	2	2	0	0	0	14^2	15	1	3	10
L Total	2	1	3	2.66	4	3	0	0	0	23^2	29	7	4	18
● Mike Smithson														
L 1988	Bos-A	0	0	0.00	1	0	0	0	0	2^1	3	0	0	1
● John Smoltz														
D 1995	Atl-N	0	0	7.94	1	1	0	0	0	5^2	5	5	1	6
D 1996	Atl-N	1	0	1.00	1	1	0	0	0	9	4	1	2	7
D 1997	Atl-N	1	0	1.00	1	1	1	0	0	9	3	1	1	11
D 1998	Atl-N	1	0	1.17	1	1	0	0	0	7^2	5	1	0	6
D 1999	Atl-N	1	0	5.14	1	1	0	0	0	7	6	4	3	3
D Total	5	4	0	2.82	5	5	1	0	0	38^1	23	12	7	33
L 1991	Atl-N	2	0	1.76	2	2	1	0	1	15^1	14	3	3	15
L 1992	Atl-N	2	0	2.66	3	3	0	0	0	20^1	14	6	10	19
L 1993	Atl-N	0	1	0.00	1	1	0	0	0	6^1	8	0	5	10
L 1995	Atl-N	0	0	2.57	1	1	0	0	0	7	7	2	2	2
L 1996	Atl-N	2	0	1.20	2	2	0	0	0	15	12	2	3	12
L 1997	Atl-N	0	1	7.50	1	1	0	0	0	6	5	5	5	9
L 1998	Atl-N	0	0	3.95	2	2	0	0	0	13^2	13	6	6	13
L 1999	Atl-N	0	0	6.23	3	1	0	1	0	8^2	8	6	0	8
L Total	8	6	2	2.92	15	13	1	1	1	92^1	81	30	34	88
W 1991	Atl-N	0	0	1.26	2	2	0	0	0	14^1	13	2	1	11
W 1992	Atl-N	1	0	2.70	2	2	0	0	0	13^1	13	4	7	12
W 1995	Atl-N	0	0	15.43	1	1	0	0	0	2^1	6	4	2	4
W 1996	Atl-N	1	1	0.64	2	2	0	0	0	14	6	1	8	14
W 1999	Atl-N	0	1	3.86	1	1	0	0	0	7	6	3	3	11
W Total	5	2	2	2.47	8	8	0	0	0	51	44	14	21	52
● Eddie Solomon														
L 1974	LA-N	0	0	0.00	1	0	0	0	0	2	2	0	1	1
● Elias Sosa														
D 1981	Mon-N	0	0	3.00	2	0	0	0	0	3	4	1	0	1
L 1977	LA-N	0	1	10.13	2	0	0	0	0	2^2	5	3	0	0
L 1981	Mon-N	0	0	0.00	1	0	0	0	0	0^1	1	0	1	0
L Total	2	0	1	9.00	3	0	0	0	0	3	6	3	1	0
W 1977	LA-N	0	0	11.57	2	0	0	0	0	2^1	3	3	1	1

YEAR	TM/L	W	L	ERA	G	GS	CG	SV	SHO	IP	H	ER	BB	SO
● Mario Soto														
L 1979	Cin-N	0	0	0.00	1	0	0	0	0	2	0	0	0	1
● Warren Spahn														
W 1948	Bos-N	1	1	3.00	3	1	0	0	0	12	10	4	3	12
W 1957	Mil-N	1	1	4.70	2	2	1	0	0	15^1	18	8	2	2
W 1958	Mil-N	2	1	2.20	3	3	2	0	1	28^2	19	7	8	18
W Total	3	4	3	3.05	8	6	3	0	1	56	47	19	13	32
● Joe Sparma														
W 1968	Det-A	0	0	54.00	1	0	0	0	0	0^1	2	2	0	0
● By Speece														
W 1924	Was-A	0	0	9.00	1	0	0	0	0	1	3	1	0	0
● George Spencer														
W 1951	NY-N	0	0	18.90	2	0	0	0	0	3^1	6	7	3	0
● Paul Splittorff														
L 1976	KC-A	1	0	1.93	2	0	0	0	0	9^1	7	2	5	2
L 1977	KC-A	1	0	2.40	2	2	0	0	0	15	14	4	3	4
L 1978	KC-A	0	0	4.91	1	1	0	0	0	7^1	9	4	0	2
L 1980	KC-A	0	0	1.69	1	1	0	0	0	5^1	5	1	2	3
L Total	4	2	0	2.68	6	4	0	0	0	37	35	11	10	11
W 1980	KC-A	0	0	5.40	1	0	0	0	0	1^2	4	1	0	0
● Paul Spoljaric														
D 1997	Sea-A	0	0	0.00	2	0	0	0	0	1^2	4	0	0	1
● Karl Spooner														
W 1955	Bro-N	0	1	13.50	2	1	0	0	0	3^1	4	5	3	6
● Russ Springer														
D 1997	Hou-N	0	0	5.40	2	0	0	0	0	1^2	2	1	1	3
D 1999	Atl-N	0	0	0.00	1	0	0	0	0	1	2	0	1	1
D Total	2	0	0	3.38	3	0	0	0	0	2^2	4	1	2	4
L 1999	Atl-N	1	0	0.00	2	0	0	0	0	2	0	0	1	1
W 1999	Atl-N	0	0	0.00	2	0	0	0	0	2^1	1	0	0	1
● Bill Stafford														
W 1960	NY-A	0	0	1.50	2	0	0	0	0	6	5	1	1	2
W 1961	NY-A	0	0	2.70	1	1	0	0	0	6^2	7	2	2	5
W 1962	NY-A	1	0	2.00	1	1	1	0	0	9	4	2	2	5
W Total	3	1	0	2.08	4	2	1	0	0	21^2	16	5	5	12
● Gerry Staley														
W 1959	Chi-A	0	1	2.16	4	0	0	1	0	8^1	8	2	0	3
● Harry Staley														
T 1892	Bos-N	1	0	3.00	1	1	1	0	0	9	10	3	1	0
● Lee Stange														
W 1967	Bos-A	0	0	0.00	1	0	0	0	0	2	3	0	0	0
● Don Stanhouse														
L 1979	Bal-A	1	1	6.00	3	0	0	0	0	3	5	2	3	0
W 1979	Bal-A	0	1	13.50	3	0	0	0	0	2	6	3	3	0
● Bob Stanley														
L 1986	Bos-A	0	0	4.76	3	0	0	0	0	5^2	7	3	3	1
L 1988	Bos-A	0	0	9.00	2	0	0	0	0	1	2	1	1	0
L Total	2	0	0	5.40	5	0	0	0	0	6^2	9	4	4	1
W 1986	Bos-A	0	0	0.00	5	0	0	1	0	6^1	5	0	1	4
● Mike Stanton														
D 1995	Bos-A	0	0	0.00	1	0	0	0	0	2^1	1	0	0	4
D 1996	Tex-A	0	1	2.70	3	0	0	0	0	3^1	2	1	3	3
D 1997	NY-A	0	0	0.00	3	0	0	0	0	1	1	0	1	3
D 2000	NY-A	1	0	2.08	3	0	0	0	0	4^1	5	1	1	3
D Total	4	1	1	1.64	10	0	0	0	0	11	9	2	5	13
L 1991	Atl-N	0	0	2.45	3	0	0	0	0	3^2	4	1	3	3
L 1992	Atl-N	0	0	0.00	5	0	0	0	0	4^1	2	0	2	5
L 1993	Atl-N	0	0	0.00	1	0	0	0	0	1	1	0	1	0
L 1998	NY-A	0	0	0.00	3	0	0	0	0	3^2	2	0	1	4
L 1999	NY-A	0	0	0.00	3	0	0	0	0	0^1	1	0	1	0
L Total	5	0	0	0.69	15	0	0	0	0	13	10	1	8	12
W 1991	Atl-N	1	0	0.00	5	0	0	0	0	7^1	5	0	2	7
W 1992	Atl-N	0	0	0.00	4	0	0	1	0	5	3	0	2	1
W 1998	NY-A	0	0	27.00	1	0	0	0	0	0^2	3	2	0	1
W 1999	NY-A	0	0	0.00	1	0	0	0	0	0^1	0	0	0	1
W 2000	NY-A	2	0	0.00	4	0	0	0	0	4^1	0	0	0	7
W Total	5	3	0	1.02	15	0	0	1	0	17^2	11	2	4	17
● Garrett Stephenson														
D 2000	StL-N	0	0	2.45	1	1	0	0	0	3^2	3	1	2	2
● Jerry Stephenson														
W 1967	Bos-A	0	0	9.00	1	0	0	0	0	2	3	2	1	0
● Dave Stewart														
D 1981	LA-N	0	2	40.50	2	0	0	0	0	0^2	4	3	0	1
L 1988	Oak-A	1	0	1.35	2	2	0	0	0	13^1	9	2	6	11
L 1989	Oak-A	2	0	2.81	2	2	0	0	0	16	13	5	3	9
L 1990	Oak-A	2	0	1.13	2	2	0	0	0	16	8	2	2	4
L 1992	Oak-A	1	0	2.70	2	2	1	0	0	16^2	14	5	6	7
L 1993	Tor-A	2	0	2.03	2	2	0	0	0	13^1	8	3	8	8
L Total	5	8	0	2.03	10	10	1	0	0	75^1	52	17	25	39
W 1981	LA-N	0	0	0.00	2	0	0	0	0	1^2	1	0	2	1
W 1988	Oak-A	0	1	3.14	2	2	0	0	0	14^1	12	5	5	5
W 1989	Oak-A	2	0	1.69	2	2	1	0	1	16	10	3	2	14
W 1990	Oak-A	0	2	3.46	2	2	1	0	0	13	10	5	6	5

YEAR	TM/L	W	L	ERA	G	GS	CG	SV	SHO	IP	H	ER	BB	SO
W 1993	Tor-A	0	1	6.75	2	2	0	0	0	12	10	9	8	8
W Total	5	2	4	3.47	10	8	2	0	1	57	43	22	23	33
● **Sammy Stewart**														
L 1983	Bal-A	0	0	0.00	2	0	0	1	0	4^1	2	0	1	2
W 1979	Bal-A	0	0	0.00	1	0	0	0	0	2^2	4	0	1	0
W 1983	Bal-A	0	0	0.00	3	0	0	0	0	5	2	0	2	6
W Total	2	0	0	0.00	4	0	0	0	0	7^2	6	0	3	6
● **Lefty Stewart**														
W 1933	Was-A	0	1	9.00	1	1	0	0	0	2	6	2	0	0
● **Dave Stieb**														
L 1985	Tor-A	1	1	3.10	3	3	0	0	0	20^1	11	7	10	18
L 1989	Tor-A	0	2	6.35	2	2	0	0	0	11^1	12	8	6	10
L Total	2	1	3	4.26	5	5	0	0	0	31^2	23	15	16	28
● **Jack Stivetts**														
T 1892	Bos-N	2	0	0.93	3	3	3	0	1	29	21	3	7	17
T 1897	Bos-N	0	1	18.47	2	1	0	0	0	6^1	16	13	7	0
T Total	2	2	1	4.08	5	4	3	0	1	35^1	37	16	14	17
● **Tim Stoddard**														
L 1984	Chi-N	0	0	4.50	2	0	0	0	0	2	1	1	2	2
W 1979	Bal-A	1	0	5.40	4	0	0	0	0	5	6	3	1	3
● **George Stone**														
L 1969	Atl-N	0	0	9.00	1	0	0	0	0	1	2	1	0	0
L 1973	NY-N	0	0	1.35	1	1	0	0	0	6^2	3	1	2	4
L Total	2	0	0	2.35	2	1	0	0	0	7^2	5	2	2	4
W 1973	NY-N	0	0	0.00	2	0	0	1	0	3	4	0	1	3
● **Steve Stone**														
W 1979	Bal-A	0	0	9.00	1	0	0	0	0	2	4	2	2	2
● **Mel Stottlemyre**														
W 1964	NY-A	1	1	3.15	3	3	1	0	0	20	18	7	6	12
● **Todd Stottlemyre**														
D 1996	StL-N	1	0	1.35	1	1	0	0	0	6^2	5	1	2	7
D 1998	Tex-A	0	1	2.25	1	1	1	0	0	8	6	2	4	8
D 1999	Ari-N	1	0	1.35	1	1	0	0	0	6^2	4	1	5	6
D Total	3	2	1	1.69	3	3	1	0	0	21^1	15	4	11	21
L 1989	Tor-A	0	1	7.20	1	1	0	0	0	5	7	4	2	3
L 1991	Tor-A	0	1	9.82	1	1	0	0	0	3^2	7	4	1	3
L 1992	Tor-A	0	0	2.45	1	0	0	0	0	3^2	3	1	0	1
L 1993	Tor-A	0	1	7.50	1	1	0	0	0	6	6	5	4	4
L 1996	StL-N	1	1	12.38	3	2	0	0	0	8	15	11	3	11
L Total	5	1	4	8.54	7	5	0	0	0	26^1	38	25	10	22
W 1992	Tor-A	0	0	0.00	4	0	0	0	0	3^2	4	0	0	4
W 1993	Tor-A	0	0	27.00	1	1	0	0	0	2	3	6	4	1
W Total	2	0	0	9.53	5	1	0	0	0	5^2	7	6	4	5
● **Les Straker**														
L 1987	Min-A	0	0	16.88	1	1	0	0	0	2^2	3	5	4	1
W 1987	Min-A	0	0	4.00	2	2	0	0	0	9	9	4	3	6
● **Scott Stratton**														
W 1890	Lou-A	1	1	2.37	3	3	1	0	0	19	26	5	4	8
● **John Stuper**														
L 1982	StL-N	0	0	3.00	1	1	0	0	0	6	4	2	1	4
W 1982	StL-N	1	0	3.46	2	2	1	0	0	13	10	5	5	5
● **Tom Sturdivant**														
W 1955	NY-A	0	0	6.00	2	0	0	0	0	3	5	2	2	0
W 1956	NY-A	1	0	2.79	2	1	1	0	0	9^2	8	3	8	9
W 1957	NY-A	0	0	6.00	2	1	0	0	0	6	6	4	1	2
W Total	3	1	0	4.34	6	2	1	0	0	18^2	19	9	11	11
● **Jim Sullivan**														
T 1897	Bos-N	0	0	3.00	1	0	0	0	0	3	6	1	0	0
● **Ed Summers**														
W 1908	Det-A	0	2	4.30	2	1	0	0	0	14^2	18	7	4	7
W 1909	Det-A	0	2	8.59	2	2	0	0	0	7^1	13	7	4	4
W Total	2	0	4	5.73	4	3	0	0	0	22	31	14	8	11
● **Steve Sundra**														
W 1939	NY-A	0	0	0.00	1	0	0	0	0	2^2	4	0	1	2
● **Rick Sutcliffe**														
L 1984	Chi-N	1	1	3.38	2	2	0	0	0	13^1	9	5	8	10
L 1989	Chi-N	0	0	4.50	1	1	0	0	0	6	5	3	4	2
L Total	2	1	1	3.72	3	3	0	0	0	19^1	14	8	12	12
● **Bruce Sutter**														
L 1982	StL-N	1	0	0.00	2	0	0	1	0	4^1	0	0	0	1
W 1982	StL-N	1	0	4.70	4	0	0	2	0	7^2	6	4	3	6
● **Don Sutton**														
L 1974	LA-N	2	0	0.53	2	2	1	0	1	17	7	1	2	13
L 1977	LA-N	1	0	1.00	1	1	1	0	0	9	9	1	0	4
L 1978	LA-N	0	1	6.35	1	1	0	0	0	5^2	7	4	2	0
L 1982	Mil-A	1	0	3.52	1	1	0	0	0	7^2	8	3	2	9
L 1986	Cal-A	0	0	1.86	2	1	0	0	0	9^2	6	2	1	4
L Total	5	4	1	2.02	7	6	2	0	1	49	37	11	7	30
W 1974	LA-N	1	0	2.77	2	2	0	0	0	13	9	4	3	12
W 1977	LA-N	1	0	3.94	2	2	1	0	0	16	17	7	1	6
W 1978	LA-N	0	2	7.50	2	2	0	0	0	12	17	10	4	8
W 1982	Mil-A	0	1	7.84	2	2	0	0	0	10^1	12	9	1	5
W Total	4	2	3	5.26	8	8	1	0	0	51^1	55	30	9	31
● **Bill Swift**														
D 1995	Col-N	0	0	6.00	1	1	0	0	0	6	7	4	2	3
● **Greg Swindell**														
D 1998	Bos-A	0	0	0.00	1	0	0	0	0	1^1	0	0	1	1
D 1999	Ari-N	0	0	0.00	3	0	0	0	0	3^1	1	0	3	1
D Total	2	0	0	0.00	4	0	0	0	0	4^2	1	0	4	2
● **Jeff Tam**														
D 2000	Oak-A	0	0	0.00	3	0	0	0	0	2	3	0	1	1
● **Frank Tanana**														
L 1979	Cal-A	0	0	3.60	1	1	0	0	0	5	6	2	2	3
L 1987	Det-A	0	1	5.06	1	1	0	0	0	5^1	6	3	4	1
L Total	2	0	1	4.35	2	2	0	0	0	10^1	12	5	6	4
● **Kevin Tapani**														
D 1995	LA-N	0	0	81.00	2	0	0	0	0	0^1	0	3	4	1
D 1998	Chi-N	0	0	1.00	1	1	0	0	0	9	5	1	3	6
D Total	2	0	0	3.86	3	1	0	0	0	9^1	5	4	7	7
L 1991	Min-A	0	1	7.84	2	2	0	0	0	10^1	16	9	3	9
W 1991	Min-A	1	1	4.50	2	2	0	0	0	12	13	6	2	7
● **Julian Tavarez**														
D 1995	Cle-A	0	0	6.75	3	0	0	0	0	2^2	5	2	0	3
D 1996	Cle-A	0	0	0.00	2	0	0	0	0	1^1	1	0	2	1
D 1997	SF-N	0	1	4.50	3	0	0	0	0	4	4	2	2	0
D Total	3	0	1	4.50	8	0	0	0	0	8	10	4	4	4
L 1995	Cle-A	0	1	2.70	4	0	0	0	0	3^1	3	1	1	2
W 1995	Cle-A	0	0	0.00	5	0	0	0	0	4^1	3	0	2	1
● **Harry Taylor**														
W 1947	Bro-N	0	0	—	1	1	0	0	0	0	2	0	1	0
● **Ron Taylor**														
L 1969	NY-N	1	0	0.00	2	0	0	1	0	3^1	3	0	0	4
W 1964	StL-N	0	0	0.00	2	0	0	1	0	4^2	0	0	1	2
W 1969	NY-N	0	0	0.00	2	0	0	1	0	2^1	0	0	1	3
W Total	2	0	0	0.00	4	0	0	2	0	7	0	0	2	5
● **Kent Tekulve**														
L 1975	Pit-N	0	0	6.75	2	0	0	0	0	1^1	3	1	1	2
L 1979	Pit-N	0	0	3.38	2	0	0	0	0	2^2	2	1	2	2
L Total	2	0	0	4.50	4	0	0	0	0	4	5	2	3	4
W 1979	Pit-N	0	1	2.89	5	0	0	3	0	9^1	4	3	3	10
● **Walt Terrell**														
L 1987	Det-A	0	0	9.00	1	1	0	0	0	6	7	6	4	4
● **Ralph Terry**														
W 1960	NY-A	0	2	5.40	2	1	0	0	0	6^2	7	4	1	5
W 1961	NY-A	0	1	4.82	2	2	0	0	0	9^1	12	5	2	7
W 1962	NY-A	2	1	1.80	3	3	2	0	1	25	17	5	2	16
W 1963	NY-A	0	0	3.00	1	0	0	0	0	3	3	1	1	0
W 1964	NY-A	0	0	0.00	1	0	0	0	0	2	2	0	0	3
W Total	5	2	4	2.93	9	6	2	0	1	46	41	15	6	31
● **Adonis Terry**														
W 1889	Bro-A	2	3	6.14	5	5	4	0	0	36^2	47	25	18	14
W 1890	Bro-N	1	1	3.60	3	3	3	0	1	25	25	10	10	8
W Total	2	3	4	5.11	8	8	7	0	1	61^2	72	35	28	22
● **Jeff Tesreau**														
W 1912	NY-N	1	2	3.13	3	3	1	0	0	23	19	8	11	15
W 1913	NY-N	0	1	6.48	2	1	0	0	0	8^1	11	6	1	4
W 1917	NY-N	0	0	0.00	1	0	0	0	0	1	0	0	1	1
W Total	3	1	3	3.90	6	4	1	0	0	32^1	30	14	13	20
● **Bobby Thigpen**														
L 1993	Phi-N	0	0	5.40	2	0	0	0	0	1^2	1	1	1	3
W 1993	Phi-N	0	0	0.00	2	0	0	0	0	2^2	1	0	1	0
● **Tommy Thomas**														
W 1933	Was-A	0	0	0.00	2	0	0	0	0	1^1	1	0	0	2
● **Myles Thomas**														
W 1926	NY-A	0	0	3.00	2	0	0	0	0	3	3	1	0	0
● **Junior Thompson**														
W 1939	Cin-N	0	1	13.50	1	1	0	0	0	4^2	5	7	4	3
W 1940	Cin-N	0	1	16.20	1	1	0	0	0	3^1	8	6	4	2
W Total	2	0	2	14.63	2	2	0	0	0	8	13	13	8	5
● **Gus Thompson**														
W 1903	Pit-N	0	0	4.50	1	0	0	0	0	2	3	1	0	1
● **Mark Thompson**														
D 1995	Col-N	0	0	0.00	1	0	0	1	0	1	0	0	0	0
● **Mark Thurmond**														
L 1984	SD-N	0	1	9.82	1	1	0	0	0	3^2	7	4	2	1
L 1987	Det-A	0	0	0.00	1	0	0	0	0	0^1	0	0	0	0
L Total	2	0	1	9.00	2	1	0	0	0	4	7	4	2	1
W 1984	SD-N	0	1	10.13	2	2	0	0	0	5^1	12	6	3	2
● **Luis Tiant**														
L 1970	Min-A	0	0	13.50	1	0	0	0	0	0^2	1	1	0	0
L 1975	Bos-A	1	0	0.00	1	1	1	0	0	9	3	0	3	8
L Total	2	1	0	0.93	2	1	1	0	0	9^2	4	1	3	8
W 1975	Bos-A	2	0	3.60	3	3	2	0	1	25	25	10	8	12
● **Dick Tidrow**														
L 1976	NY-A	1	0	3.68	3	0	0	0	0	7^1	6	3	4	0

YEAR	TM/L	W	L	ERA	G	GS	CG	SV	SHO	IP	H	ER	BB	SO
L 1977	NY-A	0	0	3.86	2	0	0	0	0	7	6	3	3	3
L 1978	NY-A	0	0	4.76	1	0	0	0	0	5^{2}	8	3	2	1
L 1983	Chi-A	0	0	3.00	1	0	0	0	0	3	1	1	3	3
L Total	4	1	0	3.91	7	0	0	0	0	23	21	10	12	7
W 1976	NY-A	0	0	7.71	2	0	0	0	0	2^{1}	5	2	1	1
W 1977	NY-A	0	0	4.91	2	0	0	0	0	3^{2}	5	2	0	1
W 1978	NY-A	0	0	1.93	2	0	0	0	0	4^{2}	4	1	0	5
W Total	3	0	0	4.22	6	0	0	0	0	10^{2}	14	5	1	7
● Mike Timlin														
D 1997	Sea-A	0	0	54.00	1	0	0	0	0	0^{2}	3	4	1	1
D 2000	StL-N	0	0	10.80	2	0	0	0	0	1^{2}	5	2	1	2
D Total	2	0	0	23.14	3	0	0	0	0	2^{1}	8	6	2	3
L 1991	Tor-A	0	1	3.18	4	0	0	0	0	5^{2}	5	2	2	5
L 1992	Tor-A	0	0	6.75	2	0	0	0	0	1^{1}	4	1	0	1
L 1993	Tor-A	0	0	3.86	1	0	0	0	0	2^{1}	3	1	0	2
L 2000	StL-N	0	1	0.00	3	0	0	0	0	3^{1}	1	0	2	0
L Total	4	0	2	2.84	10	0	0	0	0	12^{2}	13	4	4	8
W 1992	Tor-A	0	0	0.00	2	0	0	1	0	1^{1}	0	0	0	0
W 1993	Tor-A	0	0	0.00	2	0	0	0	0	2^{1}	2	0	0	4
W Total	2	0	0	0.00	4	0	0	1	0	3^{2}	2	0	0	4
● Bud Tinning														
W 1932	Chi-N	0	0	0.00	2	0	0	0	0	2^{1}	0	0	0	3
● Ledell Titcomb														
W 1888	NY-N	0	1	6.75	1	1	0	0	0	4	5	3	2	2
● Jim Tobin														
W 1945	Det-A	0	0	6.00	1	0	0	0	0	3	4	2	1	0
● Jim Todd														
L 1975	Oak-A	0	0	9.00	3	0	0	0	0	1	3	1	0	0
● Brett Tomko														
D 2000	Sea-A	0	0	0.00	1	0	0	0	0	2^{2}	1	0	1	0
L 2000	Sea-A	0	0	7.20	2	0	0	0	0	5	3	4	4	4
● Dave Tomlin														
L 1973	Cin-N	0	0	16.20	1	0	0	0	0	1^{2}	5	3	1	1
L 1979	Cin-N	0	0	0.00	3	0	0	0	0	3	3	0	2	3
L Total	2	0	0	5.79	4	0	0	0	0	4^{2}	8	3	3	4
● Randy Tomlin														
L 1991	Pit-N	0	0	3.00	1	1	0	0	0	6	6	2	2	1
L 1992	Pit-N	0	0	6.75	2	0	0	0	0	2^{2}	5	2	1	0
L Total	2	0	0	4.15	3	1	0	0	0	8^{2}	11	4	3	1
● Fred Toney														
W 1921	NY-N	0	0	23.63	2	2	0	0	0	2^{2}	7	7	3	1
● Mike Torrez														
L 1977	NY-A	0	1	4.09	2	1	0	0	0	11	11	5	5	5
W 1977	NY-A	2	0	2.50	2	2	2	0	0	18	16	5	5	15
● Dizzy Trout														
W 1940	Det-A	0	1	9.00	1	1	0	0	0	2	6	2	1	1
W 1945	Det-A	1	1	0.66	2	1	1	0	0	13^{2}	9	1	3	9
W Total	2	1	2	1.72	3	2	1	0	0	15^{2}	15	3	4	10
● Steve Trout														
L 1984	Chi-N	1	0	2.00	2	1	0	0	0	9	5	2	3	3
● Bob Trowbridge														
W 1957	Mil-N	0	0	45.00	1	0	0	0	0	1	2	5	3	1
● Virgil Trucks														
W 1945	Det-A	1	0	3.38	2	2	1	0	0	13^{1}	14	5	5	7
● John Tudor														
L 1985	StL-N	1	1	2.84	2	2	0	0	0	12^{2}	10	4	3	8
L 1987	StL-N	1	1	1.76	2	2	0	0	0	15^{1}	16	3	5	12
L 1988	LA-N	0	0	7.20	1	1	0	0	0	5	8	4	1	1
L Total	3	2	2	3.00	5	5	0	0	0	33	34	11	9	21
W 1985	StL-N	2	1	3.00	3	3	1	0	1	18	15	6	7	14
W 1987	StL-N	1	1	5.73	2	2	0	0	0	11	15	7	3	8
W 1988	LA-N	0	0	0.00	1	1	0	0	0	1^{1}	0	0	0	1
W Total	3	3	2	3.86	6	6	1	0	1	30^{1}	30	13	10	23
● Lee Tunnell														
W 1987	StL-N	0	0	2.08	2	0	0	0	0	4^{1}	4	1	2	1
● Bob Turley														
W 1955	NY-A	0	1	8.44	3	1	0	0	0	5^{1}	7	5	4	7
W 1956	NY-A	0	1	0.82	3	1	1	0	0	11	4	1	8	14
W 1957	NY-A	1	0	2.31	3	2	1	0	0	11^{2}	7	3	6	12
W 1958	NY-A	2	1	2.76	4	2	1	1	1	16^{1}	10	5	7	13
W 1960	NY-A	1	0	4.82	2	2	0	0	0	9^{1}	15	5	4	0
W Total	5	4	3	3.19	15	8	3	1	1	53^{2}	43	19	29	46
● Jim Turner														
W 1940	Cin-N	0	1	7.50	1	1	0	0	0	6	8	5	0	4
W 1942	NY-A	0	0	0.00	1	0	0	0	0	1	0	0	1	0
W Total	2	0	1	6.43	2	1	0	0	0	7	8	5	1	4
● Lefty Tyler														
W 1914	Bos-N	0	0	3.60	1	1	0	0	0	10	8	4	3	4
W 1918	Chi-N	1	1	1.17	3	3	1	0	0	23	14	3	11	4
W Total	2	1	1	1.91	4	4	1	0	0	33	22	7	14	8
● George Uhle														
W 1920	Cle-A	0	0	0.00	2	0	0	0	0	3	1	0	0	3

YEAR	TM/L	W	L	ERA	G	GS	CG	SV	SHO	IP	H	ER	BB	SO
● Tom Underwood														
D 1981	Oak-A	0	0	0.00	1	0	0	0	0	0^{1}	0	0	0	1
L 1976	Phi-N	0	0	0.00	1	0	0	0	0	0^{1}	1	0	2	0
L 1980	NY-A	0	0	0.00	2	0	0	0	0	3	3	0	0	3
L 1981	Oak-A	0	0	13.50	2	0	0	0	0	1^{1}	4	2	2	0
L Total	3	0	0	3.86	5	0	0	0	0	4^{2}	8	2	4	3
● Cecil Upshaw														
L 1969	Atl-N	0	0	2.84	3	0	0	0	0	6^{1}	5	2	1	4
● Ismael Valdes														
D 1995	LA-N	0	0	0.00	1	1	0	0	0	7	3	0	1	6
D 1996	LA-N	0	1	4.26	1	1	0	0	0	6^{1}	5	3	0	5
D Total	2	0	1	2.03	2	2	0	0	0	13^{1}	8	3	1	11
● Fernando Valenzuela														
D 1981	LA-N	1	0	1.06	2	2	1	0	0	17	10	2	3	10
D 1996	SD-N	0	0	0.00	1	0	0	0	0	0^{2}	0	0	2	0
D Total	2	1	0	1.02	3	2	1	0	0	17^{2}	10	2	5	10
L 1981	LA-N	1	1	2.45	2	2	0	0	0	14^{2}	10	4	5	10
L 1983	LA-N	1	0	1.13	1	1	0	0	0	8	7	1	4	5
L 1985	LA-N	1	0	1.88	2	2	0	0	0	14^{1}	11	3	10	13
L Total	3	3	1	1.95	5	5	0	0	0	37	28	8	19	28
W 1981	LA-N	1	0	4.00	1	1	1	0	0	9	9	4	7	6
● Dazzy Vance														
W 1934	StL-N	0	0	0.00	1	0	0	0	0	1^{1}	2	0	1	3
● Hy Vandenberg														
W 1945	Chi-N	0	0	0.00	3	0	0	0	0	6	1	0	3	3
● Johnny Vander Meer														
W 1940	Cin-N	0	0	0.00	1	0	0	0	0	3	2	0	3	2
● Hippo Vaughn														
W 1918	Chi-N	1	2	1.00	3	3	3	0	1	27	17	3	5	17
● Bob Veale														
W 1971	Pit-N	0	0	13.50	1	0	0	0	0	0^{2}	1	1	2	0
● Bucky Veil														
W 1903	Pit-N	0	0	1.29	1	0	0	0	0	7	6	1	5	1
● Mike Venafro														
D 1999	Tex-A	0	0	0.00	2	0	0	0	0	1	2	0	1	0
● Dario Veras														
D 1996	SD-N	0	0	0.00	2	0	0	0	0	1	1	0	0	1
● Dave Veres														
D 2000	StL-N	0	0	0.00	2	0	0	0	0	2	1	0	0	4
L 2000	StL-N	0	0	0.00	3	0	0	0	0	2^{1}	2	0	0	3
● Frank Viola														
L 1987	Min-A	1	0	5.25	2	2	0	0	0	12	14	7	5	9
W 1987	Min-A	2	1	3.72	3	3	0	0	0	19^{1}	17	8	3	16
● Bill Voiselle														
W 1948	Bos-N	0	1	2.53	2	1	0	0	0	10^{2}	8	3	2	2
● Ed Vosberg														
D 1996	Tex-A	0	0	—	1	0	0	0	0	0	1	0	0	0
L 1997	Fla-N	0	0	0.00	2	0	0	0	0	2^{2}	2	0	1	3
W 1997	Fla-N	0	0	6.00	2	0	0	0	0	3	3	2	3	2
● Pete Vuckovich														
D 1981	Mil-A	1	0	0.00	2	1	0	0	0	5^{1}	2	0	3	4
L 1982	Mil-A	0	1	4.40	2	2	1	0	0	14^{1}	15	7	7	8
W 1982	Mil-A	0	1	4.50	2	2	0	0	0	14	16	7	5	4
● Rube Waddell														
T 1900	Pit-N	0	1	1.93	2	1	1	0	0	14	15	3	3	7
● Ben Wade														
W 1953	Bro-N	0	0	15.43	2	0	0	0	0	2^{1}	4	4	1	2
● Terrell Wade														
L 1996	Atl-N	0	0	0.00	1	0	0	0	0	0^{1}	0	0	0	1
W 1996	Atl-N	0	0	0.00	2	0	0	0	0	0^{2}	0	0	1	0
● Billy Wagner														
D 1997	Hou-N	0	0	18.00	1	0	0	0	0	1	3	2	0	2
D 1998	Hou-N	1	0	18.00	1	0	0	0	0	1	4	2	0	1
D 1999	Hou-N	0	0	0.00	1	0	0	0	0	1	0	0	0	1
D Total	3	1	0	12.00	3	0	0	0	0	3	7	4	0	4
● Tim Wakefield														
D 1995	Bos-A	0	1	11.81	1	1	0	0	0	5^{1}	5	7	5	4
D 1998	Bos-A	0	1	33.75	1	1	0	0	0	1^{1}	3	5	2	1
D 1999	Bos-A	0	0	13.50	2	0	0	0	0	2	3	3	4	4
D Total	3	0	2	15.58	4	2	0	0	0	8^{2}	11	15	11	9
L 1992	Pit-N	2	0	3.00	2	2	2	0	0	18	14	6	5	7
● Rube Walberg														
W 1929	Phi-A	1	0	0.00	2	0	0	0	0	6^{1}	3	0	0	8
W 1930	Phi-A	0	1	3.86	1	1	0	0	0	4^{2}	4	2	1	3
W 1931	Phi-A	0	0	3.00	2	0	0	0	0	3	3	1	2	4
W Total	3	1	1	1.93	5	1	0	0	0	14	10	3	3	15
● Bob Walk														
L 1982	Atl-N	0	0	9.00	1	0	0	0	0	1	2	1	1	1
L 1990	Pit-N	1	1	4.85	2	2	0	0	0	13	11	7	2	8
L 1991	Pit-N	0	0	1.93	3	0	0	1	0	9^{1}	5	2	3	5

YEAR	TM/L	W	L	ERA	G	GS	CG	SV	SHO	IP	H	ER	BB	SO
L 1992	Pit-N	1	0	3.86	2	1	1	0	0	11^2	6	5	7	6
L Total	4	2	1	3.86	8	3	1	1	0	35	24	15	13	20
W 1980	Phi-N	1	0	7.71	1	1	0	0	0	7	8	6	3	3
● Luke Walker														
L 1970	Pit-N	0	1	1.29	1	1	0	0	0	7	5	1	1	5
L 1972	Pit-N	0	0	18.00	1	0	0	0	0	1	3	2	0	0
L Total	2	0	1	3.38	2	1	0	0	0	8	8	3	1	5
W 1971	Pit-N	0	0	40.50	1	1	0	0	0	0^2	3	3	1	0
● Bill Walker														
W 1934	StL-N	0	2	7.11	2	0	0	0	0	6^1	6	5	6	2
● Donne Wall														
D 1998	SD-N	0	0	9.00	1	0	0	0	0	1	2	1	0	2
L 1998	SD-N	0	0	3.00	3	0	0	1	0	3	3	1	4	4
W 1998	SD-N	0	1	6.75	2	0	0	0	0	2^2	3	2	3	0
● Bobby Wallace														
T 1896	Cle-N	0	1	4.50	1	1	1	0	0	8	10	4	2	4
● Ed Walsh														
W 1906	Chi-A	2	0	1.20	2	2	1	0	1	15	7	2	6	17
● Bucky Walters														
W 1939	Cin-N	0	2	4.91	2	1	1	0	0	11	13	6	1	6
W 1940	Cin-N	2	0	1.50	2	2	2	0	1	18	8	3	6	6
W Total	2	2	2	2.79	4	3	3	0	1	29	21	9	7	12
● Duane Ward														
L 1989	Tor-A	0	0	7.36	2	0	0	0	0	3^2	6	3	3	5
L 1991	Tor-A	0	1	6.23	2	0	0	0	0	4^1	4	3	1	6
L 1992	Tor-A	1	0	6.75	3	0	0	0	0	4	6	3	1	2
L 1993	Tor-A	0	0	5.79	4	0	0	2	0	4^2	4	3	3	8
L Total	4	1	1	6.48	11	0	0	3	0	16^2	20	12	8	21
W 1992	Tor-A	2	0	0.00	4	0	0	0	0	3^1	1	0	1	6
W 1993	Tor-A	1	0	1.93	4	0	0	2	0	4^2	3	1	0	7
W Total	2	3	0	1.13	8	0	0	2	0	8	4	1	1	13
● Lon Warneke														
W 1932	Chi-N	0	1	5.91	2	1	1	0	0	10^2	15	7	5	8
W 1935	Chi-N	2	0	0.54	3	2	1	0	1	16^2	9	1	4	5
W Total	2	2	1	2.63	5	3	2	0	1	27^1	24	8	9	13
● John Wasdin														
D 1998	Bos-A	0	0	10.80	1	0	0	0	0	1^2	2	2	1	2
D 1999	Bos-A	0	0	27.00	2	0	0	0	0	1^2	2	5	4	1
D Total	2	0	0	18.90	3	0	0	0	0	3^1	4	7	5	3
● Ray Washburn														
W 1967	StL-N	0	0	0.00	2	0	0	0	0	2^1	1	0	1	2
W 1968	StL-N	1	1	9.82	2	2	0	0	0	7^1	7	8	7	6
W 1970	Cin-N	0	0	13.50	1	0	0	0	0	1^1	2	2	2	0
W Total	3	1	1	8.18	5	2	0	0	0	11	10	10	10	8
● Gary Waslewski														
W 1967	Bos-A	0	0	2.16	2	1	0	0	0	8^1	4	2	2	7
● Allen Watson														
L 1999	NY-A	0	0	0.00	3	0	0	0	0	1	2	0	2	1
● Mule Watson														
W 1923	NY-N	0	0	13.50	1	1	0	0	0	2	4	3	1	1
W 1924	NY-N	0	0	0.00	1	0	0	1	0	0^2	0	0	0	0
W Total	2	0	0	10.13	2	1	0	1	0	2^2	4	3	1	1
● Eddie Watt														
L 1969	Bal-A	0	0	0.00	1	0	0	0	0	2	0	0	0	2
L 1971	Bal-A	0	0	0.00	1	0	0	1	0	2	2	0	0	1
L 1973	Bal-A	0	0	0.00	1	0	0	0	0	0^1	0	0	0	0
L Total	3	0	0	0.00	3	0	0	1	0	4^1	2	0	0	3
W 1969	Bal-A	0	1	3.00	2	0	0	0	0	3	4	1	0	3
W 1970	Bal-A	0	1	9.00	1	0	0	0	0	1	2	1	1	3
W 1971	Bal-A	0	1	3.86	2	0	0	0	0	2^1	4	1	0	2
W Total	3	0	3	4.26	5	0	0	0	0	6^1	10	3	1	8
● Dave Weathers														
D 1996	NY-A	1	0	0.00	2	0	0	0	0	5	1	0	0	5
L 1996	NY-A	1	0	0.00	2	0	0	0	0	3	3	0	0	0
W 1996	NY-A	0	0	3.00	3	0	0	0	0	3	2	1	3	3
● Monte Weaver														
W 1933	Was-A	0	1	1.74	1	1	0	0	0	10^1	11	2	4	3
● Mickey Welch														
W 1888	NY-N	1	1	2.65	2	2	2	0	0	17	10	5	9	2
W 1889	NY-N	0	1	9.00	1	1	0	0	0	5	11	5	3	1
W Total	2	1	2	4.09	3	3	2	0	0	22	21	10	12	3
● Bob Welch														
D 1981	LA-N	0	0	0.00	1	0	0	0	0	1	0	0	1	1
L 1978	LA-N	1	0	2.08	1	0	0	0	0	4^1	2	1	0	5
L 1981	LA-N	0	0	5.40	3	0	0	1	0	1^2	2	1	0	2
L 1983	LA-N	0	1	6.75	1	1	0	0	0	1^1	0	1	2	0
L 1985	LA-N	0	1	6.75	1	1	0	0	0	2^2	5	2	6	2
L 1988	Oak-A	0	0	27.00	1	1	0	0	0	1^2	6	5	2	0
L 1989	Oak-A	1	0	3.18	1	1	0	0	0	5^2	8	2	1	4
L 1990	Oak-A	1	0	1.23	1	1	0	0	0	7^1	6	1	3	4
L 1992	Oak-A	0	0	2.57	1	1	0	0	0	7	7	2	1	7
L Total	8	3	2	4.26	10	6	0	1	0	31^2	36	15	15	24
W 1978	LA-N	0	1	6.23	3	0	0	1	0	4^1	4	3	2	6

YEAR	TM/L	W	L	ERA	G	GS	CG	SV	SHO	IP	H	ER	BB	SO
W 1981	LA-N	0	0	∞	1	1	0	0	0	0	3	2	1	0
W 1988	Oak-A	0	0	1.80	1	1	0	0	0	5	6	1	3	8
W 1990	Oak-A	0	0	4.91	1	1	0	0	0	7^1	9	4	2	2
W Total	4	0	1	5.40	6	3	0	1	0	16^2	22	10	8	16
● David Wells														
D 1995	Cin-N	1	0	0.00	1	1	0	0	0	6^1	6	0	1	8
D 1996	Bal-A	1	0	4.61	2	2	0	0	0	13^2	15	7	4	6
D 1997	NY-A	1	0	1.00	1	1	1	0	0	9	5	1	0	1
D 1998	NY-A	1	0	0.00	1	1	0	0	0	8	5	0	1	9
D Total	4	4	0	1.95	5	5	1	0	0	37	31	8	6	24
L 1989	Tor-A	0	0	0.00	1	0	0	0	0	1	0	0	2	1
L 1991	Tor-A	0	0	2.35	4	0	0	0	0	7^2	6	2	2	9
L 1995	Cin-N	0	1	4.50	1	1	0	0	0	6	8	3	2	3
L 1996	Bal-A	1	0	4.05	1	1	0	0	0	6^2	8	3	3	6
L 1998	NY-A	2	0	2.87	2	2	0	0	0	15^2	12	5	2	18
L Total	5	3	1	3.16	9	4	0	0	0	37	34	13	11	37
W 1992	Tor-A	0	0	0.00	4	0	0	0	0	4^1	1	0	2	3
W 1998	NY-A	1	0	6.43	1	1	0	0	0	7	7	5	2	4
W Total	2	1	0	3.97	5	1	0	0	0	11^1	8	5	4	7
● Bob Wells														
D 1995	Sea-A	0	0	9.00	1	0	0	0	0	1	2	1	1	0
D 1997	Sea-A	0	0	0.00	1	0	0	0	0	1^1	1	0	0	1
D Total	2	0	0	3.86	2	0	0	0	0	2^1	3	1	1	1
L 1995	Sea-A	0	0	3.00	1	0	0	0	0	3	2	1	2	2
● Turk Wendell														
D 1999	NY-N	1	0	0.00	2	0	0	0	0	2	0	0	2	0
D 2000	NY-N	0	0	0.00	2	0	0	0	0	2	0	0	1	5
D Total	2	1	0	0.00	4	0	0	0	0	4	0	0	3	5
L 1999	NY-N	1	0	4.76	5	0	0	0	0	5^2	2	3	4	5
L 2000	NY-N	1	0	0.00	2	0	0	0	0	1^1	1	0	1	2
L Total	2	2	0	3.86	7	0	0	0	0	7	3	3	5	7
W 2000	NY-N	0	1	5.40	2	0	0	0	0	1^2	3	1	2	2
● Butch Wensloff														
W 1947	NY-A	0	0	0.00	1	0	0	0	0	2	0	0	0	0
● David West														
L 1991	Min-A	1	0	0.00	2	0	0	0	0	5^2	1	0	4	4
L 1993	Phi-N	0	0	13.50	3	0	0	0	0	2^2	5	4	2	5
L Total	2	1	0	4.32	5	0	0	0	0	8^1	6	4	6	9
W 1991	Min-A	0	0	∞	2	0	0	0	0	0	2	4	4	0
W 1993	Phi-N	0	0	27.00	3	0	0	0	0	1	5	3	1	0
W Total	2	0	0	63.00	5	0	0	0	0	1	7	7	5	0
● John Wetteland														
D 1995	NY-A	0	1	14.54	3	0	0	0	0	4^1	8	7	2	5
D 1996	NY-A	0	0	0.00	3	0	0	2	0	4	2	0	4	4
D 1998	Tex-A	0	0	0.00	1	0	0	0	0	1	0	0	1	1
D 1999	Tex-A	0	0	0.00	1	0	0	0	0	1	1	0	0	1
D Total	4	0	1	6.10	8	0	0	2	0	10^1	10	7	7	11
L 1996	NY-A	0	0	4.50	4	0	0	1	0	4	2	2	1	5
W 1996	NY-A	0	0	2.08	5	0	0	4	0	4^1	4	1	1	6
● Ernie White														
W 1942	StL-N	1	0	0.00	1	1	1	0	1	9	6	0	0	6
● Doc White														
W 1906	Chi-A	1	1	1.80	3	2	1	1	0	15	12	3	7	4
● Rick White														
D 2000	NY-N	1	0	0.00	2	0	0	0	0	2^2	6	0	2	4
L 2000	NY-N	0	0	9.00	1	0	0	0	0	3	5	3	3	1
W 2000	NY-N	0	0	6.75	1	0	0	0	0	1^1	1	1	1	1
● Earl Whitehill														
W 1933	Was-A	1	0	0.00	1	1	1	0	1	9	5	0	2	2
● Ed Whitson														
L 1984	SD-N	1	0	1.13	1	1	0	0	0	8	5	1	2	6
W 1984	SD-N	0	0	40.50	1	1	0	0	0	0^2	5	3	0	0
● Kemp Wicker														
W 1937	NY-A	0	0	0.00	1	0	0	0	0	1	0	0	0	0
● Bob Wickman														
D 1995	NY-A	0	0	0.00	3	0	0	0	0	3	5	0	0	3
● Milt Wilcox														
L 1970	Cin-N	1	0	0.00	1	0	0	0	0	3	1	0	2	5
L 1984	Det-A	1	0	0.00	1	1	0	0	0	8	2	0	2	8
L Total	2	2	0	0.00	2	1	0	0	0	11	3	0	4	13
W 1970	Cin-N	0	1	9.00	2	0	0	0	0	2	3	2	0	2
W 1984	Det-A	1	0	1.50	1	1	0	0	0	6	7	1	2	4
W Total	2	1	1	3.38	3	1	0	0	0	8	10	3	2	6
● Hoyt Wilhelm														
W 1954	NY-N	0	0	0.00	2	0	0	1	0	2^1	1	0	0	3
● Roy Wilkinson														
W 1919	Chi-A	0	0	1.23	2	0	0	0	0	7^1	9	1	4	3
● Ted Wilks														
W 1944	StL-N	0	1	5.68	2	1	0	1	0	6^1	5	4	3	7
W 1946	StL-N	0	0	0.00	1	0	0	0	0	1	2	0	0	0
W Total	2	0	1	4.91	3	1	0	1	0	7^1	7	4	3	7
● Ed Willett														
W 1909	Det-A	0	0	0.00	2	0	0	0	0	7^2	3	0	0	1

YEAR	TM/L	W	L	ERA	G	GS	CG	SV	SHO	IP	H	ER	BB	SO
● Carl Willey														
W 1958	Mil-N	0	0	0.00	1	0	0	0	0	1	0	0	0	2
● Lefty Williams														
W 1917	Chi-A	0	0	9.00	1	0	0	0	0	1	2	1	0	3
W 1919	Chi-A	0	3	6.61	3	3	1	0	0	16^1	12	12	8	4
W Total	2	0	3	6.75	4	3	1	0	0	17^1	14	13	8	7
● Mitch Williams														
L 1989	Chi-N	0	0	0.00	2	0	0	0	0	1	1	0	0	2
L 1993	Phi-N	2	0	1.69	4	0	0	2	0	5^1	6	1	2	5
L Total	2	2	0	1.42	6	0	0	2	0	6^1	7	1	2	7
W 1993	Phi-N	0	2	20.25	3	0	0	1	0	2^2	5	6	4	1
● Stan Williams														
L 1970	Min-A	0	0	0.00	2	0	0	0	0	6	2	0	1	2
W 1959	LA-N	0	0	0.00	1	0	0	0	0	2	0	0	2	1
W 1963	NY-A	0	0	0.00	1	0	0	0	0	3	1	0	0	5
W Total	2	0	0	0.00	2	0	0	0	0	5	1	0	2	6
● Ned Williamson														
W 1886	Chi-N	0	1	4.50	2	1	0	0	0	2	4	1	1	2
● Carl Willis														
L 1991	Min-A	0	0	0.00	3	0	0	0	0	5^1	2	0	0	3
W 1991	Min-A	0	0	5.14	4	0	0	0	0	7	6	4	2	2
● Ron Willis														
W 1967	StL-N	0	0	27.00	3	0	0	0	0	1	2	3	4	1
W 1968	StL-N	0	0	8.31	3	0	0	0	0	4^1	2	4	4	3
W Total	2	0	0	11.81	6	0	0	0	0	5^1	4	7	8	4
● Vic Willis														
W 1909	Pit-N	0	1	3.97	2	1	0	0	0	11^1	10	5	8	3
● Jim Willoughby														
W 1975	Bos-A	0	1	0.00	3	0	0	0	0	6^1	3	0	0	2
● Earl Wilson														
W 1968	Det-A	0	1	6.23	1	1	0	0	0	4^1	4	3	6	3
● Steve Wilson														
L 1989	Chi-N	0	1	4.91	2	0	0	0	0	3^2	3	2	1	4
● Hooks Wiltse														
W 1911	NY-N	0	0	18.90	2	0	0	0	0	3^1	8	7	0	2
● George Winter														
W 1908	Det-A	0	0	0.00	1	0	0	0	0	1	1	0	1	0
● Rick Wise														
L 1975	Bos-A	1	0	2.45	1	1	0	0	0	7^1	6	2	3	2
W 1975	Bos-A	1	0	8.44	2	1	0	0	0	5^1	6	5	2	2
● George Witt														
W 1960	Pit-N	0	0	0.00	3	0	0	0	0	2^2	5	0	2	1
● Mike Witt														
L 1982	Cal-A	0	0	6.00	1	0	0	0	0	3	2	2	2	3
L 1986	Cal-A	1	0	2.55	2	2	1	0	0	17^2	13	5	2	8
L Total	2	1	0	3.05	3	2	1	0	0	20^2	15	7	4	11
● Bobby Witt														
D 1996	Tex-A	0	0	8.10	1	1	0	0	0	3^1	4	3	2	3
L 1992	Oak-A	0	0	18.00	1	0	0	0	0	1	2	2	1	1
● Mark Wohlers														
D 1995	Atl-N	0	1	6.75	3	0	0	2	0	2^2	6	2	2	4
D 1996	Atl-N	0	0	0.00	3	0	0	3	0	3^1	1	0	0	4
D 1997	Atl-N	0	0	0.00	1	0	0	0	0	1	1	0	0	1
D Total	3	0	1	2.57	7	0	0	5	0	7	8	2	2	9
L 1991	Atl-N	0	0	0.00	3	0	0	0	0	1^2	3	0	1	1
L 1992	Atl-N	0	0	0.00	3	0	0	0	0	3	2	0	1	2
L 1993	Atl-N	0	1	3.38	4	0	0	0	0	5^1	2	2	3	10
L 1995	Atl-N	1	0	1.80	4	0	0	0	0	5	2	1	0	8
L 1996	Atl-N	0	0	0.00	3	0	0	2	0	3	0	0	0	4
L 1997	Atl-N	0	0	0.00	1	0	0	0	0	1	0	0	1	1
L Total	6	1	1	1.42	18	0	0	2	0	19	9	3	6	26
W 1991	Atl-N	0	0	0.00	3	0	0	0	0	1^2	2	0	2	1
W 1992	Atl-N	0	0	0.00	2	0	0	0	0	0^2	0	0	1	0
W 1995	Atl-N	0	0	1.80	4	0	0	2	0	5	4	1	3	3
W 1996	Atl-N	0	0	6.23	4	0	0	0	0	4^1	7	3	2	4
W Total	4	0	0	3.09	13	0	0	2	0	11^2	13	4	8	8
● Bob Wolcott														
L 1995	Sea-A	1	0	2.57	1	1	0	0	0	7	8	2	5	2
● Joe Wood														
W 1912	Bos-A	3	1	3.68	4	3	2	0	0	22	27	9	3	21
● Kerry Wood														
D 1998	Chi-N	0	1	1.80	1	1	0	0	0	5	3	1	4	5
● Hal Woodeshick														
W 1967	StL-N	0	0	0.00	1	0	0	0	0	1	1	0	0	0
● Dick Woodson														
L 1969	Min-A	0	0	10.80	1	0	0	0	0	1^2	3	2	3	2
L 1970	Min-A	0	0	9.00	1	0	0	0	0	1	2	1	1	0
L Total	2	0	0	10.13	2	0	0	0	0	2^2	5	3	4	2
● Ralph Works														
W 1909	Det-A	0	0	9.00	1	0	0	0	0	2	4	2	0	2
● Tim Worrell														
D 1996	SD-N	0	0	2.45	2	0	0	0	0	3^2	4	1	1	2
● Todd Worrell														
D 1996	LA-N	0	0	0.00	1	0	0	0	0	1	0	0	1	1
L 1985	StL-N	1	0	1.42	4	0	0	0	0	6^1	4	1	2	3
L 1987	StL-N	0	0	2.08	3	0	0	1	0	4^1	4	1	1	6
L Total	2	1	0	1.69	7	0	0	1	0	10^2	8	2	3	9
W 1985	StL-N	0	1	3.86	3	0	0	1	0	4^2	4	2	2	6
W 1987	StL-N	0	0	1.29	4	0	0	2	0	7	6	1	4	3
W Total	2	0	1	2.31	7	0	0	3	0	11^2	10	3	6	9
● Al Worthington														
L 1969	Min-A	0	0	6.75	1	0	0	0	0	1^1	3	1	0	1
W 1965	Min-A	0	0	0.00	2	0	0	0	0	4	2	0	2	2
● Jaret Wright														
D 1997	Cle-A	2	0	3.97	2	2	0	0	0	11^1	11	5	7	10
D 1998	Cle-A	0	1	12.46	1	1	0	0	0	4^1	7	6	2	6
D 1999	Cle-A	0	1	22.50	1	0	0	0	0	2	4	5	1	1
D Total	3	2	2	8.15	4	3	0	0	0	17^2	22	16	10	17
L 1997	Cle-A	0	0	15.00	1	1	0	0	0	3	6	5	2	3
L 1998	Cle-A	0	1	8.10	2	1	0	0	0	6^2	7	6	8	4
L Total	2	0	1	10.24	3	2	0	0	0	9^2	13	11	10	7
W 1997	Cle-A	1	0	2.92	2	2	0	0	0	12^1	7	4	10	12
● Kelly Wunsch														
D 2000	Chi-A	0	1	0.00	3	0	0	0	0	0^2	2	0	0	0
● John Wyatt														
W 1967	Bos-A	1	0	4.91	2	0	0	0	0	3^2	1	2	3	1
● Whit Wyatt														
W 1941	Bro-N	1	1	2.50	2	2	2	0	0	18	15	5	10	14
● Weldon Wyckoff														
W 1914	Phi-A	0	0	2.45	1	0	0	0	0	3^2	3	1	1	2
● Early Wynn														
W 1954	Cle-A	0	1	3.86	1	1	0	0	0	7	4	3	2	5
W 1959	Chi-A	1	1	5.54	3	3	0	0	0	13	19	8	4	10
W Total	2	1	2	4.95	4	4	0	0	0	20	23	11	6	15
● Hank Wyse														
W 1945	Chi-N	0	1	7.04	3	1	0	0	0	7^2	8	6	4	1
● Emil Yde														
W 1925	Pit-N	0	1	11.57	1	1	0	0	0	2^1	5	3	3	1
● Masato Yoshii														
D 1999	NY-N	0	0	6.75	1	1	0	0	0	5^1	6	4	0	3
L 1999	NY-N	0	1	4.70	2	2	0	0	0	7^2	9	4	3	4
● Curt Young														
L 1988	Oak-A	0	0	0.00	1	0	0	0	0	1^1	1	0	0	2
W 1988	Oak-A	0	0	0.00	1	0	0	0	0	1	1	0	0	0
W 1990	Oak-A	0	0	0.00	1	0	0	0	0	1	1	0	0	0
W Total	2	0	0	0.00	2	0	0	0	0	2	2	0	0	0
● Cy Young														
T 1892	Cle-N	0	2	3.00	3	3	3	0	1	27	26	9	3	9
T 1895	Cle-N	3	0	2.33	3	3	3	0	0	27	28	7	4	2
T 1896	Cle-N	0	1	6.00	1	1	1	0	0	9	13	6	1	0
T Total	3	3	3	3.14	7	7	7	0	1	63	67	22	8	11
W 1903	Bos-A	2	1	1.85	4	3	3	0	0	34	31	7	4	17
● Matt Young														
L 1989	Oak-A	0	0	0.00	1	0	0	0	0	0^1	0	0	2	0
● Tom Zachary														
W 1924	Was-A	2	0	2.04	2	2	1	0	0	17^2	13	4	3	3
W 1925	Was-A	0	0	10.80	1	0	0	0	0	1^2	3	2	1	0
W 1928	NY-A	1	0	3.00	1	1	1	0	0	9	9	3	1	7
W Total	3	3	0	2.86	4	3	2	0	0	28^1	25	9	5	10
● Chris Zachary														
L 1972	Det-A	0	0	∞	1	0	0	0	0	0	0	1	1	0
● Pat Zachry														
L 1976	Cin-N	1	0	3.60	1	1	0	0	0	5	6	2	3	3
L 1983	LA-N	0	0	2.25	2	0	0	0	0	4	4	1	2	2
L Total	2	1	0	3.00	3	1	0	0	0	9	10	3	5	5
W 1976	Cin-N	1	0	2.70	1	1	0	0	0	6^2	6	2	5	6
● Geoff Zahn														
L 1982	Cal-A	0	1	7.36	1	1	0	0	0	3^2	4	3	1	2
● Bill Zepp														
L 1970	Min-A	0	0	6.75	2	0	0	0	0	1^1	2	1	2	2
● Jeff Zimmerman														
D 1999	Tex-A	0	0	0.00	1	0	0	0	0	1	1	0	0	1

The Annual Record

This section contains the season-by-season standings and records for all teams since 1871, plus 28 statistical categories for each team's batting and baserunning, and 26 categories for its pitching and fielding. In those years in which major league play consisted of more than one league, the statistics are presented in the order of the leagues' founding: that is, the National Association comes first; the National League record precedes those of all its rivals; the American Association precedes the Union Association and Players League; and the American League follows the National League but precedes the Federal League.

The figure for the leading team in a given category is displayed in boldface. Where data are unavailable, the statistical column is blank. Also presented here are the top three to five players/pitchers in up to 48 categories per season. When fewer than 48 categories are shown, it means that official records are lacking; that data is not reconstructible at present; or that available data is not meaningful, such as for Relief Runs or Relief Ranking in the early years of this century. When fewer than five individuals appear in a given category, credible standouts are lacking, as in the case of Stolen Base Wins in most years. The criterion used for identifying pitching leaders is a minimum of one inning pitched per scheduled game; for batters the criterion employed is the one officially in place at the time or, in the absence of any known practice, 3.1 plate appearances per scheduled game.

Ties in counting stats are common, and occasionally they are so numerous that space does not permit listing all the players by name; ties for fifth place are not shown. Highly uncommon are ties in stats based on a large array of data, as with batting averages, on-base percentages, earned run averages, and sabermetric stats such as Runs Created, Total Average, or the various Linear Weights measures. Where rounding off has created the appearance of a tie, the true leader—as extra decimal places for a complete calculation would have revealed—is listed first. An example is the AL batting race of 1949, in which George Kell and Ted Williams are both shown as hitting .343; Kell in fact hit .3429 and Williams .3428. Both men are credited with batting averages of .343, but Kell, the actual leader, is listed first. (This procedure does not hold for calculated stats based on pitchers' won-lost percentages, where the narrow array of data frequently produces actual ties.)

For additional useful information about a team in a given year, we refer the reader to the various registers and the rosters. Team abbreviations used in the Annual Record are to be found on the last page of this book.

Following are the abbreviations employed in the team statistical reviews of the Annual Record, aside from those that are defined adequately in the introductions to the Player or Pitcher Registers, plus brief descriptions of what the less common statistics measure. For information about formulas and computation, see the Glossary.

Batting and Baserunning

PCT	Percentage of games won
GB	Games Behind the league or division leader
OR	Opponents' Runs scored
OPS	Production (On-Base Percentage plus Slugging Average)
OPS+	Normalized and park-adjusted Production. A figure of 100 is a league-average performance.
BR	Batting Runs (Linear Weights measure of runs contributed beyond what a league-average batter or team might have contributed, defined as zero.)
BR+	Adjusted Batting Runs (Normalized to league average and adjusted for home-park factor. A mark of 100 is a league-average performance. Pitcher batting is removed from all league batting statistics before normalization for a variety of reasons expanded upon in the Glossary.)
PF	Park Factor (Calculated separately for batters and pitchers: above 100 signifies a park favorable to hitters, below 100 signifies a park favorable to pitchers; see Glossary for further data and technical information.)
CHI	Clutch Hitting Index (Calculated for individuals, actual RBI over expected RBI, adjusted for league average and position in batting order; calculated for teams, actual runs scored divided by Batting Runs. Marks above the median of 100 are superior. See Glossary for precise formula.)
RC	Runs Created (Bill James's formulation for run contribution from a variety of batting and baserunning events; many different formulas are applied, depending on data available; see Glossary.)
SBA	Stolen Base Average (Stolen bases divided by attempts; availability dependent upon CS, as shown above.)

SBR Stolen Base Runs (Linear Weights measure of runs contributed *beyond* what a league-average base stealer or team might have gained, defined as zero; individual SBRs are calculated on the basis of a 66.7 percent success rate, the rate necessary to produce benefit, while team SBRs are normalized to the success rate for the league in that season; availability dependent upon CS.)

Pitching and Fielding

SH Shutouts (Individual and combined when calculated for teams; individual only for top five leaders.)

H/G Hits allowed per Game (Game defined as nine innings.)

CPI Clutch Pitching Index (Expected runs over actual runs, with 100 being a league-average performance and marks above 100 indicating better than expected results. See Glossary.)

E Errors

DP Double Plays

FW Fielding Wins (Fielding Runs divided by the number of runs required to create an additional win beyond average; average is defined as a team record of .500 because a league won-lost average must be .500. For more technical data about Runs Per Win and Fielding Run formulas, see Glossary.)

PW Pitching Wins (Adjusted Pitching Runs divided by the number of runs required to create an additional win beyond average; average is defined as a team record of .500 because a league won-lost average must be .500. For more technical data about Runs Per Win and Pitching Run formulas, see Glossary.)

BW Batting Wins (Adjusted Batting Runs divided by the number of runs required to create an additional win beyond average; average is defined as a team record of .500 because a league won-lost average must be .500. For more technical data about Runs Per Win and Batting Run formulas, see Glossary.)

SBW Stolen Base Wins (Stolen Base Runs divided by the number of runs required to create an additional win beyond average; average is defined as a team record of .500. For more technical data about Runs Per Win and Stolen Base Run formulas, see Glossary.)

DIF Differential (Difference between the team's actual won-lost record and that predicted by the total of its Pitching Wins, Batting Wins, Fielding Wins, and Stolen Base Wins; indicates the extent to which a team outperformed or underperformed its talent.)

Other stats carried only on an individual basis in the Annual Record portion of *Total Baseball* are as follows (definitions supplied only when not available from Player or Pitcher Register introductions):

Total Average Tom Boswell's formulation for offensive contribution from a variety of batting and baserunning events; calculated to make use of the maximum available data.

Fielding Runs

Total Player Rating

Bases on Balls Per Game Game defined as nine innings; league leaders calculated on the basis of fewest walks per nine innings.

Strikeouts Per Game Game defined as nine innings; league leaders calculated on the basis of most strikeouts per nine innings.

Starter Runs Identical to Pitching Runs but confined to starting pitchers, defined as pitchers who average more than three innings per appearance.

Relief Runs Identical to Pitching Runs but confined to relief pitchers.

Relief Ranking Adjusted Relief Runs, weighted for the greater value of a bullpen "closer" who limits his opponents' scoring in the late innings; see Glossary for formula. Relief Runs will tend to benefit long and middle relievers, who are effective over many innings, while Relief Ranking will tend to benefit relievers with perhaps fewer innings but more saves and decisions.

Total Pitcher Index

Total Baseball Ranking The "MVP" of statistics, this ranks pitchers and position players by the total runs contributed in all their endeavors, revealing the most valuable performers in a given year. For rare individuals like Babe Ruth in his Red Sox years, or Bob Caruthers, both of whom played a position in the field when they were not pitching, the TPR will sum up their records in both endeavors.

How to Read a Team Line

TEAM	G	W	L	PCT	GB	R	OR	AB	H	2B	3B	HR	BB	SO	AVG	OBP	SLG	PRO	PRO+	BR	/A	PF	CHI	RC	SB	CS	SBA	SBR
EAST																												
NY	160	100	60	.625		**703**	**532**	5408	1387	251	24	**152**	544	842	.256	**.328**	**.396**	**.724**	**120**	**95**	**131**	95	97	**717**	140	51	73	11
PIT	160	85	75	.531	15	651	616	5379	1327	240	45	110	**553**	947	.247	.321	.369	.690	105	33	42	99	99	648	119	60	66	0
MON	163	81	81	.500	20	628	592	5573	1400	260	**48**	107	454	1053	.251	.311	.373	.684	98	12	-18	105	97	636	189	89	68	3
CHI	163	77	85	.475	24	660	694	5675	**1481**	**262**	46	113	403	910	**.261**	.312	.383	.695	100	31	1	105	99	673	120	46	72	8
STL	162	76	86	.469	25	578	633	5518	1373	207	33	71	484	**827**	.249	.312	.337	.649	92	-47	-53	101	98	601	**234**	64	**79**	**32**
PHI	162	65	96	.404	35.5	597	734	5403	1294	246	31	106	489	981	.239	.308	.355	.663	94	-22	-35	102	100	599	112	49	70	4
WEST																												
LA	162	94	67	.584		628	544	5431	1346	217	25	99	437	947	.248	.308	.352	.660	99	-32	-14	97	**107**	590	131	46	74	12
CIN	161	87	74	.540	7	641	596	5426	1334	246	25	122	479	922	.246	.311	.368	.679	97	6	-19	104	102	639	207	56	**79**	29
SD	161	83	78	.516	11	594	583	5366	1325	205	35	94	494	892	.247	.313	.351	.664	99	-19	-8	98	99	594	123	50	71	7
SF	162	83	79	.512	11.5	670	626	5450	1353	227	44	113	550	1023	.248	.321	.368	.689	109	32	61	96	101	650	121	78	61	-11
HOU	162	82	80	.506	12.5	617	631	5494	1338	239	31	96	474	840	.244	.308	.351	.659	99	-32	-9	96	103	604	198	71	74	17
ATL	160	54	106	.338	39.5	555	741	5440	1319	228	28	96	432	848	.242	.301	.348	.649	88	-56	-84	105	99	549	95	69	58	-13
TOT	969					7522		65563	16277	2828	415	1279	5793	11032	.248	.313	.363	.675							1789	729	71	99

TEAM	CG	SH	SV	IP	H	H/G	HR	BB	SO	RAT	ERA	ERA+	OAV	OOB	PR	/A	PF	CPI	FA	E	DP	FW	PW	BW	SBW	DIF
EAST																										
NY	31	22	46	1439	**1253**	**7.8**	**78**	**404**	**1100**	**10.6**	**2.91**	111	**.235**	**.293**	**86**	50	93	97	**.981**	**115**	127	**.9**	5.4	**14.1**	.3	-.7
PIT	12	11	46	1440[2]	1349	8.4	108	469	790	11.6	3.47	98	.250	.314	-3	-10	99	101	.980	125	128	.3	-1.1	4.5	-.9	2.1
MON	18	12	43	1482[2]	1310	8.0	122	476	923	11.1	3.08	**117**	.238	.303	60	**84**	104	**105**	.978	142	145	-.5	**9.1**	-1.9	-.6	-6.0
CHI	30	10	29	1464[1]	1494	9.2	115	490	897	12.4	3.84	94	.265	.327	-64	-38	105	102	.980	125	128	.5	-4.1	.1	-.0	-.4
STL	17	14	42	1470[2]	1387	8.5	91	486	881	11.6	3.47	100	.252	.314	-4	1	101	99	**.981**	121	131	.6	.1	-5.7	**2.6**	-2.6
PHI	16	6	36	1433	1447	9.1	118	628	859	13.3	4.14	86	.265	.344	-110	-92	103	102	.976	145	139	-.7	-9.9	-3.8	-.5	-.6
WEST																										
LA	**32**	**24**	**49**	1463[1]	1291	7.9	84	473	1029	11.0	2.96	112	.237	.301	78	59	97	102	.977	142	126	-.5	6.4	-1.5	.4	8.8
CIN	24	13	43	1455	1271	7.9	121	504	934	11.1	3.35	107	.237	.306	16	38	104	98	.980	125	131	.4	4.1	-2.0	2.2	1.9
SD	30	9	39	1449	1332	8.3	112	439	885	11.1	3.28	104	.247	.306	27	19	99	102	**.981**	120	**147**	.6	2.0	-.9	-.1	.8
SF	25	13	42	1462[1]	1323	8.1	99	422	875	10.9	3.39	96	.242	.300	10	-20	95	93	.980	129	145	.2	-2.2	6.6	-2.1	-.5
HOU	21	15	40	1474[2]	1339	8.2	123	478	1049	11.3	3.41	97	.242	.307	7	-14	96	99	.978	138	124	-.3	-1.5	-1.0	.9	2.9
ATL	14	4	25	1446	1481	9.2	108	524	810	12.7	4.09	90	.268	.336	-103	-67	107	100	.976	151	138	-1.1	-7.2	-9.1	-2.3	-6.3
TOT	270	153	480	17480[2]		8.4				11.6	3.45		.248	.313					.979	1578	1609					

The Los Angeles Dodgers had a miracle season in 1988, winning the National League pennant and the World Series against seemingly far superior opponents, the New York Mets and the Oakland Athletics, respectively. But their first miracle was to win the National League's Western Division title after finishing 73-89 in each of the previous two seasons. How did they win the West so easily? With mirrors, mostly, for they had below-average fielding and hitting that should have partially negated their outstanding pitching.

Let's just track the Dodgers' performance in some of the key categories to show how illuminating a close examination of team data in the Annual Record can be. The Dodgers' on base percentage (OBP) and slugging average (SLG) reveal them to have been a weak hitting club, though their Adjusted Production (OPS+) is a bit better, for they scored more runs in their park than might have been expected from the total run-scoring picture at Chavez Ravine (Park Factor 97). However, their Clutch Hitting Index (CHI) was the best in their division. Their Stolen Base Average was above average, but still only accounted for 12 extra runs over the course of the season, so this wasn't the secret of their success.

The pitching numbers are superlative—fewest runs allowed in the West and lowest ERA—despite the fact that Cincinnati held opponents to the same batting average (OAV) and San Francisco to the same on base percentage (OOB). Their Clutch Pitching Index (CPI) suggests that Dodgers hurlers pulled their belts a notch tighter when men were on base, and their Home Runs allowed (HR) gives another tip that they knew how to stay away from the big inning. And maybe all those Shutouts (SH) are indicative of the many games they won while scoring few runs themselves.

Look at their batting (which cost them 1.5 wins in the BW, or Batting Wins, column) and baserunning and fielding (which are a virtual wash at +0.4 and – 0.5, respectively, in the SBW and FW columns), and notice that their pitching, good as it was, only supplied 6.4 wins beyond average (.500). On balance, then, their offense and defense combined to produce only five wins beyond average. They should have finished with a record of 86–76, or five games beyond the 81–81 league average. Instead they finished 94–67, eight wins beyond their expectations, as indicated in the Differential (DIF) column. Maybe it was manager Tommy Lasorda's doing after all.

TEAM	G	W	L	PCT	GB	R	OR	AB	H	2B	3B	HR	BB	SO	AVG	OBP	SLG	OPS	OPS+	BR	BR+	PF	CHI	RC	SB	CS	SBA	SBR
ATH	28	21	7	.750		376	266	1281	410	66	27	9	46	23	**.320**	**.344**	**.435**	**779**	**125**	**38**	**42**	99	107	206	56	12	82	8
BOS	31	20	10	.667	2	**401**	303	1372	**426**	**70**	37	3	**60**	19	.310	.339	.422	761	115	33	21	103	**108**	**216**	**73**	16	82	**10**
CHI	28	19	9	.679	2	302	**241**	1196	323	52	21	**10**	**60**	22	.270	.305	.374	679	86	-7	-35	111	104	150	69	21	77	8
MUT	33	16	17	.485	7.5	302	313	1404	403	43	21	1	33	15	.287	.303	.350	653	97	-20	11	91	94	159	46	15	75	5
OLY	32	15	15	.500	7	310	303	1353	375	54	26	6	48	**13**	.277	.302	.369	671	98	-12	5	95	97	160	48	13	79	6
TRO	29	13	15	.464	8	351	362	1248	384	51	34	6	49	19	.308	.334	.417	751	114	25	20	101	106	184	62	24	72	5
CLE	29	10	19	.345	11.5	249	341	1186	328	35	**40**	7	26	25	.277	.292	.391	683	102	-7	9	95	89	136	18	8	69	1
KEK	19	7	12	.368	9.5	137	243	746	178	19	8	2	33	9	.239	.271	.294	565	63	-34	-37	102	91	63	16	4	80	2
ROK	25	4	21	.160	15.5	231	287	1036	274	44	25	3	38	30	.264	.291	.364	655	92	-16	-5	96	97	121	53	10	**84**	8
TOT	127					2659		10822	3101	434	239	47	393	175	.287	.312	.384	695							441	123	78	54

TEAM	CG	SH	SV	IP	H	H/G	HR	BB	SO	RAT	ERA	ERA+	OAV	OOB	PR	PR+	PF	CPI	FA	E	DP	FW	PW	BW	SBW	DIF
ATH	27	0	0	249	329	11.9	3	53	16	13.9	4.96	81	.284	.315	-20	-27	95	85	.845	**194**	13	1.2	-1.7	**2.8**	.1	4.8
BOS	22	**1**	**3**	276	367	12.0	**2**	42	23	13.4	3.56	117	.273	.296	20	19	99	101	.834	243	**24**	-.2	1.3	1.4	**.3**	2.5
CHI	25	0	1	251	**308**	**11.1**	6	**28**	22	**12.1**	**2.77**	**166**	**.264**	**.281**	**41**	**47**	109	**121**	.829	229	16	-.7	**3.1**	-2.2	.1	4.9
MUT	**32**	**1**	0	293	373	11.5	7	42	22	12.8	3.72	102	.271	.292	16	3	90	98	.840	235	14	1.0	.2	.8	-.0	-2.3
OLY	**32**	0	0	282	371	11.9	4	45	13	13.3	4.38	95	.281	.305	-5	-6	99	90	**.850**	218	20	**1.5**	-.3	.4	.0	-1.4
TRO	28	0	0	250	431	15.6	4	75	12	18.3	5.51	76	.342	.378	-36	-36	100	118	.845	198	22	1.4	-2.3	1.4	-.0	-1.2
CLE	23	0	0	254	346	12.3	13	53	**34**	14.2	4.12	100	.283	.312	3	0	98	107	.818	234	15	-.6	.0	.6	-.3	-4.1
KEK	19	**1**	0	169	261	13.9	5	21	17	15.1	5.17	88	.305	.322	-18	-10	108	93	.803	163	8	-.9	-.6	-2.4	-.3	1.8
ROK	23	**1**	0	226	315	12.6	3	34	16	13.9	4.31	95	.282	.303	-2	-6	97	91	.821	220	14	-1.5	-.3	-.3	.1	-6.3
TOT	231	4	4	2250		12.5				14.0	4.22		.287	.312					.834	1934	146					

Runs
- Barnes-Bos 66
- Birdsall-Bos 51
- Radcliff-Ath 47
- Cuthbert-Ath 47
- Waterman-Oly 46

Hits
- McVey-Bos 66
- Meyerle-Ath 64
- Barnes-Bos 63
- Start-Mut 58
- King-Tro 57

Doubles
- Anson-Rok 11

Triples
- Bass-Cle 10
- Wolters-Mut 9
- Barnes-Bos 9
- Pratt-Cle 8

Home Runs
- Treacey-Chi 4
- Pike-Tro 4
- Meyerle-Ath 4

Total Bases
- Meyerle-Ath 91
- Barnes-Bos 91
- Pike-Tro 85
- McVey-Bos 85
- King-Tro 79

Runs Batted In
- Wolters-Mut 44
- McVey-Bos 43
- Meyerle-Ath 40
- Pike-Tro 39

Runs Produced
- Barnes-Bos 100
- McVey-Bos 86
- Meyerle-Ath 81
- King-Tro 79
- Pike-Tro 78

Bases On Balls
- Pinkham-Chi 18
- H.Wright-Bos 13
- Barnes-Bos 13
- Wood-Chi 11

Batting Average
- Meyerle-Ath .... .492
- McVey-Bos .... .431
- Barnes-Bos .... .401
- King-Tro .... .396
- Wood-Chi .... .378

On-Base Percentage
- Meyerle-Ath .... .500
- G.Wright-Bos .... .453
- Barnes-Bos .... .447
- McVey-Bos .... .435
- Wood-Chi .... .425

Slugging Average
- Meyerle-Ath .... .700
- Pike-Tro .... .654
- Bass-Cle .... .640
- Barnes-Bos .... .580
- Treacey-Chi .... .573

On-Base Plus Slugging
- Meyerle-Ath 1200
- G.Wright-Bos 1078
- Pike-Tro 1054
- Barnes-Bos 1027
- McVey-Bos 991

Adjusted OPS
- Meyerle-Ath 243
- G.Wright-Bos 200
- Pike-Tro 194
- Wolters-Mut 189
- Barnes-Bos 186

Batter Runs
- Meyerle-Ath 22.6
- Barnes-Bos 18.9
- Pike-Tro 15.5
- McVey-Bos 15.5
- Wood-Chi 14.2

Adjusted Batter Runs
- Meyerle-Ath 23.2
- Wolters-Mut 17.5
- Barnes-Bos 17.0
- Pike-Tro 14.9
- McVey-Bos 13.9

Clutch Hitting Index
- Goldsmith-Kek 169
- Barrows-Bos 150
- McMullin-Tro 149
- Brainard-Oly 143
- Fisher-Rok 137

Runs Created
- Meyerle-Ath 49
- Barnes-Bos 42
- McVey-Bos 41
- Wood-Chi 40
- Pike-Tro 33

Total Average
- Meyerle-Ath 1.470
- G.Wright-Bos 1.306
- Wood-Chi 1.198
- Barnes-Bos 1.079
- Pike-Tro 1.071

Stolen Bases
- McGeary-Tro 20
- Wood-Chi 18
- Cuthbert-Ath 16
- Leonard-Oly 14
- Eggler-Mut 14

Stolen Base Average
- Wood-Chi 90.0
- Cuthbert-Ath 88.9
- McGeary-Tro 83.3

Stolen Base Runs
- Wood-Chi 3.3
- McGeary-Tro 3.0
- Cuthbert-Ath 2.8
- Mack-Rok 2.6
- Cone-Bos 2.3

Fielding Runs
- Force-Oly 17.6
- Barnes-Bos 13.4
- Pinkham-Chi 9.4
- Malone-Ath 9.1
- Wood-Chi 8.6

Total Player Rating
- Barnes-Bos 1.9
- Wood-Chi 1.3
- Force-Oly 1.2
- Malone-Ath 1.1
- McVey-Bos 1.1

Wins
- Spalding-Bos 19
- Zettlein-Chi 18
- McBride-Ath 18
- Wolters-Mut 16

Win Percentage
- McBride-Ath .... .783
- Zettlein-Chi .... .667
- Spalding-Bos .... .655
- Wolters-Mut .... .500

Games
- Wolters-Mut 32
- Spalding-Bos 31
- Brainard-Oly 30
- McMullin-Tro 29

Complete Games
- Wolters-Mut 31
- Brainard-Oly 30
- McMullin-Tro 28
- Zettlein-Chi 25
- McBride-Ath 25

Shutouts
- Wolters-Mut 1
- Spalding-Bos 1
- Mathews-Kek 1
- Fisher-Rok 1

Saves
- H.Wright-Bos 3
- Pinkham-Chi 1

Innings Pitched
- Wolters-Mut 283.0
- Brainard-Oly 264.0
- Spalding-Bos 257.1
- McMullin-Tro 249.0
- Zettlein-Chi 240.2

Fewest Hits/Game
- Wolters-Mut 10.97
- Zettlein-Chi 11.14
- McBride-Ath 11.55
- Spalding-Bos 11.65
- Pratt-Cle 11.86

Fewest BB/Game
- Zettlein-Chi .... .93
- Mathews-Kek 1.12
- Wolters-Mut 1.24
- Brainard-Oly 1.26
- Fisher-Rok 1.31

Strikeouts
- Pratt-Cle 34
- Spalding-Bos 23
- Zettlein-Chi 22
- Wolters-Mut 22
- Mathews-Kek 17

Strikeouts/Game
- Pratt-Cle 1.36
- Mathews-Kek .... .91
- Zettlein-Chi .... .82
- Spalding-Bos .... .80
- Wolters-Mut .... .70

Ratio
- Zettlein-Chi 12.08
- Wolters-Mut 12.21
- Spalding-Bos 12.98
- McBride-Ath 13.18
- Brainard-Oly 13.57

Earned Run Average
- Zettlein-Chi 2.73
- Spalding-Bos 3.36
- Wolters-Mut 3.43
- Pratt-Cle 3.77
- Fisher-Rok 4.35

Adjusted ERA
- Zettlein-Chi 168
- Spalding-Bos 124
- Wolters-Mut 110
- Pratt-Cle 110
- Fisher-Rok 94

Opponents' Batting Avg.
- Wolters-Mut .... .263
- Zettlein-Chi .... .267
- Spalding-Bos .... .268
- Pratt-Cle .... .277
- McBride-Ath .... .280

Opponents' On-Base Pct.
- Zettlein-Chi .... .283
- Wolters-Mut .... .285
- Spalding-Bos .... .290
- Fisher-Rok .... .302
- McBride-Ath .... .307

Starter Runs
- Zettlein-Chi 39.8
- Wolters-Mut 24.7
- Spalding-Bos 24.7
- Pratt-Cle 11.3
- Stearns-Oly 3.4

Adjusted Starter Runs
- Zettlein-Chi 45.7
- Spalding-Bos 23.2
- Wolters-Mut 12.4
- Pratt-Cle 9.2
- Stearns-Oly 3.4

Clutch Pitching Index
- Zettlein-Chi 124
- McMullin-Tro 118
- Pratt-Cle 110
- Spalding-Bos 101
- Wolters-Mut 99

Relief Runs
- Pinkham-Chi 8

Adjusted Relief Runs
- Pinkham-Chi 1.2

Relief Ranking
- Pinkham-Chi 1.3

Total Pitcher Index
- Zettlein-Chi 2.6
- Wolters-Mut 2.0
- Spalding-Bos 1.6
- Pratt-Cle 1.0
- Stearns-Oly 1

Total Baseball Ranking
- Zettlein-Chi 2.5
- Wolters-Mut 2.0
- Barnes-Bos 1.9
- Spalding-Bos 1.4
- Wood-Chi 1.3

TEAM	G	W	L	PCT	GB	R	OR	AB	H	2B	3B	HR	BB	SO	AVG	OBP	SLG	OPS	OPS+	BR	BR+	PF	CHI	RC	SB	CS	SBA	SBR
BOS	48	39	8	.830		521	**236**	2122	672	**106**	**30**	7	29	26	**.317**	.326	**.405**	**731**	120	**61**	35	105	100	293	47	14	77	5
BAL	58	35	19	.648	7.5	**617**	434	2576	**753**	105	**30**	**15**	27	28	.292	.300	.374	674	104	23	-2	105	**107**	**296**	37	18	67	2
MUT	56	34	20	.630	8.5	523	362	2431	674	85	12	4	55	52	.277	.293	.327	620	99	-18	17	94	102	242	59	21	74	6
ATH	47	30	14	.682	7.5	539	349	2141	679	79	25	4	**69**	47	**.317**	**.338**	.383	721	**124**	60	**58**	100	102	287	58	31	65	2
TRO	25	15	10	.600	13	273	191	1098	330	58	8	5	7	14	.301	.305	.382	687	111	15	12	101	109	127	9	7	56	0
ATL	37	9	28	.243	25	237	473	1460	374	37	10	0	19	**24**	.256	.266	.295	561	63	-41	-81	117	87	117	19	14	58	-1
CLE	22	6	16	.273	20.5	174	254	943	272	28	5	0	17	13	.288	.301	.329	630	102	-4	8	95	87	96	12	3	80	2
MAN	24	5	19	.208	22.5	220	348	1022	294	29	9	1	5	12	.288	.291	.337	628	101	-6	7	94	103	101	5	3	63	0
ECK	29	3	26	.103	27	152	413	1070	241	24	6	0	14	29	.225	.235	.259	494	64	-55	-24	85	86	66	8	4	67	0
OLY	9	2	7	.222	18	54	140	365	91	10	3	0	4	4	.249	.257	.293	550	75	-12	-8	95	81	26	0	3	0	-1
NAT	11	0	11	.0	21	80	190	451	108	6	1	0	1	3	.239	.241	.257	498	47	-23	-33	117	109	29				
TOT	183					3390		15679	4488	567	139	36	247	252	.287	.298	.348	644							254	118	68	15

TEAM	CG	SH	SV	IP	H	H/G	HR	BB	SO	RAT	ERA	ERA+	OAV	OOB	PR	PR+	PF	CPI	FA	E	DP	FW	PW	BW	SBW	DIF
BOS	41	**4**	**4**	430[1]	**443**	**9.3**	**0**	27	28	**9.9**	**1.89**	**194**	**.243**	**.254**	**84**	**84**	100	**124**	**.876**	**278**	**43**	4.5	**5.9**	2.5	**.3**	2.5
BAL	48	1	1	516	573	10.0	3	63	**75**	11.1	2.90	127	.245	.264	43	44	101	85	.829	432	22	.5	3.1	-.0	.0	4.6
MUT	**54**	3	1	512	623	11.0	2	32	44	11.6	2.99	113	.272	.282	37	23	93	105	.867	326	33	**5.2**	1.7	1.2	**.3**	-1.2
ATH	47	1	0	419[1]	508	11.0	3	26	44	11.5	2.86	124	.265	.275	37	33	98	102	.858	298	20	3.1	2.3	**4.1**	.0	-1.4
TRO	17	2	1	225	277	11.1	2	10	18	11.5	2.61	140	.269	.276	26	26	100	117	.859	154	9	1.9	1.9	.9	-.0	-1.9
ATL	37	0	0	336	570	15.3	6	**19**	13	15.8	4.34	104	.328	.335	-26	5	124	117	.810	358	14	-4.0	.4	-5.6	-.2	.0
CLE	15	0	0	199	285	12.9	6	24	11	14.0	5.75	62	.290	.307	-47	-49	98	70	.816	184	17	-.8	-3.4	.6	.0	-1.3
MAN	20	0	0	211	374	16.0	6	14	5	16.6	5.68	63	.333	.341	-48	-49	99	95	.804	226	11	-2.2	-3.4	.5	-.0	-1.7
ECK	28	0	0	259[1]	494	17.2	6	24	11	18.0	5.52	61	.348	.358	-54	-66	93	109	.797	284	5	-3.3	-4.5	-1.6	-.0	-1.8
OLY	9	0	0	79	148	16.9	**0**	5	1	17.5	6.38	56	.333	.341	-24	-25	99	82	.786	96	7	-1.4	-1.7	-.5	-.2	1.4
NAT	11	0	0	99	193	17.6	2	3	2	17.9	6.19	75	.339	.343	-28	-14	127	90	.774	120	2	-1.8	-.9	-2.2	-.0	-.2
TOT	327	11	7	3286		12.3				13.0	3.64		.287	.298					.837	2756	183					

Runs
Eggler-Mut 94
G.Wright-Bos 87
Cuthbert-Ath 83
Barnes-Bos 81
Hatfield-Mut 76

Hits
Barnes-Bos 99
Eggler-Mut 98
Force-Tro-Bal 94
Hatfield-Mut 92
Anson-Ath 90

Doubles
Barnes-Bos 28
Eggler-Mut 20
Hall-Bal 17
G.Wright-Bos 16

Triples
Gould-Bos 8
Anson-Ath 7
G.Wright-Bos 6
Hall-Bal 6

Home Runs
Pike-Bal 7
Gedney-Tro-Eck 3

Total Bases
Barnes-Bos 134
Pike-Bal 131
G.Wright-Bos 120
Eggler-Mut 118
Hall-Bal 116

Runs Batted In
Pike-Bal 61
Start-Mut 50
Anson-Ath 50
Fisler-Ath 48

Runs Produced
Cuthbert-Ath 129
Barnes-Bos 124
Pike-Bal 122
Hatfield-Mut 120
G.Wright-Bos 117

Bases On Balls
Mack-Ath 23
Anson-Ath 16
McMullin-Mut 11

Batting Average
Barnes-Bos .432
Force-Tro-Bal .418
Anson-Ath .415
Murnane-Man .363
Hastings-Cle-Bal .362

On-Base Percentage
Anson-Ath .455
Barnes-Bos .454
Force-Tro-Bal .423
Hastings-Cle-Bal .376
McGeary-Ath .366

Slugging Average
Barnes-Bos .585
Anson-Ath .525
Wood-Tro-Eck .503
Force-Tro-Bal .493
Meyerle-Ath .486

On-Base Plus Slugging
Barnes-Bos 1039
Anson-Ath 980
Force-Tro-Bal 916
Wood-Tro-Eck 839
G.Wright-Bos 816

Adjusted OPS
Barnes-Bos 206
Anson-Ath 200
Force-Tro-Bal 176
Wood-Tro-Eck 158
Meyerle-Ath 147

Batter Runs
Barnes-Bos 30.8
Anson-Ath 26.0
Force-Tro-Bal 20.5
G.Wright-Bos 13.7
Hall-Bal 12.8

Adjusted Batter Runs
Barnes-Bos 26.7
Anson-Ath 25.7
Force-Tro-Bal 18.6
Eggler-Mut 16.5
Hatfield-Mut 12.8

Clutch Hitting Index
Start-Mut 168
White-Cle 150
Zettlein-Tro-Eck 144
Cuthbert-Ath 135
Boyd-Mut 135

Runs Created
Barnes-Bos 65
Anson-Ath 52
Force-Tro-Bal 49
Eggler-Mut 47
G.Wright-Bos 45

Total Average
Barnes-Bos 1.133
Anson-Ath .963
Force-Tro-Bal .866
Wood-Tro-Eck .828
G.Wright-Bos .769

Stolen Bases
Eggler-Mut 18
G.Wright-Bos 14
Cuthbert-Ath 14
McGeary-Ath 13

Stolen Base Average
Eggler-Mut 78.3

Stolen Base Runs
Eggler-Mut 2.2
Barnes-Bos 1.9
G.Wright-Bos 1.7
Cuthbert-Ath 1.7
Bechtel-Mut 1.6

Fielding Runs
Ferguson-Atl 36.3
Barnes-Bos 25.3
G.Wright-Bos 21.8
Eggler-Mut 15.4
York-Bal 10.5

Total Player Rating
Barnes-Bos 3.5
Eggler-Mut 2.3
G.Wright-Bos 2.2
Ferguson-Atl 1.9
Force-Tro-Bal 1.8

Wins
Spalding-Bos 38
Cummings-Mut 33
McBride-Ath 30
Mathews-Bal 25
Zettlein-Tro-Eck 15

Win Percentage
Spalding-Bos .826
McBride-Ath .682
Cummings-Mut .623
Mathews-Bal .581
Zettlein-Tro-Eck .484

Games
Cummings-Mut 55
Mathews-Bal 49
Spalding-Bos 48
McBride-Ath 47
Britt-Atl 37

Complete Games
Cummings-Mut 53
McBride-Ath 47
Spalding-Bos 41
Mathews-Bal 39
Britt-Atl 37

Shutouts
Spalding-Bos 3
Cummings-Mut 3
Zettlein-Tro-Eck 2
McBride-Ath 1
Fisher-Bal 1

Saves
H.Wright-Bos 4
Zettlein-Tro-Eck 1
McMullin-Mut 1
Fisher-Bal 1

Innings Pitched
Cummings-Mut 497.0
McBride-Ath 419.1
Mathews-Bal 406.0
Spalding-Bos 404.2
Britt-Atl 336.0

Fewest Hits/Game
Fisher-Bal 7.61
Spalding-Bos 9.27
Mathews-Bal 10.64
Zettlein-Tro-Eck 10.71
McBride-Ath 10.90

Fewest BB/Game
Stearns-Nat .27
Buttery-Man .31
P.Martin-Tro-Eck .44
Zettlein-Tro-Eck .48
Britt-Atl .51

Strikeouts
Mathews-Bal 55
McBride-Ath 44
Cummings-Mut 43
Spalding-Bos 27
Zettlein-Tro-Eck 25

Strikeouts/Game
Fisher-Bal 1.64
Mathews-Bal 1.22
McBride-Ath .94
Zettlein-Tro-Eck .86
Cummings-Mut .78

Ratio
Fisher-Bal 8.51
Spalding-Bos 9.87
Zettlein-Tro-Eck 11.19
McBride-Ath 11.46
Cummings-Mut 11.50

Earned Run Average
Fisher-Bal 1.80
Spalding-Bos 1.87
Zettlein-Tro-Eck 2.33
McBride-Ath 2.85
Cummings-Mut 2.97

Adjusted ERA
Fisher-Bal 204
Spalding-Bos 195
Zettlein-Tro-Eck 153
McBride-Ath 124
Mathews-Bal 115

Opponents' Batting Avg.
Fisher-Bal .197
Spalding-Bos .244
Mathews-Bal .257
McBride-Ath .265
Zettlein-Tro-Eck .265

Opponents' On-Base Pct.
Fisher-Bal .216
Spalding-Bos .255
Zettlein-Tro-Eck .274
McBride-Ath .275
Mathews-Bal .277

Starter Runs
Spalding-Bos 79.7
Zettlein-Tro-Eck 38.4
Cummings-Mut 37.0
McBride-Ath 36.6
Fisher-Bal 22.5

Adjusted Starter Runs
Spalding-Bos 79.9
Zettlein-Tro-Eck 36.9
McBride-Ath 33.2
Cummings-Mut 23.9
Fisher-Bal 22.7

Clutch Pitching Index
Zettlein-Tro-Eck 127
Spalding-Bos 126
Britt-Atl 117
P.Martin-Tro-Eck 115
Cummings-Mut 106

Relief Runs
H.Wright-Bos 4.4

Adjusted Relief Runs
H.Wright-Bos 4.4

Relief Ranking
H.Wright-Bos 3.1

Total Pitcher Index
Spalding-Bos 7.1
Zettlein-Tro-Eck 2.6
McBride-Ath 2.5
Fisher-Bal 1.4
Cummings-Mut 1.3

Total Baseball Ranking
Spalding-Bos 7.0
Barnes-Bos 3.5
Zettlein-Tro-Eck 2.6
McBride-Ath 2.5
Eggler-Mut 2.3

TEAM	G	W	L	PCT	GB	R	OR	AB	H	2B	3B	HR	BB	SO	AVG	OBP	SLG	OPS	OPS+	BR	BR+	PF	CHI	RC	SB	CS	SBA	SBR
BOS	60	43	16	.729		**739**	460	2755	**930**	**146**	**44**	**12**	**62**	24	**.338**	**.352**	**.436**	**788**	**128**	**122**	**68**	108	105	**428**	39	27	59	-1
PHI	53	36	17	.679	4	526	396	2325	645	83	20	8	**62**	39	.277	.296	.341	637	91	-17	-34	104	**110**	243	44	14	76	5
BAL	57	34	22	.607	7.5	644	451	2562	810	106	38	9	41	25	.316	.327	.398	725	121	57	60	100	108	340	22	11	67	1
MUT	53	29	24	.547	11	424	**385**	2214	622	51	36	5	42	**22**	.281	.294	.343	637	94	-16	-13	99	94	227	15	6	71	1
ATH	52	28	23	.549	11	474	403	2266	683	71	20	4	35	32	.301	.312	.356	668	96	8	-26	108	98	251	29	24	55	-2
ATL	55	17	37	.315	23.5	366	549	2210	588	42	23	6	53	43	.266	.283	.314	597	92	-46	4	89	87	198	19	11	63	0
WAS	39	8	31	.205	25	283	485	1563	408	38	19	2	19	33	.261	.270	.313	583	80	-41	-32	97	99	132	5	5	50	-1
RES	23	2	21	.87	23	98	299	868	204	18	8	0	8	**22**	.235	.242	.274	516	62	-43	-31	92	71	58	2	1	67	0
MAR	6	0	6	.0	16.5	26	152	211	33	1	0	0	0	3	.156	.156	.161	317	-4	-25	-19	77	139	5				
TOT	199					3580		16974	4923	556	208	46	322	243	.291	.304	.356	659							175	99	64	4

TEAM	CG	SH	SV	IP	H	H/G	HR	BB	SO	RAT	ERA	ERA+	OAV	OOB	PR	PR+	PF	CPI	FA	E	DP	FW	PW	BW	SBW	DIF
BOS	47	1	**6**	536	708	11.9	5	**35**	31	12.5	**2.59**	**128**	.287	.297	**40**	**43**	102	**118**	.838	465	**46**	.8	**3.1**	**4.9**	-.1	5.0
PHI	50	0	0	481	627	11.8	**3**	44	28	12.6	2.77	119	.284	.298	26	28	101	110	.848	379	43	2.4	2.0	-2.4	**.3**	7.3
BAL	**55**	1	0	508^2	680	12.1	4	42	37	12.8	3.01	108	.285	.297	14	14	100	101	**.855**	**366**	33	**4.7**	1.0	4.3	.0	-3.8
MUT	48	2	0	477	**539**	**10.2**	5	69	**76**	**11.5**	2.63	121	**.254**	.278	33	29	97	88	.821	419	28	.3	2.1	-.9	.0	1.1
ATH	44	**3**	2	475	553	10.5	4	58	41	11.6	3.04	113	.257	**.276**	12	19	105	75	.842	383	30	1.8	1.4	-1.8	-.2	1.5
ATL	52	1	0	500	737	13.3	8	42	15	14.1	3.98	76	.303	.315	-40	-56	93	93	.820	505	30	-3.2	-3.9	.3	-.0	-3.0
WAS	39	0	0	346	593	15.5	10	22	7	16.0	4.71	71	.335	.343	-56	-51	103	103	.818	334	27	-1.1	-3.6	-2.2	-.1	-4.4
RES	22	0	0	207	342	14.9	6	9	8	15.3	3.22	104	.310	.316	1	3	103	123	.787	247	9	-3.1	.3	-2.1	-.0	-4.2
MAR	6	0	0	54	144	24.0	1	1	0	24.2	8.01	40	.393	.395	-28	-29	100	97	.761	74	0	-1.3	-2.0	-1.3	-.0	1.8
TOT	363	8	8	3584^2		12.4				13.2	3.26		.291	.304					.832	3172	246					

Runs
Barnes-Bos 125
G.Wright-Bos 99
Spalding-Bos 83
Eggler-Mut 82
Leonard-Bos 81

Hits
Barnes-Bos 137
G.Wright-Bos 126
White-Bos 121
Spalding-Bos 106
Anson-Ath 101

Doubles
Barnes-Bos 29
G.Wright-Bos 19
O'Rourke-Bos 19
Mills-Bal 19
Carey-Bal 19

Triples
Mills-Bal 9
G.Wright-Bos 8
Pike-Bal 8
Holdsworth-Mut 8
Barnes-Bos 8

Home Runs
Pike-Bal 4
G.Wright-Bos 3
Meyerle-Phi 3

Total Bases
Barnes-Bos 188
G.Wright-Bos 170
White-Bos 148
Pike-Bal 132
Spalding-Bos 131

Runs Batted In
White-Bos 66
Barnes-Bos 62
Leonard-Bos 61
Spalding-Bos 60
Meyerle-Phi 58

Runs Produced
Barnes-Bos 185
G.Wright-Bos 146
White-Bos 145
Spalding-Bos 142
Leonard-Bos 142

Bases On Balls
Barnes-Bos 18
Mack-Phi 15
O'Rourke-Bos 14
Malone-Phi 14

Batting Average
Barnes-Bos .... .425
Anson-Ath .... .398
White-Bos .... .390
G.Wright-Bos .... .388
McVey-Bal .... .380

On-Base Percentage
Barnes-Bos .... .456
Anson-Ath .... .409
G.Wright-Bos .... .402
Force-Bal .... .391
White-Bos .... .390

Slugging Average
Barnes-Bos .... .584
G.Wright-Bos .... .523
McVey-Bal .... .484
Meyerle-Phi .... .479
White-Bos .... .477

On-Base Plus Slugging
Barnes-Bos 1040
G.Wright-Bos 925
McVey-Bal 874
White-Bos 868
Anson-Ath 858

Adjusted OPS
Barnes-Bos 191
G.Wright-Bos 160
McVey-Bal 159
Pabor-Atl 153
White-Bos 144

Batter Runs
Barnes-Bos 41.9
G.Wright-Bos 28.1
White-Bos 20.4
Anson-Ath 16.8
O'Rourke-Bos 15.9

Adjusted Batter Runs
Barnes-Bos 33.3
G.Wright-Bos 20.7
Pabor-Atl 17.0
White-Bos 13.9
McVey-Bal 13.5

Clutch Hitting Index
Cummings-Bal 168
McBride-Ath 156
Donnelly-Was 136
Hollingshead-Was 131
Addy-Phi-Bos 131

Runs Created
Barnes-Bos 91
G.Wright-Bos 69
White-Bos 61
O'Rourke-Bos 49
Pike-Bal 47

Total Average
Barnes-Bos 1.132
G.Wright-Bos .... .863
McVey-Bal .... .808
White-Bos .... .796
Meyerle-Phi .... .771

Stolen Bases
Cuthbert-Phi 13
Barnes-Bos 13
McMullin-Ath 9
Wood-Phi 8
Pike-Bal 8

Stolen Base Average

Stolen Base Runs
Cuthbert-Phi 2.2
McMullin-Ath 1.6
Barnes-Bos 1.5
Pike-Bal 1.4

Fielding Runs
Ferguson-Atl 31.5
Barnes-Bos 19.9
Fulmer-Phi 18.5
Gedney-Mut 14.6
G.Wright-Bos 14.5

Total Player Rating
Barnes-Bos 3.5
G.Wright-Bos 2.3
Ferguson-Atl 1.9
York-Bal 1.2
White-Bos 1.2

Wins
Spalding-Bos 41
Zettlein-Phi 36
Mathews-Mut 29
Cummings-Bal 28
McBride-Ath 24

Win Percentage
Spalding-Bos .... .745
Zettlein-Phi .... .706
Cummings-Bal .... .667
McBride-Ath .... .558
Mathews-Mut .... .558

Games
Spalding-Bos 60
Britt-Atl 54
Mathews-Mut 52
Zettlein-Phi 51
McBride-Ath 46

Complete Games
Britt-Atl 51
Zettlein-Phi 49
Spalding-Bos 47
Mathews-Mut 47
Cummings-Bal 42

Shutouts
McBride-Ath 3
Mathews-Mut 2
Spalding-Bos 1
Cummings-Bal 1
Britt-Atl 1

Saves
H.Wright-Bos 4
Spalding-Bos 2
Fisher-Ath 2

Innings Pitched
Spalding-Bos 497.2
Britt-Atl 480.2
Zettlein-Phi 460.0
Mathews-Mut 443.0
McBride-Ath 382.2

Fewest Hits/Game
Fisher-Ath 9.60
Mathews-Mut 9.93
McBride-Ath 10.65
Cummings-Bal 11.19
Zettlein-Phi 11.60

Fewest BB/Game
H.Campbell-Res .... .38
Stearns-Was .... .48
Spalding-Bos .... .51
Brainard-Bal .... .75
Britt-Atl .... .75

Strikeouts
Mathews-Mut 75
Cummings-Bal 34
Spalding-Bos 31
Zettlein-Phi 28
McBride-Ath 25

Strikeouts/Game
Mathews-Mut 1.52
Fisher-Ath 1.49
Cummings-Bal .... .80
McBride-Ath .... .59
Spalding-Bos .... .56

Ratio
Fisher-Ath 10.67
Mathews-Mut 11.19
McBride-Ath 11.76
Cummings-Bal 11.97
Spalding-Bos 12.13

Earned Run Average
Fisher-Ath 1.81
Spalding-Bos 2.46
Mathews-Mut 2.56
Cummings-Bal 2.66
Zettlein-Phi 2.70

Adjusted ERA
Fisher-Ath 188
Spalding-Bos 135
Mathews-Mut 123
Cummings-Bal 122
Zettlein-Phi 122

Opponents' Batting Avg.
Fisher-Ath .... .227
Mathews-Mut .... .251
McBride-Ath .... .263
Cummings-Bal .... .274
Zettlein-Phi .... .283

Opponents' On-Base Pct.
Fisher-Ath .... .246
Mathews-Mut .... .274
McBride-Ath .... .282
Cummings-Bal .... .287
Spalding-Bos .... .292

Starter Runs
Spalding-Bos 43.8
Mathews-Mut 34.0
Zettlein-Phi 28.2
Cummings-Bal 25.0
Fisher-Ath 13.5

Adjusted Starter Runs
Spalding-Bos 46.5
Mathews-Mut 30.4
Zettlein-Phi 30.1
Cummings-Bal 25.0
Fisher-Ath 14.3

Clutch Pitching Index
H.Campbell-Res 123
Spalding-Bos 119
Zettlein-Phi 111
Greason -Was 108
Brainard-Bal 103

Relief Runs

Adjusted Relief Runs

Relief Ranking

Total Pitcher Index
Spalding-Bos 5.4
Mathews-Mut 1.9
Zettlein-Phi 1.9
Cummings-Bal 1.7
Fisher-Ath 8

Total Baseball Ranking
Spalding-Bos 5.1
Barnes-Bos 3.5
G.Wright-Bos 2.3
Zettlein-Phi 1.9
Mathews-Mut 1.8

TEAM	G	W	L	PCT	GB	R	OR	AB	H	2B	3B	HR	BB	SO	AVG	OBP	SLG	OPS	OPS+	BR	BR+	PF	CHI	RC	SB	CS	SBA	SBR
BOS	71	52	18	.743		**735**	415	3129	**977**	**121**	**61**	**17**	34	**28**	**.312**	**.320**	**.406**	**726**	**128**	**114**	**78**	106	**108**	**417**	**45**	19	70	3
MUT	65	42	23	.646	7.5	501	377	2730	714	89	28	7	**36**	40	.262	.271	.322	593	90	-21	-35	103	105	252	36	4	**90**	**7**
ATH	55	33	22	.600	11.5	441	**344**	2259	647	83	18	6	24	51	.286	.294	.347	641	99	19	-15	109	103	237	36	14	72	3
PHI	58	29	29	.500	17	476	428	2435	677	78	50	2	28	33	.278	.286	.354	640	104	19	3	104	103	248	27	18	60	0
CHI	59	28	31	.475	18.5	418	480	2462	685	87	4	4	32	54	.278	.287	.322	609	97	-4	-8	101	94	232	32	12	73	3
ATL	56	22	33	.400	22.5	301	450	2169	498	45	8	1	31	51	.230	.240	.259	499	71	-84	-43	88	97	137	12	4	75	1
HAR	53	16	37	.302	27.5	371	471	2144	591	86	18	2	31	63	.276	.286	.335	621	97	4	-15	105	94	211	42	21	67	2
BAL	47	9	38	.191	31.5	227	505	1776	435	45	7	1	22	37	.245	.254	.280	534	75	-48	-46	99	83	127	12	5	71	1
TOT	232					3470		19104	5224	634	194	40	238	357	.274	.283	.334	616							242	97	71	19

TEAM	CG	SH	SV	IP	H	H/G	HR	BB	SO	RAT	ERA	ERA+	OAV	OOB	PR	PR+	PF	CPI	FA	E	DP	FW	PW	BW	SBW	DIF
BOS	**65**	**4**	**3**	634	779	11.1	**1**	23	31	11.4	1.94	112	.274	.280	18	17	99	109	**.850**	489	**53**	4.5	1.4	**6.1**	.0	5.2
MUT	62	**4**	0	586	663	10.2	3	41	**101**	10.9	1.91	118	.261	.273	19	22	103	97	.847	438	22	**4.6**	1.8	-2.7	**.4**	5.6
ATH	55	0	0	487	**514**	**9.5**	6	32	37	**10.1**	**1.65**	**141**	**.240**	**.251**	**30**	**34**	106	78	.839	**396**	34	2.6	**2.7**	-1.1	.0	1.4
PHI	56	3	0	522	673	11.7	4	19	61	12.0	1.94	115	.278	.284	15	17	101	**117**	.809	518	38	-2.3	1.4	.3	-.2	1.0
CHI	58	3	0	533[2]	684	11.6	7	45	26	12.3	2.65	84	.279	.292	-27	-24	102	93	.829	477	27	.2	-1.8	-.6	.0	.8
ATL	56	1	0	506	618	11.0	15	**11**	42	11.2	2.07	100	.266	.269	7	0	94	98	.822	500	15	-2.2	.0	-3.3	-.1	.2
HAR	45	0	0	481	653	12.3	**1**	28	39	12.8	2.53	91	.284	.293	-18	-11	105	98	.797	521	17	-4.5	-.8	-1.1	-.0	-3.9
BAL	42	0	0	420	640	13.8	3	39	20	14.6	3.13	71	.305	.318	-44	-41	102	106	.812	436	15	-2.7	-3.1	-3.5	-.1	-4.9
TOT	439	15	3	4169[2]		11.3				11.8	2.20		.274	.283					.827	3775	221					

Runs
McVey-Bos 91
O'Rourke-Bos 82
Spalding-Bos 80
G.Wright-Bos 76
White-Bos 75

Hits
McVey-Bos 123
Spalding-Bos 119
White-Bos 106
Leonard-Bos 106
O'Rourke-Bos 104

Doubles
Pike-Har 22
McVey-Bos 21
Meyerle-Chi 19
Craver-Phi 19
Leonard-Bos 18

Triples
G.Wright-Bos 15
Craver-Phi 11
Holdsworth-Phi 9

Home Runs
O'Rourke-Bos 5
White-Bos 3
McVey-Bos 3
Clapp-Ath 3

Total Bases
McVey-Bos 165
O'Rourke-Bos 150
G.Wright-Bos 149
White-Bos 134
Spalding-Bos 134

Runs Batted In
McVey-Bos 71
O'Rourke-Bos 61
Craver-Phi 56
Spalding-Bos 54
White-Bos 52

Runs Produced
McVey-Bos 159
O'Rourke-Bos 138
Spalding-Bos 134
White-Bos 124
Craver-Phi 124

Bases On Balls
Nelson-Mut 9
McMullin-Ath 8
Barnes-Bos 8

Batting Average
Meyerle-Chi .394
McVey-Bos .359
Pike-Har .355
Manning-Bal-Har .346
McMullin-Ath .346

On-Base Percentage
Meyerle-Chi .401
Pike-Har .368
McMullin-Ath .366
McVey-Bos .360
Barnes-Bos .360

Slugging Average
Pike-Har .504
Craver-Phi .498
Meyerle-Chi .488
McVey-Bos .481
G.Wright-Bos .476

On-Base Plus Slugging
Meyerle-Chi 889
Pike-Har 872
Craver-Phi 851
McVey-Bos 842
G.Wright-Bos 816

Adjusted OPS
Meyerle-Chi 182
Pike-Har 168
Craver-Phi 164
McVey-Bos 158
G.Wright-Bos 150

Batter Runs
McVey-Bos 24.3
Meyerle-Chi 22.6
Craver-Phi 19.7
G.Wright-Bos 19.6
Pike-Har 19.3

Adjusted Batter Runs
Meyerle-Chi 22.0
McVey-Bos 19.8
Craver-Phi 17.4
Pike-Har 16.3
G.Wright-Bos 15.5

Clutch Hitting Index
McBride-Ath 151
Fisher-Har 149
York-Phi 138
Malone-Chi 135
Fulmer-Phi 130

Runs Created
McVey-Bos 62
G.Wright-Bos 52
O'Rourke-Bos 51
Meyerle-Chi 51
Craver-Phi 49

Total Average
Pike-Har .824
Meyerle-Chi .822
Craver-Phi .804
McVey-Bos .774
G.Wright-Bos .739

Stolen Bases
Barlow-Har 17
O'Rourke-Bos 11
Leonard-Bos 11
Craver-Phi 11

Stolen Base Average
Barlow-Har 81.0

Stolen Base Runs
Barlow-Har 2.3
Cuthbert-Chi 1.8
O'Rourke-Bos 1.7
McGeary-Ath 1.5

Fielding Runs
White-Bal 25.0
Barnes-Bos 18.8
Pike-Har 13.6
Ryan-Bal 12.7
Force-Chi 11.0

Total Player Rating
Pike-Har 2.2
Barnes-Bos 1.9
McVey-Bos 1.7
Craver-Phi 1.6
White-Bal 1.5

Wins
Spalding-Bos 52
Mathews-Mut 42
McBride-Ath 33
Cummings-Phi 28
Zettlein-Chi 27

Win Percentage
Spalding-Bos .765
Mathews-Mut .656
McBride-Ath .600
Cummings-Phi .519
Zettlein-Chi .474

Games
Spalding-Bos 71
Mathews-Mut 65
Zettlein-Chi 57
McBride-Ath 55
Bond-Atl 55

Complete Games
Spalding-Bos 65
Mathews-Mut 62
Zettlein-Chi 57
McBride-Ath 55
Bond-Atl 55

Shutouts
Spalding-Bos 4
Mathews-Mut 4
Zettlein-Chi 3
Cummings-Phi 3
Bond-Atl 1

Saves
H.Wright-Bos 3

Innings Pitched
Spalding-Bos 617.1
Mathews-Mut 578.0
Zettlein-Chi 515.2
Bond-Atl 497.0
McBride-Ath 487.0

Fewest Hits/Game
McBride-Ath 9.50
Mathews-Mut 10.15
Bond-Atl 10.97
Spalding-Bos 11.01
Zettlein-Chi 11.17

Fewest BB/Game
Bond-Atl .14
Spalding-Bos .28
Cummings-Phi .34
Fisher-Har .36
McBride-Ath .59

Strikeouts
Mathews-Mut 101
Cummings-Phi 61
Bond-Atl 42
McBride-Ath 37
Spalding-Bos 31

Strikeouts/Game
Mathews-Mut 1.57
Cummings-Phi 1.14
Stearns-Har .79
Bond-Atl .76
Fisher-Har .70

Ratio
McBride-Ath 10.09
Mathews-Mut 10.79
Bond-Atl 11.12
Spalding-Bos 11.28
Cummings-Phi 11.81

Earned Run Average
McBride-Ath 1.64
Mathews-Mut 1.90
Spalding-Bos 1.92
Cummings-Phi 1.96
Bond-Atl 2.03

Adjusted ERA
McBride-Ath 141
Mathews-Mut 118
Cummings-Phi 113
Spalding-Bos 113
Bond-Atl 102

Opponents' Batting Avg.
McBride-Ath .240
Mathews-Mut .261
Bond-Atl .266
Spalding-Bos .273
Zettlein-Chi .273

Opponents' On-Base Pct.
McBride-Ath .251
Bond-Atl .268
Mathews-Mut .273
Spalding-Bos .278
Cummings-Phi .282

Starter Runs
McBride-Ath 29.5
Mathews-Mut 18.7
Spalding-Bos 18.3
Cummings-Phi 12.6
Bond-Atl 9.0

Adjusted Starter Runs
McBride-Ath 34.3
Mathews-Mut 21.7
Spalding-Bos 16.8
Cummings-Phi 13.9
Bechtel-Phi 2.6

Clutch Pitching Index
Cummings-Phi 113
Brainard-Bal 110
Spalding-Bos 106
Stearns-Har 101
Bond-Atl 99

Relief Runs

Adjusted Relief Runs

Relief Ranking

Total Pitcher Index
Spalding-Bos 3.0
McBride-Ath 1.7
Mathews-Mut 1.4
Bond-Atl 1.0
Cummings-Phi .4

Total Baseball Ranking
Spalding-Bos 2.9
Pike-Har 2.2
Barnes-Bos 1.9
McBride-Ath 1.7
McVey-Bos 1.7

TEAM	G	W	L	PCT	GB	R	OR	AB	H	2B	3B	HR	BB	SO	AVG	OBP	SLG	OPS	OPS+	BR	BR+	PF	CHI	RC	SB	CS	SBA	SBR
BOS	82	71	8	.899		**831**	**343**	3515	**1128**	**167**	51	**15**	33	52	**.321**	**.327**	**.410**	**737**	**153**	**191**	**165**	104	111	**494**	93	37	72	8
HAR	86	54	28	.659	18.5	557	**343**	3356	871	92	35	2	34	64	.260	.267	.310	577	97	7	-19	105	104	284	65	33	66	3
ATH	77	53	20	.726	15	699	402	3250	941	124	**57**	7	**38**	55	.290	.298	.369	667	120	102	40	111	**113**	365	75	46	62	0
STL	70	39	29	.574	26.5	386	369	2674	643	85	29	0	32	102	.240	.249	.294	543	99	-23	17	91	96	210	**108**	36	**75**	**11**
PHI	70	37	31	.544	28.5	470	376	2721	683	67	27	5	21	58	.251	.257	.301	558	92	-12	-28	104	**113**	220	105	51	67	5
MUT	71	30	38	.441	35.5	328	425	2685	633	82	21	7	19	**47**	.236	.241	.290	531	82	-36	-55	105	85	185	20	24	45	-4
CHI	69	30	37	.448	35	379	416	2685	699	83	16	0	21	65	.260	.266	.303	569	99	-1	-5	101	90	220	69	50	58	-2
NH	47	7	40	.149	48	170	397	1714	373	41	13	2	14	62	.218	.224	.260	484	80	-49	-17	87	77	103	35	16	69	2
WAS	28	5	23	.179	40.5	107	338	1004	194	14	8	0	6	42	.193	.198	.223	421	50	-49	-45	96	98	47	23	7	77	3
RS	19	4	15	.211	37	60	161	688	137	20	1	0	12	45	.199	.213	.231	444	62	-28	-19	90	74	37	27	9	**75**	3
CEN	14	2	12	.143	36.5	70	138	530	125	22	3	0	10	25	.236	.250	.289	539	97	-5	2	92	88	40	4			
ATL	44	2	42	. 45	51.5	132	438	1562	304	33	6	2	8	36	.195	.199	.227	426	57	-74	-49	87	77	69	1	5	17	-2
WES	13	1	12	. 77	37	45	88	449	81	9	6	0	1	22	.180	.182	.227	409	41	-24	-26	105	97	17	4	6	40	-1
TOT	345					4234		26833	6812	839	273	40	249	675	.254	.261	.310	571							629	320	66	26

TEAM	CG	SH	SV	IP	H	H/G	HR	BB	SO	RAT	ERA	ERA+	OAV	OOB	PR	PR+	PF	CPI	FA	E	DP	FW	PW	BW	SBW	DIF
BOS	60	10	**17**	732	751	9.3	2	33	110	9.7	1.87	115	.248	.256	29	23	96	110	.870	483	**56**	4.3	2.0	**14.2**	.5	10.7
HAR	**83**	**13**	0	770	708	**8.3**	4	**11**	**152**	**8.5**	**1.57**	**150**	**.228**	**.231**	**56**	**63**	105	94	**.881**	438	47	**7.8**	**5.4**	-1.6	.0	1.4
ATH	75	6	0	687	776	10.2	4	39	45	10.7	2.40	100	.268	.278	-13	0	107	111	.876	**419**	51	5.7	.0	3.5	-.2	7.6
STL	67	5	1	630	**636**	9.1	3	21	71	9.4	2.11	96	.241	.247	9	-7	90	87	.869	425	36	3.1	-.5	1.5	**.8**	.4
PHI	64	5	0	628	652	9.4	6	30	42	9.8	2.13	107	.243	.251	7	11	102	93	.848	477	32	.6	1.0	-2.3	.3	3.7
MUT	70	3	0	636[2]	718	10.2	4	21	77	10.5	2.46	95	.258	.264	-17	-9	105	95	.838	526	30	-1.4	-.7	-4.7	-.5	3.5
CHI	65	7	0	625	649	9.4	**0**	26	55	9.8	1.63	139	.243	.250	42	44	102	**115**	.853	478	30	.2	3.8	-.4	-.3	-6.6
NH	40	0	0	425	501	10.7	5	21	54	11.1	2.65	78	.254	.262	-20	-29	93	87	.814	447	24	-5.7	-2.4	-1.4	-.0	-6.8
WAS	23	0	0	250[2]	397	14.3	6	10	6	14.7	3.77	63	.311	.317	-43	-37	107	112	.791	285	8	-4.3	-3.1	-3.8	.0	2.3
RS	16	2	0	171	209	11.1	**0**	3	21	11.2	2.64	83	.267	.269	-8	-9	98	94	.833	150	6	-.8	-.7	-1.6	.0	-2.3
CEN	14	0	0	126	169	12.1	**0**	5	6	12.5	2.72	80	.274	.280	-7	-8	98	103	.769	164	5	-3.1	-.6	.2	-.2	-1.1
ATL	31	0	0	396	535	12.2	6	17	16	12.6	3.16	66	.285	.291	-41	-51	94	103	.801	432	20	-6.0	-4.3	-4.1	-.3	-5.0
WES	13	0	0	113	111	8.9	**0**	12	20	9.8	1.84	133	.225	.243	5	7	110	84	.860	78	5	.7	.6	-2.2	-.3	-4.2
TOT	621	51	18	6190[1]		10.0				10.3	2.23		.254	.261					.849	4802	350					

Runs
Barnes-Bos 115
G.Wright-Bos 106
O'Rourke-Bos 97
McVey-Bos 89
Leonard-Bos 87

Hits
Barnes-Bos 143
McVey-Bos 138
G.Wright-Bos 136
White-Bos 136
Leonard-Bos 127

Doubles
McVey-Bos 36
White-Bos 23
Pike-StL 22
Force-Ath 22

Triples
Craver-Cen-Ath 13
Pike-StL 12
Hall-Ath 12
McVey-Bos 9
Meyerle-Phi 8

Home Runs
O'Rourke-Bos 6
Start-Mut 4
Hall-Ath 4
Hallinan-Wes-Mut 3
McVey-Bos 3

Total Bases
McVey-Bos 201
G.Wright-Bos 176
Barnes-Bos 174
White-Bos 168
Leonard-Bos 156

Runs Batted In
McVey-Bos 87
Leonard-Bos 74
O'Rourke-Bos 72
Hall-Ath 62
G.Wright-Bos 61

Runs Produced
McVey-Bos 173
Barnes-Bos 172
G.Wright-Bos 165
O'Rourke-Bos 163
Leonard-Bos 160

Bases On Balls
Dehlman-StL 11
O'Rourke-Bos 9
Nelson-Mut 9
Hastings-Chi 9
Harbidge-Har 9

Batting Average
White-Bos .367
Barnes-Bos .364
McVey-Bos .355
Pike-StL .346
G.Wright-Bos .333

On-Base Percentage
Barnes-Bos .375
White-Bos .372
McVey-Bos .356
Pike-StL .352
G.Wright-Bos .337

Slugging Average
McVey-Bos .517
Pike-StL .494
Craver-Cen-Ath .455
White-Bos .453
Barnes-Bos .443

On-Base Plus Slugging
McVey-Bos 873
Pike-StL 846
White-Bos 824
Barnes-Bos 818
Craver-Cen-Ath 779

Adjusted OPS
Pike-StL 210
McVey-Bos 193
White-Bos 178
Barnes-Bos 177
G.Wright-Bos 159

Batter Runs
McVey-Bos 36.9
Barnes-Bos 31.4
White-Bos 30.0
Pike-StL 27.1
G.Wright-Bos 25.1

Adjusted Batter Runs
Pike-StL 34.8
McVey-Bos 33.5
Barnes-Bos 28.1
White-Bos 26.9
G.Wright-Bos 22.0

Clutch Hitting Index
Chapman-StL 189
McBride-Ath 164
Leonard-Bos 148
Addy-Phi 142
Clapp-Ath 136

Runs Created
McVey-Bos 76
Barnes-Bos 75
White-Bos 62
G.Wright-Bos 62
Pike-StL 58

Total Average
McVey-Bos .833
Pike-StL .800
Barnes-Bos .797
White-Bos .708
Craver-Cen-Ath .694

Stolen Bases
Murnane-Phi 30
Barnes-Bos 29
Pike-StL 25
Dehlman-StL 23
Burdock-Har 20

Stolen Base Average
Cuthbert-StL 94.7
Barnes-Bos 82.9
McGeary-Phi 82.6
O'Rourke-Bos 77.3
Murnane-Phi 76.9

Stolen Base Runs
Barnes-Bos 4.3
Cuthbert-StL 3.6
Murnane-Phi 3.5
McGeary-Phi 2.8
Battin-StL 2.3

Fielding Runs
Barnes-Bos 19.2
Clapp-Ath 18.1
D.Allison-Har 17.3
White-Bos 14.5
Sutton-Ath 13.9

Total Player Rating
Barnes-Bos 3.9
McVey-Bos 3.5
White-Bos 3.5
Pike-StL 2.9
G.Wright-Bos 2.1

Wins
Spalding-Bos 54
McBride-Ath 44
Cummings-Har 35
Bradley-StL 33

Win Percentage
Spalding-Bos .915
Manning-Bos .889
McBride-Ath .759
Cummings-Har .745
Zettlein-Chi-Phi .569

Games
Spalding-Bos 72
Mathews-Mut 70
McBride-Ath 60
Bradley-StL 60
Zettlein-Chi-Phi 52

Complete Games
Mathews-Mut 69
McBride-Ath 59
Bradley-StL 57
Spalding-Bos 52
Zettlein-Chi-Phi 49

Shutouts
Zettlein-Chi-Phi 7
Spalding-Bos 7
Cummings-Har 7
McBride-Ath 6
Bond-Har 6

Saves
Spalding-Bos 9
Manning-Bos 6
McVey-Bos 1
Heifer-Bos 1
Galvin-StL 1

Innings Pitched
Mathews-Mut 625.2
Spalding-Bos 570.2
McBride-Ath 538.0
Bradley-StL 535.2
Zettlein-Chi-Phi 463.1

Fewest Hits/Game
Borden-Phi 6.41
Galvin-StL 7.69
Bond-Har 7.72
Cummings-Har 8.59
Fisher-Phi 8.67

Fewest BB/Game
Cummings-Har .09
Blong-RS .14
Galvin-StL .15
Bond-Har .18
Fisher-Phi .23

Strikeouts
Cummings-Har 82
Spalding-Bos 75
Mathews-Mut 75
Bond-Har 70
Bradley-StL 60

Strikeouts/Game
Manning-Bos 2.13
Bond-Har 1.79
Cummings-Har 1.77
Nichols-NH 1.50
Golden-Wes-Chi 1.32

Ratio
Borden-Phi 7.36
Galvin-StL 7.84
Bond-Har 7.90
Cummings-Har 8.68
Fisher-Phi 8.90

Earned Run Average
Galvin-StL 1.16
Bond-Har 1.41
Borden-Phi 1.50
Zettlein-Chi-Phi 1.59
Spalding-Bos 1.59

Adjusted ERA
Galvin-StL 173
Bond-Har 167
Borden-Phi 152
Cummings-Har 146
Zettlein-Chi-Phi 143

Opponents' Batting Avg.
Borden-Phi .181
Galvin-StL .209
Bond-Har .216
Fisher-Phi .229
Cummings-Har .235

Opponents' On-Base Pct.
Borden-Phi .203
Galvin-StL .212
Bond-Har .219
Fisher-Phi .233
Cummings-Har .236

Starter Runs
Spalding-Bos 40.1
Zettlein-Chi-Phi 32.6
Bond-Har 32.1
Cummings-Har 28.9
Fisher-Phi 9.5

Adjusted Starter Runs
Spalding-Bos 36.3
Bond-Har 34.8
Zettlein-Chi-Phi 34.2
Cummings-Har 32.6
Golden-Wes-Chi 12.0

Clutch Pitching Index
Stearns-Was 123
Spalding-Bos 122
Zettlein-Chi-Phi 118
Devlin-Chi 117
McBride-Ath 113

Relief Runs

Adjusted Relief Runs

Relief Ranking

Total Pitcher Index
Spalding-Bos 4.8
Bond-Har 3.5
Cummings-Har 2.6
Zettlein-Chi-Phi 2.3
Devlin-Chi 1.3

Total Baseball Ranking
Spalding-Bos 4.5
Bond-Har 3.9
Barnes-Bos 3.9
White-Bos 3.5
McVey-Bos 3.2

TEAM	G	W	L	PCT	GB	R	OR	AB	H	2B	3B	HR	BB	SO	AVG	OBP	SLG	OPS	OPS+	BR	BR+	PF	CHI	RC	SB	CS	SBA	SBR
CHI	66	52	14	.788		**624**	257	2818	**926**	**131**	32	8	**70**	45	**.329**	**.353**	**.417**	**770**	**140**	**160**	**99**	112	107	**415**				
STL	64	45	19	.703	6	386	**229**	2537	642	73	27	2	59	63	.253	.276	.313	589	102	-6	15	95	103	219				
HAR	69	47	21	.691	6	429	261	2703	711	96	22	2	39	78	.263	.277	.322	599	92	1	-30	108	106	244				
BOS	70	39	31	.557	15	471	450	2780	723	96	24	**9**	58	98	.260	.281	.328	609	102	11	4	102	**110**	257				
LOU	69	30	36	.455	22	280	344	2594	641	68	14	6	24	98	.247	.256	.294	550	71	-42	-95	118	81	198				
NY	57	21	35	.375	26	260	412	2198	494	39	15	2	18	**35**	.225	.233	.261	494	75	-76	-38	87	103	136				
PHI	60	14	45	.237	34.5	378	534	2414	646	79	**35**	7	27	36	.268	.279	.342	621	108	16	19	99	100	233				
CIN	65	9	56	.138	42.5	238	579	2413	555	51	12	4	41	136	.230	.247	.271	518	86	-63	-13	86	80	163				
TOT	260					3066		20457	5338	633	181	40	336	589	.261	.278	.321	598										

TEAM	CG	SH	SV	IP	H	H/G	HR	BB	SO	RAT	ERA	ERA+	OAV	OOB	PR	PR+	PF	CPI	FA	E	DP	FW	PW	BW	SBW	DIF
CHI	58	9	4	592[1]	608	9.3	6	29	51	9.7	1.77	139	.244	.256	36	42	106	100	.899	282	33	6.0	3.7	**8.8**		.7
STL	63	**16**	0	577	**472**	**7.4**	3	39	103	**8.0**	**1.22**	**175**	**.207**	**.224**	**70**	**64**	93	74	**.902**	**268**	33	**6.1**	**5.7**	1.4		.0
HAR	**69**	11	0	624	570	8.3	**2**	27	114	8.7	1.68	142	.225	.235	44	47	103	72	.888	337	27	4.1	4.2	-2.6		7.5
BOS	49	3	**7**	632	732	10.5	7	104	77	12.0	2.51	90	.258	.295	-14	-18	98	106	.860	442	42	-1.1	-1.5	.4		6.4
LOU	67	5	0	643	605	8.5	3	38	**125**	9.1	1.70	160	.226	.240	44	62	118	75	.875	397	44	1.0	5.5	-8.3		-1.0
NY	56	2	0	530	718	12.2	8	**24**	37	12.7	2.94	73	.299	.309	-37	-50	93	**114**	.825	473	18	-6.8	-4.3	-3.3		7.6
PHI	53	1	2	550	783	12.9	**2**	41	22	13.5	3.23	75	.305	.321	-56	-46	105	112	.839	456	32	-4.9	-4.0	1.7		-8.1
CIN	57	0	0	591	850	13.0	9	34	60	13.5	3.63	61	.309	.322	-86	-99	95	103	.841	469	**45**	-4.0	-8.7	-1.1		-9.5
TOT	472	47	13	4739[1]		10.2				10.8	2.31		.261	.278					.867	3124	274					

Runs
Barnes-Chi 126
G.Wright-Bos 72
Peters-Chi 70
White-Chi 66
Burdock-Har 66

Hits
Barnes-Chi 138
Peters-Chi 111
Anson-Chi 110
McVey-Chi 107
White-Chi 104

Doubles
Hines-Chi 21
Higham-Har 21
Barnes-Chi 21
Pike-StL 19

Triples
Barnes-Chi 14
Hall-Phi 13
Pike-StL 10
Meyerle-Phi 8

Home Runs
Hall-Phi 5
Jones-Cin 4

Total Bases
Barnes-Chi 190
Hall-Phi 146
Anson-Chi 139
Hines-Chi 134

Runs Batted In
White-Chi 60
Hines-Chi 59
Barnes-Chi 59
Anson-Chi 59
McVey-Chi 53

Runs Produced
Barnes-Chi 184
White-Chi 125
Anson-Chi 120
Hines-Chi 119
Peters-Chi 116

Bases On Balls
Barnes-Chi 20
O'Rourke-Bos 15
Burdock-Har 13
Glenn-Chi 12
Anson-Chi 12

Batting Average
Barnes-Chi .404
Hall-Phi .355
Peters-Chi .348
McVey-Chi .345
Anson-Chi .343

On-Base Percentage
Barnes-Chi .462
Hall-Phi .384
Anson-Chi .380
White-Chi .358
O'Rourke-Bos .358

Slugging Average
Barnes-Chi .590
Hall-Phi .545
Pike-StL .472
Anson-Chi .450
Meyerle-Phi .449

On-Base Plus Slugging
Barnes-Chi 1052
Hall-Phi 929
Anson-Chi 830
Pike-StL 813
Meyerle-Phi 797

Adjusted OPS
Barnes-Chi 222
Hall-Phi 208
Pike-StL 178
Meyerle-Phi 165
Jones-Cin 162

Batter Runs
Barnes-Chi 50.0
Hall-Phi 29.1
Anson-Chi 24.2
Pike-StL 19.7
O'Rourke-Bos 19.1

Adjusted Batter Runs
Barnes-Chi 39.3
Hall-Phi 29.7
Pike-StL 23.2
Jones-Cin 19.9
O'Rourke-Bos 18.1

Clutch Hitting Index
Battin-StL 150
White-Chi 142
McVey-Chi 140
Anson-Chi 138
McGeary-StL 135

Runs Created
Barnes-Chi 90
Hall-Phi 57
Anson-Chi 54
Peters-Chi 48
O'Rourke-Bos 48

Total Average
Barnes-Chi 1.141
Hall-Phi .906
Anson-Chi .759
Pike-StL .738
Meyerle-Phi .698

Stolen Bases

Stolen Base Average

Stolen Base Runs

Fielding Runs
Somerville-Lou 29.7
Force-Phi-NY 21.3
Battin-StL 13.6
G.Wright-Bos 13.1
Anson-Chi 12.8

Total Player Rating
Barnes-Chi 4.0
Anson-Chi 2.7
G.Wright-Bos 2.4
Battin-StL 2.3
Hall-Phi 2.1

Wins
Spalding-Chi 47
Bradley-StL 45
Bond-Har 31
Devlin-Lou 30
Mathews-NY 21

Win Percentage
Spalding-Chi .797
Manning-Bos .783
Bond-Har .705
Bradley-StL .703
Cummings-Har .667

Games
Devlin-Lou 68
Bradley-StL 64
Spalding-Chi 61
Mathews-NY 56
Bond-Har 45

Complete Games
Devlin-Lou 66
Bradley-StL 63
Mathews-NY 55
Spalding-Chi 53
Bond-Har 45

Shutouts
Bradley-StL 16
Spalding-Chi 8
Bond-Har 6
Devlin-Lou 5
Cummings-Har 5

Saves
Manning-Bos 5
Zettlein-Phi 2
McVey-Chi 2

Innings Pitched
Devlin-Lou 622.0
Bradley-StL 573.0
Spalding-Chi 528.2
Mathews-NY 516.0
Bond-Har 408.0

Fewest Hits/Game
Bradley-StL 7.38
Bond-Har 7.83
Devlin-Lou 8.19
Cummings-Har 8.96
Spalding-Chi 9.23

Fewest BB/Game
Zettlein-Phi .23
Fisher-Cin .24
Bond-Har .29
Mathews-NY .42
Williams-Cin .43

Strikeouts
Devlin-Lou 122
Bradley-StL 103
Bond-Har 88
Spalding-Chi 39
Mathews-NY 37

Strikeouts/Game
Bond-Har 1.94
Devlin-Lou 1.77
Bradley-StL 1.62
Borden-Bos 1.40
Fisher-Cin 1.14

Ratio
Bradley-StL 7.98
Bond-Har 8.12
Devlin-Lou 8.73
Cummings-Har 9.54
Spalding-Chi 9.67

Earned Run Average
Bradley-StL 1.23
Devlin-Lou 1.56
Cummings-Har 1.67
Bond-Har 1.68
Spalding-Chi 1.75

Adjusted ERA
Bradley-StL 174
Devlin-Lou 174
Cummings-Har 142
Bond-Har 141
Spalding-Chi 139

Opponents' Batting Avg.
Bradley-StL .207
Bond-Har .219
Devlin-Lou .220
Cummings-Har .235
Manning-Bos .243

Opponents' On-Base Pct.
Bradley-StL .224
Bond-Har .227
Devlin-Lou .235
Cummings-Har .251
Spalding-Chi .256

Starter Runs
Bradley-StL 68.9
Devlin-Lou 51.5
Spalding-Chi 32.5
Bond-Har 28.6
Cummings-Har 15.4

Adjusted Starter Runs
Devlin-Lou 67.8
Bradley-StL 62.6
Spalding-Chi 38.3
Bond-Har 30.7
Cummings-Har 16.5

Clutch Pitching Index
Knight-Phi 126
Mathews-NY 116
Borden-Bos 108
Dean-Cin 108
Zettlein-Phi 107

Relief Runs

Adjusted Relief Runs

Relief Ranking

Total Pitcher Index
Devlin-Lou 6.3
Bradley-StL 6.2
Spalding-Chi 4.4
Bond-Har 3.1
McVey-Chi .7

Total Baseball Ranking
Devlin-Lou 6.3
Bradley-StL 6.2
Spalding-Chi 4.2
Barnes-Chi 3.9
Bond-Har 3.1

TEAM	G	W	L	PCT	GB	R	OR	AB	H	2B	3B	HR	BB	SO	AVG	OBP	SLG	OPS	OPS+	BR	BR+	PF	CHI	RC	SB	CS	SBA	SBR
BOS	61	42	18	.700		**419**	**263**	2368	**700**	**91**	**37**	4	65	121	**.296**	**.314**	**.370**	**684**	**114**	**47**	**33**	104	104	**283**				
LOU	61	35	25	.583	7	339	288	2355	659	75	36	**9**	58	140	.280	.297	.354	651	92	19	-37	118	92	254				
HAR	60	31	27	.534	10	341	311	2358	637	63	31	4	30	**97**	.270	.279	.328	607	105	-17	23	89	103	222				
STL	60	28	32	.467	14	284	318	2178	531	51	36	1	57	147	.244	.263	.302	565	84	-46	-30	95	102	177				
CHI	60	26	33	.441	15.5	366	375	2273	633	79	30	0	57	111	.278	.296	.340	636	92	8	-29	112	**105**	234				
CIN	58	15	42	.263	25.5	291	485	2135	545	72	34	6	**78**	110	.255	.282	.329	611	107	-11	28	89	94	203				
TOT	180					2040		13667	3705	431	204	24	345	726	.272	.290	.338	627										

TEAM	CG	SH	SV	IP	H	H/G	HR	BB	SO	RAT	ERA	ERA+	OAV	OOB	PR	PR+	PF	CPI	FA	E	DP	FW	PW	BW	SBW	DIF
BOS	**61**	**7**	0	548	**557**	**9.2**	5	**38**	**177**	**9.8**	**2.16**	130	**.249**	**.261**	**40**	40	100	98	.889	290	36	1.3	3.6	**3.0**		4.3
LOU	**61**	4	0	559	617	10.0	4	41	141	10.6	2.26	**147**	.270	.283	34	**56**	118	**119**	**.904**	**267**	37	**2.4**	**5.0**	-3.2		1.0
HAR	59	4	0	544	572	9.5	**2**	56	99	10.4	2.32	105	.253	.271	30	8	87	97	.885	313	32	-.1	.8	2.1		-.5
STL	52	1	0	541	582	9.7	**2**	92	132	11.3	2.67	98	.262	.291	9	-4	93	102	.892	281	29	1.5	-.3	-2.6		-.3
CHI	45	3	**3**	534	630	10.7	7	58	92	11.6	3.38	88	.274	.292	-33	-22	106	87	.883	313	**43**	-.1	-1.9	-2.5		1.3
CIN	48	1	1	515	747	13.1	4	61	85	14.2	4.20	63	.318	.335	-79	-94	94	102	.851	394	33	-4.6	-8.3	2.5		-2.9
TOT	326	20	4	3241		10.3				11.3	2.81		.272	.290					.885	1858	210					

Runs
O'Rourke-Bos 68
G.Wright-Bos 58
McVey-Chi 58
Start-Har 55

Hits
D.White-Bos 103
McVey-Chi 98
O'Rourke-Bos 96
Cassidy-Har 95
Start-Har 90

Doubles
Anson-Chi 19
York-Har 16
Manning-Cin 16
G.Wright-Bos 15
Hall-Lou 15

Triples
D.White-Bos 11
Jones-Cin-Chi-Cin ... 10
Hall-Lou 8
Brown-Bos 8

Home Runs
Pike-Cin 4
Shaffer-Lou 3
Jones-Cin-Chi-Cin 2
D.White-Bos 2
Snyder-Lou 2

Total Bases
D.White-Bos 145
McVey-Chi 121
O'Rourke-Bos 118
Hall-Lou 118
Cassidy-Har 115

Runs Batted In
D.White-Bos 49
Peters-Chi 41
Sutton-Bos 39
Jones-Cin-Chi-Cin 38
York-Har 37

Runs Produced
D.White-Bos 98
McVey-Chi 94
G.Wright-Bos 93
O'Rourke-Bos 91
Jones-Cin-Chi-Cin 89

Bases On Balls
O'Rourke-Bos 20
Jones-Cin-Chi-Cin 15
Hall-Lou 12
Booth-Cin 12
Force-StL 11

Batting Average
D.White-Bos .... .387
Cassidy-Har .... .378
McVey-Chi .... .368
O'Rourke-Bos .... .362
Anson-Chi .... .337

On-Base Percentage
O'Rourke-Bos ...... .407
D.White-Bos .... .405
McVey-Chi .... .387
Cassidy-Har .... .386
Anson-Chi .... .360

Slugging Average
D.White-Bos .... .545
Jones-Cin-Chi-Cin .... .471
Cassidy-Har .... .458
McVey-Chi .... .455
O'Rourke-Bos ...... .445

On-Base Plus Slugging
D.White-Bos 950
O'Rourke-Bos 852
Cassidy-Har 844
McVey-Chi 842
Jones-Cin-Chi-Cin 824

Adjusted OPS
D.White-Bos 190
Cassidy-Har 184
Jones-Cin-Chi-Cin 175
O'Rourke-Bos 162
Manning-Cin 157

Batter Runs
D.White-Bos 28.2
O'Rourke-Bos 21.2
McVey-Chi 18.9
Cassidy-Har 17.6
Jones-Cin-Chi-Cin 15.6

Adjusted Batter Runs
D.White-Bos 25.9
Cassidy-Har 24.2
Jones-Cin-Chi-Cin 21.7
O'Rourke-Bos 19.0
Manning-Cin 16.9

Clutch Hitting Index
Ferguson-Har 142
Peters-Chi 139
Bond-Bos 139
Croft-StL 139
Addy-Cin 138

Runs Created
D.White-Bos 60
O'Rourke-Bos 49
McVey-Chi 48
Cassidy-Har 45
Hall-Lou 43

Total Average
D.White-Bos .... .939
O'Rourke-Bos ...... .817
Jones-Cin-Chi-Cin .... .776
McVey-Chi .... .768
Cassidy-Har .... .756

Stolen Bases

Stolen Base Average

Stolen Base Runs

Fielding Runs
Gerhardt-Lou 19.8
Peters-Chi 19.1
Ferguson-Har 17.2
Brown-Bos 15.4
Snyder-Lou 15.2

Total Player Rating
Jones-Cin-Chi-Cin 2.6
D.White-Bos 2.2
Peters-Chi 1.9
Gerhardt-Lou 1.9
Cassidy-Har 1.7

Wins
Bond-Bos 40
Devlin-Lou 35
Larkin-Har 29
Nichols-StL 18
Bradley-Chi 18

Win Percentage
Bond-Bos .... .702
Devlin-Lou .... .583
Larkin-Har .... .537
Nichols-StL .... .439
Bradley-Chi .... .439

Games
Devlin-Lou 61
Bond-Bos 58
Larkin-Har 56
Bradley-Chi 50
Nichols-StL 42

Complete Games
Devlin-Lou 61
Bond-Bos 58
Larkin-Har 55
Nichols-StL 35
Bradley-Chi 35

Shutouts
Bond-Bos 6
Larkin-Har 4
Devlin-Lou 4
Bradley-Chi 2

Saves
McVey-Chi 2
Spalding-Chi 1
Manning-Cin 1

Innings Pitched
Devlin-Lou 559.0
Bond-Bos 521.0
Larkin-Har 501.0
Bradley-Chi 394.0
Nichols-StL 350.0

Fewest Hits/Game
Bond-Bos 9.16
Larkin-Har 9.16
Nichols-StL 9.67
Blong-StL 9.75
Devlin-Lou 9.93

Fewest BB/Game
Bond-Bos .... .62
Devlin-Lou .... .66
Cummings-Cin ...... .75
Bradley-Chi .... .89
Larkin-Har .... .95

Strikeouts
Bond-Bos 170
Devlin-Lou 141
Larkin-Har 96
Nichols-StL 80
Bradley-Chi 59

Strikeouts/Game
Mitchell-Cin 3.69
Bond-Bos 2.94
Blong-StL 2.45
Devlin-Lou 2.27
Nichols-StL 2.06

Ratio
Bond-Bos 9.78
Larkin-Har 10.11
Devlin-Lou 10.59
Nichols-StL 11.03
Bradley-Chi 11.22

Earned Run Average
Bond-Bos 2.11
Larkin-Har 2.14
Devlin-Lou 2.25
Nichols-StL 2.60
Blong-StL 2.74

Adjusted ERA
Devlin-Lou 147
Bond-Bos 133
Larkin-Har 114
Nichols-StL 100
Blong-StL 95

Opponents' Batting Avg.
Larkin-Har .... .245
Bond-Bos .... .249
Blong-StL .... .262
Nichols-StL .... .263
Bradley-Chi .... .269

Opponents' On-Base Pct.
Bond-Bos .... .261
Larkin-Har .... .264
Devlin-Lou .... .283
Bradley-Chi .... .286
Nichols-StL .... .289

Starter Runs
Bond-Bos 40.5
Larkin-Har 37.3
Devlin-Lou 34.4
Reis-Chi 8.2
Nichols-StL 8.2

Adjusted Starter Runs
Devlin-Lou 55.5
Bond-Bos 40.5
Larkin-Har 18.9
Reis-Chi 8.4

Clutch Pitching Index
Mathews-Cin 123
Devlin-Lou 119
Booth-Cin 104
Nichols-StL 104
Blong-StL 101

Relief Runs

Adjusted Relief Runs

Relief Ranking

Total Pitcher Index
Devlin-Lou 5.1
Bond-Bos 3.5
Larkin-Har 2.0
Reis-Chi 6
Spalding-Chi 0

Total Baseball Ranking
Devlin-Lou 5.1
Bond-Bos 3.4
Jones-Cin-Chi-Cin 2.6
D.White-Bos 2.2
Larkin-Har 2.0

TEAM	G	W	L	PCT	GB	R	OR	AB	H	2B	3B	HR	BB	SO	AVG	OBP	SLG	OPS	OPS+	BR	BR+	PF	CHI	RC	SB	CS	SBA	SBR
BOS	60	41	19	.683		298	**241**	2220	535	75	25	2	35	154	.241	.253	.300	553	79	-35	-54	108	**110**	173				
CIN	61	37	23	.617	4	333	281	2281	629	67	22	5	58	**141**	.276	.294	.331	625	**120**	21	**57**	91	98	227				
PRO	62	33	27	.550	8	353	337	2298	604	**107**	**30**	**8**	50	218	.263	.279	.346	625	109	19	20	100	104	227				
CHI	61	30	30	.500	11	**371**	331	2333	**677**	91	20	3	**88**	157	**.290**	**.316**	**.350**	**666**	115	**56**	32	107	96	**265**				
IND	63	24	36	.400	17	293	328	2300	542	76	15	3	64	197	.236	.256	.286	542	95	-43	0	87	105	173				
MIL	61	15	45	.250	26	256	386	2212	552	65	20	2	69	214	.250	.272	.300	572	86	-18	-36	107	88	185				
TOT	184					1904		13644	3539	481	132	23	364	1081	.260	.279	.320	598										

TEAM	CG	SH	SV	IP	H	H/G	HR	BB	SO	RAT	ERA	ERA+	OAV	OOB	PR	PR+	PF	CPI	FA	E	DP	FW	PW	BW	SBW	DIF
BOS	58	**9**	0	544	595	9.9	6	38	184	10.5	2.32	102	.272	.284	-1	2	102	**111**	**.914**	**228**	**48**	**3.6**	.2	-5.0		12.4
CIN	**61**	6	0	548	**546**	**9.0**	**2**	63	**220**	10.1	**1.84**	**116**	**.248**	.269	**28**	**19**	92	108	.900	269	37	1.6	**1.8**	**5.4**		-1.6
PRO	59	6	0	556	609	9.9	5	86	173	11.3	2.38	93	.265	.291	-5	-12	96	108	.892	311	42	-.5	-1.1	1.9		2.8
CHI	**61**	1	0	551	577	9.5	4	**35**	175	**10.0**	2.37	102	.253	**.265**	-4	3	105	85	.891	304	37	-.4	.3	3.0		-2.8
IND	59	2	**1**	578	621	9.7	3	87	182	11.1	2.33	87	.262	.288	-1	-22	88	106	.898	290	37	.9	-2.0	.0		-4.8
MIL	54	1	0	547	589	9.7	3	55	147	10.6	2.60	101	.255	.272	-18	1	114	82	.866	376	32	-4.4	.1	-3.3		-7.3
TOT	352	25	1	3324		9.6				10.6	2.31		.260	.279					.894	1778	233					

Runs
Higham-Pro 60
Start-Chi 58
York-Pro 56
Anson-Chi 55
Dalrymple-Mil 52

Hits
Start-Chi 100
Dalrymple-Mil 96
Hines-Pro 92
Ferguson-Chi 91

Doubles
Higham-Pro 22
Brown-Pro 21
York-Pro 19
Shaffer-Ind 19
O'Rourke-Bos 17

Triples
York-Pro 10
O'Rourke-Bos 7
Jones-Cin 7

Home Runs
Hines-Pro 4
Jones-Cin 3
McVey-Cin 2
McKelvy-Ind 2

Total Bases
York-Pro 125
Start-Chi 125
Hines-Pro 125
Shaffer-Ind 121
Higham-Pro 117

Runs Batted In
Hines-Pro 50
Brown-Pro 43
Anson-Chi 40
Jones-Cin 39
Ferguson-Chi 39

Runs Produced
Anson-Chi 95
Hines-Pro 88
Higham-Pro 88
Jones-Cin 86
Brown-Pro 86

Bases On Balls
Remsen-Chi 17
Larkin-Chi 17
Shaffer-Ind 13
Clapp-Ind 13
Anson-Chi 13

Batting Average
Dalrymple-Mil .354
Hines-Pro .358
Ferguson-Chi .351
Start-Chi .351
Anson-Chi .341

On-Base Percentage
Ferguson-Chi .375
Anson-Chi .372
Shaffer-Ind .369
Dalrymple-Mil .368
Hines-Pro .363

Slugging Average
Hines-Pro .486
York-Pro .465
Shaffer-Ind .455
Brown-Pro .453
Jones-Cin .441

On-Base Plus Slugging
Hines-Pro 849
Shaffer-Ind 824
Start-Chi 794
York-Pro 793
Dalrymple-Mil 789

Adjusted OPS
Shaffer-Ind 196
Hines-Pro 177
Jones-Cin 163
York-Pro 159
Brown-Pro 153

Batter Runs
Hines-Pro 20.0
Shaffer-Ind 19.6
Start-Chi 17.2
Dalrymple-Mil 16.4
York-Pro 16.1

Adjusted Batter Runs
Shaffer-Ind 28.6
Hines-Pro 20.2
Jones-Cin 17.8
York-Pro 16.3
Clapp-Ind 15.3

Clutch Hitting Index
McClellan-Chi 165
Harbidge-Chi 151
Hague-Pro 142
McKelvy-Ind 140
Bond-Bos 131

Runs Created
Hines-Pro 47
Shaffer-Ind 46
Start-Chi 46
Dalrymple-Mil 43
York-Pro 42

Total Average
Hines-Pro .770
Shaffer-Ind .761
York-Pro .715
Brown-Pro .692
Start-Chi .686

Stolen Bases

Stolen Base Average

Stolen Base Runs

Fielding Runs
Burdock-Bos 21.3
Hague-Pro 18.7
Ferguson-Chi 15.9
Kelly-Cin 11.1
Wright-Bos 10.5

Total Player Rating
Shaffer-Ind 3.3
Ferguson-Chi 2.8
Burdock-Bos 2.1
Hines-Pro 1.9
Jones-Cin 1.8

Wins
Bond-Bos 40
W.White-Cin 30
Larkin-Chi 29
Ward-Pro 22
Nolan-Ind 13

Win Percentage
Bond-Bos .678
Ward-Pro .629
W.White-Cin .588
Larkin-Chi .527

Games
Bond-Bos 59
Larkin-Chi 56
W.White-Cin 52
Weaver-Mil 45
Nolan-Ind 38

Complete Games
Bond-Bos 57
Larkin-Chi 56
W.White-Cin 52
Weaver-Mil 39

Shutouts
Bond-Bos 9
Ward-Pro 6
W.White-Cin 5

Saves
Healey-Pro-Ind 1

Innings Pitched
Bond-Bos 532.2
Larkin-Chi 506.0
W.White-Cin 468.0
Weaver-Mil 383.0
Nolan-Ind 347.0

Fewest Hits/Game
Mitchell-Cin 7.76
Ward-Pro 8.30
Weaver-Mil 8.72
Larkin-Chi 9.09
W.White-Cin 9.17

Fewest BB/Game
Weaver-Mil .49
Larkin-Chi .55
Bond-Bos .56
Nichols-Pro .73
W.White-Cin .87

Strikeouts
Bond-Bos 182
W.White-Cin 169
Larkin-Chi 163
Nolan-Ind 125
Ward-Pro 116

Strikeouts/Game
Mitchell-Cin 5.74
Wheeler-Pro 3.63
W.White-Cin 3.25
Nolan-Ind 3.24
Ward-Pro 3.13

Ratio
Weaver-Mil 9.21
Ward-Pro 9.22
Larkin-Chi 9.64
Mitchell-Cin 9.79
W.White-Cin 10.04

Earned Run Average
Ward-Pro 1.51
McCormick-Ind 1.69
W.White-Cin 1.79
Weaver-Mil 1.95
Bond-Bos 2.06

Adjusted ERA
Ward-Pro 146
Weaver-Mil 134
McCormick-Ind 120
W.White-Cin 119
Bond-Bos 114

Opponents' Batting Avg.
Mitchell-Cin .223
Ward-Pro .231
Weaver-Mil .237
Larkin-Chi .246
W.White-Cin .252

Opponents' On-Base Pct.
Weaver-Mil .247
Ward-Pro .251
Larkin-Chi .257
Mitchell-Cin .265
W.White-Cin .269

Starter Runs
Ward-Pro 29.5
W.White-Cin 26.8
Weaver-Mil 15.1
Bond-Bos 14.4
McCormick-Ind 8.0

Adjusted Starter Runs
Ward-Pro 26.9
Weaver-Mil 25.1
W.White-Cin 19.1
Bond-Bos 17.2
Larkin-Chi 9.7

Clutch Pitching Index
McCormick-Ind 152
Healey-Pro-Ind 122
Bond-Bos 119
W.White-Cin 114
Nichols-Pro 112

Relief Runs

Adjusted Relief Runs

Relief Ranking

Total Pitcher Index
Ward-Pro 2.7
Weaver-Mil 2.3
Larkin-Chi 1.7
Bond-Bos 1.3
W.White-Cin .8

Total Baseball Ranking
Shaffer-Ind 3.3
Ferguson-Chi 2.8
Ward-Pro 2.7
Weaver-Mil 2.1
Burdock-Bos 2.1

TEAM	G	W	L	PCT	GB	R	OR	AB	H	2B	3B	HR	BB	SO	AVG	OBP	SLG	OPS	OPS+	BR	BR+	PF	CHI	RC	SB	CS	SBA	SBR
PRO	85	59	25	.702		**612**	355	3392	**1003**	142	**55**	12	**91**	**172**	**.296**	**.314**	**.381**	**695**	**134**	**110**	**120**	98	103	**416**				
BOS	84	54	30	.643	5	562	**348**	3217	883	138	51	**20**	90	222	.274	.294	.368	662	118	68	57	102	**107**	357				
BUF	79	46	32	.590	10	394	365	2906	733	105	54	2	78	314	.252	.272	.328	600	98	1	-9	102	95	265				
CHI	83	46	33	.582	10.5	437	411	3116	808	**167**	32	3	73	294	.259	.276	.336	612	98	14	-12	106	96	297				
CIN	81	43	37	.538	14	485	464	3085	813	127	53	8	66	207	.264	.279	.347	626	115	27	51	95	105	306				
CLE	82	27	55	.329	31	322	461	2987	666	116	29	4	37	214	.223	.232	.285	517	73	-83	-80	99	96	203				
SYR	71	22	48	.314	30	276	462	2611	592	61	19	5	28	238	.227	.235	.270	505	78	-82	-46	89	98	170				
TRO	77	19	56	.253	35.5	321	543	2841	673	102	24	4	45	182	.237	.249	.294	543	87	-54	-29	93	93	213				
TOT	321					3409		24155	6171	958	317	58	508	1843	.256	.271	.329	599										

TEAM	CG	SH	SV	IP	H	H/G	HR	BB	SO	RAT	ERA	ERA+	OAV	OOB	PR	PR+	PF	CPI	FA	E	DP	FW	PW	BW	SBW	DIF
PRO	73	3	**2**	776	765	**8.9**	9	62	**329**	9.6	**2.19**	108	.243	.258	**27**	16	94	99	.902	382	41	1.8	1.5	**11.1**		2.7
BOS	80	**13**	0	753	757	9.1	9	**46**	230	9.6	**2.19**	**114**	.251	.262	26	**25**	100	107	**.913**	**319**	58	**4.9**	**2.4**	5.3		-.4
BUF	78	8	0	713	**698**	**8.9**	**3**	47	198	**9.5**	2.34	112	**.242**	**.254**	13	21	105	87	.906	331	**62**	3.0	2.0	-.8		3.0
CHI	**82**	6	0	744	762	9.3	5	57	211	10.0	2.46	105	.244	.258	3	9	103	86	.900	381	52	1.4	.9	-1.1		5.5
CIN	79	4	0	726	756	9.4	11	81	246	10.4	2.30	102	.248	.267	16	4	93	104	.877	454	48	-3.0	.4	4.8		1.0
CLE	79	3	0	741	818	10.0	4	116	287	11.4	2.65	95	.265	.292	-12	-12	100	**111**	.889	406	42	-.2	-1.1	-7.3		-5.2
SYR	64	5	0	649	775	10.8	4	52	132	11.5	3.19	74	.277	.290	-50	-62	95	96	.873	398	37	-2.6	-5.7	-4.2		-.3
TRO	75	3	0	695	840	10.9	13	47	210	11.5	2.80	89	.275	.286	-23	-22	100	110	.875	460	44	-4.4	-2.0	-2.6		-9.3
TOT	610	45	2	5797		9.6				10.4	2.50		.256	.271					.893	3131	384					

Runs
Jones-Bos 85
Hines-Pro 81
Wright-Pro 79
Kelly-Cin 78
Dickerson-Cin 73

Hits
Hines-Pro 146
O'Rourke-Pro 126
Kelly-Cin 120
Jones-Bos 112
D.White-Cin 110

Doubles
Eden-Cle 31
York-Pro 25
Hines-Pro 25
Dalrymple-Chi 25
Houck-Bos 24

Triples
Dickerson-Cin 14
Williamson-Chi 13
Kelly-Cin 12
O'Rourke-Bos 11

Home Runs
Jones-Bos 9
O'Rourke-Bos 6
Brouthers-Tro 4
Eden-Cle 3

Total Bases
Hines-Pro 197
Jones-Bos 181
Kelly-Cin 170
O'Rourke-Pro 166
O'Rourke-Bos 165

Runs Batted In
O'Rourke-Bos 62
Jones-Bos 62
Dickerson-Cin 57
McVey-Cin 55

Runs Produced
Jones-Bos 138
Hines-Pro 131
Dickerson-Cin 128
O'Rourke-Bos 125
Kelly-Cin 123

Bases On Balls
Jones-Bos 29
Williamson-Chi 24
York-Pro 19
Richardson-Buf 16
Barnes-Cin 16

Batting Average
Anson-Chi .317
Hines-Pro .357
O'Rourke-Pro .348
Kelly-Cin .348
O'Rourke-Bos .341

On-Base Percentage
O'Rourke-Pro .371
Hines-Pro .369
Jones-Bos .367
Kelly-Cin .363
O'Rourke-Bos .357

Slugging Average
O'Rourke-Bos .521
Jones-Bos .510
Kelly-Cin .493
Hines-Pro .482
O'Rourke-Pro .459

On-Base Plus Slugging
O'Rourke-Bos 877
Jones-Bos 877
Kelly-Cin 855
Hines-Pro 851
O'Rourke-Pro 829

Adjusted OPS
Kelly-Cin 188
Jones-Bos 182
O'Rourke-Bos 181
Hines-Pro 181
O'Rourke-Pro 174

Batter Runs
Jones-Bos 33.1
Hines-Pro 32.9
Kelly-Cin 28.1
O'Rourke-Bos 28.0
O'Rourke-Pro 27.2

Adjusted Batter Runs
Hines-Pro 34.3
Kelly-Cin 32.2
Jones-Bos 31.2
O'Rourke-Pro 28.4
O'Rourke-Bos 26.4

Clutch Hitting Index
Gerhardt-Cin 150
McVey-Cin 143
Brown-Pro-Chi 137
Morrill-Bos 124
W.White-Cin 122

Runs Created
Hines-Pro 75
Jones-Bos 68
Kelly-Cin 63
O'Rourke-Pro 63
O'Rourke-Bos 60

Total Average
Jones-Bos .864
O'Rourke-Bos .828
Kelly-Cin .791
Hines-Pro .779
O'Rourke-Pro .758

Stolen Bases

Stolen Base Average

Stolen Base Runs

Fielding Runs
Snyder-Bos 23.9
Wright-Pro 20.5
Shaffer-Chi 20.3
Evans-Tro 17.7
Fulmer-Buf 17.4

Total Player Rating
Kelly-Cin 4.1
Jones-Bos 3.4
Hines-Pro 3.4
Williamson-Chi 3.2
Wright-Pro 3.0

Wins
Ward-Pro 47
W.White-Cin 43
Bond-Bos 43
Galvin-Buf 37
Larkin-Chi 31

Win Percentage
Ward-Pro .712
Bond-Bos .694
Hankinson-Chi .600
W.White-Cin .581
Galvin-Buf .578

Games
W.White-Cin 76
Ward-Pro 70
Galvin-Buf 66
Bond-Bos 64
McCormick-Cle 62

Complete Games
W.White-Cin 75
Galvin-Buf 65
McCormick-Cle 59
Bond-Bos 59
Ward-Pro 58

Shutouts
Bond-Bos 11
Galvin-Buf 6
McCormick-Syr 5
W.White-Cin 4
Larkin-Chi 4

Saves
Ward-Pro 1
Mathews-Pro 1

Innings Pitched
W.White-Cin 680.0
Galvin-Buf 593.0
Ward-Pro 587.0
Bond-Bos 555.1
McCormick-Cle 546.1

Fewest Hits/Game
McGunnigle-Buf 8.48
Ward-Pro 8.75
Bond-Bos 8.80
Galvin-Buf 8.88
W.White-Cin 8.95

Fewest BB/Game
Bond-Bos .39
Galvin-Buf .47
Bradley-Tro .48
Larkin-Chi .53
Ward-Pro .55

Strikeouts
Ward-Pro 239
W.White-Cin 232
McCormick-Cle 197
Bond-Bos 155
Larkin-Chi 142

Strikeouts/Game
McGunnigle-Buf 4.65
Mathews-Pro 4.29
Mitchell-Cle 4.16
Ward-Pro 3.66
McCormick-Cle 3.25

Ratio
Bond-Bos 9.19
Ward-Pro 9.31
Galvin-Buf 9.35
Larkin-Chi 9.54
McGunnigle-Buf 9.68

Earned Run Average
Bond-Bos 1.96
W.White-Cin 1.99
Ward-Pro 2.15
Salisbury-Tro 2.22
Galvin-Buf 2.28

Adjusted ERA
Bond-Bos 127
W.White-Cin 117
Galvin-Buf 115
Salisbury-Tro 112
Ward-Pro 110

Opponents' Batting Avg.
McGunnigle-Buf .235
W.White-Cin .238
Ward-Pro .239
Larkin-Chi .240
Galvin-Buf .243

Opponents' On-Base Pct.
Larkin-Chi .250
Ward-Pro .250
Galvin-Buf .253
W.White-Cin .256
Bond-Bos .259

Starter Runs
W.White-Cin 38.6
Bond-Bos 33.0
Ward-Pro 22.8
Galvin-Buf 14.5
Goldsmith-Tro 6.5

Adjusted Starter Runs
Bond-Bos 32.4
W.White-Cin 28.0
Galvin-Buf 21.2
Ward-Pro 14.5
Larkin-Chi 7.2

Clutch Pitching Index
Salisbury-Tro 125
Mathews-Pro 122
Bond-Bos 117
McCormick-Cle 111
Mitchell-Cle 109

Relief Runs

Adjusted Relief Runs

Relief Ranking

Total Pitcher Index
Bond-Bos 3.8
Ward-Pro 3.0
Galvin-Buf 2.7
McCormick-Cle .7
Goldsmith-Tro .6

Total Baseball Ranking
Kelly-Cin 4.1
Bond-Bos 3.6
Jones-Bos 3.4
Hines-Pro 3.4
Williamson-Chi 3.2

TEAM	G	W	L	PCT	GB	R	OR	AB	H	2B	3B	HR	BB	SO	AVG	OBP	SLG	OPS	OPS+	BR	BR+	PF	CHI	RC	SB	CS	SBA	SBR
CHI	86	67	17	.798		**538**	317	3135	**876**	**164**	39	4	104	217	**.279**	**.303**	**.360**	**663**	**119**	**81**	**53**	106	109	**350**				
PRO	87	52	32	.619	15	419	**299**	3196	793	114	34	8	89	**186**	.248	.268	.313	581	101	-6	8	97	102	275				
CLE	85	47	37	.560	20	387	337	3002	726	130	**52**	7	76	237	.242	.261	.327	588	102	-1	7	98	99	262				
TRO	83	41	42	.494	25.5	392	438	3007	755	114	37	5	**120**	260	.251	.280	.319	599	100	15	-5	105	95	275				
WOR	85	40	43	.482	26.5	412	370	3024	699	129	**52**	8	81	278	.231	.251	.316	567	86	-21	-51	109	**110**	246				
BOS	86	40	44	.476	27	416	456	3080	779	134	41	**20**	105	221	.253	.278	.343	621	115	34	49	97	95	300				
BUF	85	24	58	.293	42	331	502	2962	669	104	37	3	90	327	.226	.249	.289	538	82	-48	-54	102	97	218				
CIN	83	21	59	.263	44	296	472	2895	649	91	36	7	75	267	.224	.244	.288	532	82	-54	-50	99	91	208				
TOT	340					3191		24301	5946	980	328	62	740	1993	.245	.268	.320	587										

TEAM	CG	SH	SV	IP	H	H/G	HR	BB	SO	RAT	ERA	ERA+	OAV	OOB	PR	PR+	PF	CPI	FA	E	DP	FW	PW	BW	SBW	DIF
CHI	80	8	3	775	**622**	**7.3**	8	129	**367**	8.8	1.93	126	**.209**	.242	38	42	102	83	**.913**	**329**	41	**2.4**	4.1	**5.2**		13.5
PRO	75	**13**	3	799	663	7.5	7	**51**	286	**8.1**	**1.65**	**134**	.215	**.228**	**65**	**53**	93	87	.910	357	53	1.1	**5.2**	.8		3.0
CLE	**83**	7	1	759^2	685	8.2	4	98	289	9.3	1.90	124	.228	.253	40	39	99	101	.910	330	52	2.1	3.8	.7		-1.5
TRO	81	4	0	738	760	9.3	8	112	169	10.7	2.75	92	.255	.282	-30	-17	106	100	.900	366	**58**	-.3	-1.6	-.4		2.0
WOR	68	7	**5**	762^2	709	8.4	13	97	297	9.6	2.27	115	.233	.257	9	26	109	94	.906	355	49	.8	2.6	-4.9		.3
BOS	70	4	0	744^2	840	10.2	**2**	86	187	11.2	3.09	74	.276	.296	-59	-70	96	102	.901	367	54	.4	-6.8	4.8		-.2
BUF	72	6	1	739	879	10.8	10	78	186	11.7	3.10	79	.279	.297	-59	-50	104	108	.891	408	55	-2.0	-4.8	-5.2		-4.8
CIN	79	3	0	713^1	785	10.0	10	88	208	11.1	2.44	102	.259	.280	-5	5	105	**116**	.877	437	49	-4.0	.5	-4.8		-10.5
TOT	608	52	13	6031^1		8.9				10.0	2.38		.245	.268					.901	2949	411					

Runs
Dalrymple-Chi 91
Stovey-Wor......... 76
Kelly-Chi 72
J.O'Rourke-Bos 71
Gore-Chi 70

Hits
Dalrymple-Chi....... 126
Anson-Chi.......... 120
Gore-Chi 116
Hines-Pro 115
Connor-Tro 113

Doubles
Dunlap-Cle 27
Dalrymple-Chi....... 25
Anson-Chi 24
Gore-Chi 23
J.O'Rourke-Bos 22

Triples
Stovey-Wor 14
Dalrymple-Chi 12
J.O'Rourke-Bos 11
Hornung-Buf 11
Phillips-Cle 10

Home Runs
Stovey-Wor 6
J.O'Rourke-Bos 6
Jones-Bos 5
Dunlap-Cle 4

Total Bases
Dalrymple-Chi 175
Stovey-Wor 161
J.O'Rourke-Bos 160
Dunlap-Cle.......... 160
Connor-Tro 156

Runs Batted In
Anson-Chi.......... 74
Kelly-Chi 60
Gore-Chi 47
Connor-Tro 47
J.O'Rourke-Bos 45

Runs Produced
Kelly-Chi 131
Dalrymple-Chi....... 127
Anson-Chi.......... 127
Gore-Chi 115
J.O'Rourke-Bos 110

Bases On Balls
Ferguson-Tro 24
J.O'Rourke-Bos 21
Gore-Chi 21
Clapp-Cin 21
Crowley-Buf 19

Batting Average
Gore-Chi 360
Anson-Chi 337
Connor-Tro 332
Dalrymple-Chi......330
Burns-Chi 309

On-Base Percentage
Gore-Chi .... .399
Anson-Chi .... .362
Connor-Tro .... .357
Dalrymple-Chi..... .335
Burns-Chi .... .333

Slugging Average
Gore-Chi .... .463
Connor-Tro .... .459
Dalrymple-Chi .... .458
Stovey-Wor .... .454
J.O'Rourke-Bos ... .441

On-Base Plus Slugging
Gore-Chi 862
Connor-Tro 816
Dalrymple-Chi 793
Anson-Chi......... 781
J.O'Rourke-Bos 756

Adjusted OPS
Gore-Chi 180
Connor-Tro 166
Jones-Bos 159
J.O'Rourke-Bos 158
Dalrymple-Chi...... 156

Batter Runs
Gore-Chi 30.4
Connor-Tro 25.4
Dalrymple-Chi......24.5
Anson-Chi 22.9
J.O'Rourke-Bos 19.9

Adjusted Batter Runs
Gore-Chi 26.2
J.O'Rourke-Bos 22.2
Connor-Tro 22.0
Dalrymple-Chi......20.4
Hines-Pro 19.1

Clutch Hitting Index
Anson-Chi.......... 178
Hotaling-Cle 147
Kelly-Chi 141
Richmond-Wor 131
Creamer-Wor 127

Runs Created
Gore-Chi 61
Dalrymple-Chi 60
Connor-Tro 57
Anson-Chi 55
J.O'Rourke-Bos 52

Total Average
Gore-Chi 825
Connor-Tro 744
Dalrymple-Chi 695
Anson-Chi...........691
J.O'Rourke-Bos 688

Stolen Bases

Stolen Base Average

Stolen Base Runs

Fielding Runs
Irwin-Wor 31.2
Force-Buf.......... 30.9
Bradley-Pro 19.2
Shaffer-Cle 17.2
Clapp-Cin 17.1

Total Player Rating
Irwin-Wor 3.3
Clapp-Cin 3.0
Gore-Chi 2.8
Dunlap-Cle........... 2.6
Shaffer-Cle 2.6

Wins
McCormick-Cle 45
Corcoran-Chi 43
Ward-Pro 39
Welch-Tro 34
Richmond-Wor 32

Win Percentage
Goldsmith-Chi 875
Corcoran-Chi 754
Ward-Pro............619
McCormick-Cle 616
Welch-Tro 531

Games
Richmond-Wor 74
McCormick-Cle 74
Ward-Pro 70
Welch-Tro 65

Complete Games
McCormick-Cle....... 72
Welch-Tro 64
Ward-Pro 59
W.White-Cin 58

Shutouts
Ward-Pro 8
McCormick-Cle 7
Richmond-Wor 5
Galvin-Buf 5

Saves
Richmond-Wor 3
Corey-Wor 2
Corcoran-Chi......... 2
Bradley-Pro 2

Innings Pitched
McCormick-Cle ... 657.2
Ward-Pro 595.0
Richmond-Wor.... 590.2
Welch-Tro 574.0
Corcoran-Chi 536.1

Fewest Hits/Game
Keefe-Tro 5.83
Corcoran-Chi 6.78
Bradley-Pro........ 7.26
Ward-Pro........... 7.58
Corey-Wor.......... 7.95

Fewest BB/Game
Bradley-Pro..........28
Galvin-Buf...........63
Ward-Pro.............68
Wiedman-Buf 71
Goldsmith-Chi 77

Strikeouts
Corcoran-Chi 268
McCormick-Cle...... 260
Richmond-Wor 243
Ward-Pro 230
W.White-Cin 161

Strikeouts/Game
Corcoran-Chi....... 4.50
Goldsmith-Chi...... 3.85
Richmond-Wor 3.70
McCormick-Cle 3.56
Ward-Pro 3.48

Ratio
Keefe-Tro 7.20
Bradley-Pro 7.53
Ward-Pro 8.26
Corcoran-Chi....... 8.44
Goldsmith-Chi 8.86

Earned Run Average
Keefe-Tro 86
Bradley-Pro 1.38
Ward-Pro 1.74
Goldsmith-Chi 1.75
McCormick-Cle 1.85

Adjusted ERA
Keefe-Tro 294
Bradley-Pro........ 160
Goldsmith-Chi 138
McCormick-Cle 127
Ward-Pro........... 127

Opponents' Batting Avg.
Keefe-Tro 178
Corcoran-Chi 199
Bradley-Pro.........210
Ward-Pro............217
Corey-Wor...........219

Opponents' On-Base Pct.
Keefe-Tro...........212
Bradley-Pro.........217
Ward-Pro............232
Corcoran-Chi 236
Corey-Wor...........239

Starter Runs
Ward-Pro 42.0
McCormick-Cle...... 38.5
Corcoran-Chi....... 25.5
Bradley-Pro 21.7
Keefe-Tro 17.7

Adjusted Starter Runs
McCormick-Cle 37.1
Ward-Pro 33.2
Corcoran-Chi....... 27.8
Richmond-Wor 26.9
Bradley-Pro 19.4

Clutch Pitching Index
W.White-Cin 124
Bond-Bos 114
Poorman-Buf-Chi... 112
Galvin-Buf......... 111
Goldsmith-Chi 109

Relief Runs

Adjusted Relief Runs

Relief Ranking

Total Pitcher Index
McCormick-Cle......4.0
Ward-Pro 3.6
Corcoran-Chi....... 3.1
Keefe-Tro 2.1
Bradley-Pro.........2.1

Total Baseball Ranking
Ward-Pro 4.4
McCormick-Cle 3.8
Bradley-Pro 3.5
Irwin-Wor 3.3
Clapp-Cin 3.0

TEAM	G	W	L	PCT	GB	R	OR	AB	H	2B	3B	HR	BB	SO	AVG	OBP	SLG	OPS	OPS+	BR	BR+	PF	CHI	RC	SB	CS	SBA	SBR
CHI	84	56	28	.667		**550**	**379**	3114	**918**	**157**	36	12	140	224	**.295**	**.325**	**.380**	**705**	**119**	**85**	**61**	105	**105**	**394**				
PRO	85	47	37	.560	9	447	426	3077	780	144	37	11	**146**	214	.253	.287	.335	622	100	-4	3	98	104	304				
BUF	83	45	38	.542	10.5	440	447	3019	797	**157**	50	12	108	270	.264	.289	.361	650	109	22	28	99	99	323				
DET	84	41	43	.488	15	439	429	2995	780	131	**53**	**17**	136	250	.260	.293	.357	650	103	22	5	104	99	320				
TRO	85	39	45	.464	17	399	429	3046	754	124	31	5	140	240	.248	.281	.314	595	86	-32	-52	105	100	275				
BOS	83	38	45	.458	17.5	349	410	2916	733	121	27	5	110	193	.251	.279	.317	596	94	-31	-13	95	93	264				
CLE	85	36	48	.429	20	392	414	3117	796	120	39	7	132	224	.255	.286	.326	612	100	-16	8	95	93	297				
WOR	83	32	50	.390	23	410	492	3093	781	114	31	7	121	**169**	.253	.281	.316	597	86	-31	-53	106	102	281				
TOT	336					3426		24377	6339	1068	304	76	1033	1784	.261	.289	.339	627										

TEAM	CG	SH	SV	IP	H	H/G	HR	BB	SO	RAT	ERA	ERA+	OAV	OOB	PR	PR+	PF	CPI	FA	E	DP	FW	PW	BW	SBW	DIF
CHI	81	9	0	744^{2}	**722**	**8.8**	14	122	228	**10.3**	2.43	**113**	**.243**	**.273**	29	**26**	99	97	.916	**309**	54	2.1	**2.5**	**5.8**		3.9
PRO	76	7	0	757^{2}	756	9.0	**5**	138	264	10.7	**2.40**	111	**.243**	.275	**32**	22	96	94	.896	390	66	-2.0	2.1	.3		4.7
BUF	72	5	0	742^{1}	881	10.7	9	**89**	185	11.8	2.84	98	.281	.301	-5	-5	100	**113**	.892	408	48	-3.4	-.4	2.7		4.8
DET	83	**10**	0	744^{2}	785	9.5	8	137	**265**	11.2	2.65	110	.257	.289	11	21	105	102	.906	338	**80**	.6	2.0	.5		-3.9
TRO	**85**	8	0	771	805	9.4	11	161	207	11.3	2.97	99	.263	.299	-16	-2	106	100	**.917**	311	70	**2.2**	-.1	-4.8		-.0
BOS	72	6	**3**	730^{2}	763	9.4	9	143	199	11.2	2.71	98	.258	.292	5	-4	96	103	.909	325	54	1.0	-.3	-1.2		-2.8
CLE	82	2	0	760	737	**8.8**	9	126	240	**10.3**	2.68	98	.244	.274	8	-5	94	87	.904	348	68	.3	-.4	.8		-6.4
WOR	80	5	0	737^{1}	882	10.8	11	120	196	12.3	3.54	85	.288	.315	-63	-39	109	101	.903	353	50	-.4	-3.6	-4.9		.1
TOT	631	52	3	5988^{1}		9.6				11.1	2.78		.261	.289					.906	2782	490					

Runs
Gore-Chi 86
Kelly-Chi 84
Dalrymple-Chi 72
O'Rourke-Buf 71
Farrell-Pro 69

Hits
Anson-Chi 137
Dalrymple-Chi 117
Dickerson-Wor 116

Doubles
Kelly-Chi 27
Hines-Pro 27
Stovey-Wor 25
Dunlap-Cle 25
White-Buf 24

Triples
Rowe-Buf 11
Phillips-Cle 10

Home Runs
Brouthers-Buf 8
Bennett-Det 7
Farrell-Pro 5
Burns-Chi 4

Total Bases
Anson-Chi 175
Dunlap-Cle 156
Kelly-Chi 153
Dalrymple-Chi 150
Dickerson-Wor 149

Runs Batted In
Anson-Chi 82
Bennett-Det 64
Kelly-Chi 55

Runs Produced
Anson-Chi 148
Kelly-Chi 137
Gore-Chi 129
Knight-Det 118
Richardson-Buf 113

Bases On Balls
Clapp-Cle 35
York-Pro 29
Ferguson-Tro 29
Farrell-Pro 29

Batting Average
Anson-Chi 399
Powell-Det 338
Rowe-Buf 333
Start-Pro 328
Dunlap-Cle 325

On-Base Percentage
Anson-Chi 442
York-Pro 362
Brouthers-Buf 361
Dunlap-Cle 358
Gore-Chi 354

Slugging Average
Brouthers-Buf 541
Anson-Chi 510
Rowe-Buf 480
Bennett-Det 478
Dunlap-Cle 444

On-Base Plus Slugging
Anson-Chi 952
Brouthers-Buf 902
Bennett-Det 819
Dunlap-Cle 802
York-Pro 790

Adjusted OPS
Anson-Chi 189
Brouthers-Buf 182
Dunlap-Cle 159
York-Pro 150
Bennett-Det 149

Batter Runs
Anson-Chi 38.9
Brouthers-Buf 24.1
Dunlap-Cle 20.0
Bennett-Det 18.3
Kelly-Chi 18.0

Adjusted Batter Runs
Anson-Chi 34.8
Brouthers-Buf 25.0
Dunlap-Cle 23.9
York-Pro 18.9
O'Rourke-Buf 16.0

Clutch Hitting Index
Knight-Det 164
Anson-Chi 145
Ward-Pro 143
Radbourn-Pro 135
White-Buf 128

Runs Created
Anson-Chi 79
Dunlap-Cle 57
Kelly-Chi 55
Brouthers-Buf 54
Dalrymple-Chi 54

Total Average
Anson-Chi 976
Brouthers-Buf 891
Bennett-Det 770
York-Pro 745
Dunlap-Cle 734

Stolen Bases

Stolen Base Average

Stolen Base Runs

Fielding Runs
Ewing-Tro 25.3
Richardson-Buf 24.6
Force-Buf 24.3
Williamson-Chi 22.2
Bennett-Det 18.3

Total Player Rating
Anson-Chi 3.5
Bennett-Det 3.3
Dunlap-Cle 3.1
Richardson-Buf 3.0
Williamson-Chi 2.3

Wins
Whitney-Bos 31
Corcoran-Chi 31
Derby-Det 29
Galvin-Buf 28
McCormick-Cle 26

Win Percentage
Radbourn-Pro 694
Corcoran-Chi 689
Goldsmith-Chi 649
Welch-Tro 538
Galvin-Buf 538

Games
Whitney-Bos 66
McCormick-Cle 59
Galvin-Buf 56
Derby-Det 56
Richmond-Wor 53

Complete Games
Whitney-Bos 57
McCormick-Cle 57
Derby-Det 55
Richmond-Wor 50
Galvin-Buf 48

Shutouts
Derby-Det 9
Whitney-Bos 6
Goldsmith-Chi 5
Galvin-Buf 5

Saves
Mathews-Pro-Bos 2
Morrill-Bos 1

Innings Pitched
Whitney-Bos 552.1
McCormick-Cle . . . 526.0
Derby-Det 494.2
Galvin-Buf 474.0
Richmond-Wor 462.1

Fewest Hits/Game
McCormick-Cle 8.28
Wiedman-Det 8.45
Radbourn-Pro 8.55
Corcoran-Chi 8.62
Ward-Pro 8.89

Fewest BB/Game
Galvin-Buf 87
Wiedman-Det 94
Goldsmith-Chi 1.20
Richmond-Wor 1.32
McCormick-Cle 1.44

Strikeouts
Derby-Det 212
McCormick-Cle 178
Whitney-Bos 162
Richmond-Wor 156
Corcoran-Chi 150

Strikeouts/Game
Derby-Det 3.86
Corcoran-Chi 3.40
Ward-Pro 3.25
Radbourn-Pro 3.24
McCormick-Cle 3.05

Ratio
Wiedman-Det 9.39
McCormick-Cle 9.72
Goldsmith-Chi 10.15
Radbourn-Pro 10.32
Ward-Pro 10.34

Earned Run Average
Wiedman-Det 1.80
Ward-Pro 2.13
Derby-Det 2.20
Corcoran-Chi 2.31
Galvin-Buf 2.37

Adjusted ERA
Wiedman-Det 162
Derby-Det 132
Ward-Pro 125
Corcoran-Chi 118
Galvin-Buf 117

Opponents' Batting Avg.
Radbourn-Pro 235
McCormick-Cle 235
Wiedman-Det 238
Corcoran-Chi 242
Ward-Pro 242

Opponents' On-Base Pct.
Wiedman-Det 258
McCormick-Cle 265
Radbourn-Pro 270
Goldsmith-Chi 271
Ward-Pro 271

Starter Runs
Derby-Det 31.5
Ward-Pro 23.7
Galvin-Buf 21.1
Corcoran-Chi 20.3
McCormick-Cle 19.1

Adjusted Starter Runs
Derby-Det 37.4
Galvin-Buf 21.2
Ward-Pro 20.2
Corcoran-Chi 18.9
Wiedman-Det 13.6

Clutch Pitching Index
Galvin-Buf 123
Derby-Det 112
Wiedman-Det 109
Fox-Bos 108
Lynch-Buf 106

Relief Runs

Adjusted Relief Runs

Relief Ranking

Total Pitcher Index
Derby-Det 2.8
Ward-Pro 2.6
Galvin-Buf 2.6
Whitney-Bos 1.9
Corcoran-Chi 1.4

Total Baseball Ranking
Anson-Chi 3.5
Bennett-Det 3.3
Dunlap-Cle 3.1
Richardson-Buf 3.0
Derby-Det 2.6

TEAM	G	W	L	PCT	GB	R	OR	AB	H	2B	3B	HR	BB	SO	AVG	OBP	SLG	OPS	OPS+	BR	BR+	PF	CHI	RC	SB	CS	SBA	SBR
CHI	84	55	29	.655		**604**	**353**	3225	**892**	**209**	54	15	**142**	262	**.277**	**.307**	**.389**	**696**	**119**	**82**	**57**	105	**108**	**395**				
PRO	84	52	32	.619	3	463	356	3104	776	121	53	11	102	255	.250	.274	.334	608	96	-16	-15	100	105	291				
BUF	84	45	39	.536	10	500	461	3128	858	146	47	18	116	**228**	.274	.300	.368	668	113	50	41	102	98	355				
BOS	85	45	39	.536	10	472	414	3118	823	114	50	15	134	244	.264	.294	.347	641	107	23	22	100	97	326				
CLE	84	42	40	.512	12	402	411	3009	716	139	40	**20**	122	261	.238	.268	.331	599	96	-24	-10	97	95	273				
DET	86	42	41	.506	12.5	407	488	3144	724	117	44	19	122	308	.230	.259	.314	573	84	-53	-52	100	99	262				
TRO	85	35	48	.422	19.5	430	522	3057	747	116	**59**	12	109	298	.244	.270	.333	603	99	-20	2	95	100	282				
WOR	84	18	66	.214	37	379	652	2984	689	109	57	16	113	303	.231	.259	.322	581	85	-43	-52	102	95	255				
TOT	338					3657		24769	6225	1071	404	126	960	2159	.252	.280	.343	622										

TEAM	CG	SH	SV	IP	H	H/G	HR	BB	SO	RAT	ERA	ERA+	OAV	OOB	PR	PR+	PF	CPI	FA	E	DP	FW	PW	BW	SBW	DIF
CHI	**83**	7	0	763^{2}	**667**	**7.9**	13	102	279	**9.1**	**2.22**	**129**	**.221**	**.246**	**57**	**52**	99	87	.898	376	54	.2	**4.8**	**5.2**		3.0
PRO	80	**10**	**1**	752	690	8.3	12	87	273	9.3	2.28	123	.228	.250	51	48	97	94	.901	371	67	.4	4.4	-1.3		6.7
BUF	79	3	0	737	778	9.6	16	114	287	10.9	3.25	90	.254	.280	-30	-30	101	89	**.910**	315	42	3.3	-2.7	3.8		-1.2
BOS	81	4	0	749	738	8.9	**10**	**77**	352	9.8	2.80	102	.239	.258	7	4	99	83	**.910**	**314**	37	**3.6**	.4	2.0		-2.9
CLE	81	4	0	751^{2}	743	8.9	22	132	232	10.5	2.76	101	.249	.280	11	1	97	106	.905	358	**71**	1.1	.1	-.9		.8
DET	82	7	0	793	808	9.2	19	129	**354**	10.7	2.99	98	.248	.277	-9	-8	101	94	.893	396	44	-.4	-.7	-4.7		6.4
TRO	81	6	0	758	836	10.0	13	165	184	11.9	3.08	91	.267	.304	-16	-24	98	112	.887	432	70	-2.5	-2.1	.2		-1.9
WOR	75	0	0	738^{1}	964	11.8	21	151	195	13.6	3.76	83	.294	.325	-71	-51	107	**115**	.878	468	66	-4.6	-4.6	-4.7		-10.0
TOT	642	41	1	6042^{2}		9.3				10.7	2.89		.252	.280					.898	3030	451					

Runs
Gore-Chi 99
Dalrymple-Chi 96
Stovey-Wor 90
Kelly-Chi 81
Purcell-Buf 79

Hits
Brouthers-Buf 129
Anson-Chi 126

Doubles
Kelly-Chi 37
Anson-Chi 29
Hines-Pro 28
Williamson-Chi 27
Glasscock-Cle 27

Triples
Connor-Tro 18
Wood-Det 12
Corey-Wor 12

Home Runs
Wood-Det 7
Muldoon-Cle 6
Brouthers-Buf 6

Total Bases
Brouthers-Buf 192
Connor-Tro 185
Hines-Pro 177
Anson-Chi 174
Dalrymple-Chi 167

Runs Batted In
Anson-Chi 83
Brouthers-Buf 63
Williamson-Chi 60
Richardson-Buf 57
Kelly-Chi 55

Runs Produced
Anson-Chi 151
Gore-Chi 147
Kelly-Chi 135
Dalrymple-Chi 131
Brouthers-Buf 128

Bases On Balls
Gore-Chi 29
Williamson-Chi 27
Shaffer-Cle 27
Hanlon-Det 26

Batting Average
Brouthers-Buf .... .368
Anson-Chi .... .362
Connor-Tro .... .330
Start-Pro .... .329
Whitney-Bos .... .323

On-Base Percentage
Brouthers-Buf .... .403
Anson-Chi .... .397
Whitney-Bos .... .382
Gore-Chi .... .369
Connor-Tro .... .354

Slugging Average
Brouthers-Buf .... .547
Connor-Tro .... .530
Whitney-Bos .... .510
Anson-Chi .... .500
Hines-Pro .... .467

On-Base Plus Slugging
Brouthers-Buf 950
Anson-Chi 897
Whitney-Bos 892
Connor-Tro 884
Hines-Pro 793

Adjusted OPS
Brouthers-Buf 198
Connor-Tro 188
Whitney-Bos 183
Anson-Chi 177
Hines-Pro 151

Batter Runs
Brouthers-Buf 39.1
Anson-Chi 32.7
Connor-Tro 29.7
Whitney-Bos 23.7
Gore-Chi 22.2

Adjusted Batter Runs
Brouthers-Buf 37.5
Connor-Tro 33.7
Anson-Chi 29.0
Whitney-Bos 23.5
Hines-Pro 20.7

Clutch Hitting Index
Pfeffer-Tro 147
Holbert-Tro 146
Anson-Chi 143
Rowen-Bos 129
Hayes-Wor 128

Runs Created
Brouthers-Buf 79
Anson-Chi 71
Connor-Tro 67
Hines-Pro 59
Gore-Chi 59

Total Average
Brouthers-Buf .... .959
Whitney-Bos .... .894
Anson-Chi .... .874
Connor-Tro .... .846
Gore-Chi .... .736

Stolen Bases

Stolen Base Average

Stolen Base Runs

Fielding Runs
Glasscock-Cle 24.1
A.Irwin-Wor 20.5
Evans-Wor 19.8
Dunlap-Cle 17.6
Williamson-Chi 16.2

Total Player Rating
Glasscock-Cle 4.0
Connor-Tro 2.9
Bennett-Det 2.8
Brouthers-Buf 2.8
Dunlap-Cle 2.7

Wins
McCormick-Cle 36
Radbourn-Pro 33
Goldsmith-Chi 28
Galvin-Buf 28
Corcoran-Chi 27

Win Percentage
Corcoran-Chi .... .692
Radbourn-Pro .... .635
Goldsmith-Chi ...... .622
Ward-Pro .... .594
Mathews-Bos .... .559

Games
McCormick-Cle 68
Radbourn-Pro 54
Galvin-Buf 52
Whitney-Bos 49
Richmond-Wor 48

Complete Games
McCormick-Cle 65
Radbourn-Pro 50
Galvin-Buf 48
Whitney-Bos 46
Goldsmith-Chi 45

Shutouts
Radbourn-Pro 6
Welch-Tro 5

Saves
Ward-Pro 1

Innings Pitched
McCormick-Cle ... 595.2
Radbourn-Pro 466.0
Galvin-Buf 445.1
Whitney-Bos 420.0

Fewest Hits/Game
Corcoran-Chi 7.11
Radbourn-Pro 8.15
McCormick-Cle 8.31
Goldsmith-Chi 8.38
Ward-Pro 8.43

Fewest BB/Game
Mathews-Bos .... .69
Galvin-Buf .... .81
Goldsmith-Chi .... .84
Wiedman-Det .... .85
Whitney-Bos .... .88

Strikeouts
Radbourn-Pro 201
McCormick-Cle 200
Derby-Det 182
Whitney-Bos 180
Corcoran-Chi 170

Strikeouts/Game
Mathews-Bos 4.83
Derby-Det 4.52
Corcoran-Chi 4.30
Daily-Buf 4.08
Radbourn-Pro 3.88

Ratio
Corcoran-Chi 8.70
Radbourn-Pro 9.14
Goldsmith-Chi 9.22
Wiedman-Det 9.42
Mathews-Bos 9.47

Earned Run Average
Corcoran-Chi 1.95
Radbourn-Pro 2.11
McCormick-Cle 2.37
Goldsmith-Chi 2.42
Keefe-Tro 2.49

Adjusted ERA
Corcoran-Chi 147
Radbourn-Pro 133
Goldsmith-Chi 118
McCormick-Cle 117
Keefe-Tro 113

Opponents' Batting Avg.
Corcoran-Chi .... .200
Radbourn-Pro ...... .226
Ward-Pro .... .232
Mathews-Bos ...... .232
Daily-Buf .... .234

Opponents' On-Base Pct.
Corcoran-Chi .... .234
Mathews-Bos ...... .246
Radbourn-Pro ...... .247
Wiedman-Det ...... .253
Goldsmith-Chi ...... .254

Starter Runs
Radbourn-Pro 40.4
Corcoran-Chi 37.0
McCormick-Cle 33.9
Goldsmith-Chi 20.8
Keefe-Tro 16.5

Adjusted Starter Runs
Radbourn-Pro 37.1
Corcoran-Chi 36.2
McCormick-Cle 28.4
Goldsmith-Chi 19.7
Keefe-Tro 13.9

Clutch Pitching Index
Egan-Tro 120
Richmond-Wor 116
Mountain-Wor 115
Welch-Tro 113
Corey-Wor 112

Relief Runs

Adjusted Relief Runs

Relief Ranking

Total Pitcher Index
Radbourn-Pro 3.4
Corcoran-Chi 3.2
Whitney-Bos 3.1
Keefe-Tro 2.3
McCormick-Cle 2.1

Total Baseball Ranking
Glasscock-Cle 4.0
Radbourn-Pro 3.2
Corcoran-Chi 3.2
Whitney-Bos 3.1
Connor-Tro 2.9

TEAM	G	W	L	PCT	GB	R	OR	AB	H	2B	3B	HR	BB	SO	AVG	OBP	SLG	OPS	OPS+	BR	BR+	PF	CHI	RC	SB	CS	SBA	SBR
CIN	80	55	25	.688		**489**	**268**	3007	**795**	95	47	5	102	204	**.264**	.289	.332	621	107	**38**	13	106	**104**	**295**				
PHI	75	41	34	.547	11.5	406	389	2707	660	89	21	5	125	**164**	.244	.277	.298	575	88	-4	-45	112	**104**	229				
LOU	80	42	38	.525	13	443	352	2806	728	**110**	28	9	**128**	193	.259	**.292**	.328	620	**120**	37	**63**	95	99	275				
PIT	79	39	39	.500	15	428	418	2904	730	**110**	**59**	**18**	90	183	.251	.274	**.348**	**622**	118	35	57	95	95	284				
STL	80	37	43	.463	18	399	496	2865	663	87	41	11	112	226	.231	.260	.302	562	90	-19	-34	104	101	231				
BAL	74	19	54	.260	32.5	273	515	2583	535	60	24	4	72	215	.207	.229	.254	483	72	-87	-63	92	97	153				
TOT	234					2438		16872	4111	551	220	52	629	1185	.244	.271	.312	582										

TEAM	CG	SH	SV	IP	H	H/G	HR	BB	SO	RAT	ERA	ERA+	OAV	OOB	PR	PR+	PF	CPI	FA	E	DP	FW	PW	BW	SBW	DIF
CIN	**77**	**11**	0	721^1	**609**	**7.6**	7	125	165	**9.2**	**1.65**	**160**	**.214**	**.247**	**83**	**80**	98	**119**	**.907**	**332**	41	**3.8**	**7.4**	1.2		2.8
PHI	72	2	0	663	682	9.3	13	99	190	10.7	2.98	100	.249	.275	-21	0	111	97	.895	361	36	1.2	.0	-4.1		6.5
LOU	73	6	0	693^1	637	8.3	6	112	240	9.8	2.03	122	.229	.259	51	37	92	113	.893	385	**57**	1.3	3.4	**5.8**		-8.4
PIT	**77**	2	0	696^2	694	9.0	**4**	**82**	**252**	10.1	2.80	93	.243	.264	-8	-15	97	90	.889	397	40	.5	-1.3	5.3		-4.3
STL	75	3	**1**	688^1	729	9.6	7	103	225	10.9	2.92	96	.254	.280	-18	-8	105	101	.875	446	41	-1.5	-.7	-3.1		2.5
BAL	64	1	0	646^1	760	10.6	15	108	113	12.1	3.89	71	.275	.302	-86	-80	102	94	.859	490	41	-5.0	-7.3	-5.7		.7
TOT	438	25	1	4109		9.1				10.4	2.69		.244	.271					.887	2411	256					

Runs
Swartwood-Pit 86
Sommer-Cin 82
Carpenter-Cin 78
Browning-Lou 67
Birchall-Phi 65

Hits
Carpenter-Cin 120
Browning-Lou 109
Swartwood-Pit 107
Sommer-Cin 102
B.Gleason-StL 100

Doubles
Swartwood-Pit 18
Mansell-Pit 18
Browning-Lou 17
Taylor-Pit 16
Cuthbert-StL 16

Triples
Mansell-Pit 16
Taylor-Pit 13
Wheeler-Cin 11
Swartwood-Pit 11
Wolf-Lou 8

Home Runs
Walker-StL 7
Browning-Lou 5
Swartwood-Pit 4

Total Bases
Swartwood-Pit 159
Mansell-Pit 152
Carpenter-Cin 148
Browning-Lou 147
Taylor-Pit 135

Runs Batted In

Runs Produced
Carpenter-Cin 144
Sommer-Cin 110
Comiskey-StL 102
Snyder-Cin 98
Birchall-Phi 92

Bases On Balls
J.Gleason-StL 27
Browning-Lou 26
Sommer-Cin 24
J.Reccius-Lou 23
Swartwood-Pit 21

Batting Average
Browning-Lou .... .378
Carpenter-Cin ...... .342
Swartwood-Pit ...... .329
O'Brien-Phi .... .303
Wolf-Lou .... .299

On-Base Percentage
Browning-Lou ...... .430
Swartwood-Pit ..... .370
Carpenter-Cin ...... .360
O'Brien-Phi .... .339
Sommer-Cin .... .333

Slugging Average
Browning-Lou ...... .510
Swartwood-Pit ..... .489
Taylor-Pit .... .452
Mansell-Pit .... .438
Carpenter-Cin ...... .422

On-Base Plus Slugging
Browning-Lou 940
Swartwood-Pit 859
Carpenter-Cin 782
O'Brien-Phi 758
Taylor-Pit 749

Adjusted OPS
Browning-Lou 228
Swartwood-Pit 197
Taylor-Pit 157
Carpenter-Cin 154
Mansell-Pit 150

Batter Runs
Browning-Lou 35.3
Swartwood-Pit 29.3
Carpenter-Cin 22.0
Taylor-Pit 14.5
Mansell-Pit 14.5

Adjusted Batter Runs
Browning-Lou 39.9
Swartwood-Pit 33.1
Carpenter-Cin 18.2
Mansell-Pit 17.5
Taylor-Pit 17.2

Clutch Hitting Index

Runs Created
Browning-Lou 65
Swartwood-Pit 60
Carpenter-Cin 55
Mansell-Pit 45
Sommer-Cin 44

Total Average
Browning-Lou ...... .966
Swartwood-Pit ..... .826
Carpenter-Cin ...... .684
O'Brien-Phi .... .679
Taylor-Pit .... .660

Stolen Bases

Stolen Base Average

Stolen Base Runs

Fielding Runs
Stricker-Phi 22.5
Snyder-Cin 19.4
White-Cin 12.0
Browning-Lou 11.8
O'Brien-Phi 11.4

Total Player Rating
Browning-Lou 4.8
Snyder-Cin 2.7
O'Brien-Phi 2.1
Swartwood-Pit 2.1
Mansell-Pit 1.7

Wins
White-Cin 40
Mullane-Lou 30
Weaver-Phi 26
McGinnis-StL 25
Salisbury-Pit 20

Win Percentage
White-Cin .... .769
Weaver-Phi .... .634
McGinnis-StL .... .581
Mullane-Lou .... .556
Salisbury-Pit .... .526

Games
Mullane-Lou 55
White-Cin 54
McGinnis-StL 45
Landis-Phi-Bal 44
Weaver-Phi 42

Complete Games
White-Cin 52
Mullane-Lou 51
McGinnis-StL 43
Weaver-Phi 41
Salisbury-Pit 38

Shutouts
White-Cin 8
Mullane-Lou 5
McGinnis-StL 3
McCormick-Cin 3
Weaver-Phi 2

Saves
Fusselback-StL 1

Innings Pitched
White-Cin 480.0
Mullane-Lou 460.1
McGinnis-StL 388.1
Weaver-Phi 371.0
Landis-Phi-Bal 360.0

Fewest Hits/Game
Hecker-Lou 6.49
McCormick-Cin 7.25
Driscoll-Pit 7.25
White-Cin 7.71
Geis-Bal 7.90

Fewest BB/Game
Hecker-Lou .... .43
Driscoll-Pit .... .54
Weaver-Phi .... .85
Salisbury-Pit .... .99
Landis-Phi-Bal 1.17

Strikeouts
Mullane-Lou 170
Salisbury-Pit 135
McGinnis-StL 134
White-Cin 122
Weaver-Phi 104

Strikeouts/Game
Salisbury-Pit 3.63
Arundel-Pit 3.53
Mullane-Lou 3.32
McGinnis-StL 3.11
J.Reccius-Lou 2.94

Ratio
Hecker-Lou 6.92
Driscoll-Pit 7.79
McCormick-Cin 8.97
White-Cin 9.04
Salisbury-Pit 9.46

Earned Run Average
Driscoll-Pit 1.21
Hecker-Lou 1.30
McCormick-Cin 1.52
White-Cin 1.54
Mullane-Lou 1.88

Adjusted ERA
Driscoll-Pit 216
Hecker-Lou 191
McCormick-Cin 174
White-Cin 172
Mullane-Lou 132

Opponents' Batting Avg.
Hecker-Lou .... .188
McCormick-Cin .... .206
Driscoll-Pit .... .206
White-Cin .... .216
Geis-Bal .... .220

Opponents' On-Base Pct.
Hecker-Lou .... .199
Driscoll-Pit .... .218
McCormick-Cin ..... .243
White-Cin .... .244
Salisbury-Pit .... .253

Starter Runs
White-Cin 61.1
Mullane-Lou 41.2
Driscoll-Pit 32.9
McCormick-Cin 28.5
Hecker-Lou 16.0

Adjusted Starter Runs
White-Cin 59.7
Mullane-Lou 33.2
Driscoll-Pit 32.1
McCormick-Cin 27.8
Hecker-Lou 14.8

Clutch Pitching Index
White-Cin 124
McCormick-Cin 124
Mullane-Lou 120
J.Reccius-Lou 119
Driscoll-Pit 113

Relief Runs

Adjusted Relief Runs

Relief Ranking

Total Pitcher Index
White-Cin 7.4
Mullane-Lou 5.4
Driscoll-Pit 2.5
Hecker-Lou 2.2
McCormick-Cin 2.2

Total Baseball Ranking
White-Cin 7.3
Mullane-Lou 5.3
Browning-Lou 4.8
Snyder-Cin 2.7
Hecker-Lou 2.5

TEAM	G	W	L	PCT	GB	R	OR	AB	H	2B	3B	HR	BB	SO	AVG	OBP	SLG	OPS	OPS+	BR	BR+	PF	CHI	RC	SB	CS	SBA	SBR
BOS	98	63	35	.643		669	456	3657	1010	209	**86**	**34**	123	423	.276	.300	**.408**	**708**	**114**	**68**	**53**	102	104	**459**				
CHI	98	59	39	.602	4	**679**	540	3658	1000	**277**	61	13	129	399	.273	.298	.393	691	104	49	2	108	**109**	439				
PRO	98	58	40	.592	5	636	**436**	3685	1001	189	59	21	149	309	.272	.300	.372	672	104	29	13	103	104	422				
CLE	100	55	42	.567	7.5	476	443	3457	852	184	38	8	139	374	.246	.276	.329	605	88	-53	-47	99	97	321				
BUF	98	52	45	.536	10.5	614	576	3729	**1058**	184	59	8	147	342	**.284**	**.311**	.371	682	108	44	30	102	97	441				
NY	98	46	50	.479	16	530	577	3524	900	139	69	24	127	**297**	.255	.281	.354	635	96	-18	-12	99	99	360				
DET	101	40	58	.408	23	524	650	3726	931	164	48	13	**166**	378	.250	.282	.330	612	93	-46	-20	95	96	355				
PHI	99	17	81	.173	46	437	887	3576	859	181	48	3	141	355	.240	.269	.320	589	90	-74	-27	91	89	316				
TOT	395					4565		29012	7611	1527	468	124	1121	2877	.263	.290	.361	650										

TEAM	CG	SH	SV	IP	H	H/G	HR	BB	SO	RAT	ERA	ERA+	OAV	OOB	PR	PR+	PF	CPI	FA	E	DP	FW	PW	BW	SBW	DIF
BOS	89	**6**	**3**	860	853	9.0	11	**90**	**538**	9.9	2.56	121	.245	.264	56	53	99	96	.901	409	58	3.2	4.7	**4.7**		1.6
CHI	91	5	1	862	942	9.9	21	123	299	11.2	2.78	119	.260	.284	34	45	105	109	.879	543	76	-3.4	4.0	.2		9.4
PRO	88	4	1	871	827	8.6	12	111	376	**9.7**	2.37	130	.238	**.262**	75	70	98	99	.903	419	75	2.7	6.2	1.2		-.8
CLE	**92**	5	2	879	**818**	**8.4**	**7**	217	402	10.6	**2.23**	**142**	**.237**	.282	**89**	**92**	100	**118**	**.909**	**389**	69	**4.7**	**8.1**	-4.1		-2.0
BUF	90	5	2	859[1]	971	10.2	12	101	362	11.3	3.33	96	.268	.288	-17	-8	101	97	.896	445	52	1.4	-.6	2.7		.3
NY	87	5	0	866	907	9.5	19	170	323	11.2	2.95	105	.253	.287	19	11	99	101	.889	468	52	.3	1.0	-1.0		-2.1
DET	89	5	2	894[1]	1026	10.4	22	184	324	12.2	3.59	87	.270	.303	-44	-49	99	98	.893	470	**77**	.9	-4.2	-1.7		-3.8
PHI	91	3	0	864[2]	1267	13.2	20	125	253	14.5	5.34	58	.318	.338	-212	-219	98	92	.858	639	62	-7.9	-19.1	-2.3		-2.5
TOT	717	38	11	6956[1]		9.9				11.3	3.14		.263	.290					.891	3782	521					

Runs
Hornung-Bos 107
Gore-Chi 105
O'Rourke-Buf 102
Sutton-Bos 101
Hines-Pro 94

Hits
Brouthers-Buf 159
Connor-NY 146
O'Rourke-Buf 143
Sutton-Bos 134
Wood-Det 133

Doubles
Williamson-Chi 49
Brouthers-Buf 41
Burns-Chi 37
Anson-Chi 36

Triples
Brouthers-Buf 17
Morrill-Bos 16
Sutton-Bos 15
Connor-NY 15

Home Runs
Ewing-NY 10
Hornung-Bos 8
Denny-Pro 8
Ward-NY 7
Morrill-Bos 6

Total Bases
Brouthers-Buf 243
Morrill-Bos 212
Connor-NY 207
Sutton-Bos 201
Hornung-Bos 199

Runs Batted In
Brouthers-Buf 97
Burdock-Bos 88
Sutton-Bos 73
Morrill-Bos 68
Anson-Chi 68

Runs Produced
Brouthers-Buf 179
Sutton-Bos 171
Hornung-Bos 165
Burdock-Bos 163
Gore-Chi 155

Bases On Balls
York-Cle 37
Hanlon-Det 34
Powell-Det 28
Shaffer-Buf 27
Gore-Chi 27

Batting Average
Brouthers-Buf 374
Connor-NY 357
Gore-Chi 334
Burdock-Bos 330
O'Rourke-Buf 328

On-Base Percentage
Brouthers-Buf 397
Connor-NY 394
Gore-Chi 377
Dunlap-Cle 361
Burdock-Bos 353

Slugging Average
Brouthers-Buf 572
Morrill-Bos 525
Connor-NY 506
Sutton-Bos 486
Ewing-NY 481

On-Base Plus Slugging
Brouthers-Buf 969
Connor-NY 900
Morrill-Bos 868
Gore-Chi 849
Sutton-Bos 836

Adjusted OPS
Brouthers-Buf 186
Connor-NY 173
Morrill-Bos 155
Bennett-Det 155
Sutton-Bos 147

Batter Runs
Brouthers-Buf 44.4
Connor-NY 34.6
Morrill-Bos 27.6
Gore-Chi 26.5
Sutton-Bos 24.4

Adjusted Batter Runs
Brouthers-Buf 42.0
Connor-NY 35.7
Morrill-Bos 25.4
Bennett-Det 25.1
Wood-Det 23.0

Clutch Hitting Index
Start-Pro 140
Burdock-Bos 135
Kelly-Chi 131
Sutton-Bos 131
Anson-Chi 124

Runs Created
Brouthers-Buf 99
Connor-NY 84
Morrill-Bos 75
Sutton-Bos 72
Gore-Chi 72

Total Average
Brouthers-Buf 974
Connor-NY 882
Morrill-Bos 825
Gore-Chi 812
Bennett-Det 783

Stolen Bases

Stolen Base Average

Stolen Base Runs

Fielding Runs
Farrell-Pro 24.9
Shaffer-Buf 20.0
Ward-NY 19.3
Richardson-Buf 18.7
Williamson-Chi 17.8

Total Player Rating
Farrell-Pro 3.5
Richardson-Buf 3.3
Brouthers-Buf 3.0
Dunlap-Cle 2.9
Connor-NY 2.5

Wins
Radbourn-Pro 48
Galvin-Buf 46
Whitney-Bos 37
Corcoran-Chi 34
McCormick-Cle 28

Win Percentage
McCormick-Cle 700
Radbourn-Pro 658
Buffinton-Bos 641
Whitney-Bos 638
Corcoran-Chi 630

Games
Radbourn-Pro 76
Galvin-Buf 76
Coleman-Phi 65
Whitney-Bos 62
Corcoran-Chi 56

Complete Games
Galvin-Buf 72
Radbourn-Pro 66
Coleman-Phi 59
Whitney-Bos 54
Corcoran-Chi 51

Shutouts
Galvin-Buf 5
Welch-NY 4
Radbourn-Pro 4
Daily-Cle 4
Buffinton-Bos 4

Saves
Wiedman-Det 2
Whitney-Bos 2

Innings Pitched
Galvin-Buf 656.1
Radbourn-Pro 632.1
Coleman-Phi 538.1
Whitney-Bos 514.0
Corcoran-Chi 473.2

Fewest Hits/Game
Sawyer-Cle 7.60
Radbourn-Pro 8.01
McCormick-Cle 8.32
Daily-Cle 8.56
Whitney-Bos 8.61

Fewest BB/Game
Whitney-Bos 61
Galvin-Buf 69
Radbourn-Pro 80
Coleman-Phi 80
Goldsmith-Chi 92

Strikeouts
Whitney-Bos 345
Radbourn-Pro 315
Galvin-Buf 279
Corcoran-Chi 216
Buffinton-Bos 188

Strikeouts/Game
Whitney-Bos 6.04
Buffinton-Bos 5.08
Sawyer-Cle 4.85
Radbourn-Pro 4.48
Corcoran-Chi 4.10

Ratio
Radbourn-Pro 8.81
Whitney-Bos 9.23
Galvin-Buf 9.96
McCormick-Cle 10.03
Ward-NY 10.04

Earned Run Average
McCormick-Cle 1.84
Radbourn-Pro 2.05
Whitney-Bos 2.24
Sawyer-Cle 2.36
Daily-Cle 2.42

Adjusted ERA
McCormick-Cle 171
Radbourn-Pro 150
Whitney-Bos 138
Sawyer-Cle 133
Corcoran-Chi 132

Opponents' Batting Avg.
Sawyer-Cle 217
Radbourn-Pro 227
McCormick-Cle 233
Sweeney-Pro 237
Whitney-Bos 238

Opponents' On-Base Pct.
Radbourn-Pro 244
Whitney-Bos 251
Galvin-Buf 265
Ward-NY 267
McCormick-Cle 268

Starter Runs
Radbourn-Pro 76.4
Whitney-Bos 51.2
McCormick-Cle 49.2
Corcoran-Chi 34.1
Galvin-Buf 30.8

Adjusted Starter Runs
Radbourn-Pro 73.9
Whitney-Bos 49.6
McCormick-Cle 49.5
Corcoran-Chi 40.5
Galvin-Buf 33.1

Clutch Pitching Index
McCormick-Cle 125
Shaw-Det 121
Daily-Cle 119
O'Neill-NY 118
Goldsmith-Chi 113

Relief Runs

Adjusted Relief Runs

Relief Ranking

Total Pitcher Index
Radbourn-Pro 8.5
Whitney-Bos 6.1
McCormick-Cle 5.4
Corcoran-Chi 3.6
Galvin-Buf 2.6

Total Baseball Ranking
Radbourn-Pro 8.2
Whitney-Bos 6.1
McCormick-Cle 5.3
Farrell-Pro 3.5
Richardson-Buf 3.3

TEAM	G	W	L	PCT	GB	R	OR	AB	H	2B	3B	HR	BB	SO	AVG	OBP	SLG	OPS	OPS+	BR	BR+	PF	CHI	RC	SB	CS	SBA	SBR
PHI	98	66	32	.673		**720**	547	3712	**974**	**149**	50	20	**200**	268	**.262**	**.300**	.346	646	102	45	-8	109	**114**	**395**				
STL	98	65	33	.663	1	549	409	3495	891	118	46	7	124	**240**	.255	.280	.321	601	91	-14	-42	106	104	323				
CIN	98	61	37	.622	5	662	413	3669	961	122	74	**34**	139	261	**.262**	.289	**.363**	**652**	106	**46**	14	106	108	**395**				
NY	97	54	42	.563	11	498	**405**	3534	883	111	58	6	142	259	.250	.279	.319	598	91	-17	-39	104	93	322				
LOU	98	52	45	.536	13.5	564	562	3553	892	114	64	14	141	304	.251	.280	.331	611	**107**	-3	**41**	93	103	337				
COL	97	32	65	.330	33.5	476	659	3553	854	101	**79**	15	134	409	.240	.268	.326	594	102	-25	21	92	90	318				
PIT	98	31	67	.316	35	525	728	3607	892	120	58	13	164	345	.247	.280	.324	604	101	-10	14	96	95	335				
BAL	96	28	68	.292	37	471	742	3532	870	125	49	5	164	331	.246	.280	.314	594	91	-21	-36	103	89	318				
TOT	390					4465		28655	7217	960	478	114	1208	2417	.252	.283	.331	613										

TEAM	CG	SH	SV	IP	H	H/G	HR	BB	SO	RAT	ERA	ERA+	OAV	OOB	PR	PR+	PF	CPI	FA	E	DP	FW	PW	BW	SBW	DIF
PHI	92	1	0	873	921	9.5	22	**95**	347	10.5	2.88	123	.254	.273	41	59	107	113	.865	584	40	-4.0	5.2	-.7		16.6
STL	93	**9**	**1**	879^1	**729**	**7.5**	**7**	150	325	**9.0**	**2.24**	**156**	**.211**	**.244**	**104**	**115**	106	97	**.909**	388	62	4.5	**10.2**	-3.6		5.1
CIN	96	8	0	866^2	766	8.0	17	168	215	9.7	2.27	143	.222	.258	100	95	98	**114**	.905	**383**	57	**4.8**	8.4	1.3		-2.3
NY	**97**	6	0	874	751	7.8	12	123	**490**	9.1	2.91	115	.218	**.244**	38	41	101	78	.905	391	45	4.2	3.7	-3.4		1.7
LOU	96	7	0	873^2	987	10.2	**7**	110	269	11.4	3.51	85	.267	.288	-20	-56	91	101	.886	478	67	.6	-4.9	**3.7**		4.3
COL	90	4	0	840^1	980	10.5	16	211	222	12.8	3.97	78	.274	.314	-62	-89	93	105	.874	535	**69**	-2.1	-7.8	1.9		-8.3
PIT	82	1	**1**	867^2	1140	11.9	21	151	271	13.4	4.62	70	.298	.325	-127	-135	99	102	.884	504	55	-.5	-11.8	1.3		-6.7
BAL	86	1	0	844^2	943	10.1	12	190	290	12.1	4.09	85	.265	.303	-74	-55	105	93	.855	624	44	-6.2	-4.8	-3.1		-5.7
TOT	732	37	2	6919^1		9.4				11.0	3.30		.252	.283					.886	3887	439					

Runs
Stovey-Phi 110
Reilly-Cin 103
Carpenter-Cin 99
Knight-Phi 98

Hits
Swartwood-Pit 147
Reilly-Cin 136
Carpenter-Cin 130
Stovey-Phi 128
Nelson-NY 127

Doubles
Stovey-Phi 31
Swartwood-Pit 24
Knight-Phi 23
Hayes-Pit 23

Triples
Smith-Col 17
Reilly-Cin 14
Kuehne-Col 14
Mansell-Pit 13
Mann-Col 13

Home Runs
Stovey-Phi 14
Jones-Cin 10
Reilly-Cin 9
Fulmer-Cin 5
Brown-Col 5

Total Bases
Stovey-Phi 213
Reilly-Cin 212
Swartwood-Pit 196
Jones-Cin 184
B.Gleason-StL 167

Runs Batted In

Runs Produced
Reilly-Cin 173
Stovey-Phi 162
Moynahan-Phi 156
Jones-Cin 154
Knight-Phi 150

Bases On Balls
Stearns-Bal 34
Nelson-NY 31
Moynahan-Phi 31
J.Gleason-StL-Lou . . 29

Batting Average
Swartwood-Pit 357
Browning-Lou 338
Clinton-Bal 313
Rowe-Bal 313
Reilly-Cin 311

On-Base Percentage
Swartwood-Pit 394
Browning-Lou 378
Moynahan-Phi 360
Clinton-Bal 357
Nelson-NY 353

Slugging Average
Stovey-Phi 506
Reilly-Cin 485
Swartwood-Pit 476
Jones-Cin 471
Browning-Lou 464

On-Base Plus Slugging
Swartwood-Pit 869
Stovey-Phi 852
Browning-Lou 842
Reilly-Cin 810
Jones-Cin 799

Adjusted OPS
Swartwood-Pit 186
Browning-Lou 183
Stovey-Phi 156
Reilly-Cin 149
Jones-Cin 146

Batter Runs
Swartwood-Pit 35.5
Stovey-Phi 32.4
Browning-Lou 27.4
Reilly-Cin 26.1
Jones-Cin 22.8

Adjusted Batter Runs
Swartwood-Pit 39.9
Browning-Lou 34.1
Stovey-Phi 24.0
Reilly-Cin 21.2
Jones-Cin 18.4

Clutch Hitting Index

Runs Created
Swartwood-Pit 79
Stovey-Phi 76
Reilly-Cin 71
Browning-Lou 64
Jones-Cin 62

Total Average
Swartwood-Pit 834
Stovey-Phi 819
Browning-Lou 797
Jones-Cin 739
Reilly-Cin 734

Stolen Bases

Stolen Base Average

Stolen Base Runs

Fielding Runs
Holbert-NY 34.4
Battin-Pit 28.9
Richmond-Col 25.5
Latham-StL 21.8
Gerhardt-Lou 20.3

Total Player Rating
Richmond-Col 3.6
Smith-Col 3.4
Swartwood-Pit 3.0
Gerhardt-Lou 2.6
Holbert-NY 2.4

Wins
White-Cin 43
Keefe-NY 41
Mullane-StL 35
Mathews-Phi 30

Win Percentage
Mullane-StL 700
Mathews-Phi 698
Bradley-Phi 696
White-Cin 662
McGinnis-StL 636

Games
Keefe-NY 68
White-Cin 65
Mountain-Col 59
Mullane-StL 53
Hecker-Lou 53

Complete Games
Keefe-NY 68
White-Cin 64
Mountain-Col 57
Hecker-Lou 51
Mullane-StL 49

Shutouts
White-Cin 6
McGinnis-StL 6
Keefe-NY 5
Weaver-Lou 4
Mountain-Col 4

Saves
Mullane-StL 1
Barr-Pit 1

Innings Pitched
Keefe-NY 619.0
White-Cin 577.0
Mountain-Col 503.0
Hecker-Lou 469.0
Mullane-StL 460.2

Fewest Hits/Game
Keefe-NY 7.10
Mullane-StL 7.27
White-Cin 7.38
McGinnis-StL 7.64
Deagle-Cin 8.27

Fewest BB/Game
Mathews-Phi 73
Weaver-Lou 79
Lynch-NY 88
Bradley-Phi 92
Driscoll-Pit 1.04

Strikeouts
Keefe-NY 359
Mathews-Phi 203
Mullane-StL 191
Hecker-Lou 164
Mountain-Col 159

Strikeouts/Game
Keefe-NY 5.22
Mathews-Phi 4.80
Lynch-NY 4.20
Mullane-StL 3.73
Henderson-Bal 3.64

Ratio
Keefe-NY 8.67
Mullane-StL 8.71
White-Cin 9.00
McGinnis-StL 9.27
Bradley-Phi 9.95

Earned Run Average
White-Cin 2.09
Mullane-StL 2.19
Deagle-Cin 2.31
McGinnis-StL 2.33
Keefe-NY 2.41

Adjusted ERA
Mullane-StL 159
White-Cin 155
McGinnis-StL 149
Mathews-Phi 144
Deagle-Cin 140

Opponents' Batting Avg.
Keefe-NY 203
Mullane-StL 207
White-Cin 209
McGinnis-StL 215
Deagle-Cin 229

Opponents' On-Base Pct.
Keefe-NY 237
Mullane-StL 238
White-Cin 244
McGinnis-StL 249
Bradley-Phi 263

Starter Runs
White-Cin 77.4
Keefe-NY 60.8
Mullane-StL 56.8
McGinnis-StL 41.2
Mathews-Phi 35.6

Adjusted Starter Runs
White-Cin 75.1
Keefe-NY 62.7
Mullane-StL 62.6
McGinnis-StL 46.4
Mathews-Phi 42.6

Clutch Pitching Index
Mathews-Phi 127
Corey-Phi 124
McCormick-Cin 123
Valentine-Col 122
Deagle-Cin 117

Relief Runs

Adjusted Relief Runs

Relief Ranking

Total Pitcher Index
White-Cin 6.8
Keefe-NY 6.5
Mullane-StL 5.9
McGinnis-StL 3.9
Mathews-Phi 3.2

Total Baseball Ranking
White-Cin 6.8
Keefe-NY 6.5
Mullane-StL 5.6
McGinnis-StL 3.8
Richmond-Col 3.6

TEAM	G	W	L	PCT	GB	R	OR	AB	H	2B	3B	HR	BB	SO	AVG	OBP	SLG	OPS	OPS+	BR	BR+	PF	CHI	RC	SB	CS	SBA	SBR
PRO	114	84	28	.750		665	**388**	4093	987	153	43	21	**300**	469	.241	.293	.315	608	97	-18	-7	98	**107**	387				
BOS	116	73	38	.658	10.5	684	468	4189	1063	**179**	60	36	207	660	.254	.289	.351	640	105	17	20	100	104	435				
BUF	115	64	47	.577	19.5	700	626	4197	1099	163	**69**	39	215	**458**	.262	.298	.361	659	106	46	23	103	102	463				
NY	116	62	50	.554	22	693	623	4124	1053	149	68	22	249	492	.255	.298	.340	638	102	20	5	102	105	428				
CHI	113	62	50	.554	22	**834**	647	4182	**1176**	162	50	**142**	264	469	**.281**	**.324**	**.446**	**770**	**133**	**201**	**137**	108	98	**619**				
PHI	113	39	73	.348	45	549	824	3998	934	149	39	14	209	512	.234	.272	.301	573	88	-72	-45	95	101	335				
CLE	113	35	77	.313	49	458	716	3934	934	147	49	16	170	576	.237	.269	.312	581	83	-63	-81	103	86	338				
DET	114	28	84	.250	56	445	736	3970	825	114	47	31	207	699	.208	.247	.284	531	74	-132	-102	94	93	285				
TOT	457					5028		32687	8071	1216	425	321	1821	4335	.247	.287	.340	626										

TEAM	CG	SH	SV	IP	H	H/G	HR	BB	SO	RAT	ERA	ERA+	OAV	OOB	PR	PR+	PF	CPI	FA	E	DP	FW	PW	BW	SBW	DIF
PRO	107	**16**	**2**	1036[1]	**825**	**7.2**	**26**	172	639	**8.7**	**1.61**	**177**	**.209**	**.242**	**158**	**150**	96	110	.918	398	50	5.2	**13.5**	-.6		10.1
BOS	109	14	**2**	1037	932	8.1	30	**135**	**742**	9.3	2.48	117	.226	.250	58	51	97	84	**.922**	**384**	46	**6.4**	4.6	1.8		4.8
BUF	108	14	1	1001	1041	9.4	46	189	534	11.1	2.95	107	.254	.286	3	20	106	105	.905	462	71	2.0	1.8	2.1		2.8
NY	**111**	4	0	1014	1011	9.0	28	326	567	11.9	3.12	95	.245	.300	-16	-19	100	98	.895	514	69	-.6	-1.6	.5		7.9
CHI	106	9	0	997[1]	1028	9.3	83	231	472	11.4	3.04	103	.250	.290	-6	10	105	**112**	.886	595	**107**	-5.6	.9	**12.3**		-1.5
PHI	106	3	1	981	1090	10.1	37	254	411	12.4	3.93	76	.261	.304	-103	-105	100	87	.888	536	67	-2.4	-9.3	-4.0		-1.0
CLE	107	7	0	994[2]	1046	9.5	35	269	482	11.9	3.43	92	.256	.302	-50	-30	106	97	.897	512	75	-1.2	-2.6	-7.2		-9.8
DET	109	3	0	984[2]	1097	10.1	36	245	488	12.3	3.39	86	.262	.302	-44	-55	97	100	.886	550	62	-3.0	-4.9	-9.1		-10.9
TOT	863	70	6	8046		9.1				11.1	2.98		.247	.287					.900	3951	547					

Runs
Kelly-Chi 120
O'Rourke-Buf 119
Hornung-Bos 119
Dalrymple-Chi 111
Anson-Chi 108

Hits
Sutton-Bos 162
O'Rourke-Buf 162
Dalrymple-Chi 161
Kelly-Chi 160
Anson-Chi 159

Doubles
Hines-Pro 36
O'Rourke-Buf 33
Anson-Chi 30
Manning-Phi 29

Triples
Ewing-NY 20
Brouthers-Buf 15
Rowe-Buf 14
McKinnon-NY 13
Phillips-Cle 12

Home Runs
Williamson-Chi 27
Pfeffer-Chi 25
Dalrymple-Chi 22
Anson-Chi 21
Brouthers-Buf 14

Total Bases
Dalrymple-Chi 263
Anson-Chi 258
Pfeffer-Chi 240
Kelly-Chi 237
Williamson-Chi 231

Runs Batted In
Anson-Chi 102
Pfeffer-Chi 101
Kelly-Chi 95
Williamson-Chi 84
Connor-NY 82

Runs Produced
Kelly-Chi 202
Anson-Chi 189
Pfeffer-Chi 181
O'Rourke-Buf 177
Connor-NY 176

Bases On Balls
Gore-Chi 61
Kelly-Chi 46
Hines-Pro 44
Williamson-Chi 42

Batting Average
O'Rourke-Buf .347
Kelly-Chi .354
Sutton-Bos .346
Anson-Chi .335
Brouthers-Buf .327

On-Base Percentage
Kelly-Chi .414
Gore-Chi .404
O'Rourke-Buf .392
Sutton-Bos .384
Brouthers-Buf .378

Slugging Average
Brouthers-Buf .563
Williamson-Chi .554
Anson-Chi .543
Kelly-Chi .524
Pfeffer-Chi .514

On-Base Plus Slugging
Brouthers-Buf 941
Kelly-Chi 938
Anson-Chi 916
Williamson-Chi 898
O'Rourke-Buf 872

Adjusted OPS
Brouthers-Buf 186
Kelly-Chi 178
Anson-Chi 170
O'Rourke-Buf 167
Williamson-Chi 164

Batter Runs
Kelly-Chi 48.8
Anson-Chi 44.6
Brouthers-Buf 41.3
O'Rourke-Buf 38.8
Williamson-Chi 36.7

Adjusted Batter Runs
Kelly-Chi 39.6
Brouthers-Buf 37.8
Anson-Chi 35.6
O'Rourke-Buf 35.1
Sutton-Bos 33.9

Clutch Hitting Index
Connor-NY 148
Radbourn-Pro 132
Caskin-NY 131
Kelly-Chi 131
Dorgan-NY 124

Runs Created
Kelly-Chi 100
Anson-Chi 99
O'Rourke-Buf 90
Dalrymple-Chi 88
Brouthers-Buf 87

Total Average
Kelly-Chi .969
Brouthers-Buf .959
Anson-Chi .908
Williamson-Chi .907
O'Rourke-Buf .849

Stolen Bases

Stolen Base Average

Stolen Base Runs

Fielding Runs
Pfeffer-Chi 45.5
Williamson-Chi 23.8
Gilligan-Pro 17.4
Lillie-Buf 16.0
Hanlon-Det 13.3

Total Player Rating
Pfeffer-Chi 6.3
Williamson-Chi 4.8
Kelly-Chi 3.2
Sutton-Bos 2.8
Brouthers-Buf 2.6

Wins
Radbourn-Pro 59
Buffinton-Bos 48
Galvin-Buf 46
Welch-NY 39
L.Corcoran-Chi 35

Win Percentage
Radbourn-Pro .831
Buffinton-Bos .750
Sweeney-Pro .680
Galvin-Buf .676
Welch-NY .650

Games
Radbourn-Pro 75
Galvin-Buf 72
Buffinton-Bos 67
Welch-NY 65
L.Corcoran-Chi 60

Complete Games
Radbourn-Pro 73
Galvin-Buf 71
Buffinton-Bos 63
Welch-NY 62
L.Corcoran-Chi 57

Shutouts
Galvin-Buf 12
Radbourn-Pro 11
Buffinton-Bos 8
L.Corcoran-Chi 7
Whitney-Bos 6

Saves
Morrill-Bos 2
Sweeney-Pro 1
Radbourn-Pro 1
O'Rourke-Buf 1
Ferguson-Phi 1

Innings Pitched
Radbourn-Pro 678.2
Galvin-Buf 636.1
Buffinton-Bos 587.0
Welch-NY 557.1
L.Corcoran-Chi 516.2

Fewest Hits/Game
Sweeney-Pro 6.23
Radbourn-Pro 7.00
Clarkson-Chi 7.17
Getzien-Det 7.21
Whitney-Bos 7.29

Fewest BB/Game
Whitney-Bos .72
Galvin-Buf .89
Buffinton-Bos 1.17
Sweeney-Pro 1.18
Coleman-Phi 1.28

Strikeouts
Radbourn-Pro 441
Buffinton-Bos 417
Galvin-Buf 369
Welch-NY 345
L.Corcoran-Chi 272

Strikeouts/Game
Clarkson-Chi 7.78
Whitney-Bos 7.23
Getzien-Det 6.54
Buffinton-Bos 6.39
Sweeney-Pro 5.90

Ratio
Sweeney-Pro 7.41
Whitney-Bos 8.01
Radbourn-Pro 8.30
Getzien-Det 8.74
Galvin-Buf 8.90

Earned Run Average
Radbourn-Pro 1.38
Sweeney-Pro 1.55
Getzien-Det 1.95
Galvin-Buf 1.99
Whitney-Bos 2.09

Adjusted ERA
Radbourn-Pro 206
Sweeney-Pro 184
Galvin-Buf 158
Getzien-Det 148
Clarkson-Chi 147

Opponents' Batting Avg.
Sweeney-Pro .187
Getzien-Det .204
Radbourn-Pro .205
Whitney-Bos .207
Clarkson-Chi .208

Opponents' On-Base Pct.
Sweeney-Pro .215
Whitney-Bos .223
Radbourn-Pro .234
Getzien-Det .237
Buffinton-Bos .244

Starter Runs
Radbourn-Pro 120.5
Galvin-Buf 69.5
Buffinton-Bos 54.2
Sweeney-Pro 35.1
Whitney-Bos 33.2

Adjusted Starter Runs
Radbourn-Pro 115.6
Galvin-Buf 77.1
Buffinton-Bos 49.7
L.Corcoran-Chi 39.6
Sweeney-Pro 33.3

Clutch Pitching Index
Radbourn-Pro 117
Meinke-Det 116
L.Corcoran-Chi 113
Moffett-Cle 110
Welch-NY 108

Relief Runs

Adjusted Relief Runs

Relief Ranking

Total Pitcher Index
Radbourn-Pro 10.4
Galvin-Buf 6.4
Buffinton-Bos 5.8
L.Corcoran-Chi 4.4
Sweeney-Pro 4.2

Total Baseball Ranking
Radbourn-Pro 10.2
Galvin-Buf 6.3
Pfeffer-Chi 6.3
Buffinton-Bos 5.4
Williamson-Chi 4.7

TEAM	G	W	L	PCT	GB	R	OR	AB	H	2B	3B	HR	BB	SO	AVG	OBP	SLG	OPS	OPS+	BR	BR+	PF	CHI	RC	SB	CS	SBA	SBR
NY	112	75	32	.701		734	**423**	4012	1052	155	64	22	203	**315**	.262	**.304**	.349	653	120	70	87	98	109	436				
COL	110	69	39	.639	6.5	585	459	3759	901	107	96	**40**	196	629	.240	.288	.351	639	**121**	47	**101**	92	95	390				
LOU	110	68	40	.630	7.5	573	425	3957	1004	152	69	17	146	408	.254	.286	.340	626	112	29	58	96	93	395				
STL	110	67	40	.626	8	658	539	3952	987	151	60	11	172	339	.250	.288	.327	615	100	16	-4	104	109	381				
CIN	112	68	41	.624	8	**754**	512	4090	1037	109	96	36	154	409	.254	.289	.354	643	108	53	23	105	**114**	429				
BAL	108	63	43	.594	11.5	636	515	3845	896	133	84	32	**211**	545	.233	.284	.336	620	101	25	2	104	105	377				
PHI	108	61	46	.570	14	700	546	3959	**1057**	**167**	**100**	26	153	434	**.267**	.301	**.379**	**680**	117	**100**	59	106	102	**463**				
TOL	110	46	58	.442	27.5	463	571	3712	859	153	48	8	157	545	.231	.268	.305	573	87	-39	-56	104	90	310				
BRO	109	40	64	.385	33.5	476	644	3763	845	112	47	16	179	417	.225	.263	.292	555	83	-61	-64	101	95	296				
RIC	46	12	30	.286	30.5	194	294	1469	326	40	33	7	53	282	.222	.261	.308	569	89	-18	-16	99	97	121				
PIT	110	30	78	.278	45.5	406	725	3689	777	105	50	2	143	411	.211	.248	.268	516	73	-109	-104	99	92	251				
IND	110	29	78	.271	46	462	755	3813	890	129	62	20	125	561	.233	.262	.315	577	93	-38	-24	97	88	323				
WAS	63	12	51	.190	41	248	481	2166	434	61	24	6	100	377	.200	.241	.259	500	75	-75	-42	88	100	139				
TOT	659					6889		46186	11065	1574	833	243	1992	5672	.240	.279	.326	604										

TEAM	CG	SH	SV	IP	H	H/G	HR	BB	SO	RAT	ERA	ERA+	OAV	OOB	PR	PR+	PF	CPI	FA	E	DP	FW	PW	BW	SBW	DIF
NY	110	9	0	985	**802**	**7.4**	15	115	628	**8.7**	2.46	127	**.209**	**.237**	86	75	96	89	.907	441	42	2.4	6.9	8.0		4.4
COL	102	8	**1**	962^1	815	7.7	22	172	526	9.5	2.69	113	.217	.256	60	38	93	98	.908	433	74	2.4	3.5	**9.3**		.0
LOU	101	6	0	989^2	836	7.7	**9**	**97**	470	8.8	**2.18**	**142**	.216	.241	**118**	**105**	95	106	**.912**	**426**	**84**	2.7	**9.6**	5.3		-3.4
STL	99	8	0	987	881	8.1	16	172	477	10.0	2.68	122	.226	.266	63	63	100	106	.900	490	65	-.1	5.8	-.3		8.3
CIN	**111**	**11**	0	983^2	956	8.8	27	181	308	11.2	3.34	100	.243	.290	-10	-1	103	106	.909	430	82	**2.9**	-.0	2.2		8.7
BAL	105	8	**1**	955^2	869	8.2	16	219	**635**	10.6	2.72	128	.224	.271	56	74	107	**107**	.899	461	61	.8	6.8	.2		2.4
PHI	105	5	0	948^2	920	8.8	16	127	530	10.4	3.42	99	.237	.269	-18	-4	104	89	.901	457	63	.9	-.3	5.4		1.6
TOL	103	9	**1**	946	885	8.5	12	169	501	10.6	3.07	111	.233	.275	19	34	105	99	.900	469	67	.8	3.2	-5.1		-4.7
BRO	105	6	0	948^2	996	9.5	20	163	378	11.3	3.80	87	.254	.288	-58	-50	102	94	.889	520	68	-1.6	-4.5	-5.8		.1
RIC	45	1	0	370^1	402	9.8	14	52	167	11.5	4.53	73	.257	.288	-53	-49	102	83	.874	239	27	-1.5	-4.4	-1.4		-1.5
PIT	108	4	0	943^1	1059	10.2	25	216	338	12.7	4.36	76	.265	.312	-116	-109	102	96	.889	523	71	-1.5	-9.9	-9.5		-2.9
IND	107	2	0	937^2	1001	9.7	30	199	479	11.8	4.21	78	.255	.295	-100	-96	101	90	.889	515	45	-1.2	-8.7	-2.1		-12.2
WAS	62	3	0	543^2	643	10.7	21	110	235	12.8	4.01	76	.273	.311	-46	-64	93	109	.858	400	40	-5.2	-5.8	-3.8		-4.5
TOT	1263	80	3	11501^2		8.7				10.6	3.25		.240	.279					.898	5804	789					

Runs
Stovey-Phi 124
Jones-Cin 117
Latham-StL 115
Reilly-Cin 114
Nelson-NY 114

Hits
Orr-NY 162
Reilly-Cin 152
Esterbrook-NY 150
Browning-Lou 150
Jones-Cin 148

Doubles
Barkley-Tol 39
Browning-Lou 33
Orr-NY 32
Esterbrook-NY 29
Lewis-StL 25

Triples
Stovey-Phi 23
Reilly-Cin 19
Mann-Col 18
Peltz-Ind 17
Jones-Cin 17

Home Runs
Reilly-Cin 11
Stovey-Phi 10
Orr-NY 9
Mann-Col 7
Jones-Cin 7

Total Bases
Reilly-Cin 247
Orr-NY 247
Stovey-Phi 244
Jones-Cin 222
Browning-Lou 211

Runs Batted In

Runs Produced
Stovey-Phi 197
Reilly-Cin 194
Orr-NY 185
Jones-Cin 181
McPhee-Cin 166

Bases On Balls
Nelson-NY 74
Geer-Bro 38
Jones-Cin 37
Macullar-Bal 36
Richmond-Col 35

Batting Average
Orr-NY .... .354
Reilly-Cin .... .339
Browning-Lou .... .336
Stovey-Phi .... .326
Lewis-StL .... .323

On-Base Percentage
Jones-Cin .... .376
Nelson-NY .... .375
Stovey-Phi .... .368
Fennelly-Was-Cin .... .367
Reilly-Cin .... .366

Slugging Average
Reilly-Cin .... .551
Stovey-Phi .... .545
Orr-NY .... .539
Fennelly-Was-Cin .... .480
Browning-Lou .... .472

On-Base Plus Slugging
Reilly-Cin 918
Stovey-Phi 913
Orr-NY 901
Fennelly-Was-Cin 847
Jones-Cin 846

Adjusted OPS
Orr-NY 195
Reilly-Cin 186
Fennelly-Was-Cin 186
Stovey-Phi 182
Browning-Lou 176

Batter Runs
Stovey-Phi 44.8
Reilly-Cin 44.6
Orr-NY 42.1
Jones-Cin 39.0
Browning-Lou 31.6

Adjusted Batter Runs
Orr-NY 44.9
Reilly-Cin 39.5
Stovey-Phi 38.1
Fennelly-Was-Cin 36.9
Browning-Lou 36.2

Clutch Hitting Index

Runs Created
Reilly-Cin 93
Stovey-Phi 92
Orr-NY 92
Jones-Cin 85
Browning-Lou 77

Total Average
Stovey-Phi .... .907
Reilly-Cin .... .899
Orr-NY .... .855
Jones-Cin .... .830
Fennelly-Was-Cin .... .824

Stolen Bases

Stolen Base Average

Stolen Base Runs

Fielding Runs
Latham-StL 39.5
Smith-Col 29.0
Snyder-Cin 27.5
Gerhardt-Lou 27.2
Barkley-Tol 24.5

Total Player Rating
Barkley-Tol 4.5
Latham-StL 4.3
Fennelly-Was-Cin 4.2
Smith-Col 4.1
Esterbrook-NY 3.5

Wins
Hecker-Lou 52
Lynch-NY 37
Keefe-NY 37
Mullane-Tol 36

Win Percentage
Morris-Col .... .723
Hecker-Lou .... .722
Foutz-StL .... .714
Lynch-NY .... .712
Keefe-NY .... .685

Games
Hecker-Lou 75
Mullane-Tol 67
McKeon-Ind 61
Keefe-NY 58
Terry-Bro 56

Complete Games
Hecker-Lou 72
Mullane-Tol 64
McKeon-Ind 59
Keefe-NY 56
Terry-Bro 54

Shutouts
White-Cin 7
Mullane-Tol 7
Hecker-Lou 6

Saves
O'Day-Tol 1
Mountain-Col 1
O.Burns-Bal 1

Innings Pitched
Hecker-Lou 670.2
Mullane-Tol 567.0
McKeon-Ind 512.0
Lynch-NY 496.0
Keefe-NY 483.0

Fewest Hits/Game
Morris-Col 7.02
Hecker-Lou 7.06
Keefe-NY 7.08
Mountain-Col 7.21
Foutz-StL 7.27

Fewest BB/Game
Driscoll-Lou .... .62
Hecker-Lou .... .75
Lynch-NY .... .76
E.Dugan-Ric .... .81
McGinnis-StL .... .89

Strikeouts
Hecker-Lou 385
Henderson-Bal 346
Keefe-NY 334
Mullane-Tol 325
McKeon-Ind 308

Strikeouts/Game
Henderson-Bal 7.09
Davis-StL 6.49
Morris-Col 6.33
Keefe-NY 6.22
Mathews-Phi 5.98

Ratio
Hecker-Lou 8.02
Morris-Col 8.36
Lynch-NY 8.56
Keefe-NY 8.68
Foutz-StL 9.23

Earned Run Average
Hecker-Lou 1.80
Foutz-StL 2.18
Morris-Col 2.18
Keefe-NY 2.25
Mountain-Col 2.45

Adjusted ERA
Hecker-Lou 171
Foutz-StL 150
Morris-Col 139
Keefe-NY 138
Mullane-Tol 135

Opponents' Batting Avg.
Keefe-NY .... .204
Hecker-Lou .... .204
Morris-Col .... .204
Mountain-Col .... .209
Foutz-StL .... .212

Opponents' On-Base Pct.
Hecker-Lou .... .226
Morris-Col .... .234
Lynch-NY .... .236
Keefe-NY .... .239
Foutz-StL .... .255

Starter Runs
Hecker-Lou 107.6
Keefe-NY 53.0
Morris-Col 50.8
Mullane-Tol 45.3
Mountain-Col 31.9

Adjusted Starter Runs
Hecker-Lou 100.6
Mullane-Tol 53.0
Keefe-NY 48.1
Morris-Col 43.2
Henderson-Bal 38.3

Clutch Pitching Index
Comiskey-StL 127
Foutz-StL 122
Davis-StL 120
O'Neill-StL 118
White-Cin 116

Relief Runs

Adjusted Relief Runs

Relief Ranking

Total Pitcher Index
Hecker-Lou 13.1
Mullane-Tol 7.4
Keefe-NY 5.7
Morris-Col 4.5
Henderson-Bal 4.1

Total Baseball Ranking
Hecker-Lou 13.1
Mullane-Tol 7.4
Keefe-NY 5.9
Barkley-Tol 4.5
Latham-StL 4.3

TEAM	G	W	L	PCT	GB	R	OR	AB	H	2B	3B	HR	BB	SO	AVG	OBP	SLG	OPS	OPS+	BR	BR+	PF	CHI	RC	SB	CS	SBA	SBR
STL	114	94	19	.832		**887**	**429**	4285	**1251**	**259**	41	**32**	**181**	542	**.292**	**.321**	**.394**	**715**	**113**	**-33**	**-55**	104	103	**555**				
MIL	12	8	4	.667	35.5	53	34	395	88	25	0	0	20	70	.223	.260	.286	546	124	-27	4	54	91	30				
CIN	105	69	36	.657	21	703	466	3786	1027	118	**63**	26	147	**482**	.271	.298	.356	654	92	-111	-147	108	102	413				
BAL	106	58	47	.552	32	662	627	3883	952	150	26	17	144	652	.245	.272	.310	582	71	-215	-253	110	**109**	336				
BOS	111	58	51	.532	34	636	558	3940	928	168	32	19	128	787	.236	.260	.309	569	74	-242	-236	98	107	324				
CP	93	41	50	.451	42	438	482	3212	742	127	26	10	119	505	.231	.258	.296	554	69	-211	-209	99	93	252				
WAS	114	47	65	.420	46.5	572	679	3926	931	120	26	4	118	558	.237	.259	.284	543	68	-271	-259	97	102	296				
PHI	67	21	46	.313	50	414	545	2518	618	108	35	7	103	405	.245	.275	.324	599	89	-125	-103	93	101	230				
STP	9	2	6	.250	39.5	24	57	272	49	13	1	0	7	47	.180	.201	.235	436	61	-30	-19	54	84	13				
ALT	25	6	19	.240	44	90	216	899	223	30	6	2	22	130	.248	.266	.301	567	72	-55	-56	101	67	74				
KC	82	16	63	.203	61	311	618	2802	557	104	15	6	123	529	.199	.232	.253	485	55	-255	-226	87	88	169				
WIL	18	2	16	.111	44.5	35	114	521	91	8	8	2	22	123	.175	.208	.232	440	33	-56	-57	103	61	26				
TOT	428					4825		30439	7457	1230	279	125	1134	4830	.245	.273	.317	588										

TEAM	CG	SH	SV	IP	H	H/G	HR	BB	SO	RAT	ERA	ERA+	OAV	OOB	PR	PR+	PF	CPI	FA	E	DP	FW	PW	BW	SBW	DIF
STL	**104**	8	**6**	993	838	**7.6**	**9**	110	550	**8.6**	**1.96**	**153**	**.214**	**.235**	**120**	**115**	98	106	**.888**	554	**79**	**3.8**	**10.1**	-4.8		28.6
MIL	12	3	0	104	49	4.3	1	13	139	5.4	2.26	73	.132	.161	9	-13	54	12	.892	53	4	.7	-1.1	.4		2.2
CIN	95	**11**	1	914[1]	831	8.2	17	**90**	503	9.1	2.39	134	.226	.245	68	79	105	102	.882	532	45	2.6	7.0	-12.8		20.0
BAL	92	4	0	946[2]	1002	9.6	24	177	628	11.3	3.02	111	.254	.286	3	31	110	**115**	.872	616	53	-.7	2.8	-22.1		25.8
BOS	100	5	1	953[1]	885	8.4	17	110	**753**	9.4	2.71	110	.231	.252	37	28	98	95	.868	633	39	-.3	2.5	-20.6		22.1
CP	86	6	0	803[2]	**743**	8.4	12	137	679	9.9	2.73	112	.230	.261	29	29	100	98	.882	**459**	38	2.8	2.6	-18.2		8.6
WAS	94	5	0	953[2]	992	9.4	16	168	684	11.0	3.44	87	.251	.282	-41	-48	98	95	.869	625	55	.8	-4.2	-22.6		17.2
PHI	64	1	0	593[1]	726	11.1	7	105	310	12.7	4.63	63	.283	.311	-104	-120	95	89	.841	501	36	-5.2	-10.5	-9.0		12.3
STP	7	1	0	71	72	9.2	1	27	44	12.6	3.17	52	.248	.312	-1	-22	54	117	.872	47	6	.2	-1.9	-1.6		1.5
ALT	20	0	0	219[2]	292	12.0	3	52	93	14.1	4.68	71	.300	.335	-40	-31	109	104	.862	156	4	-.6	-2.7	-4.9		1.8
KC	70	0	0	702[2]	862	11.1	14	127	334	12.7	4.08	68	.283	.312	-80	-110	92	104	.861	520	51	-2.4	-9.6	-19.7		8.4
WIL	15	0	0	142	165	10.5	4	18	113	11.6	3.05	109	.273	.294	0	4	109	126	.860	104	10	-.0	.4	-4.9		-2.2
TOT	759	44	8	7397[1]		9.1				10.5	3.05		.245	.273					.872	4800	420					

Runs
Dunlap-StL 160
Shaffer-StL 130
Seery-Bal-KC 115
Robinson-Bal 101
Rowe-StL 95

Hits
Dunlap-StL 185
Shaffer-StL 168
Moore-Was 155
Seery-Bal-KC 146
Rowe-StL 142

Doubles
Shaffer-StL 40
Dunlap-StL 39
Rowe-StL 32
O'Brien-Bos 31
Gleason-StL 30

Triples
Burns-Cin 12
Rowe-StL 11
Shaffer-StL 10

Home Runs
Dunlap-StL 13
Crane-Bos 12
Levis-Bal-Was 5

Total Bases
Dunlap-StL 279
Shaffer-StL 234
Rowe-StL 208
Crane-Bos 193
Seery-Bal-KC 192

Runs Batted In

Runs Produced
Dunlap-StL 147
Shaffer-StL 128
Seery-Bal-KC 113
Robinson-Bal 98
Rowe-StL 91

Bases On Balls
Robinson-Bal 37
Shaffer-StL 30
Dunlap-StL 29
Harbidge-Cin 25
Gleason-StL 23

Batting Average
Dunlap-StL .412
Taylor-StL .366
Dickerson-StL .365
Hoover-Phi .364
Shaffer-StL .360

On-Base Percentage
Dunlap-StL .448
Shaffer-StL .398
Hoover-Phi .390
Moore-Was .363
Gleason-StL .361

Slugging Average
Dunlap-StL .621
Taylor-StL .548
Shaffer-StL .501
Hoover-Phi .495
Burns-Cin .457

On-Base Plus Slugging
Dunlap-StL 1069
Shaffer-StL 899
Hoover-Phi 885
Gleason-StL 802
Moore-Was 777

Adjusted OPS
Dunlap-StL 213
Hoover-Phi 180
Shaffer-StL 165
Moore-Was 139
Gleason-StL 137

Batter Runs
Dunlap-StL 53.4
Shaffer-StL 27.6
Glasscock-Cin 16.9
Hoover-Phi 14.4
Taylor-StL 12.6

Adjusted Batter Runs
Dunlap-StL 49.2
Shaffer-StL 24.1
Hoover-Phi 19.0
Glasscock-Cin 13.7
Taylor-StL 11.2

Clutch Hitting Index

Runs Created
Dunlap-StL 128
Shaffer-StL 96
Moore-Was 71
Seery-Bal-KC 67
Rowe-StL 65

Total Average
Dunlap-StL 1.167
Shaffer-StL .883
Hoover-Phi .846
Gleason-StL .738
Moore-Was .686

Stolen Bases

Stolen Base Average

Stolen Base Runs

Fielding Runs
Dunlap-StL 30.5
Fusselback-Bal 19.3
Baker-StL 16.3
Robinson-Bal 16.1
Krieg-CP 14.9

Total Player Rating
Dunlap-StL 7.1
Shaffer-StL 1.8
Hoover-Phi 1.5
Briody-Cin 1.5
Glasscock-Cin 1.3

Wins
B.Sweeney-Bal 40
Daily-CP-Was 28
Taylor-StL 25
Bradley-Cin 25
Sweeney-StL 24

Win Percentage
McCormick-Cin .875
Taylor-StL .862
Boyle-StL .833
Sweeney-StL .774
B.Sweeney-Bal .656

Games
B.Sweeney-Bal 62
Daily-CP-Was 58
Wise-Was 50
Bakely-Phi-Wil-KC 46
Bradley-Cin 41

Complete Games
B.Sweeney-Bal 58
Daily-CP-Was 56
Bakely-Phi-Wil-KC 43
Bradley-Cin 36
Shaw-Bos 35

Shutouts
McCormick-Cin 7
Daily-CP-Was 5
Shaw-Bos 5
Wise-Was 4
B.Sweeney-Bal 4

Saves
Taylor-StL 4
Sylvester-Cin 1
Dunlap-StL 1
Brown-Bos 1
Boyle-StL 1

Innings Pitched
B.Sweeney-Bal 538.0
Daily-CP-Was 500.2
Bakely-Phi-Wil-KC 394.2
Wise-Was 364.1
Bradley-Cin 342.0

Fewest Hits/Game
McCormick-Cin 6.47
Shaw-Bos 6.47
Sweeney-StL 6.87
Boyle-StL 7.08
Werden-StL 7.20

Fewest BB/Game
Sweeney-StL .43
McCormick-Cin .60
Boyle-StL .60
Bradley-Cin .61
Murphy-Wil-Alt .62

Strikeouts
Daily-CP-Was 483
B.Sweeney-Bal 374
Shaw-Bos 309
Wise-Was 268
Burke-Bos 255

Strikeouts/Game
Shaw-Bos 8.81
Daily-CP-Was 8.68
Gagus-Was 7.92
Robinson-Bal 7.32
Burke-Bos 7.13

Ratio
McCormick-Cin 7.07
Sweeney-StL 7.31
Shaw-Bos 7.53
Boyle-StL 7.68
Werden-StL 8.60

Earned Run Average
McCormick-Cin 1.54
Taylor-StL 1.68
Boyle-StL 1.74
Shaw-Bos 1.77
Sweeney-StL 1.83

Adjusted ERA
McCormick-Cin 166
Taylor-StL 143
Boyle-StL 137
Shaw-Bos 134
Sweeney-StL 131

Opponents' Batting Avg.
McCormick-Cin .188
Shaw-Bos .188
Sweeney-StL .197
Boyle-StL .202
Werden-StL .205

Opponents' On-Base Pct.
McCormick-Cin .202
Sweeney-StL .207
Shaw-Bos .212
Boyle-StL .215
Werden-StL .235

Starter Runs
Shaw-Bos 23.5
Taylor-StL 22.2
McCormick-Cin 20.9
Sweeney-StL 18.4
Boyle-StL 11.6

Adjusted Starter Runs
McCormick-Cin 22.5
Shaw-Bos 21.9
Taylor-StL 21.3
Sweeney-StL 17.3
Boyle-StL 11.1

Clutch Pitching Index
Hodnett-StL 140
Robinson-Bal 132
Taylor-StL 129
B.Sweeney-Bal 111
Murphy-Wil-Alt 110

Relief Runs

Adjusted Relief Runs

Relief Ranking

Total Pitcher Index
Taylor-StL 2.8
Sweeney-StL 2.5
McCormick-Cin 1.7
Shaw-Bos 1.5
Boyle-StL .9

Total Baseball Ranking
Dunlap-StL 6.9
Taylor-StL 3.2
Sweeney-StL 2.4
Shaffer-StL 1.8
McCormick-Cin 1.7

TEAM	G	W	L	PCT	GB	R	OR	AB	H	2B	3B	HR	BB	SO	AVG	OBP	SLG	OPS	OPS+	BR	BR+	PF	CHI	RC	SB	CS	SBA	SBR
CHI	113	87	25	.777		**834**	470	4093	1079	**184**	75	**54**	**340**	429	.264	**.320**	**.385**	**705**	116	**143**	53	114	**113**	**517**				
NY	112	85	27	.759	2	691	**370**	4029	**1085**	150	**82**	16	221	**312**	**.269**	.307	.359	666	**122**	82	**91**	99	106	456				
PHI	111	56	54	.509	30	513	511	3893	891	156	35	20	220	401	.229	.270	.302	572	91	-45	-35	98	102	326				
PRO	110	53	57	.482	33	442	531	3727	820	114	30	6	265	430	.220	.272	.272	544	82	-74	-60	97	96	282				
BOS	113	46	66	.411	41	528	589	3950	915	144	53	22	190	522	.232	.267	.312	579	94	-41	-22	96	103	337				
DET	108	41	67	.380	44	514	582	3773	917	149	66	25	216	451	.243	.284	.337	621	105	17	16	100	93	371				
BUF	112	38	74	.339	49	495	761	3900	980	149	50	23	179	380	.251	.284	.333	617	100	11	-7	103	89	378				
STL	111	36	72	.333	49	390	593	3758	829	121	21	8	214	412	.221	.263	.270	533	81	-92	-62	94	89	273				
TOT	445					4407		31123	7516	1167	412	174	1845	3337	.242	.284	.323	606										

TEAM	CG	SH	SV	IP	H	H/G	HR	BB	SO	RAT	ERA	ERA+	OAV	OOB	PR	PR+	PF	CPI	FA	E	DP	FW	PW	BW	SBW	DIF
CHI	108	14	**4**	1015^{2}	868	7.7	37	202	458	9.5	2.24	134	.221	.259	66	80	107	102	.903	496	80	-2.4	7.6	5.0		21.0
NY	109	**16**	1	994	**758**	**6.9**	**11**	265	**516**	**9.3**	**1.73**	**155**	**.205**	**.258**	**121**	**112**	95	**114**	**.929**	**331**	**85**	**6.1**	**10.6**	**8.6**		3.9
PHI	108	10	0	976	860	8.0	18	218	378	10.0	2.39	117	.224	.266	46	41	99	96	.905	447	66	-.2	3.9	-3.2		.8
PRO	108	8	0	960^{2}	912	8.6	18	235	371	10.8	2.71	99	.235	.278	12	-4	95	96	.903	459	70	-1.1	-.3	-5.6		5.2
BOS	**111**	10	0	981	1045	9.6	26	**188**	480	11.4	3.03	89	.261	.294	-23	-40	95	107	.901	478	79	-1.4	-3.7	-2.0		-2.6
DET	105	6	1	954^{1}	966	9.2	18	224	475	11.3	2.88	99	.249	.290	-6	-5	101	103	.901	462	61	-1.6	-.4	1.6		-12.3
BUF	107	4	1	956	1175	11.1	31	234	320	13.3	4.30	69	.289	.328	-157	-132	106	99	.901	464	65	-.9	-12.4	-.6		-3.9
STL	107	4	0	965^{1}	935	8.8	15	278	337	11.4	3.37	82	.245	.296	-59	-69	97	89	.916	398	67	2.3	-6.4	-5.8		-7.9
TOT	863	72	7	7803		8.7				10.8	2.82		.242	.284					.908	3535	573					

Runs
Kelly-Chi 124
O'Rourke-NY 119
Gore-Chi 115
Dalrymple-Chi 109
Connor-NY 102

Hits
Connor-NY 169
Brouthers-Buf 146
Anson-Chi 144
Sutton-Bos 143
O'Rourke-NY 143

Doubles
Anson-Chi 35
Brouthers-Buf 32
Rowe-Buf 28
Dalrymple-Chi 27
Mulvey-Phi 25

Triples
O'Rourke-NY 16
Connor-NY 15
Gore-Chi 13
Bennett-Det 13

Home Runs
Dalrymple-Chi 11
Kelly-Chi 9

Total Bases
Connor-NY 225
Brouthers-Buf 221
Dalrymple-Chi 219
Anson-Chi 214
O'Rourke-NY 211

Runs Batted In
Anson-Chi 108
Kelly-Chi 75
Pfeffer-Chi 73
Burns-Chi 71

Runs Produced
Anson-Chi 201
Kelly-Chi 190
Gore-Chi 167
Connor-NY 166
Dalrymple-Chi 159

Bases On Balls
Williamson-Chi 75
Gore-Chi 68
Morrill-Bos 64
Connor-NY 51

Batting Average
Connor-NY .371
Brouthers-Buf .359
Dorgan-NY .326
Richardson-Buf .319
Gore-Chi .313

On-Base Percentage
Connor-NY .435
Brouthers-Buf .408
Gore-Chi .405
Hanlon-Det .372
Anson-Chi .357

Slugging Average
Brouthers-Buf .543
Connor-NY .495
Ewing-NY .471
Anson-Chi .461
Richardson-Buf .458

On-Base Plus Slugging
Brouthers-Buf 951
Connor-NY 929
Gore-Chi 858
Anson-Chi 819
Bennett-Det 812

Adjusted OPS
Connor-NY 203
Brouthers-Buf 199
Bennett-Det 161
Ewing-NY 159
O'Rourke-NY 158

Batter Runs
Connor-NY 51.7
Brouthers-Buf 46.8
Gore-Chi 40.6
Anson-Chi 31.7
O'Rourke-NY 29.5

Adjusted Batter Runs
Connor-NY 53.3
Brouthers-Buf 43.3
O'Rourke-NY 30.9
Gore-Chi 27.3
Sutton-Bos 24.5

Clutch Hitting Index
White-Buf 146
Williamson-Chi 146
Anson-Chi 145
Gerhardt-NY 139
Pfeffer-Chi 136

Runs Created
Connor-NY 100
Brouthers-Buf 92
Gore-Chi 83
Anson-Chi 78
O'Rourke-NY 77

Total Average
Brouthers-Buf .977
Connor-NY .965
Gore-Chi .884
Bennett-Det .808
Anson-Chi .775

Stolen Bases

Stolen Base Average

Stolen Base Runs

Fielding Runs
Dunlap-StL 25.6
Pfeffer-Chi 25.2
Fogarty-Phi 24.7
Glasscock-StL 19.2
Richardson-Buf 12.9

Total Player Rating
Connor-NY 4.4
Dunlap-StL 4.0
Richardson-Buf 3.4
Glasscock-StL 3.3
Ewing-NY 3.3

Wins
Clarkson-Chi 53
Welch-NY 44
Keefe-NY 32
Radbourn-Pro 28

Win Percentage
Welch-NY .800
Clarkson-Chi .768
McCormick-Pro-Chi .750
Keefe-NY .711
Radbourn-Pro .571

Games
Clarkson-Chi 70
Welch-NY 56
Whitney-Bos 51
Buffinton-Bos 51
Daily-Phi 50

Complete Games
Clarkson-Chi 68
Welch-NY 55
Whitney-Bos 50

Shutouts
Clarkson-Chi 10
Welch-NY 7
Keefe-NY 7
Shaw-Pro 6
Buffinton-Bos 6

Saves
Williamson-Chi 2
Pfeffer-Chi 2
Welch-NY 1
Galvin-Buf 1
Baldwin-Det 1

Innings Pitched
Clarkson-Chi 623.0
Welch-NY 492.0
Radbourn-Pro 445.2
Whitney-Bos 441.1
Daily-Phi 440.0

Fewest Hits/Game
Keefe-NY 6.75
Welch-NY 6.80
Baldwin-Det 6.88
Clarkson-Chi 7.18
Daily-Phi 7.57

Fewest BB/Game
Whitney-Bos .75
Galvin-Buf 1.17
Clarkson-Chi 1.40
Baldwin-Det 1.41
C.Sweeney-StL 1.64

Strikeouts
Clarkson-Chi 308
Welch-NY 258
Buffinton-Bos 242
Keefe-NY 227
Whitney-Bos 200

Strikeouts/Game
Baldwin-Det 6.78
Keefe-NY 5.11
Buffinton-Bos 5.01
Welch-NY 4.72
Clarkson-Chi 4.45

Ratio
Baldwin-Det 8.28
Clarkson-Chi 8.58
Keefe-NY 9.05
Welch-NY 9.20
Daily-Phi 9.41

Earned Run Average
Keefe-NY 1.58
Welch-NY 1.66
Clarkson-Chi 1.85
Baldwin-Det 1.86
Radbourn-Pro 2.20

Adjusted ERA
Keefe-NY 169
Clarkson-Chi 162
Welch-NY 160
Baldwin-Det 153
Daily-Phi 126

Opponents' Batting Avg.
Baldwin-Det .197
Welch-NY .203
Keefe-NY .203
Clarkson-Chi .208
Shaw-Pro .209

Opponents' On-Base Pct.
Baldwin-Det .228
Clarkson-Chi .239
Shaw-Pro .254
Keefe-NY .255
Daily-Phi .256

Starter Runs
Clarkson-Chi 67.0
Welch-NY 63.0
Keefe-NY 55.2
Radbourn-Pro 30.5
Daily-Phi 29.7

Adjusted Starter Runs
Clarkson-Chi 74.9
Welch-NY 57.8
Keefe-NY 51.2
Daily-Phi 28.5
Ferguson-Phi 25.6

Clutch Pitching Index
Keefe-NY 121
Getzien-Det 118
Radbourn-Pro 116
Welch-NY 112
Whitney-Bos 111

Relief Runs

Adjusted Relief Runs

Relief Ranking

Total Pitcher Index
Clarkson-Chi 8.2
Welch-NY 5.3
Keefe-NY 5.0
Ferguson-Phi 4.3
Radbourn-Pro 3.8

Total Baseball Ranking
Clarkson-Chi 8.1
Welch-NY 5.3
Keefe-NY 5.0
Ferguson-Phi 4.5
Connor-NY 4.4

TEAM	G	W	L	PCT	GB	R	OR	AB	H	2B	3B	HR	BB	SO	AVG	OBP	SLG	OPS	OPS+	BR	BR+	PF	CHI	RC	SB	CS	SBA	SBR
STL	112	79	33	.705		677	**461**	3972	979	132	57	17	234	**282**	.246	.297	.321	618	96	1	-26	105	**109**	388				
CIN	112	63	49	.563	16	642	575	4050	1046	108	77	26	153	420	.258	.294	.342	636	103	18	6	102	101	417				
PIT	111	56	55	.505	22.5	547	539	3975	955	123	79	5	189	537	.240	.282	.315	597	94	-32	-24	99	94	362				
PHI	113	55	57	.491	24	**764**	691	4142	**1099**	**169**	76	**30**	223	410	**.265**	**.310**	**.365**	**675**	**111**	**77**	36	106	106	**480**				
LOU	112	53	59	.473	26	564	598	3969	986	126	**83**	19	152	448	.248	.281	.336	617	99	-11	-10	100	95	384				
BRO	112	53	59	.473	26	624	650	3943	966	121	65	14	238	324	.245	.295	.319	614	97	-4	-8	101	102	381				
NY	108	44	64	.407	33	526	688	3731	921	123	57	21	217	428	.247	.295	.327	622	110	4	**54**	92	90	369				
BAL	110	41	68	.376	36.5	541	683	3820	837	124	59	17	**279**	529	.219	.280	.296	576	87	-53	-45	99	99	324				
TOT	445					4885		31602	7789	1026	553	149	1685	3378	.247	.292	.329	620										

TEAM	CG	SH	SV	IP	H	H/G	HR	BB	SO	RAT	ERA	ERA+	OAV	OOB	PR	PR+	PF	CPI	FA	E	DP	FW	PW	BW	SBW	DIF
STL	**111**	**11**	0	1002	**879**	**7.9**	12	**168**	378	**9.8**	**2.45**	**134**	**.228**	**.268**	**89**	**91**	101	106	**.920**	**381**	64	**3.1**	**8.2**	-2.3		14.2
CIN	102	7	1	999^{1}	998	9.0	24	250	330	11.9	3.27	100	.253	.309	-2	-1	100	**112**	.911	423	**86**	.8	-.0	.6		5.8
PIT	104	8	0	1011	918	8.2	14	201	454	10.3	2.92	110	.232	.275	36	33	99	95	.912	422	77	.7	3.0	-2.1		-.9
PHI	105	5	0	1003^{1}	1038	9.4	**11**	212	**506**	11.7	3.23	106	.254	.298	2	21	106	104	.901	483	79	-2.1	1.9	3.3		-3.9
LOU	109	3	1	1002	927	8.4	13	217	462	10.7	2.68	120	.232	.278	63	61	99	104	.905	460	75	-1.1	5.5	-.9		-6.4
BRO	110	3	1	991^{2}	955	8.7	27	211	436	10.9	3.46	95	.240	.283	-24	-18	102	89	.910	434	56	.3	-1.6	-.7		-.8
NY	103	2	0	937	1015	9.8	36	204	408	12.0	4.15	71	.262	.303	-94	-137	91	91	.901	452	62	-1.5	-12.3	**4.9**		-.9
BAL	103	2	**4**	971	1059	9.9	12	222	395	12.4	3.91	83	.269	.316	-71	-70	100	100	.910	418	71	.7	-6.3	-4.0		-3.7
TOT	847	41	7	7917^{1}		8.9				11.2	3.25		.247	.292					.909	3473	570					

Runs
Stovey-Phi 130
Larkin-Phi 114
Jones-Cin 108
Nelson-NY 98
Browning-Lou 98

Hits
Browning-Lou 174
Jones-Cin 157
Stovey-Phi 153
Orr-NY 152
Larkin-Phi 149

Doubles
Larkin-Phi 37
Browning-Lou 34
Orr-NY 29
Stovey-Phi 27

Triples
Orr-NY 21
Kuehne-Pit 19
Wolf-Lou 17
Jones-Cin 17
Fennelly-Cin 17

Home Runs
Stovey-Phi 13
Fennelly-Cin 10
Browning-Lou 9
Larkin-Phi 8
Orr-NY 6

Total Bases
Browning-Lou 255
Orr-NY 241
Larkin-Phi 238
Stovey-Phi 237
Jones-Cin 225

Runs Batted In
Fennelly-Cin 89
Larkin-Phi 88
Orr-NY 77
Stovey-Phi 75
Browning-Lou 73

Runs Produced
Larkin-Phi 194
Stovey-Phi 192
Browning-Lou 162
Fennelly-Cin 161
Welch-StL 150

Bases On Balls
Nelson-NY 61
Macullar-Bal 49
Hotaling-Bro 49
Stovey-Phi 39

Batting Average
Browning-Lou .362
Orr-NY .342
Larkin-Phi .329
Jones-Cin .322
Stovey-Phi .315

On-Base Percentage
Browning-Lou .393
Larkin-Phi .372
Stovey-Phi .371
Brown-Pit .366
Phillips-Bro .364

Slugging Average
Orr-NY .543
Browning-Lou .530
Larkin-Phi .525
Stovey-Phi .488
Jones-Cin .462

On-Base Plus Slugging
Browning-Lou 923
Orr-NY 901
Larkin-Phi 897
Stovey-Phi 858
Jones-Cin 824

Adjusted OPS
Orr-NY 197
Browning-Lou 190
Larkin-Phi 171
Stovey-Phi 160
Jones-Cin 156

Batter Runs
Browning-Lou 47.0
Larkin-Phi 40.3
Orr-NY 38.1
Stovey-Phi 37.9
Jones-Cin 31.5

Adjusted Batter Runs
Browning-Lou 47.3
Orr-NY 47.1
Larkin-Phi 34.0
Stovey-Phi 31.4
Jones-Cin 29.5

Clutch Hitting Index
Nicol-StL 131
Swartwood-Bro 131
Houck-Phi 125
Fennelly-Cin 125
Gleason-StL 123

Runs Created
Browning-Lou 103
Larkin-Phi 91
Stovey-Phi 90
Orr-NY 88
Jones-Cin 83

Total Average
Browning-Lou .912
Larkin-Phi .885
Orr-NY .863
Stovey-Phi .841
Jones-Cin .773

Stolen Bases

Stolen Base Average

Stolen Base Runs

Fielding Runs
G.Smith-Bro 39.9
Smith-Pit 33.2
Houck-Phi 21.8
Hankinson-NY 18.0
Corkhill-Cin 17.1

Total Player Rating
Browning-Lou 4.3
G.Smith-Bro 3.9
Larkin-Phi 3.8
Jones-Cin 3.4
Smith-Pit 3.2

Wins
Caruthers-StL 40
Morris-Pit 39
Porter-Bro 33
Foutz-StL 33

Win Percentage
Caruthers-StL .755
Foutz-StL .702
Mathews-Phi .638
Morris-Pit .619
Porter-Bro .611

Games
Morris-Pit 63
Henderson-Bal 61
Porter-Bro 54
Hecker-Lou 53
Caruthers-StL 53

Complete Games
Morris-Pit 63
Henderson-Bal 59
Porter-Bro 53
Caruthers-StL 53
Hecker-Lou 51

Shutouts
Morris-Pit 7
Caruthers-StL 6
McGinnis-StL 3

Saves
Burns-Bal 3
Terry-Bro 1
Sommer-Bal 1
Reccius-Lou 1
Corkhill-Cin 1

Innings Pitched
Morris-Pit 581.0
Henderson-Bal 539.1
Caruthers-StL 482.1
Porter-Bro 481.2
Hecker-Lou 480.0

Fewest Hits/Game
Morris-Pit 7.11
Mays-Lou 7.74
Foutz-StL 7.75
McGinnis-StL 7.87
Porter-Bro 7.98

Fewest BB/Game
Lynch-NY 1.00
Hecker-Lou 1.01
Caruthers-StL 1.06
Mathews-Phi 1.21
McGinnis-StL 1.53

Strikeouts
Morris-Pit 298
Mathews-Phi 286
Henderson-Bal 263
Hecker-Lou 209
Porter-Bro 197

Strikeouts/Game
Mathews-Phi 6.09
Cushman-Phi-NY 5.50
Morris-Pit 4.62
Henderson-Bal 4.39
Harkins-Bro 4.33

Ratio
Morris-Pit 8.89
Caruthers-StL 9.44
Hecker-Lou 9.86
McGinnis-StL 9.88
Mathews-Phi 10.04

Earned Run Average
Caruthers-StL 2.07
Hecker-Lou 2.17
Morris-Pit 2.35
Mathews-Phi 2.43
Foutz-StL 2.63

Adjusted ERA
Caruthers-StL 158
Hecker-Lou 148
Mathews-Phi 141
Morris-Pit 137
Foutz-StL 124

Opponents' Batting Avg.
Morris-Pit .208
Mays-Lou .219
Porter-Bro .223
McGinnis-StL .225
Foutz-StL .227

Opponents' On-Base Pct.
Morris-Pit .247
Caruthers-StL .260
Hecker-Lou .265
Cushman-Phi-NY .266
Mathews-Phi .267

Starter Runs
Caruthers-StL 62.9
Morris-Pit 57.4
Hecker-Lou 57.0
Mathews-Phi 38.2
Foutz-StL 28.0

Adjusted Starter Runs
Caruthers-StL 63.6
Hecker-Lou 56.2
Morris-Pit 56.1
Mathews-Phi 44.6
Foutz-StL 28.8

Clutch Pitching Index
Knight-Phi 283
Hecker-Lou 121
Caruthers-StL 118
Mountjoy-Cin-Bal 111
Foutz-StL 107

Relief Runs

Adjusted Relief Runs

Relief Ranking

Total Pitcher Index
Hecker-Lou 6.7
Caruthers-StL 6.5
Morris-Pit 4.6
Foutz-StL 3.8
Mathews-Phi 3.5

Total Baseball Ranking
Caruthers-StL 6.4
Hecker-Lou 6.3
Morris-Pit 4.5
Browning-Lou 4.3
G.Smith-Bro 3.9

TEAM	G	W	L	PCT	GB	R	OR	AB	H	2B	3B	HR	BB	SO	AVG	OBP	SLG	OPS	OPS+	BR	BR+	PF	CHI	RC	SB	CS	SBA	SBR
CHI	126	90	34	.726		**900**	555	4378	1223	**198**	**87**	**53**	**460**	513	.279	**.348**	**.401**	**749**	116	**176**	66	115	104	**701**	213			
DET	126	87	36	.707	2.5	829	538	4501	**1260**	176	81	**53**	374	426	**.280**	.335	.390	725	**122**	137	**114**	103	100	670	194			
NY	124	75	44	.630	12.5	692	558	4298	1156	175	68	21	237	**410**	.269	.307	.356	663	106	29	22	101	102	531	155			
PHI	119	71	43	.623	14	621	**498**	4072	976	145	66	26	282	516	.240	.289	.327	616	91	-37	-42	101	**106**	461	**226**			
BOS	118	56	61	.479	30.5	657	661	4180	1085	151	59	24	250	537	.260	.301	.341	642	104	0	24	96	104	489	156			
STL	126	43	79	.352	46	547	712	4250	1001	183	46	30	235	656	.236	.276	.321	597	92	-71	-32	94	96	430	156			
KC	126	30	91	.248	58.5	494	872	4236	967	177	48	19	269	608	.228	.274	.306	580	76	-92	-125	106	90	392	96			
WAS	125	28	92	.233	60	445	791	4082	856	135	51	23	265	582	.210	.258	.285	543	73	-143	-114	94	93	345	143			
TOT	495					5185		33997	8524	1340	506	249	2372	4248	.251	.300	.342	641							1339			

TEAM	CG	SH	SV	IP	H	H/G	HR	BB	SO	RAT	ERA	ERA+	OAV	OOB	PR	PR+	PF	CPI	FA	E	DP	FW	PW	BW	SBW	DIF
CHI	116	8	**3**	1097^{2}	988	8.2	49	262	**647**	**10.3**	2.55	**141**	.232	.277	91	**117**	109	**111**	.912	475	82	-1.7	**10.7**	6.0		13.2
DET	**122**	8	0	1103^{2}	995	8.2	**20**	270	592	10.4	2.86	115	.231	.276	53	52	100	90	**.928**	373	82	3.8	4.8	**10.4**		6.7
NY	119	3	1	1062	1029	8.8	23	280	588	11.1	2.87	111	.247	.294	50	27	97	104	.927	**359**	70	**4.2**	2.5	2.0		6.9
PHI	110	**10**	2	1045^{2}	**923**	**8.0**	29	264	540	**10.3**	**2.46**	134	**.224**	**.271**	**97**	95	100	101	.921	393	46	1.4	8.7	-3.8		7.9
BOS	116	3	0	1029	1049	9.2	33	298	511	11.8	3.25	98	.252	.302	5	-8	97	104	.905	465	63	-2.7	-.7	2.2		-1.2
STL	118	6	0	1077^{1}	1050	8.8	34	392	501	12.1	3.25	99	.246	.309	5	-7	97	105	.914	452	**92**	-.5	-.6	-2.9		-13.9
KC	117	4	0	1066^{2}	1345	11.4	27	**246**	442	13.5	4.85	77	.295	.331	-184	-116	114	90	.910	482	79	-2.1	-10.5	-11.3		-6.5
WAS	115	4	0	1041	1147	10.0	34	379	500	13.2	4.30	76	.271	.331	-117	-125	99	95	.910	458	69	-1.0	-11.3	-10.3		-9.3
TOT	933	46	6	8523		9.1				11.6	3.29		.251	.300					.916	3457	583					

Runs
Kelly-Chi 155
Gore-Chi 150
Brouthers-Det 139
Richardson-Det 125
Anson-Chi 117

Hits
Richardson-Det 189
Anson-Chi 187
Brouthers-Det 181
Kelly-Chi 175
Connor-NY 172

Doubles
Brouthers-Det 40
Anson-Chi 35
Kelly-Chi 32
Hines-Was 30

Triples
Connor-NY 20
Wood-Phi 15
Brouthers-Det 15
Thompson-Det 13

Home Runs
Richardson-Det 11
Brouthers-Det 11
Anson-Chi 10
Hines-Was 9
Denny-StL 9

Total Bases
Brouthers-Det 284
Anson-Chi 274
Richardson-Det 271
Connor-NY 262
Kelly-Chi 241

Runs Batted In
Anson-Chi 147
Pfeffer-Chi 95
Thompson-Det 89
Rowe-Det 87
Ward-NY 81

Runs Produced
Anson-Chi 254
Kelly-Chi 230
Gore-Chi 207
Brouthers-Det 200
Thompson-Det 182

Bases On Balls
Gore-Chi 102
Kelly-Chi 83
Williamson-Chi 80
Brouthers-Det 66
Radford-KC 58

Batting Average
Kelly-Chi .388
Anson-Chi .371
Brouthers-Det .370
Connor-NY .355
Richardson-Det .351

On-Base Percentage
Kelly-Chi .483
Brouthers-Det .445
Gore-Chi .434
Anson-Chi .433
Connor-NY .405

Slugging Average
Brouthers-Det .581
Anson-Chi .544
Connor-NY .540
Kelly-Chi .534
Richardson-Det .504

On-Base Plus Slugging
Brouthers-Det 1026
Kelly-Chi 1018
Anson-Chi 977
Connor-NY 945
Richardson-Det 906

Adjusted OPS
Brouthers-Det 204
Connor-NY 183
Kelly-Chi 183
Anson-Chi 171
Richardson-Det 169

Batter Runs
Brouthers-Det 65.9
Kelly-Chi 64.3
Anson-Chi 58.3
Connor-NY 48.7
Richardson-Det 47.4

Adjusted Batter Runs
Brouthers-Det 61.8
Connor-NY 47.5
Kelly-Chi 46.5
Richardson-Det 43.7
Anson-Chi 40.8

Clutch Hitting Index
Anson-Chi 158
Ward-NY 153
Pfeffer-Chi 141
Dorgan-NY 139
Gillespie-NY 138

Runs Created
Kelly-Chi 146
Brouthers-Det 139
Anson-Chi 134
Richardson-Det 129
Connor-NY 116

Total Average
Kelly-Chi 1.366
Brouthers-Det 1.205
Anson-Chi 1.129
Gore-Chi 1.042
Richardson-Det 1.029

Stolen Bases
Andrews-Phi 56
Kelly-Chi 53
Hanlon-Det 50
Richardson-Det 42
Radford-KC 39

Stolen Base Average

Stolen Base Runs

Fielding Runs
Knowles-Was 27.7
Denny-StL 22.7
Dunlap-StL-Det 19.3
Johnston-Bos 16.6
Glasscock-StL 13.8

Total Player Rating
Richardson-Det 4.7
Kelly-Chi 4.7
Glasscock-StL 4.5
Connor-NY 4.2
Brouthers-Det 3.8

Wins
Keefe-NY 42
Baldwin-Det 42
Clarkson-Chi 36
Welch-NY 33
McCormick-Chi 31

Win Percentage
Flynn-Chi .793
Ferguson-Phi .769
Baldwin-Det .764
McCormick-Chi .738
Getzien-Det .732

Games
Keefe-NY 64
Welch-NY 59
Radbourn-Bos 58
Baldwin-Det 56
Clarkson-Chi 55

Complete Games
Keefe-NY 62
Radbourn-Bos 57
Welch-NY 56
Baldwin-Det 55
Clarkson-Chi 50

Shutouts
Baldwin-Det 7
Ferguson-Phi 4
Casey-Phi 4

Saves
Ferguson-Phi 2
Williamson-Chi 1
Ryan-Chi 1
Flynn-Chi 1
Devlin-NY 1

Innings Pitched
Keefe-NY 535.0
Radbourn-Bos 509.1
Welch-NY 500.0
Baldwin-Det 487.0
Clarkson-Chi 466.2

Fewest Hits/Game
Baldwin-Det 6.86
Ferguson-Phi 7.21
Flynn-Chi 7.25
Stemmeyer-Bos 7.74
Boyle-StL 7.84

Fewest BB/Game
Whitney-KC 1.26
Ferguson-Phi 1.57
Clarkson-Chi 1.66
Keefe-NY 1.72
Baldwin-Det 1.85

Strikeouts
Baldwin-Det 323
Clarkson-Chi 313
Keefe-NY 297
Welch-NY 272
Stemmeyer-Bos 239

Strikeouts/Game
Stemmeyer-Bos 6.17
Clarkson-Chi 6.04
Baldwin-Det 5.97
Healy-StL 5.42
Flynn-Chi 5.11

Ratio
Baldwin-Det 8.70
Ferguson-Phi 8.78
Flynn-Chi 9.46
Clarkson-Chi 9.74
Keefe-NY 9.77

Earned Run Average
Boyle-StL 1.76
Ferguson-Phi 1.98
Baldwin-Det 2.24
Flynn-Chi 2.24
Clarkson-Chi 2.41

Adjusted ERA
Boyle-StL 182
Ferguson-Phi 166
Flynn-Chi 160
Clarkson-Chi 149
Baldwin-Det 147

Opponents' Batting Avg.
Baldwin-Det .202
Ferguson-Phi .210
Flynn-Chi .210
Stemmeyer-Bos .218
Boyle-StL .220

Opponents' On-Base Pct.
Baldwin-Det .243
Ferguson-Phi .244
Flynn-Chi .257
Boyle-StL .261
Clarkson-Chi .264

Starter Runs
Ferguson-Phi 57.5
Baldwin-Det 56.9
Clarkson-Chi 45.4
Keefe-NY 43.4
Casey-Phi 35.8

Adjusted Starter Runs
Ferguson-Phi 57.3
Baldwin-Det 57.0
Clarkson-Chi 56.2
Keefe-NY 38.7
Casey-Phi 35.5

Clutch Pitching Index
Boyle-StL 127
McCormick-Chi 126
Welch-NY 121
Kirby-StL 112
Radbourn-Bos 108

Relief Runs

Adjusted Relief Runs

Relief Ranking

Total Pitcher Index
Ferguson-Phi 6.5
Baldwin-Det 6.1
Clarkson-Chi 5.9
Boyle-StL 4.1
Keefe-NY 3.8

Total Baseball Ranking
Ferguson-Phi 6.4
Baldwin-Det 6.0
Clarkson-Chi 5.7
Kelly-Chi 4.7
Richardson-Det 4.5

TEAM	G	W	L	PCT	GB	R	OR	AB	H	2B	3B	HR	BB	SO	AVG	OBP	SLG	OPS	OPS+	BR	BR+	PF	CHI	RC	SB	CS	SBA	SBR
STL	139	93	46	.669		**944**	**592**	5009	**1365**	**206**	85	20	400	**425**	**.273**	**.333**	**.360**	**693**	**116**	**114**	**72**	105	102	**729**	**336**			
PIT	140	80	57	.584	12	810	647	4854	1171	186	**96**	16	**478**	713	.241	.314	.329	643	106	31	35	100	97	598	260			
BRO	141	76	61	.555	16	832	832	5053	1261	196	80	16	433	523	.250	.311	.330	641	103	22	14	101	99	610	248			
LOU	138	66	70	.485	25.5	833	805	4921	1294	182	88	20	410	558	.263	.323	.348	671	108	74	27	106	95	634	202			
CIN	141	65	73	.471	27.5	883	865	4915	1225	145	95	**45**	374	633	.249	.311	.345	656	106	45	19	103	105	599	185			
PHI	139	63	72	.467	28	772	942	4856	1142	192	82	21	378	697	.235	.296	.321	617	95	-22	-30	101	101	560	284			
NY	137	53	82	.393	38	628	766	4683	1047	108	72	18	330	578	.224	.279	.289	568	85	-101	-71	96	96	422	120			
BAL	139	48	83	.366	41	625	878	4639	945	124	51	8	379	603	.204	.269	.258	527	70	-163	-148	98	**106**	404	269			
TOT	557					6327		38930	9450	1339	649	164	3182	4730	.243	.306	.324	628							1904			

TEAM	CG	SH	SV	IP	H	H/G	HR	BB	SO	RAT	ERA	ERA+	OAV	OOB	PR	PR+	PF	CPI	FA	E	DP	FW	PW	BW	SBW	DIF
STL	134	14	**2**	1229[1]	**1087**	**8.0**	13	329	583	**10.6**	**2.49**	**138**	**.227**	**.281**	**130**	**128**	100	**113**	.915	494	96	3.3	**11.3**	**6.4**		2.7
PIT	137	**15**	1	1226	1130	8.3	**10**	**299**	515	10.8	2.83	120	.235	.285	84	76	98	104	**.917**	**487**	90	**3.9**	6.7	3.1		-2.1
BRO	**138**	6	0	1234[2]	1202	8.8	17	464	540	12.4	3.42	102	.243	.312	3	8	101	104	.900	610	87	-2.2	.8	1.3		7.8
LOU	131	5	**2**	1209[2]	1109	8.3	16	432	720	11.7	3.07	118	.230	.297	51	71	106	101	.901	593	89	-1.9	6.3	2.4		-8.6
CIN	129	3	0	1247[2]	1267	9.2	25	481	495	13.0	4.19	84	.255	.327	-103	-92	102	95	.905	582	**122**	-.7	-8.0	1.7		3.2
PHI	134	4	0	1218[2]	1308	9.7	35	388	513	13.0	3.98	88	.259	.319	-72	-65	102	100	.894	637	99	-3.9	-5.7	-2.6		7.9
NY	134	5	0	1186[1]	1148	8.8	23	386	559	11.9	3.51	97	.243	.304	-8	-14	99	98	.907	544	81	.4	-1.2	-6.2		-7.3
BAL	134	5	0	1206[2]	1197	9.0	25	403	**805**	12.4	4.08	84	.244	.308	-85	-91	99	87	.910	523	59	1.9	-7.9	-12.9		1.7
TOT	1071	57	5	9759		8.8				12.0	3.45		.243	.306					.906	4470	723					

Runs
Latham-StL 152
McPhee-Cin 139
Larkin-Phi 133
McClellan-Bro 131
Pinkney-Bro 119

Hits
Orr-NY 193
O'Neill-StL 190
Larkin-Phi 180
Latham-StL 174
Phillips-Bro 160

Doubles
Larkin-Phi 36
McClellan-Bro 33
Welch-StL 31
Barkley-Pit 31
Browning-Lou 29

Triples
Orr-NY 31
Coleman-Phi-Pit 17
Kuehne-Pit 17
Fennelly-Cin 17
Larkin-Phi 16

Home Runs
McPhee-Cin 8
Stovey-Phi 7
Orr-NY 7

Total Bases
Orr-NY 301
O'Neill-StL 255
Larkin-Phi 254
Welch-StL 221
McPhee-Cin 221

Runs Batted In
O'Neill-StL 107
Corkhill-Cin 97
Welch-StL 95
Orr-NY 91
Reilly-Cin 79

Runs Produced
O'Neill-StL 210
Welch-StL 207
Larkin-Phi 205
McPhee-Cin 201

Bases On Balls
Swartwood-Bro 70
Pinkney-Bro 70
Mack-Lou 68
Kerins-Lou 66

Batting Average
Hecker-Lou .341
Browning-Lou .340
Orr-NY .338
Caruthers-StL .334
O'Neill-StL .328

On-Base Percentage
Larkin-Phi .390
Browning-Lou .389
O'Neill-StL .385
Stovey-Phi .377
Swartwood-Bro .377

Slugging Average
Orr-NY .527
Caruthers-StL .527
Larkin-Phi .450
Hecker-Lou .446
Browning-Lou .441

On-Base Plus Slugging
Orr-NY 890
Larkin-Phi 839
Browning-Lou 830
O'Neill-StL 826
Stovey-Phi 817

Adjusted OPS
Orr-NY 186
Larkin-Phi 161
Stovey-Phi 154
O'Neill-StL 151
Browning-Lou 151

Batter Runs
Orr-NY 45.9
Caruthers-StL 41.4
Larkin-Phi 41.3
O'Neill-StL 38.6
Stovey-Phi 32.1

Adjusted Batter Runs
Orr-NY 52.1
Larkin-Phi 40.0
Caruthers-StL 36.9
O'Neill-StL 32.6
Stovey-Phi 31.0

Clutch Hitting Index
Corkhill-Cin 151
Carpenter-Cin 142
Coleman-Phi-Pit 129
O'Brien-Phi 128
O'Neill-StL 124

Runs Created
Orr-NY 118
Larkin-Phi 114
Stovey-Phi 109
O'Neill-StL 104
Latham-StL 104

Total Average
Stovey-Phi 1.009
Larkin-Phi .914
Robinson-StL .903
Orr-NY .897
Browning-Lou .873

Stolen Bases
Stovey-Phi 68
Latham-StL 60
Welch-StL 59
Robinson-StL 51
McClellan-Bro 43

Stolen Base Average

Stolen Base Runs

Fielding Runs
Kerins-Lou 39.0
McPhee-Cin 30.5
Hankinson-NY 25.4
Smith-Pit 21.0
Peoples-Bro 18.5

Total Player Rating
Kerins-Lou 4.6
McPhee-Cin 4.5
Larkin-Phi 3.6
Carroll-Pit 3.5
Orr-NY 3.4

Wins
Morris-Pit 41
Foutz-StL 41
Ramsey-Lou 38
Mullane-Cin 33
Caruthers-StL 30

Win Percentage
Foutz-StL .719
Caruthers-StL .682
Morris-Pit .672
Hudson-StL .615
Atkinson-Phi .595

Games
Kilroy-Bal 68
Ramsey-Lou 67
Morris-Pit 64
Mullane-Cin 63
Foutz-StL 59

Complete Games
Ramsey-Lou 66
Kilroy-Bal 66
Morris-Pit 63
Mullane-Cin 55
Foutz-StL 55

Shutouts
Morris-Pit 12
Foutz-StL 11
Terry-Bro 5
Kilroy-Bal 5
Ramsey-Lou 3

Saves
Morris-Pit 1
Hudson-StL 1
Foutz-StL 1
Ely-Lou 1

Innings Pitched
Ramsey-Lou 588.2
Kilroy-Bal 583.0
Morris-Pit 555.1
Mullane-Cin 529.2
Foutz-StL 504.0

Fewest Hits/Game
Ramsey-Lou 6.83
Kilroy-Bal 7.35
Morris-Pit 7.37
Foutz-StL 7.46
Caruthers-StL 7.51

Fewest BB/Game
Galvin-Pit 1.55
Morris-Pit 1.91
Caruthers-StL 2.00
McGinnis-StL-Bal 2.27
Atkinson-Phi 2.29

Strikeouts
Kilroy-Bal 513
Ramsey-Lou 499
Morris-Pit 326
Foutz-StL 283
Mullane-Cin 250

Strikeouts/Game
Kilroy-Bal 7.92
Ramsey-Lou 7.63
Morris-Pit 5.28
Miller-Phi 5.25
Terry-Bro 5.06

Ratio
Morris-Pit 9.40
Caruthers-StL 9.67
Ramsey-Lou 10.18
Foutz-StL 10.21
Cushman-NY 10.45

Earned Run Average
Foutz-StL 2.11
Caruthers-StL 2.32
Ramsey-Lou 2.45
Morris-Pit 2.45
Galvin-Pit 2.67

Adjusted ERA
Foutz-StL 163
Ramsey-Lou 148
Caruthers-StL 148
Morris-Pit 138
Hecker-Lou 127

Opponents' Batting Avg.
Ramsey-Lou .198
Kilroy-Bal .210
Morris-Pit .214
Foutz-StL .216
Caruthers-StL .217

Opponents' On-Base Pct.
Morris-Pit .258
Caruthers-StL .263
Ramsey-Lou .269
Foutz-StL .274
Kilroy-Bal .274

Starter Runs
Foutz-StL 74.8
Ramsey-Lou 65.2
Morris-Pit 61.4
Caruthers-StL 48.2
Galvin-Pit 37.3

Adjusted Starter Runs
Foutz-StL 74.4
Ramsey-Lou 73.5
Morris-Pit 58.7
Caruthers-StL 47.9
Galvin-Pit 34.9

Clutch Pitching Index
Galvin-Pit 130
McGinnis-StL-Bal 127
Foutz-StL 122
Miller-Phi 119
Mays-NY 107

Relief Runs

Adjusted Relief Runs

Relief Ranking

Total Pitcher Index
Foutz-StL 8.1
Caruthers-StL 6.8
Ramsey-Lou 6.2
Hecker-Lou 5.1
Morris-Pit 4.5

Total Baseball Ranking
Foutz-StL 8.2
Caruthers-StL 7.9
Ramsey-Lou 6.2
Hecker-Lou 5.1
Kerins-Lou 4.6

TEAM	G	W	L	PCT	GB	R	OR	AB	H	2B	3B	HR	BB	SO	AVG	OBP	SLG	OPS	OPS+	BR	BR+	PF	CHI	RC	SB	CS	SBA	SBR
DET	127	79	45	.637		**969**	714	5041	**1756**	**213**	**126**	55	352	**258**	**.348**	**.353**	**.434**	**787**	**118**	**134**	**105**	103	103	**833**	267			
PHI	128	75	48	.610	3.5	901	**702**	5015	1654	**213**	89	47	385	346	.330	.337	.389	726	99	35	-10	106	**107**	744	355			
CHI	127	71	50	.587	6.5	813	716	4757	1584	178	98	**80**	**407**	400	.333	.336	.412	748	98	62	-33	113	99	748	382			
NY	129	68	55	.553	10.5	816	723	4877	1620	167	93	48	361	326	.332	.339	.389	728	111	37	77	95	100	753	**415**			
BOS	127	61	60	.504	16.5	831	792	4871	1595	185	94	53	340	392	.327	.333	.394	727	106	32	31	100	102	736	373			
PIT	125	55	69	.444	24	621	750	4733	1460	183	78	20	319	381	.308	.314	.349	663	94	-69	-24	94	90	567	221			
WAS	126	46	76	.377	32	601	818	4583	1308	149	63	47	269	339	.285	.292	.337	629	82	-126	-93	95	99	535	334			
IND	127	37	89	.294	43	628	965	4668	1380	162	70	33	300	379	.296	.302	.339	641	85	-105	-81	96	97	562	334			
TOT	508					6180		38545	12357	1450	711	383	2733	2821	.321	.327	.382	707							2681			

TEAM	CG	SH	SV	IP	H	H/G	HR	BB	SO	RAT	ERA	ERA+	OAV	OOB	PR	PR+	PF	CPI	FA	E	DP	FW	PW	BW	SBW	DIF
DET	122	3	1	1116[1]	1516	12.3	52	344	337	12.5	3.96	102	.317	.322	12	-3	99	97	**.925**	**394**	92	**3.4**	-.2	**8.9**		5.1
PHI	119	**7**	1	1132[2]	1478	**11.8**	48	305	435	**12.1**	3.48	121	**.306**	**.311**	72	86	104	104	.912	471	76	-.3	7.3	-.8		7.5
CHI	117	4	**3**	1126	1494	12.0	55	338	**510**	12.4	**3.47**	**129**	.309	.317	**73**	**109**	110	**108**	.914	472	99	-.6	**9.3**	-2.7		4.7
NY	123	5	1	1113[2]	**1469**	11.9	**27**	373	415	12.2	3.58	105	.309	.314	59	19	93	96	.920	431	83	1.9	1.7	6.6		-3.4
BOS	123	4	1	1100[2]	1622	13.3	55	396	254	13.7	4.41	91	.332	.338	-44	-46	100	99	.905	522	94	-3.1	-3.8	2.7		5.0
PIT	123	4	0	1108[2]	1533	12.5	39	**246**	248	12.8	4.12	94	.317	.322	-9	-33	95	99	.921	425	70	1.4	-2.7	-2.0		-3.5
WAS	**124**	3	0	1090[1]	1515	12.6	47	299	396	12.9	4.20	96	.317	.323	-18	-21	100	96	.909	483	77	-1.3	-1.7	-7.8		-3.9
IND	118	4	1	1088	1720	14.3	60	431	245	14.6	5.25	79	.347	.352	-145	-137	102	92	.912	479	**105**	-.9	-11.6	-6.8		-6.5
TOT	969	34	8	8876[1]		12.6				12.9	4.05		.321	.327					.915	3677	696					

Runs
Brouthers-Det 153
Rowe-Det 135
Richardson-Det 131
Kelly-Bos 120

Hits
Brouthers-Det 240
Thompson-Det 235
Anson-Chi 224
Ward-NY 213

Doubles
Brouthers-Det 36
Kelly-Bos 34
Denny-Ind 34
Anson-Chi 33

Triples
Thompson-Det 23
Connor-NY 22
Johnston-Bos 20
Brouthers-Det 20
Wood-Phi 19

Home Runs
B.O'Brien-Was 19
Connor-NY 17
Pfeffer-Chi 16
Wood-Phi 14

Total Bases
Brouthers-Det 352
Thompson-Det 340
Connor-NY 330
Anson-Chi 304
Richardson-Det 294

Runs Batted In
Thompson-Det 166
Connor-NY 104
Anson-Chi 102
Brouthers-Det 101
Denny-Ind 97

Runs Produced
Thompson-Det 274
Brouthers-Det 242
Rowe-Det 225
Richardson-Det 217
Anson-Chi 202

Bases On Balls
Fogarty-Phi 82
Connor-NY 75
Williamson-Chi 73
Seery-Ind 71
Brouthers-Det 71

Batting Average
Anson-Chi 421
Brouthers-Det 420
Thompson-Det 407
Kelly-Bos 391
Schomberg-Ind 389

On-Base Percentage
Brouthers-Det 426
Anson-Chi 422
Thompson-Det 416
Schomberg-Ind 397
Kelly-Bos 393

Slugging Average
Thompson-Det 565
Brouthers-Det 562
Connor-NY 541
Wise-Bos 522
Anson-Chi 517

On-Base Plus Slugging
Brouthers-Det 988
Thompson-Det 982
Anson-Chi 939
Connor-NY 933
Wise-Bos 913

Adjusted OPS
Brouthers-Det 167
Thompson-Det 165
Connor-NY 164
Carroll-Pit 152
Wise-Bos 151

Batter Runs
Brouthers-Det 50.5
Thompson-Det 50.2
Anson-Chi 39.4
Connor-NY 37.1
Wise-Bos 31.7

Adjusted Batter Runs
Brouthers-Det 46.1
Thompson-Det 45.8
Connor-NY 43.3
Wise-Bos 31.6
Carroll-Pit 30.4

Clutch Hitting Index
Thompson-Det 151
O'Rourke-NY 143
Nash-Bos 129
Rowe-Det 125
Schomberg-Ind 122

Runs Created
Thompson-Det 141
Brouthers-Det 138
Kelly-Bos 129
Ward-NY 125
Connor-NY 120

Total Average
Brouthers-Det 1.184
Kelly-Bos 1.146
Connor-NY 1.131
Thompson-Det 1.085
Fogarty-Phi 1.085

Stolen Bases
Ward-NY 111
Fogarty-Phi 102
Kelly-Bos 84
Hanlon-Det 69
Glasscock-Ind 62

Stolen Base Average

Stolen Base Runs

Fielding Runs
Glasscock-Ind 35.0
Fogarty-Phi 31.7
Ward-NY 29.8
Johnston-Bos 25.3
Pfeffer-Chi 24.6

Total Player Rating
Thompson-Det 4.3
Ward-NY 4.1
Denny-Ind 4.0
Glasscock-Ind 3.7
Fogarty-Phi 3.4

Wins
Clarkson-Chi 38
Keefe-NY 35
Getzien-Det 29
Galvin-Pit 28
Casey-Phi 28

Win Percentage
Getzien-Det 690
Ferguson-Phi 688
Casey-Phi 683
Keefe-NY 648
Clarkson-Chi 644

Games
Clarkson-Chi 60
Keefe-NY 56
Radbourn-Bos 50
Galvin-Pit 49
Whitney-Was 47

Complete Games
Clarkson-Chi 56
Keefe-NY 54
Radbourn-Bos 48
Galvin-Pit 47
Whitney-Was 46

Shutouts
Casey-Phi 4
Madden-Bos 3
Healy-Ind 3
Galvin-Pit 3

Saves
VanHaltren-Chi 1
Twitchell-Det 1
Tiernan-NY 1
Stemmeyer-Bos 1
Pettit-Chi 1
Ferguson-Phi 1
Fast -Ind 1
Baldwin-Chi 1

Innings Pitched
Clarkson-Chi 523.0
Keefe-NY 476.2
Galvin-Pit 440.2
Radbourn-Bos 425.0
Whitney-Was 404.2

Fewest Hits/Game
Keefe-NY 10.12
Clarkson-Chi 10.41
Ferguson-Phi 10.41
Whitney-Was 10.50
Conway-Det 11.03

Fewest BB/Game
Whitney-Was 93
Galvin-Pit 1.37
Ferguson-Phi 1.42
Clarkson-Chi 1.58
Boyle-Ind 1.89

Strikeouts
Clarkson-Chi 237
Keefe-NY 189
Baldwin-Chi 164
Buffinton-Phi 160
Whitney-Was 146

Strikeouts/Game
Baldwin-Chi 4.42
Gilmore-Was 4.37
Buffinton-Phi 4.33
VanHaltren-Chi 4.25
Clarkson-Chi 4.08

Ratio
Keefe-NY 10.33
Clarkson-Chi 10.55
Ferguson-Phi 10.75
Whitney-Was 10.85
Welch-NY 11.32

Earned Run Average
Casey-Phi 2.86
Conway-Det 2.90
Ferguson-Phi 3.00
Clarkson-Chi 3.08
Keefe-NY 3.12

Adjusted ERA
Casey-Phi 147
Clarkson-Chi 145
Ferguson-Phi 140
Conway-Det 139
Baldwin-Chi 131

Opponents' Batting Avg.
Keefe-NY 272
Whitney-Was 277
Clarkson-Chi 278
Ferguson-Phi 283
Conway-Det 294

Opponents' On-Base Pct.
Keefe-NY 276
Clarkson-Chi 281
Whitney-Was 284
Ferguson-Phi 289
Galvin-Pit 299

Starter Runs
Clarkson-Chi 56.1
Casey-Phi 51.5
Keefe-NY 49.3
Galvin-Pit 37.1
Whitney-Was 36.9

Adjusted Starter Runs
Clarkson-Chi 72.7
Casey-Phi 56.1
Ferguson-Phi 38.4
Whitney-Was 36.5
Keefe-NY 35.9

Clutch Pitching Index
VanHaltren-Chi 123
Casey-Phi 117
Baldwin-Chi 114
Ferguson-Phi 108
Madden-Bos 105

Relief Runs

Adjusted Relief Runs

Relief Ranking

Total Pitcher Index
Clarkson-Chi 7.6
Whitney-Was 4.7
Ferguson-Phi 4.6
Keefe-NY 4.1
Casey-Phi 3.6

Total Baseball Ranking
Clarkson-Chi 7.5
Ferguson-Phi 4.6
Whitney-Was 4.5
Thompson-Det 4.3
Ward-NY 4.1

TEAM	G	W	L	PCT	GB	R	OR	AB	H	2B	3B	HR	BB	SO	AVG	OBP	SLG	OPS	OPS+	BR	BR+	PF	CHI	RC	SB	CS	SBA	SBR
STL	138	95	40	.704		**1131**	761	5490	**1992**	**261**	78	**39**	442	340	**.363**	**.371**	**.413**	**784**	111	**151**	46	111	**103**	**1012**	**581**			
CIN	136	81	54	.600	14	892	**745**	5179	1667	179	**102**	37	382	366	.322	.329	.371	700	97	-11	-31	102	102	778	527			
BAL	141	77	58	.570	18	975	861	5294	1806	202	100	31	**469**	**334**	.341	.349	.380	729	**114**	50	**109**	94	102	852	545			
LOU	139	76	60	.559	19.5	956	854	5352	1856	194	98	27	436	356	.347	.352	.385	737	107	61	42	102	98	850	466			
PHI	137	64	69	.481	30	893	890	5275	1691	231	84	29	321	388	.321	.327	.375	702	99	-13	-14	100	100	782	476			
BRO	138	60	74	.448	34.5	904	918	5369	1737	200	82	25	456	365	.324	.330	.350	680	92	-40	-50	101	**103**	720	409			
NY	138	44	89	.331	50	754	1093	5259	1636	193	66	21	439	463	.311	.318	.329	647	88	-98	-61	96	94	615	305			
CLE	133	39	92	.298	54	729	1112	5024	1545	178	77	14	375	463	.308	.314	.332	646	87	-99	-76	97	96	611	355			
TOT	550					7234		42242	13930	1638	687	223	3320	3075	.330	.337	.368	704							3664			

TEAM	CG	SH	SV	IP	H	H/G	HR	BB	SO	RAT	ERA	ERA+	OAV	OOB	PR	PR+	PF	CPI	FA	E	DP	FW	PW	BW	SBW	DIF
STL	132	6	2	1199[1]	**1577**	**11.9**	19	**323**	334	**12.3**	3.78	120	**.304**	**.311**	69	94	106	94	**.916**	**481**	86	**3.6**	7.7	3.8		12.6
CIN	129	**11**	1	1182[2]	1598	12.2	28	396	330	12.7	**3.59**	**121**	.315	.322	**93**	**98**	101	107	**.916**	484	**106**	3.1	**8.0**	-2.5		5.1
BAL	132	8	0	1220	1706	12.6	**16**	418	470	13.0	3.87	106	.320	.326	58	31	95	100	.907	549	66	.8	2.6	**8.9**		-2.6
LOU	**133**	3	1	1205[2]	1631	12.2	31	357	**544**	12.5	3.83	115	.310	.316	63	73	102	98	.903	574	83	-.8	6.0	3.5		-.4
PHI	131	5	1	1186[1]	1660	12.6	29	433	417	13.2	4.59	93	.322	.331	-39	-41	100	88	.907	528	95	1.1	-3.3	-1.1		1.0
BRO	132	3	**3**	1185[1]	1802	13.7	27	454	332	14.1	4.48	96	.343	.348	-24	-24	100	103	.905	562	88	-.4	-1.9	-4.0		-.5
NY	132	1	0	1180[1]	1951	14.9	39	406	316	15.3	5.29	80	.360	.365	-130	-139	99	102	.894	632	102	-3.9	-11.2	-4.9		-2.3
CLE	127	2	1	1136	2005	15.9	34	533	332	16.4	5.00	87	.377	.384	-88	-83	101	**115**	.898	576	97	-2.1	-6.7	-6.1		-11.4
TOT	1048	39	9	9495[2]		13.3				13.7	4.30		.330	.337					.906	4386	723					

Runs
O'Neill-StL 167
Latham-StL 163
Griffin-Bal 142
Poorman-Phi 140
Comiskey-StL 139

Hits
O'Neill-StL 275
Browning-Lou 275
Lyons-Phi 256
Burns-Bal 251
Latham-StL 243

Doubles
O'Neill-StL 52
Lyons-Phi 43
Reilly-Cin 35
Latham-StL 35
Browning-Lou 35

Triples
Poorman-Phi 19
O'Neill-StL 19
McPhee-Cin 19
Kerins-Lou 19
Davis-Bal 19
Burns-Bal 19

Home Runs
O'Neill-StL 14
Reilly-Cin 10
Burns-Bal 9

Total Bases
O'Neill-StL 407
Browning-Lou 354
Burns-Bal 349
Lyons-Phi 345
Latham-StL 304

Runs Batted In
O'Neill-StL 123
Browning-Lou 118
Davis-Bal 109
Welch-StL 108
Foutz-StL 108

Runs Produced
O'Neill-StL 276
Browning-Lou 251
Latham-StL 244
Comiskey-StL 238
Griffin-Bal 233

Bases On Balls
Radford-NY 106
Robinson-StL 92
Nicol-Cin 86
Mack-Lou 83
Fennelly-Cin 82

Batting Average
O'Neill-StL .485
Browning-Lou .457
Caruthers-StL .456
Robinson-StL .427
Lyons-Phi .415

On-Base Percentage
O'Neill-StL .490
Browning-Lou .464
Caruthers-StL .463
Robinson-StL .445
Lyons-Phi .421

Slugging Average
O'Neill-StL .691
Caruthers-StL .547
Browning-Lou .547
Lyons-Phi .523
Burns-Bal .519

On-Base Plus Slugging
O'Neill-StL 1180
Browning-Lou 1011
Caruthers-StL 1010
Lyons-Phi 943
Burns-Bal 933

Adjusted OPS
O'Neill-StL 205
Browning-Lou 178
Burns-Bal 169
Caruthers-StL 164
Lyons-Phi 162

Batter Runs
O'Neill-StL 86.4
Browning-Lou 60.9
Lyons-Phi 46.7
Burns-Bal 43.7
Caruthers-StL 42.9

Adjusted Batter Runs
O'Neill-StL 68.9
Browning-Lou 57.6
Burns-Bal 52.9
Lyons-Phi 46.5
Caruthers-StL 31.7

Clutch Hitting Index
Purcell-Bal 140
Hotaling-Cle 128
Greenwood-Bal 127
Welch-StL 127
Wolf-Lou 126

Runs Created
O'Neill-StL 194
Browning-Lou 191
Lyons-Phi 160
Burns-Bal 146
Latham-StL 146

Total Average
O'Neill-StL 1.514
Browning-Lou 1.422
Caruthers-StL 1.368
Robinson-StL 1.197
Lyons-Phi 1.175

Stolen Bases
Nicol-Cin 138
Latham-StL 129
Comiskey-StL 117
Browning-Lou 103
McPhee-Cin 95

Stolen Base Average

Stolen Base Runs

Fielding Runs
Smith-Bro 32.0
McPhee-Cin 26.2
Kerins-Lou 24.8
White-Lou 21.5
Welch-StL 19.4

Total Player Rating
O'Neill-StL 4.7
Browning-Lou 4.0
Lyons-Phi 3.5
McPhee-Cin 3.1
Burns-Bal 3.0

Wins
Kilroy-Bal 46
Ramsey-Lou 37
Smith-Cin 34
King-StL 32
Mullane-Cin 31

Win Percentage
Caruthers-StL .763
King-StL .727
Kilroy-Bal .708
Foutz-StL .676
Smith-Cin .667

Games
Kilroy-Bal 69
Ramsey-Lou 65
Smith-Bal 58
Weyhing-Phi 55
Seward-Phi 55

Complete Games
Kilroy-Bal 66
Ramsey-Lou 61
Smith-Bal 54
Weyhing-Phi 53
Seward-Phi 52

Shutouts
Mullane-Cin 6
Kilroy-Bal 6
Smith-Cin 3
Seward-Phi 3

Saves
Terry-Bro 3

Innings Pitched
Kilroy-Bal 589.1
Ramsey-Lou 561.0
Smith-Bal 491.1
Seward-Phi 470.2
Weyhing-Phi 466.1

Fewest Hits/Game
Caruthers-StL 10.50
Smith-Cin 10.58
Seward-Phi 11.19
Kilroy-Bal 11.33
Ramsey-Lou 11.41

Fewest BB/Game
Hecker-Lou 1.58
Caruthers-StL 1.61
Lynch-NY 1.73
Foutz-StL 2.39
Kilroy-Bal 2.40

Strikeouts
Ramsey-Lou 355
Kilroy-Bal 217
Smith-Bal 206
Weyhing-Phi 193
Smith-Cin 176

Strikeouts/Game
Ramsey-Lou 5.70
Morrison-Cle 4.49
Terry-Bro 3.91
Smith-Bal 3.77
Weyhing-Phi 3.72

Ratio
Smith-Cin 10.76
Caruthers-StL 10.93
Kilroy-Bal 11.64
Seward-Phi 11.65
Ramsey-Lou 11.66

Earned Run Average
Smith-Cin 2.94
Kilroy-Bal 3.07
Mullane-Cin 3.24
Caruthers-StL 3.30
Ramsey-Lou 3.43

Adjusted ERA
Smith-Cin 148
Caruthers-StL 137
Mullane-Cin 134
Kilroy-Bal 133
Ramsey-Lou 128

Opponents' Batting Avg.
Caruthers-StL .279
Smith-Cin .282
Ramsey-Lou .295
Seward-Phi .298
Kilroy-Bal .300

Opponents' On-Base Pct.
Smith-Cin .286
Caruthers-StL .287
Ramsey-Lou .299
Kilroy-Bal .306
Foutz-StL .306

Starter Runs
Kilroy-Bal 80.0
Smith-Cin 67.3
Ramsey-Lou 53.5
Mullane-Cin 48.5
Caruthers-StL 37.6

Adjusted Starter Runs
Kilroy-Bal 70.3
Smith-Cin 68.9
Ramsey-Lou 58.1
Mullane-Cin 50.1
Caruthers-StL 44.2

Clutch Pitching Index
Daily-Cle 140
Crowell-Cle 122
Morrison-Cle 121
Mullane-Cin 119
Chamberlain-Lou 117

Relief Runs

Adjusted Relief Runs

Relief Ranking

Total Pitcher Index
Kilroy-Bal 7.6
Caruthers-StL 6.0
Smith-Cin 5.9
Mullane-Cin 4.5
Ramsey-Lou 3.4

Total Baseball Ranking
Caruthers-StL 7.6
Kilroy-Bal 7.4
Smith-Cin 5.9
O'Neill-StL 4.7
Mullane-Cin 4.3

TEAM	G	W	L	PCT	GB	R	OR	AB	H	2B	3B	HR	BB	SO	AVG	OBP	SLG	OPS	OPS+	BR	BR+	PF	CHI	RC	SB	CS	SBA	SBR
NY	138	84	47	.641		659	**479**	4747	1149	130	76	55	270	456	.242	.287	.336	623	105	21	29	99	102	562	314			
CHI	136	77	58	.570	9	**734**	659	4616	1201	147	**95**	**77**	290	563	.260	.308	**.383**	**691**	118	**127**	77	107	99	**649**	287			
PHI	132	69	61	.531	14.5	535	509	4528	1021	151	46	16	268	485	.225	.276	.290	566	82	-63	-90	105	100	441	246			
BOS	137	70	64	.522	15.5	669	619	4834	1183	167	89	56	282	524	.245	.291	.351	642	108	51	39	102	97	593	293			
DET	134	68	63	.519	16	721	629	4849	**1275**	177	72	51	**307**	**396**	**.263**	**.313**	.361	674	**121**	110	**111**	100	96	623	193			
PIT	139	66	68	.493	19.5	534	580	4713	1070	150	49	14	194	583	.227	.264	.289	553	89	-93	-50	92	**103**	446	287			
IND	136	50	85	.370	36	603	731	4623	1100	**180**	33	34	236	492	.238	.281	.313	594	93	-24	-35	102	**103**	518	**350**			
WAS	136	48	86	.358	37.5	482	731	4546	944	98	49	30	246	499	.208	.255	.271	526	77	-129	-101	94	**103**	408	331			
TOT	544					4937		37456	8943	1200	509	333	2093	3998	.239	.285	.325	609							2301			

TEAM	CG	SH	SV	IP	H	H/G	HR	BB	SO	RAT	ERA	ERA+	OAV	OOB	PR	PR+	PF	CPI	FA	E	DP	FW	PW	BW	SBW	DIF
NY	133	**20**	1	1208	**907**	**6.8**	27	307	**726**	**9.4**	**1.96**	**139**	**.199**	**.255**	**117**	**107**	96	95	.924	432	76	1.3	**10.6**	2.9		3.9
CHI	123	13	1	1186[1]	1139	8.7	63	308	588	11.5	2.96	102	.246	.301	-17	5	106	**112**	**.927**	417	**112**	1.7	.5	7.6		-.2
PHI	125	16	**3**	1167	1072	8.3	26	196	519	10.0	2.39	124	.236	.271	58	67	104	103	.923	424	70	.7	6.6	-8.8		5.7
BOS	134	7	0	1225[1]	1104	8.2	36	269	484	10.5	2.61	109	.232	.280	30	27	100	100	.917	494	91	-2.2	2.7	3.9		-1.2
DET	130	10	1	1199	1115	8.4	44	**183**	522	10.0	2.74	100	.234	.266	12	-2	97	90	.919	463	83	-1.1	-.1	**11.0**		-7.1
PIT	**135**	13	0	1203[1]	1190	9.0	**23**	223	367	10.8	2.68	99	.249	.287	22	-5	94	107	**.927**	**416**	88	**2.3**	-.4	-4.9		2.2
IND	132	6	0	1187[2]	1260	9.6	64	308	388	12.3	3.82	77	.263	.313	-129	-113	104	98	.921	449	84	.0	-11.1	-3.4		-2.9
WAS	133	6	0	1179[1]	1157	8.9	50	298	406	11.5	3.55	79	.248	.300	-93	-105	98	91	.912	494	69	-2.4	-10.3	-9.9		3.7
TOT	1045	91	6	9556		8.5				10.7	2.84		.239	.285					.922	3589	673					

Runs
- Brouthers-Det 118
- Ryan-Chi 115
- Johnston-Bos 102
- Anson-Chi 101
- Connor-NY 98

Hits
- Ryan-Chi 182
- Anson-Chi 177
- Johnston-Bos 173
- Brouthers-Det 160
- White-Det 157

Doubles
- Ryan-Chi 33
- Brouthers-Det 33
- Johnston-Bos 31
- Denny-Ind 27
- Hines-Ind 26

Triples
- Johnston-Bos 18
- Connor-NY 17
- Nash-Bos 15
- Ewing-NY 15

Home Runs
- Ryan-Chi 16
- Connor-NY 14
- Johnston-Bos 12
- Denny-Ind 12
- Anson-Chi 12

Total Bases
- Ryan-Chi 283
- Johnston-Bos 276
- Anson-Chi 257
- Brouthers-Det 242
- Connor-NY 231

Runs Batted In
- Anson-Chi 84
- Nash-Bos 75
- Rowe-Det 74
- Williamson-Chi 73

Runs Produced
- Brouthers-Det 175
- Anson-Chi 173
- Ryan-Chi 163
- Johnston-Bos 158
- Connor-NY 155

Bases On Balls
- Connor-NY 73
- Hoy-Was 69
- Brouthers-Det 68
- Williamson-Chi 65
- Seery-Ind 64

Batting Average
- Anson-Chi .... .344
- Ryan-Chi .... .332
- Kelly-Bos .... .318
- Brouthers-Det ..... .307
- Ewing-NY .... .306

On-Base Percentage
- Anson-Chi .... .400
- Brouthers-Det ..... .399
- Connor-NY .... .389
- Ryan-Chi .... .377
- Hoy-Was .... .374

Slugging Average
- Ryan-Chi .... .515
- Anson-Chi .... .499
- Connor-NY .... .480
- Kelly-Bos .... .480
- Johnston-Bos ..... .472

On-Base Plus Slugging
- Anson-Chi 899
- Ryan-Chi 892
- Connor-NY 869
- Brouthers-Det 862
- Kelly-Bos 848

Adjusted OPS
- Connor-NY 178
- Brouthers-Det 174
- Anson-Chi 173
- Ryan-Chi 170
- Kelly-Bos 166

Batter Runs
- Ryan-Chi 49.4
- Anson-Chi 49.3
- Brouthers-Det 46.6
- Connor-NY 43.7
- Kelly-Bos 33.4

Adjusted Batter Runs
- Brouthers-Det 46.8
- Connor-NY 45.0
- Anson-Chi 41.3
- Ryan-Chi 41.2
- Kelly-Bos 31.8

Clutch Hitting Index
- Rowe-Det 153
- Burns-Chi 150
- Bassett-Ind 126
- Wood-Phi 122
- Nash-Bos 121

Runs Created
- Ryan-Chi 133
- Anson-Chi 117
- Brouthers-Det 113
- Connor-NY 103
- Kelly-Bos 101

Total Average
- Ryan-Chi 1.044
- Kelly-Bos 1.007
- Anson-Chi .... .985
- Brouthers-Det ..... .983
- Connor-NY .... .982

Stolen Bases
- Hoy-Was 82
- Seery-Ind 80
- Sunday-Pit 71
- Pfeffer-Chi 64
- Ryan-Chi 60

Stolen Base Average

Stolen Base Runs

Fielding Runs
- Pfeffer-Chi 38.3
- Nash-Bos 25.6
- Denny-Ind 24.5
- Burns-Chi 17.1
- Sunday-Pit 16.6

Total Player Rating
- Nash-Bos 4.8
- Pfeffer-Chi 4.4
- Ewing-NY 3.8
- Ryan-Chi 3.8
- Anson-Chi 3.7

Wins
- Keefe-NY 35
- Clarkson-Bos 33
- Conway-Det 30
- Morris-Pit 29
- Buffinton-Phi 28

Win Percentage
- Keefe-NY .... .745
- Conway-Det .... .682
- Sanders-Phi .... .655
- Krock-Chi .... .641
- Clarkson-Bos ..... .623

Games
- Morris-Pit 55
- Clarkson-Bos 54
- Keefe-NY 51
- Galvin-Pit 50
- Welch-NY 47

Complete Games
- Morris-Pit 54
- Clarkson-Bos 53
- Galvin-Pit 49
- Keefe-NY 48
- Welch-NY 47

Shutouts
- Sanders-Phi 8
- Keefe-NY 8
- Galvin-Pit 6
- Buffinton-Phi 6

Saves
- Wood-Phi 2
- VanHaltren-Chi 1
- Tyng-Phi 1
- Twitchell-Det 1
- Crane-NY 1

Innings Pitched
- Clarkson-Bos 483.1
- Morris-Pit 480.0
- Galvin-Pit 437.1
- Keefe-NY 434.1
- Welch-NY 425.1

Fewest Hits/Game
- Keefe-NY 6.57
- Titcomb-NY 6.81
- Welch-NY 6.94
- Conway-Det 7.25
- Buffinton-Phi 7.28

Fewest BB/Game
- Sanders-Phi 1.08
- Galvin-Pit 1.09
- Krock-Chi 1.19
- Getzien-Det 1.20
- Madden-Bos 1.31

Strikeouts
- Keefe-NY 335
- Clarkson-Bos 223
- Getzien-Det 202
- Buffinton-Phi 199
- O'Day-Was 186

Strikeouts/Game
- Keefe-NY 6.94
- Titcomb-NY 5.89
- Baldwin-Chi 5.63
- VanHaltren-Chi 5.09
- Getzien-Det 4.50

Ratio
- Keefe-NY 8.68
- Buffinton-Phi 8.70
- Conway-Det 8.86
- Sanders-Phi 9.02
- Gruber-Det 9.04

Earned Run Average
- Keefe-NY 1.74
- Sanders-Phi 1.90
- Buffinton-Phi 1.91
- Welch-NY 1.93
- Sowders-Bos 2.07

Adjusted ERA
- Keefe-NY 156
- Sanders-Phi 156
- Buffinton-Phi 154
- Welch-NY 141
- Sowders-Bos 137

Opponents' Batting Avg.
- Keefe-NY .... .196
- Titcomb-NY .... .201
- Welch-NY .... .207
- Conway-Det .... .208
- Buffinton-Phi ..... .213

Opponents' On-Base Pct.
- Conway-Det .... .243
- Keefe-NY .... .243
- Buffinton-Phi ..... .244
- Gruber-Det .... .249
- Titcomb-NY .... .253

Starter Runs
- Keefe-NY 52.6
- Welch-NY 42.8
- Buffinton-Phi 40.9
- Sanders-Phi 28.6
- Morris-Pit 28.0

Adjusted Starter Runs
- Keefe-NY 49.2
- Buffinton-Phi 44.4
- Welch-NY 39.1
- Sanders-Phi 30.9
- Sowders-Bos 26.7

Clutch Pitching Index
- Baldwin-Chi 137
- Gleason-Phi 125
- Burdick-Ind 116
- Sowders-Bos 113
- Morris-Pit 112

Relief Runs

Adjusted Relief Runs

Relief Ranking

Total Pitcher Index
- Buffinton-Phi 5.6
- Keefe-NY 4.4
- Sanders-Phi 4.0
- Conway-Det 4.0
- Welch-NY 3.4

Total Baseball Ranking
- Buffinton-Phi 5.5
- Nash-Bos 4.8
- Pfeffer-Chi 4.4
- Keefe-NY 4.3
- Ryan-Chi 4.0

TEAM	G	W	L	PCT	GB	R	OR	AB	H	2B	3B	HR	BB	SO	AVG	OBP	SLG	OPS	OPS+	BR	BR+	PF	CHI	RC	SB	CS	SBA	SBR
STL	137	92	43	.681		789	**501**	4755	1189	149	47	**36**	**410**	521	**.250**	**.316**	.324	640	98	54	-22	111	102	651	468			
BRO	143	88	52	.629	6.5	758	584	4871	1177	172	70	25	353	**439**	.242	.300	.321	621	103	17	19	100	101	584	334			
PHI	136	81	52	.609	10	**827**	594	4828	**1209**	**183**	**89**	31	303	473	**.250**	.305	**.344**	**649**	**113**	**60**	**66**	99	**106**	**656**	434			
CIN	137	80	54	.597	11.5	745	628	4801	1161	132	82	32	345	555	.242	.301	.323	624	99	21	-16	105	100	623	**469**			
BAL	137	57	80	.416	36	653	779	4656	1068	162	70	19	298	479	.229	.284	.306	590	96	-37	-19	97	99	511	326			
CLE	135	50	82	.379	40.5	651	839	4603	1076	128	59	12	315	559	.234	.294	.295	589	96	-32	-12	97	99	516	353			
LOU	139	48	87	.356	44	689	870	4881	1177	**183**	67	14	322	604	.241	.297	.315	612	102	1	17	98	94	565	318			
KC	132	43	89	.326	47.5	579	896	4588	1000	142	61	19	288	604	.218	.273	.288	561	78	-84	-119	106	97	441	257			
TOT	548					5691		37983	9057	1251	545	188	2634	4234	.239	.297	.315	612							2959			

TEAM	CG	SH	SV	IP	H	H/G	HR	BB	SO	RAT	ERA	ERA+	OAV	OOB	PR	PR+	PF	CPI	FA	E	DP	FW	PW	BW	SBW	DIF
STL	132	12	0	1212^2	**939**	**7.0**	19	**225**	517	**9.2**	**2.10**	**156**	**.206**	**.254**	**130**	**147**	107	96	**.924**	**430**	73	**3.5**	**13.6**	-2.0		9.6
BRO	**138**	9	0	1286^1	1059	7.5	15	285	577	9.7	2.33	128	.217	.266	104	94	97	97	.918	502	88	.6	8.7	1.8		7.0
PHI	133	**13**	0	1208^2	988	7.4	**14**	324	596	10.4	2.42	124	.216	.279	87	78	98	102	.919	475	73	.7	7.3	**6.1**		.6
CIN	132	10	**2**	1237^2	1103	8.1	19	310	539	10.9	2.73	116	.230	.288	46	58	104	102	.923	456	**100**	2.0	5.4	-1.4		7.2
BAL	130	3	0	1200^1	1162	8.8	23	419	525	12.5	3.78	79	.245	.318	-96	-111	97	93	.920	461	88	1.7	-10.2	-1.7		-1.1
CLE	131	6	1	1171	1235	9.5	38	389	500	12.9	3.72	83	.261	.324	-86	-82	101	**105**	.915	488	87	-.2	-7.5	-1.1		-7.0
LOU	133	6	0	1231^1	1264	9.3	28	281	**599**	11.8	3.25	95	.256	.304	-26	-24	100	**105**	.900	609	75	-6.2	-2.2	1.6		-12.6
KC	128	4	0	1157^2	1306	10.2	32	401	381	13.8	4.30	80	.275	.340	-159	-100	112	101	.914	507	95	-1.9	-9.2	-10.9		-.8
TOT	1057	63	3	9705^2		8.4				11.4	3.06		.239	.297					.917	3928	679					

Runs
Pinkney-Bro 134
Collins-Lou-Bro 133
Stovey-Phi 127
Welch-Phi 125
Latham-StL 119

Hits
O'Neill-StL 177
Reilly-Cin 169
McKean-Cle 164
Collins-Lou-Bro 162
Corkhill-Cin-Bro 160

Doubles
Collins-Lou-Bro 31
Wolf-Lou 28
Reilly-Cin 28
Larkin-Phi 28

Triples
Stovey-Phi 20
Burns-Bal-Bro 15
McKean-Cle 15
Reilly-Cin 14
Foutz-Bro 13

Home Runs
Reilly-Cin 13
Stovey-Phi 9
Larkin-Phi 7

Total Bases
Reilly-Cin 264
Stovey-Phi 244
O'Neill-StL 236
McKean-Cle 233
Burns-Bal-Bro 230

Runs Batted In
Reilly-Cin 103
Larkin-Phi 101
Foutz-Bro 99
O'Neill-StL 98
Corkhill-Cin-Bro 93

Runs Produced
Reilly-Cin 202
O'Neill-StL 189
Foutz-Bro 187
Larkin-Phi 186
Welch-Phi 185

Bases On Balls
Robinson-StL 116
Fennelly-Cin-Phi 72
Nicol-Cin 67
McTamany-KC 67
Pinkney-Bro 66

Batting Average
O'Neill-StL .335
Reilly-Cin .321
Browning-Lou .313
Collins-Lou-Bro .307
Orr-Bro .305

On-Base Percentage
Robinson-StL .400
O'Neill-StL .390
Browning-Lou .380
Collins-Lou-Bro .373
Stovey-Phi .365

Slugging Average
Reilly-Cin .501
Stovey-Phi .460
O'Neill-StL .446
Browning-Lou .436
Burns-Bal-Bro .435

On-Base Plus Slugging
Reilly-Cin 864
O'Neill-StL 836
Stovey-Phi 825
Browning-Lou 816
Collins-Lou-Bro 796

Adjusted OPS
Reilly-Cin 167
Stovey-Phi 165
Browning-Lou 164
Collins-Lou-Bro 158
Burns-Bal-Bro 152

Batter Runs
Reilly-Cin 41.7
O'Neill-StL 39.7
Stovey-Phi 37.8
Collins-Lou-Bro 32.6
Burns-Bal-Bro 27.7

Adjusted Batter Runs
Stovey-Phi 38.6
Reilly-Cin 35.7
Collins-Lou-Bro 34.8
Burns-Bal-Bro 29.6
McKean-Cle 28.5

Clutch Hitting Index
Hotaling-Cle 153
Foutz-Bro 135
Lyons-Phi 133
Gleason-Phi 132
Smith-Bro 130

Runs Created
Reilly-Cin 129
Stovey-Phi 124
Collins-Lou-Bro 112
Welch-Phi 106
O'Neill-StL 105

Total Average
Reilly-Cin 1.064
Stovey-Phi 1.048
Collins-Lou-Bro .956
Robinson-StL .934
Browning-Lou .928

Stolen Bases
Latham-StL 109
Nicol-Cin 103
Welch-Phi 95
McCarthy-StL 93
Stovey-Phi 87

Stolen Base Average

Stolen Base Runs

Fielding Runs
Shindle-Bal 36.8
McPhee-Cin 31.3
Davis-KC 29.8
McCarthy-StL 29.8
Easterday-KC 26.4

Total Player Rating
Collins-Lou-Bro 4.0
Stovey-Phi 3.5
McPhee-Cin 3.3
Davis-KC 3.0
McKean-Cle 3.0

Wins
King-StL 45
Seward-Phi 35
Caruthers-Bro 29
Weyhing-Phi 28
Viau-Cin 27

Win Percentage
Hudson-StL .714
Chamberlain-Lou-SL .694
King-StL .692
Caruthers-Bro .659
Viau-Cin .659

Games
King-StL 66
Bakely-Cle 61
Seward-Phi 57
Porter-KC 55
Cunningham-Bal 51

Complete Games
King-StL 64
Bakely-Cle 60
Seward-Phi 57
Porter-KC 53
Cunningham-Bal 50

Shutouts
Seward-Phi 6
King-StL 6
Smith-Cin 5
Hudson-StL 5

Saves
Mullane-Cin 1
Gilks-Cle 1

Innings Pitched
King-StL 584.2
Bakely-Cle 532.2
Seward-Phi 518.2
Porter-KC 474.0
Cunningham-Bal 453.1

Fewest Hits/Game
Terry-Bro 6.69
King-StL 6.70
Seward-Phi 6.73
Chamberlain-Lou-SL 6.95
Hughes-Bro 6.97

Fewest BB/Game
King-StL 1.17
Caruthers-Bro 1.22
Hudson-StL 1.59
Ewing-Lou 1.60
Hecker-Lou 1.73

Strikeouts
Seward-Phi 272
King-StL 258
Ramsey-Lou 228
Bakely-Cle 212
Weyhing-Phi 204

Strikeouts/Game
Terry-Bro 6.37
Ramsey-Lou 5.99
Chamberlain-Lou-SL 5.14
Smith-Bal-Phi 4.90
Seward-Phi 4.72

Ratio
King-StL 8.33
Caruthers-Bro 9.19
Seward-Phi 9.32
Foutz-Bro 9.51
Hughes-Bro 9.55

Earned Run Average
King-StL 1.63
Seward-Phi 2.01
Terry-Bro 2.03
Hughes-Bro 2.13
Chamberlain-Lou-SL 2.19

Adjusted ERA
King-StL 200
Seward-Phi 148
Terry-Bro 147
Chamberlain-Lou-SL 143
Hughes-Bro 140

Opponents' Batting Avg.
Terry-Bro .200
King-StL .200
Seward-Phi .201
Chamberlain-Lou-SL .206
Hughes-Bro .206

Opponents' On-Base Pct.
King-StL .237
Caruthers-Bro .255
Seward-Phi .258
Foutz-Bro .262
Hughes-Bro .262

Starter Runs
King-StL 92.7
Seward-Phi 60.2
Hughes-Bro 37.3
Weyhing-Phi 36.3
Chamberlain-Lou-SL 29.7

Adjusted Starter Runs
King-StL 99.1
Seward-Phi 57.4
Hughes-Bro 35.1
Weyhing-Phi 33.8
Chamberlain-Lou-SL 31.6

Clutch Pitching Index
Sullivan-KC 115
Hecker-Lou 112
Terry-Bro 110
Ramsey-Lou 106
Bakely-Cle 106

Relief Runs

Adjusted Relief Runs

Relief Ranking

Total Pitcher Index
King-StL 10.6
Seward-Phi 5.0
Weyhing-Phi 3.8
Caruthers-Bro 3.6
Chamberlain-Lou-SL 3.0

Total Baseball Ranking
King-StL 10.6
Seward-Phi 5.0
Collins-Lou-Bro 4.0
Caruthers-Bro 3.7
Weyhing-Phi 3.7

TEAM	G	W	L	PCT	GB	R	OR	AB	H	2B	3B	HR	BB	SO	AVG	OBP	SLG	OPS	OPS+	BR	BR+	PF	CHI	RC	SB	CS	SBA	SBR
NY	131	83	43	.659		**935**	708	4671	1319	208	**77**	52	**538**	386	**.282**	**.360**	**.393**	**753**	**117**	**108**	**106**	100	**105**	**785**	292			
BOS	133	83	45	.648	1	826	**626**	4628	1251	196	54	42	471	450	.270	.343	.363	706	98	26	-19	106	104	707	**331**			
CHI	136	67	65	.508	19	867	814	4849	1274	184	66	**79**	518	516	.263	.338	.377	715	101	36	-4	105	103	716	243			
PHI	130	63	64	.496	20.5	742	748	4695	1248	215	52	44	393	**353**	.266	.327	.362	689	91	-12	-72	109	98	660	269			
PIT	134	61	71	.462	25	726	801	4748	1202	209	65	42	420	467	.253	.320	.351	671	104	-44	34	90	99	622	231			
CLE	136	61	72	.459	25.5	656	720	4673	1167	131	59	25	429	417	.250	.318	.319	637	86	-93	-80	98	97	563	237			
IND	135	59	75	.440	28	819	894	4879	**1356**	**228**	35	62	377	447	.278	.335	.377	712	103	27	12	102	100	719	252			
WAS	127	41	83	.331	41	632	892	4395	1105	151	57	25	466	456	.251	.329	.329	658	96	-49	-5	94	92	566	232			
TOT	531					6203		37538	9922	1522	465	371	3612	3492	.265	.334	.360	693							2087			

TEAM	CG	SH	SV	IP	H	H/G	HR	BB	SO	RAT	ERA	ERA+	OAV	OOB	PR	PR+	PF	CPI	FA	E	DP	FW	PW	BW	SBW	DIF
NY	119	6	3	1151	**1073**	**8.4**	38	523	**558**	12.9	3.48	114	**.241**	.327	71	57	98	102	.919	437	90	-.3	5.0	**9.2**		6.3
BOS	121	**10**	**5**	1166	1152	8.9	41	413	497	**12.5**	**3.36**	**124**	.250	**.317**	**86**	**102**	104	105	.926	413	105	1.3	**8.9**	-1.6		10.6
CHI	123	6	2	1237	1313	9.6	71	408	434	12.9	3.73	112	.262	.323	41	61	104	**106**	.923	463	91	-.8	5.3	-.3		-3.1
PHI	106	4	2	1153[1]	1288	10.1	**33**	428	443	13.7	4.01	109	.275	.339	3	39	108	103	.915	466	92	-1.9	3.4	-6.2		4.4
PIT	125	5	1	1130[2]	1296	10.4	42	**374**	345	13.6	4.51	83	.272	.329	-60	-84	93	92	.931	385	94	2.9	-7.2	3.0		-3.4
CLE	**132**	6	1	1191[2]	1182	9.0	36	519	435	13.3	3.67	110	.251	.332	48	47	100	102	**.936**	**365**	**108**	**4.2**	4.1	-6.9		-6.8
IND	109	3	2	1174[1]	1365	10.5	73	420	408	14.1	4.86	86	.282	.344	-108	-85	104	95	.926	420	102	1.2	-7.3	1.1		-2.8
WAS	113	1	0	1103	1261	10.3	37	527	388	15.0	4.68	85	.279	.359	-80	-92	98	99	.904	519	91	-5.1	-7.9	-.4		-7.4
TOT	948	41	16	9307		9.7				13.5	4.03		.265	.334					.923	3468	773					

Runs
Tiernan-NY 147
Duffy-Chi 144
Ryan-Chi 140
Gore-NY 132
Glasscock-Ind 128

Hits
Glasscock-Ind 205
Brouthers-Bos 181
Ryan-Chi 177
Duffy-Chi 172
VanHaltren-Chi 168

Doubles
Kelly-Bos 41
Glasscock-Ind 40
Thompson-Phi 36
O'Rourke-NY 36
Richardson-Bos 33

Triples
Wilmot-Was 19
Fogarty-Phi 17
Connor-NY 17
Tiernan-NY 14
Ryan-Chi 14

Home Runs
Thompson-Phi 20
Denny-Ind 18
Ryan-Chi 17
Connor-NY 13
Duffy-Chi 12

Total Bases
Ryan-Chi 287
Glasscock-Ind 272
Thompson-Phi 262
Connor-NY 262
Tiernan-NY 248

Runs Batted In
Connor-NY 130
Brouthers-Bos 118
Anson-Chi 117
Denny-Ind 112
Thompson-Phi 111

Runs Produced
Connor-NY 234
Duffy-Chi 221
Brouthers-Bos 216
Tiernan-NY 210
Anson-Chi 210

Bases On Balls
Tiernan-NY 96
Connor-NY 93
Radford-Cle 91
Anson-Chi 86
Carroll-Pit 85

Batting Average
Brouthers-Bos ..... .373
Glasscock-Ind ..... .352
Tiernan-NY .... .335
Carroll-Pit .... .330
Ewing-NY .... .327

On-Base Percentage
Carroll-Pit .... .486
Brouthers-Bos ..... .462
Tiernan-NY .... .447
Connor-NY .... .426
Gore-NY .... .416

Slugging Average
Connor-NY .... .528
Brouthers-Bos ..... .507
Ryan-Chi .... .498
Tiernan-NY .... .497
Thompson-Phi ...... .492

On-Base Plus Slugging
Carroll-Pit 970
Brouthers-Bos 969
Connor-NY 955
Tiernan-NY 944
Ryan-Chi 886

Adjusted OPS
Carroll-Pit 190
Connor-NY 166
Tiernan-NY 163
Brouthers-Bos 161
Wilmot-Was 146

Batter Runs
Brouthers-Bos 49.6
Tiernan-NY 47.0
Connor-NY 46.1
Carroll-Pit 37.9
Ryan-Chi 35.3

Adjusted Batter Runs
Carroll-Pit 48.5
Tiernan-NY 46.8
Connor-NY 45.8
Brouthers-Bos 42.0
Ryan-Chi 28.9

Clutch Hitting Index
Anson-Chi 140
Dunlap-Pit 133
Twitchell-Cle 133
Whitney-NY 133
Brouthers-Bos 132

Runs Created
Ryan-Chi 132
Glasscock-Ind 132
Tiernan-NY 129
Brouthers-Bos 127
Connor-NY 124

Total Average
Carroll-Pit 1.263
Tiernan-NY 1.151
Brouthers-Bos 1.145
Connor-NY 1.115
Ryan-Chi 1.023

Stolen Bases
Fogarty-Phi 99
Kelly-Bos 68
Brown-Bos 63
Ward-NY 62
Glasscock-Ind 57

Stolen Base Average

Stolen Base Runs

Fielding Runs
Glasscock-Ind 35.5
Fogarty-Phi 19.4
Pfeffer-Chi 19.3
Ewing-NY 15.5
Wilmot-Was 14.5

Total Player Rating
Glasscock-Ind 5.6
Ewing-NY 3.7
Tiernan-NY 3.7
Carroll-Pit 3.2
Wilmot-Was 3.2

Wins
Clarkson-Bos 49
Keefe-NY 28
Buffinton-Phi 28
Welch-NY 27
Galvin-Pit 23

Win Percentage
Clarkson-Bos ...... .721
Welch-NY .... .692
Keefe-NY .... .683
Radbourn-Bos ...... .645
Buffinton-Phi ..... .636

Games
Clarkson-Bos 73
Staley-Pit 49
Keefe-NY 47
Buffinton-Phi 47
Boyle-Ind 46

Complete Games
Clarkson-Bos 68
Staley-Pit 46
Welch-NY 39
O'Brien-Cle 39
Keefe-NY 39

Shutouts
Clarkson-Bos 8
Galvin-Pit 4

Saves
Sowders-Bos-Pit ... 3
Welch-NY 2
Bishop-Chi 2

Innings Pitched
Clarkson-Bos 620.0
Staley-Pit 420.0
Buffinton-Phi 380.0
Boyle-Ind 378.2
Welch-NY 375.0

Fewest Hits/Game
Keefe-NY 7.89
Welch-NY 8.16
Clarkson-Bos 8.55
Crane-NY 8.65
Hutchison-Chi 8.66

Fewest BB/Game
Galvin-Pit 2.06
Boyle-Ind 2.26
Radbourn-Bos 2.34
Dwyer-Chi 2.35
Sanders-Phi 2.47

Strikeouts
Clarkson-Bos 284
Keefe-NY 225
Staley-Pit 159
Buffinton-Phi 153
Getzien-Ind 139

Strikeouts/Game
Keefe-NY 5.56
Crane-NY 5.09
Rusie-Ind 4.36
Healy-Was-Chi 4.35
Clarkson-Bos 4.12

Ratio
Clarkson-Bos 11.74
Radbourn-Bos 11.76
Staley-Pit 11.94
Welch-NY 11.98
Keefe-NY 12.07

Earned Run Average
Clarkson-Bos 2.73
Bakely-Cle 2.96
Welch-NY 3.02
Buffinton-Phi 3.24
Keefe-NY 3.31

Adjusted ERA
Clarkson-Bos 153
Bakely-Cle 136
Buffinton-Phi 134
Welch-NY 131
Sanders-Phi 123

Opponents' Batting Avg.
Keefe-NY .... .228
Welch-NY .... .234
Clarkson-Bos ..... .243
Crane-NY .... .245
Hutchison-Chi .... .245

Opponents' On-Base Pct.
Clarkson-Bos ..... .305
Radbourn-Bos ..... .306
Staley-Pit .... .309
Welch-NY .... .310
Keefe-NY .... .311

Starter Runs
Clarkson-Bos 89.2
Welch-NY 41.7
Bakely-Cle 36.1
Buffinton-Phi 32.9
Keefe-NY 28.7

Adjusted Starter Runs
Clarkson-Bos 95.9
Buffinton-Phi 43.4
Welch-NY 39.2
Bakely-Cle 36.4
Sanders-Phi 28.9

Clutch Pitching Index
Casey-Phi 118
Clarkson-Bos 116
Bakely-Cle 113
Sanders-Phi 113
Crane-NY 112

Relief Runs

Adjusted Relief Runs

Relief Ranking

Total Pitcher Index
Clarkson-Bos 9.8
Buffinton-Phi 4.0
Bakely-Cle 3.4
Welch-NY 2.9
Sanders-Phi 2.8

Total Baseball Ranking
Clarkson-Bos 9.7
Glasscock-Ind 5.6
Buffinton-Phi 3.9
Ewing-NY 3.8
Tiernan-NY 3.7

TEAM	G	W	L	PCT	GB	R	OR	AB	H	2B	3B	HR	BB	SO	AVG	OBP	SLG	OPS	OPS+	BR	BR+	PF	CHI	RC	SB	CS	SBA	SBR
BRO	140	93	44	.679		**995**	706	4815	1265	188	79	47	**550**	**401**	.263	.344	.364	708	106	43	40	100	**111**	756	389			
STL	141	90	45	.667	2	957	**680**	4939	1312	211	64	**58**	493	477	.266	.339	.370	709	94	38	-66	113	106	751	336			
PHI	138	75	58	.564	16	880	787	4868	**1339**	**239**	65	43	534	496	**.275**	**.354**	.377	**731**	**114**	**85**	**97**	99	93	758	252			
CIN	141	76	63	.547	18	897	769	4844	1307	197	**96**	52	452	511	.270	.340	**.382**	722	107	57	31	103	100	**806**	462			
BAL	139	70	65	.519	22	791	795	4756	1209	155	68	20	418	536	.254	.325	.328	653	88	-56	-69	102	103	624	311			
COL	140	60	78	.435	33.5	779	924	4816	1247	171	95	36	507	609	.259	.335	.356	691	106	8	53	95	91	693	304			
KC	139	55	82	.401	38	852	1031	4947	1256	162	76	18	430	626	.254	.322	.328	650	84	-66	-109	106	108	692	**472**			
LOU	140	27	111	.196	66.5	632	1091	4955	1249	170	75	22	320	521	.252	.303	.330	633	86	-109	-95	98	87	571	203			
TOT	559					6783		38940	10184	1493	618	296	3704	4177	.262	.333	.355	687							2729			

TEAM	CG	SH	SV	IP	H	H/G	HR	BB	SO	RAT	ERA	ERA+	OAV	OOB	PR	PR+	PF	CPI	FA	E	DP	FW	PW	BW	SBW	DIF
BRO	120	**10**	1	1212^{2}	1205	9.0	33	**400**	471	12.3	3.62	103	.251	.315	31	15	97	93	**.928**	**421**	92	**4.6**	1.3	3.4		15.3
STL	121	7	4	1237^{2}	**1166**	**8.5**	39	413	**617**	**11.9**	**3.01**	**141**	**.242**	**.309**	**116**	**152**	110	106	.925	438	100	3.9	**12.9**	-5.5		11.5
PHI	**130**	9	1	1199^{1}	1200	9.1	35	509	479	13.4	3.53	107	.253	.335	42	34	98	**107**	.920	465	120	1.7	2.9	**8.3**		-4.2
CIN	114	3	**8**	1243	1270	9.2	35	475	562	13.1	3.51	111	.257	.328	47	53	102	105	.926	440	**121**	3.7	4.5	2.7		-4.3
BAL	128	**10**	1	1192	1168	8.9	**27**	424	540	12.7	3.56	111	.249	.322	38	48	103	97	.907	536	104	-2.0	4.1	-5.8		6.4
COL	114	9	4	1199	1274	9.6	33	551	610	14.1	4.40	82	.264	.346	-73	-110	94	93	.915	497	92	.4	-9.3	4.5		-4.4
KC	128	0	2	1204^{1}	1373	10.3	51	457	447	14.2	4.36	96	.278	.347	-69	-23	109	101	.899	611	109	-6.2	-1.9	-9.2		4.0
LOU	127	2	1	1226^{1}	1529	11.3	43	475	451	15.1	4.82	80	.297	.362	-132	-133	100	101	.906	584	117	-4.5	-11.2	-8.0		-18.1
TOT	982	50	22	9714^{1}		9.5				13.4	3.85		.262	.333					.916	3992	855					

Runs
Stovey-Phi 152
Griffin-Bal 152
O'Brien-Bro 146
Hamilton-KC 144
Collins-Bro 139

Hits
Tucker-Bal 196
Orr-Col 183
Holliday-Cin 181
O'Neill-StL 179
Shindle-Bal 178

Doubles
Welch-Phi 39
Stovey-Phi 38
Lyons-Phi 36
O'Neill-StL 33
Long-KC 32

Triples
Marr-Col 15
Griffin-Bal 14
Beard-Cin 14

Home Runs
Stovey-Phi 19
Holliday-Cin 19
Duffee-StL 16
Milligan-StL 12

Total Bases
Stovey-Phi 292
Holliday-Cin 280
Tucker-Bal 255
O'Neill-StL 255
Orr-Col 250

Runs Batted In
Stovey-Phi 119
Foutz-Bro 113
O'Neill-StL 110
Bierbauer-Phi 105
Holliday-Cin 104

Runs Produced
Stovey-Phi 252
Foutz-Bro 225
O'Neill-StL 224
O'Brien-Bro 221
Hamilton-KC 218

Bases On Balls
Robinson-StL 118
McTamany-Col 116
Griffin-Bal 91
Marr-Col 87
Hamilton-KC 87

Batting Average
Tucker-Bal .372
O'Neill-StL .335
Lyons-Phi .329
Orr-Col .327
Holliday-Cin .321

On-Base Percentage
Tucker-Bal .450
Larkin-Phi .428
Lyons-Phi .426
O'Neill-StL .419
Hamilton-KC .413

Slugging Average
Stovey-Phi .525
Holliday-Cin .497
Tucker-Bal .484
O'Neill-StL .478
Lyons-Phi .469

On-Base Plus Slugging
Tucker-Bal 934
Stovey-Phi 918
O'Neill-StL 897
Lyons-Phi 895
Holliday-Cin 869

Adjusted OPS
Tucker-Bal 163
Stovey-Phi 162
Lyons-Phi 157
Larkin-Phi 145
Holliday-Cin 142

Batter Runs
Tucker-Bal 48.2
Stovey-Phi 42.6
O'Neill-StL 39.9
Lyons-Phi 39.3
Larkin-Phi 34.2

Adjusted Batter Runs
Tucker-Bal 45.8
Stovey-Phi 44.5
Lyons-Phi 41.1
Larkin-Phi 35.9
Marr-Col 34.5

Clutch Hitting Index
Mack-Bal 147
Foutz-Bro 145
Johnson-Col 128
Hornung-Bal 127
Collins-Bro 126

Runs Created
Tucker-Bal 147
Stovey-Phi 143
Hamilton-KC 136
O'Brien-Bro 129
Holliday-Cin 124

Total Average
Tucker-Bal 1.187
Hamilton-KC 1.134
Stovey-Phi 1.125
O'Brien-Bro 1.020
O'Neill-StL 1.014

Stolen Bases
Hamilton-KC 111
O'Brien-Bro 91
Long-KC 89
Nicol-Cin 80
Latham-StL 69

Stolen Base Average

Stolen Base Runs

Fielding Runs
McPhee-Cin 41.1
Bierbauer-Phi 36.6
Long-KC 32.2
Tomney-Lou 26.7
Shindle-Bal 20.3

Total Player Rating
Stovey-Phi 4.9
Bierbauer-Phi 4.3
Lyons-Phi 4.3
Marr-Col 4.0
McPhee-Cin 3.8

Wins
Caruthers-Bro 40
King-StL 35
Duryea-Cin 32
Chamberlain-StL 32
Weyhing-Phi 30

Win Percentage
Caruthers-Bro .784
King-StL .686
Chamberlain-StL .681
Lovett-Bro .630
Duryea-Cin .627

Games
Baldwin-Col 63
Kilroy-Bal 59
King-StL 56
Caruthers-Bro 56
Weyhing-Phi 54

Complete Games
Kilroy-Bal 55
Baldwin-Col 54
Weyhing-Phi 50
King-StL 47
Caruthers-Bro 46

Shutouts
Caruthers-Bro 7
Baldwin-Col 6
Kilroy-Bal 5
Foreman-Bal 5
Weyhing-Phi 4

Saves
Mullane-Cin 5
Stivetts-StL 2

Innings Pitched
Baldwin-Col 513.2
Kilroy-Bal 480.2
King-StL 458.0
Weyhing-Phi 449.0
Caruthers-Bro 445.0

Fewest Hits/Game
Stivetts-StL 7.18
Weyhing-Phi 7.66
Terry-Bro 7.87
Foreman-Bal 7.91
Baldwin-Col 8.02

Fewest BB/Game
Caruthers-Bro 2.10
Conway-KC 2.42
King-StL 2.46
Lovett-Bro 2.55
Swartzel-KC 2.57

Strikeouts
Baldwin-Col 368
Kilroy-Bal 217
Weyhing-Phi 213
Chamberlain-StL 202
King-StL 188

Strikeouts/Game
Stivetts-StL 6.71
Baldwin-Col 6.45
Terry-Bro 5.13
Sowders-KC 5.06
Gastright-Col 4.65

Ratio
Stivetts-StL 10.61
Caruthers-Bro 11.35
Duryea-Cin 11.56
Foreman-Bal 11.76
Conway-KC 11.77

Earned Run Average
Stivetts-StL 2.25
Duryea-Cin 2.56
Kilroy-Bal 2.85
Weyhing-Phi 2.95
Chamberlain-StL 2.97

Adjusted ERA
Stivetts-StL 187
Duryea-Cin 152
Chamberlain-StL 142
Kilroy-Bal 138
King-StL 134

Opponents' Batting Avg.
Stivetts-StL .212
Weyhing-Phi .223
Terry-Bro .228
Foreman-Bal .229
Baldwin-Col .231

Opponents' On-Base Pct.
Stivetts-StL .285
Caruthers-Bro .299
Duryea-Cin .303
Foreman-Bal .306
Conway-KC .306

Starter Runs
Duryea-Cin 57.3
Kilroy-Bal 53.3
Weyhing-Phi 44.8
Chamberlain-StL 41.1
King-StL 35.6

Adjusted Starter Runs
Duryea-Cin 59.0
Kilroy-Bal 57.0
Chamberlain-StL 53.5
King-StL 49.9
Weyhing-Phi 42.2

Clutch Pitching Index
Mullane-Cin 119
Duryea-Cin 116
Kilroy-Bal 114
Hughes-Bro 110
Weyhing-Phi 109

Relief Runs

Adjusted Relief Runs

Relief Ranking

Total Pitcher Index
Kilroy-Bal 6.8
Duryea-Cin 6.6
Caruthers-Bro 4.3
Chamberlain-StL 4.3
King-StL 4.1

Total Baseball Ranking
Kilroy-Bal 6.8
Duryea-Cin 6.5
Stovey-Phi 4.9
Bierbauer-Phi 4.3
Lyons-Phi 4.3

TEAM	G	W	L	PCT	GB	R	OR	AB	H	2B	3B	HR	BB	SO	AVG	OBP	SLG	OPS	OPS+	BR	BR+	PF	CHI	RC	SB	CS	SBA	SBR
BRO	129	86	43	.667		**884**	620	4419	1166	184	75	43	517	**361**	.264	.346	**.369**	**715**	**113**	74	**71**	100	**112**	702	**349**			
CHI	139	84	53	.613	6	847	692	4891	**1271**	147	60	**67**	516	514	.260	.336	.356	692	102	37	5	104	103	713	329			
PHI	133	78	54	.591	9.5	823	707	4707	1267	**220**	78	23	522	403	**.269**	**.350**	.364	714	110	**79**	59	103	98	**735**	335			
CIN	134	77	55	.583	10.5	753	633	4644	1203	150	**120**	27	433	377	.259	.329	.360	689	106	25	29	100	99	670	312			
BOS	134	76	57	.571	12	763	**593**	4722	1220	175	62	31	**530**	515	.258	.342	.341	683	96	30	-29	108	96	665	285			
NY	135	63	68	.481	24	713	698	4832	1250	208	89	25	350	479	.259	.315	.354	669	99	-16	-17	100	97	647	289			
CLE	136	44	88	.333	43.5	630	832	4633	1073	132	59	21	497	474	.232	.312	.299	611	84	-96	-83	98	97	491	152			
PIT	138	23	113	.169	66.5	597	1235	4739	1088	160	43	20	408	458	.230	.300	.294	594	87	-134	-53	88	97	492	208			
TOT	539					6010		37587	9538	1376	586	257	3773	3581	.254	.329	.343	671							2259			

TEAM	CG	SH	SV	IP	H	H/G	HR	BB	SO	RAT	ERA	ERA+	OAV	OOB	PR	PR+	PF	CPI	FA	E	DP	FW	PW	BW	SBW	DIF
BRO	115	6	2	1145	1102	8.7	27	401	403	12.2	3.06	112	.246	.315	64	49	96	104	**.940**	**320**	92	4.5	4.4	**6.4**		6.4
CHI	126	6	**3**	1237^{1}	1103	8.1	41	481	504	11.9	3.25	113	.234	.311	44	48	103	93	**.940**	344	89	**4.9**	4.3	.5		6.0
PHI	122	9	2	1194^{2}	1210	9.2	22	486	507	13.2	3.33	110	.255	.331	32	42	102	107	.929	398	**122**	.5	3.8	5.3		2.6
CIN	124	9	1	1190^{2}	1097	8.3	41	407	488	11.8	**2.79**	127	.238	.307	**102**	**100**	100	**109**	.932	382	106	1.6	**8.9**	2.6		-2.0
BOS	**132**	**13**	1	1187	1132	8.6	27	**354**	506	**11.5**	2.94	**128**	.245	**.303**	83	99	105	101	.935	359	77	3.1	8.8	-2.5		.3
NY	115	6	1	1177	**1029**	**7.9**	**14**	607	**612**	13.1	3.06	114	**.230**	.331	66	53	98	104	.921	449	104	-2.3	4.8	-1.5		-3.3
CLE	129	2	0	1184^{1}	1322	10.1	33	462	306	14.0	4.14	86	.273	.342	-75	-70	100	99	.930	405	108	.6	-6.2	-7.3		-8.9
PIT	119	3	0	1176^{1}	1520	11.7	52	573	381	16.7	5.97	55	.304	.384	-315	-379	92	91	.897	607	94	-11.4	-33.6	-4.7		4.9
TOT	982	54	10	9492^{1}		9.1				13.1	3.57		.254	.329					.928	3264	792					

Runs
Collins-Bro 148
Carroll-Chi 134
Hamilton-Phi 133
Tiernan-NY 132
McPhee-Cin 125

Hits
Thompson-Phi 172
Glasscock-NY 172
Tiernan-NY 168
Reilly-Cin 166
Carroll-Chi 166

Doubles
Thompson-Phi 41
Glasscock-NY 32
Collins-Bro 32
Myers-Phi 29
O'Brien-Bro 28

Triples
Reilly-Cin 26
McPhee-Cin 22
Tiernan-NY 21
Beard-Cin 15

Home Runs
Wilmot-Chi 13
Tiernan-NY 13
Burns-Bro 13
Long-Bos 8

Total Bases
Tiernan-NY 274
Reilly-Cin 261
Thompson-Phi 243
Wilmot-Chi 239
Glasscock-NY 225

Runs Batted In
Burns-Bro 128
Anson-Chi 107
Thompson-Phi 102
Wilmot-Chi 99
Foutz-Bro 98

Runs Produced
Burns-Bro 217
Thompson-Phi 214
Collins-Bro 214
Wilmot-Chi 200
Foutz-Bro 199

Bases On Balls
Anson-Chi 113
McKean-Cle 87
Allen-Phi 87
Collins-Bro 85
Hamilton-Phi 83

Batting Average
Glasscock-NY .336
Hamilton-Phi .325
Clements-Phi .315
O'Brien-Bro .314
Thompson-Phi .313

On-Base Percentage
Anson-Chi .443
Hamilton-Phi .430
Pinkney-Bro .411
McKean-Cle .401
Glasscock-NY .395

Slugging Average
Tiernan-NY .495
Clements-Phi .472
Reilly-Cin .472
Burns-Bro .464
Burkett-NY .461

On-Base Plus Slugging
Tiernan-NY 880
Clements-Phi 864
Anson-Chi 844
Pinkney-Bro 842
Glasscock-NY 834

Adjusted OPS
Tiernan-NY 156
Clements-Phi 148
Pinkney-Bro 145
Glasscock-NY 143
McKean-Cle 141

Batter Runs
Tiernan-NY 37.9
Anson-Chi 37.6
Hamilton-Phi 31.7
Pinkney-Bro 30.8
McKean-Cle 28.9

Adjusted Batter Runs
Tiernan-NY 37.7
Anson-Chi 32.7
McKean-Cle 31.2
Pinkney-Bro 30.4
Hamilton-Phi 28.8

Clutch Hitting Index
Burns-Bro 150
Anson-Chi 145
Myers-Phi 140
Hines-Pit-Bos 138
Bassett-NY 129

Runs Created
Hamilton-Phi 132
Tiernan-NY 130
Wilmot-Chi 114
Glasscock-NY 113
Collins-Bro 111

Total Average
Hamilton-Phi 1.170
Tiernan-NY 1.047
Pinkney-Bro 1.015
Anson-Chi 1.009
Collins-Bro 1.005

Stolen Bases
Hamilton-Phi 102
Collins-Bro 85
Sunday-Pit-Phi 84
Wilmot-Chi 76
Tiernan-NY 56

Stolen Base Average

Stolen Base Runs

Fielding Runs
Allen-Phi 38.6
McPhee-Cin 30.0
Glasscock-NY 22.0
Smalley-Cle 16.6
Carroll-Chi 14.5

Total Player Rating
Glasscock-NY 4.6
McPhee-Cin 4.3
Allen-Phi 3.7
Clements-Phi 2.8
Hamilton-Phi 2.6

Wins
Hutchison-Chi 42
Gleason-Phi 38
Lovett-Bro 30
Rusie-NY 29
Rhines-Cin 28

Win Percentage
Lovett-Bro .732
Gleason-Phi .691
Luby-Chi .690
Caruthers-Bro .676
Hutchison-Chi .627

Games
Hutchison-Chi 71
Rusie-NY 67
Gleason-Phi 60
Beatin-Cle 54
Nichols-Bos 48

Complete Games
Hutchison-Chi 65
Rusie-NY 56
Gleason-Phi 54
Beatin-Cle 53
Nichols-Bos 47

Shutouts
Nichols-Bos 7
Rhines-Cin 6
Gleason-Phi 6
Hutchison-Chi 5

Saves
Hutchison-Chi 2
Gleason-Phi 2
Foutz-Bro 2

Innings Pitched
Hutchison-Chi 603.0
Rusie-NY 548.2
Gleason-Phi 506.0
Beatin-Cle 474.1
Nichols-Bos 424.0

Fewest Hits/Game
Rusie-NY 7.15
Mullane-Cin 7.54
Hutchison-Chi 7.54
Rhines-Cin 7.56
Luby-Chi 7.60

Fewest BB/Game
Young-Cle 1.83
Duryea-Cin 1.97
Getzien-Bos 2.11
Nichols-Bos 2.38
Rhines-Cin 2.53

Strikeouts
Rusie-NY 341
Hutchison-Chi 289
Nichols-Bos 222
Gleason-Phi 222
Terry-Bro 185

Strikeouts/Game
Rusie-NY 5.59
Nichols-Bos 4.71
Terry-Bro 4.50
Hutchison-Chi 4.31
Sharrott-NY 4.11

Ratio
Rhines-Cin 10.43
Nichols-Bos 10.55
Hutchison-Chi 10.70
Getzien-Bos 10.98
Duryea-Cin 11.10

Earned Run Average
Rhines-Cin 1.95
Nichols-Bos 2.23
Mullane-Cin 2.24
Rusie-NY 2.56
Gleason-Phi 2.63

Adjusted ERA
Rhines-Cin 182
Nichols-Bos 168
Mullane-Cin 159
Gleason-Phi 139
Rusie-NY 137

Opponents' Batting Avg.
Rusie-NY .212
Mullane-Cin .221
Hutchison-Chi .221
Rhines-Cin .221
Luby-Chi .222

Opponents' On-Base Pct.
Rhines-Cin .282
Nichols-Bos .284
Hutchison-Chi .287
Getzien-Bos .292
Duryea-Cin .295

Starter Runs
Rhines-Cin 71.8
Nichols-Bos 62.8
Rusie-NY 61.1
Hutchison-Chi 57.6
Gleason-Phi 52.2

Adjusted Starter Runs
Rhines-Cin 71.5
Nichols-Bos 67.9
Hutchison-Chi 62.0
Rusie-NY 58.1
Gleason-Phi 55.7

Clutch Pitching Index
Mullane-Cin 131
Vickery-Phi 120
Rhines-Cin 118
Gleason-Phi 112
Nichols-Bos 110

Relief Runs

Adjusted Relief Runs

Relief Ranking

Total Pitcher Index
Rusie-NY 7.0
Rhines-Cin 6.5
Nichols-Bos 6.3
Hutchison-Chi 5.8
Gleason-Phi 4.5

Total Baseball Ranking
Rusie-NY 6.8
Rhines-Cin 6.5
Nichols-Bos 6.2
Hutchison-Chi 5.8
Glasscock-NY 4.6

TEAM	G	W	L	PCT	GB	R	OR	AB	H	2B	3B	HR	BB	SO	AVG	OBP	SLG	OPS	OPS+	BR	BR+	PF	CHI	RC	SB	CS	SBA	SBR
LOU	136	88	44	.667		819	**588**	4687	**1310**	156	65	15	410	**460**	**.279**	.344	.350	694	**113**	53	72	98	101	699	341			
COL	140	79	55	.590	10	831	617	4741	1225	159	77	16	**545**	557	.258	.341	.335	676	112	29	**89**	93	**103**	677	353			
STL	139	78	58	.574	12	**870**	736	4800	1308	178	73	**48**	474	490	.273	**.350**	**.370**	**720**	103	**100**	-10	114	98	**746**	307			
TOL	134	68	64	.515	20	739	689	4575	1152	152	**108**	24	486	558	.252	.333	.348	681	103	31	10	103	94	687	**421**			
ROC	133	63	63	.500	22	709	711	4553	1088	131	64	31	446	538	.239	.315	.316	631	98	-53	3	93	**103**	564	310			
BAL	38	15	19	.441	24	182	192	1213	278	34	16	2	125	152	.229	.316	.289	605	79	-23	-31	105	**103**	146	101			
SYR	128	55	72	.433	30.5	698	831	4469	1158	151	59	14	457	482	.259	.333	.329	662	112	1	85	90	96	600	292			
PHI	132	54	78	.409	34	702	945	4490	1057	**181**	51	24	475	540	.235	.320	.314	634	93	-41	-37	99	100	564	305			
BRO	100	26	73	.263	45.5	492	733	3475	769	116	47	13	328	456	.221	.294	.293	587	80	-98	-82	97	106	362	182			
TOT	540					6042		37003	9345	1258	560	187	3746	4233	.253	.330	.332	662							2612			

TEAM	CG	SH	SV	IP	H	H/G	HR	BB	SO	RAT	ERA	ERA+	OAV	OOB	PR	PR+	PF	CPI	FA	E	DP	FW	PW	BW	SBW	DIF
LOU	114	13	**7**	1206	1120	8.4	18	**293**	587	**11.0**	**2.58**	**149**	.239	**.291**	**173**	**170**	100	**117**	**.934**	**380**	79	**2.8**	**15.0**	6.4		-2.0
COL	120	**14**	3	1214^{2}	**976**	**7.3**	20	471	624	11.3	2.99	120	**.214**	.297	118	87	93	95	.932	396	**101**	2.7	7.7	**7.9**		-6.1
STL	118	4	1	1195^{1}	1127	8.5	38	447	**733**	12.3	3.68	117	.242	.316	25	74	112	98	.916	478	93	-1.7	6.6	-.8		6.2
TOL	**122**	4	2	1159^{1}	1122	8.8	23	429	533	12.6	3.57	111	.247	.321	39	48	102	102	.925	419	75	.5	4.3	.9		-3.5
ROC	**122**	5	2	1161^{2}	1115	8.7	19	530	477	13.2	3.57	100	.246	.331	39	-2	92	106	.926	416	95	.5	-.1	.3		-.5
BAL	36	1	0	315^{1}	307	8.8	3	123	134	13.0	4.00	101	.248	.328	-5	2	105	92	.928	109	21	.7	.2	-2.7		-.0
SYR	115	5	0	1089^{2}	1158	9.6	28	518	454	14.4	4.99	71	.265	.351	-135	-193	91	89	.925	391	90	.9	-16.9	7.5		.2
PHI	119	3	2	1132	1405	11.2	**17**	514	461	15.8	5.23	74	.296	.373	-171	-170	100	99	.918	452	93	-1.6	-14.9	-3.2		7.9
BRO	96	0	0	879	1011	10.4	21	421	230	15.3	4.71	83	.281	.365	-83	-80	101	104	.909	404	92	-4.4	-7.0	-7.2		-4.8
TOT	962	49	17	9353		9.0				13.1	3.87		.253	.330					.924	3445	739					

Runs
McTamany-Col 140
McCarthy-StL 137
Fuller-StL 118
Sneed-Tol-Col 117
Welch-Phi-Bal 116

Hits
Wolf-Lou 197
McCarthy-StL 192
Johnson-Col 186
Childs-Syr 170
Taylor-Lou 169

Doubles
Childs-Syr 33
Wolf-Lou 29
Lyons-Phi 29

Triples
Werden-Tol 20
Johnson-Col 18
Alvord-Tol 16
Sneed-Tol-Col 15

Home Runs
Campau-StL 9
Cartwright-StL 8
Stivetts-StL 7
Lyons-Phi 7

Total Bases
Wolf-Lou 260
McCarthy-StL 256
Johnson-Col 248
Childs-Syr 237
Werden-Tol 227

Runs Batted In
Johnson-Col 113
Wolf-Lou 98
Childs-Syr 89
Knowles-Roc 84
Shinnick-Lou 82

Runs Produced
Johnson-Col 218
McCarthy-StL 200
Childs-Syr 196
Wolf-Lou 194
McTamany-Col 187

Bases On Balls
McTamany-Col 112
Crooks-Col 96
Swartwood-Tol 80
Werden-Tol 78
Scheffler-Roc 78

Batting Average
Wolf-Lou .363
Lyons-Phi .354
McCarthy-StL .350
Johnson-Col .346
Childs-Syr .345

On-Base Percentage
Lyons-Phi .461
Swartwood-Tol .444
Childs-Syr .434
McCarthy-StL .430
Wright-Syr .428

Slugging Average
Lyons-Phi .531
Campau-StL .513
Childs-Syr .481
Wolf-Lou .479
McCarthy-StL .467

On-Base Plus Slugging
Lyons-Phi 992
Childs-Syr 915
Wolf-Lou 900
McCarthy-StL 898
Swartwood-Tol 887

Adjusted OPS
Lyons-Phi 193
Childs-Syr 189
Wolf-Lou 169
Johnson-Col 168
Swartwood-Tol 157

Batter Runs
McCarthy-StL 45.6
Childs-Syr 44.7
Wolf-Lou 43.3
Lyons-Phi 41.4
Swartwood-Tol 40.6

Adjusted Batter Runs
Childs-Syr 59.6
Johnson-Col 46.5
Wolf-Lou 46.4
Lyons-Phi 42.0
Swartwood-Tol 37.2

Clutch Hitting Index
Crooks-Col 148
Knowles-Roc 141
O'Brien-Phi 139
Johnson-Col 136
Shinnick-Lou 132

Runs Created
McCarthy-StL 150
Wolf-Lou 132
Childs-Syr 130
Johnson-Col 122
Werden-Tol 118

Total Average
Lyons-Phi 1.224
McCarthy-StL 1.169
Childs-Syr 1.149
Swartwood-Tol 1.141
Werden-Tol 1.074

Stolen Bases
McCarthy-StL 83
Scheffler-Roc 77
VanDyke-Tol 73
Welch-Phi-Bal 72

Stolen Base Average

Stolen Base Runs

Fielding Runs
Gerhardt-Bro-StL 41.5
Reilly-Col 28.2
Ely-Syr 19.3
Tomney-Lou 17.6
Welch-Phi-Bal 15.7

Total Player Rating
Childs-Syr 6.6
Lyons-Phi 4.5
Wolf-Lou 3.8
Swartwood-Tol 3.8
O'Connor-Col 3.7

Wins
McMahon-Phi-Bal 36
Stratton-Lou 34
Gastright-Col 30
Barr-Roc 28
Stivetts-StL 27

Win Percentage
Stratton-Lou .708
Chamberlain-SL-Col .682
Gastright-Col .682
Ehret-Lou .641
McMahon-Phi-Bal .632

Games
McMahon-Phi-Bal 60
Barr-Roc 57
Stivetts-StL 54
Stratton-Lou 50
Gastright-Col 48

Complete Games
McMahon-Phi-Bal 55
Barr-Roc 52
Stratton-Lou 44
Healy-Tol 44

Shutouts
Chamberlain-SL-Col 6
Stratton-Lou 4
Gastright-Col 4
Ehret-Lou 4

Saves
Goodall-Lou 4
Knauss-Col 2
Ehret-Lou 2

Innings Pitched
McMahon-Phi-Bal 509.0
Barr-Roc 493.1
Stratton-Lou 431.0
Stivetts-StL 419.1
Gastright-Col 401.1

Fewest Hits/Game
Knauss-Col 6.73
Gastright-Col 7.00
Easton-Col 7.50
Chamberlain-SL-Col 7.50
Healy-Tol 7.54

Fewest BB/Game
Stratton-Lou 1.27
Ehret-Lou 1.98
Ramsey-StL 2.63
Smith-Tol 2.83
McMahon-Phi-Bal 2.94

Strikeouts
McMahon-Phi-Bal 291
Stivetts-StL 289
Ramsey-StL 257
Healy-Tol 225
Barr-Roc 209

Strikeouts/Game
Ramsey-StL 6.63
Stivetts-StL 6.20
Meakim-Lou 5.77
Chamberlain-SL-Col 5.49
Healy-Tol 5.21

Ratio
Stratton-Lou 9.86
Gastright-Col 10.43
Knauss-Col 10.87
Healy-Tol 11.04
Ehret-Lou 11.21

Earned Run Average
Stratton-Lou 2.36
Ehret-Lou 2.53
Knauss-Col 2.81
Chamberlain-SL-Col 2.83
Healy-Tol 2.89

Adjusted ERA
Stratton-Lou 163
Ehret-Lou 152
Healy-Tol 136
Meakim-Lou 132
Chamberlain-SL-Col 131

Opponents' Batting Avg.
Knauss-Col .202
Gastright-Col .208
Easton-Col .220
Chamberlain-SL-Col .220
Healy-Tol .221

Opponents' On-Base Pct.
Stratton-Lou .270
Gastright-Col .282
Knauss-Col .290
Healy-Tol .293
Ehret-Lou .296

Starter Runs
Stratton-Lou 72.0
Ehret-Lou 53.1
Healy-Tol 42.0
Gastright-Col 41.3
Barr-Roc 33.8

Adjusted Starter Runs
Stratton-Lou 71.4
Ehret-Lou 52.6
Healy-Tol 44.6
McMahon-Phi-Bal 35.5
Stivetts-StL 32.9

Clutch Pitching Index
Ehret-Lou 126
Titcomb-Roc 121
Daily-Bro-Lou 113
Stratton-Lou 110
Chamberlain-SL-Col 110

Relief Runs

Adjusted Relief Runs

Relief Ranking

Total Pitcher Index
Stratton-Lou 9.0
Healy-Tol 4.6
Stivetts-StL 4.5
Ehret-Lou 4.3
McMahon-Phi-Bal 4.2

Total Baseball Ranking
Stratton-Lou 9.0
Childs-Syr 6.6
Stivetts-StL 4.6
Healy-Tol 4.5
Lyons-Phi 4.5

TEAM	G	W	L	PCT	GB	R	OR	AB	H	2B	3B	HR	BB	SO	AVG	OBP	SLG	OPS	OPS+	BR	BR+	PF	CHI	RC	SB	CS	SBA	SBR
BOS	130	81	48	.628		992	**767**	4626	1306	**223**	76	54	**652**	435	.282	**.376**	.398	**774**	105	**90**	28	107	100	**869**	**412**			
BRO	133	76	56	.576	6.5	964	893	4887	1352	186	93	34	502	369	.277	.349	.374	723	92	-13	-65	106	**106**	751	272			
NY	132	74	57	.565	8	**1018**	875	4913	**1393**	204	97	**66**	486	364	.284	.352	**.405**	757	98	40	-38	109	**106**	800	231			
CHI	138	75	62	.547	10	886	770	4968	1311	200	95	31	492	410	.264	.335	.361	696	87	-65	-99	104	102	712	276			
PHI	132	68	63	.519	14	941	855	4855	1350	187	**113**	49	431	**321**	.278	.343	.393	736	100	2	-18	102	104	743	203			
PIT	128	60	68	.469	20.5	835	892	4577	1192	168	**113**	35	569	375	.260	.349	.369	718	106	-15	62	92	97	694	249			
CLE	131	55	75	.423	26.5	849	1027	4804	1370	213	94	27	509	345	**.285**	.360	.386	746	**114**	30	**114**	92	91	749	180			
BUF	134	36	96	.273	46.5	793	1199	4795	1249	180	64	20	541	367	.260	.347	.337	684	96	-68	9	92	93	632	160			
TOT	529					7278		38425	10523	1561	745	316	4182	2986	.274	.352	.378	729							1983			

TEAM	CG	SH	SV	IP	H	H/G	HR	BB	SO	RAT	ERA	ERA+	OAV	OOB	PR	PR+	PF	CPI	FA	E	DP	FW	PW	BW	SBW	DIF
BOS	105	6	4	1137^{1}	1291	10.3	49	467	345	14.4	3.80	116	.274	.346	55	73	104	111	.918	460	109	1.8	5.9	2.3		6.7
BRO	111	4	**7**	1184	1334	10.2	**26**	570	377	15.0	3.95	113	.273	.356	37	62	105	106	.909	531	114	-1.7	5.0	-5.1		12.0
NY	111	3	6	1172^{1}	**1216**	9.4	37	569	449	14.2	4.17	109	.257	.343	8	44	107	92	**.921**	**450**	94	**2.8**	3.6	-3.0		5.3
CHI	124	5	2	1219^{1}	1238	**9.2**	27	503	**460**	**13.2**	**3.39**	**128**	**.252**	**.327**	**114**	**125**	103	100	.918	492	107	1.7	**10.0**	-7.8		2.8
PHI	118	4	2	1154^{1}	1292	10.1	33	495	361	14.4	4.06	105	.271	.347	22	27	101	100	.910	510	**118**	-.7	2.2	-1.4		2.6
PIT	121	**7**	0	1116^{2}	1267	10.3	32	**334**	318	13.3	4.22	93	.274	.328	2	-43	92	89	.907	512	80	-1.7	-3.4	5.0		-3.7
CLE	115	1	0	1143^{2}	1386	11.0	45	571	325	15.9	4.23	94	.287	.369	0	-35	94	**114**	.907	533	103	-2.3	-2.7	**9.1**		-13.9
BUF	**125**	2	0	1141	1499	11.9	67	673	351	17.6	6.12	67	.304	.393	-239	-265	97	93	.914	491	116	.9	-21.1	.8		-10.3
TOT	930	32	21	9268^{2}		10.3				14.7	4.23		.274	.352					.913	3979	841					

Runs
Duffy-Chi 161
Brown-Bos 146
Stovey-Bos 142
Ward-Bro 134
Connor-NY 133

Hits
Duffy-Chi 191
Shindle-Phi 189
Ward-Bro 188
Browning-Cle 184
Richardson-Bos 181

Doubles
Browning-Cle 40
Beckley-Pit 38
O'Rourke-NY 37
Duffy-Chi 36
Brouthers-Bos 36

Triples
Visner-Pit 22
Beckley-Pit 22
Shindle-Phi 21
Fields-Pit 20
Joyce-Bro 18

Home Runs
Connor-NY 14
Richardson-Bos 13
Stovey-Bos 12
Shindle-Phi 10
Gore-NY 10

Total Bases
Shindle-Phi 282
Duffy-Chi 280
Beckley-Pit 276
Richardson-Bos 274
Connor-NY 265

Runs Batted In
Richardson-Bos 146
Orr-Bro 124
Beckley-Pit 120
O'Rourke-NY 115
Larkin-Cle 112

Runs Produced
Richardson-Bos 259
Duffy-Chi 236
Connor-NY 222
Bierbauer-Bro 220
Beckley-Pit 220

Bases On Balls
Joyce-Bro 123
Robinson-Pit 101
Brouthers-Bos 99
Hoy-Buf 94

Batting Average
Browning-Cle .... .373
Orr-Bro .... .371
O'Rourke-NY .... .360
Connor-NY .... .349
Ryan-Chi .... .340

On-Base Percentage
Brouthers-Bos .... .466
Browning-Cle .... .459
Connor-NY .... .450
Robinson-Pit .... .434
Gore-NY .... .432

Slugging Average
Connor-NY .... .548
B.Ewing-NY .... .545
Beckley-Pit .... .535
Orr-Bro .... .534
Browning-Cle .... .517

On-Base Plus Slugging
Connor-NY 998
Browning-Cle 976
Orr-Bro 948
Gore-NY 931
O'Rourke-NY 925

Adjusted OPS
Browning-Cle 175
Beckley-Pit 156
Larkin-Cle 153
Connor-NY 152
Orr-Bro 144

Batter Runs
Connor-NY 47.6
Browning-Cle 45.2
Brouthers-Bos 38.2
Orr-Bro 32.3
Larkin-Cle 30.3

Adjusted Batter Runs
Browning-Cle 57.9
Larkin-Cle 41.8
Beckley-Pit 39.4
Connor-NY 35.9
Brouthers-Bos 29.7

Clutch Hitting Index
Richardson-Bos 128
Orr-Bro 128
Brouthers-Bos 125
Wise-Buf 122
Larkin-Cle 118

Runs Created
Duffy-Chi 141
Browning-Cle 136
Stovey-Bos 135
Connor-NY 132
Shindle-Phi 127

Total Average
Stovey-Bos 1.217
Connor-NY 1.194
Browning-Cle 1.191
Brouthers-Bos 1.149
Gore-NY 1.129

Stolen Bases
Stovey-Bos 97
Brown-Bos 79
Duffy-Chi 78
Hanlon-Pit 65
Ward-Bro 63

Stolen Base Average

Stolen Base Runs

Fielding Runs
Farrell-Chi 26.5
Richardson-NY 25.3
Bierbauer-Bro 24.8
Pfeffer-Chi 24.1
Ward-Bro 21.3

Total Player Rating
Browning-Cle 4.6
B.Ewing-NY 3.0
Connor-NY 2.8
Ward-Bro 2.6
Radford-Cle 2.5

Wins
Baldwin-Chi 33
Weyhing-Bro 30
King-Chi 30
Radbourn-Bos 27
Gumbert-Bos 23

Win Percentage
Daley-Bos .... .720
Radbourn-Bos .... .692
Knell-Phi .... .667
Gumbert-Bos .... .657
Weyhing-Bro .... .652

Games
Baldwin-Chi 58
King-Chi 56
Weyhing-Bro 49
Gruber-Cle 48
Staley-Pit 46

Complete Games
Baldwin-Chi 53
King-Chi 48
Staley-Pit 44
Gruber-Cle 39
Weyhing-Bro 38

Shutouts
King-Chi 4
Weyhing-Bro 3
Staley-Pit 3

Saves
Hemming-Cle-Bro 3
O'Day-NY 3

Innings Pitched
Baldwin-Chi 492.0
King-Chi 461.0
Weyhing-Bro 390.0
Staley-Pit 387.2
Gruber-Cle 383.1

Fewest Hits/Game
King-Chi 8.20
Crane-NY 8.80
Keefe-NY 8.84
Hemming-Cle-Bro 8.88
Knell-Phi 9.01

Fewest BB/Game
Staley-Pit 1.72
Sanders-Phi 1.79
Galvin-Pit 2.03
Morris-Pit 2.18
Radbourn-Bos 2.62

Strikeouts
Baldwin-Chi 206
King-Chi 185
Weyhing-Bro 177
Staley-Pit 145
J.Ewing-NY 145

Strikeouts/Game
J.Ewing-NY 4.88
Daley-Bos 4.21
Weyhing-Bro 4.08
McGill-Cle 4.02
Haddock-Buf 3.81

Ratio
Staley-Pit 11.07
King-Chi 11.67
Radbourn-Bos 12.15
Keefe-NY 12.66
Sanders-Phi 12.75

Earned Run Average
King-Chi 2.69
Staley-Pit 3.23
Radbourn-Bos 3.31
Baldwin-Chi 3.35
Keefe-NY 3.38

Adjusted ERA
King-Chi 161
Keefe-NY 134
Radbourn-Bos 133
Baldwin-Chi 130
Weyhing-Bro 124

Opponents' Batting Avg.
King-Chi .... .232
Crane-NY .... .245
Keefe-NY .... .246
Hemming-Cle-Bro .... .247
Knell-Phi .... .250

Opponents' On-Base Pct.
Staley-Pit .... .290
King-Chi .... .301
Radbourn-Bos .... .310
Keefe-NY .... .318
Sanders-Phi .... .320

Starter Runs
King-Chi 78.6
Baldwin-Chi 48.2
Staley-Pit 43.2
Radbourn-Bos 35.2
Weyhing-Bro 27.2

Adjusted Starter Runs
King-Chi 82.1
Baldwin-Chi 52.8
Radbourn-Bos 39.9
Weyhing-Bro 35.1
Staley-Pit 31.6

Clutch Pitching Index
O'Brien-Cle 127
Daley-Bos 124
McGill-Cle 117
Kilroy-Bos 114
Gruber-Cle 114

Relief Runs

Adjusted Relief Runs

Relief Ranking

Total Pitcher Index
King-Chi 6.9
Baldwin-Chi 4.7
Radbourn-Bos 3.5
Staley-Pit 2.7
Sanders-Phi 2.4

Total Baseball Ranking
King-Chi 6.9
Baldwin-Chi 4.7
Browning-Cle 4.6
Radbourn-Bos 3.4
B.Ewing-NY 3.1

TEAM	G	W	L	PCT	GB	R	OR	AB	H	2B	3B	HR	BB	SO	AVG	OBP	SLG	OPS	OPS+	BR	BR+	PF	CHI	RC	SB	CS	SBA	SBR
BOS	140	87	51	.630		**847**	**658**	4956	1264	181	81	53	**533**	537	.255	**.337**	.356	**693**	97	**52**	-37	112	101	**710**	289			
CHI	137	82	53	.607	3.5	832	730	4873	1231	159	88	**60**	526	457	.253	.332	.358	690	107	41	42	100	102	674	238			
NY	136	71	61	.538	13	754	711	4833	1271	189	72	46	438	**394**	**.263**	.329	**.360**	689	**111**	34	**68**	96	96	663	224			
PHI	138	68	69	.496	18.5	756	773	4929	1244	180	51	21	482	412	.252	.326	.322	648	92	-27	-45	103	101	609	232			
CLE	141	65	74	.468	22.5	835	888	5074	**1295**	183	88	22	519	464	.255	.330	.339	669	97	7	-25	104	**104**	663	242			
BRO	137	61	76	.445	25.5	765	820	4748	1233	**200**	69	23	465	435	.260	.330	.345	675	103	16	21	99	101	669	**337**			
CIN	138	56	81	.409	30.5	646	790	4791	1158	148	**90**	40	414	439	.242	.308	.335	643	92	-49	-54	101	93	584	244			
PIT	137	55	80	.407	30.5	679	744	4794	1148	148	71	29	427	503	.239	.308	.318	626	90	-73	-56	98	101	547	205			
TOT	552					6114		38998	9844	1388	610	294	3804	3641	.253	.326	.342	667							2011			

TEAM	CG	SH	SV	IP	H	H/G	HR	BB	SO	RAT	ERA	ERA+	OAV	OOB	PR	PR+	PF	CPI	FA	E	DP	FW	PW	BW	SBW	DIF
BOS	**126**	9	**6**	1241^2	1223	8.9	51	**364**	525	**11.8**	**2.77**	**132**	.248	**.305**	**80**	**112**	109	**109**	**.938**	**358**	96	**4.7**	**10.1**	-3.3		6.7
CHI	114	6	3	1220^2	1207	8.9	53	475	477	12.8	3.48	96	.249	.322	-17	-21	100	96	.932	397	**119**	1.5	-1.8	3.8		11.2
NY	117	**11**	3	1204	**1098**	**8.3**	26	593	**651**	13.1	3.00	107	**.234**	.327	47	29	96	104	.933	384	104	2.2	2.6	**6.1**		-5.8
PHI	105	3	5	1229^1	1279	9.4	29	507	342	13.4	3.74	91	.259	.333	-53	-46	102	94	.925	443	108	-1.3	-4.1	-4.0		9.0
CLE	118	1	3	1244	1371	10.0	**24**	466	400	13.7	3.51	99	.270	.336	-22	-6	103	105	.920	485	86	-3.4	-.5	-2.2		1.8
BRO	121	8	3	1204^2	1272	9.6	40	459	407	13.4	3.86	86	.261	.332	-68	-76	99	93	.924	432	73	-.8	-6.7	1.9		-1.7
CIN	125	6	1	1218^2	1234	9.2	40	465	393	13.1	3.56	95	.253	.326	-28	-25	101	96	.931	409	101	1.0	-2.2	-4.8		-6.3
PIT	122	7	3	1197^2	1160	8.8	31	465	446	12.7	2.89	114	.245	.320	61	52	98	**109**	.917	475	76	-3.6	4.7	-5.0		-8.5
TOT	948	51	27	9760^2		9.1				13.0	3.35		.253	.326					.928	3383	763					

Runs
Hamilton-Phi 141
Long-Bos 129
Childs-Cle 120
Latham-Cin 119
Stovey-Bos 118

Hits
Hamilton-Phi 179
McKean-Cle 170
Tiernan-NY 166
Davis-Cle 165
O'Rourke-NY 164

Doubles
Griffin-Bro 36
Davis-Cle 35
Stovey-Bos 31
Tiernan-NY 30

Triples
Stovey-Bos 20
Beckley-Pit 19
McPhee-Cin 16
Ryan-Chi 15
Virtue-Cle 14

Home Runs
Tiernan-NY 16
Stovey-Bos 16
Wilmot-Chi 11

Total Bases
Stovey-Bos 271
Tiernan-NY 268
Long-Bos 235
Davis-Cle 233
Beckley-Pit 232

Runs Batted In
Anson-Chi 120
Stovey-Bos 95
O'Rourke-NY 95
Nash-Bos 95
Connor-NY 94

Runs Produced
Davis-Cle 201
Childs-Cle 201
Hamilton-Phi 199
Connor-NY 199
Stovey-Bos 197

Bases On Balls
Hamilton-Phi 102
Childs-Cle 97
Connor-NY 83
Long-Bos 80

Batting Average
Hamilton-Phi .340
Holliday-Cin .319
Browning-Pit-Cin .317
Clements-Phi .310
Tiernan-NY .306

On-Base Percentage
Hamilton-Phi .453
Connor-NY .399
Childs-Cle .395
Browning-Pit-Cin .395
Tiernan-NY .388

Slugging Average
Stovey-Bos .498
Tiernan-NY .494
Holliday-Cin .473
Connor-NY .449
Ryan-Chi .434

On-Base Plus Slugging
Tiernan-NY 882
Hamilton-Phi 874
Stovey-Bos 871
Holliday-Cin 848
Connor-NY 848

Adjusted OPS
Tiernan-NY 163
Connor-NY 153
Hamilton-Phi 151
Holliday-Cin 145
Browning-Pit-Cin 139

Batter Runs
Hamilton-Phi 44.1
Tiernan-NY 37.8
Stovey-Bos 35.2
Connor-NY 30.7
Holliday-Cin 24.4

Adjusted Batter Runs
Tiernan-NY 43.1
Hamilton-Phi 40.8
Connor-NY 35.4
Holliday-Cin 23.7
Stovey-Bos 22.2

Clutch Hitting Index
Anson-Chi 130
Delahanty-Phi 126
Brodie-Bos 119
Zimmer-Cle 119
Allen-Phi 119

Runs Created
Hamilton-Phi 155
Tiernan-NY 128
Stovey-Bos 125
Long-Bos 114
Latham-Cin 112

Total Average
Hamilton-Phi 1.270
Tiernan-NY 1.045
Stovey-Bos 1.043
Latham-Cin .974
Connor-NY .968

Stolen Bases
Hamilton-Phi 111
Latham-Cin 87
Griffin-Bro 65
Long-Bos 60

Stolen Base Average

Stolen Base Runs

Fielding Runs
Richardson-NY 49.1
Griffin-Bro 25.7
Pfeffer-Chi 25.0
McPhee-Cin 23.4
Latham-Cin 20.4

Total Player Rating
Richardson-NY 4.4
Hamilton-Phi 3.8
Latham-Cin 3.4
Pfeffer-Chi 3.1
McPhee-Cin 3.0

Wins
Hutchison-Chi 44
Rusie-NY 33
Clarkson-Bos 33
Nichols-Bos 30
Young-Cle 27

Win Percentage
J.Ewing-NY .724
Hutchison-Chi .698
Staley-Pit-Bos .649
Nichols-Bos .638
Clarkson-Bos .635

Games
Hutchison-Chi 66
Rusie-NY 61
Young-Cle 55
Clarkson-Bos 55

Complete Games
Hutchison-Chi 56
Rusie-NY 52
Baldwin-Pit 48
Clarkson-Bos 47
Nichols-Bos 45

Shutouts
Rusie-NY 6
Nichols-Bos 5
J.Ewing-NY 5
Hutchison-Chi 4

Saves
Nichols-Bos 3
Clarkson-Bos 3
Young-Cle 2
Thornton-Phi 2

Innings Pitched
Hutchison-Chi 561.0
Rusie-NY 500.1
Clarkson-Bos 460.2
Baldwin-Pit 437.2
Mullane-Cin 426.1

Fewest Hits/Game
Rusie-NY 7.03
Baldwin-Pit 7.92
J.Ewing-NY 7.92
Hutchison-Chi 8.15
Mullane-Cin 8.23

Fewest BB/Game
Nichols-Bos 2.18
Staley-Pit-Bos 2.22
Galvin-Pit 2.26
Radbourn-Cin 2.56
Hutchison-Chi 2.86

Strikeouts
Rusie-NY 337
Hutchison-Chi 261
Nichols-Bos 240
Baldwin-Pit 197
King-Pit 160

Strikeouts/Game
Rusie-NY 6.06
Nichols-Bos 5.08
J.Ewing-NY 4.61
Hutchison-Chi 4.19
Baldwin-Pit 4.05

Ratio
Staley-Pit-Bos 11.08
Hutchison-Chi 11.12
Nichols-Bos 11.28
J.Ewing-NY 11.80
Clarkson-Bos 11.80

Earned Run Average
J.Ewing-NY 2.27
Nichols-Bos 2.39
Rusie-NY 2.55
Staley-Pit-Bos 2.58
Baldwin-Pit 2.76

Adjusted ERA
Nichols-Bos 153
J.Ewing-NY 141
Staley-Pit-Bos 138
Clarkson-Bos 131
Rusie-NY 125

Opponents' Batting Avg.
Rusie-NY .207
Baldwin-Pit .228
J.Ewing-NY .228
Hutchison-Chi .233
Mullane-Cin .234

Opponents' On-Base Pct.
Staley-Pit-Bos .292
Hutchison-Chi .293
Nichols-Bos .296
J.Ewing-NY .305
Clarkson-Bos .305

Starter Runs
Nichols-Bos 45.1
Rusie-NY 43.9
Hutchison-Chi 33.5
J.Ewing-NY 32.1
Baldwin-Pit 28.6

Adjusted Starter Runs
Nichols-Bos 54.6
Clarkson-Bos 40.2
Rusie-NY 37.4
Staley-Pit-Bos 33.2
Hutchison-Chi 32.6

Clutch Pitching Index
Viau-Cle 117
Nichols-Bos 116
Caruthers-Bro 116
Galvin-Pit 112
J.Ewing-NY 111

Relief Runs

Adjusted Relief Runs

Relief Ranking

Total Pitcher Index
Nichols-Bos 5.3
Clarkson-Bos 4.5
Rusie-NY 3.8
Staley-Pit-Bos 2.9
Hutchison-Chi 2.7

Total Baseball Ranking
Nichols-Bos 5.3
Clarkson-Bos 4.4
Richardson-NY 4.4
Hamilton-Phi 3.8
Rusie-NY 3.8

TEAM	G	W	L	PCT	GB	R	OR	AB	H	2B	3B	HR	BB	SO	AVG	OBP	SLG	OPS	OPS+	BR	BR+	PF	CHI	RC	SB	CS	SBA	SBR
BOS	139	93	42	.689		**1028**	**675**	4889	**1341**	163	100	52	**651**	499	**.274**	**.367**	**.380**	**747**	**121**	**127**	**142**	99	**106**	**868**	**447**			
STL	139	85	51	.625	8.5	959	738	4942	1311	165	51	**57**	612	**436**	.265	.356	.354	710	94	61	-57	115	**106**	740	279			
MIL	36	21	15	.583	22.5	227	156	1271	332	58	15	13	107	114	.261	.333	.361	694	86	3	-33	120	**106**	173	47			
BAL	139	71	64	.526	22	850	798	4771	1217	142	99	30	551	553	.255	.346	.345	691	102	23	14	101	101	705	342			
PHI	143	73	66	.525	22	817	794	5039	1301	**182**	**123**	55	447	548	.258	.328	.376	704	106	23	20	100	95	686	149			
COL	138	61	76	.445	33	702	777	4697	1113	154	61	20	529	530	.237	.319	.308	627	89	-93	-51	94	101	565	280			
CIN	102	43	57	.430	32.5	549	643	3574	838	105	58	28	428	385	.234	.322	.320	642	81	-51	-96	109	99	432	164			
LOU	139	54	83	.394	40	698	873	4764	1229	127	68	17	438	465	.258	.329	.324	653	93	-51	-41	99	94	597	227			
WAS	139	44	91	.326	49	691	1067	4715	1183	147	84	19	468	485	.251	.328	.330	658	97	-42	-7	96	93	597	219			
TOT	557					6521		38662	9865	1243	659	291	4231	4015	.256	.338	.344	682							2154			

TEAM	CG	SH	SV	IP	H	H/G	HR	BB	SO	RAT	ERA	ERA+	OAV	OOB	PR	PR+	PF	CPI	FA	E	DP	FW	PW	BW	SBW	DIF
BOS	108	**9**	**7**	1219^2	1158	8.6	42	497	524	**12.7**	**3.03**	115	.242	**.321**	**92**	64	94	**109**	.934	392	115	4.1	5.6	**12.3**		3.7
STL	101	8	5	1206^2	**1088**	**8.2**	50	571	**613**	12.9	3.23	**130**	**.233**	.325	64	**113**	113	102	.920	459	91	.2	**9.8**	-4.9		12.1
MIL	35	3	0	309^2	291	8.5	6	120	137	12.3	2.50	175	.241	.314	42	54	118	121	.922	116	20	.2	4.7	-2.8		1.0
BAL	118	6	2	1217	1238	9.2	33	472	408	13.2	3.44	108	.255	.329	37	39	100	103	.915	503	103	-2.5	3.4	1.3		1.5
PHI	**135**	3	0	1233^2	1274	9.3	35	520	533	13.7	4.02	94	.258	.338	-42	-31	102	93	.933	389	109	**5.1**	-2.6	1.8		-.6
COL	118	6	0	1213^1	1141	8.5	**29**	588	502	13.6	3.75	92	.241	.336	-5	-44	93	92	**.935**	**379**	**126**	4.7	-3.7	-4.3		-3.9
CIN	86	2	1	902	921	9.2	20	446	331	14.2	3.44	119	.256	.347	28	60	111	111	.913	389	68	-3.0	5.2	-8.2		-.8
LOU	126	**9**	1	1210	1334	10.0	32	**451**	481	13.8	4.22	86	.271	.340	-69	-80	98	93	.922	454	112	.5	-6.8	-3.5		-4.4
WAS	123	2	2	1181	1420	10.9	44	566	486	16.0	4.84	77	.288	.374	-147	-145	101	101	.900	589	95	-7.6	-12.5	-.6		-2.7
TOT	950	48	18	9693		9.2				13.7	3.71		.256	.338					.922	3670	839					

Runs
Brown-Bos 177
VanHaltren-Bal 136
Hoy-StL 134
Duffy-Bos 134

Hits
Brown-Bos 189
VanHaltren-Bal 180
Duffy-Bos 180
McCarthy-StL 176
Brouthers-Bos 170

Doubles
Milligan-Phi 35
Brown-Bos 30
O'Neill-StL 28
Duffee-Col 28
Larkin-Phi 27

Triples
Brown-Bos 21
Brouthers-Bos 19
Canavan-Cin-Mil 18
Werden-Bal 18

Home Runs
Farrell-Bos 12
Milligan-Phi 11
Lyons-StL 11

Total Bases
Brown-Bos 276
VanHaltren-Bal 251
Brouthers-Bos 249
Duffy-Bos 243
Werden-Bal 234

Runs Batted In
Farrell-Bos 110
Duffy-Bos 110
Brouthers-Bos 109
Milligan-Phi 106
Werden-Bal 104

Runs Produced
Brown-Bos 244
Duffy-Bos 235
Brouthers-Bos 221
VanHaltren-Bal 210
McCarthy-StL 208

Bases On Balls
Hoy-StL 117
Crooks-Col 103
McTamany-Col-Phi ... 101
Radford-Bos 96
Johnson-Bal 89

Batting Average
Brouthers-Bos ...... .350
Duffy-Bos .... .336
O'Neill-StL .... .323
Brown-Bos .... .321
VanHaltren-Bal ..... .318

On-Base Percentage
Brouthers-Bos ..... .471
Lyons-StL .... .445
Hoy-StL .... .424
Seery-Cin .... .423
Duffy-Bos .... .408

Slugging Average
Brouthers-Bos ...... .512
Milligan-Phi .... .505
Farrell-Bos .... .474
Brown-Bos .... .469
Cross-Phi .... .458

On-Base Plus Slugging
Brouthers-Bos 983
Milligan-Phi 903
Lyons-StL 900
Brown-Bos 865
Duffy-Bos 861

Adjusted OPS
Brouthers-Bos 184
Milligan-Phi 158
Brown-Bos 150
Duffy-Bos 149
Farrell-Bos 148

Batter Runs
Brouthers-Bos 57.0
Lyons-StL 39.2
Brown-Bos 35.3
Milligan-Phi 33.4
Duffy-Bos 32.2

Adjusted Batter Runs
Brouthers-Bos 59.3
Brown-Bos 37.3
Duffy-Bos 34.0
Milligan-Phi 32.9
Joyce-Bos 28.9

Clutch Hitting Index
Sneed-Col 133
Duffy-Bos 129
Comiskey-StL 129
Ray-Bal 128
Radford-Bos 128

Runs Created
Brown-Bos 155
Duffy-Bos 137
Brouthers-Bos 135
VanHaltren-Bal 133
Hoy-StL 113

Total Average
Brouthers-Bos 1.237
Brown-Bos 1.140
Duffy-Bos 1.104
VanHaltren-Bal 1.039
Lyons-StL 1.036

Stolen Bases
Brown-Bos 106
Duffy-Bos 85
VanHaltren-Bal 75
Hoy-StL 59
Radford-Bos 55

Stolen Base Average

Stolen Base Runs

Fielding Runs
Stricker-Bos 24.3
Radford-Bos 19.8
Crooks-Col 19.7
Farrell-Bos 19.0
Wheelock-Col 18.6

Total Player Rating
Farrell-Bos 4.3
Brouthers-Bos 3.4
Crooks-Col 3.2
Milligan-Phi 3.2
Duffy-Bos 2.8

Wins
McMahon-Bal 35
Haddock-Bos 34
Stivetts-StL 33
Weyhing-Phi 31
Buffinton-Bos 29

Win Percentage
Buffinton-Bos ...... .763
Haddock-Bos .... .756
Weyhing-Phi .... .608
Stivetts-StL .... .600
McMahon-Bal .... .593

Games
Stivetts-StL 64
McMahon-Bal 61
Knell-Col 58
Carsey-Was 54
Weyhing-Phi 52

Complete Games
McMahon-Bal 53
Weyhing-Phi 51
Knell-Col 47
Carsey-Was 46
Chamberlain-Phi 44

Shutouts
McMahon-Bal 5
Knell-Col 5
Haddock-Bos 5

Saves
O'Brien-Bos 2
Daley-Bos 2

Innings Pitched
McMahon-Bal 503.0
Knell-Col 462.0
Weyhing-Phi 450.0
Stivetts-StL 440.0
Carsey-Was 415.0

Fewest Hits/Game
Knell-Col 7.07
Stivetts-StL 7.30
Buffinton-Bos 7.50
Crane-Cin 7.78
Haddock-Bos 7.82

Fewest BB/Game
Stratton-Lou 1.78
Sanders-Phi 2.30
McMahon-Bal 2.67
Ehret-Lou 2.85
Griffith-StL-Bos 2.90

Strikeouts
Stivetts-StL 259
Knell-Col 228
Weyhing-Phi 219
McMahon-Bal 219
Chamberlain-Phi 204

Strikeouts/Game
Meekin-Lou 5.73
Stivetts-StL 5.30
McGill-Cin-StL 4.98
Daley-Bos 4.83
Chamberlain-Phi ... 4.53

Ratio
Buffinton-Bos 10.64
Haddock-Bos 11.40
McMahon-Bal 11.79
Fitzgerald-Lou ... 12.32
Weyhing-Phi 12.40

Earned Run Average
Crane-Cin 2.45
Haddock-Bos 2.49
Buffinton-Bos 2.55
McMahon-Bal 2.81
Stivetts-StL 2.86

Adjusted ERA
Crane-Cin 168
Stivetts-StL 146
Haddock-Bos 140
Buffinton-Bos 136
Mains-Cin-Mil 134

Opponents' Batting Avg.
Knell-Col .... .209
Stivetts-StL .... .215
Buffinton-Bos ...... .219
Crane-Cin .... .225
Haddock-Bos .... .226

Opponents' On-Base Pct.
Buffinton-Bos ...... .285
Haddock-Bos .... .299
McMahon-Bal ...... .306
Fitzgerald-Lou ..... .315
Weyhing-Phi .... .317

Starter Runs
Haddock-Bos 51.4
McMahon-Bal 50.2
Buffinton-Bos 46.8
Stivetts-StL 41.3
Knell-Col 40.3

Adjusted Starter Runs
Stivetts-StL 57.4
McMahon-Bal 50.8
Haddock-Bos 44.3
Crane-Cin 41.5
Buffinton-Bos 39.9

Clutch Pitching Index
Daley-Bos 134
Crane-Cin 128
O'Brien-Bos 123
Mains-Cin-Mil 122
Foreman-Was 113

Relief Runs

Adjusted Relief Runs

Relief Ranking

Total Pitcher Index
Stivetts-StL 6.9
Haddock-Bos 5.5
McMahon-Bal 4.9
Buffinton-Bos 3.8
Crane-Cin 3.1

Total Baseball Ranking
Stivetts-StL 6.8
Haddock-Bos 5.3
McMahon-Bal 4.8
Farrell-Bos 4.3
Brouthers-Bos 3.4

TEAM	G	W	L	PCT	GB	R	OR	AB	H	2B	3B	HR	BB	SO	AVG	OBP	SLG	OPS	OPS+	BR	BR+	PF	CHI	RC	SB	CS	SBA	SBR
BOS	152	102	48	.680		862	649	5301	1325	203	51	34	526	492	.250	.325	.327	652	93	18	-49	109	108	689	338			
CLE	153	93	56	.624	8.5	855	**613**	5412	1376	196	96	26	552	538	.254	.328	.340	668	103	48	15	104	101	694	225			
BRO	158	95	59	.617	9	**935**	733	5485	**1439**	183	105	30	**629**	508	**.262**	**.344**	.350	694	**119**	**109**	**145**	96	101	**822**	**409**			
PHI	155	87	66	.569	16.5	860	690	5413	1420	**225**	95	**50**	528	515	**.262**	.334	**.367**	**701**	117	106	109	100	95	753	216			
CIN	155	82	68	.547	20	766	731	5349	1291	155	75	44	503	476	.241	.311	.323	634	98	-22	-11	99	101	637	270			
PIT	155	80	73	.523	23.5	802	796	5469	1288	143	108	38	435	**453**	.236	.297	.322	619	92	-60	-63	100	**110**	604	222			
CHI	147	70	76	.479	30	635	735	5063	1189	149	92	26	427	482	.235	.299	.316	615	90	-60	-67	101	94	562	233			
NY	153	71	80	.470	31.5	811	826	5291	1329	173	85	39	510	474	.251	.321	.338	659	106	26	39	98	101	688	301			
LOU	154	63	89	.414	40	649	804	5334	1209	133	61	18	433	508	.227	.290	.285	575	86	-135	-80	92	102	534	275			
WAS	153	58	93	.384	44.5	731	869	5204	1246	149	78	37	529	555	.239	.314	.319	633	99	-18	4	97	98	624	276			
STL	155	56	94	.373	46	703	922	5259	1188	138	53	45	607	492	.226	.312	.298	610	94	-55	-17	95	96	568	209			
BAL	152	46	101	.313	54.5	779	1020	5296	1343	160	**111**	30	499	480	.254	.325	.343	668	104	44	22	103	95	680	227			
TOT	921					9388		63876	15643	2007	1010	417	6178	5973	.245	.317	.328	644							3201			

TEAM	CG	SH	SV	IP	H	H/G	HR	BB	SO	RAT	ERA	ERA+	OAV	OOB	PR	PR+	PF	CPI	FA	E	DP	FW	PW	BW	SBW	DIF
BOS	142	**15**	1	1336	**1156**	**7.8**	41	460	514	11.1	2.86	123	**.224**	.292	64	90	107	93	.929	454	127	.5	8.4	-4.5		22.8
CLE	140	11	2	1336	1178	8.0	28	**413**	472	**11.0**	**2.42**	**140**	.228	**.289**	**130**	**139**	103	**107**	.935	407	95	3.4	**12.9**	1.4		.9
BRO	132	12	**5**	1405^{2}	1285	8.3	26	600	597	12.4	3.25	97	.234	.315	6	-14	96	94	**.940**	398	98	**4.8**	-1.2	**13.5**		1.1
PHI	131	10	**5**	1379	1309	8.6	**24**	492	511	12.2	2.94	111	.241	.310	54	48	99	104	.939	**393**	128	4.6	4.5	10.1		-8.5
CIN	130	8	2	1377^{1}	1327	8.7	39	535	437	12.6	3.17	103	.243	.317	18	15	99	104	.939	402	**140**	4.1	1.4	-1.0		2.7
PIT	130	3	1	1347^{1}	1300	8.7	28	537	455	12.7	3.10	106	.244	.320	28	27	100	106	.927	483	113	-.6	2.6	-5.8		7.6
CHI	133	6	1	1298	1269	8.8	35	424	518	12.1	3.17	105	.246	.308	18	22	101	100	.932	424	85	1.4	2.1	-6.2		-.1
NY	139	5	1	1322^{2}	1165	8.0	32	635	**650**	12.6	3.30	98	.227	.318	-1	-12	98	94	.912	565	97	-5.8	-1.1	3.7		-1.1
LOU	**147**	9	0	1346	1358	9.1	26	447	430	12.3	3.34	92	.252	.313	-8	-44	93	97	.928	471	133	-.1	-4.0	-7.4		-1.3
WAS	129	5	3	1315^{1}	1293	8.9	40	556	479	13.1	3.47	94	.247	.327	-26	-32	99	102	.916	547	122	-4.7	-2.9	.4		-10.1
STL	139	4	1	1344^{2}	1466	9.9	47	543	478	13.9	4.21	76	.267	.339	-137	-156	97	96	.929	452	100	1.2	-14.4	-1.5		-4.0
BAL	131	2	2	1298^{2}	1537	10.7	51	536	437	14.8	4.29	80	.284	.353	-144	-119	104	106	.910	584	100	-7.1	-11.0	2.1		-11.4
TOT	1623	90	24	16106^{2}		8.8				12.6	3.29		.245	.317					.929	5580	1338					

Split Season: First-half Winner BOS (52-22); Second-half Winner CLE (53-23)

Runs
Childs-Cle 136
Hamilton-Phi 132
Duffy-Bos 125
Connor-Phi 123
Brouthers-Bro 121

Hits
Brouthers-Bro 197
Thompson-Phi 186
Duffy-Bos 184
Hamilton-Phi 183
Long-Bos 181

Doubles
Connor-Phi 37
Long-Bos 33
Delahanty-Phi 30
Brouthers-Bro 30
Zimmer-Cle 29

Triples
Delahanty-Phi 21
Virtue-Cle 20
Brouthers-Bro 20
Dahlen-Chi 19
Beckley-Pit 19

Home Runs
Holliday-Cin 13
Connor-Phi 12
Ryan-Chi 10
Beckley-Pit 10
Thompson-Phi 9

Total Bases
Brouthers-Bro 282
Holliday-Cin 271
Thompson-Phi 263
Connor-Phi 261
Duffy-Bos 251

Runs Batted In
Brouthers-Bro 124
Thompson-Phi 104
Larkin-Was 96
Burns-Bro 96
Beckley-Pit 96

Runs Produced
Brouthers-Bro 240
Thompson-Phi 204
Duffy-Bos 201
Holliday-Cin 192

Bases On Balls
Crooks-StL 136
Childs-Cle 117
Connor-Phi 116
McCarthy-Bos 93

Batting Average
Brouthers-Bro .335
Hamilton-Phi .330
Childs-Cle .317
Burns-Bro .315
Ewing-NY .310

On-Base Percentage
Childs-Cle .443
Brouthers-Bro .432
Hamilton-Phi .423
Connor-Phi .420
Crooks-StL .400

Slugging Average
Delahanty-Phi .495
Brouthers-Bro .480
Ewing-NY .473
Connor-Phi .463
Burns-Bro .454

On-Base Plus Slugging
Brouthers-Bro 911
Connor-Phi 883
Delahanty-Phi 855
Burns-Bro 849
Childs-Cle 841

Adjusted OPS
Brouthers-Bro 182
Connor-Phi 167
Burns-Bro 162
Delahanty-Phi 158
Hamilton-Phi 152

Batter Runs
Brouthers-Bro 56.8
Connor-Phi 50.5
Childs-Cle 45.5
Hamilton-Phi 38.9
Burns-Bro 37.3

Adjusted Batter Runs
Brouthers-Bro 62.5
Connor-Phi 50.9
Burns-Bro 41.8
Childs-Cle 40.2
Hamilton-Phi 39.3

Clutch Hitting Index
McKean-Cle 165
Pfeffer-Lou 142
Nash-Bos 135
Larkin-Was 131
Brouthers-Bro 128

Runs Created
Brouthers-Bro 138
Hamilton-Phi 123
Connor-Phi 122
VanHaltren-Bal-Pit 117
Holliday-Cin 115

Total Average
Brouthers-Bro 1.056
Connor-Phi 1.018
Hamilton-Phi 1.005
Childs-Cle .982
Burns-Bro .943

Stolen Bases
Ward-Bro 88
Brown-Lou 78
Latham-Cin 66
Hoy-Was 60
Dahlen-Chi 60

Stolen Base Average

Stolen Base Runs

Fielding Runs
D.Richardson-Was 57.4
Shindle-Bal 35.4
Bierbauer-Pit 31.6
McPhee-Cin 25.2
Dahlen-Chi 25.1

Total Player Rating
Brouthers-Bro 6.7
McPhee-Cin 4.9
Dahlen-Chi 4.5
D.Richardson-Was 4.2
Connor-Phi 4.1

Wins
Young-Cle 36
Hutchison-Chi 36
Stivetts-Bos 35
Nichols-Bos 35

Win Percentage
Young-Cle .750
Terry-Bal-Pit .692
Haddock-Bro .690
Staley-Bos .688

Games
Hutchison-Chi 75
Rusie-NY 65
Killen-Was 60
Weyhing-Phi 59
Baldwin-Pit 56

Complete Games
Hutchison-Chi 67
Rusie-NY 59
Nichols-Bos 49
Young-Cle 48

Shutouts
Young-Cle 9
Weyhing-Phi 6
Stein-Bro 6

Saves
Weyhing-Phi 3
Duryea-Cin-Was 2

Innings Pitched
Hutchison-Chi 622.0
Rusie-NY 541.0
Weyhing-Phi 469.2
Killen-Was 459.2

Fewest Hits/Game
Mullane-Cin 6.77
Rusie-NY 6.82
Terry-Bal-Pit 6.94
Young-Cle 7.21
Duryea-Cin-Was 7.25

Fewest BB/Game
Stratton-Lou 1.79
Dwyer-StL-Cin 1.98
Sanders-Lou 2.08
Young-Cle 2.34
Ehret-Pit 2.36

Strikeouts
Hutchison-Chi 314
Rusie-NY 304
Weyhing-Phi 202
Nichols-Bos 192
Stein-Bro 190

Strikeouts/Game
Kennedy-Bro 5.09
Rusie-NY 5.06
Hutchison-Chi 4.54
Stein-Bro 4.53
Crane-NY 4.30

Ratio
Young-Cle 9.77
Nichols-Bos 10.63
Stratton-Lou 10.77
Mullane-Cin 11.01
Duryea-Cin-Was 11.08

Earned Run Average
Young-Cle 1.93
Keefe-Phi 2.36
J.Clarkson-Bos-Cle 2.48
Cuppy-Cle 2.51
Terry-Bal-Pit 2.57

Adjusted ERA
Young-Cle 176
J.Clarkson-Bos-Cle 139
Keefe-Phi 138
Cuppy-Cle 135
Davies-Cle 131

Opponents' Batting Avg.
Mullane-Cin .201
Rusie-NY .202
Terry-Bal-Pit .205
Young-Cle .211
Duryea-Cin-Was .212

Opponents' On-Base Pct.
Young-Cle .266
Nichols-Bos .283
Stratton-Lou .286
Mullane-Cin .290
Duryea-Cin-Was .291

Starter Runs
Young-Cle 68.3
Hutchison-Chi 36.0
J.Clarkson-Bos-Cle 35.0
Weyhing-Phi 32.4
Keefe-Phi 32.3

Adjusted Starter Runs
Young-Cle 71.2
J.Clarkson-Bos-Cle 39.6
Hutchison-Chi 38.1
Cuppy-Cle 35.4
Nichols-Bos 31.4

Clutch Pitching Index
Sullivan-Cin 136
Galvin-Pit-StL 121
Vickery-Bal 116
McMahon-Bal 115
Luby-Chi 115

Relief Runs

Adjusted Relief Runs

Relief Ranking

Total Pitcher Index
Young-Cle 6.4
Hutchison-Chi 4.5
Cuppy-Cle 3.7
Stivetts-Bos 3.6
J.Clarkson-Bos-Cle 3.1

Total Baseball Ranking
Brouthers-Bro 6.7
Young-Cle 6.4
McPhee-Cin 4.9
Dahlen-Chi 4.5
Hutchison-Chi 4.4

TEAM	G	W	L	PCT	GB	R	OR	AB	H	2B	3B	HR	BB	SO	AVG	OBP	SLG	OPS	OPS+	BR	BR+	PF	CHI	RC	SB	CS	SBA	SBR
BOS	131	86	43	.667		1008	795	4678	1358	178	50	65	**561**	292	.290	.372	.391	763	99	54	-13	108	**111**	790	243			
PIT	131	81	48	.628	5	970	**766**	4834	1447	176	**127**	37	537	274	.299	**.377**	.411	788	116	96	**115**	98	99	848	210			
CLE	129	73	55	.570	12.5	976	839	4747	1425	222	98	32	532	**229**	.300	.374	.408	782	106	84	31	106	103	841	252			
PHI	133	72	57	.558	14	**1011**	841	5151	**1553**	**246**	90	**80**	468	335	**.301**	.368	**.431**	**799**	**117**	**108**	111	100	98	**912**	202			
NY	136	68	64	.515	19.5	941	845	4858	1424	182	101	61	504	281	.293	.366	.410	776	111	69	66	100	99	860	**299**			
CIN	131	65	63	.508	20.5	759	814	4617	1195	161	65	29	532	256	.259	.342	.341	683	84	-88	-106	102	101	634	238			
BRO	130	65	63	.508	20.5	775	845	4511	1200	173	83	45	473	296	.266	.341	.371	712	97	-46	-9	95	101	659	213			
BAL	130	60	70	.462	26.5	820	893	4651	1281	164	86	27	539	323	.275	.359	.365	724	95	-12	-25	102	98	711	233			
CHI	128	56	71	.441	29	829	874	4664	1299	186	93	32	465	262	.279	.348	.379	727	99	-20	-8	99	102	722	255			
STL	135	57	75	.432	30.5	745	829	4879	1288	152	98	10	524	251	.264	.343	.341	684	86	-89	-91	100	94	674	250			
LOU	126	50	75	.400	34	759	942	4566	1185	177	73	19	485	306	.260	.338	.343	681	92	-94	-32	92	104	612	203			
WAS	130	40	89	.310	46	722	1032	4742	1258	180	83	23	523	237	.265	.346	.353	699	92	-62	-40	97	90	648	154			
TOT	785					10315		56898	15913	2197	1047	460	6143	3342	.280	.357	.380	736							2752			

TEAM	CG	SH	SV	IP	H	H/G	HR	BB	SO	RAT	ERA	ERA+	OAV	OOB	PR	PR+	PF	CPI	FA	E	DP	FW	PW	BW	SBW	DIF
BOS	**114**	2	2	1163^{2}	1314	10.2	66	402	253	**13.6**	4.44	111	.277	**.339**	30	60	106	100	.936	353	118	1.8	5.0	-1.0		15.9
PIT	104	**8**	2	1167	**1232**	9.6	29	504	280	13.9	4.08	112	.263	.342	75	61	98	101	.938	347	112	2.2	5.1	**9.5**		.0
CLE	110	2	2	1140^{1}	1361	10.8	35	**356**	242	13.8	4.20	**116**	.288	.342	59	82	105	**106**	.929	395	92	-.9	6.8	2.6		.7
PHI	107	4	2	1189	1357	10.3	30	522	286	14.8	4.68	98	.279	.357	-2	-15	98	98	**.944**	**318**	121	**4.1**	-1.2	9.1		-4.4
NY	111	6	4	1211^{1}	1271	**9.5**	36	581	**395**	14.2	4.30	108	**.262**	.347	49	48	100	99	.927	432	95	-1.8	4.0	5.5		-5.5
CIN	97	4	**5**	1172	1305	10.1	38	549	258	14.8	4.55	105	.274	.357	15	29	103	101	.943	321	**138**	3.6	2.4	-8.6		3.8
BRO	109	3	3	1154	1262	9.9	41	547	297	14.5	4.55	97	.270	.352	15	-17	95	98	.930	385	88	-.1	-1.3	-.7		3.4
BAL	104	1	2	1123^{2}	1325	10.7	29	534	275	15.3	4.98	95	.285	.364	-39	-29	102	97	.929	384	95	-.0	-2.3	-2.0		-.4
CHI	101	4	**5**	1117^{1}	1278	10.3	**26**	553	273	15.3	4.81	96	.279	.365	-18	-24	99	99	.922	421	92	-2.5	-1.9	-.6		-2.3
STL	**114**	3	4	1207	1292	9.7	38	542	301	14.1	**4.07**	**116**	.266	.346	**80**	**87**	101	105	.930	398	110	-.0	**7.2**	-7.4		-8.5
LOU	113	4	1	1080	1431	12.0	38	479	190	16.4	5.91	74	.310	.380	-149	-192	94	94	.937	330	111	2.3	-15.7	-2.6		3.7
WAS	110	2	0	1139	1485	11.8	54	574	292	16.8	5.57	83	.306	.387	-114	-121	99	103	.912	497	96	-6.4	-9.9	-3.2		-4.8
TOT	1294	43	32	13864^{1}		10.4				14.8	4.67		.280	.357					.932	4581	1268					

Runs
Long-Bos 149
Duffy-Bos 147
Delahanty-Phi 145
Childs-Cle 145
Burkett-Cle 145

Hits
Thompson-Phi 222
Delahanty-Phi 219
Duffy-Bos 203
Davis-NY 195
Ward-NY 193

Doubles
Thompson-Phi 37
Delahanty-Phi 35
Tebeau-Cle 32
Beckley-Pit 32

Triples
Werden-StL 29
Davis-NY 27
McKean-Cle 24
Smith-Pit 23
Beckley-Pit 19

Home Runs
Delahanty-Phi 19
Clements-Phi 17
Tiernan-NY 14
Lowe-Bos 14

Total Bases
Delahanty-Phi 347
Thompson-Phi 318
Davis-NY 304
Smith-Pit 272

Runs Batted In
Delahanty-Phi 146
McKean-Cle 133
Thompson-Phi 126
Nash-Bos 123
Ewing-Cle 122

Runs Produced
Delahanty-Phi 272
Duffy-Bos 259
Thompson-Phi 245
Ewing-Cle 233
McKean-Cle 232

Bases On Balls
Crooks-StL 121
Childs-Cle 120
Radford-Was 104
McGraw-Bal 101
Burkett-Cle 98

Batting Average
Duffy-Bos .363
Hamilton-Phi .380
Thompson-Phi .370
Delahanty-Phi .368
Davis-NY .355

On-Base Percentage
Hamilton-Phi .490
Childs-Cle .463
Burkett-Cle .459
McGraw-Bal .454
Smith-Pit .435

Slugging Average
Delahanty-Phi .583
Davis-NY .554
Thompson-Phi .530
Smith-Pit .525
Hamilton-Phi .524

On-Base Plus Slugging
Hamilton-Phi 1014
Delahanty-Phi 1007
Davis-NY 964
Smith-Pit 960
Thompson-Phi 954

Adjusted OPS
Hamilton-Phi 170
Delahanty-Phi 167
Smith-Pit 158
Davis-NY 155
Thompson-Phi 153

Batter Runs
Delahanty-Phi 52.7
Burkett-Cle 43.6
Thompson-Phi 43.3
Smith-Pit 41.4
Davis-NY 40.0

Adjusted Batter Runs
Delahanty-Phi 53.2
Smith-Pit 44.1
Thompson-Phi 43.8
Hamilton-Phi 40.2
Davis-NY 39.6

Clutch Hitting Index
Anson-Chi 148
Vaughn-Cin 147
McKean-Cle 135
Glasscock-StL-Pit 132
O'Rourke-Was 129

Runs Created
Delahanty-Phi 167
Thompson-Phi 146
Davis-NY 143
Burkett-Cle 137
Smith-Pit 133

Total Average
Hamilton-Phi 1.386
Burkett-Cle 1.186
Delahanty-Phi 1.173
Smith-Pit 1.121
Davis-NY 1.107

Stolen Bases
T.Brown-Lou 66
Dowd-StL 59
Latham-Cin 57
Burke-NY 54
Brodie-StL-Bal 49

Stolen Base Average

Stolen Base Runs

Fielding Runs
McPhee-Cin 33.9
Delahanty-Phi 30.9
T.Brown-Lou 27.1
G.Smith-Cin 19.5
Allen-Phi 18.6

Total Player Rating
Delahanty-Phi 6.0
McPhee-Cin 3.8
Davis-NY 3.4
Childs-Cle 3.4
Hamilton-Phi 3.1

Wins
Killen-Pit 36
Young-Cle 34
Nichols-Bos 34
Rusie-NY 33
Kennedy-Bro 25

Win Percentage
Gastright-Pit-Bos .750
Killen-Pit .720
Nichols-Bos .708
Young-Cle .680
Staley-Bos .643

Games
Rusie-NY 56
Killen-Pit 55
Young-Cle 53
Nichols-Bos 52
Mullane-Cin-Bal 49

Complete Games
Rusie-NY 50
Nichols-Bos 43
Young-Cle 42
Kennedy-Bro 40

Shutouts
Rusie-NY 4
Ehret-Pit 4

Saves
Mullane-Cin-Bal 2
Baldwin-Pit-NY 2
Dwyer-Cin 2
Donnelly-Chi 2
Colcolough-Pit 2

Innings Pitched
Rusie-NY 482.0
Nichols-Bos 425.0
Young-Cle 422.2
Killen-Pit 415.0

Fewest Hits/Game
Rusie-NY 8.42
Breitenstein-StL 8.44
Killen-Pit 8.70
Kennedy-Bro 8.84
Stein-Bro 8.87

Fewest BB/Game
Young-Cle 2.19
Nichols-Bos 2.50
Cuppy-Cle 2.77
Staley-Bos 2.77
Stratton-Lou 2.86

Strikeouts
Rusie-NY 208
Kennedy-Bro 107
Young-Cle 102
Breitenstein-StL 102
Weyhing-Phi 101

Strikeouts/Game
Rusie-NY 3.88
Meekin-Was 3.34
Hawley-StL 2.89
Keefe-Phi 2.83
Terry-Pit 2.75

Ratio
Young-Cle 11.82
Nichols-Bos 11.84
Killen-Pit 12.06
Breitenstein-StL 12.30
Stein-Bro 12.70

Earned Run Average
Breitenstein-StL 3.18
Rusie-NY 3.23
Young-Cle 3.36
Ehret-Pit 3.44
Clarkson-StL 3.48

Adjusted ERA
Breitenstein-StL 149
Young-Cle 145
Rusie-NY 144
Nichols-Bos 140
Clarkson-StL 136

Opponents' Batting Avg.
Rusie-NY .240
Breitenstein-StL .241
Killen-Pit .246
Kennedy-Bro .249
Stein-Bro .250

Opponents' On-Base Pct.
Young-Cle .308
Nichols-Bos .308
Killen-Pit .312
Breitenstein-StL .316
Stein-Bro .323

Starter Runs
Rusie-NY 76.6
Breitenstein-StL 63.2
Young-Cle 60.9
Nichols-Bos 54.1
Killen-Pit 46.9

Adjusted Starter Runs
Rusie-NY 76.3
Young-Cle 68.0
Breitenstein-StL 65.0
Nichols-Bos 63.2
Killen-Pit 42.8

Clutch Pitching Index
Esper-Was 120
Clarkson-StL 117
McNabb-Bal 113
Cuppy-Cle 111
Rusie-NY 111

Relief Runs

Adjusted Relief Runs

Relief Ranking

Total Pitcher Index
Rusie-NY 7.2
Young-Cle 6.1
Breitenstein-StL 5.5
Killen-Pit 5.3
Nichols-Bos 5.1

Total Baseball Ranking
Rusie-NY 7.2
Young-Cle 6.1
Delahanty-Phi 6.0
Breitenstein-StL 5.4
Killen-Pit 5.3

TEAM	G	W	L	PCT	GB	R	OR	AB	H	2B	3B	HR	BB	SO	AVG	OBP	SLG	OPS	OPS+	BR	BR+	PF	CHI	RC	SB	CS	SBA	SBR
BAL	129	89	39	.695		1171	819	4799	1647	271	**150**	33	516	**200**	.343	**.418**	.483	**901**	116	**172**	122	104	99	1146	324			
NY	139	88	44	.667	3	962	**801**	4879	1469	199	96	45	489	219	.301	.369	.409	778	92	-67	-60	99	104	885	325			
BOS	133	83	49	.629	8	**1220**	1002	5011	1658	**272**	94	**103**	535	261	.331	.401	**.484**	885	108	134	49	108	**105**	1102	241			
PHI	132	71	57	.555	18	1179	995	5089	**1780**	259	137	40	508	254	**.350**	.415	.478	893	**122**	165	**197**	97	97	**1169**	285			
BRO	135	70	61	.534	20.5	1024	1020	4851	1514	231	130	42	467	295	.312	.376	.439	815	108	-1	74	93	104	942	282			
CLE	130	68	61	.527	21.5	932	896	4764	1442	241	90	37	471	301	.303	.368	.414	782	89	-58	-91	104	103	837	220			
PIT	133	65	65	.500	25	965	1001	4700	1465	223	125	48	444	210	.312	.379	.443	822	103	12	22	99	98	927	257			
CHI	137	57	75	.432	34	1056	1080	5022	1574	268	87	65	507	306	.313	.381	.440	821	97	12	-41	105	102	999	**329**			
STL	133	56	76	.424	35	771	953	4610	1320	171	113	54	442	289	.286	.354	.408	762	87	-101	-101	100	92	763	190			
CIN	134	55	75	.423	35	936	1108	4753	1407	228	71	61	517	255	.296	.370	.412	782	89	-56	-90	104	102	836	223			
WAS	132	45	87	.341	46	882	1122	4581	1317	218	118	59	**617**	375	.287	.381	.425	806	101	-8	24	97	92	864	249			
LOU	131	36	94	.277	54	698	1019	4518	1216	173	89	42	355	368	.269	.330	.375	705	78	-202	-150	93	99	657	219			
TOT	799					11796		57577	17809	2754	1300	629	5868	3333	.310	.380	.436	814							3144			

TEAM	CG	SH	SV	IP	H	H/G	HR	BB	SO	RAT	ERA	ERA+	OAV	OOB	PR	PR+	PF	CPI	FA	E	DP	FW	PW	BW	SBW	DIF
BAL	97	1	**11**	1116^{1}	1371	11.1	**31**	472	275	15.3	5.00	109	.299	.371	40	55	103	98	**.944**	**293**	105	**5.7**	4.3	9.4		5.8
NY	113	5	5	1230	**1310**	**9.6**	37	546	**403**	**13.9**	**3.81**	**138**	**.271**	**.349**	**207**	**197**	99	107	.923	454	103	-1.7	**15.1**	-4.5		13.4
BOS	108	3	2	1166	1529	11.9	89	**411**	262	15.3	5.42	105	.314	.372	-12	31	107	101	.925	415	120	-.6	2.4	3.8		11.5
PHI	103	3	4	1151^{2}	1522	11.9	62	479	266	16.2	5.63	91	.315	.385	-39	-72	96	99	.934	351	114	2.9	-5.5	**15.1**		-5.4
BRO	106	3	5	1171^{1}	1465	11.3	41	558	290	16.1	5.53	89	.303	.383	-27	-82	93	95	.928	393	85	1.0	-6.2	5.7		4.2
CLE	106	**6**	2	1124^{1}	1390	11.2	54	435	254	14.9	4.98	110	.301	.366	44	58	103	99	.935	344	107	3.0	4.5	-6.9		3.1
PIT	106	2	0	1170^{2}	1563	12.1	39	466	308	15.9	5.62	93	.318	.381	-39	-53	98	96	.936	355	106	2.9	-4.0	1.7		-.4
CHI	**118**	0	0	1163	1575	12.2	43	569	284	17.1	5.72	98	.321	.398	-51	-13	106	102	.918	458	115	-2.3	-.9	-3.1		-2.4
STL	114	2	0	1161	1418	11.0	48	500	319	15.3	5.29	102	.299	.371	4	14	102	94	.923	426	109	-1.2	1.1	-7.7		-2.1
CIN	112	4	3	1165^{1}	1615	12.5	85	500	223	16.8	5.99	93	.326	.394	-86	-55	104	101	.925	430	122	-1.2	-4.2	-6.8		2.4
WAS	101	0	4	1107	1573	12.8	59	446	190	17.0	5.52	95	.331	.396	-24	-32	99	**110**	.908	499	81	-5.5	-2.4	1.9		-14.8
LOU	114	2	1	1104^{2}	1478	12.1	41	486	259	16.4	5.46	93	.318	.387	-17	-47	96	102	.919	435	**131**	-2.0	-3.5	-11.4		-11.8
TOT	1298	31	37	13831^{1}		11.6				15.9	5.32		.310	.380					.927	4853	1298					

Runs
Hamilton-Phi 198
Kelley-Bal 165
Keeler-Bal 165
Duffy-Bos 160
Lowe-Bos 158

Hits
Duffy-Bos 237
Hamilton-Phi 225
Keeler-Bal 219
Lowe-Bos 212

Doubles
Duffy-Bos 51
Kelley-Bal 48
Wilmot-Chi 45

Triples
Reitz-Bal 31
Thompson-Phi 28
Treadway-Bro 26
Connor-NY-StL 25
Brouthers-Bal 23

Home Runs
Duffy-Bos 18
Lowe-Bos 17
Joyce-Was 17
Dahlen-Chi 15

Total Bases
Duffy-Bos 374
Lowe-Bos 319
Thompson-Phi 314
Kelley-Bal 305
Keeler-Bal 305

Runs Batted In
Thompson-Phi 147
Duffy-Bos 145
E.Delahanty-Phi 133
Cross-Phi 132
Wilmot-Chi 130

Runs Produced
Duffy-Bos 287
Hamilton-Phi 284
E.Delahanty-Phi 277
Kelley-Bal 270
Wilmot-Chi 261

Bases On Balls
Hamilton-Phi 128
Kelley-Bal 107
Childs-Cle 107

Batting Average
Duffy-Bos .440
Turner-Phi .418
Thompson-Phi .415
E.Delahanty-Phi .404
Hamilton-Phi .403

On-Base Percentage
Hamilton-Phi .522
Kelley-Bal .502
Duffy-Bos .502
Joyce-Was .496
Childs-Cle .475

Slugging Average
Thompson-Phi .696
Duffy-Bos .694
Joyce-Was .648
Kelley-Bal .602
E.Delahanty-Phi .584

On-Base Plus Slugging
Duffy-Bos 1196
Thompson-Phi 1161
Joyce-Was 1143
Kelley-Bal 1104
E.Delahanty-Phi 1059

Adjusted OPS
Thompson-Phi 181
Joyce-Was 179
Duffy-Bos 172
E.Delahanty-Phi 158
Kelley-Bal 158

Batter Runs
Duffy-Bos 75.6
Kelley-Bal 60.1
Hamilton-Phi 60.1
Thompson-Phi 53.7
Joyce-Was 47.0

Adjusted Batter Runs
Hamilton-Phi 65.1
Duffy-Bos 61.9
Thompson-Phi 57.5
Kelley-Bal 52.7
Joyce-Was 51.3

Clutch Hitting Index
Robinson-Bal 141
Wilmot-Chi 131
McGraw-Bal 122
Bierbauer-Pit 122
Reitz-Bal 118

Runs Created
Duffy-Bos 217
Hamilton-Phi 210
Kelley-Bal 182
Stenzel-Pit 164
Thompson-Phi 163

Total Average
Duffy-Bos 1.619
Hamilton-Phi 1.592
Joyce-Was 1.528
Kelley-Bal 1.503
Thompson-Phi 1.451

Stolen Bases
Hamilton-Phi 100
McGraw-Bal 78
Wilmot-Chi 76
T.Brown-Lou 66
Lange-Chi 65

Stolen Base Average

Stolen Base Runs

Fielding Runs
Dahlen-Chi 34.9
McPhee-Cin 33.7
Jennings-Bal 32.9
Farrell-NY 30.4
Reitz-Bal 26.9

Total Player Rating
Dahlen-Chi 5.1
Hamilton-Phi 4.6
E.Delahanty-Phi 4.5
Duffy-Bos 4.4
Cross-Phi 4.1

Wins
Rusie-NY 36
Meekin-NY 33
Nichols-Bos 32
Breitenstein-StL 27

Win Percentage
Meekin-NY .786
McMahon-Bal .758
Rusie-NY .735
Nichols-Bos .711

Games
Breitenstein-StL 56
Rusie-NY 54
Meekin-NY 53
Hawley-StL 53
Young-Cle 52

Complete Games
Breitenstein-StL 46
Rusie-NY 45
Young-Cle 44
Meekin-NY 41
Nichols-Bos 40

Shutouts
Rusie-NY 3
Nichols-Bos 3
Cuppy-Cle 3

Saves
Mullane-Bal-Cle 4
Mercer-Was 3
Hawke-Bal 3

Innings Pitched
Breitenstein-StL 447.1
Rusie-NY 444.0
Meekin-NY 418.1
Young-Cle 408.2
Nichols-Bos 407.0

Fewest Hits/Game
Rusie-NY 8.64
Meekin-NY 8.91
Stein-Bro 9.98
Breitenstein-StL 10.00
Clarkson-Cle 10.33

Fewest BB/Game
Young-Cle 2.33
Menefee-Lou-Pit 2.48
Gleason-StL-Bal 2.54
Staley-Bos 2.63
Nichols-Bos 2.68

Strikeouts
Rusie-NY 195
Breitenstein-StL 140
Meekin-NY 137
Hawley-StL 120
Nichols-Bos 113

Strikeouts/Game
Rusie-NY 3.95
Hawke-Bal 2.97
Wadsworth-Lou 2.97
Meekin-NY 2.95
Chamberlain-Cin 2.89

Ratio
Rusie-NY 12.79
Meekin-NY 12.93
Clarkson-Cle 13.08
Young-Cle 13.19
Nichols-Bos 13.67

Earned Run Average
Rusie-NY 2.78
Meekin-NY 3.66
Mercer-Was 3.85
Young-Cle 3.94
Taylor-Phi 4.08

Adjusted ERA
Rusie-NY 189
Meekin-NY 143
Young-Cle 138
Mercer-Was 137
McMahon-Bal 129

Opponents' Batting Avg.
Rusie-NY .250
Meekin-NY .256
Stein-Bro .278
Breitenstein-StL .279
Clarkson-Cle .285

Opponents' On-Base Pct.
Rusie-NY .331
Meekin-NY .333
Clarkson-Cle .336
Young-Cle .338
Nichols-Bos .346

Starter Runs
Rusie-NY 125.4
Meekin-NY 77.3
Young-Cle 62.5
Mercer-Was 55.6
Taylor-Phi 41.1

Adjusted Starter Runs
Rusie-NY 123.3
Meekin-NY 74.7
Young-Cle 67.1
Mercer-Was 53.9
Nichols-Bos 39.1

Clutch Pitching Index
Mercer-Was 134
Rusie-NY 124
Terry-Pit-Chi 121
Hemming-Lou-Bal 111
Killen-Pit 111

Relief Runs

Adjusted Relief Runs

Relief Ranking

Total Pitcher Index
Rusie-NY 11.1
Meekin-NY 5.7
Young-Cle 5.4
Mercer-Was 5.1
Taylor-Phi 3.9

Total Baseball Ranking
Rusie-NY 11.1
Meekin-NY 5.7
Young-Cle 5.4
Dahlen-Chi 5.1
Mercer-Was 5.0

TEAM	G	W	L	PCT	GB	R	OR	AB	H	2B	3B	HR	BB	SO	AVG	OBP	SLG	OPS	OPS+	BR	BR+	PF	CHI	RC	SB	CS	SBA	SBR
BAL	132	87	43	.669		1009	**646**	4725	1530	235	89	25	355	243	.324	.384	.427	811	110	92	66	103	104	930	310			
CLE	132	84	46	.646	3	921	725	4692	1433	194	69	29	476	365	.305	.375	.395	770	97	26	-24	106	102	796	188			
PHI	133	78	53	.595	9.5	**1068**	957	5037	**1664**	**272**	73	**61**	463	262	**.330**	**.394**	**.450**	**844**	**122**	**161**	**157**	100	97	**1040**	276			
CHI	133	72	58	.554	15	866	854	4708	1401	171	85	55	422	344	.298	.361	.405	766	95	5	-47	106	99	810	260			
BRO	134	71	60	.542	16.5	879	838	4757	1346	191	78	41	397	319	.283	.346	.382	728	99	-63	8	92	**108**	718	184			
BOS	133	71	60	.542	16.5	911	829	4750	1377	198	57	54	505	**239**	.290	.364	.390	754	91	-6	-71	108	102	782	200			
PIT	135	71	61	.538	17	815	799	4677	1355	192	89	27	378	301	.290	.351	.386	737	99	-44	3	95	99	755	257			
CIN	132	66	64	.508	21	903	854	4684	1395	235	**105**	36	414	249	.298	.359	.416	775	99	18	-17	104	103	844	**326**			
NY	132	66	65	.504	21.5	852	834	4605	1324	191	90	32	454	292	.288	.355	.389	744	98	-29	-9	98	104	763	292			
WAS	133	43	85	.336	43	840	1052	4615	1326	209	101	55	**522**	403	.287	.366	.412	778	105	31	43	99	93	811	238			
STL	136	39	92	.298	48.5	752	1036	4814	1356	155	88	39	388	283	.282	.339	.375	714	89	-91	-81	99	96	707	208			
LOU	133	35	96	.267	52.5	698	1090	4724	1320	171	73	34	346	323	.279	.339	.368	707	92	-100	-49	94	92	665	156			
TOT	799					10514		56788	16827	2414	997	488	5120	3623	.297	.362	.400	761							2895			

TEAM	CG	SH	SV	IP	H	H/G	HR	BB	SO	RAT	ERA	ERA+	OAV	OOB	PR	PR+	PF	CPI	FA	E	DP	FW	PW	BW	SBW	DIF
BAL	104	**10**	4	1134^{1}	**1216**	**9.7**	31	430	244	13.4	**3.81**	125	**.271**	.340	**123**	118	100	104	**.946**	**288**	108	**5.3**	9.6	5.4		1.9
CLE	109	6	3	1151^{2}	1284	10.1	34	**350**	330	**13.1**	3.92	**127**	.278	**.334**	110	**130**	104	102	.936	351	77	1.8	**10.6**	-1.9		8.7
PHI	106	2	**7**	1161	1467	11.4	36	485	330	15.7	5.47	88	.304	.375	-89	-88	100	93	.933	369	93	.9	-7.1	**12.8**		6.1
CHI	**119**	3	1	1150^{2}	1422	11.2	38	432	297	15.1	4.67	109	.300	.366	13	48	106	105	.928	401	**113**	-.9	3.9	-3.8		7.9
BRO	104	5	6	1159^{2}	1366	10.7	42	397	218	14.1	4.93	89	.289	.350	-20	-76	92	91	.941	326	97	3.5	-6.1	.7		7.6
BOS	117	4	4	1185^{1}	1376	10.5	56	367	377	13.7	4.26	120	.287	.343	69	103	107	103	.935	365	106	1.2	8.4	-5.7		1.8
PIT	107	4	6	1179^{2}	1279	9.8	**19**	500	383	14.3	4.10	110	.273	.353	89	57	95	102	.930	394	95	-.1	4.7	.3		.4
CIN	97	2	6	1147^{1}	1451	11.4	39	362	245	14.8	4.81	103	.304	.361	-5	18	104	101	.931	377	112	.3	1.5	-1.3		.7
NY	115	6	1	1147^{1}	1359	10.7	34	415	**409**	14.3	4.52	103	.291	.354	33	16	97	100	.922	438	106	-3.1	1.3	-.7		3.1
WAS	99	0	5	1111^{1}	1515	12.3	55	470	261	16.7	5.26	91	.321	.390	-60	-59	100	**110**	.917	450	97	-3.6	-4.7	3.5		-16.0
STL	106	1	1	1161^{1}	1572	12.2	64	443	284	16.0	5.73	84	.319	.381	-123	-115	101	98	.930	383	94	.6	-9.3	-6.5		-11.2
LOU	104	3	1	1117^{1}	1520	12.3	40	469	245	16.6	5.90	78	.320	.388	-139	-164	97	96	.913	477	104	-5.1	-13.2	-3.9		-8.0
TOT	1287	46	45	13807		11.0				14.8	4.78		.297	.362					.931	4619	1202					

Runs
Hamilton-Phi 166
Keeler-Bal 162
Jennings-Bal 159
Burkett-Cle 153
Delahanty-Phi 149

Hits
Burkett-Cle 225
Keeler-Bal 213
Thompson-Phi 211
Jennings-Bal 204
Hamilton-Phi 201

Doubles
Delahanty-Phi 49
Thompson-Phi 45
Jennings-Bal 41
Stenzel-Pit 38
Griffin-Bro 38

Triples
Selbach-Was 22
Tiernan-NY 21
Thompson-Phi 21
Cooley-StL 20

Home Runs
Thompson-Phi 18
Joyce-Was 17
Clements-Phi 13
Delahanty-Phi 11

Total Bases
Thompson-Phi 352
Delahanty-Phi 296
Burkett-Cle 288
McKean-Cle 284
Kelley-Bal 283

Runs Batted In
Thompson-Phi 165
Kelley-Bal 134
Brodie-Bal 134
Jennings-Bal 125
McKean-Cle 119

Runs Produced
Jennings-Bal 280
Thompson-Phi 278
Kelley-Bal 272
Delahanty-Phi 244
McKean-Cle 242

Bases On Balls
Joyce-Was 96
Hamilton-Phi 96
Griffin-Bro 93
Delahanty-Phi 86
Kelley-Bal 77

Batting Average
Burkett-Cle .... .405
Delahanty-Phi ..... .404
Clements-Phi ...... .394
Thompson-Phi ...... .392
Lange-Chi .... .389

On-Base Percentage
Delahanty-Phi ..... .500
Hamilton-Phi ...... .490
Burkett-Cle .... .482
McGraw-Bal .... .459
Lange-Chi .... .456

Slugging Average
Thompson-Phi ...... .654
Delahanty-Phi ..... .617
Clements-Phi ...... .612
Lange-Chi .... .575
Kelley-Bal .... .546

On-Base Plus Slugging
Delahanty-Phi 1117
Thompson-Phi 1085
Lange-Chi 1032
Kelley-Bal 1003
Burkett-Cle 1001

Adjusted OPS
Delahanty-Phi 186
Thompson-Phi 177
Stenzel-Pit 160
Lange-Chi 155
Hamilton-Phi 154

Batter Runs
Delahanty-Phi 66.4
Thompson-Phi 56.9
Burkett-Cle 52.7
Hamilton-Phi 49.6
Kelley-Bal 47.2

Adjusted Batter Runs
Delahanty-Phi 65.7
Thompson-Phi 56.3
Hamilton-Phi 49.0
Stenzel-Pit 48.8
Burkett-Cle 44.0

Clutch Hitting Index
Brodie-Bal 140
Childs-Cle 139
Kelley-Bal 131
Cross-Phi 128
Jennings-Bal 124

Runs Created
Hamilton-Phi 178
Delahanty-Phi 176
Thompson-Phi 167
Burkett-Cle 163
Lange-Chi 160

Total Average
Delahanty-Phi 1.517
Hamilton-Phi 1.443
Lange-Chi 1.373
Kelley-Bal 1.289
Thompson-Phi 1.269

Stolen Bases
Hamilton-Phi 97
Lange-Chi 67
McGraw-Bal 61
Kelley-Bal 54

Stolen Base Average

Stolen Base Runs

Fielding Runs
Jennings-Bal 36.0
Dahlen-Chi 35.9
Fuller-NY 34.3
Cross-Phi 33.5
Corcoran-Bro 20.1

Total Player Rating
Jennings-Bal 6.1
Thompson-Phi 5.0
Delahanty-Phi 4.6
Kelley-Bal 3.8
Griffin-Bro 3.8

Wins
Young-Cle 35
Hoffer-Bal 31
Hawley-Pit 31

Win Percentage
Hoffer-Bal .... .838
Young-Cle .... .778
Rhines-Cin .... .655

Games
Hawley-Pit 56
Breitenstein-StL .. 55
Rusie-NY 49
Nichols-Bos 48

Complete Games
Breitenstein-StL .. 47
Hawley-Pit 44
Nichols-Bos 43
Rusie-NY 42
Griffith-Chi 39

Shutouts
Young-Cle 4
Rusie-NY 4
McMahon-Bal 4
Hoffer-Bal 4
Hawley-Pit 4

Saves
Parrott-Cin 3
Nichols-Bos 3
Beam-Phi 3

Innings Pitched
Hawley-Pit 444.1
Breitenstein-StL .. 438.2
Rusie-NY 393.1
Nichols-Bos 389.2
Young-Cle 369.2

Fewest Hits/Game
Foreman-Pit 8.44
Hoffer-Bal 8.48
Rusie-NY 8.79
Young-Cle 8.84
Maul-Was 9.02

Fewest BB/Game
Young-Cle 1.83
Clarke-NY 1.92
Nichols-Bos 2.08
Staley-StL 2.21
Taylor-Phi 2.23

Strikeouts
Rusie-NY 201
Nichols-Bos 147
Hawley-Pit 142
Breitenstein-StL .. 131
Young-Cle 121

Strikeouts/Game
Rusie-NY 4.60
McGill-Phi 4.32
Foreman-Pit 3.48
Stivetts-Bos 3.43
Nichols-Bos 3.40

Ratio
Young-Cle 10.86
Maul-Was 11.68
Nichols-Bos 12.10
Hawley-Pit 12.23
Cuppy-Cle 12.42

Earned Run Average
Maul-Was 2.45
McMahon-Bal 2.94
Hawley-Pit 3.18
Hoffer-Bal 3.21
Foreman-Pit 3.22

Adjusted ERA
Maul-Was 195
Young-Cle 153
Nichols-Bos 151
Hoffer-Bal 148
Hawley-Pit 142

Opponents' Batting Avg.
Foreman-Pit .... .245
Hoffer-Bal .... .246
Rusie-NY .... .252
Young-Cle .... .253
Maul-Was .... .257

Opponents' On-Base Pct.
Young-Cle .... .294
Maul-Was .... .310
Nichols-Bos .... .317
Hawley-Pit .... .320
Cuppy-Cle .... .323

Starter Runs
Hawley-Pit 78.6
Young-Cle 62.0
Nichols-Bos 60.6
Hoffer-Bal 54.5
Cuppy-Cle 48.2

Adjusted Starter Runs
Nichols-Bos 69.8
Hawley-Pit 69.5
Young-Cle 67.6
Hoffer-Bal 54.0
Cuppy-Cle 53.9

Clutch Pitching Index
Maul-Was 137
Mercer-Was 126
Clarke-NY 119
Foreman-Cin 116
Griffith-Chi 115

Relief Runs

Adjusted Relief Runs

Relief Ranking

Total Pitcher Index
Hawley-Pit 7.8
Young-Cle 6.7
Cuppy-Cle 5.6
Nichols-Bos 5.4
Hoffer-Bal 4.3

Total Baseball Ranking
Hawley-Pit 7.8
Young-Cle 6.7
Jennings-Bal 6.1
Cuppy-Cle 5.6
Nichols-Bos 5.4

TEAM	G	W	L	PCT	GB	R	OR	AB	H	2B	3B	HR	BB	SO	AVG	OBP	SLG	OPS	OPS+	BR	BR+	PF	CHI	RC	SB	CS	SBA	SBR
BAL	132	90	39	.698		**995**	662	4719	**1548**	207	**100**	23	386	**201**	**.328**	**.393**	**.429**	**822**	**120**	**151**	**138**	101	103	**1003**	**441**			
CLE	135	80	48	.625	9.5	840	650	4856	1463	207	72	28	436	316	.301	.363	.391	754	97	26	-20	106	98	785	175			
CIN	128	77	50	.606	12	783	**620**	4360	1283	204	73	20	382	226	.294	.357	.388	745	95	6	-41	107	103	761	350			
BOS	132	74	57	.565	17	865	761	4723	1421	175	75	36	414	275	.301	.364	.393	757	98	29	-18	106	102	795	243			
CHI	132	71	57	.555	18.5	815	804	4582	1311	182	97	34	409	290	.286	.349	.390	739	95	-7	-36	104	**105**	769	332			
PIT	131	66	63	.512	24	787	741	4701	1371	169	94	27	387	286	.292	.353	.385	738	103	-7	26	96	98	746	217			
NY	133	64	67	.489	27	829	821	4661	1383	159	87	40	439	271	.297	.364	.394	758	107	32	56	97	99	795	274			
PHI	130	62	68	.477	28.5	890	891	4680	1382	**234**	84	**49**	438	297	.295	.363	.413	776	110	58	69	99	103	801	191			
WAS	133	58	73	.443	33	818	920	4639	1328	179	79	45	**516**	365	.286	.365	.388	753	103	29	30	100	97	783	258			
BRO	133	58	73	.443	33	692	764	4548	1292	174	87	28	344	269	.284	.340	.379	719	100	-45	-1	94	95	680	198			
STL	131	40	90	.308	50.5	593	929	4520	1162	134	78	37	332	300	.257	.313	.346	659	81	-149	-123	96	96	572	185			
LOU	134	38	93	.290	53	653	997	4588	1197	142	80	37	371	427	.261	.322	.351	673	85	-123	-96	96	100	603	195			
TOT	792					9560		55577	16141	2166	1006	404	4854	3523	.291	.355	.388	742							3059			

TEAM	CG	SH	SV	IP	H	H/G	HR	BB	SO	RAT	ERA	ERA+	OAV	OOB	PR	PR+	PF	CPI	FA	E	DP	FW	PW	BW	SBW	DIF
BAL	115	9	1	1168^1	1281	9.9	22	339	302	12.8	3.68	116	.277	.331	89	79	98	100	.945	296	114	2.7	6.8	**11.8**		4.5
CLE	113	9	**5**	1195^2	1363	10.3	27	**280**	336	**12.7**	**3.47**	**131**	.285	**.329**	**119**	**136**	104	**109**	.949	288	**117**	3.6	**11.6**	-1.6		2.6
CIN	105	**12**	4	1108	**1240**	10.1	27	310	219	13.0	3.68	125	.281	.335	85	108	106	105	**.951**	**252**	107	**4.7**	9.2	-3.4		3.2
BOS	110	6	3	1155^2	1254	**9.8**	57	397	277	13.2	3.78	120	**.275**	.337	75	93	104	106	.934	368	94	-1.6	7.9	-1.5		3.9
CHI	**118**	2	1	1161^1	1307	10.2	30	467	354	14.4	4.45	102	.282	.358	-11	11	104	97	.933	367	115	-1.6	1.0	-3.0		10.8
PIT	108	8	1	1159^1	1286	10.0	**18**	439	**362**	14.0	4.31	98	.280	.351	7	-15	96	94	.941	317	103	1.3	-1.2	2.3		-.6
NY	104	1	2	1136^2	1303	10.4	33	403	312	14.1	4.55	92	.286	.352	-24	-46	96	94	.933	365	90	-1.3	-3.9	4.8		-1.0
PHI	107	3	2	1117	1473	11.9	39	387	243	15.5	5.20	83	.316	.375	-104	-113	99	99	.941	313	112	1.4	-9.5	5.9		-.5
WAS	106	2	3	1136^2	1435	11.4	24	435	292	15.3	4.61	96	.306	.372	-32	-27	101	105	.927	398	99	-3.3	-2.2	2.6		-4.4
BRO	97	3	1	1144	1353	10.7	39	400	259	14.2	4.25	97	.292	.354	14	-18	95	104	.945	297	104	2.8	-1.5	-.0		-8.6
STL	115	1	1	1130^2	1448	11.6	40	456	279	15.6	5.33	82	.309	.376	-121	-124	100	95	.936	345	73	-.4	-10.5	-10.4		-3.5
LOU	108	1	4	1148^2	1398	11.0	48	541	288	15.9	5.13	84	.298	.381	-98	-104	99	99	.916	475	110	-7.8	-8.8	-8.1		-2.7
TOT	1306	57	28	13762		10.6				14.2	4.36		.291	.355					.938	4081	1238					

Runs
Burkett-Cle 160
Keeler-Bal 153
Hamilton-Bos 153
Kelley-Bal 148
Dahlen-Chi 137

Hits
Burkett-Cle 240
Keeler-Bal 210
Jennings-Bal 209
Delahanty-Phi 198
VanHaltren-NY 197

Doubles
Delahanty-Phi 44
Miller-Cin 38
Kelley-Bal 31
Dahlen-Chi 30

Triples
VanHaltren-NY 21
McCreery-Lou 21
Kelley-Bal 19
Dahlen-Chi 19
Clarke-Lou 18

Home Runs
Joyce-Was-NY 13
Delahanty-Phi 13
Thompson-Phi 12
Connor-StL 11

Total Bases
Burkett-Cle 317
Delahanty-Phi 315
Kelley-Bal 282
VanHaltren-NY 272
Keeler-Bal 270

Runs Batted In
Delahanty-Phi 126
Jennings-Bal 121
Duffy-Bos 113
McKean-Cle 112

Runs Produced
Jennings-Bal 246
Delahanty-Phi 244
Kelley-Bal 240
Keeler-Bal 231
Burkett-Cle 226

Bases On Balls
Hamilton-Bos 110
Joyce-Was-NY 101
Childs-Cle 100
Kelley-Bal 91
Tiernan-NY 77

Batting Average
Burkett-Cle .... .410
Jennings-Bal .... .401
Delahanty-Phi ...... .397
Keeler-Bal .... .386
Tiernan-NY .... .369

On-Base Percentage
Hamilton-Bos ...... .478
Jennings-Bal ...... .472
Delahanty-Phi ..... .472
Joyce-Was-NY ..... .470
Kelley-Bal .... .469

Slugging Average
Delahanty-Phi ..... .631
Dahlen-Chi .... .553
McCreery-Lou ..... .546
Kelley-Bal .... .543
Burkett-Cle .... .541

On-Base Plus Slugging
Delahanty-Phi 1103
Kelley-Bal 1013
Burkett-Cle 1002
Dahlen-Chi 990
Joyce-Was-NY 988

Adjusted OPS
Delahanty-Phi 192
Kelley-Bal 164
Joyce-Was-NY 162
Tiernan-NY 159
E.Smith-Pit 158

Batter Runs
Delahanty-Phi 64.7
Kelley-Bal 54.6
Burkett-Cle 54.4
Joyce-Was-NY 48.4
Hamilton-Bos 45.8

Adjusted Batter Runs
Delahanty-Phi 66.5
Kelley-Bal 52.5
Joyce-Was-NY 50.0
Tiernan-NY 47.8
Burkett-Cle 46.1

Clutch Hitting Index
Reitz-Bal 151
Duffy-Bos 148
Anson-Chi 141
Doyle-Bal 140
Cross-Phi 139

Runs Created
Kelley-Bal 178
Delahanty-Phi 170
Burkett-Cle 166
Hamilton-Bos 161
Jennings-Bal 158

Total Average
Kelley-Bal 1.430
Delahanty-Phi 1.405
Hamilton-Bos 1.325
Joyce-Was-NY 1.306
Jennings-Bal 1.263

Stolen Bases
Kelley-Bal 87
Lange-Chi 84
Hamilton-Bos 83
Miller-Cin 76
Doyle-Bal 73

Stolen Base Average

Stolen Base Runs

Fielding Runs
Childs-Cle 42.4
Jennings-Bal 34.2
Dahlen-Chi 24.5
Clingman-Lou 23.7
Corcoran-Bro 23.5

Total Player Rating
Jennings-Bal 6.9
Childs-Cle 6.5
Delahanty-Phi 5.9
Dahlen-Chi 5.6
Joyce-Was-NY 3.9

Wins
Nichols-Bos 30
Killen-Pit 30
Young-Cle 28
Meekin-NY 26

Win Percentage
Hoffer-Bal .... .781
Hemming-Bal .... .714
Dwyer-Cin .... .686
Nichols-Bos .... .682
Griffith-Chi .... .676

Games
Killen-Pit 52
Young-Cle 51
Nichols-Bos 49
Hawley-Pit 49
Clarke-NY 48

Complete Games
Killen-Pit 44
Young-Cle 42
Mercer-Was 38

Shutouts
Young-Cle 5
Killen-Pit 5

Saves
Young-Cle 3
Hill-Lou 2
Fisher-Cin 2

Innings Pitched
Killen-Pit 432.1
Young-Cle 414.1
Hawley-Pit 378.0
Nichols-Bos 372.1
Mercer-Was 366.1

Fewest Hits/Game
Rhines-Cin 8.06
Hawley-Pit 9.10
Sullivan-NY 9.13
Friend-Chi 9.23
Hoffer-Bal 9.23

Fewest BB/Game
Young-Cle 1.35
Clarke-NY 1.54
Dwyer-Cin 1.87
Cuppy-Cle 1.89
Griffith-Chi 1.98

Strikeouts
Young-Cle 140
Hawley-Pit 137
Killen-Pit 134
Breitenstein-StL 114
Meekin-NY 110

Strikeouts/Game
Briggs-Chi 3.90
Pond-Bal 3.36
McJames-Was 3.31
Hawley-Pit 3.26
Young-Cle 3.04

Ratio
Rhines-Cin 11.64
Cuppy-Cle 11.82
Young-Cle 11.95
Nichols-Bos 11.97
Esper-Bal 12.08

Earned Run Average
Rhines-Cin 2.45
Nichols-Bos 2.83
Cuppy-Cle 3.12
Dwyer-Cin 3.15
Young-Cle 3.24

Adjusted ERA
Rhines-Cin 188
Nichols-Bos 160
Dwyer-Cin 146
Cuppy-Cle 145
Young-Cle 140

Opponents' Batting Avg.
Rhines-Cin .... .238
Hawley-Pit .... .261
Sullivan-NY .... .261
Friend-Chi .... .264
Hoffer-Bal .... .264

Opponents' On-Base Pct.
Rhines-Cin .... .311
Cuppy-Cle .... .314
Young-Cle .... .317
Nichols-Bos .... .317
Esper-Bal .... .319

Starter Runs
Nichols-Bos 63.3
Young-Cle 51.7
Cuppy-Cle 49.4
Killen-Pit 45.4
Dwyer-Cin 38.8

Adjusted Starter Runs
Nichols-Bos 67.9
Young-Cle 57.4
Cuppy-Cle 54.2
Dwyer-Cin 44.2
Killen-Pit 39.1

Clutch Pitching Index
Nichols-Bos 122
Wallace-Cle 120
Payne-Bro 116
Dwyer-Cin 115
Rhines-Cin 114

Relief Runs

Adjusted Relief Runs

Relief Ranking

Total Pitcher Index
Nichols-Bos 6.4
Young-Cle 6.2
Cuppy-Cle 5.7
Dwyer-Cin 4.5
Killen-Pit 4.4

Total Baseball Ranking
Jennings-Bal 6.9
Childs-Cle 6.5
Nichols-Bos 6.3
Young-Cle 6.2
Delahanty-Phi 5.9

TEAM	G	W	L	PCT	GB	R	OR	AB	H	2B	3B	HR	BB	SO	AVG	OBP	SLG	OPS	OPS+	BR	BR+	PF	CHI	RC	SB	CS	SBA	SBR
BOS	135	93	39	.705		**1025**	**665**	4937	1574	230	83	**45**	423	262	.319	.378	**.426**	804	110	118	63	106	108	919	233			
BAL	136	90	40	.692	2	964	674	4872	**1584**	**243**	66	19	**437**	256	**.325**	**.394**	.414	**808**	**119**	**138**	**138**	100	100	**984**	**401**			
NY	138	83	48	.634	9.5	901	696	4871	1452	188	84	31	412	327	.298	.361	.390	751	106	23	47	97	108	831	332			
CIN	134	76	56	.576	17	763	705	4524	1311	219	69	22	380	**218**	.290	.353	.383	736	93	-5	-52	107	100	715	194			
CLE	132	69	62	.527	23.5	773	680	4604	1374	192	88	16	435	344	.298	.364	.389	753	99	26	-15	105	96	747	181			
WAS	135	61	71	.462	32	781	793	4636	1376	194	77	36	374	348	.297	.357	.395	752	104	19	23	100	98	755	208			
BRO	136	61	71	.462	32	802	845	4810	1343	202	72	24	351	255	.279	.336	.366	702	95	-73	-30	95	**110**	684	187			
PIT	135	60	71	.458	32.5	676	835	4590	1266	140	**108**	25	359	334	.276	.337	.370	707	95	-60	-32	96	95	657	170			
CHI	138	59	73	.447	34	832	894	4803	1356	189	97	38	430	317	.282	.347	.386	733	94	-15	-44	104	104	766	264			
PHI	134	55	77	.417	38	752	792	4756	1392	213	83	40	399	299	.293	.353	.398	751	106	13	35	97	93	754	163			
LOU	136	52	78	.400	40	675	869	4587	1209	161	70	40	375	460	.264	.328	.355	683	88	-100	-76	97	100	628	200			
STL	133	29	102	.221	63.5	592	1088	4673	1285	151	67	32	354	314	.275	.336	.357	693	89	-84	-70	98	85	643	172			
TOT	811					9536		56663	16522	2322	964	368	4729	3734	.292	.355	.387	740							2705			

TEAM	CG	SH	SV	IP	H	H/G	HR	BB	SO	RAT	ERA	ERA+	OAV	OOB	PR	PR+	PF	CPI	FA	E	DP	FW	PW	BW	SBW	DIF
BOS	115	**8**	**7**	1194^1	1273	9.6	39	393	329	**12.9**	3.66	**122**	.271	**.333**	86	**102**	104	102	**.951**	272	80	3.9	**8.8**	5.4		9.1
BAL	118	3	0	1197^2	1296	9.8	**18**	382	361	13.2	3.56	117	.274	.338	99	83	97	104	**.951**	277	110	3.8	7.2	**11.9**		2.4
NY	119	**8**	3	1196^1	**1217**	**9.2**	26	490	**463**	13.4	**3.45**	120	**.262**	.341	**114**	96	96	107	.930	399	109	-3.3	8.3	4.1		8.7
CIN	100	4	2	1156^2	1375	10.7	**18**	329	270	13.8	4.09	111	.294	.347	28	54	106	101	.948	273	100	3.7	4.7	-4.4		6.2
CLE	111	6	0	1119^1	1297	10.5	32	**289**	277	13.2	3.95	114	.288	.337	44	63	104	100	.950	**261**	74	**4.1**	5.4	-1.2		-4.6
WAS	102	7	6	1148	1383	10.9	27	400	348	14.7	4.02	108	.296	.362	37	39	101	**112**	.933	369	103	-2.0	3.4	2.0		-8.3
BRO	114	4	2	1194^2	1417	10.7	34	410	256	14.2	4.61	89	.293	.354	-40	-72	95	94	.936	364	99	-1.5	-6.1	-2.5		5.3
PIT	112	2	2	1153^1	1397	11.0	22	318	342	13.9	4.68	89	.297	.350	-48	-69	97	91	.936	346	70	-.6	-5.9	-2.7		3.8
CHI	**131**	2	1	1197	1485	11.2	30	433	361	15.0	4.54	98	.303	.367	-31	-12	104	103	.932	393	**111**	-3.0	-1.0	-3.7		.9
PHI	115	4	2	1155^1	1415	11.1	28	364	253	14.3	4.61	91	.300	.356	-39	-55	97	96	.944	296	72	2.3	-4.7	3.0		-11.5
LOU	115	2	0	1155	1374	10.8	40	467	267	15.0	4.42	96	.294	.368	-14	-22	99	106	.930	399	87	-3.6	-1.8	-6.5		-.9
STL	110	1	1	1136^1	1594	12.7	54	454	207	16.8	6.17	71	.329	.394	-236	-221	102	93	.932	380	86	-2.9	-18.9	-5.9		-8.5
TOT	1362	51	26	14004		10.7				14.2	4.31		.292	.355					.940	4029	1101					

Runs
Hamilton-Bos 152
Keeler-Bal 145
Griffin-Bro 136
Jones-Bro 134
Jennings-Bal 133

Hits
Keeler-Bal 239
F.Clarke-Lou 205
Delahanty-Phi 200
Burkett-Cle 198
Lajoie-Phi 197

Doubles
Stenzel-Bal 43
Lajoie-Phi 40
Delahanty-Phi 40
Wallace-Cle 33
Ryan-Chi 33

Triples
Davis-Pit 28
Lajoie-Phi 23
Wallace-Cle 21
Keeler-Bal 19

Home Runs
Duffy-Bos 11
Davis-NY 10
Lajoie-Phi 9
Grady-Phi-StL 8
Beckley-NY-Cin 8

Total Bases
Lajoie-Phi 310
Keeler-Bal 304
Delahanty-Phi 285
F.Clarke-Lou 279

Runs Batted In
Davis-NY 136
Collins-Bos 132
Duffy-Bos 129
Lajoie-Phi 127
Kelley-Bal 118

Runs Produced
Duffy-Bos 248
Davis-NY 238
Collins-Bos 229
Kelley-Bal 226

Bases On Balls
Hamilton-Bos 105
McGraw-Bal 99
Joyce-NY 81
Griffin-Bro 81
Selbach-Was 80

Batting Average
Keeler-Bal .424
F.Clarke-Lou .390
Burkett-Cle .383
Delahanty-Phi .377
Kelley-Bal .362

On-Base Percentage
McGraw-Bal .471
Burkett-Cle .468
Keeler-Bal .464
Jennings-Bal .463
F.Clarke-Lou .461

Slugging Average
Lajoie-Phi .569
Keeler-Bal .539
Delahanty-Phi .538
F.Clarke-Lou .530
Davis-NY .509

On-Base Plus Slugging
Keeler-Bal 1003
F.Clarke-Lou 992
Delahanty-Phi 981
Lajoie-Phi 960
Burkett-Cle 944

Adjusted OPS
F.Clarke-Lou 167
Keeler-Bal 164
Delahanty-Phi 163
Lajoie-Phi 156
Kelley-Bal 147

Batter Runs
Keeler-Bal 52.2
F.Clarke-Lou 48.9
Delahanty-Phi 45.2
Burkett-Cle 42.1
Kelley-Bal 37.3

Adjusted Batter Runs
F.Clarke-Lou 53.8
Keeler-Bal 52.2
Delahanty-Phi 48.8
Lajoie-Phi 39.4
Kelley-Bal 37.3

Clutch Hitting Index
Gleason-NY 139
Shindle-Bro 138
Collins-Bos 133
Reitz-Bal 131
Tenney-Bos 128

Runs Created
Keeler-Bal 176
F.Clarke-Lou 160
Delahanty-Phi 142
Davis-NY 139
Stenzel-Bal 136

Total Average
F.Clarke-Lou 1.271
Keeler-Bal 1.262
Jennings-Bal 1.251
Hamilton-Bos 1.162
Kelley-Bal 1.143

Stolen Bases
Lange-Chi 73
Stenzel-Bal 69
Hamilton-Bos 66
Davis-NY 65
Keeler-Bal 64

Stolen Base Average

Stolen Base Runs

Fielding Runs
Clingman-Lou 30.6
Cross-StL 28.8
Jennings-Bal 27.1
Davis-NY 23.9
Reitz-Bal 21.7

Total Player Rating
Jennings-Bal 5.7
Davis-NY 5.4
F.Clarke-Lou 4.0
Delahanty-Phi 3.9
Keeler-Bal 3.7

Wins
Nichols-Bos 31
Rusie-NY 28
Klobedanz-Bos 26
Corbett-Bal 24
Breitenstein-Cin 23

Win Percentage
Klobedanz-Bos .788
Nops-Bal .769
Corbett-Bal .750
Nichols-Bos .738
Rusie-NY .737

Games
Mercer-Was 47
Young-Cle 46
Nichols-Bos 46
Donahue-StL 46

Complete Games
Killen-Pit 38
Griffith-Chi 38
Donahue-StL 38
Nichols-Bos 37
Kennedy-Bro 36

Shutouts
Mercer-Was 3
McJames-Was 3

Saves
Nichols-Bos 3
Mercer-Was 3

Innings Pitched
Nichols-Bos 368.0
Donahue-StL 348.0
Griffith-Chi 343.2
Kennedy-Bro 343.1
Mercer-Was 342.0

Fewest Hits/Game
Seymour-NY 8.07
Rusie-NY 8.77
Nichols-Bos 8.85
Hill-Lou 9.45
Corbett-Bal 9.49

Fewest BB/Game
Young-Cle 1.31
Tannehill-Pit 1.52
Nichols-Bos 1.66
Cuppy-Cle 1.70
Killen-Pit 2.03

Strikeouts
Seymour-NY 156
McJames-Was 156
Corbett-Bal 149
Rusie-NY 135
Nichols-Bos 127

Strikeouts/Game
Seymour-NY 4.90
McJames-Was 4.34
Corbett-Bal 4.28
Rusie-NY 3.77
Nichols-Bos 3.11

Ratio
Nichols-Bos 10.59
Rusie-NY 11.48
Cuppy-Cle 11.80
Young-Cle 12.04
Nops-Bal 12.07

Earned Run Average
Rusie-NY 2.54
Nichols-Bos 2.64
Nops-Bal 2.81
Corbett-Bal 3.11
Powell-Cle 3.16

Adjusted ERA
Nichols-Bos 169
Rusie-NY 163
Nops-Bal 148
Powell-Cle 142
Cuppy-Cle 140

Opponents' Batting Avg.
Seymour-NY .238
Rusie-NY .254
Nichols-Bos .255
Hill-Lou .268
Corbett-Bal .269

Opponents' On-Base Pct.
Nichols-Bos .291
Rusie-NY .308
Cuppy-Cle .314
Young-Cle .318
Nops-Bal .319

Starter Runs
Nichols-Bos 67.9
Rusie-NY 63.1
Mercer-Was 42.5
Corbett-Bal 41.6
Nops-Bal 36.5

Adjusted Starter Runs
Nichols-Bos 71.7
Rusie-NY 59.7
Mercer-Was 43.3
Corbett-Bal 37.9
Nops-Bal 34.1

Clutch Pitching Index
Mercer-Was 132
Nops-Bal 120
Corbett-Bal 117
Rusie-NY 117
McJames-Was 117

Relief Runs

Adjusted Relief Runs

Relief Ranking

Total Pitcher Index
Nichols-Bos 7.0
Rusie-NY 6.3
Mercer-Was 4.9
Seymour-NY 3.4
Corbett-Bal 3.2

Total Baseball Ranking
Nichols-Bos 7.0
Rusie-NY 6.3
Jennings-Bal 5.7
Davis-NY 5.4
Mercer-Was 4.9

TEAM	G	W	L	PCT	GB	R	OR	AB	H	2B	3B	HR	BB	SO	AVG	OBP	SLG	OPS	OPS+	BR	BR+	PF	CHI	RC	SB	CS	SBA	SBR
BOS	152	102	47	.685		872	**614**	5276	1531	190	55	**53**	405	303	.290	.344	**.377**	721	106	72	30	105	104	780	172			
BAL	154	96	53	.644	6	**933**	623	5242	**1584**	154	77	12	519	316	**.302**	**.382**	.368	**750**	**118**	**157**	**140**	102	99	**864**	**250**			
CIN	157	92	60	.605	11.5	831	740	5334	1448	207	**101**	19	455	**300**	.271	.335	.359	694	97	24	-28	107	103	732	165			
CHI	152	85	65	.567	17.5	828	679	5219	1431	175	84	18	476	394	.274	.343	.350	693	104	29	31	100	104	735	220			
CLE	156	81	68	.544	21	730	683	5246	1379	162	56	18	**545**	306	.263	.338	.325	663	96	-23	-13	99	97	641	93			
PHI	150	78	71	.523	24	823	784	5118	1431	**238**	81	33	472	382	.280	.348	**.377**	725	**118**	84	122	96	98	769	182			
NY	157	77	73	.513	25.5	837	800	5349	1422	190	86	34	428	372	.266	.328	.353	681	103	-5	20	97	**109**	714	214			
PIT	152	72	76	.486	29.5	634	694	5087	1313	140	88	14	336	343	.258	.313	.328	641	90	-78	-65	98	96	589	107			
LOU	154	70	81	.464	33	728	833	5193	1389	150	71	32	375	429	.267	.325	.342	667	98	-31	-19	98	101	687	235			
BRO	149	54	91	.372	46	638	811	5126	1314	156	66	17	328	314	.256	.309	.322	631	85	-98	-95	100	101	577	130			
WAS	155	51	101	.336	52.5	704	939	5257	1423	177	80	36	370	386	.271	.327	.355	682	100	-5	-3	100	94	703	197			
STL	154	39	111	.260	63.5	571	929	5214	1290	149	55	13	383	402	.247	.309	.305	614	78	-127	-141	102	91	552	104			
TOT	921					9129		62661	16955	2088	900	299	5092	4247	.271	.334	.347	681							2069			

TEAM	CG	SH	SV	IP	H	H/G	HR	BB	SO	RAT	ERA	ERA+	OAV	OOB	PR	PR+	PF	CPI	FA	E	DP	FW	PW	BW	SBW	DIF
BOS	127	9	**8**	1340	**1186**	**8.0**	37	470	432	**11.6**	2.98	124	**.236**	**.310**	93	103	102	97	.950	310	102	3.2	9.7	2.9		12.0
BAL	138	12	0	1323	1236	8.5	17	400	422	**11.6**	2.90	123	.246	**.310**	104	99	99	99	.947	326	105	2.5	9.3	**13.1**		-3.2
CIN	131	10	2	1385^1	1484	9.7	16	449	294	13.1	3.50	110	.272	.336	17	48	106	103	.950	325	128	3.0	4.5	-2.6		11.3
CHI	137	**13**	0	1342^2	1357	9.1	17	364	323	12.1	**2.83**	**126**	.261	.319	**115**	**112**	99	**113**	.936	412	**149**	-2.8	**10.5**	2.9		-.5
CLE	**142**	9	0	1334	1429	9.7	26	**309**	339	12.2	3.21	113	.272	.320	59	60	100	105	**.952**	**301**	95	**4.2**	5.7	-1.2		-2.0
PHI	129	10	0	1288^1	1440	10.1	23	399	325	13.5	3.73	92	.281	.342	-17	-45	95	104	.937	379	102	-1.2	-4.2	11.5		-2.4
NY	141	9	1	1353^2	1359	9.1	21	587	**558**	13.6	3.44	101	.260	.344	25	5	96	106	.932	447	113	-4.1	.5	1.9		3.9
PIT	131	10	3	1323^2	1400	9.6	**14**	346	330	12.4	3.41	104	.270	.323	29	22	99	98	.946	340	105	1.4	2.1	-6.0		.7
LOU	137	4	0	1334	1457	9.9	33	470	271	13.7	4.25	84	.276	.346	-95	-102	99	93	.939	382	114	-.8	-9.5	-1.7		6.7
BRO	134	1	0	1298^2	1446	10.1	34	476	294	13.8	4.02	89	.280	.348	-59	-63	99	100	.947	334	125	1.3	-5.8	-8.8		-5.0
WAS	129	0	1	1307	1577	10.9	29	450	371	14.5	4.53	81	.297	.360	-134	-125	102	98	.929	443	119	-4.2	-11.6	-.2		-8.7
STL	133	0	2	1324^1	1584	10.8	32	372	288	13.9	4.54	83	.295	.350	-137	-106	105	93	.939	388	97	-1.1	-9.9	-13.1		-11.7
TOT	1609	87	17	15954^2		9.6				13.0	3.61		.271	.334					.943	4387	1354					

Runs
McGraw-Bal 143
Jennings-Bal 135
VanHaltren-NY 129
Keeler-Bal 126
Cooley-Phi 123

Hits
Keeler-Bal 216
Burkett-Cle 213
VanHaltren-NY 204
Lajoie-Phi 197

Doubles
Lajoie-Phi 43
Delahanty-Phi 36
Dahlen-Chi 35
Collins-Bos 35
Anderson-Br-Ws-Br 33

Triples
Anderson-Br-Ws-Br 22
VanHaltren-NY 16
Hoy-Lou 16

Home Runs
Collins-Bos 15
Wagner-Lou 10
Joyce-NY 10
Anderson-Br-Ws-Br 9
McKean-Cle 9

Total Bases
Collins-Bos 286
Lajoie-Phi 280
VanHaltren-NY 270
Anderson-Br-Ws-Br 257
Cooley-Phi 256

Runs Batted In
Lajoie-Phi 127
Collins-Bos 111
Kelley-Bal 110
Duffy-Bos 108
McGann-Bal 106

Runs Produced
Lajoie-Phi 234
Jennings-Bal 221
Delahanty-Phi 203
Collins-Bos 203
McGann-Bal 200

Bases On Balls
McGraw-Bal 112
Joyce-NY 88
Hamilton-Bos 87
Flick-Phi 86
Jennings-Bal 78

Batting Average
Keeler-Bal .385
Hamilton-Bos .369
McGraw-Bal .342
Smith-Cin .342
Burkett-Cle .341

On-Base Percentage
Hamilton-Bos .480
McGraw-Bal .475
Jennings-Bal .454
Flick-Phi .430
Delahanty-Phi .426

Slugging Average
Anderson-Br-Ws-Br .494
Collins-Bos .479
Lajoie-Phi .461
Delahanty-Phi .454
Hamilton-Bos .453

On-Base Plus Slugging
Hamilton-Bos 933
Delahanty-Phi 880
Flick-Phi 878
Jennings-Bal 876
McGraw-Bal 871

Adjusted OPS
Hamilton-Bos 159
Delahanty-Phi 159
Flick-Phi 158
Jennings-Bal 149
McGraw-Bal 148

Batter Runs
McGraw-Bal 45.1
Jennings-Bal 44.2
Hamilton-Bos 43.4
Delahanty-Phi 40.2
Flick-Phi 35.2

Adjusted Batter Runs
Delahanty-Phi 45.8
McGraw-Bal 42.8
Jennings-Bal 41.9
Flick-Phi 40.1
Hamilton-Bos 37.9

Clutch Hitting Index
Kelley-Bal 145
Grey-Pit 137
Davis-NY 136
Connor-Chi 136
Hartman-NY 135

Runs Created
Delahanty-Phi 135
McGraw-Bal 121
Hamilton-Bos 120
Jennings-Bal 119
Ryan-Chi 119

Total Average
Hamilton-Bos 1.262
McGraw-Bal 1.115
Delahanty-Phi 1.082
Jennings-Bal 1.050
Flick-Phi 1.035

Stolen Bases
Delahanty-Phi 58
Hamilton-Bos 54
DeMontreville-Bal 49
Dexter-Lou 44
McGraw-Bal 43

Stolen Base Average

Stolen Base Runs

Fielding Runs
Davis-NY 34.6
Dahlen-Chi 25.5
Gleason-NY 20.5
Selbach-Was 19.9
Cross-StL 18.4

Total Player Rating
Dahlen-Chi 4.7
Jennings-Bal 4.5
Davis-NY 4.4
Collins-Bos 4.0
Flick-Phi 3.7

Wins
Nichols-Bos 31
Cunningham-Lou 28
McJames-Bal 27
Hawley-Cin 27
Lewis-Bos 26

Win Percentage
Lewis-Bos .765
Maul-Bal .741
Nichols-Bos .721
Hawley-Cin .711
Griffith-Chi .706

Games
Taylor-StL 50
Nichols-Bos 50
Young-Cle 46

Complete Games
Taylor-StL 42
Cunningham-Lou 41
Young-Cle 40
Nichols-Bos 40
McJames-Bal 40

Shutouts
Powell-Cle 6
Piatt-Phi 6
Tannehill-Pit 5
Nichols-Bos 5
Hughes-Bal 5

Saves
Nichols-Bos 4
Tannehill-Pit 2
Lewis-Bos 2
Hickman-Bos 2
Dammann-Cin 2

Innings Pitched
Taylor-StL 397.1
Nichols-Bos 388.0
Young-Cle 377.2
McJames-Bal 374.0
Cunningham-Lou 362.0

Fewest Hits/Game
Nichols-Bos 7.33
Willis-Bos 7.64
Lewis-Bos 7.67
Maul-Bal 7.77
McJames-Bal 7.87

Fewest BB/Game
Young-Cle .98
Dwyer-Cin 1.58
Cunningham-Lou 1.62
Tannehill-Pit 1.74
Griffith-Chi 1.77

Strikeouts
Seymour-NY 239
McJames-Bal 178
Willis-Bos 160
Nichols-Bos 138
Piatt-Phi 121

Strikeouts/Game
Seymour-NY 6.03
Willis-Bos 4.63
McJames-Bal 4.28
Doheny-NY 4.06
Piatt-Phi 3.56

Ratio
Nichols-Bos 9.63
Maul-Bal 9.76
Young-Cle 10.41
Griffith-Chi 10.75
McJames-Bal 10.88

Earned Run Average
Griffith-Chi 1.88
Maul-Bal 2.10
Nichols-Bos 2.13
McJames-Bal 2.36
Callahan-Chi 2.46

Adjusted ERA
Griffith-Chi 190
Nichols-Bos 173
Maul-Bal 170
McJames-Bal 152
Callahan-Chi 145

Opponents' Batting Avg.
Nichols-Bos .221
Willis-Bos .229
Lewis-Bos .229
Maul-Bal .232
McJames-Bal .234

Opponents' On-Base Pct.
Nichols-Bos .272
Maul-Bal .275
Young-Cle .288
Griffith-Chi .294
McJames-Bal .297

Starter Runs
Nichols-Bos 63.3
Griffith-Chi 62.4
McJames-Bal 51.7
Young-Cle 45.2
Maul-Bal 39.9

Adjusted Starter Runs
Nichols-Bos 65.5
Griffith-Chi 61.9
McJames-Bal 50.9
Young-Cle 45.5
Maul-Bal 39.5

Clutch Pitching Index
Griffith-Chi 135
Orth-Phi 120
Dammann-Cin 118
Doheny-NY 117
Callahan-Chi 116

Relief Runs

Adjusted Relief Runs

Relief Ranking

Total Pitcher Index
Nichols-Bos 6.7
Griffith-Chi 5.8
Young-Cle 5.3
McJames-Bal 4.3
Callahan-Chi 3.9

Total Baseball Ranking
Nichols-Bos 6.7
Griffith-Chi 5.8
Young-Cle 5.3
Dahlen-Chi 4.7
Jennings-Bal 4.5

TEAM	G	W	L	PCT	GB	R	OR	AB	H	2B	3B	HR	BB	SO	AVG	OBP	SLG	OPS	OPS+	BR	BR+	PF	CHI	RC	SB	CS	SBA	SBR
BRO	150	100	47	.680		892	658	4937	1436	178	97	27	477	263	.291	**.368**	.383	751	110	87	68	102	103	824	271			
BOS	153	95	57	.625	7.5	858	**645**	5290	1517	178	90	39	431	269	.287	.345	.377	722	94	21	-52	110	103	787	185			
PHI	154	94	58	.618	8.5	**916**	743	5353	**1613**	**241**	83	31	441	341	**.301**	.363	**.395**	**758**	**118**	**96**	**129**	97	99	**879**	212			
BAL	152	86	62	.581	14.5	827	691	5073	1509	204	71	17	418	383	.297	.365	.376	741	104	68	26	105	97	861	**364**			
STL	155	84	67	.556	18	819	739	5304	1514	172	88	**47**	468	**262**	.285	.347	.378	725	102	28	9	102	97	801	210			
CIN	157	83	67	.553	18.5	861	777	5258	1448	195	106	13	**487**	300	.275	.344	.360	704	96	-5	-19	102	**105**	766	228			
PIT	155	76	73	.510	25	841	771	5486	1582	196	**121**	29	386	346	.288	.342	.384	726	104	25	28	100	97	819	179			
CHI	152	75	73	.507	25.5	812	763	5148	1428	173	82	27	406	342	.277	.338	.359	697	99	-26	-5	97	**105**	743	247			
LOU	156	75	76	.497	27	833	782	5336	1491	195	70	40	437	379	.279	.343	.365	708	100	-3	-2	100	101	786	234			
NY	153	60	90	.400	41.5	741	868	5125	1441	165	66	23	389	361	.281	.337	.353	690	98	-37	-10	97	100	714	235			
WAS	155	54	98	.355	48.5	743	983	5256	1429	162	87	**47**	350	341	.272	.328	.363	691	96	-45	-37	99	99	710	176			
CLE	154	20	134	.130	83.5	529	1252	5279	1333	142	50	12	289	280	.253	.299	.305	604	76	-209	-164	93	92	541	127			
TOT	923					9672		62845	17741	2201	1011	352	4979	3867	.283	.344	.367	710							2668			

TEAM	CG	SH	SV	IP	H	H/G	HR	BB	SO	RAT	ERA	ERA+	OAV	OOB	PR	PR+	PF	CPI	FA	E	DP	FW	PW	BW	SBW	DIF
BRO	121	9	**9**	1269^{1}	1320	9.4	32	463	331	13.0	**3.25**	120	.268	.337	84	90	102	**111**	.948	314	125	3.0	8.2	6.2		9.3
BOS	138	13	4	1348	**1273**	**8.5**	44	432	385	**11.9**	3.27	**127**	**.250**	**.317**	**87**	**123**	108	95	**.952**	**303**	124	**4.1**	**11.2**	-4.7		8.6
PHI	129	**15**	2	1333^{1}	1398	9.5	17	370	281	12.5	3.47	106	.270	.329	56	31	96	97	.940	379	110	-.3	2.9	**11.7**		3.9
BAL	132	9	4	1304^{1}	1403	9.7	**13**	349	294	12.6	3.32	119	.275	.330	77	90	103	103	.949	308	96	3.6	8.2	2.4		-2.0
STL	134	7	1	1340^{2}	1476	10.0	41	**321**	331	12.5	3.36	118	.280	.328	73	88	103	107	.939	397	117	-1.2	8.0	.9		1.0
CIN	131	8	5	1373	1494	9.8	26	372	361	12.8	3.68	106	.278	.334	26	33	102	97	.947	341	113	2.4	3.0	-1.7		-4.4
PIT	118	9	4	1373	1471	9.7	27	438	338	13.0	3.62	105	.274	.337	36	29	99	100	.945	363	100	.8	2.7	2.6		-4.4
CHI	**147**	8	1	1331^{1}	1433	9.7	20	330	313	12.5	3.37	111	.275	.328	71	56	97	102	.935	428	**145**	-3.4	5.1	-.4		-.1
LOU	135	5	2	1360^{1}	1517	10.1	35	325	288	12.7	3.44	112	.282	.331	62	62	100	106	.939	399	103	-1.1	5.7	-.1		-4.7
NY	139	4	0	1290^{2}	1463	10.3	19	630	**402**	15.3	4.27	88	.286	.375	-61	-79	97	104	.932	434	142	-3.6	-7.1	-.9		-3.2
WAS	131	3	0	1300^{1}	1649	11.5	35	422	328	14.9	4.94	79	.309	.368	-157	-148	102	95	.935	403	99	-1.5	-13.4	-3.3		-3.6
CLE	138	0	0	1264	1844	13.2	43	527	215	17.7	6.37	58	.340	.409	-354	-396	96	94	.937	388	121	-.8	-35.8	-14.8		-5.4
TOT	1593	90	32	15888^{1}		10.1				13.4	3.85		.283	.344					.942	4457	1395					

Runs
McGraw-Bal 140
Keeler-Bro 140
Thomas-Phi 137
Delahanty-Phi 135
Williams-Pit 126

Hits
Delahanty-Phi 238
Burkett-StL 221
Williams-Pit 220
Keeler-Bro 216
Tenney-Bos 209

Doubles
Delahanty-Phi 55
Wagner-Lou 45
Holmes-Bal 31
Long-Bos 30
Duffy-Bos 29

Triples
Williams-Pit 27
Freeman-Was 25
Stahl-Bos 19
Tenney-Bos 17
McCarthy-Pit 17

Home Runs
Freeman-Was 25
Wallace-StL 12
Williams-Pit 9
Mertes-Chi 9
Delahanty-Phi 9

Total Bases
Delahanty-Phi 338
Freeman-Was 331
Williams-Pit 329
Wagner-Lou 288
Stahl-Bos 284

Runs Batted In
Delahanty-Phi 137
Freeman-Was 122
Williams-Pit 116
Wagner-Lou 114
Wallace-StL 108

Runs Produced
Delahanty-Phi 263
Williams-Pit 233
Wagner-Lou 207
Freeman-Was 204

Bases On Balls
McGraw-Bal 124
Thomas-Phi 115
VanHaltren-NY 75
Childs-StL 74

Batting Average
Delahanty-Phi .... .410
Burkett-StL .... .396
McGraw-Bal .... .391
Keeler-Bro .... .379
Williams-Pit .... .354

On-Base Percentage
McGraw-Bal .... .547
Delahanty-Phi .... .464
Burkett-StL .... .463
Thomas-Phi .... .457
Stahl-Bos .... .426

Slugging Average
Delahanty-Phi .... .582
Freeman-Was .... .563
Williams-Pit .... .530
Wagner-Lou .... .501
Burkett-StL .... .500

On-Base Plus Slugging
Delahanty-Phi 1046
McGraw-Bal 994
Burkett-StL 963
Williams-Pit 946
Freeman-Was 925

Adjusted OPS
Delahanty-Phi 193
McGraw-Bal 165
Burkett-StL 160
Williams-Pit 159
Freeman-Was 154

Batter Runs
Delahanty-Phi 67.9
McGraw-Bal 56.8
Burkett-StL 51.6
Williams-Pit 48.6
Stahl-Bos 42.2

Adjusted Batter Runs
Delahanty-Phi 73.5
McGraw-Bal 50.3
Williams-Pit 49.2
Burkett-StL 48.4
Freeman-Was 37.5

Clutch Hitting Index
Brodie-Bal 139
Long-Bos 131
Magoon-Bal-Chi 129
Lauder-Phi 128
Lowe-Bos 128

Runs Created
Delahanty-Phi 175
Williams-Pit 152
Burkett-StL 145
McGraw-Bal 141
Stahl-Bos 139

Total Average
McGraw-Bal 1.601
Delahanty-Phi 1.245
Burkett-StL 1.107
Stahl-Bos 1.051
Williams-Pit 1.050

Stolen Bases
Sheckard-Bal 77
McGraw-Bal 73
Heidrick-StL 55
Holmes-Bal 50
Clarke-Lou 49

Stolen Base Average

Stolen Base Runs

Fielding Runs
G.Davis-NY 48.9
Wallace-StL 38.8
Cross-Cle-StL 32.7
Gleason-NY 28.7
Collins-Bos 20.8

Total Player Rating
G.Davis-NY 6.3
Delahanty-Phi 5.4
Williams-Pit 5.2
Wallace-StL 5.1
McGraw-Bal 4.9

Wins
McGinnity-Bal 28
Hughes-Bro 28
Willis-Bos 27
Young-StL 26
Tannehill-Pit 24

Win Percentage
Hughes-Bro .... .824
Willis-Bos .... .771
Hahn-Cin .... .742
Donahue-Phi .... .724
Kennedy-Bro .... .710

Games
Leever-Pit 51
Powell-StL 48
McGinnity-Bal 48
Young-StL 44
Carrick-NY 44

Complete Games
Young-StL 40
Powell-StL 40
Carrick-NY 40
Taylor-Chi 39
McGinnity-Bal 38

Shutouts
Willis-Bos 5

Saves
Leever-Pit 3

Innings Pitched
Leever-Pit 379.0
Powell-StL 373.0
Young-StL 369.1
McGinnity-Bal 366.1
Carrick-NY 361.2

Fewest Hits/Game
Willis-Bos 7.28
Hughes-Bro 7.71
Hahn-Cin 8.16
Seymour-NY 8.28
Leever-Pit 8.38

Fewest BB/Game
Young-StL 1.07
Cuppy-StL 1.36
Tannehill-Pit 1.45
Woods-Lou 1.79
Kitson-Bal 1.79

Strikeouts
Hahn-Cin 145
Seymour-NY 142
Leever-Pit 121
Willis-Bos 120
Doheny-NY 120

Strikeouts/Game
Seymour-NY 4.76
Hahn-Cin 4.22
Doheny-NY 3.89
McJames-Bro 3.43
Willis-Bos 3.15

Ratio
Young-StL 10.19
Hahn-Cin 10.43
Nichols-Bos 10.85
Kitson-Bal 11.13
Willis-Bos 11.14

Earned Run Average
Orth-Phi 2.49
Willis-Bos 2.50
Young-StL 2.58
Bernhard-Phi 2.65
McGinnity-Bal 2.68

Adjusted ERA
Willis-Bos 166
Young-StL 154
McGinnity-Bal 148
Hahn-Cin 146
Hughes-Bro 145

Opponents' Batting Avg.
Willis-Bos .... .222
Hughes-Bro .... .232
Hahn-Cin .... .242
Seymour-NY .... .245
Leever-Pit .... .247

Opponents' On-Base Pct.
Young-StL .... .285
Hahn-Cin .... .290
Nichols-Bos .... .298
Kitson-Bal .... .303
Willis-Bos .... .304

Starter Runs
Young-StL 51.8
Willis-Bos 51.4
McGinnity-Bal 47.5
Hahn-Cin 40.0
Kitson-Bal 38.6

Adjusted Starter Runs
Willis-Bos 58.4
Young-StL 55.2
McGinnity-Bal 50.5
Hahn-Cin 41.6
Kitson-Bal 41.3

Clutch Pitching Index
Kennedy-Bro 130
Dowling-Lou 124
Callahan-Chi 121
Woods-Lou 118
Tannehill-Pit 118

Relief Runs

Adjusted Relief Runs

Relief Ranking

Total Pitcher Index
Young-StL 6.0
Willis-Bos 4.9
McGinnity-Bal 4.8
Hughes-Bro 4.6
Griffith-Chi 4.6

Total Baseball Ranking
G.Davis-NY 6.3
Young-StL 6.0
Delahanty-Phi 5.4
Williams-Pit 5.2
Wallace-StL 5.1

TEAM	G	W	L	PCT	GB	R	OR	AB	H	2B	3B	HR	BB	SO	AVG	OBP	SLG	OPS	OPS+	BR	BR+	PF	CHI	RC	SB	CS	SBA	SBR
BRO	142	82	54	.603		**816**	722	4860	1423	199	81	26	421	**272**	**.293**	**.359**	**.383**	**742**	104	**72**	26	106	100	**795**	**274**			
PIT	140	79	60	.568	4.5	733	**612**	4817	1312	185	**100**	26	327	321	.272	.327	.368	695	96	-25	-30	101	**105**	666	174			
PHI	141	75	63	.543	8	810	792	4969	**1439**	187	82	29	**440**	374	.290	.356	.378	734	**109**	58	**65**	99	99	774	205			
BOS	142	66	72	.478	17	778	739	4952	1403	163	68	**48**	395	278	.283	.342	.373	715	92	16	-68	112	102	724	182			
STL	142	65	75	.464	19	744	748	4877	1420	141	81	36	406	318	.291	.356	.375	731	108	52	58	99	94	766	243			
CHI	146	65	75	.464	19	635	751	4907	1276	**202**	51	33	343	383	.260	.317	.342	659	90	-87	-62	96	97	622	189			
CIN	144	62	77	.446	21.5	703	745	5026	1335	178	83	33	333	408	.266	.318	.354	672	92	-71	-54	98	103	651	183			
NY	141	60	78	.435	23	713	823	4724	1317	177	61	23	369	343	.279	.338	.357	695	102	-16	18	95	102	676	236			
TOT	569					5932		39132	10925	1432	607	254	3034	2697	.280	.340	.367	705							1686			

TEAM	CG	SH	SV	IP	H	H/G	HR	BB	SO	RAT	ERA	ERA+	OAV	OOB	PR	PR+	PF	CPI	FA	E	DP	FW	PW	BW	SBW	DIF
BRO	104	8	**4**	1225^{2}	1370	10.1	30	405	300	13.6	3.90	99	.282	.346	-27	-8	104	99	.948	303	102	2.6	-.7	2.4		9.8
PIT	114	11	1	1229	**1232**	**9.1**	24	**295**	**415**	**11.7**	**3.07**	**119**	**.261**	**.313**	**87**	**79**	98	97	.945	322	106	1.1	**7.3**	-2.7		4.0
PHI	116	7	3	1248^{2}	1506	10.9	29	402	284	14.3	4.13	88	.298	.357	-59	-73	98	103	.945	330	**125**	.8	-6.6	**6.0**		6.0
BOS	116	8	2	1240^{1}	1263	9.2	59	463	340	13.0	3.73	111	.264	.335	-4	49	112	97	**.953**	**273**	86	**4.5**	4.5	-6.2		-5.6
STL	117	**12**	0	1217^{1}	1373	10.2	37	299	325	12.7	3.75	97	.284	.331	-7	-17	98	97	.943	331	73	.9	-1.5	5.4		-9.5
CHI	**137**	9	1	1271	1375	9.8	**21**	324	357	12.7	3.23	112	.276	.330	66	53	98	106	.933	418	98	-3.9	4.9	-5.6		-.2
CIN	118	9	1	1274^{2}	1383	9.8	28	404	399	13.1	3.84	96	.276	.338	-20	-24	99	94	.945	341	120	.6	-2.1	-4.9		-.8
NY	113	4	0	1207^{1}	1423	10.7	26	442	277	14.7	3.96	91	.293	.363	-35	-49	98	**108**	.928	439	124	-5.9	-4.4	1.7		-.1
TOT	935	68	12	9914		10.0				13.2	3.70		.280	.340					.943	2757	834					

Runs
Thomas-Phi 132
Slagle-Phi 115
VanHaltren-NY 114
Barrett-Cin 114
Wagner-Pit 107

Hits
Keeler-Bro 204
Burkett-StL.......... 203
Wagner-Pit 201
Flick-Phi 200
Beckley-Cin 190

Doubles
Wagner-Pit 45
Lajoie-Phi 33
Flick-Phi 32
Delahanty-Phi 32
VanHaltren-NY 30

Triples
Wagner-Pit 22
Kelley-Bro 17
Hickman-NY 17
Stahl-Bos 16
Flick-Phi 16

Home Runs
Long-Bos 12
Flick-Phi 11
Donlin-StL 10
Hickman-NY 9
Sullivan-Bos 8

Total Bases
Wagner-Pit 302
Flick-Phi 297
Burkett-StL 265
Keeler-Bro 253
Beckley-Cin 242

Runs Batted In
Flick-Phi 110
Delahanty-Phi....... 109
Wagner-Pit 100
Collins-Bos 95
Beckley-Cin 94

Runs Produced
Flick-Phi 205
Wagner-Pit 203
Collins-Bos 193
Beckley-Cin 190
Delahanty-Phi 189

Bases On Balls
Thomas-Phi 115
Hamilton-Bos 107
McGraw-StL 85
Dahlen-Bro 73

Batting Average
Wagner-Pit 381
Flick-Phi 367
Burkett-StL 363
Keeler-Bro 362
McGraw-StL 344

On-Base Percentage
McGraw-StL .... .505
Thomas-Phi......... .451
Hamilton-Bos .... .449
Flick-Phi............ .441
Wagner-Pit.......... .434

Slugging Average
Wagner-Pit .... .573
Flick-Phi .... .545
Lajoie-Phi .... .510
Kelley-Bro .... .485
Hickman-NY .... .482

On-Base Plus Slugging
Wagner-Pit 1007
Flick-Phi 986
McGraw-StL........ 921
Burkett-StL......... 904
Selbach-NY 885

Adjusted OPS
Wagner-Pit 175
Flick-Phi 172
McGraw-StL.......... 157
Selbach-NY 151
Burkett-StL 150

Batter Runs
Flick-Phi 53.5
Wagner-Pit 53.2
Burkett-StL 39.0
McGraw-StL 36.0
Selbach-NY 34.3

Adjusted Batter Runs
Flick-Phi 54.7
Wagner-Pit 52.3
Burkett-StL 40.0
Selbach-NY 40.0
McGraw-StL 36.8

Clutch Hitting Index
Delahanty-Phi 143
Cross-Phi 142
Jennings-Bro 138
Lowe-Bos 122
Collins-Bos 119

Runs Created
Wagner-Pit 152
Flick-Phi 151
Burkett-StL 133
Keeler-Bro 123
Selbach-NY 121

Total Average
McGraw-StL...... 1.260
Wagner-Pit 1.193
Flick-Phi 1.171
Selbach-NY 1.029
Burkett-StL 1.017

Stolen Bases
VanHaltren-NY 45
Donovan-StL 45
Barrett-Cin 44
Keeler-Bro............ 41

Stolen Base Average

Stolen Base Runs

Fielding Runs
Steinfeldt-Cin 35.6
Lajoie-Phi........... 29.5
Davis-NY 29.3
Dahlen-Bro 19.8
Bradley-Chi 16.8

Total Player Rating
Lajoie-Phi 5.0
Flick-Phi 4.6
Davis-NY 4.3
Wagner-Pit 3.5
Selbach-NY 3.3

Wins
McGinnity-Bro 28
Tannehill-Pit 20
Phillippe-Pit 20
Kennedy-Bro 20
Dinneen-Bos 20

Win Percentage
McGinnity-Bro 778
Tannehill-Pit 769
Fraser-Phi 625
Phillippe-Pit 606
Kennedy-Bro 606

Games
Carrick-NY 45
McGinnity-Bro 44
Scott-Cin 42
Kennedy-Bro.......... 42

Complete Games
Hawley-NY 34
Dinneen-Bos 33

Shutouts
Young-StL 4
Nichols-Bos 4
Hahn-Cin 4
Griffith-Chi 4

Saves
Kitson-Bro 4
Bernhard-Phi 2

Innings Pitched
McGinnity-Bro 343.0
Carrick-NY 341.2
Hawley-NY 329.1
Young-StL......... 321.1
Dinneen-Bos 320.2

Fewest Hits/Game
Waddell-Pit 7.59
Garvin-Chi........... 8.22
Nichols-Bos 8.36
Dinneen-Bos 8.53
Phillippe-Pit 8.84

Fewest BB/Game
Young-StL 1.01
Phillippe-Pit......... 1.35
Tannehill-Pit 1.65
Griffith-Chi 1.85
Leever-Pit 1.86

Strikeouts
Hahn-Cin 132
Waddell-Pit 130
Young-StL 115
Garvin-Chi 107
Dinneen-Bos 107

Strikeouts/Game
Waddell-Pit 5.61
Garvin-Chi 3.91
Hahn-Cin 3.82
Newton-Cin 3.38
Leever-Pit 3.25

Ratio
Phillippe-Pit 10.42
Waddell-Pit 10.52
Young-StL 10.53
Garvin-Chi 11.18
Leever-Pit 11.30

Earned Run Average
Waddell-Pit 2.37
Garvin-Chi 2.41
Taylor-Chi 2.55
Leever-Pit........... 2.71
Sudhoff-StL 2.76

Adjusted ERA
Waddell-Pit 153
Garvin-Chi........... 149
Taylor-Chi 141
Nichols-Bos 134
Leever-Pit 134

Opponents' Batting Avg.
Waddell-Pit 229
Garvin-Chi 243
Nichols-Bos 246
Dinneen-Bos 250
Phillippe-Pit 257

Opponents' On-Base Pct.
Phillippe-Pit.........289
Waddell-Pit 291
Young-StL 291
Garvin-Chi 304
Leever-Pit 306

Starter Runs
Garvin-Chi 35.1
Waddell-Pit 30.7
McGinnity-Bro....... 28.8
Taylor-Chi 28.3
Phillippe-Pit 26.5

Adjusted Starter Runs
Garvin-Chi 33.4
McGinnity-Bro 32.9
Dinneen-Bos 32.2
Waddell-Pit 29.7
Taylor-Chi 26.7

Clutch Pitching Index
Fraser-Phi 131
Taylor-Chi 119
McGinnity-Bro 118
Carrick-NY 115
Donahue-Phi 113

Relief Runs

Adjusted Relief Runs

Relief Ranking

Total Pitcher Index
Dinneen-Bos 3.3
Garvin-Chi 3.2
Taylor-Chi 2.8
Tannehill-Pit.........2.7
Waddell-Pit 2.5

Total Baseball Ranking
Lajoie-Phi 5.0
Flick-Phi 4.6
Davis-NY 4.3
Wagner-Pit........... 3.6
Selbach-NY 3.3

TEAM	G	W	L	PCT	GB	R	OR	AB	H	2B	3B	HR	BB	SO	AVG	OBP	SLG	OPS	OPS+	BR	BR+	PF	CHI	RC	SB	CS	SBA	SBR
PIT	140	90	49	.647		776	**534**	4913	1407	182	92	29	386	493	.286	**.345**	.379	**724**	113	**99**	77	103	102	743	203			
PHI	140	83	57	.593	7.5	668	543	4793	1275	194	58	24	**430**	549	.266	.334	.346	680	101	29	16	102	98	652	199			
BRO	137	79	57	.581	9.5	744	600	4879	1399	**206**	93	32	312	**449**	**.287**	.335	**.387**	722	112	86	67	103	102	718	178			
STL	142	76	64	.543	14.5	**792**	689	5039	**1430**	187	**94**	**39**	314	540	.284	.337	.381	718	**120**	87	**127**	95	**104**	**744**	190			
BOS	140	69	69	.500	20.5	531	556	4746	1180	135	36	28	303	519	.249	.298	.310	608	75	-104	-148	109	101	515	158			
CHI	140	53	86	.381	37	578	699	4844	1250	153	61	18	314	532	.258	.310	.326	636	94	-57	-34	96	99	575	**204**			
NY	141	52	85	.380	37	544	755	4839	1225	167	46	19	303	575	.253	.303	.318	621	89	-83	-61	96	98	529	133			
CIN	142	52	87	.374	38	561	818	4914	1232	173	70	38	323	584	.251	.303	.338	641	97	-56	-14	93	94	570	137			
TOT	561					5194		38967	10398	1397	550	227	2685	4241	.267	.321	.349	669							1402			

TEAM	CG	SH	SV	IP	H	H/G	HR	BB	SO	RAT	ERA	ERA+	OAV	OOB	PR	PR+	PF	CPI	FA	E	DP	FW	PW	BW	SBW	DIF
PIT	119	**15**	4	1244^{2}	1198	8.7	20	**244**	505	**10.9**	**2.59**	**126**	.252	**.297**	**102**	**95**	98	104	.950	287	97	1.3	**9.4**	7.6		2.5
PHI	125	**15**	2	1246^{2}	1221	8.9	19	259	480	11.1	2.87	119	.255	.300	63	71	102	97	**.954**	**262**	65	**2.8**	7.0	1.6		1.8
BRO	111	7	**5**	1213^{2}	1244	9.3	**18**	435	583	12.9	3.15	107	.264	.333	24	27	101	**109**	.950	281	99	1.2	2.7	6.6		.7
STL	118	5	**5**	1269^{2}	1333	9.5	39	332	445	12.3	3.68	86	.268	.321	-51	-74	96	93	.949	305	**108**	.4	-7.2	**12.5**		.5
BOS	128	11	0	1263	**1196**	**8.6**	29	349	558	11.3	2.91	125	**.249**	.305	59	91	109	98	.952	282	89	1.6	9.0	-14.5		4.1
CHI	**131**	2	0	1241^{2}	1348	9.8	27	324	**586**	12.6	3.34	97	.275	.327	-2	-14	97	105	.943	336	87	-1.7	-1.3	-3.3		-10.0
NY	118	11	1	1232	1389	10.2	24	377	542	13.4	3.88	85	.283	.342	-75	-79	100	99	.941	348	81	-2.3	-7.7	-5.9		-.4
CIN	126	4	0	1265^{2}	1469	10.5	51	365	542	13.6	4.18	77	.289	.345	-120	-143	96	99	.940	355	102	-2.6	-14.0	-1.3		.6
TOT	976	70	17	9977		9.4				12.2	3.33		.267	.321					.948	2456	728					

Runs
- Burkett-StL 142
- Keeler-Bro 123
- Beaumont-Pit 120
- Clarke-Pit 118
- Sheckard-Bro 116

Hits
- Burkett-StL 226
- Keeler-Bro 202
- Sheckard-Bro 196
- Wagner-Pit 194
- Delahanty-Phi 192

Doubles
- Delahanty-Phi 38
- Daly-Bro 38
- Wagner-Pit 37
- Beckley-Cin 36
- Wallace-StL 34

Triples
- Sheckard-Bro 19
- Flick-Phi 17

Home Runs
- Crawford-Cin 16
- Sheckard-Bro 11
- Burkett-StL 10

Total Bases
- Burkett-StL 306
- Sheckard-Bro 296
- Delahanty-Phi 286
- Wagner-Pit 271

Runs Batted In
- Wagner-Pit 126
- Delahanty-Phi 108
- Sheckard-Bro 104
- Crawford-Cin 104

Runs Produced
- Wagner-Pit 221
- Sheckard-Bro 209
- Burkett-StL 207
- Delahanty-Phi 206
- Flick-Phi 192

Bases On Balls
- Thomas-Phi 100
- Hartsel-Chi 74
- Davis-Bro-Pit 66
- Delahanty-Phi 65
- Hamilton-Bos 64

Batting Average
- Burkett-StL .... .376
- Delahanty-Phi ...... .354
- Sheckard-Bro ...... .354
- Wagner-Pit .... .353
- Keeler-Bro .... .339

On-Base Percentage
- Burkett-StL .... .440
- Thomas-Phi .... .437
- Delahanty-Phi ...... .427
- Wagner-Pit .... .417
- Hartsel-Chi .... .414

Slugging Average
- Sheckard-Bro ...... .534
- Delahanty-Phi ...... .528
- Crawford-Cin ...... .524
- Burkett-StL .... .509
- Flick-Phi .... .500

On-Base Plus Slugging
- Delahanty-Phi 955
- Burkett-StL 949
- Sheckard-Bro 944
- Wagner-Pit 911
- Crawford-Cin 903

Adjusted OPS
- Burkett-StL 184
- Delahanty-Phi 173
- Crawford-Cin 172
- Sheckard-Bro 168
- Hartsel-Chi 163

Batter Runs
- Burkett-StL 58.7
- Delahanty-Phi 53.3
- Sheckard-Bro 49.8
- Wagner-Pit 44.9
- Hartsel-Chi 42.6

Adjusted Batter Runs
- Burkett-StL 66.1
- Delahanty-Phi 50.8
- Hartsel-Chi 47.3
- Sheckard-Bro 46.5
- Crawford-Cin 44.5

Clutch Hitting Index
- Ganzel-NY 139
- Dexter-Chi 136
- Wagner-Pit 133
- Long-Bos 133
- Krueger-StL 128

Runs Created
- Burkett-StL 151
- Sheckard-Bro 139
- Delahanty-Phi 139
- Wagner-Pit 138
- Hartsel-Chi 130

Total Average
- Delahanty-Phi 1.097
- Burkett-StL 1.072
- Wagner-Pit 1.070
- Sheckard-Bro 1.070
- Hartsel-Chi 1.027

Stolen Bases
- Wagner-Pit 49
- Hartsel-Chi 41
- Strang-NY 40
- Harley-Cin 37
- Beaumont-Pit 36

Stolen Base Average

Stolen Base Runs

Fielding Runs
- Wallace-StL 29.6
- Davis-NY 23.1
- Flick-Phi 14.9
- Dahlen-Bro 13.7
- Kittridge-Bos 12.0

Total Player Rating
- Wallace-StL 5.6
- Burkett-StL 5.5
- Wagner-Pit 5.0
- Flick-Phi 4.5
- Sheckard-Bro 4.5

Wins
- Donovan-Bro 25
- Harper-StL 23
- Phillippe-Pit 22
- Hahn-Cin 22
- Chesbro-Pit 21

Win Percentage
- Chesbro-Pit .... .677
- Phillippe-Pit .... .647
- Tannehill-Pit .... .643
- Harper-StL .... .639
- Kitson-Bro .... .633

Games
- Taylor-NY 45
- Powell-StL 45
- Donovan-Bro 45
- Hahn-Cin 42
- Mathewson-NY 40

Complete Games
- Hahn-Cin 41
- Taylor-NY 37
- Mathewson-NY 36
- Donovan-Bro 36

Shutouts
- Willis-Bos 6
- Orth-Phi 6
- Chesbro-Pit 6

Saves
- Powell-StL 3
- Donovan-Bro 3
- Sudhoff-StL 2
- Phillippe-Pit 2
- Kitson-Bro 2

Innings Pitched
- Hahn-Cin 375.1
- Taylor-NY 353.1
- Donovan-Bro 351.0
- Powell-StL 338.1
- Mathewson-NY ... 336.0

Fewest Hits/Game
- Townsend-Phi 7.39
- Mathewson-NY 7.71
- Willis-Bos 7.72
- Orth-Phi 7.99
- Chesbro-Pit 8.17

Fewest BB/Game
- Orth-Phi 1.02
- Phillippe-Pit 1.16
- Tannehill-Pit 1.28
- Duggleby-Phi 1.30
- Powell-StL 1.33

Strikeouts
- Hahn-Cin 239
- Donovan-Bro 226
- Hughes-Chi 225
- Mathewson-NY 221
- Waddell-Pit-Chi 172

Strikeouts/Game
- Hughes-Chi 6.57
- Waddell-Pit-Chi 6.16
- Mathewson-NY 5.92
- Donovan-Bro 5.79
- Hahn-Cin 5.73

Ratio
- Orth-Phi 9.27
- Phillippe-Pit 9.79
- Tannehill-Pit 10.20
- Chesbro-Pit 10.23
- Willis-Bos 10.35

Earned Run Average
- Tannehill-Pit 2.18
- Phillippe-Pit 2.22
- Orth-Phi 2.27
- Willis-Bos 2.36
- Chesbro-Pit 2.38

Adjusted ERA
- Willis-Bos 153
- Tannehill-Pit 150
- Orth-Phi 150
- Phillippe-Pit 147
- Chesbro-Pit 137

Opponents' Batting Avg.
- Townsend-Phi ...... .223
- Mathewson-NY ...... .230
- Willis-Bos .... .231
- Orth-Phi .... .237
- Chesbro-Pit .... .241

Opponents' On-Base Pct.
- Orth-Phi .... .264
- Phillippe-Pit .... .275
- Tannehill-Pit .... .284
- Chesbro-Pit .... .284
- Willis-Bos .... .286

Starter Runs
- Phillippe-Pit 36.2
- Mathewson-NY 34.0
- Orth-Phi 32.9
- Willis-Bos 32.7
- Tannehill-Pit 32.1

Adjusted Starter Runs
- Willis-Bos 39.1
- Phillippe-Pit 34.9
- Orth-Phi 34.5
- Mathewson-NY 33.5
- Tannehill-Pit 31.0

Clutch Pitching Index
- Kitson-Bro 122
- Taylor-Chi 116
- Hughes-Bro 114
- Taylor-NY 113
- Donahue-Phi 109

Relief Runs

Adjusted Relief Runs

Relief Ranking

Total Pitcher Index
- Orth-Phi 4.7
- Phillippe-Pit 4.5
- Willis-Bos 4.2
- Mathewson-NY 4.2
- Tannehill-Pit 3.3

Total Baseball Ranking
- Wallace-StL 5.6
- Burkett-StL 5.5
- Wagner-Pit 5.0
- Flick-Phi 4.5
- Orth-Phi 4.5

TEAM	G	W	L	PCT	GB	R	OR	AB	H	2B	3B	HR	BB	SO	AVG	OBP	SLG	OPS	OPS+	BR	BR+	PF	CHI	RC	SB	CS	SBA	SBR
CHI	137	83	53	.610		**819**	631	4725	1303	173	89	32	**475**	337	.276	.350	.370	720	**108**	41	**63**	97	103	744	**280**			
BOS	138	79	57	.581	4	759	**608**	4866	1353	183	104	**37**	331	**282**	.278	.330	.381	711	104	9	23	98	101	693	157			
DET	136	74	61	.548	8.5	741	694	4676	1303	180	80	29	380	346	.279	.340	.370	710	98	15	-17	105	99	690	204			
PHI	137	74	62	.544	9	805	760	4882	**1409**	**239**	87	35	301	344	.289	.337	.395	732	103	42	9	104	103	734	173			
BAL	135	68	65	.511	13.5	760	750	4589	1348	179	**111**	24	369	377	**.294**	**.353**	**.397**	**750**	**108**	**80**	47	104	96	**746**	207			
WAS	138	61	72	.459	20.5	682	771	4772	1282	191	83	33	356	340	.269	.326	.364	690	97	-24	-13	99	96	633	127			
CLE	138	54	82	.397	29	666	831	4833	1311	197	68	12	243	326	.271	.313	.348	661	92	-82	-55	96	**104**	588	125			
MIL	139	48	89	.350	35.5	641	828	4795	1250	192	66	26	325	384	.261	.314	.345	659	91	-81	-47	95	98	602	176			
TOT	549					5873		38138	10559	1534	688	228	2780	2736	.277	.333	.372	704							1449			

TEAM	CG	SH	SV	IP	H	H/G	HR	BB	SO	RAT	ERA	ERA+	OAV	OOB	PR	PR+	PF	CPI	FA	E	DP	FW	PW	BW	SBW	DIF
CHI	110	**11**	2	1218[1]	1250	9.3	27	312	394	12.0	**2.98**	**117**	.263	.315	**93**	**71**	95	106	.941	345	100	.9	**6.5**	**5.7**		2.1
BOS	123	7	1	1217	**1178**	**8.8**	33	294	**396**	**11.2**	3.04	116	**.251**	**.301**	84	68	96	93	**.943**	337	104	1.6	6.2	2.1		1.3
DET	118	8	2	1188[2]	1328	10.1	22	313	307	12.8	3.31	116	.280	.330	48	68	105	**109**	.930	410	**127**	-3.3	6.2	-1.5		5.3
PHI	**124**	6	1	1200[2]	1346	10.1	**20**	374	350	13.3	4.01	94	.280	.339	-45	-31	103	94	.942	337	93	1.4	-2.7	.9		6.6
BAL	115	4	3	1158	1313	10.3	21	344	271	13.3	3.74	104	.282	.338	-9	16	106	101	.926	401	76	-2.9	1.5	4.3		-1.2
WAS	118	8	2	1183	1396	10.7	51	**284**	308	13.3	4.10	89	.291	.339	-57	-58	100	100	**.943**	**323**	97	**2.5**	-5.2	-1.1		-1.5
CLE	122	7	**4**	1182[1]	1365	10.4	22	464	334	14.5	4.12	86	.286	.358	-60	-78	97	102	.942	329	99	2.1	-7.0	-4.9		-4.0
MIL	107	3	3	1218	1383	10.3	32	395	376	13.7	4.06	89	.283	.344	-53	-65	98	98	.934	393	106	-1.7	-5.8	-4.2		-8.6
TOT	937	54	18	9566		10.0				13.0	3.67		.277	.333					.938	2875	802					

Runs
Lajoie-Phi 145
Jones-Chi 120
Williams-Bal 113
Hoy-Chi 112
Barrett-Det 110

Hits
Lajoie-Phi 232
Anderson-Mil 190
Collins-Bos 187
Waldron-Mil-Was 186
Dungan-Was 179

Doubles
Lajoie-Phi 48
Anderson-Mil 46
Collins-Bos 42
Farrell-Was 32

Triples
Williams-Bal 21
Keister-Bal 21
Mertes-Chi 17
Stahl-Bos 16
Collins-Bos 16

Home Runs
Lajoie-Phi 14
Freeman-Bos 12
Grady-Was 9

Total Bases
Lajoie-Phi 350
Collins-Bos 279
Anderson-Mil 274
Freeman-Bos 255
Williams-Bal 248

Runs Batted In
Lajoie-Phi 125
Freeman-Bos 114
Anderson-Mil 99
Mertes-Chi 98
Williams-Bal 96

Runs Produced
Lajoie-Phi 256
Williams-Bal 202
Collins-Bos 196
Freeman-Bos 190
Mertes-Chi 187

Bases On Balls
Hoy-Chi 86
Jones-Chi 84
Barrett-Det 76
McFarland-Chi 75
McGraw-Bal 61

Batting Average
Lajoie-Phi .426
Donlin-Bal .340
Freeman-Bos .339
Seybold-Phi .334
Collins-Bos .332

On-Base Percentage
Lajoie-Phi .463
Jones-Chi .412
Donlin-Bal .409
Hoy-Chi .407
Freeman-Bos .400

Slugging Average
Lajoie-Phi .643
Freeman-Bos .520
Seybold-Phi .503
Williams-Bal .495
Collins-Bos .495

On-Base Plus Slugging
Lajoie-Phi 1106
Freeman-Bos 920
Seybold-Phi 901
Donlin-Bal 883
Williams-Bal 883

Adjusted OPS
Lajoie-Phi 196
Freeman-Bos 157
Seybold-Phi 142
Collins-Bos 142
Donlin-Bal 138

Batter Runs
Lajoie-Phi 74.1
Freeman-Bos 34.9
McGraw-Bal 31.1
Donlin-Bal 29.5
Williams-Bal 29.3

Adjusted Batter Runs
Lajoie-Phi 67.6
Freeman-Bos 37.0
Collins-Bos 30.3
McGraw-Bal 28.0
Anderson-Mil 26.5

Clutch Hitting Index
Burke-Mil-Chi 140
Mertes-Chi 134
Keister-Bal 122
Hartman-Chi 120
Seymour-Bal 117

Runs Created
Lajoie-Phi 179
Collins-Bos 116
Anderson-Mil 114
Freeman-Bos 112
Donlin-Bal 109

Total Average
Lajoie-Phi 1.327
Donlin-Bal 1.000
Freeman-Bos .994
Seybold-Phi .963
Williams-Bal .956

Stolen Bases
Isbell-Chi 52
Mertes-Chi 46
Seymour-Bal 38
Jones-Chi 38

Stolen Base Average

Stolen Base Runs

Fielding Runs
Lajoie-Phi 28.7
Elberfeld-Det 22.0
Conroy-Mil 19.4
Clingman-Was 17.8
Farrell-Was 16.6

Total Player Rating
Lajoie-Phi 8.5
Collins-Bos 4.2
Elberfeld-Det 3.7
Freeman-Bos 2.7
Donlin-Bal 2.6

Wins
Young-Bos 33
McGinnity-Bal 26
Griffith-Chi 24
Miller-Det 23
Fraser-Phi 22

Win Percentage
Griffith-Chi .774
Young-Bos .767
Callahan-Chi .652
Patten-Was .643
Miller-Det .639

Games
McGinnity-Bal 48
Dowling-Mil-Cle 43
Young-Bos 43
Carrick-Was 42
Patterson-Chi 41

Complete Games
McGinnity-Bal 39
Young-Bos 38
Miller-Det 35
Fraser-Phi 35
Carrick-Was 34

Shutouts
Young-Bos 5
Griffith-Chi 5
Patterson-Chi 4
Patten-Was 4
Moore-Cle 4

Saves
Hoffer-Cle 3

Innings Pitched
McGinnity-Bal 382.0
Young-Bos 371.1
Miller-Det 332.0
Fraser-Phi 331.0
Carrick-Was 324.0

Fewest Hits/Game
Young-Bos 7.85
Callahan-Chi 8.15
Moore-Cle 8.38
Lewis-Bos 8.51
Winter-Bos 8.74

Fewest BB/Game
Young-Bos .90
Gear-Was 1.21
Lee-Was 1.55
Griffith-Chi 1.69
Cronin-Det 1.72

Strikeouts
Young-Bos 158
Patterson-Chi 127
Dowling-Mil-Cle 124
Garvin-Mil 122
Fraser-Phi 110

Strikeouts/Game
Garvin-Mil 4.27
Patten-Was 3.86
Young-Bos 3.83
Patterson-Chi 3.66
Dowling-Mil-Cle 3.65

Ratio
Young-Bos 8.92
Callahan-Chi 10.62
Griffith-Chi 11.10
Lewis-Bos 11.32
Winter-Bos 11.35

Earned Run Average
Young-Bos 1.62
Callahan-Chi 2.42
Yeager-Det 2.61
Griffith-Chi 2.67
Winter-Bos 2.80

Adjusted ERA
Young-Bos 217
Yeager-Det 147
Callahan-Chi 143
Griffith-Chi 130
Miller-Det 130

Opponents' Batting Avg.
Young-Bos .232
Callahan-Chi .239
Moore-Cle .244
Lewis-Bos .247
Winter-Bos .252

Opponents' On-Base Pct.
Young-Bos .256
Callahan-Chi .290
Griffith-Chi .300
Lewis-Bos .304
Winter-Bos .304

Starter Runs
Young-Bos 84.1
Callahan-Chi 29.6
Griffith-Chi 29.5
Miller-Det 26.1
Yeager-Det 23.2

Adjusted Starter Runs
Young-Bos 81.5
Miller-Det 31.3
Callahan-Chi 26.6
Yeager-Det 26.0
Griffith-Chi 25.3

Clutch Pitching Index
Katoll-Chi 126
Yeager-Det 121
Siever-Det 116
Sparks-Mil 116
Young-Bos 113

Relief Runs

Adjusted Relief Runs

Relief Ranking

Total Pitcher Index
Young-Bos 8.6
Callahan-Chi 4.1
Griffith-Chi 3.8
Yeager-Det 3.4
Miller-Det 3.3

Total Baseball Ranking
Young-Bos 8.6
Lajoie-Phi 8.5
Collins-Bos 4.2
Callahan-Chi 4.1
Griffith-Chi 3.8

TEAM	G	W	L	PCT	GB	R	OR	AB	H	2B	3B	HR	BB	SO	AVG	OBP	SLG	OPS	OPS+	BR	BR+	PF	CHI	RC	SB	CS	SBA	SBR
PIT	142	103	36	.741		**775**	**440**	4926	**1410**	**189**	**95**	18	372	446	**.286**	**.344**	**.374**	**718**	**124**	**152**	**127**	104	**105**	**743**	222			
BRO	141	75	63	.543	27.5	564	519	4845	1242	147	49	**19**	319	489	.256	.311	.319	630	99	-4	-8	101	100	553	145			
BOS	142	73	64	.533	29	572	516	4726	1178	142	39	14	**398**	481	.249	.313	.305	618	95	-15	-20	101	104	540	189			
CIN	141	70	70	.500	33.5	633	566	4908	1383	188	77	18	297	465	.282	.328	.362	690	109	95	37	110	95	654	131			
CHI	143	68	69	.496	34	544	505	4870	1224	133	40	6	358	572	.251	.308	.299	607	95	-37	-21	97	101	552	**229**			
STL	140	56	78	.418	44.5	517	695	4751	1226	116	37	10	273	**438**	.258	.306	.304	610	97	-37	-16	96	100	516	158			
PHI	138	56	81	.409	46	484	649	4615	1139	110	43	5	356	481	.247	.305	.293	598	90	-50	-50	100	98	473	108			
NY	141	48	88	.353	53.5	405	604	4632	1097	147	34	6	254	540	.237	.282	.287	569	81	-105	-102	99	94	452	187			
TOT	564					4494		38273	9899	1172	414	96	2627	3912	.259	.313	.319	631							1369			

TEAM	CG	SH	SV	IP	H	H/G	HR	BB	SO	RAT	ERA	ERA+	OAV	OOB	PR	PR+	PF	CPI	FA	E	DP	FW	PW	BW	SBW	DIF
PIT	131	**21**	3	1264^2	1142	8.2	**4**	**250**	**564**	**10.4**	2.30	119	.241	**.288**	68	62	98	94	.958	247	87	3.4	6.6	**13.4**		10.3
BRO	131	14	3	1256	**1113**	**8.0**	10	363	536	10.9	2.70	103	**.238**	.298	12	9	99	86	.952	275	79	1.5	1.0	-.8		4.4
BOS	124	14	**4**	1259^2	1233	8.9	16	372	523	11.8	2.61	108	.257	.316	24	29	102	109	**.959**	**240**	90	**3.8**	3.1	-2.1		-.2
CIN	130	9	1	1239	1228	9.0	15	352	430	11.9	2.68	112	.259	.318	15	41	108	108	.945	322	**118**	-1.4	4.4	4.0		-6.8
CHI	**134**	17	2	1293^1	1244	8.7	7	281	447	11.0	**2.20**	**123**	.253	.300	**85**	**75**	97	**113**	.946	331	113	-1.7	**8.0**	-2.2		-4.4
STL	112	7	**4**	1227^2	1399	10.3	16	338	400	13.1	3.48	79	.287	.338	-95	-103	99	102	.944	336	107	-2.4	-10.8	-1.6		4.0
PHI	118	8	3	1211	1323	9.9	12	334	504	12.8	3.51	80	.278	.333	-97	-92	101	95	.946	305	81	-.7	-9.7	-5.2		3.3
NY	120	11	1	1242^1	1217	8.9	16	337	508	11.7	2.87	98	.257	.313	-11	-8	101	98	.943	337	107	-2.3	-.8	-10.7		-6.0
TOT	1000	101	21	9993^2		9.0				11.7	2.79		.259	.313					.950	2393	782					

Runs
Wagner-Pit 105
Clarke-Pit 103
Beaumont-Pit 100
Leach-Pit 97
Crawford-Cin 92

Hits
Beaumont-Pit 193
Keeler-Bro 186
Crawford-Cin 185
Wagner-Pit 176
Beckley-Cin 175

Doubles
Wagner-Pit 30
Clarke-Pit 27
Cooley-Bos 26
Dahlen-Bro 25
Beckley-Cin 23

Triples
Leach-Pit 22
Crawford-Cin 22
Wagner-Pit 16
Clarke-Pit 14
Gremminger-Bos 12

Home Runs
Leach-Pit 6
Beckley-Cin 5
Sheckard-Bro 4
McCreery-Bro 4

Total Bases
Crawford-Cin 256
Wagner-Pit 247
Beckley-Cin 227
Beaumont-Pit 226
Leach-Pit 219

Runs Batted In
Wagner-Pit 91
Leach-Pit 85
Crawford-Cin 78
Dahlen-Bro 74

Runs Produced
Wagner-Pit 193
Leach-Pit 176
Crawford-Cin 167
Beaumont-Pit 167
Clarke-Pit 154

Bases On Balls
R.Thomas-Phi 107
Lush-Bos 76
Tenney-Bos 73
Sheckard-Bro 57

Batting Average
Beaumont-Pit 357
Crawford-Cin 333
Keeler-Bro 333
Wagner-Pit 330
Beckley-Cin 330

On-Base Percentage
R.Thomas-Phi 414
Tenney-Bos 409
Beaumont-Pit 404
Clarke-Pit 401
Wagner-Pit 394

Slugging Average
Wagner-Pit 463
Crawford-Cin 461
Clarke-Pit 449
Beckley-Cin 427
Leach-Pit 426

On-Base Plus Slugging
Wagner-Pit 857
Clarke-Pit 850
Crawford-Cin 848
Beaumont-Pit 822
Beckley-Cin 804

Adjusted OPS
Wagner-Pit 159
Clarke-Pit 157
Beaumont-Pit 148
Crawford-Cin 147
Tenney-Bos 141

Batter Runs
Wagner-Pit 40.0
Crawford-Cin 38.6
Clarke-Pit 34.9
Beaumont-Pit 34.1
Beckley-Cin 28.8

Adjusted Batter Runs
Wagner-Pit 36.5
Clarke-Pit 31.8
Beaumont-Pit 30.8
Crawford-Cin 29.7
Tenney-Bos 27.8

Clutch Hitting Index
Hartman-StL 160
Bransfield-Pit 133
Ritchey-Pit 124
McCreery-Bro 123
Wagner-Pit 123

Runs Created
Wagner-Pit 118
Beaumont-Pit 109
Crawford-Cin 108
Clarke-Pit 97
Beckley-Cin 94

Total Average
Wagner-Pit 966
Clarke-Pit 955
Beaumont-Pit 868
Crawford-Cin 865
Tenney-Bos 845

Stolen Bases
Wagner-Pit 42
Slagle-Chi 41
Donovan-StL 34
Beaumont-Pit 33
Smith-NY 32

Stolen Base Average

Stolen Base Runs

Fielding Runs
Farrell-StL 33.5
Lowe-Chi 29.1
H.Long-Bos 23.0
Steinfeldt-Cin 22.1
Leach-Pit 13.0

Total Player Rating
Wagner-Pit 4.4
Tenney-Bos 3.9
Leach-Pit 3.6
Farrell-StL 2.9
Crawford-Cin 2.8

Wins
Chesbro-Pit 28
Willis-Bos 27
Pittinger-Bos 27
Taylor-Chi 23
Hahn-Cin 23

Win Percentage
Chesbro-Pit 824
Doheny-Pit 800
Tannehill-Pit 769
Phillippe-Pit 690
Leever-Pit 682

Games
Willis-Bos 51
Pittinger-Bos 46
Yerkes-StL 39
Taylor-Chi 37

Complete Games
Willis-Bos 45
Pittinger-Bos 36
Hahn-Cin 35
White-Phi 34
Taylor-Chi 34

Shutouts
Taylor-Chi 8
Mathewson-NY 8
Chesbro-Pit 8
Pittinger-Bos 7
Hahn-Cin 6

Saves
Willis-Bos 3
M.O'Neill-StL 2
Newton-Bro 2
Leever-Pit 2

Innings Pitched
Willis-Bos 410.0
Pittinger-Bos 389.1
Taylor-Chi 333.2
Hahn-Cin 321.0
White-Phi 306.0

Fewest Hits/Game
Newton-Bro 7.08
McGinnity-NY 7.18
Taylor-Chi 7.36
Donovan-Bro 7.56
Chesbro-Pit 7.61

Fewest BB/Game
Phillippe-Pit 86
Tannehill-Pit 97
Menefee-Chi 1.19
Taylor-Chi 1.21
Leever-Pit 1.26

Strikeouts
Willis-Bos 225
White-Phi 185
Pittinger-Bos 174
Donovan-Bro 170
Mathewson-NY 164

Strikeouts/Game
White-Phi 5.44
Mathewson-NY 5.19
Donovan-Bro 5.14
Willis-Bos 4.94
Wicker-StL 4.61

Ratio
Taylor-Chi 8.90
Tannehill-Pit 9.27
McGinnity-NY 9.59
Hahn-Cin 9.70
Phillippe-Pit 9.76

Earned Run Average
Taylor-Chi 1.29
Hahn-Cin 1.77
Tannehill-Pit 1.95
Lundgren-Chi 1.97
Phillippe-Pit 2.05

Adjusted ERA
Taylor-Chi 208
Hahn-Cin 170
Poole-Pit-Cin 142
Tannehill-Pit 140
Lundgren-Chi 137

Opponents' Batting Avg.
Newton-Bro 217
McGinnity-NY 219
Taylor-Chi 224
Donovan-Bro 228
Chesbro-Pit 229

Opponents' On-Base Pct.
Taylor-Chi 258
Tannehill-Pit 266
McGinnity-NY 273
Hahn-Cin 275
Phillippe-Pit 276

Starter Runs
Taylor-Chi 55.1
Hahn-Cin 36.2
Willis-Bos 26.6
Phillippe-Pit 22.0
Tannehill-Pit 21.4

Adjusted Starter Runs
Taylor-Chi 53.6
Hahn-Cin 40.7
Willis-Bos 28.1
Mathewson-NY 21.5
Phillippe-Pit 21.0

Clutch Pitching Index
Lundgren-Chi 144
Poole-Pit-Cin 140
Eason-Chi-Bos 136
Taylor-NY 126
Taylor-Chi 121

Relief Runs

Adjusted Relief Runs

Relief Ranking

Total Pitcher Index
Taylor-Chi 6.7
Hahn-Cin 4.3
Tannehill-Pit 3.2
Willis-Bos 3.1
Phillips-Cin 3.0

Total Baseball Ranking
Taylor-Chi 6.3
Wagner-Pit 4.5
Hahn-Cin 4.2
Tenney-Bos 3.9
Leach-Pit 3.6

TEAM	G	W	L	PCT	GB	R	OR	AB	H	2B	3B	HR	BB	SO	AVG	OBP	SLG	OPS	OPS+	BR	BR+	PF	CHI	RC	SB	CS	SBA	SBR
PHI	137	83	53	.610		**775**	636	4762	1369	235	67	38	343	293	.287	.340	.389	729	104	50	21	104	**107**	**729**	201			
STL	140	78	58	.574	5	619	607	4736	1254	208	61	29	373	327	.265	.323	.353	676	94	-38	-29	99	97	612	137			
BOS	138	77	60	.562	6.5	664	**600**	4875	1356	195	95	42	275	375	.278	.322	.383	705	98	0	-19	103	98	671	132			
CHI	138	74	60	.552	8	675	602	4654	1248	170	50	14	411	381	.268	.332	.335	667	95	-43	-14	96	**107**	641	**265**			
CLE	137	69	67	.507	14	686	667	4840	**1401**	248	68	33	308	356	**.289**	.336	.389	725	**111**	41	**71**	96	95	712	140			
WAS	138	61	75	.449	22	707	790	4734	1338	**261**	66	**47**	329	296	.283	.335	**.395**	**730**	107	48	42	101	99	694	121			
DET	137	52	83	.385	30.5	566	657	4644	1167	141	55	22	359	**287**	.251	.312	.320	632	79	-109	-119	102	103	527	130			
BAL	141	50	88	.362	34	715	848	4760	1318	202	**107**	33	**417**	429	.277	**.342**	.385	727	103	**51**	20	104	97	723	189			
TOT	553					5407		38005	10451	1660	569	258	2815	2744	.275	.331	.369	700							1315			

TEAM	CG	SH	SV	IP	H	H/G	HR	BB	SO	RAT	ERA	ERA+	OAV	OOB	PR	PR+	PF	CPI	FA	E	DP	FW	PW	BW	SBW	DIF
PHI	114	5	2	1216^{1}	1292	9.6	33	368	**455**	12.8	3.29	111	.273	.334	39	49	103	**110**	.953	270	75	1.4	4.7	2.0		7.0
STL	120	7	2	1244	1273	9.3	36	343	348	12.1	3.34	106	.266	.321	32	26	99	99	.953	274	122	1.6	2.5	-2.7		8.8
BOS	123	6	1	1238	1217	**8.9**	27	326	431	**11.6**	**3.03**	**118**	**.258**	**.311**	**75**	**75**	100	99	**.955**	263	101	2.0	**7.2**	-1.8		1.3
CHI	116	11	0	1221^{2}	1269	9.4	30	331	346	12.2	3.42	99	.269	.323	22	-5	95	98	**.955**	**257**	**125**	**2.4**	-.4	-1.3		6.5
CLE	116	**16**	**3**	1204^{1}	**1199**	9.0	26	411	361	12.4	3.29	105	.260	.327	39	21	96	101	.950	287	96	.4	2.0	**6.8**		-8.0
WAS	**130**	2	0	1207^{2}	1403	10.5	56	**312**	300	13.2	4.36	85	.291	.341	-106	-85	104	94	.945	316	70	-1.3	-8.0	4.0		-1.5
DET	116	9	**3**	1190^{2}	1267	9.6	**20**	370	245	12.8	3.57	102	.274	.333	1	10	102	99	.943	332	111	-2.4	1.0	-11.2		-2.6
BAL	119	3	1	1210^{1}	1531	11.4	30	354	258	14.3	4.33	87	.309	.360	-102	-73	106	104	.938	357	109	-3.4	-6.9	1.9		-10.4
TOT	954	59	12	9733		9.7				12.7	3.58		.275	.331					.950	2356	809					

Runs
- Hartsel-Phi 109
- Fultz-Phi 109
- Strang-Chi 108
- Bradley-Cle 104
- Delahanty-Was 103

Hits
- Hickman-Bos-Cle ... 193
- L.Cross-Phi 191
- Bradley-Cle 187
- Delahanty-Was 178
- Freeman-Bos 174

Doubles
- Delahanty-Was 43
- Davis-Phi 43
- L.Cross-Phi 39
- Bradley-Cle 39
- Freeman-Bos 38

Triples
- Williams-Bal 21
- Freeman-Bos 19
- Ferris-Bos 14
- Delahanty-Was 14
- Hickman-Bos-Cle 13

Home Runs
- Seybold-Phi 16
- Hickman-Bos-Cle 11
- Freeman-Bos 11
- Bradley-Cle 11
- Delahanty-Was 10

Total Bases
- Hickman-Bos-Cle ... 288
- Freeman-Bos 283
- Bradley-Cle 283
- Delahanty-Was 279
- Seybold-Phi 264

Runs Batted In
- Freeman-Bos 121
- Hickman-Bos-Cle .. 110
- L.Cross-Phi 108
- Seybold-Phi 97

Runs Produced
- L.Cross-Phi 198
- Delahanty-Was 186
- Freeman-Bos 185
- Davis-Phi 175
- Hickman-Bos-Cle ... 173

Bases On Balls
- Hartsel-Phi 87
- Strang-Chi 76
- Barrett-Det 74
- Burkett-StL 71
- Davis-Chi 65

Batting Average
- Delahanty-Was ...... .376
- Lajoie-Phi-Cle ...... .378
- Hickman-Bos-Cle ... .361
- Dougherty-Bos ...... .342
- L.Cross-Phi .... .342

On-Base Percentage
- Delahanty-Was ...... .453
- Dougherty-Bos ...... .407
- Barrett-Det .... .397
- Selbach-Bal .... .393
- Jones-Chi .... .390

Slugging Average
- Delahanty-Was ...... .590
- Lajoie-Phi-Cle ...... .565
- Hickman-Bos-Cle ... .539
- Bradley-Cle .... .515
- Seybold-Phi .... .506

On-Base Plus Slugging
- Delahanty-Was ... 1043
- Hickman-Bos-Cle .. 926
- Bradley-Cle 890
- Seybold-Phi 881
- Williams-Bal 861

Adjusted OPS
- Delahanty-Was 186
- Hickman-Bos-Cle ... 159
- Bradley-Cle 151
- Seybold-Phi 137
- Freeman-Bos 131

Batter Runs
- Delahanty-Was 57.0
- Hickman-Bos-Cle ... 36.3
- Lajoie-Phi-Cle 32.5
- Bradley-Cle 30.7
- Seybold-Phi 28.5

Adjusted Batter Runs
- Delahanty-Was 56.0
- Hickman-Bos-Cle ... 39.1
- Lajoie-Phi-Cle 35.8
- Bradley-Cle 35.2
- Seybold-Phi 24.3

Clutch Hitting Index
- Davis-Chi 136
- L.Cross-Phi 131
- Anderson-StL 131
- Elberfeld-Det 130
- Mertes-Chi 129

Runs Created
- Delahanty-Was 137
- Hickman-Bos-Cle ... 118
- Bradley-Cle 114
- Freeman-Bos 109
- L.Cross-Phi 105

Total Average
- Delahanty-Was 1.224
- Hickman-Bos-Cle ... .935
- Bradley-Cle .... .895
- Seybold-Phi .... .894
- Hartsel-Phi .... .893

Stolen Bases
- Hartsel-Phi 47
- Mertes-Chi 46
- Fultz-Phi 44

Stolen Base Average

Stolen Base Runs

Fielding Runs
- Ferris-Bos 26.5
- Schreck-Cle-Phi ... 20.9
- Padden-StL 18.2
- Jones-Chi 12.5
- Coughlin-Was 11.8

Total Player Rating
- Lajoie-Phi-Cle 6.0
- Delahanty-Was 4.8
- Bradley-Cle 4.7
- Hickman-Bos-Cle ... 2.8
- Schreck-Cle-Phi 2.7

Wins
- Young-Bos 32
- Waddell-Phi 24
- Powell-StL 22
- R.Donahue-StL 22
- Dinneen-Bos 21

Win Percentage
- Bernhard-Phi-Cle ... .783
- Waddell-Phi .... .774
- Young-Bos .... .744
- R.Donahue-StL ..... .667
- Griffith-Chi .... .625

Games
- Young-Bos 45
- Powell-StL 42
- Dinneen-Bos 42
- Wiltse-Phi-Bal 38
- Orth-Was 38

Complete Games
- Young-Bos 41
- Dinneen-Bos 39
- Powell-StL 36
- Orth-Was 36

Shutouts
- Joss-Cle 5
- Siever-Det 4
- Moore-Cle 4
- Mercer-Det 4

Saves
- Powell-StL 2

Innings Pitched
- Young-Bos 384.2
- Dinneen-Bos 371.1
- Powell-StL 328.1
- Orth-Was 324.0
- R.Donahue-StL ... 316.1

Fewest Hits/Game
- Bernhard-Phi-Cle ... 7.01
- Waddell-Phi 7.30
- Joss-Cle 7.52
- Siever-Det 7.93
- Winter-Bos 7.97

Fewest BB/Game
- Orth-Was 1.11
- Young-Bos 1.24
- Bernhard-Phi-Cle ... 1.47
- Siever-Det 1.53
- Plank-Phi 1.83

Strikeouts
- Waddell-Phi 210
- Young-Bos 160
- Powell-StL 137
- Dinneen-Bos 136
- Plank-Phi 107

Strikeouts/Game
- Waddell-Phi 6.84
- Powell-StL 3.76
- Young-Bos 3.74
- Joss-Cle 3.54
- Piatt-Chi 3.51

Ratio
- Bernhard-Phi-Cle ... 8.68
- Siever-Det 9.56
- Waddell-Phi 9.71
- Young-Bos 9.73
- Joss-Cle 10.46

Earned Run Average
- Siever-Det 1.91
- Waddell-Phi 2.05
- Bernhard-Phi-Cle ... 2.15
- Young-Bos 2.15
- Garvin-Chi 2.21

Adjusted ERA
- Siever-Det 191
- Waddell-Phi 179
- Young-Bos 166
- Bernhard-Phi-Cle ... 160
- Garvin-Chi 153

Opponents' Batting Avg.
- Bernhard-Phi-Cle ... .216
- Waddell-Phi .... .223
- Joss-Cle .... .228
- Siever-Det .... .237
- Winter-Bos .... .238

Opponents' On-Base Pct.
- Bernhard-Phi-Cle ... .254
- Siever-Det .... .273
- Waddell-Phi .... .276
- Young-Bos .... .276
- Joss-Cle .... .291

Starter Runs
- Young-Bos 60.6
- Waddell-Phi 46.6
- Bernhard-Phi-Cle ... 35.7
- Siever-Det 34.7
- R.Donahue-StL 28.5

Adjusted Starter Runs
- Young-Bos 60.6
- Waddell-Phi 48.2
- Siever-Det 35.5
- Bernhard-Phi-Cle ... 33.7
- R.Donahue-StL 27.2

Clutch Pitching Index
- Garvin-Chi 129
- Shields-Bal-StL 123
- Husting-Bos-Phi 120
- Moore-Cle 119
- Sudhoff-StL 110

Relief Runs

Adjusted Relief Runs

Relief Ranking

Total Pitcher Index
- Young-Bos 5.8
- Waddell-Phi 5.7
- Bernhard-Phi-Cle ... 3.0
- Garvin-Chi 2.5
- Siever-Det 2.5

Total Baseball Ranking
- Lajoie-Phi-Cle 6.0
- Young-Bos 5.8
- Waddell-Phi 5.7
- Delahanty-Was 4.8
- Bradley-Cle 4.7

TEAM	G	W	L	PCT	GB	R	OR	AB	H	2B	3B	HR	BB	SO	AVG	OBP	SLG	OPS	OPS+	BR	BR+	PF	CHI	RC	SB	CS	SBA	SBR
PIT	141	91	49	.650		**793**	613	4988	**1429**	208	**110**	**34**	364		.286	.341	**.393**	734	**113**	89	**65**	103	101	**758**	172			
NY	142	84	55	.604	6.5	729	**567**	4741	1290	181	49	20	379		.272	.338	.344	682	97	9	-16	104	**106**	678	264			
CHI	139	82	56	.594	8	695	599	4733	1300	191	62	9	422		.275	.340	.347	687	105	19	39	97	101	678	259			
CIN	141	74	65	.532	16.5	765	656	4857	1399	**228**	92	28	403		**.288**	.346	.390	**736**	104	**95**	18	111	99	735	144			
BRO	139	70	66	.515	19	667	682	4534	1201	177	56	15	**522**		.265	**.348**	.339	687	105	27	47	97	97	661	**273**			
BOS	140	58	80	.420	32	578	699	4682	1145	176	47	25	398		.245	.312	.318	630	90	-83	-59	96	100	540	159			
PHI	139	49	86	.363	39.5	617	738	4781	1283	186	62	12	338		.268	.322	.341	663	98	-33	-11	97	97	596	120			
STL	139	43	94	.314	46.5	505	795	4689	1176	138	65	8	277		.251	.297	.313	610	83	-124	-107	97	98	511	171			
TOT	560					5349		38005	10223	1485	543	151	3103	3767	.269	.331	.349	679							1562			

TEAM	CG	SH	SV	IP	H	H/G	HR	BB	SO	RAT	ERA	ERA+	OAV	OOB	PR	PR+	PF	CPI	FA	E	DP	FW	PW	BW	SBW	DIF
PIT	117	**16**	5	1251^{1}	1215	8.8	**9**	384	454	11.8	2.92	111	.255	.316	48	44	99	95	**.951**	295	100	1.6	4.3	**6.3**		9.0
NY	115	8	**8**	1262^{2}	1257	9.0	20	371	**628**	11.9	2.96	113	.258	.316	43	55	102	98	**.951**	287	87	**2.3**	5.3	-1.5		8.5
CHI	117	6	6	1240^{1}	**1182**	**8.6**	14	**354**	451	**11.5**	**2.78**	113	**.250**	**.307**	**67**	48	96	93	.942	338	78	-1.6	4.7	3.8		6.3
CIN	**126**	11	1	1230	1277	9.4	14	378	480	12.6	3.08	**116**	.268	.331	26	**60**	109	105	.946	312	84	.5	**5.8**	1.8		-3.4
BRO	118	11	4	1221^{1}	1276	9.5	18	377	438	12.7	3.45	92	.275	.339	-25	-39	98	100	**.951**	**284**	98	2.1	-3.7	4.6		-.7
BOS	125	8	1	1228^{2}	1310	9.6	30	460	516	13.4	3.35	96	.278	.348	-11	-21	98	**112**	.939	361	89	-3.0	-2.0	-5.6		-.3
PHI	**126**	5	3	1212^{1}	1347	10.0	21	425	381	13.7	3.97	82	.285	.352	-95	-97	100	97	.947	300	76	1.0	-9.3	-1.0		-9.0
STL	111	4	2	1212^{1}	1353	10.1	25	430	419	13.7	3.67	89	.284	.350	-55	-56	100	104	.940	354	**111**	-2.6	-5.3	-10.2		-7.1
TOT	955	69	30	9859		9.4				12.7	3.27		.269	.331					.946	2531	723					

Runs
Beaumont-Pit 137
Donlin-Cin 110
Browne-NY 105
Slagle-Chi 104
Strang-Bro 101

Hits
Beaumont-Pit 209
Seymour-Cin 191
Browne-NY 185
Wagner-Pit 182
Donlin-Cin 174

Doubles
Steinfeldt-Cin 32
Mertes-NY 32
Clarke-Pit 32

Triples
Wagner-Pit 19
Donlin-Cin 18
Leach-Pit 17

Home Runs
Sheckard-Bro 9

Total Bases
Beaumont-Pit 272
Seymour-Cin 267
Wagner-Pit 265
Donlin-Cin 256
Sheckard-Bro 245

Runs Batted In
Mertes-NY 104
Wagner-Pit 101
Doyle-Bro 91
Leach-Pit 87
Steinfeldt-Cin 83

Runs Produced
Beaumont-Pit 198
Mertes-NY 197
Wagner-Pit 193
Leach-Pit 177
Doyle-Bro 175

Bases On Balls
Thomas-Phi 107
Dahlen-Bro 82
Slagle-Chi 81
Chance-Chi 78

Batting Average
Wagner-Pit 355
Clarke-Pit 351
Donlin-Cin 351
Bresnahan-NY 350
Seymour-Cin 342

On-Base Percentage
Thomas-Phi 453
Bresnahan-NY 443
Chance-Chi 439
Sheckard-Bro 423
Donlin-Cin 420

Slugging Average
Clarke-Pit 532
Wagner-Pit 518
Donlin-Cin 516
Bresnahan-NY 493
Steinfeldt-Cin 481

On-Base Plus Slugging
Clarke-Pit 946
Donlin-Cin 936
Bresnahan-NY 936
Wagner-Pit 931
Sheckard-Bro 899

Adjusted OPS
Clarke-Pit 164
Sheckard-Bro 160
Bresnahan-NY 160
Wagner-Pit 160
Chance-Chi 155

Batter Runs
Donlin-Cin 42.6
Wagner-Pit 42.1
Sheckard-Bro 39.8
Bresnahan-NY 37.8
Clarke-Pit 37.3

Adjusted Batter Runs
Sheckard-Bro 43.4
Wagner-Pit 38.7
Chance-Chi 36.9
Clarke-Pit 34.3
Bresnahan-NY 34.2

Clutch Hitting Index
Corcoran-Cin 141
Doyle-Bro 131
Mertes-NY 123
Chance-Chi 118
Dobbs-Chi-Bro 118

Runs Created
Sheckard-Bro 137
Wagner-Pit 133
Donlin-Cin 122
Beaumont-Pit 119
Chance-Chi 118

Total Average
Chance-Chi 1.175
Bresnahan-NY 1.144
Sheckard-Bro 1.142
Wagner-Pit 1.097
Clarke-Pit 1.061

Stolen Bases
Sheckard-Bro 67
Chance-Chi 67
Wagner-Pit 46
Strang-Bro 46
Mertes-NY 45

Stolen Base Average

Stolen Base Runs

Fielding Runs
Farrell-StL 28.1
Wagner-Pit 24.6
Sheckard-Bro 23.4
Moran-Bos 19.3
Ritchey-Pit 19.0

Total Player Rating
Wagner-Pit 6.2
Sheckard-Bro 5.5
Thomas-Phi 4.0
Moran-Bos 3.4
Tenney-Bos 3.1

Wins
McGinnity-NY 31
Mathewson-NY 30
Phillippe-Pit 25
Leever-Pit 25

Win Percentage
Leever-Pit 781
Phillippe-Pit 735
Weimer-Chi 714
Mathewson-NY 698
Wicker-StL-Chi 690

Games
McGinnity-NY 55
Mathewson-NY 45
Pittinger-Bos 44
Schmidt-Bro 40

Complete Games
McGinnity-NY 44
Mathewson-NY 37
Pittinger-Bos 35
Hahn-Cin 34
Taylor-Chi 33

Shutouts
Leever-Pit 7
Schmidt-Bro 5
Hahn-Cin 5
Phillippe-Pit 4
Jones-Bro 4

Saves
Miller-NY 3
Lundgren-Chi 3

Innings Pitched
McGinnity-NY 434.0
Mathewson-NY 366.1
Pittinger-Bos 351.2
Jones-Bro 324.1
Taylor-Chi 312.1

Fewest Hits/Game
Weimer-Chi 7.69
Mathewson-NY 7.89
Taylor-Chi 7.98
Leever-Pit 8.07
McGinnity-NY 8.11

Fewest BB/Game
Phillippe-Pit 90
Hahn-Cin 1.43
Taylor-Chi 1.64
McFarland-StL 1.89
Leever-Pit 1.90

Strikeouts
Mathewson-NY 267
McGinnity-NY 171
Garvin-Bro 154
Pittinger-Bos 140
Weimer-Chi 128

Strikeouts/Game
Mathewson-NY 6.56
Piatt-Bos 4.97
Garvin-Bro 4.65
Weimer-Chi 4.09
Willis-Bos 4.05

Ratio
Phillippe-Pit 9.39
Taylor-Chi 9.77
Leever-Pit 10.13
Mathewson-NY 10.59
Hahn-Cin 10.70

Earned Run Average
Leever-Pit 2.06
Mathewson-NY 2.26
Weimer-Chi 2.30
Phillippe-Pit 2.43
McGinnity-NY 2.43

Adjusted ERA
Leever-Pit 157
Mathewson-NY 148
Hahn-Cin 141
McGinnity-NY 138
Weimer-Chi 136

Opponents' Batting Avg.
Weimer-Chi 225
Mathewson-NY 231
Taylor-Chi 235
McGinnity-NY 236
Leever-Pit 238

Opponents' On-Base Pct.
Phillippe-Pit 263
Taylor-Chi 273
Leever-Pit 282
Mathewson-NY 287
McGinnity-NY 291

Starter Runs
Mathewson-NY 40.7
McGinnity-NY 40.2
Leever-Pit 38.0
Weimer-Chi 30.2
Taylor-Chi 28.2

Adjusted Starter Runs
McGinnity-NY 43.0
Mathewson-NY 42.9
Leever-Pit 37.4
Hahn-Cin 31.0
Weimer-Chi 27.1

Clutch Pitching Index
Brown-StL 153
Pittinger-Bos 126
Malarkey-Bos 115
Piatt-Bos 115
Poole-Cin 113

Relief Runs

Adjusted Relief Runs

Relief Ranking

Total Pitcher Index
Mathewson-NY 5.1
McGinnity-NY 3.9
Leever-Pit 3.4
Taylor-Chi 3.0
Hahn-Cin 2.9

Total Baseball Ranking
Wagner-Pit 6.2
Sheckard-Bro 5.5
Mathewson-NY 5.1
Thomas-Phi 4.0
McGinnity-NY 3.9

TEAM	G	W	L	PCT	GB	R	OR	AB	H	2B	3B	HR	BB	SO	AVG	OBP	SLG	OPS	OPS+	BR	BR+	PF	CHI	RC	SB	CS	SBA	SBR
BOS	141	91	47	.659		**708**	**504**	4919	**1336**	222	**113**	**48**	262	561	**.272**	.313	**.392**	**705**	111	**91**	57	105	103	**680**	141			
PHI	137	75	60	.556	14.5	597	519	4673	1236	227	68	32	268	513	.264	.309	.363	672	102	36	10	105	100	598	157			
CLE	140	77	63	.550	15	639	579	4773	1265	**231**	95	31	259	595	.265	.308	.373	681	**112**	51	**63**	98	102	634	175			
NY	136	72	62	.537	17	579	573	4565	1136	193	62	18	**332**	465	.249	.309	.330	639	92	-6	-39	106	**104**	544	160			
DET	137	65	71	.478	25	567	539	4582	1229	162	91	12	292	526	.268	**.318**	.351	669	110	39	57	97	94	587	128			
STL	139	65	74	.468	26.5	500	525	4639	1133	166	68	12	271	539	.244	.290	.317	607	90	-66	-52	97	102	480	101			
CHI	138	60	77	.438	30.5	516	613	4670	1152	176	49	14	325	537	.247	.301	.314	615	94	-46	-22	96	98	526	**180**			
WAS	140	43	94	.314	47.5	437	691	4613	1066	172	72	17	257	**463**	.231	.277	.311	588	80	-98	-107	102	96	454	131			
TOT	554					4543		37434	9553	1549	618	184	2266	4199	.256	.304	.345	648							1173			

TEAM	CG	SH	SV	IP	H	H/G	HR	BB	SO	RAT	ERA	ERA+	OAV	OOB	PR	PR+	PF	CPI	FA	E	DP	FW	PW	BW	SBW	DIF
BOS	123	**20**	**4**	1255	1142	**8.2**	23	269	579	**10.4**	**2.57**	**118**	**.242**	**.288**	**55**	**63**	102	100	.959	239	86	2.3	**6.6**	6.0		7.3
PHI	112	10	1	1207	**1124**	8.4	20	315	**728**	11.3	2.98	103	.246	.305	-2	10	103	97	**.960**	**217**	66	**3.2**	1.1	1.1		2.3
CLE	**125**	**20**	0	1243^{2}	1161	8.5	**16**	271	521	10.7	2.73	105	.247	.293	32	18	96	97	.946	322	**99**	-3.1	1.9	**6.6**		1.8
NY	111	7	2	1201^{1}	1171	8.8	19	245	463	11.0	3.08	101	.255	.299	-16	5	105	93	.953	264	87	.0	.6	-4.0		8.5
DET	123	15	2	1196	1169	8.8	19	336	554	11.6	2.76	106	.256	.310	28	21	98	**111**	.950	281	82	-.9	2.2	6.0		-10.1
STL	124	12	3	1222^{1}	1220	9.0	26	**237**	511	11.0	2.77	105	.260	.300	26	19	98	108	.953	268	94	.2	2.0	-5.3		-1.2
CHI	114	9	**4**	1235	1233	9.0	23	287	391	11.5	3.02	93	.260	.309	-8	-30	95	103	.949	297	85	-1.8	-3.1	-2.2		-1.2
WAS	122	6	3	1223^{2}	1333	9.9	38	306	452	12.4	3.82	82	.277	.325	-116	-89	106	96	.954	260	86	.8	-9.2	-11.1		-5.9
TOT	954	99	19	9784		8.8				11.2	2.97		.256	.304					.954	2148	685					

Runs
Dougherty-Bos 107
Bradley-Cle 101
Keeler-NY 95
Barrett-Det 95
Bay-Cle 94

Hits
Dougherty-Bos 195
Crawford-Det 184
Parent-Bos 170
Bay-Cle 169
Bradley-Cle 168

Doubles
Seybold-Phi 45
Lajoie-Cle 41
Freeman-Bos 39
Bradley-Cle 36
Anderson-StL 34

Triples
Crawford-Det 25
Bradley-Cle 22
Freeman-Bos 20
Parent-Bos 17
Collins-Bos 17

Home Runs
Freeman-Bos 13
Hickman-Cle 12
Ferris-Bos 9
Seybold-Phi 8

Total Bases
Freeman-Bos 281
Crawford-Det 269
Bradley-Cle 266
Lajoie-Cle 251
Dougherty-Bos 250

Runs Batted In
Freeman-Bos 104
Hickman-Cle 97
Lajoie-Cle 93
L.Cross-Phi 90
Crawford-Det 89

Runs Produced
Lajoie-Cle 176
Crawford-Det 173
Freeman-Bos 165
Bradley-Cle 163
Dougherty-Bos 162

Bases On Balls
Barrett-Det 74
Lush-Det 70
Pickering-Phi 57
Burkett-StL 52
Flick-Cle 51

Batting Average
Lajoie-Cle 344
Crawford-Det 335
Dougherty-Bos 331
Barrett-Det 315
Bradley-Cle 313

On-Base Percentage
Barrett-Det 407
Hartsel-Phi 391
Lajoie-Cle 379
Lush-Det 379
Green-Chi 375

Slugging Average
Lajoie-Cle 518
Bradley-Cle 496
Freeman-Bos 496
Crawford-Det 489
Hartsel-Phi 477

On-Base Plus Slugging
Lajoie-Cle 896
Hartsel-Phi 868
Crawford-Det 855
Bradley-Cle 844
Freeman-Bos 823

Adjusted OPS
Lajoie-Cle 170
Crawford-Det 159
Bradley-Cle 154
Hartsel-Phi 152
Green-Chi 146

Batter Runs
Lajoie-Cle 37.6
Crawford-Det 34.5
Bradley-Cle 30.8
Barrett-Det 29.6
Hartsel-Phi 28.0

Adjusted Batter Runs
Lajoie-Cle 39.3
Crawford-Det 37.5
Bradley-Cle 32.6
Barrett-Det 32.6
Green-Chi 29.1

Clutch Hitting Index
Gochnauer-Cle 155
L.Cross-Phi 144
Carr-Det 135
Williams-NY 130
Anderson-StL 129

Runs Created
Dougherty-Bos 111
Crawford-Det 110
Lajoie-Cle 107
Bradley-Cle 104
Barrett-Det 98

Total Average
Lajoie-Cle 940
Hartsel-Phi 934
Barrett-Det 873
Crawford-Det 858
Bradley-Cle 856

Stolen Bases
Bay-Cle 45
Pickering-Phi 40
Holmes-Was-Chi 35
Dougherty-Bos 35
Conroy-NY 33

Stolen Base Average

Stolen Base Runs

Fielding Runs
Lajoie-Cle 40.1
Criger-Bos 22.8
Schreckengost-Phi 18.2
Wallace-StL 17.9
Williams-NY 15.6

Total Player Rating
Lajoie-Cle 8.1
Bradley-Cle 4.8
Crawford-Det 3.5
Barrett-Det 3.4
Elberfeld-Det-NY 3.1

Wins
Young-Bos 28
Plank-Phi 23

Win Percentage
Young-Bos 757
Hughes-Bos 741
Moore-Cle 714
Dinneen-Bos 618
Plank-Phi 590

Games
Plank-Phi 43
Mullin-Det 41
Young-Bos 40
Flaherty-Chi 40
Chesbro-NY 40

Complete Games
Young-Bos 34
Waddell-Phi 34
Donovan-Det 34

Shutouts
Young-Bos 7
Mullin-Det 6
Dinneen-Bos 6
Sudhoff-StL 5
Hughes-Bos 5

Saves
Young-Bos 2
Powell-StL 2
Orth-Was 2
Mullin-Det 2
Dinneen-Bos 2

Innings Pitched
Young-Bos 341.2
Plank-Phi 336.0
Chesbro-NY 324.2
Waddell-Phi 324.0
Mullin-Det 320.2

Fewest Hits/Game
Moore-Cle 7.12
Donovan-Det 7.24
Joss-Cle 7.36
Waddell-Phi 7.61
Dinneen-Bos 7.68

Fewest BB/Game
Young-Bos 97
Bernhard-Cle 1.14
Donahue-StL-Cle 1.14
Joss-Cle 1.17
Tannehill-NY 1.28

Strikeouts
Waddell-Phi 302
Donovan-Det 187
Young-Bos 176
Plank-Phi 176
Mullin-Det 170

Strikeouts/Game
Waddell-Phi 8.39
Donovan-Det 5.48
Moore-Cle 5.38
Powell-StL 4.97
Mullin-Det 4.77

Ratio
Joss-Cle 8.82
Young-Bos 8.96
Bernhard-Cle 9.34
Moore-Cle 9.56
Dinneen-Bos 9.78

Earned Run Average
Moore-Cle 1.74
Young-Bos 2.08
Bernhard-Cle 2.12
White-Chi 2.13
Joss-Cle 2.19

Adjusted ERA
Moore-Cle 164
Young-Bos 146
Bernhard-Cle 135
Dinneen-Bos 134
White-Chi 132

Opponents' Batting Avg.
Moore-Cle 217
Donovan-Det 220
Joss-Cle 223
Waddell-Phi 229
Dinneen-Bos 230

Opponents' On-Base Pct.
Joss-Cle 256
Young-Bos 259
Bernhard-Cle 267
Moore-Cle 271
Dinneen-Bos 276

Starter Runs
Moore-Cle 33.5
Young-Bos 33.4
White-Chi 27.7
Mullin-Det 25.5
Joss-Cle 24.4

Adjusted Starter Runs
Young-Bos 35.3
Moore-Cle 31.7
Dinneen-Bos 25.2
Plank-Phi 24.2
Mullin-Det 24.1

Clutch Pitching Index
Kitson-Det 127
Mullin-Det 121
Donahue-StL-Cle . . . 119
Plank-Phi 116
Hughes-Bos 112

Relief Runs

Adjusted Relief Runs

Relief Ranking

Total Pitcher Index
Young-Bos 4.8
Mullin-Det 4.2
White-Chi 3.5
Sudhoff-StL 2.8
Joss-Cle 2.8

Total Baseball Ranking
Lajoie-Cle 8.1
Bradley-Cle 4.8
Young-Bos 4.8
Mullin-Det 4.1
Crawford-Det 3.5

TEAM	G	W	L	PCT	GB	R	OR	AB	H	2B	3B	HR	BB	SO	AVG	OBP	SLG	OPS	OPS+	BR	BR+	PF	CHI	RC	SB	CS	SBA	SBR
NY	158	106	47	.693		**744**	**474**	5150	**1347**	**202**	65	**31**	**434**		**.262**	**.328**	**.344**	**672**	**109**	**87**	**58**	104	**104**	**712**	**283**			
CHI	156	93	60	.608	13	597	517	5210	1294	157	62	22	298		.248	.295	.315	610	94	-38	-39	100	**104**	582	227			
CIN	157	88	65	.575	18	695	547	5231	1332	189	92	21	399		.255	.313	.338	651	98	42	-12	109	**104**	642	179			
PIT	156	87	66	.569	19	675	592	5160	1333	164	**102**	15	391		.258	.316	.338	654	105	48	31	103	102	639	178			
STL	155	75	79	.487	31.5	602	595	5104	1292	175	66	24	343		.253	.306	.327	633	106	7	36	96	99	602	199			
BRO	154	56	97	.366	50	497	614	4917	1142	159	53	15	411		.232	.297	.295	592	91	-57	-43	98	93	521	205			
BOS	155	55	98	.359	51	491	749	5135	1217	153	50	24	316		.237	.287	.300	587	90	-78	-59	96	94	508	143			
PHI	155	52	100	.342	53.5	571	784	5103	1268	170	54	23	377		.248	.305	.316	621	102	-11	11	96	96	570	159			
TOT	623					4872		41010	10225	1369	544	175	2969	4277	.250	.307	.323	628							1573			

TEAM	CG	SH	SV	IP	H	H/G	HR	BB	SO	RAT	ERA	ERA+	OAV	OOB	PR	PR+	PF	CPI	FA	E	DP	FW	PW	BW	SBW	DIF
NY	127	**21**	**15**	1396^2	1151	**7.5**	36	349	**707**	**9.9**	**2.18**	**125**	**.222**	**.276**	**86**	**83**	100	93	**.956**	294	**93**	**2.4**	**8.8**	**6.2**		12.3
CHI	139	18	6	1383^2	**1150**	**7.5**	16	402	618	10.4	2.31	115	.224	.285	65	55	97	90	.954	298	89	1.8	5.9	-4.1		13.1
CIN	142	12	2	1392^2	1256	8.2	**13**	343	502	10.7	2.34	**125**	.241	.295	60	82	107	102	.954	301	81	1.8	8.7	-1.2		2.4
PIT	133	15	1	1348^1	1273	8.5	**13**	379	455	11.4	2.90	95	.248	.306	-24	-24	100	92	.955	**291**	**93**	2.3	-2.5	3.3		7.6
STL	**146**	7	2	1368	1286	8.5	23	**319**	529	10.9	2.64	102	.239	.286	13	5	99	85	.952	307	83	1.1	.6	3.9		-7.4
BRO	135	12	2	1337^1	1281	8.7	27	414	453	11.9	2.70	101	.255	.319	4	4	100	**112**	.945	343	87	-1.3	.5	-4.5		-15.0
BOS	136	13	0	1348^1	1405	9.4	25	500	544	13.1	3.44	80	.272	.343	-105	-104	101	105	.945	353	91	-1.8	-11.0	-6.2		-2.3
PHI	131	10	2	1339^1	1418	9.6	22	425	469	12.9	3.40	79	.270	.332	-99	-112	98	100	.937	403	**93**	-5.0	-11.8	1.2		-8.2
TOT	1089	108	30	10914^1		8.5				11.4	2.73		.250	.307					.950	2590	710					

Runs
- Browne-NY 99
- Wagner-Pit 97
- Beaumont-Pit 97
- Huggins-Cin 96

Hits
- Beaumont-Pit 185
- Beckley-StL 179
- Wagner-Pit 171
- Browne-NY 169
- Seymour-Cin 166

Doubles
- Wagner-Pit 44
- Mertes-NY 28
- Delahanty-Bos 27
- Seymour-Cin 26
- Dahlen-NY 26

Triples
- Lumley-Bro 18
- Wagner-Pit 14
- Tinker-Chi 13
- Seymour-Cin 13
- Kelley-Cin 13

Home Runs
- Lumley-Bro 9
- Brain-StL 7

Total Bases
- Wagner-Pit 255
- Lumley-Bro 247
- Seymour-Cin 233
- Beaumont-Pit 230
- Beckley-StL 222

Runs Batted In
- Dahlen-NY 80
- Mertes-NY 78
- Lumley-Bro 78
- Wagner-Pit 75
- Corcoran-Cin 74

Runs Produced
- Wagner-Pit 168
- Mertes-NY 157
- Lumley-Bro 148
- Dahlen-NY 148
- Beaumont-Pit 148

Bases On Balls
- Thomas-Phi 102
- Huggins-Cin 88
- Devlin-NY 62
- Wagner-Pit 59
- Ritchey-Pit 59

Batting Average
- Wagner-Pit .349
- Donlin-Cin-NY .329
- Beckley-StL .325
- Grady-StL .313
- Seymour-Cin .313

On-Base Percentage
- Wagner-Pit .423
- Thomas-Phi .416
- Chance-Chi .382
- Huggins-Cin .377
- Beckley-StL .375

Slugging Average
- Wagner-Pit .520
- Grady-StL .474
- Donlin-Cin-NY .457
- Seymour-Cin .439
- Chance-Chi .430

On-Base Plus Slugging
- Wagner-Pit 944
- Chance-Chi 812
- Seymour-Cin 790
- Beckley-StL 778
- Thomas-Phi 761

Adjusted OPS
- Wagner-Pit 186
- Chance-Chi 150
- Beckley-StL 147
- Thomas-Phi 141
- Lumley-Bro 137

Batter Runs
- Wagner-Pit 52.7
- Thomas-Phi 28.4
- Chance-Chi 27.2
- Beckley-StL 25.7
- Seymour-Cin 24.9

Adjusted Batter Runs
- Wagner-Pit 49.7
- Thomas-Phi 31.9
- Beckley-StL 30.0
- Chance-Chi 27.2
- Grady-StL 25.7

Clutch Hitting Index
- Devlin-NY 154
- Dahlen-NY 146
- Corcoran-Cin 137
- Bransfield-Pit 132
- Gilbert-NY 128

Runs Created
- Wagner-Pit 134
- Lumley-Bro 95
- Beckley-StL 94
- Chance-Chi 93
- Mertes-NY 93

Total Average
- Wagner-Pit 1.163
- Chance-Chi .926
- Thomas-Phi .869
- Mertes-NY .813
- McGann-NY .802

Stolen Bases
- Wagner-Pit 53
- Mertes-NY 47
- Dahlen-NY 47
- McGann-NY 42
- Chance-Chi 42

Stolen Base Average

Stolen Base Runs

Fielding Runs
- Leach-Pit 35.8
- Evers-Chi 31.3
- Dahlen-NY 27.6
- Tinker-Chi 19.3
- Farrell-StL 16.3

Total Player Rating
- Wagner-Pit 4.9
- Thomas-Phi 4.2
- Leach-Pit 4.0
- Chance-Chi 3.8
- Dahlen-NY 3.4

Wins
- McGinnity-NY 35
- Mathewson-NY 33
- Harper-Cin 23
- Taylor-NY 21
- Nichols-StL 21

Win Percentage
- McGinnity-NY .814
- Mathewson-NY .733
- Harper-Cin .719
- Flaherty-Pit .679

Games
- McGinnity-NY 51
- Mathewson-NY 48
- Jones-Bro 46
- Willis-Bos 43
- Fraser-Phi 42

Complete Games
- Willis-Bos 39
- Taylor-StL 39
- McGinnity-NY 38
- Jones-Bro 38

Shutouts
- McGinnity-NY 9
- Harper-Cin 6

Saves
- McGinnity-NY 5
- Wiltse-NY 3
- Briggs-Chi 3
- Ames-NY 3

Innings Pitched
- McGinnity-NY 408.0
- Jones-Bro 377.0
- Mathewson-NY 367.2
- Taylor-StL 352.0
- Willis-Bos 350.0

Fewest Hits/Game
- Brown-Chi 6.57
- Weimer-Chi 6.71
- McGinnity-NY 6.77
- Garvin-Bro 6.99
- Taylor-NY 7.02

Fewest BB/Game
- Hahn-Cin 1.06
- Phillippe-Pit 1.40
- Nichols-StL 1.42
- Kellum-Cin 1.84
- McFarland-StL 1.87

Strikeouts
- Mathewson-NY 212
- Willis-Bos 196
- Weimer-Chi 177
- Pittinger-Bos 146
- McGinnity-NY 144

Strikeouts/Game
- Wiltse-NY 5.74
- Mathewson-NY 5.19
- Weimer-Chi 5.19
- Willis-Bos 5.04
- Phillippe-Pit 4.43

Ratio
- Brown-Chi 8.94
- McGinnity-NY 8.96
- Hahn-Cin 9.07
- Nichols-StL 9.17
- Mathewson-NY 9.50

Earned Run Average
- McGinnity-NY 1.61
- Garvin-Bro 1.68
- Brown-Chi 1.86
- Weimer-Chi 1.91
- Nichols-StL 2.02

Adjusted ERA
- McGinnity-NY 169
- Garvin-Bro 162
- Brown-Chi 142
- Hahn-Cin 142
- Weimer-Chi 139

Opponents' Batting Avg.
- Brown-Chi .199
- Weimer-Chi .204
- McGinnity-NY .206
- Taylor-NY .214
- Garvin-Bro .218

Opponents' On-Base Pct.
- Brown-Chi .253
- Nichols-StL .256
- McGinnity-NY .256
- Hahn-Cin .262
- Mathewson-NY .270

Starter Runs
- McGinnity-NY 50.6
- Mathewson-NY 28.4
- Weimer-Chi 28.0
- Nichols-StL 25.0
- Hahn-Cin 22.2

Adjusted Starter Runs
- McGinnity-NY 50.3
- Mathewson-NY 28.1
- Hahn-Cin 26.6
- Weimer-Chi 26.3
- Nichols-StL 24.0

Clutch Pitching Index
- Garvin-Bro 153
- O'Neill-StL 131
- Briggs-Chi 128
- Jones-Bro 117
- Mitchell-Phi-Bro 116

Relief Runs

Adjusted Relief Runs

Relief Ranking

Total Pitcher Index
- McGinnity-NY 5.6
- Mathewson-NY 4.7
- Flaherty-Pit 3.4
- Hahn-Cin 3.1
- Weimer-Chi 3.0

Total Baseball Ranking
- McGinnity-NY 5.6
- Wagner-Pit 4.9
- Mathewson-NY 4.7
- Thomas-Phi 4.2
- Leach-Pit 4.0

TEAM	G	W	L	PCT	GB	R	OR	AB	H	2B	3B	HR	BB	SO	AVG	OBP	SLG	OPS	OPS+	BR	BR+	PF	CHI	RC	SB	CS	SBA	SBR
BOS	157	95	59	.617		608	**466**	5231	1294	194	**105**	26	347	570	.247	.301	.340	641	102	42	10	106	101	597	101			
NY	155	92	59	.609	1.5	598	526	5220	**1354**	195	91	27	312	**548**	.259	**.308**	.347	655	107	69	41	105	96	640	163			
CHI	156	89	65	.578	6	600	482	5027	1217	193	68	14	**373**	586	.242	.300	.316	616	104	4	27	96	**109**	578	**216**			
CLE	154	86	65	.570	7.5	**647**	482	5152	1340	**225**	90	27	307	714	**.260**	**.308**	**.354**	**662**	**116**	**78**	**84**	99	103	**650**	178			
PHI	155	81	70	.536	12.5	557	503	5088	1266	197	77	**31**	313	605	.249	.298	.336	634	101	28	0	105	98	579	137			
STL	156	65	87	.428	29	481	604	5291	1266	153	53	10	332	609	.239	.291	.294	585	96	-52	-18	94	94	526	150			
DET	162	62	90	.408	32	505	627	5321	1231	154	69	11	344	635	.231	.282	.292	574	90	-75	-59	97	102	502	112			
WAS	157	38	113	.252	55.5	437	743	5149	1170	171	57	10	283	759	.227	.275	.288	563	84	-94	-87	98	97	475	150			
TOT	626					4433		41479	10138	1482	610	156	2611	5026	.245	.296	.321	616							1207			

TEAM	CG	SH	SV	IP	H	H/G	HR	BB	SO	RAT	ERA	ERA+	OAV	OOB	PR	PR+	PF	CPI	FA	E	DP	FW	PW	BW	SBW	DIF
BOS	**148**	21	1	1406	1208	7.8	31	**233**	612	**9.5**	**2.12**	**126**	.233	**.270**	**75**	**84**	103	101	.962	242	83	1.6	**9.4**	1.2		6.0
NY	123	15	1	1380[2]	1180	7.7	29	311	684	10.0	2.57	106	.232	.282	4	21	104	90	.958	275	90	-.8	2.4	4.6		10.4
CHI	134	**26**	**3**	1380	1161	**7.6**	13	303	550	9.9	2.31	107	**.229**	.279	45	24	95	93	**.964**	**238**	95	**1.8**	2.7	3.1		4.6
CLE	141	20	0	1356[2]	1273	8.5	**10**	285	627	10.6	2.23	114	.249	.294	56	48	98	**116**	.959	255	86	.4	5.4	**9.4**		-4.6
PHI	136	**26**	0	1361[1]	**1149**	**7.6**	13	366	**887**	10.5	2.35	114	.230	.291	38	48	103	100	.959	250	67	.9	5.4	.0		-.6
STL	135	13	1	1410	1335	8.6	25	333	577	11.1	2.83	88	.251	.303	-36	-58	96	100	.960	267	78	-.1	-6.4	-2.0		-2.3
DET	143	15	0	1430	1345	8.5	16	433	556	11.7	2.77	92	.250	.314	-27	-36	98	106	.959	273	92	.1	-4.0	-6.5		-3.4
WAS	137	7	**3**	1359[2]	1487	9.9	19	347	533	12.6	3.63	73	.279	.330	-155	-142	102	99	.951	314	**97**	-3.1	-15.8	-9.7		-8.7
TOT	1097	143	9	11084[1]		8.3				10.7	2.60		.245	.296					.960	2114	688					

Runs
Dougherty-Bos-NY . 113
Flick-Cle 97
Bradley-Cle 94
Lajoie-Cle 92

Hits
Lajoie-Cle 208
Keeler-NY 186
Bradley-Cle 183
Dougherty-Bos-NY . 181
Flick-Cle 177

Doubles
Lajoie-Cle 49
Collins-Bos 33
Bradley-Cle 32

Triples
Stahl-Bos 19
Freeman-Bos 19
Cassidy-Was 19
Murphy-Phi 17
Flick-Cle 17

Home Runs
Davis-Phi 10
Murphy-Phi 7
Freeman-Bos 7

Total Bases
Lajoie-Cle 302
Flick-Cle 260
Bradley-Cle 249
Freeman-Bos 246

Runs Batted In
Lajoie-Cle 102
Freeman-Bos 84
Bradley-Cle 83
Anderson-NY 82

Runs Produced
Lajoie-Cle 189
Bradley-Cle 171
Parent-Bos 156
Collins-Bos 149
Murphy-Phi 148

Bases On Balls
Barrett-Det 79
Burkett-StL 78
Hartsel-Phi 75
Selbach-Was-Bos . . . 72
Lush-Cle 72

Batting Average
Lajoie-Cle 376
Keeler-NY 343
Davis-Phi 309
Flick-Cle 306
Bradley-Cle 300

On-Base Percentage
Lajoie-Cle 413
Keeler-NY 390
Flick-Cle 371
Stahl-Bos 366
Burkett-StL 363

Slugging Average
Lajoie-Cle 546
Davis-Phi 490
Flick-Cle 449
Murphy-Phi 440
Hickman-Cle-Det . . .437

On-Base Plus Slugging
Lajoie-Cle 959
Flick-Cle 820
Keeler-NY 799
Stahl-Bos 782
Murphy-Phi 760

Adjusted OPS
Lajoie-Cle 204
Flick-Cle 160
Keeler-NY 146
Stahl-Bos 139
Hickman-Cle-Det . . . 137

Batter Runs
Lajoie-Cle 61.5
Flick-Cle 38.7
Keeler-NY 32.7
Stahl-Bos 32.7
Davis-Phi 27.5

Adjusted Batter Runs
Lajoie-Cle 62.6
Flick-Cle 39.6
Keeler-NY 28.6
Stahl-Bos 27.5
Burkett-StL 24.7

Clutch Hitting Index
Callahan-Chi 132
Wallace-StL 130
Tannehill-Chi 129
Bradley-Cle 126
Anderson-NY 124

Runs Created
Lajoie-Cle 141
Flick-Cle 115
Keeler-NY 100
Stahl-Bos 99
Bradley-Cle 96

Total Average
Lajoie-Cle 1.061
Flick-Cle 891
Keeler-NY 798
Stahl-Bos 782
Murphy-Phi 741

Stolen Bases
Flick-Cle 38
Bay-Cle 38
Heidrick-StL 35
Davis-Chi 32
Conroy-NY 30

Stolen Base Average

Stolen Base Runs

Fielding Runs
Tannehill-Chi 27.8
Davis-Chi 16.8
Williams-NY 16.8
Carr-Det-Cle 15.8
Elberfeld-NY 15.3

Total Player Rating
Lajoie-Cle 7.0
Flick-Cle 4.7
Bradley-Cle 3.9
Murphy-Phi 3.6
Davis-Chi 3.5

Wins
Chesbro-NY 41
Young-Bos 26
Plank-Phi 26
Waddell-Phi 25

Win Percentage
Chesbro-NY 774
Tannehill-Bos 656
Smith-Chi 640
Bernhard-Cle 639
Dinneen-Bos 622

Games
Chesbro-NY 55
Powell-NY 47
Waddell-Phi 46
Patten-Was 45
Mullin-Det 45

Complete Games
Chesbro-NY 48
Mullin-Det 42
Young-Bos 40
Waddell-Phi 39
Powell-NY 38

Shutouts
Young-Bos 10
Waddell-Phi 8
White-Chi 7
Plank-Phi 7
Mullin-Det 7

Saves
Patten-Was 3

Innings Pitched
Chesbro-NY 454.2
Powell-NY 390.1
Waddell-Phi 383.0
Mullin-Det 382.1
Young-Bos 380.0

Fewest Hits/Game
Chesbro-NY 6.69
Owen-Chi 6.94
Smith-Chi 6.98
Gibson-Bos 7.12
Waddell-Phi 7.21

Fewest BB/Game
Young-Bos 69
Tannehill-Bos 1.05
Patterson-Chi 1.31
Joss-Cle 1.40
Altrock-Chi 1.41

Strikeouts
Waddell-Phi 349
Chesbro-NY 239
Powell-NY 202
Plank-Phi 201
Young-Bos 200

Strikeouts/Game
Waddell-Phi 8.20
Bender-Phi 6.58
Moore-Cle 5.49
Plank-Phi 5.06
Glade-StL 4.86

Ratio
Young-Bos 8.53
Chesbro-NY 8.57
Owen-Chi 9.00
Joss-Cle 9.22
Dinneen-Bos 9.33

Earned Run Average
Joss-Cle 1.59
Waddell-Phi 1.62
Hess-Cle 1.67
White-Chi 1.78
Chesbro-NY 1.82

Adjusted ERA
Waddell-Phi 165
Joss-Cle 159
Chesbro-NY 149
White-Chi 138
Young-Bos 136

Opponents' Batting Avg.
Chesbro-NY 208
Owen-Chi 214
Smith-Chi 215
Gibson-Bos 219
Waddell-Phi 221

Opponents' On-Base Pct.
Young-Bos 251
Chesbro-NY 252
Owen-Chi 261
Joss-Cle 266
Dinneen-Bos 268

Starter Runs
Waddell-Phi 41.5
Chesbro-NY 39.2
Young-Bos 26.6
Owen-Chi 22.9
Joss-Cle 21.5

Adjusted Starter Runs
Waddell-Phi 43.6
Chesbro-NY 43.1
Young-Bos 29.0
Joss-Cle 20.7
Plank-Phi 19.7

Clutch Pitching Index
White-Chi 153
Siever-StL 134
Bernhard-Cle 130
Waddell-Phi 126
Donahue-Cle 118

Relief Runs

Adjusted Relief Runs

Relief Ranking

Total Pitcher Index
Chesbro-NY 6.7
Waddell-Phi 4.7
Owen-Chi 3.7
Mullin-Det 3.2
Tannehill-Bos 3.0

Total Baseball Ranking
Lajoie-Cle 7.0
Chesbro-NY 6.7
Waddell-Phi 4.7
Flick-Cle 4.7
Bradley-Cle 3.9

TEAM	G	W	L	PCT	GB	R	OR	AB	H	2B	3B	HR	BB	SO	AVG	OBP	SLG	OPS	OPS+	BR	BR+	PF	CHI	RC	SB	CS	SBA	SBR
NY	155	105	48	.686		**780**	505	5094	1392	**191**	88	**39**	**517**		**.273**	**.351**	**.368**	**719**	**119**	**143**	**127**	102	99	**796**	**291**			
PIT	155	96	57	.627	9	692	570	5213	1385	190	91	22	382		.266	.320	.350	670	104	38	21	103	102	683	202			
CHI	155	92	61	.601	13	667	**442**	5108	1249	157	82	12	448		.245	.313	.314	627	90	-30	-53	104	**109**	625	267			
PHI	155	83	69	.546	21.5	708	603	5243	1362	187	82	16	406		.260	.318	.336	654	106	13	38	96	107	655	180			
CIN	155	79	74	.516	26	736	698	5205	**1401**	160	**101**	27	434		.269	.332	.354	686	101	74	4	111	102	710	181			
STL	154	58	96	.377	47.5	535	734	5066	1254	140	85	20	391		.248	.307	.321	628	97	-36	-17	97	92	576	162			
BOS	156	51	103	.331	54.5	468	733	5190	1217	148	52	17	302		.234	.284	.293	577	80	-135	-124	98	96	491	132			
BRO	155	48	104	.316	56.5	506	807	5100	1255	154	60	29	327		.246	.297	.317	614	97	-66	-21	93	91	564	186			
TOT	620					5092		41219	10515	1327	641	182	3207	4462	.256	.316	.332	647							1601			

TEAM	CG	SH	SV	IP	H	H/G	HR	BB	SO	RAT	ERA	ERA+	OAV	OOB	PR	PR+	PF	CPI	FA	E	DP	FW	PW	BW	SBW	DIF
NY	117	18	**15**	1370	1160	7.7	25	**364**	**760**	10.3	2.40	122	.229	**.284**	91	82	98	92	.960	258	93	2.3	8.6	**13.3**		4.5
PIT	113	12	6	1382[2]	1270	8.3	**12**	389	512	11.2	2.87	104	.248	.308	20	16	100	95	.961	255	112	2.5	1.7	2.2		13.2
CHI	133	**23**	2	1407[1]	**1135**	**7.3**	14	385	627	**10.1**	**2.05**	**146**	**.224**	.286	**149**	**145**	99	105	**.962**	**248**	99	**3.0**	**15.1**	-5.5		3.1
PHI	119	12	5	1398[2]	1303	8.4	21	411	516	11.5	2.82	104	.252	.316	28	13	97	104	.957	275	99	1.3	1.4	4.0		.5
CIN	119	10	2	1365[2]	1409	9.3	22	439	547	12.6	3.02	109	.272	.335	-3	38	110	**116**	.953	310	**122**	-1.0	4.0	.5		-.8
STL	135	10	2	1347[2]	1431	9.6	28	367	411	12.4	3.59	83	.276	.329	-89	-93	99	97	.957	274	83	1.2	-9.6	-1.7		-8.7
BOS	**139**	14	0	1383	1390	9.1	36	433	533	12.2	3.53	88	.265	.326	-81	-66	103	95	.951	325	89	-1.8	-6.8	-12.8		-4.4
BRO	125	7	3	1347	1416	9.5	24	476	556	13.1	3.76	77	.274	.343	-114	-137	96	98	.937	408	101	-7.2	-14.2	-2.1		-4.3
TOT	1000	106	35	11002		8.7				11.7	3.00		.256	.316					.955	2353	798					

Runs
Donlin-NY 124
Thomas-Phi 118
Huggins-Cin 117
Wagner-Pit 114

Hits
Seymour-Cin 219
Donlin-NY 216
Wagner-Pit 199
Barry-Chi-Cin 182
Magee-Phi 180

Doubles
Seymour-Cin 40
Titus-Phi 36
Wagner-Pit 32
Donlin-NY 31
Ritchey-Pit 29

Triples
Seymour-Cin 21
Mertes-NY 17
Magee-Phi 17
Smoot-StL 16
Donlin-NY 16

Home Runs
Odwell-Cin 9
Seymour-Cin 8
Lumley-Bro 7
Donlin-NY 7
Dahlen-NY 7

Total Bases
Seymour-Cin 325
Donlin-NY 300
Wagner-Pit 277
Magee-Phi 253
Titus-Phi 239

Runs Batted In
Seymour-Cin 121
Mertes-NY 108
Wagner-Pit 101
Magee-Phi 98
Titus-Phi 89

Runs Produced
Wagner-Pit 209
Seymour-Cin 208
Donlin-NY 197
Magee-Phi 193
Titus-Phi 186

Bases On Balls
Huggins-Cin 103
Slagle-Chi 97
Thomas-Phi 93
Chance-Chi 78
Titus-Phi 69

Batting Average
Seymour-Cin .377
Wagner-Pit .363
Donlin-NY .356
Beaumont-Pit .328
Thomas-Phi .317

On-Base Percentage
Chance-Chi .450
Seymour-Cin .429
Wagner-Pit .427
Thomas-Phi .417
Donlin-NY .413

Slugging Average
Seymour-Cin .559
Wagner-Pit .505
Donlin-NY .495
Titus-Phi .436
Grady-StL .434

On-Base Plus Slugging
Seymour-Cin 988
Wagner-Pit 932
Donlin-NY 908
Chance-Chi 883
Titus-Phi 834

Adjusted OPS
Seymour-Cin 175
Wagner-Pit 173
Donlin-NY 166
Chance-Chi 157
Titus-Phi 154

Batter Runs
Seymour-Cin 64.8
Wagner-Pit 52.3
Donlin-NY 51.3
Chance-Chi 37.2
Titus-Phi 34.7

Adjusted Batter Runs
Seymour-Cin 51.5
Wagner-Pit 49.4
Donlin-NY 48.7
Titus-Phi 38.7
Chance-Chi 33.8

Clutch Hitting Index
Mertes-NY 139
Dahlen-NY 136
Wolverton-Bos 132
Corcoran-Cin 131
Courtney-Phi 131

Runs Created
Seymour-Cin 153
Wagner-Pit 147
Donlin-NY 142
Magee-Phi 111
Mertes-NY 103

Total Average
Wagner-Pit 1.132
Chance-Chi 1.131
Seymour-Cin 1.102
Donlin-NY 1.003
McGann-NY .898

Stolen Bases
Maloney-Chi 59
Devlin-NY 59
Wagner-Pit 57
Mertes-NY 52
Magee-Phi 48

Stolen Base Average

Stolen Base Runs

Fielding Runs
Huggins-Cin 36.2
Gilbert-NY 25.4
Tenney-Bos 22.2
Wagner-Pit 20.3
Dahlen-NY 19.8

Total Player Rating
Wagner-Pit 7.5
Seymour-Cin 5.7
Huggins-Cin 4.6
Thomas-Phi 4.5
Titus-Phi 4.1

Wins
Mathewson-NY 31
Pittinger-Phi 23
Ames-NY 22
McGinnity-NY 21

Win Percentage
Leever-Pit .800
Mathewson-NY .775
Ames-NY .733
Wiltse-NY .714
Lynch-Pit .680

Games
Pittinger-Phi 46
McGinnity-NY 46
Young-Bos 43
Mathewson-NY 43
Overall-Cin 42

Complete Games
Young-Bos 41
Willis-Bos 36
Fraser-Bos 35
Taylor-StL 34

Shutouts
Mathewson-NY 8
Young-Bos 7
Reulbach-Chi 5
Phillippe-Pit 5
Briggs-Chi 5

Saves
Elliott-NY 6
Wiltse-NY 3
McGinnity-NY 3
Mathewson-NY 3

Innings Pitched
Young-Bos 378.0
Willis-Bos 342.0
Mathewson-NY 338.2
Pittinger-Phi 337.1
Fraser-Bos 334.1

Fewest Hits/Game
Reulbach-Chi 6.42
Mathewson-NY 6.70
Lundgren-Chi 7.02
Wicker-Chi 7.03
Wiltse-NY 7.22

Fewest BB/Game
Phillippe-Pit 1.55
Brown-Chi 1.59
Young-Bos 1.69
Mathewson-NY 1.70
McGinnity-NY 1.99

Strikeouts
Mathewson-NY 206
Ames-NY 198
Overall-Cin 173
Ewing-Cin 164
Young-Bos 156

Strikeouts/Game
Ames-NY 6.78
Wiltse-NY 5.48
Mathewson-NY 5.47
Overall-Cin 4.90
Scanlan-Bro 4.87

Ratio
Mathewson-NY 8.42
Reulbach-Chi 9.23
Phillippe-Pit 9.45
Wicker-Chi 9.46
Brown-Chi 9.54

Earned Run Average
Mathewson-NY 1.28
Reulbach-Chi 1.42
Wicker-Chi 2.02
Briggs-Chi 2.14
Brown-Chi 2.17

Adjusted ERA
Mathewson-NY 229
Reulbach-Chi 209
Wicker-Chi 147
Briggs-Chi 139
Brown-Chi 137

Opponents' Batting Avg.
Reulbach-Chi .201
Mathewson-NY .205
Wiltse-NY .219
Lundgren-Chi .220
Wicker-Chi .221

Opponents' On-Base Pct.
Mathewson-NY .245
Reulbach-Chi .266
Brown-Chi .271
Phillippe-Pit .274
Wicker-Chi .276

Starter Runs
Mathewson-NY 64.6
Reulbach-Chi 50.9
Phillippe-Pit 24.7
Sparks-Phi 23.3
Brown-Chi 22.8

Adjusted Starter Runs
Mathewson-NY 63.4
Reulbach-Chi 50.6
Phillippe-Pit 24.7
Ewing-Cin 24.6
Brown-Chi 22.3

Clutch Pitching Index
Chech-Cin 133
Duggleby-Phi 126
Overall-Cin 119
Briggs-Chi 119
Case-Pit 115

Relief Runs

Adjusted Relief Runs

Relief Ranking

Total Pitcher Index
Mathewson-NY 9.9
Reulbach-Chi 4.9
Ewing-Cin 2.5
Brown-Chi 2.4
Wiltse-NY 2.4

Total Baseball Ranking
Mathewson-NY 9.9
Wagner-Pit 7.5
Seymour-Cin 5.7
Reulbach-Chi 4.9
Huggins-Cin 4.6

TEAM	G	W	L	PCT	GB	R	OR	AB	H	2B	3B	HR	BB	SO	AVG	OBP	SLG	OPS	OPS+	BR	BR+	PF	CHI	RC	SB	CS	SBA	SBR
PHI	152	92	56	.622		**623**	488	5146	1310	**256**	51	24	376	644	**.255**	**.310**	**.338**	**648**	**109**	**60**	**49**	102	98	**632**	190			
CHI	158	92	60	.605	2	612	**451**	5114	1213	200	55	11	439	613	.237	.305	.304	609	103	0	25	96	104	577	194			
DET	154	79	74	.516	15.5	512	604	4971	1209	190	54	13	375	583	.243	.302	.311	613	99	1	-3	101	92	540	129			
BOS	153	78	74	.513	16	579	565	5049	1179	165	69	**29**	**486**	553	.234	.305	.311	616	100	14	8	101	99	550	131			
CLE	155	76	78	.494	19	564	587	5166	**1318**	211	**72**	18	286	712	**.255**	.301	.334	635	106	33	25	101	94	608	188			
NY	152	71	78	.477	21.5	586	621	4957	1228	163	61	23	360	**537**	.248	.307	.319	626	93	26	-33	111	101	580	**200**			
WAS	154	64	87	.424	29.5	559	623	5015	1121	193	68	22	298	824	.224	.274	.302	576	92	-70	-50	96	**115**	492	169			
STL	156	54	99	.353	40.5	512	608	5204	1205	153	49	16	362	639	.232	.288	.289	577	93	-64	-35	95	100	502	130			
TOT	617					4547		40622	9783	1531	479	156	2982	5105	.241	.300	.314	613							1331			

TEAM	CG	SH	SV	IP	H	H/G	HR	BB	SO	RAT	ERA	ERA+	OAV	OOB	PR	PR+	PF	CPI	FA	E	DP	FW	PW	BW	SBW	DIF
PHI	117	**19**	0	1383^{1}	**1137**	**7.4**	21	409	**895**	10.5	2.20	121	.227	.294	70	68	100	**110**	.957	265	64	.4	7.5	**5.4**		4.9
CHI	131	16	0	1427	1163	**7.4**	**11**	329	613	**9.7**	**1.99**	**124**	**.226**	**.277**	**105**	**78**	93	105	**.967**	**218**	**95**	**4.2**	**8.6**	2.8		.6
DET	124	17	1	1348	1226	8.2	**11**	474	578	11.7	2.84	96	.246	.318	-27	-18	103	104	.957	267	80	.5	-1.9	-.3		4.4
BOS	124	15	1	1356^{1}	1198	8.0	33	**292**	652	10.2	2.85	95	.238	.286	-29	-20	102	88	.953	296	75	-1.6	-2.1	.9		5.0
CLE	**140**	16	0	1363^{1}	1251	8.3	23	334	555	10.9	2.85	92	.245	.299	-30	-32	99	96	.963	233	84	2.8	-3.5	2.8		-3.0
NY	88	**19**	**4**	1353^{2}	1235	8.3	26	396	642	11.2	2.93	100	.246	.307	-42	-2	111	97	.952	293	88	-1.5	-.2	-3.6		1.9
WAS	118	12	1	1362^{1}	1250	8.3	12	385	539	11.3	2.87	92	.247	.308	-33	-36	100	98	.951	318	76	-2.9	-3.9	-5.4		1.0
STL	134	11	2	1384^{2}	1245	8.1	19	389	633	11.1	2.74	93	.243	.304	-14	-34	96	100	.955	296	78	-1.2	-3.7	-3.8		-13.6
TOT	976	125	9	10978^{2}		8.0				10.8	2.65		.241	.300					.957	2186	640					

Runs
Davis-Phi 93
Jones-Chi 91
Bay-Cle 90
Hartsel-Phi 88
Keeler-NY 81

Hits
Stone-StL 187
Davis-Phi 173
Crawford-Det 171
Keeler-NY 169
Bay-Cle 166

Doubles
Davis-Phi 47
Crawford-Det 38
Hickman-Det-Was 37
Seybold-Phi 37

Triples
Flick-Cle 18
Ferris-Bos 16
Turner-Cle 14
Stone-StL 13
Burkett-Bos 13

Home Runs
Davis-Phi 8
Stone-StL 7

Total Bases
Stone-StL 259
Davis-Phi 256
Crawford-Det 247
Hickman-Det-Was 232
Flick-Cle 231

Runs Batted In
Davis-Phi 83
L.Cross-Phi 77
Donahue-Chi 76
Crawford-Det 75
Turner-Cle 72

Runs Produced
Davis-Phi 168
Donahue-Chi 146
L.Cross-Phi 146
Crawford-Det 142
Murphy-Phi 136

Bases On Balls
Hartsel-Phi 121
Jones-Chi 73
Selbach-Bos 67
Burkett-Bos 67
Davis-Chi 60

Batting Average
Flick-Cle .308
Keeler-NY .302
Bay-Cle .301
Crawford-Det .297
Isbell-Chi .296

On-Base Percentage
Hartsel-Phi .409
Flick-Cle .383
Keeler-NY .357
Crawford-Det .357
Selbach-Bos .355

Slugging Average
Flick-Cle .462
Isbell-Chi .440
Crawford-Det .430
Davis-Phi .422
Stone-StL .410

On-Base Plus Slugging
Flick-Cle 845
Crawford-Det 786
Stone-StL 756
Davis-Phi 756
Hartsel-Phi 755

Adjusted OPS
Flick-Cle 165
Crawford-Det 148
Stone-StL 147
Hartsel-Phi 138
Davis-Phi 137

Batter Runs
Flick-Cle 38.6
Hartsel-Phi 32.9
Crawford-Det 31.0
Stone-StL 26.9
Davis-Phi 24.9

Adjusted Batter Runs
Flick-Cle 37.4
Stone-StL 32.3
Hartsel-Phi 31.2
Crawford-Det 30.3
Davis-Phi 23.4

Clutch Hitting Index
Gleason-StL 134
Donahue-Chi 131
L.Cross-Phi 128
Fultz-NY 121
Collins-Bos 116

Runs Created
Flick-Cle 106
Stone-StL 102
Davis-Phi 101
Crawford-Det 99
Hartsel-Phi 96

Total Average
Flick-Cle .945
Hartsel-Phi .885
Crawford-Det .797
Davis-Phi .776
Stone-StL .751

Stolen Bases
Hoffman-Phi 46
Fultz-NY 44
Stahl-Was 41
Hartsel-Phi 37

Stolen Base Average

Stolen Base Runs

Fielding Runs
Cassidy-Was 33.9
Tannehill-Chi 28.1
Wallace-StL 19.8
Davis-Chi 16.7
McIntyre-Det 16.5

Total Player Rating
Davis-Chi 4.3
Wallace-StL 4.1
Crawford-Det 4.0
Flick-Cle 3.5
Stone-StL 2.7

Wins
Waddell-Phi 27
Plank-Phi 24
Killian-Det 23
Altrock-Chi 23
Tannehill-Bos 22

Win Percentage
Waddell-Phi .730
Tannehill-Bos .710
Coakley-Phi .692
Plank-Phi .667
Altrock-Chi .657

Games
Waddell-Phi 46
Mullin-Det 44
Patten-Was 42
Owen-Chi 42

Complete Games
Plank-Phi 35
Mullin-Det 35
Howell-StL 35
Killian-Det 33
Owen-Chi 32

Shutouts
Killian-Det 8
Waddell-Phi 7
Tannehill-Bos 6
Orth-NY 6
Hughes-Was 6

Saves
Buchanan-StL 2

Innings Pitched
Mullin-Det 347.2
Plank-Phi 346.2
Owen-Chi 334.0
Waddell-Phi 328.2
Howell-StL 323.0

Fewest Hits/Game
Waddell-Phi 6.33
Smith-Chi 6.63
Young-Bos 6.96
Howell-StL 7.02
White-Chi 7.05

Fewest BB/Game
Young-Bos .84
Joss-Cle 1.45
Owen-Chi 1.51
Bernhard-Cle 1.76
Altrock-Chi 1.80

Strikeouts
Waddell-Phi 287
Young-Bos 210
Plank-Phi 210
Howell-StL 198
Smith-Chi 171

Strikeouts/Game
Waddell-Phi 7.86
Young-Bos 5.89
Bender-Phi 5.58
Howell-StL 5.52
Hogg-NY 5.49

Ratio
Young-Bos 8.03
Waddell-Phi 9.06
Owen-Chi 9.19
White-Chi 9.37
Joss-Cle 9.53

Earned Run Average
Waddell-Phi 1.48
White-Chi 1.76
Young-Bos 1.82
Coakley-Phi 1.84
Altrock-Chi 1.88

Adjusted ERA
Waddell-Phi 179
Young-Bos 147
Coakley-Phi 144
White-Chi 140
Chesbro-NY 133

Opponents' Batting Avg.
Waddell-Phi .200
Smith-Chi .208
Young-Bos .216
Howell-StL .217
White-Chi .218

Opponents' On-Base Pct.
Young-Bos .241
Waddell-Phi .264
Owen-Chi .267
White-Chi .270
Joss-Cle .274

Starter Runs
Waddell-Phi 42.7
Young-Bos 29.3
Altrock-Chi 26.9
White-Chi 25.6
Howell-StL 24.0

Adjusted Starter Runs
Waddell-Phi 42.7
Young-Bos 30.4
Coakley-Phi 23.1
Chesbro-NY 22.3
Altrock-Chi 21.8

Clutch Pitching Index
Coakley-Phi 142
Altrock-Chi 118
Waddell-Phi 116
Townsend-Was 115
Mullin-Det 113

Relief Runs

Adjusted Relief Runs

Relief Ranking

Total Pitcher Index
Howell-StL 5.0
Waddell-Phi 4.9
Young-Bos 3.2
Altrock-Chi 3.0
Joss-Cle 2.8

Total Baseball Ranking
Howell-StL 5.0
Waddell-Phi 4.9
Davis-Chi 4.3
Wallace-StL 4.1
Crawford-Det 4.0

TEAM	G	W	L	PCT	GB	R	OR	AB	H	2B	3B	HR	BB	SO	AVG	OBP	SLG	OPS	OPS+	BR	BR+	PF	CHI	RC	SB	CS	SBA	SBR
CHI	155	116	36	.763		**704**	**381**	5018	**1316**	181	**71**	20	448		**.262**	.328	**.339**	**667**	109	83	48	106	**109**	**695**	283			
NY	153	96	56	.632	20	625	509	4768	1217	162	53	15	**563**		.255	**.343**	.321	664	**112**	**92**	**78**	102	98	659	**288**			
PIT	154	93	60	.608	23.5	623	470	5030	1313	164	67	12	424		.261	.324	.327	651	105	55	29	104	102	625	162			
PHI	154	71	82	.464	45.5	528	564	4911	1183	**197**	47	12	432		.241	.307	.307	614	98	-10	-11	100	99	550	180			
BRO	153	66	86	.434	50	496	625	4897	1156	141	68	**25**	388		.236	.297	.308	605	103	-31	12	92	98	532	175			
CIN	155	64	87	.424	51.5	533	582	5025	1198	140	**71**	16	395		.238	.301	.304	605	91	-28	-50	104	101	545	170			
STL	154	52	98	.347	63	470	607	5075	1195	137	69	10	361		.235	.291	.296	587	93	-66	-45	96	97	498	110			
BOS	152	49	102	.325	66.5	408	649	4925	1115	136	43	16	356		.226	.286	.281	567	85	-96	-84	97	93	449	95			
TOT	615					4387		39649	9693	1258	489	126	3367	4537	.245	.310	.311	620							1463			

TEAM	CG	SH	SV	IP	H	H/G	HR	BB	SO	RAT	ERA	ERA+	OAV	OOB	PR	PR+	PF	CPI	FA	E	DP	FW	PW	BW	SBW	DIF
CHI	125	**30**	10	1388[1]	**1018**	**6.6**	**12**	446	**702**	**9.9**	**1.76**	**150**	**.207**	**.280**	**135**	**135**	100	100	**.969**	**194**	100	**4.6**	**15.1**	5.4		15.2
NY	105	19	**18**	1334[1]	1207	8.2	13	394	639	11.0	2.49	105	.241	.300	20	15	99	96	.963	233	84	1.8	1.7	**8.7**		7.9
PIT	116	27	2	1358	1234	8.2	13	**309**	532	10.6	2.22	120	.245	.294	62	69	102	**107**	.964	228	**109**	2.3	7.7	3.3		3.5
PHI	108	21	5	1354[1]	1201	8.0	18	436	500	11.4	2.58	101	.235	.304	7	0	99	94	.956	271	83	-.6	.0	-1.2		-3.6
BRO	119	22	11	1348[2]	1255	8.4	15	453	476	11.7	3.13	80	.249	.316	-76	-97	96	88	.955	283	73	-1.5	-10.7	1.4		1.0
CIN	126	12	5	1369[2]	1248	8.3	14	470	567	11.7	2.69	102	.250	.320	-10	5	105	105	.959	262	97	.1	.6	-5.5		-6.5
STL	118	4	2	1354	1246	8.3	17	479	559	11.9	3.05	86	.246	.318	-63	-65	100	91	.957	272	92	-.6	-7.2	-5.0		-10.0
BOS	**137**	10	0	1334[1]	1291	8.8	24	436	562	12.1	3.14	85	.261	.328	-76	-69	102	100	.947	337	102	-5.1	-7.6	-9.3		-4.3
TOT	954	145	53	10841[2]		8.1				11.3	2.63		.245	.310					.959	2080	740					

Runs
Wagner-Pit 103
Chance-Chi 103
Sheckard-Chi 90
Nealon-Pit 82

Hits
Steinfeldt-Chi 176
Wagner-Pit 175
Seymour-Cin-NY 165
Magee-Phi 159
Huggins-Cin 159

Doubles
Wagner-Pit 38
Magee-Phi 36
Bransfield-Phi 28
Steinfeldt-Chi 27
Sheckard-Chi 27

Triples
Schulte-Chi 13
Clarke-Pit 13
Nealon-Pit 12
Lumley-Bro 12

Home Runs
Jordan-Bro 12
Lumley-Bro 9
Seymour-Cin-NY 8
Schulte-Chi 7

Total Bases
Wagner-Pit 237
Steinfeldt-Chi 232
Lumley-Bro 231
Magee-Phi 229
Schulte-Chi 223

Runs Batted In
Steinfeldt-Chi 83
Nealon-Pit 83
Seymour-Cin-NY 80
Jordan-Bro 78

Runs Produced
Wagner-Pit 172
Chance-Chi 171
Nealon-Pit 162
Steinfeldt-Chi 161
Seymour-Cin-NY 142

Bases On Balls
Thomas-Phi 107
Bresnahan-NY 81
Titus-Phi 78
Dahlen-NY 76
Devlin-NY 74

Batting Average
Wagner-Pit .339
Steinfeldt-Chi .327
Lumley-Bro .324
Strang-NY .319
Chance-Chi .319

On-Base Percentage
Bresnahan-NY .419
Chance-Chi .419
Wagner-Pit .416
Devlin-NY .396
Steinfeldt-Chi .395

Slugging Average
Lumley-Bro .477
Wagner-Pit .459
Strang-NY .435
Steinfeldt-Chi .430
Chance-Chi .430

On-Base Plus Slugging
Wagner-Pit 875
Lumley-Bro 864
Chance-Chi 849
Steinfeldt-Chi 825
Devlin-NY 786

Adjusted OPS
Lumley-Bro 184
Wagner-Pit 166
Chance-Chi 156
Jordan-Bro 153
Steinfeldt-Chi 149

Batter Runs
Wagner-Pit 44.7
Chance-Chi 39.1
Lumley-Bro 37.2
Steinfeldt-Chi 36.1
Devlin-NY 29.1

Adjusted Batter Runs
Lumley-Bro 45.0
Wagner-Pit 40.4
Chance-Chi 33.8
Steinfeldt-Chi 30.8
Jordan-Bro 27.3

Clutch Hitting Index
Tinker-Chi 138
Nealon-Pit 134
Ritchey-Pit 128
Kelley-Cin 126
Shannon-StL-NY 125

Runs Created
Wagner-Pit 124
Chance-Chi 114
Steinfeldt-Chi 109
Lumley-Bro 107
Magee-Phi 102

Total Average
Chance-Chi 1.062
Wagner-Pit 1.050
Lumley-Bro .963
Devlin-NY .940
Bresnahan-NY .911

Stolen Bases
Chance-Chi 57
Magee-Phi 55
Devlin-NY 54
Wagner-Pit 53
Evers-Chi 49

Stolen Base Average

Stolen Base Runs

Fielding Runs
Devlin-NY 28.0
Brain-Bos 25.7
Wagner-Pit 23.8
Gilbert-NY 22.6
Huggins-Cin 21.5

Total Player Rating
Wagner-Pit 7.4
Devlin-NY 6.4
Lumley-Bro 4.4
Huggins-Cin 4.0
Bresnahan-NY 3.9

Wins
McGinnity-NY 27
Brown-Chi 26
Willis-Pit 23
Mathewson-NY 22
Leever-Pit 22

Win Percentage
Reulbach-Chi .826
Brown-Chi .813
Leever-Pit .759
Lundgren-Chi .739
Pfiester-Chi .714

Games
McGinnity-NY 45
Young-Bos 43
Sparks-Phi 42
Duggleby-Phi 42

Complete Games
Young-Bos 37
Pfeffer-Bos 33

Shutouts
Brown-Chi 9
Leifield-Pit 8

Saves
Ferguson-NY 7
Wiltse-NY 6
Stricklett-Bro 5

Innings Pitched
Young-Bos 358.1
McGinnity-NY 339.2
Willis-Pit 322.0
Sparks-Phi 316.2
Lindaman-Bos 307.1

Fewest Hits/Game
Reulbach-Chi 5.33
Pfiester-Chi 6.21
Brown-Chi 6.43
Beebe-Chi-StL 6.67
Lundgren-Chi 6.93

Fewest BB/Game
Phillippe-Pit 1.07
Leever-Pit 1.66
Sparks-Phi 1.76
Ewing-Cin 1.88
McGinnity-NY 1.88

Strikeouts
Beebe-Chi-StL 171
Pfeffer-Bos 158
Ames-NY 156
Pfiester-Chi 153

Strikeouts/Game
Ames-NY 6.90
Beebe-Chi-StL 6.67
Pfiester-Chi 5.49
Overall-Cin-Chi 5.05
Lush-Phi 4.84

Ratio
Brown-Chi 8.53
Pfiester-Chi 8.94
Sparks-Phi 8.98
Reulbach-Chi 9.66
Ewing-Cin 9.70

Earned Run Average
Brown-Chi 1.04
Pfiester-Chi 1.51
Reulbach-Chi 1.65
Willis-Pit 1.73
Leifield-Pit 1.87

Adjusted ERA
Brown-Chi 253
Pfiester-Chi 174
Reulbach-Chi 159
Willis-Pit 154
Leifield-Pit 143

Opponents' Batting Avg.
Reulbach-Chi .175
Pfiester-Chi .194
Brown-Chi .202
Beebe-Chi-StL .209
Sparks-Phi .211

Opponents' On-Base Pct.
Brown-Chi .252
Sparks-Phi .257
Pfiester-Chi .258
Phillippe-Pit .276
Reulbach-Chi .278

Starter Runs
Brown-Chi 48.9
Willis-Pit 31.9
Pfiester-Chi 31.1
Reulbach-Chi 23.6
Leifield-Pit 21.6

Adjusted Starter Runs
Brown-Chi 48.9
Willis-Pit 32.8
Pfiester-Chi 31.2
Reulbach-Chi 23.7
Leifield-Pit 22.3

Clutch Pitching Index
Willis-Pit 139
Lindaman-Bos 126
Brown-Chi 122
Leifield-Pit 120
Lush-Phi 114

Relief Runs
Ferguson-NY 3

Adjusted Relief Runs
Ferguson-NY 1

Relief Ranking
Ferguson-NY 0

Total Pitcher Index
Brown-Chi 6.8
Willis-Pit 4.5
Taylor-StL-Chi 2.9
Reulbach-Chi 2.8
Weimer-Cin 2.8

Total Baseball Ranking
Wagner-Pit 7.4
Brown-Chi 6.8
Devlin-NY 6.4
Willis-Pit 4.5
Lumley-Bro 4.4

TEAM	G	W	L	PCT	GB	R	OR	AB	H	2B	3B	HR	BB	SO	AVG	OBP	SLG	OPS	OPS+	BR	BR+	PF	CHI	RC	SB	CS	SBA	SBR
CHI	154	93	58	.616		570	**460**	4925	1133	152	52	7	**453**		.230	.301	.286	587	91	-47	-33	97	**110**	531	214			
NY	155	90	61	.596	3	640	543	5095	1354	166	**77**	17	331		.266	.316	.339	655	101	58	0	110	103	644	192			
CLE	157	89	64	.582	5	**663**	481	5425	**1514**	**240**	73	12	330		**.279**	**.325**	**.357**	**682**	**121**	**111**	**121**	99	93	**735**	203			
PHI	149	78	67	.538	12	561	539	4883	1206	213	49	**32**	385		.247	.308	.330	638	102	30	13	103	97	581	165			
STL	154	76	73	.510	16	560	499	5030	1244	145	60	20	366		.247	.304	.312	616	102	-6	19	96	101	579	221			
DET	151	71	78	.477	21	518	598	4930	1195	154	64	10	333		.242	.295	.306	601	91	-37	-50	103	102	539	206			
WAS	151	55	95	.367	37.5	519	665	4956	1180	144	65	26	306		.238	.289	.309	598	97	-44	-19	95	104	539	**233**			
BOS	155	49	105	.318	45.5	463	706	5168	1223	160	75	13	298		.237	.284	.304	588	89	-66	-65	100	93	503	99			
TOT	613					4494		40412	10049	1374	515	137	2802	4561	.249	.304	.319	621							1533			

TEAM	CG	SH	SV	IP	H	H/G	HR	BB	SO	RAT	ERA	ERA+	OAV	OOB	PR	PR+	PF	CPI	FA	E	DP	FW	PW	BW	SBW	DIF
CHI	117	**32**	4	1375[1]	1212	8.0	11	**255**	543	**9.9**	2.14	119	.239	**.280**	85	66	94	103	.963	243	80	1.9	7.3	-3.6		12.1
NY	99	18	5	1357[2]	1236	8.2	21	351	605	10.9	2.78	107	.246	.301	-13	25	110	95	.957	272	69	.2	2.8	.0		11.7
CLE	**133**	27	4	1412[2]	1197	7.7	16	365	530	10.3	**2.09**	**125**	.232	.289	**94**	**87**	97	110	**.967**	**217**	**111**	**3.9**	**9.6**	**13.4**		-14.1
PHI	107	19	4	1322	1135	7.8	**9**	425	**749**	11.1	2.61	105	.236	.305	13	16	101	98	.956	267	86	-.2	1.8	1.5		2.6
STL	**133**	17	5	1357[2]	**1132**	**7.6**	14	314	558	10.0	2.23	116	**.230**	.284	70	56	96	98	.954	290	80	-1.1	6.2	2.1		-5.6
DET	128	7	4	1334[1]	1398	9.5	14	389	469	12.5	3.07	90	.272	.330	-55	-42	103	**111**	.959	260	86	.5	-4.6	-5.4		6.2
WAS	115	13	1	1322[2]	1331	9.1	15	451	558	12.5	3.26	81	.265	.331	-83	-93	98	102	.955	279	78	-.7	-10.2	-2.0		-6.9
BOS	124	6	**6**	1382	1360	8.9	37	285	549	11.0	3.42	81	.262	.306	-111	-103	102	87	.949	335	84	-3.8	-11.3	-7.1		-5.6
TOT	956	139	33	10864[1]		8.3				11.0	2.69		.249	.304					.958	2163	674					

Runs
Flick-Cle 98
Keeler-NY 96
Hartsel-Phi 96
Davis-Phi 94
Stone-StL 91

Hits
Lajoie-Cle 214
Stone-StL 208
Flick-Cle 194
Chase-NY 193
Keeler-NY 180

Doubles
Lajoie-Cle 48
Davis-Phi 42
Flick-Cle 34
Murphy-Phi 28
Turner-Cle 27

Triples
Flick-Cle 22
Stone-StL 20
Crawford-Det 16
Ferris-Bos 13

Home Runs
Davis-Phi 12
Hickman-Was 9
Stone-StL 6
Seybold-Phi 5

Total Bases
Stone-StL 291
Lajoie-Cle 280
Flick-Cle 275
Davis-Phi 253
Chase-NY 236

Runs Batted In
Davis-Phi 96
Lajoie-Cle 91
Davis-Chi 80
Williams-NY 77
Chase-NY 76

Runs Produced
Lajoie-Cle 179
Davis-Phi 178
Chase-NY 160
Flick-Cle 159
Stone-StL 156

Bases On Balls
Hartsel-Phi 88
Jones-Chi 83
E.Hahn-NY-Chi 72
Wallace-StL 58
McIntyre-Det 56

Batting Average
Stone-StL .358
Lajoie-Cle .355
Chase-NY .323
Congalton-Cle .320
Seybold-Phi .316

On-Base Percentage
Stone-StL .417
Lajoie-Cle .392
Flick-Cle .372
Hartsel-Phi .363
Davis-Phi .355

Slugging Average
Stone-StL .501
Lajoie-Cle .465
Davis-Phi .459
Flick-Cle .441
Hickman-Was .421

On-Base Plus Slugging
Stone-StL 918
Lajoie-Cle 857
Davis-Phi 815
Flick-Cle 813
Crawford-Det 747

Adjusted OPS
Stone-StL 195
Lajoie-Cle 170
Flick-Cle 156
Davis-Phi 150
Hickman-Was 135

Batter Runs
Stone-StL 57.8
Lajoie-Cle 44.9
Flick-Cle 38.4
Davis-Phi 33.1
Seybold-Phi 21.1

Adjusted Batter Runs
Stone-StL 63.4
Lajoie-Cle 46.4
Flick-Cle 39.9
Davis-Phi 30.3
Hemphill-StL 19.8

Clutch Hitting Index
Davis-Chi 154
Coughlin-Det 134
Stahl-Was 133
Wallace-StL 131
Williams-NY 130

Runs Created
Stone-StL 141
Lajoie-Cle 122
Flick-Cle 121
Davis-Phi 101
Chase-NY 95

Total Average
Stone-StL 1.032
Flick-Cle .872
Lajoie-Cle .866
Davis-Phi .846
Hartsel-Phi .753

Stolen Bases
Flick-Cle 39
Anderson-Was 39
Isbell-Chi 37
Altizer-Was 37
Donahue-Chi 36

Stolen Base Average

Stolen Base Runs

Fielding Runs
Tannehill-Chi 39.3
Lajoie-Cle 30.9
Turner-Cle 22.6
Schlafly-Was 14.8
McIntyre-Det 11.9

Total Player Rating
Lajoie-Cle 8.4
Stone-StL 5.7
Turner-Cle 4.6
Davis-Phi 3.0
Schlafly-Was 2.9

Wins
Orth-NY 27
Chesbro-NY 23
Rhoads-Cle 22
Owen-Chi 22

Win Percentage
Plank-Phi .760
White-Chi .750
Joss-Cle .700
Rhoads-Cle .688
Owen-Chi .629

Games
Chesbro-NY 49
Orth-NY 45
Waddell-Phi 43
Hess-Cle 43
Owen-Chi 42

Complete Games
Orth-NY 36
Mullin-Det 35
Hess-Cle 33
Rhoads-Cle 31

Shutouts
Walsh-Chi 10
Joss-Cle 9
Waddell-Phi 8

Saves
Hess-Cle 3
Bender-Phi 3

Innings Pitched
Orth-NY 338.2
Hess-Cle 333.2
Mullin-Det 330.0
Chesbro-NY 325.0
Rhoads-Cle 315.0

Fewest Hits/Game
Pelty-StL 6.53
White-Chi 6.57
Walsh-Chi 6.95
Joss-Cle 7.02
Powell-StL 7.23

Fewest BB/Game
Young-Bos .78
Altrock-Chi 1.31
Joss-Cle 1.37
White-Chi 1.56
Jacobson-StL 1.57

Strikeouts
Waddell-Phi 196
Falkenberg-Was 178
Walsh-Chi 171
Hess-Cle 167
Bender-Phi 159

Strikeouts/Game
Waddell-Phi 6.47
Bender-Phi 6.00
Walsh-Chi 5.53
Falkenberg-Was 5.36
Powell-StL 4.87

Ratio
White-Chi 8.33
Joss-Cle 8.49
Walsh-Chi 9.05
Pelty-StL 9.18
Powell-StL 9.55

Earned Run Average
White-Chi 1.52
Pelty-StL 1.59
Joss-Cle 1.72
Powell-StL 1.77
Rhoads-Cle 1.80

Adjusted ERA
White-Chi 167
Pelty-StL 163
Joss-Cle 152
Powell-StL 146
Rhoads-Cle 145

Opponents' Batting Avg.
Pelty-StL .206
White-Chi .207
Walsh-Chi .217
Joss-Cle .218
Powell-StL .223

Opponents' On-Base Pct.
White-Chi .249
Joss-Cle .252
Walsh-Chi .265
Pelty-StL .267
Powell-StL .275

Starter Runs
Pelty-StL 31.9
Hess-Cle 31.7
Rhoads-Cle 31.1
Joss-Cle 30.3
White-Chi 28.6

Adjusted Starter Runs
Pelty-StL 30.0
Hess-Cle 29.8
Rhoads-Cle 29.4
Joss-Cle 28.8
White-Chi 26.4

Clutch Pitching Index
Rhoads-Cle 126
Siever-Det 125
Hess-Cle 124
Smith-Was 121
Donahue-Det 121

Relief Runs

Adjusted Relief Runs

Relief Ranking

Total Pitcher Index
White-Chi 3.8
Joss-Cle 3.7
Pelty-StL 3.5
Orth-NY 3.5
Hess-Cle 3.4

Total Baseball Ranking
Lajoie-Cle 8.4
Stone-StL 5.7
Turner-Cle 4.6
Joss-Cle 3.8
White-Chi 3.7

TEAM	G	W	L	PCT	GB	R	OR	AB	H	2B	3B	HR	BB	SO	AVG	OBP	SLG	OPS	OPS+	BR	BR+	PF	CHI	RC	SB	CS	SBA	SBR
CHI	155	107	45	.704		574	**390**	4892	1224	**162**	48	13	435		.250	.318	.311	629	98	25	-8	106	104	596	235			
PIT	157	91	63	.591	17	**634**	510	4957	**1261**	133	78	19	469		**.254**	.325	**.324**	**649**	**109**	62	**54**	101	**106**	**645**	**264**			
PHI	149	83	64	.565	21.5	514	476	4725	1113	**162**	65	12	424		.236	.304	.305	609	99	-11	-4	99	105	514	154			
NY	155	82	71	.536	25.5	574	510	4874	1222	160	48	**23**	**516**		.251	**.331**	.317	648	107	**68**	49	103	96	617	205			
BRO	153	65	83	.439	40	446	522	4895	1135	142	63	18	336		.232	.287	.298	585	98	-62	-22	92	98	488	121			
CIN	156	66	87	.431	41.5	526	519	4966	1226	126	**90**	15	372		.247	.304	.318	622	98	3	-18	104	99	564	158			
BOS	152	58	90	.392	47	502	652	5020	1222	142	61	22	413		.243	.308	.309	617	100	2	4	100	94	545	118			
STL	155	52	101	.340	55.5	419	610	5008	1163	121	52	18	312		.232	.283	.288	571	88	-87	-72	97	96	474	125			
TOT	616					4189		39337	9566	1148	505	140	3277	4217	.244	.308	.309	616							1380			

TEAM	CG	SH	SV	IP	H	H/G	HR	BB	SO	RAT	ERA	ERA+	OAV	OOB	PR	PR+	PF	CPI	FA	E	DP	FW	PW	BW	SBW	DIF
CHI	114	**32**	8	1373[1]	**1054**	**7.0**	**11**	402	586	**9.8**	**1.74**	**144**	**.216**	**.281**	**112**	**114**	101	101	**.967**	**211**	110	**3.1**	**13.0**	-.9		15.9
PIT	111	24	5	1363	1207	8.0	12	**368**	497	10.8	2.30	106	.241	.299	25	19	99	99	.959	256	75	.3	2.2	**6.2**		5.5
PHI	110	21	4	1299[1]	1095	7.6	13	422	499	10.9	2.44	99	.233	.304	5	-3	98	94	.957	256	104	-.6	-.3	-.4		11.0
NY	109	22	**13**	1371	1219	8.1	24	369	**655**	10.7	2.45	101	.238	.294	2	1	100	90	.963	232	75	1.7	.2	5.6		-1.8
BRO	125	20	1	1356[1]	1218	8.1	16	463	479	11.5	2.39	98	.249	.319	12	-9	95	113	.959	262	94	-.6	-1.0	-2.4		-4.8
CIN	118	10	2	1351[1]	1223	8.2	16	444	481	11.6	2.42	107	.251	.322	8	24	105	**114**	.963	227	118	2.1	2.8	-2.0		-13.2
BOS	121	9	2	1338[2]	1324	9.0	28	458	426	12.5	3.34	76	.268	.339	-129	-115	103	98	.961	249	**128**	.2	-13.0	.5		-3.5
STL	**127**	19	2	1365[2]	1212	8.0	20	500	594	11.7	2.70	93	.243	.318	-35	-32	101	98	.948	340	105	-5.7	-3.6	-8.1		-6.9
TOT	935	157	37	10818[2]		8.0				11.2	2.47		.244	.308					.960	2033	809					

Runs
Shannon-NY 104
Leach-Pit 102
Wagner-Pit 98
Clarke-Pit 97
Tenney-Bos 83

Hits
Beaumont-Bos 187
Wagner-Pit 180
Leach-Pit 166
Magee-Phi 165
Mitchell-Cin 163

Doubles
Wagner-Pit 38
Magee-Phi 28
Steinfeldt-Chi 25
Seymour-NY 25
Brain-Bos 24

Triples
Ganzel-Cin 16
Alperman-Bro 16
Wagner-Pit 14
Beaumont-Bos 14
Clarke-Pit 13

Home Runs
Brain-Bos 10
Lumley-Bro 9
Murray-StL 7
Wagner-Pit 6
Browne-NY 5

Total Bases
Wagner-Pit 264
Beaumont-Bos 246
Magee-Phi 229
Leach-Pit 221
Brain-Bos 214

Runs Batted In
Magee-Phi 85
Wagner-Pit 82
Abbaticchio-Pit 82
Seymour-NY 75
Steinfeldt-Chi 70

Runs Produced
Wagner-Pit 174
Magee-Phi 156
Clarke-Pit 154
Abbaticchio-Pit 143
Leach-Pit 141

Bases On Balls
Thomas-Phi 83
Huggins-Cin 83
Tenney-Bos 82
Shannon-NY 82
Anderson-Pit 80

Batting Average
Wagner-Pit .350
Magee-Phi .328
Beaumont-Bos .322
Leach-Pit .303
Seymour-NY .294

On-Base Percentage
Wagner-Pit .408
Magee-Phi .396
Clarke-Pit .383
Devlin-NY .376
Thomas-Phi .374

Slugging Average
Wagner-Pit .513
Magee-Phi .455
Lumley-Bro .425
Beaumont-Bos .424
Brain-Bos .420

On-Base Plus Slugging
Wagner-Pit 921
Magee-Phi 852
Beaumont-Bos 790
Clarke-Pit 772
Leach-Pit 756

Adjusted OPS
Wagner-Pit 186
Magee-Phi 169
Beaumont-Bos 148
Lumley-Bro 144
Jordan-Bro 141

Batter Runs
Wagner-Pit 50.5
Magee-Phi 38.5
Beaumont-Bos 29.5
Clarke-Pit 26.5
Leach-Pit 21.4

Adjusted Batter Runs
Wagner-Pit 49.1
Magee-Phi 39.9
Beaumont-Bos 29.8
Jordan-Bro 25.7
Clarke-Pit 25.4

Clutch Hitting Index
Abbaticchio-Pit 166
Seymour-NY 130
Steinfeldt-Chi 130
Devlin-NY 126
Magee-Phi 121

Runs Created
Wagner-Pit 137
Magee-Phi 113
Beaumont-Bos 103
Leach-Pit 98
Clarke-Pit 93

Total Average
Wagner-Pit 1.122
Magee-Phi .982
Clarke-Pit .865
Leach-Pit .801
Beaumont-Bos .791

Stolen Bases
Wagner-Pit 61
Magee-Phi 46
Evers-Chi 46
Leach-Pit 43
Devlin-NY 38

Stolen Base Average

Stolen Base Runs

Fielding Runs
Evers-Chi 27.7
Brain-Bos 24.8
Mitchell-Cin 22.2
Byrne-StL 22.1
Tinker-Chi 15.7

Total Player Rating
Wagner-Pit 6.4
Brain-Bos 5.0
Magee-Phi 4.3
Mitchell-Cin 3.1
Beaumont-Bos 3.1

Wins
Mathewson-NY 24
Overall-Chi 23
Sparks-Phi 22
Willis-Pit 21

Win Percentage
Reulbach-Chi .810
Brown-Chi .769
Overall-Chi .767
Sparks-Phi .733
Lundgren-Chi .720

Games
McGinnity-NY 47
McGlynn-StL 45
Mathewson-NY 41
Ewing-Cin 41

Complete Games
McGlynn-StL 33
Ewing-Cin 32
Mathewson-NY 31
Karger-StL 29
Willis-Pit 27

Shutouts
Overall-Chi 8
Mathewson-NY 8
Lundgren-Chi 7

Saves
McGinnity-NY 4
Overall-Chi 3
Brown-Chi 3

Innings Pitched
McGlynn-StL 352.1
Ewing-Cin 332.2
Mathewson-NY 315.0
Karger-StL 314.0
McGinnity-NY 310.1

Fewest Hits/Game
Lundgren-Chi 5.65
Pfiester-Chi 6.60
Overall-Chi 6.74
Camnitz-Pit 6.75
Reulbach-Chi 6.89

Fewest BB/Game
Phillippe-Pit 1.51
Mathewson-NY 1.51
Brown-Chi 1.55
McGinnity-NY 1.68
Sparks-Phi 1.73

Strikeouts
Mathewson-NY 178
Ewing-Cin 147
Ames-NY 146
Overall-Chi 141
Beebe-StL 141

Strikeouts/Game
Ames-NY 5.63
Beebe-StL 5.32
Mathewson-NY 5.09
Overall-Chi 4.73
Reulbach-Chi 4.50

Ratio
Mathewson-NY 8.71
Brown-Chi 8.73
Pfiester-Chi 9.05
Overall-Chi 9.42
Sparks-Phi 9.48

Earned Run Average
Pfiester-Chi 1.15
Lundgren-Chi 1.17
Brown-Chi 1.39
Leever-Pit 1.66
Overall-Chi 1.68

Adjusted ERA
Pfiester-Chi 215
Lundgren-Chi 212
Brown-Chi 179
Ewing-Cin 149
Overall-Chi 148

Opponents' Batting Avg.
Lundgren-Chi .185
Pfiester-Chi .207
Overall-Chi .208
Camnitz-Pit .211
Mathewson-NY .212

Opponents' On-Base Pct.
Mathewson-NY .247
Brown-Chi .262
Pfiester-Chi .263
Overall-Chi .268
Karger-StL .270

Starter Runs
Lundgren-Chi 29.7
Pfiester-Chi 28.4
Brown-Chi 27.8
Ewing-Cin 27.1
Overall-Chi 23.5

Adjusted Starter Runs
Ewing-Cin 30.1
Lundgren-Chi 29.9
Pfiester-Chi 28.6
Brown-Chi 28.1
Overall-Chi 23.9

Clutch Pitching Index
Coakley-Cin 133
Pastorius-Bro 129
Brown-StL-Phi 126
McIntire-Bro 125
Leifield-Pit 123

Relief Runs

Adjusted Relief Runs

Relief Ranking

Total Pitcher Index
Brown-Chi 3.9
Lundgren-Chi 3.6
Overall-Chi 3.5
Pfiester-Chi 3.1
Ewing-Cin 2.7

Total Baseball Ranking
Wagner-Pit 6.4
Brain-Bos 5.0
Magee-Phi 4.3
Brown-Chi 3.9
Lundgren-Chi 3.6

TEAM	G	W	L	PCT	GB	R	OR	AB	H	2B	3B	HR	BB	SO	AVG	OBP	SLG	OPS	OPS+	BR	BR+	PF	CHI	RC	SB	CS	SBA	SBR
DET	153	92	58	.613		**693**	531	5204	**1383**	179	**75**	11	315		**.266**	**.313**	**.335**	**648**	**108**	**63**	**41**	104	110	**641**	192			
PHI	150	88	57	.607	1.5	584	511	5010	1276	**220**	44	**22**	384		.255	.311	.329	640	106	51	37	102	96	592	137			
CHI	157	87	64	.576	5.5	588	**474**	5070	1205	149	33	5	**421**		.238	.302	.283	585	95	-37	-18	97	**111**	523	175			
CLE	158	85	67	.559	8	531	525	5068	1221	182	68	11	335		.241	.295	.310	605	97	-12	-16	101	97	555	193			
NY	152	70	78	.473	21	605	667	5044	1258	150	67	15	304		.249	.299	.315	614	93	1	-40	108	110	565	206			
STL	155	69	83	.454	24	541	555	5224	1324	154	63	10	370		.253	.308	.313	621	103	18	20	100	91	580	144			
BOS	155	59	90	.396	32.5	466	558	5235	1224	154	48	18	305		.234	.281	.292	573	89	-76	-72	99	95	493	125			
WAS	154	49	102	.325	43.5	506	693	5112	1243	134	57	12	390		.243	.304	.299	603	105	-9	38	92	91	563	**223**			
TOT	617					4514		40967	10134	1322	455	104	2824	4479	.248	.302	.310	611							1395			

TEAM	CG	SH	SV	IP	H	H/G	HR	BB	SO	RAT	ERA	ERA+	OAV	OOB	PR	PR+	PF	CPI	FA	E	DP	FW	PW	BW	SBW	DIF
DET	120	15	6	1370^2	1281	8.5	**8**	380	512	11.3	2.34	**112**	.251	.309	32	**39**	102	**114**	.959	260	79	1.0	**4.4**	**4.6**		7.3
PHI	106	**27**	6	1354^2	**1106**	**7.4**	13	378	**789**	10.3	2.35	111	**.226**	.290	29	37	102	91	.958	263	67	.4	4.1	4.1		7.0
CHI	112	17	**9**	1406^1	1279	8.2	13	**305**	604	10.3	**2.23**	108	.245	.290	**50**	28	94	105	**.966**	**233**	101	**3.4**	3.1	-1.9		7.1
CLE	127	20	5	1392^2	1253	8.1	**8**	362	513	10.8	2.27	111	.244	.300	43	36	99	108	.960	264	**137**	1.4	4.0	-1.7		5.5
NY	93	10	6	1333^2	1327	9.0	13	428	511	12.2	3.03	92	.262	.325	-73	-32	110	102	.947	334	79	-4.3	-3.5	-4.4		8.4
STL	**129**	15	**9**	1381^1	1254	8.2	17	352	463	10.8	2.61	96	.245	.300	-10	-16	99	96	.959	266	97	.8	-1.7	2.3		-8.2
BOS	100	17	7	1414	1222	7.8	22	337	517	**10.2**	2.46	105	.236	**.288**	14	18	101	92	.959	274	100	.3	2.0	-7.9		-9.7
WAS	106	12	5	1351^1	1383	9.3	10	344	570	11.9	3.12	78	.268	.320	-86	-111	95	97	.951	310	69	-2.4	-12.2	4.2		-16.0
TOT	893	133	53	11004^2		8.3				11.0	2.55		.248	.302					.958	2204	729					

Runs
Crawford-Det 102
D.Jones-Det 101
Cobb-Det 97
Hartsel-Phi 93
Hahn-Chi 87

Hits
Cobb-Det 212
Stone-StL 191
Crawford-Det 188
Ganley-Was 167
Flick-Cle 166

Doubles
Davis-Phi 35
Crawford-Det 34
Lajoie-Cle 30
J.Collins-Bos-Phi . . . 29
Seybold-Phi 29

Triples
Flick-Cle 18
Crawford-Det 17
Cobb-Det 14
Unglaub-Bos 13

Home Runs
Davis-Phi 8
Seybold-Phi 5
Hoffman-NY 5
Cobb-Det 5

Total Bases
Cobb-Det 283
Crawford-Det 268
Stone-StL 238
Davis-Phi 230
Flick-Cle 226

Runs Batted In
Cobb-Det 119
Seybold-Phi 92
Davis-Phi 87
Crawford-Det 81
Wallace-StL 70

Runs Produced
Cobb-Det 211
Crawford-Det 179
Davis-Phi 163
Seybold-Phi 145
Donahue-Chi 143

Bases On Balls
Hartsel-Phi 106
Hahn-Chi 84
Jones-Chi 67
Flick-Cle 64
D.Jones-Det 60

Batting Average
Cobb-Det 350
Crawford-Det 323
Stone-StL 320
Flick-Cle 302
Nicholls-Phi 302

On-Base Percentage
Hartsel-Phi 405
Stone-StL 387
Flick-Cle 386
Cobb-Det 380
Crawford-Det 366

Slugging Average
Cobb-Det 468
Crawford-Det 460
Flick-Cle 412
Stone-StL 399
Davis-Phi 395

On-Base Plus Slugging
Cobb-Det 848
Crawford-Det 826
Flick-Cle 798
Stone-StL 787
Hartsel-Phi 771

Adjusted OPS
Cobb-Det 164
Crawford-Det 157
Flick-Cle 153
Stone-StL 151
Hartsel-Phi 143

Batter Runs
Cobb-Det 44.2
Crawford-Det 38.6
Flick-Cle 35.7
Stone-StL 35.4
Hartsel-Phi 33.0

Adjusted Batter Runs
Cobb-Det 40.5
Stone-StL 35.7
Crawford-Det 35.1
Flick-Cle 34.9
Hartsel-Phi 30.8

Clutch Hitting Index
Seybold-Phi 150
Cobb-Det 143
Donahue-Chi 134
Chase-NY 133
Wallace-StL 133

Runs Created
Cobb-Det 130
Crawford-Det 108
Flick-Cle 107
Stone-StL 105
Hartsel-Phi 87

Total Average
Cobb-Det 919
Flick-Cle 893
Hartsel-Phi 855
Crawford-Det 825
Stone-StL 805

Stolen Bases
Cobb-Det 49
Flick-Cle 41
Conroy-NY 41
Ganley-Was 40
Altizer-Was 38

Stolen Base Average

Stolen Base Runs

Fielding Runs
Lajoie-Cle 45.9
Donahue-Chi 20.6
Murphy-Phi 13.5
Ferris-Bos 13.4
D.Jones-Det 13.2

Total Player Rating
Lajoie-Cle 7.0
Cobb-Det 4.9
Crawford-Det 4.0
Flick-Cle 3.2
Schreckengost-Phi 2.8

Wins
White-Chi 27
Joss-Cle 27
Killian-Det 25
Donovan-Det 25

Win Percentage
Donovan-Det 862
Dygert-Phi 724
Joss-Cle 711
Smith-Chi 697
White-Chi 675

Games
Walsh-Chi 56
White-Chi 46
Mullin-Det 46
Waddell-Phi 44

Complete Games
Walsh-Chi 37
Mullin-Det 35
Joss-Cle 34
Young-Bos 33
Plank-Phi 33

Shutouts
Plank-Phi 8
Waddell-Phi 7
Young-Bos 6
White-Chi 6
Joss-Cle 6

Saves
Dinneen-Bos-StL 4
Walsh-Chi 4
Hughes-Was 4

Innings Pitched
Walsh-Chi 422.1
Mullin-Det 357.1
Plank-Phi 343.2
Young-Bos 343.1
Joss-Cle 338.2

Fewest Hits/Game
Dygert-Phi 6.88
Winter-Bos 6.94
Walsh-Chi 7.27
Howell-StL 7.34
Donovan-Det 7.37

Fewest BB/Game
White-Chi 1.18
Altrock-Chi 1.31
Young-Bos 1.34
Bender-Phi 1.40
Joss-Cle 1.44

Strikeouts
Waddell-Phi 232
Walsh-Chi 206
Plank-Phi 183
Dygert-Phi 151
Young-Bos 147

Strikeouts/Game
Waddell-Phi 7.33
Dygert-Phi 5.19
Plank-Phi 4.79
Bender-Phi 4.60
Walsh-Chi 4.39

Ratio
Young-Bos 9.02
Joss-Cle 9.04
Bender-Phi 9.11
Winter-Bos 9.19
Walsh-Chi 9.29

Earned Run Average
Walsh-Chi 1.60
Killian-Det 1.78
Joss-Cle 1.83
Howell-StL 1.93
Young-Bos 1.99

Adjusted ERA
Walsh-Chi 150
Killian-Det 146
Joss-Cle 136
Howell-StL 130
Young-Bos 129

Opponents' Batting Avg.
Dygert-Phi 214
Winter-Bos 216
Walsh-Chi 224
Howell-StL 225
Donovan-Det 226

Opponents' On-Base Pct.
Young-Bos 263
Joss-Cle 264
Bender-Phi 265
Winter-Bos 267
Walsh-Chi 269

Starter Runs
Walsh-Chi 44.2
Killian-Det 26.6
Joss-Cle 26.6
Howell-StL 21.3
Young-Bos 20.9

Adjusted Starter Runs
Walsh-Chi 39.6
Killian-Det 28.1
Joss-Cle 25.5
Young-Bos 21.8
Howell-StL 20.5

Clutch Pitching Index
Killian-Det 144
Hogg-NY 125
Liebhardt-Cle 125
Rhoads-Cle 119
Walsh-Chi 112

Relief Runs

Adjusted Relief Runs

Relief Ranking

Total Pitcher Index
Walsh-Chi 6.7
Killian-Det 4.5
Howell-StL 3.8
Joss-Cle 3.4
Plank-Phi 1.9

Total Baseball Ranking
Lajoie-Cle 7.0
Walsh-Chi 6.7
Cobb-Det 4.9
Killian-Det 4.7
Crawford-Det 4.0

TEAM	G	W	L	PCT	GB	R	OR	AB	H	2B	3B	HR	BB	SO	AVG	OBP	SLG	OPS	OPS+	BR	BR+	PF	CHI	RC	SB	CS	SBA	SBR
CHI	158	99	55	.643		624	461	5085	1267	**196**	56	19	418		.249	.311	.321	632	105	49	26	104	**107**	584	**212**			
PIT	155	98	56	.636	1	585	468	5109	1263	162	**98**	25	420		.247	.309	.332	641	112	63	63	100	99	582	186			
NY	157	98	56	.636	1	**651**	455	5006	**1339**	182	43	20	**494**		**.267**	**.342**	**.333**	**675**	**117**	**138**	**107**	105	97	**646**	181			
PHI	155	83	71	.539	16	504	**445**	5012	1223	194	68	11	334		.244	.298	.316	614	100	12	-5	103	96	535	200			
CIN	155	73	81	.474	26	488	543	4879	1108	129	77	14	372		.227	.288	.294	582	95	-41	-28	97	105	474	196			
BOS	156	63	91	.409	36	537	622	5131	1228	137	43	17	414		.239	.303	.293	596	99	-12	-4	98	104	501	134			
BRO	154	53	101	.344	46	375	516	4897	1044	110	60	**28**	323		.213	.266	.277	543	82	-112	-96	96	98	391	113			
STL	154	49	105	.318	50	372	626	4959	1105	134	57	17	282		.223	.271	.283	554	87	-96	-76	95	92	420	150			
TOT	622					4136		40078	9577	1244	502	151	3057	4180	.239	.300	.307	605							1372			

TEAM	CG	SH	SV	IP	H	H/G	HR	BB	SO	RAT	ERA	ERA+	OAV	OOB	PR	PR+	PF	CPI	FA	E	DP	FW	PW	BW	SBW	DIF
CHI	108	**29**	12	1433^{2}	**1137**	**7.2**	20	437	**668**	10.2	2.15	109	**.221**	.287	33	30	100	93	**.969**	**205**	76	**3.8**	3.5	3.1		11.8
PIT	100	24	9	1402^{1}	1142	7.4	16	406	468	10.3	2.13	108	.223	.287	34	25	97	92	.964	226	74	1.9	3.0	7.4		8.9
NY	95	25	**18**	1411	1214	7.8	26	**288**	656	**9.9**	2.15	112	.233	**.277**	32	38	102	92	.962	250	79	.5	4.5	**12.5**		3.8
PHI	116	22	6	1393	1167	7.6	**8**	379	476	10.3	**2.10**	**115**	.234	.294	**38**	**44**	103	103	.963	238	75	1.1	**5.2**	-.5		.5
CIN	110	17	8	1384	1218	8.0	19	415	433	10.9	2.38	96	.243	.307	-4	-19	98	**104**	.959	255	72	-.1	-2.2	-3.2		1.7
BOS	92	14	1	1404^{2}	1262	8.1	29	423	416	11.2	2.80	86	.245	.310	-70	-66	102	93	.962	253	**90**	.1	-7.6	-.4		-5.9
BRO	**118**	20	4	1369	1165	7.7	17	444	535	11.0	2.47	94	.235	.306	-18	-24	99	97	.961	247	66	.3	-2.7	-11.1		-10.3
STL	97	13	4	1368	1217	8.1	16	430	528	11.2	2.64	89	.232	.296	-44	-51	100	82	.946	348	68	-6.8	-5.9	-8.8		-6.4
TOT	836	164	62	11165^{2}		7.7				10.6	2.35		.239	.300					.961	2022	600					

Runs
Tenney-NY 101
Wagner-Pit 100
Leach-Pit 93
Evers-Chi 83
Clarke-Pit 83

Hits
Wagner-Pit 201
Donlin-NY 198
Murray-StL 167
Lobert-Cin 167
Bransfield-Phi 160

Doubles
Wagner-Pit 39
Magee-Phi 30
Chance-Chi 27
Knabe-Phi 26
Donlin-NY 26

Triples
Wagner-Pit 19
Lobert-Cin 18
Magee-Phi 16
Leach-Pit 16

Home Runs
Jordan-Bro 12
Wagner-Pit 10
Murray-StL 7
Tinker-Chi 6
Donlin-NY 6

Total Bases
Wagner-Pit 308
Donlin-NY 268
Murray-StL 237
Lobert-Cin 232
Leach-Pit 222

Runs Batted In
Wagner-Pit 109
Donlin-NY 106
Seymour-NY 92
Bransfield-Phi 71
Tinker-Chi 68

Runs Produced
Wagner-Pit 199
Donlin-NY 171
Tenney-NY 148
Seymour-NY 147

Bases On Balls
Bresnahan-NY 83
Tenney-NY 72
Evers-Chi 66
Clarke-Pit 65

Batting Average
Wagner-Pit .354
Donlin-NY .334
Doyle-NY .308
Bransfield-Phi .304
Evers-Chi .300

On-Base Percentage
Wagner-Pit .415
Evers-Chi .402
Bresnahan-NY .401
Titus-Phi .365
Donlin-NY .364

Slugging Average
Wagner-Pit .542
Donlin-NY .452
Magee-Phi .417
Lobert-Cin .407
Murray-StL .400

On-Base Plus Slugging
Wagner-Pit 957
Donlin-NY 816
Evers-Chi 777
Magee-Phi 776
Bresnahan-NY 760

Adjusted OPS
Wagner-Pit 205
Donlin-NY 153
Lobert-Cin 145
Magee-Phi 143
Evers-Chi 143

Batter Runs
Wagner-Pit 65.2
Donlin-NY 36.6
Magee-Phi 27.3
Bresnahan-NY 27.0
Evers-Chi 26.4

Adjusted Batter Runs
Wagner-Pit 65.2
Donlin-NY 32.2
Lobert-Cin 27.3
Magee-Phi 24.7
Murray-StL 24.5

Clutch Hitting Index
Seymour-NY 150
McGann-Bos 133
Abbaticchio-Pit 132
Donlin-NY 129
Steinfeldt-Chi 129

Runs Created
Wagner-Pit 148
Donlin-NY 108
Lobert-Cin 97
Murray-StL 92
Magee-Phi 90

Total Average
Wagner-Pit 1.144
Evers-Chi .904
Magee-Phi .857
Donlin-NY .825
Bresnahan-NY .820

Stolen Bases
Wagner-Pit 53
Murray-StL 48
Lobert-Cin 47
Magee-Phi 40
Evers-Chi 36

Stolen Base Average

Stolen Base Runs

Fielding Runs
Dahlen-Bos 37.5
Tinker-Chi 30.4
Ritchey-Bos 15.6
Devlin-NY 12.8
Burch-Bro 12.6

Total Player Rating
Wagner-Pit 7.2
Tinker-Chi 5.0
Dahlen-Bos 4.4
Ritchey-Bos 3.3
Donlin-NY 2.9

Wins
Mathewson-NY 37
Brown-Chi 29
Reulbach-Chi 24

Win Percentage
Reulbach-Chi .774
Mathewson-NY .771
Brown-Chi .763
Maddox-Pit .742
Leever-Pit .682

Games
Mathewson-NY 56
Raymond-StL 48
McQuillan-Phi 48
Reulbach-Chi 46

Complete Games
Mathewson-NY 34
Wilhelm-Bro 33
McQuillan-Phi 32
Wiltse-NY 30
Rucker-Bro 30

Shutouts
Mathewson-NY 11
Brown-Chi 9

Saves
McGinnity-NY 5
Mathewson-NY 5
Brown-Chi 5
Overall-Chi 4
Ewing-Cin 3

Innings Pitched
Mathewson-NY 390.2
McQuillan-Phi 359.2
Rucker-Bro 333.1
Wilhelm-Bro 332.0
Wiltse-NY 330.0

Fewest Hits/Game
Brown-Chi 6.17
Raymond-StL 6.55
Mathewson-NY 6.57
McQuillan-Phi 6.58
Overall-Chi 6.60

Fewest BB/Game
Mathewson-NY .97
Brown-Chi 1.41
Sparks-Phi 1.74
Ewing-Cin 1.75
Campbell-Cin 1.79

Strikeouts
Mathewson-NY 259
Rucker-Bro 199
Overall-Chi 167
Raymond-StL 145
Reulbach-Chi 133

Strikeouts/Game
Overall-Chi 6.68
Mathewson-NY 5.97
Rucker-Bro 5.37
Camnitz-Pit 4.49
Ferguson-Bos 4.24

Ratio
Mathewson-NY 7.60
Brown-Chi 7.72
McQuillan-Phi 9.01
Willis-Pit 9.28
Ewing-Cin 9.47

Earned Run Average
Mathewson-NY 1.43
Brown-Chi 1.47
McQuillan-Phi 1.53
Camnitz-Pit 1.56
Coakley-Cin-Chi 1.78

Adjusted ERA
Mathewson-NY 168
Brown-Chi 159
McQuillan-Phi 158
Camnitz-Pit 147
Richie-Phi 132

Opponents' Batting Avg.
Beebe-StL .193
Brown-Chi .195
Mathewson-NY .200
McQuillan-Phi .207
Raymond-StL .207

Opponents' On-Base Pct.
Mathewson-NY .225
Brown-Chi .232
Willis-Pit .262
McQuillan-Phi .263
Beebe-StL .267

Starter Runs
Mathewson-NY 39.8
McQuillan-Phi 32.7
Brown-Chi 30.4
Camnitz-Pit 20.7
Wilhelm-Bro 17.5

Adjusted Starter Runs
Mathewson-NY 41.2
McQuillan-Phi 34.3
Brown-Chi 30.2
Camnitz-Pit 19.6
Wilhelm-Bro 17.0

Clutch Pitching Index
Coakley-Cin-Chi 134
McGinnity-NY 134
Richie-Phi 126
Fraser-Chi 126
Rucker-Bro 118

Relief Runs

Adjusted Relief Runs

Relief Ranking

Total Pitcher Index
Mathewson-NY 7.2
Brown-Chi 4.2
McQuillan-Phi 3.8
Raymond-StL 2.1
Wilhelm-Bro 1.9

Total Baseball Ranking
Mathewson-NY 7.2
Wagner-Pit 7.2
Tinker-Chi 5.0
Dahlen-Bos 4.4
Brown-Chi 4.2

TEAM	G	W	L	PCT	GB	R	OR	AB	H	2B	3B	HR	BB	SO	AVG	OBP	SLG	OPS	OPS+	BR	BR+	PF	CHI	RC	SB	CS	SBA	SBR
DET	154	90	63	.588		**647**	547	5115	**1347**	**199**	86	19	320		**.263**	**.312**	**.347**	**659**	**115**	**102**	**76**	104	101	**604**	165			
CLE	157	90	64	.584	0.5	569	**459**	5108	1221	188	58	18	364		.239	.297	.309	606	103	14	12	100	102	528	177			
CHI	156	88	64	.579	1.5	537	470	5027	1127	145	41	3	**463**		.224	.298	.271	569	91	-37	-29	98	**105**	479	209			
STL	155	83	69	.546	6.5	544	483	5151	1261	173	52	20	343		.245	.296	.310	606	102	13	10	101	98	514	126			
BOS	155	75	79	.487	15.5	564	513	5048	1239	117	**88**	14	289		.245	.295	.312	607	100	13	-2	103	104	513	167			
PHI	157	68	85	.444	22	486	562	5065	1131	183	50	**21**	368		.223	.281	.292	573	86	-46	-77	107	100	450	116			
WAS	155	67	85	.441	22.5	479	539	5041	1186	132	74	8	368		.235	.293	.296	589	106	-15	32	92	92	490	170			
NY	155	51	103	.331	39.5	460	713	5047	1190	142	50	13	288		.236	.283	.291	574	91	-45	-50	101	96	478	**231**			
TOT	622					4286		40602	9702	1279	499	116	2803	4930	.239	.295	.304	598							1361			

TEAM	CG	SH	SV	IP	H	H/G	HR	BB	SO	RAT	ERA	ERA+	OAV	OOB	PR	PR+	PF	CPI	FA	E	DP	FW	PW	BW	SBW	DIF
DET	**119**	15	5	1374^1	1313	8.6	12	318	553	11.1	2.41	100	.255	.306	-3	2	101	**113**	.953	305	95	-2.0	.3	**8.7**		6.7
CLE	108	18	5	1424^1	1172	**7.5**	16	328	548	9.7	**2.02**	**118**	.229	.280	**59**	**56**	100	102	.962	257	95	1.6	**6.4**	1.4		3.7
CHI	107	**23**	**10**	1414	1165	**7.5**	11	**284**	623	**9.5**	2.23	104	**.225**	**.269**	26	14	97	82	**.966**	**232**	82	**3.2**	1.6	-3.3		10.6
STL	107	15	5	1397	**1151**	**7.5**	**7**	387	607	10.4	2.15	111	.230	.294	37	36	100	105	.964	237	**97**	2.8	4.2	1.2		-.9
BOS	102	12	7	1380^1	1200	7.9	18	364	624	10.5	2.28	108	.238	.295	17	26	103	105	.955	297	71	-1.4	3.0	-.2		-3.3
PHI	102	**23**	4	1400^1	1194	7.7	10	410	**741**	10.7	2.56	100	.235	.298	-27	-4	107	92	.957	272	68	.6	-.4	-8.7		.2
WAS	106	15	7	1391^2	1236	8.0	16	348	649	10.6	2.35	97	.241	.294	7	-13	96	102	.958	275	89	.2	-1.4	3.7		-11.2
NY	90	11	3	1366	1293	8.6	26	458	585	12.1	3.16	78	.252	.322	-117	-102	104	96	.947	337	78	-4.1	-11.6	-5.7		-4.5
TOT	841	132	46	11148		7.9				10.6	2.39		.239	.295					.958	2212	675					

Runs
McIntyre-Det 105
Crawford-Det 102
Schaefer-Det 96
Jones-Chi 92
Stone-StL 89

Hits
Cobb-Det 188
Crawford-Det 184
McIntyre-Det 168
Lajoie-Cle 168
Stone-StL 165

Doubles
Cobb-Det 36
Rossman-Det 33
Crawford-Det 33
Lajoie-Cle 32
Stovall-Cle 29

Triples
Cobb-Det 20
Stahl-NY-Bos 16
Crawford-Det 16
Gessler-Bos 14

Home Runs
Crawford-Det 7
Hinchman-Cle 6
Niles-NY-Bos 5
Stone-StL 5
Davis-Phi 5

Total Bases
Cobb-Det 276
Crawford-Det 270
Rossman-Det 219
McIntyre-Det 218
Lajoie-Cle 218

Runs Batted In
Cobb-Det 108
Crawford-Det 80
Lajoie-Cle 74
Ferris-StL 74
Rossman-Det 71

Runs Produced
Cobb-Det 192
Crawford-Det 175
Lajoie-Cle 149
Schaefer-Det 145
Jones-Chi 141

Bases On Balls
Hartsel-Phi 93
Jones-Chi 86
McIntyre-Det 83
J.Clarke-Cle 76
Davis-Phi 61

Batting Average
Cobb-Det .... .324
Crawford-Det ..... .311
Gessler-Bos ...... .308
Hemphill-NY ..... .297
McIntyre-Det ..... .295

On-Base Percentage
Gessler-Bos .... .394
McIntyre-Det ..... .392
Hemphill-NY ...... .374
Hartsel-Phi .... .371
Dougherty-Chi .... .367

Slugging Average
Cobb-Det .... .475
Crawford-Det ...... .457
Gessler-Bos .... .423
Rossman-Det ...... .418
McIntyre-Det ...... .383

On-Base Plus Slugging
Cobb-Det 842
Gessler-Bos 817
Crawford-Det 812
McIntyre-Det 775
Rossman-Det 748

Adjusted OPS
Cobb-Det 166
Gessler-Bos 161
Crawford-Det 157
McIntyre-Det 146
Rossman-Det 137

Batter Runs
Cobb-Det 43.8
Crawford-Det 38.3
McIntyre-Det 36.5
Gessler-Bos 33.2
Lajoie-Cle 23.3

Adjusted Batter Runs
Cobb-Det 39.7
Crawford-Det 34.3
McIntyre-Det 32.4
Gessler-Bos 31.0
Lajoie-Cle 23.0

Clutch Hitting Index
Cobb-Det 141
Wallace-StL 127
Ferris-StL 125
Lajoie-Cle 124
Jones-Chi 124

Runs Created
Cobb-Det 114
Crawford-Det 100
McIntyre-Det 93
Lajoie-Cle 83
Hemphill-NY 83

Total Average
Cobb-Det .... .903
Gessler-Bos ...... .880
McIntyre-Det ..... .818
Hemphill-NY ..... .800
Crawford-Det ..... .799

Stolen Bases
Dougherty-Chi 47
Hemphill-NY 42
Schaefer-Det 40
Cobb-Det 39
J.Clarke-Cle 37

Stolen Base Average

Stolen Base Runs

Fielding Runs
Lajoie-Cle 49.4
McBride-Was 32.0
Wagner-Bos 31.8
Wallace-StL 18.1
Tannehill-Chi 17.8

Total Player Rating
Lajoie-Cle 8.1
McIntyre-Det 4.4
Cobb-Det 4.2
McBride-Was 3.7
Wallace-StL 3.3

Wins
Walsh-Chi 40
Summers-Det 24
Joss-Cle 24
Young-Bos 21
Waddell-StL 19

Win Percentage
Walsh-Chi .... .727
Donovan-Det ...... .720
Joss-Cle .... .686
Summers-Det ...... .667
Young-Bos .... .656

Games
Walsh-Chi 66
Vickers-Phi 53
Chesbro-NY 45
Waddell-StL 43
Hughes-Was 43

Complete Games
Walsh-Chi 42
Young-Bos 30
Joss-Cle 29
Howell-StL 27
Mullin-Det 26

Shutouts
Walsh-Chi 11
Joss-Cle 9
Vickers-Phi 6
Johnson-Was 6
Donovan-Det 6

Saves
Walsh-Chi 6
Hughes-Was 4
Waddell-StL 3

Innings Pitched
Walsh-Chi 464.0
Joss-Cle 325.0
Howell-StL 324.1
Vickers-Phi 317.0
Summers-Det 301.0

Fewest Hits/Game
Joss-Cle 6.42
Smith-Chi 6.44
Walsh-Chi 6.65
Johnson-Was 6.81
Berger-Cle 6.86

Fewest BB/Game
Joss-Cle .... .83
Burns-Was .... .99
Walsh-Chi 1.09
Young-Bos 1.11
Summers-Det 1.64

Strikeouts
Walsh-Chi 269
Waddell-StL 232
Hughes-Was 165
Dygert-Phi 164
Johnson-Was 160

Strikeouts/Game
Waddell-StL 7.31
Dygert-Phi 6.18
Johnson-Was 5.62
Hughes-Was 5.37
Donovan-Det 5.23

Ratio
Joss-Cle 7.31
Walsh-Chi 7.91
Young-Bos 8.07
Burns-Was 8.62
Smith-Chi 8.71

Earned Run Average
Joss-Cle 1.16
Young-Bos 1.26
Walsh-Chi 1.42
Summers-Det 1.64
Johnson-Was 1.65

Adjusted ERA
Joss-Cle 205
Young-Bos 194
Walsh-Chi 163
Summers-Det 147
Johnson-Was 138

Opponents' Batting Avg.
Joss-Cle .... .197
Smith-Chi .... .203
Walsh-Chi .... .203
Johnson-Was .... .211
Young-Bos .... .213

Opponents' On-Base Pct.
Joss-Cle .... .218
Walsh-Chi .... .232
Young-Bos .... .240
Smith-Chi .... .256
Burns-Was .... .257

Starter Runs
Walsh-Chi 50.0
Joss-Cle 44.2
Young-Bos 37.3
Summers-Det 24.8
Johnson-Was 21.0

Adjusted Starter Runs
Walsh-Chi 47.5
Joss-Cle 44.1
Young-Bos 38.4
Summers-Det 25.4
Johnson-Was 18.8

Clutch Pitching Index
Summers-Det 142
Willett-Det 140
Rhoads-Cle 137
Howell-StL 122
Chech-Cle 119

Relief Runs

Adjusted Relief Runs

Relief Ranking

Total Pitcher Index
Walsh-Chi 8.4
Joss-Cle 6.0
Young-Bos 4.0
Rhoads-Cle 2.9
Summers-Det 2.4

Total Baseball Ranking
Walsh-Chi 8.4
Lajoie-Cle 8.1
Joss-Cle 6.0
McIntyre-Det 4.4
Cobb-Det 4.2

TEAM	G	W	L	PCT	GB	R	OR	AB	H	2B	3B	HR	BB	SO	AVG	OBP	SLG	OPS	OPS+	BR	BR+	PF	CHI	RC	SB	CS	SBA	SBR
PIT	154	110	42	.724		**699**	447	5129	**1332**	**218**	**92**	25	479		**.260**	.327	**.353**	**680**	**109**	**100**	48	108	103	**656**	185			
CHI	155	104	49	.680	6.5	635	**390**	4999	1227	203	60	20	420		.245	.308	.322	630	100	7	-6	102	**112**	562	187			
NY	158	92	61	.601	18.5	624	547	5218	1327	173	68	**26**	530		.254	**.329**	.328	657	**109**	70	60	102	95	640	234			
CIN	157	77	76	.503	33.5	606	599	5088	1273	159	72	22	478		.250	.319	.323	642	107	35	40	99	100	618	**280**			
PHI	154	74	79	.484	36.5	517	519	5034	1228	185	53	12	369		.244	.303	.309	612	95	-26	-30	101	97	534	185			
BRO	155	55	98	.359	55.5	444	627	5056	1157	176	59	16	330		.229	.279	.296	575	87	-98	-81	96	98	456	141			
STL	154	54	98	.355	56	583	731	5108	1242	148	56	15	**568**		.243	.326	.303	629	**109**	25	**65**	94	97	556	161			
BOS	155	45	108	.294	65.5	435	683	5017	1121	125	43	14	400		.223	.285	.274	559	76	-117	-136	105	99	435	135			
TOT	621					4543		40649	9907	1387	503	150	3574	4437	.244	.310	.314	624							1508			

TEAM	CG	SH	SV	IP	H	H/G	HR	BB	SO	RAT	ERA	ERA+	OAV	OOB	PR	PR+	PF	CPI	FA	E	DP	FW	PW	BW	SBW	DIF
PIT	93	21	11	1401^{2}	1174	7.6	12	**320**	490	10.0	2.07	131	.232	.284	81	95	105	97	**.964**	**228**	100	**3.6**	10.6	5.4		14.7
CHI	111	**32**	11	1399^{1}	**1094**	**7.1**	6	364	680	**9.7**	**1.75**	**145**	**.215**	**.272**	**131**	**127**	98	94	.962	244	95	2.7	**14.1**	-.6		11.5
NY	105	17	**15**	1440^{2}	1248	7.8	28	397	**735**	10.5	2.28	112	.238	.295	51	43	98	102	.954	307	99	-1.1	4.8	6.7		5.2
CIN	91	10	8	1407	1233	7.9	**5**	510	477	11.5	2.53	103	.240	.314	11	9	100	100	.952	309	**120**	-1.3	1.0	4.5		-3.5
PHI	89	17	6	1391	1190	7.7	23	472	612	11.0	2.44	106	.235	.304	23	20	100	99	.962	241	97	2.7	2.3	-3.3		-4.0
BRO	**126**	18	3	1384^{1}	1277	8.4	31	528	594	12.1	3.11	83	.256	.333	-79	-82	100	102	.955	282	86	.2	-9.0	-8.9		-3.5
STL	84	5	4	1379^{2}	1368	9.0	22	483	435	12.4	3.42	74	.263	.331	-126	-142	97	92	.950	322	90	-2.5	-15.7	**7.3**		-10.9
BOS	98	13	6	1370^{2}	1329	8.8	23	543	414	12.6	3.20	88	.263	.339	-93	-56	109	**103**	.948	342	101	-3.7	-6.2	-15.0		-6.4
TOT	797	133	64	11174^{1}		8.0				11.2	2.60		.244	.310					.956	2275	788					

Runs
Leach-Pit 126
Clarke-Pit 97
Byrne-StL-Pit 92
Wagner-Pit 92

Hits
Doyle-NY 172
Grant-Phi 170
Wagner-Pit 168
Konetchy-StL 165
Burch-Bro 163

Doubles
Wagner-Pit 39
Magee-Phi 33
D.Miller-Pit 31
Sheckard-Chi 29
Leach-Pit 29

Triples
Mitchell-Cin 17
Magee-Phi 14
Konetchy-StL 14
D.Miller-Pit 13

Home Runs
Murray-NY 7
Leach-Pit 6
Doyle-NY 6
Becker-Bos 6
Wagner-Pit 5

Total Bases
Wagner-Pit 242
Doyle-NY 239
Konetchy-StL 228
Mitchell-Cin 225
D.Miller-Pit 222

Runs Batted In
Wagner-Pit 100
Murray-NY 91
D.Miller-Pit 87
Mitchell-Cin 86
Konetchy-StL 80

Runs Produced
Wagner-Pit 187
Mitchell-Cin 165
Konetchy-StL 164
Leach-Pit 163
Clarke-Pit 162

Bases On Balls
Clarke-Pit 80
Byrne-StL-Pit 78
Evers-Chi 73
Sheckard-Chi 72
Bridwell-NY 67

Batting Average
Wagner-Pit 339
Mitchell-Cin 310
Hoblitzel-Cin 308
Doyle-NY 302
Bridwell-NY 294

On-Base Percentage
Wagner-Pit .... .420
Bridwell-NY .... .386
Clarke-Pit .... .384
Mitchell-Cin .... .378
Evers-Chi .... .369

Slugging Average
Wagner-Pit .... .489
Mitchell-Cin .... .430
Doyle-NY .... .419
Hoblitzel-Cin .... .418
McCormick-NY ...... .402

On-Base Plus Slugging
Wagner-Pit 909
Mitchell-Cin 808
Hoblitzel-Cin 782
Doyle-NY 779
Konetchy-StL 762

Adjusted OPS
Wagner-Pit 168
Mitchell-Cin 152
Konetchy-StL 145
Hoblitzel-Cin 144
Doyle-NY 140

Batter Runs
Wagner-Pit 48.1
Mitchell-Cin 30.4
Doyle-NY 26.2
Clarke-Pit 25.4
Konetchy-StL 24.9

Adjusted Batter Runs
Wagner-Pit 40.0
Mitchell-Cin 31.1
Konetchy-StL 30.9
Hoblitzel-Cin 25.0
Doyle-NY 24.9

Clutch Hitting Index
Murray-NY 130
Abstein-Pit 129
Wagner-Pit 128
Lobert-Cin 125
D.Miller-Pit 124

Runs Created
Wagner-Pit 117
Mitchell-Cin 98
Doyle-NY 96
Clarke-Pit 92
Konetchy-StL 92

Total Average
Wagner-Pit 1.058
Mitchell-Cin .... .884
Clarke-Pit .... .821
Doyle-NY .... .809
Konetchy-StL .... .791

Stolen Bases
Bescher-Cin 54
Murray-NY 48
Egan-Cin 39
Magee-Phi 38
Burch-Bro 38

Stolen Base Average

Stolen Base Runs

Fielding Runs
Doolan-Phi 24.6
Egan-Cin 24.1
Byrne-StL-Pit 22.8
Bergen-Bro 21.7
Tinker-Chi 19.7

Total Player Rating
Wagner-Pit 5.4
Devlin-NY 3.6
Konetchy-StL 3.6
Mitchell-Cin 3.3
Egan-Cin 3.1

Wins
M.Brown-Chi 27
Mathewson-NY 25
H.Camnitz-Pit 25
Willis-Pit 22

Win Percentage
Mathewson-NY 806
H.Camnitz-Pit 806
M.Brown-Chi 750
Pfiester-Chi 739
Leifield-Pit 704

Games
M.Brown-Chi 50
Mattern-Bos 47
Gaspar-Cin 44
Beebe-StL 44

Complete Games
M.Brown-Chi 32
Bell-Bro 29
Rucker-Bro 28
Mathewson-NY 26

Shutouts
Overall-Chi 9
Mathewson-NY 8
M.Brown-Chi 8

Saves
M.Brown-Chi 7
Crandall-NY 6

Innings Pitched
M.Brown-Chi 342.2
Mattern-Bos 316.1
Rucker-Bro 309.1
Moore-Phi 299.2
Willis-Pit 289.2

Fewest Hits/Game
Mathewson-NY 6.28
Fromme-Cin 6.28
Overall-Chi 6.44
M.Brown-Chi 6.46
H.Camnitz-Pit 6.58

Fewest BB/Game
Mathewson-NY 1.18
M.Brown-Chi 1.39
Wiltse-NY 1.70
Maddox-Pit 1.73
McQuillan-Phi 1.96

Strikeouts
Overall-Chi 205
Rucker-Bro 201
Moore-Phi 173
M.Brown-Chi 172
Ames-NY 156

Strikeouts/Game
Overall-Chi 6.47
Rucker-Bro 5.85
Ames-NY 5.75
Marquard-NY 5.67
Moore-Phi 5.20

Ratio
Mathewson-NY 7.45
M.Brown-Chi 8.04
H.Camnitz-Pit 8.97
Overall-Chi 9.22
McQuillan-Phi 9.34

Earned Run Average
Mathewson-NY 1.14
M.Brown-Chi 1.31
Overall-Chi 1.42
H.Camnitz-Pit 1.62
Kroh-Chi 1.65

Adjusted ERA
Mathewson-NY 223
M.Brown-Chi 193
Overall-Chi 178
H.Camnitz-Pit 167
Reulbach-Chi 142

Opponents' Batting Avg.
Overall-Chi 198
Mathewson-NY 200
Fromme-Cin 201
M.Brown-Chi 202
Moore-Phi 210

Opponents' On-Base Pct.
Mathewson-NY 228
M.Brown-Chi 239
Overall-Chi 262
H.Camnitz-Pit 267
McQuillan-Phi 271

Starter Runs
M.Brown-Chi 48.6
Mathewson-NY 44.2
Overall-Chi 37.0
H.Camnitz-Pit 30.4
Reulbach-Chi 23.6

Adjusted Starter Runs
M.Brown-Chi 47.5
Mathewson-NY 43.7
Overall-Chi 36.0
H.Camnitz-Pit 32.7
Reulbach-Chi 22.4

Clutch Pitching Index
Richie-Phi-Bos 126
Corridon-Phi 123
Sallee-StL 119
Wilhelm-Bro 117
Marquard-NY 117

Relief Runs

Adjusted Relief Runs

Relief Ranking

Total Pitcher Index
Mathewson-NY 7.1
M.Brown-Chi 5.5
Overall-Chi 5.2
H.Camnitz-Pit 3.5
Fromme-Cin 3.1

Total Baseball Ranking
Mathewson-NY 7.1
M.Brown-Chi 5.5
Wagner-Pit 5.4
Overall-Chi 5.2
Devlin-NY 3.6

TEAM	G	W	L	PCT	GB	R	OR	AB	H	2B	3B	HR	BB	SO	AVG	OBP	SLG	OPS	OPS+	BR	BR+	PF	CHI	RC	SB	CS	SBA	SBR
DET	158	98	54	.645		**666**	493	5095	**1360**	**209**	58	19	397		**.267**	**.325**	.342	**667**	113	**98**	71	104	103	**660**	**280**			
PHI	153	95	58	.621	3.5	605	**411**	4906	1257	186	**88**	**21**	403		.256	.321	**.343**	664	**115**	91	**79**	102	97	613	205			
BOS	152	88	63	.583	9.5	601	549	4980	1309	151	69	20	348		.263	.321	.333	654	112	74	61	102	100	600	215			
CHI	159	78	74	.513	20	492	464	5018	1109	145	56	4	**441**		.221	.291	.275	566	89	-73	-52	96	104	474	211			
NY	153	74	77	.490	23.5	589	587	4981	1234	143	61	16	407		.248	.313	.311	624	103	25	21	101	**105**	547	187			
CLE	155	71	82	.464	27.5	493	532	5048	1216	173	81	10	283		.241	.288	.313	601	92	-28	-48	104	99	501	174			
STL	154	61	89	.407	36	441	575	4964	1151	116	45	10	331		.232	.287	.279	566	91	-79	-45	93	100	436	136			
WAS	156	42	110	.276	56	380	656	4983	1113	149	41	9	321		.223	.276	.275	551	84	-108	-87	95	91	420	136			
TOT	620					4267		39975	9749	1272	499	109	2931	4918	.244	.303	.309	612							1544			

TEAM	CG	SH	SV	IP	H	H/G	HR	BB	SO	RAT	ERA	ERA+	OAV	OOB	PR	PR+	PF	CPI	FA	E	DP	FW	PW	BW	SBW	DIF
DET	**117**	17	12	1420[1]	1254	8.0	16	359	528	10.6	2.27	111	.238	.293	33	39	102	100	.959	276	87	.4	4.5	8.1		9.2
PHI	110	**27**	3	1378	**1069**	**7.0**	9	386	**728**	**10.0**	**1.94**	**124**	**.217**	**.282**	**82**	**74**	97	96	.961	**245**	92	1.8	**8.5**	**9.0**		-.6
BOS	75	11	**14**	1360[1]	1213	8.1	18	384	555	10.9	2.60	96	.243	.303	-19	-15	101	96	.955	292	95	-1.3	-1.7	7.0		8.6
CHI	115	26	4	1430[1]	1182	7.5	**8**	**340**	669	**10.0**	2.06	114	.229	.283	67	47	95	96	**.964**	246	101	**2.5**	5.4	-5.9		.2
NY	94	18	8	1350[1]	1223	8.2	21	422	597	11.5	2.65	95	.248	.316	-26	-21	102	104	.948	330	94	-3.6	-2.3	2.4		2.2
CLE	110	15	3	1361	1212	8.1	9	348	568	10.7	2.41	106	.250	.307	11	20	103	**107**	.957	278	**110**	-.0	2.3	-5.4		-2.2
STL	105	21	4	1354[2]	1287	8.6	16	383	620	11.4	2.88	84	.261	.319	-61	-74	98	101	.958	267	107	.6	-8.4	-5.1		-.9
WAS	99	11	2	1374[2]	1288	8.5	12	424	653	11.7	3.04	80	.248	.312	-87	-98	98	87	.957	280	100	-.0	-11.1	-9.8		-12.8
TOT	825	146	50	11029[2]		8.0				10.8	2.48		.244	.303					.958	2214	786					

Runs
- Cobb-Det 116
- Bush-Det 114
- Collins-Phi 104
- Lord-Bos 89
- Crawford-Det 83

Hits
- Cobb-Det 216
- Collins-Phi 198
- Crawford-Det 185
- Speaker-Bos 168
- Lord-Bos 168

Doubles
- Crawford-Det 35
- Lajoie-Cle 33
- Cobb-Det 33
- Collins-Phi 30
- Murphy-Phi 28

Triples
- Baker-Phi 19
- Murphy-Phi 14
- Crawford-Det 14

Home Runs
- Cobb-Det 9
- Speaker-Bos 7
- Stahl-Bos 6
- Crawford-Det 6
- Murphy-Phi 5

Total Bases
- Cobb-Det 296
- Crawford-Det 266
- Collins-Phi 257
- Baker-Phi 242
- Speaker-Bos 241

Runs Batted In
- Cobb-Det 107
- Crawford-Det 97
- Baker-Phi 85
- Speaker-Bos 77
- Davis-Phi 75

Runs Produced
- Cobb-Det 214
- Crawford-Det 174
- Collins-Phi 157
- Baker-Phi 154
- Bush-Det 147

Bases On Balls
- Bush-Det 88
- Collins-Phi 62
- Demmitt-NY 55
- McIntyre-Det 54

Batting Average
- Cobb-Det .377
- Collins-Phi .347
- Lajoie-Cle .324
- Lord-Bos .315
- Crawford-Det .314

On-Base Percentage
- Cobb-Det .431
- Collins-Phi .416
- Bush-Det .380
- Lajoie-Cle .378
- Stahl-Bos .377

Slugging Average
- Cobb-Det .517
- Crawford-Det .452
- Collins-Phi .450
- Baker-Phi .447
- Speaker-Bos .443

On-Base Plus Slugging
- Cobb-Det 947
- Collins-Phi 866
- Crawford-Det 817
- Stahl-Bos 812
- Lajoie-Cle 809

Adjusted OPS
- Cobb-Det 190
- Collins-Phi 170
- Stahl-Bos 153
- Crawford-Det 151
- Speaker-Bos 151

Batter Runs
- Cobb-Det 63.3
- Collins-Phi 49.1
- Crawford-Det 36.7
- Speaker-Bos 31.5
- Lajoie-Cle 28.8

Adjusted Batter Runs
- Cobb-Det 58.0
- Collins-Phi 46.9
- Crawford-Det 32.5
- Speaker-Bos 29.6
- Stahl-Bos 26.8

Clutch Hitting Index
- Chase-NY 143
- Engle-NY 132
- Crawford-Det 129
- Cobb-Det 125
- Davis-Phi 122

Runs Created
- Cobb-Det 159
- Collins-Phi 134
- Crawford-Det 108
- Speaker-Bos 99
- Baker-Phi 90

Total Average
- Cobb-Det 1.193
- Collins-Phi 1.051
- Stahl-Bos .857
- Speaker-Bos .854
- Crawford-Det .851

Stolen Bases
- Cobb-Det 76
- Collins-Phi 67
- Bush-Det 53
- Lord-Bos 36
- Dougherty-Chi 36

Stolen Base Average

Stolen Base Runs

Fielding Runs
- Speaker-Bos 23.0
- Lajoie-Cle 18.6
- Parent-Chi 16.6
- McConnell-Bos 14.5
- Wagner-Bos 14.0

Total Player Rating
- Collins-Phi 6.2
- Cobb-Det 6.0
- Speaker-Bos 5.1
- Lajoie-Cle 5.0
- Bush-Det 2.6

Wins
- Mullin-Det 29
- Smith-Chi 25
- Willett-Det 21

Win Percentage
- Mullin-Det .784
- Krause-Phi .692
- Bender-Phi .692
- Summers-Det .679
- Willett-Det .677

Games
- Smith-Chi 51
- Arellanes-Bos 45
- Groom-Was 44
- Willett-Det 41

Complete Games
- Smith-Chi 37
- Young-Cle 30
- Mullin-Det 29
- Johnson-Was 27
- Morgan-Bos-Phi 26

Shutouts
- Walsh-Chi 8
- Smith-Chi 7
- Krause-Phi 7
- Coombs-Phi 6

Saves
- Arellanes-Bos 8
- Powell-StL 3

Innings Pitched
- Smith-Chi 365.0
- Mullin-Det 303.2
- Johnson-Was 296.1
- Young-Cle 294.1
- Morgan-Bos-Phi 293.1

Fewest Hits/Game
- Morgan-Bos-Phi 6.26
- Krause-Phi 6.38
- Walsh-Chi 6.49
- Cicotte-Bos 6.49
- Wood-Bos 6.78

Fewest BB/Game
- Joss-Cle 1.15
- White-Chi 1.57
- Powell-StL 1.58
- Bender-Phi 1.62
- Summers-Det 1.66

Strikeouts
- Smith-Chi 177
- Johnson-Was 164
- Berger-Cle 162
- Bender-Phi 161
- Waddell-StL 141

Strikeouts/Game
- Berger-Cle 5.90
- Krause-Phi 5.87
- Bender-Phi 5.80
- Waddell-StL 5.76
- Bailey-StL 5.16

Ratio
- Walsh-Chi 8.60
- Joss-Cle 8.64
- Smith-Chi 8.73
- Bender-Phi 8.86
- Krause-Phi 9.00

Earned Run Average
- Krause-Phi 1.39
- Walsh-Chi 1.41
- Bender-Phi 1.66
- Joss-Cle 1.71
- Killian-Det 1.71

Adjusted ERA
- Krause-Phi 172
- Walsh-Chi 166
- Joss-Cle 149
- Killian-Det 147
- Bender-Phi 145

Opponents' Batting Avg.
- Morgan-Bos-Phi .202
- Walsh-Chi .203
- Krause-Phi .204
- Cicotte-Bos .207
- Wood-Bos .209

Opponents' On-Base Pct.
- Walsh-Chi .253
- Bender-Phi .254
- Joss-Cle .255
- Smith-Chi .257
- Krause-Phi .266

Starter Runs
- Walsh-Chi 27.2
- Smith-Chi 27.2
- Krause-Phi 25.5
- Bender-Phi 22.6
- Morgan-Bos-Phi 21.5

Adjusted Starter Runs
- Walsh-Chi 25.1
- Krause-Phi 24.5
- Smith-Chi 23.0
- Joss-Cle 22.0
- Bender-Phi 21.3

Clutch Pitching Index
- Burns-Was-Chi 142
- Killian-Det 132
- Brockett-NY 132
- Waddell-StL 125
- Bailey-StL 117

Relief Runs

Adjusted Relief Runs

Relief Ranking

Total Pitcher Index
- Smith-Chi 4.7
- Walsh-Chi 4.6
- Bender-Phi 3.0
- Plank-Phi 2.7
- Krause-Phi 2.7

Total Baseball Ranking
- Collins-Phi 6.2
- Cobb-Det 6.0
- Speaker-Bos 5.1
- Lajoie-Cle 5.0
- Smith-Chi 4.7

TEAM	G	W	L	PCT	GB	R	OR	AB	H	2B	3B	HR	BB	SO	AVG	OBP	SLG	OPS	OPS+	BR	BR+	PF	CHI	RC	SB	CS	SBA	SBR
CHI	154	104	50	.675		712	**499**	4977	1333	219	**84**	**34**	542	501	.268	.344	**.366**	710	114	81	87	99	101	696	173			
NY	155	91	63	.591	13	**715**	567	5061	**1391**	204	83	31	562	**489**	**.275**	**.354**	**.366**	**720**	**116**	**106**	**105**	100	97	**759**	282			
PIT	154	86	67	.562	17.5	655	576	5125	1364	214	83	33	437	524	.266	.328	.360	688	100	30	-6	106	100	655	148			
PHI	157	78	75	.510	25.5	674	639	5171	1319	**223**	71	22	506	559	.255	.327	.338	665	97	-4	-24	103	**106**	641	199			
CIN	156	75	79	.487	29	620	684	5121	1326	150	79	23	529	515	.259	.332	.333	665	105	0	29	96	98	669	**310**			
BRO	156	64	90	.416	40	497	623	5125	1174	166	73	25	434	706	.229	.294	.305	599	82	-132	-117	97	101	506	151			
STL	153	63	90	.412	40.5	639	718	4912	1217	167	70	15	**655**	581	.248	.345	.319	664	103	19	44	96	99	609	179			
BOS	157	53	100	.346	50.5	495	701	5123	1260	173	49	31	359	540	.246	.301	.317	618	81	-99	-121	105	96	536	152			
TOT	621					5007		40615	10384	1516	592	214	4024	4415	.256	.329	.338	666							1594			

TEAM	CG	SH	SV	IP	H	H/G	HR	BB	SO	RAT	ERA	ERA+	OAV	OOB	PR	PR+	PF	CPI	FA	E	DP	FW	PW	BW	SBW	DIF
CHI	100	**25**	13	1378[2]	**1171**	**7.7**	18	474	609	**11.1**	**2.51**	**115**	**.235**	**.307**	**79**	**57**	95	95	.963	**230**	110	**2.1**	**6.0**	9.2		9.8
NY	96	9	10	1391[2]	1290	8.4	30	397	**717**	11.2	2.68	110	.250	.308	54	45	98	99	.955	291	117	-1.6	4.8	**11.1**		-.0
PIT	73	13	12	1376	1254	8.3	20	**392**	479	11.2	2.84	109	.250	.311	29	37	102	93	.961	245	102	1.2	3.9	-.6		5.2
PHI	84	17	9	1411[1]	1297	8.3	36	547	657	12.1	3.06	102	.253	.330	-5	9	103	101	.960	258	132	.7	1.0	-2.5		2.5
CIN	86	16	11	1386[2]	1334	8.7	27	528	497	12.6	3.09	94	.261	.338	-9	-30	96	105	.955	291	103	-1.5	-3.1	3.1		-.3
BRO	**103**	15	5	1420[1]	1331	8.5	**17**	545	555	12.2	3.07	99	.259	.335	-7	-9	100	101	**.964**	235	125	2.0	-.9	-12.3		-1.7
STL	81	4	**14**	1337[1]	1396	9.4	30	541	466	13.4	3.78	79	.275	.350	-112	-122	98	96	.959	261	109	.0	-12.8	4.7		-5.2
BOS	72	12	9	1390[1]	1328	8.6	36	599	531	12.8	3.22	103	.265	.349	-30	13	110	**110**	.954	305	**137**	-2.3	1.4	-12.7		-9.7
TOT	695	111	83	11092[1]		8.5				12.1	3.03		.256	.329					.959	2116	935					

Runs
Magee-Phi 110
Huggins-StL 101
Byrne-Pit 101
Doyle-NY 97
Bescher-Cin 95

Hits
Wagner-Pit 178
Byrne-Pit 178
Wheat-Bro 172
Magee-Phi 172
Hoblitzel-Cin 170

Doubles
Byrne-Pit 43
Magee-Phi 39
Wheat-Bro 36
Merkle-NY 35
Wagner-Pit 34

Triples
Mitchell-Cin 18
Magee-Phi 17
Konetchy-StL 16
Hofman-Chi 16

Home Runs
Schulte-Chi 10
Beck-Bos 10
Doyle-NY 8
Daubert-Bro 8

Total Bases
Magee-Phi 263
Schulte-Chi 257
Byrne-Pit 251
Wheat-Bro 244
Wagner-Pit 240

Runs Batted In
Magee-Phi 123
Mitchell-Cin 88
Murray-NY 87
Hofman-Chi 86
Wagner-Pit 81

Runs Produced
Magee-Phi 227
Wagner-Pit 167
Hofman-Chi 166
Mitchell-Cin 162
Konetchy-StL 162

Bases On Balls
Huggins-StL 116
Evers-Chi 108
Magee-Phi 94
Titus-Phi 93
Sheckard-Chi 83

Batting Average
Magee-Phi 331
Campbell-Pit 326
Hofman-Chi 325
Snodgrass-NY 321
Wagner-Pit 320

On-Base Percentage
Magee-Phi 445
Snodgrass-NY 440
Evers-Chi 413
Hofman-Chi 406
Huggins-StL 399

Slugging Average
Magee-Phi 507
Hofman-Chi 461
Schulte-Chi 460
Merkle-NY 441
Campbell-Pit 436

On-Base Plus Slugging
Magee-Phi 952
Snodgrass-NY 871
Hofman-Chi 867
Konetchy-StL 822
Wagner-Pit 822

Adjusted OPS
Magee-Phi 172
Snodgrass-NY 154
Hofman-Chi 154
Konetchy-StL 145
Schulte-Chi 137

Batter Runs
Magee-Phi 54.9
Hofman-Chi 32.4
Snodgrass-NY 31.9
Konetchy-StL 28.0
Wagner-Pit 27.9

Adjusted Batter Runs
Magee-Phi 50.9
Hofman-Chi 33.2
Snodgrass-NY 31.8
Konetchy-StL 31.6
Wagner-Pit 22.6

Clutch Hitting Index
Magee-Phi 139
Evans-StL 135
Devlin-NY 132
Murray-NY 125
Steinfeldt-Chi 124

Runs Created
Magee-Phi 139
Byrne-Pit 104
Wagner-Pit 103
Hofman-Chi 102
Doyle-NY 101

Total Average
Magee-Phi 1.205
Snodgrass-NY 1.071
Hofman-Chi 975
Konetchy-StL 884
Paskert-Cin 884

Stolen Bases
Bescher-Cin 70
Murray-NY 57
Paskert-Cin 51
Magee-Phi 49
Devore-NY 43

Stolen Base Average

Stolen Base Runs

Fielding Runs
Shean-Bos 42.5
Doolan-Phi 20.7
Tinker-Chi 15.5
Paskert-Cin 14.1
Knabe-Phi 13.9

Total Player Rating
Konetchy-StL 3.9
Hofman-Chi 3.4
Mowrey-StL 3.2
Wagner-Pit 3.2
Magee-Phi 3.1

Wins
Mathewson-NY 27
Brown-Chi 25
Moore-Phi 22
Suggs-Cin 20
Cole-Chi 20

Win Percentage
Cole-Chi 833
Crandall-NY 810
Mathewson-NY 750
Adams-Pit 667
Brown-Chi 641

Games
Mattern-Bos 51
Gaspar-Cin 48

Complete Games
Rucker-Bro 27
Mathewson-NY 27
Brown-Chi 27
Bell-Bro 25
Barger-Bro 25

Shutouts
Rucker-Bro 6
Moore-Phi 6
Mattern-Bos 6
Brown-Chi 6

Saves
Gaspar-Cin 7
Brown-Chi 7
Crandall-NY 5
Richie-Bos-Chi 4
Phillippe-Pit 4

Innings Pitched
Rucker-Bro 320.1
Mathewson-NY 318.1
Bell-Bro 310.0
Mattern-Bos 305.0
Brown-Chi 295.1

Fewest Hits/Game
Cole-Chi 6.53
Scanlan-Bro 7.25
Moore-Phi 7.25
Drucke-NY 7.27
Ames-NY 7.61

Fewest BB/Game
Suggs-Cin 1.62
Mathewson-NY 1.70
Crandall-NY 1.86
Brown-Chi 1.95
Wiltse-NY 1.99

Strikeouts
Moore-Phi 185
Mathewson-NY 184
Frock-Pit-Bos 171
Drucke-NY 151
Rucker-Bro 147

Strikeouts/Game
Drucke-NY 6.31
Frock-Pit-Bos 5.98
Moore-Phi 5.88
Mathewson-NY 5.20
Ames-NY 4.44

Ratio
Brown-Chi 9.87
Mathewson-NY 10.04
Bell-Bro 10.25
Adams-Pit 10.40
Crandall-NY 10.44

Earned Run Average
McQuillan-Phi 1.60
Cole-Chi 1.80
Brown-Chi 1.86
Mathewson-NY 1.89
Ames-NY 2.22

Adjusted ERA
Cole-Chi 159
Mathewson-NY 156
Brown-Chi 155
Adams-Pit 138
Ames-NY 133

Opponents' Batting Avg.
Cole-Chi 211
Drucke-NY 228
Moore-Phi 228
Brown-Chi 232
Scanlan-Bro 234

Opponents' On-Base Pct.
Brown-Chi 277
Mathewson-NY 286
Crandall-NY 289
Adams-Pit 291
Bell-Bro 296

Starter Runs
Mathewson-NY 40.0
Brown-Chi 38.2
Cole-Chi 32.5
McQuillan-Phi 24.2
Adams-Pit 21.3

Adjusted Starter Runs
Mathewson-NY 38.5
Brown-Chi 35.0
Cole-Chi 30.0
McQuillan-Phi 25.0
Adams-Pit 22.6

Clutch Pitching Index
Cole-Chi 136
Brown-Bos 122
Barger-Bro 122
Mathewson-NY 117
Curtis-Bos 116

Relief Runs

Adjusted Relief Runs

Relief Ranking

Total Pitcher Index
Mathewson-NY 6.1
Brown-Chi 5.1
Cole-Chi 3.2
McQuillan-Phi 2.4
Brown-Bos 2.3

Total Baseball Ranking
Mathewson-NY 6.1
Brown-Chi 5.1
Konetchy-StL 3.8
Hofman-Chi 3.4
Mowrey-StL 3.2

TEAM	G	W	L	PCT	GB	R	OR	AB	H	2B	3B	HR	BB	SO	AVG	OBP	SLG	OPS	OPS+	BR	BR+	PF	CHI	RC	SB	CS	SBA	SBR
PHI	155	102	48	.680		674	**442**	5154	**1373**	**191**	**105**	19	409		**.266**	.326	**.355**	**681**	**120**	**105**	**112**	99	99	**665**	207			
NY	156	88	63	.583	14.5	626	557	5051	1254	164	75	20	**464**		.248	.320	.322	642	101	44	10	106	102	614	**288**			
DET	155	86	68	.558	18	**679**	584	5039	1317	190	72	28	459		.261	**.329**	.344	673	110	96	54	107	102	655	249			
BOS	158	81	72	.529	22.5	641	564	5204	1350	175	87	**43**	430		.259	.323	.351	674	114	94	78	102	94	656	194			
CLE	161	71	81	.467	32	548	657	5395	1316	188	64	9	366		.244	.296	.308	604	94	-39	-46	101	99	548	189			
CHI	156	68	85	.444	35.5	457	479	5024	1058	115	58	7	403		.211	.275	.261	536	76	-150	-132	96	**111**	415	183			
WAS	157	66	85	.437	36.5	501	551	4989	1175	145	47	9	449		.236	.309	.289	598	98	-32	-6	95	94	508	192			
STL	158	47	107	.305	57	451	743	5077	1105	131	60	12	415		.218	.281	.274	555	84	-117	-87	94	101	438	169			
TOT	628					4577		40933	9948	1299	568	147	3395	5278	.244	.308	.314	621							1671			

TEAM	CG	SH	SV	IP	H	H/G	HR	BB	SO	RAT	ERA	ERA+	OAV	OOB	PR	PR+	PF	CPI	FA	E	DP	FW	PW	BW	SBW	DIF
PHI	**123**	**24**	5	1421^2	**1103**	**7.0**	**8**	450	**789**	10.2	**1.79**	**133**	**.221**	.292	**116**	**97**	94	**112**	**.965**	**230**	**117**	**3.9**	**10.8**	**12.5**		-.0
NY	110	14	**8**	1399	1238	8.0	16	**364**	654	10.7	2.62	102	.243	.300	-15	5	106	91	.956	286	95	.2	.6	1.2		10.7
DET	108	17	5	1380^1	1257	8.2	34	460	532	11.7	2.83	93	.248	.319	-47	-26	104	101	.956	288	79	-.0	-2.8	6.0		6.0
BOS	100	12	6	1430	1236	7.8	30	414	670	10.7	2.46	104	.235	.297	10	14	101	94	.954	309	80	-1.1	1.6	8.7		-4.5
CLE	92	13	5	1467	1392	8.6	10	488	617	12.0	2.89	90	.261	.330	-60	-49	103	104	.964	248	112	3.4	-5.4	-5.1		2.2
CHI	103	23	7	1421	1130	7.2	16	381	785	**9.9**	2.03	118	.222	**.281**	77	59	95	92	.954	314	100	-1.7	6.6	-14.6		1.4
WAS	119	19	3	1373^1	1215	8.0	19	375	674	10.8	2.47	101	.244	.304	8	5	99	101	.959	264	99	1.9	.6	-.6		-11.1
STL	101	9	3	1391	1356	8.8	14	532	557	12.6	3.10	80	.265	.341	-89	-97	98	106	.943	385	113	-6.2	-10.7	-9.6		-3.2
TOT	856	131	42	11283^1		8.0				11.1	2.52		.244	.308					.957	2324	795					

Runs
Cobb-Det 106
Lajoie-Cle 94
Speaker-Bos 92
Bush-Det 90
Milan-Was 89

Hits
Lajoie-Cle 227
Cobb-Det 194
Collins-Phi 188
Speaker-Bos 183
Crawford-Det 170

Doubles
Lajoie-Cle 51
Cobb-Det 35
Lewis-Bos 29
Murphy-Phi 28
Oldring-Phi 27

Triples
Crawford-Det 19
Lord-Cle-Phi 18
Murphy-Phi 18
Stahl-Bos 16
Cree-NY 16

Home Runs
Stahl-Bos 10
Lewis-Bos 8
Cobb-Det 8
Speaker-Bos 7
Crawford-Det 5

Total Bases
Lajoie-Cle 304
Cobb-Det 279
Speaker-Bos 252
Crawford-Det 249
Murphy-Phi 244

Runs Batted In
Crawford-Det 120
Cobb-Det 91
Collins-Phi 81
Stahl-Bos 77
Lajoie-Cle 76

Runs Produced
Crawford-Det 198
Cobb-Det 189
Lajoie-Cle 166
Collins-Phi 159
Baker-Phi 155

Bases On Balls
Bush-Det 78
Milan-Was 71
Wolter-NY 66
Cobb-Det 64

Batting Average
Cobb-Det .383
Lajoie-Cle .384
Speaker-Bos .340
Collins-Phi .324
Knight-NY .312

On-Base Percentage
Cobb-Det .456
Lajoie-Cle .445
Speaker-Bos .404
Collins-Phi .382
Milan-Was .379

Slugging Average
Cobb-Det .551
Lajoie-Cle .514
Speaker-Bos .468
Murphy-Phi .436
Oldring-Phi .430

On-Base Plus Slugging
Cobb-Det 1008
Lajoie-Cle 960
Speaker-Bos 873
Collins-Phi 800
Cree-NY 775

Adjusted OPS
Cobb-Det 202
Lajoie-Cle 198
Speaker-Bos 169
Collins-Phi 152
Murphy-Phi 143

Batter Runs
Lajoie-Cle 68.2
Cobb-Det 67.9
Speaker-Bos 44.9
Collins-Phi 33.4
Murphy-Phi 23.6

Adjusted Batter Runs
Lajoie-Cle 66.5
Cobb-Det 60.0
Speaker-Bos 42.5
Collins-Phi 34.4
Murphy-Phi 24.5

Clutch Hitting Index
LaPorte-NY 154
Crawford-Det 153
Chase-NY 135
Moriarty-Det 127
McBride-Was 122

Runs Created
Cobb-Det 156
Lajoie-Cle 147
Collins-Phi 123
Speaker-Bos 115
Crawford-Det 89

Total Average
Cobb-Det 1.321
Lajoie-Cle 1.085
Speaker-Bos .972
Collins-Phi .964
Cree-NY .820

Stolen Bases
Collins-Phi 81
Cobb-Det 65
Zeider-Chi 49
Bush-Det 49
Milan-Was 44

Stolen Base Average

Stolen Base Runs

Fielding Runs
Collins-Phi 33.7
McBride-Was 26.7
Wallace-StL 22.0
Speaker-Bos 15.1
Lajoie-Cle 14.8

Total Player Rating
Lajoie-Cle 8.8
Collins-Phi 7.5
Cobb-Det 6.8
Speaker-Bos 5.5
Wallace-StL 3.5

Wins
Coombs-Phi 31
Ford-NY 26
Johnson-Was 25
Bender-Phi 23
Mullin-Det 21

Win Percentage
Bender-Phi .821
Ford-NY .813
Coombs-Phi .775
Donovan-Det .708
Mullin-Det .636

Games
Walsh-Chi 45
Johnson-Was 45
Coombs-Phi 45
Scott-Chi 41

Complete Games
Johnson-Was 38
Coombs-Phi 35
Walsh-Chi 33
Ford-NY 29
Mullin-Det 27

Shutouts
Coombs-Phi 13
Johnson-Was 8
Ford-NY 8
Walsh-Chi 7

Saves
Walsh-Chi 5
Browning-Det 3

Innings Pitched
Johnson-Was 370.0
Walsh-Chi 369.2
Coombs-Phi 353.0
Ford-NY 299.2
Morgan-Phi 290.2

Fewest Hits/Game
Ford-NY 5.83
Walsh-Chi 5.89
Coombs-Phi 6.32
Johnson-Was 6.37
Bender-Phi 6.55

Fewest BB/Game
Walsh-Chi 1.49
Young-Cle 1.49
Collins-Bos 1.51
Bender-Phi 1.69
Johnson-Was 1.85

Strikeouts
Johnson-Was 313
Walsh-Chi 258
Coombs-Phi 224
Ford-NY 209
Bender-Phi 155

Strikeouts/Game
Johnson-Was 7.61
Wood-Bos 6.64
Walsh-Chi 6.28
Ford-NY 6.28
Coombs-Phi 5.71

Ratio
Walsh-Chi 7.47
Ford-NY 8.17
Johnson-Was 8.54
Bender-Phi 8.60
Collins-Bos 9.09

Earned Run Average
Walsh-Chi 1.27
Coombs-Phi 1.30
Johnson-Was 1.36
Morgan-Phi 1.55
Bender-Phi 1.58

Adjusted ERA
Walsh-Chi 189
Johnson-Was 183
Coombs-Phi 182
Ford-NY 161
Collins-Bos 158

Opponents' Batting Avg.
Walsh-Chi .187
Ford-NY .188
Coombs-Phi .201
Johnson-Was .205
Hall-Bos .207

Opponents' On-Base Pct.
Walsh-Chi .226
Ford-NY .245
Bender-Phi .255
Johnson-Was .257
Collins-Bos .264

Starter Runs
Walsh-Chi 51.4
Coombs-Phi 47.7
Johnson-Was 47.5
Morgan-Phi 31.3
Ford-NY 28.8

Adjusted Starter Runs
Walsh-Chi 48.7
Johnson-Was 46.8
Coombs-Phi 44.6
Ford-NY 31.7
Morgan-Phi 28.2

Clutch Pitching Index
Morgan-Phi 142
Olmstead-Chi 142
Vaughn-NY 122
Wood-Bos 116
Coombs-Phi 114

Relief Runs

Adjusted Relief Runs

Relief Ranking

Total Pitcher Index
Walsh-Chi 7.4
Johnson-Was 5.8
Coombs-Phi 5.2
Bender-Phi 3.9
Ford-NY 3.8

Total Baseball Ranking
Lajoie-Cle 8.8
Collins-Phi 7.5
Walsh-Chi 7.4
Cobb-Det 6.8
Johnson-Was 5.8

TEAM	G	W	L	PCT	GB	R	OR	AB	H	2B	3B	HR	BB	SO	AVG	OBP	SLG	OPS	OPS+	BR	BR+	PF	CHI	RC	SB	CS	SBA	SBR
NY	154	99	54	.647		756	**542**	5006	1399	225	103	41	530	**506**	**.279**	**.358**	**.390**	**748**	**113**	**109**	**85**	103	96	**820**	**347**			
CHI	157	92	62	.597	7.5	**757**	607	5130	1335	218	101	54	585	617	.260	.341	.374	715	107	44	43	100	102	729	214			
PIT	155	85	69	.552	14.5	744	557	5137	1345	206	**106**	49	525	583	.262	.336	.372	708	101	28	2	104	104	698	160			
PHI	153	79	73	.520	19.5	658	669	5044	1307	214	56	**60**	490	588	.259	.328	.359	687	98	-11	-19	101	100	647	153			
STL	158	75	74	.503	22	671	745	5132	1295	199	86	26	**592**	650	.252	.337	.340	677	99	-18	1	97	99	651	175			
CIN	159	70	83	.458	29	682	706	5291	1379	180	105	21	578	594	.261	.337	.346	683	102	-10	16	96	97	716	289			
BRO	154	64	86	.427	33.5	539	659	5059	1198	151	71	28	425	.683	.237	.301	.311	612	80	-152	-130	96	**106**	528	184			
BOS	156	44	107	.291	54	699	1021	5308	**1417**	**249**	54	37	554	577	.267	.340	.355	695	93	10	-44	108	98	696	169			
TOT	623					5506		41107	10675	1642	682	316	4279	4798	.260	.336	.356	691							1691			

TEAM	CG	SH	SV	IP	H	H/G	HR	BB	SO	RAT	ERA	ERA+	OAV	OOB	PR	PR+	PF	CPI	FA	E	DP	FW	PW	BW	SBW	DIF
NY	**95**	19	13	1368	1267	8.4	33	**369**	**771**	11.0	**2.70**	**125**	.246	**.300**	**106**	**101**	99	97	.959	256	86	.5	**10.2**	**8.6**		3.4
CHI	85	12	**16**	1411	1270	**8.2**	**26**	525	582	11.8	2.90	114	**.245**	.320	78	63	97	100	.960	260	114	.6	6.4	4.4		3.9
PIT	91	13	11	1380[1]	**1249**	**8.2**	36	375	605	**10.9**	2.84	121	.248	.306	85	87	101	97	**.963**	232	**131**	**2.1**	8.8	.3		-3.0
PHI	90	**20**	10	1373[1]	1285	8.5	43	598	697	12.7	3.30	104	.255	.340	14	19	101	**104**	**.963**	**231**	113	2.0	2.0	-1.9		1.1
STL	88	6	10	1402[1]	1296	8.4	39	701	561	13.2	3.69	91	.254	.350	-46	-52	99	97	.960	261	106	.6	-5.2	.2		5.1
CIN	77	4	12	1425	1410	9.0	36	476	557	12.4	3.26	101	.265	.332	21	5	97	103	.955	295	108	-1.4	.6	1.7		-7.1
BRO	81	13	10	1371[2]	1310	8.6	27	566	533	12.6	3.40	98	.263	.344	0	-13	98	103	.962	241	112	1.5	-1.3	-13.0		2.0
BOS	73	5	7	1374	1570	10.3	76	672	486	15.1	5.09	75	.296	.381	-258	-174	113	96	.947	347	110	-4.9	-17.4	-4.4		-4.6
TOT	680	92	89	11105[2]		8.7				12.5	3.40		.260	.336					.959	2123	880					

Runs
Sheckard-Chi 121
Huggins-StL 106
Bescher-Cin 106
Schulte-Chi 105
Doyle-NY 102

Hits
Miller-Bos 192
Hoblitzel-Cin 180
Daubert-Bro 176
Schulte-Chi 173
Luderus-Phi 166

Doubles
Konetchy-StL 38
Miller-Bos 36
Wilson-Pit 34
Herzog-Bos-NY 33
Sweeney-Bos 33

Triples
Doyle-NY 25
Mitchell-Cin 22
Schulte-Chi 21
Zimmerman-Chi 17
Byrne-Pit 17

Home Runs
Schulte-Chi 21
Luderus-Phi 16
Magee-Phi 15
Doyle-NY 13

Total Bases
Schulte-Chi 308
Doyle-NY 277
Luderus-Phi 260
Hoblitzel-Cin 258
Wilson-Pit 257

Runs Batted In
Wilson-Pit 107
Schulte-Chi 107
Luderus-Phi 99
Magee-Phi 94

Runs Produced
Schulte-Chi 191
Konetchy-StL 172
Wilson-Pit 167
Wagner-Pit 167
Sheckard-Chi 167

Bases On Balls
Sheckard-Chi 147
Bates-Cin 103
Bescher-Cin 102
Huggins-StL 96
Knabe-Phi 94

Batting Average
Wagner-Pit .334
Miller-Bos .333
Meyers-NY .332
Clarke-Pit .324
Fletcher-NY .319

On-Base Percentage
Sheckard-Chi .434
Wagner-Pit .423
Bates-Cin .415
Sweeney-Bos .404
Doyle-NY .397

Slugging Average
Schulte-Chi .534
Doyle-NY .527
Wagner-Pit .507
Clarke-Pit .492
Magee-Phi .483

On-Base Plus Slugging
Wagner-Pit 930
Doyle-NY 924
Schulte-Chi 918
Magee-Phi 849
Wilson-Pit 826

Adjusted OPS
Schulte-Chi 156
Wagner-Pit 154
Doyle-NY 153
Magee-Phi 135
Konetchy-StL 132

Batter Runs
Schulte-Chi 40.6
Doyle-NY 39.3
Wagner-Pit 38.8
Sheckard-Chi 31.7
Clarke-Pit 27.0

Adjusted Batter Runs
Schulte-Chi 40.4
Doyle-NY 35.9
Wagner-Pit 35.0
Sheckard-Chi 31.6
Bates-Cin 27.6

Clutch Hitting Index
Hofman-Chi 133
Miller-Pit 128
Grant-Cin 126
Snodgrass-NY 124
Wilson-Pit 117

Runs Created
Schulte-Chi 127
Doyle-NY 124
Bescher-Cin 115
Wagner-Pit 109
Miller-Bos 107

Total Average
Doyle-NY 1.077
Wagner-Pit 1.057
Schulte-Chi 1.015
Sheckard-Chi 1.003
Bates-Cin .943

Stolen Bases
Bescher-Cin 81
Devore-NY 61
Snodgrass-NY 51
Merkle-NY 49

Stolen Base Average

Stolen Base Runs

Fielding Runs
Tinker-Chi 23.4
Doolan-Phi 20.3
Ingerton-Bos 18.2
Herzog-Bos-NY 17.8
Merkle-NY 15.3

Total Player Rating
Wagner-Pit 4.4
Sheckard-Chi 3.9
Herzog-Bos-NY 3.3
Tinker-Chi 3.1
Sweeney-Bos 2.9

Wins
Alexander-Phi 28
Mathewson-NY 26
Marquard-NY 24
Harmon-StL 23

Win Percentage
Marquard-NY .774
Crandall-NY .750
Cole-Chi .720
Alexander-Phi .683
Mathewson-NY .667

Games
Brown-Chi 53
Harmon-StL 51
Rucker-Bro 48
Alexander-Phi 48

Complete Games
Alexander-Phi 31
Mathewson-NY 29
Harmon-StL 28
Leifield-Pit 26
Adams-Pit 24

Shutouts
Alexander-Phi 7
Adams-Pit 6

Saves
Brown-Chi 13
Crandall-NY 5

Innings Pitched
Alexander-Phi 367.0
Harmon-StL 348.0
Leifield-Pit 318.0
Rucker-Bro 315.2
Moore-Phi 308.1

Fewest Hits/Game
Alexander-Phi 6.99
Marquard-NY 7.16
Rucker-Bro 7.27
Ames-NY 7.46
Harmon-StL 7.50

Fewest BB/Game
Mathewson-NY 1.11
Adams-Pit 1.29
Steele-Pit-Bro 1.71
Brown-Chi 1.83
Wiltse-NY 1.87

Strikeouts
Marquard-NY 237
Alexander-Phi 227
Rucker-Bro 190
Moore-Phi 174
Harmon-StL 144

Strikeouts/Game
Marquard-NY 7.68
Alexander-Phi 5.57
Rucker-Bro 5.42
Ames-NY 5.18
Moore-Phi 5.08

Ratio
Adams-Pit 9.30
Ames-NY 10.01
Mathewson-NY 10.03
Steele-Pit-Bro 10.33
Alexander-Phi 10.35

Earned Run Average
Mathewson-NY 1.99
Richie-Chi 2.31
Adams-Pit 2.33
Marquard-NY 2.50
Alexander-Phi 2.57

Adjusted ERA
Mathewson-NY 168
Adams-Pit 147
Richie-Chi 143
Marquard-NY 134
Alexander-Phi 133

Opponents' Batting Avg.
Alexander-Phi .219
Marquard-NY .219
Ames-NY .223
Rucker-Bro .226
Keefe-Cin .229

Opponents' On-Base Pct.
Adams-Pit .271
Ames-NY .277
Mathewson-NY .283
Wiltse-NY .292
Alexander-Phi .293

Starter Runs
Mathewson-NY 47.7
Adams-Pit 34.5
Alexander-Phi 33.3
Richie-Chi 30.3
Marquard-NY 27.6

Adjusted Starter Runs
Mathewson-NY 46.9
Adams-Pit 35.3
Alexander-Phi 34.5
Richie-Chi 28.5
Leifield-Pit 27.7

Clutch Pitching Index
Moore-Phi 130
Mathewson-NY 122
Richie-Chi 119
Leifield-Pit 117
Gaspar-Cin 115

Relief Runs
Richter-Chi 1.6

Adjusted Relief Runs
Richter-Chi 1.1

Relief Ranking
Richter-Chi .8

Total Pitcher Index
Mathewson-NY 6.7
Alexander-Phi 3.5
Adams-Pit 3.5
Leifield-Pit 3.2
Rucker-Bro 3.1

Total Baseball Ranking
Mathewson-NY 6.7
Wagner-Pit 4.4
Sheckard-Chi 3.9
Alexander-Phi 3.5
Adams-Pit 3.5

TEAM	G	W	L	PCT	GB	R	OR	AB	H	2B	3B	HR	BB	SO	AVG	OBP	SLG	OPS	OPS+	BR	BR+	PF	CHI	RC	SB	CS	SBA	SBR
PHI	152	101	50	.669		**861**	**602**	5199	1540	237	93	**35**	424		**.296**	**.357**	**.398**	**755**	**119**	**108**	**123**	98	104	821	226			
DET	154	89	65	.578	13.5	831	777	5294	**1544**	230	**96**	30	471		.292	.355	.388	743	108	91	52	105	102	**825**	**276**			
CLE	156	80	73	.523	22	693	712	5321	1501	**238**	81	20	354		.282	.333	.369	702	101	1	-7	101	97	716	209			
CHI	154	77	74	.510	24	718	624	5210	1401	179	92	20	385		.269	.325	.350	675	97	-46	-24	97	**108**	660	201			
BOS	153	78	75	.510	24	680	643	5014	1379	203	66	**35**	**506**		.275	.350	.363	713	106	39	46	99	91	710	190			
NY	153	76	76	.500	25.5	684	723	5052	1374	190	**96**	25	493		.272	.344	.362	706	97	24	-20	107	94	724	269			
WAS	154	64	90	.416	38.5	624	765	5065	1308	159	54	16	466		.258	.330	.320	650	89	-75	-63	98	100	607	215			
STL	152	45	107	.296	56.5	567	812	4996	1192	187	63	17	460		.239	.307	.311	618	81	-142	-120	96	105	515	125			
TOT	614					5658		41151	11239	1623	641	198	3559	5093	.274	.338	.359	696							1711			

TEAM	CG	SH	SV	IP	H	H/G	HR	BB	SO	RAT	ERA	ERA+	OAV	OOB	PR	PR+	PF	CPI	FA	E	DP	FW	PW	BW	SBW	DIF
PHI	97	13	**13**	1375^{2}	1343	**8.8**	**17**	487	739	12.6	3.01	105	.264	.338	50	22	94	106	**.964**	**225**	100	**4.9**	2.2	**12.1**		6.4
DET	**108**	8	3	1387^{2}	1514	9.9	28	460	538	13.3	3.73	93	.283	.348	-60	-43	104	97	.951	318	78	-.9	-4.2	5.2		12.1
CLE	93	6	6	1390^{2}	1382	9.0	**17**	552	675	13.0	3.36	101	.267	.345	-3	7	102	100	.954	303	**108**	.3	.7	-.6		3.3
CHI	85	**17**	11	1386^{1}	1349	**8.8**	22	**384**	**752**	**11.5**	2.97	108	**.255**	**.310**	57	39	96	88	.961	252	98	3.4	3.9	-2.3		-3.3
BOS	87	10	8	1351^{2}	**1309**	**8.8**	21	473	711	12.2	**2.75**	**119**	.262	.332	**89**	**80**	98	**113**	.949	323	93	-1.4	**7.9**	4.6		-9.4
NY	90	5	3	1360^{2}	1404	9.3	26	406	667	12.4	3.54	101	.270	.329	-30	9	108	89	.949	328	99	-1.7	.9	-1.9		2.9
WAS	106	13	3	1353^{1}	1471	9.8	39	410	628	12.9	3.52	93	.277	.334	-27	-38	98	96	.953	305	90	-.0	-3.7	-6.1		-2.9
STL	92	8	1	1332^{1}	1465	9.9	28	463	383	13.4	3.86	87	.278	.342	-77	-73	101	90	.945	358	104	-3.8	-7.1	-11.7		-8.2
TOT	758	80	48	10938^{1}		9.3				12.7	3.34		.274	.338					.954	2412	770					

Runs
Cobb-Det 147
Jackson-Cle 126
Bush-Det 126
Milan-Was 109
Crawford-Det 109

Hits
Cobb-Det 248
Jackson-Cle 233
Crawford-Det 217
Baker-Phi 198
Milan-Was 194

Doubles
Cobb-Det 47
Jackson-Cle 45
Baker-Phi 42
Lord-Phi 37
LaPorte-StL 37

Triples
Cobb-Det 24
Cree-NY 22
Jackson-Cle 19
Lord-Chi 18
Wolter-NY 15

Home Runs
Baker-Phi 11
Speaker-Bos 8
Cobb-Det 8

Total Bases
Cobb-Det 367
Jackson-Cle 337
Crawford-Det 302
Baker-Phi 301
Cree-NY 267

Runs Batted In
Cobb-Det 127
Crawford-Det 115
Baker-Phi 115
Bodie-Chi 97
Delahanty-Det 94

Runs Produced
Cobb-Det 266
Crawford-Det 217
Jackson-Cle 202
Baker-Phi 200

Bases On Balls
Bush-Det 98
Milan-Was 74
Gessler-Was 74
Hooper-Bos 73
Austin-StL 69

Batting Average
Cobb-Det .420
Jackson-Cle .408
Crawford-Det .378
Collins-Phi .365
Cree-NY .348

On-Base Percentage
Jackson-Cle .468
Cobb-Det .467
Collins-Phi .451
Crawford-Det .438
Speaker-Bos .418

Slugging Average
Cobb-Det .621
Jackson-Cle .590
Crawford-Det .526
Cree-NY .513
Baker-Phi .508

On-Base Plus Slugging
Cobb-Det 1088
Jackson-Cle 1058
Crawford-Det 964
Collins-Phi 932
Cree-NY 928

Adjusted OPS
Cobb-Det 193
Jackson-Cle 192
Collins-Phi 163
Crawford-Det 160
Speaker-Bos 158

Batter Runs
Cobb-Det 78.4
Jackson-Cle 71.8
Crawford-Det 52.4
Collins-Phi 43.0
Cree-NY 39.9

Adjusted Batter Runs
Cobb-Det 70.9
Jackson-Cle 70.1
Crawford-Det 46.1
Collins-Phi 45.1
Speaker-Bos 39.3

Clutch Hitting Index
Stovall-Cle 163
Gessler-Was 147
Hartzell-NY 131
Barry-Phi 130
Moriarty-Det 128

Runs Created
Cobb-Det 207
Jackson-Cle 175
Crawford-Det 147
Cree-NY 129
Baker-Phi 127

Total Average
Cobb-Det 1.464
Jackson-Cle 1.308
Collins-Phi 1.125
Crawford-Det 1.120
Cree-NY 1.103

Stolen Bases
Cobb-Det 83
Milan-Was 58
Cree-NY 48
Callahan-Chi 45
Lord-Chi 43

Stolen Base Average

Stolen Base Runs

Fielding Runs
Tannehill-Chi 42.5
Gardner-Bos 23.6
McBride-Was 23.5
Bush-Det 16.7
Austin-StL 16.2

Total Player Rating
Cobb-Det 6.8
Jackson-Cle 6.7
Collins-Phi 4.9
Baker-Phi 3.8
Speaker-Bos 3.5

Wins
Coombs-Phi 28
Walsh-Chi 27
Johnson-Was 25

Win Percentage
Bender-Phi .773
Gregg-Cle .767
Plank-Phi .742
Coombs-Phi .700
Morgan-Phi .682

Games
Walsh-Chi 56
Coombs-Phi 47
Wood-Bos 44
Caldwell-NY 41

Complete Games
Johnson-Was 36
Walsh-Chi 33
Ford-NY 26
Coombs-Phi 26

Shutouts
Plank-Phi 6
Johnson-Was 6
Wood-Bos 5
Walsh-Chi 5
Gregg-Cle 5

Saves
Walsh-Chi 4
Plank-Phi 4
Hall-Bos 4
Wood-Bos 3
Bender-Phi 3

Innings Pitched
Walsh-Chi 368.2
Coombs-Phi 336.2
Johnson-Was 322.1
Ford-NY 281.1
Wood-Bos 275.2

Fewest Hits/Game
Gregg-Cle 6.33
Wood-Bos 7.38
Krapp-Cle 7.62
Morgan-Phi 7.82
Scott-Chi 7.91

Fewest BB/Game
White-Chi 1.47
Lake-StL 1.67
Walsh-Chi 1.76
Warhop-NY 1.89
Powell-StL 1.91

Strikeouts
Walsh-Chi 255
Wood-Bos 231
Johnson-Was 207
Coombs-Phi 185
Ford-NY 158

Strikeouts/Game
Wood-Bos 7.54
Walsh-Chi 6.23
Lange-Chi 5.79
Johnson-Was 5.78
Kahler-Cle 5.66

Ratio
Gregg-Cle 9.86
Walsh-Chi 9.91
Wood-Bos 10.22
Johnson-Was 10.33
Ford-NY 10.59

Earned Run Average
Gregg-Cle 1.80
Johnson-Was 1.90
Wood-Bos 2.02
Plank-Phi 2.10
Bender-Phi 2.16

Adjusted ERA
Gregg-Cle 189
Johnson-Was 173
Wood-Bos 162
Ford-NY 158
Plank-Phi 150

Opponents' Batting Avg.
Gregg-Cle .205
Wood-Bos .223
Krapp-Cle .232
Ford-NY .237
Johnson-Was .238

Opponents' On-Base Pct.
Walsh-Chi .280
Johnson-Was .283
Wood-Bos .284
Gregg-Cle .286
Ford-NY .291

Starter Runs
Johnson-Was 51.6
Walsh-Chi 45.8
Gregg-Cle 41.8
Wood-Bos 40.3
Plank-Phi 35.2

Adjusted Starter Runs
Johnson-Was 50.3
Gregg-Cle 42.7
Walsh-Chi 42.4
Wood-Bos 39.0
Ford-NY 38.3

Clutch Pitching Index
Plank-Phi 133
Pape-Bos 130
Cicotte-Bos 122
Bender-Phi 117
Willett-Det 111

Relief Runs

Adjusted Relief Runs

Relief Ranking

Total Pitcher Index
Wood-Bos 6.6
Johnson-Was 6.5
Walsh-Chi 6.4
Gregg-Cle 4.6
Ford-NY 3.9

Total Baseball Ranking
Cobb-Det 6.8
Jackson-Cle 6.7
Wood-Bos 6.6
Johnson-Was 6.5
Walsh-Chi 6.4

TEAM	G	W	L	PCT	GB	R	OR	AB	H	2B	3B	HR	BB	SO	AVG	OBP	SLG	OPS	OPS+	BR	BR+	PF	CHI	RC	SB	CS	SBA	SBR
NY	154	103	48	.682		**823**	571	5067	1451	231	89	**47**	514	497	**.286**	**.360**	.395	**755**	**110**	**89**	**66**	103	104	**830**	**319**			
PIT	152	93	58	.616	10	751	**565**	5252	**1493**	222	**129**	39	420	514	.284	.340	**.398**	738	**110**	44	56	99	99	767	177			
CHI	152	91	59	.607	11.5	756	668	5048	1398	**245**	91	42	**560**	615	.277	.354	.386	740	109	62	65	100	98	750	164			
CIN	155	75	78	.490	29	656	722	5115	1310	183	89	21	479	**492**	.256	.323	.339	662	90	-90	-71	97	**107**	639	248			
PHI	152	73	79	.480	30.5	670	688	5077	1354	244	68	43	464	615	.267	.332	.367	699	91	-23	-65	107	99	671	159			
STL	153	63	90	.412	41	659	830	5092	1366	190	77	27	508	620	.268	.340	.352	692	97	-27	-10	98	97	675	193			
BRO	153	58	95	.379	46	651	744	5141	1377	220	73	32	490	584	.268	.336	.358	694	100	-28	0	96	96	677	179			
BOS	155	52	101	.340	52	693	871	5361	1465	227	68	35	454	690	.273	.335	.361	696	94	-28	-40	102	99	693	137			
TOT	613					5659		41153	11214	1762	684	286	3889	4627	.273	.341	.370	710							1576			

TEAM	CG	SH	SV	IP	H	H/G	HR	BB	SO	RAT	ERA	ERA+	OAV	OOB	PR	PR+	PF	CPI	FA	E	DP	FW	PW	BW	SBW	DIF
NY	93	8	**16**	1369^2	1352	8.9	35	**338**	652	**11.3**	**2.59**	**130**	.259	**.307**	**124**	**120**	99	103	.956	280	123	-2.0	**11.9**	**6.5**		11.3
PIT	**94**	**18**	7	1385	**1268**	**8.3**	**28**	497	**664**	11.8	2.86	114	**.251**	.324	84	63	96	99	**.972**	**169**	125	**6.0**	6.2	5.6		-.1
CHI	80	15	9	1358^2	1307	8.7	33	493	554	12.3	3.43	97	.259	.331	-4	-20	98	89	.960	249	125	.0	-1.9	6.4		11.6
CIN	86	13	10	1377^2	1455	9.6	**28**	452	561	12.9	3.43	98	.279	.344	-4	-14	99	102	.960	249	102	.4	-1.3	-6.9		6.6
PHI	81	10	9	1355	1381	9.2	43	515	616	12.9	3.25	111	.272	.344	23	50	106	**107**	.963	231	98	1.4	5.0	-6.3		-2.8
STL	61	6	12	1353	1466	9.8	31	560	487	13.8	3.86	89	.286	.361	-68	-63	101	102	.957	274	113	-1.7	-6.1	-.9		-4.5
BRO	71	10	8	1357	1399	9.3	45	510	553	12.9	3.65	92	.273	.343	-37	-50	98	96	.959	255	96	-.3	-4.9	.0		-13.2
BOS	88	5	5	1390^2	1544	10.0	43	521	542	13.7	4.17	86	.291	.359	-119	-94	105	95	.954	297	**129**	-3.2	-9.2	-3.9		-8.0
TOT	654	85	76	10946^2		9.2				12.7	3.40		.273	.341					.961	2004	911					

Runs
Bescher-Cin 120
Carey-Pit 114
Paskert-Phi 102
Campbell-Bos 102

Hits
Zimmerman-Chi 207
Sweeney-Bos 204
Campbell-Bos 185
Doyle-NY 184
Wagner-Pit 181

Doubles
Zimmerman-Chi 41
Paskert-Phi 37
Wagner-Pit 35
Miller-Pit 33
Doyle-NY 33

Triples
Wilson-Pit 36
Wagner-Pit 20
Murray-NY 20
Daubert-Bro 16

Home Runs
Zimmerman-Chi 14
Schulte-Chi 12
Wilson-Pit 11
Merkle-NY 11
Cravath-Phi 11

Total Bases
Zimmerman-Chi 318
Wilson-Pit 299
Wagner-Pit 277
Sweeney-Bos 264
Doyle-NY 263

Runs Batted In
Wagner-Pit 102
Sweeney-Bos 100
Zimmerman-Chi 99
Wilson-Pit 95
Murray-NY 92

Runs Produced
Wagner-Pit 186
Sweeney-Bos 183
Zimmerman-Chi 180
Doyle-NY 178
Carey-Pit 175

Bases On Balls
Sheckard-Chi 122
Paskert-Phi 91
Huggins-StL 87
Bescher-Cin 83
Titus-Phi-Bos 82

Batting Average
Zimmerman-Chi .... .372
Meyers-NY .... .358
Sweeney-Bos ...... .344
Evers-Chi .... .341
Doyle-NY .... .330

On-Base Percentage
Evers-Chi .... .431
Huggins-StL .... .422
Paskert-Phi .... .420
Zimmerman-Chi ... .418
Sweeney-Bos ...... .416

Slugging Average
Zimmerman-Chi .... .571
Wilson-Pit .... .513
Wagner-Pit .... .496
Meyers-NY .... .477
Doyle-NY .... .471

On-Base Plus Slugging
Zimmerman-Chi 989
Wagner-Pit 891
Evers-Chi 873
Doyle-NY 864
Titus-Phi-Bos 862

Adjusted OPS
Zimmerman-Chi 170
Wagner-Pit 145
Evers-Chi 139
Wilson-Pit 134
Konetchy-StL 134

Batter Runs
Zimmerman-Chi ... 49.8
Wagner-Pit 32.1
Sweeney-Bos 30.9
Evers-Chi 29.1
Meyers-NY 28.2

Adjusted Batter Runs
Zimmerman-Chi ... 50.3
Wagner-Pit 33.7
Evers-Chi 29.5
Sweeney-Bos 29.0
Meyers-NY 25.9

Clutch Hitting Index
Sweeney-Bos 138
Tinker-Chi 131
Hoblitzel-Cin 124
Murray-NY 119
Snodgrass-NY 114

Runs Created
Zimmerman-Chi 141
Sweeney-Bos 123
Wagner-Pit 118
Doyle-NY 116
Paskert-Phi 108

Total Average
Zimmerman-Chi ... 1.100
Wagner-Pit .... .976
Paskert-Phi .... .965
Evers-Chi .... .962
Doyle-NY .... .955

Stolen Bases
Bescher-Cin 67
Carey-Pit 45
Snodgrass-NY 43
Murray-NY 38

Stolen Base Average

Stolen Base Runs

Fielding Runs
Sweeney-Bos 30.2
Tinker-Chi 24.7
Wagner-Pit 22.9
Herzog-NY 19.2
Fletcher-NY 15.8

Total Player Rating
Wagner-Pit 6.4
Sweeney-Bos 5.9
Zimmerman-Chi 5.3
Evers-Chi 3.7
Konetchy-StL 2.6

Wins
Marquard-NY 26
Cheney-Chi 26
Hendrix-Pit 24
Mathewson-NY 23
Camnitz-Pit 22

Win Percentage
Hendrix-Pit .... .727
Cheney-Chi .... .722
Tesreau-NY .... .708
Marquard-NY ...... .703
Richie-Chi .... .667

Games
Benton-Cin 50
Sallee-StL 48
Alexander-Phi 46
Rucker-Bro 45
Seaton-Phi 44

Complete Games
Cheney-Chi 28
Mathewson-NY 27
Suggs-Cin 25
Hendrix-Pit 25
Alexander-Phi 25

Shutouts
Rucker-Bro 6
O'Toole-Pit 6
Suggs-Cin 5

Saves
Sallee-StL 6
Mathewson-NY 5
Rucker-Bro 4
Reulbach-Chi 4

Innings Pitched
Alexander-Phi 310.1
Mathewson-NY ... 310.0
Cheney-Chi 303.1
Suggs-Cin 303.0
Benton-Cin 302.0

Fewest Hits/Game
Tesreau-NY 6.56
Robinson-Pit 7.51
O'Toole-Pit 7.75
Cheney-Chi 7.77
Brown-Bos 7.81

Fewest BB/Game
Mathewson-NY ...... .99
Robinson-Pit 1.54
Suggs-Cin 1.66
Ames-NY 1.76
Adams-Pit 1.85

Strikeouts
Alexander-Phi 195
Hendrix-Pit 176
Marquard-NY 175
Benton-Cin 162
Rucker-Bro 151

Strikeouts/Game
Alexander-Phi 5.66
Hendrix-Pit 5.49
Marquard-NY 5.35
Tyler-Bos 5.06
O'Toole-Pit 4.90

Ratio
Robinson-Pit 9.57
Mathewson-NY ... 10.07
Rucker-Bro 10.49
Tesreau-NY 10.85
Adams-Pit 10.94

Earned Run Average
Tesreau-NY 1.96
Mathewson-NY 2.12
Rucker-Bro 2.21
Robinson-Pit 2.26
Ames-NY 2.46

Adjusted ERA
Tesreau-NY 172
Mathewson-NY 159
Rucker-Bro 151
Rixey-Phi 145
Robinson-Pit 144

Opponents' Batting Avg.
Tesreau-NY .... .204
Cheney-Chi .... .234
Robinson-Pit ...... .237
Brown-Bos .... .239
O'Toole-Pit .... .241

Opponents' On-Base Pct.
Mathewson-NY .... .281
Robinson-Pit ...... .284
Rucker-Bro .... .298
Tesreau-NY .... .298
Adams-Pit .... .303

Starter Runs
Mathewson-NY 44.1
Rucker-Bro 39.4
Tesreau-NY 38.8
Marquard-NY 27.3
Sallee-StL 26.0

Adjusted Starter Runs
Mathewson-NY 43.4
Tesreau-NY 38.3
Rucker-Bro 38.1
Marquard-NY 26.5
Sallee-StL 26.5

Clutch Pitching Index
Ames-NY 125
Geyer-StL 125
Benton-Cin 116
Dickson-Bos 116
Yingling-Bro 114

Relief Runs

Adjusted Relief Runs

Relief Ranking

Total Pitcher Index
Rucker-Bro 5.3
Mathewson-NY 5.3
Hendrix-Pit 4.4
Tesreau-NY 3.4
Alexander-Phi 2.9

Total Baseball Ranking
Wagner-Pit 6.4
Sweeney-Bos 5.9
Rucker-Bro 5.3
Zimmerman-Chi 5.3
Mathewson-NY 5.3

TEAM	G	W	L	PCT	GB	R	OR	AB	H	2B	3B	HR	BB	SO	AVG	OBP	SLG	OPS	OPS+	BR	BR+	PF	CHI	RC	SB	CS	SBA	SBR
BOS	154	105	47	.691		**799**	**544**	5071	1404	**269**	84	**29**	**565**		.277	**.355**	**.380**	**735**	110	**104**	66	105	100	752	185			
WAS	154	91	61	.599	14	699	581	5075	1298	202	86	20	472		.256	.324	.341	665	94	-32	-36	101	**108**	645	**274**			
PHI	153	90	62	.592	15	779	658	5111	**1442**	204	**108**	22	485		**.282**	.349	.377	726	**117**	83	**112**	96	101	**763**	258			
CHI	158	78	76	.506	28	639	648	5182	1321	174	80	17	423		.255	.317	.329	646	93	-68	-47	97	102	610	205			
CLE	155	75	78	.490	30.5	677	681	5132	1403	219	77	12	407		.273	.333	.353	686	98	5	-16	103	98	671	194			
DET	154	69	84	.451	36.5	720	777	5143	1376	189	86	19	530		.268	.343	.349	692	106	26	50	97	100	705	270			
STL	157	53	101	.344	53	552	764	5080	1262	166	71	19	449		.248	.315	.320	635	90	-86	-64	96	94	565	176			
NY	153	50	102	.329	55	630	842	5092	1320	168	79	18	463		.259	.329	.334	663	90	-31	-68	106	97	638	247			
TOT	619					5495		40886	10826	1591	671	156	3794	5157	.265	.333	.348	681							1809			

TEAM	CG	SH	SV	IP	H	H/G	HR	BB	SO	RAT	ERA	ERA+	OAV	OOB	PR	PR+	PF	CPI	FA	E	DP	FW	PW	BW	SBW	DIF
BOS	**108**	**18**	6	1362	1243	8.3	18	**385**	712	**11.0**	2.76	124	.248	**.306**	88	101	103	98	.957	267	88	2.5	10.1	6.6		10.0
WAS	98	11	7	1376[2]	**1219**	**8.0**	24	525	**828**	11.8	**2.70**	**125**	**.242**	.320	**99**	**104**	101	108	.954	297	92	.7	**10.4**	-3.5		7.6
PHI	95	11	9	1357	1273	8.5	**12**	518	601	12.3	3.33	93	.258	.336	2	-33	93	99	**.959**	**263**	115	**2.6**	-3.2	**11.2**		3.7
CHI	85	14	**16**	1413	1398	9.0	26	426	698	11.9	3.06	105	.264	.322	44	27	96	104	.956	291	102	1.5	2.7	-4.6		1.6
CLE	94	7	7	1352[2]	1367	9.1	15	523	622	12.9	3.31	104	.272	.346	6	20	103	**110**	.954	287	124	1.4	2.0	-1.5		-3.2
DET	107	7	5	1367[1]	1438	9.5	16	521	512	13.3	3.78	87	.277	.350	-66	-72	98	100	.950	338	91	-1.7	-7.1	5.0		-3.5
STL	85	8	5	1369[2]	1433	9.5	17	442	547	12.8	3.71	90	.277	.341	-56	-55	100	97	.947	341	**127**	-1.5	-5.4	-6.3		-10.5
NY	105	5	3	1335	1448	9.8	28	436	637	13.1	4.13	88	.282	.344	-117	-66	108	92	.940	382	77	-4.4	-6.5	-6.7		-8.2
TOT	777	81	58	10933[1]		9.0				12.4	3.34		.265	.333					.953	2466	816					

Runs
Collins-Phi 137
Speaker-Bos 136
Jackson-Cle 121
Cobb-Det 120
Baker-Phi 116

Hits
Jackson-Cle 226
Cobb-Det 226
Speaker-Bos 222
Baker-Phi 200

Doubles
Speaker-Bos 53
Jackson-Cle 44
Baker-Phi 40
Lewis-Bos 36

Triples
Jackson-Cle 26
Cobb-Det 23
Crawford-Det 21
Baker-Phi 21
Gardner-Bos 18

Home Runs
Speaker-Bos 10
Baker-Phi 10
Cobb-Det 7

Total Bases
Jackson-Cle 331
Speaker-Bos 329
Cobb-Det 323
Baker-Phi 312
Crawford-Det 273

Runs Batted In
Baker-Phi 130
Lewis-Bos 109
Crawford-Det 109
McInnis-Phi 101

Runs Produced
Baker-Phi 236
Speaker-Bos 216
Jackson-Cle 208
Collins-Phi 201
Cobb-Det 196

Bases On Balls
Bush-Det 117
Collins-Phi 101
Rath-Chi 95
Shotton-StL 86
Speaker-Bos 82

Batting Average
Cobb-Det .409
Jackson-Cle .395
Speaker-Bos .383
Lajoie-Cle .368
Collins-Phi .348

On-Base Percentage
Speaker-Bos .464
Jackson-Cle .458
Cobb-Det .456
Collins-Phi .450
Lajoie-Cle .414

Slugging Average
Cobb-Det .584
Jackson-Cle .579
Speaker-Bos .567
Baker-Phi .541
Crawford-Det .470

On-Base Plus Slugging
Cobb-Det 1040
Jackson-Cle 1036
Speaker-Bos 1031
Baker-Phi 945
Collins-Phi 885

Adjusted OPS
Cobb-Det 203
Jackson-Cle 190
Speaker-Bos 185
Baker-Phi 176
Collins-Phi 159

Batter Runs
Speaker-Bos 72.8
Jackson-Cle 70.3
Cobb-Det 67.1
Baker-Phi 49.2
Collins-Phi 43.7

Adjusted Batter Runs
Cobb-Det 71.7
Jackson-Cle 65.9
Speaker-Bos 65.5
Baker-Phi 53.9
Collins-Phi 48.3

Clutch Hitting Index
Lajoie-Cle 145
Lewis-Bos 130
Gandil-Was 125
Milan-Was 124
McInnis-Phi 120

Runs Created
Speaker-Bos 175
Cobb-Det 173
Jackson-Cle 166
Baker-Phi 140
Collins-Phi 136

Total Average
Cobb-Det 1.321
Speaker-Bos 1.310
Jackson-Cle 1.249
Collins-Phi 1.130
Baker-Phi 1.082

Stolen Bases
Milan-Was 88
Collins-Phi 63
Cobb-Det 61
Speaker-Bos 52
Zeider-Chi 47

Stolen Base Average

Stolen Base Runs

Fielding Runs
McBride-Was 31.1
Bush-Det 29.4
Louden-Det 22.8
Speaker-Bos 21.6
Rath-Chi 18.3

Total Player Rating
Speaker-Bos 7.4
Jackson-Cle 6.8
Baker-Phi 6.6
Collins-Phi 6.4
Cobb-Det 6.1

Wins
Wood-Bos 34
Johnson-Was 33
Walsh-Chi 27
Plank-Phi 26
Groom-Was 24

Win Percentage
Wood-Bos .872
Plank-Phi .813
Johnson-Was .733
Bedient-Bos .690
Coombs-Phi .677

Games
Walsh-Chi 62
Johnson-Was 50
Wood-Bos 43
Groom-Was 43
Benz-Chi 42

Complete Games
Wood-Bos 35
Johnson-Was 34
Walsh-Chi 32
Ford-NY 30

Shutouts
Wood-Bos 10
Johnson-Was 7
Walsh-Chi 6
Plank-Phi 5
Collins-Bos 4

Saves
Walsh-Chi 10
Warhop-NY 3
Mogridge-Chi 3
Lange-Chi 3
Dubuc-Det 3

Innings Pitched
Walsh-Chi 393.0
Johnson-Was 369.0
Wood-Bos 344.0
Groom-Was 316.0
Ford-NY 291.2

Fewest Hits/Game
Johnson-Was 6.32
Wood-Bos 6.99
Houck-Phi 7.37
Walsh-Chi 7.60
O'Brien-Bos 7.74

Fewest BB/Game
Bender-Phi 1.74
Johnson-Was 1.85
Collins-Bos 1.90
Powell-StL 1.99
Warhop-NY 2.06

Strikeouts
Johnson-Was 303
Wood-Bos 258
Walsh-Chi 254
Gregg-Cle 184
Groom-Was 179

Strikeouts/Game
Johnson-Was 7.39
Wood-Bos 6.75
Gregg-Cle 6.10
Walsh-Chi 5.82
Lange-Chi 5.23

Ratio
Johnson-Was 8.56
Wood-Bos 9.44
Walsh-Chi 9.78
Bedient-Bos 10.29
Collins-Bos 10.66

Earned Run Average
Johnson-Was 1.39
Wood-Bos 1.91
Walsh-Chi 2.15
Plank-Phi 2.22
Collins-Bos 2.53

Adjusted ERA
Johnson-Was 241
Wood-Bos 179
Walsh-Chi 149
Plank-Phi 140
Collins-Bos 135

Opponents' Batting Avg.
Johnson-Was .196
Wood-Bos .216
Walsh-Chi .231
Houck-Phi .234
Dubuc-Det .235

Opponents' On-Base Pct.
Johnson-Was .248
Wood-Bos .272
Walsh-Chi .279
Bedient-Bos .288
Collins-Bos .297

Starter Runs
Johnson-Was 79.9
Wood-Bos 54.6
Walsh-Chi 51.8
Plank-Phi 32.3
Groom-Was 25.2

Adjusted Starter Runs
Johnson-Was 80.1
Wood-Bos 56.4
Walsh-Chi 48.2
Plank-Phi 27.3
Groom-Was 25.7

Clutch Pitching Index
Hughes-Was 129
McConnell-NY 121
Cashion-Was 120
Kahler-Cle 120
Plank-Phi 119

Relief Runs

Adjusted Relief Runs

Relief Ranking

Total Pitcher Index
Johnson-Was 11.1
Wood-Bos 8.4
Walsh-Chi 6.8
Plank-Phi 3.5
McConnell-NY 2.8

Total Baseball Ranking
Johnson-Was 11.1
Wood-Bos 8.4
Speaker-Bos 7.4
Jackson-Cle 6.8
Walsh-Chi 6.8

TEAM	G	W	L	PCT	GB	R	OR	AB	H	2B	3B	HR	BB	SO	AVG	OBP	SLG	OPS	OPS+	BR	BR+	PF	CHI	RC	SB	CS	SBA	SBR
NY	156	101	51	.664		684	**515**	5218	1427	226	71	31	444	**501**	**.273**	**.338**	.362	700	105	43	38	101	99	**701**	**296**			
PHI	159	88	63	.583	12.5	693	636	5400	**1433**	**257**	78	**73**	383	578	.265	.318	**.382**	700	102	29	2	104	100	683	156			
CHI	155	88	65	.575	13.5	**720**	630	5022	1289	195	**96**	59	**554**	634	.257	.335	.369	**704**	**107**	**52**	**51**	100	104	661	181			
PIT	155	78	71	.523	21.5	673	585	5252	1383	210	86	35	391	545	.263	.319	.356	675	103	-13	15	96	**106**	629	181			
BOS	154	69	82	.457	31.5	641	690	5145	1318	191	60	32	488	640	.256	.326	.335	661	93	-26	-38	102	103	603	177			
BRO	152	65	84	.436	34.5	595	613	5165	1394	193	86	39	361	555	.270	.321	.363	684	98	4	-13	103	94	637	188			
CIN	156	64	89	.418	37.5	607	717	5132	1339	170	**96**	27	458	579	.261	.325	.347	672	98	-10	-7	100	96	630	226			
STL	153	51	99	.340	49	528	755	4967	1229	152	72	15	451	573	.247	.316	.316	632	88	-78	-70	99	97	534	171			
TOT	620					5141		41301	10812	1594	645	311	3530	4605	.262	.325	.355	679							1576			

TEAM	CG	SH	SV	IP	H	H/G	HR	BB	SO	RAT	ERA	ERA+	OAV	OOB	PR	PR+	PF	CPI	FA	E	DP	FW	PW	BW	SBW	DIF
NY	82	12	**17**	1422	**1276**	**8.1**	38	**315**	651	**10.2**	**2.43**	**128**	**.243**	**.289**	**122**	**110**	97	99	.961	254	107	-.6	**11.5**	4.0		10.3
PHI	77	**20**	11	1455[1]	1407	8.8	40	512	**667**	12.2	3.16	105	.261	.330	7	26	104	103	**.968**	**214**	112	**2.3**	2.8	.3		7.4
CHI	89	12	15	1373	1330	8.8	39	478	556	12.2	3.14	101	.260	.328	10	5	99	103	.959	260	106	-1.1	.6	**5.4**		6.8
PIT	74	9	7	1400	1344	8.7	**26**	434	590	11.7	2.90	104	.260	.320	46	18	94	**104**	.964	226	94	1.1	1.9	1.6		-.9
BOS	**105**	13	3	1373[1]	1343	8.9	38	419	597	11.9	3.20	103	.263	.324	1	11	103	100	.957	273	82	-2.0	1.2	-3.9		-1.6
BRO	71	9	7	1373	1287	8.5	33	439	548	11.7	3.13	105	.255	.321	11	22	103	97	.961	243	**125**	-.3	2.3	-1.3		-10.1
CIN	71	10	10	1380	1398	9.2	40	456	522	12.5	3.46	94	.273	.338	-40	-35	101	102	.961	251	104	-.4	-3.6	-.7		-7.6
STL	74	6	11	1351[2]	1426	9.5	57	477	465	13.1	4.24	76	.280	.348	-156	-150	101	92	.965	219	113	1.3	-15.6	-7.2		-2.4
TOT	643	91	81	11128[1]		8.8				11.9	3.20		.262	.325					.963	1940	843					

Runs
Leach-Chi 99
Carey-Pit 99
Lobert-Phi 98
Saier-Chi 94
Magee-Phi 92

Hits
Cravath-Phi 179
Daubert-Bro 178
Burns-NY 173
Lobert-Phi 172
Carey-Pit 172

Doubles
Smith-Bro 40
Burns-NY 37
Magee-Phi 36
Cravath-Phi 34

Triples
Saier-Chi 21
Miller-Pit 20
Konetchy-StL 17
Wilson-Pit 14
Cravath-Phi 14

Home Runs
Cravath-Phi 19
Luderus-Phi 18
Saier-Chi 14
Magee-Phi 11
Wilson-Pit 10

Total Bases
Cravath-Phi 298
Luderus-Phi 254
Saier-Chi 249
Miller-Pit 243
Lobert-Phi 243

Runs Batted In
Cravath-Phi 128
Zimmerman-Chi 95
Saier-Chi 92
Miller-Pit 90
Luderus-Phi 86

Runs Produced
Cravath-Phi 187
Saier-Chi 172
Miller-Pit 158
Zimmerman-Chi 155
Magee-Phi 151

Bases On Balls
Bescher-Cin 94
Huggins-StL 92
Leach-Chi 77
Bridwell-Chi 74

Batting Average
Daubert-Bro .... .350
Cravath-Phi .... .341
Viox-Pit .... .317
Tinker-Cin .... .317
Becker-Cin-Phi .... .316

On-Base Percentage
Huggins-StL .... .432
Cravath-Phi .... .407
Daubert-Bro .... .405
Viox-Pit .... .399
Leach-Chi .... .391

Slugging Average
Cravath-Phi .... .568
Becker-Cin-Phi .... .502
Zimmerman-Chi .... .490
Saier-Chi .... .480
Magee-Phi .... .479

On-Base Plus Slugging
Cravath-Phi 974
Zimmerman-Chi 868
Saier-Chi 850
Magee-Phi 848
Daubert-Bro 829

Adjusted OPS
Cravath-Phi 169
Zimmerman-Chi 147
Viox-Pit 142
Saier-Chi 141
Magee-Phi 135

Batter Runs
Cravath-Phi 50.4
Saier-Chi 27.5
Zimmerman-Chi 26.3
Daubert-Bro 25.2
Viox-Pit 24.8

Adjusted Batter Runs
Cravath-Phi 45.9
Viox-Pit 28.8
Saier-Chi 27.4
Zimmerman-Chi 26.2
Daubert-Bro 22.9

Clutch Hitting Index
Zimmerman-Chi 132
Cutshaw-Bro 127
Cravath-Phi 124
Doyle-NY 119
Fletcher-NY 116

Runs Created
Cravath-Phi 120
Saier-Chi 97
Lobert-Phi 96
Daubert-Bro 94
Carey-Pit 92

Total Average
Cravath-Phi 1.058
Saier-Chi .... .927
Zimmerman-Chi .... .925
Magee-Phi .... .905
Leach-Chi .... .895

Stolen Bases
Carey-Pit 61
Myers-Bos 57
Lobert-Phi 41
Burns-NY 40
Cutshaw-Bro 39

Stolen Base Average

Stolen Base Runs

Fielding Runs
Evers-Chi 29.9
Paskert-Phi 17.7
Cutshaw-Bro 17.5
Tinker-Cin 17.3
Doolan-Phi 17.2

Total Player Rating
Evers-Chi 3.9
Tinker-Cin 3.7
Cravath-Phi 3.6
Zimmerman-Chi 3.5
Wagner-Pit 2.8

Wins
Seaton-Phi 27
Mathewson-NY 25
Marquard-NY 23
Tesreau-NY 22
Alexander-Phi 22

Win Percentage
Humphries-Chi .... .800
Alexander-Phi .... .733
Marquard-NY .... .697
Mathewson-NY .... .694
Seaton-Phi .... .692

Games
Cheney-Chi 54
Seaton-Phi 52
Sallee-StL 50
Alexander-Phi 47
Camnitz-Pit-Phi 45

Complete Games
Tyler-Bos 28
Mathewson-NY 25
Cheney-Chi 25
Adams-Pit 24
Alexander-Phi 23

Shutouts
Alexander-Phi 9
Seaton-Phi 5

Saves
Cheney-Chi 11
Crandall-NY 6
Brown-Cin 6
Sallee-StL 5

Innings Pitched
Seaton-Phi 322.1
Adams-Pit 313.2
Alexander-Phi 306.1
Mathewson-NY 306.0
Cheney-Chi 305.0

Fewest Hits/Game
Tesreau-NY 7.09
Seaton-Phi 7.32
Allen-Bro 7.42
Pearce-Chi 7.52
Tyler-Bos 7.59

Fewest BB/Game
Mathewson-NY .... .62
Humphries-Chi 1.19
Adams-Pit 1.41
Marquard-NY 1.53
Suggs-Cin 1.58

Strikeouts
Seaton-Phi 168
Tesreau-NY 167
Alexander-Phi 159
Marquard-NY 151
Adams-Pit 144

Strikeouts/Game
Tesreau-NY 5.33
Hendrix-Pit 5.15
Marquard-NY 4.72
Seaton-Phi 4.69
Alexander-Phi 4.67

Ratio
Mathewson-NY 9.18
Adams-Pit 9.18
Marquard-NY 9.38
Humphries-Chi 9.70
Demaree-NY 9.87

Earned Run Average
Mathewson-NY 2.06
Adams-Pit 2.15
Tesreau-NY 2.17
Demaree-NY 2.21
Pearce-Chi 2.30

Adjusted ERA
Mathewson-NY 151
Tesreau-NY 143
Demaree-NY 141
Adams-Pit 140
Brennan-Phi 139

Opponents' Batting Avg.
Tesreau-NY .... .220
Seaton-Phi .... .226
Allen-Bro .... .231
Pearce-Chi .... .234
Tyler-Bos .... .235

Opponents' On-Base Pct.
Mathewson-NY .... .266
Adams-Pit .... .267
Marquard-NY .... .273
Humphries-Chi .... .277
Demaree-NY .... .286

Starter Runs
Mathewson-NY 38.7
Adams-Pit 36.4
Tesreau-NY 32.1
Marquard-NY 22.3
Demaree-NY 21.9

Adjusted Starter Runs
Mathewson-NY 36.8
Adams-Pit 31.8
Tesreau-NY 30.3
Seaton-Phi 25.1
Brennan-Phi 20.7

Clutch Pitching Index
Brennan-Phi 128
Packard-Cin 127
Brown-Cin 119
Ames-NY-Cin 119
Pearce-Chi 113

Relief Runs
Crandall-NY 3.7

Adjusted Relief Runs
Crandall-NY 2.9

Relief Ranking
Crandall-NY 2.5

Total Pitcher Index
Mathewson-NY 4.8
Tesreau-NY 4.0
Adams-Pit 3.9
Tyler-Bos 2.9
Cheney-Chi 2.6

Total Baseball Ranking
Mathewson-NY 4.8
Tesreau-NY 4.0
Evers-Chi 3.9
Adams-Pit 3.9
Tinker-Cin 3.7

TEAM	G	W	L	PCT	GB	R	OR	AB	H	2B	3B	HR	BB	SO	AVG	OBP	SLG	OPS	OPS+	BR	BR+	PF	CHI	RC	SB	CS	SBA	SBR
PHI	153	96	57	.627		**794**	592	5044	**1412**	**223**	80	**33**	**534**	547	**.280**	**.356**	**.375**	**731**	**124**	**135**	**152**	98	**105**	**732**	221			
WAS	155	90	64	.584	6.5	596	562	5074	1281	156	81	19	440	595	.252	.317	.326	643	93	-34	-46	102	**105**	585	**287**			
CLE	155	86	66	.566	9.5	633	536	5031	1349	206	74	16	420	557	.268	.331	.348	679	102	30	12	103	99	630	191			
BOS	151	79	71	.527	15.5	631	610	4969	1334	220	**101**	17	467	534	.268	.336	.364	700	109	66	50	103	95	652	189			
CHI	153	78	74	.513	17.5	488	**498**	4822	1139	157	66	24	398	550	.236	.299	.311	610	86	-94	-89	99	100	487	156			
DET	153	66	87	.431	30	625	716	5064	1344	180	**101**	24	496	**501**	.265	.336	.355	691	111	56	66	99	93	655	218			
NY	153	57	94	.377	38	529	668	4880	1157	155	45	8	**534**	617	.237	.320	.292	612	85	-75	-77	100	101	505	203			
STL	155	57	96	.373	39	528	642	5031	1193	179	73	18	455	769	.237	.306	.312	618	90	-80	-65	97	101	524	209			
TOT	614					4824		39915	10209	1476	621	159	3744	4670	.256	.326	.336	661							1674			

TEAM	CG	SH	SV	IP	H	H/G	HR	BB	SO	RAT	ERA	ERA+	OAV	OOB	PR	PR+	PF	CPI	FA	E	DP	FW	PW	BW	SBW	DIF
PHI	69	17	**22**	1351^{1}	1200	8.0	24	532	630	11.8	3.20	87	.229	.304	-39	-69	94	70	**.966**	**212**	108	**3.3**	-7.3	**16.2**		7.4
WAS	78	**23**	20	1396^{1}	**1177**	**7.6**	35	465	**758**	**11.1**	2.74	108	**.225**	**.297**	31	34	101	80	.960	261	122	.4	3.7	-4.8		14.0
CLE	93	18	5	1386^{2}	1278	8.3	19	502	689	11.9	2.55	119	.249	.321	59	71	104	**108**	.962	242	124	1.6	7.6	1.3		-.4
BOS	83	12	10	1358^{1}	1323	8.8	**6**	442	710	12.0	2.95	100	.260	.323	-2	-3	100	96	.961	238	84	1.4	-.3	5.4		-2.3
CHI	84	17	8	1360^{1}	1190	7.9	10	**438**	602	**11.1**	**2.33**	**125**	.237	.302	**91**	**89**	100	97	.960	255	104	.6	**9.5**	-9.4		1.5
DET	90	4	7	1360	1359	9.0	13	504	468	12.7	3.39	86	.265	.336	-68	-71	100	94	.954	303	105	-2.5	-7.5	7.1		-7.4
NY	75	8	7	1344	1318	8.9	31	455	530	12.3	3.28	91	.260	.327	-51	-41	102	94	.954	293	94	-1.9	-4.3	-8.1		-4.0
STL	**104**	14	5	1382^{1}	1369	9.0	21	454	476	12.3	3.07	96	.266	.332	-20	-22	100	103	.954	301	**125**	-2.2	-2.3	-6.9		-8.0
TOT	676	113	84	10939^{1}		8.5				11.9	2.93		.256	.326					.959	2105	866					

Runs
Collins-Phi 125
Baker-Phi 116
Jackson-Cle 109
Shotton-StL 105
E.Murphy-Phi 105

Hits
Jackson-Cle 197
Crawford-Det 193
Baker-Phi 190
Speaker-Bos 189
Collins-Phi 184

Doubles
Jackson-Cle 39
Speaker-Bos 35
Baker-Phi 34
Crawford-Det 32

Triples
Crawford-Det 23
Speaker-Bos 22
Jackson-Cle 17
Williams-StL 16
Cobb-Det 16

Home Runs
Baker-Phi 12
Crawford-Det 9
Bodie-Chi 8
Jackson-Cle 7

Total Bases
Crawford-Det 298
Jackson-Cle 291
Baker-Phi 278
Speaker-Bos 277
Collins-Phi 242

Runs Batted In
Baker-Phi 117
McInnis-Phi 90
Lewis-Bos 90
Pratt-StL 87
Barry-Phi 85

Runs Produced
Baker-Phi 221
Collins-Phi 195
Jackson-Cle 173
Oldring-Phi 167
McInnis-Phi 165

Bases On Balls
Shotton-StL 99
Collins-Phi 85
Wolter-NY 80
Jackson-Cle 80
Bush-Det 80

Batting Average
Cobb-Det .... .390
Jackson-Cle .... .373
Speaker-Bos .... .363
Collins-Phi .... .345
Baker-Phi .... .337

On-Base Percentage
Cobb-Det .... .467
Jackson-Cle .... .460
Collins-Phi .... .441
Speaker-Bos .... .441
Baker-Phi .... .413

Slugging Average
Jackson-Cle .... .551
Cobb-Det .... .535
Speaker-Bos .... .533
Baker-Phi .... .493
Crawford-Det ...... .489

On-Base Plus Slugging
Jackson-Cle 1011
Cobb-Det 1002
Speaker-Bos 974
Baker-Phi 906
Collins-Phi 894

Adjusted OPS
Cobb-Det 196
Jackson-Cle 190
Speaker-Bos 180
Baker-Phi 168
Collins-Phi 165

Batter Runs
Jackson-Cle 65.5
Speaker-Bos 55.9
Cobb-Det 51.9
Baker-Phi 46.0
Collins-Phi 45.7

Adjusted Batter Runs
Jackson-Cle 61.8
Cobb-Det 53.5
Speaker-Bos 53.0
Baker-Phi 48.5
Collins-Phi 48.3

Clutch Hitting Index
Barry-Phi 163
Lewis-Bos 133
Pratt-StL 127
McInnis-Phi 122
Turner-Cle 121

Runs Created
Jackson-Cle 140
Speaker-Bos 136
Collins-Phi 126
Cobb-Det 124
Baker-Phi 122

Total Average
Cobb-Det 1.310
Jackson-Cle 1.215
Speaker-Bos 1.193
Collins-Phi 1.111
Baker-Phi 1.029

Stolen Bases
Milan-Was 75
Moeller-Was 62
Collins-Phi 55
Cobb-Det 51
Speaker-Bos 46

Stolen Base Average

Stolen Base Runs

Fielding Runs
Weaver-Chi 33.9
Speaker-Bos 23.6
Turner-Cle 16.2
Collins-Phi 15.6
Shotton-StL 12.7

Total Player Rating
Speaker-Bos 6.9
Collins-Phi 6.9
Baker-Phi 6.3
Jackson-Cle 5.8
Cobb-Det 4.9

Wins
Johnson-Was 36
Falkenberg-Cle 23
Russell-Chi 22
Bender-Phi 21

Win Percentage
Johnson-Was .... .837
Bush-Phi .... .714
Boehling-Was ...... .708
Collins-Bos .... .704
Falkenberg-Cle ..... .697

Games
Russell-Chi 52
Scott-Chi 48
Johnson-Was 48
Bender-Phi 48
V.Gregg-Cle 44

Complete Games
Johnson-Was 29
Russell-Chi 26
Scott-Chi 25

Shutouts
Johnson-Was 11
Russell-Chi 8
Plank-Phi 7
Falkenberg-Cle 6

Saves
Bender-Phi 13
Hughes-Was 6
Bedient-Bos 5

Innings Pitched
Johnson-Was 346.0
Russell-Chi 316.2
Scott-Chi 312.1
V.Gregg-Cle 285.2
Falkenberg-Cle ... 276.0

Fewest Hits/Game
Johnson-Was 6.03
Mitchell-Cle 6.35
Engel-Was 6.78
Leverenz-StL 7.06
Russell-Chi 7.11

Fewest BB/Game
Johnson-Was .... .99
Collins-Bos 1.35
Mitchell-StL 1.72
Plank-Phi 2.11
Weilman-StL 2.15

Strikeouts
Johnson-Was 243
V.Gregg-Cle 166
Falkenberg-Cle 166
Scott-Chi 158
Groom-Was 156

Strikeouts/Game
Johnson-Was 6.32
Mitchell-Cle 5.85
Plank-Phi 5.60
Falkenberg-Cle 5.41
Groom-Was 5.31

Ratio
Johnson-Was 7.26
Russell-Chi 9.55
Scott-Chi 10.00
Cicotte-Chi 10.07
Plank-Phi 10.13

Earned Run Average
Johnson-Was 1.14
Cicotte-Chi 1.58
Scott-Chi 1.90
Russell-Chi 1.90
Mitchell-Cle 1.91

Adjusted ERA
Johnson-Was 258
Cicotte-Chi 185
Mitchell-Cle 159
Scott-Chi 154
Russell-Chi 153

Opponents' Batting Avg.
Johnson-Was ...... .187
Mitchell-Cle ...... .199
Engel-Was .... .207
Houck-Phi .... .214
Russell-Chi ...... .219

Opponents' On-Base Pct.
Johnson-Was ...... .217
Russell-Chi ...... .273
Bender-Phi .... .277
Cicotte-Chi ...... .281
Scott-Chi .... .281

Starter Runs
Johnson-Was 68.6
Cicotte-Chi 40.2
Russell-Chi 36.1
Scott-Chi 35.7
Mitchell-Cle 24.6

Adjusted Starter Runs
Johnson-Was 68.9
Cicotte-Chi 40.1
Russell-Chi 35.9
Scott-Chi 35.5
Mitchell-Cle 26.2

Clutch Pitching Index
Blanding-Cle 141
V.Gregg-Cle 130
Ford-NY 123
Baumgardner-StL ... 118
Cicotte-Chi 114

Relief Runs

Adjusted Relief Runs

Relief Ranking

Total Pitcher Index
Johnson-Was 10.8
Cicotte-Chi 5.0
Russell-Chi 4.2
Scott-Chi 3.9
Boehling-Was 2.7

Total Baseball Ranking
Johnson-Was 10.8
Speaker-Bos 6.9
Collins-Phi 6.9
Baker-Phi 6.3
Jackson-Cle 5.8

TEAM	G	W	L	PCT	GB	R	OR	AB	H	2B	3B	HR	BB	SO	AVG	OBP	SLG	OPS	OPS+	BR	BR+	PF	CHI	RC	SB	CS	SBA	SBR
BOS	158	94	59	.614		657	548	5206	1307	213	60	35	**502**	617	.251	.323	.335	658	103	17	21	99	103	602	139			
NY	156	84	70	.545	10.5	**672**	576	5146	1363	**222**	59	30	447	**479**	.265	**.330**	.348	678	**112**	53	**76**	97	103	**644**	**239**			
STL	157	81	72	.529	13	558	**540**	5046	1249	203	65	33	445	618	.248	.314	.333	647	100	-9	-2	99	95	576	204			
CHI	156	78	76	.506	16.5	605	638	5050	1229	199	74	42	501	577	.243	.317	.337	654	101	7	9	100	100	579	164			
BRO	154	75	79	.487	19.5	622	618	5152	**1386**	172	**90**	31	376	559	**.269**	.323	.355	678	106	43	29	102	97	629	173			
PHI	154	74	80	.481	20.5	651	687	5110	1345	211	52	**62**	472	570	.263	.329	**.361**	**690**	105	**69**	28	107	97	636	145			
PIT	158	69	85	.448	25.5	503	**540**	5145	1197	148	79	18	416	608	.233	.295	.303	598	88	-101	-79	96	101	488	147			
CIN	157	60	94	.390	34.5	530	651	4991	1178	142	64	16	441	627	.236	.305	.300	605	83	-79	-94	103	**105**	506	224			
TOT	625					4798		40846	10254	1510	543	267	3600	4655	.252	.317	.335	651							1435			

TEAM	CG	SH	SV	IP	H	H/G	HR	BB	SO	RAT	ERA	ERA+	OAV	OOB	PR	PR+	PF	CPI	FA	E	DP	FW	PW	BW	SBW	DIF
BOS	**104**	19	6	1421	1272	8.1	38	477	606	11.4	2.75	100	.249	.319	7	1	99	102	.963	246	**143**	1.9	.2	2.3		13.4
NY	88	**20**	9	1390^{2}	1298	8.5	47	**367**	563	11.0	2.95	90	.253	**.306**	-25	-49	95	92	.961	254	119	1.1	-5.2	**8.2**		3.1
STL	84	16	12	1424^{2}	1279	8.1	**26**	422	531	11.1	**2.39**	**117**	.250	.313	**64**	**64**	100	**112**	.964	239	109	2.2	**7.0**	-.2		-4.3
CHI	70	14	11	1389^{1}	**1169**	**7.6**	37	528	**651**	11.3	2.71	103	**.233**	.311	12	9	100	92	.951	310	87	-2.7	1.0	1.0		1.8
BRO	80	11	11	1368^{1}	1282	8.5	36	466	605	11.8	2.82	101	.255	.323	-5	7	103	105	.961	248	112	1.3	.8	3.2		-7.1
PHI	85	14	7	1379^{1}	1403	9.2	**26**	452	650	12.5	3.07	96	.270	.335	-42	-20	105	106	.950	324	81	-3.8	-2.1	3.1		.0
PIT	86	10	11	1405	1272	8.2	27	392	488	**10.9**	2.71	98	.249	.308	13	-10	95	95	**.966**	**223**	96	**3.4**	-1.0	-8.5		-1.7
CIN	74	15	**15**	1387^{1}	1259	8.2	30	489	607	11.7	2.94	100	.248	.320	-24	-3	105	95	.952	314	113	-2.8	-.3	-10.1		-3.6
TOT	671	119	82	11165^{2}		8.3				11.5	2.79		.252	.317					.959	2158	860					

Runs
Burns-NY 100
Magee-Phi 96
Daubert-Bro 89
Saier-Chi 87
Doyle-NY 87

Hits
Magee-Phi 171
Wheat-Bro 170
Burns-NY 170
Zimmerman-Chi 167
Becker-Phi 167

Doubles
Magee-Phi 39
Zimmerman-Chi 36
Burns-NY 35
Connolly-Bos 28

Triples
Carey-Pit 17
Zimmerman-Chi 12
Wilson-StL 12
Cutshaw-Bro 12

Home Runs
Cravath-Phi 19
Saier-Chi 18
Magee-Phi 15
Luderus-Phi 12

Total Bases
Magee-Phi 277
Cravath-Phi 249
Wheat-Bro 241
Zimmerman-Chi 239
Burns-NY 234

Runs Batted In
Magee-Phi 103
Cravath-Phi 100
Wheat-Bro 89
D.Miller-StL 88
Zimmerman-Chi 87

Runs Produced
Magee-Phi 184
Zimmerman-Chi 158
Cravath-Phi 157
Burns-NY 157
D.Miller-StL 151

Bases On Balls
Huggins-StL 105
Saier-Chi 94
Burns-NY 89
Evers-Bos 87
Cravath-Phi 83

Batting Average
Daubert-Bro .... .329
Becker-Phi .... .325
Dalton-Bro .... .319
Wheat-Bro .... .319
Stengel-Bro .... .316

On-Base Percentage
Stengel-Bro .... .404
Burns-NY .... .403
Cravath-Phi .... .402
Huggins-StL .... .396
Dalton-Bro .... .396

Slugging Average
Magee-Phi .... .509
Cravath-Phi .... .499
Connolly-Bos .... .494
Wheat-Bro .... .452
Becker-Phi .... .446

On-Base Plus Slugging
Cravath-Phi 901
Magee-Phi 890
Wheat-Bro 830
Stengel-Bro 829
Burns-NY 820

Adjusted OPS
Cravath-Phi 157
Magee-Phi 154
Burns-NY 149
Stengel-Bro 143
Wheat-Bro 143

Batter Runs
Cravath-Phi 42.7
Magee-Phi 40.7
Burns-NY 34.0
Connolly-Bos 31.0
Wheat-Bro 29.3

Adjusted Batter Runs
Burns-NY 37.6
Cravath-Phi 36.3
Magee-Phi 34.3
Connolly-Bos 31.5
Wheat-Bro 27.3

Clutch Hitting Index
Fletcher-NY 129
Maranville-Bos 127
Cutshaw-Bro 123
D.Miller-StL 122
Schmidt-Bos 121

Runs Created
Burns-NY 113
Magee-Phi 110
Cravath-Phi 103
Wheat-Bro 95
Becker-Phi 87

Total Average
Burns-NY .... .997
Cravath-Phi .... .997
Magee-Phi .... .965
Stengel-Bro .... .904
Wheat-Bro .... .857

Stolen Bases
Burns-NY 62
Herzog-Cin 46
Dolan-StL 42
Carey-Pit 38

Stolen Base Average

Stolen Base Runs

Fielding Runs
Maranville-Bos 51.8
Herzog-Cin 30.6
Cutshaw-Bro 27.5
Smith-Bro-Bos 22.6
Wheat-Bro 18.2

Total Player Rating
Maranville-Bos 5.7
Herzog-Cin 4.6
Magee-Phi 4.5
Wheat-Bro 4.2
Smith-Bro-Bos 4.1

Wins
Alexander-Phi 27
Tesreau-NY 26
Rudolph-Bos 26
James-Bos 26
Mathewson-NY 24

Win Percentage
James-Bos .... .788
Doak-StL .... .760
Tesreau-NY .... .722
Rudolph-Bos .... .722
Pfeffer-Bro .... .657

Games
Cheney-Chi 50
Mayer-Phi 48
Ames-Cin 47

Complete Games
Alexander-Phi 32
Rudolph-Bos 31
James-Bos 30
Mathewson-NY 29
Pfeffer-Bro 27

Shutouts
Tesreau-NY 8
Doak-StL 7
Rudolph-Bos 6
Cheney-Chi 6
Alexander-Phi 6

Saves
Sallee-StL 6
Ames-Cin 6
Cheney-Chi 5
Pfeffer-Bro 4
McQuillan-Pit 4

Innings Pitched
Alexander-Phi 355.0
Rudolph-Bos 336.1
James-Bos 332.1
Tesreau-NY 322.1
Mayer-Phi 321.0

Fewest Hits/Game
Tesreau-NY 6.65
Doak-StL 6.79
Cheney-Chi 6.91
Douglas-Cin 6.99
James-Bos 7.07

Fewest BB/Game
Mathewson-NY .... .66
Adams-Pit 1.24
Marquard-NY 1.58
Rudolph-Bos 1.63
Alexander-Phi 1.93

Strikeouts
Alexander-Phi 214
Tesreau-NY 189
Vaughn-Chi 165
Cheney-Chi 157
James-Bos 156

Strikeouts/Game
Alexander-Phi 5.43
Tesreau-NY 5.28
Vaughn-Chi 5.06
L.Tyler-Bos 4.64
Ragan-Bro 4.58

Ratio
Rudolph-Bos 9.45
Adams-Pit 9.51
Mathewson-NY 9.78
Doak-StL 10.09
Pfeffer-Bro 10.34

Earned Run Average
Doak-StL 1.72
James-Bos 1.90
Pfeffer-Bro 1.97
Vaughn-Chi 2.05
Sallee-StL 2.10

Adjusted ERA
Doak-StL 162
James-Bos 145
Pfeffer-Bro 145
Vaughn-Chi 135
Sallee-StL 133

Opponents' Batting Avg.
Tesreau-NY .... .209
Cheney-Chi .... .215
Doak-StL .... .216
Vaughn-Chi .... .222
Douglas-Cin .... .223

Opponents' On-Base Pct.
Adams-Pit .... .276
Rudolph-Bos .... .276
Mathewson-NY .... .278
Alexander-Phi .... .290
Doak-StL .... .290

Starter Runs
James-Bos 32.8
Doak-StL 30.2
Pfeffer-Bro 28.5
Vaughn-Chi 23.9
Sallee-StL 21.4

Adjusted Starter Runs
James-Bos 32.0
Doak-StL 30.3
Pfeffer-Bro 30.2
Vaughn-Chi 23.7
Sallee-StL 21.5

Clutch Pitching Index
Cooper-Pit 126
James-Bos 121
Crutcher-Bos 120
Perritt-StL 116
Sallee-StL 116

Relief Runs

Adjusted Relief Runs

Relief Ranking

Total Pitcher Index
James-Bos 3.7
Doak-StL 3.2
Alexander-Phi 3.2
Pfeffer-Bro 3.0
Sallee-StL 2.9

Total Baseball Ranking
Maranville-Bos 5.7
Herzog-Cin 4.6
Magee-Phi 4.5
Wheat-Bro 4.2
Smith-Bro-Bos 4.1

TEAM	G	W	L	PCT	GB	R	OR	AB	H	2B	3B	HR	BB	SO	AVG	OBP	SLG	OPS	OPS+	BR	BR+	PF	CHI	RC	SB	CS	SBA	SBR
PHI	158	99	53	.651		**749**	529	5126	**1392**	165	80	**29**	545	**517**	**.272**	**.348**	**.352**	**700**	**123**	**112**	**141**	96	**107**	**662**	231	188	55	-15
BOS	159	91	62	.595	8.5	589	**510**	5117	1278	**226**	**85**	18	490	549	.250	.320	.338	658	105	26	26	100	98	567	177	176	50	-23
WAS	158	81	73	.526	19	572	519	5108	1245	176	81	18	470	640	.244	.313	.320	633	93	-17	-38	104	102	544	220	163	57	-9
DET	157	80	73	.523	19.5	615	618	5102	1318	195	84	25	557	537	.258	.336	.344	680	109	76	56	103	93	630	211	154	**58**	**-7**
STL	159	71	82	.464	28.5	523	615	5101	1241	185	75	17	423	863	.243	.306	.319	625	99	-38	-17	96	99	516	233	189	55	-15
NY	157	70	84	.455	30	537	550	4992	1144	149	52	12	**577**	711	.229	.315	.287	602	88	-60	-58	100	105	484	**251**	191	57	-12
CHI	157	70	84	.455	30	487	560	5040	1205	161	71	19	408	609	.239	.302	.311	613	92	-59	-52	99	96	497	167	152	52	-16
CLE	157	51	102	.333	48.5	538	709	5157	1262	178	70	10	450	685	.245	.310	.312	622	90	-39	-59	104	100	517	167	157	52	-18
TOT	631					4610		40743	10085	1435	598	148	3920	5111	.248	.319	.324	642							1657	1370	55	-115

TEAM	CG	SH	SV	IP	H	H/G	HR	BB	SO	RAT	ERA	ERA+	OAV	OOB	PR	PR+	PF	CPI	FA	E	DP	FW	PW	BW	SBW	DIF
PHI	89	24	16	1404	1264	8.2	18	521	720	11.7	2.78	94	.249	.322	-6	-29	95	100	**.966**	**213**	116	**3.6**	-3.2	**15.6**	-.0	7.2
BOS	88	24	7	1427^{1}	1207	7.7	18	393	602	**10.3**	**2.37**	**114**	.236	**.295**	**59**	**51**	98	94	.963	242	99	1.9	**5.7**	2.9	-1.0	5.2
WAS	75	**25**	**19**	1420^{2}	**1170**	**7.5**	20	520	**784**	11.1	2.55	111	**.233**	.311	31	40	103	97	.961	254	116	1.0	4.5	-4.1	.6	2.2
DET	81	14	11	1412	1285	8.2	17	498	567	11.8	2.86	98	.249	.322	-19	-10	103	97	.958	286	101	-1.0	-1.1	6.2	**.8**	-1.3
STL	81	15	9	1410^{2}	1309	8.4	20	540	553	12.2	2.85	95	.251	.327	-17	-23	99	103	.952	317	114	-2.7	-2.5	-1.8	-.0	1.8
NY	**98**	9	2	1397^{1}	1277	8.3	30	**390**	563	11.0	2.82	98	.250	.308	-12	-10	101	94	.963	238	93	1.9	-1.1	-6.4	.3	-1.6
CHI	74	17	11	1398^{2}	1207	7.8	15	401	660	10.6	2.48	108	.239	.298	40	31	98	92	.955	299	90	-1.8	3.5	-5.7	-.2	-2.6
CLE	69	9	2	1391^{2}	1365	8.9	**10**	666	688	13.5	3.22	90	.267	.357	-74	-53	105	**110**	.953	300	**119**	-1.9	-5.8	-6.5	-.4	-10.8
TOT	655	137	77	11262^{1}		8.1				11.5	2.74		.248	.319					.959	2149	848					

Runs

Collins-Phi	122
Speaker-Bos	101
Murphy-Phi	101
Bush-Det	97

Hits

Speaker-Bos	193
Crawford-Det	183
Baker-Phi	182
McInnis-Phi	181
Collins-Phi	181

Doubles

Speaker-Bos	46
Lewis-Bos	37
Pratt-StL	34
Collins-Chi	34
Leary-StL	28

Triples

Crawford-Det	26
Gardner-Bos	19
Speaker-Bos	18
T.Walker-StL	16
Hooper-Bos	15

Home Runs

Baker-Phi	9
Crawford-Det	8
T.Walker-StL	6
Fournier-Chi	6

Total Bases

Speaker-Bos	287
Crawford-Det	281
Baker-Phi	252
Pratt-StL	240
Collins-Phi	238

Runs Batted In

Crawford-Det	104
McInnis-Phi	95
Speaker-Bos	90
Baker-Phi	89
Collins-Phi	85

Runs Produced

Collins-Phi	205
Speaker-Bos	187
Crawford-Det	170
McInnis-Phi	168
Baker-Phi	164

Bases On Balls

Bush-Det	112
Collins-Phi	97
Murphy-Phi	87
Speaker-Bos	77
Maisel-NY	76

Batting Average

Cobb-Det	.368
Collins-Phi	.344
Speaker-Bos	.338
Jackson-Cle	.338
Baker-Phi	.319

On-Base Percentage

Collins-Phi	.452
Speaker-Bos	.423
Jackson-Cle	.399
Crawford-Det	.388
Baker-Phi	.380

Slugging Average

Cobb-Det	.513
Speaker-Bos	.503
Crawford-Det	.483
Jackson-Cle	.464
Collins-Phi	.452

On-Base Plus Slugging

Speaker-Bos	926
Collins-Phi	904
Crawford-Det	871
Jackson-Cle	862
Baker-Phi	822

Adjusted OPS

Collins-Phi	179
Speaker-Bos	178
Crawford-Det	157
Baker-Phi	153
Jackson-Cle	153

Batter Runs

Speaker-Bos	54.9
Collins-Phi	51.6
Cobb-Det	42.3
Crawford-Det	42.1
Jackson-Cle	31.6

Adjusted Batter Runs

Collins-Phi	56.5
Speaker-Bos	54.9
Cobb-Det	39.8
Crawford-Det	38.8
Baker-Phi	35.2

Clutch Hitting Index

McInnis-Phi	147
Gandil-Was	138
Collins-Phi	127
Lewis-Bos	125
Crawford-Det	125

Runs Created

Speaker-Bos	124
Collins-Phi	120
Crawford-Det	113
Baker-Phi	95
Cobb-Det	89

Total Average

Collins-Phi	.984
Speaker-Bos	.943
Crawford-Det	.867
Jackson-Cle	.835
T.Walker-StL	.776

Stolen Bases

Maisel-NY	74
Collins-Phi	58
Speaker-Bos	42
Shotton-StL	40

Stolen Base Average

Maisel-NY	81.3
Sweeney-NY	76.0
Chapman-Cle	72.7
Moriarty-Det	69.4
Peckinpaugh-NY	69.1

Stolen Base Runs

Maisel-NY	10.3
Peckinpaugh-NY	2.4
Collins-Phi	2.3
Moriarty-Det	2.2
Chapman-Cle	2.1

Fielding Runs

Bush-Det	33.5
Speaker-Bos	27.7
Gandil-Was	23.7
Boone-NY	22.7
Turner-Cle	21.3

Total Player Rating

Speaker-Bos	7.6
Collins-Phi	6.6
Bush-Det	5.1
Baker-Phi	5.0
T.Walker-StL	4.1

Wins

Johnson-Was	28
Coveleski-Det	22
Collins-Bos	20
Leonard-Bos	19
Dauss-Det	19

Win Percentage

Bender-Phi	.850
Leonard-Bos	.792
Plank-Phi	.682
Caldwell-NY	.667
Shawkey-Phi	.652

Games

Johnson-Was	51
Ayers-Was	49
Shaw-Was	48
Benz-Chi	48

Complete Games

Johnson-Was	33
Coveleski-Det	23
Dauss-Det	22
Caldwell-NY	22

Shutouts

Johnson-Was	9
Leonard-Bos	7
Bender-Phi	7
Collins-Bos	6

Saves

Shaw-Was	4
Mitchell-StL	4
Faber-Chi	4
Bentley-Was	4

Innings Pitched

Johnson-Was	371.2
Coveleski-Det	303.1
Hamilton-StL	302.1
Dauss-Det	302.0
Weilman-StL	299.0

Fewest Hits/Game

Leonard-Bos	5.57
Caldwell-NY	6.46
Shaw-Was	6.93
Johnson-Was	6.95
Foster-Bos	6.97

Fewest BB/Game

McHale-NY	1.55
Russell-Chi	1.77
Johnson-Was	1.79
Warhop-NY	1.83
Ayers-Was	1.83

Strikeouts

Johnson-Was	225
Mitchell-Cle	179
Leonard-Bos	176
Shaw-Was	164
Dauss-Det	150

Strikeouts/Game

Leonard-Bos	7.05
Mitchell-Cle	6.27
Shaw-Was	5.74
Johnson-Was	5.45
Bender-Phi	5.38

Ratio

Leonard-Bos	8.29
Caldwell-NY	8.79
Johnson-Was	9.01
Foster-Bos	9.48
Ayers-Was	9.60

Earned Run Average

Leonard-Bos	.96
Foster-Bos	1.70
Johnson-Was	1.72
Caldwell-NY	1.94
Shore-Bos	2.00

Adjusted ERA

Leonard-Bos	279
Johnson-Was	163
Foster-Bos	158
Caldwell-NY	142
Cicotte-Chi	131

Opponents' Batting Avg.

Leonard-Bos	.180
Caldwell-NY	.205
Shaw-Was	.216
Johnson-Was	.217
Foster-Bos	.218

Opponents' On-Base Pct.

Leonard-Bos	.246
Caldwell-NY	.260
Johnson-Was	.265
Foster-Bos	.274
Benz-Chi	.282

Starter Runs

Leonard-Bos	44.3
Johnson-Was	41.9
Foster-Bos	24.3
Weilman-StL	21.8
Cicotte-Chi	20.8

Adjusted Starter Runs

Leonard-Bos	43.8
Johnson-Was	43.8
Foster-Bos	23.6
Weilman-StL	20.9
Cicotte-Chi	19.5

Clutch Pitching Index

Hagerman-Cle	126
Steen-Cle	123
Shawkey-Phi	109
James-StL	106
Bender-Phi	106

Relief Runs

Adjusted Relief Runs

Relief Ranking

Total Pitcher Index

Johnson-Was	7.1
Leonard-Bos	4.7
Cicotte-Chi	2.7
Foster-Bos	2.6
Caldwell-NY	2.5

Total Baseball Ranking

Speaker-Bos	7.6
Johnson-Was	7.1
Collins-Phi	6.6
Bush-Det	5.1
Baker-Phi	5.0

TEAM	G	W	L	PCT	GB	R	OR	AB	H	2B	3B	HR	BB	SO	AVG	OBP	SLG	OPS	OPS+	BR	BR+	PF	CHI	RC	SB	CS	SBA	SBR
IND	157	88	65	.575		**762**	622	5176	**1474**	**230**	**90**	33	470	668	**.285**	**.349**	**.383**	**732**	95	**-36**	-96	111	100	**765**	**273**			
CHI	157	87	67	.565	1.5	621	**517**	5098	1314	227	50	**52**	**520**	645	.258	.331	.352	683	**98**	-125	**-92**	94	94	634	171			
BAL	160	84	70	.545	4.5	645	628	5120	1374	222	67	32	487	589	.268	.337	.357	694	92	-105	-121	103	94	652	152			
BUF	155	80	71	.530	7	620	602	5064	1264	177	74	37	430	761	.250	.311	.336	647	80	-202	-211	102	**109**	574	228			
BRO	157	77	77	.500	11.5	662	677	5221	1402	225	85	42	404	665	.269	.326	.368	694	96	-117	-113	99	99	669	220			
KC	154	67	84	.444	20	644	683	5127	1369	226	77	39	399	621	.267	.324	.364	688	97	-127	-105	96	99	637	171			
PIT	154	64	86	.427	22.5	605	698	5114	1339	180	**90**	34	410	**575**	.262	.321	.352	673	90	-152	-148	99	96	613	153			
STL	154	62	89	.411	25	565	697	5078	1254	193	65	26	503	662	.247	.319	.326	645	77	-198	-220	105	96	554	113			
TOT	624					5124		40998	10790	1680	598	295	3623	5186	.264	.323	.355	678							1481			

TEAM	CG	SH	SV	IP	H	H/G	HR	BB	SO	RAT	ERA	ERA+	OAV	OOB	PR	PR+	PF	CPI	FA	E	DP	FW	PW	BW	SBW	DIF
IND	**104**	15	9	1397^{2}	1352	8.8	**29**	476	664	12.1	3.06	113	.258	.325	23	58	108	100	.956	289	113	-1.2	6.1	-9.9		16.7
CHI	93	**17**	8	1420^{1}	**1204**	**7.7**	43	393	650	**10.4**	**2.44**	**121**	**.233**	**.291**	**121**	**87**	92	94	**.962**	249	114	1.1	**9.1**	-9.5		9.5
BAL	88	15	13	1392	1389	9.0	34	**392**	**732**	11.8	3.13	108	.268	.323	12	35	105	101	.960	263	105	.6	3.7	-12.5		15.4
BUF	89	15	**16**	1387	1249	8.2	45	505	662	11.7	3.17	104	.245	.318	7	19	103	91	**.962**	**242**	109	**1.4**	2.0	-21.9		23.2
BRO	91	11	9	1385^{1}	1375	9.0	31	559	636	13.0	3.34	96	.264	.341	-20	-22	100	**102**	.956	283	120	-.8	-2.2	-11.7		14.9
KC	82	10	12	1361	1387	9.2	37	445	600	12.5	3.41	91	.268	.331	-30	-50	96	98	.957	279	**135**	-.9	-5.1	-10.9		8.6
PIT	97	9	6	1370	1416	9.4	38	444	510	12.4	3.57	89	.273	.333	-54	-59	99	96	.960	253	92	.6	-6.1	-15.3		10.0
STL	97	9	6	1367^{2}	1418	9.4	38	409	661	12.3	3.59	94	.267	.324	-58	-31	105	89	.957	273	94	-.5	-3.2	-22.8		13.2
TOT	741	101	79	11081		8.8				12.0	3.21		.264	.323					.959	2131	882					

Runs
Kauff-Ind 120
McKechnie-Ind 107
Duncan-Bal 99
Kenworthy-KC 93
Evans-Bro 93

Hits
Kauff-Ind 211
Zwilling-Chi 185
Evans-Bro 179
Oakes-Pit 178
Hanford-Buf 174

Doubles
Kauff-Ind 44
Evans-Bro 41
Kenworthy-KC 40
Zwilling-Chi 38

Triples
Evans-Bro 15
Esmond-Ind 15
Kenworthy-KC 14

Home Runs
Zwilling-Chi 16
Kenworthy-KC 15
Hanford-Buf 12
Evans-Bro 12

Total Bases
Kauff-Ind 305
Zwilling-Chi 287
Kenworthy-KC 286
Evans-Bro 286
Hanford-Buf 264

Runs Batted In
LaPorte-Ind 107
Evans-Bro 96
Zwilling-Chi 95
Kauff-Ind 95
Kenworthy-KC 91

Runs Produced
Kauff-Ind 207
LaPorte-Ind 189
Evans-Bro 177
Zwilling-Chi 170
Kenworthy-KC 169

Bases On Balls
Wickland-Chi 81
Agler-Buf 77
Kauff-Ind 72

Batting Average
Kauff-Ind .... .370
Evans-Bro .... .348
Easterly-KC .... .335
Shaw-Bro .... .324
Campbell-Ind ...... .318

On-Base Percentage
Kauff-Ind .... .447
Evans-Bro .... .416
Lennox-Pit .... .414
Meyer-Bal .... .395
Wilson-Chi .... .394

Slugging Average
Evans-Bro .... .556
Kauff-Ind .... .534
Kenworthy-KC ...... .525
Lennox-Pit .... .493
Zwilling-Chi ...... .485

On-Base Plus Slugging
Kauff-Ind 981
Evans-Bro 973
Lennox-Pit 907
Kenworthy-KC 896
Wilson-Chi 860

Adjusted OPS
Evans-Bro 165
Kauff-Ind 150
Kenworthy-KC 148
Lennox-Pit 148
Wilson-Chi 142

Batter Runs
Kauff-Ind 47.0
Evans-Bro 37.2
Lennox-Pit 23.2
Kenworthy-KC 21.3
Wilson-Chi 15.3

Adjusted Batter Runs
Evans-Bro 38.0
Kauff-Ind 35.2
Kenworthy-KC 25.1
Lennox-Pit 23.9
Wilson-Chi 20.0

Clutch Hitting Index
LaPorte-Ind 151
Swacina-Bal 137
Wisterzil-Bro 128
Stovall-KC 128
Carr-Ind 127

Runs Created
Kauff-Ind 160
Evans-Bro 121
Kenworthy-KC 114
Zwilling-Chi 106
McKechnie-Ind 94

Total Average
Kauff-Ind 1.278
Evans-Bro 1.087
Lennox-Pit 1.034
Kenworthy-KC ...... .995
Wilson-Chi .... .939

Stolen Bases
Kauff-Ind 75
McKechnie-Ind 47
Myers-Bro 43
Chadbourne-KC 42

Stolen Base Average

Stolen Base Runs

Fielding Runs
Doolan-Bal 29.3
McKechnie-Ind 22.9
Kenworthy-KC 20.8
Rariden-Ind 20.1
Tinker-Chi 19.1

Total Player Rating
Kenworthy-KC 4.9
Wilson-Chi 4.6
Kauff-Ind 4.3
Evans-Bro 2.8
McKechnie-Ind 1.6

Wins
Hendrix-Chi 29
Quinn-Bal 26
Seaton-Bro 25
Falkenberg-Ind 25
Suggs-Bal 24

Win Percentage
Ford-Buf .... .778
Hendrix-Chi .... .744
Quinn-Bal .... .650
Seaton-Bro .... .641
Suggs-Bal .... .632

Games
Hendrix-Chi 49
Falkenberg-Ind 49
Wilhelm-Bal 47
Suggs-Bal 46
Quinn-Bal 46

Complete Games
Hendrix-Chi 34
Falkenberg-Ind 33
Moseley-Ind 29
Quinn-Bal 27

Shutouts
Falkenberg-Ind 9
Seaton-Bro 7
Suggs-Bal 6
Hendrix-Chi 6

Saves
Ford-Buf 6
Wilhelm-Bal 5
Packard-KC 5
Hendrix-Chi 5

Innings Pitched
Falkenberg-Ind 377.1
Hendrix-Chi 362.0
Quinn-Bal 342.2
Suggs-Bal 319.1
Moseley-Ind 316.2

Fewest Hits/Game
Hendrix-Chi 6.51
Ford-Buf 6.91
Krapp-Buf 7.05
Fiske-Chi 7.32
Watson-Chi-StL 7.34

Fewest BB/Game
Ford-Buf 1.49
Suggs-Bal 1.61
Quinn-Bal 1.71
Hendrix-Chi 1.91
Keupper-StL 2.07

Strikeouts
Falkenberg-Ind 236
Moseley-Ind 205
Hendrix-Chi 189
Seaton-Bro 172
Groom-StL 167

Strikeouts/Game
Davenport-StL 5.93
Moseley-Ind 5.83
Falkenberg-Ind 5.63
Groom-StL 5.36
Seaton-Bro 5.11

Ratio
Hendrix-Chi 8.55
Ford-Buf 8.66
Falkenberg-Ind ... 10.16
Fiske-Chi 10.32
Lange-Chi 10.42

Earned Run Average
Johnson-Chi 1.57
Hendrix-Chi 1.69
Ford-Buf 1.82
Watson-Chi-StL 2.01
Falkenberg-Ind 2.22

Adjusted ERA
Ford-Buf 163
Hendrix-Chi 157
Falkenberg-Ind 141
Watson-Chi-StL 137
Lange-Chi 119

Opponents' Batting Avg.
Hendrix-Chi .... .203
Krapp-Buf .... .210
Ford-Buf .... .214
Lange-Chi .... .224
Watson-Chi-StL .... .230

Opponents' On-Base Pct.
Hendrix-Chi .... .251
Ford-Buf .... .254
Lange-Chi .... .282
Falkenberg-Ind .... .284
Anderson-Buf ...... .297

Starter Runs
Hendrix-Chi 48.0
Ford-Buf 29.3
Falkenberg-Ind 27.9
Watson-Chi-StL 22.1
Cullop-KC 17.8

Adjusted Starter Runs
Hendrix-Chi 42.1
Falkenberg-Ind 34.9
Ford-Buf 30.5
Watson-Chi-StL 19.6
Johnson-Chi 15.6

Clutch Pitching Index
Mullin-Ind 128
Lafitte-Bro 122
Watson-Chi-StL 114
Kaiserling-Ind 109
Quinn-Bal 106

Relief Runs

Adjusted Relief Runs

Relief Ranking

Total Pitcher Index
Hendrix-Chi 5.8
Falkenberg-Ind 3.5
Ford-Buf 3.0
Quinn-Bal 2.6
Krapp-Buf 1.8

Total Baseball Ranking
Hendrix-Chi 5.8
Kenworthy-KC 4.9
Wilson-Chi 4.6
Kauff-Ind 4.3
Falkenberg-Ind 3.5

TEAM	G	W	L	PCT	GB	R	OR	AB	H	2B	3B	HR	BB	SO	AVG	OBP	SLG	OPS	OPS+	BR	BR+	PF	CHI	RC	SB	CS	SBA	SBR
PHI	153	90	62	.592		589	**463**	4916	1216	202	39	**58**	460	600	.247	.316	.340	**656**	104	**31**	25	101	101	550	121	113	52	-13
BOS	157	83	69	.546	7	582	545	5070	1219	**231**	57	17	**549**	620	.240	**.321**	.319	640	**105**	15	**43**	96	98	554	121	98	55	-8
BRO	154	80	72	.526	10	536	560	5120	1268	165	75	14	313	**496**	.248	.295	.317	612	89	-56	-65	102	107	496	131	126	51	-15
CHI	156	73	80	.477	17.5	570	620	5114	1246	212	66	53	393	639	.244	.303	**.342**	645	102	4	3	100	100	555	166	124	57	-7
PIT	156	73	81	.474	18	557	520	5113	1259	197	91	24	419	656	.246	.309	.334	643	102	8	16	99	97	563	**182**	111	**62**	**1**
STL	157	72	81	.471	18.5	**590**	601	5106	1297	159	**92**	20	457	658	**.254**	.320	.333	653	104	30	29	100	98	**568**	162	144	53	-15
CIN	160	71	83	.461	20	516	585	5231	**1323**	194	84	15	360	512	.253	.308	.331	639	98	-5	-15	102	91	553	156	142	52	-15
NY	155	69	83	.454	21	582	628	5218	1312	195	68	24	315	547	.251	.300	.329	629	103	-27	6	94	**109**	526	155	137	53	-14
TOT	624					4522		40888	10140	1555	572	225	3266	4728	.248	.310	.331	640							1194	995	55	-86

TEAM	CG	SH	SV	IP	H	H/G	HR	BB	SO	RAT	ERA	ERA+	OAV	OOB	PR	PR+	PF	CPI	FA	E	DP	FW	PW	BW	SBW	DIF
PHI	**98**	**20**	8	1374^{1}	**1161**	**7.7**	26	342	652	**10.1**	**2.18**	**126**	**.234**	**.288**	**87**	**85**	100	103	**.966**	216	99	.9	**9.5**	2.8	-.3	1.3
BOS	95	17	**13**	1405^{2}	1257	8.1	23	366	630	10.7	2.58	100	.246	.302	27	1	94	100	**.966**	**213**	115	**1.5**	.2	**4.8**	.3	.4
BRO	87	16	8	1389^{2}	1252	8.2	29	473	499	11.7	2.66	104	.245	.318	14	17	101	**108**	.963	238	96	-.5	1.9	-7.2	-.5	10.4
CHI	71	18	8	1399	1272	8.2	28	480	**657**	11.6	3.12	89	.247	.316	-57	-54	101	91	.958	268	94	-2.3	-6.0	.4	.4	4.2
PIT	91	18	11	1380	1229	8.1	**21**	384	544	10.8	2.60	105	.246	.304	23	19	99	100	**.966**	214	100	1.3	2.2	1.8	**1.3**	-10.4
STL	79	13	9	1400^{2}	1320	8.5	30	402	538	11.3	2.89	96	.256	.314	-22	-17	101	101	.964	235	109	.0	-1.8	3.3	-.5	-5.3
CIN	80	19	12	1432^{1}	1304	8.2	28	497	572	11.7	2.85	101	.250	.321	-15	1	104	104	**.966**	222	**148**	1.2	.2	-1.6	-.5	-5.0
NY	78	15	9	1385	1350	8.8	40	**325**	637	11.2	3.12	82	.260	.308	-57	-92	93	94	.960	256	119	-1.6	-10.2	.7	-.4	4.6
TOT	679	136	78	11166^{2}		8.2				11.1	2.75		.248	.310					.964	1862	880					

Runs
- Cravath-Phi 89
- Doyle-NY 86
- Bancroft-Phi 85
- Burns-NY 83
- O'Mara-Bro 77

Hits
- Doyle-NY 189
- Griffith-Cin 179
- Hinchman-Pit 177
- Groh-Cin 170
- Burns-NY 169

Doubles
- Doyle-NY 40
- Luderus-Phi 36
- Saier-Chi 35
- Smith-Bos 34
- Magee-Bos 34

Triples
- Long-StL 25
- H.Wagner-Pit 17
- Griffith-Cin 16
- Hinchman-Pit 14
- Burns-NY 14

Home Runs
- Cravath-Phi 24
- Williams-Chi 13
- Schulte-Chi 12
- Saier-Chi 11
- Becker-Phi 11

Total Bases
- Cravath-Phi 266
- Doyle-NY 261
- Griffith-Cin 254
- Hinchman-Pit 253
- H.Wagner-Pit 239

Runs Batted In
- Cravath-Phi 115
- Magee-Bos 87
- Griffith-Cin 85
- H.Wagner-Pit 78
- Hinchman-Pit 77

Runs Produced
- Cravath-Phi 180
- Magee-Bos 157
- Doyle-NY 152
- Hinchman-Pit 144
- Miller-StL 143

Bases On Balls
- Cravath-Phi 86
- Bancroft-Phi 77
- Viox-Pit 75
- Huggins-StL 74
- Smith-Bos 67

Batting Average
- Doyle-NY .320
- Luderus-Phi .315
- Griffith-Cin .307
- Hinchman-Pit .307
- Daubert-Bro .301

On-Base Percentage
- Cravath-Phi .393
- Luderus-Phi .376
- Daubert-Bro .369
- Hinchman-Pit .368
- Doyle-NY .358

Slugging Average
- Cravath-Phi .510
- Luderus-Phi .457
- Long-StL .446
- Saier-Chi .445
- Doyle-NY .442

On-Base Plus Slugging
- Cravath-Phi 902
- Luderus-Phi 833
- Hinchman-Pit 807
- Doyle-NY 799
- Saier-Chi 795

Adjusted OPS
- Cravath-Phi 170
- Doyle-NY 150
- Luderus-Phi 150
- Hinchman-Pit 146
- Saier-Chi 140

Batter Runs
- Cravath-Phi 46.8
- Luderus-Phi 30.3
- Hinchman-Pit 29.7
- Doyle-NY 27.1
- Griffith-Cin 25.4

Adjusted Batter Runs
- Cravath-Phi 45.6
- Doyle-NY 32.7
- Hinchman-Pit 31.0
- Luderus-Phi 29.3
- Griffith-Cin 23.8

Clutch Hitting Index
- Fletcher-NY 134
- Magee-Bos 131
- Miller-StL 128
- Schmidt-Bos 125
- Cutshaw-Bro 123

Runs Created
- Cravath-Phi 105
- Doyle-NY 94
- Hinchman-Pit 94
- Luderus-Phi 87
- Griffith-Cin 85

Total Average
- Cravath-Phi .942
- Saier-Chi .819
- Luderus-Phi .799
- Hinchman-Pit .741
- Doyle-NY .714

Stolen Bases
- Carey-Pit 36
- Herzog-Cin 35
- Saier-Chi 29
- Baird-Pit 29
- Cutshaw-Bro 28

Stolen Base Average
- Bresnahan-Chi 86.4
- Saier-Chi 76.3
- Baird-Pit 70.7
- Robertson-NY 68.8
- Herzog-Cin 68.6

Stolen Base Runs
- Saier-Chi 3.2
- Bresnahan-Chi 3.1
- Baird-Pit 2.2
- Herzog-Cin 2.1
- Carey-Pit 2.0

Fielding Runs
- Fletcher-NY 32.5
- Herzog-Cin 30.9
- Maranville-Bos 19.3
- Cutshaw-Bro 16.8
- Magee-Bos 15.2

Total Player Rating
- Cravath-Phi 5.0
- Herzog-Cin 4.2
- Luderus-Phi 3.9
- Snyder-StL 3.2
- Fletcher-NY 3.2

Wins
- Alexander-Phi 31
- Rudolph-Bos 22
- Mayer-Phi 21
- Mamaux-Pit 21
- Vaughn-Chi 20

Win Percentage
- Alexander-Phi .756
- Toney-Cin .739
- Mamaux-Pit .724
- Vaughn-Chi .625
- Coombs-Bro .600

Games
- Hughes-Bos 50
- Dale-Cin 49
- Alexander-Phi 49
- Schneider-Cin 48
- Sallee-StL 46

Complete Games
- Alexander-Phi 36
- Rudolph-Bos 30
- Pfeffer-Bro 26
- Harmon-Pit 25
- Tesreau-NY 24

Shutouts
- Alexander-Phi 12
- Tesreau-NY 8
- Mamaux-Pit 8
- Toney-Cin 6
- Pfeffer-Bro 6

Saves
- Hughes-Bos 9
- Benton-Cin-NY 5
- Lavender-Chi 4
- Cooper-Pit 4

Innings Pitched
- Alexander-Phi 376.1
- Rudolph-Bos 341.1
- Tesreau-NY 306.0
- Dale-Cin 296.2
- Pfeffer-Bro 291.2

Fewest Hits/Game
- Alexander-Phi 6.05
- Toney-Cin 6.47
- Mamaux-Pit 6.51
- Hughes-Bos 6.68
- Zabel-Chi 6.85

Fewest BB/Game
- Mathewson-NY .97
- Humphries-Chi 1.21
- Adams-Pit 1.25
- Alexander-Phi 1.53
- Rudolph-Bos 1.69

Strikeouts
- Alexander-Phi 241
- Tesreau-NY 176
- Hughes-Bos 171
- Mamaux-Pit 152
- Vaughn-Chi 148

Strikeouts/Game
- Alexander-Phi 5.76
- Hughes-Bos 5.49
- Mamaux-Pit 5.44
- Douglas-Cin-Br-Chi 5.26
- Tesreau-NY 5.18

Ratio
- Alexander-Phi 7.82
- Hughes-Bos 8.89
- Tesreau-NY 9.26
- Toney-Cin 9.54
- Adams-Pit 9.73

Earned Run Average
- Alexander-Phi 1.22
- Toney-Cin 1.58
- Mamaux-Pit 2.04
- Pfeffer-Bro 2.10
- Hughes-Bos 2.12

Adjusted ERA
- Alexander-Phi 224
- Toney-Cin 181
- Mamaux-Pit 134
- Pfeffer-Bro 132
- Hughes-Bos 122

Opponents' Batting Avg.
- Alexander-Phi .191
- Toney-Cin .207
- Mamaux-Pit .208
- Hughes-Bos .213
- Tesreau-NY .215

Opponents' On-Base Pct.
- Alexander-Phi .234
- Hughes-Bos .265
- Tesreau-NY .269
- Toney-Cin .278
- Adams-Pit .280

Starter Runs
- Alexander-Phi 63.8
- Toney-Cin 28.9
- Pfeffer-Bro 21.0
- Mamaux-Pit 19.8
- Hughes-Bos 19.5

Adjusted Starter Runs
- Alexander-Phi 63.6
- Toney-Cin 30.4
- Pfeffer-Bro 21.6
- Mamaux-Pit 19.4
- Hughes-Bos 15.4

Clutch Pitching Index
- Humphries-Chi 139
- Perritt-NY 122
- Schneider-Cin 121
- Rixey-Phi 120
- Stroud-NY 118

Relief Runs

Adjusted Relief Runs

Relief Ranking

Total Pitcher Index
- Alexander-Phi 8.7
- Toney-Cin 2.9
- Pfeffer-Bro 2.6
- Mayer-Phi 2.2
- Schneider-Cin 1.9

Total Baseball Ranking
- Alexander-Phi 8.7
- Cravath-Phi 5.0
- Herzog-Cin 4.2
- Luderus-Phi 3.9
- Snyder-StL 3.2

TEAM	G	W	L	PCT	GB	R	OR	AB	H	2B	3B	HR	BB	SO	AVG	OBP	SLG	OPS	OPS+	BR	BR+	PF	CHI	RC	SB	CS	SBA	SBR
BOS	155	101	50	.669		669	499	5024	1308	202	76	14	527	**476**	.260	.336	.339	675	110	46	67	97	100	611	118	117	50	-15
DET	156	100	54	.649	2.5	**778**	597	5128	**1372**	**207**	94	23	**681**	527	**.268**	**.357**	**.358**	**715**	**114**	**131**	**94**	105	101	**711**	**241**	146	62	2
CHI	155	93	61	.604	9.5	717	509	4914	1269	163	**102**	25	583	575	.258	.345	.348	693	110	83	63	103	102	637	233	183	56	-13
WAS	155	85	68	.556	17	569	**491**	5029	1225	152	79	12	458	541	.244	.312	.312	624	90	-52	-62	102	**103**	535	186	106	**64**	**4**
NY	154	69	83	.454	32.5	584	588	4982	1162	167	50	**31**	570	669	.233	.317	.305	622	91	-46	-45	100	**103**	523	198	133	60	-3
STL	159	63	91	.409	39.5	522	680	5112	1255	166	65	19	472	765	.246	.315	.315	630	98	-44	-21	96	92	535	202	160	56	-12
CLE	154	57	95	.375	44.5	539	670	5034	1210	169	79	20	490	681	.240	.312	.317	629	91	-43	-54	102	95	526	138	117	54	-11
PHI	154	43	109	.283	58.5	545	889	5081	1204	183	72	16	436	634	.237	.304	.311	615	92	-74	-55	97	**103**	507	127	89	59	-3
TOT	621					4923		40304	10005	1409	617	160	4217	4868	.249	.326	.326	651							1443	1051	58	-50

TEAM	CG	SH	SV	IP	H	H/G	HR	BB	SO	RAT	ERA	ERA+	OAV	OOB	PR	PR+	PF	CPI	FA	E	DP	FW	PW	BW	SBW	DIF
BOS	81	19	15	1397	1164	**7.5**	18	446	634	10.7	2.40	116	**.231**	.300	84	62	95	97	.964	226	95	2.5	6.6	7.2	-.9	10.3
DET	86	10	**19**	1413[1]	1259	8.1	14	492	550	11.6	2.86	106	.243	.316	11	24	103	94	.961	258	107	.5	2.6	**10.0**	.9	9.2
CHI	91	16	9	1401	1242	8.0	14	**350**	635	**10.5**	2.43	122	.241	**.294**	78	83	101	95	.965	222	95	2.8	8.9	6.7	-.7	-1.5
WAS	87	**21**	13	1393[2]	**1161**	**7.5**	**12**	455	**715**	10.8	**2.31**	**129**	.232	.302	**97**	**101**	101	102	.964	230	101	2.2	**10.8**	-6.5	**1.1**	1.1
NY	**101**	12	1	1382[2]	1272	8.3	41	517	559	12.0	3.06	96	.254	.329	-20	-20	100	**104**	**.966**	**217**	118	**3.0**	-2.1	-4.7	.4	-3.3
STL	76	6	6	1403	1256	8.1	21	612	566	12.4	3.05	94	.249	.338	-17	-32	98	103	.949	336	**144**	-4.3	-3.3	-2.2	-.6	-3.4
CLE	62	11	10	1372	1287	8.5	18	518	610	12.1	3.13	97	.256	.329	-30	-13	104	98	.957	280	82	-1.2	-1.3	-5.7	-.5	-10.1
PHI	78	6	2	1348[1]	1358	9.1	22	827	588	15.0	4.30	68	.278	.388	-204	-207	100	102	.947	338	118	-5.0	-21.9	-5.8	.4	-.5
TOT	662	101	75	11111		8.1				11.9	2.94		.249	.326					.960	2107	860					

Runs
Cobb-Det 144
E.Collins-Chi 118
Vitt-Det 116
Speaker-Bos 108
Chapman-Cle 101

Hits
Cobb-Det 208
Crawford-Det 183
Veach-Det 178
Speaker-Bos 176
Pratt-StL 175

Doubles
Veach-Det 40
Pratt-StL 31
Lewis-Bos 31
Crawford-Det 31
Cobb-Det 31

Triples
Crawford-Det 19
Fournier-Chi 18
Roth-Chi-Cle 17
S.Collins-Chi 17
Chapman-Cle 17

Home Runs
Roth-Chi-Cle 7
Oldring-Phi 6

Total Bases
Cobb-Det 274
Crawford-Det 264
Veach-Det 247
Pratt-StL 237
E.Collins-Chi 227

Runs Batted In
Veach-Det 112
Crawford-Det 112
Cobb-Det 99
S.Collins-Chi 85
J.Jackson-Cle-Chi 81

Runs Produced
Cobb-Det 240
E.Collins-Chi 191
Veach-Det 190
Crawford-Det 189
Speaker-Bos 177

Bases On Balls
E.Collins-Chi 119
Shotton-StL 118
Cobb-Det 118
Bush-Det 118
Hooper-Bos 89

Batting Average
Cobb-Det .369
E.Collins-Chi .332
Fournier-Chi .322
Speaker-Bos .322
McInnis-Phi .314

On-Base Percentage
Cobb-Det .486
E.Collins-Chi .460
Fournier-Chi .429
Speaker-Bos .416
Shotton-StL .409

Slugging Average
Fournier-Chi .491
Cobb-Det .487
Kavanagh-Det .452
J.Jackson-Cle-Chi .445
Roth-Chi-Cle .438

On-Base Plus Slugging
Cobb-Det 973
Fournier-Chi 920
E.Collins-Chi 896
J.Jackson-Cle-Chi 830
Speaker-Bos 827

Adjusted OPS
Cobb-Det 182
Fournier-Chi 170
E.Collins-Chi 163
Speaker-Bos 152
J.Jackson-Cle-Chi 145

Batter Runs
Cobb-Det 71.6
E.Collins-Chi 51.9
Fournier-Chi 40.9
Speaker-Bos 35.0
Veach-Det 32.3

Adjusted Batter Runs
Cobb-Det 64.7
E.Collins-Chi 48.3
Speaker-Bos 38.3
Fournier-Chi 38.1
Shotton-StL 31.4

Clutch Hitting Index
Crawford-Det 138
Veach-Det 135
Schalk-Chi 128
Gardner-Bos 123
S.Collins-Chi 120

Runs Created
Cobb-Det 155
E.Collins-Chi 116
Crawford-Det 101
Speaker-Bos 97
Veach-Det 97

Total Average
Cobb-Det 1.170
E.Collins-Chi .971
Fournier-Chi .964
Speaker-Bos .801
Veach-Det .771

Stolen Bases
Cobb-Det 96
Maisel-NY 51
E.Collins-Chi 46
Shotton-StL 43
C.Milan-Was 40

Stolen Base Average
Schang-Phi 85.7
Maisel-NY 81.0
Foster-Was 76.9
Moeller-Was 76.2
Roth-Chi-Cle 72.2

Stolen Base Runs
Cobb-Det 7.8
Maisel-NY 7.0
Moeller-Was 3.5
Schang-Phi 2.9
Chapman-Cle 2.7

Fielding Runs
Boone-NY 20.8
T.Walker-StL 14.8
Vitt-Det 14.4
Lajoie-Phi 14.1
Speaker-Bos 13.4

Total Player Rating
E.Collins-Chi 6.6
Cobb-Det 6.1
Speaker-Bos 4.1
Fournier-Chi 3.7
Chapman-Cle 3.4

Wins
Johnson-Was 27
Scott-Chi 24
Faber-Chi 24
Dauss-Det 24
Coveleski-Det 22

Win Percentage
Wood-Bos .750
Shore-Bos .704
Foster-Bos .704
Ruth-Bos .692
Scott-Chi .686

Games
Faber-Chi 50
Coveleski-Det 50
Scott-Chi 48
Jones-Cle 48

Complete Games
Johnson-Was 35
Caldwell-NY 31
Dauss-Det 27
Scott-Chi 23
Dubuc-Det 22

Shutouts
Scott-Chi 7
Johnson-Was 7
Morton-Cle 6
Foster-Bos 5
Dubuc-Det 5

Saves
Mays-Bos 7

Innings Pitched
Johnson-Was 336.2
Coveleski-Det 312.2
Dauss-Det 309.2
Caldwell-NY 305.0
Faber-Chi 299.2

Fewest Hits/Game
Leonard-Bos 6.38
Ruth-Bos 6.86
Wood-Bos 6.86
Johnson-Was 6.90
Morton-Cle 7.09

Fewest BB/Game
Johnson-Was 1.50
Ayers-Was 1.62
Benz-Chi 1.62
Russell-Chi 1.84
Cicotte-Chi 1.93

Strikeouts
Johnson-Was 203
Faber-Chi 182
Wyckoff-Phi 157
Coveleski-Det 150
Mitchell-Cle 149

Strikeouts/Game
Leonard-Bos 5.69
Mitchell-Cle 5.68
Faber-Chi 5.47
Johnson-Was 5.43
Lowdermilk-StL-Det 5.32

Ratio
Johnson-Was 8.90
Morton-Cle 9.41
Wood-Bos 9.44
Ayers-Was 9.50
Benz-Chi 9.63

Earned Run Average
Wood-Bos 1.49
Johnson-Was 1.55
Shore-Bos 1.64
Scott-Chi 2.03
Fisher-NY 2.11

Adjusted ERA
Johnson-Was 191
Wood-Bos 186
Shore-Bos 169
Scott-Chi 146
Morton-Cle 142

Opponents' Batting Avg.
Leonard-Bos .208
Ruth-Bos .212
Johnson-Was .214
Morton-Cle .216
Wood-Bos .216

Opponents' On-Base Pct.
Johnson-Was .260
Morton-Cle .268
Wood-Bos .275
Benz-Chi .276
Ayers-Was .276

Starter Runs
Johnson-Was 51.7
Shore-Bos 35.5
Scott-Chi 29.5
Wood-Bos 25.2
Foster-Bos 23.2

Adjusted Starter Runs
Johnson-Was 52.3
Shore-Bos 32.9
Scott-Chi 30.4
Wood-Bos 23.8
Morton-Cle 23.3

Clutch Pitching Index
Hamilton-StL 125
Shore-Bos 122
Foster-Bos 121
Fisher-NY 119
Wood-Bos 118

Relief Runs

Adjusted Relief Runs

Relief Ranking

Total Pitcher Index
Johnson-Was 7.7
Wood-Bos 3.8
Shore-Bos 3.7
Scott-Chi 3.4
Dauss-Det 3.2

Total Baseball Ranking
Johnson-Was 7.5
E.Collins-Chi 6.6
Cobb-Det 6.1
Speaker-Bos 4.1
Wood-Bos 3.8

TEAM	G	W	L	PCT	GB	R	OR	AB	H	2B	3B	HR	BB	SO	AVG	OBP	SLG	OPS	OPS+	BR	BR+	PF	CHI	RC	SB	CS	SBA	SBR
CHI	155	86	66	.566		640	538	5133	1320	185	77	**50**	444	590	.257	.320	.352	672	101	-110	-79	94	102	650	161			
STL	159	87	67	.565		634	527	5145	1344	199	**81**	23	**576**	**502**	.261	**.340**	.345	685	94	-71	-98	105	92	698	195			
PIT	156	86	67	.562	0.5	592	**524**	5040	1318	180	80	20	448	561	.262	.326	.341	667	94	-110	-106	99	95	655	224			
KC	153	81	72	.529	5.5	547	551	4937	1206	200	66	28	368	503	.244	.303	.329	632	87	-182	-165	96	**103**	559	144			
NEW	155	80	72	.526	6	585	562	5097	1283	**210**	80	17	438	550	.252	.315	.334	649	93	-148	-120	94	99	618	184			
BUF	153	74	78	.487	12	574	634	5065	1261	193	68	40	420	587	.249	.309	.338	647	85	-158	-167	102	102	594	184			
BRO	153	70	82	.461	16	**647**	673	5035	**1348**	205	75	36	473	654	**.268**	.336	**.360**	**696**	**103**	**-56**	**-52**	99	97	**704**	**249**			
BAL	154	47	107	.305	40	550	760	5060	1235	196	53	36	470	641	.244	.313	.325	638	82	-167	-180	103	97	578	128			
TOT	619					4769		40512	10315	1568	580	250	3637	4588	.255	.317	.341	656							1469			

TEAM	CG	SH	SV	IP	H	H/G	HR	BB	SO	RAT	ERA	ERA+	OAV	OOB	PR	PR+	PF	CPI	FA	E	DP	FW	PW	BW	SBW	DIF
STL	94	**24**	9	1426	1267	**8.0**	22	396	**698**	**10.7**	2.74	**117**	.243	.300	47	**69**	105	92	.967	212	111	2.1	**7.5**	-10.5		11.2
PIT	88	16	12	1382[1]	1273	8.3	37	441	517	11.4	2.80	108	.253	.317	37	33	99	107	**.971**	**182**	98	**3.6**	3.6	-11.4		13.9
KC	95	16	11	1359	**1210**	8.1	29	**390**	526	10.9	2.83	103	.242	.301	32	15	96	91	.962	246	96	-.5	1.7	-17.7		21.2
NEW	**100**	16	7	1406[2]	1308	8.4	**15**	453	581	11.7	**2.61**	109	.253	.319	**67**	40	94	**111**	.963	239	124	.1	4.4	-12.9		12.6
BUF	79	14	11	1360	1271	8.5	35	553	594	12.3	3.39	92	.254	.331	-53	-40	103	95	.964	232	112	.3	-4.3	-17.9		20.0
BRO	78	10	**16**	1355[2]	1299	8.7	27	536	467	12.4	3.37	90	.258	.332	-50	-53	100	97	.955	290	103	-3.1	-5.7	-5.5		8.5
BAL	85	5	7	1360[1]	1455	9.7	52	466	570	13.0	3.96	81	.284	.349	-140	-111	105	100	.957	273	**140**	-2.0	-11.9	-19.3		3.4
TOT	716	122	83	11047[2]		8.5				11.6	3.04		.255	.317					.963	1907	886					

Runs
Borton-StL 97
Berghammer-Pit 96
Evans-Bro-Bal 94
Tobin-StL 92
Kauff-Bro 92

Hits
Tobin-StL 184
Konetchy-Pit 181
Evans-Bro-Bal 171
Kauff-Bro 165
Chase-Buf 165

Doubles
Evans-Bro-Bal 34
Zwilling-Chi 32
Konetchy-Pit 31
Chase-Buf 31

Triples
Mann-Chi 19
Konetchy-Pit 18
Kelly-Pit 17
Gilmore-KC 15

Home Runs
Chase-Buf 17
Zwilling-Chi 13
Kauff-Bro 12
Konetchy-Pit 10
Walsh-Bal-StL 9

Total Bases
Konetchy-Pit 278
Chase-Buf 267
Tobin-StL 254
Kauff-Bro 246
Zwilling-Chi 242

Runs Batted In
Zwilling-Chi 94
Konetchy-Pit 93
Chase-Buf 89
Kauff-Bro 83
Borton-StL 83

Runs Produced
Borton-StL 177
Kauff-Bro 163
Konetchy-Pit 162
Evans-Bro-Bal 157
Chase-Buf 157

Bases On Balls
Borton-StL 92
Kauff-Bro 85
Berghammer-Pit 83
W.Miller-StL 79

Batting Average
Kauff-Bro 342
Fischer-Chi 329
Magee-Bro 323
Konetchy-Pit 314
Flack-Chi 314

On-Base Percentage
Kauff-Bro 446
W.Miller-StL 400
Borton-StL 395
Evans-Bro-Bal 392
Cooper-Bro 388

Slugging Average
Kauff-Bro 509
Konetchy-Pit 483
Chase-Buf 471
Fischer-Chi 449
Zwilling-Chi 442

On-Base Plus Slugging
Kauff-Bro 955
Konetchy-Pit 846
Evans-Bro-Bal 818
Zwilling-Chi 808
Mann-Chi 795

Adjusted OPS
Kauff-Bro 170
Konetchy-Pit 138
Zwilling-Chi 135
Mann-Chi 131
Flack-Chi 129

Batter Runs
Kauff-Bro 41.3
Konetchy-Pit 17.5
Wilson-Chi 17.5
Evans-Bro-Bal 16.3
Crandall-StL 13.9

Adjusted Batter Runs
Kauff-Bro 42.1
Wilson-Chi 20.9
Konetchy-Pit 18.3
Zwilling-Chi 16.3
Evans-Bro-Bal 15.1

Clutch Hitting Index
Oakes-Pit 152
Engle-Buf 129
F.Smith-Buf-Bro 123
Borton-StL 122
Halt-Bro 118

Runs Created
Kauff-Bro 132
Konetchy-Pit 111
Tobin-StL 106
Zwilling-Chi 99
Evans-Bro-Bal 99

Total Average
Kauff-Bro 1.233
Konetchy-Pit 884
Cooper-Bro 868
W.Miller-StL 863
Zwilling-Chi 857

Stolen Bases
Kauff-Bro 55
Mowrey-Pit 40
Kelly-Pit 38
Flack-Chi 37
Magee-Bro 34

Stolen Base Average

Stolen Base Runs

Fielding Runs
Doolan-Bal-Chi 33.0
Rariden-New 23.0
Cooper-Bro 18.3
Johnson-StL 17.7
Perring-KC 14.8

Total Player Rating
Kauff-Bro 5.0
Rariden-New 3.9
Cooper-Bro 2.5
Wilson-Chi 2.1
Louden-Buf 1.8

Wins
McConnell-Chi 25
Allen-Pit 23
Davenport-StL 22
Cullop-KC 22

Win Percentage
McConnell-Chi 714
Brown-Chi 680
Reulbach-New 677
Cullop-KC 667
Plank-StL 656

Games
Davenport-StL 55
Bedient-Buf 53
Crandall-StL 51
Johnson-KC 46

Complete Games
Davenport-StL 30
Hendrix-Chi 26
Schulz-Buf 25
Allen-Pit 24

Shutouts
Davenport-StL 10
Plank-StL 6
Allen-Pit 6

Saves
Bedient-Buf 10
Barger-Pit 6
Wiltse-Bro 5

Innings Pitched
Davenport-StL 392.2
Crandall-StL 312.2
Schulz-Buf 309.2
McConnell-Chi 303.0
Cullop-KC 302.1

Fewest Hits/Game
Davenport-StL 6.88
Main-KC 7.08
Plank-StL 7.11
Brown-Chi 7.20
Anderson-Buf 7.20

Fewest BB/Game
Plank-StL 1.81
Bender-Bal 1.87
Hearn-Pit 1.90
Cullop-KC 1.99
Quinn-Bal 2.07

Strikeouts
Davenport-StL 229
Schulz-Buf 160
McConnell-Chi 151
Plank-StL 147

Strikeouts/Game
Anderson-Buf 5.33
Davenport-StL 5.25
Plank-StL 4.93
Bailey-Bal-Chi 4.91
Groom-StL 4.78

Ratio
Plank-StL 9.02
Davenport-StL 9.19
Brown-Chi 9.90
Anderson-Buf 10.01
Reulbach-New 10.17

Earned Run Average
Moseley-New 1.91
Plank-StL 2.08
Brown-Chi 2.09
McConnell-Chi 2.20
Davenport-StL 2.20

Adjusted ERA
Plank-StL 138
Moseley-New 134
Davenport-StL 131
Brown-Chi 120
Reulbach-New 115

Opponents' Batting Avg.
Davenport-StL 215
Plank-StL 218
Brown-Chi 220
Main-KC 222
Anderson-Buf 222

Opponents' On-Base Pct.
Plank-StL 262
Davenport-StL 268
Brown-Chi 279
Anderson-Buf 285
Reulbach-New 287

Starter Runs
Moseley-New 24.2
Davenport-StL 23.0
Plank-StL 19.3
McConnell-Chi 17.8
Brown-Chi 16.6

Adjusted Starter Runs
Davenport-StL 27.9
Plank-StL 22.5
Moseley-New 20.5
Brown-Chi 11.9
McConnell-Chi 11.4

Clutch Pitching Index
Moran-New 129
Kaiserling-New 127
Rogge-Pit 127
Moseley-New 122
Lafitte-Bro-Buf 117

Relief Runs

Adjusted Relief Runs

Relief Ranking

Total Pitcher Index
Plank-StL 2.8
Crandall-StL 2.5
McConnell-Chi 2.2
Brown-Chi 2.1
Moseley-New 1.4

Total Baseball Ranking
Kauff-Bro 5.0
Rariden-New 3.9
Plank-StL 2.8
Crandall-StL 2.5
Cooper-Bro 2.5

TEAM	G	W	L	PCT	GB	R	OR	AB	H	2B	3B	HR	BB	SO	AVG	OBP	SLG	OPS	OPS+	BR	BR+	PF	CHI	RC	SB	CS	SBA	SBR
BRO	156	94	60	.610		585	471	5234	**1366**	195	80	28	355	**550**	**.261**	**.313**	**.345**	**658**	105	**46**	30	103	99	**645**	187			
PHI	154	91	62	.595	2.5	581	489	4985	1244	**223**	53	42	399	571	.250	.310	.341	651	102	34	15	104	104	593	149			
BOS	158	89	63	.586	4	542	**453**	5075	1181	166	73	22	**437**	646	.233	.299	.307	606	96	-38	-15	96	**108**	535	141			
NY	155	86	66	.566	7	**597**	504	5152	1305	188	74	42	356	558	.253	.307	.343	650	**112**	31	**63**	95	106	617	**206**			
CHI	156	67	86	.438	26.5	520	541	5179	1237	194	56	**46**	399	662	.239	.298	.325	623	88	-18	-69	111	99	559	133			
PIT	157	65	89	.422	29	484	586	5181	1246	147	**91**	20	372	618	.240	.298	.316	614	94	-32	-37	101	95	556	173			
STL	153	60	93	.392	33.5	476	629	5030	1223	155	74	25	335	651	.243	.295	.318	613	95	-35	-32	99	99	535	182			
CIN	155	60	93	.392	33.5	505	617	5254	1336	187	88	14	362	573	.254	.307	.331	638	105	13	27	98	91	596	157			
TOT	622					4290		41090	10138	1455	589	239	3015	4829	.247	.304	.329	632							1328			

TEAM	CG	SH	SV	IP	H	H/G	HR	BB	SO	RAT	ERA	ERA+	OAV	OOB	PR	PR+	PF	CPI	FA	E	DP	FW	PW	BW	SBW	DIF
BRO	96	22	9	1427[1]	**1201**	**7.6**	**24**	372	634	10.2	**2.12**	**126**	**.232**	.289	**78**	**84**	102	103	.965	224	90	1.3	**9.7**	3.5		2.8
PHI	**97**	**25**	9	1382[1]	1238	8.1	28	**295**	601	10.3	2.36	112	.244	.292	39	43	101	101	.963	234	119	.5	5.0	1.8		7.5
BOS	**97**	23	11	1415[2]	1206	7.7	**24**	325	**644**	**10.0**	2.20	113	.235	**.285**	66	47	95	99	**.967**	**212**	124	**2.2**	5.4	-1.7		7.3
NY	88	22	12	1397[1]	1267	8.2	41	310	638	10.5	2.61	93	.245	.293	2	-30	93	95	.966	217	108	1.6	-3.4	**7.3**		4.7
CHI	72	17	13	1416[2]	1265	8.1	32	365	616	10.7	2.65	110	.244	.298	-6	35	111	94	.957	286	104	-2.5	4.1	-7.8		-3.0
PIT	88	11	7	1419[2]	1277	8.1	**24**	443	596	11.2	2.77	97	.247	.311	-24	-14	103	97	.959	260	97	-.8	-1.6	-4.2		-5.2
STL	58	13	**15**	1355	1331	8.9	31	445	529	12.1	3.15	84	.265	.330	-80	-76	101	**104**	.957	278	124	-2.3	-8.6	-3.6		-1.7
CIN	86	7	6	1408	1356	8.7	35	461	569	11.9	3.11	84	.261	.326	-76	-82	99	102	.965	228	**126**	.9	-9.3	3.1		-11.0
TOT	682	140	82	11222		8.2				10.9	2.62		.247	.304					.963	1939	892					

Runs
Burns-NY 105
Carey-Pit 90
Robertson-NY 88
Groh-Cin 85
Paskert-Phi 82

Hits
Chase-Cin 184
Robertson-NY 180
Z.Wheat-Bro 177
Hinchman-Pit 175
Burns-NY 174

Doubles
Niehoff-Phi 42
Z.Wheat-Bro 32
Paskert-Phi 30

Triples
Hinchman-Pit 16
Roush-NY-Cin 15
Kauff-NY 15
Hornsby-StL 15

Home Runs
Williams-Chi 12
Robertson-NY 12
Cravath-Phi 11
Z.Wheat-Bro 9
Kauff-NY 9

Total Bases
Z.Wheat-Bro 262
Robertson-NY 250
Chase-Cin 249
Hinchman-Pit 237
Burns-NY 229

Runs Batted In
Zimmerman-Chi-NY .. 83
Chase-Cin 82
Hinchman-Pit 76
Kauff-NY 74
Z.Wheat-Bro 73

Runs Produced
Zimmerman-Chi-NY .. 153
Robertson-NY 145
Chase-Cin 144
Konetchy-Bos 143
Burns-NY 141

Bases On Balls
Groh-Cin 84
Saier-Chi 79
Bancroft-Phi 74
Kauff-NY 68
Cravath-Phi 64

Batting Average
Chase-Cin .... .339
Daubert-Bro .... .316
Hinchman-Pit .... .315
Hornsby-StL .... .313
Z.Wheat-Bro .... .312

On-Base Percentage
Cravath-Phi .... .379
Hinchman-Pit .... .378
Williams-Chi .... .372
Daubert-Bro .... .371
Groh-Cin .... .370

Slugging Average
Z.Wheat-Bro .... .461
Chase-Cin .... .459
Williams-Chi .... .459
Hornsby-StL .... .444
Cravath-Phi .... .440

On-Base Plus Slugging
Williams-Chi 831
Z.Wheat-Bro 828
Chase-Cin 822
Cravath-Phi 819
Hornsby-StL 814

Adjusted OPS
Chase-Cin 155
Hornsby-StL 150
Z.Wheat-Bro 149
Cravath-Phi 146
Hinchman-Pit 146

Batter Runs
Z.Wheat-Bro 34.5
Hinchman-Pit 31.1
Chase-Cin 30.2
Cravath-Phi 28.7
Hornsby-StL 28.2

Adjusted Batter Runs
Chase-Cin 32.3
Z.Wheat-Bro 32.0
Hinchman-Pit 30.3
Hornsby-StL 28.7
Cravath-Phi 26.0

Clutch Hitting Index
Mowrey-Bro 145
Zimmerman-Chi-NY .. 134
Magee-Bos 133
Smith-Bos 121
Fletcher-NY 119

Runs Created
Z.Wheat-Bro 103
Hinchman-Pit 96
Chase-Cin 93
Hornsby-StL 88
Carey-Pit 87

Total Average
Williams-Chi .... .863
Cravath-Phi .... .857
Z.Wheat-Bro .... .844
Hornsby-StL .... .826
Hinchman-Pit .... .797

Stolen Bases
Carey-Pit 63
Kauff-NY 40
Bescher-StL 39
Burns-NY 37
Herzog-Cin-NY 34

Stolen Base Average
Carey-Pit 76.8
Bescher-StL 76.5
Daubert-Bro 75.0
Maranville-Bos 68.1
Chase-Cin 66.7

Stolen Base Runs
Carey-Pit 7.2
Bescher-StL 4.4
Daubert-Bro 2.2
Maranville-Bos 1.8
Chase-Cin 1.0

Fielding Runs
Carey-Pit 29.9
Betzel-StL 28.4
Bancroft-Phi 24.5
Maranville-Bos 21.5
Doyle-NY-Chi 20.0

Total Player Rating
Groh-Cin 5.3
Fletcher-NY 4.5
Carey-Pit 4.4
Doyle-NY-Chi 4.0
Z.Wheat-Bro 3.9

Wins
Alexander-Phi 33
Pfeffer-Bro 25
Rixey-Phi 22
Mamaux-Pit 21

Win Percentage
Hughes-Bos .... .842
Alexander-Phi .... .733
Pfeffer-Bro .... .694
Rixey-Phi .... .688
Benton-NY .... .667

Games
Meadows-StL 51
Alexander-Phi 48
Mamaux-Pit 45
Ames-StL 45

Complete Games
Alexander-Phi 38
Pfeffer-Bro 30
Rudolph-Bos 27
Mamaux-Pit 26
Demaree-Phi 25

Shutouts
Alexander-Phi 16
Tyler-Bos 6
Pfeffer-Bro 6

Saves
Ames-StL 8
Packard-Chi 5
Marquard-Bro 5
Hughes-Bos 5

Innings Pitched
Alexander-Phi 389.0
Pfeffer-Bro 328.2
Rudolph-Bos 312.0
Mamaux-Pit 310.0
Toney-Cin 300.0

Fewest Hits/Game
Cheney-Bro 6.33
Hughes-Bos 6.76
Cooper-Pit 6.91
Miller-Pit 7.02
Ragan-Bos 7.07

Fewest BB/Game
Rudolph-Bos 1.10
Alexander-Phi 1.16
Demaree-Phi 1.52
Sallee-StL-NY 1.63
Marquard-Bro 1.67

Strikeouts
Alexander-Phi 167
Cheney-Bro 166
Mamaux-Pit 163
Toney-Cin 146
Vaughn-Chi 144

Strikeouts/Game
Cheney-Bro 5.91
Hughes-Bos 5.42
Hendrix-Chi 4.83
Mamaux-Pit 4.73
Marquard-Bro 4.70

Ratio
Rudolph-Bos 8.86
Alexander-Phi 8.86
Marquard-Bro 9.09
McConnell-Chi 9.30
Ragan-Bos 9.40

Earned Run Average
Alexander-Phi 1.55
Marquard-Bro 1.58
Rixey-Phi 1.85
Cooper-Pit 1.87
Pfeffer-Bro 1.92

Adjusted ERA
Alexander-Phi 171
Marquard-Bro 169
Cooper-Pit 144
Rixey-Phi 143
Pfeffer-Bro 140

Opponents' Batting Avg.
Cheney-Bro .... .198
Cooper-Pit .... .215
Hughes-Bos .... .215
Ragan-Bos .... .218
McConnell-Chi .... .223

Opponents' On-Base Pct.
Rudolph-Bos .... .261
Alexander-Phi .... .262
Marquard-Bro .... .267
Ragan-Bos .... .270
McConnell-Chi .... .271

Starter Runs
Alexander-Phi 45.9
Schupp-NY 26.7
Pfeffer-Bro 25.4
Rixey-Phi 24.3
Marquard-Bro 23.5

Adjusted Starter Runs
Alexander-Phi 46.8
Pfeffer-Bro 27.1
Schupp-NY 25.7
Rixey-Phi 25.1
Marquard-Bro 24.4

Clutch Pitching Index
Dell-Bro 124
Sallee-StL-NY 117
Meadows-StL 116
Schulz-Cin 114
Alexander-Phi 114

Relief Runs

Adjusted Relief Runs

Relief Ranking

Total Pitcher Index
Alexander-Phi 7.3
Pfeffer-Bro 3.5
Rixey-Phi 3.2
Tyler-Bos 2.6
Cheney-Bro 2.2

Total Baseball Ranking
Alexander-Phi 7.3
Groh-Cin 5.3
Fletcher-NY 4.5
Carey-Pit 4.4
Doyle-NY-Chi 4.0

TEAM	G	W	L	PCT	GB	R	OR	AB	H	2B	3B	HR	BB	SO	AVG	OBP	SLG	OPS	OPS+	BR	BR+	PF	CHI	RC	SB	CS	SBA	SBR
BOS	156	91	63	.591		550	**480**	5018	1246	197	56	14	464	**482**	.248	.317	.318	635	97	-20	-22	100	101	580	129			
CHI	155	89	65	.578	2	601	497	5081	1277	194	**100**	17	447	591	.251	.319	.339	658	103	18	12	101	102	638	197			
DET	155	87	67	.565	4	**670**	595	5193	**1371**	202	96	17	545	529	**.264**	**.337**	**.350**	**687**	**109**	**78**	**56**	104	101	**700**	190			
NY	156	80	74	.519	11	577	561	5198	1277	194	59	**35**	516	632	.246	.318	.326	644	98	-4	-16	102	100	613	179			
STL	158	79	75	.513	12	588	545	5155	1262	181	50	14	**626**	638	.245	.331	.307	638	103	2	32	95	99	620	**234**			
CLE	157	77	77	.500	14	630	602	5064	1264	**233**	66	16	522	605	.250	.324	.331	655	97	17	-16	106	**106**	625	160			
WAS	159	76	77	.497	14.5	536	543	5114	1238	170	60	12	535	597	.242	.320	.306	626	95	-30	-24	99	98	579	185			
PHI	154	36	117	.235	54.5	447	776	5010	1212	169	65	19	406	631	.242	.303	.313	616	96	-61	-36	95	91	538	151			
TOT	625					4599		40833	10147	1540	552	144	4061	4705	.249	.322	.324	645							1425			

TEAM	CG	SH	SV	IP	H	H/G	HR	BB	SO	RAT	ERA	ERA+	OAV	OOB	PR	PR+	PF	CPI	FA	E	DP	FW	PW	BW	SBW	DIF
BOS	76	**24**	16	1410^{2}	1221	7.8	**10**	463	584	11.0	2.48	112	.239	.307	55	45	98	99	**.972**	**183**	108	**3.1**	5.0	-2.4		8.5
CHI	73	20	15	1412^{1}	**1189**	**7.6**	14	**405**	644	**10.4**	**2.37**	**117**	**.236**	**.296**	**72**	**63**	98	96	.968	205	**134**	1.6	**7.0**	1.4		2.2
DET	81	8	13	1410	1254	8.1	12	578	531	12.1	2.97	96	.248	.333	-23	-18	101	100	.968	211	110	1.2	-1.9	**6.3**		4.7
NY	84	12	**17**	1428	1249	7.9	37	476	616	11.2	2.78	104	.244	.314	8	17	102	100	.967	219	119	.8	1.9	-1.7		2.2
STL	74	9	13	1443^{2}	1292	8.1	15	478	505	11.3	2.59	106	.248	.316	39	27	97	105	.963	248	120	-.9	3.0	3.6		-3.6
CLE	65	9	16	1410	1383	8.9	16	467	537	12.1	2.91	103	.264	.328	-13	15	106	**107**	.965	232	130	.0	1.7	-1.7		.2
WAS	85	11	7	1430^{2}	1271	8.0	14	490	**706**	11.4	2.67	104	.244	.314	25	18	99	99	.964	232	119	.2	2.0	-2.6		.0
PHI	**94**	11	3	1343^{2}	1311	8.8	26	715	575	13.8	3.92	73	.267	.364	-163	-159	101	97	.951	314	126	-5.4	-17.6	-3.9		-13.4
TOT	632	104	100	11289		8.2				11.7	2.83		.249	.322					.965	1844	966					

Runs
Cobb-Det 113
Graney-Cle 106
Speaker-Cle 102
Shotton-StL 97
Veach-Det 92

Hits
Speaker-Cle 211
Jackson-Chi 202
Cobb-Det 201
Sisler-StL 177
Shotton-StL 174

Doubles
Speaker-Cle 41
Graney-Cle 41
Jackson-Chi 40
Pratt-StL 35
Veach-Det 33

Triples
Jackson-Chi 21
E.Collins-Chi 17
Witt-Phi 15
Veach-Det 15

Home Runs
Pipp-NY 12
Baker-NY 10
Schang-Phi 7
Felsch-Chi 7

Total Bases
Jackson-Chi 293
Speaker-Cle 274
Cobb-Det 267
Veach-Det 245

Runs Batted In
Pratt-StL 103
Pipp-NY 93
Veach-Det 91
Speaker-Cle 79
Jackson-Chi 78

Runs Produced
Veach-Det 180
Speaker-Cle 179
Cobb-Det 176
Jackson-Chi 166
Pratt-StL 162

Bases On Balls
Shotton-StL 110
Graney-Cle 102
E.Collins-Chi 86
Speaker-Cle 82
Hooper-Bos 80

Batting Average
Speaker-Cle .386
Cobb-Det .371
Jackson-Chi .341
Strunk-Phi .316
Gardner-Bos .308

On-Base Percentage
Speaker-Cle .470
Cobb-Det .452
E.Collins-Chi .405
Jackson-Chi .393
Strunk-Phi .393

Slugging Average
Speaker-Cle .502
Jackson-Chi .495
Cobb-Det .493
Veach-Det .433
Baker-NY .428

On-Base Plus Slugging
Speaker-Cle 972
Cobb-Det 944
Jackson-Chi 888
Strunk-Phi 814
E.Collins-Chi 802

Adjusted OPS
Speaker-Cle 181
Cobb-Det 177
Jackson-Chi 165
Strunk-Phi 152
E.Collins-Chi 139

Batter Runs
Speaker-Cle 64.6
Cobb-Det 57.5
Jackson-Chi 44.9
E.Collins-Chi 30.5
Strunk-Phi 30.2

Adjusted Batter Runs
Speaker-Cle 57.4
Cobb-Det 53.4
Jackson-Chi 43.7
Strunk-Phi 34.9
E.Collins-Chi 29.5

Clutch Hitting Index
Pratt-StL 136
Heilmann-Det 132
Marsans-StL 132
Gandil-Cle 129
Burns-Det 127

Runs Created
Cobb-Det 136
Speaker-Cle 132
Jackson-Chi 119
E.Collins-Chi 99
Veach-Det 94

Total Average
Cobb-Det 1.071
Speaker-Cle 1.017
Jackson-Chi .876
E.Collins-Chi .814
Graney-Cle .761

Stolen Bases
Cobb-Det 68
Marsans-StL 46
Shotton-StL 41
E.Collins-Chi 40
Speaker-Cle 35

Stolen Base Average
Cobb-Det 73.9
Hooper-Bos 71.1
Schalk-Chi 69.8
Roth-Cle 67.4
Shanks-Was 65.7

Stolen Base Runs
Cobb-Det 6.6
Hooper-Bos 2.1
Schalk-Chi 2.0
Roth-Cle 1.5
E.Collins-Chi 1.5

Fielding Runs
Lavan-StL 34.2
Lajoie-Phi 30.4
Vitt-Det 27.6
Pratt-StL 22.4
Milan-Was 16.5

Total Player Rating
Speaker-Cle 5.8
Cobb-Det 5.2
Pratt-StL 4.2
Jackson-Chi 3.9
Lavan-StL 3.5

Wins
Johnson-Was 25
Shawkey-NY 24
Ruth-Bos 23
Coveleski-Det 21
Dauss-Det 19

Win Percentage
Cicotte-Chi .682
Ruth-Bos .657
Coveleski-Det .656
Faber-Chi .654
Shawkey-NY .632

Games
Davenport-StL 59
Russell-Chi 56
Shawkey-NY 53
Gallia-Was 49

Complete Games
Johnson-Was 36
Myers-Phi 31
Bush-Phi 25
Ruth-Bos 23
Coveleski-Det 22

Shutouts
Ruth-Bos 9
Bush-Phi 8
Leonard-Bos 6
Russell-Chi 5

Saves
Shawkey-NY 8
Russell-NY 6
Leonard-Bos 6
Cicotte-Chi 5
Bagby-Cle 5

Innings Pitched
Johnson-Was 369.2
Coveleski-Det 324.1
Ruth-Bos 323.2
Myers-Phi 315.0
Davenport-StL 290.2

Fewest Hits/Game
Ruth-Bos 6.40
Shawkey-NY 6.64
Cicotte-Chi 6.64
Bush-Phi 6.97
Russell-Chi 7.05

Fewest BB/Game
Russell-Chi 1.43
Cullop-NY 1.72
Coveleski-Det 1.75
Shore-Bos 1.95
Johnson-Was 2.00

Strikeouts
Johnson-Was 228
Myers-Phi 182
Ruth-Bos 170
Bush-Phi 157
Harper-Was 149

Strikeouts/Game
Johnson-Was 5.55
Williams-Chi 5.54
Russell-NY 5.46
Harper-Was 5.37
Myers-Phi 5.20

Ratio
Russell-Chi 8.51
Johnson-Was 9.28
Shawkey-NY 9.47
Coveleski-Det 9.77
Ruth-Bos 9.90

Earned Run Average
Ruth-Bos 1.75
Cicotte-Chi 1.78
Johnson-Was 1.90
Coveleski-Det 1.97
Faber-Chi 2.02

Adjusted ERA
Ruth-Bos 158
Cicotte-Chi 155
Johnson-Was 147
Coveleski-Det 145
Cullop-NY 141

Opponents' Batting Avg.
Ruth-Bos .201
Shawkey-NY .209
Cicotte-Chi .218
Bush-Phi .219
Johnson-Was .220

Opponents' On-Base Pct.
Russell-Chi .254
Johnson-Was .270
Shawkey-NY .273
Ruth-Bos .280
Coveleski-Det .282

Starter Runs
Ruth-Bos 38.6
Johnson-Was 38.0
Coveleski-Det 30.8
Cicotte-Chi 21.7
Weilman-StL 20.6

Adjusted Starter Runs
Ruth-Bos 37.2
Johnson-Was 37.0
Coveleski-Det 31.7
Cicotte-Chi 20.8
Shawkey-NY 20.3

Clutch Pitching Index
Cicotte-Chi 117
Gallia-Was 117
Mogridge-NY 113
Fisher-NY 113
Weilman-StL 113

Relief Runs

Adjusted Relief Runs

Relief Ranking

Total Pitcher Index
Ruth-Bos 6.0
Johnson-Was 5.2
Coveleski-Det 3.9
Mays-Bos 3.3
Cicotte-Chi 2.9

Total Baseball Ranking
Ruth-Bos 6.0
Speaker-Cle 5.8
Cobb-Det 5.2
Johnson-Was 5.2
Pratt-StL 4.2

TEAM	G	W	L	PCT	GB	R	OR	AB	H	2B	3B	HR	BB	SO	AVG	OBP	SLG	OPS	OPS+	BR	BR+	PF	CHI	RC	SB	CS	SBA	SBR
NY	158	98	56	.636		**635**	**457**	5211	1360	170	71	**39**	373	533	.261	**.317**	.343	660	113	**50**	70	97	105	**597**	**162**			
PHI	154	87	65	.572	10	578	500	5084	1262	**225**	60	38	**435**	533	.248	.310	.339	649	101	29	6	104	100	556	109			
STL	154	82	70	.539	15	531	567	5083	1271	159	93	26	359	652	.250	.303	.333	636	104	2	18	97	98	542	159			
CIN	157	78	76	.506	20	601	611	5251	**1385**	196	**100**	26	312	**477**	**.264**	.309	**.354**	**663**	**114**	48	**74**	96	101	596	153			
CHI	157	74	80	.481	24	552	567	5135	1229	194	67	17	415	599	.239	.299	.313	612	86	-35	-73	108	**107**	511	127			
BOS	157	72	81	.471	25.5	536	552	5201	1280	169	75	22	427	587	.246	.309	.320	629	105	-2	32	94	96	549	155			
BRO	156	70	81	.464	26.5	511	559	5251	1299	159	78	25	334	527	.247	.296	.322	618	93	-32	-46	103	98	522	130			
PIT	157	51	103	.331	47	464	595	5169	1230	160	61	9	399	580	.238	.298	.298	596	86	-61	-76	103	94	493	150			
TOT	625					4408		41385	10316	1432	605	202	3054	4488	.250	.306	.328	633							1145			

TEAM	CG	SH	SV	IP	H	H/G	HR	BB	SO	RAT	ERA	ERA+	OAV	OOB	PR	PR+	PF	CPI	FA	E	DP	FW	PW	BW	SBW	DIF
NY	92	18	**14**	1426^{2}	**1221**	**7.8**	29	327	551	**10.0**	**2.28**	112	**.234**	**.283**	**69**	45	94	97	**.968**	**208**	122	**1.9**	5.1	8.0		6.2
PHI	102	**22**	5	1389	1258	8.2	25	**325**	616	10.5	2.46	**114**	.246	.295	38	**51**	104	102	.967	212	112	1.2	**5.8**	.7		3.4
STL	66	16	10	1392^{2}	1257	8.2	29	421	502	11.1	3.04	89	.248	.311	-51	-55	99	92	.967	221	**153**	.7	-6.2	2.1		9.6
CIN	94	12	6	1397^{1}	1358	8.8	20	402	488	11.6	2.70	97	.260	.317	1	-15	97	**110**	.962	247	120	-.6	-1.6	**8.4**		-4.9
CHI	79	16	9	1404	1303	8.4	34	374	**654**	11.0	2.62	110	.253	.307	14	38	107	108	.959	267	121	-1.9	4.3	-8.2		2.9
BOS	**103**	21	3	1424^{2}	1309	8.3	19	371	593	10.9	2.77	92	.251	.304	-10	-40	94	96	.966	224	122	.8	-4.5	3.7		-4.3
BRO	99	8	9	1421^{1}	1288	8.2	32	405	582	11.0	2.78	100	.247	.307	-12	0	103	98	.962	245	102	-.6	.0	-5.2		.4
PIT	84	17	6	1417^{2}	1318	8.4	**14**	432	509	11.4	3.01	94	.253	.314	-48	-28	105	94	.961	251	119	-.9	-3.1	-8.5		-13.3
TOT	719	130	62	11273^{1}		8.3				10.9	2.71		.250	.306					.965	1875	971					

Runs
Burns-NY 103
Groh-Cin 91
Kauff-NY 89
Hornsby-StL 86

Hits
Groh-Cin 182
Burns-NY 180
Roush-Cin 178
Zimmerman-NY 174
Carey-Pit 174

Doubles
Groh-Cin 39
Merkle-Bro-Chi 31
Smith-Bos 31
Cravath-Phi 29
Chase-Cin 28

Triples
Hornsby-StL 17
Cravath-Phi 16
Chase-Cin 15
Roush-Cin 14
Long-StL 14

Home Runs
Robertson-NY 12
Cravath-Phi 12
Hornsby-StL 8

Total Bases
Hornsby-StL 253
Groh-Cin 246
Burns-NY 246
Cravath-Phi 238

Runs Batted In
Zimmerman-NY 102
Chase-Cin 86
Cravath-Phi 83
Stengel-Bro 73
Luderus-Phi 72

Runs Produced
Zimmerman-NY 158
Chase-Cin 153
Kauff-NY 152
Roush-Cin 145
Hornsby-StL 144

Bases On Balls
Burns-NY 75
Groh-Cin 71
Cravath-Phi 70
Luderus-Phi 65
Paskert-Phi 62

Batting Average
Roush-Cin .... .341
Hornsby-StL .... .327
Z.Wheat-Bro .... .312
Kauff-NY .... .308
Groh-Cin .... .304

On-Base Percentage
Groh-Cin .... .385
Hornsby-StL .... .385
Burns-NY .... .380
Roush-Cin .... .379
Kauff-NY .... .379

Slugging Average
Hornsby-StL .... .484
Cravath-Phi .... .473
Roush-Cin .... .454
Z.Wheat-Bro .... .423
Burns-NY .... .412

On-Base Plus Slugging
Hornsby-StL 868
Cravath-Phi 842
Roush-Cin 833
Groh-Cin 796
Burns-NY 792

Adjusted OPS
Hornsby-StL 170
Roush-Cin 162
Cravath-Phi 151
Groh-Cin 150
Burns-NY 148

Batter Runs
Hornsby-StL 39.6
Cravath-Phi 34.7
Groh-Cin 33.5
Roush-Cin 32.3
Burns-NY 32.2

Adjusted Batter Runs
Hornsby-StL 42.4
Groh-Cin 37.8
Roush-Cin 36.1
Burns-NY 35.4
Cravath-Phi 31.0

Clutch Hitting Index
Zimmerman-NY 146
Ward-Pit 133
Luderus-Phi 132
Deal-Chi 130
Chase-Cin 121

Runs Created
Burns-NY 102
Hornsby-StL 100
Groh-Cin 96
Roush-Cin 94
Carey-Pit 94

Total Average
Hornsby-StL .... .906
Cravath-Phi .... .870
Burns-NY .... .868
Roush-Cin .... .843
Groh-Cin .... .815

Stolen Bases
Carey-Pit 46
Burns-NY 40
Kauff-NY 30
Maranville-Bos 27
Baird-Pit-StL 26

Stolen Base Average

Stolen Base Runs

Fielding Runs
Bancroft-Phi 27.9
Fletcher-NY 27.4
Carey-Pit 24.5
Hornsby-StL 21.3
Miller-StL 18.6

Total Player Rating
Hornsby-StL 8.0
Groh-Cin 5.5
Fletcher-NY 4.4
Burns-NY 3.7
Carey-Pit 3.7

Wins
Alexander-Phi 30
Toney-Cin 24
Vaughn-Chi 23
Schupp-NY 21
Schneider-Cin 20

Win Percentage
Schupp-NY .... .750
Sallee-NY .... .720
Perritt-NY .... .708
Alexander-Phi .... .698
Nehf-Bos .... .680

Games
Douglas-Chi 51
Barnes-Bos 50
Schneider-Cin 46
Alexander-Phi 45
Doak-StL 44

Complete Games
Alexander-Phi 34
Toney-Cin 31
Vaughn-Chi 27
Barnes-Bos 26
Schupp-NY 25

Shutouts
Alexander-Phi 8
Toney-Cin 7
Cooper-Pit 7
Schupp-NY 6

Saves
Sallee-NY 4

Innings Pitched
Alexander-Phi 388.0
Toney-Cin 339.2
Schneider-Cin 333.2
Cooper-Pit 297.2
Vaughn-Chi 295.2

Fewest Hits/Game
Schupp-NY 6.68
Anderson-NY 6.78
Nehf-Bos 7.60
Pfeffer-Bro 7.61
Tyler-Bos 7.64

Fewest BB/Game
Alexander-Phi 1.30
Sallee-NY 1.42
Nehf-Bos 1.50
Barnes-Bos 1.53
Douglas-Chi 1.53

Strikeouts
Alexander-Phi 200
Vaughn-Chi 195
Douglas-Chi 151
Schupp-NY 147
Schneider-Cin 138

Strikeouts/Game
Vaughn-Chi 5.94
Schupp-NY 4.86
Alexander-Phi 4.64
Douglas-Chi 4.63
Marquard-Bro 4.53

Ratio
Anderson-NY 8.78
Schupp-NY 9.13
Alexander-Phi 9.23
Nehf-Bos 9.26
Barnes-Bos 9.58

Earned Run Average
Alexander-Phi 1.83
Anderson-NY 1.44
Perritt-NY 1.88
Schupp-NY 1.95
Vaughn-Chi 2.01

Adjusted ERA
Anderson-NY 176
Alexander-Phi 153
Vaughn-Chi 144
Perritt-NY 135
Schupp-NY 130

Opponents' Batting Avg.
Schupp-NY .... .209
Anderson-NY .... .209
Nehf-Bos .... .231
Marquard-Bro .... .232
Pfeffer-Bro .... .234

Opponents' On-Base Pct.
Anderson-NY .... .255
Schupp-NY .... .265
Alexander-Phi .... .266
Nehf-Bos .... .268
Barnes-Bos .... .277

Starter Runs
Alexander-Phi 37.5
Vaughn-Chi 22.8
Schupp-NY 22.7
Anderson-NY 22.7
Schneider-Cin 22.2

Adjusted Starter Runs
Alexander-Phi 40.3
Vaughn-Chi 27.1
Anderson-NY 21.0
Schneider-Cin 19.4
Schupp-NY 19.0

Clutch Pitching Index
Schneider-Cin 145
Vaughn-Chi 120
Perritt-NY 118
Hendrix-Chi 117
Mayer-Phi 114

Relief Runs

Adjusted Relief Runs

Relief Ranking

Total Pitcher Index
Alexander-Phi 5.7
Vaughn-Chi 3.8
Rixey-Phi 2.5
Anderson-NY 1.9
Schneider-Cin 1.9

Total Baseball Ranking
Hornsby-StL 8.0
Alexander-Phi 5.7
Groh-Cin 5.5
Fletcher-NY 4.4
Vaughn-Chi 3.8

TEAM	G	W	L	PCT	GB	R	OR	AB	H	2B	3B	HR	BB	SO	AVG	OBP	SLG	OPS	OPS+	BR	BR+	PF	CHI	RC	SB	CS	SBA	SBR
CHI	156	100	54	.649		**655**	463	5057	1281	152	**81**	18	522	479	.253	**.329**	.326	655	103	36	24	102	**108**	607	**219**			
BOS	157	90	62	.592	9	555	**455**	5048	1243	198	64	14	466	**473**	.246	.314	.319	633	100	-10	-4	99	99	550	105			
CLE	156	88	66	.571	12	584	543	4994	1224	**218**	64	13	**549**	596	.245	.324	.322	646	96	21	-20	107	99	588	210			
DET	154	78	75	.510	21.5	639	577	5093	**1317**	204	77	25	483	476	**.259**	.328	**.344**	**672**	**111**	**61**	**64**	100	102	**615**	163			
WAS	157	74	79	.484	25.5	544	566	5142	1238	173	70	4	500	574	.241	.313	.304	617	95	-34	-27	99	101	531	166			
NY	155	71	82	.464	28.5	524	558	5136	1226	172	52	**27**	496	535	.239	.310	.308	618	93	-34	-39	101	98	526	136			
STL	155	57	97	.370	43	510	687	5091	1250	183	63	15	405	540	.246	.305	.315	620	98	-39	-19	96	99	523	157			
PHI	154	55	98	.359	44.5	529	691	5109	1296	177	62	17	435	519	.254	.316	.323	639	101	-1	7	99	94	551	112			
TOT	622					4540		40670	10075	1477	533	133	3856	4192	.248	.318	.321	638							1268			

TEAM	CG	SH	SV	IP	H	H/G	HR	BB	SO	RAT	ERA	ERA+	OAV	OOB	PR	PR+	PF	CPI	FA	E	DP	FW	PW	BW	SBW	DIF
CHI	78	**22**	21	1424^1	1236	7.9	**10**	**413**	517	10.7	**2.17**	**123**	.238	.298	**79**	**76**	100	**102**	.967	204	117	2.3	**8.5**	2.7		9.7
BOS	**115**	15	7	1421^1	**1197**	**7.6**	12	**413**	509	**10.6**	2.20	117	**.231**	**.295**	73	62	97	95	**.972**	**183**	116	**4.0**	6.9	-.4		3.7
CLE	73	20	**22**	1412^2	1270	8.1	17	438	451	11.1	2.53	112	.247	.310	22	45	106	101	.964	242	136	-.4	5.1	-2.2		8.7
DET	78	20	15	1396^1	1209	7.8	12	504	516	11.4	2.56	103	.240	.316	16	13	99	99	.964	234	95	-.0	1.5	**7.2**		-6.9
WAS	84	21	10	1413	1217	7.8	12	537	**637**	11.5	2.76	95	.239	.316	-14	-20	99	91	.961	251	127	-1.0	-2.2	-3.0		3.8
NY	87	10	6	1411^1	1280	8.2	28	427	571	11.2	2.66	101	.252	.314	0	3	101	**102**	.965	225	129	.7	.4	-4.3		-2.1
STL	66	12	12	1385^1	1320	8.6	19	537	429	12.3	3.21	81	.257	.332	-83	-99	98	94	.957	281	**139**	-3.4	-11.0	-2.1		-3.4
PHI	80	8	8	1365^2	1310	8.7	23	562	516	12.5	3.27	84	.261	.338	-92	-77	103	97	.961	251	106	-1.3	-8.5	.8		-12.3
TOT	661	128	101	11230		8.1				11.4	2.67		.248	.318					.964	1871	965					

Runs
Bush-Det 112
Cobb-Det 107
Chapman-Cle 98
Jackson-Chi 91
E.Collins-Chi 91

Hits
Cobb-Det 225
Sisler-StL 190
Speaker-Cle 184
Veach-Det 182

Doubles
Cobb-Det 44
Speaker-Cle 42
Veach-Det 31
Sisler-StL 30
Roth-Cle 30

Triples
Cobb-Det 24
Jackson-Chi 17
Judge-Was 15
Chapman-Cle 13

Home Runs
Pipp-NY 9
Veach-Det 8
Bodie-Phi 7

Total Bases
Cobb-Det 335
Veach-Det 261
Speaker-Cle 254
Sisler-StL 244
Bodie-Phi 233

Runs Batted In
Veach-Det 103
Felsch-Chi 102
Cobb-Det 102
Heilmann-Det 86
Jackson-Chi 75

Runs Produced
Cobb-Det 203
Veach-Det 174
Felsch-Chi 171
Jackson-Chi 161
E.Collins-Chi 158

Bases On Balls
Graney-Cle 94
E.Collins-Chi 89
Hooper-Bos 80
Bush-Det 80
Leibold-Chi 74

Batting Average
Cobb-Det .... .383
Sisler-StL .... .353
Speaker-Cle .... .352
Veach-Det .... .319
Felsch-Chi .... .308

On-Base Percentage
Cobb-Det .... .444
Speaker-Cle .... .432
Veach-Det .... .393
Sisler-StL .... .390
E.Collins-Chi .... .389

Slugging Average
Cobb-Det .... .570
Speaker-Cle .... .486
Veach-Det .... .457
Sisler-StL .... .453
Jackson-Chi .... .429

On-Base Plus Slugging
Cobb-Det 1014
Speaker-Cle 918
Veach-Det 850
Sisler-StL 843
Jackson-Chi 805

Adjusted OPS
Cobb-Det 210
Speaker-Cle 168
Sisler-StL 163
Veach-Det 160
Jackson-Chi 142

Batter Runs
Cobb-Det 74.4
Speaker-Cle 51.2
Veach-Det 40.1
Sisler-StL 34.0
Jackson-Chi 28.8

Adjusted Batter Runs
Cobb-Det 75.0
Speaker-Cle 43.6
Veach-Det 40.5
Sisler-StL 37.5
Jackson-Chi 26.9

Clutch Hitting Index
Schalk-Chi 135
Bates-Phi 134
Felsch-Chi 133
Veach-Det 130
E.Collins-Chi 128

Runs Created
Cobb-Det 164
Speaker-Cle 118
Veach-Det 108
Chapman-Cle 105
Sisler-StL 104

Total Average
Cobb-Det 1.253
Speaker-Cle 1.056
Veach-Det .... .905
Sisler-StL .... .900
E.Collins-Chi .... .873

Stolen Bases
Cobb-Det 55
E.Collins-Chi 53
Chapman-Cle 52
Roth-Cle 51
Sisler-StL 37

Stolen Base Average

Stolen Base Runs

Fielding Runs
Chapman-Cle 24.4
Felsch-Chi 18.9
Wambsganss-Cle 15.3
Ainsmith-Was 14.9
Pratt-StL 14.8

Total Player Rating
Cobb-Det 8.3
Chapman-Cle 5.8
Speaker-Cle 4.5
Veach-Det 4.2
Sisler-StL 4.1

Wins
Cicotte-Chi 28
Ruth-Bos 24
Johnson-Was 23
Bagby-Cle 23
Mays-Bos 22

Win Percentage
Russell-Chi .... .750
Mays-Bos .... .710
Cicotte-Chi .... .700
Williams-Chi .... .680
Ruth-Bos .... .649

Games
Danforth-Chi 50
Cicotte-Chi 49
Bagby-Cle 49
Sothoron-StL 48

Complete Games
Ruth-Bos 35
Johnson-Was 30
Cicotte-Chi 29
Mays-Bos 27

Shutouts
Coveleski-Cle 9
Johnson-Was 8
Bagby-Cle 8
Cicotte-Chi 7

Saves
Danforth-Chi 9
Bagby-Cle 7
Boland-Det 6
Coumbe-Cle 5

Innings Pitched
Cicotte-Chi 346.2
Ruth-Bos 326.1
Johnson-Was 326.0
Bagby-Cle 320.2
Coveleski-Cle 298.1

Fewest Hits/Game
Coveleski-Cle 6.09
Cicotte-Chi 6.39
Ruth-Bos 6.73
Johnson-Was 6.85
Mays-Bos 7.16

Fewest BB/Game
Russell-Chi 1.52
Mogridge-NY 1.79
Cicotte-Chi 1.82
Johnson-Was 1.88
Bagby-Cle 2.05

Strikeouts
Johnson-Was 188
Cicotte-Chi 150
Leonard-Bos 144
Coveleski-Cle 133
Ruth-Bos 128

Strikeouts/Game
Johnson-Was 5.19
Harper-Was 4.97
Bush-Phi 4.67
Leonard-Bos 4.40
Danforth-Chi 4.11

Ratio
Cicotte-Chi 8.28
Coveleski-Cle 8.96
Johnson-Was 9.11
Russell-Chi 9.65
Mays-Bos 9.90

Earned Run Average
Cicotte-Chi 1.53
Mays-Bos 1.74
Coveleski-Cle 1.81
Faber-Chi 1.92
Russell-Chi 1.95

Adjusted ERA
Cicotte-Chi 173
Coveleski-Cle 156
Mays-Bos 148
Bagby-Cle 142
Faber-Chi 138

Opponents' Batting Avg.
Coveleski-Cle .... .194
Cicotte-Chi .... .203
Ruth-Bos .... .211
Johnson-Was .... .211
Mays-Bos .... .221

Opponents' On-Base Pct.
Cicotte-Chi .... .248
Coveleski-Cle .... .261
Johnson-Was .... .263
Russell-Chi .... .279
Mays-Bos .... .282

Starter Runs
Cicotte-Chi 43.5
Mays-Bos 29.4
Coveleski-Cle 28.2
Bagby-Cle 23.8
Ruth-Bos 23.5

Adjusted Starter Runs
Cicotte-Chi 43.4
Coveleski-Cle 31.8
Bagby-Cle 28.1
Mays-Bos 27.6
Ruth-Bos 21.1

Clutch Pitching Index
Faber-Chi 136
Ayers-Was 128
James-Det 127
Morton-Cle 117
Mitchell-Det 116

Relief Runs

Adjusted Relief Runs

Relief Ranking

Total Pitcher Index
Cicotte-Chi 5.4
Mays-Bos 4.9
Ruth-Bos 4.8
Bagby-Cle 3.4
Johnson-Was 3.0

Total Baseball Ranking
Cobb-Det 8.3
Chapman-Cle 5.8
Cicotte-Chi 5.4
Mays-Bos 4.9
Ruth-Bos 4.8

TEAM	G	W	L	PCT	GB	R	OR	AB	H	2B	3B	HR	BB	SO	AVG	OBP	SLG	OPS	OPS+	BR	BR+	PF	CHI	RC	SB	CS	SBA	SBR
CHI	131	84	45	.651		**538**	**393**	4325	1147	164	53	21	358	343	.265	.325	.342	667	106	48	35	103	102	524	159			
NY	124	71	53	.573	10.5	480	415	4164	1081	150	53	13	271	365	.260	.310	.330	640	103	1	10	98	**107**	451	130			
CIN	129	68	60	.531	15.5	530	496	4265	**1185**	**165**	**84**	15	304	303	**.278**	**.330**	**.366**	**696**	**120**	**86**	**96**	98	96	**545**	128			
PIT	126	65	60	.520	17	466	412	4091	1016	107	72	15	**371**	**285**	.248	.315	.321	636	96	1	-14	103	102	466	**200**			
BRO	126	57	69	.452	25.5	360	463	4212	1052	121	62	10	212	326	.250	.291	.315	606	90	-53	-51	100	91	405	113			
PHI	125	55	68	.447	26	430	507	4192	1022	158	28	25	346	400	.244	.305	.313	618	88	-29	-56	107	101	417	97			
BOS	124	53	71	.427	28.5	424	469	4162	1014	107	59	13	350	438	.244	.307	.307	614	97	-32	-13	96	100	412	83			
STL	131	51	78	.395	33	454	527	4369	1066	147	64	**27**	329	461	.244	.301	.325	626	99	-21	-5	97	100	450	119			
TOT	508					3682		33780	8583	1119	475	139	2541	2921	.255	.311	.328	638							1029			

TEAM	CG	SH	SV	IP	H	H/G	HR	BB	SO	RAT	ERA	ERA+	OAV	OOB	PR	PR+	PF	CPI	FA	E	DP	FW	PW	BW	SBW	DIF
CHI	92	**23**	8	1197	1050	**7.9**	**13**	296	**472**	10.3	**2.19**	**128**	**.239**	.291	**77**	**80**	101	104	.966	188	91	.5	**9.0**	4.0		6.2
NY	74	18	**11**	1111[2]	**1002**	8.2	20	**228**	330	**10.2**	2.64	100	.243	**.287**	15	-1	95	87	**.971**	**152**	78	**2.2**	-.0	1.2		5.9
CIN	84	14	6	1142[1]	1136	9.0	19	381	321	12.2	3.01	89	.268	.332	-30	-44	97	**109**	.964	192	**127**	.1	-4.9	**10.8**		-1.8
PIT	85	10	7	1140[1]	1005	8.0	**13**	299	367	10.6	2.48	116	.243	.300	36	49	104	99	.966	179	108	.6	5.5	-1.5		-2.0
BRO	85	17	2	1131[1]	1024	8.2	22	320	395	11.0	2.81	99	.248	.307	-6	-4	101	95	.963	193	74	-.2	-.4	-5.6		.5
PHI	78	10	6	1139[2]	1086	8.6	22	369	312	11.8	3.16	95	.258	.323	-49	-19	109	96	.961	211	91	-1.5	-2.1	-6.2		3.5
BOS	**96**	13	0	1117[1]	1111	9.0	14	277	340	11.4	2.90	93	.266	.316	-17	-28	97	102	.965	184	89	.1	-3.1	-1.4		-4.5
STL	72	3	5	1193	1148	8.7	16	352	361	11.7	2.97	91	.261	.321	-27	-34	98	101	.962	220	116	-1.5	-3.7	-.5		-7.6
TOT	666	108	45	9172[2]		8.5				11.1	2.77		.255	.311					.965	1519	774					

Runs
Groh-Cin 86
Burns-NY 80
Flack-Chi 74
Hollocher-Chi 72

Hits
Hollocher-Chi 161
Groh-Cin 158
Roush-Cin 145
Youngs-NY 143
Merkle-Chi 143

Doubles
Groh-Cin 28
Mann-Chi 27
Cravath-Phi 27
Meusel-Phi 25
Merkle-Chi 25

Triples
Daubert-Bro 15
Wickland-Bos 13
S.Magee-Cin 13
L.Magee-Cin 13

Home Runs
Cravath-Phi 8
Williams-Phi 6
Cruise-StL 6

Total Bases
Hollocher-Chi 202
Roush-Cin 198
Groh-Cin 195
Mann-Chi 188
Merkle-Chi 187

Runs Batted In
S.Magee-Cin 76
Cutshaw-Pit 68
Luderus-Phi 67
R.Smith-Bos 65
Merkle-Chi 65

Runs Produced
Burns-NY 127
Paskert-Chi 125
Mann-Chi 122
Groh-Cin 122
S.Magee-Cin 120

Bases On Balls
Carey-Pit 62
Flack-Chi 56
Groh-Cin 54
Cravath-Phi 54
Bancroft-Phi 54

Batting Average
Z.Wheat-Bro .335
Roush-Cin .333
Groh-Cin .320
Hollocher-Chi .316
Daubert-Bro .308

On-Base Percentage
Groh-Cin .395
Hollocher-Chi .379
R.Smith-Bos .373
S.Magee-Cin .370
Z.Wheat-Bro .369

Slugging Average
Roush-Cin .455
Daubert-Bro .429
Hornsby-StL .416
S.Magee-Cin .415
Wickland-Bos .398

On-Base Plus Slugging
Roush-Cin 823
Groh-Cin 791
Daubert-Bro 789
S.Magee-Cin 785
Hollocher-Chi 775

Adjusted OPS
Roush-Cin 153
Groh-Cin 144
S.Magee-Cin 142
Daubert-Bro 141
Wickland-Bos 139

Batter Runs
Groh-Cin 26.4
Roush-Cin 24.3
Hollocher-Chi 23.0
S.Magee-Cin 19.2
Daubert-Bro 18.2

Adjusted Batter Runs
Groh-Cin 27.9
Roush-Cin 25.6
Hollocher-Chi 21.0
S.Magee-Cin 20.3
R.Smith-Bos 18.4

Clutch Hitting Index
S.Magee-Cin 158
Konetchy-Bos 137
R.Smith-Bos 135
Z.Wheat-Bro 122
Paulette-StL 122

Runs Created
Hollocher-Chi 85
Roush-Cin 80
Groh-Cin 79
Carey-Pit 76
Burns-NY 74

Total Average
Roush-Cin .848
Carey-Pit .844
Wickland-Bos .812
Burns-NY .809
S.Magee-Cin .804

Stolen Bases
Carey-Pit 58
Burns-NY 40
Hollocher-Chi 26
Cutshaw-Pit 25
Baird-StL 25

Stolen Base Average

Stolen Base Runs

Fielding Runs
Fletcher-NY 22.3
Carey-Pit 18.6
Bancroft-Phi 17.9
Schmidt-Pit 15.7
Myers-Bro 13.0

Total Player Rating
Hornsby-StL 3.9
Groh-Cin 3.7
Fisher-StL 3.3
Fletcher-NY 2.9
Roush-Cin 2.9

Wins
Vaughn-Chi 22
Hendrix-Chi 20
Tyler-Chi 19
Grimes-Bro 19
Cooper-Pit 19

Win Percentage
Hendrix-Chi .741
Tyler-Chi .704
Mayer-Phi-Pit .696
Vaughn-Chi .688
Grimes-Bro .679

Games
Grimes-Bro 40
Cooper-Pit 38
Eller-Cin 37

Complete Games
Nehf-Bos 28
Vaughn-Chi 27
Cooper-Pit 26
Tyler-Chi 22
Hendrix-Chi 21

Shutouts
Vaughn-Chi 8
Grimes-Bro 7
Tyler-Chi 6
Perritt-NY 6

Saves
Toney-Cin-NY 3
Oeschger-Phi 3
Cooper-Pit 3
Anderson-NY 3

Innings Pitched
Vaughn-Chi 290.1
Nehf-Bos 284.1
Cooper-Pit 273.1
Grimes-Bro 269.2
Tyler-Chi 269.1

Fewest Hits/Game
Vaughn-Chi 6.70
Grimes-Bro 7.01
Cooper-Pit 7.21
Tyler-Chi 7.28
Jacobs-Pit-Phi 7.50

Fewest BB/Game
Sallee-NY .82
Perritt-NY 1.47
G.Smith-Cin-NY-Bro 1.50
Toney-Cin-NY 1.54
Demaree-NY 1.58

Strikeouts
Vaughn-Chi 148
Cooper-Pit 117
Grimes-Bro 113
Tyler-Chi 102
Nehf-Bos 96

Strikeouts/Game
Vaughn-Chi 4.59
Cooper-Pit 3.85
Grimes-Bro 3.77
Cheney-Bro 3.72
May-StL 3.60

Ratio
Sallee-NY 9.14
Vaughn-Chi 9.27
Grimes-Bro 9.68
Cooper-Pit 9.68
Tyler-Chi 9.69

Earned Run Average
Vaughn-Chi 1.74
Tyler-Chi 2.00
Cooper-Pit 2.11
Douglas-Chi 2.13
Grimes-Bro 2.14

Adjusted ERA
Vaughn-Chi 161
Tyler-Chi 139
Cooper-Pit 136
Douglas-Chi 131
Grimes-Bro 130

Opponents' Batting Avg.
Vaughn-Chi .208
Grimes-Bro .216
Cooper-Pit .223
Tyler-Chi .226
Jacobs-Pit-Phi .233

Opponents' On-Base Pct.
Sallee-NY .259
Vaughn-Chi .266
Grimes-Bro .276
Perritt-NY .278
Cooper-Pit .279

Starter Runs
Vaughn-Chi 33.1
Tyler-Chi 22.7
Cooper-Pit 19.9
Grimes-Bro 18.8
Hamilton-Pit 11.6

Adjusted Starter Runs
Vaughn-Chi 33.6
Tyler-Chi 23.2
Cooper-Pit 22.3
Grimes-Bro 19.3
Hamilton-Pit 11.8

Clutch Pitching Index
Bressler-Cin 123
Mayer-Phi-Pit 117
Schneider-Cin 113
Eller-Cin 112
Demaree-NY 112

Relief Runs

Adjusted Relief Runs

Relief Ranking

Total Pitcher Index
Vaughn-Chi 4.4
Tyler-Chi 3.0
Cooper-Pit 3.0
Grimes-Bro 2.6
Douglas-Chi 1.9

Total Baseball Ranking
Vaughn-Chi 4.4
Hornsby-StL 3.9
Groh-Cin 3.7
Fisher-StL 3.3
Tyler-Chi 3.0

TEAM	G	W	L	PCT	GB	R	OR	AB	H	2B	3B	HR	BB	SO	AVG	OBP	SLG	OPS	OPS+	BR	BR+	PF	CHI	RC	SB	CS	SBA	SBR
BOS	126	75	51	.595		474	**380**	3982	990	159	54	15	407	**324**	.249	.322	.327	649	103	6	14	98	105	455	110			
CLE	129	73	54	.575	2.5	**504**	447	4166	1084	**176**	**67**	9	**491**	386	**.260**	**.344**	**.341**	**685**	102	**68**	21	110	93	**537**	**165**			
WAS	130	72	56	.563	4	461	412	4472	**1144**	156	49	4	376	361	.256	.318	.315	633	98	-21	-12	98	99	479	137			
NY	126	60	63	.488	13.5	493	475	4224	1085	160	45	20	367	370	.257	.320	.330	650	99	2	-8	102	**106**	469	88			
STL	123	58	64	.475	15	426	448	4019	1040	152	40	5	397	340	.259	.331	.320	651	**105**	11	**26**	97	93	467	138			
CHI	124	57	67	.460	17	457	446	4132	1057	136	55	8	375	358	.256	.322	.321	643	98	-5	-9	101	102	458	116			
DET	128	55	71	.437	20	476	557	4262	1063	141	56	13	452	380	.249	.325	.318	643	103	-2	18	96	101	470	123			
PHI	130	52	76	.406	24	412	538	4278	1039	124	44	**22**	343	485	.243	.303	.308	611	88	-59	-63	101	102	415	83			
TOT	508					3703		33535	8502	1204	410	96	3208	3004	.254	.324	.323	646							960			

TEAM	CG	SH	SV	IP	H	H/G	HR	BB	SO	RAT	ERA	ERA+	OAV	OOB	PR	PR+	PF	CPI	FA	E	DP	FW	PW	BW	SBW	DIF
BOS	**105**	**26**	2	1120	**931**	**7.5**	**9**	380	392	10.8	2.31	116	**.231**	.302	58	49	97	95	**.971**	**152**	89	**2.5**	5.5	1.6		2.6
CLE	78	5	**13**	1161	1126	8.8	**9**	343	364	11.6	2.64	114	.262	.319	18	42	108	105	.962	207	82	-.6	4.7	2.4		3.2
WAS	75	19	8	1228	1021	**7.5**	10	395	**505**	**10.6**	**2.15**	**127**	**.231**	**.298**	**86**	**81**	98	99	.960	226	95	-1.7	**9.1**	-1.3		2.1
NY	59	8	**13**	1157^1	1103	8.6	25	463	370	12.5	3.01	94	.261	.340	-30	-23	102	**107**	.970	161	**137**	2.0	-2.5	-.8		.1
STL	67	8	8	1111^1	993	8.1	11	402	346	11.6	2.76	99	.246	.319	2	-2	99	95	.963	190	86	-.1	-.2	**3.0**		-5.4
CHI	76	9	8	1126	1092	8.8	**9**	**300**	349	11.3	2.74	100	.261	.314	5	-3	99	97	.967	169	98	1.3	-.3	-1.0		-4.8
DET	74	8	7	1160^2	1130	8.8	10	437	374	12.5	3.41	78	.263	.335	-81	-104	96	89	.960	212	77	-1.0	-11.6	2.1		2.7
PHI	80	13	9	1156	1106	8.7	13	486	277	12.7	3.23	91	.266	.348	-58	-37	106	103	.959	228	136	-1.8	-4.1	-7.0		1.1
TOT	614	96	68	9220^1		8.3				11.7	2.78		.254	.324					.964	1545	800					

Runs
Chapman-Cle 84
T.Cobb-Det 83
Hooper-Bos 81
Bush-Det 74
Speaker-Cle 73

Hits
Burns-Phi 178
T.Cobb-Det 161
Sisler-StL 154
Baker-NY 154
Speaker-Cle 150

Doubles
Speaker-Cle 33
Ruth-Bos 26
Hooper-Bos 26
Baker-NY 24

Triples
T.Cobb-Det 14
Veach-Det 13
Hooper-Bos 13
Roth-Cle 12

Home Runs
Walker-Phi 11
Ruth-Bos 11
Burns-Phi 6
Baker-NY 6

Total Bases
Burns-Phi 236
T.Cobb-Det 217
Baker-NY 206
Speaker-Cle 205
Sisler-StL 199

Runs Batted In
Veach-Det 78
Burns-Phi 70
Wood-Cle 66
Ruth-Bos 66
T.Cobb-Det 64

Runs Produced
T.Cobb-Det 144
Veach-Det 134
Speaker-Cle 134
Burns-Phi 125
Hooper-Bos 124

Bases On Balls
Chapman-Cle 84
Bush-Det 79
Hooper-Bos 75
E.Collins-Chi 73
Shotton-Was 67

Batting Average
T.Cobb-Det .382
Burns-Phi .352
Sisler-StL .341
Speaker-Cle .318
Baker-NY .306

On-Base Percentage
T.Cobb-Det .440
E.Collins-Chi .407
Speaker-Cle .403
Sisler-StL .400
Hooper-Bos .391

Slugging Average
Ruth-Bos .555
T.Cobb-Det .515
Burns-Phi .467
Sisler-StL .440
Speaker-Cle .435

On-Base Plus Slugging
T.Cobb-Det 955
Burns-Phi 857
Sisler-StL 841
Speaker-Cle 839
Hooper-Bos 796

Adjusted OPS
T.Cobb-Det 196
Sisler-StL 159
Burns-Phi 157
Hooper-Bos 142
Speaker-Cle 140

Batter Runs
T.Cobb-Det 44.0
Ruth-Bos 35.1
Burns-Phi 32.8
Speaker-Cle 31.3
Sisler-StL 28.8

Adjusted Batter Runs
T.Cobb-Det 47.9
Ruth-Bos 36.4
Burns-Phi 31.9
Sisler-StL 31.3
Hooper-Bos 26.5

Clutch Hitting Index
Veach-Det 140
Demmitt-StL 137
McInnis-Bos 136
Shanks-Was 133
S.Collins-Chi 132

Runs Created
T.Cobb-Det 105
Sisler-StL 92
Burns-Phi 91
Speaker-Cle 90
Hooper-Bos 82

Total Average
T.Cobb-Det 1.131
Sisler-StL .970
Speaker-Cle .931
Roth-Cle .929
Hooper-Bos .875

Stolen Bases
Sisler-StL 45
Roth-Cle 35
T.Cobb-Det 34
Chapman-Cle 30
Speaker-Cle 27

Stolen Base Average

Stolen Base Runs

Fielding Runs
Peckinpaugh-NY 25.0
Scott-Bos 17.5
Dugan-Phi 17.0
Gedeon-StL 15.8
S.Collins-Chi 14.1

Total Player Rating
T.Cobb-Det 4.7
Sisler-StL 4.0
Burns-Phi 3.8
Baker-NY 3.3
Speaker-Cle 2.9

Wins
Johnson-Was 23
Coveleski-Cle 22
Mays-Bos 21
Perry-Phi 20
Bagby-Cle 17

Win Percentage
Jones-Bos .762
Johnson-Was .639
Coveleski-Cle .629
Mays-Bos .618
Shaw-Was .571

Games
Mogridge-NY 45
Bagby-Cle 45
Perry-Phi 44
Shaw-Was 41
Ayers-Was 40

Complete Games
Perry-Phi 30
Mays-Bos 30
Johnson-Was 29
Bush-Bos 26
Coveleski-Cle 25

Shutouts
Mays-Bos 8
Johnson-Was 8
Bush-Bos 7
Jones-Bos 5

Saves
Mogridge-NY 7
Bagby-Cle 6
Russell-NY 4
Geary-Phi 4

Innings Pitched
Perry-Phi 332.1
Johnson-Was 326.0
Coveleski-Cle 311.0
Mays-Bos 293.1
Bush-Bos 272.2

Fewest Hits/Game
Sothoron-StL 6.55
Johnson-Was 6.65
Harper-Was 6.71
Ruth-Bos 6.76
Mays-Bos 7.06

Fewest BB/Game
Cicotte-Chi 1.35
Mogridge-NY 1.62
Benz-Chi 1.64
Enzmann-Cle 1.91
Johnson-Was 1.93

Strikeouts
Johnson-Was 162
Shaw-Was 129
Bush-Bos 125
Morton-Cle 123
Mays-Bos 114

Strikeouts/Game
Morton-Cle 5.16
Shaw-Was 4.81
Johnson-Was 4.47
Bush-Bos 4.13
Love-NY 3.74

Ratio
Johnson-Was 8.81
Ruth-Bos 9.52
Sothoron-StL 9.56
Coveleski-Cle 9.87
Mays-Bos 9.88

Earned Run Average
Johnson-Was 1.27
Coveleski-Cle 1.82
Sothoron-StL 1.94
Perry-Phi 1.98
Bush-Bos 2.11

Adjusted ERA
Johnson-Was 214
Coveleski-Cle 164
Perry-Phi 148
Sothoron-StL 141
Mogridge-NY 129

Opponents' Batting Avg.
Sothoron-StL .205
Johnson-Was .210
Harper-Was .212
Ruth-Bos .214
Mays-Bos .221

Opponents' On-Base Pct.
Johnson-Was .260
Sothoron-StL .274
Ruth-Bos .277
Coveleski-Cle .279
Mays-Bos .284

Starter Runs
Johnson-Was 54.4
Coveleski-Cle 32.8
Perry-Phi 29.4
Bush-Bos 20.0
Sothoron-StL 19.4

Adjusted Starter Runs
Johnson-Was 53.6
Coveleski-Cle 37.5
Perry-Phi 33.2
Sothoron-StL 18.7
Bush-Bos 17.7

Clutch Pitching Index
Perry-Phi 124
Mogridge-NY 123
Coumbe-Cle 119
Russell-NY 119
Shellenback-Chi 116

Relief Runs
Houck-StL 3.1

Adjusted Relief Runs
Houck-StL 2.8

Relief Ranking
Houck-StL 2.3

Total Pitcher Index
Johnson-Was 7.8
Coveleski-Cle 4.2
Mays-Bos 4.2
Perry-Phi 3.7
Bush-Bos 3.2

Total Baseball Ranking
Johnson-Was 7.7
Ruth-Bos 5.7
T.Cobb-Det 4.6
Coveleski-Cle 4.2
Mays-Bos 4.2

TEAM	G	W	L	PCT	GB	R	OR	AB	H	2B	3B	HR	BB	SO	AVG	OBP	SLG	OPS	OPS+	BR	BR+	PF	CHI	RC	SB	CS	SBA	SBR
CIN	140	96	44	.686		577	**401**	4577	1204	135	**83**	20	**405**	368	.263	**.327**	.342	669	110	43	58	97	104	552	143			
NY	140	87	53	.621	9	**605**	470	4664	1254	204	64	40	328	407	**.269**	.322	**.366**	**688**	**113**	**64**	**70**	99	**106**	**576**	157			
CHI	140	75	65	.536	21	454	407	4581	1174	166	58	21	298	**359**	.256	.308	.332	640	97	-14	-17	101	93	500	150			
PIT	139	71	68	.511	24.5	472	466	4538	1132	130	82	17	344	381	.249	.306	.325	631	92	-25	-42	104	100	493	**196**			
BRO	141	69	71	.493	27	525	513	4844	**1272**	167	66	25	258	405	.263	.304	.340	644	97	-13	-23	102	104	518	112			
BOS	140	57	82	.410	38.5	465	563	4746	1201	142	62	24	355	481	.253	.311	.324	635	100	-17	5	96	92	509	145			
STL	138	54	83	.394	40.5	463	552	4588	1175	163	52	18	304	418	.256	.305	.326	631	101	-28	2	94	99	485	148			
PHI	138	47	90	.343	47.5	510	699	4746	1191	**208**	50	**42**	323	469	.251	.303	.342	645	92	-9	-42	107	101	506	114			
TOT	558					4071		37284	9603	1315	517	207	2615	3288	.258	.311	.338	648							1165			

TEAM	CG	SH	SV	IP	H	H/G	HR	BB	SO	RAT	ERA	ERA+	OAV	OOB	PR	PR+	PF	CPI	FA	E	DP	FW	PW	BW	SBW	DIF
CIN	89	**23**	9	1274	**1104**	**7.8**	21	298	407	**10.1**	2.24	124	**.239**	**.288**	96	79	95	104	**.974**	**151**	98	**2.8**	8.8	6.5		8.1
NY	72	11	**13**	1256	1153	8.3	34	305	340	10.7	2.71	104	.247	.296	29	14	96	96	.964	216	96	-1.0	1.6	**7.8**		8.8
CHI	80	21	5	1265	1127	8.1	**14**	294	**495**	10.4	**2.22**	**130**	.242	.291	**98**	**94**	99	106	.969	185	87	.8	**10.5**	-1.8		-4.3
PIT	91	17	4	1249	1113	8.1	23	**263**	391	10.2	2.89	104	.244	.290	4	17	104	84	.970	165	89	1.9	1.9	-4.6		2.5
BRO	**98**	12	1	1281	1256	8.9	21	292	476	11.2	2.74	109	.262	.309	25	32	102	106	.963	219	84	-1.1	3.6	-2.5		-.8
BOS	79	5	9	1270[1]	1313	9.4	29	337	374	11.9	3.17	90	.276	.327	-36	-46	98	**107**	.966	204	111	-.3	-5.1	.6		-7.5
STL	55	6	8	1217[1]	1146	8.5	25	415	414	12.0	3.24	86	.256	.326	-44	-63	96	97	.963	214	**112**	-1.0	-7.0	.3		-6.6
PHI	93	6	2	1252	1391	10.0	40	408	397	13.3	4.15	78	.294	.356	-171	-116	111	100	.963	218	**112**	-1.3	-12.8	-4.6		-2.6
TOT	657	101	51	10064[2]		8.6				11.2	2.91		.258	.311					.967	1572	789					

Runs
Burns-NY 86
Groh-Cin 79
Daubert-Cin 79
Rath-Cin 77

Hits
Olson-Bro 164
Hornsby-StL 163
Roush-Cin 162
Burns-NY 162

Doubles
Youngs-NY 31
Luderus-Phi 30
Burns-NY 30
Kauff-NY 27
Meusel-Phi 26

Triples
Southworth-Pit 14
Myers-Bro 14

Home Runs
Cravath-Phi 12
Kauff-NY 10
Williams-Phi 9
Hornsby-StL 8
Doyle-NY 7

Total Bases
Myers-Bro 223
Hornsby-StL 220
Z.Wheat-Bro 219
Roush-Cin 217
Burns-NY 216

Runs Batted In
Myers-Bro 73
Roush-Cin 71
Hornsby-StL 71
Kauff-NY 67
Groh-Cin 63

Runs Produced
Roush-Cin 140
Groh-Cin 137
Hornsby-StL 131

Bases On Balls
Burns-NY 82
Rath-Cin 64
Groh-Cin 56
Luderus-Phi 54
Boeckel-Pit-Bos 53

Batting Average
Roush-Cin .... .321
Hornsby-StL .... .318
Youngs-NY .... .311
Groh-Cin .... .310
Stock-StL .... .307

On-Base Percentage
Burns-NY .... .396
Groh-Cin .... .392
Hornsby-StL .... .384
Youngs-NY .... .384
Roush-Cin .... .380

Slugging Average
Myers-Bro .... .436
Doyle-NY .... .433
Groh-Cin .... .431
Roush-Cin .... .431
Hornsby-StL .... .430

On-Base Plus Slugging
Groh-Cin 823
Hornsby-StL 814
Roush-Cin 811
Burns-NY 801
Youngs-NY 799

Adjusted OPS
Hornsby-StL 154
Groh-Cin 151
Roush-Cin 147
Burns-NY 142
Youngs-NY 142

Batter Runs
Cravath-Phi 32.2
Burns-NY 30.0
Hornsby-StL 28.5
Groh-Cin 27.4
Roush-Cin 26.9

Adjusted Batter Runs
Hornsby-StL 34.1
Burns-NY 31.1
Groh-Cin 29.5
Roush-Cin 29.2
Cravath-Phi 28.4

Clutch Hitting Index
Kopf-Cin 125
Southworth-Pit 123
Zimmerman-NY 121
Roush-Cin 121
Merkle-Chi 120

Runs Created
Burns-NY 96
Roush-Cin 88
Hornsby-StL 87
Youngs-NY 84
Groh-Cin 81

Total Average
Burns-NY .... .909
Groh-Cin .... .887
Youngs-NY .... .846
Hornsby-StL .... .837
Roush-Cin .... .833

Stolen Bases
Burns-NY 40
Cutshaw-Pit 36
Bigbee-Pit 31
Smith-StL 30

Stolen Base Average

Stolen Base Runs

Fielding Runs
Maranville-Bos 28.7
Fletcher-NY 24.0
Bigbee-Pit 17.9
Killefer-Chi 17.4
Stock-StL 16.8

Total Player Rating
Maranville-Bos 4.9
Hornsby-StL 4.4
Stock-StL 4.1
Groh-Cin 3.4
Fletcher-NY 3.3

Wins
J.Barnes-NY 25
Vaughn-Chi 21
Sallee-Cin 21

Win Percentage
Ruether-Cin .... .760
Sallee-Cin .... .750
J.Barnes-NY .... .735
Eller-Cin .... .679
Adams-Pit .... .630

Games
Tuero-StL 45
Meadows-StL-Phi 40
Vaughn-Chi 38
Eller-Cin 38
J.Barnes-NY 38

Complete Games
Cooper-Pit 27
Pfeffer-Bro 26
Vaughn-Chi 25
Rudolph-Bos 24

Shutouts
Alexander-Chi 9
Eller-Cin 7
Adams-Pit 6
Fisher-Cin 5

Saves
Tuero-StL 4

Innings Pitched
Vaughn-Chi 306.2
J.Barnes-NY 295.2
Cooper-Pit 286.2
Rudolph-Bos 273.2
Nehf-Bos-NY 270.2

Fewest Hits/Game
Alexander-Chi 6.89
Cooper-Pit 7.19
Ruether-Cin 7.23
Carlson-Pit 7.28
Fisher-Cin 7.28

Fewest BB/Game
Adams-Pit .... .79
Sallee-Cin .... .79
J.Barnes-NY 1.07
Cadore-Bro 1.40
Alexander-Chi 1.46

Strikeouts
Vaughn-Chi 141
Eller-Cin 137
Alexander-Chi 121
Meadows-StL-Phi 116
Cooper-Pit 106

Strikeouts/Game
Eller-Cin 4.97
Alexander-Chi 4.63
Meadows-StL-Phi 4.17
Vaughn-Chi 4.14
Grimes-Bro 4.07

Ratio
Adams-Pit 8.17
Alexander-Chi 8.35
J.Barnes-NY 9.13
Fisher-Cin 9.29
Miller-Pit 9.33

Earned Run Average
Alexander-Chi 1.72
Vaughn-Chi 1.79
Ruether-Cin 1.82
Toney-NY 1.84
Adams-Pit 1.98

Adjusted ERA
Alexander-Chi 167
Vaughn-Chi 161
Ruether-Cin 152
Toney-NY 152
Adams-Pit 152

Opponents' Batting Avg.
Alexander-Chi .... .211
Adams-Pit .... .220
Ruether-Cin .... .223
Cooper-Pit .... .225
Nehf-Bos-NY .... .225

Opponents' On-Base Pct.
Adams-Pit .... .241
Alexander-Chi .... .245
J.Barnes-NY .... .260
Fisher-Cin .... .271
Miller-Pit .... .272

Starter Runs
Vaughn-Chi 38.1
Alexander-Chi 31.0
Ruether-Cin 29.4
Adams-Pit 27.1
Rudolph-Bos 22.5

Adjusted Starter Runs
Vaughn-Chi 37.5
Alexander-Chi 30.5
Adams-Pit 29.1
Ruether-Cin 27.0
Rudolph-Bos 21.2

Clutch Pitching Index
Rudolph-Bos 141
Smith-Bro 141
Martin-Chi 122
Jacobs-Phi-StL 122
Toney-NY 120

Relief Runs

Adjusted Relief Runs

Relief Ranking

Total Pitcher Index
Alexander-Chi 4.5
Vaughn-Chi 4.3
Ruether-Cin 3.3
Rudolph-Bos 3.0
Adams-Pit 2.6

Total Baseball Ranking
Maranville-Bos 4.9
Alexander-Chi 4.5
Hornsby-StL 4.4
Vaughn-Chi 4.3
Stock-StL 4.1

TEAM	G	W	L	PCT	GB	R	OR	AB	H	2B	3B	HR	BB	SO	AVG	OBP	SLG	OPS	OPS+	BR	BR+	PF	CHI	RC	SB	CS	SBA	SBR
CHI	140	88	52	.629		**667**	534	4675	**1343**	218	70	25	427	**358**	**.287**	.351	.380	731	111	69	66	100	103	**668**	**150**			
CLE	139	84	55	.604	3.5	636	537	4565	1268	**254**	72	24	**498**	367	.278	**.354**	**.381**	**735**	107	**78**	41	106	98	651	113			
NY	141	80	59	.576	7.5	578	**506**	4775	1275	193	49	**45**	386	479	.267	.326	.356	682	96	-20	-24	101	**104**	575	101			
DET	140	80	60	.571	8	618	578	4665	1319	222	**84**	23	429	427	.283	.346	**.381**	727	**113**	60	**75**	98	97	649	121			
STL	140	67	72	.482	20.5	533	567	4672	1234	187	73	31	391	443	.264	.326	.355	681	95	-22	-35	103	97	560	74			
BOS	138	66	71	.482	20.5	564	552	4548	1188	181	49	33	471	411	.261	.336	.344	680	103	-11	23	94	102	559	108			
WAS	142	56	84	.400	32	533	570	4757	1238	177	63	24	416	511	.260	.325	.339	664	93	-47	-42	99	100	558	142			
PHI	140	36	104	.257	52	457	742	4730	1156	175	71	35	349	565	.244	.300	.334	634	82	-108	-113	101	100	487	103			
TOT	560					4586		37387	10021	1607	531	240	3367	3561	.269	.334	.359	692							912			

TEAM	CG	SH	SV	IP	H	H/G	HR	BB	SO	RAT	ERA	ERA+	OAV	OOB	PR	PR+	PF	CPI	FA	E	DP	FW	PW	BW	SBW	DIF
CHI	88	14	3	1265^{2}	1245	8.9	24	**342**	468	11.6	3.04	105	.262	.315	26	19	99	92	.969	176	116	1.7	2.0	7.0		7.5
CLE	79	10	**10**	1245	1242	9.0	19	362	432	11.9	2.95	**114**	.264	.321	39	51	104	98	.965	201	102	.0	5.4	4.3		5.0
NY	85	14	7	1287	**1143**	**8.0**	47	433	500	**11.3**	**2.82**	113	**.240**	**.309**	**58**	**54**	99	92	.968	193	108	.7	**5.7**	-2.5		6.8
DET	85	10	4	1256	1254	9.0	35	436	428	12.4	3.31	97	.266	.333	-11	-14	99	98	.964	205	81	-.2	-1.4	**7.9**		3.9
STL	78	14	4	1256	1255	9.0	35	421	415	12.4	3.14	106	.263	.328	13	23	103	99	.963	215	98	-.8	2.5	-3.6		-.3
BOS	**89**	**15**	8	1224^{1}	1251	9.2	**16**	421	381	12.5	3.31	91	.275	.341	-12	-44	94	**101**	**.975**	**140**	**118**	**3.8**	-4.6	2.5		-4.0
WAS	68	13	**10**	1274^{1}	1237	8.8	20	451	**536**	12.2	3.01	106	.259	.328	30	28	99	99	.960	227	86	-1.4	3.0	-4.3		-11.1
PHI	72	1	3	1239^{1}	1371	10.0	44	503	417	13.9	4.27	80	.292	.364	-143	-111	106	96	.956	257	96	-3.5	-11.6	-11.8		-7.0
TOT	644	91	49	10047^{2}		9.0				12.3	3.23		.269	.334					.966	1614	805					

Runs
Ruth-Bos 103
Sisler-StL 96
Cobb-Det 92
Weaver-Chi 89
Peckinpaugh-NY 89

Hits
Veach-Det 191
Cobb-Det 191
Jackson-Chi 181
Sisler-StL 180
Rice-Was 179

Doubles
Veach-Det 45
Speaker-Cle 38
Cobb-Det 36
O'Neill-Cle 35

Triples
Veach-Det 17
Sisler-StL 15
Heilmann-Det 15
Jackson-Chi 14
Cobb-Det 13

Home Runs
Ruth-Bos 29
T.Walker-Phi 10
Sisler-StL 10
Baker-NY 10
Smith-Cle 9

Total Bases
Ruth-Bos 284
Veach-Det 279
Sisler-StL 271
Jackson-Chi 261

Runs Batted In
Ruth-Bos 114
Veach-Det 101
Jackson-Chi 96
Heilmann-Det 93
Lewis-NY 89

Runs Produced
Ruth-Bos 188
Veach-Det 185
Sisler-StL 169
Jackson-Chi 168
E.Collins-Chi 163

Bases On Balls
Graney-Cle 105
Ruth-Bos 101
Judge-Was 81
Hooper-Bos 79
Bush-Det 75

Batting Average
Cobb-Det .384
Veach-Det .355
Sisler-StL .352
Jackson-Chi .351
Flagstead-Det .331

On-Base Percentage
Ruth-Bos .456
Cobb-Det .429
Jackson-Chi .422
Leibold-Chi .404
E.Collins-Chi .400

Slugging Average
Ruth-Bos .657
Sisler-StL .530
Veach-Det .519
Cobb-Det .515
Jackson-Chi .506

On-Base Plus Slugging
Ruth-Bos 1114
Cobb-Det 944
Jackson-Chi 928
Sisler-StL 921
Veach-Det 916

Adjusted OPS
Ruth-Bos 224
Cobb-Det 168
Veach-Det 160
Jackson-Chi 159
Sisler-StL 153

Batter Runs
Ruth-Bos 66.5
Jackson-Chi 41.7
Cobb-Det 41.6
Veach-Det 37.7
Sisler-StL 35.8

Adjusted Batter Runs
Ruth-Bos 74.2
Cobb-Det 44.0
Jackson-Chi 41.3
Veach-Det 40.1
Sisler-StL 33.4

Clutch Hitting Index
E.Collins-Chi 143
Lewis-NY 131
Jones-Det 130
Shanks-Was 123
Gardner-Cle 123

Runs Created
Ruth-Bos 128
Cobb-Det 116
Veach-Det 115
Sisler-StL 112
Jackson-Chi 111

Total Average
Ruth-Bos 1.358
Cobb-Det 1.056
Sisler-StL 1.000
Jackson-Chi .997
Veach-Det .968

Stolen Bases
E.Collins-Chi 33
Sisler-StL 28
Cobb-Det 28
Rice-Was 26

Stolen Base Average

Stolen Base Runs

Fielding Runs
Pratt-NY 28.0
Peckinpaugh-NY 27.7
Felsch-Chi 21.4
Speaker-Cle 19.1
Young-Det 17.3

Total Player Rating
Ruth-Bos 6.6
Peckinpaugh-NY 5.2
Veach-Det 4.6
Sisler-StL 4.4
Cobb-Det 3.4

Wins
Cicotte-Chi 29
Coveleski-Cle 24
Williams-Chi 23
Dauss-Det 21

Win Percentage
Cicotte-Chi .806
Dauss-Det .700
Williams-Chi .676
Pennock-Bos .667
Coveleski-Cle .667

Games
Shaw-Was 45
Russell-NY-Bos 44
Kinney-Phi 43
Coveleski-Cle 43

Complete Games
Cicotte-Chi 30
Williams-Chi 27
Johnson-Was 27
Mays-Bos-NY 26
Coveleski-Cle 24

Shutouts
Johnson-Was 7

Saves
Russell-NY-Bos 5
Shawkey-NY 5
Shaw-Was 5
Coveleski-Cle 4

Innings Pitched
Shaw-Was 306.2
Cicotte-Chi 306.2
Williams-Chi 297.0
Johnson-Was 290.1
Coveleski-Cle 286.0

Fewest Hits/Game
Johnson-Was 7.28
Thormahlen-NY 7.39
Shawkey-NY 7.51
Cicotte-Chi 7.51
Mays-Bos-NY 7.68

Fewest BB/Game
Cicotte-Chi 1.44
Johnson-Was 1.58
Bagby-Cle 1.64
Williams-Chi 1.76
Coveleski-Cle 1.89

Strikeouts
Johnson-Was 147
Shaw-Was 128
Williams-Chi 125
Shawkey-NY 122
Coveleski-Cle 118

Strikeouts/Game
Erickson-Det-Was 5.52
Russell-NY-Bos 4.80
Johnson-Was 4.56
Kinney-Phi 4.31
Leonard-Det 4.22

Ratio
Cicotte-Chi 9.01
Johnson-Was 9.08
Williams-Chi 10.12
Thormahlen-NY 10.49
Quinn-NY 10.59

Earned Run Average
Johnson-Was 1.49
Cicotte-Chi 1.82
Weilman-StL 2.07
Mays-Bos-NY 2.10
Sothoron-StL 2.20

Adjusted ERA
Johnson-Was 215
Cicotte-Chi 175
Weilman-StL 160
Sothoron-StL 151
Mays-Bos-NY 147

Opponents' Batting Avg.
Johnson-Was .219
Cicotte-Chi .228
Thormahlen-NY .228
Shawkey-NY .231
Mays-Bos-NY .233

Opponents' On-Base Pct.
Johnson-Was .259
Cicotte-Chi .261
Williams-Chi .289
Morton-Cle .293
Quinn-NY .295

Starter Runs
Johnson-Was 56.0
Cicotte-Chi 47.8
Mays-Bos-NY 33.3
Sothoron-StL 30.7
Coveleski-Cle 19.4

Adjusted Starter Runs
Johnson-Was 55.7
Cicotte-Chi 46.9
Sothoron-StL 32.5
Mays-Bos-NY 30.7
Coveleski-Cle 22.4

Clutch Pitching Index
Weilman-StL 119
Sothoron-StL 114
Ehmke-Det 113
Harper-Was 107
Pennock-Bos 107

Relief Runs
Phillips-Cle 1.7

Adjusted Relief Runs
Phillips-Cle 2.3

Relief Ranking
Phillips-Cle 1.9

Total Pitcher Index
Johnson-Was 7.2
Cicotte-Chi 5.3
Mays-Bos-NY 3.9
Coveleski-Cle 3.5
Sothoron-StL 2.8

Total Baseball Ranking
Ruth-Bos 8.1
Johnson-Was 7.1
Cicotte-Chi 5.3
Peckinpaugh-NY 5.2
Veach-Det 4.6

TEAM	G	W	L	PCT	GB	R	OR	AB	H	2B	3B	HR	BB	SO	AVG	OBP	SLG	OPS	OPS+	BR	BR+	PF	CHI	RC	SB	CS	SBA	SBR
BRO	155	93	61	.604		660	**528**	5399	1493	205	**99**	28	359	391	.277	.324	.367	691	100	19	-1	103	103	637	70	80	47	-13
NY	155	86	68	.558	7	**682**	543	5309	1427	210	76	46	**432**	545	.269	.327	.363	690	104	23	30	99	**107**	628	131	113	54	-11
CIN	154	82	71	.536	10.5	639	569	5176	1432	169	76	18	382	**367**	.277	.332	.349	681	102	11	20	99	104	602	158	128	55	-10
PIT	155	79	75	.513	14	530	552	5219	1342	162	90	16	374	405	.257	.310	.332	642	86	-67	-83	103	99	544	**181**	117	**61**	**-1**
STL	155	75	79	.487	18	675	682	5495	**1589**	**238**	96	32	373	484	**.289**	**.337**	**.385**	**722**	**117**	**83**	**111**	96	94	**704**	126	114	53	-12
CHI	154	75	79	.487	18	619	635	5117	1350	223	67	34	428	421	.264	.326	.354	680	98	7	-5	102	101	589	115	129	47	-20
BOS	153	62	90	.408	30	523	670	5218	1358	168	86	23	385	488	.260	.315	.339	654	97	-45	-20	96	93	557	88	98	47	-15
PHI	153	62	91	.405	30.5	565	714	5264	1385	229	54	**64**	283	531	.263	.305	.364	669	93	-30	-56	105	99	577	100	83	55	-7
TOT	617					4893		42197	11376	1604	644	261	3016	3632	.270	.323	.357	679							969	862	53	-89

TEAM	CG	SH	SV	IP	H	H/G	HR	BB	SO	RAT	ERA	ERA+	OAV	OOB	PR	PR+	PF	CPI	FA	E	DP	FW	PW	BW	SBW	DIF
BRO	89	17	10	1427^1	1381	8.8	**25**	327	**553**	11.0	**2.63**	**122**	.259	.304	**81**	**89**	102	102	.966	226	118	-.1	**9.6**	-.0	-.2	7.0
NY	86	**18**	9	1408^2	1379	8.9	44	297	380	10.9	2.81	107	.261	.303	51	32	96	99	.969	210	**137**	.8	3.5	3.3	.0	1.6
CIN	90	12	9	1391^2	**1327**	**8.6**	26	393	435	11.4	2.90	105	**.256**	.313	36	23	97	97	.968	200	125	1.3	2.5	2.2	.1	-.5
PIT	92	17	10	1415^1	1389	8.9	**25**	**280**	444	**10.8**	2.89	111	.261	**.301**	39	49	103	91	**.971**	**186**	119	**2.3**	5.3	-8.8	**1.1**	2.4
STL	72	9	**12**	1426^2	1488	9.4	30	479	529	12.8	3.44	87	.277	.343	-47	-75	95	**103**	.961	256	136	-1.9	-8.0	**11.9**	-.1	-3.8
CHI	**95**	13	9	1388^2	1459	9.5	37	382	508	12.1	3.27	98	.276	.328	-21	-10	102	102	.965	225	112	-.1	-1.0	-.5	-1.0	.8
BOS	93	14	6	1386^1	1464	9.6	39	415	368	12.5	3.54	86	.280	.337	-62	-77	97	100	.964	239	125	-1.1	-8.2	-2.1	-.4	-2.0
PHI	77	8	11	1380^2	1480	9.7	35	444	419	12.9	3.64	94	.284	.345	-76	-32	109	102	.964	232	135	-.6	-3.4	-5.9	.4	-4.8
TOT	694	108	76	11225^1		9.2				11.8	3.14		.270	.323					.967	1774	1007					

Runs
Burns-NY 115
Bancroft-Phi-NY 102
Daubert-Cin 97
Hornsby-StL 96
Youngs-NY 92

Hits
Hornsby-StL 218
Youngs-NY 204
Stock-StL 204
Roush-Cin 196
Williams-Phi 192

Doubles
Hornsby-StL 44
Bancroft-Phi-NY 36
Williams-Phi 36
Myers-Bro 36
Burns-NY 35

Triples
Myers-Bro 22
Hornsby-StL 20
Roush-Cin 16
Maranville-Bos 15
Bigbee-Pit 15

Home Runs
Williams-Phi 15
Meusel-Phi 14
Kelly-NY 11
Robertson-Chi 10
McHenry-StL 10

Total Bases
Hornsby-StL 329
Williams-Phi 293
Youngs-NY 277
Wheat-Bro 270
Myers-Bro 269

Runs Batted In
Kelly-NY 94
Hornsby-StL 94
Roush-Cin 90
Duncan-Cin 83
Myers-Bro 80

Runs Produced
Hornsby-StL 181
Roush-Cin 167
Youngs-NY 164
Stock-StL 161
Myers-Bro 159

Bases On Balls
Burns-NY 76
Youngs-NY 75
Paskert-Chi 64
Hornsby-StL 60
Groh-Cin 60

Batting Average
Hornsby-StL .370
Nicholson-Pit .360
Youngs-NY .351
Roush-Cin .339
Wheat-Bro .328

On-Base Percentage
Hornsby-StL .431
Youngs-NY .427
Roush-Cin .386
Wheat-Bro .385
Groh-Cin .375

Slugging Average
Hornsby-StL .559
Nicholson-Pit .530
Williams-Phi .497
Youngs-NY .477
Meusel-Phi .473

On-Base Plus Slugging
Hornsby-StL 990
Youngs-NY 904
Williams-Phi 861
Wheat-Bro 848
Roush-Cin 839

Adjusted OPS
Hornsby-StL 190
Youngs-NY 161
Roush-Cin 142
Williams-Phi 139
Wheat-Bro 138

Batter Runs
Hornsby-StL 62.6
Youngs-NY 47.1
Williams-Phi 32.1
Wheat-Bro 31.9
Roush-Cin 29.7

Adjusted Batter Runs
Hornsby-StL 67.7
Youngs-NY 48.4
Roush-Cin 31.1
Wheat-Bro 28.9
Williams-Phi 27.7

Clutch Hitting Index
Whitted-Pit 151
Kopf-Cin 147
Duncan-Cin 131
Roush-Cin 126
Kelly-NY 122

Runs Created
Hornsby-StL 138
Youngs-NY 118
Williams-Phi 103
Wheat-Bro 102
Roush-Cin 98

Total Average
Hornsby-StL 1.008
Youngs-NY .896
Williams-Phi .817
Wheat-Bro .801
Roush-Cin .784

Stolen Bases
Carey-Pit 52
Roush-Cin 36
Frisch-NY 34
Bigbee-Pit 31
Neale-Cin 29

Stolen Base Average
Carey-Pit 83.9
Frisch-NY 75.6
Neale-Cin 70.7
Bigbee-Pit 67.4
Meusel-Phi 60.7

Stolen Base Runs
Carey-Pit 7.9
Frisch-NY 3.6
Neale-Cin 2.2
Bigbee-Pit 1.6
Gowdy-Bos 1.0

Fielding Runs
Bancroft-Phi-NY 39.0
Lavan-StL 16.2
Roush-Cin 15.7
Maranville-Bos 14.3
Neale-Cin 14.3

Total Player Rating
Hornsby-StL 8.1
Bancroft-Phi-NY 5.7
Youngs-NY 4.2
Roush-Cin 3.8
Williams-Phi 2.9

Wins
Alexander-Chi 27
Cooper-Pit 24
Grimes-Bro 23
Toney-NY 21
Nehf-NY 21

Win Percentage
Grimes-Bro .676
Alexander-Chi .659
Toney-NY .656
Pfeffer-Bro .640
Nehf-NY .636

Games
Haines-StL 47
Douglas-NY 46
Alexander-Chi 46
Scott-Bos 44
Cooper-Pit 44

Complete Games
Alexander-Chi 33
Cooper-Pit 28
Rixey-Phi 25
Grimes-Bro 25
Vaughn-Chi 24

Shutouts
Adams-Pit 8
Alexander-Chi 7

Saves
Sherdel-StL 6
McQuillan-Bos 5
Alexander-Chi 5
Hubbell-NY-Phi 4
Mamaux-Bro 4

Innings Pitched
Alexander-Chi 363.1
Cooper-Pit 327.0
Grimes-Bro 303.2
Haines-StL 301.2
Vaughn-Chi 301.0

Fewest Hits/Game
Luque-Cin 7.28
Ruether-Cin 7.96
Grimes-Bro 8.03
Mamaux-Bro 8.12
Adams-Pit 8.21

Fewest BB/Game
Adams-Pit .62
Cooper-Pit 1.43
Nehf-NY 1.44
Benton-NY 1.44
Marquard-Bro 1.66

Strikeouts
Alexander-Chi 173
Vaughn-Chi 131
Grimes-Bro 131
Haines-StL 120
Schupp-StL 119

Strikeouts/Game
Mamaux-Bro 4.77
Alexander-Chi 4.29
Schupp-StL 4.27
Marquard-Bro 4.22
Sherdel-StL 3.92

Ratio
Adams-Pit 8.86
Alexander-Chi 10.03
Luque-Cin 10.05
J.Barnes-NY 10.12
Grimes-Bro 10.14

Earned Run Average
Alexander-Chi 1.91
Adams-Pit 2.16
Grimes-Bro 2.22
Cooper-Pit 2.39
Ruether-Cin 2.47

Adjusted ERA
Alexander-Chi 168
Adams-Pit 149
Grimes-Bro 144
Cooper-Pit 134
Vaughn-Chi 126

Opponents' Batting Avg.
Luque-Cin .225
Grimes-Bro .238
Adams-Pit .244
Ponder-Pit .246
Ruether-Cin .247

Opponents' On-Base Pct.
Adams-Pit .259
Grimes-Bro .282
Alexander-Chi .285
Luque-Cin .286
Ponder-Pit .286

Starter Runs
Alexander-Chi 49.5
Grimes-Bro 30.7
Adams-Pit 28.5
Cooper-Pit 26.8
Vaughn-Chi 19.8

Adjusted Starter Runs
Alexander-Chi 51.2
Grimes-Bro 32.3
Adams-Pit 30.1
Cooper-Pit 29.0
Vaughn-Chi 21.7

Clutch Pitching Index
Meadows-Phi 121
Alexander-Chi 120
Vaughn-Chi 119
Fillingim-Bos 118
Benton-NY 115

Relief Runs

Adjusted Relief Runs

Relief Ranking

Total Pitcher Index
Alexander-Chi 7.0
Grimes-Bro 5.3
Smith-Bro 4.0
Cooper-Pit 3.2
Adams-Pit 2.7

Total Baseball Ranking
Hornsby-StL 8.1
Alexander-Chi 7.0
Bancroft-Phi-NY 5.7
Grimes-Bro 5.3
Youngs-NY 4.2

TEAM	G	W	L	PCT	GB	R	OR	AB	H	2B	3B	HR	BB	SO	AVG	OBP	SLG	OPS	OPS+	BR	BR+	PF	CHI	RC	SB	CS	SBA	SBR
CLE	154	98	56	.636		**857**	642	5196	1574	**300**	95	35	**576**	379	.303	**.376**	.417	**793**	**113**	**125**	**99**	103	98	**827**	73	93	44	-16
CHI	154	96	58	.623	2	794	665	5328	1574	263	**98**	37	471	355	.295	.357	.402	759	107	49	49	100	100	769	109	96	53	-10
NY	154	95	59	.617	3	838	**629**	5176	1448	268	71	**115**	539	626	.280	.350	**.426**	776	107	71	44	104	105	773	64	82	44	-15
STL	154	76	77	.497	21.5	797	766	5358	**1651**	279	83	50	427	**339**	**.308**	.363	.419	782	110	93	69	103	95	822	121	79	**61**	**-1**
BOS	154	72	81	.471	25.5	650	698	5199	1397	216	71	22	533	429	.269	.342	.350	692	93	-70	-40	96	97	637	98	111	47	-17
WAS	153	68	84	.447	29	723	802	5251	1526	233	81	36	433	543	.291	.351	.386	737	104	7	27	97	98	718	**160**	114	58	-5
DET	155	61	93	.396	37	652	833	5215	1408	228	72	30	479	391	.270	.334	.359	693	91	-80	-63	98	100	639	76	68	53	-7
PHI	156	48	106	.312	50	558	834	5256	1324	220	49	44	353	593	.252	.305	.338	643	74	-188	-193	101	**106**	543	50	67	43	-12
TOT	617					5869		41979	11902	2007	620	369	3811	3655	.284	.348	.388	734							751	710	51	-83

TEAM	CG	SH	SV	IP	H	H/G	HR	BB	SO	RAT	ERA	ERA+	OAV	OOB	PR	PR+	PF	CPI	FA	E	DP	FW	PW	BW	SBW	DIF
CLE	94	11	7	1377	1448	9.5	**31**	**401**	466	**12.3**	3.42	111	.276	.331	57	58	100	98	.971	184	124	2.2	5.7	**9.7**	-.5	4.2
CHI	**109**	9	10	1386[2]	1467	9.6	45	405	438	12.4	3.59	105	.280	.335	31	24	99	98	.968	198	**142**	1.2	2.4	4.8	.0	10.8
NY	88	**15**	11	1368	**1414**	**9.4**	48	420	480	**12.3**	**3.32**	**115**	**.270**	**.328**	**72**	**75**	101	99	.969	194	129	1.5	**7.3**	4.3	-.4	5.5
STL	84	9	**14**	1378[2]	1481	9.7	53	578	444	13.7	4.04	97	.283	.359	-38	-22	103	99	.963	233	119	-1.2	-2.1	6.7	**.9**	-4.7
BOS	92	11	6	1395[1]	1481	9.6	39	461	481	12.8	3.82	95	.279	.339	-5	-31	96	93	**.972**	**183**	131	**2.3**	-3.0	-3.8	-.6	.9
WAS	81	10	10	1367	1521	10.1	51	520	418	13.8	4.17	89	.288	.357	-58	-71	98	97	.963	232	95	-1.2	-6.8	2.7	.5	-2.9
DET	74	9	7	1385	1487	9.7	46	561	**483**	13.7	4.04	92	.284	.359	-38	-52	98	99	.964	230	95	-.9	-5.0	-6.1	.3	-4.2
PHI	79	6	2	1380[1]	1612	10.6	56	461	423	13.8	3.93	102	.302	.362	-21	11	106	**110**	.959	266	125	-3.3	1.1	-18.7	-.2	-7.8
TOT	701	80	67	11038		9.8				13.1	3.79		.284	.348					.967	1720	960					

Runs
Ruth-NY 158
Speaker-Cle 137
Sisler-StL 137
E.Collins-Chi 117

Hits
Sisler-StL 257
E.Collins-Chi 224
Jackson-Chi 218
Jacobson-StL 216
Speaker-Cle 214

Doubles
Speaker-Cle 50
Sisler-StL 49
Jackson-Chi 42

Triples
Jackson-Chi 20
Sisler-StL 18
Hooper-Bos 17

Home Runs
Ruth-NY 54
Sisler-StL 19
T.Walker-Phi 17
Felsch-Chi 14

Total Bases
Sisler-StL 399
Ruth-NY 388
Jackson-Chi 336
Speaker-Cle 310
Jacobson-StL 305

Runs Batted In
Ruth-NY 137
Sisler-StL 122
Jacobson-StL 122
Jackson-Chi 121
Gardner-Cle 118

Runs Produced
Ruth-NY 241
Sisler-StL 240
Speaker-Cle 236
Jackson-Chi 214
Jacobson-StL 210

Bases On Balls
Ruth-NY 150
Speaker-Cle 97
Hooper-Bos 88
Young-Det 85
Roth-Was 75

Batting Average
Sisler-StL .407
Speaker-Cle .388
Jackson-Chi .382
Ruth-NY .376
E.Collins-Chi .372

On-Base Percentage
Ruth-NY .532
Speaker-Cle .483
Sisler-StL .449
Jackson-Chi .444
E.Collins-Chi .438

Slugging Average
Ruth-NY .847
Sisler-StL .632
Jackson-Chi .589
Speaker-Cle .562
Felsch-Chi .540

On-Base Plus Slugging
Ruth-NY 1379
Sisler-StL 1082
Speaker-Cle 1045
Jackson-Chi 1033
E.Collins-Chi 932

Adjusted OPS
Ruth-NY 252
Sisler-StL 179
Jackson-Chi 172
Speaker-Cle 171
E.Collins-Chi 146

Batter Runs
Ruth-NY 113.8
Sisler-StL 73.2
Speaker-Cle 65.7
Jackson-Chi 58.4
E.Collins-Chi 42.3

Adjusted Batter Runs
Ruth-NY 107.4
Sisler-StL 68.6
Speaker-Cle 61.3
Jackson-Chi 58.4
E.Collins-Chi 42.3

Clutch Hitting Index
Gardner-Cle 144
Roth-Was 131
Smith-Cle 123
Risberg-Chi 121
Pratt-NY 118

Runs Created
Ruth-NY 212
Sisler-StL 176
Speaker-Cle 152
Jackson-Chi 145
E.Collins-Chi 134

Total Average
Ruth-NY 1.803
Sisler-StL 1.207
Speaker-Cle 1.165
Jackson-Chi 1.088
E.Collins-Chi .984

Stolen Bases
Rice-Was 63
Sisler-StL 42
Roth-Was 24
Menosky-Bos 23
Tobin-StL 21

Stolen Base Average
E.Collins-Chi 71.4
Sisler-StL 71.2
Williams-StL 69.2
Rice-Was 67.7
Roth-Was 66.7

Stolen Base Runs
Rice-Was 3.4
Sisler-StL 3.3
E.Collins-Chi 1.6
Williams-StL 1.2
Burns-Phi-Cle 1.1

Fielding Runs
Perkins-Phi 22.8
Ward-NY 21.8
Rice-Was 21.4
Pinelli-Det 19.9
Felsch-Chi 17.7

Total Player Rating
Ruth-NY 9.1
Sisler-StL 7.8
Speaker-Cle 5.5
E.Collins-Chi 5.4
Jackson-Chi 4.7

Wins
Bagby-Cle 31
Mays-NY 26
Coveleski-Cle 24
Faber-Chi 23
Williams-Chi 22

Win Percentage
Bagby-Cle .721
Mays-NY .703
Kerr-Chi .700
Cicotte-Chi .677

Games
Bagby-Cle 48
Ayers-Det 46
Mays-NY 45
Kerr-Chi 45
Zachary-Was 44

Complete Games
Bagby-Cle 30
Faber-Chi 28
Cicotte-Chi 28
Mays-NY 26
Coveleski-Cle 26

Shutouts
Mays-NY 6
Shocker-StL 5
Shawkey-NY 5

Saves
Shocker-StL 5
Kerr-Chi 5
Burwell-StL 4

Innings Pitched
Bagby-Cle 339.2
Faber-Chi 319.0
Coveleski-Cle 315.0
Mays-NY 312.0
Cicotte-Chi 303.1

Fewest Hits/Game
Coveleski-Cle 8.11
Shocker-StL 8.21
Collins-NY 8.22
Shawkey-NY 8.27
Davis-StL 8.35

Fewest BB/Game
Quinn-NY 1.71
Coveleski-Cle 1.86
Bagby-Cle 2.09
Cicotte-Chi 2.20
Perry-Phi 2.22

Strikeouts
Coveleski-Cle 133
Williams-Chi 128
Shawkey-NY 126
Faber-Chi 108
Shocker-StL 107

Strikeouts/Game
Ayers-Det 4.44
Shawkey-NY 4.24
Harper-Bos 3.93
Shocker-StL 3.92
Williams-Chi 3.85

Ratio
Coveleski-Cle 10.09
Shocker-StL 10.92
Rommel-Phi 10.99
Shawkey-NY 11.16
Bagby-Cle 11.18

Earned Run Average
Shawkey-NY 2.45
Coveleski-Cle 2.49
Shocker-StL 2.71
Rommel-Phi 2.85
Bagby-Cle 2.89

Adjusted ERA
Shawkey-NY 155
Coveleski-Cle 153
Shocker-StL 144
Rommel-Phi 141
Bagby-Cle 131

Opponents' Batting Avg.
Coveleski-Cle .243
Collins-NY .247
Shawkey-NY .248
Shocker-StL .248
Ehmke-Det .253

Opponents' On-Base Pct.
Coveleski-Cle .285
Shocker-StL .305
Shawkey-NY .308
Quinn-NY .308
Rommel-Phi .309

Starter Runs
Coveleski-Cle 45.6
Shawkey-NY 39.6
Bagby-Cle 33.9
Shocker-StL 29.4
Faber-Chi 28.2

Adjusted Starter Runs
Coveleski-Cle 45.6
Shawkey-NY 40.1
Bagby-Cle 34.0
Shocker-StL 31.7
Faber-Chi 27.4

Clutch Pitching Index
Naylor-Phi 130
Harper-Bos 128
Davis-StL 117
Oldham-Det 116
Perry-Phi 113

Relief Runs

Adjusted Relief Runs

Relief Ranking

Total Pitcher Index
Coveleski-Cle 5.9
Shawkey-NY 4.3
Shocker-StL 3.9
Bagby-Cle 3.8
Mays-NY 3.6

Total Baseball Ranking
Ruth-NY 9.1
Sisler-StL 7.9
Coveleski-Cle 5.9
Speaker-Cle 5.5
E.Collins-Chi 5.4

TEAM	G	W	L	PCT	GB	R	OR	AB	H	2B	3B	HR	BB	SO	AVG	OBP	SLG	OPS	OPS+	BR	BR+	PF	CHI	RC	SB	CS	SBA	SBR
NY	153	94	59	.614		**840**	637	5278	1575	237	93	75	**469**	390	.298	**.359**	.421	780	112	94	92	100	**104**	795	**137**	114	55	-10
PIT	154	90	63	.588	4	692	**595**	5379	1533	231	**104**	37	341	371	.285	.330	.387	717	93	-37	-54	103	102	684	134	93	**59**	**-3**
STL	154	87	66	.569	7	809	681	5309	**1635**	**260**	88	83	382	452	**.308**	.358	**.437**	**795**	**118**	**114**	**132**	98	98	**816**	94	94	50	-12
BOS	153	79	74	.516	15	721	697	5385	1561	209	100	61	377	470	.290	.339	.400	739	107	6	48	95	100	718	94	100	48	-14
BRO	152	77	75	.507	16.5	667	681	5263	1476	209	85	59	325	400	.280	.325	.386	711	90	-52	-74	104	**104**	655	91	73	55	-6
CIN	153	70	83	.458	24	618	649	5112	1421	221	94	20	375	**308**	.278	.333	.370	703	96	-56	-26	95	98	623	117	120	49	-16
CHI	153	64	89	.418	30	668	773	5321	1553	234	56	37	343	374	.292	.339	.378	717	95	-31	-32	100	99	671	70	97	42	-19
PHI	154	51	103	.331	43.5	617	919	5329	1512	238	50	**88**	294	615	.284	.324	.397	721	89	-37	-85	108	94	668	66	80	45	-13
TOT	613					5632		42376	12266	1839	670	460	2906	3380	.290	.339	.398	736							803	771	51	-93

TEAM	CG	SH	SV	IP	H	H/G	HR	BB	SO	RAT	ERA	ERA+	OAV	OOB	PR	PR+	PF	CPI	FA	E	DP	FW	PW	BW	SBW	DIF
NY	71	9	**18**	1372^{1}	1497	9.9	79	**295**	357	11.9	3.56	103	.286	.326	34	17	97	102	.971	187	**155**	1.3	1.7	9.1	.2	5.4
PIT	**88**	10	10	1415^{2}	**1448**	**9.3**	**37**	322	**500**	**11.5**	**3.17**	**121**	**.271**	**.316**	**96**	**103**	101	96	.973	172	129	2.3	**10.2**	-5.3	**.9**	5.6
STL	70	10	16	1371^{2}	1486	9.8	61	399	464	12.7	3.63	101	.282	.337	24	5	97	102	.965	219	130	-.5	.5	**13.1**	-.0	-2.4
BOS	74	**11**	12	1385	1488	9.7	54	420	382	12.7	3.90	94	.280	.337	-18	-40	97	93	.969	199	122	.6	-3.9	4.8	-.2	1.5
BRO	82	8	12	1363^{1}	1556	10.3	46	361	471	12.9	3.70	105	.293	.342	13	27	103	**103**	.964	232	142	-1.5	2.7	-7.3	.6	6.7
CIN	83	7	9	1363	1500	10.0	**37**	305	408	12.1	3.47	103	.287	.328	48	17	95	100	.969	193	139	1.0	1.7	-2.5	-.4	-6.0
CHI	73	7	7	1363	1605	10.6	67	409	441	13.6	4.40	87	.303	.357	-93	-87	101	99	**.974**	**166**	129	**2.6**	-8.5	-3.1	-.7	-2.5
PHI	82	5	8	1348^{2}	1665	11.2	79	371	333	13.9	4.48	94	.308	.356	-105	-35	112	99	.955	295	127	-5.1	-3.4	-8.3	-.1	-8.8
TOT	623	67	92	10982^{2}		10.1				12.7	3.78		.290	.339					.968	1663	1073					

Runs
Hornsby-StL 131
Frisch-NY 121
Bancroft-NY 121
Powell-Bos 114
Burns-NY 111

Hits
Hornsby-StL 235
Frisch-NY 211
C.Bigbee-Pit 204
Johnston-Bro 203

Doubles
Hornsby-StL 44
Kelly-NY 42
Johnston-Bro 41
Grimes-Chi 38
McHenry-StL 37

Triples
Powell-Bos 18
Hornsby-StL 18
Grimm-Pit 17
Frisch-NY 17
C.Bigbee-Pit 17

Home Runs
Kelly-NY 23
Hornsby-StL 21
Williams-Phi 18
McHenry-StL 17
Fournier-StL 16

Total Bases
Hornsby-StL 378
Kelly-NY 310
McHenry-StL 305
Meusel-Phi-NY 302
Frisch-NY 300

Runs Batted In
Hornsby-StL 126
Kelly-NY 122
Youngs-NY 102
McHenry-StL 102
Frisch-NY 100

Runs Produced
Hornsby-StL 236
Frisch-NY 213
Kelly-NY 194
Youngs-NY 189
Bancroft-NY 182

Bases On Balls
Burns-NY 80
Youngs-NY 71
Grimes-Chi 70
Carey-Pit 70
Bancroft-NY 66

Batting Average
Hornsby-StL .... .397
Roush-Cin .... .352
McHenry-StL ...... .350
Cruise-Bos .... .346
Fournier-StL ...... .343

On-Base Percentage
Hornsby-StL .... .458
Youngs-NY .... .411
Fournier-StL ...... .409
Grimes-Chi .... .406
Carey-Pit .... .395

Slugging Average
Hornsby-StL .... .639
McHenry-StL ...... .531
Kelly-NY .... .528
Meusel-Phi-NY ..... .515
Mann-StL .... .512

On-Base Plus Slugging
Hornsby-StL 1097
McHenry-StL 924
Fournier-StL 914
Meusel-Phi-NY 895
Kelly-NY 884

Adjusted OPS
Hornsby-StL 191
McHenry-StL 145
Fournier-StL 144
Kelly-NY 131
Youngs-NY 129

Batter Runs
Hornsby-StL 74.4
Fournier-StL 34.5
McHenry-StL 33.5
Meusel-Phi-NY 27.6
Frisch-NY 24.8

Adjusted Batter Runs
Hornsby-StL 77.8
Fournier-StL 36.9
McHenry-StL 35.8
Cruise-Bos 28.7
Roush-Cin 26.8

Clutch Hitting Index
Youngs-NY 142
Stock-StL 142
Lavan-StL 140
Barnhart-Pit 123
Konetchy-Bro-Phi ... 115

Runs Created
Hornsby-StL 169
Frisch-NY 118
Fournier-StL 114
McHenry-StL 111
Meusel-Phi-NY 110

Total Average
Hornsby-StL 1.203
Frisch-NY .... .902
Fournier-StL ...... .888
Carey-Pit .... .868
Youngs-NY .... .860

Stolen Bases
Frisch-NY 49
Carey-Pit 37
Johnston-Bro 28
Bohne-Cin 26
Maranville-Pit 25

Stolen Base Average
Frisch-NY 79.0
Carey-Pit 75.5
Maisel-Chi 70.8
Maranville-Pit 67.6
Johnston-Bro 63.6

Stolen Base Runs
Frisch-NY 6.2
Carey-Pit 3.9
Stock-StL 1.4
Cutshaw-Pit 1.3
Maranville-Pit 1.3

Fielding Runs
Lavan-StL 18.5
Bancroft-NY 17.4
Williams-Phi 16.3
C.Bigbee-Pit 16.2
Carey-Pit 16.1

Total Player Rating
Hornsby-StL 7.4
Bancroft-NY 5.1
Frisch-NY 4.2
Johnston-Bro 3.1
Carey-Pit 2.7

Wins
Grimes-Bro 22
Cooper-Pit 22
Oeschger-Bos 20
Nehf-NY 20
Rixey-Cin 19

Win Percentage
Doak-StL .... .714
Nehf-NY .... .667
Grimes-Bro .... .629
Barnes-NY .... .625
Toney-NY .... .621

Games
Scott-Bos 47
Oeschger-Bos 46
McQuillan-Bos 45
Watson-Bos 44
Fillingim-Bos 44

Complete Games
Grimes-Bro 30
Cooper-Pit 29
Luque-Cin 25

Shutouts
Oeschger-Bos 3
J.Morrison-Pit 3
Mitchell-Bro 3
Luque-Cin 3
Haines-StL 3
Fillingim-Bos 3
Douglas-NY 3
Alexander-Chi 3

Saves
North-StL 7
Barnes-NY 6
McQuillan-Bos 5

Innings Pitched
Cooper-Pit 327.0
Luque-Cin 304.0
Grimes-Bro 302.1
Rixey-Cin 301.0
Oeschger-Bos 299.0

Fewest Hits/Game
Glazner-Pit 8.23
Adams-Pit 8.72
Oeschger-Bos 9.12
Pertica-StL 9.16
Nehf-NY 9.18

Fewest BB/Game
Adams-Pit 1.01
Alexander-Chi 1.18
Barnes-NY 1.53
Hubbell-Phi 1.55
Doak-StL 1.60

Strikeouts
Grimes-Bro 136
Cooper-Pit 134
Luque-Cin 102
McQuillan-Bos 94

Strikeouts/Game
Grimes-Bro 4.05
Cooper-Pit 3.69
Doak-StL 3.58
Martin-Chi 3.56
Glazner-Pit 3.38

Ratio
Adams-Pit 9.73
Glazner-Pit 10.92
Nehf-NY 11.15
Luque-Cin 11.34
Alexander-Chi 11.43

Earned Run Average
Doak-StL 2.59
Adams-Pit 2.64
Glazner-Pit 2.77
Rixey-Cin 2.78
Grimes-Bro 2.83

Adjusted ERA
Adams-Pit 145
Doak-StL 142
Glazner-Pit 138
Grimes-Bro 137
Mitchell-Bro 134

Opponents' Batting Avg.
Glazner-Pit .... .250
Adams-Pit .... .251
Pertica-StL .... .267
Watson-Bos .... .270
Nehf-NY .... .271

Opponents' On-Base Pct.
Adams-Pit .... .272
Glazner-Pit .... .306
Nehf-NY .... .311
Luque-Cin .... .312
Doak-StL .... .313

Starter Runs
Rixey-Cin 33.4
Grimes-Bro 32.0
Doak-StL 27.6
Glazner-Pit 26.3
Adams-Pit 20.2

Adjusted Starter Runs
Grimes-Bro 34.5
Rixey-Cin 28.1
Glazner-Pit 27.3
Doak-StL 25.7
Cooper-Pit 20.9

Clutch Pitching Index
Barnes-NY 124
Mitchell-Bro 118
Doak-StL 116
Rixey-Cin 113
Grimes-Bro 112

Relief Runs
North-StL 2.3
Sallee-NY 1.5

Adjusted Relief Runs
North-StL 1.2
Sallee-NY 2

Relief Ranking
North-StL 1.2
Sallee-NY 2

Total Pitcher Index
Grimes-Bro 4.4
Rixey-Cin 3.0
Mitchell-Bro 2.7
Adams-Pit 2.5
Doak-StL 2.3

Total Baseball Ranking
Hornsby-StL 7.4
Bancroft-NY 5.1
Grimes-Bro 4.4
Frisch-NY 4.2
Johnston-Bro 3.1

TEAM	G	W	L	PCT	GB	R	OR	AB	H	2B	3B	HR	BB	SO	AVG	OBP	SLG	OPS	OPS+	BR	BR+	PF	CHI	RC	SB	CS	SBA	SBR
NY	153	98	55	.641		**948**	708	5249	1576	285	87	**134**	588	569	.300	.375	**.464**	**839**	**116**	**142**	122	102	102	**929**	89	64	58	-3
CLE	154	94	60	.610	4.5	925	712	5383	1656	**355**	90	42	**623**	376	.308	.383	.430	813	111	112	98	102	100	916	51	42	55	-3
STL	154	81	73	.526	17.5	835	845	5442	1655	246	**106**	67	413	407	.304	.357	.425	782	98	28	-18	106	102	827	91	71	56	-5
WAS	154	80	73	.523	18	704	738	5294	1468	240	96	42	462	472	.277	.342	.383	725	95	-80	-45	95	101	712	**112**	66	**63**	**2**
BOS	154	75	79	.487	23.5	668	**696**	5206	1440	248	69	17	428	**344**	.277	.335	.361	696	84	-133	-116	97	**107**	642	83	65	56	-4
DET	154	71	82	.464	27	883	852	5461	**1724**	268	100	58	582	376	**.316**	**.385**	.433	818	115	120	**129**	99	94	921	95	89	52	-10
CHI	154	62	92	.403	36.5	683	858	5329	1509	242	82	35	445	474	.283	.343	.379	722	90	-86	-77	99	99	695	94	93	50	-12
PHI	155	53	100	.346	45	657	894	5465	1497	256	64	82	424	565	.274	.331	.389	720	88	-102	-105	101	96	710	69	56	55	-4
TOT	616					6303		42829	12525	2140	694	477	3965	3583	.293	.357	.409	765							684	546	56	-41

TEAM	CG	SH	SV	IP	H	H/G	HR	BB	SO	RAT	ERA	ERA+	OAV	OOB	PR	PR+	PF	CPI	FA	E	DP	FW	PW	BW	SBW	DIF
NY	**92**	8	15	1364	**1461**	**9.7**	51	470	**481**	**13.1**	**3.83**	**111**	**.277**	**.342**	**70**	**63**	99	99	.965	222	138	-.2	**5.9**	11.5	.2	4.3
CLE	81	**11**	14	1377	1534	10.1	**43**	**431**	475	**13.1**	3.91	109	.288	.344	58	55	100	100	.967	204	124	.9	5.2	9.2	.2	1.7
STL	77	9	9	1379	1541	10.1	71	556	477	14.0	4.62	97	.288	.360	-51	-21	105	94	.964	224	127	-.3	-1.9	-1.6	.0	8.0
WAS	80	10	10	1383[2]	1568	10.2	51	442	452	13.4	3.98	104	.291	.349	47	23	96	102	.963	235	153	-.9	2.2	-4.2	**.7**	5.9
BOS	88	9	5	1364[1]	1521	10.1	53	452	446	13.3	3.99	106	.291	.352	45	38	99	**104**	**.975**	**157**	151	**3.5**	3.6	-10.8	.1	1.8
DET	73	4	**17**	1386[1]	1634	10.7	71	495	452	14.2	4.41	97	.297	.361	-18	-20	100	102	.963	232	107	-.7	-1.8	**12.1**	-.5	-14.4
CHI	84	7	9	1365[1]	1603	10.6	52	549	392	14.5	4.94	86	.303	.372	-99	-109	99	94	.969	200	**155**	1.1	-10.1	-7.1	-.6	2.0
PHI	75	2	7	1400[1]	1645	10.6	85	548	431	14.4	4.62	97	.300	.367	-52	-24	104	102	.958	274	144	-3.0	-2.2	-9.8	.1	-8.4
TOT	650	60	86	11020		10.3				13.7	4.29		.293	.357					.966	1748	1099					

Runs
Ruth-NY 177
Tobin-StL 132
Peckinpaugh-NY ... 128
Sisler-StL 125
Cobb-Det 124

Hits
Heilmann-Det 237
Tobin-StL 236
Sisler-StL 216
Jacobson-StL 211
Veach-Det 207

Doubles
Speaker-Cle 52
Ruth-NY 44
Veach-Det 43
Heilmann-Det 43
Meusel-NY 40

Triples
Tobin-StL 18
Sisler-StL 18
Shanks-Was 18

Home Runs
Ruth-NY 59
Williams-StL 24
Meusel-NY 24
T.Walker-Phi 23
Heilmann-Det 19

Total Bases
Ruth-NY 457
Heilmann-Det 365
Meusel-NY 334
Tobin-StL 327
Sisler-StL 326

Runs Batted In
Ruth-NY 171
Heilmann-Det 139
Meusel-NY 135
Veach-Det 128
Gardner-Cle 120

Runs Produced
Ruth-NY 289
Heilmann-Det 234
Veach-Det 222
Gardner-Cle 218
Sisler-StL 217

Bases On Balls
Ruth-NY 145
Blue-Det 103
Peckinpaugh-NY 84
J.Sewell-Cle 80
Schang-NY 78

Batting Average
Heilmann-Det .... .394
Cobb-Det .... .389
Ruth-NY .... .378
Sisler-StL .... .371
Speaker-Cle .... .362

On-Base Percentage
Ruth-NY .... .512
Cobb-Det .... .452
Heilmann-Det .... .444
Speaker-Cle .... .439
Williams-StL .... .429

Slugging Average
Ruth-NY .... .846
Heilmann-Det .... .606
Cobb-Det .... .596
Williams-StL .... .561
Sisler-StL .... .560

On-Base Plus Slugging
Ruth-NY 1359
Heilmann-Det 1051
Cobb-Det 1048
Williams-StL 990
Speaker-Cle 977

Adjusted OPS
Ruth-NY 236
Heilmann-Det 167
Cobb-Det 167
Speaker-Cle 146
Williams-StL 142

Batter Runs
Ruth-NY 119.5
Heilmann-Det 58.4
Cobb-Det 50.3
Williams-StL 42.5
Speaker-Cle 38.2

Adjusted Batter Runs
Ruth-NY 115.0
Heilmann-Det 59.9
Cobb-Det 51.5
Speaker-Cle 36.5
Williams-StL 35.4

Clutch Hitting Index
Gardner-Cle 141
Severeid-StL 127
Pratt-Bos 124
O'Rourke-Was 113
Sheely-Chi 112

Runs Created
Ruth-NY 239
Heilmann-Det 159
Cobb-Det 134
Sisler-StL 133
Williams-StL 130

Total Average
Ruth-NY 1.748
Cobb-Det 1.132
Heilmann-Det 1.121
Speaker-Cle 1.040
Williams-StL 1.037

Stolen Bases
Sisler-StL 35
Harris-Was 29
Rice-Was 26
Johnson-Chi 22
Cobb-Det 22

Stolen Base Average
Judge-Was 77.8
Harris-Was 76.3
Sisler-StL 76.1
Meusel-NY 73.9
Rice-Was 68.4

Stolen Base Runs
Sisler-StL 3.8
Harris-Was 3.2
Judge-Was 2.5
Meusel-NY 1.6
Rice-Was 1.5

Fielding Runs
Scott-Bos 38.1
Collins-Chi 27.1
Dykes-Phi 25.0
Ward-NY 18.8
Johnson-Chi 18.0

Total Player Rating
Ruth-NY 9.6
Cobb-Det 5.4
Collins-Chi 4.1
Speaker-Cle 3.7
Heilmann-Det 3.3

Wins
Shocker-StL 27
Mays-NY 27
Faber-Chi 25
Jones-Bos 23
Coveleski-Cle 23

Win Percentage
Mays-NY .... .750
Shocker-StL .... .692
Bush-Bos .... .640
Coveleski-Cle .... .639
Faber-Chi .... .625

Games
Mays-NY 49
Shocker-StL 47
Bayne-StL 47
Rommel-Phi 46

Complete Games
Faber-Chi 32
Shocker-StL 30
Mays-NY 30
Coveleski-Cle 28

Shutouts
Jones-Bos 5
Shocker-StL 4
Mogridge-Was 4
Faber-Chi 4

Saves
Middleton-Det 7
Mays-NY 7

Innings Pitched
Mays-NY 336.2
Faber-Chi 330.2
Shocker-StL 326.2
Coveleski-Cle 315.0
Kerr-Chi 308.2

Fewest Hits/Game
Faber-Chi 7.97
Bush-Bos 8.63
Mays-NY 8.88
Shawkey-NY 9.00
Johnson-Was 9.03

Fewest BB/Game
Hasty-Phi 2.01
Mays-NY 2.03
Mogridge-Was 2.06
Bagby-Cle 2.07
Zachary-Was 2.12

Strikeouts
Johnson-Was 143
Shocker-StL 132
Shawkey-NY 126
Faber-Chi 124
Leonard-Det 120

Strikeouts/Game
Johnson-Was 4.88
Shawkey-NY 4.63
Bayne-StL 4.50
Leonard-Det 4.41
Mails-Cle 4.03

Ratio
Faber-Chi 10.53
Mays-NY 11.15
Mogridge-Was 11.69
Shocker-StL 12.04
Jones-Bos 12.11

Earned Run Average
Faber-Chi 2.48
Mogridge-Was 3.00
Mays-NY 3.05
Hoyt-NY 3.09
Jones-Bos 3.22

Adjusted ERA
Faber-Chi 171
Mays-NY 139
Mogridge-Was 137
Hoyt-NY 137
Jones-Bos 131

Opponents' Batting Avg.
Faber-Chi .... .242
Mays-NY .... .257
Bush-Bos .... .260
Shawkey-NY .... .263
Johnson-Was .... .263

Opponents' On-Base Pct.
Faber-Chi .... .297
Mays-NY .... .303
Mogridge-Was .... .313
Shocker-StL .... .319
Johnson-Was .... .326

Starter Runs
Faber-Chi 66.3
Mays-NY 46.2
Mogridge-Was 41.0
Hoyt-NY 37.3
Jones-Bos 35.1

Adjusted Starter Runs
Faber-Chi 65.3
Mays-NY 44.9
Mogridge-Was 37.1
Hoyt-NY 36.2
Jones-Bos 33.7

Clutch Pitching Index
Russell-Bos 122
Zachary-Was 118
Keefe-Phi 114
Uhle-Cle 108
Sothoron-SL-Bs-Cle 108

Relief Runs

Adjusted Relief Runs

Relief Ranking

Total Pitcher Index
Faber-Chi 7.1
Mays-NY 5.8
Shocker-StL 4.2
Jones-Bos 4.1
Hoyt-NY 3.4

Total Baseball Ranking
Ruth-NY 8.9
Faber-Chi 7.1
Mays-NY 5.8
Cobb-Det 5.4
Shocker-StL 4.2

TEAM	G	W	L	PCT	GB	R	OR	AB	H	2B	3B	HR	BB	SO	AVG	OBP	SLG	OPS	OPS+	BR	BR+	PF	CHI	RC	SB	CS	SBA	SBR
NY	156	93	61	.604		852	**658**	5454	1661	253	90	80	448	421	.305	**.363**	.428	791	109	77	70	101	99	848	116	83	58	-4
CIN	156	86	68	.558	7	766	677	5282	1561	226	99	45	436	381	.296	.353	.401	754	102	8	23	98	99	737	130	136	49	-19
STL	154	85	69	.552	8	863	819	5425	1634	**280**	88	107	447	425	.301	.357	**.444**	**801**	**118**	**91**	**134**	95	99	**860**	73	63	54	-6
PIT	155	85	69	.552	8	**865**	736	5521	**1698**	239	**110**	52	423	326	**.308**	.360	.419	779	106	56	46	101	102	848	**145**	59	**71**	**11**
CHI	156	80	74	.519	13	771	808	5335	1564	248	71	42	**525**	447	.293	.359	.390	749	97	7	-8	102	98	752	97	108	47	-16
BRO	155	76	78	.494	17	743	754	5413	1569	235	76	56	339	**318**	.290	.335	.392	727	94	-58	-52	99	105	709	79	60	57	-4
PHI	154	57	96	.373	35.5	738	920	5459	1537	268	55	**116**	450	611	.282	.341	.415	756	92	-3	-71	110	95	771	48	60	44	-10
BOS	154	53	100	.346	39.5	596	822	5161	1355	162	73	32	387	451	.263	.317	.341	658	78	-179	-153	96	**106**	566	67	65	51	-8
TOT	620					6194		43050	12579	1911	662	530	3455	3380	.293	.349	.405	753							755	634	54	-56

TEAM	CG	SH	SV	IP	H	H/G	HR	BB	SO	RAT	ERA	ERA+	OAV	OOB	PR	PR+	PF	CPI	FA	E	DP	FW	PW	BW	SBW	DIF
NY	76	7	**15**	1396^1	**1454**	**9.4**	71	393	388	12.1	**3.46**	**116**	**.272**	.324	**100**	**85**	98	99	**.970**	194	145	1.2	**8.1**	6.7	.3	.0
CIN	**88**	8	3	1385^2	1481	9.7	**49**	**326**	357	**11.9**	3.54	113	.278	**.322**	87	71	97	95	.968	205	147	.4	6.8	2.2	-1.1	.9
STL	60	8	12	1362^2	1609	10.7	61	447	465	13.9	4.44	87	.299	.358	-52	-93	94	98	.961	239	122	-2.0	-8.7	**12.7**	.0	6.1
PIT	**88**	**15**	7	1387^1	1613	10.5	52	358	490	13.0	3.99	102	.296	.343	18	14	99	99	**.970**	**187**	126	**1.5**	1.4	4.4	**1.7**	-.8
CHI	74	8	12	1397^2	1579	10.2	77	475	402	13.6	4.35	97	.292	.356	-38	-23	102	99	.968	204	**154**	.5	-2.1	-.7	-.9	6.4
BRO	82	12	8	1385^2	1574	10.3	74	490	**499**	13.7	4.05	100	.293	.356	8	2	99	**106**	.967	208	139	.2	.2	-4.9	.3	3.4
PHI	73	6	5	1372	1692	11.1	89	460	394	14.4	4.64	101	.307	.365	-82	6	114	102	.965	225	152	-1.1	.6	-6.7	-.3	-11.9
BOS	63	7	6	1348	1565	10.5	57	489	360	14.0	4.38	91	.298	.361	-41	-59	98	100	.965	215	121	-.4	-5.5	-14.4	-.0	-2.9
TOT	604	71	68	11035^1		10.3				13.3	4.10		.293	.349					.967	1677	1106					

Runs	Hits	Doubles	Triples	Home Runs	Total Bases
Hornsby-StL 141	Hornsby-StL 250	Hornsby-StL 46	Daubert-Cin 22	Hornsby-StL 42	Hornsby-StL 450
Carey-Pit 140	Bigbee-Pit 215	Grimes-Chi 45	Meusel-NY 17	Williams-Phi 26	Meusel-NY 314
Smith-StL 117	Bancroft-NY 209	Duncan-Cin 44	Maranville-Pit 15	Lee-Phi 17	Wheat-Bro 302
Bancroft-NY 117	Carey-Pit 207	Bancroft-NY 41	Bigbee-Pit 15	Kelly-NY 17	Williams-Phi 300
Maranville-Pit 115	Daubert-Cin 205	Hollocher-Chi 37			Daubert-Cin 300

Runs Batted In	Runs Produced	Bases On Balls	Batting Average	On-Base Percentage	Slugging Average
Hornsby-StL 152	Hornsby-StL 251	Carey-Pit 80	Hornsby-StL .401	Hornsby-StL .459	Hornsby-StL .722
Meusel-NY 132	Meusel-NY 216	O'Farrell-Chi 79	Grimes-Chi .354	Grimes-Chi .442	Grimes-Chi .572
Wheat-Bro 112	Bigbee-Pit 207	Bancroft-NY 79	Miller-Chi .352	O'Farrell-Chi .439	Lee-Phi .540
Kelly-NY 107	Carey-Pit 200	Burns-Cin 78	Bigbee-Pit .350	Carey-Pit .408	Tierney-Pit .515
	Wheat-Bro 188	Grimes-Chi 75	Tierney-Pit .345	Bigbee-Pit .405	Williams-Phi .514

On-Base Plus Slugging	Adjusted OPS	Batter Runs	Adjusted Batter Runs	Clutch Hitting Index	Runs Created
Hornsby-StL 1181	Hornsby-StL 210	Hornsby-StL 90.0	Hornsby-StL 98.9	Terry-Chi 125	Hornsby-StL 200
Grimes-Chi 1014	Grimes-Chi 157	Grimes-Chi 47.1	Grimes-Chi 44.8	Harper-Cin 117	Carey-Pit 131
Williams-Phi 905	Daubert-Cin 130	Williams-Phi 27.5	Daubert-Cin 26.9	Meusel-NY 116	Grimes-Chi 130
Miller-Chi 899	Wheat-Bro 129	Walker-Phi 26.3	Wheat-Bro 25.2	Pinelli-Cin 115	Walker-Phi 118
Walker-Phi 899	Miller-Chi 128	Daubert-Cin 24.7	Russell-Pit 23.4	Tierney-Pit 114	Bigbee-Pit 116

Total Average	Stolen Bases	Stolen Base Average	Stolen Base Runs	Fielding Runs	Total Player Rating
Hornsby-StL 1.353	Carey-Pit 51	Carey-Pit 96.2	Carey-Pit 10.5	Parkinson-Phi 31.0	Hornsby-StL 8.7
Grimes-Chi 1.107	Frisch-NY 31	Traynor-Pit 85.0	Traynor-Pit 2.7	Bancroft-NY 21.9	Bancroft-NY 4.7
Carey-Pit .995	Burns-Cin 30	Smith-StL 72.0	Kelly-NY 1.6	Pinelli-Cin 21.1	Carey-Pit 4.2
O'Farrell-Chi .951	Maranville-Pit 24	Johnston-Bro 66.7	Smith-StL 1.5	Carey-Pit 18.5	O'Farrell-Chi 4.0
Walker-Phi .918	Bigbee-Pit 24	Youngs-NY 65.4	T.Griffith-Bro 1.2	Bigbee-Pit 16.6	Grimes-Chi 3.1

Wins	Win Percentage	Games	Complete Games	Shutouts	Saves
Rixey-Cin 25	Donohue-Cin .667	North-StL 53	Cooper-Pit 27	Vance-Bro 5	Jonnard-NY 5
Cooper-Pit 23	Rixey-Cin .658	Sherdel-StL 47	Ruether-Bro 26	Morrison-Pit 5	North-StL 4
Ruether-Bro 21	Couch-Cin .640	Ryan-NY 46	Rixey-Cin 26	Cooper-Pit 4	
Pfeffer-StL 19	Ruether-Bro .636	Oeschger-Bos 46		Adams-Pit 4	
Nehf-NY 19	Cooper-Pit .622	Morrison-Pit 45		Sherdel-StL 3	

Innings Pitched	Fewest Hits/Game	Fewest BB/Game	Strikeouts	Strikeouts/Game	Ratio
Rixey-Cin 313.1	Douglas-NY 8.79	Adams-Pit .79	Vance-Bro 134	Vance-Bro 4.91	Douglas-NY 11.02
Cooper-Pit 294.2	Osborne-Chi 8.95	Alexander-Chi 1.25	Cooper-Pit 129	Ring-Phi 4.19	Adams-Pit 11.03
Morrison-Pit 286.1	Ryan-NY 9.11	Rixey-Cin 1.29	Ring-Phi 116	Osborne-Chi 3.96	Rixey-Cin 11.09
Nehf-NY 268.1	Luque-Cin 9.17	Donohue-Cin 1.60	Morrison-Pit 104	Cooper-Pit 3.94	Donohue-Cin 11.34
Ruether-Bro 267.1	Vance-Bro 9.49	J.Barnes-NY 1.61	Grimes-Bro 99	Doak-StL 3.64	Luque-Cin 11.69

Earned Run Average	Adjusted ERA	Opponents' Batting Avg.	Opponents' On-Base Pct.	Starter Runs	Adjusted Starter Runs
Douglas-NY 2.63	Douglas-NY 152	Douglas-NY .257	Douglas-NY .302	Cooper-Pit 30.2	Cooper-Pit 29.6
Ryan-NY 3.01	Weinert-Phi 137	Luque-Cin .268	Rixey-Cin .303	Donohue-Cin 26.2	Douglas-NY 24.7
Donohue-Cin 3.12	Ryan-NY 133	Ryan-NY .269	Adams-Pit .307	Douglas-NY 25.8	Donohue-Cin 23.9
Cooper-Pit 3.18	Cooper-Pit 128	Osborne-Chi .271	J.Barnes-NY .311	Nehf-NY 24.2	Nehf-NY 21.8
Nehf-NY 3.29	Donohue-Cin 128	Rixey-Cin .275	Donohue-Cin .312	Ryan-NY 23.3	Ryan-NY 21.7

Clutch Pitching Index	Relief Runs	Adjusted Relief Runs	Relief Ranking	Total Pitcher Index	Total Baseball Ranking
Weinert-Phi 129	McNamara-Bos 13.2	McNamara-Bos 12.7	McNamara-Bos 11.3	Cooper-Pit 4.1	Hornsby-StL 8.7
Ryan-NY 116	Causey-NY 7.2	Causey-NY 6.6	Causey-NY 6.1	Ryan-NY 2.9	Bancroft-NY 4.7
Cooper-Pit 113	Braxton-Bos 5.4	Braxton-Bos 4.7	Braxton-Bos 2.4	Luque-Cin 2.6	Carey-Pit 4.2
Morrison-Pit 111	Mamaux-Bro 3.9	Mamaux-Bro 3.6	Mamaux-Bro 2.1	Nehf-NY 2.6	Cooper-Pit 4.1
McQuillan-Bos-NY 110	V.Barnes-NY 3.5	V.Barnes-NY 3.0	V.Barnes-NY 1.5	Aldridge-Chi 2.4	O'Farrell-Chi 4.0

TEAM	G	W	L	PCT	GB	R	OR	AB	H	2B	3B	HR	BB	SO	AVG	OBP	SLG	OPS	OPS+	BR	BR+	PF	CHI	RC	SB	CS	SBA	SBR
NY	154	94	60	.610		758	**618**	5245	1504	220	75	95	497	532	.287	.353	.412	765	103	36	19	102	99	774	62	59	51	-7
STL	154	93	61	.604	1	**867**	643	5416	**1693**	291	**94**	98	473	381	**.313**	**.372**	**.455**	**827**	**117**	**157**	**126**	104	96	**923**	**136**	76	**64**	**3**
DET	155	79	75	.513	15	828	791	5360	1641	250	87	54	530	378	.306	**.372**	.415	787	115	94	122	97	98	847	78	62	56	-5
CLE	155	78	76	.506	16	768	817	5293	1544	**320**	73	32	**554**	**331**	.292	.364	.398	762	104	43	38	101	97	792	90	58	61	0
CHI	155	77	77	.500	17	691	691	5267	1463	243	62	45	482	463	.278	.343	.373	716	92	-52	-49	100	101	690	109	84	56	-5
WAS	154	69	85	.448	25	650	706	5201	1395	229	76	45	458	442	.268	.334	.367	701	93	-84	-51	95	103	656	97	63	61	-1
PHI	155	65	89	.422	29	705	830	5211	1409	229	63	**111**	437	591	.270	.331	.402	733	94	-36	-53	103	104	695	60	69	47	-11
BOS	154	61	93	.396	33	598	769	5288	1392	250	55	45	366	455	.263	.316	.357	673	82	-149	-144	99	**105**	599	64	67	49	-9
TOT	618					5865		42281	12041	2032	585	525	3797	3573	.285	.349	.398	746							696	538	56	-35

TEAM	CG	SH	SV	IP	H	H/G	HR	BB	SO	RAT	ERA	ERA+	OAV	OOB	PR	PR+	PF	CPI	FA	E	DP	FW	PW	BW	SBW	DIF
NY	**100**	7	14	1393^{2}	**1402**	**9.1**	73	423	458	**12.0**	3.40	118	**.268**	**.325**	99	92	99	101	**.975**	157	124	2.1	9.0	1.9	-.3	4.5
STL	79	8	**22**	1392	1412	9.2	71	**419**	**534**	12.2	**3.39**	**122**	**.268**	.327	**101**	**112**	103	103	.968	201	158	-.4	**10.9**	**12.3**	**.7**	-7.3
DET	67	7	15	1391	1554	10.1	62	473	461	13.7	4.28	91	.288	.354	-37	-67	96	97	.970	191	133	.2	-6.5	11.9	-.0	-3.4
CLE	76	**14**	7	1383^{2}	1605	10.5	58	464	489	13.8	4.59	87	.296	.356	-85	-93	99	93	.968	202	147	-.4	-9.0	3.7	.4	6.4
CHI	86	13	8	1403^{2}	1472	9.5	57	529	484	13.0	3.94	103	.278	.346	15	15	101	98	**.975**	**155**	143	**2.3**	1.5	-4.7	-.0	1.2
WAS	84	13	10	1362^{1}	1485	9.9	49	500	422	13.5	3.82	101	.286	.354	33	6	96	**107**	.969	196	**168**	-.1	.6	-4.9	.3	-3.7
PHI	73	4	6	1362^{1}	1573	10.4	107	469	373	13.8	4.60	92	.297	.357	-85	-52	105	99	.966	215	118	-1.2	-5.0	-5.1	-.6	.0
BOS	71	10	6	1373^{1}	1508	9.9	**48**	503	359	13.5	4.30	95	.287	.354	-41	-31	102	94	.965	224	145	-1.7	-3.0	-13.9	-.4	3.3
TOT	636	76	88	11062		9.8				13.2	4.04		.285	.349					.970	1541	1136					

Runs
Sisler-StL 134
Blue-Det 131
Williams-StL 128
Tobin-StL 122

Hits
Sisler-StL 246
Cobb-Det 211
Tobin-StL 207
Veach-Det 202

Doubles
Speaker-Cle 48
Pratt-Bos 44
Sisler-StL 42
Cobb-Det 42

Triples
Sisler-StL 18
Jacobson-StL 16
Cobb-Det 16
Judge-Was 15
Mostil-Chi 14

Home Runs
Williams-StL 39
Walker-Phi 37
Ruth-NY 35
Miller-Phi 21
Heilmann-Det 21

Total Bases
Williams-StL 367
Sisler-StL 348
Walker-Phi 310
Cobb-Det 297
Tobin-StL 296

Runs Batted In
Williams-StL 155
Veach-Det 126
McManus-StL 109
Sisler-StL 105
Jacobson-StL 102

Runs Produced
Williams-StL 244
Sisler-StL 231
Veach-Det 213
Cobb-Det 194
McManus-StL 186

Bases On Balls
Witt-NY 89
Ruth-NY 84
Blue-Det 82
Speaker-Cle 77
Williams-StL 74

Batting Average
Sisler-StL .420
Cobb-Det .401
Speaker-Cle .378
Heilmann-Det .356
Miller-Phi .335

On-Base Percentage
Speaker-Cle .474
Sisler-StL .467
Cobb-Det .462
Ruth-NY .434
Heilmann-Det .432

Slugging Average
Ruth-NY .672
Williams-StL .627
Speaker-Cle .606
Heilmann-Det .598
Sisler-StL .594

On-Base Plus Slugging
Ruth-NY 1106
Speaker-Cle 1080
Sisler-StL 1061
Williams-StL 1040
Heilmann-Det 1030

Adjusted OPS
Ruth-NY 181
Speaker-Cle 178
Cobb-Det 172
Heilmann-Det 172
Sisler-StL 169

Batter Runs
Sisler-StL 64.4
Williams-StL 56.1
Speaker-Cle 52.8
Cobb-Det 52.4
Ruth-NY 50.5

Adjusted Batter Runs
Sisler-StL 59.5
Cobb-Det 56.6
Speaker-Cle 52.0
Williams-StL 51.4
Ruth-NY 48.1

Clutch Hitting Index
Veach-Det 143
O'Neill-Cle 132
Johnson-Chi 127
Wood-Cle 126
Gardner-Cle 125

Runs Created
Sisler-StL 162
Williams-StL 149
Cobb-Det 133
Speaker-Cle 127
Ruth-NY 120

Total Average
Speaker-Cle 1.272
Ruth-NY 1.254
Sisler-StL 1.203
Heilmann-Det 1.135
Williams-StL 1.131

Stolen Bases
Sisler-StL 51
Williams-StL 37
Harris-Was 25
Johnson-Chi 21

Stolen Base Average
Jacobson-StL 76.0
Sisler-StL 72.9
Harris-Was 69.4
Rice-Was 69.0
Rigney-Det 68.0

Stolen Base Runs
Sisler-StL 4.6
Jacobson-StL 2.1
Evans-Cle 1.7
Harris-Was 1.7
Veach-Det 1.6

Fielding Runs
Harris-Was 26.4
Peckinpaugh-Was 20.4
Schalk-Chi 20.2
Scott-NY 17.3
Sisler-StL 12.1

Total Player Rating
Sisler-StL 6.3
Speaker-Cle 5.3
Cobb-Det 4.9
Williams-StL 4.6
Ruth-NY 3.7

Wins
Rommel-Phi 27
Bush-NY 26
Shocker-StL 24
Uhle-Cle 22
Faber-Chi 21

Win Percentage
Bush-NY .788
Rommel-Phi .675
Shawkey-NY .625
Pillette-Det .613
Hoyt-NY .613

Games
Rommel-Phi 51
Uhle-Cle 50
Shocker-StL 48
Harriss-Phi 47

Complete Games
Faber-Chi 31
Shocker-StL 29
Uhle-Cle 23
Johnson-Was 23

Shutouts
Uhle-Cle 5

Saves
Jones-NY 8
Pruett-StL 7
Wright-StL 5

Innings Pitched
Faber-Chi 352.0
Shocker-StL 348.0
Shawkey-NY 299.2
Rommel-Phi 294.0
Uhle-Cle 287.1

Fewest Hits/Game
Davis-StL 8.36
Bush-NY 8.46
Faber-Chi 8.54
Shawkey-NY 8.59
Wright-StL 8.65

Fewest BB/Game
Shocker-StL 1.47
Vangilder-StL 1.76
Mays-NY 1.88
Kolp-StL 1.91
Hasty-Phi 1.92

Strikeouts
Shocker-StL 149
Faber-Chi 148
Shawkey-NY 130
Ehmke-Det 108
Johnson-Was 105

Strikeouts/Game
Morton-Cle 4.53
Harriss-Phi 4.00
Shawkey-NY 3.90
Shocker-StL 3.85
Faber-Chi 3.78

Ratio
Faber-Chi 10.82
Shocker-StL 11.02
Rommel-Phi 11.08
Vangilder-StL 11.09
Quinn-Bos 11.43

Earned Run Average
Faber-Chi 2.81
Pillette-Det 2.85
Shawkey-NY 2.91
Wright-StL 2.92
Shocker-StL 2.97

Adjusted ERA
Faber-Chi 144
Wright-StL 141
Shocker-StL 139
Shawkey-NY 137
Pillette-Det 136

Opponents' Batting Avg.
Davis-StL .250
Bush-NY .252
Faber-Chi .252
Shawkey-NY .256
Pillette-Det .258

Opponents' On-Base Pct.
Faber-Chi .299
Shocker-StL .304
Rommel-Phi .309
Vangilder-StL .310
Quinn-Bos .311

Starter Runs
Faber-Chi 47.7
Shocker-StL 40.9
Shawkey-NY 37.2
Pillette-Det 36.0
Johnson-Was 32.4

Adjusted Starter Runs
Faber-Chi 48.4
Shocker-StL 43.7
Shawkey-NY 36.3
Pillette-Det 32.4
Rommel-Phi 30.0

Clutch Pitching Index
Mogridge-Was 124
Wright-StL 118
Johnson-Was 114
Pillette-Det 110
Shawkey-NY 109

Relief Runs
Murray-NY 4

Adjusted Relief Runs
Murray-NY 2

Relief Ranking
Murray-NY 1

Total Pitcher Index
Faber-Chi 4.9
Shocker-StL 4.7
Rommel-Phi 3.8
Vangilder-StL 3.4
Pillette-Det 3.3

Total Baseball Ranking
Sisler-StL 6.3
Speaker-Cle 5.3
Cobb-Det 4.9
Faber-Chi 4.9
Shocker-StL 4.7

TEAM	G	W	L	PCT	GB	R	OR	AB	H	2B	3B	HR	BB	SO	AVG	OBP	SLG	OPS	OPS+	BR	BR+	PF	CHI	RC	SB	CS	SBA	SBR
NY	153	95	58	.621		**854**	679	5452	**1610**	248	76	85	**487**	406	**.295**	**.356**	**.415**	**771**	**110**	**72**	**83**	99	**103**	**816**	106	70	60	-1
CIN	154	91	63	.591	4.5	708	**629**	5278	1506	237	95	45	439	367	.285	.344	.392	736	102	-1	14	98	96	707	96	105	48	-16
PIT	154	87	67	.565	8.5	786	696	5405	1592	224	**111**	49	407	**362**	**.295**	.347	.404	751	102	26	10	102	**103**	766	154	75	**67**	**8**
CHI	154	83	71	.539	12.5	756	704	5259	1516	243	52	90	455	485	.288	.348	.406	754	104	33	32	100	99	735	**181**	143	56	-10
STL	154	79	74	.516	16	746	732	5526	1582	**274**	76	63	438	446	.286	.343	.398	741	103	5	21	98	97	761	89	61	59	-2
BRO	155	76	78	.494	19.5	753	741	5476	1559	214	81	62	425	382	.285	.340	.387	727	100	-20	1	97	102	730	71	50	59	-2
BOS	155	54	100	.351	41.5	636	798	5329	1455	213	58	32	429	404	.273	.331	.353	684	90	-99	-72	96	99	625	57	80	42	-15
PHI	155	50	104	.325	45.5	748	1008	5491	1528	259	39	**112**	414	556	.278	.333	.401	734	89	-15	-91	112	101	729	70	73	49	-10
TOT	617					5987		43216	12348	1912	588	538	3494	3408	.286	.343	.395	737							824	657	56	-49

TEAM	CG	SH	SV	IP	H	H/G	HR	BB	SO	RAT	ERA	ERA+	OAV	OOB	PR	PR+	PF	CPI	FA	E	DP	FW	PW	BW	SBW	DIF
NY	62	10	**18**	1378	1440	9.5	82	424	453	12.4	3.90	98	.271	.328	15	-14	96	93	**.972**	**176**	141	**2.4**	-1.3	**8.0**	.5	9.1
CIN	88	11	9	1391^{1}	1465	9.5	**28**	**359**	450	**12.1**	**3.22**	**120**	.273	**.322**	**121**	**102**	97	101	.969	202	144	.9	**9.9**	1.4	-1.0	3.0
PIT	92	5	9	1376^{1}	1513	9.9	53	402	414	12.7	3.88	103	.284	.337	19	19	100	98	.971	179	157	2.3	1.9	1.0	**1.4**	3.6
CHI	80	8	11	1366^{2}	**1419**	**9.4**	86	435	408	12.5	3.82	105	**.269**	.329	27	25	100	96	.967	208	144	.6	2.5	3.1	-.4	.4
STL	77	9	7	1398^{1}	1539	10.0	70	456	398	13.2	3.87	101	.284	.344	20	5	98	**104**	.963	232	141	-.8	.5	2.1	.4	.5
BRO	**94**	8	5	1396^{2}	1503	9.7	55	476	**548**	13.1	3.75	103	.277	.340	39	21	97	100	.955	293	137	-4.4	2.1	.1	.4	1.0
BOS	55	**13**	7	1392^{2}	1662	10.8	64	394	351	13.5	4.22	94	.302	.352	-34	-41	100	102	.964	230	157	-.6	-3.9	-6.9	-.9	-10.5
PHI	68	3	8	1376^{1}	1801	11.8	100	549	384	15.7	5.34	86	.322	.386	-205	-100	115	102	.966	217	**172**	.1	-9.6	-8.7	-.4	-8.3
TOT	616	67	74	11076^{1}		10.1				13.1	4.00		.286	.343					.966	1737	1193					

Runs
Youngs-NY 121
Carey-Pit 120
Frisch-NY 116
Johnston-Bro 111
Statz-Chi 110

Hits
Frisch-NY 223
Statz-Chi 209
Traynor-Pit 208
Johnston-Bro 203
Youngs-NY 200

Doubles
Roush-Cin 41
Tierney-Pit-Phi 36
Grantham-Chi 36
Bottomley-StL 34

Triples
Traynor-Pit 19
Carey-Pit 19
Roush-Cin 18
Southworth-Bos 16

Home Runs
Williams-Phi 41
Fournier-Bro 22
Miller-Chi 20
Meusel-NY 19
Hornsby-StL 17

Total Bases
Frisch-NY 311
Williams-Phi 308
Fournier-Bro 303
Traynor-Pit 301
Statz-Chi 288

Runs Batted In
Meusel-NY 125
Williams-Phi 114
Frisch-NY 111
Kelly-NY 103
Fournier-Bro 102

Runs Produced
Frisch-NY 215
Meusel-NY 208
Youngs-NY 205
Traynor-Pit 197
Carey-Pit 177

Bases On Balls
Burns-Cin 101
Sand-Phi 82
Youngs-NY 73
Carey-Pit 73
Grantham-Chi 71

Batting Average
Hornsby-StL .384
Wheat-Bro .375
Bottomley-StL .371
Fournier-Bro .351
Roush-Cin .351

On-Base Percentage
Hornsby-StL .459
Bottomley-StL .425
Youngs-NY .412
Fournier-Bro .411
O'Farrell-Chi .408

Slugging Average
Hornsby-StL .627
Fournier-Bro .588
Williams-Phi .576
Barnhart-Pit .563
Bottomley-StL .535

On-Base Plus Slugging
Hornsby-StL 1086
Fournier-Bro 999
Bottomley-StL 960
Williams-Phi 947
Roush-Cin 938

Adjusted OPS
Hornsby-StL 188
Fournier-Bro 165
Bottomley-StL 155
Roush-Cin 149
Frisch-NY 133

Batter Runs
Hornsby-StL 52.1
Fournier-Bro 43.7
Bottomley-StL 39.2
Roush-Cin 34.0
Williams-Phi 33.2

Adjusted Batter Runs
Hornsby-StL 54.5
Fournier-Bro 47.1
Bottomley-StL 41.6
Roush-Cin 36.2
Frisch-NY 29.9

Clutch Hitting Index
Stock-StL 136
McInnis-Bos 124
Frisch-NY 123
Meusel-NY 117
Bigbee-Pit 114

Runs Created
Fournier-Bro 125
Frisch-NY 123
Hornsby-StL 120
Bottomley-StL 117
Carey-Pit 117

Total Average
Hornsby-StL 1.194
Fournier-Bro 1.071
Bottomley-StL .976
Williams-Phi .966
Carey-Pit .928

Stolen Bases
Carey-Pit 51
Grantham-Chi 43
Smith-StL 32
Heathcote-Chi 32

Stolen Base Average
Carey-Pit 86.4
Smith-StL 74.4
Frisch-NY 70.7
Traynor-Pit 68.3
Heathcote-Chi 65.3

Stolen Base Runs
Carey-Pit 8.4
Smith-StL 3.2
Frisch-NY 2.2
Rawlings-Pit 2.0
Traynor-Pit 1.6

Fielding Runs
Johnston-Bro 24.5
Bancroft-NY 21.1
Carey-Pit 19.7
Statz-Chi 17.7
Tierney-Pit-Phi 14.0

Total Player Rating
Johnston-Bro 4.4
Fournier-Bro 4.1
Bancroft-NY 3.8
Traynor-Pit 3.8
Carey-Pit 3.7

Wins
Luque-Cin 27
Morrison-Pit 25
Alexander-Chi 22
Grimes-Bro 21
Donohue-Cin 21

Win Percentage
Luque-Cin .771
Ryan-NY .762
Scott-NY .696
Morrison-Pit .658
Alexander-Chi .647

Games
Ryan-NY 45
Jonnard-NY 45
Oeschger-Bos 44
J.Barnes-NY-Bos 43
Genewich-Bos 43

Complete Games
Grimes-Bro 33
Luque-Cin 28
Morrison-Pit 27
Cooper-Pit 26
Alexander-Chi 26

Shutouts
Luque-Cin 6
J.Barnes-NY-Bos 5
McQuillan-NY 5

Saves
Jonnard-NY 5
Ryan-NY 4

Innings Pitched
Grimes-Bro 327.0
Luque-Cin 322.0
Rixey-Cin 309.0
Alexander-Chi 305.0
Ring-Phi 304.1

Fewest Hits/Game
Luque-Cin 7.80
Vance-Bro 8.44
Morrison-Pit 8.56
Keen-Chi 8.59
Aldridge-Chi 8.67

Fewest BB/Game
Alexander-Chi .89
B.Adams-Pit 1.42
Genewich-Bos 1.82
Rixey-Cin 1.89
Meadows-Phi-Pit 2.15

Strikeouts
Vance-Bro 197
Luque-Cin 151
Grimes-Bro 119
Morrison-Pit 114
Ring-Phi 112

Strikeouts/Game
Vance-Bro 6.32
Luque-Cin 4.22
Bentley-NY 3.93
Osborne-Chi 3.46
Morrison-Pit 3.40

Ratio
Alexander-Chi 9.97
Luque-Cin 10.40
Ryan-NY 11.31
Aldridge-Chi 11.49
McQuillan-NY 11.56

Earned Run Average
Luque-Cin 1.93
Rixey-Cin 2.80
Keen-Chi 3.00
Kaufmann-Chi 3.10
Haines-StL 3.11

Adjusted ERA
Luque-Cin 200
Rixey-Cin 138
Keen-Chi 133
Kaufmann-Chi 129
Alexander-Chi 125

Opponents' Batting Avg.
Luque-Cin .235
Vance-Bro .250
Aldridge-Chi .251
Morrison-Pit .253
Osborne-Chi .255

Opponents' On-Base Pct.
Alexander-Chi .277
Luque-Cin .291
Aldridge-Chi .307
Ryan-NY .308
McQuillan-NY .315

Starter Runs
Luque-Cin 73.9
Rixey-Cin 41.1
Alexander-Chi 27.4
Haines-StL 26.1
Kaufmann-Chi 20.6

Adjusted Starter Runs
Luque-Cin 71.5
Rixey-Cin 37.8
Alexander-Chi 27.4
Haines-StL 23.8
Ring-Phi 21.2

Clutch Pitching Index
Kaufmann-Chi 118
Rixey-Cin 116
Genewich-Bos 116
Doak-StL 116
Luque-Cin 115

Relief Runs
Decatur-Bro 15.3
Jonnard-NY 7.6
Keck-Cin 2.6
V.Barnes-NY .5

Adjusted Relief Runs
Decatur-Bro 14.5
Jonnard-NY 6.0
Keck-Cin 1.3

Relief Ranking
Decatur-Bro 9.0
Jonnard-NY 4.6
Keck-Cin 1.3

Total Pitcher Index
Luque-Cin 7.7
Rixey-Cin 3.6
Alexander-Chi 3.2
Haines-StL 2.4
Kaufmann-Chi 2.4

Total Baseball Ranking
Luque-Cin 7.7
Johnston-Bro 4.4
Fournier-Bro 4.1
Bancroft-NY 3.8
Traynor-Pit 3.8

TEAM	G	W	L	PCT	GB	R	OR	AB	H	2B	3B	HR	BB	SO	AVG	OBP	SLG	OPS	OPS+	BR	BR+	PF	CHI	RC	SB	CS	SBA	SBR
NY	152	98	54	.645		823	**622**	5347	1554	231	79	**105**	521	516	.291	.357	**.422**	779	108	73	59	102	101	811	69	74	48	-11
DET	155	83	71	.539	16	831	741	5266	1579	270	69	41	596	385	.300	.377	.401	778	113	91	108	98	98	827	87	62	58	-3
CLE	153	82	71	.536	16.5	**888**	746	5290	**1594**	**301**	75	59	**633**	**384**	**.301**	**.381**	.420	**801**	**117**	**135**	**137**	100	100	**868**	79	79	50	-10
WAS	155	75	78	.490	23.5	720	747	5244	1436	224	**93**	26	532	448	.274	.346	.367	713	98	-46	-9	95	**104**	693	102	68	60	-1
STL	154	74	78	.487	24	688	720	5298	1489	248	62	82	442	423	.281	.339	.398	737	94	-15	-53	106	96	724	64	54	54	-5
PHI	153	69	83	.454	29	661	761	5196	1407	229	64	53	445	517	.271	.333	.370	703	89	-74	-82	101	103	653	72	62	54	-6
CHI	156	69	85	.448	30	692	741	5246	1463	254	57	42	532	458	.279	.350	.373	723	97	-26	-17	99	97	707	**191**	118	**62**	**1**
BOS	154	61	91	.401	37	584	809	5181	1354	253	54	34	391	480	.261	.318	.351	669	81	-143	-146	101	**104**	579	79	91	46	-14
TOT	616					5887		42068	11876	2010	553	442	4092	3611	.283	.351	.389	739							743	608	55	-49

TEAM	CG	SH	SV	IP	H	H/G	HR	BB	SO	RAT	ERA	ERA+	OAV	OOB	PR	PR+	PF	CPI	FA	E	DP	FW	PW	BW	SBW	DIF
NY	**101**	9	10	1380^{2}	**1365**	**8.9**	68	491	**506**	**12.3**	**3.63**	**109**	**.263**	**.330**	**55**	**49**	99	96	**.977**	**144**	131	**3.3**	**4.8**	5.8	-.5	8.8
DET	61	9	12	1373^{2}	1502	9.9	58	**449**	447	13.2	4.09	94	.283	.345	-16	-35	97	96	.968	200	103	.1	-3.3	10.5	.3	-1.4
CLE	77	**10**	11	1376	1517	10.0	**36**	465	407	13.3	3.92	101	.285	.346	11	4	100	97	.964	226	143	-1.6	.4	**13.3**	-.4	-6.0
WAS	71	8	**16**	1374^{1}	1527	10.0	56	563	474	14.0	3.99	95	.291	.364	0	-32	95	**109**	.966	216	**182**	-.9	-3.0	-.8	.5	2.9
STL	83	**10**	10	1373^{1}	1430	9.4	59	528	488	13.2	3.93	106	.275	.348	9	35	105	98	.971	177	145	1.5	3.4	-5.1	.1	-1.7
PHI	65	7	12	1364^{2}	1465	9.7	68	550	400	13.5	4.09	101	.280	.352	-15	1	103	99	.965	221	127	-1.3	.1	-7.9	.0	2.2
CHI	74	5	11	1397	1512	9.8	49	534	467	13.5	4.05	98	.283	.353	-10	-13	99	99	.971	184	138	1.2	-1.2	-1.6	**.7**	-6.9
BOS	77	3	11	1372	1534	10.1	48	520	412	14.0	4.20	98	.294	.366	-33	-15	103	104	.963	232	126	-1.9	-1.4	-14.1	-.8	3.3
TOT	609	61	93	11011^{2}		9.7				13.4	3.99		.283	.351					.969	1600	1095					

Runs
Ruth-NY 151
Speaker-Cle 133
Jamieson-Cle 130
Heilmann-Det 121
Rice-Was 117

Hits
Jamieson-Cle 222
Speaker-Cle 218
Heilmann-Det 211
Ruth-NY 205
Tobin-StL 202

Doubles
Speaker-Cle 59
Burns-Bos 47
Ruth-NY 45
Heilmann-Det 44
J.Sewell-Cle 41

Triples
Rice-Was 18
Goslin-Was 18
Tobin-StL 15
Mostil-Chi 15

Home Runs
Ruth-NY 41
Williams-StL 29
Heilmann-Det 18
Speaker-Cle 17
Hauser-Phi 17

Total Bases
Ruth-NY 399
Speaker-Cle 350
Williams-StL 346
Heilmann-Det 331
Tobin-StL 303

Runs Batted In
Ruth-NY 131
Speaker-Cle 130
Heilmann-Det 115
J.Sewell-Cle 109
Pipp-NY 108

Runs Produced
Speaker-Cle 246
Ruth-NY 241
Heilmann-Det 218
J.Sewell-Cle 204
Rice-Was 189

Bases On Balls
Ruth-NY 170
J.Sewell-Cle 98
Blue-Det 96
Speaker-Cle 93
Collins-Chi 84

Batting Average
Heilmann-Det ...... .403
Ruth-NY .... .393
Speaker-Cle .... .380
Collins-Chi .... .360
Williams-StL ...... .357

On-Base Percentage
Ruth-NY .... .545
Heilmann-Det ...... .481
Speaker-Cle .... .469
J.Sewell-Cle ...... .456
Collins-Chi .... .455

Slugging Average
Ruth-NY .... .764
Heilmann-Det ...... .632
Williams-StL ...... .623
Speaker-Cle .... .610
Harris-Bos .... .520

On-Base Plus Slugging
Ruth-NY 1309
Heilmann-Det 1113
Speaker-Cle 1079
Williams-StL 1062
J.Sewell-Cle 935

Adjusted OPS
Ruth-NY 238
Heilmann-Det 195
Speaker-Cle 183
Williams-StL 168
J.Sewell-Cle 147

Batter Runs
Ruth-NY 119.1
Speaker-Cle 70.9
Heilmann-Det 70.7
Williams-StL 61.2
J.Sewell-Cle 42.8

Adjusted Batter Runs
Ruth-NY 115.7
Heilmann-Det 73.7
Speaker-Cle 71.2
Williams-StL 53.8
J.Sewell-Cle 43.0

Clutch Hitting Index
Pipp-NY 137
J.Sewell-Cle 123
Bassler-Det 122
Sheely-Chi 122
Meusel-NY 121

Runs Created
Ruth-NY 223
Speaker-Cle 166
Heilmann-Det 160
Williams-StL 148
J.Sewell-Cle 128

Total Average
Ruth-NY 1.683
Heilmann-Det 1.288
Speaker-Cle 1.222
Williams-StL 1.144
J.Sewell-Cle 1.025

Stolen Bases
Collins-Chi 48
Mostil-Chi 41
Harris-Was 23
Rice-Was 20

Stolen Base Average
Mostil-Chi 71.9
Rice-Was 71.4
Elsh-Chi 66.7
Collins-Chi 62.3
Harris-Was 59.0

Stolen Base Runs
Mostil-Chi 3.4
Rice-Was 1.6
Barrett-Chi 1.6
Veach-Det 1.1

Fielding Runs
Peckinpaugh-Was .. 22.8
Mostil-Chi 21.8
Harris-Was 19.4
Ruel-Was 18.5
Flagstead-Det-Bos ... 18.5

Total Player Rating
Ruth-NY 10.8
Speaker-Cle 6.9
J.Sewell-Cle 6.2
Heilmann-Det 6.1
Williams-StL 4.9

Wins
Uhle-Cle 26
Jones-NY 21
Dauss-Det 21
Shocker-StL 20
Ehmke-Bos 20

Win Percentage
Pennock-NY .... .760
Jones-NY .... .724
Hoyt-NY .... .654
Shocker-StL ...... .625
Uhle-Cle .... .619

Games
Rommel-Phi 56
Uhle-Cle 54
Russell-Was 52
Cole-Det 52
Dauss-Det 50

Complete Games
Uhle-Cle 29
Ehmke-Bos 28
Shocker-StL 24
Dauss-Det 22
Bush-NY 22

Shutouts
Coveleski-Cle 5
Vangilder-StL 4
Dauss-Det 4

Saves
Russell-Was 9
Quinn-Bos 7
Harriss-Phi 6

Innings Pitched
Uhle-Cle 357.2
Ehmke-Bos 316.2
Dauss-Det 316.0
Rommel-Phi 297.2
Vangilder-StL 282.1

Fewest Hits/Game
Shawkey-NY 8.07
Hoyt-NY 8.56
Bush-NY 8.59
Russell-Was 8.78
Danforth-StL 8.79

Fewest BB/Game
Shocker-StL 1.59
Coveleski-Cle 1.66
Thurston-StL-Chi . 1.75
Quinn-Bos 1.96
Dauss-Det 2.22

Strikeouts
Johnson-Was 130
Shawkey-NY 125
Bush-NY 125
Ehmke-Bos 121

Strikeouts/Game
Johnson-Det 4.75
Johnson-Was 4.48
Shawkey-NY 4.35
Bush-NY 4.08
Harriss-Phi 3.83

Ratio
Shocker-StL 11.16
Hoyt-NY 11.20
Pennock-NY 11.52
Jones-NY 11.63
Coveleski-Cle ... 11.64

Earned Run Average
Coveleski-Cle 2.76
Hoyt-NY 3.02
Russell-Was 3.03
Vangilder-StL 3.06
Mogridge-Was 3.11

Adjusted ERA
Coveleski-Cle 143
Vangilder-StL 136
Hoyt-NY 131
Thurston-StL-Chi .. 127
Rommel-Phi 126

Opponents' Batting Avg.
Shawkey-NY .... .246
Hoyt-NY .... .253
Jones-NY .... .257
Faber-Chi .... .259
Bush-NY .... .260

Opponents' On-Base Pct.
Shocker-StL ...... .306
Hoyt-NY .... .307
Faber-Chi .... .311
Jones-NY .... .312
Pennock-NY .... .314

Starter Runs
Coveleski-Cle 30.9
Vangilder-StL 28.9
Hoyt-NY 25.6
Rommel-Phi 23.7
Pennock-NY 22.4

Adjusted Starter Runs
Vangilder-StL 33.2
Coveleski-Cle 30.5
Rommel-Phi 26.9
Hoyt-NY 24.7
Shocker-StL 22.4

Clutch Pitching Index
Thurston-StL-Chi .. 139
Russell-Was 128
Mogridge-Was 122
Vangilder-StL 121
Coveleski-Cle 121

Relief Runs

Adjusted Relief Runs

Relief Ranking

Total Pitcher Index
Rommel-Phi 3.9
Vangilder-StL 3.2
Coveleski-Cle 2.9
Bush-NY 2.6
Uhle-Cle 2.5

Total Baseball Ranking
Ruth-NY 10.8
Speaker-Cle 6.9
J.Sewell-Cle 6.2
Heilmann-Det 6.1
Williams-StL 4.9

TEAM	G	W	L	PCT	GB	R	OR	AB	H	2B	3B	HR	BB	SO	AVG	OBP	SLG	OPS	OPS+	BR	BR+	PF	CHI	RC	SB	CS	SBA	SBR
NY	154	93	60	.608		**857**	641	5445	**1634**	269	81	**95**	467	479	**.300**	**.358**	**.432**	**790**	**120**	**124**	**148**	97	102	**849**	82	53	61	-1
BRO	154	92	62	.597	1.5	717	679	5339	1534	227	54	72	447	357	.287	.345	.391	736	105	19	43	97	99	725	34	46	43	-9
PIT	153	90	63	.588	3	724	586	5288	1517	222	**122**	44	366	396	.287	.336	.400	736	100	11	0	102	**103**	715	**181**	92	**66**	**8**
CIN	153	83	70	.542	10	649	**579**	5301	1539	236	111	36	349	**334**	.290	.337	.397	734	103	8	19	99	93	698	103	98	51	-12
CHI	154	81	72	.529	12	698	699	5134	1419	207	59	66	**469**	521	.276	.340	.378	718	96	-10	-16	101	**103**	652	137	149	48	-22
STL	154	65	89	.422	28.5	740	750	5349	1552	**270**	87	67	382	418	.290	.341	.411	752	108	42	56	98	100	740	86	86	50	-11
PHI	152	55	96	.364	37	676	849	5306	1459	256	56	94	382	452	.275	.328	.397	725	88	-13	-87	112	99	687	57	67	46	-11
BOS	154	53	100	.346	40	520	798	5283	1355	194	52	25	354	451	.256	.306	.327	633	77	-181	-158	96	**103**	532	74	68	52	-8
TOT	614					5581		42445	12009	1881	622	499	3216	3408	.283	.337	.392	729							754	659	53	-65

TEAM	CG	SH	SV	IP	H	H/G	HR	BB	SO	RAT	ERA	ERA+	OAV	OOB	PR	PR+	PF	CPI	FA	E	DP	FW	PW	BW	SBW	DIF
NY	71	4	**21**	1378^{2}	1464	9.6	77	392	406	12.3	3.62	101	.274	.326	38	7	95	100	.971	186	160	.4	.7	**14.7**	.7	.0
BRO	**97**	10	5	1376^{1}	1432	9.4	58	403	**638**	12.3	3.64	103	.270	.326	35	17	97	96	.968	196	121	-.1	1.7	4.3	-.0	9.4
PIT	85	**15**	5	1382	**1387**	**9.1**	42	323	364	**11.3**	3.27	117	**.267**	.313	92	88	99	97	.971	183	161	.5	8.8	.0	**1.6**	2.8
CIN	77	14	9	1378	1408	9.2	**30**	**293**	451	**11.3**	**3.12**	**121**	**.267**	**.309**	**115**	**102**	97	97	.966	217	142	-1.4	**10.2**	1.9	-.4	-3.6
CHI	85	4	6	1380^{2}	1459	9.6	89	438	416	12.6	3.83	102	.275	.333	6	11	101	101	.966	218	153	-1.4	1.1	-1.5	-1.4	7.8
STL	79	7	6	1364^{2}	1528	10.1	70	486	393	13.6	4.15	91	.290	.354	-43	-58	98	**104**	.969	188	162	.3	-5.7	5.6	-.3	-11.7
PHI	59	7	10	1354^{1}	1691	11.3	84	469	349	14.6	4.88	92	.314	.372	-151	-52	115	103	.972	175	**168**	.9	-5.1	-8.6	-.3	-7.2
BOS	66	10	4	1379^{1}	1607	10.5	49	402	364	13.3	4.47	86	.301	.353	-92	-101	99	96	**.973**	**168**	154	**1.4**	-10.0	-15.6	.0	.9
TOT	619	71	66	10994		9.9				12.7	3.87		.283	.337					.970	1531	1221					

Runs
Hornsby-StL 121
Frisch-NY 121
Carey-Pit 113
Youngs-NY 112
Williams-Phi 101

Hits
Hornsby-StL 227
Wheat-Bro 212
Frisch-NY 198
High-Bro 191
Fournier-Bro 188

Doubles
Hornsby-StL 43
Wheat-Bro 41
Kelly-NY 37

Triples
Roush-Cin 21
Maranville-Pit 20
Wright-Pit 18
Cuyler-Pit 16
Frisch-NY 15

Home Runs
Fournier-Bro 27
Hornsby-StL 25
Williams-Phi 24
Kelly-NY 21

Total Bases
Hornsby-StL 373
Wheat-Bro 311
Williams-Phi 308
Kelly-NY 303
Fournier-Bro 302

Runs Batted In
Kelly-NY 136
Fournier-Bro 116
Wright-Pit 111
Bottomley-StL 111
Meusel-NY 102

Runs Produced
Kelly-NY 206
Hornsby-StL 190
Wright-Pit 184
Bottomley-StL 184
Frisch-NY 183

Bases On Balls
Hornsby-StL 89
Fournier-Bro 83
Youngs-NY 77
Williams-Phi 67
Friberg-Chi 66

Batting Average
Hornsby-StL .424
Wheat-Bro .375
Youngs-NY .356
Cuyler-Pit .354
Roush-Cin .348

On-Base Percentage
Hornsby-StL .507
Youngs-NY .441
Fournier-Bro .428
Wheat-Bro .428
Williams-Phi .403

Slugging Average
Hornsby-StL .696
Williams-Phi .552
Wheat-Bro .549
Cuyler-Pit .539
Fournier-Bro .536

On-Base Plus Slugging
Hornsby-StL 1203
Wheat-Bro 978
Fournier-Bro 965
Youngs-NY 962
Williams-Phi 955

Adjusted OPS
Hornsby-StL 223
Wheat-Bro 165
Fournier-Bro 162
Youngs-NY 161
Cuyler-Pit 147

Batter Runs
Hornsby-StL 94.1
Wheat-Bro 48.2
Fournier-Bro 48.1
Youngs-NY 45.3
Williams-Phi 42.0

Adjusted Batter Runs
Hornsby-StL 97.2
Fournier-Bro 52.3
Wheat-Bro 52.2
Youngs-NY 48.7
Kelly-NY 32.4

Clutch Hitting Index
Friberg-Chi 141
Griffith-Bro 140
Meusel-NY 135
Wright-Pit 130
Pinelli-Cin 129

Runs Created
Hornsby-StL 186
Fournier-Bro 133
Wheat-Bro 132
Youngs-NY 123
Williams-Phi 121

Total Average
Hornsby-StL 1.424
Fournier-Bro 1.045
Youngs-NY 1.023
Wheat-Bro 1.014
Cuyler-Pit .990

Stolen Bases
Carey-Pit 49
Cuyler-Pit 32
Heathcote-Chi 26
Traynor-Pit 24
Smith-StL 24

Stolen Base Average
Carey-Pit 79.0
Cuyler-Pit 74.4
Frisch-NY 71.0
Critz-Cin 63.3
Smith-StL 60.0

Stolen Base Runs
Carey-Pit 6.2
Cuyler-Pit 3.2
Frisch-NY 1.7
Hartnett-Chi 1.5
Freigau-StL 1.1

Fielding Runs
Pinelli-Cin 26.6
Frisch-NY 24.8
Statz-Chi 14.5
Ford-Phi 12.1
Wright-Pit 10.7

Total Player Rating
Hornsby-StL 9.1
Frisch-NY 5.7
Fournier-Bro 4.8
Wheat-Bro 4.4
Youngs-NY 3.5

Wins
Vance-Bro 28
Grimes-Bro 22
Mays-Cin 20
Cooper-Pit 20
Kremer-Pit 18

Win Percentage
Yde-Pit .842
Vance-Bro .824
Bentley-NY .762
Mays-Cin .690
Kremer-Pit .643

Games
Morrison-Pit 41
Kremer-Pit 41
Keen-Chi 40
Sheehan-Cin 39

Complete Games
Vance-Bro 30
Grimes-Bro 30
Cooper-Pit 25
Barnes-Bos 21
Aldridge-Chi 20

Shutouts
Yde-Pit 4
Sothoron-StL 4
Rixey-Cin 4
Kremer-Pit 4
Cooper-Pit 4
Barnes-Bos 4

Saves
May-Cin 6
Ryan-NY 5
Jonnard-NY 5

Innings Pitched
Grimes-Bro 310.2
Vance-Bro 308.1
Cooper-Pit 268.2
Barnes-Bos 267.2
Kremer-Pit 259.1

Fewest Hits/Game
Vance-Bro 6.95
Yde-Pit 7.93
Morrison-Pit 8.07
Doak-StL-Bro 8.14
Rixey-Cin 8.27

Fewest BB/Game
Benton-Cin 1.33
Alexander-Chi 1.33
Cooper-Pit 1.34
Mays-Cin 1.43
Donohue-Cin 1.46

Strikeouts
Vance-Bro 262
Grimes-Bro 135
Luque-Cin 86
Morrison-Pit 85
Kaufmann-Chi 79

Strikeouts/Game
Vance-Bro 7.65
Grimes-Bro 3.91
Nehf-NY 3.77
Luque-Cin 3.53
Kaufmann-Chi 3.41

Ratio
Vance-Bro 9.46
Rixey-Cin 10.12
Benton-Cin 10.73
Doak-StL-Bro 10.87
McQuillan-NY 10.96

Earned Run Average
Vance-Bro 2.16
McQuillan-NY 2.69
Rixey-Cin 2.76
Benton-Cin 2.77
Yde-Pit 2.83

Adjusted ERA
Vance-Bro 173
Rixey-Cin 137
McQuillan-NY 136
Benton-Cin 136
Yde-Pit 136

Opponents' Batting Avg.
Vance-Bro .213
Yde-Pit .244
Morrison-Pit .245
Rixey-Cin .246
Doak-StL-Bro .249

Opponents' On-Base Pct.
Vance-Bro .269
Rixey-Cin .285
Benton-Cin .297
Alexander-Chi .299
Nehf-NY .301

Starter Runs
Vance-Bro 58.4
Rixey-Cin 29.4
McQuillan-NY 24.0
Yde-Pit 22.3
Barnes-NY 20.5

Adjusted Starter Runs
Vance-Bro 56.1
Rixey-Cin 27.4
Yde-Pit 21.9
McQuillan-NY 21.0
Kremer-Pit 18.7

Clutch Pitching Index
Sherdel-StL 117
Sothoron-StL 115
Ring-Phi 113
McQuillan-NY 113
Aldridge-Chi 110

Relief Runs
Jonnard-NY 14.5
May-Cin 9.5
Stone-Pit 6.5

Adjusted Relief Runs
Jonnard-NY 13.2
May-Cin 8.6
Stone-Pit 6.3

Relief Ranking
Jonnard-NY 12.3
May-Cin 5.9
Stone-Pit 5.3

Total Pitcher Index
Vance-Bro 5.9
Mays-Cin 3.5
Rixey-Cin 3.2
Cooper-Pit 2.5
Yde-Pit 2.3

Total Baseball Ranking
Hornsby-StL 9.1
Vance-Bro 5.9
Frisch-NY 5.7
Fournier-Bro 4.8
Wheat-Bro 4.4

TEAM	G	W	L	PCT	GB	R	OR	AB	H	2B	3B	HR	BB	SO	AVG	OBP	SLG	OPS	OPS+	BR	BR+	PF	CHI	RC	SB	CS	SBA	SBR
WAS	156	92	62	.597		755	**613**	5304	1558	255	**88**	22	513	392	.294	.361	.387	748	101	-8	17	97	98	762	116	85	58	-4
NY	153	89	63	.586	2	798	667	5240	1516	248	86	**98**	478	420	.289	.352	**.426**	**778**	106	29	31	100	102	789	69	67	51	-8
DET	156	86	68	.558	6	**849**	796	5389	**1604**	**315**	76	35	**607**	400	**.298**	**.373**	.404	777	**108**	**53**	**67**	98	100	**837**	100	77	56	-5
STL	153	74	78	.487	17	769	807	5236	1543	266	62	67	465	**349**	.295	.356	.408	764	96	10	-35	106	101	762	85	85	50	-11
PHI	152	71	81	.467	20	685	778	5184	1459	251	59	63	374	484	.281	.334	.389	723	90	-77	-83	101	**105**	674	77	68	53	-7
CLE	153	67	86	.438	24.5	755	814	5332	1580	306	59	41	492	371	.296	.361	.399	760	100	9	-1	101	97	784	85	57	**60**	**-1**
BOS	157	67	87	.435	25	735	806	5340	1481	302	63	30	603	417	.277	.356	.374	730	94	-42	-43	100	99	741	78	61	56	-4
CHI	154	66	87	.431	25.5	793	858	5255	1512	254	58	41	604	421	.288	.365	.382	747	101	-6	19	97	103	761	**137**	92	**60**	-2
TOT	617					6139		42280	12253	2197	551	397	4136	3254	.290	.359	.397	755							747	592	56	-43

TEAM	CG	SH	SV	IP	H	H/G	HR	BB	SO	RAT	ERA	ERA+	OAV	OOB	PR	PR+	PF	CPI	FA	E	DP	FW	PW	BW	SBW	DIF
WAS	74	**13**	**25**	1383	**1329**	**8.7**	**34**	505	469	**12.3**	**3.35**	**121**	**.259**	**.330**	**136**	**112**	95	99	.972	171	149	1.4	**10.6**	1.7	.1	1.4
NY	76	**13**	13	1359^{1}	1483	9.9	59	522	**487**	13.5	3.86	108	.284	.353	56	45	98	**107**	**.974**	**156**	131	**2.1**	4.3	3.0	-.2	4.1
DET	60	5	20	1394^{2}	1586	10.3	55	**467**	441	13.6	4.20	98	.293	.354	5	-12	97	101	.971	187	142	.4	-1.1	**6.4**	.0	3.5
STL	66	11	7	1353^{1}	1511	10.1	68	517	386	13.8	4.57	99	.289	.358	-51	-9	107	95	.969	184	142	.4	-.8	-3.3	-.5	2.4
PHI	68	8	10	1345	1527	10.3	43	597	371	14.5	4.39	98	.292	.368	-24	-15	101	101	.971	180	**157**	.5	-1.4	-7.8	-.2	4.0
CLE	**87**	7	7	1349	1603	10.7	43	503	315	14.3	4.40	97	.300	.365	-25	-20	101	101	.967	205	130	-.9	-1.8	-.0	**.4**	-6.9
BOS	73	8	16	1391^{1}	1563	10.2	43	523	414	14.0	4.36	100	.290	.359	-19	2	103	97	.967	210	126	-.9	.2	-4.0	.1	-5.2
CHI	76	1	11	1370^{2}	1635	10.8	52	512	360	14.3	4.75	87	.305	.368	-78	-98	97	98	.963	229	136	-2.3	-9.2	1.8	.3	-.9
TOT	580	66	109	10946^{1}		10.1				13.8	4.23		.290	.359					.970	1522	1113					

Runs
Ruth-NY 143
Cobb-Det 115
Collins-Chi 108
Hooper-Chi 107
Heilmann-Det 107

Hits
Rice-Was 216
Jamieson-Cle 213
Cobb-Det 211
Ruth-NY 200
Goslin-Was 199

Doubles
J.Sewell-Cle 45
Heilmann-Det 45
Wambsganss-Bos 41
Jacobson-StL 41
Meusel-NY 40

Triples
Pipp-NY 19
Goslin-Was 17
Heilmann-Det 16
Rice-Was 14
Jacobson-StL 12

Home Runs
Ruth-NY 46
Hauser-Phi 27
Jacobson-StL 19
Williams-StL 18
Boone-Bos 13

Total Bases
Ruth-NY 391
Jacobson-StL 306
Heilmann-Det 304
Goslin-Was 299
Hauser-Phi 290

Runs Batted In
Goslin-Was 129
Ruth-NY 121
Meusel-NY 120
Hauser-Phi 115

Runs Produced
Ruth-NY 218
Goslin-Was 217
Heilmann-Det 211
J.Sewell-Cle 201
Meusel-NY 201

Bases On Balls
Ruth-NY 142
Rigney-Det 102
Sheely-Chi 95
Collins-Chi 89
Cobb-Det 85

Batting Average
Ruth-NY 378
Jamieson-Cle 359
Falk-Chi 352
Collins-Chi 349
Bassler-Det 346

On-Base Percentage
Ruth-NY 513
Collins-Chi 441
Speaker-Cle 432
Heilmann-Det 428
Sheely-Chi 426

Slugging Average
Ruth-NY 739
Heilmann-Det 533
Williams-StL 533
Jacobson-StL 528
Myatt-Cle 518

On-Base Plus Slugging
Ruth-NY 1252
Heilmann-Det 961
Williams-StL 958
Speaker-Cle 943
Goslin-Was 937

Adjusted OPS
Ruth-NY 221
Heilmann-Det 149
Goslin-Was 145
Speaker-Cle 141
Williams-StL 138

Batter Runs
Ruth-NY 100.8
Heilmann-Det 40.4
Goslin-Was 35.6
Speaker-Cle 32.4
Collins-Chi 30.5

Adjusted Batter Runs
Ruth-NY 101.2
Heilmann-Det 42.5
Goslin-Was 39.4
Collins-Chi 34.2
Speaker-Cle 31.1

Clutch Hitting Index
Sheely-Chi 149
Kamm-Chi 138
Pratt-Det 138
Rigney-Det 136
Veach-Bos 131

Runs Created
Ruth-NY 205
Heilmann-Det 134
Goslin-Was 125
Cobb-Det 121
Collins-Chi 119

Total Average
Ruth-NY 1.558
Heilmann-Det 1.042
Williams-StL 1.039
Speaker-Cle 988
Collins-Chi 976

Stolen Bases
Collins-Chi 42
Meusel-NY 26
Rice-Was 24
Cobb-Det 23
Jamieson-Cle 21

Stolen Base Average
Collins-Chi 71.2
Harris-Was 66.7
Meusel-NY 65.0
Rice-Was 64.9
Williams-StL 64.5

Stolen Base Runs
Collins-Chi 3.3
Manush-Det 1.3
Burns-Cle 1.3
Heilmann-Det 1.1

Fielding Runs
J.Sewell-Cle 21.4
Lutzke-Cle 19.4
Dykes-Phi 15.9
Jacobson-StL 15.8
Wambsganss-Bos . . . 14.4

Total Player Rating
Ruth-NY 8.6
J.Sewell-Cle 4.3
Heilmann-Det 3.8
Rigney-Det 3.6
Collins-Chi 3.2

Wins
Johnson-Was 23
Pennock-NY 21
Thurston-Chi 20
Shaute-Cle 20
Ehmke-Bos 19

Win Percentage
Johnson-Was 767
Pennock-NY 700
Whitehill-Det 654
Zachary-Was 625

Games
Marberry-Was 50
Holloway-Det 49
Shaute-Cle 46
Hoyt-NY 46
Ehmke-Bos 45

Complete Games
Thurston-Chi 28
Ehmke-Bos 26
Pennock-NY 25
Shaute-Cle 21
Rommel-Phi 21

Shutouts
Johnson-Was 6
Davis-StL 5
Shocker-StL 4
Pennock-NY 4
Ehmke-Bos 4

Saves
Marberry-Was 15
Russell-Was 8
Quinn-Bos 7
Dauss-Det 6
Connally-Chi 6

Innings Pitched
Ehmke-Bos 315.0
Thurston-Chi 291.0
Pennock-NY 286.1
Shaute-Cle 283.0
Rommel-Phi 278.0

Fewest Hits/Game
Johnson-Was 7.55
Collins-Det 8.29
Marberry-Was 8.75
Zachary-Was 8.79
Wingard-StL 8.88

Fewest BB/Game
Smith-Cle 1.53
Thurston-Chi 1.86
Shocker-StL 1.90
Pennock-NY 2.01
Quinn-Bos 2.05

Strikeouts
Johnson-Was 158
Ehmke-Bos 119
Shawkey-NY 114
Pennock-NY 101
Shocker-StL 88

Strikeouts/Game
Johnson-Was 5.12
Shawkey-NY 4.94
Ehmke-Bos 3.40
Shocker-StL 3.22
Pennock-NY 3.17

Ratio
Johnson-Was 10.37
Collins-Det 11.08
Zachary-Was 11.28
Smith-Cle 11.48
Pennock-NY 11.54

Earned Run Average
Johnson-Was 2.72
Zachary-Was 2.75
Pennock-NY 2.83
Baumgartner-Phi . . . 2.88
Smith-Cle 3.02

Adjusted ERA
Baumgartner-Phi . . . 149
Johnson-Was 148
Pennock-NY 147
Zachary-Was 147
Smith-Cle 142

Opponents' Batting Avg.
Johnson-Was 224
Collins-Det 249
Marberry-Was 262
Wingard-StL 262
Davis-StL 263

Opponents' On-Base Pct.
Johnson-Was 284
Collins-Det 307
Smith-Cle 312
Pennock-NY 314
Zachary-Was 315

Starter Runs
Johnson-Was 46.5
Pennock-NY 44.6
Smith-Cle 33.4
Zachary-Was 33.2
Baumgartner-Phi . . . 27.1

Adjusted Starter Runs
Pennock-NY 43.0
Johnson-Was 42.4
Smith-Cle 34.2
Ehmke-Bos 30.9
Zachary-Was 30.2

Clutch Pitching Index
Baumgartner-Phi . . . 132
Pennock-NY 117
Zachary-Was 113
Ferguson-Bos 113
Hoyt-NY 112

Relief Runs
Speece-Was 9.5

Adjusted Relief Runs
Speece-Was 8.8

Relief Ranking
Speece-Was 4.4

Total Pitcher Index
Johnson-Was 4.7
Pennock-NY 3.8
Zachary-Was 3.8
Bush-NY 3.5
Smith-Cle 3.4

Total Baseball Ranking
Ruth-NY 8.6
Johnson-Was 4.7
J.Sewell-Cle 4.3
Pennock-NY 3.8
Zachary-Was 3.8

TEAM	G	W	L	PCT	GB	R	OR	AB	H	2B	3B	HR	BB	SO	AVG	OBP	SLG	OPS	OPS+	BR	BR+	PF	CHI	RC	SB	CS	SBA	SBR
PIT	153	95	58	.621		**912**	715	5372	**1651**	**316**	**105**	78	**499**	363	**.307**	**.369**	**.449**	**818**	**108**	**116**	**59**	107	101	**909**	**159**	63	**72**	**13**
NY	152	86	66	.566	8.5	736	702	5327	1507	239	61	**114**	411	494	.283	.337	.415	752	101	-26	5	96	100	742	79	65	55	-5
CIN	153	80	73	.523	15	690	**643**	5233	1490	221	90	44	409	**327**	.285	.339	.387	726	93	-66	-49	98	100	680	108	107	50	-14
STL	153	77	76	.503	18	828	764	5329	1592	292	80	109	446	414	.299	.356	.445	801	**108**	72	53	102	98	846	70	51	58	-2
BOS	153	70	83	.458	25	708	802	5365	1567	260	70	41	405	380	.292	.345	.390	735	102	-48	22	91	98	722	77	72	52	-8
PHI	153	68	85	.444	27	812	930	5412	1598	288	58	100	456	542	.295	.354	.425	779	96	35	-31	109	99	814	48	59	45	-10
BRO	153	68	85	.444	27	786	866	5468	1617	250	80	64	437	383	.296	.351	.406	757	102	-6	16	97	101	787	37	30	55	-2
CHI	154	68	86	.442	27.5	723	773	5353	1473	254	70	86	397	470	.275	.329	.397	726	89	-77	-87	102	**104**	700	94	70	57	-4
TOT	612					6195		42859	12495	2120	614	636	3460	3373	.292	.348	.415	762							672	517	57	-33

TEAM	CG	SH	SV	IP	H	H/G	HR	BB	SO	RAT	ERA	ERA+	OAV	OOB	PR	PR+	PF	CPI	FA	E	DP	FW	PW	BW	SBW	DIF
PIT	77	2	**13**	1354^{2}	1526	10.2	81	387	386	13.0	3.88	115	.287	.339	59	84	105	**105**	.964	224	**171**	-.8	7.9	**5.6**	**1.6**	4.5
NY	80	6	8	1354	1532	10.2	73	408	446	13.1	3.95	102	.289	.342	49	18	95	104	.968	199	129	.5	1.7	.5	-.0	7.5
CIN	**92**	**11**	12	1375^{1}	**1447**	**9.5**	**35**	**324**	437	**11.9**	**3.39**	**121**	**.272**	**.317**	**135**	**115**	96	95	.968	203	161	.4	**10.8**	-4.5	-.9	-2.0
STL	82	8	7	1335^{2}	1480	10.0	86	470	428	13.5	4.36	99	.283	.347	-14	-7	101	96	.966	204	156	.3	-.6	5.0	.2	-4.2
BOS	77	5	4	1366^{2}	1567	10.4	67	458	351	13.5	4.40	91	.291	.348	-19	-62	94	96	.964	221	145	-.7	-5.8	2.1	-.4	-1.6
PHI	69	8	9	1350^{2}	1753	11.7	117	444	371	14.8	5.03	95	.315	.368	-114	-34	112	103	.966	211	147	-.0	-3.1	-2.9	-.5	-1.7
BRO	82	4	4	1350^{2}	1608	10.8	75	477	**518**	14.2	4.78	88	.301	.362	-76	-92	98	97	.966	210	130	-.0	-8.6	1.5	.2	-1.5
CHI	75	5	10	1370	1575	10.4	102	485	435	13.8	4.41	98	.292	.353	-21	-13	101	102	**.969**	**198**	161	**.8**	-1.2	-8.1	.0	-.3
TOT	634	49	67	10857^{2}		10.4				13.5	4.27		.292	.348					.967	1670	1200					

Runs
Cuyler-Pit 144
Hornsby-StL 133
Wheat-Bro 125
Traynor-Pit 114
Blades-StL 112

Hits
Bottomley-StL 227
Wheat-Bro 221
Cuyler-Pit 220
Hornsby-StL 203
Stock-Bro 202

Doubles
Bottomley-StL 44
Cuyler-Pit 43
Wheat-Bro 42
Hornsby-StL 41
Burrus-Bos 41

Triples
Cuyler-Pit 26
Walker-Cin 16
Roush-Cin 16
Fournier-Bro 16

Home Runs
Hornsby-StL 39
Hartnett-Chi 24
Fournier-Bro 22
Meusel-NY 21
Bottomley-StL 21

Total Bases
Hornsby-StL 381
Cuyler-Pit 369
Bottomley-StL 358
Wheat-Bro 333
Fournier-Bro 310

Runs Batted In
Hornsby-StL 143
Fournier-Bro 130
Bottomley-StL 128
Wright-Pit 121
Barnhart-Pit 114

Runs Produced
Hornsby-StL 237
Cuyler-Pit 228
Wheat-Bro 214
Traynor-Pit 214
Fournier-Bro 207

Bases On Balls
Fournier-Bro 86
Hornsby-StL 83
Moore-Pit 73
Youngs-NY 66
Carey-Pit 66

Batting Average
Hornsby-StL .403
Bottomley-StL .367
Wheat-Bro .359
Cuyler-Pit .357
Fournier-Bro .350

On-Base Percentage
Hornsby-StL .489
Fournier-Bro .446
Blades-StL .423
Cuyler-Pit .423
Carey-Pit .418

Slugging Average
Hornsby-StL .756
Cuyler-Pit .598
Wrightstone-Phi .591
Bottomley-StL .578
Fournier-Bro .569

On-Base Plus Slugging
Hornsby-StL 1245
Cuyler-Pit 1021
Fournier-Bro 1015
Bottomley-StL 992
Blades-StL 958

Adjusted OPS
Hornsby-StL 208
Fournier-Bro 162
Cuyler-Pit 148
Bottomley-StL 147
Wheat-Bro 143

Batter Runs
Hornsby-StL 87.1
Cuyler-Pit 53.1
Fournier-Bro 50.1
Bottomley-StL 45.5
Wheat-Bro 35.0

Adjusted Batter Runs
Hornsby-StL 83.4
Fournier-Bro 53.9
Cuyler-Pit 43.9
Bottomley-StL 42.5
Wheat-Bro 38.4

Clutch Hitting Index
Barnhart-Pit 146
Traynor-Pit 117
Felix-Bos 115
E.Brown-Bro 114
Moore-Pit 112

Runs Created
Hornsby-StL 187
Cuyler-Pit 158
Bottomley-StL 145
Fournier-Bro 141
Wheat-Bro 134

Total Average
Hornsby-StL 1.539
Cuyler-Pit 1.141
Fournier-Bro 1.117
Bottomley-StL 1.025
Carey-Pit 1.011

Stolen Bases
Carey-Pit 46
Cuyler-Pit 41
Adams-Chi 26
Roush-Cin 22
Frisch-NY 21

Stolen Base Average
Smith-StL 90.9
Carey-Pit 80.7
Cuyler-Pit 75.9
Moore-Pit 73.1
Adams-Chi 68.4

Stolen Base Runs
Carey-Pit 6.3
Cuyler-Pit 4.5
Smith-StL 3.7
Moore-Pit 1.7
Grantham-Pit 1.7

Fielding Runs
Adams-Chi 28.1
Traynor-Pit 22.9
Critz-Cin 21.6
Pinelli-Cin 20.8
Kelly-NY 16.2

Total Player Rating
Hornsby-StL 6.2
Fournier-Bro 4.2
Cuyler-Pit 4.0
Bancroft-Bos 3.9
Traynor-Pit 3.6

Wins
Vance-Bro 22
Rixey-Cin 21
Donohue-Cin 21
Meadows-Pit 19

Win Percentage
Sherdel-StL .714
Vance-Bro .710
Aldridge-Pit .682
Kremer-Pit .680
Rixey-Cin .656

Games
Morrison-Pit 44
Donohue-Cin 42
Bush-Chi 42
Osborne-Bro 41
Kremer-Pit 40

Complete Games
Donohue-Cin 27
Vance-Bro 26
Rixey-Cin 22
Luque-Cin 22
Ring-Phi 21

Shutouts
Vance-Bro 4
Luque-Cin 4
Carlson-Phi 4
Donohue-Cin 3

Saves
Morrison-Pit 4
Bush-Chi 4

Innings Pitched
Donohue-Cin 301.0
Luque-Cin 291.0
Rixey-Cin 287.1
Ring-Phi 270.0
Vance-Bro 265.1

Fewest Hits/Game
Luque-Cin 8.13
Benton-Bos 8.35
Vance-Bro 8.38
Aldridge-Pit 9.20
Donohue-Cin 9.27

Fewest BB/Game
Alexander-Chi 1.11
Donohue-Cin 1.47
Rixey-Cin 1.47
Cooney-Bos 1.83
Sherdel-StL 1.89

Strikeouts
Vance-Bro 221
Luque-Cin 140
Ring-Phi 93
Blake-Chi 93
Aldridge-Pit 88

Strikeouts/Game
Vance-Bro 7.50
Luque-Cin 4.33
Sothoron-StL 3.87
Bush-Chi 3.76
Aldridge-Pit 3.71

Ratio
Luque-Cin 10.61
Donohue-Cin 10.79
Vance-Bro 10.96
Rixey-Cin 11.15
Alexander-Chi 11.52

Earned Run Average
Luque-Cin 2.63
Rixey-Cin 2.88
Reinhart-StL 3.05
Donohue-Cin 3.08
Benton-Bos 3.09

Adjusted ERA
Luque-Cin 156
Rixey-Cin 143
Sherdel-StL 139
Donohue-Cin 133
Benton-Bos 130

Opponents' Batting Avg.
Luque-Cin .239
Benton-Bos .249
Vance-Bro .250
Donohue-Cin .268
Scott-NY .269

Opponents' On-Base Pct.
Luque-Cin .291
Donohue-Cin .299
Vance-Bro .304
Rixey-Cin .307
Cooney-Bos .312

Starter Runs
Luque-Cin 53.0
Rixey-Cin 44.2
Donohue-Cin 39.7
Scott-NY 29.6
Sherdel-StL 25.8

Adjusted Starter Runs
Luque-Cin 49.7
Rixey-Cin 40.7
Donohue-Cin 35.8
Sherdel-StL 26.6
Scott-NY 24.8

Clutch Pitching Index
Nehf-NY 122
Yde-Pit 117
Sherdel-StL 109
Rixey-Cin 108
Morrison-Pit 107

Relief Runs
Huntzinger-NY 5.5

Adjusted Relief Runs
Huntzinger-NY 4.1

Relief Ranking
Huntzinger-NY 3.4

Total Pitcher Index
Luque-Cin 6.3
Donohue-Cin 4.2
Rixey-Cin 3.8
Scott-NY 3.5
Sherdel-StL 2.6

Total Baseball Ranking
Luque-Cin 6.3
Hornsby-StL 6.2
Fournier-Bro 4.2
Donohue-Cin 4.2
Cuyler-Pit 4.0

TEAM	G	W	L	PCT	GB	R	OR	AB	H	2B	3B	HR	BB	SO	AVG	OBP	SLG	OPS	OPS+	BR	BR+	PF	CHI	RC	SB	CS	SBA	SBR
WAS	152	96	55	.636		829	**670**	5206	1577	251	71	56	533	427	.303	.373	.411	784	106	39	56	98	100	815	**135**	92	59	-2
PHI	153	88	64	.579	8.5	831	713	5399	**1659**	298	79	76	453	432	**.307**	.364	.434	798	101	54	1	107	97	856	67	60	53	-6
STL	154	82	71	.536	15	900	906	5440	1620	**304**	68	**110**	498	**375**	.298	.360	**.439**	**799**	103	52	10	105	**105**	859	85	78	52	-9
DET	156	81	73	.526	16.5	**903**	829	5371	1621	277	**84**	50	640	386	.302	**.379**	.413	792	**109**	**63**	**77**	99	102	**872**	97	63	**61**	**-1**
CHI	154	79	75	.513	18.5	811	770	5224	1482	299	59	38	**662**	405	.284	.370	.385	755	102	-7	38	95	101	782	131	87	60	-2
CLE	155	70	84	.455	27.5	782	817	5436	1613	285	58	52	520	379	.297	.361	.399	760	97	-12	-18	101	98	795	90	77	54	-7
NY	156	69	85	.448	28.5	706	774	5353	1471	247	74	**110**	470	482	.275	.336	.410	746	96	-61	-48	98	97	739	69	73	49	-10
BOS	152	47	105	.309	49.5	639	922	5166	1375	257	64	41	513	422	.266	.336	.364	700	83	-131	-130	100	100	647	42	56	43	-10
TOT	616					6401		42595	12418	2218	557	533	4289	3308	.292	.361	.408	768							716	586	55	-48

TEAM	CG	SH	SV	IP	H	H/G	HR	BB	SO	RAT	ERA	ERA+	OAV	OOB	PR	PR+	PF	CPI	FA	E	DP	FW	PW	BW	SBW	DIF
WAS	69	10	**21**	1358^1	**1434**	**9.6**	49	543	463	**13.4**	**3.70**	114	.278	.351	**105**	82	96	**107**	.972	170	**166**	1.8	7.6	5.2	.4	5.6
PHI	61	8	18	1381^2	1468	**9.6**	60	544	**495**	**13.4**	3.87	**120**	**.276**	**.347**	81	**113**	106	101	.966	211	148	-.5	**10.5**	.1	.0	2.1
STL	67	7	10	1379^2	1588	10.4	99	675	419	15.0	4.92	95	.298	.380	-80	-37	106	102	.964	226	164	-1.3	-3.4	1.0	-.3	9.7
DET	66	2	18	1383^2	1582	10.3	70	556	419	14.2	4.61	94	.296	.366	-32	-47	98	99	.972	173	143	2.0	-4.3	**7.2**	**.5**	-1.1
CHI	71	**12**	13	1385^2	1579	10.3	69	**489**	374	13.6	4.29	97	.295	.356	17	-23	95	102	.968	200	162	.2	-2.1	3.6	.4	.1
CLE	**93**	6	9	1372^1	1604	10.6	**41**	493	345	14.1	4.50	98	.296	.359	-15	-9	101	95	.967	210	146	-.3	-.8	-1.6	-.0	-4.0
NY	80	8	13	1387^2	1560	10.2	78	505	492	13.6	4.34	98	.289	.353	10	-11	97	99	**.974**	**160**	150	**2.7**	-1.0	-4.4	-.4	-4.8
BOS	68	6	6	1326^2	1615	11.0	67	510	310	14.7	4.97	92	.308	.374	-84	-60	103	98	.957	271	150	-4.2	-5.5	-12.0	-.4	-6.8
TOT	575	59	108	10975^2		10.2				14.0	4.40		.292	.361					.968	1621	1229					

Runs
Mostil-Chi 135
Simmons-Phi 122
Combs-NY 117
Goslin-Was 116
Rice-Was 111

Hits
Simmons-Phi 253
Rice-Was 227
Heilmann-Det 225
Sisler-StL 224
J.Sewell-Cle 204

Doubles
McManus-StL 44
Simmons-Phi 43
Sheely-Chi 43
Burns-Cle 41

Triples
Goslin-Was 20
Mostil-Chi 16
Sisler-StL 15

Home Runs
Meusel-NY 33
Williams-StL 25
Ruth-NY 25
Simmons-Phi 24
Gehrig-NY 20

Total Bases
Simmons-Phi 392
Meusel-NY 338
Goslin-Was 329
Heilmann-Det 326
Sisler-StL 311

Runs Batted In
Meusel-NY 138
Heilmann-Det 134
Simmons-Phi 129
Goslin-Was 113
Sheely-Chi 111

Runs Produced
Simmons-Phi 227
Heilmann-Det 218
Goslin-Was 211
Meusel-NY 206
Rice-Was 197

Bases On Balls
Mostil-Chi 90
Kamm-Chi 90
Collins-Chi 87
Bishop-Phi 87
Blue-Det 83

Batting Average
Heilmann-Det .393
Speaker-Cle .389
Simmons-Phi .387
Cobb-Det .378
Wingo-Det .370

On-Base Percentage
Speaker-Cle .479
Cobb-Det .468
Collins-Chi .461
Heilmann-Det .457
Wingo-Det .456

Slugging Average
Williams-StL .613
Simmons-Phi .599
Cobb-Det .598
Speaker-Cle .578
Heilmann-Det .569

On-Base Plus Slugging
Cobb-Det 1066
Speaker-Cle 1057
Heilmann-Det 1026
Simmons-Phi 1018
Wingo-Det 983

Adjusted OPS
Cobb-Det 171
Speaker-Cle 166
Heilmann-Det 161
Wingo-Det 151
Simmons-Phi 146

Batter Runs
Heilmann-Det 52.5
Simmons-Phi 51.4
Speaker-Cle 47.0
Cobb-Det 45.3
Wingo-Det 35.3

Adjusted Batter Runs
Heilmann-Det 54.6
Cobb-Det 47.0
Speaker-Cle 46.1
Simmons-Phi 42.5
Wingo-Det 36.9

Clutch Hitting Index
Galloway-Phi 149
Blue-Det 136
Sheely-Chi 127
Collins-Chi 123
B.Harris-Was 120

Runs Created
Simmons-Phi 155
Heilmann-Det 149
Goslin-Was 131
Speaker-Cle 123
Cobb-Det 118

Total Average
Speaker-Cle 1.231
Cobb-Det 1.206
Heilmann-Det 1.113
Wingo-Det 1.041
Collins-Chi 1.028

Stolen Bases
Mostil-Chi 43
Goslin-Was 27
Rice-Was 26

Stolen Base Average
Blue-Det 79.2
Goslin-Was 77.1
Collins-Chi 76.0
Rice-Was 70.3
Mostil-Chi 68.3

Stolen Base Runs
Goslin-Was 3.1
Mostil-Chi 2.5
Blue-Det 2.4
Collins-Chi 2.1
Haney-Det 2.1

Fielding Runs
Flagstead-Bos 19.9
J.Sewell-Cle 16.3
O'Rourke-Det 14.6
Goslin-Was 13.6
Ruel-Was 11.6

Total Player Rating
Speaker-Cle 4.7
J.Sewell-Cle 3.9
Cobb-Det 3.6
Heilmann-Det 3.6
Goslin-Was 3.6

Wins
Rommel-Phi 21
Lyons-Chi 21
Johnson-Was 20
Coveleski-Was 20
Harriss-Phi 19

Win Percentage
Coveleski-Was .800
Johnson-Was .741
Ruether-Was .720
Blankenship-Chi .680
Rommel-Phi .677

Games
Marberry-Was 55
Walberg-Phi 53
Vangilder-StL 52
Rommel-Phi 52
Pennock-NY 47

Complete Games
Smith-Cle 22
Ehmke-Bos 22
Pennock-NY 21
Lyons-Chi 19
Wingfield-Bos 18

Shutouts
Lyons-Chi 5
Gray-Phi 4
Giard-StL 4

Saves
Marberry-Was 15
Doyle-Det 8
Connally-Chi 8
Walberg-Phi 7

Innings Pitched
Pennock-NY 277.0
Lyons-Chi 262.2
Rommel-Phi 261.0
Ehmke-Bos 260.2
Wingfield-Bos 254.1

Fewest Hits/Game
Blankenship-Chi 8.46
Johnson-Was 8.53
Coveleski-Was 8.59
Pennock-NY 8.68
Gray-Phi 8.79

Fewest BB/Game
Smith-Cle 1.82
Quinn-Bos-Phi 1.85
Shocker-NY 2.14
Faber-Chi 2.23
Pennock-NY 2.31

Strikeouts
Grove-Phi 116
Johnson-Was 108
Harriss-Phi 95
Ehmke-Bos 95
Jones-NY 92

Strikeouts/Game
Grove-Phi 5.30
Johnson-Was 4.24
Shawkey-NY 3.92
Walberg-Phi 3.85
Gray-Phi 3.54

Ratio
Pennock-NY 11.05
Blankenship-Chi 11.13
Coveleski-Was 11.39
Gray-Phi 11.71
Johnson-Was 11.87

Earned Run Average
Coveleski-Was 2.84
Pennock-NY 2.96
Blankenship-Chi 3.03
Johnson-Was 3.07
Dauss-Det 3.16

Adjusted ERA
Coveleski-Was 149
Pennock-NY 144
Gray-Phi 142
Johnson-Was 138
Blankenship-Chi 137

Opponents' Batting Avg.
Johnson-Was .250
Blankenship-Chi .253
Pennock-NY .254
Coveleski-Was .255
Gray-Phi .260

Opponents' On-Base Pct.
Pennock-NY .303
Blankenship-Chi .308
Coveleski-Was .312
Johnson-Was .317
Gray-Phi .319

Starter Runs
Pennock-NY 44.2
Coveleski-Was 41.7
Blankenship-Chi 35.3
Johnson-Was 33.8
Lyons-Chi 33.3

Adjusted Starter Runs
Pennock-NY 41.4
Coveleski-Was 38.7
Harriss-Phi 30.7
Blankenship-Chi 30.7
Johnson-Was 30.7

Clutch Pitching Index
Dauss-Det 119
Shocker-NY 114
Zachary-Was 113
Lyons-Chi 111
Shawkey-NY 110

Relief Runs
Marberry-Was 9.6
Gregg-Was 2.3

Adjusted Relief Runs
Marberry-Was 8.1
Gregg-Was 1.0

Relief Ranking
Marberry-Was 13.9
Gregg-Was .5

Total Pitcher Index
Johnson-Was 4.5
Pennock-NY 3.8
Harriss-Phi 3.4
Rommel-Phi 3.1
Dauss-Det 3.1

Total Baseball Ranking
Speaker-Cle 4.7
Johnson-Was 4.5
J.Sewell-Cle 3.9
Pennock-NY 3.8
Cobb-Det 3.7

TEAM	G	W	L	PCT	GB	R	OR	AB	H	2B	3B	HR	BB	SO	AVG	OBP	SLG	OPS	OPS+	BR	BR+	PF	CHI	RC	SB	CS	SBA	SBR
STL	156	89	65	.578		**817**	678	5381	**1541**	259	82	**90**	**478**	518	.286	.348	**.415**	**763**	107	**76**	47	104	102	**770**	83			
CIN	157	87	67	.565	2	747	651	5320	**1541**	242	**120**	35	454	**333**	**.290**	**.349**	.400	749	**110**	52	**73**	97	97	738	51			
PIT	157	84	69	.549	4.5	769	689	5312	1514	243	106	44	434	350	.285	.343	.396	739	99	28	-9	105	**104**	713	91			
CHI	155	82	72	.532	7	682	**602**	5229	1453	**291**	49	66	445	447	.278	.338	.390	728	100	7	-1	101	96	685	85			
NY	151	74	77	.490	13.5	663	668	5167	1435	214	58	73	339	420	.278	.325	.384	709	97	-36	-28	99	**104**	631	**94**			
BRO	155	71	82	.464	17.5	623	705	5130	1348	246	62	40	475	464	.263	.328	.358	686	91	-65	-56	99	100	607	76			
BOS	153	66	86	.434	22	624	719	5216	1444	209	62	16	426	348	.277	.335	.350	685	99	-66	-4	91	99	612	81			
PHI	152	58	93	.384	29.5	687	900	5254	1479	244	50	75	422	479	.281	.337	.390	727	96	5	-29	105	98	683	47			
TOT	618					5612		42009	11755	1948	589	439	3473	3359	.280	.339	.386	724							608			

TEAM	CG	SH	SV	IP	H	H/G	HR	BB	SO	RAT	ERA	ERA+	OAV	OOB	PR	PR+	PF	CPI	FA	E	DP	FW	PW	BW	SBW	DIF
STL	**90**	10	6	1398[2]	1423	**9.2**	76	397	365	11.9	3.67	106	**.269**	.322	24	35	102	96	.969	198	141	.4	3.5	4.7		3.6
CIN	88	**14**	8	1408[2]	1449	9.3	40	**324**	424	**11.6**	3.42	108	.271	**.316**	64	44	97	95	.972	183	160	1.3	4.4	**7.3**		-2.8
PIT	83	12	**18**	1379[1]	1422	9.3	50	455	387	12.5	3.67	107	.272	.334	24	41	103	99	.965	220	161	-.8	4.1	-.8		5.3
CHI	77	13	14	1378[1]	1407	**9.2**	**39**	486	508	12.6	**3.26**	**118**	.273	.340	**87**	**89**	101	**113**	**.974**	**162**	**174**	**2.4**	**8.8**	-.0		-6.0
NY	61	4	15	1341[2]	**1370**	**9.2**	70	427	419	12.2	3.77	100	**.269**	.328	8	-3	98	96	.970	186	150	.7	-.2	-2.7		1.0
BRO	83	5	9	1361[2]	1440	9.6	50	472	**517**	12.8	3.83	100	.276	.339	1	0	100	98	.963	229	95	-1.5	.0	-5.5		1.6
BOS	60	9	9	1365[1]	1536	10.2	46	455	408	13.4	4.01	88	.294	.354	-28	-76	93	105	.967	208	150	-.4	-7.5	-.3		-1.6
PHI	68	5	5	1334[1]	1699	11.5	68	454	331	14.7	5.04	82	.315	.371	-179	-123	108	98	.964	224	153	-1.4	-12.1	-2.8		-.9
TOT	610	72	84	10968		9.7				12.7	3.83		.280	.339					.968	1610	1184					

Runs
Cuyler-Pit 113
Waner-Pit 101
Southworth-NY-StL 99
Sand-Phi 99

Hits
Brown-Bos 201
Cuyler-Pit 197
Adams-Chi 193
L.Bell-StL 189

Doubles
Bottomley-StL 40
Roush-Cin 37
Wilson-Chi 36

Triples
Waner-Pit 22
Walker-Cin 20
Traynor-Pit 17

Home Runs
Wilson-Chi 21
Bottomley-StL 19
Williams-Phi 18
L.Bell-StL 17
Southworth-NY-StL 16

Total Bases
Bottomley-StL 305
L.Bell-StL 301
Wilson-Chi 285
Waner-Pit 283
Cuyler-Pit 282

Runs Batted In
Bottomley-StL 120
Wilson-Chi 109
L.Bell-StL 100
Southworth-NY-StL 99
Pipp-Cin 99

Runs Produced
Bottomley-StL 199
Cuyler-Pit 197
Wilson-Chi 185
Southworth-NY-StL 182
Hornsby-StL 178

Bases On Balls
Wilson-Chi 69
Waner-Pit 66
Sand-Phi 66
Bancroft-Bos 64
Blades-StL 62

Batting Average
Hargrave-Cin .353
Christensen-Cin .350
Smith-Pit .346
Williams-Phi .345
Waner-Pit .336

On-Base Percentage
Waner-Pit .413
Blades-StL .409
Wilson-Chi .406
Grantham-Pit .400
Bancroft-Bos .399

Slugging Average
Williams-Phi .568
Wilson-Chi .539
Waner-Pit .528
Hargrave-Cin .525
L.Bell-StL .518

On-Base Plus Slugging
Wilson-Chi 944
Waner-Pit 941
L.Bell-StL 901
Grantham-Pit 890
Herman-Bro 875

Adjusted OPS
Wilson-Chi 150
Waner-Pit 144
Herman-Bro 136
L.Bell-StL 135
Grantham-Pit 131

Batter Runs
Waner-Pit 39.5
Wilson-Chi 39.2
L.Bell-StL 31.6
Williams-Phi 29.8
Bottomley-StL 25.2

Adjusted Batter Runs
Wilson-Chi 37.9
Waner-Pit 33.8
L.Bell-StL 27.5
Williams-Phi 26.1
Herman-Bro 23.7

Clutch Hitting Index
Butler-Bro 125
Pipp-Cin 122
Hornsby-StL 116
Thevenow-StL 116
Burrus-Bos 116

Runs Created
Waner-Pit 115
Wilson-Chi 115
L.Bell-StL 112
Bottomley-StL 109
Cuyler-Pit 105

Total Average
Wilson-Chi 1.031
Waner-Pit 1.022
Grantham-Pit .938
Blades-StL .938
L.Bell-StL .929

Stolen Bases
Cuyler-Pit 35
Adams-Chi 27
Frisch-NY 23
Douthit-StL 23
Youngs-NY 21

Stolen Base Average

Stolen Base Runs

Fielding Runs
Critz-Cin 24.0
Friberg-Phi 22.4
Cooney-Chi 19.4
Thevenow-StL 18.4
Douthit-StL 17.8

Total Player Rating
Wilson-Chi 3.3
Waner-Pit 3.0
Bancroft-Bos 2.8
O'Farrell-StL 2.7
Jackson-NY 2.6

Wins
Rhem-StL 20
Meadows-Pit 20
Kremer-Pit 20
Donohue-Cin 20
Mays-Cin 19

Win Percentage
Kremer-Pit .769
Rhem-StL .741
Meadows-Pit .690
Mays-Cin .613
Donohue-Cin .588

Games
Scott-NY 50
Willoughby-Phi 47
Donohue-Cin 47
Ulrich-Phi 45
May-Cin 45

Complete Games
Mays-Cin 24
Petty-Bro 23
Root-Chi 21
Rhem-StL 20
Carlson-Phi 20

Shutouts
Donohue-Cin 5
B.Smith-Bos 4
Blake-Chi 4

Saves
Davies-NY 6
Scott-NY 5
Kremer-Pit 5
Ehrhardt-Bro 4

Innings Pitched
Donohue-Cin 285.2
Mays-Cin 281.0
Petty-Bro 275.2
Root-Chi 271.1
Carlson-Phi 267.1

Fewest Hits/Game
Petty-Bro 8.03
Greenfield-NY 8.33
Rhem-StL 8.41
Jones-Chi 8.48
Bush-Chi 8.52

Fewest BB/Game
Donohue-Cin 1.23
Alexander-Chi-StL 1.39
Carlson-Phi 1.58
Mays-Cin 1.70
Lucas-Cin 1.75

Strikeouts
Vance-Bro 140
Root-Chi 127
May-Cin 103
Benton-Bos 103
Petty-Bro 101

Strikeouts/Game
Vance-Bro 7.46
May-Cin 5.53
Jones-Chi 4.49
Blake-Chi 4.33
Root-Chi 4.21

Ratio
Alexander-Chi-StL 10.06
Petty-Bro 10.71
Kremer-Pit 10.74
Donohue-Cin 10.90
Mays-Cin 10.99

Earned Run Average
Kremer-Pit 2.61
Root-Chi 2.82
Petty-Bro 2.84
Bush-Chi 2.86
Barnes-NY 2.87

Adjusted ERA
Kremer-Pit 151
Root-Chi 136
Petty-Bro 134
Bush-Chi 134
Barnes-NY 131

Opponents' Batting Avg.
Petty-Bro .240
Alexander-Chi-StL .250
Rhem-StL .250
Greenfield-NY .251
Kremer-Pit .252

Opponents' On-Base Pct.
Alexander-Chi-StL .281
Petty-Bro .296
Kremer-Pit .296
Donohue-Cin .298
Rhem-StL .305

Starter Runs
Kremer-Pit 31.3
Root-Chi 30.3
Petty-Bro 30.1
Fitzsimmons-NY 23.0
Mays-Cin 21.4

Adjusted Starter Runs
Kremer-Pit 33.2
Root-Chi 30.7
Petty-Bro 30.0
Carlson-Phi 24.9
Fitzsimmons-NY 21.7

Clutch Pitching Index
Jones-Chi 122
Blake-Chi 119
Fitzsimmons-NY 118
Werts-Bos 117
Root-Chi 111

Relief Runs
Hallahan-StL 1.1

Adjusted Relief Runs
Hallahan-StL 1.5

Relief Ranking
Hallahan-StL 1.2

Total Pitcher Index
Kremer-Pit 3.6
Root-Chi 3.2
Mays-Cin 3.1
Petty-Bro 2.7
Carlson-Phi 2.4

Total Baseball Ranking
Kremer-Pit 3.6
Wilson-Chi 3.3
Root-Chi 3.2
Mays-Cin 3.1
Waner-Pit 3.0

TEAM	G	W	L	PCT	GB	R	OR	AB	H	2B	3B	HR	BB	SO	AVG	OBP	SLG	OPS	OPS+	BR	BR+	PF	CHI	RC	SB	CS	SBA	SBR
NY	155	91	63	.591		**847**	713	5221	1508	262	75	**121**	**642**	580	.289	**.369**	**.437**	**806**	**119**	**123**	**137**	98	98	**866**	79	62	56	-4
CLE	154	88	66	.571	3	738	612	5293	1529	**333**	49	27	455	**332**	.289	.349	.386	735	97	-17	-23	101	**103**	735	88	42	**68**	**5**
PHI	150	83	67	.553	6	677	**570**	5046	1359	259	65	61	523	452	.269	.341	.383	724	90	-39	-75	106	101	682	56	45	55	-3
WAS	152	81	69	.540	8	802	761	5223	1525	244	**97**	43	555	369	**.292**	.364	.401	765	109	48	68	98	**103**	779	117	91	56	-6
CHI	155	81	72	.529	9.5	730	665	5220	1508	314	60	32	556	381	.289	.361	.390	751	106	24	52	96	96	761	**123**	78	61	0
DET	157	79	75	.513	12	793	830	5315	**1547**	281	90	36	599	423	.291	.367	.398	765	105	52	42	101	99	801	88	71	55	-5
STL	155	62	92	.403	29	682	845	5259	1449	253	78	72	437	472	.276	.335	.394	729	92	-38	-69	105	100	700	64	66	49	-9
BOS	154	46	107	.301	44.5	562	835	5185	1325	249	54	32	465	454	.256	.321	.343	664	82	-155	-137	97	101	588	52	48	52	-5
TOT	616					5831		41762	11750	2195	568	424	4232	3463	.282	.352	.392	743							667	503	57	-29

TEAM	CG	SH	SV	IP	H	H/G	HR	BB	SO	RAT	ERA	ERA+	OAV	OOB	PR	PR+	PF	CPI	FA	E	DP	FW	PW	BW	SBW	DIF
NY	63	4	20	1372[1]	1442	9.5	56	478	486	12.8	3.86	100	.274	.337	24	-1	96	96	.966	210	117	-1.0	-.0	**13.3**	-.0	2.0
CLE	**96**	**11**	4	1374	1412	9.3	49	**450**	381	12.5	3.40	119	.271	.334	94	100	101	105	.972	173	153	1.1	9.7	-2.2	**.8**	1.7
PHI	62	10	16	1346	**1362**	**9.2**	**38**	451	**571**	**12.3**	**3.00**	**139**	**.268**	**.331**	**153**	**168**	104	**114**	.972	171	131	.9	**16.3**	-7.2	.0	-1.9
WAS	65	5	**26**	1348[1]	1489	10.0	45	566	418	14.0	4.34	89	.287	.361	-48	-74	96	98	.969	184	129	.3	-7.1	6.6	-.2	6.6
CHI	85	**11**	12	1380	1426	9.4	47	506	458	12.7	3.74	103	.271	.336	43	17	96	96	**.973**	**165**	122	**1.7**	1.7	5.1	.4	-4.1
DET	57	10	18	1394[2]	1570	10.2	58	555	469	14.1	4.41	92	.292	.363	-61	-53	101	99	.969	193	151	.1	-5.1	4.1	-.1	3.2
STL	64	5	9	1368	1549	10.2	86	654	337	14.8	4.67	92	.297	.379	-98	-55	107	105	.963	235	**167**	-2.6	-5.3	-6.6	-.5	.2
BOS	53	6	5	1362	1520	10.1	45	546	336	13.9	4.73	86	.294	.365	-107	-99	101	92	.970	193	143	-.1	-9.5	-13.2	-.1	-7.3
TOT	545	62	110	10945[1]		9.7				13.4	4.02		.282	.352					.970	1524	1113					

Runs
Ruth-NY 139
Gehrig-NY 135
Mostil-Chi 120
Combs-NY 113
Goslin-Was 105

Hits
Rice-Was 216
Burns-Cle 216
Goslin-Was 201
Simmons-Phi 199
Mostil-Chi 197

Doubles
Burns-Cle 64
Simmons-Phi 53
Speaker-Cle 52
Jacobson-StL-Bos 51
Gehrig-NY 47

Triples
Gehrig-NY 20
Gehringer-Det 17
Mostil-Chi 15
Goslin-Was 15

Home Runs
Ruth-NY 47
Simmons-Phi 19
Lazzeri-NY 18
Williams-StL 17
Goslin-Was 17

Total Bases
Ruth-NY 365
Simmons-Phi 329
Gehrig-NY 314
Goslin-Was 308
Burns-Cle 298

Runs Batted In
Ruth-NY 146
Lazzeri-NY 114
Burns-Cle 114
Gehrig-NY 112
Simmons-Phi 109

Runs Produced
Ruth-NY 238
Gehrig-NY 231
Burns-Cle 207
Goslin-Was 196
Falk-Chi 186

Bases On Balls
Ruth-NY 144
Bishop-Phi 116
Rigney-Bos 108
Gehrig-NY 105
Speaker-Cle 94

Batting Average
Manush-Det .378
Ruth-NY .372
Fothergill-Det .367
Heilmann-Det .367
Burns-Cle .358

On-Base Percentage
Ruth-NY .516
Heilmann-Det .445
Bishop-Phi .431
Goslin-Was .425
Manush-Det .421

Slugging Average
Ruth-NY .737
Simmons-Phi .564
Manush-Det .564
Gehrig-NY .549
Goslin-Was .542

On-Base Plus Slugging
Ruth-NY 1253
Manush-Det 985
Heilmann-Det 979
Gehrig-NY 969
Goslin-Was 967

Adjusted OPS
Ruth-NY 228
Goslin-Was 155
Gehrig-NY 154
Manush-Det 153
Heilmann-Det 153

Batter Runs
Ruth-NY 97.5
Gehrig-NY 44.2
Goslin-Was 42.3
Heilmann-Det 41.8
Manush-Det 38.2

Adjusted Batter Runs
Ruth-NY 100.3
Gehrig-NY 46.3
Goslin-Was 45.4
Heilmann-Det 40.3
Manush-Det 36.9

Clutch Hitting Index
Judge-Was 134
Dugan-NY 131
Haney-Bos 127
Myer-Was 121
Lutzke-Cle 118

Runs Created
Ruth-NY 196
Gehrig-NY 137
Goslin-Was 131
Simmons-Phi 129
Mostil-Chi 122

Total Average
Ruth-NY 1.606
Gehrig-NY 1.058
Heilmann-Det 1.040
Manush-Det 1.029
Goslin-Was 1.008

Stolen Bases
Mostil-Chi 35
Rice-Was 24
Hunnefield-Chi 24
McNeely-Was 18
J.Sewell-Cle 17

Stolen Base Average
McNeely-Was 75.0
Hunnefield-Chi 72.7
Mostil-Chi 71.4
J.Sewell-Cle 70.8
Lazzeri-NY 69.6

Stolen Base Runs
Mostil-Chi 2.8
Hunnefield-Chi 2.1
McNeely-Was 1.9
Simmons-Phi 1.4
J.Sewell-Cle 1.3

Fielding Runs
Dykes-Phi 26.4
Rigney-Bos 19.6
Goslin-Was 18.5
Regan-Bos 17.4
Mostil-Chi 17.1

Total Player Rating
Ruth-NY 8.4
Goslin-Was 5.1
Mostil-Chi 4.4
Rigney-Bos 4.1
J.Sewell-Cle 3.4

Wins
Uhle-Cle 27
Pennock-NY 23
Shocker-NY 19
Lyons-Chi 18

Win Percentage
Uhle-Cle .711
Pennock-NY .676
Shocker-NY .633
Faber-Chi .625
Hoyt-NY .571

Games
Marberry-Was 64
Pate-Phi 47
Grove-Phi 45
Thomas-Chi 44

Complete Games
Uhle-Cle 32
Lyons-Chi 24
Johnson-Was 22
Grove-Phi 20
Pennock-NY 19

Shutouts
Wells-Det 4

Saves
Marberry-Was 22
Dauss-Det 9
Pate-Phi 6
Grove-Phi 6
Jones-NY 5

Innings Pitched
Uhle-Cle 318.1
Lyons-Chi 283.2
Pennock-NY 266.1
Johnson-Was 260.2
Shocker-NY 258.1

Fewest Hits/Game
Grove-Phi 7.92
Thomas-Chi 8.13
Uhle-Cle 8.48
Lyons-Chi 8.50
Buckeye-Cle 8.69

Fewest BB/Game
Pennock-NY 1.45
Smith-Cle 1.48
Quinn-Phi 1.98
Rommel-Phi 2.22
Wingfield-Bos 2.36

Strikeouts
Grove-Phi 194
Uhle-Cle 159
Thomas-Chi 127
Johnson-Was 125
Whitehill-Det 109

Strikeouts/Game
Grove-Phi 6.77
Thomas-Chi 4.59
Uhle-Cle 4.50
Johnson-Was 4.32
Whitehill-Det 3.89

Ratio
Pennock-NY 11.52
Rommel-Phi 11.55
Johnson-Was 11.64
Grove-Phi 11.65
Lyons-Chi 11.90

Earned Run Average
Grove-Phi 2.51
Uhle-Cle 2.83
Lyons-Chi 3.01
Rommel-Phi 3.08
Buckeye-Cle 3.10

Adjusted ERA
Grove-Phi 166
Uhle-Cle 143
Rommel-Phi 135
Buckeye-Cle 131
Lyons-Chi 128

Opponents' Batting Avg.
Thomas-Chi .244
Grove-Phi .244
Lyons-Chi .252
Uhle-Cle .253
Levsen-Cle .261

Opponents' On-Base Pct.
Pennock-NY .313
Rommel-Phi .314
Hoyt-NY .316
Johnson-Was .317
Shocker-NY .318

Starter Runs
Grove-Phi 43.1
Uhle-Cle 42.1
Lyons-Chi 31.6
Coveleski-Was 24.5
Rommel-Phi 22.7

Adjusted Starter Runs
Grove-Phi 45.7
Uhle-Cle 43.0
Lyons-Chi 27.7
Rommel-Phi 25.4
Walberg-Phi 22.1

Clutch Pitching Index
Wingard-StL 128
Zachary-StL 122
Grove-Phi 119
Coveleski-Was 117
Buckeye-Cle 114

Relief Runs
Pate-Phi 16.4
Marberry-Was 15.6
Braxton-NY 10.1
Russell-Bos 4.7

Adjusted Relief Runs
Pate-Phi 17.6
Marberry-Was 13.8
Braxton-NY 9.2
Russell-Bos 5.2

Relief Ranking
Marberry-Was 22.0
Pate-Phi 14.8
Braxton-NY 8.0
Russell-Bos 2.6

Total Pitcher Index
Uhle-Cle 5.2
Grove-Phi 3.9
Lyons-Chi 3.4
Walberg-Phi 2.7
Zachary-StL 2.6

Total Baseball Ranking
Ruth-NY 8.4
Uhle-Cle 5.2
Goslin-Was 5.1
Mostil-Chi 4.4
Rigney-Bos 4.1

TEAM	G	W	L	PCT	GB	R	OR	AB	H	2B	3B	HR	BB	SO	AVG	OBP	SLG	OPS	OPS+	BR	BR+	PF	CHI	RC	SB	CS	SBA	SBR
PIT	156	94	60	.610		**817**	659	5397	**1648**	258	78	54	437	355	**.305**	**.361**	.412	773	106	99	45	107	99	791	65			
STL	153	92	61	.601	1.5	754	665	5207	1450	264	**79**	84	**484**	511	.278	.343	.408	751	104	47	25	103	101	723	**110**			
NY	155	92	62	.597	2	**817**	720	5372	1594	251	62	**109**	461	462	.297	.356	**.427**	**783**	**116**	**113**	**115**	100	98	**805**	73			
CHI	153	85	68	.556	8.5	750	661	5303	1505	**266**	63	74	481	492	.284	.346	.400	746	106	43	41	100	99	730	65			
CIN	153	75	78	.490	18.5	643	653	5185	1439	222	77	29	402	**332**	.278	.332	.367	699	96	-47	-26	97	100	628	62			
BRO	154	65	88	.425	28.5	541	**619**	5193	1314	195	74	39	368	494	.253	.306	.342	648	79	-152	-154	100	102	539	106			
BOS	155	60	94	.390	34	651	771	5370	1498	216	61	37	346	363	.279	.326	.363	689	98	-73	-19	92	**103**	626	100			
PHI	155	51	103	.331	43	678	903	5317	1487	216	46	57	434	482	.280	.337	.370	707	94	-30	-39	101	100	660	68			
TOT	617					5651		42344	11935	1888	540	483	3413	3491	.282	.339	.387	725							649			

TEAM	CG	SH	SV	IP	H	H/G	HR	BB	SO	RAT	ERA	ERA+	OAV	OOB	PR	PR+	PF	CPI	FA	E	DP	FW	PW	BW	SBW	DIF
PIT	**90**	10	10	1385	1400	**9.1**	58	418	435	12.0	3.66	112	.267	.324	39	65	105	95	.969	187	130	.7	6.5	4.5		5.6
STL	89	**14**	11	1367^1	1416	9.4	72	363	394	**11.9**	3.58	110	.271	**.320**	52	56	101	99	.966	213	**170**	-.9	5.6	2.5		8.5
NY	65	7	**16**	1381^2	1520	10.0	77	453	442	13.1	3.97	97	.283	.341	-8	-18	98	102	.969	195	160	.2	-1.7	**11.4**		5.3
CHI	75	11	5	1385	1439	9.4	50	514	465	13.0	3.66	106	.273	.342	40	32	99	**104**	.971	181	152	.8	3.2	4.1		.6
CIN	87	12	12	1368	1472	9.7	**36**	**316**	407	12.0	3.54	107	.281	.325	57	38	97	100	**.973**	**165**	160	**1.7**	3.8	-2.5		-4.3
BRO	74	7	10	1375^1	**1382**	**9.1**	63	418	**574**	12.0	**3.36**	**118**	**.265**	.323	**85**	**89**	101	103	.963	229	117	-1.7	**8.8**	-15.1		-3.3
BOS	52	3	11	1390	1602	10.4	43	468	402	13.6	4.23	88	.296	.356	-48	-83	95	102	.963	231	130	-1.8	-8.1	-1.8		-5.1
PHI	81	5	6	1355^1	1710	11.4	84	462	377	14.7	5.36	77	.317	.374	-218	-177	106	96	.972	169	152	1.6	-17.4	-3.8		-6.2
TOT	613	69	81	11007^2		9.8				12.8	3.92		.282	.339					.969	1570	1171					

Runs
- L.Waner-Pit 133
- Hornsby-NY 133
- Wilson-Chi 119
- P.Waner-Pit 114
- Frisch-StL 112

Hits
- P.Waner-Pit 237
- L.Waner-Pit 223
- Frisch-StL 208
- Hornsby-NY 205
- Stephenson-Chi 199

Doubles
- Stephenson-Chi 46
- P.Waner-Pit 42
- Lindstrom-NY 36
- Dressen-Cin 36
- Brown-Bos 35

Triples
- P.Waner-Pit 18
- Bottomley-StL 15
- Thompson-Phi 14
- Terry-NY 13
- Wilson-Chi 12

Home Runs
- Wilson-Chi 30
- Williams-Phi 30
- Hornsby-NY 26
- Terry-NY 20
- Bottomley-StL 19

Total Bases
- P.Waner-Pit 342
- Hornsby-NY 333
- Wilson-Chi 319
- Terry-NY 307
- Bottomley-StL 292

Runs Batted In
- P.Waner-Pit 131
- Wilson-Chi 129
- Hornsby-NY 125
- Bottomley-StL 124
- Terry-NY 121

Runs Produced
- P.Waner-Pit 236
- Hornsby-NY 232
- Wilson-Chi 218
- Terry-NY 202
- Bottomley-StL 200

Bases On Balls
- Hornsby-NY 86
- Harper-NY 84
- Grantham-Pit 74
- Bottomley-StL 74

Batting Average
- P.Waner-Pit .380
- Hornsby-NY .361
- L.Waner-Pit .355
- Stephenson-Chi .344
- Traynor-Pit .342

On-Base Percentage
- Hornsby-NY .448
- P.Waner-Pit .437
- Harper-NY .435
- Stephenson-Chi .415
- Harris-Pit .402

Slugging Average
- Hafey-StL .590
- Hornsby-NY .586
- Wilson-Chi .579
- P.Waner-Pit .549
- Terry-NY .529

On-Base Plus Slugging
- Hornsby-NY 1035
- P.Waner-Pit 986
- Wilson-Chi 980
- Harper-NY 930
- Terry-NY 907

Adjusted OPS
- Hornsby-NY 175
- Wilson-Chi 159
- P.Waner-Pit 152
- Harper-NY 149
- Stephenson-Chi 141

Batter Runs
- Hornsby-NY 62.5
- P.Waner-Pit 55.6
- Wilson-Chi 45.7
- Harper-NY 37.1
- Stephenson-Chi 35.7

Adjusted Batter Runs
- Hornsby-NY 62.8
- P.Waner-Pit 46.5
- Wilson-Chi 45.5
- Harper-NY 37.3
- Stephenson-Chi 35.5

Clutch Hitting Index
- P.Waner-Pit 135
- Wright-Pit 134
- Bressler-Cin 133
- Farrell-NY-Bos 131
- Bottomley-StL 124

Runs Created
- Hornsby-NY 148
- P.Waner-Pit 145
- Wilson-Chi 126
- Stephenson-Chi 117
- Bottomley-StL 112

Total Average
- Hornsby-NY 1.190
- Wilson-Chi 1.088
- P.Waner-Pit 1.062
- Harper-NY 1.037
- Stephenson-Chi .955

Stolen Bases
- Frisch-StL 48
- Carey-Bro 32
- Hendrick-Bro 29
- Adams-Chi 26
- Richbourg-Bos 24

Stolen Base Average

Stolen Base Runs

Fielding Runs
- Frisch-StL 48.6
- Jackson-NY 27.9
- Friberg-Phi 25.3
- Beck-Chi 22.0
- Statz-Bro 15.3

Total Player Rating
- Frisch-StL 7.2
- Hornsby-NY 6.8
- Jackson-NY 5.5
- P.Waner-Pit 4.0
- Wilson-Chi 3.8

Wins
- Root-Chi 26
- Haines-StL 24
- Hill-Pit 22
- Alexander-StL 21

Win Percentage
- Benton-Bos-NY .708
- Haines-StL .706
- Kremer-Pit .704
- Grimes-NY .704
- Alexander-StL .677

Games
- Scott-Phi 48
- Root-Chi 48
- Ehrhardt-Bro 46
- Henry-NY 45
- May-Cin 44

Complete Games
- Vance-Bro 25
- Meadows-Pit 25
- Haines-StL 25
- Hill-Pit 22
- Alexander-StL 22

Shutouts
- Haines-StL 6
- Root-Chi 4
- Lucas-Cin 4
- Kremer-Pit 3

Saves
- Sherdel-StL 6
- Nehf-Cin-Chi 5
- Mogridge-Bos 5
- Henry-NY 4

Innings Pitched
- Root-Chi 309.0
- Haines-StL 300.2
- Meadows-Pit 299.1
- Hill-Pit 277.2
- Vance-Bro 273.1

Fewest Hits/Game
- Vance-Bro 7.97
- Kremer-Pit 8.16
- Haines-StL 8.17
- Bush-Chi 8.24
- Hill-Pit 8.43

Fewest BB/Game
- Alexander-StL 1.28
- Lucas-Cin 1.46
- Donohue-Cin 1.51
- Carlson-Phi-Chi 1.63
- Henry-NY 1.70

Strikeouts
- Vance-Bro 184
- Root-Chi 145
- May-Cin 121
- Grimes-NY 102
- Petty-Bro 101

Strikeouts/Game
- Vance-Bro 6.06
- Elliott-Bro 4.73
- May-Cin 4.62
- Pruett-Phi 4.35
- Root-Chi 4.22

Ratio
- Alexander-StL 10.07
- Lucas-Cin 10.14
- Kremer-Pit 10.27
- Vance-Bro 10.44
- Petty-Bro 10.60

Earned Run Average
- Kremer-Pit 2.47
- Alexander-StL 2.52
- Vance-Bro 2.70
- Haines-StL 2.72
- Petty-Bro 2.98

Adjusted ERA
- Kremer-Pit 166
- Alexander-StL 157
- Vance-Bro 147
- Haines-StL 145
- Petty-Bro 133

Opponents' Batting Avg.
- Vance-Bro .239
- Kremer-Pit .244
- Haines-StL .245
- Hill-Pit .249
- Bush-Chi .250

Opponents' On-Base Pct.
- Alexander-StL .286
- Lucas-Cin .287
- Kremer-Pit .289
- Vance-Bro .291
- Petty-Bro .293

Starter Runs
- Alexander-StL 41.5
- Haines-StL 39.8
- Vance-Bro 36.9
- Kremer-Pit 36.3
- Petty-Bro 28.1

Adjusted Starter Runs
- Alexander-StL 42.1
- Haines-StL 40.5
- Kremer-Pit 39.2
- Vance-Bro 37.8
- Petty-Bro 29.1

Clutch Pitching Index
- Blake-Chi 117
- McWeeny-Bro 116
- B.Smith-Bos 114
- Donohue-Cin 111
- Alexander-StL 109

Relief Runs
- Clark-Bro 13.0
- Ehrhardt-Bro 3.6
- Cvengros-Pit 3.3
- Songer-Pit-NY 1.9

Adjusted Relief Runs
- Clark-Bro 13.2
- Cvengros-Pit 4.3
- Ehrhardt-Bro 4.0
- Songer-Pit-NY 1.7
- H.Bell-StL .1

Relief Ranking
- Clark-Bro 15.4
- Ehrhardt-Bro 4.0
- Cvengros-Pit 2.3
- Songer-Pit-NY 2.3
- H.Bell-StL .0

Total Pitcher Index
- Alexander-StL 5.2
- Haines-StL 4.3
- Kremer-Pit 4.0
- Vance-Bro 3.8
- Hill-Pit 3.0

Total Baseball Ranking
- Frisch-StL 7.2
- Hornsby-NY 6.8
- Jackson-NY 5.5
- Alexander-StL 5.2
- Haines-StL 4.3

TEAM	G	W	L	PCT	GB	R	OR	AB	H	2B	3B	HR	BB	SO	AVG	OBP	SLG	OPS	OPS+	BR	BR+	PF	CHI	RC	SB	CS	SBA	SBR
NY	155	110	44	.714		**975**	**599**	5347	**1644**	291	**103**	**158**	**635**	605	**.307**	**.383**	**.489**	**872**	**135**	**235**	**267**	97	95	**1016**	90	64	58	-3
PHI	155	91	63	.591	19	841	726	5296	1606	281	70	56	551	**326**	.303	.372	.414	786	103	79	34	106	99	839	101	63	62	0
WAS	157	85	69	.552	25	782	730	5389	1549	268	87	29	498	359	.287	.351	.386	737	97	-25	-16	99	104	758	133	52	**72**	**11**
DET	156	82	71	.536	27.5	845	805	5299	1533	282	100	51	587	420	.289	.363	.409	772	105	47	36	101	103	813	**139**	73	66	5
CHI	153	70	83	.458	39.5	662	708	5157	1433	285	61	36	493	389	.278	.344	.378	722	94	-54	-36	98	95	685	89	75	54	-7
CLE	153	66	87	.431	43.5	668	766	5202	1471	**321**	52	26	381	366	.283	.337	.379	716	90	-70	-75	101	100	669	65	72	47	-11
STL	155	59	94	.386	50.5	724	904	5220	1440	262	59	55	443	420	.276	.338	.380	718	88	-68	-90	103	**106**	683	90	66	58	-3
BOS	154	51	103	.331	59	597	856	5207	1348	271	78	28	430	456	.259	.320	.357	677	82	-149	-136	98	100	614	81	46	64	2
TOT	619					6094		42117	12024	2261	610	439	4018	3341	.286	.352	.400	751							788	511	61	-5

TEAM	CG	SH	SV	IP	H	H/G	HR	BB	SO	RAT	ERA	ERA+	OAV	OOB	PR	PR+	PF	CPI	FA	E	DP	FW	PW	BW	SBW	DIF
NY	82	**11**	20	1389^2	**1403**	**9.1**	42	**409**	431	**11.9**	**3.20**	**120**	**.267**	**.323**	**145**	**107**	93	104	.969	195	123	.7	**10.2**	**25.4**	-.2	-3.0
PHI	65	8	**24**	1384	1467	9.6	65	442	**553**	12.7	3.97	107	.278	.338	26	44	103	97	.970	190	124	1.0	4.2	3.3	.0	5.6
WAS	62	10	23	1402	1434	9.3	53	491	497	12.7	3.97	102	.269	.335	26	14	98	91	.969	195	125	.9	1.4	-1.5	**1.1**	6.3
DET	75	5	17	1387^2	1542	10.1	52	577	421	14.1	4.14	102	.290	.364	0	9	102	**106**	.968	206	**173**	.2	.9	3.5	.5	.6
CHI	**85**	10	8	1367	1467	9.7	55	440	365	12.8	3.92	103	.283	.342	34	20	98	101	**.971**	**178**	131	**1.6**	2.0	-3.4	-.6	-5.9
CLE	72	5	8	1353^1	1542	10.3	**37**	508	366	13.9	4.27	98	.295	.361	-20	-11	102	102	.968	201	146	.2	-1.0	-7.1	-1.0	-1.5
STL	80	4	8	1353^1	1592	10.6	79	604	385	14.8	4.95	88	.304	.378	-122	-87	105	101	.960	248	166	-2.4	-8.2	-8.5	-.2	2.1
BOS	63	6	7	1366^1	1603	10.6	56	558	381	14.6	4.72	89	.305	.376	-88	-76	102	102	.964	228	167	-1.3	-7.2	-12.9	.3	-4.7
TOT	584	59	115	11003^1		9.9				13.4	4.14		.286	.352					.968	1641	1155					

Runs
Ruth-NY 158
Gehrig-NY 149
Combs-NY 137
Gehringer-Det 110
Heilmann-Det 106

Hits
Combs-NY 231
Gehrig-NY 218
Sisler-StL 201
Heilmann-Det 201
Goslin-Was 194

Doubles
Gehrig-NY 52
Burns-Cle 51
Heilmann-Det 50
J.Sewell-Cle 48
Meusel-NY 47

Triples
Combs-NY 23
Manush-Det 18
Gehrig-NY 18
Goslin-Was 15
Rice-Was 14

Home Runs
Ruth-NY 60
Gehrig-NY 47
Lazzeri-NY 18
Williams-StL 17
Simmons-Phi 15

Total Bases
Gehrig-NY 447
Ruth-NY 417
Combs-NY 331
Heilmann-Det 311
Goslin-Was 300

Runs Batted In
Gehrig-NY 175
Ruth-NY 164
Heilmann-Det 120
Goslin-Was 120
Fothergill-Det 114

Runs Produced
Gehrig-NY 277
Ruth-NY 262
Heilmann-Det 212
Goslin-Was 203
Fothergill-Det 198

Bases On Balls
Ruth-NY 137
Gehrig-NY 109
Bishop-Phi 105
Heilmann-Det 72
Blue-Det 71

Batting Average
Heilmann-Det .398
Simmons-Phi .392
Gehrig-NY .373
Fothergill-Det .359
Cobb-Phi .357

On-Base Percentage
Ruth-NY .486
Heilmann-Det .475
Gehrig-NY .474
Bishop-Phi .442
Cobb-Phi .440

Slugging Average
Ruth-NY .772
Gehrig-NY .765
Simmons-Phi .645
Heilmann-Det .616
Williams-StL .525

On-Base Plus Slugging
Ruth-NY 1258
Gehrig-NY 1240
Heilmann-Det 1091
Fothergill-Det 929
Williams-StL 928

Adjusted OPS
Ruth-NY 229
Gehrig-NY 224
Heilmann-Det 179
Combs-NY 143
Fothergill-Det 138

Batter Runs
Gehrig-NY 100.8
Ruth-NY 100.4
Heilmann-Det 62.3
Simmons-Phi 44.1
Combs-NY 37.1

Adjusted Batter Runs
Gehrig-NY 106.7
Ruth-NY 106.2
Heilmann-Det 60.4
Combs-NY 41.1
Simmons-Phi 38.7

Clutch Hitting Index
Fothergill-Det 119
Goslin-Was 118
Sisler-StL 116
Harris-Was 115
J.Sewell-Cle 114

Runs Created
Gehrig-NY 212
Ruth-NY 208
Heilmann-Det 150
Combs-NY 138
Goslin-Was 119

Total Average
Ruth-NY 1.568
Gehrig-NY 1.500
Heilmann-Det 1.265
Williams-StL .959
Combs-NY .955

Stolen Bases
Sisler-StL 27
Meusel-NY 24
Neun-Det 22
Lazzeri-NY 22
Cobb-Phi 22

Stolen Base Average
Harris-Was 85.7
Sisler-StL 79.4
Goslin-Was 77.8
Rice-Was 76.0
Neun-Det 75.9

Stolen Base Runs
Sisler-StL 3.5
Harris-Was 2.9
Goslin-Was 2.5
Neun-Det 2.4
Rice-Was 2.1

Fielding Runs
Gehringer-Det 19.8
Falk-Chi 18.2
Metzler-Chi 15.7
Bluege-Was 15.0
Koenig-NY 13.8

Total Player Rating
Ruth-NY 9.0
Gehrig-NY 8.3
Heilmann-Det 4.0
Simmons-Phi 3.5
Combs-NY 3.5

Wins
Lyons-Chi 22
Hoyt-NY 22
Grove-Phi 20

Win Percentage
Hoyt-NY .759
Shocker-NY .750
Moore-NY .731
Pennock-NY .704
Lisenbee-Was .667

Games
Braxton-Was 58
Marberry-Was 56
Grove-Phi 51
Moore-NY 50
Walberg-Phi 46

Complete Games
Lyons-Chi 30
Thomas-Chi 24
Hoyt-NY 23
Gaston-StL 21

Shutouts
Lisenbee-Was 4

Saves
Moore-NY 13
Braxton-Was 13
Marberry-Was 9
Grove-Phi 9

Innings Pitched
Thomas-Chi 307.2
Lyons-Chi 307.2
Hudlin-Cle 264.2
Grove-Phi 262.1
Hoyt-NY 256.1

Fewest Hits/Game
Moore-NY 7.82
Thomas-Chi 7.93
Pipgras-NY 8.01
Hadley-Was 8.02
Lisenbee-Was 8.22

Fewest BB/Game
Quinn-Phi 1.65
Shocker-NY 1.85
Hoyt-NY 1.90
Braxton-Was 1.91
Lyons-Chi 1.96

Strikeouts
Grove-Phi 174
Walberg-Phi 136
Thomas-Chi 107
Lisenbee-Was 105
Braxton-Was 96

Strikeouts/Game
Grove-Phi 5.97
Braxton-Was 5.56
Walberg-Phi 4.91
Pipgras-NY 4.38
Ruffing-Bos 4.38

Ratio
Moore-NY 10.35
Braxton-Was 10.37
Lyons-Chi 10.47
Hoyt-NY 10.53
Thomas-Chi 10.71

Earned Run Average
Moore-NY 2.28
Hoyt-NY 2.63
Shocker-NY 2.84
Lyons-Chi 2.84
Hadley-Was 2.85

Adjusted ERA
Moore-NY 169
Hoyt-NY 146
Lyons-Chi 143
Hadley-Was 142
Braxton-Was 137

Opponents' Batting Avg.
Moore-NY .234
Thomas-Chi .244
Hadley-Was .244
Lisenbee-Was .245
Braxton-Was .246

Opponents' On-Base Pct.
Moore-NY .289
Braxton-Was .289
Lyons-Chi .292
Hoyt-NY .294
Thomas-Chi .303

Starter Runs
Lyons-Chi 44.4
Moore-NY 43.9
Hoyt-NY 42.8
Thomas-Chi 39.4
Shocker-NY 28.9

Adjusted Starter Runs
Lyons-Chi 42.2
Moore-NY 39.9
Hoyt-NY 37.2
Thomas-Chi 37.1
Grove-Phi 30.3

Clutch Pitching Index
Ruether-NY 119
Gibson-Det 119
Pennock-NY 118
Zachary-StL-Was 115
Stoner-Det 114

Relief Runs
Braxton-Was 20.4
Burke-Was 1.9
G.Smith-Det 1.8

Adjusted Relief Runs
Braxton-Was 19.4
G.Smith-Det 2.3
Burke-Was 1.1

Relief Ranking
Braxton-Was 25.1
G.Smith-Det 1.4
Burke-Was .6

Total Pitcher Index
Lyons-Chi 5.2
Moore-NY 5.1
Hoyt-NY 3.8
Grove-Phi 3.2
Thomas-Chi 3.0

Total Baseball Ranking
Ruth-NY 9.0
Gehrig-NY 8.3
Lyons-Chi 5.2
Moore-NY 5.1
Heilmann-Det 4.0

TEAM	G	W	L	PCT	GB	R	OR	AB	H	2B	3B	HR	BB	SO	AVG	OBP	SLG	OPS	OPS+	BR	BR+	PF	CHI	RC	SB	CS	SBA	SBR
STL	154	95	59	.617		807	636	5357	1505	**292**	70	113	**568**	438	.281	.353	.425	778	108	73	59	102	99	802	82			
NY	155	93	61	.604	2	807	653	5459	1600	276	59	**118**	444	376	.293	.349	**.430**	779	**110**	68	**65**	100	100	805	62			
CHI	154	91	63	.591	4	714	**615**	5260	1460	251	64	92	508	517	.278	.345	.402	747	103	11	21	99	97	728	**83**			
PIT	152	85	67	.559	9	**837**	704	5371	**1659**	246	**100**	52	435	352	**.309**	**.364**	.421	**785**	108	**89**	58	104	103	**809**	64			
CIN	153	78	74	.513	16	648	686	5184	1449	229	67	32	386	**330**	.280	.333	.368	701	91	-76	-66	98	**104**	630	**83**			
BRO	155	77	76	.503	17.5	665	640	5243	1393	229	70	66	557	510	.266	.340	.374	714	94	-46	-36	99	98	673	81			
BOS	153	50	103	.327	44.5	631	878	5228	1439	241	41	52	447	377	.275	.335	.367	702	95	-70	-35	95	99	643	60			
PHI	152	43	109	.283	51	660	957	5234	1396	257	47	85	503	510	.267	.333	.382	715	90	-49	-71	103	99	667	53			
TOT	614					5769		42336	11901	2021	518	610	3848	3410	.282	.345	.397	741							568			

TEAM	CG	SH	SV	IP	H	H/G	HR	BB	SO	RAT	ERA	ERA+	OAV	OOB	PR	PR+	PF	CPI	FA	E	DP	FW	PW	BW	SBW	DIF
STL	**83**	4	**21**	1415^{1}	1470	9.4	86	**399**	422	**12.1**	3.38	118	.270	**.323**	97	98	100	105	.974	160	134	1.4	9.6	5.8		1.4
NY	79	7	16	1394	1454	9.4	77	405	399	12.2	3.67	107	.273	.327	50	38	98	98	.972	178	175	.4	3.8	**6.4**		5.7
CHI	75	12	14	1380^{2}	1383	9.1	**56**	508	531	12.6	3.40	113	.267	.336	91	72	96	**106**	**.975**	**156**	176	**1.6**	7.1	2.1		3.4
PIT	82	8	11	1354	1422	9.5	66	446	385	12.6	3.95	103	.274	.335	7	16	102	94	.967	201	123	-1.2	1.6	5.7		3.1
CIN	68	11	11	1371^{2}	1516	10.0	58	410	355	12.8	3.94	100	.289	.342	8	2	99	101	.974	162	**194**	1.2	.2	-6.4		7.2
BRO	75	**16**	15	1396	**1378**	**8.9**	59	468	**551**	12.2	**3.25**	**122**	**.261**	.324	**115**	**113**	100	101	.965	217	113	-2.0	**11.1**	-3.5		-5.0
BOS	54	1	6	1360	1596	10.6	100	524	343	14.3	4.84	81	.298	.363	-127	-142	98	97	.969	193	141	-.7	-13.8	-3.4		-8.4
PHI	42	4	11	1346^{2}	1664	11.2	108	675	402	16.0	5.61	76	.315	.397	-242	-188	107	100	.971	181	171	-.0	-18.3	-6.9		-7.6
TOT	558	63	105	11018^{1}		9.8				13.1	4.00		.282	.345					.971	1448	1227					

Runs
- P.Waner-Pit 142
- Bottomley-StL 123
- L.Waner-Pit 121
- Douthit-StL 111
- Frisch-StL 107

Hits
- Lindstrom-NY 231
- P.Waner-Pit 223
- L.Waner-Pit 221
- Richbourg-Bos 206
- Traynor-Pit 192

Doubles
- P.Waner-Pit 50
- Hafey-StL 46
- Hornsby-Bos 42
- Bottomley-StL 42
- Lindstrom-NY 39

Triples
- Bottomley-StL 20
- P.Waner-Pit 19
- L.Waner-Pit 14
- Bressler-Bro 13
- Bissonette-Bro 13

Home Runs
- Wilson-Chi 31
- Bottomley-StL 31
- Hafey-StL 27
- Bissonette-Bro 25
- Hornsby-Bos 21

Total Bases
- Bottomley-StL 362
- Lindstrom-NY 330
- P.Waner-Pit 329
- Bissonette-Bro 319
- Hafey-StL 314

Runs Batted In
- Bottomley-StL 136
- Traynor-Pit 124
- Wilson-Chi 120
- Hafey-StL 111
- Lindstrom-NY 107

Runs Produced
- Bottomley-StL 228
- P.Waner-Pit 222
- Traynor-Pit 212
- Lindstrom-NY 192
- Hafey-StL 185

Bases On Balls
- Hornsby-Bos 107
- Douthit-StL 84
- Bressler-Bro 80
- Wilson-Chi 77
- P.Waner-Pit 77

Batting Average
- Hornsby-Bos .... .387
- P.Waner-Pit .... .370
- Lindstrom-NY .... .358
- Sisler-Bos .... .340
- Herman-Bro .... .340

On-Base Percentage
- Hornsby-Bos .... .498
- P.Waner-Pit .... .446
- Grantham-Pit .... .408
- Stephenson-Chi ..... .407
- Wilson-Chi .... .404

Slugging Average
- Hornsby-Bos .... .632
- Bottomley-StL ...... .628
- Hafey-StL .... .604
- Wilson-Chi .... .588
- P.Waner-Pit .... .547

On-Base Plus Slugging
- Hornsby-Bos 1130
- Bottomley-StL 1030
- Wilson-Chi 992
- P.Waner-Pit 992
- Hafey-StL 990

Adjusted OPS
- Hornsby-Bos 204
- Bottomley-StL 163
- Wilson-Chi 159
- Hafey-StL 152
- P.Waner-Pit 152

Batter Runs
- Hornsby-Bos 72.5
- P.Waner-Pit 53.4
- Bottomley-StL 52.5
- Wilson-Chi 42.1
- Hafey-StL 38.5

Adjusted Batter Runs
- Hornsby-Bos 80.5
- Bottomley-StL 50.1
- P.Waner-Pit 48.1
- Wilson-Chi 43.8
- Bissonette-Bro 38.1

Clutch Hitting Index
- Traynor-Pit 147
- Walker-Cin 126
- Whitney-Phi 124
- Ford-Cin 123
- Wilson-Phi-StL 121

Runs Created
- Hornsby-Bos 154
- P.Waner-Pit 145
- Bottomley-StL 142
- Bissonette-Bro 125
- Wilson-Chi 122

Total Average
- Hornsby-Bos 1.409
- Bottomley-StL 1.147
- P.Waner-Pit 1.100
- Wilson-Chi 1.090
- Hafey-StL 1.055

Stolen Bases
- Cuyler-Chi 37
- Frisch-StL 29
- Walker-Cin 19
- Thompson-Phi 19

Stolen Base Average

Stolen Base Runs

Fielding Runs
- Maguire-Chi 50.5
- Jackson-NY 28.3
- Douthit-StL 24.3
- Lindstrom-NY 15.1
- Ford-Cin 11.9

Total Player Rating
- Hornsby-Bos 5.8
- Lindstrom-NY 5.0
- Jackson-NY 4.2
- Hartnett-Chi 4.0
- P.Waner-Pit 3.9

Wins
- Grimes-Pit 25
- Benton-NY 25
- Vance-Bro 22
- Sherdel-StL 21

Win Percentage
- Benton-NY .... .735
- Haines-StL .... .714
- Bush-Chi .... .714
- Fitzsimmons-NY .... .690
- Vance-Bro .... .688

Games
- Grimes-Pit 48
- Kolp-Cin 44
- Rixey-Cin 43

Complete Games
- Grimes-Pit 28
- Benton-NY 28
- Vance-Bro 24
- Sherdel-StL 20
- Haines-StL 20

Shutouts
- Vance-Bro 4
- McWeeny-Bro 4
- Lucas-Cin 4
- Grimes-Pit 4
- Blake-Chi 4

Saves
- Sherdel-StL 5
- Haid-StL 5
- Carlson-Chi 4
- Benton-NY 4

Innings Pitched
- Grimes-Pit 330.2
- Benton-NY 310.1
- Rixey-Cin 291.1
- Vance-Bro 280.1
- Fitzsimmons-NY ... 261.1

Fewest Hits/Game
- Vance-Bro 7.26
- Blake-Chi 7.82
- Malone-Chi 7.83
- McWeeny-Bro 8.04
- Root-Chi 8.13

Fewest BB/Game
- Alexander-StL 1.37
- Sherdel-StL 2.03
- Benton-NY 2.06
- Rixey-Cin 2.07
- Grimes-Pit 2.10

Strikeouts
- Vance-Bro 200
- Malone-Chi 155
- Root-Chi 122
- Grimes-Pit 97
- Benton-NY 90

Strikeouts/Game
- Vance-Bro 6.42
- Malone-Chi 5.57
- Root-Chi 4.63
- Clark-Bro 3.93
- Ring-Phi 3.58

Ratio
- Vance-Bro 9.79
- Benton-NY 10.73
- Grimes-Pit 10.81
- Lucas-Cin 11.08
- Alexander-StL 11.12

Earned Run Average
- Vance-Bro 2.09
- Blake-Chi 2.47
- Nehf-Chi 2.65
- Clark-Bro 2.68
- Benton-NY 2.73

Adjusted ERA
- Vance-Bro 191
- Blake-Chi 156
- Clark-Bro 148
- Nehf-Chi 145
- Benton-NY 144

Opponents' Batting Avg.
- Vance-Bro .... .221
- McWeeny-Bro .... .235
- Malone-Chi .... .236
- Blake-Chi .... .240
- Root-Chi .... .242

Opponents' On-Base Pct.
- Vance-Bro .... .277
- Grimes-Pit .... .297
- Benton-NY .... .300
- Sherdel-StL .... .303
- Lucas-Cin .... .304

Starter Runs
- Vance-Bro 59.3
- Benton-NY 43.6
- Blake-Chi 40.7
- Grimes-Pit 36.7
- Malone-Chi 32.2

Adjusted Starter Runs
- Vance-Bro 59.1
- Benton-NY 41.7
- Grimes-Pit 38.5
- Blake-Chi 38.3
- Sherdel-StL 31.4

Clutch Pitching Index
- Nehf-Chi 133
- Bush-Chi 118
- Blake-Chi 115
- Kolp-Cin 115
- Rhem-StL 114

Relief Runs

Adjusted Relief Runs

Relief Ranking

Total Pitcher Index
- Vance-Bro 7.0
- Grimes-Pit 6.0
- Blake-Chi 4.0
- Benton-NY 4.0
- Sherdel-StL 3.7

Total Baseball Ranking
- Vance-Bro 7.0
- Grimes-Pit 6.0
- Hornsby-Bos 5.8
- Lindstrom-NY 5.0
- Jackson-NY 4.2

TEAM	G	W	L	PCT	GB	R	OR	AB	H	2B	3B	HR	BB	SO	AVG	OBP	SLG	OPS	OPS+	BR	BR+	PF	CHI	RC	SB	CS	SBA	SBR
NY	154	101	53	.656		**894**	685	5337	**1578**	269	79	**133**	**562**	544	**.296**	**.365**	**.450**	**815**	**124**	**146**	**176**	97	100	**888**	51	51	50	-7
PHI	153	98	55	.641	2.5	829	**615**	5226	1540	**323**	75	89	533	442	.295	.363	.436	799	112	115	93	103	97	843	59	48	55	-4
STL	154	82	72	.532	19	772	742	5217	1431	276	76	63	548	479	.274	.346	.393	739	97	2	-20	103	**104**	736	76	43	64	2
WAS	155	75	79	.487	26	718	705	5320	1510	277	93	40	481	**390**	.284	.346	.393	739	101	1	6	99	97	743	110	59	**65**	**4**
CHI	155	72	82	.468	29	656	725	5207	1405	231	77	24	469	488	.270	.334	.358	692	88	-88	-79	99	102	641	**139**	82	63	2
DET	154	68	86	.442	33	744	804	5292	1476	265	**97**	62	469	438	.279	.340	.401	741	99	-2	-13	102	102	730	113	77	59	-2
CLE	155	62	92	.403	39	674	830	5386	1535	299	61	34	377	426	.285	.335	.382	717	93	-49	-56	101	98	693	50	52	49	-7
BOS	154	57	96	.373	43.5	589	770	5132	1356	260	62	38	389	512	.264	.319	.361	680	86	-119	-108	98	100	602	99	64	61	-1
TOT	617					5876		42117	11831	2200	620	483	3828	3719	.281	.344	.397	741							697	476	59	-13

TEAM	CG	SH	SV	IP	H	H/G	HR	BB	SO	RAT	ERA	ERA+	OAV	OOB	PR	PR+	PF	CPI	FA	E	DP	FW	PW	BW	SBW	DIF
NY	82	13	**21**	1375^1	1466	9.6	59	452	487	12.7	3.74	101	.276	.335	46	3	93	102	.968	194	136	.0	.3	**17.1**	-.5	7.3
PHI	81	**15**	16	1367^2	**1349**	**8.9**	66	**424**	**607**	**11.9**	**3.37**	**119**	**.259**	**.318**	**103**	**98**	99	99	.970	181	124	.7	**9.5**	9.0	-.2	2.7
STL	80	6	15	1374^1	1487	9.8	93	454	456	12.9	4.18	101	.282	.340	-20	3	104	100	.969	189	146	.3	.3	-1.9	.4	6.1
WAS	77	**15**	10	1384	1420	9.3	**40**	466	462	12.5	3.88	103	.272	.335	25	19	99	94	**.972**	**178**	146	**1.0**	1.9	.6	**.5**	-5.9
CHI	**88**	6	11	1378	1518	10.0	66	501	418	13.4	3.99	102	.287	.352	8	8	100	**108**	.970	186	149	.5	.8	-7.6	.4	1.1
DET	65	5	16	1372	1481	9.8	58	567	451	13.7	4.32	95	.281	.355	-42	-33	102	97	.965	218	140	-1.4	-3.1	-1.2	-.0	-3.0
CLE	71	4	15	1378	1615	10.6	52	511	416	14.2	4.47	93	.303	.369	-66	-51	103	105	.965	221	**187**	-1.5	-4.9	-5.4	-.5	-2.5
BOS	70	5	9	1352	1492	10.0	49	452	407	13.3	4.40	93	.288	.349	-53	-44	102	94	.971	**178**	139	.9	-4.2	-10.4	.0	-5.7
TOT	614	69	113	10981^1		9.7				13.1	4.04		.281	.344					.969	1545	1167					

Runs
Ruth-NY 163
Gehrig-NY 139
Combs-NY 118
Blue-StL 116
Gehringer-Det 108

Hits
Manush-StL 241
Gehrig-NY 210
Rice-Was 202
Combs-NY 194
Gehringer-Det 193

Doubles
Manush-StL 47
Gehrig-NY 47
Meusel-NY 45
Schulte-StL 44
Lind-Cle 42

Triples
Combs-NY 21
Manush-StL 20
Gehringer-Det 16

Home Runs
Ruth-NY 54
Gehrig-NY 27
Goslin-Was 17
Hauser-Phi 16
Simmons-Phi 15

Total Bases
Ruth-NY 380
Manush-StL 367
Gehrig-NY 364
Combs-NY 290
Heilmann-Det 283

Runs Batted In
Ruth-NY 142
Gehrig-NY 142
Meusel-NY 113
Manush-StL 108

Runs Produced
Gehrig-NY 254
Ruth-NY 251
Manush-StL 199
Blue-StL 182
Meusel-NY 179

Bases On Balls
Ruth-NY 137
Blue-StL 105
Bishop-Phi 97
Gehrig-NY 95
Judge-Was 80

Batting Average
Goslin-Was .379
Manush-StL .378
Gehrig-NY .374
Simmons-Phi .351
Lazzeri-NY .332

On-Base Percentage
Gehrig-NY .467
Ruth-NY .463
Goslin-Was .442
Bishop-Phi .435
Manush-StL .414

Slugging Average
Ruth-NY .709
Gehrig-NY .648
Goslin-Was .614
Manush-StL .575
Simmons-Phi .558

On-Base Plus Slugging
Ruth-NY 1172
Gehrig-NY 1115
Goslin-Was 1056
Manush-StL 989
Simmons-Phi 954

Adjusted OPS
Ruth-NY 211
Gehrig-NY 196
Goslin-Was 176
Manush-StL 153
Simmons-Phi 144

Batter Runs
Ruth-NY 84.6
Gehrig-NY 76.0
Manush-StL 50.3
Goslin-Was 49.0
Foxx-Phi 30.5

Adjusted Batter Runs
Ruth-NY 90.1
Gehrig-NY 81.2
Goslin-Was 49.8
Manush-StL 46.2
Foxx-Phi 28.1

Clutch Hitting Index
Cissell-Chi 130
Meusel-NY 128
Judge-Was 123
Hodapp-Cle 118
Boley-Phi 117

Runs Created
Ruth-NY 183
Gehrig-NY 169
Manush-StL 150
Goslin-Was 125
Combs-NY 114

Total Average
Ruth-NY 1.410
Gehrig-NY 1.256
Goslin-Was 1.203
Manush-StL 1.040
Simmons-Phi .951

Stolen Bases
Myer-Bos 30
Mostil-Chi 23
Rice-Det 20
Cissell-Chi 18
Bluege-Was 18

Stolen Base Average
Rice-Was 84.2
Goslin-Was 84.2
Judge-Was 80.0
Manush-StL 77.3

Stolen Base Runs
Rice-Was 2.5
Goslin-Was 2.5
Reynolds-Chi 2.3
Judge-Was 2.1
Manush-StL 2.0

Fielding Runs
Gerber-StL-Bos 32.0
J.Sewell-Cle 27.0
Jamieson-Cle 19.9
Mostil-Chi 17.8
Schulte-StL 17.3

Total Player Rating
Ruth-NY 7.0
Gehrig-NY 5.7
J.Sewell-Cle 5.3
Goslin-Was 4.3
Manush-StL 3.6

Wins
Pipgras-NY 24
Grove-Phi 24
Hoyt-NY 23
Crowder-StL 21
Gray-StL 20

Win Percentage
Crowder-StL .808
Hoyt-NY .767
Grove-Phi .750
Pennock-NY .739
Quinn-Phi .720

Games
Marberry-Was 48
Morris-Bos 47
Pipgras-NY 46
Rommel-Phi 43

Complete Games
Ruffing-Bos 25
Thomas-Chi 24
Grove-Phi 24
Pipgras-NY 22

Shutouts
Pennock-NY 5
Quinn-Phi 4
Pipgras-NY 4
Jones-Was 4
Grove-Phi 4

Saves
Hoyt-NY 8
Hudlin-Cle 7
Lyons-Chi 6
Braxton-Was 6

Innings Pitched
Pipgras-NY 300.2
Ruffing-Bos 289.1
Thomas-Chi 283.0
Hoyt-NY 273.0
Gray-StL 262.2

Fewest Hits/Game
Braxton-Was 7.30
Grove-Phi 7.84
Earnshaw-Phi 8.13
Jones-Was 8.37
Johnson-NY 8.50

Fewest BB/Game
Rommel-Phi 1.35
Quinn-Phi 1.45
Pennock-NY 1.71
Braxton-Was 1.81
Russell-Bos 1.83

Strikeouts
Grove-Phi 183
Pipgras-NY 139
Thomas-Chi 129
Ruffing-Bos 118
Earnshaw-Phi 117

Strikeouts/Game
Earnshaw-Phi 6.65
Grove-Phi 6.29
Johnson-NY 4.97
Walberg-Phi 4.28
Whitehill-Det 4.26

Ratio
Braxton-Was 9.32
Grove-Phi 10.08
Rommel-Phi 10.62
Pennock-NY 10.88
Hoyt-NY 11.21

Earned Run Average
Braxton-Was 2.51
Pennock-NY 2.56
Grove-Phi 2.58
Jones-Was 2.84
Quinn-Phi 2.90

Adjusted ERA
Braxton-Was 159
Grove-Phi 155
Pennock-NY 147
Jones-Was 141
Quinn-Phi 138

Opponents' Batting Avg.
Braxton-Was .222
Grove-Phi .229
Earnshaw-Phi .240
Johnson-NY .250
Jones-Was .252

Opponents' On-Base Pct.
Braxton-Was .267
Grove-Phi .277
Rommel-Phi .295
Pennock-NY .302
Thomas-Chi .310

Starter Runs
Grove-Phi 42.4
Braxton-Was 37.0
Pennock-NY 34.7
Thomas-Chi 30.0
Jones-Was 29.8

Adjusted Starter Runs
Grove-Phi 41.8
Braxton-Was 36.5
Thomas-Chi 30.2
Pennock-NY 30.2
Jones-Was 29.2

Clutch Pitching Index
Miller-Cle 119
Quinn-Phi 119
Blankenship-Chi 114
Pennock-NY 113
Adkins-Chi 113

Relief Runs

Adjusted Relief Runs
Simmons-Bos 5

Relief Ranking
Simmons-Bos 2

Total Pitcher Index
Grove-Phi 4.7
Jones-Was 3.6
Braxton-Was 3.5
Gray-StL 3.4
Thomas-Chi 3.3

Total Baseball Ranking
Ruth-NY 7.0
Gehrig-NY 5.7
J.Sewell-Cle 5.3
Grove-Phi 4.7
Goslin-Was 4.3

TEAM	G	W	L	PCT	GB	R	OR	AB	H	2B	3B	HR	BB	SO	AVG	OBP	SLG	OPS	OPS+	BR	BR+	PF	CHI	RC	SB	CS	SBA	SBR
CHI	156	98	54	.645		**982**	758	5471	1655	**310**	46	139	**589**	567	.303	.373	.452	825	**111**	92	**90**	100	104	916	103			
PIT	154	88	65	.575	10.5	904	780	5490	1663	285	**116**	60	503	**335**	.303	.364	.430	794	101	28	8	102	104	850	94			
NY	152	84	67	.556	13.5	897	**709**	5388	1594	251	47	136	482	405	.296	.358	.436	794	103	18	21	100	**106**	827	85			
STL	154	78	74	.513	20	831	806	5364	1569	**310**	84	100	490	455	.293	.354	.438	792	101	12	4	101	100	819	72			
PHI	154	71	82	.464	27.5	897	1032	5484	**1693**	305	51	**153**	573	470	**.309**	**.377**	**.467**	**844**	108	**125**	66	107	92	**951**	59			
BRO	153	70	83	.458	28.5	755	888	5273	1535	282	69	99	504	454	.291	.355	.427	782	102	-1	16	98	93	792	80			
CIN	155	66	88	.429	33	686	760	5269	1478	258	79	34	412	347	.281	.336	.379	715	87	-133	-100	95	103	664	**134**			
BOS	154	56	98	.364	43	657	876	5291	1481	252	77	33	408	432	.280	.335	.375	710	85	-142	-114	96	99	659	65			
TOT	616					6609		43030	12668	2253	569	754	3961	3465	.295	.357	.426	783							692			

TEAM	CG	SH	SV	IP	H	H/G	HR	BB	SO	RAT	ERA	ERA+	OAV	OOB	PR	PR+	PF	CPI	FA	E	DP	FW	PW	BW	SBW	DIF
CHI	79	**14**	21	1398[2]	1542	**10.0**	77	537	548	13.6	4.16	111	**.284**	.350	86	71	98	104	**.975**	**154**	**169**	**1.5**	6.5	**8.2**		6.0
PIT	79	5	13	1379	**1530**	**10.0**	96	439	409	13.0	4.36	109	**.284**	.340	54	61	101	98	.970	181	136	-.2	5.6	.8		5.5
NY	68	9	13	1372	1536	10.1	102	**387**	431	**12.8**	**3.97**	**115**	.287	**.337**	**113**	**96**	97	**109**	**.975**	158	163	1.0	**8.8**	2.0		-3.0
STL	**83**	6	8	1359[2]	1604	10.7	101	474	453	14.0	4.66	100	.297	.357	8	-1	99	102	.971	174	149	.2	-.0	.4		1.6
PHI	45	5	**24**	1348	1743	11.7	122	616	369	16.1	6.13	85	.319	.391	-212	-129	110	96	.969	191	153	-.7	-11.7	6.1		1.1
BRO	59	8	16	1358	1553	10.3	92	549	**549**	14.2	4.93	94	.290	.360	-32	-49	98	95	.968	192	113	-.9	-4.4	1.5		-2.5
CIN	75	5	8	1369[1]	1558	10.3	**61**	413	347	13.1	4.42	103	.292	.345	46	23	97	97	.974	162	148	1.0	2.1	-9.0		-4.9
BOS	78	4	12	1352[2]	1604	10.7	103	530	366	14.4	5.13	91	.302	.367	-62	-69	99	99	.967	204	146	-1.5	-6.2	-10.3		-2.8
TOT	566	56	115	10937[1]		10.5				13.9	4.72		.295	.357					.972	1416	1177					

Runs
Hornsby-Chi 156
O'Doul-Phi 152
Ott-NY 138
Wilson-Chi 135
L.Waner-Pit 134

Hits
O'Doul-Phi 254
L.Waner-Pit 234
Hornsby-Chi 229
Terry-NY 226
Klein-Phi 219

Doubles
Frederick-Bro 52
Hornsby-Chi 47
Hafey-StL 47
Klein-Phi 45
Kelly-Cin 45

Triples
L.Waner-Pit 20
P.Waner-Pit 15
Walker-Cin 15
Whitney-Phi 14

Home Runs
Klein-Phi 43
Ott-NY 42
Wilson-Chi 39
Hornsby-Chi 39
O'Doul-Phi 32

Total Bases
Hornsby-Chi 409
Klein-Phi 405
O'Doul-Phi 397
Wilson-Chi 355
Herman-Bro 348

Runs Batted In
Wilson-Chi 159
Ott-NY 151
Hornsby-Chi 149
Klein-Phi 145
Bottomley-StL 137

Runs Produced
Hornsby-Chi 266
Wilson-Chi 255
Ott-NY 247
O'Doul-Phi 242
Klein-Phi 228

Bases On Balls
Ott-NY 113
Grantham-Pit 93
P.Waner-Pit 89
Hornsby-Chi 87
Walker-Cin 85

Batting Average
O'Doul-Phi .... .398
Herman-Bro .... .381
Hornsby-Chi .... .380
Terry-NY .... .372
Stephenson-Chi .... .362

On-Base Percentage
O'Doul-Phi .... .465
Hornsby-Chi .... .459
Ott-NY .... .449
Stephenson-Chi .... .445
Cuyler-Chi .... .438

Slugging Average
Hornsby-Chi .... .679
Klein-Phi .... .657
Ott-NY .... .635
Hafey-StL .... .632
O'Doul-Phi .... .622

On-Base Plus Slugging
Hornsby-Chi 1139
O'Doul-Phi 1087
Ott-NY 1084
Klein-Phi 1065
Herman-Bro 1047

Adjusted OPS
Hornsby-Chi 178
Ott-NY 166
Herman-Bro 160
O'Doul-Phi 157
Wilson-Chi 155

Batter Runs
Hornsby-Chi 74.1
O'Doul-Phi 68.5
Ott-NY 58.4
Klein-Phi 53.3
Herman-Bro 49.6

Adjusted Batter Runs
Hornsby-Chi 73.8
Ott-NY 58.9
O'Doul-Phi 58.2
Herman-Bro 52.4
Wilson-Chi 48.7

Clutch Hitting Index
Traynor-Pit 139
Sheely-Pit 137
Comorosky-Pit 133
Grimm-Chi 127
Kelly-Cin 122

Runs Created
Hornsby-Chi 183
O'Doul-Phi 180
Klein-Phi 158
Ott-NY 157
Wilson-Chi 148

Total Average
Hornsby-Chi 1.338
Ott-NY 1.287
O'Doul-Phi 1.247
Herman-Bro 1.205
Cuyler-Chi 1.181

Stolen Bases
Cuyler-Chi 43
Swanson-Cin 33
Frisch-StL 24
Herman-Bro 21
Allen-Cin 21

Stolen Base Average

Stolen Base Runs

Fielding Runs
Whitney-Phi 21.3
Maranville-Bos 19.5
Jackson-NY 19.2
L.Waner-Pit 15.7
English-Chi 15.4

Total Player Rating
Hornsby-Chi 7.0
Ott-NY 5.0
O'Doul-Phi 4.5
Jackson-NY 3.9
Wilson-Chi 3.6

Wins
Malone-Chi 22
Root-Chi 19
Lucas-Cin 19

Win Percentage
Root-Chi .... .760
Bush-Chi .... .720
Grimes-Pit .... .708
Malone-Chi .... .688
Kremer-Pit .... .643

Games
Bush-Chi 50
Willoughby-Phi 49
Sweetland-Phi 43
Root-Chi 43
Collins-Phi 43

Complete Games
Lucas-Cin 28

Shutouts
Malone-Chi 5
Root-Chi 4
Fitzsimmons-NY 4

Saves
Morrison-Bro 8
Bush-Chi 8
Koupal-Bro-Phi 6

Innings Pitched
Clark-Bro 279.0
Root-Chi 272.0
Bush-Chi 270.2
Lucas-Cin 270.0
Hubbell-NY 268.0

Fewest Hits/Game
Lucas-Cin 8.90
Hubbell-NY 9.17
Kremer-Pit 9.18
Johnson-StL 9.18
Bush-Chi 9.21

Fewest BB/Game
Vance-Bro 1.83
Lucas-Cin 1.93
Petty-Pit 2.05
Hubbell-NY 2.25
Clark-Bro 2.29

Strikeouts
Malone-Chi 166
Clark-Bro 140
Vance-Bro 126
Root-Chi 124
Hubbell-NY 106

Strikeouts/Game
Malone-Chi 5.60
Vance-Bro 4.90
Clark-Bro 4.52
May-Cin 4.16
Root-Chi 4.10

Ratio
Lucas-Cin 10.87
Hubbell-NY 11.62
Kremer-Pit 11.65
Petty-Pit 11.67
Vance-Bro 11.67

Earned Run Average
Walker-NY 3.09
Grimes-Pit 3.13
Root-Chi 3.47
Malone-Chi 3.57
Lucas-Cin 3.60

Adjusted ERA
Grimes-Pit 152
Walker-NY 148
Root-Chi 133
Johnson-StL 129
Malone-Chi 129

Opponents' Batting Avg.
Lucas-Cin .... .257
Johnson-StL .... .265
Hubbell-NY .... .265
Bush-Chi .... .265
Grimes-Pit .... .269

Opponents' On-Base Pct.
Lucas-Cin .... .297
Hubbell-NY .... .313
Clark-Bro .... .316
Vance-Bro .... .316
Petty-Pit .... .317

Starter Runs
Grimes-Pit 40.8
Root-Chi 37.4
Malone-Chi 33.8
Lucas-Cin 33.3
Walker-NY 32.0

Adjusted Starter Runs
Grimes-Pit 41.7
Root-Chi 35.1
Malone-Chi 31.5
Walker-NY 30.2
Lucas-Cin 29.8

Clutch Pitching Index
Mitchell-StL 129
Walker-NY 129
Sweetland-Phi 116
Grimes-Pit 116
Malone-Chi 115

Relief Runs
Hill-Pit-StL 2.9
Cvengros-Chi 5

Adjusted Relief Runs
Hill-Pit-StL 3.3

Relief Ranking
Hill-Pit-StL 1.9

Total Pitcher Index
Grimes-Pit 4.7
Lucas-Cin 4.1
Malone-Chi 3.1
Clark-Bro 2.6
Root-Chi 2.5

Total Baseball Ranking
Hornsby-Chi 7.0
Ott-NY 5.0
Grimes-Pit 4.7
O'Doul-Phi 4.5
Lucas-Cin 4.1

TEAM	G	W	L	PCT	GB	R	OR	AB	H	2B	3B	HR	BB	SO	AVG	OBP	SLG	OPS	OPS+	BR	BR+	PF	CHI	RC	SB	CS	SBA	SBR
PHI	151	104	46	.693		901	**615**	5204	1539	288	76	122	543	440	.296	**.365**	.451	**816**	111	**113**	82	104	**102**	875	61	38	62	0
NY	154	88	66	.571	18	899	775	5379	1587	262	74	**142**	554	518	.295	.364	.450	814	**123**	111	**174**	93	101	892	51	44	54	-4
CLE	152	81	71	.533	24	717	736	5187	1525	294	79	62	453	**363**	.294	.354	.417	771	100	26	-1	104	92	763	75	85	47	-13
STL	154	79	73	.520	26	733	713	5174	1426	277	64	46	**589**	431	.276	.352	.381	733	91	-33	-60	104	100	723	72	46	61	0
WAS	153	71	81	.467	34	730	776	5237	1445	244	66	48	556	400	.276	.347	.375	722	90	-55	-60	101	**102**	706	86	61	59	-2
DET	155	70	84	.455	36	**926**	928	5592	**1671**	**339**	**97**	110	521	496	**.299**	.360	**.453**	813	114	110	106	100	101	**914**	95	72	57	-4
CHI	152	59	93	.388	46	627	792	5248	1406	240	74	37	425	436	.268	.325	.363	688	83	-133	-125	99	101	633	**109**	65	**63**	**1**
BOS	155	58	96	.377	48	605	803	5160	1377	285	69	28	413	494	.267	.325	.365	690	85	-130	-115	98	99	616	85	80	52	-9
TOT	613					6138		42181	11976	2229	599	595	4054	3578	.284	.350	.408	756							634	491	56	-32

TEAM	CG	SH	SV	IP	H	H/G	HR	BB	SO	RAT	ERA	ERA+	OAV	OOB	PR	PR+	PF	CPI	FA	E	DP	FW	PW	BW	SBW	DIF
PHI	70	9	**24**	1357	**1371**	**9.1**	73	487	**573**	**12.5**	**3.44**	**123**	**.264**	**.329**	**121**	**119**	100	105	**.975**	**146**	117	**2.6**	**11.3**	7.8	.4	7.1
NY	64	12	18	1366^{2}	1475	9.8	83	485	484	13.1	4.20	92	.278	.341	7	-57	91	96	.971	178	153	.9	-5.3	**16.5**	.0	-.8
CLE	80	8	10	1352	1570	10.5	56	488	389	13.9	4.06	109	.295	.357	28	54	105	**109**	.968	198	**162**	-.5	5.1	-.0	-.8	1.5
STL	83	**15**	10	1371	1469	9.7	100	**462**	415	12.8	4.08	108	.279	.340	25	49	104	102	**.975**	156	148	2.2	4.7	-5.6	.4	1.5
WAS	62	3	17	1354^{2}	1429	9.5	**48**	496	494	13.0	4.34	98	.276	.342	-15	-16	100	89	.968	195	156	-.3	-1.5	-5.6	.2	2.3
DET	82	5	9	1390^{1}	1641	10.7	73	646	467	15.0	4.96	86	.301	.377	-111	-104	101	100	.961	242	149	-3.0	-9.8	10.0	.0	-4.1
CHI	78	5	7	1357^{2}	1481	9.9	84	505	328	13.4	4.42	97	.284	.351	-26	-22	101	98	.970	188	153	.1	-2.0	-11.7	**.5**	-3.6
BOS	**84**	9	5	1366^{2}	1537	10.2	78	496	416	13.6	4.43	96	.291	.355	-28	-25	101	100	.965	218	159	-1.5	-2.3	-10.8	-.5	-3.7
TOT	603	66	100	10916		9.9				13.4	4.24		.284	.350					.969	1521	1197					

Runs
Gehringer-Det 131
Johnson-Det 128
Gehrig-NY 127
Foxx-Phi 123
Ruth-NY 121

Hits
Gehringer-Det 215
Alexander-Det 215
Simmons-Phi 212
Fonseca-Cle 209
Manush-StL 204

Doubles
Manush-StL 45
Johnson-Det 45
Gehringer-Det 45
Fonseca-Cle 44

Triples
Gehringer-Det 19
Scarritt-Bos 17
B.Miller-Phi 16

Home Runs
Ruth-NY 46
Gehrig-NY 35
Simmons-Phi 34
Foxx-Phi 33
Alexander-Det 25

Total Bases
Simmons-Phi 373
Alexander-Det 363
Ruth-NY 348
Gehringer-Det 337

Runs Batted In
Simmons-Phi 157
Ruth-NY 154
Alexander-Det 137
Gehrig-NY 126
Heilmann-Det 120

Runs Produced
Simmons-Phi 237
Ruth-NY 229
Gehringer-Det 224
Alexander-Det 222
Gehrig-NY 218

Bases On Balls
Bishop-Phi 128
Blue-StL 126
Gehrig-NY 122
Foxx-Phi 103
Cronin-Was 85

Batting Average
Fonseca-Cle .... .369
Simmons-Phi .... .365
Manush-StL .... .355
Lazzeri-NY .... .354
Foxx-Phi .... .354

On-Base Percentage
Foxx-Phi .... .463
Gehrig-NY .... .431
Ruth-NY .... .430
Lazzeri-NY .... .429
Fonseca-Cle .... .427

Slugging Average
Ruth-NY .... .697
Simmons-Phi .... .642
Foxx-Phi .... .625
Gehrig-NY .... .584
Alexander-Det ..... .580

On-Base Plus Slugging
Ruth-NY 1128
Foxx-Phi 1088
Simmons-Phi 1040
Gehrig-NY 1015
Lazzeri-NY 991

Adjusted OPS
Ruth-NY 199
Foxx-Phi 171
Gehrig-NY 170
Lazzeri-NY 164
Simmons-Phi 158

Batter Runs
Foxx-Phi 63.2
Ruth-NY 61.9
Gehrig-NY 51.6
Simmons-Phi 50.3
Lazzeri-NY 43.9

Adjusted Batter Runs
Ruth-NY 71.6
Gehrig-NY 61.5
Foxx-Phi 58.1
Lazzeri-NY 52.8
Simmons-Phi 45.8

Clutch Hitting Index
West-Was 130
Heilmann-Det 129
Kress-StL 123
Myer-Was 119
Falk-Cle 118

Runs Created
Foxx-Phi 154
Ruth-NY 150
Gehrig-NY 146
Simmons-Phi 145
Alexander-Det 140

Total Average
Ruth-NY 1.288
Foxx-Phi 1.261
Gehrig-NY 1.151
Simmons-Phi 1.097
Lazzeri-NY 1.041

Stolen Bases
Gehringer-Det 27
Cissell-Chi 25
B.Miller-Phi 24
Rothrock-Bos 23
Johnson-Det 20

Stolen Base Average
Gehringer-Det 75.0
B.Miller-Phi 72.7
Myer-Was 72.0
Reynolds-Chi 67.9
Rice-Was 66.7

Stolen Base Runs
Gehringer-Det 2.8
B.Miller-Phi 2.1
Myer-Was 1.5
Goslin-Was 1.1
Reynolds-Chi 1.0

Fielding Runs
Durocher-NY 26.2
Kerr-Chi 24.0
Melillo-StL 22.5
Simmons-Phi 17.3
West-Was 15.0

Total Player Rating
Ruth-NY 4.9
Simmons-Phi 4.8
Lazzeri-NY 4.8
Gehrig-NY 4.3
Foxx-Phi 4.2

Wins
Earnshaw-Phi 24
Ferrell-Cle 21
Grove-Phi 20
Marberry-Was 19

Win Percentage
Grove-Phi .... .769
Earnshaw-Phi ...... .750
Ferrell-Cle .... .677
Walberg-Phi .... .621
Marberry-Was ...... .613

Games
Marberry-Was 49
Earnshaw-Phi 44
Gray-StL 43
Ferrell-Cle 43

Complete Games
Thomas-Chi 24
Uhle-Det 23
Gray-StL 23
Hudlin-Cle 22
Lyons-Chi 21

Shutouts
MacFayden-Bos 4
Gray-StL 4
Crowder-StL 4
Blaeholder-StL 4

Saves
Marberry-Was 11
Moore-NY 8
Shores-Phi 7
Ferrell-Cle 5

Innings Pitched
Gray-StL 305.0
Hudlin-Cle 280.1
Grove-Phi 275.1
Walberg-Phi 267.2
Crowder-StL 266.2

Fewest Hits/Game
Earnshaw-Phi 8.23
Wells-NY 8.33
Marberry-Was 8.38
Walberg-Phi 8.61
McKain-Chi 9.00

Fewest BB/Game
Russell-Bos 1.58
Pennock-NY 1.60
Thomas-Chi 2.08
Uhle-Det 2.10
Quinn-Phi 2.18

Strikeouts
Grove-Phi 170
Earnshaw-Phi 149
Pipgras-NY 125
Marberry-Was 121

Strikeouts/Game
Grove-Phi 5.56
Earnshaw-Phi 5.27
Pipgras-NY 4.99
Hadley-Was 4.52
Marberry-Was 4.35

Ratio
Marberry-Was 11.07
Thomas-Chi 11.44
Grove-Phi 11.83
Walberg-Phi 11.94
Faber-Chi 11.96

Earned Run Average
Grove-Phi 2.81
Marberry-Was 3.06
Thomas-Chi 3.19
Earnshaw-Phi 3.29
Hudlin-Cle 3.34

Adjusted ERA
Grove-Phi 150
Marberry-Was 139
Thomas-Chi 134
Hudlin-Cle 133
Earnshaw-Phi 129

Opponents' Batting Avg.
Earnshaw-Phi ...... .241
Wells-NY .... .248
Marberry-Was ...... .252
Walberg-Phi .... .254
Grove-Phi .... .262

Opponents' On-Base Pct.
Marberry-Was ...... .308
Thomas-Chi .... .310
Grove-Phi .... .316
Hudlin-Cle .... .318
Walberg-Phi .... .320

Starter Runs
Grove-Phi 43.7
Marberry-Was 32.9
Thomas-Chi 30.3
Hudlin-Cle 28.1
Earnshaw-Phi 27.0

Adjusted Starter Runs
Grove-Phi 43.4
Marberry-Was 32.8
Hudlin-Cle 32.7
Thomas-Chi 31.1
Earnshaw-Phi 26.7

Clutch Pitching Index
McKain-Chi 130
M.Gaston-Bos 116
Shaute-Cle 116
Ferrell-Cle 116
Collins-StL 113

Relief Runs
Moore-NY 7

Adjusted Relief Runs

Relief Ranking

Total Pitcher Index
Marberry-Was 3.8
Hudlin-Cle 3.7
Grove-Phi 3.5
Thomas-Chi 3.4
Ferrell-Cle 3.2

Total Baseball Ranking
Ruth-NY 4.9
Simmons-Phi 4.8
Lazzeri-NY 4.8
Gehrig-NY 4.3
Foxx-Phi 4.2

TEAM	G	W	L	PCT	GB	R	OR	AB	H	2B	3B	HR	BB	SO	AVG	OBP	SLG	OPS	OPS+	BR	BR+	PF	CHI	RC	SB	CS	SBA	SBR
STL	154	92	62	.597		**1004**	784	5512	1732	**373**	89	104	479	496	.314	.372	.471	843	105	72	41	103	104	944	72			
CHI	156	90	64	.584	2	998	870	5581	1722	305	72	**171**	**588**	635	.309	**.378**	**.481**	**859**	**111**	**110**	**103**	101	98	**1001**	70			
NY	154	87	67	.565	5	959	814	5553	1769	264	83	143	422	**382**	**.319**	.369	.473	842	110	67	87	98	101	941	59			
BRO	154	86	68	.558	6	871	**738**	5433	1654	303	73	122	481	541	.304	.364	.454	818	103	21	32	99	97	881	53			
PIT	154	80	74	.519	12	891	928	5346	1622	285	**119**	86	494	449	.303	.365	.449	814	101	15	12	100	101	862	**76**			
BOS	154	70	84	.455	22	693	835	5356	1503	246	78	66	332	397	.281	.326	.393	719	81	-186	-163	97	**105**	669	69			
CIN	154	59	95	.383	33	665	857	5245	1475	265	67	74	445	489	.281	.339	.400	739	87	-135	-98	95	94	703	48			
PHI	156	52	102	.338	40	944	1199	5667	**1783**	345	44	126	450	459	.315	.367	.458	825	97	37	-26	107	100	929	34			
TOT	618					7025		43693	13260	2386	625	892	3691	3848	.304	.361	.448	808							481			

TEAM	CG	SH	SV	IP	H	H/G	HR	BB	SO	RAT	ERA	ERA+	OAV	OOB	PR	PR+	PF	CPI	FA	E	DP	FW	PW	BW	SBW	DIF
STL	63	5	**21**	1380^{2}	1594	10.4	87	476	**639**	13.7	4.40	114	.293	.353	89	94	101	**104**	.970	183	**176**	.2	8.3	3.7		3.0
CHI	67	6	12	1403^{2}	1642	10.6	111	528	601	14.1	4.81	102	.294	.357	26	14	98	99	.973	170	167	1.1	1.3	**9.1**		1.7
NY	64	6	19	1363^{1}	1546	10.3	117	439	522	13.4	4.62	103	.290	.348	54	19	95	99	**.974**	164	144	1.3	1.7	7.7		-.6
BRO	74	**13**	15	1372	**1480**	**9.8**	115	**394**	526	**12.5**	**4.03**	**122**	**.278**	**.330**	**144**	**136**	99	102	.972	174	167	.7	**12.1**	2.9		-6.5
PIT	**80**	7	13	1361^{1}	1730	11.5	128	438	393	14.6	5.25	95	.313	.367	-41	-40	100	101	.965	216	164	-1.7	-3.5	1.1		7.3
BOS	71	6	11	1361	1624	10.8	117	475	424	14.0	4.92	100	.302	.360	9	3	99	102	.971	178	167	.5	.3	-14.3		6.7
CIN	61	6	11	1335	1650	11.2	**75**	**394**	361	14.0	5.08	95	.310	.361	-15	-38	97	96	.973	**161**	164	**1.5**	-3.3	-8.6		-7.4
PHI	54	3	7	1372^{2}	1993	13.1	142	543	384	16.9	6.72	81	.346	.405	-266	-172	110	99	.962	239	169	-2.9	-15.1	-2.2		-4.5
TOT	534	52	109	10949^{2}		10.9				14.1	4.98		.304	.361					.970	1485	1318					

Runs
Klein-Phi 158
Cuyler-Chi 155
English-Chi 152
Wilson-Chi 146
Herman-Bro 143

Hits
Terry-NY 254
Klein-Phi 250
Herman-Bro 241
Lindstrom-NY 231
Cuyler-Chi 228

Doubles
Klein-Phi 59
Cuyler-Chi 50
Herman-Bro 48
Comorosky-Pit 47
Frisch-StL 46

Triples
Comorosky-Pit 23
P.Waner-Pit 18
English-Chi 17
Cuyler-Chi 17
Terry-NY 15

Home Runs
Wilson-Chi 56
Klein-Phi 40
Berger-Bos 38
Hartnett-Chi 37
Herman-Bro 35

Total Bases
Klein-Phi 445
Wilson-Chi 423
Herman-Bro 416
Terry-NY 392
Cuyler-Chi 351

Runs Batted In
Wilson-Chi 191
Klein-Phi 170
Cuyler-Chi 134
Herman-Bro 130
Terry-NY 129

Runs Produced
Klein-Phi 288
Wilson-Chi 281
Cuyler-Chi 276
Terry-NY 245
Herman-Bro 238

Bases On Balls
Wilson-Chi 105
Ott-NY 103
English-Chi 100
Grantham-Pit 81
Suhr-Pit 80

Batting Average
Terry-NY .... .401
Herman-Bro .... .393
Klein-Phi .... .386
O'Doul-Phi .... .383
Lindstrom-NY .... .379

On-Base Percentage
Ott-NY .... .458
Herman-Bro .... .455
Wilson-Chi .... .454
O'Doul-Phi .... .453
Terry-NY .... .452

Slugging Average
Wilson-Chi .... .723
Klein-Phi .... .687
Herman-Bro .... .678
Hafey-StL .... .652
Hartnett-Chi .... .630

On-Base Plus Slugging
Wilson-Chi 1177
Herman-Bro 1132
Klein-Phi 1123
Terry-NY 1071
Hafey-StL 1059

Adjusted OPS
Wilson-Chi 177
Herman-Bro 171
Terry-NY 159
Klein-Phi 155
Ott-NY 152

Batter Runs
Wilson-Chi 75.4
Herman-Bro 68.7
Klein-Phi 67.3
Terry-NY 57.6
O'Doul-Phi 46.9

Adjusted Batter Runs
Wilson-Chi 74.2
Herman-Bro 70.7
Terry-NY 61.1
Klein-Phi 55.8
Ott-NY 48.4

Clutch Hitting Index
Thevenow-Phi 138
Traynor-Pit 133
Cuyler-Chi 129
Frisch-StL 126
Whitney-Phi 120

Runs Created
Wilson-Chi 189
Klein-Phi 186
Herman-Bro 183
Terry-NY 170
Cuyler-Chi 148

Total Average
Wilson-Chi 1.411
Herman-Bro 1.351
Klein-Phi 1.274
Ott-NY 1.224
Terry-NY 1.208

Stolen Bases
Cuyler-Chi 37
P.Waner-Pit 18
Herman-Bro 18

Stolen Base Average

Stolen Base Runs

Fielding Runs
Frisch-StL 27.5
Klein-Phi 23.0
Whitney-Phi 20.3
Terry-NY 12.6
Cuyler-Chi 12.2

Total Player Rating
Klein-Phi 5.7
Terry-NY 5.5
Wilson-Chi 5.2
Lindstrom-NY 4.9
Frisch-StL 4.2

Wins
Malone-Chi 20
Kremer-Pit 20
Fitzsimmons-NY 19

Win Percentage
Fitzsimmons-NY .... .731
Malone-Chi .... .690
Brame-Pit .... .680
Kremer-Pit .... .625
Hallahan-StL .... .625

Games
Elliott-Phi 48
Collins-Phi 47
Bush-Chi 46
Pruett-NY 45
Malone-Chi 45

Complete Games
Malone-Chi 22
Brame-Pit 22
French-Pit 21
Vance-Bro 20
Seibold-Bos 20

Shutouts
Vance-Bro 4
Root-Chi 4
Hubbell-NY 3
French-Pit 3

Saves
Bell-StL 8
Heving-NY 6
Clark-Bro 6

Innings Pitched
Kremer-Pit 276.0
French-Pit 274.2
Malone-Chi 271.2
Vance-Bro 258.2
Seibold-Bos 251.0

Fewest Hits/Game
Vance-Bro 8.39
Hallahan-StL 8.84
Fitzsimmons-NY 9.23
Elliott-Bro 9.26
Clark-Bro 9.41

Fewest BB/Game
Clark-Bro 1.71
Kolp-Cin 1.82
Johnson-StL 1.82
Lucas-Cin 1.88
Vance-Bro 1.91

Strikeouts
Hallahan-StL 177
Vance-Bro 173
Malone-Chi 142
Root-Chi 124
Hubbell-NY 117

Strikeouts/Game
Hallahan-StL 6.71
Vance-Bro 6.02
Root-Chi 5.07
Malone-Chi 4.70
Johnson-StL 4.41

Ratio
Vance-Bro 10.47
Clark-Bro 11.11
Kolp-Cin 11.44
Fitzsimmons-NY .. 11.63
Johnson-StL 12.33

Earned Run Average
Vance-Bro 2.61
Hubbell-NY 3.87
Walker-NY 3.93
Malone-Chi 3.94
Elliott-Bro 3.95

Adjusted ERA
Vance-Bro 188
Elliott-Bro 124
Malone-Chi 124
Grimes-Bos-StL 123
Hubbell-NY 122

Opponents' Batting Avg.
Vance-Bro .... .246
Hallahan-StL .... .260
Fitzsimmons-NY ..... .266
Walker-NY .... .268
Malone-Chi .... .271

Opponents' On-Base Pct.
Vance-Bro .... .289
Clark-Bro .... .306
Fitzsimmons-NY ..... .314
Kolp-Cin .... .314
Hubbell-NY .... .327

Starter Runs
Vance-Bro 67.9
Malone-Chi 31.1
Hubbell-NY 29.5
Walker-NY 28.5
Seibold-Bos 23.7

Adjusted Starter Runs
Vance-Bro 67.0
Malone-Chi 29.0
Hubbell-NY 24.3
Walker-NY 23.1
Seibold-Bos 22.9

Clutch Pitching Index
Grimes-Bos-StL 119
Smith-Bos 117
Haines-StL 109
Vance-Bro 108
Seibold-Bos 107

Relief Runs
Bell-StL 13.7
Lindsey-StL 6.4
Johnson-Cin 3

Adjusted Relief Runs
Bell-StL 14.2
Lindsey-StL 6.8

Relief Ranking
Bell-StL 9.9
Lindsey-StL 7.7

Total Pitcher Index
Vance-Bro 6.7
Malone-Chi 2.8
Grimes-Bos-StL 2.6
Walker-NY 2.3
Fitzsimmons-NY 2.2

Total Baseball Ranking
Vance-Bro 6.7
Klein-Phi 5.7
Terry-NY 5.5
Wilson-Chi 5.2
Lindstrom-NY 4.9

TEAM	G	W	L	PCT	GB	R	OR	AB	H	2B	3B	HR	BB	SO	AVG	OBP	SLG	OPS	OPS+	BR	BR+	PF	CHI	RC	SB	CS	SBA	SBR
PHI	154	102	52	.662		951	751	5345	1573	319	74	125	599	531	.294	.369	.452	821	108	102	62	104	100	913	48	33	59	-1
WAS	154	94	60	.610	8	892	**689**	5370	1620	300	98	57	537	**438**	.302	.369	.426	795	106	59	55	100	99	860	**101**	67	60	-1
NY	154	86	68	.558	16	**1062**	898	5448	**1683**	298	**110**	**152**	**644**	569	**.309**	**.384**	**.488**	**872**	**131**	**206**	**256**	96	99	**1035**	91	60	60	-1
CLE	154	81	73	.526	21	890	915	5439	1654	**358**	59	72	490	461	.304	.364	.431	795	102	54	21	104	99	863	51	47	52	-5
DET	154	75	79	.487	27	783	833	5297	1504	298	90	82	461	508	.284	.344	.421	765	96	-18	-33	102	98	771	98	70	58	-3
STL	154	64	90	.416	38	751	886	5278	1415	289	67	75	497	550	.268	.333	.391	724	85	-96	-120	103	**104**	696	93	71	57	-4
CHI	154	62	92	.403	40	729	884	5419	1496	256	90	63	389	479	.276	.328	.391	719	89	-111	-86	97	102	706	74	40	**65**	**2**
BOS	154	52	102	.338	50	612	814	5286	1393	257	68	47	358	552	.264	.313	.365	678	79	-192	-167	96	100	608	42	35	55	-3
TOT	616					6670		42882	12338	2375	656	673	3975	4088	.288	.351	.421	772							598	423	59	-16

TEAM	CG	SH	SV	IP	H	H/G	HR	BB	SO	RAT	ERA	ERA+	OAV	OOB	PR	PR+	PF	CPI	FA	E	DP	FW	PW	BW	SBW	DIF
PHI	72	**8**	**21**	1371	1457	9.6	84	488	**672**	12.9	4.29	109	.274	.337	56	58	101	98	**.975**	**145**	121	**3.0**	5.3	5.7	.0	11.1
WAS	**78**	6	14	1369	**1367**	**9.0**	**52**	504	524	**12.5**	**3.97**	**116**	**.264**	**.332**	**104**	**97**	99	97	.974	157	150	2.3	**8.8**	5.0	.0	.9
NY	65	7	15	1367^2	1566	10.4	93	524	572	14.0	4.89	88	.287	.352	-36	-98	93	96	.965	207	132	-.7	-8.8	**23.2**	.0	-4.6
CLE	68	5	14	1360	1663	11.1	85	528	442	14.7	4.89	99	.305	.368	-36	-9	104	**107**	.962	237	156	-2.5	-.8	1.9	-.3	5.8
DET	68	4	17	1351^2	1507	10.1	86	570	574	14.1	4.71	102	.286	.359	-8	13	103	102	.967	192	156	.2	1.2	-2.9	-.0	-.2
STL	68	5	10	1371^2	1639	10.8	124	449	470	13.9	5.08	96	.300	.356	-65	-29	105	101	.970	188	152	.4	-2.6	-10.8	-.2	.3
CHI	63	2	10	1361	1629	10.8	74	**407**	471	13.7	4.72	98	.300	.352	-10	-15	99	101	.962	235	136	-2.4	-1.3	-7.7	**.4**	-3.8
BOS	**78**	4	5	1360^1	1515	10.1	75	488	356	13.4	4.69	98	.286	.348	-6	-12	99	97	.968	196	**161**	-.0	-1.0	-15.1	-.0	-8.6
TOT	560	41	106	10912^1		10.2				13.7	4.65		.288	.351					.968	1557	1164					

Runs
Simmons-Phi 152
Ruth-NY 150
Gehringer-Det 144
Gehrig-NY 143
Combs-NY 129

Hits
Hodapp-Cle 225
Gehrig-NY 220
Simmons-Phi 211
Rice-Was 207
Morgan-Cle 204

Doubles
Hodapp-Cle 51
Manush-StL-Was 49
Morgan-Cle 47
Gehringer-Det 47

Triples
Combs-NY 22
Reynolds-Chi 18
Gehrig-NY 17
Simmons-Phi 16

Home Runs
Ruth-NY 49
Gehrig-NY 41
Goslin-Was-StL 37
Foxx-Phi 37
Simmons-Phi 36

Total Bases
Gehrig-NY 419
Simmons-Phi 392
Ruth-NY 379
Foxx-Phi 358

Runs Batted In
Gehrig-NY 174
Simmons-Phi 165
Foxx-Phi 156
Ruth-NY 153
Goslin-Was-StL 138

Runs Produced
Simmons-Phi 281
Gehrig-NY 276
Ruth-NY 254
Foxx-Phi 246
Cronin-Was 240

Bases On Balls
Ruth-NY 136
Bishop-Phi 128
Gehrig-NY 101
Foxx-Phi 93
Blue-StL 81

Batting Average
Simmons-Phi .... .381
Gehrig-NY .... .379
Ruth-NY .... .359
Reynolds-Chi ...... .359
Cochrane-Phi ...... .357

On-Base Percentage
Ruth-NY .... .493
Gehrig-NY .... .473
Foxx-Phi .... .429
Bishop-Phi .... .426
Combs-NY .... .424

Slugging Average
Ruth-NY .... .732
Gehrig-NY .... .721
Simmons-Phi ..... .708
Foxx-Phi .... .637

On-Base Plus Slugging
Ruth-NY 1225
Gehrig-NY 1194
Simmons-Phi 1130
Foxx-Phi 1066
Morgan-Cle 1014

Adjusted OPS
Ruth-NY 216
Gehrig-NY 207
Simmons-Phi 173
Foxx-Phi 159
Morgan-Cle 148

Batter Runs
Ruth-NY 89.5
Gehrig-NY 88.4
Simmons-Phi 64.2
Foxx-Phi 57.0
Morgan-Cle 46.3

Adjusted Batter Runs
Ruth-NY 98.1
Gehrig-NY 97.1
Simmons-Phi 57.9
Foxx-Phi 50.7
Morgan-Cle 41.2

Clutch Hitting Index
Rice-Det-NY 137
Lazzeri-NY 125
Dykes-Phi 113
Cronin-Was 112
Alexander-Det 112

Runs Created
Gehrig-NY 195
Ruth-NY 191
Simmons-Phi 163
Foxx-Phi 154
Morgan-Cle 144

Total Average
Ruth-NY 1.509
Gehrig-NY 1.389
Simmons-Phi 1.272
Foxx-Phi 1.184
Morgan-Cle 1.089

Stolen Bases
McManus-Det 23
Gehringer-Det 19
Goslin-Was-StL 17
Johnson-Det 17
Cronin-Was 17

Stolen Base Average
Reynolds-Chi 80.0
McManus-Det 74.2
Cissell-Chi 64.0
Johnson-Det 63.0
Cronin-Was 63.0

Stolen Base Runs
Lary-NY 2.4
McManus-Det 2.3
Reynolds-Chi 2.1
Simmons-Phi 1.3
Dickey-NY 1.2

Fielding Runs
Melillo-StL 26.8
Cronin-Was 26.1
Goldman-Cle 20.7
Oliver-Bos 15.2
Kamm-Chi 14.9

Total Player Rating
Gehrig-NY 7.6
Ruth-NY 7.4
Cronin-Was 6.8
Simmons-Phi 4.8
Cochrane-Phi 3.7

Wins
Grove-Phi 28
Ferrell-Cle 25
Lyons-Chi 22
Earnshaw-Phi 22
Stewart-StL 20

Win Percentage
Grove-Phi .... .848
Marberry-Was ..... .750
Jones-Was .... .682
Ferrell-Cle ...... .658
Ruffing-Bos-NY ... .652

Games
Grove-Phi 50
Earnshaw-Phi 49
Pipgras-NY 44
Johnson-NY 44
Ferrell-Cle 43

Complete Games
Lyons-Chi 29
Crowder-StL-Was ... 25
Ferrell-Cle 25
Stewart-StL 23
Grove-Phi 22

Shutouts
Pipgras-NY 3
Earnshaw-Phi 3
Brown-Cle 3

Saves
Grove-Phi 9
Braxton-Was-Chi 6
Quinn-Phi 6
Sullivan-Det 5
McKain-Chi 5

Innings Pitched
Lyons-Chi 297.2
Ferrell-Cle 296.2
Earnshaw-Phi 296.0
Grove-Phi 291.0
Crowder-StL-Was . 279.2

Fewest Hits/Game
Hadley-Was 8.37
Grove-Phi 8.44
Collins-StL 8.81
Crowder-StL-Was .. 8.88
Gaston-Bos 8.97

Fewest BB/Game
Pennock-NY 1.15
Lyons-Chi 1.72
Grove-Phi 1.86
Russell-Bos 2.08
Brown-Cle 2.15

Strikeouts
Grove-Phi 209
Earnshaw-Phi 193
Hadley-Was 162
Ferrell-Cle 143
Ruffing-Bos-NY ... 131

Strikeouts/Game
Grove-Phi 6.46
Johnson-NY 5.90
Earnshaw-Phi 5.87
Hadley-Was 5.60
Ruffing-Bos-NY .. 5.32

Ratio
Grove-Phi 10.45
Stewart-StL 11.69
Lyons-Chi 11.79
Marberry-Was ... 11.82
Caraway-Chi 11.82

Earned Run Average
Grove-Phi 2.54
Ferrell-Cle 3.31
Stewart-StL 3.45
Uhle-Det 3.65
Hadley-Was 3.73

Adjusted ERA
Grove-Phi 184
Ferrell-Cle 146
Stewart-StL 141
Uhle-Det 131
Sorrell-Det 124

Opponents' Batting Avg.
Grove-Phi .... .247
Hadley-Was .... .247
Crowder-StL-Was .. .259
Collins-StL ...... .259
Gaston-Bos .... .259

Opponents' On-Base Pct.
Grove-Phi .... .288
Stewart-StL ...... .315
Lyons-Chi .... .319
Marberry-Was ..... .321
Crowder-StL-Was .. .321

Starter Runs
Grove-Phi 68.3
Ferrell-Cle 44.2
Stewart-StL 35.9
Lyons-Chi 28.7
Hadley-Was 26.4

Adjusted Starter Runs
Grove-Phi 68.7
Ferrell-Cle 48.2
Stewart-StL 40.7
Uhle-Det 29.4
Lyons-Chi 28.0

Clutch Pitching Index
Henry-Chi 122
Harder-Cle 115
Sorrell-Det 115
Hoyt-NY-Det 113
Ferrell-Cle 113

Relief Runs
Quinn-Phi 2.3

Adjusted Relief Runs
Quinn-Phi 2.5

Relief Ranking
Quinn-Phi 4.4

Total Pitcher Index
Grove-Phi 7.2
Ferrell-Cle 6.0
Stewart-StL 4.4
Lyons-Chi 4.1
Uhle-Det 3.1

Total Baseball Ranking
Ruth-NY 7.7
Gehrig-NY 7.6
Grove-Phi 7.2
Cronin-Was 6.8
Ferrell-Cle 6.0

TEAM	G	W	L	PCT	GB	R	OR	AB	H	2B	3B	HR	BB	SO	AVG	OBP	SLG	OPS	OPS+	BR	BR+	PF	CHI	RC	SB	CS	SBA	SBR
STL	154	101	53	.656		815	614	5435	1554	**353**	74	60	432	475	.286	.342	.411	753	105	61	32	104	**107**	787	**114**			
NY	153	87	65	.572	13	768	**599**	5372	1554	251	64	**101**	383	**395**	**.289**	.340	.416	756	112	61	80	98	103	776	83			
CHI	156	84	70	.545	17	**828**	710	5451	**1578**	340	66	84	**577**	641	**.289**	**.360**	**.422**	**782**	**115**	**131**	**117**	102	97	**865**	49			
BRO	153	79	73	.520	21	681	673	5309	1464	240	**77**	71	409	512	.276	.331	.390	721	101	-3	2	99	101	705	45			
PIT	155	75	79	.487	26	636	691	5360	1425	243	70	41	493	454	.266	.330	.360	690	93	-54	-47	99	98	667	59			
PHI	155	66	88	.429	35	684	828	5375	1502	299	52	81	437	492	.279	.336	.400	736	96	27	-26	108	95	745	42			
BOS	156	64	90	.416	37	533	680	5296	1367	221	59	34	368	430	.258	.309	.341	650	84	-137	-117	96	98	580	46			
CIN	154	58	96	.377	43	592	742	5343	1439	241	70	21	403	463	.269	.323	.352	675	94	-85	-47	94	99	631	24			
TOT	618					5537		42941	11883	2188	532	493	3502	3862	.277	.335	.387	721							462			

TEAM	CG	SH	SV	IP	H	H/G	HR	BB	SO	RAT	ERA	ERA+	OAV	OOB	PR	PR+	PF	CPI	FA	E	DP	FW	PW	BW	SBW	DIF
STL	80	**17**	**20**	1384^2	1470	9.6	65	449	**626**	12.7	3.46	**114**	.273	.332	63	**72**	102	**110**	**.974**	160	169	**1.0**	**7.2**	3.2		12.7
NY	**90**	**17**	12	1360^2	**1341**	**8.9**	71	422	570	**11.9**	**3.31**	112	**.255**	**.313**	**85**	61	96	100	**.974**	**159**	126	**1.0**	6.1	8.0		-3.9
CHI	80	8	8	1385^2	1448	9.5	54	524	541	13.1	3.98	97	.268	.337	-17	-19	100	94	.973	169	141	.6	-1.8	**11.7**		-3.3
BRO	64	9	18	1356	1520	10.1	56	**351**	546	12.6	3.85	99	.283	.329	3	-5	99	100	.969	187	154	-.6	-.4	.2		4.0
PIT	89	9	5	1390	1489	9.7	55	442	345	12.7	3.66	105	.274	.331	32	28	100	102	.968	194	167	-.9	2.8	-4.6		.9
PHI	60	6	16	1360^1	1603	10.7	75	511	499	14.3	4.58	93	.293	.358	-108	-46	110	100	.966	210	149	-1.8	-4.5	-2.5		-1.9
BOS	78	12	9	1380^1	1465	9.6	66	406	419	12.4	3.90	97	.272	.325	-5	-18	98	94	.973	170	141	.6	-1.7	-11.6		-.0
CIN	70	7	6	1345	1545	10.4	**51**	399	317	13.2	4.22	89	.294	.346	-53	-75	97	101	.973	165	**194**	.7	-7.4	-4.6		-7.5
TOT	611	85	94	10962^2		9.8				12.8	3.87		.277	.335					.972	1414	1241					

Runs
Terry-NY 121
Klein-Phi 121
English-Chi 117
Cuyler-Chi 110
Ott-NY 104

Hits
L.Waner-Pit 214
Terry-NY 213
English-Chi 202
Cuyler-Chi 202
Klein-Phi 200

Doubles
Adams-StL 46
Berger-Bos 44
Terry-NY 43
Herman-Bro 43
Bartell-Phi 43

Triples
Terry-NY 20
Herman-Bro 16
Traynor-Pit 15
Bissonette-Bro 14

Home Runs
Klein-Phi 31
Ott-NY 29
Berger-Bos 19
Herman-Bro 18
Arlett-Phi 18

Total Bases
Klein-Phi 347
Terry-NY 323
Herman-Bro 320
Berger-Bos 316
Cuyler-Chi 290

Runs Batted In
Klein-Phi 121
Ott-NY 115
Terry-NY 112
Traynor-Pit 103
Herman-Bro 97

Runs Produced
Terry-NY 224
Klein-Phi 211
Ott-NY 190
Cuyler-Chi 189
Traynor-Pit 182

Bases On Balls
Ott-NY 80
P.Waner-Pit 73
Cuyler-Chi 72
Grantham-Pit 71
English-Chi 68

Batting Average
Hafey-StL .349
Terry-NY .349
Bottomley-StL .348
Klein-Phi .337
O'Doul-Bro .336

On-Base Percentage
Hafey-StL .404
Cuyler-Chi .404
P.Waner-Pit .404
Grantham-Pit .400
Klein-Phi .398

Slugging Average
Klein-Phi .584
Hornsby-Chi .574
Hafey-StL .569
Ott-NY .545
Arlett-Phi .538

On-Base Plus Slugging
Klein-Phi 982
Hafey-StL 973
Ott-NY 937
Terry-NY 926
Berger-Bos 892

Adjusted OPS
Ott-NY 153
Hafey-StL 153
Terry-NY 150
Klein-Phi 149
Berger-Bos 143

Batter Runs
Klein-Phi 48.9
Terry-NY 39.0
Hafey-StL 36.2
Ott-NY 35.0
Hornsby-Chi 33.5

Adjusted Batter Runs
Terry-NY 42.0
Klein-Phi 39.7
Ott-NY 37.6
Berger-Bos 35.7
Hafey-StL 32.7

Clutch Hitting Index
Sheely-Bos 150
Traynor-Pit 127
Frisch-StL 122
Gelbert-StL 122
Hendrick-Bro-Cin 120

Runs Created
Klein-Phi 140
Terry-NY 130
Cuyler-Chi 122
Berger-Bos 122
Herman-Bro 118

Total Average
Hafey-StL 1.055
Klein-Phi 1.051
Ott-NY 1.031
Terry-NY .955
Cuyler-Chi .925

Stolen Bases
Frisch-StL 28
Herman-Bro 17
Martin-StL 16
Adams-StL 16
Watkins-StL 15

Stolen Base Average

Stolen Base Runs

Fielding Runs
L.Waner-Pit 18.3
Frisch-StL 16.3
P.Waner-Pit 14.6
Gelbert-StL 12.9
Hurst-Phi 11.4

Total Player Rating
Berger-Bos 4.2
Ott-NY 3.9
Terry-NY 3.6
Cuccinello-Cin 3.3
P.Waner-Pit 3.2

Wins
Meine-Pit 19
Hallahan-StL 19
J.Elliott-Phi 19

Win Percentage
Derringer-StL .692
Hallahan-StL .679
Bush-Chi .667
Grimes-StL .654

Games
J.Elliott-Phi 52
Johnson-Cin 42
Collins-Phi 42

Complete Games
Lucas-Cin 24
Brandt-Bos 23
Meine-Pit 22
Hubbell-NY 21
French-Pit 20

Shutouts
Walker-NY 6
Hubbell-NY 4
Fitzsimmons-NY 4
Derringer-StL 4

Saves
Quinn-Bro 15
Lindsey-StL 7
J.Elliott-Phi 5
Hallahan-StL 4
Collins-Phi 4

Innings Pitched
Meine-Pit 284.0
French-Pit 275.2
Johnson-Cin 262.1
Fitzsimmons-NY 253.2
Root-Chi 251.0

Fewest Hits/Game
Hubbell-NY 7.66
Walker-NY 7.97
Brandt-Bos 8.21
Fitzsimmons-NY 8.59
Root-Chi 8.61

Fewest BB/Game
Johnson-StL 1.40
Lucas-Cin 1.47
Cantwell-Bos 1.96
Clark-Bro 2.01
Zachary-Bos 2.08

Strikeouts
Hallahan-StL 159
Hubbell-NY 155
Vance-Bro 150
Derringer-StL 134
Root-Chi 131

Strikeouts/Game
Vance-Bro 6.17
Hallahan-StL 5.75
Derringer-StL 5.70
Hubbell-NY 5.63
Root-Chi 4.70

Ratio
Hubbell-NY 10.23
Walker-NY 10.49
Johnson-StL 10.50
Fitzsimmons-NY 10.79
Brandt-Bos 11.12

Earned Run Average
Walker-NY 2.26
Hubbell-NY 2.65
Brandt-Bos 2.92
Meine-Pit 2.98
Johnson-StL 3.00

Adjusted ERA
Walker-NY 164
Hubbell-NY 139
Benge-Phi 134
Johnson-StL 131
Brandt-Bos 130

Opponents' Batting Avg.
Hubbell-NY .227
Walker-NY .231
Brandt-Bos .244
Fitzsimmons-NY .251
Root-Chi .252

Opponents' On-Base Pct.
Hubbell-NY .282
Walker-NY .283
Johnson-StL .286
Fitzsimmons-NY .296
Cantwell-Bos .301

Starter Runs
Walker-NY 42.7
Hubbell-NY 33.5
Meine-Pit 27.9
Brandt-Bos 26.3
Fitzsimmons-NY 22.9

Adjusted Starter Runs
Walker-NY 39.9
Hubbell-NY 30.0
Meine-Pit 27.4
Benge-Phi 26.8
Brandt-Bos 24.7

Clutch Pitching Index
Benton-Cin 125
Dudley-Phi 120
Grimes-StL 114
Hallahan-StL 113
Derringer-StL 112

Relief Runs
Lindsey-StL 9.1
Quinn-Bro 8.6
Moore-Bro .5

Adjusted Relief Runs
Lindsey-StL 9.5
Quinn-Bro 8.3
Moore-Bro .1

Relief Ranking
Quinn-Bro 14.9
Lindsey-StL 13.4
Moore-Bro .0

Total Pitcher Index
Fitzsimmons-NY 3.8
Brandt-Bos 3.6
Hubbell-NY 3.3
Walker-NY 3.0
Benge-Phi 2.9

Total Baseball Ranking
Berger-Bos 4.2
Ott-NY 3.9
Fitzsimmons-NY 3.8
Brandt-Bos 3.6
Terry-NY 3.6

TEAM	G	W	L	PCT	GB	R	OR	AB	H	2B	3B	HR	BB	SO	AVG	OBP	SLG	OPS	OPS+	BR	BR+	PF	CHI	RC	SB	CS	SBA	SBR
PHI	153	107	45	.704		858	**626**	5377	1544	311	64	118	528	543	.287	.355	.435	790	107	93	42	106	98	843	25	23	52	-3
NY	155	94	59	.614	13.5	**1067**	760	5608	**1667**	277	78	**155**	**748**	554	**.297**	**.383**	**.457**	**840**	**135**	**220**	**283**	94	100	**1016**	**138**	68	67	**7**
WAS	156	92	62	.597	16	843	690	5576	1588	308	**93**	49	481	459	.285	.345	.400	745	100	8	4	101	103	774	72	64	53	-7
CLE	155	78	76	.506	30	885	833	5445	1612	**321**	69	71	555	**433**	.296	.363	.419	782	105	91	44	106	100	840	63	60	51	-7
STL	154	63	91	.409	45	721	870	5374	1455	287	62	76	488	580	.271	.333	.390	723	92	-40	-65	104	98	696	73	80	48	-12
BOS	153	62	90	.408	45	625	800	5379	1409	289	34	37	405	565	.262	.315	.349	664	85	-154	-118	95	102	596	42	43	49	-6
DET	154	61	93	.396	47	651	836	5430	1456	292	69	43	480	468	.268	.330	.371	701	87	-79	-102	103	93	675	117	75	61	-1
CHI	156	56	97	.366	51.5	704	939	5481	1423	238	69	27	483	445	.260	.323	.343	666	86	-146	-105	94	**108**	632	94	39	**71**	**7**
TOT	618					6354		43670	12154	2323	538	576	4168	4047	.279	.345	.396	740							624	452	58	-21

TEAM	CG	SH	SV	IP	H	H/G	HR	BB	SO	RAT	ERA	ERA+	OAV	OOB	PR	PR+	PF	CPI	FA	E	DP	FW	PW	BW	SBW	DIF
PHI	**97**	**12**	16	1365^{1}	**1342**	**8.9**	73	457	574	**12.0**	**3.47**	**130**	**.256**	**.316**	**138**	**152**	103	**105**	**.976**	**141**	151	3.2	**14.2**	4.0	-.0	9.9
NY	78	4	17	1410^{1}	1461	9.4	67	543	**686**	13.0	4.20	94	.263	.332	28	-41	91	94	.972	169	131	1.7	-3.8	**26.4**	**.9**	-7.6
WAS	60	7	**24**	1394^{1}	1434	9.3	73	498	582	12.6	3.77	114	.264	.327	95	83	98	104	**.976**	142	148	**3.4**	7.8	.4	-.4	4.0
CLE	76	6	9	1354^{2}	1577	10.5	64	561	470	14.4	4.64	100	.286	.355	-38	-2	106	100	.963	232	143	-2.0	-.1	4.1	-.4	-.4
STL	65	4	10	1362	1623	10.8	84	**448**	436	13.9	4.76	97	.293	.348	-57	-17	106	99	.963	232	**160**	-2.1	-1.5	-6.0	-.9	-3.3
BOS	61	5	10	1366^{2}	1559	10.3	**54**	473	365	13.6	4.60	94	.285	.344	-33	-45	98	95	.970	188	127	.5	-4.1	-10.9	-.3	1.1
DET	86	5	6	1384^{1}	1549	10.1	79	597	511	14.2	4.59	100	.282	.355	-32	-1	105	102	.964	220	139	-1.4	-.0	-9.5	.2	-5.1
CHI	54	6	10	1390^{1}	1613	10.5	82	588	421	14.5	5.04	85	.287	.358	-101	-125	97	96	.961	245	131	-2.7	-11.6	-9.7	**.9**	2.8
TOT	577	49	102	11028		10.0				13.5	4.38		.279	.345					.969	1569	1130					

Runs
Gehrig-NY 163
Ruth-NY 149
Averill-Cle 140
Combs-NY 120
Chapman-NY 120

Hits
Gehrig-NY 211
Averill-Cle 209
Simmons-Phi 200
Ruth-NY 199
Webb-Bos 196

Doubles
Webb-Bos 67
Alexander-Det 47
Kress-StL 46
Cronin-Was 44

Triples
Johnson-Det 19
Gehrig-NY 15
Blue-Chi 15
Vosmik-Cle 14
Reynolds-Chi 14

Home Runs
Ruth-NY 46
Gehrig-NY 46
Averill-Cle 32
Foxx-Phi 30
Goslin-StL 24

Total Bases
Gehrig-NY 410
Ruth-NY 374
Averill-Cle 361
Simmons-Phi 329
Goslin-StL 328

Runs Batted In
Gehrig-NY 184
Ruth-NY 163
Averill-Cle 143
Simmons-Phi 128
Cronin-Was 126

Runs Produced
Gehrig-NY 301
Ruth-NY 266
Averill-Cle 251
Chapman-NY 225
Cronin-Was 217

Bases On Balls
Ruth-NY 128
Blue-Chi 127
Gehrig-NY 117
Bishop-Phi 112
Lary-NY 88

Batting Average
Simmons-Phi .390
Ruth-NY .373
Morgan-Cle .351
Cochrane-Phi .349
Gehrig-NY .341

On-Base Percentage
Ruth-NY .495
Morgan-Cle .451
Gehrig-NY .446
Simmons-Phi .444
Blue-Chi .430

Slugging Average
Ruth-NY .700
Gehrig-NY .662
Simmons-Phi .641
Averill-Cle .576
Foxx-Phi .567

On-Base Plus Slugging
Ruth-NY 1195
Gehrig-NY 1108
Simmons-Phi 1085
Averill-Cle 979
Cochrane-Phi 976

Adjusted OPS
Ruth-NY 223
Gehrig-NY 199
Simmons-Phi 172
Webb-Bos 151
Goslin-StL 147

Batter Runs
Ruth-NY 91.5
Gehrig-NY 79.9
Simmons-Phi 59.6
Averill-Cle 48.2
Goslin-StL 44.7

Adjusted Batter Runs
Ruth-NY 102.1
Gehrig-NY 90.4
Simmons-Phi 51.9
Webb-Bos 43.7
Averill-Cle 40.8

Clutch Hitting Index
Bluege-Was 126
Kamm-Chi-Cle 124
Vosmik-Cle 119
Lazzeri-NY 118
Spencer-Was 118

Runs Created
Ruth-NY 192
Gehrig-NY 185
Simmons-Phi 145
Averill-Cle 144
Goslin-StL 137

Total Average
Ruth-NY 1.487
Gehrig-NY 1.267
Simmons-Phi 1.199
Morgan-Cle 1.046
Cochrane-Phi 1.033

Stolen Bases
Chapman-NY 61
Johnson-Det 33
Burns-StL 19
Lazzeri-NY 18
Cissell-Chi 18

Stolen Base Average
Cissell-Chi 75.0
Reynolds-Chi 73.9
Chapman-NY 72.6
Lazzeri-NY 66.7
Bluege-Was 61.5

Stolen Base Runs
Chapman-NY 5.4
Cissell-Chi 1.9
H.Walker-Det 1.9
Blue-Chi 1.8
Reynolds-Chi 1.6

Fielding Runs
Melillo-StL 33.1
McManus-Det-Bos 21.1
West-Was 21.0
Burns-StL 18.4
Rhyne-Bos 16.9

Total Player Rating
Ruth-NY 7.4
Gehrig-NY 5.9
Simmons-Phi 4.8
Cronin-Was 4.4
Cochrane-Phi 4.3

Wins
Grove-Phi 31
Ferrell-Cle 22
Gomez-NY 21
Earnshaw-Phi 21
Walberg-Phi 20

Win Percentage
Grove-Phi .886
Marberry-Was .800
Mahaffey-Phi .789
Earnshaw-Phi .750
Gomez-NY .700

Games
Hadley-Was 55
Moore-Bos 53
Caraway-Chi 51
Frasier-Chi 46
Fischer-Was 46

Complete Games
Grove-Phi 27
Ferrell-Cle 27
Earnshaw-Phi 23
Whitehill-Det 22
Stewart-StL 20

Shutouts
Grove-Phi 4
Earnshaw-Phi 3

Saves
Moore-Bos 10
Hadley-Was 8
Marberry-Was 7
Kimsey-StL 7
Earnshaw-Phi 6

Innings Pitched
Walberg-Phi 291.0
Grove-Phi 288.2
Earnshaw-Phi 281.2
Ferrell-Cle 276.1
Whitehill-Det 271.1

Fewest Hits/Game
Hadley-Was 7.26
Gomez-NY 7.63
Grove-Phi 7.76
Johnson-NY 8.07
Earnshaw-Phi 8.15

Fewest BB/Game
Pennock-NY 1.43
Gray-StL 1.88
Grove-Phi 1.93
Brown-Cle 2.12
Blaeholder-StL 2.23

Strikeouts
Grove-Phi 175
Earnshaw-Phi 152
Gomez-NY 150
Ruffing-NY 132
Hadley-Was 124

Strikeouts/Game
Hadley-Was 6.21
Gomez-NY 5.56
Bridges-Det 5.46
Grove-Phi 5.46
Ruffing-NY 5.01

Ratio
Grove-Phi 9.73
Earnshaw-Phi 10.64
Gomez-NY 10.93
Coffman-StL 11.27
Uhle-Det 11.33

Earned Run Average
Grove-Phi 2.06
Gomez-NY 2.67
Hadley-Was 3.06
Brown-Was 3.20
Marberry-Was 3.45

Adjusted ERA
Grove-Phi 218
Gomez-NY 149
Hadley-Was 140
Brown-Was 134
Uhle-Det 131

Opponents' Batting Avg.
Hadley-Was .218
Gomez-NY .226
Grove-Phi .229
Johnson-NY .234
Earnshaw-Phi .236

Opponents' On-Base Pct.
Grove-Phi .271
Earnshaw-Phi .288
Gomez-NY .295
Coffman-StL .298
Uhle-Det .304

Starter Runs
Grove-Phi 74.5
Gomez-NY 46.2
Brown-Was 33.9
Hadley-Was 26.4
Marberry-Was 22.6

Adjusted Starter Runs
Grove-Phi 76.1
Gomez-NY 38.8
Brown-Was 32.0
Ferrell-Cle 25.5
Hadley-Was 25.2

Clutch Pitching Index
Grove-Phi 118
Faber-Chi 116
Whitehill-Det 115
Pennock-NY 110
Brown-Was 110

Relief Runs

Adjusted Relief Runs
Kimsey-StL 2.4

Relief Ranking
Kimsey-StL 2.7

Total Pitcher Index
Grove-Phi 8.4
Ferrell-Cle 5.0
Gomez-NY 3.9
Brown-Was 3.5
Earnshaw-Phi 2.8

Total Baseball Ranking
Grove-Phi 8.4
Ruth-NY 7.4
Gehrig-NY 5.9
Ferrell-Cle 5.0
Simmons-Phi 4.8

TEAM	G	W	L	PCT	GB	R	OR	AB	H	2B	3B	HR	BB	SO	AVG	OBP	SLG	OPS	OPS+	BR	BR+	PF	CHI	RC	SB	CS	SBA	SBR
CHI	154	90	64	.584		720	**633**	5462	1519	296	60	69	398	514	.278	.330	.392	722	101	0	7	99	101	728	48			
PIT	154	86	68	.558	4	701	711	5421	1543	274	**90**	48	358	**385**	.285	.333	.395	728	103	9	22	98	99	729	71			
BRO	154	81	73	.526	9	752	747	5433	1538	296	59	110	388	574	.283	.334	.420	754	**110**	55	**71**	98	99	778	61			
PHI	154	78	76	.506	12	**844**	796	5510	**1608**	**330**	67	**122**	**446**	547	**.292**	**.348**	**.442**	**790**	105	**132**	41	112	98	**870**	71			
BOS	155	77	77	.500	13	649	655	5506	1460	262	53	63	347	496	.265	.311	.366	677	90	-94	-70	96	105	643	36			
STL	156	72	82	.468	18	684	717	5458	1467	307	51	76	420	514	.269	.324	.385	709	93	-27	-46	103	100	702	**92**			
NY	154	72	82	.468	18	755	706	5530	1527	263	54	116	348	391	.276	.322	.406	728	103	1	16	98	**107**	735	31			
CIN	155	60	94	.390	30	575	715	5443	1429	265	68	47	436	436	.263	.320	.362	682	92	-77	-55	97	91	654	35			
TOT	618					5680		43763	12091	2293	502	651	3141	3857	.277	.328	.397	724							445			

TEAM	CG	SH	SV	IP	H	H/G	HR	BB	SO	RAT	ERA	ERA+	OAV	OOB	PR	PR+	PF	CPI	FA	E	DP	FW	PW	BW	SBW	DIF
CHI	79	9	7	1401	**1444**	**9.3**	68	409	527	12.1	**3.45**	**109**	**.264**	.319	**68**	**51**	97	102	.973	173	146	.4	**5.1**	.7		7.0
PIT	71	12	12	1377	1472	9.7	86	338	377	12.0	3.75	102	.270	.314	20	11	98	96	.969	185	124	-.3	1.1	2.2		6.2
BRO	61	7	16	1379^{2}	1538	10.1	72	403	497	12.9	4.28	89	.282	.334	-60	-69	98	94	.971	183	**169**	-.2	-6.8	**7.1**		4.1
PHI	59	4	**17**	1384	1589	10.4	107	450	459	13.5	4.47	99	.287	.344	-91	-8	114	100	.968	194	133	-.9	-.7	4.1		-1.3
BOS	72	8	8	1414	1483	9.5	**61**	420	440	12.3	3.53	107	.272	.328	55	37	97	105	**.976**	**152**	145	**1.8**	3.7	-6.9		1.6
STL	70	**13**	9	1396	1533	9.9	76	455	**681**	13.0	3.98	99	.282	.340	-14	-5	101	104	.971	175	155	.4	-.4	-4.5		-.3
NY	57	3	16	1375^{1}	1533	10.1	112	387	506	12.8	3.83	97	.280	.330	8	-19	96	**108**	.969	191	143	-.7	-1.8	1.6		-3.9
CIN	**83**	6	6	1394^{2}	1505	9.8	69	**276**	359	**11.7**	3.79	102	.274	**.311**	14	10	99	92	.971	178	129	.2	1.0	-5.4		-12.6
TOT	552	62	91	11121^{2}		9.8				12.5	3.88		.277	.328					.972	1431	1144					

Runs
Klein-Phi 152
Terry-NY 124
O'Doul-Bro 120
Ott-NY 119
Bartell-Phi 118

Hits
Klein-Phi 226
Terry-NY 225
O'Doul-Bro 219
P.Waner-Pit 215
Herman-Chi 206

Doubles
P.Waner-Pit 62
Klein-Phi 50
Stephenson-Chi 49
Bartell-Phi 48

Triples
Herman-Cin 19
Suhr-Pit 16
Klein-Phi 15

Home Runs
Ott-NY 38
Klein-Phi 38
Terry-NY 28
Hurst-Phi 24
Wilson-Bro 23

Total Bases
Klein-Phi 420
Terry-NY 373
Ott-NY 340
O'Doul-Bro 330
P.Waner-Pit 321

Runs Batted In
Hurst-Phi 143
Klein-Phi 137
Whitney-Phi 124
Wilson-Bro 123
Ott-NY 123

Runs Produced
Klein-Phi 251
Hurst-Phi 228
Terry-NY 213
Whitney-Phi 204
Ott-NY 204

Bases On Balls
Ott-NY 100
Hurst-Phi 65
Bartell-Phi 64
Suhr-Pit 63

Batting Average
O'Doul-Bro .368
Terry-NY .350
Klein-Phi .348
P.Waner-Pit .341
Hurst-Phi .339

On-Base Percentage
Ott-NY .424
O'Doul-Bro .423
Hurst-Phi .412
Klein-Phi .404
P.Waner-Pit .397

Slugging Average
Klein-Phi .646
Ott-NY .601
Terry-NY .580
O'Doul-Bro .555
Hurst-Phi .547

On-Base Plus Slugging
Klein-Phi 1050
Ott-NY 1025
O'Doul-Bro 978
Terry-NY 962
Hurst-Phi 959

Adjusted OPS
Ott-NY 175
O'Doul-Bro 164
Klein-Phi 158
Terry-NY 158
Herman-Cin 152

Batter Runs
Klein-Phi 68.2
Ott-NY 59.8
O'Doul-Bro 51.2
Terry-NY 46.4
Hurst-Phi 46.2

Adjusted Batter Runs
Ott-NY 62.8
O'Doul-Bro 53.9
Klein-Phi 51.9
Terry-NY 49.1
Herman-Cin 41.9

Clutch Hitting Index
Wilson-Bro 132
Whitney-Phi 131
Hogan-NY 129
Cuyler-Chi 126
Hurst-Phi 124

Runs Created
Klein-Phi 171
Ott-NY 151
O'Doul-Bro 142
Terry-NY 142
Hurst-Phi 134

Total Average
Klein-Phi 1.182
Ott-NY 1.166
O'Doul-Bro 1.059
Hurst-Phi 1.042
Terry-NY .981

Stolen Bases
Klein-Phi 20
Piet-Pit 19
Watkins-StL 18
Frisch-StL 18
K.Davis-Phi 16

Stolen Base Average

Stolen Base Runs

Fielding Runs
Jurges-Chi 31.7
Cuccinello-Bro 19.0
Herman-Chi 16.8
Frisch-StL 16.4
Stripp-Bro 15.9

Total Player Rating
Ott-NY 5.4
Klein-Phi 5.0
Herman-Cin 4.7
Terry-NY 4.7
O'Doul-Bro 4.0

Wins
Warneke-Chi 22
Clark-Bro 20
Bush-Chi 19

Win Percentage
Warneke-Chi .786
Bush-Chi .633
Rhem-StL-Phi .625
Clark-Bro .625
Hubbell-NY .621

Games
French-Pit 47
Dean-StL 46
Carleton-StL 44
Collins-Phi 43

Complete Games
Lucas-Cin 28
Warneke-Chi 25
Hubbell-NY 22

Shutouts
Warneke-Chi 4
Swetonic-Pit 4
Dean-StL 4

Saves
Quinn-Bro 8
Benge-Phi 6
Luque-NY 5
Cantwell-Bos 5

Innings Pitched
Dean-StL 286.0
Hubbell-NY 284.0
Warneke-Chi 277.0
French-Pit 274.1
Clark-Bro 273.0

Fewest Hits/Game
Swetonic-Pit 7.41
Brown-Bos 7.90
Warneke-Chi 8.03
Hubbell-NY 8.24
Malone-Chi 8.43

Fewest BB/Game
Swift-Pit 1.09
Lucas-Cin 1.17
Hubbell-NY 1.27
Benton-Cin 1.35
Betts-Bos 1.42

Strikeouts
Dean-StL 191
Hubbell-NY 137
Malone-Chi 120
Carleton-StL 113
Brown-Bos 110

Strikeouts/Game
Dean-StL 6.01
Hallahan-StL 5.51
Vance-Bro 5.28
Carleton-StL 5.18
Brown-Bos 4.65

Ratio
Hubbell-NY 9.63
Swift-Pit 9.78
Lucas-Cin 9.92
Warneke-Chi 10.17
Swetonic-Pit 10.46

Earned Run Average
Warneke-Chi 2.37
Hubbell-NY 2.50
Betts-Bos 2.80
Swetonic-Pit 2.82
Lucas-Cin 2.94

Adjusted ERA
Warneke-Chi 159
Hubbell-NY 148
Swetonic-Pit 135
Betts-Bos 134
Lucas-Cin 131

Opponents' Batting Avg.
Swetonic-Pit .221
Warneke-Chi .237
Hubbell-NY .238
Brown-Bos .238
Malone-Chi .244

Opponents' On-Base Pct.
Hubbell-NY .268
Swift-Pit .272
Lucas-Cin .274
Warneke-Chi .283
Swetonic-Pit .286

Starter Runs
Warneke-Chi 46.4
Hubbell-NY 43.4
Lucas-Cin 28.1
Betts-Bos 26.5
French-Pit 26.2

Adjusted Starter Runs
Warneke-Chi 44.2
Hubbell-NY 39.8
Lucas-Cin 27.5
French-Pit 24.6
Betts-Bos 24.3

Clutch Pitching Index
Bush-Chi 123
French-Pit 123
Zachary-Bos 117
Hallahan-StL 113
Derringer-StL 113

Relief Runs
Quinn-Bro 5.6
Frankhouse-Bos 3.8

Adjusted Relief Runs
Quinn-Bro 5.1
Frankhouse-Bos 2.5

Relief Ranking
Quinn-Bro 6.3
Frankhouse-Bos 2.0

Total Pitcher Index
Hubbell-NY 5.0
Lucas-Cin 4.5
Warneke-Chi 4.2
Cantwell-Bos 2.7
French-Pit 2.6

Total Baseball Ranking
Ott-NY 5.4
Klein-Phi 5.0
Hubbell-NY 5.0
Herman-Cin 4.7
Terry-NY 4.7

TEAM	G	W	L	PCT	GB	R	OR	AB	H	2B	3B	HR	BB	SO	AVG	OBP	SLG	OPS	OPS+	BR	BR+	PF	CHI	RC	SB	CS	SBA	SBR
NY	156	107	47	.695		**1002**	724	5477	1564	279	82	160	**766**	527	.286	**.376**	.454	**830**	**128**	**172**	**227**	95	99	**961**	77	66	54	-6
PHI	154	94	60	.610	13	981	752	5537	**1606**	303	52	**172**	647	630	**.290**	.366	**.457**	823	115	148	114	104	100	951	38	23	62	0
WAS	154	93	61	.604	14	840	**716**	5515	1565	303	**100**	61	505	442	.284	.347	.408	755	102	8	19	99	103	793	70	47	60	-1
CLE	153	87	65	.572	19	845	747	5412	1544	**310**	74	78	566	454	.285	.357	.413	770	99	44	-8	107	99	811	52	54	49	-7
DET	153	76	75	.503	29.5	799	787	5409	1479	291	80	80	486	523	.273	.335	.401	736	92	-35	-64	104	**106**	741	**103**	49	**68**	**6**
STL	154	63	91	.409	44	736	898	5449	1502	274	69	67	507	528	.276	.339	.388	727	89	-45	-86	106	97	726	69	62	53	-7
CHI	152	49	102	.325	56.5	667	897	5336	1426	274	56	36	459	**386**	.267	.327	.360	687	90	-122	-76	94	101	642	89	58	61	-1
BOS	154	43	111	.279	64	566	915	5295	1331	253	57	53	469	539	.251	.314	.351	665	80	-171	-154	97	94	593	46	46	50	-6
TOT	615					6436		43430	12017	2287	570	707	4405	4029	.277	.346	.405	750							544	405	57	-22

TEAM	CG	SH	SV	IP	H	H/G	HR	BB	SO	RAT	ERA	ERA+	OAV	OOB	PR	PR+	PF	CPI	FA	E	DP	FW	PW	BW	SBW	DIF
NY	**96**	**11**	15	1408	1425	**9.2**	93	561	**780**	**12.9**	**3.99**	102	**.260**	.331	**78**	17	91	101	.969	188	124	.2	1.6	**21.0**	-.3	7.6
PHI	95	10	10	1386	1477	9.6	112	511	595	13.1	4.46	102	.271	.336	4	11	101	98	**.979**	**124**	142	**3.9**	1.1	10.6	.3	1.4
WAS	66	10	**22**	1383[1]	1463	9.6	73	526	437	13.0	4.16	104	.271	.337	49	25	96	100	**.979**	125	157	3.8	2.4	1.8	.2	8.1
CLE	94	6	8	1377[1]	1506	9.9	**70**	**446**	439	**12.9**	4.12	**115**	.273	**.329**	55	**90**	106	98	.969	191	129	-.2	**8.4**	-.7	-.4	4.1
DET	67	9	17	1362[2]	**1421**	9.4	89	592	521	13.6	4.30	109	.269	.346	27	58	105	**102**	.969	187	154	.0	5.4	-5.9	**.8**	.3
STL	63	8	11	1376[2]	1592	10.5	103	574	496	14.3	5.01	97	.290	.359	-81	-22	108	100	.969	188	156	.0	-2.0	-7.9	-.4	-3.6
CHI	50	2	12	1348[2]	1551	10.4	88	580	379	14.5	4.83	90	.287	.359	-52	-77	97	101	.958	264	**170**	-4.5	-7.1	-7.0	.2	-7.9
BOS	42	3	7	1362	1574	10.5	79	612	365	14.7	5.02	90	.289	.364	-81	-79	100	99	.963	233	165	-2.6	-7.3	-14.2	-.3	-9.5
TOT	573	59	102	11004[2]		9.9				13.6	4.48		.277	.346					.970	1500	1197					

Runs
Foxx-Phi 151
Simmons-Phi 144
Combs-NY 143
Gehrig-NY 138
Manush-Was 121

Hits
Simmons-Phi 216
Manush-Was 214
Foxx-Phi 213
Gehrig-NY 208
Averill-Cle 198

Doubles
McNair-Phi 47
Gehringer-Det 44
Cronin-Was 43

Triples
Cronin-Was 18
Myer-Was 16
Lazzeri-NY 16
Chapman-NY 15

Home Runs
Foxx-Phi 58
Ruth-NY 41
Simmons-Phi 35
Gehrig-NY 34
Averill-Cle 32

Total Bases
Foxx-Phi 438
Gehrig-NY 370
Simmons-Phi 367
Averill-Cle 359
Manush-Was 325

Runs Batted In
Foxx-Phi 169
Simmons-Phi 151
Gehrig-NY 151
Ruth-NY 137
Averill-Cle 124

Runs Produced
Foxx-Phi 262
Simmons-Phi 260
Gehrig-NY 255
Manush-Was 223
Ruth-NY 216

Bases On Balls
Ruth-NY 130
Foxx-Phi 116
Bishop-Phi 110
Gehrig-NY 108
Cochrane-Phi 100

Batting Average
Alexander-Det-Bos .... .367
Foxx-Phi .... .364
Gehrig-NY .... .349
Manush-Was .... .342
Ruth-NY .... .341

On-Base Percentage
Ruth-NY .... .489
Foxx-Phi .... .469
Gehrig-NY .... .451
Bishop-Phi .... .412
Cochrane-Phi ...... .412

Slugging Average
Foxx-Phi .... .749
Ruth-NY .... .661
Gehrig-NY .... .621
Averill-Cle .... .569
Simmons-Phi .... .548

On-Base Plus Slugging
Foxx-Phi 1218
Ruth-NY 1150
Gehrig-NY 1072
Averill-Cle 961
Cochrane-Phi 921

Adjusted OPS
Ruth-NY 206
Foxx-Phi 203
Gehrig-NY 184
Lazzeri-NY 140
Averill-Cle 137

Batter Runs
Foxx-Phi 96.7
Ruth-NY 71.2
Gehrig-NY 68.6
Averill-Cle 41.1
Alexander-Det-Bos 31.8

Adjusted Batter Runs
Foxx-Phi 90.2
Ruth-NY 79.4
Gehrig-NY 77.5
Alexander-Det-Bos 33.3
Averill-Cle 32.9

Clutch Hitting Index
Dykes-Phi 124
Cronin-Was 121
Kamm-Cle 119
Lazzeri-NY 118
Davis-Det 114

Runs Created
Foxx-Phi 207
Gehrig-NY 168
Ruth-NY 157
Averill-Cle 140
Simmons-Phi 134

Total Average
Foxx-Phi 1.451
Ruth-NY 1.432
Gehrig-NY 1.188
Cochrane-Phi 1.000
Averill-Cle .... .991

Stolen Bases
Chapman-NY 38
Walker-Det 30
Johnson-Det-Bos ... 20
Cissell-Chi-Cle ... 18

Stolen Base Average
Walker-Det 83.3
Johnson-Det-Bos ... 76.9
Blue-Chi 73.9
Chapman-NY 67.9
Burns-StL 60.7

Stolen Base Runs
Walker-Det 4.5
Johnson-Det-Bos ... 2.3
Chapman-NY 2.1
Blue-Chi 1.6
Schuble-Det 1.3

Fielding Runs
Warstler-Bos 27.9
Vosmik-Cle 23.8
West-Was 19.3
Appling-Chi 18.1
Kress-StL-Chi 12.8

Total Player Rating
Foxx-Phi 6.4
Ruth-NY 5.8
Gehrig-NY 4.9
Cochrane-Phi 4.1
Lazzeri-NY 4.1

Wins
Crowder-Was 26
Grove-Phi 25
Gomez-NY 24
Ferrell-Cle 23
Weaver-Was 22

Win Percentage
Allen-NY .... .810
Gomez-NY .... .774
Ruffing-NY .... .720
Grove-Phi .... .714
Weaver-Was .... .688

Games
Marberry-Was 54
Gray-StL 52
Crowder-Was 50

Complete Games
Grove-Phi 27
Ferrell-Cle 26
Ruffing-NY 22

Shutouts
Grove-Phi 4
Bridges-Det 4

Saves
Marberry-Was 13
Moore-Bos-NY 8
Hogsett-Det 7
Grove-Phi 7
Faber-Chi 6

Innings Pitched
Crowder-Was 327.0
Grove-Phi 291.2
Ferrell-Cle 287.2
Walberg-Phi 272.0
Gomez-NY 265.1

Fewest Hits/Game
Allen-NY 7.59
Ruffing-NY 7.61
Bridges-Det 7.79
Grove-Phi 8.30
Crowder-Was 8.78

Fewest BB/Game
Brown-Cle 1.71
Crowder-Was 2.12
Gray-StL 2.31
Harder-Cle 2.40
Grove-Phi 2.44

Strikeouts
Ruffing-NY 190
Grove-Phi 188
Gomez-NY 176
Hadley-Chi-StL 145
Pipgras-NY 111

Strikeouts/Game
Ruffing-NY 6.60
Gomez-NY 5.97
Grove-Phi 5.80
Hadley-Chi-StL 5.26
Allen-NY 5.11

Ratio
Grove-Phi 10.77
Crowder-Was 10.90
Allen-NY 11.39
Ruffing-NY 11.71
Sorrell-Det 12.06

Earned Run Average
Grove-Phi 2.84
Ruffing-NY 3.09
Lyons-Chi 3.28
Crowder-Was 3.33
Bridges-Det 3.36

Adjusted ERA
Grove-Phi 159
Bridges-Det 140
Hogsett-Det 133
Lyons-Chi 132
Ruffing-NY 132

Opponents' Batting Avg.
Ruffing-NY .... .226
Allen-NY .... .228
Bridges-Det .... .233
Grove-Phi .... .241
Crowder-Was .... .252

Opponents' On-Base Pct.
Grove-Phi .... .292
Crowder-Was .... .295
Allen-NY .... .306
Ruffing-NY .... .311
Brown-Cle .... .314

Starter Runs
Grove-Phi 53.2
Crowder-Was 41.7
Ruffing-NY 39.9
Lyons-Chi 30.8
Ferrell-Cle 26.2

Adjusted Starter Runs
Grove-Phi 54.1
Crowder-Was 37.1
Ferrell-Cle 32.7
Ruffing-NY 31.1
Bridges-Det 28.6

Clutch Pitching Index
Hogsett-Det 129
Lyons-Chi 120
Weiland-Bos 117
Bridges-Det 116
Gaston-Chi 115

Relief Runs
Faber-Chi 8.8
Kimsey-StL-Chi 6.5

Adjusted Relief Runs
Kimsey-StL-Chi 8.9
Faber-Chi 7.2

Relief Ranking
Faber-Chi 8.9
Kimsey-StL-Chi 8.3

Total Pitcher Index
Grove-Phi 5.8
Ferrell-Cle 4.1
Ruffing-NY 3.8
Crowder-Was 3.7
Lyons-Chi 3.1

Total Baseball Ranking
Foxx-Phi 6.4
Ruth-NY 5.8
Grove-Phi 5.8
Gehrig-NY 4.9
Cochrane-Phi 4.1

TEAM	G	W	L	PCT	GB	R	OR	AB	H	2B	3B	HR	BB	SO	AVG	OBP	SLG	OPS	OPS+	BR	BR+	PF	CHI	RC	SB	CS	SBA	SBR
NY	156	91	61	.599		636	**515**	5461	1437	204	41	**82**	377	477	.263	.312	.361	673	100	-14	-4	98	**104**	617	31			
PIT	154	87	67	.565	5	667	619	5429	**1548**	249	**84**	39	366	**334**	**.285**	**.333**	**.383**	**716**	**111**	**71**	**72**	100	96	**709**	34			
CHI	154	86	68	.558	6	646	536	5255	1422	**256**	51	72	392	475	.271	.325	.380	705	107	47	49	100	99	643	52			
BOS	156	83	71	.539	9	552	531	5243	1320	217	56	54	326	428	.252	.299	.345	644	98	-70	-22	92	**104**	538	25			
STL	154	82	71	.536	9.5	**687**	609	5387	1486	**256**	61	57	391	528	.276	.329	.378	707	103	53	20	105	102	676	**99**			
BRO	157	65	88	.425	26.5	617	695	5367	1413	224	51	62	**397**	453	.263	.316	.359	675	103	-8	19	96	101	612	82			
PHI	152	60	92	.395	31	607	760	5261	1439	240	41	60	381	479	.274	.326	.369	695	93	32	-40	113	95	642	55			
CIN	153	58	94	.382	33	496	643	5156	1267	208	37	34	349	354	.246	.298	.320	618	83	-111	-104	99	103	487	30			
TOT	618					4908		42559	11332	1854	422	460	2979	3528	.267	.318	.363	679							408			

TEAM	CG	SH	SV	IP	H	H/G	HR	BB	SO	RAT	ERA	ERA+	OAV	OOB	PR	PR+	PF	CPI	FA	E	DP	FW	PW	BW	SBW	DIF
NY	75	**23**	15	1408^2	**1280**	**8.2**	61	400	555	**10.9**	**2.71**	**118**	**.242**	**.299**	**98**	**81**	96	102	.973	178	156	-.4	**8.6**	-.4		7.4
PIT	70	16	12	1373^1	1417	9.3	54	313	401	11.5	3.28	101	.264	.308	10	7	99	95	.972	166	133	.2	.8	**7.7**		1.5
CHI	**95**	16	9	1362	1316	8.7	51	413	488	11.7	2.93	112	.254	.312	62	53	98	**105**	.973	168	**163**	.0	5.7	5.2		-1.8
BOS	85	15	**16**	1403	1391	9.0	54	355	383	11.3	2.97	103	.261	.309	58	15	92	**105**	**.978**	**138**	148	**2.2**	1.6	-2.3		4.7
STL	73	11	**16**	1382^2	1391	9.1	55	452	**635**	12.2	3.38	103	.261	.321	-5	15	104	98	.973	162	119	.5	1.6	2.2		1.4
BRO	71	9	10	1386^1	1502	9.8	51	374	415	12.5	3.73	86	.275	.326	-60	-82	96	95	.971	177	120	-.3	-8.6	2.1		-4.4
PHI	52	10	13	1336^2	1563	10.6	87	410	341	13.6	4.35	88	.293	.348	-150	-69	114	101	.970	183	156	-1.0	-7.3	-4.2		-3.3
CIN	74	13	8	1352	1470	9.8	**47**	**257**	310	11.6	3.43	99	.279	.314	-13	-5	102	99	.971	177	139	-.6	-.5	-11.0		-5.8
TOT	595	113	99	11004^2		9.3				11.9	3.34		.267	.318					.973	1349	1134					

Runs		Hits		Doubles		Triples		Home Runs		Total Bases	
Martin-StL	122	Klein-Phi	223	Klein-Phi	44	Vaughan-Pit	19	Klein-Phi	28	Klein-Phi	365
P.Waner-Pit	101	Fullis-Phi	200	Medwick-StL	40	P.Waner-Pit	16	Berger-Bos	27	Berger-Bos	299
Klein-Phi	101	P.Waner-Pit	191	Lindstrom-Pit	39	Martin-StL	12	Ott-NY	23	Medwick-StL	296
Ott-NY	98	Traynor-Pit	190	P.Waner-Pit	38	B.Herman-Chi	12	Medwick-StL	18	P.Waner-Pit	282
Medwick-StL	92	Martin-StL	189	Berger-Bos	37					Vaughan-Pit	274

Runs Batted In		Runs Produced		Bases On Balls		Batting Average		On-Base Percentage		Slugging Average	
Klein-Phi	120	Klein-Phi	193	Ott-NY	75	Klein-Phi	.368	Klein-Phi	.422	Klein-Phi	.602
Berger-Bos	106	Ott-NY	178	Suhr-Pit	72	Davis-Phi	.349	Davis-Phi	.395	Berger-Bos	.566
Ott-NY	103	Vaughan-Pit	173	Martin-StL	67	Stephenson-Chi	.329	Vaughan-Pit	.388	B.Herman-Chi	.502
Medwick-StL	98	Medwick-StL	172	Vaughan-Pit	64	Piet-Pit	.323	Martin-StL	.387	Medwick-StL	.497
Vaughan-Pit	97	Martin-StL	171	P.Waner-Pit	60	Terry-NY	.322	Terry-NY	.375	Vaughan-Pit	.478

On-Base Plus Slugging		Adjusted OPS		Batter Runs		Adjusted Batter Runs		Clutch Hitting Index		Runs Created	
Klein-Phi	1025	Berger-Bos	177	Klein-Phi	69.1	Klein-Phi	53.4	Hartnett-Chi	120	Klein-Phi	162
Berger-Bos	932	Klein-Phi	168	Berger-Bos	40.5	Berger-Bos	49.5	Traynor-Pit	119	Berger-Bos	113
Davis-Phi	867	Vaughan-Pit	146	Vaughan-Pit	35.2	Vaughan-Pit	35.4	Rice-Cin	117	Vaughan-Pit	112
Vaughan-Pit	866	B.Herman-Chi	142	Martin-StL	32.3	Ott-NY	30.0	Ott-NY	114	Martin-StL	111
B.Herman-Chi	855	Ott-NY	139	Davis-Phi	29.8	P.Waner-Pit	28.9	Bottomley-Cin	111	P.Waner-Pit	109

Total Average		Stolen Bases		Stolen Base Average		Stolen Base Runs		Fielding Runs		Total Player Rating	
Klein-Phi	1.132	Martin-StL	26					Critz-NY	46.5	Klein-Phi	5.4
Berger-Bos	.935	Fullis-Phi	18					B.Herman-Chi	29.1	Berger-Bos	5.1
Martin-StL	.881	Frisch-StL	18					Jurges-Chi	20.1	Vaughan-Pit	3.9
Vaughan-Pit	.861	Klein-Phi	15					Lopez-Bro	18.4	B.Herman-Chi	3.6
B.Herman-Chi	.827	Orsatti-StL	14					Ryan-NY	17.4	Critz-NY	3.3

Wins		Win Percentage		Games		Complete Games		Shutouts		Saves	
Hubbell-NY	23	Cantwell-Bos	.667	Dean-StL	48	Warneke-Chi	26	Hubbell-NY	10	Collins-Phi	6
Dean-StL	20	Hubbell-NY	.657	French-Pit	47	Dean-StL	26	Schumacher-NY	7	Hubbell-NY	5
Cantwell-Bos	20	Meine-Pit	.652	Liska-Phi	45	Brandt-Bos	23	French-Pit	5	Harris-Pit	5
Bush-Chi	20	Bush-Chi	.625	Hubbell-NY	45	Hubbell-NY	22			Bell-NY	5
Schumacher-NY	19	Schumacher-NY	.613	Carleton-StL	44						

Innings Pitched		Fewest Hits/Game		Fewest BB/Game		Strikeouts		Strikeouts/Game		Ratio	
Hubbell-NY	308.2	Schumacher-NY	6.92	Lucas-Cin	.74	Dean-StL	199	Dean-StL	6.11	Hubbell-NY	8.92
Dean-StL	293.0	Hubbell-NY	7.46	Hubbell-NY	1.37	Hubbell-NY	156	Parmelee-NY	5.44	Schumacher-NY	9.88
French-Pit	291.1	Parmelee-NY	7.87	Swift-Pit	1.48	Carleton-StL	147	Carleton-StL	4.78	Betts-Bos	10.41
Brandt-Bos	287.2	Brandt-Bos	8.01	Hansen-Phi	1.60	Warneke-Chi	133	Hubbell-NY	4.55	Swift-Pit	10.47
Warneke-Chi	287.1	Mungo-Bro	8.09	French-Pit	1.70	Parmelee-NY	132	Warneke-Chi	4.17	Brandt-Bos	10.51

Earned Run Average		Adjusted ERA		Opponents' Batting Avg.		Opponents' On-Base Pct.		Starter Runs		Adjusted Starter Runs	
Hubbell-NY	1.66	Hubbell-NY	193	Schumacher-NY	.214	Hubbell-NY	.260	Hubbell-NY	57.4	Hubbell-NY	55.2
Warneke-Chi	2.00	Warneke-Chi	163	Hubbell-NY	.227	Schumacher-NY	.280	Warneke-Chi	42.5	Warneke-Chi	41.2
Schumacher-NY	2.16	Schumacher-NY	149	Parmelee-NY	.232	Swift-Pit	.285	Schumacher-NY	33.9	Schumacher-NY	31.4
Brandt-Bos	2.60	Root-Chi	126	Mungo-Bro	.236	Betts-Bos	.290	Brandt-Bos	23.6	French-Pit	19.5
Root-Chi	2.60	French-Pit	122	Warneke-Chi	.244	Cantwell-Bos	.291	Cantwell-Bos	20.4	Root-Chi	18.4

Clutch Pitching Index		Relief Runs		Adjusted Relief Runs		Relief Ranking		Total Pitcher Index		Total Baseball Ranking	
Warneke-Chi	131	Bell-NY	15.0	Bell-NY	14.1	Bell-NY	14.8	Hubbell-NY	7.8	Hubbell-NY	7.8
Root-Chi	120	Luque-NY	5.8	Luque-NY	4.8	Luque-NY	6.0	Warneke-Chi	6.3	Warneke-Chi	6.3
Walker-StL	117	Harris-Pit	.7	Harris-Pit	.6	Harris-Pit	.9	Schumacher-NY	4.4	Klein-Phi	5.4
Holley-Phi	115							Brandt-Bos	2.9	Berger-Bos	5.1
Hubbell-NY	112							Bush-Chi	2.2	Schumacher-NY	4.4

TEAM	G	W	L	PCT	GB	R	OR	AB	H	2B	3B	HR	BB	SO	AVG	OBP	SLG	OPS	OPS+	BR	BR+	PF	CHI	RC	SB	CS	SBA	SBR
WAS	153	99	53	.651		850	**665**	5524	**1586**	281	**86**	60	539	**395**	**.287**	.353	.402	755	107	47	56	99	102	798	65	50	57	-3
NY	152	91	59	.607	7	**927**	768	5274	1495	241	75	**144**	**700**	506	.283	**.369**	**.440**	**809**	**129**	**155**	**214**	94	100	**880**	**76**	59	56	-4
PHI	152	79	72	.523	19.5	875	853	5330	1519	**297**	57	139	625	618	.285	.362	**.440**	802	118	135	126	101	97	868	34	34	50	-4
CLE	151	75	76	.497	23.5	654	669	5240	1366	218	77	50	448	426	.261	.321	.360	681	82	-103	-130	105	**103**	616	36	40	47	-6
DET	155	75	79	.487	25	722	733	5502	1479	283	78	57	475	523	.269	.329	.380	709	92	-54	-67	102	101	698	68	50	58	-3
CHI	151	67	83	.447	31	683	814	5318	1448	231	53	43	538	416	.272	.342	.360	702	96	-50	-19	96	96	674	43	46	48	-7
BOS	149	63	86	.423	34.5	700	758	5201	1407	294	56	50	525	464	.271	.339	.377	716	97	-29	-22	99	98	687	58	37	**61**	0
STL	153	55	96	.364	43.5	669	820	5285	1337	244	64	64	520	556	.253	.322	.360	682	81	-102	-140	106	**103**	625	72	60	55	-5
TOT	608					6080		42674	11637	2089	546	607	4370	3904	.273	.343	.391	732							452	376	55	-32

TEAM	CG	SH	SV	IP	H	H/G	HR	BB	SO	RAT	ERA	ERA+	OAV	OOB	PR	PR+	PF	CPI	FA	E	DP	FW	PW	BW	SBW	DIF
WAS	68	5	**26**	1389^{2}	1415	**9.2**	64	**452**	447	**12.2**	3.83	109	**.263**	**.322**	71	57	98	98	**.979**	**131**	149	**2.6**	5.4	5.4	.0	9.7
NY	70	8	22	1354^{2}	1426	9.5	66	612	**711**	13.7	4.37	89	.267	.344	-13	-80	91	96	.972	165	122	.5	-7.5	**20.3**	.0	3.0
PHI	69	6	14	1343^{2}	1523	10.3	77	644	423	14.7	4.81	89	.283	.361	-79	-78	100	99	.966	203	121	-1.9	-7.3	12.0	.0	1.0
CLE	**74**	**12**	7	1350	**1382**	9.3	**60**	465	437	12.5	**3.71**	**120**	.264	.325	**86**	**107**	104	102	.974	156	127	.9	**10.2**	-12.3	-.2	1.0
DET	69	6	17	1398	1415	**9.2**	84	561	575	12.9	3.95	109	**.263**	.335	52	56	101	**103**	.971	178	**167**	-.1	5.4	-6.3	.0	-.8
CHI	53	8	13	1371^{1}	1505	9.9	85	519	423	13.5	4.45	95	.277	.343	-26	-33	99	99	.970	186	143	-.9	-3.1	-1.7	-.3	-1.8
BOS	60	4	14	1327^{2}	1396	9.5	75	591	467	13.7	4.36	101	.271	.348	-10	4	102	100	.966	204	133	-2.2	.4	-2.0	**.4**	-7.9
STL	55	7	10	1360^{2}	1574	10.5	96	531	426	14.1	4.83	97	.289	.354	-82	-23	109	100	.976	149	162	1.5	-2.1	-13.2	-.0	-6.4
TOT	518	56	123	10895^{2}		9.7				13.4	4.29		.273	.343					.972	1372	1124					

Runs
Gehrig-NY 138
Foxx-Phi 125
Manush-Was 115
Chapman-NY 112
Cramer-Phi 109

Hits
Manush-Was 221
Gehringer-Det 204
Foxx-Phi 204
Simmons-Chi 200
Gehrig-NY 198

Doubles
Cronin-Was 45
Johnson-Phi 44
Burns-StL 43
Rogell-Det 42
Gehringer-Det 42

Triples
Manush-Was 17
Combs-NY 16
Averill-Cle 16
Myer-Was 15
Reynolds-StL 14

Home Runs
Foxx-Phi 48
Ruth-NY 34
Gehrig-NY 32
Johnson-Phi 21
Lazzeri-NY 18

Total Bases
Foxx-Phi 403
Gehrig-NY 359
Manush-Was 302
Gehringer-Det 294
Simmons-Chi 291

Runs Batted In
Foxx-Phi 163
Gehrig-NY 139
Simmons-Chi 119
Cronin-Was 118
Kuhel-Was 107

Runs Produced
Gehrig-NY 245
Foxx-Phi 240
Manush-Was 205
Cronin-Was 202
Chapman-NY 201

Bases On Balls
Ruth-NY 114
Cochrane-Phi 106
Bishop-Phi 106
Foxx-Phi 96
Swanson-Chi 93

Batting Average
Foxx-Phi .356
Manush-Was .336
Gehrig-NY .334
Simmons-Chi .331
Gehringer-Det .325

On-Base Percentage
Cochrane-Phi .459
Foxx-Phi .449
Bishop-Phi .446
Ruth-NY .442
Gehrig-NY .424

Slugging Average
Foxx-Phi .703
Gehrig-NY .605
Ruth-NY .582
Cochrane-Phi .515
Johnson-Phi .505

On-Base Plus Slugging
Foxx-Phi 1153
Gehrig-NY 1030
Ruth-NY 1023
Cochrane-Phi 974
Johnson-Phi 892

Adjusted OPS
Foxx-Phi 199
Gehrig-NY 181
Ruth-NY 180
Cochrane-Phi 156
Dickey-NY 138

Batter Runs
Foxx-Phi 82.7
Gehrig-NY 59.5
Ruth-NY 49.5
Cochrane-Phi 41.6
Johnson-Phi 26.8

Adjusted Batter Runs
Foxx-Phi 81.1
Gehrig-NY 68.8
Ruth-NY 57.3
Cochrane-Phi 40.5
Lazzeri-NY 28.0

Clutch Hitting Index
Cronin-Was 126
Melillo-StL 125
Ferrell-StL-Bos 124
Bluege-Was 123
Kress-Chi 121

Runs Created
Foxx-Phi 184
Gehrig-NY 151
Ruth-NY 124
Gehringer-Det 117
Manush-Was 111

Total Average
Foxx-Phi 1.348
Ruth-NY 1.172
Cochrane-Phi 1.118
Gehrig-NY 1.098
Johnson-Phi .940

Stolen Bases
Chapman-NY 27
Walker-Det 26
Swanson-Chi 19
Kuhel-Was 17

Stolen Base Average
Walker-Det 74.3
Kuhel-Was 68.0
Swanson-Chi 63.3
Chapman-NY 60.0

Stolen Base Runs
Walker-Det 2.6
Werber-NY-Bos 1.5
Kuhel-Was .9
Stumpf-Bos .9
Lazzeri-NY .9

Fielding Runs
Melillo-StL 23.3
Rogell-Det 19.5
Schulte-Was 15.8
Simmons-Chi 14.3
Scharein-StL 14.0

Total Player Rating
Foxx-Phi 6.7
Gehrig-NY 4.5
Cronin-Was 4.1
Ruth-NY 3.9
Cochrane-Phi 3.8

Wins
Grove-Phi 24
Crowder-Was 24
Whitehill-Was 22

Win Percentage
Grove-Phi .750
Whitehill-Was .733
Stewart-Was .714
Allen-NY .682

Games
Crowder-Was 52
Russell-Was 50
Welch-Bos 47
Kline-Bos 46

Complete Games
Grove-Phi 21
Whitehill-Was 19
Hadley-StL 19
Ruffing-NY 18

Shutouts
Hildebrand-Cle 6
Gomez-NY 4
Blaeholder-StL 3

Saves
Russell-Was 13
Hogsett-Det 9
Moore-NY 8
Heving-Chi 6
Grove-Phi 6

Innings Pitched
Hadley-StL 316.2
Crowder-Was 299.1
Grove-Phi 275.1
Whitehill-Was 270.0
Blaeholder-StL 255.2

Fewest Hits/Game
Bridges-Det 7.42
Weiland-Bos 8.20
Allen-NY 8.33
Gomez-NY 8.36
Hildebrand-Cle 8.37

Fewest BB/Game
Brown-Cle 1.65
Marberry-Det 2.30
Stewart-Was 2.34
Harder-Cle 2.38
Blaeholder-StL 2.43

Strikeouts
Gomez-NY 163
Hadley-StL 149
Ruffing-NY 122
Bridges-Det 120
Allen-NY 119

Strikeouts/Game
Gomez-NY 6.25
Allen-NY 5.80
Ruffing-NY 4.67
Bridges-Det 4.64
Fischer-Det 4.58

Ratio
Marberry-Det 11.10
Stewart-Was 11.24
Harder-Cle 11.53
Brown-Cle 11.58
Weaver-Was 11.88

Earned Run Average
Pearson-Cle 2.33
Harder-Cle 2.95
Bridges-Det 3.09
Gomez-NY 3.18
Grove-Phi 3.20

Adjusted ERA
Harder-Cle 151
Bridges-Det 140
Grove-Phi 134
Marberry-Det 131
Brown-Cle 130

Opponents' Batting Avg.
Bridges-Det .226
Gomez-NY .240
Allen-NY .242
Weiland-Bos .244
Hildebrand-Cle .245

Opponents' On-Base Pct.
Marberry-Det .302
Stewart-Was .304
Harder-Cle .309
Brown-Cle .310
Grove-Phi .316

Starter Runs
Harder-Cle 37.4
Grove-Phi 33.0
Bridges-Det 30.8
Pearson-Cle 29.4
Gomez-NY 28.6

Adjusted Starter Runs
Harder-Cle 40.4
Grove-Phi 33.1
Bridges-Det 31.4
Pearson-Cle 30.7
Marberry-Det 27.0

Clutch Pitching Index
Cain-Phi 125
Jones-Chi 124
Harder-Cle 115
Whitehill-Was 112
Grove-Phi 111

Relief Runs
Russell-Was 22.0
Heving-Chi 21.1
Faber-Chi 8.1
Burke-Was 7.4
Herring-Det 3.0

Adjusted Relief Runs
Russell-Was 21.1
Heving-Chi 20.8
Faber-Chi 7.7
Burke-Was 6.9
Gray-StL 6.4

Relief Ranking
Russell-Was 32.6
Heving-Chi 21.4
Burke-Was 6.8
Faber-Chi 6.7
Gray-StL 6.1

Total Pitcher Index
Harder-Cle 5.5
Russell-Was 3.5
Bridges-Det 3.5
Pearson-Cle 3.2
Grove-Phi 2.9

Total Baseball Ranking
Foxx-Phi 6.7
Harder-Cle 5.5
Gehrig-NY 4.5
Cronin-Was 4.1
Cochrane-Phi 3.8

TEAM	G	W	L	PCT	GB	R	OR	AB	H	2B	3B	HR	BB	SO	AVG	OBP	SLG	OPS	OPS+	BR	BR+	PF	CHI	RC	SB	CS	SBA	SBR
STL	154	95	58	.621		**799**	656	5502	**1582**	**294**	75	104	392	535	**.288**	.337	**.425**	**762**	102	**63**	15	107	101	**796**	**69**			
NY	153	93	60	.608	2	760	**583**	5396	1485	240	41	**126**	406	526	.275	.329	.405	734	105	8	26	98	**105**	736	19			
CHI	152	86	65	.570	8	705	639	5347	1494	263	44	101	375	630	.279	.330	.402	732	103	5	20	98	99	719	59			
BOS	152	78	73	.517	16	683	714	5370	1460	233	44	83	375	440	.272	.323	.378	701	101	-52	1	93	104	660	30			
PIT	151	74	76	.493	19.5	735	713	5361	1541	281	**77**	52	440	**398**	.287	.344	.398	742	102	34	17	102	99	742	44			
BRO	153	71	81	.467	23.5	748	795	5427	1526	284	52	79	**548**	555	.281	**.350**	.396	746	**112**	51	**92**	95	95	782	55			
PHI	149	56	93	.376	37	675	794	5218	1480	286	35	56	398	534	.284	.338	.384	722	87	-3	-84	113	98	685	52			
CIN	152	52	99	.344	42	590	801	5361	1428	227	65	55	313	532	.266	.311	.364	675	88	-105	-90	98	99	603	34			
TOT	608					5695		42982	11996	2108	433	656	3247	4150	.280	.333	.395	727							362			

TEAM	CG	SH	SV	IP	H	H/G	HR	BB	SO	RAT	ERA	ERA+	OAV	OOB	PR	PR+	PF	CPI	FA	E	DP	FW	PW	BW	SBW	DIF
STL	**78**	**15**	16	1386[2]	1463	9.5	77	411	**689**	12.4	3.69	115	.268	.323	58	79	104	101	.972	166	**141**	.4	7.7	1.5		9.1
NY	68	13	**30**	1370	**1384**	**9.1**	75	**351**	499	**11.6**	**3.20**	**121**	**.260**	**.308**	**132**	**107**	95	**105**	.972	179	**141**	-.5	**10.5**	2.6		4.1
CHI	73	11	9	1361[1]	1432	9.5	80	417	633	12.4	3.76	103	.269	.325	46	19	95	101	**.977**	**137**	135	**1.9**	1.9	2.0		4.9
BOS	62	12	20	1359[2]	1512	10.1	78	405	462	12.9	4.12	93	.279	.331	-7	-47	94	97	.972	169	120	.0	-4.5	.1		7.0
PIT	63	8	8	1329[2]	1523	10.4	78	354	487	13.0	4.20	98	.284	.332	-20	-13	101	98	.975	145	118	1.4	-1.2	1.7		-2.7
BRO	66	6	12	1354[1]	1540	10.3	81	475	520	13.6	4.48	87	.285	.346	-63	-91	96	97	.970	180	**141**	-.5	-8.8	**9.0**		-4.5
PHI	52	8	15	1297	1501	10.5	126	437	416	13.7	4.77	99	.288	.347	-101	-3	116	99	.966	197	140	-1.8	-.2	-8.1		-8.1
CIN	51	3	19	1347[2]	1645	11.0	**61**	389	438	13.8	4.37	93	.299	.348	-46	-43	101	102	.970	181	136	-.6	-4.1	-8.7		-9.8
TOT	513	76	129	10806[1]		10.0				12.9	4.07		.280	.333					.972	1354	1072					

Runs
P.Waner-Pit 122
Ott-NY 119
Collins-StL 116
Vaughan-Pit 115
Medwick-StL 110

Hits
P.Waner-Pit 217
Terry-NY 213
Collins-StL 200
Medwick-StL 198

Doubles
Cuyler-Chi 42
Allen-Phi 42
Vaughan-Pit 41
Medwick-StL 40
Collins-StL 40

Triples
Medwick-StL 18
P.Waner-Pit 16
Suhr-Pit 13
Collins-StL 12

Home Runs
Ott-NY 35
Collins-StL 35
Berger-Bos 34
Hartnett-Chi 22
Klein-Chi 20

Total Bases
Collins-StL 369
Ott-NY 344
Berger-Bos 336
Medwick-StL 328
P.Waner-Pit 323

Runs Batted In
Ott-NY 135
Collins-StL 128
Berger-Bos 121
Medwick-StL 106
Suhr-Pit 103

Runs Produced
Ott-NY 219
Collins-StL 209
P.Waner-Pit 198
Medwick-StL 198
Vaughan-Pit 197

Bases On Balls
Vaughan-Pit 94
Ott-NY 85
Koenecke-Bro 70
Leslie-Bro 69
P.Waner-Pit 68

Batting Average
P.Waner-Pit .... .362
Terry-NY .... .354
Cuyler-Chi .... .338
Vaughan-Pit .... .333
Collins-StL .... .333

On-Base Percentage
Vaughan-Pit .... .431
P.Waner-Pit .... .429
Ott-NY .... .415
Terry-NY .... .414
Koenecke-Bro .... .411

Slugging Average
Collins-StL .... .615
Ott-NY .... .591
DeLancey-StL .... .565
Berger-Bos .... .546
P.Waner-Pit .... .539

On-Base Plus Slugging
Collins-StL 1008
Ott-NY 1006
P.Waner-Pit 968
Vaughan-Pit 942
Koenecke-Bro 919

Adjusted OPS
Ott-NY 170
Collins-StL 155
P.Waner-Pit 154
Koenecke-Bro 152
Berger-Bos 148

Batter Runs
Ott-NY 55.2
Collins-StL 53.3
P.Waner-Pit 50.2
Vaughan-Pit 44.3
Terry-NY 31.5

Adjusted Batter Runs
Ott-NY 58.5
P.Waner-Pit 47.2
Collins-StL 45.2
Vaughan-Pit 41.5
Berger-Bos 38.2

Clutch Hitting Index
Thevenow-Pit 133
Durocher-StL 132
Leslie-Bro 126
Jackson-NY 124
Cuccinello-Bro 124

Runs Created
Ott-NY 150
Collins-StL 148
P.Waner-Pit 142
Vaughan-Pit 135
Terry-NY 122

Total Average
Ott-NY 1.075
Collins-StL 1.046
Vaughan-Pit 1.043
P.Waner-Pit 1.010
Koenecke-Bro .... .981

Stolen Bases
Martin-StL 23
Cuyler-Chi 15
Bartell-Phi 13
Taylor-Bro 12

Stolen Base Average

Stolen Base Runs

Fielding Runs
Critz-NY 25.0
K.Davis-StL-Phi 17.8
B.Herman-Chi 15.6
Bartell-Phi 13.5
Hartnett-Chi 13.5

Total Player Rating
Vaughan-Pit 5.3
P.Waner-Pit 4.4
Ott-NY 3.9
Hartnett-Chi 3.7
Collins-StL 3.7

Wins
D.Dean-StL 30
Schumacher-NY 23
Warneke-Chi 22
Hubbell-NY 21

Win Percentage
D.Dean-StL .... .811
Hoyt-Pit .... .714
Schumacher-NY ...... .697
Warneke-Chi .... .688
Frankhouse-Bos ..... .654

Games
C.Davis-Phi 51
Hansen-Phi 50
D.Dean-StL 50
Hubbell-NY 49
French-Pit 49

Complete Games
Hubbell-NY 25
D.Dean-StL 24
Warneke-Chi 23
Mungo-Bro 22
Brandt-Bos 20

Shutouts
D.Dean-StL 7
Hubbell-NY 5
P.Dean-StL 5
Lee-Chi 4

Saves
Hubbell-NY 8
Luque-NY 7
D.Dean-StL 7
Bell-NY 6

Innings Pitched
Mungo-Bro 315.1
Hubbell-NY 313.0
D.Dean-StL 311.2
Schumacher-NY 297.0
Warneke-Chi 291.1

Fewest Hits/Game
Parmelee-NY 7.90
Hubbell-NY 8.22
D.Dean-StL 8.32
Warneke-Chi 8.43
Mungo-Bro 8.56

Fewest BB/Game
Hubbell-NY 1.06
Freitas-Cin 1.47
Frey-Cin 1.54
Leonard-Bro 1.62
Fitzsimmons-NY 1.74

Strikeouts
D.Dean-StL 195
Mungo-Bro 184
P.Dean-StL 150
Warneke-Chi 143
Derringer-Cin 122

Strikeouts/Game
P.Dean-StL 5.79
D.Dean-StL 5.63
Weaver-Chi 5.55
Mungo-Bro 5.25
Malone-Chi 5.23

Ratio
Hubbell-NY 9.35
Warneke-Chi 10.53
D.Dean-StL 10.66
Hoyt-Pit 10.81
Fitzsimmons-NY 10.87

Earned Run Average
Hubbell-NY 2.30
D.Dean-StL 2.66
Hoyt-Pit 2.93
C.Davis-Phi 2.95
Fitzsimmons-NY 3.04

Adjusted ERA
Hubbell-NY 168
C.Davis-Phi 160
D.Dean-StL 159
Hoyt-Pit 141
Walker-StL 135

Opponents' Batting Avg.
Parmelee-NY .... .238
Hubbell-NY .... .239
D.Dean-StL .... .241
Warneke-Chi .... .244
P.Dean-StL .... .248

Opponents' On-Base Pct.
Hubbell-NY .... .263
Warneke-Chi .... .287
D.Dean-StL .... .289
P.Dean-StL .... .292
Hoyt-Pit .... .296

Starter Runs
Hubbell-NY 61.3
D.Dean-StL 48.7
C.Davis-Phi 33.8
Fitzsimmons-NY 29.8
Schumacher-NY 29.0

Adjusted Starter Runs
Hubbell-NY 57.2
D.Dean-StL 52.2
C.Davis-Phi 46.4
Fitzsimmons-NY 25.4
Hoyt-Pit 24.8

Clutch Pitching Index
Walker-StL 137
Leonard-Bro 121
C.Davis-Phi 120
Freitas-Cin 111
Frankhouse-Bos 110

Relief Runs
Haines-StL 5.6
Bell-NY 2.4
Brennan-Cin 2.2

Adjusted Relief Runs
Haines-StL 7.0
Brennan-Cin 2.4
Bell-NY 1.3

Relief Ranking
Haines-StL 5.7
Brennan-Cin 2.0
Bell-NY 1.8

Total Pitcher Index
C.Davis-Phi 6.8
Hubbell-NY 6.3
D.Dean-StL 6.2
Fitzsimmons-NY 3.8
Schumacher-NY 3.7

Total Baseball Ranking
C.Davis-Phi 6.8
Hubbell-NY 6.3
D.Dean-StL 6.2
Vaughan-Pit 5.3
P.Waner-Pit 4.4

TEAM	G	W	L	PCT	GB	R	OR	AB	H	2B	3B	HR	BB	SO	AVG	OBP	SLG	OPS	OPS+	BR	BR+	PF	CHI	RC	SB	CS	SBA	SBR
DET	154	101	53	.656		**958**	708	5475	**1644**	**349**	53	74	639	528	**.300**	**.376**	.424	**800**	113	**112**	110	100	104	**905**	**125**	55	69	8
NY	154	94	60	.610	7	842	**669**	5368	1494	226	61	135	**700**	597	.278	.364	.419	783	**117**	70	**134**	93	96	848	71	46	61	0
CLE	154	85	69	.552	16	814	763	5396	1550	340	46	100	526	**433**	.287	.353	.423	776	105	44	32	102	98	820	52	32	62	0
BOS	153	76	76	.500	24	820	775	5339	1465	287	**70**	51	610	535	.274	.350	.383	733	90	-28	-78	107	**108**	748	116	47	**71**	**9**
PHI	153	68	82	.453	31	764	838	5317	1491	236	50	**144**	491	584	.280	.343	**.425**	768	108	20	50	96	97	785	57	35	62	0
STL	154	67	85	.441	33	674	800	5288	1417	252	59	62	514	631	.268	.335	.373	708	82	-84	-137	108	98	680	43	31	58	-1
WAS	155	66	86	.434	34	729	806	5448	1512	278	**70**	51	570	447	.278	.348	.382	730	99	-35	-5	96	95	747	47	42	53	-4
CHI	153	53	99	.349	47	704	946	5301	1395	237	40	71	565	524	.263	.336	.363	699	84	-97	-117	103	103	672	36	27	57	-2
TOT	615					6305		42932	11968	2205	449	688	4615	4279	.279	.351	.400	750							547	315	63	10

TEAM	CG	SH	SV	IP	H	H/G	HR	BB	SO	RAT	ERA	ERA+	OAV	OOB	PR	PR+	PF	CPI	FA	E	DP	FW	PW	BW	SBW	DIF
DET	74	**13**	14	1370[2]	1467	9.7	86	**488**	640	13.0	4.06	108	.273	.335	67	52	98	102	**.974**	159	150	1.2	4.9	10.3	.6	7.2
NY	**83**	**13**	10	1382[2]	**1349**	**8.8**	71	542	**656**	**12.4**	**3.76**	108	**.254**	**.324**	**114**	53	90	97	.973	**157**	151	**1.3**	5.0	**12.5**	-.1	-1.5
CLE	72	8	19	1367	1476	9.8	**70**	582	554	13.8	4.28	106	.275	.349	33	40	101	101	.972	172	164	.5	3.8	3.0	-.1	1.0
BOS	68	9	9	1361	1527	10.1	**70**	543	538	13.9	4.32	**111**	.283	.351	27	**68**	107	103	.969	188	141	-.5	**6.4**	-7.2	**.7**	.8
PHI	68	8	8	1337	1429	9.7	84	693	480	14.5	5.02	87	.275	.363	-77	-97	97	94	.967	196	166	-.9	-9.0	4.7	-.1	-1.5
STL	50	6	**20**	1350	1499	10.0	94	632	499	14.3	4.50	**111**	.283	.361	1	**68**	111	**107**	.969	187	160	-.4	**6.4**	-12.7	-.2	-1.9
WAS	61	4	12	1381[1]	1622	10.6	74	503	412	14.0	4.68	92	.295	.355	-28	-57	96	101	**.974**	162	**167**	1.1	-5.3	-.4	-.5	-4.7
CHI	72	5	8	1355	1599	10.7	139	628	506	15.0	5.41	88	.292	.367	-137	-96	105	97	.966	207	126	-1.5	-8.9	-10.8	-.3	-1.3
TOT	548	66	100	10904[2]		9.9				13.9	4.50		.279	.351					.971	1428	1225					

Runs	Hits	Doubles	Triples	Home Runs	Total Bases
Gehringer-Det 134	Gehringer-Det 214	Greenberg-Det 63	Chapman-NY 13	Gehrig-NY 49	Gehrig-NY 409
Werber-Bos 129	Gehrig-NY 210	Gehringer-Det 50	Manush-Was 11	Foxx-Phi 44	Trosky-Cle 374
Gehrig-NY 128	Trosky-Cle 206	Averill-Cle 48		Trosky-Cle 35	Greenberg-Det 356
Averill-Cle 128	Cramer-Phi 202	Trosky-Cle 45		Johnson-Phi 34	Foxx-Phi 352
Foxx-Phi 120	Greenberg-Det 201	Hale-Cle 44		Averill-Cle 31	Averill-Cle 340

Runs Batted In	Runs Produced	Bases On Balls	Batting Average	On-Base Percentage	Slugging Average
Gehrig-NY 165	Gehringer-Det 250	Foxx-Phi 111	Gehrig-NY .363	Gehrig-NY .465	Gehrig-NY .706
Trosky-Cle 142	Gehrig-NY 244	Gehrig-NY 109	Gehringer-Det .356	Gehringer-Det .450	Foxx-Phi .653
Greenberg-Det 139	Greenberg-Det 231	Ruth-NY 104	Manush-Was .349	Foxx-Phi .449	Greenberg-Det .600
Foxx-Phi 130	Trosky-Cle 224	Myer-Was 102	Simmons-Chi .344	Cochrane-Det .428	Trosky-Cle .598
Gehringer-Det 127	Rogell-Det 211		Vosmik-Cle .341	Myer-Was .419	Averill-Cle .569

On-Base Plus Slugging	Adjusted OPS	Batter Runs	Adjusted Batter Runs	Clutch Hitting Index	Runs Created
Gehrig-NY 1172	Gehrig-NY 213	Gehrig-NY 85.6	Gehrig-NY 98.4	Dykes-Chi 137	Gehrig-NY 195
Foxx-Phi 1102	Foxx-Phi 188	Foxx-Phi 66.4	Foxx-Phi 72.2	Cronin-Was 131	Foxx-Phi 165
Greenberg-Det 1005	Greenberg-Det 156	Gehringer-Det 47.8	Gehringer-Det 47.5	Pepper-StL 129	Averill-Cle 145
Trosky-Cle 987	Trosky-Cle 149	Greenberg-Det 46.7	Greenberg-Det 46.4	Cochrane-Det 129	Trosky-Cle 145
Averill-Cle 982	Averill-Cle 149	Averill-Cle 45.6	Averill-Cle 43.6	Rogell-Det 126	Gehringer-Det 144

Total Average	Stolen Bases	Stolen Base Average	Stolen Base Runs	Fielding Runs	Total Player Rating
Gehrig-NY 1.401	Werber-Bos 40	White-Det 82.4	White-Det 4.1	Hale-Cle 25.7	Gehrig-NY 7.7
Foxx-Phi 1.310	White-Det 28	Werber-Bos 72.7	Werber-Bos 3.5	Hemsley-StL 23.3	Foxx-Phi 5.9
Averill-Cle 1.075	Chapman-NY 26	Fox-Det 71.4	Lazzeri-NY 2.1	Werber-Bos 20.3	Gehringer-Det 5.9
Greenberg-Det 1.071	Fox-Det 25	Walker-Det 69.0	Fox-Det 2.0	Cronin-Was 18.4	Averill-Cle 4.4
Gehringer-Det 1.053	Walker-Det 20	Chapman-NY 61.9	Rogell-Det 1.8	Melillo-StL 18.1	Werber-Bos 4.1

Wins	Win Percentage	Games	Complete Games	Shutouts	Saves
Gomez-NY 26	Gomez-NY .839	Russell-Was 54	Gomez-NY 25	Harder-Cle 6	Russell-Was 7
Rowe-Det 24	Rowe-Det .750	Newsom-StL 47	Bridges-Det 23	Gomez-NY 6	L.Brown-Cle 6
Bridges-Det 22	Marberry-Det .750	Rowe-Det 45	Lyons-Chi 21	Ruffing-NY 5	Newsom-StL 5
Harder-Cle 20	Auker-Det .682	Knott-StL 45	Rowe-Det 20	Dietrich-Phi 4	
Ruffing-NY 19	Bridges-Det .667				

Innings Pitched	Fewest Hits/Game	Fewest BB/Game	Strikeouts	Strikeouts/Game	Ratio
Gomez-NY 281.2	Gomez-NY 7.13	W.Ferrell-Bos 2.44	Gomez-NY 158	Ruffing-NY 5.23	Gomez-NY 10.19
Bridges-Det 275.0	Ruffing-NY 8.15	Auker-Det 2.46	Bridges-Det 151	Gomez-NY 5.05	Rowe-Det 11.54
Rowe-Det 266.0	Bridges-Det 8.15	Blaeholder-StL 2.61	Ruffing-NY 149	Rowe-Det 5.04	Bridges-Det 11.65
Newsom-StL 262.1	Burke-Was 8.30	Rowe-Det 2.74	Rowe-Det 149	Pearson-Cle 4.95	Murphy-NY 11.66
Ruffing-NY 256.1	Murphy-NY 8.36	Weaver-Was 2.77	Pearson-Cle 140	Bridges-Det 4.94	Harder-Cle 11.77

Earned Run Average	Adjusted ERA	Opponents' Batting Avg.	Opponents' On-Base Pct.	Starter Runs	Adjusted Starter Runs
Gomez-NY 2.33	Harder-Cle 174	Gomez-NY .215	Gomez-NY .282	Gomez-NY 67.7	Gomez-NY 60.0
Harder-Cle 2.61	Gomez-NY 174	Ruffing-NY .236	Ruffing-NY .310	Harder-Cle 53.6	Harder-Cle 54.4
Murphy-NY 3.12	Ostermueller-Bos 138	Bridges-Det .241	Rowe-Det .312	Murphy-NY 31.8	Rowe-Det 28.4
Burke-Was 3.21	Burke-Was 134	Burke-Was .245	Bridges-Det .312	Rowe-Det 30.9	Ostermueller-Bos 27.2
Auker-Det 3.42	W.Ferrell-Bos 132	Benton-Phi .249	Harder-Cle .316	Bridges-Det 25.4	Newsom-StL 25.8

Clutch Pitching Index	Relief Runs	Adjusted Relief Runs	Relief Ranking	Total Pitcher Index	Total Baseball Ranking
Harder-Cle 127	Pennock-Bos 10.0	Pennock-Bos 11.3	Pennock-Bos 5.7	Harder-Cle 6.4	Gehrig-NY 7.7
Auker-Det 123	McColl-Was 8.0	McColl-Was 6.0	Bean-Cle 4.1	Gomez-NY 5.5	Harder-Cle 6.4
Ostermueller-Bos 116	Russell-Was 5.8	Bean-Cle 3.9	McColl-Was 3.5	Rowe-Det 4.1	Foxx-Phi 5.9
Murphy-NY 113	Bean-Cle 3.7	Russell-Was 2.7	Russell-Was 2.6	Ostermueller-Bos 2.9	Gehringer-Det 5.9
Coffman-StL 109		Wells-StL 1.9	Wells-StL 1.5	Newsom-StL 2.9	Gomez-NY 5.5

TEAM	G	W	L	PCT	GB	R	OR	AB	H	2B	3B	HR	BB	SO	AVG	OBP	SLG	OPS	OPS+	BR	BR+	PF	CHI	RC	SB	CS	SBA	SBR
CHI	154	100	54	.649		**847**	**597**	5486	1581	**303**	62	88	**464**	471	**.288**	**.347**	.414	**761**	**110**	**81**	**76**	101	102	**812**	66			
STL	154	96	58	.623	4	829	625	5457	1548	286	59	86	404	521	.284	.335	.405	740	101	33	4	104	**109**	759	71			
NY	156	91	62	.595	8.5	770	675	5623	**1608**	248	56	**123**	392	479	.286	.336	**.416**	752	**110**	54	69	98	96	797	32			
PIT	153	86	67	.562	13.5	743	647	5415	1543	255	**90**	66	457	437	.285	.343	.402	745	103	49	25	103	96	758	30			
BRO	154	70	83	.458	29.5	711	767	5410	1496	235	62	59	430	520	.277	.333	.376	709	99	-21	-5	98	101	691	60			
CIN	154	68	85	.444	31.5	646	772	5296	1403	244	68	73	392	547	.265	.319	.378	697	96	-51	-30	97	99	658	**72**			
PHI	156	64	89	.418	35.5	685	871	5442	1466	249	32	92	392	661	.269	.322	.378	700	85	-47	-109	110	101	681	52			
BOS	153	38	115	.248	61.5	575	852	5309	1396	233	33	75	353	**436**	.263	.311	.362	673	93	-98	-46	92	95	596	20			
TOT	617					5806		43438	12041	2053	462	662	3284	4072	.278	.332	.392	722							403			

TEAM	CG	SH	SV	IP	H	H/G	HR	BB	SO	RAT	ERA	ERA+	OAV	OOB	PR	PR+	PF	CPI	FA	E	DP	FW	PW	BW	SBW	DIF
CHI	**81**	12	14	1394[1]	**1417**	**9.2**	85	400	589	11.9	**3.26**	**121**	.263	.317	**118**	**106**	98	**111**	.970	186	**163**	.4	**10.4**	**7.4**		5.1
STL	73	10	18	1384[2]	1445	9.4	68	377	**602**	12.1	3.53	116	.267	.318	76	87	102	101	**.972**	**164**	133	**1.6**	8.5	.4		8.6
NY	76	10	11	1403[2]	1433	**9.2**	106	411	524	12.1	3.79	102	**.262**	.318	37	12	96	98	**.972**	174	129	1.2	1.2	6.8		5.5
PIT	76	**15**	11	1365[2]	1428	9.5	**63**	**312**	549	**11.6**	3.43	120	.265	**.307**	91	101	102	98	.968	190	94	.0	9.9	2.5		-2.7
BRO	62	11	**20**	1358	1519	10.1	88	436	480	13.1	4.23	94	.281	.337	-31	-37	99	100	.969	188	146	.2	-3.5	-.4		-2.6
CIN	59	9	12	1356	1490	9.9	65	438	500	13.0	4.31	93	.278	.336	-43	-50	99	94	.966	204	139	-.7	-4.8	-2.9		.0
PHI	53	8	15	1374[2]	1652	10.9	106	505	475	14.5	4.76	95	.295	.358	-113	-31	113	102	.963	228	145	-1.9	-3.0	-10.5		3.1
BOS	54	6	5	1330	1645	11.2	81	404	355	14.1	4.94	77	.303	.354	-135	-180	94	96	.967	197	101	-.3	-17.4	-4.4		-16.1
TOT	534	81	106	10967		9.9				12.8	4.02		.278	.332					.969	1531	1050					

Runs
Galan-Chi 133
Medwick-StL 132
Martin-StL 121
Ott-NY 113
Herman-Chi 113

Hits
Herman-Chi 227
Medwick-StL 224

Doubles
Herman-Chi 57
Medwick-StL 46
Allen-Phi 46
Martin-StL 41
Galan-Chi 41

Triples
Goodman-Cin 18
L.Waner-Pit 14
Medwick-StL 13

Home Runs
Berger-Bos 34
Ott-NY 31
Camilli-Phi 25
Medwick-StL 23
R.Collins-StL 23

Total Bases
Medwick-StL 365
Ott-NY 329
Berger-Bos 323
Herman-Chi 317
Leiber-NY 314

Runs Batted In
Berger-Bos 130
Medwick-StL 126
R.Collins-StL 122
Ott-NY 114
Leiber-NY 107

Runs Produced
Medwick-StL 235
R.Collins-StL 208
Galan-Chi 200
Ott-NY 196
Leiber-NY 195

Bases On Balls
Vaughan-Pit 97
Galan-Chi 87
Ott-NY 82
Suhr-Pit 70
Frey-Bro 66

Batting Average
Vaughan-Pit .... .385
Medwick-StL .... .353
Hartnett-Chi .... .344
Lombardi-Cin .... .343
Herman-Chi .... .341

On-Base Percentage
Vaughan-Pit .... .491
Ott-NY .... .407
Hack-Chi .... .406
Galan-Chi .... .399
P.Waner-Pit .... .392

Slugging Average
Vaughan-Pit .... .607
Medwick-StL .... .576
Ott-NY .... .555
Berger-Bos .... .548
Hartnett-Chi .... .545

On-Base Plus Slugging
Vaughan-Pit 1098
Medwick-StL 962
Ott-NY 962
R.Collins-StL 915
Berger-Bos 903

Adjusted OPS
Vaughan-Pit 187
Ott-NY 159
Berger-Bos 151
Medwick-StL 149
Leiber-NY 143

Batter Runs
Vaughan-Pit 71.9
Ott-NY 47.6
Medwick-StL 46.0
R.Collins-StL 35.0
Leiber-NY 34.3

Adjusted Batter Runs
Vaughan-Pit 67.4
Ott-NY 50.0
Medwick-StL 41.1
Berger-Bos 39.2
Leiber-NY 36.4

Clutch Hitting Index
Leslie-Bro 135
Young-Pit 128
Durocher-StL 125
Jurges-Chi 121
Whitney-Bos 113

Runs Created
Vaughan-Pit 163
Ott-NY 144
Medwick-StL 139
Galan-Chi 133
R.Collins-StL 125

Total Average
Vaughan-Pit 1.317
Ott-NY 1.037
Medwick-StL .... .948
Galan-Chi .... .937
R.Collins-StL .... .930

Stolen Bases
Galan-Chi 22
Martin-StL 20
Bordagaray-Bro 18
Hack-Chi 14
Goodman-Cin 14

Stolen Base Average

Stolen Base Runs

Fielding Runs
Jurges-Chi 30.2
Herman-Chi 18.9
Allen-Phi 16.5
Hartnett-Chi 14.5
T.Moore-StL 13.8

Total Player Rating
Vaughan-Pit 6.3
Herman-Chi 5.3
Hartnett-Chi 4.9
Ott-NY 4.6
Berger-Bos 4.3

Wins
D.Dean-StL 28
Hubbell-NY 23
Derringer-Cin 22
Warneke-Chi 20
Lee-Chi 20

Win Percentage
Lee-Chi .... .769
Castleman-NY .... .714
D.Dean-StL .... .700
Schumacher-NY .... .679
Hubbell-NY .... .657

Games
Jorgens-Phi 53
D.Dean-StL 50
Bivin-Phi 47
Smith-Bos 46
P.Dean-StL 46

Complete Games
D.Dean-StL 29
Hubbell-NY 24
Blanton-Pit 23
Warneke-Chi 20
Derringer-Cin 20

Shutouts
Weaver-Pit 4
Mungo-Bro 4
French-Chi 4
Fitzsimmons-NY 4
Blanton-Pit 4

Saves
Leonard-Bro 8
Johnson-Phi 6
Hoyt-Pit 6

Innings Pitched
D.Dean-StL 325.1
Hubbell-NY 302.2
Derringer-Cin 276.2
P.Dean-StL 269.2

Fewest Hits/Game
Blanton-Pit 7.79
Schumacher-NY 8.08
Parmelee-NY 8.52
Swift-Pit 8.53
Hollingsworth-Cin 8.57

Fewest BB/Game
Clark-Bro 1.22
Hubbell-NY 1.46
Hoyt-Pit 1.48
Derringer-Cin 1.59
Johnson-Phi 1.60

Strikeouts
D.Dean-StL 190
Hubbell-NY 150
Mungo-Bro 143
P.Dean-StL 143
Blanton-Pit 142

Strikeouts/Game
Mungo-Bro 6.00
D.Dean-StL 5.26
Blanton-Pit 5.02
P.Dean-StL 4.77
Hollingsworth-Cin 4.62

Ratio
Blanton-Pit 9.80
Swift-Pit 10.21
Clark-Bro 10.61
Warneke-Chi 10.66
Schumacher-NY 10.66

Earned Run Average
Blanton-Pit 2.58
Swift-Pit 2.70
Schumacher-NY 2.89
French-Chi 2.96
Lee-Chi 2.96

Adjusted ERA
Blanton-Pit 159
Swift-Pit 152
D.Dean-StL 135
Schumacher-NY 133
French-Chi 133

Opponents' Batting Avg.
Blanton-Pit .... .229
Schumacher-NY .... .238
Hollingsworth-Cin .... .243
Swift-Pit .... .247
P.Dean-StL .... .249

Opponents' On-Base Pct.
Blanton-Pit .... .272
Swift-Pit .... .282
Clark-Bro .... .289
Schumacher-NY .... .292
P.Dean-StL .... .292

Starter Runs
Blanton-Pit 40.6
D.Dean-StL 35.3
Schumacher-NY 32.8
Swift-Pit 29.9
Lee-Chi 29.5

Adjusted Starter Runs
Blanton-Pit 42.1
D.Dean-StL 37.4
Swift-Pit 31.2
Schumacher-NY 29.2
Lee-Chi 27.7

Clutch Pitching Index
French-Chi 126
Zachary-Bro 121
Walker-StL 116
Lee-Chi 111
Hallahan-StL 111

Relief Runs

Adjusted Relief Runs

Relief Ranking

Total Pitcher Index
Blanton-Pit 4.6
D.Dean-StL 4.2
Schumacher-NY 3.8
Swift-Pit 3.1
Warneke-Chi 3.0

Total Baseball Ranking
Vaughan-Pit 6.3
Herman-Chi 5.3
Hartnett-Chi 4.9
Blanton-Pit 4.6
Ott-NY 4.6

TEAM	G	W	L	PCT	GB	R	OR	AB	H	2B	3B	HR	BB	SO	AVG	OBP	SLG	OPS	OPS+	BR	BR+	PF	CHI	RC	SB	CS	SBA	SBR
DET	152	93	58	.616		**919**	665	5423	1573	301	83	106	**627**	456	**.290**	**.366**	**.435**	**801**	**116**	**95**	**127**	97	**104**	**885**	70	45	61	0
NY	149	89	60	.597	3	818	**632**	5214	1462	255	70	104	604	469	.280	.358	.416	774	111	42	89	94	102	799	68	46	60	-1
CLE	156	82	71	.536	12	776	739	5534	1573	**324**	77	93	460	567	.284	.341	.421	762	100	3	-11	102	99	796	63	54	54	-5
BOS	154	78	75	.510	16	718	732	5288	1458	281	63	69	609	470	.276	.353	.392	745	92	-11	-59	107	94	757	**91**	59	61	-1
CHI	153	74	78	.487	19.5	738	750	5314	1460	262	42	74	580	**405**	.275	.348	.382	730	92	-41	-59	103	101	733	46	28	62	0
WAS	154	67	86	.438	27	823	903	5592	**1591**	255	**95**	32	596	406	.285	.357	.381	738	99	-18	9	97	**104**	788	54	37	59	-1
STL	155	65	87	.428	28.5	718	930	5365	1446	291	51	73	593	561	.270	.344	.384	728	90	-49	-81	105	98	735	45	25	**64**	**1**
PHI	149	58	91	.389	34	710	869	5269	1470	243	44	**112**	475	602	.279	.341	.406	747	99	-23	-17	99	98	738	43	35	55	-3
TOT	611					6220		42999	12033	2212	525	663	4544	3936	.280	.352	.402	753							480	329	59	-10

TEAM	CG	SH	SV	IP	H	H/G	HR	BB	SO	RAT	ERA	ERA+	OAV	OOB	PR	PR+	PF	CPI	FA	E	DP	FW	PW	BW	SBW	DIF
DET	**87**	**16**	11	1364	1440	9.6	78	522	584	13.2	3.83	109	.271	.339	96	57	94	**107**	**.978**	**128**	154	**2.3**	5.4	**11.9**	.1	-2.1
NY	76	12	13	1331	**1276**	**8.7**	91	516	**594**	**12.2**	**3.61**	112	**.251**	**.321**	**126**	72	91	101	.974	151	114	.8	6.8	8.4	.0	-1.3
CLE	67	12	**21**	1396	1527	9.9	68	**457**	498	13.0	4.16	108	.278	.335	47	54	101	97	.972	177	147	-.2	5.1	-1.0	-.4	2.1
BOS	82	6	11	1376	1520	10.0	**67**	520	470	13.5	4.05	**117**	.280	.346	62	**100**	107	105	.969	194	136	-1.3	**9.4**	-5.5	.0	-1.0
CHI	80	8	8	1360[2]	1443	9.6	105	574	436	13.5	4.38	106	.272	.346	12	35	104	100	.976	146	133	1.4	3.3	-5.5	.1	-1.1
WAS	67	5	12	1378[2]	1672	11.0	89	613	456	15.1	5.25	82	.302	.374	-122	-146	97	99	.972	171	**186**	.0	-13.6	.9	.0	3.4
STL	42	4	15	1380[1]	1667	10.9	92	641	435	15.2	5.27	91	.297	.371	-124	-67	108	97	.970	187	138	-.8	-6.2	-7.5	**.2**	3.6
PHI	58	7	10	1326[1]	1486	10.1	73	704	469	15.1	5.12	89	.285	.372	-97	-83	102	96	.968	190	150	-1.4	-7.7	-1.5	-.2	-5.5
TOT	559	70	101	10913		10.0				13.9	4.46		.280	.352					.973	1344	1158					

Runs
Gehrig-NY 125
Gehringer-Det 123
Greenberg-Det 121
Foxx-Phi 118
Chapman-NY 118

Hits
Vosmik-Cle 216
Myer-Was 215
Cramer-Phi 214
Greenberg-Det 203

Doubles
Vosmik-Cle 47
Greenberg-Det 46
Solters-Bos-StL 45
Fox-Det 38
Chapman-NY 38

Triples
Vosmik-Cle 20
Stone-Was 18
Greenberg-Det 16
Cronin-Bos 14
Averill-Cle 13

Home Runs
Greenberg-Det 36
Foxx-Phi 36
Gehrig-NY 30
Johnson-Phi 28
Trosky-Cle 26

Total Bases
Greenberg-Det 389
Foxx-Phi 340
Vosmik-Cle 333
Solters-Bos-StL 314
Gehrig-NY 312

Runs Batted In
Greenberg-Det 170
Gehrig-NY 119
Foxx-Phi 115
Trosky-Cle 113
Solters-Bos-StL 112

Runs Produced
Greenberg-Det 255
Gehrig-NY 214
Gehringer-Det 212
Myer-Was 210
Foxx-Phi 197

Bases On Balls
Gehrig-NY 132
Appling-Chi 122
Foxx-Phi 114
Myer-Was 96
Cochrane-Det 96

Batting Average
Myer-Was .349
Vosmik-Cle .348
Foxx-Phi .346
Cramer-Phi .332
Gehringer-Det .330

On-Base Percentage
Gehrig-NY .466
Foxx-Phi .461
Cochrane-Det .452
Myer-Was .440
Appling-Chi .437

Slugging Average
Foxx-Phi .636
Greenberg-Det .628
Gehrig-NY .583
Vosmik-Cle .537
Fox-Det .513

On-Base Plus Slugging
Foxx-Phi 1096
Gehrig-NY 1049
Greenberg-Det 1039
Vosmik-Cle 946
Gehringer-Det 911

Adjusted OPS
Foxx-Phi 182
Gehrig-NY 180
Greenberg-Det 171
Vosmik-Cle 140
Myer-Was 139

Batter Runs
Foxx-Phi 67.2
Gehrig-NY 61.6
Greenberg-Det 57.5
Vosmik-Cle 38.3
Myer-Was 36.5

Adjusted Batter Runs
Gehrig-NY 70.3
Foxx-Phi 68.4
Greenberg-Det 62.9
Myer-Was 40.9
Gehringer-Det 36.4

Clutch Hitting Index
Owen-Det 134
Kuhel-Was 124
Goslin-Det 124
Powell-Was 124
Myer-Was 122

Runs Created
Foxx-Phi 163
Greenberg-Det 161
Gehrig-NY 154
Vosmik-Cle 137
Myer-Was 132

Total Average
Foxx-Phi 1.288
Gehrig-NY 1.230
Greenberg-Det 1.138
Cochrane-Det 1.000
Vosmik-Cle .980

Stolen Bases
Werber-Bos 29
Lary-Was-StL 28
Almada-Bos 20
White-Det 19
Chapman-NY 17

Stolen Base Average
Lary-Was-StL 87.5
Werber-Bos 80.6
Almada-Bos 69.0
White-Det 65.5
Chapman-NY 63.0

Stolen Base Runs
Lary-Was-StL 4.8
Werber-Bos 3.9
Hughes-Cle 1.8
Solters-Bos-StL 1.7

Fielding Runs
Appling-Chi 21.3
Travis-Was 21.3
Solters-Bos-StL 18.6
Melillo-StL-Bos 18.6
Werber-Bos 17.2

Total Player Rating
Foxx-Phi 5.9
Myer-Was 5.3
Gehrig-NY 5.1
Greenberg-Det 5.0
Appling-Chi 4.6

Wins
W.Ferrell-Bos 25
Harder-Cle 22
Bridges-Det 21
Grove-Bos 20
Rowe-Det 19

Win Percentage
Auker-Det .720
Broaca-NY .682
Bridges-Det .677
Harder-Cle .667
Lyons-Chi .652

Games
VanAtta-NY-StL 58
Walkup-StL 55
Andrews-StL 50
Thomas-StL 49
Knott-StL 48

Complete Games
W.Ferrell-Bos 31
Grove-Bos 23
Bridges-Det 23
Rowe-Det 21

Shutouts
Rowe-Det 6
Harder-Cle 4
Bridges-Det 4

Saves
Knott-StL 7

Innings Pitched
W.Ferrell-Bos 322.1
Harder-Cle 287.1
Whitehill-Was 279.1
Rowe-Det 275.2
Bridges-Det 274.1

Fewest Hits/Game
Allen-NY 8.03
Ruffing-NY 8.15
Gomez-NY 8.16
Whitehead-Chi 8.46
Grove-Bos 8.87

Fewest BB/Game
Harder-Cle 1.66
Grove-Bos 2.14
Rowe-Det 2.22
Andrews-StL 2.24
Hudlin-Cle 2.37

Strikeouts
Bridges-Det 163
Rowe-Det 140
Gomez-NY 138
Grove-Bos 121
Allen-NY 113

Strikeouts/Game
Allen-NY 6.09
Bridges-Det 5.35
Gomez-NY 5.05
VanAtta-NY-StL 4.63
Rowe-Det 4.57

Ratio
Grove-Bos 11.11
Rowe-Det 11.17
Ruffing-NY 11.27
Allen-NY 11.37
Gomez-NY 11.38

Earned Run Average
Grove-Bos 2.70
Lyons-Chi 3.02
Ruffing-NY 3.12
Gomez-NY 3.18
Harder-Cle 3.29

Adjusted ERA
Grove-Bos 176
Lyons-Chi 153
Harder-Cle 137
Andrews-StL 135
W.Ferrell-Bos 135

Opponents' Batting Avg.
Allen-NY .238
Ruffing-NY .239
Gomez-NY .242
Whitehead-Chi .250
Broaca-NY .254

Opponents' On-Base Pct.
Rowe-Det .301
Grove-Bos .302
Ruffing-NY .303
Allen-NY .307
Harder-Cle .307

Starter Runs
Grove-Bos 53.1
Harder-Cle 37.2
Gomez-NY 34.8
W.Ferrell-Bos 33.6
Ruffing-NY 32.9

Adjusted Starter Runs
Grove-Bos 58.1
W.Ferrell-Bos 41.2
Harder-Cle 38.4
Lyons-Chi 32.7
Andrews-StL 27.5

Clutch Pitching Index
Lyons-Chi 124
Bridges-Det 113
Auker-Det 112
Grove-Bos 112
Tietje-Chi 110

Relief Runs
L.Brown-Cle 11.4
Hogsett-Det 9.9
DeShong-NY 9.2
Murphy-NY 4.9
Wilson-Bos 1.7

Adjusted Relief Runs
L.Brown-Cle 11.9
Hogsett-Det 7.3
DeShong-NY 6.7
Wilson-Bos 3.5

Relief Ranking
L.Brown-Cle 14.1
Hogsett-Det 8.9
DeShong-NY 5.0
Wilson-Bos 3.6

Total Pitcher Index
W.Ferrell-Bos 6.8
Grove-Bos 6.0
Harder-Cle 4.3
Ruffing-NY 3.8
Lyons-Chi 3.5

Total Baseball Ranking
W.Ferrell-Bos 6.8
Grove-Bos 6.0
Foxx-Phi 5.9
Myer-Was 5.3
Gehrig-NY 5.1

TEAM	G	W	L	PCT	GB	R	OR	AB	H	2B	3B	HR	BB	SO	AVG	OBP	SLG	OPS	OPS+	BR	BR+	PF	CHI	RC	SB	CS	SBA	SBR
NY	154	92	62	.597		742	621	5449	1529	237	48	97	431	**452**	.281	.337	.395	732	104	19	27	99	99	744	31			
STL	155	87	67	.565	5	795	794	5537	1554	**332**	60	88	442	577	.281	.336	**.410**	**746**	**106**	40	**43**	100	103	772	**69**			
CHI	154	87	67	.565	5	755	**603**	5409	1545	275	36	76	491	462	**.286**	**.349**	.392	741	104	44	27	102	97	757	68			
PIT	156	84	70	.545	8	**804**	718	5586	**1596**	283	**80**	60	**517**	502	**.286**	**.349**	.397	**746**	105	**56**	38	102	100	**798**	37			
CIN	154	74	80	.481	18	722	760	5393	1476	224	73	82	410	584	.274	.329	.388	717	**106**	-14	33	94	**104**	699	68			
BOS	157	71	83	.461	21	631	715	5478	1450	207	45	67	433	582	.265	.322	.356	678	94	-86	-42	94	98	635	23			
BRO	156	67	87	.435	25	662	752	5574	1518	263	43	33	390	458	.272	.323	.353	676	87	-92	-98	101	**104**	649	55			
PHI	154	54	100	.351	38	726	874	5465	1538	250	46	**103**	451	586	.281	.339	.401	740	95	32	-37	110	96	757	50			
TOT	620					5837		43891	12206	2071	431	606	3565	4203	.279	.336	.387	722							401			

TEAM	CG	SH	SV	IP	H	H/G	HR	BB	SO	RAT	ERA	ERA+	OAV	OOB	PR	PR+	PF	CPI	FA	E	DP	FW	PW	BW	SBW	DIF
NY	60	12	22	1385^{2}	1458	9.5	75	401	500	12.3	**3.46**	**113**	.273	.327	**86**	**69**	97	**110**	.974	168	164	1.2	**6.8**	2.7		4.6
STL	65	5	**24**	1398	1610	10.4	89	434	559	13.4	4.48	88	.289	.344	-71	-85	98	98	.974	156	134	1.9	-8.2	**4.2**		12.3
CHI	**77**	**18**	10	1382^{1}	**1413**	**9.2**	77	434	597	12.3	3.54	**113**	**.265**	.324	74	**69**	99	104	**.976**	**146**	156	**2.4**	**6.8**	2.7		-1.7
PIT	67	5	12	1395^{1}	1475	9.6	74	**379**	559	**12.2**	3.89	104	.269	**.319**	20	25	101	92	.967	199	113	-.5	2.5	3.8		1.4
CIN	50	6	23	1367^{1}	1576	10.4	**51**	418	459	13.4	4.22	91	.287	.341	-31	-64	95	97	.969	191	150	-.2	-6.2	3.3		.3
BOS	61	7	13	1413^{1}	1566	10.0	69	451	421	13.0	3.95	97	.281	.337	12	-18	95	103	.971	189	**175**	.2	-1.7	-4.0		-.2
BRO	59	7	18	1403	1466	9.5	84	528	**651**	13.0	3.99	104	.266	.333	5	21	103	97	.966	208	107	-1.0	2.1	-9.5		-1.4
PHI	51	7	14	1365^{1}	1630	10.8	87	515	454	14.4	4.65	98	.292	.356	-95	-15	113	100	.959	252	144	-3.6	-1.4	-3.6		-14.2
TOT	490	67	136	11110^{1}		9.9				13.0	4.02		.279	.336					.970	1509	1143					

Runs
Vaughan-Pit 122
P.Martin-StL 121
Ott-NY 120
Medwick-StL 115
Suhr-Pit 111

Hits
Medwick-StL 223
P.Waner-Pit 218
Demaree-Chi 212
Herman-Chi 211
Moore-NY 205

Doubles
Medwick-StL 64
Herman-Chi 57
P.Waner-Pit 53
Moore-StL 39
Moore-Bos 38

Triples
Goodman-Cin 14
Medwick-StL 13
Camilli-Phi 13

Home Runs
Ott-NY 33
Camilli-Phi 28
Klein-Chi-Phi 25
Berger-Bos 25
Mize-StL 19

Total Bases
Medwick-StL 367
Ott-NY 314
Klein-Chi-Phi 308
Camilli-Phi 306
P.Waner-Pit 304

Runs Batted In
Medwick-StL 138
Ott-NY 135
Suhr-Pit 118
Klein-Chi-Phi 104

Runs Produced
Medwick-StL 235
Ott-NY 222
Suhr-Pit 218
P.Waner-Pit 196
Vaughan-Pit 191

Bases On Balls
Vaughan-Pit 118
Camilli-Phi 116
Ott-NY 111
Suhr-Pit 95
Hack-Chi 89

Batting Average
P.Waner-Pit .373
Phelps-Bro .367
Medwick-StL .351
Demaree-Chi .350
Vaughan-Pit .335

On-Base Percentage
Vaughan-Pit .453
Ott-NY .448
P.Waner-Pit .446
Camilli-Phi .441
Suhr-Pit .410

Slugging Average
Ott-NY .588
Camilli-Phi .577
Mize-StL .577
Medwick-StL .577
P.Waner-Pit .520

On-Base Plus Slugging
Ott-NY 1036
Camilli-Phi 1018
P.Waner-Pit 965
Medwick-StL 964
Vaughan-Pit 927

Adjusted OPS
Ott-NY 179
Medwick-StL 157
Camilli-Phi 156
P.Waner-Pit 156
Vaughan-Pit 146

Batter Runs
Ott-NY 61.9
Camilli-Phi 58.0
P.Waner-Pit 51.4
Vaughan-Pit 47.3
Medwick-StL 46.9

Adjusted Batter Runs
Ott-NY 63.5
P.Waner-Pit 48.4
Medwick-StL 47.4
Camilli-Phi 45.6
Vaughan-Pit 44.3

Clutch Hitting Index
Brubaker-Pit 147
Young-Pit 131
Suhr-Pit 124
Herman-Chi 115
Whitney-Bos-Phi 114

Runs Created
Ott-NY 153
Camilli-Phi 148
Medwick-StL 141
P.Waner-Pit 140
Vaughan-Pit 137

Total Average
Ott-NY 1.188
Camilli-Phi 1.162
Vaughan-Pit 1.034
P.Waner-Pit 1.016
Medwick-StL .956

Stolen Bases
P.Martin-StL 23
S.Martin-StL 17
Hack-Chi 17
Chiozza-Phi 17

Stolen Base Average

Stolen Base Runs

Fielding Runs
Bartell-NY 44.8
Whitehead-NY 29.2
Kampouris-Cin 28.0
Berres-Bro 23.0

Total Player Rating
Bartell-NY 5.9
Medwick-StL 5.1
Ott-NY 4.9
Herman-Chi 4.8
P.Waner-Pit 4.7

Wins
Hubbell-NY 26
D.Dean-StL 24
Derringer-Cin 19

Win Percentage
Hubbell-NY .813
Lucas-Pit .789
French-Chi .667
D.Dean-StL .649
Lee-Chi .621

Games
Derringer-Cin 51
D.Dean-StL 51
Passeau-Phi 49
Brown-Pit 47

Complete Games
D.Dean-StL 28
Hubbell-NY 25
Mungo-Bro 22
MacFayden-Bos 21
Lee-Chi 20

Shutouts
Warneke-Chi 4
Walters-Phi 4
Smith-NY 4
Lee-Chi 4
French-Chi 4
Carleton-Chi 4
Blanton-Pit 4

Saves
D.Dean-StL 11
Brennan-Cin 9
Smith-Bos 8
Johnson-Phi 7
Coffman-NY 7

Innings Pitched
D.Dean-StL 315.0
Mungo-Bro 311.2
Hubbell-NY 304.0
Derringer-Cin 282.1
MacFayden-Bos 266.2

Fewest Hits/Game
Hubbell-NY 7.85
Mungo-Bro 7.94
Lee-Chi 8.28
D.Dean-StL 8.86
Blanton-Pit 8.97

Fewest BB/Game
Lucas-Pit 1.33
Derringer-Cin 1.34
D.Dean-StL 1.51
Hubbell-NY 1.69
Gabler-NY 1.89

Strikeouts
Mungo-Bro 238
D.Dean-StL 195
Blanton-Pit 127
Hubbell-NY 123
Derringer-Cin 121

Strikeouts/Game
Mungo-Bro 6.87
D.Dean-StL 5.57
Blanton-Pit 4.85
Weaver-Pit 4.31
Warneke-Chi 4.23

Ratio
Hubbell-NY 9.68
D.Dean-StL 10.46
Lucas-Pit 10.61
Blanton-Pit 11.19
Davis-Phi-Chi 11.35

Earned Run Average
Hubbell-NY 2.31
MacFayden-Bos 2.87
Gabler-NY 3.12
D.Dean-StL 3.17
Lucas-Pit 3.18

Adjusted ERA
Hubbell-NY 169
MacFayden-Bos 134
Passeau-Phi 130
Lucas-Pit 128
Gabler-NY 125

Opponents' Batting Avg.
Mungo-Bro .234
Hubbell-NY .236
Lee-Chi .246
D.Dean-StL .253
Blanton-Pit .257

Opponents' On-Base Pct.
Hubbell-NY .276
D.Dean-StL .285
Lucas-Pit .287
Blanton-Pit .301
Mungo-Bro .305

Starter Runs
Hubbell-NY 57.7
MacFayden-Bos 34.0
D.Dean-StL 29.6
Mungo-Bro 23.1
Lee-Chi 20.4

Adjusted Starter Runs
Hubbell-NY 55.2
MacFayden-Bos 29.9
D.Dean-StL 27.4
Mungo-Bro 26.2
Passeau-Phi 22.5

Clutch Pitching Index
Schumacher-NY 120
Gabler-NY 119
Chaplin-Bos 111
Smith-NY 110
Carleton-Chi 109

Relief Runs
Bryant-Chi 4.6
Coffman-NY 1.4

Adjusted Relief Runs
Bryant-Chi 4.4
Johnson-Phi 2.5

Relief Ranking
Johnson-Phi 2.8
Bryant-Chi 2.2

Total Pitcher Index
Hubbell-NY 5.7
Passeau-Phi 3.0
MacFayden-Bos 2.9
D.Dean-StL 2.9
Mungo-Bro 2.7

Total Baseball Ranking
Bartell-NY 5.9
Hubbell-NY 5.7
Medwick-StL 5.1
Ott-NY 4.9
Herman-Chi 4.8

TEAM	G	W	L	PCT	GB	R	OR	AB	H	2B	3B	HR	BB	SO	AVG	OBP	SLG	OPS	OPS+	BR	BR+	PF	CHI	RC	SB	CS	SBA	SBR
NY	155	102	51	.667		**1065**	**731**	5591	1676	315	83	**182**	**700**	594	.300	**.381**	**.483**	**864**	**124**	**162**	**201**	97	100	**1056**	77	40	66	3
DET	154	83	71	.539	19.5	921	871	5464	1638	326	55	94	640	462	.300	.377	.431	808	106	57	54	100	98	912	73	49	60	-1
CHI	153	81	70	.536	20	920	873	5466	1597	282	56	60	684	417	.292	.374	.397	771	94	-9	-40	104	**104**	851	66	29	69	4
WAS	153	82	71	.536	20	889	799	5433	1601	293	**84**	62	576	**398**	.295	.365	.414	779	105	-7	44	94	**104**	847	**104**	42	71	**8**
CLE	157	80	74	.519	22.5	921	862	5646	**1715**	**357**	82	123	514	470	**.304**	.364	.461	825	109	70	62	101	96	948	66	53	55	-4
BOS	155	74	80	.481	28.5	775	764	5383	1485	288	62	86	584	465	.276	.349	.400	749	86	-72	-115	106	98	773	55	44	56	-3
STL	155	57	95	.375	44.5	804	1064	5391	1502	299	66	79	625	627	.279	.356	.403	759	91	-51	-73	103	99	804	62	20	**76**	7
PHI	154	53	100	.346	49	714	1045	5373	1443	240	60	72	524	590	.269	.336	.376	712	84	-151	-137	98	102	694	59	43	58	-2
TOT	618					7009		43747	12657	2400	548	758	4847	4023	.290	.363	.422	784							562	320	64	12

TEAM	CG	SH	SV	IP	H	H/G	HR	BB	SO	RAT	ERA	ERA+	OAV	OOB	PR	PR+	PF	CPI	FA	E	DP	FW	PW	BW	SBW	DIF
NY	77	6	**21**	1400[1]	**1474**	**9.5**	84	663	**624**	13.9	**4.18**	112	**.271**	.351	**135**	81	92	**108**	.973	163	148	.8	7.2	**17.8**	.1	-.3
DET	76	**13**	13	1360	1568	10.4	100	562	526	14.3	5.00	99	.289	.358	6	-7	98	100	**.975**	**153**	159	**1.3**	-.6	4.8	-.2	.8
CHI	**80**	5	8	1365	1603	10.6	104	578	414	14.6	5.07	103	.293	.363	-4	20	103	102	.973	168	**174**	.4	1.8	-3.5	.2	6.7
WAS	78	8	14	1345[2]	1484	10.0	**73**	588	462	14.1	4.59	104	.279	.353	68	31	95	101	.970	182	163	-.4	2.8	3.9	**.6**	-1.2
CLE	74	6	12	1389[1]	1604	10.4	**73**	607	619	14.5	4.84	104	.289	.362	32	32	100	102	.971	178	154	.1	2.9	5.5	-.5	-4.8
BOS	78	11	9	1372[1]	1501	9.9	78	**552**	584	**13.6**	4.39	**121**	.277	**.346**	99	**134**	106	102	.972	165	139	.7	**11.9**	-10.1	-.4	-4.9
STL	54	3	13	1348[1]	1776	11.9	115	609	399	16.3	6.25	86	.314	.385	-180	-122	107	95	.969	188	143	-.6	-10.7	-6.4	.5	-1.6
PHI	68	3	12	1352[1]	1645	11.0	131	696	405	15.8	6.08	84	.300	.381	-156	-144	101	94	.965	209	152	-1.8	-12.7	-12.0	-.3	3.5
TOT	585	55	102	10933[1]		10.5				14.6	5.04		.290	.363					.971	1406	1232					

Runs
Gehrig-NY 167
Clift-StL 145
Gehringer-Det 144
Crosetti-NY 137
Averill-Cle 136

Hits
Averill-Cle 232
Gehringer-Det 227
Trosky-Cle 216
Bell-StL 212
Radcliff-Chi 207

Doubles
Gehringer-Det 60
Walker-Det 55
Chapman-NY-Was 50
Hale-Cle 50

Triples
Rolfe-NY 15
DiMaggio-NY 15
Averill-Cle 15
B.Johnson-Phi 14

Home Runs
Gehrig-NY 49
Trosky-Cle 42
Foxx-Bos 41
DiMaggio-NY 29
Averill-Cle 28

Total Bases
Trosky-Cle 405
Gehrig-NY 403
Averill-Cle 385
Foxx-Bos 369
DiMaggio-NY 367

Runs Batted In
Trosky-Cle 162
Gehrig-NY 152
Foxx-Bos 143
Bonura-Chi 138
Solters-StL 134

Runs Produced
Gehrig-NY 270
Bonura-Chi 246
Gehringer-Det 245
Trosky-Cle 244
Averill-Cle 234

Bases On Balls
Gehrig-NY 130
Lary-StL 117
Clift-StL 115
Foxx-Bos 105
Lazzeri-NY 97

Batting Average
Appling-Chi 388
Averill-Cle 378
Dickey-NY 362
Gehringer-Det 354
Gehrig-NY 354

On-Base Percentage
Gehrig-NY 478
Appling-Chi 474
Foxx-Bos 440
Averill-Cle 438
Gehringer-Det 431

Slugging Average
Gehrig-NY 696
Trosky-Cle 644
Foxx-Bos 631
Averill-Cle 627
Dickey-NY 617

On-Base Plus Slugging
Gehrig-NY 1174
Foxx-Bos 1071
Averill-Cle 1065
Trosky-Cle 1026
Gehringer-Det 987

Adjusted OPS
Gehrig-NY 193
Averill-Cle 159
Foxx-Bos 153
Trosky-Cle 148
Stone-Was 145

Batter Runs
Gehrig-NY 82.2
Foxx-Bos 56.8
Averill-Cle 56.4
Gehringer-Det 43.0
Trosky-Cle 41.9

Adjusted Batter Runs
Gehrig-NY 88.9
Averill-Cle 55.2
Foxx-Bos 48.5
Gehringer-Det 42.6
Trosky-Cle 40.8

Clutch Hitting Index
Appling-Chi 132
Sewell-Chi 131
Bonura-Chi 127
Owen-Det 126
Vosmik-Cle 125

Runs Created
Gehrig-NY 199
Averill-Cle 168
Foxx-Bos 168
Gehringer-Det 157
Trosky-Cle 150

Total Average
Gehrig-NY 1.426
Foxx-Bos 1.238
Averill-Cle 1.171
Appling-Chi 1.088
Gehringer-Det 1.075

Stolen Bases
Lary-StL 37
Powell-Was-NY 26
Werber-Bos 23
Chapman-NY-Was 20
Hughes-Cle 20

Stolen Base Average
Lary-StL 80.4
Crosetti-NY 72.0
Powell-Was-NY 70.3
Chapman-NY-Was 69.0
Hughes-Cle 69.0

Stolen Base Runs
Lary-StL 5.0
Hill-Was 2.4
Powell-Was-NY 1.9
Stone-Was 1.8
Sewell-Chi 1.7

Fielding Runs
Hayes-Chi 17.1
Hale-Cle 16.5
Cramer-Bos 16.3
Gehringer-Det 15.7
Appling-Chi 15.2

Total Player Rating
Gehrig-NY 6.5
Gehringer-Det 6.0
Appling-Chi 5.3
Averill-Cle 4.1
Dickey-NY 3.9

Wins
Bridges-Det 23
Kennedy-Chi 21
Ruffing-NY 20
W.Ferrell-Bos 20
Allen-Cle 20

Win Percentage
Pearson-NY 731
Kennedy-Chi 700
Bridges-Det 676
Allen-Cle 667
Rowe-Det 655

Games
VanAtta-StL 52
Knott-StL 47

Complete Games
W.Ferrell-Bos 28
Bridges-Det 26
Ruffing-NY 25
Newsom-Was 24
Grove-Bos 22

Shutouts
Grove-Bos 6
Bridges-Det 5
Rowe-Det 4
Newsom-Was 4
Allen-Cle 4

Saves
Malone-NY 9
Knott-StL 6
Murphy-NY 5
Brown-Chi 5
Hildebrand-Cle 4

Innings Pitched
W.Ferrell-Bos 301.0
Bridges-Det 294.2
Newsom-Was 285.2
Kennedy-Chi 274.1
Ruffing-NY 271.0

Fewest Hits/Game
Pearson-NY 7.71
Grove-Bos 8.42
Allen-Cle 8.67
Gomez-NY 8.78
Bridges-Det 8.83

Fewest BB/Game
Lyons-Chi 2.23
Grove-Bos 2.31
Rowe-Det 2.35
Andrews-StL 2.35
Marcum-Bos 2.69

Strikeouts
Bridges-Det 175
Allen-Cle 165
Newsom-Was 156
Grove-Bos 130
Pearson-NY 118

Strikeouts/Game
Allen-Cle 6.11
Bridges-Det 5.35
Gomez-NY 5.01
Newsom-Was 4.91
Pearson-NY 4.76

Ratio
Grove-Bos 10.87
Rowe-Det 12.18
Ruffing-NY 12.19
Allen-Cle 12.30
Appleton-Was 12.45

Earned Run Average
Grove-Bos 2.81
Allen-Cle 3.44
Appleton-Was 3.53
Bridges-Det 3.60
Pearson-NY 3.71

Adjusted ERA
Grove-Bos 189
Allen-Cle 146
Bridges-Det 137
Appleton-Was 135
Kelley-Phi 132

Opponents' Batting Avg.
Pearson-NY 233
Grove-Bos 246
Gomez-NY 254
Appleton-Was 254
Bridges-Det 255

Opponents' On-Base Pct.
Grove-Bos 297
Rowe-Det 321
Ruffing-NY 323
Appleton-Was 324
Bridges-Det 326

Starter Runs
Grove-Bos 62.8
Bridges-Det 46.9
Allen-Cle 43.0
Ruffing-NY 35.7
Appleton-Was 33.9

Adjusted Starter Runs
Grove-Bos 66.9
Bridges-Det 44.9
Allen-Cle 43.0
W.Ferrell-Bos 35.8
Kelley-Phi 32.0

Clutch Pitching Index
Hadley-NY 116
Kelley-Phi 115
Grove-Bos 115
Bridges-Det 109
Thomas-StL 107

Relief Runs
Lee-Cle 2.1
Gumpert-Phi 1.9
Kimsey-Det 1.1
Brown-Chi 5

Adjusted Relief Runs
Gumpert-Phi 2.3
Lee-Cle 2.1
Brown-Chi 1.9
Kimsey-Det 6

Relief Ranking
Brown-Chi 1.9
Lee-Cle 1.3
Gumpert-Phi 1.2
Kimsey-Det 6

Total Pitcher Index
Grove-Bos 6.6
Bridges-Det 4.5
Allen-Cle 4.5
W.Ferrell-Bos 4.3
Ruffing-NY 4.1

Total Baseball Ranking
Grove-Bos 6.6
Gehrig-NY 6.5
Gehringer-Det 6.0
Appling-Chi 5.3
Bridges-Det 4.5

TEAM	G	W	L	PCT	GB	R	OR	AB	H	2B	3B	HR	BB	SO	AVG	OBP	SLG	OPS	OPS+	BR	BR+	PF	CHI	RC	SB	CS	SBA	SBR
NY	152	95	57	.625		732	602	5329	1484	251	41	**111**	412	492	.278	.334	.403	737	105	40	31	101	100	734	45			
CHI	154	93	61	.604	3	**811**	682	5349	1537	253	74	96	**538**	496	**.287**	**.355**	**.416**	**771**	**111**	**117**	**84**	104	98	**816**	71			
PIT	154	86	68	.558	10	704	647	5433	**1550**	223	**86**	47	463	**480**	.285	.343	.384	727	104	30	30	100	96	734	32			
STL	157	81	73	.526	15	789	733	5476	1543	**264**	67	94	385	569	.282	.331	.406	737	104	36	22	102	**107**	744	**78**			
BOS	152	79	73	.520	16	579	**556**	5124	1265	200	41	63	485	707	.247	.314	.339	653	91	-109	-53	91	102	565	45			
BRO	155	62	91	.405	33.5	616	772	5295	1401	258	53	37	469	583	.265	.327	.354	681	90	-57	-67	102	97	629	69			
PHI	155	61	92	.399	34.5	724	869	5424	1482	258	37	103	478	640	.273	.334	.391	725	95	21	-33	108	100	730	66			
CIN	155	56	98	.364	40	612	706	5230	1329	215	59	73	437	586	.254	.315	.360	675	94	-78	-47	95	102	599	53			
TOT	617					5567		42660	11591	1922	458	624	3667	4553	.272	.332	.383	714							459			

TEAM	CG	SH	SV	IP	H	H/G	HR	BB	SO	RAT	ERA	ERA+	OAV	OOB	PR	PR+	PF	CPI	FA	E	DP	FW	PW	BW	SBW	DIF
NY	67	11	17	1361	**1341**	**8.9**	86	404	**653**	11.7	3.43	**113**	**.258**	.314	73	**70**	99	102	.974	159	143	1.0	**7.0**	3.1		8.1
CHI	73	11	13	1381^1	1434	9.4	91	502	596	12.8	3.98	100	.267	.332	-10	0	102	99	**.975**	**151**	141	**1.5**	.0	**8.4**		6.2
PIT	67	12	17	1366^1	1398	9.3	71	428	643	12.2	3.57	108	.264	.321	53	46	99	101	.970	181	135	-.1	4.6	3.0		1.7
STL	81	10	4	1392	1546	10.0	95	448	571	13.0	3.98	100	.281	.337	-10	-1	102	**105**	.973	164	127	1.0	-.0	2.2		1.0
BOS	**85**	**16**	10	1359^1	1344	**8.9**	60	**372**	387	**11.5**	**3.22**	111	.259	**.310**	**105**	60	92	103	**.975**	157	128	1.1	6.0	-5.2		1.3
BRO	63	5	8	1362^2	1470	9.8	68	476	592	13.1	4.13	98	.274	.336	-33	-14	103	96	.964	217	127	-2.1	-1.3	-6.6		-4.3
PHI	59	6	15	1373^2	1629	10.7	115	501	529	14.2	5.06	86	.297	.359	-174	-103	111	97	.970	184	**157**	-.2	-10.2	-3.2		-1.7
CIN	64	10	**18**	1358^1	1428	9.5	**38**	533	581	13.2	3.94	95	.270	.339	-4	-33	95	97	.966	208	139	-1.6	-3.2	-4.6		-11.4
TOT	559	81	102	10954^2		9.6				12.7	3.92		.272	.332					.971	1421	1097					

Runs
Medwick-StL 111
Herman-Chi 106
Hack-Chi 106
Galan-Chi 104
Demaree-Chi 104

Hits
Medwick-StL 237
P.Waner-Pit 219
Mize-StL 204
Demaree-Chi 199
Herman-Chi 189

Doubles
Medwick-StL 56
Mize-StL 40
Bartell-NY 38
Phelps-Bro 37
Moore-NY 37

Triples
Vaughan-Pit 17
Suhr-Pit 14
Handley-Pit 12
Goodman-Cin 12
Herman-Chi 11

Home Runs
Ott-NY 31
Medwick-StL 31
Camilli-Phi 27
Mize-StL 25
Galan-Chi 18

Total Bases
Medwick-StL 406
Mize-StL 333
Demaree-Chi 298
Ott-NY 285
Camilli-Phi 279

Runs Batted In
Medwick-StL 154
Demaree-Chi 115
Mize-StL 113
Suhr-Pit 97
Ott-NY 95

Runs Produced
Medwick-StL 234
Demaree-Chi 202
Mize-StL 191
Hack-Chi 167
P.Waner-Pit 166

Bases On Balls
Ott-NY 102
Camilli-Phi 90
Suhr-Pit 83
Hack-Chi 83
Galan-Chi 79

Batting Average
Medwick-StL .374
Mize-StL .364
Hartnett-Chi .354
P.Waner-Pit .354
Whitney-Phi .341

On-Base Percentage
Camilli-Phi .446
Mize-StL .427
Medwick-StL .414
P.Waner-Pit .413
Ott-NY .408

Slugging Average
Medwick-StL .641
Mize-StL .595
Camilli-Phi .587
Hartnett-Chi .548
Ott-NY .523

On-Base Plus Slugging
Medwick-StL 1056
Camilli-Phi 1034
Mize-StL 1021
Ott-NY 931
Herman-Chi 875

Adjusted OPS
Medwick-StL 179
Mize-StL 171
Camilli-Phi 165
Ott-NY 149
P.Waner-Pit 132

Batter Runs
Medwick-StL 68.8
Mize-StL 57.4
Camilli-Phi 54.9
Ott-NY 41.2
Hartnett-Chi 31.1

Adjusted Batter Runs
Medwick-StL 65.9
Mize-StL 54.9
Camilli-Phi 45.8
Ott-NY 39.8
P.Waner-Pit 29.8

Clutch Hitting Index
Scharein-Phi 136
Durocher-StL 133
Suhr-Pit 129
Jurges-Chi 124
Todd-Pit 120

Runs Created
Medwick-StL 170
Mize-StL 150
Camilli-Phi 137
Ott-NY 128
P.Waner-Pit 118

Total Average
Camilli-Phi 1.189
Medwick-StL 1.113
Mize-StL 1.097
Ott-NY 1.021
Vaughan-Pit .864

Stolen Bases
Galan-Chi 23
Hack-Chi 16

Stolen Base Average

Stolen Base Runs

Fielding Runs
Bartell-NY 37.5
Whitehead-NY 26.1
Riggs-Cin 19.5
Herman-Chi 18.6
Young-Pit 18.1

Total Player Rating
Bartell-NY 6.2
Medwick-StL 5.9
Herman-Chi 5.1
Camilli-Phi 3.7
Ott-NY 3.6

Wins
Hubbell-NY 22
Turner-Bos 20
Melton-NY 20
Fette-Bos 20
Warneke-StL 18

Win Percentage
Hubbell-NY .733
Melton-NY .690
Fette-Bos .667
Carleton-Chi .667
Turner-Bos .645

Games
Mulcahy-Phi 56
Jorgens-Phi 52

Complete Games
Turner-Bos 24
Fette-Bos 23
Weiland-StL 21

Shutouts
Turner-Bos 5
Grissom-Cin 5
Fette-Bos 5

Saves
Melton-NY 7
Brown-Pit 7
Grissom-Cin 6
Root-Chi 5
Hollingsworth-Cin 5

Innings Pitched
Passeau-Phi 292.1
Lee-Chi 272.1
Weiland-StL 264.1
Hubbell-NY 261.2
Fette-Bos 259.0

Fewest Hits/Game
Mungo-Bro 7.60
Grissom-Cin 7.77
Melton-NY 7.84
Carleton-Chi 7.91
Turner-Bos 7.99

Fewest BB/Game
D.Dean-StL 1.51
Root-Chi 1.61
Hoyt-Pit-Bro 1.66
Turner-Bos 1.82
Castleman-NY 1.85

Strikeouts
Hubbell-NY 159
Grissom-Cin 149
Blanton-Pit 143
Melton-NY 142

Strikeouts/Game
Mungo-Bro 6.82
Grissom-Cin 6.00
Bauers-Pit 5.66
Henshaw-Bro 5.64
LaMaster-Phi 5.51

Ratio
Turner-Bos 9.82
Melton-NY 10.05
Castleman-NY 10.16
Root-Chi 10.53
D.Dean-StL 10.72

Earned Run Average
Turner-Bos 2.38
Melton-NY 2.61
D.Dean-StL 2.69
Bauers-Pit 2.88
Fette-Bos 2.88

Adjusted ERA
Turner-Bos 150
Melton-NY 149
D.Dean-StL 148
Mungo-Bro 139
Bauers-Pit 134

Opponents' Batting Avg.
Mungo-Bro .229
Grissom-Cin .232
Melton-NY .233
Turner-Bos .235
Carleton-Chi .236

Opponents' On-Base Pct.
Turner-Bos .274
Melton-NY .280
Castleman-NY .287
Root-Chi .290
D.Dean-StL .291

Starter Runs
Turner-Bos 43.5
Melton-NY 35.8
Fette-Bos 29.5
MacFayden-Bos 26.9
D.Dean-StL 26.7

Adjusted Starter Runs
Turner-Bos 37.3
Melton-NY 35.3
D.Dean-StL 27.7
Fette-Bos 21.9
Bauers-Pit 20.8

Clutch Pitching Index
Johnson-StL 128
Brandt-Pit 124
Weiland-StL 115
Frankhouse-Bro 113
MacFayden-Bos 112

Relief Runs
Coffman-NY 7.8
Hutchinson-Bos 1.8

Adjusted Relief Runs
Coffman-NY 7.6

Relief Ranking
Coffman-NY 10.0

Total Pitcher Index
Turner-Bos 4.9
Melton-NY 3.9
Mungo-Bro 3.0
D.Dean-StL 2.9
Fette-Bos 2.8

Total Baseball Ranking
Bartell-NY 6.2
Medwick-StL 5.9
Herman-Chi 5.1
Turner-Bos 4.9
Melton-NY 3.9

TEAM	G	W	L	PCT	GB	R	OR	AB	H	2B	3B	HR	BB	SO	AVG	OBP	SLG	OPS	OPS+	BR	BR+	PF	CHI	RC	SB	CS	SBA	SBR
NY	157	102	52	.662		**979**	**671**	5487	1554	282	73	**174**	**709**	607	.283	.369	**.456**	**825**	**113**	**112**	**106**	101	**103**	**952**	60	36	63	1
DET	155	89	65	.578	13	935	841	5516	**1611**	309	62	150	656	711	**.292**	**.370**	.452	822	111	106	86	102	100	947	89	45	66	**4**
CHI	154	86	68	.558	16	780	730	5277	1478	280	76	67	549	**447**	.280	.350	.400	750	95	-38	-37	100	**103**	763	70	34	**67**	**4**
CLE	156	83	71	.539	19	817	768	5353	1499	304	76	103	570	551	.280	.352	.423	775	100	4	-1	101	101	813	78	51	60	-1
BOS	154	80	72	.526	21	821	775	5354	1506	269	64	100	601	557	.281	.357	.411	768	96	-1	-31	104	102	804	79	61	56	-4
WAS	158	73	80	.477	28.5	757	841	5578	1559	245	**84**	47	591	503	.279	.351	.379	730	94	-74	-38	96	100	767	61	35	64	1
PHI	154	54	97	.358	46.5	699	854	5228	1398	278	60	94	583	557	.267	.341	.397	738	93	-63	-51	98	97	732	**95**	48	66	**4**
STL	156	46	108	.299	56	715	1023	5510	1573	**327**	44	71	514	510	.285	.348	.399	747	93	-47	-52	101	93	780	30	27	53	-3
TOT	622					6503		43303	12178	2294	539	806	4773	4443	.282	.355	.415	770							562	337	63	6

TEAM	CG	SH	SV	IP	H	H/G	HR	BB	SO	RAT	ERA	ERA+	OAV	OOB	PR	PR+	PF	CPI	FA	E	DP	FW	PW	BW	SBW	DIF
NY	**82**	**15**	**21**	1396	**1417**	**9.2**	92	**506**	652	**12.5**	**3.65**	**122**	**.261**	**.325**	**151**	**128**	96	103	.972	170	134	.2	**11.8**	**9.8**	.0	3.4
DET	70	6	11	1378	1521	10.0	102	635	485	14.3	4.88	96	.279	.357	-38	-30	101	95	**.976**	**147**	149	**1.5**	-2.7	7.9	**.3**	5.2
CHI	70	**15**	**21**	1351[1]	1435	9.6	115	532	533	13.3	4.17	110	.273	.341	68	65	100	**104**	.971	174	173	-.2	6.0	-3.3	**.3**	6.4
CLE	64	4	15	1364[2]	1529	10.1	**61**	566	630	14.0	4.40	105	.285	.356	35	33	100	102	.974	159	153	.8	3.1	-.0	-.2	2.5
BOS	74	6	14	1366	1518	10.1	92	597	**682**	14.1	4.49	106	.279	.352	21	39	103	100	.970	177	139	-.4	3.6	-2.8	-.4	4.2
WAS	75	5	14	1398[2]	1498	9.7	96	671	524	14.1	4.58	97	.275	.357	7	-24	96	99	.972	170	**181**	.3	-2.2	-3.4	.0	2.0
PHI	65	6	9	1335	1490	10.1	105	613	469	14.4	4.86	97	.281	.358	-35	-20	102	97	.967	198	150	-1.6	-1.8	-4.6	**.3**	-13.6
STL	55	2	8	1363	1768	11.7	143	653	468	16.2	6.01	80	.315	.390	-209	-170	105	100	.972	173	166	.0	-15.6	-4.7	-.3	-10.2
TOT	555	59	113	10952[2]		10.1				14.1	4.63		.282	.355					.972	1368	1245					

Runs
DiMaggio-NY 151
Rolfe-NY 143
Gehrig-NY 138
Greenberg-Det 137
Gehringer-Det 133

Hits
Bell-StL 218
DiMaggio-NY 215
Walker-Det 213
Lewis-Was 210
Gehringer-Det 209

Doubles
Bell-StL 51
Greenberg-Det 49
Moses-Phi 48
Vosmik-StL 47
Lary-Cle 46

Triples
Walker-Chi 16
Kreevich-Chi 16
Stone-Was 15
DiMaggio-NY 15
Greenberg-Det 14

Home Runs
DiMaggio-NY 46
Greenberg-Det 40
Gehrig-NY 37
Foxx-Bos 36
York-Det 35

Total Bases
DiMaggio-NY 418
Greenberg-Det 397
Gehrig-NY 366
Moses-Phi 357
Trosky-Cle 329

Runs Batted In
Greenberg-Det 183
DiMaggio-NY 167
Gehrig-NY 159
Dickey-NY 133
Trosky-Cle 128

Runs Produced
Greenberg-Det 280
DiMaggio-NY 272
Gehrig-NY 260
Gehringer-Det 215
Foxx-Bos 202

Bases On Balls
Gehrig-NY 127
Greenberg-Det 102
Foxx-Bos 99
Johnson-Phi 98
Clift-StL 98

Batting Average
Gehringer-Det 371
Gehrig-NY 351
DiMaggio-NY 346
Bonura-Chi 345
Travis-Was 344

On-Base Percentage
Gehrig-NY 473
Gehringer-Det 458
Greenberg-Det 436
Johnson-Phi 425
Dickey-NY 417

Slugging Average
DiMaggio-NY 673
Greenberg-Det 668
York-Det 651
Gehrig-NY 643
Bonura-Chi 573

On-Base Plus Slugging
Gehrig-NY 1116
Greenberg-Det 1105
DiMaggio-NY 1085
Dickey-NY 987
Bonura-Chi 984

Adjusted OPS
Gehrig-NY 177
Greenberg-Det 171
DiMaggio-NY 168
Johnson-Phi 147
Bonura-Chi 146

Batter Runs
Gehrig-NY 73.3
Greenberg-Det 67.2
DiMaggio-NY 61.3
Gehringer-Det 44.0
Dickey-NY 37.5

Adjusted Batter Runs
Gehrig-NY 72.3
Greenberg-Det 63.8
DiMaggio-NY 60.4
Gehringer-Det 41.2
Johnson-Phi 36.9

Clutch Hitting Index
Hayes-Chi 152
Higgins-Bos 127
Myer-Was 125
Hale-Cle 117
Werber-Phi 116

Runs Created
Gehrig-NY 181
Greenberg-Det 178
DiMaggio-NY 173
Gehringer-Det 140
Clift-StL 134

Total Average
Gehrig-NY 1.339
Greenberg-Det 1.277
DiMaggio-NY 1.207
Gehringer-Det 1.089
Johnson-Phi 1.083

Stolen Bases
Chapman-Was-Bos .. 35
Werber-Phi 35
Walker-Det 23

Stolen Base Average
Hill-Was-Phi 81.8
Walker-Det 76.7
Pytlak-Cle 76.2
Chapman-Was-Bos . 74.5
Werber-Phi 72.9

Stolen Base Runs
Chapman-Was-Bos ..3.5
Werber-Phi 3.2
Walker-Det 2.6
Hill-Was-Phi 2.6
Kreevich-Chi 1.9

Fielding Runs
Clift-StL 41.0
Hale-Cle 25.9
Hayes-Chi 20.5
Appling-Chi 13.8
Dickey-NY 12.3

Total Player Rating
Clift-StL 7.3
DiMaggio-NY 6.2
Dickey-NY 5.2
Gehringer-Det 5.2
Greenberg-Det 5.0

Wins
Gomez-NY 21
Ruffing-NY 20
Lawson-Det 18
Grove-Bos 17
Auker-Det 17

Win Percentage
Allen-Cle 938
Stratton-Chi 750
Ruffing-NY 741
Lawson-Det 720
Gomez-NY 656

Games
Brown-Chi 53
Wilson-Bos 51
Newsom-Was-Bos ... 41
Kelley-Phi 41
Heving-Cle 40

Complete Games
W.Ferrell-Bos-Was ... 26
Gomez-NY 25
Ruffing-NY 22
Grove-Bos 21
DeShong-Was 20

Shutouts
Gomez-NY 6
Stratton-Chi 5
Whitehead-Chi 4
Ruffing-NY 4
Appleton-Was 4

Saves
Brown-Chi 18
Murphy-NY 10
Wilson-Bos 7
Malone-NY 6

Innings Pitched
W.Ferrell-Bos-Was 281.0
Gomez-NY 278.1
Newsom-Was-Bos . 275.1
DeShong-Was 264.1
Grove-Bos 262.0

Fewest Hits/Game
Gomez-NY 7.53
Stratton-Chi 7.76
Smith-Phi 8.15
Allen-Cle 8.17
Ruffing-NY 8.50

Fewest BB/Game
Stratton-Chi 2.02
Hudlin-Cle 2.20
Marcum-Bos 2.30
Ruffing-NY 2.39
Lyons-Chi 2.39

Strikeouts
Gomez-NY 194
Newsom-Was-Bos .. 166
Grove-Bos 153
Feller-Cle 150
Bridges-Det 138

Strikeouts/Game
Gomez-NY 6.27
Wilson-Bos 5.57
Newsom-Was-Bos . 5.43
Grove-Bos 5.26
Bridges-Det 5.06

Ratio
Stratton-Chi 9.89
Gomez-NY 10.57
Ruffing-NY 10.92
Allen-Cle 11.55
Lee-Chi 11.87

Earned Run Average
Gomez-NY 2.33
Stratton-Chi 2.40
Allen-Cle 2.55
Ruffing-NY 2.98
Grove-Bos 3.02

Adjusted ERA
Stratton-Chi 191
Gomez-NY 191
Allen-Cle 181
Grove-Bos 157
Ruffing-NY 149

Opponents' Batting Avg.
Gomez-NY 223
Stratton-Chi 234
Smith-Phi 242
Allen-Cle 244
Ruffing-NY 247

Opponents' On-Base Pct.
Stratton-Chi 280
Gomez-NY 287
Ruffing-NY 296
Lee-Chi 312
Allen-Cle 313

Starter Runs
Gomez-NY 70.9
Ruffing-NY 46.6
Grove-Bos 46.5
Stratton-Chi 40.6
Allen-Cle 39.8

Adjusted Starter Runs
Gomez-NY 68.1
Grove-Bos 48.8
Ruffing-NY 43.3
Stratton-Chi 40.4
Allen-Cle 39.7

Clutch Pitching Index
Allen-Cle 120
Whitehead-Chi 119
Knott-StL 112
Grove-Bos 111
Galehouse-Cle 110

Relief Runs
Brown-Chi 13.3
Cohen-Was 9.2
Murphy-NY 5.5
Fink-Phi 5.1
Wyatt-Cle 1.5

Adjusted Relief Runs
Brown-Chi 13.2
Cohen-Was 8.4
Fink-Phi 5.8
Murphy-NY 3.5
Wyatt-Cle 1.4

Relief Ranking
Brown-Chi 22.0
Cohen-Was 9.6
Murphy-NY 5.5
Fink-Phi 2.9
Wyatt-Cle 8

Total Pitcher Index
Gomez-NY 6.7
Stratton-Chi 4.6
Grove-Bos 3.9
Ruffing-NY 3.8
Auker-Det 2.9

Total Baseball Ranking
Clift-StL 7.3
Gomez-NY 6.7
DiMaggio-NY 6.2
Dickey-NY 5.2
Gehringer-Det 5.2

TEAM	G	W	L	PCT	GB	R	OR	AB	H	2B	3B	HR	BB	SO	AVG	OBP	SLG	OPS	OPS+	BR	BR+	PF	CHI	RC	SB	CS	SBA	SBR
CHI	154	89	63	.586		713	**597**	5333	1435	242	70	65	522	476	.269	.338	.377	715	100	25	6	103	101	689	49			
PIT	152	86	64	.573	2	707	630	5422	1511	265	66	65	485	**409**	**.279**	**.340**	.388	728	106	48	43	101	96	727	47			
NY	152	83	67	.553	5	705	637	5255	1424	210	36	**125**	465	528	.271	.334	.396	730	106	45	39	101	99	715	31			
CIN	151	82	68	.547	6	723	634	5391	1495	251	57	110	366	518	.277	.327	.406	733	**110**	43	**63**	97	101	720	19			
BOS	153	77	75	.507	12	561	618	5250	1311	199	39	54	424	548	.250	.309	.333	642	91	-119	-59	90	**104**	549	49			
STL	156	71	80	.470	17.5	**725**	722	5528	**1542**	**288**	74	91	412	492	**.279**	.331	**.407**	**738**	103	**56**	16	106	97	**752**	55			
BRO	151	69	80	.463	18.5	704	710	5142	1322	225	**79**	61	**611**	615	.257	.338	.367	705	98	13	-2	102	103	671	**66**			
PHI	151	45	105	.300	43	550	840	5192	1318	233	29	40	423	507	.254	.312	.333	645	85	-111	-95	97	101	549	38			
TOT	610					5388		42513	11358	1913	450	611	3708	4093	.268	.329	.377	705							354			

TEAM	CG	SH	SV	IP	H	H/G	HR	BB	SO	RAT	ERA	ERA+	OAV	OOB	PR	PR+	PF	CPI	FA	E	DP	FW	PW	BW	SBW	DIF
CHI	67	**16**	**18**	1396[2]	1414	9.2	71	454	**583**	12.2	**3.38**	**113**	.262	.322	**64**	**66**	101	105	**.978**	**135**	151	**2.3**	**6.7**	.7		3.6
PIT	57	8	15	1379[2]	1406	9.2	71	432	557	12.2	3.47	109	.266	.324	49	50	100	**106**	.974	163	**168**	.5	5.1	4.4		1.2
NY	59	8	**18**	1349	1370	9.2	87	**389**	497	**11.9**	3.63	104	.261	**.314**	24	20	99	97	.973	168	147	.2	2.1	4.0		1.9
CIN	72	11	16	1362	**1329**	**8.8**	75	463	542	12.0	3.63	101	**.254**	.316	25	3	96	94	.971	172	133	-.0	.4	**6.4**		.5
BOS	**83**	15	12	1380	1375	9.0	**66**	465	413	12.2	3.41	101	.258	.322	58	3	91	103	.972	173	136	.0	.4	-5.9		6.7
STL	58	10	16	1384[2]	1482	9.7	77	474	534	12.9	3.85	103	.272	.333	-9	16	104	102	.967	199	145	-1.3	1.7	1.7		-6.3
BRO	56	12	14	1332	1464	9.9	88	446	469	13.2	4.07	96	.278	.338	-42	-25	103	102	.973	157	148	.8	-2.5	-.2		-3.5
PHI	68	3	6	1329[1]	1516	10.3	76	582	492	14.4	4.93	79	.285	.358	-169	-151	103	92	.966	201	135	-1.8	-15.1	-9.5		-3.4
TOT	520	83	115	10913[1]		9.4				12.6	3.79		.268	.329					.972	1368	1163					

Runs
Ott-NY 116
Hack-Chi 109
Camilli-Bro 106
Goodman-Cin 103
Medwick-StL 100

Hits
McCormick-Cin 209
Hack-Chi 195
L.Waner-Pit 194
Medwick-StL 190
Mize-StL 179

Doubles
Medwick-StL 47
McCormick-Cin 40
Young-Pit 36
Martin-Phi 36

Triples
Mize-StL 16
Gutteridge-StL 15
Suhr-Pit 14
Riggs-Cin 13
Koy-Bro 13

Home Runs
Ott-NY 36
Goodman-Cin 30
Mize-StL 27
Camilli-Bro 24
Rizzo-Pit 23

Total Bases
Mize-StL 326
Medwick-StL 316
Ott-NY 307
Goodman-Cin 303
Rizzo-Pit 285

Runs Batted In
Medwick-StL 122
Ott-NY 116
Rizzo-Pit 111
McCormick-Cin 106
Mize-StL 102

Runs Produced
Medwick-StL 201
Ott-NY 196
McCormick-Cin 190
Rizzo-Pit 185
Camilli-Bro 182

Bases On Balls
Camilli-Bro 119
Ott-NY 118
Vaughan-Pit 104
Hack-Chi 94
Suhr-Pit 87

Batting Average
Lombardi-Cin .342
Mize-StL .337
McCormick-Cin .327
Medwick-StL .322
Vaughan-Pit .322

On-Base Percentage
Ott-NY .442
Vaughan-Pit .433
Mize-StL .422
Hack-Chi .411
Suhr-Pit .394

Slugging Average
Mize-StL .614
Ott-NY .583
Medwick-StL .536
Goodman-Cin .533
Lombardi-Cin .524

On-Base Plus Slugging
Mize-StL 1036
Ott-NY 1024
Lombardi-Cin 915
Medwick-StL 905
Goodman-Cin 901

Adjusted OPS
Ott-NY 178
Mize-StL 172
Lombardi-Cin 154
Goodman-Cin 149
Vaughan-Pit 140

Batter Runs
Ott-NY 61.9
Mize-StL 59.2
Vaughan-Pit 36.4
Medwick-StL 34.4
Goodman-Cin 33.5

Adjusted Batter Runs
Ott-NY 60.8
Mize-StL 52.4
Goodman-Cin 36.5
Vaughan-Pit 35.6
Lombardi-Cin 34.5

Clutch Hitting Index
Durocher-Bro 140
McCormick-Cin 134
Arnovich-Phi 128
Todd-Pit 127
Lavagetto-Bro 125

Runs Created
Ott-NY 149
Mize-StL 141
Hack-Chi 119
Goodman-Cin 116
Vaughan-Pit 115

Total Average
Ott-NY 1.164
Mize-StL 1.104
Camilli-Bro .964
Vaughan-Pit .960
Goodman-Cin .908

Stolen Bases
Hack-Chi 16
Lavagetto-Bro 15
Koy-Bro 15
Vaughan-Pit 14
Gutteridge-StL 14

Stolen Base Average

Stolen Base Runs

Fielding Runs
Young-Pit 31.8
Herman-Chi 24.8
Bartell-NY 22.4
Vaughan-Pit 18.3
Arnovich-Phi 16.7

Total Player Rating
Vaughan-Pit 6.4
Ott-NY 6.3
Hack-Chi 3.9
Lombardi-Cin 3.9
Mize-StL 3.7

Wins
Lee-Chi 22
Derringer-Cin 21
Bryant-Chi 19
Weiland-StL 16

Win Percentage
Lee-Chi .710
Bryant-Chi .633
Brown-Pit .625
VanderMeer-Cin .600
Derringer-Cin .600

Games
Coffman-NY 51
Brown-Pit 51
McGee-StL 47
Mulcahy-Phi 46

Complete Games
Derringer-Cin 26
Turner-Bos 22
Walters-Phi-Cin 20
MacFayden-Bos 19
Lee-Chi 19

Shutouts
Lee-Chi 9
MacFayden-Bos 5
Warneke-StL 4
Derringer-Cin 4

Saves
Coffman-NY 12
Root-Chi 8
Hamlin-Bro 6
Errickson-Bos 6

Innings Pitched
Derringer-Cin 307.0
Lee-Chi 291.0
Bryant-Chi 270.1
Turner-Bos 268.0
Mulcahy-Phi 267.1

Fewest Hits/Game
VanderMeer-Cin 7.07
Bauers-Pit 7.67
Bryant-Chi 7.82
MacFayden-Bos 8.52
Klinger-Pit 8.59

Fewest BB/Game
Davis-StL 1.40
Derringer-Cin 1.44
Hubbell-NY 1.66
Root-Chi 1.68
Turner-Bos 1.81

Strikeouts
Bryant-Chi 135
Derringer-Cin 132
VanderMeer-Cin 125
Lee-Chi 121

Strikeouts/Game
Hubbell-NY 5.23
VanderMeer-Cin 4.99
Weiland-StL 4.61
Bryant-Chi 4.49

Ratio
Hubbell-NY 10.36
Derringer-Cin 10.67
Root-Chi 10.92
Turner-Bos 10.95
Lee-Chi 11.04

Earned Run Average
Lee-Chi 2.66
Root-Chi 2.86
Derringer-Cin 2.93
MacFayden-Bos 2.95
Klinger-Pit 2.99

Adjusted ERA
Lee-Chi 144
Root-Chi 134
Fitzsimmons-Bro 129
Klinger-Pit 127
Derringer-Cin 124

Opponents' Batting Avg.
VanderMeer-Cin .213
Bauers-Pit .233
Bryant-Chi .235
MacFayden-Bos .247
Schumacher-NY .248

Opponents' On-Base Pct.
Hubbell-NY .285
Derringer-Cin .291
Root-Chi .294
Lohrman-NY .294
Schumacher-NY .299

Starter Runs
Lee-Chi 36.3
Derringer-Cin 29.1
Bryant-Chi 20.6
MacFayden-Bos 20.3
Bauers-Pit 19.2

Adjusted Starter Runs
Lee-Chi 37.2
Derringer-Cin 25.2
Bryant-Chi 21.6
Bauers-Pit 19.3
Fitzsimmons-Bro 19.2

Clutch Pitching Index
Lee-Chi 119
Pressnell-Bro 111
Blanton-Pit 111
Tamulis-Bro 110
Fette-Bos 110

Relief Runs
Brown-NY 19.8
Russell-Chi 5.0
Coffman-NY 3.8

Adjusted Relief Runs
Brown-NY 19.7
Russell-Chi 5.4
Coffman-NY 3.5

Relief Ranking
Brown-NY 18.2
Coffman-NY 4.3
Russell-Chi 3.7

Total Pitcher Index
Lee-Chi 4.0
Derringer-Cin 2.5
Bryant-Chi 2.4
Fitzsimmons-Bro 2.2
Bauers-Pit 2.1

Total Baseball Ranking
Vaughan-Pit 6.4
Ott-NY 6.3
Lee-Chi 4.0
Hack-Chi 3.9
Lombardi-Cin 3.9

TEAM	G	W	L	PCT	GB	R	OR	AB	H	2B	3B	HR	BB	SO	AVG	OBP	SLG	OPS	OPS+	BR	BR+	PF	CHI	RC	SB	CS	SBA	SBR
NY	157	99	53	.651		**966**	**710**	5410	1480	283	63	**174**	**749**	616	.274	.366	**.446**	**812**	**111**	77	**82**	100	**104**	**926**	**91**	28	**76**	**10**
BOS	150	88	61	.591	9.5	902	751	5229	1566	298	56	98	650	463	**.299**	**.378**	.434	**812**	105	**87**	47	105	100	881	55	51	52	-6
CLE	153	86	66	.566	13	847	782	5356	1506	**300**	**89**	113	550	605	.281	.350	.434	784	104	9	26	98	102	832	83	36	70	6
DET	155	84	70	.545	16	862	795	5270	1434	219	52	137	693	581	.272	.359	.411	770	94	0	-45	106	**104**	812	76	41	65	2
WAS	152	75	76	.497	23.5	814	873	5474	**1602**	278	72	85	573	**379**	.293	.362	.416	778	108	12	75	93	96	845	65	37	64	1
CHI	149	65	83	.439	32	709	752	5199	1439	239	55	67	514	489	.277	.343	.383	726	86	-91	-107	102	101	700	56	39	59	-1
STL	156	55	97	.362	44	755	962	5333	1498	273	36	92	590	528	.281	.355	.397	752	95	-38	-36	100	96	774	51	40	56	-3
PHI	154	53	99	.349	46	726	956	5229	1410	243	62	98	605	590	.270	.348	.396	744	95	-57	-37	97	97	741	65	53	55	-4
TOT	613					6581		42500	11935	2133	485	864	4924	4251	.281	.358	.415	773							542	325	63	5

TEAM	CG	SH	SV	IP	H	H/G	HR	BB	SO	RAT	ERA	ERA+	OAV	OOB	PR	PR+	PF	CPI	FA	E	DP	FW	PW	BW	SBW	DIF
NY	**91**	**11**	13	1382	1436	**9.4**	**85**	566	567	**13.1**	**3.92**	**116**	**.268**	**.339**	**134**	**101**	95	**106**	.973	169	177	.5	**9.2**	**7.5**	**.8**	5.2
BOS	67	10	15	1316[1]	1472	10.1	102	**528**	484	13.9	4.46	111	.281	.349	48	67	103	103	.968	190	172	-1.1	6.1	4.3	-.6	5.0
CLE	68	5	**17**	1353	**1416**	9.5	100	681	**717**	14.2	4.60	101	**.268**	.355	29	7	97	99	.974	151	145	1.3	.7	2.4	.5	5.3
DET	75	3	11	1348[1]	1532	10.3	110	608	435	14.4	4.79	104	.287	.361	1	31	104	103	**.976**	147	172	1.6	2.9	-4.0	.1	6.6
WAS	59	6	11	1360[1]	1472	9.8	92	655	515	14.3	4.94	91	.276	.358	-22	-68	94	94	.970	180	**179**	-.4	-6.1	6.8	.0	-.7
CHI	83	5	9	1316[1]	1449	10.0	101	550	432	13.8	4.37	112	.279	.350	62	76	102	**106**	.967	196	155	-1.5	6.9	-9.6	-.2	-4.4
STL	71	3	7	1344[2]	1584	10.7	132	737	632	15.8	5.81	86	.295	.382	-151	-120	104	96	.975	**145**	163	**1.8**	-10.8	-3.2	-.3	-8.3
PHI	56	4	12	1324	1573	10.7	142	599	473	14.9	5.48	88	.292	.365	-101	-94	101	96	.965	206	119	-1.7	-8.4	-3.3	-.4	-8.9
TOT	570	47	95	10745		10.0				14.3	4.79		.281	.358					.971	1384	1282					

Runs
Greenberg-Det 144
Foxx-Bos 139
Gehringer-Det 133
Rolfe-NY 132
DiMaggio-NY 129

Hits
Vosmik-Bos 201
Cramer-Bos 198
Almada-Was-StL 197
Foxx-Bos 197
Rolfe-NY 196

Doubles
Cronin-Bos 51
McQuinn-StL 42
Trosky-Cle 40
Chapman-Bos 40
Vosmik-Bos 37

Triples
Heath-Cle 18
Averill-Cle 15
DiMaggio-NY 13

Home Runs
Greenberg-Det 58
Foxx-Bos 50
Clift-StL 34
York-Det 33
DiMaggio-NY 32

Total Bases
Foxx-Bos 398
Greenberg-Det 380
DiMaggio-NY 348
Johnson-Phi 311
Heath-Cle 302

Runs Batted In
Foxx-Bos 175
Greenberg-Det 146
DiMaggio-NY 140
York-Det 127
Clift-StL 118

Runs Produced
Foxx-Bos 264
DiMaggio-NY 237
Greenberg-Det 232
Gehringer-Det 220
Clift-StL 203

Bases On Balls
Greenberg-Det 119
Foxx-Bos 119
Clift-StL 118
Gehringer-Det 113
Gehrig-NY 107

Batting Average
Foxx-Bos .349
Heath-Cle .343
Chapman-Bos .340
Myer-Was .336
Travis-Was .335

On-Base Percentage
Foxx-Bos .462
Myer-Was .454
Greenberg-Det .438
Averill-Cle .429
Cronin-Bos .428

Slugging Average
Foxx-Bos .704
Greenberg-Det .683
Heath-Cle .602
DiMaggio-NY .581
York-Det .579

On-Base Plus Slugging
Foxx-Bos 1166
Greenberg-Det 1122
York-Det 995
Heath-Cle 985
Dickey-NY 981

Adjusted OPS
Foxx-Bos 180
Greenberg-Det 167
Heath-Cle 146
Dickey-NY 144
Clift-StL 143

Batter Runs
Foxx-Bos 78.2
Greenberg-Det 66.0
Clift-StL 37.7
Cronin-Bos 34.8
York-Det 33.9

Adjusted Batter Runs
Foxx-Bos 70.6
Greenberg-Det 57.4
Clift-StL 38.0
Johnson-Phi 35.9
Averill-Cle 33.9

Clutch Hitting Index
Higgins-Bos 140
Heffner-StL 138
R.Ferrell-Was 116
Doerr-Bos 116
Bonura-Was 111

Runs Created
Foxx-Bos 189
Greenberg-Det 172
DiMaggio-NY 136
Clift-StL 133
Gehrig-NY 131

Total Average
Foxx-Bos 1.392
Greenberg-Det 1.306
Clift-StL 1.104
York-Det 1.104
Dickey-NY 1.083

Stolen Bases
Crosetti-NY 27
Lary-Cle 23
Werber-Phi 19
Lewis-Was 17
Fox-Det 16

Stolen Base Average
Lary-Cle 79.3
Fox-Det 69.6
Crosetti-NY 69.2
Lewis-Was 65.4
Werber-Phi 55.9

Stolen Base Runs
Lary-Cle 3.0
Gehringer-Det 2.7
Rolfe-NY 2.5
Crosetti-NY 1.7
Moses-Phi 1.5

Fielding Runs
Gordon-NY 23.7
Crosetti-NY 17.6
Clift-StL 14.0
Johnson-Phi 10.3
Cramer-Bos 8.7

Total Player Rating
Foxx-Bos 5.5
Clift-StL 5.1
Greenberg-Det 4.4
Cronin-Bos 4.2
Myer-Was 3.8

Wins
Ruffing-NY 21
Newsom-StL 20
Gomez-NY 18
Harder-Cle 17
Feller-Cle 17

Win Percentage
Ruffing-NY .750
Pearson-NY .696
Harder-Cle .630
Stratton-Chi .625
Feller-Cle .607

Games
Humphries-Cle 45
Newsom-StL 44
E.Smith-Phi 43
Bagby-Bos 43
Appleton-Was 43

Complete Games
Newsom-StL 31
Ruffing-NY 22
Gomez-NY 20
Feller-Cle 20
Caster-Phi 20

Shutouts
Gomez-NY 4
Wilson-Bos 3
Ruffing-NY 3
Leonard-Was 3

Saves
Murphy-NY 11
McKain-Bos 6
Humphries-Cle 6
Potter-Phi 5
Appleton-Was 5

Innings Pitched
Newsom-StL 329.2
Caster-Phi 281.1
Feller-Cle 277.2
Ruffing-NY 247.1
Lee-Chi 245.1

Fewest Hits/Game
Feller-Cle 7.29
Allen-Cle 8.51
Pearson-NY 8.82
Rigney-Chi 8.84
Hadley-NY 8.87

Fewest BB/Game
Leonard-Was 2.14
Harder-Cle 2.33
Lyons-Chi 2.40
Chandler-NY 2.46
Thomas-Phi 2.63

Strikeouts
Feller-Cle 240
Newsom-StL 226
L.Mills-StL 134
Gomez-NY 129
Ruffing-NY 127

Strikeouts/Game
Feller-Cle 7.78
Newsom-StL 6.17
L.Mills-StL 5.73
Grove-Bos 5.44
Allen-Cle 5.04

Ratio
Leonard-Was 11.32
Ruffing-NY 11.94
Stratton-Chi 12.03
Chandler-NY 12.14
Harder-Cle 12.15

Earned Run Average
Grove-Bos 3.08
Ruffing-NY 3.31
Gomez-NY 3.35
Leonard-Was 3.43
Lee-Chi 3.49

Adjusted ERA
Grove-Bos 160
Lee-Chi 140
Rigney-Chi 138
Ruffing-NY 137
Gomez-NY 135

Opponents' Batting Avg.
Feller-Cle .220
Allen-Cle .246
Hadley-NY .254
Stratton-Chi .255
Rigney-Chi .256

Opponents' On-Base Pct.
Leonard-Was .305
Stratton-Chi .315
Ruffing-NY .317
Harder-Cle .319
Grove-Bos .319

Starter Runs
Ruffing-NY 40.6
Gomez-NY 38.2
Lee-Chi 35.6
Leonard-Was 33.8
Grove-Bos 31.1

Adjusted Starter Runs
Lee-Chi 37.6
Ruffing-NY 35.5
Gomez-NY 33.2
Grove-Bos 32.7
Leonard-Was 28.6

Clutch Pitching Index
Lyons-Chi 125
Gill-Det 119
Grove-Bos 118
Rigney-Chi 117
Ruffing-NY 110

Relief Runs
Murphy-NY 5.6
McKain-Bos 3.0

Adjusted Relief Runs
McKain-Bos 4.5
Murphy-NY 3.2

Relief Ranking
McKain-Bos 4.3
Murphy-NY 4.0

Total Pitcher Index
Ruffing-NY 4.2
Lee-Chi 3.7
Gomez-NY 3.5
Leonard-Was 3.3
Grove-Bos 3.0

Total Baseball Ranking
Foxx-Bos 5.5
Clift-StL 5.1
Greenberg-Det 4.4
Ruffing-NY 4.2
Cronin-Bos 4.2

TEAM	G	W	L	PCT	GB	R	OR	AB	H	2B	3B	HR	BB	SO	AVG	OBP	SLG	OPS	OPS+	BR	BR+	PF	CHI	RC	SB	CS	SBA	SBR
CIN	156	97	57	.630		767	**595**	5378	1493	269	60	98	500	538	.278	.343	.405	748	106	51	47	101	102	759	46			
STL	155	92	61	.601	4.5	**779**	633	5447	**1601**	**332**	**62**	98	475	566	**.294**	**.354**	**.432**	**786**	**110**	**122**	**74**	106	94	**834**	44			
BRO	157	84	69	.549	12.5	708	645	5350	1420	265	57	78	**564**	639	.265	.338	.380	718	96	0	-24	104	102	697	59			
CHI	156	84	70	.545	13	724	678	5293	1407	263	**62**	91	523	553	.266	.336	.391	727	99	10	-2	102	103	702	**61**			
NY	151	77	74	.510	18.5	703	685	5129	1395	211	38	**116**	498	499	.272	.340	.396	736	103	28	22	101	101	683	26			
PIT	153	68	85	.444	28.5	666	721	5269	1453	261	60	63	477	**420**	.276	.338	.384	722	102	4	15	98	97	687	44			
BOS	152	63	88	.417	32.5	572	659	5286	1395	199	39	56	366	494	.264	.314	.348	662	91	-117	-74	93	**104**	575	41			
PHI	152	45	106	.298	50.5	553	856	5133	1341	232	40	49	421	486	.261	.318	.351	669	89	-98	-81	97	99	570	47			
TOT	616					5472		42285	11505	2032	418	649	3824	4195	.273	.336	.386	721							368			

TEAM	CG	SH	SV	IP	H	H/G	HR	BB	SO	RAT	ERA	ERA+	OAV	OOB	PR	PR+	PF	CPI	FA	E	DP	FW	PW	BW	SBW	DIF
CIN	**86**	13	9	1403^{2}	**1340**	**8.6**	81	499	**637**	12.0	**3.28**	**117**	**.255**	.322	**101**	**89**	98	**107**	.974	162	170	.7	**9.0**	4.8		5.8
STL	45	**18**	**32**	1384^{2}	1377	9.0	76	498	603	12.4	3.59	115	.260	.326	50	76	105	100	.971	177	140	-.2	7.7	**7.5**		.8
BRO	69	9	13	1410^{1}	1431	9.2	93	**399**	528	**11.9**	3.65	110	.263	**.317**	43	58	103	97	.972	176	157	.0	5.9	-2.4		4.2
CHI	72	8	13	1392^{1}	1504	9.8	74	430	584	12.7	3.81	104	.276	.331	18	20	101	101	.970	186	126	-.6	2.1	-.2		5.9
NY	55	6	20	1319	1412	9.7	86	477	505	13.1	4.07	96	.275	.340	-22	-20	100	100	**.975**	**153**	151	**.8**	-2.0	2.3		.6
PIT	53	10	15	1354	1537	10.3	70	423	464	13.2	4.16	92	.287	.342	-36	-51	98	100	.972	168	153	.2	-5.1	1.6		-5.0
BOS	68	11	15	1358^{1}	1400	9.3	**63**	513	430	12.9	3.72	100	.271	.339	31	-3	94	104	.971	181	**178**	-.5	-.3	-7.4		-4.2
PHI	67	3	12	1326^{2}	1502	10.2	106	579	447	14.5	5.17	77	.289	.365	-185	-167	102	93	.970	171	136	-.0	-16.7	-8.1		-5.6
TOT	515	78	129	10949		9.5				12.8	3.92		.273	.336					.972	1374	1211					

Runs
Werber-Cin 115
Hack-Chi 112
Herman-Chi 111
Camilli-Bro 105

Hits
McCormick-Cin 209
Medwick-StL 201
Mize-StL 197
Slaughter-StL 193
Brown-StL 192

Doubles
Slaughter-StL 52
Medwick-StL 48
Mize-StL 44
McCormick-Cin 41

Triples
Herman-Chi 18
Goodman-Cin 16
Mize-StL 14
Camilli-Bro 12

Home Runs
Mize-StL 28
Ott-NY 27
Camilli-Bro 26
Leiber-Chi 24
Lombardi-Cin 20

Total Bases
Mize-StL 353
McCormick-Cin 312
Medwick-StL 307
Camilli-Bro 296
Slaughter-StL 291

Runs Batted In
McCormick-Cin 128
Medwick-StL 117
Mize-StL 108
Camilli-Bro 104
Leiber-Chi 88

Runs Produced
McCormick-Cin 209
Medwick-StL 201
Mize-StL 184
Camilli-Bro 183
Herman-Chi 174

Bases On Balls
Camilli-Bro 110
Ott-NY 100
Mize-StL 92
Werber-Cin 91
Lavagetto-Bro 78

Batting Average
Mize-StL 349
McCormick-Cin 332
Medwick-StL 332
P.Waner-Pit 328
Arnovich-Phi 324

On-Base Percentage
Ott-NY 449
Mize-StL 444
Camilli-Bro 409
Goodman-Cin 401
Arnovich-Phi 397

Slugging Average
Mize-StL 626
Ott-NY 581
Leiber-Chi 556
Camilli-Bro 524
Goodman-Cin 515

On-Base Plus Slugging
Mize-StL 1070
Ott-NY 1030
Camilli-Bro 933
Goodman-Cin 916
Medwick-StL 886

Adjusted OPS
Mize-StL 174
Ott-NY 173
Camilli-Bro 144
Goodman-Cin 144
West-Bos 139

Batter Runs
Mize-StL 68.7
Ott-NY 45.9
Camilli-Bro 41.8
Leiber-Chi 30.5
Goodman-Cin 29.8

Adjusted Batter Runs
Mize-StL 60.3
Ott-NY 45.1
Camilli-Bro 37.7
Goodman-Cin 29.4
Leiber-Chi 29.1

Clutch Hitting Index
May-Phi 120
Lavagetto-Bro 116
McCormick-Cin 116
R.Russell-Chi 116
Bonura-NY 113

Runs Created
Mize-StL 162
Camilli-Bro 128
Medwick-StL 114
Ott-NY 112
McCormick-Cin 110

Total Average
Mize-StL 1.194
Ott-NY 1.194
Camilli-Bro 995
Goodman-Cin 941
Frey-Cin 860

Stolen Bases
Handley-Pit 17
Hack-Chi 17
Werber-Cin 15
Lavagetto-Bro 14
Hassett-Bos 13

Stolen Base Average

Stolen Base Runs

Fielding Runs
Slaughter-StL 15.8
Frey-Cin 15.1
Arnovich-Phi 14.9
Jurges-NY 14.9
Werber-Cin 12.6

Total Player Rating
Mize-StL 4.1
Frey-Cin 4.1
Vaughan-Pit 3.7
Ott-NY 3.4
Camilli-Bro 3.2

Wins
Walters-Cin 27
Derringer-Cin 25
Davis-StL 22
Hamlin-Bro 20
Lee-Chi 19

Win Percentage
Derringer-Cin 781
Walters-Cin 711
French-Chi 652
Gumbert-NY 621
Hamlin-Bro 606

Games
Shoun-StL 53
Sewell-Pit 52
Bowman-StL 51
Davis-StL 49
Brown-Pit 47

Complete Games
Walters-Cin 31
Derringer-Cin 28
Lee-Chi 20
Hamlin-Bro 19
Posedel-Bos 18

Shutouts
Fette-Bos 6
Posedel-Bos 5
Derringer-Cin 5
McGee-StL 4

Saves
Shoun-StL 9
Bowman-StL 9
Davis-StL 7
Brown-NY 7
Brown-Pit 7

Innings Pitched
Walters-Cin 319.0
Derringer-Cin 301.0
Lee-Chi 282.1
Passeau-Phi-Chi . . . 274.1
Hamlin-Bro 269.2

Fewest Hits/Game
Walters-Cin 7.05
Bowman-StL 7.49
Moore-Cin 8.49
Hamlin-Bro 8.51
Hubbell-NY 8.77

Fewest BB/Game
Derringer-Cin 1.05
Hubbell-NY 1.40
Davis-StL 1.74
Hamlin-Bro 1.80
Root-Chi 1.83

Strikeouts
Passeau-Phi-Chi 137
Walters-Cin 137
Cooper-StL 130
Derringer-Cin 128
Lee-Chi 105

Strikeouts/Game
Cooper-StL 5.55
Tamulis-Bro 4.71
French-Chi 4.55
Passeau-Phi-Chi 4.49
Bowman-StL 4.15

Ratio
Hubbell-NY 10.29
Walters-Cin 10.30
Hamlin-Bro 10.31
Derringer-Cin 10.73
Bowman-StL 10.74

Earned Run Average
Walters-Cin 2.29
Bowman-StL 2.60
Hubbell-NY 2.75
Casey-Bro 2.93
Derringer-Cin 2.93

Adjusted ERA
Walters-Cin 168
Bowman-StL 158
Hubbell-NY 143
Casey-Bro 137
Derringer-Cin 131

Opponents' Batting Avg.
Walters-Cin 220
Bowman-StL 232
Hamlin-Bro 248
Hubbell-NY 249
Moore-Cin 254

Opponents' On-Base Pct.
Hubbell-NY 280
Hamlin-Bro 285
Walters-Cin 291
Derringer-Cin 295
Bowman-StL 302

Starter Runs
Walters-Cin 57.8
Derringer-Cin 33.0
Casey-Bro 24.9
Bowman-StL 24.7
Thompson-Cin 23.3

Adjusted Starter Runs
Walters-Cin 56.0
Derringer-Cin 30.8
Bowman-StL 27.0
Casey-Bro 26.9
Thompson-Cin 22.3

Clutch Pitching Index
Brown-Pit 120
Shoffner-Bos-Cin . . . 115
Casey-Bro 113
Cooper-StL 113
Moore-Cin 113

Relief Runs
J.Russell-Chi 1.9
Shoun-StL 1.8

Adjusted Relief Runs
Shoun-StL 3.9
J.Russell-Chi 2.0

Relief Ranking
Shoun-StL 2.1
J.Russell-Chi 2.0

Total Pitcher Index
Walters-Cin 8.6
Davis-StL 3.2
Casey-Bro 3.1
Derringer-Cin 2.7
Bowman-StL 2.6

Total Baseball Ranking
Walters-Cin 8.6
Mize-StL 4.1
Frey-Cin 4.1
Vaughan-Pit 3.7
Ott-NY 3.4

TEAM	G	W	L	PCT	GB	R	OR	AB	H	2B	3B	HR	BB	SO	AVG	OBP	SLG	OPS	OPS+	BR	BR+	PF	CHI	RC	SB	CS	SBA	SBR
NY	152	106	45	.702		**967**	**556**	5300	1521	259	55	**166**	**701**	543	.287	**.374**	**.451**	**825**	**119**	**134**	**149**	98	102	**923**	72	37	66	3
BOS	152	89	62	.589	17	890	795	5308	**1543**	287	57	124	591	505	**.291**	.363	.436	799	106	78	46	104	101	831	42	44	49	-6
CLE	154	87	67	.565	20.5	797	700	5316	1490	**291**	**79**	85	557	574	.280	.350	.413	763	105	4	33	97	100	775	72	46	61	0
CHI	155	85	69	.552	22.5	755	737	5279	1451	220	56	64	579	502	.275	.349	.374	723	89	-62	-81	103	**103**	708	**113**	61	65	4
DET	155	81	73	.526	26.5	849	762	5326	1487	277	67	124	620	592	.279	.356	.426	782	99	43	-16	108	100	821	88	38	**70**	**6**
WAS	153	65	87	.428	41.5	702	797	5334	1483	249	**79**	44	547	**460**	.278	.346	.379	725	98	-62	-3	93	96	718	94	47	67	4
PHI	153	55	97	.362	51.5	711	1022	5309	1438	282	55	98	503	532	.271	.336	.400	736	96	-55	-39	98	97	713	60	34	64	1
STL	156	43	111	.279	64.5	733	1035	5422	1453	242	50	91	559	606	.268	.339	.381	720	88	-79	-94	102	100	706	48	38	56	-3
TOT	615					6404		42594	11866	2107	498	796	4657	4314	.279	.352	.408	759							589	345	63	9

TEAM	CG	SH	SV	IP	H	H/G	HR	BB	SO	RAT	ERA	ERA+	OAV	OOB	PR	PR+	PF	CPI	FA	E	DP	FW	PW	BW	SBW	DIF
NY	**87**	**15**	**26**	1348^2	**1208**	**8.1**	85	567	565	**12.0**	**3.31**	**132**	**.241**	**.319**	**196**	**166**	94	**107**	**.978**	**126**	159	**2.9**	**15.3**	**13.8**	.2	-1.5
BOS	52	4	20	1350^2	1533	10.3	77	543	539	14.0	4.56	104	.287	.355	9	25	102	102	.970	180	147	.1	2.4	4.3	-.7	7.6
CLE	69	10	13	1364^2	1394	9.2	**75**	602	614	13.3	4.09	108	.267	.344	81	51	95	103	.970	180	148	.3	4.7	3.1	-.1	2.2
CHI	62	5	21	1377	1470	9.7	99	**454**	535	12.7	4.31	110	.275	.333	48	63	102	98	.972	167	140	1.0	5.9	-7.4	.3	8.5
DET	64	8	16	1367^1	1430	9.5	104	574	**633**	13.4	4.30	114	.268	.341	50	86	106	100	.967	198	147	-.6	8.0	-1.4	**.5**	-2.2
WAS	72	4	10	1354^2	1420	9.5	**75**	602	521	13.6	4.61	94	.271	.348	2	-41	94	94	.966	205	**167**	-1.1	-3.7	-.2	.3	-6.0
PHI	50	6	12	1342^2	1687	11.4	148	579	397	15.4	5.80	81	.307	.375	-175	-159	102	99	.964	210	131	-1.3	-14.6	-3.5	.0	-1.3
STL	56	3	3	1371^1	1724	11.4	133	739	516	16.4	6.02	81	.310	.393	-212	-166	105	100	.968	199	144	-.6	-15.2	-8.6	-.4	-9.0
TOT	512	55	121	10877		9.9				13.8	4.62		.279	.352					.970	1465	1183					

Runs
Rolfe-NY 139
Williams-Bos 131
Foxx-Bos 130
McCosky-Det 120
Johnson-Phi 115

Hits
Rolfe-NY 213
McQuinn-StL 195
Keltner-Cle 191
McCosky-Det 190
Williams-Bos 185

Doubles
Rolfe-NY 46
Williams-Bos 44
Greenberg-Det 42
McQuinn-StL 37
Keltner-Cle 35

Triples
Lewis-Was 16
McCosky-Det 14
McQuinn-StL 13
Campbell-Cle 13

Home Runs
Foxx-Bos 35
Greenberg-Det 33
Williams-Bos 31
DiMaggio-NY 30
Gordon-NY 28

Total Bases
Williams-Bos 344
Foxx-Bos 324
Rolfe-NY 321
McQuinn-StL 318
Greenberg-Det 311

Runs Batted In
Williams-Bos 145
DiMaggio-NY 126
Johnson-Phi 114
Greenberg-Det 112

Runs Produced
Williams-Bos 245
Johnson-Phi 206
Rolfe-NY 205
DiMaggio-NY 204
Foxx-Bos 200

Bases On Balls
Clift-StL 111
Williams-Bos 107
Appling-Chi 105
Selkirk-NY 103
Johnson-Phi 99

Batting Average
DiMaggio-NY ...... .381
Foxx-Bos .... .360
Johnson-Phi .... .338
Trosky-Cle .... .335
Rolfe-NY .... .329

On-Base Percentage
Foxx-Bos .... .464
Selkirk-NY .... .452
DiMaggio-NY ...... .448
Keller-NY .... .447
Johnson-Phi .... .440

Slugging Average
Foxx-Bos .... .694
DiMaggio-NY ...... .671
Greenberg-Det ..... .622
Williams-Bos .... .609
Trosky-Cle .... .589

On-Base Plus Slugging
Foxx-Bos 1158
DiMaggio-NY 1119
Williams-Bos 1045
Greenberg-Det 1042
Trosky-Cle 994

Adjusted OPS
DiMaggio-NY 185
Foxx-Bos 185
Williams-Bos 158
Trosky-Cle 157
Johnson-Phi 156

Batter Runs
Foxx-Bos 66.1
Williams-Bos 56.3
DiMaggio-NY 56.0
Greenberg-Det 47.3
Johnson-Phi 45.7

Adjusted Batter Runs
Foxx-Bos 60.9
DiMaggio-NY 58.1
Williams-Bos 51.0
Johnson-Phi 48.5
Greenberg-Det 38.4

Clutch Hitting Index
Wright-Was 129
McNair-Chi 116
Dahlgren-NY 116
Selkirk-NY 115
Higgins-Det 115

Runs Created
Williams-Bos 157
Foxx-Bos 150
DiMaggio-NY 139
Johnson-Phi 138
Greenberg-Det 136

Total Average
Foxx-Bos 1.304
DiMaggio-NY 1.242
Williams-Bos 1.161
Greenberg-Det 1.152
Selkirk-NY 1.121

Stolen Bases
Case-Was 51
Kreevich-Chi 23
Fox-Det 23
McCosky-Det 20

Stolen Base Average
McCosky-Det 83.3
Kuhel-Chi 78.3
Chapman-Cle 75.0
Case-Was 75.0
Walker-Chi 73.9

Stolen Base Runs
Case-Was 5.3
McCosky-Det 3.0
Kuhel-Chi 2.2
Welaj-Was 2.2
Chapman-Cle 1.9

Fielding Runs
Doerr-Bos 27.3
Kreevich-Chi 16.1
Tebbetts-Det 14.5
Lewis-Was 13.6
Clift-StL 12.0

Total Player Rating
DiMaggio-NY 5.8
Foxx-Bos 5.1
Johnson-Phi 4.5
Lewis-Was 4.2
Williams-Bos 4.0

Wins
Feller-Cle 24
Ruffing-NY 21
Newsom-StL-Det 20
Leonard-Was 20
Bridges-Det 17

Win Percentage
Grove-Bos .... .789
Ruffing-NY .... .750
Feller-Cle .... .727
Leonard-Was .... .714
Bridges-Det .... .708

Games
Brown-Chi 61
Dean-Phi 54
Dickman-Bos 48
Heving-Bos 46

Complete Games
Newsom-StL-Det 24
Feller-Cle 24
Ruffing-NY 22
Leonard-Was 21
Grove-Bos 17

Shutouts
Ruffing-NY 5
Feller-Cle 4
Newsom-StL-Det 3

Saves
Murphy-NY 19
Brown-Chi 18
Heving-Bos 7
Dean-Phi 7
Appleton-Was 6

Innings Pitched
Feller-Cle 296.2
Newsom-StL-Det .. 291.2
Leonard-Was 269.1
Lee-Chi 235.0
Ruffing-NY 233.1

Fewest Hits/Game
Feller-Cle 6.89
Hadley-NY 7.71
Gomez-NY 7.86
Ruffing-NY 8.14
Chase-Was 8.34

Fewest BB/Game
Lyons-Chi 1.36
Leonard-Was 1.97
Beckmann-Phi 2.38
Lee-Chi 2.68
Grove-Bos 2.73

Strikeouts
Feller-Cle 246
Newsom-StL-Det ... 192
Bridges-Det 129
Rigney-Chi 119
Chase-Was 118

Strikeouts/Game
Feller-Cle 7.46
Newsom-StL-Det .. 5.92
Bridges-Det 5.86
Rigney-Chi 4.90
Gomez-NY 4.64

Ratio
Lyons-Chi 9.85
Ruffing-NY 11.11
Leonard-Was 11.26
Grove-Bos 11.26
Feller-Cle 11.29

Earned Run Average
Grove-Bos 2.54
Lyons-Chi 2.76
Feller-Cle 2.85
Ruffing-NY 2.93
Hadley-NY 2.98

Adjusted ERA
Grove-Bos 186
Lyons-Chi 171
Feller-Cle 154
Ruffing-NY 149
Hadley-NY 146

Opponents' Batting Avg.
Feller-Cle .... .210
Gomez-NY .... .235
Hadley-NY .... .237
Ruffing-NY .... .240
Bridges-Det .... .243

Opponents' On-Base Pct.
Lyons-Chi .... .276
Ruffing-NY .... .301
Feller-Cle .... .303
Bridges-Det .... .304
Leonard-Was .... .305

Starter Runs
Feller-Cle 58.3
Grove-Bos 44.0
Ruffing-NY 43.8
Lyons-Chi 35.6
Newsom-StL-Det .. 33.7

Adjusted Starter Runs
Feller-Cle 53.6
Grove-Bos 45.3
Newsom-StL-Det .. 40.0
Ruffing-NY 39.2
Lyons-Chi 36.9

Clutch Pitching Index
Hadley-NY 132
Grove-Bos 126
Trout-Det 116
Harder-Cle 116
Milnar-Cle 110

Relief Runs
Heving-Bos 10.9
Brown-Chi 9.7
Dickman-Bos 2.3
Murphy-NY 1.5
Appleton-Was 7

Adjusted Relief Runs
Heving-Bos 11.9
Brown-Chi 10.9
Dickman-Bos 3.6

Relief Ranking
Brown-Chi 21.2
Heving-Bos 15.8
Dickman-Bos 3.5

Total Pitcher Index
Feller-Cle 5.9
Ruffing-NY 4.9
Lyons-Chi 4.2
Grove-Bos 3.6
Newsom-StL-Det 3.3

Total Baseball Ranking
Feller-Cle 5.9
DiMaggio-NY 5.8
Foxx-Bos 5.1
Ruffing-NY 4.9
Johnson-Phi 4.5

TEAM	G	W	L	PCT	GB	R	OR	AB	H	2B	3B	HR	BB	SO	AVG	OBP	SLG	OPS	OPS+	BR	BR+	PF	CHI	RC	SB	CS	SBA	SBR
CIN	155	100	53	.654		707	**528**	5372	1427	264	38	89	453	503	.266	.327	.379	706	100	6	-1	101	103	672	72			
BRO	156	88	65	.575	12	697	621	5470	1421	256	**70**	93	522	570	.260	.327	.383	710	96	15	-26	106	98	692	56			
STL	156	84	69	.549	16	747	699	5499	**1514**	266	61	**119**	479	610	.275	.336	**.411**	**747**	106	83	41	106	96	**764**	**97**			
PIT	156	78	76	.506	22.5	**809**	783	5466	1511	**276**	68	76	**553**	494	**.276**	**.346**	.394	740	**112**	**84**	**90**	99	104	757	69			
CHI	154	75	79	.487	25.5	681	636	5389	1441	272	48	86	482	566	.267	.331	.384	715	106	25	39	98	97	691	63			
NY	152	72	80	.474	27.5	663	659	5324	1423	201	46	91	453	**478**	.267	.329	.374	703	99	3	-2	101	98	653	45			
BOS	152	65	87	.428	34.5	623	745	5329	1366	219	50	59	402	581	.256	.311	.349	660	93	-83	-49	95	**108**	581	48			
PHI	153	50	103	.327	50	494	750	5137	1225	180	35	75	435	527	.238	.300	.331	631	83	-133	-112	96	96	512	25			
TOT	617					5421		42986	11328	1934	416	688	3779	4329	.264	.327	.376	702							475			

TEAM	CG	SH	SV	IP	H	H/G	HR	BB	SO	RAT	ERA	ERA+	OAV	OOB	PR	PR+	PF	CPI	FA	E	DP	FW	PW	BW	SBW	DIF
CIN	**91**	10	11	1407^{2}	**1263**	**8.1**	73	445	557	**11.1**	**3.05**	**124**	**.240**	**.302**	**125**	**117**	98	102	**.981**	**117**	158	**2.9**	**11.9**	-.0		8.9
BRO	65	**17**	14	1433	1366	8.6	101	**393**	**639**	11.3	3.50	114	.248	**.302**	56	76	104	95	.970	183	110	-.3	7.7	-2.6		6.8
STL	71	10	14	1396	1457	9.4	83	488	550	12.7	3.83	104	.266	.329	3	23	104	102	.971	174	134	.2	2.4	4.2		1.0
PIT	49	8	**24**	1388^{2}	1569	10.2	**72**	492	491	13.6	4.37	87	.283	.345	-79	-86	99	99	.966	217	161	-1.9	-8.6	**9.2**		2.6
CHI	69	12	14	1392	1418	9.2	74	430	564	12.1	3.55	106	.262	.319	47	33	97	103	.968	199	143	-1.2	3.4	4.0		-8.0
NY	57	11	18	1360^{1}	1383	9.2	110	473	606	12.4	3.80	102	.262	.325	9	14	101	**104**	.977	139	132	1.7	1.5	-.2		-6.8
BOS	76	9	12	1359	1444	9.6	83	573	435	13.6	4.36	85	.274	.349	-77	-100	97	100	.970	184	**169**	-.5	-10.1	-4.9		4.7
PHI	66	5	8	1357	1429	9.5	92	475	485	12.9	4.40	89	.270	.333	-83	-74	101	93	.970	181	136	-.3	-7.4	-11.3		-7.2
TOT	544	82	115	11093^{2}		9.2				12.5	3.85		.264	.327					.972	1394	1143					

Runs
Vaughan-Pit 113
Mize-StL 111
Werber-Cin 105
Frey-Cin 102
Hack-Chi 101

Hits
F.McCormick-Cin 191
Hack-Chi 191
Mize-StL 182
Vaughan-Pit 178
Medwick-StL-Bro 175

Doubles
F.McCormick-Cin 44
Vaughan-Pit 40
Gleeson-Chi 39
Hack-Chi 38
Walker-Bro 37

Triples
Vaughan-Pit 15
Ross-Bos 14
Slaughter-StL 13
Mize-StL 13
Camilli-Bro 13

Home Runs
Mize-StL 43
Nicholson-Chi 25
Rizzo-Pit-Cin-Phi 24
Camilli-Bro 23

Total Bases
Mize-StL 368
F.McCormick-Cin 298
Medwick-StL-Bro 280
Camilli-Bro 271
Vaughan-Pit 269

Runs Batted In
Mize-StL 137
F.McCormick-Cin 127
VanRobays-Pit 116
Fletcher-Pit 104
Young-NY 101

Runs Produced
Mize-StL 205
Vaughan-Pit 201
F.McCormick-Cin 201
VanRobays-Pit 187
Fletcher-Pit 182

Bases On Balls
Fletcher-Pit 119
Ott-NY 100
Camilli-Bro 89
Vaughan-Pit 88
Mize-StL 82

Batting Average
Garms-Pit .355
Davis-Pit .326
Lombardi-Cin .319
Cooney-Bos .318
Hack-Chi .317

On-Base Percentage
Fletcher-Pit .418
Ott-NY .407
Mize-StL .404
Camilli-Bro .397
Hack-Chi .395

Slugging Average
Mize-StL .636
Nicholson-Chi .534
Camilli-Bro .529
DiMaggio-Cin-Pit .519
Slaughter-StL .504

On-Base Plus Slugging
Mize-StL 1039
Camilli-Bro 926
Nicholson-Chi 899
Slaughter-StL 874
Ott-NY 864

Adjusted OPS
Mize-StL 173
Nicholson-Chi 148
Camilli-Bro 144
Gleeson-Chi 139
Fletcher-Pit 137

Batter Runs
Mize-StL 63.9
Camilli-Bro 38.7
Fletcher-Pit 31.8
Ott-NY 31.7
Vaughan-Pit 28.8

Adjusted Batter Runs
Mize-StL 56.4
Fletcher-Pit 32.6
Camilli-Bro 32.5
Ott-NY 30.8
Nicholson-Chi 30.5

Clutch Hitting Index
VanRobays-Pit 154
Fletcher-Pit 129
F.McCormick-Cin 121
Young-NY 115
Danning-NY 115

Runs Created
Mize-StL 152
Camilli-Bro 114
Vaughan-Pit 113
Hack-Chi 112
Ott-NY 107

Total Average
Mize-StL 1.135
Camilli-Bro 1.005
Fletcher-Pit .930
Ott-NY .915
Nicholson-Chi .901

Stolen Bases
Frey-Cin 22
Hack-Chi 21
Moore-StL 18
Werber-Cin 16
Reese-Bro 15

Stolen Base Average

Stolen Base Runs

Fielding Runs
Witek-NY 19.0
Herman-Chi 18.9
Frey-Cin 18.2
Moore-StL 16.8
Miller-Bos 14.7

Total Player Rating
Vaughan-Pit 4.9
Hack-Chi 4.7
Mize-StL 3.5
Miller-Bos 3.3
Frey-Cin 3.1

Wins
Walters-Cin 22
Passeau-Chi 20
Derringer-Cin 20

Win Percentage
Fitzsimmons-Bro .889
Sewell-Pit .762
Walters-Cin .688
Thompson-Cin .640
Derringer-Cin .625

Games
Shoun-StL 54
Brown-Pit 48
Passeau-Chi 46
Casey-Bro 44
Raffensberger-Chi 43

Complete Games
Walters-Cin 29
Derringer-Cin 26
Mulcahy-Phi 21
Passeau-Chi 20
Higbe-Phi 20

Shutouts
Wyatt-Bro 5
Salvo-Bos 5

Saves
Brown-NY 7
Brown-Pit 7
Beggs-Cin 7
Shoun-StL 5
Passeau-Chi 5

Innings Pitched
Walters-Cin 305.0
Derringer-Cin 296.2
Higbe-Phi 283.0
Passeau-Chi 280.2
Mulcahy-Phi 280.0

Fewest Hits/Game
Walters-Cin 7.11
Higbe-Phi 7.70
Thompson-Cin 7.87
Casey-Bro 7.95
Sullivan-Bos 7.97

Fewest BB/Game
Derringer-Cin 1.46
Turner-Cin 1.54
Hamlin-Bro 1.68
Davis-StL-Bro 1.79
Warneke-StL 1.82

Strikeouts
Higbe-Phi 137
Wyatt-Bro 124
Passeau-Chi 124
Schumacher-NY 123

Strikeouts/Game
Melton-NY 4.91
Schumacher-NY 4.88
Wyatt-Bro 4.66
Hamlin-Bro 4.49
Higbe-Phi 4.36

Ratio
Derringer-Cin 9.95
Walters-Cin 9.97
Passeau-Chi 10.33
Turner-Cin 10.54
Tamulis-Bro 10.73

Earned Run Average
Walters-Cin 2.48
Passeau-Chi 2.50
Sewell-Pit 2.80
Fitzsimmons-Bro 2.81
Turner-Cin 2.89

Adjusted ERA
Walters-Cin 153
Passeau-Chi 150
Sewell-Pit 136
Turner-Cin 131
Hamlin-Bro 131

Opponents' Batting Avg.
Walters-Cin .220
Higbe-Phi .232
Thompson-Cin .233
Passeau-Chi .237
Casey-Bro .237

Opponents' On-Base Pct.
Derringer-Cin .276
Passeau-Chi .278
Walters-Cin .283
Tamulis-Bro .288
Hamlin-Bro .292

Starter Runs
Walters-Cin 46.4
Passeau-Chi 42.0
Derringer-Cin 25.8
Sewell-Pit 22.1
Turner-Cin 20.0

Adjusted Starter Runs
Walters-Cin 45.0
Passeau-Chi 39.9
Derringer-Cin 24.2
Sewell-Pit 21.5
Warneke-StL 21.0

Clutch Pitching Index
Errickson-Bos 124
Olsen-Chi 119
Schumacher-NY 113
Turner-Cin 113
Hamlin-Bro 111

Relief Runs
Beggs-Cin 15.8
Russell-StL 8.1
Raffensberger-Chi 6.0
MacFayden-Pit 3.0
Joiner-NY 2.7

Adjusted Relief Runs
Beggs-Cin 15.5
Russell-StL 8.6
Raffensberger-Chi 4.9
Brown-NY 2.8
Joiner-NY 2.8

Relief Ranking
Beggs-Cin 30.5
Russell-StL 10.4
Raffensberger-Chi 6.4
Brown-NY 3.6
Pressnell-Bro 3.4

Total Pitcher Index
Passeau-Chi 5.5
Walters-Cin 4.7
Beggs-Cin 3.3
Sewell-Pit 2.7
Olsen-Chi 2.6

Total Baseball Ranking
Passeau-Chi 5.5
Vaughan-Pit 4.9
Walters-Cin 4.7
Hack-Chi 4.7
Mize-StL 3.5

TEAM	G	W	L	PCT	GB	R	OR	AB	H	2B	3B	HR	BB	SO	AVG	OBP	SLG	OPS	OPS+	BR	BR+	PF	CHI	RC	SB	CS	SBA	SBR
DET	155	90	64	.584		**888**	717	5418	1549	**312**	65	134	**664**	556	**.286**	**.366**	.442	**808**	105	**124**	45	110	97	**913**	66	39	63	1
CLE	155	89	65	.578	1	710	**637**	5361	1422	287	61	101	519	597	.265	.332	.398	730	98	-43	-22	97	99	724	53	36	60	-1
NY	155	88	66	.571	2	817	671	5286	1371	243	66	**155**	648	606	.259	.344	.418	762	107	25	58	96	**103**	789	59	36	62	0
CHI	155	82	72	.532	8	735	672	5386	1499	238	63	73	496	569	.278	.340	.387	727	93	-41	-50	101	102	713	52	60	46	-10
BOS	154	82	72	.532	8	872	825	5481	**1566**	301	**80**	145	590	597	**.286**	.356	**.449**	805	**110**	109	**75**	104	97	889	55	49	53	-5
STL	156	67	87	.435	23	757	882	5416	1423	278	58	118	556	642	.263	.333	.401	734	94	-35	-50	102	**103**	744	51	40	56	-3
WAS	154	64	90	.416	26	665	811	5365	1453	266	67	52	468	**504**	.271	.331	.374	705	95	-85	-39	94	100	690	**94**	40	**70**	**7**
PHI	154	54	100	.351	36	703	932	5304	1391	242	53	105	556	656	.262	.334	.387	721	95	-53	-38	98	100	704	48	33	59	-1
TOT	619					6147		43017	11674	2167	513	883	4497	4727	.272	.343	.408	750							478	333	59	-11

TEAM	CG	SH	SV	IP	H	H/G	HR	BB	SO	RAT	ERA	ERA+	OAV	OOB	PR	PR+	PF	CPI	FA	E	DP	FW	PW	BW	SBW	DIF
DET	59	10	**23**	1375[1]	1425	9.4	102	570	**752**	13.2	4.02	**119**	.266	.338	57	**105**	109	**105**	.968	194	116	-.6	**10.0**	4.3	.2	-.7
CLE	72	**13**	22	1375	**1328**	**8.7**	**86**	512	686	12.3	**3.64**	116	.254	.324	**115**	93	96	102	**.975**	**149**	164	**1.8**	8.8	-2.0	.0	3.6
NY	76	10	14	1373	1389	9.2	119	511	559	12.6	3.89	104	.261	.328	76	24	92	104	**.975**	152	158	1.6	2.3	5.5	.1	1.6
CHI	**83**	10	18	1386[2]	1335	**8.7**	111	**480**	574	**11.9**	3.74	118	**.250**	**.313**	99	**105**	101	96	.969	185	125	-.1	**10.0**	-4.7	-.8	.9
BOS	51	4	16	1379[2]	1568	10.3	124	625	613	14.5	4.89	92	.284	.359	-77	-58	103	101	.972	173	156	.4	-5.4	**7.1**	-.3	3.4
STL	64	4	9	1373[1]	1592	10.5	113	646	439	14.8	5.13	89	.290	.367	-113	-79	105	100	.974	158	**179**	1.4	-7.4	-4.7	-.1	1.1
WAS	74	6	7	1350	1494	10.0	93	618	618	14.3	4.60	91	.281	.359	-31	-67	95	103	.968	194	166	-.7	-6.3	-3.6	**.8**	-3.0
PHI	72	4	12	1345	1543	10.4	135	534	488	14.0	5.22	85	.283	.348	-125	-114	101	91	.960	238	131	-3.0	-10.7	-3.5	.0	-5.6
TOT	551	61	121	10958		9.6				13.5	4.39		.272	.343					.971	1443	1195					

Runs
Williams-Bos 134
Greenberg-Det 129
McCosky-Det 123
Gordon-NY 112
Kuhel-Chi 111

Hits
Radcliff-StL 200
McCosky-Det 200
Cramer-Bos 200
Appling-Chi 197
Wright-Chi 196

Doubles
Greenberg-Det 50
York-Det 46
Boudreau-Cle 46
Williams-Bos 43
Moses-Phi 41

Triples
McCosky-Det 19
Keller-NY 15
Finney-Bos 15
Williams-Bos 14
Appling-Chi 13

Home Runs
Greenberg-Det 41
Foxx-Bos 36
York-Det 33
Johnson-Phi 31
DiMaggio-NY 31

Total Bases
Greenberg-Det 384
York-Det 343
Williams-Bos 333
DiMaggio-NY 318
Gordon-NY 315

Runs Batted In
Greenberg-Det 150
York-Det 134
DiMaggio-NY 133
Foxx-Bos 119
Williams-Bos 113

Runs Produced
Greenberg-Det 238
Williams-Bos 224
York-Det 206
DiMaggio-NY 195
Cronin-Bos 191

Bases On Balls
Keller-NY 106
Clift-StL 104
Gehringer-Det 101
Foxx-Bos 101
Williams-Bos 96

Batting Average
DiMaggio-NY .352
Appling-Chi .348
Williams-Bos .344
Radcliff-StL .342
Greenberg-Det .340

On-Base Percentage
Williams-Bos .442
Greenberg-Det .433
Gehringer-Det .428
DiMaggio-NY .425
Appling-Chi .420

Slugging Average
Greenberg-Det .670
DiMaggio-NY .626
Williams-Bos .594
York-Det .583
Foxx-Bos .581

On-Base Plus Slugging
Greenberg-Det 1103
DiMaggio-NY 1051
Williams-Bos 1036
York-Det 993
Foxx-Bos 993

Adjusted OPS
DiMaggio-NY 176
Greenberg-Det 166
Williams-Bos 159
Foxx-Bos 148
Keller-NY 142

Batter Runs
Greenberg-Det 68.8
Williams-Bos 57.2
DiMaggio-NY 50.8
York-Det 47.3
Foxx-Bos 42.6

Adjusted Batter Runs
DiMaggio-NY 56.0
Greenberg-Det 55.4
Williams-Bos 51.7
Foxx-Bos 37.9
York-Det 35.7

Clutch Hitting Index
Tresh-Chi 131
Boudreau-Cle 130
Walker-Was 117
Bell-Cle 114
Cronin-Bos 109

Runs Created
Greenberg-Det 171
Williams-Bos 154
York-Det 147
DiMaggio-NY 135
Foxx-Bos 124

Total Average
Greenberg-Det 1.215
Williams-Bos 1.122
DiMaggio-NY 1.098
York-Det 1.050
Foxx-Bos 1.026

Stolen Bases
Case-Was 35
Walker-Was 21
Gordon-NY 18
Lewis-Was 15
Kreevich-Chi 15

Stolen Base Average
Walker-Was 84.0
Case-Was 77.8
Gordon-NY 69.2

Stolen Base Runs
Case-Was 4.2
Walker-Was 3.2
Gehringer-Det 2.2
Bartell-Det 1.9
Rosar-NY 1.2

Fielding Runs
Heffner-StL 19.1
Doerr-Bos 18.3
Tebbetts-Det 18.2
Travis-Was 15.7
Gordon-NY 14.0

Total Player Rating
DiMaggio-NY 4.9
Greenberg-Det 4.5
Williams-Bos 4.0
Gordon-NY 3.9
Doerr-Bos 3.6

Wins
Feller-Cle 27
Newsom-Det 21
Milnar-Cle 18
Hudson-Was 17

Win Percentage
Rowe-Det .842
Newsom-Det .808
Feller-Cle .711
Smith-Cle .682
Milnar-Cle .643

Games
Feller-Cle 43
Benton-Det 42
Wilson-Bos 41
Heusser-Phi 41
Dobson-Cle 40

Complete Games
Feller-Cle 31
Lee-Chi 24
Leonard-Was 23

Shutouts
Milnar-Cle 4
Lyons-Chi 4
Feller-Cle 4

Saves
Benton-Det 17
Brown-Chi 10
Murphy-NY 9

Innings Pitched
Feller-Cle 320.1
Leonard-Was 289.0
Rigney-Chi 280.2
Newsom-Det 264.0
Auker-StL 263.2

Fewest Hits/Game
Feller-Cle 6.88
Rigney-Chi 7.70
Smith-Chi 7.77
Bridges-Det 7.79
Newsom-Det 8.01

Fewest BB/Game
Lyons-Chi 1.79
Lee-Chi 2.21
Rowe-Det 2.29
Leonard-Was 2.43
Russo-NY 2.61

Strikeouts
Feller-Cle 261
Newsom-Det 164
Rigney-Chi 141
Bridges-Det 133
Chase-Was 129

Strikeouts/Game
Feller-Cle 7.33
Bridges-Det 6.06
Wilson-Bos 5.82
Newsom-Det 5.59
Smith-Chi 5.17

Ratio
Feller-Cle 10.34
Rigney-Chi 10.65
Lyons-Chi 10.87
Lee-Chi 11.09
Russo-NY 11.27

Earned Run Average
Feller-Cle 2.61
Newsom-Det 2.83
Rigney-Chi 3.11
Smith-Chi 3.21
Chase-Was 3.23

Adjusted ERA
Newsom-Det 168
Feller-Cle 161
Rigney-Chi 142
Bridges-Det 141
Smith-Chi 138

Opponents' Batting Avg.
Feller-Cle .210
Smith-Chi .228
Bridges-Det .229
Rigney-Chi .230
Newsom-Det .238

Opponents' On-Base Pct.
Feller-Cle .285
Lyons-Chi .287
Rigney-Chi .292
Lee-Chi .300
Russo-NY .303

Starter Runs
Feller-Cle 63.0
Newsom-Det 45.6
Rigney-Chi 39.7
Chase-Was 33.4
Milnar-Cle 30.0

Adjusted Starter Runs
Feller-Cle 59.3
Newsom-Det 52.1
Rigney-Chi 40.6
Chase-Was 28.6
Bridges-Det 28.1

Clutch Pitching Index
Chase-Was 134
Leonard-Was 122
Newsom-Det 119
Smith-Cle 117
Milnar-Cle 115

Relief Runs
Eisenstat-Cle 9.9
Trotter-StL 6.7
Brown-Chi 5.1
Murphy-NY 4.8

Adjusted Relief Runs
Eisenstat-Cle 8.9
Trotter-StL 8.5
Brown-Chi 5.4
Benton-Det 2.7
Murphy-NY 2.6

Relief Ranking
Trotter-StL 10.6
Brown-Chi 9.2
Eisenstat-Cle 6.7
Benton-Det 5.4
Murphy-NY 5.2

Total Pitcher Index
Feller-Cle 6.4
Newsom-Det 4.2
Rigney-Chi 4.2
Chase-Was 3.0
Smith-Chi 2.9

Total Baseball Ranking
Feller-Cle 6.4
DiMaggio-NY 4.9
Greenberg-Det 4.5
Newsom-Det 4.2
Rigney-Chi 4.2

TEAM	G	W	L	PCT	GB	R	OR	AB	H	2B	3B	HR	BB	SO	AVG	OBP	SLG	OPS	OPS+	BR	BR+	PF	CHI	RC	SB	CS	SBA	SBR
BRO	157	100	54	.649		**800**	581	5485	**1494**	**286**	**69**	**101**	**600**	535	**.272**	**.347**	**.405**	**752**	**113**	**128**	**94**	104	98	**792**	36			
STL	155	97	56	.634	2.5	734	589	5457	1482	254	56	70	540	543	**.272**	.340	.377	717	102	62	16	107	99	719	47			
CIN	154	88	66	.571	12	616	**564**	5218	1288	213	33	64	477	**428**	.247	.313	.337	650	89	-72	-74	100	**108**	556	**68**			
PIT	156	81	73	.526	19	690	643	5297	1417	233	65	56	547	516	.268	.338	.368	706	105	39	42	100	99	670	59			
NY	156	74	79	.484	25.5	667	706	5395	1401	248	35	95	504	518	.260	.326	.371	697	101	15	2	102	98	659	36			
CHI	155	70	84	.455	30	666	670	5230	1323	239	25	99	559	670	.253	.327	.365	692	105	9	34	96	101	642	39			
BOS	156	62	92	.403	38	592	720	5414	1357	231	38	48	471	608	.251	.312	.334	646	92	-82	-57	96	103	568	61			
PHI	155	43	111	.279	57	501	793	5233	1277	188	38	64	451	596	.244	.307	.331	638	89	-97	-76	96	93	528	65			
TOT	622					5266		42729	11039	1892	359	597	4149	4414	.259	.327	.362	688							411			

TEAM	CG	SH	SV	IP	H	H/G	HR	BB	SO	RAT	ERA	ERA+	OAV	OOB	PR	PR+	PF	CPI	FA	E	DP	FW	PW	BW	SBW	DIF
BRO	66	17	**22**	1421	**1236**	**7.9**	81	495	603	**11.1**	**3.15**	117	**.233**	**.300**	**78**	82	101	93	.974	162	125	.9	8.5	**9.7**		4.1
STL	64	15	20	1416[1]	1289	8.2	85	502	**659**	11.6	3.19	**118**	.242	.310	70	**87**	104	101	.973	172	146	.2	**9.0**	1.7		9.8
CIN	**89**	**19**	10	1386[2]	1300	8.5	61	510	627	11.9	3.17	114	.250	.319	72	67	99	**106**	**.975**	**152**	147	**1.3**	6.9	-7.6		10.5
PIT	71	8	12	1374[1]	1392	9.2	66	492	410	12.5	3.49	104	.260	.323	23	19	99	102	.968	196	130	-1.1	2.0	4.4		-1.1
NY	55	12	18	1391[2]	1455	9.5	90	539	566	13.0	3.95	94	.269	.337	-48	-38	102	102	.974	160	144	1.0	-3.9	.3		.3
CHI	74	8	9	1364[2]	1431	9.5	**60**	**449**	548	12.6	3.72	94	.267	.327	-13	-34	97	98	.970	180	139	-.2	-3.4	3.5		-6.7
BOS	62	10	9	1385[2]	1440	9.4	75	554	446	13.2	3.95	90	.269	.341	-49	-59	98	102	.969	191	**174**	-.8	-6.0	-5.8		-2.2
PHI	35	4	9	1372[1]	1499	9.9	79	606	552	14.0	4.50	82	.279	.355	-132	-119	102	98	.969	187	147	-.6	-12.2	-7.8		-13.2
TOT	516	93	109	11112[2]		9.0				12.5	3.64		.259	.327					.972	1400	1152					

Runs
Reiser-Bro 117
Hack-Chi 111
Medwick-Bro 100
Rucker-NY 95
Fletcher-Pit 95

Hits
Hack-Chi 186
Reiser-Bro 184
Litwhiler-Phi 180
Rucker-NY 179
Medwick-Bro 171

Doubles
Reiser-Bro 39
Mize-StL 39
Rucker-NY 38
Dallessandro-Chi 36

Triples
Reiser-Bro 17
Fletcher-Pit 13
Hopp-StL 11
Medwick-Bro 10
Elliott-Pit 10

Home Runs
Camilli-Bro 34
Ott-NY 27
Nicholson-Chi 26
Young-NY 25
Dahlgren-Bos-Chi 23

Total Bases
Reiser-Bro 299
Camilli-Bro 294
Medwick-Bro 278
Litwhiler-Phi 275
Young-NY 265

Runs Batted In
Camilli-Bro 120
Young-NY 104
Mize-StL 100
DiMaggio-Pit 100
Nicholson-Chi 98

Runs Produced
Reiser-Bro 179
Camilli-Bro 178
Medwick-Bro 170
Young-NY 169
Fletcher-Pit 158

Bases On Balls
Fletcher-Pit 118
Camilli-Bro 104
Ott-NY 100
Hack-Chi 99

Batting Average
Reiser-Bro .343
Cooney-Bos .319
Medwick-Bro .318
Hack-Chi .317
Mize-StL .317

On-Base Percentage
Fletcher-Pit .421
Hack-Chi .417
Camilli-Bro .407
Reiser-Bro .406
Mize-StL .406

Slugging Average
Reiser-Bro .558
Camilli-Bro .556
Mize-StL .535
Medwick-Bro .517
Slaughter-StL .496

On-Base Plus Slugging
Reiser-Bro 964
Camilli-Bro 962
Mize-StL 941
Ott-NY 898
Slaughter-StL 886

Adjusted OPS
Reiser-Bro 163
Camilli-Bro 162
Mize-StL 153
Ott-NY 149
Fletcher-Pit 148

Batter Runs
Camilli-Bro 50.2
Reiser-Bro 48.0
Mize-StL 40.2
Ott-NY 38.7
Fletcher-Pit 38.2

Adjusted Batter Runs
Camilli-Bro 45.2
Reiser-Bro 43.3
Fletcher-Pit 38.6
Hack-Chi 38.0
Ott-NY 36.6

Clutch Hitting Index
Lavagetto-Bro 160
VanRobays-Pit 143
Dallessandro-Chi 139
Bragan-Phi 124
Elliott-Pit 121

Runs Created
Camilli-Bro 128
Reiser-Bro 124
Ott-NY 115
Hack-Chi 114
Fletcher-Pit 111

Total Average
Camilli-Bro 1.057
Reiser-Bro 1.006
Mize-StL .991
Ott-NY .976
Fletcher-Pit .965

Stolen Bases
Murtaugh-Phi 18
Benjamin-Phi 17
Handley-Pit 16
Frey-Cin 16
Hopp-StL 15

Stolen Base Average

Stolen Base Runs

Fielding Runs
May-Phi 25.2
Stringer-Chi 20.1
Litwhiler-Phi 17.1
Werber-Cin 12.5
Miller-Bos 12.2

Total Player Rating
Reiser-Bro 5.2
Camilli-Bro 3.4
Fletcher-Pit 3.4
Ott-NY 3.3
Litwhiler-Phi 3.2

Wins
Wyatt-Bro 22
Higbe-Bro 22
Walters-Cin 19
E.Riddle-Cin 19

Win Percentage
E.Riddle-Cin .826
Higbe-Bro .710
White-StL .708
Wyatt-Bro .688
Warneke-StL .654

Games
Higbe-Bro 48
Pearson-Phi 46
Casey-Bro 45
Hutchings-Cin-Bos 44
Johnson-Bos 43

Complete Games
Walters-Cin 27
Wyatt-Bro 23
Tobin-Bos 20
Passeau-Chi 20

Shutouts
Wyatt-Bro 7
VanderMeer-Cin 6
Walters-Cin 5
Davis-Bro 5

Saves
Brown-NY 8
Crouch-Phi-StL 7
Casey-Bro 7
Pearson-Phi 6

Innings Pitched
Walters-Cin 302.0
Higbe-Bro 298.0
Wyatt-Bro 288.1
Sewell-Pit 249.0
Warneke-StL 246.0

Fewest Hits/Game
VanderMeer-Cin 6.84
Wyatt-Bro 6.96
White-StL 7.24
Higbe-Bro 7.37
E.Riddle-Cin 7.48

Fewest BB/Game
Passeau-Chi 2.03
Derringer-Cin 2.13
Lohrman-NY 2.26
Tobin-Bos 2.27
Lee-Chi 2.31

Strikeouts
VanderMeer-Cin 202
Wyatt-Bro 176
Walters-Cin 129
Higbe-Bro 121
M.Cooper-StL 118

Strikeouts/Game
VanderMeer-Cin 8.03
M.Cooper-StL 5.69
Wyatt-Bro 5.49
White-StL 5.01
Melton-NY 4.63

Ratio
Wyatt-Bro 9.58
E.Riddle-Cin 10.14
White-StL 10.50
Tobin-Bos 10.93
Sewell-Pit 11.28

Earned Run Average
E.Riddle-Cin 2.24
Wyatt-Bro 2.34
White-StL 2.40
VanderMeer-Cin 2.82
Walters-Cin 2.83

Adjusted ERA
E.Riddle-Cin 160
White-StL 157
Wyatt-Bro 157
VanderMeer-Cin 127
Walters-Cin 127

Opponents' Batting Avg.
Wyatt-Bro .212
VanderMeer-Cin .214
White-StL .217
Higbe-Bro .220
E.Riddle-Cin .224

Opponents' On-Base Pct.
Wyatt-Bro .270
E.Riddle-Cin .282
White-StL .287
Sewell-Pit .299
Tobin-Bos .300

Starter Runs
Wyatt-Bro 41.4
E.Riddle-Cin 33.5
White-StL 28.8
Walters-Cin 26.9
VanderMeer-Cin 20.4

Adjusted Starter Runs
Wyatt-Bro 42.1
E.Riddle-Cin 32.9
White-StL 30.7
Walters-Cin 26.0
VanderMeer-Cin 19.6

Clutch Pitching Index
V.Olsen-Chi 120
Heintzelman-Pit 117
Butcher-Pit 112
Johnson-Bos 111
Walters-Cin 111

Relief Runs
Pressnell-Chi 4.3
Brown-NY 2.0
Pearson-Phi .9
Sullivan-Bos-Pit .0

Adjusted Relief Runs
Pressnell-Chi 3.4
Brown-NY 2.4
Pearson-Phi 1.9

Relief Ranking
Pressnell-Chi 3.6
Brown-NY 3.0
Pearson-Phi 2.5

Total Pitcher Index
Wyatt-Bro 5.3
E.Riddle-Cin 3.7
Walters-Cin 3.3
White-StL 3.1
VanderMeer-Cin 2.3

Total Baseball Ranking
Wyatt-Bro 5.3
Reiser-Bro 5.2
E.Riddle-Cin 3.7
Camilli-Bro 3.4
Fletcher-Pit 3.4

TEAM	G	W	L	PCT	GB	R	OR	AB	H	2B	3B	HR	BB	SO	AVG	OBP	SLG	OPS	OPS+	BR	BR+	PF	CHI	RC	SB	CS	SBA	SBR
NY	156	101	53	.656		830	**631**	5444	1464	243	60	**151**	616	565	.269	.346	.419	765	111	64	75	99	103	822	51	33	61	0
BOS	155	84	70	.545	17	**865**	750	5359	**1517**	**304**	55	124	683	567	**.283**	**.366**	**.430**	**796**	**115**	**136**	**115**	102	98	**872**	67	51	57	-3
CHI	156	77	77	.500	24	638	649	5404	1376	245	47	47	510	**476**	.255	.322	.343	665	84	-128	-120	99	106	612	**91**	53	63	1
DET	155	75	79	.487	26	686	743	5370	1412	247	55	81	602	584	.263	.340	.375	715	87	-27	-92	110	97	713	43	28	61	0
CLE	155	75	79	.487	26	677	668	5283	1350	249	**84**	103	512	605	.256	.323	.393	716	101	-40	-5	95	100	691	63	47	57	-3
WAS	156	70	84	.455	31	728	798	5521	1502	257	80	52	470	488	.272	.331	.376	707	99	-53	-19	95	**107**	702	79	36	**69**	**5**
STL	157	70	84	.455	31	765	823	5408	1440	281	58	91	**775**	552	.266	.360	.390	750	103	56	30	103	93	804	50	39	56	-3
PHI	154	64	90	.416	37	713	840	5336	1431	240	69	85	574	588	.268	.340	.387	727	102	-7	11	98	99	711	27	36	43	-7
TOT	622					5902		43125	11492	2066	508	734	4742	4425	.267	.342	.390	730							471	323	59	-9

TEAM	CG	SH	SV	IP	H	H/G	HR	BB	SO	RAT	ERA	ERA+	OAV	OOB	PR	PR+	PF	CPI	FA	E	DP	FW	PW	BW	SBW	DIF
NY	75	13	**26**	1396[1]	**1309**	**8.5**	81	598	589	12.4	**3.53**	112	**.248**	.325	96	66	95	102	.973	165	**196**	.5	6.4	7.3	.1	9.8
BOS	70	8	11	1372	1453	9.6	88	611	574	13.7	4.19	100	.270	.347	-6	-3	101	102	.972	172	139	.0	-.2	**11.2**	-.2	-3.7
CHI	**106**	**14**	4	1416	1362	8.7	89	**521**	564	**12.2**	**3.53**	**116**	.252	**.320**	**99**	**92**	99	102	.971	180	145	-.3	**9.0**	-11.6	.2	2.9
DET	52	8	16	1381[2]	1399	9.2	80	645	**697**	13.4	4.18	109	.260	.341	-4	52	110	96	.969	186	129	-.7	5.1	-8.9	.1	2.5
CLE	68	10	19	1377	1366	9.0	71	660	617	13.4	3.90	101	.259	.344	39	7	95	**103**	**.976**	**142**	158	**1.8**	.7	-.4	-.2	-3.7
WAS	69	8	7	1389[1]	1524	9.9	**69**	603	544	13.9	4.36	93	.279	.353	-32	-49	98	101	.969	187	169	-.7	-4.7	-1.8	**.6**	-.2
STL	65	7	10	1389	1563	10.2	120	549	454	13.9	4.72	91	.283	.350	-88	-62	104	99	.975	151	156	1.4	-6.0	3.0	-.2	-5.0
PHI	64	3	18	1365[1]	1516	10.0	136	557	386	13.8	4.84	87	.279	.348	-104	-97	101	97	.967	200	150	-1.5	-9.4	1.1	-.6	-2.5
TOT	569	71	111	11086[2]		9.4				13.4	4.15		.267	.342					.972	1383	1242					

Runs
Williams-Bos 135
DiMaggio-NY 122
DiMaggio-Bos 117
Clift-StL 108

Hits
Travis-Was 218
Heath-Cle 199
DiMaggio-NY 193
Appling-Chi 186
Williams-Bos 185

Doubles
Boudreau-Cle 45
DiMaggio-NY 43
Judnich-StL 40
Travis-Was 39
Kuhel-Chi 39

Triples
Heath-Cle 20
Travis-Was 19
Keltner-Cle 13

Home Runs
Williams-Bos 37
Keller-NY 33
Henrich-NY 31
DiMaggio-NY 30
York-Det 27

Total Bases
DiMaggio-NY 348
Heath-Cle 343
Williams-Bos 335
Travis-Was 316
S.Chapman-Phi 300

Runs Batted In
DiMaggio-NY 125
Heath-Cle 123
Keller-NY 122
Williams-Bos 120
York-Det 111

Runs Produced
Williams-Bos 218
DiMaggio-NY 217
Travis-Was 200
Keller-NY 191
Heath-Cle 188

Bases On Balls
Williams-Bos 145
Cullenbine-StL 121
Clift-StL 113
Keller-NY 102

Batting Average
Williams-Bos .... .406
Travis-Was .... .359
DiMaggio-NY .... .357
Heath-Cle .... .340
Siebert-Phi .... .334

On-Base Percentage
Williams-Bos .... .551
Cullenbine-StL ..... .452
DiMaggio-NY .... .440
Keller-NY .... .416
Foxx-Bos .... .412

Slugging Average
Williams-Bos .... .735
DiMaggio-NY .... .643
Heath-Cle .... .586
Keller-NY .... .580
S.Chapman-Phi ..... .543

On-Base Plus Slugging
Williams-Bos 1286
DiMaggio-NY 1083
Keller-NY 996
Heath-Cle 982
Travis-Was 930

Adjusted OPS
Williams-Bos 232
DiMaggio-NY 186
Heath-Cle 165
Keller-NY 163
Travis-Was 152

Batter Runs
Williams-Bos 102.0
DiMaggio-NY 64.3
Keller-NY 45.7
Heath-Cle 44.8
Cullenbine-StL 38.3

Adjusted Batter Runs
Williams-Bos 97.9
DiMaggio-NY 66.3
Heath-Cle 51.2
Keller-NY 47.4
Travis-Was 43.9

Clutch Hitting Index
Berardino-StL 152
Cullenbine-StL 126
Tabor-Bos 125
Foxx-Bos 116
Wright-Chi 116

Runs Created
Williams-Bos 202
DiMaggio-NY 162
Heath-Cle 138
Keller-NY 134
Travis-Was 131

Total Average
Williams-Bos 1.688
DiMaggio-NY 1.208
Keller-NY 1.099
Cullenbine-StL 1.023
Heath-Cle 1.000

Stolen Bases
Case-Was 33
Kuhel-Chi 20
Heath-Cle 18
Tabor-Bos 17
Kreevich-Chi 17

Stolen Base Average
Kuhel-Chi 80.0
Case-Was 78.6
Kreevich-Chi 77.3
Tabor-Bos 65.4
Heath-Cle 60.0

Stolen Base Runs
Case-Was 4.1
Kuhel-Chi 2.7
Kreevich-Chi 2.0
Rizzuto-NY 1.3
Fox-Bos 1.3

Fielding Runs
Bloodworth-Was 34.7
Keltner-Cle 22.5
Rizzuto-NY 15.6
Case-Was 15.2
S.Chapman-Phi 14.4

Total Player Rating
Williams-Bos 8.0
DiMaggio-NY 6.9
Travis-Was 5.3
Keller-NY 4.2
S.Chapman-Phi 4.0

Wins
Feller-Cle 25
Lee-Chi 22
D.Newsome-Bos 19
Leonard-Was 18

Win Percentage
Gomez-NY .... .750
Ruffing-NY .... .714
Benton-Det .... .714
Lee-Chi .... .667
Feller-Cle .... .658

Games
Feller-Cle 44
Newsom-Det 43
Brown-Cle 41
Ryba-Bos 40
Benton-Det 38

Complete Games
Lee-Chi 30
Feller-Cle 28
Smith-Chi 21
Lyons-Chi 19
Leonard-Was 19

Shutouts
Feller-Cle 6
Leonard-Was 4
Humphries-Chi 4
Chandler-NY 4

Saves
Murphy-NY 15
Ferrick-Phi 7
Benton-Det 7
Ryba-Bos 6

Innings Pitched
Feller-Cle 343.0
Lee-Chi 300.1
Smith-Chi 263.1
Leonard-Was 256.0
Newsom-Det 250.1

Fewest Hits/Game
Benton-Det 7.42
Feller-Cle 7.45
Lee-Chi 7.73
Donald-NY 7.98
Chandler-NY 8.03

Fewest BB/Game
Lyons-Chi 1.78
Leonard-Was 1.90
Muncrief-StL 2.23
Ruffing-NY 2.62
Lee-Chi 2.76

Strikeouts
Feller-Cle 260
Newsom-Det 175
Lee-Chi 130
Rigney-Chi 119

Strikeouts/Game
Feller-Cle 6.82
Newsom-Det 6.29
Newhouser-Det 5.51
Harris-Bos 5.15
Rigney-Chi 4.52

Ratio
Lee-Chi 10.61
Ruffing-NY 11.25
Benton-Det 11.30
Chandler-NY 11.33
Lyons-Chi 11.53

Earned Run Average
Lee-Chi 2.37
Benton-Det 2.97
Wagner-Bos 3.07
Russo-NY 3.09
Feller-Cle 3.15

Adjusted ERA
Lee-Chi 173
Benton-Det 153
Wagner-Bos 136
Smith-Chi 129
Harris-Bos 128

Opponents' Batting Avg.
Benton-Det .... .221
Feller-Cle .... .226
Lee-Chi .... .232
Donald-NY .... .237
Chandler-NY .... .239

Opponents' On-Base Pct.
Lee-Chi .... .293
Benton-Det .... .302
Ruffing-NY .... .306
Chandler-NY .... .307
Lyons-Chi .... .308

Starter Runs
Lee-Chi 59.4
Feller-Cle 38.1
Smith-Chi 28.4
Russo-NY 24.6
Wagner-Bos 22.3

Adjusted Starter Runs
Lee-Chi 58.4
Feller-Cle 31.7
Smith-Chi 27.2
Benton-Det 25.2
Wagner-Bos 22.6

Clutch Pitching Index
Lee-Chi 122
Wagner-Bos 120
Gomez-NY 115
Marchildon-Phi 115
Smith-Chi 112

Relief Runs
Murphy-NY 18.6
Heving-Cle 14.6
Carrasquel-Was 7.5
Brown-Cle 7.3

Adjusted Relief Runs
Murphy-NY 17.7
Heving-Cle 13.6
Carrasquel-Was 6.6
Brown-Cle 5.8
Thomas-Det 2.5

Relief Ranking
Murphy-NY 30.4
Heving-Cle 14.3
Carrasquel-Was 5.2
Brown-Cle 5.1
Thomas-Det 1.4

Total Pitcher Index
Lee-Chi 6.7
Feller-Cle 3.3
Smith-Chi 3.3
Murphy-NY 2.8
Benton-Det 2.8

Total Baseball Ranking
Williams-Bos 8.0
DiMaggio-NY 6.9
Lee-Chi 6.7
Travis-Was 5.3
Keller-NY 4.2

TEAM	G	W	L	PCT	GB	R	OR	AB	H	2B	3B	HR	BB	SO	AVG	OBP	SLG	OPS	OPS+	BR	BR+	PF	CHI	RC	SB	CS	SBA	SBR
STL	156	106	48	.688		**755**	**480**	5421	**1454**	**282**	**69**	60	551	507	**.268**	**.338**	**.379**	**717**	109	**109**	58	108	103	**718**	71			
BRO	155	104	50	.675	2	742	512	5285	1398	263	34	62	**572**	**484**	.265	**.338**	.362	700	**110**	80	**69**	102	**107**	671	**81**			
NY	154	85	67	.559	20	675	600	5210	1323	162	35	**109**	558	511	.254	.330	.361	691	108	59	56	101	102	627	39			
CIN	154	76	76	.500	29	527	545	5260	1216	198	39	66	483	549	.231	.299	.321	620	88	-81	-80	100	102	519	42			
PIT	151	66	81	.449	36.5	585	631	5104	1250	173	49	54	537	536	.245	.320	.330	650	95	-15	-29	103	102	556	41			
CHI	155	68	86	.442	38	591	665	5352	1360	224	41	75	509	607	.254	.321	.353	674	108	23	48	96	93	619	63			
BOS	150	59	89	.399	44	515	645	5077	1216	210	19	68	474	507	.240	.307	.329	636	94	-48	-37	98	97	520	49			
PHI	151	42	109	.278	62.5	394	706	5060	1174	168	37	44	392	488	.232	.289	.306	595	84	-125	-102	95	89	451	37			
TOT	613					4784		41769	10391	1680	323	538	4076	4189	.249	.319	.344	661							423			

TEAM	CG	SH	SV	IP	H	H/G	HR	BB	SO	RAT	ERA	ERA+	OAV	OOB	PR	PR+	PF	CPI	FA	E	DP	FW	PW	BW	SBW	DIF
STL	70	**18**	15	1410^1	**1192**	**7.7**	49	473	**651**	**10.8**	**2.55**	**134**	**.228**	**.294**	**120**	**133**	103	102	.972	169	137	-.0	**14.3**	6.3		8.7
BRO	67	16	**24**	1398^2	1205	7.8	73	493	612	11.2	2.85	115	.231	.302	73	65	98	101	**.977**	**138**	150	**1.7**	7.0	**7.5**		11.0
NY	70	12	13	1370	1299	8.6	94	493	497	11.9	3.32	101	.250	.316	0	7	101	104	**.977**	**138**	128	**1.7**	.8	6.1		.7
CIN	**80**	12	8	1411^2	1213	7.8	**47**	526	616	11.3	2.82	117	.230	.302	78	74	99	97	.971	177	**158**	-.7	8.0	-8.5		1.4
PIT	64	13	11	1351^1	1376	9.2	62	**435**	426	12.2	3.59	94	.262	.320	-41	-30	102	97	.969	184	128	-1.3	-3.2	-3.1		.2
CHI	71	10	14	1400^2	1447	9.3	70	525	507	12.8	3.60	89	.267	.334	-44	-65	97	**105**	.973	170	136	-.2	-6.9	5.2		-6.9
BOS	68	9	8	1334	1326	9.0	82	518	414	12.7	3.76	89	.260	.331	-66	-62	101	100	.976	142	138	1.2	-6.6	-3.9		-5.4
PHI	51	2	6	1341	1328	9.0	61	605	472	13.2	4.13	80	.260	.342	-120	-122	100	93	.968	194	147	-1.9	-13.0	-10.9		-7.5
TOT	541	92	99	11017^2		8.5				12.0	3.32		.249	.319					.973	1312	1122					

Runs
Ott-NY 118
Slaughter-StL 100
Mize-NY 97
Hack-Chi 91

Hits
Slaughter-StL 188
Nicholson-Chi 173
Medwick-Bro 166
Hack-Chi 166
Elliott-Pit 166

Doubles
Marion-StL 38
Medwick-Bro 37
Hack-Chi 36
Herman-Bro 34
Reiser-Bro 33

Triples
Slaughter-StL 17
Nicholson-Chi 11
Musial-StL 10
Litwhiler-Phi 9

Home Runs
Ott-NY 30
Mize-NY 26
Camilli-Bro 26
Nicholson-Chi 21
West-Bos 16

Total Bases
Slaughter-StL 292
Mize-NY 282
Nicholson-Chi 280
Ott-NY 273
Camilli-Bro 247

Runs Batted In
Mize-NY 110
Camilli-Bro 109
Slaughter-StL 98
Medwick-Bro 96
Ott-NY 93

Runs Produced
Slaughter-StL 185
Ott-NY 183
Mize-NY 181
Camilli-Bro 172
Medwick-Bro 161

Bases On Balls
Ott-NY 109
Fletcher-Pit 105
Camilli-Bro 97
Hack-Chi 94
Slaughter-StL 88

Batting Average
Lombardi-Bos 330
Slaughter-StL 318
Musial-StL 315
Reiser-Bro 310
Mize-NY 305

On-Base Percentage
Fletcher-Pit 417
Ott-NY 415
Slaughter-StL 412
Hack-Chi 402
Musial-StL 397

Slugging Average
Mize-NY 521
Ott-NY 497
Slaughter-StL 494
Musial-StL 490
Lombardi-Bos 482

On-Base Plus Slugging
Ott-NY 912
Slaughter-StL 906
Mize-NY 901
Musial-StL 888
Nicholson-Chi 859

Adjusted OPS
Ott-NY 165
Mize-NY 161
Nicholson-Chi 156
Slaughter-StL 153
Musial-StL 148

Batter Runs
Slaughter-StL 49.8
Ott-NY 49.3
Mize-NY 40.8
Nicholson-Chi 37.6
Musial-StL 35.0

Adjusted Batter Runs
Ott-NY 48.7
Nicholson-Chi 41.8
Slaughter-StL 41.5
Mize-NY 40.2
Hack-Chi 33.6

Clutch Hitting Index
Brown-StL 146
Medwick-Bro 143
Owen-Bro 120
Camilli-Bro 117
F.McCormick-Cin 116

Runs Created
Slaughter-StL 128
Ott-NY 122
Nicholson-Chi 112
Mize-NY 110
Hack-Chi 100

Total Average
Ott-NY 990
Slaughter-StL 966
Musial-StL 926
Mize-NY 911
Camilli-Bro 888

Stolen Bases
Reiser-Bro 20
Reese-Bro 15
Fernandez-Bos 15
Merullo-Chi 14
Hopp-StL 14

Stolen Base Average

Stolen Base Runs

Fielding Runs
DiMaggio-Pit 19.8
Reese-Bro 17.4
May-Phi 17.2
Holmes-Bos 14.8
Fletcher-Pit 11.5

Total Player Rating
Nicholson-Chi 4.6
Ott-NY 4.0
Slaughter-StL 3.8
Reese-Bro 3.2
Hack-Chi 3.0

Wins
M.Cooper-StL 22
Beazley-StL 21
Wyatt-Bro 19
Passeau-Chi 19
VanderMeer-Cin 18

Win Percentage
French-Bro 789
Beazley-StL 778
M.Cooper-StL 759
Wyatt-Bro 731
Davis-Bro 714

Games
Adams-NY 61
Casey-Bro 50
Podgajny-Phi 43
Beazley-StL 43

Complete Games
Tobin-Bos 28
Passeau-Chi 24
M.Cooper-StL 22
Walters-Cin 21
VanderMeer-Cin 21

Shutouts
M.Cooper-StL 10
Sewell-Pit 5
Javery-Bos 5
Davis-Bro 5

Saves
Casey-Bro 13
Adams-NY 11
Beggs-Cin 8
Sain-Bos 6
Gumbert-StL 5

Innings Pitched
Tobin-Bos 287.2
M.Cooper-StL 278.2
Passeau-Chi 278.1
Starr-Cin 276.2
Javery-Bos 261.0

Fewest Hits/Game
M.Cooper-StL 6.69
VanderMeer-Cin 6.93
Higbe-Bro 7.31
Starr-Cin 7.42
Beazley-StL 7.57

Fewest BB/Game
Warneke-StL-Chi 1.79
Lohrman-StL-NY 1.85
Hubbell-NY 1.94
Derringer-Cin 2.11
M.Cooper-StL 2.20

Strikeouts
VanderMeer-Cin 186
M.Cooper-StL 152
Higbe-Bro 115
Walters-Cin 109
Melton-Phi 107

Strikeouts/Game
VanderMeer-Cin 6.86
Lanier-StL 5.20
M.Cooper-StL 4.91
Higbe-Bro 4.67
Melton-Phi 4.60

Ratio
M.Cooper-StL 9.04
Lohrman-StL-NY 10.07
Davis-Bro 10.35
Warneke-StL-Chi 10.39
Wyatt-Bro 10.56

Earned Run Average
M.Cooper-StL 1.78
Beazley-StL 2.13
Davis-Bro 2.36
VanderMeer-Cin 2.43
Lohrman-StL-NY 2.48

Adjusted ERA
M.Cooper-StL 193
Beazley-StL 161
Davis-Bro 138
Lohrman-StL-NY 136
VanderMeer-Cin 135

Opponents' Batting Avg.
M.Cooper-StL 204
VanderMeer-Cin 208
Higbe-Bro 223
Wyatt-Bro 225
Starr-Cin 226

Opponents' On-Base Pct.
M.Cooper-StL 258
Lohrman-StL-NY 281
Wyatt-Bro 286
Warneke-StL-Chi 286
Davis-Bro 287

Starter Runs
M.Cooper-StL 47.6
Beazley-StL 28.3
French-Bro 24.4
VanderMeer-Cin 23.8
Davis-Bro 21.8

Adjusted Starter Runs
M.Cooper-StL 49.3
Beazley-StL 29.9
French-Bro 23.9
VanderMeer-Cin 23.2
Davis-Bro 21.0

Clutch Pitching Index
Bithorn-Chi 130
Passeau-Chi 121
Beazley-StL 114
Schumacher-NY 113
Carpenter-NY 112

Relief Runs
Adams-NY 14.4
Casey-Bro 13.2
Beggs-Cin 11.6
Shoun-StL-Cin 9.4
Webber-Bro 2.0

Adjusted Relief Runs
Adams-NY 14.6
Casey-Bro 12.8
Beggs-Cin 11.5
Shoun-StL-Cin 9.2
Webber-Bro 1.7

Relief Ranking
Adams-NY 20.6
Beggs-Cin 15.1
Casey-Bro 12.6
Shoun-StL-Cin 4.6
Webber-Bro 1.6

Total Pitcher Index
M.Cooper-StL 4.9
Beazley-StL 3.8
French-Bro 3.4
Walters-Cin 3.0
VanderMeer-Cin 2.9

Total Baseball Ranking
M.Cooper-StL 4.9
Nicholson-Chi 4.6
Ott-NY 4.0
Beazley-StL 3.8
Slaughter-StL 3.8

TEAM	G	W	L	PCT	GB	R	OR	AB	H	2B	3B	HR	BB	SO	AVG	OBP	SLG	OPS	OPS+	BR	BR+	PF	CHI	RC	SB	CS	SBA	SBR
NY	154	103	51	.669		**801**	**507**	5305	1429	223	57	**108**	591	556	.269	.346	.394	740	**118**	104	**120**	98	**104**	759	69	33	68	4
BOS	152	93	59	.612	9	761	594	5248	**1451**	**244**	55	103	591	508	**.276**	**.352**	**.403**	**755**	116	**132**	106	103	96	**774**	68	61	53	-6
STL	151	82	69	.543	19.5	730	637	5229	1354	239	**62**	98	**609**	607	.259	.338	.385	723	109	68	57	102	101	703	37	38	49	-5
CLE	156	75	79	.487	28	590	659	5317	1344	223	58	50	500	544	.253	.320	.345	665	100	-43	-5	94	96	596	69	74	48	-11
DET	156	73	81	.474	30	589	587	5327	1313	217	37	76	509	476	.246	.314	.344	658	85	-57	-102	108	98	582	39	40	49	-5
CHI	148	66	82	.446	34	538	609	4949	1215	214	36	25	497	**427**	.246	.316	.318	634	87	-87	-75	98	102	520	**114**	70	62	1
WAS	151	62	89	.411	39.5	653	817	5295	1364	224	49	40	581	536	.258	.333	.341	674	98	-14	-7	99	101	641	98	29	**77**	**11**
PHI	154	55	99	.357	48	549	801	5285	1315	213	46	33	440	490	.249	.309	.325	634	86	-101	-98	99	101	536	44	45	49	-6
TOT	611					5211		41955	10785	1797	400	533	4318	4144	.258	.329	.358	686							538	390	58	-18

TEAM	CG	SH	SV	IP	H	H/G	HR	BB	SO	RAT	ERA	ERA+	OAV	OOB	PR	PR+	PF	CPI	FA	E	DP	FW	PW	BW	SBW	DIF
NY	**88**	**18**	**17**	1375	**1259**	**8.3**	71	**431**	558	**11.2**	**2.91**	118	**.244**	**.304**	**115**	87	94	108	**.976**	**142**	**190**	**2.1**	9.0	**12.3**	.6	2.2
BOS	84	11	**17**	1358^{2}	1260	8.4	65	553	500	12.2	3.45	108	.247	.322	32	42	102	99	.974	157	156	1.1	4.4	10.9	-.4	1.2
STL	68	12	13	1363	1387	9.2	63	505	488	12.7	3.60	103	.262	.330	10	17	101	103	.972	167	143	.5	1.8	5.9	-.3	-1.2
CLE	61	12	11	1402^{2}	1353	8.7	61	560	448	12.5	3.60	96	.254	.327	10	-24	94	99	.974	163	175	1.0	-2.4	-.5	-.9	.9
DET	65	12	14	1399^{1}	1321	8.5	60	598	**671**	12.5	3.14	**126**	.248	.326	82	**118**	108	**111**	.969	194	142	-.7	**12.1**	-10.4	-.3	-4.5
CHI	86	8	8	1314^{1}	1304	9.0	74	473	432	12.4	3.59	100	.258	.325	11	3	98	102	.970	173	144	-.0	.4	-7.6	.3	-.8
WAS	68	12	11	1346^{2}	1496	10.0	**50**	558	496	13.9	4.59	80	.279	.349	-139	-139	100	91	.962	222	133	-2.6	-14.2	-.7	**1.4**	2.8
PHI	67	5	9	1374^{2}	1404	9.2	89	639	546	13.6	4.45	85	.263	.344	-120	-99	103	93	.969	188	124	-.5	-10.1	-10.0	-.4	-.8
TOT	587	90	100	10934^{1}		8.9				12.6	3.66		.258	.329					.971	1406	1207					

Runs
Williams-Bos 141
DiMaggio-NY 123
DiMaggio-Bos 110
Clift-StL 108
Keller-NY 106

Hits
Pesky-Bos 205
Spence-Was 203
Williams-Bos 186
DiMaggio-NY 186
Keltner-Cle 179

Doubles
Kolloway-Chi 40
Clift-StL 39
Heath-Cle 37
DiMaggio-Bos 36

Triples
Spence-Was 15
Heath-Cle 13
DiMaggio-NY 13
McQuillen-StL 12

Home Runs
Williams-Bos 36
Laabs-StL 27
Keller-NY 26
York-Det 21
DiMaggio-NY 21

Total Bases
Williams-Bos 338
DiMaggio-NY 304
Keller-NY 279
Spence-Was 272
DiMaggio-Bos 272

Runs Batted In
Williams-Bos 137
DiMaggio-NY 114
Keller-NY 108
Gordon-NY 103
Doerr-Bos 102

Runs Produced
Williams-Bos 242
DiMaggio-NY 216
Keller-NY 188
Gordon-NY 173
Spence-Was 169

Bases On Balls
Williams-Bos 145
Keller-NY 114
Fleming-Cle 106
Clift-StL 106
Cullenbine-SL-W-NY 92

Batting Average
Williams-Bos .... .356
Pesky-Bos .... .331
Spence-Was .... .323
Gordon-NY .... .322
Case-Was .... .320

On-Base Percentage
Williams-Bos .... .499
Keller-NY .... .417
Judnich-StL .... .413
Fleming-Cle .... .412
Gordon-NY .... .409

Slugging Average
Williams-Bos .... .648
Keller-NY .... .513
Judnich-StL .... .499
DiMaggio-NY .... .498
Laabs-StL .... .498

On-Base Plus Slugging
Williams-Bos 1147
Keller-NY 930
Judnich-StL 912
Gordon-NY 900
Laabs-StL 878

Adjusted OPS
Williams-Bos 214
Keller-NY 164
Gordon-NY 156
Judnich-StL 153
DiMaggio-NY 148

Batter Runs
Williams-Bos 92.6
Keller-NY 46.9
Gordon-NY 38.6
Judnich-StL 35.4
DiMaggio-NY 34.5

Adjusted Batter Runs
Williams-Bos 87.1
Keller-NY 49.5
Gordon-NY 40.9
Fleming-Cle 38.6
DiMaggio-NY 36.8

Clutch Hitting Index
Lupien-Bos 124
Cullenbine-SL-W-NY 116
Vernon-Was 113
Siebert-Phi 113
Tabor-Bos 112

Runs Created
Williams-Bos 185
Keller-NY 131
DiMaggio-NY 120
Spence-Was 111
Gordon-NY 108

Total Average
Williams-Bos 1.394
Keller-NY 1.038
Judnich-StL .... .950
Gordon-NY .... .891
Laabs-StL .... .878

Stolen Bases
Case-Was 44
Vernon-Was 25
Rizzuto-NY 22
Kuhel-Chi 22

Stolen Base Average
Case-Was 88.0
Vernon-Was 80.6
Rizzuto-NY 78.6
Appling-Chi 77.3
Kuhel-Chi 71.0

Stolen Base Runs
Case-Was 7.6
Vernon-Was 3.4
Rizzuto-NY 2.7
Keller-NY 2.4
Appling-Chi 2.0

Fielding Runs
Rizzuto-NY 25.0
Pesky-Bos 17.7
DiMaggio-Bos 16.9
Keltner-Cle 15.6
York-Det 15.4

Total Player Rating
Williams-Bos 8.0
Gordon-NY 5.5
Pesky-Bos 4.4
Keller-NY 4.3
Rizzuto-NY 4.1

Wins
Hughson-Bos 22
Bonham-NY 21
Marchildon-Phi 17
Bagby-Cle 17
Chandler-NY 16

Win Percentage
Bonham-NY .... .808
Borowy-NY .... .789
Hughson-Bos .... .786
Chandler-NY .... .762
Bagby-Cle .... .654

Games
Haynes-Chi 40
Caster-StL 39

Complete Games
Hughson-Bos 22
Bonham-NY 22
Lyons-Chi 20
Hudson-Was 19

Shutouts
Bonham-NY 6

Saves
Murphy-NY 11
Haynes-Chi 6
Brown-Bos 6
Newhouser-Det 5
Caster-StL 5

Innings Pitched
Hughson-Bos 281.0
Bagby-Cle 270.2
Auker-StL 249.0
Marchildon-Phi 244.0
Hudson-Was 239.1

Fewest Hits/Game
Newhouser-Det 6.71
Niggeling-StL 7.55
Dobson-Bos 7.64
Trucks-Det 7.89
Chandler-NY 7.89

Fewest BB/Game
Bonham-NY .... .96
Lyons-Chi 1.30
Ruffing-NY 1.91
Breuer-NY 2.03
Bagby-Cle 2.13

Strikeouts
Newsom-Was 113
Hughson-Bos 113
Marchildon-Phi 110
Benton-Det 110
Niggeling-StL 107

Strikeouts/Game
Newhouser-Det 5.05
Bridges-Det 5.02
Trucks-Det 4.88
Newsom-Was 4.76
Niggeling-StL 4.67

Ratio
Bonham-NY 8.92
Lyons-Chi 9.73
Ruffing-NY 10.55
Breuer-NY 10.68
Hughson-Bos 10.70

Earned Run Average
Lyons-Chi 2.10
Bonham-NY 2.27
Chandler-NY 2.38
Newhouser-Det 2.45
Borowy-NY 2.52

Adjusted ERA
Lyons-Chi 172
Newhouser-Det 161
Bonham-NY 152
Chandler-NY 145
Trucks-Det 144

Opponents' Batting Avg.
Newhouser-Det .... .207
Niggeling-StL .... .226
Dobson-Bos .... .231
Trucks-Det .... .231
Borowy-NY .... .233

Opponents' On-Base Pct.
Bonham-NY .... .259
Lyons-Chi .... .275
Ruffing-NY .... .292
Breuer-NY .... .295
Hughson-Bos .... .296

Starter Runs
Bonham-NY 34.8
Hughson-Bos 33.2
Lyons-Chi 31.3
Chandler-NY 28.5
Humphries-Chi 24.8

Adjusted Starter Runs
Hughson-Bos 34.8
Bonham-NY 31.3
Lyons-Chi 30.6
Newhouser-Det 28.3
Chandler-NY 25.2

Clutch Pitching Index
Chandler-NY 136
Lyons-Chi 131
Hollingsworth-StL 123
Humphries-Chi 121
Niggeling-StL 119

Relief Runs
Ferrick-Cle 15.0
Haynes-Chi 11.9
Caster-StL 7.5
Murphy-NY 1.6
Brown-Bos 1.5

Adjusted Relief Runs
Ferrick-Cle 14.0
Haynes-Chi 11.4
Caster-StL 7.8
Brown-Bos 2.0
Murphy-NY 2

Relief Ranking
Haynes-Chi 14.4
Caster-StL 9.9
Ferrick-Cle 8.9
Brown-Bos 3.9
Murphy-NY 4

Total Pitcher Index
Lyons-Chi 4.0
Hughson-Bos 3.7
Newhouser-Det 3.7
Chandler-NY 3.3
Bonham-NY 2.8

Total Baseball Ranking
Williams-Bos 8.0
Gordon-NY 5.5
Pesky-Bos 4.4
Keller-NY 4.3
Rizzuto-NY 4.1

TEAM	G	W	L	PCT	GB	R	OR	AB	H	2B	3B	HR	BB	SO	AVG	OBP	SLG	OPS	OPS+	BR	BR+	PF	CHI	RC	SB	CS	SBA	SBR
STL	157	105	49	.682		679	**475**	5438	**1515**	259	72	70	428	438	**.279**	.333	**.391**	**724**	**110**	**92**	62	104	95	**720**	40			
CIN	155	87	67	.565	18	608	543	5329	1362	229	47	43	445	476	.256	.315	.340	655	96	-35	-27	99	**106**	581	49			
BRO	153	81	72	.529	23.5	**716**	675	5309	1444	**263**	35	39	**580**	**422**	.272	**.346**	.357	703	**110**	70	**69**	100	104	675	58			
PIT	157	80	74	.519	25	669	605	5353	1401	240	**73**	42	573	566	.262	.335	.357	692	103	45	23	103	100	657	**64**			
CHI	154	74	79	.484	30.5	632	599	5279	1380	207	56	52	574	522	.261	.336	.351	687	107	38	48	99	97	641	53			
BOS	153	68	85	.444	36.5	465	612	5196	1213	202	36	39	469	609	.233	.299	.309	608	82	-121	-114	99	98	491	56			
PHI	157	64	90	.416	41	571	676	5297	1321	186	36	66	499	556	.249	.316	.335	651	98	-38	-14	96	100	565	29			
NY	156	55	98	.359	49.5	558	713	5290	1309	153	33	**81**	480	470	.247	.313	.335	648	92	-48	-52	101	100	552	35			
TOT	621					4898		42491	10945	1739	388	432	4048	4059	.258	.325	.348	672							384			

TEAM	CG	SH	SV	IP	H	H/G	HR	BB	SO	RAT	ERA	ERA+	OAV	OOB	PR	PR+	PF	CPI	FA	E	DP	FW	PW	BW	SBW	DIF
STL	**94**	**21**	15	1427	**1246**	**7.9**	**33**	477	**639**	**11.0**	**2.57**	**131**	**.237**	**.303**	**129**	**127**	99	105	.976	151	183	.9	**13.6**	6.7		7.0
CIN	78	18	17	1404	1299	8.4	38	579	498	12.2	3.14	106	.251	.328	39	28	98	105	**.980**	**125**	**193**	**2.3**	3.0	-2.8		7.7
BRO	50	13	**22**	1369^{2}	1326	8.8	59	637	588	13.1	3.89	86	.254	.338	-76	-80	99	93	.972	168	137	-.3	-8.5	**7.4**		6.1
PIT	74	11	12	1404	1424	9.2	44	422	396	12.0	3.09	113	.264	.319	47	58	103	**107**	.973	170	159	-.2	6.2	2.5		-5.4
CHI	67	13	14	1386	1379	9.0	53	**394**	513	11.7	3.32	101	.258	.311	11	4	99	95	.973	168	138	-.2	.5	5.2		-7.7
BOS	87	13	4	1397^{2}	1361	8.8	66	441	409	11.8	3.26	105	.255	.314	20	25	101	100	.972	176	139	-.7	2.7	-12.1		1.8
PHI	66	10	14	1392^{2}	1436	9.3	59	451	431	12.4	3.79	89	.267	.326	-62	-64	100	93	.969	189	143	-1.2	-6.8	-1.4		-3.3
NY	35	6	19	1394^{2}	1474	9.6	80	626	588	13.7	4.08	84	.272	.350	-108	-97	102	101	.973	166	140	.0	-10.3	-5.5		-5.5
TOT	551	105	117	11175^{2}		8.9				12.2	3.39		.258	.325					.974	1313	1232					

Runs
Vaughan-Bro 112
Musial-StL 108
Nicholson-Chi 95
Cavarretta-Chi 93
Stanky-Chi 92

Hits
Musial-StL 220
Witek-NY 195
Herman-Bro 193
Nicholson-Chi 188
Vaughan-Bro 186

Doubles
Musial-StL 48
Herman-Bro 41
DiMaggio-Pit 41
Vaughan-Bro 39
Holmes-Bos 33

Triples
Musial-StL 20
Klein-StL 14
Lowrey-Chi 12
Elliott-Pit 12

Home Runs
Nicholson-Chi 29
Ott-NY 18
Northey-Phi 16
Triplett-StL-Phi 15
DiMaggio-Pit 15

Total Bases
Musial-StL 347
Nicholson-Chi 323
Elliott-Pit 258
Klein-StL 257

Runs Batted In
Nicholson-Chi 128
Elliott-Pit 101
Herman-Bro 100
DiMaggio-Pit 88

Runs Produced
Nicholson-Chi 194
Musial-StL 176
Elliott-Pit 176
Herman-Bro 174
Vaughan-Bro 173

Bases On Balls
Galan-Bro 103
Ott-NY 95
Fletcher-Pit 95
Stanky-Chi 92
Tipton-Cin 85

Batting Average
Musial-StL .357
Herman-Bro .330
W.Cooper-StL .318
Elliott-Pit .315
Witek-NY .314

On-Base Percentage
Musial-StL .425
Galan-Bro .412
Herman-Bro .398
Fletcher-Pit .395
Tipton-Cin .395

Slugging Average
Musial-StL .562
Nicholson-Chi .531
W.Cooper-StL .463
Elliott-Pit .444
Triplett-StL-Phi .439

On-Base Plus Slugging
Musial-StL 988
Nicholson-Chi 917
Elliott-Pit 820
Tipton-Cin 819
Galan-Bro 818

Adjusted OPS
Musial-StL 176
Nicholson-Chi 166
Tipton-Cin 138
Galan-Bro 136
Herman-Bro 135

Batter Runs
Musial-StL 65.5
Nicholson-Chi 47.7
Galan-Bro 28.5
Herman-Bro 28.0
Elliott-Pit 26.5

Adjusted Batter Runs
Musial-StL 59.7
Nicholson-Chi 49.5
Galan-Bro 28.3
Herman-Bro 27.8
Tipton-Cin 27.1

Clutch Hitting Index
Miller-Cin 138
Herman-Bro 131
Elliott-Pit 123
Wasdell-Pit-Phi 121
Medwick-Bro-NY 117

Runs Created
Musial-StL 147
Nicholson-Chi 129
Herman-Bro 97
Vaughan-Bro 96
Elliott-Pit 96

Total Average
Musial-StL 1.039
Nicholson-Chi .944
Ott-NY .895
Galan-Bro .876
Tipton-Cin .825

Stolen Bases
Vaughan-Bro 20
Lowrey-Chi 13
Workman-Bos 12
Russell-Pit 12
Gustine-Pit 12

Stolen Base Average

Stolen Base Runs

Fielding Runs
Miller-Cin 26.6
Marion-StL 25.3
Mueller-Cin 20.2
Wietelmann-Bos 20.0
Galan-Bro 16.1

Total Player Rating
Musial-StL 6.3
Nicholson-Chi 4.7
Galan-Bro 4.1
Mueller-Cin 3.7
Witek-NY 3.3

Wins
Sewell-Pit 21
Riddle-Cin 21
M.Cooper-StL 21
Bithorn-Chi 18
Javery-Bos 17

Win Percentage
M.Cooper-StL .724
Sewell-Pit .700
Lanier-StL .682
Riddle-Cin .656
Bithorn-Chi .600

Games
Adams-NY 70
Webber-Bro 54
Head-Bro 47
Shoun-Cin 45
Mungo-NY 45

Complete Games
Sewell-Pit 25
Tobin-Bos 24
M.Cooper-StL 24
Andrews-Bos 23

Shutouts
Bithorn-Chi 7
M.Cooper-StL 6

Saves
Webber-Bro 10
Adams-NY 9
Shoun-Cin 7
Head-Bro 6
Beggs-Cin 6

Innings Pitched
Javery-Bos 303.0
VanderMeer-Cin 289.0
Andrews-Bos 283.2
M.Cooper-StL 274.0
Sewell-Pit 265.1

Fewest Hits/Game
Wyatt-Bro 6.92
VanderMeer-Cin 7.10
M.Cooper-StL 7.49
Krist-StL 7.72
Barrett-Chi-Phi 7.94

Fewest BB/Game
Rowe-Phi 1.31
Wyse-Chi 1.96
Derringer-Chi 2.02
Davis-Bro 2.14
Wyatt-Bro 2.14

Strikeouts
VanderMeer-Cin 174
M.Cooper-StL 141
Javery-Bos 134
Lanier-StL 123
Higbe-Bro 108

Strikeouts/Game
VanderMeer-Cin 5.42
Higbe-Bro 5.25
Lanier-StL 5.19
M.Cooper-StL 4.63
Head-Bro 4.40

Ratio
Wyatt-Bro 9.07
M.Cooper-StL 10.25
Rowe-Phi 10.31
Andrews-Bos 10.60
Bithorn-Chi 10.60

Earned Run Average
Pollet-StL 1.75
Lanier-StL 1.90
M.Cooper-StL 2.30
Wyatt-Bro 2.49
Sewell-Pit 2.54

Adjusted ERA
Lanier-StL 177
M.Cooper-StL 146
Sewell-Pit 137
Wyatt-Bro 135
Butcher-Pit 134

Opponents' Batting Avg.
Wyatt-Bro .207
VanderMeer-Cin .224
M.Cooper-StL .226
Krist-StL .233
Barrett-Chi-Phi .237

Opponents' On-Base Pct.
Wyatt-Bro .255
Rowe-Phi .279
M.Cooper-StL .286
Andrews-Bos .291
Bithorn-Chi .294

Starter Runs
Lanier-StL 35.2
M.Cooper-StL 33.0
Andrews-Bos 25.6
Sewell-Pit 24.7
Riddle-Cin 21.9

Adjusted Starter Runs
Lanier-StL 34.9
M.Cooper-StL 32.6
Sewell-Pit 26.8
Andrews-Bos 26.4
Pollet-StL 21.3

Clutch Pitching Index
Lanier-StL 151
Butcher-Pit 122
Sewell-Pit 121
Riddle-Cin 118
Tobin-Bos 113

Relief Runs
Beggs-Cin 13.4
Adams-NY 8.8
Prim-Chi 5.6
Brandt-Pit 1.6

Adjusted Relief Runs
Beggs-Cin 12.7
Adams-NY 9.5
Prim-Chi 5.3
Brandt-Pit 2.1

Relief Ranking
Beggs-Cin 14.4
Adams-NY 12.4
Prim-Chi 5.8
Brandt-Pit 1.6

Total Pitcher Index
Sewell-Pit 3.9
Lanier-StL 3.6
Tobin-Bos 3.5
Andrews-Bos 3.4
M.Cooper-StL 3.2

Total Baseball Ranking
Musial-StL 6.3
Nicholson-Chi 4.7
Galan-Bro 4.1
Sewell-Pit 3.9
Mueller-Cin 3.7

TEAM	G	W	L	PCT	GB	R	OR	AB	H	2B	3B	HR	BB	SO	AVG	OBP	SLG	OPS	OPS+	BR	BR+	PF	CHI	RC	SB	CS	SBA	SBR
NY	155	98	56	.636		**669**	**542**	5282	1350	218	**59**	**100**	**624**	562	.256	**.337**	**.376**	**713**	**114**	**97**	**92**	101	95	**683**	46	60	43	-11
WAS	153	84	69	.549	13.5	666	595	5233	1328	245	50	47	605	579	.254	.336	.347	683	110	45	70	96	103	656	142	55	**72**	**12**
CLE	153	82	71	.536	15.5	600	577	5269	1344	**246**	45	55	567	521	.255	.329	.350	679	112	32	73	94	95	626	47	58	45	-10
CHI	155	82	72	.532	16	573	594	5254	1297	193	46	33	561	581	.247	.322	.320	642	94	-33	-32	100	102	570	**173**	87	67	8
DET	155	78	76	.506	20	632	560	5364	**1401**	200	47	77	483	553	**.261**	.324	.359	683	98	32	-13	108	99	620	40	43	48	-6
STL	153	72	80	.474	25	596	604	5175	1269	229	36	78	569	646	.245	.322	.349	671	100	14	2	102	98	603	37	43	46	-7
BOS	155	68	84	.447	29	563	607	5392	1314	223	42	57	486	591	.244	.308	.332	640	92	-48	-57	102	101	570	86	61	59	-2
PHI	155	49	105	.318	49	497	717	5244	1219	174	44	26	430	**465**	.232	.294	.297	591	78	-137	-135	100	**111**	466	55	42	57	-3
TOT	617					4796		42213	10522	1728	369	473	4325	4498	.250	.322	.342	663							626	449	58	-19

TEAM	CG	SH	SV	IP	H	H/G	HR	BB	SO	RAT	ERA	ERA+	OAV	OOB	PR	PR+	PF	CPI	FA	E	DP	FW	PW	BW	SBW	DIF
NY	**83**	14	13	1415[1]	1229	**7.9**	60	489	653	**11.1**	**2.93**	110	**.234**	**.301**	**58**	47	98	95	.974	160	166	.3	5.1	**10.0**	-.9	6.7
WAS	61	16	**21**	1388	1293	8.4	**48**	540	495	12.0	3.19	101	.246	.318	17	3	97	99	.971	179	145	-.9	.4	7.6	**1.6**	-1.0
CLE	64	14	20	1406[1]	1234	**7.9**	52	606	585	12.0	3.15	99	.239	.322	23	-7	94	100	.975	157	**183**	.3	-.7	7.9	-.8	-1.1
CHI	70	12	19	1400[1]	1352	8.7	54	501	476	12.2	3.21	104	.255	.324	15	21	101	105	.973	166	167	-.0	2.3	-3.4	1.1	5.2
DET	67	**18**	20	1411[2]	**1226**	**7.9**	51	549	**706**	11.5	3.01	**117**	**.234**	.308	46	**76**	107	95	.971	177	130	-.7	**8.3**	-1.4	-.4	-4.7
STL	64	10	14	1385	1397	9.1	74	**488**	572	12.4	3.42	97	.263	.327	-18	-13	101	**106**	.975	**152**	127	.6	-1.4	.3	-.5	-2.8
BOS	62	13	16	1426[1]	1369	8.7	61	615	513	12.7	3.46	96	.257	.335	-25	-22	101	105	**.976**	153	179	**.7**	-2.3	-6.1	.0	-.0
PHI	73	5	13	1394	1421	9.2	73	536	503	12.9	4.05	84	.265	.336	-117	-98	103	94	.973	162	148	.2	-10.6	-14.6	-.0	-2.8
TOT	544	102	136	11227		8.5				12.1	3.30		.250	.322					.974	1306	1245					

Runs
Case-Was 102
Keller-NY 97
Wakefield-Det 91
York-Det 90
Vernon-Was 89

Hits
Wakefield-Det 200
Appling-Chi 192
Cramer-Det 182
Case-Was 180

Doubles
Wakefield-Det 38
Case-Was 36
Gutteridge-StL 35
Etten-NY 35

Triples
Moses-Chi 12
Lindell-NY 12
York-Det 11
Keller-NY 11
Spence-Was 10

Home Runs
York-Det 34
Keller-NY 31
Stephens-StL 22
Heath-Cle 18

Total Bases
York-Det 301
Wakefield-Det 275
Keller-NY 269
Doerr-Bos 249
Stephens-StL 247

Runs Batted In
York-Det 118
Etten-NY 107
Johnson-NY 94
Stephens-StL 91
Spence-Was 88

Runs Produced
York-Det 174
Etten-NY 171
Wakefield-Det 163
Johnson-NY 159
Case-Was 153

Bases On Balls
Keller-NY 106
Gordon-NY 98
Cullenbine-Cle 96
Boudreau-Cle 90
Appling-Chi 90

Batting Average
Appling-Chi .328
Wakefield-Det .316
Hodgin-Chi .314
Cramer-Det .300
Case-Was .294

On-Base Percentage
Appling-Chi .419
Cullenbine-Cle .407
Keller-NY .396
Boudreau-Cle .388
Curtright-Chi .382

Slugging Average
York-Det .527
Keller-NY .525
Stephens-StL .482
Heath-Cle .481
Wakefield-Det .434

On-Base Plus Slugging
Keller-NY 922
York-Det 893
Heath-Cle 850
Stephens-StL 839
Appling-Chi 825

Adjusted OPS
Keller-NY 167
Heath-Cle 157
York-Det 148
Cullenbine-Cle 146
Appling-Chi 142

Batter Runs
Keller-NY 45.8
York-Det 41.0
Appling-Chi 35.0
Wakefield-Det 28.8
Cullenbine-Cle 27.4

Adjusted Batter Runs
Keller-NY 45.0
Appling-Chi 35.1
York-Det 33.3
Cullenbine-Cle 33.1
Heath-Cle 29.9

Clutch Hitting Index
Sullivan-Was 162
Johnson-NY 134
Siebert-Phi 128
Early-Was 125
McQuinn-StL 125

Runs Created
Keller-NY 116
Appling-Chi 109
York-Det 108
Wakefield-Det 101
Spence-Was 93

Total Average
Keller-NY .979
York-Det .871
Appling-Chi .841
Heath-Cle .828
Cullenbine-Cle .816

Stolen Bases
Case-Was 61
Moses-Chi 56
Tucker-Chi 29
Appling-Chi 27
Vernon-Was 24

Stolen Base Average
Case-Was 81.3
Moses-Chi 80.0
Appling-Chi 77.1
Vernon-Was 75.0
Fox-Bos 73.3

Stolen Base Runs
Case-Was 8.5
Moses-Chi 7.4
Appling-Chi 3.1
Culberson-Bos 3.1
Vernon-Was 2.5

Fielding Runs
Boudreau-Cle 28.4
Gordon-NY 25.7
Clift-StL-Was 18.3
York-Det 17.6
Bloodworth-Det 17.2

Total Player Rating
Boudreau-Cle 6.9
Appling-Chi 6.1
Gordon-NY 5.6
York-Det 4.5
Keller-NY 4.2

Wins
Trout-Det 20
Chandler-NY 20
Wynn-Was 18
Smith-Cle 17
Bagby-Cle 17

Win Percentage
Chandler-NY .833
Smith-Cle .708
Bonham-NY .652
Trout-Det .625
Grove-Chi .625

Games
Brown-Bos 49
Trout-Det 44
Wolff-Phi 41
Ryba-Bos 40
Carrasquel-Was 39

Complete Games
Hughson-Bos 20
Chandler-NY 20
Wensloff-NY 18
Trout-Det 18
Grove-Chi 18

Shutouts
Trout-Det 5
Chandler-NY 5
Hughson-Bos 4
Bonham-NY 4

Saves
Maltzberger-Chi 14
Heving-Cle 9
Brown-Bos 9
Murphy-NY 8
Caster-StL 8

Innings Pitched
Bagby-Cle 273.0
Hughson-Bos 266.0
Wynn-Was 256.2
Chandler-NY 253.0
Trout-Det 246.2

Fewest Hits/Game
Reynolds-Cle 6.34
Niggeling-StL-Was 6.66
Haefner-Was 6.86
Chandler-NY 7.01
Wensloff-NY 7.21

Fewest BB/Game
Leonard-Was 1.88
Chandler-NY 1.92
Bonham-NY 2.07
Muncrief-StL 2.11
Trucks-Det 2.31

Strikeouts
Reynolds-Cle 151
Newhouser-Det 144
Chandler-NY 134
Bridges-Det 124
Trucks-Det 118

Strikeouts/Game
Reynolds-Cle 6.84
Newhouser-Det 6.62
Bridges-Det 5.82
Trucks-Det 5.24
Chandler-NY 4.77

Ratio
Chandler-NY 9.07
Trucks-Det 9.90
Bonham-NY 9.97
Wensloff-NY 10.07
Niggeling-StL-Was 10.24

Earned Run Average
Chandler-NY 1.64
Bonham-NY 2.27
Haefner-Was 2.29
Bridges-Det 2.39
Trout-Det 2.48

Adjusted ERA
Chandler-NY 197
Bridges-Det 147
Trout-Det 142
Bonham-NY 141
Haefner-Was 140

Opponents' Batting Avg.
Reynolds-Cle .202
Niggeling-StL-Was .204
Haefner-Was .208
Chandler-NY .215
Wensloff-NY .219

Opponents' On-Base Pct.
Chandler-NY .261
Trucks-Det .276
Wensloff-NY .282
Bonham-NY .282
Niggeling-StL-Was .282

Starter Runs
Chandler-NY 46.6
Bonham-NY 25.6
Trout-Det 22.3
Hughson-Bos 19.4
Bridges-Det 19.2

Adjusted Starter Runs
Chandler-NY 45.5
Trout-Det 26.7
Bonham-NY 24.2
Bridges-Det 22.4
Hughson-Bos 19.8

Clutch Pitching Index
Hughson-Bos 124
Muncrief-StL 120
Bonham-NY 116
Galehouse-StL 115
Candini-Was 115

Relief Runs
Brown-Bos 12.2
Caster-StL 10.0
Maltzberger-Chi 9.1
Naymick-Cle 6.9
Murphy-NY 5.9

Adjusted Relief Runs
Brown-Bos 12.3
Caster-StL 10.1
Maltzberger-Chi 9.5
Naymick-Cle 6.0
Murphy-NY 5.4

Relief Ranking
Caster-StL 19.1
Brown-Bos 16.9
Maltzberger-Chi 12.5
Murphy-NY 10.9
Naymick-Cle 7.3

Total Pitcher Index
Chandler-NY 5.8
Trout-Det 4.4
Bridges-Det 2.4
Caster-StL 2.1
Bonham-NY 2.0

Total Baseball Ranking
Boudreau-Cle 6.9
Appling-Chi 6.1
Chandler-NY 5.8
Gordon-NY 5.6
York-Det 4.5

TEAM	G	W	L	PCT	GB	R	OR	AB	H	2B	3B	HR	BB	SO	AVG	OBP	SLG	OPS	OPS+	BR	BR+	PF	CHI	RC	SB	CS	SBA	SBR
STL	157	105	49	.682		**772**	**490**	5475	**1507**	**274**	59	**100**	544	473	**.275**	**.344**	**.402**	**746**	**114**	**110**	**96**	102	98	**775**	37			
PIT	158	90	63	.588	14.5	744	662	5428	1441	248	**80**	70	**573**	616	.265	.338	.379	717	104	58	29	104	102	707	**87**			
CIN	155	89	65	.578	16	573	537	5271	1340	229	31	51	423	**391**	.254	.313	.338	651	92	-74	-52	96	101	558	51			
CHI	157	75	79	.487	30	702	669	5462	1425	236	46	71	520	521	.261	.328	.360	688	101	-2	2	99	**104**	658	53			
NY	155	67	87	.435	38	682	773	5306	1398	191	47	93	512	480	.263	.331	.370	701	103	22	24	100	100	656	39			
BOS	155	65	89	.422	40	593	674	5282	1299	250	39	79	456	509	.246	.308	.353	661	88	-61	-84	104	101	586	37			
BRO	155	63	91	.409	42	690	832	5393	1450	255	51	56	486	451	.269	.331	.366	697	104	16	28	98	101	664	45			
PHI	154	61	92	.399	43.5	539	658	5301	1331	199	42	55	470	500	.251	.316	.336	652	92	-70	-50	97	92	571	32			
TOT	623					5295		42918	11191	1882	395	575	3984	3941	.261	.327	.364	689							381			

TEAM	CG	SH	SV	IP	H	H/G	HR	BB	SO	RAT	ERA	ERA+	OAV	OOB	PR	PR+	PF	CPI	FA	E	DP	FW	PW	BW	SBW	DIF
STL	89	**26**	12	1427	**1228**	**7.8**	55	468	**637**	**10.9**	**2.68**	**132**	**.233**	**.298**	**148**	**138**	98	103	**.982**	**112**	**162**	**3.8**	**14.2**	**9.9**		.3
PIT	77	10	19	1414^{1}	1466	9.4	65	435	452	12.3	3.44	108	.265	.321	27	43	103	103	.970	191	122	-1.0	4.5	3.0		7.2
CIN	**93**	17	12	1398^{1}	1292	8.4	60	**390**	369	11.0	2.98	117	.246	.300	99	83	97	99	.978	137	153	2.1	8.6	-5.3		6.8
CHI	70	11	13	1400^{2}	1484	9.6	75	458	545	12.6	3.59	98	.274	.331	4	-9	98	**108**	.970	186	151	-.8	-.9	.3		-.4
NY	47	4	**21**	1363^{2}	1413	9.4	116	587	499	13.5	4.29	85	.265	.342	-103	-93	102	98	.971	179	128	-.5	-9.5	2.5		-2.3
BOS	70	13	12	1388^{1}	1430	9.3	80	527	454	12.9	3.67	104	.267	.335	-9	21	106	106	.971	182	160	-.7	2.2	-8.6		-4.7
BRO	50	4	13	1367^{2}	1471	9.7	75	660	487	14.3	4.68	76	.274	.357	-162	-175	98	93	.966	197	112	-1.6	-17.9	2.9		2.8
PHI	66	11	6	1395^{1}	1407	9.1	**49**	459	496	12.2	3.64	99	.261	.321	-4	-4	100	93	.972	177	138	-.4	-.4	-5.1		-9.4
TOT	562	96	108	11155^{1}		9.1				12.4	3.62		.261	.327					.973	1361	1126					

Runs
- Nicholson-Chi 116
- Musial-StL 112
- Russell-Pit 109
- Hopp-StL 106
- Cavarretta-Chi 106

Hits
- Musial-StL 197
- Cavarretta-Chi 197
- Holmes-Bos 195
- Walker-Bro 191
- Russell-Pit 181

Doubles
- Musial-StL 51
- Galan-Bro 43
- Holmes-Bos 42

Triples
- Barrett-Pit 19
- Elliott-Pit 16
- Cavarretta-Chi 15
- Russell-Pit 14
- Musial-StL 14

Home Runs
- Nicholson-Chi 33
- Ott-NY 26
- Northey-Phi 22
- McCormick-Cin 20
- Kurowski-StL 20

Total Bases
- Nicholson-Chi 317
- Musial-StL 312
- Holmes-Bos 288
- Walker-Bro 283
- Northey-Phi 283

Runs Batted In
- Nicholson-Chi 122
- Elliott-Pit 108
- Northey-Phi 104
- Sanders-StL 102
- McCormick-Cin 102

Runs Produced
- Nicholson-Chi 205
- Musial-StL 194
- Elliott-Pit 183
- Cavarretta-Chi 183

Bases On Balls
- Galan-Bro 101
- Nicholson-Chi 93
- Ott-NY 90
- Musial-StL 90
- Barrett-Pit 86

Batting Average
- Walker-Bro .357
- Musial-StL .347
- Medwick-NY .337
- Hopp-StL .336
- Cavarretta-Chi .321

On-Base Percentage
- Musial-StL .440
- Walker-Bro .434
- Galan-Bro .426
- Ott-NY .423
- Hopp-StL .404

Slugging Average
- Musial-StL .549
- Nicholson-Chi .545
- Ott-NY .544
- Walker-Bro .529
- Weintraub-NY .524

On-Base Plus Slugging
- Musial-StL 990
- Ott-NY 967
- Walker-Bro 963
- Nicholson-Chi 935
- Galan-Bro 922

Adjusted OPS
- Musial-StL 174
- Walker-Bro 173
- Ott-NY 171
- Nicholson-Chi 162
- Galan-Bro 162

Batter Runs
- Musial-StL 60.9
- Walker-Bro 51.2
- Nicholson-Chi 47.4
- Galan-Bro 46.5
- Ott-NY 40.4

Adjusted Batter Runs
- Musial-StL 58.6
- Walker-Bro 53.4
- Galan-Bro 48.7
- Nicholson-Chi 48.2
- Ott-NY 40.7

Clutch Hitting Index
- Olmo-Bro 132
- Elliott-Pit 126
- Dahlgren-Pit 119
- Schultz-Bro 118
- Medwick-NY 117

Runs Created
- Musial-StL 145
- Nicholson-Chi 132
- Walker-Bro 128
- Galan-Bro 123
- Russell-Pit 112

Total Average
- Musial-StL 1.095
- Ott-NY 1.087
- Walker-Bro 1.034
- Nicholson-Chi 1.002
- Galan-Bro .992

Stolen Bases
- Barrett-Pit 28
- Lupien-Phi 18
- Hughes-Chi 16
- Hopp-StL 15
- Kerr-NY 14

Stolen Base Average

Stolen Base Runs

Fielding Runs
- Kerr-NY 16.8
- Luby-NY 16.4
- Williams-Cin 15.0
- Pafko-Chi 14.7
- Russell-Pit 13.3

Total Player Rating
- Musial-StL 5.4
- Walker-Bro 4.2
- Nicholson-Chi 4.0
- Galan-Bro 3.9
- McCormick-Cin 3.7

Wins
- Walters-Cin 23
- M.Cooper-StL 22
- Voiselle-NY 21
- Sewell-Pit 21
- Tobin-Bos 18

Win Percentage
- Wilks-StL .810
- Brecheen-StL .762
- M.Cooper-StL .759
- Walters-Cin .742
- Sewell-Pit .636

Games
- Adams-NY 65
- Webber-Bro 48
- Rescigno-Pit 48
- Voiselle-NY 43
- Tobin-Bos 43

Complete Games
- Tobin-Bos 28
- Walters-Cin 27
- Voiselle-NY 25
- Sewell-Pit 24
- M.Cooper-StL 22

Shutouts
- M.Cooper-StL 7
- Walters-Cin 6
- Tobin-Bos 5
- Lanier-StL 5
- Butcher-Pit 5

Saves
- Adams-NY 13
- Schmidt-StL 5
- Rescigno-Pit 5
- Davis-Bro 4
- Cuccurullo-Pit 4

Innings Pitched
- Voiselle-NY 312.2
- Tobin-Bos 299.1
- Sewell-Pit 286.0
- Walters-Cin 285.0
- Raffensberger-Phi 258.2

Fewest Hits/Game
- Walters-Cin 7.36
- Wilks-StL 7.50
- Lanier-StL 7.70
- Heusser-Cin 7.71
- Voiselle-NY 7.94

Fewest BB/Game
- Raffensberger-Phi 1.57
- Strincevich-Pit 1.75
- Davis-Bro 1.81
- Shoun-Cin 1.87
- Derringer-Chi 1.95

Strikeouts
- Voiselle-NY 161
- Lanier-StL 141
- Javery-Bos 137
- Raffensberger-Phi 136

Strikeouts/Game
- Lanier-StL 5.66
- Javery-Bos 4.85
- Raffensberger-Phi 4.73
- Voiselle-NY 4.63
- Melton-Bro 4.37

Ratio
- Wilks-StL 9.66
- Heusser-Cin 9.72
- De LaCruz-Cin 10.16
- Walters-Cin 10.23
- M.Cooper-StL 10.41

Earned Run Average
- Heusser-Cin 2.38
- Walters-Cin 2.40
- M.Cooper-StL 2.46
- Wilks-StL 2.64
- Lanier-StL 2.65

Adjusted ERA
- Heusser-Cin 146
- Walters-Cin 145
- M.Cooper-StL 143
- Wilks-StL 133
- Lanier-StL 133

Opponents' Batting Avg.
- Walters-Cin .219
- Wilks-StL .227
- Heusser-Cin .231
- Voiselle-NY .232
- Lanier-StL .234

Opponents' On-Base Pct.
- Wilks-StL .275
- Heusser-Cin .275
- Walters-Cin .281
- De LaCruz-Cin .284
- Raffensberger-Phi .285

Starter Runs
- Walters-Cin 38.3
- M.Cooper-StL 32.2
- Munger-StL 30.5
- Heusser-Cin 26.3
- Lanier-StL 24.0

Adjusted Starter Runs
- Walters-Cin 35.7
- M.Cooper-StL 30.5
- Munger-StL 30.1
- Tobin-Bos 25.6
- Heusser-Cin 24.5

Clutch Pitching Index
- Fleming-Chi 121
- Ostermueller-Br-Pt 120
- Chipman-Bro-Chi 119
- Wyse-Chi 113
- Javery-Bos 111

Relief Runs
- Karl-Phi 12.7
- Donnelly-StL 12.6

Adjusted Relief Runs
- Karl-Phi 12.7
- Donnelly-StL 12.2

Relief Ranking
- Karl-Phi 7.1
- Donnelly-StL 6.1

Total Pitcher Index
- Walters-Cin 4.9
- Tobin-Bos 4.5
- Munger-StL 3.7
- M.Cooper-StL 3.1
- Heusser-Cin 3.0

Total Baseball Ranking
- Musial-StL 5.4
- Walters-Cin 4.9
- Tobin-Bos 4.5
- Walker-Bro 4.2
- Nicholson-Chi 4.0

TEAM	G	W	L	PCT	GB	R	OR	AB	H	2B	3B	HR	BB	SO	AVG	OBP	SLG	OPS	OPS+	BR	BR+	PF	CHI	RC	SB	CS	SBA	SBR
STL	154	89	65	.578		684	587	5269	1328	223	45	72	531	604	.252	.323	.352	675	94	-4	-38	106	**110**	629	44	33	57	-2
DET	156	88	66	.571	1	658	**581**	5344	1405	220	44	60	**532**	500	.263	.332	.354	686	97	21	-13	106	100	641	61	55	53	-6
NY	154	83	71	.539	6	674	617	5331	1410	216	**74**	**96**	523	627	.264	.333	**.387**	**720**	108	**75**	52	103	95	707	91	31	**75**	**9**
BOS	156	77	77	.500	12	**739**	676	5400	1456	**277**	56	69	522	505	**.270**	**.336**	.380	716	**112**	73	**82**	99	103	**710**	60	40	60	-1
PHI	155	72	82	.468	17	525	594	5312	1364	169	47	36	422	490	.257	.314	.327	641	90	-73	-65	99	96	547	42	32	57	-2
CLE	155	72	82	.468	17	643	677	5481	**1458**	270	50	70	512	593	.266	.331	.372	703	111	46	73	96	93	684	48	42	53	-4
CHI	154	71	83	.461	18	543	662	5292	1307	210	55	23	439	**448**	.247	.307	.320	627	86	-97	-90	99	104	533	66	47	58	-2
WAS	154	64	90	.416	25	592	664	5319	1386	186	42	33	470	477	.261	.324	.330	654	97	-41	-13	96	101	594	**127**	59	68	7
TOT	619					5058		42748	11114	1771	413	459	3951	4244	.260	.326	.353	678							539	339	61	0

TEAM	CG	SH	SV	IP	H	H/G	HR	BB	SO	RAT	ERA	ERA+	OAV	OOB	PR	PR+	PF	CPI	FA	E	DP	FW	PW	BW	SBW	DIF
STL	71	16	17	1397^{1}	1392	9.0	58	469	**581**	12.1	3.17	114	.259	.320	41	63	105	**105**	.972	171	142	.5	6.7	-3.9	-.2	9.2
DET	**87**	**20**	8	1400	1373	8.9	**39**	452	568	11.9	**3.09**	**116**	.257	.318	**54**	**72**	104	103	.970	190	184	-.5	**7.6**	-1.3	-.6	6.0
NY	78	9	13	1390^{1}	1351	8.8	82	532	529	12.3	3.39	103	.257	.326	7	15	102	**105**	**.974**	**156**	170	**1.4**	1.6	5.5	**.9**	-3.3
BOS	58	7	17	1394^{1}	1404	9.1	66	592	524	13.1	3.83	89	.263	.339	-60	-66	99	98	.972	171	154	.6	-6.9	**8.7**	-.1	-2.1
PHI	72	10	14	1397^{1}	**1345**	**8.7**	58	**390**	534	**11.4**	3.26	107	**.252**	**.307**	27	35	102	93	.971	176	127	.3	3.7	-6.8	-.2	-1.8
CLE	48	7	**18**	1419^{1}	1428	9.1	40	621	524	13.2	3.66	90	.265	.344	-35	-58	96	102	**.974**	165	**192**	.9	-6.0	7.7	-.4	-7.0
CHI	64	5	17	1390^{2}	1411	9.2	68	420	481	12.0	3.58	96	.264	.320	-23	-23	100	97	.970	183	154	-.2	-2.4	-9.4	-.2	6.4
WAS	83	13	11	1381	1410	9.2	48	475	503	12.5	3.50	93	.264	.327	-10	-38	95	99	.964	218	156	-2.3	-3.9	-1.3	.7	-6.0
TOT	561	87	115	11170^{1}		9.0				12.3	3.44		.260	.326					.972	1430	1279					

Runs
Stirnweiss-NY 125
B.Johnson-Bos 106
Cullenbine-Cle 98
Doerr-Bos 95
Metkovich-Bos 94

Hits
Stirnweiss-NY 205
Boudreau-Cle 191
Spence-Was 187
Lindell-NY 178
Rocco-Cle 174

Doubles
Boudreau-Cle 45
Keltner-Cle 41
B.Johnson-Bos 40
Fox-Bos 37
Stirnweiss-NY 35

Triples
Stirnweiss-NY 16
Lindell-NY 16
Gutteridge-StL 11
Doerr-Bos 10

Home Runs
Etten-NY 22
Stephens-StL 20
York-Det 18
Spence-Was 18
Lindell-NY 18

Total Bases
Lindell-NY 297
Stirnweiss-NY 296
Spence-Was 288
B.Johnson-Bos 277

Runs Batted In
Stephens-StL 109
B.Johnson-Bos 106
Lindell-NY 103
Spence-Was 100
York-Det 98

Runs Produced
B.Johnson-Bos 195
Stephens-StL 180
Lindell-NY 176
Spence-Was 165
Cullenbine-Cle 162

Bases On Balls
Etten-NY 97
B.Johnson-Bos 95
Cullenbine-Cle 87
McQuinn-StL 85
Higgins-Det 81

Batting Average
Boudreau-Cle ...... .327
Doerr-Bos .... .325
B.Johnson-Bos ..... .324
Stirnweiss-NY ..... .319
Spence-Was .... .316

On-Base Percentage
B.Johnson-Bos ..... .431
Boudreau-Cle ...... .406
Doerr-Bos .... .399
Etten-NY .... .399
Byrnes-StL .... .396

Slugging Average
Doerr-Bos .... .528
B.Johnson-Bos ..... .528
Lindell-NY .... .500
Spence-Was .... .486

On-Base Plus Slugging
B.Johnson-Bos 959
Doerr-Bos 927
Spence-Was 877
Etten-NY 865
Lindell-NY 851

Adjusted OPS
B.Johnson-Bos 175
Doerr-Bos 166
Spence-Was 157
Boudreau-Cle 146
Etten-NY 142

Batter Runs
B.Johnson-Bos 52.9
Spence-Was 38.1
Doerr-Bos 38.0
Etten-NY 37.3
Wakefield-Det 36.7

Adjusted Batter Runs
B.Johnson-Bos 54.4
Spence-Was 43.3
Doerr-Bos 39.2
Boudreau-Cle 37.3
Etten-NY 33.8

Clutch Hitting Index
Christman-StL 134
Carnett-Chi 123
Mayo-Det 121
Torres-Was 115
Stephens-StL 112

Runs Created
Stirnweiss-NY 128
B.Johnson-Bos 124
Spence-Was 118
Etten-NY 114
Boudreau-Cle 112

Total Average
B.Johnson-Bos ..... .987
Doerr-Bos .... .945
Stirnweiss-NY ..... .910
Etten-NY .... .879
Spence-Was .... .856

Stolen Bases
Stirnweiss-NY 55
Case-Was 49
Myatt-Was 26
Moses-Chi 21
Gutteridge-StL 20

Stolen Base Average
Stirnweiss-NY 83.3
Moses-Chi 75.0
Case-Was 73.1
Myatt-Was 72.2
Gutteridge-StL 71.4

Stolen Base Runs
Stirnweiss-NY 8.3
Case-Was 4.5
Myatt-Was 2.2
Moses-Chi 2.2
Gutteridge-StL 1.6

Fielding Runs
Mayo-Det 29.4
Boudreau-Cle 25.8
Stirnweiss-NY 18.9
Spence-Was 18.6
Tucker-Chi 17.7

Total Player Rating
Boudreau-Cle 7.8
Stirnweiss-NY 6.9
Spence-Was 5.7
Doerr-Bos 5.2
B.Johnson-Bos 4.9

Wins
Newhouser-Det 29
Trout-Det 27
Potter-StL 19
Hughson-Bos 18

Win Percentage
Hughson-Bos .... .783
Newhouser-Det ..... .763
Potter-StL .... .731
Trout-Det .... .659
Borowy-NY .... .586

Games
Heving-Cle 63
Berry-Phi 53
Trout-Det 49
Newhouser-Det 47
Klieman-Cle 47

Complete Games
Trout-Det 33
Newhouser-Det 25

Shutouts
Trout-Det 7
Newhouser-Det 6
Jakucki-StL 4

Saves
Maltzberger-Chi 12
Caster-StL 12
Berry-Phi 12
Heving-Cle 10
Barrett-Bos 8

Innings Pitched
Trout-Det 352.1
Newhouser-Det 312.1
Newsom-Phi 265.0
Kramer-StL 257.0
Borowy-NY 252.2

Fewest Hits/Game
Gromek-Cle 7.07
Niggeling-Was 7.17
Newhouser-Det 7.61
Hughson-Bos 7.61
Borowy-NY 7.98

Fewest BB/Game
Harris-Phi 1.34
Leonard-Was 1.45
Bonham-NY 1.73
Gorsica-Det 1.78
Hamlin-Phi 1.80

Strikeouts
Newhouser-Det 187
Trout-Det 144
Newsom-Phi 142
Kramer-StL 124
Niggeling-Was 121

Strikeouts/Game
Newhouser-Det 5.39
Niggeling-Was 5.29
Gromek-Cle 5.08
Hughson-Bos 4.96
Newsom-Phi 4.82

Ratio
Hughson-Bos 9.52
Trout-Det 10.24
Leonard-Was 10.28
Gromek-Cle 10.30
Newhouser-Det 10.58

Earned Run Average
Trout-Det 2.12
Newhouser-Det 2.22
Hughson-Bos 2.26
Niggeling-Was 2.32
Kramer-StL 2.49

Adjusted ERA
Trout-Det 168
Newhouser-Det 161
Hughson-Bos 151
Kramer-StL 145
Niggeling-Was 141

Opponents' Batting Avg.
Gromek-Cle .... .219
Niggeling-Was ..... .221
Hughson-Bos .... .225
Newhouser-Det ..... .230
Borowy-NY .... .236

Opponents' On-Base Pct.
Hughson-Bos .... .267
Leonard-Was .... .284
Trout-Det .... .284
Gromek-Cle .... .290
Newhouser-Det ..... .293

Starter Runs
Trout-Det 51.3
Newhouser-Det 42.1
Kramer-StL 27.0
Hughson-Bos 26.5
Niggeling-Was 25.5

Adjusted Starter Runs
Trout-Det 54.5
Newhouser-Det 45.0
Kramer-StL 30.3
Hughson-Bos 26.0
Borowy-NY 23.5

Clutch Pitching Index
Donald-NY 129
Woods-Bos 122
Smith-Cle 116
Haynes-Chi 116
Bonham-NY 115

Relief Runs
Heving-Cle 19.6
Berry-Phi 18.4
Caster-StL 8.9
Maltzberger-Chi 4.8

Adjusted Relief Runs
Berry-Phi 18.8
Heving-Cle 18.6
Caster-StL 9.9
Maltzberger-Chi 4.8

Relief Ranking
Berry-Phi 31.9
Heving-Cle 18.9
Caster-StL 16.5
Maltzberger-Chi 8.5

Total Pitcher Index
Trout-Det 8.8
Newhouser-Det 6.2
Kramer-StL 4.1
Berry-Phi 3.6
Hughson-Bos 3.0

Total Baseball Ranking
Trout-Det 8.8
Boudreau-Cle 7.8
Stirnweiss-NY 6.9
Newhouser-Det 6.2
Spence-Was 5.7

TEAM	G	W	L	PCT	GB	R	OR	AB	H	2B	3B	HR	BB	SO	AVG	OBP	SLG	OPS	OPS+	BR	BR+	PF	CHI	RC	SB	CS	SBA	SBR
CHI	155	98	56	.636		735	**532**	5298	1465	229	52	57	554	462	**.277**	**.349**	.372	721	**109**	53	69	98	99	714	69			
STL	155	95	59	.617	3	756	582	5487	**1498**	256	44	64	515	488	.273	.338	.371	709	102	25	8	102	**103**	716	55			
BRO	155	87	67	.565	11	**795**	724	5418	1468	257	**71**	57	**629**	**434**	.271	**.349**	.376	**725**	**109**	**66**	**72**	99	102	**746**	75			
PIT	155	82	72	.532	16	753	686	5343	1425	**259**	56	72	590	480	.267	.342	.377	719	102	45	17	104	102	701	81			
NY	154	78	74	.513	19	668	701	5350	1439	175	35	**114**	501	457	.269	.336	**.379**	715	103	33	22	102	93	692	38			
BOS	154	67	85	.441	30	721	728	5441	1453	229	25	101	520	510	.267	.334	.374	708	102	20	16	101	100	692	**82**			
CIN	154	61	93	.396	37	536	694	5283	1317	221	26	56	392	532	.249	.304	.333	637	85	-122	-110	98	99	537	71			
PHI	154	46	108	.299	52	548	865	5203	1278	197	27	56	449	501	.246	.307	.326	633	84	-122	-107	97	102	527	54			
TOT	618					5512		42823	11343	1823	336	577	4150	3864	.265	.333	.364	696							525			

TEAM	CG	SH	SV	IP	H	H/G	HR	BB	SO	RAT	ERA	ERA+	OAV	OOB	PR	PR+	PF	CPI	FA	E	DP	FW	PW	BW	SBW	DIF
CHI	**86**	15	14	1366^1	**1301**	**8.6**	**57**	**385**	541	**11.3**	**2.98**	**123**	**.249**	**.304**	**125**	**106**	96	102	**.980**	**121**	124	**3.4**	**10.7**	7.0		.2
STL	77	**18**	9	1408^2	1351	8.7	70	497	510	12.0	3.24	116	.253	.320	88	80	99	**106**	.977	137	150	2.5	8.1	.9		6.8
BRO	61	7	18	1392^1	1357	8.8	74	586	**557**	12.8	3.71	101	.253	.331	15	7	99	98	.962	230	144	-3.2	.8	**7.3**		5.4
PIT	73	8	16	1387^1	1477	9.6	61	455	518	12.7	3.77	105	.272	.331	6	26	104	100	.971	178	141	-.0	2.7	1.8		.8
NY	53	13	21	1374^2	1401	9.2	85	528	529	12.8	4.06	96	.263	.332	-40	-22	103	95	.973	166	112	.6	-2.2	2.3		1.5
BOS	57	7	13	1391^2	1474	9.6	99	557	404	13.3	4.04	95	.272	.342	-37	-32	101	104	.969	193	**160**	-1.0	-3.2	1.7		-6.3
CIN	77	11	6	1365^2	1438	9.5	70	534	372	13.2	4.01	94	.271	.340	-31	-37	99	100	.976	146	138	1.8	-3.7	-11.0		-3.0
PHI	31	4	**26**	1352^2	1544	10.3	61	608	432	14.6	4.64	83	.285	.360	-126	-122	101	97	.962	234	150	-3.5	-12.2	-10.7		-4.5
TOT	515	83	123	11039^1		9.3				12.8	3.80		.265	.333					.972	1405	1119					

Runs
Stanky-Bro 128
Rosen-Bro 126
Holmes-Bos 125
Galan-Bro 114
Hack-Chi 110

Hits
Holmes-Bos 224
Rosen-Bro 197
Hack-Chi 193
Clay-Cin 184

Doubles
Holmes-Bos 47
Walker-Bro 42
Galan-Bro 36
Elliott-Pit 36
Cavarretta-Chi 34

Triples
Olmo-Bro 13
Pafko-Chi 12
Rucker-NY 11
Rosen-Bro 11
Cavarretta-Chi 10

Home Runs
Holmes-Bos 28
Workman-Bos 25
Adams-Phi-StL 22
Ott-NY 21
Kurowski-StL 21

Total Bases
Holmes-Bos 367
Adams-Phi-StL 279
Rosen-Bro 279
Walker-Bro 266
Kurowski-StL 261

Runs Batted In
Walker-Bro 124
Holmes-Bos 117
Pafko-Chi 110
Olmo-Bro 110
Adams-Phi-StL 109

Runs Produced
Walker-Bro 218
Holmes-Bos 214
Galan-Bro 197
Adams-Phi-StL 191
Rosen-Bro 189

Bases On Balls
Stanky-Bro 148
Galan-Bro 114
Hack-Chi 99
Nicholson-Chi 92
Sanders-StL 83

Batting Average
Cavarretta-Chi .... .355
Holmes-Bos .... .352
Rosen-Bro .... .325
Hack-Chi .... .323
Kurowski-StL .... .323

On-Base Percentage
Cavarretta-Chi .... .449
Galan-Bro .... .423
Hack-Chi .... .420
Holmes-Bos .... .420
Stanky-Bro .... .417

Slugging Average
Holmes-Bos .... .577
Kurowski-StL .... .511
Cavarretta-Chi .... .500
Ott-NY .... .499
Olmo-Bro .... .462

On-Base Plus Slugging
Holmes-Bos 997
Cavarretta-Chi 949
Ott-NY 910
Kurowski-StL 894
Galan-Bro 864

Adjusted OPS
Holmes-Bos 175
Cavarretta-Chi 167
Ott-NY 150
Kurowski-StL 144
Galan-Bro 142

Batter Runs
Holmes-Bos 62.9
Cavarretta-Chi 46.4
Galan-Bro 36.8
Ott-NY 33.4
Kurowski-StL 30.7

Adjusted Batter Runs
Holmes-Bos 62.1
Cavarretta-Chi 48.8
Galan-Bro 37.7
Ott-NY 32.0
Hack-Chi 31.7

Clutch Hitting Index
Walker-Bro 135
Elliott-Pit 135
Lowrey-Chi 129
Cavarretta-Chi 126
Olmo-Bro 125

Runs Created
Holmes-Bos 156
Cavarretta-Chi 119
Galan-Bro 116
Hack-Chi 111
Rosen-Bro 110

Total Average
Holmes-Bos 1.078
Cavarretta-Chi 1.037
Ott-NY .... .959
Galan-Bro .... .936
Kurowski-StL .... .876

Stolen Bases
Schoendienst-StL 26
Barrett-Pit 25
Clay-Cin 19

Stolen Base Average

Stolen Base Runs

Fielding Runs
Kerr-NY 28.2
Gillenwater-Bos 23.8
Coscarart-Pit 21.1
Hack-Chi 18.0
Walker-Bro 12.4

Total Player Rating
Holmes-Bos 5.2
Hack-Chi 5.0
Cavarretta-Chi 4.0
Stanky-Bro 3.5
Kurowski-StL 3.1

Wins
Barrett-Bos-StL 23
Wyse-Chi 22
Gregg-Bro 18
Burkhart-StL 18
Passeau-Chi 17

Win Percentage
Brecheen-StL .... .789
Burkhart-StL .... .692
Wyse-Chi .... .688
Barrett-Bos-StL .... .657
Passeau-Chi .... .654

Games
Karl-Phi 67
Adams-NY 65
Hutchings-Bos 57
Barrett-Bos-StL 45
Fox-Cin 45

Complete Games
Barrett-Bos-StL 24
Wyse-Chi 23
Passeau-Chi 19
Strincevich-Pit 18
Heusser-Cin 18

Shutouts
Passeau-Chi 5
Voiselle-NY 4
Heusser-Cin 4
Donnelly-StL 4
Burkhart-StL 4

Saves
Karl-Phi 15
Adams-NY 15
Rescigno-Pit 9

Innings Pitched
Barrett-Bos-StL 284.2
Wyse-Chi 278.1
Gregg-Bro 254.1
Roe-Pit 235.0
Voiselle-NY 232.1

Fewest Hits/Game
Prim-Chi 7.73
Brecheen-StL 7.78
Gregg-Bro 7.82
Mungo-NY 7.92
Passeau-Chi 8.13

Fewest BB/Game
Prim-Chi 1.25
Barrett-Bos-StL 1.71
Roe-Pit 1.76
Wyse-Chi 1.78
Strincevich-Pit 1.93

Strikeouts
Roe-Pit 148
Gregg-Bro 139
Voiselle-NY 115
Mungo-NY 101
Hutchings-Bos 99

Strikeouts/Game
Roe-Pit 5.67
Mungo-NY 4.97
Gregg-Bro 4.92
Hutchings-Bos 4.82
Prim-Chi 4.79

Ratio
Prim-Chi 9.04
Roe-Pit 10.53
Passeau-Chi 10.55
Brecheen-StL 10.58
Wyse-Chi 10.74

Earned Run Average
Borowy-Chi 2.13
Prim-Chi 2.40
Passeau-Chi 2.46
Brecheen-StL 2.52
Walters-Cin 2.68

Adjusted ERA
Prim-Chi 152
Brecheen-StL 149
Passeau-Chi 149
Walters-Cin 140
Roe-Pit 137

Opponents' Batting Avg.
Prim-Chi .... .228
Gregg-Bro .... .232
Brecheen-StL .... .238
Mungo-NY .... .238
Passeau-Chi .... .238

Opponents' On-Base Pct.
Prim-Chi .... .256
Passeau-Chi .... .289
Barrett-Bos-StL .... .295
Wyse-Chi .... .296
Roe-Pit .... .296

Starter Runs
Wyse-Chi 34.5
Passeau-Chi 33.8
Prim-Chi 25.8
Barrett-Bos-StL 25.2
Roe-Pit 24.2

Adjusted Starter Runs
Passeau-Chi 31.3
Wyse-Chi 31.1
Roe-Pit 26.9
Barrett-Bos-StL 24.0
Prim-Chi 24.0

Clutch Pitching Index
Butcher-Pit 124
Logan-Bos 124
Walters-Cin 124
Lee-Phi-Bos 123
Wyse-Chi 117

Relief Runs
Karl-Phi 16.3
Buker-Bro 4.9
Adams-NY 4.7
Chipman-Chi 2.4

Adjusted Relief Runs
Karl-Phi 16.7
Adams-NY 5.9
Buker-Bro 4.5
Chipman-Chi 1.3

Relief Ranking
Karl-Phi 16.5
Adams-NY 11.2
Buker-Bro 4.7
Chipman-Chi 1.4

Total Pitcher Index
Passeau-Chi 3.9
Wyse-Chi 3.4
Prim-Chi 3.2
Walters-Cin 2.9
Roe-Pit 2.7

Total Baseball Ranking
Holmes-Bos 5.2
Hack-Chi 5.0
Cavarretta-Chi 4.0
Passeau-Chi 3.9
Stanky-Bro 3.5

TEAM	G	W	L	PCT	GB	R	OR	AB	H	2B	3B	HR	BB	SO	AVG	OBP	SLG	OPS	OPS+	BR	BR+	PF	CHI	RC	SB	CS	SBA	SBR
DET	155	88	65	.575		633	565	5257	1345	**227**	47	77	517	533	.256	.324	.361	685	98	20	-17	106	102	627	60	54	53	-6
WAS	156	87	67	.565	1.5	622	562	5326	1375	197	**63**	27	545	489	.258	.330	.334	664	107	-8	48	92	103	612	**110**	65	**63**	**1**
STL	154	81	70	.536	6	597	**548**	5227	1302	215	37	63	500	555	.249	.316	.341	657	91	-29	-56	105	**105**	584	25	31	45	-5
NY	152	81	71	.533	6.5	**676**	606	5176	1343	189	61	**93**	**618**	567	.259	**.343**	**.373**	**716**	108	**90**	**59**	105	97	**698**	64	43	60	-1
CLE	147	73	72	.503	11	557	**548**	4898	1249	216	48	65	505	578	.255	.326	.359	685	**109**	23	49	96	95	588	19	31	38	-7
CHI	150	71	78	.477	15	596	633	5077	1330	204	55	22	470	467	**.262**	.326	.337	663	101	-13	3	97	**105**	571	78	54	59	-2
BOS	157	71	83	.461	17.5	599	674	5367	**1393**	225	44	50	541	534	.260	.330	.346	676	100	12	-2	102	96	634	72	50	59	-2
PHI	153	52	98	.347	34.5	494	638	5296	1297	201	37	33	449	**463**	.245	.306	.316	622	86	-96	-94	100	98	523	25	45	36	-10
TOT	612					4774		41624	10634	1674	392	430	4145	4186	.256	.326	.346	671							453	373	55	-31

TEAM	CG	SH	SV	IP	H	H/G	HR	BB	SO	RAT	ERA	ERA+	OAV	OOB	PR	PR+	PF	CPI	FA	E	DP	FW	PW	BW	SBW	DIF
DET	78	**19**	**16**	1393^{2}	1305	8.5	48	538	**588**	12.1	2.99	**118**	.250	.322	58	**78**	105	**108**	.975	158	173	.4	**8.4**	-1.8	-.2	4.9
WAS	82	**19**	11	1412^{1}	1307	**8.4**	42	**440**	550	**11.3**	**2.93**	106	**.242**	**.301**	**69**	30	92	93	.970	183	124	-.9	3.3	5.2	**.5**	2.1
STL	**91**	10	8	1382^{2}	1307	8.6	59	506	570	11.9	3.15	112	.249	.316	34	55	105	101	.976	143	123	1.2	5.9	-5.9	-.1	4.6
NY	78	9	14	1355	1277	8.5	66	485	474	11.8	3.46	100	.250	.316	-13	1	103	93	.971	175	170	-.7	.2	**6.4**	.3	-.9
CLE	76	14	12	1302^{1}	**1269**	8.8	**39**	501	497	12.4	3.32	98	.257	.328	8	-9	97	102	**.977**	**126**	149	**1.8**	-.9	5.3	-.3	-5.1
CHI	84	13	13	1330^{2}	1400	9.5	63	448	486	12.8	3.70	90	.270	.332	-49	-56	99	100	.970	180	139	-1.1	-5.9	.4	.2	3.2
BOS	71	15	13	1390^{2}	1389	9.0	58	656	490	13.5	3.80	90	.264	.348	-67	-60	101	102	.973	169	**198**	-.0	-6.4	-.2	.2	.6
PHI	65	11	8	1381	1380	9.0	55	571	531	12.9	3.63	95	.262	.337	-40	-29	102	101	.973	168	160	-.2	-3.1	-10.0	-.7	-8.8
TOT	625	110	95	10948^{1}		8.8				12.3	3.37		.256	.326					.974	1302	1236					

Runs
Stirnweiss-NY 107
Stephens-StL 90
Cullenbine-Cle-Det 83

Hits
Stirnweiss-NY 195
Moses-Chi 168
Stephens-StL 165
Hall-Phi 161
Etten-NY 161

Doubles
Moses-Chi 35
Stirnweiss-NY 32
Binks-Was 32
McQuinn-StL 31

Triples
Stirnweiss-NY 22
Moses-Chi 15
Kuhel-Was 13
Dickshot-Chi 10
Peck-Phi 9

Home Runs
Stephens-StL 24
Cullenbine-Cle-Det 18
York-Det 18
Etten-NY 18
Heath-Cle 15

Total Bases
Stirnweiss-NY 301
Stephens-StL 270
Etten-NY 247
York-Det 246
Moses-Chi 239

Runs Batted In
Etten-NY 111
Cullenbine-Cle-Det 93
Stephens-StL 89
York-Det 87
Binks-Was 81

Runs Produced
Etten-NY 170
Stirnweiss-NY 161
Cullenbine-Cle-Det 158
Stephens-StL 155
Kuhel-Was 146

Bases On Balls
Cullenbine-Cle-Det 113
Lake-Bos 106
Grimes-NY 97
Etten-NY 90
Kuhel-Was 79

Batting Average
Stirnweiss-NY 309
Cuccinello-Chi 308
Dickshot-Chi 302
Estalella-Phi 299
Myatt-Was 296

On-Base Percentage
Lake-Bos 412
Cullenbine-Cle-Det 402
Estalella-Phi 399
Grimes-NY 395
Etten-NY 387

Slugging Average
Stirnweiss-NY 476
Stephens-StL 473
Cullenbine-Cle-Det 444
Etten-NY 437
Estalella-Phi 435

On-Base Plus Slugging
Stirnweiss-NY 862
Cullenbine-Cle-Det 846
Estalella-Phi 834
Stephens-StL 825
Etten-NY 824

Adjusted OPS
Stirnweiss-NY 143
Estalella-Phi 142
Kuhel-Was 137
Cullenbine-Cle-Det 137
Lake-Bos 136

Batter Runs
Stirnweiss-NY 39.1
Cullenbine-Cle-Det 35.1
Etten-NY 29.9
Heath-Cle 29.4
Lake-Bos 28.7

Adjusted Batter Runs
Stirnweiss-NY 34.2
Heath-Cle 32.7
Cullenbine-Cle-Det 29.4
Kuhel-Was 27.0
Lake-Bos 26.7

Clutch Hitting Index
Schalk-Chi 135
Michaels-Chi 132
Tresh-Chi 130
Etten-NY 121
Binks-Was 119

Runs Created
Stirnweiss-NY 121
Cullenbine-Cle-Det 106
Etten-NY 98
Stephens-StL 98
Moses-Chi 97

Total Average
Cullenbine-Cle-Det 888
Stirnweiss-NY 855
Lake-Bos 849
Etten-NY 794
Estalella-Phi 789

Stolen Bases
Stirnweiss-NY 33
Myatt-Was 30
Case-Was 30
Metkovich-Bos 19
Dickshot-Chi 18

Stolen Base Average
Dickshot-Chi 85.7
Metkovich-Bos 76.0
Myatt-Was 73.2
Stirnweiss-NY 66.0
Case-Was 65.2

Stolen Base Runs
Dickshot-Chi 2.9
Myatt-Was 2.8
Metkovich-Bos 2.1
Stirnweiss-NY 1.3
Crosetti-NY 1.2

Fielding Runs
Hall-Phi 26.1
Stirnweiss-NY 25.5
Webb-Det 23.0
Newsome-Bos 22.2
Kell-Phi 21.7

Total Player Rating
Stirnweiss-NY 7.2
Lake-Bos 5.9
Cullenbine-Cle-Det 3.2
Mayo-Det 3.1
Newsome-Bos 2.8

Wins
Newhouser-Det 25
Ferriss-Bos 21
Wolff-Was 20
Gromek-Cle 19

Win Percentage
Newhouser-Det 735
Leonard-Was 708
Gromek-Cle 679
Ferriss-Bos 677
Wolff-Was 667

Games
Berry-Phi 52
Reynolds-Cle 44
Pieretti-Was 44
Trout-Det 41
Newhouser-Det 40

Complete Games
Newhouser-Det 29
Ferriss-Bos 26
Wolff-Was 21
Potter-StL 21
Gromek-Cle 21

Shutouts
Newhouser-Det 8
Ferriss-Bos 5
Benton-Det 5

Saves
Turner-NY 10
Berry-Phi 5

Innings Pitched
Newhouser-Det . . . 313.1
Ferriss-Bos 264.2
Newsom-Phi 257.1
Potter-StL 255.1
Gromek-Cle 251.0

Fewest Hits/Game
Newhouser-Det 6.86
Wolff-Was 7.20
Potter-StL 7.47
Lee-Chi 8.20
Niggeling-Was 8.20

Fewest BB/Game
Bonham-NY 1.10
Leonard-Was 1.46
Wolff-Was 1.91
Overmire-Det 2.33
Gromek-Cle 2.37

Strikeouts
Newhouser-Det 212
Potter-StL 129
Newsom-Phi 127
Reynolds-Cle 112

Strikeouts/Game
Newhouser-Det 6.09
Kramer-StL 4.62
Niggeling-Was 4.58
Potter-StL 4.55
Newsom-Phi 4.44

Ratio
Wolff-Was 9.14
Potter-StL 9.90
Newhouser-Det . . . 10.02
Leonard-Was 10.21
Bonham-NY 10.41

Earned Run Average
Newhouser-Det 1.81
Benton-Det 2.02
Wolff-Was 2.12
Leonard-Was 2.13
Lee-Chi 2.44

Adjusted ERA
Newhouser-Det 194
Benton-Det 174
Wolff-Was 146
Leonard-Was 146
Potter-StL 143

Opponents' Batting Avg.
Newhouser-Det 211
Wolff-Was 215
Potter-StL 226
Niggeling-Was 240
Benton-Det 241

Opponents' On-Base Pct.
Wolff-Was 258
Potter-StL 279
Leonard-Was 279
Newhouser-Det 281
Bonham-NY 288

Starter Runs
Newhouser-Det 54.1
Wolff-Was 34.5
Leonard-Was 29.8
Benton-Det 28.7
Potter-StL 25.5

Adjusted Starter Runs
Newhouser-Det 56.9
Benton-Det 30.5
Wolff-Was 29.5
Potter-StL 28.5
Leonard-Was 25.4

Clutch Pitching Index
Benton-Det 139
Lee-Chi 121
Shirley-StL 116
Hollingsworth-StL . . . 116
Ferriss-Bos 114

Relief Runs
Berry-Phi 14.7
Holcombe-NY 9.7
Barrett-Bos 7.2
Zoldak-StL 0

Adjusted Relief Runs
Berry-Phi 15.4
Holcombe-NY 10.0
Barrett-Bos 7.4
Zoldak-StL 1.2

Relief Ranking
Berry-Phi 17.3
Holcombe-NY 9.8
Barrett-Bos 6.0
Zoldak-StL 8

Total Pitcher Index
Newhouser-Det 7.5
Potter-StL 3.3
Ferriss-Bos 3.3
Benton-Det 3.0
Leonard-Was 3.0

Total Baseball Ranking
Newhouser-Det 7.5
Stirnweiss-NY 7.2
Lake-Bos 5.9
Potter-StL 3.3
Ferriss-Bos 3.3

TEAM	G	W	L	PCT	GB	R	OR	AB	H	2B	3B	HR	BB	SO	AVG	OBP	SLG	OPS	OPS+	BR	BR+	PF	CHI	RC	SB	CS	SBA	SBR
STL	156	98	58	.628		**712**	**545**	5372	**1426**	**265**	56	81	530	537	**.265**	.334	**.381**	**715**	105	54	26	104	**105**	**702**	58			
BRO	157	96	60	.615	2	701	570	5285	1376	233	**66**	55	**691**	575	.260	**.348**	.361	709	**106**	**60**	**53**	101	101	699	**100**			
CHI	155	82	71	.536	14.5	626	581	5298	1344	223	50	56	586	599	.254	.331	.346	677	100	-9	4	98	102	622	43			
BOS	154	81	72	.529	15.5	630	592	5225	1377	238	48	44	558	**468**	.264	.337	.353	690	101	16	9	101	100	641	60			
PHI	155	69	85	.448	28	560	705	5233	1351	209	40	80	417	590	.258	.315	.359	674	100	-30	-13	97	99	598	41			
CIN	156	67	87	.435	30	523	570	5291	1262	206	33	65	493	604	.239	.307	.327	634	88	-101	-81	96	102	546	82			
PIT	155	63	91	.409	34	552	668	5199	1300	202	52	60	592	555	.250	.328	.344	672	95	-18	-32	103	93	602	48			
NY	154	61	93	.396	36	612	685	5191	1326	176	37	**121**	532	546	.255	.328	.374	702	104	27	23	101	97	644	46			
TOT	621					4916		42094	10762	1752	382	562	4399	4474	.256	.329	.356	684							478			

TEAM	CG	SH	SV	IP	H	H/G	HR	BB	SO	RAT	ERA	ERA+	OAV	OOB	PR	PR+	PF	CPI	FA	E	DP	FW	PW	BW	SBW	DIF
STL	**75**	**18**	15	1397	1326	8.6	63	493	607	12.0	**3.01**	**115**	.254	.322	**63**	**69**	101	**108**	**.980**	**124**	167	**2.1**	**7.4**	2.8		7.9
BRO	52	14	**28**	1418	**1280**	**8.2**	58	671	**647**	12.6	3.05	111	**.243**	.331	58	53	99	107	.972	174	154	-.8	5.7	**5.7**		7.7
CHI	59	15	11	1393	1370	8.9	58	527	619	12.4	3.25	102	.256	.325	26	15	97	102	.976	146	119	.7	1.6	.5		2.8
BOS	74	10	12	1371	1291	8.5	76	478	566	11.8	3.35	102	.249	**.314**	10	13	101	93	.972	169	129	-.7	1.4	1.0		3.0
PHI	55	11	23	1369	1442	9.5	73	542	490	13.3	4.00	86	.273	.344	-88	-85	101	98	.975	148	144	.6	-9.0	-1.3		1.9
CIN	69	17	11	1413[1]	1334	8.5	70	**467**	506	**11.6**	3.08	109	.252	**.314**	53	43	98	101	.975	155	**192**	.3	4.6	-8.6		-6.1
PIT	61	10	6	1370	1406	9.3	**50**	561	458	13.1	3.72	95	.269	.342	-46	-28	103	99	.970	184	127	-1.5	-2.9	-3.3		-6.0
NY	47	8	13	1353[1]	1313	8.8	114	660	581	13.3	3.92	88	.256	.343	-76	-71	101	100	.973	159	121	-.1	-7.5	2.5		-10.7
TOT	492	103	119	11084[2]		8.8				12.5	3.42		.256	.329					.975	1259	1153					

Runs
Musial-StL 124
Slaughter-StL 100
Stanky-Bro 98
Schoendienst-StL . . . 94
Cavarretta-Chi 89

Hits
Musial-StL 228
Walker-Bro 184
Slaughter-StL 183
Holmes-Bos 176
Schoendienst-StL . . . 170

Doubles
Musial-StL 50
Holmes-Bos 35
Kurowski-StL 32
Herman-Bro-Bos 31

Triples
Musial-StL 20
Reese-Bro 10
Cavarretta-Chi 10
Walker-Bro 9

Home Runs
Kiner-Pit 23
Mize-NY 22
Slaughter-StL 18
Ennis-Phi 17

Total Bases
Musial-StL 366
Slaughter-StL 283
Ennis-Phi 262
Walker-Bro 258
Holmes-Bos 241

Runs Batted In
Slaughter-StL 130
Walker-Bro 116
Musial-StL 103
Kurowski-StL 89
Kiner-Pit 81

Runs Produced
Slaughter-StL 212
Musial-StL 211
Walker-Bro 187
Cavarretta-Chi 159
Holmes-Bos 153

Bases On Balls
Stanky-Bro 137
Fletcher-Pit 111
Cavarretta-Chi 88
Reese-Bro 87
Hack-Chi 83

Batting Average
Musial-StL 365
Hopp-Bos 333
Walker-Bro 319
Ennis-Phi 313
Holmes-Bos 310

On-Base Percentage
Stanky-Bro 436
Musial-StL 434
Cavarretta-Chi 401
Herman-Bro-Bos 395
Walker-Bro 391

Slugging Average
Musial-StL 587
Ennis-Phi 485
Slaughter-StL 465
Kurowski-StL 462
Walker-Bro 448

On-Base Plus Slugging
Musial-StL 1021
Kurowski-StL 853
Ennis-Phi 849
Walker-Bro 839
Slaughter-StL 838

Adjusted OPS
Musial-StL 180
Ennis-Phi 144
Cavarretta-Chi 140
Walker-Bro 136
Kurowski-StL 136

Batter Runs
Musial-StL 70.9
Mize-NY 43.6
Kurowski-StL 29.1
Walker-Bro 28.9
Slaughter-StL 28.6

Adjusted Batter Runs
Musial-StL 64.9
Mize-NY 43.0
Cavarretta-Chi 29.6
Ennis-Phi 28.0
Walker-Bro 27.9

Clutch Hitting Index
Walker-Bro 138
Slaughter-StL 131
Elliott-Pit 127
Fletcher-Pit 123
Reiser-Bro 120

Runs Created
Musial-StL 164
Slaughter-StL 110
Walker-Bro 104
Mize-NY 100
Kurowski-StL 97

Total Average
Musial-StL 1.114
Stanky-Bro 890
Reiser-Bro 877
Kurowski-StL 855
Walker-Bro 848

Stolen Bases
Reiser-Bro 34
Haas-Cin 22
Hopp-Bos 21
Adams-Cin 16
Walker-Bro 14

Stolen Base Average

Stolen Base Runs

Fielding Runs
Marion-StL 18.8
Wyrostek-Phi 17.2
Ennis-Phi 13.6
Handley-Pit 13.2
Mueller-Cin 9.8

Total Player Rating
Musial-StL 5.9
Mize-NY 4.6
Ennis-Phi 3.3
Stanky-Bro 2.9
Cavarretta-Chi 2.7

Wins
Pollet-StL 21
Sain-Bos 20
Higbe-Bro 17
Dickson-StL 15
Brecheen-StL 15

Win Percentage
Dickson-StL 714
Higbe-Bro 680
Pollet-StL 677
Sain-Bos 588
Brecheen-StL 500

Games
Trinkle-NY 48
Dickson-StL 47
Behrman-Bro 47
Casey-Bro 46

Complete Games
Sain-Bos 24
Pollet-StL 22
Koslo-NY 17
Ostermueller-Pit 16
Cooper-Bos 15

Shutouts
Brecheen-StL 5
Blackwell-Cin 5
VanderMeer-Cin 4
Pollet-StL 4
Cooper-Bos 4

Saves
Raffensberger-Phi 6
Pollet-StL 5
Karl-Phi 5
Herring-Bro 5
Casey-Bro 5

Innings Pitched
Pollet-StL 266.0
Koslo-NY 265.1
Sain-Bos 265.0
Brecheen-StL 231.1
Schmitz-Chi 224.1

Fewest Hits/Game
Kennedy-NY 7.38
Schmitz-Chi 7.38
Blackwell-Cin 7.41
Higbe-Bro 7.60
Sain-Bos 7.64

Fewest BB/Game
Cooper-Bos 1.76
Raffensberger-Phi 1.79
Beggs-Cin 1.85
Heusser-Cin 2.09
Strincevich-Pit 2.25

Strikeouts
Schmitz-Chi 135
Higbe-Bro 134
Sain-Bos 129
Koslo-NY 121
Brecheen-StL 117

Strikeouts/Game
Higbe-Bro 5.72
Schmitz-Chi 5.42
Blackwell-Cin 4.63
Brecheen-StL 4.55
Voiselle-NY 4.50

Ratio
Cooper-Bos 9.95
Beggs-Cin 10.18
Sain-Bos 10.66
Dickson-StL 10.74
Pollet-StL 10.79

Earned Run Average
Pollet-StL 2.10
Sain-Bos 2.21
Beggs-Cin 2.32
Blackwell-Cin 2.45
Brecheen-StL 2.49

Adjusted ERA
Pollet-StL 165
Sain-Bos 155
Beggs-Cin 144
Brecheen-StL 139
Blackwell-Cin 136

Opponents' Batting Avg.
Schmitz-Chi 221
Kennedy-NY 224
Blackwell-Cin 226
Higbe-Bro 229
Sain-Bos 230

Opponents' On-Base Pct.
Cooper-Bos 276
Beggs-Cin 287
Sain-Bos 294
Dickson-StL 295
Pollet-StL 300

Starter Runs
Pollet-StL 38.9
Sain-Bos 35.5
Brecheen-StL 23.7
Beggs-Cin 23.1
Blackwell-Cin 20.7

Adjusted Starter Runs
Pollet-StL 39.6
Sain-Bos 35.8
Brecheen-StL 24.5
Beggs-Cin 22.1
Rowe-Phi 19.8

Clutch Pitching Index
Hatten-Bro 129
Pollet-StL 127
Beggs-Cin 124
Wyse-Chi 117
Ostermueller-Pit 110

Relief Runs
Casey-Bro 15.8
Thompson-NY 14.8
Malloy-Cin 5.3
Budnick-NY 2.5
Herring-Bro 6

Adjusted Relief Runs
Casey-Bro 15.6
Thompson-NY 14.8
Malloy-Cin 4.9
Budnick-NY 2.8
Wilks-StL 5

Relief Ranking
Casey-Bro 24.3
Thompson-NY 23.5
Malloy-Cin 4.6
Budnick-NY 1.6
Wilks-StL 4

Total Pitcher Index
Sain-Bos 5.9
Pollet-StL 5.0
Brecheen-StL 3.1
Beggs-Cin 3.0
Casey-Bro 2.9

Total Baseball Ranking
Musial-StL 5.9
Sain-Bos 5.9
Pollet-StL 5.0
Mize-NY 4.6
Ennis-Phi 3.3

TEAM	G	W	L	PCT	GB	R	OR	AB	H	2B	3B	HR	BB	SO	AVG	OBP	SLG	OPS	OPS+	BR	BR+	PF	CHI	RC	SB	CS	SBA	SBR
BOS	156	104	50	.675		**792**	594	5318	**1441**	**268**	50	109	**687**	661	**.271**	**.356**	**.402**	**758**	**113**	**136**	**94**	106	101	**790**	45	36	56	-3
DET	155	92	62	.597	12	704	567	5318	1373	212	41	108	622	616	.258	.337	.374	711	100	42	3	106	103	698	65	41	**61**	0
NY	154	87	67	.565	17	684	**547**	5139	1275	208	50	**136**	627	706	.248	.334	.387	721	107	55	46	101	101	695	48	35	58	-2
WAS	155	76	78	.494	28	608	706	5337	1388	260	**63**	60	511	641	.260	.327	.366	693	106	1	41	94	96	653	51	50	50	-6
CHI	155	74	80	.481	30	562	595	5312	1364	206	44	37	501	600	.257	.323	.333	656	94	-64	-42	96	100	579	**78**	64	55	-5
CLE	156	68	86	.442	36	537	638	5242	1285	233	56	79	506	697	.245	.313	.356	669	99	-49	-9	94	94	596	57	49	54	-5
STL	156	66	88	.429	38	621	710	5373	1350	220	46	84	465	713	.251	.313	.356	669	89	-53	-80	105	**108**	601	23	35	40	-7
PHI	155	49	105	.318	55	529	680	5200	1317	220	51	40	482	**594**	.253	.318	.338	656	91	-68	-65	99	97	574	39	30	57	-2
TOT	621					5037		42239	10793	1827	401	653	4401	5228	.256	.328	.365	692							406	340	54	-30

TEAM	CG	SH	SV	IP	H	H/G	HR	BB	SO	RAT	ERA	ERA+	OAV	OOB	PR	PR+	PF	CPI	FA	E	DP	FW	PW	BW	SBW	DIF
BOS	79	15	**20**	1396[2]	1359	8.8	89	501	667	12.1	3.39	108	.254	.319	19	42	105	100	**.977**	**139**	163	**1.5**	4.5	**9.9**	.0	11.3
DET	**94**	**18**	15	1402	1277	**8.2**	97	**497**	**896**	**11.5**	3.22	**114**	**.241**	**.307**	45	**65**	104	95	.974	155	138	.5	**6.9**	.4	**.4**	7.1
NY	68	17	17	1361	**1232**	**8.2**	**66**	552	653	11.9	3.14	110	.243	.319	56	49	99	100	.975	150	**174**	.7	5.2	4.9	.2	-.8
WAS	71	8	10	1396[1]	1459	9.5	81	547	537	13.2	3.74	89	.269	.339	-36	-64	96	103	.966	211	162	-2.8	-6.7	4.3	-.2	4.5
CHI	62	9	16	1392[1]	1348	8.8	80	508	550	12.2	**3.10**	110	.255	.323	**63**	50	97	**110**	.972	175	170	-.7	5.3	-4.4	-.1	-2.9
CLE	63	16	13	1388[2]	1282	8.4	84	649	789	12.7	3.62	91	.245	.331	-17	-51	94	96	.975	147	147	1.0	-5.3	-.9	-.1	-3.5
STL	63	13	12	1382[1]	1465	9.6	73	573	574	13.4	3.96	94	.272	.343	-69	-32	107	99	.974	159	157	.3	-3.3	-8.3	-.3	.8
PHI	61	10	5	1342[2]	1371	9.2	83	577	562	13.3	3.91	91	.264	.340	-59	-52	101	98	.971	167	141	-.2	-5.4	-6.8	.2	-15.6
TOT	561	106	108	11062		8.8				12.5	3.51		.256	.328					.973	1303	1252					

Runs
Williams-Bos 142
Pesky-Bos 115
Lake-Det 105
Keller-NY 98
Doerr-Bos 95

Hits
Pesky-Bos 208
Vernon-Was 207
Appling-Chi 180
Williams-Bos 176
Lewis-Was 170

Doubles
Vernon-Was 51
Spence-Was 50
Pesky-Bos 43
Williams-Bos 37
Doerr-Bos 34

Triples
Edwards-Cle 16
Lewis-Was 13
Kell-Phi-Det 10
Spence-Was 10
Keller-NY 10

Home Runs
Greenberg-Det 44
Williams-Bos 38
Keller-NY 30
Seerey-Cle 26
DiMaggio-NY 25

Total Bases
Williams-Bos 343
Greenberg-Det 316
Vernon-Was 298
Spence-Was 287
Keller-NY 287

Runs Batted In
Greenberg-Det 127
Williams-Bos 123
York-Bos 119
Doerr-Bos 116
Keller-NY 101

Runs Produced
Williams-Bos 227
Doerr-Bos 193
York-Bos 180
Greenberg-Det 174
Keller-NY 169

Bases On Balls
Williams-Bos 156
Keller-NY 113
Lake-Det 103
Cullenbine-Det 88
Henrich-NY 87

Batting Average
Vernon-Was .... .353
Williams-Bos .... .342
Pesky-Bos .... .335
Kell-Phi-Det .... .322
DiMaggio-Bos .... .316

On-Base Percentage
Williams-Bos .... .497
Keller-NY .... .405
Vernon-Was .... .403
Pesky-Bos .... .401
DiMaggio-Bos .... .393

Slugging Average
Williams-Bos .... .667
Greenberg-Det ..... .604
Keller-NY .... .533
DiMaggio-NY .... .511
Edwards-Cle .... .509

On-Base Plus Slugging
Williams-Bos 1164
Greenberg-Det 977
Keller-NY 938
Vernon-Was 910
DiMaggio-NY 878

Adjusted OPS
Williams-Bos 211
Vernon-Was 163
Greenberg-Det 160
Keller-NY 158
Edwards-Cle 151

Batter Runs
Williams-Bos 94.2
Greenberg-Det 46.1
Keller-NY 45.9
Cullenbine-Det 42.2
Vernon-Was 40.3

Adjusted Batter Runs
Williams-Bos 85.4
Vernon-Was 47.2
Keller-NY 44.4
Greenberg-Det 39.8
Cullenbine-Det 37.2

Clutch Hitting Index
Travis-Was 136
York-Bos 135
Doerr-Bos 126
Henrich-NY 119
Heath-Was-StL 109

Runs Created
Williams-Bos 188
Keller-NY 127
Vernon-Was 120
Greenberg-Det 119
Pesky-Bos 111

Total Average
Williams-Bos 1.431
Greenberg-Det 1.010
Keller-NY 1.005
Vernon-Was .... .873
DiMaggio-NY .... .862

Stolen Bases
Case-Cle 28
Stirnweiss-NY 18
Lake-Det 15

Stolen Base Average
Stirnweiss-NY 75.0
Case-Cle 71.8

Stolen Base Runs
Case-Cle 2.3
Stirnweiss-NY 1.9
Dillinger-StL 1.4
Evers-Det 1.2
Wright-Chi 1.1

Fielding Runs
Doerr-Bos 26.8
Gordon-NY 21.5
Boudreau-Cle 16.2
Rizzuto-NY 13.1
Pesky-Bos 12.0

Total Player Rating
Williams-Bos 7.5
Doerr-Bos 4.7
Pesky-Bos 4.4
Vernon-Was 4.2
Greenberg-Det 3.9

Wins
Newhouser-Det 26
Feller-Cle 26
Ferriss-Bos 25
Hughson-Bos 20
Chandler-NY 20

Win Percentage
Ferriss-Bos .... .806
Newhouser-Det ..... .743
Chandler-NY .... .714
Harris-Bos .... .654
Hughson-Bos .... .645

Games
Feller-Cle 48
Savage-Phi 40
Ferriss-Bos 40
Hughson-Bos 39
Caldwell-Chi 39

Complete Games
Feller-Cle 36
Newhouser-Det 29
Ferriss-Bos 26
Trout-Det 23
Hughson-Bos 21

Shutouts
Feller-Cle 10
Newhouser-Det 6
Hughson-Bos 6
Ferriss-Bos 6
Chandler-NY 6

Saves
Klinger-Bos 9
Caldwell-Chi 8
Murphy-NY 7
Ferrick-Cle-StL 6

Innings Pitched
Feller-Cle 371.1
Newhouser-Det 292.2
Hughson-Bos 278.0
Trout-Det 276.1
Ferriss-Bos 274.0

Fewest Hits/Game
Newhouser-Det 6.61
Feller-Cle 6.71
Chandler-NY 6.99
Embree-Cle 7.65
Bevens-NY 7.68

Fewest BB/Game
Hughson-Bos 1.65
Lopat-Chi 1.87
Leonard-Was 2.00
Flores-Phi 2.21
Ferriss-Bos 2.33

Strikeouts
Feller-Cle 348
Newhouser-Det 275
Hughson-Bos 172
Trucks-Det 161
Trout-Det 151

Strikeouts/Game
Newhouser-Det 8.46
Feller-Cle 8.43
Trucks-Det 6.12
Hutchinson-Det 6.00
Hughson-Bos 5.57

Ratio
Newhouser-Det 9.66
Hughson-Bos 9.87
Chandler-NY 10.18
Lopat-Chi 10.32
Feller-Cle 10.49

Earned Run Average
Newhouser-Det 1.94
Chandler-NY 2.10
Feller-Cle 2.18
Bevens-NY 2.23
Flores-Phi 2.32

Adjusted ERA
Newhouser-Det 189
Chandler-NY 164
Trout-Det 156
Bevens-NY 154
Flores-Phi 153

Opponents' Batting Avg.
Newhouser-Det ..... .201
Feller-Cle .... .208
Chandler-NY .... .218
Embree-Cle .... .227
Bevens-NY .... .232

Opponents' On-Base Pct.
Newhouser-Det ..... .269
Hughson-Bos .... .274
Chandler-NY .... .288
Lopat-Chi .... .288
Feller-Cle .... .291

Starter Runs
Feller-Cle 54.5
Newhouser-Det 50.9
Chandler-NY 40.2
Trout-Det 35.6
Bevens-NY 35.2

Adjusted Starter Runs
Newhouser-Det 53.5
Feller-Cle 49.2
Chandler-NY 39.3
Trout-Det 38.5
Bevens-NY 34.2

Clutch Pitching Index
Grove-Chi 126
Flores-Phi 121
Trout-Det 119
Haynes-Chi 118
Bevens-NY 115

Relief Runs
Caldwell-Chi 14.3
Lemon-Cle 10.6
Klinger-Bos 7.2
Kinder-StL 1.7

Adjusted Relief Runs
Caldwell-Chi 13.7
Lemon-Cle 9.0
Klinger-Bos 7.8
Kinder-StL 3.7

Relief Ranking
Caldwell-Chi 25.9
Klinger-Bos 9.0
Lemon-Cle 8.0
Kinder-StL 2.4

Total Pitcher Index
Newhouser-Det 6.8
Feller-Cle 5.3
Trout-Det 5.1
Chandler-NY 4.9
Bevens-NY 3.1

Total Baseball Ranking
Williams-Bos 7.5
Newhouser-Det 6.8
Feller-Cle 5.3
Trout-Det 5.1
Chandler-NY 4.9

TEAM	G	W	L	PCT	GB	R	OR	AB	H	2B	3B	HR	BB	SO	AVG	OBP	SLG	OPS	OPS+	BR	BR+	PF	CHI	RC	SB	CS	SBA	SBR
BRO	155	94	60	.610		774	667	5249	1428	241	50	83	**732**	561	.272	**.364**	.384	748	102	62	33	104	98	781	**88**			
STL	156	89	65	.578	5	780	634	5422	**1462**	235	**65**	115	612	511	.270	.347	.401	748	101	41	9	104	102	762	28			
BOS	154	86	68	.558	8	701	**626**	5253	1444	**265**	42	85	558	**500**	**.275**	.346	.390	736	105	19	37	98	97	717	58			
NY	155	81	73	.526	13	**830**	761	5343	1446	220	48	**221**	494	568	.271	.335	**.454**	**789**	**114**	**95**	**90**	101	**104**	**809**	29			
CIN	154	73	81	.474	21	681	755	5299	1372	242	43	95	539	530	.259	.330	.375	705	95	-48	-43	99	103	672	46			
CHI	155	69	85	.448	25	569	722	5305	1373	231	48	71	471	578	.259	.321	.361	682	91	-93	-68	96	95	620	22			
PIT	156	62	92	.403	32	745	817	5307	1385	216	44	156	607	687	.261	.340	.406	746	102	31	11	103	100	738	30			
PHI	155	62	92	.403	32	589	687	5256	1354	210	52	60	464	594	.258	.321	.352	673	88	-108	-86	96	101	597	60			
TOT	620					5669		42434	11264	1860	392	886	4477	4529	.266	.339	.391	729							361			

TEAM	CG	SH	SV	IP	H	H/G	HR	BB	SO	RAT	ERA	ERA+	OAV	OOB	PR	PR+	PF	CPI	FA	E	DP	FW	PW	BW	SBW	DIF
BRO	47	**14**	**34**	1375	**1299**	**8.6**	104	626	592	12.9	3.82	108	**.251**	.336	37	48	102	100	.978	129	**169**	1.0	4.8	3.3		8.1
STL	65	12	20	1397[2]	1417	9.2	106	495	**642**	12.5	**3.53**	**117**	.266	.330	**83**	**92**	102	**110**	**.979**	**128**	**169**	**1.1**	**9.1**	.9		1.1
BOS	**74**	**14**	13	1362[2]	1342	8.9	**93**	**453**	494	**12.0**	3.62	108	.255	**.316**	67	43	96	95	.974	153	124	-.5	4.3	3.7		1.8
NY	58	6	14	1363[2]	1428	9.5	122	590	553	13.5	4.45	92	.267	.342	-58	-56	100	94	.974	155	136	-.6	-5.5	**8.9**		1.4
CIN	54	13	13	1365[1]	1442	9.6	102	589	633	13.6	4.41	93	.274	.349	-53	-46	101	98	.977	138	134	.4	-4.5	-4.2		4.5
CHI	46	8	15	1367	1449	9.6	106	618	571	13.8	4.04	98	.274	.353	4	-13	97	109	.975	150	159	-.3	-1.2	-6.6		.4
PIT	44	9	13	1374	1488	9.8	155	592	530	13.9	4.69	90	.278	.354	-95	-68	104	101	.975	149	131	-.2	-6.6	1.1		-9.1
PHI	70	8	14	1362	1399	9.3	98	513	514	12.8	3.96	101	.276	.346	15	8	99	108	.974	152	140	-.4	.8	-8.4		-6.8
TOT	458	84	136	10967[1]		9.3				13.1	4.07		.266	.339					.976	1154	1162					

Runs
Mize-NY 137
Robinson-Bro 125
Kiner-Pit 118
Musial-StL 113
Kurowski-StL 108

Hits
Holmes-Bos 191
Walker-StL-Phi 186
Musial-StL 183
Gustine-Pit 183
Baumholtz-Cin 182

Doubles
Miller-Cin 38
B.Elliott-Bos 35
Ryan-Bos 33
Holmes-Bos 33
Baumholtz-Cin 32

Triples
Walker-StL-Phi 16
Slaughter-StL 13
Musial-StL 13
Schoendienst-StL 9
Baumholtz-Cin 9

Home Runs
Mize-NY 51
Kiner-Pit 51
Marshall-NY 36
W.Cooper-NY 35
Thomson-NY 29

Total Bases
Kiner-Pit 361
Mize-NY 360
Marshall-NY 310
W.Cooper-NY 302
Musial-StL 296

Runs Batted In
Mize-NY 138
Kiner-Pit 127
W.Cooper-NY 122
B.Elliott-Bos 113
Marshall-NY 107

Runs Produced
Mize-NY 224
Kiner-Pit 194
Musial-StL 189
Kurowski-StL 185
B.Elliott-Bos 184

Bases On Balls
Reese-Bro 104
Greenberg-Pit 104
Stanky-Bro 103
Kiner-Pit 98
Walker-Bro 97

Batting Average
Walker-StL-Phi .363
B.Elliott-Bos .317
Cavarretta-Chi .314
Kiner-Pit .313
Musial-StL .312

On-Base Percentage
Galan-Cin .449
Walker-StL-Phi .436
Kurowski-StL .420
Kiner-Pit .417
Walker-Bro .415

Slugging Average
Kiner-Pit .639
Mize-NY .614
W.Cooper-NY .586
Kurowski-StL .544
Marshall-NY .528

On-Base Plus Slugging
Kiner-Pit 1055
Mize-NY 998
Kurowski-StL 964
B.Elliott-Bos 927
W.Cooper-NY 926

Adjusted OPS
Kiner-Pit 172
Mize-NY 160
Walker-StL-Phi 150
B.Elliott-Bos 148
Kurowski-StL 148

Batter Runs
Kiner-Pit 61.4
Mize-NY 48.3
Kurowski-StL 41.8
B.Elliott-Bos 36.8
Walker-StL-Phi 35.4

Adjusted Batter Runs
Kiner-Pit 57.5
Mize-NY 47.5
B.Elliott-Bos 39.6
Walker-StL-Phi 38.9
Kurowski-StL 36.9

Clutch Hitting Index
Marion-StL 128
Haas-Cin 125
Walker-Bro 125
Edwards-Bro 125
Jorgensen-Bro 122

Runs Created
Kiner-Pit 154
Mize-NY 143
B.Elliott-Bos 120
Kurowski-StL 118
Musial-StL 118

Total Average
Kiner-Pit 1.155
Mize-NY 1.060
Kurowski-StL 1.019
Walker-StL-Phi .979
Torgeson-Bos .973

Stolen Bases
Robinson-Bro 29
Reiser-Bro 14
Walker-StL-Phi 13
Hopp-Bos 13
Torgeson-Bos 11

Stolen Base Average

Stolen Base Runs

Fielding Runs
Marion-StL 20.1
Verban-Phi 16.9
Gustine-Pit 14.8
Kiner-Pit 13.2
Kerr-NY 12.1

Total Player Rating
Kiner-Pit 5.7
Mize-NY 4.9
Walker-StL-Phi 4.5
B.Elliott-Bos 3.6
Marshall-NY 3.2

Wins
Blackwell-Cin 22
Spahn-Bos 21
Sain-Bos 21
Jansen-NY 21
Branca-Bro 21

Win Percentage
Jansen-NY .808
Munger-StL .762
Blackwell-Cin .733
Hatten-Bro .680
Spahn-Bos .677

Games
Trinkle-NY 62
Higbe-Bro-Pit 50
Behrman-Bro-Pt-Bro 50
Kush-Chi 47
Dickson-StL 47

Complete Games
Blackwell-Cin 23
Spahn-Bos 22
Sain-Bos 22
Jansen-NY 20
Leonard-Phi 19

Shutouts
Spahn-Bos 7
Munger-StL 6
Blackwell-Cin 6
Dickson-StL 4
Branca-Bro 4

Saves
Casey-Bro 18
Trinkle-NY 10
Gumbert-Cin 10
Behrman-Bro-Pt-Bro 8

Innings Pitched
Spahn-Bos 289.2
Branca-Bro 280.0
Blackwell-Cin 273.0
Sain-Bos 266.0
Jansen-NY 248.0

Fewest Hits/Game
Taylor-Bro 7.22
Blackwell-Cin 7.48
Spahn-Bos 7.61
Lombardi-Bro 8.04
Branca-Bro 8.07

Fewest BB/Game
Jansen-NY 2.07
Rowe-Phi 2.07
Leonard-Phi 2.18
Barrett-Bos 2.26
Brazle-StL 2.57

Strikeouts
Blackwell-Cin 193
Branca-Bro 148
Sain-Bos 132
Spahn-Bos 123
Munger-StL 123

Strikeouts/Game
Blackwell-Cin 6.36
Munger-StL 4.93
Branca-Bro 4.76
Brazle-StL 4.55
Sain-Bos 4.47

Ratio
Spahn-Bos 10.25
Blackwell-Cin 10.75
Leonard-Phi 10.84
Jansen-NY 10.85
Barrett-Bos 10.89

Earned Run Average
Spahn-Bos 2.33
Blackwell-Cin 2.47
Branca-Bro 2.67
Leonard-Phi 2.68
Brazle-StL 2.84

Adjusted ERA
Spahn-Bos 167
Blackwell-Cin 166
Branca-Bro 155
Leonard-Phi 149
Brazle-StL 146

Opponents' Batting Avg.
Taylor-Bro .225
Spahn-Bos .226
Blackwell-Cin .234
Branca-Bro .240
Lombardi-Bro .241

Opponents' On-Base Pct.
Spahn-Bos .283
Barrett-Bos .292
Blackwell-Cin .304
Leonard-Phi .306
Jansen-NY .306

Starter Runs
Spahn-Bos 55.7
Blackwell-Cin 48.2
Branca-Bro 43.3
Leonard-Phi 36.0
Dickson-StL 25.5

Adjusted Starter Runs
Spahn-Bos 52.5
Blackwell-Cin 49.0
Branca-Bro 44.8
Leonard-Phi 35.1
Dickson-StL 26.9

Clutch Pitching Index
Brazle-StL 139
Leonard-Phi 123
Branca-Bro 122
Blackwell-Cin 115
Jansen-NY 114

Relief Runs
Lanfranconi-Bos 7.9
Kush-Chi 7.1
Trinkle-NY 3.3
Gumbert-Cin 1.8
Casey-Bro .6

Adjusted Relief Runs
Lanfranconi-Bos 7.0
Kush-Chi 6.1
Trinkle-NY 3.4
Gumbert-Cin 2.2
Casey-Bro 1.2

Relief Ranking
Lanfranconi-Bos 8.1
Kush-Chi 7.4
Trinkle-NY 4.7
Gumbert-Cin 4.4
Casey-Bro 2.4

Total Pitcher Index
Spahn-Bos 5.3
Blackwell-Cin 5.2
Leonard-Phi 4.4
Branca-Bro 4.3
Brazle-StL 3.3

Total Baseball Ranking
Kiner-Pit 5.7
Spahn-Bos 5.3
Blackwell-Cin 5.2
Mize-NY 4.9
Walker-StL-Phi 4.5

TEAM	G	W	L	PCT	GB	R	OR	AB	H	2B	3B	HR	BB	SO	AVG	OBP	SLG	OPS	OPS+	BR	BR+	PF	CHI	RC	SB	CS	SBA	SBR
NY	155	97	57	.630		**794**	**568**	5308	**1439**	230	**72**	**115**	610	581	**.271**	.349	**.407**	**756**	**117**	**110**	**118**	99	104	**780**	27	23	54	-2
DET	158	85	69	.552	12	714	642	5276	1363	**234**	42	103	**762**	565	.258	**.353**	.377	730	106	77	56	103	96	735	52	60	46	-10
BOS	157	83	71	.539	14	720	669	5322	1412	206	54	103	666	590	.265	.349	.382	731	102	71	21	107	98	734	41	35	54	-3
CLE	157	80	74	.519	17	687	588	5367	1392	**234**	51	112	502	609	.259	.324	.385	709	106	9	27	97	**105**	687	29	25	54	-2
PHI	156	78	76	.506	19	633	614	5198	1311	218	52	61	605	563	.252	.333	.349	682	94	-24	-36	102	102	635	37	33	53	-3
CHI	155	70	84	.455	27	553	661	5274	1350	211	41	53	492	**527**	.256	.321	.342	663	93	-69	-47	96	98	584	**91**	57	**61**	0
WAS	154	64	90	.416	33	496	675	5112	1234	186	48	42	525	534	.241	.313	.321	634	84	-118	-104	97	99	523	53	51	51	-6
STL	154	59	95	.383	38	564	744	5145	1238	189	52	90	583	664	.241	.320	.350	670	90	-55	-66	102	98	596	69	49	58	-2
TOT	623					5161		42002	10739	1708	412	679	4745	4633	.256	.334	.365	698							399	333	55	-29

TEAM	CG	SH	SV	IP	H	H/G	HR	BB	SO	RAT	ERA	ERA+	OAV	OOB	PR	PR+	PF	CPI	FA	E	DP	FW	PW	BW	SBW	DIF
NY	73	14	21	1374[1]	**1221**	**8.0**	95	628	**691**	12.3	**3.40**	104	**.238**	**.323**	**48**	23	95	100	.981	109	151	1.5	2.4	**12.3**	.2	3.8
DET	**77**	**15**	18	1398[2]	1382	8.9	79	**531**	648	12.5	3.58	106	.258	.326	21	30	102	100	.975	155	142	-1.0	3.2	5.9	-.7	.8
BOS	64	13	19	1391[1]	1383	9.0	84	575	586	12.8	3.82	102	.261	.335	-16	11	105	100	.977	137	172	.0	1.2	2.2	.0	2.7
CLE	55	13	**29**	1402[1]	1244	**8.0**	94	628	590	**12.2**	3.44	101	.240	.325	41	7	94	100	**.983**	**104**	178	**1.9**	.8	2.8	.2	-2.5
PHI	70	12	15	1391[1]	1291	8.4	85	597	493	12.4	3.52	**109**	.247	.326	30	**45**	103	99	.976	143	161	-.4	**4.7**	-3.7	.0	.5
CHI	47	11	27	1391	1384	9.0	76	603	522	13.0	3.64	100	.261	.339	11	3	99	**105**	.975	155	**180**	-1.1	.4	-4.8	**.4**	-1.6
WAS	67	**15**	12	1362	1408	9.4	**63**	579	551	13.3	3.98	94	.267	.342	-40	-37	101	98	.976	143	151	-.5	-3.8	-10.7	-.2	2.4
STL	50	7	13	1365	1426	9.5	103	604	552	13.5	4.33	90	.272	.348	-94	-65	105	98	.977	134	169	.0	-6.7	-6.8	.2	-4.6
TOT	503	100	154	11076		8.8				12.7	3.71		.256	.334					.978	1080	1304					

Runs
Williams-Bos 125
Henrich-NY 109
Pesky-Bos 106
Stirnweiss-NY 102
DiMaggio-NY 97

Hits
Pesky-Bos 207
Kell-Det 188
Williams-Bos 181
McCosky-Phi 179

Doubles
Boudreau-Cle 45
Williams-Bos 40
Henrich-NY 35
DiMaggio-NY 31

Triples
Henrich-NY 13
Vernon-Was 12
Philley-Chi 11

Home Runs
Williams-Bos 32
Gordon-Cle 29
Heath-StL 27
Cullenbine-Det 24
York-Bos-Chi 21

Total Bases
Williams-Bos 335
Gordon-Cle 279
DiMaggio-NY 279
Henrich-NY 267
Pesky-Bos 250

Runs Batted In
Williams-Bos 114
Henrich-NY 98
DiMaggio-NY 97
Jones-Chi-Bos 96

Runs Produced
Williams-Bos 207
Henrich-NY 191
DiMaggio-NY 174
Kell-Det 163
Doerr-Bos 157

Bases On Balls
Williams-Bos 162
Cullenbine-Det 137
Lake-Det 120
Joost-Phi 114
Fain-Phi 95

Batting Average
Williams-Bos ...... .343
McCosky-Phi ...... .328
Pesky-Bos .... .324
Wright-Chi .... .324
Kell-Det .... .320

On-Base Percentage
Williams-Bos ...... .499
Fain-Phi .... .414
Cullenbine-Det .... .401
McCosky-Phi ...... .395
McQuinn-NY ...... .395

Slugging Average
Williams-Bos ...... .634
DiMaggio-NY ..... .522
Gordon-Cle .... .496
Henrich-NY .... .485
Heath-StL .... .485

On-Base Plus Slugging
Williams-Bos 1133
DiMaggio-NY 913
Henrich-NY 857
Heath-StL 850
Gordon-Cle 842

Adjusted OPS
Williams-Bos 199
DiMaggio-NY 154
Henrich-NY 139
Gordon-Cle 136
Heath-StL 133

Batter Runs
Williams-Bos 91.1
DiMaggio-NY 36.5
Henrich-NY 26.4
Fain-Phi 24.7
Cullenbine-Det 23.8

Adjusted Batter Runs
Williams-Bos 79.6
DiMaggio-NY 37.5
Henrich-NY 27.4
McQuinn-NY 24.2
Gordon-Cle 23.9

Clutch Hitting Index
B.Johnson-NY 140
Kell-Det 121
Jones-Chi-Bos 119
Joost-Phi 118
Majeski-Phi 115

Runs Created
Williams-Bos 186
DiMaggio-NY 112
Henrich-NY 104
Pesky-Bos 103
McQuinn-NY 97

Total Average
Williams-Bos 1.391
DiMaggio-NY ..... .918
Cullenbine-Det .... .898
Heath-StL .... .856
Henrich-NY .... .849

Stolen Bases
Dillinger-StL 34
Philley-Chi 21
Vernon-Was 12
Pesky-Bos 12

Stolen Base Average
Dillinger-StL 72.3
Philley-Chi 56.8

Stolen Base Runs
Dillinger-StL 2.9
Valo-Phi 1.4
Binks-Phi 1.1
Kolloway-Chi 1.0
Tucker-Chi 8

Fielding Runs
Doerr-Bos 23.8
DiMaggio-Bos 19.0
Baker-Chi 18.3
Kell-Det 17.9
Boudreau-Cle 16.7

Total Player Rating
Williams-Bos 6.9
Boudreau-Cle 4.9
Cullenbine-Det 3.3
Kell-Det 3.2
Doerr-Bos 3.2

Wins
Feller-Cle 20
Reynolds-NY 19
Marchildon-Phi 19
Hutchinson-Det 18
Dobson-Bos 18

Win Percentage
Reynolds-NY ...... .704
Dobson-Bos .... .692
Marchildon-Phi .... .679
Feller-Cle .... .645
Hutchinson-Det .... .643

Games
Klieman-Cle 58
Page-NY 56
Johnson-Bos 45
Savage-Phi 44
Christopher-Phi 44

Complete Games
Newhouser-Det 24
Wynn-Was 22
Lopat-Chi 22
Marchildon-Phi 21
Feller-Cle 20

Shutouts
Feller-Cle 5
Reynolds-NY 4
Masterson-Was 4
Haefner-Was 4

Saves
Page-NY 17
Klieman-Cle 17
Christopher-Phi 12
Ferrick-Was 9

Innings Pitched
Feller-Cle 299.0
Newhouser-Det ... 285.0
Marchildon-Phi ... 276.2
Masterson-Was ... 253.0
Lopat-Chi 252.2

Fewest Hits/Game
Shea-NY 6.40
Feller-Cle 6.92
Marchildon-Phi 7.42
Embree-Cle 7.58
Masterson-Was 7.65

Fewest BB/Game
Galehouse-StL-Bos .. 2.48
Hutchinson-Det 2.50
Lopat-Chi 2.60
Muncrief-StL 2.60
Dobson-Bos 2.87

Strikeouts
Feller-Cle 196
Newhouser-Det 176
Masterson-Was 135
Reynolds-NY 129
Marchildon-Phi 128

Strikeouts/Game
Feller-Cle 5.90
Hughson-Bos 5.66
Newhouser-Det 5.56
Trucks-Det 5.38
Kinder-StL 5.09

Ratio
Feller-Cle 10.87
Dobson-Bos 10.90
Shea-NY 11.08
Masterson-Was ... 11.17
Hutchinson-Det ... 11.23

Earned Run Average
Haynes-Chi 2.42
Chandler-NY 2.46
Feller-Cle 2.68
Fowler-Phi 2.81
Lopat-Chi 2.81

Adjusted ERA
Haynes-Chi 151
Fowler-Phi 136
Dobson-Bos 132
Newhouser-Det 131
Feller-Cle 130

Opponents' Batting Avg.
Shea-NY .... .200
Feller-Cle .... .215
Marchildon-Phi .... .224
Reynolds-NY ...... .227
Embree-Cle .... .233

Opponents' On-Base Pct.
Dobson-Bos .... .299
Feller-Cle .... .300
Shea-NY .... .303
Hutchinson-Det .... .304
Lopat-Chi .... .307

Starter Runs
Feller-Cle 34.1
Newhouser-Det 26.3
Haynes-Chi 25.9
Lopat-Chi 25.0
Fowler-Phi 22.6

Adjusted Starter Runs
Feller-Cle 28.4
Newhouser-Det 27.9
Haynes-Chi 25.2
Fowler-Phi 24.6
Lopat-Chi 23.9

Clutch Pitching Index
Haynes-Chi 124
Fowler-Phi 119
Lopat-Chi 116
Ferriss-Bos 114
Newsom-Was-NY ... 112

Relief Runs
Page-NY 19.2
Christopher-Phi 7.2
Klieman-Cle 6.9
Murphy-Bos 5.5
Ferrick-Was 3.7

Adjusted Relief Runs
Page-NY 17.3
Christopher-Phi 7.9
Murphy-Bos 6.3
Klieman-Cle 4.9
Ferrick-Was 3.8

Relief Ranking
Page-NY 28.9
Christopher-Phi ... 15.9
Klieman-Cle 6.3
Ferrick-Was 5.9
Murphy-Bos 3.2

Total Pitcher Index
Newhouser-Det 3.9
Hutchinson-Det 3.7
Feller-Cle 3.3
Page-NY 3.2
Haynes-Chi 3.0

Total Baseball Ranking
Williams-Bos 6.9
Boudreau-Cle 4.9
Newhouser-Det 3.9
Hutchinson-Det 3.7
Cullenbine-Det 3.3

TEAM	G	W	L	PCT	GB	R	OR	AB	H	2B	3B	HR	BB	SO	AVG	OBP	SLG	OPS	OPS+	BR	BR+	PF	CHI	RC	SB	CS	SBA	SBR
BOS	154	91	62	.595		739	**584**	5297	**1458**	**272**	49	95	**671**	536	**.275**	**.359**	.399	**758**	**114**	**95**	**109**	98	92	**784**	43			
STL	155	85	69	.552	6.5	742	646	5302	1396	238	**58**	105	594	**521**	.263	.340	.389	729	98	31	-8	106	103	713	24			
BRO	155	84	70	.545	7.5	744	669	5328	1393	256	54	91	601	684	.261	.338	.381	719	98	13	-10	103	105	709	**114**			
PIT	156	83	71	.539	8.5	706	701	5286	1388	191	54	108	580	578	.263	.338	.380	718	99	10	-4	102	101	698	68			
NY	155	78	76	.506	13.5	**780**	703	5277	1352	210	49	**164**	599	648	.256	.334	**.408**	742	106	46	42	101	**106**	731	51			
PHI	155	66	88	.429	25.5	591	728	5287	1367	227	39	91	440	598	.259	.318	.368	686	94	-63	-52	98	97	625	68			
CIN	153	64	89	.418	27	588	751	5127	1266	221	37	104	478	586	.247	.313	.365	678	92	-76	-55	97	101	587	42			
CHI	155	64	90	.416	27.5	597	705	5352	1402	225	44	87	443	578	.262	.322	.369	691	97	-52	-26	96	95	641	39			
TOT	619					5487		42256	11022	1840	384	845	4406	4729	.261	.333	.383	715							449			

TEAM	CG	SH	SV	IP	H	H/G	HR	BB	SO	RAT	ERA	ERA+	OAV	OOB	PR	PR+	PF	CPI	FA	E	DP	FW	PW	BW	SBW	DIF
BOS	**70**	10	17	1389^1	1354	8.8	93	**430**	579	**11.7**	**3.38**	**114**	**.249**	**.306**	**89**	**73**	97	96	.976	143	132	.8	**7.3**	**10.9**		-4.4
STL	60	13	18	1368	1392	9.2	103	476	625	12.4	3.91	105	.262	.324	7	27	103	97	**.980**	**119**	138	**2.1**	2.7	-.7		4.1
BRO	52	9	**22**	1392^2	**1328**	**8.6**	119	633	**670**	12.9	3.76	106	.253	.337	31	36	101	107	.973	161	151	-.1	3.6	-.9		4.6
PIT	65	5	19	1371^2	1373	9.1	120	564	543	12.9	4.15	98	.261	.335	-29	-12	103	98	.977	137	150	1.2	-1.1	-.3		6.5
NY	54	**15**	21	1373	1425	9.4	122	556	527	13.2	3.93	100	.269	.342	4	0	100	**109**	.974	156	134	.2	.0	4.2		-3.3
PHI	61	6	15	1362^1	1385	9.2	95	556	550	13.0	4.08	97	.262	.335	-18	-20	100	97	.964	210	126	-2.7	-1.9	-5.1		-1.0
CIN	40	8	20	1343^1	1410	9.5	104	572	599	13.4	4.47	87	.270	.344	-77	-86	99	95	.973	158	135	-.0	-8.5	-5.4		1.7
CHI	51	7	10	1355^1	1355	9.0	**89**	619	636	13.3	4.01	97	.261	.342	-7	-15	99	101	.972	172	**152**	-.7	-1.4	-2.5		-8.1
TOT	453	73	142	10955^2		9.1				12.9	3.96		.261	.333					.974	1256	1118					

Runs
Musial-StL 135
Lockman-NY 117
Mize-NY 110
Robinson-Bro 108
Kiner-Pit 104

Hits
Musial-StL 230
Holmes-Bos 190
Rojek-Pit 186
Slaughter-StL 176
Dark-Bos 175

Doubles
Musial-StL 46
Ennis-Phi 40
Dark-Bos 39
Robinson-Bro 38
Holmes-Bos 35

Triples
Musial-StL 18
Hopp-Pit 12
Slaughter-StL 11
Waitkus-Chi 10
Lockman-NY 10

Home Runs
Mize-NY 40
Kiner-Pit 40
Musial-StL 39
Sauer-Cin 35

Total Bases
Musial-StL 429
Mize-NY 316
Ennis-Phi 309
Kiner-Pit 296
Pafko-Chi 283

Runs Batted In
Musial-StL 131
Mize-NY 125
Kiner-Pit 123
Gordon-NY 107
Pafko-Chi 101

Runs Produced
Musial-StL 227
Mize-NY 195
Kiner-Pit 187
Robinson-Bro 181
Gordon-NY 177

Bases On Balls
B.Elliott-Bos 131
Kiner-Pit 112
Mize-NY 94

Batting Average
Musial-StL 376
Ashburn-Phi 333
Holmes-Bos 325
Dark-Bos 322
Slaughter-StL 321

On-Base Percentage
Musial-StL 450
B.Elliott-Bos 423
Ashburn-Phi 410
Slaughter-StL 409
Mize-NY 395

Slugging Average
Musial-StL 702
Mize-NY 564
Gordon-NY 537
Kiner-Pit 533
Ennis-Phi 525

On-Base Plus Slugging
Musial-StL 1152
Mize-NY 959
Gordon-NY 927
Kiner-Pit 924
B.Elliott-Bos 897

Adjusted OPS
Musial-StL 196
Mize-NY 156
Gordon-NY 148
Kiner-Pit 145
B.Elliott-Bos 145

Batter Runs
Musial-StL 90.2
Mize-NY 44.6
Kiner-Pit 38.5
B.Elliott-Bos 37.8
Gordon-NY 35.1

Adjusted Batter Runs
Musial-StL 81.0
Mize-NY 43.9
B.Elliott-Bos 39.8
Kiner-Pit 36.2
Gordon-NY 34.4

Clutch Hitting Index
Murtaugh-Pit 135
Jones-StL 129
Stallcup-Cin 128
Lowrey-Chi 123
Torgeson-Bos 118

Runs Created
Musial-StL 191
Mize-NY 131
Kiner-Pit 120
B.Elliott-Bos 117
Slaughter-StL 110

Total Average
Musial-StL 1.298
Mize-NY 1.032
B.Elliott-Bos 980
Kiner-Pit 974
Gordon-NY 953

Stolen Bases
Ashburn-Phi 32
Reese-Bro 25
Rojek-Pit 24
Robinson-Bro 22
Torgeson-Bos 19

Stolen Base Average

Stolen Base Runs

Fielding Runs
Ashburn-Phi 17.8
Pafko-Chi 12.8
Reese-Bro 10.3
Marion-StL 9.4
Gustine-Pit 9.0

Total Player Rating
Musial-StL 6.6
Pafko-Chi 4.4
Mize-NY 4.2
Kiner-Pit 3.1
Ashburn-Phi 3.1

Wins
Sain-Bos 24
Brecheen-StL 20
Schmitz-Chi 18
Jansen-NY 18
VanderMeer-Cin 17

Win Percentage
Brecheen-StL 741
Jones-NY 667
Sain-Bos 615
Jansen-NY 600
Schmitz-Chi 581

Games
Gumbert-Cin 61
Wilks-StL 57
Higbe-Pit 56
Jones-NY 55
Dobernic-Chi 54

Complete Games
Sain-Bos 28
Brecheen-StL 21
Schmitz-Chi 18
Spahn-Bos 16
Leonard-Phi 16

Shutouts
Brecheen-StL 7
Sain-Bos 4
Raffensberger-Cin 4
Jansen-NY 4
Barney-Bro 4

Saves
Gumbert-Cin 17
Wilks-StL 13
Higbe-Pit 10
Trinkle-NY 7
Behrman-Bro 7

Innings Pitched
Sain-Bos 314.2
Jansen-NY 277.0
Spahn-Bos 257.0
Dickson-StL 252.1
Barney-Bro 246.2

Fewest Hits/Game
Schmitz-Chi 6.92
Barney-Bro 7.04
Brecheen-StL 7.44
Branca-Bro 7.89
Roe-Bro 7.90

Fewest BB/Game
Roe-Bro 1.67
Jansen-NY 1.75
Raffensberger-Cin 1.85
Brecheen-StL 1.89
Leonard-Phi 2.15

Strikeouts
Brecheen-StL 149
Barney-Bro 138
Sain-Bos 137
Jansen-NY 126
Branca-Bro 122

Strikeouts/Game
Brecheen-StL 5.75
Branca-Bro 5.09
Barney-Bro 5.04
Higbe-Pit 4.90
Meyer-Chi 4.86

Ratio
Brecheen-StL 9.41
Roe-Bro 9.68
Schmitz-Chi 10.60
Sain-Bos 11.01
Spahn-Bos 11.03

Earned Run Average
Brecheen-StL 2.24
Leonard-Phi 2.51
Sain-Bos 2.60
Roe-Bro 2.63
Schmitz-Chi 2.64

Adjusted ERA
Brecheen-StL 183
Leonard-Phi 157
Roe-Bro 152
Schmitz-Chi 148
Sain-Bos 147

Opponents' Batting Avg.
Schmitz-Chi 215
Barney-Bro 217
Brecheen-StL 222
Branca-Bro 232
Roe-Bro 233

Opponents' On-Base Pct.
Brecheen-StL 265
Roe-Bro 271
Schmitz-Chi 295
Sain-Bos 296
Raffensberger-Cin 296

Starter Runs
Sain-Bos 47.3
Brecheen-StL 44.5
Leonard-Phi 36.2
Schmitz-Chi 35.3
Roe-Bro 26.1

Adjusted Starter Runs
Brecheen-StL 46.4
Sain-Bos 44.4
Leonard-Phi 36.0
Schmitz-Chi 34.4
Roe-Bro 26.6

Clutch Pitching Index
Leonard-Phi 134
Jones-NY 126
Hatten-Bro 124
Voiselle-Bos 120
Sain-Bos 115

Relief Runs
Wilks-StL 19.4
Hansen-NY 10.9
Minner-Bro 10.5
Higbe-Pit 10.4
Dobernic-Chi 7.6

Adjusted Relief Runs
Wilks-StL 20.7
Higbe-Pit 12.1
Hansen-NY 10.8
Minner-Bro 10.7
Dobernic-Chi 7.2

Relief Ranking
Wilks-StL 21.7
Higbe-Pit 12.1
Minner-Bro 11.1
Gumbert-Cin 9.8
Trinkle-NY 8.1

Total Pitcher Index
Sain-Bos 5.4
Brecheen-StL 5.3
Schmitz-Chi 4.7
Leonard-Phi 4.6
Roe-Bro 2.6

Total Baseball Ranking
Musial-StL 6.6
Sain-Bos 5.4
Brecheen-StL 5.3
Schmitz-Chi 4.7
Leonard-Phi 4.6

TEAM	G	W	L	PCT	GB	R	OR	AB	H	2B	3B	HR	BB	SO	AVG	OBP	SLG	OPS	OPS+	BR	BR+	PF	CHI	RC	SB	CS	SBA	SBR
CLE	156	97	58	.626		840	**568**	5446	**1534**	242	54	**155**	646	575	**.282**	.360	.431	**791**	**119**	112	**135**	97	97	868	54	44	55	-4
BOS	155	96	59	.619	1	**907**	720	5363	1471	**277**	40	121	**823**	552	.274	**.374**	.409	783	109	**116**	74	105	104	**869**	38	17	**69**	**2**
NY	154	94	60	.610	2.5	857	633	5324	1480	251	**75**	139	623	**478**	.278	.356	**.432**	788	116	99	107	99	103	838	24	24	50	-3
PHI	154	84	70	.545	12.5	729	735	5181	1345	231	47	68	726	523	.260	.353	.362	715	96	-20	-21	100	102	699	40	32	56	-2
DET	154	78	76	.506	18.5	700	726	5235	1396	219	58	78	671	504	.267	.353	.375	728	96	0	-19	103	95	723	22	32	41	-6
STL	155	59	94	.386	37	671	849	5303	1438	251	62	63	578	572	.271	.345	.378	723	96	-21	-39	103	95	711	63	44	59	-2
WAS	154	56	97	.366	40	578	796	5111	1245	203	**75**	31	568	572	.244	.322	.331	653	81	-151	-135	97	**105**	566	**76**	48	61	0
CHI	154	51	101	.336	44.5	559	814	5192	1303	172	39	55	595	528	.251	.329	.331	660	84	-134	-114	97	97	588	46	47	49	-6
TOT	618					5841		42155	11212	1846	450	710	5230	4304	.266	.350	.382	731							363	288	56	-21

TEAM	CG	SH	SV	IP	H	H/G	HR	BB	SO	RAT	ERA	ERA+	OAV	OOB	PR	PR+	PF	CPI	FA	E	DP	FW	PW	BW	SBW	DIF
CLE	66	**26**	**30**	1409^1	**1246**	**8.0**	82	625	593	**12.1**	**3.23**	**126**	**.239**	**.323**	**167**	**138**	95	**108**	**.982**	114	183	**1.4**	**13.4**	**13.1**	-.1	-8.1
BOS	70	11	13	1379^1	1445	9.5	83	592	513	13.5	4.27	103	.270	.345	4	20	102	99	.981	116	174	1.3	2.0	7.2	**.4**	7.8
NY	62	16	24	1365^2	1289	8.5	94	641	654	12.9	3.75	109	.250	.336	82	53	95	104	.979	120	161	1.0	5.2	10.4	-.0	.6
PHI	**74**	7	18	1368^2	1456	9.6	86	638	486	13.9	4.43	97	.275	.355	-21	-20	100	101	.981	**113**	180	**1.4**	-1.9	-2.0	.0	9.6
DET	60	5	22	1377	1367	9.0	92	**589**	**678**	12.9	4.16	105	.259	.335	21	33	102	95	.974	155	143	-.9	3.2	-1.8	-.3	1.0
STL	35	4	20	1373^1	1513	10.0	103	737	531	15.0	5.01	91	.281	.371	-109	-65	106	99	.972	168	**190**	-1.5	-6.3	-3.7	.0	-5.8
WAS	42	4	22	1357^1	1439	9.6	**81**	734	446	14.6	4.66	93	.273	.364	-55	-46	101	99	.974	154	144	-.8	-4.4	-13.0	.3	-2.3
CHI	35	2	23	1345^2	1454	9.8	89	673	403	14.5	4.89	87	.280	.365	-90	-95	99	97	.974	160	176	-1.2	-9.2	-11.0	-.3	-3.2
TOT	444	75	172	10976^1		9.2				13.7	4.29		.266	.350					.977	1100	1351					

Runs
Henrich-NY 138
DiMaggio-Bos 127
Williams-Bos 124
Pesky-Bos 124
Boudreau-Cle 116

Hits
Dillinger-StL 207
Mitchell-Cle 204
Boudreau-Cle 199
DiMaggio-NY 190
Williams-Bos 188

Doubles
Williams-Bos 44
Henrich-NY 42
Majeski-Phi 41
Priddy-StL 40
DiMaggio-Bos 40

Triples
Henrich-NY 14
Stewart-NY-Was 13
Yost-Was 11
Mullin-Det 11
DiMaggio-NY 11

Home Runs
DiMaggio-NY 39
Gordon-Cle 32
Keltner-Cle 31
Stephens-Bos 29
Doerr-Bos 27

Total Bases
DiMaggio-NY 355
Henrich-NY 326
Williams-Bos 313
Stephens-Bos 299
Boudreau-Cle 299

Runs Batted In
DiMaggio-NY 155
Stephens-Bos 137
Williams-Bos 127
Gordon-Cle 124
Majeski-Phi 120

Runs Produced
Williams-Bos 226
DiMaggio-NY 226
Stephens-Bos 222
Henrich-NY 213
DiMaggio-Bos 205

Bases On Balls
Williams-Bos 126
Joost-Phi 119
Fain-Phi 113
DiMaggio-Bos 101
Pesky-Bos 99

Batting Average
Williams-Bos .369
Boudreau-Cle .355
Mitchell-Cle .336
Zarilla-StL .329
McCosky-Phi .326

On-Base Percentage
Williams-Bos .497
Boudreau-Cle .453
Appling-Chi .423
Goodman-Bos .414
Fain-Phi .412

Slugging Average
Williams-Bos .615
DiMaggio-NY .598
Henrich-NY .554
Boudreau-Cle .534
Keltner-Cle .522

On-Base Plus Slugging
Williams-Bos 1112
DiMaggio-NY 994
Boudreau-Cle 987
Henrich-NY 945
Keltner-Cle 917

Adjusted OPS
Williams-Bos 185
Boudreau-Cle 166
DiMaggio-NY 164
Henrich-NY 151
Keltner-Cle 146

Batter Runs
Williams-Bos 75.7
Boudreau-Cle 52.7
DiMaggio-NY 48.6
Henrich-NY 38.9
Keltner-Cle 33.0

Adjusted Batter Runs
Williams-Bos 68.4
Boudreau-Cle 56.3
DiMaggio-NY 49.9
Henrich-NY 40.1
Keltner-Cle 36.0

Clutch Hitting Index
Platt-StL 126
Majeski-Phi 121
Goodman-Bos 120
Stephens-Bos 120
Tebbetts-Bos 119

Runs Created
Williams-Bos 172
Boudreau-Cle 143
DiMaggio-NY 140
Henrich-NY 130
Keltner-Cle 116

Total Average
Williams-Bos 1.347
Boudreau-Cle 1.058
DiMaggio-NY 1.012
Henrich-NY .955
Keltner-Cle .918

Stolen Bases
Dillinger-StL 28
Coan-Was 23
Vernon-Was 15
Mitchell-Cle 13

Stolen Base Average
Coan-Was 71.9
Dillinger-StL 71.8

Stolen Base Runs
Dillinger-StL 2.3
Coan-Was 1.9
Robertson-Was 1.8
Tucker-Cle 1.7
DiMaggio-Bos 1.5

Fielding Runs
Pellagrini-StL 24.0
Priddy-StL 23.5
Hegan-Cle 21.6
DiMaggio-Bos 15.8
Philley-Chi 15.1

Total Player Rating
Boudreau-Cle 7.0
Williams-Bos 5.6
DiMaggio-NY 4.7
Priddy-StL 4.5
Doerr-Bos 3.6

Wins
Newhouser-Det 21
Lemon-Cle 20
Bearden-Cle 20
Raschi-NY 19
Feller-Cle 19

Win Percentage
Kramer-Bos .783
Bearden-Cle .741
Raschi-NY .704
Reynolds-NY .696

Games
Page-NY 55
Widmar-StL 49
Biscan-StL 47
Thompson-Was 46

Complete Games
Lemon-Cle 20
Newhouser-Det 19
Raschi-NY 18
Feller-Cle 18

Shutouts
Lemon-Cle 10
Raschi-NY 6
Bearden-Cle 6
Dobson-Bos 5

Saves
Christopher-Cle 17
Page-NY 16
Houtteman-Det 10
Ferrick-Was 10
Judson-Chi 8

Innings Pitched
Lemon-Cle 293.2
Feller-Cle 280.1
Newhouser-Det 272.1
Dobson-Bos 245.1
Reynolds-NY 236.1

Fewest Hits/Game
Shea-NY 6.76
Lemon-Cle 7.08
Bearden-Cle 7.33
Scarborough-Was 8.06
Trucks-Det 8.08

Fewest BB/Game
Hutchinson-Det 1.95
Zoldak-StL-Cle 2.42
Lopat-NY 2.62
Kramer-Bos 2.81
Houtteman-Det 2.85

Strikeouts
Feller-Cle 164
Lemon-Cle 147
Newhouser-Det 143
Brissie-Phi 127
Raschi-NY 124

Strikeouts/Game
Brissie-Phi 5.89
Feller-Cle 5.27
Trucks-Det 5.23
Raschi-NY 5.01
Newhouser-Det 4.73

Ratio
Hutchinson-Det 11.08
Lemon-Cle 11.12
Raschi-NY 11.52
Newhouser-Det 11.53
Bearden-Cle 11.60

Earned Run Average
Bearden-Cle 2.43
Scarborough-Was 2.82
Lemon-Cle 2.82
Newhouser-Det 3.01
Parnell-Bos 3.14

Adjusted ERA
Bearden-Cle 167
Scarborough-Was 154
Newhouser-Det 145
Lemon-Cle 144
Parnell-Bos 140

Opponents' Batting Avg.
Shea-NY .208
Lemon-Cle .216
Bearden-Cle .229
Scarborough-Was .233
Trucks-Det .240

Opponents' On-Base Pct.
Hutchinson-Det .297
Lemon-Cle .302
Scarborough-Was .307
Newhouser-Det .309
Raschi-NY .310

Starter Runs
Lemon-Cle 48.0
Bearden-Cle 47.5
Newhouser-Det 38.8
Scarborough-Was 30.3
Parnell-Bos 27.1

Adjusted Starter Runs
Bearden-Cle 43.9
Lemon-Cle 42.7
Newhouser-Det 40.4
Scarborough-Was 31.1
Parnell-Bos 28.8

Clutch Pitching Index
Bearden-Cle 132
Garver-StL 129
Fowler-Phi 119
Lopat-NY 118
Reynolds-NY 117

Relief Runs
Klieman-Cle 15.0
Christopher-Cle 9.1
Thompson-Was 6.6
Hiller-NY 1.7
Harris-Phi 1.6

Adjusted Relief Runs
Klieman-Cle 13.7
Christopher-Cle 8.0
Thompson-Was 7.3
Harris-Phi 1.6
Ferrick-Was 1.6

Relief Ranking
Christopher-Cle 11.3
Klieman-Cle 9.3
Thompson-Was 8.5
Ferrick-Was 1.8
Harris-Phi 1.3

Total Pitcher Index
Lemon-Cle 7.0
Bearden-Cle 5.8
Newhouser-Det 4.8
Scarborough-Was 3.8
Parnell-Bos 2.6

Total Baseball Ranking
Lemon-Cle 7.0
Boudreau-Cle 7.0
Bearden-Cle 5.8
Williams-Bos 5.6
Newhouser-Det 4.8

TEAM	G	W	L	PCT	GB	R	OR	AB	H	2B	3B	HR	BB	SO	AVG	OBP	SLG	OPS	OPS+	BR	BR+	PF	CHI	RC	SB	CS	SBA	SBR
BRO	156	97	57	.630		**879**	651	5400	1477	236	47	**152**	638	570	.274	**.354**	**.419**	**773**	**110**	**103**	**70**	104	**106**	**815**	**117**			
STL	157	96	58	.623	1	766	**616**	5463	**1513**	**281**	54	102	569	**482**	**.277**	.348	.404	752	103	61	26	105	98	777	17			
PHI	154	81	73	.526	16	662	668	5307	1349	232	**55**	122	528	670	.254	.325	.388	713	100	-27	-8	97	99	674	27			
BOS	157	75	79	.487	22	706	719	5336	1376	246	33	103	**684**	656	.258	.345	.374	719	105	6	47	95	97	710	28			
NY	156	73	81	.474	24	736	693	5308	1383	203	52	147	613	523	.261	.340	.401	741	105	36	37	100	99	735	43			
PIT	154	71	83	.461	26	681	760	5214	1350	191	41	126	548	554	.259	.332	.384	716	96	-14	-31	103	101	682	48			
CIN	156	62	92	.403	35	627	770	5469	1423	264	35	86	429	559	.260	.316	.368	684	88	-84	-91	101	101	636	31			
CHI	154	61	93	.396	36	593	773	5214	1336	212	53	97	396	573	.256	.312	.373	685	91	-83	-67	97	100	601	53			
TOT	622					5650		42711	11207	1865	370	935	4405	4587	.263	.335	.390	723							364			

TEAM	CG	SH	SV	IP	H	H/G	HR	BB	SO	RAT	ERA	ERA+	OAV	OOB	PR	PR+	PF	CPI	FA	E	DP	FW	PW	BW	SBW	DIF
BRO	62	**15**	17	1408^2	**1306**	**8.4**	132	582	**743**	12.3	3.81	108	**.246**	.324	37	46	102	99	**.980**	**122**	162	**1.6**	4.6	**7.0**		7.0
STL	64	13	**19**	1407^2	1356	8.7	**87**	507	606	**12.1**	**3.44**	**121**	.252	**.319**	**94**	**110**	103	101	.976	146	149	.3	**11.0**	2.6		5.3
PHI	58	12	15	1391^2	1389	9.0	104	**502**	495	12.4	3.90	101	.268	.335	23	9	98	**105**	.974	156	141	-.4	.9	-.7		4.4
BOS	**68**	12	11	1400	1466	9.5	110	520	589	13.0	3.99	95	.268	.334	8	-35	94	102	.976	148	144	.2	-3.4	4.7		-3.3
NY	**68**	10	9	1374^1	1328	8.7	132	544	516	12.4	3.83	104	.249	.321	33	25	99	97	.973	161	134	-.6	2.5	3.7		-9.5
PIT	53	9	15	1356	1452	9.7	142	535	556	13.5	4.57	92	.274	.344	-79	-53	104	99	.978	132	**173**	.9	-5.2	-3.0		1.5
CIN	55	10	6	1401^2	1423	9.2	124	640	538	13.5	4.35	96	.264	.345	-47	-24	104	99	.977	138	150	.7	-2.3	-9.0		-4.2
CHI	44	8	17	1357^2	1487	9.9	104	575	544	13.9	4.51	90	.279	.351	-70	-71	100	100	.970	186	160	-2.1	-7.0	-6.6		-.1
TOT	472	89	109	11097^2		9.1				12.9	4.05		.263	.335					.976	1189	1213					

Runs
Reese-Bro 132
Musial-StL 128
Robinson-Bro 122
Kiner-Pit 116
Schoendienst-StL ... 102

Hits
Musial-StL 207
Robinson-Bro 203
Thomson-NY 198
Slaughter-StL 191
Schoendienst-StL ... 190

Doubles
Musial-StL 41
Ennis-Phi 39
Robinson-Bro 38
Hatton-Cin 38

Triples
Slaughter-StL 13
Musial-StL 13
Robinson-Bro 12
Ennis-Phi 11
Ashburn-Phi 11

Home Runs
Kiner-Pit 54
Musial-StL 36
Sauer-Cin-Chi 31
Thomson-NY 27
Gordon-NY 26

Total Bases
Musial-StL 382
Kiner-Pit 361
Thomson-NY 332
Ennis-Phi 320
Robinson-Bro 313

Runs Batted In
Kiner-Pit 127
Robinson-Bro 124
Musial-StL 123
Hodges-Bro 115
Ennis-Phi 110

Runs Produced
Robinson-Bro 230
Musial-StL 215
Reese-Bro 189
Kiner-Pit 189
Hodges-Bro 186

Bases On Balls
Kiner-Pit 117
Reese-Bro 116
Stanky-Bos 113
Musial-StL 107
Gordon-NY 95

Batting Average
Robinson-Bro ...... .342
Musial-StL .... .338
Slaughter-StL ..... .336
Furillo-Bro .... .322
Kiner-Pit .... .310

On-Base Percentage
Musial-StL .... .438
Robinson-Bro ...... .432
Kiner-Pit .... .432
Slaughter-StL ..... .418
Stanky-Bos .... .417

Slugging Average
Kiner-Pit .... .658
Musial-StL .... .624
Robinson-Bro ...... .528
Ennis-Phi .... .525
Thomson-NY .... .518

On-Base Plus Slugging
Kiner-Pit 1089
Musial-StL 1062
Robinson-Bro 960
Slaughter-StL 929
Gordon-NY 909

Adjusted OPS
Kiner-Pit 183
Musial-StL 174
Robinson-Bro 150
Gordon-NY 142
Slaughter-StL 141

Batter Runs
Musial-StL 72.4
Kiner-Pit 70.0
Robinson-Bro 49.9
Slaughter-StL 40.1
Gordon-NY 31.6

Adjusted Batter Runs
Kiner-Pit 66.2
Musial-StL 65.5
Robinson-Bro 44.7
Slaughter-StL 35.0
Ennis-Phi 32.4

Clutch Hitting Index
Robinson-Bro 130
Marion-StL 117
Russell-Bos 116
Hodges-Bro 116
Cooper-NY-Cin 114

Runs Created
Musial-StL 173
Kiner-Pit 163
Robinson-Bro 135
Slaughter-StL 127
Ennis-Phi 118

Total Average
Kiner-Pit 1.247
Musial-StL 1.185
Robinson-Bro 1.078
Slaughter-StL ..... .971
Gordon-NY .... .925

Stolen Bases
Robinson-Bro 37
Reese-Bro 26

Stolen Base Average

Stolen Base Runs

Fielding Runs
Ashburn-Phi 24.7
Schoendienst-StL .. 24.0
Thomson-NY 19.5
Marion-StL 16.6
Reich-Chi 14.1

Total Player Rating
Kiner-Pit 5.2
Robinson-Bro 5.1
Musial-StL 4.1
Thomson-NY 4.0
B.Elliott-Bos 3.8

Wins
Spahn-Bos 21
Pollet-StL 20
Raffensberger-Cin .. 18

Win Percentage
Roe-Bro .... .714
Pollet-StL .... .690
Newcombe-Bro ...... .680
Meyer-Phi .... .680
Munger-StL .... .652

Games
Wilks-StL 59
Konstanty-Phi 53
Palica-Bro 49
Banta-Bro 48
Muncrief-Pit-Chi .. 47

Complete Games
Spahn-Bos 25
Raffensberger-Cin .. 20
Newcombe-Bro 19
Pollet-StL 17
Jansen-NY 17

Shutouts
Raffensberger-Cin .. 5
Pollet-StL 5
Newcombe-Bro 5
Heintzelman-Phi ... 5

Saves
Wilks-StL 9
Potter-Bos 7
Konstanty-Phi 7
Staley-StL 6
Palica-Bro 6

Innings Pitched
Spahn-Bos 302.1
Raffensberger-Cin .. 284.0
Jansen-NY 259.2
Heintzelman-Phi ... 250.0
Newcombe-Bro 244.1

Fewest Hits/Game
Staley-StL 8.09
Koslo-NY 8.19
Newcombe-Bro 8.21
Kennedy-NY 8.38
Meyer-Phi 8.41

Fewest BB/Game
Koslo-NY 1.83
Roe-Bro 1.86
Werle-Pit 2.08
Jansen-NY 2.15
Leonard-Chi 2.15

Strikeouts
Spahn-Bos 151
Newcombe-Bro 149
Jansen-NY 113
Roe-Bro 109
Branca-Bro 109

Strikeouts/Game
Newcombe-Bro 5.49
Branca-Bro 5.26
Chambers-Pit 4.72
Roe-Bro 4.61
Spahn-Bos 4.50

Ratio
Koslo-NY 10.02
Staley-StL 10.40
Roe-Bro 10.45
Newcombe-Bro 11.01
Spahn-Bos 11.07

Earned Run Average
Koslo-NY 2.50
Staley-StL 2.73
Pollet-StL 2.77
Roe-Bro 2.79
Heintzelman-Phi ... 3.02

Adjusted ERA
Koslo-NY 159
Staley-StL 152
Pollet-StL 150
Roe-Bro 147
Brazle-StL 131

Opponents' Batting Avg.
Staley-StL .... .238
Koslo-NY .... .239
Kennedy-NY .... .242
Newcombe-Bro ...... .243
Spahn-Bos .... .245

Opponents' On-Base Pct.
Koslo-NY .... .278
Staley-StL .... .286
Roe-Bro .... .293
Spahn-Bos .... .299
Newcombe-Bro ...... .301

Starter Runs
Koslo-NY 36.2
Spahn-Bos 32.7
Pollet-StL 32.6
Roe-Bro 29.5
Heintzelman-Phi ... 28.2

Adjusted Starter Runs
Koslo-NY 35.3
Pollet-StL 34.6
Roe-Bro 30.4
Staley-StL 26.4
Heintzelman-Phi ... 26.2

Clutch Pitching Index
Roe-Bro 126
Heintzelman-Phi ... 123
Brazle-StL 121
Jones-NY 116
Dickson-Pit 113

Relief Runs
Erautt-Cin 8.6
Konstanty-Phi 8.5
Hogue-Bos 7.3
Palica-Bro 4.5
Wilks-StL 4.1

Adjusted Relief Runs
Erautt-Cin 10.0
Konstanty-Phi 7.7
Hogue-Bos 5.6
Wilks-StL 5.5
Palica-Bro 5.1

Relief Ranking
Erautt-Cin 12.2
Konstanty-Phi 11.2
Palica-Bro 8.8
Wilks-StL 6.4
Hogue-Bos 3.3

Total Pitcher Index
Koslo-NY 4.2
Pollet-StL 4.1
Staley-StL 3.4
Dickson-Pit 2.9
Newcombe-Bro 2.7

Total Baseball Ranking
Kiner-Pit 5.2
Robinson-Bro 5.1
Koslo-NY 4.2
Musial-StL 4.1
Pollet-StL 4.1

TEAM	G	W	L	PCT	GB	R	OR	AB	H	2B	3B	HR	BB	SO	AVG	OBP	SLG	OPS	OPS+	BR	BR+	PF	CHI	RC	SB	CS	SBA	SBR
NY	155	97	57	.630		829	637	5196	1396	215	60	115	731	539	.269	.362	.400	762	108	58	58	100	**106**	790	58	30	**66**	**2**
BOS	155	96	58	.623	1	**896**	667	5320	**1500**	**272**	36	**131**	**835**	510	**.282**	**.381**	**.420**	**801**	**111**	**147**	**87**	107	100	**890**	43	25	63	1
CLE	154	89	65	.578	8	675	**574**	5221	1358	194	58	112	601	534	.260	.339	.384	723	99	-30	-16	98	99	696	44	40	52	-4
DET	155	87	67	.565	10	751	655	5259	1405	215	51	88	751	502	.267	.361	.378	739	102	20	18	100	99	739	39	52	43	-10
PHI	154	81	73	.526	16	726	725	5123	1331	214	49	82	783	**493**	.260	.361	.369	730	104	6	32	97	99	719	36	25	59	-1
CHI	154	63	91	.409	34	648	737	5204	1340	207	**66**	43	702	596	.257	.347	.347	694	93	-66	-44	97	99	657	**62**	55	53	-6
STL	155	53	101	.344	44	667	913	5112	1301	213	30	117	631	700	.254	.339	.377	716	92	-41	-68	104	101	670	38	39	49	-5
WAS	154	50	104	.325	47	584	868	5234	1330	207	41	81	593	495	.254	.333	.356	689	90	-93	-79	98	95	640	46	33	58	-1
TOT	618					5776		41669	10961	1737	391	769	5627	4369	.264	.354	.379	732							366	299	55	-24

TEAM	CG	SH	SV	IP	H	H/G	HR	BB	SO	RAT	ERA	ERA+	OAV	OOB	PR	PR+	PF	CPI	FA	E	DP	FW	PW	BW	SBW	DIF
NY	59	12	**36**	1371[1]	**1231**	**8.1**	98	812	**671**	13.7	3.70	110	**.242**	.351	77	56	96	**107**	.977	138	195	.0	5.5	5.7	**.5**	8.4
BOS	84	16	16	1377	1375	9.0	82	661	598	13.5	3.98	110	.262	.347	34	57	104	101	.980	120	207	1.1	5.6	**8.5**	.4	3.5
CLE	65	10	19	1383[2]	1275	8.3	82	**611**	594	**12.4**	**3.36**	**119**	.247	**.329**	**129**	**103**	95	104	**.983**	**103**	192	**2.1**	**10.1**	-1.5	-.0	1.6
DET	70	**19**	12	1393[2]	1338	8.7	102	628	631	12.9	3.78	110	.254	.335	66	61	99	100	.978	131	174	.5	6.0	1.8	-.7	2.6
PHI	**85**	9	11	1365	1359	9.0	105	758	490	14.1	4.24	97	.263	.360	-5	-19	98	103	.976	140	**217**	-.0	-1.8	3.2	.2	2.7
CHI	57	10	17	1363[1]	1362	9.0	108	693	502	13.7	4.30	97	.264	.353	-15	-19	99	99	.977	141	180	-.2	-1.8	-4.2	-.3	-7.3
STL	43	3	16	1341[1]	1583	10.7	113	685	432	15.4	5.22	87	.294	.377	-151	-94	108	98	.971	166	154	-1.6	-9.1	-6.6	-.2	-6.3
WAS	44	9	9	1345[2]	1438	9.7	**79**	779	451	15.0	5.10	84	.276	.373	-134	-124	101	91	.973	161	168	-1.3	-12.0	-7.6	.2	-6.0
TOT	507	88	136	10941		9.1				13.8	4.20		.264	.354					.977	1100	1487					

Runs
Williams-Bos 150
Joost-Phi 128
DiMaggio-Bos 126
Stephens-Bos 113
Pesky-Bos 111

Hits
Mitchell-Cle 203
Williams-Bos 194
DiMaggio-Bos 186
Wertz-Det 185
Pesky-Bos 185

Doubles
Williams-Bos 39
Kell-Det 38
DiMaggio-Bos 34
Zarilla-StL-Bos 33
Stephens-Bos 31

Triples
Mitchell-Cle 23
Dillinger-StL 13
Valo-Phi 12

Home Runs
Williams-Bos 43
Stephens-Bos 39

Total Bases
Williams-Bos 368
Stephens-Bos 329
Wertz-Det 283
Mitchell-Cle 274
Doerr-Bos 269

Runs Batted In
Williams-Bos 159
Stephens-Bos 159
Wertz-Det 133
Doerr-Bos 109
Chapman-Phi 108

Runs Produced
Williams-Bos 266
Stephens-Bos 233
Wertz-Det 209
Joost-Phi 186
Doerr-Bos 182

Bases On Balls
Williams-Bos 162
Joost-Phi 149
Fain-Phi 136
Appling-Chi 121
Valo-Phi 119

Batting Average
Kell-Det .... .343
Williams-Bos .... .343
Dillinger-StL .... .324
Mitchell-Cle .... .317
Doerr-Bos .... .309

On-Base Percentage
Williams-Bos .... .490
Appling-Chi .... .439
Joost-Phi .... .429
Kell-Det .... .424
Michaels-Chi .... .417

Slugging Average
Williams-Bos .... .650
Stephens-Bos ...... .539
Henrich-NY .... .526
Doerr-Bos .... .497
Berra-NY .... .480

On-Base Plus Slugging
Williams-Bos 1141
Henrich-NY 942
Stephens-Bos 930
Kell-Det 892
Doerr-Bos 890

Adjusted OPS
Williams-Bos 187
Henrich-NY 148
Joost-Phi 138
Kell-Det 136
Stephens-Bos 135

Batter Runs
Williams-Bos 88.9
Stephens-Bos 36.9
Joost-Phi 31.9
DiMaggio-NY 31.7
Henrich-NY 29.7

Adjusted Batter Runs
Williams-Bos 77.0
Joost-Phi 35.9
DiMaggio-NY 31.7
Henrich-NY 29.7
Stephens-Bos 28.7

Clutch Hitting Index
Fain-Phi 143
Lipon-Det 124
Valo-Phi 124
Wertz-Det 121
Williams-Bos 120

Runs Created
Williams-Bos 193
Stephens-Bos 132
Joost-Phi 119
DiMaggio-Bos 110
Wertz-Det 110

Total Average
Williams-Bos 1.347
Henrich-NY 1.017
Joost-Phi .... .995
Stephens-Bos .... .947
Kell-Det .... .877

Stolen Bases
Dillinger-StL 20
Rizzuto-NY 18
Valo-Phi 14
Philley-Chi 13

Stolen Base Average
Rizzuto-NY 75.0
Dillinger-StL 58.8

Stolen Base Runs
Rizzuto-NY 1.9
Philley-Chi 1.5
Tebbetts-Bos 1.4
Fain-Phi 1.4
Mapes-NY 1.3

Fielding Runs
Doerr-Bos 27.8
Pesky-Bos 21.4
Vernon-Cle 18.8
DiMaggio-Bos 14.3
Baker-Chi 11.8

Total Player Rating
Williams-Bos 6.4
Doerr-Bos 5.2
Joost-Phi 5.1
Michaels-Chi 4.2
Stephens-Bos 4.0

Wins
Parnell-Bos 25
Kinder-Bos 23
Lemon-Cle 22
Raschi-NY 21
Kellner-Phi 20

Win Percentage
Kinder-Bos .... .793
Parnell-Bos .... .781
Reynolds-NY .... .739
Lemon-Cle .... .688

Games
Page-NY 60
Welteroth-Was 52
Ferrick-StL 50
Kennedy-StL 48
Surkont-Chi 44

Complete Games
Parnell-Bos 27
Newhouser-Det 22
Lemon-Cle 22
Raschi-NY 21

Shutouts
Trucks-Det 6
Kinder-Bos 6
Garcia-Cle 5

Saves
Page-NY 27
Benton-Cle 10
Ferrick-StL 6
Paige-Cle 5

Innings Pitched
Parnell-Bos 295.1
Newhouser-Det ... 292.0
Lemon-Cle 279.2
Trucks-Det 275.0
Raschi-NY 274.2

Fewest Hits/Game
Byrne-NY 5.74
Lemon-Cle 6.79
Trucks-Det 6.84
Gray-Det 7.52
Pierce-Chi 7.60

Fewest BB/Game
Hutchinson-Det 2.48
Houtteman-Det 2.61
Lopat-NY 2.88
Garcia-Cle 3.07
Wynn-Cle 3.12

Strikeouts
Trucks-Det 153
Newhouser-Det 144
Lemon-Cle 138
Kinder-Bos 138
Byrne-NY 129

Strikeouts/Game
Byrne-NY 5.92
Trucks-Det 5.01
Pierce-Chi 4.98
Kinder-Bos 4.93
Garcia-Cle 4.82

Ratio
Hutchinson-Det ... 10.49
Trucks-Det 11.03
Garcia-Cle 11.07
Lemon-Cle 11.39
Gumpert-Chi 11.81

Earned Run Average
Garcia-Cle 2.36
Parnell-Bos 2.77
Trucks-Det 2.81
Hutchinson-Det 2.96
Lemon-Cle 2.99

Adjusted ERA
Garcia-Cle 169
Parnell-Bos 157
Trucks-Det 148
Hutchinson-Det 141
Lemon-Cle 133

Opponents' Batting Avg.
Byrne-NY .... .183
Lemon-Cle .... .211
Trucks-Det .... .211
Gray-Det .... .227
Pierce-Chi .... .228

Opponents' On-Base Pct.
Hutchinson-Det ...... .290
Trucks-Det .... .301
Garcia-Cle .... .308
Lemon-Cle .... .309
Gumpert-Chi .... .318

Starter Runs
Parnell-Bos 46.7
Trucks-Det 42.3
Lemon-Cle 37.4
Garcia-Cle 35.9
Benton-Cle 31.3

Adjusted Starter Runs
Parnell-Bos 50.2
Trucks-Det 41.5
Garcia-Cle 33.6
Lemon-Cle 32.6
Benton-Cle 29.6

Clutch Pitching Index
Garcia-Cle 123
Lopat-NY 122
Wight-Chi 118
Houtteman-Det 115
Kinder-Bos 114

Relief Runs
Page-NY 24.1
Paige-Cle 10.7
Papish-Cle 6.9
Ferrick-StL 3.7

Adjusted Relief Runs
Page-NY 22.7
Paige-Cle 9.3
Ferrick-StL 7.0
Papish-Cle 5.8
Starr-StL 1.8

Relief Ranking
Page-NY 41.8
Paige-Cle 12.3
Ferrick-StL 6.9
Papish-Cle 2.9
Starr-StL 1.6

Total Pitcher Index
Lemon-Cle 5.8
Parnell-Bos 5.3
Page-NY 3.9
Garcia-Cle 3.8
Hutchinson-Det 3.4

Total Baseball Ranking
Williams-Bos 6.4
Lemon-Cle 5.8
Parnell-Bos 5.3
Doerr-Bos 5.2
Joost-Phi 5.1

TEAM	G	W	L	PCT	GB	R	OR	AB	H	2B	3B	HR	BB	SO	AVG	OBP	SLG	OPS	OPS+	BR	BR+	PF	CHI	RC	SB	CS	SBA	SBR
PHI	157	91	63	.591		722	**624**	5426	1440	225	55	125	535	569	.265	.334	.396	730	100	-14	-2	98	101	714	33			
BRO	155	89	65	.578	2	**847**	724	5364	**1461**	247	46	**194**	607	632	**.272**	**.349**	**.444**	**793**	**113**	**107**	**91**	102	101	**833**	**77**			
NY	154	86	68	.558	5	735	643	5238	1352	204	50	133	**627**	629	.258	.342	.392	734	100	4	0	101	101	726	42			
BOS	156	83	71	.539	8	785	736	5363	1411	246	36	148	615	616	.263	.342	.405	747	110	24	76	94	**104**	750	71			
STL	153	78	75	.510	12.5	693	670	5215	1353	255	50	102	606	604	.259	.339	.386	725	93	-15	-47	105	99	696	23			
CIN	153	66	87	.431	24.5	654	734	5253	1366	**257**	27	99	504	**497**	.260	.327	.376	703	91	-65	-67	100	102	643	37			
CHI	154	64	89	.418	26.5	643	772	5230	1298	224	47	161	479	767	.248	.315	.401	716	95	-53	-45	99	100	658	46			
PIT	154	57	96	.373	33.5	681	857	5327	1404	227	**59**	138	564	693	.264	.338	.406	744	99	13	-10	103	93	729	43			
TOT	618					5760		42416	11085	1885	370	1100	4537	5007	.262	.336	.402	737							372			

TEAM	CG	SH	SV	IP	H	H/G	HR	BB	SO	RAT	ERA	ERA+	OAV	OOB	PR	PR+	PF	CPI	FA	E	DP	FW	PW	BW	SBW	DIF
PHI	57	13	**27**	1406	1324	8.5	122	**530**	620	**12.0**	**3.50**	**116**	.250	**.320**	**101**	**88**	98	**105**	.975	151	155	.2	**8.7**	-.1		5.5
BRO	62	10	21	1389²	1397	9.1	163	591	**772**	13.1	4.29	96	.263	.339	-22	-29	99	102	**.979**	**127**	**183**	**1.4**	-2.8	**8.9**		4.6
NY	70	**19**	15	1375	**1268**	**8.3**	140	536	596	12.1	3.72	110	**.246**	**.320**	66	59	99	100	.977	137	181	.8	5.8	.0		2.5
BOS	**88**	7	10	1385¹	1411	9.2	129	554	615	13.0	4.14	93	.263	.336	0	-48	93	99	.970	182	146	-1.6	-4.6	7.5		5.0
STL	57	10	14	1356	1398	9.3	**119**	535	603	13.0	3.97	108	.268	.339	26	47	104	**105**	.978	130	172	1.2	4.6	-4.5		.4
CIN	67	7	13	1357²	1363	9.1	145	582	686	13.2	4.32	98	.259	.338	-26	-13	102	97	.976	140	132	.6	-1.2	-6.5		-3.2
CHI	55	9	19	1371¹	1452	9.6	130	593	559	13.6	4.28	98	.271	.347	-21	-11	101	103	.968	201	169	-2.8	-1.0	-4.3		-4.1
PIT	42	6	16	1368²	1472	9.7	152	616	556	14.0	4.96	88	.275	.353	-124	-83	106	95	.977	136	165	.9	-8.1	-.9		-11.2
TOT	498	81	135	11009²		9.1				13.0	4.15		.262	.336					.976	1204	1303					

Runs
Torgeson-Bos 120
Stanky-NY 115
Kiner-Pit 112
Snider-Bro 109
Musial-StL 105

Hits
Snider-Bro 199
Musial-StL 192
Furillo-Bro 189
Ennis-Phi 185
Waitkus-Phi 182

Doubles
Schoendienst-StL 43
Musial-StL 41
Robinson-Bro 39
Kluszewski-Cin 37
Dark-NY 36

Triples
Ashburn-Phi 14
Bell-Pit 11
Snider-Bro 10
Smalley-Chi 9
Schoendienst-StL 9

Home Runs
Kiner-Pit 47
Pafko-Chi 36
Sauer-Chi 32
Hodges-Bro 32

Total Bases
Snider-Bro 343
Musial-StL 331
Ennis-Phi 328
Kiner-Pit 323
Pafko-Chi 304

Runs Batted In
Ennis-Phi 126
Kiner-Pit 118
Hodges-Bro 113
Kluszewski-Cin 111
Musial-StL 109

Runs Produced
Furillo-Bro 187
Ennis-Phi 187
Musial-StL 186
Snider-Bro 185
Torgeson-Bos 184

Bases On Balls
Stanky-NY 144
Kiner-Pit 122
Torgeson-Bos 119
Westrum-NY 92
Reese-Bro 91

Batting Average
Musial-StL .346
Robinson-Bro .328
Snider-Bro .321
Ennis-Phi .311
Kluszewski-Cin .307

On-Base Percentage
Stanky-NY .460
Musial-StL .437
Robinson-Bro .423
Glaviano-StL .421
Torgeson-Bos .412

Slugging Average
Musial-StL .596
Pafko-Chi .591
Kiner-Pit .590
Gordon-Bos .557
Snider-Bro .553

On-Base Plus Slugging
Musial-StL 1034
Kiner-Pit 998
Pafko-Chi 989
Gordon-Bos 960
Snider-Bro 932

Adjusted OPS
Musial-StL 161
Gordon-Bos 160
Pafko-Chi 158
Kiner-Pit 154
Elliott-Bos 143

Batter Runs
Musial-StL 57.3
Kiner-Pit 48.7
Pafko-Chi 41.5
Snider-Bro 35.6
Gordon-Bos 35.3

Adjusted Batter Runs
Musial-StL 51.1
Kiner-Pit 44.6
Pafko-Chi 42.8
Gordon-Bos 42.4
Torgeson-Bos 39.0

Clutch Hitting Index
D.Mueller-NY 138
Slaughter-StL 136
Westlake-Pit 115
Wyrostek-Cin 112
Thompson-NY 111

Runs Created
Musial-StL 149
Kiner-Pit 133
Snider-Bro 131
Pafko-Chi 124
Torgeson-Bos 121

Total Average
Musial-StL 1.139
Kiner-Pit 1.071
Pafko-Chi 1.057
Stanky-NY 1.013
Gordon-Bos 1.003

Stolen Bases
Jethroe-Bos 35
Reese-Bro 17
Snider-Bro 16
Torgeson-Bos 15
Ashburn-Phi 14

Stolen Base Average

Stolen Base Runs

Fielding Runs
Smalley-Chi 21.3
Cox-Bro 12.0
Ryan-Bos-Cin 11.6
Robinson-Bro 10.6
Westrum-NY 10.4

Total Player Rating
Robinson-Bro 4.8
Stanky-NY 4.3
Gordon-Bos 3.7
Pafko-Chi 3.7
Snider-Bro 3.7

Wins
Spahn-Bos 21
Sain-Bos 20
Roberts-Phi 20

Win Percentage
Maglie-NY .818
Konstanty-Phi .696
Simmons-Phi .680
Roberts-Phi .645

Games
Konstanty-Phi 74
Dickson-Pit 51
Werle-Pit 48
Maglie-NY 47
Brazle-StL 46

Complete Games
Bickford-Bos 27
Spahn-Bos 25
Sain-Bos 25
Roberts-Phi 21
Jansen-NY 21

Shutouts
Hearn-StL-NY 5
Roberts-Phi 5
Maglie-NY 5
Jansen-NY 5

Saves
Konstanty-Phi 22
Werle-Pit 8
Hogue-Bos 7
Branca-Bro 7

Innings Pitched
Bickford-Bos 311.2
Roberts-Phi 304.1
Spahn-Bos 293.0
Sain-Bos 278.1
Jansen-NY 275.0

Fewest Hits/Game
Blackwell-Cin 7.00
Maglie-NY 7.38
Simmons-Phi 7.46
Spahn-Bos 7.62
Jansen-NY 7.79

Fewest BB/Game
Raffensberger-Cin 1.51
Jansen-NY 1.80
Sain-Bos 2.26
Roberts-Phi 2.28
Roe-Bro 2.37

Strikeouts
Spahn-Bos 191
Blackwell-Cin 188
Jansen-NY 161
Simmons-Phi 146
Roberts-Phi 146

Strikeouts/Game
Blackwell-Cin 6.48
Simmons-Phi 6.12
Spahn-Bos 5.87
Palica-Bro 5.86
Jansen-NY 5.27

Ratio
Jansen-NY 9.62
Roberts-Phi 10.68
Brecheen-StL 10.97
Spahn-Bos 11.06
Simmons-Phi 11.24

Earned Run Average
Hearn-StL-NY 2.49
Maglie-NY 2.71
Blackwell-Cin 2.97
Jansen-NY 3.01
Roberts-Phi 3.02

Adjusted ERA
Maglie-NY 151
Blackwell-Cin 143
Lanier-StL 137
Jansen-NY 136
Roberts-Phi 134

Opponents' Batting Avg.
Blackwell-Cin .210
Simmons-Phi .223
Maglie-NY .226
Spahn-Bos .227
Jansen-NY .232

Opponents' On-Base Pct.
Jansen-NY .271
Roberts-Phi .297
Brecheen-StL .298
Spahn-Bos .299
Blackwell-Cin .301

Starter Runs
Roberts-Phi 38.0
Jansen-NY 34.5
Blackwell-Cin 34.1
Maglie-NY 32.8
Spahn-Bos 31.8

Adjusted Starter Runs
Blackwell-Cin 35.9
Roberts-Phi 35.6
Jansen-NY 33.5
Maglie-NY 32.1
Pollet-StL 24.9

Clutch Pitching Index
Brazle-StL 125
Roe-Bro 118
Maglie-NY 116
Ramsdell-Bro-Cin 115
Minner-Chi 113

Relief Runs
Konstanty-Phi 24.9
Kramer-NY 5.9
Leonard-Chi 3.1
VanderMeer-Chi 2.9
Smith-Cin 2.7

Adjusted Relief Runs
Konstanty-Phi 23.9
Kramer-NY 5.5
Smith-Cin 3.6
Leonard-Chi 3.5
VanderMeer-Chi 3.3

Relief Ranking
Konstanty-Phi 40.3
Kramer-NY 5.3
Smith-Cin 3.4
Leonard-Chi 3.2
VanderMeer-Chi 2.9

Total Pitcher Index
Blackwell-Cin 4.2
Jansen-NY 3.8
Konstanty-Phi 3.7
Maglie-NY 3.3
Spahn-Bos 3.3

Total Baseball Ranking
Robinson-Bro 4.8
Stanky-NY 4.3
Blackwell-Cin 4.2
Jansen-NY 3.8
Konstanty-Phi 3.7

TEAM	G	W	L	PCT	GB	R	OR	AB	H	2B	3B	HR	BB	SO	AVG	OBP	SLG	OPS	OPS+	BR	BR+	PF	CHI	RC	SB	CS	SBA	SBR
NY	155	98	56	.636		914	691	5361	1511	234	**70**	159	687	**463**	.282	.367	.441	808	**116**	92	**118**	97	**104**	902	41	28	59	-1
DET	157	95	59	.617	3	837	713	5381	1518	285	50	114	**722**	480	.282	.369	.417	786	104	60	33	103	97	846	23	40	37	-9
BOS	154	94	60	.610	4	**1027**	804	5516	**1665**	**287**	61	161	719	582	**.302**	**.385**	**.464**	**849**	112	**185**	97	110	103	**1014**	32	17	**65**	**1**
CLE	155	92	62	.597	6	806	**654**	5263	1417	222	46	**164**	693	624	.269	.358	.422	780	109	39	67	97	98	820	40	34	54	-3
WAS	155	67	87	.435	31	690	813	5251	1365	190	53	76	671	606	.260	.347	.360	707	91	-93	-59	95	101	690	**42**	25	63	0
CHI	156	60	94	.390	38	625	749	5260	1368	172	47	93	551	566	.260	.333	.364	697	86	-125	-107	97	98	648	19	22	46	-4
STL	154	58	96	.377	40	684	916	5163	1269	235	43	106	690	744	.246	.337	.370	707	84	-102	-126	104	103	667	39	40	49	-5
PHI	154	52	102	.338	46	670	913	5212	1361	204	53	100	685	493	.261	.349	.378	727	94	-56	-42	98	94	708	**42**	25	63	0
TOT	620					6253		42407	11474	1829	423	973	5418	4558	.271	.357	.403	759							278	231	55	-20

TEAM	CG	SH	SV	IP	H	H/G	HR	BB	SO	RAT	ERA	ERA+	OAV	OOB	PR	PR+	PF	CPI	FA	E	DP	FW	PW	BW	SBW	DIF
NY	66	**12**	**31**	1372[2]	1322	8.7	118	708	**712**	13.6	4.16	103	.255	.348	65	23	94	102	.980	119	188	1.3	2.2	**11.1**	.1	6.4
DET	**72**	9	20	1407[1]	1444	9.3	141	**553**	576	13.0	4.13	114	.267	.339	71	86	102	**105**	**.981**	120	194	1.4	8.1	3.1	-.6	6.2
BOS	66	6	28	1362[1]	1413	9.4	121	748	630	14.5	4.89	100	.270	.364	-46	2	107	97	**.981**	**111**	181	**1.7**	.2	9.1	**.3**	5.8
CLE	69	11	16	1378[2]	**1289**	**8.5**	120	647	674	**12.8**	**3.76**	**115**	**.248**	**.333**	**126**	**94**	95	103	.978	129	160	.8	**8.9**	6.3	-.0	-.7
WAS	59	7	18	1364[2]	1479	9.8	**99**	648	486	14.2	4.66	96	.278	.359	-12	-25	98	99	.972	167	181	-1.3	-2.3	-5.5	.2	-.9
CHI	62	7	9	1365[2]	1370	9.1	107	734	566	14.1	4.41	102	.263	.356	26	12	98	100	.977	140	181	.2	1.2	-10.0	-.1	-8.1
STL	56	7	14	1365[1]	1629	10.8	129	651	448	15.3	5.21	95	.295	.372	-94	-35	108	100	.967	196	155	-3.0	-3.2	-11.7	-.2	-.6
PHI	50	3	18	1346[1]	1528	10.3	138	729	466	15.3	5.49	83	.287	.376	-136	-141	99	96	.974	155	**208**	-.7	-13.2	-3.9	.2	-7.3
TOT	500	62	154	10963		9.5				14.1	4.58		.271	.357					.977	1137	1448					

Runs
DiMaggio-Bos 131
Stephens-Bos 125
Rizzuto-NY 125
Berra-NY 116

Hits
Kell-Det 218
Rizzuto-NY 200
DiMaggio-Bos 193
Berra-NY 192
Stephens-Bos 185

Doubles
Kell-Det 56
Wertz-Det 37
Rizzuto-NY 36
Evers-Det 35
Stephens-Bos 34

Triples
Evers-Det 11
Doerr-Bos 11
DiMaggio-Bos 11

Home Runs
Rosen-Cle 37
Dropo-Bos 34
DiMaggio-NY 32
Stephens-Bos 30
Zernial-Chi 29

Total Bases
Dropo-Bos 326
Stephens-Bos 321
Berra-NY 318
Kell-Det 310
DiMaggio-NY 307

Runs Batted In
Stephens-Bos 144
Dropo-Bos 144
Berra-NY 124
Wertz-Det 123
DiMaggio-NY 122

Runs Produced
Stephens-Bos 239
Berra-NY 212
Dropo-Bos 211
Kell-Det 207
DiMaggio-NY 204

Bases On Balls
Yost-Was 141
Fain-Phi 133
Pesky-Bos 104
Joost-Phi 103
Rosen-Cle 100

Batting Average
Goodman-Bos ...... .354
Kell-Det .... .340
DiMaggio-Bos ..... .328
Doby-Cle .... .326
Zarilla-Bos ...... .325

On-Base Percentage
Doby-Cle .... .442
Yost-Was .... .440
Pesky-Bos .... .437
Fain-Phi .... .430
Goodman-Bos ...... .427

Slugging Average
DiMaggio-NY ...... .585
Dropo-Bos .... .583
Evers-Det .... .551
Doby-Cle .... .545
Rosen-Cle .... .543

On-Base Plus Slugging
Doby-Cle 986
DiMaggio-NY 979
Dropo-Bos 961
Evers-Det 959
Rosen-Cle 948

Adjusted OPS
Doby-Cle 156
DiMaggio-NY 152
Rosen-Cle 146
Evers-Det 139
Berra-NY 136

Batter Runs
Doby-Cle 41.7
Williams-Bos 40.9
DiMaggio-NY 35.4
Rosen-Cle 34.3
Evers-Det 33.5

Adjusted Batter Runs
Doby-Cle 45.8
DiMaggio-NY 38.8
Rosen-Cle 38.4
Williams-Bos 32.6
Evers-Det 30.1

Clutch Hitting Index
Vernon-Cle-Was ... 126
Mele-Was 125
Noren-Was 116
Stephens-Bos 110
Fain-Phi 108

Runs Created
Doby-Cle 130
Wertz-Det 128
DiMaggio-NY 125
Berra-NY 125
Rizzuto-NY 124

Total Average
Doby-Cle 1.073
DiMaggio-NY 1.018
Wertz-Det .... .978
Zarilla-Bos ...... .954
Rosen-Cle .... .953

Stolen Bases
DiMaggio-Bos 15
Valo-Phi 12
Rizzuto-NY 12
Coan-Was 10
Lipon-Det 9

Stolen Base Average

Stolen Base Runs
DiMaggio-Bos 1.9
Vernon-Cle-Was ... 1.4
Collins-NY 1.1
Avila-Cle 1.1
Jensen-NY 9

Fielding Runs
Priddy-Det 31.3
Hegan-Cle 24.2
Pesky-Bos 21.5
Noren-Was 15.9
Carrasquel-Chi ... 11.2

Total Player Rating
Rizzuto-NY 4.0
Berra-NY 3.6
Rosen-Cle 3.4
Doby-Cle 3.3
DiMaggio-NY 3.3

Wins
B.Lemon-Cle 23
Raschi-NY 21
Houtteman-Det 19

Win Percentage
Raschi-NY .... .724
Wynn-Cle .... .692
Lopat-NY .... .692
Hutchinson-Det ... .680
B.Lemon-Cle ...... .676

Games
Harris-Was 53
Kinder-Bos 48
Ferrick-StL-NY ... 46
Judson-Chi 46
Brissie-Phi 46

Complete Games
B.Lemon-Cle 22
Garver-StL 22
Parnell-Bos 21
Houtteman-Det 21

Shutouts
Houtteman-Det 4

Saves
Harris-Was 15
Page-NY 13
Ferrick-StL-NY ... 11
Kinder-Bos 9
Brissie-Phi 8

Innings Pitched
B.Lemon-Cle 288.0
Houtteman-Det 274.2
Garver-StL 260.0
Raschi-NY 256.2
Parnell-Bos 249.0

Fewest Hits/Game
Wynn-Cle 6.99
Pierce-Chi 7.76
Cain-Chi 8.02
Reynolds-NY 8.04
Raschi-NY 8.14

Fewest BB/Game
Hutchinson-Det ... 1.86
Lopat-NY 2.48
Overmire-StL 2.52
Trout-Det 3.12
Houtteman-Det 3.24

Strikeouts
B.Lemon-Cle 170
Reynolds-NY 160
Raschi-NY 155
Wynn-Cle 143
Feller-Cle 119

Strikeouts/Game
Wynn-Cle 6.02
Reynolds-NY 5.98
Raschi-NY 5.44
B.Lemon-Cle 5.31
Byrne-NY 5.22

Ratio
Wynn-Cle 11.41
Lopat-NY 11.92
Houtteman-Det 11.93
Raschi-NY 12.31
Feller-Cle 12.32

Earned Run Average
Wynn-Cle 3.20
Garver-StL 3.39
Feller-Cle 3.43
Lopat-NY 3.47
Houtteman-Det 3.54

Adjusted ERA
Garver-StL 146
Parnell-Bos 136
Wynn-Cle 135
Houtteman-Det 132
Feller-Cle 126

Opponents' Batting Avg.
Wynn-Cle .... .212
Pierce-Chi .... .228
Reynolds-NY ...... .242
Raschi-NY .... .243
Cain-Chi .... .244

Opponents' On-Base Pct.
Wynn-Cle .... .305
Lopat-NY .... .317
Houtteman-Det .... .322
Feller-Cle .... .325
Raschi-NY .... .327

Starter Runs
Garver-StL 34.3
Wynn-Cle 32.7
Houtteman-Det 31.7
Feller-Cle 31.7
Lopat-NY 29.2

Adjusted Starter Runs
Garver-StL 41.6
Houtteman-Det 34.3
Parnell-Bos 33.2
Wynn-Cle 28.4
Feller-Cle 26.3

Clutch Pitching Index
Garver-StL 119
Hudson-Was 113
B.Lemon-Cle 111
Houtteman-Det 110
Parnell-Bos 110

Relief Runs
Judson-Chi 8.0
Aloma-Chi 7.6
Benton-Cle 7.0
Ferrick-StL-NY ... 7.0
Flores-Cle 5.0

Adjusted Relief Runs
Judson-Chi 7.0
Aloma-Chi 6.8
Ferrick-StL-NY ... 6.4
Benton-Cle 5.6
Flores-Cle 3.7

Relief Ranking
Ferrick-StL-NY ... 12.7
Aloma-Chi 7.0
Benton-Cle 5.6
Flores-Cle 4.4
Judson-Chi 3.5

Total Pitcher Index
Garver-StL 5.3
B.Lemon-Cle 3.8
Wynn-Cle 3.8
Parnell-Bos 3.7
Houtteman-Det 3.5

Total Baseball Ranking
Garver-StL 5.3
Rizzuto-NY 4.0
B.Lemon-Cle 3.8
Wynn-Cle 3.8
Parnell-Bos 3.7

TEAM	G	W	L	PCT	GB	R	OR	AB	H	2B	3B	HR	BB	SO	AVG	OBP	SLG	OPS	OPS+	BR	BR+	PF	CHI	RC	SB	CS	SBA	SBR
NY	157	98	59	.624		781	**641**	5360	1396	201	53	179	**671**	624	.260	.347	.418	765	111	91	85	101	97	812	55	34	62	0
BRO	158	97	60	.618	1	**855**	672	5492	**1511**	**249**	37	**184**	603	649	**.275**	**.352**	**.434**	**786**	**116**	**130**	**113**	102	101	**843**	**89**	70	56	-5
STL	155	81	73	.526	15.5	683	671	5317	1404	230	**57**	95	569	**492**	.264	.339	.382	721	99	7	3	101	97	705	30	30	50	-4
BOS	155	76	78	.494	20.5	723	662	5293	1385	234	37	130	565	617	.262	.336	.394	730	111	20	74	93	102	719	80	34	**70**	**6**
PHI	154	73	81	.474	23.5	648	644	5332	1384	199	47	108	505	525	.260	.326	.375	701	96	-38	-28	99	99	676	63	28	69	4
CIN	155	68	86	.442	28.5	559	667	5285	1309	215	33	88	415	577	.248	.304	.351	655	81	-134	-142	102	**104**	562	44	40	52	-4
PIT	155	64	90	.416	32.5	689	845	5318	1372	218	56	137	557	615	.258	.331	.397	728	99	11	-9	103	98	712	29	27	52	-3
CHI	155	62	92	.403	34.5	614	750	5307	1327	200	47	103	477	647	.250	.315	.364	679	86	-86	-96	102	103	613	63	30	68	3
TOT	622					5552		42704	11088	1746	367	1024	4362	4746	.260	.332	.390	721							453	293	61	-3

TEAM	CG	SH	SV	IP	H	H/G	HR	BB	SO	RAT	ERA	ERA+	OAV	OOB	PR	PR+	PF	CPI	FA	E	DP	FW	PW	BW	SBW	DIF
NY	64	9	18	1412^2	**1334**	**8.5**	148	**482**	625	**11.7**	**3.48**	**113**	**.248**	**.313**	**75**	**69**	99	**104**	.972	171	175	-1.0	**7.0**	8.6	.0	5.1
BRO	64	10	13	1423^1	1360	8.6	150	549	**693**	12.3	3.88	101	.253	.326	13	8	99	101	.979	129	**192**	1.3	.9	**11.4**	-.5	5.6
STL	58	9	**23**	1387^2	1391	9.1	119	568	546	12.9	3.95	100	.264	.338	1	2	100	103	**.980**	**125**	187	**1.4**	.3	.4	-.4	2.6
BOS	**73**	16	12	1389	1378	9.0	**96**	595	604	13.0	3.75	98	.259	.337	33	-12	93	**104**	.976	145	157	.3	-1.2	7.5	**.6**	-8.1
PHI	57	**19**	15	1384^2	1373	9.0	110	497	570	12.3	3.81	101	.258	.324	23	6	97	98	.977	138	146	.6	.7	-2.8	.4	-2.8
CIN	55	14	**23**	1390^2	1357	8.8	119	490	584	12.3	3.71	110	.255	.323	40	56	103	100	.977	140	141	.6	5.7	-14.2	-.4	-.5
PIT	40	9	22	1380^1	1479	9.7	157	609	580	13.9	4.80	88	.274	.350	-128	-82	107	97	.972	170	178	-1.0	-8.2	-.9	-.3	-2.5
CHI	48	10	10	1385^2	1416	9.2	125	572	544	13.2	4.34	94	.265	.340	-58	-36	103	96	.971	181	161	-1.6	-3.6	-9.6	.3	-.4
TOT	459	96	136	11154		9.0				12.7	3.96		.260	.332					.976	1199	1337					

Runs
Musial-StL 124
Kiner-Pit 124
Hodges-Bro 118
Dark-NY 114
Robinson-Bro 106

Hits
Ashburn-Phi 221
Musial-StL 205
Furillo-Bro 197
Dark-NY 196
Robinson-Bro 185

Doubles
Dark-NY 41
Kluszewski-Cin 35
Robinson-Bro 33
Campanella-Bro 33

Triples
Musial-StL 12
Bell-Pit 12
Irvin-NY 11
Jethroe-Bos 10
Baumholtz-Chi 10

Home Runs
Kiner-Pit 42
Hodges-Bro 40
Campanella-Bro 33
Thomson-NY 32
Musial-StL 32

Total Bases
Musial-StL 355
Kiner-Pit 333
Hodges-Bro 307
Campanella-Bro 298

Runs Batted In
Irvin-NY 121
Kiner-Pit 109
Gordon-Bos 109
Musial-StL 108
Campanella-Bro 108

Runs Produced
Musial-StL 200
Kiner-Pit 191
Irvin-NY 191
Hodges-Bro 181
Gordon-Bos 176

Bases On Balls
Kiner-Pit 137
Stanky-NY 127
Westrum-NY 104
Torgeson-Bos 102
Musial-StL 98

Batting Average
Musial-StL .355
Ashburn-Phi .344
Robinson-Bro .338
Campanella-Bro .325
Irvin-NY .312

On-Base Percentage
Kiner-Pit .452
Musial-StL .449
Robinson-Bro .429
Irvin-NY .415
Stanky-NY .401

Slugging Average
Kiner-Pit .627
Musial-StL .614
Campanella-Bro .590
Thomson-NY .562
Hodges-Bro .527

On-Base Plus Slugging
Kiner-Pit 1079
Musial-StL 1063
Campanella-Bro 983
Robinson-Bro 957
Thomson-NY 947

Adjusted OPS
Musial-StL 182
Kiner-Pit 182
Campanella-Bro 158
Robinson-Bro 153
Thomson-NY 150

Batter Runs
Kiner-Pit 70.8
Musial-StL 70.1
Robinson-Bro 45.8
Campanella-Bro 41.7
Irvin-NY 40.7

Adjusted Batter Runs
Musial-StL 69.2
Kiner-Pit 66.6
Robinson-Bro 43.4
Irvin-NY 39.8
Campanella-Bro 39.6

Clutch Hitting Index
Slaughter-StL 136
Reese-Bro 130
Irvin-NY 118
Westlake-Pit-StL 112
Torgeson-Bos 109

Runs Created
Musial-StL 169
Kiner-Pit 165
Robinson-Bro 133
Irvin-NY 127
Hodges-Bro 119

Total Average
Kiner-Pit 1.251
Musial-StL 1.180
Robinson-Bro 1.034
Irvin-NY .985
Campanella-Bro .978

Stolen Bases
Jethroe-Bos 35
Ashburn-Phi 29
Robinson-Bro 25
Torgeson-Bos 20
Reese-Bro 20

Stolen Base Average
Jethroe-Bos 87.5
Ashburn-Phi 82.9
Robinson-Bro 75.8
Torgeson-Bos 64.5
Reese-Bro 58.8

Stolen Base Runs
Jethroe-Bos 5.9
Ashburn-Phi 4.3
Robinson-Bro 2.7
Jackson-Chi 2.0
Irvin-NY 1.9

Fielding Runs
Ashburn-Phi 32.3
Robinson-Bro 16.5
Furillo-Bro 16.1
Schoendienst-StL 15.5
Hemus-StL 13.4

Total Player Rating
Robinson-Bro 6.9
Musial-StL 6.2
Campanella-Bro 5.4
Ashburn-Phi 5.2
Kiner-Pit 5.1

Wins
Maglie-NY 23
Jansen-NY 23
Spahn-Bos 22
Roe-Bro 22
Roberts-Phi 21

Win Percentage
Roe-Bro .880
Maglie-NY .793
Newcombe-Bro .690
Jansen-NY .676
Hearn-NY .654

Games
Wilks-StL-Pit 65
Werle-Pit 59
Konstanty-Phi 58
Spencer-NY 57
Brazle-StL 56

Complete Games
Spahn-Bos 26
Roberts-Phi 22
Maglie-NY 22
Roe-Bro 19
Dickson-Pit 19

Shutouts
Spahn-Bos 7
Roberts-Phi 6
Raffensberger-Cin 5

Saves
Wilks-StL-Pit 13
Smith-Cin 11
Konstanty-Phi 9
Brazle-StL 7

Innings Pitched
Roberts-Phi 315.0
Spahn-Bos 310.2
Maglie-NY 298.0
Dickson-Pit 288.2
Jansen-NY 278.2

Fewest Hits/Game
Maglie-NY 7.67
Newcombe-Bro 7.78
Blackwell-Cin 7.89
Branca-Bro 7.94
Queen-Pit 7.97

Fewest BB/Game
Raffensberger-Cin 1.38
Jansen-NY 1.81
Roberts-Phi 1.83
Roe-Bro 2.24
Sain-Bos 2.53

Strikeouts
Spahn-Bos 164
Newcombe-Bro 164
Maglie-NY 146
Jansen-NY 145
Rush-Chi 129

Strikeouts/Game
Queen-Pit 6.58
Rush-Chi 5.49
Newcombe-Bro 5.43
Branca-Bro 5.21
Spahn-Bos 4.75

Ratio
Raffensberger-Cin 9.99
Roberts-Phi 10.03
Jansen-NY 10.11
Maglie-NY 10.45
Roe-Bro 10.86

Earned Run Average
Nichols-Bos 2.88
Maglie-NY 2.93
Spahn-Bos 2.98
Roberts-Phi 3.03
Jansen-NY 3.04

Adjusted ERA
Maglie-NY 134
Roe-Bro 129
Jansen-NY 129
Nichols-Bos 127
Roberts-Phi 127

Opponents' Batting Avg.
Maglie-NY .230
Newcombe-Bro .230
Blackwell-Cin .233
Queen-Pit .233
Branca-Bro .237

Opponents' On-Base Pct.
Roberts-Phi .278
Jansen-NY .279
Raffensberger-Cin .279
Maglie-NY .289
Newcombe-Bro .297

Starter Runs
Maglie-NY 34.1
Spahn-Bos 33.7
Roberts-Phi 32.6
Jansen-NY 28.6
Roe-Bro 26.4

Adjusted Starter Runs
Maglie-NY 33.0
Roberts-Phi 29.5
Jansen-NY 27.5
Spahn-Bos 25.7
Roe-Bro 25.6

Clutch Pitching Index
Roe-Bro 122
Sain-Bos 113
Nichols-Bos 112
Minner-Chi 111
Bickford-Bos 108

Relief Runs
Brazle-StL 14.9
Kennedy-NY 12.9
Perkowski-Cin 12.9
Wilks-StL-Pit 12.3
Leonard-Chi 11.9

Adjusted Relief Runs
Brazle-StL 14.9
Wilks-StL-Pit 14.0
Perkowski-Cin 13.8
Kennedy-NY 12.7
Leonard-Chi 12.7

Relief Ranking
Leonard-Chi 23.5
Wilks-StL-Pit 14.0
Perkowski-Cin 11.3
Brazle-StL 11.1
Smith-Cin 10.9

Total Pitcher Index
Roberts-Phi 3.5
Spahn-Bos 3.1
Maglie-NY 3.0
Jansen-NY 2.9
Blackwell-Cin 2.9

Total Baseball Ranking
Robinson-Bro 6.9
Musial-StL 6.2
Campanella-Bro 5.4
Ashburn-Phi 5.2
Kiner-Pit 5.1

TEAM	G	W	L	PCT	GB	R	OR	AB	H	2B	3B	HR	BB	SO	AVG	OBP	SLG	OPS	OPS+	BR	BR+	PF	CHI	RC	SB	CS	SBA	SBR
NY	154	98	56	.636		798	621	5194	1395	208	48	**140**	605	547	.269	.349	**.408**	**757**	**113**	62	**91**	96	**104**	762	78	39	**67**	**4**
CLE	155	93	61	.604	5	696	**594**	5250	1346	208	35	**140**	606	632	.256	.336	.389	725	106	0	42	94	98	710	52	35	60	-1
BOS	154	87	67	.565	11	**804**	725	5378	1428	233	32	127	**756**	594	.266	**.358**	.392	750	98	**64**	-7	110	100	**778**	20	21	49	-3
CHI	155	81	73	.526	17	714	644	5378	**1453**	229	**64**	86	596	524	**.270**	.349	.385	734	105	23	39	98	95	745	**99**	70	59	-3
DET	154	73	81	.474	25	685	741	5336	1413	231	35	104	568	525	.265	.338	.380	718	99	-14	-17	100	98	697	37	34	52	-4
PHI	154	70	84	.455	28	736	745	5277	1381	**262**	43	102	677	565	.262	.349	.386	735	101	29	14	102	98	745	47	36	57	-2
WAS	154	62	92	.403	36	672	764	5329	1399	242	45	54	560	**515**	.263	.336	.355	691	93	-60	-48	98	103	648	45	38	54	-3
STL	154	52	102	.338	46	611	882	5219	1288	223	47	86	521	693	.247	.317	.357	674	84	-102	-119	103	103	592	35	38	48	-6
TOT	617					5716		42361	11103	1836	349	839	4889	4595	.263	.342	.382	723							413	311	57	-18

TEAM	CG	SH	SV	IP	H	H/G	HR	BB	SO	RAT	ERA	ERA+	OAV	OOB	PR	PR+	PF	CPI	FA	E	DP	FW	PW	BW	SBW	DIF
NY	66	**24**	22	1367	1290	8.5	92	562	**664**	12.4	3.57	107	.250	.328	85	44	93	103	.975	144	190	.4	4.4	**9.0**	**.6**	6.8
CLE	**76**	10	19	1391[1]	**1287**	**8.4**	**85**	577	642	12.3	**3.39**	112	**.245**	**.323**	**114**	68	92	103	**.978**	**134**	151	**1.0**	6.7	4.2	.1	4.2
BOS	46	7	**24**	1399	1413	9.1	99	599	658	13.2	4.14	108	.264	.342	-2	46	108	99	.977	141	184	.5	4.6	-.6	-.0	5.8
CHI	74	11	14	1418[1]	1353	8.6	109	**549**	572	**12.2**	3.51	**115**	.252	**.323**	97	**86**	98	**105**	.975	151	176	.0	**8.5**	3.9	-.0	-8.2
DET	51	8	17	1384	1385	9.1	103	602	597	13.2	4.30	97	.262	.342	-26	-18	101	96	.973	163	166	-.6	-1.7	-1.6	-.2	.4
PHI	52	7	22	1358	1421	9.5	109	569	437	13.5	4.47	96	.272	.347	-52	-27	104	98	**.978**	136	**204**	.8	-2.6	1.4	.0	-6.5
WAS	58	6	13	1366[1]	1429	9.5	110	630	475	13.7	4.49	91	.269	.348	-55	-59	99	97	.973	160	148	-.5	-5.8	-4.7	-.0	-3.8
STL	56	5	9	1370[1]	1525	10.1	132	801	550	15.6	5.18	85	.282	.379	-160	-112	107	101	.971	172	179	-1.1	-11.0	-11.7	-.4	-.7
TOT	479	78	140	11054[1]		9.1				13.3	4.13		.263	.342					.976	1201	1398					

Runs
- DiMaggio-Bos 113
- Minoso-Cle-Chi 112
- Yost-Was 109
- Williams-Bos 109
- Joost-Phi 107

Hits
- Kell-Det 191
- Fox-Chi 189
- DiMaggio-Bos 189
- Minoso-Cle-Chi 173
- Williams-Bos 169

Doubles
- Yost-Was 36
- Mele-Was 36
- Kell-Det 36

Triples
- Minoso-Cle-Chi 14
- Coleman-StL-Chi 12
- Fox-Chi 12
- Young-StL 9

Home Runs
- Zernial-Chi-Phi 33
- Williams-Bos 30
- Robinson-Chi 29

Total Bases
- Williams-Bos 295
- Zernial-Chi-Phi 292
- Robinson-Chi 279
- Berra-NY 269
- DiMaggio-Bos 267

Runs Batted In
- Zernial-Chi-Phi 129
- Williams-Bos 126
- Robinson-Chi 117
- Easter-Cle 103
- Rosen-Cle 102

Runs Produced
- Williams-Bos 205
- Zernial-Chi-Phi 188
- Minoso-Cle-Chi 178
- Robinson-Chi 173
- DiMaggio-Bos 173

Bases On Balls
- Williams-Bos 144
- Yost-Was 126
- Joost-Phi 106
- Doby-Cle 101
- Rosen-Cle 85

Batting Average
- Fain-Phi .... .344
- Minoso-Cle-Chi ..... .326
- Kell-Det .... .319
- Williams-Bos .... .318
- Fox-Chi .... .313

On-Base Percentage
- Williams-Bos .... .464
- Fain-Phi .... .451
- Doby-Cle .... .428
- Yost-Was .... .423
- Minoso-Cle-Chi ..... .422

Slugging Average
- Williams-Bos .... .556
- Doby-Cle .... .512
- Zernial-Chi-Phi .... .511
- Wertz-Det .... .511
- Minoso-Cle-Chi ..... .500

On-Base Plus Slugging
- Williams-Bos 1019
- Doby-Cle 941
- Minoso-Cle-Chi 922
- Fain-Phi 921
- Wertz-Det 894

Adjusted OPS
- Doby-Cle 163
- Williams-Bos 159
- Minoso-Cle-Chi 152
- Fain-Phi 146
- Wertz-Det 140

Batter Runs
- Williams-Bos 62.8
- Minoso-Cle-Chi 38.2
- Doby-Cle 37.0
- Fain-Phi 33.8
- Joost-Phi 30.5

Adjusted Batter Runs
- Williams-Bos 50.2
- Doby-Cle 43.1
- Minoso-Cle-Chi 40.8
- Yost-Was 32.3
- Fain-Phi 31.8

Clutch Hitting Index
- Mele-Was 136
- Busby-Chi 127
- Noren-Was 120
- Zernial-Chi-Phi 118
- DiMaggio-NY 113

Runs Created
- Williams-Bos 152
- Minoso-Cle-Chi 120
- Yost-Was 117
- Joost-Phi 115
- Doby-Cle 108

Total Average
- Williams-Bos 1.177
- Doby-Cle 1.031
- Minoso-Cle-Chi .... .987
- Fain-Phi .... .959
- Yost-Was .... .909

Stolen Bases
- Minoso-Cle-Chi 31
- Busby-Chi 26
- Rizzuto-NY 18

Stolen Base Average
- Rizzuto-NY 85.7
- Minoso-Cle-Chi 75.6
- Busby-Chi 70.3

Stolen Base Runs
- Minoso-Cle-Chi 3.3
- Rizzuto-NY 2.9
- Busby-Chi 1.9
- Carrasquel-Chi 1.7
- McDougald-NY 1.3

Fielding Runs
- Coan-Was 22.0
- Noren-Was 21.1
- Stephens-Bos 14.1
- Fain-Phi 12.6
- Carrasquel-Chi 12.5

Total Player Rating
- Williams-Bos 4.0
- Joost-Phi 3.9
- Fain-Phi 3.8
- Doby-Cle 3.8
- Berra-NY 3.5

Wins
- Feller-Cle 22
- Raschi-NY 21
- Lopat-NY 21

Win Percentage
- Feller-Cle .... .733
- Lopat-NY .... .700
- Reynolds-NY .... .680
- Raschi-NY .... .677
- Shantz-Phi .... .643

Games
- Kinder-Bos 63
- Brissie-Phi-Cle 56
- Garcia-Cle 47
- Scheib-Phi 46

Complete Games
- Garver-StL 24
- Wynn-Cle 21
- Lopat-NY 20
- Pierce-Chi 18

Shutouts
- Reynolds-NY 7
- Raschi-NY 4
- Lopat-NY 4
- Feller-Cle 4

Saves
- Kinder-Bos 14
- Scheib-Phi 10
- Brissie-Phi-Cle 9
- Reynolds-NY 7
- Garcia-Cle 6

Innings Pitched
- Wynn-Cle 274.1
- Lemon-Cle 263.1
- Raschi-NY 258.1
- Garcia-Cle 254.0
- Feller-Cle 249.2

Fewest Hits/Game
- Reynolds-NY 6.96
- McDermott-Bos 7.38
- Wynn-Cle 7.45
- Rogovin-Det-Chi 7.85
- Lopat-NY 8.02

Fewest BB/Game
- Hutchinson-Det 1.29
- Lopat-NY 2.72
- Pierce-Chi 2.73
- Hooper-Phi 2.90
- Garcia-Cle 2.91

Strikeouts
- Raschi-NY 164
- Wynn-Cle 133
- Lemon-Cle 132
- Gray-Det 131
- McDermott-Bos 127

Strikeouts/Game
- McDermott-Bos 6.65
- Gray-Det 5.97
- Raschi-NY 5.71
- Reynolds-NY 5.13
- Lemon-Cle 4.51

Ratio
- Lopat-NY 10.85
- Rogovin-Det-Chi .. 10.97
- Wynn-Cle 11.06
- Hutchinson-Det ... 11.13
- Reynolds-NY 11.24

Earned Run Average
- Rogovin-Det-Chi .. 2.78
- Lopat-NY 2.91
- Wynn-Cle 3.02
- Pierce-Chi 3.03
- Reynolds-NY 3.05

Adjusted ERA
- Rogovin-Det-Chi .. 146
- Parnell-Bos 137
- McDermott-Bos 133
- Pierce-Chi 133
- Lopat-NY 131

Opponents' Batting Avg.
- Reynolds-NY ...... .213
- Wynn-Cle .... .225
- McDermott-Bos .... .226
- Rogovin-Det-Chi .. .235
- Lopat-NY .... .239

Opponents' On-Base Pct.
- Lopat-NY .... .298
- Rogovin-Det-Chi .. .301
- Wynn-Cle .... .301
- Hutchinson-Det ... .302
- Reynolds-NY ...... .304

Starter Runs
- Wynn-Cle 33.6
- Rogovin-Det-Chi ... 32.2
- Lopat-NY 31.5
- Pierce-Chi 29.1
- Garcia-Cle 27.3

Adjusted Starter Runs
- Rogovin-Det-Chi ... 31.0
- Pierce-Chi 27.3
- Parnell-Bos 27.3
- Lopat-NY 25.7
- Wynn-Cle 25.5

Clutch Pitching Index
- Parnell-Bos 119
- Pierce-Chi 113
- Rogovin-Det-Chi ... 111
- Feller-Cle 109
- Raschi-NY 108

Relief Runs
- Kinder-Bos 22.2
- Aloma-Chi 17.7
- Brissie-Phi-Cle 7.5
- Ostrowski-NY 6.7
- Masterson-Bos 5.2

Adjusted Relief Runs
- Kinder-Bos 24.9
- Aloma-Chi 17.4
- Masterson-Bos 6.8
- Brissie-Phi-Cle 3.9
- Ostrowski-NY 3.8

Relief Ranking
- Kinder-Bos 29.1
- Aloma-Chi 15.3
- Harris-Was 4.3
- Ostrowski-NY 4.1
- Masterson-Bos 3.6

Total Pitcher Index
- Parnell-Bos 3.8
- Lopat-NY 3.3
- Pierce-Chi 3.0
- Garver-StL 3.0
- Wynn-Cle 2.9

Total Baseball Ranking
- Williams-Bos 4.0
- Joost-Phi 3.9
- Fain-Phi 3.8
- Parnell-Bos 3.8
- Doby-Cle 3.8

TEAM	G	W	L	PCT	GB	R	OR	AB	H	2B	3B	HR	BB	SO	AVG	OBP	SLG	OPS	OPS+	BR	BR+	PF	CHI	RC	SB	CS	SBA	SBR
BRO	155	96	57	.627		**775**	603	5266	1380	199	32	**153**	**663**	699	.262	**.348**	**.399**	**747**	**113**	**107**	**99**	101	100	**754**	**90**	49	**65**	**3**
NY	154	92	62	.597	4.5	722	639	5229	1337	186	**56**	151	536	672	.256	.329	**.399**	728	107	56	51	101	103	712	30	31	49	-4
STL	154	88	66	.571	8.5	677	630	5200	1386	**247**	54	97	537	**479**	**.267**	.340	.391	731	110	68	67	100	95	708	33	32	51	-4
PHI	154	87	67	.565	9.5	657	**552**	5205	1353	237	45	93	540	534	.260	.332	.376	708	104	26	33	99	98	671	60	41	59	-1
CHI	155	77	77	.500	19.5	628	631	5330	**1408**	223	45	107	422	712	.264	.321	.383	704	101	5	-3	101	97	652	50	40	56	-3
CIN	154	69	85	.448	27.5	615	659	5234	1303	212	45	104	480	709	.249	.314	.366	680	95	-36	-34	100	102	610	32	42	43	-8
BOS	155	64	89	.418	32	569	651	5221	1214	187	31	110	483	711	.233	.301	.343	644	88	-102	-82	97	**106**	555	58	34	63	1
PIT	155	42	112	.273	54.5	515	793	5193	1201	181	30	92	486	724	.231	.300	.331	631	79	-125	-138	103	101	530	43	41	51	-5
TOT	618					5158		41878	10582	1672	338	907	4147	5240	.253	.324	.374	697							396	310	56	-21

TEAM	CG	SH	SV	IP	H	H/G	HR	BB	SO	RAT	ERA	ERA+	OAV	OOB	PR	PR+	PF	CPI	FA	E	DP	FW	PW	BW	SBW	DIF
BRO	45	11	24	1399^{1}	1295	8.4	121	544	**773**	12.1	3.54	103	.247	.321	31	17	98	103	**.982**	**106**	169	**2.1**	1.8	**10.3**	**.6**	5.0
NY	49	12	**31**	1371	1282	8.5	121	538	655	12.2	3.60	103	.248	.323	22	17	99	103	.974	158	**175**	-.7	1.8	5.3	-.1	8.9
STL	49	12	27	1361^{1}	1274	8.5	119	501	712	12.0	3.67	101	.247	.317	11	8	100	98	.977	141	159	.2	.9	7.0	-.1	3.3
PHI	**80**	**17**	16	1386^{2}	1306	8.5	**96**	**373**	609	**11.1**	**3.07**	**119**	.249	**.301**	**102**	**92**	98	**104**	.975	150	145	-.3	**9.6**	3.5	.2	-2.7
CHI	59	15	15	1386^{1}	**1265**	**8.3**	101	534	661	11.9	3.59	107	**.240**	.314	23	40	103	94	.976	146	123	-.0	4.2	-.3	-.0	-3.6
CIN	56	11	12	1363^{1}	1377	9.1	111	517	579	12.8	4.02	94	.267	.338	-43	-36	101	103	**.982**	107	145	2.0	-3.7	-3.5	-.6	-2.1
BOS	63	11	13	1396	1388	9.0	106	525	687	12.6	3.78	96	.259	.329	-7	-27	97	102	.975	154	143	-.5	-2.7	-8.4	.4	-1.0
PIT	43	5	8	1363^{2}	1395	9.3	132	615	564	13.5	4.65	86	.265	.345	-139	-92	107	94	.970	182	167	-2.0	-9.5	-14.2	-.2	-8.9
TOT	444	94	146	11027^{2}		8.7				12.3	3.74		.253	.324					.977	1144	1226					

Runs
Musial-StL 105
Hemus-StL 105
Robinson-Bro 104
Lockman-NY 99
Reese-Bro 94

Hits
Musial-StL 194
Schoendienst-StL .. 188
Adams-Cin 180
Dark-NY 177
Lockman-NY 176

Doubles
Musial-StL 42
Schoendienst-StL.... 40
McMillan-Cin 32
Sauer-Chi 31
Ashburn-Phi 31

Triples
Thomson-NY 14
Slaughter-StL 12
Kluszewski-Cin 11
Ennis-Phi 10

Home Runs
Sauer-Chi 37
Kiner-Pit 37
Hodges-Bro 32
Mathews-Bos 25
Gordon-Bos 25

Total Bases
Musial-StL 311
Sauer-Chi 301
Thomson-NY 293
Ennis-Phi 281
Snider-Bro 264

Runs Batted In
Sauer-Chi 121
Thomson-NY 108
Ennis-Phi 107
Hodges-Bro 102
Slaughter-StL 101

Runs Produced
Ennis-Phi 177
Musial-StL 175
Thomson-NY 173
Sauer-Chi 173
Slaughter-StL 163

Bases On Balls
Kiner-Pit 110
Hodges-Bro 107
Robinson-Bro 106
Musial-StL 96
Hemus-StL 96

Batting Average
Musial-StL .... .336
Baumholtz-Chi ..... .325
Kluszewski-Cin ..... .320
Robinson-Bro .... .308
Snider-Bro .... .303

On-Base Percentage
Robinson-Bro ...... .440
Musial-StL .... .432
Hemus-StL .... .392
Hodges-Bro .... .386
Slaughter-StL ..... .386

Slugging Average
Musial-StL .... .538
Sauer-Chi .... .531
Kluszewski-Cin ..... .509
Kiner-Pit .... .500
Hodges-Bro .... .500

On-Base Plus Slugging
Musial-StL 970
Robinson-Bro 904
Kluszewski-Cin 892
Sauer-Chi 892
Hodges-Bro 886

Adjusted OPS
Musial-StL 167
Robinson-Bro 149
Kluszewski-Cin 146
Gordon-Bos 144
Sauer-Chi 143

Batter Runs
Musial-StL 55.7
Robinson-Bro 41.9
Sauer-Chi 32.8
Kiner-Pit 32.7
Hodges-Bro 32.4

Adjusted Batter Runs
Musial-StL 55.6
Robinson-Bro 40.7
Gordon-Bos 31.8
Sauer-Chi 31.5
Hodges-Bro 31.3

Clutch Hitting Index
Slaughter-StL 138
Hatton-Cin 129
Campanella-Bro 128
Sauer-Chi 115
Wyrostek-Cin-Phi ... 112

Runs Created
Musial-StL 141
Robinson-Bro 116
Sauer-Chi 111
Kiner-Pit 111
Hodges-Bro 106

Total Average
Musial-StL 1.017
Robinson-Bro .... .995
Kiner-Pit .... .955
Hodges-Bro .... .921
Sauer-Chi .... .886

Stolen Bases
Reese-Bro 30
Jethroe-Bos 28
Robinson-Bro 24
Ashburn-Phi 16

Stolen Base Average
Reese-Bro 85.7
Robinson-Bro 77.4
Jethroe-Bos 75.7
Ashburn-Phi 59.3

Stolen Base Runs
Reese-Bro 4.8
Jethroe-Bos 3.0
Robinson-Bro 2.8
Davis-Pit 1.3
Ryan-Phi 1.1

Fielding Runs
Schoendienst-StL .. 32.9
Logan-Bos 17.6
Sauer-Chi 16.6
Ashburn-Phi 15.1
McMillan-Cin 10.6

Total Player Rating
Robinson-Bro 5.6
Schoendienst-StL 5.1
Musial-StL 4.3
Hemus-StL 3.7
Sauer-Chi 3.7

Wins
Roberts-Phi 28
Maglie-NY 18
Staley-StL 17
Rush-Chi 17
Raffensberger-Cin ... 17

Win Percentage
Wilhelm-NY .... .833
Roberts-Phi .... .800
Black-Bro .... .789
Maglie-NY .... .692
Hacker-Chi .... .625

Games
Wilhelm-NY 71
Black-Bro 56
Yuhas-StL 54
Smith-Cin 53
Main-Pit 48

Complete Games
Roberts-Phi 30
Dickson-Pit 21
Spahn-Bos 19
Raffensberger-Cin ... 18
Rush-Chi 17

Shutouts
Simmons-Phi 6
Raffensberger-Cin 6

Saves
Brazle-StL 16
Black-Bro 15
Wilhelm-NY 11
Leonard-Chi 11

Innings Pitched
Roberts-Phi 330.0
Spahn-Bos 290.0
Dickson-Pit 277.2
Rush-Chi 250.1
Raffensberger-Cin ... 247.0

Fewest Hits/Game
Hacker-Chi 7.01
Wilhelm-NY 7.17
Erskine-Bro 7.27
Rush-Chi 7.37
Loes-Bro 7.40

Fewest BB/Game
Roberts-Phi 1.23
Hacker-Chi 1.51
Raffensberger-Cin 1.64
Staley-StL 1.95
Drews-Phi 2.05

Strikeouts
Spahn-Bos 183
Rush-Chi 157
Roberts-Phi 148
Mizell-StL 146
Simmons-Phi 141

Strikeouts/Game
Mizell-StL 6.92
Simmons-Phi 6.30
Wilhelm-NY 6.10
Wade-Bro 5.90
Erskine-Bro 5.70

Ratio
Hacker-Chi 8.56
Roberts-Phi 9.33
Erskine-Bro 10.45
Rush-Chi 10.50
Drews-Phi 10.59

Earned Run Average
Wilhelm-NY 2.43
Hacker-Chi 2.58
Roberts-Phi 2.59
Loes-Bro 2.69
Rush-Chi 2.70

Adjusted ERA
Wilhelm-NY 152
Hacker-Chi 149
Rush-Chi 143
Roberts-Phi 141
Loes-Bro 135

Opponents' Batting Avg.
Hacker-Chi .... .212
Rush-Chi .... .216
Wilhelm-NY .... .220
Erskine-Bro .... .220
Loes-Bro .... .224

Opponents' On-Base Pct.
Hacker-Chi .... .247
Roberts-Phi .... .263
Rush-Chi .... .282
Erskine-Bro .... .289
Spahn-Bos .... .291

Starter Runs
Roberts-Phi 41.8
Rush-Chi 28.8
Drews-Phi 25.8
Raffensberger-Cin 25.4
Spahn-Bos 24.3

Adjusted Starter Runs
Roberts-Phi 39.8
Rush-Chi 31.1
Raffensberger-Cin 26.3
Hacker-Chi 25.4
Drews-Phi 24.3

Clutch Pitching Index
Roe-Bro 127
Church-Phi-Cin 119
Wilhelm-NY 119
Raffensberger-Cin ... 117
Maglie-NY 116

Relief Runs
Black-Bro 25.0
Wilhelm-NY 23.1
Brazle-StL 12.3
Leonard-Chi 11.6
Yuhas-StL 11.2

Adjusted Relief Runs
Black-Bro 24.2
Wilhelm-NY 22.7
Brazle-StL 12.2
Leonard-Chi 12.1
Yuhas-StL 11.0

Relief Ranking
Black-Bro 34.7
Wilhelm-NY 26.6
Brazle-StL 21.0
Yuhas-StL 15.5
Leonard-Chi 11.1

Total Pitcher Index
Rush-Chi 4.8
Roberts-Phi 4.1
Black-Bro 3.4
Wilhelm-NY 2.9
Drews-Phi 2.8

Total Baseball Ranking
Robinson-Bro 5.6
Schoendienst-StL 5.1
Rush-Chi 4.8
Musial-StL 4.3
Roberts-Phi 4.1

TEAM	G	W	L	PCT	GB	R	OR	AB	H	2B	3B	HR	BB	SO	AVG	OBP	SLG	OPS	OPS+	BR	BR+	PF	CHI	RC	SB	CS	SBA	SBR
NY	154	95	59	.617		727	**557**	5294	**1411**	221	**56**	129	566	652	**.267**	.341	.403	744	121	89	136	94	99	758	52	42	55	-3
CLE	155	93	61	.604	2	**763**	606	5330	1399	211	49	**148**	626	749	.262	.342	**.404**	**746**	**122**	**95**	**147**	94	102	**759**	46	39	54	-4
CHI	156	81	73	.526	14	610	568	5316	1337	199	38	80	541	**521**	.252	.327	.348	675	93	-35	-40	101	99	633	**61**	38	**62**	0
PHI	155	79	75	.513	16	664	723	5163	1305	212	35	89	**683**	561	.253	**.343**	.359	702	96	26	-14	106	99	659	52	43	55	-4
WAS	157	78	76	.506	17	598	608	5357	1282	225	44	50	580	607	.239	.317	.326	643	88	-98	-78	97	**107**	572	48	37	56	-2
BOS	154	76	78	.494	19	668	658	5246	1338	**233**	34	113	542	739	.255	.328	.377	705	96	14	-33	108	103	659	59	47	56	-3
STL	155	64	90	.416	31	604	733	5353	1340	225	46	82	540	720	.250	.322	.356	678	92	-39	-56	103	99	631	30	34	47	-5
DET	156	50	104	.325	45	557	738	5258	1278	190	37	103	553	605	.243	.318	.352	670	92	-52	-57	101	95	594	27	38	42	-7
TOT	621					5191		42317	10690	1716	339	794	4631	5154	.253	.330	.366	695							375	318	54	-29

TEAM	CG	SH	SV	IP	H	H/G	HR	BB	SO	RAT	ERA	ERA+	OAV	OOB	PR	PR+	PF	CPI	FA	E	DP	FW	PW	BW	SBW	DIF
NY	72	**21**	27	1381	**1240**	8.1	94	581	666	12.1	**3.15**	106	.243	.324	**82**	31	90	**110**	.979	127	**199**	.8	3.3	14.2	.0	-.1
CLE	**80**	19	18	1407	1278	8.2	94	556	671	11.9	3.32	101	.241	**.316**	55	4	91	99	.975	155	141	-.7	.5	**15.3**	-.0	1.2
CHI	53	15	**28**	1416[2]	1251	**8.0**	86	578	**774**	**11.8**	3.26	**112**	**.238**	**.316**	66	**63**	99	98	**.980**	**123**	158	**1.1**	**6.6**	-4.1	**.4**	.2
PHI	73	11	15	1384[1]	1402	9.2	113	**526**	562	12.8	4.16	95	.263	.333	-74	-28	108	94	.977	140	148	.1	-2.9	-1.4	-.0	6.4
WAS	75	10	15	1429[2]	1405	8.9	**78**	577	574	12.7	3.38	105	.258	.332	48	30	97	108	.978	132	152	.7	3.2	-8.0	.2	5.2
BOS	53	7	24	1372[1]	1332	8.8	107	623	624	13.1	3.81	104	.256	.340	-20	19	107	104	.976	145	181	-.2	2.0	-3.4	.0	.7
STL	48	6	18	1399	1388	9.0	111	598	581	13.1	4.12	95	.260	.339	-69	-30	107	97	.974	155	176	-.7	-3.1	-5.8	-.1	-3.1
DET	51	10	14	1388[1]	1394	9.1	111	591	702	13.1	4.26	90	.262	.338	-89	-66	104	94	.975	152	145	-.5	-6.8	-5.9	-.4	-13.3
TOT	505	99	159	11178[1]		8.7				12.6	3.68		.253	.330					.977	1129	1300					

Runs
Doby-Cle 104
Avila-Cle 102
Rosen-Cle 101
Berra-NY 97
Minoso-Chi 96

Hits
Fox-Chi 192
Avila-Cle 179
Robinson-Chi 176
Fain-Phi 176

Doubles
Fain-Phi 43
Mantle-NY 37
Vernon-Was 33
Robinson-Chi 33

Triples
Avila-Cle 11
Simpson-Cle 10
Rizzuto-NY 10
Fox-Chi 10

Home Runs
Doby-Cle 32
Easter-Cle 31
Berra-NY 30
Dropo-Bos-Det 29
Zernial-Phi 29

Total Bases
Rosen-Cle 297
Mantle-NY 291
Dropo-Bos-Det 282
Doby-Cle 281
Robinson-Chi 277

Runs Batted In
Rosen-Cle 105
Robinson-Chi 104
Doby-Cle 104
Zernial-Phi 100
Berra-NY 98

Runs Produced
Rosen-Cle 178
Doby-Cle 176
Berra-NY 165
Robinson-Chi 161
Mantle-NY 158

Bases On Balls
Yost-Was 129
Joost-Phi 122
Fain-Phi 105
Valo-Phi 101
Doby-Cle 90

Batting Average
Fain-Phi .327
Mitchell-Cle .323
Mantle-NY .311
Kell-Det-Bos .311
Woodling-NY .309

On-Base Percentage
Fain-Phi .438
Valo-Phi .432
Mantle-NY .394
Joost-Phi .388
Rosen-Cle .387

Slugging Average
Doby-Cle .541
Mantle-NY .530
Rosen-Cle .524
Easter-Cle .513
Wertz-Det-StL .506

On-Base Plus Slugging
Mantle-NY 924
Doby-Cle 924
Rosen-Cle 911
Wertz-Det-StL 887
Fain-Phi 867

Adjusted OPS
Doby-Cle 166
Mantle-NY 166
Rosen-Cle 162
Easter-Cle 144
Wertz-Det-StL 143

Batter Runs
Mantle-NY 40.3
Rosen-Cle 38.6
Doby-Cle 37.9
Fain-Phi 36.3
Robinson-Chi 28.3

Adjusted Batter Runs
Mantle-NY 47.2
Rosen-Cle 46.2
Doby-Cle 45.1
Fain-Phi 30.0
Woodling-NY 28.3

Clutch Hitting Index
Runnels-Was 120
Philley-Phi 116
McDougald-NY 115
Easter-Cle 110
Joost-Phi 107

Runs Created
Mantle-NY 123
Doby-Cle 116
Rosen-Cle 115
Robinson-Chi 113
Fain-Phi 107

Total Average
Doby-Cle .974
Mantle-NY .961
Wertz-Det-StL .912
Rosen-Cle .900
Valo-Phi .873

Stolen Bases
Minoso-Chi 22
Rivera-StL-Chi 21
Jensen-NY-Was 18
Rizzuto-NY 17
Throneberry-Bos 16

Stolen Base Average
Jensen-NY-Was 75.0
Rizzuto-NY 73.9
Rivera-StL-Chi 70.0
Throneberry-Bos 69.6
Minoso-Chi 57.9

Stolen Base Runs
Jensen-NY-Was 1.9
Rizzuto-NY 1.6
Rivera-StL-Chi 1.5
Throneberry-Bos 1.1
Goodman-Bos 1.1

Fielding Runs
Goodman-Bos 20.1
Rizzuto-NY 18.9
Martin-NY 18.3
Hatfield-Bos-Det 17.8
Fain-Phi 16.0

Total Player Rating
Doby-Cle 5.3
Mantle-NY 4.8
Fain-Phi 4.1
Berra-NY 3.7
Goodman-Bos 3.1

Wins
Shantz-Phi 24
Wynn-Cle 23
Lemon-Cle 22
Garcia-Cle 22
Reynolds-NY 20

Win Percentage
Shantz-Phi .774
Raschi-NY .727
Reynolds-NY .714
Lemon-Cle .667
Garcia-Cle .667

Games
Kennedy-Chi 47
Paige-StL 46
Garcia-Cle 46
Hooper-Phi 43

Complete Games
Lemon-Cle 28
Shantz-Phi 27
Reynolds-NY 24
Wynn-Cle 19
Garcia-Cle 19

Shutouts
Reynolds-NY 6
Garcia-Cle 6
Shantz-Phi 5
Lemon-Cle 5

Saves
Dorish-Chi 11
Paige-StL 10
Sain-NY 7

Innings Pitched
Lemon-Cle 309.2
Garcia-Cle 292.1
Wynn-Cle 285.2
Shantz-Phi 279.2
Pierce-Chi 255.1

Fewest Hits/Game
Lemon-Cle 6.86
Raschi-NY 7.02
Reynolds-NY 7.15
Dobson-Chi 7.36
Shantz-Phi 7.40

Fewest BB/Game
Shantz-Phi 2.03
Pillette-StL 2.41
Marrero-Was 2.59
Houtteman-Det 2.65
Garcia-Cle 2.68

Strikeouts
Reynolds-NY 160
Wynn-Cle 153
Shantz-Phi 152
Pierce-Chi 144
Garcia-Cle 143

Strikeouts/Game
McDermott-Bos 6.50
Reynolds-NY 5.89
Trucks-Det 5.89
Gray-Det 5.54
Grissom-Chi 5.26

Ratio
Shantz-Phi 9.56
Dobson-Chi 10.05
Lemon-Cle 10.09
Pierce-Chi 10.43
Raschi-NY 10.94

Earned Run Average
Reynolds-NY 2.06
Garcia-Cle 2.37
Shantz-Phi 2.48
Lemon-Cle 2.50
Dobson-Chi 2.51

Adjusted ERA
Reynolds-NY 161
Shantz-Phi 160
Dobson-Chi 145
Pierce-Chi 142
Garcia-Cle 141

Opponents' Batting Avg.
Lemon-Cle .208
Raschi-NY .216
Reynolds-NY .218
Dobson-Chi .222
Shantz-Phi .225

Opponents' On-Base Pct.
Shantz-Phi .272
Lemon-Cle .279
Dobson-Chi .280
Pierce-Chi .289
Reynolds-NY .300

Starter Runs
Reynolds-NY 43.8
Garcia-Cle 42.4
Lemon-Cle 40.4
Shantz-Phi 37.2
Pierce-Chi 31.3

Adjusted Starter Runs
Shantz-Phi 42.7
Reynolds-NY 37.8
Garcia-Cle 34.7
Lemon-Cle 31.9
Pierce-Chi 30.7

Clutch Pitching Index
Garcia-Cle 127
Byrd-Phi 126
Reynolds-NY 125
Porterfield-Was 120
Hudson-Was-Bos 117

Relief Runs
Dorish-Chi 12.2
Kennedy-Chi 6.9
Consuegra-Was 5.1
Brissie-Cle 1.8
Littlefield-Det-SL 1.4

Adjusted Relief Runs
Dorish-Chi 12.0
Kennedy-Chi 6.7
Consuegra-Was 4.3
Littlefield-Det-SL 3.1
White-Det .8

Relief Ranking
Dorish-Chi 17.5
Kennedy-Chi 4.5
Consuegra-Was 3.8
Littlefield-Det-SL 2.5
White-Det 1.1

Total Pitcher Index
Shantz-Phi 5.2
Lemon-Cle 4.9
Reynolds-NY 4.4
Garcia-Cle 4.0
Pierce-Chi 3.2

Total Baseball Ranking
Doby-Cle 5.3
Shantz-Phi 5.2
Lemon-Cle 4.9
Mantle-NY 4.8
Reynolds-NY 4.4

TEAM	G	W	L	PCT	GB	R	OR	AB	H	2B	3B	HR	BB	SO	AVG	OBP	SLG	OPS	OPS+	BR	BR+	PF	CHI	RC	SB	CS	SBA	SBR
BRO	155	105	49	.682		**955**	689	5373	**1529**	274	59	**208**	**655**	686	**.285**	**.366**	**.474**	**840**	**121**	**188**	**168**	102	101	**963**	**90**	47	66	**3**
MIL	157	92	62	.597	13	738	**589**	5349	1422	227	52	156	439	637	.266	.325	.415	740	104	-22	25	94	**104**	727	46	27	63	1
STL	157	83	71	.539	22	768	713	5397	1474	**281**	56	140	574	617	.273	.347	.424	771	107	53	54	100	95	806	18	22	45	-4
PHI	156	83	71	.539	22	716	666	5290	1400	228	**62**	115	530	**597**	.265	.335	.396	731	97	-25	-21	99	101	727	42	21	67	2
NY	155	70	84	.455	35	768	747	5362	1452	195	45	176	499	608	.271	.336	.422	758	101	20	7	102	101	771	31	21	60	-1
CIN	155	68	86	.442	37	714	788	5343	1396	190	34	166	485	701	.261	.325	.403	728	94	-42	-47	101	103	711	25	20	56	-1
CHI	155	65	89	.422	40	633	835	5272	1372	204	57	137	514	746	.260	.328	.399	727	93	-41	-56	102	92	697	49	21	**70**	**3**
PIT	154	50	104	.325	55	622	887	5253	1297	178	49	99	524	715	.247	.319	.356	675	82	-130	-126	99	103	614	41	39	51	-5
TOT	622					5914		42639	11342	1777	414	1197	4220	5307	.267	.336	.412	747							342	218	61	-1

TEAM	CG	SH	SV	IP	H	H/G	HR	BB	SO	RAT	ERA	ERA+	OAV	OOB	PR	PR+	PF	CPI	FA	E	DP	FW	PW	BW	SBW	DIF
BRO	51	11	29	1380[2]	1337	8.8	169	509	**817**	12.2	4.11	104	.253	.320	29	25	99	97	**.980**	**118**	161	**1.7**	2.5	**16.2**	**.3**	7.5
MIL	72	**14**	15	1387	**1282**	**8.4**	**107**	539	738	**12.0**	**3.30**	**119**	**.245**	**.318**	**153**	**105**	92	**106**	.976	143	169	.4	**10.2**	2.5	.1	2.0
STL	51	11	**36**	1386[2]	1406	9.2	139	533	732	12.9	4.23	101	.262	.333	9	5	99	98	.977	138	161	.7	.5	5.3	-.4	.0
PHI	**76**	13	15	1369[2]	1410	9.3	138	**410**	637	12.2	3.80	111	.265	.320	74	63	98	104	.975	147	161	.1	6.1	-2.0	.2	1.7
NY	46	10	20	1365[2]	1403	9.3	146	610	647	13.5	4.26	101	.264	.343	5	6	100	103	.975	151	151	-.1	.6	.7	-.0	-7.9
CIN	47	7	15	1365	1484	9.8	179	488	506	13.3	4.64	94	.279	.343	-53	-42	102	102	.978	129	**176**	1.1	-4.0	-4.5	-.0	-1.3
CHI	38	3	22	1359	1491	9.9	151	554	623	13.8	4.79	93	.276	.347	-76	-49	104	97	.967	193	141	-2.5	-4.7	-5.3	**.3**	.4
PIT	49	4	10	1358	1529	10.2	168	577	607	14.1	5.23	86	.285	.356	-141	-108	104	96	.973	163	139	-.9	-10.4	-12.1	-.5	-3.0
TOT	430	73	162	10971[2]		9.4				13.0	4.29		.267	.336					.976	1182	1259					

Runs
Snider-Bro 132
Musial-StL 127
Dark-NY 126
Gilliam-Bro 125

Hits
Ashburn-Phi 205
Musial-StL 200
Snider-Bro 198
Dark-NY 194
Schoendienst-StL 193

Doubles
Musial-StL 53
Dark-NY 41
Snider-Bro 38
Furillo-Bro 38
Bell-Cin 37

Triples
Gilliam-Bro 17
Bruton-Mil 14
Hemus-StL 11
Fondy-Chi 11

Home Runs
Mathews-Mil 47
Snider-Bro 42
Campanella-Bro 41
Kluszewski-Cin 40
Kiner-Pit-Chi 35

Total Bases
Snider-Bro 370
Mathews-Mil 363
Musial-StL 361
Kluszewski-Cin 325
Bell-Cin 320

Runs Batted In
Campanella-Bro 142
Mathews-Mil 135
Snider-Bro 126
Ennis-Phi 125
Hodges-Bro 122

Runs Produced
Snider-Bro 216
Musial-StL 210
Campanella-Bro 204
Mathews-Mil 198

Bases On Balls
Musial-StL 105
Kiner-Pit-Chi 100
Gilliam-Bro 100
Mathews-Mil 99
Hemus-StL 86

Batting Average
Furillo-Bro .344
Schoendienst-StL .342
Musial-StL .337
Snider-Bro .336
Mueller-NY .333

On-Base Percentage
Musial-StL .437
Robinson-Bro .425
Snider-Bro .419
Irvin-NY .406
Mathews-Mil .406

Slugging Average
Snider-Bro .627
Mathews-Mil .627
Campanella-Bro .611
Musial-StL .609
Furillo-Bro .580

On-Base Plus Slugging
Snider-Bro 1046
Musial-StL 1046
Mathews-Mil 1033
Campanella-Bro 1006
Furillo-Bro 973

Adjusted OPS
Mathews-Mil 175
Musial-StL 169
Snider-Bro 165
Campanella-Bro 154
Furillo-Bro 146

Batter Runs
Musial-StL 62.7
Snider-Bro 59.3
Mathews-Mil 54.9
Campanella-Bro 42.9
Kluszewski-Cin 35.0

Adjusted Batter Runs
Mathews-Mil 64.1
Musial-StL 62.9
Snider-Bro 56.2
Campanella-Bro 40.4
Kluszewski-Cin 34.2

Clutch Hitting Index
Slaughter-StL 142
Jablonski-StL 128
Robinson-Bro 125
Ennis-Phi 121
Campanella-Bro 119

Runs Created
Musial-StL 166
Snider-Bro 161
Mathews-Mil 157
Campanella-Bro 128
Kluszewski-Cin 126

Total Average
Musial-StL 1.143
Snider-Bro 1.134
Mathews-Mil 1.119
Campanella-Bro 1.048
Robinson-Bro .988

Stolen Bases
Bruton-Mil 26
Reese-Bro 22
Gilliam-Bro 21
Robinson-Bro 17
Snider-Bro 16

Stolen Base Average
Robinson-Bro 81.0
Reese-Bro 78.6
Bruton-Mil 70.3
Snider-Bro 69.6
Gilliam-Bro 60.0

Stolen Base Runs
Reese-Bro 2.7
Robinson-Bro 2.3
Bruton-Mil 1.9
Miksis-Chi 1.5
Torgeson-Phi 1.2

Fielding Runs
Ashburn-Phi 25.7
Schoendienst-StL 25.3
Logan-Mil 20.6
Crandall-Mil 14.8
Bell-Cin 13.7

Total Player Rating
Mathews-Mil 6.2
Schoendienst-StL 6.1
Campanella-Bro 4.8
Snider-Bro 4.5
Musial-StL 4.2

Wins
Spahn-Mil 23
Roberts-Phi 23
Haddix-StL 20
Erskine-Bro 20
Staley-StL 18

Win Percentage
Erskine-Bro .769
Spahn-Mil .767
Meyer-Bro .750
Burdette-Mil .750
Haddix-StL .690

Games
Wilhelm-NY 68
Brazle-StL 60
Hetki-Pit 54
Smith-Cin 50

Complete Games
Roberts-Phi 33
Spahn-Mil 24
Simmons-Phi 19
Haddix-StL 19
Erskine-Bro 16

Shutouts
Haddix-StL 6
Spahn-Mil 5
Roberts-Phi 5
Simmons-Phi 4
Erskine-Bro 4

Saves
Brazle-StL 18
Wilhelm-NY 15
Hughes-Bro 9
Leonard-Chi 8
Burdette-Mil 8

Innings Pitched
Roberts-Phi 346.2
Spahn-Mil 265.2
Haddix-StL 253.0
Erskine-Bro 246.2
Simmons-Phi 238.0

Fewest Hits/Game
Spahn-Mil 7.15
Gomez-NY 7.32
Mizell-StL 7.74
Erskine-Bro 7.77
Haddix-StL 7.83

Fewest BB/Game
Roberts-Phi 1.58
Raffensberger-Cin 1.71
Minner-Chi 1.79
Staley-StL 2.11
Hacker-Chi 2.19

Strikeouts
Roberts-Phi 198
Erskine-Bro 187
Mizell-StL 173
Haddix-StL 163
Spahn-Mil 148

Strikeouts/Game
Mizell-StL 6.94
Erskine-Bro 6.82
Antonelli-Mil 6.72
Klippstein-Chi 6.07
Haddix-StL 5.80

Ratio
Spahn-Mil 9.55
Roberts-Phi 10.05
Haddix-StL 10.42
Simmons-Phi 11.19
Erskine-Bro 11.35

Earned Run Average
Spahn-Mil 2.10
Roberts-Phi 2.75
Haddix-StL 3.06
Antonelli-Mil 3.18
Simmons-Phi 3.21

Adjusted ERA
Spahn-Mil 187
Roberts-Phi 153
Haddix-StL 139
Simmons-Phi 131
Gomez-NY 126

Opponents' Batting Avg.
Spahn-Mil .217
Gomez-NY .218
Mizell-StL .227
Erskine-Bro .230
Haddix-StL .232

Opponents' On-Base Pct.
Spahn-Mil .270
Roberts-Phi .276
Haddix-StL .287
Hacker-Chi .299
Simmons-Phi .302

Starter Runs
Spahn-Mil 64.5
Roberts-Phi 59.1
Haddix-StL 34.5
Simmons-Phi 28.3
Buhl-Mil 22.5

Adjusted Starter Runs
Spahn-Mil 58.8
Roberts-Phi 57.1
Haddix-StL 33.9
Simmons-Phi 26.8
Gomez-NY 20.2

Clutch Pitching Index
Raffensberger-Cin 115
Dickson-Pit 112
Drews-Phi 112
Burdette-Mil 110
Roe-Bro 108

Relief Runs
Wilhelm-NY 20.1
Labine-Bro 18.5
Johnson-Mil 14.6
White-StL 12.3
Hughes-Bro 7.8

Adjusted Relief Runs
Wilhelm-NY 20.0
Labine-Bro 18.3
Johnson-Mil 12.3
White-StL 12.1
Hughes-Bro 7.6

Relief Ranking
Labine-Bro 28.0
Wilhelm-NY 23.4
White-StL 16.4
Johnson-Mil 9.6
Hughes-Bro 7.4

Total Pitcher Index
Spahn-Mil 7.3
Roberts-Phi 6.2
Haddix-StL 4.7
Labine-Bro 2.7
Simmons-Phi 2.4

Total Baseball Ranking
Spahn-Mil 7.3
Roberts-Phi 6.2
Mathews-Mil 6.2
Schoendienst-StL 6.1
Campanella-Bro 4.8

TEAM	G	W	L	PCT	GB	R	OR	AB	H	2B	3B	HR	BB	SO	AVG	OBP	SLG	OPS	OPS+	BR	BR+	PF	CHI	RC	SB	CS	SBA	SBR
NY	151	99	52	.656		**801**	**547**	5194	1420	226	52	139	**656**	644	**.273**	**.359**	**.417**	**776**	**120**	**113**	**142**	97	100	**809**	34	44	44	-8
CLE	155	92	62	.597	8.5	770	627	5285	1426	201	29	**160**	609	683	.270	.349	.410	759	114	77	98	97	100	780	33	29	53	-3
CHI	156	89	65	.578	11.5	716	592	5212	1345	226	**53**	74	601	**530**	.258	.341	.364	705	93	-17	-37	103	**106**	666	**73**	55	57	-3
BOS	153	84	69	.549	16	656	632	5246	1385	255	37	101	496	601	.264	.332	.384	716	94	-10	-44	105	98	683	33	45	42	-8
WAS	152	76	76	.500	23.5	687	614	5149	1354	230	**53**	69	596	604	.263	.343	.368	711	100	-6	10	98	103	675	65	36	**64**	**2**
DET	158	60	94	.390	40.5	695	923	5553	**1479**	**259**	44	108	506	603	.266	.331	.387	718	100	-10	-1	99	99	716	30	35	46	-6
PHI	157	59	95	.383	41.5	632	799	5455	1398	205	38	116	498	602	.256	.321	.372	693	89	-61	-84	104	100	658	41	24	63	1
STL	154	54	100	.351	46.5	555	778	5264	1310	214	25	112	507	644	.249	.317	.363	680	87	-83	-94	102	93	606	17	34	33	-8
TOT	618					5512		42358	11117	1816	331	879	4469	4911	.263	.337	.384	720							326	302	52	-34

TEAM	CG	SH	SV	IP	H	H/G	HR	BB	SO	RAT	ERA	ERA+	OAV	OOB	PR	PR+	PF	CPI	FA	E	DP	FW	PW	BW	SBW	DIF
NY	50	**18**	**39**	1358[1]	**1286**	8.6	94	500	604	**12.1**	**3.21**	115	.251	**.321**	**120**	80	92	**110**	.979	126	182	.3	8.1	**14.3**	-.4	1.4
CLE	**81**	11	15	1373	1311	8.6	**92**	519	586	12.3	3.65	103	.253	.325	53	17	94	99	.979	127	**197**	.5	1.8	9.9	.1	3.0
CHI	57	17	33	1403[2]	1299	**8.4**	113	583	**714**	12.3	3.42	**118**	**.246**	.324	91	**95**	101	105	**.980**	125	144	.6	**9.6**	-3.7	.1	5.5
BOS	41	15	37	1373	1333	8.8	**92**	584	642	12.8	3.58	**118**	.254	.331	63	91	105	104	.975	148	173	-.8	9.2	-4.4	-.4	4.1
WAS	76	16	10	1344[2]	1313	8.8	112	**478**	515	12.2	3.67	106	.258	.324	50	36	98	103	.979	**120**	173	**.7**	3.7	1.1	**.6**	-5.9
DET	50	2	16	1415	1633	10.4	154	585	645	14.4	5.26	77	.291	.363	-198	-183	102	96	.978	135	149	.2	-18.3	-.0	-.2	1.5
PHI	51	7	11	1409	1475	9.5	121	594	566	13.6	4.67	92	.271	.349	-106	-56	107	93	.977	137	161	.0	-5.6	-8.4	.5	-4.4
STL	28	10	24	1383[2]	1467	9.6	101	626	639	13.8	4.48	94	.273	.351	-74	-40	105	97	.974	152	165	-1.0	-4.0	-9.4	-.4	-8.1
TOT	434	96	185	11060[1]		9.1				12.9	4.00		.263	.337					.978	1070	1344					

Runs
Rosen-Cle 115
Yost-Was 107
Mantle-NY 105
Minoso-Chi 104
Vernon-Was 101

Hits
Kuenn-Det 209
Vernon-Was 205
Rosen-Cle 201
Philley-Phi 188
Busby-Was 183

Doubles
Vernon-Was 43
Kell-Bos 41
White-Bos 34
Kuenn-Det 33
Goodman-Bos 33

Triples
Rivera-Chi 16
Vernon-Was 11
Piersall-Bos 9
Philley-Phi 9

Home Runs
Rosen-Cle 43
Zernial-Phi 42
Doby-Cle 29
Berra-NY 27
Boone-Cle-Det 26

Total Bases
Rosen-Cle 367
Vernon-Was 315
Zernial-Phi 311
Philley-Phi 263
Berra-NY 263

Runs Batted In
Rosen-Cle 145
Vernon-Was 115
Boone-Cle-Det 114
Zernial-Phi 108
Berra-NY 108

Runs Produced
Rosen-Cle 217
Vernon-Was 201
Minoso-Chi 193
Boone-Cle-Det 182
Mantle-NY 176

Bases On Balls
Yost-Was 123
Fain-Chi 108
Doby-Cle 96
Gernert-Bos 88
Rosen-Cle 85

Batting Average
Vernon-Was .337
Rosen-Cle .336
Goodman-Bos .313
Minoso-Chi .313
Busby-Was .312

On-Base Percentage
Woodling-NY .429
Rosen-Cle .422
Minoso-Chi .410
Fain-Chi .405
Yost-Was .403

Slugging Average
Rosen-Cle .613
Zernial-Phi .559
Berra-NY .523
Boone-Cle-Det .519
Vernon-Was .518

On-Base Plus Slugging
Rosen-Cle 1034
Vernon-Was 921
Zernial-Phi 914
Boone-Cle-Det 909
Woodling-NY 898

Adjusted OPS
Rosen-Cle 181
Vernon-Was 151
Woodling-NY 147
Boone-Cle-Det 146
Mantle-NY 145

Batter Runs
Rosen-Cle 63.3
Vernon-Was 39.7
Minoso-Chi 30.6
Boone-Cle-Det 30.5
Zernial-Phi 30.4

Adjusted Batter Runs
Rosen-Cle 67.3
Vernon-Was 42.6
Boone-Cle-Det 32.0
Mantle-NY 30.5
Woodling-NY 30.2

Clutch Hitting Index
Rizzuto-NY 128
Dropo-Det 122
Fox-Chi 120
Vernon-Was 119
Robinson-Phi 118

Runs Created
Rosen-Cle 155
Vernon-Was 127
Zernial-Phi 113
Boone-Cle-Det 106
Minoso-Chi 106

Total Average
Rosen-Cle 1.078
Mantle-NY .943
Boone-Cle-Det .925
Zernial-Phi .917
Doby-Cle .912

Stolen Bases
Minoso-Chi 25
Rivera-Chi 22
Jensen-Was 18
Philley-Phi 13
Busby-Was 13

Stolen Base Average
Jensen-Was 69.2
Minoso-Chi 61.0
Rivera-Chi 59.5

Stolen Base Runs
Michaels-Phi 1.5
Coan-Was 1.5
Jensen-Was 1.2
Philley-Phi 1.1
Zernial-Phi .9

Fielding Runs
Busby-Was 18.9
Groth-StL 17.1
Piersall-Bos 16.1
Strickland-Cle 15.6
Hunter-StL 14.6

Total Player Rating
Rosen-Cle 6.5
Berra-NY 3.5
Boone-Cle-Det 3.4
Zernial-Phi 3.2
Vernon-Was 2.9

Wins
Porterfield-Was 22
Parnell-Bos 21
B.Lemon-Cle 21
Trucks-StL-Chi 20

Win Percentage
Lopat-NY .800
Ford-NY .750
Parnell-Bos .724
Porterfield-Was .688

Games
Kinder-Bos 69
Stuart-StL 60
Martin-Phi 58
Paige-StL 57
Dorish-Chi 55

Complete Games
Porterfield-Was 24
B.Lemon-Cle 23
Garcia-Cle 21
Pierce-Chi 19
Trucks-StL-Chi 17

Shutouts
Porterfield-Was 9
Pierce-Chi 7
Trucks-StL-Chi 5
Parnell-Bos 5
B.Lemon-Cle 5

Saves
Kinder-Bos 27
Dorish-Chi 18
Reynolds-NY 13
Paige-StL 11
Sain-NY 9

Innings Pitched
B.Lemon-Cle 286.2
Garcia-Cle 271.2
Pierce-Chi 271.1
Trucks-StL-Chi 264.1
Porterfield-Was 255.0

Fewest Hits/Game
Pierce-Chi 7.16
McDermott-Bos 7.37
Raschi-NY 7.46
Masterson-Was 7.85
Trucks-StL-Chi 7.97

Fewest BB/Game
Lopat-NY 1.61
Sain-NY 2.14
A.Kellner-Phi 2.28
Porterfield-Was 2.58
Hoeft-Det 2.64

Strikeouts
Pierce-Chi 186
Trucks-StL-Chi 149
Wynn-Cle 138
Parnell-Bos 136
Garcia-Cle 134

Strikeouts/Game
Pierce-Chi 6.17
Gray-Det 5.88
Masterson-Was 5.14
Parnell-Bos 5.08
Trucks-StL-Chi 5.07

Ratio
Raschi-NY 10.24
Lopat-NY 10.35
Pierce-Chi 10.65
Porterfield-Was 11.19
Sain-NY 11.29

Earned Run Average
Lopat-NY 2.42
Pierce-Chi 2.72
Trucks-StL-Chi 2.93
Sain-NY 3.00
Ford-NY 3.00

Adjusted ERA
Lopat-NY 152
Pierce-Chi 148
McDermott-Bos 140
Trucks-StL-Chi 139
Parnell-Bos 137

Opponents' Batting Avg.
Pierce-Chi .218
McDermott-Bos .224
Raschi-NY .224
Masterson-Was .232
Trucks-StL-Chi .238

Opponents' On-Base Pct.
Raschi-NY .283
Lopat-NY .288
Pierce-Chi .292
Masterson-Was .304
Garcia-Cle .307

Starter Runs
Pierce-Chi 38.4
Trucks-StL-Chi 31.3
Lopat-NY 31.2
Parnell-Bos 25.0
Ford-NY 22.9

Adjusted Starter Runs
Pierce-Chi 39.0
Trucks-StL-Chi 33.1
Parnell-Bos 29.1
Lopat-NY 27.2
McDermott-Bos 26.1

Clutch Pitching Index
Ford-NY 127
Lopat-NY 123
Sain-NY 118
B.Lemon-Cle 113
Parnell-Bos 112

Relief Runs
Kinder-Bos 25.5
Dorish-Chi 9.7
Kuzava-NY 7.0
Bearden-Chi 6.9
Paige-StL 6.1

Adjusted Relief Runs
Kinder-Bos 26.6
Dorish-Chi 10.0
Paige-StL 8.3
Bearden-Chi 7.0
Kuzava-NY 4.2

Relief Ranking
Kinder-Bos 50.9
Dorish-Chi 12.7
Paige-StL 9.4
Bearden-Chi 6.5
Kuzava-NY 4.9

Total Pitcher Index
Kinder-Bos 5.6
McDermott-Bos 4.2
Trucks-StL-Chi 3.8
Pierce-Chi 3.5
B.Lemon-Cle 3.3

Total Baseball Ranking
Rosen-Cle 6.5
Kinder-Bos 5.6
McDermott-Bos 4.2
Trucks-StL-Chi 3.8
Berra-NY 3.5

TEAM	G	W	L	PCT	GB	R	OR	AB	H	2B	3B	HR	BB	SO	AVG	OBP	SLG	OPS	OPS+	BR	BR+	PF	CHI	RC	SB	CS	SBA	SBR
NY	154	97	57	.630		732	**550**	5245	1386	194	42	**186**	522	**561**	.264	.335	.424	759	102	17	13	101	102	747	30	23	57	-1
BRO	154	92	62	.597	5	778	740	5251	1418	246	56	**186**	**634**	625	.270	.353	**.444**	**797**	**110**	**100**	**76**	103	96	**821**	46	39	54	-4
MIL	154	89	65	.578	8	670	556	5261	1395	217	41	139	471	619	.265	.330	.401	731	103	-33	13	94	101	697	54	31	**64**	**1**
PHI	154	75	79	.487	22	659	614	5184	1384	243	**58**	102	604	620	.267	.345	.395	740	99	-2	-1	100	95	707	30	27	53	-3
CIN	154	74	80	.481	23	729	763	5234	1369	221	46	147	557	645	.262	.336	.406	742	96	-8	-27	103	**105**	726	47	30	61	0
STL	154	72	82	.468	25	**799**	790	5405	**1518**	**285**	**58**	119	582	586	**.281**	**.354**	.421	775	107	65	59	101	102	807	**63**	46	58	-2
CHI	154	64	90	.416	33	700	766	5359	1412	229	45	159	478	693	.263	.327	.412	739	97	-21	-28	101	103	717	46	31	60	-1
PIT	154	53	101	.344	44	557	845	5088	1260	181	57	76	566	737	.248	.326	.350	676	83	-119	-110	99	98	596	21	13	62	0
TOT	616					5624		42027	11142	1816	403	1114	4414	5086	.266	.339	.408	745							337	240	58	-10

TEAM	CG	SH	SV	IP	H	H/G	HR	BB	SO	RAT	ERA	ERA+	OAV	OOB	PR	PR+	PF	CPI	FA	E	DP	FW	PW	BW	SBW	DIF
NY	45	**19**	33	1390	**1258**	**8.2**	113	613	692	12.4	**3.10**	**130**	**.243**	.328	**151**	**147**	99	**113**	.975	154	172	-.5	**14.6**	1.3	.0	4.7
BRO	39	8	**36**	1393[2]	1399	9.1	164	533	**762**	12.6	4.31	95	.261	.330	-36	-34	100	93	.978	129	138	.9	-3.3	**7.6**	-.3	10.3
MIL	63	13	21	1394[2]	1296	8.4	**106**	553	698	12.2	3.19	117	.250	.326	137	91	92	110	**.981**	**116**	171	**1.6**	9.1	1.3	**.2**	.0
PHI	**78**	14	12	1365[1]	1329	8.8	133	**450**	570	**11.9**	3.60	112	.256	**.318**	73	68	99	100	.975	145	133	.0	6.8	-.0	-.2	-8.4
CIN	34	8	27	1367[1]	1491	9.9	169	547	537	13.7	4.51	93	.282	.354	-65	-45	103	105	.977	137	**194**	.4	-4.4	-2.6	.1	3.7
STL	40	11	18	1390[1]	1484	9.7	170	535	680	13.4	4.50	91	.275	.346	-66	-59	101	100	.976	146	178	-.0	-5.8	5.9	-.0	-4.8
CHI	41	6	19	1374[1]	1375	9.1	131	619	622	13.3	4.51	93	.264	.345	-66	-45	103	92	.974	154	164	-.5	-4.4	-2.7	.0	-5.2
PIT	37	4	15	1346	1510	10.1	128	564	525	14.1	4.93	85	.287	.359	-127	-106	103	95	.971	173	136	-1.5	-10.4	-10.8	.1	-1.1
TOT	377	83	181	11021[2]		9.1				12.9	4.08		.266	.339					.976	1154	1286					

Runs
Snider-Bro 120
Musial-StL 120
Mays-NY 119
Ashburn-Phi 111
Gilliam-Bro 107

Hits
Mueller-NY 212
Snider-Bro 199
Musial-StL 195
Mays-NY 195
Moon-StL 193

Doubles
Musial-StL 41
Snider-Bro 39
Repulski-StL 39
Hamner-Phi 39

Triples
Mays-NY 13
Hamner-Phi 11
Snider-Bro 10

Home Runs
Kluszewski-Cin 49
Hodges-Bro 42
Sauer-Chi 41
Mays-NY 41

Total Bases
Snider-Bro 378
Mays-NY 377
Kluszewski-Cin 368
Musial-StL 359
Hodges-Bro 335

Runs Batted In
Kluszewski-Cin 141
Snider-Bro 130
Hodges-Bro 130
Musial-StL 126
Ennis-Phi 119

Runs Produced
Musial-StL 211
Snider-Bro 210
Kluszewski-Cin 196
Hodges-Bro 194

Bases On Balls
Ashburn-Phi 125
Mathews-Mil 113
Musial-StL 103
Thompson-NY 90
Reese-Bro 90

Batting Average
Mays-NY 345
Mueller-NY 342
Snider-Bro 341
Musial-StL 330
Kluszewski-Cin 326

On-Base Percentage
Ashburn-Phi 442
Musial-StL 433
Mathews-Mil 428
Snider-Bro 427
Mays-NY 415

Slugging Average
Mays-NY 667
Snider-Bro 647
Kluszewski-Cin 642
Musial-StL 607
Mathews-Mil 603

On-Base Plus Slugging
Mays-NY 1083
Snider-Bro 1074
Kluszewski-Cin 1052
Musial-StL 1040
Mathews-Mil 1031

Adjusted OPS
Mathews-Mil 177
Mays-NY 176
Snider-Bro 170
Musial-StL 166
Kluszewski-Cin 165

Batter Runs
Snider-Bro 64.6
Mays-NY 61.8
Musial-StL 60.7
Kluszewski-Cin 57.1
Mathews-Mil 48.6

Adjusted Batter Runs
Mays-NY 61.1
Snider-Bro 60.2
Musial-StL 59.6
Mathews-Mil 56.9
Kluszewski-Cin 53.4

Clutch Hitting Index
Ennis-Phi 132
Jablonski-StL 127
Post-Cin 126
Furillo-Bro 119
Bell-Cin 117

Runs Created
Snider-Bro 161
Mays-NY 155
Musial-StL 153
Kluszewski-Cin 151
Mathews-Mil 131

Total Average
Mathews-Mil 1.169
Mays-NY 1.158
Snider-Bro 1.156
Kluszewski-Cin 1.117
Musial-StL 1.087

Stolen Bases
Bruton-Mil 34
Temple-Cin 21
Fondy-Chi 20
Moon-StL 18
Ashburn-Phi 11

Stolen Base Average
Fondy-Chi 80.0
Temple-Cin 75.0
Bruton-Mil 72.3
Moon-StL 64.3

Stolen Base Runs
Bruton-Mil 2.9
Fondy-Chi 2.7
Temple-Cin 2.2
Torgeson-Phi 1.2
Mathews-Mil 1.1

Fielding Runs
Schoendienst-StL 32.9
Grammas-StL 29.8
Ashburn-Phi 17.2
Mays-NY 15.5
Logan-Mil 14.4

Total Player Rating
Mays-NY 6.7
Mathews-Mil 5.4
Schoendienst-StL 4.9
Musial-StL 4.8
Snider-Bro 4.6

Wins
Roberts-Phi 23
Spahn-Mil 21
Antonelli-NY 21
Haddix-StL 18
Erskine-Bro 18

Win Percentage
Antonelli-NY 750
Lawrence-StL 714
Gomez-NY 654
Spahn-Mil 636
Roberts-Phi 605

Games
Hughes-Bro 60
Hetki-Pit 58
Brazle-StL 58
Wilhelm-NY 57
Grissom-NY 56

Complete Games
Roberts-Phi 29
Spahn-Mil 23
Simmons-Phi 21
Antonelli-NY 18

Shutouts
Antonelli-NY 6

Saves
Hughes-Bro 24
Smith-Cin 20
Grissom-NY 19
Jolly-Mil 10
Hetki-Pit 9

Innings Pitched
Roberts-Phi 336.2
Spahn-Mil 283.1
Erskine-Bro 260.1
Haddix-StL 259.2
Antonelli-NY 258.2

Fewest Hits/Game
Antonelli-NY 7.27
Roberts-Phi 7.73
Conley-Mil 7.92
Lawrence-StL 8.00
Wehmeier-Cin-Phi 8.02

Fewest BB/Game
Roberts-Phi 1.50
Minner-Chi 2.06
Hacker-Chi 2.10
Burdette-Mil 2.34
Meyer-Bro 2.45

Strikeouts
Roberts-Phi 185
Haddix-StL 184
Erskine-Bro 166
Antonelli-NY 152
Spahn-Mil 136

Strikeouts/Game
Haddix-StL 6.38
Erskine-Bro 5.74
Littlefield-Pit 5.34
Antonelli-NY 5.29
Conley-Mil 5.23

Ratio
Roberts-Phi 9.36
Antonelli-NY 10.72
Burdette-Mil 10.97
Spahn-Mil 11.09
Hacker-Chi 11.23

Earned Run Average
Antonelli-NY 2.30
Burdette-Mil 2.76
Simmons-Phi 2.81
Gomez-NY 2.88
Conley-Mil 2.96

Adjusted ERA
Antonelli-NY 176
Simmons-Phi 144
Gomez-NY 140
Roberts-Phi 136
Burdette-Mil 135

Opponents' Batting Avg.
Antonelli-NY 219
Roberts-Phi 231
Simmons-Phi 239
Littlefield-Pit 239
Wehmeier-Cin-Phi 239

Opponents' On-Base Pct.
Roberts-Phi 267
Antonelli-NY 293
Spahn-Mil 302
Burdette-Mil 302
Hacker-Chi 304

Starter Runs
Antonelli-NY 51.0
Roberts-Phi 41.3
Simmons-Phi 35.5
Burdette-Mil 34.7
Gomez-NY 29.3

Adjusted Starter Runs
Antonelli-NY 50.4
Roberts-Phi 40.4
Simmons-Phi 34.8
Gomez-NY 28.7
Burdette-Mil 27.9

Clutch Pitching Index
Gomez-NY 130
Dickson-Phi 123
Fowler-Cin 116
Conley-Mil 116
Antonelli-NY 115

Relief Runs
Wilhelm-NY 24.4
Grissom-NY 23.4
Jolly-Mil 20.4
Johnson-Mil 13.9
Smith-Cin 12.7

Adjusted Relief Runs
Wilhelm-NY 24.1
Grissom-NY 23.1
Jolly-Mil 17.6
Smith-Cin 13.3
Johnson-Mil 11.1

Relief Ranking
Grissom-NY 36.9
Wilhelm-NY 34.6
Jolly-Mil 27.7
Smith-Cin 26.7
Hughes-Bro 15.5

Total Pitcher Index
Antonelli-NY 5.5
Grissom-NY 3.7
Roberts-Phi 3.7
Wilhelm-NY 3.4
Simmons-Phi 3.3

Total Baseball Ranking
Mays-NY 6.7
Antonelli-NY 5.5
Mathews-Mil 5.4
Schoendienst-StL 4.9
Musial-StL 4.8

TEAM	G	W	L	PCT	GB	R	OR	AB	H	2B	3B	HR	BB	SO	AVG	OBP	SLG	OPS	OPS+	BR	BR+	PF	CHI	RC	SB	CS	SBA	SBR
CLE	156	111	43	.721		746	**504**	5222	1368	188	39	**156**	637	668	.262	.345	.403	748	109	76	64	102	102	739	30	33	48	-5
NY	155	103	51	.669	8	**805**	563	5226	1400	215	59	133	650	632	**.268**	**.351**	**.408**	**759**	**118**	**101**	**128**	97	**106**	**768**	34	41	45	-7
CHI	155	94	60	.610	17	711	521	5168	1382	203	47	94	604	**536**	.267	.350	.379	729	103	51	28	103	101	700	**98**	58	63	**1**
BOS	156	69	85	.448	42	700	728	5399	**1436**	**244**	41	123	**654**	660	.266	.348	.395	743	99	73	-1	111	93	749	51	30	63	**1**
DET	155	68	86	.442	43	584	664	5233	1351	215	41	90	492	603	.258	.324	.367	691	97	-37	-25	98	97	609	48	44	52	-5
WAS	155	66	88	.429	45	632	680	5249	1292	188	**69**	81	610	719	.246	.328	.355	683	98	-44	-9	95	104	631	37	21	**64**	**1**
BAL	154	54	100	.351	57	483	668	5206	1309	195	49	52	468	634	.251	.316	.338	654	92	-104	-61	93	91	553	30	31	49	-4
PHI	156	51	103	.331	60	542	875	5206	1228	191	41	94	504	677	.236	.307	.342	649	84	-117	-119	100	105	553	30	29	51	-4
TOT	621					5203		41909	10766	1639	386	823	4619	5129	.257	.334	.374	707							358	287	56	-22

TEAM	CG	SH	SV	IP	H	H/G	HR	BB	SO	RAT	ERA	ERA+	OAV	OOB	PR	PR+	PF	CPI	FA	E	DP	FW	PW	BW	SBW	DIF
CLE	**77**	12	36	1419[1]	**1220**	**7.8**	89	**486**	678	**11.0**	**2.79**	**132**	**.232**	**.299**	**148**	**142**	99	100	.979	128	148	.8	**14.7**	6.7	-.2	12.3
NY	51	16	**37**	1379[1]	1284	8.4	86	552	655	12.2	3.27	105	.251	.328	71	29	92	**107**	.979	126	**198**	.8	3.0	**13.3**	-.4	9.5
CHI	60	**23**	33	1383	1255	8.2	94	517	701	11.7	3.06	122	.244	.314	103	105	100	105	**.982**	**108**	149	**1.8**	10.9	2.9	**.4**	1.1
BOS	41	10	22	1412[1]	1434	9.2	118	612	**707**	13.3	4.02	102	.265	.344	-46	14	110	101	.972	176	163	-1.9	1.5	-.0	**.4**	-7.7
DET	58	13	13	1383	1375	9.0	138	506	603	12.5	3.81	97	.261	.330	-13	-18	99	103	.978	129	131	.7	-1.8	-2.5	-.2	-4.9
WAS	69	10	7	1383[1]	1396	9.1	79	573	562	13.0	3.84	93	.265	.340	-18	-46	96	99	.977	137	172	.2	-4.7	-.9	**.4**	-5.8
BAL	58	6	8	1373[1]	1279	8.4	**78**	688	668	13.1	3.88	92	.250	.341	-24	-47	96	94	.975	147	152	-.4	-4.8	-6.3	-.1	-11.2
PHI	49	3	13	1371[1]	1523	10.0	141	685	555	14.8	5.18	75	.285	.370	-222	-185	105	95	.972	169	163	-1.5	-19.1	-12.2	-.1	7.2
TOT	463	93	169	11105		8.8				12.7	3.73		.257	.334					.977	1120	1276					

Runs
Mantle-NY 129
Minoso-Chi 119
Avila-Cle 112
Fox-Chi 111
Carrasquel-Chi 106

Hits
Kuenn-Det 201
Fox-Chi 201
Avila-Cle 189
Busby-Was 187
Minoso-Chi 182

Doubles
Vernon-Was 33
Smith-Cle 29
Minoso-Chi 29

Triples
Minoso-Chi 18
Runnels-Was 15
Vernon-Was 14
Mantle-NY 12
Tuttle-Det 11

Home Runs
Doby-Cle 32
Williams-Bos 29
Mantle-NY 27
Jensen-Bos 25

Total Bases
Minoso-Chi 304
Vernon-Was 294
Mantle-NY 285
Berra-NY 285
Doby-Cle 279

Runs Batted In
Doby-Cle 126
Berra-NY 125
Jensen-Bos 117
Minoso-Chi 116

Runs Produced
Minoso-Chi 216
Mantle-NY 204
Berra-NY 191
Doby-Cle 188
Jensen-Bos 184

Bases On Balls
Williams-Bos 136
Yost-Was 131
Mantle-NY 102
Smith-Cle 88

Batting Average
Avila-Cle .341
Minoso-Chi .320
Noren-NY .319
Fox-Chi .319
Berra-NY .307

On-Base Percentage
Williams-Bos .516
Minoso-Chi .416
Rosen-Cle .412
Mantle-NY .411
Yost-Was .406

Slugging Average
Minoso-Chi .535
Mantle-NY .525
Rosen-Cle .506
Vernon-Was .492
Berra-NY .488

On-Base Plus Slugging
Williams-Bos 1151
Minoso-Chi 951
Mantle-NY 936
Rosen-Cle 918
Avila-Cle 882

Adjusted OPS
Williams-Bos 193
Mantle-NY 160
Minoso-Chi 154
Rosen-Cle 148
Noren-NY 140

Batter Runs
Williams-Bos 70.9
Minoso-Chi 47.3
Mantle-NY 42.8
Rosen-Cle 34.2
Avila-Cle 31.5

Adjusted Batter Runs
Williams-Bos 58.2
Mantle-NY 46.9
Minoso-Chi 43.3
Rosen-Cle 32.6
Avila-Cle 29.8

Clutch Hitting Index
Berra-NY 123
Minoso-Chi 122
Rosen-Cle 118
Sievers-Was 117
Doby-Cle 116

Runs Created
Williams-Bos 139
Mantle-NY 127
Minoso-Chi 125
Avila-Cle 109
Doby-Cle 108

Total Average
Williams-Bos 1.452
Mantle-NY 1.013
Minoso-Chi .969
Rosen-Cle .959
Doby-Cle .862

Stolen Bases
Jensen-Bos 22
Rivera-Chi 18
Minoso-Chi 18
Jacobs-Phi 17
Busby-Was 17

Stolen Base Average
Busby-Was 89.5
Jacobs-Phi 85.0
Jensen-Bos 75.9
Rivera-Chi 64.3
Fox-Chi 64.0

Stolen Base Runs
Busby-Was 3.0
Jacobs-Phi 2.7
Jensen-Bos 2.4
Cavarretta-Chi .9
Michaels-Chi .8

Fielding Runs
Coleman-NY 17.9
Carey-NY 16.7
Lepcio-Bos 16.1
Bolling-Bos 15.3
Minoso-Chi 13.4

Total Player Rating
Avila-Cle 4.9
Minoso-Chi 4.9
Williams-Bos 4.9
Mantle-NY 4.0
Berra-NY 3.7

Wins
Wynn-Cle 23
Lemon-Cle 23
Grim-NY 20
Trucks-Chi 19
Garcia-Cle 19

Win Percentage
Consuegra-Chi .842
Grim-NY .769
Lemon-Cle .767
Garcia-Cle .704
Houtteman-Cle .682

Games
Dixon-Was-Phi 54
Martin-Phi-Chi 48
Pascual-Was 48
Kinder-Bos 48

Complete Games
Porterfield-Was 21
Lemon-Cle 21
Wynn-Cle 20
Gromek-Det 17

Shutouts
Trucks-Chi 5
Garcia-Cle 5

Saves
Sain-NY 22
Kinder-Bos 15
Narleski-Cle 13

Innings Pitched
Wynn-Cle 270.2
Trucks-Chi 264.2
Garcia-Cle 258.2
Lemon-Cle 258.1
Gromek-Det 252.2

Fewest Hits/Game
Turley-Bal 6.48
Ford-NY 7.26
Wynn-Cle 7.48
Coleman-Bal 7.48
Reynolds-NY 7.61

Fewest BB/Game
Lopat-NY 1.75
Gromek-Det 2.03
Garver-Det 2.27
Garcia-Cle 2.47
Zuverink-Det 2.75

Strikeouts
Turley-Bal 185
Wynn-Cle 155
Trucks-Chi 152
Pierce-Chi 148
Harshman-Chi 134

Strikeouts/Game
Pierce-Chi 7.06
Harshman-Chi 6.81
Turley-Bal 6.73
Hoeft-Det 5.86
Reynolds-NY 5.72

Ratio
Garcia-Cle 10.19
Wynn-Cle 10.24
Garver-Det 10.30
Gromek-Det 10.86
Trucks-Chi 10.88

Earned Run Average
Garcia-Cle 2.64
Lemon-Cle 2.72
Wynn-Cle 2.73
Gromek-Det 2.74
Trucks-Chi 2.79

Adjusted ERA
Garcia-Cle 139
Lemon-Cle 135
Wynn-Cle 135
Gromek-Det 135
Trucks-Chi 134

Opponents' Batting Avg.
Turley-Bal .203
Wynn-Cle .225
Ford-NY .227
Trucks-Chi .228
Garcia-Cle .229

Opponents' On-Base Pct.
Garcia-Cle .284
Wynn-Cle .284
Garver-Det .287
Gromek-Det .297
Trucks-Chi .297

Starter Runs
Garcia-Cle 31.0
Wynn-Cle 30.0
Lemon-Cle 28.9
Gromek-Det 27.5
Trucks-Chi 27.5

Adjusted Starter Runs
Garcia-Cle 30.0
Wynn-Cle 28.9
Lemon-Cle 27.8
Trucks-Chi 27.7
Gromek-Det 26.9

Clutch Pitching Index
Keegan-Chi 126
Gromek-Det 116
Houtteman-Cle 114
Lopat-NY 114
Harshman-Chi 114

Relief Runs
Mossi-Cle 18.5
Narleski-Cle 14.8
Dorish-Chi 12.1
Miller-Det 9.8
Sain-NY 4.9

Adjusted Relief Runs
Mossi-Cle 18.2
Narleski-Cle 14.5
Dorish-Chi 12.2
Miller-Det 9.7
Kinder-Bos 5.3

Relief Ranking
Mossi-Cle 15.4
Narleski-Cle 13.6
Dorish-Chi 11.6
Kinder-Bos 8.8
Sain-NY 5.2

Total Pitcher Index
Lemon-Cle 4.2
Gromek-Det 3.4
Wynn-Cle 3.3
Trucks-Chi 3.2
Garcia-Cle 2.9

Total Baseball Ranking
Avila-Cle 4.9
Minoso-Chi 4.9
Williams-Bos 4.9
Lemon-Cle 4.2
Mantle-NY 4.0

TEAM	G	W	L	PCT	GB	R	OR	AB	H	2B	3B	HR	BB	SO	AVG	OBP	SLG	OPS	OPS+	BR	BR+	PF	CHI	RC	SB	CS	SBA	SBR
BRO	154	98	55	.641		**857**	**650**	5193	1406	**230**	44	**201**	**674**	718	**.271**	**.359**	**.448**	**807**	**116**	**142**	**119**	103	100	**834**	**79**	56	59	-2
MIL	154	85	69	.552	13.5	743	668	5277	1377	219	55	182	504	735	.261	.329	.427	756	109	27	65	95	102	733	42	27	61	0
NY	154	80	74	.519	18.5	702	673	5288	1377	173	34	169	497	**581**	.260	.328	.402	730	98	-15	-16	100	102	699	38	22	**63**	**1**
PHI	154	77	77	.500	21.5	675	666	5092	1300	214	50	132	652	673	.255	.343	.395	738	103	14	27	98	95	692	44	32	58	-2
CIN	154	75	79	.487	23.5	761	684	5270	**1424**	216	28	181	556	657	.270	.344	.425	769	103	63	21	106	99	773	51	36	59	-1
CHI	154	72	81	.471	26	626	713	5214	1287	187	55	164	428	806	.247	.307	.398	705	91	-75	-73	100	**103**	623	37	35	51	-4
STL	154	68	86	.442	30.5	654	757	5266	1375	228	36	143	458	597	.261	.324	.400	724	96	-30	-29	100	99	662	64	59	52	-7
PIT	154	60	94	.390	38.5	560	767	5173	1262	210	**60**	91	471	652	.244	.310	.361	671	84	-127	-119	99	100	567	22	22	50	-3
TOT	616					5578		41773	10808	1677	362	1263	4240	5419	.259	.331	.407	737							377	289	57	-18

TEAM	CG	SH	SV	IP	H	H/G	HR	BB	SO	RAT	ERA	ERA+	OAV	OOB	PR	PR+	PF	CPI	FA	E	DP	FW	PW	BW	SBW	DIF
BRO	46	11	**37**	1378	1296	**8.5**	168	483	**773**	**11.8**	**3.69**	**110**	**.248**	**.314**	**54**	**58**	101	100	.978	133	156	.6	**5.8**	**11.9**	.0	3.5
MIL	**61**	5	12	1383	1339	8.8	**138**	591	654	12.7	3.85	98	.256	.333	29	-15	93	102	.975	152	155	-.5	-1.4	6.5	.2	3.4
NY	52	6	14	1386[2]	1347	8.8	155	560	721	12.7	3.78	107	.257	.334	41	39	100	**107**	.976	142	165	.0	3.9	-1.5	**.3**	.4
PHI	58	11	21	1356[2]	**1291**	8.6	161	477	657	11.9	3.93	101	.251	.318	17	6	98	96	**.981**	**110**	117	**1.9**	.6	2.7	.0	-5.1
CIN	38	**12**	22	1363	1373	9.1	161	**443**	576	12.2	3.95	107	.264	.324	13	41	105	102	.977	139	169	.2	4.1	2.1	.1	-8.4
CHI	47	10	23	1378[1]	1306	8.6	153	601	686	12.7	4.18	98	.251	.332	-21	-13	101	95	.975	147	147	-.2	-1.2	-7.2	-.2	4.5
STL	42	10	15	1376[2]	1376	9.0	185	549	730	12.9	4.57	89	.262	.337	-80	-76	101	95	.975	146	152	-.2	-7.5	-2.8	-.5	2.2
PIT	41	5	16	1362	1480	9.8	142	536	622	13.5	4.40	94	.281	.350	-54	-41	102	104	.972	166	**175**	-1.3	-4.0	-11.8	-.0	.4
TOT	385	70	160	10984[1]		8.9				12.6	4.04		.259	.331					.977	1135	1236					

Runs
Snider-Bro 126
Mays-NY 123
Post-Cin 116
Kluszewski-Cin 116
Gilliam-Bro 110

Hits
Kluszewski-Cin 192
Aaron-Mil 189
Bell-Cin 188
Post-Cin 186

Doubles
Logan-Mil 37
Aaron-Mil........... 37
Snider-Bro.......... 34
Post-Cin 33
Ashburn-Phi 32

Triples
Mays-NY 13
Long-Pit............ 13
Bruton-Mil 12
Clemente-Pit 11

Home Runs
Mays-NY 51
Kluszewski-Cin 47
Banks-Chi 44
Snider-Bro.......... 42
Mathews-Mil 41

Total Bases
Mays-NY 382
Kluszewski-Cin 358
Banks-Chi 355
Post-Cin 345
Snider-Bro 338

Runs Batted In
Snider-Bro 136
Mays-NY 127
Ennis-Phi 120
Banks-Chi 117
Kluszewski-Cin 113

Runs Produced
Snider-Bro 220
Mays-NY 199
Post-Cin 185
Aaron-Mil 184
Kluszewski-Cin 182

Bases On Balls
Mathews-Mil 109
Ashburn-Phi 105
Snider-Bro......... 104
Thompson-NY 84

Batting Average
Ashburn-Phi .... .338
Mays-NY .... .319
Musial-StL......... .319
Campanella-Bro .... .318
Aaron-Mil.......... .314

On-Base Percentage
Ashburn-Phi .... .449
Snider-Bro .... .421
Mathews-Mil .... .417
Musial-StL......... .411
Mays-NY .... .404

Slugging Average
Mays-NY .... .659
Snider-Bro .... .628
Mathews-Mil .... .601
Banks-Chi .... .596
Kluszewski-Cin ..... .585

On-Base Plus Slugging
Mays-NY 1063
Snider-Bro 1050
Mathews-Mil 1018
Campanella-Bro 985
Musial-StL 977

Adjusted OPS
Mays-NY 176
Mathews-Mil 175
Snider-Bro 169
Musial-StL 156
Campanella-Bro 153

Batter Runs
Mays-NY 62.3
Snider-Bro 58.9
Mathews-Mil 50.0
Musial-StL 46.5
Kluszewski-Cin 44.9

Adjusted Batter Runs
Mays-NY 62.0
Mathews-Mil 56.5
Snider-Bro 55.2
Musial-StL 46.6
Ashburn-Phi 38.9

Clutch Hitting Index
Long-Pit 117
Jones-Phi 117
Mueller-NY 116
Ennis-Phi 116
Temple-Cin 115

Runs Created
Mays-NY 157
Snider-Bro 145
Kluszewski-Cin 136
Musial-StL 131
Mathews-Mil 131

Total Average
Mays-NY 1.180
Snider-Bro 1.147
Mathews-Mil 1.124
Musial-StL 1.020
Campanella-Bro ... 1.000

Stolen Bases
Bruton-Mil 25
Mays-NY 24
Boyer-StL 22
Temple-Cin 19
Gilliam-Bro 15

Stolen Base Average
Mays-NY 85.7
Temple-Cin 82.6
Bruton-Mil 69.4
Boyer-StL 56.4

Stolen Base Runs
Mays-NY 3.9
Temple-Cin 2.8
Bruton-Mil 1.7
Robinson-Bro 1.6
Blaylock-Phi 1.0

Fielding Runs
Mays-NY 19.8
McMillan-Cin 16.6
O'Connell-Mil 15.8
Groat-Pit 15.4
Bruton-Mil 14.7

Total Player Rating
Mays-NY 7.6
Banks-Chi 5.3
Mathews-Mil 5.0
Snider-Bro 4.7
Ashburn-Phi 4.2

Wins
Roberts-Phi 23
Newcombe-Bro 20
Spahn-Mil 17
Nuxhall-Cin 17

Win Percentage
Newcombe-Bro ..... .800
Roberts-Phi .... .622
Nuxhall-Cin .... .586
Spahn-Mil .... .548

Games
Labine-Bro 60
Wilhelm-NY 59
LaPalme-StL 56
Grissom-NY 55
Freeman-Cin 52

Complete Games
Roberts-Phi 26
Newcombe-Bro 17
Spahn-Mil 16

Shutouts
Nuxhall-Cin 5
Jones-Chi 4
Dickson-Phi 4

Saves
Meyer-Phi 16
Roebuck-Bro 12
Labine-Bro 11
Freeman-Cin 11
Grissom-NY 8

Innings Pitched
Roberts-Phi 305.0
Nuxhall-Cin 257.0
Spahn-Mil 245.2
Jones-Chi 241.2
Antonelli-NY 235.1

Fewest Hits/Game
Jones-Chi 6.52
Buhl-Mil 7.50
Rush-Chi 7.85
Antonelli-NY 7.88
Dickson-Phi 7.92

Fewest BB/Game
Newcombe-Bro 1.46
Roberts-Phi 1.56
Hacker-Chi 1.82
Friend-Pit 2.34
Spahn-Mil 2.38

Strikeouts
Jones-Chi 198
Roberts-Phi 160
Haddix-StL 150
Newcombe-Bro 143
Antonelli-NY 143

Strikeouts/Game
Jones-Chi 7.37
Haddix-StL 6.49
Podres-Bro 6.44
Conley-Mil 6.09
Newcombe-Bro 5.51

Ratio
Newcombe-Bro ... 10.05
Roberts-Phi 10.24
Friend-Pit 10.42
Hacker-Chi 10.44
Rush-Chi 10.73

Earned Run Average
Friend-Pit 2.83
Newcombe-Bro 3.20
Buhl-Mil 3.21
Spahn-Mil 3.26
Roberts-Phi 3.28

Adjusted ERA
Friend-Pit 145
Newcombe-Bro 127
Nuxhall-Cin 122
Roberts-Phi 121
Antonelli-NY 121

Opponents' Batting Avg.
Jones-Chi .... .206
Buhl-Mil .... .227
Rush-Chi .... .234
Antonelli-NY ...... .234
Dickson-Phi .... .238

Opponents' On-Base Pct.
Roberts-Phi .... .280
Newcombe-Bro ..... .280
Hacker-Chi .... .285
Friend-Pit .... .294
Rush-Chi .... .295

Starter Runs
Friend-Pit 26.9
Roberts-Phi 25.8
Newcombe-Bro 21.8
Spahn-Mil 21.2
Antonelli-NY 18.6

Adjusted Starter Runs
Friend-Pit 28.1
Roberts-Phi 23.9
Newcombe-Bro 22.3
Nuxhall-Cin 20.9
Schmidt-StL 18.4

Clutch Pitching Index
Minner-Chi 122
Spahn-Mil 114
Jackson-StL 113
Law-Pit 109
Friend-Pit 109

Relief Runs
Freeman-Cin 19.1
Miller-Phi 16.2
LaPalme-StL 13.1
Labine-Bro 12.8
Jeffcoat-Chi 12.2

Adjusted Relief Runs
Freeman-Cin 20.2
Miller-Phi 15.8
LaPalme-StL 13.3
Labine-Bro 13.1
Jeffcoat-Chi 12.6

Relief Ranking
Freeman-Cin 27.2
Miller-Phi 19.4
Jeffcoat-Chi 17.4
Labine-Bro 16.9
Bessent-Bro 13.2

Total Pitcher Index
Newcombe-Bro 4.1
Roberts-Phi 3.8
Friend-Pit 3.2
Freeman-Cin 3.0
Antonelli-NY 2.6

Total Baseball Ranking
Mays-NY 7.6
Banks-Chi 5.3
Mathews-Mil 5.0
Snider-Bro 4.7
Ashburn-Phi 4.2

TEAM	G	W	L	PCT	GB	R	OR	AB	H	2B	3B	HR	BB	SO	AVG	OBP	SLG	OPS	OPS+	BR	BR+	PF	CHI	RC	SB	CS	SBA	SBR
NY	154	96	58	.623		762	569	5161	1342	179	**55**	**175**	609	658	.260	.343	**.418**	**761**	**113**	71	**83**	98	101	759	55	25	69	3
CLE	154	93	61	.604	3	698	601	5146	1325	195	31	148	**723**	715	.257	.353	.394	747	104	60	33	104	93	741	28	24	54	-2
CHI	155	91	63	.591	5	725	**557**	5220	1401	204	36	116	567	595	**.268**	.347	.388	735	101	31	11	103	101	712	**69**	45	61	-1
BOS	154	84	70	.545	12	755	652	5273	1392	**241**	39	137	707	733	.264	**.354**	.402	756	101	**77**	13	109	97	**773**	43	17	**72**	**4**
DET	154	79	75	.513	17	**775**	658	5283	**1407**	211	38	130	641	**583**	.266	.348	.394	742	108	46	63	98	**104**	736	41	22	65	1
KC	155	63	91	.409	33	638	911	5335	1395	189	46	121	463	725	.261	.323	.382	705	95	-40	-47	101	100	637	22	36	38	-8
BAL	156	57	97	.370	39	540	754	5257	1263	177	39	54	560	742	.240	.316	.320	636	83	-159	-120	93	**104**	532	34	46	43	-9
WAS	154	53	101	.344	43	598	789	5142	1277	178	54	80	538	654	.248	.324	.351	675	93	-86	-53	95	103	586	25	32	44	-6
TOT	618					5491		41817	10802	1574	338	961	4808	5405	.259	.339	.382	720							317	247	56	-17

TEAM	CG	SH	SV	IP	H	H/G	HR	BB	SO	RAT	ERA	ERA+	OAV	OOB	PR	PR+	PF	CPI	FA	E	DP	FW	PW	BW	SBW	DIF
NY	52	19	33	1372[1]	**1163**	**7.7**	108	688	731	12.4	**3.24**	116	**.232**	.328	**111**	82	95	**107**	.978	128	**180**	.5	8.3	**8.4**	.5	1.5
CLE	45	15	**36**	1386[1]	1285	8.4	111	558	**877**	12.2	3.39	**118**	.245	.320	88	**92**	101	101	**.981**	**108**	152	**1.7**	**9.3**	3.4	.0	1.9
CHI	55	**20**	23	1378	1301	8.5	111	**497**	720	**11.9**	3.38	117	.251	**.319**	90	89	100	103	**.981**	111	147	1.6	9.0	1.2	.1	2.4
BOS	44	9	34	1384[1]	1333	8.7	128	582	674	12.7	3.72	115	.253	.331	37	81	108	102	.977	136	140	.0	8.2	1.4	**.6**	-3.0
DET	**66**	16	12	1380[1]	1381	9.1	126	517	629	12.7	3.80	101	.261	.331	26	8	97	102	.976	139	159	-.1	.9	6.4	.3	-5.2
KC	29	9	23	1382	1486	9.7	175	707	572	14.6	5.36	78	.278	.367	-214	-172	105	94	.976	146	174	-.5	-17.2	-4.7	-.6	9.1
BAL	35	10	22	1388[2]	1403	9.1	103	625	595	13.4	4.22	91	.266	.348	-39	-64	96	98	.972	167	159	-1.7	-6.4	-12.0	-.7	.9
WAS	37	10	16	1354[2]	1450	9.7	**99**	634	607	14.2	4.63	83	.279	.362	-100	-124	97	98	.974	154	170	-1.0	-12.4	-5.3	-.4	-4.8
TOT	363	108	199	11026[2]		8.9				13.0	3.97		.259	.339					.978	1089	1281					

Runs
Smith-Cle 123
Mantle-NY 121
Kaline-Det 121
Tuttle-Det 102
Kuenn-Det 101

Hits
Kaline-Det 200
Fox-Chi 198
Power-KC 190
Kuenn-Det 190
Smith-Cle 186

Doubles
Kuenn-Det 38
Power-KC 34
Goodman-Bos 31
White-Bos 30
Finigan-KC 30

Triples
Mantle-NY 11
Carey-NY 11
Power-KC 10

Home Runs
Mantle-NY 37
Zernial-KC 30
Williams-Bos 28

Total Bases
Kaline-Det 321
Mantle-NY 316
Power-KC 301
Smith-Cle 287
Jensen-Bos 275

Runs Batted In
Jensen-Bos 116
Boone-Det 116
Berra-NY 108
Sievers-Was 106
Kaline-Det 102

Runs Produced
Kaline-Det 196
Jensen-Bos 185
Mantle-NY 183
Smith-Cle 178
Tuttle-Det 166

Bases On Balls
Mantle-NY 113
Goodman-Bos 99
Yost-Was 95
Fain-Det-Cle 94
Smith-Cle 93

Batting Average
Kaline-Det .340
Power-KC .319
Kell-Chi .312
Fox-Chi .311
Kuenn-Det .306

On-Base Percentage
Mantle-NY .433
Kaline-Det .425
Smith-Cle .411
Yost-Was .410
Goodman-Bos .397

Slugging Average
Mantle-NY .611
Kaline-Det .546
Zernial-KC .508
Doby-Cle .505
Power-KC .505

On-Base Plus Slugging
Mantle-NY 1044
Kaline-Det 971
Smith-Cle 884
Doby-Cle 877
Power-KC 862

Adjusted OPS
Mantle-NY 181
Kaline-Det 163
Sievers-Was 136
Vernon-Was 133
Smith-Cle 132

Batter Runs
Williams-Bos 59.3
Mantle-NY 59.0
Kaline-Det 50.2
Smith-Cle 34.7
Valo-KC 24.8

Adjusted Batter Runs
Mantle-NY 61.2
Kaline-Det 53.2
Williams-Bos 50.5
Smith-Cle 30.5
Vernon-Was 25.5

Clutch Hitting Index
Kell-Chi 137
Boone-Det 137
Zauchin-Bos 114
Jensen-Bos 111
Sievers-Was 111

Runs Created
Mantle-NY 148
Kaline-Det 135
Smith-Cle 128
Williams-Bos 118
Power-KC 103

Total Average
Mantle-NY 1.206
Kaline-Det .993
Smith-Cle .928
Doby-Cle .884
Jensen-Bos .849

Stolen Bases
Rivera-Chi 25
Minoso-Chi 19
Jensen-Bos 16
Busby-Was-Chi 12
Smith-Cle 11

Stolen Base Average
Minoso-Chi 70.4
Jensen-Bos 69.6
Rivera-Chi 61.0

Stolen Base Runs
Torgeson-Det 2.0
Busby-Was-Chi 1.6
Mantle-NY 1.4
Minoso-Chi 1.4
Klaus-Bos 1.3

Fielding Runs
Fox-Chi 26.9
McDougald-NY 19.4
Miranda-Bal 19.0
Lopez-KC 15.1
Tuttle-Det 14.9

Total Player Rating
Mantle-NY 6.2
Kaline-Det 5.3
Williams-Bos 4.3
Fox-Chi 4.0
McDougald-NY 3.5

Wins
F.Sullivan-Bos 18
Lemon-Cle 18
Ford-NY 18
Wynn-Cle 17
Turley-NY 17

Win Percentage
Byrne-NY .762
Ford-NY .720
Hoeft-Det .696
Lemon-Cle .643
Donovan-Chi .625

Games
Narleski-Cle 60
Mossi-Cle 57
Gorman-KC 57
Dorish-Chi-Bal 48
Moore-Bal 46

Complete Games
Ford-NY 18
Hoeft-Det 17

Shutouts
Hoeft-Det 7
Wynn-Cle 6
Turley-NY 6
Pierce-Chi 6

Saves
Narleski-Cle 19
Kinder-Bos 18
Gorman-KC 18
Konstanty-NY 11
Morgan-NY 10

Innings Pitched
F.Sullivan-Bos 260.0
Ford-NY 253.2
Turley-NY 246.2
Wilson-Bal 235.1
Lary-Det 235.0

Fewest Hits/Game
Turley-NY 6.13
Score-Cle 6.26
Ford-NY 6.67
Pierce-Chi 7.09
Harshman-Chi 7.23

Fewest BB/Game
Gromek-Det 1.84
Donovan-Chi 2.31
Garcia-Cle 2.39
Garver-Det 2.61
Porterfield-Was 2.73

Strikeouts
Score-Cle 245
Turley-NY 210
Pierce-Chi 157
Ford-NY 137
Hoeft-Det 133

Strikeouts/Game
Score-Cle 9.70
Turley-NY 7.66
Pierce-Chi 6.87
Harshman-Chi 5.82
Hoeft-Det 5.44

Ratio
Pierce-Chi 10.02
Ford-NY 10.71
Hoeft-Det 10.96
Wilson-Bal 11.13
Wynn-Cle 11.35

Earned Run Average
Pierce-Chi 1.97
Ford-NY 2.63
Wynn-Cle 2.82
Score-Cle 2.85
F.Sullivan-Bos 2.91

Adjusted ERA
Pierce-Chi 201
F.Sullivan-Bos 148
Ford-NY 143
Wynn-Cle 142
Score-Cle 140

Opponents' Batting Avg.
Turley-NY .193
Score-Cle .194
Ford-NY .208
Pierce-Chi .213
Harshman-Chi .224

Opponents' On-Base Pct.
Pierce-Chi .277
Ford-NY .297
Hoeft-Det .298
Wilson-Bal .300
Wynn-Cle .307

Starter Runs
Pierce-Chi 45.5
Ford-NY 37.6
F.Sullivan-Bos 30.4
Wynn-Cle 29.2
Score-Cle 28.1

Adjusted Starter Runs
Pierce-Chi 45.4
F.Sullivan-Bos 36.9
Ford-NY 33.3
Wynn-Cle 29.7
Score-Cle 28.6

Clutch Pitching Index
Pierce-Chi 119
Byrne-NY 119
F.Sullivan-Bos 116
Lary-Det 115
Schmitz-Was 115

Relief Runs
Consuegra-Chi 18.6
Mossi-Cle 13.9
Konstanty-NY 13.4
Kiely-Bos 11.6
Dorish-Chi-Bal 10.4

Adjusted Relief Runs
Consuegra-Chi 18.5
Mossi-Cle 14.1
Kiely-Bos 13.8
Konstanty-NY 12.3
Hurd-Bos 10.6

Relief Ranking
Kinder-Bos 19.5
Hurd-Bos 18.0
Konstanty-NY 17.7
Consuegra-Chi 16.8
Mossi-Cle 14.4

Total Pitcher Index
Pierce-Chi 5.3
F.Sullivan-Bos 3.8
Ford-NY 3.3
Wynn-Cle 3.3
Lary-Det 2.6

Total Baseball Ranking
Mantle-NY 6.2
Pierce-Chi 5.3
Kaline-Det 5.3
Williams-Bos 4.3
Fox-Chi 4.0

TEAM	G	W	L	PCT	GB	R	OR	AB	H	2B	3B	HR	BB	SO	AVG	OBP	SLG	OPS	OPS+	BR	BR+	PF	CHI	RC	SB	CS	SBA	SBR
BRO	154	93	61	.604		720	601	5098	1315	212	36	179	**649**	738	.258	**.344**	.419	763	103	81	27	108	97	728	65	37	64	1
MIL	155	92	62	.597	1	709	**569**	5207	1350	212	54	177	486	714	.259	.325	.423	748	**113**	38	**83**	94	101	714	29	20	59	-1
CIN	155	91	63	.591	2	**775**	658	5291	1406	201	32	**221**	528	760	.266	.338	**.441**	**779**	107	**103**	56	106	100	**789**	45	22	**67**	2
STL	156	76	78	.494	17	678	698	5378	**1443**	**234**	49	124	503	**622**	**.268**	.335	.399	734	103	25	25	100	97	707	41	35	54	-3
PHI	154	71	83	.461	22	668	738	5204	1313	207	49	121	585	673	.252	.331	.381	712	99	-12	1	98	**103**	658	45	23	66	2
NY	154	67	87	.435	26	540	650	5190	1268	192	45	145	402	659	.244	.301	.382	683	89	-85	-81	99	97	586	**67**	34	66	**3**
PIT	157	66	88	.429	27	588	653	5221	1340	199	**57**	110	383	752	.257	.310	.380	690	93	-70	-56	98	102	594	24	33	42	-6
CHI	157	60	94	.390	33	597	708	5260	1281	202	50	142	446	776	.244	.304	.382	686	91	-79	-68	98	**103**	606	55	38	59	-1
TOT	621					5275		41849	10716	1659	372	1219	3982	5694	.257	.324	.401	725							371	242	61	-3

TEAM	CG	SH	SV	IP	H	H/G	HR	BB	SO	RAT	ERA	ERA+	OAV	OOB	PR	PR+	PF	CPI	FA	E	DP	FW	PW	BW	SBW	DIF
BRO	46	**12**	**30**	1368^2	**1251**	**8.3**	171	441	**772**	**11.3**	3.58	**111**	**.244**	**.307**	31	57	105	97	**.981**	**111**	149	**1.5**	5.9	2.8	.1	5.9
MIL	**64**	**12**	27	1393^1	1295	8.4	**133**	467	639	11.6	**3.12**	**111**	.247	.311	**102**	**59**	92	**107**	.979	130	159	.4	**6.1**	**8.5**	-.0	.3
CIN	47	4	29	1389	1406	9.2	141	458	653	12.3	3.85	103	.265	.327	-12	19	106	101	**.981**	113	147	1.4	2.0	5.8	.2	4.8
STL	41	**12**	**30**	1388^2	1339	8.7	155	546	709	12.4	3.97	95	.257	.329	-30	-28	100	98	.978	134	**172**	.2	-2.8	2.6	-.3	-.5
PHI	57	4	15	1377^1	1407	9.2	172	**437**	750	12.3	4.21	89	.266	.325	-66	-74	99	95	.975	144	140	-.5	-7.5	.2	.2	1.9
NY	31	9	28	1378	1287	8.5	144	551	765	12.3	3.78	100	.250	.326	-1	1	100	98	.976	144	143	-.5	.2	-8.2	**.3**	-1.5
PIT	37	8	24	1376^1	1406	9.2	142	469	662	12.4	3.75	101	.267	.329	5	5	100	105	.973	162	140	-1.5	.6	-5.7	-.6	-3.6
CHI	37	6	17	1392	1325	8.6	161	613	744	12.8	3.96	95	.252	.334	-29	-29	100	100	.976	144	141	-.4	-2.9	-6.9	-.0	-6.5
TOT	360	67	200	11063^1		8.8				12.2	3.78		.257	.324					.978	1082	1191					

Runs
Robinson-Cin 122
Snider-Bro 112
Aaron-Mil 106
Mathews-Mil 103
Gilliam-Bro 102

Hits
Aaron-Mil 200
Ashburn-Phi 190
Virdon-StL-Pit 185
Musial-StL 184
Boyer-StL 182

Doubles
Aaron-Mil 34
Snider-Bro 33
Musial-StL 33
Lopata-Phi 33
Bell-Cin 31

Triples
Bruton-Mil 15
Aaron-Mil 14
Walls-Pit 11
Moon-StL 11
Virdon-StL-Pit 10

Home Runs
Snider-Bro 43
Robinson-Cin 38
Adcock-Mil 38
Mathews-Mil 37

Total Bases
Aaron-Mil 340
Snider-Bro 324
Mays-NY 322
Robinson-Cin 319
Musial-StL 310

Runs Batted In
Musial-StL 109
Adcock-Mil 103
Kluszewski-Cin 102
Snider-Bro 101
Boyer-StL 98

Runs Produced
Aaron-Mil 172
Snider-Bro 170
Musial-StL 169
Robinson-Cin 167
Boyer-StL 163

Bases On Balls
Snider-Bro 99
Gilliam-Bro 95
Jones-Phi 92
Mathews-Mil 91
Moon-StL 80

Batting Average
Aaron-Mil .328
Virdon-StL-Pit .319
Clemente-Pit .311
Musial-StL .310
Boyer-StL .306

On-Base Percentage
Snider-Bro .402
Gilliam-Bro .400
Musial-StL .390
Moon-StL .390
Jones-Phi .387

Slugging Average
Snider-Bro .598
Adcock-Mil .597
Aaron-Mil .558
Robinson-Cin .558
Mays-NY .557

On-Base Plus Slugging
Snider-Bro 1000
Robinson-Cin 939
Adcock-Mil 936
Mays-NY 928
Aaron-Mil 927

Adjusted OPS
Adcock-Mil 154
Aaron-Mil 154
Snider-Bro 152
Mays-NY 146
Mathews-Mil 146

Batter Runs
Snider-Bro 50.5
Robinson-Cin 39.1
Aaron-Mil 36.3
Musial-StL 36.3
Mays-NY 35.9

Adjusted Batter Runs
Aaron-Mil 43.3
Snider-Bro 41.5
Mays-NY 36.7
Mathews-Mil 36.5
Musial-StL 36.3

Clutch Hitting Index
McMillan-Cin 145
Thomson-Mil 123
Ennis-Phi 115
Jones-Phi 109
Long-Pit 109

Runs Created
Snider-Bro 128
Robinson-Cin 121
Musial-StL 119
Mays-NY 118
Aaron-Mil 115

Total Average
Snider-Bro 1.052
Mays-NY .972
Robinson-Cin .960
Mathews-Mil .946
Adcock-Mil .916

Stolen Bases
Mays-NY 40
Gilliam-Bro 21
White-NY 15
Temple-Cin 14
Reese-Bro 13

Stolen Base Average
Mays-NY 80.0
Gilliam-Bro 70.0

Stolen Base Runs
Mays-NY 5.3
Ashburn-Phi 1.9
Temple-Cin 1.7
Gilliam-Bro 1.5
Reese-Bro 1.5

Fielding Runs
McMillan-Cin 29.9
Ashburn-Phi 25.3
Blasingame-StL 21.9
Gilliam-Bro 17.7
Baker-Chi 17.2

Total Player Rating
Aaron-Mil 4.7
Mays-NY 4.7
McMillan-Cin 3.8
Musial-StL 3.5
Snider-Bro 3.4

Wins
Newcombe-Bro 27
Spahn-Mil 20
Antonelli-NY 20

Win Percentage
Newcombe-Bro .794
Buhl-Mil .692
Lawrence-Cin .655
Burdette-Mil .655
Spahn-Mil .645

Games
Face-Pit 68
Wilhelm-NY 64
Freeman-Cin 64
Labine-Bro 62
Lown-Chi 61

Complete Games
Roberts-Phi 22
Spahn-Mil 20
Friend-Pit 19
Newcombe-Bro 18
Burdette-Mil 16

Shutouts
Burdette-Mil 6
Newcombe-Bro 5
Antonelli-NY 5
Friend-Pit 4

Saves
Labine-Bro 19
Freeman-Cin 18
Lown-Chi 13
Jackson-StL 9
Bessent-Bro 9

Innings Pitched
Friend-Pit 314.1
Roberts-Phi 297.1
Spahn-Mil 281.1
Newcombe-Bro 268.0
Kline-Pit 264.0

Fewest Hits/Game
Maglie-Bro 7.26
Newcombe-Bro 7.35
Jones-Chi 7.39
Mizell-StL 7.42
Craig-Bro 7.64

Fewest BB/Game
Roberts-Phi 1.21
Newcombe-Bro 1.54
Spahn-Mil 1.66
Fowler-Cin 1.77
Burdette-Mil 1.83

Strikeouts
Jones-Chi 176
Haddix-StL-Phi 170
Friend-Pit 166
Roberts-Phi 157
Mizell-StL 153

Strikeouts/Game
Jones-Chi 8.40
Haddix-StL-Phi 6.64
Mizell-StL 6.60
Nuxhall-Cin 5.38
Worthington-NY 5.16

Ratio
Newcombe-Bro 9.00
Spahn-Mil 9.73
Maglie-Bro 9.94
Burdette-Mil 10.15
Rush-Chi 10.18

Earned Run Average
Burdette-Mil 2.70
Spahn-Mil 2.78
Antonelli-NY 2.86
Maglie-Bro 2.87
Newcombe-Bro 3.06

Adjusted ERA
Maglie-Bro 138
Antonelli-NY 132
Newcombe-Bro 130
Burdette-Mil 128
Spahn-Mil 124

Opponents' Batting Avg.
Newcombe-Bro .221
Jones-Chi .221
Mizell-StL .222
Maglie-Bro .222
Craig-Bro .231

Opponents' On-Base Pct.
Newcombe-Bro .257
Spahn-Mil .276
Maglie-Bro .281
Burdette-Mil .282
Rush-Chi .282

Starter Runs
Spahn-Mil 30.9
Burdette-Mil 30.4
Antonelli-NY 26.3
Newcombe-Bro 21.3
Maglie-Bro 19.0

Adjusted Starter Runs
Antonelli-NY 26.5
Newcombe-Bro 25.8
Burdette-Mil 23.5
Spahn-Mil 23.1
Maglie-Bro 22.1

Clutch Pitching Index
Conley-Mil 127
Klippstein-Cin 111
Kline-Pit 110
Poholsky-StL 108
Jeffcoat-Cin 105

Relief Runs
Grissom-NY 19.8
Acker-Cin 13.1
Bessent-Bro 11.2
B.Miller-Phi 7.3
Labine-Bro 5.5

Adjusted Relief Runs
Grissom-NY 19.8
Acker-Cin 14.2
Bessent-Bro 12.3
Labine-Bro 7.6
B.Miller-Phi 6.7

Relief Ranking
Freeman-Cin 13.0
Bessent-Bro 12.9
Labine-Bro 12.3
Acker-Cin 11.1
Grissom-NY 9.9

Total Pitcher Index
Newcombe-Bro 4.1
Antonelli-NY 3.6
Spahn-Mil 3.1
Burdette-Mil 2.8
Dickson-Phi-StL 2.2

Total Baseball Ranking
Aaron-Mil 4.7
Mays-NY 4.7
Newcombe-Bro 4.1
McMillan-Cin 3.8
Antonelli-NY 3.6

TEAM	G	W	L	PCT	GB	R	OR	AB	H	2B	3B	HR	BB	SO	AVG	OBP	SLG	OPS	OPS+	BR	BR+	PF	CHI	RC	SB	CS	SBA	SBR
NY	154	97	57	.630		**857**	631	5312	1433	193	55	**190**	615	755	.270	.349	**.434**	783	**116**	80	**107**	97	**106**	814	51	37	58	-2
CLE	155	88	66	.571	9	712	**581**	5148	1256	199	23	153	681	764	.244	.337	.381	718	93	-35	-50	102	105	681	40	32	56	-2
CHI	154	85	69	.552	12	776	634	5286	1412	218	43	128	619	660	.267	.352	.397	749	102	30	19	101	102	756	**70**	33	**68**	**4**
BOS	155	84	70	.545	13	780	751	5349	1473	**261**	45	139	**727**	687	.275	**.365**	.419	**784**	101	**100**	8	112	93	**826**	28	19	60	0
DET	155	82	72	.532	15	789	699	5364	**1494**	209	50	150	644	**618**	**.279**	.359	.420	779	111	84	82	100	97	816	43	26	62	0
BAL	154	69	85	.448	28	571	705	5090	1242	198	34	91	563	725	.244	.322	.350	672	90	-123	-76	92	101	572	39	42	48	-6
WAS	155	59	95	.383	38	652	924	5202	1302	198	**62**	112	690	877	.250	.343	.377	720	96	-27	-26	100	94	681	37	34	52	-4
KC	154	52	102	.338	45	619	831	5256	1325	204	41	112	480	727	.252	.317	.370	687	86	-108	-110	100	105	610	40	30	57	-2
TOT	618					5756		42007	10937	1680	353	1075	5019	5813	.261	.344	.394	737							348	253	58	-12

TEAM	CG	SH	SV	IP	H	H/G	HR	BB	SO	RAT	ERA	ERA+	OAV	OOB	PR	PR+	PF	CPI	FA	E	DP	FW	PW	BW	SBW	DIF
NY	50	10	**35**	1382	1285	8.4	114	652	732	12.9	3.63	107	.249	.337	82	40	93	105	.977	136	**214**	.6	4.0	**10.5**	-.0	5.1
CLE	**67**	**17**	24	1384	**1233**	**8.1**	116	564	**845**	**11.9**	**3.33**	**127**	**.238**	**.316**	**129**	**134**	101	100	.978	129	130	1.1	**13.2**	-4.8	-.0	1.9
CHI	65	11	13	1389	1351	8.8	118	**524**	722	12.4	3.73	110	.255	.325	67	59	99	99	**.979**	**122**	160	**1.4**	5.8	1.9	**.5**	-1.5
BOS	50	8	20	1398	1354	8.8	130	668	712	13.4	4.17	111	.254	.342	-1	64	111	96	.972	169	168	-1.2	6.3	.8	.1	1.1
DET	62	10	15	1379	1389	9.1	140	655	788	13.7	4.06	101	.264	.351	15	9	99	**108**	.976	140	151	.4	.9	8.1	.1	-4.4
BAL	38	10	24	1360[2]	1362	9.1	**99**	547	715	12.8	4.21	93	.263	.337	-6	-45	94	93	.977	137	142	.6	-4.4	-7.4	-.4	3.8
WAS	36	1	18	1368[2]	1539	10.2	171	730	663	15.2	5.34	81	.287	.376	-179	-147	104	99	.972	171	173	-1.3	-14.3	-2.5	-.2	.5
KC	30	3	18	1370[1]	1424	9.4	187	679	636	14.1	4.87	89	.271	.359	-107	-78	104	101	.973	166	187	-1.0	-7.6	-10.7	-.0	-5.4
TOT	398	70	167	11031[2]		9.0				13.3	4.16		.261	.344					.976	1170	1325					

Runs
Mantle-NY 132
Fox-Chi 109
Minoso-Chi 106

Hits
Kuenn-Det 196
Kaline-Det 194
Fox-Chi 192
Mantle-NY 188
Jensen-Bos 182

Doubles
Piersall-Bos 40
Kuenn-Det 32
Kaline-Det 32

Triples
Simpson-KC 11
Minoso-Chi 11
Lemon-Was 11
Jensen-Bos 11

Home Runs
Mantle-NY 52
Wertz-Cle 32
Berra-NY 30
Sievers-Was 29
Maxwell-Det 28

Total Bases
Mantle-NY 376
Kaline-Det 327
Jensen-Bos 287
Minoso-Chi 286

Runs Batted In
Mantle-NY 130
Kaline-Det 128
Wertz-Cle 106
Simpson-KC 105
Berra-NY 105

Runs Produced
Mantle-NY 210
Kaline-Det 197
Minoso-Chi 173
Kuenn-Det 172
Berra-NY 168

Bases On Balls
Yost-Was 151
Mantle-NY 112
Williams-Bos 102
Doby-Chi 102
Sievers-Was 100

Batting Average
Mantle-NY .353
Williams-Bos .345
Kuenn-Det .332
Maxwell-Det .326
Nieman-Chi-Bal .320

On-Base Percentage
Williams-Bos .479
Mantle-NY .467
Nieman-Chi-Bal .438
Minoso-Chi .430
Maxwell-Det .420

Slugging Average
Mantle-NY .705
Williams-Bos .605
Maxwell-Det .534
Berra-NY .534
Kaline-Det .530

On-Base Plus Slugging
Mantle-NY 1172
Williams-Bos 1084
Minoso-Chi 954
Maxwell-Det 954
Nieman-Chi-Bal 934

Adjusted OPS
Mantle-NY 213
Williams-Bos 164
Nieman-Chi-Bal 156
Maxwell-Det 150
Minoso-Chi 149

Batter Runs
Mantle-NY 83.3
Williams-Bos 54.1
Minoso-Chi 43.2
Maxwell-Det 37.5
Kaline-Det 33.4

Adjusted Batter Runs
Mantle-NY 88.8
Williams-Bos 41.7
Minoso-Chi 41.6
Nieman-Chi-Bal 39.1
Maxwell-Det 37.3

Clutch Hitting Index
Kaline-Det 117
Lollar-Chi 117
Triandos-Bal 114
Doby-Chi 113
Carey-NY 109

Runs Created
Mantle-NY 188
Minoso-Chi 130
Kaline-Det 129
Williams-Bos 121
Maxwell-Det 118

Total Average
Mantle-NY 1.426
Williams-Bos 1.255
Minoso-Chi 1.031
Maxwell-Det 1.015
Nieman-Chi-Bal .955

Stolen Bases
Aparicio-Chi 21
Rivera-Chi 20
Avila-Cle 17
Minoso-Chi 12

Stolen Base Average
Aparicio-Chi 84.0
Avila-Cle 81.0
Rivera-Chi 69.0

Stolen Base Runs
Aparicio-Chi 3.2
Avila-Cle 2.3
Mantle-NY 1.9
Jensen-Bos 1.4
Pilarcik-KC 1.3

Fielding Runs
Piersall-Bos 17.6
Kaline-Det 17.3
Hegan-Cle 15.6
Buddin-Bos 13.9
Maxwell-Det 13.1

Total Player Rating
Mantle-NY 8.7
Kaline-Det 4.4
Berra-NY 4.4
Maxwell-Det 4.0
Nieman-Chi-Bal 3.6

Wins
Lary-Det 21

Win Percentage
Ford-NY .760
Wynn-Cle .690
Score-Cle .690
Pierce-Chi .690
Brewer-Bos .679

Games
Zuverink-Bal 62
Crimian-KC 54
Gorman-KC 52
Mossi-Cle 48
Delock-Bos 48

Complete Games
Pierce-Chi 21
Lemon-Cle 21
Lary-Det 20

Shutouts
Score-Cle 5

Saves
Zuverink-Bal 16
Mossi-Cle 11
Morgan-NY 11
Shantz-KC 9
Delock-Bos 9

Innings Pitched
Lary-Det 294.0
Wynn-Cle 277.2
Pierce-Chi 276.1
Foytack-Det 256.0
Lemon-Cle 255.1

Fewest Hits/Game
Score-Cle 5.85
Larsen-NY 6.66
Harshman-Chi 7.27
Brewer-Bos 7.37
Foytack-Det 7.42

Fewest BB/Game
Stobbs-Was 2.03
Donovan-Chi 2.26
Kucks-NY 2.89
Wynn-Cle 2.95
Sturdivant-NY 2.96

Strikeouts
Score-Cle 263
Pierce-Chi 192
Foytack-Det 184
Hoeft-Det 172
Lary-Det 165

Strikeouts/Game
Score-Cle 9.49
Pascual-Was 7.73
Foytack-Det 6.47
Pierce-Chi 6.25
Sturdivant-NY 6.25

Ratio
Score-Cle 10.58
Donovan-Chi 10.62
Wynn-Cle 10.66
Sturdivant-NY 10.80
Ford-NY 10.97

Earned Run Average
Ford-NY 2.47
Score-Cle 2.53
Wynn-Cle 2.72
Lemon-Cle 3.03
Harshman-Chi 3.10

Adjusted ERA
Score-Cle 166
Ford-NY 156
Wynn-Cle 154
Lemon-Cle 139
Sullivan-Bos 135

Opponents' Batting Avg.
Score-Cle .186
Larsen-NY .204
Brewer-Bos .220
Harshman-Chi .221
Sturdivant-NY .224

Opponents' On-Base Pct.
Sturdivant-NY .291
Donovan-Chi .292
Score-Cle .292
Wynn-Cle .294
Ford-NY .303

Starter Runs
Score-Cle 45.2
Wynn-Cle 44.3
Ford-NY 42.3
Lary-Det 32.9
Lemon-Cle 32.0

Adjusted Starter Runs
Score-Cle 46.0
Wynn-Cle 45.2
Ford-NY 37.6
Lemon-Cle 32.9
Lary-Det 31.8

Clutch Pitching Index
Lary-Det 117
Sullivan-Bos 116
Hoeft-Det 116
Ford-NY 114
Stobbs-Was 114

Relief Runs
Narleski-Cle 17.4
Grim-NY 11.5
Byrne-NY 9.7
Byerly-Was 6.9
Mossi-Cle 5.5

Adjusted Relief Runs
Narleski-Cle 17.5
Grim-NY 9.8
Byerly-Was 7.5
Byrne-NY 6.6
Mossi-Cle 5.9

Relief Ranking
Narleski-Cle 16.0
Grim-NY 9.7
Byerly-Was 9.2
Mossi-Cle 8.3
Delock-Bos 8.3

Total Pitcher Index
Lemon-Cle 5.2
Wynn-Cle 5.0
Ford-NY 4.8
Score-Cle 4.8
Brewer-Bos 3.8

Total Baseball Ranking
Mantle-NY 8.7
Lemon-Cle 5.2
Wynn-Cle 5.0
Ford-NY 4.8
Score-Cle 4.8

TEAM	G	W	L	PCT	GB	R	OR	AB	H	2B	3B	HR	BB	SO	AVG	OBP	SLG	OPS	OPS+	BR	BR+	PF	CHI	RC	SB	CS	SBA	SBR
MIL	155	95	59	.617		**772**	613	5458	1469	221	**62**	**199**	461	729	.269	.329	**.442**	771	**121**	82	**142**	93	101	787	35	16	**69**	2
STL	154	87	67	.565	8	737	666	5472	**1497**	235	43	132	493	672	**.274**	.336	.405	741	103	36	22	102	102	731	58	44	57	-3
BRO	154	84	70	.545	11	690	**591**	5242	1325	188	38	147	**550**	848	.253	.328	.387	715	89	-11	-69	110	104	664	60	34	64	1
CIN	154	80	74	.519	15	747	781	5389	1452	**251**	33	187	546	752	.269	**.341**	.432	**773**	106	**97**	45	107	95	**794**	51	36	59	-1
PHI	156	77	77	.500	18	623	656	5241	1311	213	44	117	534	758	.250	.325	.375	700	97	-39	-19	97	99	635	57	26	**69**	**3**
NY	154	69	85	.448	26	643	701	5346	1349	171	54	157	447	**669**	.252	.313	.393	706	95	-42	-40	100	103	646	**64**	38	63	1
PIT	155	62	92	.403	33	586	696	5402	1447	231	60	92	374	733	.268	.318	.384	702	97	-46	-27	97	93	649	46	35	57	-2
CHI	156	62	92	.403	33	628	722	5369	1312	223	31	147	461	989	.244	.307	.380	687	91	-78	-68	98	**105**	623	28	25	53	-3
TOT	619					5426		42919	11162	1733	365	1178	3866	6150	.261	.325	.400	724							399	254	61	-1

TEAM	CG	SH	SV	IP	H	H/G	HR	BB	SO	RAT	ERA	ERA+	OAV	OOB	PR	PR+	PF	CPI	FA	E	DP	FW	PW	BW	SBW	DIF
MIL	**60**	9	24	1411	1347	8.6	**124**	570	693	12.4	3.47	101	.253	.327	64	5	90	**107**	.981	120	173	1.1	.6	**14.5**	.2	1.9
STL	46	11	**29**	1413[1]	1385	8.9	140	506	778	12.3	3.78	105	.257	.324	16	29	102	100	.979	131	168	.4	3.0	2.3	-.3	4.8
BRO	44	**18**	**29**	1399	**1285**	**8.3**	144	456	**891**	**11.4**	**3.36**	**124**	**.244**	**.307**	**82**	**118**	107	101	.979	127	136	.6	**12.0**	-7.0	.1	1.4
CIN	40	5	**29**	1395[2]	1486	9.6	179	429	707	12.7	4.63	89	.275	.334	-116	-75	106	95	**.982**	**107**	139	**1.7**	-7.6	4.6	-.0	4.5
PHI	54	9	23	1401[2]	1363	8.8	139	**412**	858	11.6	3.80	100	.254	.310	13	1	98	92	.976	136	117	.2	.2	-1.9	**.3**	1.4
NY	35	9	20	1398[2]	1436	9.3	150	471	701	12.6	4.01	98	.267	.330	-20	-12	101	101	.974	161	**180**	-1.2	-1.2	-4.0	.1	-1.5
PIT	47	9	15	1395	1463	9.5	158	421	663	12.4	3.88	98	.270	.325	0	-14	98	105	.972	170	143	-1.7	-1.4	-2.7	-.2	-8.9
CHI	30	5	26	1403[1]	1397	9.0	144	601	859	13.1	4.14	94	.261	.339	-39	-41	100	100	.975	149	140	-.5	-4.1	-6.9	-.3	-3.1
TOT	356	75	195	11217[2]		9.0				12.3	3.88		.261	.325					.978	1101	1196					

Runs
Aaron-Mil 118
Banks-Chi 113
Mays-NY 112
Mathews-Mil 109
Blasingame-StL 108

Hits
Schoendienst-NY-Mil 200
Aaron-Mil 198
Robinson-Cin 197
Mays-NY 195
Ashburn-Phi 186

Doubles
Hoak-Cin 39
Musial-StL 38
Bouchee-Phi 35
Banks-Chi 34
Moryn-Chi 33

Triples
Mays-NY 20
Virdon-Pit 11
Mathews-Mil 9
Bruton-Mil 9

Home Runs
Aaron-Mil 44
Banks-Chi 43
Snider-Bro 40
Mays-NY 35
Mathews-Mil 32

Total Bases
Aaron-Mil 369
Mays-NY 366
Banks-Chi 344
Robinson-Cin 323
Mathews-Mil 309

Runs Batted In
Aaron-Mil 132
Ennis-StL 105
Musial-StL 102
Banks-Chi 102
Hodges-Bro 98

Runs Produced
Aaron-Mil 206
Mays-NY 174
Banks-Chi 172
Mathews-Mil 171
Hodges-Bro 165

Bases On Balls
Temple-Cin 94
Ashburn-Phi 94
Mathews-Mil 90
Bouchee-Phi 84
Snider-Bro 77

Batting Average
Musial-StL .351
Mays-NY .333
Robinson-Cin .322
Aaron-Mil .322
Groat-Pit .315

On-Base Percentage
Musial-StL .428
Mays-NY .411
Bouchee-Phi .396
Ashburn-Phi .392
Temple-Cin .391

Slugging Average
Mays-NY .626
Musial-StL .612
Aaron-Mil .600
Snider-Bro .587
Banks-Chi .579

On-Base Plus Slugging
Musial-StL 1040
Mays-NY 1037
Aaron-Mil 979
Snider-Bro 957
Banks-Chi 942

Adjusted OPS
Mays-NY 174
Musial-StL 172
Aaron-Mil 170
Mathews-Mil 157
Banks-Chi 150

Batter Runs
Mays-NY 60.5
Musial-StL 54.1
Aaron-Mil 48.3
Banks-Chi 38.6
Mathews-Mil 38.3

Adjusted Batter Runs
Mays-NY 61.0
Aaron-Mil 58.0
Musial-StL 51.8
Mathews-Mil 47.1
Banks-Chi 40.5

Clutch Hitting Index
McMillan-Cin 134
Ennis-StL 131
Hamner-Phi 115
Post-Cin 112
Hoak-Cin 112

Runs Created
Mays-NY 145
Aaron-Mil 136
Musial-StL 129
Mathews-Mil 126
Banks-Chi 123

Total Average
Musial-StL 1.103
Mays-NY 1.092
Aaron-Mil .988
Mathews-Mil .973
Snider-Bro .962

Stolen Bases
Mays-NY 38
Gilliam-Bro 26
Blasingame-StL 21
Temple-Cin 19
Fernandez-Phi 18

Stolen Base Average
Temple-Cin 79.2
Fernandez-Phi 78.3
Gilliam-Bro 72.2
Blasingame-StL 70.0
Mays-NY 66.7

Stolen Base Runs
Temple-Cin 2.4
Gilliam-Bro 2.2
Fernandez-Phi 2.2
Mays-NY 1.7
Robinson-Cin 1.5

Fielding Runs
Ashburn-Phi 32.4
Blasingame-StL 25.8
Logan-Mil 23.9
Robinson-Cin 18.7
Campanella-Bro 16.0

Total Player Rating
Mays-NY 6.6
Aaron-Mil 5.4
Musial-StL 4.6
Mathews-Mil 4.5
Robinson-Cin 3.8

Wins
Spahn-Mil 21
Sanford-Phi 19
Buhl-Mil 18
Drysdale-Bro 17
Burdette-Mil 17

Win Percentage
Buhl-Mil .720
Sanford-Phi .704
Spahn-Mil .656
Drysdale-Bro .654
Burdette-Mil .654

Games
Lown-Chi 67
Face-Pit 59
Labine-Bro 58
Worthington-NY 55
Grissom-NY 55

Complete Games
Spahn-Mil 18
Friend-Pit 17
Gomez-NY 16
Sanford-Phi 15

Shutouts
Podres-Bro 6
Spahn-Mil 4
Newcombe-Bro 4
Drysdale-Bro 4

Saves
Labine-Bro 17
Grissom-NY 14
Lown-Chi 12
Wilhelm-StL 11

Innings Pitched
Friend-Pit 277.0
Spahn-Mil 271.0
Burdette-Mil 256.2
Lawrence-Cin 250.1
Roberts-Phi 249.2

Fewest Hits/Game
Sanford-Phi 7.38
Podres-Bro 7.71
Drott-Chi 7.86
Buhl-Mil 7.93
Worthington-NY 7.99

Fewest BB/Game
Newcombe-Bro 1.49
Roberts-Phi 1.55
Law-Pit 1.67
Purkey-Pit 1.90
Jeffcoat-Cin 2.00

Strikeouts
Sanford-Phi 188
Drott-Chi 170
Drabowsky-Chi 170
Jones-StL 154
Drysdale-Bro 148

Strikeouts/Game
Jones-StL 7.59
Haddix-Phi 7.17
Sanford-Phi 7.15
Drott-Chi 6.68
Drabowsky-Chi 6.38

Ratio
Podres-Bro 9.78
Roberts-Phi 10.45
Newcombe-Bro 10.56
Spahn-Mil 10.66
Law-Pit 10.74

Earned Run Average
Podres-Bro 2.66
Drysdale-Bro 2.69
Spahn-Mil 2.69
Buhl-Mil 2.74
Law-Pit 2.87

Adjusted ERA
Podres-Bro 156
Drysdale-Bro 155
Law-Pit 132
Spahn-Mil 130
Buhl-Mil 128

Opponents' Batting Avg.
Sanford-Phi .221
Podres-Bro .230
Drott-Chi .234
Drysdale-Bro .236
Spahn-Mil .237

Opponents' On-Base Pct.
Podres-Bro .274
Roberts-Phi .284
Newcombe-Bro .290
Law-Pit .291
Spahn-Mil .293

Starter Runs
Spahn-Mil 35.8
Drysdale-Bro 29.2
Buhl-Mil 27.4
Podres-Bro 26.5
Sanford-Phi 21.0

Adjusted Starter Runs
Drysdale-Bro 33.8
Podres-Bro 30.5
Spahn-Mil 27.0
Buhl-Mil 20.2
Sanford-Phi 19.4

Clutch Pitching Index
Buhl-Mil 135
Barclay-NY 117
Law-Pit 113
Spahn-Mil 109
Antonelli-NY 108

Relief Runs
Farrell-Phi 13.9
Roebuck-Bro 12.5
Grissom-NY 11.6
Face-Pit 8.4
Miller-Phi 8.0

Adjusted Relief Runs
Roebuck-Bro 14.5
Farrell-Phi 13.5
Grissom-NY 12.0
Labine-Bro 7.9
Miller-Phi 7.7

Relief Ranking
Farrell-Phi 21.1
Roebuck-Bro 16.3
Grissom-NY 15.0
Labine-Bro 11.0
Miller-Phi 9.7

Total Pitcher Index
Drysdale-Bro 4.4
Podres-Bro 3.3
Spahn-Mil 3.3
Farrell-Phi 2.3
Roebuck-Bro 2.2

Total Baseball Ranking
Mays-NY 6.6
Aaron-Mil 5.4
Musial-StL 4.6
Mathews-Mil 4.5
Drysdale-Bro 4.4

TEAM	G	W	L	PCT	GB	R	OR	AB	H	2B	3B	HR	BB	SO	AVG	OBP	SLG	OPS	OPS+	BR	BR+	PF	CHI	RC	SB	CS	SBA	SBR
NY	154	98	56	.636		**723**	**534**	5271	**1412**	200	**54**	145	562	709	**.268**	.341	**.409**	**750**	**113**	**76**	**88**	98	99	**729**	49	38	56	-3
CHI	155	90	64	.584	8	707	566	5265	1369	208	41	106	**633**	745	.260	**.347**	.375	722	103	40	36	101	100	708	**109**	51	**68**	**6**
BOS	154	82	72	.532	16	721	668	5267	1380	**231**	32	153	624	739	.262	.343	.405	748	104	**76**	36	106	98	725	29	21	58	-1
DET	154	78	76	.506	20	614	614	5348	1376	224	37	116	504	**643**	.257	.324	.378	702	96	-18	-34	103	96	644	36	47	43	-9
BAL	154	76	76	.500	21	597	588	5264	1326	191	39	87	504	699	.252	.321	.353	674	96	-66	-27	94	101	600	57	35	62	0
CLE	153	76	77	.497	21.5	682	722	5171	1304	199	26	140	591	786	.252	.332	.382	714	102	10	17	99	**103**	661	40	47	46	-8
KC	154	59	94	.386	38.5	563	710	5170	1262	195	40	**166**	364	760	.244	.297	.394	691	92	-60	-69	102	100	578	35	27	56	-2
WAS	154	55	99	.357	43	603	808	5231	1274	215	38	111	527	733	.244	.318	.363	681	93	-56	-49	99	102	592	13	38	25	-10
TOT	616					5210		41987	10703	1663	307	1024	4309	5814	.255	.329	.383	710							368	304	55	-25

TEAM	CG	SH	SV	IP	H	H/G	HR	BB	SO	RAT	ERA	ERA+	OAV	OOB	PR	PR+	PF	CPI	FA	E	DP	FW	PW	BW	SBW	DIF
NY	41	13	**42**	1395^{1}	**1198**	**7.8**	110	580	**810**	11.8	**3.00**	**120**	**.234**	.317	**122**	**96**	95	**109**	.980	123	**183**	.3	**10.0**	**9.1**	.0	1.8
CHI	**59**	**16**	27	1401^{2}	1305	8.4	124	**470**	665	11.6	3.35	112	.248	.313	69	62	99	102	**.982**	**107**	169	**1.2**	6.5	3.8	**.9**	.8
BOS	55	9	23	1376^{2}	1391	9.1	116	498	692	12.6	3.88	103	.264	.331	-14	16	105	100	.976	149	179	-1.1	1.7	3.8	.2	.6
DET	52	9	21	1417^{2}	1330	8.5	147	505	756	12.0	3.56	108	.250	.320	37	46	102	104	.980	121	151	.4	4.8	-3.5	-.6	.0
BAL	44	13	25	1408	1272	8.2	**95**	493	767	**11.5**	3.47	104	.243	**.312**	51	21	95	92	.981	112	159	.9	2.2	-2.7	.3	-.5
CLE	46	7	23	1380^{2}	1381	9.1	130	618	807	13.4	4.07	92	.261	.343	-42	-54	98	101	.974	153	154	-1.4	-5.5	1.8	-.5	5.3
KC	26	6	19	1369^{2}	1344	8.9	153	565	626	12.8	4.19	94	.260	.336	-61	-34	104	99	.979	125	162	.2	-3.5	-7.1	.1	-7.0
WAS	31	5	16	1377	1482	9.7	149	580	691	13.8	4.85	80	.278	.353	-162	-142	103	95	.979	128	159	.0	-14.6	-5.0	-.7	-1.5
TOT	354	78	196	11126^{2}		8.7				12.4	3.79		.255	.329					.979	1018	1316					

Runs
Mantle-NY 121
Fox-Chi 110
Piersall-Bos 103
Sievers-Was 99

Hits
Fox-Chi 196
Malzone-Bos 185
Minoso-Chi 176
Mantle-NY 173
Kuenn-Det 173

Doubles
Minoso-Chi 36
Gardner-Bal 36
Malzone-Bos 31
Kuenn-Det 30

Triples
Simpson-KC-NY 9
McDougald-NY 9
Bauer-NY 9
Fox-Chi 8
Boyd-Bal 8

Home Runs
Sievers-Was 42
Williams-Bos 38
Mantle-NY 34
Wertz-Cle 28
Zernial-KC 27

Total Bases
Sievers-Was 331
Mantle-NY 315
Williams-Bos 307
Kaline-Det 276
Malzone-Bos 271

Runs Batted In
Sievers-Was 114
Wertz-Cle 105
Minoso-Chi 103
Malzone-Bos 103
Jensen-Bos 103

Runs Produced
Minoso-Chi 187
Mantle-NY 181
Sievers-Was 171
Malzone-Bos 170
Fox-Chi 165

Bases On Balls
Mantle-NY 146
Williams-Bos 119
Smith-Cle 79
Minoso-Chi 79
Wertz-Cle 78

Batting Average
Williams-Bos .388
Mantle-NY .365
Woodling-Cle .321
Boyd-Bal .318
Fox-Chi .317

On-Base Percentage
Williams-Bos .528
Mantle-NY .515
Minoso-Chi .413
Woodling-Cle .412
Fox-Chi .404

Slugging Average
Williams-Bos .731
Mantle-NY .665
Sievers-Was .579
Woodling-Cle .521
Wertz-Cle .485

On-Base Plus Slugging
Williams-Bos 1259
Mantle-NY 1179
Sievers-Was 968
Woodling-Cle 933
Minoso-Chi 867

Adjusted OPS
Williams-Bos 227
Mantle-NY 223
Sievers-Was 163
Woodling-Cle 155
Minoso-Chi 136

Batter Runs
Williams-Bos 89.9
Mantle-NY 88.9
Sievers-Was 47.3
Woodling-Cle 33.0
Minoso-Chi 32.7

Adjusted Batter Runs
Mantle-NY 91.4
Williams-Bos 81.7
Sievers-Was 48.7
Woodling-Cle 33.9
Minoso-Chi 32.2

Clutch Hitting Index
Minoso-Chi 126
Doby-Chi 125
Skowron-NY 123
Malzone-Bos 117
Jensen-Bos 114

Runs Created
Mantle-NY 178
Williams-Bos 167
Sievers-Was 131
Fox-Chi 109
Minoso-Chi 106

Total Average
Williams-Bos 1.599
Mantle-NY 1.534
Sievers-Was 1.010
Woodling-Cle .944
Maxwell-Det .876

Stolen Bases
Aparicio-Chi 28
Rivera-Chi 18
Minoso-Chi 18
Mantle-NY 16

Stolen Base Average
Rivera-Chi 90.0
Mantle-NY 84.2
Aparicio-Chi 77.8
Minoso-Chi 54.5

Stolen Base Runs
Aparicio-Chi 3.4
Rivera-Chi 3.3
Mantle-NY 2.5
Landis-Chi 1.7
Martin-NY-KC 1.3

Fielding Runs
Bridges-Was 29.3
Fox-Chi 20.9
Berra-NY 15.6
Phillips-Chi 15.5
McDougald-NY 15.1

Total Player Rating
Mantle-NY 8.7
Williams-Bos 7.1
Fox-Chi 5.6
Sievers-Was 4.4
McDougald-NY 4.2

Wins
Pierce-Chi 20
Bunning-Det 20
Sturdivant-NY 16
Donovan-Chi 16
Brewer-Bos 16

Win Percentage
Sturdivant-NY .727
Donovan-Chi .727
Bunning-Det .714
Wilson-Chi .652
Pierce-Chi .625

Games
Zuverink-Bal 56
Hyde-Was 53
Clevenger-Was 52
Delock-Bos 49
Trucks-KC 48

Complete Games
Pierce-Chi 16
Donovan-Chi 16
Brewer-Bos 15

Shutouts
Wilson-Chi 5
Turley-NY 4
Pierce-Chi 4

Saves
Grim-NY 19
Narleski-Cle 16
Delock-Bos 11
Zuverink-Bal 9
Clevenger-Was 8

Innings Pitched
Bunning-Det 267.1
Wynn-Cle 263.0
Pierce-Chi 257.0
Johnson-Bal 242.0
F.Sullivan-Bos 240.2

Fewest Hits/Game
Turley-NY 6.12
Bunning-Det 7.20
Foytack-Det 7.43
Sturdivant-NY 7.59
F.Sullivan-Bos 7.70

Fewest BB/Game
F.Sullivan-Bos 1.80
Donovan-Chi 1.84
Shantz-NY 2.08
Loes-Bal 2.14
Bunning-Det 2.42

Strikeouts
Wynn-Cle 184
Bunning-Det 182
Johnson-Bal 177
Pierce-Chi 171
Turley-NY 152

Strikeouts/Game
Turley-NY 7.76
Johnson-Bal 6.58
Wynn-Cle 6.30
Bunning-Det 6.13
Pierce-Chi 5.99

Ratio
F.Sullivan-Bos 9.76
Bunning-Det 10.00
Donovan-Chi 10.44
Johnson-Bal 10.45
Pierce-Chi 10.51

Earned Run Average
Shantz-NY 2.45
Sturdivant-NY 2.54
Bunning-Det 2.69
Turley-NY 2.71
F.Sullivan-Bos 2.73

Adjusted ERA
Shantz-NY 147
F.Sullivan-Bos 146
Bunning-Det 143
Sturdivant-NY 141
Donovan-Chi 135

Opponents' Batting Avg.
Turley-NY .194
Bunning-Det .218
Foytack-Det .226
F.Sullivan-Bos .230
Sturdivant-NY .232

Opponents' On-Base Pct.
F.Sullivan-Bos .275
Bunning-Det .279
Pierce-Chi .287
Johnson-Bal .289
Donovan-Chi .293

Starter Runs
Bunning-Det 32.5
F.Sullivan-Bos 28.3
Sturdivant-NY 27.9
Shantz-NY 25.8
Donovan-Chi 24.9

Adjusted Starter Runs
Bunning-Det 33.9
F.Sullivan-Bos 31.9
Sturdivant-NY 24.7
Donovan-Chi 23.9
Shantz-NY 23.2

Clutch Pitching Index
Shantz-NY 131
Sturdivant-NY 121
Narleski-Cle 113
Kemmerer-Bos-Was 110
Donovan-Chi 108

Relief Runs
Staley-Chi 20.2
Zuverink-Bal 16.4
Trucks-KC 9.8
Grim-NY 9.3
Lehman-Bal 7.6

Adjusted Relief Runs
Staley-Chi 19.9
Zuverink-Bal 14.7
Trucks-KC 11.5
Grim-NY 8.1
Byerly-Was 7.9

Relief Ranking
Zuverink-Bal 21.5
Grim-NY 16.3
Trucks-KC 15.8
Staley-Chi 13.2
Lehman-Bal 10.7

Total Pitcher Index
F.Sullivan-Bos 3.3
Bunning-Det 3.2
Shantz-NY 3.2
Donovan-Chi 2.5
Sturdivant-NY 2.5

Total Baseball Ranking
Mantle-NY 8.7
Williams-Bos 7.1
Fox-Chi 5.6
Sievers-Was 4.4
McDougald-NY 4.2

TEAM	G	W	L	PCT	GB	R	OR	AB	H	2B	3B	HR	BB	SO	AVG	OBP	SLG	OPS	OPS+	BR	BR+	PF	CHI	RC	SB	CS	SBA	SBR
MIL	154	92	62	.597		675	**541**	5225	1388	221	21	167	478	646	**.266**	.331	.412	743	**111**	14	**78**	92	98	705	26	8	**76**	3
PIT	154	84	70	.545	8	662	607	5247	1386	229	**68**	134	396	753	.264	.319	.410	729	101	-21	-3	97	103	669	30	15	67	1
SF	154	80	74	.519	12	**727**	698	5318	1399	**250**	42	170	531	817	.263	.334	.422	756	107	37	54	98	100	**747**	64	29	69	**4**
CIN	154	76	78	.494	16	695	621	5273	1359	242	40	123	572	765	.258	.333	.389	722	92	-19	-53	105	104	690	61	38	62	0
STL	154	72	82	.468	20	619	704	5255	1371	216	39	111	533	**637**	.261	.331	.380	711	90	-38	-62	104	97	638	44	43	51	-5
CHI	154	72	82	.468	20	709	725	5289	1402	207	49	**182**	487	853	.265	.332	**.426**	**758**	108	**39**	51	98	99	737	39	23	63	1
LA	154	71	83	.461	21	668	761	5173	1297	166	50	172	495	850	.251	.319	.402	721	93	-32	-52	103	**106**	650	**73**	47	61	0
PHI	154	69	85	.448	23	664	762	5363	**1424**	238	56	124	**573**	871	**.266**	**.341**	.400	741	103	20	30	99	93	729	51	33	61	0
TOT	616					5419		42143	11026	1769	365	1183	4065	6192	.262	.331	.406	735							388	236	62	3

TEAM	CG	SH	SV	IP	H	H/G	HR	BB	SO	RAT	ERA	ERA+	OAV	OOB	PR	PR+	PF	CPI	FA	E	DP	FW	PW	BW	SBW	DIF
MIL	**72**	**16**	17	1376	**1261**	**8.3**	125	426	773	**11.3**	**3.22**	110	**.244**	**.305**	**113**	53	89	99	.980	120	152	.9	5.4	**7.9**	.3	.7
PIT	43	10	**41**	1367	1344	8.9	**123**	470	679	12.1	3.57	109	.261	.325	59	47	98	**105**	.978	133	173	.2	4.8	-.3	.0	2.4
SF	38	7	25	1389[1]	1400	9.1	166	512	775	12.7	3.98	96	.263	.332	-4	-26	97	103	.975	152	156	-.8	-2.6	5.5	**.4**	.8
CIN	50	7	20	1385[1]	1422	9.3	148	**419**	705	12.2	3.73	**111**	.267	.324	34	**61**	105	**105**	**.983**	**100**	148	**2.0**	**6.2**	-5.3	-.0	-3.6
STL	45	6	25	1381[2]	1398	9.2	158	567	822	13.1	4.12	100	.264	.340	-25	2	105	102	.974	153	163	-.9	.3	-6.2	-.5	2.6
CHI	27	5	24	1361	1322	8.8	142	619	805	13.1	4.22	93	.254	.338	-40	-46	99	94	.975	150	161	-.7	-4.6	5.2	.0	-4.7
LA	30	7	31	1368[1]	1399	9.3	173	606	**855**	13.5	4.48	92	.267	.347	-79	-55	104	100	.975	146	**198**	-.5	-5.5	-5.2	-.0	5.4
PHI	51	6	15	1397	1480	9.6	148	446	778	12.6	4.33	92	.272	.329	-58	-56	100	93	.978	129	136	.4	-5.6	3.1	-.0	-5.6
TOT	356	64	198	11025[2]		9.1				12.6	3.96		.262	.331					.978	1083	1287					

Runs
- Mays-SF 121
- Banks-Chi 119
- Aaron-Mil 109
- Boyer-StL 101
- Ashburn-Phi 98

Hits
- Ashburn-Phi 215
- Mays-SF 208
- Aaron-Mil 196
- Banks-Chi 193
- Cepeda-SF 188

Doubles
- Cepeda-SF 38
- Groat-Pit 36
- Musial-StL 35
- H.Anderson-Phi 34
- Aaron-Mil 34

Triples
- Ashburn-Phi 13
- Virdon-Pit 11
- Mays-SF 11
- Banks-Chi 11

Home Runs
- Banks-Chi 47
- Thomas-Pit 35
- Robinson-Cin 31
- Mathews-Mil 31
- Aaron-Mil 30

Total Bases
- Banks-Chi 379
- Mays-SF 350
- Aaron-Mil 328
- Cepeda-SF 309
- Thomas-Pit 297

Runs Batted In
- Banks-Chi 129
- Thomas-Pit 109
- H.Anderson-Phi 97
- Mays-SF 96
- Cepeda-SF 96

Runs Produced
- Banks-Chi 201
- Mays-SF 188
- Aaron-Mil 174
- Boyer-StL 168
- Thomas-Pit 163

Bases On Balls
- Ashburn-Phi 97
- Temple-Cin 91
- Mathews-Mil 85
- Cunningham-StL 82

Batting Average
- Ashburn-Phi .350
- Mays-SF .347
- Musial-StL .337
- Aaron-Mil .326
- Skinner-Pit .321

On-Base Percentage
- Ashburn-Phi .441
- Musial-StL .426
- Mays-SF .423
- Temple-Cin .406
- Skinner-Pit .390

Slugging Average
- Banks-Chi .614
- Mays-SF .583
- Aaron-Mil .546
- Thomas-Pit .528
- Musial-StL .528

On-Base Plus Slugging
- Mays-SF 1006
- Banks-Chi 984
- Musial-StL 953
- Aaron-Mil 933
- H.Anderson-Phi 900

Adjusted OPS
- Mays-SF 167
- Banks-Chi 157
- Aaron-Mil 157
- Musial-StL 145
- H.Anderson-Phi 137

Batter Runs
- Mays-SF 55.3
- Banks-Chi 45.7
- Aaron-Mil 37.0
- Musial-StL 36.7
- Ashburn-Phi 36.5

Adjusted Batter Runs
- Mays-SF 58.5
- Banks-Chi 47.7
- Aaron-Mil 47.5
- Ashburn-Phi 38.2
- Musial-StL 32.9

Clutch Hitting Index
- H.Anderson-Phi 111
- Fernandez-Phi 110
- Long-Chi 103
- Spencer-SF 103
- Banks-Chi 103

Runs Created
- Mays-SF 152
- Banks-Chi 135
- Ashburn-Phi 129
- Aaron-Mil 121
- Skinner-Pit 102

Total Average
- Mays-SF 1.110
- Banks-Chi .984
- Musial-StL .970
- Ashburn-Phi .929
- Aaron-Mil .916

Stolen Bases
- Mays-SF 31
- Ashburn-Phi 30
- T.Taylor-Chi 21
- Blasingame-StL 20
- Gilliam-LA 18

Stolen Base Average
- Mays-SF 83.8
- Blasingame-StL 80.0
- T.Taylor-Chi 77.8
- Ashburn-Phi 71.4
- Gilliam-LA 62.1

Stolen Base Runs
- Mays-SF 4.7
- Blasingame-StL 2.7
- T.Taylor-Chi 2.5
- Ashburn-Phi 2.4
- Zimmer-LA 2.4

Fielding Runs
- Zimmer-LA 32.6
- Clemente-Pit 25.2
- Boyer-StL 23.4
- Ashburn-Phi 22.1
- Flood-StL 19.3

Total Player Rating
- Mays-SF 7.2
- Banks-Chi 5.8
- Ashburn-Phi 5.5
- Aaron-Mil 4.3
- Boyer-StL 3.9

Wins
- Spahn-Mil 22
- Friend-Pit 22
- Burdette-Mil 20
- Roberts-Phi 17
- Purkey-Cin 17

Win Percentage
- Spahn-Mil .667
- Burdette-Mil .667
- Friend-Pit .611
- Purkey-Cin .607
- Antonelli-SF .552

Games
- Elston-Chi 69
- Klippstein-Cin-LA 57
- Face-Pit 57
- Hobbie-Chi 55

Complete Games
- Spahn-Mil 23
- Roberts-Phi 21
- Burdette-Mil 19
- Purkey-Cin 17
- Friend-Pit 16

Shutouts
- Willey-Mil 4
- Witt-Pit 3
- Purkey-Cin 3
- Jay-Mil 3
- Burdette-Mil 3

Saves
- Face-Pit 20
- Labine-LA 14
- Farrell-Phi 11

Innings Pitched
- Spahn-Mil 290.0
- Burdette-Mil 275.1
- Friend-Pit 274.0
- Roberts-Phi 269.2

Fewest Hits/Game
- Jones-StL 7.34
- Koufax-LA 7.49
- Miller-SF 7.91
- Spahn-Mil 7.98
- Brosnan-Chi-StL 7.99

Fewest BB/Game
- Burdette-Mil 1.63
- Roberts-Phi 1.70
- Law-Pit 1.73
- Purkey-Cin 1.76
- Newcombe-LA-Cin 1.93

Strikeouts
- Jones-StL 225
- Spahn-Mil 150
- Podres-LA 143
- Antonelli-SF 143
- Friend-Pit 135

Strikeouts/Game
- Jones-StL 8.10
- Koufax-LA 7.43
- Drott-Chi 6.83
- Podres-LA 6.12
- Miller-SF 5.88

Ratio
- Spahn-Mil 10.40
- Miller-SF 10.43
- Roberts-Phi 10.78
- Burdette-Mil 10.92
- Purkey-Cin 11.23

Earned Run Average
- Miller-SF 2.47
- Jones-StL 2.88
- Burdette-Mil 2.91
- Spahn-Mil 3.07
- Roberts-Phi 3.24

Adjusted ERA
- Miller-SF 154
- Jones-StL 143
- Roberts-Phi 122
- Brosnan-Chi-StL 121
- Burdette-Mil 121

Opponents' Batting Avg.
- Koufax-LA .220
- Jones-StL .223
- Miller-SF .233
- Spahn-Mil .237
- Antonelli-SF .239

Opponents' On-Base Pct.
- Miller-SF .286
- Spahn-Mil .288
- Roberts-Phi .294
- Burdette-Mil .301
- Purkey-Cin .306

Starter Runs
- Burdette-Mil 31.9
- Miller-SF 29.9
- Jones-StL 29.8
- Spahn-Mil 28.3
- Witt-Pit 27.5

Adjusted Starter Runs
- Jones-StL 33.2
- Miller-SF 28.1
- Witt-Pit 27.1
- Roberts-Phi 21.6
- Burdette-Mil 21.0

Clutch Pitching Index
- Haddix-Cin 116
- Newcombe-LA-Cin 115
- Mizell-StL 114
- Miller-SF 110
- Podres-LA 109

Relief Runs
- Elston-Chi 11.6
- Face-Pit 9.9
- Henry-Chi 9.7
- Schmidt-Cin 8.4
- Porterfield-Pit 6.5

Adjusted Relief Runs
- Elston-Chi 11.3
- Henry-Chi 9.5
- Schmidt-Cin 9.5
- Face-Pit 9.3
- Farrell-Phi 6.3

Relief Ranking
- Elston-Chi 20.5
- Farrell-Phi 12.0
- Face-Pit 11.9
- Henry-Chi 11.0
- Schmidt-Cin 9.8

Total Pitcher Index
- Spahn-Mil 4.1
- Burdette-Mil 3.3
- Jones-StL 2.8
- Witt-Pit 2.6
- Roberts-Phi 2.5

Total Baseball Ranking
- Mays-SF 7.2
- Banks-Chi 5.8
- Ashburn-Phi 5.5
- Aaron-Mil 4.3
- Spahn-Mil 4.1

TEAM	G	W	L	PCT	GB	R	OR	AB	H	2B	3B	HR	BB	SO	AVG	OBP	SLG	OPS	OPS+	BR	BR+	PF	CHI	RC	SB	CS	SBA	SBR
NY	155	92	62	.597		**759**	577	5294	**1418**	212	39	**164**	537	822	**.268**	.338	**.416**	**754**	**117**	**88**	**116**	96	102	**746**	48	32	60	-1
CHI	155	82	72	.532	10	634	615	5249	1348	191	42	101	518	**669**	.257	.329	.367	696	99	-13	0	98	99	647	**101**	33	**75**	**11**
BOS	155	79	75	.513	13	697	691	5218	1335	**229**	30	155	**638**	820	.256	**.340**	.400	740	102	70	24	107	96	708	29	22	57	-1
CLE	153	77	76	.503	14.5	694	635	5201	1340	210	31	161	494	819	.258	.327	.403	730	109	38	55	98	102	677	50	49	51	-6
DET	154	77	77	.500	15	659	606	5194	1384	**229**	41	109	463	678	.266	.329	.389	718	96	20	-25	107	100	657	48	32	60	-1
BAL	154	74	79	.484	17.5	521	**575**	5111	1233	195	19	108	483	731	.241	.310	.350	660	92	-85	-55	95	96	546	33	35	49	-5
KC	156	73	81	.474	19	642	713	5261	1297	196	**50**	138	452	747	.247	.309	.381	690	93	-40	-51	102	**106**	601	22	36	38	-8
WAS	156	61	93	.396	31	553	747	5156	1240	161	38	121	477	751	.240	.309	.357	666	91	-78	-67	98	99	555	22	41	35	-10
TOT	619					5159		41684	10595	1623	290	1057	4062	6037	.255	.325	.384	707							353	280	56	-20

TEAM	CG	SH	SV	IP	H	H/G	HR	BB	SO	RAT	ERA	ERA+	OAV	OOB	PR	PR+	PF	CPI	FA	E	DP	FW	PW	BW	SBW	DIF
NY	53	**21**	**33**	1379	**1201**	**7.9**	116	557	796	11.8	**3.22**	110	**.235**	.315	**85**	51	94	103	.978	128	**182**	-.0	5.3	**12.0**	.2	-2.3
CHI	55	15	25	1389^{2}	1296	8.4	152	515	751	11.9	3.61	101	.250	.320	25	5	97	**104**	.981	114	160	.7	.6	.0	**1.4**	2.5
BOS	44	5	28	1380	1396	9.2	121	521	695	12.8	3.92	102	.264	.334	-23	13	106	102	.976	145	172	-1.0	1.4	2.5	.2	-.9
CLE	51	2	20	1373^{1}	1283	8.5	123	604	766	12.6	3.73	98	.249	.331	6	-13	97	101	.974	152	171	-1.5	-1.3	5.7	-.4	-1.9
DET	**59**	8	19	1357^{1}	1294	8.6	133	437	**797**	11.8	3.60	**112**	.252	.316	26	**62**	107	101	**.982**	**106**	140	**1.1**	**6.5**	-2.5	.2	-5.0
BAL	55	15	28	1369^{2}	1277	8.4	**106**	**403**	749	**11.3**	3.40	106	.249	**.308**	57	32	95	97	.980	114	159	.7	3.4	-5.6	-.3	-.4
KC	42	9	25	1398^{1}	1405	9.1	150	467	721	12.3	4.16	94	.262	.324	-59	-36	104	95	.979	125	166	.2	-3.7	-5.2	-.6	5.5
WAS	28	6	28	1376^{2}	1443	9.5	156	558	762	13.3	4.54	84	.272	.344	-116	-108	101	98	.980	118	163	.5	-11.1	-6.9	-.8	2.4
TOT	387	81	206	11024		8.7				12.2	3.77		.255	.325					.979	1002	1313					

Runs
Mantle-NY 127
Runnels-Bos 103
Power-KC-Cle 98
Minoso-Cle 94
Cerv-KC 93

Hits
Fox-Chi 187
Malzone-Bos 185
Power-KC-Cle 184
Runnels-Bos 183
Kuenn-Det 179

Doubles
Kuenn-Det 39
Power-KC-Cle 37
Kaline-Det 34
Runnels-Bos 32
Jensen-Bos 31

Triples
Power-KC-Cle 10
Tuttle-KC 9
Lemon-Was 9
Aparicio-Chi 9
Harris-Det 8

Home Runs
Mantle-NY 42
Colavito-Cle 41
Sievers-Was 39
Cerv-KC 38
Jensen-Bos 35

Total Bases
Mantle-NY 307
Cerv-KC 305
Colavito-Cle 303
Sievers-Was 299
Jensen-Bos 293

Runs Batted In
Jensen-Bos 122
Colavito-Cle 113
Sievers-Was 108
Cerv-KC 104
Mantle-NY 97

Runs Produced
Mantle-NY 182
Jensen-Bos 170
Power-KC-Cle 162
Cerv-KC 159

Bases On Balls
Mantle-NY 129
Jensen-Bos 99
Williams-Bos 98
Runnels-Bos 87
Colavito-Cle 84

Batting Average
Williams-Bos .328
Runnels-Bos .322
Kuenn-Det .319
Kaline-Det .313
Power-KC-Cle .312

On-Base Percentage
Williams-Bos .462
Mantle-NY .445
Runnels-Bos .418
Colavito-Cle .407
Jensen-Bos .398

Slugging Average
Colavito-Cle .620
Cerv-KC .592
Mantle-NY .592
Williams-Bos .584
Sievers-Was .544

On-Base Plus Slugging
Williams-Bos 1046
Mantle-NY 1036
Colavito-Cle 1027
Cerv-KC 964
Jensen-Bos 933

Adjusted OPS
Mantle-NY 189
Colavito-Cle 183
Williams-Bos 174
Cerv-KC 158
Sievers-Was 148

Batter Runs
Mantle-NY 64.2
Williams-Bos 53.6
Colavito-Cle 52.8
Jensen-Bos 42.7
Cerv-KC 40.7

Adjusted Batter Runs
Mantle-NY 69.3
Colavito-Cle 55.8
Williams-Bos 46.5
Cerv-KC 38.8
Jensen-Bos 35.4

Clutch Hitting Index
Courtney-Was 131
Lollar-Chi 127
F.Bolling-Det 117
Harris-Det 116
Skowron-NY 116

Runs Created
Mantle-NY 147
Colavito-Cle 122
Jensen-Bos 120
Williams-Bos 112
Runnels-Bos 107

Total Average
Mantle-NY 1.208
Williams-Bos 1.163
Colavito-Cle 1.078
Jensen-Bos .980
Cerv-KC .947

Stolen Bases
Aparicio-Chi 29
Rivera-Chi 21
Landis-Chi 19
Mantle-NY 18
Minoso-Cle 14

Stolen Base Average
Rivera-Chi 87.5
Mantle-NY 85.7
Aparicio-Chi 82.9
Landis-Chi 73.1

Stolen Base Runs
Aparicio-Chi 4.3
Rivera-Chi 3.6
Mantle-NY 2.9
Wilson-Det 2.2

Fielding Runs
Kaline-Det 23.0
Kubek-NY 20.0
Cerv-KC 20.0
Malzone-Bos 16.6
Kuenn-Det 15.1

Total Player Rating
Mantle-NY 6.5
Colavito-Cle 5.3
Cerv-KC 5.1
Runnels-Bos 3.9
Kaline-Det 3.9

Wins
Turley-NY 21
Pierce-Chi 17
McLish-Cle 16
Lary-Det 16

Win Percentage
Turley-NY .750
McLish-Cle .667
Pierce-Chi .607
Portocarrero-Bal .577
Foytack-Det .536

Games
Clevenger-Was 55
Tomanek-Cle-KC 54
Hyde-Was 53
Wall-Bos 52

Complete Games
Turley-NY 19
Pierce-Chi 19
Lary-Det 19
Harshman-Bal 17

Shutouts
Ford-NY 7
Turley-NY 6
Wynn-Chi 4
Ramos-Was 4
Donovan-Chi 4

Saves
Duren-NY 20
Hyde-Was 18
Kiely-Bos 12
Wall-Bos 10

Innings Pitched
Lary-Det 260.1
Ramos-Was 259.1
Donovan-Chi 248.0
Turley-NY 245.1
Pierce-Chi 245.0

Fewest Hits/Game
Turley-NY 6.53
Bell-Cle 6.97
Ford-NY 7.14
Pierce-Chi 7.49
Portocarrero-Bal 7.61

Fewest BB/Game
Donovan-Chi 1.92
O'Dell-Bal 2.07
Sullivan-Bos 2.21
Lary-Det 2.35
Pierce-Chi 2.42

Strikeouts
Wynn-Chi 179
Bunning-Det 177
Turley-NY 168
Harshman-Bal 161
Pascual-Was 146

Strikeouts/Game
Pascual-Was 7.41
Bunning-Det 7.25
Wynn-Chi 6.72
Turley-NY 6.16
Harshman-Bal 6.13

Ratio
Ford-NY 9.81
Pierce-Chi 9.96
Portocarrero-Bal 10.25
O'Dell-Bal 10.41
Harshman-Bal 10.74

Earned Run Average
Ford-NY 2.01
Pierce-Chi 2.68
Harshman-Bal 2.89
Lary-Det 2.90
O'Dell-Bal 2.97

Adjusted ERA
Ford-NY 176
Lary-Det 139
Pierce-Chi 136
Harshman-Bal 124
McLish-Cle 122

Opponents' Batting Avg.
Turley-NY .206
Bell-Cle .213
Ford-NY .217
Pierce-Chi .227
Grant-Cle .228

Opponents' On-Base Pct.
Ford-NY .276
Pierce-Chi .280
Portocarrero-Bal .286
O'Dell-Bal .288
Harshman-Bal .294

Starter Runs
Ford-NY 42.9
Pierce-Chi 29.6
Lary-Det 25.0
Harshman-Bal 23.0
Turley-NY 21.7

Adjusted Starter Runs
Ford-NY 39.6
Lary-Det 30.6
Pierce-Chi 27.0
Wilhelm-Cle-Bal 19.6
Harshman-Bal 19.3

Clutch Pitching Index
McLish-Cle 120
Ford-NY 117
Pierce-Chi 114
Lary-Det 113
Wilson-Chi 110

Relief Runs
Hyde-Was 23.1
Duren-NY 14.7
Kiely-Bos 6.9
Staley-Chi 5.7
Morgan-Det 4.2

Adjusted Relief Runs
Hyde-Was 23.4
Duren-NY 13.5
Kiely-Bos 8.5
Morgan-Det 5.7
Staley-Chi 4.7

Relief Ranking
Hyde-Was 35.7
Duren-NY 24.2
Kiely-Bos 9.5
Wall-Bos 7.1
Morgan-Det 5.9

Total Pitcher Index
Ford-NY 4.2
Hyde-Was 3.8
Harshman-Bal 3.5
Lary-Det 3.4
Pierce-Chi 3.0

Total Baseball Ranking
Mantle-NY 6.5
Colavito-Cle 5.4
Cerv-KC 5.1
Ford-NY 4.2
Runnels-Bos 3.9

TEAM	G	W	L	PCT	GB	R	OR	AB	H	2B	3B	HR	BB	SO	AVG	OBP	SLG	OPS	OPS+	BR	BR+	PF	CHI	RC	SB	CS	SBA	SBR
LA	156	88	68	.564		705	670	5282	1360	196	46	148	**591**	891	.257	.335	.396	731	94	17	-31	107	99	706	**84**	51	62	1
MIL	157	86	70	.551	2	724	623	5388	1426	216	36	**177**	488	765	.265	.329	.417	746	**115**	32	**98**	92	100	729	41	14	**75**	4
SF	154	83	71	.539	4	705	**613**	5281	1377	239	35	167	473	875	.261	.324	.414	738	105	16	32	98	101	711	81	34	70	**6**
PIT	155	78	76	.506	9	651	680	5369	1414	230	42	112	442	**715**	.263	.322	.384	706	95	-39	-33	99	101	653	32	26	55	-2
CIN	154	74	80	.481	13	**764**	738	5288	**1448**	**258**	34	161	499	763	**.274**	**.340**	**.427**	**767**	108	**76**	55	103	101	**764**	65	28	70	5
CHI	155	74	80	.481	13	673	688	5296	1321	209	44	163	498	911	.249	.319	.398	717	98	-23	-16	99	102	673	32	19	63	0
STL	154	71	83	.461	16	641	725	5317	1432	244	**49**	118	485	747	.269	.333	.400	733	96	14	-28	106	92	699	65	53	55	-4
PHI	155	64	90	.416	23	599	725	5109	1237	196	38	113	498	858	.242	.314	.362	676	86	-92	-101	102	**105**	574	39	46	46	-8
TOT	620					5462		42330	11015	1788	324	1159	3974	6525	.261	.328	.400	727							439	271	62	2

TEAM	CG	SH	SV	IP	H	H/G	HR	BB	SO	RAT	ERA	ERA+	OAV	OOB	PR	PR+	PF	CPI	FA	E	DP	FW	PW	BW	SBW	DIF
LA	43	14	**26**	1411^{2}	1317	**8.4**	157	614	**1077**	12.7	3.80	**111**	.247	.331	24	**64**	107	103	**.981**	**114**	154	**1.5**	**6.5**	-3.1	.0	5.2
MIL	**69**	**18**	18	1400^{2}	1406	9.1	**128**	429	775	12.0	3.51	101	.260	.317	68	6	90	**104**	.979	127	138	.8	.7	**9.9**	.4	-3.6
SF	52	12	23	1376^{1}	**1279**	**8.4**	139	500	873	**11.9**	**3.47**	110	**.246**	**.316**	**74**	54	97	103	.974	152	118	-.7	5.5	3.3	**.6**	-2.4
PIT	48	7	17	1393^{1}	1432	9.3	134	**418**	730	12.1	3.91	99	.267	.323	7	-5	98	100	.975	154	**165**	-.8	-.5	-3.3	-.2	5.9
CIN	44	7	**26**	1357^{1}	1460	9.7	162	456	690	13.0	4.31	94	.275	.337	-55	-38	103	102	.978	126	157	.7	-3.8	5.6	.5	-5.8
CHI	30	11	25	1391	1337	8.7	152	519	765	12.2	4.02	98	.254	.323	-10	-10	100	96	.977	140	142	.0	-1.0	-1.6	-.0	-.3
STL	36	8	21	1363	1427	9.5	137	564	846	13.3	4.34	98	.271	.344	-59	-14	107	100	.975	146	158	-.4	-1.4	-2.8	-.4	-.9
PHI	54	8	15	1354	1357	9.1	150	474	769	12.4	4.28	96	.261	.326	-49	-24	104	93	.973	154	132	-.8	-2.4	-10.1	-.8	1.3
TOT	376	85	171	11047^{1}		9.0				12.5	3.95		.261	.328					.977	1113	1164					

Runs
Pinson-Cin 131
Mays-SF 125
Mathews-Mil 118
Aaron-Mil 116
Robinson-Cin 106

Hits
Aaron-Mil 223
Pinson-Cin 205
Cepeda-SF 192
Temple-Cin 186
Mathews-Mil 182

Doubles
Pinson-Cin 47
Aaron-Mil 46
Mays-SF 43
Cimoli-StL 40

Triples
Neal-LA 11
Moon-LA 11
White-StL 9
Pinson-Cin 9
Dark-Chi 9

Home Runs
Mathews-Mil 46
Banks-Chi 45
Aaron-Mil 39
Robinson-Cin 36
Mays-SF 34

Total Bases
Aaron-Mil 400
Mathews-Mil 352
Banks-Chi 351
Mays-SF 335
Pinson-Cin 330

Runs Batted In
Banks-Chi 143
Robinson-Cin 125
Aaron-Mil 123
Bell-Cin 115
Mathews-Mil 114

Runs Produced
Aaron-Mil 200
Robinson-Cin 195
Pinson-Cin 195
Mays-SF 195
Banks-Chi 195

Bases On Balls
Gilliam-LA 96
Cunningham-StL 88
Moon-LA 81
Mathews-Mil 80
Ashburn-Phi 79

Batting Average
Aaron-Mil .355
Cunningham-StL .345
Cepeda-SF .317
Pinson-Cin .316
Mays-SF .313

On-Base Percentage
Cunningham-StL .456
Aaron-Mil .406
Robinson-Cin .397
Moon-LA .396
Mathews-Mil .391

Slugging Average
Aaron-Mil .636
Banks-Chi .596
Mathews-Mil .593
Robinson-Cin .583
Mays-SF .583

On-Base Plus Slugging
Aaron-Mil 1042
Mathews-Mil 984
Robinson-Cin 980
Banks-Chi 975
Mays-SF 967

Adjusted OPS
Aaron-Mil 188
Mathews-Mil 172
Mays-SF 157
Banks-Chi 156
Robinson-Cin 152

Batter Runs
Aaron-Mil 62.8
Mathews-Mil 48.4
Banks-Chi 44.4
Robinson-Cin 44.0
Mays-SF 42.6

Adjusted Batter Runs
Aaron-Mil 75.9
Mathews-Mil 60.0
Banks-Chi 45.8
Mays-SF 45.3
Robinson-Cin 40.7

Clutch Hitting Index
Bell-Cin 134
Post-Phi 128
Mazeroski-Pit 120
Bouchee-Phi 111
Cimoli-StL 111

Runs Created
Aaron-Mil 156
Mathews-Mil 143
Mays-SF 131
Banks-Chi 126
Pinson-Cin 124

Total Average
Aaron-Mil 1.089
Mathews-Mil 1.041
Mays-SF 1.037
Robinson-Cin 1.015
Cunningham-StL .978

Stolen Bases
Mays-SF 27
T.Taylor-Chi 23
Gilliam-LA 23
Cepeda-SF 23
Pinson-Cin 21

Stolen Base Average
Mays-SF 87.1
Pinson-Cin 77.8
Neal-LA 73.9
T.Taylor-Chi 71.9
Cepeda-SF 71.9

Stolen Base Runs
Mays-SF 4.5
Pinson-Cin 2.5
Temple-Cin 2.0
T.Taylor-Chi 1.9
Cepeda-SF 1.9

Fielding Runs
Virdon-Pit 23.5
Blasingame-StL 20.5
Neal-LA 20.0
Pinson-Cin 19.7
H.Anderson-Phi 18.3

Total Player Rating
Aaron-Mil 6.8
Banks-Chi 6.3
Mathews-Mil 6.2
Mays-SF 4.9
Pinson-Cin 4.0

Wins
Spahn-Mil 21
S.Jones-SF 21
Burdette-Mil 21
Antonelli-SF 19

Win Percentage
Face-Pit .947
Law-Pit .667
Antonelli-SF .655
Buhl-Mil .625

Games
Henry-Chi 65
Elston-Chi 65
McDaniel-StL 62
McMahon-Mil 60
Miller-SF 59

Complete Games
Spahn-Mil 21
Law-Pit 20
Burdette-Mil 20
Roberts-Phi 19

Shutouts
Spahn-Mil 4
S.Jones-SF 4
Drysdale-LA 4
Craig-LA 4
Burdette-Mil 4
Buhl-Mil 4
Antonelli-SF 4

Saves
McMahon-Mil 15
McDaniel-StL 15
Elston-Chi 13
Henry-Chi 12

Innings Pitched
Spahn-Mil 292.0
Burdette-Mil 289.2
Antonelli-SF 282.0
S.Jones-SF 270.2
Drysdale-LA 270.2

Fewest Hits/Game
Haddix-Pit 7.58
S.Jones-SF 7.71
Hobbie-Chi 7.85
Drysdale-LA 7.88
Antonelli-SF 7.88

Fewest BB/Game
Newcombe-Cin 1.09
Burdette-Mil 1.18
Roberts-Phi 1.22
Purkey-Cin 1.78
Law-Pit 1.79

Strikeouts
Drysdale-LA 242
S.Jones-SF 209
Koufax-LA 173
Antonelli-SF 165
McCormick-SF 151

Strikeouts/Game
Drysdale-LA 8.05
S.Jones-SF 6.95
Podres-LA 6.69
Broglio-StL 6.60
McCormick-SF 6.02

Ratio
Haddix-Pit 9.63
Newcombe-Cin 10.05
Conley-Phi 10.15
Law-Pit 10.15
Antonelli-SF 10.40

Earned Run Average
S.Jones-SF 2.83
Miller-SF 2.84
Buhl-Mil 2.86
Spahn-Mil 2.96
Law-Pit 2.98

Adjusted ERA
Conley-Phi 137
S.Jones-SF 135
Miller-SF 134
Law-Pit 130
Jackson-StL 128

Opponents' Batting Avg.
S.Jones-SF .228
Haddix-Pit .228
Antonelli-SF .233
Drysdale-LA .233
Conley-Phi .235

Opponents' On-Base Pct.
Haddix-Pit .273
Newcombe-Cin .280
Conley-Phi .281
Law-Pit .282
Antonelli-SF .286

Starter Runs
S.Jones-SF 33.7
Spahn-Mil 32.1
Craig-LA 32.0
Law-Pit 28.7
Antonelli-SF 26.7

Adjusted Starter Runs
Craig-LA 34.3
S.Jones-SF 30.6
Law-Pit 26.9
Jackson-StL 24.7
Antonelli-SF 23.2

Clutch Pitching Index
Miller-SF 134
Buhl-Mil 120
Spahn-Mil 105
Jackson-StL 104
S.Jones-SF 104

Relief Runs
Miller-SF 20.5
Henry-Chi 18.9
Face-Pit 12.9
McMahon-Mil 12.4
Elston-Chi 6.8

Adjusted Relief Runs
Henry-Chi 18.9
Miller-SF 18.6
Face-Pit 12.4
McMahon-Mil 9.7
Meyer-Phi 7.4

Relief Ranking
Henry-Chi 25.3
Face-Pit 24.7
Miller-SF 17.0
Elston-Chi 13.4
McMahon-Mil 12.8

Total Pitcher Index
S.Jones-SF 3.6
Newcombe-Cin 3.4
Spahn-Mil 3.1
Craig-LA 3.0
Drysdale-LA 2.8

Total Baseball Ranking
Aaron-Mil 6.8
Banks-Chi 6.3
Mathews-Mil 6.2
Mays-SF 4.9
Pinson-Cin 4.0

TEAM	G	W	L	PCT	GB	R	OR	AB	H	2B	3B	HR	BB	SO	AVG	OBP	SLG	OPS	OPS+	BR	BR+	PF	CHI	RC	SB	CS	SBA	SBR
CHI	156	94	60	.610		669	**588**	5297	1325	220	**46**	97	580	**634**	.250	.330	.364	694	97	-20	-11	99	100	653	**113**	53	68	**6**
CLE	154	89	65	.578	5	**745**	646	5288	1390	216	25	**167**	433	721	**.263**	.323	**.408**	731	**110**	32	**60**	96	**107**	682	33	36	48	-5
NY	155	79	75	.513	15	687	647	5379	**1397**	224	40	153	457	828	.260	.321	.402	723	107	17	42	97	98	695	45	22	67	2
DET	154	76	78	.494	18	713	732	5211	1346	196	30	160	580	737	.258	**.338**	.400	**738**	102	**57**	19	105	97	**720**	34	17	67	2
BOS	154	75	79	.487	19	726	696	5225	1335	**248**	28	125	**626**	810	.256	**.338**	.385	723	99	36	4	105	101	697	68	25	**73**	**6**
BAL	155	74	80	.481	20	551	621	5208	1240	182	23	109	536	690	.238	.312	.345	657	88	-96	-82	98	96	563	36	24	60	0
KC	154	66	88	.429	28	681	760	5264	1383	231	43	117	481	780	**.263**	.328	.390	718	100	16	4	102	99	669	34	24	59	-1
WAS	154	63	91	.409	31	619	701	5092	1205	173	32	163	517	881	.237	.310	.379	689	94	-43	-40	100	101	594	51	34	60	-1
TOT	618					5391		41964	10621	1690	267	1091	4210	6081	.254	.326	.385	709							414	235	64	9

TEAM	CG	SH	SV	IP	H	H/G	HR	BB	SO	RAT	ERA	ERA+	OAV	OOB	PR	PR+	PF	CPI	FA	E	DP	FW	PW	BW	SBW	DIF
CHI	44	13	**36**	1425^1	1297	8.2	129	525	761	11.8	**3.29**	**114**	.242	**.313**	**91**	**76**	97	**106**	**.979**	130	141	.7	**7.7**	-1.1	**.5**	9.3
CLE	**58**	7	23	1383^2	**1230**	**8.1**	148	635	799	12.3	3.75	98	**.239**	.325	18	-10	95	101	.978	127	138	.8	-1.0	**6.1**	-.6	6.9
NY	38	**15**	28	1399	1281	8.3	120	594	**836**	12.3	3.61	101	.244	.324	40	7	94	102	.978	131	160	.6	.8	4.3	.0	-3.5
DET	53	9	24	1360	1327	8.8	177	**432**	829	12.0	4.21	97	.254	.316	-52	-20	105	94	.978	**124**	131	**.9**	-2.0	2.0	.0	-1.8
BOS	38	9	25	1364	1386	9.2	135	589	724	13.3	4.18	97	.266	.343	-47	-16	105	104	.978	131	**167**	.5	-1.6	.5	**.5**	-1.7
BAL	45	**15**	30	1400^1	1290	8.3	**111**	476	735	**11.6**	3.57	106	.246	**.313**	47	35	98	96	.976	146	163	-.3	3.6	-8.3	-.1	2.3
KC	44	8	21	1360^2	1452	9.7	148	492	703	13.2	4.36	92	.274	.341	-74	-51	104	102	.973	160	156	-1.2	-5.1	.5	-.2	-4.7
WAS	46	10	21	1360	1358	9.0	123	467	694	12.4	4.02	98	.259	.324	-23	-14	101	96	.973	162	140	-1.3	-1.4	-4.0	-.2	-6.9
TOT	366	86	208	11053		8.7				12.3	3.87		.254	.326					.977	1111	1196					

Runs
Yost-Det 115
Mantle-NY 104
Power-Cle 102
Jensen-Bos 101
Kuenn-Det 99

Hits
Kuenn-Det 198
Fox-Chi 191
Runnels-Bos 176
Power-Cle 172
Minoso-Cle 172

Doubles
Kuenn-Det 42
Malzone-Bos 34
Fox-Chi 34
Williams-KC 33
Runnels-Bos 33

Triples
Allison-Was 9
McDougald-NY 8

Home Runs
Killebrew-Was 42
Colavito-Cle 42
Lemon-Was 33
Maxwell-Det 31
Mantle-NY 31

Total Bases
Colavito-Cle 301
Killebrew-Was 282
Kuenn-Det 281
Mantle-NY 278
Allison-Was 275

Runs Batted In
Jensen-Bos 112
Colavito-Cle 111
Killebrew-Was 105
Lemon-Was 100
Maxwell-Det 95

Runs Produced
Jensen-Bos 185
Minoso-Cle 163
Malzone-Bos 163
Kuenn-Det 161
Killebrew-Was 161

Bases On Balls
Yost-Det 135
Runnels-Bos 95
Mantle-NY 93
Buddin-Bos 92
Killebrew-Was 90

Batting Average
Kuenn-Det 353
Kaline-Det 327
Runnels-Bos 314
Fox-Chi 306
Minoso-Cle 302

On-Base Percentage
Yost-Det 437
Runnels-Bos 415
Kaline-Det 414
Woodling-Bal 405
Kuenn-Det 405

Slugging Average
Kaline-Det 530
Killebrew-Was 516
Mantle-NY 514
Colavito-Cle 512
Lemon-Was 510

On-Base Plus Slugging
Kaline-Det 944
Kuenn-Det 906
Mantle-NY 905
Yost-Det 873
Killebrew-Was 873

Adjusted OPS
Mantle-NY 152
Kaline-Det 149
Kuenn-Det 140
Woodling-Bal 139
Killebrew-Was 137

Batter Runs
Kaline-Det 41.6
Yost-Det 37.9
Francona-Cle 36.6
Kuenn-Det 36.2
Mantle-NY 36.0

Adjusted Batter Runs
Francona-Cle 40.1
Mantle-NY 39.9
Kaline-Det 36.0
Yost-Det 32.0
Kuenn-Det 30.7

Clutch Hitting Index
Strickland-Cle 125
Fox-Chi 121
Woodling-Bal 120
Jensen-Bos 115
Cerv-KC 115

Runs Created
Mantle-NY 117
Kuenn-Det 117
Yost-Det 115
Kaline-Det 114
Killebrew-Was 103

Total Average
Yost-Det 992
Mantle-NY 985
Kaline-Det 983
Kuenn-Det 903
Jensen-Bos 888

Stolen Bases
Aparicio-Chi 56
Mantle-NY 21
Landis-Chi 20
Jensen-Bos 20
Allison-Was 13

Stolen Base Average
Mantle-NY 87.5
Aparicio-Chi 81.2
Jensen-Bos 80.0
Landis-Chi 69.0

Stolen Base Runs
Aparicio-Chi 7.8
Mantle-NY 3.6
Jensen-Bos 2.7
Malzone-Bos 1.3
Yost-Det 1.3

Fielding Runs
Gardner-Bal 30.5
Minoso-Cle 16.2
Landis-Chi 15.8
Jensen-Bos 15.1
Colavito-Cle 11.6

Total Player Rating
Mantle-NY 4.5
Kaline-Det 4.1
Jensen-Bos 3.6
Runnels-Bos 3.5
Minoso-Cle 3.4

Wins
Wynn-Chi 22
McLish-Cle 19
Shaw-Chi 18

Win Percentage
Shaw-Chi 750
McLish-Cle 704
Wynn-Chi 688
Mossi-Det 654

Games
Staley-Chi 67
Lown-Chi 60
Clevenger-Was 50
Shaw-Chi 47

Complete Games
Pascual-Was 17
Pappas-Bal 15
Mossi-Det 15
Wynn-Chi 14
Bunning-Det 14

Shutouts
Pascual-Was 6
Wynn-Chi 5
Pappas-Bal 4

Saves
Lown-Chi 15
Staley-Chi 14
Loes-Bal 14
Duren-NY 14
Fornieles-Bos 11

Innings Pitched
Wynn-Chi 255.2
Bunning-Det 249.2
Foytack-Det 240.1
Pascual-Was 238.2
McLish-Cle 235.1

Fewest Hits/Game
Score-Cle 6.89
Ditmar-NY 6.95
Wilhelm-Bal 7.09
Wynn-Chi 7.11
O'Dell-Bal 7.36

Fewest BB/Game
Brown-Bal 1.76
Lary-Det 1.86
Garver-KC 1.88
Mossi-Det 1.93
Ramos-Was 2.00

Strikeouts
Bunning-Det 201
Pascual-Was 185
Wynn-Chi 179
Score-Cle 147
Wilhelm-Bal 139

Strikeouts/Game
Score-Cle 8.23
Bunning-Det 7.25
Pascual-Was 6.98
Turley-NY 6.47
Wynn-Chi 6.30

Ratio
Ditmar-NY 9.62
Pascual-Was 10.33
Mossi-Det 10.34
O'Dell-Bal 10.43
Brown-Bal 10.48

Earned Run Average
Wilhelm-Bal 2.19
Pascual-Was 2.64
Shaw-Chi 2.69
Ditmar-NY 2.90
Walker-Bal 2.92

Adjusted ERA
Wilhelm-Bal 173
Pascual-Was 148
Shaw-Chi 140
Walker-Bal 130
O'Dell-Bal 129

Opponents' Batting Avg.
Score-Cle 210
Ditmar-NY 211
Wynn-Chi 216
O'Dell-Bal 220
Wilhelm-Bal 224

Opponents' On-Base Pct.
Ditmar-NY 270
Pascual-Was 284
O'Dell-Bal 286
Mossi-Det 286
Brown-Bal 290

Starter Runs
Wilhelm-Bal 42.0
Pascual-Was 32.4
Shaw-Chi 30.0
Ditmar-NY 21.7
Perry-Cle 20.6

Adjusted Starter Runs
Wilhelm-Bal 40.8
Pascual-Was 33.4
Shaw-Chi 28.0
Daley-KC 19.5
O'Dell-Bal 19.2

Clutch Pitching Index
Wilhelm-Bal 132
Daley-KC 122
Ford-NY 119
Shaw-Chi 114
McLish-Cle 114

Relief Runs
Staley-Chi 20.9
Duren-NY 16.9
Shantz-NY 15.6
Coates-NY 11.0
Lown-Chi 10.0

Adjusted Relief Runs
Staley-Chi 20.1
Duren-NY 15.9
Shantz-NY 14.1
Stobbs-Was 9.3
Lown-Chi 9.2

Relief Ranking
Staley-Chi 25.7
Duren-NY 23.4
Shantz-NY 14.4
Lown-Chi 13.1
Fornieles-Bos 10.1

Total Pitcher Index
Pascual-Was 5.0
Wilhelm-Bal 3.8
Daley-KC 3.4
Perry-Cle 3.0
Ford-NY 2.9

Total Baseball Ranking
Pascual-Was 5.0
Mantle-NY 4.5
Kaline-Det 4.1
Wilhelm-Bal 3.8
Jensen-Bos 3.6

TEAM	G	W	L	PCT	GB	R	OR	AB	H	2B	3B	HR	BB	SO	AVG	OBP	SLG	OPS	OPS+	BR	BR+	PF	CHI	RC	SB	CS	SBA	SBR
PIT	155	95	59	.617		**734**	**593**	5406	**1493**	**236**	56	120	486	**747**	**.276**	**.338**	.407	**745**	109	**72**	68	101	99	**737**	34	24	59	-1
MIL	154	88	66	.571	7	724	658	5263	1393	198	48	**170**	463	793	.265	.327	**.417**	744	**118**	60	**118**	93	102	714	69	37	65	2
STL	155	86	68	.558	9	639	616	5187	1317	213	48	138	501	792	.254	.323	.393	716	94	13	-39	109	97	652	48	35	58	-2
LA	154	82	72	.532	13	662	**593**	5227	1333	216	38	126	529	837	.255	.327	.383	710	94	6	-34	106	99	659	**95**	53	64	2
SF	156	79	75	.513	16	671	631	5324	1357	220	**62**	130	467	846	.255	.319	.393	712	106	1	43	94	102	663	86	45	**66**	**3**
CIN	154	67	87	.435	28	640	692	5289	1324	230	40	140	512	858	.250	.320	.388	708	98	-1	-12	102	97	661	73	37	**66**	**3**
CHI	156	60	94	.390	35	634	776	5311	1293	213	48	119	**531**	897	.243	.314	.369	683	94	-48	-41	99	**103**	617	51	34	60	-1
PHI	154	59	95	.383	36	546	691	5169	1235	196	44	99	448	1054	.239	.304	.351	655	85	-102	-103	100	102	546	45	48	48	-7
TOT	619					5250		42176	10745	1722	384	1042	3937	6824	.255	.322	.388	710							501	313	62	1

TEAM	CG	SH	SV	IP	H	H/G	HR	BB	SO	RAT	ERA	ERA+	OAV	OOB	PR	PR+	PF	CPI	FA	E	DP	FW	PW	BW	SBW	DIF
PIT	47	11	33	1399[2]	1363	8.8	**105**	**386**	811	**11.4**	3.50	107	.257	**.309**	42	41	100	99	**.979**	128	**163**	.8	4.3	7.0	-.1	6.2
MIL	**55**	13	28	1387[1]	1327	8.7	130	518	807	12.2	3.77	91	.251	.322	0	-57	91	99	.976	141	137	.0	-5.8	**12.2**	.2	4.6
STL	37	11	30	1371	1316	8.7	127	511	906	12.1	3.65	112	.253	.322	18	64	109	**103**	.976	141	152	.0	6.6	-4.0	-.2	6.7
LA	46	13	20	1398	**1218**	**7.9**	154	564	**1122**	11.7	**3.40**	**117**	**.234**	.312	**56**	**84**	106	**103**	**.979**	**125**	142	**.9**	**8.7**	-3.4	.2	-1.1
SF	**55**	**16**	26	1396	1288	8.4	107	512	897	11.8	3.45	101	.245	.315	50	6	93	99	.972	166	117	-1.3	.7	4.5	**.3**	-2.0
CIN	33	8	**35**	1390[1]	1417	9.2	134	442	740	12.4	4.01	96	.267	.328	-37	-27	102	101	**.979**	**125**	155	**.9**	-2.7	-1.2	**.3**	-7.1
CHI	36	6	25	1402[2]	1393	9.0	152	565	805	12.9	4.36	87	.260	.335	-92	-89	100	96	.977	143	133	.0	-9.1	-4.2	-.1	-3.4
PHI	45	6	16	1375[1]	1423	9.4	133	439	736	12.4	4.02	97	.270	.328	-38	-19	103	101	.974	155	129	-.7	-1.9	-10.5	-.7	-3.9
TOT	354	84	213	11120[1]		8.7				12.1	3.77		.255	.322					.977	1124	1128					

Runs
Bruton-Mil 112
Mathews-Mil 108
Pinson-Cin 107
Mays-SF 107
Aaron-Mil 102

Hits
Mays-SF 190
Pinson-Cin 187
Groat-Pit 186
Bruton-Mil 180
Clemente-Pit 179

Doubles
Pinson-Cin 37
Cepeda-SF 36
Skinner-Pit 33
Robinson-Cin 33
Banks-Chi 32

Triples
Bruton-Mil 13
Pinson-Cin 12
Mays-SF 12
Aaron-Mil 11

Home Runs
Banks-Chi 41
Aaron-Mil 40
Mathews-Mil 39
Boyer-StL 32
Robinson-Cin 31

Total Bases
Aaron-Mil 334
Banks-Chi 331
Mays-SF 330
Boyer-StL 310
Pinson-Cin 308

Runs Batted In
Aaron-Mil 126
Mathews-Mil 124
Banks-Chi 117
Mays-SF 103
Boyer-StL 97

Runs Produced
Mathews-Mil 193
Aaron-Mil 188
Mays-SF 181
Banks-Chi 170
Clemente-Pit 167

Bases On Balls
Ashburn-Chi 116
Mathews-Mil 111
Gilliam-LA 96
Robinson-Cin 82
Spencer-StL 81

Batting Average
Groat-Pit .325
Larker-LA .323
Mays-SF .319
Clemente-Pit .314
Boyer-StL .304

On-Base Percentage
Ashburn-Chi .416
Robinson-Cin .413
Mathews-Mil .401
Moon-LA .387
Mays-SF .386

Slugging Average
Robinson-Cin .595
Aaron-Mil .566
Boyer-StL .562
Mays-SF .555
Banks-Chi .554

On-Base Plus Slugging
Robinson-Cin 1007
Mathews-Mil 952
Mays-SF 941
Boyer-StL 934
Aaron-Mil 925

Adjusted OPS
Mathews-Mil 170
Robinson-Cin 169
Mays-SF 164
Aaron-Mil 161
Banks-Chi 145

Batter Runs
Robinson-Cin 47.8
Mathews-Mil 46.0
Mays-SF 43.5
Boyer-StL 37.9
Aaron-Mil 37.4

Adjusted Batter Runs
Mathews-Mil 55.8
Mays-SF 51.0
Aaron-Mil 46.4
Robinson-Cin 46.0
Banks-Chi 35.7

Clutch Hitting Index
Larker-LA 149
Mathews-Mil 120
Bailey-Cin 120
Stuart-Pit 114
Clemente-Pit 112

Runs Created
Mathews-Mil 128
Mays-SF 124
Aaron-Mil 119
Banks-Chi 113
Robinson-Cin 113

Total Average
Robinson-Cin 1.069
Mathews-Mil 1.029
Mays-SF .953
Aaron-Mil .935
Boyer-StL .918

Stolen Bases
Wills-LA 50
Pinson-Cin 32
T.Taylor-Chi-Phi 26
Mays-SF 25
Bruton-Mil 22

Stolen Base Average
Javier-StL 82.6
Wills-LA 80.6
Ashburn-Chi 80.0
Pinson-Cin 72.7
Mays-SF 71.4

Stolen Base Runs
Wills-LA 6.8
Pinson-Cin 2.8
Javier-StL 2.8
Blasingame-SF 2.4
Ashburn-Chi 2.1

Fielding Runs
Mazeroski-Pit 25.4
Wills-LA 20.5
Grammas-StL 19.8
Smith-StL 18.0
Mays-SF 13.7

Total Player Rating
Mays-SF 6.0
Banks-Chi 5.9
Aaron-Mil 5.1
Robinson-Cin 4.6
Mathews-Mil 4.3

Wins
Spahn-Mil 21
Broglio-StL 21
Law-Pit 20
Burdette-Mil 19

Win Percentage
Broglio-StL .700
Law-Pit .690
Spahn-Mil .677
Buhl-Mil .640
Purkey-Cin .607

Games
Face-Pit 68
McDaniel-StL 65
Elston-Chi 60
Farrell-Phi 59
Roebuck-LA 58

Complete Games
Spahn-Mil 18
Law-Pit 18
Burdette-Mil 18
Hobbie-Chi 16
Friend-Pit 16

Shutouts
Sanford-SF 6
Drysdale-LA 5

Saves
McDaniel-StL 26
Face-Pit 24
Henry-Cin 17
Brosnan-Cin 12

Innings Pitched
Jackson-StL 282.0
Friend-Pit 275.2
Burdette-Mil 275.2
Law-Pit 271.2
Drysdale-LA 269.0

Fewest Hits/Game
Broglio-StL 6.84
Koufax-LA 6.84
Williams-LA 7.03
Drysdale-LA 7.16
Buhl-Mil 7.62

Fewest BB/Game
Burdette-Mil 1.14
Roberts-Phi 1.29
Law-Pit 1.33
Friend-Pit 1.47
Haddix-Pit 1.98

Strikeouts
Drysdale-LA 246
Koufax-LA 197
S.Jones-SF 190
Broglio-StL 188
Friend-Pit 183

Strikeouts/Game
Koufax-LA 10.13
Drysdale-LA 8.23
Williams-LA 7.60
Broglio-StL 7.48
S.Jones-SF 7.31

Ratio
Drysdale-LA 9.90
Friend-Pit 10.15
Law-Pit 10.27
Burdette-Mil 10.35
Williams-LA 10.37

Earned Run Average
McCormick-SF 2.70
Broglio-StL 2.74
Drysdale-LA 2.84
Williams-LA 3.00
Friend-Pit 3.00

Adjusted ERA
Broglio-StL 149
Drysdale-LA 140
Simmons-Phi-StL 134
Williams-LA 133
Podres-LA 129

Opponents' Batting Avg.
Koufax-LA .207
Williams-LA .210
Broglio-StL .213
Drysdale-LA .215
Buhl-Mil .229

Opponents' On-Base Pct.
Drysdale-LA .275
Friend-Pit .281
Williams-LA .282
Law-Pit .287
Burdette-Mil .287

Starter Runs
McCormick-SF 29.8
Drysdale-LA 27.5
Broglio-StL 25.6
Friend-Pit 23.2
Law-Pit 20.6

Adjusted Starter Runs
Drysdale-LA 31.9
Broglio-StL 31.3
McCormick-SF 23.6
Friend-Pit 23.0
Williams-LA 21.3

Clutch Pitching Index
Simmons-Phi-StL 121
Podres-LA 117
O'Dell-SF 110
Sadecki-StL 109
Buhl-Mil 108

Relief Runs
McDaniel-StL 21.6
Brosnan-Cin 15.4
Roebuck-LA 12.8
Farrell-Phi 12.2
Face-Pit 10.9

Adjusted Relief Runs
McDaniel-StL 23.8
Brosnan-Cin 15.8
Roebuck-LA 14.7
Farrell-Phi 13.2
Face-Pit 10.8

Relief Ranking
McDaniel-StL 41.5
Farrell-Phi 21.5
Face-Pit 20.4
Brosnan-Cin 17.2
Roebuck-LA 14.7

Total Pitcher Index
McDaniel-StL 4.6
Broglio-StL 4.4
Drysdale-LA 4.1
McCormick-SF 2.9
Law-Pit 2.6

Total Baseball Ranking
Mays-SF 6.0
Banks-Chi 5.9
Aaron-Mil 5.1
Robinson-Cin 4.6
McDaniel-StL 4.6

TEAM	G	W	L	PCT	GB	R	OR	AB	H	2B	3B	HR	BB	SO	AVG	OBP	SLG	OPS	OPS+	BR	BR+	PF	CHI	RC	SB	CS	SBA	SBR
NY	155	97	57	.630		**746**	627	5290	1377	215	40	**193**	537	818	.260	.332	**.426**	**758**	**117**	**63**	**107**	94	100	**747**	37	23	62	0
BAL	154	89	65	.578	8	682	**606**	5170	1307	206	33	123	596	801	.253	.334	.377	711	99	-8	1	99	**103**	659	37	24	61	0
CHI	154	87	67	.565	10	741	617	5191	1402	**242**	38	112	567	648	**.270**	**.348**	.396	744	108	57	64	99	101	726	**122**	48	**72**	**10**
CLE	154	76	78	.494	21	667	693	5296	**1415**	218	20	127	444	**573**	.267	.328	.388	716	102	-11	10	97	101	673	58	25	70	4
WAS	154	73	81	.474	24	672	696	5248	1283	205	**43**	147	584	883	.244	.326	.384	710	99	-18	-11	99	101	656	52	43	55	-4
DET	154	71	83	.461	26	633	644	5202	1243	188	34	150	**636**	728	.239	.326	.375	701	93	-32	-49	103	97	651	66	32	67	3
BOS	154	65	89	.422	32	658	775	5215	1359	234	32	124	570	798	.261	.336	.389	725	99	16	-7	104	95	674	34	28	55	-2
KC	155	58	96	.377	39	615	756	5226	1303	212	34	110	513	744	.249	.318	.366	684	90	-68	-72	101	**103**	598	16	11	59	0
TOT	617					5414		41838	10689	1720	274	1086	4447	5993	.256	.331	.388	718							422	234	64	11

TEAM	CG	SH	SV	IP	H	H/G	HR	BB	SO	RAT	ERA	ERA+	OAV	OOB	PR	PR+	PF	CPI	FA	E	DP	FW	PW	BW	SBW	DIF
NY	38	**16**	**42**	1398	1225	**7.9**	123	609	712	12.1	**3.52**	102	**.238**	.322	**55**	11	93	98	.979	129	162	.2	1.2	**10.9**	-.1	8.1
BAL	**48**	11	22	1375[2]	**1222**	8.0	**117**	552	785	**11.9**	**3.52**	108	.241	.320	54	45	98	98	**.982**	**108**	172	**1.5**	4.6	.2	-.1	6.1
CHI	42	11	26	1381	1338	8.8	127	533	695	12.3	3.61	105	.258	.329	41	28	98	**106**	**.982**	109	**175**	1.4	2.9	6.5	**.9**	-1.5
CLE	32	10	30	1382[1]	1308	8.6	161	636	771	12.9	3.96	95	.252	.336	-12	-34	97	103	.978	128	165	.2	-3.4	1.1	.3	1.0
WAS	34	10	35	1405[1]	1392	9.0	130	538	775	12.6	3.78	103	.260	.331	16	18	100	103	.973	165	159	-2.1	1.9	-1.1	-.5	-2.0
DET	40	7	25	1405[2]	1336	8.6	141	**474**	**824**	**11.9**	3.64	**109**	.251	**.317**	37	**49**	102	99	.977	138	138	-.4	**5.0**	-4.9	.2	-5.7
BOS	34	6	23	1361	1440	9.6	127	580	767	13.6	4.63	87	.273	.349	-113	-84	104	94	.976	141	156	-.6	-8.4	-.7	-.3	-1.8
KC	44	4	14	1374	1428	9.4	160	525	664	13.1	4.38	91	.271	.342	-77	-59	103	100	.979	127	149	.3	-5.9	-7.2	-.1	-5.8
TOT	312	75	217	11083		8.7				12.6	3.88		.256	.331					.979	1045	1276					

Runs
Mantle-NY 119
Maris-NY 98
Minoso-Chi 89
Landis-Chi 89
Sievers-Chi 87

Hits
Minoso-Chi 184
Robinson-Bal 175
Fox-Chi 175
Smith-Chi 169
Runnels-Bos 169

Doubles
Francona-Cle 36
Skowron-NY 34
Minoso-Chi 32
Freese-Chi 32

Triples
Fox-Chi 10
Robinson-Bal 9

Home Runs
Mantle-NY 40
Maris-NY 39
Lemon-Was 38
Colavito-Det 35
Killebrew-Was 31

Total Bases
Mantle-NY 294
Maris-NY 290
Skowron-NY 284
Minoso-Chi 284
Lemon-Was 268

Runs Batted In
Maris-NY 112
Minoso-Chi 105
Wertz-Bos 103
Lemon-Was 100
Gentile-Bal 98

Runs Produced
Minoso-Chi 174
Mantle-NY 173
Maris-NY 171
Sievers-Chi 152
Robinson-Bal 148

Bases On Balls
Yost-Det 125
Mantle-NY 111
Allison-Was 92
Woodling-Bal 84
Landis-Chi 80

Batting Average
Runnels-Bos .... .320
Smith-Chi .... .315
Minoso-Chi .... .311
Skowron-NY .... .309
Kuenn-Cle .... .308

On-Base Percentage
Yost-Det .... .416
Woodling-Bal .... .403
Runnels-Bos .... .403
Mantle-NY .... .402
Sievers-Chi .... .399

Slugging Average
Maris-NY .... .581
Mantle-NY .... .558
Killebrew-Was .... .534
Sievers-Chi .... .534
Skowron-NY .... .528

On-Base Plus Slugging
Mantle-NY 960
Maris-NY 955
Sievers-Chi 933
Killebrew-Was 911
Skowron-NY 884

Adjusted OPS
Mantle-NY 166
Maris-NY 164
Sievers-Chi 152
Killebrew-Was 145
Skowron-NY 144

Batter Runs
Mantle-NY 43.9
Williams-Bos 43.5
Maris-NY 36.5
Sievers-Chi 32.1
Killebrew-Was 26.9

Adjusted Batter Runs
Mantle-NY 50.8
Maris-NY 42.6
Williams-Bos 40.5
Sievers-Chi 33.0
Skowron-NY 29.9

Clutch Hitting Index
Wertz-Bos 149
Power-Cle 115
Woodling-Bal 110
Fox-Chi 109
Minoso-Chi 109

Runs Created
Mantle-NY 125
Maris-NY 111
Minoso-Chi 104
Lemon-Was 99
Francona-Cle 96

Total Average
Mantle-NY 1.053
Maris-NY .... .992
Sievers-Chi .... .960
Killebrew-Was .... .936
Lemon-Was .... .871

Stolen Bases
Aparicio-Chi 51
Landis-Chi 23
Green-Was 21
Kaline-Det 19
Piersall-Cle 18

Stolen Base Average
Aparicio-Chi 86.4
Kaline-Det 82.6
Landis-Chi 79.3
Piersall-Cle 78.3
Green-Was 72.4

Stolen Base Runs
Aparicio-Chi 8.4
Landis-Chi 3.0
Kaline-Det 2.8
Piersall-Cle 2.2
Mantle-NY 2.0

Fielding Runs
Aparicio-Chi 30.4
Boyer-NY 27.6
Power-Cle 21.0
Tuttle-KC 17.1
Landis-Chi 12.9

Total Player Rating
Mantle-NY 4.5
Maris-NY 4.0
Aparicio-Chi 3.7
Williams-Bos 3.3
Skowron-NY 3.0

Wins
Perry-Cle 18
Estrada-Bal 18
B.Daley-KC 16

Win Percentage
Perry-Cle .... .643
Ditmar-NY .... .625
Estrada-Bal .... .621
Pappas-Bal .... .577

Games
Fornieles-Bos 70
Staley-Chi 64
Clevenger-Was 53
Moore-Chi-Was 51
Kutyna-KC 51

Complete Games
Lary-Det 15
Ramos-Was 14
Herbert-KC 14
Wynn-Chi 13
B.Daley-KC 13

Shutouts
Wynn-Chi 4
Perry-Cle 4
Ford-NY 4

Saves
Klippstein-Cle 14
Fornieles-Bos 14
Moore-Chi-Was 13
B.Shantz-NY 11

Innings Pitched
Lary-Det 274.1
Ramos-Was 274.0
Perry-Cle 261.1
Herbert-KC 252.2
Bunning-Det 252.0

Fewest Hits/Game
Estrada-Bal 6.99
Turley-NY 7.17
Barber-Bal 7.33
Bunning-Det 7.75
Ford-NY 7.85

Fewest BB/Game
Brown-Bal 1.25
Mossi-Det 1.82
Hall-KC 1.88
Lary-Det 2.03
Pierce-Chi 2.11

Strikeouts
Bunning-Det 201
Ramos-Was 160
Wynn-Chi 158
Lary-Det 149
Estrada-Bal 144

Strikeouts/Game
Bunning-Det 7.18
Bell-Cle 6.34
Estrada-Bal 6.21
Wynn-Chi 5.99
Monbouquette-Bos 5.61

Ratio
Brown-Bal 10.08
Bunning-Det 10.43
Baumann-Chi 10.83
Mossi-Det 10.86
Ford-NY 10.93

Earned Run Average
Baumann-Chi 2.67
Bunning-Det 2.79
Brown-Bal 3.06
Ditmar-NY 3.06
Ford-NY 3.08

Adjusted ERA
Bunning-Det 142
Baumann-Chi 141
Brown-Bal 125
Herbert-KC 121
Barber-Bal 118

Opponents' Batting Avg.
Estrada-Bal .... .218
Turley-NY .... .222
Barber-Bal .... .226
Ford-NY .... .235
Bunning-Det .... .236

Opponents' On-Base Pct.
Brown-Bal .... .286
Bunning-Det .... .293
Mossi-Det .... .296
Ford-NY .... .299
Terry-NY .... .300

Starter Runs
Bunning-Det 30.4
Baumann-Chi 24.7
Ditmar-NY 18.0
Ford-NY 16.9
Herbert-KC 16.7

Adjusted Starter Runs
Bunning-Det 32.1
Baumann-Chi 23.4
Herbert-KC 19.2
Pascual-Was 14.5
Kralick-Was 14.2

Clutch Pitching Index
Ditmar-NY 121
Perry-Cle 113
Lee-Was 113
Baumann-Chi 113
Herbert-KC 111

Relief Runs
Staley-Chi 18.6
Fornieles-Bos 14.9
Sisler-Det 12.4
Aguirre-Det 10.7
B.Shantz-NY 8.1

Adjusted Relief Runs
Staley-Chi 17.9
Fornieles-Bos 16.2
Sisler-Det 12.9
Aguirre-Det 11.4
Stobbs-Was 7.5

Relief Ranking
Staley-Chi 32.7
Fornieles-Bos 24.8
Sisler-Det 19.6
Klippstein-Cle 11.6
Aguirre-Det 11.4

Total Pitcher Index
Staley-Chi 3.8
Fornieles-Bos 2.8
Bunning-Det 2.6
Herbert-KC 2.5
Baumann-Chi 2.2

Total Baseball Ranking
Mantle-NY 4.5
Maris-NY 4.0
Staley-Chi 3.8
Aparicio-Chi 3.7
Williams-Bos 3.3

TEAM	G	W	L	PCT	GB	R	OR	AB	H	2B	3B	HR	BB	SO	AVG	OBP	SLG	OPS	OPS+	BR	BR+	PF	CHI	RC	SB	CS	SBA	SBR
CIN	154	93	61	.604		710	**653**	5243	1414	**247**	35	158	423	761	.270	.328	.421	749	102	19	10	101	101	713	70	33	**68**	**4**
LA	154	89	65	.578	4	735	697	5189	1358	193	40	157	**596**	796	.262	**.340**	.405	745	95	29	-30	109	100	722	**86**	45	66	3
SF	155	85	69	.552	8	**773**	655	5233	1379	219	32	183	506	764	.264	.332	**.423**	**755**	109	**35**	63	96	**106**	719	79	54	59	-2
MIL	155	83	71	.539	10	712	656	5288	1365	199	34	**188**	534	880	.258	.330	.415	745	**110**	19	**66**	94	98	714	70	43	62	0
STL	155	80	74	.519	13	703	668	5307	1436	236	51	103	494	745	.271	.336	.393	729	90	-3	-66	110	100	702	46	28	62	0
PIT	154	75	79	.487	18	694	675	5311	**1448**	232	**57**	128	428	**721**	**.273**	.330	.410	740	101	8	6	100	99	694	26	30	46	-5
CHI	156	64	90	.416	29	689	800	5344	1364	238	51	176	539	1027	.255	.327	.418	745	101	16	7	101	95	**726**	35	25	58	-1
PHI	155	47	107	.305	46	584	796	5213	1265	185	50	103	475	928	.243	.311	.357	668	84	-123	-115	99	102	577	56	30	65	2
TOT	619					5600		42128	11029	1749	350	1196	3995	6622	.262	.330	.406	735							468	288	62	2

TEAM	CG	SH	SV	IP	H	H/G	HR	BB	SO	RAT	ERA	ERA+	OAV	OOB	PR	PR+	PF	CPI	FA	E	DP	FW	PW	BW	SBW	DIF
CIN	46	**12**	**40**	1370	**1300**	8.6	147	500	829	12.1	3.79	107	.250	.320	38	42	101	98	.977	134	124	.7	4.2	1.0	**.4**	9.9
LA	40	10	35	1378[1]	1346	8.8	167	544	**1105**	12.7	4.05	107	.256	.331	-2	43	108	101	.975	144	162	.2	4.3	-2.9	.3	10.4
SF	39	9	30	1388	1306	**8.5**	152	502	924	**12.0**	3.78	101	**.249**	**.318**	40	6	95	98	.977	133	126	.8	.6	6.3	-.2	.7
MIL	**57**	8	16	1391[1]	1357	8.8	153	493	652	12.2	3.90	96	.258	.324	21	-26	93	101	**.982**	**111**	152	**2.1**	-2.5	**6.6**	-.0	.0
STL	49	10	24	1368[2]	1334	8.8	136	570	823	12.7	**3.75**	**118**	.256	.333	**44**	**92**	109	**106**	.972	166	165	-1.0	**9.2**	-6.5	-.0	1.6
PIT	34	9	29	1362	1442	9.6	**121**	**400**	759	12.4	3.92	102	.274	.328	17	10	99	102	.975	150	**187**	-.2	1.0	.6	-.5	-2.8
CHI	34	6	25	1385	1492	9.7	165	465	755	13.0	4.49	93	.277	.338	-70	-45	104	99	.970	183	175	-1.9	-4.4	.7	-.1	-7.1
PHI	29	9	13	1383[1]	1452	9.5	155	521	775	13.1	4.61	88	.273	.342	-88	-81	101	96	.976	146	179	.0	-8.0	-11.4	.2	-10.7
TOT	328	73	212	11026[2]		9.1				12.5	4.04		.262	.330					.976	1167	1270					

Runs
Mays-SF 129
Robinson-Cin 117
Aaron-Mil 115
Boyer-StL 109

Hits
Pinson-Cin 208
Clemente-Pit 201
Aaron-Mil 197
Boyer-StL 194
Cepeda-SF 182

Doubles
Aaron-Mil 39
Pinson-Cin 34
Santo-Chi 32
Robinson-Cin 32
Mays-SF 32

Triples
Altman-Chi 12
White-StL 11
Callison-Phi 11
Boyer-StL 11

Home Runs
Cepeda-SF 46
Mays-SF 40
Robinson-Cin 37
Stuart-Pit 35
Adcock-Mil 35

Total Bases
Aaron-Mil 358
Cepeda-SF 356
Mays-SF 334
Robinson-Cin 333
Clemente-Pit 320

Runs Batted In
Cepeda-SF 142
Robinson-Cin 124
Mays-SF 123
Aaron-Mil 120
Stuart-Pit 117

Runs Produced
Mays-SF 212
Robinson-Cin 204
Cepeda-SF 201
Aaron-Mil 201
Boyer-StL 180

Bases On Balls
Mathews-Mil 93
Moon-LA 89
Mays-SF 81
Gilliam-LA 79

Batting Average
Clemente-Pit .351
Pinson-Cin .343
Boyer-StL .329
Moon-LA .328
Aaron-Mil .327

On-Base Percentage
Moon-LA .438
Robinson-Cin .411
Mathews-Mil .405
Boyer-StL .400
Mays-SF .395

Slugging Average
Robinson-Cin .611
Cepeda-SF .609
Aaron-Mil .594
Mays-SF .584
Stuart-Pit .581

On-Base Plus Slugging
Robinson-Cin 1022
Aaron-Mil 979
Mays-SF 979
Cepeda-SF 972
Clemente-Pit 951

Adjusted OPS
Aaron-Mil 165
Robinson-Cin 164
Mays-SF 162
Cepeda-SF 158
Mathews-Mil 156

Batter Runs
Robinson-Cin 52.4
Aaron-Mil 46.0
Mays-SF 45.8
Cepeda-SF 40.7
Mathews-Mil 40.4

Adjusted Batter Runs
Aaron-Mil 54.1
Robinson-Cin 50.8
Mays-SF 50.5
Mathews-Mil 48.2
Cepeda-SF 45.2

Clutch Hitting Index
Moon-LA 113
McMillan-Mil 110
Davenport-SF 110
Adcock-Mil 105
Cepeda-SF 105

Runs Created
Robinson-Cin 137
Aaron-Mil 132
Mays-SF 130
Mathews-Mil 128
Boyer-StL 126

Total Average
Robinson-Cin 1.119
Mays-SF 1.017
Moon-LA 1.003
Aaron-Mil .993
Mathews-Mil .981

Stolen Bases
Wills-LA 35
Pinson-Cin 23
Robinson-Cin 22
Aaron-Mil 21
Mays-SF 18

Stolen Base Average
Robinson-Cin 88.0
Wills-LA 70.0
Aaron-Mil 70.0
Pinson-Cin 69.7
Mays-SF 66.7

Stolen Base Runs
Robinson-Cin 3.8
Wills-LA 2.5
Maye-Mil 1.9
Pinson-Cin 1.6
Gonzalez-Phi 1.5

Fielding Runs
Mazeroski-Pit 30.5
Pinson-Cin 19.2
Malkmus-Phi 16.3
Clemente-Pit 14.4
Amaro-Phi 14.1

Total Player Rating
Aaron-Mil 5.8
Mays-SF 5.5
Robinson-Cin 5.3
Clemente-Pit 4.2
Pinson-Cin 4.2

Wins
Spahn-Mil 21
Jay-Cin 21
O'Toole-Cin 19

Win Percentage
Podres-LA .783
O'Toole-Cin .679
Jay-Cin .677
Burdette-Mil .621
Spahn-Mil .618

Games
Baldschun-Phi 65
Miller-SF 63
Face-Pit 62
Elston-Chi 58
Anderson-Chi 57

Complete Games
Spahn-Mil 21
Koufax-LA 15
Jay-Cin 14
Burdette-Mil 14

Shutouts
Spahn-Mil 4
Jay-Cin 4

Saves
Miller-SF 17
Face-Pit 17
Henry-Cin 16
Brosnan-Cin 16
L.Sherry-LA 15

Innings Pitched
Burdette-Mil 272.1
Spahn-Mil 262.2
Cardwell-Chi 259.1
Koufax-LA 255.2
O'Toole-Cin 252.2

Fewest Hits/Game
Koufax-LA 7.46
Jay-Cin 7.90
Gibson-StL 7.92
Sadecki-StL 7.92
Spahn-Mil 8.09

Fewest BB/Game
Burdette-Mil 1.09
Friend-Pit 1.72
Purkey-Cin 1.86
Spahn-Mil 2.19
Ellsworth-Chi 2.31

Strikeouts
Koufax-LA 269
Williams-LA 205
Drysdale-LA 182
O'Toole-Cin 178
Gibson-StL 166

Strikeouts/Game
Koufax-LA 9.47
Williams-LA 7.84
Gibson-StL 7.07
Drysdale-LA 6.71
Gibbon-Pit 6.68

Ratio
Spahn-Mil 10.42
Burdette-Mil 10.94
Koufax-LA 10.95
Purkey-Cin 11.03
Jackson-StL 11.22

Earned Run Average
Spahn-Mil 3.02
O'Toole-Cin 3.10
Simmons-StL 3.13
McCormick-SF 3.20
Gibson-StL 3.24

Adjusted ERA
Simmons-StL 141
Gibson-StL 136
O'Toole-Cin 131
Spahn-Mil 124
Koufax-LA 123

Opponents' Batting Avg.
Koufax-LA .222
Jay-Cin .236
Sadecki-StL .238
Gibson-StL .239
O'Toole-Cin .240

Opponents' On-Base Pct.
Spahn-Mil .293
Koufax-LA .295
Burdette-Mil .296
Purkey-Cin .297
Jackson-StL .303

Starter Runs
Spahn-Mil 29.7
O'Toole-Cin 26.2
McCormick-SF 23.0
Simmons-StL 19.6
Gibson-StL 18.7

Adjusted Starter Runs
O'Toole-Cin 26.9
Simmons-StL 25.3
Gibson-StL 25.0
Spahn-Mil 22.8
Koufax-LA 21.7

Clutch Pitching Index
Simmons-StL 122
Ellsworth-Chi 121
Podres-LA 116
McCormick-SF 115
Gibson-StL 114

Relief Runs
Miller-SF 18.6
Perranoski-LA 14.1
McMahon-Mil 12.2
Henry-Cin 10.9
Schultz-Chi 9.9

Adjusted Relief Runs
Miller-SF 16.6
Perranoski-LA 16.0
Henry-Cin 11.0
Schultz-Chi 10.6
McMahon-Mil 10.0

Relief Ranking
Miller-SF 28.4
Perranoski-LA 21.2
Schultz-Chi 21.1
Brosnan-Cin 18.1
Henry-Cin 13.0

Total Pitcher Index
Spahn-Mil 4.2
Miller-SF 3.3
Gibson-StL 3.0
Simmons-StL 2.8
O'Toole-Cin 2.7

Total Baseball Ranking
Aaron-Mil 5.8
Mays-SF 5.5
Robinson-Cin 5.3
Clemente-Pit 4.2
Pinson-Cin 4.2

TEAM	G	W	L	PCT	GB	R	OR	AB	H	2B	3B	HR	BB	SO	AVG	OBP	SLG	OPS	OPS+	BR	BR+	PF	CHI	RC	SB	CS	SBA	SBR
NY	163	109	53	.673		827	612	5559	1461	194	40	**240**	543	785	.263	.332	**.442**	**774**	**118**	82	**127**	95	101	811	28	18	61	0
DET	163	101	61	.623	8	**841**	671	5561	1481	215	**53**	180	673	867	**.266**	**.349**	.421	770	109	**96**	73	103	99	**835**	98	36	73	**9**
BAL	163	95	67	.586	14	691	**588**	5481	1393	227	36	149	581	902	.254	.328	.390	718	102	-16	10	97	97	699	39	30	57	-2
CHI	163	86	76	.531	23	765	726	5556	1475	216	46	138	550	**612**	.265	.338	.395	733	104	17	29	98	101	754	**100**	40	71	8
CLE	161	78	83	.484	30.5	737	752	5609	**1493**	**257**	39	150	492	720	**.266**	.328	.406	734	105	9	30	97	99	743	34	11	**76**	4
BOS	163	76	86	.469	33	729	792	5508	1401	251	37	112	647	847	.254	.336	.374	710	94	-22	-39	102	101	704	56	36	61	0
MIN	161	70	90	.438	38	707	778	5417	1353	215	40	167	597	840	.250	.328	.397	725	95	-5	-43	106	98	698	47	43	52	-5
LA	162	70	91	.435	38.5	744	784	5424	1331	218	22	189	**681**	1068	.245	.333	.398	731	91	12	-64	111	99	734	37	28	57	-2
WAS	161	61	100	.379	47.5	618	776	5366	1307	217	44	119	558	917	.244	.317	.367	684	90	-83	-73	99	98	625	81	47	63	1
KC	162	61	100	.379	47.5	683	863	5423	1342	216	47	90	580	772	.247	.323	.354	677	85	-90	-101	102	**107**	642	58	22	73	5
TOT	811					7342		54904	14037	2226	404	1534	5902	8330	.256	.332	.395	726							578	311	65	18

TEAM	CG	SH	SV	IP	H	H/G	HR	BB	SO	RAT	ERA	ERA+	OAV	OOB	PR	PR+	PF	CPI	FA	E	DP	FW	PW	BW	SBW	DIF
NY	47	14	**39**	1451	1288	8.0	137	542	866	11.6	3.47	107	.239	.312	91	45	92	99	**.980**	**124**	**180**	**1.7**	4.5	**12.6**	-.2	9.6
DET	**62**	12	30	1459[1]	1404	8.7	170	**469**	836	11.8	3.55	116	.252	.313	78	88	102	**106**	.976	146	147	.4	8.8	7.3	**.7**	3.1
BAL	54	**21**	33	1471[1]	**1226**	**7.5**	**109**	617	926	**11.5**	**3.22**	**120**	**.227**	**.310**	**132**	**108**	96	97	**.980**	128	173	1.4	**10.8**	1.0	-.4	1.4
CHI	39	3	33	1448[2]	1491	9.3	158	498	814	12.5	4.06	97	.268	.329	-5	-23	97	102	**.980**	128	138	1.4	-2.2	2.9	.6	2.5
CLE	35	12	23	1443[1]	1426	8.9	178	599	801	12.9	4.15	95	.258	.334	-20	-34	98	102	.977	139	142	.7	-3.3	3.0	.2	-2.9
BOS	35	6	30	1442[2]	1472	9.2	167	679	831	13.6	4.30	97	.266	.348	-43	-19	104	105	.977	144	170	.5	-1.8	-3.8	-.2	.5
MIN	49	14	23	1432[1]	1415	8.9	163	570	914	12.8	4.28	99	.256	.331	-41	-6	105	95	.972	174	150	-1.4	-.5	-4.2	-.7	-3.0
LA	25	5	34	1438	1391	8.8	180	713	**973**	13.4	4.32	105	.254	.343	-46	28	112	101	.969	192	154	-2.4	2.8	-6.3	-.4	-4.1
WAS	39	8	21	1425	1405	8.9	131	586	666	12.8	4.24	95	.260	.336	-33	-34	100	96	.975	156	171	-.3	-3.3	-7.2	-.0	-8.4
KC	32	5	23	1415	1519	9.7	141	629	703	14.0	4.75	88	.275	.355	-113	-85	104	97	.972	175	160	-1.4	-8.4	-10.0	.3	.1
TOT	417	100	289	14426[2]		8.8				12.7	4.03		.256	.332					.976	1506	1585					

Runs
Maris-NY . . . 132
Mantle-NY . . . 132
Colavito-Det . . . 129
Cash-Det . . . 119
Kaline-Det . . . 116

Hits
Cash-Det . . . 193
B.Robinson-Bal . . . 192
Kaline-Det . . . 190
Francona-Cle . . . 178
Richardson-NY . . . 173

Doubles
Kaline-Det . . . 41
B.Robinson-Bal . . . 38
Kubek-NY . . . 38
Siebern-KC . . . 36
Power-Cle . . . 34

Triples
Wood-Det . . . 14
Lumpe-KC . . . 9
Keough-Was . . . 9

Home Runs
Maris-NY . . . 61
Mantle-NY . . . 54
Killebrew-Min . . . 46
Gentile-Bal . . . 46
Colavito-Det . . . 45

Total Bases
Maris-NY . . . 366
Cash-Det . . . 354
Mantle-NY . . . 353
Colavito-Det . . . 338
Killebrew-Min . . . 328

Runs Batted In
Maris-NY . . . 142
Gentile-Bal . . . 141
Colavito-Det . . . 140
Cash-Det . . . 132
Mantle-NY . . . 128

Runs Produced
Colavito-Det . . . 224
Maris-NY . . . 213
Cash-Det . . . 210
Mantle-NY . . . 206
Gentile-Bal . . . 191

Bases On Balls
Mantle-NY . . . 126
Cash-Det . . . 124
Colavito-Det . . . 113
Killebrew-Min . . . 107
Allison-Min . . . 103

Batting Average
Cash-Det 361
Kaline-Det 324
Piersall-Cle 322
Mantle-NY 317
Gentile-Bal 302

On-Base Percentage
Cash-Det 488
Mantle-NY 452
Gentile-Bal 428
Pearson-LA 422
Killebrew-Min 409

Slugging Average
Mantle-NY 687
Cash-Det 662
Gentile-Bal 646
Maris-NY 620
Killebrew-Min 606

On-Base Plus Slugging
Cash-Det . . . 1150
Mantle-NY . . . 1138
Gentile-Bal . . . 1074
Killebrew-Min . . . 1015
Maris-NY . . . 997

Adjusted OPS
Mantle-NY . . . 210
Cash-Det . . . 198
Gentile-Bal . . . 189
Maris-NY . . . 170
Killebrew-Min . . . 159

Batter Runs
Cash-Det . . . 86.1
Mantle-NY . . . 76.3
Gentile-Bal . . . 59.1
Killebrew-Min . . . 52.9
Colavito-Det . . . 51.5

Adjusted Batter Runs
Mantle-NY . . . 84.6
Cash-Det . . . 81.6
Gentile-Bal . . . 63.8
Maris-NY . . . 56.7
Colavito-Det . . . 47.9

Clutch Hitting Index
Schilling-Bos . . . 120
Gentile-Bal . . . 115
Malzone-Bos . . . 115
Allison-Min . . . 111
Siebern-KC . . . 109

Runs Created
Cash-Det . . . 178
Mantle-NY . . . 174
Colavito-Det . . . 141
Gentile-Bal . . . 138
Maris-NY . . . 138

Total Average
Mantle-NY . . . 1.384
Cash-Det . . . 1.358
Gentile-Bal . . . 1.196
Killebrew-Min . . . 1.098
Colavito-Det . . . 1.051

Stolen Bases
Aparicio-Chi . . . 53
Howser-KC . . . 37
Wood-Det . . . 30
Hinton-Was . . . 22
Bruton-Det . . . 22

Stolen Base Average
Hinton-Was . . . 81.5
Howser-KC . . . 80.4
Aparicio-Chi . . . 80.3
Geiger-Bos . . . 80.0
Landis-Chi . . . 79.2

Stolen Base Runs
Aparicio-Chi . . . 7.1
Howser-KC . . . 5.0
Wood-Det . . . 3.5
Hinton-Was . . . 3.1
Bruton-Det . . . 2.7

Fielding Runs
Boyer-NY . . . 30.3
Landis-Chi . . . 19.3
Power-Cle . . . 18.1
Cottier-Det-Was . . . 16.9
Lumpe-KC . . . 16.0

Total Player Rating
Mantle-NY . . . 8.3
Cash-Det . . . 7.5
Gentile-Bal . . . 5.6
Colavito-Det . . . 4.7
Howard-NY . . . 4.3

Wins
Ford-NY . . . 25
Lary-Det . . . 23
Barber-Bal . . . 18
Bunning-Det . . . 17
Terry-NY . . . 16

Win Percentage
Ford-NY 862
Terry-NY 842
Arroyo-NY 750
Lary-Det 719

Games
Arroyo-NY . . . 65
Morgan-LA . . . 59
Lown-Chi . . . 59
Kunkel-KC . . . 58
Fornieles-Bos . . . 57

Complete Games
Lary-Det . . . 22
Pascual-Min . . . 15
Barber-Bal . . . 14

Shutouts
Pascual-Min . . . 8
Barber-Bal . . . 8
Pappas-Bal . . . 4
Lary-Det . . . 4
Bunning-Det . . . 4

Saves
Arroyo-NY . . . 29
Wilhelm-Bal . . . 18
Fornieles-Bos . . . 15
Moore-Min . . . 14
Fox-Det . . . 12

Innings Pitched
Ford-NY . . . 283.0
Lary-Det . . . 275.1
Bunning-Det . . . 268.0
Ramos-Min . . . 264.1
Pascual-Min . . . 252.1

Fewest Hits/Game
Estrada-Bal . . . 6.75
Pappas-Bal . . . 6.79
Barber-Bal . . . 7.03
Pascual-Min . . . 7.31
Donovan-Was . . . 7.36

Fewest BB/Game
Mossi-Det . . . 1.76
Brown-Bal . . . 1.78
Donovan-Was . . . 1.87
Terry-NY . . . 2.01
McClain-Was . . . 2.04

Strikeouts
Pascual-Min . . . 221
Ford-NY . . . 209
Bunning-Det . . . 194
Pizarro-Chi . . . 188
McBride-LA . . . 180

Strikeouts/Game
Pizarro-Chi . . . 8.69
Pascual-Min . . . 7.88
Estrada-Bal . . . 6.79
McBride-LA . . . 6.70
Ford-NY . . . 6.65

Ratio
Donovan-Was . . . 9.39
Terry-NY . . . 9.80
Brown-Bal . . . 10.10
Bunning-Det . . . 10.48
Lary-Det . . . 10.59

Earned Run Average
Donovan-Was . . . 2.40
Stafford-NY . . . 2.68
Mossi-Det . . . 2.96
Pappas-Bal . . . 3.04
Pizarro-Chi . . . 3.05

Adjusted ERA
Donovan-Was . . . 167
Stafford-NY . . . 139
Mossi-Det . . . 139
Archer-KC . . . 131
Schwall-Bos . . . 129

Opponents' Batting Avg.
Estrada-Bal 207
Pappas-Bal 208
Pascual-Min 217
Barber-Bal 218
Donovan-Was 224

Opponents' On-Base Pct.
Donovan-Was 269
Terry-NY 277
Bunning-Det 285
Brown-Bal 286
Ford-NY 292

Starter Runs
Hoeft-Bal . . . 30.7
Donovan-Was . . . 30.4
Stafford-NY . . . 29.2
Mossi-Det . . . 28.5
Ford-NY . . . 25.5

Adjusted Starter Runs
Donovan-Was . . . 30.3
Mossi-Det . . . 29.9
Hoeft-Bal . . . 29.3
Bunning-Det . . . 26.6
Lary-Det . . . 26.0

Clutch Pitching Index
Schwall-Bos . . . 131
Mossi-Det . . . 119
Shaw-Chi-KC . . . 116
Monbouquette-Bos . . . 115
McBride-LA . . . 112

Relief Runs
Arroyo-NY . . . 24.2
Wilhelm-Bal . . . 21.0
Morgan-LA . . . 17.0
Fox-Det . . . 16.6
Lown-Chi . . . 14.2

Adjusted Relief Runs
Arroyo-NY . . . 21.8
Wilhelm-Bal . . . 19.7
Morgan-LA . . . 19.6
Fox-Det . . . 16.8
Lown-Chi . . . 13.3

Relief Ranking
Arroyo-NY . . . 43.7
Wilhelm-Bal . . . 33.2
Fox-Det . . . 26.4
Morgan-LA . . . 24.0
Lown-Chi . . . 17.5

Total Pitcher Index
Arroyo-NY . . . 4.6
Donovan-Was . . . 3.7
Lary-Det . . . 3.6
Wilhelm-Bal . . . 3.4
Stafford-NY . . . 2.8

Total Baseball Ranking
Mantle-NY . . . 8.3
Cash-Det . . . 7.5
Gentile-Bal . . . 5.6
Colavito-Det . . . 4.7
Arroyo-NY . . . 4.6

TEAM	G	W	L	PCT	GB	R	OR	AB	H	2B	3B	HR	BB	SO	AVG	OBP	SLG	OPS	OPS+	BR	BR+	PF	CHI	RC	SB	CS	SBA	SBR
SF	165	103	62	.624		**878**	690	5588	**1552**	235	32	**204**	523	822	**.278**	**.344**	**.441**	**785**	**119**	**123**	**138**	98	102	**838**	73	50	59	-1
LA	165	102	63	.618	1	842	697	5628	1510	192	**65**	140	572	886	.268	.339	.400	739	112	41	92	94	**107**	783	**198**	43	**82**	**29**
CIN	162	98	64	.605	3.5	802	685	5645	1523	**252**	40	167	498	903	.270	.333	.417	750	104	54	30	103	102	779	66	39	63	1
PIT	161	93	68	.578	8	706	**626**	5483	1468	240	**65**	108	432	836	.268	.323	.394	717	99	-15	-16	100	102	682	50	39	56	-3
MIL	162	86	76	.531	15.5	730	665	5458	1376	204	38	181	581	975	.252	.328	.403	731	105	16	36	97	99	720	57	27	68	3
STL	163	84	78	.519	17.5	774	664	5643	1528	221	31	137	515	846	.271	.337	.394	731	94	22	-45	110	102	747	86	41	68	5
PHI	161	81	80	.503	20	705	759	5420	1410	199	39	142	531	923	.260	.332	.390	722	103	4	26	97	98	705	79	42	65	3
HOU	162	64	96	.400	36.5	592	717	5558	1370	170	47	105	493	**806**	.246	.312	.351	663	91	-117	-68	93	97	605	42	30	58	-1
CHI	162	59	103	.364	42.5	632	827	5534	1398	196	56	126	504	1044	.253	.319	.377	696	90	-53	-76	104	94	657	78	50	61	0
NY	161	40	120	.250	60.5	617	948	5492	1318	166	40	139	**616**	991	.240	.320	.361	681	88	-75	-85	102	94	640	59	48	55	-4
TOT	812					7278		55449	14453	2075	453	1449	5265	9032	.261	.329	.393	722							788	409	66	30

TEAM	CG	SH	SV	IP	H	H/G	HR	BB	SO	RAT	ERA	ERA+	OAV	OOB	PR	PR+	PF	CPI	FA	E	DP	FW	PW	BW	SBW	DIF
SF	**62**	10	39	1461^{2}	1399	8.7	148	503	886	**11.9**	3.80	100	.251	**.316**	24	0	96	95	.977	142	153	1.0	.0	**13.8**	-.4	6.2
LA	44	8	**46**	1488^{2}	**1386**	**8.4**	115	588	**1104**	12.2	3.62	100	**.245**	.319	54	3	92	94	.970	193	144	-2.0	.3	9.2	**2.6**	9.6
CIN	51	13	35	1460^{2}	1397	8.7	149	567	964	12.4	3.76	107	.254	.329	31	43	102	104	.977	145	144	.7	4.3	3.0	-.2	9.3
PIT	40	13	41	1432^{1}	1433	9.1	118	466	897	12.1	**3.38**	117	.262	.322	**90**	89	100	**110**	.976	152	**177**	.2	8.9	-1.5	-.6	5.7
MIL	59	10	24	1434^{2}	1443	9.1	151	**407**	802	**11.9**	3.68	103	.262	.317	42	20	96	103	**.980**	**124**	154	**1.9**	2.0	3.6	.0	-2.4
STL	53	**17**	25	1463^{1}	1394	8.6	149	517	914	12.0	3.55	**120**	.252	.319	64	**108**	108	104	.979	132	170	1.5	**10.8**	-4.4	.2	-4.9
PHI	43	7	24	1426^{2}	1469	9.3	155	574	863	13.2	4.28	90	.268	.343	-53	-66	98	102	.977	138	167	1.0	-6.5	2.6	.0	3.6
HOU	34	9	19	1453^{2}	1446	9.0	**113**	471	1047	12.1	3.83	98	.259	.321	19	-15	95	95	.973	173	149	-1.0	-1.4	-6.7	-.4	-6.2
CHI	29	4	26	1438^{1}	1509	9.5	159	601	783	13.5	4.54	91	.272	.348	-95	-59	105	99	.977	146	171	.6	-5.8	-7.5	-.3	-8.7
NY	43	4	10	1430	1577	10.0	192	571	772	13.9	5.05	83	.281	.352	-175	-129	106	96	.967	210	167	-3.3	-12.8	-8.4	-.7	-14.6
TOT	458	95	289	14490		9.0				12.5	3.95		.261	.329					.976	1555	1596					

Runs
Robinson-Cin 134
Wills-LA. 130
Mays-SF 130
H.Aaron-Mil 127
T.Davis-LA 120

Hits
T.Davis-LA 230
Wills-LA. 208
Robinson-Cin 208
White-StL 199
Groat-Pit 199

Doubles
Robinson-Cin 51
Mays-SF 36
Groat-Pit 34

Triples
Wills-LA 10
Virdon-Pit 10
W.Davis-LA 10
Callison-Phi 10

Home Runs
Mays-SF 49
H.Aaron-Mil 45
Robinson-Cin 39
Banks-Chi 37
Cepeda-SF 35

Total Bases
Mays-SF 382
Robinson-Cin 380
H.Aaron-Mil 366
T.Davis-LA 356
Cepeda-SF 324

Runs Batted In
T.Davis-LA 153
Mays-SF 141
Robinson-Cin 136
H.Aaron-Mil 128
Howard-LA 119

Runs Produced
T.Davis-LA 246
Robinson-Cin 231
Mays-SF 222
H.Aaron-Mil 210

Bases On Balls
Mathews-Mil 101
Gilliam-LA 93
Ashburn-NY 81
Mays-SF 78

Batting Average
T.Davis-LA 346
Robinson-Cin 342
Musial-StL 330
White-StL 324
H.Aaron-Mil 323

On-Base Percentage
Robinson-Cin 424
Musial-StL 420
Skinner-Pit 397
Altman-Chi 394
H.Aaron-Mil 393

Slugging Average
Robinson-Cin 624
H.Aaron-Mil 618
Mays-SF 615
Howard-LA 560
T.Davis-LA 535

On-Base Plus Slugging
Robinson-Cin 1048
H.Aaron-Mil 1012
Mays-SF 1001
Musial-StL 928
T.Davis-LA 914

Adjusted OPS
Robinson-Cin 172
H.Aaron-Mil 171
Mays-SF 167
T.Davis-LA 151
Howard-LA 149

Batter Runs
Robinson-Cin 66.6
Mays-SF 54.1
H.Aaron-Mil 54.0
T.Davis-LA 37.2
Altman-Chi 31.5

Adjusted Batter Runs
Robinson-Cin 62.0
H.Aaron-Mil 57.7
Mays-SF 56.4
T.Davis-LA 45.0
Howard-LA 30.6

Clutch Hitting Index
T.Davis-LA 125
Howard-LA 122
Musial-StL 112
Fairly-LA 112
Santo-Chi 111

Runs Created
Robinson-Cin 160
Mays-SF 146
H.Aaron-Mil 140
T.Davis-LA 129
White-StL 114

Total Average
Robinson-Cin 1.125
Mays-SF 1.060
H.Aaron-Mil 1.050
Musial-StL 957
Skinner-Pit 930

Stolen Bases
Wills-LA 104
W.Davis-LA 32
Pinson-Cin 26
Javier-StL 26
Taylor-Phi 20

Stolen Base Average
Mays-SF 90.0
Wills-LA 88.9
W.Davis-LA 82.1
Clendenon-Pit 80.0
Pinson-Cin 76.5

Stolen Base Runs
Wills-LA 18.3
W.Davis-LA 4.6
Mays-SF 3.3
Pinson-Cin 2.9
Javier-StL 2.6

Fielding Runs
Mazeroski-Pit 41.1
Callison-Phi 22.9
Flood-StL 15.7
Williams-Chi 15.5
Kanehl-NY 14.5

Total Player Rating
Mays-SF 6.7
Robinson-Cin 5.9
H.Aaron-Mil 5.7
Mazeroski-Pit 4.8
T.Davis-LA 3.9

Wins
Drysdale-LA 25
Sanford-SF 24
Purkey-Cin 23
Jay-Cin 21

Win Percentage
Purkey-Cin 821
Sanford-SF 774
Drysdale-LA 735
Pierce-SF 727
Shaw-Mil 625

Games
Perranoski-LA 70
Baldschun-Phi 67
Roebuck-LA 64
Face-Pit 63
Olivo-Pit 62

Complete Games
Spahn-Mil 22
O'Dell-SF 20
Mahaffey-Phi 20
Drysdale-LA 19

Shutouts
Gibson-StL 5
Friend-Pit 5

Saves
Face-Pit 28
Perranoski-LA 20
Miller-SF 19
McDaniel-StL 14

Innings Pitched
Drysdale-LA 314.1
Purkey-Cin 288.1
O'Dell-SF 280.2
Mahaffey-Phi 274.0
Jay-Cin 273.0

Fewest Hits/Game
Koufax-LA 6.54
Gibson-StL 6.70
Bennett-Phi 7.42
Drysdale-LA 7.79
Broglio-StL 7.81

Fewest BB/Game
Shaw-Mil 1.76
Friend-Pit 1.82
Spahn-Mil 1.84
Pierce-SF 1.94
Purkey-Cin 2.00

Strikeouts
Drysdale-LA 232
Koufax-LA 216
Gibson-StL 208
Farrell-Hou 203
O'Dell-SF 195

Strikeouts/Game
Koufax-LA 10.55
Johnson-Hou 8.13
Gibson-StL 8.01
Bennett-Phi 7.68
Farrell-Hou 7.56

Ratio
Koufax-LA 9.42
Farrell-Hou 10.06
Spahn-Mil 10.23
Pierce-SF 10.26
Drysdale-LA 10.34

Earned Run Average
Koufax-LA 2.54
Shaw-Mil 2.80
Purkey-Cin 2.81
Drysdale-LA 2.83
Gibson-StL 2.85

Adjusted ERA
Gibson-StL 150
Purkey-Cin 143
Koufax-LA 143
Broglio-StL 142
Shaw-Mil 136

Opponents' Batting Avg.
Koufax-LA 197
Gibson-StL 204
Bennett-Phi 224
Drysdale-LA 230
Farrell-Hou 233

Opponents' On-Base Pct.
Koufax-LA 261
Farrell-Hou 280
Drysdale-LA 283
Pierce-SF 284
Spahn-Mil 287

Starter Runs
Drysdale-LA 38.6
Purkey-Cin 36.3
Koufax-LA 28.7
Shaw-Mil 28.5
Gibson-StL 28.3

Adjusted Starter Runs
Purkey-Cin 38.1
Gibson-StL 34.0
Drysdale-LA 30.2
Broglio-StL 29.0
Shaw-Mil 25.8

Clutch Pitching Index
Shaw-Mil 123
Friend-Pit 119
Broglio-StL 116
McBean-Pit 114
Koonce-Chi 111

Relief Runs
Face-Pit 20.8
McMahon-Mil-Hou . . 19.9
Shantz-Hou-StL 17.3
Umbricht-Hou 14.3
Perranoski-LA 13.0

Adjusted Relief Runs
Face-Pit 20.8
McMahon-Mil-Hou . . 19.1
Shantz-Hou-StL 18.1
Umbricht-Hou 13.5
Elston-Chi 11.9

Relief Ranking
Face-Pit 41.6
McMahon-Mil-Hou . . 28.0
Shantz-Hou-StL 22.8
Elston-Chi 22.7
Baldschun-Phi 20.7

Total Pitcher Index
Gibson-StL 4.7
Face-Pit 4.1
Drysdale-LA 3.7
Purkey-Cin 3.5
Spahn-Mil 3.2

Total Baseball Ranking
Mays-SF 6.7
Robinson-Cin 5.9
H.Aaron-Mil 5.7
Mazeroski-Pit 4.8
Gibson-StL 4.7

TEAM	G	W	L	PCT	GB	R	OR	AB	H	2B	3B	HR	BB	SO	AVG	OBP	SLG	OPS	OPS+	BR	BR+	PF	CHI	RC	SB	CS	SBA	SBR
NY	162	96	66	.593		**817**	680	5644	**1509**	240	29	199	584	842	**.267**	.339	**.426**	**765**	**116**	**87**	**114**	97	99	**816**	42	29	59	-1
MIN	163	91	71	.562	5	798	713	5561	1445	215	39	185	649	823	.260	**.340**	.412	752	104	67	38	104	100	789	33	20	62	0
LA	162	86	76	.531	10	718	706	5499	1377	232	35	137	602	917	.250	.328	.380	708	100	-23	0	97	**103**	698	46	27	63	1
DET	161	85	76	.528	10.5	758	692	5456	1352	191	36	**209**	**651**	894	.248	.332	.411	743	102	41	15	104	100	757	69	21	77	8
CHI	162	85	77	.525	11	707	**658**	5514	1415	250	56	92	620	**674**	.257	.336	.372	708	97	-13	-9	100	99	701	76	40	66	3
CLE	162	80	82	.494	16	682	745	5484	1341	202	22	180	502	939	.245	.314	.388	702	97	-46	-25	97	**103**	671	35	16	69	2
BAL	162	77	85	.475	19	652	680	5491	1363	225	34	156	516	931	.248	.316	.387	703	101	-42	3	94	98	665	45	32	58	-1
BOS	160	76	84	.475	19	707	756	5530	1429	**257**	53	146	525	923	.258	.326	.403	729	99	9	-13	103	98	716	39	33	54	-3
KC	162	72	90	.444	24	745	837	5576	1467	220	**58**	116	556	803	.263	.334	.386	720	96	3	-30	105	102	738	76	21	**78**	**9**
WAS	162	60	101	.373	35.5	599	716	5484	1370	206	38	132	466	789	.250	.310	.373	683	90	-82	-77	99	97	623	**99**	53	65	3
TOT	809					7183		55239	14068	2238	400	1552	5671	8535	.255	.328	.394	722							560	292	66	21

TEAM	CG	SH	SV	IP	H	H/G	HR	BB	SO	RAT	ERA	ERA+	OAV	OOB	PR	PR+	PF	CPI	FA	E	DP	FW	PW	BW	SBW	DIF
NY	33	10	42	1470[1]	1375	**8.5**	146	499	838	**11.7**	3.71	101	**.247**	**.312**	44	8	94	96	.979	131	151	.4	.9	**11.5**	-.3	2.7
MIN	**53**	11	27	1463[1]	1400	8.7	166	**493**	**948**	12.0	3.90	105	.253	.319	13	30	103	99	.980	129	**173**	.6	3.1	3.9	-.2	2.9
LA	23	**15**	**47**	1466	1412	8.7	**118**	616	858	12.8	**3.70**	104	.253	.332	**45**	27	97	104	.973	175	153	-2.1	2.8	.0	-.1	4.6
DET	46	8	35	1443[2]	1452	9.1	169	503	873	12.4	3.81	**107**	.259	.323	26	**41**	103	**105**	.974	156	114	-1.1	**4.2**	1.6	.6	-.5
CHI	50	13	28	1451[2]	1380	8.6	123	537	821	12.1	3.74	105	.251	.320	38	29	98	97	**.982**	**110**	153	**1.6**	3.0	-.9	.0	.4
CLE	45	12	31	1441	1410	8.9	174	594	780	12.8	4.15	94	.258	.334	-27	-44	98	102	.978	139	168	-.0	-4.4	-2.5	-.0	6.1
BAL	32	8	33	1462[1]	**1373**	**8.5**	147	549	898	12.1	**3.70**	100	.249	.320	**45**	1	93	101	.980	122	152	.9	.2	.4	-.3	-4.9
BOS	34	12	40	1437[2]	1416	8.9	159	632	923	13.1	4.22	98	.258	.339	-40	-14	104	101	.979	131	152	.3	-1.4	-1.3	-.5	-1.0
KC	32	4	33	1434	1450	9.2	199	655	825	13.5	4.80	88	.263	.346	-131	-85	106	97	.979	132	131	.4	-8.5	-3.0	**.7**	1.6
WAS	38	11	13	1445	1400	8.8	151	593	771	12.6	4.05	100	.256	.331	-12	-1	102	100	.978	139	160	-.0	-.0	-7.7	.0	-12.6
TOT	386	104	329	14515		8.8				12.5	3.98		.255	.328					.979	1364	1507					

Runs
Pearson-LA 115
Siebern-KC 114
Allison-Min 102
Yastrzemski-Bos 99
Richardson-NY 99

Hits
Richardson-NY 209
Lumpe-KC 193
B.Robinson-Bal 192
Yastrzemski-Bos ... 191
Robinson-Chi 187

Doubles
Robinson-Chi 45
Yastrzemski-Bos 43
Bressoud-Bos 40
Richardson-NY 38

Triples
Cimoli-KC 15
Robinson-Chi 10
Lumpe-KC 10
Clinton-Bos 10

Home Runs
Killebrew-Min 48
Cash-Det 39
Wagner-LA 37
Colavito-Det 37

Total Bases
Colavito-Det 309
B.Robinson-Bal 308
Wagner-LA 306
Yastrzemski-Bos 303
Killebrew-Min 301

Runs Batted In
Killebrew-Min 126
Siebern-KC 117
Colavito-Det 112
Robinson-Chi 109
Wagner-LA 107

Runs Produced
Siebern-KC 206
Robinson-Chi 187
Rollins-Min 176
Allison-Min 175
Yastrzemski-Bos ... 174

Bases On Balls
Mantle-NY 122
Siebern-KC 110
Killebrew-Min 106
Cash-Det 104
Cunningham-Chi ... 101

Batting Average
Runnels-Bos .... .326
Mantle-NY .... .321
Robinson-Chi .... .312
Hinton-Was .... .310
Siebern-KC .... .308

On-Base Percentage
Mantle-NY .... .488
Siebern-KC .... .416
Cunningham-Chi ... .415
Runnels-Bos .... .411
Robinson-Chi ..... .387

Slugging Average
Mantle-NY .... .605
Killebrew-Min ...... .545
Colavito-Det .... .514
Cash-Det .... .513
Allison-Min .... .511

On-Base Plus Slugging
Mantle-NY 1093
Killebrew-Min 914
Siebern-KC 911
Cash-Det 897
Colavito-Det 889

Adjusted OPS
Mantle-NY 198
Siebern-KC 138
Killebrew-Min 137
Cash-Det 134
Colavito-Det 132

Batter Runs
Mantle-NY 57.3
Siebern-KC 41.1
Killebrew-Min 33.1
Colavito-Det 31.4
Kaline-Det 30.7

Adjusted Batter Runs
Mantle-NY 61.1
Siebern-KC 35.6
Killebrew-Min 29.2
Kaline-Det 27.9
Colavito-Det 27.6

Clutch Hitting Index
Siebern-KC 125
Robinson-Chi 124
Rollins-Min 121
Howard-NY 115
L.Thomas-LA 111

Runs Created
Siebern-KC 129
Mantle-NY 126
Colavito-Det 117
Killebrew-Min 113
Robinson-Chi 113

Total Average
Mantle-NY 1.385
Siebern-KC .... .956
Cash-Det .... .950
Killebrew-Min ...... .945
Allison-Min .... .901

Stolen Bases
Aparicio-Chi 31
Hinton-Was 28
Wood-Det 24
Charles-KC 20

Stolen Base Average
Howser-KC 90.5
Wood-Det 88.9
Charles-KC 83.3
Tartabull-KC 79.2
Hinton-Was 73.7

Stolen Base Runs
Wood-Det 4.2
Howser-KC 3.5
Charles-KC 3.0
Hinton-Was 2.7
Aparicio-Chi 2.6

Fielding Runs
Boyer-NY 36.2
Versalles-Min 31.6
Bressoud-Bos 24.5
Kindall-Cle 20.7
Cottier-Was 20.5

Total Player Rating
Mantle-NY 5.2
Bressoud-Bos 3.8
Boyer-NY 3.7
Colavito-Det 3.6
Kaline-Det 3.3

Wins
Terry-NY 23
Pascual-Min 20
Herbert-Chi 20
Donovan-Cle 20
Bunning-Det 19

Win Percentage
Herbert-Chi .... .690
Ford-NY .... .680
Donovan-Cle .... .667
Aguirre-Det .... .667
Terry-NY .... .657

Games
Radatz-Bos 62
Wyatt-KC 59

Complete Games
Pascual-Min 18
Kaat-Min 16
Donovan-Cle 16
Terry-NY 14

Shutouts
Pascual-Min 5
Kaat-Min 5
Donovan-Cle 5
Monbouquette-Bos 4
McBride-LA 4

Saves
Radatz-Bos 24
Bridges-NY 18
Fox-Det 16
Wilhelm-Bal 15
Bell-Cle 12

Innings Pitched
Terry-NY 298.2
Kaat-Min 269.0
Bunning-Det 258.0
Pascual-Min 257.2
Ford-NY 257.2

Fewest Hits/Game
Aguirre-Det 6.75
Cheney-Was 6.96
Belinsky-LA 7.16
Wilson-Bos 7.67
Stenhouse-Was 7.72

Fewest BB/Game
Donovan-Cle 1.69
Terry-NY 1.72
Mossi-Det 1.80
Roberts-Bal 1.93
Pascual-Min 2.06

Strikeouts
Pascual-Min 206
Bunning-Det 184
Terry-NY 176
Pizarro-Chi 173
Kaat-Min 173

Strikeouts/Game
Pizarro-Chi 7.66
Cheney-Was 7.63
Pascual-Min 7.20
Belinsky-LA 6.97
Estrada-Bal 6.65

Ratio
Terry-NY 9.55
Aguirre-Det 9.67
Pascual-Min 10.37
Roberts-Bal 10.40
Fisher-Chi 10.59

Earned Run Average
Aguirre-Det 2.21
Roberts-Bal 2.78
Ford-NY 2.90
Chance-LA 2.96
Fisher-Chi 3.10

Adjusted ERA
Aguirre-Det 184
Roberts-Bal 133
Chance-LA 130
Kaat-Min 130
Ford-NY 129

Opponents' Batting Avg.
Aguirre-Det .... .205
Cheney-Was .... .213
Belinsky-LA .... .216
Terry-NY .... .231
Wilson-Bos .... .231

Opponents' On-Base Pct.
Aguirre-Det .... .269
Terry-NY .... .270
Pascual-Min .... .286
Roberts-Bal .... .289
Fisher-Chi .... .293

Starter Runs
Aguirre-Det 42.3
Ford-NY 30.7
Terry-NY 25.8
Roberts-Bal 25.4
Kaat-Min 24.7

Adjusted Starter Runs
Aguirre-Det 43.6
Kaat-Min 27.3
Ford-NY 25.7
Pascual-Min 21.3
Chance-LA 21.2

Clutch Pitching Index
Chance-LA 114
Roberts-Bal 111
Ramos-Cle 110
Ford-NY 110
Perry-Cle 109

Relief Runs
Radatz-Bos 24.0
Hall-Bal 22.2
Wilhelm-Bal 21.0
Fox-Det 14.6
Fowler-LA 10.0

Adjusted Relief Runs
Radatz-Bos 25.2
Hall-Bal 20.0
Wilhelm-Bal 19.6
Fox-Det 14.9
Fowler-LA 9.3

Relief Ranking
Wilhelm-Bal 39.1
Radatz-Bos 38.0
Hall-Bal 20.5
Fox-Det 18.3
Bridges-NY 10.3

Total Pitcher Index
Wilhelm-Bal 4.1
Kaat-Min 4.1
Aguirre-Det 3.6
Radatz-Bos 3.6
Pascual-Min 3.3

Total Baseball Ranking
Mantle-NY 5.2
Wilhelm-Bal 4.1
Kaat-Min 4.1
Bressoud-Bos 3.8
Boyer-NY 3.7

TEAM	G	W	L	PCT	GB	R	OR	AB	H	2B	3B	HR	BB	SO	AVG	OBP	SLG	OPS	OPS+	BR	BR+	PF	CHI	RC	SB	CS	SBA	SBR
LA	163	99	63	.611		640	**550**	5428	1361	178	34	110	453	**867**	.251	.311	.357	668	106	-3	42	93	105	596	**124**	70	64	**3**
STL	162	93	69	.574	6	**747**	628	5678	**1540**	**231**	**66**	128	458	915	**.271**	**.328**	.403	731	107	**119**	55	109	99	**751**	77	42	**65**	2
SF	162	88	74	.543	11	725	641	5579	1442	206	35	**197**	441	889	.258	.318	**.414**	**732**	**118**	111	**119**	99	98	712	55	49	53	-5
PHI	162	87	75	.537	12	642	578	5524	1390	228	54	126	403	955	.252	.308	.381	689	106	28	36	99	99	640	56	39	59	-1
CIN	162	86	76	.531	13	648	594	5416	1333	225	44	122	474	960	.246	.312	.371	683	100	25	6	103	101	630	92	58	61	0
MIL	163	84	78	.519	15	677	603	5518	1345	204	39	139	**525**	954	.244	.314	.370	684	105	30	37	99	102	643	75	52	59	-2
CHI	162	82	80	.506	17	570	578	5404	1286	205	44	127	439	1049	.238	.300	.363	663	92	-21	-51	105	97	573	68	60	53	-6
PIT	162	74	88	.457	25	567	595	5536	1385	181	49	108	454	940	.250	.310	.359	669	98	-2	-6	101	92	603	57	41	58	-2
HOU	162	66	96	.407	33	464	640	5384	1184	170	39	62	456	938	.220	.284	.301	585	80	-159	-129	94	103	461	39	30	57	-2
NY	162	51	111	.315	48	501	774	5336	1168	156	35	96	457	1078	.219	.286	.315	601	79	-129	-136	102	**106**	477	41	52	44	-9
TOT	811					6181		54803	13434	1984	439	1215	4560	9545	.246	.308	.364	671							684	493	58	-22

TEAM	CG	SH	SV	IP	H	H/G	HR	BB	SO	RAT	ERA	ERA+	OAV	OOB	PR	PR+	PF	CPI	FA	E	DP	FW	PW	BW	SBW	DIF
LA	51	**24**	29	1469^2	1329	8.2	111	402	**1095**	**10.9**	**2.86**	106	.239	**.294**	**71**	30	92	103	.975	159	129	.0	3.3	4.6	**.6**	9.7
STL	49	17	32	1463	1329	8.2	124	463	978	11.4	3.33	107	.241	.305	-5	34	108	97	.976	147	136	.7	3.7	6.0	.5	1.3
SF	46	9	30	1469	1380	8.5	126	464	954	11.6	3.35	96	.246	.307	-9	-24	97	99	.975	156	113	.2	-2.6	**13.0**	-.3	-3.1
PHI	45	12	31	1457^1	**1262**	**7.8**	113	553	1052	11.5	3.09	105	**.235**	.311	32	24	98	104	.978	142	147	1.0	2.7	4.0	.1	-1.5
CIN	55	22	**36**	1439^2	1307	8.2	117	425	1048	11.1	3.30	102	.242	.302	-1	8	102	96	.978	135	127	1.4	.9	.7	.2	1.9
MIL	**56**	18	25	1471^2	1327	8.2	149	489	924	11.3	3.27	99	.241	.306	4	-8	98	103	**.980**	**129**	161	**1.8**	-.8	4.1	.0	-1.9
CHI	45	15	28	1457	1357	8.4	119	400	851	11.1	3.08	**114**	.249	.303	34	**66**	107	105	.976	155	172	.2	**7.2**	-5.5	-.4	-.3
PIT	34	16	33	1448	1350	8.4	99	457	900	11.6	3.10	107	.249	.313	31	33	100	**107**	.972	182	**195**	-1.4	3.6	-.6	.0	-8.5
HOU	36	16	20	1450^1	1341	8.4	**95**	**378**	937	**10.9**	3.44	92	.245	.298	-24	-48	96	87	.974	162	100	-.2	-5.2	-13.9	.0	4.5
NY	42	5	12	1427^2	1452	9.2	162	529	806	12.8	4.13	85	.263	.332	-132	-95	106	100	.967	210	151	-3.1	-10.3	-14.7	-.7	-1.0
TOT	459	154	276	14553^1		8.4				11.4	3.29		.246	.308					.975	1577	1431					

Runs	Hits	Doubles	Triples	Home Runs	Total Bases
H.Aaron-Mil 121	Pinson-Cin 204	Groat-StL 43	Pinson-Cin 14	McCovey-SF 44	H.Aaron-Mil 370
Mays-SF 115	Groat-StL 201	Pinson-Cin 37	Gonzalez-Phi 12	H.Aaron-Mil 44	Mays-SF 347
Flood-StL 112	H.Aaron-Mil 201	Williams-Chi 36	Groat-StL 11	Mays-SF 38	Pinson-Cin 335
White-StL 106	White-StL 200	Gonzalez-Phi 36	Callison-Phi 11	Cepeda-SF 34	Cepeda-SF 326
McCovey-SF 103	Flood-StL 200	Callison-Phi 36	Brock-Chi 11	Howard-LA 28	White-StL 323

Runs Batted In	Runs Produced	Bases On Balls	Batting Average	On-Base Percentage	Slugging Average
H.Aaron-Mil 130	H.Aaron-Mil 207	Mathews-Mil 124	T.Davis-LA .326	Mathews-Mil .400	H.Aaron-Mil .586
Boyer-StL 111	White-StL 188	Robinson-Cin 81	Clemente-Pit .320	H.Aaron-Mil .394	Mays-SF .582
White-StL 109	Pinson-Cin 180	H.Aaron-Mil 78	Groat-StL .319	Mays-SF .384	McCovey-SF .566
Pinson-Cin 106	Mays-SF 180	Boyer-StL 70	H.Aaron-Mil .319	Robinson-Cin .381	Cepeda-SF .563
Mays-SF 103	Boyer-StL 173	Schofield-Pit 69	Cepeda-SF .316	Groat-StL .380	Pinson-Cin .514

On-Base Plus Slugging	Adjusted OPS	Batter Runs	Adjusted Batter Runs	Clutch Hitting Index	Runs Created
H.Aaron-Mil 980	H.Aaron-Mil 180	H.Aaron-Mil 63.0	H.Aaron-Mil 64.5	Sievers-Phi 135	H.Aaron-Mil 149
Mays-SF 966	Mays-SF 176	Mays-SF 55.8	Mays-SF 57.2	Fairly-LA 135	Mays-SF 131
Cepeda-SF 930	Cepeda-SF 166	Cepeda-SF 45.4	Cepeda-SF 46.6	Robinson-Cin 126	White-StL 117
McCovey-SF 916	McCovey-SF 161	McCovey-SF 41.1	McCovey-SF 42.2	Boyer-StL 120	Cepeda-SF 113
Pinson-Cin 864	Mathews-Mil 147	Mathews-Mil 37.4	Mathews-Mil 38.6	Edwards-Cin 120	Pinson-Cin 113

Total Average	Stolen Bases	Stolen Base Average	Stolen Base Runs	Fielding Runs	Total Player Rating
H.Aaron-Mil 1.063	Wills-LA 40	H.Aaron-Mil 86.1	H.Aaron-Mil 5.1	Mazeroski-Pit 56.7	Mays-SF 7.0
Mays-SF .984	H.Aaron-Mil 31	Gilliam-LA 79.2	Pinson-Cin 3.1	Callison-Phi 22.7	H.Aaron-Mil 6.0
McCovey-SF .911	Pinson-Cin 27	Pinson-Cin 77.1	Gilliam-LA 2.4	Hubbs-Chi 20.1	Mazeroski-Pit 5.9
Cepeda-SF .906	Robinson-Cin 26	Robinson-Cin 72.2	Maye-Mil 2.4	Flood-StL 19.5	Mathews-Mil 5.3
Mathews-Mil .894	W.Davis-LA 25	Taylor-Phi 71.9	Harper-Cin 2.3	Harkness-NY 16.4	Callison-Phi 4.6

Wins	Win Percentage	Games	Complete Games	Shutouts	Saves
Marichal-SF 25	Perranoski-LA .842	Perranoski-LA 69	Spahn-Mil 22	Koufax-LA 11	McDaniel-Chi 22
Koufax-LA 25	Koufax-LA .833	Baldschun-Phi 65	Koufax-LA 20	Spahn-Mil 7	Perranoski-LA 21
Spahn-Mil 23	Spahn-Mil .767	Bearnarth-NY 58	Ellsworth-Chi 19	Simmons-StL 6	Face-Pit 16
Maloney-Cin 23	Maloney-Cin .767	Sisk-Pit 57	Marichal-SF 18	Maloney-Cin 6	Baldschun-Phi 16
Ellsworth-Chi 22	Marichal-SF .758	McDaniel-Chi 57	Drysdale-LA 17		Henry-Cin 14

Innings Pitched	Fewest Hits/Game	Fewest BB/Game	Strikeouts	Strikeouts/Game	Ratio
Marichal-SF 321.1	Koufax-LA 6.19	Friend-Pit 1.47	Koufax-LA 306	Maloney-Cin 9.53	Koufax-LA 7.96
Drysdale-LA 315.1	Culp-Phi 6.55	Farrell-Hou 1.56	Maloney-Cin 265	Koufax-LA 8.86	Farrell-Hou 8.81
Koufax-LA 311.0	Maloney-Cin 6.58	Nuxhall-Cin 1.62	Drysdale-LA 251	Culp-Phi 7.79	Marichal-SF 9.02
Ellsworth-Chi 290.2	Ellsworth-Chi 6.90	Drysdale-LA 1.63	Marichal-SF 248	Short-Phi 7.27	Ellsworth-Chi 9.29
Sanford-SF 284.1	Farrell-Hou 7.16	Koufax-LA 1.68	Gibson-StL 204	Lemaster-Mil 7.22	Friend-Pit 9.55

Earned Run Average	Adjusted ERA	Opponents' Batting Avg.	Opponents' On-Base Pct.	Starter Runs	Adjusted Starter Runs
Koufax-LA 1.88	Ellsworth-Chi 167	Koufax-LA .189	Koufax-LA .230	Koufax-LA 48.6	Koufax-LA 42.9
Ellsworth-Chi 2.11	Koufax-LA 161	Maloney-Cin .202	Marichal-SF .256	Ellsworth-Chi 38.2	Ellsworth-Chi 42.5
Friend-Pit 2.34	Simmons-StL 143	Culp-Phi .206	Farrell-Hou .256	Marichal-SF 31.4	Marichal-SF 29.0
Marichal-SF 2.41	Friend-Pit 141	Ellsworth-Chi .210	Ellsworth-Chi .263	Friend-Pit 28.2	Friend-Pit 28.4
Simmons-StL 2.48	Jackson-Chi 137	Broglio-StL .216	Friend-Pit .269	Drysdale-LA 23.2	Jackson-Chi 27.4

Clutch Pitching Index	Relief Runs	Adjusted Relief Runs	Relief Ranking	Total Pitcher Index	Total Baseball Ranking
Schwall-Pit 118	Perranoski-LA 23.1	Perranoski-LA 21.0	Perranoski-LA 35.6	Ellsworth-Chi 4.9	Mays-SF 7.0
Spahn-Mil 115	Veale-Pit 19.4	Veale-Pit 19.4	Woodeshick-Hou 27.7	Perranoski-LA 4.0	H.Aaron-Mil 6.0
Short-Phi 111	Klippstein-Phi 16.9	Klippstein-Phi 16.5	Baldschun-Phi 20.9	Jackson-Chi 3.9	Mazeroski-Pit 5.9
Cardwell-Pit 110	Woodeshick-Hou 16.6	Woodeshick-Hou 15.6	Veale-Pit 17.4	Woodeshick-Hou 3.4	Mathews-Mil 5.3
Buhl-Chi 109	Baldschun-Phi 12.5	Baldschun-Phi 12.0	Klippstein-Phi 17.2	Koufax-LA 3.4	Ellsworth-Chi 4.9

TEAM	G	W	L	PCT	GB	R	OR	AB	H	2B	3B	HR	BB	SO	AVG	OBP	SLG	OPS	OPS+	BR	BR+	PF	CHI	RC	SB	CS	SBA	SBR
NY	161	104	57	.646		714	547	5506	1387	197	35	188	434	**808**	.252	.310	.403	713	106	27	33	99	**105**	686	42	26	62	0
CHI	162	94	68	.580	10.5	683	**544**	5508	1379	208	**40**	114	571	896	.250	.325	.365	690	101	4	16	98	101	675	64	28	70	4
MIN	161	91	70	.565	13	**767**	602	5531	**1408**	223	35	**225**	547	912	**.255**	.326	**.430**	**756**	**115**	**116**	**101**	102	98	**777**	32	14	70	2
BAL	162	86	76	.531	18.5	644	621	5448	1359	207	32	146	469	940	.249	.312	.380	692	103	-7	18	96	100	645	**97**	34	**74**	**9**
DET	162	79	83	.488	25.5	700	703	5500	1388	195	36	148	**592**	908	.252	**.329**	.382	711	102	43	20	103	98	699	73	32	70	5
CLE	162	79	83	.488	25.5	635	702	5496	1314	214	29	169	469	1102	.239	.304	.381	685	98	-26	-20	99	100	634	59	36	62	0
BOS	161	76	85	.472	28	666	704	5575	1403	**247**	34	171	475	954	.252	.313	.400	713	102	31	10	103	96	684	27	16	63	0
KC	162	73	89	.451	31.5	615	704	5495	1356	225	38	95	529	829	.247	.316	.353	669	88	-41	-74	106	99	616	47	26	64	1
LA	161	70	91	.435	34	597	660	5506	1378	208	38	95	448	916	.250	.312	.354	666	98	-53	-15	94	99	608	43	30	59	-1
WAS	162	56	106	.346	48.5	578	812	5446	1237	190	35	138	497	963	.227	.295	.351	646	86	-95	-93	100	104	569	68	28	71	5
TOT	808					6599		55011	13609	2114	352	1489	5031	9228	.248	.315	.380	694							552	270	67	27

TEAM	CG	SH	SV	IP	H	H/G	HR	BB	SO	RAT	ERA	ERA+	OAV	OOB	PR	PR+	PF	CPI	FA	E	DP	FW	PW	BW	SBW	DIF
NY	**59**	19	31	1449	**1239**	**7.7**	115	476	965	**10.8**	3.08	114	**.232**	**.297**	89	73	97	98	.982	110	162	1.5	7.7	3.5	-.3	11.3
CHI	49	**21**	39	1469	1311	8.1	**100**	**440**	932	11.0	**2.98**	**118**	.239	.299	**107**	**90**	97	102	.979	131	163	.3	**9.5**	1.7	.1	1.5
MIN	58	13	30	1446[1]	1322	8.3	162	459	941	11.3	3.28	111	.242	.303	56	58	100	**105**	.976	144	140	-.5	6.1	**10.7**	-.0	-5.5
BAL	35	8	**43**	1452	1353	8.4	137	507	913	11.8	3.46	101	.248	.316	29	4	96	104	**.984**	**99**	157	**2.1**	.5	1.9	**.7**	.0
DET	42	7	28	1456[1]	1407	8.7	195	477	930	12.0	3.90	96	.253	.317	-44	-25	103	102	.982	113	124	1.3	-2.6	2.2	.2	-2.9
CLE	40	14	25	1469	1390	8.6	176	478	**1018**	11.7	3.80	95	.249	.311	-27	-28	100	98	.977	143	129	-.4	-2.9	-2.1	-.3	3.8
BOS	29	7	32	1449[2]	1367	8.5	152	539	1009	12.1	3.98	95	.248	.318	-55	-29	104	93	.978	135	119	.0	-3.0	1.1	-.3	-2.2
KC	35	11	29	1458	1417	8.8	156	540	887	12.4	3.92	100	.256	.327	-47	-3	108	101	.980	127	131	.5	-.3	-7.7	-.2	-.2
LA	30	13	31	1455[1]	1317	8.2	120	578	889	12.1	3.53	97	.242	.320	17	-17	94	100	.974	163	155	-1.6	-1.7	-1.5	-.4	-5.1
WAS	29	8	25	1447	1486	9.3	176	537	744	12.9	4.42	84	.266	.334	-126	-111	102	98	.971	182	**165**	-2.6	-11.6	-9.7	.2	-1.1
TOT	406	121	313	14551[2]		8.5				11.8	3.63		.248	.315					.979	1347	1445					

Runs
Allison-Min 99
Pearson-LA 92
Yastrzemski-Bos 91
Tresh-NY 91
Colavito-Det 91

Hits
Yastrzemski-Bos 183
Ward-Chi 177
Pearson-LA 176
Kaline-Det 172
Fregosi-LA 170

Doubles
Yastrzemski-Bos 40
Ward-Chi 34
Torres-LA 32
Causey-KC 32
Alvis-Cle 32

Triples
Versalles-Min 13
Hinton-Was 12
Fregosi-LA 12
Cimoli-KC 11

Home Runs
Killebrew-Min 45
Stuart-Bos 42
Allison-Min 35
Hall-Min 33
Howard-NY 28

Total Bases
Stuart-Bos 319
Ward-Chi 289
Killebrew-Min 286
Kaline-Det 283
Allison-Min 281

Runs Batted In
Stuart-Bos 118
Kaline-Det 101
Killebrew-Min 96
Colavito-Det 91
Allison-Min 91

Runs Produced
Kaline-Det 163
Colavito-Det 160
Stuart-Bos 157
Allison-Min 155
Siebern-KC 147

Bases On Balls
Yastrzemski-Bos 95
Pearson-LA 92
Allison-Min 90
Cash-Det 89
Colavito-Det 84

Batting Average
Yastrzemski-Bos .321
Kaline-Det .312
Rollins-Min .307
Pearson-LA .304
Ward-Chi .295

On-Base Percentage
Yastrzemski-Bos .419
Pearson-LA .403
Cash-Det .388
Allison-Min .381
Kaline-Det .378

Slugging Average
Killebrew-Min .555
Allison-Min .533
Howard-NY .528
Stuart-Bos .521
Hall-Min .521

On-Base Plus Slugging
Allison-Min 914
Killebrew-Min 908
Yastrzemski-Bos 894
Kaline-Det 891
Howard-NY 871

Adjusted OPS
Allison-Min 150
Killebrew-Min 147
Yastrzemski-Bos 145
Kaline-Det 142
Howard-NY 141

Batter Runs
Yastrzemski-Bos 42.0
Allison-Min 38.6
Kaline-Det 34.3
Killebrew-Min 33.5
Cash-Det 28.7

Adjusted Batter Runs
Yastrzemski-Bos 38.5
Allison-Min 36.6
Killebrew-Min 31.7
Kaline-Det 31.0
Pearson-LA 30.1

Clutch Hitting Index
Hansen-Chi 127
Torres-LA 115
Siebern-KC 114
L.Thomas-LA 112
Phillips-Det 112

Runs Created
Yastrzemski-Bos 118
Allison-Min 113
Kaline-Det 105
Ward-Chi 104
Pearson-LA 100

Total Average
Allison-Min .967
Yastrzemski-Bos .916
Killebrew-Min .907
Tresh-NY .879
Cash-Det .876

Stolen Bases
Aparicio-Bal 40
Hinton-Was 25
Wood-Det 18
Snyder-Bal 18
Pearson-LA 17

Stolen Base Average
Tartabull-KC 94.1
Aparicio-Bal 87.0
Wood-Det 78.3
Snyder-Bal 78.3
Hinton-Was 73.5

Stolen Base Runs
Aparicio-Bal 6.7
Tartabull-KC 3.2
Weis-Chi 3.0
Richardson-NY 3.0
Hinton-Was 2.3

Fielding Runs
Hansen-Chi 27.0
Boyer-NY 22.3
Moran-LA 15.2
Lock-Was 14.8
Geiger-Bos 13.7

Total Player Rating
Yastrzemski-Bos 4.5
Allison-Min 4.0
Hansen-Chi 3.8
Pearson-LA 3.3
Battey-Min 3.2

Wins
Ford-NY 24
Pascual-Min 21
Bouton-NY 21
Monbouquette-Bos 20
Barber-Bal 20

Win Percentage
Ford-NY .774
Bouton-NY .750
Radatz-Bos .714
Peters-Chi .704
Pascual-Min .700

Games
S.Miller-Bal 71
Radatz-Bos 66
Dailey-Min 66
Lamabe-Bos 65
Wyatt-KC 63

Complete Games
Terry-NY 18
Pascual-Min 18
Stigman-Min 15
Herbert-Chi 14
Aguirre-Det 14

Shutouts
Herbert-Chi 7
Bouton-NY 6

Saves
S.Miller-Bal 27
Radatz-Bos 25
Wyatt-KC 21
Wilhelm-Chi 21
Dailey-Min 21

Innings Pitched
Ford-NY 269.1
Terry-NY 268.0
Monbouquette-Bos 266.2
Barber-Bal 258.2
Roberts-Bal 251.1

Fewest Hits/Game
Downing-NY 5.84
Bouton-NY 6.89
Drabowsky-KC 6.97
Morehead-Bos 7.06
McBride-LA 7.10

Fewest BB/Game
Donovan-Cle 1.22
Terry-NY 1.31
Herbert-Chi 1.40
Monbouquette-Bos 1.42
Roberts-Bal 1.43

Strikeouts
Pascual-Min 202
Bunning-Det 196
Stigman-Min 193
Peters-Chi 189
Ford-NY 189

Strikeouts/Game
Downing-NY 8.76
Ramos-Cle 8.24
Pascual-Min 7.32
Stigman-Min 7.21
Bunning-Det 7.10

Ratio
Terry-NY 9.71
Roberts-Bal 9.78
Ramos-Cle 9.80
Peters-Chi 9.93
Downing-NY 9.94

Earned Run Average
Peters-Chi 2.33
Pizarro-Chi 2.39
Pascual-Min 2.46
Bouton-NY 2.53
Downing-NY 2.56

Adjusted ERA
Peters-Chi 150
Pascual-Min 148
Pizarro-Chi 147
Bouton-NY 139
Stange-Min 139

Opponents' Batting Avg.
Downing-NY .184
Morehead-Bos .211
Bouton-NY .212
Drabowsky-KC .214
Peters-Chi .216

Opponents' On-Base Pct.
Roberts-Bal .272
Terry-NY .273
Ramos-Cle .273
Downing-NY .277
Peters-Chi .278

Starter Runs
Peters-Chi 35.0
Pascual-Min 32.2
Bouton-NY 30.6
Pizarro-Chi 29.6
Ford-NY 26.6

Adjusted Starter Runs
Peters-Chi 32.8
Pascual-Min 32.4
Bouton-NY 28.2
Pizarro-Chi 27.6
Ford-NY 23.9

Clutch Pitching Index
Barber-Bal 126
Osteen-Was 120
Stange-Min 120
Segui-KC 115
Pascual-Min 115

Relief Runs
Radatz-Bos 24.4
Dailey-Min 19.8
S.Miller-Bal 17.3
Wilhelm-Chi 15.0
Fowler-LA 12.0

Adjusted Relief Runs
Radatz-Bos 25.6
Dailey-Min 19.9
S.Miller-Bal 16.0
Wilhelm-Chi 13.6
Fowler-LA 10.6

Relief Ranking
Radatz-Bos 47.4
S.Miller-Bal 25.4
Dailey-Min 23.5
Wilhelm-Chi 16.4
Kline-Was 13.8

Total Pitcher Index
Radatz-Bos 4.8
Peters-Chi 4.6
Pascual-Min 4.6
S.Miller-Bal 3.1
Pizarro-Chi 3.1

Total Baseball Ranking
Radatz-Bos 4.8
Peters-Chi 4.6
Pascual-Min 4.6
Yastrzemski-Bos 4.5
Allison-Min 4.0

TEAM	G	W	L	PCT	GB	R	OR	AB	H	2B	3B	HR	BB	SO	AVG	OBP	SLG	OPS	OPS+	BR	BR+	PF	CHI	RC	SB	CS	SBA	SBR
STL	162	93	69	.574		715	652	5625	**1531**	240	53	109	427	925	**.272**	.326	.392	718	100	62	4	109	99	711	73	51	59	-2
PHI	162	92	70	.568	1	693	632	5493	1415	241	51	130	440	924	.258	.317	.391	708	107	41	50	99	100	672	30	35	46	-6
CIN	163	92	70	.568	1	660	**566**	5561	1383	220	38	130	457	974	.249	.310	.372	682	96	-10	-32	104	102	642	90	36	**71**	7
SF	162	90	72	.556	3	656	587	5535	1360	185	38	**165**	**505**	900	.246	.313	.382	695	100	16	2	102	97	657	64	35	65	2
MIL	162	88	74	.543	5	**803**	744	5591	1522	**274**	32	159	486	**825**	**.272**	**.335**	**.418**	**753**	**118**	**132**	**127**	101	101	**764**	53	41	56	-3
PIT	162	80	82	.494	13	663	636	5566	1469	225	**54**	121	408	970	.264	.317	.389	706	105	35	36	100	97	668	39	33	54	-3
LA	164	80	82	.494	13	614	572	5499	1375	180	39	79	438	893	.250	.308	.340	648	96	-70	-25	93	105	581	**141**	60	70	**10**
CHI	162	76	86	.469	17	649	724	5545	1391	239	50	145	499	1041	.251	.316	.390	706	101	37	10	104	94	679	70	49	59	-2
HOU	162	66	96	.407	27	495	628	5303	1214	162	41	70	381	872	.229	.287	.315	602	81	-158	-130	94	**106**	469	40	48	45	-8
NY	163	53	109	.327	40	569	776	5566	1372	195	31	103	353	932	.246	.297	.348	645	90	-84	-70	98	102	552	36	31	54	-3
TOT	812					6517		55284	14032	2161	427	1211	4394	9256	.254	.313	.375	687							636	419	60	-7

TEAM	CG	SH	SV	IP	H	H/G	HR	BB	SO	RAT	ERA	ERA+	OAV	OOB	PR	PR+	PF	CPI	FA	E	DP	FW	PW	BW	SBW	DIF
STL	47	10	38	1445[1]	1405	8.8	133	410	877	11.5	3.44	111	.255	.310	17	56	108	104	.973	172	147	-.7	6.0	.5	-.1	6.6
PHI	37	17	**41**	1461	1402	8.7	129	440	1009	11.7	3.37	103	.252	.313	28	17	98	**106**	.975	157	150	.1	1.8	5.3	-.6	4.5
CIN	54	14	35	1467	1306	8.1	112	436	**1122**	10.9	3.08	**118**	.238	.298	75	**86**	102	100	**.979**	**130**	137	**1.6**	**9.1**	-3.3	.8	2.9
SF	48	17	30	1476[1]	1348	8.3	118	480	1023	11.4	3.19	112	.241	.306	57	61	101	102	.975	159	136	.0	6.5	.3	.3	2.1
MIL	45	14	39	1434[2]	1411	8.9	160	452	906	11.9	4.12	86	.257	.316	-92	-95	100	94	.977	143	139	.9	-10.0	**13.5**	-.2	3.1
PIT	42	14	29	1443[2]	1429	9.0	92	476	951	12.1	3.53	100	.260	.322	2	-2	99	103	.972	177	**179**	-.9	-.2	3.9	-.2	-3.3
LA	47	**19**	27	1483[2]	**1289**	**7.9**	**88**	458	1062	**10.8**	**2.96**	110	**.232**	**.294**	**96**	51	92	95	.973	170	126	-.5	5.4	-2.6	**1.1**	-4.3
CHI	**58**	11	19	1445	1510	9.5	144	423	737	12.2	4.08	91	.270	.323	-87	-56	105	98	.975	162	147	-.1	-5.9	1.1	-.1	.2
HOU	30	9	31	1428	1421	9.0	105	**353**	852	11.4	3.41	100	.260	.309	20	1	97	102	.976	149	124	.6	.2	-13.7	-.8	-1.1
NY	40	10	15	1438[2]	1511	9.5	130	466	717	12.7	4.26	84	.272	.334	-115	-107	101	98	.974	167	154	-.4	-11.2	-7.3	-.2	-8.6
TOT	448	135	304	14523[1]		8.7				11.7	3.54		.254	.313					.975	1586	1439					

Runs
Allen-Phi 125
Mays-SF 121
Brock-Chi-StL 111
Robinson-Cin 103
Aaron-Mil 103

Hits
Flood-StL 211
Clemente-Pit 211
Williams-Chi 201
Allen-Phi 201
Brock-Chi-StL 200

Doubles
Maye-Mil 44
Clemente-Pit 40
Williams-Chi 39
Robinson-Cin 38
Allen-Phi 38

Triples
Santo-Chi 13
Allen-Phi 13
Brock-Chi-StL 11
Pinson-Cin 11

Home Runs
Mays-SF 47
Williams-Chi 33
Hart-SF 31
Cepeda-SF 31
Callison-Phi 31

Total Bases
Allen-Phi 352
Mays-SF 351
Williams-Chi 343
Santo-Chi 334
Callison-Phi 322

Runs Batted In
Boyer-StL 119
Santo-Chi 114
Mays-SF 111
Torre-Mil 109
Callison-Phi 104

Runs Produced
Boyer-StL 195
Allen-Phi 187
Mays-SF 185
Santo-Chi 178
Torre-Mil 176

Bases On Balls
Santo-Chi 86
Mathews-Mil 85
Mays-SF 82
Robinson-Cin 79
Boyer-StL 70

Batting Average
Clemente-Pit ...... .339
Carty-Mil .... .330
Aaron-Mil .... .328
Torre-Mil .... .321
Allen-Phi .... .318

On-Base Percentage
Santo-Chi .... .401
Robinson-Cin ..... .399
Aaron-Mil .... .394
Carty-Mil .... .391
Clemente-Pit ..... .391

Slugging Average
Mays-SF .... .607
Santo-Chi .... .564
Allen-Phi .... .557
Carty-Mil .... .554
Robinson-Cin ..... .548

On-Base Plus Slugging
Mays-SF 992
Santo-Chi 966
Robinson-Cin 947
Carty-Mil 945
Allen-Phi 940

Adjusted OPS
Mays-SF 171
Allen-Phi 163
Santo-Chi 162
Carty-Mil 162
Robinson-Cin 158

Batter Runs
Mays-SF 56.5
Santo-Chi 55.1
Allen-Phi 50.5
Robinson-Cin 49.5
Williams-Chi 42.5

Adjusted Batter Runs
Mays-SF 53.9
Allen-Phi 52.1
Santo-Chi 50.0
Robinson-Cin 45.4
Aaron-Mil 40.2

Clutch Hitting Index
Fairly-LA 142
Boyer-StL 117
T.Davis-LA 116
Torre-Mil 113
Javier-StL 111

Runs Created
Mays-SF 136
Santo-Chi 135
Allen-Phi 135
Robinson-Cin 127
Williams-Chi 125

Total Average
Mays-SF 1.059
Robinson-Cin 1.012
Santo-Chi .... .998
Allen-Phi .... .944
Carty-Mil .... .920

Stolen Bases
Wills-LA 53
Brock-Chi-StL 43
W.Davis-LA 42
Harper-Cin 24
Robinson-Cin 23

Stolen Base Average
Harper-Cin 88.9
Aaron-Mil 84.6
Robinson-Cin 82.1
Mays-SF 79.2
W.Davis-LA 76.4

Stolen Base Runs
Wills-LA 5.7
W.Davis-LA 4.7
Harper-Cin 4.2
Aaron-Mil 3.4
Robinson-Cin 3.3

Fielding Runs
Mazeroski-Pit 33.9
W.Davis-LA 24.9
Edwards-Cin 22.6
Callison-Phi 19.4
Rodgers-Chi 19.4

Total Player Rating
Mays-SF 6.7
Santo-Chi 6.7
Allen-Phi 6.0
Aaron-Mil 4.7
Robinson-Cin 4.3

Wins
Jackson-Chi 24
Marichal-SF 21
Sadecki-StL 20

Win Percentage
Koufax-LA .... .792
Marichal-SF .... .724
O'Toole-Cin .... .708
Bunning-Phi .... .704
Jackson-Chi .... .686

Games
B.Miller-LA 74
Perranoski-LA 72
Baldschun-Phi 71
Taylor-StL 63
McDaniel-Chi 63

Complete Games
Marichal-SF 22
Drysdale-LA 21
Jackson-Chi 19
Gibson-StL 17
Ellsworth-Chi 16

Shutouts
Koufax-LA 7
Law-Pit 5
Fischer-Mil 5
Drysdale-LA 5
Bunning-Phi 5

Saves
Woodeshick-Hou ... 23
McBean-Pit 22
Baldschun-Phi 21
McDaniel-Chi 15

Innings Pitched
Drysdale-LA 321.1
Jackson-Chi 297.2
Gibson-StL 287.1
Bunning-Phi 284.1
Veale-Pit 279.2

Fewest Hits/Game
Koufax-LA 6.22
Drysdale-LA 6.78
Short-Phi 7.10
Veale-Pit 7.14
Maloney-Cin 7.29

Fewest BB/Game
Bunning-Phi 1.46
Bruce-Hou 1.47
Law-Pit 1.50
Marichal-SF 1.74
Jackson-Chi 1.75

Strikeouts
Veale-Pit 250
Gibson-StL 245
Drysdale-LA 237
Koufax-LA 223
Bunning-Phi 219

Strikeouts/Game
Koufax-LA 9.00
Maloney-Cin 8.92
Veale-Pit 8.05
Gibson-StL 7.67
Lemaster-Mil 7.53

Ratio
Koufax-LA 8.35
Drysdale-LA 8.96
Short-Phi 9.34
Bunning-Phi 9.75
Jackson-Chi 9.80

Earned Run Average
Koufax-LA 1.74
Drysdale-LA 2.18
Short-Phi 2.20
Marichal-SF 2.48
Bunning-Phi 2.63

Adjusted ERA
Koufax-LA 187
Short-Phi 157
Drysdale-LA 148
Marichal-SF 144
O'Toole-Cin 136

Opponents' Batting Avg.
Koufax-LA .... .191
Drysdale-LA ...... .207
Veale-Pit .... .217
Short-Phi .... .217
Bolin-SF .... .220

Opponents' On-Base Pct.
Koufax-LA .... .241
Drysdale-LA ...... .256
Short-Phi .... .268
Jackson-Chi ...... .273
Marichal-SF ...... .273

Starter Runs
Drysdale-LA 48.2
Koufax-LA 44.6
Short-Phi 32.7
Marichal-SF 31.7
Bunning-Phi 28.7

Adjusted Starter Runs
Drysdale-LA 41.1
Koufax-LA 40.7
Marichal-SF 32.3
Short-Phi 31.6
Bunning-Phi 27.1

Clutch Pitching Index
Craig-StL 122
D.Bennett-Phi 119
Farrell-Hou 115
Tsitouris-Cin 115
Hendley-SF 110

Relief Runs
McBean-Pit 16.2
B.Miller-LA 14.1
Ellis-Cin 13.1
Roebuck-Phi 11.4
McCool-Cin 11.1

Adjusted Relief Runs
McBean-Pit 16.1
Ellis-Cin 13.8
McCool-Cin 11.6
Roebuck-Phi 11.0
B.Miller-LA 10.4

Relief Ranking
McBean-Pit 26.6
Ellis-Cin 16.8
McCool-Cin 14.9
Roebuck-Phi 14.1
Woodeshick-Hou ... 11.4

Total Pitcher Index
Drysdale-LA 5.2
Koufax-LA 4.0
Short-Phi 3.5
Marichal-SF 3.4
McBean-Pit 3.3

Total Baseball Ranking
Mays-SF 6.7
Santo-Chi 6.7
Allen-Phi 6.0
Drysdale-LA 5.2
Aaron-Mil 4.7

TEAM	G	W	L	PCT	GB	R	OR	AB	H	2B	3B	HR	BB	SO	AVG	OBP	SLG	OPS	OPS+	BR	BR+	PF	CHI	RC	SB	CS	SBA	SBR
NY	164	99	63	.611		730	577	5705	**1442**	208	35	162	520	976	.253	.319	.387	706	100	13	2	102	**105**	705	54	18	**75**	**6**
CHI	162	98	64	.605	1	642	**501**	5491	1356	184	40	106	**562**	**902**	.247	.323	.353	676	98	-32	-14	97	101	643	75	39	66	3
BAL	163	97	65	.599	2	679	567	5463	1357	229	20	162	537	1019	.248	.319	.387	706	102	14	17	100	101	671	78	38	67	4
DET	163	85	77	.525	14	699	678	5513	1394	199	**57**	157	517	912	.253	.321	.395	716	103	35	25	102	100	707	60	27	69	4
LA	162	82	80	.506	17	544	551	5362	1297	186	27	102	472	920	.242	.306	.344	650	97	-89	-29	90	99	552	49	39	56	-3
MIN	163	79	83	.488	20	**737**	678	5610	1413	227	46	**221**	553	1019	.252	**.324**	**.427**	**751**	**113**	**98**	**93**	101	95	**775**	46	22	68	2
CLE	164	79	83	.488	20	689	693	5603	1386	208	22	164	500	1063	.247	.315	.380	695	100	-8	-3	99	104	666	**79**	51	61	0
BOS	162	72	90	.444	27	688	793	5513	1425	**253**	29	186	504	917	**.258**	**.324**	.416	740	106	76	42	105	94	725	18	16	53	-2
WAS	162	62	100	.383	37	578	733	5396	1246	199	28	125	514	1124	.231	.301	.348	649	86	-95	-92	100	**105**	566	47	30	61	0
KC	163	57	105	.352	42	621	836	5524	1321	216	29	166	548	1104	.239	.313	.379	692	95	-14	-33	103	96	645	34	20	63	0
TOT	814					6607		55180	13637	2109	333	1551	5227	9956	.248	.317	.382	698							540	300	64	14

TEAM	CG	SH	SV	IP	H	H/G	HR	BB	SO	RAT	ERA	ERA+	OAV	OOB	PR	PR+	PF	CPI	FA	E	DP	FW	PW	BW	SBW	DIF
NY	46	18	**45**	1506^{2}	1312	7.9	129	504	989	11.0	3.16	115	.234	.300	79	78	100	97	.983	109	158	1.2	8.3	.3	**.5**	8.0
CHI	44	20	**45**	1467^{2}	**1216**	**7.5**	124	**401**	955	**10.2**	**2.73**	**127**	**.226**	**.283**	**147**	**125**	95	100	.981	122	164	.3	**13.2**	-1.4	.2	5.0
BAL	44	17	41	1458^{2}	1292	8.0	129	456	939	11.1	3.16	113	.239	.302	76	68	99	100	**.985**	**95**	159	**2.0**	7.2	1.8	.3	4.9
DET	35	11	35	1453	1343	8.4	164	536	993	12.0	3.85	95	.244	.317	-35	-29	101	95	.982	111	137	1.0	-3.0	2.7	.3	3.2
LA	30	**28**	41	1450^{2}	1273	7.9	**100**	530	965	11.5	2.91	113	.236	.310	115	67	91	**107**	.978	138	**168**	-.7	7.1	-3.0	-.5	-1.8
MIN	**47**	4	29	1477^{2}	1361	8.3	181	545	1099	11.8	3.58	100	.243	.314	8	1	99	102	.977	145	131	-1.0	.2	**9.8**	.0	-10.8
CLE	37	16	37	1487^{2}	1443	8.8	154	565	**1162**	12.4	3.76	96	.255	.326	-21	-25	99	103	.981	118	149	.6	-2.6	-.3	-.1	.6
BOS	21	9	38	1422	1464	9.3	178	571	1094	13.1	4.51	86	.266	.339	-138	-95	106	97	.977	138	123	-.7	-9.9	4.5	-.4	-2.3
WAS	27	5	26	1435^{1}	1417	8.9	172	505	794	12.3	3.99	93	.259	.324	-57	-44	102	100	.979	127	145	.0	-4.6	-9.6	-.1	-4.4
KC	18	6	27	1455^{2}	1516	9.4	220	614	966	13.6	4.71	81	.269	.346	-175	-136	105	101	.975	158	152	-1.8	-14.3	-3.4	-.1	-4.2
TOT	349	134	364	14615		8.4				11.9	3.63		.248	.317					.980	1261	1486					

Runs	Hits	Doubles	Triples	Home Runs	Total Bases
Oliva-Min 109	Oliva-Min 217	Oliva-Min 43	Versalles-Min 10	Killebrew-Min 49	Oliva-Min 374
Howser-Cle 101	B.Robinson-Bal 194	Bressoud-Bos 41	Rollins-Min 10	Powell-Bal 39	B.Robinson-Bal 319
Killebrew-Min 95	Richardson-NY 181	B.Robinson-Bal 35	Yastrzemski-Bos 9	Mantle-NY 35	Killebrew-Min 316
Wagner-Cle 94	Howard-NY 172	Versalles-Min 33	Oliva-Min 9	Colavito-KC 34	Colavito-KC 298
Versalles-Min 94	Versalles-Min 171		Fregosi-LA 9	Stuart-Bos 33	Stuart-Bos 296

Runs Batted In	Runs Produced	Bases On Balls	Batting Average	On-Base Percentage	Slugging Average
B.Robinson-Bal 118	B.Robinson-Bal 172	Siebern-Bal 106	Oliva-Min .323	Mantle-NY .426	Powell-Bal .606
Stuart-Bos 114	Oliva-Min 171	Mantle-NY 99	B.Robinson-Bal .317	Allison-Min .406	Mantle-NY .591
Mantle-NY 111	Mantle-NY 168	Killebrew-Min 93	Howard-NY .313	Powell-Bal .400	Oliva-Min .557
Killebrew-Min 111	Wagner-Cle 163	Allison-Min 92	Mantle-NY .303	Robinson-Chi .388	Allison-Min .553
Colavito-KC 102		Causey-KC 88	Robinson-Chi .301	Kaline-Det .385	Killebrew-Min .548

On-Base Plus Slugging	Adjusted OPS	Batter Runs	Adjusted Batter Runs	Clutch Hitting Index	Runs Created
Mantle-NY 1017	Mantle-NY 177	Mantle-NY 53.0	Mantle-NY 51.2	Rodgers-LA 125	Oliva-Min 132
Powell-Bal 1007	Powell-Bal 176	Allison-Min 45.0	Powell-Bal 44.5	Boyer-NY 118	Killebrew-Min 122
Allison-Min 959	Allison-Min 163	Powell-Bal 44.1	Allison-Min 44.2	Pepitone-NY 118	Mantle-NY 121
Killebrew-Min 927	Killebrew-Min 153	Killebrew-Min 43.1	Killebrew-Min 42.3	Mantle-NY 117	Allison-Min 119
Oliva-Min 918	Oliva-Min 150	Oliva-Min 43.0	Oliva-Min 42.2	Cash-Det 116	B.Robinson-Bal 115

Total Average	Stolen Bases	Stolen Base Average	Stolen Base Runs	Fielding Runs	Total Player Rating
Mantle-NY 1.122	Aparicio-Bal 57	Aparicio-Bal 77.0	Aparicio-Bal 6.6	Knoop-LA 37.2	Fregosi-LA 4.6
Powell-Bal 1.081	Weis-Chi 22	Weis-Chi 75.9	Tresh-NY 2.9	Yastrzemski-Bos 27.7	Hansen-Chi 4.5
Allison-Min 1.058	Davalillo-Cle 21	Howser-Cle 74.1	Weis-Chi 2.4	Boyer-NY 19.3	Powell-Bal 4.3
Killebrew-Min .956	Howser-Cle 20	Hinton-Was 73.9	Wagner-Cle 2.4	Green-KC 16.5	Yastrzemski-Bos 4.2
Oliva-Min .894	Hinton-Was 17	Davalillo-Cle 65.6	Howser-Cle 2.0	Brandt-Bal 16.1	Howard-NY 4.0

Wins	Win Percentage	Games	Complete Games	Shutouts	Saves
Peters-Chi 20	Bunker-Bal .792	Wyatt-KC 81	Chance-LA 15	Chance-LA 11	Radatz-Bos 29
Chance-LA 20	Ford-NY .739	Radatz-Bos 79	Pascual-Min 14	Ford-NY 8	Wilhelm-Chi 27
Wickersham-Det 19	Peters-Chi .714	Wilhelm-Chi 73	Pappas-Bal 13	Pappas-Bal 7	Miller-Bal 23
Pizarro-Chi 19	Pappas-Bal .696	McMahon-Cle 70	Osteen-Was 13	Lolich-Det 6	Wyatt-KC 20
Bunker-Bal 19	Chance-LA .690	Miller-Bal 66	Kaat-Min 13	Monbouquette-Bos 5	B.Lee-LA 19

Innings Pitched	Fewest Hits/Game	Fewest BB/Game	Strikeouts	Strikeouts/Game	Ratio
Chance-LA 278.1	Horlen-Chi 6.07	Monbouquette-Bos 1.54	Downing-NY 217	McDowell-Cle 9.19	Horlen-Chi 8.59
Peters-Chi 273.2	Chance-LA 6.27	Pappas-Bal 1.72	Pascual-Min 213	Downing-NY 8.00	Chance-LA 9.12
Bouton-NY 271.1	Bunker-Bal 6.77	Newman-LA 1.85	Chance-LA 207	Pena-KC 7.55	Pizarro-Chi 9.45
Pascual-Min 267.1	Peters-Chi 7.14	Bouton-NY 1.99	Peters-Chi 205	Stigman-Min 7.53	Bunker-Bal 9.50
Osteen-Was 257.0	Pizarro-Chi 7.27	Pizarro-Chi 2.07	Lolich-Det 192	Morehead-Bos 7.51	Bouton-NY 9.72

Earned Run Average	Adjusted ERA	Opponents' Batting Avg.	Opponents' On-Base Pct.	Starter Runs	Adjusted Starter Runs
Chance-LA 1.65	Chance-LA 199	Horlen-Chi .190	Horlen-Chi .250	Chance-LA 61.1	Chance-LA 55.8
Horlen-Chi 1.88	Horlen-Chi 184	Chance-LA .195	Chance-LA .261	Horlen-Chi 40.9	Ford-NY 40.5
Ford-NY 2.13	Ford-NY 170	Bunker-Bal .207	Pizarro-Chi .267	Ford-NY 40.6	Horlen-Chi 38.7
Peters-Chi 2.50	Peters-Chi 138	Peters-Chi .219	Bunker-Bal .269	Peters-Chi 34.2	Peters-Chi 30.5
Pizarro-Chi 2.56	Pizarro-Chi 135	Pizarro-Chi .219	Bouton-NY .273	Pizarro-Chi 28.3	Pizarro-Chi 24.9

Clutch Pitching Index	Relief Runs	Adjusted Relief Runs	Relief Ranking	Total Pitcher Index	Total Baseball Ranking
McDowell-Cle 123	B.Lee-LA 32.2	B.Lee-LA 29.8	Radatz-Bos 46.2	Chance-LA 5.3	Chance-LA 5.3
Roberts-Bal 121	Wilhelm-Chi 23.9	Radatz-Bos 25.6	Wilhelm-Chi 41.6	Radatz-Bos 4.8	Radatz-Bos 4.8
Kralick-Cle 118	Radatz-Bos 23.2	Wilhelm-Chi 22.5	Worthington-Min 31.6	Wilhelm-Chi 4.4	Fregosi-LA 4.6
Grant-Cle-Min 112	Worthington-Min 18.1	Worthington-Min 18.0	B.Lee-LA 29.8	Horlen-Chi 4.4	Hansen-Chi 4.5
Peters-Chi 111	Hall-Bal 17.3	Stock-Bal-KC 17.9	Kline-Was 24.4	Ford-NY 4.2	Wilhelm-Chi 4.4

TEAM	G	W	L	PCT	GB	R	OR	AB	H	2B	3B	HR	BB	SO	AVG	OBP	SLG	OPS	OPS+	BR	BR+	PF	CHI	RC	SB	CS	SBA	SBR
LA	162	97	65	.599		608	**521**	5425	1329	193	32	78	492	891	.245	.314	.335	649	96	-61	-19	93	103	593	**172**	77	69	**11**
SF	163	95	67	.586	2	682	593	5495	1384	169	43	159	476	**844**	.252	.315	.385	700	101	24	6	103	101	649	47	27	64	1
PIT	163	90	72	.556	7	675	580	5686	1506	217	57	111	419	1008	.265	.319	.382	701	103	27	24	101	97	671	51	38	57	-2
CIN	162	89	73	.549	8	**825**	704	5658	**1544**	**268**	**61**	183	**538**	1003	**.273**	**.341**	**.439**	**780**	**118**	**188**	**132**	107	95	**842**	82	40	67	4
MIL	162	86	76	.531	11	708	633	5542	1419	243	28	**196**	408	976	.256	.311	.416	727	110	67	63	101	99	699	64	37	63	1
PHI	162	85	76	.528	11.5	654	667	5528	1380	205	53	144	494	1091	.250	.315	.384	699	105	24	36	98	96	665	46	32	59	-1
STL	162	80	81	.497	16.5	707	674	5579	1415	234	46	109	477	882	.254	.316	.371	687	91	3	-54	109	**107**	659	100	52	66	4
CHI	164	72	90	.444	25	635	723	5540	1316	202	33	134	532	948	.238	.309	.358	667	92	-34	-49	102	101	613	65	47	58	-2
HOU	162	65	97	.401	32	569	711	5483	1299	188	42	97	502	877	.237	.306	.340	646	96	-73	-30	93	98	574	90	37	**71**	7
NY	164	50	112	.309	47	495	752	5441	1202	203	27	107	392	1129	.221	.278	.327	605	79	-164	-146	96	105	480	28	42	40	-9
TOT	813					6558		55377	13794	2122	422	1318	4730	9649	.250	.313	.375	687							745	429	63	14

TEAM	CG	SH	SV	IP	H	H/G	HR	BB	SO	RAT	ERA	ERA+	OAV	OOB	PR	PR+	PF	CPI	FA	E	DP	FW	PW	BW	SBW	DIF
LA	**58**	**23**	34	1476	**1223**	**7.5**	127	425	1079	**10.3**	**2.82**	116	**.224**	**.284**	**119**	80	92	99	.979	134	135	.9	8.5	-2.0	**1.0**	7.8
SF	42	17	**42**	1465[1]	1325	8.2	137	408	1060	10.9	3.20	112	.238	.295	55	64	102	98	.976	148	124	.1	6.8	.7	-.0	6.6
PIT	49	17	27	1479	1324	8.1	**89**	469	882	11.2	3.02	**117**	.241	.306	87	**83**	99	103	.977	152	**189**	-.0	**8.8**	2.6	-.4	-1.8
CIN	43	9	34	1457[1]	1355	8.4	136	587	**1113**	12.3	3.89	96	.247	.325	-56	-21	106	96	**.981**	**117**	142	**1.8**	-2.2	**14.0**	.3	-5.8
MIL	43	4	38	1447[2]	1336	8.4	123	541	966	11.9	3.52	100	.246	.318	3	1	100	101	.978	140	145	.5	.2	6.7	-.0	-2.2
PHI	50	18	21	1468[2]	1426	8.8	116	466	1071	12.0	3.53	98	.256	.320	2	-12	98	**104**	.975	157	153	-.4	-1.2	3.9	-.3	2.7
STL	40	11	35	1461[1]	1414	8.8	166	467	916	11.9	3.77	102	.255	.317	-37	11	109	102	.979	130	152	1.1	1.2	-5.7	.3	2.8
CHI	33	9	35	1472	1470	9.0	154	481	855	12.1	3.78	98	.260	.321	-39	-15	104	**104**	.974	171	166	-1.1	-1.5	-5.1	-.4	-.7
HOU	29	7	26	1461	1459	9.0	123	**388**	931	11.7	3.85	87	.260	.312	-49	-84	95	94	.974	166	130	-.9	-8.8	-3.1	.6	-3.5
NY	29	11	14	1454[2]	1462	9.1	147	498	776	12.5	4.06	87	.262	.328	-84	-86	100	99	.974	171	153	-1.1	-9.0	-15.4	-1.1	-4.2
TOT	416	126	306	14643		8.5				11.7	3.54		.250	.313					.977	1486	1489					

Runs
Harper-Cin 126
Mays-SF 118
Rose-Cin 117
Williams-Chi 115

Hits
Rose-Cin 209
Pinson-Cin 204
Williams-Chi 203
Clemente-Pit 194
Flood-StL 191

Doubles
H.Aaron-Mil 40
Williams-Chi 39
Rose-Cin 35
Brock-StL 35
Pinson-Cin 34

Triples
Callison-Phi 16
Clendenon-Pit 14
Clemente-Pit 14
Allen-Phi 14
Morgan-Hou 12

Home Runs
Mays-SF 52
McCovey-SF 39
Williams-Chi 34
Santo-Chi 33
Robinson-Cin 33

Total Bases
Mays-SF 360
Williams-Chi 356
Pinson-Cin 324
H.Aaron-Mil 319
Johnson-Cin 317

Runs Batted In
Johnson-Cin 130
Robinson-Cin 113
Mays-SF 112
Williams-Chi 108
Stargell-Pit 107

Runs Produced
Johnson-Cin 190
Williams-Chi 189
Robinson-Cin 189
Rose-Cin 187
Mays-SF 178

Bases On Balls
Morgan-Hou 97
Santo-Chi 88
McCovey-SF 88
Wynn-Hou 84
Harper-Cin 78

Batting Average
Clemente-Pit 329
H.Aaron-Mil 318
Mays-SF 317
Williams-Chi 315
Rose-Cin 312

On-Base Percentage
Mays-SF 399
Robinson-Cin 388
H.Aaron-Mil 384
McCovey-SF 383
Rose-Cin 383

Slugging Average
Mays-SF 645
H.Aaron-Mil 560
Williams-Chi 552
Robinson-Cin 540
McCovey-SF 539

On-Base Plus Slugging
Mays-SF 1044
H.Aaron-Mil 943
Williams-Chi 932
Robinson-Cin 928
McCovey-SF 922

Adjusted OPS
Mays-SF 184
H.Aaron-Mil 161
Williams-Chi 155
McCovey-SF 152
Robinson-Cin 148

Batter Runs
Mays-SF 64.7
Williams-Chi 49.3
H.Aaron-Mil 45.9
Robinson-Cin 45.9
McCovey-SF 41.8

Adjusted Batter Runs
Mays-SF 61.2
Williams-Chi 46.4
H.Aaron-Mil 45.4
McCovey-SF 38.9
Allen-Phi 38.4

Clutch Hitting Index
Stargell-Pit 120
Johnson-Cin 118
Boyer-StL 118
Stuart-Phi 118
Flood-StL 118

Runs Created
Mays-SF 143
Williams-Chi 132
H.Aaron-Mil 122
Santo-Chi 121
Robinson-Cin 120

Total Average
Mays-SF 1.114
H.Aaron-Mil 980
McCovey-SF 945
Robinson-Cin 938
Williams-Chi 935

Stolen Bases
Wills-LA 94
Brock-StL 63
Wynn-Hou 43
Harper-Cin 35
W.Davis-LA 25

Stolen Base Average
Wynn-Hou 91.5
H.Aaron-Mil 85.7
Harper-Cin 85.4
Wills-LA 75.2
W.Davis-LA 73.5

Stolen Base Runs
Wills-LA 9.8
Wynn-Hou 8.1
Harper-Cin 5.6
Brock-StL 4.4
H.Aaron-Mil 3.9

Fielding Runs
Alley-Pit 29.5
Mazeroski-Pit 25.6
Wine-Phi 21.7
Wills-LA 21.2
Wynn-Hou 20.1

Total Player Rating
Mays-SF 7.5
Wynn-Hou 6.1
Santo-Chi 5.7
H.Aaron-Mil 5.0
Morgan-Hou 4.3

Wins
Koufax-LA 26
Cloninger-Mil 24
Drysdale-LA 23
Marichal-SF 22
Ellis-Cin 22

Win Percentage
Koufax-LA 765
Maloney-Cin 690
Ellis-Cin 688
Cloninger-Mil 686
Bunning-Phi 679

Games
Abernathy-Chi 84
Woodeshick-Hou-StL . . . 78
McDaniel-Chi 71
Baldschun-Phi 65

Complete Games
Koufax-LA 27
Marichal-SF 24
Gibson-StL 20
Drysdale-LA 20
Cloninger-Mil 16

Shutouts
Marichal-SF 10
Koufax-LA 8
Veale-Pit 7
Drysdale-LA 7
Bunning-Phi 7

Saves
Abernathy-Chi 31
McCool-Cin 21
Linzy-SF 21

Innings Pitched
Koufax-LA 335.2
Drysdale-LA 308.1
Gibson-StL 299.0
Short-Phi 297.1
Marichal-SF 295.1

Fewest Hits/Game
Koufax-LA 5.79
Maloney-Cin 6.66
Marichal-SF 6.83
Bolin-SF 6.90
Gibson-StL 7.31

Fewest BB/Game
Marichal-SF 1.40
Law-Pit 1.45
Bruce-Hou 1.49
Farrell-Hou 1.51
Johnson-Hou-Mil 1.87

Strikeouts
Koufax-LA 382
Veale-Pit 276
Gibson-StL 270
Bunning-Phi 268
Maloney-Cin 244

Strikeouts/Game
Koufax-LA 10.24
Veale-Pit 9.34
Maloney-Cin 8.60
Bunning-Phi 8.29
Gibson-StL 8.13

Ratio
Koufax-LA 7.83
Marichal-SF 8.35
Law-Pit 9.11
Bunning-Phi 10.11
Drysdale-LA 10.16

Earned Run Average
Koufax-LA 2.04
Marichal-SF 2.13
Law-Pit 2.15
Maloney-Cin 2.54
Bunning-Phi 2.60

Adjusted ERA
Marichal-SF 169
Law-Pit 163
Koufax-LA 160
Maloney-Cin 148
Shaw-SF 136

Opponents' Batting Avg.
Koufax-LA 179
Marichal-SF 205
Maloney-Cin 206
Bolin-SF 214
Gibson-StL 222

Opponents' On-Base Pct.
Koufax-LA 228
Marichal-SF 240
Law-Pit 264
Drysdale-LA 280
Shaw-SF 280

Starter Runs
Koufax-LA 56.0
Marichal-SF 46.1
Law-Pit 33.5
Bunning-Phi 30.4
Maloney-Cin 28.4

Adjusted Starter Runs
Koufax-LA 49.6
Marichal-SF 47.3
Law-Pit 33.0
Maloney-Cin 32.4
Bunning-Phi 28.5

Clutch Pitching Index
Law-Pit 115
Koonce-Chi 112
Culp-Phi 108
Spahn-NY-SF 107
Buhl-Chi 107

Relief Runs
Linzy-SF 19.1
O'Dell-Mil 16.8
McBean-Pit 15.8
Perranoski-LA 15.2
Abernathy-Chi 14.6

Adjusted Relief Runs
Linzy-SF 19.3
O'Dell-Mil 16.6
Abernathy-Chi 16.1
McBean-Pit 15.6
McDaniel-Chi 15.1

Relief Ranking
Linzy-SF 36.7
O'Dell-Mil 27.6
Woodeshick-Hou-StL . . 22.6
McBean-Pit 20.3
Abernathy-Chi 18.9

Total Pitcher Index
Marichal-SF 5.9
Koufax-LA 5.5
Linzy-SF 4.8
Law-Pit 4.7
Drysdale-LA 4.6

Total Baseball Ranking
Mays-SF 7.5
Wynn-Hou 6.1
Marichal-SF 5.9
Santo-Chi 5.7
Koufax-LA 5.5

TEAM	G	W	L	PCT	GB	R	OR	AB	H	2B	3B	HR	BB	SO	AVG	OBP	SLG	OPS	OPS+	BR	BR+	PF	CHI	RC	SB	CS	SBA	SBR
MIN	162	102	60	.630		**774**	600	5488	**1396**	**257**	42	150	554	969	**.254**	.327	.399	726	**107**	84	**53**	104	**106**	**730**	92	33	**74**	**9**
CHI	162	95	67	.586	7	647	**555**	5509	1354	200	38	125	533	916	.246	.317	.364	681	106	1	43	94	99	636	50	33	60	-1
BAL	162	94	68	.580	8	641	578	5450	1299	227	38	125	529	907	.238	.309	.363	672	95	-21	-33	102	103	607	67	31	68	4
DET	162	89	73	.549	13	680	602	5368	1278	190	27	162	554	952	.238	.314	.374	688	101	10	3	101	**106**	628	57	41	58	-2
CLE	162	87	75	.537	15	663	613	5469	1367	198	21	156	506	**857**	.250	.317	.379	696	103	26	21	101	99	667	109	46	70	8
NY	162	77	85	.475	25	611	604	5470	1286	196	31	149	489	951	.235	.300	.364	664	95	-42	-38	99	103	593	35	20	64	1
CAL	162	75	87	.463	27	527	569	5354	1279	200	36	92	443	973	.239	.300	.341	641	90	-81	-68	98	97	549	107	59	64	3
WAS	162	70	92	.432	32	591	721	5374	1227	179	33	136	570	1125	.228	.306	.350	656	94	-47	-38	99	101	586	30	19	61	0
BOS	162	62	100	.383	40	669	791	5487	1378	244	40	**165**	**607**	964	.251	**.329**	**.400**	**729**	**107**	**95**	**53**	106	90	715	47	24	66	2
KC	162	59	103	.364	43	585	755	5393	1294	186	**59**	110	521	1020	.240	.311	.358	669	97	-25	-16	99	96	604	**110**	51	68	6
TOT	810					6388		54362	13158	2077	365	1370	5306	9634	.243	.314	.370	682							704	357	66	30

TEAM	CG	SH	SV	IP	H	H/G	HR	BB	SO	RAT	ERA	ERA+	OAV	OOB	PR	PR+	PF	CPI	FA	E	DP	FW	PW	BW	SBW	DIF
MIN	32	12	45	1457[1]	1278	7.9	166	503	934	11.2	3.14	113	.235	.303	52	66	103	**107**	.973	172	158	-2.2	7.1	**5.7**	**.6**	10.0
CHI	21	14	**53**	1481[2]	1261	**7.7**	122	**460**	946	**10.7**	3.00	107	**.231**	**.294**	76	35	92	98	.980	127	156	.6	3.8	4.6	-.4	5.6
BAL	32	**15**	41	1477[2]	1268	7.8	120	510	939	11.0	**2.99**	**116**	.233	.302	**78**	**79**	100	104	.980	126	152	.7	**8.5**	-3.5	.1	7.4
DET	**45**	14	31	1455	1283	8.0	137	509	1069	11.4	3.36	104	.237	.308	17	20	101	99	**.981**	116	126	1.3	2.2	.4	-.5	4.9
CLE	41	13	41	1458[1]	**1254**	7.8	129	500	**1156**	11.0	3.30	106	.232	.300	26	30	101	94	**.981**	**114**	127	**1.4**	3.3	2.3	.5	-1.3
NY	41	11	31	1459[2]	1337	8.3	126	511	1001	11.6	3.29	104	.245	.313	29	20	98	104	.978	137	**166**	-.0	2.2	-4.0	-.2	-1.7
CAL	39	14	33	1441[2]	1259	7.9	**91**	563	847	11.6	3.18	107	.237	.313	46	37	98	100	**.981**	123	149	.9	4.0	-7.2	.0	-3.5
WAS	21	8	40	1435[2]	1376	8.7	160	633	867	12.9	3.94	88	.254	.336	-75	-72	101	105	.977	143	148	-.4	-7.6	-4.0	-.3	1.6
BOS	33	9	25	1439[1]	1443	9.1	158	543	993	12.7	4.24	88	.260	.329	-125	-76	108	95	.974	162	129	-1.6	-8.1	**5.7**	-.1	-14.7
KC	18	7	32	1433	1399	8.8	161	574	882	12.7	4.24	82	.256	.331	-124	-118	101	96	.977	139	142	-.1	-12.5	-1.7	.3	-7.8
TOT	323	117	372	14539[1]		8.2				11.7	3.46		.243	.314					.979	1359	1453					

Runs
Versalles-Min 126
Oliva-Min 107
Tresh-NY 94
Buford-Chi 93
Colavito-Cle 92

Hits
Oliva-Min 185
Versalles-Min 182
Colavito-Cle 170
Tresh-NY 168
Fregosi-Cal 167

Doubles
Yastrzemski-Bos 45
Versalles-Min 45
Oliva-Min 40
Tresh-NY 29
Richardson-NY 28

Triples
Versalles-Min 12
Campaneris-KC 12
Aparicio-Bal 10
W.Smith-Cal 9

Home Runs
Conigliaro-Bos 32
Cash-Det 30
Horton-Det 29
Wagner-Cle 28

Total Bases
Versalles-Min 308
Tresh-NY 287
Oliva-Min 283
Colavito-Cle 277
Conigliaro-Bos 267

Runs Batted In
Colavito-Cle 108
Horton-Det 104
Oliva-Min 98
Mantilla-Bos 92
Whitfield-Cle 90

Runs Produced
Oliva-Min 189
Versalles-Min 184
Colavito-Cle 174
Hall-Min 147
Horton-Det 144

Bases On Balls
Colavito-Cle 93
Blefary-Bal 88
Mantilla-Bos 79
Cash-Det 77
Robinson-Chi 76

Batting Average
Oliva-Min .... .321
Yastrzemski-Bos ..... .312
Davalillo-Cle .... .301
Robinson-Bal .... .297
Wagner-Cle .... .294

On-Base Percentage
Yastrzemski-Bos ..... .398
Colavito-Cle .... .387
Oliva-Min .... .384
Blefary-Bal .... .382
Mantilla-Bos .... .377

Slugging Average
Yastrzemski-Bos ..... .536
Conigliaro-Bos ..... .512
Cash-Det .... .512
Wagner-Cle .... .495
Oliva-Min .... .491

On-Base Plus Slugging
Yastrzemski-Bos 935
Cash-Det 886
Oliva-Min 876
Wagner-Cle 866
Colavito-Cle 855

Adjusted OPS
Yastrzemski-Bos 154
Cash-Det 147
Wagner-Cle 143
Oliva-Min 141
Colavito-Cle 140

Batter Runs
Yastrzemski-Bos 41.6
Oliva-Min 35.3
Colavito-Cle 34.6
Cash-Det 31.0
Wagner-Cle 29.6

Adjusted Batter Runs
Yastrzemski-Bos 35.8
Colavito-Cle 33.7
Oliva-Min 31.0
Cash-Det 30.1
Wagner-Cle 28.8

Clutch Hitting Index
Mantilla-Bos 126
Horton-Det 120
Powell-Bal 116
Allison-Min 116
Adair-Bal 115

Runs Created
Colavito-Cle 110
Oliva-Min 109
Yastrzemski-Bos 102
Versalles-Min 102
Tresh-NY 101

Total Average
Yastrzemski-Bos .... .931
Cash-Det .... .894
Wagner-Cle .... .882
Blefary-Bal .... .876
Oliva-Min .... .863

Stolen Bases
Campaneris-KC 51
Cardenal-Cal 37
Versalles-Min 27
Davalillo-Cle 26
Aparicio-Bal 26

Stolen Base Average
Hinton-Cle 85.0
Versalles-Min 84.4
Howser-Cle 81.0
Davalillo-Cle 78.8
Aparicio-Bal 78.8

Stolen Base Runs
Campaneris-KC 4.6
Versalles-Min 4.2
Davalillo-Cle 3.3
Aparicio-Bal 3.3
Hinton-Cle 2.7

Fielding Runs
Boyer-NY 25.9
Hansen-Chi 16.7
Davalillo-Cle 14.7
Conigliaro-Bos 13.5
Knoop-Cal 12.8

Total Player Rating
Yastrzemski-Bos 3.6
Weis-Chi 3.4
Buford-Chi 3.4
Fregosi-Cal 3.3
Versalles-Min 3.3

Wins
Grant-Min 21
Stottlemyre-NY 20
Kaat-Min 18
McDowell-Cle 17

Win Percentage
Grant-Min .... .750
McLain-Det .... .727
Stottlemyre-NY ..... .690
Fisher-Chi .... .682
Siebert-Cle .... .667

Games
Fisher-Chi 82
Kline-Was 74
B.Lee-Cal 69
Dickson-KC 68
S.Miller-Bal 67

Complete Games
Stottlemyre-NY 18
McDowell-Cle 14
Grant-Min 14
McLain-Det 13

Shutouts
Grant-Min 6
Stottlemyre-NY 4
McLain-Det 4
Horlen-Chi 4
Chance-Cal 4

Saves
Kline-Was 29
S.Miller-Bal 24
Fisher-Chi 24
B.Lee-Cal 23
Radatz-Bos 22

Innings Pitched
Stottlemyre-NY ... 291.0
McDowell-Cle 273.0
Grant-Min 270.1
Kaat-Min 264.1
Newman-Cal 260.2

Fewest Hits/Game
McDowell-Cle 5.87
Fisher-Chi 6.42
Siebert-Cle 6.63
Richert-Was 6.77
Brunet-Cal 6.81

Fewest BB/Game
Terry-Cle 1.25
Monbouquette-Bos ... 1.57
Horlen-Chi 1.60
Ford-NY 1.84
Grant-Min 2.03

Strikeouts
McDowell-Cle 325
Lolich-Det 226
McLain-Det 192
Siebert-Cle 191
Downing-NY 179

Strikeouts/Game
McDowell-Cle 10.71
Siebert-Cle 9.11
Lolich-Det 8.35
McLain-Det 7.84
Morehead-Bos 7.61

Ratio
Fisher-Chi 8.87
Siebert-Cle 9.06
Terry-Cle 9.67
McLain-Det 9.72
Newman-Cal 10.01

Earned Run Average
McDowell-Cle 2.18
Fisher-Chi 2.40
Siebert-Cle 2.43
Brunet-Cal 2.56
Richert-Was 2.60

Adjusted ERA
McDowell-Cle 160
Siebert-Cle 143
Perry-Min 135
Richert-Was 134
Pappas-Bal 133

Opponents' Batting Avg.
McDowell-Cle ...... .185
Fisher-Chi .... .205
Siebert-Cle .... .206
Brunet-Cal .... .209
Richert-Was .... .210

Opponents' On-Base Pct.
Siebert-Cle .... .262
Fisher-Chi .... .262
Terry-Cle .... .269
McLain-Det .... .273
Pappas-Bal .... .281

Starter Runs
McDowell-Cle 38.9
Stottlemyre-NY 26.8
Siebert-Cle 21.5
Pappas-Bal 21.1
McLain-Det 20.7

Adjusted Starter Runs
McDowell-Cle 39.3
Stottlemyre-NY 25.4
Siebert-Cle 21.8
Pappas-Bal 21.2
McLain-Det 21.0

Clutch Pitching Index
Kaat-Min 123
Perry-Min 117
Peters-Chi 113
Richert-Was 110
Pappas-Bal 110

Relief Runs
Wilhelm-Chi 26.3
B.Lee-Cal 22.5
S.Miller-Bal 20.9
Fisher-Chi 19.5
Hamilton-NY 13.4

Adjusted Relief Runs
Wilhelm-Chi 23.9
B.Lee-Cal 22.0
S.Miller-Bal 20.9
Fisher-Chi 15.9
Hamilton-NY 13.3

Relief Ranking
S.Miller-Bal 41.4
B.Lee-Cal 31.6
Wilhelm-Chi 27.4
Worthington-Min 24.8
Fisher-Chi 23.5

Total Pitcher Index
S.Miller-Bal 4.6
McDowell-Cle 4.0
B.Lee-Cal 3.4
Kaat-Min 3.4
Stottlemyre-NY 3.3

Total Baseball Ranking
S.Miller-Bal 4.6
McDowell-Cle 4.0
Yastrzemski-Bos 3.6
B.Lee-Cal 3.4
Weis-Chi 3.4

TEAM	G	W	L	PCT	GB	R	OR	AB	H	2B	3B	HR	BB	SO	AVG	OBP	SLG	OPS	OPS+	BR	BR+	PF	CHI	RC	SB	CS	SBA	SBR
LA	162	95	67	.586		606	**490**	5471	1399	201	27	108	430	**830**	.256	.316	.362	678	103	-37	16	92	98	615	94	64	59	-2
SF	161	93	68	.578	1.5	675	626	5539	1373	195	31	181	414	860	.248	.304	.392	696	96	-14	-32	103	105	633	29	30	49	-4
PIT	162	92	70	.568	3	759	641	5676	**1586**	**238**	**66**	158	405	1011	**.279**	**.331**	**.428**	**759**	**116**	**117**	**116**	100	96	**779**	64	60	52	-7
PHI	162	87	75	.537	8	696	640	5607	1448	224	49	117	510	969	.258	.323	.378	701	101	12	11	100	101	683	56	42	57	-2
ATL	163	85	77	.525	10	**782**	683	5617	1476	220	32	**207**	**512**	913	.263	.329	.424	753	113	106	94	102	100	775	59	47	56	-3
STL	162	83	79	.512	12	571	577	5480	1377	196	61	108	345	977	.251	.300	.368	668	91	-66	-69	101	99	592	**144**	61	**70**	**10**
CIN	160	76	84	.475	18	692	702	5521	1434	232	33	149	394	877	.260	.311	.395	706	94	7	-46	109	105	658	70	50	58	-2
HOU	163	72	90	.444	23	612	695	5511	1405	203	35	112	491	885	.255	.320	.365	685	104	-19	28	93	94	640	90	47	66	3
NY	161	66	95	.410	28.5	587	761	5371	1286	187	35	98	446	992	.239	.303	.342	645	87	-99	-86	98	**108**	546	55	46	54	-4
CHI	162	59	103	.364	36	644	809	5592	1418	203	43	140	457	998	.254	.315	.380	695	98	-6	-14	101	97	665	76	47	62	0
TOT	809					6624		55385	14202	2099	412	1378	4404	9312	.257	.316	.384	699							737	494	60	-11

TEAM	CG	SH	SV	IP	H	H/G	HR	BB	SO	RAT	ERA	ERA+	OAV	OOB	PR	PR+	PF	CPI	FA	E	DP	FW	PW	BW	SBW	DIF
LA	**52**	**20**	35	1458	**1287**	**8.0**	**84**	**356**	**1084**	**10.4**	**2.63**	**126**	**.237**	**.288**	**159**	**119**	91	102	.979	133	128	.9	**12.5**	1.7	-.0	-.9
SF	**52**	14	27	1476[2]	1370	8.4	140	359	973	10.8	3.24	113	.244	.294	61	69	102	96	.974	168	131	-1.1	7.3	-3.3	-.3	10.1
PIT	35	12	**43**	1463[1]	1445	8.9	125	463	898	12.0	3.53	101	.261	.322	13	8	99	105	.978	141	**215**	.5	.9	**12.2**	-.6	-1.7
PHI	**52**	15	23	1459[2]	1439	8.9	137	412	928	11.8	3.57	101	.258	.316	6	4	100	102	**.982**	**113**	147	**2.0**	.5	1.2	-.0	2.6
ATL	37	10	36	1469[1]	1430	8.8	129	485	884	12.0	3.69	99	.257	.319	-12	-7	101	98	.976	154	139	-.2	-.7	9.9	-.2	-4.6
STL	47	19	32	1459[2]	1345	8.3	130	448	892	11.3	3.12	115	.246	.307	80	77	100	**107**	.977	145	166	.2	8.1	-7.2	**1.2**	-.1
CIN	28	10	35	1436	1408	8.9	153	490	1043	12.2	4.09	96	.258	.324	-76	-26	108	94	.980	122	133	1.4	-2.7	-4.8	-.0	2.3
HOU	34	13	26	1443[2]	1468	9.2	130	391	929	11.9	3.76	91	.262	.314	-24	-57	95	96	.972	174	126	-1.3	-5.9	3.0	.4	-4.9
NY	37	9	22	1427	1497	9.5	166	521	773	13.0	4.17	87	.272	.339	-89	-84	101	104	.975	159	171	-.6	-8.8	-9.0	-.3	4.3
CHI	28	6	24	1458	1513	9.4	184	479	908	12.5	4.34	85	.268	.328	-118	-104	102	97	.974	166	132	-.9	-10.8	-1.4	.1	-8.7
TOT	402	128	303	14551[1]		8.8				11.8	3.61		.257	.316					.977	1475	1488					

Runs
Alou-Atl 122
Aaron-Atl 117
Allen-Phi 112
Clemente-Pit 105
Williams-Chi 100

Hits
Alou-Atl 218
Rose-Cin 205
Clemente-Pit 202
Beckert-Chi 188

Doubles
Callison-Phi 40
Rose-Cin 38
Pinson-Cin 35
Alou-Atl 32

Triples
McCarver-StL 13
Brock-StL 12
Clemente-Pit 11

Home Runs
Aaron-Atl 44
Allen-Phi 40
Mays-SF 37
Torre-Atl 36
McCovey-SF 36

Total Bases
Alou-Atl 355
Clemente-Pit 342
Allen-Phi 331
Aaron-Atl 325
Mays-SF 307

Runs Batted In
Aaron-Atl 127
Clemente-Pit 119
Allen-Phi 110
White-Phi 103
Mays-SF 103

Runs Produced
Aaron-Atl 200
Clemente-Pit 195
Allen-Phi 182
White-Phi 166

Bases On Balls
Santo-Chi 95
Morgan-Hou 89
McCovey-SF 76
Aaron-Atl 76
Menke-Atl 71

Batting Average
Alou-Pit .342
Alou-Atl .327
Carty-Atl .326
Allen-Phi .317
Clemente-Pit .317

On-Base Percentage
Santo-Chi .417
Morgan-Hou .412
Allen-Phi .398
Carty-Atl .396
McCovey-SF .394

Slugging Average
Allen-Phi .632
McCovey-SF .586
Stargell-Pit .581
Torre-Atl .560
Mays-SF .556

On-Base Plus Slugging
Allen-Phi 1030
McCovey-SF 979
Stargell-Pit 965
Santo-Chi 955
Torre-Atl 945

Adjusted OPS
Allen-Phi 181
Stargell-Pit 164
McCovey-SF 163
Santo-Chi 161
Torre-Atl 157

Batter Runs
Allen-Phi 56.8
Santo-Chi 51.2
McCovey-SF 46.9
Torre-Atl 43.0
Stargell-Pit 41.1

Adjusted Batter Runs
Allen-Phi 56.7
Santo-Chi 49.7
McCovey-SF 43.8
Torre-Atl 41.4
Stargell-Pit 41.0

Clutch Hitting Index
White-Phi 125
Beckert-Chi 117
Clemente-Pit 117
Woodward-Atl 117
Staub-Hou 116

Runs Created
Allen-Phi 131
Santo-Chi 127
Alou-Atl 123
McCovey-SF 119
Clemente-Pit 119

Total Average
Allen-Phi 1.088
McCovey-SF 1.039
Santo-Chi .988
Stargell-Pit .980
Mays-SF .941

Stolen Bases
Brock-StL 74
Jackson-Hou 49
Wills-LA 38
Phillips-Phi-Chi 32
Harper-Cin 29

Stolen Base Average
Aaron-Atl 87.5
Brock-StL 80.4
Jackson-Hou 77.8
Harper-Cin 74.4
White-Phi 72.7

Stolen Base Runs
Brock-StL 10.0
Jackson-Hou 5.9
Aaron-Atl 3.6
Harper-Cin 2.9
Phillips-Phi-Chi 1.8

Fielding Runs
Mazeroski-Pit 40.8
Santo-Chi 28.8
Lanier-SF 28.2
Maxvill-StL 23.8
Clemente-Pit 15.4

Total Player Rating
Santo-Chi 7.9
Mazeroski-Pit 4.8
Allen-Phi 4.7
Mays-SF 4.5
Clemente-Pit 4.3

Wins
Koufax-LA 27
Marichal-SF 25
Perry-SF 21
Gibson-StL 21
Short-Phi 20

Win Percentage
Marichal-SF .806
Koufax-LA .750
Perry-SF .724
Short-Phi .667
Maloney-Cin .667

Games
Carroll-Atl 73
Mikkelsen-Pit 71
Knowles-Phi 69
Regan-LA 65
McDaniel-SF 64

Complete Games
Koufax-LA 27
Marichal-SF 25
Gibson-StL 20
Short-Phi 19
Bunning-Phi 16

Shutouts
L.Jackson-Chi-Phi 5
Maloney-Cin 5
Koufax-LA 5
Jaster-StL 5
Gibson-StL 5
Bunning-Phi 5

Saves
Regan-LA 21
McCool-Cin 18
Face-Pit 18
Raymond-Hou 16
Linzy-SF 16

Innings Pitched
Koufax-LA 323.0
Bunning-Phi 314.0
Marichal-SF 307.1
Gibson-StL 280.1
Drysdale-LA 273.2

Fewest Hits/Game
Marichal-SF 6.68
Koufax-LA 6.72
Gibson-StL 6.74
Maloney-Cin 6.97
Bolin-SF 6.98

Fewest BB/Game
Marichal-SF 1.05
Law-Pit 1.22
Perry-SF 1.41
Drysdale-LA 1.48
Bunning-Phi 1.58

Strikeouts
Koufax-LA 317
Bunning-Phi 252
Veale-Pit 229
Gibson-StL 225
Marichal-SF 222

Strikeouts/Game
Koufax-LA 8.83
Maloney-Cin 8.65
Sutton-LA 8.34
Veale-Pit 7.68
Jenkins-Phi-Chi 7.32

Ratio
Marichal-SF 7.88
Koufax-LA 8.86
Gibson-StL 9.41
Bunning-Phi 9.57
Cuellar-Hou 9.70

Earned Run Average
Koufax-LA 1.73
Cuellar-Hou 2.22
Marichal-SF 2.23
Bunning-Phi 2.41
Gibson-StL 2.44

Adjusted ERA
Koufax-LA 191
Marichal-SF 165
Cuellar-Hou 154
Bunning-Phi 149
Gibson-StL 147

Opponents' Batting Avg.
Marichal-SF .202
Koufax-LA .205
Gibson-StL .207
Bolin-SF .211
Maloney-Cin .214

Opponents' On-Base Pct.
Marichal-SF .230
Koufax-LA .253
Gibson-StL .267
Bunning-Phi .270
Cuellar-Hou .274

Starter Runs
Koufax-LA 67.4
Marichal-SF 47.2
Bunning-Phi 41.8
Gibson-StL 36.3
Cuellar-Hou 35.1

Adjusted Starter Runs
Koufax-LA 61.6
Marichal-SF 48.4
Bunning-Phi 41.6
Gibson-StL 36.0
Cuellar-Hou 32.1

Clutch Pitching Index
Jackson-StL 117
L.Jackson-Chi-Phi 110
Ellsworth-Chi 108
Johnson-Atl 108
Osteen-LA 107

Relief Runs
Regan-LA 25.8
Carroll-Atl 19.8
Hoerner-StL 17.5
McCool-Cin 13.2
Woodeshick-StL 13.2

Adjusted Relief Runs
Regan-LA 23.8
Carroll-Atl 20.2
Hoerner-StL 17.4
McCool-Cin 15.4
McDaniel-SF 13.4

Relief Ranking
Regan-LA 37.1
McCool-Cin 27.0
Carroll-Atl 22.3
Hoerner-StL 19.0
McDaniel-SF 16.3

Total Pitcher Index
Koufax-LA 6.0
Marichal-SF 5.7
Gibson-StL 4.5
Jackson-StL 4.2
Regan-LA 4.1

Total Baseball Ranking
Santo-Chi 7.9
Koufax-LA 6.0
Marichal-SF 5.7
Mazeroski-Pit 4.8
Allen-Phi 4.7

TEAM	G	W	L	PCT	GB	R	OR	AB	H	2B	3B	HR	BB	SO	AVG	OBP	SLG	OPS	OPS+	BR	BR+	PF	CHI	RC	SB	CS	SBA	SBR
BAL	160	97	63	.606		**755**	601	5529	**1426**	**243**	35	175	514	926	**.258**	**.325**	**.409**	**734**	**119**	**114**	**126**	98	100	**727**	55	43	56	-3
MIN	162	89	73	.549	9	663	581	5390	1341	219	33	144	513	844	.249	.319	.382	701	101	49	8	106	98	643	67	42	61	0
DET	162	88	74	.543	10	719	698	5507	1383	224	45	**179**	**551**	987	.251	.323	.406	729	112	102	85	102	96	714	41	34	55	-3
CHI	163	83	79	.512	15	574	**517**	5348	1235	193	40	87	476	872	.231	.299	.331	630	93	-83	-44	93	106	539	**153**	78	66	6
CLE	162	81	81	.500	17	574	586	5474	1300	156	25	155	450	914	.237	.299	.360	659	95	-38	-38	100	97	579	53	41	56	-3
CAL	162	80	82	.494	18	604	643	5360	1244	179	54	122	525	1062	.232	.305	.354	659	98	-29	-12	97	101	582	80	54	60	-1
KC	160	74	86	.463	23	564	648	5328	1259	212	**56**	70	421	982	.236	.295	.337	632	90	-84	-67	97	**107**	535	132	50	**73**	**12**
WAS	159	71	88	.447	25.5	557	659	5318	1245	185	40	126	450	1069	.234	.296	.355	651	94	-50	-44	99	99	548	53	37	59	-1
BOS	162	72	90	.444	26	655	731	5498	1318	228	44	145	542	1020	.240	.312	.376	688	93	24	-38	110	98	640	35	24	59	-1
NY	160	70	89	.440	26.5	611	612	5330	1254	182	36	162	485	**817**	.235	.302	.374	676	104	-5	18	96	100	598	49	29	63	1
TOT	806					6276		54082	13005	2021	408	1365	4927	9493	.241	.308	.369	676							718	432	62	7

TEAM	CG	SH	SV	IP	H	H/G	HR	BB	SO	RAT	ERA	ERA+	OAV	OOB	PR	PR+	PF	CPI	FA	E	DP	FW	PW	BW	SBW	DIF
BAL	23	13	**51**	1466[1]	1267	7.8	127	514	1070	11.2	3.33	100	.233	.303	19	2	97	97	**.981**	**115**	142	**1.4**	.3	**13.6**	-.4	2.4
MIN	**52**	11	28	1438[2]	1246	7.8	139	**392**	1015	10.5	3.14	115	.232	.287	48	71	105	97	.977	139	118	.0	7.7	.9	-.0	-.4
DET	36	11	38	1454[1]	1356	8.4	185	520	1026	11.9	3.85	90	.247	.317	-67	-59	101	102	.980	120	142	1.2	-6.3	9.2	-.4	3.5
CHI	38	**22**	34	1475[1]	**1229**	**7.5**	**101**	403	896	**10.2**	**2.69**	**118**	**.226**	**.283**	**123**	**86**	92	100	.976	159	149	-1.0	**9.3**	-4.7	.6	-2.0
CLE	49	15	28	1467[1]	1260	7.8	129	489	**1111**	11.0	3.23	107	.232	.299	34	35	100	98	.978	138	132	.1	3.8	-4.0	-.4	.7
CAL	31	12	40	1457[1]	1364	8.5	136	511	836	11.9	3.57	94	.251	.320	-21	-34	98	**105**	.979	136	**186**	.2	-3.6	-1.2	-.2	4.0
KC	19	11	47	1435	1281	8.1	106	630	854	12.3	3.56	96	.241	.326	-19	-25	99	101	.977	139	154	-.0	-2.6	-7.1	**1.2**	2.8
WAS	25	6	35	1419	1282	8.2	154	448	866	11.2	3.71	93	.242	.304	-42	-38	101	95	.977	142	139	-.3	-4.0	-4.7	-.2	.8
BOS	32	10	31	1463[2]	1402	8.7	164	577	977	12.4	3.92	97	.253	.327	-78	-16	111	103	.975	155	153	-.9	-1.7	-4.0	-.2	-2.1
NY	29	7	32	1415[2]	1318	8.4	124	443	842	11.4	3.42	97	.248	.308	3	-15	97	102	.977	142	142	-.2	-1.6	2.0	.0	-9.6
TOT	334	118	364	14492[2]		8.1				11.4	3.44		.241	.308					.978	1385	1457					

Runs
F.Robinson-Bal 122
Oliva-Min 99
Cash-Det 98
Agee-Chi 98

Hits
Oliva-Min 191
F.Robinson-Bal 182
Aparicio-Bal 182
Agee-Chi 172
Cash-Det 168

Doubles
Yastrzemski-Bos 39
B.Robinson-Bal 35
F.Robinson-Bal 34
Oliva-Min 32
Fregosi-Cal 32

Triples
Knoop-Cal 11
Campaneris-KC 10
Brinkman-Was 9

Home Runs
F.Robinson-Bal 49
Killebrew-Min 39
Powell-Bal 34
Cash-Det 32
Pepitone-NY 31

Total Bases
F.Robinson-Bal 367
Oliva-Min 312
Killebrew-Min 306
Cash-Det 288
Agee-Chi 281

Runs Batted In
F.Robinson-Bal 122
Killebrew-Min 110
Powell-Bal 109
B.Robinson-Bal 100
Horton-Det 100

Runs Produced
F.Robinson-Bal 195
B.Robinson-Bal 168
Agee-Chi 162
Oliva-Min 161
Killebrew-Min 160

Bases On Balls
Killebrew-Min 103
Foy-Bos 91
F.Robinson-Bal 87
Tresh-NY 86
Yastrzemski-Bos 84

Batting Average
F.Robinson-Bal .316
Oliva-Min .307
Kaline-Det .288
Powell-Bal .287
Killebrew-Min .281

On-Base Percentage
F.Robinson-Bal .415
Kaline-Det .396
Killebrew-Min .393
McAuliffe-Det .375
Powell-Bal .374

Slugging Average
F.Robinson-Bal .637
Killebrew-Min .538
Kaline-Det .534
Powell-Bal .532
McAuliffe-Det .509

On-Base Plus Slugging
F.Robinson-Bal 1052
Killebrew-Min 931
Kaline-Det 931
Powell-Bal 905
McAuliffe-Det 884

Adjusted OPS
F.Robinson-Bal 200
Kaline-Det 161
Powell-Bal 159
Killebrew-Min 155
McAuliffe-Det 148

Batter Runs
F.Robinson-Bal 73.6
Killebrew-Min 49.9
Kaline-Det 42.1
Powell-Bal 36.3
Oliva-Min 33.2

Adjusted Batter Runs
F.Robinson-Bal 76.0
Killebrew-Min 42.6
Kaline-Det 39.8
Powell-Bal 37.8
Mantle-NY 31.4

Clutch Hitting Index
Powell-Bal 119
Horton-Det 119
Green-KC 116
Hershberger-KC 115
D.Johnson-Bal 113

Runs Created
F.Robinson-Bal 146
Killebrew-Min 122
Oliva-Min 106
Kaline-Det 105
Cash-Det 101

Total Average
F.Robinson-Bal 1.104
Kaline-Det .969
Killebrew-Min .967
Powell-Bal .898
McAuliffe-Det .877

Stolen Bases
Campaneris-KC 52
Buford-Chi 51
Agee-Chi 44
Aparicio-Bal 25
Cardenal-Cal 24

Stolen Base Average
Campaneris-KC 83.9
Tartabull-KC-Bos 82.6
Tovar-Min 72.7
Agee-Chi 71.0
Buford-Chi 69.9

Stolen Base Runs
Campaneris-KC 7.9
Buford-Chi 3.5
Agee-Chi 3.4
Tartabull-KC-Bos 2.8
Salmon-Cle 1.9

Fielding Runs
Weis-Chi 36.9
Tresh-NY 27.7
Boyer-NY 19.9
Yastrzemski-Bos 16.6
Knoop-Cal 16.5

Total Player Rating
F.Robinson-Bal 6.5
Tresh-NY 4.3
Kaline-Det 4.0
Fregosi-Cal 3.9
Oliva-Min 3.3

Wins
Kaat-Min 25
McLain-Det 20
Wilson-Bos-Det 18
Siebert-Cle 16
Palmer-Bal 15

Win Percentage
Siebert-Cle .667
Kaat-Min .658
Wilson-Bos-Det .621
Palmer-Bal .600
McLain-Det .588

Games
Fisher-Chi-Bal 67
Cox-Was 66
Aker-KC 66
Worthington-Min 65
Kline-Was 63

Complete Games
Kaat-Min 19
McLain-Det 14
Wilson-Bos-Det 13
Bell-Cle 12

Shutouts
Tiant-Cle 5
McDowell-Cle 5
John-Chi 5

Saves
Aker-KC 32
Kline-Was 23
Sherry-Det 20
Fisher-Chi-Bal 19
S.Miller-Bal 18

Innings Pitched
Kaat-Min 304.2
McLain-Det 264.1
Wilson-Bos-Det 264.0
Chance-Cal 259.2
Bell-Cle 254.1

Fewest Hits/Game
McDowell-Cle 6.02
Boswell-Min 6.38
Peters-Chi 6.86
McLain-Det 6.98
Chance-Cal 7.14

Fewest BB/Game
Kaat-Min 1.62
Peterson-NY 1.67
Grant-Min 1.77
Peters-Chi 1.98
Hargan-Cle 2.11

Strikeouts
McDowell-Cle 225
Kaat-Min 205
Wilson-Bos-Det 200
Richert-Was 195
Bell-Cle 194

Strikeouts/Game
McDowell-Cle 10.42
Boswell-Min 9.19
Lolich-Det 7.64
Richert-Was 7.14
Bell-Cle 6.87

Ratio
Peters-Chi 8.97
Kaat-Min 9.72
Richert-Was 9.74
Siebert-Cle 9.75
Ortega-Was 9.85

Earned Run Average
Peters-Chi 1.98
Horlen-Chi 2.43
Hargan-Cle 2.48
Perry-Min 2.54
John-Chi 2.62

Adjusted ERA
Peters-Chi 160
Perry-Min 142
Hargan-Cle 138
Kaat-Min 131
Horlen-Chi 130

Opponents' Batting Avg.
McDowell-Cle .188
Boswell-Min .197
Peters-Chi .212
McLain-Det .214
Richert-Was .215

Opponents' On-Base Pct.
Peters-Chi .261
Richert-Was .271
Kaat-Min .271
Ortega-Was .276
Siebert-Cle .278

Starter Runs
Peters-Chi 33.1
Horlen-Chi 23.5
Kaat-Min 23.3
Hargan-Cle 20.3
John-Chi 20.1

Adjusted Starter Runs
Peters-Chi 29.4
Kaat-Min 27.5
Perry-Min 20.7
Hargan-Cle 20.3
Nash-KC 19.2

Clutch Pitching Index
McNally-Bal 118
Horlen-Chi 114
Brunet-Cal 114
Perry-Min 113
Hargan-Cle 110

Relief Runs
Aker-KC 18.1
Wilhelm-Chi 16.0
S.Miller-Bal 12.1
Fisher-Chi-Bal 10.8
Lines-Was 10.7

Adjusted Relief Runs
Aker-KC 17.9
Wilhelm-Chi 14.8
S.Miller-Bal 11.4
Worthington-Min 11.0
Lines-Was 10.8

Relief Ranking
Aker-KC 27.1
S.Miller-Bal 18.9
McMahon-Cle-Bos 18.7
Kline-Was 16.0
Locker-Chi 15.1

Total Pitcher Index
Peters-Chi 4.2
Kaat-Min 3.9
Aker-KC 3.2
Wilson-Bos-Det 3.2
Horlen-Chi 2.4

Total Baseball Ranking
F.Robinson-Bal 6.5
Tresh-NY 4.3
Peters-Chi 4.2
Kaline-Det 4.0
Kaat-Min 3.9

TEAM	G	W	L	PCT	GB	R	OR	AB	H	2B	3B	HR	BB	SO	AVG	OBP	SLG	OPS	OPS+	BR	BR+	PF	CHI	RC	SB	CS	SBA	SBR
STL	161	101	60	.627		695	557	5566	1462	225	40	115	443	919	.263	.322	.379	701	**109**	52	**61**	99	103	676	**102**	54	65	4
SF	162	91	71	.562	10.5	652	**551**	5524	1354	201	39	140	520	978	.245	.315	.372	687	104	24	33	99	100	641	22	30	42	-6
CHI	162	87	74	.540	14	**702**	624	5463	1373	211	49	128	509	912	.251	.319	.378	697	101	44	15	105	**105**	654	63	50	56	-4
CIN	162	87	75	.537	14.5	604	563	5519	1366	251	54	109	372	969	.248	.299	.372	671	88	-20	-80	111	102	592	92	63	59	-2
PHI	162	82	80	.506	19.5	612	581	5401	1306	221	47	103	**545**	1033	.242	.314	.357	671	98	-1	-7	101	99	604	79	62	56	-4
PIT	163	81	81	.500	20.5	679	693	5724	**1585**	193	**62**	91	387	914	**.277**	**.327**	**.380**	**707**	108	**63**	60	101	97	**693**	79	37	68	4
ATL	162	77	85	.475	24.5	631	640	5450	1307	191	29	**158**	512	947	.240	.309	.372	681	102	10	19	99	100	615	55	45	55	-4
LA	162	73	89	.451	28.5	519	595	5456	1285	203	38	82	485	**881**	.236	.303	.332	635	97	-74	-25	92	95	541	56	47	54	-4
HOU	162	69	93	.426	32.5	626	742	5506	1372	**259**	46	93	537	934	.249	.319	.364	683	107	20	43	97	97	640	88	38	**70**	**6**
NY	162	61	101	.377	40.5	498	672	5417	1288	178	23	83	362	981	.238	.290	.325	615	83	-118	-110	98	103	500	58	44	57	-3
TOT	810					6218		55026	13698	2133	427	1102	4672	9468	.249	.312	.364	675							694	470	60	-12

TEAM	CG	SH	SV	IP	H	H/G	HR	BB	SO	RAT	ERA	ERA+	OAV	OOB	PR	PR+	PF	CPI	FA	E	DP	FW	PW	BW	SBW	DIF
STL	44	17	**45**	1465	1313	8.1	97	431	956	11.0	3.05	108	.239	.299	54	40	97	98	.978	140	127	.0	4.4	**6.7**	.6	9.1
SF	**64**	17	25	1474^{1}	**1283**	**7.9**	113	453	990	**10.8**	**2.92**	113	**.234**	**.296**	**75**	62	97	101	.979	134	149	.4	6.8	3.6	-.5	-.1
CHI	47	7	28	1457	1352	8.4	142	463	888	11.4	3.49	102	.246	.308	-17	9	105	99	**.981**	**121**	143	**1.2**	1.0	1.7	-.3	3.1
CIN	34	**18**	39	1468	1328	8.2	101	498	**1065**	11.5	3.05	**123**	.241	.309	54	**103**	111	**104**	.980	**121**	124	**1.2**	**11.2**	-8.6	-.0	2.5
PHI	46	17	23	1453^{2}	1372	8.5	**86**	403	967	11.3	3.11	110	.250	.306	44	49	101	102	.978	137	174	.3	5.4	-.7	-.3	-3.4
PIT	35	5	35	1458^{1}	1439	8.9	108	561	820	12.6	3.74	90	.261	.332	-59	-61	100	103	.978	141	**186**	.0	-6.6	6.5	.6	-.4
ATL	35	5	32	1454	1377	8.6	118	449	862	11.6	3.48	96	.251	.313	-16	-25	98	100	.978	138	148	.2	-2.7	2.1	-.3	-3.2
LA	41	17	24	1473	1421	8.7	93	**393**	967	11.4	3.22	96	.254	.308	27	-20	92	102	.975	160	144	-1.1	-2.1	-2.7	-.3	-1.7
HOU	35	8	21	1445^{2}	1444	9.0	120	485	1060	12.3	4.03	82	.260	.324	-105	-117	98	93	.974	159	120	-1.0	-12.6	4.7	**.8**	-3.7
NY	36	10	19	1433^{2}	1369	8.6	124	536	893	12.2	3.73	91	.253	.323	-56	-54	100	99	.975	157	147	-.9	-5.8	-11.9	-.2	-1.1
TOT	417	121	291	14582^{2}		8.5				11.6	3.38		.249	.312					.978	1408	1462					

Runs
Brock-StL 113
Aaron-Atl 113
Santo-Chi 107
Clemente-Pit 103
Wynn-Hou 102

Hits
Clemente-Pit 209
Brock-StL 206
Pinson-Cin 187
Wills-Pit 186
Alou-Pit 186

Doubles
Staub-Hou 44
Cepeda-StL 37
Aaron-Atl 37

Triples
Pinson-Cin 13
Williams-Chi 12
Brock-StL 12
Morgan-Hou 11

Home Runs
Aaron-Atl 39
Wynn-Hou 37
Santo-Chi 31
McCovey-SF 31
Hart-SF 29

Total Bases
Aaron-Atl 344
Brock-StL 325
Clemente-Pit 324
Williams-Chi 305
Santo-Chi 300

Runs Batted In
Cepeda-StL 111
Clemente-Pit 110
Aaron-Atl 109
Wynn-Hou 107
Perez-Cin 102

Runs Produced
Clemente-Pit 190
Aaron-Atl 183
Cepeda-StL 177
Santo-Chi 174
Wynn-Hou 172

Bases On Balls
Santo-Chi 96
Morgan-Hou 81
Phillips-Chi 80
Hart-SF 77
Allen-Phi 75

Batting Average
Clemente-Pit 357
Gonzalez-Phi 339
Alou-Pit 338
Flood-StL 335
Staub-Hou 333

On-Base Percentage
Allen-Phi 404
Cepeda-StL 403
Staub-Hou 402
Clemente-Pit 402
Santo-Chi 401

Slugging Average
Aaron-Atl 573
Allen-Phi 566
Clemente-Pit 554
McCovey-SF 535
Cepeda-StL 524

On-Base Plus Slugging
Allen-Phi 970
Clemente-Pit 956
Aaron-Atl 946
Cepeda-StL 927
McCovey-SF 916

Adjusted OPS
Allen-Phi 173
Clemente-Pit 170
Aaron-Atl 169
Cepeda-StL 166
McCovey-SF 162

Batter Runs
Clemente-Pit 52.1
Aaron-Atl 50.1
Santo-Chi 47.9
Cepeda-StL 47.3
Allen-Phi 46.1

Adjusted Batter Runs
Aaron-Atl 51.8
Clemente-Pit 51.6
Cepeda-StL 48.8
Allen-Phi 45.1
Santo-Chi 42.6

Clutch Hitting Index
Shannon-StL 141
Lanier-SF 125
Maxvill-StL 120
Fairly-LA 118
Boyer-Atl 117

Runs Created
Clemente-Pit 126
Aaron-Atl 126
Santo-Chi 120
Cepeda-StL 118
Hart-SF 111

Total Average
Allen-Phi 1.054
Aaron-Atl 965
Clemente-Pit 959
Cepeda-StL 950
McCovey-SF 941

Stolen Bases
Brock-StL 52
Wills-Pit 29
Morgan-Hou 29
Pinson-Cin 26
Phillips-Chi 24

Stolen Base Average
Morgan-Hou 85.3
Wynn-Hou 80.0
Allen-Phi 80.0
Davis-LA 76.9
Pinson-Cin 76.5

Stolen Base Runs
Brock-StL 5.1
Morgan-Hou 4.6
Pinson-Cin 2.9
Wills-Pit 2.9
Allen-Phi 2.7

Fielding Runs
Santo-Chi 30.6
Lanier-SF 28.9
Wine-Phi 28.9
Fuentes-SF 24.5
Mazeroski-Pit 16.7

Total Player Rating
Santo-Chi 7.5
Aaron-Atl 5.8
Clemente-Pit 5.5
Allen-Phi 4.4
Cepeda-StL 4.3

Wins
McCormick-SF 22
Jenkins-Chi 20
Osteen-LA 17
Bunning-Phi 17

Win Percentage
Hughes-StL 727
McCormick-SF 688
Veale-Pit 667
Jenkins-Chi 606
Jarvis-Atl 600

Games
Perranoski-LA 70
Abernathy-Cin 70
Willis-StL 65
Face-Pit 61

Complete Games
Jenkins-Chi 20
Seaver-NY 18
Perry-SF 18
Marichal-SF 18

Shutouts
Bunning-Phi 6
Osteen-LA 5
Nolan-Cin 5
McCormick-SF 5
L.Jackson-Phi 4

Saves
Abernathy-Cin 28
Linzy-SF 17
Face-Pit 17
Perranoski-LA 16
Hoerner-StL 15

Innings Pitched
Bunning-Phi 302.1
Perry-SF 293.0
Jenkins-Chi 289.1
Osteen-LA 288.1
Drysdale-LA 282.0

Fewest Hits/Game
Hughes-StL 6.64
Wilson-Hou 6.90
Perry-SF 7.10
Queen-Cin 7.13
Niekro-Atl 7.13

Fewest BB/Game
Pappas-Cin 1.57
Osteen-LA 1.62
Johnson-Atl 1.63
Niekro-Chi 1.70
L.Jackson-Phi 1.86

Strikeouts
Bunning-Phi 253
Jenkins-Chi 236
Perry-SF 230
Nolan-Cin 206
Cuellar-Hou 203

Strikeouts/Game
Nolan-Cin 8.18
Veale-Pit 7.94
Carlton-StL 7.83
Wilson-Hou 7.78
Gibson-StL 7.55

Ratio
Hughes-StL 8.78
Bunning-Phi 9.73
Queen-Cin 9.80
Perry-SF 9.80
Niekro-Atl 9.83

Earned Run Average
Niekro-Atl 1.87
Bunning-Phi 2.29
Short-Phi 2.39
Nolan-Cin 2.58
Perry-SF 2.61

Adjusted ERA
Niekro-Atl 178
Bunning-Phi 149
Nolan-Cin 145
Short-Phi 142
Queen-Cin 136

Opponents' Batting Avg.
Hughes-StL 203
Wilson-Hou 209
Perry-SF 214
Queen-Cin 215
Bunning-Phi 217

Opponents' On-Base Pct.
Hughes-StL 252
Bunning-Phi 273
Queen-Cin 273
Perry-SF 274
Jenkins-Chi 277

Starter Runs
Bunning-Phi 36.4
Niekro-Atl 34.6
Perry-SF 24.9
Short-Phi 21.8
Nolan-Cin 20.0

Adjusted Starter Runs
Bunning-Phi 37.2
Niekro-Atl 33.9
Nolan-Cin 26.5
Jenkins-Chi 22.8
Perry-SF 22.6

Clutch Pitching Index
Ellis-Cin 123
Niekro-Atl 121
Seaver-NY 114
Marichal-SF 114
Short-Phi 114

Relief Runs
Abernathy-Cin 24.9
Linzy-SF 19.9
Nottebart-Cin 12.8
McBean-Pit 12.1
Farrell-Hou-Phi 11.9

Adjusted Relief Runs
Abernathy-Cin 26.4
Linzy-SF 19.5
Nottebart-Cin 14.5
Farrell-Hou-Phi 12.1
McBean-Pit 12.0

Relief Ranking
Abernathy-Cin 35.7
Linzy-SF 33.4
Hall-Phi 22.9
Farrell-Hou-Phi 19.9
Face-Pit 15.4

Total Pitcher Index
Abernathy-Cin 4.0
Bunning-Phi 4.0
Linzy-SF 4.0
Niekro-Atl 3.8
Jenkins-Chi 3.0

Total Baseball Ranking
Santo-Chi 7.5
Aaron-Atl 5.8
Clemente-Pit 5.5
Allen-Phi 4.4
Cepeda-StL 4.3

TEAM	G	W	L	PCT	GB	R	OR	AB	H	2B	3B	HR	BB	SO	AVG	OBP	SLG	OPS	OPS+	BR	BR+	PF	CHI	RC	SB	CS	SBA	SBR
BOS	162	92	70	.568		**722**	614	5471	**1394**	**216**	39	**158**	522	1020	**.255**	.323	**.395**	**718**	109	**118**	64	108	100	**694**	68	59	54	-6
MIN	164	91	71	.562	1	671	590	5458	1309	**216**	48	131	512	976	.240	.310	.369	679	99	44	-5	108	104	625	55	37	60	-1
DET	163	91	71	.562	1	683	587	5410	1315	192	36	152	**626**	994	.243	**.327**	.376	703	**111**	100	**81**	103	96	681	37	21	64	1
CHI	162	89	73	.549	3	531	**491**	5383	1209	181	34	89	480	**849**	.225	.293	.320	613	90	-80	-60	96	104	504	124	82	60	-1
CAL	161	84	77	.522	7.5	567	587	5307	1265	170	37	114	453	1021	.238	.302	.349	651	102	-12	11	96	99	553	40	36	53	-4
WAS	161	76	85	.472	15.5	550	637	5441	1211	168	25	115	472	1037	.223	.289	.326	615	92	-81	-60	96	**107**	512	53	37	59	-1
BAL	161	76	85	.472	15.5	654	592	5456	1312	215	44	138	531	1002	.240	.313	.372	685	110	54	59	99	99	639	54	37	59	-1
CLE	162	75	87	.463	17	559	613	5461	1282	213	35	131	413	984	.235	.295	.359	654	98	-15	-20	101	96	563	53	65	45	-11
NY	163	72	90	.444	20	522	621	5443	1225	166	17	100	532	1043	.225	.298	.317	615	91	-74	-54	96	98	522	63	37	63	1
KC	161	62	99	.385	29.5	533	660	5349	1244	212	**50**	69	452	1019	.233	.297	.330	627	94	-54	-36	97	100	539	**132**	59	**69**	**8**
TOT	810					5992		54179	12766	1949	365	1197	4993	9945	.236	.305	.352	656							679	470	59	-15

TEAM	CG	SH	SV	IP	H	H/G	HR	BB	SO	RAT	ERA	ERA+	OAV	OOB	PR	PR+	PF	CPI	FA	E	DP	FW	PW	BW	SBW	DIF
BOS	41	9	44	1459^1	1307	8.1	142	477	1010	11.3	3.37	104	.239	.306	-21	19	108	101	.977	142	142	-.5	2.1	7.1	-.5	3.0
MIN	**58**	18	24	1461	1336	8.3	115	**396**	1089	11.0	3.14	110	.243	.298	15	49	107	101	.978	132	123	.2	5.5	-.5	.0	5.0
DET	46	17	40	1443^2	1230	7.7	151	472	1038	10.9	3.32	98	.230	.297	-14	-9	101	97	.978	132	126	.1	-.9	**9.0**	.3	1.7
CHI	36	**24**	39	1490^1	**1197**	**7.3**	**87**	465	927	**10.4**	**2.46**	**127**	**.219**	**.288**	**129**	**112**	96	**106**	.979	138	149	-.3	**12.4**	-6.6	.0	2.6
CAL	19	14	**46**	1430^1	1246	7.9	118	525	892	11.4	3.20	98	.237	.311	6	-8	97	105	**.982**	**111**	135	**1.3**	-.8	1.3	-.3	2.2
WAS	24	14	39	1473^1	1334	8.2	113	495	878	11.4	3.39	93	.242	.309	-25	-37	98	98	.978	144	**167**	-.7	-4.0	-6.6	.0	7.0
BAL	29	17	36	1457^1	1218	7.6	116	566	1034	11.3	3.33	95	.228	.305	-15	-28	98	95	.980	124	144	.5	-3.0	6.6	.0	-8.4
CLE	49	14	27	1477^2	1258	7.7	120	559	**1189**	11.3	3.25	101	.231	.307	-3	3	101	99	.981	116	138	1.1	.4	-2.2	-1.0	-4.1
NY	37	16	27	1480^2	1375	8.4	110	480	898	11.6	3.24	97	.249	.313	-2	-19	97	**106**	.976	154	144	-1.2	-2.0	-5.9	.3	.1
KC	26	10	34	1428	1265	8.0	125	558	990	11.8	3.69	87	.238	.315	-71	-80	99	94	.978	132	120	.0	-8.8	-3.9	**1.0**	-6.7
TOT	365	153	356	14601^2		7.9				11.2	3.24		.236	.305					.979	1325	1388					

Runs
Yastrzemski-Bos . . . 112
Killebrew-Min 105
Tovar-Min 98
Kaline-Det 94
McAuliffe-Det 92

Hits
Yastrzemski-Bos . . . 189
Tovar-Min 173
Scott-Bos 171
Fregosi-Cal 171
B.Robinson-Bal 164

Doubles
Oliva-Min 34
Tovar-Min 32
Yastrzemski-Bos 31
D.Johnson-Bal 30
Campaneris-KC 29

Triples
Blair-Bal 12
Buford-Chi 9

Home Runs
Yastrzemski-Bos 44
Killebrew-Min 44
Howard-Was 36
F.Robinson-Bal 30

Total Bases
Yastrzemski-Bos 360
Killebrew-Min 305
F.Robinson-Bal 276
B.Robinson-Bal 265
Howard-Was 265

Runs Batted In
Yastrzemski-Bos 121
Killebrew-Min 113
F.Robinson-Bal 94
Howard-Was 89
Oliva-Min 83

Runs Produced
Yastrzemski-Bos . . . 189
Killebrew-Min 174
F.Robinson-Bal 147
Kaline-Det 147
B.Robinson-Bal 143

Bases On Balls
Killebrew-Min 131
Mantle-NY 107
McAuliffe-Det 105
Yastrzemski-Bos 91
Kaline-Det 83

Batting Average
Yastrzemski-Bos 326
F.Robinson-Bal 311
Kaline-Det 308
Scott-Bos 303
Blair-Bal 293

On-Base Percentage
Yastrzemski-Bos 421
Kaline-Det 415
Killebrew-Min 413
F.Robinson-Bal 408
Mantle-NY 394

Slugging Average
Yastrzemski-Bos 622
F.Robinson-Bal 576
Killebrew-Min 558
Kaline-Det 541
Howard-Was 511

On-Base Plus Slugging
Yastrzemski-Bos . . 1043
F.Robinson-Bal 984
Killebrew-Min 970
Kaline-Det 957
Mincher-Cal 855

Adjusted OPS
Yastrzemski-Bos . . . 189
F.Robinson-Bal 189
Kaline-Det 176
Killebrew-Min 170
Mincher-Cal 156

Batter Runs
Yastrzemski-Bos 76.4
Killebrew-Min 62.3
F.Robinson-Bal 53.3
Kaline-Det 48.4
Scott-Bos 33.8

Adjusted Batter Runs
Yastrzemski-Bos 65.7
F.Robinson-Bal 54.2
Killebrew-Min 52.6
Kaline-Det 45.7
Mincher-Cal 34.7

Clutch Hitting Index
Hershberger-KC 124
D.Johnson-Bal 113
Hansen-Chi 111
Northrup-Det 109
Versalles-Min 108

Runs Created
Yastrzemski-Bos 155
Killebrew-Min 131
F.Robinson-Bal 113
Kaline-Det 104
Scott-Bos 97

Total Average
Yastrzemski-Bos . . . 1.134
Killebrew-Min 1.058
F.Robinson-Bal . . . 1.029
Kaline-Det 1.009
Mantle-NY 874

Stolen Bases
Campaneris-KC 55
Buford-Chi 34
Agee-Chi 28
McCraw-Chi 24
Clarke-NY 21

Stolen Base Average
Valentine-Was 85.0
Clarke-NY 84.0
Aparicio-Bal 78.3
Campaneris-KC 77.5
Agee-Chi 73.7

Stolen Base Runs
Campaneris-KC 6.5
Clarke-NY 3.2
Valentine-Was 2.7
Agee-Chi 2.7
Aparicio-Bal 2.2

Fielding Runs
B.Robinson-Bal 30.8
Blair-Bal 20.9
Smith-Bos 16.5
Monday-KC 15.2
Clarke-NY 15.2

Total Player Rating
Yastrzemski-Bos 7.4
B.Robinson-Bal 5.2
Kaline-Det 4.9
F.Robinson-Bal 4.7
Blair-Bal 4.5

Wins
Wilson-Det 22
Lonborg-Bos 22
Chance-Min 20
Horlen-Chi 19
McLain-Det 17

Win Percentage
Horlen-Chi 731
Lonborg-Bos 710
Wilson-Det 667
Sparma-Det 640
Peters-Chi 593

Games
Locker-Chi 77
Rojas-Cal 72
Kelso-Cal 69
Womack-NY 65
McMahon-Bos-Chi . . . 63

Complete Games
Chance-Min 18
Lonborg-Bos 15
Hargan-Cle 15

Shutouts
McGlothlin-Cal 6
Lolich-Det 6
John-Chi 6
Horlen-Chi 6
Hargan-Cle 6

Saves
Rojas-Cal 27
Wyatt-Bos 20
Locker-Chi 20
Womack-NY 18
Worthington-Min 16

Innings Pitched
Chance-Min 283.2
Lonborg-Bos 273.1
Wilson-Det 264.0
Kaat-Min 263.1
Peters-Chi 260.0

Fewest Hits/Game
Peters-Chi 6.47
Boswell-Min 6.55
Horlen-Chi 6.56
Siebert-Cle 6.60
Downing-NY 7.05

Fewest BB/Game
Merritt-Min 1.19
Kaat-Min 1.44
Stange-Bos 1.59
Horlen-Chi 2.02
Peterson-NY 2.13

Strikeouts
Lonborg-Bos 246
McDowell-Cle 236
Chance-Min 220
Tiant-Cle 219
Peters-Chi 215

Strikeouts/Game
Tiant-Cle 9.22
McDowell-Cle 8.99
Boswell-Min 8.25
Lonborg-Bos 8.10
Phoebus-Bal 7.75

Ratio
Horlen-Chi 8.72
Merritt-Min 9.21
Siebert-Cle 9.52
John-Chi 9.84
Peters-Chi 10.00

Earned Run Average
Horlen-Chi 2.06
Peters-Chi 2.28
Siebert-Cle 2.38
John-Chi 2.47
Merritt-Min 2.53

Adjusted ERA
Horlen-Chi 151
Siebert-Cle 137
Merritt-Min 137
Peters-Chi 136
Chance-Min 127

Opponents' Batting Avg.
Peters-Chi 199
Boswell-Min 202
Siebert-Cle 202
Horlen-Chi 203
Downing-NY 217

Opponents' On-Base Pct.
Horlen-Chi 253
Merritt-Min 262
Siebert-Cle 268
John-Chi 277
Peters-Chi 277

Starter Runs
Horlen-Chi 33.6
Peters-Chi 27.3
Merritt-Min 17.7
Siebert-Cle 17.5
Chance-Min 15.8

Adjusted Starter Runs
Horlen-Chi 31.2
Peters-Chi 24.6
Merritt-Min 22.0
Chance-Min 21.5
Siebert-Cle 18.1

Clutch Pitching Index
Clark-Cal 121
Stottlemyre-NY 117
Kaat-Min 108
Tiant-Cle 107
Stange-Bos 105

Relief Runs
Wilhelm-Chi 18.9
Drabowsky-Bal 17.2
Locker-Chi 15.7
McMahon-Bos-Chi . 15.2
Baldwin-Was 11.6

Adjusted Relief Runs
Wilhelm-Chi 18.4
Drabowsky-Bal 16.8
McMahon-Bos-Chi . . 14.8
Locker-Chi 14.6
Baldwin-Was 11.4

Relief Ranking
Wilhelm-Chi 25.6
Drabowsky-Bal 23.4
Locker-Chi 17.4
Rojas-Cal 17.4
Wyatt-Bos 17.0

Total Pitcher Index
Peters-Chi 3.8
Horlen-Chi 3.7
Drabowsky-Bal 3.0
Wilhelm-Chi 2.7
John-Chi 2.4

Total Baseball Ranking
Yastrzemski-Bos 7.4
B.Robinson-Bal 5.2
Kaline-Det 4.9
F.Robinson-Bal 4.7
Blair-Bal 4.5

TEAM	G	W	L	PCT	GB	R	OR	AB	H	2B	3B	HR	BB	SO	AVG	OBP	SLG	OPS	OPS+	BR	BR+	PF	CHI	RC	SB	CS	SBA	SBR
STL	162	97	65	.599		583	**472**	5561	1383	227	**48**	73	378	897	.249	.300	.346	646	102	2	9	99	**104**	581	110	45	**71**	**8**
SF	163	88	74	.543	9	599	529	5441	1301	162	33	108	**508**	904	.239	.310	.341	651	103	20	21	100	103	577	50	37	57	-2
CHI	163	84	78	.519	13	612	611	5458	1319	203	43	**130**	415	854	.242	.300	.366	666	100	36	-1	107	**104**	593	41	30	58	-1
CIN	163	83	79	.512	14	**690**	673	5767	**1573**	**281**	36	106	379	938	**.273**	**.322**	**.389**	**711**	**114**	**130**	**87**	106	98	**688**	59	55	52	-6
ATL	163	81	81	.500	16	514	549	5552	1399	179	31	80	414	**782**	.252	.308	.339	647	101	9	7	100	90	564	83	44	65	3
PIT	163	80	82	.494	17	583	532	5569	1404	180	44	80	422	953	.252	.309	.343	652	105	19	28	99	100	580	**130**	59	69	**8**
PHI	162	76	86	.469	21	543	615	5372	1253	178	30	100	462	1003	.233	.297	.333	630	96	-24	-24	100	**104**	527	58	51	53	-5
LA	162	76	86	.469	21	470	509	5354	1234	202	36	67	439	980	.230	.291	.319	610	97	-61	-21	92	97	501	57	43	57	-3
NY	163	73	89	.451	24	473	499	5503	1252	178	30	81	379	1203	.228	.283	.315	598	86	-91	-93	101	102	486	72	45	62	0
HOU	162	72	90	.444	25	510	588	5336	1233	205	28	66	479	988	.231	.300	.317	617	94	-41	-31	98	100	505	44	51	46	-8
TOT	813					5577		54913	13351	1995	359	891	4275	9502	.244	.302	.342	643							704	460	60	-6

TEAM	CG	SH	SV	IP	H	H/G	HR	BB	SO	RAT	ERA	ERA+	OAV	OOB	PR	PR+	PF	CPI	FA	E	DP	FW	PW	BW	SBW	DIF
STL	63	**30**	32	1479[1]	1282	7.8	82	375	971	**10.3**	**2.49**	**116**	.234	.286	**82**	**69**	97	105	.978	140	135	-.0	**8.0**	1.1	**1.0**	6.2
SF	**77**	20	16	1469	1302	8.0	86	**344**	942	**10.3**	2.71	109	.236	**.283**	45	39	99	96	.975	162	125	-1.2	4.5	2.5	-.2	1.6
CHI	46	12	32	1453[2]	1399	8.7	138	392	894	11.3	3.42	93	.254	.306	-69	-38	106	100	**.981**	**119**	149	**1.3**	-4.3	-.0	-.0	6.4
CIN	24	16	**38**	1490[1]	1399	8.5	114	573	963	12.2	3.57	89	.250	.324	-96	-63	106	100	.978	144	144	-.2	-7.2	**10.0**	-.6	.2
ATL	44	16	29	1474[2]	1326	8.1	87	362	871	10.6	2.92	103	.241	.292	11	12	100	96	.980	125	139	.9	1.4	.9	.4	-3.4
PIT	42	19	30	1487	1322	8.1	73	485	897	11.2	2.75	107	.240	.306	40	31	98	**107**	.979	139	162	.0	3.6	3.3	**1.0**	-8.8
PHI	42	12	27	1448[1]	1416	8.8	91	421	935	11.7	3.37	89	.257	.315	-61	-57	101	100	.980	127	**163**	.7	-6.5	-2.7	-.5	4.2
LA	38	23	31	1448[2]	1293	8.1	**65**	414	994	10.9	2.70	103	.241	.300	48	13	93	104	.977	144	144	-.2	1.5	-2.4	-.3	-3.5
NY	45	25	32	1483[1]	**1250**	**7.6**	87	430	1014	10.5	2.73	111	**.230**	.292	43	48	101	98	.979	133	142	.4	5.6	-10.6	.0	-3.3
HOU	50	12	23	1446[2]	1362	8.5	68	479	**1021**	11.7	3.26	91	.249	.313	-44	-49	99	96	.975	156	129	-.9	-5.6	-3.5	-.8	2.1
TOT	471	185	290	14681		8.2				11.1	2.99		.244	.302					.979	1389	1432					

Runs
Beckert-Chi 98
Rose-Cin 94
Perez-Cin 93
Brock-StL 92
Williams-Chi 91

Hits
Rose-Cin 210
Alou-Atl 210
Beckert-Chi 189
A.Johnson-Cin 188
Flood-StL 186

Doubles
Brock-StL 46
Rose-Cin 42
Bench-Cin 40
Staub-Hou 37
Alou-Atl 37

Triples
Brock-StL 14
Clemente-Pit 12
Davis-LA 10
Allen-Phi 9
Williams-Chi 8

Home Runs
McCovey-SF 36
Allen-Phi 33
Banks-Chi 32
Williams-Chi 30
H.Aaron-Atl 29

Total Bases
Williams-Chi 321
H.Aaron-Atl 302
Rose-Cin 294
Alou-Atl 290
McCovey-SF 285

Runs Batted In
McCovey-SF 105
Williams-Chi 98
Santo-Chi 98
Perez-Cin 92
Allen-Phi 90

Runs Produced
Perez-Cin 167
Williams-Chi 159
Santo-Chi 158
McCovey-SF 150
Allen-Phi 144

Bases On Balls
Santo-Chi 96
Wynn-Hou 90
Hunt-SF 78
Allen-Phi 74
Staub-Hou 73

Batting Average
Rose-Cin 335
Alou-Pit 332
Alou-Atl 317
A.Johnson-Cin 312
Flood-StL 301

On-Base Percentage
Rose-Cin 394
McCovey-SF 383
Wynn-Hou 378
Mays-SF 376
Staub-Hou 376

Slugging Average
McCovey-SF 545
Allen-Phi 520
Williams-Chi 500
H.Aaron-Atl 498
Mays-SF 488

On-Base Plus Slugging
McCovey-SF 928
Allen-Phi 876
Mays-SF 864
Rose-Cin 863
H.Aaron-Atl 855

Adjusted OPS
McCovey-SF 176
Allen-Phi 160
Mays-SF 158
Wynn-Hou 158
H.Aaron-Atl 154

Batter Runs
McCovey-SF 48.8
Rose-Cin 44.5
H.Aaron-Atl 39.0
Wynn-Hou 38.4
Allen-Phi 38.0

Adjusted Batter Runs
McCovey-SF 48.9
Wynn-Hou 40.4
H.Aaron-Atl 38.7
Rose-Cin 38.0
Allen-Phi 38.0

Clutch Hitting Index
Hundley-Chi 134
Staub-Hou 123
Clendenon-Pit 122
Santo-Chi 117
Swoboda-NY 117

Runs Created
Rose-Cin 113
McCovey-SF 110
Williams-Chi 107
H.Aaron-Atl 104
Alou-Atl 103

Total Average
McCovey-SF 953
Allen-Phi 869
Mays-SF 853
H.Aaron-Atl 852
Wynn-Hou 826

Stolen Bases
Brock-StL 62
Wills-Pit 52
Davis-LA 36
H.Aaron-Atl 28
Jones-NY 23

Stolen Base Average
H.Aaron-Atl 84.8
Brock-StL 83.8
Taylor-Phi 81.5
Davis-LA 78.3

Stolen Base Runs
Brock-StL 9.4
Davis-LA 4.4
H.Aaron-Atl 4.4
Wills-Pit 4.1
Taylor-Phi 3.1

Fielding Runs
Mazeroski-Pit 25.7
Alley-Pit 25.6
Kessinger-Chi 17.9
Flood-StL 17.5
Santo-Chi 17.3

Total Player Rating
H.Aaron-Atl 5.1
Wynn-Hou 5.1
McCovey-SF 4.8
Santo-Chi 4.0
Alou-Atl 3.8

Wins
Marichal-SF 26
Gibson-StL 22
Jenkins-Chi 20

Win Percentage
Blass-Pit 750
Marichal-SF 743
Gibson-StL 710
Briles-StL 633

Games
Abernathy-Cin 78
Regan-LA-Chi 73
Carroll-Atl-Cin 68
Taylor-NY 58
Linzy-SF 57

Complete Games
Marichal-SF 30
Gibson-StL 28
Jenkins-Chi 20
Perry-SF 19
Koosman-NY 17

Shutouts
Gibson-StL 13
Drysdale-LA 8
Koosman-NY 7
Blass-Pit 7

Saves
Regan-LA-Chi 25
Carroll-Atl-Cin 17
Hoerner-StL 17
Brewer-LA 14

Innings Pitched
Marichal-SF 326.0
Jenkins-Chi 308.0
Gibson-StL 304.2
Perry-SF 291.0
Seaver-NY 277.2

Fewest Hits/Game
Gibson-StL 5.85
Bolin-SF 6.52
Veale-Pit 6.86
Jarvis-Atl 7.10
Moose-Pit 7.14

Fewest BB/Game
Hands-Chi 1.25
Marichal-SF 1.27
Seaver-NY 1.56
Pappas-Cin-Atl 1.57
Niekro-Atl 1.58

Strikeouts
Gibson-StL 268
Jenkins-Chi 260
Singer-LA 227
Marichal-SF 218
Sadecki-SF 206

Strikeouts/Game
Singer-LA 7.97
Gibson-StL 7.92
Maloney-Cin 7.87
Jenkins-Chi 7.60
Wilson-Hou 7.55

Ratio
Gibson-StL 7.89
Jarvis-Atl 8.93
Bolin-SF 9.07
Seaver-NY 9.08
Hands-Chi 9.15

Earned Run Average
Gibson-StL 1.12
Bolin-SF 1.99
Veale-Pit 2.05
Koosman-NY 2.08
Blass-Pit 2.12

Adjusted ERA
Gibson-StL 258
Bolin-SF 148
Koosman-NY 145
Veale-Pit 142
Blass-Pit 138

Opponents' Batting Avg.
Gibson-StL 184
Bolin-SF 200
Veale-Pit 211
Jarvis-Atl 214
Moose-Pit 218

Opponents' On-Base Pct.
Gibson-StL 233
Jarvis-Atl 255
Bolin-SF 258
Seaver-NY 262
Hands-Chi 264

Starter Runs
Gibson-StL 63.1
Koosman-NY 26.5
Veale-Pit 25.4
Seaver-NY 24.1
Drysdale-LA 22.3

Adjusted Starter Runs
Gibson-StL 61.9
Koosman-NY 27.2
Seaver-NY 24.9
Veale-Pit 24.2
Blass-Pit 20.0

Clutch Pitching Index
Blass-Pit 125
Briles-StL 124
Koosman-NY 123
Lemaster-Hou 122
Drysdale-LA 117

Relief Runs
Kline-Pit 16.4
Regan-LA-Chi 10.7
Linzy-SF 9.4
Grant-LA 9.4
Abernathy-Cin 7.7

Adjusted Relief Runs
Kline-Pit 15.9
Regan-LA-Chi 12.3
Abernathy-Cin 9.7
Linzy-SF 9.1
Grant-LA 7.6

Relief Ranking
Kline-Pit 23.9
Regan-LA-Chi 19.2
Linzy-SF 17.3
Abernathy-Cin 13.2
Upshaw-Atl 9.6

Total Pitcher Index
Gibson-StL 7.6
Seaver-NY 3.0
Koosman-NY 3.0
Marichal-SF 2.7
Drysdale-LA 2.5

Total Baseball Ranking
Gibson-StL 7.6
H.Aaron-Atl 5.1
Wynn-Hou 5.1
McCovey-SF 4.8
Santo-Chi 4.0

TEAM	G	W	L	PCT	GB	R	OR	AB	H	2B	3B	HR	BB	SO	AVG	OBP	SLG	OPS	OPS+	BR	BR+	PF	CHI	RC	SB	CS	SBA	SBR
DET	164	103	59	.636		**671**	**492**	5490	1292	190	39	**185**	521	964	.235	.309	**.385**	**694**	**114**	**102**	**82**	103	100	**646**	26	32	45	-5
BAL	162	91	71	.562	12	579	497	5275	1187	**215**	28	133	570	1019	.225	.306	.352	658	106	41	40	100	97	585	78	32	**71**	6
CLE	162	86	75	.534	16.5	516	504	5416	1266	210	36	75	427	858	.234	.294	.327	621	96	-34	-26	99	100	525	115	61	65	4
BOS	162	86	76	.531	17	614	611	5303	1253	207	17	125	**582**	974	.236	**.316**	.352	668	102	62	24	107	99	590	76	62	55	-5
NY	164	83	79	.512	20	536	531	5310	1137	154	34	109	566	958	.214	.293	.318	611	95	-46	-30	97	**106**	507	90	50	64	2
OAK	163	82	80	.506	21	569	544	5406	**1300**	192	40	94	472	1022	**.240**	.306	.343	649	108	19	48	95	99	580	**147**	61	**71**	**11**
MIN	162	79	83	.488	24	562	546	5373	1274	207	**41**	105	445	966	.237	.301	.350	651	99	20	-7	105	99	564	98	54	64	3
CAL	162	67	95	.414	36	498	615	5331	1209	170	33	83	447	1080	.227	.293	.318	611	96	-51	-32	96	100	498	62	50	55	-4
CHI	162	67	95	.414	36	463	527	5405	1233	169	33	71	397	**840**	.228	.286	.311	597	86	-82	-87	101	99	480	90	50	64	2
WAS	161	65	96	.404	37.5	524	665	5400	1208	160	37	124	454	960	.224	.289	.336	625	99	-31	-14	97	101	518	29	19	60	0
TOT	812					5532		53709	12359	1874	338	1104	4881	9641	.231	.300	.340	639							811	471	63	14

TEAM	CG	SH	SV	IP	H	H/G	HR	BB	SO	RAT	ERA	ERA+	OAV	OOB	PR	PR+	PF	CPI	FA	E	DP	FW	PW	BW	SBW	DIF
DET	**59**	19	29	1489^2	1180	7.2	129	486	1115	**10.3**	2.72	**111**	.217	**.285**	44	49	101	100	**.983**	**105**	133	**2.1**	5.7	**9.5**	-.7	5.7
BAL	53	16	31	1451	1111	6.9	101	502	1044	**10.3**	2.67	110	.212	.287	51	43	98	96	.981	120	131	1.1	5.0	4.6	.5	-1.0
CLE	48	**23**	32	1464^1	**1087**	**6.7**	98	540	**1157**	10.4	**2.66**	**111**	**.206**	.286	**53**	**50**	99	93	.979	127	130	.7	**5.8**	-2.9	.3	1.9
BOS	55	17	31	1447	1303	8.2	115	523	972	11.7	3.34	95	.241	.313	-57	-27	106	100	.979	128	147	.6	-3.0	2.8	-.7	5.6
NY	45	14	27	1467^1	1308	8.1	99	424	831	10.9	2.80	104	.240	.298	31	19	97	108	.979	139	142	.0	2.2	-3.4	.0	3.2
OAK	45	18	29	1455^2	1220	7.6	124	505	997	10.9	2.95	96	.227	.297	6	-21	95	101	.977	145	136	-.4	-2.4	5.6	**1.1**	-2.7
MIN	46	14	29	1433^1	1224	7.7	**92**	**414**	996	10.6	2.90	107	.229	.290	13	30	104	94	.973	170	117	-1.9	3.5	-.8	.2	-2.8
CAL	29	11	31	1437	1234	7.8	131	519	869	11.2	3.44	85	.233	.306	-72	-85	98	94	.977	140	**156**	-.1	-9.7	-3.6	-.6	.2
CHI	20	11	**40**	1468	1290	8.0	97	451	834	11.1	2.75	110	.236	.303	38	45	102	**110**	.977	151	152	-.8	5.2	-9.9	.0	-8.4
WAS	26	11	28	1439^2	1402	8.8	118	517	826	12.3	3.65	80	.258	.327	-106	-119	98	104	.976	148	144	-.6	-13.6	-1.6	-.2	.6
TOT	426	154	307	14553		7.7				11.0	2.98		.231	.300					.978	1373	1388					

Runs
McAuliffe-Det 95
Yastrzemski-Bos 90
White-NY 89
Tovar-Min 89
Stanley-Det 88

Hits
Campaneris-Oak 177
Tovar-Min 167
F.Howard-Was 164
Aparicio-Chi 164
Yastrzemski-Bos 162

Doubles
Smith-Bos 37
B.Robinson-Bal 36
Yastrzemski-Bos 32
Tovar-Min 31

Triples
Fregosi-Cal 13
McCraw-Chi 12
Stroud-Was 10
McAuliffe-Det 10
Campaneris-Oak 9

Home Runs
F.Howard-Was 44
Horton-Det 36
Harrelson-Bos 35
Jackson-Oak 29

Total Bases
F.Howard-Was 330
Horton-Det 278
Harrelson-Bos 277
Yastrzemski-Bos 267
Northrup-Det 259

Runs Batted In
Harrelson-Bos 109
F.Howard-Was 106
Northrup-Det 90
Powell-Bal 85
Horton-Det 85

Runs Produced
Harrelson-Bos 153
Northrup-Det 145
Yastrzemski-Bos 141
F.Howard-Was 141
Stanley-Det 137

Bases On Balls
Yastrzemski-Bos 119
Mantle-NY 106
Foy-Bos 84
McAuliffe-Det 82
Andrews-Bos 81

Batting Average
Yastrzemski-Bos .301
Cater-Oak .290
Oliva-Min .289
Horton-Det .285
Uhlaender-Min .283

On-Base Percentage
Yastrzemski-Bos .429
F.Robinson-Bal .391
Mantle-NY .387
Monday-Oak .373
Andrews-Bos .369

Slugging Average
F.Howard-Was .552
Horton-Det .543
Harrelson-Bos .518
Yastrzemski-Bos .495
Oliva-Min .477

On-Base Plus Slugging
Yastrzemski-Bos 924
Horton-Det 900
F.Howard-Was 892
Harrelson-Bos 877
Oliva-Min 837

Adjusted OPS
F.Howard-Was 172
Yastrzemski-Bos 168
Horton-Det 165
Harrelson-Bos 153
F.Robinson-Bal 153

Batter Runs
Yastrzemski-Bos 57.5
F.Howard-Was 45.1
Horton-Det 41.1
Harrelson-Bos 40.2
Freehan-Det 32.7

Adjusted Batter Runs
Yastrzemski-Bos 50.2
F.Howard-Was 48.6
Horton-Det 38.4
Harrelson-Bos 34.2
Freehan-Det 30.0

Clutch Hitting Index
Foy-Bos 118
Cater-Oak 116
Powell-Bal 113
Tresh-NY 111
Harrelson-Bos 111

Runs Created
Yastrzemski-Bos 121
F.Howard-Was 110
Horton-Det 95
Harrelson-Bos 94
Freehan-Det 94

Total Average
Yastrzemski-Bos 1.000
F.Howard-Was .872
Horton-Det .867
F.Robinson-Bal .865
Harrelson-Bos .835

Stolen Bases
Campaneris-Oak 62
Cardenal-Cle 40
Tovar-Min 35
Buford-Bal 27
Foy-Bos 26

Stolen Base Average
McCraw-Chi 80.0
Nelson-Cle 76.7
Foy-Bos 76.5
Clarke-NY 74.1
Campaneris-Oak 73.8

Stolen Base Runs
Campaneris-Oak 5.9
Tovar-Min 3.2
Foy-Bos 2.9
McCraw-Chi 2.7
Nelson-Cle 2.6

Fielding Runs
Clarke-NY 29.5
Aparicio-Chi 24.7
Unser-Was 18.8
Yastrzemski-Bos 17.3
B.Robinson-Bal 16.6

Total Player Rating
Yastrzemski-Bos 6.6
F.Howard-Was 4.7
Freehan-Det 4.6
Campaneris-Oak 3.6
Aparicio-Chi 3.5

Wins
McLain-Det 31
McNally-Bal 22
Tiant-Cle 21
Stottlemyre-NY 21
Hardin-Bal 18

Win Percentage
McLain-Det .838
Culp-Bos .727
Tiant-Cle .700
Ellsworth-Bos .696
McNally-Bal .688

Games
Wood-Chi 88
Wilhelm-Chi 72
Locker-Chi 70
Perranoski-Min 66

Complete Games
McLain-Det 28
Tiant-Cle 19
Stottlemyre-NY 19
McNally-Bal 18
Hardin-Bal 16

Shutouts
Tiant-Cle 9

Saves
Worthington-Min 18
Wood-Chi 16
Higgins-Was 13

Innings Pitched
McLain-Det 336.0
Chance-Min 292.0
Stottlemyre-NY 278.2
McNally-Bal 273.0
McDowell-Cle 269.0

Fewest Hits/Game
Tiant-Cle 5.30
McNally-Bal 5.77
McDowell-Cle 6.06
Siebert-Cle 6.33
McLain-Det 6.46

Fewest BB/Game
Peterson-NY 1.23
McLain-Det 1.69
Ellsworth-Bos 1.70
Kaat-Min 1.73
McNally-Bal 1.81

Strikeouts
McDowell-Cle 283
McLain-Det 280
Tiant-Cle 264
Chance-Min 234
McNally-Bal 202

Strikeouts/Game
McDowell-Cle 9.47
Tiant-Cle 9.20
Lolich-Det 8.06
Culp-Bos 7.90
McLain-Det 7.50

Ratio
McNally-Bal 7.91
Tiant-Cle 7.98
McLain-Det 8.30
Chance-Min 9.15
Peterson-NY 9.32

Earned Run Average
Tiant-Cle 1.60
McDowell-Cle 1.81
McNally-Bal 1.95
McLain-Det 1.96
John-Chi 1.98

Adjusted ERA
Tiant-Cle 185
McDowell-Cle 164
McLain-Det 154
John-Chi 153
McNally-Bal 150

Opponents' Batting Avg.
Tiant-Cle .168
McNally-Bal .182
McDowell-Cle .189
Siebert-Cle .198
McLain-Det .200

Opponents' On-Base Pct.
Tiant-Cle .233
McNally-Bal .234
McLain-Det .243
Chance-Min .261
Nash-Oak .270

Starter Runs
Tiant-Cle 39.5
McLain-Det 38.2
McDowell-Cle 35.0
McNally-Bal 31.4
Bahnsen-NY 27.5

Adjusted Starter Runs
Tiant-Cle 39.2
McLain-Det 38.9
McDowell-Cle 34.7
McNally-Bal 30.3
Bahnsen-NY 25.9

Clutch Pitching Index
Horlen-Chi 133
John-Chi 119
Fisher-Chi 116
McDowell-Cle 113
Bahnsen-NY 111

Relief Runs
Wood-Chi 19.6
Wilhelm-Chi 13.0
Romo-Cle 12.6
McMahon-Chi-Det 9.0
Drabowsky-Bal 7.3

Adjusted Relief Runs
Wood-Chi 20.1
Wilhelm-Chi 13.3
Romo-Cle 12.5
McMahon-Chi-Det 9.3
Locker-Chi 7.3

Relief Ranking
Wood-Chi 33.1
Romo-Cle 14.8
Wilhelm-Chi 14.0
Drabowsky-Bal 10.1
Watt-Bal 8.5

Total Pitcher Index
McLain-Det 4.8
Tiant-Cle 4.2
McDowell-Cle 4.1
McNally-Bal 4.0
Wood-Chi 3.8

Total Baseball Ranking
Yastrzemski-Bos 6.6
McLain-Det 4.8
F.Howard-Was 4.7
Freehan-Det 4.6
Tiant-Cle 4.2

TEAM	G	W	L	PCT	GB	R	OR	AB	H	2B	3B	HR	BB	SO	AVG	OBP	SLG	OPS	OPS+	BR	BR+	PF	CHI	RC	SB	CS	SBA	SBR
EAST																												
NY	162	100	62	.617		632	541	5427	1311	184	41	109	527	1089	.242	.313	.351	664	91	-52	-64	102	**105**	601	66	43	61	-1
CHI	163	92	70	.568	8	720	611	5530	1400	215	40	142	559	928	.253	.326	.384	710	94	37	-43	113	102	693	30	32	48	-5
PIT	162	88	74	.543	12	725	652	5626	1557	220	**52**	119	454	944	**.277**	.336	.398	734	**115**	84	**100**	98	97	742	74	34	**69**	**4**
STL	162	87	75	.537	13	595	**540**	5536	1403	**228**	44	90	503	876	.253	.318	.359	677	96	-25	-27	100	94	632	87	49	64	2
PHI	162	63	99	.389	37	645	745	5408	1304	227	35	137	549	1130	.241	.314	.372	686	102	-12	6	97	101	629	73	49	60	-1
MON	162	52	110	.321	48	582	791	5419	1300	202	33	125	529	962	.240	.312	.359	671	94	-40	-42	100	96	596	52	52	50	-7
WEST																												
ATL	162	93	69	.574		691	631	5460	1411	195	22	141	485	**665**	.258	.323	.380	703	104	20	18	100	103	655	59	48	55	-4
SF	162	90	72	.556	3	713	636	5474	1325	187	28	136	**711**	1054	.242	.336	.361	697	104	32	45	98	100	690	71	32	**69**	**4**
CIN	163	89	73	.549	4	**798**	768	5634	**1558**	224	42	**171**	474	1042	**.277**	**.338**	**.422**	**760**	114	**133**	94	105	99	**791**	79	56	59	-2
LA	162	85	77	.525	8	645	561	5532	1405	185	**52**	97	484	823	.254	.316	.359	675	103	-31	17	93	103	626	80	51	61	0
HOU	162	81	81	.500	12	676	668	5348	1284	208	40	104	699	972	.240	.332	.352	684	101	7	21	98	101	649	**101**	58	64	2
SD	162	52	110	.321	41	468	746	5357	1203	180	42	99	423	1143	.225	.286	.329	615	81	-153	-133	96	98	491	45	44	51	-5
TOT	973					7890		65751	16461	2455	471	1470	6397	11628	.251	.321	.370	690							817	548	60	-12

TEAM	CG	SH	SV	IP	H	H/G	HR	BB	SO	RAT	ERA	ERA+	OAV	OOB	PR	PR+	PF	CPI	FA	E	DP	FW	PW	BW	SBW	DIF
EAST																										
NY	51	**28**	35	1468^1	**1217**	**7.5**	119	517	1012	**10.9**	2.99	**122**	**.227**	**.298**	99	**107**	102	99	.980	122	146	1.4	**11.3**	-6.7	.0	13.1
CHI	58	22	27	1454^1	1366	8.5	118	475	1017	11.6	3.35	120	.248	.311	41	98	112	101	.979	136	149	.7	10.3	-4.5	-.4	5.0
PIT	39	9	33	1445^2	1348	8.4	**96**	553	1124	12.1	3.62	97	.248	.322	-3	-21	97	96	.975	155	169	-.4	-2.2	**10.5**	**.5**	-1.3
STL	63	12	26	1460^1	1289	8.0	99	511	1004	11.3	**2.94**	121	.237	.307	**106**	103	99	**105**	.978	138	144	.5	10.9	-2.8	.3	-2.7
PHI	47	14	21	1434	1494	9.4	134	570	921	13.2	4.15	86	.270	.342	-88	-97	99	103	.978	137	157	.6	-10.1	.7	.0	-8.9
MON	26	8	21	1426	1429	9.1	145	702	973	13.8	4.33	85	.263	.353	-117	-101	102	102	.971	184	**179**	-2.1	-10.6	-4.4	-.6	-11.2
WEST																										
ATL	38	7	42	1445	1334	8.4	144	438	893	11.3	3.53	102	.245	.304	11	13	100	95	**.981**	**115**	114	**1.8**	1.4	1.9	-.3	7.3
SF	**71**	15	17	1473^2	1381	8.5	120	461	906	11.5	3.26	108	.248	.309	55	41	97	103	.974	169	155	-1.2	4.4	4.8	**.5**	.8
CIN	23	11	**44**	1465	1478	9.1	149	611	818	13.2	4.11	92	.262	.340	-84	-54	105	102	.974	167	158	-1.1	-5.6	9.9	-.1	5.1
LA	47	20	31	1457	1324	8.2	122	**420**	975	11.1	3.09	108	.242	.301	83	42	93	103	.980	126	130	1.2	4.5	1.8	.1	-3.4
HOU	52	11	34	1435^2	1347	8.5	111	547	**1221**	12.1	3.60	98	.247	.319	-1	-10	99	96	.975	153	136	-.3	-1.0	2.3	.3	-1.1
SD	16	9	25	1422^1	1454	9.3	113	592	764	13.2	4.24	83	.267	.343	-102	-113	98	97	.975	156	140	-.5	-11.8	-13.9	-.4	-2.2
TOT	531	166	356	17387^1		8.6				12.1	3.60		.251	.321					.977	1758	1777					

Runs
Rose-Cin 120
Bonds-SF 120
Wynn-Hou 113
Kessinger-Chi 109
Alou-Pit 105

Hits
Alou-Pit 231
Rose-Cin 218
Brock-StL 195
Tolan-Cin 194
Williams-Chi 188

Doubles
Alou-Pit 41
Kessinger-Chi 38
Williams-Chi 33
Rose-Cin 33
Brock-StL 33

Triples
Clemente-Pit 12
Rose-Cin 11
Williams-Chi 10
Tolan-Cin 10
Brock-StL 10

Home Runs
McCovey-SF 45
H.Aaron-Atl 44
May-Cin 38
Perez-Cin 37
Wynn-Hou 33

Total Bases
H.Aaron-Atl 332
Perez-Cin 331
McCovey-SF 322
Rose-Cin 321
May-Cin 321

Runs Batted In
McCovey-SF 126
Santo-Chi 123
Perez-Cin 122
May-Cin 110
Banks-Chi 106

Runs Produced
Santo-Chi 191
Perez-Cin 188
Rose-Cin 186
McCovey-SF 182
Bonds-SF 178

Bases On Balls
Wynn-Hou 148
McCovey-SF 121
Staub-Mon 110
Morgan-Hou 110
Santo-Chi 96

Batting Average
Rose-Cin 348
Clemente-Pit 345
Jones-NY 340
Alou-Pit 331
McCovey-SF 320

On-Base Percentage
McCovey-SF 458
Wynn-Hou 440
Rose-Cin 432
Staub-Mon 427
Jones-NY 424

Slugging Average
McCovey-SF 656
H.Aaron-Atl 607
Allen-Phi 573
Stargell-Pit 556
Clemente-Pit 544

On-Base Plus Slugging
McCovey-SF 1114
H.Aaron-Atl 1005
Clemente-Pit 958
Staub-Mon 953
Allen-Phi 952

Adjusted OPS
McCovey-SF 212
H.Aaron-Atl 177
Clemente-Pit 170
Wynn-Hou 168
Allen-Phi 168

Batter Runs
McCovey-SF 76.1
H.Aaron-Atl 56.3
Rose-Cin 56.0
Staub-Mon 52.6
Wynn-Hou 51.0

Adjusted Batter Runs
McCovey-SF 78.7
H.Aaron-Atl 55.9
Wynn-Hou 53.4
Staub-Mon 52.2
Rose-Cin 49.5

Clutch Hitting Index
Menke-Hou 134
Rader-Hou 132
Banks-Chi 132
Santo-Chi 122
D.Johnson-Phi 121

Runs Created
McCovey-SF 151
Rose-Cin 138
Staub-Mon 128
H.Aaron-Atl 128
Wynn-Hou 126

Total Average
McCovey-SF 1.296
Wynn-Hou 1.118
H.Aaron-Atl 1.032
Staub-Mon 1.018
Allen-Phi 988

Stolen Bases
Brock-StL 53
Morgan-Hou 49
Bonds-SF 45
Wills-Mon-LA 40
Tolan-Cin 26

Stolen Base Average
Bonds-SF 91.8
Brock-StL 79.1
Morgan-Hou 77.8
Wynn-Hou 76.7
Alou-Pit 73.3

Stolen Base Runs
Bonds-SF 8.5
Brock-StL 6.8
Morgan-Hou 5.9
Wynn-Hou 2.6
Alou-Pit 2.0

Fielding Runs
Lanier-SF 28.6
Kessinger-Chi 24.6
Maxvill-StL 21.1
Grote-NY 19.3
Money-Phi 17.3

Total Player Rating
Wynn-Hou 6.4
McCovey-SF 6.3
H.Aaron-Atl 5.4
Staub-Mon 5.1
Clemente-Pit 4.9

Wins
Seaver-NY 25
Niekro-Atl 23
Marichal-SF 21
Jenkins-Chi 21

Win Percentage
Seaver-NY 781
Marichal-SF 656
Merritt-Cin 654
Koosman-NY 654
Reed-Atl 643

Games
Granger-Cin 90
McGinn-Mon 74
Regan-Chi 71
Carroll-Cin 71
Reberger-SD 67

Complete Games
Gibson-StL 28
Marichal-SF 27
Perry-SF 26
Jenkins-Chi 23
Niekro-Atl 21

Shutouts
Marichal-SF 8
Osteen-LA 7
Jenkins-Chi 7
Koosman-NY 6
Holtzman-Chi 6

Saves
Gladding-Hou 29
Upshaw-Atl 27
Granger-Cin 27
Brewer-LA 20
Regan-Chi 17

Innings Pitched
Perry-SF 325.1
Osteen-LA 321.0
Singer-LA 315.2
Gibson-StL 314.0
Jenkins-Chi 311.1

Fewest Hits/Game
Seaver-NY 6.65
Maloney-Cin 6.80
Singer-LA 6.96
Koosman-NY 6.98
Carlton-StL 7.05

Fewest BB/Game
Marichal-SF 1.62
Niekro-Atl 1.80
Jenkins-Chi 2.05
Niekro-Chi-SD 2.07
Osteen-LA 2.07

Strikeouts
Jenkins-Chi 273
Gibson-StL 269
Singer-LA 247
Wilson-Hou 235
Perry-SF 233

Strikeouts/Game
Griffin-Hou 9.56
Wilson-Hou 9.40
Moose-Pit 8.74
Selma-SD-Chi 8.54
Veale-Pit 8.49

Ratio
Marichal-SF 9.13
Dierker-Hou 9.23
Singer-LA 9.35
Niekro-Atl 9.40
Seaver-NY 9.58

Earned Run Average
Marichal-SF 2.10
Carlton-StL 2.17
Gibson-StL 2.18
Seaver-NY 2.21
Koosman-NY 2.28

Adjusted ERA
Marichal-SF 167
Seaver-NY 166
Carlton-StL 165
Gibson-StL 164
Hands-Chi 162

Opponents' Batting Avg.
Seaver-NY 207
Maloney-Cin 208
Singer-LA 210
Dierker-Hou 214
Carlton-StL 216

Opponents' On-Base Pct.
Dierker-Hou 262
Marichal-SF 263
Singer-LA 263
Niekro-Atl 264
Seaver-NY 273

Starter Runs
Marichal-SF 49.8
Gibson-StL 49.5
Singer-LA 44.2
Dierker-Hou 43.1
Seaver-NY 42.3

Adjusted Starter Runs
Gibson-StL 49.1
Marichal-SF 47.9
Hands-Chi 45.8
Seaver-NY 43.4
Dierker-Hou 41.9

Clutch Pitching Index
Carlton-StL 122
Perry-SF 117
Veale-Pit 114
Robertson-Mon 113
Hands-Chi 112

Relief Runs
McGraw-NY 15.1
Granger-Cin 12.8
Brewer-LA 10.3
Gibbon-SF-Pit 9.5
DiLauro-NY 8.5

Adjusted Relief Runs
McGraw-NY 15.5
Granger-Cin 14.9
Gibbon-SF-Pit 9.0
DiLauro-NY 8.7
Brewer-LA 8.3

Relief Ranking
McGraw-NY 20.9
Granger-Cin 20.1
Brewer-LA 15.2
Taylor-NY 15.0
Gibbon-SF-Pit 14.4

Total Pitcher Index
Gibson-StL 6.1
Marichal-SF 5.6
Seaver-NY 5.5
Carlton-StL 5.0
Hands-Chi 4.8

Total Baseball Ranking
Wynn-Hou 6.4
McCovey-SF 6.3
Gibson-StL 6.1
Marichal-SF 5.6
Seaver-NY 5.5

TEAM	G	W	L	PCT	GB	R	OR	AB	H	2B	3B	HR	BB	SO	AVG	OBP	SLG	OPS	OPS+	BR	BR+	PF	CHI	RC	SB	CS	SBA	SBR
EAST																												
BAL	162	109	53	.673		779	**517**	5518	1465	234	29	175	634	**806**	.265	**.346**	.414	**760**	**118**	**135**	**128**	101	96	791	82	45	65	2
DET	162	90	72	.556	19	701	601	5441	1316	188	29	182	578	922	.242	.318	.387	705	99	17	-11	104	104	674	35	28	56	-2
BOS	162	87	75	.537	22	743	736	5494	1381	234	37	**197**	**658**	923	.251	.335	**.415**	750	110	110	71	105	95	761	41	47	47	-7
WAS	162	86	76	.531	23	694	644	5447	1365	171	40	148	630	900	.251	.332	.378	710	111	38	77	95	99	675	52	40	57	-3
NY	162	80	81	.497	28.5	562	587	5308	1247	210	**44**	94	565	840	.235	.310	.344	654	92	-74	-52	96	99	572	119	74	62	0
CLE	161	62	99	.385	46.5	573	717	5365	1272	173	24	119	535	906	.237	.309	.345	654	86	-77	-95	103	101	568	85	37	70	6
WEST																												
MIN	162	97	65	.599		**790**	618	5677	**1520**	**246**	32	163	599	906	**.268**	.342	.408	750	114	118	101	102	98	**794**	115	70	62	1
OAK	162	88	74	.543	9	740	678	5614	1400	210	28	148	617	953	.249	.330	.376	706	109	32	64	96	103	712	100	39	72	8
CAL	163	71	91	.438	26	528	652	5316	1221	151	29	88	516	929	.230	.302	.319	621	84	-137	-110	95	**105**	518	54	39	58	-2
KC	163	69	93	.426	28	586	688	5462	1311	179	32	98	522	901	.240	.311	.338	649	87	-84	-87	101	102	577	129	70	65	4
CHI	162	68	94	.420	29	625	723	5450	1346	210	27	112	552	844	.247	.322	.357	679	92	-25	-55	105	98	638	54	22	71	4
SEA	163	64	98	.395	33	639	799	5444	1276	179	27	125	626	1015	.234	.317	.346	663	94	-53	-42	98	104	622	**167**	59	**74**	**16**
TOT	973					7960		65536	16120	2385	378	1649	7032	10845	.246	.324	.370	693							1033	570	64	28

TEAM	CG	SH	SV	IP	H	H/G	HR	BB	SO	RAT	ERA	ERA+	OAV	OOB	PR	PR+	PF	CPI	FA	E	DP	FW	PW	BW	SBW	DIF
EAST																										
BAL	50	**20**	36	1473^{2}	**1194**	**7.3**	**117**	**498**	897	**10.5**	**2.83**	**126**	**.223**	**.291**	**130**	**123**	98	97	**.984**	**101**	145	**2.2**	**12.9**	**13.5**	-.0	-.4
DET	**55**	**20**	28	1455^{1}	1250	7.8	128	586	**1032**	11.6	3.32	113	.232	.312	50	65	103	98	.979	130	130	.6	6.9	-1.1	-.5	3.3
BOS	30	7	41	1466^{2}	1423	8.8	155	685	935	13.3	3.93	97	.256	.343	-49	-18	105	106	.975	157	**178**	-1.0	-1.8	7.5	-1.0	2.5
WAS	28	10	41	1447^{1}	1310	8.2	135	656	835	12.5	3.49	99	.244	.330	22	-4	96	**107**	.978	140	159	.0	-.4	8.1	-.6	-2.0
NY	53	13	20	1440^{2}	1258	7.9	118	522	801	11.3	3.23	108	.236	.306	63	41	96	97	.979	131	158	.5	4.3	-5.4	-.2	.5
CLE	35	7	22	1437	1330	8.4	134	681	1000	12.9	3.94	96	.248	.338	-51	-26	104	99	.976	145	153	-.3	-2.7	-9.9	.4	-5.8
WEST																										
MIN	41	8	**43**	1497^{2}	1388	8.4	119	524	906	11.8	3.24	113	.246	.315	64	68	101	104	.977	150	177	-.6	7.2	10.6	-.1	-.9
OAK	42	14	36	1480^{2}	1356	8.3	163	586	887	12.1	3.72	93	.245	.322	-15	-48	95	100	.979	136	162	.2	-5.0	6.8	.6	4.6
CAL	25	9	39	1438^{1}	1294	8.1	126	517	885	11.7	3.55	98	.242	.315	13	-9	96	96	.978	136	164	.3	-.9	-11.5	-.5	2.7
KC	42	10	25	1464^{2}	1357	8.4	136	560	894	12.0	3.72	99	.246	.319	-15	-5	102	95	.975	157	114	-.9	-.5	-9.1	.2	-1.5
CHI	29	10	25	1437^{2}	1470	9.3	146	564	810	13.0	4.21	92	.267	.339	-93	-52	107	100	.981	122	163	1.0	-5.4	-5.7	.2	-2.9
SEA	21	6	33	1463^{2}	1490	9.2	172	653	963	13.5	4.35	84	.264	.345	-118	-116	100	101	.974	167	149	-1.5	-12.1	-4.4	**1.4**	-.3
TOT	451	134	389	17503^{1}		8.3				12.2	3.63		.246	.324					.978	1672	1852					

Runs
Jackson-Oak 123
F.Robinson-Bal 111
Howard-Was 111
Killebrew-Min 106
Bando-Oak 106

Hits
Oliva-Min 197
Clarke-NY 183
Blair-Bal 178
Howard-Was 175
Horton-Cle 174

Doubles
Oliva-Min 39
Jackson-Oak 36
Johnson-Bal 34
Petrocelli-Bos 32
Blair-Bal 32

Triples
Unser-Was 8
Smith-Bos 7
Clarke-NY 7

Home Runs
Killebrew-Min 49
Howard-Was 48
Jackson-Oak 47
Yastrzemski-Bos 40
Petrocelli-Bos 40

Total Bases
Howard-Was 340
Jackson-Oak 334
Killebrew-Min 324
Oliva-Min 316
Petrocelli-Bos 315

Runs Batted In
Killebrew-Min 140
Powell-Bal 121
Jackson-Oak 118
Bando-Oak 113

Runs Produced
Killebrew-Min 197
Jackson-Oak 194
Bando-Oak 188
F.Robinson-Bal 179

Bases On Balls
Killebrew-Min 145
Jackson-Oak 114
Bando-Oak 111
Howard-Was 102
Yastrzemski-Bos 101

Batting Average
Carew-Min .332
Smith-Bos .309
Oliva-Min .309
F.Robinson-Bal .308
Powell-Bal .304

On-Base Percentage
Killebrew-Min .430
F.Robinson-Bal .417
Jackson-Oak .410
Petrocelli-Bos .407
Howard-Was .403

Slugging Average
Jackson-Oak .608
Petrocelli-Bos .589
Killebrew-Min .584
Howard-Was .574
Powell-Bal .559

On-Base Plus Slugging
Jackson-Oak 1019
Killebrew-Min 1014
Petrocelli-Bos 996
Howard-Was 978
F.Robinson-Bal 957

Adjusted OPS
Jackson-Oak 190
Howard-Was 180
Killebrew-Min 177
Petrocelli-Bos 167
F.Robinson-Bal 164

Batter Runs
Killebrew-Min 65.6
Jackson-Oak 62.0
Howard-Was 56.8
Petrocelli-Bos 54.8
F.Robinson-Bal 49.9

Adjusted Batter Runs
Jackson-Oak 68.0
Howard-Was 64.0
Killebrew-Min 62.7
F.Robinson-Bal 48.8
Petrocelli-Bos 48.6

Clutch Hitting Index
White-NY 128
Cater-Oak 120
Bando-Oak 118
Foy-KC 116
T.Conigliaro-Bos 113

Runs Created
Killebrew-Min 146
Jackson-Oak 144
Howard-Was 132
Petrocelli-Bos 129
F.Robinson-Bal 126

Total Average
Killebrew-Min 1.143
Jackson-Oak 1.139
Petrocelli-Bos 1.048
F.Robinson-Bal 1.026
Howard-Was 1.004

Stolen Bases
Harper-Sea 73
Campaneris-Oak 62
Tovar-Min 45
Kelly-KC 40
Foy-KC 37

Stolen Base Average
Campaneris-Oak 88.6
Alomar-Chi-Cal 87.0
Cardenal-Cle 85.7
Aparicio-Chi 85.7
Davis-Sea 82.6

Stolen Base Runs
Campaneris-Oak 10.8
Harper-Sea 9.8
Cardenal-Cle 5.8
Tovar-Min 5.7
Kelly-KC 4.3

Fielding Runs
Cardenas-Min 33.5
Aparicio-Chi 29.3
Blair-Bal 24.8
Knoop-Cal-Chi 24.5
Quilici-Min 24.2

Total Player Rating
Petrocelli-Bos 7.2
Jackson-Oak 6.7
Cardenas-Min 5.9
Aparicio-Chi 5.1
F.Robinson-Bal 4.2

Wins
McLain-Det 24
Cuellar-Bal 23

Win Percentage
Palmer-Bal .800
Perry-Min .769
McNally-Bal .741
McLain-Det .727
Odom-Oak .714

Games
Wood-Chi 76
Perranoski-Min 75
Lyle-Bos 71
Locker-Chi-Sea 68
Segui-Sea 66

Complete Games
Stottlemyre-NY 24
McLain-Det 23
McDowell-Cle 18
Cuellar-Bal 18
Peterson-NY 16

Shutouts
McLain-Det 9
Palmer-Bal 6
Cuellar-Bal 5

Saves
Perranoski-Min 31
K.Tatum-Cal 22
Lyle-Bos 17
Watt-Bal 16
Higgins-Was 16

Innings Pitched
McLain-Det 325.0
Stottlemyre-NY 303.0
Cuellar-Bal 290.2
McDowell-Cle 285.0
Lolich-Det 280.2

Fewest Hits/Game
Messersmith-Cal 6.08
Palmer-Bal 6.51
Cuellar-Bal 6.60
Lolich-Det 6.86
Odom-Oak 6.96

Fewest BB/Game
Peterson-NY 1.42
Bosman-Was 1.82
McLain-Det 1.86
Perry-Min 2.27
Cuellar-Bal 2.45

Strikeouts
McDowell-Cle 279
Lolich-Det 271
Messersmith-Cal 211
Boswell-Min 190

Strikeouts/Game
McDowell-Cle 8.81
Lolich-Det 8.69
Messersmith-Cal 7.60
Butler-KC 7.25
Williams-Cle 7.01

Ratio
Peterson-NY 9.07
Cuellar-Bal 9.07
Bosman-Was 9.19
Palmer-Bal 9.75
Messersmith-Cal 9.86

Earned Run Average
Bosman-Was 2.19
Palmer-Bal 2.34
Cuellar-Bal 2.38
Messersmith-Cal 2.52
Peterson-NY 2.55

Adjusted ERA
Bosman-Was 158
Palmer-Bal 153
Cuellar-Bal 150
Messersmith-Cal 138
Peterson-NY 137

Opponents' Batting Avg.
Messersmith-Cal .190
Palmer-Bal .200
Cuellar-Bal .204
Lolich-Det .210
McDowell-Cle .213

Opponents' On-Base Pct.
Cuellar-Bal .261
Bosman-Was .262
Peterson-NY .263
Palmer-Bal .272
Messersmith-Cal .276

Starter Runs
Cuellar-Bal 40.2
Peterson-NY 32.6
Bosman-Was 30.8
Messersmith-Cal 30.8
McLain-Det 30.0

Adjusted Starter Runs
Cuellar-Bal 38.9
McLain-Det 32.9
Peterson-NY 29.4
Bosman-Was 28.7
Messersmith-Cal 28.0

Clutch Pitching Index
Cox-Was 128
Nagy-Bos 119
Tiant-Cle 118
John-Chi 114
Wilson-Det 112

Relief Runs
K.Tatum-Cal 21.8
Perranoski-Min 20.2
Watt-Bal 15.6
Roland-Oak 13.8
Knowles-Was 13.0

Adjusted Relief Runs
K.Tatum-Cal 21.3
Perranoski-Min 20.5
Watt-Bal 15.4
Lyle-Bos 13.8
Roland-Oak 12.7

Relief Ranking
Perranoski-Min 40.9
K.Tatum-Cal 32.2
Watt-Bal 21.5
Wood-Chi 19.9
Lyle-Bos 18.4

Total Pitcher Index
Perranoski-Min 4.4
Cuellar-Bal 4.2
Stottlemyre-NY 4.0
K.Tatum-Cal 3.9
Peterson-NY 3.8

Total Baseball Ranking
Petrocelli-Bos 7.2
Jackson-Oak 6.7
Cardenas-Min 5.9
Aparicio-Chi 5.1
Perranoski-Min 4.4

TEAM	G	W	L	PCT	GB	R	OR	AB	H	2B	3B	HR	BB	SO	AVG	OBP	SLG	OPS	OPS+	BR	BR+	PF	CHI	RC	SB	CS	SBA	SBR
EAST																												
PIT	162	89	73	.549		729	664	5637	**1522**	235	**70**	130	444	871	**.270**	.328	.406	734	105	12	28	98	99	740	66	34	66	3
CHI	162	84	78	.519	5	806	679	5491	1424	228	44	179	607	844	.259	.335	.415	750	95	49	-35	112	**104**	773	39	16	71	3
NY	162	83	79	.512	6	695	**630**	5443	1358	211	42	120	684	1062	.249	.336	.370	706	96	-23	-24	100	98	689	118	54	69	7
STL	162	76	86	.469	13	744	747	5689	1497	218	51	113	569	961	.263	.333	.379	712	95	-20	-35	102	103	719	117	47	71	9
PHI	161	73	88	.453	15.5	594	730	5456	1299	224	58	101	519	1066	.238	.307	.356	663	85	-125	-108	97	101	582	72	64	53	-7
MON	162	73	89	.451	16	687	807	5411	1284	211	35	136	659	972	.237	.324	.365	689	91	-62	-61	100	103	658	65	45	59	-1
WEST																												
CIN	162	102	60	.630		775	681	5540	1498	253	45	**191**	547	984	**.270**	.339	**.436**	**775**	**113**	**94**	92	100	94	814	115	52	69	7
LA	161	87	74	.540	14.5	749	684	5606	1515	233	67	87	541	841	**.270**	.337	.382	719	104	-4	30	96	102	730	**138**	57	71	10
SF	162	86	76	.531	16	**831**	826	5578	1460	**257**	35	165	**729**	1005	.262	**.353**	.409	762	112	92	**102**	99	98	**821**	83	27	**75**	9
HOU	162	79	83	.488	23	744	763	5574	1446	250	47	129	598	911	.259	.334	.391	725	104	5	38	96	100	728	114	41	74	**11**
ATL	162	76	86	.469	26	736	772	5546	1495	215	24	160	522	**736**	**.270**	.337	.404	741	99	32	-10	106	97	742	58	34	63	1
SD	162	63	99	.389	39	681	788	5494	1353	208	36	172	500	1164	.246	.314	.391	705	98	-49	-21	96	102	669	60	45	57	-3
TOT	971					8771		66465	17151	2743	554	1683	6919	11417	.259	.332	.392	724							1045	516	67	49

TEAM	CG	SH	SV	IP	H	H/G	HR	BB	SO	RAT	ERA	ERA+	OAV	OOB	PR	PR+	PF	CPI	FA	E	DP	FW	PW	BW	SBW	DIF
EAST																										
PIT	36	13	43	1453^2	1386	8.6	106	625	990	12.7	3.70	106	.255	.336	56	34	96	**106**	.979	137	**195**	.3	3.4	2.8	-.1	1.7
CHI	**59**	9	25	1435	1402	8.8	143	**475**	1000	12.0	3.76	**120**	.256	.318	46	**106**	111	102	.978	137	146	.3	**10.6**	-3.4	-.1	-4.2
NY	47	10	32	1459^2	**1260**	**7.8**	135	575	**1064**	**11.5**	**3.45**	117	**.233**	**.310**	**97**	94	99	98	.979	124	136	1.1	9.4	-2.3	.3	-6.2
STL	51	11	20	1475^2	1483	9.1	**102**	632	960	13.1	4.06	101	.263	.340	-2	9	102	100	.977	150	159	-.4	.9	-3.4	.5	-2.4
PHI	24	8	36	1461	1483	9.2	132	538	1047	12.7	4.18	96	.265	.333	-20	-30	99	99	**.981**	**114**	134	**1.6**	-2.9	-10.7	-1.1	5.9
MON	29	10	32	1438^2	1434	9.0	162	716	914	13.8	4.51	91	.261	.351	-73	-62	102	101	.977	141	193	.1	-6.1	-6.0	-.5	4.7
WEST																										
CIN	32	15	**60**	1444^2	1370	8.6	118	592	843	12.5	3.69	109	.251	.327	57	56	100	102	.976	151	173	-.4	5.6	9.2	.3	6.5
LA	37	**17**	42	1458^2	1394	8.7	164	496	880	11.9	3.82	100	.250	.316	37	2	95	100	.978	135	135	.4	.2	3.0	.6	2.4
SF	50	7	30	1457^2	1514	9.4	156	604	931	13.3	4.51	88	.267	.341	-74	-87	98	98	.973	170	153	-1.5	-8.6	**10.2**	.5	4.6
HOU	36	6	35	1456	1491	9.3	131	577	942	13.1	4.24	92	.265	.338	-30	-61	96	99	.978	140	144	.2	-6.0	3.8	**.7**	-.5
ATL	45	9	24	1430^2	1451	9.2	185	478	960	12.4	4.33	99	.261	.322	-45	-6	106	96	.977	141	118	.1	-.5	-.9	-.3	-3.1
SD	24	9	32	1440^1	1483	9.3	149	611	886	13.4	4.36	91	.267	.344	-50	-62	98	102	.975	158	159	-.8	-6.1	-2.0	-.7	-8.1
TOT	470	124	411	17411^2		8.9				12.7	4.05		.259	.332					.978	1698	1845					

Runs
Williams-Chi 137
Bonds-SF 134
Rose-Cin 120
Brock-StL 114
Tolan-Cin 112

Hits
Williams-Chi 205
Rose-Cin 205
Torre-StL 203
Brock-StL 202
Alou-Pit 201

Doubles
Parker-LA 47
McCovey-SF 39
Rose-Cin 37
Dietz-SF 36
Bonds-SF 36

Triples
Davis-LA 16
Kessinger-Chi 14
Clemente-Pit 10
Bonds-SF 10

Home Runs
Bench-Cin 45
Williams-Chi 42
Perez-Cin 40
McCovey-SF 39

Total Bases
Williams-Chi 373
Bench-Cin 355
Perez-Cin 346
Bonds-SF 334
Gaston-SD 317

Runs Batted In
Bench-Cin 148
Williams-Chi 129
Perez-Cin 129
McCovey-SF 126
H.Aaron-Atl 118

Runs Produced
Williams-Chi 224
Bench-Cin 200
Perez-Cin 196
Bonds-SF 186

Bases On Balls
McCovey-SF 137
Staub-Mon 112
Dietz-SF 109
Wynn-Hou 106
Morgan-Hou 102

Batting Average
Carty-Atl .... .366
Torre-StL .... .325
Sanguillen-Pit .... .325
Williams-Chi .... .322
Parker-LA .... .319

On-Base Percentage
Carty-Atl .... .456
McCovey-SF .... .446
Dietz-SF .... .430
Hickman-Chi .... .421
Perez-Cin .... .405

Slugging Average
McCovey-SF .... .612
Perez-Cin .... .589
Bench-Cin .... .587
Williams-Chi .... .586
Carty-Atl .... .584

On-Base Plus Slugging
McCovey-SF 1058
Carty-Atl 1040
Hickman-Chi 1003
Perez-Cin 994
Williams-Chi 979

Adjusted OPS
McCovey-SF 183
Carty-Atl 167
Perez-Cin 162
Dietz-SF 154
Hickman-Chi 148

Batter Runs
McCovey-SF 62.0
Carty-Atl 54.4
Perez-Cin 52.1
Williams-Chi 51.1
Hickman-Chi 49.5

Adjusted Batter Runs
McCovey-SF 63.6
Perez-Cin 51.7
Carty-Atl 47.7
Dietz-SF 42.2
Carbo-Cin 40.2

Clutch Hitting Index
Parker-LA 126
Dietz-SF 122
Wine-Mon 118
Santo-Chi 117
Davis-LA 115

Runs Created
Williams-Chi 147
McCovey-SF 140
Perez-Cin 140
Bonds-SF 134
Hickman-Chi 129

Total Average
McCovey-SF 1.214
Carty-Atl 1.102
Hickman-Chi 1.080
Perez-Cin 1.045
Williams-Chi 1.018

Stolen Bases
Tolan-Cin 57
Brock-StL 51
Bonds-SF 48
Morgan-Hou 42
Davis-LA 38

Stolen Base Average
Henderson-SF 87.0
Harrelson-NY 85.2
Wynn-Hou 82.8
Bonds-SF 82.8
Cedeno-Hou 81.0

Stolen Base Runs
Bonds-SF 7.1
Brock-StL 6.0
Tolan-Cin 5.5
Morgan-Hou 4.7
Harrelson-NY 3.7

Fielding Runs
Maxvill-StL 37.5
Alley-Pit 33.7
Mazeroski-Pit 23.9
Rader-Hou 23.8
Wine-Mon 19.7

Total Player Rating
McCovey-SF 6.3
Bench-Cin 4.4
Perez-Cin 4.4
Wynn-Hou 4.3
Carty-Atl 4.1

Wins
Perry-SF 23
Gibson-StL 23
Jenkins-Chi 22
Merritt-Cin 20

Win Percentage
Gibson-StL .... .767
Nolan-Cin .... .720
Walker-Pit .... .714
Perry-SF .... .639
Merritt-Cin .... .625

Games
Herbel-SD-NY 76
Selma-Phi 73
Linzy-SF-StL 67
Granger-Cin 67
Giusti-Pit 66

Complete Games
Jenkins-Chi 24
Perry-SF 23
Gibson-StL 23
Seaver-NY 19
Dierker-Hou 17

Shutouts
Perry-SF 5
Sutton-LA 4
Osteen-LA 4
Morton-Mon 4
Ellis-Pit 4

Saves
Granger-Cin 35
Giusti-Pit 26
Brewer-LA 24
Raymond-Mon 23
Selma-Phi 22

Innings Pitched
Perry-SF 328.2
Jenkins-Chi 313.0
Gibson-StL 294.0
Seaver-NY 290.2
Holtzman-Chi 287.2

Fewest Hits/Game
Simpson-Cin 6.39
Seaver-NY 7.12
Walker-Pit 7.12
Gentry-NY 7.41
Jenkins-Chi 7.62

Fewest BB/Game
Jenkins-Chi 1.73
Marichal-SF 1.78
Osteen-LA 1.81
McAndrew-NY 1.86
Merritt-Cin 2.04

Strikeouts
Seaver-NY 283
Jenkins-Chi 274
Gibson-StL 274
Perry-SF 214
Holtzman-Chi 202

Strikeouts/Game
Seaver-NY 8.76
Gibson-StL 8.39
Veale-Pit 7.93
Jenkins-Chi 7.88
Stoneman-Mon 7.63

Ratio
Jenkins-Chi 9.55
Seaver-NY 9.82
McAndrew-NY 10.06
Perry-SF 10.52
Gibson-StL 10.84

Earned Run Average
Seaver-NY 2.82
Simpson-Cin 3.02
Walker-Pit 3.04
Gibson-StL 3.12
Koosman-NY 3.14

Adjusted ERA
Seaver-NY 143
Simpson-Cin 134
Pappas-Atl-Chi 134
Holtzman-Chi 133
Jenkins-Chi 133

Opponents' Batting Avg.
Simpson-Cin .... .198
Seaver-NY .... .214
Walker-Pit .... .219
Jenkins-Chi .... .224
Gentry-NY .... .224

Opponents' On-Base Pct.
Jenkins-Chi .... .265
Seaver-NY .... .273
McAndrew-NY .... .281
Perry-SF .... .290
Gibson-StL .... .296

Starter Runs
Seaver-NY 39.9
Perry-SF 31.0
Gibson-StL 30.4
Jenkins-Chi 23.0
Nolan-Cin 21.9

Adjusted Starter Runs
Seaver-NY 39.4
Jenkins-Chi 34.9
Holtzman-Chi 32.5
Gibson-StL 32.1
Perry-SF 28.9

Clutch Pitching Index
Ellis-Pit 119
Morton-Mon 118
Coombs-SD 113
Pappas-Atl-Chi 109
Dobson-SD 108

Relief Runs
Selma-Phi 19.5
Carroll-Cin 17.0
Gullett-Cin 14.0
Granger-Cin 13.1
C.Taylor-StL 13.0

Adjusted Relief Runs
Selma-Phi 18.9
Carroll-Cin 16.9
Gullett-Cin 13.9
C.Taylor-StL 13.7
Granger-Cin 13.1

Relief Ranking
Selma-Phi 28.1
Granger-Cin 26.1
Carroll-Cin 24.5
McMahon-SF 19.3
Hoerner-Phi 17.5

Total Pitcher Index
Seaver-NY 4.5
Gibson-StL 4.3
Jenkins-Chi 3.6
Perry-SF 3.1
Holtzman-Chi 3.1

Total Baseball Ranking
McCovey-SF 6.3
Seaver-NY 4.5
Bench-Cin 4.4
Perez-Cin 4.4
Wynn-Hou 4.3

TEAM	G	W	L	PCT	GB	R	OR	AB	H	2B	3B	HR	BB	SO	AVG	OBP	SLG	OPS	OPS+	BR	BR+	PF	CHI	RC	SB	CS	SBA	SBR
EAST																												
BAL	162	108	54	.667		**792**	**574**	5545	1424	213	25	179	**717**	952	.257	**.346**	.401	747	**112**	101	**92**	101	99	**795**	84	39	68	5
NY	163	93	69	.574	15	680	612	5492	1381	208	**41**	111	588	**808**	.251	.327	.365	692	102	-18	18	95	103	662	105	61	63	2
BOS	162	87	75	.537	21	786	722	5535	**1450**	**252**	28	**203**	594	855	**.262**	.338	**.428**	**766**	109	**119**	67	107	98	786	50	48	51	-6
DET	162	79	83	.488	29	666	731	5377	1282	207	38	148	656	825	.238	.325	.374	699	98	-4	-9	101	99	658	29	30	49	-4
CLE	162	76	86	.469	32	649	675	5463	1358	197	23	183	503	909	.249	.316	.394	710	96	3	-28	105	97	670	25	36	41	-7
WAS	162	70	92	.432	38	626	689	5460	1302	184	28	138	635	989	.238	.323	.358	681	99	-36	-4	95	97	638	72	42	63	1
WEST																												
MIN	162	98	64	.605		744	605	5483	1438	230	**41**	153	501	905	**.262**	.329	.403	732	107	50	40	101	103	709	57	52	52	-6
OAK	162	89	73	.549	9	678	593	5376	1338	208	24	171	584	977	.249	.327	.392	719	108	28	54	96	98	689	**131**	68	66	5
CAL	162	86	76	.531	12	631	630	5532	1391	197	40	114	447	922	.251	.311	.363	674	95	-64	-42	97	104	622	69	27	**72**	**6**
MIL	163	65	97	.401	33	613	751	5395	1305	202	24	126	592	985	.242	.321	.358	679	92	-42	-46	101	97	618	91	73	55	-6
KC	162	65	97	.401	33	611	705	5503	1341	202	**41**	97	514	958	.244	.311	.348	659	88	-88	-87	100	**105**	593	97	53	65	3
CHI	162	56	106	.346	41	633	822	5514	1394	192	20	123	477	872	.253	.317	.362	679	90	-50	-73	104	102	627	53	33	62	0
TOT	973					8109		65675	16404	2492	373	1746	6808	10957	.250	.325	.379	703							863	562	61	-7

TEAM	CG	SH	SV	IP	H	H/G	HR	BB	SO	RAT	ERA	ERA+	OAV	OOB	PR	PR+	PF	CPI	FA	E	DP	FW	PW	BW	SBW	DIF
EAST																										
BAL	**60**	12	31	1478^{2}	1317	8.1	139	469	941	**11.1**	**3.15**	**116**	.240	**.302**	**93**	**84**	98	102	.981	117	148	1.1	**8.8**	**9.6**	.6	7.1
NY	36	6	49	1471^{2}	1386	8.5	**130**	**451**	777	11.4	3.25	108	.249	.308	77	47	95	**103**	.980	130	146	.4	4.9	1.9	.3	4.7
BOS	38	8	44	1446^{1}	1391	8.7	156	594	1003	12.7	3.88	102	.251	.329	-25	13	107	100	.974	156	131	-1.1	1.4	7.0	-.6	-.5
DET	33	9	39	1447^{1}	1443	9.0	153	623	1045	13.1	4.10	91	.260	.338	-61	-59	100	100	.978	133	142	.2	-6.1	-.9	-.4	5.3
CLE	34	8	35	1451^{1}	1333	8.3	163	689	**1076**	12.8	3.91	101	.247	.337	-31	8	107	**103**	.979	133	168	.2	.9	-2.9	-.7	-2.4
WAS	20	11	40	1457^{2}	1375	8.5	139	611	823	12.5	3.80	94	.252	.330	-13	-41	96	100	**.982**	**116**	173	**1.2**	-4.2	-.4	.2	-7.6
WEST																										
MIN	26	12	**58**	1448^{1}	1329	8.3	**130**	486	940	11.6	3.24	115	.244	.310	78	79	100	**103**	.980	123	130	.8	8.2	4.2	-.6	4.5
OAK	33	**15**	40	1442^{2}	**1253**	**7.9**	134	542	858	11.5	3.31	107	**.234**	.308	66	40	95	98	.977	141	152	-.3	4.2	5.7	.6	-2.0
CAL	21	10	49	1462^{1}	1280	**7.9**	154	559	922	11.6	3.49	104	.237	.313	37	22	97	99	.980	127	169	.6	2.3	-4.3	**.7**	5.9
MIL	31	2	27	1446^{2}	1397	8.7	146	587	895	12.7	4.21	90	.255	.332	-79	-66	102	93	.978	136	142	.0	-6.8	-4.7	-.6	-3.8
KC	30	11	25	1463^{2}	1346	8.3	138	641	915	12.5	3.79	99	.247	.331	-11	-7	101	100	.976	152	162	-.9	-.7	-9.0	.4	-5.6
CHI	20	6	30	1430^{1}	1554	9.8	164	556	762	13.6	4.55	86	.280	.350	-132	-98	105	101	.975	165	**187**	-1.6	-10.1	-7.5	.0	-5.6
TOT	382	110	467	17447		8.5				12.2	3.72		.250	.325					.979	1629	1850					

Runs
- Yastrzemski-Bos 125
- Tovar-Min 120
- White-NY 109
- Smith-Bos 109
- Harper-Mil 104

Hits
- Oliva-Min 204
- Johnson-Cal 202
- Tovar-Min 195
- Yastrzemski-Bos 186
- White-NY 180

Doubles
- Tovar-Min 36
- Otis-KC 36
- Oliva-Min 36
- Harper-Mil 35
- Cardenas-Min 34

Triples
- Tovar-Min 13
- Stanley-Det 11
- Otis-KC 9

Home Runs
- Howard-Was 44
- Killebrew-Min 41
- Yastrzemski-Bos 40
- T.Conigliaro-Bos 36
- Powell-Bal 35

Total Bases
- Yastrzemski-Bos 335
- Oliva-Min 323
- Harper-Mil 315
- Howard-Was 309
- Powell-Bal 289

Runs Batted In
- Howard-Was 126
- T.Conigliaro-Bos 116
- Powell-Bal 114
- Killebrew-Min 113
- Oliva-Min 107

Runs Produced
- Yastrzemski-Bos 187
- White-NY 181
- Oliva-Min 180
- Howard-Was 172
- T.Conigliaro-Bos 169

Bases On Balls
- Howard-Was 132
- Yastrzemski-Bos 128
- Killebrew-Min 128
- Bando-Oak 118
- Buford-Bal 109

Batting Average
- Johnson-Cal .329
- Yastrzemski-Bos .329
- Oliva-Min .325
- Aparicio-Chi .313
- F.Robinson-Bal .306

On-Base Percentage
- Yastrzemski-Bos .453
- Howard-Was .420
- Powell-Bal .417
- Killebrew-Min .416
- Buford-Bal .409

Slugging Average
- Yastrzemski-Bos .592
- Powell-Bal .549
- Killebrew-Min .546
- Howard-Was .546
- Harper-Mil .522

On-Base Plus Slugging
- Yastrzemski-Bos 1045
- Powell-Bal 967
- Howard-Was 966
- Killebrew-Min 962
- F.Robinson-Bal 922

Adjusted OPS
- Yastrzemski-Bos 174
- Howard-Was 173
- Powell-Bal 163
- Killebrew-Min 161
- F.Robinson-Bal 151

Batter Runs
- Yastrzemski-Bos 71.7
- Howard-Was 54.1
- Killebrew-Min 49.5
- Powell-Bal 49.2
- Harper-Mil 37.5

Adjusted Batter Runs
- Yastrzemski-Bos 62.1
- Howard-Was 60.7
- Powell-Bal 47.9
- Killebrew-Min 47.8
- White-NY 38.5

Clutch Hitting Index
- Piniella-KC 128
- Cater-NY 117
- McMullen-Was-Cal 116
- Howard-Was 116
- Belanger-Bal 115

Runs Created
- Yastrzemski-Bos 157
- Howard-Was 130
- Powell-Bal 123
- Harper-Mil 122
- Killebrew-Min 116

Total Average
- Yastrzemski-Bos 1.170
- Powell-Bal 1.034
- Howard-Was 1.026
- Killebrew-Min 1.000
- F.Robinson-Bal .944

Stolen Bases
- Campaneris-Oak 42
- Harper-Mil 38
- Alomar-Cal 35
- Kelly-KC 34
- Otis-KC 33

Stolen Base Average
- Otis-KC 94.3
- Johnson-Cal 89.5
- Campaneris-Oak 80.8
- Stroud-Was 78.4
- Kenney-NY 76.9

Stolen Base Runs
- Otis-KC 6.6
- Campaneris-Oak 5.7
- Stroud-Was 3.6
- Alomar-Cal 3.5
- Johnson-Cal 3.0

Fielding Runs
- Knoop-Chi 35.1
- Brinkman-Was 31.1
- Nettles-Cle 27.8
- Cullen-Was 26.5
- Mitterwald-Min 24.3

Total Player Rating
- Yastrzemski-Bos 5.4
- Aparicio-Chi 4.6
- Oliva-Min 4.3
- Fregosi-Cal 4.3
- Howard-Was 4.2

Wins
- Perry-Min 24
- McNally-Bal 24
- Cuellar-Bal 24
- Wright-Cal 22

Win Percentage
- Cuellar-Bal .750
- McNally-Bal .727
- Perry-Min .667
- Palmer-Bal .667
- Siebert-Bos .652

Games
- Wood-Chi 77
- Grant-Oak 72
- Knowles-Was 71
- Williams-Min 68

Complete Games
- Cuellar-Bal 21
- McDowell-Cle 19
- Palmer-Bal 17
- McNally-Bal 16
- Culp-Bos 15

Shutouts
- Palmer-Bal 5
- Dobson-Oak 5
- Peters-Bos 4
- Perry-Min 4
- Cuellar-Bal 4

Saves
- Perranoski-Min 34
- McDaniel-NY 29
- Timmermann-Det 27
- Knowles-Was 27
- Grant-Oak 24

Innings Pitched
- Palmer-Bal 305.0
- McDowell-Cle 305.0
- Cuellar-Bal 297.2
- McNally-Bal 296.0
- Perry-Min 278.2

Fewest Hits/Game
- Messersmith-Cal 6.66
- McDowell-Cle 6.96
- Segui-Oak 7.22
- Johnson-KC 7.49
- Culp-Bos 7.56

Fewest BB/Game
- Peterson-NY 1.38
- Perry-Min 1.84
- Cox-Was 2.06
- Cuellar-Bal 2.09
- Horlen-Chi 2.14

Strikeouts
- McDowell-Cle 304
- Lolich-Det 230
- Johnson-KC 206
- Palmer-Bal 199
- Culp-Bos 197

Strikeouts/Game
- McDowell-Cle 8.97
- Johnson-KC 8.66
- Cain-Det 7.77
- Lolich-Det 7.59
- Messersmith-Cal 7.49

Ratio
- Peterson-NY 10.03
- Cuellar-Bal 10.37
- Perry-Min 10.46
- Blyleven-Min 10.54
- Messersmith-Cal 10.54

Earned Run Average
- Segui-Oak 2.56
- Palmer-Bal 2.71
- Wright-Cal 2.83
- Peterson-NY 2.90
- McDowell-Cle 2.92

Adjusted ERA
- Segui-Oak 139
- McDowell-Cle 136
- Palmer-Bal 134
- Culp-Bos 130
- Wright-Cal 128

Opponents' Batting Avg.
- Messersmith-Cal .205
- McDowell-Cle .213
- Segui-Oak .222
- Culp-Bos .224
- Johnson-KC .228

Opponents' On-Base Pct.
- Peterson-NY .280
- Cuellar-Bal .286
- Perry-Min .287
- Blyleven-Min .289
- Messersmith-Cal .290

Starter Runs
- Palmer-Bal 34.0
- McDowell-Cle 27.0
- Wright-Cal 25.7
- Peterson-NY 23.6
- Perry-Min 21.1

Adjusted Starter Runs
- McDowell-Cle 33.1
- Palmer-Bal 32.3
- Culp-Bos 24.1
- Wright-Cal 23.4
- Perry-Min 21.3

Clutch Pitching Index
- Stottlemyre-NY 113
- Kaat-Min 112
- Bahnsen-NY 109
- Segui-Oak 109
- Wright-Cal 108

Relief Runs
- Grant-Oak 26.0
- Knowles-Was 22.3
- Williams-Min 21.8
- McDaniel-NY 21.1
- Hall-Min 20.2

Adjusted Relief Runs
- Grant-Oak 24.7
- Williams-Min 21.9
- Knowles-Was 21.1
- Sanders-Mil 20.5
- Hall-Min 20.3

Relief Ranking
- Knowles-Was 34.4
- McDaniel-NY 31.8
- Perranoski-Min 28.5
- Wood-Chi 27.4
- Williams-Min 24.5

Total Pitcher Index
- Knowles-Was 3.7
- McDaniel-NY 3.5
- Perry-Min 3.3
- Wood-Chi 3.1
- Wright-Cal 3.1

Total Baseball Ranking
- Yastrzemski-Bos 5.4
- Aparicio-Chi 4.6
- Oliva-Min 4.3
- Fregosi-Cal 4.3
- Howard-Was 4.2

TEAM	G	W	L	PCT	GB	R	OR	AB	H	2B	3B	HR	BB	SO	AVG	OBP	SLG	OPS	OPS+	BR	BR+	PF	CHI	RC	SB	CS	SBA	SBR
EAST																												
PIT	162	97	65	.599		**788**	599	5674	**1555**	223	**61**	**154**	469	919	.274	.333	**.416**	**749**	**119**	**121**	**125**	100	103	**776**	65	31	68	3
STL	163	90	72	.556	7	739	699	5610	1542	225	54	95	543	757	**.275**	**.342**	.385	727	108	91	63	104	100	736	**124**	53	70	9
NY	162	83	79	.512	14	588	**550**	5477	1365	203	29	98	547	958	.249	.321	.351	672	98	-20	-11	99	95	614	89	43	67	5
CHI	162	83	79	.512	14	637	648	5438	1401	202	34	128	527	772	.258	.327	.378	705	93	41	-44	115	95	663	44	32	58	-2
MON	162	71	90	.441	25.5	622	729	5335	1312	197	29	88	543	800	.246	.325	.343	668	96	-20	-22	100	102	598	51	43	54	-4
PHI	162	67	95	.414	30	558	688	5538	1289	209	35	123	499	1031	.233	.300	.350	650	90	-74	-73	100	99	586	63	39	62	0
WEST																												
SF	162	90	72	.556		706	644	5461	1348	224	36	140	**654**	1042	.247	.331	.378	709	109	57	68	98	101	699	101	36	**74**	**10**
LA	162	89	73	.549	1	663	587	5523	1469	213	38	95	489	755	.266	.328	.370	698	111	28	70	94	100	661	76	40	66	3
ATL	162	82	80	.506	8	643	699	5575	1434	192	30	153	434	**747**	.257	.314	.385	699	98	18	-21	106	98	658	57	46	55	-4
HOU	162	79	83	.488	11	585	567	5492	1319	**230**	52	71	478	888	.240	.304	.340	644	90	-81	-66	97	**107**	573	101	51	66	4
CIN	162	79	83	.488	11	586	581	5414	1306	203	28	138	438	907	.241	.301	.366	667	96	-45	-33	98	103	580	59	33	64	1
SD	161	61	100	.379	28.5	486	610	5366	1250	184	31	96	438	966	.233	.294	.332	626	89	-117	-81	93	98	513	70	45	61	0
TOT	972					7601		65903	16590	2505	457	1379	6059	10542	.252	.319	.367	685							900	492	65	26

TEAM	CG	SH	SV	IP	H	H/G	HR	BB	SO	RAT	ERA	ERA+	OAV	OOB	PR	PR+	PF	CPI	FA	E	DP	FW	PW	BW	SBW	DIF
EAST																										
PIT	43	15	**48**	1461	1426	8.8	108	470	813	11.9	3.31	102	.257	.318	26	12	98	105	.979	133	164	.1	1.3	**13.5**	.0	1.2
STL	56	14	22	1467	1482	9.1	104	576	911	12.9	3.86	93	.263	.336	-63	-39	104	99	.978	142	155	-.3	-4.1	6.8	.7	6.1
NY	42	13	22	1466[1]	**1227**	**7.6**	100	529	**1157**	**11.1**	**2.99**	**114**	**.227**	**.300**	**78**	**69**	98	95	.981	114	135	1.2	**7.4**	-1.1	.3	-5.7
CHI	**75**	17	13	1444	1458	9.1	132	411	900	11.9	3.61	109	.262	.316	-23	46	114	101	.980	126	150	.5	5.0	-4.7	-.4	1.8
MON	49	8	25	1434[1]	1418	8.9	133	658	829	13.3	4.12	86	.260	.344	-104	-92	102	100	.976	150	164	-.9	-9.8	-2.3	-.7	4.3
PHI	31	10	25	1470[2]	1396	8.6	132	525	838	12.0	3.72	95	.254	.323	-41	-30	102	98	.981	122	158	.8	-3.2	-7.8	-.2	-3.4
WEST																										
SF	45	14	30	1454[2]	1324	8.2	128	471	831	11.3	3.32	102	.242	.306	24	13	98	97	.972	179	153	-2.5	1.4	7.3	**.8**	2.1
LA	48	**18**	33	1449[2]	1363	8.5	110	**399**	853	**11.1**	3.24	100	.250	.304	37	-1	93	99	.979	131	159	.2	-.0	7.6	.0	.4
ATL	40	11	31	1474[2]	1529	9.4	152	485	823	12.5	3.75	99	.269	.330	-46	-5	107	**108**	.977	146	**180**	-.6	-.5	-2.2	-.7	5.2
HOU	43	10	25	1471[1]	1318	8.1	**75**	475	914	11.4	3.14	107	.241	.309	55	39	97	95	.983	106	152	1.7	4.2	-7.0	.2	-.9
CIN	27	11	38	1444	1298	8.1	112	501	750	11.4	3.36	100	.243	.311	18	0	97	97	**.984**	**103**	174	**1.9**	.0	-3.5	-.1	-.1
SD	47	10	17	1438	1351	8.5	93	559	923	12.2	3.23	102	.249	.323	39	12	95	106	.974	161	144	-1.5	1.3	-8.6	-.2	-10.2
TOT	546	151	329	17475[2]		8.6				11.9	3.47		.252	.319					.979	1613	1888					

Runs
Brock-StL 126
Bonds-SF 110
Stargell-Pit 104
Garr-Atl 101
Torre-StL 97

Hits
Torre-StL 230
Garr-Atl 219
Brock-StL 200
Davis-LA 198

Doubles
Cedeno-Hou 40
Brock-StL 37
Torre-StL 34
Staub-Mon 34
Davis-LA 33

Triples
Morgan-Hou 11
Metzger-Hou 11
Davis-LA 10
Gaston-SD 9

Home Runs
Stargell-Pit 48
H.Aaron-Atl 47
May-Cin 39
Johnson-Phi 34

Total Bases
Torre-StL 352
H.Aaron-Atl 331
Stargell-Pit 321
Bonds-SF 317
Williams-Chi 300

Runs Batted In
Torre-StL 137
Stargell-Pit 125
H.Aaron-Atl 118
Bonds-SF 102
Montanez-Phi 99

Runs Produced
Torre-StL 210
Stargell-Pit 181
Brock-StL 180
Bonds-SF 179
Staub-Mon 172

Bases On Balls
Mays-SF 112
Dietz-SF 97
Bailey-Mon 97
Allen-LA 93
Morgan-Hou 88

Batting Average
Torre-StL .... .363
Garr-Atl .... .343
Beckert-Chi .... .342
Clemente-Pit .... .341
H.Aaron-Atl .... .327

On-Base Percentage
Mays-SF .... .429
Torre-StL .... .424
H.Aaron-Atl .... .414
Hunt-Mon .... .403
Stargell-Pit .... .401

Slugging Average
H.Aaron-Atl .... .669
Stargell-Pit .... .628
Torre-StL .... .555
May-Cin .... .532
Bonds-SF .... .512

On-Base Plus Slugging
H.Aaron-Atl 1082
Stargell-Pit 1029
Torre-StL 979
Mays-SF 911
Williams-Chi 889

Adjusted OPS
H.Aaron-Atl 190
Stargell-Pit 188
Torre-StL 169
Mays-SF 160
Allen-LA 154

Batter Runs
H.Aaron-Atl 65.2
Torre-StL 62.5
Stargell-Pit 58.7
Williams-Chi 39.4
Staub-Mon 38.5

Adjusted Batter Runs
Stargell-Pit 59.3
H.Aaron-Atl 57.9
Torre-StL 57.4
Allen-LA 41.4
Mays-SF 39.1

Clutch Hitting Index
Fairly-Mon 129
Sanguillen-Pit 125
Bailey-Mon 123
Watson-Hou 121
Simmons-StL 120

Runs Created
Torre-StL 145
H.Aaron-Atl 137
Stargell-Pit 131
Bonds-SF 115
Brock-StL 114

Total Average
H.Aaron-Atl 1.178
Stargell-Pit 1.117
Mays-SF 1.067
Torre-StL .... .998
Bonds-SF .... .876

Stolen Bases
Brock-StL 64
Morgan-Hou 40
Garr-Atl 30

Stolen Base Average
Mays-SF 88.5
Henderson-SF 85.7
Morgan-Hou 83.3
Agee-NY 82.4
Hernandez-SD 80.8

Stolen Base Runs
Brock-StL 7.4
Morgan-Hou 6.0
Agee-NY 4.1
Mays-SF 4.0
Harrelson-NY 3.7

Fielding Runs
Maxvill-StL 29.2
Garr-Atl 16.2
Robertson-Pit 15.2
Helms-Cin 14.4
Barton-SD 14.0

Total Player Rating
Stargell-Pit 5.6
H.Aaron-Atl 4.3
Torre-StL 4.2
Mays-SF 3.7
Staub-Mon 3.6

Wins
Jenkins-Chi 24
Seaver-NY 20
Downing-LA 20
Carlton-StL 20
Ellis-Pit 19

Win Percentage
Gullett-Cin .... .727
Downing-LA .... .690
Carlton-StL .... .690
Ellis-Pit .... .679
Seaver-NY .... .667

Games
Granger-Cin 70
J.Johnson-SF 67
Marshall-Mon 66
McMahon-SF 61
Carroll-Cin 61

Complete Games
Jenkins-Chi 30
Seaver-NY 21
Stoneman-Mon 20
Gibson-StL 20

Shutouts
Pappas-Chi 5
Gibson-StL 5
Downing-LA 5
Blass-Pit 5

Saves
Giusti-Pit 30
Marshall-Mon 23
Brewer-LA 22
J.Johnson-SF 18
Upshaw-Atl 17

Innings Pitched
Jenkins-Chi 325.0
Stoneman-Mon 294.2
Seaver-NY 286.1
Perry-SF 280.0
Marichal-SF 279.0

Fewest Hits/Game
Wilson-Hou 6.55
Seaver-NY 6.60
Kirby-SD 7.17
Gentry-NY 7.39
Stoneman-Mon 7.42

Fewest BB/Game
Jenkins-Chi 1.02
Marichal-SF 1.81
Stone-Atl 1.82
Hands-Chi 1.86
Sutton-LA 1.87

Strikeouts
Seaver-NY 289
Jenkins-Chi 263
Stoneman-Mon 251
Kirby-SD 231
Sutton-LA 194

Strikeouts/Game
Seaver-NY 9.08
Kirby-SD 7.78
Stoneman-Mon 7.67
Jenkins-Chi 7.28
Gentry-NY 6.86

Ratio
Seaver-NY 8.64
Wilson-Hou 9.44
Jenkins-Chi 9.58
Marichal-SF 9.77
Sutton-LA 9.87

Earned Run Average
Seaver-NY 1.76
Roberts-SD 2.10
Wilson-Hou 2.45
Forsch-Hou 2.53
Sutton-LA 2.54

Adjusted ERA
Seaver-NY 194
Roberts-SD 157
Jenkins-Chi 142
Wilson-Hou 137
Forsch-Hou 133

Opponents' Batting Avg.
Wilson-Hou .... .202
Seaver-NY .... .206
Kirby-SD .... .216
Cumberland-SF ...... .223
Gentry-NY .... .224

Opponents' On-Base Pct.
Seaver-NY .... .253
Wilson-Hou .... .268
Jenkins-Chi .... .271
Marichal-SF .... .274
Nolan-Cin .... .275

Starter Runs
Seaver-NY 54.4
Roberts-SD 41.0
Wilson-Hou 30.3
Sutton-LA 27.3
Jenkins-Chi 25.3

Adjusted Starter Runs
Seaver-NY 53.4
Roberts-SD 37.7
Jenkins-Chi 37.2
Wilson-Hou 28.2
Sutton-LA 21.8

Clutch Pitching Index
Roberts-SD 120
Downing-LA 116
Short-Phi 115
Johnson-Pit 112
Wise-Phi 112

Relief Runs
McGraw-NY 21.8
Miller-Chi-SD-Pit 20.0
Frisella-NY 15.0
Ray-Hou 14.7
Brewer-LA 14.4

Adjusted Relief Runs
McGraw-NY 21.4
Miller-Chi-SD-Pit 19.5
Frisella-NY 14.6
Ray-Hou 14.0
Brewer-LA 13.1

Relief Ranking
McGraw-NY 29.5
Miller-Chi-SD-Pit 27.6
Brewer-LA 24.0
Frisella-NY 23.2
Ray-Hou 19.0

Total Pitcher Index
Seaver-NY 6.6
Jenkins-Chi 5.8
Roberts-SD 4.9
McGraw-NY 3.4
Wise-Phi 3.4

Total Baseball Ranking
Seaver-NY 6.6
Jenkins-Chi 5.8
Stargell-Pit 5.6
Roberts-SD 4.9
H.Aaron-Atl 4.3

TEAM	G	W	L	PCT	GB	R	OR	AB	H	2B	3B	HR	BB	SO	AVG	OBP	SLG	OPS	OPS+	BR	BR+	PF	CHI	RC	SB	CS	SBA	SBR
EAST																												
BAL	158	101	57	.639		**742**	**530**	5303	1382	207	25	158	**672**	844	**.261**	**.349**	.398	**747**	**120**	**133**	**140**	99	97	**750**	66	38	63	1
DET	162	91	71	.562	12	701	645	5502	1399	214	38	**179**	540	854	.254	.327	**.405**	732	110	88	61	104	97	715	35	43	45	-7
BOS	162	85	77	.525	18	691	667	5401	1360	**246**	28	161	552	871	.252	.325	.397	722	104	68	22	107	100	686	51	34	60	-1
NY	162	82	80	.506	21	648	641	5413	1377	195	**43**	97	581	**717**	.254	.331	.360	691	109	22	64	94	99	643	75	55	58	-3
WAS	159	63	96	.396	38.5	537	660	5290	1219	189	30	86	575	956	.230	.309	.326	635	91	-86	-54	94	102	538	68	45	60	-1
CLE	162	60	102	.370	43	543	747	5467	1303	200	20	109	467	868	.238	.302	.342	644	81	-83	-128	109	101	558	57	37	61	0
WEST																												
OAK	161	101	60	.627		691	564	5494	1383	195	25	160	542	1018	.252	.323	.384	707	109	42	56	98	102	681	80	53	60	-1
KC	161	85	76	.528	16	603	566	5295	1323	225	40	80	490	819	.250	.316	.353	669	97	-28	-23	99	**104**	594	**130**	46	**74**	**13**
CHI	162	79	83	.488	22.5	617	597	5382	1346	185	30	138	562	870	.250	.327	.373	700	102	33	13	103	94	661	83	65	56	-4
CAL	162	76	86	.469	25.5	511	576	5495	1271	213	18	96	441	827	.231	.292	.329	621	88	-131	-93	93	**104**	518	72	34	68	4
MIN	160	74	86	.463	26.5	654	670	5414	**1406**	197	31	116	512	846	.260	.326	.372	698	101	28	8	103	101	641	66	44	60	-1
MIL	161	69	92	.429	27.5	534	609	5185	1188	160	23	104	543	924	.229	.306	.329	635	87	-88	-82	99	103	534	82	53	61	-1
TOT	966					7472		64641	15957	2426	351	1484	6477	10414	.247	.320	.365	684							865	547	61	-1

TEAM	CG	SH	SV	IP	H	H/G	HR	BB	SO	RAT	ERA	ERA+	OAV	OOB	PR	PR+	PF	CPI	FA	E	DP	FW	PW	BW	SBW	DIF
EAST																										
BAL	**71**	15	22	1415^1	1257	8.0	125	**416**	793	**10.8**	**2.99**	112	.239	**.297**	**74**	59	97	101	.981	112	148	.7	6.4	**15.1**	.1	-.2
DET	53	11	32	1468^1	1355	8.4	126	609	**1000**	12.4	3.64	99	.247	.327	-28	-7	104	99	**.983**	**106**	156	**1.3**	-.7	6.6	-.7	3.8
BOS	44	11	35	1443	1424	8.9	136	535	871	12.5	3.81	97	.259	.329	-55	-17	107	100	.981	116	149	.7	-1.8	2.4	-.0	3.0
NY	67	15	12	1452	1382	8.6	126	423	707	11.4	3.44	94	.252	.308	4	-35	93	97	.981	125	159	.2	-3.7	6.9	-.3	-1.9
WAS	30	10	26	1418^2	1376	8.8	132	554	762	12.6	3.70	89	.258	.333	-37	-65	96	105	.977	141	170	-.9	-6.9	-5.8	-.0	-2.6
CLE	21	7	32	1440	1352	8.5	154	770	937	13.6	4.28	89	.252	.351	-130	-65	111	99	.981	116	159	.7	-6.9	-13.7	.0	-.8
WEST																										
OAK	57	18	36	1469^1	**1229**	**7.6**	131	501	999	**10.8**	3.06	109	**.228**	.298	67	48	96	97	.981	117	157	.6	5.2	6.1	-.0	8.9
KC	34	15	**44**	1420^1	1301	8.3	**84**	496	775	11.7	3.26	106	.247	.316	33	29	99	98	.979	132	**178**	-.3	3.2	-2.4	**1.4**	2.8
CHI	46	19	32	1450^1	1348	8.4	100	468	976	11.5	3.13	**115**	.247	.309	55	**73**	104	101	.975	160	128	-1.9	**7.9**	1.4	-.4	-8.8
CAL	39	11	32	1481	1246	**7.6**	101	607	904	11.5	3.10	104	.230	.312	60	24	94	98	.980	131	159	-.2	2.6	-10.0	.4	2.3
MIN	43	9	25	1416^2	1384	8.8	139	529	895	12.5	3.82	93	.257	.328	-55	-40	103	100	.980	118	134	.5	-4.3	.9	-.0	-2.8
MIL	32	**23**	32	1416^1	1303	8.3	130	569	795	12.1	3.39	103	.247	.324	13	14	100	**106**	.977	138	152	-.7	1.6	-8.8	-.0	-3.3
TOT	537	164	360	17291^1		8.4				11.9	3.47		.247	.320					.980	1512	1849					

Runs
Buford-Bal 99
Tovar-Min 94
Murcer-NY 94
Carew-Min 88
Jackson-Oak 87

Hits
Tovar-Min 204
Alomar-Cal 179
Carew-Min 177
Smith-Bos 175
Murcer-NY 175

Doubles
Smith-Bos 33
Schaal-KC 31
Rodriguez-Det 30
Oliva-Min 30

Triples
Patek-KC 11
Carew-Min 10
Blair-Bal 8

Home Runs
Melton-Chi 33
Jackson-Oak 32
Cash-Det 32
Smith-Bos 30

Total Bases
Smith-Bos 302
Jackson-Oak 288
Murcer-NY 287
Melton-Chi 267
Oliva-Min 266

Runs Batted In
Killebrew-Min 119
F.Robinson-Bal 99
Smith-Bos 96
Murcer-NY 94
Bando-Oak 94

Runs Produced
Murcer-NY 163
F.Robinson-Bal 153
Killebrew-Min 152
White-NY 151
Smith-Bos 151

Bases On Balls
Killebrew-Min 114
Yastrzemski-Bos 106
Schaal-KC 103
Petrocelli-Bos 91
Murcer-NY 91

Batting Average
Oliva-Min .337
Murcer-NY .331
Rettenmund-Bal .318
Tovar-Min .311
Carew-Min .307

On-Base Percentage
Murcer-NY .429
Rettenmund-Bal .424
Kaline-Det .421
Buford-Bal .415
White-NY .399

Slugging Average
Oliva-Min .546
Murcer-NY .543
Cash-Det .531
F.Robinson-Bal .510
Jackson-Oak .508

On-Base Plus Slugging
Murcer-NY 972
Oliva-Min 918
Cash-Det 905
F.Robinson-Bal 900
Buford-Bal 891

Adjusted OPS
Murcer-NY 185
White-NY 155
F.Robinson-Bal 154
Buford-Bal 153
Oliva-Min 152

Batter Runs
Murcer-NY 53.7
Rettenmund-Bal 34.8
Buford-Bal 34.5
White-NY 33.7
Oliva-Min 33.6

Adjusted Batter Runs
Murcer-NY 61.3
White-NY 40.1
Rettenmund-Bal 35.7
Buford-Bal 35.3
F.Robinson-Bal 33.8

Clutch Hitting Index
Killebrew-Min 140
Powell-Bal 137
Alou-Oak-NY 123
F.Robinson-Bal 121
May-Chi 120

Runs Created
Murcer-NY 126
Smith-Bos 106
Jackson-Oak 103
White-NY 103
Rettenmund-Bal 99

Total Average
Murcer-NY 1.035
Buford-Bal .970
Cash-Det .933
F.Robinson-Bal .905
Rettenmund-Bal .904

Stolen Bases
Otis-KC 52
Patek-KC 49
Alomar-Cal 39
Campaneris-Oak 34

Stolen Base Average
Harper-Mil 89.3
Otis-KC 86.7
Campaneris-Oak 82.9
Pinson-Cle 80.6
Alomar-Cal 79.6

Stolen Base Runs
Otis-KC 8.6
Patek-KC 5.9
Alomar-Cal 5.1
Campaneris-Oak 5.0
Harper-Mil 4.4

Fielding Runs
Nettles-Cle 42.3
Melton-Chi 27.0
Alomar-Cal 21.4
Cullen-Was 20.5
Otis-KC 19.8

Total Player Rating
Murcer-NY 6.0
Nettles-Cle 5.5
Melton-Chi 5.2
White-NY 4.4
Otis-KC 4.3

Wins
Lolich-Det 25
Blue-Oak 24
Wood-Chi 22
McNally-Bal 21
Hunter-Oak 21

Win Percentage
McNally-Bal .808
Dobson-Oak .750
Blue-Oak .750
Dobson-Bal .714

Games
Sanders-Mil 83
Scherman-Det 69
Burgmeier-KC 67
Abernathy-KC 63

Complete Games
Lolich-Det 29
Blue-Oak 24
Wood-Chi 22
Cuellar-Bal 21
Palmer-Bal 20

Shutouts
Blue-Oak 8
Wood-Chi 7
Stottlemyre-NY 7
Bradley-Chi 6

Saves
Sanders-Mil 31
Abernathy-KC 23
Scherman-Det 20
Fingers-Oak 17
Burgmeier-KC 17

Innings Pitched
Lolich-Det 376.0
Wood-Chi 334.0
Blue-Oak 312.0
Cuellar-Bal 292.1
Coleman-Det 286.0

Fewest Hits/Game
Blue-Oak 6.03
McDowell-Cle 6.71
May-Cal 6.91
Messersmith-Cal 7.29
Wright-Cal 7.32

Fewest BB/Game
Peterson-NY 1.38
Kline-NY 1.50
Kaat-Min 1.62
Wood-Chi 1.67
Drago-KC 1.72

Strikeouts
Lolich-Det 308
Blue-Oak 301
Coleman-Det 236
Blyleven-Min 224
Wood-Chi 210

Strikeouts/Game
Blue-Oak 8.68
McDowell-Cle 8.05
Johnson-Chi 7.74
Coleman-Det 7.43
Lolich-Det 7.37

Ratio
Blue-Oak 8.68
Wood-Chi 9.19
Kline-NY 9.84
Dobson-Bal 9.98
McNally-Bal 10.07

Earned Run Average
Blue-Oak 1.82
Wood-Chi 1.91
Palmer-Bal 2.68
Hedlund-KC 2.71
Blyleven-Min 2.81

Adjusted ERA
Wood-Chi 188
Blue-Oak 184
Siebert-Bos 127
Hedlund-KC 127
Blyleven-Min 126

Opponents' Batting Avg.
Blue-Oak .189
McDowell-Cle .207
May-Cal .213
Messersmith-Cal .218
Palmer-Bal .221

Opponents' On-Base Pct.
Blue-Oak .252
Wood-Chi .264
Kline-NY .276
Dobson-Bal .279
Hunter-Oak .282

Starter Runs
Wood-Chi 57.7
Blue-Oak 57.2
Palmer-Bal 24.6
Lolich-Det 22.9
Blyleven-Min 20.2

Adjusted Starter Runs
Wood-Chi 60.2
Blue-Oak 54.8
Lolich-Det 27.2
Blyleven-Min 22.4
Palmer-Bal 21.9

Clutch Pitching Index
Drago-KC 119
Krausse-Mil 118
Johnson-Chi 117
Wood-Chi 112
Bosman-Was 112

Relief Runs
Sanders-Mil 23.5
Burgmeier-KC 17.0
Mingori-Cle 12.8
Queen-Cal 12.3
Grzenda-Was 12.1

Adjusted Relief Runs
Sanders-Mil 23.6
Burgmeier-KC 16.9
Mingori-Cle 13.7
Queen-Cal 11.4
Grzenda-Was 11.4

Relief Ranking
Sanders-Mil 41.6
Burgmeier-KC 33.8
Scherman-Det 18.8
Abernathy-KC 14.0
Grzenda-Was 12.0

Total Pitcher Index
Wood-Chi 6.4
Blue-Oak 5.1
Sanders-Mil 4.7
Burgmeier-KC 4.3
Siebert-Bos 3.4

Total Baseball Ranking
Wood-Chi 6.4
Murcer-NY 6.0
Nettles-Cle 5.5
Melton-Chi 5.2
Blue-Oak 5.1

TEAM	G	W	L	PCT	GB	R	OR	AB	H	2B	3B	HR	BB	SO	AVG	OBP	SLG	OPS	OPS+	BR	BR+	PF	CHI	RC	SB	CS	SBA	SBR
EAST																												
PIT	155	96	59	.619		691	**512**	5490	**1505**	**251**	**47**	110	404	871	**.274**	.327	**.397**	**724**	114	74	89	98	100	**701**	49	30	62	0
CHI	156	85	70	.548	11	685	567	5247	1346	206	40	133	565	815	.257	.332	.387	719	100	74	8	111	100	670	69	47	59	-1
NY	156	83	73	.532	13.5	528	578	5135	1154	175	31	105	589	990	.225	.309	.332	641	91	-68	-54	97	99	530	41	41	50	-5
STL	156	75	81	.481	21.5	568	600	5326	1383	214	42	70	437	793	.260	.319	.355	674	99	-14	-6	99	96	591	104	48	68	6
MON	156	70	86	.449	26.5	513	609	5156	1205	156	22	91	474	828	.234	.304	.325	629	84	-92	-100	102	102	513	68	66	51	-8
PHI	156	59	97	.378	37.5	503	635	5248	1240	200	36	98	487	930	.236	.304	.344	648	88	-65	-78	103	94	545	42	50	46	-8
WEST																												
CIN	154	95	59	.617		707	557	5241	1317	214	44	124	**606**	914	.251	**.333**	.380	713	**116**	67	**109**	94	104	676	**140**	63	69	9
HOU	153	84	69	.549	10.5	**708**	636	5267	1359	233	38	134	524	907	.258	.329	.393	722	114	**75**	90	98	103	686	111	56	66	5
LA	155	85	70	.548	10.5	584	527	5270	1349	178	39	98	480	786	.256	.321	.360	681	102	1	16	98	96	610	82	39	68	4
ATL	155	70	84	.455	25	628	730	5278	1363	186	17	144	532	**770**	.258	.330	.382	712	100	60	4	109	94	661	47	35	57	-2
SF	155	69	86	.445	26.5	662	649	5245	1281	211	36	**150**	480	964	.244	.311	.384	695	102	17	8	101	**107**	630	123	45	**73**	**11**
SD	153	58	95	.379	36.5	488	665	5213	1181	168	38	102	407	976	.227	.284	.332	616	87	-130	-95	93	106	489	78	46	63	1
TOT	930					7265		63116	15683	2392	430	1359	5985	10544	.249	.318	.365	682							954	566	63	12

TEAM	CG	SH	SV	IP	H	H/G	HR	BB	SO	RAT	ERA	ERA+	OAV	OOB	PR	PR+	PF	CPI	FA	E	DP	FW	PW	BW	SBW	DIF
EAST																										
PIT	39	15	48	1414^1	1282	8.2	90	433	838	11.1	2.81	118	.243	.304	102	84	96	**108**	.978	136	**171**	.0	9.1	9.6	-.1	.1
CHI	54	19	32	1398^2	1329	8.6	112	**421**	824	11.5	3.22	118	.251	.311	37	83	110	105	.979	132	148	.3	9.0	.9	-.2	-2.2
NY	32	12	41	1414^2	1263	8.1	118	486	**1059**	11.4	3.27	103	.240	.308	30	16	97	99	.980	116	122	1.1	1.8	-5.8	-.6	8.7
STL	**64**	13	13	1399^2	1290	8.3	87	531	912	11.9	3.43	99	.247	.319	5	-3	99	97	.977	141	146	-.2	-.3	-.6	.5	-2.2
MON	39	11	23	1401^1	1281	8.3	103	579	888	12.2	3.60	99	.245	.323	-21	-6	103	97	.978	134	141	.1	-.6	-10.7	-1.0	4.3
PHI	43	13	15	1400	1318	8.5	117	536	927	12.2	3.67	98	.251	.324	-33	-11	104	99	.981	116	142	1.1	-1.1	-8.3	-1.0	-9.5
WEST																										
CIN	25	15	**60**	1412^2	1313	8.4	129	435	806	11.3	3.22	100	.247	.307	38	0	93	104	**.982**	**110**	143	**1.4**	.0	**11.8**	.9	4.2
HOU	38	14	31	1385^1	1340	8.8	114	498	971	12.2	3.77	89	.256	.325	-48	-64	97	98	.980	116	151	1.0	-6.8	9.7	.4	3.4
LA	50	**23**	29	1403	**1196**	**7.7**	**83**	429	856	**10.7**	**2.79**	**120**	**.230**	**.292**	**104**	**89**	97	96	.974	162	145	-1.4	**9.6**	1.8	.3	-2.6
ATL	40	4	27	1377	1412	9.3	155	512	732	12.8	4.28	89	.266	.333	-126	-67	110	97	.974	156	130	-1.1	-7.2	.5	-.3	1.3
SF	44	8	23	1386^1	1309	8.5	130	507	771	12.0	3.70	94	.250	.320	-37	-32	101	98	.974	156	121	-1.1	-3.4	.9	**1.1**	-5.8
SD	39	17	19	1403^2	1350	8.7	121	618	960	12.9	3.78	87	.255	.337	-50	-80	95	104	.976	144	146	-.5	-8.6	-10.2	.0	1.0
TOT	507	164	361	16796^2		8.5				11.9	3.46		.249	.318					.978	1619	1706					

Runs
Morgan-Cin 122
Bonds-SF 118
Wynn-Hou 117
Rose-Cin 107
Cedeno-Hou 103

Hits
Rose-Cin 198
Brock-StL 193
Williams-Chi 191
Simmons-StL 180
Garr-Atl 180

Doubles
Montanez-Phi 39
Cedeno-Hou 39
Simmons-StL 36
Williams-Chi 34

Triples
Bowa-Phi 13
Rose-Cin 11
Sanguillen-Pit 8
Cedeno-Hou 8
Brock-StL 8

Home Runs
Bench-Cin 40
Colbert-SD 38
Williams-Chi 37
Aaron-Atl 34
Stargell-Pit 33

Total Bases
Williams-Chi 348
Cedeno-Hou 300
Bench-Cin 291
May-Hou 290
Colbert-SD 286

Runs Batted In
Bench-Cin 125
Williams-Chi 122
Stargell-Pit 112
Colbert-SD 111
May-Hou 98

Runs Produced
Wynn-Hou 183
Williams-Chi 180
Morgan-Cin 179
Bonds-SF 172
Bench-Cin 172

Bases On Balls
Morgan-Cin 115
Wynn-Hou 103
Bench-Cin 100
Aaron-Atl 92
Evans-Atl 90

Batting Average
Williams-Chi .333
Garr-Atl .325
Baker-Atl .321
Cedeno-Hou .320
Watson-Hou .312

On-Base Percentage
Morgan-Cin .419
Williams-Chi .403
Santo-Chi .397
Aaron-Atl .391
Wynn-Hou .391

Slugging Average
Williams-Chi .606
Stargell-Pit .558
Bench-Cin .541
Cedeno-Hou .537
Aaron-Atl .514

On-Base Plus Slugging
Williams-Chi 1010
Stargell-Pit 935
Bench-Cin 927
Cedeno-Hou 924
Aaron-Atl 906

Adjusted OPS
Bench-Cin 171
Stargell-Pit 166
Williams-Chi 166
Cedeno-Hou 163
Hebner-Pit 155

Batter Runs
Williams-Chi 61.1
Bench-Cin 44.0
Cedeno-Hou 42.9
Stargell-Pit 39.6
Morgan-Cin 37.2

Adjusted Batter Runs
Bench-Cin 50.9
Williams-Chi 48.9
Cedeno-Hou 45.2
Morgan-Cin 43.8
Stargell-Pit 41.7

Clutch Hitting Index
Parker-LA 140
Tolan-Cin 131
Helms-Hou 120
Sanguillen-Pit 119
Oliver-Pit 117

Runs Created
Williams-Chi 137
Morgan-Cin 117
Cedeno-Hou 115
Bench-Cin 110
Rose-Cin 109

Total Average
Williams-Chi 1.050
Morgan-Cin .973
Cedeno-Hou .959
Stargell-Pit .958
Aaron-Atl .945

Stolen Bases
Brock-StL 63
Morgan-Cin 58
Cedeno-Hou 55
Bonds-SF 44
Tolan-Cin 42

Stolen Base Average
Hernandez-SD 88.9
Bonds-SF 88.0
Davis-LA 87.0
Brock-StL 77.8
Morgan-Cin 77.3

Stolen Base Runs
Bonds-SF 7.6
Brock-StL 7.6
Morgan-Cin 6.8
Cedeno-Hou 4.8
Hernandez-SD 4.2

Fielding Runs
Helms-Hou 26.5
Money-Phi 20.3
Rader-Hou 18.0
Rose-Cin 16.1
Russell-LA 15.0

Total Player Rating
Cedeno-Hou 6.0
Morgan-Cin 5.6
Bench-Cin 5.3
Rose-Cin 4.1
Williams-Chi 3.9

Wins
Carlton-Phi 27
Seaver-NY 21
Osteen-LA 20
Jenkins-Chi 20

Win Percentage
Nolan-Cin .750
Carlton-Phi .730
Pappas-Chi .708
Blass-Pit .704
Ellis-Pit .682

Games
Marshall-Mon 65
Carroll-Cin 65
Borbon-Cin 62
Ross-SD 60

Complete Games
Carlton-Phi 30
Jenkins-Chi 23
Gibson-StL 23
Wise-StL 20
Sutton-LA 18

Shutouts
Sutton-LA 9
Carlton-Phi 8
Norman-SD 6
Jenkins-Chi 5
Dierker-Hou 5

Saves
Carroll-Cin 37
McGraw-NY 27
Giusti-Pit 22
Marshall-Mon 18

Innings Pitched
Carlton-Phi 346.1
Jenkins-Chi 289.1
Niekro-Atl 282.1
Gibson-StL 278.0
Sutton-LA 272.2

Fewest Hits/Game
Sutton-LA 6.14
Carlton-Phi 6.68
Gibson-StL 7.32
Seaver-NY 7.39
Bryant-SF 7.40

Fewest BB/Game
Pappas-Chi 1.34
Nolan-Cin 1.53
Niekro-Atl 1.69
Ellis-Pit 1.82
Moose-Pit 1.87

Strikeouts
Carlton-Phi 310
Seaver-NY 249
Gibson-StL 208
Sutton-LA 207
Jenkins-Chi 184

Strikeouts/Game
Seaver-NY 8.55
Reuss-Hou 8.16
Koosman-NY 8.12
Carlton-Phi 8.06
Norman-SD 7.10

Ratio
Sutton-LA 8.35
Carlton-Phi 8.97
Nolan-Cin 9.10
McAndrew-NY 9.86
Niekro-Atl 9.95

Earned Run Average
Carlton-Phi 1.97
Nolan-Cin 1.99
Sutton-LA 2.08
Matlack-NY 2.32
Gibson-StL 2.46

Adjusted ERA
Carlton-Phi 182
Nolan-Cin 161
Sutton-LA 160
Matlack-NY 145
Gibson-StL 138

Opponents' Batting Avg.
Sutton-LA .189
Carlton-Phi .206
Gibson-StL .224
Seaver-NY .224
Bryant-SF .224

Opponents' On-Base Pct.
Sutton-LA .240
Carlton-Phi .259
Nolan-Cin .262
Niekro-Atl .275
McAndrew-NY .278

Starter Runs
Carlton-Phi 57.0
Sutton-LA 41.7
Gibson-StL 30.8
Matlack-NY 30.7
Nolan-Cin 28.6

Adjusted Starter Runs
Carlton-Phi 59.9
Sutton-LA 39.4
Gibson-StL 29.6
Matlack-NY 29.0
Nolan-Cin 25.7

Clutch Pitching Index
Blass-Pit 131
Nolan-Cin 115
Hooton-Chi 115
Matlack-NY 115
Downing-LA 115

Relief Runs
Marshall-Mon 21.6
McGraw-NY 20.7
Brewer-LA 19.1
R.Hernandez-Pit 13.9
Carroll-Cin 12.9

Adjusted Relief Runs
Marshall-Mon 22.2
McGraw-NY 20.2
Brewer-LA 18.7
R.Hernandez-Pit 13.4
Giusti-Pit 12.0

Relief Ranking
Marshall-Mon 44.4
Brewer-LA 37.4
McGraw-NY 35.5
Giusti-Pit 24.0
Carroll-Cin 20.0

Total Pitcher Index
Carlton-Phi 7.1
Marshall-Mon 5.0
Gibson-StL 4.3
Brewer-LA 4.2
Sutton-LA 4.0

Total Baseball Ranking
Carlton-Phi 7.1
Cedeno-Hou 6.0
Morgan-Cin 5.6
Bench-Cin 5.3
Marshall-Mon 5.0

TEAM	G	W	L	PCT	GB	R	OR	AB	H	2B	3B	HR	BB	SO	AVG	OBP	SLG	OPS	OPS+	BR	BR+	PF	CHI	RC	SB	CS	SBA	SBR
EAST																												
DET	156	86	70	.551		558	514	5099	1206	179	32	122	483	793	.237	.306	.356	662	100	18	1	103	101	549	17	21	45	-4
BOS	155	85	70	.548	0.5	**640**	620	5208	1289	**229**	**34**	124	522	858	.248	.320	**.376**	**696**	108	**83**	50	106	102	**634**	66	30	**69**	**4**
BAL	154	80	74	.519	5	519	**430**	5028	1153	193	29	100	507	935	.229	.304	.339	643	96	-12	-25	103	100	523	78	41	66	3
NY	155	79	76	.510	6.5	557	527	5168	1288	201	24	103	491	**689**	.249	.318	.357	675	111	45	66	97	95	588	71	42	63	1
CLE	156	72	84	.462	14	472	519	5207	1220	187	18	91	420	762	.234	.295	.330	625	89	-54	-69	103	98	495	49	53	48	-8
MIL	156	65	91	.417	21	493	595	5124	1204	167	22	88	472	868	.235	.303	.328	631	96	-35	-25	98	99	495	64	57	53	-6
WEST																												
OAK	155	93	62	.600		604	457	5200	1248	195	29	**134**	463	886	.240	.308	.366	674	**113**	37	**69**	95	104	584	87	48	64	2
CHI	154	87	67	.565	5.5	566	538	5083	1208	170	28	108	511	991	.238	.311	.346	657	100	14	3	102	103	550	100	52	66	**4**
MIN	154	77	77	.500	15.5	537	535	5234	1277	182	31	93	478	905	.244	.311	.344	655	96	9	-17	105	97	554	53	41	56	-3
KC	154	76	78	.494	16.5	580	545	5167	**1317**	220	26	78	**534**	711	**.255**	**.329**	.353	682	111	65	68	100	95	601	85	44	66	3
CAL	155	75	80	.484	18	454	533	5165	1249	171	26	78	358	850	.242	.294	.330	624	98	-55	-27	94	97	487	57	37	61	0
TEX	154	54	100	.351	39	461	628	5029	1092	166	17	56	503	926	.217	.292	.290	582	83	-115	-96	96	**111**	438	**126**	73	63	2
TOT	929					6441		61712	14751	2260	316	1175	5742	10174	.240	.308	.344	651							853	539	61	-1

TEAM	CG	SH	SV	IP	H	H/G	HR	BB	SO	RAT	ERA	ERA+	OAV	OOB	PR	PR+	PF	CPI	FA	E	DP	FW	PW	BW	SBW	DIF
EAST																										
DET	46	11	33	1388^1	1212	7.9	101	465	952	11.2	2.97	106	.236	.306	15	28	103	102	**.984**	**96**	137	**2.0**	3.2	.2	-.4	3.3
BOS	48	20	25	1382^2	1309	8.6	101	512	918	12.2	3.47	93	.251	.323	-63	-37	105	100	.978	130	141	-.0	-4.2	5.7	**.5**	5.7
BAL	**62**	20	21	1371^2	1116	7.4	**85**	**395**	788	**10.1**	**2.54**	**121**	.224	**.283**	**81**	**82**	100	97	.983	100	150	1.7	**9.4**	-2.8	.4	-5.4
NY	35	19	39	1373^1	1306	8.6	87	419	625	11.6	3.05	97	.252	.312	2	-16	96	106	.978	134	**179**	-.3	-1.8	7.6	.1	-4.0
CLE	47	13	25	1410	1232	7.9	123	534	846	11.6	2.92	110	.237	.313	23	45	105	**112**	.981	116	157	.8	5.2	-7.8	-.9	-3.1
MIL	37	14	32	1391^2	1289	8.4	116	486	740	11.7	3.46	88	.247	.315	-61	-66	99	97	.977	139	145	-.5	-7.5	-2.8	-.7	-1.4
WEST																										
OAK	42	**23**	**43**	1417^2	1170	7.5	96	418	862	10.3	2.58	110	.226	.286	76	45	93	99	.979	130	146	-.0	5.2	**7.9**	.2	2.4
CHI	36	14	42	1385^1	1269	8.3	94	431	936	11.3	3.12	100	.245	.307	-9	1	102	99	.977	135	136	-.4	.2	.4	**.5**	9.5
MIN	37	17	34	1399^1	1188	7.7	105	444	838	10.8	2.84	113	.230	.296	35	55	105	99	.974	159	133	-1.7	6.3	-1.9	-.3	-2.1
KC	44	16	28	1381^1	1293	8.5	**85**	405	801	11.3	3.24	94	.251	.309	-27	-32	99	97	.981	116	164	.7	-3.6	7.8	.4	-6.1
CAL	57	18	16	1377^2	**1109**	**7.3**	90	620	**1000**	11.5	3.07	95	**.222**	.312	0	-25	95	96	.981	114	135	.9	-2.8	-3.0	.0	2.6
TEX	11	8	34	1374^2	1258	8.3	92	613	868	12.6	3.53	85	.246	.332	-71	-81	98	100	.972	166	147	-2.1	-9.2	-10.9	.2	-.9
TOT	502	193	372	16653^2		8.0				11.3	3.07		.240	.308					.979	1535	1770					

Runs
Murcer-NY 102
Rudi-Oak 94
Harper-Bos 92
D.Allen-Chi 90
Tovar-Min 86

Hits
Rudi-Oak 181
Piniella-KC 179
Murcer-NY 171
Carew-Min 170
May-Chi 161

Doubles
Piniella-KC 33
Rudi-Oak 32
Murcer-NY 30
White-NY 29
Harper-Bos 29

Triples
Rudi-Oak 9
Fisk-Bos 9
Blair-Bal 8
Murcer-NY 7
Kelly-Chi 7

Home Runs
D.Allen-Chi 37
Murcer-NY 33
Killebrew-Min 26
Epstein-Oak 26

Total Bases
Murcer-NY 314
D.Allen-Chi 305
Rudi-Oak 288
Mayberry-KC 255
Piniella-KC 253

Runs Batted In
D.Allen-Chi 113
Mayberry-KC 100
Murcer-NY 96
Scott-Mil 88
Powell-Bal 81

Runs Produced
D.Allen-Chi 166
Murcer-NY 165
Rudi-Oak 150
Mayberry-KC 140

Bases On Balls
White-NY 99
D.Allen-Chi 99
Killebrew-Min 94
May-Chi 79

Batting Average
Carew-Min .... .318
Piniella-KC .... .312
D.Allen-Chi .... .308
May-Chi .... .308
Rudi-Oak .... .305

On-Base Percentage
D.Allen-Chi .... .422
May-Chi .... .408
Mayberry-KC .... .396
White-NY .... .385
Scheinblum-KC ..... .385

Slugging Average
D.Allen-Chi .... .603
Fisk-Bos .... .538
Murcer-NY .... .537
Mayberry-KC .... .507
Epstein-Oak .... .490

On-Base Plus Slugging
D.Allen-Chi 1025
Fisk-Bos 909
Mayberry-KC 903
Murcer-NY 900
Epstein-Oak 868

Adjusted OPS
D.Allen-Chi 199
Murcer-NY 171
Mayberry-KC 168
Epstein-Oak 166
Fisk-Bos 159

Batter Runs
D.Allen-Chi 66.1
Murcer-NY 44.9
Mayberry-KC 43.0
Fisk-Bos 37.1
May-Chi 36.7

Adjusted Batter Runs
D.Allen-Chi 63.6
Murcer-NY 48.7
Mayberry-KC 43.5
Epstein-Oak 37.7
Rudi-Oak 35.9

Clutch Hitting Index
Billings-Tex 138
Rojas-KC 123
Scheinblum-KC 123
Petrocelli-Bos 122
Bando-Oak 121

Runs Created
D.Allen-Chi 131
Murcer-NY 114
Mayberry-KC 101
May-Chi 96
Rudi-Oak 95

Total Average
D.Allen-Chi 1.121
Mayberry-KC .... .910
Fisk-Bos .... .908
Murcer-NY .... .888
Epstein-Oak .... .885

Stolen Bases
Campaneris-Oak 52
Nelson-Tex 51
Patek-KC 33
Kelly-Chi 32
Otis-KC 28

Stolen Base Average
Baylor-Bal 92.3
Patek-KC 82.5
Scott-Mil 80.0
Campaneris-Oak 78.8
Harper-Bos 78.1

Stolen Base Runs
Campaneris-Oak 6.5
Nelson-Tex 5.3
Patek-KC 4.8
Baylor-Bal 4.6
Kelly-Chi 3.9

Fielding Runs
Patek-KC 29.5
Rodriguez-Det 24.0
Michael-NY 23.7
Belanger-Bal 20.8
May-Mil 14.9

Total Player Rating
Murcer-NY 6.0
D.Allen-Chi 5.5
Fisk-Bos 4.5
Mayberry-KC 3.5
Patek-KC 3.4

Wins
Wood-Chi 24
Perry-Cle 24
Lolich-Det 22

Win Percentage
Hunter-Oak .... .750
Tiant-Bos .... .714
Odom-Oak .... .714
Palmer-Bal .... .677
Kline-NY .... .640

Games
Lindblad-Tex 66
Fingers-Oak 65
Granger-Min 63

Complete Games
Perry-Cle 29
Lolich-Det 23
Wood-Chi 20
Ryan-Cal 20
Palmer-Bal 18

Shutouts
Ryan-Cal 9
Wood-Chi 8
Stottlemyre-NY 7

Saves
Lyle-NY 35
Forster-Chi 29
Fingers-Oak 21
Granger-Min 19
Sanders-Mil 17

Innings Pitched
Wood-Chi 376.2
Perry-Cle 342.2
Lolich-Det 327.1
Hunter-Oak 295.1
Blyleven-Min 287.1

Fewest Hits/Game
Ryan-Cal 5.26
Hunter-Oak 6.09
Nelson-KC 6.23
Tiant-Bos 6.44
Messersmith-Cal ... 6.63

Fewest BB/Game
Peterson-NY 1.58
Nelson-KC 1.61
Kline-NY 1.68
Holtzman-Oak 1.76
Wood-Chi 1.77

Strikeouts
Ryan-Cal 329
Lolich-Det 250
Perry-Cle 234
Blyleven-Min 228
Coleman-Det 222

Strikeouts/Game
Ryan-Cal 10.43
Messersmith-Cal ... 7.53
May-Cal 7.41
Bradley-Chi 7.23
Blyleven-Min 7.14

Ratio
Nelson-KC 7.89
Hunter-Oak 8.32
Perry-Cle 9.11
Palmer-Bal 9.51
Wood-Chi 9.70

Earned Run Average
Tiant-Bos 1.91
Perry-Cle 1.92
Hunter-Oak 2.04
Palmer-Bal 2.07
Nelson-KC 2.08

Adjusted ERA
Tiant-Bos 169
Perry-Cle 168
Palmer-Bal 149
Nelson-KC 146
Hunter-Oak 140

Opponents' Batting Avg.
Ryan-Cal .... .171
Hunter-Oak .... .189
Nelson-KC .... .196
Tiant-Bos .... .202
Perry-Cle .... .205

Opponents' On-Base Pct.
Nelson-KC .... .236
Hunter-Oak .... .242
Perry-Cle .... .261
Palmer-Bal .... .269
Tiant-Bos .... .277

Starter Runs
Perry-Cle 43.9
Hunter-Oak 33.8
Palmer-Bal 30.6
Ryan-Cal 24.9
Wood-Chi 23.5

Adjusted Starter Runs
Perry-Cle 47.5
Palmer-Bal 30.8
Hunter-Oak 28.6
Wood-Chi 25.7
Tiant-Bos 24.9

Clutch Pitching Index
Paul-Tex 129
Odom-Oak 124
Wilcox-Cle 120
Lonborg-Mil 112
Lolich-Det 112

Relief Runs
Lyle-NY 13.7
Knowles-Oak 12.4
Bell-Mil 11.1
Forster-Chi 9.1
Abernathy-KC 8.9

Adjusted Relief Runs
Lyle-NY 12.9
Knowles-Oak 11.6
Bell-Mil 11.0
Forster-Chi 9.6
Abernathy-KC 8.8

Relief Ranking
Lyle-NY 24.4
Forster-Chi 15.8
Knowles-Oak 14.0
Abernathy-KC 11.2
Fingers-Oak 9.2

Total Pitcher Index
Perry-Cle 6.7
Palmer-Bal 4.2
Wood-Chi 3.1
Hunter-Oak 2.9
Tiant-Bos 2.9

Total Baseball Ranking
Perry-Cle 6.7
Murcer-NY 6.0
D.Allen-Chi 5.5
Fisk-Bos 4.5
Palmer-Bal 4.2

TEAM	G	W	L	PCT	GB	R	OR	AB	H	2B	3B	HR	BB	SO	AVG	OBP	SLG	OPS	OPS+	BR	BR+	PF	CHI	RC	SB	CS	SBA	SBR
EAST																												
NY	161	82	79	.509		608	588	5457	1345	198	24	85	540	805	.246	.317	.338	655	89	-81	-71	98	104	583	27	22	55	-2
STL	162	81	81	.500	1.5	643	603	5478	1418	240	35	75	531	796	.259	.328	.357	685	96	-24	-22	100	100	635	100	46	68	6
PIT	162	80	82	.494	2.5	704	693	5608	1465	**257**	44	154	432	842	.261	.317	.405	722	109	30	49	97	101	697	23	30	43	-5
MON	162	79	83	.488	3.5	668	702	5369	1345	190	23	125	**695**	**777**	.251	**.341**	.364	705	98	30	5	104	94	672	77	68	53	-7
CHI	161	77	84	.478	5	614	655	5363	1322	201	21	117	575	855	.247	.322	.357	679	88	-35	-78	107	99	605	65	58	53	-6
PHI	162	71	91	.438	11.5	642	717	5546	1381	218	29	134	476	979	.249	.312	.371	683	93	-40	-56	103	102	641	51	47	52	-5
WEST																												
CIN	162	99	63	.611		741	621	5505	1398	232	34	137	639	947	.254	.335	.383	718	**111**	43	**83**	95	102	724	**148**	55	**73**	**13**
LA	162	95	66	.590	3.5	675	**565**	5604	1473	219	29	110	497	795	.263	.326	.371	697	104	-5	26	96	100	676	109	50	69	6
SF	162	88	74	.543	11	739	702	5537	1452	212	**52**	161	590	913	.262	.337	.407	744	108	87	57	104	96	765	112	52	68	6
HOU	162	82	80	.506	17	681	672	5532	1391	216	35	134	469	962	.251	.314	.376	690	97	-28	-26	100	**107**	639	92	48	66	3
ATL	162	76	85	.472	22.5	**799**	774	5631	**1497**	219	34	**206**	608	870	**.266**	**.341**	**.427**	**768**	**111**	**134**	76	108	97	**826**	84	40	68	4
SD	162	60	102	.370	39	548	770	5457	1330	198	26	112	401	966	.244	.298	.351	649	92	-110	-62	92	102	566	88	36	71	7
TOT	971					8062		66087	16817	2600	386	1550	6453	10507	.255	.325	.376	700							976	552	64	22

TEAM	CG	SH	SV	IP	H	H/G	HR	BB	SO	RAT	ERA	ERA+	OAV	OOB	PR	PR+	PF	CPI	FA	E	DP	FW	PW	BW	SBW	DIF
EAST																										
NY	47	15	40	1465	1345	8.3	127	490	**1027**	11.5	3.27	111	.245	.309	65	58	99	101	.980	126	140	1.2	6.1	-7.3	-.4	2.2
STL	42	14	36	1460^{2}	1366	8.5	**105**	486	867	11.6	3.26	112	.248	.312	66	63	100	100	.975	159	149	-.7	6.6	-2.2	.4	-3.9
PIT	26	11	**44**	1450^{2}	1426	8.9	110	564	839	12.6	3.74	94	.258	.331	-12	-36	96	100	.976	151	156	-.2	-3.7	5.2	-.7	-1.3
MON	26	6	38	1451^{2}	1356	8.5	128	681	866	12.9	3.72	103	.250	.337	-9	16	104	104	.974	163	156	-.9	1.7	.6	-.9	-2.3
CHI	27	13	40	1437^{2}	1471	9.3	128	**438**	885	12.2	3.66	108	.267	.325	1	43	108	104	.975	157	155	-.6	4.5	-8.1	-.8	1.7
PHI	**49**	11	22	1447^{1}	1435	9.0	131	632	919	13.1	4.00	95	.263	.343	-53	-30	104	103	.979	134	**179**	.7	-3.1	-5.8	-.7	-1.0
WEST																										
CIN	39	**17**	43	1473	1389	8.5	135	518	801	11.9	3.41	100	.252	.319	42	0	93	**106**	**.982**	**115**	162	**1.8**	.0	**8.7**	**1.2**	6.5
LA	45	15	38	1491	**1270**	**7.7**	129	461	961	**10.7**	**3.01**	**115**	**.231**	**.294**	**109**	**77**	94	97	.981	125	166	1.3	**8.1**	2.8	.4	2.2
SF	33	8	**44**	1452^{1}	1442	9.0	145	485	787	12.2	3.80	101	.257	.320	-21	4	104	97	.974	163	138	-.9	.5	6.0	.4	1.2
HOU	45	14	26	1460^{2}	1389	8.6	111	575	907	12.3	3.75	97	.252	.325	-14	-19	99	95	.981	116	140	**1.8**	-1.9	-2.7	.1	3.9
ATL	34	9	35	1462	1467	9.1	144	575	803	12.8	4.25	93	.263	.335	-95	-48	107	95	.974	166	142	-1.1	-4.9	8.0	.2	-6.5
SD	34	10	23	1430	1461	9.2	157	548	845	12.9	4.17	83	.267	.336	-79	-116	95	100	.973	170	152	-1.3	-12.0	-6.4	.5	-1.6
TOT	447	143	429	17482		8.7				12.2	3.67		.255	.325					.977	1745	1835					

Runs
Bonds-SF 131
Morgan-Cin 116
Rose-Cin 115
Evans-Atl 114
Brock-StL 110

Hits
Rose-Cin 230
Garr-Atl 200
Brock-StL 193
Simmons-StL 192
Oliver-Pit 191

Doubles
Stargell-Pit 43
Oliver-Pit 38
Staub-NY 36
Simmons-StL 36
Rose-Cin 36

Triples
Metzger-Hou 14
Matthews-SF 10
Maddox-SF 10
Davis-LA 9

Home Runs
Stargell-Pit 44
Johnson-Atl 43
Evans-Atl 41
Aaron-Atl 40
Bonds-SF 39

Total Bases
Bonds-SF 341
Stargell-Pit 337
Evans-Atl 331
Johnson-Atl 305
Oliver-Pit 303

Runs Batted In
Stargell-Pit 119
May-Hou 105
Evans-Atl 104
Bench-Cin 104
Singleton-Mon 103

Runs Produced
Bonds-SF 188
Stargell-Pit 181
Singleton-Mon 180
Baker-Atl 179
Evans-Atl 177

Bases On Balls
Evans-Atl 124
Singleton-Mon 123
Morgan-Cin 111
McCovey-SF 105
Monday-Chi 92

Batting Average
Rose-Cin 338
Cedeno-Hou 320
Maddox-SF 319
Perez-Cin 314
Watson-Hou 312

On-Base Percentage
Singleton-Mon 429
Fairly-Mon 422
Morgan-Cin 408
Evans-Atl 407
Watson-Hou 405

Slugging Average
Stargell-Pit 646
Evans-Atl 556
Johnson-Atl 546
Cedeno-Hou 537
Bonds-SF 530

On-Base Plus Slugging
Stargell-Pit 1041
Evans-Atl 964
Perez-Cin 923
Johnson-Atl 917
Cedeno-Hou 914

Adjusted OPS
Stargell-Pit 189
Perez-Cin 162
Morgan-Cin 157
Evans-Atl 153
Cedeno-Hou 151

Batter Runs
Stargell-Pit 57.8
Evans-Atl 54.8
Aaron-Atl 45.5
Singleton-Mon 44.8
Morgan-Cin 41.6

Adjusted Batter Runs
Stargell-Pit 61.1
Morgan-Cin 48.0
Perez-Cin 47.4
Evans-Atl 45.4
Singleton-Mon 40.7

Clutch Hitting Index
Cey-LA 126
Sizemore-StL 123
Bench-Cin 121
Speier-SF 119
Tolan-Cin 116

Runs Created
Evans-Atl 143
Stargell-Pit 136
Bonds-SF 130
Morgan-Cin 128
Rose-Cin 119

Total Average
Stargell-Pit 1.129
Evans-Atl 1.048
Morgan-Cin 1.034
Cedeno-Hou 949
Johnson-Atl 947

Stolen Bases
Brock-StL 70
Morgan-Cin 67
Cedeno-Hou 56
Bonds-SF 43
Lopes-LA 36

Stolen Base Average
Baker-Atl 88.9
Morgan-Cin 81.7
Concepcion-Cin 81.5
Cedeno-Hou 78.9
Brock-StL 77.8

Stolen Base Runs
Morgan-Cin 9.5
Brock-StL 8.4
Cedeno-Hou 7.1
Baker-Atl 4.2
Garr-Atl 3.8

Fielding Runs
Schmidt-Phi 21.2
Kessinger-Chi 17.0
Unser-Phi 16.7
Rose-Cin 16.7
Cey-LA 16.2

Total Player Rating
Morgan-Cin 6.1
Stargell-Pit 6.1
Cedeno-Hou 5.4
Evans-Atl 5.2
Rose-Cin 4.5

Wins
Bryant-SF 24
Seaver-NY 19
Billingham-Cin 19
Sutton-LA 18
Gullett-Cin 18

Win Percentage
John-LA 696
Gullett-Cin 692
Bryant-SF 667
Seaver-NY 655
Billingham-Cin 655

Games
Marshall-Mon 92
Borbon-Cin 80
Sosa-SF 71
Giusti-Pit 67
Segui-StL 65

Complete Games
Seaver-NY 18
Carlton-Phi 18
Billingham-Cin 16

Shutouts
Billingham-Cin 7
Roberts-Hou 6
Wise-StL 5
Twitchell-Phi 5

Saves
Marshall-Mon 31
McGraw-NY 25
Giusti-Pit 20
Brewer-LA 20

Innings Pitched
Carlton-Phi 293.1
Billingham-Cin 293.1
Seaver-NY 290.0
Reuss-Hou 279.1
Jenkins-Chi 271.0

Fewest Hits/Game
Seaver-NY 6.80
Sutton-LA 6.88
Twitchell-Phi 6.93
Wilson-Hou 7.03
Messersmith-LA 7.07

Fewest BB/Game
Marichal-SF 1.61
Jenkins-Chi 1.89
Barr-SF 1.91
Sutton-LA 1.97
Seaver-NY 1.99

Strikeouts
Seaver-NY 251
Carlton-Phi 223
Matlack-NY 205
Sutton-LA 200

Strikeouts/Game
Seaver-NY 7.79
Moore-Mon 7.71
Matlack-NY 7.62
Sutton-LA 7.02
Carlton-Phi 6.84

Ratio
Seaver-NY 8.91
Sutton-LA 9.02
Messersmith-LA 10.06
Gibson-StL 10.11
Rooker-Pit 10.41

Earned Run Average
Seaver-NY 2.08
Sutton-LA 2.42
Twitchell-Phi 2.50
Marshall-Mon 2.66
Messersmith-LA 2.70

Adjusted ERA
Seaver-NY 174
Twitchell-Phi 152
Marshall-Mon 144
Sutton-LA 142
Renko-Mon 136

Opponents' Batting Avg.
Seaver-NY 206
Sutton-LA 209
Wilson-Hou 213
Messersmith-LA 214
Renko-Mon 218

Opponents' On-Base Pct.
Seaver-NY 254
Sutton-LA 258
Messersmith-LA 279
Gibson-StL 284
Briles-Pit 288

Starter Runs
Seaver-NY 51.3
Sutton-LA 35.5
Rogers-Mon 31.6
Twitchell-Phi 29.1
Messersmith-LA 26.8

Adjusted Starter Runs
Seaver-NY 50.4
Rogers-Mon 32.6
Twitchell-Phi 31.3
Sutton-LA 31.0
Renko-Mon 27.0

Clutch Pitching Index
Marshall-Mon 134
Roberts-Hou 122
Twitchell-Phi 121
Grimsley-Cin 116
Moose-Pit 113

Relief Runs
Borbon-Cin 20.3
Marshall-Mon 20.0
Giusti-Pit 14.2
Moffitt-SF 13.9
Locker-Chi 13.4

Adjusted Relief Runs
Marshall-Mon 22.1
Borbon-Cin 18.2
Locker-Chi 15.5
Moffitt-SF 15.0
Giusti-Pit 13.2

Relief Ranking
Marshall-Mon 35.6
Locker-Chi 26.3
Borbon-Cin 24.5
Giusti-Pit 18.7
Scarce-Phi 15.7

Total Pitcher Index
Seaver-NY 5.5
Marshall-Mon 4.2
Rogers-Mon 3.9
Renko-Mon 3.5
Sutton-LA 3.1

Total Baseball Ranking
Morgan-Cin 6.1
Stargell-Pit 6.1
Seaver-NY 5.5
Cedeno-Hou 5.4
Evans-Atl 5.2

TEAM	G	W	L	PCT	GB	R	OR	AB	H	2B	3B	HR	BB	SO	AVG	OBP	SLG	OPS	OPS+	BR	BR+	PF	CHI	RC	SB	CS	SBA	SBR
EAST																												
BAL	162	97	65	.599		754	**561**	5537	1474	229	**48**	119	**648**	752	.266	**.348**	.389	737	108	**61**	67	99	98	**765**	**146**	64	70	**10**
BOS	162	89	73	.549	8	738	647	5513	1472	235	30	147	581	799	.267	.340	**.401**	**741**	102	58	16	106	98	751	114	45	**72**	9
DET	162	85	77	.525	12	642	674	5508	1400	213	32	157	509	722	.254	.322	.390	712	94	-9	-51	107	95	674	28	30	48	-4
NY	162	80	82	.494	17	641	610	5492	1435	212	17	131	489	**680**	.261	.324	.378	702	101	-25	-1	97	98	655	47	43	52	-5
MIL	162	74	88	.457	23	708	731	5526	1399	229	40	145	563	977	.253	.327	.388	715	103	2	18	98	101	702	110	66	63	1
CLE	162	71	91	.438	26	680	826	5592	1429	205	29	**158**	471	793	.256	.317	.387	704	95	-27	-38	102	103	666	60	68	47	-11
WEST																												
OAK	162	94	68	.580		**758**	615	5507	1431	216	28	147	595	919	.260	.336	.389	725	**110**	28	**68**	95	**104**	730	128	57	69	8
KC	162	88	74	.543	6	755	752	5508	1440	239	40	114	644	696	.261	.342	.381	723	96	31	-21	108	103	720	105	69	60	-1
MIN	162	81	81	.500	13	738	692	5625	**1521**	**240**	44	120	598	954	**.270**	.344	.393	737	103	56	27	104	97	756	87	46	65	3
CAL	162	79	83	.488	15	629	657	5505	1395	183	29	93	509	816	.253	.320	.348	668	95	-84	-34	92	**104**	609	59	47	56	-3
CHI	162	77	85	.475	17	652	705	5475	1400	228	38	111	537	952	.256	.326	.372	698	93	-28	-50	103	99	647	83	73	53	-7
TEX	162	57	105	.352	40	619	844	5488	1397	195	29	110	503	791	.255	.320	.361	681	95	-63	-36	96	100	629	91	53	63	1
TOT	972					8314		66276	17193	2624	404	1552	6647	9851	.260	.331	.382	712							1058	661	62	1

TEAM	CG	SH	SV	IP	H	H/G	HR	BB	SO	RAT	ERA	ERA+	OAV	OOB	PR	PR+	PF	CPI	FA	E	DP	FW	PW	BW	SBW	DIF
EAST																										
BAL	67	14	26	1461^2	**1297**	**8.0**	124	475	715	**11.1**	**3.07**	**122**	**.240**	**.303**	**122**	**111**	98	102	.981	119	184	1.3	**11.4**	6.9	**1.0**	-4.5
BOS	67	10	33	1440^1	1417	8.9	158	499	808	12.2	3.65	110	.259	.325	27	56	105	**106**	.979	127	162	.9	5.8	1.7	.9	-1.1
DET	39	11	**46**	1447^2	1468	9.2	154	493	911	12.4	3.90	105	.265	.328	-13	28	107	102	**.982**	**112**	144	**1.7**	2.9	-5.2	-.4	5.1
NY	47	16	39	1427^2	1379	8.7	109	**457**	708	11.8	3.35	110	.254	.315	75	53	96	102	.976	156	172	-.7	5.5	-.0	-.5	-4.9
MIL	50	11	28	1454	1476	9.2	119	623	671	13.2	3.99	94	.265	.342	-27	-36	99	101	.977	145	167	-.1	-3.6	1.9	.0	-5.0
CLE	55	9	21	1464^2	1532	9.5	172	602	883	13.4	4.59	85	.271	.345	-125	-105	103	96	.978	139	174	.2	-10.7	-3.8	-1.1	5.7
WEST																										
OAK	46	16	41	1457^1	1311	8.1	143	494	797	11.4	3.29	108	.241	.308	86	45	93	101	.978	137	170	.3	4.7	**7.0**	.8	.4
KC	40	7	41	1449^1	1521	9.5	114	617	790	13.5	4.20	98	.273	.349	-60	-12	108	100	.974	167	**192**	-1.4	-1.2	-2.1	-.1	12.0
MIN	48	**18**	34	1451^2	1443	9.0	115	519	879	12.4	3.77	105	.259	.327	7	29	104	97	.978	139	147	.2	3.0	2.8	.3	-6.1
CAL	**72**	13	19	1456^1	1351	8.4	**104**	614	**1010**	12.4	3.53	100	.246	.326	46	3	93	98	.975	156	153	-.7	.4	-3.4	-.3	2.3
CHI	48	15	35	1456	1484	9.2	110	574	848	13.0	3.87	102	.266	.338	-8	15	104	101	.977	144	165	-.0	1.6	-5.1	-.7	.5
TEX	35	10	27	1430	1514	9.6	130	680	831	14.1	4.64	80	.273	.357	-131	-150	98	96	.974	161	164	-1.0	-15.3	-3.6	.0	-3.9
TOT	614	150	390	17396^2		8.9				12.6	3.82		.260	.331					.978	1702	1994					

Runs
Jackson-Oak 99
Scott-Mil 98
North-Oak 98
Carew-Min 98
Bando-Oak 97

Hits
Carew-Min 203
May-Mil 189
Murcer-NY 187
Scott-Mil 185
Johnson-Tex 179

Doubles
Garcia-Mil 32
Bando-Oak 32
Scott-Mil 30
Chambliss-Cle 30
Carew-Min 30

Triples
Carew-Min 11
Bumbry-Bal 11
Orta-Chi 10
Coggins-Bal 9
Coluccio-Mil 8

Home Runs
Jackson-Oak 32
Robinson-Cal 30
Burroughs-Tex 30
Bando-Oak 29

Total Bases
Scott-Mil 295
May-Mil 295
Bando-Oak 295
Murcer-NY 286
Jackson-Oak 286

Runs Batted In
Jackson-Oak 117
Scott-Mil 107
Mayberry-KC 100
Bando-Oak 98
Robinson-Cal 97

Runs Produced
Jackson-Oak 184
Scott-Mil 181
Bando-Oak 166
May-Mil 164
Mayberry-KC 161

Bases On Balls
Mayberry-KC 122
Grich-Bal 107
Yastrzemski-Bos 105
Tenace-Oak 101
Briggs-Mil 87

Batting Average
Carew-Min .350
Scott-Mil .306
Davis-Bal .306
Murcer-NY .304
May-Mil .303

On-Base Percentage
Mayberry-KC .420
Carew-Min .415
Yastrzemski-Bos .411
Tenace-Oak .391
Jackson-Oak .387

Slugging Average
Jackson-Oak .531
Bando-Oak .498
Robinson-Cal .489
Scott-Mil .488
Munson-NY .487

On-Base Plus Slugging
Jackson-Oak 918
Mayberry-KC 898
Carew-Min 885
Bando-Oak 876
Yastrzemski-Bos 874

Adjusted OPS
Jackson-Oak 165
Robinson-Cal 153
Bando-Oak 153
Scott-Mil 144
Carew-Min 143

Batter Runs
Mayberry-KC 41.0
Jackson-Oak 40.5
Carew-Min 38.9
Yastrzemski-Bos 36.8
Bando-Oak 35.5

Adjusted Batter Runs
Jackson-Oak 46.6
Bando-Oak 41.7
Robinson-Cal 38.5
Carew-Min 34.6
Scott-Mil 34.0

Clutch Hitting Index
Davis-Bal 134
Robinson-Bal 124
Piniella-KC 123
Johnson-Oak 122
May-Chi 119

Runs Created
Bando-Oak 113
Carew-Min 113
Mayberry-KC 113
Jackson-Oak 112
Scott-Mil 106

Total Average
Mayberry-KC .995
Jackson-Oak .953
Carew-Min .885
Yastrzemski-Bos .879
Bando-Oak .876

Stolen Bases
Harper-Bos 54
North-Oak 53
Nelson-Tex 43
Carew-Min 41
Patek-KC 36

Stolen Base Average
Rojas-KC 81.8
Money-Mil 81.5
Harper-Bos 79.4
Baylor-Bal 78.0
Campaneris-Oak 77.3

Stolen Base Runs
Harper-Bos 7.0
North-Oak 4.7
Campaneris-Oak 4.0
Baylor-Bal 3.9
Nelson-Tex 3.9

Fielding Runs
Patek-KC 35.3
Nettles-NY 26.0
Bell-Cle 24.3
North-Oak 23.6
Grich-Bal 21.0

Total Player Rating
Carew-Min 5.5
Grich-Bal 4.9
Jackson-Oak 4.5
Munson-NY 4.0
Robinson-Cal 3.8

Wins
Wood-Chi 24
Coleman-Det 23
Palmer-Bal 22

Win Percentage
Hunter-Oak .808
Palmer-Bal .710
Blue-Oak .690
Splittorff-KC .645
Colborn-Mil .625

Games
Hiller-Det 65
Fingers-Oak 62
Bird-KC 54
Knowles-Oak 52

Complete Games
Perry-Cle 29
Ryan-Cal 26
Blyleven-Min 25
Tiant-Bos 23
Colborn-Mil 22

Shutouts
Blyleven-Min 9
Perry-Cle 7
Palmer-Bal 6

Saves
Hiller-Det 38
Lyle-NY 27
Fingers-Oak 22
Bird-KC 20
Acosta-Chi 18

Innings Pitched
Wood-Chi 359.1
Perry-Cle 344.0
Ryan-Cal 326.0
Blyleven-Min 325.0
Singer-Cal 315.2

Fewest Hits/Game
Bibby-Tex 6.04
Ryan-Cal 6.57
Palmer-Bal 6.83
Tiant-Bos 7.18
Blue-Oak 7.30

Fewest BB/Game
Kaat-Min-Chi 1.73
Blyleven-Min 1.86
Holtzman-Oak 2.00
Wood-Chi 2.28
Lolich-Det 2.30

Strikeouts
Ryan-Cal 383
Blyleven-Min 258
Singer-Cal 241
Perry-Cle 238
Lolich-Det 214

Strikeouts/Game
Ryan-Cal 10.57
Bibby-Tex 7.74
Blyleven-Min 7.14
Stone-Chi 7.04
Singer-Cal 6.87

Ratio
Tiant-Bos 9.99
Hunter-Oak 10.25
Blyleven-Min 10.30
Palmer-Bal 10.36
Holtzman-Oak 10.44

Earned Run Average
Palmer-Bal 2.40
Blyleven-Min 2.52
Lee-Bos 2.75
Ryan-Cal 2.87
Medich-NY 2.95

Adjusted ERA
Blyleven-Min 157
Palmer-Bal 156
Lee-Bos 146
Medich-NY 124
Ryan-Cal 124

Opponents' Batting Avg.
Bibby-Tex .192
Ryan-Cal .203
Palmer-Bal .211
Tiant-Bos .219
Blue-Oak .224

Opponents' On-Base Pct.
Tiant-Bos .281
Hunter-Oak .284
Blyleven-Min .287
Holtzman-Oak .287
Palmer-Bal .289

Starter Runs
Blyleven-Min 47.0
Palmer-Bal 46.9
Ryan-Cal 34.5
Lee-Bos 33.9
Holtzman-Oak 28.3

Adjusted Starter Runs
Blyleven-Min 50.3
Palmer-Bal 45.1
Lee-Bos 38.3
Ryan-Cal 26.5
Beene-NY 20.9

Clutch Pitching Index
Lee-Bos 120
Forster-Chi 117
Curtis-Bos 113
Drago-KC 112
Bahnsen-Chi 112

Relief Runs
Hiller-Det 33.2
Fingers-Oak 26.8
Reynolds-Bal 23.1
Acosta-Chi 17.2
Jackson-Bal 17.1

Adjusted Relief Runs
Hiller-Det 34.6
Fingers-Oak 24.7
Reynolds-Bal 22.6
Acosta-Chi 18.1
Jackson-Bal 16.7

Relief Ranking
Hiller-Det 60.7
Fingers-Oak 36.0
Acosta-Chi 34.3
Reynolds-Bal 26.1
Lyle-NY 22.0

Total Pitcher Index
Hiller-Det 6.6
Blyleven-Min 5.5
Palmer-Bal 4.5
Lee-Bos 3.8
Fingers-Oak 3.7

Total Baseball Ranking
Hiller-Det 6.6
Carew-Min 5.5
Blyleven-Min 5.5
Grich-Bal 4.9
Palmer-Bal 4.5

TEAM	G	W	L	PCT	GB	R	OR	AB	H	2B	3B	HR	BB	SO	AVG	OBP	SLG	OPS	OPS+	BR	BR+	PF	CHI	RC	SB	CS	SBA	SBR
EAST																												
PIT	162	88	74	.543		751	657	5702	**1560**	238	46	114	514	828	**.274**	.338	.391	729	114	66	95	96	100	745	55	31	64	1
STL	161	86	75	.534	1.5	677	643	5620	1492	216	46	83	531	752	.265	.334	.365	699	102	9	15	99	98	687	**172**	62	74	**16**
PHI	162	80	82	.494	8	676	701	5494	1434	233	**50**	95	469	822	.261	.322	.373	695	96	-7	-33	104	**104**	658	115	58	66	5
MON	161	79	82	.491	8.5	662	657	5343	1355	201	29	86	652	812	.254	.338	.350	688	93	2	-33	106	99	657	124	49	72	10
NY	162	71	91	.438	17	572	646	5468	1286	183	22	96	597	**735**	.235	.314	.329	643	86	-99	-89	98	100	571	43	23	65	1
CHI	162	66	96	.407	22	669	826	5574	1397	221	42	110	621	857	.251	.329	.365	694	96	-1	-28	104	98	668	78	73	52	-8
WEST																												
LA	162	102	60	.630		**798**	**561**	5557	1511	231	34	**139**	597	820	.272	**.346**	**.401**	**747**	**120**	**103**	**137**	96	102	774	149	75	67	7
CIN	163	98	64	.605	4	776	631	5535	1437	**271**	35	135	**693**	940	.260	.345	.394	739	115	95	107	99	99	**776**	146	49	**75**	15
ATL	163	88	74	.543	14	661	563	5533	1375	202	37	120	571	772	.249	.321	.363	684	93	-23	-50	104	101	649	72	44	62	0
HOU	162	81	81	.500	21	653	632	5489	1441	222	41	110	471	864	.263	.324	.378	702	107	6	36	96	98	663	108	65	62	1
SF	162	72	90	.444	30	634	723	5482	1380	228	38	93	548	869	.252	.323	.358	681	92	-28	-57	105	100	642	107	51	68	6
SD	162	60	102	.370	42	541	830	5415	1239	196	27	99	564	900	.229	.304	.330	634	87	-122	-98	96	101	555	85	45	65	3
TOT	972					8070		66212	16907	2642	447	1280	6828	9971	.256	.329	.367	695							1254	625	67	57

TEAM	CG	SH	SV	IP	H	H/G	HR	BB	SO	RAT	ERA	ERA+	OAV	OOB	PR	PR+	PF	CPI	FA	E	DP	FW	PW	BW	SBW	DIF
EAST																										
PIT	**51**	9	17	1466	1428	8.8	93	543	721	12.4	3.49	99	.256	.326	21	-7	95	101	.975	162	154	-.4	-.7	9.9	-.4	-1.3
STL	37	13	20	1473[1]	1399	8.6	97	616	794	12.5	3.49	103	.254	.331	22	15	99	**104**	.977	147	**192**	.4	1.6	1.6	**1.2**	.9
PHI	46	4	19	1447[1]	1394	8.7	111	682	892	13.2	3.92	97	.257	.343	-47	-21	104	101	.976	148	168	.4	-2.1	-3.4	.0	4.3
MON	35	8	**27**	1429	1340	8.5	99	544	822	12.1	3.60	107	.249	.321	3	36	106	95	.976	153	157	.0	3.8	-3.4	.5	-2.3
NY	46	15	14	1470[1]	1433	8.8	99	504	908	12.1	3.42	104	.257	.322	33	24	99	102	.975	158	150	-.2	2.5	-9.2	-.4	-2.6
CHI	23	6	26	1466[1]	1593	9.8	122	576	895	13.6	4.28	89	.277	.347	-108	-72	105	100	.969	199	141	-2.6	-7.4	-2.9	-1.3	-.6
WEST																										
LA	33	19	23	1465[1]	**1272**	**7.9**	112	**464**	**943**	**10.9**	**2.98**	114	**.233**	**.296**	**105**	74	94	97	.975	157	122	-.1	7.8	**14.3**	.2	-1.0
CIN	34	11	**27**	1466[1]	1364	8.4	126	536	875	11.8	3.42	102	.247	.316	33	13	96	101	.979	134	151	1.3	1.4	11.2	1.1	2.3
ATL	46	**21**	22	1474[1]	1343	8.2	97	488	772	11.4	3.06	**124**	.244	.309	93	**114**	104	102	.979	132	161	1.4	**11.9**	-5.2	-.5	-.5
HOU	36	18	18	1450[2]	1396	8.7	**84**	601	738	12.7	3.47	100	.255	.333	25	0	96	**104**	**.982**	**113**	161	**2.4**	.0	3.8	-.4	-5.7
SF	27	11	25	1439	1409	8.9	116	559	756	12.5	3.78	101	.257	.328	-26	3	105	98	.972	175	153	-1.2	.4	-5.9	.1	-2.2
SD	25	7	19	1445[2]	1536	9.6	124	715	855	14.4	4.59	78	.275	.362	-155	-168	98	99	.973	170	126	-.9	-17.4	-10.2	-.2	7.9
TOT	439	142	257	17493[2]		8.7				12.4	3.62		.256	.329					.976	1848	1836					

Runs
Rose-Cin 110
Schmidt-Phi 108
Bench-Cin 108
Morgan-Cin 107
Brock-StL 105

Hits
Garr-Atl 214
Cash-Phi 206
Garvey-LA 200
Oliver-Pit 198
Stennett-Pit 196

Doubles
Rose-Cin 45
Oliver-Pit 38
Bench-Cin 38
Stargell-Pit 37

Triples
Garr-Atl 17
Oliver-Pit 12
Cash-Phi 11
Metzger-Hou 10
Bowa-Phi 10

Home Runs
Schmidt-Phi 36
Bench-Cin 33
Wynn-LA 32
Perez-Cin 28
Cedeno-Hou 26

Total Bases
Bench-Cin 315
Schmidt-Phi 310
Garr-Atl 305
Garvey-LA 301
Oliver-Pit 293

Runs Batted In
Bench-Cin 129
Schmidt-Phi 116
Garvey-LA 111
Wynn-LA 108
Simmons-StL 103

Runs Produced
Bench-Cin 204
Schmidt-Phi 188
Garvey-LA 185
Wynn-LA 180
Cedeno-Hou 171

Bases On Balls
Evans-Atl 126
Morgan-Cin 120
Wynn-LA 108
Schmidt-Phi 106
Rose-Cin 106

Batting Average
Garr-Atl .353
Oliver-Pit .321
Gross-Hou .314
Buckner-LA .314
Madlock-Chi .313

On-Base Percentage
Morgan-Cin .430
Stargell-Pit .409
Bailey-Mon .400
Schmidt-Phi .398
Smith-StL .394

Slugging Average
Schmidt-Phi .546
Stargell-Pit .537
Smith-StL .528
Bench-Cin .507
Garr-Atl .503

On-Base Plus Slugging
Stargell-Pit 947
Schmidt-Phi 944
Morgan-Cin 924
Smith-StL 922
Wynn-LA 891

Adjusted OPS
Stargell-Pit 169
Morgan-Cin 160
Smith-StL 158
Schmidt-Phi 156
Wynn-LA 154

Batter Runs
Schmidt-Phi 48.3
Morgan-Cin 45.2
Stargell-Pit 44.4
Smith-StL 38.5
Wynn-LA 36.4

Adjusted Batter Runs
Stargell-Pit 48.6
Morgan-Cin 46.9
Schmidt-Phi 43.5
Wynn-LA 40.9
Smith-StL 39.4

Clutch Hitting Index
Sizemore-StL 128
Singleton-Mon 123
Montanez-Phi 121
Cey-LA 120
Zisk-Pit 119

Runs Created
Schmidt-Phi 130
Morgan-Cin 125
Stargell-Pit 115
Bench-Cin 114
Garr-Atl 113

Total Average
Morgan-Cin 1.108
Schmidt-Phi 1.017
Stargell-Pit .997
Smith-StL .920
Wynn-LA .915

Stolen Bases
Brock-StL 118
Lopes-LA 59
Morgan-Cin 58
Cedeno-Hou 57
Lintz-Mon 50

Stolen Base Average
Lintz-Mon 87.7
Concepcion-Cin 87.2
Morgan-Cin 82.9
Bonds-SF 78.8
Hernandez-SD 78.7

Stolen Base Runs
Brock-StL 14.4
Morgan-Cin 8.6
Lintz-Mon 8.6
Concepcion-Cin 6.9
Lopes-LA 6.7

Fielding Runs
Cash-Phi 29.1
Schmidt-Phi 26.3
Cedeno-Hou 20.9
Foli-Mon 19.4
Rose-Cin 17.6

Total Player Rating
Schmidt-Phi 7.1
Morgan-Cin 5.3
Wynn-LA 4.8
Cedeno-Hou 4.5
Cash-Phi 4.3

Wins
P.Niekro-Atl 20
Messersmith-LA 20
Sutton-LA 19
Billingham-Cin 19

Win Percentage
Messersmith-LA .769
Sutton-LA .679
Capra-Atl .667
Torrez-Mon .652
Billingham-Cin .633

Games
Marshall-LA 106
Hardy-SD 76
Borbon-Cin 73
Forsch-Hou 70
Sosa-SF 68

Complete Games
P.Niekro-Atl 18
Carlton-Phi 17
Lonborg-Phi 16
Rooker-Pit 15

Shutouts
Matlack-NY 7
P.Niekro-Atl 6

Saves
Marshall-LA 21
Moffitt-SF 15
Borbon-Cin 14
Giusti-Pit 12

Innings Pitched
P.Niekro-Atl 302.1
Messersmith-LA 292.1
Carlton-Phi 291.0
Lonborg-Phi 283.0
Sutton-LA 276.0

Fewest Hits/Game
Capra-Atl 6.76
Messersmith-LA 6.99
P.Niekro-Atl 7.41
Gullett-Cin 7.44
Wilson-Hou 7.48

Fewest BB/Game
Barr-SF 1.76
Reed-Atl 1.98
Ellis-Pit 2.09
Lonborg-Phi 2.23
Marshall-LA 2.42

Strikeouts
Carlton-Phi 240
Messersmith-LA 221
Seaver-NY 201
P.Niekro-Atl 195
Matlack-NY 195

Strikeouts/Game
Seaver-NY 7.67
Carlton-Phi 7.42
Bonham-Chi 7.08
D'Acquisto-SF 6.99
Norman-Cin 6.81

Ratio
Messersmith-LA 9.97
P.Niekro-Atl 10.21
Barr-SF 10.21
Matlack-NY 10.24
Reed-Atl 10.35

Earned Run Average
Capra-Atl 2.28
P.Niekro-Atl 2.38
Matlack-NY 2.41
Marshall-LA 2.42
Messersmith-LA 2.59

Adjusted ERA
Capra-Atl 166
P.Niekro-Atl 159
Matlack-NY 148
Marshall-LA 141
Barr-SF 139

Opponents' Batting Avg.
Capra-Atl .208
Messersmith-LA .212
Gullett-Cin .222
P.Niekro-Atl .225
Matlack-NY .226

Opponents' On-Base Pct.
Messersmith-LA .278
Matlack-NY .285
P.Niekro-Atl .286
Reed-Atl .286
Capra-Atl .287

Starter Runs
P.Niekro-Atl 41.9
Matlack-NY 36.0
Messersmith-LA 33.9
Capra-Atl 32.5
Rooker-Pit 24.9

Adjusted Starter Runs
P.Niekro-Atl 45.3
Matlack-NY 34.9
Capra-Atl 34.8
Messersmith-LA 28.5
Barr-SF 27.1

Clutch Pitching Index
Caldwell-SF 118
Morton-Atl 117
Marshall-LA 117
Schueler-Phi 113
McGlothen-StL 113

Relief Runs
Marshall-LA 28.0
Murray-Mon 20.1
House-Atl 19.4
Taylor-Mon 17.4
C.Carroll-Cin 16.6

Adjusted Relief Runs
Marshall-LA 24.4
Murray-Mon 20.6
House-Atl 20.3
Taylor-Mon 18.9
C.Carroll-Cin 15.7

Relief Ranking
Marshall-LA 34.1
C.Carroll-Cin 26.0
House-Atl 19.2
Taylor-Mon 17.0
Leon-Atl 12.9

Total Pitcher Index
P.Niekro-Atl 5.1
Marshall-LA 3.7
Capra-Atl 3.6
Messersmith-LA 3.5
Rooker-Pit 3.3

Total Baseball Ranking
Schmidt-Phi 7.1
Morgan-Cin 5.3
P.Niekro-Atl 5.1
Wynn-LA 4.8
Cedeno-Hou 4.5

TEAM	G	W	L	PCT	GB	R	OR	AB	H	2B	3B	HR	BB	SO	AVG	OBP	SLG	OPS	OPS+	BR	BR+	PF	CHI	RC	SB	CS	SBA	SBR
EAST																												
BAL	162	91	71	.562		659	612	5535	1418	226	27	116	509	770	.256	.325	.370	695	103	-2	19	97	98	671	145	58	**71**	**12**
NY	162	89	73	.549	2	671	623	5524	1451	220	30	101	515	**690**	.263	.328	.368	696	102	1	13	98	100	666	53	35	60	-1
BOS	162	84	78	.519	7	**696**	661	5499	1449	**236**	31	109	**569**	811	.264	.336	.377	713	98	39	-7	107	98	699	104	58	64	3
CLE	162	77	85	.475	14	662	694	5474	1395	201	19	131	432	756	.255	.312	.370	682	97	-36	-30	99	**108**	610	79	68	54	-6
MIL	162	76	86	.469	15	647	660	5472	1335	228	**49**	120	500	909	.244	.310	.369	679	96	-41	-37	99	105	622	106	75	59	-3
DET	162	72	90	.444	19	620	768	5568	1375	200	35	131	436	784	.247	.304	.366	670	89	-64	-84	104	104	607	67	38	64	1
WEST																												
OAK	162	90	72	.556		689	**551**	5331	1315	205	37	132	568	876	.247	.324	.373	697	107	1	46	94	105	648	**164**	93	64	4
TEX	161	84	76	.525	5	690	698	5449	1482	198	39	99	508	710	**.272**	**.338**	.377	715	**108**	42	**60**	98	98	677	113	80	59	-3
MIN	163	82	80	.506	8	673	669	5632	**1530**	190	37	111	520	791	**.272**	**.338**	.378	716	103	44	22	103	93	**707**	74	45	62	1
CHI	163	80	80	.500	9	684	721	5577	1492	225	23	**135**	519	858	.268	.333	**.389**	**722**	104	**49**	32	102	95	701	64	53	55	-4
KC	162	77	85	.475	13	667	662	5582	1448	232	42	89	550	768	.259	.329	.364	693	94	-2	-38	106	99	668	146	76	66	6
CAL	163	68	94	.420	29	618	657	5401	1372	203	31	95	509	801	.254	.323	.356	679	101	-30	8	94	99	615	119	79	60	-1
TOT	973					7976		66044	17062	2564	400	1369	6135	9524	.259	.326	.372	697							1234	758	62	6

TEAM	CG	SH	SV	IP	H	H/G	HR	BB	SO	RAT	ERA	ERA+	OAV	OOB	PR	PR+	PF	CPI	FA	E	DP	FW	PW	BW	SBW	DIF
EAST																										
BAL	57	**16**	25	1474	1393	8.6	101	480	701	11.6	3.28	105	.253	.316	56	31	95	102	**.980**	128	174	**1.1**	3.3	2.0	**1.2**	2.6
NY	53	13	24	1455^{1}	1402	8.7	104	528	829	12.2	3.31	106	.256	.325	50	36	97	**107**	.977	142	158	.3	3.8	1.4	-.2	2.9
BOS	**71**	12	18	1455^{1}	1462	9.1	126	463	751	12.1	3.72	103	.262	.322	-16	19	106	99	.977	145	156	.0	2.0	-.7	.3	1.5
CLE	45	9	27	1445^{2}	1419	8.9	138	479	650	12.1	3.81	95	.260	.323	-30	-31	100	98	.977	146	157	.0	-3.2	-3.1	-.7	3.1
MIL	43	11	24	1457^{2}	1476	9.2	126	493	621	12.4	3.77	96	.266	.329	-23	-23	100	102	**.980**	**127**	168	**1.1**	-2.4	-3.8	-.4	.6
DET	54	7	15	1455^{2}	1443	9.0	148	621	869	13.0	4.17	91	.262	.341	-88	-55	105	99	.975	158	155	-.7	-5.7	-8.7	.0	6.3
WEST																										
OAK	49	12	28	1439^{2}	**1322**	**8.3**	**90**	**430**	755	**11.2**	**2.96**	**112**	**.246**	**.305**	**107**	**64**	92	103	.977	141	154	.3	**6.7**	4.9	.4	-3.1
TEX	62	**16**	12	1433^{2}	1423	9.0	126	449	871	12.1	3.83	93	.260	.321	-33	-42	99	95	.974	163	164	-1.0	-4.3	**6.3**	-.4	3.6
MIN	43	11	**29**	1455^{1}	1436	8.9	115	513	934	12.3	3.65	102	.260	.327	-4	13	103	101	.976	151	164	-.2	1.4	2.4	.0	-2.4
CHI	55	11	**29**	1465^{2}	1470	9.1	103	548	826	12.8	3.94	95	.263	.334	-52	-33	103	96	.977	147	**188**	.0	-3.4	3.4	-.5	.7
KC	54	13	17	1471^{2}	1477	9.1	91	482	731	12.2	3.52	109	.263	.325	17	47	106	101	.976	152	166	-.3	5.0	-3.9	.6	-5.1
CAL	64	13	12	1439	1339	8.4	101	649	**986**	12.8	3.53	98	.248	.334	15	-14	95	102	.976	147	150	.0	-1.4	.9	-.2	-12.1
TOT	650	144	260	17448^{2}		8.9				12.2	3.62		.259	.326					.977	1747	1954					

Runs
Yastrzemski-Bos 93
Grich-Bal 92
Jackson-Oak 90
Otis-KC 87
Carew-Min 86

Hits
Carew-Min 218
Davis-Bal 181
Money-Mil 178
K.Henderson-Chi . . . 176
Rudi-Oak 174

Doubles
Rudi-Oak 39
Scott-Mil 36
McRae-KC 36
K.Henderson-Chi 35
Burroughs-Tex 33

Triples
Rivers-Cal 11
Otis-KC 9

Home Runs
D.Allen-Chi 32
Jackson-Oak 29
Tenace-Oak 26
Darwin-Min 25
Burroughs-Tex 25

Total Bases
Rudi-Oak 287
K.Henderson-Chi . . . 281
Burroughs-Tex 279
Carew-Min 267

Runs Batted In
Burroughs-Tex 118
Bando-Oak 103
Rudi-Oak 99
K.Henderson-Chi 95
Darwin-Min 94

Runs Produced
Burroughs-Tex 177
Bando-Oak 165
Yastrzemski-Bos 157
Grich-Bal 155
Jackson-Oak 154

Bases On Balls
Tenace-Oak 110
Yastrzemski-Bos 104
Burroughs-Tex 91
Grich-Bal 90

Batting Average
Carew-Min 364
Orta-Chi 316
McRae-KC 310
Piniella-NY 305
Maddox-NY 303

On-Base Percentage
Carew-Min 435
Yastrzemski-Bos 421
Burroughs-Tex 405
Maddox-NY 397
Jackson-Oak 396

Slugging Average
D.Allen-Chi 563
Jackson-Oak 514
Burroughs-Tex 504
Rudi-Oak 484
Freehan-Det 479

On-Base Plus Slugging
D.Allen-Chi 942
Jackson-Oak 910
Burroughs-Tex 908
Carew-Min 880
Yastrzemski-Bos 866

Adjusted OPS
Jackson-Oak 171
Burroughs-Tex 164
D.Allen-Chi 164
Carew-Min 149
Robinson-Cal-Cle . . . 143

Batter Runs
Burroughs-Tex 45.3
Carew-Min 44.7
Jackson-Oak 41.0
D.Allen-Chi 39.3
Yastrzemski-Bos 38.1

Adjusted Batter Runs
Jackson-Oak 48.4
Burroughs-Tex 48.3
Carew-Min 41.0
D.Allen-Chi 37.0
Grich-Bal 31.4

Clutch Hitting Index
Murcer-NY 134
Bando-Oak 132
Burroughs-Tex 131
Petrocelli-Bos 119
Evans-Bos 115

Runs Created
Carew-Min 118
Burroughs-Tex 113
Jackson-Oak 109
Yastrzemski-Bos 102
K.Henderson-Chi 100

Total Average
Jackson-Oak 992
D.Allen-Chi 953
Burroughs-Tex 919
Yastrzemski-Bos 900
Carew-Min 879

Stolen Bases
North-Oak 54
Carew-Min 38
Lowenstein-Cle 36
Campaneris-Oak 34
Patek-KC 33

Stolen Base Average
Jackson-Oak 83.3
Coggins-Bal 81.3
Pinson-KC 80.8
Otis-KC 78.3
Money-Mil 76.0

Stolen Base Runs
Jackson-Oak 3.8
Coggins-Bal 3.6
Pinson-KC 2.9
Blair-Bal 2.8
North-Oak 2.8

Fielding Runs
Terrell-Min 23.3
Rodriguez-Det 21.6
Robinson-Bal 20.5
North-Oak 18.4
Doyle-Cal 16.4

Total Player Rating
Carew-Min 6.4
Jackson-Oak 5.5
Grich-Bal 5.2
K.Henderson-Chi 3.2
Burroughs-Tex 3.2

Wins
Jenkins-Tex 25
Hunter-Oak 25

Win Percentage
Cuellar-Bal 688
Jenkins-Tex 676
Hunter-Oak 676
Tiant-Bos 629

Games
Fingers-Oak 76
Murphy-Mil 70
Foucault-Tex 69
Lyle-NY 66
Campbell-Min 63

Complete Games
Jenkins-Tex 29
G.Perry-Cle 28
Lolich-Det 27
Ryan-Cal 26
Tiant-Bos 25

Shutouts
Tiant-Bos 7
Jenkins-Tex 6
Hunter-Oak 6
Cuellar-Bal 5
Bibby-Tex 5

Saves
Forster-Chi 24
Murphy-Mil 20
Campbell-Min 19
Buskey-NY-Cle 18
Fingers-Oak 18

Innings Pitched
Ryan-Cal 332.2
Jenkins-Tex 328.1
G.Perry-Cle 322.1
Wood-Chi 320.1
Hunter-Oak 318.1

Fewest Hits/Game
Ryan-Cal 5.98
G.Perry-Cle 6.42
DalCanton-KC 6.93
Hassler-Cal 7.33
Hunter-Oak 7.58

Fewest BB/Game
Jenkins-Tex 1.23
Hunter-Oak 1.30
Holtzman-Oak 1.80
Kaat-Chi 2.04
Wright-Mil 2.09

Strikeouts
Ryan-Cal 367
Blyleven-Min 249
Jenkins-Tex 225
G.Perry-Cle 216
Lolich-Det 202

Strikeouts/Game
Ryan-Cal 9.93
Blyleven-Min 7.98
Jenkins-Tex 6.17
Busby-KC 6.10
G.Perry-Cle 6.03

Ratio
Hunter-Oak 8.99
Jenkins-Tex 9.29
G.Perry-Cle 9.35
Grimsley-Bal 10.53
Blyleven-Min 10.57

Earned Run Average
Hunter-Oak 2.49
G.Perry-Cle 2.51
Hassler-Cal 2.61
Blyleven-Min 2.66
Fitzmorris-KC 2.79

Adjusted ERA
G.Perry-Cle 144
Blyleven-Min 140
Fitzmorris-KC 137
Hunter-Oak 134
Hassler-Cal 132

Opponents' Batting Avg.
Ryan-Cal 190
G.Perry-Cle 204
DalCanton-KC 211
Hassler-Cal 225
Hunter-Oak 229

Opponents' On-Base Pct.
Hunter-Oak 260
Jenkins-Tex 264
G.Perry-Cle 272
Blyleven-Min 292
Tiant-Bos 293

Starter Runs
Hunter-Oak 40.2
G.Perry-Cle 39.8
Blyleven-Min 30.2
Jenkins-Tex 29.2
Ryan-Cal 27.0

Adjusted Starter Runs
G.Perry-Cle 39.7
Blyleven-Min 32.6
Hunter-Oak 32.3
Tiant-Bos 30.3
Jenkins-Tex 27.7

Clutch Pitching Index
Goltz-Min 124
Hassler-Cal 122
Lee-Bos 119
Fitzmorris-KC 116
Tanana-Cal 113

Relief Runs
Lyle-NY 24.9
Murphy-Mil 23.5
Foucault-Tex 22.1
Lindblad-Oak 17.5
Hiller-Det 16.4

Adjusted Relief Runs
Lyle-NY 24.4
Murphy-Mil 23.5
Foucault-Tex 21.6
Hiller-Det 18.6
Lindblad-Oak 15.5

Relief Ranking
Murphy-Mil 43.1
Hiller-Det 37.1
Lyle-NY 30.3
Foucault-Tex 26.9
Campbell-Min 21.4

Total Pitcher Index
Murphy-Mil 5.0
G.Perry-Cle 4.4
Blyleven-Min 4.0
Hiller-Det 3.8
Hunter-Oak 3.3

Total Baseball Ranking
Carew-Min 6.4
Jackson-Oak 5.5
Grich-Bal 5.2
Murphy-Mil 5.0
G.Perry-Cle 4.4

TEAM	G	W	L	PCT	GB	R	OR	AB	H	2B	3B	HR	BB	SO	AVG	OBP	SLG	OPS	OPS+	BR	BR+	PF	CHI	RC	SB	CS	SBA	SBR
EAST																												
PIT	161	92	69	.571		712	565	5489	1444	255	47	**138**	468	832	.263	.325	**.402**	727	109	44	50	99	102	709	49	28	64	1
PHI	162	86	76	.531	6.5	735	694	5592	1506	**283**	42	125	610	960	.269	.344	**.402**	746	109	98	68	104	94	785	126	57	69	8
NY	162	82	80	.506	10.5	646	625	5587	1430	217	34	101	501	805	.256	.321	.361	682	100	-36	-6	95	102	639	32	26	55	-2
STL	163	82	80	.506	10.5	662	689	5597	**1527**	239	46	81	444	**649**	**.273**	.329	.375	704	99	7	-16	104	99	683	116	49	70	8
MON	162	75	87	.463	17.5	601	690	5518	1346	216	31	98	579	954	.244	.319	.348	667	87	-63	-88	104	99	623	108	58	65	3
CHI	162	75	87	.463	17.5	712	827	5470	1419	229	41	95	650	802	.259	.341	.368	709	99	33	3	104	100	702	67	55	55	-5
WEST																												
CIN	162	108	54	.667		**840**	586	5581	1515	278	37	124	**691**	916	.271	**.355**	.401	**756**	**114**	**128**	**114**	102	103	**829**	**168**	36	**82**	**24**
LA	162	88	74	.543	20	648	**534**	5453	1355	217	31	118	611	825	.248	.328	.365	693	103	-10	20	96	98	667	138	52	73	12
SF	161	80	81	.497	27.5	659	671	5447	1412	235	45	84	604	775	.259	.336	.365	701	97	11	-16	104	98	673	99	47	68	5
SD	162	71	91	.438	37	552	683	5429	1324	215	22	78	506	754	.244	.313	.335	648	92	-100	-63	94	99	571	85	50	63	1
ATL	161	67	94	.416	40.5	583	739	5424	1323	179	28	107	543	759	.244	.315	.346	661	86	-75	-96	104	101	587	55	38	59	-1
HOU	162	64	97	.398	43.5	664	711	5515	1401	218	**54**	84	523	762	.254	.322	.359	681	102	-36	13	93	**106**	643	133	62	68	8
TOT	971					8014		66102	17002	2781	458	1233	6730	9793	.258	.330	.370	698							1176	558	68	63

TEAM	CG	SH	SV	IP	H	H/G	HR	BB	SO	RAT	ERA	ERA+	OAV	OOB	PR	PR+	PF	CPI	FA	E	DP	FW	PW	BW	SBW	DIF
EAST																										
PIT	43	14	31	1437[1]	1302	8.2	**79**	551	768	11.8	3.01	**118**	.243	.315	98	**87**	98	104	.976	151	147	.3	**9.1**	5.3	-.4	-2.5
PHI	33	11	30	1455	1353	8.4	111	546	897	12.0	3.83	98	.249	.320	-33	-15	103	90	.976	152	156	.3	-1.5	7.1	.3	-1.0
NY	40	14	31	1466	1344	8.3	99	580	**989**	12.0	3.39	102	.246	.321	38	11	95	99	.976	151	144	.3	1.2	-.6	-.8	1.0
STL	33	13	36	1454[2]	1452	9.0	98	571	824	12.7	3.57	105	.260	.331	8	29	104	103	.973	171	140	-.7	3.1	-1.6	.3	.2
MON	30	12	25	1480	1448	8.9	102	665	831	13.1	3.73	103	.259	.341	-17	16	106	103	.973	180	**179**	-1.3	1.7	-9.1	-.2	3.1
CHI	27	8	33	1444[1]	1587	9.9	130	551	850	13.6	4.50	86	.281	.349	-140	-99	106	98	.972	179	152	-1.2	-10.3	.4	-1.1	6.4
WEST																										
CIN	22	8	**50**	1459	1422	8.8	112	487	663	12.0	3.37	107	.257	.321	41	37	99	105	**.984**	**102**	173	**3.1**	3.9	**11.9**	**2.0**	6.3
LA	**51**	**18**	21	1469[2]	**1215**	**7.5**	104	**448**	894	**10.4**	**2.93**	116	**.225**	**.287**	**114**	83	94	89	.979	127	106	1.7	8.7	2.1	.7	-6.0
SF	37	9	24	1432[2]	1406	8.9	92	612	856	13.0	3.74	102	.259	.339	-19	9	105	101	.976	146	164	.5	1.0	-1.6	-.0	-.2
SD	40	12	20	1463[1]	1494	9.2	99	521	713	12.6	3.49	100	.266	.331	23	-2	96	**108**	.971	188	163	-1.7	-.2	-6.5	-.4	-.9
ATL	32	4	24	1430	1543	9.8	101	519	669	13.3	3.92	96	.278	.344	-47	-22	104	105	.972	175	147	-1.1	-2.2	-10.0	-.7	.6
HOU	39	6	25	1458[1]	1436	8.9	106	679	839	13.3	4.04	83	.262	.347	-67	-117	93	99	.979	137	166	1.1	-12.2	1.4	.3	-6.9
TOT	427	129	350	17450[1]		8.8				12.5	3.63		.258	.330					.976	1859	1837					

Runs
- Rose-Cin 112
- Cash-Phi 111
- Lopes-LA 108
- Morgan-Cin 107
- Thomas-SF 99

Hits
- Cash-Phi 213
- Rose-Cin 210
- Garvey-LA 210
- Simmons-StL 193
- Millan-NY 191

Doubles
- Rose-Cin 47
- Cash-Phi 40
- Oliver-Pit 39
- Bench-Cin 39
- Garvey-LA 38

Triples
- Garr-Atl 11
- Parker-Pit 10
- Kessinger-Chi 10
- Joshua-SF 10
- Gross-Hou 10

Home Runs
- Schmidt-Phi 38
- Kingman-NY 36
- Luzinski-Phi 34
- Bench-Cin 28

Total Bases
- Luzinski-Phi 322
- Garvey-LA 314
- Parker-Pit 302
- Schmidt-Phi 294
- Rose-Cin 286

Runs Batted In
- Luzinski-Phi 120
- Bench-Cin 110
- Perez-Cin 109
- Staub-NY 105

Runs Produced
- Morgan-Cin 184
- Staub-NY 179
- Rose-Cin 179
- Luzinski-Phi 171
- Bench-Cin 165

Bases On Balls
- Morgan-Cin 132
- Wynn-LA 110
- Evans-Atl 105
- Schmidt-Phi 101

Batting Average
- Madlock-Chi .354
- Simmons-StL .332
- Sanguillen-Pit .328
- Morgan-Cin .327
- Watson-Hou .324

On-Base Percentage
- Morgan-Cin .471
- Wynn-LA .407
- Rose-Cin .407
- Madlock-Chi .406
- Murcer-SF .404

Slugging Average
- Parker-Pit .541
- Luzinski-Phi .540
- Schmidt-Phi .523
- Bench-Cin .519
- Foster-Cin .518

On-Base Plus Slugging
- Morgan-Cin 979
- Luzinski-Phi 939
- Parker-Pit 899
- Stargell-Pit 894
- Schmidt-Phi 890

Adjusted OPS
- Morgan-Cin 168
- Luzinski-Phi 152
- Watson-Hou 152
- Parker-Pit 148
- Stargell-Pit 147

Batter Runs
- Morgan-Cin 57.1
- Luzinski-Phi 47.5
- Simmons-StL 35.7
- Thornton-Chi 35.4
- Schmidt-Phi 33.7

Adjusted Batter Runs
- Morgan-Cin 54.9
- Luzinski-Phi 42.7
- Parker-Pit 32.5
- Simmons-StL 32.2
- Watson-Hou 31.9

Clutch Hitting Index
- Perez-Cin 133
- Morales-Chi 133
- Trillo-Chi 132
- Montanez-Phi-SF 127
- Murcer-SF 123

Runs Created
- Morgan-Cin 145
- Luzinski-Phi 128
- Rose-Cin 120
- Schmidt-Phi 113
- Simmons-StL 108

Total Average
- Morgan-Cin 1.279
- Luzinski-Phi .956
- Schmidt-Phi .943
- Bench-Cin .901
- Stargell-Pit .895

Stolen Bases
- Lopes-LA 77
- Morgan-Cin 67
- Brock-StL 56
- Cedeno-Hou 50
- Cardenal-Chi 34

Stolen Base Average
- Morgan-Cin 87.0
- Lopes-LA 86.5
- Maddox-SF-Phi 86.2
- Winfield-SD 85.2
- Concepcion-Cin 84.6

Stolen Base Runs
- Lopes-LA 12.7
- Morgan-Cin 11.2
- Brock-StL 6.7
- Concepcion-Cin 5.2
- Cedeno-Hou 5.1

Fielding Runs
- Schmidt-Phi 24.0
- Evans-Atl 23.4
- Maddox-SF-Phi 21.0
- Mackanin-Mon 18.2
- Trillo-Chi 16.0

Total Player Rating
- Morgan-Cin 7.0
- Schmidt-Phi 5.7
- Bench-Cin 3.8
- Parker-Pit 3.6
- Evans-Atl 3.4

Wins
- Seaver-NY 22
- Jones-SD 20
- Messersmith-LA 19
- Hooton-Chi-LA 18
- Reuss-Pit 18

Win Percentage
- Gullett-Cin .789
- Seaver-NY .710
- Hooton-Chi-LA .667
- Murray-Mon .652

Games
- Garber-Phi 71
- McEnaney-Cin 70
- Tomlin-SD 67
- Borbon-Cin 67
- Garman-StL 66

Complete Games
- Messersmith-LA 19
- Jones-SD 18
- Seaver-NY 15
- Reuss-Pit 15

Shutouts
- Messersmith-LA 7
- Reuss-Pit 6
- Jones-SD 6
- Seaver-NY 5

Saves
- Hrabosky-StL 22
- Eastwick-Cin 22
- Giusti-Pit 17
- McEnaney-Cin 15
- Knowles-Chi 15

Innings Pitched
- Messersmith-LA 321.2
- Jones-SD 285.0
- Seaver-NY 280.1
- Morton-Atl 277.2
- Niekro-Atl 275.2

Fewest Hits/Game
- Messersmith-LA 6.83
- Seaver-NY 6.97
- Warthen-Mon 6.98
- Sutton-LA 7.15
- Hooton-Chi-LA 7.29

Fewest BB/Game
- Nolan-Cin 1.24
- Jones-SD 1.77
- Reed-Atl-StL 1.91
- Rau-LA 2.13
- Barr-SF 2.14

Strikeouts
- Seaver-NY 243
- Montefusco-SF 215
- Messersmith-LA 213
- Carlton-Phi 192
- Richard-Hou 176

Strikeouts/Game
- Montefusco-SF 7.94
- Richard-Hou 7.80
- Seaver-NY 7.80
- Warthen-Mon 6.87
- Carlton-Phi 6.77

Ratio
- Jones-SD 9.41
- Sutton-LA 9.45
- Messersmith-LA 9.65
- Hooton-Chi-LA 9.89
- Nolan-Cin 9.91

Earned Run Average
- Jones-SD 2.24
- Messersmith-LA 2.29
- Seaver-NY 2.38
- Reuss-Pit 2.54
- Forsch-StL 2.86

Adjusted ERA
- Jones-SD 155
- Messersmith-LA 149
- Seaver-NY 146
- Reuss-Pit 140
- Montefusco-SF 132

Opponents' Batting Avg.
- Messersmith-LA .213
- Sutton-LA .213
- Seaver-NY .214
- Warthen-Mon .217
- Hooton-Chi-LA .219

Opponents' On-Base Pct.
- Sutton-LA .264
- Jones-SD .271
- Hooton-Chi-LA .276
- Messersmith-LA .276
- Nolan-Cin .278

Starter Runs
- Messersmith-LA 47.8
- Jones-SD 44.0
- Seaver-NY 39.2
- Reuss-Pit 28.8
- Sutton-LA 21.7

Adjusted Starter Runs
- Messersmith-LA 42.5
- Jones-SD 41.0
- Seaver-NY 35.5
- Reuss-Pit 27.3
- Montefusco-SF 24.0

Clutch Pitching Index
- Reuss-Pit 122
- Niekro-Atl 122
- Blair-Mon 115
- Koosman-NY 114
- Barr-SF 111

Relief Runs
- Hrabosky-StL 21.3
- Apodaca-NY 20.2
- Hilgendorf-Phi 16.0
- McEnaney-Cin 11.7
- Garman-StL 10.9

Adjusted Relief Runs
- Hrabosky-StL 21.9
- Apodaca-NY 19.5
- Hilgendorf-Phi 16.7
- Garman-StL 11.6
- McEnaney-Cin 11.5

Relief Ranking
- Hrabosky-StL 43.6
- Apodaca-NY 21.2
- Garman-StL 17.9
- Hilgendorf-Phi 15.5
- C.Carroll-Cin 13.7

Total Pitcher Index
- Jones-SD 5.2
- Hrabosky-StL 4.6
- Seaver-NY 4.6
- Messersmith-LA 4.4
- Reuss-Pit 3.8

Total Baseball Ranking
- Morgan-Cin 7.0
- Schmidt-Phi 5.7
- Jones-SD 5.2
- Hrabosky-StL 4.6
- Seaver-NY 4.5

TEAM	G	W	L	PCT	GB	R	OR	AB	H	2B	3B	HR	BB	SO	AVG	OBP	SLG	OPS	OPS+	BR	BR+	PF	CHI	RC	SB	CS	SBA	SBR
EAST																												
BOS	160	95	65	.594		**796**	709	5448	**1500**	**284**	44	134	565	741	**.275**	**.347**	**.417**	**764**	106	**108**	45	109	99	**776**	66	58	53	-6
BAL	159	90	69	.566	4.5	682	**553**	5474	1382	224	33	124	580	834	.252	.328	.373	701	105	-14	33	94	100	680	104	55	65	4
NY	160	83	77	.519	12	681	588	5415	1430	230	39	110	486	710	.264	.328	.382	710	102	-3	9	98	101	665	102	59	63	2
CLE	159	79	80	.497	15.5	688	703	5404	1409	201	25	**153**	525	**667**	.261	.329	.392	721	103	17	18	100	99	672	106	89	54	-8
MIL	162	68	94	.420	28	675	792	5378	1343	242	34	146	553	922	.250	.323	.389	712	100	-2	-5	101	99	663	65	64	50	-8
DET	159	57	102	.358	37.5	570	786	5366	1338	171	39	125	383	872	.249	.303	.366	669	84	-94	-118	104	101	573	63	57	53	-6
WEST																												
OAK	162	98	64	.605		758	606	5415	1376	220	33	151	609	846	.254	.335	.391	726	**107**	34	**51**	98	104	725	183	82	**69**	**12**
KC	162	91	71	.562	7	710	649	5491	1431	263	**58**	118	591	675	.261	.336	.394	730	103	40	21	103	96	736	155	75	67	8
TEX	162	79	83	.488	19	714	733	5599	1431	208	17	134	**613**	863	.256	.332	.371	703	99	-10	-4	99	102	693	102	62	62	1
MIN	159	76	83	.478	20.5	724	736	5514	1497	215	28	121	563	746	.271	.343	.386	729	105	46	36	101	97	732	81	48	63	1
CHI	161	75	86	.466	22.5	655	703	5490	1400	209	38	94	611	800	.255	.334	.358	692	95	-24	-33	101	97	659	101	54	65	3
CAL	161	72	89	.447	24.5	628	723	5377	1324	195	41	55	593	811	.246	.324	.328	652	91	-99	-55	93	**106**	596	**220**	108	67	11
TOT	963					8281		65371	16861	2662	429	1465	6672	9487	.258	.331	.380	709							1348	811	62	13

TEAM	CG	SH	SV	IP	H	H/G	HR	BB	SO	RAT	ERA	ERA+	OAV	OOB	PR	PR+	PF	CPI	FA	E	DP	FW	PW	BW	SBW	DIF
EAST																										
BOS	62	11	31	1436^{2}	1463	9.2	145	**490**	720	12.4	3.99	102	.265	.327	-33	13	108	99	.977	139	142	.9	1.4	4.6	-.7	9.0
BAL	**70**	**19**	21	1451	1285	8.0	110	500	717	**11.2**	**3.17**	111	.242	**.308**	**98**	59	93	101	**.983**	**107**	**175**	**2.7**	6.1	3.4	.3	-1.8
NY	**70**	11	20	1424	1325	8.4	104	502	809	11.7	3.29	**112**	.249	.317	78	**64**	97	103	.978	135	148	1.1	**6.6**	1.0	.0	-5.6
CLE	37	6	33	1435^{1}	1395	8.8	136	599	800	12.8	3.85	98	.258	.335	-10	-10	100	103	.978	134	156	1.1	-1.0	1.9	-.9	-1.4
MIL	36	10	34	1431^{2}	1496	9.5	133	624	643	13.7	4.34	88	.271	.351	-89	-79	101	100	.971	180	162	-1.3	-8.0	-.5	-.9	-2.1
DET	52	10	17	1396	1496	9.7	137	533	787	13.3	4.28	94	.275	.343	-77	-38	106	101	.972	173	141	-1.1	-3.8	-12.0	-.7	-4.7
WEST																										
OAK	36	10	**44**	1448	**1267**	**7.9**	**102**	523	784	11.4	3.27	111	**.236**	**.308**	82	60	96	94	.977	143	140	.8	6.2	**5.3**	**1.1**	3.8
KC	52	11	25	1456^{2}	1422	8.8	108	498	815	12.1	3.47	111	.258	.322	50	61	102	103	.976	155	151	.1	6.3	2.2	.7	.9
TEX	60	16	17	1465^{2}	1456	9.0	123	518	792	12.4	3.87	97	.261	.329	-14	-18	99	98	.971	191	173	-1.9	-1.8	-.4	.0	2.3
MIN	57	7	22	1423	1381	8.8	137	617	846	12.9	4.05	94	.257	.337	-43	-35	101	99	.973	170	147	-.9	-3.5	3.7	.0	-2.6
CHI	34	7	39	1452^{1}	1489	9.3	107	655	799	13.5	3.93	99	.268	.349	-24	-9	103	**106**	.978	140	155	.9	-.9	-3.3	.2	-2.2
CAL	59	**19**	16	1453^{1}	1386	8.6	123	613	**975**	12.7	3.89	91	.253	.333	-18	-59	94	97	.971	184	164	-1.6	-6.0	-5.6	1.0	3.8
TOT	625	137	319	17273^{2}		8.8				12.5	3.78		.258	.331					.976	1851	1854					

Runs
Lynn-Bos 103
Mayberry-KC 95
Bonds-NY 93
Rice-Bos 92

Hits
Brett-KC 195
Carew-Min 192
Munson-NY 190
C.Washington-Oak .. 182

Doubles
Lynn-Bos 47
Jackson-Oak 39
McRae-KC 38
Mayberry-KC 38
Chambliss-NY 38

Triples
Rivers-Cal 13
Brett-KC 13
Orta-Chi 10
Cowens-KC 8

Home Runs
Scott-Mil 36
Jackson-Oak 36
Mayberry-KC 34
Bonds-NY 32

Total Bases
Scott-Mil 318
Mayberry-KC 303
Jackson-Oak 303
Lynn-Bos 299
Brett-KC 289

Runs Batted In
Scott-Mil 109
Mayberry-KC 106
Lynn-Bos 105
Jackson-Oak 104

Runs Produced
Lynn-Bos 187
Munson-NY 173
Rice-Bos 172
Mayberry-KC 167
Brett-KC 162

Bases On Balls
Mayberry-KC 119
Singleton-Bal 118
Grich-Bal 107
Tenace-Oak 106
Harrah-Tex 98

Batting Average
Carew-Min .... .359
Lynn-Bos .... .331
Munson-NY .... .318
Rice-Bos .... .309
C.Washington-Oak ... .308

On-Base Percentage
Carew-Min .... .428
Mayberry-KC .... .419
Singleton-Bal .... .418
Harrah-Tex .... .406
Lynn-Bos .... .405

Slugging Average
Lynn-Bos .... .566
Mayberry-KC .... .547
Powell-Cle .... .524
Scott-Mil .... .515
Bonds-NY .... .512

On-Base Plus Slugging
Lynn-Bos 971
Mayberry-KC 966
Carew-Min 926
Powell-Cle 906
Bonds-NY 891

Adjusted OPS
Mayberry-KC 167
Carew-Min 159
Lynn-Bos 158
Singleton-Bal 156
Powell-Cle 154

Batter Runs
Mayberry-KC 56.0
Lynn-Bos 49.4
Carew-Min 44.4
Singleton-Bal 41.3
Bonds-NY 35.4

Adjusted Batter Runs
Mayberry-KC 52.6
Singleton-Bal 49.6
Carew-Min 42.9
Lynn-Bos 40.2
Bonds-NY 37.2

Clutch Hitting Index
Stanton-Cal 135
Robinson-Bal 130
Munson-NY 122
Duffy-Cle 116
Bando-Oak 115

Runs Created
Mayberry-KC 135
Lynn-Bos 120
Singleton-Bal 118
Carew-Min 118
Harrah-Tex 105

Total Average
Mayberry-KC 1.059
Lynn-Bos 1.000
Carew-Min .... .986
Tenace-Oak .... .919
Harrah-Tex .... .914

Stolen Bases
Rivers-Cal 70
C.Washington-Oak ... 40
Otis-KC 39
Carew-Min 35
Remy-Cal 34

Stolen Base Average
Hisle-Min 85.0
Bumbry-Bal 84.2
Rivers-Cal 83.3
Alomar-NY 82.4
Patek-KC 82.1

Stolen Base Runs
Rivers-Cal 10.5
Otis-KC 4.7
Patek-KC 4.6
Carew-Min 4.6
Alomar-NY 4.1

Fielding Runs
Belanger-Bal 28.0
Dent-Chi 27.2
Grich-Bal 24.0
Rodriguez-Det 20.7
North-Oak 19.6

Total Player Rating
Harrah-Tex 6.4
Grich-Bal 6.2
Carew-Min 5.8
Lynn-Bos 5.0
Mayberry-KC 4.5

Wins
Palmer-Bal 23
Hunter-NY 23
Blue-Oak 22
Torrez-Bal 20
Kaat-Chi 20

Win Percentage
Torrez-Bal .... .690
Leonard-KC .... .682
Palmer-Bal .... .676
Blue-Oak .... .667
Lee-Bos .... .654

Games
Fingers-Oak 75
Lindblad-Oak 68
Gossage-Chi 62
LaRoche-Cle 61
Foucault-Tex 59

Complete Games
Hunter-NY 30
G.Perry-Cle-Tex 25
Palmer-Bal 25
Jenkins-Tex 22
Blyleven-Min 20

Shutouts
Palmer-Bal 10
Hunter-NY 7

Saves
Gossage-Chi 26
Fingers-Oak 24
Murphy-Mil 20
LaRoche-Cle 17
Drago-Bos 15

Innings Pitched
Hunter-NY 328.0
Palmer-Bal 323.0
G.Perry-Cle-Tex ... 305.2
Kaat-Chi 303.2
Wood-Chi 291.1

Fewest Hits/Game
Hunter-NY 6.80
Ryan-Cal 6.91
Palmer-Bal 7.05
Eckersley-Cle 7.09
Blyleven-Min 7.15

Fewest BB/Game
Jenkins-Tex 1.87
G.Perry-Cle-Tex 2.06
Grimsley-Bal 2.15
Palmer-Bal 2.23
Hunter-NY 2.28

Strikeouts
Tanana-Cal 269
G.Perry-Cle-Tex 233
Blyleven-Min 233
Palmer-Bal 193
Blue-Oak 189

Strikeouts/Game
Tanana-Cal 9.41
Ryan-Cal 8.45
Blyleven-Min 7.61
Eckersley-Cle 7.33
G.Perry-Cle-Tex 6.86

Ratio
Hunter-NY 9.22
Palmer-Bal 9.33
Blyleven-Min 10.02
Tanana-Cal 10.18
G.Perry-Cle-Tex 10.33

Earned Run Average
Palmer-Bal 2.09
Hunter-NY 2.58
Eckersley-Cle 2.60
Tanana-Cal 2.62
Figueroa-Cal 2.91

Adjusted ERA
Palmer-Bal 168
Eckersley-Cle 146
Hunter-NY 143
Tanana-Cal 136
Blyleven-Min 128

Opponents' Batting Avg.
Hunter-NY .... .208
Ryan-Cal .... .213
Eckersley-Cle .... .215
Palmer-Bal .... .216
Blyleven-Min .... .219

Opponents' On-Base Pct.
Hunter-NY .... .263
Palmer-Bal .... .267
Blyleven-Min .... .283
G.Perry-Cle-Tex .... .284
Tanana-Cal .... .288

Starter Runs
Palmer-Bal 61.0
Hunter-NY 44.1
Tanana-Cal 33.3
Eckersley-Cle 24.6
Blyleven-Min 24.1

Adjusted Starter Runs
Palmer-Bal 55.2
Hunter-NY 41.6
Tanana-Cal 28.5
Kaat-Chi 25.4
Blyleven-Min 25.1

Clutch Pitching Index
Kaat-Chi 119
Eckersley-Cle 116
Torrez-Bal 111
Osteen-Chi 111
Hargan-Tex 108

Relief Runs
Gossage-Chi 30.6
Todd-Oak 20.4
LaRoche-Cle 14.7
Lindblad-Oak 14.5
Hiller-Det 12.7

Adjusted Relief Runs
Gossage-Chi 31.3
Todd-Oak 19.1
LaRoche-Cle 14.7
Hiller-Det 13.8
Lindblad-Oak 13.0

Relief Ranking
Gossage-Chi 46.8
Todd-Oak 19.7
LaRoche-Cle 19.7
Fingers-Oak 15.0
Hiller-Det 14.9

Total Pitcher Index
Palmer-Bal 6.1
Gossage-Chi 5.1
Hunter-NY 4.1
Tanana-Cal 3.0
Busby-KC 2.8

Total Baseball Ranking
Harrah-Tex 6.4
Grich-Bal 6.2
Palmer-Bal 6.1
Carew-Min 5.8
Gossage-Chi 5.1

TEAM	G	W	L	PCT	GB	R	OR	AB	H	2B	3B	HR	BB	SO	AVG	OBP	SLG	OPS	OPS+	BR	BR+	PF	CHI	RC	SB	CS	SBA	SBR
EAST																												
PHI	162	101	61	.623		770	557	5528	1505	259	45	110	542	793	.272	.342	.395	737	112	106	84	103	101	746	127	70	64	3
PIT	162	92	70	.568	9	708	630	5604	1499	249	56	110	433	807	.267	.323	.391	714	107	50	44	101	102	700	130	45	74	13
NY	162	86	76	.531	15	615	**538**	5415	1334	198	34	102	561	797	.246	.320	.352	672	103	-19	19	94	99	608	66	58	53	-6
CHI	162	75	87	.463	26	611	728	5519	1386	216	24	105	490	834	.251	.316	.356	672	89	-27	-78	109	99	605	74	74	50	-10
STL	162	72	90	.444	29	629	671	5516	1432	243	57	63	512	860	.260	.325	.359	684	99	1	-5	101	97	644	123	55	69	8
MON	162	55	107	.340	46	531	734	5428	1275	224	32	94	433	841	.235	.293	.340	633	82	-109	-130	104	102	539	86	44	66	4
WEST																												
CIN	162	102	60	.630		**857**	633	5702	**1599**	**271**	**63**	**141**	**681**	902	**.280**	**.360**	**.424**	**784**	**126**	**214**	**193**	102	95	**907**	**210**	57	**79**	**26**
LA	162	92	70	.568	10	608	543	5472	1371	200	34	91	486	744	.251	.315	.349	664	96	-39	-27	98	101	604	144	55	72	12
HOU	162	80	82	.494	22	625	657	5464	1401	195	50	66	530	719	.256	.325	.347	672	107	-20	41	91	101	622	150	57	72	13
SF	162	74	88	.457	28	595	686	5452	1340	211	37	85	518	778	.246	.314	.345	659	90	-48	-65	103	100	591	88	55	62	0
SD	162	73	89	.451	29	570	662	5369	1327	216	37	64	488	**716**	.247	.313	.337	650	98	-65	-15	92	100	570	92	46	67	4
ATL	162	70	92	.432	32	620	700	5345	1309	170	30	82	589	811	.245	.322	.334	656	87	-44	-79	106	**104**	579	74	61	55	-5
TOT	972					7739		65814	16778	2652	499	1113	6263	9602	.255	.323	.362	684							1364	677	67	63

TEAM	CG	SH	SV	IP	H	H/G	HR	BB	SO	RAT	ERA	ERA+	OAV	OOB	PR	PR+	PF	CPI	FA	E	DP	FW	PW	BW	SBW	DIF
EAST																										
PHI	34	9	44	1459	1377	8.5	98	**397**	918	11.1	3.08	**115**	.250	.303	69	**75**	101	102	.981	115	148	1.8	**8.0**	9.0	-.2	1.7
PIT	45	12	35	1466[1]	1402	8.7	95	460	762	11.6	3.37	104	.253	.313	22	20	100	99	.975	163	142	-1.0	2.2	4.7	.8	4.5
NY	**53**	**18**	25	1449	**1248**	**7.8**	97	419	**1025**	**10.5**	**2.94**	112	**.233**	**.292**	**91**	61	94	95	.979	131	116	.9	6.5	2.1	-1.2	-3.1
CHI	27	12	33	1471[1]	1511	9.3	123	490	850	12.5	3.94	98	.268	.330	-71	-11	110	100	.978	140	145	.3	-1.1	-8.2	-1.6	4.8
STL	35	15	26	1453[2]	1416	8.8	91	581	731	12.6	3.61	98	.258	.332	-16	-11	101	103	.973	174	163	-1.6	-1.1	-.5	.3	-5.9
MON	26	10	21	1440	1442	9.1	89	659	783	13.4	4.00	93	.266	.350	-79	-41	106	103	.976	155	**179**	-.5	-4.3	-13.8	-.1	-7.1
WEST																										
CIN	33	12	**45**	1471	1436	8.8	100	491	790	12.0	3.51	100	.258	.321	-1	0	100	101	**.984**	**102**	157	**2.5**	.0	**20.5**	**2.2**	-4.1
LA	47	17	28	1470[2]	1330	8.2	97	479	747	11.3	3.02	112	.243	.307	79	62	97	**104**	.980	128	154	1.0	6.6	-2.8	.7	5.6
HOU	42	17	29	1444[1]	1349	8.5	82	662	780	12.7	3.56	90	.250	.335	-9	-64	91	101	.978	140	155	.3	-6.7	4.4	.8	.4
SF	27	**18**	31	1461[2]	1464	9.1	**68**	518	746	12.4	3.53	103	.263	.328	-4	16	104	100	.971	186	153	-2.3	1.7	-6.9	-.6	1.2
SD	47	11	18	1432[1]	1368	8.6	87	543	652	12.2	3.66	90	.253	.323	-24	-65	93	95	.978	141	148	.3	-6.9	-1.5	-.1	.4
ATL	33	13	27	1438	1435	9.0	86	564	818	12.8	3.87	98	.261	.335	-58	-11	108	97	.973	167	151	-1.2	-1.1	-8.3	-1.1	1.0
TOT	449	164	362	17457[1]		8.7				12.1	3.51		.255	.323					.978	1742	1811					

Runs
Rose-Cin 130
Morgan-Cin 113
Schmidt-Phi 112
Griffey-Cin 111
Monday-Chi 107

Hits
Rose-Cin 215
Montanez-SF-Atl ... 206
Garvey-LA 200
Buckner-LA 193

Doubles
Rose-Cin 42
Johnstone-Phi 38
Maddox-Phi 37
Garvey-LA 37

Triples
Cash-Phi 12
Geronimo-Cin 11
Parker-Pit 10
W.Davis-SD 10

Home Runs
Schmidt-Phi 38
Kingman-NY 37
Monday-Chi 32
Foster-Cin 29
Morgan-Cin 27

Total Bases
Schmidt-Phi 306
Rose-Cin 299
Foster-Cin 298
Garvey-LA 284

Runs Batted In
Foster-Cin 121
Morgan-Cin 111
Schmidt-Phi 107
Watson-Hou 102
Luzinski-Phi 95

Runs Produced
Morgan-Cin 197
Rose-Cin 183
Schmidt-Phi 181
Griffey-Cin 179
Foster-Cin 178

Bases On Balls
Wynn-Atl 127
Morgan-Cin 114
Schmidt-Phi 100
Cey-LA 89
Rose-Cin 86

Batting Average
Madlock-Chi .... .339
Griffey-Cin .... .336
Maddox-Phi .... .330
Rose-Cin .... .323
Morgan-Cin .... .320

On-Base Percentage
Morgan-Cin .... .453
Madlock-Chi .... .415
Rose-Cin .... .406
Griffey-Cin .... .403
Cey-LA .... .389

Slugging Average
Morgan-Cin .... .576
Foster-Cin .... .530
Schmidt-Phi .... .524
Monday-Chi .... .507
Kingman-NY .... .506

On-Base Plus Slugging
Morgan-Cin 1029
Madlock-Chi 915
Schmidt-Phi 904
Foster-Cin 899
Rose-Cin 855

Adjusted OPS
Morgan-Cin 186
Watson-Hou 151
Schmidt-Phi 150
Foster-Cin 149
Madlock-Chi 146

Batter Runs
Morgan-Cin 61.4
Schmidt-Phi 42.7
Madlock-Chi 40.6
Rose-Cin 39.6
Foster-Cin 36.7

Adjusted Batter Runs
Morgan-Cin 58.5
Schmidt-Phi 39.3
Watson-Hou 38.9
Rose-Cin 36.8
Foster-Cin 34.3

Clutch Hitting Index
Cruz-StL 119
Brock-StL 117
Milner-NY 117
Bench-Cin 116
Reitz-SF 116

Runs Created
Morgan-Cin 144
Rose-Cin 123
Schmidt-Phi 121
Foster-Cin 111
Griffey-Cin 109

Total Average
Morgan-Cin 1.319
Schmidt-Phi .... .944
Foster-Cin .... .911
Madlock-Chi .... .882
Griffey-Cin .... .876

Stolen Bases
Lopes-LA 63
Morgan-Cin 60
Taveras-Pit 58
Cedeno-Hou 58
Brock-StL 56

Stolen Base Average
Morgan-Cin 87.0
Lopes-LA 86.3
Foster-Cin 85.0
Taveras-Pit 84.1
Geronimo-Cin 81.5

Stolen Base Runs
Lopes-LA 10.4
Morgan-Cin 10.1
Taveras-Pit 8.9
Cedeno-Hou 7.5
Brock-StL 5.7

Fielding Runs
Schmidt-Phi 24.7
Maddox-Phi 24.3
Trillo-Chi 18.3
Stennett-Pit 17.4
Royster-Atl 16.6

Total Player Rating
Schmidt-Phi 6.5
Morgan-Cin 5.6
Maddox-Phi 4.8
Cedeno-Hou 4.5
Concepcion-Cin 4.2

Wins
Jones-SD 22
Sutton-LA 21
Koosman-NY 21
Richard-Hou 20
Carlton-Phi 20

Win Percentage
Carlton-Phi .... .741
Candelaria-Pit ..... .696
Sutton-LA .... .677
Koosman-NY .... .677
Rooker-Pit .... .652

Games
Murray-Mon 81
Metzger-SD 77
Hough-LA 77
Eastwick-Cin 71
Borbon-Cin 69

Complete Games
Jones-SD 25
Koosman-NY 17
Matlack-NY 16
Sutton-LA 15
Richard-Hou 14

Shutouts
Montefusco-SF 6
Matlack-NY 6
Seaver-NY 5
Jones-SD 5

Saves
Eastwick-Cin 26
Lockwood-NY 19
Forsch-Hou 19
Hough-LA 18
Metzger-SD 16

Innings Pitched
Jones-SD 315.1
Richard-Hou 291.0
Seaver-NY 271.0
Niekro-Atl 270.2
Sutton-LA 267.2

Fewest Hits/Game
Richard-Hou 6.84
Seaver-NY 7.01
Candelaria-Pit 7.08
Messersmith-Atl 7.21
Falcone-StL 7.34

Fewest BB/Game
Nolan-Cin 1.02
Kaat-Phi 1.27
Jones-SD 1.43
Matlack-NY 1.96
Lonborg-Phi 2.03

Strikeouts
Seaver-NY 235
Richard-Hou 214
Koosman-NY 200
Carlton-Phi 195
Niekro-Atl 173

Strikeouts/Game
Seaver-NY 7.80
Koosman-NY 7.28
Carlton-Phi 6.95
Richard-Hou 6.62
Zachry-Cin 6.31

Ratio
Jones-SD 9.36
Candelaria-Pit 9.61
Seaver-NY 9.70
Nolan-Cin 9.78
Koosman-NY 9.90

Earned Run Average
Denny-StL 2.52
Rau-LA 2.57
Seaver-NY 2.59
Koosman-NY 2.69
Zachry-Cin 2.74

Adjusted ERA
Denny-StL 140
Rau-LA 132
Zachry-Cin 128
Montefusco-SF 128
Seaver-NY 127

Opponents' Batting Avg.
Richard-Hou .... .212
Seaver-NY .... .213
Candelaria-Pit ...... .216
Messersmith-Atl ..... .219
Falcone-StL .... .222

Opponents' On-Base Pct.
Jones-SD .... .267
Candelaria-Pit ...... .273
Seaver-NY .... .273
Nolan-Cin .... .276
Koosman-NY .... .279

Starter Runs
Seaver-NY 27.6
Jones-SD 26.8
Richard-Hou 24.4
Rau-LA 24.0
Denny-StL 22.6

Adjusted Starter Runs
Denny-StL 23.2
Seaver-NY 22.7
Rau-LA 21.7
Montefusco-SF 21.5
Barr-SF 20.1

Clutch Pitching Index
Rau-LA 139
Denny-StL 129
Burris-Chi 118
Christenson-Phi 112
Fryman-Mon 112

Relief Runs
Hough-LA 20.6
Eastwick-Cin 16.9
Reed-Phi 14.9
Moffitt-SF 14.1
Forsch-Hou 13.8

Adjusted Relief Runs
Hough-LA 19.3
Eastwick-Cin 17.0
Reed-Phi 15.3
Moffitt-SF 15.0
Twitchell-Phi 12.2

Relief Ranking
Eastwick-Cin 31.9
Hough-LA 29.9
Moffitt-SF 20.3
Reed-Phi 19.9
Lavelle-SF 17.2

Total Pitcher Index
Hough-LA 3.4
Eastwick-Cin 3.1
Barr-SF 2.7
Rau-LA 2.7
Denny-StL 2.6

Total Baseball Ranking
Schmidt-Phi 6.5
Morgan-Cin 5.6
Maddox-Phi 4.8
Cedeno-Hou 4.5
Concepcion-Cin 4.2

TEAM	G	W	L	PCT	GB	R	OR	AB	H	2B	3B	HR	BB	SO	AVG	OBP	SLG	OPS	OPS+	BR	BR+	PF	CHI	RC	SB	CS	SBA	SBR
EAST																												
NY	159	97	62	.610		730	**575**	5555	1496	231	36	120	470	**616**	.269	.330	.389	719	**111**	64	**71**	99	103	723	163	65	71	13
BAL	162	88	74	.543	10.5	619	598	5457	1326	213	28	119	519	883	.243	.311	.358	669	102	-33	7	94	102	612	150	61	71	12
BOS	162	83	79	.512	15.5	716	660	5511	1448	257	53	**134**	500	832	.263	.327	**.402**	**729**	101	**80**	1	112	98	709	95	70	58	-4
CLE	159	81	78	.509	16	615	615	5412	1423	189	38	85	479	631	.263	.324	.359	683	101	-2	5	99	97	611	75	69	52	-8
DET	161	74	87	.460	24	609	709	5441	1401	207	38	101	450	730	.257	.318	.365	683	96	-7	-31	104	97	611	107	59	64	3
MIL	161	66	95	.410	32	570	655	5396	1326	170	38	88	511	909	.246	.314	.340	654	93	-57	-46	98	98	575	62	61	50	-8
WEST																												
KC	162	90	72	.556		713	611	5540	1490	**259**	**57**	65	484	650	.269	.331	.371	702	104	37	32	101	103	687	218	106	67	11
OAK	161	87	74	.540	2.5	686	598	5353	1319	208	33	113	**592**	818	.246	.327	.361	688	105	13	41	96	**105**	663	**341**	123	**73**	**32**
MIN	162	85	77	.525	5	**743**	704	5574	**1526**	222	51	81	550	714	**.274**	**.343**	.375	718	108	78	63	102	100	**727**	146	75	66	6
TEX	162	76	86	.469	14	616	652	5555	1390	213	26	80	568	809	.250	.323	.341	664	93	-32	-45	102	98	616	87	45	66	3
CAL	162	76	86	.469	14	550	631	5385	1265	210	23	63	534	812	.235	.309	.318	627	90	-105	-69	94	102	531	126	80	61	0
CHI	161	64	97	.398	32.5	586	745	5532	1410	209	46	73	471	739	.255	.317	.349	666	94	-36	-40	101	96	622	120	53	69	8
TOT	967					7753		65711	16820	2588	467	1122	6128	9143	.256	.323	.361	684							1690	867	66	68

TEAM	CG	SH	SV	IP	H	H/G	HR	BB	SO	RAT	ERA	ERA+	OAV	OOB	PR	PR+	PF	CPI	FA	E	DP	FW	PW	BW	SBW	DIF
EAST																										
NY	62	15	37	1455	**1300**	**8.1**	97	448	674	**11.0**	**3.20**	107	**.241**	**.301**	**53**	37	97	95	.980	126	141	.9	4.0	**7.6**	.8	4.4
BAL	59	16	23	1468[2]	1396	8.6	**80**	489	678	11.7	3.32	99	.255	.318	33	-8	93	101	**.982**	**118**	157	**1.5**	-.8	.8	.7	5.0
BOS	49	13	27	1458	1495	9.3	109	**409**	673	12.0	3.53	**111**	.267	.320	-1	**56**	111	104	.978	141	148	.2	**6.0**	.2	-1.0	-3.1
CLE	30	**17**	**46**	1432	1361	8.6	**80**	533	928	12.2	3.47	101	.255	.326	8	3	99	101	.980	121	159	1.2	.4	.6	-1.5	1.0
DET	55	12	20	1431[1]	1426	9.0	101	550	738	12.7	3.87	96	.263	.334	-56	-24	105	99	.974	168	161	-1.4	-2.5	-3.2	-.3	1.1
MIL	45	10	27	1435[1]	1406	8.9	99	567	677	12.7	3.65	96	.260	.334	-20	-24	99	104	.975	152	160	-.5	-2.5	-4.8	-1.5	-5.1
WEST																										
KC	41	12	35	1472[1]	1356	8.3	83	493	735	11.5	3.21	109	.247	.312	51	48	100	99	.978	139	147	.3	5.1	3.4	.6	-.3
OAK	39	15	29	1459[1]	1412	8.8	96	415	711	11.5	3.26	103	.255	.310	42	16	95	102	.977	144	130	.0	1.7	4.4	**2.8**	-2.2
MIN	29	11	23	1459	1421	8.8	89	610	762	12.8	3.70	97	.259	.337	-29	-19	102	102	.973	172	**182**	-1.6	-2.0	6.7	.0	1.0
TEX	63	15	15	1472	1464	9.0	106	461	773	12.0	3.46	104	.262	.322	10	21	102	**105**	.976	156	142	-.6	2.3	-4.7	-.3	-1.4
CAL	**64**	15	17	1477[1]	1323	**8.1**	95	553	**992**	11.7	3.36	99	**.241**	.315	26	-6	95	97	.977	150	139	-.3	-.6	-7.3	-.6	4.0
CHI	54	10	22	1448	1460	9.1	87	600	802	13.1	4.26	84	.266	.342	-118	-109	101	92	.979	130	155	.8	-11.5	-4.2	.2	-1.6
TOT	590	161	321	17468[1]		8.7				12.1	3.52		.256	.323					.978	1717	1821					

Runs
White-NY 104
Carew-Min 97
Rivers-NY 95
Brett-KC 94

Hits
Brett-KC 215
Carew-Min 200
Chambliss-NY 188
Munson-NY 186
Rivers-NY 184

Doubles
Otis-KC 40
McRae-KC 34
Evans-Bos 34
Carty-Cle 34
Brett-KC 34

Triples
Brett-KC 14
Garner-Oak 12
Carew-Min 12
Poquette-KC 10
Bostock-Min 9

Home Runs
Nettles-NY 32
R.Jackson-Bal 27
Bando-Oak 27

Total Bases
Brett-KC 298
Chambliss-NY 283
Rice-Bos 280
Carew-Min 280
Nettles-NY 277

Runs Batted In
L.May-Bal 109
Munson-NY 105
Yastrzemski-Bos 102

Runs Produced
Carew-Min 178
Munson-NY 167
Hisle-Min 163
Otis-KC 161

Bases On Balls
Hargrove-Tex 97
Harrah-Tex 91
Grich-Bal 86
White-NY 83
Staub-Det 83

Batting Average
Brett-KC .333
McRae-KC .332
Carew-Min .331
Bostock-Min .323
LeFlore-Det .316

On-Base Percentage
McRae-KC .412
Hargrove-Tex .401
Carew-Min .398
Staub-Det .392
Carty-Cle .384

Slugging Average
R.Jackson-Bal .502
Rice-Bos .482
Nettles-NY .475
Lynn-Bos .467
Carew-Min .463

On-Base Plus Slugging
McRae-KC 873
Carew-Min 861
R.Jackson-Bal 855
Brett-KC 843
Lynn-Bos 842

Adjusted OPS
R.Jackson-Bal 158
McRae-KC 154
Tenace-Oak 150
Carew-Min 149
Brett-KC 145

Batter Runs
Carew-Min 40.0
McRae-KC 38.8
Brett-KC 36.2
Staub-Det 33.2
Carty-Cle 29.8

Adjusted Batter Runs
McRae-KC 38.1
Carew-Min 37.8
Brett-KC 35.4
R.Jackson-Bal 34.5
Carty-Cle 30.8

Clutch Hitting Index
Mayberry-KC 137
Rudi-Oak 131
L.May-Bal 127
Yastrzemski-Bos 124
Hisle-Min 124

Runs Created
Brett-KC 114
Carew-Min 111
McRae-KC 101
Staub-Det 99
White-NY 98

Total Average
McRae-KC .862
R.Jackson-Bal .857
Tenace-Oak .855
Carew-Min .854
Brett-KC .797

Stolen Bases
North-Oak 75
LeFlore-Det 58
Campaneris-Oak 54
Baylor-Oak 52
Patek-KC 51

Stolen Base Average
Rivers-NY 86.0
Campaneris-Oak 81.8
Baylor-Oak 81.3
Bumbry-Bal 80.8
R.Jackson-Bal 80.0

Stolen Base Runs
Campaneris-Oak 7.7
Baylor-Oak 7.2
Rivers-NY 7.0
North-Oak 6.3
Patek-KC 6.0

Fielding Runs
White-KC 21.1
Kuiper-Cle 20.0
Beniquez-Tex 19.5
Brohamer-Chi 18.0
Nettles-NY 17.2

Total Player Rating
Nettles-NY 4.2
Brett-KC 4.1
Grich-Bal 4.0
Belanger-Bal 3.8
LeFlore-Det 3.8

Wins
Palmer-Bal 22
Tiant-Bos 21
Garland-Bal 20

Win Percentage
Campbell-Min .773
Garland-Bal .741
Ellis-NY .680
Fidrych-Det .679

Games
Campbell-Min 78
Fingers-Oak 70
Lindblad-Oak 65
Lyle-NY 64
LaRoche-Cle 61

Complete Games
Fidrych-Det 24
Tanana-Cal 23
Palmer-Bal 23

Shutouts
Ryan-Cal 7
Blyleven-Min-Tex 6
Palmer-Bal 6
Blue-Oak 6

Saves
Lyle-NY 23
LaRoche-Cle 21
Fingers-Oak 20
Campbell-Min 20
Littell-KC 16

Innings Pitched
Palmer-Bal 315.0
Hunter-NY 298.2
Blue-Oak 298.1
Blyleven-Min-Tex 297.2
Slaton-Mil 292.2

Fewest Hits/Game
Ryan-Cal 6.11
Tanana-Cal 6.62
Eckersley-Cle 7.00
Palmer-Bal 7.29
Brett-NY-Chi 7.67

Fewest BB/Game
Bird-KC 1.41
Jenkins-Bos 1.85
Perry-Tex 1.87
Blue-Oak 1.90
Fidrych-Det 1.91

Strikeouts
Ryan-Cal 327
Tanana-Cal 261
Blyleven-Min-Tex 219
Eckersley-Cle 200
Hunter-NY 173

Strikeouts/Game
Ryan-Cal 10.35
Eckersley-Cle 9.03
Tanana-Cal 8.15
Blyleven-Min-Tex 6.62
Campbell-Min 6.17

Ratio
Tanana-Cal 9.18
Fidrych-Det 9.81
Palmer-Bal 9.91
Blue-Oak 10.02
Perry-Tex 10.21

Earned Run Average
Fidrych-Det 2.34
Blue-Oak 2.35
Tanana-Cal 2.43
Torrez-Oak 2.50
Palmer-Bal 2.51

Adjusted ERA
Fidrych-Det 159
Blue-Oak 143
Tanana-Cal 137
Torrez-Oak 134
Palmer-Bal 130

Opponents' Batting Avg.
Ryan-Cal .195
Tanana-Cal .203
Eckersley-Cle .214
Palmer-Bal .224
Brett-NY-Chi .233

Opponents' On-Base Pct.
Tanana-Cal .261
Fidrych-Det .279
Blue-Oak .280
Palmer-Bal .282
Bird-KC .283

Starter Runs
Blue-Oak 38.8
Palmer-Bal 35.3
Tanana-Cal 34.9
Fidrych-Det 33.0
Torrez-Oak 30.2

Adjusted Starter Runs
Fidrych-Det 36.3
Blue-Oak 34.9
Tanana-Cal 30.3
Palmer-Bal 28.7
Torrez-Oak 26.6

Clutch Pitching Index
Hartzell-Cal 124
Travers-Mil 120
Umbarger-Tex 118
Garland-Bal 116
Torrez-Oak 115

Relief Runs
Littell-KC 16.7
Fingers-Oak 15.7
Hiller-Det 15.4
Kern-Cle 15.1
Lyle-NY 14.6

Adjusted Relief Runs
Hiller-Det 17.0
Littell-KC 16.6
Kern-Cle 14.8
Thomas-Cle 14.1
Fingers-Oak 13.9

Relief Ranking
Hiller-Det 29.4
Fingers-Oak 26.9
Lyle-NY 24.9
Kern-Cle 23.5
Littell-KC 23.0

Total Pitcher Index
Fidrych-Det 4.8
Palmer-Bal 3.3
Blue-Oak 3.3
Tanana-Cal 3.2
Hiller-Det 3.1

Total Baseball Ranking
Fidrych-Det 4.8
Nettles-NY 4.2
Brett-KC 4.1
Grich-Bal 4.0
Belanger-Bal 3.8

TEAM	G	W	L	PCT	GB	R	OR	AB	H	2B	3B	HR	BB	SO	AVG	OBP	SLG	OPS	OPS+	BR	BR+	PF	CHI	RC	SB	CS	SBA	SBR
EAST																												
PHI	162	101	61	.623		**847**	668	5546	1548	266	56	186	573	806	**.279**	**.351**	**.448**	**799**	**114**	**143**	**107**	104	98	**865**	135	68	67	6
PIT	162	96	66	.593	5	734	665	5662	**1550**	278	57	133	474	878	.274	.334	.413	747	102	37	17	103	98	776	**260**	120	68	15
STL	162	83	79	.512	18	737	688	5527	1490	252	56	96	489	823	.270	.332	.388	720	100	-13	0	98	**107**	690	134	112	54	-10
CHI	162	81	81	.500	20	692	739	5604	1489	271	37	111	534	**796**	.266	.333	.387	720	88	-11	-82	111	98	709	64	45	59	-2
MON	162	75	87	.463	26	665	736	5675	1474	**294**	50	138	478	877	.260	.320	.402	722	101	-20	1	97	95	715	88	50	64	2
NY	162	64	98	.395	37	587	663	5410	1319	227	30	88	529	887	.244	.315	.346	661	87	-125	-97	95	103	577	98	81	55	-7
WEST																												
LA	162	98	64	.605		769	**582**	5589	1484	223	28	**191**	588	896	.266	.338	.418	756	109	58	62	100	98	794	114	62	65	3
CIN	162	88	74	.543	10	802	725	5524	1513	269	42	181	600	911	.274	.348	.436	784	113	115	100	102	97	847	170	64	**73**	15
HOU	162	81	81	.500	17	680	650	5530	1405	263	**60**	114	515	839	.254	.322	.385	707	104	-41	24	91	102	697	187	72	72	**16**
SF	162	75	87	.463	23	673	711	5497	1392	227	41	134	568	842	.253	.326	.383	709	95	-35	-32	100	100	683	90	59	60	-1
SD	162	69	93	.426	29	692	834	5602	1397	245	49	120	**602**	1057	.249	.325	.375	700	104	-49	30	90	102	700	133	57	70	9
ATL	162	61	101	.377	37	678	895	5534	1404	218	20	139	537	876	.254	.322	.376	698	82	-58	-127	112	104	660	82	53	61	-1
TOT	972					8556		66700	17465	3033	526	1631	6487	10488	.262	.331	.397	727							1555	843	65	47

TEAM	CG	SH	SV	IP	H	H/G	HR	BB	SO	RAT	ERA	ERA+	OAV	OOB	PR	PR+	PF	CPI	FA	E	DP	FW	PW	BW	SBW	DIF
EAST																										
PHI	31	7	**47**	1455^2	1451	9.0	134	482	856	12.1	3.71	108	.263	.325	32	46	102	103	.981	120	168	1.4	4.7	**10.9**	.2	3.0
PIT	25	**15**	39	1481^2	1406	8.6	149	485	890	11.7	3.61	110	.252	.314	50	61	102	99	.977	145	137	-.0	6.2	1.8	1.1	6.1
STL	26	10	31	1446	1420	8.9	139	532	768	12.4	3.81	101	.260	.329	16	6	98	102	.978	139	**174**	.3	.7	.0	-1.4	2.6
CHI	16	10	44	1468	1500	9.2	128	489	**942**	12.4	4.01	109	.266	.327	-16	55	112	96	.977	153	147	-.5	5.6	-8.2	-.6	3.9
MON	31	11	33	1481	1426	8.7	135	579	856	12.4	4.02	95	.255	.327	-17	-34	97	94	.980	129	128	.9	-3.4	.2	-.2	-3.2
NY	27	12	28	1433^2	**1378**	8.7	118	490	911	12.0	3.78	99	.254	.319	22	-6	96	94	.978	134	132	.6	-.6	-9.8	-1.1	-6.0
WEST																										
LA	34	13	39	1475^1	1393	**8.5**	119	**438**	930	**11.4**	**3.23**	**119**	**.251**	**.309**	**113**	**101**	98	104	.981	124	160	1.1	**10.3**	6.3	-.0	-.4
CIN	33	12	32	1437^1	1469	9.2	156	544	868	12.8	4.22	93	.267	.337	-49	-45	101	100	**.984**	**95**	154	**2.8**	-4.5	10.2	1.1	-2.3
HOU	**37**	11	28	1465^2	1384	**8.5**	**110**	545	871	12.0	3.54	101	**.251**	.321	61	5	91	99	.978	142	136	.1	.6	2.5	**1.2**	-4.2
SF	27	10	33	1459	1501	9.3	114	529	854	12.7	3.76	104	.267	.333	26	26	100	104	.972	179	136	-1.9	2.7	-3.2	-.5	-2.9
SD	6	5	44	1466^1	1556	9.6	160	673	827	13.9	4.44	80	.276	.355	-85	-161	91	**105**	.971	189	142	-2.5	-16.2	3.1	.5	3.3
ATL	28	5	31	1445^1	1581	9.9	169	701	915	14.5	4.86	92	.279	.363	-151	-57	114	101	.972	175	127	-1.7	-5.7	-12.8	-.5	.9
TOT	321	121	429	17515		9.0				12.5	3.91		.262	.331					.978	1724	1741					

Runs
Foster-Cin 124
Griffey-Cin 117
Schmidt-Phi 114
Morgan-Cin 113
Parker-Pit 107

Hits
Parker-Pit 215
Rose-Cin 204
Templeton-StL 200
Foster-Cin 197
Garvey-LA 192

Doubles
Parker-Pit 44
Cash-Mon 42
Hernandez-StL 41
Cromartie-Mon 41

Triples
Templeton-StL 18
Schmidt-Phi 11
Richards-SD 11
Almon-SD 11

Home Runs
Foster-Cin 52
Burroughs-Atl 41
Luzinski-Phi 39
Schmidt-Phi 38
Garvey-LA 33

Total Bases
Foster-Cin 388
Parker-Pit 338
Luzinski-Phi 329
Garvey-LA 322
Schmidt-Phi 312

Runs Batted In
Foster-Cin 149
Luzinski-Phi 130
Garvey-LA 115
Burroughs-Atl 114

Runs Produced
Foster-Cin 221
Luzinski-Phi 190
Schmidt-Phi 177
Parker-Pit 174
Garvey-LA 173

Bases On Balls
Tenace-SD 125
Morgan-Cin 117
Smith-LA 104
Schmidt-Phi 104
Cey-LA 93

Batting Average
Parker-Pit .338
Templeton-StL .322
Foster-Cin .320
Griffey-Cin .318
Simmons-StL .318

On-Base Percentage
Smith-LA .432
Morgan-Cin .420
Tenace-SD .417
Simmons-StL .410
Parker-Pit .399

Slugging Average
Foster-Cin .631
Luzinski-Phi .594
Smith-LA .576
Schmidt-Phi .574
Bench-Cin .540

On-Base Plus Slugging
Foster-Cin 1017
Smith-LA 1008
Luzinski-Phi 993
Schmidt-Phi 972
Parker-Pit 929

Adjusted OPS
Smith-LA 168
Foster-Cin 165
Luzinski-Phi 155
Schmidt-Phi 151
Hendrick-SD 148

Batter Runs
Foster-Cin 56.0
Smith-LA 50.3
Luzinski-Phi 48.6
Schmidt-Phi 45.8
Parker-Pit 42.0

Adjusted Batter Runs
Foster-Cin 53.7
Smith-LA 50.9
Luzinski-Phi 43.4
Schmidt-Phi 40.6
Parker-Pit 38.8

Clutch Hitting Index
Watson-Hou 121
Cey-LA 116
Bench-Cin 114
Robinson-Pit 114
Evans-SF 114

Runs Created
Foster-Cin 144
Luzinski-Phi 132
Parker-Pit 130
Schmidt-Phi 129
Smith-LA 129

Total Average
Smith-LA 1.121
Morgan-Cin 1.054
Schmidt-Phi 1.046
Luzinski-Phi 1.043
Foster-Cin 1.039

Stolen Bases
Taveras-Pit 70
Cedeno-Hou 61
Richards-SD 56
Moreno-Pit 53
Morgan-Cin 49

Stolen Base Average
Bowa-Phi 91.4
McBride-StL-Phi 83.7
Morgan-Cin 83.1
Richards-SD 82.4
Cedeno-Hou 81.3

Stolen Base Runs
Taveras-Pit 9.1
Cedeno-Hou 8.5
Richards-SD 8.1
Morgan-Cin 7.3
Lopes-LA 6.1

Fielding Runs
DeJesus-Chi 35.8
Parker-Pit 32.5
Trillo-Chi 30.1
Schmidt-Phi 28.8
Tyson-StL 22.0

Total Player Rating
Schmidt-Phi 6.7
Foster-Cin 6.2
Parker-Pit 5.9
Hendrick-SD 4.2
Cedeno-Hou 3.7

Wins
Carlton-Phi 23
Seaver-NY-Cin 21

Win Percentage
Candelaria-Pit .800
Seaver-NY-Cin .778
Christenson-Phi .760
John-LA .741
Forsch-StL .741

Games
Fingers-SD 78
Tomlin-SD 76
Spillner-SD 76
Metzger-SD-StL 75

Complete Games
Niekro-Atl 20
Seaver-NY-Cin 19
Rogers-Mon 17
Carlton-Phi 17
Richard-Hou 13

Shutouts
Seaver-NY-Cin 7
Rogers-Mon 4
R.Reuschel-Chi 4

Saves
Fingers-SD 35
Sutter-Chi 31
Gossage-Pit 26
Hough-LA 22

Innings Pitched
Niekro-Atl 330.1
Rogers-Mon 301.2
Carlton-Phi 283.0
Richard-Hou 267.0
Seaver-NY-Cin 261.1

Fewest Hits/Game
Seaver-NY-Cin 6.85
Richard-Hou 7.15
Carlton-Phi 7.28
Hooton-LA 7.41
Candelaria-Pit 7.69

Fewest BB/Game
Candelaria-Pit 1.95
John-LA 2.04
Rau-LA 2.08
Barr-SF 2.15
Lemongello-Hou 2.18

Strikeouts
Niekro-Atl 262
Richard-Hou 214
Rogers-Mon 206
Carlton-Phi 198
Seaver-NY-Cin 196

Strikeouts/Game
Koosman-NY 7.62
Richard-Hou 7.21
Niekro-Atl 7.14
Seaver-NY-Cin 6.75
Matlack-NY 6.55

Ratio
Seaver-NY-Cin 9.13
Candelaria-Pit 9.72
Hooton-LA 9.95
Carlton-Phi 10.24
Sutton-LA 10.45

Earned Run Average
Candelaria-Pit 2.34
Seaver-NY-Cin 2.58
Hooton-LA 2.62
Carlton-Phi 2.64
John-LA 2.78

Adjusted ERA
Candelaria-Pit 170
R.Reuschel-Chi 158
Carlton-Phi 152
Seaver-NY-Cin 150
Hooton-LA 146

Opponents' Batting Avg.
Seaver-NY-Cin .209
Richard-Hou .218
Carlton-Phi .223
Hooton-LA .225
Koosman-NY .232

Opponents' On-Base Pct.
Seaver-NY-Cin .260
Candelaria-Pit .276
Hooton-LA .281
Carlton-Phi .287
Sutton-LA .291

Starter Runs
Candelaria-Pit 40.3
Carlton-Phi 40.1
Seaver-NY-Cin 38.6
Hooton-LA 32.1
R.Reuschel-Chi 31.6

Adjusted Starter Runs
Carlton-Phi 41.9
Candelaria-Pit 41.4
R.Reuschel-Chi 40.1
Seaver-NY-Cin 37.7
Hooton-LA 30.7

Clutch Pitching Index
Candelaria-Pit 126
John-LA 121
Rooker-Pit 119
Lemongello-Hou 116
Rau-LA 114

Relief Runs
Gossage-Pit 33.8
Sutter-Chi 30.7
Lavelle-SF 24.5
Garber-Phi 17.9
Reed-Phi 16.1

Adjusted Relief Runs
Gossage-Pit 34.3
Sutter-Chi 32.4
Lavelle-SF 24.5
Garber-Phi 18.5
Reed-Phi 16.9

Relief Ranking
Gossage-Pit 60.1
Sutter-Chi 46.3
Lavelle-SF 34.5
Garber-Phi 29.6
W.Hernandez-Chi 19.3

Total Pitcher Index
Gossage-Pit 6.3
Carlton-Phi 5.9
R.Reuschel-Chi 5.2
Sutter-Chi 5.0
Candelaria-Pit 4.6

Total Baseball Ranking
Schmidt-Phi 6.7
Gossage-Pit 6.3
Foster-Cin 6.2
Parker-Pit 5.9
Carlton-Phi 5.9

TEAM	G	W	L	PCT	GB	R	OR	AB	H	2B	3B	HR	BB	SO	AVG	OBP	SLG	OPS	OPS+	BR	BR+	PF	CHI	RC	SB	CS	SBA	SBR
EAST																												
NY	162	100	62	.617		831	**651**	5605	1576	267	47	184	533	681	.281	.347	.444	791	**115**	104	**113**	99	98	853	93	57	62	1
BAL	161	97	64	.602	2.5	719	653	5494	1433	231	25	148	560	945	.261	.332	.393	725	103	-23	24	94	102	711	90	51	64	2
BOS	161	97	64	.602	2.5	859	712	5510	1551	258	56	**213**	528	905	.281	.349	**.465**	**814**	107	**144**	52	112	98	**875**	66	47	58	-2
DET	162	74	88	.457	26	714	751	5604	1480	228	45	166	452	764	.264	.321	.410	731	93	-25	-61	105	101	717	60	46	57	-3
CLE	161	71	90	.441	28.5	676	739	5491	1476	221	46	100	531	688	.269	.337	.380	717	98	-31	-8	97	96	682	87	87	50	-11
MIL	162	67	95	.414	33	639	765	5517	1425	255	46	125	443	862	.258	.316	.389	705	91	-73	-72	100	99	660	85	67	56	-5
TOR	161	54	107	.335	45.5	605	822	5418	1367	230	41	100	499	819	.252	.318	.365	683	85	-106	-114	101	99	610	65	55	54	-5
WEST																												
KC	162	102	60	.630		822	**651**	5594	1549	**299**	**77**	146	522	687	.277	.343	.436	779	110	82	75	101	100	835	170	87	**66**	7
TEX	162	94	68	.580	8	767	657	5541	1497	265	39	135	**596**	904	.270	.345	.405	750	103	34	26	101	98	780	154	85	64	4
CHI	162	90	72	.556	12	844	771	5633	1568	254	52	192	559	**666**	.278	.347	.444	791	114	107	109	100	99	858	42	44	49	-6
MIN	161	84	77	.522	17.5	**867**	776	5639	**1588**	273	60	123	563	754	**.282**	**.351**	.417	768	110	71	84	99	105	827	105	65	62	0
CAL	162	74	88	.457	23	675	695	5410	1380	233	40	131	542	880	.255	.327	.386	713	97	-47	-19	96	100	681	159	89	64	4
SEA	162	64	98	.395	33	624	855	5460	1398	218	33	133	426	769	.256	.314	.381	695	89	-91	-85	99	100	643	110	67	62	1
OAK	161	63	98	.391	33.5	605	749	5358	1284	176	37	117	516	910	.240	.311	.352	663	81	-145	-136	99	**107**	589	**176**	89	**66**	**8**
TOT	1131					10247		77274	20572	3408	644	2013	7270	11234	.267	.333	.406	738							1462	936	61	-6

TEAM	CG	SH	SV	IP	H	H/G	HR	BB	SO	RAT	ERA	ERA+	OAV	OOB	PR	PR+	PF	CPI	FA	E	DP	FW	PW	BW	SBW	DIF
EAST																										
NY	52	16	34	1449[1]	1395	8.7	139	486	758	11.9	3.61	109	.254	.318	73	55	97	101	.979	132	151	.7	5.5	**11.3**	.1	1.6
BAL	**65**	11	23	1451	1414	8.8	124	494	737	12.1	3.75	101	.260	.325	51	9	93	101	**.983**	**106**	**189**	**2.1**	.9	2.4	.2	11.0
BOS	40	13	40	1428	1555	9.9	158	**378**	758	12.4	4.11	109	.278	.327	-8	54	111	102	.978	133	162	.5	5.4	5.2	-.2	5.7
DET	44	3	23	1457	1526	9.5	162	470	784	12.5	4.13	104	.271	.329	-11	24	106	100	.978	142	153	.0	2.4	-6.0	-.3	-3.1
CLE	45	8	30	1452[1]	1441	9.0	136	550	876	12.6	4.10	96	.261	.331	-6	-26	97	96	.979	130	145	.7	-2.5	-.7	-1.1	-5.7
MIL	38	6	25	1431	1461	9.2	136	566	719	13.0	4.33	94	.268	.341	-42	-40	100	97	.978	139	165	.3	-3.9	-7.1	-.5	-2.6
TOR	40	3	20	1428[1]	1538	9.7	152	623	771	13.8	4.57	92	.278	.354	-81	-57	103	102	.974	164	133	-1.2	-5.6	-11.3	-.5	-7.8
WEST																										
KC	41	15	**42**	1460[2]	**1377**	**8.5**	**110**	499	850	11.8	**3.52**	**115**	**.251**	.318	**88**	**84**	99	98	.978	137	145	.4	**8.4**	7.5	.7	4.2
TEX	49	**17**	31	1472[1]	1412	8.7	134	471	864	**11.7**	3.57	114	.255	**.317**	81	**84**	101	101	.982	117	156	1.5	**8.4**	2.6	.4	.2
CHI	34	3	40	1444[2]	1557	9.7	136	516	842	13.2	4.25	96	.277	.342	-31	-27	101	102	.974	159	125	-.9	-2.6	10.9	-.6	2.4
MIN	35	4	25	1442	1546	9.7	151	507	737	13.1	4.36	91	.278	.342	-48	-61	98	101	.978	143	184	-.0	-6.0	8.4	.0	1.3
CAL	53	13	26	1437[2]	1383	8.7	136	572	**965**	12.6	3.72	105	.256	.333	54	32	96	**106**	.976	147	137	-.2	3.2	-1.8	.4	-8.4
SEA	18	1	31	1433	1508	9.5	194	578	785	13.5	4.83	85	.272	.347	-123	-113	101	96	.976	147	162	-.2	-11.2	-8.4	.1	2.8
OAK	32	4	26	1436[2]	1459	9.2	145	560	788	12.8	4.05	100	.265	.336	3	-3	99	102	.970	190	136	-2.7	-.2	-13.5	**.8**	-1.8
TOT	586	117	416	20224		9.2				12.6	4.06		.267	.333					.978	1986	2143					

Runs
Carew-Min 128
Fisk-Bos 106
Brett-KC 105

Hits
Carew-Min 239
LeFlore-Det 212
Rice-Bos 206
Bostock-Min 199
Burleson-Bos 194

Doubles
McRae-KC 54
Jackson-NY 39
Lemon-Chi 38
Carew-Min 38

Triples
Carew-Min 16
Rice-Bos 15
Cowens-KC 14
Brett-KC 13
Bostock-Min 12

Home Runs
Rice-Bos 39
Nettles-NY 37
Bonds-Cal 37
Scott-Bos 33
Jackson-NY 32

Total Bases
Rice-Bos 382
Carew-Min 351
McRae-KC 330
Cowens-KC 318
LeFlore-Det 310

Runs Batted In
Hisle-Min 119
Bonds-Cal 115
Rice-Bos 114
Hobson-Bos 112
Cowens-KC 112

Runs Produced
Carew-Min 214
Cowens-KC 187
Hisle-Min 186
Fisk-Bos 182
Bonds-Cal 181

Bases On Balls
Harrah-Tex 109
Singleton-Bal 107
Hargrove-Tex 103
Gross-Oak 86
Mayberry-KC 83

Batting Average
Carew-Min .388
Bostock-Min .336
Singleton-Bal .328
Rivers-NY .326
LeFlore-Det .325

On-Base Percentage
Carew-Min .452
Singleton-Bal .442
Hargrove-Tex .424
Fisk-Bos .408
Page-Oak .407

Slugging Average
Rice-Bos .593
Carew-Min .570
Jackson-NY .550
Hisle-Min .533
Brett-KC .532

On-Base Plus Slugging
Carew-Min 1022
Rice-Bos 972
Singleton-Bal 949
Fisk-Bos 929
Page-Oak 928

Adjusted OPS
Carew-Min 179
Singleton-Bal 168
Page-Oak 153
Jackson-NY 151
Thornton-Cle 149

Batter Runs
Carew-Min 67.0
Rice-Bos 51.4
Singleton-Bal 48.5
Fisk-Bos 39.9
Hargrove-Tex 37.8

Adjusted Batter Runs
Carew-Min 69.3
Singleton-Bal 56.8
Page-Oak 39.0
Bostock-Min 37.6
Rice-Bos 37.2

Clutch Hitting Index
Wynegar-Min 130
Doyle-Bos 128
Sundberg-Tex 128
Carty-Cle 123
Staub-Det 116

Runs Created
Carew-Min 160
Rice-Bos 136
Singleton-Bal 124
McRae-KC 119
Page-Oak 117

Total Average
Carew-Min 1.093
Page-Oak 1.064
Singleton-Bal 1.011
Jackson-NY .997
Harrah-Tex .964

Stolen Bases
Patek-KC 53
Page-Oak 42
Remy-Cal 41
Bonds-Cal 41
LeFlore-Det 39

Stolen Base Average
Page-Oak 89.4
Jackson-NY 85.0
Harrah-Tex 84.4
White-KC 82.1
Patek-KC 80.3

Stolen Base Runs
Page-Oak 7.5
Patek-KC 7.1
Harrah-Tex 4.2
White-KC 3.3
Remy-Cal 3.1

Fielding Runs
Lemon-Chi 34.9
Sundberg-Tex 22.9
R.Jones-Sea 22.0
Belanger-Bal 20.7
Smalley-Min 18.7

Total Player Rating
Carew-Min 6.4
Singleton-Bal 4.8
Page-Oak 4.6
Brett-KC 4.5
Lemon-Chi 4.5

Wins
Palmer-Bal 20
Leonard-KC 20
Goltz-Min 20
Ryan-Cal 19

Win Percentage
Splittorff-KC .727
T.Johnson-Min .696
Guidry-NY .696
Rozema-Det .682

Games
Lyle-NY 72
T.Johnson-Min 71
Campbell-Bos 69
McClure-Mil 68
LaGrow-Chi 66

Complete Games
Ryan-Cal 22
Palmer-Bal 22
Leonard-KC 21
Garland-Cle 21
Tanana-Cal 20

Shutouts
Tanana-Cal 7
Leonard-KC 5
Guidry-NY 5
Blyleven-Tex 5

Saves
Campbell-Bos 31
Lyle-NY 26
LaGrow-Chi 25
Kern-Cle 18
LaRoche-Cle-Cal 17

Innings Pitched
Palmer-Bal 319.0
Goltz-Min 303.0
Ryan-Cal 299.0
Leonard-KC 292.2
Garland-Cle 282.2

Fewest Hits/Game
Ryan-Cal 5.96
Blyleven-Tex 6.94
Palmer-Bal 7.42
Guidry-NY 7.43
Tanana-Cal 7.50

Fewest BB/Game
Rozema-Det 1.40
Jenkins-Bos 1.68
Hartzell-Cal 1.81
Eckersley-Cle 1.96
Cleveland-Bos 2.03

Strikeouts
Ryan-Cal 341
Leonard-KC 244
Tanana-Cal 205
Palmer-Bal 193
Eckersley-Cle 191

Strikeouts/Game
Ryan-Cal 10.26
Tanana-Cal 7.65
Guidry-NY 7.52
Leonard-KC 7.50
Blyleven-Tex 6.98

Ratio
Blyleven-Tex 9.86
Eckersley-Cle 10.01
Guidry-NY 10.21
Tanana-Cal 10.22
Leonard-KC 10.24

Earned Run Average
Tanana-Cal 2.54
Blyleven-Tex 2.72
Ryan-Cal 2.77
Guidry-NY 2.82
Palmer-Bal 2.91

Adjusted ERA
Tanana-Cal 155
Blyleven-Tex 150
Ryan-Cal 142
Guidry-NY 140
Rozema-Det 139

Opponents' Batting Avg.
Ryan-Cal .193
Blyleven-Tex .214
Guidry-NY .224
Tanana-Cal .227
Leonard-KC .227

Opponents' On-Base Pct.
Eckersley-Cle .278
Blyleven-Tex .279
Guidry-NY .284
Leonard-KC .285
Tanana-Cal .286

Starter Runs
Ryan-Cal 43.3
Palmer-Bal 41.4
Tanana-Cal 41.2
Blyleven-Tex 35.2
Leonard-KC 33.5

Adjusted Starter Runs
Ryan-Cal 39.9
Tanana-Cal 38.7
Blyleven-Tex 35.6
Palmer-Bal 34.1
Leonard-KC 32.9

Clutch Pitching Index
Slaton-Mil 118
Rozema-Det 116
Grimsley-Bal 110
Splittorff-KC 108
Tanana-Cal 107

Relief Runs
Lyle-NY 29.0
Torrealba-Oak 18.8
LaGrow-Chi 17.7
Campbell-Bos 17.4
Coleman-Oak 15.8

Adjusted Relief Runs
Lyle-NY 28.0
Campbell-Bos 21.8
Torrealba-Oak 18.5
LaGrow-Chi 17.8
Romo-Sea 16.2

Relief Ranking
Lyle-NY 45.1
Campbell-Bos 41.6
Romo-Sea 28.1
LaGrow-Chi 26.4
T.Johnson-Min 23.6

Total Pitcher Index
Lyle-NY 4.6
Ryan-Cal 4.5
Campbell-Bos 4.4
Tanana-Cal 3.8
Blyleven-Tex 3.8

Total Baseball Ranking
Carew-Min 6.4
Singleton-Bal 4.8
Page-Oak 4.6
Lyle-NY 4.6
Brett-KC 4.5

TEAM	G	W	L	PCT	GB	R	OR	AB	H	2B	3B	HR	BB	SO	AVG	OBP	SLG	OPS	OPS+	BR	BR+	PF	CHI	RC	SB	CS	SBA	SBR
EAST																												
PHI	162	90	72	.556		708	586	5448	1404	248	32	133	552	866	.258	.331	.388	719	106	49	43	101	101	715	152	58	72	13
PIT	161	88	73	.547	1.5	684	637	5406	1390	239	**54**	115	480	874	.257	.323	.385	708	100	21	-7	105	104	676	**213**	90	70	15
CHI	162	79	83	.488	11	664	724	5532	**1461**	224	48	72	562	746	**.264**	.334	.361	695	90	11	-62	112	99	673	110	58	65	4
MON	162	76	86	.469	14	633	611	5530	1404	269	31	121	396	881	.254	.308	.379	687	98	-27	-20	99	103	629	80	42	66	3
STL	162	69	93	.426	21	600	657	5415	1351	263	44	79	420	**713**	.249	.306	.358	664	92	-66	-57	99	**106**	583	97	42	70	7
NY	162	66	96	.407	24	607	690	5433	1332	227	47	86	549	829	.245	.317	.352	669	96	-47	-25	96	101	600	100	77	56	-5
WEST																												
LA	162	95	67	.586		**727**	**573**	5437	1435	251	27	**149**	610	818	**.264**	**.340**	**.402**	**742**	**114**	**98**	**101**	100	96	**763**	137	52	72	12
CIN	161	92	69	.571	2.5	710	688	5392	1378	**270**	32	136	**636**	899	.256	.337	.393	730	110	75	75	100	97	730	137	58	70	10
SF	162	89	73	.549	6	613	594	5364	1331	240	41	117	554	814	.248	.320	.374	694	104	-1	25	96	95	647	87	54	62	0
SD	162	84	78	.519	11	591	598	5360	1349	208	42	75	536	848	.252	.323	.348	671	102	-37	14	92	98	624	152	70	68	9
HOU	162	74	88	.457	21	605	634	5458	1408	231	45	70	434	743	.258	.315	.355	670	101	-49	-1	93	103	608	178	59	**75**	**19**
ATL	162	69	93	.426	26	600	750	5381	1313	191	39	123	550	874	.244	.317	.363	680	86	-28	-90	111	98	608	90	65	58	-3
TOT	971					7742		65156	16556	2861	482	1276	6279	9905	.255	.323	.372	694							1533	725	68	84

TEAM	CG	SH	SV	IP	H	H/G	HR	BB	SO	RAT	ERA	ERA+	OAV	OOB	PR	PR+	PF	CPI	FA	E	DP	FW	PW	BW	SBW	DIF
EAST																										
PHI	38	9	29	1436^1	1343	8.5	118	**393**	813	**11.1**	3.34	107	.251	**.305**	39	37	100	100	**.983**	**104**	156	**2.0**	4.0	4.6	.6	-2.1
PIT	30	13	44	1444^2	1366	8.6	103	499	880	11.9	3.42	108	.249	.315	26	44	104	99	.973	167	133	-1.4	4.7	-.7	.9	4.2
CHI	24	7	38	1455^1	1475	9.2	125	539	768	12.7	4.06	99	.265	.333	-77	-4	113	98	.978	144	154	-.1	-.4	-6.5	-.3	5.5
MON	42	13	32	1446	1332	8.3	117	572	740	12.1	3.43	103	.249	.325	24	16	99	**106**	.979	134	150	.4	1.7	-2.1	-.4	-4.5
STL	32	13	22	1437^2	**1300**	**8.2**	94	600	859	12.1	3.59	98	**.245**	.326	-1	-11	98	97	.978	136	155	.3	-1.1	-6.0	.0	-5.0
NY	21	7	26	1455^1	1447	9.0	114	531	775	12.5	3.88	90	.265	.334	-48	-64	98	102	.979	132	160	.5	-6.7	-2.6	-1.3	-4.8
WEST																										
LA	46	16	38	1440^1	1362	8.6	107	440	800	11.5	**3.12**	**112**	.250	.309	**73**	**63**	98	**106**	.978	140	138	.1	**6.7**	**10.7**	.5	-3.9
CIN	16	10	46	1448^1	1437	9.0	122	567	908	12.6	3.81	93	.261	.332	-38	-43	99	102	.978	134	120	.4	-4.5	8.0	.3	7.5
SF	42	**17**	29	1455	1377	8.6	84	453	840	11.5	3.31	104	.252	.311	44	24	96	98	.977	146	118	-.2	2.6	2.7	-.7	3.9
SD	21	10	**55**	1433^2	1385	8.7	**74**	483	744	11.9	3.28	101	.257	.320	47	8	93	104	.975	160	**171**	-1.0	.9	1.5	.2	1.5
HOU	**48**	**17**	23	1440^1	1328	8.3	86	578	**930**	12.2	3.64	91	.247	.323	-9	-56	93	94	.978	133	109	.5	-5.9	-.0	**1.3**	-2.6
ATL	29	12	32	1440^1	1404	8.8	132	624	848	13.0	4.09	99	.257	.337	-81	-5	113	98	.975	153	126	-.6	-.5	-9.5	-1.1	-.2
TOT	389	144	414	17333^1		8.6				12.1	3.58		.255	.323					.978	1683	1690					

Runs
DeJesus-Chi....... 104
Rose-Cin.......... 103
Parker-Pit........ 102
Foster-Cin........ 97
Moreno-Pit........ 95

Hits
Garvey-LA......... 202
Rose-Cin.......... 198
Cabell-Hou........ 195
Parker-Pit........ 194
Bowa-Phi.......... 192

Doubles
Rose-Cin.......... 51
Clark-SF.......... 46
Simmons-StL....... 40
Parrish-Mon....... 39
Perez-Mon......... 38

Triples
Templeton-StL..... 13
Richards-SD....... 12
Parker-Pit........ 12

Home Runs
Foster-Cin........ 40
Luzinski-Phi...... 35
Parker-Pit........ 30
Smith-LA.......... 29

Total Bases
Parker-Pit........ 340
Foster-Cin........ 330
Garvey-LA......... 319
Clark-SF.......... 318
Winfield-SD....... 293

Runs Batted In
Foster-Cin........ 120
Parker-Pit........ 117
Garvey-LA......... 113
Luzinski-Phi...... 101
Clark-SF.......... 98

Runs Produced
Parker-Pit........ 189
Garvey-LA......... 181
Foster-Cin........ 177
Clark-SF.......... 163
Winfield-SD....... 161

Bases On Balls
Burroughs-Atl..... 117
Evans-SF.......... 105
Tenace-SD......... 101
Luzinski-Phi...... 100
Cey-LA............ 96

Batting Average
Parker-Pit........ .334
Garvey-LA......... .316
Cruz-Hou.......... .315
Madlock-SF........ .309
Winfield-SD....... .308

On-Base Percentage
Burroughs-Atl..... .436
Parker-Pit........ .395
Tenace-SD......... .394
Smith-LA.......... .392
Luzinski-Phi...... .390

Slugging Average
Parker-Pit........ .585
Smith-LA.......... .559
Foster-Cin........ .546
Clark-SF.......... .537
Burroughs-Atl..... .529

On-Base Plus Slugging
Parker-Pit........ 981
Burroughs-Atl..... 965
Smith-LA.......... 951
Luzinski-Phi...... 916
Foster-Cin........ 909

Adjusted OPS
Smith-LA.......... 164
Parker-Pit........ 163
Clark-SF.......... 155
Winfield-SD....... 153
Luzinski-Phi...... 152

Batter Runs
Parker-Pit........ 52.9
Burroughs-Atl..... 50.1
Luzinski-Phi...... 40.9
Foster-Cin........ 39.2
Smith-LA.......... 37.8

Adjusted Batter Runs
Parker-Pit........ 47.7
Clark-SF.......... 40.1
Luzinski-Phi...... 39.9
Foster-Cin........ 39.2
Winfield-SD....... 39.0

Clutch Hitting Index
Morgan-Cin........ 134
Reitz-StL......... 126
Montanez-NY....... 119
Watson-Hou........ 118
B.Robinson-Pit.... 117

Runs Created
Parker-Pit........ 134
Burroughs-Atl..... 116
Foster-Cin........ 115
Luzinski-Phi...... 114
Clark-SF.......... 109

Total Average
Burroughs-Atl..... 1.042
Parker-Pit........ 1.025
Smith-LA.......... 1.009
Luzinski-Phi...... .957
Foster-Cin........ .893

Stolen Bases
Moreno-Pit........ 71
Taveras-Pit....... 46
Lopes-LA.......... 45
DeJesus-Chi....... 41
Smith-SD.......... 40

Stolen Base Average
Cedeno-Hou........ 92.0
Lopes-LA.......... 91.8
McBride-Phi....... 90.3
Sexton-Hou........ 88.9
Bowa-Phi.......... 84.4

Stolen Base Runs
Lopes-LA.......... 8.5
Moreno-Pit........ 7.9
McBride-Phi....... 5.1
Cruz-Hou.......... 5.0
DeJesus-Chi....... 4.8

Fielding Runs
Trillo-Chi........ 28.9
Smith-SD.......... 25.6
Cromartie-Mon..... 24.7
Templeton-StL..... 22.9
Dawson-Mon........ 21.1

Total Player Rating
Parker-Pit........ 5.1
Clark-SF.......... 4.7
Foster-Cin........ 4.1
Simmons-StL....... 3.6
Templeton-StL..... 3.5

Wins
Perry-SD.......... 21
Grimsley-Mon...... 20
Niekro-Atl........ 19
Hooton-LA......... 19

Win Percentage
Perry-SD.......... .778
Hooton-LA......... .655
Grimsley-Mon...... .645
Blue-SF........... .643
John-LA........... .630

Games
Tekulve-Pit....... 91
Littell-StL....... 72
Moore-Chi......... 71
Moffitt-SF........ 70
Bair-Cin.......... 70

Complete Games
Niekro-Atl........ 22
Grimsley-Mon...... 19
Richard-Hou....... 16
Knepper-SF........ 16

Shutouts
Knepper-SF........ 6
Niekro-Atl........ 4
Halicki-SF........ 4
Blyleven-Pit...... 4
Blue-SF........... 4

Saves
Fingers-SD........ 37
Tekulve-Pit....... 31
Bair-Cin.......... 28
Sutter-Chi........ 27
Garber-Phi-Atl.... 25

Innings Pitched
Niekro-Atl........ 334.1
Richard-Hou....... 275.1
Grimsley-Mon...... 263.0
Perry-SD.......... 260.2
Knepper-SF........ 260.0

Fewest Hits/Game
Richard-Hou....... 6.28
Swan-NY........... 7.12
Hooton-LA......... 7.47
Halicki-SF........ 7.51
Knepper-SF........ 7.55

Fewest BB/Game
Christenson-Phi... 1.86
Barr-SF........... 1.93
R.Reuschel-Chi.... 2.00
Halicki-SF........ 2.04
Sutton-LA......... 2.04

Strikeouts
Richard-Hou....... 303
Niekro-Atl........ 248
Seaver-Cin........ 226
Blyleven-Pit...... 182
Montefusco-SF..... 177

Strikeouts/Game
Richard-Hou....... 9.90
Seaver-Cin........ 7.83
Vuckovich-StL..... 6.76
Blyleven-Pit...... 6.72
Niekro-Atl........ 6.68

Ratio
Swan-NY........... 9.72
Hooton-LA......... 9.80
Halicki-SF........ 9.86
Christenson-Phi... 10.14
Rogers-Mon........ 10.36

Earned Run Average
Swan-NY........... 2.43
Rogers-Mon........ 2.47
Vuckovich-StL..... 2.54
Knepper-SF........ 2.63
Hooton-LA......... 2.71

Adjusted ERA
Swan-NY........... 144
Rogers-Mon........ 143
Niekro-Atl........ 141
Vuckovich-StL..... 139
Knepper-SF........ 131

Opponents' Batting Avg.
Richard-Hou....... .196
Swan-NY........... .219
Halicki-SF........ .221
Hooton-LA......... .226
Seaver-Cin........ .227

Opponents' On-Base Pct.
Halicki-SF........ .271
Swan-NY........... .277
Hooton-LA......... .277
Christenson-Phi... .284
D.Robinson-Pit.... .286

Starter Runs
Knepper-SF........ 27.4
Rogers-Mon........ 27.1
Swan-NY........... 26.5
Niekro-Atl........ 26.0
Perry-SD.......... 24.7

Adjusted Starter Runs
Niekro-Atl........ 38.5
Rogers-Mon........ 26.2
Swan-NY........... 25.1
Knepper-SF........ 24.6
Vuckovich-StL..... 21.9

Clutch Pitching Index
Rau-LA............ 135
Vuckovich-StL..... 124
Carlton-Phi....... 121
Jones-SD.......... 114
Rogers-Mon........ 113

Relief Runs
Tekulve-Pit....... 18.8
Garber-Phi-Atl.... 18.5
Bair-Cin.......... 17.9
Reed-Phi.......... 16.2
D'Acquisto-SD..... 15.0

Adjusted Relief Runs
Garber-Phi-Atl.... 20.8
Tekulve-Pit....... 20.0
Bair-Cin.......... 17.7
Reed-Phi.......... 16.2
D'Acquisto-SD..... 13.3

Relief Ranking
Bair-Cin.......... 31.1
Tekulve-Pit....... 29.7
Garber-Phi-Atl.... 27.0
Forster-LA........ 22.9
Fingers-SD........ 20.9

Total Pitcher Index
Niekro-Atl........ 5.1
Tekulve-Pit....... 3.4
Carlton-Phi....... 3.3
Bair-Cin.......... 3.3
Garber-Phi-Atl.... 2.9

Total Baseball Ranking
Parker-Pit........ 5.1
Niekro-Atl........ 5.1
Clark-SF.......... 4.7
Foster-Cin........ 4.1
Simmons-StL....... 3.6

TEAM	G	W	L	PCT	GB	R	OR	AB	H	2B	3B	HR	BB	SO	AVG	OBP	SLG	OPS	OPS+	BR	BR+	PF	CHI	RC	SB	CS	SBA	SBR
EAST																												
NY	163	100	63	.613		735	**582**	5583	1489	228	38	125	505	695	.267	.332	.388	720	105	14	31	98	**105**	720	98	42	70	7
BOS	163	99	64	.607	1	796	657	5587	1493	270	46	172	582	835	.267	.339	.424	763	102	96	19	111	100	793	74	51	59	-2
MIL	162	93	69	.574	6.5	**804**	650	5536	**1530**	265	38	**173**	520	805	**.276**	**.342**	**.432**	**774**	**116**	**114**	**112**	100	100	**822**	95	53	64	2
BAL	161	90	71	.559	9	659	633	5422	1397	248	19	154	552	864	.258	.329	.396	725	110	18	64	94	95	691	75	61	55	-5
DET	162	86	76	.531	13.5	714	653	5601	1520	218	34	129	563	695	.271	.341	.392	733	103	45	24	103	96	748	90	38	70	7
CLE	159	69	90	.434	29	639	694	5365	1400	223	45	106	488	698	.261	.326	.379	705	99	-19	-11	99	99	649	64	63	50	-8
TOR	161	59	102	.366	40	590	775	5430	1358	217	39	98	448	645	.250	.310	.359	669	86	-93	-104	102	103	587	28	52	35	-12
WEST																												
KC	162	92	70	.568		743	634	5474	1469	**305**	**59**	98	498	644	.268	.333	.399	732	102	34	16	103	104	739	**216**	84	**72**	**18**
TEX	162	87	75	.537	5	692	632	5347	1353	216	36	132	**624**	779	.253	.335	.381	716	101	11	10	100	100	696	196	91	68	11
CAL	162	87	75	.537	5	691	666	5472	1417	226	28	108	539	682	.259	.333	.370	703	101	-14	13	96	103	669	86	69	55	-5
MIN	162	73	89	.451	19	666	678	5522	1472	259	47	82	604	684	.267	**.342**	.375	717	99	21	8	102	92	715	99	56	64	2
CHI	161	71	90	.441	25.5	634	731	5393	1423	221	41	106	409	**625**	.264	.320	.379	699	95	-35	-41	101	102	635	83	68	55	-6
OAK	162	69	93	.426	28	532	690	5321	1304	200	31	100	433	800	.245	.305	.351	656	89	-117	-87	95	99	552	144	117	55	-9
SEA	160	56	104	.350	40	614	834	5358	1327	229	37	97	522	702	.248	.317	.359	676	91	-73	-69	99	103	620	123	47	**72**	11
TOT	1131					9509		76411	19952	3325	538	1680	7287	10153	.262	.329	.385	714							1471	892	62	11

TEAM	CG	SH	SV	IP	H	H/G	HR	BB	SO	RAT	ERA	ERA+	OAV	OOB	PR	PR+	PF	CPI	FA	E	DP	FW	PW	BW	SBW	DIF
EAST																										
NY	39	16	**36**	1460^2	**1321**	**8.2**	111	478	817	**11.3**	**3.18**	114	**.243**	**.308**	**95**	74	96	100	**.982**	113	134	1.6	7.7	3.2	.6	5.6
BOS	57	15	26	1472^2	1530	9.4	137	464	706	12.4	3.54	**116**	.270	.329	37	**86**	109	**111**	.977	146	171	-.3	**8.9**	2.0	-.3	7.4
MIL	62	**19**	24	1436	1442	9.1	109	**398**	577	11.8	3.66	103	.262	.316	17	17	100	96	.977	150	144	-.6	1.8	**11.6**	.1	-.7
BAL	**65**	16	33	1429	1340	8.5	107	509	754	11.8	3.57	98	.251	.318	32	-12	93	96	**.982**	**110**	166	**1.7**	-1.2	6.6	-.6	3.2
DET	60	12	21	1455^2	1441	9.0	135	503	684	12.3	3.65	106	.263	.329	20	35	103	106	.981	118	**177**	1.3	3.7	2.5	.6	-2.9
CLE	36	6	28	1407^1	1397	9.0	**100**	568	739	12.8	3.98	94	.261	.335	-33	-37	99	95	.980	123	142	.8	-3.8	-1.1	-.9	-5.4
TOR	35	5	23	1429^1	1529	9.7	149	614	758	13.7	4.54	86	.279	.353	-123	-94	104	101	.979	131	163	.5	-9.6	-10.7	-1.3	-.2
WEST																										
KC	53	14	33	1439	1350	8.5	108	478	657	11.7	3.44	111	.251	.316	52	60	102	98	.976	150	153	-.6	6.2	1.7	**1.8**	2.1
TEX	54	12	25	1456^1	1431	8.9	108	421	776	11.6	3.36	112	.259	.315	66	63	100	102	.976	153	140	-.7	6.5	1.1	1.0	-1.7
CAL	44	13	33	1455^2	1382	8.6	125	599	**892**	12.5	3.65	99	.253	.330	19	-7	96	102	.978	136	136	.2	-.7	1.4	-.6	5.9
MIN	48	9	26	1459^2	1468	9.1	102	520	703	12.5	3.70	103	.266	.333	11	20	102	103	.977	146	171	-.3	2.1	.9	.1	-10.6
CHI	38	9	33	1409^1	1380	8.9	128	586	710	12.9	4.22	90	.259	.337	-71	-64	101	94	.977	139	130	.0	-6.5	-4.2	-.7	2.1
OAK	26	11	29	1433^1	1401	8.8	106	582	750	12.7	3.63	100	.259	.333	22	3	97	104	.971	179	145	-2.2	.4	-8.9	-1.0	.0
SEA	28	4	20	1419^1	1540	9.8	155	567	630	13.7	4.68	81	.280	.352	-144	-135	101	98	.978	141	174	-.2	-13.9	-7.1	1.0	-3.8
TOT	645	161	390	20163^1		9.0				12.4	3.77		.262	.329					.978	1935	2146					

Runs
LeFlore-Det 126
Rice-Bos 121
Baylor-Cal 103
Thornton-Cle 97
Hisle-Mil 96

Hits
Rice-Bos 213
LeFlore-Det 198
Carew-Min 188
Munson-NY 183
Staub-Det 175

Doubles
Brett-KC 45
McRae-KC 39
Fisk-Bos 39
DeCinces-Bal 37
Ford-Min 36

Triples
Rice-Bos 15
Ford-Min 10
Carew-Min 10
Yount-Mil 9
Garr-Chi 9

Home Runs
Rice-Bos 46
Hisle-Mil 34
Baylor-Cal 34
Thornton-Cle 33
Thomas-Mil 32

Total Bases
Rice-Bos 406
Murray-Bal 293
Staub-Det 279
Baylor-Cal 279
Thompson-Det 278

Runs Batted In
Rice-Bos 139
Staub-Det 121
Hisle-Mil 115
Thornton-Cle 105

Runs Produced
Rice-Bos 214
Hisle-Mil 177
LeFlore-Det 176
Staub-Det 172
Thornton-Cle 169

Bases On Balls
Hargrove-Tex 107
Singleton-Bal 98
Kemp-Det 97
Thornton-Cle 93
Smalley-Min 85

Batting Average
Carew-Min .333
Oliver-Tex .324
Rice-Bos .315
Piniella-NY .314
Oglivie-Mil .303

On-Base Percentage
Carew-Min .415
Singleton-Bal .410
Hargrove-Tex .391
Otis-KC .387
Randolph-NY .385

Slugging Average
Rice-Bos .600
Hisle-Mil .533
DeCinces-Bal .526
Otis-KC .525
Thornton-Cle .516

On-Base Plus Slugging
Rice-Bos 973
Otis-KC 911
Hisle-Mil 909
Thornton-Cle 898
Roberts-Sea 881

Adjusted OPS
Singleton-Bal 154
Rice-Bos 153
Hisle-Mil 153
Thornton-Cle 152
DeCinces-Bal 152

Batter Runs
Rice-Bos 58.7
Hisle-Mil 36.3
Thornton-Cle 35.6
Otis-KC 35.2
Singleton-Bal 34.0

Adjusted Batter Runs
Rice-Bos 45.0
Singleton-Bal 40.7
Thornton-Cle 36.8
Hisle-Mil 36.0
Murray-Bal 34.0

Clutch Hitting Index
Staub-Det 136
L.Johnson-Chi 127
Whitaker-Det 119
Chambliss-NY 117
Cowens-KC 116

Runs Created
Rice-Bos 147
LeFlore-Det 105
Carew-Min 105
Thompson-Det 104
Murray-Bal 104

Total Average
Rice-Bos .973
Otis-KC .972
Hisle-Mil .907
Singleton-Bal .900
Thornton-Cle .897

Stolen Bases
LeFlore-Det 68
Cruz-Sea 59
Wills-Tex 52
Dilone-Oak 50
Wilson-KC 46

Stolen Base Average
Cruz-Sea 85.5
Campaneris-Tex 84.6
Lowenstein-Tex 84.2
Randolph-NY 83.7
Rivers-NY 83.3

Stolen Base Runs
Cruz-Sea 9.5
LeFlore-Det 9.4
Wills-Tex 6.5
Wilson-KC 5.9
Randolph-NY 5.5

Fielding Runs
Belanger-Bal 33.8
Bell-Cle 28.3
Bosetti-Tor 25.1
Yount-Mil 21.9
Wills-Tex 21.3

Total Player Rating
Smalley-Min 5.2
Rice-Bos 4.9
Otis-KC 4.6
Yount-Mil 4.3
DeCinces-Bal 4.1

Wins
Guidry-NY 25
Caldwell-Mil 22
Palmer-Bal 21
Leonard-KC 21

Win Percentage
Guidry-NY .893
Stanley-Bos .882
Gura-KC .800
Eckersley-Bos .714
Caldwell-Mil .710

Games
Lacey-Oak 74
Heaverlo-Oak 69
Sosa-Oak 68
Gossage-NY 63

Complete Games
Caldwell-Mil 23
Leonard-KC 20
Palmer-Bal 19
Matlack-Tex 18

Shutouts
Guidry-NY 9
Palmer-Bal 6
Caldwell-Mil 6
Tiant-Bos 5

Saves
Gossage-NY 27
LaRoche-Cal 25
Stanhouse-Bal 24
Marshall-Min 21
Hrabosky-KC 20

Innings Pitched
Palmer-Bal 296.0
Leonard-KC 294.2
Caldwell-Mil 293.1
Flanagan-Bal 281.1
Sorensen-Mil 280.2

Fewest Hits/Game
Guidry-NY 6.15
Ryan-Cal 7.02
Gura-KC 7.43
Palmer-Bal 7.48
Tiant-Bos 7.84

Fewest BB/Game
Jenkins-Tex 1.48
Sorensen-Mil 1.60
Caldwell-Mil 1.66
Matlack-Tex 1.70
Rozema-Det 1.76

Strikeouts
Ryan-Cal 260
Guidry-NY 248
Leonard-KC 183
Flanagan-Bal 167
Eckersley-Bos 162

Strikeouts/Game
Ryan-Cal 9.97
Guidry-NY 8.16
Kravec-Chi 6.83
Underwood-Tor 6.33
Knapp-Cal 6.02

Ratio
Guidry-NY 8.55
Caldwell-Mil 9.79
Jenkins-Tex 9.83
Gura-KC 10.03
Matlack-Tex 10.23

Earned Run Average
Guidry-NY 1.74
Matlack-Tex 2.27
Caldwell-Mil 2.36
Palmer-Bal 2.46
Goltz-Min 2.49

Adjusted ERA
Guidry-NY 209
Matlack-Tex 166
Caldwell-Mil 160
Goltz-Min 154
Palmer-Bal 143

Opponents' Batting Avg.
Guidry-NY .193
Ryan-Cal .220
Palmer-Bal .227
Gura-KC .229
Tiant-Bos .234

Opponents' On-Base Pct.
Guidry-NY .250
Caldwell-Mil .274
Jenkins-Tex .279
Matlack-Tex .284
Gura-KC .286

Starter Runs
Guidry-NY 61.9
Caldwell-Mil 46.1
Matlack-Tex 45.4
Palmer-Bal 43.3
Goltz-Min 31.5

Adjusted Starter Runs
Guidry-NY 59.8
Caldwell-Mil 46.1
Matlack-Tex 45.0
Palmer-Bal 37.1
Goltz-Min 32.4

Clutch Pitching Index
Lee-Bos 131
Zahn-Min 129
Goltz-Min 126
Gale-KC 115
Eckersley-Bos 115

Relief Runs
Gossage-NY 26.4
Stanley-Bos 18.5
Hiller-Det 14.8
Marshall-Min 14.6
Sosa-Oak 13.8

Adjusted Relief Runs
Gossage-NY 25.2
Stanley-Bos 22.0
Hiller-Det 15.4
Marshall-Min 15.0
Sosa-Oak 12.7

Relief Ranking
Gossage-NY 46.9
Marshall-Min 29.9
Stanley-Bos 27.2
Hiller-Det 25.1
LaRoche-Cal 17.8

Total Pitcher Index
Guidry-NY 6.5
Caldwell-Mil 5.0
Gossage-NY 4.9
Matlack-Tex 4.8
Palmer-Bal 4.2

Total Baseball Ranking
Guidry-NY 6.5
Smalley-Min 5.2
Caldwell-Mil 5.0
Gossage-NY 4.9
Rice-Bos 4.9

TEAM	G	W	L	PCT	GB	R	OR	AB	H	2B	3B	HR	BB	SO	AVG	OBP	SLG	OPS	OPS+	BR	BR+	PF	CHI	RC	SB	CS	SBA	SBR
EAST																												
PIT	163	98	64	.605		**775**	643	5661	1541	264	52	148	483	855	.272	.333	**.416**	**749**	105	**68**	34	105	101	**781**	180	66	**73**	**17**
MON	160	95	65	.594	2	701	**581**	5465	1445	273	42	143	432	890	.264	.321	.408	729	105	23	29	99	102	701	121	56	68	7
STL	163	86	76	.531	12	731	693	5734	**1594**	**279**	**63**	100	460	838	**.278**	.335	.401	736	106	46	40	101	98	757	116	69	63	1
PHI	163	84	78	.519	14	683	718	5463	1453	250	53	119	602	764	.266	**.343**	.396	739	105	63	40	103	91	743	128	76	63	2
CHI	162	80	82	.494	18	706	707	5550	1494	250	43	135	478	762	.269	.331	.403	734	97	40	-23	110	98	726	73	52	58	-2
NY	163	63	99	.389	35	593	706	5591	1399	255	41	74	498	817	.250	.315	.350	665	90	-90	-67	96	99	615	135	79	63	2
WEST																												
CIN	161	90	71	.559		731	644	5477	1445	266	31	132	**614**	902	.264	.340	.396	736	106	55	51	101	99	741	99	47	68	5
HOU	162	89	73	.549	1.5	583	582	5394	1382	224	52	49	461	**745**	.256	.317	.344	661	91	-93	-58	94	102	591	**190**	95	67	9
LA	162	79	83	.488	11.5	739	717	5490	1443	220	24	**183**	556	834	.263	.333	.412	745	**111**	62	**73**	99	99	743	106	46	70	7
SF	162	71	91	.438	19.5	672	751	5395	1328	192	36	125	580	925	.246	.322	.365	687	100	-46	0	93	**106**	644	140	73	66	5
SD	161	68	93	.422	22	603	681	5446	1316	193	53	93	534	770	.242	.313	.348	661	91	-97	-60	94	103	600	100	58	63	2
ATL	160	66	94	.413	23.5	669	763	5422	1389	220	28	126	490	818	.256	.320	.377	697	89	-31	-75	107	105	654	98	50	66	4
TOT	971					8186		66088	17229	2886	518	1427	6188	9920	.261	.328	.385	712							1486	767	66	58

TEAM	CG	SH	SV	IP	H	H/G	HR	BB	SO	RAT	ERA	ERA+	OAV	OOB	PR	PR+	PF	CPI	FA	E	DP	FW	PW	BW	SBW	DIF
EAST																										
PIT	24	7	**52**	1493[1]	1424	8.6	125	504	904	11.9	3.42	114	.254	.318	53	74	104	103	.979	134	163	.5	7.7	3.6	**1.3**	4.3
MON	33	18	39	1447[1]	1379	8.6	116	**450**	813	11.6	**3.15**	**117**	.253	.312	**95**	**86**	98	**108**	.979	131	123	.5	**8.9**	3.0	.2	2.5
STL	38	10	25	1486[2]	1449	8.8	127	501	788	12.0	3.73	101	.258	.321	1	6	101	98	.980	132	166	.6	.7	4.2	-.4	.2
PHI	33	14	29	1441[1]	1455	9.1	135	477	787	12.3	4.16	92	.266	.328	-69	-52	103	94	**.983**	**106**	148	**2.1**	-5.3	4.2	-.3	2.5
CHI	20	11	44	1446[2]	1500	9.4	127	521	**933**	12.9	3.89	106	.270	.338	-24	34	110	105	.975	159	163	-1.1	3.6	-2.3	-.7	-.2
NY	16	10	36	1482[2]	1486	9.1	120	607	819	12.9	3.85	95	.266	.341	-18	-35	98	105	.978	140	**168**	.0	-3.6	-6.9	-.3	-7.2
WEST																										
CIN	27	10	40	1440[1]	1415	8.9	103	485	773	12.0	3.59	104	.260	.322	24	24	100	100	.980	124	152	.9	2.5	5.3	.0	.9
HOU	**55**	**19**	31	1447[2]	**1278**	**8.0**	**90**	504	854	**11.3**	3.20	110	**.237**	**.306**	86	54	94	93	.978	138	146	.2	5.6	-5.9	.4	7.9
LA	30	6	34	1444	1425	8.9	101	555	811	12.6	3.83	95	.260	.331	-15	-32	97	97	.981	118	123	1.4	-3.3	**7.6**	.2	-7.7
SF	25	6	34	1436	1484	9.4	143	577	880	13.1	4.17	84	.269	.341	-69	-114	94	101	.974	163	138	-1.3	-11.7	.0	.0	3.2
SD	29	7	25	1453	1438	9.0	108	513	779	12.3	3.70	96	.263	.328	6	-28	95	101	.978	141	154	-.0	-2.8	-6.1	-.3	-3.0
ATL	32	3	34	1407[2]	1496	9.6	132	494	779	13.1	4.19	97	.272	.337	-70	-19	109	99	.970	183	139	-2.6	-1.9	-7.7	-.0	-1.5
TOT	362	121	423	17426[2]		8.9				12.3	3.74		.261	.328					.978	1669	1783					

Runs
Hernandez-StL 116
Moreno-Pit 110
Schmidt-Phi 109
Parker-Pit 109
Lopes-LA 109

Hits
Templeton-StL 211
Hernandez-StL 210
Rose-Phi 208
Garvey-LA 204
Moreno-Pit 196

Doubles
Hernandez-StL 48
Cromartie-Mon 46
Parker-Pit 45
Reitz-StL 41
Rose-Phi 40

Triples
Templeton-StL 19
Moreno-Pit 12
McBride-Phi 12
Dawson-Mon 12

Home Runs
Kingman-Chi 48
Schmidt-Phi 45
Winfield-SD 34
Horner-Atl 33
Stargell-Pit 32

Total Bases
Winfield-SD 333
Parker-Pit 327
Kingman-Chi 326
Garvey-LA 322
Matthews-Atl 317

Runs Batted In
Winfield-SD 118
Kingman-Chi 115
Schmidt-Phi 114
Garvey-LA 110
Hernandez-StL 105

Runs Produced
Hernandez-StL 210
Winfield-SD 181
Schmidt-Phi 178
Parker-Pit 178
Garvey-LA 174

Bases On Balls
Schmidt-Phi 120
Tenace-SD 105
Lopes-LA 97
North-SF 96
Rose-Phi 95

Batting Average
Hernandez-StL ...... .344
Rose-Phi .... .331
Knight-Cin .... .318
Garvey-LA .... .315
Horner-Atl .... .314

On-Base Percentage
Hernandez-StL .... .421
Rose-Phi .... .421
Tenace-SD .... .407
Mazzilli-NY .... .397
Winfield-SD .... .396

Slugging Average
Kingman-Chi .... .613
Schmidt-Phi .... .564
Foster-Cin .... .561
Winfield-SD .... .558
Horner-Atl .... .552

On-Base Plus Slugging
Kingman-Chi 960
Schmidt-Phi 955
Winfield-SD 954
Foster-Cin 950
Hernandez-StL 934

Adjusted OPS
Winfield-SD 167
Foster-Cin 155
Schmidt-Phi 153
Hernandez-StL 152
Parrish-Mon 146

Batter Runs
Winfield-SD 47.4
Hernandez-StL 47.1
Schmidt-Phi 44.9
Parker-Pit 39.3
Kingman-Chi 37.8

Adjusted Batter Runs
Winfield-SD 55.3
Hernandez-StL 46.1
Schmidt-Phi 41.2
Parker-Pit 34.0
Foster-Cin 33.1

Clutch Hitting Index
Foli-NY-Pit 140
Hebner-NY 137
Flynn-NY 124
Luzinski-Phi 122
Concepcion-Cin ... 114

Runs Created
Hernandez-StL 135
Winfield-SD 132
Parker-Pit 131
Schmidt-Phi 123
Matthews-Atl 118

Total Average
Schmidt-Phi 1.024
Winfield-SD .... .988
Kingman-Chi .... .972
Hernandez-StL ..... .961
Foster-Cin .... .959

Stolen Bases
Moreno-Pit 77
North-SF 58
Taveras-Pit-NY 44
Lopes-LA 44
Scott-Mon 39

Stolen Base Average
Lopes-LA 91.7
Parker-Pit 83.3
Morgan-Cin 82.4
Royster-Atl 81.4
Smith-SD 80.0

Stolen Base Runs
Moreno-Pit 9.6
Lopes-LA 8.3
Royster-Atl 4.9
Scott-Mon 4.4
North-SF 4.4

Fielding Runs
Maddox-Phi 26.9
Moreno-Pit 22.8
Evans-SF 22.4
Smith-SD 21.0
Cromartie-Mon 20.4

Total Player Rating
Winfield-SD 5.8
Schmidt-Phi 5.8
Hernandez-StL 5.6
Templeton-StL 4.6
Mazzilli-NY 4.2

Wins
Niekro-Atl 21
Niekro-Hou 21
Richard-Hou 18
Reuschel-Chi 18
Carlton-Phi 18

Win Percentage
Seaver-Cin .... .727
Niekro-Hou .... .656
Martinez-StL .... .652
Sutcliffe-LA .... .630
Carlton-Phi .... .621

Games
Tekulve-Pit 94
Romo-Pit 84
Jackson-Pit 72
Lavelle-SF 70
Garber-Atl 68

Complete Games
Niekro-Atl 23
Richard-Hou 19
Rogers-Mon 13
Carlton-Phi 13
Hooton-LA 12

Shutouts
Seaver-Cin 5
Rogers-Mon 5
Niekro-Hou 5
Richard-Hou 4
Carlton-Phi 4

Saves
Sutter-Chi 37
Tekulve-Pit 31
Garber-Atl 25
Sambito-Hou 22
Lavelle-SF 20

Innings Pitched
Niekro-Atl 342.0
Richard-Hou 292.1
Niekro-Hou 263.2
Jones-SD 263.0
Swan-NY 251.1

Fewest Hits/Game
Richard-Hou 6.77
Carlton-Phi 7.24
Niekro-Hou 7.54
Schatzeder-Mon ... 7.56
Andujar-Hou 7.79

Fewest BB/Game
Forsch-Hou 1.77
Candelaria-Pit 1.78
Hume-Cin 1.82
Lee-Mon 1.86
Swan-NY 2.04

Strikeouts
Richard-Hou 313
Carlton-Phi 213
Niekro-Atl 208
Blyleven-Pit 172
McGlothen-Chi 147

Strikeouts/Game
Richard-Hou 9.64
Carlton-Phi 7.64
Sanderson-Mon ... 7.39
Blyleven-Pit 6.52
Krukow-Chi 6.50

Ratio
Forsch-Hou 9.62
Richard-Hou 9.88
Seaver-Cin 10.38
Sutton-LA 10.47
Carlton-Phi 10.61

Earned Run Average
Richard-Hou 2.71
Hume-Cin 2.76
Schatzeder-Mon ... 2.83
Hooton-LA 2.97
Niekro-Hou 3.00

Adjusted ERA
Hume-Cin 135
Richard-Hou 130
Schatzeder-Mon ... 130
Hooton-LA 123
Rogers-Mon 122

Opponents' Batting Avg.
Richard-Hou .... .209
Carlton-Phi .... .219
Schatzeder-Mon ... .225
Niekro-Hou .... .228
Andujar-Hou .... .233

Opponents' On-Base Pct.
Forsch-Hou .... .275
Richard-Hou .... .278
Seaver-Cin .... .291
Sutton-LA .... .291
Carlton-Phi .... .292

Starter Runs
Richard-Hou 33.5
Niekro-Hou 21.6
Rogers-Mon 20.4
Fulgham-StL 19.7
Hooton-LA 18.1

Adjusted Starter Runs
Richard-Hou 28.0
Niekro-Atl 23.3
Fulgham-StL 20.0
Rogers-Mon 18.8
Hooton-LA 16.2

Clutch Pitching Index
Hume-Cin 117
Lamp-Chi 114
Lee-Mon 113
Kobel-NY 113
Blyleven-Pit 112

Relief Runs
Sambito-Hou 20.0
Sosa-Mon 19.2
Hume-Cin 17.7
Sutter-Chi 17.1
Minton-SF 17.1

Adjusted Relief Runs
Sutter-Chi 19.5
Sambito-Hou 18.8
Sosa-Mon 18.8
Hume-Cin 17.7
Tekulve-Pit 16.4

Relief Ranking
Sambito-Hou 37.2
Sutter-Chi 35.4
Sosa-Mon 33.5
Tekulve-Pit 27.5
Littell-StL 25.1

Total Pitcher Index
Sambito-Hou 4.3
Sutter-Chi 4.0
Sosa-Mon 3.4
Niekro-Atl 3.2
Tekulve-Pit 3.0

Total Baseball Ranking
Winfield-SD 5.8
Schmidt-Phi 5.8
Hernandez-StL 5.6
Templeton-StL 4.6
Sambito-Hou 4.3

TEAM	G	W	L	PCT	GB	R	OR	AB	H	2B	3B	HR	BB	SO	AVG	OBP	SLG	OPS	OPS+	BR	BR+	PF	CHI	RC	SB	CS	SBA	SBR
EAST																												
BAL	159	102	57	.642		757	**582**	5371	1401	258	24	181	608	847	.261	.339	.419	758	107	25	55	96	98	758	99	49	67	5
MIL	161	95	66	.590	8	807	722	5536	1552	291	41	185	549	745	.280	.347	.448	795	113	95	95	100	94	**850**	100	53	65	3
BOS	160	91	69	.569	11.5	841	711	5538	1567	**310**	34	**194**	512	708	**.283**	.347	**.456**	**803**	109	**108**	63	106	97	848	60	43	58	-2
NY	160	89	71	.556	13.5	734	672	5421	1443	226	40	150	509	**590**	.266	.331	.406	737	100	-21	-5	98	102	708	65	46	59	-2
DET	161	85	76	.528	18	770	738	5375	1446	221	35	164	575	814	.269	.342	.415	757	100	24	0	103	101	754	176	86	67	9
CLE	161	81	80	.503	22	760	805	5376	1388	206	29	138	**657**	786	.258	.344	.384	728	96	-21	-24	100	103	720	143	90	61	0
TOR	162	53	109	.327	50.5	613	862	5423	1362	253	34	95	448	663	.251	.313	.363	676	81	-142	-148	101	104	602	75	56	57	-3
WEST																												
CAL	162	88	74	.543		**866**	768	5550	1563	242	43	164	589	843	.282	**.354**	.429	783	**114**	83	**113**	97	101	842	100	53	65	3
KC	162	85	77	.525	3	851	816	5653	**1596**	286	**79**	116	528	675	.282	.347	.422	769	104	51	36	102	103	836	**207**	76	**73**	**19**
TEX	162	83	79	.512	5	750	698	5562	1549	252	26	140	461	607	.278	.337	.409	746	101	-1	8	99	99	750	79	51	61	0
MIN	162	82	80	.506	6	764	725	5544	1544	256	46	112	526	693	.278	.344	.402	746	96	7	-21	104	99	770	66	45	59	-1
CHI	160	73	87	.456	23	730	748	5463	1505	290	33	127	454	668	.275	.335	.410	745	100	-4	-4	100	99	726	97	62	61	0
SEA	162	67	95	.414	30	711	820	5544	1490	250	52	132	515	725	.269	.334	.404	738	96	-17	-29	102	96	733	126	52	71	10
OAK	162	54	108	.333	43	573	860	5348	1276	188	32	108	482	751	.239	.304	.346	650	79	-189	-158	95	**106**	552	104	69	60	-1
TOT	1128					10527		76704	20682	3529	548	2006	7413	10115	.270	.338	.409	746							1497	831	64	38

TEAM	CG	SH	SV	IP	H	H/G	HR	BB	SO	RAT	ERA	ERA+	OAV	OOB	PR	PR+	PF	CPI	FA	E	DP	FW	PW	BW	SBW	DIF
EAST																										
BAL	52	**12**	30	1434^{1}	**1279**	**8.1**	133	467	786	**11.1**	**3.27**	**123**	**.241**	**.304**	**152**	**125**	95	101	.980	125	161	.8	**12.2**	5.4	.2	4.0
MIL	**61**	**12**	23	1439^{2}	1563	9.8	162	**381**	580	12.3	4.04	103	.279	.327	29	22	99	105	.980	127	153	.8	2.2	9.3	.0	2.4
BOS	47	11	29	1431^{1}	1487	9.4	133	463	731	12.5	4.04	110	.270	.330	29	58	105	100	.977	142	166	-.1	5.7	6.2	-.5	-.1
NY	43	10	37	1432^{1}	1446	9.1	123	455	731	12.1	3.84	106	.268	.326	61	39	97	102	**.981**	122	183	1.0	3.9	-.4	-.5	5.2
DET	25	5	37	1423^{1}	1429	9.1	167	547	802	12.8	4.28	101	.265	.338	-9	8	103	101	**.981**	**120**	184	**1.2**	.8	.0	.6	2.0
CLE	28	7	32	1431^{2}	1502	9.5	138	570	781	13.2	4.58	93	.272	.343	-56	-50	101	95	.978	134	149	.4	-4.8	-2.3	-.3	7.7
TOR	44	7	11	1417	1537	9.8	165	594	613	13.8	4.83	90	.281	.356	-95	-73	103	100	.975	159	187	-1.0	-7.1	-14.4	-.6	-4.8
WEST																										
CAL	46	9	33	1436	1463	9.2	131	573	**820**	13.0	4.34	94	.267	.340	-19	-44	97	96	.978	135	172	.4	-4.2	**11.1**	.0	-.0
KC	42	7	27	1448^{1}	1477	9.2	165	536	640	12.7	4.45	96	.267	.335	-38	-30	101	96	.977	146	160	-.2	-2.9	3.6	**1.6**	2.2
TEX	26	10	**42**	1437	1371	8.6	135	532	773	12.1	3.87	107	.253	.323	56	46	98	97	.979	130	151	.7	4.5	.8	-.3	-3.6
MIN	31	6	33	1444^{1}	1590	10.0	128	452	721	12.9	4.14	106	.285	.340	14	38	104	**106**	.979	134	**203**	.4	3.8	-2.0	-.4	-.6
CHI	28	9	37	1409	1365	8.8	**114**	618	675	13.0	4.11	104	.256	.338	18	23	101	96	.972	173	142	-1.9	2.3	-.3	-.3	-6.6
SEA	37	7	26	1438	1567	9.9	165	571	736	13.6	4.58	95	.281	.351	-57	-33	103	103	.978	141	170	.0	-3.2	-2.8	.7	-8.6
OAK	41	4	20	1429^{1}	1606	10.2	147	654	726	14.6	4.75	85	.288	.367	-84	-117	96	**106**	.972	174	137	-1.8	-11.4	-15.4	-.4	2.1
TOT	551	116	417	20051^{2}		9.3				12.8	4.22		.270	.338					.978	1962	2318					

Runs
Baylor-Cal 120
Brett-KC 119
Rice-Bos 117
Lynn-Bos 116
Lansford-Cal 114

Hits
Brett-KC 212
Rice-Bos 201
Bell-Tex 200
Molitor-Mil 188
Lansford-Cal 188

Doubles
Lemon-Chi 44
Cooper-Mil 44
Lynn-Bos 42
Brett-KC 42
Bell-Tex 42

Triples
Brett-KC 20
Molitor-Mil 16
Wilson-KC 13
Randolph-NY 13

Home Runs
Thomas-Mil 45
Rice-Bos 39
Lynn-Bos 39
Baylor-Cal 36
Singleton-Bal 35

Total Bases
Rice-Bos 369
Brett-KC 363
Lynn-Bos 338
Baylor-Cal 333
Singleton-Bal 304

Runs Batted In
Baylor-Cal 139
Rice-Bos 130
Thomas-Mil 123
Lynn-Bos 122
Porter-KC 112

Runs Produced
Baylor-Cal 223
Rice-Bos 208
Brett-KC 203
Lynn-Bos 199
Porter-KC 193

Bases On Balls
Porter-KC 121
Singleton-Bal 109
Thomas-Mil 98
Randolph-NY 95
Thornton-Cle 90

Batting Average
Lynn-Bos .... .333
Brett-KC .... .329
Downing-Cal .... .326
Rice-Bos .... .325
Oliver-Tex .... .323

On-Base Percentage
Porter-KC .... .429
Lynn-Bos .... .426
Downing-Cal .... .420
Lezcano-Mil .... .420
Singleton-Bal ..... .409

Slugging Average
Lynn-Bos .... .637
Rice-Bos .... .596
Lezcano-Mil .... .573
Brett-KC .... .563
Jackson-NY .... .544

On-Base Plus Slugging
Lynn-Bos 1063
Lezcano-Mil 992
Rice-Bos 981
Kemp-Det 946
Singleton-Bal 942

Adjusted OPS
Lynn-Bos 173
Lezcano-Mil 165
Singleton-Bal 158
Rice-Bos 152
Jackson-NY 151

Batter Runs
Lynn-Bos 62.1
Rice-Bos 50.2
Lezcano-Mil 44.6
Singleton-Bal 44.4
Brett-KC 42.8

Adjusted Batter Runs
Lynn-Bos 54.9
Singleton-Bal 49.3
Lezcano-Mil 44.6
Rice-Bos 43.2
Baylor-Cal 40.9

Clutch Hitting Index
Porter-KC 123
Baylor-Cal 121
Sundberg-Tex 120
Cerone-Tor 117
Dauer-Bal 114

Runs Created
Lynn-Bos 147
Rice-Bos 138
Brett-KC 134
Singleton-Bal 127
Baylor-Cal 126

Total Average
Lynn-Bos 1.162
Lezcano-Mil 1.051
Rice-Bos .... .993
Singleton-Bal ..... .993
Porter-KC .... .982

Stolen Bases
Wilson-KC 83
LeFlore-Det 78
Cruz-Sea 49
Bumbry-Bal 37
Wills-Tex 35

Stolen Base Average
Wilson-KC 87.4
Otis-KC 85.7
LeFlore-Det 84.8
Cruz-Sea 84.5
Lowenstein-Bal 80.0

Stolen Base Runs
Wilson-KC 14.1
LeFlore-Det 12.3
Cruz-Sea 7.6
Otis-KC 4.8
Bumbry-Bal 3.9

Fielding Runs
Smalley-Min 33.1
Dent-NY 32.0
Mendoza-Sea 27.5
Burleson-Bos 21.7
Wilfong-Min 20.7

Total Player Rating
Lynn-Bos 5.7
Smalley-Min 5.6
Brett-KC 4.9
Grich-Cal 4.1
Porter-KC 4.0

Wins
Flanagan-Bal 23
John-NY 21
Koosman-Min 20
Guidry-NY 18

Win Percentage
Caldwell-Mil ...... .727
Flanagan-Bal ...... .719
Morris-Det .... .708
John-NY .... .700
Guidry-NY .... .692

Games
Marshall-Min 90
Monge-Cle 76
Kern-Tex 71
Lyle-Tex 67
Heaverlo-Oak 62

Complete Games
D.Martinez-Bal 18
Ryan-Cal 17
John-NY 17
Eckersley-Bos 17

Shutouts
Ryan-Cal 5
Leonard-KC 5
Flanagan-Bal 5
Stanley-Bos 4
Caldwell-Mil 4

Saves
Marshall-Min 32
Kern-Tex 29
Stanhouse-Bal 21
Lopez-Det 21
Monge-Cle 19

Innings Pitched
D.Martinez-Bal 292.1
John-NY 276.1
Flanagan-Bal 265.2
Koosman-Min 263.2
Jenkins-Tex 259.0

Fewest Hits/Game
Ryan-Cal 6.83
Kravec-Chi 7.49
Guidry-NY 7.73
Morris-Det 8.15
Baumgarten-Chi 8.26

Fewest BB/Game
McGregor-Bal 1.19
Caldwell-Mil 1.49
Sorensen-Mil 1.61
Stanley-Bos 1.83
John-NY 2.12

Strikeouts
Ryan-Cal 223
Guidry-NY 201
Flanagan-Bal 190
Jenkins-Tex 164
Koosman-Min 157

Strikeouts/Game
Ryan-Cal 9.01
Guidry-NY 7.65
Flanagan-Bal 6.44
Jenkins-Tex 5.70
Bannister-Sea 5.68

Ratio
McGregor-Bal 9.79
Guidry-NY 10.43
Flanagan-Bal 10.77
Leonard-KC 10.83
Eckersley-Bos 10.91

Earned Run Average
Guidry-NY 2.78
John-NY 2.96
Eckersley-Bos 2.99
Flanagan-Bal 3.08
Morris-Det 3.28

Adjusted ERA
Eckersley-Bos 148
Guidry-NY 147
John-NY 138
Morris-Det 132
Flanagan-Bal 131

Opponents' Batting Avg.
Ryan-Cal .... .212
Kravec-Chi .... .233
Guidry-NY .... .236
Baumgarten-Chi .... .243
Morris-Det .... .244

Opponents' On-Base Pct.
McGregor-Bal ...... .275
Guidry-NY .... .294
Flanagan-Bal ...... .297
Eckersley-Bos ..... .298
Leonard-KC .... .299

Starter Runs
John-NY 38.9
Guidry-NY 38.1
Eckersley-Bos 34.0
Flanagan-Bal 33.9
Koosman-Min 24.9

Adjusted Starter Runs
Eckersley-Bos 37.6
John-NY 35.7
Guidry-NY 35.5
Flanagan-Bal 29.2
Koosman-Min 28.7

Clutch Pitching Index
Eckersley-Bos 116
Keough-Oak 114
McCatty-Oak 114
Travers-Mil 114
Koosman-Min 113

Relief Runs
Kern-Tex 42.2
Monge-Cle 26.6
Lopez-Det 25.7
Marshall-Min 25.1
Stoddard-Bal 16.3

Adjusted Relief Runs
Kern-Tex 41.8
Monge-Cle 26.9
Marshall-Min 26.6
Lopez-Det 26.6
Burgmeier-Bos 15.9

Relief Ranking
Kern-Tex 66.5
Marshall-Min 53.3
Monge-Cle 49.4
Lopez-Det 38.1
Drago-Bos 25.7

Total Pitcher Index
Kern-Tex 6.8
Marshall-Min 5.6
Monge-Cle 5.0
Eckersley-Bos 3.9
Lopez-Det 3.8

Total Baseball Ranking
Kern-Tex 6.8
Lynn-Bos 5.7
Marshall-Min 5.6
Smalley-Min 5.6
Monge-Cle 5.0

TEAM	G	W	L	PCT	GB	R	OR	AB	H	2B	3B	HR	BB	SO	AVG	OBP	SLG	OPS	OPS+	BR	BR+	PF	CHI	RC	SB	CS	SBA	SBR
EAST																												
PHI	162	91	71	.562		728	639	5625	1517	272	54	117	472	**708**	.270	.330	**.400**	730	103	61	23	106	100	**736**	140	62	69	9
MON	162	90	72	.556	1	694	629	5465	1407	250	61	114	547	865	.257	.327	.388	715	105	36	35	100	101	709	237	82	74	23
PIT	162	83	79	.512	8	666	646	5517	1469	249	38	116	452	760	.266	.325	.388	713	102	27	17	102	98	686	209	102	67	10
STL	162	74	88	.457	17	**738**	710	5608	**1541**	**300**	49	101	451	781	**.275**	**.331**	**.400**	**731**	106	**63**	41	103	102	724	117	54	68	7
NY	162	67	95	.414	24	611	702	5478	1407	218	41	61	501	840	.257	.322	.345	667	95	-52	-35	97	102	601	158	99	61	0
CHI	162	64	98	.395	27	614	728	5619	1411	251	35	107	471	912	.251	.311	.365	676	88	-47	-89	107	100	627	93	64	59	-2
WEST																												
HOU	163	93	70	.571		637	**589**	5566	1455	231	**67**	75	540	755	.261	.328	.367	695	**109**	2	**59**	92	96	688	194	74	72	17
LA	163	92	71	.564	1	663	591	5568	1462	209	24	**148**	492	846	.263	.325	.388	713	106	29	42	98	96	699	123	72	63	2
CIN	163	89	73	.549	3.5	707	670	5516	1445	256	45	113	537	852	.262	.330	.386	716	105	39	39	100	101	716	156	43	**78**	19
ATL	161	81	80	.503	11	630	660	5402	1352	226	22	144	434	899	.250	.308	.380	688	94	-27	-46	103	**104**	616	73	52	58	-2
SF	161	75	86	.466	17	573	634	5368	1310	199	44	80	509	840	.244	.311	.342	653	90	-82	-69	98	102	571	100	58	63	2
SD	163	73	89	.451	19.5	591	654	5540	1410	195	43	67	**563**	791	.255	.326	.342	668	98	-48	-10	94	96	641	**239**	73	77	**27**
TOT	973					7852		66272	17186	2856	523	1243	5969	9849	.260	.323	.375	697							1839	835	69	112

TEAM	CG	SH	SV	IP	H	H/G	HR	BB	SO	RAT	ERA	ERA+	OAV	OOB	PR	PR+	PF	CPI	FA	E	DP	FW	PW	BW	SBW	DIF
EAST																										
PHI	25	8	40	1480	1419	8.7	87	530	889	12.0	3.43	**110**	.255	.322	28	**56**	105	100	.979	136	136	.3	**6.0**	2.5	-.0	1.5
MON	33	15	36	1456[2]	1447	9.0	100	460	823	12.0	3.48	102	.261	.320	20	14	99	102	.977	144	126	-.1	1.5	3.7	1.4	2.6
PIT	25	8	**43**	1458[1]	1422	8.8	110	**451**	832	11.8	3.58	102	.259	.318	4	10	101	99	.978	137	154	.2	1.1	1.8	.0	-1.1
STL	**34**	9	27	1447	1454	9.1	90	495	664	12.3	3.94	94	.265	.329	-53	-38	103	94	.981	122	**174**	1.0	-4.0	4.4	-.2	-8.0
NY	17	9	33	1451[1]	1473	9.2	140	510	886	12.5	3.86	92	.267	.331	-40	-49	99	104	.975	154	132	-.6	-5.1	-3.6	-1.0	-3.4
CHI	13	6	35	1479	1525	9.3	109	589	923	13.1	3.89	101	.272	.344	-47	4	109	**106**	.974	174	149	-1.7	.5	-9.4	-1.2	-5.0
WEST																										
HOU	31	18	41	1482[2]	1367	**8.3**	**69**	466	**929**	**11.3**	**3.11**	106	**.246**	**.307**	**82**	34	91	97	.978	140	145	.1	3.6	**6.3**	.8	.8
LA	24	**19**	42	1472[2]	**1358**	**8.3**	105	480	835	11.4	3.25	108	.247	.309	58	42	97	100	.981	123	149	1.0	4.5	4.5	-.8	1.5
CIN	30	12	37	1459[1]	1404	8.7	113	506	833	11.9	3.85	93	.255	.319	-40	-44	99	92	**.983**	**106**	144	**1.9**	-4.6	4.2	1.0	5.7
ATL	29	9	37	1428	1397	8.9	131	454	696	11.9	3.77	99	.258	.318	-27	-4	104	97	.975	162	156	-1.1	-.4	-4.8	-1.2	8.2
SF	27	10	35	1448[1]	1446	9.0	92	492	811	12.3	3.46	102	.261	.325	24	13	98	104	.975	159	124	-1.0	1.4	-7.2	-.8	2.2
SD	19	9	39	1466[1]	1474	9.1	97	536	728	12.5	3.66	94	.267	.333	-8	-38	95	105	.980	132	157	.6	-4.0	-1.0	**1.9**	-5.2
TOT	307	132	445	17529[2]		8.9				12.1	3.61		.260	.323					.978	1689	1746					

Runs
Hernandez-StL 111
Schmidt-Phi 104
Murphy-Atl 98
Dawson-Mon 96

Hits
Garvey-LA 200
Richards-SD 193
Hernandez-StL 191
Buckner-Chi 187

Doubles
Rose-Phi 42
Dawson-Mon 41
Buckner-Chi 41
Knight-Cin 39
Hernandez-StL 39

Triples
Scott-Mon 13
Moreno-Pit 13
LeFlore-Mon 11
Herndon-SF 11

Home Runs
Schmidt-Phi 48
Horner-Atl 35
Murphy-Atl 33
Carter-Mon 29
Baker-LA 29

Total Bases
Schmidt-Phi 342
Garvey-LA 307
Hernandez-StL 294
Baker-LA 291
Murphy-Atl 290

Runs Batted In
Schmidt-Phi 121
Hendrick-StL 109
Garvey-LA 106
Carter-Mon 101
Hernandez-StL 99

Runs Produced
Hernandez-StL 194
Schmidt-Phi 177
Dawson-Mon 166
Simmons-StL 161
Griffey-Cin 161

Bases On Balls
Morgan-Hou 93
Driessen-Cin 93
Tenace-SD 92
Schmidt-Phi 89
Hernandez-StL 86

Batting Average
Buckner-Chi .... .324
Hernandez-StL ..... .321
Templeton-StL ..... .319
McBride-Phi .... .309
Cedeno-Hou .... .309

On-Base Percentage
Hernandez-StL ..... .410
Cedeno-Hou .... .390
Clark-SF .... .390
Schmidt-Phi .... .388
Driessen-Cin .... .382

Slugging Average
Schmidt-Phi .... .624
Clark-SF .... .517
Murphy-Atl .... .510
Simmons-StL .... .505
Baker-LA .... .503

On-Base Plus Slugging
Schmidt-Phi 1012
Clark-SF 907
Hernandez-StL 904
Simmons-StL 885
Murphy-Atl 859

Adjusted OPS
Schmidt-Phi 169
Clark-SF 155
Cedeno-Hou 150
Hernandez-StL 147
Simmons-StL 140

Batter Runs
Schmidt-Phi 56.5
Hernandez-StL 43.3
Easler-Pit 37.2
Clark-SF 31.1
Simmons-StL 29.6

Adjusted Batter Runs
Schmidt-Phi 49.9
Hernandez-StL 39.8
Easler-Pit 36.0
Cedeno-Hou 34.0
Clark-SF 33.2

Clutch Hitting Index
Montanez-SD-Mon .. 124
Rose-Phi 117
Youngblood-NY 117
Simmons-StL 117
Concepcion-Cin 116

Runs Created
Schmidt-Phi 137
Hernandez-StL 122
Dawson-Mon 105
Murphy-Atl 101
Griffey-Cin 99

Total Average
Schmidt-Phi 1.095
Hernandez-StL ..... .915
Clark-SF .... .906
Cedeno-Hou .... .890
Simmons-StL .... .872

Stolen Bases
LeFlore-Mon 97
Moreno-Pit 96
Collins-Cin 79
Scott-Mon 63
Richards-SD 61

Stolen Base Average
Griffey-Cin 95.8
Mumphrey-SD 91.2
LeFlore-Mon 83.6
Maddox-Phi 83.3
Scott-Mon 82.9

Stolen Base Runs
LeFlore-Mon 14.7
Collins-Cin 10.0
Mumphrey-SD 9.7
Moreno-Pit 9.6
Scott-Mon 9.3

Fielding Runs
Smith-SD 40.8
Templeton-StL 27.6
Moreno-Pit 27.4
Schmidt-Phi 23.2
Dawson-Mon 20.1

Total Player Rating
Schmidt-Phi 7.3
Dawson-Mon 5.2
Cedeno-Hou 4.7
Templeton-StL 4.7
Smith-SD 4.4

Wins
Carlton-Phi 24
Niekro-Hou 20
Bibby-Pit 19
Reuss-LA 18
Ruthven-Phi 17

Win Percentage
Bibby-Pit .... .760
Reuss-LA .... .750
Carlton-Phi .... .727
Ruthven-Phi .... .630
Niekro-Hou .... .625

Games
Tidrow-Chi 84
Tekulve-Pit 78
Hume-Cin 78
Camp-Atl 77
Romo-Pit 74

Complete Games
Rogers-Mon 14
Carlton-Phi 13
Niekro-Atl 11
Niekro-Hou 11

Shutouts
Reuss-LA 6
Rogers-Mon 4
Richard-Hou 4

Saves
Sutter-Chi 28
Hume-Cin 25
Fingers-SD 23
Camp-Atl 22
Allen-NY 22

Innings Pitched
Carlton-Phi 304.0
Rogers-Mon 281.0
Niekro-Atl 275.0
Reuschel-Chi 257.0
Niekro-Hou 256.0

Fewest Hits/Game
Soto-Cin 5.96
Sutton-LA 6.91
Carlton-Phi 7.19
Seaver-Cin 7.50
Reuss-LA 7.57

Fewest BB/Game
Forsch-StL 1.38
Reuss-LA 1.57
Forsch-Hou 1.66
Candelaria-Pit 1.93
Sutton-LA 1.99

Strikeouts
Carlton-Phi 286
Ryan-Hou 200
Soto-Cin 182
Niekro-Atl 176
Blyleven-Pit 168

Strikeouts/Game
Soto-Cin 8.61
Carlton-Phi 8.47
Ryan-Hou 7.70
Blyleven-Pit 6.98
Welch-LA 5.94

Ratio
Sutton-LA 8.99
Reuss-LA 9.14
Pastore-Cin 9.89
Carlton-Phi 9.92
Soto-Cin 10.02

Earned Run Average
Sutton-LA 2.20
Carlton-Phi 2.34
Reuss-LA 2.51
Blue-SF 2.97
Rogers-Mon 2.98

Adjusted ERA
Carlton-Phi 162
Sutton-LA 159
Reuss-LA 140
Rogers-Mon 120
Blue-SF 119

Opponents' Batting Avg.
Soto-Cin .... .187
Sutton-LA .... .211
Carlton-Phi .... .218
Seaver-Cin .... .225
Reuss-LA .... .227

Opponents' On-Base Pct.
Sutton-LA .... .258
Reuss-LA .... .261
Pastore-Cin .... .277
Carlton-Phi .... .278
Soto-Cin .... .279

Starter Runs
Carlton-Phi 42.9
Sutton-LA 33.1
Reuss-LA 28.0
Ruhle-Hou 21.9
Richard-Hou 21.6

Adjusted Starter Runs
Carlton-Phi 46.8
Sutton-LA 31.6
Reuss-LA 26.0
Richard-Hou 19.3
Rogers-Mon 18.7

Clutch Pitching Index
Reuschel-Chi 119
Bomback-NY 117
Zachry-NY 114
Ruthven-Phi 112
Sanderson-Mon 111

Relief Runs
McGraw-Phi 22.0
Camp-Atl 20.4
Caudill-Chi 20.2
Smith-Hou 19.2
Holland-SF 17.0

Adjusted Relief Runs
McGraw-Phi 22.8
Caudill-Chi 22.7
Camp-Atl 21.3
Smith-Hou 17.1
Holland-SF 16.7

Relief Ranking
McGraw-Phi 29.7
Camp-Atl 26.2
Hume-Cin 25.2
Sutter-Chi 22.6
Smith-Hou 21.2

Total Pitcher Index
Carlton-Phi 5.0
McGraw-Phi 3.3
Camp-Atl 3.2
Hume-Cin 3.0
Reuss-LA 2.8

Total Baseball Ranking
Schmidt-Phi 7.3
Dawson-Mon 5.2
Carlton-Phi 5.0
Cedeno-Hou 4.7
Templeton-StL 4.7

TEAM	G	W	L	PCT	GB	R	OR	AB	H	2B	3B	HR	BB	SO	AVG	OBP	SLG	OPS	OPS+	BR	BR+	PF	CHI	RC	SB	CS	SBA	SBR
EAST																												
NY	162	103	59	.636		820	662	5553	1484	239	34	189	643	739	.267	.346	.425	771	112	79	93	98	100	820	86	36	70	6
BAL	162	100	62	.617	3	805	**640**	5585	1523	258	29	156	587	766	.273	.344	.413	757	107	52	60	99	102	788	111	38	74	11
MIL	162	86	76	.531	17	811	682	5653	1555	**298**	36	**203**	455	745	.275	.332	**.448**	**780**	**116**	78	**105**	97	100	**834**	131	56	70	9
BOS	160	83	77	.519	19	757	767	5603	1588	297	36	162	475	720	.283	.343	.436	779	107	**86**	47	105	93	810	79	48	62	1
DET	163	84	78	.519	19	**830**	757	5648	1543	232	53	143	**645**	844	.273	.351	.409	760	106	66	48	102	101	804	75	68	52	-7
CLE	160	79	81	.494	23	738	807	5470	1517	221	40	89	617	625	.277	**.355**	.381	736	102	26	23	100	97	739	118	58	67	6
TOR	162	67	95	.414	36	624	762	5571	1398	249	53	126	448	813	.251	.310	.383	693	85	-92	-120	105	99	640	67	72	48	-10
WEST																												
KC	162	97	65	.599		809	694	5714	**1633**	266	**59**	115	508	709	**.286**	.348	.413	761	107	62	56	101	100	826	**185**	43	**81**	**26**
OAK	162	83	79	.512	14	686	642	5495	1424	212	35	137	506	824	.259	.324	.385	709	100	-51	-1	93	102	680	175	82	68	10
MIN	161	77	84	.478	19.5	670	724	5530	1468	252	46	99	436	703	.265	.322	.381	703	86	-65	-109	107	103	655	62	46	57	-2
TEX	163	76	85	.472	20.5	756	752	5690	1616	263	27	124	480	**589**	.284	.342	.405	747	107	30	54	97	98	768	91	49	65	3
CHI	162	70	90	.438	26	587	722	5444	1408	255	38	91	399	670	.259	.314	.370	684	87	-104	-101	100	98	608	68	54	56	-4
CAL	160	65	95	.406	31	698	797	5443	1442	236	32	106	539	889	.265	.335	.378	713	97	-33	-15	98	102	681	91	63	59	-2
SEA	163	59	103	.364	38	610	793	5489	1359	211	35	104	483	727	.248	.311	.356	667	81	-136	-141	101	**105**	598	116	62	65	4
TOT	1132					10201		77888	20958	3489	553	1844	7221	10363	.270	.335	.400	733							1455	775	65	49

TEAM	CG	SH	SV	IP	H	H/G	HR	BB	SO	RAT	ERA	ERA+	OAV	OOB	PR	PR+	PF	CPI	FA	E	DP	FW	PW	BW	SBW	DIF
EAST																										
NY	29	**15**	**50**	1464[1]	1433	8.9	**102**	463	845	11.8	3.59	109	.259	.319	73	56	97	98	.978	138	160	.0	5.6	9.3	.3	6.9
BAL	42	10	41	1460	1438	8.9	134	507	789	12.2	3.65	109	.261	.325	63	51	98	105	**.985**	**95**	178	**2.5**	5.1	6.0	.7	4.8
MIL	48	14	30	1450	1530	9.5	137	**420**	575	12.3	3.71	104	.273	.326	53	27	96	**107**	.977	147	189	-.5	2.7	**10.5**	.6	-8.2
BOS	30	8	43	1441[1]	1557	9.8	129	481	696	13.0	4.38	96	.279	.340	-55	-25	105	97	.977	149	**206**	-.7	-2.4	4.7	-.2	1.8
DET	40	9	30	1467[1]	1505	9.3	152	558	741	12.9	4.26	97	.267	.336	-35	-22	102	98	.979	133	165	.4	-2.1	4.8	-1.0	1.2
CLE	35	8	32	1428	1519	9.6	137	552	843	13.3	4.69	87	.275	.344	-103	-96	101	92	.983	105	143	1.8	-9.5	2.3	.3	4.3
TOR	39	9	23	1466	1523	9.4	135	635	705	13.5	4.20	103	.274	.351	-26	16	107	105	.979	133	**206**	.3	1.6	-11.9	-1.3	-2.5
WEST																										
KC	37	10	42	1459[1]	1496	9.3	129	465	614	12.3	3.83	106	.267	.325	33	36	100	100	.978	141	150	-.1	3.6	5.6	**2.2**	4.8
OAK	**94**	9	13	1471[2]	**1347**	**8.3**	142	521	769	**11.7**	**3.47**	109	**.244**	**.312**	**94**	54	93	99	.979	130	115	.5	5.4	-.0	.6	-4.3
MIN	35	9	30	1451	1502	9.4	120	468	744	12.4	3.94	**111**	.272	.331	16	**63**	108	101	.977	148	192	-.6	**6.3**	-10.8	-.5	2.3
TEX	35	6	25	1451[2]	1561	9.7	119	519	**890**	13.2	4.03	97	.277	.342	2	-22	97	105	.977	147	169	-.4	-2.1	5.4	-.0	-7.1
CHI	32	12	42	1435[1]	1434	9.0	108	563	724	12.8	3.92	103	.263	.337	18	17	100	100	.973	171	162	-1.8	1.7	-10.0	-.7	1.1
CAL	22	6	30	1428[1]	1548	9.8	141	529	725	13.4	4.52	87	.278	.345	-77	-96	97	97	.978	134	144	.2	-9.5	-1.4	-.5	-3.5
SEA	31	7	26	1457[1]	1565	9.7	159	540	703	13.2	4.38	94	.278	.344	-56	-39	102	102	.977	149	189	-.5	-3.8	-14.0	.0	-3.5
TOT	549	132	457	20331[2]		9.3				12.7	4.04		.270	.335					.979	1920	2368					

Runs
Wilson-KC 133
Yount-Mil 121
Bumbry-Bal 118
Henderson-Oak 111
Trammell-Det 107

Hits
Wilson-KC 230
Cooper-Mil 219
Rivers-Tex 210
Oliver-Tex 209
Bumbry-Bal 205

Doubles
Yount-Mil 49
Oliver-Tex 43
Morrison-Chi 40
McRae-KC 39
Evans-Bos 37

Triples
Wilson-KC 15
Griffin-Tor 15
Washington-KC 11
Landreaux-Min 11
Yount-Mil 10

Home Runs
Oglivie-Mil 41
Jackson-NY 41
Thomas-Mil 38
Armas-Oak 35
Murray-Bal 32

Total Bases
Cooper-Mil 335
Oglivie-Mil 333
Murray-Bal 322
Yount-Mil 317
Oliver-Tex 315

Runs Batted In
Cooper-Mil 122
Oglivie-Mil 118
G.Brett-KC 118
Oliver-Tex 117
Murray-Bal 116

Runs Produced
Oliver-Tex 194
Cooper-Mil 193
Yount-Mil 185
Murray-Bal 184
G.Brett-KC 181

Bases On Balls
Randolph-NY 119
Henderson-Oak 117
Hargrove-Cle 111
Murphy-Oak 102
Harrah-Cle 98

Batting Average
G.Brett-KC .... .390
Cooper-Mil .... .352
Dilone-Cle .... .341
Rivers-Tex .... .333
Carew-Cal .... .331

On-Base Percentage
G.Brett-KC .... .461
Randolph-NY .... .429
Henderson-Oak ...... .422
Hargrove-Cle .... .421
Thompson-Det-Cal ... .402

Slugging Average
G.Brett-KC .... .664
Jackson-NY .... .597
Oglivie-Mil .... .563
Cooper-Mil .... .539
Yount-Mil .... .519

On-Base Plus Slugging
G.Brett-KC 1124
Jackson-NY 996
Cooper-Mil 931
Oglivie-Mil 930
Singleton-Bal 885

Adjusted OPS
G.Brett-KC 202
Jackson-NY 172
Cooper-Mil 157
Oglivie-Mil 156
Singleton-Bal 143

Batter Runs
G.Brett-KC 64.8
Jackson-NY 49.1
Cooper-Mil 42.9
Oglivie-Mil 39.2
Singleton-Bal 35.4

Adjusted Batter Runs
G.Brett-KC 63.8
Jackson-NY 51.1
Cooper-Mil 47.0
Oglivie-Mil 43.1
Henderson-Oak 37.0

Clutch Hitting Index
Manning-Cle 125
Thompson-Det-Cal ... 125
Hargrove-Cle 122
Whitaker-Det 122
Aikens-KC 122

Runs Created
G.Brett-KC 135
Cooper-Mil 126
Jackson-NY 125
Oglivie-Mil 121
Henderson-Oak 120

Total Average
G.Brett-KC 1.258
Jackson-NY 1.060
Henderson-Oak .... .973
Randolph-NY ...... .952
Oglivie-Mil ...... .925

Stolen Bases
Henderson-Oak 100
Wilson-KC 79
Dilone-Cle 61
Cruz-Sea 45
Bumbry-Bal 44

Stolen Base Average
Otis-KC 94.1
Harrah-Cle 89.5
Kelly-Bal 88.9
Wilson-KC 88.8
Cruz-Sea 86.5

Stolen Base Runs
Wilson-KC 13.9
Henderson-Oak 12.9
Cruz-Sea 7.4
Dilone-Cle 7.1
Bumbry-Bal 5.8

Fielding Runs
Castino-Min 27.8
Burleson-Bos 25.5
DeCinces-Bal 24.5
Murphy-Oak 23.9
Henderson-Oak 23.3

Total Player Rating
G.Brett-KC 6.5
Henderson-Oak 6.4
Oglivie-Mil 5.5
Bell-Tex 4.7
Bumbry-Bal 4.6

Wins
Stone-Bal 25
Norris-Oak 22
John-NY 22
McGregor-Bal 20
Leonard-KC 20

Win Percentage
Stone-Bal .... .781
May-NY .... .750
McGregor-Bal .... .714
Norris-Oak .... .710
John-NY .... .710

Games
Quisenberry-KC 75
Corbett-Min 73
Monge-Cle 67
Lopez-Det 67

Complete Games
Langford-Oak 28
Norris-Oak 24
Keough-Oak 20
John-NY 16
Gura-KC 16

Shutouts
John-NY 6
Zahn-Min 5
Stieb-Tor 4
McGregor-Bal 4
Gura-KC 4

Saves
Quisenberry-KC 33
Gossage-NY 33
Farmer-Chi 30
Stoddard-Bal 26
Burgmeier-Bos 24

Innings Pitched
Langford-Oak 290.0
Norris-Oak 284.1
Gura-KC 283.1
Leonard-KC 280.1
John-NY 265.1

Fewest Hits/Game
Norris-Oak 6.81
May-NY 7.39
Clancy-Tor 7.79
Underwood-NY 7.84
Keough-Oak 7.85

Fewest BB/Game
Matlack-Tex 1.84
Splittorff-KC 1.90
John-NY 1.90
Tanana-Cal 1.99
Langford-Oak 1.99

Strikeouts
Barker-Cle 187
Norris-Oak 180
Guidry-NY 166
Leonard-KC 155
Bannister-Sea 155

Strikeouts/Game
Barker-Cle 6.83
May-NY 6.83
Guidry-NY 6.80
Bannister-Sea 6.41
Perry-Tex-NY 5.91

Ratio
May-NY 9.39
Norris-Oak 9.62
Langford-Oak 10.58
Burns-Chi 10.59
Eckersley-Bos 10.65

Earned Run Average
May-NY 2.46
Norris-Oak 2.53
Burns-Chi 2.84
Keough-Oak 2.92
Gura-KC 2.95

Adjusted ERA
May-NY 159
Norris-Oak 149
Burns-Chi 142
Gura-KC 137
Erickson-Min 135

Opponents' Batting Avg.
Norris-Oak .... .209
May-NY .... .224
Clancy-Tor .... .233
Keough-Oak .... .236
Underwood-NY .... .237

Opponents' On-Base Pct.
May-NY .... .268
Norris-Oak .... .272
Eckersley-Bos ...... .291
Burns-Chi .... .295
Bannister-Sea ...... .296

Starter Runs
Norris-Oak 47.7
Gura-KC 34.3
Burns-Chi 31.9
Keough-Oak 31.3
May-NY 30.8

Adjusted Starter Runs
Norris-Oak 42.1
Gura-KC 34.6
Burns-Chi 31.8
May-NY 29.4
Clancy-Tor 26.3

Clutch Pitching Index
Sorensen-Mil 126
Stanley-Bos 118
Keough-Oak 113
Trout-Chi 113
Perry-Tex-NY 112

Relief Runs
Corbett-Min 31.2
Burgmeier-Bos 22.5
Gossage-NY 19.5
Darwin-Tex 17.3
Garvin-Tor 16.1

Adjusted Relief Runs
Corbett-Min 33.5
Burgmeier-Bos 23.4
Gossage-NY 18.8
Garvin-Tor 17.4
Darwin-Tex 16.1

Relief Ranking
Corbett-Min 43.5
Burgmeier-Bos 31.8
Gossage-NY 27.5
Quisenberry-KC 26.3
Darwin-Tex 25.1

Total Pitcher Index
Norris-Oak 4.8
Corbett-Min 4.8
Burgmeier-Bos 3.6
Burns-Chi 3.5
Gura-KC 3.3

Total Baseball Ranking
G.Brett-KC 6.5
Henderson-Oak 6.4
Oglivie-Mil 5.5
Norris-Oak 4.8
Corbett-Min 4.8

TEAM	G	W	L	PCT	GB	R	OR	AB	H	2B	3B	HR	BB	SO	AVG	OBP	SLG	OPS	OPS+	BR	BR+	PF	CHI	RC	SB	CS	SBA	SBR
EAST																												
Split Season: First-half Winner PHI (34-21); Second-half Winner MON (30-23)																												
STL	103	59	43	.578		464	417	3537	936	158	**45**	50	379	495	.265	.339	.377	716	106	43	31	103	102	454	88	45	66	4
MON	108	60	48	.556	2	443	394	3591	883	146	28	81	368	498	.246	.319	.370	689	100	3	-2	101	**105**	435	**138**	40	**78**	**16**
PHI	107	59	48	.551	2.5	**491**	472	3665	**1002**	165	25	69	372	**432**	**.273**	**.344**	**.389**	**733**	**109**	**66**	**45**	104	100	**495**	103	46	69	7
PIT	103	46	56	.451	13	407	425	3576	920	176	30	55	278	494	.257	.314	.369	683	96	-9	-21	103	102	417	122	52	70	9
NY	105	41	62	.398	18.5	348	432	3493	868	136	35	57	304	603	.248	.311	.356	667	96	-26	-20	98	93	387	103	42	71	8
CHI	106	38	65	.369	21.5	370	483	3546	838	138	29	57	342	611	.236	.306	.340	646	84	-52	-67	104	104	368	72	41	64	1
WEST																												
Split Season: First-half Winner LA (36-21); Second-half Winner HOU (33-20)																												
CIN	108	66	42	.611		464	440	3637	972	**190**	24	64	375	553	.267	.339	.385	724	**109**	53	**45**	102	97	469	58	37	61	0
LA	110	63	47	.573	4	450	356	3751	984	133	20	**82**	331	550	.262	.325	.374	699	108	16	33	96	101	450	73	46	61	0
HOU	110	61	49	.555	6	394	**331**	3693	948	160	35	45	340	488	.257	.321	.356	677	103	-12	10	95	95	425	81	43	65	3
SF	111	56	55	.505	11.5	427	414	3766	941	161	26	63	**386**	543	.250	.322	.357	679	100	-8	0	98	99	431	89	50	64	2
ATL	107	50	56	.472	15	395	416	3642	886	148	22	64	321	540	.243	.308	.349	657	90	-41	-51	103	**105**	391	98	39	72	8
SD	110	41	69	.373	26	382	455	3757	963	170	35	32	311	525	.256	.316	.346	662	100	-33	-2	93	96	400	83	62	57	-3
TOT	644					5035		43654	11141	1881	354	719	4107	6332	.256	.322	.364	686							1108	543	67	54

TEAM	CG	SH	SV	IP	H	H/G	HR	BB	SO	RAT	ERA	ERA+	OAV	OOB	PR	PR+	PF	CPI	FA	E	DP	FW	PW	BW	SBW	DIF
EAST																										
STL	11	5	**33**	943	902	8.7	52	290	388	11.6	3.63	98	.255	.314	-14	-7	102	91	**.981**	82	108	.7	-.7	3.4	-.0	4.9
MON	20	12	23	975	902	8.4	58	**268**	520	11.0	3.30	106	.247	.302	21	21	100	92	.980	81	88	**1.0**	2.3	-.2	**1.2**	1.9
PHI	19	5	23	960[1]	967	9.1	72	347	580	12.5	4.05	90	.267	.333	-60	-43	104	97	.980	86	90	.7	-4.6	**4.9**	.3	4.4
PIT	11	5	29	942	953	9.2	60	346	492	12.6	3.57	101	.266	.333	-8	3	103	107	.979	86	106	.5	.4	-2.2	.5	-3.9
NY	7	3	24	926[1]	906	8.9	74	336	490	12.2	3.55	98	.259	.326	-6	-7	100	105	.968	130	89	-1.6	-.7	-2.1	.4	-6.3
CHI	6	2	20	956[2]	983	9.3	59	388	532	13.1	4.01	92	.270	.344	-55	-31	106	101	.974	113	103	-.7	-3.3	-7.2	-.4	-1.8
WEST																										
CIN	25	14	20	965[2]	863	8.1	67	393	593	11.9	3.73	95	.241	.318	-26	-18	102	90	**.981**	**80**	99	**1.0**	-1.9	**4.9**	-.5	8.7
LA	**26**	**19**	24	997	904	8.2	54	302	603	11.1	3.01	110	.245	.304	54	36	95	101	.980	87	101	.8	3.9	3.6	-.5	.4
HOU	23	**19**	25	990	**842**	**7.7**	**40**	300	**610**	**10.5**	**2.67**	**124**	**.231**	**.291**	**91**	**74**	94	96	.980	87	81	.8	**8.0**	1.1	-.2	-3.5
SF	8	9	**33**	1009[1]	970	8.7	57	393	561	12.4	3.29	105	.256	.330	23	17	98	**109**	.977	102	102	.0	1.9	.0	-.3	-1.0
ATL	11	4	24	968	936	8.8	62	330	471	11.9	3.45	104	.257	.321	4	14	103	102	.976	102	93	-.1	1.6	-5.4	.4	.8
SD	9	6	23	1002	1013	9.1	64	414	492	13.0	3.72	88	.268	.343	-25	-55	93	108	.977	102	**117**	.0	-5.9	-.2	-.8	-7.0
TOT	176	103	301	11635[1]		8.7				12.0	3.50		.256	.322					.978	1138	1177					

Runs
Schmidt-Phi 78
Rose-Phi 73
Dawson-Mon 71
Hendrick-StL 67

Hits
Rose-Phi 140
Buckner-Chi 131
Concepcion-Cin 129
Baker-LA 128
Griffey-Cin 123

Doubles
Buckner-Chi 35
Jones-SD 34
Concepcion-Cin 28
Hernandez-StL 27
Chambliss-Atl 25

Triples
Richards-SD 12
Reynolds-Hou 12
Herr-StL 9

Home Runs
Schmidt-Phi 31
Dawson-Mon 24
Kingman-NY 22
Foster-Cin 22
Hendrick-StL 18

Total Bases
Schmidt-Phi 228
Dawson-Mon 218
Foster-Cin 215
Buckner-Chi 202
Hendrick-StL 191

Runs Batted In
Schmidt-Phi 91
Foster-Cin 90
Buckner-Chi 75
Carter-Mon 68

Runs Produced
Schmidt-Phi 138
Foster-Cin 132
Matthews-Phi 120
Concepcion-Cin 119
Garvey-LA 117

Bases On Balls
Schmidt-Phi 73
Morgan-SF 66
Hernandez-StL 61
Thompson-Pit 59
Matthews-Phi 59

Batting Average
Madlock-Pit 341
Rose-Phi 325
Baker-LA 320
Schmidt-Phi 316
Buckner-Chi 311

On-Base Percentage
Schmidt-Phi 439
Madlock-Pit 418
Hernandez-StL 405
Matthews-Phi 404
Raines-Mon 394

Slugging Average
Schmidt-Phi 644
Dawson-Mon 553
Foster-Cin 519
Madlock-Pit 495
Hendrick-StL 485

On-Base Plus Slugging
Schmidt-Phi 1083
Dawson-Mon 923
Madlock-Pit 912
Foster-Cin 895
Hernandez-StL 868

Adjusted OPS
Schmidt-Phi 195
Dawson-Mon 157
Madlock-Pit 153
Foster-Cin 150
Cey-LA 145

Batter Runs
Schmidt-Phi 50.1
Dawson-Mon 28.8
Foster-Cin 27.7
Hernandez-StL 24.6
Matthews-Phi 22.0

Adjusted Batter Runs
Schmidt-Phi 46.1
Dawson-Mon 28.0
Foster-Cin 26.5
Hernandez-StL 22.8
Madlock-Pit 20.4

Clutch Hitting Index
Concepcion-Cin 141
Herr-StL 127
Matthews-Phi 126
Foster-Cin 126
Maddox-Phi 122

Runs Created
Schmidt-Phi 102
Dawson-Mon 83
Foster-Cin 81
Hernandez-StL 73
Matthews-Phi 71

Total Average
Schmidt-Phi 1.227
Raines-Mon 1.034
Dawson-Mon 989
Madlock-Pit 959
Matthews-Phi 908

Stolen Bases
Raines-Mon 71
Moreno-Pit 39
Scott-Mon 30

Stolen Base Average
Lopes-LA 90.9
Lacy-Pit 88.9
Dawson-Mon 86.7
Raines-Mon 86.6
Puhl-Hou 84.6

Stolen Base Runs
Raines-Mon 11.8
Dawson-Mon 4.3
Lacy-Pit 4.2
Scott-Mon 4.2
Lopes-LA 3.7

Fielding Runs
Smith-SD 25.9
Schmidt-Phi 22.5
Dawson-Mon 17.8
Flynn-NY 12.2
Clark-SF 11.9

Total Player Rating
Schmidt-Phi 7.0
Dawson-Mon 5.1
Foster-Cin 3.2
Raines-Mon 2.7
Concepcion-Cin 2.5

Wins
Seaver-Cin 14
Valenzuela-LA 13
Carlton-Phi 13

Win Percentage
Seaver-Cin 875
Carlton-Phi 765
Ryan-Hou 688
Valenzuela-LA 650
Hooton-LA 647

Games
Lucas-SD 57
Minton-SF 55
Tidrow-Chi 51
Hume-Cin 51
Sambito-Hou 49

Complete Games
Valenzuela-LA 11
Soto-Cin 10
Carlton-Phi 10
Reuss-LA 8
Rogers-Mon 7

Shutouts
Valenzuela-LA 8
Knepper-Hou 5
Hooton-LA 4

Saves
Sutter-StL 25
Minton-SF 21
Allen-NY 18
Camp-Atl 17

Innings Pitched
Valenzuela-LA 192.1
Carlton-Phi 190.0
Soto-Cin 175.0
Seaver-Cin 166.1
Niekro-Hou 166.0

Fewest Hits/Game
Ryan-Hou 5.98
Seaver-Cin 6.49
Valenzuela-LA 6.55
Berenyi-Cin 6.93
Blue-SF 7.00

Fewest BB/Game
Perry-Atl 1.43
Reuss-LA 1.59
Sutton-Hou 1.64
Sorensen-StL 1.67
Solomon-Pit 1.91

Strikeouts
Valenzuela-LA 180
Carlton-Phi 179
Soto-Cin 151
Ryan-Hou 140
Gullickson-Mon 115

Strikeouts/Game
Carlton-Phi 8.48
Ryan-Hou 8.46
Valenzuela-LA 8.42
Soto-Cin 7.77
Berenyi-Cin 7.57

Ratio
Sutton-Hou 9.19
Valenzuela-LA 9.45
Knepper-Hou 9.77
Reuss-LA 9.96
Hooton-LA 10.05

Earned Run Average
Ryan-Hou 1.69
Knepper-Hou 2.18
Hooton-LA 2.28
Reuss-LA 2.30
Carlton-Phi 2.42

Adjusted ERA
Ryan-Hou 195
Knepper-Hou 151
Carlton-Phi 150
Hooton-LA 146
Reuss-LA 144

Opponents' Batting Avg.
Ryan-Hou 188
Valenzuela-LA 205
Seaver-Cin 205
Berenyi-Cin 211
Blue-SF 217

Opponents' On-Base Pct.
Sutton-Hou 268
Valenzuela-LA 271
Knepper-Hou 280
Sanderson-Mon 281
Ryan-Hou 281

Starter Runs
Ryan-Hou 29.8
Knepper-Hou 22.8
Carlton-Phi 22.7
Valenzuela-LA 21.6
Reuss-LA 20.2

Adjusted Starter Runs
Ryan-Hou 28.1
Carlton-Phi 24.6
Knepper-Hou 20.5
Valenzuela-LA 18.9
Seaver-Cin 18.4

Clutch Pitching Index
Mahler-Atl 124
Solomon-Pit 124
Alexander-SF 123
Blue-SF 112
Zachry-NY 111

Relief Runs
Lucas-SD 14.9
Camp-Atl 14.5
Holland-SF 12.1
Sambito-Hou 11.7
Reardon-NY-Mon 10.3

Adjusted Relief Runs
Camp-Atl 14.9
Lucas-SD 13.5
Holland-SF 11.6
Sambito-Hou 10.9
Reardon-NY-Mon 10.3

Relief Ranking
Camp-Atl 27.5
Lucas-SD 22.6
Sambito-Hou 18.7
Fryman-Mon 15.3
Holland-SF 14.0

Total Pitcher Index
Ryan-Hou 3.5
Camp-Atl 2.9
Valenzuela-LA 2.6
Lucas-SD 2.5
Hooton-LA 2.3

Total Baseball Ranking
Schmidt-Phi 7.0
Dawson-Mon 5.1
Ryan-Hou 3.5
Foster-Cin 3.2
Camp-Atl 2.9

TEAM	G	W	L	PCT	GB	R	OR	AB	H	2B	3B	HR	BB	SO	AVG	OBP	SLG	OPS	OPS+	BR	BR+	PF	CHI	RC	SB	CS	SBA	SBR
EAST																												
Split Season: First-half Winner NY (34-22); Second-half Winner MIL (31-22)																												
MIL	109	62	47	.569		493	459	3743	961	173	20	96	300	461	.257	.317	.391	708	109	9	34	95	108	451	39	36	52	-4
BAL	105	59	46	.562	1	429	437	3516	883	165	11	88	**404**	454	.251	.331	.379	710	104	22	23	100	95	431	41	34	55	-3
NY	107	59	48	.551	2	421	**343**	3529	889	148	22	100	391	434	.252	.328	.391	719	108	29	36	99	92	445	47	30	61	0
DET	109	60	49	.550	2	427	404	3600	922	148	29	65	**404**	500	.256	.334	.368	702	98	14	-2	104	94	442	61	37	62	0
BOS	108	59	49	.546	2.5	**519**	481	3820	**1052**	168	17	90	378	520	**.275**	**.343**	**.399**	**742**	107	**65**	35	106	99	**514**	32	31	51	-4
CLE	103	52	51	.505	7	431	442	3507	922	150	21	39	343	**379**	.263	.331	.351	682	98	-11	-5	99	104	414	**119**	37	**76**	**13**
TOR	106	37	69	.349	23.5	329	466	3521	797	137	23	61	284	556	.226	.288	.330	618	73	-103	-122	106	105	326	66	57	54	-5
WEST																												
Split Season: First-half Winner OAK (37-23); Second-half Winner KC (30-23)																												
OAK	109	64	45	.587		458	403	3677	910	119	26	**104**	342	647	.247	.314	.379	693	104	-8	14	95	106	438	98	47	68	5
TEX	105	57	48	.543	5	452	389	3581	968	**178**	15	49	295	396	.270	.329	.369	698	107	5	29	95	105	425	46	41	53	-4
CHI	106	54	52	.509	8.5	476	423	3615	982	135	27	76	322	518	.272	.338	.387	725	**110**	41	**51**	98	100	471	86	44	66	4
KC	103	50	53	.485	11	397	405	3560	952	169	29	61	301	419	.267	.327	.383	710	105	17	21	99	90	437	100	53	65	3
CAL	110	51	59	.464	20	476	453	3688	944	134	16	97	393	571	.256	.332	.380	712	105	26	26	100	100	463	44	33	57	-2
SEA	110	44	65	.404	26.5	426	521	3780	950	148	13	89	329	553	.251	.316	.368	684	93	-19	-36	104	98	441	100	50	67	5
MIN	110	41	68	.376	29.5	378	486	3676	884	147	**36**	47	275	497	.240	.295	.338	633	77	-87	-109	107	**109**	355	34	27	56	-2
TOT	750					6112		50813	13016	2119	305	1062	4761	6905	.257	.324	.373	696							913	557	62	6

TEAM	CG	SH	SV	IP	H	H/G	HR	BB	SO	RAT	ERA	ERA+	OAV	OOB	PR	PR+	PF	CPI	FA	E	DP	FW	PW	BW	SBW	DIF
EAST																										
MIL	11	4	**35**	986	994	9.1	72	352	448	12.4	3.91	88	.266	.331	-27	-57	94	99	.982	79	**135**	.4	-5.9	3.6	-.5	10.1
BAL	25	10	23	940	923	8.9	83	347	489	12.3	3.70	98	.260	.328	-4	-7	99	**105**	.983	68	114	.8	-.7	2.5	-.4	4.4
NY	16	**13**	30	948	**827**	7.9	**64**	287	**606**	**10.7**	**2.90**	**123**	**.235**	**.295**	**80**	**73**	98	100	.982	72	100	.7	**7.7**	3.8	-.0	-6.5
DET	33	**13**	22	969[1]	840	**7.8**	83	373	476	11.6	3.53	107	.236	.313	14	25	103	95	**.984**	**67**	109	**1.1**	2.7	-.2	-.0	2.1
BOS	19	4	24	987[1]	983	9.0	90	354	536	12.5	3.82	102	.262	.330	-17	6	106	103	.979	91	108	-.4	-.7	3.7	-.5	1.6
CLE	33	10	13	931	989	9.6	67	311	569	12.7	3.88	94	.274	.333	-23	-26	99	102	.978	87	91	-.3	-2.7	-.5	**1.3**	2.9
TOR	20	4	18	953[1]	908	8.6	72	377	451	12.5	3.82	103	.252	.329	-17	12	108	97	.975	105	102	-1.2	1.3	-12.8	-.6	-2.5
WEST																										
OAK	**60**	11	10	993	883	8.1	80	370	505	11.7	3.30	105	.240	.314	40	21	95	101	.980	81	74	.3	2.3	1.5	.5	5.2
TEX	23	**13**	18	940[1]	851	8.2	67	322	488	11.4	3.40	102	.243	.310	27	8	95	96	**.984**	69	102	.8	.9	3.1	.5	.4
CHI	20	8	23	940[2]	891	8.6	73	336	529	12.0	3.48	103	.252	.321	19	11	98	102	.979	87	113	-.2	1.2	**5.4**	.4	-5.6
KC	24	8	24	922[1]	909	8.9	75	**273**	404	11.8	3.57	101	.260	.317	10	5	99	101	.982	72	94	.5	.6	2.3	.3	-4.9
CAL	27	8	19	971[1]	958	8.9	81	323	426	12.1	3.70	99	.261	.324	-4	-5	100	102	.977	101	120	-.8	-.5	2.8	-.3	-5.0
SEA	10	5	23	997[1]	1039	9.4	76	360	478	12.8	4.24	91	.271	.336	-64	-40	105	95	.979	91	122	-.3	-4.1	-3.7	.5	-2.6
MIN	13	6	22	979[2]	1021	9.4	79	376	500	13.0	3.98	99	.272	.341	-35	-3	108	104	.978	96	103	-.5	-.3	-11.4	-.3	-.8
TOT	334	117	304	13459[2]		8.8				12.1	3.66		.257	.324					.981	1166	1487					

Runs
Henderson-Oak 89
Evans-Bos 84
Cooper-Mil 70
Harrah-Cle 64
Rivers-Tex 62

Hits
Henderson-Oak 135
Lansford-Bos 134
Wilson-KC 133
Cooper-Mil 133
Paciorek-Sea 132

Doubles
Cooper-Mil 35
Oliver-Tex 29
Paciorek-Sea 28
Dauer-Bal 27
G.Brett-KC 27

Triples
Castino-Min 9
Wilson-KC 7
Henderson-Oak 7
G.Brett-KC 7
Baines-Chi 7

Home Runs
Murray-Bal 22
Grich-Cal 22
Evans-Bos 22
Armas-Oak 22

Total Bases
Evans-Bos 215
Armas-Oak 211
Paciorek-Sea 206
Cooper-Mil 206
Murray-Bal 202

Runs Batted In
Murray-Bal 78
Armas-Oak 76
Oglivie-Mil 72
Evans-Bos 71
Winfield-NY 68

Runs Produced
Evans-Bos 133
Henderson-Oak 118
Cooper-Mil 118
Murray-Bal 113
Oglivie-Mil 111

Bases On Balls
Evans-Bos 85
Murphy-Oak 73
Kemp-Det 70
Henderson-Oak 64
Aikens-KC 62

Batting Average
Lansford-Bos .... .336
Paciorek-Sea .... .326
Cooper-Mil .... .320
Henderson-Oak ..... .319
Hargrove-Cle .... .317

On-Base Percentage
Hargrove-Cle .... .432
Evans-Bos .... .418
Henderson-Oak ..... .411
Kemp-Det .... .393
Lansford-Bos .... .391

Slugging Average
Grich-Cal .... .543
Murray-Bal .... .534
Evans-Bos .... .522
Paciorek-Sea .... .509
Cooper-Mil .... .495

On-Base Plus Slugging
Evans-Bos 940
Grich-Cal 924
Murray-Bal 897
Paciorek-Sea 894
Lemon-Chi 879

Adjusted OPS
Grich-Cal 164
Evans-Bos 160
Murray-Bal 156
Lemon-Chi 155
Cooper-Mil 154

Batter Runs
Evans-Bos 39.8
Paciorek-Sea 28.4
Grich-Cal 28.3
Henderson-Oak 26.9
Murray-Bal 25.9

Adjusted Batter Runs
Evans-Bos 34.4
Henderson-Oak 30.9
Grich-Cal 28.3
Cooper-Mil 27.5
Murray-Bal 26.0

Clutch Hitting Index
Yastrzemski-Bos 139
Wills-Tex 132
Hargrove-Cle 129
Oglivie-Mil 128
Murphy-Oak 125

Runs Created
Evans-Bos 95
Henderson-Oak 81
Paciorek-Sea 76
Grich-Cal 73
Murray-Bal 70

Total Average
Evans-Bos 1.007
Grich-Cal .... .917
Henderson-Oak ..... .899
Murray-Bal .... .864
Paciorek-Sea ...... .846

Stolen Bases
Henderson-Oak 56
Cruz-Sea 43
LeFlore-Chi 36
Wilson-KC 34
Dilone-Cle 29

Stolen Base Average
Manning-Cle 89.3
Bannister-Cle 88.9
Cruz-Sea 84.3
Wilson-KC 81.0
Gibson-Det 77.3

Stolen Base Runs
Cruz-Sea 6.7
Wilson-KC 4.7
Henderson-Oak 4.6
Manning-Cle 4.4
LeFlore-Chi 4.1

Fielding Runs
Bell-Tex 30.0
Yount-Mil 27.5
Wilson-KC 22.1
Burleson-Cal 21.0
Henderson-Oak 20.1

Total Player Rating
Henderson-Oak 5.2
Bell-Tex 4.7
Yount-Mil 4.6
Grich-Cal 4.5
Evans-Bos 4.3

Wins
Vuckovich-Mil 14
Morris-Det 14
McCatty-Oak 14
D.Martinez-Bal 14

Win Percentage
Vuckovich-Mil ...... .778
D.Martinez-Bal ..... .737
McGregor-Bal .... .722
Guidry-NY .... .688

Games
Corbett-Min 54
Fingers-Mil 47
Rawley-Sea 46
Easterly-Mil 44

Complete Games
Langford-Oak 18
McCatty-Oak 16
Morris-Det 15
Norris-Oak 12
Gura-KC 12

Shutouts
Medich-Tex 4
McCatty-Oak 4
Forsch-Cal 4
Dotson-Chi 4

Saves
Fingers-Mil 28
Gossage-NY 20
Quisenberry-KC 18
Corbett-Min 17
Saucier-Det 13

Innings Pitched
Leonard-KC 201.2
Morris-Det 198.0
Langford-Oak 195.1
McCatty-Oak 185.2
Stieb-Tor 183.2

Fewest Hits/Game
McCatty-Oak 6.79
Morris-Det 6.95
Guidry-NY 7.09
Darwin-Tex 7.09
Stewart-Bal 7.13

Fewest BB/Game
Honeycutt-Tex 1.20
Forsch-Cal 1.59
Gura-KC 1.83
Leonard-KC 1.83
Guidry-NY 1.84

Strikeouts
Barker-Cle 127
Burns-Chi 108
Leonard-KC 107
Blyleven-Cle 107
Guidry-NY 104

Strikeouts/Game
Barker-Cle 7.41
Guidry-NY 7.37
Bannister-Sea 6.30
Burns-Chi 6.20
Blyleven-Cle 6.04

Ratio
Guidry-NY 9.00
Gura-KC 9.30
Honeycutt-Tex 9.66
McCatty-Oak 9.84
Forsch-Cal 10.24

Earned Run Average
McCatty-Oak 2.33
Stewart-Bal 2.32
Lamp-Chi 2.41
John-NY 2.63
Burns-Chi 2.64

Adjusted ERA
Stewart-Bal 156
McCatty-Oak 150
Lamp-Chi 149
John-NY 136
Burns-Chi 136

Opponents' Batting Avg.
McCatty-Oak .... .211
Guidry-NY .... .214
Darwin-Tex .... .218
Morris-Det .... .218
Lamp-Chi .... .222

Opponents' On-Base Pct.
Guidry-NY .... .257
Gura-KC .... .269
Honeycutt-Tex ...... .272
McCatty-Oak .... .279
Forsch-Cal .... .289

Starter Runs
McCatty-Oak 27.6
Righetti-NY 18.9
Gura-KC 18.1
Burns-Chi 17.8
Lamp-Chi 17.7

Adjusted Starter Runs
McCatty-Oak 25.1
Righetti-NY 18.3
Gura-KC 17.4
Lamp-Chi 16.9
Burns-Chi 16.7

Clutch Pitching Index
Stewart-Bal 145
John-NY 129
Burns-Chi 121
Denny-Cle 119
McGregor-Bal 116

Relief Runs
Fingers-Mil 22.7
Gossage-NY 15.0
Quisenberry-KC 13.4
Saucier-Det 10.9
Corbett-Min 10.7

Adjusted Relief Runs
Fingers-Mil 22.1
Gossage-NY 14.9
Quisenberry-KC 13.2
Corbett-Min 12.5
Saucier-Det 11.2

Relief Ranking
Fingers-Mil 40.6
Gossage-NY 28.5
Saucier-Det 19.0
Quisenberry-KC 18.0
Corbett-Min 15.7

Total Pitcher Index
Fingers-Mil 4.5
Gossage-NY 3.2
McCatty-Oak 2.8
Quisenberry-KC 2.3
Saucier-Det 2.1

Total Baseball Ranking
Henderson-Oak 5.2
Bell-Tex 4.7
Yount-Mil 4.6
Fingers-Mil 4.5
Grich-Cal 4.5

TEAM	G	W	L	PCT	GB	R	OR	AB	H	2B	3B	HR	BB	SO	AVG	OBP	SLG	OPS	OPS+	BR	BR+	PF	CHI	RC	SB	CS	SBA	SBR
EAST																												
STL	162	92	70	.568		685	**609**	5455	1439	239	**52**	67	569	805	.264	**.337**	.364	701	101	24	17	101	99	682	**200**	91	69	12
PHI	162	89	73	.549	3	664	654	5454	1417	245	25	112	506	831	.260	.325	.376	701	100	14	0	102	99	654	128	76	63	2
MON	162	86	76	.531	6	697	616	5557	1454	270	38	133	503	816	.262	.327	.396	723	106	52	39	102	97	725	156	56	**74**	**15**
PIT	162	84	78	.519	8	724	696	5614	**1535**	**272**	40	134	447	862	**.273**	.330	**.408**	**738**	109	**80**	58	103	97	**745**	161	75	68	9
CHI	162	73	89	.451	19	676	709	5531	1436	239	46	102	460	869	.260	.319	.375	694	97	-4	-21	103	103	662	132	70	65	5
NY	162	65	97	.401	27	609	723	5510	1361	227	26	97	456	1005	.247	.307	.350	657	90	-75	-71	99	105	595	137	58	70	10
WEST																												
ATL	162	89	73	.549		**739**	702	5507	1411	215	22	**146**	554	869	.256	.327	.383	710	100	33	5	104	105	697	151	77	66	6
LA	162	88	74	.543	1	691	612	5642	1487	222	32	138	528	**804**	.264	.330	.388	718	**110**	47	**66**	98	95	735	151	56	73	14
SF	162	87	75	.537	2	673	687	5499	1393	213	30	133	**607**	915	.253	.329	.376	705	103	27	28	100	97	685	130	56	70	9
SD	162	81	81	.500	8	675	658	5575	1435	217	**52**	81	429	877	.257	.313	.359	672	99	-49	-15	95	**110**	626	165	77	68	9
HOU	162	77	85	.475	12	569	620	5440	1342	236	48	74	435	830	.247	.305	.349	654	95	-84	-38	92	102	578	140	61	70	9
CIN	162	61	101	.377	28	545	661	5479	1375	228	34	82	470	817	.251	.313	.350	663	89	-63	-75	102	92	588	131	69	66	5
TOT	972					7947		66263	17085	2823	445	1299	5964	10300	.258	.322	.373	695							1782	822	68	104

TEAM	CG	SH	SV	IP	H	H/G	HR	BB	SO	RAT	ERA	ERA+	OAV	OOB	PR	PR+	PF	CPI	FA	E	DP	FW	PW	BW	SBW	DIF
EAST																										
STL	25	10	47	1465^{1}	1420	8.8	94	502	689	12.0	3.38	107	.258	.322	37	40	101	105	**.981**	124	169	1.0	4.3	1.8	.3	3.8
PHI	**38**	13	33	1456^{1}	1395	8.7	86	472	**1002**	11.8	3.61	102	.255	.317	-1	9	102	93	**.981**	**121**	138	**1.2**	1.0	.0	-.7	6.7
MON	34	10	43	1460^{2}	1371	8.5	110	**448**	936	11.4	3.32	**110**	.250	.309	46	**52**	101	100	.980	122	117	1.1	**5.5**	4.1	**.7**	-6.2
PIT	19	7	39	1466^{2}	1434	8.8	118	521	933	12.2	3.82	97	.257	.324	-34	-17	103	97	.977	145	133	-.2	-1.7	6.1	.0	-1.0
CHI	9	7	43	1447^{1}	1510	9.4	125	452	764	12.4	3.92	95	.272	.330	-51	-28	104	102	.979	132	110	.5	-2.9	-2.2	-.4	-2.9
NY	15	5	37	1447^{1}	1508	9.4	119	582	759	13.2	3.89	94	.273	.344	-45	-40	101	**109**	.972	175	134	-2.0	-4.2	-7.4	.1	-2.4
WEST																										
ATL	15	11	**51**	1463	1484	9.2	126	502	813	12.4	3.83	98	.267	.331	-36	-14	104	104	.979	137	**186**	.2	-1.4	.6	-.3	9.1
LA	37	**16**	28	1488^{1}	1356	**8.2**	**81**	468	932	**11.2**	**3.26**	106	**.244**	**.305**	**56**	36	96	93	.979	139	131	.1	3.8	**7.0**	.6	-4.3
SF	18	4	45	1465^{1}	1507	9.3	109	466	810	12.3	3.64	99	.270	.329	-6	-7	100	106	.973	173	125	-1.8	-.7	3.0	.0	5.7
SD	20	11	41	1476	1348	8.3	139	502	765	11.5	3.53	97	**.244**	.310	13	-17	95	96	.976	152	142	-.6	-1.7	-1.5	.0	4.1
HOU	37	**16**	31	1446^{2}	**1338**	8.4	87	479	899	11.6	3.42	97	.247	.312	30	-17	92	94	.978	136	154	.3	-1.7	-3.9	.0	1.5
CIN	22	7	31	1460^{1}	1414	8.8	105	570	998	12.4	3.67	101	.258	.330	-10	6	103	102	.980	128	158	.8	.7	-7.8	-.4	-13.0
TOT	289	117	469	17543^{1}		8.8				12.0	3.61		.258	.322					.979	1684	1697					

Runs
L.Smith-StL 120
Murphy-Atl 113
Schmidt-Phi 108
Dawson-Mon 107
Sandberg-Chi 103

Hits
Oliver-Mon 204
Buckner-Chi 201
Dawson-Mon 183
L.Smith-StL 182
Ray-Pit 182

Doubles
Oliver-Mon 43
Kennedy-SD 42
Dawson-Mon 37
Knight-Hou 36

Triples
Thon-Hou 10
Wilson-NY 9
Puhl-Hou 9
Moreno-Pit 9

Home Runs
Kingman-NY 37
Murphy-Atl 36
Schmidt-Phi 35
Horner-Atl 32
Guerrero-LA 32

Total Bases
Oliver-Mon 317
Guerrero-LA 308
Murphy-Atl 303
Dawson-Mon 303
Buckner-Chi 290

Runs Batted In
Oliver-Mon 109
Murphy-Atl 109
Buckner-Chi 105
Hendrick-StL 104
Clark-SF 103

Runs Produced
Murphy-Atl 186
Buckner-Chi 183
L.Smith-StL 181
Oliver-Mon 177
Madlock-Pit 168

Bases On Balls
Schmidt-Phi 107
Thompson-Pit 101
Hernandez-StL 100
Murphy-Atl 93
Clark-SF 90

Batting Average
Oliver-Mon 331
Madlock-Pit 319
Durham-Chi 312
L.Smith-StL 307
Buckner-Chi 306

On-Base Percentage
Schmidt-Phi .... .407
Hernandez-StL .... .404
Morgan-SF .... .402
Thompson-Pit ..... .397
Oliver-Mon .... .394

Slugging Average
Schmidt-Phi........ .547
Guerrero-LA .... .536
Durham-Chi .... .521
Oliver-Mon .... .514
Thompson-Pit ..... .511

On-Base Plus Slugging
Schmidt-Phi 954
Guerrero-LA 915
Durham-Chi 910
Oliver-Mon 908
Thompson-Pit 908

Adjusted OPS
Schmidt-Phi 161
Guerrero-LA 157
Oliver-Mon 149
Lezcano-SD 149
Durham-Chi 148

Batter Runs
Schmidt-Phi 47.2
Oliver-Mon 42.7
Thompson-Pit 40.7
Guerrero-LA 40.3
Murphy-Atl 37.8

Adjusted Batter Runs
Schmidt-Phi 44.7
Guerrero-LA 43.1
Oliver-Mon 40.6
Thompson-Pit 37.4
Durham-Chi 35.1

Clutch Hitting Index
Hernandez-StL 129
Hendrick-StL 128
DeJesus-Phi 123
Buckner-Chi 123
Lezcano-SD 115

Runs Created
Oliver-Mon 125
Guerrero-LA 120
Murphy-Atl 118
Schmidt-Phi 118
Thompson-Pit 117

Total Average
Schmidt-Phi 1.026
Guerrero-LA .... .959
Thompson-Pit ...... .951
Morgan-SF .... .923
Durham-Chi .... .917

Stolen Bases
Raines-Mon 78
L.Smith-StL 68
Moreno-Pit 60
Wilson-NY 58
S.Sax-LA 49

Stolen Base Average
Bailor-NY 87.0
Morgan-SF 85.7
Wiggins-SD 84.6
Matthews-Phi 84.0
O.Smith-StL 83.3

Stolen Base Runs
Raines-Mon 11.6
Wilson-NY 7.2
L.Smith-StL 5.9
Thon-Hou 5.3
Wiggins-SD 5.2

Fielding Runs
O.Smith-StL 33.1
Dawson-Mon 20.8
Hubbard-Atl 19.9
Schmidt-Phi 18.8
Davis-SF 17.9

Total Player Rating
Schmidt-Phi............ 6.3
Carter-Mon 5.6
Dawson-Mon 4.9
O.Smith-StL 4.5
Guerrero-LA 4.4

Wins
Carlton-Phi 23
Valenzuela-LA 19
Rogers-Mon 19
Reuss-LA 18

Win Percentage
Niekro-Atl 810
Rogers-Mon 704
Carlton-Phi 676
Lollar-SD 640
Forsch-StL 625

Games
Tekulve-Pit 85
Minton-SF 78
Scurry-Pit 76
Reardon-Mon 75
Hernandez-Chi 75

Complete Games
Carlton-Phi 19
Valenzuela-LA 18
Niekro-Hou 16
Rogers-Mon 14
Soto-Cin 13

Shutouts
Carlton-Phi 6
Niekro-Hou 5
Andujar-StL 5

Saves
Sutter-StL 36
Minton-SF 30
Garber-Atl 30
Reardon-Mon 26
Tekulve-Pit 20

Innings Pitched
Carlton-Phi 295.2
Valenzuela-LA..... 285.0
Rogers-Mon 277.0
Niekro-Hou 270.0
Andujar-StL 265.2

Fewest Hits/Game
Ryan-Hou 7.05
Soto-Cin 7.06
Lea-Mon 7.35
Lollar-SD 7.43
Niekro-Hou 7.47

Fewest BB/Game
Bird-Chi 1.41
Hammaker-SF 1.44
Andujar-StL 1.69
Reuss-LA 1.77
Candelaria-Pit 1.91

Strikeouts
Carlton-Phi 286
Soto-Cin 274
Ryan-Hou 245
Valenzuela-LA 199
Rogers-Mon 179

Strikeouts/Game
Soto-Cin 9.57
Ryan-Hou 8.81
Carlton-Phi 8.71
Candelaria-Pit 6.85
Welch-LA 6.72

Ratio
Soto-Cin............. 9.68
Niekro-Hou 9.77
Andujar-StL 9.96
Sutton-Hou 9.97
Reuss-LA 10.04

Earned Run Average
Rogers-Mon 2.40
Niekro-Hou 2.47
Andujar-StL 2.47
Soto-Cin 2.79
Valenzuela-LA 2.87

Adjusted ERA
Rogers-Mon 152
Andujar-StL 147
Niekro-Hou 135
Soto-Cin 133
Candelaria-Pit 126

Opponents' Batting Avg.
Ryan-Hou 213
Soto-Cin 215
Lea-Mon 222
Lollar-SD 224
Niekro-Hou 229

Opponents' On-Base Pct.
Soto-Cin 273
Reuss-LA 278
Sutton-Hou 279
Niekro-Hou 279
Andujar-StL 282

Starter Runs
Rogers-Mon 37.1
Niekro-Hou 34.3
Andujar-StL 33.5
Soto-Cin 23.3
Valenzuela-LA 23.3

Adjusted Starter Runs
Rogers-Mon 37.9
Andujar-StL 33.9
Niekro-Hou 27.9
Soto-Cin 25.4
Valenzuela-LA 19.8

Clutch Pitching Index
Camp-Atl 124
Jenkins-Chi 121
Krukow-Phi 120
Gale-SF 115
Mura-StL 110

Relief Runs
Minton-SF 24.3
Scurry-Pit 21.6
Reardon-Mon 18.7
Bedrosian-Atl 18.2
DeLeon-SD 17.9

Adjusted Relief Runs
Minton-SF 24.3
Scurry-Pit 22.1
Bedrosian-Atl 19.5
Reardon-Mon 19.0
Garber-Atl 17.9

Relief Ranking
Minton-SF 35.9
Garber-Atl 32.7
Reardon-Mon 25.7
DeLeon-SD 25.2
Scurry-Pit 22.9

Total Pitcher Index
Minton-SF 4.0
Garber-Atl 3.8
Rogers-Mon 3.7
Andujar-StL 3.2
DeLeon-SD 2.8

Total Baseball Ranking
Schmidt-Phi 6.3
Carter-Mon 5.6
Dawson-Mon 4.9
O.Smith-StL 4.5
Guerrero-LA 4.4

TEAM	G	W	L	PCT	GB	R	OR	AB	H	2B	3B	HR	BB	SO	AVG	OBP	SLG	OPS	OPS+	BR	BR+	PF	CHI	RC	SB	CS	SBA	SBR
EAST																												
MIL	163	95	67	.586		**891**	717	5733	1599	277	41	**216**	484	714	.279	.337	**.455**	**792**	**123**	**109**	**165**	94	105	**865**	84	52	62	0
BAL	163	94	68	.580	1	774	687	5557	1478	259	27	179	634	796	.266	.344	.419	763	108	67	70	100	96	795	49	38	56	-3
BOS	162	89	73	.549	6	753	713	5596	1536	271	31	136	547	736	.274	.342	.407	749	99	39	-3	106	98	755	42	39	52	-4
DET	162	83	79	.512	12	729	685	5590	1489	237	40	177	470	807	.266	.326	.418	744	103	15	12	100	99	752	93	66	58	-3
NY	162	79	83	.488	16	709	716	5526	1417	225	37	161	590	719	.256	.331	.398	729	101	-5	7	98	98	716	69	45	61	-1
TOR	162	78	84	.481	17	651	701	5526	1447	262	45	106	415	749	.262	.317	.383	700	83	-70	-124	109	102	655	**118**	81	59	-2
CLE	162	78	84	.481	17	683	748	5559	1458	225	32	109	**651**	**625**	.262	.343	.373	716	97	-13	-9	100	94	723	151	68	69	9
WEST																												
CAL	162	93	69	.574		814	**670**	5532	1518	268	26	186	613	760	.274	**.350**	.433	783	114	108	108	100	96	834	55	53	51	-6
KC	162	90	72	.556	3	784	717	5629	**1603**	**295**	**58**	132	442	758	**.285**	.340	.428	768	109	67	66	100	99	802	133	48	**73**	12
CHI	162	87	75	.537	6	786	710	5575	1523	266	52	136	533	866	.273	.340	.413	753	106	43	43	100	102	784	136	58	70	10
SEA	162	76	86	.469	17	651	712	5626	1431	259	33	130	456	806	.254	.313	.381	694	87	-84	-101	103	102	657	131	82	62	0
OAK	162	68	94	.420	29	691	819	5448	1286	211	27	149	582	948	.236	.312	.367	679	90	-106	-78	96	**113**	644	**232**	87	**73**	**21**
TEX	162	64	98	.395	33	590	749	5445	1354	204	26	115	447	750	.249	.309	.359	668	87	-128	-98	95	103	593	63	45	58	-2
MIN	162	60	102	.370	37	657	819	5544	1427	234	44	148	474	887	.257	.319	.396	715	93	-43	-61	103	98	676	38	33	54	-3
TOT	1135					10163		77886	20566	3493	519	2080	7338	10921	.265	.331	.403	733							1394	795	64	28

TEAM	CG	SH	SV	IP	H	H/G	HR	BB	SO	RAT	ERA	ERA+	OAV	OOB	PR	PR+	PF	CPI	FA	E	DP	FW	PW	BW	SBW	DIF
EAST																										
MIL	34	6	**47**	1467^{1}	1514	9.3	152	511	717	12.6	3.99	95	.270	.333	15	-35	93	106	.980	125	**185**	.2	-3.5	**16.6**	-.2	1.1
BAL	38	8	34	1462^{1}	1436	8.9	147	488	719	**12.0**	3.99	101	.257	**.320**	14	7	99	95	**.984**	**101**	140	**1.5**	.8	7.1	-.5	4.4
BOS	23	11	33	1453	1557	9.7	155	478	816	12.9	4.04	107	.276	.336	7	42	106	**108**	.981	121	172	.3	4.3	-.3	-.6	4.5
DET	**45**	5	27	1451	**1371**	**8.6**	172	554	740	12.1	**3.81**	107	**.251**	.323	**44**	42	100	104	.981	117	165	.6	4.3	1.3	-.5	-3.4
NY	24	8	39	1459	1471	9.1	113	491	939	12.3	4.00	100	.264	.326	13	-1	98	95	.979	128	158	-.0	-.0	.8	-.3	-2.2
TOR	41	**13**	25	1443^{2}	1428	9.0	147	493	776	12.2	3.95	**113**	.257	.321	20	**77**	110	97	.978	136	146	-.5	**7.8**	-12.4	-.4	2.7
CLE	31	9	30	1468^{1}	1433	8.8	122	589	882	12.6	4.11	99	.257	.330	-5	-5	100	94	.980	123	129	.2	-.5	-.9	.7	-2.4
WEST																										
CAL	40	10	27	1464	1436	8.9	124	482	728	12.1	3.82	106	.259	.322	42	38	100	98	.983	108	171	1.0	3.9	10.9	-.8	-2.7
KC	16	12	45	1431	1443	9.1	163	471	650	12.3	4.09	100	.262	.323	-1	0	100	98	.979	127	140	.0	.0	6.7	1.0	1.5
CHI	30	10	41	1439	1502	9.4	**99**	**460**	753	12.5	3.87	104	.270	.329	33	27	99	100	.976	154	173	-1.5	2.8	4.4	.8	-.2
SEA	23	11	39	1476^{1}	1431	8.8	173	547	**1002**	12.3	3.88	109	.256	.325	32	57	104	104	.978	139	158	-.6	5.8	-10.1	-.2	.3
OAK	42	6	22	1456	1506	9.4	177	648	697	13.6	4.55	86	.268	.346	-76	-107	96	100	.974	160	140	-1.8	-10.7	-7.8	**1.9**	5.5
TEX	32	5	24	1431	1554	9.8	128	483	690	13.1	4.29	90	.280	.342	-33	-69	95	102	.981	121	169	.3	-6.9	-9.8	-.4	-.1
MIN	26	7	30	1433	1484	9.4	208	643	812	13.5	4.73	90	.269	.347	-103	-74	104	101	.982	108	162	1.0	-7.4	-6.1	-.5	-7.9
TOT	445	121	463	20335		9.2				12.6	4.08		.265	.331					.980	1768	2208					

Runs
Molitor-Mil 136
Yount-Mil 129
Evans-Bos 122
Henderson-Oak 119
Downing-Cal 109

Hits
Yount-Mil 210
Cooper-Mil 205
Molitor-Mil 201
Wilson-KC 194
McRae-KC 189

Doubles
Yount-Mil 46
McRae-KC 46
White-KC 45
DeCinces-Cal 42
Cowens-Sea 39

Triples
Wilson-KC 15
Herndon-Det 13
Yount-Mil 12
Mumphrey-NY 10

Home Runs
Thomas-Mil 39
R.Jackson-Cal 39
Winfield-NY 37
Oglivie-Mil 34

Total Bases
Yount-Mil 367
Cooper-Mil 345
McRae-KC 332
Evans-Bos 325
DeCinces-Cal 315

Runs Batted In
McRae-KC 133
Cooper-Mil 121
Thornton-Cle 116
Yount-Mil 114
Thomas-Mil 112

Runs Produced
Yount-Mil 214
McRae-KC 197
Cooper-Mil 193
Molitor-Mil 188
Evans-Bos 188

Bases On Balls
Henderson-Oak 116
Evans-Bos 112
Thornton-Cle 109
Hargrove-Cle 101
Murphy-Oak 94

Batting Average
Wilson-KC .332
Yount-Mil .331
Carew-Cal .319
Murray-Bal .316
Cooper-Mil .313

On-Base Percentage
Evans-Bos .403
Harrah-Cle .400
Henderson-Oak .399
Carew-Cal .399
Murray-Bal .395

Slugging Average
Yount-Mil .578
Winfield-NY .560
Murray-Bal .549
DeCinces-Cal .548
McRae-KC .542

On-Base Plus Slugging
Yount-Mil 962
Murray-Bal 944
Evans-Bos 937
DeCinces-Cal 922
McRae-KC 912

Adjusted OPS
Yount-Mil 170
Murray-Bal 157
DeCinces-Cal 149
R.Jackson-Cal 147
McRae-KC 146

Batter Runs
Yount-Mil 50.3
Evans-Bos 48.5
Murray-Bal 42.5
DeCinces-Cal 38.1
Harrah-Cle 38.0

Adjusted Batter Runs
Yount-Mil 59.0
Murray-Bal 42.9
Evans-Bos 41.2
Harrah-Cle 38.6
DeCinces-Cal 38.1

Clutch Hitting Index
Otis-KC 137
Foli-Cal 137
Hayes-Cle 128
Boone-Cal 124
Murphy-Oak 122

Runs Created
Yount-Mil 136
Evans-Bos 134
Harrah-Cle 123
McRae-KC 123
Cooper-Mil 118

Total Average
Evans-Bos .976
Yount-Mil .969
Murray-Bal .957
Henderson-Oak .934
Harrah-Cle .931

Stolen Bases
Henderson-Oak 130
Garcia-Tor 54
J.Cruz-Sea 46
Molitor-Mil 41
Wilson-KC 37

Stolen Base Average
Sexton-Oak 100.0
Fisk-Chi 89.5
Dilone-Cle 86.8
Harrah-Cle 85.0
Brown-Sea 82.4

Stolen Base Runs
Henderson-Oak 13.9
Molitor-Mil 5.9
J.Cruz-Sea 5.6
Dilone-Cle 5.5
Garcia-Tor 4.9

Fielding Runs
Bell-Tex 34.4
Bernazard-Chi 24.6
Murphy-Oak 21.8
DeCinces-Cal 20.6
Almon-Chi 20.0

Total Player Rating
Yount-Mil 7.2
DeCinces-Cal 5.5
Bell-Tex 5.3
Evans-Bos 3.8
Henderson-Oak 3.8

Wins
Hoyt-Chi 19
Zahn-Cal 18
Vuckovich-Mil 18
Gura-KC 18

Win Percentage
Vuckovich-Mil .750
Palmer-Bal .750
Zahn-Cal .692
Petry-Det .625
Gura-KC .600

Games
VandeBerg-Sea 78
T.Martinez-Bal 76
Quisenberry-KC 72
Caudill-Sea 70
Spillner-Cle 65

Complete Games
Stieb-Tor 19
Morris-Det 17
Langford-Oak 15
Hoyt-Chi 14

Shutouts
Stieb-Tor 5
Zahn-Cal 4
Forsch-Cal 4

Saves
Quisenberry-KC 35
Gossage-NY 30
Fingers-Mil 29
Caudill-Sea 26
Davis-Min 22

Innings Pitched
Stieb-Tor 288.1
Clancy-Tor 266.2
Morris-Det 266.1
Caldwell-Mil 258.0
D.Martinez-Bal 252.0

Fewest Hits/Game
Sutcliffe-Cle 7.25
Ujdur-Det 7.58
Righetti-NY 7.62
Palmer-Bal 7.73
Barker-Cle 7.76

Fewest BB/Game
John-NY-Cal 1.58
Eckersley-Bos 1.73
Hoyt-Chi 1.80
Haas-Mil 1.82
Langford-Oak 1.86

Strikeouts
Bannister-Sea 209
Barker-Cle 187
Righetti-NY 163
Guidry-NY 162
Tudor-Bos 146

Strikeouts/Game
Righetti-NY 8.02
Bannister-Sea 7.62
Beattie-Sea 7.31
Barker-Cle 6.88
Tudor-Bos 6.72

Ratio
Palmer-Bal 10.39
Eckersley-Bos 10.95
Stieb-Tor 10.96
Barker-Cle 11.11
Bannister-Sea 11.11

Earned Run Average
Sutcliffe-Cle 2.96
Stanley-Bos 3.10
Palmer-Bal 3.13
Petry-Det 3.22
Stieb-Tor 3.25

Adjusted ERA
Stanley-Bos 139
Stieb-Tor 138
Sutcliffe-Cle 138
Palmer-Bal 129
Beattie-Sea 127

Opponents' Batting Avg.
Sutcliffe-Cle .226
Righetti-NY .229
Ujdur-Det .230
Palmer-Bal .231
Barker-Cle .232

Opponents' On-Base Pct.
Palmer-Bal .287
Eckersley-Bos .297
Stieb-Tor .299
Barker-Cle .301
Clancy-Tor .302

Starter Runs
Sutcliffe-Cle 27.0
Stieb-Tor 26.8
Palmer-Bal 24.0
Petry-Det 23.6
Vuckovich-Mil 18.5

Adjusted Starter Runs
Stieb-Tor 36.2
Sutcliffe-Cle 27.0
Petry-Det 23.3
Palmer-Bal 23.2
Bannister-Sea 21.7

Clutch Pitching Index
Vuckovich-Mil 131
Tudor-Bos 121
Dotson-Chi 119
Wilcox-Det 113
Stanley-Bos 110

Relief Runs
Spillner-Cle 23.6
Quisenberry-KC 23.1
Burgmeier-Bos 20.4
Gossage-NY 19.2
Caudill-Sea 18.4

Adjusted Relief Runs
Spillner-Cle 23.7
Quisenberry-KC 23.1
Burgmeier-Bos 21.8
Stanley-Bos 21.5
Caudill-Sea 19.4

Relief Ranking
Spillner-Cle 43.3
Caudill-Sea 38.8
Quisenberry-KC 37.3
Gossage-NY 29.5
Clear-Bos 29.0

Total Pitcher Index
Quisenberry-KC 4.5
Spillner-Cle 4.2
Stieb-Tor 4.1
Caudill-Sea 3.9
Stanley-Bos 3.1

Total Baseball Ranking
Yount-Mil 7.2
DeCinces-Cal 5.5
Bell-Tex 5.3
Quisenberry-KC 4.5
Spillner-Cle 4.2

TEAM	G	W	L	PCT	GB	R	OR	AB	H	2B	3B	HR	BB	SO	AVG	OBP	SLG	OPS	OPS+	BR	BR+	PF	CHI	RC	SB	CS	SBA	SBR
EAST																												
PHI	163	90	72	.556		696	635	5426	1352	209	45	125	**640**	906	.249	.331	.373	704	102	17	25	99	101	676	143	75	66	5
PIT	162	84	78	.519	6	659	648	5531	1460	238	29	121	497	873	.264	.327	.383	710	100	17	0	103	96	682	124	77	62	0
MON	163	82	80	.506	8	677	646	5611	1482	**297**	41	102	509	**733**	.264	.329	.386	715	105	30	34	99	95	716	138	44	**76**	15
STL	162	79	83	.488	11	679	710	5550	**1496**	262	**63**	83	543	879	.270	.337	.384	721	**106**	47	**47**	100	94	725	**207**	89	70	14
CHI	162	71	91	.438	19	701	719	5512	1436	272	42	140	470	868	.261	.322	**.401**	723	101	35	3	105	100	707	84	40	68	4
NY	162	68	94	.420	22	575	680	5444	1314	172	26	112	436	1031	.241	.301	.344	645	85	-112	-107	99	107	562	141	64	69	9
WEST																												
LA	163	91	71	.562		654	**609**	5440	1358	197	34	**146**	541	925	.250	.320	.379	699	100	-6	-2	99	100	663	166	76	69	10
ATL	162	88	74	.543	3	**746**	640	5472	1489	218	45	130	582	847	**.272**	**.344**	.400	**744**	104	**91**	39	107	98	**744**	146	88	62	1
HOU	162	85	77	.525	6	643	646	5502	1412	239	60	97	517	869	.257	.323	.375	698	**106**	-7	37	94	97	673	164	95	63	3
SD	163	81	81	.500	10	653	653	5527	1384	207	34	93	482	822	.250	.313	.351	664	93	-74	-53	97	**110**	609	179	67	73	**16**
SF	162	79	83	.488	12	687	697	5369	1324	206	30	142	619	990	.247	.328	.375	703	104	11	33	97	102	662	140	78	64	4
CIN	162	74	88	.457	17	623	710	5333	1274	236	35	107	588	1006	.239	.317	.356	673	89	-49	-69	104	103	606	154	77	67	7
TOT	974					7993		65717	16781	2753	484	1398	6424	10749	.256	.325	.376	700							1786	870	67	88

TEAM	CG	SH	SV	IP	H	H/G	HR	BB	SO	RAT	ERA	ERA+	OAV	OOB	PR	PR+	PF	CPI	FA	E	DP	FW	PW	BW	SBW	DIF
EAST																										
PHI	20	10	41	1461^{2}	1429	8.8	111	**464**	**1092**	11.8	3.34	107	.256	.316	47	38	98	104	.976	152	117	-.7	4.0	2.7	-.2	3.4
PIT	25	14	41	1462^{1}	1378	8.5	109	563	1061	12.1	3.56	104	.252	.323	12	24	102	100	**.982**	115	165	**1.5**	2.6	.0	-.8	-.1
MON	**38**	**15**	34	1471	1406	8.7	120	479	899	11.8	3.58	100	.254	.317	8	1	99	98	.981	116	130	**1.5**	.2	3.6	.8	-4.8
STL	22	10	27	1460^{2}	1479	9.2	115	525	709	12.5	3.79	96	.266	.332	-26	-28	100	103	.976	152	173	-.7	-2.9	**5.0**	.7	-3.8
CHI	9	10	42	1428^{2}	1496	9.5	117	498	807	12.8	4.08	93	.274	.337	-71	-43	105	100	**.982**	115	164	**1.5**	-4.4	.4	-.4	-6.9
NY	18	7	33	1451	1384	8.6	97	615	717	12.6	3.68	99	.256	.334	-8	-8	100	101	.976	151	171	-.7	-.8	-11.1	.2	-.4
WEST																										
LA	27	12	40	1464	1336	8.3	97	495	1000	**11.4**	**3.11**	**116**	.244	**.309**	**85**	**80**	99	101	.974	168	132	-1.6	**8.4**	-.2	.3	3.3
ATL	18	4	**48**	1440^{2}	1412	8.9	132	540	895	12.4	3.68	106	.260	.329	-7	30	107	**105**	.978	137	**176**	.2	3.2	4.1	-.7	.4
HOU	22	14	**48**	1466^{1}	**1276**	**7.9**	**94**	570	904	11.5	3.45	99	**.236**	.312	29	-8	94	90	.977	147	165	-.4	-.8	3.9	-.5	2.0
SD	23	5	44	1467^{2}	1389	8.6	144	528	850	12.0	3.62	96	.253	.322	1	-23	96	103	.979	129	135	.7	-2.4	-5.5	**.9**	6.4
SF	20	9	47	1445^{2}	1431	9.0	127	520	881	12.4	3.70	96	.259	.326	-11	-27	97	102	.973	171	109	-1.9	-2.8	3.5	-.4	-.3
CIN	34	5	29	1441^{1}	1365	8.6	135	627	934	12.6	3.99	95	.253	.333	-57	-27	105	97	.981	**114**	121	**1.5**	-2.8	-7.2	-.0	1.6
TOT	276	115	474	17461		8.7				12.2	3.63		.256	.325					.978	1667	1758					

Runs
Raines-Mon 133
Murphy-Atl 131
Schmidt-Phi 104
Dawson-Mon 104

Hits
Dawson-Mon 189
Cruz-Hou 189
Ramirez-Atl 185
Oliver-Mon 184
Raines-Mon 183

Doubles
Ray-Pit 38
Oliver-Mon 38
Buckner-Chi 38
Carter-Mon 37

Triples
Butler-Atl 13
Moreno-Hou 11
Green-StL 10
Dawson-Mon 10

Home Runs
Schmidt-Phi 40
Murphy-Atl 36
Guerrero-LA 32
Dawson-Mon 32
Evans-SF 30

Total Bases
Dawson-Mon 341
Murphy-Atl 318
Guerrero-LA 310
Thon-Hou 283
Schmidt-Phi 280

Runs Batted In
Murphy-Atl 121
Dawson-Mon 113
Schmidt-Phi 109
Guerrero-LA 103
Kennedy-SD 98

Runs Produced
Murphy-Atl 216
Raines-Mon 193
Dawson-Mon 185
Schmidt-Phi 173
Cruz-Hou 163

Bases On Balls
Schmidt-Phi 128
Thompson-Pit 99
Raines-Mon 97
Murphy-Atl 90
Morgan-Phi 89

Batting Average
Madlock-Pit .... .323
L.Smith-StL .... .321
Cruz-Hou .... .318
Hendrick-StL .... .318
Knight-Hou .... .304

On-Base Percentage
Schmidt-Phi .... .402
Hernandez-StL-NY . .398
Murphy-Atl .... .396
Raines-Mon .... .395
Madlock-Pit .... .389

Slugging Average
Murphy-Atl .... .540
Dawson-Mon .... .539
Guerrero-LA .... .531
Schmidt-Phi .... .524
Evans-SF .... .516

On-Base Plus Slugging
Murphy-Atl 936
Schmidt-Phi 926
Guerrero-LA 908
Evans-SF 896
Dawson-Mon 886

Adjusted OPS
Schmidt-Phi 156
Evans-SF 151
Guerrero-LA 150
Murphy-Atl 146
Cruz-Hou 143

Batter Runs
Murphy-Atl 46.2
Schmidt-Phi 43.2
Guerrero-LA 37.8
Evans-SF 33.0
Dawson-Mon 32.4

Adjusted Batter Runs
Schmidt-Phi 44.7
Guerrero-LA 38.4
Murphy-Atl 37.9
Evans-SF 36.2
Cruz-Hou 34.8

Clutch Hitting Index
Kennedy-SD 122
Rose-Phi 121
Garner-Hou 115
Hendrick-StL 115
McGee-StL 112

Runs Created
Murphy-Atl 131
Raines-Mon 120
Guerrero-LA 118
Schmidt-Phi 117
Dawson-Mon 113

Total Average
Murphy-Atl 1.014
Schmidt-Phi .... .986
Raines-Mon .... .959
Guerrero-LA .... .935
Evans-SF .... .908

Stolen Bases
Raines-Mon 90
Wiggins-SD 66
S.Sax-LA 56
Wilson-NY 54
L.Smith-StL 43

Stolen Base Average
Morgan-Phi 90.0
Murphy-Atl 88.2
Raines-Mon 86.5
Bailor-NY 85.7
Wiggins-SD 83.5

Stolen Base Runs
Raines-Mon 14.9
Wiggins-SD 10.0
Wilson-NY 6.3
McGee-StL 5.8
Dernier-Phi 5.3

Fielding Runs
Sandberg-Chi 41.1
Schmidt-Phi 23.3
Hubbard-Atl 21.6
Buckner-Chi 21.0
Thon-Hou 20.8

Total Player Rating
Schmidt-Phi 6.6
Thon-Hou 6.2
Raines-Mon 5.3
Dawson-Mon 4.9
Murphy-Atl 4.7

Wins
Denny-Phi 19
Soto-Cin 17
Rogers-Mon 17
Gullickson-Mon 17
Lea-Mon 16

Win Percentage
Denny-Phi .... .760
Perez-Atl .... .652
McWilliams-Pit ...... .652
Candelaria-Pit ...... .652
McMurtry-Atl .... .625

Games
Campbell-Chi 82
Tekulve-Pit 76
Hernandez-Chi-Phi .. 74
Scherrer-Cin 73
Minton-SF 73

Complete Games
Soto-Cin 18
Rogers-Mon 13
Gullickson-Mon 10

Shutouts
Rogers-Mon 5
Valenzuela-LA 4
McWilliams-Pit 4
Lea-Mon 4

Saves
Smith-Chi 29
Holland-Phi 25
Minton-SF 22
Sutter-StL 21
Reardon-Mon 21

Innings Pitched
Carlton-Phi 283.2
Soto-Cin 273.2
Rogers-Mon 273.0
Niekro-Hou 263.2
Valenzuela-LA 257.0

Fewest Hits/Game
Ryan-Hou 6.14
Soto-Cin 6.81
Welch-LA 7.24
Hammaker-SF 7.68
Pena-LA 7.73

Fewest BB/Game
Hammaker-SF 1.67
Ruthven-Phi-Chi 1.87
Denny-Phi 1.97
Reuss-LA 2.01
Candelaria-Pit 2.05

Strikeouts
Carlton-Phi 275
Soto-Cin 242
McWilliams-Pit 199
Valenzuela-LA 189
Ryan-Hou 183

Strikeouts/Game
Carlton-Phi 8.73
Ryan-Hou 8.39
Soto-Cin 7.96
McWilliams-Pit 7.53
Berenyi-Cin 7.29

Ratio
Hammaker-SF 9.50
Soto-Cin 10.10
Pena-LA 10.37
Welch-LA 10.54
Denny-Phi 10.61

Earned Run Average
Hammaker-SF 2.25
Denny-Phi 2.37
Welch-LA 2.65
Soto-Cin 2.70
Pena-LA 2.75

Adjusted ERA
Hammaker-SF 158
Denny-Phi 151
Soto-Cin 141
Welch-LA 136
Pena-LA 131

Opponents' Batting Avg.
Ryan-Hou .... .195
Soto-Cin .... .208
Welch-LA .... .222
Hammaker-SF .... .228
Pena-LA .... .229

Opponents' On-Base Pct.
Hammaker-SF .... .267
Soto-Cin .... .280
Pena-LA .... .285
Welch-LA .... .294
Denny-Phi .... .294

Starter Runs
Denny-Phi 34.1
Soto-Cin 28.6
Hammaker-SF 26.6
Welch-LA 22.4
Smith-Mon 19.8

Adjusted Starter Runs
Denny-Phi 33.0
Soto-Cin 32.4
Hammaker-SF 25.5
Welch-LA 21.8
Smith-Mon 19.3

Clutch Pitching Index
Rhoden-Pit 120
Niekro-Atl 117
Reuss-LA 116
Denny-Phi 116
Knepper-Hou 111

Relief Runs
Orosco-NY 26.5
Smith-Chi 22.8
Tekulve-Pit 22.0
Niedenfuer-LA 18.3
Howe-LA 16.7

Adjusted Relief Runs
Orosco-NY 26.5
Smith-Chi 23.6
Tekulve-Pit 22.4
Niedenfuer-LA 18.1
Howe-LA 16.6

Relief Ranking
Orosco-NY 50.8
Smith-Chi 41.0
Howe-LA 32.0
Tekulve-Pit 31.9
Holland-Phi 22.9

Total Pitcher Index
Orosco-NY 5.8
Smith-Chi 4.4
Howe-LA 3.6
Denny-Phi 3.6
Tekulve-Pit 3.4

Total Baseball Ranking
Schmidt-Phi 6.6
Thon-Hou 6.2
Orosco-NY 5.8
Raines-Mon 5.3
Dawson-Mon 4.9

TEAM	G	W	L	PCT	GB	R	OR	AB	H	2B	3B	HR	BB	SO	AVG	OBP	SLG	OPS	OPS+	BR	BR+	PF	CHI	RC	SB	CS	SBA	SBR
EAST																												
BAL	162	98	64	.605		799	652	5546	1492	283	27	**168**	601	800	.269	**.343**	.421	764	111	70	86	98	99	794	61	33	65	2
DET	162	92	70	.568	6	789	679	5592	1530	283	53	156	508	831	.274	.338	.427	765	112	67	88	97	99	799	93	53	64	2
NY	162	91	71	.562	7	770	703	5631	1535	269	40	153	533	686	.273	.339	.416	755	110	52	82	96	98	783	84	42	67	4
TOR	162	89	73	.549	9	795	726	5581	1546	268	**58**	167	510	810	**.277**	.341	**.436**	**777**	106	**89**	42	106	97	**818**	131	72	65	4
MIL	162	87	75	.537	11	764	708	5620	**1556**	281	57	132	475	**665**	**.277**	.336	.418	754	**115**	44	**108**	92	98	774	101	49	67	5
BOS	162	78	84	.481	20	724	775	5590	1512	**287**	32	142	536	758	.270	.337	.409	746	97	-35	-17	107	94	749	30	26	54	-2
CLE	162	70	92	.432	28	704	785	5476	1451	249	31	86	**605**	691	.265	.341	.369	710	92	-23	-49	104	100	687	109	71	61	-1
WEST																												
CHI	162	99	63	.611		**800**	650	5484	1439	270	42	157	527	888	.262	.332	.413	745	100	26	-1	104	**107**	762	165	50	77	19
KC	163	79	83	.488	20	696	767	5598	1515	273	54	109	397	722	.271	.322	.397	719	97	-31	-32	100	102	711	182	47	**79**	**24**
TEX	163	77	85	.475	22	639	**609**	5610	1429	242	33	106	442	767	.255	.312	.366	678	88	-108	-95	98	104	633	119	60	66	5
OAK	162	74	88	.457	25	708	782	5516	1447	237	28	121	524	872	.262	.330	.381	711	101	-34	9	94	102	694	**235**	98	71	17
CAL	162	70	92	.432	27	722	779	5640	1467	241	22	154	509	835	.260	.325	.393	718	98	-29	-23	99	102	702	41	39	51	-5
MIN	162	70	92	.432	27	709	822	5601	1463	280	41	141	467	802	.261	.321	.401	722	94	-23	-47	104	101	701	44	29	60	0
SEA	162	60	102	.370	37	558	740	5336	1280	247	31	111	460	840	.240	.303	.360	663	79	-135	-155	104	100	574	144	80	64	4
TOT	1135					10177		77821	20662	3710	549	1903	7094	10967	.266	.331	.401	731							1539	749	67	76

TEAM	CG	SH	SV	IP	H	H/G	HR	BB	SO	RAT	ERA	ERA+	OAV	OOB	PR	PR+	PF	CPI	FA	E	DP	FW	PW	BW	SBW	DIF
EAST																										
BAL	36	**15**	38	1452^1	1451	9.0	130	452	774	11.9	3.63	109	.261	.318	70	54	97	104	.981	121	159	.6	5.4	8.6	-.3	2.9
DET	42	9	28	1451	**1318**	**8.2**	170	522	875	11.6	3.81	103	**.242**	.312	42	17	96	96	.980	125	142	.4	1.7	8.8	-.3	.6
NY	**47**	12	32	1456^2	1449	9.0	116	455	892	11.9	3.86	101	.260	.318	33	6	96	96	.978	139	157	-.4	.6	8.2	-.1	1.9
TOR	43	8	32	1445^1	1434	9.0	145	517	835	12.5	4.13	104	.259	.327	-10	27	106	97	.981	115	148	.9	2.7	4.2	-.1	.4
MIL	35	10	43	1454	1513	9.4	133	491	689	12.6	4.03	93	.270	.332	6	-50	92	103	**.982**	**113**	162	1.0	-4.9	**10.8**	-.0	-.7
BOS	29	7	42	1446^1	1572	9.8	158	493	767	13.1	4.34	100	.279	.340	-44	2	107	104	.979	130	168	.0	.2	-1.6	-.7	-.8
CLE	34	8	25	1441^2	1531	9.6	120	529	794	13.1	4.44	96	.275	.342	-60	-30	104	97	.980	122	174	.5	-2.9	-4.8	-.6	-2.9
WEST																										
CHI	35	12	48	1445^1	1355	8.5	128	**447**	877	**11.5**	3.67	114	.248	**.309**	63	81	103	95	.981	120	158	.7	8.1	-.0	1.4	8.1
KC	19	8	**49**	1437^2	1535	9.7	133	471	593	12.8	4.26	96	.274	.333	-30	-28	100	99	.974	165	178	-1.8	-2.7	-3.1	**1.9**	4.1
TEX	43	11	32	1466^2	1392	8.6	**97**	471	826	11.7	**3.32**	**121**	.252	.315	**122**	**114**	99	104	**.982**	**113**	151	**1.1**	**11.4**	-9.4	-.0	-6.8
OAK	22	12	33	1454^1	1462	9.1	135	626	719	13.2	4.35	89	.263	.340	-46	-84	95	97	.974	157	157	-1.4	-8.3	.9	1.2	.9
CAL	39	7	23	1474	1636	10.0	130	496	668	13.3	4.32	93	.284	.344	-41	-49	99	104	.977	154	**190**	-1.2	-4.8	-2.2	-1.0	-1.4
MIN	20	5	39	1437^1	1559	9.8	163	580	748	13.7	4.67	91	.280	.351	-96	-64	105	102	.980	121	170	.6	-6.3	-4.6	-.5	.1
SEA	25	9	39	1418^1	1455	9.3	145	544	**910**	13.0	4.12	103	.268	.339	-9	21	105	**105**	.978	136	159	-.2	2.1	-15.4	-.1	-7.1
TOT	469	133	503	20281		9.2				12.6	4.07		.266	.331					.980	1831	2273					

Runs
Ripken-Bal 121
Murray-Bal 115
Cooper-Mil 106
Henderson-Oak 105
Moseby-Tor 104

Hits
Ripken-Bal 211
Boggs-Bos 210
Whitaker-Det 206
Cooper-Mil 203
Rice-Bos 191

Doubles
Ripken-Bal 47
Boggs-Bos 44
Yount-Mil 42
Parrish-Det 42

Triples
Yount-Mil 10
Herndon-Det 9
Griffin-Tor 9
Gibson-Det 9

Home Runs
Rice-Bos 39
Armas-Bos 36
Kittle-Chi 35
Murray-Bal 33

Total Bases
Rice-Bos 344
Ripken-Bal 343
Cooper-Mil 336
Murray-Bal 313
Winfield-NY 307

Runs Batted In
Rice-Bos 126
Cooper-Mil 126
Winfield-NY 116
Parrish-Det 114
Murray-Bal 111

Runs Produced
Cooper-Mil 202
Ripken-Bal 196
Murray-Bal 193
Winfield-NY 183
Rice-Bos 177

Bases On Balls
Henderson-Oak 103
Singleton-Bal 99
Boggs-Bos 92
Thornton-Cle 87
Murray-Bal 86

Batting Average
Boggs-Bos 361
Carew-Cal 339
Whitaker-Det 320
Trammell-Det 319
Ripken-Bal 318

On-Base Percentage
Boggs-Bos 449
Henderson-Oak 415
Carew-Cal 411
Murray-Bal 398
Singleton-Bal 395

Slugging Average
Brett-KC 563
Rice-Bos 550
Murray-Bal 538
Fisk-Chi 518
Ripken-Bal 517

On-Base Plus Slugging
Brett-KC 949
Murray-Bal 936
Boggs-Bos 935
Rice-Bos 914
Upshaw-Tor 891

Adjusted OPS
Murray-Bal 158
Brett-KC 157
Yount-Mil 155
Boggs-Bos 147
Ripken-Bal 145

Batter Runs
Boggs-Bos 50.6
Murray-Bal 44.9
Rice-Bos 38.7
Ripken-Bal 37.1
Brett-KC 36.3

Adjusted Batter Runs
Murray-Bal 47.4
Yount-Mil 44.1
Boggs-Bos 41.8
Ripken-Bal 39.4
Brett-KC 36.1

Clutch Hitting Index
Simmons-Mil 124
Franco-Cle 122
Murphy-Oak 116
Cooper-Mil 116
Singleton-Bal 113

Runs Created
Boggs-Bos 130
Murray-Bal 127
Ripken-Bal 120
Yount-Mil 115
Whitaker-Det 114

Total Average
Henderson-Oak 1.048
Murray-Bal 971
Boggs-Bos 964
Brett-KC 964
Yount-Mil 897

Stolen Bases
Henderson-Oak 108
R.Law-Chi 77
Wilson-KC 59
J.Cruz-Sea-Chi 57
Sample-Tex 44

Stolen Base Average
Wilson-KC 88.1
R.Law-Chi 86.5
Washington-KC 85.1
Henderson-Oak 85.0

Stolen Base Runs
Henderson-Oak 17.1
R.Law-Chi 12.7
Wilson-KC 10.2
J.Cruz-Sea-Chi 8.3
Sample-Tex 6.9

Fielding Runs
Ward-Min 25.9
T.Cruz-Sea-Bal 25.4
Dempsey-Bal 20.6
Fletcher-Chi 18.2
Brunansky-Min 17.8

Total Player Rating
Ripken-Bal 7.0
Yount-Mil 5.4
Henderson-Oak 5.2
Grich-Cal 4.7
Boggs-Bos 4.6

Wins
Hoyt-Chi 24
Dotson-Chi 22
Guidry-NY 21
Morris-Det 20
Petry-Det 19

Win Percentage
Dotson-Chi 759
McGregor-Bal 720
Hoyt-Chi 706
Guidry-NY 700
Boddicker-Bal 667

Games
Quisenberry-KC 69
VandeBerg-Sea 68
Davis-Min 66
T.Martinez-Bal 65
Stanley-Bos 64

Complete Games
Guidry-NY 21
Morris-Det 20
Stieb-Tor 14
Rawley-NY 13
McGregor-Bal 12

Shutouts
Boddicker-Bal 5
Stieb-Tor 4
Burns-Chi 4

Saves
Quisenberry-KC 45
Stanley-Bos 33
Davis-Min 30
Caudill-Sea 26
Ladd-Mil 25

Innings Pitched
Morris-Det 293.2
Stieb-Tor 278.0
Petry-Det 266.1
Hoyt-Chi 260.2
McGregor-Bal 260.0

Fewest Hits/Game
Boddicker-Bal 7.09
Stieb-Tor 7.22
Conroy-Oak 7.82
Hough-Tex 7.82
Dotson-Chi 7.84

Fewest BB/Game
Hoyt-Chi 1.07
McGregor-Bal 1.56
John-Cal 1.88
Honeycutt-Tex 1.91
Eckersley-Bos 1.99

Strikeouts
Morris-Det 232
Bannister-Chi 193
Stieb-Tor 187
Righetti-NY 169
Sutcliffe-Cle 160

Strikeouts/Game
Bannister-Chi 7.99
Morris-Det 7.11
Righetti-NY 7.01
Conroy-Oak 6.21
Gott-Tor 6.16

Ratio
Hoyt-Chi 9.25
Boddicker-Bal 9.70
Morris-Det 10.51
Guidry-NY 10.57
Stieb-Tor 10.68

Earned Run Average
Honeycutt-Tex 2.42
Boddicker-Bal 2.77
Stieb-Tor 3.04
Hough-Tex 3.18
McGregor-Bal 3.18

Adjusted ERA
Honeycutt-Tex 166
Boddicker-Bal 143
Stieb-Tor 142
Young-Sea 131
Dotson-Chi 130

Opponents' Batting Avg.
Boddicker-Bal 216
Stieb-Tor 219
Conroy-Oak 232
Bannister-Chi 233
Morris-Det 233

Opponents' On-Base Pct.
Hoyt-Chi 262
Boddicker-Bal 274
Morris-Det 289
Guidry-NY 291
Stieb-Tor 293

Starter Runs
Honeycutt-Tex 32.1
Stieb-Tor 31.9
Boddicker-Bal 26.1
McGregor-Bal 25.8
Hough-Tex 25.1

Adjusted Starter Runs
Stieb-Tor 37.1
Honeycutt-Tex 31.4
Dotson-Chi 25.3
Boddicker-Bal 24.5
Hough-Tex 23.9

Clutch Pitching Index
Honeycutt-Tex 140
Zahn-Cal 119
Hurst-Bos 114
Dotson-Chi 113
McGregor-Bal 113

Relief Runs
Quisenberry-KC 33.0
Stanley-Bos 19.8
T.Martinez-Bal 19.8
Gossage-NY 17.6
Lopez-Det 16.2

Adjusted Relief Runs
Quisenberry-KC 33.0
Stanley-Bos 22.9
T.Martinez-Bal 19.0
Gossage-NY 16.6
Barojas-Chi 16.3

Relief Ranking
Quisenberry-KC 38.8
Stanley-Bos 36.0
Gossage-NY 33.2
T.Martinez-Bal 27.8
Lopez-Det 24.3

Total Pitcher Index
Honeycutt-Tex 4.2
Quisenberry-KC 4.2
Stieb-Tor 3.7
Stanley-Bos 3.7
Boddicker-Bal 3.5

Total Baseball Ranking
Ripken-Bal 7.0
Yount-Mil 5.4
Henderson-Oak 5.2
Grich-Cal 4.7
Boggs-Bos 4.6

TEAM	G	W	L	PCT	GB	R	OR	AB	H	2B	3B	HR	BB	SO	AVG	OBP	SLG	OPS	OPS+	BR	BR+	PF	CHI	RC	SB	CS	SBA	SBR
EAST																												
CHI	161	96	65	.596		**762**	658	5437	1415	240	47	136	**567**	967	.260	.333	.397	730	102	78	17	109	104	729	154	66	70	11
NY	162	90	72	.556	6.5	652	676	5438	1400	235	25	107	500	1001	.257	.322	.369	691	102	1	11	99	100	645	149	54	73	14
STL	162	84	78	.519	12.5	652	645	5433	1369	225	44	75	516	924	.252	.319	.351	670	97	-35	-19	97	**106**	623	**220**	71	76	**24**
PHI	162	81	81	.500	15.5	720	690	5614	1494	**248**	51	**147**	555	1084	**.266**	**.335**	**.407**	**742**	**112**	**102**	**90**	102	93	**766**	186	60	76	20
MON	161	78	83	.484	18	593	585	5439	1367	242	36	96	470	**782**	.251	.314	.362	676	101	-32	-3	96	96	630	131	38	**78**	16
PIT	162	75	87	.463	21.5	615	**567**	5537	1412	237	33	98	438	841	.255	.312	.363	675	95	-37	-37	100	99	611	96	62	61	-1
WEST																												
SD	162	92	70	.568		686	634	5504	1425	207	42	109	472	810	.259	.320	.371	691	100	-1	0	100	105	645	152	68	69	10
HOU	162	80	82	.494	12	693	630	5548	1465	222	**67**	79	494	837	.264	.326	.371	697	110	14	67	93	102	679	105	61	63	2
ATL	162	80	82	.494	12	632	655	5422	1338	234	27	111	555	896	.247	.319	.361	680	90	-18	-61	107	99	623	140	85	62	1
LA	162	79	83	.488	13	580	600	5399	1316	213	23	102	488	829	.244	.308	.348	656	91	-68	-62	99	100	573	109	69	61	0
CIN	162	70	92	.432	22	627	747	5498	1342	238	30	106	566	978	.244	.316	.356	672	91	-34	-61	105	100	635	160	63	72	13
SF	162	66	96	.407	26	682	807	5650	**1499**	229	26	112	528	980	.265	.330	.375	705	108	31	55	97	97	686	126	76	62	1
TOT	971					7894		65919	16842	2770	451	1278	6149	10929	.256	.322	.370	691							1728	773	69	110

TEAM	CG	SH	SV	IP	H	H/G	HR	BB	SO	RAT	ERA	ERA+	OAV	OOB	PR	PR+	PF	CPI	FA	E	DP	FW	PW	BW	SBW	DIF
EAST																										
CHI	19	8	50	1434	1458	9.2	99	**442**	879	12.1	3.76	104	.267	.324	-26	23	109	99	.981	121	137	1.1	2.5	1.8	.2	10.1
NY	12	15	50	1442^{2}	1371	8.6	104	573	1028	12.3	3.60	98	.252	.326	-2	-11	99	101	.979	129	154	.7	-1.1	1.2	.5	7.9
STL	19	12	**51**	1449	1427	8.9	94	494	808	12.1	3.59	97	.262	.326	1	-19	97	103	**.982**	**118**	**184**	**1.4**	-1.9	-1.9	**1.6**	4.2
PHI	11	6	35	1458^{1}	1416	8.8	101	448	904	11.7	3.62	100	.253	**.310**	-5	2	101	92	.975	161	112	-1.2	.3	**9.5**	1.1	-9.5
MON	19	10	48	1431	1333	8.4	114	474	861	11.5	3.31	103	.249	.312	45	19	95	103	.978	132	147	.5	2.0	-.3	.7	-5.3
PIT	27	13	34	1470	1344	8.3	102	502	995	**11.4**	**3.12**	**116**	.246	**.310**	**78**	**80**	100	**105**	.980	128	142	.8	**8.5**	-3.8	-1.1	-10.1
WEST																										
SD	13	**17**	44	1460^{1}	**1327**	**8.2**	122	563	812	11.8	3.49	102	**.244**	.317	17	14	99	100	.978	138	144	.2	1.5	.0	.0	9.3
HOU	24	13	29	1449^{1}	1350	8.4	91	502	950	11.7	3.32	100	.248	.314	44	1	93	100	.979	133	160	.5	.2	7.1	-.7	-7.8
ATL	17	7	49	1447	1401	8.8	122	525	859	12.1	3.58	108	.257	.324	3	42	107	**105**	.978	139	153	.1	4.5	-6.4	-.9	1.8
LA	**39**	16	27	1460^{2}	1381	8.6	**76**	499	**1033**	11.7	3.17	111	.250	.314	68	60	98	103	.975	163	146	-1.3	6.4	-6.5	-1.0	.6
CIN	25	6	25	1461^{1}	1445	8.9	128	578	946	12.6	4.16	91	.259	.330	-92	-58	105	94	.977	139	116	.1	-6.0	-6.4	.4	1.1
SF	9	7	38	1461	1589	9.8	125	549	854	13.4	4.40	80	.278	.345	-131	-147	98	99	.973	173	134	-1.9	-15.4	5.8	-.9	-2.5
TOT	234	130	480	17424^{2}		8.7				12.1	3.59		.256	.322					.978	1674	1729					

Runs
- Sandberg-Chi 114
- Wiggins-SD 106
- Raines-Mon 106
- Samuel-Phi 105
- Matthews-Chi 101

Hits
- Gwynn-SD 213
- Sandberg-Chi 200
- Raines-Mon 192
- Samuel-Phi 191
- Cruz-Hou 187

Doubles
- Ray-Pit 38
- Raines-Mon 38
- Sandberg-Chi 36
- Samuel-Phi 36

Triples
- Sandberg-Chi 19
- Samuel-Phi 19
- Cruz-Hou 13

Home Runs
- Schmidt-Phi 36
- Murphy-Atl 36
- Carter-Mon 27
- Strawberry-NY 26
- Cey-Chi 25

Total Bases
- Murphy-Atl 332
- Sandberg-Chi 331
- Samuel-Phi 310
- Carter-Mon 290
- Schmidt-Phi 283

Runs Batted In
- Schmidt-Phi 106
- Carter-Mon 106
- Murphy-Atl 100
- Strawberry-NY 97
- Cey-Chi 97

Runs Produced
- Sandberg-Chi 179
- Cruz-Hou 179
- Matthews-Chi 169
- Schmidt-Phi 163
- Hernandez-NY 162

Bases On Balls
- Matthews-Chi 103
- Hernandez-NY 97
- Schmidt-Phi 92
- Thompson-Pit 87
- Raines-Mon 87

Batting Average
- Gwynn-SD .351
- Lacy-Pit .321
- C.Davis-SF .315
- Sandberg-Chi .314
- Ray-Pit .312

On-Base Percentage
- Matthews-Chi .417
- Hernandez-NY .415
- Gwynn-SD .411
- Raines-Mon .395
- Schmidt-Phi .388

Slugging Average
- Murphy-Atl .547
- Schmidt-Phi .536
- Sandberg-Chi .520
- C.Davis-SF .507
- Durham-Chi .505

On-Base Plus Slugging
- Schmidt-Phi 924
- Murphy-Atl 920
- Sandberg-Chi 889
- Durham-Chi 877
- C.Davis-SF 876

Adjusted OPS
- Schmidt-Phi 155
- C.Davis-SF 149
- Cruz-Hou 148
- Murphy-Atl 145
- Hernandez-NY 145

Batter Runs
- Murphy-Atl 43.8
- Schmidt-Phi 41.2
- Sandberg-Chi 37.9
- Hernandez-NY 35.5
- Gwynn-SD 33.9

Adjusted Batter Runs
- Schmidt-Phi 39.5
- Cruz-Hou 38.8
- Hernandez-NY 37.1
- Murphy-Atl 35.9
- Raines-Mon 35.5

Clutch Hitting Index
- Mumphrey-Hou 132
- Davis-Chi 125
- Garvey-SD 125
- Cey-Chi 120
- Concepcion-Cin 118

Runs Created
- Sandberg-Chi 126
- Raines-Mon 124
- Murphy-Atl 123
- Cruz-Hou 111
- Carter-Mon 108

Total Average
- Raines-Mon .953
- Murphy-Atl .942
- Schmidt-Phi .933
- Sandberg-Chi .913
- Matthews-Chi .888

Stolen Bases
- Raines-Mon 75
- Samuel-Phi 72
- Wiggins-SD 70
- L.Smith-StL 50

Stolen Base Average
- Dilone-Mon 93.1
- Raines-Mon 88.2
- Cedeno-Cin 86.4
- VanSlyke-StL 84.8
- Stone-Phi 84.4

Stolen Base Runs
- Raines-Mon 13.0
- Samuel-Phi 10.6
- Wiggins-SD 8.1
- Wilson-NY 7.0
- Redus-Cin 6.7

Fielding Runs
- O.Smith-StL 26.2
- Sandberg-Chi 23.3
- Garner-Hou 23.1
- Martinez-SD 20.6
- Hubbard-Atl 19.6

Total Player Rating
- Sandberg-Chi 6.7
- Raines-Mon 5.8
- Schmidt-Phi 4.9
- Cruz-Hou 4.8
- Hernandez-NY 4.6

Wins
- Andujar-StL 20
- Soto-Cin 18
- Gooden-NY 17
- Sutcliffe-Chi 16
- Niekro-Hou 16

Win Percentage
- Sutcliffe-Chi .941
- Soto-Cin .720
- Gooden-NY .654
- Show-SD .625

Games
- Power-Cin 78
- Lavelle-SF 77
- Minton-SF 74
- Tekulve-Pit 72
- Sutter-StL 71

Complete Games
- Soto-Cin 13
- Valenzuela-LA 12
- Andujar-StL 12
- Knepper-Hou 11
- Mahler-Atl 9

Shutouts
- Pena-LA 4
- Hershiser-LA 4
- Andujar-StL 4

Saves
- Sutter-StL 45
- Smith-Chi 33
- Orosco-NY 31
- Holland-Phi 29
- Gossage-SD 25

Innings Pitched
- Andujar-StL 261.1
- Valenzuela-LA 261.0
- Niekro-Hou 248.1
- Rhoden-Pit 238.1
- Soto-Cin 237.1

Fewest Hits/Game
- Gooden-NY 6.65
- Soto-Cin 6.86
- DeLeon-Pit 6.88
- Ryan-Hou 7.01
- Andujar-StL 7.51

Fewest BB/Game
- Gullickson-Mon 1.47
- Candelaria-Pit 1.65
- Whitson-SD 2.00
- Pena-LA 2.08
- Knepper-Hou 2.12

Strikeouts
- Gooden-NY 276
- Valenzuela-LA 240
- Ryan-Hou 197
- Soto-Cin 185
- Carlton-Phi 163

Strikeouts/Game
- Gooden-NY 11.39
- Ryan-Hou 9.65
- Valenzuela-LA 8.28
- Berenyi-Cin-NY 7.27
- DeLeon-Pit 7.16

Ratio
- Gooden-NY 9.74
- Hershiser-LA 10.15
- Andujar-StL 10.16
- Soto-Cin 10.35
- Candelaria-Pit 10.39

Earned Run Average
- Pena-LA 2.48
- Gooden-NY 2.60
- Hershiser-LA 2.66
- Rhoden-Pit 2.72
- Candelaria-Pit 2.72

Adjusted ERA
- Pena-LA 142
- Gooden-NY 136
- Hershiser-LA 133
- Rhoden-Pit 133
- Candelaria-Pit 133

Opponents' Batting Avg.
- Gooden-NY .202
- Soto-Cin .209
- Ryan-Hou .211
- DeLeon-Pit .214
- Hershiser-LA .225

Opponents' On-Base Pct.
- Gooden-NY .270
- Hershiser-LA .279
- Soto-Cin .286
- Andujar-StL .286
- Ryan-Hou .288

Starter Runs
- Pena-LA 24.6
- Gooden-NY 24.0
- Rhoden-Pit 23.1
- Hershiser-LA 19.7
- Denny-Phi 19.6

Adjusted Starter Runs
- Pena-LA 23.7
- Rhoden-Pit 23.4
- Gooden-NY 23.1
- Denny-Phi 20.1
- Hershiser-LA 18.8

Clutch Pitching Index
- McWilliams-Pit 130
- Terrell-NY 124
- Candelaria-Pit 122
- Honeycutt-LA 117
- Trout-Chi 117

Relief Runs
- Sutter-StL 28.0
- Dawley-Hou 18.1
- Lefferts-SD 17.2
- Sisk-NY 13.0
- Andersen-Phi 12.2

Adjusted Relief Runs
- Sutter-StL 27.3
- Lefferts-SD 17.0
- Dawley-Hou 16.4
- Bedrosian-Atl 12.9
- Sisk-NY 12.7

Relief Ranking
- Sutter-StL 42.2
- Dawley-Hou 24.1
- Bedrosian-Atl 23.9
- Orosco-NY 18.7
- Power-Cin 16.7

Total Pitcher Index
- Sutter-StL 4.6
- Rhoden-Pit 3.5
- Gooden-NY 2.9
- Dawley-Hou 2.7
- Sutcliffe-Chi 2.6

Total Baseball Ranking
- Sandberg-Chi 6.7
- Raines-Mon 5.8
- Schmidt-Phi 4.9
- Cruz-Hou 4.8
- Hernandez-NY 4.6

TEAM	G	W	L	PCT	GB	R	OR	AB	H	2B	3B	HR	BB	SO	AVG	OBP	SLG	OPS	OPS+	BR	BR+	PF	CHI	RC	SB	CS	SBA	SBR
EAST																												
DET	162	104	58	.642		**829**	**643**	5644	1529	254	46	**187**	602	941	.271	**.345**	.432	777	**114**	103	**109**	99	99	**843**	106	68	61	0
TOR	163	89	73	.549	15	750	696	5687	1555	**275**	**68**	143	460	816	.273	.333	.421	754	103	52	25	104	96	808	**193**	67	**74**	**19**
NY	162	87	75	.537	17	758	679	5661	1560	**275**	32	130	534	**673**	.276	.342	.404	746	110	47	79	96	97	773	62	38	62	0
BOS	162	86	76	.531	18	810	764	5648	**1598**	259	45	181	500	842	**.283**	.343	**.441**	**784**	110	**113**	76	105	97	832	38	25	60	0
BAL	162	85	77	.525	19	681	667	5456	1374	234	23	160	**620**	884	.252	.331	.391	722	101	-4	12	98	96	705	51	36	59	-1
CLE	163	75	87	.463	29	761	766	5643	1498	222	39	123	600	815	.265	.339	.384	723	98	4	-8	102	103	732	126	77	62	1
MIL	161	67	94	.416	36.5	641	734	5511	1446	232	36	96	432	**673**	.262	.319	.370	689	94	-75	-49	96	103	621	52	57	48	-9
WEST																												
KC	162	84	78	.519		673	686	5543	1487	269	52	117	400	832	.268	.320	.399	719	97	-23	-28	101	99	685	106	64	62	1
CAL	162	81	81	.500	3	696	697	5470	1363	211	30	150	556	928	.249	.322	.381	703	95	-46	-41	99	**105**	663	80	51	61	0
MIN	162	81	81	.500	3	673	675	5562	1473	259	33	114	437	735	.265	.321	.385	706	90	-45	-74	105	102	669	39	30	57	-2
OAK	162	77	85	.475	7	738	796	5457	1415	257	29	158	568	871	.259	.332	.404	736	109	18	70	93	101	736	145	64	69	10
SEA	162	74	88	.457	23	682	774	5546	1429	244	34	129	519	871	.258	.326	.384	710	97	-32	-23	99	100	700	116	62	65	4
CHI	162	74	88	.457	23	679	736	5513	1360	225	38	172	523	883	.247	.316	.395	711	91	-37	-66	105	101	690	109	49	69	7
TEX	161	69	92	.429	27.5	656	714	5569	1452	227	29	120	420	807	.261	.315	.377	692	88	-75	-95	103	104	643	81	50	62	0
TOT	1134					10027		77910	20539	3443	534	1980	7171	11571	.264	.329	.398	727							1304	738	64	29

TEAM	CG	SH	SV	IP	H	H/G	HR	BB	SO	RAT	ERA	ERA+	OAV	OOB	PR	PR+	PF	CPI	FA	E	DP	FW	PW	BW	SBW	DIF
EAST																										
DET	19	8	**51**	1464	**1358**	**8.4**	130	489	914	**11.6**	**3.50**	**112**	**.246**	**.311**	**81**	**71**	98	98	.979	127	162	.4	**7.2**	**11.0**	-.2	4.9
TOR	34	10	33	1464	1433	8.9	140	528	875	12.3	3.87	106	.257	.325	21	37	103	100	.980	123	166	.6	3.8	2.6	**1.7**	-.5
NY	15	12	43	1465[1]	1485	9.2	**120**	518	**992**	12.5	3.78	100	.264	.328	35	2	95	103	.977	142	**177**	-.5	.3	8.0	-.2	-1.3
BOS	40	12	32	1442	1524	9.6	141	517	927	13.0	4.18	100	.270	.334	-29	-2	104	100	.977	143	128	-.5	-.2	7.7	-.2	-1.6
BAL	**48**	**13**	32	1439[1]	1393	8.8	137	512	714	12.1	3.72	104	.256	.323	44	26	97	102	**.981**	123	166	.6	2.7	1.3	-.3	.0
CLE	21	7	35	1467[2]	1523	9.4	141	545	803	12.9	4.26	96	.269	.336	-43	-27	102	98	.977	146	163	-.7	-2.7	-.8	-.1	-1.6
MIL	13	7	41	1433	1532	9.7	137	480	785	12.8	4.06	95	.274	.334	-10	-35	96	103	.978	136	156	-.2	-3.5	-4.9	-1.1	-3.6
WEST																										
KC	18	9	50	1444	1426	8.9	136	**433**	724	11.8	3.93	103	.258	.315	11	17	101	94	.979	131	157	.1	1.8	-2.8	-.1	4.2
CAL	36	12	26	1458	1526	9.5	143	474	754	12.6	3.96	100	.271	.331	6	2	99	**104**	.980	128	170	.3	.3	-4.1	-.2	3.9
MIN	32	9	38	1437[2]	1429	9.0	159	463	713	12.1	3.85	109	.260	.321	23	54	105	102	.980	**120**	134	**.7**	5.5	-7.4	-.4	1.8
OAK	15	6	44	1430	1554	9.8	155	592	695	13.8	4.49	84	.278	.351	-78	-125	94	103	.975	146	159	-.7	-12.5	7.1	.8	1.5
SEA	26	4	35	1442	1497	9.4	138	619	972	13.5	4.31	93	.270	.348	-50	-51	100	102	.979	128	143	.3	-5.1	-2.3	.2	.0
CHI	43	9	32	1454[1]	1416	8.8	155	483	840	12.0	4.14	101	.256	.320	-23	4	104	93	**.981**	122	160	.6	.5	-6.6	.5	-1.8
TEX	38	6	21	1438[2]	1443	9.1	148	518	863	12.5	3.91	106	.260	.327	13	36	104	101	.977	138	138	-.3	3.7	-9.5	-.2	-4.9
TOT	398	124	513	20280		9.2				12.5	4.00		.264	.329					.979	1853	2179					

Runs
Evans-Bos 121
Henderson-Oak 113
Boggs-Bos 109
Butler-Cle 108
Armas-Bos 107

Hits
Mattingly-NY 207
Boggs-Bos 203
Ripken-Bal 195
Winfield-NY 193

Doubles
Mattingly-NY 44
Parrish-Tex 42
Bell-Tor 39
Ripken-Bal 37
Evans-Bos 37

Triples
Moseby-Tor 15
Collins-Tor 15
Gibson-Det 10
Baines-Chi 10

Home Runs
Armas-Bos 43
Kingman-Oak 35
Thornton-Cle 33
Parrish-Det 33
Murphy-Oak 33

Total Bases
Armas-Bos 339
Evans-Bos 335
Ripken-Bal 327
Mattingly-NY 324
Easler-Bos 310

Runs Batted In
Armas-Bos 123
Rice-Bos 122
Kingman-Oak 118
Davis-Sea 116

Runs Produced
Evans-Bos 193
Rice-Bos 192
Winfield-NY 187
Armas-Bos 187

Bases On Balls
Murray-Bal 107
Davis-Sea 97
Evans-Bos 96
Thornton-Cle 91
Boggs-Bos 89

Batting Average
Mattingly-NY .... .343
Winfield-NY .... .340
Boggs-Bos .... .325
Bell-Tex .... .315
Trammell-Det .... .314

On-Base Percentage
Murray-Bal .... .415
Boggs-Bos .... .409
Henderson-Oak ..... .401
Winfield-NY .... .397
Davis-Sea .... .395

Slugging Average
Baines-Chi .... .541
Mattingly-NY .... .537
Evans-Bos .... .532
Armas-Bos .... .531
Hrbek-Min .... .522

On-Base Plus Slugging
Evans-Bos 924
Mattingly-NY 923
Murray-Bal 923
Winfield-NY 912
Hrbek-Min 909

Adjusted OPS
Mattingly-NY 159
Murray-Bal 157
Winfield-NY 156
Henderson-Oak 147
Davis-Sea 147

Batter Runs
Murray-Bal 46.8
Evans-Bos 46.6
Mattingly-NY 41.3
Winfield-NY 38.4
Davis-Sea 37.5

Adjusted Batter Runs
Murray-Bal 49.7
Mattingly-NY 46.1
Winfield-NY 42.9
Evans-Bos 40.8
Ripken-Bal 39.4

Clutch Hitting Index
Franco-Cle 132
Davis-Sea 127
Rice-Bos 124
Simmons-Mil 121
Tabler-Cle 116

Runs Created
Evans-Bos 132
Murray-Bal 130
Ripken-Bal 122
Mattingly-NY 120
Easler-Bos 118

Total Average
Murray-Bal .... .993
Henderson-Oak ..... .971
Evans-Bos .... .942
Davis-Sea .... .928
Gibson-Det .... .926

Stolen Bases
Henderson-Oak 66
Collins-Tor 60
Butler-Cle 52
Pettis-Cal 48
Wilson-KC 47

Stolen Base Average
Wilson-KC 90.4
Tolleson-Tex 84.6
Perconte-Sea 82.9
Moseby-Tor 81.3
Collins-Tor 81.1

Stolen Base Runs
Wilson-KC 8.6
Collins-Tor 8.3
Henderson-Oak 8.2
Garcia-Tor 5.9
Moseby-Tor 5.4

Fielding Runs
Ripken-Bal 38.8
Puckett-Min 30.1
Cruz-Chi 22.1
Boggs-Bos 21.0
Murphy-Oak 21.0

Total Player Rating
Ripken-Bal 9.3
Yount-Mil 5.1
Murray-Bal 4.9
Mattingly-NY 4.9
Henderson-Oak 4.5

Wins
Boddicker-Bal 20
Morris-Det 19
Blyleven-Cle 19
Viola-Min 18
Petry-Det 18

Win Percentage
Alexander-Tor ...... .739
Blyleven-Cle .... .731
Petry-Det .... .692
Wilcox-Det .... .680

Games
Hernandez-Det 80
Quisenberry-KC 72
Lopez-Det 71
Camacho-Cle 69
Caudill-Oak 68

Complete Games
Hough-Tex 17
Boddicker-Bal 16
Dotson-Chi 14
Blyleven-Cle 12
Beattie-Sea 12

Shutouts
Zahn-Cal 5
Ojeda-Bos 5

Saves
Quisenberry-KC 44
Caudill-Oak 36
Hernandez-Det 32
Righetti-NY 31
Davis-Min 29

Innings Pitched
Stieb-Tor 267.0
Hough-Tex 266.0
Alexander-Tor 261.2
Boddicker-Bal 261.1
Viola-Min 257.2

Fewest Hits/Game
Stieb-Tor 7.25
Blyleven-Cle 7.49
Boddicker-Bal 7.51
Langston-Sea 7.52
Mason-Tex 7.76

Fewest BB/Game
Hoyt-Chi 1.64
Smithson-Min 1.93
Guidry-NY 2.02
Alexander-Tor 2.03
Haas-Mil 2.04

Strikeouts
Langston-Sea 204
Stieb-Tor 198
Witt-Cal 196
Blyleven-Cle 170
Hough-Tex 164

Strikeouts/Game
Langston-Sea 8.16
Witt-Cal 7.15
Moore-Sea 6.71
Stieb-Tor 6.67
Berenguer-Det 6.31

Ratio
Black-KC 10.30
Alexander-Tor 10.32
Mason-Tex 10.35
Blyleven-Cle 10.43
Boddicker-Bal 10.47

Earned Run Average
Boddicker-Bal 2.79
Stieb-Tor 2.83
Blyleven-Cle 2.87
Niekro-NY 3.09
Zahn-Cal 3.12

Adjusted ERA
Stieb-Tor 145
Blyleven-Cle 143
Boddicker-Bal 139
Alexander-Tor 131
Viola-Min 131

Opponents' Batting Avg.
Stieb-Tor .... .221
Blyleven-Cle ...... .224
Boddicker-Bal ..... .228
Langston-Sea ...... .230
Berenguer-Det ..... .232

Opponents' On-Base Pct.
Black-KC .... .283
Blyleven-Cle ...... .287
Alexander-Tor ..... .287
Mason-Tex .... .288
Seaver-Chi .... .290

Starter Runs
Boddicker-Bal 35.1
Stieb-Tor 34.6
Blyleven-Cle 30.8
Alexander-Tor 25.2
Black-KC 25.2

Adjusted Starter Runs
Stieb-Tor 36.7
Blyleven-Cle 32.7
Boddicker-Bal 32.6
Alexander-Tor 27.5
Viola-Min 27.1

Clutch Pitching Index
Niekro-NY 125
Fontenot-NY 120
Cocanower-Mil 115
Hurst-Bos 113
Burris-Oak 113

Relief Runs
Hernandez-Det 32.3
Quisenberry-KC 19.5
Righetti-NY 17.8
Corbett-Cal 17.8
Camacho-Cle 17.4

Adjusted Relief Runs
Hernandez-Det 31.8
Quisenberry-KC 19.8
Camacho-Cle 18.1
Corbett-Cal 17.6
Righetti-NY 16.5

Relief Ranking
Hernandez-Det 38.9
Camacho-Cle 31.0
Righetti-NY 27.5
Quisenberry-KC 25.8
Caudill-Oak 23.8

Total Pitcher Index
Boddicker-Bal 4.4
Hernandez-Det 3.9
Blyleven-Cle 3.4
Stieb-Tor 3.3
Camacho-Cle 3.2

Total Baseball Ranking
Ripken-Bal 9.3
Yount-Mil 5.1
Murray-Bal 4.9
Mattingly-NY 4.9
Henderson-Oak 4.5

TEAM	G	W	L	PCT	GB	R	OR	AB	H	2B	3B	HR	BB	SO	AVG	OBP	SLG	OPS	OPS+	BR	BR+	PF	CHI	RC	SB	CS	SBA	SBR
EAST																												
STL	162	101	61	.623		**747**	572	5467	1446	245	**59**	87	**586**	853	**.264**	**.338**	.379	**717**	**108**	**52**	58	99	**105**	**733**	**314**	96	77	**35**
NY	162	98	64	.605	3	695	**568**	5549	1425	239	35	134	546	872	.257	.326	.385	711	**108**	31	49	98	99	691	117	53	69	7
MON	161	84	77	.522	16.5	633	636	5429	1342	242	49	118	492	880	.247	.313	.375	688	104	-19	20	94	101	633	169	77	69	10
CHI	162	77	84	.478	23.5	686	729	5492	1397	239	28	**150**	562	937	.254	.326	**.390**	716	95	40	-29	111	98	710	182	49	**79**	23
PHI	162	75	87	.463	26	667	673	5477	1343	238	47	141	527	1095	.245	.314	.383	697	97	0	-17	103	102	657	122	51	71	9
PIT	161	57	104	.354	43.5	568	708	5436	1340	251	28	80	514	842	.247	.313	.347	660	91	-64	-58	99	97	587	110	60	65	3
WEST																												
LA	162	95	67	.586		682	579	5502	1434	226	28	129	539	846	.261	.330	.382	712	**108**	38	**60**	97	97	704	136	58	70	10
CIN	162	89	72	.553	5.5	677	666	5431	1385	249	34	114	576	856	.255	.329	.376	705	98	26	-7	105	99	672	159	70	69	10
SD	162	83	79	.512	12	650	622	5507	1405	241	28	109	513	**809**	.255	.321	.368	689	101	-9	1	99	100	645	60	39	61	0
HOU	162	83	79	.512	12	706	691	5582	**1457**	**261**	42	121	477	873	.261	.322	.388	710	107	25	46	97	103	684	96	56	63	2
ATL	162	66	96	.407	29	632	781	5526	1359	213	28	126	553	849	.246	.317	.363	680	91	-28	-64	106	99	622	72	52	58	-2
SF	162	62	100	.383	33	556	674	5420	1263	217	31	115	488	962	.233	.301	.348	649	91	-93	-64	95	100	564	99	55	64	3
TOT	971					7899		65818	16596	2861	437	1424	6373	10674	.253	.321	.374	695							1636	716	70	109

TEAM	CG	SH	SV	IP	H	H/G	HR	BB	SO	RAT	ERA	ERA+	OAV	OOB	PR	PR+	PF	CPI	FA	E	DP	FW	PW	BW	SBW	DIF
EAST																										
STL	**37**	20	44	1464	1343	8.3	**98**	453	798	11.3	3.11	114	.246	.307	79	71	98	102	**.983**	**108**	166	**1.7**	7.5	6.2	**2.7**	2.1
NY	32	19	37	1488	1306	**7.9**	111	515	**1039**	11.2	3.11	111	.237	.304	80	59	96	100	.982	115	138	1.3	6.3	5.2	-.2	4.7
MON	13	13	**53**	1457	1346	8.4	99	509	870	11.6	3.55	96	.247	.313	7	-27	94	93	.981	121	152	.9	-2.8	2.2	.0	3.3
CHI	20	8	42	1442[1]	1492	9.4	156	519	820	12.7	4.16	96	.271	.336	-91	-24	111	103	.979	134	150	.2	-2.5	-3.0	1.5	.5
PHI	24	9	30	1447	1424	8.9	115	596	899	12.8	3.69	100	.259	.334	-15	0	103	105	.978	139	142	-.1	.0	-1.7	-.0	-4.0
PIT	15	6	29	1445[1]	1406	8.8	107	584	962	12.6	3.98	90	.255	.330	-61	-64	100	94	.979	133	127	.2	-6.7	-6.1	-.6	-10.1
WEST																										
LA	**37**	**21**	36	1465	**1280**	**7.9**	102	462	979	**10.9**	**2.97**	**117**	**.234**	**.296**	**102**	**86**	97	98	.974	166	131	-1.8	**9.1**	**6.4**	.0	.4
CIN	24	11	45	1451[1]	1347	8.4	131	535	910	11.8	3.71	102	.248	.317	-19	12	105	96	.980	122	142	.9	1.3	-.7	.0	7.1
SD	26	19	44	1451[1]	1399	8.7	127	**443**	727	11.6	3.41	104	.257	.316	30	21	98	**106**	.980	124	158	.8	2.3	.2	-1.0	-.0
HOU	17	9	42	1458	1393	8.6	119	543	909	12.2	3.67	95	.254	.324	-11	-34	96	100	.976	152	159	-.9	-3.5	4.9	-.7	2.5
ATL	9	9	29	1457[1]	1512	9.4	134	642	776	13.5	4.20	92	.271	.349	-98	-53	107	105	.976	159	**197**	-1.3	-5.5	-6.7	-1.2	-.0
SF	13	5	24	1448	1348	8.4	125	572	985	12.1	3.62	95	.247	.321	-3	-29	96	99	.976	148	134	-.7	-3.0	-6.7	-.6	-7.8
TOT	267	149	455	17474[2]		8.6				12.0	3.60		.253	.321					.979	1621	1796					

Runs
Murphy-Atl 118
Raines-Mon 115
McGee-StL 114
Sandberg-Chi 113
Coleman-StL 107

Hits
McGee-StL 216
Parker-Cin 198
Gwynn-SD 197
Sandberg-Chi 186
Murphy-Atl 185

Doubles
Parker-Cin 42
Wilson-Phi 39
Herr-StL 38
Wallach-Mon 36

Triples
McGee-StL 18
Samuel-Phi 13
Raines-Mon 13
Garner-Hou 10
Coleman-StL 10

Home Runs
Murphy-Atl 37
Parker-Cin 34
Schmidt-Phi 33
Guerrero-LA 33
Carter-NY 32

Total Bases
Parker-Cin 350
Murphy-Atl 332
McGee-StL 308
Sandberg-Chi 307
Schmidt-Phi 292

Runs Batted In
Parker-Cin 125
Murphy-Atl 111
Herr-StL 110
Moreland-Chi 106
Wilson-Phi 102

Runs Produced
Herr-StL 199
Murphy-Atl 192
McGee-StL 186
Parker-Cin 179
Sandberg-Chi 170

Bases On Balls
Murphy-Atl 90
Schmidt-Phi 87
Martinez-SD 87
Rose-Cin 86
Law-Mon 86

Batting Average
McGee-StL 353
Guerrero-LA 320
Raines-Mon 320
Gwynn-SD 317
Parker-Cin 312

On-Base Percentage
Guerrero-LA .... .425
Scioscia-LA .... .409
Raines-Mon .... .407
Rose-Cin .... .398
Clark-StL .... .397

Slugging Average
Guerrero-LA .... .577
Parker-Cin .... .551
Murphy-Atl .... .539
Schmidt-Phi .... .532
Marshall-LA .... .515

On-Base Plus Slugging
Guerrero-LA 1002
Murphy-Atl 929
Parker-Cin 918
Schmidt-Phi 911
Clark-StL 899

Adjusted OPS
Guerrero-LA 183
Raines-Mon 155
Clark-StL 151
McGee-StL 148
Murphy-Atl 148

Batter Runs
Guerrero-LA 52.8
Murphy-Atl 47.6
Parker-Cin 42.5
Schmidt-Phi 38.5
Raines-Mon 37.5

Adjusted Batter Runs
Guerrero-LA 56.3
Raines-Mon 44.2
Murphy-Atl 40.6
McGee-StL 37.6
Parker-Cin 37.0

Clutch Hitting Index
Herr-StL 161
Pendleton-StL 139
Moreland-Chi 128
Wilson-Phi 128
Brooks-Mon 125

Runs Created
Murphy-Atl 131
Raines-Mon 124
McGee-StL 123
Guerrero-LA 121
Sandberg-Chi 117

Total Average
Guerrero-LA 1.086
Raines-Mon 1.022
Murphy-Atl .... .960
Schmidt-Phi .... .927
McGee-StL .... .920

Stolen Bases
Coleman-StL 110
Raines-Mon 70
McGee-StL 56
Sandberg-Chi 54
Samuel-Phi 53

Stolen Base Average
Lopes-Chi 92.2
Herr-StL 91.2
Raines-Mon 88.6
VanSlyke-StL 85.0
Davis-Cin 84.2

Stolen Base Runs
Coleman-StL 15.4
Raines-Mon 12.3
Lopes-Chi 8.9
Sandberg-Chi 8.0
McGee-StL 6.7

Fielding Runs
Hubbard-Atl 61.8
Wallach-Mon 36.7
McReynolds-SD ... 23.1
Pendleton-StL 22.7
Wilson-Phi 20.4

Total Player Rating
Guerrero-LA 6.3
Raines-Mon 6.1
McGee-StL 5.7
Hubbard-Atl 5.7
Sandberg-Chi 4.8

Wins
Gooden-NY 24
Tudor-StL 21
Andujar-StL 21
Browning-Cin 20
Hershiser-LA 19

Win Percentage
Hershiser-LA 864
Gooden-NY 857
Smith-Mon 783
Darling-NY 727
Tudor-StL 724

Games
Burke-Mon 78
M.Davis-SF 77
Garrelts-SF 74
Carman-Phi 71
Minton-SF 68

Complete Games
Gooden-NY 16
Valenzuela-LA 14
Tudor-StL 14
Cox-StL 10
Andujar-StL 10

Shutouts
Tudor-StL 10
Gooden-NY 8
Valenzuela-LA 5
Hershiser-LA 5

Saves
Reardon-Mon 41
Smith-Chi 33
Smith-Hou 27
Power-Cin 27
Gossage-SD 26

Innings Pitched
Gooden-NY 276.2
Tudor-StL 275.0
Valenzuela-LA 272.1
Andujar-StL 269.2
Mahler-Atl 266.2

Fewest Hits/Game
Fernandez-NY 5.71
Gooden-NY 6.44
Hershiser-LA 6.72
Tudor-StL 6.84
Soto-Cin 6.85

Fewest BB/Game
Hoyt-SD 86
Eckersley-Chi 1.01
Lynch-NY 1.27
Tudor-StL 1.60
Smith-Mon 1.66

Strikeouts
Gooden-NY 268
Soto-Cin 214
Ryan-Hou 209
Valenzuela-LA 208
Fernandez-NY 180

Strikeouts/Game
Fernandez-NY 9.51
Gooden-NY 8.72
DeLeon-Pit 8.24
Ryan-Hou 8.11
Soto-Cin 7.50

Ratio
Tudor-StL 8.61
Gooden-NY 8.75
Eckersley-Chi 8.88
Hershiser-LA 9.50
Smith-Mon 9.51

Earned Run Average
Gooden-NY 1.53
Tudor-StL 1.93
Hershiser-LA 2.03
Reuschel-Pit 2.27
Welch-LA 2.31

Adjusted ERA
Gooden-NY 226
Tudor-StL 183
Hershiser-LA 172
Reuschel-Pit 158
Welch-LA 151

Opponents' Batting Avg.
Fernandez-NY 181
Gooden-NY 201
Hershiser-LA 206
Tudor-StL 209
Soto-Cin 211

Opponents' On-Base Pct.
Tudor-StL 249
Gooden-NY 254
Eckersley-Chi 255
Hershiser-LA 268
Smith-Mon 269

Starter Runs
Gooden-NY 63.6
Tudor-StL 51.0
Hershiser-LA 41.8
Valenzuela-LA 34.9
Reuschel-Pit 28.6

Adjusted Starter Runs
Gooden-NY 61.8
Tudor-StL 50.0
Hershiser-LA 40.0
Valenzuela-LA 32.4
Reuschel-Pit 28.4

Clutch Pitching Index
Darling-NY 120
Hawkins-SD 119
Show-SD 119
Reuss-LA 116
Gooden-NY 115

Relief Runs
Burke-Mon 16.1
Gossage-SD 15.6
Franco-Cin 15.6
Garrelts-SF 15.2
Carman-Phi 14.5

Adjusted Relief Runs
Franco-Cin 16.8
Gossage-SD 15.3
Carman-Phi 15.0
Burke-Mon 14.2
Garrelts-SF 14.0

Relief Ranking
Franco-Cin 26.8
Gossage-SD 23.6
Carman-Phi 22.7
Smith-Hou 21.9
Garrelts-SF 21.2

Total Pitcher Index
Gooden-NY 7.6
Tudor-StL 5.7
Hershiser-LA 4.3
Reuschel-Pit 4.0
Valenzuela-LA 3.8

Total Baseball Ranking
Gooden-NY 7.6
Guerrero-LA 6.3
Raines-Mon 6.1
McGee-StL 5.7
Hubbard-Atl 5.7

TEAM	G	W	L	PCT	GB	R	OR	AB	H	2B	3B	HR	BB	SO	AVG	OBP	SLG	OPS	OPS+	BR	BR+	PF	CHI	RC	SB	CS	SBA	SBR
EAST																												
TOR	161	99	62	.615		759	**588**	5508	1482	281	**53**	158	503	807	.269	.334	.425	759	103	43	24	103	98	767	144	77	65	5
NY	161	97	64	.602	2	**839**	660	5458	1458	272	31	176	620	771	.267	.347	.425	772	**113**	82	**102**	98	102	821	**155**	53	**75**	**16**
DET	161	84	77	.522	15	729	688	5575	1413	254	45	202	526	926	.253	.321	.424	745	103	8	13	99	97	765	75	41	65	2
BAL	161	83	78	.516	16	818	764	5517	1451	234	22	**214**	604	908	.263	.338	**.430**	768	112	64	86	97	102	794	69	43	62	0
BOS	163	81	81	.500	18.5	800	720	5720	**1615**	**292**	31	162	562	816	**.282**	**.350**	.429	**779**	108	**96**	62	104	93	**844**	66	27	71	5
MIL	161	71	90	.441	28	690	802	5568	1467	250	44	101	462	**746**	.263	.322	.379	701	91	-68	-65	100	103	666	69	34	67	3
CLE	162	60	102	.370	39.5	729	861	5527	1465	254	31	116	492	817	.265	.327	.385	712	95	-44	-38	99	106	681	132	72	65	4
WEST																												
KC	162	91	71	.562		687	639	5500	1384	261	49	154	473	840	.252	.315	.401	716	94	-47	-49	100	101	687	128	48	73	11
CAL	162	90	72	.556	1	732	703	5442	1364	215	31	153	**648**	902	.251	.335	.386	721	97	-17	-13	100	100	711	106	51	68	5
CHI	163	85	77	.525	6	736	720	5470	1386	247	37	146	471	843	.253	.318	.392	710	90	-55	-80	104	**110**	674	108	56	66	4
MIN	162	77	85	.475	14	705	782	5509	1453	282	41	141	502	779	.264	.329	.407	736	95	-1	-40	106	97	729	68	44	61	0
OAK	162	77	85	.475	20	757	787	5581	1475	230	34	155	508	861	.264	.327	.401	728	106	-15	43	93	104	725	117	58	67	5
SEA	162	74	88	.457	23	719	818	5521	1410	277	38	171	564	942	.255	.328	.412	740	100	7	3	101	96	739	94	35	73	8
TEX	161	62	99	.385	34.5	617	785	5361	1359	213	41	129	530	819	.253	.324	.381	705	91	-54	-63	101	93	652	130	76	63	2
TOT	1132					10317		77257	20182	3562	528	2178	7465	11777	.262	.330	.406	735							1461	715	67	71

TEAM	CG	SH	SV	IP	H	H/G	HR	BB	SO	RAT	ERA	ERA+	OAV	OOB	PR	PR+	PF	CPI	FA	E	DP	FW	PW	BW	SBW	DIF
EAST																										
TOR	18	9	47	1448	**1312**	**8.2**	147	484	823	**11.4**	**3.31**	**127**	.243	**.308**	**135**	**143**	102	107	.980	125	164	.3	**14.2**	2.4	.0	1.8
NY	25	9	**49**	1440[1]	1373	8.6	157	518	907	11.9	3.69	109	.251	.318	74	52	97	104	.979	126	172	.2	5.2	**10.1**	**1.1**	.0
DET	31	**11**	40	1456	1313	**8.2**	141	556	943	11.7	3.79	108	**.240**	.313	59	48	98	94	.977	143	152	-.7	4.8	1.3	-.3	-1.4
BAL	32	6	33	1427[1]	1480	9.4	160	568	793	13.1	4.38	92	.270	.341	-36	-56	97	102	.979	129	168	.0	-5.5	8.6	-.5	.0
BOS	35	8	29	1461[1]	1487	9.2	130	540	913	12.7	4.06	106	.265	.333	14	35	103	101	.977	145	161	-.8	3.5	6.2	.0	-8.7
MIL	34	5	37	1437	1510	9.5	175	499	777	12.8	4.40	95	.271	.334	-39	-36	100	101	.977	142	153	-.7	-3.5	-6.4	-.2	1.5
CLE	24	7	28	1421	1556	9.9	170	547	702	13.6	4.92	84	.281	.350	-121	-124	100	98	.977	141	161	-.6	-12.2	-3.7	-.1	-4.2
WEST																										
KC	27	**11**	41	1461	1433	8.9	**103**	463	846	11.9	3.49	119	.257	.317	107	109	100	103	.980	127	160	.2	10.8	-4.8	.6	3.4
CAL	22	8	41	1457[1]	1453	9.0	171	514	767	12.4	3.91	105	.263	.328	38	33	99	**108**	**.982**	112	**202**	1.0	3.3	-1.2	.0	6.1
CHI	20	8	39	1451[2]	1411	8.8	161	569	**1023**	12.5	4.07	106	.256	.330	13	39	104	101	**.982**	**111**	152	**1.1**	3.9	-7.9	-.1	7.1
MIN	**41**	7	34	1426[1]	1468	9.3	164	**462**	767	12.4	4.49	98	.268	.329	-53	-11	106	95	.980	120	139	.6	-1.0	-3.9	-.5	1.1
OAK	10	6	41	1453	1451	9.0	172	607	785	13.0	4.42	87	.259	.334	-43	-96	93	97	.977	140	137	-.5	-9.4	4.3	.0	1.9
SEA	23	8	30	1432	1456	9.2	154	637	868	13.5	4.68	90	.265	.346	-84	-72	102	96	.980	122	156	.5	-7.1	.3	.3	-.8
TEX	18	5	33	1411[2]	1479	9.5	173	501	863	12.9	4.56	93	.269	.334	-65	-51	102	97	.980	120	145	.5	-5.0	-6.2	-.3	-7.4
TOT	360	108	522	20184		9.0				12.6	4.15		.262	.330					.980	1803	2222					

Runs
Henderson-NY 146
Ripken-Bal 116
Murray-Bal 111
Evans-Bos 110
Brett-KC 108

Hits
Boggs-Bos 240
Mattingly-NY 211
Buckner-Bos 201
Puckett-Min 199
Baines-Chi 198

Doubles
Mattingly-NY 48
Buckner-Bos 46
Boggs-Bos 42
Cooper-Mil 39

Triples
Wilson-KC 21
Butler-Cle 14
Puckett-Min 13
Fernandez-Tor 10

Home Runs
Evans-Det 40
Fisk-Chi 37
Balboni-KC 36
Mattingly-NY 35
G.Thomas-Sea 32

Total Bases
Mattingly-NY 370
Brett-KC 322
Bradley-Sea 319
Boggs-Bos 312
Murray-Bal 305

Runs Batted In
Mattingly-NY 145
Murray-Bal 124
Winfield-NY 114
Baines-Chi 113
Brett-KC 112

Runs Produced
Mattingly-NY 217
Murray-Bal 204
Ripken-Bal 200
Henderson-NY 194
Winfield-NY 193

Bases On Balls
Evans-Bos 114
Harrah-Tex 113
Brett-KC 103
Henderson-NY 99
Boggs-Bos 96

Batting Average
Boggs-Bos .... .368
Brett-KC .... .335
Mattingly-NY ...... .324
Henderson-NY ...... .314
Butler-Cle .... .311

On-Base Percentage
Boggs-Bos .... .452
Brett-KC .... .442
Harrah-Tex .... .437
Henderson-NY ..... .422
Murray-Bal .... .387

Slugging Average
Brett-KC .... .585
Mattingly-NY ...... .567
Barfield-Tor .... .536
Murray-Bal .... .523
Evans-Det .... .519

On-Base Plus Slugging
Brett-KC 1028
Mattingly-NY 946
Henderson-NY 938
Boggs-Bos 929
Murray-Bal 910

Adjusted OPS
Brett-KC 178
Henderson-NY 159
Mattingly-NY 159
Murray-Bal 150
Boggs-Bos 149

Batter Runs
Brett-KC 63.4
Boggs-Bos 54.8
Mattingly-NY 47.5
Henderson-NY 45.5
Murray-Bal 38.4

Adjusted Batter Runs
Brett-KC 63.0
Mattingly-NY 50.8
Boggs-Bos 49.1
Henderson-NY 48.5
Murray-Bal 41.7

Clutch Hitting Index
Franco-Cle 137
Meacham-NY 137
Mattingly-NY 132
Boone-Cal 130
Thornton-Cle 125

Runs Created
Brett-KC 146
Boggs-Bos 143
Henderson-NY 138
Mattingly-NY 136
Murray-Bal 122

Total Average
Henderson-NY 1.155
Brett-KC 1.150
Gibson-Det .... .953
Boggs-Bos .... .952
Murray-Bal .... .938

Stolen Bases
Henderson-NY 80
Pettis-Cal 56
Butler-Cle 47
Wilson-KC 43
Smith-KC 40

Stolen Base Average
Perconte-Sea 93.9
Henderson-NY 88.9
Gibson-Det 88.2
Pettis-Cal 86.2
Smith-KC 85.1

Stolen Base Runs
Henderson-NY 14.1
Pettis-Cal 9.2
Smith-KC 6.3
Perconte-Sea 6.1
Wilson-KC 5.6

Fielding Runs
Owen-Sea 30.3
Buckner-Bos 25.4
Barfield-Tor 21.9
Butler-Cle 21.8
Puckett-Min 21.2

Total Player Rating
Henderson-NY 7.4
Brett-KC 7.1
Boggs-Bos 5.3
Barfield-Tor 4.5
Ripken-Bal 4.5

Wins
Guidry-NY 22
Saberhagen-KC 20
Viola-Min 18
Burns-Chi 18

Win Percentage
Guidry-NY .... .786
Saberhagen-KC .... .769
Leibrandt-KC ...... .654
Higuera-Mil .... .652

Games
Quisenberry-KC 84
VandeBerg-Sea 76
Righetti-NY 74
Hernandez-Det 74
Nunez-Sea 70

Complete Games
Blyleven-Cle-Min ... 24
Moore-Sea 14
Hough-Tex 14
Morris-Det 13
Boyd-Bos 13

Shutouts
Blyleven-Cle-Min 5
Morris-Det 4
Burns-Chi 4

Saves
Quisenberry-KC 37
James-Chi 32
Moore-Cal 31
Hernandez-Det 31

Innings Pitched
Blyleven-Cle-Min 293.2
Boyd-Bos 272.1
Stieb-Tor 265.0
Alexander-Tor 260.2
Guidry-NY 259.0

Fewest Hits/Game
Stieb-Tor 7.00
Hough-Tex 7.12
Petry-Det 7.16
Morris-Det 7.42
Higuera-Mil 7.88

Fewest BB/Game
Haas-Mil 1.39
Saberhagen-KC 1.45
Guidry-NY 1.46
Butcher-Min 1.86
Key-Tor 2.12

Strikeouts
Blyleven-Cle-Min ... 206
Bannister-Chi 198
Morris-Det 191
Hurst-Bos 189
Witt-Cal 180

Strikeouts/Game
Bannister-Chi 8.46
Hurst-Bos 7.42
Burns-Chi 6.82
Morris-Det 6.69
Tanana-Tex-Det 6.66

Ratio
Saberhagen-KC 9.56
Guidry-NY 9.90
Key-Tor 10.16
Petry-Det 10.33
Hough-Tex 10.35

Earned Run Average
Stieb-Tor 2.48
Leibrandt-KC 2.69
Saberhagen-KC 2.87
Key-Tor 3.00
Blyleven-Cle-Min ... 3.16

Adjusted ERA
Stieb-Tor 170
Leibrandt-KC 155
Saberhagen-KC 145
Key-Tor 140
Seaver-Chi 136

Opponents' Batting Avg.
Stieb-Tor .... .213
Hough-Tex .... .215
Petry-Det .... .217
Morris-Det .... .225
Higuera-Mil .... .235

Opponents' On-Base Pct.
Saberhagen-KC .... .273
Guidry-NY .... .279
Key-Tor .... .284
Hough-Tex .... .285
Petry-Det .... .285

Starter Runs
Stieb-Tor 49.2
Leibrandt-KC 38.6
Saberhagen-KC 33.5
Blyleven-Cle-Min ... 32.4
Key-Tor 27.0

Adjusted Starter Runs
Stieb-Tor 50.2
Leibrandt-KC 38.8
Blyleven-Cle-Min ... 34.7
Saberhagen-KC 33.7
Seaver-Chi 29.3

Clutch Pitching Index
Leibrandt-KC 121
Romanick-Cal 117
Boddicker-Bal 115
Alexander-Tor 114
Stieb-Tor 112

Relief Runs
Moore-Cal 25.5
Quisenberry-KC 25.5
James-Chi 24.7
Cliburn-Cal 22.6
Harris-Tex 21.1

Adjusted Relief Runs
James-Chi 25.7
Quisenberry-KC 25.6
Moore-Cal 25.3
Cliburn-Cal 22.4
Harris-Tex 21.7

Relief Ranking
Moore-Cal 50.2
James-Chi 46.2
Quisenberry-KC 44.6
Hernandez-Det 33.2
Righetti-NY 30.3

Total Pitcher Index
Stieb-Tor 5.5
Moore-Cal 5.1
James-Chi 4.7
Quisenberry-KC 4.6
Leibrandt-KC 4.5

Total Baseball Ranking
Henderson-NY 7.4
Brett-KC 7.1
Stieb-Tor 5.5
Boggs-Bos 5.3
Moore-Cal 5.1

TEAM	G	W	L	PCT	GB	R	OR	AB	H	2B	3B	HR	BB	SO	AVG	OBP	SLG	OPS	OPS+	BR	BR+	PF	CHI	RC	SB	CS	SBA	SBR
EAST																												
NY	162	108	54	.667		**783**	578	5558	**1462**	261	31	148	**631**	968	**.263**	**.341**	**.401**	**742**	**114**	**84**	**107**	97	101	**773**	118	48	71	9
PHI	161	86	75	.534	21.5	739	713	5483	1386	266	39	154	589	1154	.253	.330	.400	730	103	50	25	104	101	739	153	59	72	13
STL	161	79	82	.491	28.5	601	611	5378	1270	216	48	58	568	905	.236	.311	.327	638	83	-119	-114	99	**109**	584	**262**	78	**77**	**30**
MON	161	78	83	.484	29.5	637	688	5508	1401	255	**50**	110	537	1016	.254	.324	.379	703	101	-1	5	99	94	676	193	95	67	9
CHI	160	70	90	.438	37	680	781	5499	1409	258	27	**155**	508	966	.256	.321	.398	719	96	21	-29	108	98	697	132	62	68	7
PIT	162	64	98	.395	44	663	700	5456	1366	**273**	33	111	569	929	.250	.323	.374	697	96	-12	-27	102	100	654	152	84	64	4
WEST																												
HOU	162	96	66	.593		654	**569**	5441	1388	244	32	125	536	916	.255	.325	.381	706	104	3	22	97	98	668	163	75	68	10
CIN	162	86	76	.531	10	732	717	5536	1404	237	35	144	586	920	.254	.327	.387	714	99	21	-8	104	104	712	177	53	**77**	20
SF	162	83	79	.512	13	698	618	5501	1394	269	29	114	536	1087	.253	.324	.375	699	104	-9	26	95	104	674	148	93	61	0
SD	162	74	88	.457	22	656	723	5515	1442	239	25	136	484	917	.261	.323	.388	711	104	9	24	98	97	671	96	68	59	-3
LA	162	73	89	.451	23	638	679	5471	1373	232	14	130	478	966	.251	.315	.370	685	102	-42	5	93	102	639	155	67	70	11
ATL	161	72	89	.447	23.5	615	719	5384	1348	241	24	138	538	**904**	.250	.321	.381	702	94	-5	-40	106	93	646	93	76	55	-6
TOT	969					8096		65730	16643	2991	387	1523	6560	11648	.254	.324	.380	704							1842	858	68	105

TEAM	CG	SH	SV	IP	H	H/G	HR	BB	SO	RAT	ERA	ERA+	OAV	OOB	PR	PR+	PF	CPI	FA	E	DP	FW	PW	BW	SBW	DIF
EAST																										
NY	27	11	46	1484	1304	8.0	**103**	509	1083	11.2	**3.12**	**114**	.236	.304	**100**	73	95	99	.978	138	145	.2	7.6	**11.2**	.0	8.2
PHI	22	11	39	1451[2]	1473	9.2	130	553	874	12.7	3.86	100	.265	.334	-22	0	104	105	.978	137	157	.2	.0	2.6	.4	2.4
STL	17	4	46	1466[1]	1364	8.4	135	**485**	761	11.5	3.37	108	.250	.314	56	45	98	**106**	**.981**	**123**	178	**.9**	4.7	-11.8	**2.2**	2.6
MON	15	9	50	1466[1]	1350	8.3	119	566	1051	12.0	3.79	98	.246	.320	-11	-15	99	93	.979	133	132	.4	-1.5	.6	.0	-1.8
CHI	11	6	42	1445	1546	9.7	143	557	962	13.3	4.50	90	.279	.346	-124	-67	109	100	.980	124	147	.8	-6.9	-3.0	-.2	-.6
PIT	17	9	30	1450[2]	1397	8.7	138	570	924	12.5	3.91	98	.255	.329	-30	-11	103	100	.978	143	134	-.1	-1.1	-2.8	-.5	-12.3
WEST																										
HOU	18	**19**	**51**	1456[1]	**1203**	**7.5**	116	523	**1160**	**10.9**	3.15	**114**	**.225**	**.297**	92	**76**	97	93	.979	130	108	.6	**7.9**	2.3	.1	4.2
CIN	14	8	45	1468	1465	9.0	136	524	924	12.3	3.92	99	.264	.329	-32	-7	104	102	.978	140	160	.0	-.7	-.8	1.2	5.4
SF	18	10	35	1460[1]	1264	7.8	121	591	992	11.7	3.34	106	.236	.316	62	32	95	101	.977	143	149	-.1	3.4	2.8	-.9	-2.9
SD	13	7	32	1443[1]	1406	8.8	150	607	934	12.8	4.00	92	.258	.335	-44	-55	98	102	.978	137	135	.2	-5.7	2.5	-1.2	-2.7
LA	**35**	14	25	1454[1]	1428	8.9	115	499	1051	12.1	3.77	92	.256	.320	-7	-55	93	96	.971	181	118	-2.2	-5.7	.6	.2	-.7
ATL	17	5	39	1424[2]	1443	9.2	117	576	932	13.0	3.98	100	.266	.340	-41	0	107	103	.978	141	**181**	-.0	.0	-4.1	-1.5	-2.7
TOT	224	113	480	17471		8.6				12.2	3.72		.254	.324					.978	1670	1744					

Runs	
Hayes-Phi	107
Gwynn-SD	107
Schmidt-Phi	97
Davis-Cin	97

Hits	
Gwynn-SD	211
Sax-LA	210
Raines-Mon	194
Hayes-Phi	186
Bass-Hou	184

Doubles	
Hayes-Phi	46
Sax-LA	43
Dunston-Chi	37
Bream-Pit	37
Samuel-Phi	36

Triples	
Webster-Mon	13
Samuel-Phi	12
Raines-Mon	10
Coleman-StL	8

Home Runs	
Schmidt-Phi	37
Parker-Cin	31
Davis-Hou	31
Murphy-Atl	29

Total Bases	
Parker-Cin	304
Schmidt-Phi	302
Gwynn-SD	300
Murphy-Atl	293
Hayes-Phi	293

Runs Batted In	
Schmidt-Phi	119
Parker-Cin	116
Carter-NY	105
Davis-Hou	101
Hayes-Phi	98

Runs Produced	
Hayes-Phi	186
Schmidt-Phi	179
Parker-Cin	174
Hernandez-NY	164
Carter-NY	162

Bases On Balls	
Hernandez-NY	94
Schmidt-Phi	89
C.Davis-SF	84
Oberkfell-Atl	83
Doran-Hou	81

Batting Average	
Raines-Mon	.334
Sax-LA	.332
Gwynn-SD	.329
Bass-Hou	.311
Hernandez-NY	.310

On-Base Percentage	
Raines-Mon	.415
Hernandez-NY	.414
Schmidt-Phi	.395
Sax-LA	.391
Gwynn-SD	.382

Slugging Average	
Schmidt-Phi	.547
Strawberry-NY	.507
McReynolds-SD	.504
Davis-Hou	.493
Bass-Hou	.486

On-Base Plus Slugging	
Schmidt-Phi	942
Raines-Mon	891
Strawberry-NY	871
McReynolds-SD	867
Hayes-Phi	861

Adjusted OPS	
Schmidt-Phi	152
Raines-Mon	146
Strawberry-NY	142
Hernandez-NY	141
McReynolds-SD	140

Batter Runs	
Schmidt-Phi	44.0
Raines-Mon	38.0
Hernandez-NY	32.2
Hayes-Phi	30.3
Gwynn-SD	28.4

Adjusted Batter Runs	
Schmidt-Phi	40.1
Raines-Mon	39.0
Hernandez-NY	35.3
Sax-LA	33.8
Gwynn-SD	30.6

Clutch Hitting Index	
Carter-NY	132
Pendleton-StL	123
Cruz-Hou	121
Uribe-SF	121
Jeltz-Phi	120

Runs Created	
Raines-Mon	130
Schmidt-Phi	122
Gwynn-SD	113
Hayes-Phi	111
Sax-LA	110

Total Average	
Raines-Mon	1.040
Schmidt-Phi	.988
Strawberry-NY	.910
Hernandez-NY	.873
McReynolds-SD	.848

Stolen Bases	
Coleman-StL	107
Davis-Cin	80
Raines-Mon	70
Duncan-LA	48

Stolen Base Average	
Dernier-Chi	93.1
Raines-Mon	88.6
Coleman-StL	88.4
Davis-Cin	87.9
Leonard-SF	84.2

Stolen Base Runs	
Coleman-StL	18.6
Davis-Cin	13.8
Raines-Mon	12.3
Duncan-LA	6.0
Bonds-Pit	5.5

Fielding Runs	
Hubbard-Atl	41.0
Pendleton-StL	24.2
Bream-Pit	22.8
Wilson-Phi	20.6
Dunston-Chi	20.3

Total Player Rating	
Raines-Mon	5.7
Gwynn-SD	4.8
Hernandez-NY	4.5
Sax-LA	4.1
Hubbard-Atl	3.8

Wins	
Valenzuela-LA	21
Krukow-SF	20
Scott-Hou	18
Ojeda-NY	18

Win Percentage	
Ojeda-NY	.783
Gooden-NY	.739
Fernandez-NY	.727
Darling-NY	.714
Krukow-SF	.690

Games	
Lefferts-SD	83
McDowell-NY	75
Worrell-StL	74
Franco-Cin	74
Tekulve-Phi	73

Complete Games	
Valenzuela-LA	20
Rhoden-Pit	12
Gooden-NY	12
Krukow-SF	10

Shutouts	
Scott-Hou	5
Knepper-Hou	5
Welch-LA	3
Valenzuela-LA	3

Saves	
Worrell-StL	36
Reardon-Mon	35
Smith-Hou	33
Smith-Chi	31

Innings Pitched	
Scott-Hou	275.1
Valenzuela-LA	269.1
Knepper-Hou	258.0
Rhoden-Pit	253.2
Gooden-NY	250.0

Fewest Hits/Game	
Scott-Hou	5.95
Youmans-Mon	5.96
Ryan-Hou	6.02
Fernandez-NY	7.09
Gooden-NY	7.09

Fewest BB/Game	
Eckersley-Chi	1.93
Sanderson-Chi	1.96
Krukow-SF	2.02
Welch-LA	2.10
Ojeda-NY	2.15

Strikeouts	
Scott-Hou	306
Valenzuela-LA	242
Youmans-Mon	202
Gooden-NY	200
Fernandez-NY	200

Strikeouts/Game	
Scott-Hou	10.00
Ryan-Hou	9.81
Fernandez-NY	8.81
Youmans-Mon	8.30
Valenzuela-LA	8.09

Ratio	
Scott-Hou	8.37
Krukow-SF	9.66
Ojeda-NY	9.90
Gooden-NY	10.12
Rhoden-Pit	10.25

Earned Run Average	
Scott-Hou	2.22
Ojeda-NY	2.57
Darling-NY	2.81
Rhoden-Pit	2.84
Gooden-NY	2.84

Adjusted ERA	
Scott-Hou	162
Ojeda-NY	138
Rhoden-Pit	135
Darling-NY	126
Cox-StL	126

Opponents' Batting Avg.	
Scott-Hou	.186
Ryan-Hou	.188
Youmans-Mon	.188
Gooden-NY	.215
Fernandez-NY	.216

Opponents' On-Base Pct.	
Scott-Hou	.244
Krukow-SF	.271
Ojeda-NY	.279
Gooden-NY	.280
Ryan-Hou	.285

Starter Runs	
Scott-Hou	46.0
Ojeda-NY	28.0
Rhoden-Pit	25.0
Gooden-NY	24.5
Darling-NY	24.1

Adjusted Starter Runs	
Scott-Hou	43.7
Rhoden-Pit	27.4
Ojeda-NY	24.8
Ruffin-Phi	22.0
Gooden-NY	20.4

Clutch Pitching Index	
Dravecky-SD	115
Darling-NY	113
Garrelts-SF	110
Tudor-StL	110
Gullickson-Cin	110

Relief Runs	
Worrell-StL	18.9
McGaffigan-Mon	17.1
Horton-StL	16.5
Tekulve-Phi	14.5
McCullers-SD	14.3

Adjusted Relief Runs	
Worrell-StL	18.4
McGaffigan-Mon	16.8
Horton-StL	16.0
Tekulve-Phi	15.6
McCullers-SD	13.6

Relief Ranking	
Worrell-StL	36.8
Orosco-NY	22.9
Tekulve-Phi	21.5
Garber-Atl	20.1
McCullers-SD	18.9

Total Pitcher Index	
Scott-Hou	4.5
Rhoden-Pit	4.0
Worrell-StL	3.8
Orosco-NY	2.4
Ojeda-NY	2.4

Total Baseball Ranking	
Raines-Mon	5.7
Gwynn-SD	4.8
Hernandez-NY	4.5
Scott-Hou	4.5
Sax-LA	4.1

TEAM	G	W	L	PCT	GB	R	OR	AB	H	2B	3B	HR	BB	SO	AVG	OBP	SLG	OPS	OPS+	BR	BR+	PF	CHI	RC	SB	CS	SBA	SBR
EAST																												
BOS	161	95	66	.590		794	696	5498	1488	**320**	21	144	595	**707**	.271	.349	.415	764	107	59	57	100	98	792	41	34	55	-3
NY	162	90	72	.556	5.5	797	738	5570	1512	275	23	188	645	911	.271	**.350**	**.430**	**780**	**112**	**89**	**99**	99	94	**843**	139	48	**74**	**14**
DET	162	87	75	.537	8.5	798	714	5512	1447	234	30	**198**	613	885	.263	.341	.424	765	107	52	55	100	99	814	138	58	70	10
TOR	163	86	76	.531	9.5	809	733	5716	1540	285	35	181	496	848	.269	.331	.427	758	102	29	11	102	103	796	110	59	65	4
CLE	163	84	78	.519	11.5	**831**	841	5702	**1620**	270	**45**	157	456	944	**.284**	.340	**.430**	770	110	57	72	98	102	822	**141**	54	72	12
MIL	161	77	84	.478	18	667	734	5461	1393	255	38	127	530	986	.255	.324	.385	709	89	-59	-79	103	98	682	100	50	67	5
BAL	162	73	89	.451	22.5	708	760	5524	1425	223	13	169	563	862	.258	.330	.395	725	97	-28	-17	99	99	708	64	34	65	2
WEST																												
CAL	162	92	70	.568		786	684	5433	1387	236	36	167	**671**	860	.255	.341	.404	745	103	22	31	99	101	765	109	42	72	9
TEX	162	87	75	.537	5	771	743	5529	1479	248	43	184	511	1088	.267	.333	.428	761	103	37	19	102	99	761	103	85	55	-7
KC	162	76	86	.469	16	654	**673**	5561	1403	264	**45**	137	474	919	.252	.315	.390	705	88	-77	-89	102	99	683	97	46	68	5
OAK	162	76	86	.469	16	731	760	5435	1370	213	25	163	553	983	.252	.325	.390	715	101	-48	8	93	106	700	139	61	70	9
CHI	162	72	90	.444	25	644	699	5406	1335	197	34	121	487	940	.247	.313	.363	676	81	-125	-143	103	**107**	614	115	54	68	6
MIN	162	71	91	.438	26	741	839	5531	1446	257	39	196	501	977	.261	.327	.428	755	100	21	2	103	97	756	81	61	57	-4
SEA	162	67	95	.414	30	718	835	5498	1392	243	41	158	572	1148	.253	.327	.399	726	95	-28	-33	101	100	706	93	76	55	-6
TOT	1134					10449		77376	20237	3520	468	2290	7667	13058	.262	.333	.408	740							1470	762	66	57

TEAM	CG	SH	SV	IP	H	H/G	HR	BB	SO	RAT	ERA	ERA+	OAV	OOB	PR	PR+	PF	CPI	FA	E	DP	FW	PW	BW	SBW	DIF
EAST																										
BOS	36	6	41	1429^2	1469	9.3	167	**474**	1033	12.4	3.94	106	.266	.327	38	36	100	**106**	.979	129	146	-.1	3.6	5.7	-.7	6.3
NY	13	8	**58**	1443^1	1461	9.2	175	492	878	12.4	4.11	99	.263	.325	11	-4	98	101	.979	127	153	.0	-.3	**9.8**	**1.0**	-1.3
DET	33	12	38	1443^2	1374	8.6	183	571	880	12.4	4.03	102	.251	.325	25	16	99	101	.982	108	163	1.2	1.6	5.5	.6	-2.7
TOR	16	12	44	1476	1467	9.0	164	487	1002	12.2	4.08	103	.261	.325	16	22	101	99	**.984**	**100**	150	**1.7**	2.2	1.1	.0	.2
CLE	31	7	34	1447^2	1548	9.7	167	605	744	13.8	4.58	91	.273	.349	-64	-70	99	102	.975	157	148	-1.7	-6.8	7.1	.8	3.8
MIL	29	12	32	1431^2	1478	9.3	158	494	952	12.6	4.02	108	.267	.330	26	48	104	104	.976	146	146	-1.1	4.8	-7.7	.0	.7
BAL	17	6	39	1436^2	1451	9.1	177	535	954	12.6	4.31	96	.263	.330	-20	-27	99	99	.978	135	163	-.4	-2.6	-1.6	-.2	-3.0
WEST																										
CAL	29	12	40	1456	1356	**8.4**	153	478	955	**11.6**	3.84	107	.248	**.311**	54	44	98	94	.983	107	156	1.2	4.4	3.1	.5	2.0
TEX	15	8	41	1450^1	1356	8.5	145	736	**1059**	13.3	4.11	105	.249	.342	11	30	103	100	.980	122	160	.4	3.0	1.9	-1.1	2.0
KC	24	**13**	31	1440^2	1413	8.9	**121**	479	888	12.1	**3.83**	**111**	.258	.322	**56**	**67**	102	98	.980	123	153	.3	**6.6**	-8.7	.0	-3.1
OAK	22	8	37	1433	**1334**	**8.4**	166	667	937	12.8	4.31	90	**.247**	.333	-21	-76	93	94	.978	135	120	-.4	-7.4	.8	.5	1.7
CHI	18	8	38	1442^1	1361	8.5	143	561	895	12.2	3.94	110	.251	.325	39	59	103	98	.981	117	142	.7	5.9	-14.0	.2	-1.5
MIN	**39**	6	24	1432^2	1579	10.0	200	503	937	13.4	4.77	90	.281	.345	-94	-72	103	101	.980	118	168	.6	-7.0	.2	-.8	-2.8
SEA	33	5	27	1439^2	1590	10.0	171	585	944	14.0	4.66	91	.283	.355	-76	-64	102	105	.975	156	**191**	-1.7	-6.2	-3.2	-1.0	-1.7
TOT	355	123	524	20203^1		9.1				12.7	4.18		.262	.333					.980	1780	2159					

Runs
Henderson-NY 130
Puckett-Min 119
Mattingly-NY 117
Carter-Cle 108

Hits
Mattingly-NY 238
Puckett-Min 223
Fernandez-Tor 213
Boggs-Bos 207

Doubles
Mattingly-NY 53
Boggs-Bos 47
Rice-Bos 39
Buckner-Bos 39
Barrett-Bos 39

Triples
Butler-Cle 14
Sierra-Tex 10
Fernandez-Tor 9
Carter-Cle 9

Home Runs
Barfield-Tor 40
Kingman-Oak 35
Gaetti-Min 34
Deer-Mil 33
Canseco-Oak 33

Total Bases
Mattingly-NY 388
Puckett-Min 365
Carter-Cle 341
Bell-Tor 341
Barfield-Tor 329

Runs Batted In
Carter-Cle 121
Canseco-Oak 117
Mattingly-NY 113
Rice-Bos 110

Runs Produced
Carter-Cle 200
Mattingly-NY 199
Rice-Bos 188
Puckett-Min 184
Bell-Tor 178

Bases On Balls
Boggs-Bos 105
Evans-Bos 97
Randolph-NY 94
Jackson-Cal 92
Evans-Det 91

Batting Average
Boggs-Bos 357
Mattingly-NY 352
Puckett-Min 328
Tabler-Cle 326
Rice-Bos 324

On-Base Percentage
Boggs-Bos .... .455
P.Bradley-Sea ...... .406
Brett-KC .... .404
Murray-Bal .... .400
Mattingly-NY ...... .399

Slugging Average
Mattingly-NY .... .573
Barfield-Tor .... .559
Puckett-Min .... .537
Bell-Tor .... .532
Gaetti-Min .... .518

On-Base Plus Slugging
Mattingly-NY 973
Boggs-Bos 942
Barfield-Tor 929
Puckett-Min 903
Brett-KC 885

Adjusted OPS
Mattingly-NY 163
Boggs-Bos 156
Barfield-Tor 145
Puckett-Min 138
Rice-Bos 137

Batter Runs
Mattingly-NY 55.6
Boggs-Bos 51.6
Barfield-Tor 39.0
Puckett-Min 37.1
Rice-Bos 32.6

Adjusted Batter Runs
Mattingly-NY 57.4
Boggs-Bos 51.1
Barfield-Tor 36.2
Puckett-Min 34.1
Rice-Bos 32.3

Clutch Hitting Index
Phillips-Oak 135
Buckner-Bos 127
Cooper-Mil 126
Canseco-Oak 125
Downing-Cal 122

Runs Created
Mattingly-NY 150
Boggs-Bos 133
Puckett-Min 127
Barfield-Tor 122
Carter-Cle 116

Total Average
Boggs-Bos 987
Mattingly-NY 969
Gibson-Det 950
Barfield-Tor 931
Henderson-NY 931

Stolen Bases
Henderson-NY 87
Pettis-Cal 50
Cangelosi-Chi 50
Wilson-KC 34
Gibson-Det 34

Stolen Base Average
Felder-Mil 88.9
Davis-Oak 87.1
Gibson-Det 85.0
Henderson-NY 82.9

Stolen Base Runs
Henderson-NY 12.8
Pettis-Cal 6.4
Gibson-Det 5.4
Cangelosi-Chi 5.1
Wilson-KC 4.7

Fielding Runs
Owen-Sea-Bos 31.9
Reynolds-Sea 29.0
Barfield-Tor 20.9
Pettis-Cal 20.7
Buckner-Bos 20.1

Total Player Rating
Barfield-Tor 4.6
Ripken-Bal 4.6
Boggs-Bos 4.5
Henderson-NY 4.3
Puckett-Min 4.3

Wins
Clemens-Bos 24
Morris-Det 21
Higuera-Mil 20
Witt-Cal 18
Rasmussen-NY 18

Win Percentage
Clemens-Bos 857
Rasmussen-NY 750
Morris-Det 724
Higuera-Mil 645
Witt-Cal 643

Games
Williams-Tex 80
Righetti-NY 74
Harris-Tex 73
Eichhorn-Tor 69

Complete Games
Candiotti-Cle 17
Blyleven-Min 16
Morris-Det 15
Higuera-Mil 15
Witt-Cal 14

Shutouts
Morris-Det 6
Hurst-Bos 4
Higuera-Mil 4

Saves
Righetti-NY 46
Aase-Bal 34
Henke-Tor 27
Hernandez-Det 24
Moore-Cal 21

Innings Pitched
Blyleven-Min 271.2
Witt-Cal 269.0
Morris-Det 267.0
Moore-Sea 266.0
Clemens-Bos 254.0

Fewest Hits/Game
Clemens-Bos 6.34
Rasmussen-NY 7.13
Witt-Cal 7.29
Hough-Tex 7.35
Cowley-Chi 7.37

Fewest BB/Game
Guidry-NY 1.78
Boyd-Bos 1.89
Blyleven-Min 1.92
Wegman-Mil 1.95
Sutton-Cal 2.13

Strikeouts
Langston-Sea 245
Clemens-Bos 238
Morris-Det 223
Blyleven-Min 215
Witt-Cal 208

Strikeouts/Game
Langston-Sea 9.21
Hurst-Bos 8.62
Clemens-Bos 8.43
Correa-Tex 8.41
Rijo-Oak 8.18

Ratio
Clemens-Bos 8.86
Witt-Cal 9.84
Morris-Det 10.48
Rasmussen-NY 10.51
Sutton-Cal 10.61

Earned Run Average
Clemens-Bos 2.48
Higuera-Mil 2.79
Witt-Cal 2.84
Hurst-Bos 2.99
D.Jackson-KC 3.20

Adjusted ERA
Clemens-Bos 168
Higuera-Mil 155
Witt-Cal 145
Hurst-Bos 139
D.Jackson-KC 133

Opponents' Batting Avg.
Clemens-Bos 195
Rasmussen-NY 217
Witt-Cal 221
Hough-Tex 221
Correa-Tex 223

Opponents' On-Base Pct.
Clemens-Bos 253
Witt-Cal 277
Morris-Det 287
Sutton-Cal 288
Rasmussen-NY 290

Starter Runs
Clemens-Bos 48.1
Witt-Cal 40.1
Higuera-Mil 38.5
Morris-Det 27.2
Hurst-Bos 23.1

Adjusted Starter Runs
Clemens-Bos 47.9
Higuera-Mil 41.2
Witt-Cal 38.7
Morris-Det 25.9
Hurst-Bos 22.9

Clutch Pitching Index
Hurst-Bos 124
D.Jackson-KC 121
Higuera-Mil 119
Stieb-Tor 119
Niekro-Cle 117

Relief Runs
Eichhorn-Tor 43.0
Righetti-NY 20.6
Harris-Tex 16.8
Clear-Mil 16.3
Mohorcic-Tex 14.7

Adjusted Relief Runs
Eichhorn-Tor 43.3
Righetti-NY 20.0
Harris-Tex 17.8
Clear-Mil 16.9
Mohorcic-Tex 15.4

Relief Ranking
Eichhorn-Tor 55.0
Righetti-NY 40.0
Harris-Tex 32.1
Clear-Mil 27.8
Plesac-Mil 26.5

Total Pitcher Index
Eichhorn-Tor 5.8
Clemens-Bos 5.0
Higuera-Mil 4.8
Witt-Cal 4.0
Righetti-NY 3.9

Total Baseball Ranking
Eichhorn-Tor 5.8
Clemens-Bos 5.0
Higuera-Mil 4.8
Barfield-Tor 4.6
Ripken-Bal 4.6

TEAM	G	W	L	PCT	GB	R	OR	AB	H	2B	3B	HR	BB	SO	AVG	OBP	SLG	OPS	OPS+	BR	BR+	PF	CHI	RC	SB	CS	SBA	SBR
EAST																												
STL	162	95	67	.586		798	693	5500	1449	252	49	94	**644**	933	.263	**.343**	.378	721	95	-9	-23	102	**109**	740	**248**	72	78	**29**
NY	162	92	70	.568	3	**823**	698	5601	**1499**	287	34	192	592	1012	**.268**	.341	**.434**	**775**	**117**	**81**	**126**	95	100	**848**	159	49	76	18
MON	162	91	71	.562	4	741	720	5527	1467	**310**	39	120	501	918	.265	.330	.401	731	96	-6	-27	103	103	734	166	74	69	11
PIT	162	80	82	.494	15	723	744	5536	1464	282	45	131	535	914	.264	.332	.403	735	99	3	-1	101	98	741	140	58	71	11
PHI	162	80	82	.494	15	702	749	5475	1390	248	**51**	169	587	1109	.254	.329	.410	739	98	8	-15	103	95	736	111	49	69	7
CHI	161	76	85	.472	18.5	720	801	5583	1475	244	33	**209**	504	1064	.264	.327	.432	759	102	40	11	104	94	785	109	48	69	7
WEST																												
SF	162	90	72	.556		783	**669**	5608	1458	274	32	205	511	1094	.260	.326	.430	756	110	33	72	95	102	768	126	97	57	-6
CIN	162	84	78	.519	6	783	752	5560	1478	262	29	192	514	928	.266	.331	.427	758	102	42	9	104	102	786	169	46	**79**	21
HOU	162	76	86	.469	14	648	678	5485	1386	238	28	122	526	936	.253	.321	.373	694	94	-78	-53	96	100	669	162	46	78	20
LA	162	73	89	.451	17	635	675	5517	1389	236	23	125	445	923	.252	.311	.371	682	88	-108	-92	97	104	627	128	59	68	8
ATL	161	69	92	.429	20.5	747	829	5428	1401	284	24	152	641	**834**	.258	.341	.403	744	98	28	-8	105	98	747	135	68	67	6
SD	162	65	97	.401	25	668	763	5456	1419	209	48	113	577	992	.260	.334	.378	712	99	-34	-8	96	96	693	198	91	69	12
TOT	971					8771		66276	17275	3126	435	1824	6577	11657	.261	.331	.404	734							1851	757	71	142

TEAM	CG	SH	SV	IP	H	H/G	HR	BB	SO	RAT	ERA	ERA+	OAV	OOB	PR	PR+	PF	CPI	FA	E	DP	FW	PW	BW	SBW	DIF
EAST																										
STL	10	7	48	1466	1484	9.2	**129**	533	873	12.6	3.92	106	.265	.332	28	39	102	103	**.982**	**116**	172	**.9**	3.9	-2.2	**1.7**	9.9
NY	16	7	**51**	1454	1407	8.8	135	510	1032	12.1	3.85	98	.254	.321	38	-12	93	98	.978	137	137	-.3	-1.1	**12.6**	.6	-.6
MON	16	8	50	1450^1	1428	8.9	145	**446**	1012	**11.8**	3.92	**107**	.257	**.315**	26	**45**	103	95	.976	147	122	-.8	**4.5**	-2.6	-.0	9.2
PIT	25	**13**	39	1445	1377	**8.6**	164	562	914	12.3	4.20	98	.253	.326	-19	-14	101	95	.980	123	147	.5	-1.3	-.0	-.0	.2
PHI	13	7	48	1448^1	1453	9.1	167	587	877	12.9	4.19	101	.263	.338	-16	9	104	103	.980	121	137	.6	.9	-1.4	-.5	-.5
CHI	11	5	48	1434^2	1524	9.6	159	628	1024	13.7	4.56	94	.275	.352	-76	-42	105	103	.979	130	154	.0	-4.1	1.1	-.5	-.9
WEST																										
SF	19	10	38	1471	1407	8.7	146	547	1038	12.2	**3.68**	105	.255	.325	**66**	29	94	**106**	.980	129	**183**	.2	2.9	7.2	-1.8	.6
CIN	7	6	44	1452^1	1486	9.3	170	485	919	12.4	4.25	100	.267	.328	-27	0	104	99	.979	130	137	.1	.0	.9	.9	1.2
HOU	13	**13**	33	1441^1	**1363**	**8.6**	141	525	**1137**	12.0	3.85	102	**.250**	.319	38	13	96	96	.981	**116**	113	**.9**	1.3	-5.2	.8	-2.7
LA	**29**	8	32	1455	1415	8.8	130	565	1097	12.5	3.72	**107**	.255	.327	59	41	97	103	.975	155	144	-1.3	4.1	-9.1	-.4	-1.2
ATL	16	4	32	1427^2	1529	9.7	163	587	837	13.6	4.63	94	.276	.350	-87	-42	107	101	**.982**	**116**	170	**.9**	-4.1	-.7	-.6	-6.7
SD	14	10	33	1433^1	1402	8.9	175	602	897	12.9	4.27	93	.256	.334	-30	-52	97	99	.976	147	135	-.8	-5.1	-.7	.0	-9.1
TOT	189	98	496	17379		9.0				12.6	4.08		.261	.331					.980	1567	1751					

Runs
Raines-Mon 123
Coleman-StL 121
Davis-Cin 120
Gwynn-SD 119
Murphy-Atl 115

Hits
Gwynn-SD 218
Guerrero-LA 184
Smith-StL 182
Coleman-StL 180

Doubles
Wallach-Mon 42
Smith-StL 40
Galarraga-Mon 40

Triples
Samuel-Phi 15
Gwynn-SD 13
VanSlyke-Pit 11
McGee-StL 11
Coleman-StL 10

Home Runs
Dawson-Chi 49
Murphy-Atl 44
Strawberry-NY 39
Davis-Cin 37
Johnson-NY 36

Total Bases
Dawson-Chi 353
Samuel-Phi 329
Murphy-Atl 328
Strawberry-NY 310
Clark-SF 307

Runs Batted In
Dawson-Chi 137
Wallach-Mon 123
Schmidt-Phi 113
Clark-StL 106

Runs Produced
Wallach-Mon 186
Samuel-Phi 185
Davis-Cin 183
Smith-StL 179
Dawson-Chi 178

Bases On Balls
Clark-StL 136
Hayes-Phi 121
Murphy-Atl 115
Strawberry-NY 97
Raines-Mon 90

Batting Average
Gwynn-SD .370
Guerrero-LA .338
Raines-Mon .330
Kruk-SD .313
James-Atl .312

On-Base Percentage
Clark-StL .461
Gwynn-SD .450
Raines-Mon .431
Guerrero-LA .421
Murphy-Atl .420

Slugging Average
Clark-StL .597
Davis-Cin .593
Strawberry-NY .583
Clark-SF .580
Murphy-Atl .580

On-Base Plus Slugging
Clark-StL 1058
Murphy-Atl 1000
Davis-Cin 994
Strawberry-NY 984
Gwynn-SD 961

Adjusted OPS
Clark-StL 174
Strawberry-NY 165
Gwynn-SD 160
Guerrero-LA 156
Clark-SF 155

Batter Runs
Clark-StL 54.3
Murphy-Atl 53.3
Gwynn-SD 49.6
Strawberry-NY 44.7
Raines-Mon 43.2

Adjusted Batter Runs
Gwynn-SD 54.4
Clark-StL 52.0
Strawberry-NY 51.3
Murphy-Atl 47.0
Guerrero-LA 45.7

Clutch Hitting Index
Herr-StL 172
Pendleton-StL 131
Smith-StL 130
McGee-StL 126
Diaz-Cin 124

Runs Created
Murphy-Atl 143
Gwynn-SD 143
Strawberry-NY 132
Raines-Mon 132
Clark-StL 127

Total Average
Clark-StL 1.258
Davis-Cin 1.182
Raines-Mon 1.133
Murphy-Atl 1.106
Strawberry-NY 1.103

Stolen Bases
Coleman-StL 109
Gwynn-SD 56
Hatcher-Hou 53
Raines-Mon 50
Davis-Cin 50

Stolen Base Average
Sandberg-Chi 91.3
Raines-Mon 90.9
Davis-Cin 89.3
Hatcher-Hou 85.5
Coleman-StL 83.2

Stolen Base Runs
Coleman-StL 16.3
Raines-Mon 9.3
Davis-Cin 8.9
Hatcher-Hou 8.5
Gwynn-SD 8.1

Fielding Runs
Hubbard-Atl 28.2
Davis-Cin 28.1
Bonds-Pit 19.7
Smith-StL 19.3
Hernandez-NY 17.7

Total Player Rating
Davis-Cin 7.0
Gwynn-SD 6.1
Raines-Mon 5.7
Murphy-Atl 5.1
Smith-StL 4.9

Wins
Sutcliffe-Chi 18
Rawley-Phi 17
Scott-Hou 16
Hershiser-LA 16

Win Percentage
Gooden-NY .682
Sutcliffe-Chi .643
Welch-LA .625
Rawley-Phi .607
Z.Smith-Atl .600

Games
Tekulve-Phi 90
Murphy-Cin 87
Williams-Cin 85
J.Robinson-SF-Pit 81
McCullers-SD 78

Complete Games
Reuschel-Pit-SF 12
Valenzuela-LA 12
Hershiser-LA 10
Z.Smith-Atl 9
Scott-Hou 8

Shutouts
Reuschel-Pit-SF 4
Welch-LA 4

Saves
Bedrosian-Phi 40
Smith-Chi 36
Worrell-StL 33
Franco-Cin 32
McDowell-NY 25

Innings Pitched
Hershiser-LA 264.2
Welch-LA 251.2
Valenzuela-LA 251.0
Scott-Hou 247.2
Z.Smith-Atl 242.0

Fewest Hits/Game
Ryan-Hou 6.55
Scott-Hou 7.23
Welch-LA 7.30
Dunne-Pit 7.88
Darling-NY 7.93

Fewest BB/Game
Reuschel-Pit-SF 1.67
Heaton-Mon 1.72
Gullickson-Cin 2.13
Forsch-StL 2.26
Drabek-Pit 2.35

Strikeouts
Ryan-Hou 270
Scott-Hou 233
Welch-LA 196
Valenzuela-LA 190
Hershiser-LA 190

Strikeouts/Game
Ryan-Hou 11.48
Scott-Hou 8.47
Sebra-Mon 7.92
Gooden-NY 7.41
Darling-NY 7.24

Ratio
Reuschel-Pit-SF 10.19
Scott-Hou 10.25
Ryan-Hou 10.42
Welch-LA 10.51
Drabek-Pit 10.77

Earned Run Average
Ryan-Hou 2.76
Dunne-Pit 3.03
Hershiser-LA 3.06
Reuschel-Pit-SF 3.09
Gooden-NY 3.21

Adjusted ERA
Ryan-Hou 142
Dunne-Pit 136
Reuschel-Pit-SF 131
Hershiser-LA 130
Welch-LA 123

Opponents' Batting Avg.
Ryan-Hou .199
Scott-Hou .217
Welch-LA .221
Darling-NY .233
Dunne-Pit .240

Opponents' On-Base Pct.
Scott-Hou .282
Ryan-Hou .284
Reuschel-Pit-SF .284
Welch-LA .291
Drabek-Pit .296

Starter Runs
Ryan-Hou 31.1
Hershiser-LA 30.2
Reuschel-Pit-SF 25.1
Welch-LA 24.3
Scott-Hou 23.4

Adjusted Starter Runs
Ryan-Hou 28.4
Hershiser-LA 27.6
Reuschel-Pit-SF 24.5
Welch-LA 21.7
Scott-Hou 19.7

Clutch Pitching Index
LaCoss-SF 124
Cox-StL 120
Dravecky-SD-SF 113
Ruffin-Phi 112
Grant-SF-SD 111

Relief Runs
Burke-Mon 29.3
McGaffigan-Mon 22.6
Williams-Cin 21.0
J.Robinson-SF-Pit 17.0
Smith-Hou 16.2

Adjusted Relief Runs
Burke-Mon 29.7
McGaffigan-Mon 23.6
Williams-Cin 22.0
Smith-Hou 15.8
Worrell-StL 15.5

Relief Ranking
Burke-Mon 30.9
Franco-Cin 30.2
Worrell-StL 30.1
Smith-Hou 23.0
J.Robinson-SF-Pit 21.9

Total Pitcher Index
Hershiser-LA 3.8
Burke-Mon 3.1
Worrell-StL 3.1
Franco-Cin 3.0
Ryan-Hou 2.6

Total Baseball Ranking
Davis-Cin 7.0
Gwynn-SD 6.1
Raines-Mon 5.7
Murphy-Atl 5.1
Smith-StL 4.9

TEAM	G	W	L	PCT	GB	R	OR	AB	H	2B	3B	HR	BB	SO	AVG	OBP	SLG	OPS	OPS+	BR	BR+	PF	CHI	RC	SB	CS	SBA	SBR
EAST																												
DET	162	98	64	.605		**896**	735	5649	1535	274	32	**225**	**653**	913	.272	.352	**.451**	**803**	**116**	**91**	**133**	96	98	**910**	106	50	68	6
TOR	162	96	66	.593	2	845	**655**	5635	1514	277	38	215	555	970	.269	.338	.446	784	103	42	26	102	100	841	126	50	72	10
MIL	162	91	71	.562	7	862	817	5625	1552	272	46	163	598	1040	.276	.349	.428	777	102	40	18	103	101	852	**176**	74	70	**13**
NY	162	89	73	.549	9	788	758	5511	1445	239	16	196	604	949	.262	.338	.418	756	100	-6	4	99	100	773	105	43	71	8
BOS	162	78	84	.481	20	842	825	5586	**1554**	273	26	174	606	**825**	**.278**	**.355**	.430	785	104	61	39	103	97	855	77	45	63	1
BAL	162	67	95	.414	31	729	880	5576	1437	219	20	211	524	939	.258	.324	.418	742	98	-47	-26	97	99	736	69	45	61	-1
CLE	162	61	101	.377	37	742	957	5606	1476	267	30	187	489	977	.263	.326	.422	748	95	-35	-40	101	98	772	140	54	72	12
WEST																												
MIN	162	85	77	.525		786	806	5441	1422	258	35	196	523	898	.261	.330	.430	760	96	-8	-34	104	103	757	113	65	63	2
KC	162	83	79	.512	2	715	691	5499	1443	239	40	168	523	1034	.262	.330	.412	742	93	-40	-57	102	97	747	125	43	**74**	12
OAK	162	81	81	.500	4	806	789	5511	1432	263	33	199	593	1056	.260	.336	.428	764	108	4	62	93	101	796	140	63	69	9
SEA	162	78	84	.481	7	760	801	5508	1499	282	**48**	161	500	863	.272	.337	.428	765	96	9	-29	105	96	788	174	73	70	**13**
CHI	162	77	85	.475	20	748	746	5538	1427	**283**	36	173	487	971	.258	.321	.415	736	91	-57	-73	102	103	737	138	52	73	12
TEX	162	75	87	.463	22	823	849	5564	1478	264	35	194	567	1081	.266	.336	.430	766	101	9	8	100	102	798	120	71	63	2
CAL	162	75	87	.463	22	770	803	5570	1406	257	26	172	590	926	.252	.328	.401	729	95	-65	-38	97	**105**	744	125	44	**74**	12
TOT	1134					11112		77819	20620	3667	461	2634	7812	13442	.265	.336	.426	761							1734	772	69	111

TEAM	CG	SH	SV	IP	H	H/G	HR	BB	SO	RAT	ERA	ERA+	OAV	OOB	PR	PR+	PF	CPI	FA	E	DP	FW	PW	BW	SBW	DIF
EAST																										
DET	33	10	31	1456	1430	8.9	180	563	976	12.6	4.03	105	.256	.328	70	33	95	103	.980	122	147	.2	3.2	**12.7**	-.2	1.3
TOR	18	8	43	1454	**1323**	**8.2**	158	567	1064	**11.9**	**3.75**	**120**	**.244**	**.318**	**115**	**120**	101	101	.982	111	148	.8	**11.5**	2.5	.2	.2
MIL	28	6	45	1464	1548	9.6	169	529	1039	13.0	4.63	99	.271	.336	-27	-8	103	96	.976	145	155	-1.3	-.7	1.8	**.5**	9.9
NY	19	10	**47**	1446^{1}	1475	9.2	179	542	900	12.8	4.36	101	.266	.334	16	5	98	101	.983	102	155	1.4	.5	.4	.0	5.9
BOS	**47**	**13**	16	1436	1584	10.0	190	517	1034	13.4	4.77	95	.282	.346	-50	-37	102	102	.982	110	158	.9	-3.5	3.8	-.7	-3.3
BAL	17	6	30	1439^{2}	1555	9.8	226	547	870	13.4	5.01	88	.276	.343	-88	-99	99	99	.982	111	**174**	.8	-9.4	-2.4	-.9	-2.0
CLE	24	8	25	1422^{2}	1566	10.0	219	606	849	14.1	5.29	86	.278	.354	-131	-118	102	97	.975	153	128	-1.7	-11.2	-3.8	.4	-3.5
WEST																										
MIN	16	4	39	1427^{1}	1465	9.3	210	564	990	13.2	4.63	100	.266	.339	-27	-2	104	101	**.984**	**98**	147	**1.6**	-.1	-3.2	-.6	6.5
KC	44	11	26	1424	1424	9.1	**128**	548	923	12.7	3.86	118	.261	.333	95	108	102	**105**	.979	131	151	-.4	10.3	-5.4	.4	-2.7
OAK	18	6	40	1445^{2}	1442	9.0	176	531	1042	12.6	4.33	96	.258	.327	22	-34	93	96	.977	142	122	-1.1	-3.2	6.0	.1	-1.6
SEA	39	10	33	1430^{2}	1503	9.5	199	**497**	919	12.8	4.49	105	.272	.335	-5	35	106	103	.980	122	150	.2	3.4	-2.7	**.5**	-4.1
CHI	29	12	37	1447^{2}	1436	9.0	189	537	792	12.5	4.30	107	.259	.329	26	45	103	100	.981	116	**174**	.5	4.3	-6.9	.4	-2.1
TEX	20	3	27	1444^{1}	1388	8.7	199	760	**1103**	13.8	4.63	97	.253	.350	-28	-25	100	100	.976	151	148	-1.6	-2.3	.8	-.6	-2.1
CAL	20	7	36	1457^{1}	1481	9.2	212	504	941	12.5	4.38	98	.264	.329	13	-13	97	102	.981	117	162	.5	-1.2	-3.6	.4	-1.9
TOT	372	114	475	20195^{2}		9.2				12.9	4.46		.265	.336					.980	1731	2119					

Runs
Molitor-Mil 114
Bell-Tor 111
Whitaker-Det 110
Downing-Cal 110

Hits
Seitzer-KC 207
Puckett-Min 207
Trammell-Det 205
Boggs-Bos 200
Yount-Mil 198

Doubles
Molitor-Mil 41
Boggs-Bos 40

Triples
Wilson-KC 15
Polonia-Oak 10
P.Bradley-Sea 10
Yount-Mil 9

Home Runs
McGwire-Oak 49
Bell-Tor 47

Total Bases
Bell-Tor 369
McGwire-Oak 344
Puckett-Min 333
Trammell-Det 329
Boggs-Bos 324

Runs Batted In
Bell-Tor 134
Evans-Bos 123
McGwire-Oak 118
Joyner-Cal 117
Mattingly-NY 115

Runs Produced
Evans-Bos 198
Bell-Tor 198
Trammell-Det 186
Joyner-Cal 183
Yount-Mil 181

Bases On Balls
Evans-Bos 106
Downing-Cal 106
Boggs-Bos 105
Evans-Det 100
Butler-Cle 91

Batting Average
Boggs-Bos .363
Molitor-Mil .353
Trammell-Det .343
Puckett-Min .332
Mattingly-NY .327

On-Base Percentage
Boggs-Bos .467
Molitor-Mil .438
Evans-Bos .422
Randolph-NY .415
Trammell-Det .406

Slugging Average
McGwire-Oak .618
Bell-Tor .605
Boggs-Bos .588
Evans-Bos .569
Molitor-Mil .566

On-Base Plus Slugging
Boggs-Bos 1055
Molitor-Mil 1004
McGwire-Oak 992
Evans-Bos 991
Bell-Tor 962

Adjusted OPS
Boggs-Bos 173
McGwire-Oak 168
Molitor-Mil 159
Trammell-Det 157
Evans-Bos 155

Batter Runs
Boggs-Bos 66.6
Evans-Bos 49.6
Molitor-Mil 44.8
McGwire-Oak 44.2
Trammell-Det 43.7

Adjusted Batter Runs
Boggs-Bos 62.7
McGwire-Oak 53.4
Trammell-Det 49.6
Evans-Bos 46.2
Molitor-Mil 41.9

Clutch Hitting Index
Randolph-NY 141
Griffin-Oak 127
Owen-Bos 118
Tabler-Cle 117
Ward-NY 117

Runs Created
Boggs-Bos 154
Trammell-Det 137
Evans-Bos 134
McGwire-Oak 131
Molitor-Mil 125

Total Average
Molitor-Mil 1.171
Boggs-Bos 1.169
Evans-Bos 1.059
McGwire-Oak 1.042
Trammell-Det 1.015

Stolen Bases
Reynolds-Sea 60
Wilson-KC 59
Redus-Chi 52
Molitor-Mil 45
Henderson-NY 41

Stolen Base Average
McDowell-Tex 92.3
Trammell-Det 91.3
Schofield-Cal 86.4
Moseby-Tor 84.8
Wilson-KC 84.3

Stolen Base Runs
Wilson-KC 9.1
Redus-Chi 7.6
Molitor-Mil 6.4
Henderson-NY 6.2
Reynolds-Sea 6.2

Fielding Runs
Barrett-Bos 32.3
Salazar-KC 21.8
Manrique-Chi 18.9
Reynolds-Sea 18.8
Gagne-Min 16.9

Total Player Rating
Boggs-Bos 5.8
Trammell-Det 5.5
McGwire-Oak 3.5
Henderson-NY 3.5
Molitor-Mil 3.4

Wins
Stewart-Oak 20
Clemens-Bos 20
Langston-Sea 19

Win Percentage
Clemens-Bos .690
Key-Tor .680
Saberhagen-KC .643
Higuera-Mil .643

Games
Eichhorn-Tor 89
Williams-Tex 85
Mohorcic-Tex 74
Henke-Tor 72
Musselman-Tor 68

Complete Games
Clemens-Bos 18
Saberhagen-KC 15
Hurst-Bos 15
Langston-Sea 14
Higuera-Mil 14

Shutouts
Clemens-Bos 7
Saberhagen-KC 4

Saves
Henke-Tor 34
Righetti-NY 31
Reardon-Min 31
Plesac-Mil 23
Buice-Cal 17

Innings Pitched
Hough-Tex 285.1
Clemens-Bos 281.2
Langston-Sea 272.0
Blyleven-Min 267.0
Morris-Det 266.0

Fewest Hits/Game
Key-Tor 7.24
Hough-Tex 7.51
Morris-Det 7.68
Stewart-Oak 7.71
DeLeon-Chi 7.73

Fewest BB/Game
Long-Chi 1.49
Saberhagen-KC 1.86
Sutton-Cal 1.93
Bannister-Chi 1.93
Young-Oak 1.95

Strikeouts
Langston-Sea 262
Clemens-Bos 256
Higuera-Mil 240
Hough-Tex 223
Morris-Det 208

Strikeouts/Game
Langston-Sea 8.67
Higuera-Mil 8.25
Clemens-Bos 8.18
Bosio-Mil 7.94
Nieves-Mil 7.50

Ratio
Key-Tor 9.59
Bannister-Chi 10.43
Saberhagen-KC 10.68
Young-Oak 10.68
Viola-Min 10.80

Earned Run Average
Key-Tor 2.76
Viola-Min 2.90
Clemens-Bos 2.97
Saberhagen-KC 3.36
Morris-Det 3.38

Adjusted ERA
Key-Tor 163
Viola-Min 160
Clemens-Bos 153
Saberhagen-KC 136
Leibrandt-KC 134

Opponents' Batting Avg.
Key-Tor .221
Hough-Tex .223
Morris-Det .228
Stewart-Oak .229
DeLeon-Chi .230

Opponents' On-Base Pct.
Key-Tor .273
Bannister-Chi .286
Viola-Min .294
Morris-Det .294
Young-Oak .295

Starter Runs
Key-Tor 49.7
Clemens-Bos 47.0
Viola-Min 44.1
Morris-Det 32.2
Saberhagen-KC 31.7

Adjusted Starter Runs
Key-Tor 50.3
Clemens-Bos 48.6
Viola-Min 46.9
Saberhagen-KC 33.8
Leibrandt-KC 30.4

Clutch Pitching Index
Viola-Min 116
Rhoden-NY 113
Terrell-Det 110
Blyleven-Min 109
Gubicza-KC 107

Relief Runs
Henke-Tor 20.7
Eckersley-Oak 18.5
Eichhorn-Tor 18.4
Thigpen-Chi 17.2
Plesac-Mil 16.4

Adjusted Relief Runs
Henke-Tor 20.9
Eichhorn-Tor 18.8
Thigpen-Chi 18.0
Plesac-Mil 17.0
Mohorcic-Tex 16.5

Relief Ranking
Plesac-Mil 31.8
Thigpen-Chi 28.7
Henke-Tor 28.3
Mohorcic-Tex 25.1
Eichhorn-Tor 22.5

Total Pitcher Index
Key-Tor 4.6
Viola-Min 4.5
Clemens-Bos 4.4
Leibrandt-KC 3.5
Saberhagen-KC 3.4

Total Baseball Ranking
Boggs-Bos 5.8
Trammell-Det 5.5
Key-Tor 4.6
Viola-Min 4.5
Clemens-Bos 4.4

TEAM	G	W	L	PCT	GB	R	OR	AB	H	2B	3B	HR	BB	SO	AVG	OBP	SLG	OPS	OPS+	BR	BR+	PF	CHI	RC	SB	CS	SBA	SBR
EAST																												
NY	160	100	60	.625		**703**	**532**	5408	1387	251	24	**152**	544	842	.256	**.328**	**.396**	**724**	**120**	**95**	**132**	95	97	**717**	140	51	73	13
PIT	160	85	75	.531	15	651	616	5379	1327	240	45	110	**553**	947	.247	.321	.369	690	105	33	42	99	99	648	119	60	66	5
MON	163	81	81	.500	20	628	592	5573	1400	260	**48**	107	454	1053	.251	.311	.373	684	98	12	-16	105	97	636	189	89	68	10
CHI	163	77	85	.475	24	660	694	5675	**1481**	**262**	46	113	403	910	**.261**	.312	.383	695	100	31	2	105	99	673	120	46	72	10
STL	162	76	86	.469	25	578	633	5518	1373	207	33	71	484	**827**	.249	.312	.337	649	92	-47	-53	101	98	601	**234**	64	**79**	**29**
PHI	162	65	96	.404	35.5	597	734	5403	1294	246	31	106	489	981	.239	.308	.355	663	94	-22	-34	102	100	599	112	49	70	7
WEST																												
LA	162	94	67	.584		628	544	5431	1346	217	25	99	437	947	.248	.308	.352	660	99	-32	-13	97	**107**	590	131	46	74	13
CIN	161	87	74	.540	7	641	596	5426	1334	246	25	122	479	922	.246	.311	.368	679	97	6	-18	104	102	639	207	56	**79**	26
SD	161	83	78	.516	11	594	583	5366	1325	205	35	94	494	892	.247	.313	.351	664	99	-19	-8	98	99	594	123	50	71	10
SF	162	83	79	.512	11.5	670	626	5450	1353	227	44	113	550	1023	.248	.321	.368	689	109	32	62	96	101	650	121	78	61	-1
HOU	162	82	80	.506	12.5	617	631	5494	1338	239	31	96	474	840	.244	.308	.351	659	99	-32	-8	96	103	604	198	71	74	19
ATL	160	54	106	.338	39.5	555	741	5440	1319	228	28	96	432	848	.242	.301	.348	649	88	-56	-83	105	99	549	95	69	58	-3
TOT	969					7522		65563	16277	2828	415	1279	5793	11032	.249	.313	.363	675							1789	729	71	138

TEAM	CG	SH	SV	IP	H	H/G	HR	BB	SO	RAT	ERA	ERA+	OAV	OOB	PR	PR+	PF	CPI	FA	E	DP	FW	PW	BW	SBW	DIF
EAST																										
NY	31	22	46	1439	**1253**	**7.9**	**78**	**404**	**1100**	**10.6**	**2.91**	111	**.235**	**.293**	**86**	53	93	98	**.981**	**115**	127	**.9**	5.8	**14.3**	.2	-.9
PIT	12	11	46	1440^{2}	1349	8.5	108	469	790	11.6	3.47	98	.250	.314	-3	-11	99	101	.980	125	128	.4	-1.1	4.6	-.7	2.1
MON	18	12	43	1482^{2}	1310	8.0	122	476	923	11.1	3.09	**117**	.238	.303	60	**81**	104	**105**	.978	142	145	-.5	**8.8**	-1.7	-.2	-6.3
CHI	30	10	29	1464^{1}	1494	9.2	115	490	897	12.4	3.85	94	.265	.327	-64	-37	105	102	.980	125	128	.5	-3.9	.3	-.2	-.5
STL	17	14	42	1470^{2}	1387	8.5	91	486	881	11.6	3.47	100	.252	.314	-4	1	101	99	**.981**	121	131	.7	.2	-5.7	**1.9**	-1.9
PHI	16	6	36	1433	1447	9.1	118	628	859	13.3	4.14	86	.265	.344	-110	-89	103	103	.976	145	139	-.7	-9.5	-3.6	-.5	-1.0
WEST																										
LA	**32**	**24**	**49**	1463^{1}	1291	8.0	84	473	1029	11.0	2.97	112	.237	.301	78	61	97	102	.977	142	126	-.5	6.6	-1.4	.2	8.8
CIN	24	13	43	1455	1271	**7.9**	121	504	934	11.2	3.35	107	.237	.306	16	37	104	98	.980	125	131	.4	4.0	-1.9	1.6	2.6
SD	30	9	39	1449	1332	8.3	112	439	885	11.2	3.28	104	.247	.306	27	19	99	103	**.981**	120	**147**	.7	2.1	-.8	-.2	.9
SF	25	13	42	1462^{1}	1323	8.2	99	422	875	11.0	3.39	96	.242	.300	10	-21	95	93	.980	129	145	.2	-2.2	6.7	-1.4	-1.2
HOU	21	15	40	1474^{2}	1339	8.2	123	478	1049	11.4	3.41	97	.242	.307	7	-15	96	99	.978	138	124	-.3	-1.6	-.8	.8	3.0
ATL	14	4	25	1446	1481	9.3	108	524	810	12.8	4.09	90	.268	.336	-103	-63	107	100	.976	151	138	-1.1	-6.7	-8.9	-1.6	-7.5
TOT	270	153	480	17480^{2}		8.4				11.6	3.45		.249	.313					.980	1578	1609					

Runs
Butler-SF 109
Gibson-LA 106
Clark-SF 102
VanSlyke-Pit 101
Strawberry-NY 101

Hits
Galarraga-Mon 184
Dawson-Chi 179
Palmeiro-Chi 178
Sax-LA 175
Larkin-Cin 174

Doubles
Galarraga-Mon 42
Palmeiro-Chi 41
Sabo-Cin 40
Bream-Pit 37

Triples
VanSlyke-Pit 15
Coleman-StL 10
Young-Hou 9
Samuel-Phi 9
Butler-SF 9

Home Runs
Strawberry-NY 39
Davis-Hou 30
Galarraga-Mon 29
Clark-SF 29
McReynolds-NY 27

Total Bases
Galarraga-Mon 329
Dawson-Chi 298
VanSlyke-Pit 297
Strawberry-NY 296
Clark-SF 292

Runs Batted In
Clark-SF 109
Strawberry-NY 101
VanSlyke-Pit 100
Bonilla-Pit 100

Runs Produced
Clark-SF 182
VanSlyke-Pit 176
Strawberry-NY 163
Bonilla-Pit 163
Galarraga-Mon 162

Bases On Balls
Clark-SF 100
Butler-SF 97
Daniels-Cin 87
Johnson-NY 86

Batting Average
Gwynn-SD .... .313
Palmeiro-Chi .... .307
Dawson-Chi .... .303
Galarraga-Mon ..... .302
Perry-Atl .... .300

On-Base Percentage
Daniels-Cin .... .400
Butler-SF .... .395
Clark-SF .... .392
Gibson-LA .... .381
Gwynn-SD .... .374

Slugging Average
Strawberry-NY ..... .545
Galarraga-Mon .... .540
Clark-SF .... .508
VanSlyke-Pit ...... .506
Dawson-Chi .... .504

On-Base Plus Slugging
Strawberry-NY 916
Clark-SF 900
Galarraga-Mon 894
Gibson-LA 864
Daniels-Cin 863

Adjusted OPS
Strawberry-NY 168
Clark-SF 163
Gibson-LA 151
Bonds-Pit 147
Galarraga-Mon 147

Batter Runs
Clark-SF 44.3
Strawberry-NY 42.0
Galarraga-Mon 39.2
Gibson-LA 33.8
Daniels-Cin 33.2

Adjusted Batter Runs
Clark-SF 49.4
Strawberry-NY 47.6
Gibson-LA 37.0
Galarraga-Mon 34.5
Bonilla-Pit 33.6

Clutch Hitting Index
Moreland-SD 131
Gwynn-SD 118
Maldonado-SF 114
Bream-Pit 114
Davis-Cin 113

Runs Created
Clark-SF 120
Galarraga-Mon 114
Strawberry-NY 111
Gibson-LA 107
VanSlyke-Pit 107

Total Average
Strawberry-NY ...... .957
Clark-SF .... .955
Gibson-LA .... .929
Davis-Cin .... .927
Daniels-Cin .... .924

Stolen Bases
Coleman-StL 81
Young-Hou 65
Smith-StL 57
Sabo-Cin 46
Nixon-Mon 46

Stolen Base Average
McReynolds-NY ... 100.0
Davis-Cin 92.1
Gibson-LA 88.6
McGee-StL 87.2
Smith-StL 86.4

Stolen Base Runs
Smith-StL 9.4
Coleman-StL 8.4
McGee-StL 6.9
Davis-Cin 6.7
Larkin-Cin 6.3

Fielding Runs
Smith-StL 22.9
Bream-Pit 20.9
Sabo-Cin 18.8
Murphy-Atl 17.5
VanSlyke-Pit 16.7

Total Player Rating
VanSlyke-Pit 5.5
Strawberry-NY 5.4
Gibson-LA 4.8
Smith-StL 4.7
Larkin-Cin 4.3

Wins
Jackson-Cin 23
Hershiser-LA 23
Cone-NY 20
Reuschel-SF 19

Win Percentage
Cone-NY .... .870
Browning-Cin .... .783
Jackson-Cin .... .742
Hershiser-LA .... .742
Maddux-Chi .... .692

Games
Murphy-Cin 76
Robinson-Pit 75
Agosto-Hou 75
Tekulve-Phi 70
Franco-Cin 70

Complete Games
Jackson-Cin 15
Hershiser-LA 15
Show-SD 13
Sutcliffe-Chi 12
Gooden-NY 10

Shutouts
Hershiser-LA 8
Leary-LA 6
Jackson-Cin 6
Scott-Hou 5
Ojeda-NY 5

Saves
Franco-Cin 39
Gott-Pit 34
Worrell-StL 32
Davis-SD 28
Bedrosian-Phi 28

Innings Pitched
Hershiser-LA 267.0
Jackson-Cin 260.2
Browning-Cin 250.2
Mahler-Atl 249.0
Maddux-Chi 249.0

Fewest Hits/Game
Fernandez-NY 6.11
Perez-Mon 6.37
Rijo-Cin 6.67
Scott-Hou 6.67
Cone-NY 6.93

Fewest BB/Game
B.Smith-Mon 1.45
Mahler-Atl 1.52
Reuschel-SF 1.54
Ojeda-NY 1.56
Tudor-StL-LA 1.87

Strikeouts
Ryan-Hou 228
Cone-NY 213
DeLeon-StL 208
Scott-Hou 190
Fernandez-NY 189

Strikeouts/Game
Ryan-Hou 9.33
Fernandez-NY 9.10
Rijo-Cin 8.89
DeLeon-StL 8.31
Cone-NY 8.29

Ratio
Perez-Mon 8.81
Scott-Hou 9.18
Ojeda-NY 9.22
Hershiser-LA 9.61
Jackson-Cin 9.63

Earned Run Average
Magrane-StL 2.18
Cone-NY 2.22
Hershiser-LA 2.26
Tudor-StL-LA 2.32
Rijo-Cin 2.39

Adjusted ERA
Magrane-StL 160
Rijo-Cin 150
Tudor-StL-LA 148
Hershiser-LA 148
Perez-Mon 148

Opponents' Batting Avg.
Fernandez-NY ...... .191
Perez-Mon .... .196
Scott-Hou .... .204
Rijo-Cin .... .209
Cone-NY .... .213

Opponents' On-Base Pct.
Perez-Mon .... .253
Scott-Hou .... .261
Ojeda-NY .... .264
Hershiser-LA ...... .271
Fernandez-NY ...... .274

Starter Runs
Hershiser-LA 35.5
Cone-NY 31.8
Tudor-StL-LA 24.9
Magrane-StL 23.5
Perez-Mon 21.2

Adjusted Starter Runs
Hershiser-LA 33.1
Cone-NY 27.8
Tudor-StL-LA 24.7
Jackson-Cin 24.0
Magrane-StL 23.8

Clutch Pitching Index
Tudor-StL-LA 135
Rawley-Phi 122
Moyer-Chi 118
Robinson-SF 113
D.Martinez-Mon 112

Relief Runs
Franco-Cin 18.0
Holton-LA 16.5
Pena-LA 16.2
Davis-SD 15.7
Myers-NY 13.1

Adjusted Relief Runs
Franco-Cin 18.6
Holton-LA 15.9
Pena-LA 15.5
Davis-SD 15.4
Harris-Phi 14.0

Relief Ranking
Franco-Cin 37.1
Davis-SD 29.1
Myers-NY 24.4
Pena-LA 22.8
Holton-LA 17.3

Total Pitcher Index
Hershiser-LA 4.7
Franco-Cin 4.2
Davis-SD 3.6
Jackson-Cin 3.1
D.Martinez-Mon 2.9

Total Baseball Ranking
VanSlyke-Pit 5.5
Strawberry-NY 5.4
Gibson-LA 4.8
Smith-StL 4.7
Hershiser-LA 4.7

TEAM	G	W	L	PCT	GB	R	OR	AB	H	2B	3B	HR	BB	SO	AVG	OBP	SLG	OPS	OPS+	BR	BR+	PF	CHI	RC	SB	CS	SBA	SBR
EAST																												
BOS	162	89	73	.549		**813**	689	5545	**1569**	**310**	39	124	**623**	**728**	**.283**	**.360**	.420	**780**	**113**	**140**	**105**	104	94	**842**	65	36	64	2
DET	162	88	74	.543	1	703	658	5433	1358	213	28	143	588	841	.250	.326	.378	704	100	-20	7	96	103	673	87	42	67	4
TOR	162	87	75	.537	2	763	680	5557	1491	271	**47**	**158**	521	935	.268	.334	.419	753	109	68	65	100	98	771	107	36	75	11
MIL	162	87	75	.537	2	682	**616**	5488	1409	258	26	113	439	911	.257	.316	.375	691	92	-56	-61	101	**107**	648	**159**	55	74	16
NY	161	85	76	.528	3.5	772	748	5592	1469	272	12	148	588	935	.263	.336	.395	731	105	33	39	99	102	754	146	39	**79**	**18**
CLE	162	78	84	.481	11	666	731	5505	1435	235	28	134	416	866	.261	.317	.387	704	94	-35	-52	103	101	667	97	50	66	4
BAL	161	54	107	.335	34.5	550	789	5358	1275	199	20	137	504	869	.238	.307	.359	666	88	-101	-84	97	94	581	69	44	61	0
WEST																												
OAK	162	104	58	.642		800	620	5602	1474	251	22	156	580	926	.263	.339	.399	738	110	50	78	97	103	763	129	54	70	9
MIN	162	91	71	.562	13	759	672	5510	1508	294	31	151	528	832	.274	.343	**.421**	764	110	94	71	103	95	785	107	63	63	1
KC	161	84	77	.522	19.5	704	648	5469	1419	275	40	121	486	944	.259	.324	.391	715	98	-9	-15	101	102	696	137	54	72	11
CAL	162	75	87	.463	29	714	771	5582	1458	258	31	124	469	819	.261	.324	.385	709	101	-18	1	97	103	690	86	52	62	1
CHI	161	71	90	.441	25.5	631	757	5449	1327	224	35	132	446	908	.244	.305	.370	675	88	-92	-90	100	105	609	98	46	68	5
TEX	161	70	91	.435	26.5	637	735	5479	1378	227	39	112	542	1022	.252	.323	.368	691	91	-47	-62	102	97	661	130	57	70	9
SEA	161	68	93	.422	28.5	664	744	5436	1397	271	27	148	461	787	.257	.319	.398	717	95	-7	-36	104	97	673	95	61	61	0
TOT	1131					9858		77005	19967	3558	425	1901	7191	12323	.260	.327	.391	718							1512	689	69	91

TEAM	CG	SH	SV	IP	H	H/G	HR	BB	SO	RAT	ERA	ERA+	OAV	OOB	PR	PR+	PF	CPI	FA	E	DP	FW	PW	BW	SBW	DIF
EAST																										
BOS	26	14	37	1426[1]	1415	9.0	143	493	**1085**	12.3	3.97	104	.259	.324	-1	22	104	100	.984	93	123	1.6	2.3	**10.7**	-.5	-5.9
DET	34	8	36	1445[2]	1361	8.5	150	497	890	11.8	3.72	103	.248	.314	41	17	96	100	.982	109	129	.7	1.8	.8	-.3	4.3
TOR	16	**17**	47	1449	1404	8.8	143	528	904	12.4	3.80	104	.256	.328	27	22	99	**105**	.982	110	170	.6	2.3	6.6	.5	-3.8
MIL	30	8	51	1449[1]	1355	8.5	125	**437**	832	**11.3**	3.45	**115**	.248	**.306**	84	**85**	100	99	.981	120	146	.0	**8.7**	-6.1	1.0	2.7
NY	16	5	43	1456	1512	9.4	157	487	861	12.7	4.26	92	.267	.331	-48	-52	99	99	.978	134	161	-.8	-5.2	4.0	**1.2**	5.6
CLE	35	10	46	1434	1501	9.5	120	442	812	12.5	4.17	99	.270	.328	-31	-8	104	97	.980	124	131	-.2	-.8	-5.2	-.3	3.6
BAL	20	7	26	1416	1506	9.6	153	523	709	13.2	4.54	86	.274	.342	-90	-102	98	100	.980	119	172	.0	-10.3	-8.4	-.7	-7.0
WEST																										
OAK	22	9	**64**	1489[1]	1376	8.4	116	553	983	11.9	**3.44**	110	.247	.318	**87**	59	95	104	.983	105	151	.9	6.0	7.9	.2	8.1
MIN	18	9	52	1431[2]	1457	9.2	146	453	897	12.3	3.93	104	.266	.327	6	22	103	**105**	**.986**	**84**	155	**2.1**	2.3	7.2	-.6	-.9
KC	29	12	32	1428[1]	1415	9.0	**102**	465	886	12.1	3.66	109	.258	.320	49	52	101	100	.980	124	147	-.2	5.3	-1.5	.5	-.3
CAL	26	9	33	1455[2]	1503	9.3	135	568	817	13.1	4.32	89	.270	.342	-57	-76	97	101	.979	135	175	-.8	-7.6	.2	-.6	3.1
CHI	11	9	43	1439	1467	9.2	138	533	754	12.8	4.13	96	.266	.334	-25	-24	100	102	.976	154	**177**	-2.0	-2.4	-9.1	-.2	4.3
TEX	**41**	11	31	1438[2]	**1310**	**8.2**	129	654	912	12.7	4.05	101	**.244**	.332	-13	5	103	95	.979	131	145	-.7	.6	-6.2	.2	-4.2
SEA	28	11	28	1428	1385	8.8	144	558	981	12.5	4.16	100	.256	.330	-30	1	105	97	.980	123	168	-.2	.2	-3.6	-.7	-8.0
TOT	352	139	569	20187		9.0				12.4	3.97		.260	.327					.981	1665	2150					

Runs
Boggs-Bos 128
Canseco-Oak 120
Henderson-NY 118
Molitor-Mil 115
Puckett-Min 109

Hits
Puckett-Min 234
Boggs-Bos 214
Greenwell-Bos 192
Yount-Mil 190
Molitor-Mil 190

Doubles
Boggs-Bos 45
Ray-Cal 42
Puckett-Min 42
Brett-KC 42
Fernandez-Tor 41

Triples
Yount-Mil 11
Wilson-KC 11
Reynolds-Sea 11
Greenwell-Bos 8

Home Runs
Canseco-Oak 42
McGriff-Tor 34
McGwire-Oak 32
Murray-Bal 28
Gaetti-Min 28

Total Bases
Puckett-Min 358
Canseco-Oak 347
Greenwell-Bos 313
Brett-KC 300
Carter-Cle 297

Runs Batted In
Canseco-Oak 124
Puckett-Min 121
Greenwell-Bos 119
Evans-Bos 111
Winfield-NY 107

Runs Produced
Puckett-Min 206
Canseco-Oak 202
Evans-Bos 186
Greenwell-Bos 183
Boggs-Bos 181

Bases On Balls
Boggs-Bos 125
Clark-NY 113
C.Ripken-Bal 102
Davis-Sea 95
Greenwell-Bos 87

Batting Average
Boggs-Bos .366
Puckett-Min .356
Greenwell-Bos .325
Winfield-NY .322
Molitor-Mil .312

On-Base Percentage
Boggs-Bos .480
Greenwell-Bos .420
Davis-Sea .416
Winfield-NY .398
Henderson-NY .397

Slugging Average
Canseco-Oak .569
McGriff-Tor .552
Gaetti-Min .551
Puckett-Min .545
Greenwell-Bos .531

On-Base Plus Slugging
Boggs-Bos 970
Canseco-Oak 963
Greenwell-Bos 950
McGriff-Tor 930
Winfield-NY 928

Adjusted OPS
Canseco-Oak 172
Boggs-Bos 165
Winfield-NY 159
Greenwell-Bos 158
McGriff-Tor 156

Batter Runs
Boggs-Bos 65.8
Canseco-Oak 54.1
Greenwell-Bos 53.4
Puckett-Min 45.5
Winfield-NY 43.4

Adjusted Batter Runs
Boggs-Bos 59.8
Canseco-Oak 59.0
Greenwell-Bos 48.1
Winfield-NY 44.4
Puckett-Min 42.0

Clutch Hitting Index
Barrett-Bos 135
Hall-Cle 123
Larkin-Min 121
Evans-Bos 120
Clark-NY 118

Runs Created
Boggs-Bos 140
Canseco-Oak 136
Greenwell-Bos 134
Puckett-Min 126
Brett-KC 119

Total Average
Boggs-Bos 1.043
Canseco-Oak 1.011
Greenwell-Bos 1.000
McGriff-Tor .958
Henderson-NY .955

Stolen Bases
Henderson-NY 93
Pettis-Det 44
Molitor-Mil 41
Canseco-Oak 40

Stolen Base Average
Javier-Oak 95.2
Redus-Chi 92.9
Cotto-Sea 90.0
Henderson-NY 87.7
Yount-Mil 84.6

Stolen Base Runs
Henderson-NY 15.9
Pettis-Det 6.2
Molitor-Mil 5.5
Wilson-KC 5.3
Redus-Chi 5.0

Fielding Runs
Guillen-Chi 42.6
Gruber-Tor 25.1
Schofield-Cal 23.2
Puckett-Min 19.5
Gladden-Min 16.3

Total Player Rating
Canseco-Oak 6.4
Puckett-Min 5.8
Boggs-Bos 5.4
Greenwell-Bos 5.0
Yount-Mil 4.4

Wins
Viola-Min 24
Stewart-Oak 21
Gubicza-KC 20

Win Percentage
Viola-Min .774
Hurst-Bos .750
Gubicza-KC .714
Davis-Oak .696
Stieb-Tor .667

Games
Crim-Mil 70
Thigpen-Chi 68
Williams-Tex 67
Henneman-Det 65

Complete Games
Stewart-Oak 14
Clemens-Bos 14
Witt-Tex 13
Witt-Cal 12
Swindell-Cle 12

Shutouts
Clemens-Bos 8
Swindell-Cle 4
Stieb-Tor 4
Gubicza-KC 4

Saves
Eckersley-Oak 45
Reardon-Min 42
Jones-Cle 37
Thigpen-Chi 34
Plesac-Mil 30

Innings Pitched
Stewart-Oak 275.2
Gubicza-KC 269.2
Clemens-Bos 264.0
Langston-Sea 261.1
Saberhagen-KC 260.2

Fewest Hits/Game
Robinson-Det 6.33
Higuera-Mil 6.65
Stieb-Tor 6.82
Witt-Tex 6.92
Hough-Tex 7.21

Fewest BB/Game
Anderson-Min 1.65
Swindell-Cle 1.67
Alexander-Det 1.81
Bosio-Mil 1.88
Viola-Min 1.90

Strikeouts
Clemens-Bos 291
Langston-Sea 235
Viola-Min 193
Stewart-Oak 192
Higuera-Mil 192

Strikeouts/Game
Clemens-Bos 9.92
Langston-Sea 8.09
Witt-Tex 7.64
Higuera-Mil 7.60
Moore-Sea 7.16

Ratio
Higuera-Mil 9.22
Clemens-Bos 9.72
Robinson-Det 10.26
Moore-Sea 10.31
Viola-Min 10.33

Earned Run Average
Anderson-Min 2.45
Higuera-Mil 2.45
Viola-Min 2.64
Gubicza-KC 2.70
Clemens-Bos 2.93

Adjusted ERA
Anderson-Min 167
Higuera-Mil 162
Viola-Min 154
Gubicza-KC 148
Clemens-Bos 141

Opponents' Batting Avg.
Robinson-Det .197
Higuera-Mil .207
Stieb-Tor .210
Witt-Tex .216
Clemens-Bos .220

Opponents' On-Base Pct.
Higuera-Mil .265
Clemens-Bos .270
Robinson-Det .284
Moore-Sea .287
Swindell-Cle .287

Starter Runs
Higuera-Mil 38.4
Gubicza-KC 38.1
Viola-Min 37.8
Anderson-Min 34.4
Clemens-Bos 30.6

Adjusted Starter Runs
Viola-Min 39.7
Higuera-Mil 38.6
Gubicza-KC 38.5
Anderson-Min 35.8
Clemens-Bos 33.7

Clutch Pitching Index
Anderson-Min 138
Davis-Oak 121
Candiotti-Cle 117
Leibrandt-KC 116
Viola-Min 115

Relief Runs
Henneman-Det 21.3
Jones-Cle 15.8
Harvey-Cal 15.6
Mirabella-Mil 15.5
Jackson-Sea 14.9

Adjusted Relief Runs
Henneman-Det 20.6
Jones-Cle 16.6
Jackson-Sea 16.2
Mirabella-Mil 15.5
Harvey-Cal 15.1

Relief Ranking
Henneman-Det 39.3
Harvey-Cal 27.4
Jones-Cle 25.7
Reardon-Min 22.6
Eckersley-Oak 22.5

Total Pitcher Index
Viola-Min 4.6
Anderson-Min 4.5
Higuera-Mil 4.3
Gubicza-KC 4.3
Henneman-Det 4.0

Total Baseball Ranking
Canseco-Oak 6.4
Puckett-Min 5.8
Boggs-Bos 5.4
Greenwell-Bos 5.0
Viola-Min 4.6

TEAM	G	W	L	PCT	GB	R	OR	AB	H	2B	3B	HR	BB	SO	AVG	OBP	SLG	OPS	OPS+	BR	BR+	PF	CHI	RC	SB	CS	SBA	SBR
EAST																												
CHI	162	93	69	.574		**702**	623	5513	**1438**	235	45	124	472	921	**.261**	.322	.387	**709**	101	**54**	6	107	101	**685**	136	57	70	10
NY	162	87	75	.537	6	683	595	5489	1351	**280**	21	**147**	504	934	.246	.313	.385	698	110	30	64	95	102	676	158	53	**75**	**16**
STL	164	86	76	.531	7	632	608	5492	1418	263	47	73	507	**848**	.258	**.323**	.363	686	99	16	-4	103	97	652	155	54	74	15
MON	162	81	81	.500	12	632	630	5482	1353	267	30	100	**572**	958	.247	.322	.361	683	100	13	4	101	96	645	**160**	70	70	11
PIT	164	74	88	.457	19	637	680	5539	1334	263	**53**	95	563	914	.241	.314	.359	673	102	-13	10	97	100	629	155	69	69	10
PHI	163	67	95	.414	26	629	735	5447	1324	215	36	123	558	926	.243	.316	.364	680	100	1	1	100	99	634	106	50	68	6
WEST																												
SF	162	92	70	.568		699	600	5469	1365	241	52	141	508	1071	.250	.318	**.390**	708	**111**	50	**70**	97	102	683	87	54	62	0
SD	162	89	73	.549	3	642	626	5422	1360	215	32	120	552	1013	.251	.321	.369	690	103	22	21	100	98	644	136	67	67	6
HOU	162	86	76	.531	6	647	669	5516	1316	239	28	97	530	860	.239	.308	.345	653	95	-50	-28	97	**109**	606	144	62	70	10
LA	160	77	83	.481	14	554	**536**	5465	1313	241	17	89	507	885	.240	.308	.339	647	93	-61	-51	98	96	576	81	54	60	-1
CIN	162	75	87	.463	17	632	691	5520	1362	243	28	128	493	1028	.247	.312	.370	682	97	1	-20	103	99	639	128	71	64	3
ATL	161	63	97	.394	28	584	680	5463	1281	201	22	128	485	996	.234	.300	.350	650	89	-64	-78	103	103	575	83	54	61	-1
TOT	973					7673		65817	16215	2903	411	1365	6251	11354	.247	.315	.366	680							1529	715	68	86

TEAM	CG	SH	SV	IP	H	H/G	HR	BB	SO	RAT	ERA	ERA+	OAV	OOB	PR	PR+	PF	CPI	FA	E	DP	FW	PW	BW	SBW	DIF
EAST																										
CHI	18	10	**55**	1460[1]	1369	8.5	106	532	918	11.9	3.43	110	.250	.319	11	50	108	104	.980	124	130	.6	5.4	.7	.3	5.2
NY	24	12	38	1454[1]	**1260**	**7.8**	115	532	**1108**	11.3	3.30	99	**.231**	**.303**	33	-5	93	96	.976	144	110	-.5	-.5	6.9	**.9**	-.6
STL	18	18	43	1461	1330	8.2	**84**	482	844	11.4	3.37	108	.243	.308	21	41	104	95	**.982**	**112**	134	**1.4**	4.4	-.4	.8	-1.1
MON	20	13	35	1468[1]	1344	8.3	120	519	1059	11.7	3.48	102	.245	.314	3	9	101	101	.979	136	126	-.0	1.0	.5	.4	-1.6
PIT	20	9	40	1487[2]	1394	8.5	121	539	827	11.9	3.65	92	.248	.317	-24	-49	96	98	.975	160	130	-1.3	-5.2	1.1	.3	-1.7
PHI	10	10	33	1433[1]	1408	8.9	127	613	899	12.9	4.05	88	.259	.337	-87	-79	101	101	.979	133	136	.2	-8.4	.2	-.1	-5.6
WEST																										
SF	12	16	47	1457	1320	8.2	120	471	802	11.3	3.31	102	.243	.307	31	11	97	102	**.982**	114	135	1.2	1.2	**7.5**	-.8	2.0
SD	21	11	52	1457[1]	1359	8.4	133	481	933	11.5	3.38	103	.249	.312	19	19	100	106	.976	154	147	-1.1	2.1	2.3	-.1	5.0
HOU	19	12	38	1479[1]	1379	8.4	105	551	965	11.9	3.65	93	.247	.318	-25	-44	97	96	.977	142	121	-.4	-4.7	-2.9	.3	12.9
LA	**25**	**19**	36	1463[1]	1278	7.9	95	504	1052	**11.2**	**2.95**	**116**	.237	.306	**89**	**78**	98	**107**	.981	118	**153**	.9	**8.4**	-5.4	-.9	-5.8
CIN	16	9	37	1464[1]	1404	8.7	125	559	981	12.3	3.74	96	.253	.326	-38	-21	103	102	.980	121	108	.8	-2.2	-2.1	-.4	-1.9
ATL	15	8	33	1447[2]	1370	8.6	114	**468**	966	11.6	3.70	99	.250	.311	-33	-8	104	94	.976	152	124	-1.0	-.8	-8.3	-.9	-5.8
TOT	218	147	487	17534		8.4				11.7	3.50		.247	.315					.979	1610	1554					

Runs
Sandberg-Chi 104
Johnson-NY 104
Clark-SF 104
Mitchell-SF 100
Butler-SF 100

Hits
Gwynn-SD 203
Clark-SF 196
R.Alomar-SD 184
Guerrero-StL 177
Sandberg-Chi 176

Doubles
Wallach-Mon 42
Guerrero-StL 42
Johnson-NY 41
Clark-SF 38
Bonilla-Pit 37

Triples
Thompson-SF 11
Bonilla-Pit 10
VanSlyke-Pit 9
Coleman-StL 9
Clark-SF 9

Home Runs
Mitchell-SF 47
Johnson-NY 36
Davis-Hou 34
Davis-Cin 34
Sandberg-Chi 30

Total Bases
Mitchell-SF 345
Clark-SF 321
Johnson-NY 319
Bonilla-Pit 302
Sandberg-Chi 301

Runs Batted In
Mitchell-SF 125
Guerrero-StL 117
Clark-SF 111
Johnson-NY 101
Davis-Cin 101

Runs Produced
Clark-SF 192
Mitchell-SF 178
Johnson-NY 169
Guerrero-StL 160
Bonilla-Pit 158

Bases On Balls
J.Clark-SD 132
V.Hayes-Phi 101
Raines-Mon 93
Bonds-Pit 93

Batting Average
Gwynn-SD .336
Clark-SF .333
L.Smith-Atl .315
Grace-Chi .314
Guerrero-StL .311

On-Base Percentage
L.Smith-Atl .420
J.Clark-SD .413
Clark-SF .412
Grace-Chi .407
Guerrero-StL .398

Slugging Average
Mitchell-SF .635
Johnson-NY .559
Clark-SF .546
Davis-Cin .541
L.Smith-Atl .533

On-Base Plus Slugging
Mitchell-SF 1027
Clark-SF 958
L.Smith-Atl 953
Johnson-NY 932
Davis-Cin 916

Adjusted OPS
Mitchell-SF 194
Clark-SF 177
Johnson-NY 171
L.Smith-Atl 166
Davis-Cin 154

Batter Runs
Mitchell-SF 62.1
Clark-SF 55.6
L.Smith-Atl 47.0
Johnson-NY 45.7
Guerrero-StL 38.3

Adjusted Batter Runs
Mitchell-SF 65.9
Clark-SF 59.2
Johnson-NY 51.5
L.Smith-Atl 44.3
Bonilla-Pit 36.2

Clutch Hitting Index
Guerrero-StL 132
Hatcher-Hou-Pit 121
J.Clark-SD 120
Doran-Hou 117
Murphy-Atl 115

Runs Created
Clark-SF 136
Mitchell-SF 136
Johnson-NY 127
L.Smith-Atl 113
Guerrero-StL 109

Total Average
Mitchell-SF 1.099
Johnson-NY 1.026
L.Smith-Atl 1.023
Clark-SF 1.010
J.Clark-SD .969

Stolen Bases
Coleman-StL 65
Samuel-Phi-NY 42
R.Alomar-SD 42
Raines-Mon 41
Johnson-NY 41

Stolen Base Average
Doran-Hou 88.0
Biggio-Hou 87.5
Coleman-StL 86.7
D.Martinez-Mon 85.2
Johnson-NY 83.7

Stolen Base Runs
Coleman-StL 10.8
Johnson-NY 6.2
Raines-Mon 5.9
Samuel-Phi-NY 5.0
Nixon-Mon 3.9

Fielding Runs
Pendleton-StL 30.2
Young-Hou 26.3
Oquendo-StL 20.4
Foley-Mon 19.8
Bonds-Pit 19.7

Total Player Rating
Mitchell-SF 7.0
L.Smith-Atl 5.2
Clark-SF 5.1
Bonilla-Pit 4.3
Bonds-Pit 4.1

Wins
Scott-Hou 20
Maddux-Chi 19
Magrane-StL 18
Bielecki-Chi 18
Reuschel-SF 17

Win Percentage
Bielecki-Chi .720
D.Martinez-Mon .696
Reuschel-SF .680
Scott-Hou .667
Magrane-StL .667

Games
Williams-Chi 76
Dibble-Cin 74
Parrett-Phi 72
Dayley-StL 71
Agosto-Hou 71

Complete Games
Hurst-SD 10
Belcher-LA 10
Scott-Hou 9
Magrane-StL 9
Browning-Cin 9

Shutouts
Belcher-LA 8
Drabek-Pit 5
Langston-Mon 4
Hershiser-LA 4
Glavine-Atl 4

Saves
Davis-SD 44
Williams-Chi 36
Franco-Cin 32
Howell-LA 28
Burke-Mon 28

Innings Pitched
Hershiser-LA 256.2
Browning-Cin 249.2
Hurst-SD 244.2
DeLeon-StL 244.2
Drabek-Pit 244.1

Fewest Hits/Game
DeLeon-StL 6.36
Fernandez-NY 6.44
Howell-Phi 6.84
Smoltz-Atl 6.92
Garrelts-SF 6.94

Fewest BB/Game
Robinson-SF 1.69
Lilliquist-Atl 1.85
D.Martinez-Mon 1.90
Whitson-SD 1.90
Glavine-Atl 1.94

Strikeouts
DeLeon-StL 201
Belcher-LA 200
Fernandez-NY 198
Cone-NY 190
Hurst-SD 179

Strikeouts/Game
Langston-Mon 8.92
Fernandez-NY 8.12
Belcher-LA 7.83
Cone-NY 7.78
DeLeon-StL 7.39

Ratio
Garrelts-SF 9.08
DeLeon-StL 9.53
Scott-Hou 9.63
Fernandez-NY 9.77
B.Smith-Mon 9.81

Earned Run Average
Garrelts-SF 2.28
Hershiser-LA 2.31
Langston-Mon 2.39
Whitson-SD 2.66
Hurst-SD 2.69

Adjusted ERA
Garrelts-SF 148
Hershiser-LA 148
Langston-Mon 148
Whitson-SD 132
Hurst-SD 130

Opponents' Batting Avg.
DeLeon-StL .197
Fernandez-NY .198
Smoltz-Atl .212
Garrelts-SF .212
Scott-Hou .212

Opponents' On-Base Pct.
Garrelts-SF .260
Scott-Hou .268
DeLeon-StL .269
Fernandez-NY .272
Smiley-Pit .276

Starter Runs
Hershiser-LA 33.9
Garrelts-SF 26.2
Hurst-SD 22.2
Langston-Mon 21.7
Whitson-SD 21.3

Adjusted Starter Runs
Hershiser-LA 32.3
Garrelts-SF 24.5
Langston-Mon 22.2
Hurst-SD 22.2
Whitson-SD 21.3

Clutch Pitching Index
Langston-Mon 135
Hershiser-LA 124
Lilliquist-Atl 117
Maddux-Chi 115
Drabek-Pit 113

Relief Runs
Andersen-Hou 19.1
Lancaster-Chi 17.3
Davis-SD 17.1
Howell-LA 17.0
Landrum-Pit 16.5

Adjusted Relief Runs
Andersen-Hou 18.6
Lancaster-Chi 18.0
Davis-SD 17.1
Howell-LA 16.7
Dibble-Cin 16.2

Relief Ranking
Davis-SD 26.1
Howell-LA 25.6
McDowell-NY-Phi 25.1
Dibble-Cin 22.7
Landrum-Pit 18.0

Total Pitcher Index
Hershiser-LA 4.7
Maddux-Chi 3.2
McDowell-NY-Phi 3.2
Howell-LA 2.8
Langston-Mon 2.7

Total Baseball Ranking
Mitchell-SF 7.0
L.Smith-Atl 5.2
Clark-SF 5.1
Hershiser-LA 4.7
Bonilla-Pit 4.3

TEAM	G	W	L	PCT	GB	R	OR	AB	H	2B	3B	HR	BB	SO	AVG	OBP	SLG	OPS	OPS+	BR	BR+	PF	CHI	RC	SB	CS	SBA	SBR
EAST																												
TOR	162	89	73	.549		731	651	5581	1449	265	40	142	521	923	.260	.326	.398	724	105	18	32	98	102	724	144	58	71	11
BAL	162	87	75	.537	2	708	686	5440	1369	238	33	129	593	957	.252	.329	.379	708	102	-6	16	97	102	678	118	55	68	7
BOS	162	83	79	.512	6	**774**	735	5666	**1571**	**326**	30	108	**643**	755	**.277**	**.355**	**.403**	**758**	**106**	**106**	**57**	106	93	**802**	56	35	62	0
MIL	162	81	81	.500	8	707	679	5473	1415	235	32	126	455	791	.259	.321	.382	703	98	-22	-15	99	**106**	677	**165**	62	73	15
NY	161	74	87	.460	14.5	698	792	5458	1470	229	23	130	502	831	.269	.334	.391	725	105	26	35	99	98	709	137	60	70	9
CLE	162	73	89	.451	16	604	654	5463	1340	221	26	127	499	934	.245	.312	.365	677	89	-72	-82	102	98	622	74	51	59	-2
DET	162	59	103	.364	30	617	816	5432	1315	198	24	116	585	899	.242	.320	.351	671	91	-74	-59	98	100	616	103	50	67	5
WEST																												
OAK	162	99	63	.611		712	**576**	5416	1414	220	25	127	562	855	.261	.334	.381	715	105	12	38	96	101	687	157	55	74	15
KC	162	92	70	.568	7	690	635	5475	1428	227	41	101	554	897	.261	.332	.373	705	98	-9	-6	100	101	682	154	51	**75**	**16**
CAL	162	91	71	.562	8	669	578	5545	1422	208	37	**145**	429	1011	.256	.313	.386	699	98	-38	-26	98	103	663	89	40	69	6
TEX	162	83	79	.512	16	695	714	5458	1433	260	**46**	122	503	989	.263	.329	.394	723	101	18	7	102	98	694	101	49	67	5
MIN	162	80	82	.494	17	740	738	5581	1542	278	35	117	478	**743**	.276	.338	.402	740	101	53	6	107	98	751	111	53	68	6
SEA	162	73	89	.451	24	694	728	5512	1417	237	29	134	489	838	.257	.323	.384	707	95	-16	-37	103	103	679	81	55	60	-1
CHI	161	69	92	.429	27.5	693	750	5504	1493	262	36	94	464	873	.271	.331	.383	714	103	4	21	98	100	696	97	52	65	3
TOT	1133					9732		77004	20078	3404	457	1718	7277	12296	.261	.329	.384	712							1587	726	69	95

TEAM	CG	SH	SV	IP	H	H/G	HR	BB	SO	RAT	ERA	ERA+	OAV	OOB	PR	PR+	PF	CPI	FA	E	DP	FW	PW	BW	SBW	DIF
EAST																										
TOR	12	12	38	1467	1408	8.7	99	478	849	11.9	3.59	105	.255	.320	49	31	97	99	.980	127	164	-.0	3.2	3.3	.4	1.3
BAL	16	7	44	1448^1	1518	9.5	134	486	676	12.7	4.01	95	.272	.333	-19	-34	98	104	**.986**	**87**	163	**2.3**	-3.4	1.7	.0	5.6
BOS	14	9	42	1460^1	1448	9.0	131	548	1054	12.6	4.01	102	.261	.331	-20	15	106	99	.980	127	162	-.0	1.6	**5.9**	-.7	-4.5
MIL	16	8	45	1432^1	1463	9.2	129	457	812	12.3	3.80	101	.265	.324	14	7	99	103	.975	155	164	-1.7	.8	-1.5	.8	1.8
NY	15	9	44	1414^2	1550	9.9	150	521	787	13.5	4.51	86	.281	.347	-98	-100	100	102	.980	122	**183**	.2	-10.1	3.6	.2	-.2
CLE	23	13	38	1453	1423	8.9	107	**452**	844	11.8	3.65	109	.257	.315	38	49	102	97	.981	118	126	.5	5.0	-8.3	-.9	-4.1
DET	24	4	26	1427^1	1514	9.6	150	652	831	14.0	4.54	84	.274	.355	-103	-116	98	103	.979	130	153	-.2	-11.8	-6.0	-.2	-3.7
WEST																										
OAK	17	**20**	**57**	1448^1	1287	**8.0**	103	510	930	**11.4**	**3.09**	**119**	**.238**	**.307**	**128**	**101**	95	103	.979	129	159	-.2	**10.3**	3.9	.8	3.3
KC	27	13	38	1451^2	1415	8.8	**86**	455	978	11.8	3.55	109	.257	.316	54	49	99	97	.982	114	139	.7	5.0	-.6	**.9**	5.1
CAL	**32**	**20**	38	1454^1	1384	8.6	113	465	897	11.7	3.28	116	.253	.315	97	88	98	**107**	.985	96	173	1.8	9.0	-2.6	-.0	2.1
TEX	26	7	44	1434^1	**1279**	8.1	119	654	**1112**	12.5	3.91	101	.239	.327	-4	9	102	92	.978	136	137	-.6	1.0	.8	-.2	1.2
MIN	19	8	38	1429^1	1495	9.5	139	500	851	12.9	4.29	97	.269	.334	-63	-21	107	98	.982	107	141	1.1	-2.1	.7	-.0	-.4
SEA	15	10	44	1438	1422	8.9	114	560	897	12.7	4.00	101	.259	.333	-19	4	104	98	.977	143	168	-1.0	.5	-3.7	-.8	-2.7
CHI	9	5	46	1422	1472	9.4	144	539	778	13.0	4.23	90	.269	.338	-54	-68	98	101	.975	151	176	-1.5	-6.9	2.2	-.4	-4.7
TOT	265	145	582	20181		9.0				12.5	3.89		.261	.329					.980	1742	2208					

Runs
R.Henderson-NY-Oak 113
Boggs-Bos 113
Yount-Mil 101
Sierra-Tex 101
McGriff-Tor 98

Hits
Puckett-Min 215
Sax-NY 205
Boggs-Bos 205
Yount-Mil 195

Doubles
Boggs-Bos 51
Puckett-Min 45
Reed-Bos 42
Bell-Tor 41
Yount-Mil 38

Triples
Sierra-Tex 14
White-Cal 13
Bradley-Bal 10

Home Runs
McGriff-Tor 36
Carter-Cle 35
McGwire-Oak 33
Jackson-KC 32
Esasky-Bos 30

Total Bases
Sierra-Tex 344
Yount-Mil 314
Carter-Cle 303
Mattingly-NY 301
Puckett-Min 295

Runs Batted In
Sierra-Tex 119
Mattingly-NY 113
Esasky-Bos 108
Jackson-KC 105
Carter-Cle 105

Runs Produced
Sierra-Tex 191
Yount-Mil 183
Bell-Tor 174
Mattingly-NY 169
Greenwell-Bos 168

Bases On Balls
R.Henderson-NY-Oak 126
McGriff-Tor 119
Boggs-Bos 107
Seitzer-KC 102
Davis-Sea 101

Batting Average
Puckett-Min .339
Lansford-Oak .336
Boggs-Bos .330
Yount-Mil .318
Franco-Tex .316

On-Base Percentage
Boggs-Bos .434
Davis-Sea .428
R.Henderson-NY-Oak .413
McGriff-Tor .402
Evans-Bos .402

Slugging Average
Sierra-Tex .543
McGriff-Tor .525
Yount-Mil .511
Esasky-Bos .500
Davis-Sea .496

On-Base Plus Slugging
McGriff-Tor 927
Davis-Sea 924
Yount-Mil 898
Sierra-Tex 895
Boggs-Bos 883

Adjusted OPS
McGriff-Tor 162
Davis-Sea 155
Yount-Mil 152
Sierra-Tex 146
Baines-Chi-Tex 144

Batter Runs
McGriff-Tor 46.8
Boggs-Bos 46.6
Davis-Sea 44.2
Yount-Mil 41.2
Sierra-Tex 37.4

Adjusted Batter Runs
McGriff-Tor 49.2
Yount-Mil 42.4
Davis-Sea 40.7
Boggs-Bos 39.0
Sierra-Tex 35.6

Clutch Hitting Index
Evans-Bos 122
Brett-KC 121
Mattingly-NY 119
Ray-Cal 118
Greenwell-Bos 113

Runs Created
Yount-Mil 125
Boggs-Bos 122
Sierra-Tex 122
McGriff-Tor 121
R.Henderson-NY-Oak 110

Total Average
McGriff-Tor .986
R.Henderson-NY-Oak .983
Davis-Sea .975
Yount-Mil .926
Boggs-Bos .882

Stolen Bases
R.Henderson-NY-Oak 77
Espy-Tex 45
White-Cal 44
Sax-NY 43
Pettis-Det 43

Stolen Base Average
Thurman-KC 100.0
Franco-Tex 87.5
Yount-Mil 86.4
Finley-Bal 85.0
R.Henderson-NY-Oak 84.6

Stolen Base Runs
R.Henderson-NY-Oak 12.0
Pettis-Det 4.2
White-Cal 4.1
Felder-Mil 4.0
Franco-Tex 3.6

Fielding Runs
Reynolds-Sea 27.0
Howell-Cal 22.5
Gruber-Tor 19.2
Snyder-Cle 18.6
Puckett-Min 18.4

Total Player Rating
R.Henderson-NY-Oak 4.9
Yount-Mil 4.8
Puckett-Min 4.2
Sierra-Tex 3.8
McGriff-Tor 3.7

Wins
Saberhagen-KC 23
Stewart-Oak 21
Moore-Oak 19
Davis-Oak 19
Ballard-Bal 18

Win Percentage
Saberhagen-KC .793
Blyleven-Cal .773
Davis-Oak .731
Stewart-Oak .700
Ballard-Bal .692

Games
Crim-Mil 76
Murphy-Bos 74
Rogers-Tex 73
Russell-Tex 71
Guetterman-NY 70

Complete Games
Saberhagen-KC 12
Morris-Det 10
Finley-Cal 9

Shutouts
Blyleven-Cal 5
Saberhagen-KC 4
McCaskill-Cal 4

Saves
Russell-Tex 38
Thigpen-Chi 34
Schooler-Sea 33
Plesac-Mil 33
Eckersley-Oak 33

Innings Pitched
Saberhagen-KC 262.1
Stewart-Oak 257.2
Gubicza-KC 255.0
Clemens-Bos 253.1
Milacki-Bal 243.0

Fewest Hits/Game
Ryan-Tex 6.09
Gordon-KC 6.74
Stieb-Tor 7.14
Saberhagen-KC 7.17
Moore-Oak 7.19

Fewest BB/Game
Key-Tor 1.13
Saberhagen-KC 1.48
Blyleven-Cal 1.64
Bosio-Mil 1.84
Witt-Cal 1.96

Strikeouts
Ryan-Tex 301
Clemens-Bos 230
Saberhagen-KC 193
Gubicza-KC 173
Bosio-Mil 173

Strikeouts/Game
Ryan-Tex 11.32
Gordon-KC 8.45
Clemens-Bos 8.17
Witt-Tex 7.69
Viola-Min 7.07

Ratio
Saberhagen-KC 8.71
Ryan-Tex 10.12
Blyleven-Cal 10.34
Moore-Oak 10.35
Key-Tor 10.67

Earned Run Average
Saberhagen-KC 2.16
Finley-Cal 2.57
Moore-Oak 2.61
Blyleven-Cal 2.73
McCaskill-Cal 2.93

Adjusted ERA
Saberhagen-KC 178
Finley-Cal 149
Moore-Oak 142
Blyleven-Cal 140
Clemens-Bos 131

Opponents' Batting Avg.
Ryan-Tex .187
Gordon-KC .210
Saberhagen-KC .217
Stieb-Tor .219
Moore-Oak .219

Opponents' On-Base Pct.
Saberhagen-KC .252
Ryan-Tex .276
Moore-Oak .288
Blyleven-Cal .289
Bosio-Mil .291

Starter Runs
Saberhagen-KC 50.5
Moore-Oak 34.5
Blyleven-Cal 31.2
Finley-Cal 29.4
Bosio-Mil 24.5

Adjusted Starter Runs
Saberhagen-KC 49.9
Moore-Oak 30.7
Blyleven-Cal 29.9
Finley-Cal 28.3
Clemens-Bos 26.2

Clutch Pitching Index
Cerutti-Tor 130
Finley-Cal 124
Ballard-Bal 124
McCaskill-Cal 116
Davis-Oak 113

Relief Runs
Montgomery-KC 25.8
Olson-Bal 20.8
Lamp-Bos 19.6
Henke-Tor 19.5
Burns-Oak 17.7

Adjusted Relief Runs
Montgomery-KC 25.7
Lamp-Bos 21.1
Olson-Bal 20.4
Henke-Tor 18.9
Minton-Cal 16.5

Relief Ranking
Montgomery-KC 33.9
Russell-Tex 31.5
Jones-Cle 28.6
Henke-Tor 28.5
Olson-Bal 26.5

Total Pitcher Index
Saberhagen-KC 5.5
Moore-Oak 3.9
Montgomery-KC 3.5
Russell-Tex 3.5
Finley-Cal 3.1

Total Baseball Ranking
Saberhagen-KC 5.5
R.Henderson-NY-Oak 4.9
Yount-Mil 4.8
Puckett-Min 4.2
Moore-Oak 3.9

TEAM	G	W	L	PCT	GB	R	OR	AB	H	2B	3B	HR	BB	SO	AVG	OBP	SLG	OPS	OPS+	BR	BR+	PF	CHI	RC	SB	CS	SBA	SBR
EAST																												
PIT	162	95	67	.586		733	619	5388	1395	**288**	42	138	**582**	914	.259	**.334**	.405	**739**	**113**	**64**	**93**	96	99	738	137	52	72	12
NY	162	91	71	.562	4	**775**	613	5504	1410	278	21	**172**	536	851	.256	.326	**.408**	734	107	48	50	100	**106**	**748**	110	33	**77**	13
MON	162	85	77	.525	10	662	598	5453	1363	227	**43**	114	576	1024	.250	.325	.370	695	101	-18	8	96	99	672	**235**	99	70	17
PHI	162	77	85	.475	18	646	729	5535	1410	237	27	103	**582**	915	.255	.329	.363	692	96	-19	-17	100	96	675	108	35	76	12
CHI	162	77	85	.475	18	690	774	5600	**1474**	240	36	136	406	869	.263	.316	.392	708	93	-7	-53	107	103	695	151	50	75	16
STL	162	70	92	.432	25	599	698	5462	1398	255	41	73	517	**844**	.256	.323	.358	681	93	-46	-49	100	95	650	221	74	75	**23**
WEST																												
CIN	162	91	71	.562		693	**597**	5525	1466	284	40	125	466	913	**.265**	.327	.399	726	101	35	6	104	97	726	166	66	72	13
LA	162	86	76	.531	5	728	685	5491	1436	222	27	129	538	952	.262	.331	.382	713	105	17	37	97	104	699	141	65	68	8
SF	162	85	77	.525	6	719	710	5573	1459	221	35	152	488	973	.262	.325	.396	721	108	24	51	96	101	724	109	56	66	4
SD	162	75	87	.463	16	673	673	5554	1429	243	35	123	509	902	.257	.323	.380	703	98	-8	-13	101	99	682	138	59	70	10
HOU	162	75	87	.463	16	573	656	5379	1301	209	32	94	548	997	.242	.315	.345	660	90	-83	-65	97	97	596	179	83	68	10
ATL	162	65	97	.401	26	682	821	5504	1376	263	26	162	473	1010	.250	.312	.396	708	95	-8	-44	106	103	675	92	55	63	1
TOT	972					8173		65968	16917	2967	405	1521	6221	11164	.257	.324	.383	707							1787	727	71	139

TEAM	CG	SH	SV	IP	H	H/G	HR	BB	SO	RAT	ERA	ERA+	OAV	OOB	PR	PR+	PF	CPI	FA	E	DP	FW	PW	BW	SBW	DIF
EAST																										
PIT	18	8	43	1447	1367	8.6	135	**413**	848	**11.3**	3.40	106	.251	.307	63	37	95	103	.979	134	125	-.4	3.9	**9.6**	.0	1.0
NY	18	**14**	41	1440	1339	8.4	119	444	**1217**	11.4	3.43	109	.246	**.306**	59	51	99	97	.978	132	107	-.3	5.3	5.2	.1	-.2
MON	18	11	**50**	1473^{1}	1349	**8.3**	127	510	991	11.6	**3.37**	108	**.245**	.313	**70**	48	96	104	.982	110	134	1.0	5.0	.9	.6	-3.2
PHI	18	7	35	1449	1381	8.6	124	651	840	12.9	4.07	94	.253	.336	-45	-39	101	97	.981	117	**150**	.6	-4.0	-1.7	.0	1.2
CHI	13	7	42	1442^{2}	1510	9.5	121	572	877	13.2	4.34	94	.271	.342	-87	-39	108	98	.980	124	136	.2	-4.0	-5.4	.5	4.9
STL	8	13	39	1443^{1}	1432	9.0	**98**	475	833	12.2	3.88	98	.261	.324	-13	-9	101	95	.979	130	114	-.2	-.9	-5.0	**1.2**	-5.9
WEST																										
CIN	14	12	**50**	1456^{1}	**1338**	**8.3**	124	543	1029	11.9	3.40	**116**	.246	.318	64	**86**	104	105	**.983**	**102**	126	**1.5**	**8.9**	.7	.1	-1.0
LA	**29**	12	29	1442	1364	8.6	137	478	1021	11.7	3.72	98	.249	.313	11	-10	97	96	.979	130	123	-.2	-1.0	3.9	-.4	2.8
SF	14	6	45	1446^{1}	1477	9.2	131	553	788	12.8	4.08	89	.267	.335	-46	-72	96	101	**.983**	107	148	1.2	-7.4	5.3	-.8	5.9
SD	21	12	35	1461^{2}	1437	8.9	147	507	928	12.1	3.68	104	.258	.322	19	23	101	**106**	.977	141	141	-.8	2.4	-1.3	-.2	-6.0
HOU	12	6	37	1450	1396	8.7	130	496	854	12.0	3.61	103	.255	.321	30	17	98	104	.978	131	124	-.2	1.8	-6.7	-.2	-.6
ATL	17	8	30	1429^{2}	1527	9.7	128	579	938	13.5	4.58	88	.275	.346	-125	-81	106	97	.974	158	133	-1.8	-8.3	-4.5	-1.1	-.1
TOT	200	116	476	17381^{1}		8.8				12.2	3.80		.257	.324					.980	1516	1561					

Runs
Sandberg-Chi 116
Bonilla-Pit 112
Butler-SF 108
Gant-Atl 107
Dykstra-Phi 106

Hits
Dykstra-Phi 192
Butler-SF 192
Sandberg-Chi 188
Wallach-Mon 185
Larkin-Cin 185

Doubles
Jefferies-NY 40
Bonilla-Pit 39
Sabo-Cin 38
Wallach-Mon 37
Johnson-NY 37

Triples
Duncan-Cin 11
Gwynn-SD 10
L.Smith-Atl 9
Coleman-StL 9
Butler-SF 9

Home Runs
Sandberg-Chi 40
Strawberry-NY 37
Mitchell-SF 35
Williams-SF 33
Bonds-Pit 33

Total Bases
Sandberg-Chi 344
Bonilla-Pit 324
Gant-Atl 310
Williams-SF 301
Wallach-Mon 295

Runs Batted In
Williams-SF 122
Bonilla-Pit 120
Carter-SD 115
Bonds-Pit 114
Strawberry-NY 108

Runs Produced
Bonilla-Pit 200
Bonds-Pit 185
Williams-SF 176
Sandberg-Chi 176
Carter-SD 170

Bases On Balls
J.Clark-SD 104
Bonds-Pit 93
Butler-SF 90
Dykstra-Phi 89
V.Hayes-Phi 87

Batting Average
McGee-StL .335
Murray-LA .330
Magadan-NY .328
Dykstra-Phi .325
Dawson-Chi .310

On-Base Percentage
Magadan-NY .425
Dykstra-Phi .420
Murray-LA .417
Bonds-Pit .410
Butler-SF .401

Slugging Average
Bonds-Pit .565
Sandberg-Chi .559
Mitchell-SF .544
Gant-Atl .539
Justice-Atl .535

On-Base Plus Slugging
Bonds-Pit 974
Murray-LA 936
Daniels-LA 923
Sandberg-Chi 918
Justice-Atl 909

Adjusted OPS
Bonds-Pit 172
Murray-LA 160
Daniels-LA 156
Mitchell-SF 151
Magadan-NY 143

Batter Runs
Bonds-Pit 48.1
Murray-LA 44.7
Sandberg-Chi 37.9
J.Clark-SD 36.5
Dykstra-Phi 34.3

Adjusted Batter Runs
Bonds-Pit 52.7
Murray-LA 48.0
J.Clark-SD 35.9
Mitchell-SF 35.0
Daniels-LA 34.9

Clutch Hitting Index
Carter-SD 130
Magadan-NY 123
Kruk-Phi 121
Guerrero-StL 119
V.Hayes-Phi 119

Runs Created
Bonds-Pit 128
Sandberg-Chi 124
Dykstra-Phi 121
Murray-LA 118
Gant-Atl 109

Total Average
Bonds-Pit 1.115
Daniels-LA .945
Murray-LA .945
Justice-Atl .941
Dykstra-Phi .941

Stolen Bases
Coleman-StL 77
Yelding-Hou 64
Bonds-Pit 52
Butler-SF 51
Nixon-Mon 50

Stolen Base Average
Gibson-LA 92.9
Grissom-Mon 91.7
Dawson-Chi 88.9
Davis-Cin 87.5
Dykstra-Phi 86.8

Stolen Base Runs
Coleman-StL 11.0
Bonds-Pit 6.9
Nixon-Mon 6.4
Roberts-SD 5.9
Dykstra-Phi 5.5

Fielding Runs
Thompson-SF 27.7
Grace-Chi 26.7
C.Hayes-Phi 23.6
Dykstra-Phi 20.1
Larkin-Cin 19.9

Total Player Rating
Bonds-Pit 7.1
Dykstra-Phi 5.9
Sandberg-Chi 4.5
Murray-LA 4.2
Larkin-Cin 4.1

Wins
Drabek-Pit 22
Viola-NY 20
Martinez-LA 20
Gooden-NY 19

Win Percentage
Drabek-Pit .786
Martinez-LA .769
Gooden-NY .731
Viola-NY .625
Browning-Cin .625

Games
Agosto-Hou 82
Assenmacher-Chi 74
Harris-SD 73
McDowell-Phi 72
Akerfelds-Phi 71

Complete Games
Martinez-LA 12
Hurst-SD 9
Drabek-Pit 9
Maddux-Chi 8

Shutouts
Morgan-LA 4
Hurst-SD 4

Saves
Franco-NY 33
Myers-Cin 31
L.Smith-StL 27
Smith-Hou 23
Lefferts-SD 23

Innings Pitched
Viola-NY 249.2
Maddux-Chi 237.0
Martinez-LA 234.1
Gooden-NY 232.2

Fewest Hits/Game
Fernandez-NY 6.52
Rijo-Cin 6.90
Martinez-LA 7.34
Drabek-Pit 7.39
Darwin-Hou 7.52

Fewest BB/Game
Darwin-Hou 1.72
Whitson-SD 1.85
Leibrandt-Atl 1.94
D.Martinez-Mon 1.95
Browning-Cin 2.06

Strikeouts
Cone-NY 233
Martinez-LA 223
Gooden-NY 223
Viola-NY 182
Fernandez-NY 181

Strikeouts/Game
Cone-NY 9.91
Fernandez-NY 9.08
Gooden-NY 8.63
Martinez-LA 8.56
DeLeon-StL 8.08

Ratio
Darwin-Hou 9.46
Drabek-Pit 9.69
D.Martinez-Mon 9.80
Martinez-LA 10.06
Fernandez-NY 10.14

Earned Run Average
Darwin-Hou 2.21
Smith-Mon-Pit 2.55
Whitson-SD 2.60
Viola-NY 2.67
Rijo-Cin 2.70

Adjusted ERA
Darwin-Hou 168
Whitson-SD 147
Rijo-Cin 147
Smith-Mon-Pit 143
Viola-NY 140

Opponents' Batting Avg.
Fernandez-NY .200
Rijo-Cin .212
Martinez-LA .220
Drabek-Pit .225
Darwin-Hou .225

Opponents' On-Base Pct.
Darwin-Hou .267
Drabek-Pit .275
D.Martinez-Mon .275
Martinez-LA .279
Fernandez-NY .280

Starter Runs
Viola-NY 31.3
Whitson-SD 30.5
Smith-Mon-Pit 29.8
Darwin-Hou 28.6
Drabek-Pit 26.6

Adjusted Starter Runs
Whitson-SD 31.0
Viola-NY 30.4
Darwin-Hou 27.8
Smith-Mon-Pit 27.3
Rijo-Cin 26.4

Clutch Pitching Index
Gullickson-Hou 121
Smith-Mon-Pit 118
Whitson-SD 115
Rasmussen-SD 114
Darwin-Hou 107

Relief Runs
Dibble-Cin 22.3
Brantley-SF 21.6
Harris-SD 19.5
Charlton-Cin 18.1
Myers-Cin 16.6

Adjusted Relief Runs
Dibble-Cin 23.1
Brantley-SF 21.0
Charlton-Cin 19.9
Harris-SD 19.7
Myers-Cin 17.3

Relief Ranking
Myers-Cin 29.4
Dibble-Cin 28.1
Harris-SD 27.0
Brantley-SF 25.9
Charlton-Cin 24.9

Total Pitcher Index
Viola-NY 3.7
Drabek-Pit 3.5
Whitson-SD 3.4
Myers-Cin 3.1
Rijo-Cin 3.0

Total Baseball Ranking
Bonds-Pit 7.1
Dykstra-Phi 5.9
Sandberg-Chi 4.5
Murray-LA 4.2
Larkin-Cin 4.1

TEAM	G	W	L	PCT	GB	R	OR	AB	H	2B	3B	HR	BB	SO	AVG	OBP	SLG	OPS	OPS+	BR	BR+	PF	CHI	RC	SB	CS	SBA	SBR
EAST																												
BOS	162	88	74	.543		699	664	5516	**1502**	298	31	106	598	795	**.272**	**.346**	.395	741	102	57	24	105	92	733	53	52	50	-7
TOR	162	86	76	.531	2	**767**	661	5589	1479	263	**50**	167	526	970	.265	.331	**.419**	**750**	106	56	43	102	101	**769**	111	52	68	6
DET	162	79	83	.488	9	750	754	5479	1418	241	32	**172**	634	952	.259	.339	.409	748	107	**62**	57	101	98	754	82	57	59	-2
CLE	162	77	85	.475	11	732	737	5485	1465	266	41	110	458	836	.267	.327	.391	718	101	-5	-2	100	107	694	107	52	67	5
BAL	161	76	85	.472	11.5	669	698	5410	1328	234	22	132	**660**	962	.245	.332	.370	702	99	-21	2	97	98	676	94	52	64	2
MIL	162	74	88	.457	14	732	760	5503	1408	247	36	128	519	821	.256	.324	.384	708	98	-24	-19	99	**109**	692	**164**	72	69	11
NY	162	67	95	.414	21	603	749	5483	1322	208	19	147	427	1027	.241	.302	.366	668	86	-109	-111	100	105	605	119	45	**73**	10
WEST																												
OAK	162	103	59	.636		733	**570**	5433	1379	209	22	164	651	992	.254	.339	.391	730	**108**	31	**62**	96	100	739	141	54	72	**12**
CHI	162	94	68	.580	9	682	633	5402	1393	251	44	106	478	903	.258	.322	.379	701	97	-35	-20	98	105	651	140	90	61	-1
TEX	162	83	79	.512	20	676	696	5469	1416	257	27	110	575	1054	.259	.333	.376	709	98	-11	-12	100	98	688	115	48	71	9
CAL	162	80	82	.494	23	690	706	5570	1448	237	27	147	566	1000	.260	.331	.391	722	103	10	25	98	96	715	69	43	62	0
SEA	162	77	85	.475	20	640	680	5474	1419	251	26	107	596	**749**	.259	.336	.373	709	97	-7	-15	101	92	691	105	51	67	5
KC	161	75	86	.466	21.5	707	709	5488	1465	**316**	44	100	498	879	.267	.331	.395	726	104	14	25	98	101	706	107	62	63	2
MIN	162	74	88	.457	23	666	729	5499	1458	281	39	100	445	**749**	.265	.326	.385	711	92	-17	-58	107	99	673	96	53	64	3
TOT	1133					9746		76800	19900	3559	460	1796	7631	12689	.260	.331	.388	718							1503	783	66	57

TEAM	CG	SH	SV	IP	H	H/G	HR	BB	SO	RAT	ERA	ERA+	OAV	OOB	PR	PR+	PF	CPI	FA	E	DP	FW	PW	BW	SBW	DIF
EAST																										
BOS	15	13	44	1442	1439	9.0	**92**	519	997	12.6	3.72	110	.261	.329	30	54	104	100	.980	123	154	-.2	5.5	2.5	-1.1	.4
TOR	6	9	48	1454	1434	8.9	143	**445**	892	11.9	3.84	103	.260	.319	11	16	101	99	**.986**	**86**	144	**2.1**	1.7	4.4	.2	-3.2
DET	15	12	45	1430[1]	1401	8.9	154	661	856	13.3	4.39	90	.259	.345	-76	-67	101	98	.979	131	178	-.6	-6.8	5.9	-.6	.4
CLE	12	10	47	1427[1]	1491	9.5	163	518	860	13.0	4.27	92	.270	.337	-57	-55	100	102	.981	117	146	.2	-5.5	-.2	.0	1.6
BAL	10	5	43	1435[1]	1445	9.1	161	537	776	12.6	4.04	94	.264	.331	-21	-40	97	103	.985	93	151	1.6	-4.0	.3	-.2	-1.9
MIL	23	13	42	1445	1558	9.8	121	469	771	12.9	4.08	95	.275	.335	-28	-34	99	101	.976	149	152	-1.7	-3.4	-1.9	.7	-.5
NY	15	6	41	1444[2]	1430	9.0	144	618	909	13.0	4.22	94	.261	.339	-49	-38	102	99	.980	126	164	-.3	-3.8	-11.2	.6	1.0
WEST																										
OAK	18	**16**	64	1456	**1287**	**8.0**	123	494	831	**11.2**	**3.18**	**117**	**.238**	**.305**	**118**	**91**	95	102	**.986**	87	152	2.0	**9.3**	**6.4**	**.8**	3.7
CHI	17	10	**68**	1449[1]	1313	8.2	106	548	914	11.8	3.61	106	.244	.318	48	35	98	95	.980	124	169	-.2	3.6	-2.0	-.5	12.3
TEX	**25**	9	36	1444[2]	1343	8.4	113	623	997	12.6	3.84	102	.248	.330	12	14	100	97	.979	133	161	-.8	1.5	-1.2	.5	2.2
CAL	21	13	42	1454	1482	9.2	106	544	944	12.8	3.80	101	.267	.337	18	4	98	**105**	.978	142	**186**	-1.3	.5	2.6	-.4	-2.1
SEA	21	7	41	1443[1]	1319	8.3	120	606	**1064**	12.3	3.70	107	.243	.324	34	42	101	97	.979	130	152	-.6	4.3	-1.5	.0	-6.2
KC	18	8	33	1420[2]	1449	9.2	116	560	1006	13.1	3.94	97	.264	.337	-5	-17	98	102	.980	122	161	-.1	-1.7	2.6	-.2	-5.9
MIN	13	13	43	1435[2]	1509	9.5	134	489	872	12.7	4.13	101	.273	.335	-35	4	106	102	.983	101	161	1.2	.5	-5.9	-.1	-2.5
TOT	229	144	637	20182[1]		8.9				12.6	3.91		.260	.331					.981	1664	2231					

Runs
R.Henderson-Oak .. 119
Fielder-Det 104
Reynolds-Sea 100
Yount-Mil 98
Phillips-Det 97

Hits
Palmeiro-Tex 191
Boggs-Bos 187
Kelly-NY 183
Greenwell-Bos 181

Doubles
J.Reed-Bos 45
Brett-KC 45
Calderon-Chi 44
Boggs-Bos 44
Harper-Min 42

Triples
Fernandez-Tor 17
Sosa-Chi 10
Polonia-NY-Cal 9
Liriano-Tor-Min 9
Johnson-Chi 9

Home Runs
Fielder-Det 51
McGwire-Oak 39
J.Canseco-Oak 37
McGriff-Tor 35
Gruber-Tor 31

Total Bases
Fielder-Det 339
Gruber-Tor 303
McGriff-Tor 295
Griffey-Sea 287
Burks-Bos 286

Runs Batted In
Fielder-Det 132
Gruber-Tor 118
McGwire-Oak 108
J.Canseco-Oak 101
Sierra-Tex 96

Runs Produced
Fielder-Det 185
Gruber-Tor 179
Yount-Mil 158
Burks-Bos 157
McGwire-Oak 156

Bases On Balls
McGwire-Oak 110
Tettleton-Bal 106
Phillips-Det 99
R.Henderson-Oak ... 97
McGriff-Tor 94

Batting Average
Brett-KC .... .329
R.Henderson-Oak .. .325
Palmeiro-Tex .... .319
Trammell-Det .... .304
Boggs-Bos .... .302

On-Base Percentage
R.Henderson-Oak .. .441
McGriff-Tor .... .403
E.Martinez-Sea .... .399
Davis-Sea .... .393
Brett-KC .... .392

Slugging Average
Fielder-Det .... .592
R.Henderson-Oak .. .577
J.Canseco-Oak .... .543
McGriff-Tor .... .530
Brett-KC .... .515

On-Base Plus Slugging
R.Henderson-Oak . 1017
Fielder-Det 972
McGriff-Tor 932
J.Canseco-Oak 917
Brett-KC 906

Adjusted OPS
R.Henderson-Oak .. 190
Fielder-Det 167
J.Canseco-Oak 160
McGriff-Tor 156
Brett-KC 154

Batter Runs
R.Henderson-Oak .. 57.5
Fielder-Det 51.3
McGriff-Tor 45.5
Brett-KC 37.0
J.Canseco-Oak 34.3

Adjusted Batter Runs
R.Henderson-Oak .. 62.9
Fielder-Det 50.4
McGriff-Tor 43.4
Brett-KC 38.7
J.Canseco-Oak 38.5

Clutch Hitting Index
Leonard-Sea 138
Guillen-Chi 122
Fletcher-Chi 121
Gaetti-Min 118
Gruber-Tor 117

Runs Created
R.Henderson-Oak .. 137
Fielder-Det 129
McGriff-Tor 124
Brett-KC 106
Griffey-Sea 103

Total Average
R.Henderson-Oak . 1.241
Fielder-Det 1.007
McGriff-Tor .... .983
J.Canseco-Oak ..... .943
McGwire-Oak .... .903

Stolen Bases
R.Henderson-Oak ... 65
Sax-NY 43
Kelly-NY 42
Cole-Cle 40
Pettis-Tex 38

Stolen Base Average
Cotto-Sea 87.5
R.Henderson-Oak .. 86.7
Molitor-Mil 85.7
Gantner-Mil 85.7
Wilson-Tor 85.2

Stolen Base Runs
R.Henderson-Oak .. 10.8
Sax-NY 6.3
Cole-Cle 5.7
Wilson-Tor 3.7
Cotto-Sea 3.6

Fielding Runs
Espinoza-NY 21.1
Reynolds-Sea 15.1
Quintana-Bos 14.5
Gaetti-Min 13.8
Gallego-Oak 13.7

Total Player Rating
R.Henderson-Oak .. 7.9
Fielder-Det 4.2
McGriff-Tor 4.2
J.Canseco-Oak 4.0
Fisk-Chi 3.4

Wins
Welch-Oak 27
Stewart-Oak 22
Clemens-Bos 21

Win Percentage
Welch-Oak .... .818
Clemens-Bos ...... .778
Stieb-Tor .... .750
Boddicker-Bos .... .680

Games
Thigpen-Chi 77
Ward-Tor 73
Montgomery-KC 73
Rogers-Tex 69
Henneman-Det 69

Complete Games
Stewart-Oak 11
Morris-Det 11

Shutouts
Stewart-Oak 4
Clemens-Bos 4
Perez-Chi 3
Morris-Det 3
Appier-KC 3

Saves
Thigpen-Chi 57
Eckersley-Oak 48
Jones-Cle 43
Olson-Bal 37
Righetti-NY 36

Innings Pitched
Stewart-Oak 267.0
Morris-Det 249.2
Welch-Oak 238.0
Hanson-Sea 236.0
Finley-Cal 236.0

Fewest Hits/Game
Ryan-Tex 6.04
Johnson-Sea 7.13
Clemens-Bos 7.61
Stewart-Oak 7.62
Stieb-Tor 7.72

Fewest BB/Game
Anderson-Min 1.86
Swindell-Cle 1.97
Clemens-Bos 2.13
Knudson-Mil 2.14
Wells-Tor 2.14

Strikeouts
Ryan-Tex 232
Witt-Tex 221
Hanson-Sea 211
Clemens-Bos 209
Langston-Cal 195

Strikeouts/Game
Ryan-Tex 10.24
Witt-Tex 8.96
Clemens-Bos 8.24
Gordon-KC 8.06
Hanson-Sea 8.05

Ratio
Ryan-Tex 9.62
Clemens-Bos 10.01
Wells-Tor 10.10
Hanson-Sea 10.49
Stewart-Oak 10.58

Earned Run Average
Clemens-Bos 1.93
Finley-Cal 2.40
Stewart-Oak 2.56
Appier-KC 2.76
Stieb-Tor 2.93

Adjusted ERA
Clemens-Bos 212
Finley-Cal 159
Stewart-Oak 145
Appier-KC 139
Stieb-Tor 135

Opponents' Batting Avg.
Ryan-Tex .... .188
Johnson-Sea ...... .216
Clemens-Bos ...... .228
Stieb-Tor .... .230
Stewart-Oak .... .231

Opponents' On-Base Pct.
Ryan-Tex .... .269
Clemens-Bos ...... .280
Wells-Tor .... .283
Hanson-Sea .... .289
Black-Cle-Tor ..... .293

Starter Runs
Clemens-Bos 50.4
Stewart-Oak 40.2
Finley-Cal 39.7
Welch-Oak 25.6
Appier-KC 23.8

Adjusted Starter Runs
Clemens-Bos 52.4
Finley-Cal 38.2
Stewart-Oak 36.3
Stieb-Tor 23.4
Appier-KC 22.7

Clutch Pitching Index
Finley-Cal 137
Appier-KC 121
Clemens-Bos 119
Welch-Oak 118
Johnson-Bal 113

Relief Runs
Farr-KC 27.3
Eckersley-Oak 26.9
Swift-Sea 21.7
Thigpen-Chi 20.6
Nelson-Oak 19.5

Adjusted Relief Runs
Farr-KC 26.7
Eckersley-Oak 26.7
Swift-Sea 22.1
Thigpen-Chi 20.2
Nelson-Oak 18.8

Relief Ranking
Eckersley-Oak 47.6
Thigpen-Chi 40.4
Farr-KC 38.2
Jones-Cle 24.1
Jones-Chi 23.6

Total Pitcher Index
Clemens-Bos 6.5
Eckersley-Oak 4.9
Thigpen-Chi 4.2
Stewart-Oak 4.2
Finley-Cal 4.1

Total Baseball Ranking
R.Henderson-Oak .. 7.9
Clemens-Bos 6.5
Eckersley-Oak 4.9
Fielder-Det 4.2
Thigpen-Chi 4.2

TEAM	G	W	L	PCT	GB	R	OR	AB	H	2B	3B	HR	BB	SO	AVG	OBP	SLG	OPS	OPS+	BR	BR+	PF	CHI	RC	SB	CS	SBA	SBR
EAST																												
PIT	162	98	64	.605		**768**	632	5449	**1433**	**259**	50	126	**620**	901	**.263**	**.342**	.398	**740**	**116**	**104**	**117**	98	98	**762**	124	46	73	11
STL	162	84	78	.519	14	651	648	5362	1366	239	**53**	68	532	857	.255	.324	.357	681	96	-13	-17	101	102	628	202	110	65	6
PHI	162	78	84	.481	20	629	680	5521	1332	248	33	111	490	1026	.241	.306	.358	664	93	-60	-53	99	**104**	609	92	30	**75**	10
CHI	160	77	83	.481	20	695	734	5522	1395	232	26	159	442	879	.253	.312	.390	702	97	11	-19	105	103	675	123	64	66	5
NY	161	77	84	.478	20.5	640	646	5359	1305	250	24	117	578	**789**	.244	.320	.365	685	99	-9	-4	99	99	641	153	70	69	9
MON	161	71	90	.441	26.5	579	655	5412	1329	236	42	95	484	1056	.246	.311	.357	668	94	-47	-38	99	95	607	**221**	100	69	**14**
WEST																												
ATL	162	94	68	.580		749	644	5456	1407	255	30	141	563	906	.258	.331	.393	724	103	65	24	106	102	719	165	76	68	10
LA	162	93	69	.574	1	665	**565**	5408	1366	191	29	108	583	957	.253	.328	.359	687	101	1	17	98	100	650	126	68	65	4
SD	162	84	78	.519	10	636	646	5408	1321	204	36	121	501	1069	.244	.312	.362	674	92	-35	-53	103	102	605	101	64	61	0
SF	162	75	87	.463	19	649	697	5463	1345	215	48	141	471	973	.246	.311	.381	692	103	-9	13	97	100	647	95	57	63	1
CIN	162	74	88	.457	20	689	691	5501	1419	250	27	**164**	488	1006	.258	.322	**.403**	725	105	57	31	104	96	721	124	56	69	8
HOU	162	65	97	.401	29	605	717	5504	1345	240	43	79	502	1027	.244	.312	.347	659	97	-64	-27	94	101	606	125	68	65	4
TOT	970					7955		65365	16363	2819	441	1430	6254	11446	.251	.320	.373	692							1651	809	67	80

TEAM	CG	SH	SV	IP	H	H/G	HR	BB	SO	RAT	ERA	ERA+	OAV	OOB	PR	PR+	PF	CPI	FA	E	DP	FW	PW	BW	SBW	DIF
EAST																										
PIT	**18**	11	**51**	1456^2	1411	8.8	117	**401**	919	11.4	3.45	104	.256	.309	39	21	97	104	.981	120	134	.4	2.2	**12.3**	.5	1.8
STL	9	5	**51**	1435^1	1367	8.6	114	454	822	11.8	3.69	101	.255	.318	0	5	101	100	**.982**	**107**	133	**1.2**	.6	-1.7	-.0	3.3
PHI	16	11	35	1463	1346	8.3	111	670	988	12.7	3.87	95	.246	.332	-29	-32	100	99	.981	119	111	.5	-3.3	-5.5	.3	5.2
CHI	12	4	40	1456^2	1415	8.8	117	542	927	12.3	4.04	96	.257	.327	-57	-23	105	96	**.982**	113	120	.7	-2.4	-1.9	-.2	.9
NY	12	11	39	1437^1	1403	8.8	108	410	1028	11.6	3.56	102	.257	.311	20	14	99	100	.977	143	112	-1.0	1.5	-.4	.2	-3.7
MON	12	**14**	39	1440^1	**1304**	8.2	111	584	909	12.0	3.65	99	.244	.322	7	-4	98	100	.979	133	128	-.4	-.4	-3.9	**.8**	-5.4
WEST																										
ATL	**18**	7	48	1452^2	**1304**	**8.1**	118	481	969	**11.3**	3.49	111	**.240**	**.305**	32	61	106	96	.978	138	122	-.6	6.4	2.6	.3	4.5
LA	15	**14**	40	1458	1312	**8.1**	**96**	500	1028	11.4	**3.07**	**117**	.241	.308	**101**	**88**	98	**107**	.980	123	126	.2	**9.2**	1.8	-.3	1.2
SD	14	11	47	1452^2	1385	8.6	139	457	921	11.5	3.58	106	.252	.311	18	35	103	102	**.982**	113	130	.8	3.7	-5.5	-.7	4.9
SF	10	10	45	1442	1397	8.8	143	544	905	12.4	4.04	89	.257	.329	-56	-74	97	101	**.982**	109	**151**	1.0	-7.7	1.4	-.6	.0
CIN	7	11	43	1440	1372	8.6	127	560	997	12.3	3.84	99	.253	.326	-24	-4	103	101	.979	125	131	.1	-.4	3.3	.1	-10.0
HOU	7	13	36	1453	1347	8.4	129	651	**1033**	12.6	4.01	88	.247	.330	-51	-84	95	97	.974	161	129	-2.0	-8.7	-2.8	-.3	-2.0
TOT	150	122	514	17387^2		8.5				11.9	3.69		.251	.320					.980	1504	1527					

Runs
Butler-LA 112
Johnson-NY 108
Sandberg-Chi 104
Bonilla-Pit 102
Gant-Atl 101

Hits
Pendleton-Atl 187
Butler-LA 182
Sabo-Cin 175
Bonilla-Pit 174
Jose-StL 173

Doubles
Bonilla-Pit 44
Jose-StL 40
Zeile-StL 36
O'Neill-Cin 36

Triples
Lankford-StL 15
Gwynn-SD 11
Finley-Hou 10
Grissom-Mon 9
Gonzalez-Hou 9

Home Runs
Johnson-NY 38
Williams-SF 34
Gant-Atl 32
McGriff-SD 31
Dawson-Chi 31

Total Bases
Pendleton-Atl 303
Clark-SF 303
Johnson-NY 302
Williams-SF 294
Sabo-Cin 294

Runs Batted In
Johnson-NY 117
Clark-SF 116
Bonds-Pit 116
McGriff-SD 106
Gant-Atl 105

Runs Produced
Johnson-NY 187
Bonds-Pit 186
Bonilla-Pit 184
Sandberg-Chi 178
Gant-Atl 174

Bases On Balls
Butler-LA 108
Bonds-Pit 107
McGriff-SD 105
DeShields-Mon 95
Bonilla-Pit 90

Batting Average
Pendleton-Atl 319
Morris-Cin 318
Gwynn-SD 317
McGee-SF 312
Jose-StL 305

On-Base Percentage
Bonds-Pit .... .419
Butler-LA .... .402
McGriff-SD .... .400
Bonilla-Pit .... .398
Bagwell-Hou .... .391

Slugging Average
Clark-SF .... .536
Johnson-NY .... .535
Pendleton-Atl ...... .517
Bonds-Pit .... .514
Larkin-Cin .... .506

On-Base Plus Slugging
Bonds-Pit 932
Clark-SF 897
McGriff-SD 894
Bonilla-Pit 890
Larkin-Cin 886

Adjusted OPS
Bonds-Pit 163
Clark-SF 154
Bonilla-Pit 151
Johnson-NY 147
McGriff-SD 146

Batter Runs
Bonds-Pit 45.5
Bonilla-Pit 39.5
McGriff-SD 38.4
Sandberg-Chi 34.8
Clark-SF 34.7

Adjusted Batter Runs
Bonds-Pit 47.3
Bonilla-Pit 41.3
Clark-SF 38.2
McGriff-SD 35.2
Johnson-NY 33.5

Clutch Hitting Index
Pagnozzi-StL 129
Bonds-Pit 127
Murray-LA 118
Magadan-NY 117
Daniels-LA 116

Runs Created
Bonds-Pit 118
Sandberg-Chi 114
Bonilla-Pit 114
Clark-SF 110
Pendleton-Atl 107

Total Average
Bonds-Pit 1.055
McGriff-SD .... .937
Larkin-Cin .... .923
Johnson-NY .... .902
Sandberg-Chi ...... .896

Stolen Bases
Grissom-Mon 76
Nixon-Atl 72
DeShields-Mon 56
Lankford-StL 44
Bonds-Pit 43

Stolen Base Average
Dykstra-Phi 85.7
Redus-Pit 85.0
Landrum-Chi 84.4
Jefferies-NY 83.9
Grissom-Mon 81.7

Stolen Base Runs
Grissom-Mon 10.8
Nixon-Atl 8.5
Bonds-Pit 4.9
O.Smith-StL 4.6
DeShields-Mon 4.3

Fielding Runs
Pendleton-Atl 27.9
Belliard-Atl 26.1
Lind-Pit 22.6
Grissom-Mon 20.4
Grace-Chi 20.0

Total Player Rating
Bonds-Pit 6.3
Pendleton-Atl 5.9
Larkin-Cin 5.7
Sandberg-Chi 4.8
Bonilla-Pit 4.1

Wins
Smiley-Pit 20
Glavine-Atl 20
Avery-Atl 18
Martinez-LA 17

Win Percentage
Smiley-Pit 714
Rijo-Cin 714
Avery-Atl 692
Hurst-SD 652
Glavine-Atl 645

Games
Jones-Mon 77
Assenmacher-Chi 75
Stanton-Atl 74
Burke-Mon-NY 72
Agosto-StL 72

Complete Games
D.Martinez-Mon 9
Glavine-Atl 9
Mulholland-Phi 8
Maddux-Chi 7

Shutouts
D.Martinez-Mon 5
Martinez-LA 4
Smith-Pit 3
Mulholland-Phi 3
Black-SF 3

Saves
L.Smith-StL 47
Dibble-Cin 31
Williams-Phi 30
Franco-NY 30
Righetti-SF 24

Innings Pitched
Maddux-Chi 263.0
Glavine-Atl 246.2
Morgan-LA 236.1
Drabek-Pit 234.2
Cone-NY 232.2

Fewest Hits/Game
Harnisch-Hou 7.02
Rijo-Cin 7.27
DeJesus-Phi 7.28
Hill-StL 7.30
Glavine-Atl 7.33

Fewest BB/Game
Smith-Pit 1.14
Tewksbury-StL 1.79
Mulholland-Phi 1.90
Smiley-Pit 1.91
B.Smith-StL 2.04

Strikeouts
Cone-NY 241
Maddux-Chi 198
Glavine-Atl 192
Rijo-Cin 172
Harnisch-Hou 172

Strikeouts/Game
Cone-NY 9.32
Rijo-Cin 7.58
Harnisch-Hou 7.14
Gooden-NY 7.11
Glavine-Atl 7.01

Ratio
Rijo-Cin 9.82
Glavine-Atl 9.92
Morgan-LA 9.94
D.Martinez-Mon ... 10.26
Benes-SD 10.37

Earned Run Average
D.Martinez-Mon 2.39
Rijo-Cin 2.51
Glavine-Atl 2.55
Belcher-LA 2.62
Harnisch-Hou 2.70

Adjusted ERA
Glavine-Atl 152
Rijo-Cin 152
D.Martinez-Mon 151
DeLeon-StL 137
Belcher-LA 137

Opponents' Batting Avg.
Harnisch-Hou 212
Rijo-Cin 219
Glavine-Atl 222
Hill-StL 224
DeJesus-Phi 224

Opponents' On-Base Pct.
Rijo-Cin 274
Glavine-Atl 279
Morgan-LA 279
D.Martinez-Mon 283
Benes-SD 286

Starter Runs
D.Martinez-Mon ... 32.0
Glavine-Atl 31.1
Rijo-Cin 26.7
Belcher-LA 24.8
Morgan-LA 23.8

Adjusted Starter Runs
Glavine-Atl 34.7
D.Martinez-Mon 30.9
Rijo-Cin 28.5
Belcher-LA 23.2
Harris-SD 22.5

Clutch Pitching Index
DeLeon-StL 132
Drabek-Pit 128
Tewksbury-StL 122
Ojeda-LA 121
Belcher-LA 118

Relief Runs
McElroy-Chi 19.5
Maddux-SD 13.4
Williams-Phi 13.2
Brantley-SF 13.1
Pena-NY-Atl 11.7

Adjusted Relief Runs
McElroy-Chi 20.6
Maddux-SD 14.2
Williams-Phi 13.1
Brantley-SF 12.3
Pena-NY-Atl 11.8

Relief Ranking
Williams-Phi 26.2
L.Smith-StL 22.2
McElroy-Chi 15.7
Pena-NY-Atl 15.3
McDowell-Phi-LA ... 14.3

Total Pitcher Index
Glavine-Atl 5.2
D.Martinez-Mon 4.0
Rijo-Cin 3.0
Williams-Phi 2.7
Maddux-Chi 2.3

Total Baseball Ranking
Bonds-Pit 6.3
Pendleton-Atl 5.9
Larkin-Cin 5.7
Glavine-Atl 5.2
Sandberg-Chi 4.8

TEAM	G	W	L	PCT	GB	R	OR	AB	H	2B	3B	HR	BB	SO	AVG	OBP	SLG	OPS	OPS+	BR	BR+	PF	CHI	RC	SB	CS	SBA	SBR
EAST																												
TOR	162	91	71	.562		684	**622**	5489	1412	295	45	133	499	1043	.257	.326	.400	726	96	-7	-32	104	96	724	148	53	74	**14**
DET	162	84	78	.519	7	817	794	5547	1372	259	26	**209**	**699**	1185	.247	.335	.416	751	105	50	39	101	103	800	109	47	70	8
BOS	162	84	78	.519	7	731	712	5530	1486	**305**	25	126	593	820	.269	.343	.401	744	100	42	6	105	95	756	59	39	60	-1
MIL	162	83	79	.512	8	799	744	5611	1523	247	**53**	116	556	802	.271	.340	.396	736	106	24	43	98	105	745	106	68	61	0
NY	162	71	91	.438	20	674	777	5541	1418	249	19	147	473	861	.256	.319	.387	706	94	-47	-48	100	101	683	109	36	**75**	11
BAL	162	67	95	.414	24	686	796	5604	1421	256	29	170	528	974	.254	.321	.401	722	102	-17	13	96	96	707	50	33	60	-1
CLE	162	57	105	.352	34	576	759	5470	1390	236	26	79	449	888	.254	.316	.350	666	83	-118	-122	101	98	591	84	58	59	-2
WEST																												
MIN	162	95	67	.586		776	652	5556	**1557**	270	42	140	526	**747**	**.280**	**.347**	.420	**767**	106	82	47	105	96	786	107	68	61	0
CHI	162	87	75	.537	8	758	681	5594	1464	226	39	139	610	896	.262	.338	.391	729	103	12	31	98	101	741	134	74	64	4
TEX	162	85	77	.525	10	**829**	814	5703	1539	288	31	177	596	1039	.270	.343	**.424**	**767**	**113**	**85**	**100**	98	99	**831**	102	50	67	5
OAK	162	84	78	.519	11	760	776	5410	1342	246	19	159	642	981	.248	.333	.389	722	105	-2	41	94	**106**	711	**151**	64	70	11
SEA	162	83	79	.512	14	702	674	5494	1400	268	29	126	588	811	.255	.331	.383	714	97	-21	-22	100	99	698	97	44	69	6
KC	162	82	80	.506	15	727	722	5584	1475	290	41	117	523	969	.264	.331	.394	725	100	-4	-7	100	101	720	119	68	64	2
CAL	162	81	81	.500	16	653	649	5470	1396	245	29	115	448	928	.255	.316	.374	690	90	-78	-77	100	104	640	94	56	63	1
TOT	1134					10172		77603	20195	3680	453	1953	7730	12944	.261	.332	.395	726							1469	758	66	58

TEAM	CG	SH	SV	IP	H	H/G	HR	BB	SO	RAT	ERA	ERA+	OAV	OOB	PR	PR+	PF	CPI	FA	E	DP	FW	PW	BW	SBW	DIF
EAST																										
TOR	10	**16**	**60**	1462^{2}	**1301**	8.1	121	523	971	**11.5**	**3.51**	**120**	**.238**	**.309**	**96**	**111**	103	96	.980	127	115	-.5	**11.2**	-3.2	**1.0**	1.8
DET	18	8	38	1450^{1}	1570	9.8	148	593	739	13.6	4.51	92	.280	.352	-66	-56	101	105	.983	104	171	.7	-5.6	4.0	.4	3.7
BOS	15	13	45	1439^{2}	1405	8.8	147	530	999	12.3	4.02	107	.257	.326	13	43	105	100	.981	116	165	.0	4.4	.7	-.5	-1.4
MIL	23	11	41	1463^{2}	1498	9.3	147	527	859	12.8	4.15	96	.266	.334	-8	-29	97	103	.981	118	176	-.0	-2.9	4.4	-.4	1.2
NY	3	11	37	1444	1510	9.5	152	506	936	12.9	4.42	94	.271	.336	-52	-44	101	99	.979	133	181	-.9	-4.4	-4.8	.7	-.5
BAL	8	8	42	1457^{2}	1534	9.5	147	504	868	12.8	4.59	86	.273	.335	-80	-107	97	95	**.985**	**91**	172	**1.4**	-10.7	1.4	-.5	-5.4
CLE	22	8	33	1441^{1}	1551	9.7	110	**441**	862	12.7	4.24	98	.276	.333	-22	-13	101	98	.976	149	150	-1.8	-1.3	-12.2	-.6	-8.0
WEST																										
MIN	21	12	53	1449^{1}	1402	8.8	139	488	876	12.0	3.70	115	.255	.319	64	88	104	104	**.985**	95	161	1.2	8.9	4.8	-.4	-.2
CHI	**28**	8	40	1478	1302	**8.0**	154	601	923	11.8	3.79	105	.239	.318	50	31	97	98	.982	116	151	.0	3.2	3.2	-.0	-.2
TEX	9	10	41	1479	1486	9.1	151	662	**1022**	13.4	4.47	90	.262	.344	-61	-73	98	98	.979	134	138	-.9	-7.3	**10.1**	.0	2.2
OAK	14	10	49	1444^{1}	1425	8.9	155	655	892	13.4	4.58	84	.260	.345	-77	-127	94	97	.982	107	150	.6	-12.7	4.2	.7	10.5
SEA	10	13	48	1464^{1}	1387	8.6	136	628	1003	12.7	3.79	109	.253	.335	50	54	101	**107**	.983	110	**187**	.4	5.5	-2.2	.2	-1.7
KC	17	12	41	1466	1473	9.1	**105**	529	1004	12.6	3.93	105	.261	.329	28	32	101	99	.980	125	141	-.4	3.3	-.7	-.2	-.8
CAL	18	10	50	1441^{2}	1351	8.5	141	543	990	12.1	3.69	111	.250	.323	65	66	100	105	.984	102	156	.8	6.7	-7.7	-.3	.7
TOT	216	150	618	20382		9.0				12.6	4.10		.261	.332					.982	1627	2214					

Runs
Molitor-Mil 133
Palmeiro-Tex 115
Canseco-Oak 115
White-Tor 110
Sierra-Tex 110

Hits
Molitor-Mil 216
C.Ripken-Bal 210
Sierra-Tex 203
Palmeiro-Tex 203
Franco-Tex 201

Doubles
Palmeiro-Tex 49
C.Ripken-Bal 46
Sierra-Tex 44

Triples
Molitor-Mil 13
Johnson-Chi 13
Alomar-Tor 11
White-Tor 10
Devereaux-Bal 10

Home Runs
Fielder-Det 44
Canseco-Oak 44
C.Ripken-Bal 34
Carter-Tor 33
Thomas-Chi 32

Total Bases
C.Ripken-Bal 368
Palmeiro-Tex 336
Sierra-Tex 332
Molitor-Mil 325
Carter-Tor 321

Runs Batted In
Fielder-Det 133
Canseco-Oak 122
Sierra-Tex 116
C.Ripken-Bal 114
Thomas-Chi 109

Runs Produced
Sierra-Tex 201
Canseco-Oak 193
Molitor-Mil 191
Fielder-Det 191
Thomas-Chi 181

Bases On Balls
Thomas-Chi 138
Tettleton-Det 101
R.Henderson-Oak 98
Clark-Bos 96
Davis-Min 95

Batting Average
Franco-Tex .341
Boggs-Bos .332
Randolph-Mil .327
Griffey-Sea .327
Molitor-Mil .325

On-Base Percentage
Thomas-Chi .454
Randolph-Mil .427
Boggs-Bos .425
Franco-Tex .409
E.Martinez-Sea .407

Slugging Average
Tartabull-KC .593
C.Ripken-Bal .566
Canseco-Oak .556
Thomas-Chi .553
Palmeiro-Tex .532

On-Base Plus Slugging
Thomas-Chi 1007
Tartabull-KC 993
C.Ripken-Bal 945
Griffey-Sea 932
Palmeiro-Tex 925

Adjusted OPS
Thomas-Chi 181
Tartabull-KC 170
C.Ripken-Bal 164
Canseco-Oak 159
Palmeiro-Tex 156

Batter Runs
Thomas-Chi 65.9
C.Ripken-Bal 48.5
Tartabull-KC 46.4
Palmeiro-Tex 45.6
Griffey-Sea 42.3

Adjusted Batter Runs
Thomas-Chi 69.5
C.Ripken-Bal 54.1
Palmeiro-Tex 47.9
Tartabull-KC 45.9
Canseco-Oak 45.0

Clutch Hitting Index
Davis-Sea 135
Surhoff-Mil 125
Yount-Mil 124
Randolph-Mil 122
Hrbek-Min 119

Runs Created
Thomas-Chi 145
C.Ripken-Bal 134
Molitor-Mil 132
Palmeiro-Tex 129
Griffey-Sea 118

Total Average
Thomas-Chi 1.109
Tartabull-KC 1.044
Griffey-Sea .969
Canseco-Oak .962
Whitaker-Det .942

Stolen Bases
R.Henderson-Oak 58
Alomar-Tor 53
Raines-Chi 51
Polonia-Cal 48
Cuyler-Det 41

Stolen Base Average
Cotto-Sea 84.2
Knoblauch-Min 83.3
Alomar-Tor 82.8
Gibson-KC 81.8
Canseco-Oak 81.3

Stolen Base Runs
Alomar-Tor 7.8
R.Henderson-Oak 6.5
Raines-Chi 6.0
Cuyler-Det 5.5
Franco-Tex 4.8

Fielding Runs
Gaetti-Cal 24.6
Vizquel-Sea 23.5
Espinoza-NY 20.3
Buechele-Tex 19.9
Sojo-Cal 19.5

Total Player Rating
C.Ripken-Bal 8.3
Thomas-Chi 5.6
Griffey-Sea 5.1
Canseco-Oak 4.1
R.Henderson-Oak 4.0

Wins
Gullickson-Det 20
Erickson-Min 20
Langston-Cal 19

Win Percentage
Erickson-Min .714
Langston-Cal .704
Gullickson-Det .690
Wegman-Mil .682
Moore-Oak .680

Games
D.Ward-Tor 81
Olson-Bal 72
Jackson-Sea 72
Swift-Sea 71

Complete Games
McDowell-Chi 15
Clemens-Bos 13
Navarro-Mil 10
Morris-Min 10
Terrell-Det 8

Shutouts
Clemens-Bos 4
McDowell-Chi 3
Holman-Sea 3
Erickson-Min 3
Appier-KC 3

Saves
Harvey-Cal 46
Eckersley-Oak 43
Aguilera-Min 42
Reardon-Bos 40
Montgomery-KC 33

Innings Pitched
Clemens-Bos 271.1
McDowell-Chi 253.2
Morris-Min 246.2
Langston-Cal 246.1
Tapani-Min 244.0

Fewest Hits/Game
Ryan-Tex 5.31
Johnson-Sea 6.75
Langston-Cal 6.94
Clemens-Bos 7.26
McDowell-Chi 7.52

Fewest BB/Game
Swindell-Cle 1.17
Sanderson-NY 1.25
Tapani-Min 1.48
Gullickson-Det 1.75
Wegman-Mil 1.86

Strikeouts
Clemens-Bos 241
Johnson-Sea 228
Ryan-Tex 203
McDowell-Chi 191
Langston-Cal 183

Strikeouts/Game
Ryan-Tex 10.56
Johnson-Sea 10.19
Clemens-Bos 7.99
Hanson-Sea 7.37
Appier-KC 6.85

Ratio
Ryan-Tex 9.31
Clemens-Bos 9.59
Tapani-Min 9.85
Sanderson-NY 10.04
Saberhagen-KC 10.04

Earned Run Average
Clemens-Bos 2.62
Candiotti-Cle-Tor 2.65
Wegman-Mil 2.84
J.Abbott-Cal 2.89
Ryan-Tex 2.91

Adjusted ERA
Clemens-Bos 164
Candiotti-Cle-Tor 158
Tapani-Min 143
J.Abbott-Cal 142
Wegman-Mil 140

Opponents' Batting Avg.
Ryan-Tex .172
Johnson-Sea .213
Langston-Cal .215
Clemens-Bos .221
Candiotti-Cle-Tor .228

Opponents' On-Base Pct.
Ryan-Tex .267
Clemens-Bos .272
Tapani-Min .278
Sanderson-NY .281
Saberhagen-KC .281

Starter Runs
Clemens-Bos 44.7
Candiotti-Cle-Tor 38.5
J.Abbott-Cal 32.8
Langston-Cal 30.3
Tapani-Min 30.2

Adjusted Starter Runs
Clemens-Bos 48.4
Candiotti-Cle-Tor 39.9
Tapani-Min 33.5
J.Abbott-Cal 32.9
Langston-Cal 30.4

Clutch Pitching Index
Krueger-Sea 131
Holman-Sea 117
Terrell-Det 117
Guzman-Tex 116
Tanana-Det 115

Relief Runs
Frohwirth-Bal 23.9
Harvey-Cal 21.9
Swift-Sea 21.2
Eichhorn-Cal 19.2
Flanagan-Bal 18.8

Adjusted Relief Runs
Frohwirth-Bal 23.2
Harvey-Cal 21.9
Swift-Sea 21.3
Eichhorn-Cal 19.3
Habyan-NY 18.3

Relief Ranking
Harvey-Cal 36.2
Aguilera-Min 28.4
Farr-NY 27.6
D.Ward-Tor 24.2
Radinsky-Chi 23.2

Total Pitcher Index
Clemens-Bos 5.0
Candiotti-Cle-Tor 4.2
J.Abbott-Cal 4.1
Harvey-Cal 3.7
Key-Tor 3.6

Total Baseball Ranking
C.Ripken-Bal 8.3
Thomas-Chi 5.6
Griffey-Sea 5.1
Clemens-Bos 5.0
Candiotti-Cle-Tor 4.2

TEAM	G	W	L	PCT	GB	R	OR	AB	H	2B	3B	HR	BB	SO	AVG	OBP	SLG	OPS	OPS+	BR	BR+	PF	CHI	RC	SB	CS	SBA	SBR
EAST																												
PIT	162	96	66	.593		**693**	595	5527	1409	272	**54**	106	569	872	.255	.327	.381	708	**107**	48	**56**	99	101	**699**	110	53	67	6
MON	162	87	75	.537	9	648	581	5477	1381	263	37	102	463	976	.252	.315	.370	685	101	-4	2	99	104	651	196	63	76	**21**
STL	162	83	79	.512	13	631	604	5594	**1464**	262	44	94	495	996	**.262**	.325	.375	700	**107**	30	51	97	94	680	**208**	118	64	4
CHI	162	78	84	.481	18	593	624	5590	1420	221	41	104	417	**816**	.254	.309	.364	673	94	-31	-46	103	99	617	77	51	60	-1
NY	162	72	90	.444	24	599	653	5340	1254	259	17	93	**572**	956	.235	.312	.342	654	92	-54	-46	99	**106**	583	129	52	71	10
PHI	162	70	92	.432	26	686	717	5500	1392	255	36	118	509	1059	.253	.322	.377	699	104	27	29	100	104	684	127	31	**80**	17
WEST																												
ATL	162	98	64	.605		682	**569**	5480	1391	223	48	**138**	493	924	.254	.318	**.388**	706	99	34	-4	106	103	686	126	60	68	7
CIN	162	90	72	.556	8	660	609	5460	1418	**281**	44	99	563	888	.260	**.331**	.382	**713**	105	**58**	40	103	96	689	125	65	66	5
SD	162	82	80	.506	16	617	636	5476	1396	255	30	135	453	864	.255	.315	.386	701	102	22	11	102	96	648	69	52	57	-3
HOU	162	81	81	.500	17	608	668	5480	1350	255	38	96	506	1025	.246	.316	.359	675	102	-20	9	96	100	636	139	54	72	12
SF	162	72	90	.444	26	574	647	5456	1330	220	36	105	435	1067	.244	.304	.355	659	97	-57	-24	94	102	584	112	64	64	2
LA	162	63	99	.389	35	548	636	5368	1333	201	34	72	503	899	.248	.316	.339	655	93	-54	-45	98	97	579	142	78	65	4
TOT	972					7539		65748	16538	2967	459	1262	5978	11342	.252	.318	.369	686							1560	741	68	84

TEAM	CG	SH	SV	IP	H	H/G	HR	BB	SO	RAT	ERA	ERA+	OAV	OOB	PR	PR+	PF	CPI	FA	E	DP	FW	PW	BW	SBW	DIF
EAST																										
PIT	20	20	43	1479[2]	1410	8.6	101	455	844	11.6	3.36	103	.254	.314	25	15	98	103	.984	101	144	.9	1.7	**6.1**	-.1	6.6
MON	11	14	49	1468	**1296**	**8.0**	92	525	1014	11.5	3.25	107	**.238**	.310	41	35	99	97	.980	124	113	-.4	3.8	.3	**1.5**	1.0
STL	10	9	47	1480	1405	8.6	118	**400**	842	**11.2**	3.39	100	.252	**.305**	20	1	97	99	**.985**	**94**	146	**1.3**	.2	5.5	-.3	-4.5
CHI	16	11	37	1469	1337	8.2	107	575	901	12.0	3.40	106	.246	.323	18	33	103	104	.982	114	142	.2	3.6	-4.9	-.9	-.8
NY	17	13	34	1446[2]	1404	8.8	98	482	1025	12.0	3.66	95	.256	.321	-25	-30	99	98	.981	116	134	.0	-3.2	-4.9	.3	-1.1
PHI	**27**	7	34	1428	1387	8.8	113	549	851	12.4	4.11	85	.257	.328	-96	-99	100	92	.978	131	128	-.7	-10.6	3.2	1.1	-3.7
WEST																										
ATL	26	**24**	41	1460	1321	8.2	89	489	948	11.4	**3.15**	**116**	.242	.307	**58**	**80**	104	100	.982	109	121	.5	**8.7**	-.4	.0	8.4
CIN	9	11	**55**	1449[2]	1362	8.5	109	470	**1060**	11.6	3.47	104	.251	.314	6	21	103	100	.984	96	128	1.2	2.3	4.4	-.2	1.5
SD	9	11	46	1461[1]	1444	8.9	111	439	971	11.8	3.56	100	.261	.318	-9	3	102	102	.982	115	127	.1	.4	1.2	-1.1	.5
HOU	5	12	45	1459[1]	1386	8.6	114	539	978	12.2	3.72	90	.252	.323	-35	-61	96	98	.981	114	125	.2	-6.5	1.0	.5	5.0
SF	9	12	30	1461	1385	8.6	128	502	927	11.9	3.61	91	.253	.320	-17	-53	94	102	.982	113	**174**	.3	-5.7	-2.5	-.5	-.3
LA	18	13	29	1438	1401	8.8	**82**	553	981	12.5	3.42	101	.257	.328	15	5	98	**106**	.972	174	136	-3.2	.6	-4.8	-.3	-10.1
TOT	177	157	490	17500[2]		8.6				11.8	3.51		.252	.318					.982	1401	1618					

Runs
- Bonds-Pit 109
- Hollins-Phi 104
- VanSlyke-Pit 103
- Sandberg-Chi 100
- Grissom-Mon 99

Hits
- VanSlyke-Pit 199
- Pendleton-Atl 199
- Sandberg-Chi 186
- Grace-Chi 185
- Sheffield-SD 184

Doubles
- VanSlyke-Pit 45
- Lankford-StL 40
- Duncan-Phi 40
- Clark-SF 40

Triples
- Sanders-Atl 14
- Finley-Hou 13
- VanSlyke-Pit 12
- Butler-LA 11
- Alicea-StL 11

Home Runs
- McGriff-SD 35
- Bonds-Pit 34
- Sheffield-SD 33
- Hollins-Phi 27
- Daulton-Phi 27

Total Bases
- Sheffield-SD 323
- Sandberg-Chi 312
- VanSlyke-Pit 310
- Pendleton-Atl 303

Runs Batted In
- Daulton-Phi 109
- Pendleton-Atl 105
- McGriff-SD 104
- Bonds-Pit 103
- Sheffield-SD 100

Runs Produced
- Pendleton-Atl 182
- VanSlyke-Pit 178
- Bonds-Pit 178
- Hollins-Phi 170
- Bagwell-Hou 165

Bases On Balls
- Bonds-Pit 127
- McGriff-SD 96
- Butler-LA 95
- Biggio-Hou 94
- Kruk-Phi 92

Batting Average
- Sheffield-SD .330
- VanSlyke-Pit .324
- Kruk-Phi .323
- Roberts-Cin .323
- Gwynn-SD .317

On-Base Percentage
- Bonds-Pit .461
- Kruk-Phi .428
- Butler-LA .413
- McGriff-SD .396
- Roberts-Cin .396

Slugging Average
- Bonds-Pit .624
- Sheffield-SD .580
- McGriff-SD .556
- Daulton-Phi .524
- Sandberg-Chi .510

On-Base Plus Slugging
- Bonds-Pit 1085
- Sheffield-SD 969
- McGriff-SD 952
- Daulton-Phi 912
- VanSlyke-Pit 891

Adjusted OPS
- Bonds-Pit 207
- Sheffield-SD 168
- McGriff-SD 164
- Daulton-Phi 157
- Clark-SF 153

Batter Runs
- Bonds-Pit 71.8
- Sheffield-SD 50.1
- McGriff-SD 48.1
- VanSlyke-Pit 40.2
- Kruk-Phi 38.6

Adjusted Batter Runs
- Bonds-Pit 73.3
- Sheffield-SD 48.2
- McGriff-SD 46.2
- VanSlyke-Pit 41.4
- Kruk-Phi 38.9

Clutch Hitting Index
- Murray-NY 126
- Daulton-Phi 124
- Lind-Pit 120
- Karros-LA 115
- Larkin-Cin 114

Runs Created
- Bonds-Pit 148
- VanSlyke-Pit 122
- Sheffield-SD 118
- Sandberg-Chi 117
- McGriff-SD 116

Total Average
- Bonds-Pit 1.335
- Daulton-Phi .994
- McGriff-SD .987
- Sheffield-SD .945
- Kruk-Phi .900

Stolen Bases
- Grissom-Mon 78
- DeShields-Mon 46
- Roberts-Cin 44
- Finley-Hou 44
- O.Smith-StL 43

Stolen Base Average
- Davis-LA 95.0
- Alou-Mon 88.9
- Duncan-Phi 88.5

Stolen Base Runs
- Grissom-Mon 12.6
- Finley-Hou 6.5
- O.Smith-StL 6.3
- Bonds-Pit 5.8
- DeShields-Mon 4.9

Fielding Runs
- Belliard-Atl 26.6
- Jackson-SD 24.2
- Thompson-SF 20.3
- Wallach-Mon 18.2
- Harris-LA 16.6

Total Player Rating
- Bonds-Pit 8.9
- Sheffield-SD 6.0
- Sandberg-Chi 5.8
- VanSlyke-Pit 5.6
- Lankford-StL 4.8

Wins
- Maddux-Chi 20
- Glavine-Atl 20

Win Percentage
- Tewksbury-StL .762
- Glavine-Atl .714
- Leibrandt-Atl .682
- Morgan-Chi .667
- Maddux-Chi .645

Games
- Boever-Hou 81
- D.Jones-Hou 80
- Perez-StL 77
- Hernandez-Hou 77
- Innis-NY 76

Complete Games
- Mulholland-Phi 12
- Schilling-Phi 10
- Drabek-Pit 10
- Smoltz-Atl 9
- Maddux-Chi 9

Shutouts
- Glavine-Atl 5
- Cone-NY 5

Saves
- L.Smith-StL 43
- Myers-SD 38
- Wetteland-Mon 37
- D.Jones-Hou 36
- M.Williams-Phi 29

Innings Pitched
- Maddux-Chi 268.0
- Drabek-Pit 256.2
- Smoltz-Atl 246.2
- Morgan-Chi 240.0
- Avery-Atl 233.2

Fewest Hits/Game
- Schilling-Phi 6.56
- Maddux-Chi 6.75
- Fernandez-NY 6.79
- Martinez-Mon 6.84
- Cone-NY 7.41

Fewest BB/Game
- Tewksbury-StL .77
- Cormier-StL 1.60
- Swindell-Cin 1.73
- Mulholland-Phi 1.81
- Tomlin-Pit 1.81

Strikeouts
- Smoltz-Atl 215
- Cone-NY 214
- Maddux-Chi 199
- Fernandez-NY 193
- Drabek-Pit 177

Strikeouts/Game
- Cone-NY 9.79
- Fernandez-NY 8.09
- Smoltz-Atl 7.84
- Rijo-Cin 7.29
- Harnisch-Hou 7.14

Ratio
- Schilling-Phi 8.95
- Tewksbury-StL 9.27
- Maddux-Chi 9.57
- Martinez-Mon 9.58
- Drabek-Pit 9.75

Earned Run Average
- Swift-SF 2.08
- Tewksbury-StL 2.16
- Maddux-Chi 2.18
- Schilling-Phi 2.35
- Martinez-Mon 2.47

Adjusted ERA
- Maddux-Chi 165
- Swift-SF 159
- Tewksbury-StL 157
- Schilling-Phi 149
- Morgan-Chi 141

Opponents' Batting Avg.
- Schilling-Phi .201
- Maddux-Chi .210
- Fernandez-NY .210
- Martinez-Mon .211
- Cone-NY .223

Opponents' On-Base Pct.
- Schilling-Phi .256
- Tewksbury-StL .267
- Martinez-Mon .273
- Maddux-Chi .273
- Drabek-Pit .277

Starter Runs
- Maddux-Chi 39.5
- Tewksbury-StL 34.8
- Schilling-Phi 29.2
- Martinez-Mon 26.2
- Swift-SF 26.2

Adjusted Starter Runs
- Maddux-Chi 41.3
- Tewksbury-StL 32.9
- Schilling-Phi 29.0
- Morgan-Chi 27.4
- Martinez-Mon 25.6

Clutch Pitching Index
- Swift-SF 131
- Tewksbury-StL 120
- Swindell-Cin 119
- Morgan-Chi 115
- Ojeda-LA 113

Relief Runs
- Rojas-Mon 23.2
- D.Jones-Hou 20.5
- Beck-SF 17.9
- Hernandez-Hou 17.3
- Perez-StL 17.3

Adjusted Relief Runs
- Rojas-Mon 23.1
- D.Jones-Hou 19.6
- Beck-SF 16.8
- Perez-StL 16.6
- Hernandez-Hou 16.2

Relief Ranking
- D.Jones-Hou 39.1
- Rojas-Mon 20.6
- Perez-StL 19.3
- Beck-SF 15.4
- Hernandez-Hou 14.9

Total Pitcher Index
- Maddux-Chi 6.1
- D.Jones-Hou 4.2
- Martinez-Mon 3.5
- Glavine-Atl 3.2
- Rijo-Cin 3.1

Total Baseball Ranking
- Bonds-Pit 8.9
- Maddux-Chi 6.1
- Sheffield-SD 6.0
- Sandberg-Chi 5.8
- VanSlyke-Pit 5.6

TEAM	G	W	L	PCT	GB	R	OR	AB	H	2B	3B	HR	BB	SO	AVG	OBP	SLG	OPS	OPS+	BR	BR+	PF	CHI	RC	SB	CS	SBA	SBR
EAST																												
TOR	162	96	66	.593		780	682	5536	1458	265	40	163	561	933	.263	.336	**.414**	**750**	104	**63**	30	105	102	**779**	129	39	**77**	15
MIL	162	92	70	.568	4	740	**604**	5504	1477	272	35	82	511	779	.268	.334	.375	709	100	-10	5	98	108	700	**256**	115	69	**16**
BAL	162	89	73	.549	7	705	656	5485	1423	243	36	148	647	827	.259	.343	.398	741	104	56	37	103	92	754	89	48	65	3
NY	162	76	86	.469	20	733	746	5593	1462	281	18	163	536	903	.261	.331	.406	737	106	33	39	99	99	742	78	37	68	4
CLE	162	76	86	.469	20	674	746	5620	1495	227	24	127	448	885	.266	.325	.383	708	100	-22	-10	98	99	686	144	67	68	8
DET	162	75	87	.463	21	**791**	794	5515	1411	256	16	**182**	675	1055	.256	.340	.407	747	107	**63**	59	101	102	769	66	45	59	-1
BOS	162	73	89	.451	23	599	669	5461	1343	259	21	84	591	865	.246	.323	.347	670	83	-84	-122	107	98	617	44	48	48	-7
WEST																												
OAK	162	96	66	.593		745	672	5387	1389	219	24	142	**707**	831	.258	**.349**	.386	735	**112**	54	**97**	95	98	748	143	59	71	11
MIN	162	90	72	.556	6	747	653	5582	**1544**	275	27	104	527	834	**.277**	.345	.391	736	103	46	23	103	99	748	123	74	62	1
CHI	162	86	76	.531	10	738	690	5498	1434	269	36	110	622	784	.261	.339	.383	722	103	19	29	99	102	728	160	57	74	15
TEX	162	77	85	.475	19	682	753	5537	1387	266	23	159	550	1036	.250	.324	.393	717	104	-5	21	96	98	708	81	44	65	2
KC	162	72	90	.444	25	610	667	5501	1411	**284**	**42**	75	439	**741**	.256	.317	.364	681	88	-73	-89	103	99	629	131	71	65	4
CAL	162	72	90	.444	25	579	671	5364	1306	202	20	88	416	882	.243	.303	.338	641	79	-152	-155	101	**112**	529	160	101	61	0
SEA	162	64	98	.395	33	679	799	5564	1466	278	24	149	474	841	.263	.326	.402	728	102	13	9	101	96	708	100	55	65	3
TOT	1134					9802		77147	20006	3596	386	1776	7704	12196	.260	.332	.386	716							1704	860	66	74

TEAM	CG	SH	SV	IP	H	H/G	HR	BB	SO	RAT	ERA	ERA+	OAV	OOB	PR	PR+	PF	CPI	FA	E	DP	FW	PW	BW	SBW	DIF
EAST																										
TOR	18	14	49	1440^2	1346	8.5	124	541	954	12.1	3.92	104	.248	.321	5	26	104	93	.985	93	109	1.5	2.7	3.1	1.0	7.0
MIL	19	14	39	1457	**1344**	**8.4**	127	**435**	793	**11.3**	**3.44**	112	**.246**	**.307**	**82**	67	97	99	**.986**	**89**	146	**1.7**	6.9	.6	**1.1**	1.0
BAL	20	**16**	48	1464	1419	8.8	124	518	846	12.2	3.79	106	.256	.324	25	38	102	100	.985	93	168	1.5	3.9	3.8	-.2	-.8
NY	20	9	44	1452^2	1453	9.1	129	612	851	13.1	4.21	93	.263	.341	-43	-47	99	99	.982	114	165	.3	-4.7	4.0	-.1	-4.2
CLE	13	7	46	1470	1507	9.3	159	566	890	13.0	4.11	95	.268	.339	-28	-34	99	106	.978	141	**176**	-1.2	-3.4	-1.0	.3	.5
DET	10	4	36	1435^2	1534	9.7	155	564	693	13.4	4.60	86	.277	.346	-105	-102	100	100	.981	116	164	.2	-10.3	6.1	-.6	-1.1
BOS	22	13	39	1448^2	1403	8.8	107	535	943	12.3	3.59	**117**	.255	.326	57	**94**	107	103	.978	139	170	-1.1	**9.6**	-12.4	-1.3	-2.7
WEST																										
OAK	8	9	**58**	1447	1396	8.7	129	601	843	12.7	3.73	100	.256	.335	34	3	95	**107**	.979	125	158	-.3	.4	**9.9**	.6	4.7
MIN	16	13	50	1453	1391	8.7	121	479	923	11.9	3.71	109	.254	.318	38	55	103	98	.985	95	155	1.3	5.7	2.4	-.4	.2
CHI	21	5	52	1461^2	1400	8.7	123	550	810	12.4	3.83	101	.252	.326	19	6	98	98	.979	129	134	-.5	.7	3.0	1.0	1.1
TEX	19	3	42	1460^1	1471	9.1	113	598	**1034**	13.1	4.09	93	.264	.341	-24	-49	96	100	.975	154	153	-1.9	-4.9	2.2	-.3	1.2
KC	9	12	44	1447^1	1426	8.9	**106**	512	834	12.3	3.82	106	.259	.327	21	38	103	99	.980	122	164	-.2	3.9	-9.0	-.1	-3.4
CAL	**26**	13	42	1446	1449	9.1	130	532	888	12.6	3.85	104	.264	.333	16	23	101	106	.979	134	172	-.8	2.4	-15.7	-.5	5.9
SEA	21	9	30	1445	1467	9.2	129	661	894	13.7	4.55	87	.266	.351	-97	-92	101	96	.982	112	170	.4	-9.3	1.0	-.2	-8.6
TOT	242	141	619	20329		8.9				12.6	3.94		.260	.332					.981	1656	2204					

Runs

Phillips-Det	114
Thomas-Chi	108
Alomar-Tor	105
Puckett-Min	104
Knoblauch-Min	104

Hits

Puckett-Min	210
Baerga-Cle	205
Molitor-Mil	195
Mack-Min	189
Thomas-Chi	185

Doubles

Thomas-Chi	46
E.Martinez-Sea	46
Yount-Mil	40
Mattingly-NY	40
Griffey-Sea	39

Triples

Johnson-Chi	12
Devereaux-Bal	11
Anderson-Bal	10
Raines-Chi	9

Home Runs

Gonzalez-Tex	43
McGwire-Oak	42
Fielder-Det	35
Carter-Tor	34
Belle-Cle	34

Total Bases

Puckett-Min	313
Carter-Tor	310
Gonzalez-Tex	309
Thomas-Chi	307
Devereaux-Bal	303

Runs Batted In

Fielder-Det	124
Carter-Tor	119
Thomas-Chi	115
Belle-Cle	112
Bell-Chi	112

Runs Produced

Thomas-Chi	199
Puckett-Min	195
Carter-Tor	182
Baerga-Cle	177
Winfield-Tor	174

Bases On Balls

Thomas-Chi	122
Tettleton-Det	122
Phillips-Det	114
Milligan-Bal	106
Tartabull-NY	103

Batting Average

E.Martinez-Sea	.343
Puckett-Min	.329
Thomas-Chi	.323
Molitor-Mil	.320
Mack-Min	.315

On-Base Percentage

Thomas-Chi	.446
Tartabull-NY	.410
E.Martinez-Sea	.408
Alomar-Tor	.406
Molitor-Mil	.396

Slugging Average

McGwire-Oak	.585
E.Martinez-Sea	.544
Thomas-Chi	.536
Griffey-Sea	.535
Gonzalez-Tex	.529

On-Base Plus Slugging

Thomas-Chi	981
McGwire-Oak	976
E.Martinez-Sea	951
Tartabull-NY	900
Griffey-Sea	898

Adjusted OPS

McGwire-Oak	180
Thomas-Chi	176
E.Martinez-Sea	164
Tartabull-NY	152
Griffey-Sea	148

Batter Runs

Thomas-Chi	62.4
E.Martinez-Sea	44.9
McGwire-Oak	44.4
Griffey-Sea	34.2
Mack-Min	33.8

Adjusted Batter Runs

Thomas-Chi	64.3
McGwire-Oak	50.5
E.Martinez-Sea	44.4
R.Henderson-Oak	35.8
Molitor-Mil	35.8

Clutch Hitting Index

Surhoff-Mil	136
Lansford-Oak	134
Devereaux-Bal	120
Felix-Cal	120
Ventura-Chi	119

Runs Created

Thomas-Chi	142
Anderson-Bal	118
E.Martinez-Sea	116
Molitor-Mil	116
Mack-Min	114

Total Average

Thomas-Chi	1.066
McGwire-Oak	1.040
Tartabull-NY	.972
E.Martinez-Sea	.970
Alomar-Tor	.915

Stolen Bases

Lofton-Cle	66
Listach-Mil	54
Anderson-Bal	53
Polonia-Cal	51
Alomar-Tor	49

Stolen Base Average

Cotto-Sea	92.0
White-Tor	90.2
Raines-Chi	88.2
R.Kelly-NY	84.8
Lofton-Cle	84.6

Stolen Base Runs

Lofton-Cle	10.3
Raines-Chi	7.8
Alomar-Tor	7.6
White-Tor	6.7
R.Henderson-Oak	6.7

Fielding Runs

Reed-Bos	23.8
Ventura-Chi	23.7
Gagne-Min	20.9
Lofton-Cle	16.7
White-Tor	15.1

Total Player Rating

Ventura-Chi	4.8
E.Martinez-Sea	4.6
R.Henderson-Oak	4.5
Thomas-Chi	4.3
Anderson-Bal	4.0

Wins

Morris-Tor	21
Brown-Tex	21
McDowell-Chi	20
Mussina-Bal	18
Clemens-Bos	18

Win Percentage

Mussina-Bal	.783
Morris-Tor	.778
Guzman-Tor	.762
Bosio-Mil	.727
McDowell-Chi	.667

Games

Rogers-Tex	81
D.Ward-Tor	79
Olin-Cle	72
Lilliquist-Cle	71
Harris-Bos	70

Complete Games

McDowell-Chi	13
Clemens-Bos	11
Brown-Tex	11
Perez-NY	10
Nagy-Cle	10

Shutouts

Clemens-Bos	5
Mussina-Bal	4
Fleming-Sea	4

Saves

Eckersley-Oak	51
Aguilera-Min	41
Montgomery-KC	39
Olson-Bal	36
Henke-Tor	34

Innings Pitched

Brown-Tex	265.2
Wegman-Mil	261.2
McDowell-Chi	260.2
Nagy-Cle	252.0
Perez-NY	247.2

Fewest Hits/Game

Johnson-Sea	6.59
Guzman-Tor	6.73
Appier-KC	7.21
Clemens-Bos	7.41
Smiley-Min	7.66

Fewest BB/Game

Bosio-Mil	1.71
Mussina-Bal	1.79
Wegman-Mil	1.89
Tapani-Min	1.96
Gullickson-Det	2.03

Strikeouts

Johnson-Sea	241
Perez-NY	218
Clemens-Bos	208
Guzman-Tex	179
McDowell-Chi	178

Strikeouts/Game

Johnson-Sea	10.31
Guzman-Tor	8.22
Perez-NY	7.92
Clemens-Bos	7.59
Guzman-Tex	7.19

Ratio

Mussina-Bal	9.78
Clemens-Bos	10.00
Appier-KC	10.24
Smiley-Min	10.31
Guzman-Tor	10.36

Earned Run Average

Clemens-Bos	2.41
Appier-KC	2.46
Mussina-Bal	2.54
Guzman-Tor	2.64
Abbott-Cal	2.77

Adjusted ERA

Clemens-Bos	175
Appier-KC	165
Mussina-Bal	159
Guzman-Tor	155
Abbott-Cal	144

Opponents' Batting Avg.

Johnson-Sea	.206
Guzman-Tor	.207
Appier-KC	.217
Clemens-Bos	.224
Smiley-Min	.231

Opponents' On-Base Pct.

Mussina-Bal	.279
Clemens-Bos	.280
Appier-KC	.282
Guzman-Tor	.287
Smiley-Min	.288

Starter Runs

Clemens-Bos	42.2
Mussina-Bal	37.8
Appier-KC	34.4
Perez-NY	29.7
Abbott-Cal	27.6

Adjusted Starter Runs

Clemens-Bos	46.5
Mussina-Bal	39.2
Appier-KC	36.0
Perez-NY	29.2
Abbott-Cal	28.3

Clutch Pitching Index

Abbott-Cal	132
Finley-Cal	125
Erickson-Min	113
Perez-NY	111
Moore-Oak	108

Relief Runs

D.Ward-Tor	22.5
Hernandez-Chi	18.2
Eckersley-Oak	18.1
Frohwirth-Bal	17.5
Harris-Bos	17.2

Adjusted Relief Runs

D.Ward-Tor	23.2
Harris-Bos	19.2
Frohwirth-Bal	18.1
Hernandez-Chi	17.9
Eckersley-Oak	17.2

Relief Ranking

Eckersley-Oak	33.6
Olin-Cle	29.0
J.Russell-Tex-Oak	28.2
Hernandez-Chi	27.7
D.Ward-Tor	27.2

Total Pitcher Index

Clemens-Bos	5.5
Appier-KC	4.0
Mussina-Bal	3.6
Eckersley-Oak	3.6
Perez-NY	3.2

Total Baseball Ranking

Clemens-Bos	5.5
Ventura-Chi	4.8
E.Martinez-Sea	4.6
R.Henderson-Oak	4.5
Thomas-Chi	4.3

TEAM	G	W	L	PCT	GB	R	OR	AB	H	2B	3B	HR	BB	SO	AVG	OBP	SLG	OPS	OPS+	BR	BR+	PF	CHI	RC	SB	CS	SBA	SBR
EAST																												
PHI	162	97	65	.599		**877**	740	5685	**1555**	**297**	51	156	**665**	1049	.274	**.354**	.426	**780**	**116**	**117**	**130**	99	99	**880**	91	32	74	9
MON	163	94	68	.580	3	732	682	5493	1410	270	36	122	542	**860**	.257	.329	.386	715	92	-25	-54	104	104	727	**228**	56	**80**	**31**
STL	162	87	75	.537	10	758	744	5551	1508	262	34	118	588	882	.272	.344	.395	739	105	32	48	98	99	759	153	72	68	8
CHI	163	84	78	.519	13	738	739	5627	1521	259	32	161	446	923	.270	.328	.414	742	105	18	31	98	99	748	100	43	70	7
PIT	162	75	87	.463	22	707	806	5549	1482	267	50	110	536	972	.267	.338	.393	731	101	10	12	100	95	734	92	55	63	1
FLA	162	64	98	.395	33	581	724	5475	1356	197	31	94	498	1054	.248	.316	.346	662	79	-124	-155	106	98	604	117	56	68	6
NY	162	59	103	.364	38	672	744	5448	1350	228	37	158	448	879	.248	.308	.390	698	92	-72	-64	99	**105**	646	79	50	61	0
WEST																												
ATL	162	104	58	.642		767	**559**	5515	1444	239	29	**169**	560	946	.262	.334	.408	742	103	26	19	101	101	754	125	48	72	11
SF	162	103	59	.636	1	808	636	5557	1534	269	33	168	516	930	**.276**	.343	**.427**	770	115	82	108	97	99	803	120	65	65	4
HOU	162	85	77	.525	19	716	630	5464	1459	288	37	138	497	911	.267	.333	.409	742	107	24	53	96	96	733	103	60	63	2
LA	162	81	81	.500	23	675	662	5588	1458	234	28	130	492	937	.261	.324	.383	707	100	-45	-2	94	98	696	126	61	67	6
CIN	162	73	89	.451	31	722	785	5517	1457	261	28	137	485	1025	.264	.327	.396	723	98	-13	-14	100	102	720	142	59	71	11
COL	162	67	95	.414	37	758	967	5517	1507	278	**59**	142	388	944	.273	.326	.422	748	90	28	-76	116	102	731	146	90	62	1
SD	162	61	101	.377	43	679	772	5503	1386	239	28	153	443	1046	.252	.314	.389	703	91	-58	-69	102	103	672	92	41	69	6
TOT	1135					10190		77489	20427	3588	513	1956	7104	13358	.264	.330	.399	729							1714	788	69	101

TEAM	CG	SH	SV	IP	H	H/G	HR	BB	SO	RAT	ERA	ERA+	OAV	OOB	PR	PR+	PF	CPI	FA	E	DP	FW	PW	BW	SBW	DIF
EAST																										
PHI	**24**	11	46	1472^{2}	1419	8.7	129	573	**1117**	12.4	3.96	100	.251	.324	14	1	98	94	.977	141	123	-.4	.1	**13.0**	.2	3.2
MON	8	7	**61**	1456^{2}	1369	8.5	119	521	934	12.0	3.55	118	.249	.319	80	98	103	101	.975	159	144	-1.3	9.8	-5.3	**2.4**	7.7
STL	5	7	54	1453	1553	9.7	152	**383**	775	12.3	4.09	97	.276	.327	-8	-21	98	102	.975	159	157	-1.4	-2.0	4.8	.0	4.7
CHI	8	5	56	1449^{2}	1514	9.4	153	470	905	12.6	4.18	95	.273	.335	-22	-31	99	103	.982	115	162	1.2	-3.0	3.1	-.0	1.9
PIT	12	5	34	1445^{2}	1557	9.7	153	485	832	13.0	4.77	85	.280	.342	-117	-116	100	95	.983	105	161	1.7	-11.5	1.2	-.6	3.4
FLA	4	5	48	1440^{1}	1437	9.0	135	598	945	13.0	4.14	105	.261	.337	-14	28	107	100	.980	125	130	.6	2.8	-15.4	-.1	-4.7
NY	16	8	22	1438	1483	9.3	139	434	867	12.4	4.05	99	.269	.328	-2	-6	99	100	.975	156	143	-1.2	-.5	-6.3	-.7	-13.0
WEST																										
ATL	18	**16**	46	1455	**1297**	**8.1**	**101**	480	1036	**11.2**	**3.14**	**128**	**.240**	**.305**	**146**	**143**	99	101	.983	108	146	1.6	**14.3**	1.9	.4	5.0
SF	4	9	50	1456^{2}	1385	8.6	168	442	982	11.6	3.62	108	.253	.315	69	49	97	**106**	**.984**	**101**	**169**	**2.0**	4.9	10.8	-.3	4.8
HOU	18	14	42	1441^{1}	1363	8.6	117	476	1056	11.8	3.50	111	.251	.316	88	63	96	101	.979	126	141	.5	6.3	5.3	-.5	-7.5
LA	17	9	36	1472^{2}	1406	8.6	103	567	1043	12.3	3.51	109	.254	.327	88	54	94	105	.979	133	141	.1	5.4	-.1	-.1	-5.1
CIN	11	8	37	1434	1510	9.5	158	508	996	13.0	4.51	89	.272	.338	-74	-77	100	97	.980	121	133	.8	-7.6	-1.3	.4	.0
COL	9	0	35	1431^{1}	1664	10.5	181	609	913	14.6	5.41	88	.294	.367	-218	-86	118	98	.973	167	149	-1.9	-8.5	-7.5	-.6	4.7
SD	8	6	32	1437^{2}	1470	9.3	148	558	957	13.0	4.23	98	.266	.337	-30	-15	102	101	.974	160	129	-1.5	-1.4	-6.8	-.1	-9.9
TOT	162	110	599	20284^{2}		9.1				12.5	4.04		.264	.330					.979	1876	2028					

Runs
Dykstra-Phi 143
Bonds-SF 129
Gant-Atl 113
McGriff-SD-Atl 111
Blauser-Atl 110

Hits
Dykstra-Phi 194
Grace-Chi 193
Grissom-Mon 188
Bell-Pit 187
Jefferies-StL 186

Doubles
Hayes-Col 45
Dykstra-Phi 44
Bichette-Col 43
Gwynn-SD 41
Biggio-Hou 41

Triples
Finley-Hou 13
Butler-LA 10
Morandini-Phi 9
Bell-Pit 9

Home Runs
Bonds-SF 46
Justice-Atl 40
Williams-SF 38
McGriff-SD-Atl 37
Gant-Atl 36

Total Bases
Bonds-SF 365
Williams-SF 325
Gant-Atl 309
Piazza-LA 307
Dykstra-Phi 307

Runs Batted In
Bonds-SF 123
Justice-Atl 120
Gant-Atl 117
Piazza-LA 112
Williams-SF 110

Runs Produced
Bonds-SF 206
Gant-Atl 194
Dykstra-Phi 190
Grissom-Mon 180
Hollins-Phi 179

Bases On Balls
Dykstra-Phi 129
Bonds-SF 126
Daulton-Phi 117
Kruk-Phi 111
Butler-LA 86

Batting Average
Galarraga-Col .370
Gwynn-SD .358
Jefferies-StL .342
Bonds-SF .336
Grace-Chi .325

On-Base Percentage
Bonds-SF .463
Kruk-Phi .433
Dykstra-Phi .423
Merced-Pit .415
Jefferies-StL .411

Slugging Average
Bonds-SF .677
Galarraga-Col .602
Williams-SF .561
Piazza-LA .561
McGriff-SD-Atl .549

On-Base Plus Slugging
Bonds-SF 1140
Galarraga-Col 1010
Piazza-LA 935
McGriff-SD-Atl 927
Bagwell-Hou 909

Adjusted OPS
Bonds-SF 207
Piazza-LA 155
Bagwell-Hou 146
Kruk-Phi 145
Dykstra-Phi 144

Batter Runs
Bonds-SF 82.0
Dykstra-Phi 43.3
Galarraga-Col 42.3
Kruk-Phi 38.1
McGriff-SD-Atl 34.8

Adjusted Batter Runs
Bonds-SF 87.1
Dykstra-Phi 45.3
Piazza-LA 40.8
Kruk-Phi 39.9
Bagwell-Hou 35.5

Clutch Hitting Index
Zeile-StL 128
King-Pit 127
May-Chi 126
Oliver-Cin 125
Daulton-Phi 122

Runs Created
Bonds-SF 172
Dykstra-Phi 142
Kruk-Phi 117
McGriff-SD-Atl 115
Jefferies-StL 113

Total Average
Bonds-SF 1.339
Galarraga-Col 1.006
Dykstra-Phi 1.000
Kruk-Phi .974
Daulton-Phi .971

Stolen Bases
Carr-Fla 58
Grissom-Mon 53
Nixon-Atl 47
Lewis-SF 46
Jefferies-StL 46

Stolen Base Average
Frazier-Mon 89.5
Davis-LA 86.8
Grissom-Mon 84.1
Bell-SD 83.9
Jefferies-StL 83.6

Stolen Base Runs
Grissom-Mon 8.2
Jefferies-StL 7.0
DeShields-Mon 6.0
Nixon-Atl 5.8
Davis-LA 5.5

Fielding Runs
Bell-Pit 25.7
King-Pit 20.5
Gonzalez-Hou 20.2
Reed-LA 19.4
O.Smith-StL 18.2

Total Player Rating
Bonds-SF 8.7
Dykstra-Phi 6.6
Bell-Pit 5.9
Piazza-LA 5.3
Wilkins-Chi 4.2

Wins
Glavine-Atl 22
Burkett-SF 22
Swift-SF 21
Maddux-Atl 20

Win Percentage
Portugal-Hou .818
Greene-Phi .800
Glavine-Atl .786
Burkett-SF .759
Avery-Atl .750

Games
Jackson-SF 81
West-Phi 76
Beck-SF 76
McMichael-Atl 74

Complete Games
Maddux-Atl 8

Shutouts
Harnisch-Hou 4
R.Martinez-LA 3

Saves
Myers-Chi 53
Beck-SF 48
Harvey-Fla 45

Innings Pitched
Maddux-Atl 267.0
Rijo-Cin 257.1
Smoltz-Atl 243.2
Glavine-Atl 239.1
Drabek-Hou 237.2

Fewest Hits/Game
Harnisch-Hou 7.07
Swift-SF 7.54
Rijo-Cin 7.62
Smoltz-Atl 7.68
Maddux-Atl 7.69

Fewest BB/Game
Tewksbury-StL .84
Arocha-StL 1.48
Burkett-SF 1.55
Avery-Atl 1.73
Maddux-Atl 1.75

Strikeouts
Rijo-Cin 227
Smoltz-Atl 208
Maddux-Atl 197
Schilling-Phi 186
Harnisch-Hou 185

Strikeouts/Game
Rijo-Cin 7.94
Smoltz-Atl 7.68
Guzman-Chi 7.68
Harnisch-Hou 7.65
Greene-Phi 7.62

Ratio
Maddux-Atl 9.64
Rijo-Cin 9.86
Swift-SF 9.90
Mulholland-Phi 10.37
Avery-Atl 10.44

Earned Run Average
Maddux-Atl 2.36
Rijo-Cin 2.48
Portugal-Hou 2.77
Swift-SF 2.82
Avery-Atl 2.94

Adjusted ERA
Maddux-Atl 170
Rijo-Cin 162
Portugal-Hou 140
Swift-SF 139
Avery-Atl 137

Opponents' Batting Avg.
Harnisch-Hou .214
Swift-SF .226
Rijo-Cin .230
Smoltz-Atl .230
Maddux-Atl .232

Opponents' On-Base Pct.
Maddux-Atl .274
Swift-SF .278
Rijo-Cin .278
Mulholland-Phi .283
Harnisch-Hou .290

Starter Runs
Maddux-Atl 50.0
Rijo-Cin 44.7
Swift-SF 31.6
Portugal-Hou 29.5
Avery-Atl 27.4

Adjusted Starter Runs
Maddux-Atl 49.5
Rijo-Cin 44.4
Swift-SF 29.1
Avery-Atl 26.9
Portugal-Hou 26.7

Clutch Pitching Index
Portugal-Hou 120
Glavine-Atl 117
R.Martinez-LA 116
Reynoso-Col 113
Avery-Atl 110

Relief Runs
Fassero-Mon 29.3
Wetteland-Mon 25.4
McMichael-Atl 20.2
Harvey-Fla 18.0
P.Martinez-LA 17.1

Adjusted Relief Runs
Fassero-Mon 30.5
Wetteland-Mon 25.8
McMichael-Atl 20.1
Harvey-Fla 18.9
Beck-SF 16.0

Relief Ranking
Wetteland-Mon 51.5
Harvey-Fla 35.7
Fassero-Mon 31.5
Gott-LA 26.6
Beck-SF 23.8

Total Pitcher Index
Maddux-Atl 6.1
Wetteland-Mon 5.2
Rijo-Cin 4.9
Swift-SF 4.4
Harvey-Fla 3.6

Total Baseball Ranking
Bonds-SF 8.7
Dykstra-Phi 6.6
Maddux-Atl 6.1
Bell-Pit 5.9
Piazza-LA 5.3

TEAM	G	W	L	PCT	GB	R	OR	AB	H	2B	3B	HR	BB	SO	AVG	OBP	SLG	OPS	OPS+	BR	BR+	PF	CHI	RC	SB	CS	SBA	SBR
EAST																												
TOR	162	95	67	.586		847	742	5579	1556	317	42	159	588	861	**.279**	.353	**.436**	789	110	85	81	101	99	867	**170**	49	**78**	**20**
NY	162	88	74	.543	7	821	761	5615	**1568**	294	24	178	629	910	**.279**	.356	.435	791	**115**	93	123	97	95	861	39	35	53	-4
BAL	162	85	77	.525	10	786	745	5508	1470	287	24	157	655	930	.267	.349	.413	762	100	36	4	104	98	796	73	54	57	-3
DET	162	85	77	.525	10	**899**	837	5620	1546	282	38	178	**765**	1122	.275	**.365**	.434	**799**	**115**	**120**	**126**	99	98	**916**	104	63	62	1
BOS	162	80	82	.494	15	686	698	5496	1451	**319**	29	114	508	871	.264	.333	.395	728	89	-41	-83	106	96	713	73	38	66	3
CLE	162	76	86	.469	19	790	813	5619	1547	264	31	141	488	843	.275	.339	.409	748	100	-5	-2	100	104	776	159	55	74	16
MIL	162	69	93	.426	26	733	792	5525	1426	240	25	125	555	932	.258	.330	.378	708	91	-77	-67	99	108	686	138	93	60	-2
WEST																												
CHI	162	94	68	.580		776	**664**	5483	1454	228	**44**	162	604	**834**	.265	.342	.411	753	103	11	28	98	100	773	106	57	65	3
TEX	162	86	76	.531	8	835	751	5510	1472	284	39	**181**	483	984	.267	.332	.431	763	107	16	47	96	**109**	777	113	67	63	1
KC	162	84	78	.519	10	675	694	5522	1455	294	35	125	428	936	.263	.322	.397	719	87	-67	-105	106	100	692	100	75	57	-4
SEA	162	82	80	.506	12	734	731	5494	1429	272	24	161	624	901	.260	.342	.406	748	99	3	-8	101	95	758	91	68	57	-4
CAL	162	71	91	.438	26	684	770	5391	1399	259	24	114	564	930	.260	.334	.380	714	88	-63	-85	103	101	679	169	100	63	2
MIN	162	71	91	.438	26	693	830	5601	1480	261	27	121	493	850	.264	.329	.385	714	91	-70	-72	100	101	692	83	59	58	-2
OAK	162	68	94	.420	29	715	846	5543	1408	260	21	158	622	1048	.254	.333	.394	727	101	-42	4	94	99	735	131	59	69	8
TOT	1134					10674		77506	20661	3861	427	2074	8006	12952	.267	.341	.408	748							1549	872	64	36

TEAM	CG	SH	SV	IP	H	H/G	HR	BB	SO	RAT	ERA	ERA+	OAV	OOB	PR	PR+	PF	CPI	FA	E	DP	FW	PW	BW	SBW	DIF
EAST																										
TOR	11	11	**50**	1441^{1}	1441	9.0	134	620	1023	13.1	4.21	103	.261	.339	18	17	100	99	.982	107	144	.5	1.7	7.9	**1.7**	2.4
NY	11	**13**	38	1438^{1}	1467	9.2	170	552	899	12.9	4.35	95	.266	.336	-5	-33	96	100	.983	105	166	.6	-3.2	12.0	-.6	-1.6
BAL	21	10	42	1442^{2}	1427	9.0	153	579	900	12.8	4.32	104	.261	.336	2	25	104	98	.984	100	171	.9	2.5	.4	-.5	.9
DET	11	7	36	1436^{2}	1547	9.7	188	542	828	13.4	4.65	92	.276	.345	-52	-58	99	102	.979	132	148	-1.0	-5.6	**12.3**	-.2	-1.4
BOS	9	11	44	1452^{1}	**1379**	**8.6**	127	552	997	**12.3**	3.78	**122**	**.252**	**.325**	88	**127**	107	100	.980	122	155	-.4	**12.4**	-8.0	.0	-4.9
CLE	7	8	45	1445^{2}	1591	10.0	182	591	888	13.9	4.58	95	.281	.353	-41	-40	100	**107**	.976	148	**174**	-1.9	-3.8	-.1	1.3	-.2
MIL	**26**	6	29	1447	1511	9.4	153	522	810	13.1	4.46	95	.271	.340	-21	-34	98	99	.979	131	148	-.9	-3.3	-6.5	-.4	-.7
WEST																										
CHI	16	11	48	1454	1398	8.7	125	566	974	12.5	**3.71**	113	.255	.330	**100**	80	97	105	.982	112	153	.2	7.8	2.8	.0	2.3
TEX	20	6	45	1438^{1}	1476	9.3	144	562	957	13.1	4.28	97	.267	.339	6	-22	96	100	.979	132	145	-1.0	-2.1	4.6	-.2	3.8
KC	16	6	48	1445^{1}	**1379**	**8.6**	**105**	571	985	12.5	4.05	113	.254	.329	45	82	106	93	.984	97	150	1.1	8.0	-10.2	-.6	4.9
SEA	22	10	41	1453^{2}	1421	8.8	135	605	**1083**	13.0	4.20	105	.259	.340	20	32	102	100	**.985**	**90**	173	**1.5**	3.2	-.7	-.6	-2.1
CAL	**26**	6	41	1430^{1}	1482	9.4	153	550	843	13.2	4.35	104	.270	.342	-3	25	104	102	.980	120	161	-.3	2.5	-8.2	-.0	-3.8
MIN	5	3	44	1444^{1}	1591	10.0	148	**514**	901	13.4	4.72	92	.283	.348	-63	-57	101	99	.984	100	160	.9	-5.5	-7.0	-.4	2.2
OAK	8	2	42	1452^{1}	1551	9.7	157	680	864	14.2	4.91	83	.276	.359	-94	-142	94	99	.982	111	161	.3	-13.8	.4	.5	-.3
TOT	209	110	593	20222^{1}		9.2				13.1	4.33		.267	.341					.982	1607	2209					

Runs
Palmeiro-Tex 124
Molitor-Tor 121
White-Tor 116
Lofton-Cle 116
Henderson-Oak-Tor 114

Hits
Molitor-Tor 211
Olerud-Tor 200
Baerga-Cle 200
Alomar-Tor 192
Lofton-Cle 185

Doubles
Olerud-Tor 54
White-Tor 42
Valentin-Bos 40
Palmeiro-Tex 40
Puckett-Min 39

Triples
Johnson-Chi 14
Cora-Chi 13
Hulse-Tex 10
McRae-KC 9
Fernandez-Tor 9

Home Runs
Gonzalez-Tex 46
Griffey-Sea 45
Thomas-Chi 41
Belle-Cle 38
Palmeiro-Tex 37

Total Bases
Griffey-Sea 359
Gonzalez-Tex 339
Thomas-Chi 333
Palmeiro-Tex 331
Olerud-Tor 330

Runs Batted In
Belle-Cle 129
Thomas-Chi 128
Carter-Tor 121
Gonzalez-Tex 118
Fielder-Det 117

Runs Produced
Molitor-Tor 210
Baerga-Cle 198
Thomas-Chi 193
Palmeiro-Tex 192
Olerud-Tor 192

Bases On Balls
Phillips-Det 132
Henderson-Oak-Tor 120
Olerud-Tor 114
Thomas-Chi 112
Tettleton-Det 109

Batting Average
Olerud-Tor .363
Molitor-Tor .332
Alomar-Tor .326
Lofton-Cle .325
Baerga-Cle .321

On-Base Percentage
Olerud-Tor .478
Phillips-Det .446
Henderson-Oak-Tor .435
Thomas-Chi .434
Hoiles-Bal .419

Slugging Average
Gonzalez-Tex .632
Griffey-Sea .617
Thomas-Chi .607
Olerud-Tor .599
Hoiles-Bal .585

On-Base Plus Slugging
Olerud-Tor 1077
Thomas-Chi 1041
Griffey-Sea 1029
Hoiles-Bal 1003
Gonzalez-Tex 1001

Adjusted OPS
Olerud-Tor 186
Thomas-Chi 180
Gonzalez-Tex 170
Griffey-Sea 170
Hoiles-Bal 160

Batter Runs
Olerud-Tor 74.4
Thomas-Chi 62.3
Griffey-Sea 60.1
Gonzalez-Tex 44.4
Molitor-Tor 41.0

Adjusted Batter Runs
Olerud-Tor 73.6
Thomas-Chi 65.6
Griffey-Sea 58.1
Gonzalez-Tex 49.1
Palmeiro-Tex 43.0

Clutch Hitting Index
McLemore-Bal 122
Surhoff-Mil 120
Baerga-Cle 119
Davis-Cal 117
Kirby-Cle 115

Runs Created
Olerud-Tor 161
Thomas-Chi 149
Griffey-Sea 147
Molitor-Tor 136
Palmeiro-Tex 128

Total Average
Olerud-Tor 1.230
Thomas-Chi 1.160
Henderson-Oak-Tor 1.106
Griffey-Sea 1.104
Hoiles-Bal 1.077

Stolen Bases
Lofton-Cle 70
Polonia-Cal 55
Alomar-Tor 55
Henderson-Oak-Tor 53
Curtis-Cal 48

Stolen Base Average
White-Tor 89.5
Palmeiro-Tex 88.0
Henderson-Oak-Tor 86.9
Molitor-Tor 84.6
Fletcher-Bos 84.2

Stolen Base Runs
Lofton-Cle 10.5
Henderson-Oak-Tor 8.9
Alomar-Tor 6.8
White-Tor 6.1
Johnson-Chi 5.3

Fielding Runs
Vizquel-Sea 23.1
Pena-Bos 21.6
Joyner-KC 20.4
Boggs-NY 19.7
Belle-Cle 19.1

Total Player Rating
Griffey-Sea 5.8
Olerud-Tor 5.7
Belle-Cle 5.1
Henderson-Oak-Tor 5.0
Gonzalez-Tex 4.7

Wins
McDowell-Chi 22
Johnson-Sea 19
Hentgen-Tor 19

Win Percentage
Key-NY .750
Johnson-Sea .704
Appier-KC .692
McDowell-Chi .688
Hentgen-Tor .679

Games
Harris-Bos 80
Radinsky-Chi 73
D.Ward-Tor 71
Nelson-Sea 71
Fossas-Bos 71

Complete Games
Finley-Cal 13
Brown-Tex 12
McDowell-Chi 10
Johnson-Sea 10
Eldred-Mil 8

Shutouts
McDowell-Chi 4
Moore-Det 3
Johnson-Sea 3
Brown-Tex 3

Saves
D.Ward-Tor 45
Montgomery-KC 45
Henke-Tex 40
Hernandez-Chi 38
Eckersley-Oak 36

Innings Pitched
Eldred-Mil 258.0
McDowell-Chi 256.2
Langston-Cal 256.1
Johnson-Sea 255.1
Cone-KC 254.0

Fewest Hits/Game
Johnson-Sea 6.52
Appier-KC 6.90
Cone-KC 7.26
Alvarez-Chi 7.28
McDonald-Bal 7.56

Fewest BB/Game
Key-NY 1.64
Darwin-Bos 1.92
Wells-Det 2.02
Tapani-Min 2.27
Doherty-Det 2.34

Strikeouts
Johnson-Sea 308
Langston-Cal 196
Guzman-Tor 194
Cone-KC 191
Finley-Cal 187

Strikeouts/Game
Johnson-Sea 10.86
Perez-NY 8.17
Guzman-Tor 7.90
Clemens-Bos 7.51
Banks-Min 7.25

Ratio
Darwin-Bos 9.73
Appier-KC 9.99
Key-NY 10.00
Johnson-Sea 10.57
Fernandez-Chi 10.70

Earned Run Average
Appier-KC 2.56
Alvarez-Chi 2.95
Key-NY 3.00
Fernandez-Chi 3.13
Viola-Bos 3.14

Adjusted ERA
Appier-KC 179
Viola-Bos 148
Finley-Cal 143
Alvarez-Chi 142
Darwin-Bos 142

Opponents' Batting Avg.
Johnson-Sea .203
Appier-KC .212
Cone-KC .223
McDonald-Bal .228
Bosio-Sea .229

Opponents' On-Base Pct.
Darwin-Bos .274
Appier-KC .280
Key-NY .282
Johnson-Sea .292
Fernandez-Chi .296

Starter Runs
Appier-KC 47.0
Key-NY 35.0
Fernandez-Chi 33.1
Finley-Cal 33.1
Langston-Cal 32.5

Adjusted Starter Runs
Appier-KC 50.8
Finley-Cal 36.7
Langston-Cal 36.2
Cone-KC 33.7
Darwin-Bos 32.8

Clutch Pitching Index
Alvarez-Chi 130
Viola-Bos 123
Pavlik-Tex 120
Banks-Min 118
Finley-Cal 116

Relief Runs
Montgomery-KC 20.1
Hernandez-Chi 17.9
D.Ward-Tor 17.5
Lilliquist-Cle 14.8
Henneman-Det 13.5

Adjusted Relief Runs
Montgomery-KC 21.3
D.Ward-Tor 17.5
Hernandez-Chi 17.2
Lilliquist-Cle 14.8
Mills-Bal 13.5

Relief Ranking
Montgomery-KC 42.6
D.Ward-Tor 29.9
Hernandez-Chi 28.1
Henke-Tex 21.6
Henneman-Det 21.1

Total Pitcher Index
Appier-KC 5.1
Montgomery-KC 4.3
Finley-Cal 3.9
Langston-Cal 3.8
Darwin-Bos 3.4

Total Baseball Ranking
Griffey-Sea 5.8
Olerud-Tor 5.7
Belle-Cle 5.1
Appier-KC 5.1
Henderson-Oak-Tor 5.0

TEAM	G	W	L	PCT	GB	R	OR	AB	H	2B	3B	HR	BB	SO	AVG	OBP	SLG	OPS	OPS+	BR	BR+	PF	CHI	RC	SB	CS	SBA	SBR
EAST																												
MON	114	74	40	.649		585	454	4000	1111	246	30	108	379	669	.278	.346	.435	781	107	47	42	101	99	615	**137**	36	**79**	**18**
ATL	114	68	46	.596	6	542	**448**	3861	1031	198	18	**137**	377	**668**	.267	.336	.434	770	103	25	14	102	99	548	48	31	61	0
NY	113	55	58	.487	18.5	506	526	3869	966	164	21	117	336	807	.250	.318	.394	712	91	-57	-52	99	**109**	484	25	26	49	-4
PHI	115	54	61	.470	20.5	521	497	3927	1028	208	28	80	396	711	.262	.334	.390	724	92	-31	-42	102	104	515	67	24	74	6
FLA	115	51	64	.443	23.5	468	576	3926	1043	180	24	94	349	746	.266	.332	.396	728	92	-29	-43	103	94	519	65	26	71	5
CENTRAL																												
CIN	115	66	48	.579		**609**	490	3999	**1142**	211	36	124	388	738	**.286**	**.353**	**.449**	**802**	115	**78**	85	99	98	**633**	119	51	70	8
HOU	115	66	49	.574	0.5	602	503	3955	1099	**252**	25	120	394	718	.278	.350	.445	795	**118**	66	**99**	95	99	624	124	44	74	12
STL	115	53	61	.465	13	535	621	3902	1026	213	27	108	**434**	686	.263	.342	.414	756	104	14	25	98	98	555	76	46	62	1
PIT	114	53	61	.465	13	466	580	3864	1001	198	23	80	349	725	.259	.324	.384	708	88	-57	-62	101	102	478	53	25	68	3
CHI	113	49	64	.434	16.5	500	549	3918	1015	189	26	109	364	750	.259	.326	.404	730	96	-29	-21	99	101	507	69	53	57	-3
WEST																												
LA	114	58	56	.509		532	509	3904	1055	160	29	115	366	687	.270	.336	.414	750	107	1	39	93	101	538	74	37	67	3
SF	115	55	60	.478	3.5	504	500	3869	963	159	32	123	364	719	.249	.320	.402	722	97	-44	-20	95	105	504	114	40	74	11
COL	117	53	64	.453	6.5	573	638	4006	1098	206	**39**	125	378	761	.274	.340	.439	779	92	40	-42	116	99	584	91	53	63	1
SD	117	47	70	.402	12.5	479	531	4068	1117	200	19	92	319	762	.275	.332	.401	733	99	-24	-8	97	93	526	79	37	68	4
TOT	803					7422		55068	14695	2784	377	1532	5193	10147	.267	.336	.415	750							1141	529	68	66

TEAM	CG	SH	SV	IP	H	H/G	HR	BB	SO	RAT	ERA	ERA+	OAV	OOB	PR	PR+	PF	CPI	FA	E	DP	FW	PW	BW	SBW	DIF
EAST																										
MON	4	**8**	**46**	1036[2]	970	8.5	100	**288**	805	**11.3**	**3.56**	**119**	.247	**.305**	**75**	**76**	100	95	.979	94	90	-.4	**7.5**	4.2	**1.3**	4.6
ATL	**16**	**8**	26	1026[1]	**929**	**8.2**	**76**	378	**865**	11.7	3.57	**119**	**.242**	.314	73	**76**	101	93	.982	81	85	.3	**7.5**	1.4	-.5	2.4
NY	7	3	35	1023	1069	9.5	117	332	640	12.6	4.14	101	.271	.331	9	4	99	103	.980	89	112	-.2	.4	-5.1	-.9	4.3
PHI	7	6	30	1024[1]	1028	9.1	98	377	699	12.6	3.85	111	.261	.330	41	49	102	103	.978	94	96	-.4	4.9	-4.1	.1	-3.9
FLA	5	7	30	1015	1069	9.5	120	428	649	13.7	4.50	97	.274	.352	-32	-14	104	104	.978	95	111	-.4	-1.3	-4.2	.0	-.4
CENTRAL																										
CIN	6	6	27	1038[1]	1037	9.0	117	339	799	12.2	3.78	109	.262	.324	50	41	98	**106**	.983	73	91	.8	4.1	8.4	.3	-4.5
HOU	9	6	29	1029[2]	1043	9.2	102	367	739	12.7	3.97	100	.265	.333	28	-2	94	104	.983	76	110	.7	-.1	**9.8**	.7	-2.3
STL	7	7	29	1018	1154	10.3	134	355	632	13.7	5.14	81	.289	.353	-105	-113	99	97	.982	80	119	.4	-11.1	2.5	-.4	4.7
PIT	8	2	24	1005[2]	1094	9.8	117	370	650	13.5	4.64	93	.281	.350	-47	-35	103	102	.980	91	**131**	-.2	-3.4	-6.0	-.2	6.0
CHI	5	5	27	1023[2]	1054	9.3	120	392	717	12.9	4.47	93	.268	.338	-29	-36	99	98	.982	81	110	.3	-3.5	-2.0	-.8	-1.3
WEST																										
LA	14	5	20	1014	1041	9.3	90	354	732	12.7	4.18	94	.267	.333	4	-30	93	97	.980	88	104	-.0	-2.9	3.9	-.2	.4
SF	2	4	33	1025[1]	1014	9.0	122	372	655	12.5	3.99	100	.262	.333	26	2	95	**106**	**.985**	**68**	113	**1.1**	.2	-1.9	.6	-2.4
COL	4	5	28	1031	1185	10.4	120	448	703	14.7	5.16	96	.292	.369	-108	-18	118	101	.981	84	117	.3	-1.7	-4.1	-.4	.6
SD	8	6	27	1045[2]	1008	8.7	99	393	862	12.3	4.08	101	.252	.323	15	3	98	92	.975	111	82	-1.3	.3	-.7	-.0	-9.6
TOT	102	78	411	14356[2]		9.3				12.8	4.22		.267	.336					.981	1205	1471					

Runs
Bagwell-Hou 104
Grissom-Mon 96
Lankford-StL 89
Bonds-SF 89
Biggio-Hou 88

Hits
Gwynn-SD 165
Bichette-Col 147
Bagwell-Hou 147
Morris-Cin 146
Conine-Fla 144

Doubles
Walker-Mon 44
Biggio-Hou 44
Gwynn-SD 35
Bell-Pit 35
Bichette-Col 33

Triples
Lewis-SF 9
Butler-LA 9
R.Sanders-Cin 8
Mondesi-LA 8
Kingery-Col 8

Home Runs
Williams-SF 43
Bagwell-Hou 39
Bonds-SF 37
McGriff-Atl 34
Galarraga-Col 31

Total Bases
Bagwell-Hou 300
Williams-SF 270
Bichette-Col 265
McGriff-Atl 264
Bonds-SF 253

Runs Batted In
Bagwell-Hou 116
Williams-SF 96
Bichette-Col 95
McGriff-Atl 94
Piazza-LA 92

Runs Produced
Bagwell-Hou 181
Walker-Mon 143
Bichette-Col 142
McGriff-Atl 141
Biggio-Hou 138

Bases On Balls
Bonds-SF 74
Justice-Atl 69
Dykstra-Phi 68
Butler-LA 68
Bagwell-Hou 65

Batting Average
Gwynn-SD .394
Bagwell-Hou .368
Alou-Mon .339
Morris-Cin .335
Mitchell-Cin .326

On-Base Percentage
Bagwell-Hou .461
Gwynn-SD .458
Mitchell-Cin .438
Bonds-SF .429
Justice-Atl .428

Slugging Average
Bagwell-Hou .750
Mitchell-Cin .681
Bonds-SF .647
McGriff-Atl .623
Williams-SF .607

On-Base Plus Slugging
Bagwell-Hou 1211
Mitchell-Cin 1119
Bonds-SF 1076
Gwynn-SD 1026
McGriff-Atl 1014

Adjusted OPS
Bagwell-Hou 220
Mitchell-Cin 188
Bonds-SF 184
Gwynn-SD 171
McGriff-Atl 156

Batter Runs
Bagwell-Hou 64.7
Bonds-SF 44.9
Gwynn-SD 42.2
Mitchell-Cin 40.3
McGriff-Atl 35.6

Adjusted Batter Runs
Bagwell-Hou 71.4
Bonds-SF 50.0
Gwynn-SD 45.2
Mitchell-Cin 41.3
McGriff-Atl 33.7

Clutch Hitting Index
Gonzalez-Hou 132
Blauser-Atl 121
Piazza-LA 120
Morris-Cin 116
Sheffield-Fla 116

Runs Created
Bagwell-Hou 137
Bonds-SF 115
Gwynn-SD 104
McGriff-Atl 103
Biggio-Hou 98

Total Average
Bagwell-Hou 1.413
Bonds-SF 1.256
Mitchell-Cin 1.244
Gwynn-SD 1.069
McGriff-Atl 1.063

Stolen Bases
Biggio-Hou 39
D.Sanders-Atl-Cin 38
Grissom-Mon 36
Carr-Fla 32
Lewis-SF 30

Stolen Base Average
Larkin-Cin 92.9
Biggio-Hou 90.7
Clayton-SF 88.5
Grissom-Mon 85.7
Cordero-Mon 84.2

Stolen Base Runs
Biggio-Hou 7.2
Grissom-Mon 5.8
Larkin-Cin 5.0
Carr-Fla 4.2
Clayton-SF 4.0

Fielding Runs
Sanchez-Chi 28.5
Bell-Pit 19.3
Bagwell-Hou 17.1
Grissom-Mon 16.3
Karros-LA 16.0

Total Player Rating
Bagwell-Hou 7.6
Bonds-SF 5.6
Gwynn-SD 4.1
Mitchell-Cin 4.1
Biggio-Hou 3.5

Wins
Maddux-Atl 16
Hill-Mon 16
Saberhagen-NY 14
Jackson-Phi 14
Glavine-Atl 13

Win Percentage
Saberhagen-NY .778
Hill-Mon .762
Maddux-Atl .727
Jackson-Phi .700
Martinez-Mon .688

Games
Reed-Col 61
Rojas-Mon 58
Bautista-Chi 58
Munoz-Col 57
Burba-SF 57

Complete Games
Maddux-Atl 10
Drabek-Hou 6
Candiotti-LA 5

Shutouts
Martinez-LA 3
Maddux-Atl 3
Drabek-Hou 2
Benes-SD 2

Saves
Franco-NY 30
Beck-SF 28
Jones-Phi 27
Wetteland-Mon 25

Innings Pitched
Maddux-Atl 202.0
Jackson-Phi 179.1
Saberhagen-NY 177.1
Rijo-Cin 172.1
Benes-SD 172.1

Fewest Hits/Game
Maddux-Atl 6.68
Martinez-Mon 7.15
Drabek-Hou 7.21
Avery-Atl 7.54
Fassero-Mon 7.72

Fewest BB/Game
Saberhagen-NY .66
Tewksbury-StL 1.27
Maddux-Atl 1.38
Reynolds-Hou 1.52
Swindell-Hou 1.58

Strikeouts
Benes-SD 189
Rijo-Cin 171
Maddux-Atl 156
Saberhagen-NY 143
Martinez-Mon 142

Strikeouts/Game
Benes-SD 9.87
Rijo-Cin 8.93
Martinez-Mon 8.83
Neagle-Pit 8.01
Reynolds-Hou 7.98

Ratio
Maddux-Atl 8.33
Saberhagen-NY 9.44
Drabek-Hou 9.78
Fassero-Mon 10.38
Ashby-SD 10.46

Earned Run Average
Maddux-Atl 1.56
Saberhagen-NY 2.74
Drabek-Hou 2.84
Fassero-Mon 2.99
Reynolds-Hou 3.05

Adjusted ERA
Maddux-Atl 272
Saberhagen-NY 153
Fassero-Mon 142
Drabek-Hou 139
Rijo-Cin 134

Opponents' Batting Avg.
Maddux-Atl .207
Martinez-Mon .220
Drabek-Hou .220
Avery-Atl .227
Fassero-Mon .229

Opponents' On-Base Pct.
Maddux-Atl .245
Saberhagen-NY .273
Drabek-Hou .277
Fassero-Mon .286
Ashby-SD .286

Starter Runs
Maddux-Atl 59.7
Saberhagen-NY 29.1
Drabek-Hou 25.2
Rijo-Cin 21.8
Henry-Mon 21.3

Adjusted Starter Runs
Maddux-Atl 59.9
Saberhagen-NY 28.6
Freeman-Col 23.2
Drabek-Hou 21.8
Henry-Mon 21.4

Clutch Pitching Index
Rijo-Cin 125
Rapp-Fla 122
Smith-Pit 118
Burkett-SF 118
Trachsel-Chi 117

Relief Runs
Jackson-SF 12.8
Brantley-Cin 12.6
Carrasco-Cin 12.4
Jones-Phi 12.3
Jones-Hou 12.1

Adjusted Relief Runs
Jones-Phi 12.5
Jackson-SF 12.5
Brantley-Cin 12.3
Carrasco-Cin 12.1
McElroy-Cin 11.7

Relief Ranking
Brantley-Cin 24.6
Carrasco-Cin 23.6
Jones-Phi 23.6
Wetteland-Mon 19.8
Hoffman-SD 18.8

Total Pitcher Index
Maddux-Atl 7.3
Saberhagen-NY 3.1
Drabek-Hou 2.8
Brantley-Cin 2.5
Jones-Phi 2.4

Total Baseball Ranking
Bagwell-Hou 7.6
Maddux-Atl 7.3
Bonds-SF 5.6
Gwynn-SD 4.1
Mitchell-Cin 4.1

TEAM	G	W	L	PCT	GB	R	OR	AB	H	2B	3B	HR	BB	SO	AVG	OBP	SLG	OPS	OPS+	BR	BR+	PF	CHI	RC	SB	CS	SBA	SBR
EAST																												
NY	113	70	43	.619		670	534	3986	1155	238	16	139	**530**	660	**.290**	**.377**	.462	**839**	**120**	**97**	**125**	96	94	**692**	55	40	58	-2
BAL	112	63	49	.563	6.5	589	**497**	3856	1047	185	20	139	438	655	.272	.352	.438	790	97	13	-15	105	99	606	69	13	**84**	11
TOR	115	55	60	.478	16	566	579	3962	1064	210	30	115	387	691	.269	.339	.424	763	95	-30	-32	100	100	570	79	26	75	8
BOS	115	54	61	.470	17	552	621	3940	1038	222	19	120	404	723	.263	.337	.421	758	90	-39	-64	105	100	558	81	38	68	5
DET	115	53	62	.461	15	652	671	3955	1048	216	25	161	520	897	.265	.355	.454	809	107	42	39	100	100	646	46	33	58	-1
CENTRAL																												
CHI	113	67	46	.593		633	498	3942	1133	175	**39**	121	497	**568**	.287	.370	.444	814	111	58	71	98	95	660	77	27	74	7
CLE	113	66	47	.584	1	**679**	562	4022	**1165**	**240**	20	**167**	382	629	**.290**	.354	**.484**	838	113	73	72	100	101	686	131	48	73	**12**
KC	115	64	51	.557	4	574	532	3911	1051	211	38	100	376	698	.269	.338	.419	757	90	-38	-60	104	105	558	**140**	62	69	9
MIN	113	53	60	.469	14	594	688	3952	1092	239	23	103	359	635	.276	.343	.427	770	97	-20	-20	100	105	578	94	30	76	10
MIL	115	53	62	.461	18	547	586	3978	1045	238	21	99	417	680	.263	.338	.408	746	87	-53	-76	105	100	549	59	37	61	0
WEST																												
TEX	114	52	62	.456		613	697	3983	1114	198	27	124	437	730	.280	.356	.436	792	103	20	22	100	98	622	82	35	70	6
OAK	114	51	63	.447	1	549	589	3885	1009	178	13	113	417	686	.260	.334	.399	733	96	-68	-20	92	**106**	527	91	39	70	6
SEA	112	49	63	.438	2	569	616	3883	1045	211	18	153	372	652	.269	.337	.451	788	99	-1	-12	102	98	585	48	21	70	3
CAL	115	47	68	.409	5.5	543	660	3943	1042	178	16	120	402	715	.264	.336	.409	745	90	-54	-61	101	101	536	65	54	55	-5
TOT	797					8330		55198	15048	2939	325	1774	5938	9619	.273	.348	.435	782							1117	503	69	70

TEAM	CG	SH	SV	IP	H	H/G	HR	BB	SO	RAT	ERA	ERA+	OAV	OOB	PR	PR+	PF	CPI	FA	E	DP	FW	PW	BW	SBW	DIF
EAST																										
NY	8	2	31	1019^{2}	1045	9.3	120	398	656	13.0	4.35	105	.267	.337	52	27	95	104	.982	80	122	.2	2.5	**11.6**	-.6	.0
BAL	13	4	37	997^{2}	1005	9.1	131	**351**	666	12.5	4.32	116	.263	.330	54	74	104	103	**.986**	**57**	103	**1.5**	6.9	-1.3	**.6**	-.4
TOR	13	4	26	1025	1053	9.3	127	482	**832**	13.8	4.70	103	.266	.351	12	14	100	102	.981	81	105	.2	1.3	-2.9	.3	-1.2
BOS	6	3	30	1029^{1}	1104	9.7	120	450	729	13.9	4.94	102	.276	.354	-15	11	105	100	.981	81	124	.2	1.1	-5.9	.0	1.3
DET	15	1	20	1018	1139	10.1	148	449	560	14.3	5.39	90	.282	.358	-66	-61	101	98	.981	82	90	.2	-5.6	3.7	-.6	-2.0
CENTRAL																										
CHI	13	**9**	20	1011^{1}	**964**	**8.6**	115	377	754	**12.1**	**3.97**	**118**	**.250**	**.320**	**94**	81	97	100	.981	79	91	.3	7.5	6.6	.2	-3.9
CLE	**17**	5	21	1018^{2}	1097	9.7	**94**	404	666	13.7	4.37	108	.275	.348	49	41	98	**105**	.980	90	119	-.4	3.8	6.7	**.6**	-1.1
KC	5	6	**38**	1031^{2}	1018	8.9	95	392	717	12.6	4.24	**118**	.260	.332	65	**85**	104	98	.982	80	102	.3	**7.9**	-5.5	.4	3.6
MIN	6	4	29	1005	1197	10.8	153	388	602	14.5	5.68	86	.299	.365	-98	-89	101	100	.982	75	99	.5	-8.2	-1.8	.5	5.7
MIL	11	3	23	1036	1071	9.4	127	421	577	13.3	4.63	109	.269	.343	20	45	105	101	.981	85	**130**	-.0	4.2	-7.0	-.5	-1.1
WEST																										
TEX	10	4	26	1023	1176	10.4	157	394	683	14.1	5.46	88	.288	.355	-75	-72	100	98	.976	106	106	-1.3	-6.6	2.1	.0	.9
OAK	12	**9**	23	1003^{1}	979	8.8	128	510	732	13.7	4.80	92	.257	.350	0	-45	92	98	.979	88	105	-.2	-4.1	-1.8	.0	.2
SEA	13	7	21	984	1051	9.7	109	486	763	14.4	5.00	98	.274	.360	-21	-12	102	99	.977	95	102	-.7	-1.1	-1.1	-.2	-3.8
CAL	11	4	21	1027	1149	10.1	150	436	682	14.3	5.42	90	.287	.363	-70	-59	102	100	.983	76	110	.5	-5.4	-5.6	-.9	1.1
TOT	153	65	366	14229^{2}		9.6				13.6	4.80		.273	.348					.981	1155	1508					

Runs		Hits		Doubles		Triples		Home Runs		Total Bases	
Thomas-Chi	106	Lofton-Cle	160	Knoblauch-Min	45	L.Johnson-Chi	14	Griffey-Sea	40	Belle-Cle	294
Lofton-Cle	105	Molitor-Tor	155	Belle-Cle	35	Coleman-KC	12	Thomas-Chi	38	Griffey-Sea	292
Griffey-Sea	94	Belle-Cle	147	Thomas-Chi	34	Lofton-Cle	9	Belle-Cle	36	Thomas-Chi	291
Phillips-Det	91	Thomas-Chi	141	Fryman-Det	34	Diaz-Mil	7	Canseco-Tex	31	Lofton-Cle	246
Belle-Cle	90							Fielder-Det	28	Palmeiro-Bal	240

Runs Batted In		Runs Produced		Bases On Balls		Batting Average		On-Base Percentage		Slugging Average	
Puckett-Min	112	Puckett-Min	171	Thomas-Chi	109	O'Neill-NY	.359	Thomas-Chi	.494	Thomas-Chi	.729
Carter-Tor	103	Thomas-Chi	169	Tettleton-Det	97	Belle-Cle	.357	O'Neill-NY	.464	Belle-Cle	.714
Thomas-Chi	101	Belle-Cle	155	Phillips-Det	95	Thomas-Chi	.353	Belle-Cle	.442	Griffey-Sea	.674
Belle-Cle	101	Lofton-Cle	150	O'Neill-NY	72	Lofton-Cle	.349	Boggs-NY	.437	O'Neill-NY	.603
Franco-Chi	98	Franco-Chi	150	Henderson-Oak	72	Boggs-NY	.342	Clark-Tex	.436	Hamelin-KC	.599

On-Base Plus Slugging		Adjusted OPS		Batter Runs		Adjusted Batter Runs		Clutch Hitting Index		Runs Created	
Thomas-Chi	1223	Thomas-Chi	214	Thomas-Chi	71.3	Thomas-Chi	74.0	Puckett-Min	143	Thomas-Chi	145
Belle-Cle	1156	Belle-Cle	191	Belle-Cle	56.3	Belle-Cle	56.0	Clark-Tex	122	Belle-Cle	131
Griffey-Sea	1078	O'Neill-NY	179	Griffey-Sea	44.7	O'Neill-NY	46.9	Sorrento-Cle	120	Griffey-Sea	117
O'Neill-NY	1067	Griffey-Sea	168	O'Neill-NY	42.8	Griffey-Sea	42.7	Franco-Chi	120	Lofton-Cle	111
Hamelin-KC	992	Davis-Cal	147	Vaughn-Bos	30.7	Lofton-Cle	30.5	Fryman-Det	118	Molitor-Tor	101

Total Average		Stolen Bases		Stolen Base Average		Stolen Base Runs		Fielding Runs		Total Player Rating	
Thomas-Chi	1.453	Lofton-Cle	60	Molitor-Tor	100.0	Lofton-Cle	9.0	Valentin-Mil	28.1	Thomas-Chi	5.0
Belle-Cle	1.304	Coleman-KC	50	Anderson-Bal	96.9	Coleman-KC	8.2	Espinoza-Cle	24.4	Belle-Cle	5.0
Griffey-Sea	1.174	Nixon-Bos	42	Hulse-Tex	90.0	Anderson-Bal	6.5	Gallego-NY	19.6	Griffey-Sea	4.5
O'Neill-NY	1.152	Knoblauch-Min	35	Coleman-KC	86.2	Nixon-Bos	5.7	Fielder-Det	15.7	Lofton-Cle	4.4
Lofton-Cle	1.101	Anderson-Bal	31	Shumpert-KC	85.7	Knoblauch-Min	5.6	Curtis-Cal	14.6	O'Neill-NY	3.9

Wins		Win Percentage		Games		Complete Games		Shutouts		Saves	
Key-NY	17	Bere-Chi	.857	Wickman-NY	53	Johnson-Sea	9	Johnson-Sea	4	L.Smith-Bal	33
Mussina-Bal	16	Key-NY	.810	Mesa-Cle	51	Martinez-Cle	7			Montgomery-KC	27
Cone-KC	16	Clark-Cle	.786	Guthrie-Min	50	Finley-Cal	7			Aguilera-Min	23
McDonald-Bal	14	Mussina-Bal	.762	Brewer-KC	50					Eckersley-Oak	19
		Cone-KC	.762	Willis-Min	49					Ayala-Sea	18

Innings Pitched		Fewest Hits/Game		Fewest BB/Game		Strikeouts		Strikeouts/Game		Ratio	
Finley-Cal	183.1	Clemens-Bos	6.54	Gubicza-KC	1.80	Johnson-Sea	204	Johnson-Sea	10.67	Ontiveros-Oak	9.75
McDowell-Chi	181.0	Cone-KC	6.82	Gullickson-Det	1.95	Clemens-Bos	168	Clemens-Bos	8.86	Cone-KC	10.01
Eldred-Mil	179.0	Johnson-Sea	6.91	Wegman-Mil	2.02	Finley-Cal	148	Appier-KC	8.42	Clemens-Bos	10.49
Martinez-Cle	176.2	Ontiveros-Oak	7.26	Ontiveros-Oak	2.03	Hentgen-Tor	147	Langston-Cal	8.22	Mussina-Bal	10.51
Mussina-Bal	176.1	Bere-Chi	7.56	McDowell-Chi	2.09	Appier-KC	145	Bere-Chi	8.07	Johnson-Sea	10.99

Earned Run Average		Adjusted ERA		Opponents' Batting Avg.		Opponents' On-Base Pct.		Starter Runs		Adjusted Starter Runs	
Ontiveros-Oak	2.65	Clemens-Bos	177	Clemens-Bos	.203	Ontiveros-Oak	.272	Clemens-Bos	37.2	Clemens-Bos	39.6
Clemens-Bos	2.85	Cone-KC	171	Cone-KC	.209	Cone-KC	.279	Cone-KC	35.7	Cone-KC	37.9
Cone-KC	2.94	Ontiveros-Oak	167	Johnson-Sea	.216	Clemens-Bos	.291	Mussina-Bal	34.2	Mussina-Bal	36.7
Mussina-Bal	3.06	Mussina-Bal	164	Ontiveros-Oak	.217	Mussina-Bal	.294	Johnson-Sea	30.9	Johnson-Sea	31.9
Johnson-Sea	3.19	Johnson-Sea	153	Bere-Chi	.229	Martinez-Cle	.301	Key-NY	28.7	Bones-Mil	29.1

Clutch Pitching Index		Relief Runs		Adjusted Relief Runs		Relief Ranking		Total Pitcher Index		Total Baseball Ranking	
Kamieniecki-NY	124	Eichhorn-Bal	20.9	Eichhorn-Bal	21.6	Eichhorn-Bal	30.7	Cone-KC	4.3	Thomas-Chi	5.0
Key-NY	122	Plunk-Cle	17.9	Plunk-Cle	17.6	Ayala-Sea	21.8	Mussina-Bal	4.1	Belle-Cle	5.0
Clark-Cle	117	Castillo-Tor	17.3	Castillo-Tor	17.4	Plunk-Cle	21.5	Johnson-Sea	3.4	Griffey-Sea	4.5
Mahomes-Min	116	Wickman-NY	13.4	Ryan-Bos	13.2	Fetters-Mil	20.7	Clemens-Bos	3.3	Lofton-Cle	4.4
Stottlemyre-Tor	114	Howe-NY	13.4	Howe-NY	13.0	Ryan-Bos	19.4	Key-NY	3.2	Cone-KC	4.3

TEAM	G	W	L	PCT	GB	R	OR	AB	H	2B	3B	HR	BB	SO	AVG	OBP	SLG	OPS	OPS+	BR	BR+	PF	CHI	RC	SB	CS	SBA	SBR
EAST																												
ATL	144	90	54	.625		645	**540**	4814	1202	210	27	168	520	933	.250	.328	.409	737	96	-10	-30	103	100	647	73	43	63	1
NY	144	69	75	.479	21	657	618	4958	1323	218	34	125	446	994	.267	.333	.400	733	101	-15	7	97	100	657	58	39	60	-1
PHI	144	69	75	.479	21	615	658	4950	1296	263	30	94	497	884	.262	.335	.384	719	94	-33	-37	101	96	648	72	25	74	7
FLA	143	67	76	.469	22.5	673	673	4886	1278	214	29	144	517	916	.262	.338	.406	744	101	9	7	100	99	681	131	53	71	10
MON	144	66	78	.458	24	621	638	4905	1268	265	24	118	400	901	.259	.322	.394	716	90	-49	-69	104	**103**	619	120	49	71	9
CENTRAL																												
CIN	144	85	59	.590		747	623	4903	1326	**277**	35	161	519	946	.270	.345	.440	785	112	77	81	100	100	757	**190**	68	74	**18**
HOU	144	76	68	.528	9	747	674	5097	1403	260	22	109	**566**	992	.275	**.356**	.399	755	**113**	43	**98**	93	100	745	176	60	**75**	**18**
CHI	144	73	71	.507	12	693	671	4963	1315	267	39	158	440	953	.265	.329	.430	759	106	23	36	98	101	698	105	37	74	10
STL	143	62	81	.434	22.5	563	658	4779	1182	238	24	107	436	920	.247	.316	.374	690	86	-89	-87	100	102	562	79	46	63	1
PIT	144	58	86	.403	27	629	736	4937	1281	245	27	125	456	972	.259	.325	.396	721	93	-39	-50	102	101	634	84	55	60	-1
WEST																												
LA	144	78	66	.542		634	609	4942	1303	191	31	140	468	1023	.264	.331	.400	731	106	-18	45	91	98	662	127	45	74	12
COL	144	77	67	.535	1	**785**	783	4994	**1406**	259	**43**	**200**	484	943	**.282**	.352	**.471**	**823**	94	**141**	-41	129	96	**815**	125	59	68	7
SD	144	70	74	.486	8	668	672	4950	1345	231	20	116	447	**872**	.272	.336	.397	733	102	-11	13	97	**103**	657	124	46	73	11
SF	144	67	77	.465	11	652	776	4971	1256	229	33	152	472	1060	.253	.325	.404	729	100	-28	-7	97	101	663	138	46	**75**	14
TOT	1007					9329		69049	18184	3367	418	1917	6668	13309	.264	.334	.408	741							1602	671	70	118

TEAM	CG	SH	SV	IP	H	H/G	HR	BB	SO	RAT	ERA	ERA+	OAV	OOB	PR	PR+	PF	CPI	FA	E	DP	FW	PW	BW	SBW	DIF
EAST																										
ATL	**18**	11	34	1291^{2}	**1184**	**8.3**	**107**	436	**1087**	**11.6**	**3.45**	**124**	.244	**.311**	**106**	**116**	102	99	.982	100	113	.7	**11.5**	-2.9	-.7	9.7
NY	9	9	36	1291	1296	9.1	133	**401**	901	12.1	3.88	104	.262	.322	44	25	97	102	.979	115	125	-.2	2.5	.7	-.9	-4.9
PHI	8	8	41	1290^{1}	1241	8.7	134	538	980	12.8	4.21	100	.254	.335	-4	3	101	97	.982	97	139	.9	.3	-3.6	-.1	-.3
FLA	12	7	29	1286	1299	9.1	139	562	994	13.4	4.27	99	.264	.345	-13	-8	101	103	.979	115	143	-.3	-.7	.7	.2	-4.2
MON	7	9	42	1283^{2}	1286	9.1	128	416	950	12.4	4.11	104	.262	.327	10	26	103	97	.980	109	119	.2	2.6	-6.7	.0	-1.9
CENTRAL																										
CIN	8	10	38	1289^{1}	1270	8.9	131	424	903	12.1	4.04	102	.260	.323	21	12	99	97	**.986**	**79**	140	**2.0**	1.2	8.0	**.9**	1.0
HOU	6	8	32	1320^{1}	1357	9.3	118	460	1056	12.8	4.07	95	.266	.333	17	-31	93	100	.979	121	120	-.6	-3.0	**9.7**	**.9**	-2.9
CHI	6	**12**	**45**	1301	1313	9.1	162	518	926	13.0	4.13	99	.262	.335	7	-4	98	**105**	.979	115	115	-.2	-.3	3.6	.2	-2.0
STL	4	6	38	1265^{2}	1290	9.2	135	445	842	12.7	4.09	102	.268	.335	13	14	100	104	.980	113	**156**	-.1	1.4	-8.5	-.7	-1.4
PIT	11	7	29	1275^{1}	1407	10.0	130	477	871	13.7	4.70	92	.283	.353	-74	-55	103	101	.978	122	138	-.6	-5.4	-4.9	-.9	-2.0
WEST																										
LA	16	11	37	1295	1188	**8.3**	125	462	1060	11.8	3.66	104	**.243**	.313	76	22	91	96	.976	130	120	-1.1	2.2	4.5	.4	.3
COL	1	1	43	1288^{1}	1443	10.1	160	512	891	14.0	4.97	108	.286	.357	-113	47	129	101	.981	107	146	.3	4.7	-4.0	-.1	4.4
SD	6	10	35	1284^{2}	1242	8.8	142	512	1047	12.7	4.14	97	.255	.332	7	-15	96	99	.980	108	130	.2	-1.4	1.3	.3	-2.2
SF	12	5	34	1293^{2}	1368	9.6	173	505	801	13.5	4.87	84	.275	.348	-98	-115	98	98	.980	108	142	.2	-11.3	-.6	.6	6.3
TOT	124	114	513	18056		9.1				12.7	4.19		.264	.334					.981	1539	1846					

Runs
Biggio-Hou 123
Bonds-SF 109
Finley-SD 104
Bichette-Col 102
Larkin-Cin 98

Hits
Gwynn-SD 197
Bichette-Col 197
Grace-Chi 180

Doubles
Grace-Chi 51
McRae-Chi 38
Bichette-Col 38
R.Sanders-Cin 36

Triples
Butler-NY-LA 9
Young-Col 9
D.Sanders-Cin-SF 8
Gonzalez-Hou-Chi 8
Finley-SD 8

Home Runs
Bichette-Col 40
Walker-Col 36
Sosa-Chi 36
Bonds-SF 33

Total Bases
Bichette-Col 359
Walker-Col 300
Castilla-Col 297
Karros-LA 295
Bonds-SF 292

Runs Batted In
Bichette-Col 128
Sosa-Chi 119
Galarraga-Col 106
Karros-LA 105
Conine-Fla 105

Runs Produced
Bichette-Col 190
Bonds-SF 180
Biggio-Hou 178
Grace-Chi 173
Sosa-Chi 172

Bases On Balls
Bonds-SF 120
Weiss-Col 98
Veras-Fla 80
Biggio-Hou 80
Bagwell-Hou 79

Batting Average
Gwynn-SD .368
Piazza-LA .346
Bichette-Col .340
Bell-Hou .334
Grace-Chi .326

On-Base Percentage
Bonds-SF .434
Biggio-Hou .411
Gwynn-SD .408
Weiss-Col .404
Bagwell-Hou .403

Slugging Average
Bichette-Col .620
Walker-Col .607
Piazza-LA .606
R.Sanders-Cin .579
Bonds-SF .577

On-Base Plus Slugging
Bonds-SF 1011
Piazza-LA 1007
Walker-Col 991
Bichette-Col 989
R.Sanders-Cin 980

Adjusted OPS
Piazza-LA 177
Bonds-SF 169
R.Sanders-Cin 155
Karros-LA 149
Gant-Cin 146

Batter Runs
Bonds-SF 51.4
Bichette-Col 42.1
Walker-Col 39.0
R.Sanders-Cin 38.6
Piazza-LA 37.0

Adjusted Batter Runs
Bonds-SF 55.5
Piazza-LA 46.2
Biggio-Hou 39.5
R.Sanders-Cin 39.2
Karros-LA 37.6

Clutch Hitting Index
Bell-Hou 138
Hayes-Phi 128
King-Pit 121
Bagwell-Hou 121
Conine-Fla 116

Runs Created
Bonds-SF 134
Bichette-Col 121
Biggio-Hou 121
R.Sanders-Cin 115
Grace-Chi 115

Total Average
Bonds-SF 1.156
R.Sanders-Cin 1.067
Walker-Col 1.047
Piazza-LA 1.034
Larkin-Cin 1.014

Stolen Bases
Veras-Fla 56
Larkin-Cin 51
DeShields-LA 39
R.Sanders-Cin 36
Finley-SD 36

Stolen Base Average
Larkin-Cin 91.1
Roberts-SD 90.9
Tarasco-Mon 88.9
Mondesi-LA 87.1
Lansing-Mon 87.1

Stolen Base Runs
Larkin-Cin 9.5
Sosa-Chi 5.0
Veras-Fla 5.0
Mondesi-LA 4.5
Lansing-Mon 4.5

Fielding Runs
Branson-Cin 21.5
Reed-SD 18.0
Bagwell-Hou 18.0
Bonds-SF 15.0
C.Garcia-Pit 14.4

Total Player Rating
Bonds-SF 6.7
Biggio-Hou 4.6
Piazza-LA 4.3
R.Sanders-Cin 4.1
Caminiti-SD 4.0

Wins
Maddux-Atl 19
Schourek-Cin 18
Martinez-LA 17
Glavine-Atl 16

Win Percentage
Maddux-Atl .905
Schourek-Cin .720
Martinez-LA .708
Glavine-Atl .696

Games
Leskanic-Col 76
Veres-Hou 72
Reed-Col 71
Perez-Fla 69

Complete Games
Maddux-Atl 10
Leiter-SF 7
Valdes-LA 6
Neagle-Pit 5

Shutouts
Nomo-LA 3
Maddux-Atl 3

Saves
Myers-Chi 38
Henke-StL 36
Beck-SF 33
Worrell-LA 32
Slocumb-Phi 32

Innings Pitched
Neagle-Pit 209.2
Maddux-Atl 209.2
Martinez-LA 206.1
Hamilton-SD 204.1
Navarro-Chi 200.1

Fewest Hits/Game
Nomo-LA 5.83
Maddux-Atl 6.31
Martinez-Mon 7.30
Schourek-Cin 7.47
Valdes-LA 7.65

Fewest BB/Game
Maddux-Atl .99
Reynolds-Hou 1.76
Neagle-Pit 1.93
Saberhagen-NY-Col 1.94
Smiley-Cin 1.99

Strikeouts
Nomo-LA 236
Smoltz-Atl 193
Maddux-Atl 181
Reynolds-Hou 175
Martinez-Mon 174

Strikeouts/Game
Nomo-LA 11.10
Smoltz-Atl 9.02
Reynolds-Hou 8.32
Martinez-Mon 8.04
Foster-Chi 7.84

Ratio
Maddux-Atl 7.47
Nomo-LA 9.74
Schourek-Cin 9.98
Valdes-LA 10.02
Martinez-Mon 10.86

Earned Run Average
Maddux-Atl 1.63
Nomo-LA 2.54
Ashby-SD 2.94
Valdes-LA 3.05
Glavine-Atl 3.08

Adjusted ERA
Maddux-Atl 262
Nomo-LA 149
Glavine-Atl 139
Ashby-SD 137
Smoltz-Atl 134

Opponents' Batting Avg.
Nomo-LA .182
Maddux-Atl .197
Martinez-Mon .227
Valdes-LA .228
Schourek-Cin .228

Opponents' On-Base Pct.
Maddux-Atl .225
Nomo-LA .271
Valdes-LA .279
Schourek-Cin .283
Reynolds-Hou .300

Starter Runs
Maddux-Atl 59.5
Nomo-LA 34.9
Ashby-SD 26.6
Hamilton-SD 25.0
Valdes-LA 24.9

Adjusted Starter Runs
Maddux-Atl 60.2
Nomo-LA 29.4
Glavine-Atl 25.7
Ashby-SD 24.2
Smoltz-Atl 22.9

Clutch Pitching Index
Ashby-SD 127
Neagle-Pit 113
Rapp-Fla 112
Swindell-Hou 111
Castillo-Chi 110

Relief Runs
Veres-Hou 22.0
Reed-Col 19.1
Bottalico-Phi 16.8
Wohlers-Atl 15.1
Worrell-LA 15.0

Adjusted Relief Runs
Reed-Col 23.5
Veres-Hou 19.9
Bottalico-Phi 17.0
Leskanic-Col 16.9
Wohlers-Atl 15.4

Relief Ranking
Wohlers-Atl 30.7
Worrell-LA 22.1
Henke-StL 21.4
Slocumb-Phi 19.2
Reed-Col 19.1

Total Pitcher Index
Maddux-Atl 6.7
Glavine-Atl 3.4
Wohlers-Atl 3.0
Schourek-Cin 2.6
Ashby-SD 2.4

Total Baseball Ranking
Maddux-Atl 6.7
Bonds-SF 6.7
Biggio-Hou 4.6
Piazza-LA 4.3
R.Sanders-Cin 4.1

TEAM	G	W	L	PCT	GB	R	OR	AB	H	2B	3B	HR	BB	SO	AVG	OBP	SLG	OPS	OPS+	BR	BR+	PF	CHI	RC	SB	CS	SBA	SBR
EAST																												
BOS	144	86	58	.597		791	698	4997	1399	**286**	31	175	560	923	.280	.360	.455	815	106	76	50	103	97	818	99	44	69	6
NY	145	79	65	.549	7	749	688	4947	1365	280	34	122	**625**	851	.276	.362	.420	782	104	28	37	99	98	755	50	30	63	1
BAL	144	71	73	.493	15	704	640	4837	1267	229	27	173	574	803	.262	.345	.428	773	99	-3	-14	102	99	716	92	45	67	4
DET	144	60	84	.417	26	654	844	4865	1204	228	29	159	551	987	.247	.329	.404	733	90	-78	-74	99	102	649	73	36	67	3
TOR	144	56	88	.389	30	642	777	5036	1309	275	27	140	492	906	.260	.331	.409	740	92	-69	-64	99	97	687	75	16	**82**	**11**
CENTRAL																												
CLE	144	100	44	.694		**840**	**607**	5028	**1461**	279	23	**207**	542	**766**	**.291**	**.364**	**.479**	**843**	**115**	**122**	**110**	101	98	**868**	**132**	53	71	10
KC	144	70	74	.486	30	629	691	4903	1275	240	35	119	475	849	.260	.331	.396	727	87	-88	-96	101	100	647	120	53	69	8
CHI	145	68	76	.472	32	755	758	5060	1417	252	37	146	576	767	.280	.357	.431	788	109	33	71	95	97	793	110	39	74	**11**
MIL	144	65	79	.451	35	740	747	5000	1329	249	**42**	128	502	800	.266	.338	.409	747	88	-50	-86	106	**109**	702	105	40	72	9
MIN	144	56	88	.389	44	703	889	5005	1398	270	34	120	471	916	.279	.348	.419	767	98	-11	-12	100	99	710	105	57	65	3
WEST																												
SEA	145	79	66	.545		796	708	4996	1377	276	20	182	549	871	.276	.352	.448	800	105	45	38	101	102	794	110	41	73	10
CAL	145	78	67	.538	1	801	697	5019	1390	252	25	186	564	889	.277	.354	.448	802	108	51	59	99	102	795	58	39	60	-1
TEX	144	74	70	.514	4.5	691	720	4913	1304	247	24	138	526	877	.265	.340	.410	750	92	-43	-58	102	102	688	90	47	66	3
OAK	144	67	77	.465	11.5	730	761	4916	1296	228	18	169	565	911	.264	.345	.420	765	104	-15	27	95	102	725	112	46	71	9
TOT	1010					10225		69522	18791	3591	406	2164	7572	12116	.271	.347	.428	774							1331	586	69	88

TEAM	CG	SH	SV	IP	H	H/G	HR	BB	SO	RAT	ERA	ERA+	OAV	OOB	PR	PR+	PF	CPI	FA	E	DP	FW	PW	BW	SBW	DIF
EAST																										
BOS	7	9	39	1292^{2}	1338	9.4	**127**	476	888	13.0	4.40	111	.268	.337	46	66	103	99	.978	120	151	-1.2	6.2	4.7	-.0	4.4
NY	18	5	35	1284^{2}	1286	9.1	159	535	908	13.0	4.57	101	.261	.337	22	8	98	97	**.986**	74	121	1.4	.8	3.5	-.5	2.0
BAL	**19**	**10**	29	1267	**1165**	**8.3**	149	523	930	12.3	4.32	110	**.245**	.325	56	61	101	93	**.986**	**72**	141	**1.5**	5.8	-1.3	-.2	-6.6
DET	5	3	38	1275	1509	10.7	170	536	729	14.8	5.50	87	.296	.368	-110	-103	101	101	.981	106	143	-.4	-9.6	-6.9	-.3	5.4
TOR	16	8	22	1292^{2}	1336	9.4	145	654	894	14.3	4.89	96	.267	.358	-24	-25	100	99	.982	97	131	.1	-2.3	-6.0	**.4**	-8.1
CENTRAL																										
CLE	10	**10**	**50**	1301	1261	8.8	135	**445**	926	**12.2**	**3.84**	**122**	.255	**.322**	**127**	**125**	100	104	.982	101	142	-.1	**11.8**	**10.4**	**.4**	5.8
KC	11	**10**	37	1288	1323	9.3	142	503	763	13.1	4.49	107	.268	.340	32	42	102	100	.984	90	168	.5	4.0	-9.0	.2	2.5
CHI	12	4	36	1284^{2}	1374	9.7	164	617	892	14.3	4.86	92	.275	.359	-20	-61	95	104	.980	108	131	-.5	-5.7	6.7	**.4**	-4.8
MIL	7	4	31	1286	1391	9.8	146	603	699	14.3	4.83	103	.280	.364	-16	22	106	**106**	.981	105	**186**	-.3	2.1	-8.0	.3	-.8
MIN	7	2	27	1272^{2}	1450	10.3	210	533	790	14.3	5.77	83	.287	.359	-149	-139	101	95	.981	100	141	-.0	-13.0	-1.1	-.3	-1.4
WEST																										
SEA	9	8	39	1289^{1}	1343	9.4	149	591	**1068**	13.9	4.50	105	.268	.350	31	34	101	105	.980	104	108	-.2	3.2	3.6	**.4**	-.3
CAL	8	9	42	1284^{1}	1310	9.2	163	486	901	12.9	4.52	104	.265	.336	28	25	100	99	.982	95	120	.3	2.4	5.6	-.7	-1.8
TEX	14	4	34	1285	1385	9.8	152	514	838	13.6	4.66	104	.278	.349	8	23	102	104	.982	98	156	.0	2.2	-5.4	-.3	5.6
OAK	8	4	34	1273	1320	9.4	153	556	890	13.7	4.94	91	.269	.350	-31	-70	95	97	.981	102	151	-.2	-6.5	2.6	.3	-1.0
TOT	151	90	493	17976		9.5				13.5	4.72		.271	.347					.983	1372	1990					

Runs
E.Martinez-Sea 121
Belle-Cle 121
Edmonds-Cal 120
Phillips-Cal 119
Salmon-Cal 111

Hits
Johnson-Chi 186
E.Martinez-Sea 182
Knoblauch-Min 179
Salmon-Cal 177
Baerga-Cle 175

Doubles
E.Martinez-Sea 52
Belle-Cle 52
Puckett-Min 39
Valentin-Bos 37
T.Martinez-Sea 35

Triples
Lofton-Cle 13
Johnson-Chi 12
Anderson-Bal 10
B.Williams-NY 9
Knoblauch-Min 8

Home Runs
Belle-Cle 50
F.Thomas-Chi 40
Buhner-Sea 40

Total Bases
Belle-Cle 377
Palmeiro-Bal 323
E.Martinez-Sea 321
Salmon-Cal 319
Vaughn-Bos 316

Runs Batted In
Vaughn-Bos 126
Belle-Cle 126
Buhner-Sea 121
E.Martinez-Sea 113

Runs Produced
E.Martinez-Sea 205
Belle-Cle 197
Edmonds-Cal 194
Vaughn-Bos 185
Valentin-Bos 183

Bases On Balls
F.Thomas-Chi 136
E.Martinez-Sea 116
Phillips-Cal 113
Tettleton-Tex 107
Thome-Cle 97

Batting Average
E.Martinez-Sea 356
Knoblauch-Min 333
Salmon-Cal 330
Boggs-NY 324
Murray-Cle 323

On-Base Percentage
E.Martinez-Sea 482
F.Thomas-Chi 463
Thome-Cle 440
Davis-Cal 437
Salmon-Cal 432

Slugging Average
Belle-Cle 690
E.Martinez-Sea 628
F.Thomas-Chi 606
Salmon-Cal 594
Palmeiro-Bal 583

On-Base Plus Slugging
E.Martinez-Sea 1110
Belle-Cle 1094
F.Thomas-Chi 1069
Salmon-Cal 1026
Thome-Cle 998

Adjusted OPS
E.Martinez-Sea 184
F.Thomas-Chi 184
Belle-Cle 175
Salmon-Cal 165
Thome-Cle 155

Batter Runs
E.Martinez-Sea 71.5
F.Thomas-Chi 61.9
Belle-Cle 60.6
Salmon-Cal 52.7
McGwire-Oak 45.0

Adjusted Batter Runs
E.Martinez-Sea 70.1
F.Thomas-Chi 69.0
Belle-Cle 58.7
Salmon-Cal 54.0
McGwire-Oak 50.8

Clutch Hitting Index
Blowers-Sea 127
Stanley-NY 121
Clark-Tex 120
Joyner-KC 118
Snow-Cal 113

Runs Created
E.Martinez-Sea 161
F.Thomas-Chi 144
Belle-Cle 144
Salmon-Cal 142
Palmeiro-Bal 123

Total Average
E.Martinez-Sea 1.300
F.Thomas-Chi 1.238
Belle-Cle 1.150
Salmon-Cal 1.112
Thome-Cle 1.106

Stolen Bases
Lofton-Cle 54
Nixon-Tex 50
Goodwin-KC 50
Knoblauch-Min 46
Coleman-KC-Sea 42

Stolen Base Average
Amaral-Sea 91.3
Alomar-Tor 90.9
Javier-Oak 87.8
Johnson-Chi 87.0
Goodwin-Bal 84.6

Stolen Base Runs
Johnson-Chi 6.7
Lofton-Cle 6.6
Javier-Oak 6.2
Alomar-Tor 5.6
Goodwin-KC 4.7

Fielding Runs
Fryman-Det 26.6
Valentin-Mil 19.7
Edmonds-Cal 19.4
Cordova-Min 18.7
Gil-Tex 16.2

Total Player Rating
Belle-Cle 5.8
Salmon-Cal 5.6
E.Martinez-Sea 5.5
Valentin-Bos 4.5
F.Thomas-Chi 4.1

Wins
Mussina-Bal 19
Cone-Tor-NY 18
Johnson-Sea 18
Rogers-Tex 17

Win Percentage
Johnson-Sea 900
Hanson-Bos 750
Nagy-Cle 727
Hershiser-Cle 727
Rogers-Tex 708

Games
Orosco-Bal 65
McDowell-Tex 64
Wickman-NY 63
Belinda-Bos 63
Ayala-Sea 63

Complete Games
McDowell-NY 8
Erickson-Min-Bal 7
Mussina-Bal 7

Shutouts
Mussina-Bal 4
Johnson-Sea 3

Saves
Mesa-Cle 46
Smith-Cal 37
Aguilera-Min-Bos 32
Hernandez-Chi 32

Innings Pitched
Cone-Tor-NY 229.1
Mussina-Bal 221.2
McDowell-NY 217.2
Johnson-Sea 214.1
Gubicza-KC 213.1

Fewest Hits/Game
Johnson-Sea 6.68
Appier-KC 7.29
Wakefield-Bos 7.51
Mussina-Bal 7.59
Cone-Tor-NY 7.65

Fewest BB/Game
Mussina-Bal 2.03
Martinez-Cle 2.21
Radke-Min 2.34
K.Brown-Bal 2.51
Gubicza-KC 2.62

Strikeouts
Johnson-Sea 294
Stottlemyre-Oak 205
Finley-Cal 195
Cone-Tor-NY 191
Appier-KC 185

Strikeouts/Game
Johnson-Sea 12.35
Stottlemyre-Oak 8.80
Finley-Cal 8.65
Appier-KC 8.27
Leiter-Tor 7.52

Ratio
Johnson-Sea 9.66
Mussina-Bal 9.66
Wakefield-Bos 11.06
K.Brown-Bal 11.07
Hershiser-Cle 11.13

Earned Run Average
Johnson-Sea 2.48
Wakefield-Bos 2.95
Martinez-Cle 3.08
Mussina-Bal 3.29
Rogers-Tex 3.38

Adjusted ERA
Johnson-Sea 191
Wakefield-Bos 165
Martinez-Cle 153
Mussina-Bal 145
Rogers-Tex 143

Opponents' Batting Avg.
Johnson-Sea 201
Appier-KC 221
Mussina-Bal 226
Wakefield-Bos 227
Cone-Tor-NY 228

Opponents' On-Base Pct.
Johnson-Sea 267
Mussina-Bal 271
Wakefield-Bos 302
K.Brown-Bal 303
Appier-KC 304

Starter Runs
Johnson-Sea 53.4
Wakefield-Bos 38.4
Mussina-Bal 35.3
Martinez-Cle 34.1
Rogers-Tex 31.1

Adjusted Starter Runs
Johnson-Sea 53.7
Wakefield-Bos 40.5
Mussina-Bal 35.9
Martinez-Cle 33.8
Rogers-Tex 32.9

Clutch Pitching Index
Bosio-Sea 117
Wakefield-Bos 116
Gubicza-KC 114
Martinez-Cle 113
Rogers-Tex 112

Relief Runs
Mesa-Cle 25.6
Percival-Cal 22.8
Nelson-Sea 22.3
Tavarez-Cle 21.6
Plunk-Cle 14.6

Adjusted Relief Runs
Mesa-Cle 25.5
Percival-Cal 22.7
Nelson-Sea 22.4
Tavarez-Cle 21.5
Plunk-Cle 14.5

Relief Ranking
Mesa-Cle 44.6
Tavarez-Cle 27.3
Aguilera-Min-Bos . . . 26.8
Nelson-Sea 26.6
Wetteland-NY 21.3

Total Pitcher Index
Johnson-Sea 4.6
Wakefield-Bos 4.4
Mesa-Cle 4.4
Mussina-Bal 4.0
Rogers-Tex 3.5

Total Baseball Ranking
Belle-Cle 5.8
Salmon-Cal 5.6
E.Martinez-Sea 5.5
Johnson-Sea 4.6
Valentin-Bos 4.5

TEAM	G	W	L	PCT	GB	R	OR	AB	H	2B	3B	HR	BB	SO	AVG	OBP	SLG	OPS	OPS+	BR	BR+	PF	CHI	RC	SB	CS	SBA	SBR
EAST																												
ATL	162	96	66	.593		773	**648**	5614	1514	264	28	197	530	1032	.270	.336	.432	768	101	49	7	106	95	798	83	43	66	3
MON	162	88	74	.543	8	741	668	5505	1441	297	27	148	492	1077	.262	.329	.406	735	96	-14	-31	102	101	739	108	34	**76**	12
FLA	162	80	82	.494	16	688	703	5498	1413	240	30	150	553	1122	.257	.331	.393	724	99	-29	-4	97	95	713	99	46	68	6
NY	162	71	91	.438	25	746	779	5618	1515	267	**47**	147	445	1069	.270	.327	.412	739	104	-10	26	95	100	748	97	48	67	5
PHI	162	67	95	.414	29	650	790	5499	1405	249	39	132	536	1092	.256	.327	.387	714	92	-52	-59	101	93	704	117	41	74	11
CENTRAL																												
STL	162	88	74	.543		759	706	5502	1468	281	31	142	495	1089	.267	.332	.407	739	101	-5	3	99	102	743	149	58	72	12
HOU	162	82	80	.506	6	753	792	5508	1445	297	29	129	554	1057	.262	.339	.397	736	**107**	-1	**63**	92	99	758	180	63	74	18
CIN	162	81	81	.500	7	778	773	5455	1398	259	36	191	604	1134	.256	.334	.422	756	104	29	26	100	99	780	171	63	73	16
CHI	162	76	86	.469	12	772	771	5531	1388	267	19	175	523	1090	.251	.322	.401	723	93	-39	-56	103	**108**	713	108	50	68	6
PIT	162	73	89	.451	15	776	833	5665	1509	**319**	33	138	510	**989**	.266	.331	.407	738	96	-6	-25	103	102	771	126	49	72	11
WEST																												
SD	162	91	71	.562		771	682	5655	1499	285	24	147	601	1014	.265	.341	.402	743	**107**	13	**63**	94	97	772	109	55	66	5
LA	162	90	72	.556	1	703	652	5538	1396	215	33	150	516	1190	.252	.318	.384	702	98	-80	-22	92	105	684	124	40	**76**	13
COL	162	83	79	.512	8	**961**	964	5590	**1607**	297	37	**221**	527	1108	**.287**	**.357**	**.472**	**829**	100	**178**	-3	124	102	**951**	**201**	66	75	**21**
SF	162	68	94	.420	23	752	862	5533	1400	245	21	153	**615**	1189	.253	.333	.388	721	99	-32	-2	96	102	730	113	53	68	6
TOT	1134					10623		77711	20398	3782	434	2220	7501	15252	.263	.333	.409	741							1785	709	72	145

TEAM	CG	SH	SV	IP	H	H/G	HR	BB	SO	RAT	ERA	ERA+	OAV	OOB	PR	PR+	PF	CPI	FA	E	DP	FW	PW	BW	SBW	DIF
EAST																										
ATL	**14**	9	46	1469	1372	**8.5**	120	**451**	**1245**	**11.3**	3.53	**125**	**.247**	**.306**	113	**137**	104	96	.980	130	143	-.0	**13.4**	.7	-.7	1.8
MON	11	7	43	1441[1]	**1353**	**8.5**	152	482	1206	11.9	3.78	114	**.247**	.315	70	84	102	98	.980	126	121	.1	8.3	-3.0	.2	1.6
FLA	8	**13**	41	1443	1386	8.7	**113**	598	1050	12.8	3.96	103	.256	.336	42	19	97	100	.982	111	**187**	1.1	1.9	-.3	-.4	-3.0
NY	10	10	41	1440	1517	9.5	159	532	999	13.1	4.22	95	.272	.340	-1	-36	95	**106**	.974	159	163	-1.9	-3.5	2.6	-.5	-6.5
PHI	12	6	42	1423[1]	1463	9.3	160	510	1044	12.7	4.48	96	.267	.333	-42	-26	102	96	.981	116	145	.8	-2.5	-5.7	.0	-6.4
CENTRAL																										
STL	13	11	43	1452[1]	1380	8.6	173	539	1050	12.2	3.98	105	.251	.322	39	34	99	100	.980	125	139	.2	3.4	.3	.2	3.1
HOU	13	4	35	1447	1541	9.6	154	539	1163	13.4	4.37	89	.274	.345	-24	-88	92	104	.978	138	130	-.6	-8.5	**6.2**	.8	3.4
CIN	6	8	**52**	1443	1447	9.1	167	591	1089	13.0	4.32	98	.263	.339	-16	-14	100	102	.980	121	145	.5	-1.3	2.6	.6	-2.1
CHI	10	10	34	1456[1]	1447	9.0	184	546	1027	12.7	4.36	99	.260	.332	-23	-5	103	99	**.983**	**104**	147	**1.5**	-.4	-5.4	-.4	-.0
PIT	5	7	37	1453[1]	1602	10.0	183	479	1044	13.2	4.61	95	.281	.342	-63	-39	103	103	.980	128	144	.0	-3.8	-2.4	.0	-1.7
WEST																										
SD	5	11	47	1489	1395	**8.5**	138	506	1194	11.8	3.73	107	.248	.315	81	43	94	97	.981	118	136	.6	4.3	**6.2**	-.5	-.4
LA	6	9	50	1466[1]	1378	**8.5**	125	534	1212	12.0	**3.47**	111	.249	.320	**123**	70	92	**106**	.980	125	143	.2	6.9	-2.1	.3	3.9
COL	5	4	34	1422[2]	1597	10.2	198	624	932	14.5	5.60	93	.285	.364	-218	-48	124	95	.976	149	167	-1.3	-4.6	-.2	**1.0**	7.3
SF	9	8	35	1442[1]	1520	9.5	194	570	997	13.5	4.72	87	.273	.348	-80	-103	97	102	.978	136	165	-.5	-10.0	-.1	-.4	-1.7
TOT	127	117	580	20289		9.1				12.7	4.22		.263	.333					.980	1786	2075					

Runs
Burks-Col 142
Finley-SD 126
Bonds-SF 122
Galarraga-Col 119
Sheffield-Fla 118

Hits
Johnson-NY 227
Burks-Col 211
Grissom-Atl 207
Grudzielanek-Mon . . . 201
Bichette-Col 198

Doubles
Bagwell-Hou 48
Finley-SD 45
Burks-Col 45
Gilkey-NY 44
Rodriguez-Mon 42

Triples
Johnson-NY 21
Howard-Cin 10
Grissom-Atl 10
Finley-SD 9

Home Runs
Galarraga-Col 47
Sheffield-Fla 42
Bonds-SF 42
Hundley-NY 41

Total Bases
Burks-Col 392
Galarraga-Col 376
Finley-SD 348
Castilla-Col 345
Caminiti-SD 339

Runs Batted In
Galarraga-Col 150
Bichette-Col 141
Caminiti-SD 130
Bonds-SF 129
Burks-Col 128

Runs Produced
Burks-Col 230
Bichette-Col 224
Galarraga-Col 222
Bonds-SF 209
Bagwell-Hou 200

Bases On Balls
Bonds-SF 151
Sheffield-Fla 142
Bagwell-Hou 135
Henderson-SD 125
Larkin-Cin 96

Batting Average
Gwynn-SD 353
Burks-Col 344
Piazza-LA 336
Johnson-NY 333
Grace-Chi 331

On-Base Percentage
Sheffield-Fla 469
Bonds-SF 465
Bagwell-Hou 454
Piazza-LA 423
Larkin-Cin 415

Slugging Average
Burks-Col 639
Sheffield-Fla 624
Caminiti-SD 621
Bonds-SF 615
Galarraga-Col 601

On-Base Plus Slugging
Sheffield-Fla 1094
Bonds-SF 1080
Burks-Col 1048
Caminiti-SD 1035
Bagwell-Hou 1025

Adjusted OPS
Sheffield-Fla 192
Bonds-SF 189
Bagwell-Hou 182
Caminiti-SD 179
Piazza-LA 171

Batter Runs
Sheffield-Fla 72.3
Bonds-SF 69.2
Bagwell-Hou 63.3
Burks-Col 61.6
Caminiti-SD 54.2

Adjusted Batter Runs
Sheffield-Fla 77.6
Bagwell-Hou 76.0
Bonds-SF 75.3
Caminiti-SD 62.5
Piazza-LA 57.6

Clutch Hitting Index
Jordan-StL 128
Bell-Hou 128
Pendleton-Fla-Atl . . . 121
Joyner-SD 121
Reed-SD 121

Runs Created
Bonds-SF 162
Sheffield-Fla 159
Burks-Col 158
Bagwell-Hou 156
Caminiti-SD 138

Total Average
Bonds-SF 1.338
Sheffield-Fla 1.268
Bagwell-Hou 1.175
Burks-Col 1.136
Caminiti-SD 1.101

Stolen Bases
Young-Col 53
Johnson-NY 50
DeShields-LA 48
Bonds-SF 40
Martin-Pit 38

Stolen Base Average
Bell-Hou 90.6
Walker-Col 90.0
Renteria-Fla 88.9
Owens-Cin 88.9
Bonds-SF 85.1

Stolen Base Runs
Johnson-NY 6.8
DeShields-LA 6.7
Bonds-SF 6.3
Bell-Hou 5.3
Lankford-StL 5.3

Fielding Runs
Young-Col 27.9
Castilla-Col 27.6
Gilkey-NY 24.1
Andrews-Mon 21.0
Lopez-Atl 18.5

Total Player Rating
Bonds-SF 8.3
Caminiti-SD 7.3
Bagwell-Hou 6.7
Gilkey-NY 6.4
Larkin-Cin 5.9

Wins
Smoltz-Atl 24
A.Benes-StL 18
Ritz-Col 17
Brown-Fla 17

Win Percentage
Smoltz-Atl 750
Martinez-LA 714
Valdes-LA 682
A.Benes-StL 643
Neagle-Pit-Atl 640

Games
Clontz-Atl 81
Patterson-Chi 79
Shaw-Cin 78
Dewey-SF 78
Wohlers-Atl 77

Complete Games
Schilling-Phi 8
Smoltz-Atl 6

Shutouts
Brown-Fla 3

Saves
Worrell-LA 44
Brantley-Cin 44
Hoffman-SD 42
Wohlers-Atl 39
Rojas-Mon 36

Innings Pitched
Smoltz-Atl 253.2
Maddux-Atl 245.0
Reynolds-Hou 239.0
Navarro-Chi 236.2
Glavine-Atl 235.1

Fewest Hits/Game
Leiter-Fla 6.39
Smoltz-Atl 7.06
Nomo-LA 7.09
Brown-Fla 7.22
Schilling-Phi 7.31

Fewest BB/Game
Maddux-Atl 1.03
Brown-Fla 1.27
Darwin-Pit-Hou 1.48
Reynolds-Hou 1.66
Tewksbury-SD 1.87

Strikeouts
Smoltz-Atl 276
Nomo-LA 234
Martinez-Mon 222
Fassero-Mon 222
Kile-Hou 219

Strikeouts/Game
Smoltz-Atl 9.79
Nomo-LA 9.22
Martinez-Mon 9.22
Kile-Hou 9.00
Schilling-Phi 8.93

Ratio
Smoltz-Atl 9.08
Brown-Fla 9.12
Maddux-Atl 9.40
Schilling-Phi 9.92
Reynolds-Hou 10.51

Earned Run Average
Brown-Fla 1.89
Maddux-Atl 2.72
Leiter-Fla 2.93
Smoltz-Atl 2.94
Glavine-Atl 2.98

Adjusted ERA
Brown-Fla 215
Maddux-Atl 162
Smoltz-Atl 150
Glavine-Atl 148
Trachsel-Chi 143

Opponents' Batting Avg.
Leiter-Fla 202
Smoltz-Atl 216
Nomo-LA 218
Brown-Fla 220
Schilling-Phi 223

Opponents' On-Base Pct.
Smoltz-Atl 261
Brown-Fla 263
Maddux-Atl 265
Schilling-Phi 280
Reynolds-Hou 290

Starter Runs
Brown-Fla 60.3
Maddux-Atl 41.0
Smoltz-Atl 36.0
Glavine-Atl 32.4
Leiter-Fla 31.0

Adjusted Starter Runs
Brown-Fla 58.6
Maddux-Atl 44.1
Smoltz-Atl 39.5
Glavine-Atl 35.7
Trachsel-Chi 29.0

Clutch Pitching Index
Trachsel-Chi 120
Valenzuela-SD 118
Martinez-LA 115
Drabek-Hou 114
Astacio-LA 114

Relief Runs
Nen-Fla 20.9
Shaw-Cin 20.1
Hoffman-SD 19.3
Ryan-Phi 17.8
Guthrie-LA 16.3

Adjusted Relief Runs
Nen-Fla 20.3
Shaw-Cin 20.2
Ryan-Phi 18.3
Hoffman-SD 17.9
Adams-Chi 15.3

Relief Ranking
Hoffman-SD 35.8
Nen-Fla 28.3
J.Franco-NY 27.5
Shaw-Cin 25.7
Brantley-Cin 21.1

Total Pitcher Index
Brown-Fla 7.6
Maddux-Atl 5.4
Smoltz-Atl 5.2
Glavine-Atl 4.6
Hoffman-SD 3.5

Total Baseball Ranking
Bonds-SF 8.3
Brown-Fla 7.6
Caminiti-SD 7.3
Bagwell-Hou 6.7
Gilkey-NY 6.4

TEAM	G	W	L	PCT	GB	R	OR	AB	H	2B	3B	HR	BB	SO	AVG	OBP	SLG	OPS	OPS+	BR	BR+	PF	CHI	RC	SB	CS	SBA	SBR
EAST																												
NY	162	92	70	.568		871	787	5628	1621	293	28	162	632	909	.288	.364	.436	800	101	16	17	100	98	890	96	46	68	5
BAL	163	88	74	.543	4	949	903	5689	1557	299	29	**257**	645	915	.274	.354	.472	826	107	50	57	99	102	948	76	40	66	3
BOS	162	85	77	.525	7	928	921	5756	1631	308	31	209	642	1020	.283	.362	.457	819	103	47	30	102	99	948	91	44	67	5
TOR	162	74	88	.457	18	766	809	5599	1451	302	35	177	529	1105	.259	.333	.420	753	89	-101	-97	100	101	794	116	38	75	12
DET	162	53	109	.327	39	783	1103	5530	1413	257	21	204	546	1268	.256	.326	.420	746	87	-121	-119	100	**108**	746	87	50	64	2
CENTRAL																												
CLE	161	99	62	.615		952	**769**	5681	**1665**	335	23	218	671	**844**	**.293**	**.372**	.475	847	**113**	109	115	99	96	1003	160	50	**76**	**18**
CHI	162	85	77	.525	14.5	898	794	5644	1586	284	33	195	**701**	927	.281	.364	.447	811	108	35	82	95	98	926	105	41	72	9
MIL	162	80	82	.494	19.5	894	899	5662	1578	304	40	178	624	986	.279	.356	.441	797	96	0	-31	104	102	899	101	48	68	5
MIN	162	78	84	.481	21.5	877	900	5673	1633	332	**47**	118	576	958	.288	.360	.425	785	96	-15	-28	102	103	860	143	53	73	13
KC	161	75	86	.466	24	746	786	5542	1477	286	38	123	529	943	.267	.335	.398	733	84	-132	-130	100	104	750	**195**	85	70	13
WEST																												
TEX	163	90	72	.556		928	799	5702	1622	323	32	221	660	1041	.284	.362	.469	831	103	67	21	105	98	975	83	26	**76**	9
SEA	161	85	76	.528	4.5	**993**	895	5668	1625	**343**	19	245	670	1052	.287	.370	**.484**	**854**	**113**	**117**	**118**	100	99	**1024**	90	39	70	6
OAK	162	78	84	.481	12	861	900	5630	1492	283	21	243	640	1114	.265	.346	.452	798	101	-8	11	98	100	880	58	35	62	1
CAL	161	70	91	.435	19.5	762	943	5686	1571	256	24	192	527	974	.276	.341	.431	772	93	-62	-64	100	96	814	53	39	58	-2
TOT	1133					12208		79090	21922	4205	421	2742	8592	14056	.278	.354	.445	798							1454	634	70	98

TEAM	CG	SH	SV	IP	H	H/G	HR	BB	SO	RAT	ERA	ERA+	OAV	OOB	PR	PR+	PF	CPI	FA	E	DP	FW	PW	BW	SBW	DIF
EAST																										
NY	6	**9**	**52**	1440	**1469**	**9.2**	**143**	610	1139	13.4	4.66	106	**.265**	.343	55	46	99	95	.985	91	146	1.3	4.2	1.6	-.2	4.3
BAL	13	1	44	1468^2	1604	9.9	209	597	1047	13.8	5.15	96	.280	.352	-25	-37	99	99	.984	97	173	1.0	-3.3	5.2	-.4	4.7
BOS	17	5	37	1458	1606	10.0	185	722	**1165**	14.7	4.99	102	.279	.364	1	14	102	103	.978	135	152	-1.2	1.3	2.8	-.2	1.5
TOR	**19**	7	35	1445^2	1476	**9.2**	187	610	1033	13.3	4.57	109	.266	.343	68	69	100	101	.982	110	187	.2	6.3	-8.8	.5	-5.0
DET	10	4	22	1432^2	1699	10.7	241	784	957	16.2	6.38	79	.296	.389	-221	-209	101	97	.978	137	157	-1.3	-19.0	-10.8	-.5	3.7
CENTRAL																										
CLE	13	**9**	46	1452^1	1530	9.5	173	484	1033	**12.8**	**4.34**	**113**	.271	**.333**	**105**	**90**	98	102	.980	124	156	-.6	**8.3**	10.5	**1.0**	-.5
CHI	7	4	43	1461	1529	9.5	174	616	1039	13.5	4.52	105	.270	.345	77	39	95	102	.982	109	145	.3	3.6	7.5	.2	-7.4
MIL	6	4	42	1447^1	1570	9.8	213	635	846	14.1	5.14	101	.278	.357	-23	8	104	101	.978	134	180	-1.1	.8	-2.8	-.2	2.5
MIN	13	5	31	1439^2	1561	9.8	233	581	959	13.7	5.28	97	.277	.348	-46	-26	102	97	.984	94	142	1.1	-2.3	-2.5	.5	.4
KC	17	8	35	1450	1563	9.8	176	**460**	926	13.0	4.55	110	.277	.338	71	73	100	101	.982	111	184	.1	6.7	-11.8	.5	-.9
WEST																										
TEX	**19**	6	43	1449^1	1569	9.8	168	582	976	13.7	4.66	**113**	.278	.350	55	**90**	105	103	**.986**	**87**	150	**1.5**	**8.3**	2.0	.2	-2.7
SEA	4	4	34	1431^2	1562	9.9	216	605	1000	14.0	5.22	95	.279	.356	-35	-43	99	99	.982	110	155	.2	-3.9	**10.8**	-.0	-2.3
OAK	7	5	34	1456^1	1638	10.2	205	644	884	14.5	5.20	95	.287	.365	-33	-45	99	**104**	.984	103	**195**	.6	-4.1	1.1	-.5	.1
CAL	12	8	38	1439	1546	9.7	219	662	1052	14.4	5.30	94	.275	.360	-49	-47	100	99	.979	128	156	-.8	-4.2	-5.8	-.8	1.4
TOT	163	79	536	20271^2		9.8				13.9	5.00		.278	.354					.982	1570	2278					

Runs
Rodriguez-Sea 141
Knoblauch-Min 140
Lofton-Cle 132
Alomar-Bal 132
Griffey-Sea 125

Hits
Molitor-Min 225
Rodriguez-Sea 215
Lofton-Cle 210
Vaughn-Bos 207
Knoblauch-Min 197

Doubles
Rodriguez-Sea 54
E.Martinez-Sea 52
Rodriguez-Tex 47
Cordova-Min 46
Cirillo-Mil 46

Triples
Knoblauch-Min 14
Vina-Mil 10

Home Runs
McGwire-Oak 52
Anderson-Bal 50
Griffey-Sea 49
Belle-Cle 48
Gonzalez-Tex 47

Total Bases
Rodriguez-Sea 379
Belle-Cle 375
Vaughn-Bos 370
Anderson-Bal 369
Gonzalez-Tex 348

Runs Batted In
Belle-Cle 148
Gonzalez-Tex 144
Vaughn-Bos 143
Palmeiro-Bal 142
Griffey-Sea 140

Runs Produced
Rodriguez-Sea 228
Belle-Cle 224
Vaughn-Bos 217
Griffey-Sea 216
Palmeiro-Bal 213

Bases On Balls
Phillips-Chi 125
Thome-Cle 123
E.Martinez-Sea 123
McGwire-Oak 116
F.Thomas-Chi 109

Batting Average
Rodriguez-Sea .358
F.Thomas-Chi .349
Molitor-Min .341
Knoblauch-Min .341
Greer-Tex .332

On-Base Percentage
McGwire-Oak .468
E.Martinez-Sea .467
F.Thomas-Chi .465
Knoblauch-Min .452
Thome-Cle .451

Slugging Average
McGwire-Oak .730
Gonzalez-Tex .643
Anderson-Bal .637
Rodriguez-Sea .631
Griffey-Sea .628

On-Base Plus Slugging
McGwire-Oak 1199
F.Thomas-Chi 1091
Thome-Cle 1063
E.Martinez-Sea 1062
Rodriguez-Sea 1049

Adjusted OPS
McGwire-Oak 201
F.Thomas-Chi 181
Thome-Cle 166
E.Martinez-Sea 166
Rodriguez-Sea 160

Batter Runs
McGwire-Oak 67.3
F.Thomas-Chi 63.3
E.Martinez-Sea 57.1
Thome-Cle 55.6
Rodriguez-Sea 54.6

Adjusted Batter Runs
F.Thomas-Chi 71.1
McGwire-Oak 70.3
E.Martinez-Sea 57.2
Thome-Cle 56.4
Rodriguez-Sea 54.7

Clutch Hitting Index
Molitor-Min 129
Cordova-Min 120
Elster-Tex 117
Tartabull-Chi 117
O'Leary-Bos 116

Runs Created
Vaughn-Bos 158
Rodriguez-Sea 157
Belle-Cle 156
Anderson-Bal 150
F.Thomas-Chi 150

Total Average
McGwire-Oak 1.420
E.Martinez-Sea 1.209
Thome-Cle 1.207
F.Thomas-Chi 1.203
Griffey-Sea 1.139

Stolen Bases
Lofton-Cle 75
Goodwin-KC 66
Nixon-Tor 54
Knoblauch-Min 45
Vizquel-Cle 35

Stolen Base Average
Griffey-Sea 94.1
Durham-Chi 88.2
Listach-Mil 83.3
Damon-KC 83.3
Frye-Bos 81.8

Stolen Base Runs
Lofton-Cle 10.6
Nixon-Tor 7.3
Goodwin-KC 6.8
Durham-Chi 5.2
Knoblauch-Min 5.0

Fielding Runs
Becker-Min 23.9
Gonzalez-Tor 22.7
McLemore-Tex 20.1
Howard-KC 18.8
Fryman-Det 17.1

Total Player Rating
Griffey-Sea 5.8
Anderson-Bal 5.3
Rodriguez-Sea 5.3
Belle-Cle 5.2
Alomar-Bal 5.2

Wins
Pettitte-NY 21
Hentgen-Tor 20
Mussina-Bal 19
Nagy-Cle 17

Win Percentage
Nagy-Cle .773
Pettitte-NY .724
Hentgen-Tor .667
Pavlik-Tex .652
Mussina-Bal .633

Games
Myers-Det 83
Guardado-Min 83
Stanton-Bos-Tex 81
Slocumb-Bos 75

Complete Games
Hentgen-Tor 10
Pavlik-Tex 7
Hill-Tex 7

Shutouts
Robertson-Min 3
Hill-Tex 3
Hentgen-Tor 3
Lira-Det 2
Clemens-Bos 2

Saves
Wetteland-NY 43
Mesa-Cle 39
Hernandez-Chi 38
Percival-Cal 36
Fetters-Mil 32

Innings Pitched
Hentgen-Tor 265.2
Fernandez-Chi 258.0
Hill-Tex 250.2
Mussina-Bal 243.1
Clemens-Bos 242.2

Fewest Hits/Game
Guzman-Tor 7.58
Clemens-Bos 8.01
Hentgen-Tor 8.06
Appier-KC 8.18
Fernandez-Chi 8.65

Fewest BB/Game
Haney-KC 2.01
Wells-Bal 2.05
Radke-Min 2.21
Nagy-Cle 2.47
Fernandez-Chi 2.51

Strikeouts
Clemens-Bos 257
Finley-Cal 215
Appier-KC 207
Mussina-Bal 204
Fernandez-Chi 200

Strikeouts/Game
Clemens-Bos 9.53
Appier-KC 8.82
Finley-Cal 8.13
Guzman-Tor 7.91
Mussina-Bal 7.55

Ratio
Guzman-Tor 10.45
Radke-Min 11.33
Nagy-Cle 11.39
Fernandez-Chi 11.41
Hentgen-Tor 11.42

Earned Run Average
Guzman-Tor 2.93
Hentgen-Tor 3.22
Nagy-Cle 3.41
Fernandez-Chi 3.45
Appier-KC 3.62

Adjusted ERA
Guzman-Tor 171
Hentgen-Tor 156
Hill-Tex 145
Nagy-Cle 144
Clemens-Bos 140

Opponents' Batting Avg.
Guzman-Tor .228
Clemens-Bos .237
Hentgen-Tor .241
Appier-KC .245
Fernandez-Chi .253

Opponents' On-Base Pct.
Guzman-Tor .290
Radke-Min .304
Nagy-Cle .307
Fernandez-Chi .309
Hentgen-Tor .310

Starter Runs
Hentgen-Tor 52.6
Fernandez-Chi 44.3
Guzman-Tor 43.2
Nagy-Cle 39.3
Hill-Tex 38.2

Adjusted Starter Runs
Hentgen-Tor 52.8
Guzman-Tor 43.4
Hill-Tex 43.0
Fernandez-Chi 39.1
Clemens-Bos 38.3

Clutch Pitching Index
Belcher-KC 117
Fernandez-Chi 113
Hill-Tex 112
Pettitte-NY 111
Boskie-Cal 111

Relief Runs
M.Rivera-NY 34.8
Hernandez-Chi 29.0
Plunk-Cle 22.1
Percival-Cal 22.1
James-Cal 21.0

Adjusted Relief Runs
M.Rivera-NY 34.5
Hernandez-Chi 28.1
Percival-Cal 22.1
Plunk-Cle 21.7
James-Cal 21.0

Relief Ranking
Hernandez-Chi 56.2
M.Rivera-NY 34.8
Slocumb-Bos 33.5
Wetteland-NY 30.1
Percival-Cal 25.9

Total Pitcher Index
Hernandez-Chi 5.2
Hentgen-Tor 5.2
Hill-Tex 4.0
Guzman-Tor 3.8
Fernandez-Chi 3.7

Total Baseball Ranking
Griffey-Sea 5.8
Anderson-Bal 5.3
Rodriguez-Sea 5.3
Belle-Cle 5.2
Hernandez-Chi 5.2

TEAM	G	W	L	PCT	GB	R	OR	AB	H	2B	3B	HR	BB	SO	AVG	OBP	SLG	OPS	OPS+	BR	BR+	PF	CHI	RC	SB	CS	SBA	SBR
EAST																												
ATL	162	101	61	.623		791	**581**	5528	1490	268	37	174	597	1160	.270	.346	.426	772	105	56	40	102	98	810	108	58	65	3
FLA	162	92	70	.568	9	740	669	5439	1410	272	28	136	**686**	**1074**	.259	.349	.395	744	105	11	48	95	97	763	115	58	66	5
NY	162	88	74	.543	13	777	709	5524	1448	274	28	153	550	1029	.262	.335	.405	740	102	-11	17	96	**106**	742	97	74	57	-5
MON	162	78	84	.481	23	691	740	5526	1423	**339**	34	172	420	1084	.258	.318	.425	743	98	-24	-20	100	97	741	75	46	62	0
PHI	162	68	94	.420	33	668	840	5443	1390	290	35	116	519	1032	.255	.325	.385	710	91	-72	-70	100	101	685	92	56	62	1
CENTRAL																												
HOU	162	84	78	.519		777	660	5502	1427	314	40	133	633	1085	.259	.346	.403	749	105	20	52	96	100	794	171	74	70	12
PIT	162	79	83	.488	5	725	760	5503	1440	291	**52**	129	481	1161	.262	.331	.404	735	96	-24	-35	102	101	753	160	50	**76**	**18**
CIN	162	76	86	.469	8	651	764	5484	1386	269	27	142	518	1113	.253	.322	.389	711	90	-72	-79	101	98	701	**190**	67	74	**18**
STL	162	73	89	.451	11	689	708	5524	1409	269	39	144	543	1191	.255	.326	.396	722	95	-50	-42	99	100	717	164	60	73	15
CHI	162	68	94	.420	16	687	759	5489	1444	269	39	127	451	1003	.263	.323	.396	719	91	-61	-76	102	103	692	116	60	66	5
WEST																												
SF	162	90	72	.556		784	793	5485	1415	266	37	172	642	1120	.258	.341	.414	755	105	21	44	97	101	789	121	49	71	9
LA	162	88	74	.543	2	742	645	5544	1488	242	33	174	498	1079	.268	.332	.418	750	**110**	3	66	92	99	768	131	64	67	6
COL	162	83	79	.512	7	**923**	908	5603	**1611**	269	40	**239**	562	1060	**.288**	**.359**	**.478**	**837**	100	**180**	6	123	98	**949**	137	65	68	7
SD	162	76	86	.469	14	795	891	5609	1519	275	16	152	604	1129	.271	.345	.407	752	**110**	21	**84**	93	102	795	140	60	70	10
TOT	1134					10440		77203	20300	3907	485	2163	7704	15320	.263	.336	.411	746							1817	841	68	105

TEAM	CG	SH	SV	IP	H	H/G	HR	BB	SO	RAT	ERA	ERA+	OAV	OOB	PR	PR+	PF	CPI	FA	E	DP	FW	PW	BW	SBW	DIF
EAST																										
ATL	21	**17**	37	1465^{2}	**1319**	**8.1**	**111**	**450**	1196	**11.1**	**3.19**	**132**	**.241**	**.303**	**166**	**166**	100	100	.982	114	136	.4	**16.4**	4.0	-.4	-.1
FLA	12	10	39	1446^{2}	1353	8.5	131	639	1188	12.8	3.83	105	.250	.336	60	34	96	103	.981	116	167	.3	3.4	4.8	-.2	3.0
NY	7	8	**49**	1459^{1}	1452	9.0	160	504	982	12.4	3.95	102	.262	.328	41	14	96	103	.981	120	165	.0	1.4	1.7	-1.2	5.2
MON	**27**	14	37	1447	1365	8.5	149	557	1138	12.4	4.14	101	.250	.327	10	9	100	94	.979	132	150	-.7	.9	-1.9	-.7	-.4
PHI	13	7	35	1420^{1}	1441	9.2	171	616	1209	13.5	4.85	88	.265	.346	-102	-95	101	93	.982	108	134	.7	-9.3	-6.8	-.6	3.3
CENTRAL																										
HOU	16	12	37	1459	1379	8.6	134	511	1138	12.0	3.67	109	.251	.321	87	56	95	101	.979	131	169	-.6	5.6	5.2	.4	-7.4
PIT	6	8	41	1436	1503	9.5	143	560	1080	13.4	4.29	100	.271	.345	-13	1	102	103	.979	131	149	-.6	.1	-3.4	**1.0**	1.0
CIN	5	8	**49**	1449	1408	8.8	173	558	1159	12.7	4.41	97	.255	.332	-34	-23	102	94	.982	**106**	129	**.8**	-2.2	-7.7	**1.0**	3.3
STL	5	3	39	1455^{2}	1422	8.8	124	536	1130	12.5	3.88	107	.259	.331	52	44	99	101	.980	123	156	-.1	4.4	-4.1	.7	-8.7
CHI	6	4	37	1429	1451	9.2	185	590	1072	13.2	4.45	97	.266	.342	-38	-22	102	102	.981	112	117	.5	-2.1	-7.4	-.2	-3.5
WEST																										
SF	5	9	45	1446	1494	9.3	160	578	1044	13.2	4.40	93	.270	.343	-31	-52	97	101	.980	125	157	-.3	-5.1	4.4	.1	10.0
LA	6	6	45	1459^{1}	1325	8.2	163	546	**1232**	11.9	3.63	106	**.241**	.315	94	41	92	100	.981	116	104	.3	4.1	6.6	-.2	-3.6
COL	9	5	38	1432^{2}	1697	10.7	196	566	870	14.7	5.26	98	.300	.370	-167	-11	123	**105**	**.983**	111	**202**	.6	-1.0	.6	-.0	2.1
SD	5	2	43	1450	1581	9.9	172	596	1059	13.9	4.98	78	.280	.355	-125	-192	92	97	.979	132	132	-.7	-18.9	**8.3**	.2	6.2
TOT	143	113	571	20255^{2}		9.0				12.8	4.21		.263	.336					.981	1677	2067					

Runs	
Biggio-Hou	146
Walker-Col	143
Bonds-SF	123
Galarraga-Col	120
Bagwell-Hou	109

Hits	
Gwynn-SD	220
Walker-Col	208
Piazza-LA	201

Doubles	
Grudzielanek-Mon	54
Gwynn-SD	49
Walker-Col	46
Lansing-Mon	45
Mondesi-LA	42

Triples	
DeShields-StL	14
Perez-Col	10
Womack-Pit	9
Randa-Pit	9
Guerrero-LA	9

Home Runs	
Walker-Col	49
Bagwell-Hou	43
Galarraga-Col	41

Total Bases	
Walker-Col	409
Piazza-LA	355
Galarraga-Col	351
Castilla-Col	335
Bagwell-Hou	335

Runs Batted In	
Galarraga-Col	140
Bagwell-Hou	135
Walker-Col	130
Piazza-LA	124
Kent-SF	121

Runs Produced	
Walker-Col	224
Galarraga-Col	219
Biggio-Hou	205
Bagwell-Hou	201
Gwynn-SD	199

Bases On Balls	
Bonds-SF	145
Bagwell-Hou	127
Sheffield-Fla	121
Snow-SF	96
Lankford-StL	95

Batting Average	
Gwynn-SD	.372
Walker-Col	.366
Piazza-LA	.362
Lofton-Atl	.333
Joyner-SD	.327

On-Base Percentage	
Walker-Col	.455
Bonds-SF	.450
Piazza-LA	.435
Bagwell-Hou	.430
Sheffield-Fla	.426

Slugging Average	
Walker-Col	.720
Piazza-LA	.638
Bagwell-Hou	.592
Galarraga-Col	.585
Lankford-StL	.585

On-Base Plus Slugging	
Walker-Col	1175
Piazza-LA	1073
Bonds-SF	1034
Bagwell-Hou	1022
Lankford-StL	999

Adjusted OPS	
Piazza-LA	191
Bonds-SF	173
Bagwell-Hou	171
Walker-Col	164
Gwynn-SD	162

Batter Runs	
Walker-Col	84.9
Piazza-LA	62.3
Bonds-SF	60.0
Bagwell-Hou	57.7
Galarraga-Col	43.6

Adjusted Batter Runs	
Piazza-LA	73.9
Bonds-SF	64.3
Bagwell-Hou	63.5
Walker-Col	54.4
Gwynn-SD	52.4

Clutch Hitting Index	
Alou-Fla	128
Kent-SF	125
Joyner-SD	121
Bichette-Col	120
Olerud-NY	118

Runs Created	
Walker-Col	187
Bagwell-Hou	153
Bonds-SF	151
Piazza-LA	150
Biggio-Hou	148

Total Average	
Walker-Col	1.373
Bonds-SF	1.239
Bagwell-Hou	1.177
Piazza-LA	1.149
Lankford-StL	1.083

Stolen Bases	
Womack-Pit	60
D.Sanders-Cin	56
DeShields-StL	55
Biggio-Hou	47
Young-Col-LA	45

Stolen Base Average	
Womack-Pit	89.6
Javier-SF	89.3
Henderson-SD	87.9
Biggio-Hou	82.5
Bonds-SF	82.2

Stolen Base Runs	
Womack-Pit	10.8
D.Sanders-Cin	7.8
DeShields-StL	7.2
Biggio-Hou	6.8
Bonds-SF	5.3

Fielding Runs	
Biggio-Hou	23.7
Young-Col	21.2
Randa-Pit	20.1
Weiss-Col	19.5
White-Mon	17.4

Total Player Rating	
Biggio-Hou	8.0
Piazza-LA	7.6
Bonds-SF	7.0
Bagwell-Hou	5.7
Lankford-StL	4.9

Wins	
Neagle-Atl	20
Maddux-Atl	19
Kile-Hou	19
Estes-SF	19

Win Percentage	
Maddux-Atl	.826
Neagle-Atl	.800
Estes-SF	.792
Kile-Hou	.731
Martinez-Mon	.680

Games	
Tavarez-SF	89
Belinda-Cin	84
Shaw-Cin	78
Rojas-Chi-NY	77

Complete Games	
Martinez-Mon	13
Perez-Mon	8
Smoltz-Atl	7
Schilling-Phi	7
Hampton-Hou	7

Shutouts	
Perez-Mon	5
Neagle-Atl	4
Martinez-Mon	4
Kile-Hou	4

Saves	
Shaw-Cin	42
Hoffman-SD	37
Beck-SF	37
J.Franco-NY	36
Eckersley-StL	36

Innings Pitched	
Smoltz-Atl	256.0
Kile-Hou	255.2
Schilling-Phi	254.1
Martinez-Mon	241.1
Glavine-Atl	240.0

Fewest Hits/Game	
Martinez-Mon	5.89
Park-LA	6.98
Estes-SF	7.25
Kile-Hou	7.32
Schilling-Phi	7.36

Fewest BB/Game	
Maddux-Atl	.77
Reed-NY	1.34
Neagle-Atl	1.89
Schilling-Phi	2.05
Perez-Mon	2.09

Strikeouts	
Schilling-Phi	319
Martinez-Mon	305
Smoltz-Atl	241
Nomo-LA	233

Strikeouts/Game	
Martinez-Mon	11.37
Schilling-Phi	11.29
Nomo-LA	10.11
A.Benes-StL	8.90
Smoltz-Atl	8.47

Ratio	
Martinez-Mon	8.73
Maddux-Atl	8.74
Schilling-Phi	9.59
Reed-NY	9.59
Neagle-Atl	9.99

Earned Run Average	
Martinez-Mon	1.90
Maddux-Atl	2.20
Kile-Hou	2.57
Valdes-LA	2.65
Brown-Fla	2.69

Adjusted ERA	
Martinez-Mon	221
Maddux-Atl	191
Kile-Hou	156
Brown-Fla	150
Valdes-LA	145

Opponents' Batting Avg.	
Martinez-Mon	.184
Park-LA	.213
Estes-SF	.223
Schilling-Phi	.224
Kile-Hou	.225

Opponents' On-Base Pct.	
Martinez-Mon	.250
Maddux-Atl	.258
Reed-NY	.273
Schilling-Phi	.273
Neagle-Atl	.279

Starter Runs	
Martinez-Mon	61.8
Maddux-Atl	51.8
Kile-Hou	46.5
Brown-Fla	39.9
Schilling-Phi	34.9

Adjusted Starter Runs	
Martinez-Mon	61.7
Maddux-Atl	51.8
Kile-Hou	42.7
Brown-Fla	36.9
Schilling-Phi	35.7

Clutch Pitching Index	
Bailey-Col	118
Kile-Hou	117
Cooke-Pit	115
Trachsel-Chi	113
Morris-StL	111

Relief Runs	
Shaw-Cin	19.2
Frascatore-StL	15.4
Hoffman-SD	14.0
Osuna-LA	13.8
Martin-Hou	13.2

Adjusted Relief Runs	
Shaw-Cin	19.6
Frascatore-StL	15.1
Martin-Hou	12.5
Osuna-LA	12.5
Hoffman-SD	12.0

Relief Ranking	
Shaw-Cin	26.9
Hoffman-SD	23.2
J.Franco-NY	20.7
McMichael-NY	20.3
Wagner-Hou	17.8

Total Pitcher Index	
Martinez-Mon	6.3
Maddux-Atl	5.2
Kile-Hou	4.4
Brown-Fla	4.0
Smoltz-Atl	4.0

Total Baseball Ranking	
Biggio-Hou	8.0
Piazza-LA	7.6
Bonds-SF	7.0
Martinez-Mon	6.3
Bagwell-Hou	5.7

TEAM	G	W	L	PCT	GB	R	OR	AB	H	2B	3B	HR	BB	SO	AVG	OBP	SLG	OPS	OPS+	BR	BR+	PF	CHI	RC	SB	CS	SBA	SBR
EAST																												
BAL	162	98	64	.605		812	**681**	5584	1498	264	22	196	586	952	.268	.345	.429	774	104	6	31	97	100	833	63	26	71	5
NY	162	96	66	.593	2	891	688	5710	1636	325	23	161	**676**	954	.287	**.366**	.436	802	110	80	88	99	98	913	99	58	63	1
DET	162	79	83	.488	19	784	790	5481	1415	268	32	176	578	1164	.258	.334	.415	749	95	-46	-39	99	**106**	764	**161**	72	69	10
BOS	162	78	84	.481	20	851	857	5781	**1684**	**373**	32	185	514	1044	**.291**	.355	.463	818	110	96	79	102	93	922	68	48	59	-2
TOR	162	76	86	.469	22	654	694	5473	1333	275	**41**	147	487	1138	.244	.312	.389	701	82	-150	-153	101	105	674	134	50	73	12
CENTRAL																												
CLE	161	86	75	.534		868	815	5556	1589	301	22	220	617	955	.286	.361	.467	828	110	118	87	104	95	923	118	59	67	5
CHI	161	80	81	.497	6	779	833	5491	1498	260	28	158	569	**901**	.273	.345	.417	762	102	-15	18	96	101	786	106	52	67	5
MIL	161	78	83	.484	8	681	742	5444	1415	294	27	135	494	967	.260	.328	.398	726	88	-92	-97	101	100	707	103	55	65	3
MIN	162	68	94	.420	18.5	772	861	5634	1522	305	40	132	495	1121	.270	.336	.409	745	92	-56	-65	101	105	779	151	52	**74**	**15**
KC	161	67	94	.416	19	747	820	5599	1478	256	35	158	561	1061	.264	.336	.407	743	91	-58	-75	102	101	770	130	66	66	6
WEST																												
SEA	162	90	72	.556		**925**	833	5614	1574	312	21	**264**	626	1110	.280	.358	**.485**	**843**	**119**	**140**	**150**	99	98	**962**	89	40	69	6
ANA	162	84	78	.519	6	829	794	5628	1531	279	25	161	617	953	.272	.349	.416	765	99	-4	-2	100	103	818	126	72	64	3
TEX	162	77	85	.475	13	807	823	5651	1547	311	27	187	500	1116	.274	.336	.438	774	95	-3	-43	105	102	824	72	37	66	3
OAK	162	65	97	.401	25	764	946	5589	1451	274	23	197	642	1181	.260	.341	.423	764	100	-14	0	98	96	811	71	36	66	3
TOT	1132					11164		78235	21171	4097	398	2477	7962	14617	.271	.344	.429	771							1491	723	67	75

TEAM	CG	SH	SV	IP	H	H/G	HR	BB	SO	RAT	ERA	ERA+	OAV	OOB	PR	PR+	PF	CPI	FA	E	DP	FW	PW	BW	SBW	DIF
EAST																										
BAL	8	10	**59**	1461	**1404**	**8.7**	164	563	1139	**12.4**	3.92	112	**.253**	**.326**	106	82	96	102	.984	97	148	.9	7.8	3.0	-.0	5.5
NY	11	10	51	1467[2]	1463	9.0	**144**	532	1165	12.6	**3.84**	116	.260	.329	**118**	102	97	104	.983	104	156	.5	9.8	8.4	-.4	-3.1
DET	13	8	42	1445[2]	1476	9.2	178	552	982	12.9	4.56	101	.266	.337	1	4	100	97	**.985**	92	146	**1.2**	.4	-3.7	.4	-.2
BOS	7	4	40	1451[2]	1569	9.8	149	611	987	14.0	4.85	96	.277	.354	-46	-34	102	97	.978	135	**179**	-1.2	-3.2	7.6	-.7	-5.2
TOR	**19**	**16**	34	1442[2]	1453	9.1	167	497	1150	12.5	3.92	**117**	.263	.328	104	**107**	101	**106**	.984	94	150	1.1	**10.2**	-14.5	.6	-2.2
CENTRAL																										
CLE	4	3	39	1425[2]	1528	9.7	181	575	1036	13.6	4.73	99	.276	.350	-26	-6	103	101	.983	106	159	.4	-.5	8.3	-.0	-2.4
CHI	6	7	52	1422[1]	1505	9.6	175	575	961	13.4	4.74	93	.271	.342	-27	-58	96	96	.978	127	131	-.8	-5.5	1.8	-.0	4.3
MIL	6	8	44	1427[1]	1419	9.0	177	542	1016	12.8	4.22	109	.261	.335	55	62	101	103	.980	121	171	-.5	5.9	-9.2	-.2	1.6
MIN	10	4	30	1434	1596	10.1	187	**495**	908	13.4	5.00	93	.283	.344	-69	-54	102	96	.983	101	170	.7	-5.1	-6.1	**.9**	-3.2
KC	11	5	29	1443	1530	9.6	186	531	961	13.2	4.70	100	.274	.343	-21	2	103	99	**.985**	**91**	168	**1.2**	.2	-7.1	.0	-7.7
WEST																										
SEA	9	8	38	1447[2]	1500	9.4	192	598	**1207**	13.5	4.79	94	.267	.344	-35	-47	99	97	.979	126	143	-.7	-4.4	**14.3**	.0	-.0
ANA	9	5	39	1454[2]	1506	9.4	202	605	1050	13.4	4.52	101	.269	.346	8	8	100	105	.980	123	140	-.6	.8	-.1	-.2	3.3
TEX	8	9	33	1429[2]	1598	10.1	169	541	925	13.8	4.69	102	.283	.350	-20	15	105	103	.980	121	155	-.4	1.5	-4.0	-.2	-.6
OAK	2	1	38	1445[1]	1734	10.8	197	642	953	15.2	5.48	83	.301	.377	-147	-155	99	104	.980	122	170	-.5	-14.7	.0	-.2	-.4
TOT	123	98	568	20198[1]		9.5				13.3	4.57		.271	.344					.982	1560	2186					

Runs
Griffey-Sea 125
Garciaparra-Bos 122
Knoblauch-Min 117
Jeter-NY 116

Hits
Garciaparra-Bos 209
Greer-Tex 193
Jeter-NY 190
Anderson-Ana 189
Rodriguez-Tex 187

Doubles
Valentin-Bos 47
Cirillo-Mil 46
Belle-Chi 45
Garciaparra-Bos 44

Triples
Garciaparra-Bos 11
Knoblauch-Min 10
Damon-KC 8
Burnitz-Mil 8

Home Runs
Griffey-Sea 56
Martinez-NY 44
Gonzalez-Tex 42
Thome-Cle 40
Buhner-Sea 40

Total Bases
Griffey-Sea 393
Garciaparra-Bos 365
Martinez-NY 343
F.Thomas-Chi 324
Greer-Tex 319

Runs Batted In
Griffey-Sea 147
Martinez-NY 141
Gonzalez-Tex 131
Salmon-Ana 129
F.Thomas-Chi 125

Runs Produced
Griffey-Sea 216
F.Thomas-Chi 200
Martinez-NY 193
Salmon-Ana 191

Bases On Balls
Thome-Cle 120
E.Martinez-Sea 119
Buhner-Sea 119
F.Thomas-Chi 109
Phillips-Chi-Ana 102

Batting Average
F.Thomas-Chi 347
E.Martinez-Sea 330
Justice-Cle 329
Williams-NY 328
Ramirez-Cle 328

On-Base Percentage
F.Thomas-Chi 461
E.Martinez-Sea 460
Thome-Cle 428
Justice-Cle 423
Vaughn-Bos 422

Slugging Average
Griffey-Sea 646
F.Thomas-Chi 611
Justice-Cle 596
Gonzalez-Tex 589
Thome-Cle 579

On-Base Plus Slugging
F.Thomas-Chi 1072
Griffey-Sea 1035
Justice-Cle 1019
E.Martinez-Sea 1013
Thome-Cle 1007

Adjusted OPS
F.Thomas-Chi 184
Griffey-Sea 165
E.Martinez-Sea 164
Justice-Cle 156
Thome-Cle 154

Batter Runs
F.Thomas-Chi 64.6
E.Martinez-Sea 57.1
Griffey-Sea 55.2
Thome-Cle 47.5
Justice-Cle 46.4

Adjusted Batter Runs
F.Thomas-Chi 70.9
E.Martinez-Sea 58.5
Griffey-Sea 56.7
Thome-Cle 43.2
Justice-Cle 42.3

Clutch Hitting Index
Molitor-Min 133
King-KC 126
O'Neill-NY 125
Carter-Tor 119
Anderson-Ana 118

Runs Created
F.Thomas-Chi 153
Griffey-Sea 152
E.Martinez-Sea 140
Greer-Tex 132
Thome-Cle 131

Total Average
F.Thomas-Chi 1.204
Thome-Cle 1.126
Griffey-Sea 1.112
E.Martinez-Sea 1.103
Justice-Cle 1.069

Stolen Bases
Hunter-Det 74
Knoblauch-Min 62
Goodwin-KC-Tex 50
Nixon-Tor 47
Vizquel-Cle 43

Stolen Base Average
Cameron-Chi 92.0
Knoblauch-Min 86.1
Roberts-KC-Cle 85.7
Fryman-Det 84.2
Rodriguez-Sea 82.9

Stolen Base Runs
Knoblauch-Min 10.1
Hunter-Det 10.0
Nixon-Tor 6.8
Goodwin-KC-Tex 5.4
Vizquel-Cle 5.3

Fielding Runs
Gil-Tex 22.0
King-KC 20.0
Salmon-Ana 18.5
Cirillo-Mil 17.9
Matheny-Mil 17.7

Total Player Rating
Griffey-Sea 6.9
F.Thomas-Chi 4.8
E.Martinez-Sea 4.5
Salmon-Ana 4.0
Valentin-Bos 3.9

Wins
Clemens-Tor 21
Radke-Min 20
Johnson-Sea 20
Pettitte-NY 18
Moyer-Sea 17

Win Percentage
Johnson-Sea 833
Moyer-Sea 773
Clemens-Tor 750
Pettitte-NY 720
Erickson-Bal 696

Games
Myers-Det 88
Groom-Oak 78
Quantrill-Tor 77
Nelson-NY 77
Slocumb-Bos-Sea 76

Complete Games
Hentgen-Tor 9
Clemens-Tor 9
Wells-NY 5
Tewksbury-Min 5
Johnson-Sea 5

Shutouts
Hentgen-Tor 3
Clemens-Tor 3

Saves
Myers-Bal 45
Rivera-NY 43
Jones-Mil 36
Wetteland-Tex 31
Jones-Det 31

Innings Pitched
Hentgen-Tor 264.0
Clemens-Tor 264.0
Pettitte-NY 240.1
Radke-Min 239.2
Appier-KC 235.2

Fewest Hits/Game
Johnson-Sea 6.21
Clemens-Tor 6.95
Cone-NY 7.15
Thompson-Det 7.58
Gordon-Bos 7.64

Fewest BB/Game
Burkett-Tex 1.43
Tewksbury-Min 1.65
Radke-Min 1.80
Wells-NY 1.86
Moyer-Sea 2.05

Strikeouts
Clemens-Tor 292
Johnson-Sea 291
Cone-NY 222
Mussina-Bal 218
Appier-KC 196

Strikeouts/Game
Johnson-Sea 12.30
Cone-NY 10.25
Clemens-Tor 9.95
Mussina-Bal 8.73
Finley-Ana 8.51

Ratio
Clemens-Tor 9.68
Johnson-Sea 9.89
Mussina-Bal 10.18
Thompson-Det 10.32
Radke-Min 10.85

Earned Run Average
Clemens-Tor 2.05
Johnson-Sea 2.28
Cone-NY 2.82
Pettitte-NY 2.88
Thompson-Det 3.02

Adjusted ERA
Clemens-Tor 225
Johnson-Sea 197
Cone-NY 158
Pettitte-NY 154
Thompson-Det 152

Opponents' Batting Avg.
Johnson-Sea 194
Clemens-Tor 213
Cone-NY 218
Gordon-Bos 226
Thompson-Det 233

Opponents' On-Base Pct.
Clemens-Tor 274
Johnson-Sea 277
Mussina-Bal 282
Thompson-Det 292
Radke-Min 296

Starter Runs
Clemens-Tor 74.1
Johnson-Sea 54.2
Pettitte-NY 45.1
Thompson-Det 38.5
Cone-NY 38.1

Adjusted Starter Runs
Clemens-Tor 74.4
Johnson-Sea 53.4
Pettitte-NY 43.0
Thompson-Det 38.8
Cone-NY 36.4

Clutch Pitching Index
Key-Bal 123
Dickson-Ana 117
Oliver-Tex 115
Witt-Tex 110
Nagy-Cle 110

Relief Runs
Quantrill-Tor 25.7
Jones-Mil 22.8
Rivera-NY 21.4
Myers-Bal 20.3
Mesa-Cle 19.8

Adjusted Relief Runs
Quantrill-Tor 25.8
Jones-Mil 23.0
Rivera-NY 21.0
Mesa-Cle 20.4
Myers-Bal 19.9

Relief Ranking
Jones-Mil 46.0
Rivera-NY 42.0
Myers-Bal 39.9
Wetteland-Tex 39.3
Quantrill-Tor 36.9

Total Pitcher Index
Clemens-Tor 8.0
Johnson-Sea 5.6
Jones-Mil 4.5
Pettitte-NY 4.3
Rivera-NY 4.2

Total Baseball Ranking
Clemens-Tor 8.0
Griffey-Sea 6.9
Johnson-Sea 5.6
F.Thomas-Chi 4.8
Jones-Mil 4.5

TEAM	G	W	L	PCT	GB	R	OR	AB	H	2B	3B	HR	BB	SO	AVG	OBP	SLG	OPS	OPS+	BR	BR+	PF	CHI	RC	SB	CS	SBA	SBR
EAST																												
ATL	162	106	56	.654		826	**581**	5484	1489	297	26	215	548	1062	.272	.344	.453	797	114	102	102	100	98	862	98	43	70	7
NY	162	88	74	.543	18	706	645	5510	1425	289	24	136	572	1049	.259	.332	.394	726	98	-30	-18	98	99	719	62	46	57	-2
PHI	162	75	87	.463	31	713	808	5617	1482	286	36	126	508	1080	.264	.330	.395	725	94	-37	-47	101	100	737	97	45	68	6
MON	162	65	97	.401	41	644	783	5418	1348	280	32	147	439	1058	.249	.312	.394	706	91	-84	-74	98	101	663	91	46	66	4
FLA	162	54	108	.333	52	667	923	5558	1381	277	36	114	525	1120	.248	.318	.373	691	91	-105	-71	95	105	662	115	57	67	5
CENTRAL																												
HOU	162	102	60	.630		**874**	620	5641	1578	326	28	166	621	1122	.280	**.359**	.436	795	**117**	116	**141**	97	99	**889**	155	51	75	16
CHI	163	90	73	.552	12.5	831	792	5649	1494	250	34	212	601	1223	.264	.339	.433	772	103	58	31	103	101	827	65	44	60	-1
STL	163	83	79	.512	19	810	782	5593	1444	292	30	**223**	676	1179	.258	.343	.441	784	111	81	90	99	96	862	133	41	**76**	15
CIN	162	77	85	.475	25	750	760	5496	1441	298	28	138	608	1107	.262	.340	.402	742	99	4	-4	101	100	757	95	42	69	6
MIL	162	74	88	.457	28	707	812	5541	1439	266	17	152	532	1039	.260	.332	.396	728	96	-28	-29	100	99	719	81	59	58	-3
PIT	163	69	93	.426	33	650	718	5493	1395	271	35	107	393	1060	.254	.314	.374	688	84	-112	-119	101	105	658	**159**	51	**76**	**17**
WEST																												
SD	162	98	64	.605		749	635	5490	1390	292	30	167	604	1072	.253	.332	.409	741	107	-4	58	92	101	757	79	37	68	4
SF	163	89	74	.546	9.5	845	739	5628	1540	292	26	161	**678**	1040	.274	.356	.421	777	116	84	138	94	99	858	102	51	67	5
LA	162	83	79	.512	15	669	678	5459	1374	209	27	159	447	1056	.252	.313	.387	700	94	-95	-55	94	**106**	666	137	53	72	12
COL	162	77	85	.475	21	826	855	5632	**1640**	**333**	36	183	469	**949**	**.291**	.350	**.461**	**811**	96	**129**	-27	122	94	878	67	47	59	-2
ARI	162	65	97	.401	33	665	812	5491	1353	235	**46**	159	489	1239	.246	.315	.393	708	90	-78	-76	100	102	675	73	38	66	3
TOT	1298					11932		88700	23213	4493	491	2565	8710	17455	.262	.334	.411	744							1609	751	68	91

TEAM	CG	SH	SV	IP	H	H/G	HR	BB	SO	RAT	ERA	ERA+	OAV	OOB	PR	PR+	PF	CPI	FA	E	DP	FW	PW	BW	SBW	DIF
EAST																										
ATL	**24**	**23**	45	1438[2]	**1291**	**8.1**	**117**	467	**1232**	**11.3**	**3.26**	**128**	**.240**	**.305**	**156**	**147**	98	101	**.985**	**91**	139	**1.4**	**14.6**	10.1	.1	-1.0
NY	9	16	46	1458	1381	8.6	152	532	1129	12.3	3.76	110	.253	.327	76	62	98	106	.984	101	151	.8	6.2	-1.7	-.8	2.7
PHI	21	10	32	1463	1476	9.1	188	544	1176	12.8	4.64	93	.262	.333	-66	-49	102	94	.982	110	131	.4	-4.8	-4.6	.0	3.2
MON	4	5	39	1427	1448	9.2	156	533	1017	12.9	4.39	96	.264	.335	-24	-29	99	98	.975	155	127	-2.1	-2.8	-7.3	-.2	-3.5
FLA	11	3	24	1449[2]	1617	10.1	182	715	1016	14.9	5.18	78	.287	.373	-153	-189	96	104	.979	129	177	-.7	-18.6	-7.0	-.0	-.5
CENTRAL																										
HOU	12	11	44	1471[1]	1435	8.8	147	**465**	1187	11.9	3.50	116	.256	.317	119	94	96	**109**	.983	108	144	.5	9.3	**14.0**	1.0	-3.6
CHI	7	7	56	1477[1]	1528	9.4	180	575	1207	13.2	4.47	99	.266	.338	-39	-11	104	100	.984	101	107	.9	-1.0	3.1	-.7	6.4
STL	6	10	44	1469[2]	1513	9.3	151	558	972	13.1	4.31	97	.268	.340	-12	-19	99	101	.978	142	160	-1.3	-1.8	8.9	.9	-4.5
CIN	6	8	42	1441[1]	1400	8.8	170	573	1098	12.7	4.44	96	.256	.333	-34	-26	101	95	.980	122	142	-.3	-2.5	-.3	.0	-.7
MIL	2	2	39	1451	1538	9.6	188	550	1063	13.4	4.63	92	.275	.347	-64	-59	101	103	.982	110	192	.4	-5.8	-2.8	-.9	2.3
PIT	7	10	41	1449	1433	9.0	147	530	1112	12.4	3.91	110	.259	.327	52	61	102	103	.977	140	161	-1.2	6.1	-11.7	**1.1**	-6.1
WEST																										
SD	14	11	**59**	1454[2]	1384	8.6	139	501	1217	12.0	3.64	108	.252	.320	97	48	92	104	.983	104	155	.7	4.8	5.8	-.2	6.1
SF	6	6	44	1477	1457	8.9	171	562	1089	12.7	4.19	95	.259	.332	8	-38	94	101	.984	101	157	.9	-3.7	13.7	-.0	-3.1
LA	16	10	47	1447[1]	1332	8.3	135	587	1178	12.3	3.81	104	.246	.326	68	26	94	100	.978	134	154	-.9	2.6	-5.4	.6	5.3
COL	9	5	36	1432[2]	1583	10.0	174	562	951	13.9	4.99	104	.285	.358	-121	23	122	101	.984	102	**193**	.8	2.3	-2.6	-.8	-3.5
ARI	7	6	37	1432[1]	1463	9.2	188	489	908	12.6	4.64	91	.266	.330	-64	-68	100	95	.984	100	125	.9	-6.7	-7.4	-.3	-2.3
TOT	161	143	675	23240		9.1				12.8	4.23		.262	.334					.982	1850	2415					

Runs
Sosa-Chi 134
McGwire-StL 130
Bagwell-Hou 124
C.Jones-Atl 123
Biggio-Hou 123

Hits
Bichette-Col 219
Biggio-Hou 210
Castilla-Col 206
V.Guerrero-Mon 202

Doubles
Biggio-Hou 51
Young-Cin 48
Bichette-Col 48
Walker-Col 46

Triples
Dellucci-Ari 12
B.Larkin-Cin 10
W.Guerrero-LA-Mon 9
Perez-Col 9

Home Runs
McGwire-StL 70
Sosa-Chi 66
Vaughn-SD 50
Castilla-Col 46
Galarraga-Atl 44

Total Bases
Sosa-Chi 416
McGwire-StL 383
Castilla-Col 380
V.Guerrero-Mon 367
Vaughn-SD 342

Runs Batted In
Sosa-Chi 158
McGwire-StL 147
Castilla-Col 144
Kent-SF 128
Burnitz-Mil 125

Runs Produced
Sosa-Chi 226
McGwire-StL 207
Castilla-Col 206
Bonds-SF 205
Bagwell-Hou 201

Bases On Balls
McGwire-StL 162
Bonds-SF 130
Bagwell-Hou 109
Olerud-NY 96
C.Jones-Atl 96

Batting Average
Walker-Col .363
Olerud-NY .354
Bichette-Col .331
Piazza-LA-Fla-NY .328
Kendall-Pit .327

On-Base Percentage
McGwire-StL .473
Olerud-NY .452
Walker-Col .446
Bonds-SF .442
Sheffield-Fla-LA .435

Slugging Average
McGwire-StL .752
Sosa-Chi .647
Walker-Col .630
Bonds-SF .609
Vaughn-SD .597

On-Base Plus Slugging
McGwire-StL 1225
Walker-Col 1076
Bonds-SF 1051
Sosa-Chi 1026
Olerud-NY 1003

Adjusted OPS
McGwire-StL 218
Bonds-SF 184
Olerud-NY 165
Bagwell-Hou 161
Sheffield-Fla-LA 160

Batter Runs
McGwire-StL 93.1
Bonds-SF 63.6
Sosa-Chi 56.4
Olerud-NY 54.8
Walker-Col 53.5

Adjusted Batter Runs
McGwire-StL 94.8
Bonds-SF 72.8
Olerud-NY 57.0
Sosa-Chi 51.7
Bagwell-Hou 51.7

Clutch Hitting Index
Brogna-Phi 125
Kent-SF 120
Lee-Fla 118
Guillen-Pit 113
Bichette-Col 109

Runs Created
McGwire-StL 193
Bonds-SF 153
Sosa-Chi 149
Biggio-Hou 142
Olerud-NY 141

Total Average
McGwire-StL 1.512
Walker-Col 1.197
Bonds-SF 1.189
Sheffield-Fla-LA 1.088
Bagwell-Hou 1.081

Stolen Bases
Womack-Pit 58
Biggio-Hou 50
Young-LA 42
Renteria-Fla 41
Bonds-SF 28

Stolen Base Average
B.Larkin-Cin 89.7
Womack-Pit 87.9
A.Jones-Atl 87.1
Martin-Pit 87.0
Biggio-Hou 86.2

Stolen Base Runs
Womack-Pit 10.0
Biggio-Hou 8.2
Young-LA 4.7
B.Larkin-Cin 4.7
A.Jones-Atl 4.5

Fielding Runs
A.Jones-Atl 31.8
Vina-Mil 28.7
Perez-Col 26.4
Cirillo-Mil 24.2
Kotsay-Fla 22.0

Total Player Rating
Bonds-SF 7.5
McGwire-StL 7.2
Sosa-Chi 5.8
Piazza-LA-Fla-NY 5.4
Vaughn-SD 5.2

Wins
Glavine-Atl 20
Tapani-Chi 19
Reynolds-Hou 19
Maddux-Atl 18
Brown-SD 18

Win Percentage
Smoltz-Atl .850
Glavine-Atl .769
Leiter-NY .739
Brown-SD .720
Reynolds-Hou .704

Games
Beck-Chi 81
Nen-SF 78
McElroy-Col 78
Kline-Mon 78
Telford-Mon 77

Complete Games
Schilling-Phi 15
Maddux-Atl 9
Hernandez-Fla 9
C.Perez-Mon-LA 7
Brown-SD 7

Shutouts
Maddux-Atl 5
R.Johnson-Hou 4
Glavine-Atl 3
Brown-SD 3

Saves
Hoffman-SD 53
Beck-Chi 51
Shaw-Cin-LA 48
Nen-SF 40
J.Franco-NY 38

Innings Pitched
Schilling-Phi 268.2
Brown-SD 257.0
Maddux-Atl 251.0
C.Perez-Mon-LA 241.0
Hernandez-Fla 234.1

Fewest Hits/Game
Wood-Chi 6.32
Leiter-NY 7.04
Maddux-Atl 7.21
Harnisch-Cin 7.58
Smoltz-Atl 7.78

Fewest BB/Game
Anderson-Ari 1.04
Reed-NY 1.23
Lima-Hou 1.23
Maddux-Atl 1.61
Brown-SD 1.72

Strikeouts
Schilling-Phi 300
Brown-SD 257
Wood-Chi 233
Reynolds-Hou 209
Maddux-Atl 204

Strikeouts/Game
Wood-Chi 12.58
Schilling-Phi 10.05
Smoltz-Atl 9.29
Brown-SD 9.00
Millwood-Atl 8.41

Ratio
Maddux-Atl 9.07
Brown-SD 9.95
Schilling-Phi 10.15
Reed-NY 10.30
Lima-Hou 10.34

Earned Run Average
Maddux-Atl 2.22
Brown-SD 2.38
Leiter-NY 2.47
Glavine-Atl 2.47
Daal-Ari 2.88

Adjusted ERA
Maddux-Atl 187
Glavine-Atl 168
Leiter-NY 167
Brown-SD 164
Daal-Ari 147

Opponents' Batting Avg.
Wood-Chi .196
Leiter-NY .216
Maddux-Atl .220
Harnisch-Cin .228
Smoltz-Atl .231

Opponents' On-Base Pct.
Maddux-Atl .262
Brown-SD .280
Schilling-Phi .284
Smoltz-Atl .286
Lima-Hou .287

Starter Runs
Maddux-Atl 56.2
Brown-SD 53.0
Glavine-Atl 45.0
Leiter-NY 37.9
Schilling-Phi 29.5

Adjusted Starter Runs
Maddux-Atl 55.0
Brown-SD 47.4
Glavine-Atl 43.8
Leiter-NY 36.6
Schilling-Phi 31.7

Clutch Pitching Index
Hampton-Hou 133
Glavine-Atl 121
Reynolds-Hou 119
Daal-Ari 117
Hernandez-Fla 117

Relief Runs
Nen-SF 26.7
Urbina-Mon 22.6
Hoffman-SD 22.4
Shaw-Cin-LA 20.0
Acevedo-StL 18.3

Adjusted Relief Runs
Nen-SF 25.7
Urbina-Mon 22.6
Hoffman-SD 21.4
Shaw-Cin-LA 19.6
Mulholland-Chi 18.1

Relief Ranking
Nen-SF 51.5
Urbina-Mon 45.1
Hoffman-SD 42.6
Shaw-Cin-LA 39.2
Acevedo-StL 22.9

Total Pitcher Index
Maddux-Atl 7.1
Glavine-Atl 5.5
Brown-SD 5.2
Nen-SF 5.2
Urbina-Mon 4.5

Total Baseball Ranking
Bonds-SF 7.5
McGwire-StL 7.2
Maddux-Atl 7.1
Sosa-Chi 5.8
Glavine-Atl 5.5

TEAM	G	W	L	PCT	GB	R	OR	AB	H	2B	3B	HR	BB	SO	AVG	OBP	SLG	OPS	OPS+	BR	BR+	PF	CHI	RC	SB	CS	SBA	SBR
EAST																												
NY	162	114	48	.704		**965**	**656**	5643	1625	290	31	207	**653**	1025	.288	**.368**	.460	**828**	**119**	**123**	**161**	96	101	**957**	153	63	71	**12**
BOS	162	92	70	.568	22	876	729	5601	1568	**338**	35	205	541	1049	.280	.351	.463	814	108	77	59	102	99	895	72	39	65	2
TOR	163	88	74	.543	26	816	768	5580	1482	316	19	221	564	1132	.266	.342	.448	790	104	28	25	100	97	861	**184**	81	69	**12**
BAL	162	79	83	.488	35	817	785	5565	1520	303	11	214	593	**903**	.273	.349	.447	796	107	46	59	99	95	863	86	48	64	2
TB	162	63	99	.389	51	620	751	5555	1450	267	**43**	111	473	1107	.261	.323	.385	708	82	-135	-147	102	94	678	120	73	62	1
CENTRAL																												
CLE	162	89	73	.549		850	779	5616	1530	334	30	198	630	1061	.272	.350	.448	798	103	51	23	103	97	887	143	60	70	10
CHI	163	80	82	.494	9	861	931	5585	1516	291	38	198	551	916	.271	.342	.444	786	106	19	43	97	104	850	127	46	73	**12**
KC	161	72	89	.447	16.5	714	899	5546	1459	274	40	134	475	984	.263	.328	.399	727	86	-96	-114	103	102	730	135	50	73	**12**
MIN	162	70	92	.432	19	734	818	5641	1499	285	32	115	506	915	.266	.331	.389	720	86	-108	-118	102	105	712	112	54	67	6
DET	162	65	97	.401	24	722	863	5664	1494	306	29	165	455	1070	.264	.325	.415	740	90	-77	-81	101	99	759	122	62	66	5
WEST																												
TEX	162	88	74	.543		940	871	5672	**1637**	314	32	201	595	1045	**.289**	.360	.462	822	108	103	66	104	101	935	82	47	64	2
ANA	162	85	77	.525	3	787	783	5630	1530	314	27	147	510	1028	.272	.337	.415	752	94	-43	-48	101	103	787	93	45	67	5
SEA	161	76	85	.472	11.5	859	855	5628	1553	321	28	**234**	558	1081	.276	.347	**.468**	815	110	76	76	100	96	923	115	39	**75**	**12**
OAK	162	74	88	.457	14	804	866	5490	1413	295	13	149	633	1122	.257	.340	.397	737	93	-64	-46	98	**108**	762	131	47	74	**12**
TOT	1134					11365		78416	21276	4248	408	2499	7737	14438	.272	.343	.432	774							1675	754	69	105

TEAM	CG	SH	SV	IP	H	H/G	HR	BB	SO	RAT	ERA	ERA+	OAV	OOB	PR	PR+	PF	CPI	FA	E	DP	FW	PW	BW	SBW	DIF
EAST																										
NY	**22**	**16**	48	1456^{2}	**1357**	**8.4**	**156**	466	1080	**11.7**	**3.83**	**114**	**.247**	**.314**	**133**	**95**	94	98	.984	98	146	.9	**9.0**	**15.2**	**.4**	7.6
BOS	5	8	**53**	1436	1406	8.9	168	504	1025	12.4	4.19	113	.255	.324	75	83	101	97	.983	105	128	.5	7.9	5.6	-.5	-2.3
TOR	10	11	47	1465	1443	8.9	169	587	1154	12.8	4.29	109	.256	.331	60	62	100	98	.979	125	131	-.5	5.9	2.4	**.4**	-1.0
BAL	16	10	37	1431^{1}	1505	9.5	169	535	1065	13.2	4.75	96	.272	.341	-15	-31	98	97	**.987**	**81**	144	**1.9**	-2.9	5.6	-.5	-5.9
TB	7	7	28	1443	1425	8.9	171	643	1008	13.5	4.36	110	.261	.347	47	68	103	105	.985	94	**178**	1.1	6.5	-13.8	-.6	-11.0
CENTRAL																										
CLE	9	4	47	1460	1552	9.6	171	563	1037	13.5	4.45	107	.274	.346	33	51	103	**106**	.982	110	146	.3	4.9	2.2	.2	.6
CHI	8	4	42	1438^{2}	1569	9.9	211	580	911	13.8	5.23	87	.278	.351	-92	-111	98	97	.977	140	161	-1.4	-10.4	4.1	**.4**	6.4
KC	6	5	46	1436^{1}	1590	10.0	196	568	999	13.9	5.16	94	.281	.353	-80	-51	104	98	.980	125	172	-.6	-4.8	-10.7	**.4**	7.3
MIN	7	8	42	1447^{2}	1622	10.1	180	**457**	952	13.2	4.75	100	.284	.341	-16	2	103	101	.982	108	135	.4	.2	-11.1	-.1	-.2
DET	9	4	32	1446^{1}	1551	9.7	185	595	947	13.7	4.93	96	.277	.351	-45	-34	101	100	.982	115	164	-.0	-3.2	-7.6	-.2	-4.8
WEST																										
TEX	10	8	46	1431^{1}	1624	10.3	164	519	994	13.8	5.00	97	.285	.350	-55	-26	104	98	.980	121	140	-.3	-2.4	6.3	-.5	4.2
ANA	3	5	52	1444	1481	9.3	164	630	1091	13.5	4.49	104	.267	.347	26	32	101	103	.983	106	146	.5	3.1	-4.5	-.2	5.4
SEA	17	7	31	1424^{1}	1530	9.7	196	528	**1156**	13.4	4.94	94	.273	.342	-45	-49	100	97	.979	125	139	-.6	-4.6	7.2	**.4**	-6.8
OAK	12	4	39	1434	1555	9.8	179	529	922	13.5	4.81	95	.276	.344	-25	-39	98	99	.977	141	155	-1.5	-3.6	-4.3	**.4**	2.1
TOT	141	101	590	20194^{2}		9.5				13.3	4.65		.272	.343					.982	1594	2085					

Runs
Jeter-NY 127
Durham-Chi 126
Rodriguez-Sea 123
Griffey-Sea 120
Knoblauch-NY 117

Hits
Rodriguez-Sea 213
Vaughn-Bos 205
Jeter-NY 203
Belle-Chi 200
Garciaparra-Bos 195

Doubles
Gonzalez-Tex 50
Belle-Chi 48
Martinez-Sea 46
Valentin-Bos 44
Delgado-Tor 43

Triples
Offerman-KC 13
Damon-KC 10
Winn-TB 9

Home Runs
Griffey-Sea 56
Belle-Chi 49
Canseco-Tor 46
M.Ramirez-Cle 45
Gonzalez-Tex 45

Total Bases
Belle-Chi 399
Griffey-Sea 387
Rodriguez-Sea 384
Gonzalez-Tex 382
Vaughn-Bos 360

Runs Batted In
Gonzalez-Tex 157
Belle-Chi 152
Griffey-Sea 146
M.Ramirez-Cle 145
Rodriguez-Sea 124

Runs Produced
Gonzalez-Tex 222
Belle-Chi 216
Griffey-Sea 210
M.Ramirez-Cle 208
Rodriguez-Sea 205

Bases On Balls
Henderson-Oak 118
Thomas-Chi 110
Martinez-Sea 106
Salmon-Ana 90

Batting Average
Williams-NY .339
Vaughn-Bos .337
Belle-Chi .328
Davis-Bal .327
Jeter-NY .324

On-Base Percentage
Martinez-Sea .433
Williams-NY .425
Salmon-Ana .417
Thome-Cle .417
Belle-Chi .408

Slugging Average
Belle-Chi .655
Gonzalez-Tex .630
Griffey-Sea .611
M.Ramirez-Cle .599
Delgado-Tor .592

On-Base Plus Slugging
Belle-Chi 1063
Gonzalez-Tex 1003
Thome-Cle 1001
Williams-NY 1000
Martinez-Sea 998

Adjusted OPS
Belle-Chi 175
Williams-NY 163
Martinez-Sea 157
Thome-Cle 151
Davis-Bal 151

Batter Runs
Belle-Chi 62.5
Martinez-Sea 50.4
Vaughn-Bos 48.6
Gonzalez-Tex 45.6
Williams-NY 43.5

Adjusted Batter Runs
Belle-Chi 66.9
Martinez-Sea 50.4
Williams-NY 48.2
Vaughn-Bos 45.8
Griffey-Sea 43.1

Clutch Hitting Index
Molitor-Min 132
Martinez-NY 129
Brosius-NY 120
Greer-Tex 120
King-KC 118

Runs Created
Belle-Chi 158
Vaughn-Bos 144
Griffey-Sea 142
Martinez-Sea 141
Rodriguez-Sea 138

Total Average
Belle-Chi 1.123
Thome-Cle 1.104
Martinez-Sea 1.082
Delgado-Tor 1.047
Salmon-Ana 1.030

Stolen Bases
Henderson-Oak 66
Lofton-Cle 54
Stewart-Tor 51
Rodriguez-Sea 46
Offerman-KC 45

Stolen Base Average
Lofton-Cle 84.4
Nixon-Min 84.1
Henderson-Oak 83.5
Jeter-NY 83.3
Curtis-NY 80.8

Stolen Base Runs
Henderson-Oak 10.0
Lofton-Cle 8.4
Offerman-KC 5.7
Nixon-Min 5.7
Rodriguez-Sea 5.6

Fielding Runs
Bell-Cle-Sea 25.8
Easley-Det 21.8
Bordick-Bal 20.8
Stocker-TB 19.6
Cruz-Det 19.4

Total Player Rating
Belle-Chi 6.3
Griffey-Sea 5.8
Rodriguez-Sea 4.8
Williams-NY 4.8
Martinez-Sea 4.0

Wins
Helling-Tex 20
Cone-NY 20
Clemens-Tor 20
Sele-Tex 19
Martinez-Bos 19

Win Percentage
Wells-NY .818
Clemens-Tor .769
Helling-Tex .741
Cone-NY .741
Martinez-Bos .731

Games
Runyan-Det 88
Quantrill-Tor 82
Swindell-Min-Bos 81
Guardado-Min 79
Plesac-Tor 78

Complete Games
Erickson-Bal 11
Wells-NY 8
Rogers-Oak 7
Fassero-Sea 7

Shutouts
Wells-NY 5
Moyer-Sea 3
Moehler-Det 3
Clemens-Tor 3

Saves
Gordon-Bos 46
Wetteland-Tex 42
Percival-Ana 42
Jackson-Cle 40
Aguilera-Min 38

Innings Pitched
Erickson-Bal 251.1
Rogers-Oak 238.2
Clemens-Tor 234.2
Moyer-Sea 234.1
Belcher-KC 234.0

Fewest Hits/Game
Clemens-Tor 6.48
Martinez-Bos 7.24
Irabu-NY 7.70
Cone-NY 8.06
Rogers-Oak 8.11

Fewest BB/Game
Wells-NY 1.22
Saberhagen-Bos 1.49
Moyer-Sea 1.61
Mussina-Bal 1.79
Radke-Min 1.81

Strikeouts
Clemens-Tor 271
Martinez-Bos 251
Johnson-Sea 213
Finley-Ana 212
Cone-NY 209

Strikeouts/Game
Clemens-Tor 10.39
Martinez-Bos 9.67
Cone-NY 9.06
Finley-Ana 8.54
Saunders-TB 8.05

Ratio
Wells-NY 9.45
Clemens-Tor 10.13
Martinez-Bos 10.13
Mussina-Bal 10.21
Rogers-Oak 10.90

Earned Run Average
Clemens-Tor 2.65
Martinez-Bos 2.89
Rogers-Oak 3.17
Finley-Ana 3.39
Wells-NY 3.49

Adjusted ERA
Clemens-Tor 176
Martinez-Bos 163
Rogers-Oak 144
Finley-Ana 139
Arrojo-TB 135

Opponents' Batting Avg.
Clemens-Tor .197
Martinez-Bos .217
Irabu-NY .233
Cone-NY .237
Wells-NY .239

Opponents' On-Base Pct.
Wells-NY .266
Clemens-Tor .278
Martinez-Bos .280
Mussina-Bal .283
Moyer-Sea .296

Starter Runs
Clemens-Tor 52.4
Martinez-Bos 45.9
Rogers-Oak 39.5
Finley-Ana 31.5
Moyer-Sea 29.2

Adjusted Starter Runs
Clemens-Tor 52.6
Martinez-Bos 46.8
Rogers-Oak 37.9
Finley-Ana 32.2
Moyer-Sea 28.8

Clutch Pitching Index
Olivares-Ana 119
Finley-Ana 117
Arrojo-TB 116
Saunders-TB 115
Burba-Cle 113

Relief Runs
Jackson-Cle 22.1
Rivera-NY 18.7
Quantrill-Tor 18.4
Lopez-TB 18.2
Wetteland-Tex 18.1

Adjusted Relief Runs
Jackson-Cle 22.4
Lopez-TB 18.9
Wetteland-Tex 18.6
Quantrill-Tor 18.5
Rivera-NY 17.9

Relief Ranking
Gordon-Bos 34.7
Wetteland-Tex 32.6
Jackson-Cle 30.5
Rivera-NY 26.1
Lopez-TB 23.9

Total Pitcher Index
Clemens-Tor 5.3
Martinez-Bos 4.5
Rogers-Oak 4.1
Arrojo-TB 3.4
Gordon-Bos 3.2

Total Baseball Ranking
Belle-Chi 6.3
Griffey-Sea 5.8
Clemens-Tor 5.3
Rodriguez-Sea 4.8
Williams-NY 4.8

TEAM	G	W	L	PCT	GB	R	OR	AB	H	2B	3B	HR	BB	SO	AVG	OBP	SLG	OPS	OPS+	BR	BR+	PF	CHI	RC	SB	CS	SBA	SBR
EAST																												
ATL	162	103	59	.636		840	**661**	5569	1481	309	23	197	608	962	.266	.344	.436	780	101	9	10	100	**102**	839	148	66	69	9
NY	163	97	66	.595	6.5	853	711	5572	1553	297	14	181	717	994	.279	**.366**	.434	800	111	71	101	97	95	897	150	61	71	12
PHI	162	77	85	.475	26	841	846	5598	1539	302	44	161	631	1081	.275	.353	.431	784	100	27	4	103	100	869	125	35	**78**	15
MON	162	68	94	.420	35	718	853	5559	1473	**320**	**47**	163	438	939	.265	.325	.427	752	97	-61	-40	97	99	745	70	51	58	-2
FLA	162	64	98	.395	39	691	852	5578	1465	266	44	128	479	1145	.263	.328	.395	723	92	-109	-67	94	101	720	92	46	67	4
CENTRAL																												
HOU	162	97	65	.599		823	675	5485	1463	293	23	168	**728**	1138	.267	.358	.420	778	104	24	38	98	98	845	166	75	69	10
CIN	163	96	67	.589	1.5	865	711	5649	1536	312	37	209	569	1125	.272	.343	.451	794	102	33	11	103	**102**	887	164	54	75	**17**
PIT	161	78	83	.484	18.5	775	782	5468	1417	282	40	171	573	1197	.259	.336	.419	755	95	-41	-38	100	**102**	782	112	44	72	9
STL	161	75	86	.466	21.5	809	838	5570	1461	274	27	194	613	1202	.262	.341	.426	767	98	-17	-20	100	**102**	824	134	48	74	13
MIL	161	74	87	.460	22.5	815	886	5582	1524	299	30	165	658	1065	.273	.355	.426	781	103	25	36	99	96	868	81	33	71	6
CHI	162	67	95	.414	30	747	920	5482	1411	255	35	189	571	1170	.257	.332	.420	752	96	-52	-39	98	101	761	60	44	58	-2
WEST																												
ARI	162	100	62	.617		**908**	676	5658	1566	289	46	216	588	1045	.277	.350	.459	809	107	65	61	101	**102**	**929**	137	39	**78**	16
SF	162	86	76	.531	14	872	831	5563	1507	307	18	188	696	1028	.271	.358	.434	792	**113**	48	**117**	93	100	878	109	56	66	4
LA	162	77	85	.475	23	793	787	5567	1480	253	23	187	594	1030	.266	.342	.420	762	103	-23	26	94	101	815	167	68	71	13
SD	162	74	88	.457	26	710	781	5394	1360	256	22	153	631	1169	.252	.334	.393	727	96	-89	-28	92	**102**	719	**174**	67	72	15
COL	162	72	90	.444	28	906	1028	5717	**1644**	305	39	**223**	508	**863**	**.288**	.350	**.472**	**822**	87	**88**	-104	127	100	**929**	70	43	62	0
TOT	1295					12966		89011	23880	4619	512	2893	9602	17153	.269	.345	.430	774							1959	830	70	140

TEAM	CG	SH	SV	IP	H	H/G	HR	BB	SO	RAT	ERA	ERA+	OAV	OOB	PR	PR+	PF	CPI	FA	E	DP	FW	PW	BW	SBW	DIF
EAST																										
ATL	9	9	45	1471	1398	8.6	142	507	1197	**11.9**	**3.63**	**124**	.251	**.316**	**152**	**143**	99	100	.982	111	127	.6	**13.6**	1.0	.0	7.0
NY	5	7	49	1456[2]	1372	8.5	167	617	1172	12.7	4.27	103	.252	.333	47	18	96	96	**.989**	**68**	147	**3.3**	1.8	9.6	.3	.7
PHI	11	6	32	1438[1]	1494	9.4	212	627	1030	13.7	4.93	96	.269	.349	-58	-32	103	98	.983	100	144	1.3	-3.0	.4	.6	-3.1
MON	6	4	44	1434[1]	1505	9.5	152	572	1043	13.5	4.70	96	.270	.345	-21	-34	98	95	.974	160	125	-2.4	-3.2	-3.7	-1.0	-2.5
FLA	6	5	33	1435[2]	1560	9.8	171	655	943	14.3	4.90	89	.281	.363	-54	-90	96	103	.979	127	150	-.4	-8.5	-6.3	-.5	-1.3
CENTRAL																										
HOU	12	8	48	1458[2]	1485	9.2	**128**	**478**	**1204**	12.4	3.83	115	.267	.329	119	98	97	**104**	.983	106	175	.9	9.3	3.6	.1	2.2
CIN	6	**11**	**55**	1462	**1309**	**8.1**	190	636	1081	12.3	3.99	117	**.241**	.326	94	107	102	100	.983	105	139	1.0	10.2	1.1	**.8**	1.6
PIT	8	3	34	1433[1]	1444	9.1	160	633	1083	13.4	4.33	106	.263	.345	37	38	100	102	.976	147	179	-1.6	3.6	-3.5	.0	-.8
STL	5	3	38	1445[1]	1519	9.5	161	667	1025	14.1	4.74	96	.273	.357	-29	-27	100	100	.978	132	163	-.7	-2.5	-1.8	.4	-.7
MIL	2	5	40	1442[2]	1618	10.1	213	616	987	14.3	5.08	89	.284	.359	-82	-87	99	102	.979	127	146	-.4	-8.2	3.5	-.3	-.9
CHI	11	6	32	1430[2]	1619	10.2	221	529	980	13.7	5.27	86	.286	.350	-112	-121	99	97	.977	139	135	-1.1	-11.4	-3.6	-1.0	3.3
WEST																										
ARI	**16**	9	42	1467[1]	1387	8.6	176	543	1198	12.2	3.78	121	.249	.321	128	130	100	103	.983	104	132	1.1	12.3	5.8	.7	-.7
SF	6	3	42	1456[1]	1486	9.2	194	655	1076	13.6	4.71	89	.265	.347	-24	-89	92	98	.983	105	155	1.0	-8.4	**11.1**	-.5	1.9
LA	8	6	37	1453	1438	9.0	192	594	1077	13.0	4.45	96	.258	.336	18	-28	94	98	.978	137	137	-1.0	-2.6	2.5	.4	-3.1
SD	5	6	43	1420[1]	1454	9.3	193	529	1078	12.8	4.47	94	.266	.334	15	-47	92	99	.979	129	151	-.5	-4.4	-2.6	.6	.0
COL	12	2	33	1429	1700	10.8	237	737	1032	15.8	6.02	97	.301	.387	-231	-26	127	101	.981	118	**189**	.2	-2.4	-9.8	-.8	4.0
TOT	128	93	647	23134[2]		9.3				13.3	4.57		.269	.345					.981	1915	2394					

Runs
Bagwell-Hou 143
Bell-Ari 132
Biggio-Hou 123
Alfonzo-NY 123

Hits
Gonzalez-Ari 206
Glanville-Phi 204
Cirillo-Mil 198
Casey-Cin 197

Doubles
Biggio-Hou 56
Vidro-Mon 45
Gonzalez-Ari 45
Grace-Chi 44
Jenkins-Mil 43

Triples
Perez-Col 11
Abreu-Phi 11
Womack-Ari 10
Finley-Ari 10

Home Runs
McGwire-StL 65
Sosa-Chi 63
Vaughn-Cin 45
C.Jones-Atl 45

Total Bases
Sosa-Chi 397
V.Guerrero-Mon 366
McGwire-StL 363
C.Jones-Atl 359
Helton-Col 339

Runs Batted In
McGwire-StL 147
Williams-Ari 142
Sosa-Chi 141
Bichette-Col 133
V.Guerrero-Mon 131

Runs Produced
Bagwell-Hou 227
Bell-Ari 206
Williams-Ari 205
Alfonzo-NY 204
Bichette-Col 203

Bases On Balls
Bagwell-Hou 149
McGwire-StL 133
C.Jones-Atl 126
Olerud-NY 125
Abreu-Phi 109

Batting Average
Walker-Col .379
Gonzalez-Ari .336
Abreu-Phi .335
Casey-Cin .332
Cirillo-Mil .326

On-Base Percentage
Walker-Col .464
Bagwell-Hou .458
Abreu-Phi .448
C.Jones-Atl .445
Olerud-NY .431

Slugging Average
Walker-Col .710
McGwire-StL .697
Sosa-Chi .635
C.Jones-Atl .633
Giles-Pit .614

On-Base Plus Slugging
Walker-Col 1174
McGwire-StL 1124
C.Jones-Atl 1078
Bagwell-Hou 1049
Giles-Pit 1037

Adjusted OPS
McGwire-StL 177
C.Jones-Atl 168
Bagwell-Hou 165
Giles-Pit 159
Walker-Col 150

Batter Runs
McGwire-StL 63.8
C.Jones-Atl 63.1
Walker-Col 62.0
Bagwell-Hou 61.6
Giles-Pit 47.8

Adjusted Batter Runs
Bagwell-Hou 64.1
C.Jones-Atl 63.3
McGwire-StL 63.2
Giles-Pit 48.3
Sosa-Chi 44.6

Clutch Hitting Index
Ordonez-NY 133
Jordan-Atl 125
Williams-Ari 113
Kent-SF 112
Everett-Hou 112

Runs Created
C.Jones-Atl 165
Bagwell-Hou 161
McGwire-StL 160
Walker-Col 143
Abreu-Phi 142

Total Average
Walker-Col 1.344
McGwire-StL 1.284
C.Jones-Atl 1.244
Bagwell-Hou 1.217
Giles-Pit 1.131

Stolen Bases
Womack-Ari 72
Cedeno-NY 66
Young-LA 51
Castillo-Fla 50

Stolen Base Average
Glanville-Phi 94.4
C.Jones-Atl 89.3
Kendall-Pit 88.0
Martin-Pit 87.0
Drew-StL 86.4

Stolen Base Runs
Womack-Ari 11.3
Cedeno-NY 8.6
Glanville-Phi 6.8
Reese-Cin 5.9
Renteria-StL 5.3

Fielding Runs
Benjamin-Pit 36.3
A.Jones-Atl 35.0
Perez-Col 28.4
Biggio-Hou 22.6
Ventura-NY 19.6

Total Player Rating
Bagwell-Hou 5.2
Giles-Pit 4.9
Sosa-Chi 4.8
A.Jones-Atl 4.6
Ventura-NY 4.5

Wins
Hampton-Hou 22
Lima-Hou 21
Maddux-Atl 19

Win Percentage
Hampton-Hou .846
Millwood-Atl .720
Bottenfield-StL .720
Schilling-Phi .714
Maddux-Atl .679

Games
Kline-Mon 82
Wendell-NY 80
Telford-Mon 79
Sullivan-Cin 79
Benitez-NY 77

Complete Games
Johnson-Ari 12
Schilling-Phi 8
Astacio-Col 7
Brown-LA 5

Shutouts
Ashby-SD 3

Saves
Urbina-Mon 41
Hoffman-SD 40
Wagner-Hou 39
Rocker-Atl 38

Innings Pitched
Johnson-Ari 271.2
Brown-LA 252.1
Lima-Hou 246.1
Hampton-Hou 239.0
Glavine-Atl 234.0

Fewest Hits/Game
Millwood-Atl 6.63
Johnson-Ari 6.86
Brown-LA 7.49
Hampton-Hou 7.76
Daal-Ari 7.88

Fewest BB/Game
Reynolds-Hou 1.44
Maddux-Atl 1.52
Lima-Hou 1.61
Woodard-Mil 1.75
Smoltz-Atl 1.93

Strikeouts
Johnson-Ari 364
Brown-LA 221
Astacio-Col 210
Millwood-Atl 205
Reynolds-Hou 197

Strikeouts/Game
Johnson-Ari 12.06
Hitchcock-SD 8.49
Lieber-Chi 8.23
Nomo-Mil 8.22
Astacio-Col 8.15

Ratio
Millwood-Atl 9.12
Johnson-Ari 9.47
Brown-LA 9.84
Smoltz-Atl 10.24
Schilling-Phi 10.38

Earned Run Average
Johnson-Ari 2.48
Millwood-Atl 2.68
Hampton-Hou 2.90
Brown-LA 3.00
Smoltz-Atl 3.19

Adjusted ERA
Johnson-Ari 184
Millwood-Atl 168
Hampton-Hou 152
Brown-LA 143
Smoltz-Atl 141

Opponents' Batting Avg.
Millwood-Atl .202
Johnson-Ari .208
Brown-LA .222
Daal-Ari .236
Schilling-Phi .237

Opponents' On-Base Pct.
Millwood-Atl .258
Johnson-Ari .267
Brown-LA .273
Schilling-Phi .288
Smoltz-Atl .290

Starter Runs
Johnson-Ari 62.8
Millwood-Atl 47.7
Hampton-Hou 44.3
Brown-LA 44.0
Smoltz-Atl 28.5

Adjusted Starter Runs
Johnson-Ari 63.0
Millwood-Atl 46.7
Hampton-Hou 41.6
Brown-LA 38.6
Smoltz-Atl 27.5

Clutch Pitching Index
Hampton-Hou 117
Bottenfield-StL 117
Maddux-Atl 115
Ortiz-SF 115
Karl-Mil 115

Relief Runs
Wagner-Hou 24.9
Benitez-NY 23.6
Williamson-Cin 22.4
Remlinger-Atl 20.5
Sullivan-Cin 19.7

Adjusted Relief Runs
Wagner-Hou 24.4
Benitez-NY 22.9
Williamson-Cin 22.9
Sullivan-Cin 20.5
Remlinger-Atl 20.1

Relief Ranking
Williamson-Cin 45.7
Wagner-Hou 37.9
Rocker-Atl 32.8
Graves-Cin 31.7
Benitez-NY 30.2

Total Pitcher Index
Hampton-Hou 5.5
Johnson-Ari 5.2
Millwood-Atl 4.5
Williamson-Cin 4.3
Brown-LA 3.7

Total Baseball Ranking
Hampton-Hou 5.5
Bagwell-Hou 5.2
Johnson-Ari 5.2
Giles-Pit 4.9
Sosa-Chi 4.8

TEAM	G	W	L	PCT	GB	R	OR	AB	H	2B	3B	HR	BB	SO	AVG	OBP	SLG	OPS	OPS+	BR	BR+	PF	CHI	RC	SB	CS	SBA	SBR
EAST																												
NY	162	98	64	.605		900	731	5568	1568	302	36	193	718	978	.282	.369	.453	822	**110**	81	**92**	99	97	938	104	57	65	3
BOS	162	94	68	.580	4	836	**718**	5579	1551	334	42	176	597	928	.278	.354	.448	802	100	25	-1	103	97	882	67	39	63	1
TOR	162	84	78	.519	14	883	862	5642	1580	**337**	14	212	578	1077	.280	.355	.457	812	103	46	33	102	99	918	119	48	71	9
BAL	162	78	84	.481	20	851	815	5637	1572	299	21	203	615	890	.279	.356	.447	803	108	32	66	96	96	896	107	46	70	7
TB	162	69	93	.426	29	772	913	5586	1531	272	29	145	544	1042	.274	.345	.411	756	91	-62	-70	101	100	779	73	49	60	-1
CENTRAL																												
CLE	162	97	65	.599		**1009**	860	5634	1629	309	32	209	743	1099	.289	**.377**	.467	**844**	109	**130**	86	105	101	**1014**	**147**	50	75	**15**
CHI	162	75	86	.466	21.5	777	870	5644	1563	298	37	162	499	**810**	.277	.339	.429	768	95	-50	-52	100	100	809	110	50	69	7
DET	161	69	92	.429	27.5	747	882	5481	1433	289	34	212	458	1049	.261	.328	.443	771	96	-57	-52	99	99	782	108	70	61	-1
KC	161	64	97	.398	32.5	856	921	5624	1584	294	**52**	151	535	932	.282	.351	.433	784	97	-9	-27	102	103	850	127	39	**77**	14
MIN	161	63	97	.394	33	686	845	5495	1450	285	30	105	500	978	.264	.331	.384	715	79	-148	-170	104	103	686	118	60	66	5
WEST																												
TEX	162	95	67	.586		945	859	5651	**1653**	304	29	230	611	937	**.293**	.364	**.479**	843	108	111	70	105	99	972	111	54	67	6
OAK	162	87	75	.537	8	893	846	5519	1430	287	20	235	**770**	1129	.259	.357	.446	803	109	35	74	96	100	899	70	37	65	2
SEA	162	79	83	.488	16	859	905	5572	1499	263	21	**244**	610	1095	.269	.346	.455	801	105	15	36	98	101	886	130	45	74	13
ANA	162	70	92	.432	25	711	826	5494	1404	248	22	158	511	1022	.256	.324	.395	719	84	-149	-145	99	**107**	692	71	45	61	0
TOT	1132					11725		78126	21447	4121	419	2635	8289	13966	.275	.350	.440	789							1462	689	68	80

TEAM	CG	SH	SV	IP	H	H/G	HR	BB	SO	RAT	ERA	ERA+	OAV	OOB	PR	PR+	PF	CPI	FA	E	DP	FW	PW	BW	SBW	DIF
EAST																										
NY	6	10	**50**	1439^{2}	1402	**8.8**	**158**	581	1111	12.8	4.14	114	.255	.332	116	97	97	100	.982	111	132	.2	9.0	**8.6**	-.3	-.4
BOS	6	**12**	**50**	1436^{2}	**1396**	**8.8**	160	**469**	**1131**	**12.1**	**4.00**	**124**	**.253**	**.317**	**137**	**151**	102	97	.979	127	132	-.6	**14.0**	-.0	-.4	.3
TOR	14	9	39	1439	1582	9.9	191	575	1009	13.9	4.93	100	.280	.352	-11	0	101	101	.983	106	165	.5	.0	3.1	.3	-.7
BAL	**17**	11	33	1435	1468	9.3	198	647	982	13.6	4.77	98	.269	.351	14	-14	96	103	**.986**	**89**	191	**1.4**	-1.2	6.2	.1	-9.2
TB	6	5	45	1433	1606	10.1	172	695	1055	15.0	5.06	98	.286	.373	-32	-15	102	**106**	.978	135	**198**	-1.0	-1.3	-6.4	-.6	-2.4
CENTRAL																										
CLE	3	6	46	1450^{1}	1503	9.4	197	634	1120	13.6	4.89	103	.268	.348	-5	22	104	98	.983	106	154	.5	2.1	8.0	**.9**	4.8
CHI	6	3	39	1438^{1}	1608	10.1	210	596	968	14.2	4.92	99	.282	.356	-10	-8	100	105	.977	136	149	-1.1	-.7	-4.8	.1	1.1
DET	4	6	33	1421	1528	9.7	209	583	976	13.9	5.18	94	.276	.353	-50	-50	100	98	.982	106	156	.5	-4.6	-4.8	-.6	-1.8
KC	11	3	29	1420^{2}	1607	10.2	202	643	831	14.7	5.35	94	.288	.369	-78	-53	103	102	.980	125	188	-.5	-4.9	-2.4	.8	-9.2
MIN	13	8	34	1423^{1}	1591	10.1	208	487	927	13.4	5.01	102	.283	.343	-23	12	105	99	.985	92	150	1.2	1.2	-15.7	-.0	-3.4
WEST																										
TEX	6	9	47	1436^{1}	1626	10.2	186	509	979	13.7	5.07	100	.286	.349	-34	0	104	98	.981	119	169	-.2	.0	6.5	.0	7.8
OAK	6	5	48	1438^{1}	1537	9.7	160	569	967	13.6	4.70	99	.274	.346	26	-9	96	99	.980	122	166	-.3	-.8	6.9	-.3	.8
SEA	7	6	40	1433^{2}	1613	10.2	191	684	980	14.9	5.24	90	.287	.371	-60	-84	97	104	.981	113	182	.1	-7.7	3.4	.7	1.7
ANA	4	7	37	1431^{1}	1472	9.3	177	624	877	13.6	4.80	101	.269	.350	10	8	100	99	.983	106	156	.5	.8	-13.4	-.5	1.8
TOT	109	100	570	20076^{2}		9.7				13.8	4.86		.275	.350					.982	1593	2288					

Runs
R.Alomar-Cle 138
Jeter-NY 134
Green-Tor 134
M.Ramirez-Cle 131
Griffey-Sea 123

Hits
Jeter-NY 219
Surhoff-Bal 207
Williams-NY 202
Velarde-Ana-Oak 200
Rodriguez-Tex 199

Doubles
Green-Tor 45
Sweeney-KC 44
Dye-KC 44
Garciaparra-Bos 42

Triples
Offerman-Bos 11
Jeter-NY 9
Febles-KC 9
Damon-KC 9

Home Runs
Griffey-Sea 48
Palmeiro-Tex 47
M.Ramirez-Cle 44
Delgado-Tor 44

Total Bases
Green-Tor 361
Palmeiro-Tex 356
Griffey-Sea 349
M.Ramirez-Cle 346
Jeter-NY 346

Runs Batted In
M.Ramirez-Cle 165
Palmeiro-Tex 148
Griffey-Sea 134
Delgado-Tor 134
Gonzalez-Tex 128

Runs Produced
M.Ramirez-Cle 252
R.Alomar-Cle 234
Green-Tor 215
Jeter-NY 212
Griffey-Sea 209

Bases On Balls
Thome-Cle 127
Giambi-Oak 105
Jaha-Oak 101
Belle-Bal 101
Williams-NY 100

Batting Average
Garciaparra-Bos ..... .357
Jeter-NY .... .349
Williams-NY .... .342
Martinez-Sea .... .337
M.Ramirez-Cle ...... .333

On-Base Percentage
Martinez-Sea .... .450
M.Ramirez-Cle ...... .448
Jeter-NY .... .441
Williams-NY .... .438
R.Alomar-Cle .... .430

Slugging Average
M.Ramirez-Cle ...... .663
Palmeiro-Tex .... .630
Garciaparra-Bos ..... .603
Gonzalez-Tex .... .601
Green-Tor .... .588

On-Base Plus Slugging
M.Ramirez-Cle 1111
Palmeiro-Tex 1056
Garciaparra-Bos 1025
Martinez-Sea 1003
Jeter-NY 993

Adjusted OPS
M.Ramirez-Cle 171
Martinez-Sea 158
Palmeiro-Tex 157
Giambi-Oak 154
Jeter-NY 153

Batter Runs
M.Ramirez-Cle 65.0
Palmeiro-Tex 56.6
Jeter-NY 52.4
Garciaparra-Bos 46.1
Williams-NY 45.7

Adjusted Batter Runs
M.Ramirez-Cle 58.4
Jeter-NY 54.2
Giambi-Oak 50.6
Palmeiro-Tex 50.3
Martinez-Sea 48.8

Clutch Hitting Index
Sexson-Cle 127
Valentin-Bos 126
M.Ramirez-Cle 126
Beltran-KC 124
Justice-Cle 122

Runs Created
Jeter-NY 158
M.Ramirez-Cle 158
Palmeiro-Tex 152
Giambi-Oak 142
Williams-NY 140

Total Average
M.Ramirez-Cle 1.245
Palmeiro-Tex 1.138
Martinez-Sea 1.112
Garciaparra-Bos 1.098
Thome-Cle 1.096

Stolen Bases
Hunter-Det-Sea 44
Vizquel-Cle 42
Goodwin-Tex 39
Stewart-Tor 37
R.Alomar-Cle 37

Stolen Base Average
Lawton-Min 86.7
R.Alomar-Cle 86.0
Damon-KC 85.7
Belle-Bal 85.0
Hunter-Det-Sea 84.6

Stolen Base Runs
Hunter-Det-Sea 6.9
Vizquel-Cle 6.1
R.Alomar-Cle 6.0
Damon-KC 5.8
Anderson-Bal 5.5

Fielding Runs
Sanchez-KC 30.4
Bordick-Bal 29.6
Cairo-TB 22.2
D.Cruz-Det 21.1
Varitek-Bos 21.0

Total Player Rating
R.Alomar-Cle 6.2
A.Rodriguez-Sea 5.4
Williams-NY 5.2
Griffey-Sea 4.7
M.Ramirez-Cle 4.5

Wins
P.Martinez-Bos 23
Sele-Tex 18
Mussina-Bal 18
Colon-Cle 18

Win Percentage
P.Martinez-Bos ..... .852
Colon-Cle .... .783
Mussina-Bal .... .720
Garcia-Sea .... .680
Sele-Tex .... .667

Games
Wells-Min 76
Groom-Oak 76
Trombley-Min 75
Lowe-Bos 74
Lloyd-Tor 74

Complete Games
D.Wells-Tor 7
Ponson-Bal 6
Erickson-Bal 6

Shutouts
Erickson-Bal 3
Witt-TB 2
Sele-Tex 2
Moehler-Det 2
Milton-Min 2

Saves
Rivera-NY 45
Wetteland-Tex 43
Hernandez-TB 43
Jackson-Cle 39
Mesa-Sea 33

Innings Pitched
D.Wells-Tor 231.2
Erickson-Bal 230.1
Moyer-Sea 228.0
Burba-Cle 220.0
Helling-Tex 219.1

Fewest Hits/Game
P.Martinez-Bos 6.75
Cone-NY 7.63
Hernandez-NY 7.85
Colon-Cle 8.12
Milton-Min 8.29

Fewest BB/Game
Heredia-Oak 1.53
P.Martinez-Bos 1.56
Radke-Min 1.81
Moyer-Sea 1.89
Mussina-Bal 2.30

Strikeouts
P.Martinez-Bos 313
Finley-Ana 200
Sele-Tex 186
Cone-NY 177
Burba-Cle 174

Strikeouts/Game
P.Martinez-Bos 13.20
Finley-Ana 8.44
Cone-NY 8.24
Sele-Tex 8.17
Clemens-NY 7.82

Ratio
P.Martinez-Bos 8.69
Milton-Min 11.17
Mussina-Bal 11.51
Moyer-Sea 11.53
Radke-Min 11.69

Earned Run Average
P.Martinez-Bos 2.07
Cone-NY 3.44
Mussina-Bal 3.50
Radke-Min 3.75
Rosado-KC 3.85

Adjusted ERA
P.Martinez-Bos 241
Cone-NY 138
Radke-Min 136
Mussina-Bal 134
Rosado-KC 130

Opponents' Batting Avg.
P.Martinez-Bos ..... .205
Cone-NY .... .229
Hernandez-NY .... .233
Colon-Cle .... .242
Milton-Min .... .243

Opponents' On-Base Pct.
P.Martinez-Bos ..... .249
Milton-Min .... .302
Moyer-Sea .... .312
Hernandez-NY .... .315
Mussina-Bal .... .315

Starter Runs
P.Martinez-Bos 66.5
Mussina-Bal 31.1
Cone-NY 30.7
Radke-Min 27.4
Moyer-Sea 25.4

Adjusted Starter Runs
P.Martinez-Bos 67.5
Radke-Min 31.4
Cone-NY 28.6
Mussina-Bal 28.1
Saberhagen-Bos 26.3

Clutch Pitching Index
Radke-Min 115
Sirotka-Chi 112
Parque-Chi 112
Olivares-Ana-Oak ... 111
Halama-Sea 111

Relief Runs
Foulke-Chi 31.0
Lowe-Bos 27.2
Zimmerman-Tex 24.5
Rivera-NY 23.4
Brocail-Det 21.4

Adjusted Relief Runs
Foulke-Chi 31.1
Lowe-Bos 27.9
Zimmerman-Tex 25.4
Rivera-NY 23.0
Brocail-Det 21.4

Relief Ranking
Rivera-NY 45.9
Zimmerman-Tex 32.9
Lowe-Bos 27.4
Hernandez-TB 25.2
Karsay-Cle 24.4

Total Pitcher Index
P.Martinez-Bos 8.1
Rivera-NY 4.5
Mussina-Bal 3.6
Radke-Min 3.5
Saberhagen-Bos 3.2

Total Baseball Ranking
P.Martinez-Bos 8.1
R.Alomar-Cle 6.2
A.Rodriguez-Sea 5.4
Williams-NY 5.2
Griffey-Sea 4.7

TEAM	G	W	L	PCT	GB	R	OR	AB	H	2B	3B	HR	BB	SO	AVG	OBP	SLG	OPS	OPS+	BR	BR+	PF	CHI	RC	SB	CS	SBA	SBR
EAST																												
ATL	162	95	67	.586		810	**714**	5489	1490	274	26	179	595	1010	.271	.349	.429	778	102	8	20	99	100	831	148	56	73	13
NY	162	94	68	.580	1	807	738	5486	1445	281	20	198	675	1037	.263	.349	.430	779	105	11	45	96	98	831	66	46	59	-2
FLA	161	79	82	.491	15.5	731	797	5509	1441	274	29	160	540	1184	.262	.334	.409	743	97	-68	-27	95	101	771	**168**	55	75	**18**
MON	162	67	95	.414	28	738	902	5535	1475	310	35	178	476	1048	.266	.328	.432	760	94	-48	-53	101	100	768	58	48	55	-4
PHI	162	65	97	.401	30	708	830	5511	1386	304	40	144	611	1117	.251	.331	.400	731	88	-92	-102	101	99	747	102	30	**77**	12
CENTRAL																												
STL	162	95	67	.586		887	771	5478	1481	259	25	235	675	1253	.270	.359	.455	814	110	83	82	100	99	911	87	51	63	1
CIN	163	85	77	.525	10	825	765	5635	1545	302	36	200	559	995	.274	.346	.447	793	100	32	1	104	97	868	100	38	72	9
MIL	163	73	89	.451	22	740	826	5563	1366	297	25	177	620	1245	.246	.328	.403	731	91	-95	-78	98	103	740	72	44	62	0
HOU	162	72	90	.444	23	938	944	5570	1547	289	36	**249**	673	1129	.278	.364	**.477**	**841**	110	**135**	87	105	98	**962**	114	52	69	7
PIT	162	69	93	.426	26	793	888	5643	1506	**320**	31	168	564	1032	.267	.341	.424	765	98	-25	-15	99	100	814	86	40	68	5
CHI	162	65	97	.401	30	764	904	5577	1426	272	23	183	632	1120	.256	.337	.411	748	95	-55	-35	97	100	790	93	37	72	8
WEST																												
SF	162	97	65	.599		925	747	5519	1535	304	44	226	**709**	1032	.278	**.366**	.472	838	**125**	130	**204**	93	97	960	79	39	67	4
LA	162	86	76	.531	11	798	729	5481	1408	265	28	211	668	1083	.257	.343	.431	774	104	-4	38	95	99	820	95	42	69	6
ARI	162	85	77	.525	12	792	754	5527	1466	282	44	179	535	975	.265	.337	.429	766	97	-27	-31	101	102	802	97	44	69	6
COL	162	82	80	.506	15	**968**	897	5660	**1664**	**320**	**53**	161	601	**907**	**.294**	**.366**	.455	821	88	101	-100	128	**104**	943	131	61	68	7
SD	162	76	86	.469	21	752	815	5560	1413	279	37	157	602	1177	.254	.332	.402	734	96	-86	-38	94	**104**	750	131	53	71	10
TOT	1296					12976		88743	23594	4632	532	3005	9735	17344	.266	.345	.432	776							1627	736	69	100

TEAM	CG	SH	SV	IP	H	H/G	HR	BB	SO	RAT	ERA	ERA+	OAV	OOB	PR	PR+	PF	CPI	FA	E	DP	FW	PW	BW	SBW	DIF
EAST																										
ATL	13	9	**53**	1440^1	1428	9.0	165	**484**	1093	**12.2**	**4.05**	112	.258	**.321**	**93**	77	98	99	.979	129	138	-.6	7.3	1.9	.6	4.9
NY	8	10	49	1450	1398	8.7	164	574	1164	12.7	4.16	106	**.252**	.329	76	42	95	98	.980	118	121	.0	4.0	4.3	-.8	5.7
FLA	5	4	48	1429^2	1477	9.3	169	650	1051	13.7	4.59	96	.269	.351	6	-29	95	103	.980	125	144	-.4	-2.7	-2.5	**1.1**	3.2
MON	4	7	39	1424^2	1575	10.0	181	579	1011	14.0	5.13	92	.282	.356	-79	-65	102	98	.978	132	151	-.7	-6.1	-5.0	-1.0	-1.0
PHI	8	6	34	1438^2	1458	9.2	201	640	1123	13.4	4.78	99	.265	.346	-23	-9	102	99	.983	100	136	1.0	-.8	-9.6	.5	-7.0
CENTRAL																										
STL	10	7	37	1433^2	1403	8.9	196	606	1100	13.1	4.39	105	.259	.341	39	38	100	104	.981	111	148	.4	3.6	7.8	-.5	2.9
CIN	8	7	42	1456^1	1446	9.0	190	659	1015	13.3	4.33	110	.261	.344	49	69	103	106	.982	111	156	.4	6.6	.1	.3	-3.2
MIL	2	7	29	1466^1	1501	9.3	174	728	967	14.1	4.64	98	.269	.360	-1	-14	98	105	.981	118	**187**	.0	-1.3	-7.3	-.6	1.3
HOU	8	2	30	1437^2	1596	10.0	234	598	1064	14.2	5.42	90	.281	.356	-125	-81	105	98	.978	133	149	-.8	-7.6	8.3	.0	-8.7
PIT	5	7	27	1449	1554	9.7	163	711	1070	14.5	4.94	93	.277	.364	-50	-56	99	101	.979	132	169	-.7	-5.2	-1.4	-.1	-4.3
CHI	10	5	39	1454^2	1505	9.4	231	658	1143	13.8	5.26	87	.268	.351	-101	-114	99	95	.983	100	139	1.0	-10.7	-3.3	.2	-3.0
WEST																										
SF	9	**15**	47	1444^1	1452	9.1	**151**	623	1076	13.2	4.21	100	.266	.346	68	4	91	**107**	**.985**	**93**	173	**1.4**	.4	**19.3**	-.2	-4.7
LA	9	11	36	1445	**1379**	**8.6**	176	600	1154	12.8	4.11	107	**.252**	.334	84	47	95	103	.978	135	151	-.9	4.5	3.6	-.0	-2.0
ARI	**16**	8	38	1443^2	1441	9.0	190	500	**1220**	12.4	4.36	106	.262	.328	45	41	100	99	.982	107	138	.6	3.9	-2.9	-.0	2.6
COL	7	2	33	1430	1568	9.9	221	588	1001	14.1	5.26	**113**	.281	.357	-99	**83**	128	100	**.985**	94	176	1.3	**7.9**	-9.4	.0	1.3
SD	5	5	46	1459^1	1443	8.9	191	649	1071	13.4	4.53	97	.258	.342	18	-27	94	100	.977	141	155	-1.2	-2.5	-3.5	.4	2.1
TOT	127	112	627	23103^1		9.3				13.4	4.63		.266	.345					.981	1879	2431					

Runs
Bagwell-Hou 152
Helton-Col 138
Edmonds-StL 129
Bonds-SF 129
A.Jones-Atl 122

Hits
Helton-Col 216
Vidro-Mon 200
A.Jones-Atl 199
V.Guerrero-Mon 197
Kent-SF 196

Doubles
Helton-Col 59
Cirillo-Col 53
Vidro-Mon 51
Gonzalez-Ari 47
Green-LA 44

Triples
Womack-Ari 14
Perez-Col 11
V.Guerrero-Mon 11
Abreu-Phi 10

Home Runs
Sosa-Chi 50
Bonds-SF 49
Bagwell-Hou 47
Hidalgo-Hou 44
V.Guerrero-Mon 44

Total Bases
Helton-Col 405
Sosa-Chi 383
V.Guerrero-Mon 379
Bagwell-Hou 363

Runs Batted In
Helton-Col 147
Sosa-Chi 138
Bagwell-Hou 132
Kent-SF 125

Runs Produced
Helton-Col 243
Bagwell-Hou 237
Cirillo-Col 215
Kent-SF 206
Giles-Pit 199

Bases On Balls
Bonds-SF 117
Giles-Pit 114
Bagwell-Hou 107
Helton-Col 103
Edmonds-StL 103

Batting Average
Helton-Col .... .372
Alou-Hou .... .355
V.Guerrero-Mon .... .345
Hammonds-Col .... .335
Castillo-Fla .... .334

On-Base Percentage
Helton-Col .... .470
Bonds-SF .... .445
Sheffield-LA .... .442
Giles-Pit .... .437
Kent-SF .... .430

Slugging Average
Helton-Col .... .698
Bonds-SF .... .688
V.Guerrero-Mon .... .664
Sheffield-LA .... .643
Hidalgo-Hou .... .636

On-Base Plus Slugging
Helton-Col 1168
Bonds-SF 1133
Sheffield-LA 1085
V.Guerrero-Mon 1077
Alou-Hou 1047

Adjusted OPS
Bonds-SF 194
Sheffield-LA 178
Kent-SF 167
V.Guerrero-Mon 164
Sosa-Chi 162

Batter Runs
Helton-Col 82.8
Bonds-SF 61.9
Bagwell-Hou 56.1
V.Guerrero-Mon 55.9
Sheffield-LA 55.8

Adjusted Batter Runs
Bonds-SF 72.8
Sheffield-LA 62.9
Kent-SF 62.8
Sosa-Chi 57.5
V.Guerrero-Mon 55.0

Clutch Hitting Index
Hammonds-Col 131
Cirillo-Col 129
Relaford-Phi-SD 126
Young-Pit 118
Snow-SF 117

Runs Created
Helton-Col 192
Sosa-Chi 157
Bagwell-Hou 156
Bonds-SF 155
Giles-Pit 151

Total Average
Helton-Col 1.356
Bonds-SF 1.339
Sheffield-LA 1.190
Giles-Pit 1.153
Bagwell-Hou 1.130

Stolen Bases
Castillo-Fla 62
Goodwin-Col-LA 55
E.Young-Chi 54
Womack-Ari 45
Furcal-Atl 40

Stolen Base Average
Reese-Cin 90.6
Floyd-Fla 88.9
E.Young-Chi 88.5
Hunter-Col-Cin 87.0
Goodwin-Col-LA 84.6

Stolen Base Runs
E.Young-Chi 9.4
Goodwin-Col-LA 8.6
Womack-Ari 6.1
Castillo-Fla 5.9
Reese-Cin 5.3

Fielding Runs
Perez-Col 38.9
Meares-Pit 25.2
A.Jones-Atl 20.3
Morris-Pit 19.8
Helton-Col 18.9

Total Player Rating
Bonds-SF 7.3
Kent-SF 6.6
Giles-Pit 5.7
Edmonds-StL 5.1
Sheffield-LA 5.0

Wins
Glavine-Atl 21
Kile-StL 20
Maddux-Atl 19
Johnson-Ari 19
Park-LA 18

Win Percentage
Johnson-Ari .... .731
Estes-SF .... .714
Elarton-Hou .... .708
Glavine-Atl .... .700
Kile-StL .... .690

Games
Kline-Mon 83
Sullivan-Cin 79
Myers-Col 78
Wendell-NY 77

Complete Games
Schilling-Phi-Ari 8
Johnson-Ari 8
Maddux-Atl 6
Lieber-Chi 6

Shutouts
Maddux-Atl 3
Johnson-Ari 3

Saves
Alfonseca-Fla 45
Hoffman-SD 43
Nen-SF 41
Benitez-NY 41
Graves-Cin 30

Innings Pitched
Lieber-Chi 251.0
Maddux-Atl 249.1
Johnson-Ari 248.2
Glavine-Atl 241.0
Hernandez-SF 240.0

Fewest Hits/Game
Park-LA 6.89
Ankiel-StL 7.05
Brown-LA 7.08
Johnson-Ari 7.31
Person-Phi 7.48

Fewest BB/Game
Maddux-Atl 1.52
Anderson-Ari 1.65
Reed-NY 1.66
Brown-LA 1.84
Schilling-Phi-Ari 1.93

Strikeouts
Johnson-Ari 347
Park-LA 217
Brown-LA 216
Dempster-Fla 209
Leiter-NY 200

Strikeouts/Game
Johnson-Ari 12.56
Ankiel-StL 9.98
Astacio-Col 8.85
Leiter-NY 8.65
Park-LA 8.64

Ratio
Brown-LA 9.27
Maddux-Atl 10.00
Johnson-Ari 10.28
Schilling-Phi-Ari 10.70
D'Amico-Mil 10.81

Earned Run Average
Brown-LA 2.58
Johnson-Ari 2.64
D'Amico-Mil 2.66
Maddux-Atl 3.00
Hampton-NY 3.14

Adjusted ERA
Johnson-Ari 175
D'Amico-Mil 171
Brown-LA 170
Maddux-Atl 151
Hampton-NY 140

Opponents' Batting Avg.
Brown-LA .... .213
Park-LA .... .214
Ankiel-StL .... .219
Johnson-Ari .... .224
Leiter-NY .... .228

Opponents' On-Base Pct.
Brown-LA .... .262
Maddux-Atl .... .277
Johnson-Ari .... .289
Schilling-Phi-Ari .... .295
Glavine-Atl .... .298

Starter Runs
Johnson-Ari 55.1
Brown-LA 52.5
Maddux-Atl 45.5
Hampton-NY 36.2
D'Amico-Mil 35.6

Adjusted Starter Runs
Johnson-Ari 54.8
Brown-LA 48.8
Maddux-Atl 43.4
D'Amico-Mil 34.8
Hampton-NY 32.3

Clutch Pitching Index
Rueter-SF 126
D'Amico-Mil 120
Wright-Mil 114
Vazquez-Mon 113
Johnson-Ari 113

Relief Runs
Nen-SF 23.0
White-Cin-Col 21.3
Graves-Cin 21.1
Rodriguez-SF 18.1
Herges-LA 18.0

Adjusted Relief Runs
White-Cin-Col 26.1
Nen-SF 22.0
Graves-Cin 21.8
Williamson-Cin 17.9
Leskanic-Mil 17.5

Relief Ranking
Nen-SF 43.9
Graves-Cin 43.6
White-Cin-Col 39.1
Benitez-NY 31.2
Leskanic-Mil 29.4

Total Pitcher Index
Maddux-Atl 5.5
Johnson-Ari 5.1
Graves-Cin 4.7
Nen-SF 4.2
Park-LA 4.2

Total Baseball Ranking
Bonds-SF 7.3
Kent-SF 6.6
Giles-Pit 5.7
Maddux-Atl 5.5
Johnson-Ari 5.1

TEAM	G	W	L	PCT	GB	R	OR	AB	H	2B	3B	HR	BB	SO	AVG	OBP	SLG	OPS	OPS+	BR	BR+	PF	CHI	RC	SB	CS	SBA	SBR
EAST																												
NY	161	87	74	.540		871	814	5556	1541	294	25	205	631	1007	.277	.357	.450	807	105	28	42	98	99	893	99	48	67	5
BOS	162	85	77	.525	2.5	792	**745**	5630	1503	316	32	167	611	1019	.267	.343	.423	766	89	-59	-90	104	99	824	43	30	59	-1
TOR	162	83	79	.512	4.5	861	908	5677	1562	328	21	**244**	526	1026	.275	.343	.469	812	102	20	9	101	99	905	89	34	72	8
BAL	162	74	88	.457	13.5	794	913	5549	1508	310	22	184	558	900	.272	.344	.435	779	99	-37	-11	97	99	814	**126**	65	66	5
TB	161	69	92	.429	18	733	842	5505	1414	253	22	162	559	1022	.257	.331	.399	730	84	-134	-131	100	104	729	90	46	66	4
CENTRAL																												
CHI	162	95	67	.586		**978**	839	5646	1615	325	33	216	591	960	.286	.359	.470	829	107	69	59	101	105	952	119	42	74	11
CLE	162	90	72	.556	5	950	816	5683	1639	310	30	221	685	1057	**.288**	**.370**	.470	**840**	108	**103**	77	103	97	**1004**	113	34	77	13
DET	162	79	83	.488	16	823	827	5644	1553	307	41	177	562	982	.275	.345	.438	783	100	-27	-1	97	99	847	83	38	69	5
KC	162	77	85	.475	18	879	930	5709	**1644**	281	27	150	511	**840**	**.288**	.351	.425	776	95	-33	-43	101	**106**	855	121	35	**78**	**14**
MIN	162	69	93	.426	26	748	880	5615	1516	325	**49**	116	556	1021	.270	.340	.407	747	84	-98	-137	106	100	769	90	45	67	4
WEST																												
OAK	161	91	70	.565		947	813	5560	1501	281	23	239	750	1159	.270	.362	.458	820	**109**	57	**80**	98	102	933	40	15	73	4
SEA	162	91	71	.562	0.5	907	780	5497	1481	300	26	198	**775**	1073	.269	.365	.442	807	107	37	59	98	100	908	122	56	69	7
ANA	162	82	80	.506	9.5	864	869	5628	1574	309	34	236	608	1024	.280	.355	**.472**	827	106	60	55	101	94	938	93	52	64	2
TEX	162	71	91	.438	20.5	848	974	5648	1601	**330**	35	173	580	922	.283	.354	.446	800	98	13	-16	103	97	872	69	47	59	-1
TOT	1132					11995		78547	21652	4269	420	2688	8503	14012	.276	.352	.444	795							1297	587	69	80

TEAM	CG	SH	SV	IP	H	H/G	HR	BB	SO	RAT	ERA	ERA+	OAV	OOB	PR	PR+	PF	CPI	FA	E	DP	FW	PW	BW	SBW	DIF
EAST																										
NY	9	6	40	1424[1]	1458	9.3	177	577	1040	13.2	4.76	101	.263	.339	24	4	97	94	.981	109	132	.2	.4	3.9	-.0	2.2
BOS	7	**12**	**46**	1452[2]	**1433**	**8.9**	173	499	1121	**12.4**	**4.24**	**120**	**.257**	**.324**	**110**	**132**	103	97	.982	109	120	.3	**12.1**	-8.2	-.6	.6
TOR	**15**	4	37	1437[1]	1615	10.2	195	560	978	14.1	5.15	97	.285	.356	-37	-26	101	100	.984	100	176	.8	-2.3	.9	.2	2.7
BAL	14	6	33	1433[1]	1547	9.8	202	665	1017	14.2	5.37	89	.275	.355	-73	-97	97	94	.981	116	151	-.1	-8.8	-1.0	-.0	3.2
TB	10	8	38	1431[1]	1553	9.8	198	533	955	13.6	4.87	102	.277	.347	8	14	101	101	.981	118	169	-.3	1.3	-12.0	-.2	-.2
CENTRAL																										
CHI	5	7	43	1450[1]	1509	9.4	195	614	1037	13.6	4.67	106	.270	.348	41	47	101	**103**	.978	133	**190**	-1.1	4.4	5.5	.5	5.0
CLE	6	5	34	1442[1]	1511	9.5	173	666	**1213**	13.9	4.84	103	.270	.352	12	24	102	98	**.988**	**72**	147	**2.4**	2.2	7.1	.7	-3.3
DET	6	6	44	1443[1]	1583	9.9	177	**496**	978	13.3	4.71	101	.280	.343	33	10	97	101	.983	105	171	.5	1.0	-.0	-.0	-3.2
KC	10	6	29	1439[1]	1585	10.0	239	693	927	14.6	5.48	91	.282	.365	-90	-76	102	100	.983	102	185	.7	-6.9	-3.9	**.8**	5.6
MIN	6	4	35	1432[2]	1634	10.3	212	516	1042	13.8	5.15	102	.287	.350	-37	15	107	100	.983	102	155	.7	1.4	-12.5	-.2	-1.2
WEST																										
OAK	7	11	43	1435[1]	1535	9.7	**158**	615	963	13.8	4.58	104	.274	.351	53	29	97	**103**	.978	134	164	-1.2	2.7	**7.4**	-.2	2.0
SEA	4	10	44	1441[2]	1442	9.1	167	634	998	13.2	4.50	106	.262	.342	67	47	97	99	.984	99	176	.9	4.4	5.5	.1	-.6
ANA	5	3	**46**	1448	1534	9.6	228	662	846	13.9	5.01	99	.273	.354	-15	-7	101	102	.978	134	182	-1.2	-.6	5.1	-.3	-1.8
TEX	3	4	39	1429	1683	10.6	202	661	918	15.2	5.52	92	.294	.373	-96	-66	104	102	.978	135	162	-1.3	-6.0	-1.4	-.6	-.5
TOT	107	92	551	20141		9.7				13.8	4.92		.276	.352					.982	1568	2280					

Runs		Hits		Doubles		Triples		Home Runs		Total Bases	
Damon-KC	136	Erstad-Ana	240	Delgado-Tor	57	Guzman-Min	20	Glaus-Ana	47	Delgado-Tor	378
A.Rodriguez-Sea	134	Damon-KC	214	Garciaparra-Bos	51	Kennedy-Ana	11	Thomas-Chi	43	Erstad-Ana	366
Erstad-Ana	121	Sweeney-KC	206	D.Cruz-Det	46	Damon-KC	10	J.Giambi-Oak	43	Thomas-Chi	364
Durham-Chi	121	Jeter-NY	201	Olerud-Sea	45	Durham-Chi	9			Glaus-Ana	340
Glaus-Ana	120	Garciaparra-Bos	197							Dye-KC	337

Runs Batted In		Runs Produced		Bases On Balls		Batting Average		On-Base Percentage		Slugging Average	
Martinez-Sea	145	A.Rodriguez-Sea	225	J.Giambi-Oak	137	Garciaparra-Bos	.372	J.Giambi-Oak	.482	M.Ramirez-Cle	.697
Sweeney-KC	144	Sweeney-KC	220	Delgado-Tor	123	Erstad-Ana	.355	Delgado-Tor	.472	Delgado-Tor	.664
Thomas-Chi	143	Thomas-Chi	215	Thome-Cle	118	M.Ramirez-Cle	.351	M.Ramirez-Cle	.460	J.Giambi-Oak	.647
J.Giambi-Oak	137	Delgado-Tor	211	Thomas-Chi	112	Delgado-Tor	.344	Thomas-Chi	.441	Thomas-Chi	.625
Delgado-Tor	137			Glaus-Ana	112	Jeter-NY	.339	Garciaparra-Bos	.439	A.Rodriguez-Sea	.606

On-Base Plus Slugging		Adjusted OPS		Batter Runs		Adjusted Batter Runs		Clutch Hitting Index		Runs Created	
M.Ramirez-Cle	1157	J.Giambi-Oak	187	Delgado-Tor	78.8	Delgado-Tor	76.6	Sweeney-KC	135	Delgado-Tor	186
Delgado-Tor	1137	M.Ramirez-Cle	183	J.Giambi-Oak	72.2	J.Giambi-Oak	76.2	Ledee-Cle-NY-Tex	131	J.Giambi-Oak	172
J.Giambi-Oak	1129	Delgado-Tor	181	Thomas-Chi	61.8	Thomas-Chi	60.0	Olerud-Sea	128	Thomas-Chi	163
Thomas-Chi	1066	Thomas-Chi	164	M.Ramirez-Cle	61.1	M.Ramirez-Cle	57.7	Randa-KC	122	Erstad-Ana	154
Garciaparra-Bos	1038	A.Rodriguez-Sea	162	A.Rodriguez-Sea	51.0	A.Rodriguez-Sea	54.5	O'Neill-NY	118	A.Rodriguez-Sea	150

Total Average		Stolen Bases		Stolen Base Average		Stolen Base Runs		Fielding Runs		Total Player Rating	
J.Giambi-Oak	1.370	Damon-KC	46	R.Alomar-Cle	90.7	R.Alomar-Cle	7.2	Sanchez-KC	19.7	A.Rodriguez-Sea	7.7
M.Ramirez-Cle	1.339	R.Alomar-Cle	39	Valentin-Chi	90.5	Damon-KC	7.0	A.Rodriguez-Sea	18.2	J.Giambi-Oak	5.1
Delgado-Tor	1.334	DeShields-Bal	37	Jeter-NY	84.6	DeShields-Bal	4.6	Gil-Ana	16.9	Delgado-Tor	4.7
Thomas-Chi	1.177	Henderson-Sea	31	Damon-KC	83.6	Lofton-Cle	4.2	Higginson-Det	16.2	Glaus-Ana	4.7
A.Rodriguez-Sea	1.155			Ordonez-Chi	81.8	Cairo-TB	3.7	R.Alomar-Cle	15.8	Erstad-Ana	4.6

Wins		Win Percentage		Games		Complete Games		Shutouts		Saves	
D.Wells-Tor	20	Hudson-Oak	.769	Wunsch-Chi	83	D.Wells-Tor	9	P.Martinez-Bos	4	Lowe-Bos	42
Hudson-Oak	20	P.Martinez-Bos	.750	Venafro-Tex	77	P.Martinez-Bos	7	Sele-Sea	2	Jones-Det	42
Pettitte-NY	19	Burba-Cle	.727	Wells-Min	76	Ponson-Bal	6	Hudson-Oak	2	Sasaki-Sea	37
P.Martinez-Bos	18	D.Wells-Tor	.714	Trombley-Bal	75	Mussina-Bal	6			Rivera-NY	36
Sele-Sea	17	Pettitte-NY	.679	Lowe-Bos	74						

Innings Pitched		Fewest Hits/Game		Fewest BB/Game		Strikeouts		Strikeouts/Game		Ratio	
Mussina-Bal	237.2	P.Martinez-Bos	5.31	D.Wells-Tor	1.21	P.Martinez-Bos	284	P.Martinez-Bos	11.78	P.Martinez-Bos	7.22
D.Wells-Tor	229.2	Hudson-Oak	7.52	P.Martinez-Bos	1.33	Colon-Cle	212	Colon-Cle	10.15	Mussina-Bal	10.79
Rogers-Tex	227.1	Colon-Cle	7.80	Mussina-Bal	1.74	Mussina-Bal	210	Nomo-Det	8.57	Hernandez-NY	11.18
Radke-Min	226.2	Clemens-NY	8.10	Milton-Min	1.98	Finley-Cle	189	Burba-Cle	8.47	Hudson-Oak	11.48
Ponson-Bal	222.0	Abbott-Sea	8.25	Moehler-Det	2.02	Clemens-NY	188	Clemens-NY	8.28	Milton-Min	11.52

Earned Run Average		Adjusted ERA		Opponents' Batting Avg.		Opponents' On-Base Pct.		Starter Runs		Adjusted Starter Runs	
P.Martinez-Bos	1.74	P.Martinez-Bos	292	P.Martinez-Bos	.167	P.Martinez-Bos	.214	P.Martinez-Bos	76.7	P.Martinez-Bos	78.0
Clemens-NY	3.70	Sirotka-Chi	131	Hudson-Oak	.227	Mussina-Bal	.293	Mussina-Bal	30.0	Mussina-Bal	27.1
Mussina-Bal	3.79	Clemens-NY	130	Colon-Cle	.233	Hernandez-NY	.300	Clemens-NY	27.7	Clemens-NY	25.5
Sirotka-Chi	3.79	Colon-Cle	129	Clemens-NY	.236	Milton-Min	.305	Sirotka-Chi	24.7	Sirotka-Chi	25.5
Colon-Cle	3.88	Mussina-Bal	126	Abbott-Sea	.243	Hudson-Oak	.309	Zito-Oak	22.7	Colon-Cle	23.0

Clutch Pitching Index		Relief Runs		Adjusted Relief Runs		Relief Ranking		Total Pitcher Index		Total Baseball Ranking	
Lopez-TB	115	Lowe-Bos	23.9	Lowe-Bos	24.8	Lowe-Bos	40.8	P.Martinez-Bos	8.5	P.Martinez-Bos	8.5
Sirotka-Chi	115	Tam-Oak	21.8	Tam-Oak	21.0	Koch-Tor	40.6	Lowe-Bos	3.9	A.Rodriguez-Sea	7.7
Parque-Chi	114	Koch-Tor	20.0	Koch-Tor	20.3	Rivera-NY	33.5	Koch-Tor	3.8	J.Giambi-Oak	5.1
Loaiza-Tex-Tor	111	Foulke-Chi	19.1	Foulke-Chi	19.4	Nelson-NY	28.8	Rivera-NY	3.3	Delgado-Tor	4.7
Moehler-Det	111	Nelson-NY	19.1	Nelson-NY	18.6	Hernandez-TB	28.6	Hernandez-TB	2.7	Glaus-Ana	4.7

The All-Time Leaders

This section is divided into two parts: lifetime leaders and single-season leaders. Both groups command our attention and convey the pleasures of the game, which lie as much in contemplation of the past as in experiencing the present: Henry Aaron, 755; Babe Ruth, 714; Willie Mays, 660—this is no mere aggregation of names and numbers, as in a telephone directory . . . it comprises the romance and lore of the home run, and of baseball itself. Jack Chesbro, 41, 1904; Bob Gibson, 1.12, 1968; Nolan Ryan, 383, 1973 . . . you can fill in the blanks that tell the story of pitching's most glorious seasons.

What follows are the all-time great achievements in 219 categories, both the traditional statistics and the new. For most of these we will give not the top 10 or 20 but the top 100, because some categories would otherwise be dominated by players of a certain era (for example, slugging average by batters of the 1920s and 1930s, earned run average by pitchers of 1900–1919). And for many stats we will offer a second kind of ranking, broken down into six distinct eras of baseball, with the top 10 or 15 leaders in each. For example, breaking down single-season home runs this way would produce lists topped by these men:

1876–1892: Ned Williamson, 27, 1884
1893–1919: Babe Ruth, 29, 1919
1920–1941: Babe Ruth, 60, 1927
1942–1960: Ralph Kiner, 54, 1949
1961–1976: Roger Maris, 61, 1961
1977–2000: Mark McGwire, 70, 1998

And for single-season Adjusted ERA (normalized to league average and adjusted for home-park factor), we get:

1876–1892: Tim Keefe, 294
(adjusted from actual 0.86), 1880
1893–1919: Dutch Leonard, 280
(adjusted from actual 0.96), 1914
1920–1941: Lefty Grove, 218
(adjusted from actual 2.06), 1931
1942–1960: Billy Pierce, 201
(adjusted from actual 1.97), 1955
1961–1976: Bob Gibson, 258
(adjusted from actual 1.12), 1968
1977–2000: Pedro Martinez, 292
(adjusted from actual 1.74), 2000

This is quite a different lineup from the traditional list of ERA leaders (which relegates pre-1900 pitching to the shadows), where of the 15 top spots, 14 are accorded to pitchers active from 1905 to 1918. Is there a baseball fan alive who thinks that all the great pitchers were created in that 14-year span and that the mold was then broken?

We also present certain categories in a per game fashion that illuminates some hidden great performers. While it is not surprising to find such names as Babe Ruth, Lou Gehrig, and Jimmie Foxx among the top 10 all-time at runs batted in per game, few fans would expect to find Cap Anson listed eighth, or to find that the best of the best was 19th-century slugger Sam Thompson.

But we go one step further and rank several batting categories by position, thus recognizing and illustrating the greater demands for fielding skill at such positions as shortstop, catcher, and second base, and the comparatively plentiful supply of batting talent in the outfield and at first base. Having Mark McGwire hit 70 home runs for you is great, but he cannot play anywhere but first base; a team of nine McGwires (or 10, in the AL) would finish dead last. For example, here is the list of the top 10 lifetime batting averages:

Ty Cobb, .366
Rogers Hornsby, .358
Joe Jackson, .356
Dan Brouthers, .349
Pete Browning, .349
Ed Delahanty, .346
Tris Speaker, .345
Billy Hamilton, .344
Ted Williams, .344
Babe Ruth, .342

This would be a formidable team indeed, but it would not win, for it includes a first baseman, a second baseman, and eight outfielders. Here, as food for thought, is a list of the top 10 lifetime leading averages among catchers, that indispensable class of men. ("You gotta have a catcher," Casey Stengel explained, "because if you don't, the ball rolls all the way to the backstop.")

Mike Piazza, .328
Mickey Cochrane, .320
Bill Dickey, .313
Spud Davis, .308
Ernie Lombardi, .306
Ivan Rodriguez, .304
Gabby Hartnett, .297
Manny Sanguillen, .296
Smoky Burgess, .295
Thurman Munson, .292

This team would not win, either. But the point is that the section that follows will, if perused carefully, make you think differently about the game and its statistics. And that's a large part of what *Total Baseball* is about.

For example, the batting average itself is a flawed measure, as we have discussed in "The History of Major League Baseball Statistics" and "Sabermetrics." While batting average is not as good as, say, Production (on-base plus slugging or OPS), it is not worthless, either. And when we report batting average in a form which relates it to the league average at the time, it becomes far more useful as an evaluative tool.

Remember that list above of the top 10 lifetime batting averages? Here are the top 10 batting averages *as compared to* the league batting averages in the years in which the men played (individual batting average divided by league batting average, expressed in three digits, so that a man who batted at exactly his league average over the course of his career would have a mark of 100):

Ty Cobb, 134.8
Joe Jackson, 133.1
Pete Browning, 130.8
Dan Brouthers, 128.3
Ted Williams, 128.1
Tony Gwynn, 127.7
Nap Lajoie, 127.4
Rod Carew, 127.0
Rogers Hornsby, 126.2
Tris Speaker, 125.4

Says something, doesn't it? But enough expostulation and fulmination. Let's set some ground rules, define some terms that may still be unfamiliar after you've browsed through the Player and Pitcher registers, and get on with the show.

To be eligible for a lifetime pitching category that is stated as an average, a man must have pitched 1,500 or more innings, or 750 or more innings if he is a relief pitcher, in the major leagues; for a counting statistic, he must simply have attained the necessary quantity to crack the list. For a single-season category expressed as an average, he must have pitched one inning per league scheduled game or have attained the necessary quantity (wins, strikeouts, saves) to head a counted list.

To be eligible for a lifetime batting category that is stated as an average, a man must have played in 1,000 or more games; for counting stats such as strikeouts, a Rob Deer earned his place on the list before he played his 1,000th game. For Pitcher Batting Average, the criterion is 1,500 innings pitched or 100 hits. And to reach the single-season batting lists, a man must have 3.1 plate appearances per scheduled game.

We provide tables of the top fielding performances, too, sorted by position as you would expect (and, in this edition, including only games played at the position, rather than combining data from secondary positions under the dominant position). As we establish a 1,000-game minimum for inclusion in all but a few batting and baserunning categories, we likewise establish for these positional rankings a minimum of 1,000 games played at the position.

For the three principal categories—Total Player Rating, Total Pitcher Index, and Total Baseball Ranking—we have introduced several variations. For example, TPR and TBR are shown 500 deep for lifetime leaders—sorted first by highest value; then alphabetically so that the reader may find a particular player without scanning 500 names; and last by the above-named eras, the top 25 in each. Total Pitcher Index is also sorted this way, but because far fewer pitchers than position players meet the longevity criteria, the lifetime groupings go 300 and 200 deep rather than 500 and 300.

Ties are calculated to as many decimal places as needed to break them, but averages are shown to only three places. When two or more players are tied in an averaged category with a narrow base of data, such as a season's won-lost percentage, the reader can presume a numerical dead heat (and obviously this goes for counting stats, too—one man's 39 doubles are as good as another's). But where there is a tie for batting average, earned run average, or any of the sabermetric measures, the reader may assume that the man listed above the other(s) has the minutely higher average.

Here are the few stats carried in this section that are not carried in the Annual Record or Registers, with definitions where the terms are not self-explanatory (see Glossary for formulas):

Batting, Baserunning, Fielding

Runs (Scored) Per Game Broken down by era

Home Run Percentage Home runs per 100 at bats

Bases on Balls Percentage Walks (most) per 100 appearances (at bats plus walks)

At Bats Per Strikeout Broken down by era

Relative Batting Average Normalized to league average

Isolated Power Slugging average minus batting average

Extra Base Hits

Pinch Hits

Pinch Hit Batting Average

Pinch Hit Home Runs

Strikeout Percentage

Total Player Rating Per 150 Games Highlighting the achievements of modern players and those with comparatively short careers (though at least 1,000 games)

Total Chances Per Game Broken down by position

Chances Accepted Per Game Broken down by position

Putouts Broken down by position

Putouts Per Game Broken down by position

Assists Broken down by position

Assists Per Game Broken down by position

Double Plays Broken down by position

Pitching

Wins Above Team How many wins a pitcher garnered beyond those expected of an average pitcher for that team; the formula is weighted so that a pitcher on a good team has a chance to compete with pitchers on poor teams who otherwise would benefit from the larger potential spread between their team's won-lost percentage and their own; see Glossary for more information.

Wins Above League A pitcher's won-lost record restated by adding his Pitching Wins above the league average to the record that a league-average pitcher would have had with the same number of decisions (for example, Tom Seaver goes 20–10 with seven Pitching Wins; applying the seven wins to a 15–15 mark in the same 30 decisions results in a WAL of 22–8).

Percentage of Team Wins

Relief Games

Pitchers' Batting Runs

Pitchers' Fielding Runs

Relief Wins This statistic, like the relief stats below, includes only games in relief.

Relief Losses

Relief Innings Pitched

Relief Points Relief wins plus saves minus losses

Games

1	Pete Rose	3562
2	Carl Yastrzemski	3308
3	Hank Aaron	3298
4	Ty Cobb	3035
5	Eddie Murray	3026
	Stan Musial	3026
7	Willie Mays	2992
8	Dave Winfield	2973
9	Rusty Staub	2951
10	Brooks Robinson	2896
11	Cal Ripken	2873
12	Rickey Henderson	2856
	Robin Yount	2856
14	Al Kaline	2834
15	Eddie Collins	2826
16	Reggie Jackson	2820
17	Frank Robinson	2808
18	Harold Baines	2798
19	Honus Wagner	2794
20	Tris Speaker	2789
21	Tony Perez	2777
22	Mel Ott	2730
23	George Brett	2707
24	Graig Nettles	2700
25	Darrell Evans	2687
26	Paul Molitor	2683
27	Rabbit Maranville	2670
28	Joe Morgan	2649
29	Andre Dawson	2627
30	Lou Brock	2616
31	Dwight Evans	2606
32	Luis Aparicio	2599
33	Willie McCovey	2588
34	Ozzie Smith	2573
35	Paul Waner	2549
36	Ernie Banks	2528
37	Bill Buckner	2517
	Sam Crawford	2517
39	Gary Gaetti	2507
40	Babe Ruth	2503
41	Carlton Fisk	2499
42	Dave Concepcion	2488
	Billy Williams	2488
44	Nap Lajoie	2480
45	Max Carey	2476
46	Rod Carew	2469
	Vada Pinson	2469
48	Dave Parker	2466
49	Ted Simmons	2456
50	Bill Dahlen	2444
51	Ron Fairly	2442
52	Wade Boggs	2440
53	Chili Davis	2436
54	Harmon Killebrew	2435
55	Roberto Clemente	2433
56	Willie Davis	2429
57	Luke Appling	2422
58	Zack Wheat	2410
59	Mickey Vernon	2409
60	Buddy Bell	2405
61	Sam Rice	2404
	Mike Schmidt	2404
63	Mickey Mantle	2401
64	Eddie Mathews	2391
65	Lou Whitaker	2390
66	Jake Beckley	2389
67	Bobby Wallace	2383
68	Enos Slaughter	2380
69	George Davis	2372
70	Tony Gwynn	2369
71	Al Oliver	2368
72	Nellie Fox	2367
73	Willie Stargell	2360
74	Jose Cruz	2353
	Tim Raines	2353
76	Brian Downing	2344
77	Steve Garvey	2332
78	Bert Campaneris	2328
79	Frank White	2324
80	Charlie Gehringer	2323
81	Jimmie Foxx	2317
82	Frankie Frisch	2311
83	Harry Hooper	2309
84	Gary Carter	2296
85	Alan Trammell	2293
86	Don Baylor	2292
	Ted Williams	2292
88	Goose Goslin	2287
89	Jimmy Dykes	2282
90	Lave Cross	2278
91	Cap Anson	2277
92	Bob Boone	2264
93	Chris Speier	2260
94	Rogers Hornsby	2259
95	Larry Bowa	2247
96	Fred Clarke	2246
97	Ron Santo	2243
98	Doc Cramer	2239
99	Red Schoendienst	2216
100	Al Simmons	2215

At Bats

Rank	Player	AB
1	Pete Rose	14053
2	Hank Aaron	12364
3	Carl Yastrzemski	11988
4	Ty Cobb	11434
5	Eddie Murray	11336
6	Cal Ripken	11074
7	Robin Yount	11008
8	Dave Winfield	11003
9	Stan Musial	10972
10	Willie Mays	10881
11	Paul Molitor	10835
12	Brooks Robinson	10654
13	Honus Wagner	10439
14	George Brett	10349
15	Lou Brock	10332
16	Rickey Henderson	10331
17	Luis Aparicio	10230
18	Tris Speaker	10195
19	Al Kaline	10116
20	Rabbit Maranville	10078
21	Frank Robinson	10006
22	Eddie Collins	9949
23	Andre Dawson	9927
24	Reggie Jackson	9864
25	Harold Baines	9824
26	Tony Perez	9778
27	Rusty Staub	9720
28	Vada Pinson	9645
29	Nap Lajoie	9589
30	Sam Crawford	9570
31	Jake Beckley	9538
32	Paul Waner	9459
33	Mel Ott	9456
34	Roberto Clemente	9454
35	Ernie Banks	9421
36	Bill Buckner	9397
37	Ozzie Smith	9396
38	Max Carey	9363
39	Dave Parker	9358
40	Billy Williams	9350
41	Rod Carew	9315
42	Joe Morgan	9277
43	Sam Rice	9269
44	Nellie Fox	9232
45	Tony Gwynn	9186
46	Wade Boggs	9180
47	Cap Anson	9176
48	Willie Davis	9174
49	Doc Cramer	9140
50	Frankie Frisch	9112
51	Zack Wheat	9106
52	Lave Cross	9100
53	Al Oliver	9049
54	George Davis	9045
55	Bill Dahlen	9036
56	Dwight Evans	8996
57	Buddy Bell	8995
58	Graig Nettles	8986
59	Darrell Evans	8973
60	Gary Gaetti	8951
61	Charlie Gehringer	8860
62	Luke Appling	8856
63	Steve Garvey	8835
64	Tommy Corcoran	8812
65	Harry Hooper	8785
66	Al Simmons	8759
67	Carlton Fisk	8756
68	Mickey Vernon	8731
69	Dave Concepcion	8723
70	Tim Raines	8694
71	Bert Campaneris	8684
72	Ted Simmons	8680
73	Chili Davis	8673
74	Goose Goslin	8656
75	Bobby Wallace	8618
76	Willie Keeler	8591
77	Fred Clarke	8584
78	Lou Whitaker	8570
79	Eddie Mathews	8537
80	Red Schoendienst	8479
81	Jesse Burkett	8426
82	Joe Carter	8422
83	Larry Bowa	8418
84	Babe Ruth	8399
85	Ryne Sandberg	8385
86	Richie Ashburn	8365
87	Bid McPhee	8358
88	Mike Schmidt	8352
89	Alan Trammell	8288
90	George Sisler	8267
91	Jim Rice	8225
	Jimmy Ryan	8225
93	Don Baylor	8198
94	Willie McCovey	8197
95	Brett Butler	8180
96	Rogers Hornsby	8173
97	Harmon Killebrew	8147
98	Ron Santo	8143
99	Jimmie Foxx	8134
100	Mickey Mantle	8102

Runs

Rank	Player	R
1	Ty Cobb	2246
2	Rickey Henderson	2178
3	Hank Aaron	2174
	Babe Ruth	2174
5	Pete Rose	2165
6	Willie Mays	2062
7	Stan Musial	1949
8	Lou Gehrig	1888
9	Tris Speaker	1882
10	Mel Ott	1859
11	Frank Robinson	1829
12	Eddie Collins	1821
13	Carl Yastrzemski	1816
14	Ted Williams	1798
15	Paul Molitor	1782
16	Charlie Gehringer	1774
17	Jimmie Foxx	1751
18	Honus Wagner	1739
19	Cap Anson	1722
20	Jesse Burkett	1720
21	Willie Keeler	1719
22	Billy Hamilton	1697
23	Bid McPhee	1684
24	Mickey Mantle	1677
25	Dave Winfield	1669
26	Joe Morgan	1650
27	Jimmy Ryan	1643
28	George Van Haltren	1642
29	Robin Yount	1632
30	Eddie Murray	1627
	Paul Waner	1627
32	Fred Clarke	1622
	Al Kaline	1622
34	Roger Connor	1620
35	Lou Brock	1610
36	Cal Ripken	1604
37	Jake Beckley	1602
38	Ed Delahanty	1600
39	Bill Dahlen	1590
40	Barry Bonds	1584
41	George Brett	1583
42	Rogers Hornsby	1579
43	Hugh Duffy	1554
44	Reggie Jackson	1551
45	Tim Raines	1548
46	Max Carey	1545
	George Davis	1545
48	Frankie Frisch	1532
49	Dan Brouthers	1523
	Tom Brown	1523
51	Sam Rice	1514
52	Wade Boggs	1513
53	Eddie Mathews	1509
54	Al Simmons	1507
55	Mike Schmidt	1506
56	Nap Lajoie	1504
57	Harry Stovey	1492
58	Goose Goslin	1483
59	Arlie Latham	1481
60	Dwight Evans	1470
61	Herman Long	1456
62	Jim O'Rourke	1446
63	Harry Hooper	1429
	Dummy Hoy	1429
65	Rod Carew	1424
66	Joe Kelley	1421
67	Roberto Clemente	1416
68	John Ward	1410
	Billy Williams	1410
70	Mike Griffin	1406
71	Sam Crawford	1391
72	Joe DiMaggio	1390
73	Lou Whitaker	1386
74	Tony Gwynn	1378
75	Andre Dawson	1373
76	Vada Pinson	1366
77	Brett Butler	1359
78	Doc Cramer	1357
	King Kelly	1357
80	Tommy Leach	1355
81	Darrell Evans	1344
82	Lave Cross	1338
	Pee Wee Reese	1338
84	Luis Aparicio	1335
85	George Gore	1327
86	Richie Ashburn	1322
87	Patsy Donovan	1321
88	Luke Appling	1319
89	Ryne Sandberg	1318
90	Mike Tiernan	1316
91	Ernie Banks	1305
	Kiki Cuyler	1305
93	Tony Phillips	1300
94	Harold Baines	1296
	Jimmy Sheckard	1296
96	Harry Heilmann	1291
97	Zack Wheat	1289
98	Heinie Manush	1287
99	George Sisler	1284
100	Harmon Killebrew	1283

Runs per Game (by era)

1876-1892

Rank	Player	R/G
1	George Gore	1.01
2	Harry Stovey	1.00
3	King Kelly	.93
4	Dan Brouthers	.91
5	Arlie Latham	.91
6	Sam Thompson	.90
7	Buck Ewing	.86
8	Tom Brown	.85
9	Hardy Richardson	.84
10	Tommy McCarthy	.84
11	Tip O'Neill	.84
12	Denny Lyons	.83
13	Curt Welch	.83
14	Jim O'Rourke	.82
15	Roger Connor	.81

1893-1919

Rank	Player	R/G
1	Billy Hamilton	1.06
2	John McGraw	.93
3	Mike Griffin	.93
4	Hugh Duffy	.89
5	Mike Tiernan	.89
6	Ed Delahanty	.87
7	Cupid Childs	.83
8	Jesse Burkett	.83
9	George Van Haltren	.83
10	Jimmy Ryan	.82
11	Willie Keeler	.81
12	Dummy Hoy	.80
13	Herman Long	.78
14	Hughie Jennings	.77
15	Joe Kelley	.77

1920-1941

Rank	Player	R/G
1	Lou Gehrig	.87
2	Babe Ruth	.87
3	Earle Combs	.82
4	Red Rolfe	.80
5	Charlie Gehringer	.76
6	Jimmie Foxx	.76
7	Hank Greenberg	.75
8	Earl Averill	.73
9	Max Bishop	.72
10	Lu Blue	.71
11	Mickey Cochrane	.70
12	Rogers Hornsby	.70
13	Kiki Cuyler	.69
14	Mel Ott	.68
15	Al Simmons	.68

1942-1960

Rank	Player	R/G
1	Joe DiMaggio	.80
2	Ted Williams	.78
3	Dom DiMaggio	.75
4	Tommy Henrich	.70
5	Mickey Mantle	.70
6	Jackie Robinson	.69
7	Johnny Pesky	.68
8	Ralph Kiner	.66
9	Eddie Stanky	.64
10	Stan Musial	.64
11	George Case	.64
12	Eddie Mathews	.63
13	Larry Doby	.63
14	Charlie Keller	.62
15	Minnie Minoso	.62

1961-1976

Rank	Player	R/G
1	Willie Mays	.69
2	Bobby Bonds	.68
3	Hank Aaron	.66
4	Frank Robinson	.65
5	Dick Allen	.63
6	Joe Morgan	.62
7	Lou Brock	.62
8	Pete Rose	.61
9	Roberto Clemente	.58
10	Rod Carew	.58
11	Jimmy Wynn	.58
12	Al Kaline	.57
13	Billy Williams	.57
14	Reggie Smith	.57
15	Roger Maris	.56

1977-2000

Rank	Player	R/G
1	Kenny Lofton	.78
2	Rickey Henderson	.76
3	Barry Bonds	.74
4	Jeff Bagwell	.73
5	Chuck Knoblauch	.72
6	Frank Thomas	.71
7	Bernie Williams	.70
8	Ken Griffey Jr.	.69
9	Larry Walker	.69
10	Jim Thome	.67
11	Ron LeFlore	.67
12	Paul Molitor	.66
13	Craig Biggio	.66
14	Tim Raines	.66
15	Roberto Alomar	.65

Hits

Rank	Player	Hits
1	Pete Rose	4256
2	Ty Cobb	4189
3	Hank Aaron	3771
4	Stan Musial	3630
5	Tris Speaker	3514
6	Honus Wagner	3420
7	Carl Yastrzemski	3419
8	Paul Molitor	3319
9	Eddie Collins	3315
10	Willie Mays	3283
11	Eddie Murray	3255
12	Nap Lajoie	3242
13	George Brett	3154
14	Paul Waner	3152
15	Robin Yount	3142
16	Dave Winfield	3110
17	Tony Gwynn	3108
18	Cal Ripken	3070
19	Cap Anson	3056
20	Rod Carew	3053
21	Lou Brock	3023
22	Wade Boggs	3010
23	Al Kaline	3007
24	Roberto Clemente	3000
25	Sam Rice	2987
26	Sam Crawford	2961
27	Frank Robinson	2943
28	Jake Beckley	2934
29	Willie Keeler	2932
30	Rogers Hornsby	2930
31	Al Simmons	2927
32	Rickey Henderson	2914
33	Zack Wheat	2884
34	Frankie Frisch	2880
35	Mel Ott	2876
36	Babe Ruth	2873
37	Harold Baines	2855
38	Jesse Burkett	2850
39	Brooks Robinson	2848
40	Charlie Gehringer	2839
41	George Sisler	2812
42	Andre Dawson	2774
43	Vada Pinson	2757
44	Luke Appling	2749
45	Al Oliver	2743
46	Goose Goslin	2735
47	Tony Perez	2732
48	Lou Gehrig	2721
49	Rusty Staub	2716
50	Bill Buckner	2715
51	Dave Parker	2712
52	Billy Williams	2711
53	Doc Cramer	2705
54	Fred Clarke	2678
55	Luis Aparicio	2677
56	Lave Cross	2666
57	Max Carey	2665
	George Davis	2665
59	Nellie Fox	2663
60	Harry Heilmann	2660
61	Ted Williams	2654
62	Jimmie Foxx	2646
63	Rabbit Maranville	2605
64	Steve Garvey	2599
65	Ed Delahanty	2597
66	Reggie Jackson	2584
67	Ernie Banks	2583
68	Richie Ashburn	2574
69	Willie Davis	2561
	Tim Raines	2561
71	Jimmy Ryan	2556
72	George Van Haltren	2552
73	Roger Connor	2542
74	Heinie Manush	2524
75	Joe Morgan	2517
76	Buddy Bell	2514
77	Mickey Vernon	2495
78	Ted Simmons	2472
79	Joe Medwick	2471
80	Harry Hooper	2466
81	Bill Dahlen	2461
82	Ozzie Smith	2460
83	Lloyd Waner	2459
84	Jim Rice	2452
85	Red Schoendienst	2449
86	Dwight Evans	2446
87	Pie Traynor	2416
88	Mickey Mantle	2415
89	Stuffy McInnis	2405
90	Ryne Sandberg	2386
91	Enos Slaughter	2383
92	Chili Davis	2380
93	Edd Roush	2376
94	Brett Butler	2375
95	Lou Whitaker	2369
96	Dan Brouthers	2367
97	Alan Trammell	2365
98	Carlton Fisk	2356
99	Joe Judge	2352
100	Orlando Cepeda	2351

Doubles

Rank	Player	Doubles
1	Tris Speaker	792
2	Pete Rose	746
3	Stan Musial	725
4	Ty Cobb	724
5	George Brett	665
6	Nap Lajoie	657
7	Carl Yastrzemski	646
8	Honus Wagner	643
9	Hank Aaron	624
10	Paul Molitor	605
	Paul Waner	605
12	Cal Ripken	587
13	Robin Yount	583
14	Wade Boggs	578
15	Charlie Gehringer	574
16	Eddie Murray	560
17	Harry Heilmann	542
18	Rogers Hornsby	541
19	Joe Medwick	540
	Dave Winfield	540
21	Al Simmons	539
22	Lou Gehrig	534
	Tony Gwynn	534
24	Cap Anson	529
	Al Oliver	529
26	Frank Robinson	528
27	Dave Parker	526
28	Ted Williams	525
29	Willie Mays	523
30	Ed Delahanty	522
31	Joe Cronin	515
32	Babe Ruth	506
33	Tony Perez	505
34	Andre Dawson	503
35	Goose Goslin	500
36	Rusty Staub	499
37	Bill Buckner	498
	Al Kaline	498
	Sam Rice	498
40	Heinie Manush	491
41	Mickey Vernon	490
42	Mel Ott	488
43	Harold Baines	487
44	Lou Brock	486
	Rickey Henderson	486
	Billy Herman	486
47	Vada Pinson	485
48	Hal McRae	484
49	Dwight Evans	483
	Ted Simmons	483
51	Brooks Robinson	482
52	Zack Wheat	476
53	Jake Beckley	473
54	Frankie Frisch	466
55	Jim Bottomley	465
56	Reggie Jackson	463
57	Dan Brouthers	460
58	Sam Crawford	458
	Jimmie Foxx	458
60	Mark Grace	456
61	Rafael Palmeiro	455
62	George Davis	453
	Jimmy Dykes	453
64	Barry Bonds	451
	Jimmy Ryan	451
66	Joe Morgan	449
67	Rod Carew	445
68	George Burns	444
69	Gary Gaetti	443
70	Dick Bartell	442
	Don Mattingly	442
72	Roger Connor	441
73	Luke Appling	440
	Will Clark	440
	Roberto Clemente	440
	Steve Garvey	440
77	Eddie Collins	438
78	Cesar Cedeno	436
	Joe Sewell	436
80	Wally Moses	435
81	Billy Williams	434
82	Joe Judge	433
83	Joe Carter	432
	Tim Wallach	432
85	Red Schoendienst	427
86	Keith Hernandez	426
87	Buddy Bell	425
	Sherry Magee	425
	George Sisler	425
90	Chili Davis	424
91	Willie Stargell	423
92	Carlton Fisk	421
93	Lou Whitaker	420
94	Max Carey	419
	Tim Raines	419
96	Paul O'Neill	418
97	Orlando Cepeda	417
98	Cecil Cooper	415
99	Jim O'Rourke	414
	Kirby Puckett	414

Triples

Rank	Player	Triples
1	Sam Crawford	309
2	Ty Cobb	295
3	Honus Wagner	252
4	Jake Beckley	244
5	Roger Connor	233
6	Tris Speaker	222
7	Fred Clarke	220
8	Dan Brouthers	205
9	Joe Kelley	194
10	Paul Waner	191
11	Bid McPhee	189
12	Eddie Collins	187
13	Ed Delahanty	186
14	Sam Rice	184
15	Jesse Burkett	182
	Ed Konetchy	182
	Edd Roush	182
18	Buck Ewing	178
19	Rabbit Maranville	177
	Stan Musial	177
21	Harry Stovey	174
22	Goose Goslin	173
23	Tommy Leach	172
	Zack Wheat	172
25	Rogers Hornsby	169
26	Joe Jackson	168
27	Roberto Clemente	166
	Sherry Magee	166
29	Jake Daubert	165
30	Elmer Flick	164
	George Sisler	164
	Pie Traynor	164
33	Bill Dahlen	163
	George Davis	163
	Lou Gehrig	163
	Nap Lajoie	163
37	Mike Tiernan	162
38	Sam Thompson	161
	George Van Haltren	161
40	Harry Hooper	160
	Heinie Manush	160
42	Max Carey	159
	Joe Judge	159
44	Ed McKean	158
45	Kiki Cuyler	157
	Jimmy Ryan	157
47	Tommy Corcoran	155
48	Earle Combs	154
49	Jim Bottomley	151
	Harry Heilmann	151
51	Kip Selbach	149
	Al Simmons	149
53	Wally Pipp	148
	Enos Slaughter	148
55	Bobby Veach	147
	Willie Wilson	147
57	Charlie Gehringer	146
58	Harry Davis	145
	Willie Keeler	145
60	Bobby Wallace	143
61	Lou Brock	141
62	Willie Mays	140
63	John Reilly	139
64	Tom Brown	138
	Willie Davis	138
	Frankie Frisch	138
	Jimmy Williams	138
68	George Brett	137
69	Lave Cross	136
	Babe Ruth	136
	Jimmy Sheckard	136
	Elmer Smith	136
73	Pete Rose	135
74	Shano Collins	133
75	Jim O'Rourke	132
	George Wood	132
77	Brett Butler	131
	Joe DiMaggio	131
	Buck Freeman	131
80	Buddy Myer	130
81	Oyster Burns	129
	Larry Gardner	129
83	Earl Averill	128
	Arky Vaughan	128
85	Vada Pinson	127
86	Hardy Richardson	126
	Robin Yount	126
88	Jimmie Foxx	125
89	John Anderson	124
	Cap Anson	124
	Hal Chase	124
	Frank Schulte	124
93	Larry Doyle	123
	Duke Farrell	123
95	Dummy Hoy	121
96	Fred Pfeffer	120
	Mickey Vernon	120
98	Hugh Duffy	119
99	3 players tied	118

Triples (by era)

1876-1892

Rank	Player	Triples
1	Roger Connor	233
2	Dan Brouthers	205
3	Bid McPhee	189
4	Buck Ewing	178
5	Harry Stovey	174
6	Sam Thompson	161
7	John Reilly	139
8	Tom Brown	138
9	Jim O'Rourke	132
	George Wood	132
11	Oyster Burns	129
12	Hardy Richardson	126
13	Cap Anson	124
14	Fred Pfeffer	120
15	Bill Kuehne	115

1893-1919

Rank	Player	Triples
1	Sam Crawford	309
2	Ty Cobb	295
3	Honus Wagner	252
4	Jake Beckley	244
5	Tris Speaker	222
6	Fred Clarke	220
7	Joe Kelley	194
8	Eddie Collins	187
9	Ed Delahanty	186
10	Jesse Burkett	182
	Ed Konetchy	182
12	Tommy Leach	172
	Zack Wheat	172
14	Joe Jackson	168
15	Sherry Magee	166

1920-1941

Rank	Player	Triples
1	Paul Waner	191
2	Sam Rice	184
3	Edd Roush	182
4	Rabbit Maranville	177
5	Goose Goslin	173
6	Rogers Hornsby	169
7	George Sisler	164
	Pie Traynor	164
9	Lou Gehrig	163
10	Heinie Manush	160
11	Max Carey	159
	Joe Judge	159
13	Kiki Cuyler	157
14	Earle Combs	154
15	2 players tied	151

1942-1960

Rank	Player	Triples
1	Stan Musial	177
2	Enos Slaughter	148
3	Joe DiMaggio	131
4	Mickey Vernon	120
5	Nellie Fox	112
6	Wally Moses	110
7	Richie Ashburn	109
8	Bill Bruton	102
	Jeff Heath	102
10	Phil Cavarretta	99
11	Dixie Walker	96
12	Bob Elliott	94
13	Bobby Doerr	89
14	Duke Snider	85
15	2 players tied	83

1961-1976

Rank	Player	Triples
1	Roberto Clemente	166
2	Lou Brock	141
3	Willie Mays	140
4	Willie Davis	138
5	Pete Rose	135
6	Vada Pinson	127
7	Rod Carew	112
8	Hank Aaron	98
9	Joe Morgan	96
10	Luis Aparicio	92
11	Ernie Banks	90
12	Johnny Callison	89
13	Billy Williams	88
14	Bert Campaneris	86
	Tony Taylor	86

1977-2000

Rank	Player	Triples
1	Willie Wilson	147
2	George Brett	137
3	Brett Butler	131
4	Robin Yount	126
5	Lance Johnson	117
6	Paul Molitor	114
7	Tim Raines	112
8	Garry Templeton	106
9	Juan Samuel	102
10	Larry Bowa	99
11	Andre Dawson	98
12	Jose Cruz	94
	Willie McGee	94
14	Tony Fernandez	92
15	Andy Van Slyke	91

Home Runs

1	Hank Aaron	755
2	Babe Ruth	714
3	Willie Mays	660
4	Frank Robinson	586
5	Harmon Killebrew	573
6	Reggie Jackson	563
7	Mark McGwire	554
8	Mike Schmidt	548
9	Mickey Mantle	536
10	Jimmie Foxx	534
11	Willie McCovey	521
	Ted Williams	521
13	Ernie Banks	512
	Eddie Mathews	512
15	Mel Ott	511
16	Eddie Murray	504
17	Barry Bonds	494
18	Lou Gehrig	493
19	Stan Musial	475
	Willie Stargell	475
21	Dave Winfield	465
22	Carl Yastrzemski	452
23	Jose Canseco	446
24	Dave Kingman	442
25	Andre Dawson	438
	Ken Griffey Jr.	438
27	Billy Williams	426
28	Fred McGriff	417
	Cal Ripken	417
30	Darrell Evans	414
31	Duke Snider	407
32	Rafael Palmeiro	400
33	Al Kaline	399
34	Dale Murphy	398
35	Joe Carter	396
36	Graig Nettles	390
37	Johnny Bench	389
38	Sammy Sosa	386
39	Dwight Evans	385
40	Harold Baines	384
41	Frank Howard	382
	Jim Rice	382
43	Albert Belle	381
44	Orlando Cepeda	379
	Tony Perez	379
46	Norm Cash	377
47	Carlton Fisk	376
48	Rocky Colavito	374
49	Gil Hodges	370
50	Ralph Kiner	369
51	Juan Gonzalez	362
52	Joe DiMaggio	361
53	Gary Gaetti	360
	Andres Galarraga	360
55	Johnny Mize	359
56	Yogi Berra	358
57	Lee May	354
58	Dick Allen	351
59	Chili Davis	350
60	George Foster	348
61	Matt Williams	346
62	Frank Thomas	344
63	Ron Santo	342
64	Jack Clark	340
65	Dave Parker	339
	Boog Powell	339
67	Don Baylor	338
68	Joe Adcock	336
69	Darryl Strawberry	335
70	Bobby Bonds	332
71	Hank Greenberg	331
72	Willie Horton	325
73	Gary Carter	324
	Lance Parrish	324
75	Greg Vaughn	320
76	Cecil Fielder	319
77	Roy Sievers	318
78	George Brett	317
79	Ron Cey	316
80	Reggie Smith	314
81	Jeff Bagwell	310
82	Jay Buhner	308
83	Greg Luzinski	307
	Al Simmons	307
85	Fred Lynn	306
86	Rogers Hornsby	301
87	Chuck Klein	300
88	Mo Vaughn	299
89	Kent Hrbek	293
90	Ron Gant	292
	Rusty Staub	292
92	Jimmy Wynn	291
93	Del Ennis	288
	Bob Johnson	288
	Hank Sauer	288
96	Frank Thomas	286
97	Ellis Burks	285
98	Will Clark	284
99	4 players tied	282

Home Runs (by era)

1876-1892

1	Roger Connor	138
2	Sam Thompson	126
3	Harry Stovey	122
4	Dan Brouthers	106
5	Cap Anson	97
6	Fred Pfeffer	94
7	Jack Clements	77
8	Jerry Denny	74
9	Buck Ewing	71
10	Hardy Richardson	70
11	King Kelly	69
	John Reilly	69
13	George Wood	68
14	Oyster Burns	65
	Bug Holliday	65

1893-1919

1	Zack Wheat	132
2	Gavvy Cravath	119
3	Jimmy Ryan	118
	Tilly Walker	118
5	Ty Cobb	117
	Tris Speaker	117
7	Hugh Duffy	106
	Mike Tiernan	106
9	Ed Delahanty	101
	Honus Wagner	101
11	Sam Crawford	97
12	Frank Baker	96
13	Frank Schulte	92
14	Herman Long	91
15	Jake Beckley	87

1920-1941

1	Babe Ruth	714
2	Jimmie Foxx	534
3	Mel Ott	511
4	Lou Gehrig	493
5	Hank Greenberg	331
6	Al Simmons	307
7	Rogers Hornsby	301
8	Chuck Klein	300
9	Bob Johnson	288
10	Cy Williams	251
11	Goose Goslin	248
12	Hack Wilson	244
13	Wally Berger	242
14	Dolph Camilli	239
15	Earl Averill	238

1942-1960

1	Mickey Mantle	536
2	Ted Williams	521
3	Eddie Mathews	512
4	Stan Musial	475
5	Duke Snider	407
6	Gil Hodges	370
7	Ralph Kiner	369
8	Joe DiMaggio	361
9	Johnny Mize	359
10	Yogi Berra	358
11	Joe Adcock	336
12	Roy Sievers	318
13	Del Ennis	288
	Hank Sauer	288
15	Frank Thomas	286

1961-1976

1	Hank Aaron	755
2	Willie Mays	660
3	Frank Robinson	586
4	Harmon Killebrew	573
5	Willie McCovey	521
6	Ernie Banks	512
7	Willie Stargell	475
8	Carl Yastrzemski	452
9	Billy Williams	426
10	Al Kaline	399
11	Johnny Bench	389
12	Frank Howard	382
13	Orlando Cepeda	379
	Tony Perez	379
15	Norm Cash	377

1977-2000

1	Reggie Jackson	563
2	Mark McGwire	554
3	Mike Schmidt	548
4	Eddie Murray	504
5	Barry Bonds	494
6	Dave Winfield	465
7	Jose Canseco	446
8	Dave Kingman	442
9	Andre Dawson	438
	Ken Griffey Jr.	438
11	Fred McGriff	417
	Cal Ripken	417
13	Darrell Evans	414
14	Rafael Palmeiro	400
15	Dale Murphy	398

Home Run Percentage

1	Mark McGwire	9.41
2	Babe Ruth	8.50
3	Ralph Kiner	7.09
4	Harmon Killebrew	7.03
5	Ken Griffey Jr.	6.90
6	Juan Gonzalez	6.84
7	Ted Williams	6.76
8	Mike Piazza	6.72
9	Barry Bonds	6.63
10	Dave Kingman	6.62
11	Mickey Mantle	6.62
12	Jimmie Foxx	6.57
13	Mike Schmidt	6.56
14	Jose Canseco	6.56
15	Sammy Sosa	6.55
16	Albert Belle	6.51
17	Jim Thome	6.41
18	Hank Greenberg	6.37
19	Willie McCovey	6.36
20	Frank Thomas	6.28
21	Jay Buhner	6.20
22	Cecil Fielder	6.19
23	Darryl Strawberry	6.18
24	Lou Gehrig	6.16
25	Hank Aaron	6.11
26	Willie Mays	6.07
27	Mo Vaughn	6.02
28	Hank Sauer	6.01
29	Greg Vaughn	6.00
30	Eddie Mathews	6.00
31	Willie Stargell	5.99
32	Rob Deer	5.93
33	Frank Howard	5.89
34	Frank Robinson	5.86
35	Jeff Bagwell	5.80
36	Bob Horner	5.77
37	Roy Campanella	5.76
38	Dean Palmer	5.75
39	Rocky Colavito	5.75
40	Gus Zernial	5.74
41	Gorman Thomas	5.73
42	Reggie Jackson	5.71
43	Dick Stuart	5.70
44	David Justice	5.70
45	Duke Snider	5.68
46	Tim Salmon	5.68
47	Fred McGriff	5.67
48	Kevin Mitchell	5.66
49	Norm Cash	5.62
50	Johnny Mize	5.57
51	Dick Allen	5.54
52	Matt Williams	5.54
53	Larry Walker	5.52
54	Ernie Banks	5.43
55	Vinny Castilla	5.43
56	Gary Sheffield	5.42
57	Mel Ott	5.40
58	Roger Maris	5.39
59	Eric Davis	5.38
60	Todd Hundley	5.33
61	Joe DiMaggio	5.29
62	Gil Hodges	5.26
63	Wally Post	5.24
64	Danny Tartabull	5.23
65	Mickey Tettleton	5.21
66	Al Rosen	5.15
67	Hack Wilson	5.13
68	Glenn Davis	5.11
69	Rafael Palmeiro	5.10
70	Bob Allison	5.09
71	Joe Adcock	5.09
72	Johnny Bench	5.08
73	Boog Powell	5.07
74	Glenallen Hill	5.07
75	Jesse Barfield	5.06
76	Nate Colbert	5.06
77	Andres Galarraga	5.05
78	Dale Murphy	5.00
79	Ron Gant	4.99
80	Charlie Keller	4.99
81	Roy Sievers	4.98
82	Cliff Johnson	4.97
83	Don Mincher	4.97
84	Jack Clark	4.97
85	George Foster	4.96
86	Pete Incaviglia	4.87
87	Paul Sorrento	4.87
88	Tony Armas	4.86
89	Raul Mondesi	4.83
90	Eric Karros	4.80
91	Tino Martinez	4.80
92	Andy Thornton	4.78
93	Orlando Cepeda	4.78
94	Leon Wagner	4.77
95	Jim Lemon	4.76
96	Yogi Berra	4.74
97	Don Demeter	4.73
98	Kent Hrbek	4.73
99	Larry Doby	4.73
100	Greg Luzinski	4.72

Home Run Pctg. (by era)

1876-1892

1	Sam Thompson	2.09
2	Harry Stovey	1.97
3	Jack Clements	1.79
4	Roger Connor	1.75
5	Dan Brouthers	1.56
6	Jerry Denny	1.49
7	John Reilly	1.47
8	Charlie Bennett	1.43
9	Denny Lyons	1.43
10	Fred Pfeffer	1.43
11	Ned Williamson	1.38
12	Oyster Burns	1.38
13	Buck Ewing	1.32
14	George Wood	1.26
15	Hardy Richardson	1.23

1893-1919

1	Gavvy Cravath	3.01
2	Tilly Walker	2.33
3	Buck Freeman	1.95
4	Mike Tiernan	1.78
5	Fred Luderus	1.73
6	Frank Baker	1.60
7	Hugh Duffy	1.50
8	Charlie Hickman	1.48
9	Zack Wheat	1.45
10	Jimmy Ryan	1.43
11	Frank Schulte	1.41
12	Casey Stengel	1.40
13	Ed Delahanty	1.34
14	Mike Donlin	1.32
15	Chief Wilson	1.28

1920-1941

1	Babe Ruth	8.50
2	Jimmie Foxx	6.57
3	Hank Greenberg	6.37
4	Lou Gehrig	6.16
5	Mel Ott	5.40
6	Hack Wilson	5.13
7	Wally Berger	4.69
8	Chuck Klein	4.63
9	Dolph Camilli	4.46
10	Hal Trosky	4.42
11	Bob Johnson	4.16
12	Ken Williams	4.03
13	Earl Averill	3.75
14	Cy Williams	3.70
15	Rogers Hornsby	3.68

1942-1960

1	Ralph Kiner	7.09
2	Ted Williams	6.76
3	Mickey Mantle	6.62
4	Hank Sauer	6.01
5	Eddie Mathews	6.00
6	Roy Campanella	5.76
7	Gus Zernial	5.74
8	Duke Snider	5.68
9	Johnny Mize	5.57
10	Joe DiMaggio	5.29
11	Gil Hodges	5.26
12	Wally Post	5.24
13	Al Rosen	5.15
14	Joe Adcock	5.09
15	Charlie Keller	4.99

1961-1976

1	Harmon Killebrew	7.03
2	Willie McCovey	6.36
3	Hank Aaron	6.11
4	Willie Mays	6.07
5	Willie Stargell	5.99
6	Frank Howard	5.89
7	Frank Robinson	5.86
8	Rocky Colavito	5.75
9	Dick Stuart	5.70
10	Norm Cash	5.62
11	Dick Allen	5.54
12	Ernie Banks	5.43
13	Roger Maris	5.39
14	Bob Allison	5.09
15	Johnny Bench	5.08

1977-2000

1	Mark McGwire	9.41
2	Ken Griffey Jr.	6.90
3	Juan Gonzalez	6.84
4	Mike Piazza	6.72
5	Barry Bonds	6.63
6	Dave Kingman	6.62
7	Mike Schmidt	6.56
8	Jose Canseco	6.56
9	Sammy Sosa	6.55
10	Albert Belle	6.51
11	Jim Thome	6.41
12	Frank Thomas	6.28
13	Jay Buhner	6.20
14	Cecil Fielder	6.19
15	Darryl Strawberry	6.18

Total Bases

Rank	Player	TB
1	Hank Aaron	6856
2	Stan Musial	6134
3	Willie Mays	6066
4	Ty Cobb	5854
5	Babe Ruth	5793
6	Pete Rose	5752
7	Carl Yastrzemski	5539
8	Eddie Murray	5397
9	Frank Robinson	5373
10	Dave Winfield	5221
11	Tris Speaker	5101
12	Lou Gehrig	5060
13	George Brett	5044
14	Mel Ott	5041
15	Cal Ripken	4996
16	Jimmie Foxx	4956
17	Ted Williams	4884
18	Honus Wagner	4870
19	Paul Molitor	4854
20	Al Kaline	4852
21	Reggie Jackson	4834
22	Andre Dawson	4787
23	Robin Yount	4730
24	Rogers Hornsby	4712
25	Ernie Banks	4706
26	Al Simmons	4685
27	Billy Williams	4599
28	Harold Baines	4592
29	Tony Perez	4532
30	Mickey Mantle	4511
31	Roberto Clemente	4492
32	Paul Waner	4478
33	Nap Lajoie	4471
34	Dave Parker	4405
35	Mike Schmidt	4404
36	Rickey Henderson	4370
37	Eddie Mathews	4349
38	Sam Crawford	4328
39	Goose Goslin	4325
40	Brooks Robinson	4270
41	Eddie Collins	4268
42	Vada Pinson	4264
43	Charlie Gehringer	4257
44	Lou Brock	4238
45	Dwight Evans	4230
46	Barry Bonds	4228
47	Willie McCovey	4219
48	Tony Gwynn	4212
49	Willie Stargell	4190
50	Rusty Staub	4185
51	Jake Beckley	4156
52	Harmon Killebrew	4143
53	Jim Rice	4129
54	Cap Anson	4124
55	Zack Wheat	4100
56	Al Oliver	4083
57	Wade Boggs	4064
58	Harry Heilmann	4053
59	Rafael Palmeiro	4048
60	Carlton Fisk	3999
61	Rod Carew	3998
62	Joe Morgan	3962
63	Orlando Cepeda	3959
64	Sam Rice	3955
65	Joe DiMaggio	3948
66	Steve Garvey	3941
67	Frankie Frisch	3937
68	Chili Davis	3914
69	Joe Carter	3910
70	Gary Gaetti	3881
71	George Sisler	3871
72	Darrell Evans	3866
73	Duke Snider	3865
74	Roger Connor	3863
75	Joe Medwick	3852
76	Bill Buckner	3833
77	Ed Delahanty	3794
78	Ted Simmons	3793
79	Ryne Sandberg	3787
80	Graig Nettles	3779
	Ron Santo	3779
82	Willie Davis	3778
83	Fred McGriff	3766
84	Jesse Burkett	3759
85	Mickey Vernon	3741
86	Jim Bottomley	3737
87	Dale Murphy	3733
88	Tim Raines	3708
89	Fred Clarke	3680
90	Jimmy Ryan	3675
91	Heinie Manush	3665
92	George Davis	3663
93	Buddy Bell	3654
94	Lou Whitaker	3651
95	Johnny Bench	3644
96	Yogi Berra	3643
97	Johnny Mize	3621
98	Max Carey	3612
99	Ken Griffey Jr.	3605
100	Andres Galarraga	3601

Runs Batted In

Rank	Player	RBI
1	Hank Aaron	2297
2	Babe Ruth	2213
3	Lou Gehrig	1995
4	Stan Musial	1951
5	Ty Cobb	1938
6	Jimmie Foxx	1922
7	Eddie Murray	1917
8	Willie Mays	1903
9	Cap Anson	1880
10	Mel Ott	1860
11	Carl Yastrzemski	1844
12	Ted Williams	1839
13	Dave Winfield	1833
14	Al Simmons	1827
15	Frank Robinson	1812
16	Honus Wagner	1733
17	Reggie Jackson	1702
18	Tony Perez	1652
19	Ernie Banks	1636
20	Cal Ripken	1627
21	Harold Baines	1622
22	Goose Goslin	1609
23	Nap Lajoie	1599
24	George Brett	1595
	Mike Schmidt	1595
26	Andre Dawson	1591
27	Rogers Hornsby	1584
	Harmon Killebrew	1584
29	Al Kaline	1583
30	Jake Beckley	1577
31	Willie McCovey	1555
32	Willie Stargell	1540
33	Harry Heilmann	1539
34	Joe DiMaggio	1537
35	Tris Speaker	1529
36	Sam Crawford	1525
37	Mickey Mantle	1509
38	Dave Parker	1493
39	Billy Williams	1475
40	Ed Delahanty	1466
	Rusty Staub	1466
42	Eddie Mathews	1453
43	Jim Rice	1451
44	Joe Carter	1445
45	George Davis	1439
46	Yogi Berra	1430
47	Charlie Gehringer	1427
48	Joe Cronin	1424
49	Jim Bottomley	1422
50	Robin Yount	1406
51	Barry Bonds	1405
52	Ted Simmons	1389
53	Dwight Evans	1384
54	Joe Medwick	1383
55	Lave Cross	1378
56	Johnny Bench	1376
57	Chili Davis	1372
58	Orlando Cepeda	1365
59	Jose Canseco	1358
60	Brooks Robinson	1357
61	Darrell Evans	1354
62	Mark McGwire	1350
63	Rafael Palmeiro	1347
64	Gary Gaetti	1341
65	Johnny Mize	1337
66	Duke Snider	1333
67	Ron Santo	1331
68	Carlton Fisk	1330
69	Al Oliver	1326
70	Roger Connor	1323
71	Graig Nettles	1314
	Pete Rose	1314
73	Mickey Vernon	1311
74	Paul Waner	1309
75	Steve Garvey	1308
76	Paul Molitor	1307
77	Roberto Clemente	1305
	Sam Thompson	1305
79	Enos Slaughter	1304
80	Hugh Duffy	1302
81	Eddie Collins	1300
82	Fred McGriff	1298
83	Dan Brouthers	1296
84	Del Ennis	1284
85	Bob Johnson	1283
86	Don Baylor	1276
	Hank Greenberg	1276
88	Gil Hodges	1274
89	Pie Traynor	1273
90	Andres Galarraga	1272
91	Ken Griffey Jr.	1270
92	Dale Murphy	1266
93	Zack Wheat	1248
94	Bobby Doerr	1247
95	Frankie Frisch	1244
	Lee May	1244
97	Albert Belle	1239
	George Foster	1239
99	Bill Dahlen	1234
100	Gary Carter	1225

Runs Batted In (by era)

1876-1892

Rank	Player	RBI
1	Cap Anson	1880
2	Roger Connor	1323
3	Sam Thompson	1305
4	Dan Brouthers	1296
5	Bid McPhee	1072
6	Fred Pfeffer	1021
7	Jim O'Rourke	1010
8	Billy Nash	979
9	King Kelly	950
10	Harry Stovey	908
11	Charlie Comiskey	883
	Buck Ewing	883
13	John Ward	869
14	Lou Bierbauer	837
15	Henry Larkin	836

1893-1919

Rank	Player	RBI
1	Ty Cobb	1938
2	Honus Wagner	1733
3	Nap Lajoie	1599
4	Jake Beckley	1577
5	Tris Speaker	1529
6	Sam Crawford	1525
7	Ed Delahanty	1466
8	George Davis	1439
9	Lave Cross	1378
10	Hugh Duffy	1302
11	Eddie Collins	1300
12	Zack Wheat	1248
13	Bill Dahlen	1234
14	Joe Kelley	1194
15	Sherry Magee	1176

1920-1941

Rank	Player	RBI
1	Babe Ruth	2213
2	Lou Gehrig	1995
3	Jimmie Foxx	1922
4	Mel Ott	1860
5	Al Simmons	1827
6	Goose Goslin	1609
7	Rogers Hornsby	1584
8	Harry Heilmann	1539
9	Charlie Gehringer	1427
10	Joe Cronin	1424
11	Jim Bottomley	1422
12	Joe Medwick	1383
13	Paul Waner	1309
14	Bob Johnson	1283
15	Hank Greenberg	1276

1942-1960

Rank	Player	RBI
1	Stan Musial	1951
2	Ted Williams	1839
3	Joe DiMaggio	1537
4	Mickey Mantle	1509
5	Eddie Mathews	1453
6	Yogi Berra	1430
7	Johnny Mize	1337
8	Duke Snider	1333
9	Mickey Vernon	1311
10	Enos Slaughter	1304
11	Del Ennis	1284
12	Gil Hodges	1274
13	Bobby Doerr	1247
14	Bob Elliott	1195
15	Vic Wertz	1178

1961-1976

Rank	Player	RBI
1	Hank Aaron	2297
2	Willie Mays	1903
3	Carl Yastrzemski	1844
4	Frank Robinson	1812
5	Tony Perez	1652
6	Ernie Banks	1636
7	Harmon Killebrew	1584
8	Al Kaline	1583
9	Willie McCovey	1555
10	Willie Stargell	1540
11	Billy Williams	1475
12	Rusty Staub	1466
13	Johnny Bench	1376
14	Orlando Cepeda	1365
15	Brooks Robinson	1357

1977-2000

Rank	Player	RBI
1	Eddie Murray	1917
2	Dave Winfield	1833
3	Reggie Jackson	1702
4	Cal Ripken	1627
5	Harold Baines	1622
6	George Brett	1595
	Mike Schmidt	1595
8	Andre Dawson	1591
9	Dave Parker	1493
10	Jim Rice	1451
11	Joe Carter	1445
12	Robin Yount	1406
13	Barry Bonds	1405
14	Ted Simmons	1389
15	Dwight Evans	1384

Runs Batted In per Game

Rank	Player	RBI/G
1	Sam Thompson	.93
2	Lou Gehrig	.92
3	Hank Greenberg	.92
4	Joe DiMaggio	.89
5	Babe Ruth	.88
6	Juan Gonzalez	.84
7	Jimmie Foxx	.83
8	Cap Anson	.83
9	Al Simmons	.82
10	Albert Belle	.81
11	Ted Williams	.80
12	Ed Delahanty	.80
13	Mike Piazza	.79
14	Hack Wilson	.79
15	Dan Brouthers	.77
16	Frank Thomas	.77
17	Mark McGwire	.76
18	Bob Meusel	.76
19	Ken Griffey Jr.	.76
20	Hal Trosky	.75
21	Jose Canseco	.75
22	Hugh Duffy	.75
23	Jeff Bagwell	.74
24	Mo Vaughn	.73
25	Tip O'Neill	.72
26	Rudy York	.72
27	Harry Heilmann	.72
28	Jim Bottomley	.71
29	Johnny Mize	.71
30	Henry Larkin	.71
31	Roy Campanella	.70
32	Goose Goslin	.70
33	Rogers Hornsby	.70
34	Oyster Burns	.70
35	Earl Averill	.70
36	Joe Medwick	.70
37	Hank Aaron	.70
38	Moises Alou	.69
39	Jim Rice	.69
40	Ralph Kiner	.69
41	Sammy Sosa	.69
42	Bob Johnson	.69
43	Al Rosen	.69
44	Cecil Fielder	.69
45	Chuck Klein	.69
46	Tony Lazzeri	.68
47	Dante Bichette	.68
48	Vern Stephens	.68
49	Mel Ott	.68
50	Tim Salmon	.68
51	Ed McKean	.68
52	Tino Martinez	.68
53	Bill Dickey	.68
54	Del Ennis	.67
55	Yogi Berra	.67
56	Denny Lyons	.67
57	Bob Horner	.67
58	Buck Ewing	.67
59	Joe Cronin	.67
60	Bobby Doerr	.67
61	Dick Stuart	.67
62	Jeff Kent	.67
63	Wally Berger	.67
64	Andres Galarraga	.66
65	David Justice	.66
66	Mike Schmidt	.66
67	Matt Williams	.66
68	Roger Connor	.66
69	Jay Buhner	.66
70	Dave Foutz	.66
71	Joe Carter	.66
72	Jake Beckley	.66
73	Danny Tartabull	.66
74	Pie Traynor	.66
75	Barry Bonds	.66
76	Hughie Jennings	.65
77	Larry Walker	.65
78	Ken Williams	.65
79	King Kelly	.65
80	Willie Stargell	.65
81	Harmon Killebrew	.65
82	Charlie Keller	.65
83	Chick Hafey	.65
84	Bernie Williams	.65
85	John Reilly	.65
86	Ernie Banks	.65
87	Glenn Wright	.65
88	Jackie Jensen	.65
89	Frank Robinson	.65
90	Nap Lajoie	.64
91	Stan Musial	.64
92	Joe Kelley	.64
93	Orlando Cepeda	.64
94	Babe Herman	.64
95	Rafael Palmeiro	.64
96	Jeff Heath	.64
97	Bobby Veach	.64
98	Dick Allen	.64
99	Ty Cobb	.64
100	Jim Thome	.64

Walks

1	Babe Ruth	2062
2	Rickey Henderson	2060
3	Ted Williams	2019
4	Joe Morgan	1865
5	Carl Yastrzemski	1845
6	Mickey Mantle	1733
7	Mel Ott	1708
8	Eddie Yost	1614
9	Darrell Evans	1605
10	Stan Musial	1599
11	Pete Rose	1566
12	Harmon Killebrew	1559
13	Barry Bonds	1547
14	Lou Gehrig	1508
15	Mike Schmidt	1507
16	Eddie Collins	1499
17	Willie Mays	1464
18	Jimmie Foxx	1452
19	Eddie Mathews	1444
20	Frank Robinson	1420
21	Wade Boggs	1412
22	Hank Aaron	1402
23	Dwight Evans	1391
24	Tris Speaker	1381
25	Reggie Jackson	1375
26	Willie McCovey	1345
27	Eddie Murray	1333
28	Tony Phillips	1319
29	Luke Appling	1302
30	Tim Raines	1290
31	Al Kaline	1277
32	Ken Singleton	1263
33	Jack Clark	1262
34	Mark McGwire	1261
35	Rusty Staub	1255
36	Ty Cobb	1249
37	Willie Randolph	1243
38	Jimmy Wynn	1224
39	Dave Winfield	1216
40	Pee Wee Reese	1210
41	Richie Ashburn	1198
42	Brian Downing	1197
	Lou Whitaker	1197
44	Chili Davis	1194
45	Billy Hamilton	1189
46	Frank Thomas	1188
47	Charlie Gehringer	1186
48	Donie Bush	1158
49	Max Bishop	1153
	Toby Harrah	1153
51	Harry Hooper	1136
	Fred McGriff	1136
53	Jimmy Sheckard	1135
54	Brett Butler	1129
55	Ron Santo	1108
56	Cal Ripken	1103
57	George Brett	1096
58	Paul Molitor	1094
59	Lu Blue	1092
	Stan Hack	1092
61	Paul Waner	1091
62	Graig Nettles	1088
63	Bobby Grich	1087
64	Bob Johnson	1075
65	Ozzie Smith	1072
66	Harlond Clift	1070
	Keith Hernandez	1070
68	Bill Dahlen	1064
69	Joe Cronin	1059
70	Harold Baines	1054
71	Ron Fairly	1052
72	Billy Williams	1045
73	Norm Cash	1043
	Eddie Joost	1043
75	Roy Thomas	1042
76	Max Carey	1040
77	Rogers Hornsby	1038
78	Jim Gilliam	1036
79	Sal Bando	1031
80	Jesse Burkett	1029
81	Rod Carew	1018
	Enos Slaughter	1018
83	Ron Cey	1012
84	Ralph Kiner	1011
85	Dummy Hoy	1006
86	Miller Huggins	1003
87	Roger Connor	1002
88	Boog Powell	1001
89	Eddie Stanky	996
90	Jeff Bagwell	992
91	Cupid Childs	991
92	Dale Murphy	986
93	Gene Tenace	984
94	Bid McPhee	983
95	Joe Kuhel	980
	Earl Torgeson	980
97	Augie Galan	979
98	Edgar Martinez	973
99	Duke Snider	971
100	Bob Elliott	967

Walk Percentage

1	Ted Williams	20.76
2	Max Bishop	20.42
3	Babe Ruth	19.71
4	Eddie Stanky	18.80
5	Ferris Fain	18.70
6	Gene Tenace	18.31
7	Roy Cullenbine	18.03
8	Eddie Yost	18.01
9	Frank Thomas	17.83
10	Mark McGwire	17.64
11	Mickey Mantle	17.62
12	John McGraw	17.56
13	Jim Thome	17.37
14	Barry Bonds	17.18
15	Charlie Keller	17.14
16	Mickey Tettleton	16.81
17	Joe Morgan	16.74
18	Rickey Henderson	16.62
19	Earl Torgeson	16.47
20	Bernie Carbo	16.45
21	Roy Thomas	16.44
22	Ralph Kiner	16.26
23	Harmon Killebrew	16.06
24	Billy Hamilton	15.91
25	Lou Gehrig	15.86
26	Elmer Valo	15.78
27	Joe Ferguson	15.77
28	Harlond Clift	15.74
29	Eddie Joost	15.69
30	Jeff Bagwell	15.64
31	Lu Blue	15.61
32	Jack Clark	15.56
33	Jimmy Wynn	15.54
34	Mel Ott	15.30
35	Miller Huggins	15.29
36	Mike Schmidt	15.29
37	Edgar Martinez	15.19
38	Darrell Evans	15.17
39	John Cangelosi	15.16
40	Jimmie Foxx	15.15
41	Joe Cunningham	15.12
42	Dolph Camilli	15.03
43	Cupid Childs	14.99
44	Ken Singleton	14.94
45	Dave Magadan	14.90
46	Elbie Fletcher	14.85
47	Merv Rettenmund	14.83
48	Mike Hargrove	14.78
49	Darren Daulton	14.77
50	Tony Phillips	14.76
51	John Olerud	14.75
52	Topsy Hartsel	14.72
53	Dwayne Murphy	14.66
54	Wayne Garrett	14.59
55	Jason Thompson	14.52
56	Eddie Mathews	14.47
57	Tim Salmon	14.43
58	Gary Sheffield	14.29
59	John Kruk	14.28
60	Mickey Cochrane	14.22
61	Andy Thornton	14.20
62	Augie Galan	14.16
63	Gene Woodling	14.15
64	Willie McCovey	14.10
65	Hank Greenberg	14.09
66	Darrell Porter	14.04
67	Larry Doby	14.01
68	John Mayberry	13.92
69	Alvin Davis	13.91
70	Johnny Briggs	13.87
71	Billy North	13.85
72	David Justice	13.85
73	Donie Bush	13.84
74	Wally Schang	13.79
75	Roger Bresnahan	13.74
76	Steve Braun	13.69
77	Norm Siebern	13.64
78	Bob Allison	13.64
79	Jay Buhner	13.63
80	Bobby Grich	13.63
81	Al Rosen	13.61
82	Toby Harrah	13.48
83	Lee Mazzilli	13.47
84	Norm Cash	13.46
85	Mike Jorgensen	13.46
86	Paul Radford	13.45
87	Bob Johnson	13.45
88	Willie Randolph	13.42
89	Tommy Henrich	13.40
90	Dwight Evans	13.39
91	Fred McGriff	13.38
92	Rick Ferrell	13.38
93	Mike Stanley	13.38
94	Wayne Gross	13.36
95	Carl Yastrzemski	13.34
96	Wade Boggs	13.33
97	Grady Hatton	13.31
98	Danny Tartabull	13.29
99	Lyn Lary	13.28
100	Brian Downing	13.23

Strikeouts

1	Reggie Jackson	2597
2	Willie Stargell	1936
3	Mike Schmidt	1883
4	Jose Canseco	1867
	Tony Perez	1867
6	Dave Kingman	1816
7	Bobby Bonds	1757
8	Dale Murphy	1748
9	Andres Galarraga	1741
10	Lou Brock	1730
11	Mickey Mantle	1710
12	Harmon Killebrew	1699
13	Chili Davis	1698
14	Dwight Evans	1697
15	Dave Winfield	1686
16	Gary Gaetti	1602
17	Fred McGriff	1592
18	Lee May	1570
19	Dick Allen	1556
20	Willie McCovey	1550
21	Rickey Henderson	1547
22	Dave Parker	1537
	Sammy Sosa	1537
24	Frank Robinson	1532
25	Lance Parrish	1527
26	Willie Mays	1526
27	Eddie Murray	1516
28	Rick Monday	1513
29	Andre Dawson	1509
30	Tony Phillips	1499
31	Greg Luzinski	1495
32	Eddie Mathews	1487
33	Mark McGwire	1478
34	Frank Howard	1460
35	Juan Samuel	1442
36	Jack Clark	1441
37	Devon White	1431
38	Jimmy Wynn	1427
39	Harold Baines	1425
40	Jim Rice	1423
41	George Foster	1419
42	George Scott	1418
43	Darrell Evans	1410
44	Rob Deer	1409
45	Jay Buhner	1397
46	Carl Yastrzemski	1393
47	Joe Carter	1387
48	Carlton Fisk	1386
49	Hank Aaron	1383
50	Danny Tartabull	1362
51	Eric Davis	1360
52	Larry Parrish	1359
53	Darryl Strawberry	1352
54	Robin Yount	1350
55	Ron Santo	1343
56	Gorman Thomas	1339
57	Babe Ruth	1330
58	Deron Johnson	1318
59	Jay Bell	1317
60	Cecil Fielder	1316
61	Willie Horton	1313
62	Jimmie Foxx	1311
63	Mickey Tettleton	1307
	Tim Wallach	1307
65	Ray Lankford	1289
66	Greg Vaughn	1288
67	Kirk Gibson	1285
68	Johnny Bench	1278
	Bobby Grich	1278
70	Pete Incaviglia	1277
71	Claudell Washington	1266
72	Ron Gant	1263
73	Mo Vaughn	1262
74	Ryne Sandberg	1260
75	Ken Singleton	1246
76	Paul Molitor	1244
77	Cal Ripken	1242
78	Dean Palmer	1240
79	Willie McGee	1238
80	Duke Snider	1237
81	Ernie Banks	1236
82	Ron Cey	1235
83	Jesse Barfield	1234
84	Roberto Clemente	1230
85	Boog Powell	1226
	Matt Williams	1226
87	Travis Fryman	1224
88	Graig Nettles	1209
89	Tony Armas	1201
90	Vada Pinson	1196
91	Will Clark	1190
92	Barry Bonds	1189
93	Tom Brunansky	1187
94	Dave Concepcion	1186
95	Orlando Cepeda	1169
96	Bobby Bonilla	1151
97	Willie Wilson	1144
98	Pete Rose	1143
99	Bert Campaneris	1142
100	Donn Clendenon	1140

At Bats per Strikeout

1	Joe Sewell	62.6
2	Lloyd Waner	44.9
3	Nellie Fox	42.7
4	Tommy Holmes	40.9
5	Andy High	33.8
6	Sam Rice	33.7
7	Frankie Frisch	33.5
8	Dale Mitchell	33.5
9	Johnny Cooney	31.5
10	Frank McCormick	30.3
11	Don Mueller	29.9
12	Billy Southworth	29.5
13	Rip Radcliff	28.9
14	Edd Roush	28.3
15	Pie Traynor	27.2
16	Doc Cramer	26.5
17	Carson Bigbee	26.0
18	Hank Severeid	25.5
19	George Sisler	25.3
20	Paul Waner	25.2
21	Jack Rowe	25.0
22	Deacon White	25.0
23	Sparky Adams	24.9
24	Lou Finney	24.9
25	Ezra Sutton	24.7
26	Irish Meusel	24.6
27	Red Schoendienst	24.5
28	Vic Power	24.5
29	Arky Vaughan	24.0
30	Felix Millan	23.9
31	Mickey Cochrane	23.8
32	Charlie Gehringer	23.8
33	John Ward	23.6
34	George Kell	23.4
35	George Cutshaw	23.2
36	Jack Tobin	23.1
37	Taffy Wright	23.1
38	Hughie Critz	23.1
39	Mark Koenig	22.5
40	Ernie Lombardi	22.3
41	Heinie Manush	22.2
42	Bobby Richardson	22.2
43	Jo-Jo Moore	22.0
44	Earl Sheely	21.8
45	Bill Dickey	21.8
46	Johnny Pesky	21.8
47	Rick Ferrell	21.8
48	Tony Gwynn	21.6
49	Glenn Beckert	21.4
50	Dick Siebert	21.2
51	Eddie Waitkus	20.9
52	Max Flack	20.8
53	Bill Buckner	20.7
54	Dixie Walker	20.7
55	Paul Hines	20.7
56	Everett Scott	20.7
57	Earle Combs	20.7
58	Freddie Lindstrom	20.3
59	Mickey Owen	20.2
60	Joe Vosmik	20.1
61	Lou Boudreau	19.5
62	Milt Stock	19.5
63	Willard Marshall	19.3
64	Debs Garms	19.3
65	Charlie Grimm	19.3
66	Harry Rice	19.3
67	Skeeter Newsome	19.2
68	Curt Walker	19.1
69	Peanuts Lowrey	19.1
70	Charlie Jamieson	19.0
71	Muddy Ruel	19.0
72	Tommy Griffith	18.9
73	Tommy Thevenow	18.8
74	Joe Stripp	18.6
75	Joe DiMaggio	18.5
76	Bob Fothergill	18.5
77	Bing Miller	18.3
78	Riggs Stephenson	18.3
79	Yogi Berra	18.2
80	Billy Herman	18.0
81	Lee Magee	18.0
82	Dave Cash	18.0
83	Elmer Valo	17.7
84	Heinie Groh	17.6
85	Luke Sewell	17.5
86	Rich Dauer	17.5
87	Buddy Lewis	17.4
88	Billy Goodman	17.2
89	Jim Gilliam	17.1
90	Harvey Kuenn	17.1
91	Gus Mancuso	17.1
92	Jimmie Wilson	17.1
93	Billy Cox	17.0
94	Ken Williams	16.9
95	George Case	16.9
96	Cecil Travis	16.9
97	Luke Appling	16.8
98	Jackie Hayes	16.8
99	Brian Harper	16.8
100	Jackie Robinson	16.8

Batting Average

Rank	Player	AVG
1	Ty Cobb	.366
2	Rogers Hornsby	.358
3	Joe Jackson	.356
4	Dan Brouthers	.349
5	Pete Browning	.349
6	Ed Delahanty	.346
7	Tris Speaker	.345
8	Billy Hamilton	.344
9	Ted Williams	.344
10	Babe Ruth	.342
11	Harry Heilmann	.342
12	Willie Keeler	.341
13	Bill Terry	.341
14	George Sisler	.340
15	Lou Gehrig	.340
16	Tony Gwynn	.338
17	Jesse Burkett	.338
18	Nap Lajoie	.338
19	Riggs Stephenson	.336
20	Sam Thompson	.335
21	Al Simmons	.334
22	Tip O'Neill	.334
23	John McGraw	.334
24	Paul Waner	.333
25	Eddie Collins	.333
26	Cap Anson	.333
27	Mike Donlin	.333
28	Stan Musial	.331
29	Heinie Manush	.330
30	Mike Piazza	.328
31	Wade Boggs	.328
32	Rod Carew	.328
33	Honus Wagner	.328
34	Bob Fothergill	.325
35	Jimmie Foxx	.325
36	Earle Combs	.325
37	Joe DiMaggio	.325
38	Babe Herman	.324
39	Hugh Duffy	.324
40	Joe Medwick	.324
41	Roger Connor	.323
42	Edd Roush	.323
43	Sam Rice	.322
44	Ross Youngs	.322
45	Kiki Cuyler	.321
46	Frank Thomas	.321
47	Charlie Gehringer	.320
48	Chuck Klein	.320
49	Edgar Martinez	.320
50	Pie Traynor	.320
51	Mickey Cochrane	.320
52	Ken Williams	.319
53	Kirby Puckett	.318
54	Earl Averill	.318
55	Denny Lyons	.318
56	Arky Vaughan	.318
57	Roberto Clemente	.317
58	Chick Hafey	.317
59	Joe Kelley	.317
60	Zack Wheat	.317
61	George Van Haltren	.317
62	Lloyd Waner	.316
63	Frankie Frisch	.316
64	Goose Goslin	.316
65	Bibb Falk	.314
66	Mike Tiernan	.314
67	Cecil Travis	.314
68	King Kelly	.314
69	Hank Greenberg	.313
70	Jack Fournier	.313
71	Elmer Flick	.313
72	Jim O'Rourke	.313
73	Bill Dickey	.313
74	Dale Mitchell	.312
75	Johnny Mize	.312
76	Joe Sewell	.312
77	Fred Clarke	.312
78	Elmer Smith	.312
79	Barney McCosky	.312
80	Hughie Jennings	.312
81	Larry Walker	.311
82	Freddie Lindstrom	.311
83	Bing Miller	.311
84	Jackie Robinson	.311
85	Baby Doll Jacobson	.311
86	Taffy Wright	.311
87	Rip Radcliff	.311
88	Ginger Beaumont	.311
89	Jimmy Ryan	.310
90	Luke Appling	.310
91	Irish Meusel	.310
92	Bobby Veach	.310
93	Henry Larkin	.310
94	Jim Bottomley	.310
95	John Stone	.310
96	Sam Crawford	.309
97	Bob Meusel	.309
98	Oyster Burns	.309
99	Jack Tobin	.309
100	Spud Davis	.308

Batting Average (by era)

1876-1892

Rank	Player	AVG
1	Dan Brouthers	.349
2	Pete Browning	.349
3	Sam Thompson	.335
4	Tip O'Neill	.334
5	Cap Anson	.333
6	Roger Connor	.323
7	Denny Lyons	.318
8	King Kelly	.314
9	Jim O'Rourke	.313
10	Henry Larkin	.310
11	Oyster Burns	.309
12	Buck Ewing	.307
13	Deacon White	.306
14	George Gore	.306
15	Paul Hines	.306

1893-1919

Rank	Player	AVG
1	Ty Cobb	.366
2	Joe Jackson	.356
3	Ed Delahanty	.346
4	Tris Speaker	.345
5	Billy Hamilton	.344
6	Willie Keeler	.341
7	Jesse Burkett	.338
8	Nap Lajoie	.338
9	John McGraw	.334
10	Eddie Collins	.333
11	Mike Donlin	.333
12	Honus Wagner	.328
13	Hugh Duffy	.324
14	Joe Kelley	.317
15	Zack Wheat	.317

1920-1941

Rank	Player	AVG
1	Rogers Hornsby	.358
2	Babe Ruth	.342
3	Harry Heilmann	.342
4	Bill Terry	.341
5	George Sisler	.340
6	Lou Gehrig	.340
7	Riggs Stephenson	.336
8	Al Simmons	.334
9	Paul Waner	.333
10	Heinie Manush	.330
11	Bob Fothergill	.325
12	Jimmie Foxx	.325
13	Earle Combs	.325
14	Babe Herman	.324
15	Joe Medwick	.324

1942-1960

Rank	Player	AVG
1	Ted Williams	.344
2	Stan Musial	.331
3	Joe DiMaggio	.325
4	Dale Mitchell	.312
5	Johnny Mize	.312
6	Barney McCosky	.312
7	Jackie Robinson	.311
8	Taffy Wright	.311
9	Richie Ashburn	.308
10	Johnny Pesky	.307
11	George Kell	.306
12	Dixie Walker	.306
13	Harvey Kuenn	.303
14	Tommy Holmes	.302
15	Enos Slaughter	.300

1961-1976

Rank	Player	AVG
1	Rod Carew	.328
2	Roberto Clemente	.317
3	Matty Alou	.307
4	Ralph Garr	.306
5	Hank Aaron	.305
6	Tony Oliva	.304
7	Manny Mota	.304
8	Pete Rose	.303
9	Willie Mays	.302
10	Rico Carty	.299
11	Joe Torre	.297
12	Al Kaline	.297
13	Orlando Cepeda	.297
14	Manny Sanguillen	.296
15	Bob Watson	.295

1977-2000

Rank	Player	AVG
1	Tony Gwynn	.338
2	Mike Piazza	.328
3	Wade Boggs	.328
4	Frank Thomas	.321
5	Edgar Martinez	.320
6	Kirby Puckett	.318
7	Larry Walker	.311
8	Mark Grace	.308
9	Don Mattingly	.307
10	Paul Molitor	.306
11	Kenny Lofton	.306
12	George Brett	.305
13	Jeff Bagwell	.305
14	Bill Madlock	.305
15	Bernie Williams	.304

Batting Average (by position)

First Base

Rank	Player	AVG
1	Dan Brouthers	.349
2	Bill Terry	.341
3	George Sisler	.340
4	Lou Gehrig	.340
5	Cap Anson	.333
6	Rod Carew	.328
7	Jimmie Foxx	.325
8	Roger Connor	.323
9	Hank Greenberg	.313
10	Jack Fournier	.313

Second Base

Rank	Player	AVG
1	Rogers Hornsby	.358
2	Nap Lajoie	.338
3	Eddie Collins	.333
4	Charlie Gehringer	.320
5	Frankie Frisch	.316
6	Cupid Childs	.306
7	Billy Herman	.304
8	Roberto Alomar	.304
9	Buddy Myer	.303
10	Chuck Knoblauch	.297

Shortstop

Rank	Player	AVG
1	Honus Wagner	.328
2	Arky Vaughan	.318
3	Joe Sewell	.312
4	Luke Appling	.310
5	Ed McKean	.308
6	Joe Cronin	.301
7	Barry Larkin	.300
8	Lou Boudreau	.295
9	George Davis	.295
10	Jack Glasscock	.294

Third Base

Rank	Player	AVG
1	Wade Boggs	.328
2	Pie Traynor	.320
3	Denny Lyons	.318
4	Frank Baker	.307
5	George Kell	.306
6	George Brett	.305
7	Bill Madlock	.305
8	Stan Hack	.301
9	Pinky Whitney	.295
10	Kevin Seitzer	.295

Outfield

Rank	Player	AVG
1	Ty Cobb	.366
2	Joe Jackson	.356
3	Ed Delahanty	.346
4	Tris Speaker	.345
5	Billy Hamilton	.344
6	Ted Williams	.344
7	Babe Ruth	.342
8	Harry Heilmann	.342
9	Willie Keeler	.341
10	Tony Gwynn	.338
11	Jesse Burkett	.338
12	Sam Thompson	.335
13	Al Simmons	.334
14	Tip O'Neill	.334
15	Paul Waner	.333
16	Stan Musial	.331
17	Heinie Manush	.330
18	Earle Combs	.325
19	Joe DiMaggio	.325
20	Babe Herman	.324

Catcher

Rank	Player	AVG
1	Mike Piazza	.328
2	Mickey Cochrane	.320
3	Bill Dickey	.313
4	Spud Davis	.308
5	Ernie Lombardi	.306
6	Ivan Rodriguez	.304
7	Gabby Hartnett	.297
8	Manny Sanguillen	.296
9	Smoky Burgess	.295
10	Thurman Munson	.292

Relative Batting Average

Rank	Player	RBA
1	Ty Cobb	134.8
2	Joe Jackson	133.1
3	Pete Browning	130.8
4	Dan Brouthers	128.3
5	Ted Williams	128.1
6	Tony Gwynn	127.7
7	Nap Lajoie	127.4
8	Rod Carew	127.0
9	Rogers Hornsby	126.2
10	Tris Speaker	125.4
11	Tip O'Neill	124.8
12	Willie Keeler	124.6
13	Stan Musial	123.9
14	Wade Boggs	123.7
15	Mike Donlin	123.6
16	Honus Wagner	123.1
17	Cap Anson	122.8
18	Billy Hamilton	122.7
19	Ed Delahanty	122.6
20	Eddie Collins	121.8
21	Jesse Burkett	121.6
22	Kirby Puckett	121.0
23	Mike Piazza	120.8
24	Roberto Clemente	120.7
25	Tony Oliva	120.4
26	Sam Thompson	120.3
27	Harry Heilmann	119.4
28	Babe Ruth	119.2
29	Edgar Martinez	119.1
30	Frank Thomas	119.0
31	George Sisler	118.9
32	Sam Crawford	118.8
33	King Kelly	118.5
34	Roger Connor	118.1
35	Matty Alou	117.9
36	Joe Medwick	117.8
37	Paul Waner	117.8
38	Jim O'Rourke	117.7
39	Elmer Flick	117.4
40	Bill Terry	117.3
41	Lou Gehrig	117.2
42	Joe DiMaggio	117.1
43	Ginger Beaumont	117.0
44	Don Mattingly	116.9
45	Ralph Garr	116.7
46	Manny Mota	116.4
47	George Brett	116.3
48	Dale Mitchell	116.3
49	John McGraw	116.2
50	Larry Walker	116.2
51	Hank Aaron	116.0
52	Henry Larkin	115.8
53	Paul Hines	115.8
54	Jackie Robinson	115.7
55	George Gore	115.6
56	Pete Rose	115.6
57	Paul Molitor	115.5
58	Mark Grace	115.4
59	Al Simmons	115.4
60	Frank Baker	115.4
61	Al Kaline	115.4
62	Bill Madlock	115.2
63	Arky Vaughan	115.1
64	Deacon White	115.1
65	Al Oliver	115.1
66	Riggs Stephenson	115.0
67	Mickey Mantle	115.0
68	Johnny Mize	115.0
69	Zack Wheat	114.9
70	Hugh Duffy	114.8
71	George Kell	114.8
72	Barney McCosky	114.7
73	Richie Ashburn	114.6
74	Mike Greenwell	114.6
75	Pedro Guerrero	114.5
76	Johnny Pesky	114.5
77	Harvey Kuenn	114.5
78	Rico Carty	114.4
79	Willie Mays	114.3
80	John Kruk	114.2
81	Fred Clarke	114.1
82	Heinie Manush	114.0
83	Will Clark	113.9
84	Cy Seymour	113.9
85	Roberto Alomar	113.9
86	Jimmie Foxx	113.8
87	Joe Torre	113.8
88	Hardy Richardson	113.8
89	Edd Roush	113.8
90	Julio Franco	113.7
91	Cecil Cooper	113.5
92	Jim Rice	113.5
93	Frank Robinson	113.4
94	Tommy Davis	113.4
95	Taffy Wright	113.4
96	Jeff Bagwell	113.4
97	Hal Morris	113.3
98	Kenny Lofton	113.1
99	Minnie Minoso	113.1
100	Denny Lyons	113.0

On-Base Percentage

Rank	Player	OBP
1	Ted Williams	.483
2	Babe Ruth	.474
3	John McGraw	.466
4	Billy Hamilton	.455
5	Lou Gehrig	.447
6	Frank Thomas	.446
7	Rogers Hornsby	.434
8	Ty Cobb	.433
9	Edgar Martinez	.429
10	Jimmie Foxx	.428
	Tris Speaker	.428
12	Ferris Fain	.425
13	Eddie Collins	.424
14	Max Bishop	.423
	Dan Brouthers	.423
	Joe Jackson	.423
	Mickey Mantle	.423
18	Jeff Bagwell	.422
19	Wade Boggs	.419
	Mickey Cochrane	.419
21	Stan Musial	.418
22	Cupid Childs	.416
23	Barry Bonds	.415
	Jesse Burkett	.415
25	Mel Ott	.414
26	Roy Thomas	.413
	Jim Thome	.413
28	Hank Greenberg	.412
29	Ed Delahanty	.411
30	Harry Heilmann	.410
	Charlie Keller	.410
	Jackie Robinson	.410
	Eddie Stanky	.410
34	John Olerud	.409
35	Roy Cullenbine	.408
36	Denny Lyons	.407
	Riggs Stephenson	.407
38	Joe Cunningham	.406
	Rickey Henderson	.406
	Arky Vaughan	.406
41	Charlie Gehringer	.404
	Paul Waner	.404
43	Pete Browning	.403
44	Lu Blue	.402
	Joe Kelley	.402
	Mark McGwire	.402
	Gary Sheffield	.402
48	Mike Hargrove	.400
	John Kruk	.400
50	Luke Appling	.399
	Elmer Valo	.399
	Ross Youngs	.399
53	Joe DiMaggio	.398
	Ralph Kiner	.398
	Tim Salmon	.398
	Elmer Smith	.398
57	Richie Ashburn	.397
	Earle Combs	.397
	Roger Connor	.397
	Johnny Mize	.397
61	Dave Magadan	.396
62	Cap Anson	.395
	Earl Averill	.395
	Rod Carew	.395
	Joe Morgan	.395
	Mike Piazza	.395
	Hack Wilson	.395
	Eddie Yost	.395
69	Frank Chance	.394
	Stan Hack	.394
	Johnny Pesky	.394
	Larry Walker	.394
73	Bob Johnson	.393
	Wally Schang	.393
	Bill Terry	.393
	Ken Williams	.393
77	Jack Fournier	.392
	George Grantham	.392
	Tony Gwynn	.392
	Tip O'Neill	.392
	Frank Robinson	.392
	Mike Tiernan	.392
	Bernie Williams	.392
84	Mark Grace	.391
	Hughie Jennings	.391
	Minnie Minoso	.391
	Joe Sewell	.391
	Ken Singleton	.391
	Gene Tenace	.391
	Honus Wagner	.391
91	Harlond Clift	.390
	Joe Cronin	.390
	Augie Galan	.390
	Mo Vaughn	.390
95	Bernie Carbo	.389
	Elmer Flick	.389
	Chuck Knoblauch	.389
	Buddy Myer	.389
99	7 players tied	.388

Slugging Average

Rank	Player	SLG
1	Babe Ruth	.690
2	Ted Williams	.634
3	Lou Gehrig	.632
4	Jimmie Foxx	.609
5	Hank Greenberg	.605
6	Mark McGwire	.593
7	Mike Piazza	.580
8	Joe DiMaggio	.579
9	Frank Thomas	.579
10	Rogers Hornsby	.577
11	Ken Griffey Jr.	.568
12	Barry Bonds	.567
13	Juan Gonzalez	.566
14	Albert Belle	.564
15	Larry Walker	.563
16	Johnny Mize	.562
17	Stan Musial	.559
18	Willie Mays	.557
19	Mickey Mantle	.557
20	Hank Aaron	.555
21	Jeff Bagwell	.552
22	Ralph Kiner	.548
23	Jim Thome	.545
24	Hack Wilson	.545
25	Chuck Klein	.543
26	Duke Snider	.540
27	Frank Robinson	.537
28	Al Simmons	.535
29	Dick Allen	.534
30	Earl Averill	.534
31	Mel Ott	.533
32	Mo Vaughn	.533
33	Babe Herman	.532
34	Ken Williams	.530
35	Edgar Martinez	.529
36	Willie Stargell	.529
37	Mike Schmidt	.527
38	Tim Salmon	.527
39	Chick Hafey	.526
40	Dan Brouthers	.524
41	Sammy Sosa	.523
42	Hal Trosky	.522
43	Wally Berger	.522
44	Harry Heilmann	.520
45	Moises Alou	.520
46	Kevin Mitchell	.520
47	Charlie Keller	.518
48	Joe Jackson	.517
49	Jose Canseco	.516
50	Rafael Palmeiro	.516
51	Willie McCovey	.515
52	Gary Sheffield	.515
53	David Justice	.513
54	Fred McGriff	.512
55	Ty Cobb	.512
56	Ellis Burks	.510
57	Vinny Castilla	.509
58	Eddie Mathews	.509
59	Jeff Heath	.509
60	Harmon Killebrew	.509
61	Sam Thompson	.508
62	Bob Johnson	.506
63	Bill Terry	.506
64	Raul Mondesi	.506
65	Andres Galarraga	.506
66	Darryl Strawberry	.505
67	Ed Delahanty	.505
68	Joe Medwick	.505
69	Jim Rice	.502
70	Dante Bichette	.501
71	Tris Speaker	.500
72	Jim Bottomley	.500
73	Goose Goslin	.500
74	Roy Campanella	.500
75	Ernie Banks	.500
76	Orlando Cepeda	.499
77	Bob Horner	.499
78	Frank Howard	.499
79	Ted Kluszewski	.498
80	Bob Meusel	.497
81	Will Clark	.497
82	Hank Sauer	.496
83	Bernie Williams	.496
84	Danny Tartabull	.496
85	Al Rosen	.495
86	Jay Buhner	.494
87	Jeff Kent	.493
88	Matt Williams	.492
89	Billy Williams	.492
90	Ripper Collins	.492
91	Dolph Camilli	.492
92	Tommy Henrich	.491
93	Roger Connor	.491
94	Larry Doby	.490
95	Reggie Jackson	.490
96	Dick Stuart	.489
97	Reggie Smith	.489
98	Gabby Hartnett	.489
99	Rocky Colavito	.489
100	Norm Cash	.488

On-Base Plus Slugging

Rank	Player	OPS
1	Babe Ruth	1164
2	Ted Williams	1116
3	Lou Gehrig	1080
4	Jimmie Foxx	1038
5	Frank Thomas	1024
6	Hank Greenberg	1017
7	Rogers Hornsby	1010
8	Mark McGwire	995
9	Barry Bonds	982
10	Mickey Mantle	979
11	Joe DiMaggio	977
	Stan Musial	977
13	Jeff Bagwell	975
14	Mike Piazza	974
15	Johnny Mize	959
16	Edgar Martinez	958
	Jim Thome	958
18	Larry Walker	957
19	Ken Griffey Jr.	951
20	Mel Ott	947
21	Ralph Kiner	946
22	Ty Cobb	945
23	Willie Mays	944
24	Dan Brouthers	942
25	Joe Jackson	940
	Hack Wilson	940
27	Albert Belle	938
28	Hank Aaron	932
29	Harry Heilmann	930
30	Frank Robinson	929
31	Earl Averill	928
	Charlie Keller	928
	Tris Speaker	928
34	Tim Salmon	925
35	Ken Williams	924
36	Mo Vaughn	923
37	Chuck Klein	922
38	Duke Snider	921
39	Ed Delahanty	916
	Gary Sheffield	916
41	Babe Herman	915
	Al Simmons	915
43	Dick Allen	914
44	Juan Gonzalez	912
	Mike Schmidt	912
46	Bob Johnson	899
	Bill Terry	899
48	Chick Hafey	898
	David Justice	898
50	Mickey Cochrane	897
51	Fred McGriff	896
52	Moises Alou	893
53	Willie McCovey	892
	Willie Stargell	892
	Hal Trosky	892
56	Rafael Palmeiro	891
57	Sam Thompson	890
58	Billy Hamilton	888
	Eddie Mathews	888
	Bernie Williams	888
61	Goose Goslin	887
	Harmon Killebrew	887
63	John Olerud	886
64	Will Clark	885
65	Charlie Gehringer	884
66	Roger Connor	883
	Kevin Mitchell	883
	Jackie Robinson	883
69	Al Rosen	882
70	Wally Berger	881
71	Dolph Camilli	880
	Riggs Stephenson	880
73	Jeff Heath	879
74	Paul Waner	878
75	Larry Doby	877
76	Ellis Burks	876
	John McGraw	876
78	Jack Fournier	875
79	Tommy Henrich	873
80	Jose Canseco	872
81	Jim Bottomley	869
	Pete Browning	869
83	Bill Dickey	868
84	Joe Medwick	867
	Danny Tartabull	867
86	Norm Cash	865
	Darryl Strawberry	865
88	Wade Boggs	861
	George Brett	861
	Jesse Burkett	861
	Roy Campanella	861
92	Kiki Cuyler	860
93	Earle Combs	859
	Al Kaline	859
	Reggie Smith	859
	Arky Vaughan	859
97	6 players tied	858

Adjusted OPS

Rank	Player	Adj. OPS
1	Babe Ruth	209
2	Ted Williams	186
3	Lou Gehrig	182
4	Rogers Hornsby	176
5	Mickey Mantle	173
6	Frank Thomas	171
7	Dan Brothers	169
	Joe Jackson	169
9	Mark McGwire	168
10	Barry Bonds	167
	Ty Cobb	167
12	Pete Browning	164
13	Jeff Bagwell	161
	Jimmie Foxx	161
15	Mike Piazza	159
16	Hank Greenberg	157
	Willie Mays	157
	Johnny Mize	157
	Stan Musial	157
20	Hank Aaron	156
	Dick Allen	156
	Joe DiMaggio	156
	Tris Speaker	156
24	Mel Ott	155
25	Roger Connor	154
	Frank Robinson	154
27	Ed Delahanty	152
	Charlie Keller	152
29	Edgar Martinez	151
30	Nap Lajoie	150
	Honus Wagner	150
32	Gavvy Cravath	149
	Elmer Flick	149
34	Harry Heilmann	148
	Ralph Kiner	148
	Willie McCovey	148
37	Ken Griffey Jr.	147
	Mike Schmidt	147
	Willie Stargell	147
40	Sam Thompson	146
41	Eddie Mathews	145
	Gary Sheffield	145
	Hack Wilson	145
44	Albert Belle	144
45	Sam Crawford	143
	Jack Fournier	143
	Frank Howard	143
	Kevin Mitchell	143
49	Eddie Collins	142
	Mike Donlin	142
	Harmon Killebrew	142
	Jim Thome	142
53	Babe Herman	141
	Henry Larkin	141
	Harry Stovey	141
56	Wally Berger	140
	Jesse Burkett	140
	Jeff Heath	140
	Reggie Jackson	140
	Tip O'Neill	140
61	Billy Hamilton	139
	Bob Johnson	139
	Darryl Strawberry	139
64	Cap Anson	138
	Norm Cash	138
	Jack Clark	138
	Will Clark	138
	Pedro Guerrero	138
	Denny Lyons	138
	Al Rosen	138
	Duke Snider	138
	Mike Tiernan	138
73	Larry Doby	137
	Sherry Magee	137
	Gene Tenace	137
	Bill Terry	137
77	Frank Baker	136
	King Kelly	136
	Tim Salmon	136
	Reggie Smith	136
	Arky Vaughan	136
	Ken Williams	136
83	George Brett	135
	Oyster Burns	135
	Frank Chance	135
	Chuck Klein	135
	John McGraw	135
	Fred McGriff	135
89	Dolph Camilli	134
	Juan Gonzalez	134
	George Gore	134
	Tony Gwynn	134
	Al Kaline	134
	John Kruk	134
	Rafael Palmeiro	134
	Boog Powell	134
	Mo Vaughn	134
	Larry Walker	134
99	11 players tied	133

Batting Runs

1	Babe Ruth	1324
2	Ted Williams	1166
3	Ty Cobb	1031
4	Stan Musial	983
5	Lou Gehrig	918
6	Hank Aaron	878
7	Rogers Hornsby	844
8	Tris Speaker	843
9	Willie Mays	827
10	Jimmie Foxx	803
	Mickey Mantle	803
12	Frank Robinson	773
13	Mel Ott	767
14	Barry Bonds	687
15	Honus Wagner	666
16	Dan Brouthers	635
17	Carl Yastrzemski	617
18	Eddie Collins	608
19	Mike Schmidt	592
20	Frank Thomas	582
21	Nap Lajoie	556
22	Cap Anson	548
23	Roger Connor	547
24	Mark McGwire	543
25	Harmon Killebrew	532
26	Ed Delahanty	525
27	Willie McCovey	524
28	Johnny Mize	520
29	Harry Heilmann	517
30	Al Kaline	513
31	George Brett	511
32	Joe DiMaggio	507
33	Jesse Burkett	502
34	Sam Crawford	493
35	Paul Waner	491
36	Wade Boggs	490
37	Willie Stargell	483
38	Eddie Mathews	480
39	Billy Hamilton	473
40	Dick Allen	470
41	Hank Greenberg	468
42	Reggie Jackson	466
43	Billy Williams	463
44	Jeff Bagwell	461
45	Joe Jackson	452
46	Rickey Henderson	448
47	Edgar Martinez	441
	Duke Snider	441
49	Joe Morgan	438
50	Ken Griffey Jr.	433
51	Rod Carew	431
52	Eddie Murray	420
53	Dwight Evans	418
54	Pete Rose	416
55	Fred McGriff	404
56	Al Simmons	399
57	Tony Gwynn	396
58	Ralph Kiner	391
59	Norm Cash	390
60	Rafael Palmeiro	387
61	Dave Winfield	382
62	Reggie Smith	379
63	Will Clark	377
	Fred Clarke	377
65	Charlie Gehringer	376
66	Joe Kelley	375
	Chuck Klein	375
68	Jack Clark	367
	Jim Rice	367
70	Bob Johnson	366
71	Sam Thompson	363
72	Arky Vaughan	361
	Larry Walker	361
74	Pete Browning	356
75	Roberto Clemente	354
	Joe Medwick	354
77	Albert Belle	347
	Harry Stovey	347
79	Ron Santo	345
80	Elmer Flick	342
81	Goose Goslin	341
	Willie Keeler	341
83	Orlando Cepeda	337
84	Earl Averill	334
	Zack Wheat	334
86	Ken Singleton	332
87	Sherry Magee	331
	Paul Molitor	331
	Gary Sheffield	331
90	Frank Howard	324
91	Dolph Camilli	319
92	Rusty Staub	318
	Bill Terry	318
94	King Kelly	313
95	Tim Raines	311
96	Keith Hernandez	310
97	Fred Lynn	309
98	Enos Slaughter	306
99	Boog Powell	305
	Hack Wilson	305

Adjusted Batting Runs

1	Babe Ruth	1386
2	Ted Williams	1029
3	Lou Gehrig	1007
4	Ty Cobb	1006
5	Hank Aaron	919
6	Stan Musial	902
7	Rogers Hornsby	875
8	Mickey Mantle	865
9	Willie Mays	845
10	Tris Speaker	795
11	Mel Ott	777
12	Barry Bonds	749
13	Jimmie Foxx	748
14	Frank Robinson	746
15	Honus Wagner	635
16	Eddie Collins	623
17	Frank Thomas	617
18	Dan Brouthers	611
19	Mark McGwire	590
20	Eddie Mathews	562
21	Nap Lajoie	559
22	Roger Connor	550
23	Ed Delahanty	544
	Mike Schmidt	544
25	Willie McCovey	541
26	Rickey Henderson	536
27	Harry Heilmann	533
28	Joe DiMaggio	529
29	Reggie Jackson	520
30	Jeff Bagwell	506
31	Johnny Mize	491
32	George Brett	489
33	Willie Stargell	488
34	Harmon Killebrew	484
35	Carl Yastrzemski	482
36	Joe Morgan	480
37	Jesse Burkett	475
38	Dick Allen	470
	Al Kaline	470
40	Sam Crawford	467
41	Paul Waner	466
42	Eddie Murray	463
43	Edgar Martinez	444
44	Dave Winfield	443
45	Wade Boggs	441
46	Tony Gwynn	438
47	Joe Jackson	433
48	Cap Anson	425
	Ken Griffey Jr.	425
50	Hank Greenberg	424
51	Billy Hamilton	418
52	Rod Carew	412
53	Will Clark	399
54	Duke Snider	390
55	Bob Johnson	388
56	Pete Browning	386
57	Fred McGriff	382
58	Rafael Palmeiro	380
59	Jack Clark	378
60	Billy Williams	376
61	Pete Rose	370
62	Fred Clarke	368
63	Albert Belle	364
	Ralph Kiner	364
65	Roberto Clemente	363
	Al Simmons	363
67	Ken Singleton	361
68	Frank Howard	360
69	Norm Cash	356
	Gary Sheffield	356
71	Elmer Flick	353
72	Mike Piazza	352
	Arky Vaughan	352
74	Goose Goslin	349
75	Sam Thompson	348
76	Paul Molitor	347
77	Reggie Smith	344
78	Orlando Cepeda	340
79	Bill Terry	338
80	Rusty Staub	336
	Zack Wheat	336
82	Dwight Evans	335
	Charlie Gehringer	335
84	Tim Raines	332
85	Sherry Magee	325
86	Babe Herman	324
	Joe Kelley	324
88	Keith Hernandez	321
89	Mike Tiernan	316
90	Joe Medwick	312
	Hack Wilson	312
92	Boog Powell	311
93	Jack Fournier	309
94	Jose Canseco	308
95	Jake Beckley	305
96	Chuck Klein	303
97	Joe Torre	299
98	Earl Averill	298
	Harold Baines	298
	Minnie Minoso	298

Batting Wins

1	Babe Ruth	124.2
2	Ted Williams	112.7
3	Ty Cobb	104.0
4	Stan Musial	97.8
5	Hank Aaron	89.6
6	Tris Speaker	84.4
7	Willie Mays	84.1
8	Lou Gehrig	83.7
9	Rogers Hornsby	83.0
10	Mickey Mantle	81.2
11	Frank Robinson	79.3
12	Mel Ott	75.0
13	Jimmie Foxx	74.0
14	Barry Bonds	68.0
15	Honus Wagner	67.5
16	Carl Yastrzemski	63.5
17	Eddie Collins	61.4
18	Mike Schmidt	60.9
19	Nap Lajoie	56.1
20	Harmon Killebrew	55.0
21	Dan Brouthers	54.5
22	Frank Thomas	54.4
23	Willie McCovey	54.2
24	Al Kaline	52.8
25	Mark McGwire	52.1
26	Sam Crawford	51.7
27	Johnny Mize	51.4
28	George Brett	50.9
29	Willie Stargell	50.4
30	Harry Heilmann	50.0
31	Dick Allen	49.1
32	Eddie Mathews	48.6
33	Billy Williams	48.0
34	Paul Waner	48.0
35	Cap Anson	47.9
36	Joe DiMaggio	47.9
37	Reggie Jackson	47.4
38	Wade Boggs	47.4
39	Roger Connor	47.2
40	Joe Jackson	46.4
41	Ed Delahanty	45.6
42	Joe Morgan	45.4
43	Jesse Burkett	45.3
44	Jeff Bagwell	44.9
45	Rod Carew	44.2
46	Duke Snider	43.9
47	Hank Greenberg	43.7
48	Rickey Henderson	43.7
49	Pete Rose	43.5
50	Dwight Evans	41.8
51	Edgar Martinez	41.6
52	Eddie Murray	41.6
53	Ken Griffey Jr.	41.1
54	Billy Hamilton	40.6
55	Norm Cash	40.6
56	Tony Gwynn	40.0
57	Reggie Smith	39.8
58	Fred McGriff	39.4
59	Ralph Kiner	38.5
60	Dave Winfield	38.3
61	Jack Clark	37.6
62	Rafael Palmeiro	37.2
63	Al Simmons	37.0
64	Will Clark	37.0
65	Jim Rice	36.5
66	Roberto Clemente	36.5
67	Chuck Klein	36.3
68	Fred Clarke	36.2
69	Arky Vaughan	36.0
70	Ron Santo	35.9
71	Larry Walker	35.5
72	Joe Medwick	35.4
73	Sherry Magee	35.4
74	Charlie Gehringer	34.8
75	Bob Johnson	34.8
76	Orlando Cepeda	34.7
77	Elmer Flick	34.3
78	Zack Wheat	34.1
79	Frank Howard	34.0
80	Joe Kelley	34.0
81	Ken Singleton	33.6
82	Rusty Staub	33.1
83	Albert Belle	32.6
84	Willie Keeler	32.4
85	Gary Sheffield	32.4
86	Paul Molitor	32.3
87	Keith Hernandez	32.1
88	Boog Powell	32.1
89	Dolph Camilli	31.8
90	Goose Goslin	31.7
91	Tim Raines	31.1
92	Joe Torre	31.1
93	Sam Thompson	31.1
94	Fred Lynn	30.8
95	Enos Slaughter	30.7
96	Pete Browning	30.6
97	Earl Averill	30.5
98	Rocky Colavito	30.5
99	Bill Terry	30.4
100	Tony Perez	30.4

Adjusted Batting Wins

1	Babe Ruth	130.0
2	Ty Cobb	101.5
3	Ted Williams	99.4
4	Hank Aaron	93.8
5	Lou Gehrig	91.8
6	Stan Musial	89.7
7	Mickey Mantle	87.5
8	Rogers Hornsby	86.0
9	Willie Mays	85.9
10	Tris Speaker	79.6
11	Frank Robinson	76.6
12	Mel Ott	76.0
13	Barry Bonds	74.1
14	Jimmie Foxx	68.9
15	Honus Wagner	64.4
16	Eddie Collins	63.0
17	Frank Thomas	57.7
18	Eddie Mathews	56.9
19	Mark McGwire	56.6
20	Nap Lajoie	56.4
21	Mike Schmidt	56.0
22	Willie McCovey	56.0
23	Reggie Jackson	52.9
24	Dan Brouthers	52.4
25	Rickey Henderson	52.2
26	Harry Heilmann	51.5
27	Willie Stargell	50.9
28	Harmon Killebrew	50.1
29	Joe DiMaggio	49.9
30	Joe Morgan	49.8
31	Carl Yastrzemski	49.6
32	Jeff Bagwell	49.3
33	Dick Allen	49.1
34	Sam Crawford	49.0
35	George Brett	48.7
36	Johnny Mize	48.5
37	Al Kaline	48.4
38	Roger Connor	47.4
39	Ed Delahanty	47.3
40	Eddie Murray	45.8
41	Paul Waner	45.6
42	Dave Winfield	44.4
43	Joe Jackson	44.4
44	Tony Gwynn	44.2
45	Jesse Burkett	42.8
46	Wade Boggs	42.7
47	Rod Carew	42.3
48	Edgar Martinez	41.9
49	Ken Griffey Jr.	40.4
50	Hank Greenberg	39.6
51	Will Clark	39.2
52	Billy Williams	39.0
53	Duke Snider	38.8
54	Jack Clark	38.7
55	Pete Rose	38.7
56	Frank Howard	37.8
57	Roberto Clemente	37.4
58	Fred McGriff	37.3
59	Cap Anson	37.2
60	Norm Cash	37.1
61	Bob Johnson	36.9
62	Ken Singleton	36.6
63	Rafael Palmeiro	36.5
64	Reggie Smith	36.1
65	Billy Hamilton	35.9
66	Ralph Kiner	35.8
67	Elmer Flick	35.4
68	Fred Clarke	35.3
69	Arky Vaughan	35.1
70	Orlando Cepeda	35.0
71	Rusty Staub	35.0
72	Gary Sheffield	34.8
73	Sherry Magee	34.8
74	Zack Wheat	34.3
75	Albert Belle	34.2
76	Mike Piazza	33.9
77	Paul Molitor	33.8
78	Al Simmons	33.7
79	Dwight Evans	33.5
80	Tim Raines	33.3
81	Keith Hernandez	33.2
82	Pete Browning	33.2
83	Boog Powell	32.7
84	Goose Goslin	32.4
85	Bill Terry	32.4
86	Joe Medwick	31.2
87	Joe Torre	31.2
88	Babe Herman	31.1
89	Charlie Gehringer	31.0
90	Jack Fournier	30.8
91	Jimmy Wynn	30.4
92	Minnie Minoso	29.9
93	Hack Wilson	29.8
94	Sam Thompson	29.8
95	Rocky Colavito	29.6
96	Jose Canseco	29.5
97	Joe Kelley	29.4
98	Chuck Klein	29.3
99	Darryl Strawberry	29.3
100	Harold Baines	29.0

Runs Created

1	Babe Ruth	2849
2	Ty Cobb	2810
3	Stan Musial	2625
4	Hank Aaron	2550
5	Ted Williams	2538
6	Willie Mays	2372
7	Tris Speaker	2325
8	Lou Gehrig	2321
9	Honus Wagner	2240
10	Mel Ott	2235
11	Pete Rose	2220
12	Jimmie Foxx	2191
13	Carl Yastrzemski	2147
14	Frank Robinson	2126
15	Rickey Henderson	2075
16	Rogers Hornsby	2074
17	Mickey Mantle	2069
18	Eddie Collins	2063
19	Eddie Murray	1939
20	Nap Lajoie	1906
21	George Brett	1878
22	Barry Bonds	1875
23	Paul Molitor	1872
24	Paul Waner	1853
25	Al Kaline	1846
26	Ed Delahanty	1832
27	Dave Winfield	1813
28	Joe Morgan	1804
29	Jesse Burkett	1802
30	Charlie Gehringer	1787
31	Al Simmons	1777
32	Reggie Jackson	1772
33	Cap Anson	1757
	Mike Schmidt	1757
35	Wade Boggs	1751
36	Eddie Mathews	1738
37	Sam Crawford	1716
38	Billy Hamilton	1711
39	Goose Goslin	1707
40	Harry Heilmann	1698
41	Jake Beckley	1688
	Willie Keeler	1688
43	Cal Ripken	1683
44	Fred Clarke	1681
45	Billy Williams	1671
46	Robin Yount	1655
47	Roger Connor	1648
48	George Davis	1639
49	Willie McCovey	1638
50	Dan Brouthers	1624
51	Tony Gwynn	1615
52	Dwight Evans	1611
53	Harmon Killebrew	1609
54	Tim Raines	1608
55	Joe DiMaggio	1606
56	Harold Baines	1605
57	Rod Carew	1595
58	George Van Haltren	1568
59	Jimmy Ryan	1561
60	Roberto Clemente	1557
61	Zack Wheat	1540
62	Joe Kelley	1535
63	Rusty Staub	1534
64	Willie Stargell	1531
65	Rafael Palmeiro	1524
66	Tony Perez	1523
67	Andre Dawson	1519
68	Ernie Banks	1513
69	Lou Brock	1512
70	Bill Dahlen	1510
71	Hugh Duffy	1509
72	Johnny Mize	1502
73	Sam Rice	1501
74	Darrell Evans	1499
75	George Sisler	1498
76	Luke Appling	1493
77	Duke Snider	1487
78	Mark McGwire	1481
79	Max Carey	1472
80	Frankie Frisch	1464
81	Fred McGriff	1458
82	Frank Thomas	1454
83	Dave Parker	1452
84	Enos Slaughter	1432
85	Joe Cronin	1426
86	Bob Johnson	1418
87	Will Clark	1417
88	Chili Davis	1416
89	Ken Griffey Jr.	1397
90	Lou Whitaker	1396
91	Vada Pinson	1394
92	Heinie Manush	1389
93	Mickey Vernon	1387
94	Richie Ashburn	1386
95	Jim Bottomley	1384
96	Jim Rice	1382
97	Ron Santo	1379
98	Chuck Klein	1378
99	Carlton Fisk	1375
100	Joe Medwick	1372

Total Average

1	Babe Ruth	1.400
2	Ted Williams	1.320
3	Lou Gehrig	1.229
4	Billy Hamilton	1.192
5	John McGraw	1.153
6	Jimmie Foxx	1.143
7	Frank Thomas	1.129
8	Barry Bonds	1.110
9	Hank Greenberg	1.105
	Rogers Hornsby	1.105
11	Mickey Mantle	1.091
12	Mark McGwire	1.081
13	Ty Cobb	1.066
14	Dan Brouthers	1.061
15	Jeff Bagwell	1.055
16	Jim Thome	1.037
17	Mel Ott	1.036
18	Ed Delahanty	1.035
19	Stan Musial	1.028
20	Edgar Martinez	1.017
21	Joe DiMaggio	1.012
22	Tris Speaker	1.011
23	Joe Jackson	1.008
24	Ralph Kiner	1.006
25	Johnny Mize	1.005
	Hack Wilson	1.005
27	Larry Walker	1.004
28	Charlie Keller	1.000
29	Ken Griffey Jr.	.992
30	Willie Mays	.982
31	Mike Piazza	.976
32	Mike Tiernan	.970
33	Harry Heilmann	.963
34	Tim Salmon	.962
35	Joe Kelley	.961
	Frank Robinson	.961
37	Earl Averill	.957
	Rickey Henderson	.957
39	Gary Sheffield	.956
40	Denny Lyons	.954
	Mike Schmidt	.954
42	Roger Connor	.952
43	Honus Wagner	.948
44	Mickey Cochrane	.947
45	Pete Browning	.946
46	Chuck Klein	.944
47	Eddie Collins	.943
	Ken Williams	.943
49	Jesse Burkett	.942
	Babe Herman	.942
	Sam Thompson	.942
52	Hank Aaron	.940
	Mo Vaughn	.940
54	Jackie Robinson	.939
55	Albert Belle	.937
56	Duke Snider	.933
57	Hugh Duffy	.931
58	Dick Allen	.930
59	Dolph Camilli	.928
60	Harry Stovey	.924
61	Frank Chance	.922
62	Bob Johnson	.920
63	Eddie Mathews	.916
64	Elmer Flick	.915
65	Mike Donlin	.914
	David Justice	.914
67	Willie McCovey	.912
68	Elmer Smith	.911
69	Charlie Gehringer	.910
	Harmon Killebrew	.910
	Joe Morgan	.910
72	Chick Hafey	.908
	Fred McGriff	.908
74	Gavvy Cravath	.905
	Mike Griffin	.905
	Al Simmons	.905
77	John Olerud	.903
78	Eric Davis	.902
79	Kiki Cuyler	.901
	Goose Goslin	.901
81	Cupid Childs	.900
82	Riggs Stephenson	.899
	Bill Terry	.899
84	Tip O'Neill	.898
85	Arky Vaughan	.894
86	Larry Doby	.893
	Tommy Henrich	.893
88	Will Clark	.890
89	Willie Stargell	.889
	Darryl Strawberry	.889
	Hal Trosky	.889
92	Tim Raines	.888
	Paul Waner	.888
94	Rafael Palmeiro	.887
95	Hughie Jennings	.885
96	Fred Clarke	.884
	Jack Fournier	.884
98	Bernie Williams	.883
99	George Grantham	.882
100	2 players tied	.881

Runs Produced

1	Ty Cobb	4067
2	Hank Aaron	3716
3	Babe Ruth	3673
4	Cap Anson	3505
5	Stan Musial	3425
6	Lou Gehrig	3390
7	Honus Wagner	3371
8	Pete Rose	3319
9	Willie Mays	3305
10	Tris Speaker	3294
11	Mel Ott	3208
	Carl Yastrzemski	3208
13	Jimmie Foxx	3139
14	Ted Williams	3116
15	Jake Beckley	3092
16	Eddie Collins	3074
17	Frank Robinson	3055
18	Eddie Murray	3040
19	Dave Winfield	3037
20	Al Simmons	3027
21	Nap Lajoie	3021
22	Charlie Gehringer	3017
23	Ed Delahanty	2965
24	Rickey Henderson	2948
25	George Davis	2911
26	Rogers Hornsby	2862
27	George Brett	2861
28	Paul Molitor	2855
29	Goose Goslin	2844
30	Paul Waner	2823
31	Sam Crawford	2819
32	Cal Ripken	2814
33	Al Kaline	2806
34	Roger Connor	2805
35	Robin Yount	2787
36	Hugh Duffy	2750
37	Bill Dahlen	2740
38	Dan Brouthers	2713
39	Bid McPhee	2703
40	Reggie Jackson	2690
41	Frankie Frisch	2671
42	Lave Cross	2669
43	Mickey Mantle	2650
44	Harry Heilmann	2647
45	Jimmy Ryan	2618
46	Jesse Burkett	2597
47	George Van Haltren	2587
48	Fred Clarke	2570
49	Joe DiMaggio	2566
50	Sam Rice	2558
51	Mike Schmidt	2553
52	Joe Kelley	2550
53	Tony Perez	2545
54	Harold Baines	2534
55	Andre Dawson	2526
56	Joe Morgan	2515
57	Willie Keeler	2496
58	Barry Bonds	2495
59	Joe Cronin	2487
60	Roberto Clemente	2481
61	Dwight Evans	2469
62	Billy Williams	2459
63	Eddie Mathews	2450
64	Sam Thompson	2441
65	Ernie Banks	2429
66	Dave Parker	2426
67	Herman Long	2420
68	Wade Boggs	2409
69	Jim O'Rourke	2406
70	Zack Wheat	2405
71	Billy Hamilton	2399
72	Pie Traynor	2398
73	Luke Appling	2390
74	Enos Slaughter	2382
75	Jim Bottomley	2380
76	Joe Medwick	2376
77	Tony Gwynn	2365
78	Rusty Staub	2363
79	Lou Brock	2361
80	Heinie Manush	2360
81	George Sisler	2357
82	Rod Carew	2347
83	Tim Raines	2344
84	Mickey Vernon	2335
85	Brooks Robinson	2321
86	Jim Rice	2318
87	Al Oliver	2296
88	Harmon Killebrew	2294
89	Tommy Corcoran	2289
90	Darrell Evans	2284
	Ed McKean	2284
92	Vada Pinson	2280
93	Harry Stovey	2278
94	Max Carey	2275
95	Willie McCovey	2263
96	Chili Davis	2262
97	Willie Stargell	2260
98	John Ward	2253
99	Yogi Berra	2247
100	Kiki Cuyler	2242

Clutch Hitting Index

1	Cap Anson	132
2	Earl Sheely	127
3	Tommy Thevenow	126
4	Bobby Veach	124
5	Pat Tabler	120
	Pie Traynor	120
7	Sam Mertes	119
8	Hughie Jennings	118
	Duffy Lewis	118
	Jack Rowe	118
	Luke Sewell	118
12	Rube Bressler	117
	Tommy Davis	117
	Bob Fothergill	117
	Chick Gandil	117
	King Kelly	117
	Cookie Lavagetto	117
	Muddy Ruel	117
	Ray Schalk	117
	Billy Sullivan	117
21	John Anderson	116
	Frank Bowerman	116
	Sherry Magee	116
	Elmer Smith	116
	Red Smith	116
26	Kitty Bransfield	115
	Lou Criger	115
	Ron Fairly	115
	Jeff King	115
	Sam Mele	115
	Lee Tannehill	115
	Pinky Whitney	115
	Possum Whitted	115
34	Roy Campanella	114
	Sam Crawford	114
	George Cutshaw	114
	Art Devlin	114
	Jack Doyle	114
	Ferris Fain	114
	Carl Furillo	114
	Red Murray	114
	Denny Walling	114
	Deacon White	114
	Jimmie Wilson	114
	Heinie Zimmerman	114
46	Bob Elliott	113
	Larry Gardner	113
	Frank LaPorte	113
	Frank McCormick	113
	Stuffy McInnis	113
	Terry Pendleton	113
	Enos Slaughter	113
	Frank Snyder	113
	Sam Thompson	113
	Vic Wertz	113
	Taffy Wright	113
57	Alan Ashby	112
	Frank Baker	112
	Larry Biittner	112
	Smoky Burgess	112
	Frank Chance	112
	Darren Daulton	112
	Johnny Edwards	112
	Kid Elberfeld	112
	Art Fletcher	112
	Sherm Lollar	112
	Ed McKean	112
	Keith Moreland	112
	Manny Mota	112
	Jack O'Connor	112
	Joe Oliver	112
	Mickey Owen	112
	Fred Pfeffer	112
	Boog Powell	112
	Cy Seymour	112
	Ted Simmons	112
	Mike Tresh	112
78	Bob Boone	111
	Sid Bream	111
	Steve Brodie	111
	Gavvy Cravath	111
	Joe Cronin	111
	Lave Cross	111
	Hugh Duffy	111
	Hank Gowdy	111
	Ron Hassey	111
	Charlie Hayes	111
	Jim Kaat	111
	Willie Kamm	111
	Ed Kirkpatrick	111
	Steve O'Neill	111
	Del Pratt	111
	Wilbert Robinson	111
	Rusty Staub	111
	Harry Steinfeldt	111
	Riggs Stephenson	111
	Patsy Tebeau	111
	Joe Tinker	111
	Jimmy Williams	111
	Glenn Wright	111

Isolated Power

1	Babe Ruth	.348
2	Mark McGwire	.326
3	Lou Gehrig	.292
4	Hank Greenberg	.292
5	Ted Williams	.289
6	Jimmie Foxx	.284
7	Barry Bonds	.278
8	Juan Gonzalez	.272
9	Ken Griffey Jr.	.271
10	Ralph Kiner	.269
11	Albert Belle	.269
12	Jim Thome	.261
13	Mike Schmidt	.260
14	Mickey Mantle	.259
15	Frank Thomas	.258
16	Willie Mays	.256
17	Joe DiMaggio	.254
18	Harmon Killebrew	.252
19	Mike Piazza	.252
20	Larry Walker	.252
21	Sammy Sosa	.250
22	Johnny Mize	.250
23	Jose Canseco	.250
24	Hank Aaron	.250
25	Jeff Bagwell	.248
26	Willie Stargell	.247
27	Darryl Strawberry	.247
28	Willie McCovey	.245
29	Duke Snider	.244
30	Frank Robinson	.243
31	Dave Kingman	.242
32	Dick Allen	.242
33	Jay Buhner	.240
34	Eddie Mathews	.238
35	Hack Wilson	.238
36	Kevin Mitchell	.236
37	Tim Salmon	.235
38	Mo Vaughn	.235
39	Greg Vaughn	.234
40	Charlie Keller	.231
41	David Justice	.230
42	Hank Sauer	.230
43	Mel Ott	.229
44	Stan Musial	.228
45	Reggie Jackson	.228
46	Cecil Fielder	.227
47	Dean Palmer	.227
48	Fred McGriff	.226
49	Dick Stuart	.225
50	Ernie Banks	.225
51	Frank Howard	.225
52	Matt Williams	.224
53	Roy Campanella	.224
54	Danny Tartabull	.223
55	Chuck Klein	.223
56	Gorman Thomas	.223
57	Rob Deer	.223
58	Rocky Colavito	.223
59	Bob Horner	.222
60	Gary Sheffield	.222
61	Wally Berger	.221
62	Gus Zernial	.221
63	Rafael Palmeiro	.220
64	Wally Post	.220
65	Raul Mondesi	.220
66	Hal Trosky	.219
67	Rogers Hornsby	.218
68	Vinny Castilla	.218
69	Moises Alou	.217
70	Ellis Burks	.217
71	Norm Cash	.217
72	Bob Allison	.217
73	Roger Maris	.216
74	Earl Averill	.216
75	Jeff Heath	.216
76	Eric Davis	.215
77	Andres Galarraga	.215
78	Glenallen Hill	.215
79	Dolph Camilli	.215
80	Gil Hodges	.214
81	Ron Gant	.213
82	Ken Williams	.211
83	Todd Hundley	.210
84	Jesse Barfield	.210
85	Al Rosen	.210
86	Bob Johnson	.210
87	Tommy Henrich	.209
88	Jeff Kent	.209
89	Edgar Martinez	.209
90	Chick Hafey	.209
91	Jack Clark	.209
92	Johnny Bench	.208
93	Roy Sievers	.208
94	Rudy York	.208
95	Mickey Tettleton	.208
96	Glenn Davis	.208
97	Joe Adcock	.208
98	Nate Colbert	.207
99	Babe Herman	.207
100	Reggie Sanders	.207

Extra Base Hits

1	Hank Aaron	1477
2	Stan Musial	1377
3	Babe Ruth	1356
4	Willie Mays	1323
5	Lou Gehrig	1190
6	Frank Robinson	1186
7	Carl Yastrzemski	1157
8	Ty Cobb	1136
9	Tris Speaker	1131
10	George Brett	1119
11	Jimmie Foxx	1117
	Ted Williams	1117
13	Eddie Murray	1099
14	Dave Winfield	1093
15	Reggie Jackson	1075
16	Mel Ott	1071
17	Cal Ripken	1048
18	Pete Rose	1041
19	Andre Dawson	1039
20	Mike Schmidt	1015
21	Barry Bonds	1014
22	Rogers Hornsby	1011
23	Ernie Banks	1009
24	Honus Wagner	996
25	Al Simmons	995
26	Al Kaline	972
27	Tony Perez	963
28	Robin Yount	960
29	Paul Molitor	953
	Willie Stargell	953
31	Mickey Mantle	952
32	Billy Williams	948
33	Dwight Evans	941
34	Dave Parker	940
35	Eddie Mathews	938
36	Goose Goslin	921
37	Harold Baines	920
	Willie McCovey	920
39	Paul Waner	909
40	Charlie Gehringer	904
41	Nap Lajoie	902
42	Rafael Palmeiro	891
43	Harmon Killebrew	887
44	Joe Carter	881
	Joe DiMaggio	881
46	Harry Heilmann	876
47	Vada Pinson	868
48	Sam Crawford	864
49	Joe Medwick	858
50	Duke Snider	850
51	Roberto Clemente	846
52	Carlton Fisk	844
53	Gary Gaetti	842
54	Rusty Staub	838
55	Jim Bottomley	835
56	Jim Rice	834
57	Rickey Henderson	830
58	Al Oliver	825
59	Orlando Cepeda	823
60	Brooks Robinson	818
61	Ken Griffey Jr.	813
	Joe Morgan	813
63	Roger Connor	812
64	Ed Delahanty	809
	Fred McGriff	809
	Johnny Mize	809
67	Mark McGwire	808
68	Jake Beckley	804
	Chili Davis	804
70	Joe Cronin	803
71	Johnny Bench	794
72	Jose Canseco	792
73	Albert Belle	791
74	Dale Murphy	787
75	Mickey Vernon	782
76	Hank Greenberg	781
77	Andres Galarraga	780
	Zack Wheat	780
79	Darrell Evans	779
	Bob Johnson	779
81	Ted Simmons	778
82	Lou Brock	776
83	Ron Santo	774
84	Chuck Klein	772
85	Dan Brouthers	771
	Will Clark	771
87	Earl Averill	767
88	Heinie Manush	761
	Ryne Sandberg	761
90	Wade Boggs	757
91	Steve Garvey	755
92	Tony Gwynn	752
93	Dick Allen	750
	Cap Anson	750
95	Graig Nettles	746
96	Bobby Bonilla	744
97	Hal McRae	741
98	Fred Lynn	737
99	Reggie Smith	734
100	Don Baylor	732

Pinch Hits

1	Manny Mota	150
2	Smoky Burgess	145
3	Greg Gross	143
4	Lenny Harris	130
5	Jose Morales	123
6	Jerry Lynch	116
	John Vander Wal	116
8	Red Lucas	114
9	Steve Braun	113
10	Terry Crowley	108
	Denny Walling	108
12	Gates Brown	107
13	Mike Lum	103
14	Jim Dwyer	102
15	Dave Hansen	101
16	Rusty Staub	100
17	Dave Clark	96
18	Larry Biittner	95
	Vic Davalillo	95
	Gerald Perry	95
21	Jerry Hairston	94
22	Dave Philley	93
	Joel Youngblood	93
24	Jay Johnstone	92
25	Ed Kranepool	90
	Elmer Valo	90

Pinch Hit Average (150 at-bats minimum)

1	Harold Baines	.324
2	Alex Arias	.321
3	Tommy Davis	.320
4	Frenchy Bordagaray	.312
5	Frankie Baumholtz	.307
6	Willie McGee	.307
7	Sid Bream	.306
8	Mark Carreon	.306
9	Red Schoendienst	.303
10	Bob Fothergill	.300
11	Dave Philley	.299
12	Manny Mota	.297
13	Ted Easterly	.296
14	Harvey Hendrick	.295
15	Larry Herndon	.294
16	Rance Mulliniks	.292
17	Terry Puhl	.289
18	Chip Hale	.289
19	Manny Sanguillen	.288
20	Smoky Burgess	.286
21	Rick Miller	.286
22	Johnny Mize	.283
23	Ken Griffey Sr.	.282
24	Bubba Morton	.281
25	Steve Braun	.281

Pinch Hit Home Runs

1	Cliff Johnson	20
2	Jerry Lynch	18
3	Gates Brown	16
	Smoky Burgess	16
	Willie McCovey	16
	John Vander Wal	16
7	George Crowe	14
8	Dave Hansen	13
	Glenallen Hill	13
10	Joe Adcock	12
	Bob Cerv	12
	Jose Morales	12
	Graig Nettles	12
14	Jeff Burroughs	11
	Jay Johnstone	11
	Candy Maldonado	11
	Fred Whitfield	11
	Cy Williams	11
19	Mark Carreon	10
	Dave Clark	10
	Jim Dwyer	10
	Mike Lum	10
	Ken McMullen	10
	Don Mincher	10
	Wally Post	10
	Champ Summers	10
	Jerry Turner	10
	Gus Zernial	10

Total Player Rating / 150g

1	Babe Ruth	6.53
2	Barry Bonds	6.26
3	Nap Lajoie	5.78
4	Rogers Hornsby	5.49
5	Ted Williams	5.43
6	Mike Schmidt	4.97
7	Mickey Mantle	4.84
8	Mike Piazza	4.83
9	Willie Mays	4.81
10	Lou Gehrig	4.78
11	Tris Speaker	4.74
12	Ken Griffey Jr.	4.61
13	Jeff Bagwell	4.59
14	Ty Cobb	4.55
15	Joe Jackson	4.39
16	Honus Wagner	4.39
17	Joe DiMaggio	4.34
18	Hank Aaron	4.05
19	Rickey Henderson	4.04
20	Frank Thomas	3.99
21	Eddie Collins	3.89
22	Lou Boudreau	3.87
23	Dan Brouthers	3.77
24	Jimmie Foxx	3.62
25	Pete Browning	3.61
26	Frank Robinson	3.61
27	Stan Musial	3.54
28	Ed Delahanty	3.50
29	Edgar Martinez	3.48
30	Jackie Robinson	3.47
31	Bernie Williams	3.47
32	Bobby Grich	3.42
33	Barry Larkin	3.42
34	Hank Greenberg	3.39
35	Buck Ewing	3.38
36	Mel Ott	3.37
37	Albert Belle	3.34
38	Frank Baker	3.30
39	Arky Vaughan	3.28
40	Eddie Mathews	3.27
41	Sam Thompson	3.27
42	Bobby Doerr	3.26
43	Lenny Dykstra	3.25
44	Roger Connor	3.25
45	George Davis	3.25
46	Mark McGwire	3.24
47	Mickey Cochrane	3.22
48	Tim Salmon	3.15
49	Bill Dahlen	3.14
50	Jack Glasscock	3.11
51	Joe Morgan	3.10
52	Cupid Childs	3.09
53	Hardy Richardson	3.09
54	Dick Allen	3.08
55	Elmer Flick	3.07
56	Hughie Jennings	3.07
57	Tim Raines	3.05
58	Gabby Hartnett	3.04
59	Bill Dickey	2.97
60	Craig Biggio	2.97
61	Dave Bancroft	2.94
62	Charlie Gehringer	2.91
63	Tony Gwynn	2.89
64	Charlie Keller	2.88
65	Johnny Mize	2.88
66	Bid McPhee	2.88
67	Ray Lankford	2.86
68	Gary Sheffield	2.85
69	Reggie Smith	2.83
70	Joe Cronin	2.82
71	Bob Johnson	2.81
72	Jimmy Wynn	2.80
73	Joe Sewell	2.80
74	Charlie Bennett	2.80
75	Roy Campanella	2.78
76	Kenny Lofton	2.77
77	Joe Gordon	2.76
78	Ron Santo	2.74
79	Wade Boggs	2.73
80	Larry Walker	2.72
81	Kirby Puckett	2.72
82	Roberto Alomar	2.70
83	King Kelly	2.69
84	Wally Berger	2.67
85	Yogi Berra	2.65
86	Ralph Kiner	2.64
87	Luke Appling	2.63
88	Roberto Clemente	2.60
89	Billy Hamilton	2.58
90	Art Fletcher	2.56
91	Denny Lyons	2.55
92	Ryne Sandberg	2.54
93	Bill Mazeroski	2.52
94	Heinie Groh	2.51
95	Darryl Strawberry	2.51
96	Frankie Frisch	2.51
97	Keith Hernandez	2.50
98	Billy Herman	2.48
99	Jim Thome	2.47
100	Ozzie Smith	2.47

Stolen Bases

1	Rickey Henderson	1370
2	Lou Brock	938
3	Billy Hamilton	914
4	Ty Cobb	892
5	Tim Raines	807
6	Vince Coleman	752
7	Eddie Collins	745
8	Arlie Latham	742
9	Max Carey	738
10	Honus Wagner	723
11	Joe Morgan	689
12	Willie Wilson	668
13	Tom Brown	657
14	Bert Campaneris	649
15	Otis Nixon	620
16	George Davis	619
17	Dummy Hoy	596
18	Maury Wills	586
19	George Van Haltren	583
20	Ozzie Smith	580
21	Hugh Duffy	574
22	Bid McPhee	568
23	Brett Butler	558
24	Davey Lopes	557
25	Cesar Cedeno	550
26	Bill Dahlen	547
27	John Ward	540
28	Herman Long	537
29	Patsy Donovan	518
30	Jack Doyle	517
31	Fred Clarke	509
	Harry Stovey	509
33	Luis Aparicio	506
34	Paul Molitor	504
35	Willie Keeler	495
	Clyde Milan	495
37	Omar Moreno	487
38	Mike Griffin	473
39	Barry Bonds	471
40	Tommy McCarthy	468
41	Jimmy Sheckard	465
42	Kenny Lofton	463
43	Bobby Bonds	461
44	Ed Delahanty	455
	Ron LeFlore	455
46	Curt Welch	453
47	Steve Sax	444
48	Joe Kelley	443
49	Sherry Magee	441
50	John McGraw	436
51	Tris Speaker	432
52	Delino DeShields	430
53	Bob Bescher	428
	Mike Tiernan	428
55	Frankie Frisch	419
56	Jimmy Ryan	418
57	Roberto Alomar	416
	Charlie Comiskey	416
59	Tommy Harper	408
60	Donie Bush	404
61	Frank Chance	403
62	Marquis Grissom	402
63	Bill Lange	399
64	Willie Davis	398
65	Sam Mertes	396
	Juan Samuel	396
67	Dave Collins	395
	Billy North	395
69	Jesse Burkett	389
70	Tommy Corcoran	387
71	Tom Daly	385
	Freddie Patek	385
73	George Burns	383
	Hugh Nicol	383
	Fred Pfeffer	383
	Walt Wilmot	383
77	Nap Lajoie	380
78	Harry Hooper	375
	George Sisler	375
80	Jack Glasscock	372
81	Lonnie Smith	370
82	Tommy Dowd	368
	King Kelly	368
84	Sam Crawford	366
85	Hal Chase	363
86	Tommy Leach	361
87	Hughie Jennings	359
	Fielder Jones	359
	Barry Larkin	359
90	Craig Biggio	358
91	Buck Ewing	354
	Gary Pettis	354
93	Rod Carew	353
94	Willie McGee	352
	Tommy Tucker	352
96	Sam Rice	351
97	Chuck Knoblauch	350
98	George Case	349
99	Eric Davis	348
100	2 players tied	346

Stolen Base Average

1	Tony Womack	86.0
2	Tim Raines	84.7
3	Eric Davis	84.3
4	Barry Larkin	83.5
5	Henry Cotto	83.3
6	Willie Wilson	83.3
7	Davey Lopes	83.0
8	Stan Javier	82.5
9	Julio Cruz	81.5
10	Joe Morgan	81.0
11	Vince Coleman	80.9
12	Rickey Henderson	80.8
13	Roberto Alomar	80.6
14	Brian Hunter	80.6
15	Andy Van Slyke	80.6
16	Kenny Lofton	80.2
17	Doug Glanville	80.1
18	Mickey Mantle	80.1
19	Lenny Dykstra	79.8
20	Ozzie Smith	79.7
21	Enzo Hernandez	79.6
22	Gary Redus	79.5
23	Paul Molitor	79.4
24	Marquis Grissom	79.3
25	R. J. Reynolds	79.0
26	Luis Aparicio	78.8
27	Johnny Damon	78.8
28	Alex Rodriguez	78.7
29	Amos Otis	78.6
30	Kirk Gibson	78.5
31	Roger Cedeno	78.1
32	Alan Wiggins	78.1
33	Tommy Harper	77.9
34	Rudy Law	77.8
35	Joe Carter	77.8
	Mike Felder	77.8
37	Barry Bonds	77.7
38	Derek Bell	77.6
39	Bob Dernier	77.6
40	Devon White	77.5
41	Miguel Dilone	77.4
42	Gary Pettis	77.3
43	Mike Cameron	77.2
44	Craig Biggio	77.2
45	Mookie Wilson	76.9
46	Chuck Knoblauch	76.9
	Otis Nixon	76.9
48	Mike Lansing	76.8
49	Rodney Scott	76.8
50	Hank Aaron	76.7

Stolen Base Runs

1	Rickey Henderson	187
2	Tim Raines	126
3	Vince Coleman	103
4	Willie Wilson	100
5	Lou Brock	99
6	Joe Morgan	95
7	Davey Lopes	83
8	Ozzie Smith	76
9	Bert Campaneris	73
10	Otis Nixon	71
11	Paul Molitor	65
12	Luis Aparicio	64
13	Kenny Lofton	62
14	Cesar Cedeno	58
15	Roberto Alomar	57
16	Barry Bonds	56
	Maury Wills	56
18	Eric Davis	54
	Barry Larkin	54
20	Marquis Grissom	52
21	Ron LeFlore	50
22	Tommy Harper	49
23	Julio Cruz	48
24	Delino DeShields	44
25	Omar Moreno	43
26	Craig Biggio	42
	Bobby Bonds	42
	Willie Davis	42
	Amos Otis	42
	Gary Redus	42
31	Gary Pettis	41
32	Chuck Knoblauch	40
33	George Case	39
	Freddie Patek	39
	Devon White	39
	Tony Womack	39
37	Dave Collins	38
	Lenny Dykstra	38
	Willie Mays	38
	Ryne Sandberg	38
	Mookie Wilson	38
42	Juan Samuel	37
43	Eric Young	36
44	Kirk Gibson	35
	Lance Johnson	35
	Willie McGee	35
	Steve Sax	35
48	Stan Javier	34
49	4 players tied	33

Stolen Base Wins

1	Rickey Henderson	18.2
2	Tim Raines	12.6
3	Vince Coleman	10.5
4	Lou Brock	10.4
5	Willie Wilson	10.0
6	Joe Morgan	9.8
7	Davey Lopes	8.6
8	Ozzie Smith	7.9
9	Bert Campaneris	7.7
10	Otis Nixon	7.0
11	Luis Aparicio	6.7
12	Paul Molitor	6.3
13	Cesar Cedeno	6.0
14	Maury Wills	5.9
15	Kenny Lofton	5.9
16	Barry Bonds	5.5
17	Roberto Alomar	5.5
18	Eric Davis	5.4
19	Barry Larkin	5.4
20	Tommy Harper	5.2
21	Marquis Grissom	5.2
22	Ron LeFlore	5.1
23	Julio Cruz	4.8
24	Omar Moreno	4.5
25	Willie Davis	4.4
26	Delino DeShields	4.4
27	Bobby Bonds	4.3
28	Amos Otis	4.3
29	Gary Redus	4.3
30	Craig Biggio	4.2
31	Gary Pettis	4.1
32	Freddie Patek	4.1
33	Mookie Wilson	4.0
34	Ryne Sandberg	3.9
35	Dave Collins	3.9
36	George Case	3.9
37	Lenny Dykstra	3.9
38	Willie Mays	3.9
39	Devon White	3.8
40	Tony Womack	3.8
41	Chuck Knoblauch	3.8
42	Juan Samuel	3.8
43	Steve Sax	3.6
44	Willie McGee	3.6
45	Eric Young	3.5
46	Larry Bowa	3.5
47	Kirk Gibson	3.5
48	Lance Johnson	3.4
49	Andy Van Slyke	3.4
50	Dave Concepcion	3.4

Games

First Base

	Player	G
1	Eddie Murray	2413
2	Jake Beckley	2380
3	Mickey Vernon	2237
4	Lou Gehrig	2137
5	Charlie Grimm	2131
6	Joe Judge	2084
7	Ed Konetchy	2073
8	Cap Anson	2059
	Steve Garvey	2059
10	Joe Kuhel	2057

Second Base

	Player	G
1	Eddie Collins	2650
2	Joe Morgan	2527
3	Lou Whitaker	2308
4	Nellie Fox	2295
5	Charlie Gehringer	2206
6	Willie Randolph	2152
7	Frank White	2150
8	Bid McPhee	2129
9	Bill Mazeroski	2094
10	Nap Lajoie	2035

Shortstop

	Player	G
1	Luis Aparicio	2581
2	Ozzie Smith	2511
3	Cal Ripken	2302
4	Larry Bowa	2222
5	Luke Appling	2218
6	Dave Concepcion	2178
7	Rabbit Maranville	2153
8	Alan Trammell	2139
9	Bill Dahlen	2133
10	Bert Campaneris	2097

Third Base

	Player	G
1	Brooks Robinson	2870
2	Graig Nettles	2412
3	Gary Gaetti	2282
4	Wade Boggs	2215
5	Mike Schmidt	2212
6	Buddy Bell	2183
7	Eddie Mathews	2181
8	Ron Santo	2130
9	Tim Wallach	2054
10	Eddie Yost	2008

Outfield

	Player	G
1	Ty Cobb	2934
2	Willie Mays	2842
3	Hank Aaron	2760
4	Tris Speaker	2698
5	Rickey Henderson	2650
6	Lou Brock	2507
7	Al Kaline	2488
8	Dave Winfield	2469
9	Max Carey	2421
10	Vada Pinson	2403
11	Roberto Clemente	2370
12	Zack Wheat	2337
13	Willie Davis	2323
	Andre Dawson	2323
15	Mel Ott	2313
16	Tony Gwynn	2309
17	Sam Crawford	2299
18	Paul Waner	2288
19	Harry Hooper	2284
20	Sam Rice	2270

Catcher

	Player	G
1	Carlton Fisk	2226
2	Bob Boone	2225
3	Gary Carter	2056
4	Tony Pena	1950
5	Jim Sundberg	1927
6	Al Lopez	1918
7	Lance Parrish	1818
8	Rick Ferrell	1806
9	Gabby Hartnett	1793
10	Ted Simmons	1771

Pitcher

	Player	G
1	Jesse Orosco	1096
2	Dennis Eckersley	1071
3	Hoyt Wilhelm	1070
4	Kent Tekulve	1050
5	Lee Smith	1022
6	Rich Gossage	1002
7	Lindy McDaniel	987
8	Rollie Fingers	944
9	John Franco	940
10	Gene Garber	931

Fielding Average

First Base

1	David Segui	.996
2	Steve Garvey	.996
3	Don Mattingly	.996
4	Wes Parker	.996
5	J. T. Snow	.996
6	Dan Driessen	.995
7	John Olerud	.995
8	Jim Spencer	.995
9	Tino Martinez	.995
10	Mark Grace	.995
11	Frank McCormick	.995

Second Base

1	Ryne Sandberg	.989
2	Tom Herr	.989
3	Mickey Morandini	.989
4	Jose Lind	.988
5	Jody Reed	.988
6	Bret Boone	.986
7	Jim Gantner	.985
8	Frank White	.984
9	Bobby Grich	.984
10	Craig Biggio	.984

Shortstop

1	Omar Vizquel	.983
2	Mike Bordick	.981
3	Larry Bowa	.980
4	Tony Fernandez	.980
5	Cal Ripken	.979
6	Ozzie Smith	.978
7	Spike Owen	.977
8	Alan Trammell	.977
9	Mark Belanger	.977
10	Bucky Dent	.976

Third Base

1	Brooks Robinson	.971
2	Ken Reitz	.970
3	George Kell	.969
4	Steve Buechele	.968
5	Don Money	.968
6	Don Wert	.968
7	Willie Kamm	.967
8	Heinie Groh	.967
9	Travis Fryman	.967
10	Carney Lansford	.966

Outfield

1	Darryl Hamilton	.995
2	Darren Lewis	.994
3	Terry Puhl	.993
4	Brett Butler	.993
5	Pete Rose	.991
6	Amos Otis	.991
7	Joe Rudi	.991
8	Mickey Stanley	.991
9	Robin Yount	.990
10	Jim Piersall	.990
11	Brian McRae	.990
12	Jim Landis	.989
13	Ken Berry	.989
14	Otis Nixon	.989
15	Brady Anderson	.989
16	Tommy Holmes	.989
17	Kirby Puckett	.989
18	Bernie Williams	.989
19	Paul O'Neill	.989
20	Gene Woodling	.989

Catcher

1	Bill Freehan	.993
2	Elston Howard	.993
3	Jim Sundberg	.993
4	Sherm Lollar	.992
5	Mike Macfarlane	.992
6	Johnny Edwards	.992
7	Tom Haller	.992
8	Lance Parrish	.991
9	Jerry Grote	.991
10	Ernie Whitt	.991

Pitcher

1	Don Mossi	.990
2	Gary Nolan	.990
3	Rick Rhoden	.989
4	Lon Warneke	.988
5	Jim Wilson	.988
6	Woodie Fryman	.988
7	Mike Mussina	.986
8	Larry Gura	.986
9	Grover Alexander	.985
10	Alvin Crowder	.984

Total Chances per Game

First Base

1	Tom Jones	11.38
2	George Stovall	11.30
3	George Kelly	11.09
4	Wally Pipp	11.05
5	Ed Konetchy	11.04
6	Candy LaChance	11.04
7	George Burns	10.92
8	Bill Terry	10.91
9	Cap Anson	10.85
10	Walter Holke	10.83
11	Bill Phillips	10.83
12	Fred Tenney	10.83

Second Base

1	Fred Pfeffer	6.95
2	Bid McPhee	6.70
3	Cub Stricker	6.59
4	Lou Bierbauer	6.49
5	Cupid Childs	6.32
6	Ski Melillo	6.16
7	Hughie Critz	6.07
8	Frankie Frisch	6.05
9	Bobby Lowe	6.01
10	Bucky Harris	6.00
11	Nap Lajoie	6.00

Shortstop

1	Herman Long	6.38
2	Dave Bancroft	6.33
3	Bill Dahlen	6.26
4	George Davis	6.22
5	Rabbit Maranville	6.10
6	Bobby Wallace	6.10
7	Tommy Corcoran	6.09
8	Monte Cross	6.06
9	Bones Ely	6.06
10	Honus Wagner	5.99

Third Base

1	Jerry Denny	4.21
2	Billy Shindle	4.15
3	Billy Nash	4.07
4	Arlie Latham	4.04
5	Denny Lyons	3.98
6	Jimmy Collins	3.89
7	Hick Carpenter	3.81
8	Jimmy Austin	3.74
9	Lave Cross	3.73
10	Frank Baker	3.64

Outfield

1	Taylor Douthit	3.16
2	Richie Ashburn	3.04
3	Dom DiMaggio	2.99
4	Mike Kreevich	2.95
5	Dwayne Murphy	2.92
6	Sam Chapman	2.91
7	Sam West	2.88
8	Max Carey	2.87
9	Fred Schulte	2.84
10	Lloyd Waner	2.81
11	Vince DiMaggio	2.80
12	Joe DiMaggio	2.78
13	Tris Speaker	2.77
14	Billy North	2.76
15	Terry Moore	2.75
16	Garry Maddox	2.74
17	Jimmy McAleer	2.73
18	Wally Berger	2.71
19	Gary Pettis	2.71
20	Kirby Puckett	2.71

Catcher

1	Mike Piazza	7.46
2	Johnny Edwards	6.98
3	Johnny Roseboro	6.83
4	Bill Freehan	6.79
5	Joe Girardi	6.64
6	Ivan Rodriguez	6.59
7	Mike Scioscia	6.59
8	Jerry Grote	6.53
9	Tim McCarver	6.41
10	Gary Carter	6.38

Pitcher

1	Nick Altrock	3.70
2	Harry Howell	3.61
3	Addie Joss	3.59
4	Ed Walsh	3.48
5	Nixey Callahan	3.47
6	Willie Sudhoff	3.33
7	George Mullin	3.20
8	Barney Pelty	3.17
9	Chick Fraser	3.12
10	Red Donahue	2.95
11	Ed Willett	2.95

Chances Accepted per Game

First Base

1	Tom Jones	11.21
2	George Stovall	11.14
3	George Kelly	11.00
4	Wally Pipp	10.96
5	Ed Konetchy	10.93
6	Candy LaChance	10.87
7	Bill Terry	10.82
8	George Burns	10.77
9	Walter Holke	10.75
10	Fred Tenney	10.65

Second Base

1	Fred Pfeffer	6.40
2	Bid McPhee	6.33
3	Lou Bierbauer	6.07
4	Ski Melillo	6.00
5	Cub Stricker	5.97
6	Hughie Critz	5.91
7	Frankie Frisch	5.89
8	Cupid Childs	5.88
9	Bucky Harris	5.79
10	Nap Lajoie	5.78

Shortstop

1	Dave Bancroft	5.98
2	George Davis	5.85
3	Rabbit Maranville	5.81
4	Bill Dahlen	5.80
5	Herman Long	5.78
6	Bobby Wallace	5.73
7	Travis Jackson	5.67
8	Dick Bartell	5.64
9	Tommy Corcoran	5.63
10	Honus Wagner	5.63

Third Base

1	Jerry Denny	3.72
2	Billy Shindle	3.70
3	Billy Nash	3.65
4	Jimmy Collins	3.61
5	Arlie Latham	3.52
6	Denny Lyons	3.51
7	Lave Cross	3.50
8	Jimmy Austin	3.49
9	Frank Baker	3.43
10	Bill Bradley	3.38

Outfield

1	Taylor Douthit	3.07
2	Richie Ashburn	2.98
3	Dom DiMaggio	2.92
4	Mike Kreevich	2.89
5	Dwayne Murphy	2.88
6	Sam Chapman	2.83
7	Sam West	2.83
8	Max Carey	2.77
9	Fred Schulte	2.77
10	Lloyd Waner	2.76
11	Vince DiMaggio	2.75
12	Joe DiMaggio	2.72
13	Terry Moore	2.71
14	Billy North	2.71
15	Garry Maddox	2.70
16	Tris Speaker	2.69
17	Kirby Puckett	2.68
18	Robin Yount	2.68
19	Gary Pettis	2.67
20	Chet Lemon	2.66

Catcher

1	Mike Piazza	7.38
2	Johnny Edwards	6.92
3	Johnny Roseboro	6.76
4	Bill Freehan	6.75
5	Joe Girardi	6.58
6	Ivan Rodriguez	6.53
7	Mike Scioscia	6.51
8	Jerry Grote	6.47
9	Tim McCarver	6.35
10	Gary Carter	6.32

Pitcher

1	Nick Altrock	3.57
2	Addie Joss	3.47
3	Harry Howell	3.46
4	Ed Walsh	3.35
5	Nixey Callahan	3.25
6	Willie Sudhoff	3.13
7	George Mullin	3.03
8	Barney Pelty	2.97
9	Chick Fraser	2.90
10	Doc White	2.82

Putouts

First Base

1	Jake Beckley	23731
2	Ed Konetchy	21361
3	Eddie Murray	21255
4	Cap Anson	20798
5	Charlie Grimm	20711
6	Stuffy McInnis	19962
7	Mickey Vernon	19808
8	Jake Daubert	19634
9	Lou Gehrig	19510
10	Joe Kuhel	19386

Second Base

1	Bid McPhee	6550
2	Eddie Collins	6526
3	Nellie Fox	6090
4	Joe Morgan	5742
5	Nap Lajoie	5496
6	Charlie Gehringer	5369
7	Bill Mazeroski	4974
8	Bobby Doerr	4928
9	Willie Randolph	4859
10	Billy Herman	4780

Shortstop

1	Rabbit Maranville	5139
2	Bill Dahlen	4856
3	Dave Bancroft	4623
4	Honus Wagner	4576
5	Tommy Corcoran	4553
6	Luis Aparicio	4548
7	Luke Appling	4398
8	Ozzie Smith	4249
9	Herman Long	4229
10	Bobby Wallace	4142

Third Base

1	Brooks Robinson	2697
2	Jimmy Collins	2372
3	Eddie Yost	2356
4	Lave Cross	2310
5	Pie Traynor	2289
6	Billy Nash	2222
7	Frank Baker	2154
8	Willie Kamm	2151
9	Eddie Mathews	2049
10	Willie Jones	2045

Outfield

1	Willie Mays	7095
2	Tris Speaker	6788
3	Max Carey	6363
4	Ty Cobb	6361
5	Rickey Henderson	6207
6	Richie Ashburn	6089
7	Hank Aaron	5539
8	Willie Davis	5449
9	Doc Cramer	5412
10	Brett Butler	5296
11	Andre Dawson	5158
12	Vada Pinson	5097
13	Willie Wilson	5060
14	Al Kaline	5035
15	Zack Wheat	4996
16	Chet Lemon	4993
17	Al Simmons	4988
18	Dave Winfield	4975
19	Amos Otis	4936
20	Paul Waner	4872

Catcher

1	Gary Carter	11785
2	Carlton Fisk	11369
3	Bob Boone	11260
4	Tony Pena	11212
5	Bill Freehan	9941
6	Jim Sundberg	9767
7	Lance Parrish	9647
8	Johnny Roseboro	9291
9	Johnny Bench	9249
10	Johnny Edwards	8925

Pitcher

1	Greg Maddux	403
2	Jack Morris	387
3	Phil Niekro	386
4	Fergie Jenkins	363
5	Gaylord Perry	349
6	Kevin Brown	347
7	Don Sutton	334
8	Orel Hershiser	332
9	Tony Mullane	328
	Rick Reuschel	328
	Tom Seaver	328

Putouts per Game

First Base

1	Tom Jones	10.53
2	Candy LaChance	10.48
3	George Stovall	10.45
4	George Kelly	10.37
5	Wally Pipp	10.33
6	Ed Konetchy	10.31
7	Bill Phillips	10.22
8	Walter Holke	10.20
9	Charlie Comiskey	10.15
10	John Reilly	10.12
11	Bill Terry	10.12

Second Base

1	Bid McPhee	3.08
2	Fred Pfeffer	3.07
3	Cub Stricker	3.02
4	Jerry Priddy	2.74
5	Lou Bierbauer	2.73
6	Bucky Harris	2.73
7	Nap Lajoie	2.71
8	Bobby Doerr	2.67
9	Cupid Childs	2.66
10	Nellie Fox	2.66

Shortstop

1	Dave Bancroft	2.47
2	Honus Wagner	2.43
3	Rabbit Maranville	2.39
4	Monte Cross	2.38
5	George Davis	2.36
6	Herman Long	2.36
7	Dick Bartell	2.31
8	Bill Dahlen	2.28
9	Ivy Olson	2.27
10	Bobby Wallace	2.27

Third Base

1	Jerry Denny	1.61
2	Denny Lyons	1.55
3	Billy Nash	1.52
4	Jimmy Austin	1.43
5	Billy Shindle	1.43
6	Jimmy Collins	1.41
7	Frank Baker	1.40
8	Hick Carpenter	1.37
9	Lave Cross	1.34
10	Hans Lobert	1.30

Outfield

1	Taylor Douthit	3.01
2	Richie Ashburn	2.90
3	Dom DiMaggio	2.82
4	Dwayne Murphy	2.82
5	Mike Kreevich	2.81
6	Sam Chapman	2.74
7	Sam West	2.74
8	Fred Schulte	2.70
9	Lloyd Waner	2.68
10	Billy North	2.65
11	Garry Maddox	2.64
12	Max Carey	2.63
13	Joe DiMaggio	2.63
14	Vince DiMaggio	2.63
15	Terry Moore	2.63
16	Robin Yount	2.63
17	Gary Pettis	2.62
18	Chet Lemon	2.60
19	Kirby Puckett	2.59
20	Omar Moreno	2.58
21	Devon White	2.58

Catcher

1	Mike Piazza	6.90
2	Johnny Edwards	6.42
3	Johnny Roseboro	6.30
4	Bill Freehan	6.29
5	Joe Girardi	6.09
6	Jerry Grote	6.00
7	Mike Scioscia	5.98
8	Ivan Rodriguez	5.97
9	Tim McCarver	5.92
10	Tom Haller	5.85

Pitcher

1	Kevin Brown	0.91
2	Greg Maddux	0.86
3	Dave Foutz	0.78
4	Nick Altrock	0.77
5	Chick Fraser	0.74
6	Al Spalding	0.73
7	Mike Boddicker	0.72
8	Carl Morton	0.72
9	Jack Morris	0.71
10	Dan Petry	0.69

Assists

First Base

1	Eddie Murray	1865
2	Keith Hernandez	1682
3	Mark Grace	1550
4	George Sisler	1529
5	Wally Joyner	1452
6	Mickey Vernon	1448
7	Fred Tenney	1363
8	Bill Buckner	1351
	Chris Chambliss	1351
10	Norm Cash	1317

Second Base

1	Eddie Collins	7630
2	Charlie Gehringer	7068
3	Joe Morgan	6967
4	Bid McPhee	6915
5	Bill Mazeroski	6685
6	Lou Whitaker	6653
7	Nellie Fox	6373
8	Ryne Sandberg	6363
9	Willie Randolph	6336
10	Nap Lajoie	6262

Shortstop

1	Ozzie Smith	8375
2	Luis Aparicio	8016
3	Bill Dahlen	7505
4	Rabbit Maranville	7354
5	Luke Appling	7218
6	Tommy Corcoran	7110
7	Cal Ripken	6977
8	Larry Bowa	6857
9	Dave Concepcion	6594
10	Dave Bancroft	6561

Third Base

1	Brooks Robinson	6205
2	Graig Nettles	5279
3	Mike Schmidt	5045
4	Buddy Bell	4925
5	Ron Santo	4581
6	Gary Gaetti	4531
7	Eddie Mathews	4322
8	Wade Boggs	4246
9	Aurelio Rodriguez	4150
10	Ron Cey	4018

Outfield

1	Tris Speaker	449
2	Ty Cobb	392
3	Jimmy Ryan	375
4	George Van Haltren	349
5	Tom Brown	348
6	Harry Hooper	344
7	Max Carey	339
8	Jimmy Sheckard	307
9	Clyde Milan	294
10	Orator Shaffer	289
11	King Kelly	285
12	Sam Thompson	283
13	Sam Rice	278
14	Dummy Hoy	274
15	Jesse Burkett	270
16	Sam Crawford	268
	Tommy McCarthy	268
18	Roberto Clemente	266
19	Patsy Donovan	265
20	Willie Keeler	258

Catcher

1	Deacon McGuire	1860
2	Ray Schalk	1811
3	Steve O'Neill	1698
4	Red Dooin	1590
5	Chief Zimmer	1580
6	Johnny Kling	1554
7	Ivey Wingo	1487
8	Wilbert Robinson	1454
9	Bill Bergen	1444
10	Wally Schang	1420

Pitcher

1	Cy Young	2014
2	Christy Mathewson	1503
3	Grover Alexander	1419
4	Jim Galvin	1382
5	Walter Johnson	1351
6	Burleigh Grimes	1252
7	George Mullin	1244
8	Jack Quinn	1240
9	Ed Walsh	1207
10	Eppa Rixey	1195

Assists per Game

First Base

1	Bill Buckner	0.87
2	Eric Karros	0.85
3	Jeff Bagwell	0.84
4	Ferris Fain	0.84
5	Keith Hernandez	0.84
6	Mark Grace	0.83
7	Vic Power	0.83
8	Wally Joyner	0.78
9	Eddie Murray	0.78
10	Pete O'Brien	0.78
11	George Sisler	0.78

Second Base

1	Hughie Critz	3.54
2	Frankie Frisch	3.42
3	Ski Melillo	3.38
4	Lou Bierbauer	3.35
5	Glenn Hubbard	3.34
6	Fred Pfeffer	3.33
7	Rogers Hornsby	3.31
8	Bid McPhee	3.25
9	Tony Cuccinello	3.23
10	Cupid Childs	3.22

Shortstop

1	Germany Smith	3.70
2	Art Fletcher	3.55
3	Bill Dahlen	3.52
4	Dave Bancroft	3.51
5	Bones Ely	3.50
6	Travis Jackson	3.50
7	George Davis	3.49
8	Jack Glasscock	3.46
9	Bobby Wallace	3.46
10	Tommy Corcoran	3.43

Third Base

1	Mike Schmidt	2.29
2	Billy Shindle	2.27
3	Buddy Bell	2.26
4	Arlie Latham	2.26
5	Clete Boyer	2.24
6	Jimmy Collins	2.20
7	Graig Nettles	2.19
8	George Brett	2.18
9	Terry Pendleton	2.18
10	Darrell Evans	2.17
11	Brooks Robinson	2.17

Outfield

1	Tommy McCarthy	0.23
2	Pop Corkhill	0.22
3	Jimmy Wolf	0.22
4	Sam Thompson	0.21
5	Tom Brown	0.20
6	Jimmy Ryan	0.20
7	George Van Haltren	0.20
8	Curt Welch	0.20
9	Ed Delahanty	0.19
10	George Gore	0.19
11	Paul Hines	0.18
12	Gavvy Cravath	0.17
13	Mike Griffin	0.17
14	Ned Hanlon	0.17
15	Joe Hornung	0.17
16	Mike Mitchell	0.17
17	Tris Speaker	0.17
18	Tilly Walker	0.17
19	George Wood	0.17
20	Johnny Bates	0.16
21	Ira Flagstead	0.16
22	Harry Hooper	0.16
23	Dummy Hoy	0.16
24	Nemo Leibold	0.16
25	Clyde Milan	0.16

Catcher

1	Duke Farrell	1.42
2	Red Dooin	1.34
3	Johnny Kling	1.33
4	Bill Killefer	1.32
5	Oscar Stanage	1.29
6	Chief Zimmer	1.28
7	John Warner	1.27
8	Ivey Wingo	1.21
9	Billy Sullivan	1.18
10	George Gibson	1.17

Pitcher

1	Addie Joss	2.96
2	Harry Howell	2.84
3	Ed Walsh	2.81
4	Nick Altrock	2.80
5	Willie Sudhoff	2.75
6	Nixey Callahan	2.60
7	George Mullin	2.56
8	Ed Willett	2.54
9	Barney Pelty	2.48
10	Red Donahue	2.47

Double Plays

First Base

1	Mickey Vernon	2044
2	Eddie Murray	2033
3	Joe Kuhel	1769
4	Charlie Grimm	1733
5	Chris Chambliss	1687
6	Keith Hernandez	1654
7	Gil Hodges	1614
8	Wally Joyner	1584
9	Lou Gehrig	1575
10	Will Clark	1571

Second Base

1	Bill Mazeroski	1706
2	Nellie Fox	1619
3	Willie Randolph	1547
4	Lou Whitaker	1527
5	Bobby Doerr	1507
6	Joe Morgan	1505
7	Charlie Gehringer	1444
8	Frank White	1382
9	Red Schoendienst	1368
10	Bobby Grich	1302

Shortstop

1	Ozzie Smith	1590
2	Cal Ripken	1565
3	Luis Aparicio	1553
4	Luke Appling	1424
5	Alan Trammell	1307
6	Roy McMillan	1304
7	Dave Concepcion	1290
8	Larry Bowa	1265
9	Pee Wee Reese	1246
10	Dick Groat	1237

Third Base

1	Brooks Robinson	618
2	Graig Nettles	470
3	Gary Gaetti	460
4	Mike Schmidt	450
5	Buddy Bell	430
6	Wade Boggs	423
7	Aurelio Rodriguez	408
8	Ron Santo	395
9	Eddie Mathews	369
10	Ken Boyer	355

Outfield

1	Tris Speaker	139
2	Ty Cobb	107
3	Max Carey	86
4	Tom Brown	85
5	Harry Hooper	81
6	Jimmy Sheckard	80
7	Mike Griffin	75
8	Dummy Hoy	72
9	Jimmy Ryan	71
10	Fielder Jones	70
11	Patsy Donovan	69
12	Sam Rice	67
13	George Van Haltren	64
14	Jesse Burkett	62
15	Sam Thompson	61
16	Willie Keeler	60
	Willie Mays	60
	Tommy McCarthy	60
	Mel Ott	60
20	Sam Crawford	59

Catcher

1	Ray Schalk	226
2	Steve O'Neill	193
3	Yogi Berra	175
4	Gabby Hartnett	163
5	Tony Pena	156
6	Bob Boone	154
7	Jimmie Wilson	153
8	Gary Carter	149
	Wally Schang	149
10	Carlton Fisk	147

Pitcher

1	Phil Niekro	83
2	Warren Spahn	82
3	Freddie Fitzsimmons	79
4	Bob Lemon	78
5	Bucky Walters	76
6	Burleigh Grimes	74
7	Walter Johnson	72
8	Tommy John	69
9	Jim Kaat	65
10	Dizzy Trout	63

Fielding Runs

1	Nap Lajoie	366
2	Bill Mazeroski	362
3	Bill Dahlen	352
4	Bid McPhee	318
5	Fred Pfeffer	268
6	Mike Schmidt	265
7	George Davis	256
8	Tris Speaker	248
9	Ozzie Smith	243
10	Jack Glasscock	242
11	Clete Boyer	233
12	Glenn Hubbard	229
13	Richie Ashburn	227
14	Joe Tinker	214
15	Bobby Wallace	212
16	Dave Bancroft	197
	Max Carey	197
18	Buddy Bell	191
19	Aurelio Rodriguez	183
20	Bobby Doerr	181
	Terry Pendleton	181
22	Willie Mays	180
23	Dick Bartell	178
	Mickey Doolan	178
25	Roberto Clemente	175
26	Joe Gerhardt	173
27	George McBride	170
28	Barry Bonds	169
29	Mark Belanger	167
30	Darrell Evans	165
	Lee Tannehill	165
32	Germany Smith	162
33	Rey Sanchez	161
34	Art Fletcher	160
	Dal Maxvill	160
36	Danny Richardson	155
37	Lou Bierbauer	154
	Rickey Henderson	154
	Rabbit Maranville	154
40	Ski Melillo	151
	Brooks Robinson	151
42	Lave Cross	150
	Bobby Knoop	150
44	Jim Hegan	149
	Carl Yastrzemski	149
46	Frankie Frisch	148
	Keith Hernandez	148
	Pop Snyder	148
49	Hughie Jennings	147
50	Rafael Belliard	146
51	Garry Maddox	142
52	Billy Jurges	140
53	Bill Holbert	138
	Ron Santo	138
55	Jimmy Collins	137
	Willie Davis	137
	Fred Dunlap	137
	Kirby Puckett	137
	Bobby Wine	137
60	John Ward	136
61	Mike Benjamin	135
62	Lou Boudreau	134
63	Hal Lanier	132
	Graig Nettles	132
65	Bill Killefer	131
66	Lou Criger	130
67	Manny Trillo	129
68	Mick Kelleher	128
69	Bill Buckner	127
70	Gene Alley	125
	Neifi Perez	125
72	Andre Dawson	123
	Vic Power	123
	Fred Tenney	123
75	Tony Pena	122
76	Al Weis	121
77	Bill Bergen	119
78	Chet Lemon	116
	Harold Reynolds	116
	Devon White	116
81	Everett Scott	115
82	Jesse Barfield	114
	Curt Flood	114
	Tommy Leach	114
85	Johnny Callison	113
	Hank DeBerry	113
	Hardy Richardson	113
88	Hughie Critz	111
	Jose Cruz	111
	Hobe Ferris	111
91	Brett Butler	110
	Jimmy Wynn	110
93	Jerry Denny	109
	Charlie O'Brien	109
95	Tim Bogar	108
	Tommy Corcoran	108
	Alvaro Espinoza	108
	Matt Williams	108
99	3 players tied	107

Fielding Runs (by position)

First Base

1	Keith Hernandez	150
2	Fred Tenney	128
3	Vic Power	124
4	Bill Buckner	121
5	George Sisler	89
6	Mark Grace	85
7	Eric Karros	84
8	Jeff Bagwell	81
9	Sid Bream	76
	Darrell Evans	76

Second Base

1	Nap Lajoie	368
2	Bill Mazeroski	363
3	Bid McPhee	319
4	Fred Pfeffer	259
5	Glenn Hubbard	229
6	Bobby Doerr	180
7	Joe Gerhardt	160
8	Lou Bierbauer	157
9	Bobby Knoop	150
10	Ski Melillo	148

Shortstop

1	Bill Dahlen	304
2	Jack Glasscock	245
3	Ozzie Smith	242
4	Joe Tinker	216
5	Dave Bancroft	198
6	George Davis	192
7	George McBride	174
8	Rabbit Maranville	173
9	Mickey Doolan	168
10	Mark Belanger	164
	Germany Smith	164

Third Base

1	Mike Schmidt	265
2	Clete Boyer	201
3	Buddy Bell	199
4	Aurelio Rodriguez	184
5	Terry Pendleton	181
6	Brooks Robinson	152
7	Lave Cross	137
8	Jimmy Collins	136
	Graig Nettles	136
10	Ron Santo	135

Outfield

1	Tris Speaker	248
2	Richie Ashburn	227
3	Max Carey	201
4	Willie Mays	184
5	Roberto Clemente	173
6	Barry Bonds	169
7	Rickey Henderson	154
8	Carl Yastrzemski	143
9	Garry Maddox	142
10	Kirby Puckett	139
11	Willie Davis	137
12	Andre Dawson	124
13	Chet Lemon	119
14	Jimmy Wynn	118
15	Curt Flood	116
16	Johnny Callison	114
	Devon White	114
18	Jesse Barfield	112
19	Jose Cruz	111
20	Jim Fogarty	110

Catcher

1	Pop Snyder	151
2	Jim Hegan	150
3	Lou Criger	133
4	Bill Killefer	131
5	Tony Pena	120
6	Bill Bergen	119
7	Charlie O'Brien	110
8	Chief Zimmer	105
9	Ossee Schreckengost	98
	Jim Sundberg	98

Pitcher

1	Ed Walsh	84
2	Greg Maddux	81
3	Carl Mays	74
4	Christy Mathewson	69
5	Freddie Fitzsimmons	61
6	Bob Lemon	59
7	Burleigh Grimes	58
8	Tommy John	56
9	Harry Gumbert	51
10	Harry Howell	50

Fielding Wins

1	Bill Mazeroski	37.8
2	Nap Lajoie	36.9
3	Bill Dahlen	33.2
4	Bid McPhee	27.5
5	Mike Schmidt	27.3
6	Ozzie Smith	25.4
7	Tris Speaker	24.8
8	Clete Boyer	24.3
9	Glenn Hubbard	23.9
10	George Davis	23.8
11	Fred Pfeffer	23.4
12	Richie Ashburn	22.6
13	Joe Tinker	22.6
14	Jack Glasscock	21.4
15	Bobby Wallace	21.3
16	Max Carey	20.1
17	Dave Bancroft	20.0
18	Buddy Bell	19.5
19	Aurelio Rodriguez	19.2
20	Mickey Doolan	19.2
21	Terry Pendleton	18.6
22	George McBride	18.4
23	Willie Mays	18.3
24	Lee Tannehill	18.1
25	Roberto Clemente	18.0
26	Bobby Doerr	17.7
27	Mark Belanger	17.6
28	Dick Bartell	17.5
29	Dal Maxvill	17.1
30	Art Fletcher	17.0
31	Darrell Evans	16.9
32	Barry Bonds	16.7
33	Bobby Knoop	16.2
34	Brooks Robinson	15.8
35	Rey Sanchez	15.8
36	Rabbit Maranville	15.6
37	Joe Gerhardt	15.6
38	Carl Yastrzemski	15.3
39	Keith Hernandez	15.3
40	Rafael Belliard	15.1
41	Rickey Henderson	15.0
42	Jim Hegan	15.0
43	Garry Maddox	14.9
44	Bobby Wine	14.5
45	Frankie Frisch	14.4
46	Willie Davis	14.4
47	Ron Santo	14.4
48	Bill Killefer	14.3
49	Billy Jurges	14.2
50	Hal Lanier	14.2
51	Ski Melillo	14.2
52	Germany Smith	14.0
53	Lave Cross	13.7
54	Graig Nettles	13.6
55	Danny Richardson	13.5
56	Manny Trillo	13.5
57	Mick Kelleher	13.5
58	Kirby Puckett	13.4
59	Lou Boudreau	13.4
60	Gene Alley	13.3
61	Pop Snyder	13.3
62	Mike Benjamin	13.2
63	Lou Criger	13.2
64	Jimmy Collins	13.1
65	Bill Buckner	13.1
66	Lou Bierbauer	13.1
67	Al Weis	13.0
68	Bill Bergen	12.8
69	Hughie Jennings	12.8
70	Andre Dawson	12.7
71	Vic Power	12.6
72	Bill Holbert	12.5
73	Tony Pena	12.5
74	Fred Dunlap	12.3
75	Neifi Perez	12.1
76	Fred Tenney	12.1
77	John Ward	12.0
78	Curt Flood	11.9
79	Tommy Leach	11.9
80	Johnny Callison	11.8
81	Hobe Ferris	11.8
82	Everett Scott	11.8
83	Chet Lemon	11.6
84	Harold Reynolds	11.5
85	Jose Cruz	11.5
86	Jimmy Wynn	11.5
87	Devon White	11.4
88	Jesse Barfield	11.3
89	Brett Butler	11.2
90	Hank DeBerry	10.9
91	Hughie Critz	10.8
92	Charlie O'Brien	10.8
93	Matt Williams	10.8
94	Omar Moreno	10.7
95	Alvaro Espinoza	10.6
96	Mike Gallego	10.6
97	Johnny Logan	10.6
98	Al Kaline	10.6
99	Tim Bogar	10.6
100	Lenny Dykstra	10.5

Total Player Rating

1	Babe Ruth	108.9
2	Willie Mays	95.9
3	Nap Lajoie	95.5
4	Ty Cobb	92.0
5	Barry Bonds	89.4
6	Hank Aaron	89.1
7	Tris Speaker	88.2
8	Ted Williams	83.0
9	Rogers Hornsby	82.7
10	Honus Wagner	81.8
11	Mike Schmidt	79.6
12	Mickey Mantle	77.4
13	Rickey Henderson	77.0
14	Eddie Collins	73.3
15	Stan Musial	71.5
16	Lou Gehrig	68.9
17	Frank Robinson	67.6
18	Mel Ott	61.4
19	Jimmie Foxx	55.9
20	Joe Morgan	54.8
21	Eddie Mathews	52.2
22	Ken Griffey Jr.	51.6
23	George Davis	51.4
24	Bill Dahlen	51.1
25	Joe DiMaggio	50.2
26	Tim Raines	47.9
27	Carl Yastrzemski	46.7
28	Robin Yount	46.0
29	Bobby Grich	45.8
30	Tony Gwynn	45.6
31	Jeff Bagwell	45.2
	Al Kaline	45.2
33	Charlie Gehringer	45.0
34	Wade Boggs	44.4
35	Roger Connor	43.3
36	Ed Delahanty	42.9
37	Lou Boudreau	42.5
38	Luke Appling	42.4
	Ozzie Smith	42.4
40	Roberto Clemente	42.2
	Reggie Jackson	42.2
	Cal Ripken	42.2
43	Dan Brouthers	42.1
44	Barry Larkin	41.2
45	Bid McPhee	41.0
46	Ron Santo	40.9
47	Frank Thomas	40.7
48	Bobby Doerr	40.5
49	Gabby Hartnett	40.3
50	George Brett	40.0
51	Joe Cronin	39.9
52	Arky Vaughan	39.7
53	Joe Jackson	39.0
54	Frankie Frisch	38.6
55	Mark McGwire	38.4
56	Dave Bancroft	37.5
	Reggie Smith	37.5
58	Yogi Berra	37.4
59	Willie McCovey	37.3
60	Dave Winfield	36.9
61	Ryne Sandberg	36.6
62	Bill Mazeroski	36.3
63	Johnny Mize	36.2
64	Jack Glasscock	36.0
	Mike Piazza	36.0
66	Dick Allen	35.9
	Jimmy Wynn	35.9
68	Edgar Martinez	35.7
	Bobby Wallace	35.7
70	Craig Biggio	35.6
71	Darrell Evans	35.5
	Joe Sewell	35.5
73	Bill Dickey	35.4
74	Bob Johnson	34.9
75	Keith Hernandez	34.8
76	Frank Baker	34.6
77	Albert Belle	34.3
78	Rod Carew	34.2
79	Eddie Murray	34.1
80	Roberto Alomar	33.8
81	Paul Waner	33.5
82	Richie Ashburn	32.8
83	Cap Anson	32.6
	Paul Molitor	32.6
85	Kirby Puckett	32.3
86	Harry Heilmann	32.2
87	Jackie Robinson	32.0
88	Mickey Cochrane	31.8
	Billy Herman	31.8
90	Willie Stargell	31.6
91	Hank Greenberg	31.5
92	Cesar Cedeno	31.3
	Sam Crawford	31.3
94	Andre Dawson	31.0
95	Jack Clark	30.7
	Sam Thompson	30.7
97	Elmer Flick	30.4
98	Gary Carter	30.1
	Billy Williams	30.1
100	Cupid Childs	30.0

Total Player Rating

101	Bobby Bonds	29.6
	Buck Ewing	29.6
103	Norm Cash	28.8
	Joe Gordon	28.8
105	Brett Butler	28.7
106	Bernie Williams	28.6
107	Pete Browning	28.5
	Jose Cruz	28.5
	Dwight Evans	28.5
110	Dick Bartell	28.3
111	Stan Hack	28.2
112	Heinie Groh	28.1
113	Fred Dunlap	27.8
114	Lenny Dykstra	27.7
115	Gary Sheffield	27.5
116	Billy Hamilton	27.4
	Hardy Richardson	27.4
118	Harmon Killebrew	27.3
119	Chet Lemon	27.1
120	Jesse Burkett	27.0
121	Ernie Banks	26.9
	Fred Lynn	26.9
	Al Simmons	26.9
124	Fred Clarke	26.7
125	Ray Lankford	26.6
126	Rafael Palmeiro	26.5
	Darryl Strawberry	26.5
128	Jim Rice	26.4
	Rusty Staub	26.4
130	Hughie Jennings	26.3
	Lou Whitaker	26.3
132	Art Fletcher	26.2
133	King Kelly	26.1
	Bill Terry	26.1
135	Sherry Magee	26.0
	Minnie Minoso	26.0
137	Ralph Kiner	25.9
138	Zack Wheat	25.7
139	Johnny Bench	25.6
140	Rocky Colavito	25.5
141	Jose Canseco	25.3
	Alex Rodriguez	25.3
143	Larry Walker	25.1
144	Goose Goslin	25.0
	Joe Medwick	25.0
146	Carlton Fisk	24.9
147	George Sisler	24.7
148	Buddy Bell	24.6
149	Jack Fournier	24.5
150	Harlond Clift	24.4
151	Eric Davis	24.1
	Duke Snider	24.1
153	Wally Berger	24.0
	Jimmy Collins	24.0
	Tony Oliva	24.0
156	Travis Jackson	23.7
157	Roy Thomas	23.6
158	Willie Randolph	23.5
159	Max Carey	23.4
	Will Clark	23.4
	Tim Salmon	23.4
	Joe Tinker	23.4
163	Alan Trammell	23.3
164	Amos Otis	23.1
165	Kenny Lofton	22.8
	Fred Pfeffer	22.8
167	Larry Doby	22.7
168	Jake Beckley	22.6
	Matt Williams	22.6
170	Roy Campanella	22.5
	Ron Cey	22.5
	Charlie Keller	22.5
173	Harry Stovey	22.4
174	Graig Nettles	22.2
175	Del Pratt	21.7
176	George Foster	21.6
	Andy Van Slyke	21.6
178	Glenn Hubbard	21.5
	Dave Parker	21.5
180	Ed Konetchy	21.4
	Dale Murphy	21.4
	Pete Rose	21.4
183	Jim Fregosi	21.3
184	Fred Tenney	21.2
185	Earl Averill	21.1
186	Frank Chance	21.0
	Miller Huggins	21.0
188	Robin Ventura	20.8
	Roy White	20.8
190	Vern Stephens	20.7
191	Frank Howard	20.6
192	Ken Singleton	20.4
193	Art Devlin	20.3
	Mike Griffin	20.3
195	Dwayne Murphy	20.2
196	Ken Boyer	20.1
	Kevin Mitchell	20.1
	Brooks Robinson	20.1
199	Roger Bresnahan	20.0
	Chuck Klein	20.0

Total Player Rating

	Manny Ramirez	20.0
202	Tony Fernandez	19.9
	Charley Jones	19.9
204	Charlie Bennett	19.8
205	Pie Traynor	19.7
206	Bob Elliott	19.6
	Joe Kelley	19.6
	Joe Torre	19.6
209	Fred McGriff	19.5
210	Jay Bell	19.2
	David Justice	19.2
212	Brian Downing	19.1
	Denny Lyons	19.1
	Paul O'Neill	19.1
215	Sammy Sosa	19.0
216	Ken Caminiti	18.9
	Gavvy Cravath	18.9
218	Wally Schang	18.8
219	Chili Davis	18.7
	Bill Joyce	18.7
	Bill Nicholson	18.7
222	Jimmy Sheckard	18.5
223	Ted Simmons	18.4
	Eddie Stanky	18.4
225	Orlando Cepeda	18.3
226	Ken Williams	18.2
227	Roy Cullenbine	18.0
	Gil McDougald	18.0
229	Hack Wilson	17.9
230	Johnny Logan	17.7
	Jim Thome	17.7
232	Gene Alley	17.6
	Rico Carty	17.6
	Jeff Kent	17.6
235	Tony Lazzeri	17.5
	Ernie Lombardi	17.5
237	Jim Edmonds	17.4
	Ferris Fain	17.4
239	Thurman Munson	17.2
240	Luis Gonzalez	17.0
241	Harold Baines	16.9
	Pedro Guerrero	16.9
	Bobby Veach	16.9
244	Steve Finley	16.8
	Mark Grace	16.8
	John Olerud	16.8
247	Tommy Leach	16.7
248	Ellis Burks	16.6
249	John McGraw	16.5
	Gene Tenace	16.5
251	Kiki Cuyler	16.4
	Babe Herman	16.4
253	Edd Roush	16.3
254	Ray Chapman	16.2
	Jocko Milligan	16.2
256	Willie Davis	16.1
	Davey Johnson	16.1
	Phil Rizzuto	16.1
259	Bobby Knoop	16.0
260	Al Oliver	15.9
	Jimmy Williams	15.9
262	Enos Slaughter	15.8
263	Paul Hines	15.7
264	Mike Hargrove	15.6
	Tommy Holmes	15.6
	Chief Zimmer	15.6
267	Jeff Heath	15.5
268	Ben Chapman	15.4
	Lave Cross	15.4
	George Gore	15.4
	Boog Powell	15.4
272	Earle Combs	15.3
	Bobby Murcer	15.3
	Jim O'Rourke	15.3
	John Valentin	15.3
276	Jesse Barfield	15.2
277	Johnny Evers	15.1
	Juan Gonzalez	15.1
	Ron Hansen	15.1
	Kevin McReynolds	15.1
	Ivan Rodriguez	15.1
282	Jason Kendall	15.0
	Roger Peckinpaugh	15.0
284	Dom DiMaggio	14.9
	Kirk Gibson	14.9
286	Bobby Bonilla	14.8
287	Mark Belanger	14.7
	Pee Wee Reese	14.7
	Mike Scioscia	14.7
	Danny Tartabull	14.7
291	Tommy Henrich	14.6
	Chipper Jones	14.6
	Henry Larkin	14.6
294	Johnny Pesky	14.5
295	Mike Tiernan	14.3
296	Andruw Jones	14.2
	Benny Kauff	14.2
	Roy Smalley	14.2
299	Duke Farrell	14.1
300	Bob Allison	14.0

Total Player Rating

	Greg Luzinski	14.0
	Rabbit Maranville	14.0
	Stan Spence	14.0
304	Doug DeCinces	13.9
	Jimmy Ryan	13.9
306	Augie Galan	13.8
	Nomar Garciaparra	13.8
	Vladimir Guerrero	13.8
	Harry Hooper	13.8
310	Fred Carroll	13.6
	Willie Kamm	13.6
	Dave Orr	13.6
	Darrell Porter	13.6
	Al Rosen	13.6
315	Sid Gordon	13.5
	Gil Hodges	13.5
317	Sixto Lezcano	13.4
	Chief Meyers	13.4
319	Dolph Camilli	13.3
	Ken Keltner	13.3
	Garry Maddox	13.3
	Raul Mondesi	13.3
	Kip Selbach	13.3
324	Willie Keeler	13.2
	Orator Shaffer	13.2
	Red Smith	13.2
327	Robby Thompson	13.1
328	Clete Boyer	13.0
	Rick Burleson	13.0
	Bill Freehan	13.0
	Brian Giles	13.0
	Rick Monday	13.0
	John Titus	13.0
334	Jeff Cirillo	12.9
	Richie Zisk	12.9
336	Chick Hafey	12.8
337	Johnny Callison	12.7
	Jack Clements	12.7
	Roy Sievers	12.7
340	Nellie Fox	12.6
	Ron Gant	12.6
	Vada Pinson	12.6
	Jerry Priddy	12.6
344	Jackie Jensen	12.5
	Hal McRae	12.5
346	Moises Alou	12.4
	Kid Elberfeld	12.4
	Julio Franco	12.4
	Deacon McGuire	12.4
	Lance Parrish	12.4
	Riggs Stephenson	12.4
352	Kal Daniels	12.3
	Freddie Lindstrom	12.3
	Billy Nash	12.3
	George Stone	12.3
356	Lonny Frey	12.2
	Scott Rolen	12.2
	Maury Wills	12.2
359	Jim Gentile	12.0
	Ossee Schreckengost	12.0
361	Jay Buhner	11.9
	Don Mattingly	11.9
	Ed Swartwood	11.9
364	Jake Daubert	11.8
	George Van Haltren	11.8
	Jimmy Wolf	11.8
367	Buddy Myer	11.7
	Andy Thornton	11.7
369	Lou Criger	11.6
	Wally Joyner	11.6
	Dan McGann	11.6
	Bob Watson	11.6
373	Lefty O'Doul	11.5
	Ross Youngs	11.5
375	Brady Anderson	11.4
	Johnny Kling	11.4
	Red Schoendienst	11.4
378	Luis Aparicio	11.3
	Ken Griffey Sr.	11.3
	Andy Seminick	11.3
	Cy Seymour	11.3
382	Tom Haller	11.2
	Toby Harrah	11.2
	Roger Maris	11.2
	Rico Petrocelli	11.2
386	Earl Battey	11.1
	Larry Hisle	11.1
	Lonnie Smith	11.1
	Vic Wertz	11.1
	Ned Williamson	11.1
391	Bobby Abreu	11.0
	Tony Cuccinello	11.0
	Bernard Gilkey	11.0
	Devon White	11.0
	Deacon White	11.0
	Rudy York	11.0
397	Mike Donlin	10.9
	Rick Ferrell	10.9
399	John Kruk	10.8
	Cecil Travis	10.8

Total Player Rating

	Dixie Walker	10.8
402	Joe Harris	10.7
	Billy Jurges	10.7
	Marty McManus	10.7
	Bill Melton	10.7
	Danny Murphy	10.7
407	Don Baylor	10.6
	Harry Davis	10.6
	Mike Greenwell	10.6
	Johnny Mostil	10.6
	Greg Vaughn	10.6
	Heinie Zimmerman	10.6
413	Lou Brock	10.5
	Tip O'Neill	10.5
	Doug Rader	10.5
	Sam Rice	10.5
417	Don Buford	10.4
	Travis Fryman	10.4
	Buck Herzog	10.4
	Javy Lopez	10.4
	Gary Matthews	10.4
	Ben Oglivie	10.4
423	Ed McFarland	10.2
424	Charlie Hickman	10.1
	Whitey Kurowski	10.1
	Tony Perez	10.1
	Tony Phillips	10.1
	Reggie Sanders	10.1
429	Oyster Burns	10.0
	Monte Irvin	10.0
	Bill Sweeney	10.0
432	Jack Crooks	9.9
	Hank Gowdy	9.9
	Pinky May	9.9
435	Jerry Denny	9.8
	Kent Hrbek	9.8
	Johnny Romano	9.8
438	Sherm Lollar	9.7
	Billy North	9.7
440	Oscar Gamble	9.6
	Bill Lange	9.6
	Terry Pendleton	9.6
	Curt Welch	9.6
	Wes Westrum	9.6
445	George Burns	9.5
446	Jim Sundberg	9.4
447	Donie Bush	9.3
	Del Crandall	9.3
	Tom Daly	9.3
450	Bill Bradley	9.2
	Buddy Lewis	9.2
	Jody Reed	9.2
	Cy Williams	9.2
454	Dave Concepcion	9.1
	Billy Werber	9.1
456	Mickey Rivers	9.0
	Rondell White	9.0
458	Sal Bando	8.8
	Walker Cooper	8.8
	Charlie Hollocher	8.8
	Bob Nieman	8.8
462	Jimmy Barrett	8.7
	Chris Hoiles	8.7
	Johnny Ray	8.7
	Ray Schalk	8.7
466	Fred Luderus	8.6
	Hank Sauer	8.6
468	Jimmy Dykes	8.5
	Derek Jeter	8.5
	Eddie Joost	8.5
	Ron LeFlore	8.5
	Jose Valentin	8.5
	Bump Wills	8.5
474	Johnny Bassler	8.4
	John Farrell	8.4
	Claude Ritchey	8.4
	Rey Sanchez	8.4
	John Ward	8.4
479	Happy Felsch	8.3
	Socks Seybold	8.3
481	Bernie Carbo	8.2
	Frank Fennelly	8.2
	Dal Maxvill	8.2
	Elmer Smith	8.2
	Pinky Whitney	8.2
486	Phil Garner	8.1
	Jason Giambi	8.1
	Ken McMullen	8.1
489	Hank DeBerry	8.0
	Elbie Fletcher	8.0
	Pop Snyder	8.0
	Snuffy Stirnweiss	8.0
	Mo Vaughn	8.0
	Al Weis	8.0
495	Larry Gardner	7.9
	Solly Hemus	7.9
	Bobby Higginson	7.9
	Harry Steinfeldt	7.9
	Elmer Valo	7.9
	Gene Woodling	7.9

Total Player Rating (alpha.)

Hank Aaron	89.1
Bobby Abreu	11.0
Dick Allen	35.9
Gene Alley	17.6
Bob Allison	14.0
Roberto Alomar	33.8
Moises Alou	12.4
Brady Anderson	11.4
Cap Anson	32.6
Luis Aparicio	11.3
Luke Appling	42.4
Richie Ashburn	32.8
Earl Averill	21.1
Jeff Bagwell	45.2
Harold Baines	16.9
Frank Baker	34.6
Dave Bancroft	37.5
Sal Bando	8.8
Ernie Banks	26.9
Jesse Barfield	15.2
Jimmy Barrett	8.7
Dick Bartell	28.3
Johnny Bassler	8.4
Earl Battey	11.1
Don Baylor	10.6
Jake Beckley	22.6
Mark Belanger	14.7
Buddy Bell	24.6
Jay Bell	19.2
Albert Belle	34.3
Johnny Bench	25.6
Charlie Bennett	19.8
Wally Berger	24.0
Yogi Berra	37.4
Craig Biggio	35.6
Wade Boggs	44.4
Barry Bonds	89.4
Bobby Bonds	29.6
Bobby Bonilla	14.8
Lou Boudreau	42.5
Clete Boyer	13.0
Ken Boyer	20.1
Bill Bradley	9.2
Roger Bresnahan	20.0
George Brett	40.0
Lou Brock	10.5
Dan Brouthers	42.1
Pete Browning	28.5
Don Buford	10.4
Jay Buhner	11.9
Jesse Burkett	27.0
Ellis Burks	16.6
Rick Burleson	13.0
George Burns	9.5
Oyster Burns	10.0
Donie Bush	9.3
Brett Butler	28.7
Johnny Callison	12.7
Dolph Camilli	13.3
Ken Caminiti	18.9
Roy Campanella	22.5
Jose Canseco	25.3
Bernie Carbo	8.2
Rod Carew	34.2
Max Carey	23.4
Fred Carroll	13.6
Gary Carter	30.1
Rico Carty	17.6
Norm Cash	28.8
Cesar Cedeno	31.3
Orlando Cepeda	18.3
Ron Cey	22.5
Frank Chance	21.0
Ray Chapman	16.2
Ben Chapman	15.4
Cupid Childs	30.0
Jeff Cirillo	12.9
Jack Clark	30.7
Will Clark	23.4
Fred Clarke	26.7
Roberto Clemente	42.2
Jack Clements	12.7
Harlond Clift	24.4
Ty Cobb	92.0
Mickey Cochrane	31.8
Rocky Colavito	25.5
Eddie Collins	73.3
Jimmy Collins	24.0
Earle Combs	15.3
Dave Concepcion	9.1
Roger Connor	43.3
Walker Cooper	8.8
Del Crandall	9.3
Gavvy Cravath	18.9
Sam Crawford	31.3
Lou Criger	11.6
Joe Cronin	39.9
Jack Crooks	9.9
Lave Cross	15.4
Jose Cruz	28.5

Total Player Rating (alpha.)

Tony Cuccinello	11.0
Roy Cullenbine	18.0
Kiki Cuyler	16.4
Bill Dahlen	51.1
Tom Daly	9.3
Kal Daniels	12.3
Jake Daubert	11.8
Chili Davis	18.7
Eric Davis	24.1
George Davis	51.4
Harry Davis	10.6
Willie Davis	16.1
Andre Dawson	31.0
Hank DeBerry	8.0
Doug DeCinces	13.9
Ed Delahanty	42.9
Jerry Denny	9.8
Art Devlin	20.3
Bill Dickey	35.4
Dom DiMaggio	14.9
Joe DiMaggio	50.2
Larry Doby	22.7
Bobby Doerr	40.5
Mike Donlin	10.9
Brian Downing	19.1
Fred Dunlap	27.8
Jimmy Dykes	8.5
Lenny Dykstra	27.7
Jim Edmonds	17.4
Kid Elberfeld	12.4
Bob Elliott	19.6
Darrell Evans	35.5
Dwight Evans	28.5
Johnny Evers	15.1
Buck Ewing	29.6
Ferris Fain	17.4
Duke Farrell	14.1
John Farrell	8.4
Happy Felsch	8.3
Frank Fennelly	8.2
Tony Fernandez	19.9
Rick Ferrell	10.9
Steve Finley	16.8
Carlton Fisk	24.9
Art Fletcher	26.2
Elbie Fletcher	8.0
Elmer Flick	30.4
George Foster	21.6
Jack Fournier	24.5
Nellie Fox	12.6
Jimmie Foxx	55.9
Julio Franco	12.4
Bill Freehan	13.0
Jim Fregosi	21.3
Lonny Frey	12.2
Frankie Frisch	38.6
Travis Fryman	10.4
Augie Galan	13.8
Oscar Gamble	9.6
Ron Gant	12.6
Nomar Garciaparra	13.8
Larry Gardner	7.9
Phil Garner	8.1
Lou Gehrig	68.9
Charlie Gehringer	45.0
Jim Gentile	12.0
Jason Giambi	8.1
Kirk Gibson	14.9
Brian Giles	13.0
Bernard Gilkey	11.0
Jack Glasscock	36.0
Juan Gonzalez	15.1
Luis Gonzalez	17.0
Joe Gordon	28.8
Sid Gordon	13.5
George Gore	15.4
Goose Goslin	25.0
Hank Gowdy	9.9
Mark Grace	16.8
Hank Greenberg	31.5
Mike Greenwell	10.6
Bobby Grich	45.8
Ken Griffey Jr.	51.6
Ken Griffey Sr.	11.3
Mike Griffin	20.3
Heinie Groh	28.1
Pedro Guerrero	16.9
Vladimir Guerrero	13.8
Tony Gwynn	45.6
Stan Hack	28.2
Chick Hafey	12.8
Tom Haller	11.2
Billy Hamilton	27.4
Ron Hansen	15.1
Mike Hargrove	15.6
Toby Harrah	11.2
Joe Harris	10.7
Gabby Hartnett	40.3
Jeff Heath	15.5
Harry Heilmann	32.2

Total Player Rating (alpha.)

Solly Hemus	7.9
Rickey Henderson	77.0
Tommy Henrich	14.6
Babe Herman	16.4
Billy Herman	31.8
Keith Hernandez	34.8
Buck Herzog	10.4
Charlie Hickman	10.1
Bobby Higginson	7.9
Paul Hines	15.7
Larry Hisle	11.1
Gil Hodges	13.5
Chris Hoiles	8.7
Charlie Hollocher	8.8
Tommy Holmes	15.6
Harry Hooper	13.8
Rogers Hornsby	82.7
Frank Howard	20.6
Kent Hrbek	9.8
Glenn Hubbard	21.5
Miller Huggins	21.0
Monte Irvin	10.0
Joe Jackson	39.0
Reggie Jackson	42.2
Travis Jackson	23.7
Hughie Jennings	26.3
Jackie Jensen	12.5
Derek Jeter	8.5
Davey Johnson	16.1
Bob Johnson	34.9
Andruw Jones	14.2
Charley Jones	19.9
Chipper Jones	14.6
Eddie Joost	8.5
Bill Joyce	18.7
Wally Joyner	11.6
Billy Jurges	10.7
David Justice	19.2
Al Kaline	45.2
Willie Kamm	13.6
Benny Kauff	14.2
Willie Keeler	13.2
Charlie Keller	22.5
Joe Kelley	19.6
King Kelly	26.1
Ken Keltner	13.3
Jason Kendall	15.0
Jeff Kent	17.6
Harmon Killebrew	27.3
Ralph Kiner	25.9
Chuck Klein	20.0
Johnny Kling	11.4
Bobby Knoop	16.0
Ed Konetchy	21.4
John Kruk	10.8
Whitey Kurowski	10.1
Nap Lajoie	95.5
Bill Lange	9.6
Ray Lankford	26.6
Barry Larkin	41.2
Henry Larkin	14.6
Tony Lazzeri	17.5
Tommy Leach	16.7
Chet Lemon	27.1
Buddy Lewis	9.2
Sixto Lezcano	13.4
Freddie Lindstrom	12.3
Kenny Lofton	22.8
Johnny Logan	17.7
Sherm Lollar	9.7
Ernie Lombardi	17.5
Javy Lopez	10.4
Fred Luderus	8.6
Greg Luzinski	14.0
Fred Lynn	26.9
Denny Lyons	19.1
Ron LeFlore	8.5
Garry Maddox	13.3
Sherry Magee	26.0
Mickey Mantle	77.4
Rabbit Maranville	14.0
Roger Maris	11.2
Edgar Martinez	35.7
Eddie Mathews	52.2
Gary Matthews	10.4
Don Mattingly	11.9
Dal Maxvill	8.2
Pinky May	9.9
Willie Mays	95.9
Bill Mazeroski	36.3
Willie McCovey	37.3
Gil McDougald	18.0
Ed McFarland	10.2
Dan McGann	11.6
John McGraw	16.5
Fred McGriff	19.5
Deacon McGuire	12.4
Mark McGwire	38.4
Marty McManus	10.7
Ken McMullen	8.1

Total Player Rating (alpha.)

Bid McPhee	41.0
Hal McRae	12.5
Kevin McReynolds	15.1
Joe Medwick	25.0
Bill Melton	10.7
Chief Meyers	13.4
Jocko Milligan	16.2
Minnie Minoso	26.0
Kevin Mitchell	20.1
Johnny Mize	36.2
Paul Molitor	32.6
Rick Monday	13.0
Raul Mondesi	13.3
Joe Morgan	54.8
Johnny Mostil	10.6
Thurman Munson	17.2
Bobby Murcer	15.3
Dale Murphy	21.4
Danny Murphy	10.7
Dwayne Murphy	20.2
Eddie Murray	34.1
Stan Musial	71.5
Buddy Myer	11.7
Billy Nash	12.3
Graig Nettles	22.2
Bill Nicholson	18.7
Bob Nieman	8.8
Billy North	9.7
Lefty O'Doul	11.5
Ben Oglivie	10.4
John Olerud	16.8
Tony Oliva	24.0
Al Oliver	15.9
Tip O'Neill	10.5
Paul O'Neill	19.1
Jim O'Rourke	15.3
Dave Orr	13.6
Amos Otis	23.1
Mel Ott	61.4
Rafael Palmeiro	26.5
Dave Parker	21.5
Lance Parrish	12.4
Roger Peckinpaugh	15.0
Terry Pendleton	9.6
Tony Perez	10.1
Johnny Pesky	14.5
Rico Petrocelli	11.2
Fred Pfeffer	22.8
Tony Phillips	10.1
Mike Piazza	36.0
Vada Pinson	12.6
Darrell Porter	13.6
Boog Powell	15.4
Del Pratt	21.7
Jerry Priddy	12.6
Kirby Puckett	32.3
Doug Rader	10.5
Tim Raines	47.9
Manny Ramirez	20.0
Willie Randolph	23.5
Johnny Ray	8.7
Jody Reed	9.2
Pee Wee Reese	14.7
Sam Rice	10.5
Jim Rice	26.4
Hardy Richardson	27.4
Cal Ripken	42.2
Claude Ritchey	8.4
Mickey Rivers	9.0
Phil Rizzuto	16.1
Brooks Robinson	20.1
Frank Robinson	67.6
Jackie Robinson	32.0
Alex Rodriguez	25.3
Ivan Rodriguez	15.1
Scott Rolen	12.2
Johnny Romano	9.8
Pete Rose	21.4
Al Rosen	13.6
Edd Roush	16.3
Babe Ruth	108.9
Jimmy Ryan	13.9
Tim Salmon	23.4
Rey Sanchez	8.4
Ryne Sandberg	36.6
Reggie Sanders	10.1
Ron Santo	40.9
Hank Sauer	8.6
Ray Schalk	8.7
Wally Schang	18.8
Mike Schmidt	79.6
Red Schoendienst	11.4
Ossee Schreckengost	12.0
Mike Scioscia	14.7
Kip Selbach	13.3
Andy Seminick	11.3
Joe Sewell	35.5
Socks Seybold	8.3
Cy Seymour	11.3
Orator Shaffer	13.2

Total Player Rating (alpha.)

Jimmy Sheckard	18.5
Gary Sheffield	27.5
Roy Sievers	12.7
Al Simmons	26.9
Ted Simmons	18.4
Ken Singleton	20.4
George Sisler	24.7
Enos Slaughter	15.8
Roy Smalley	14.2
Reggie Smith	37.5
Elmer Smith	8.2
Red Smith	13.2
Lonnie Smith	11.1
Ozzie Smith	42.4
Duke Snider	24.1
Pop Snyder	8.0
Sammy Sosa	19.0
Tris Speaker	88.2
Stan Spence	14.0
Eddie Stanky	18.4
Willie Stargell	31.6
Rusty Staub	26.4
Harry Steinfeldt	7.9
Vern Stephens	20.7
Riggs Stephenson	12.4
Snuffy Stirnweiss	8.0
George Stone	12.3
Harry Stovey	22.4
Darryl Strawberry	26.5
Jim Sundberg	9.4
Ed Swartwood	11.9
Bill Sweeney	10.0
Danny Tartabull	14.7
Gene Tenace	16.5
Fred Tenney	21.2
Bill Terry	26.1
Frank Thomas	40.7
Roy Thomas	23.6
Jim Thome	17.7
Robby Thompson	13.1
Sam Thompson	30.7
Andy Thornton	11.7
Mike Tiernan	14.3
Joe Tinker	23.4
John Titus	13.0
Joe Torre	19.6
Alan Trammell	23.3
Cecil Travis	10.8
Pie Traynor	19.7
John Valentin	15.3
Jose Valentin	8.5
Elmer Valo	7.9
George Van Haltren	11.8
Andy Van Slyke	21.6
Arky Vaughan	39.7
Greg Vaughn	10.6
Mo Vaughn	8.0
Bobby Veach	16.9
Robin Ventura	20.8
Honus Wagner	81.8
Dixie Walker	10.8
Larry Walker	25.1
Bobby Wallace	35.7
Paul Waner	33.5
John Ward	8.4
Bob Watson	11.6
Al Weis	8.0
Curt Welch	9.6
Billy Werber	9.1
Vic Wertz	11.1
Wes Westrum	9.6
Zack Wheat	25.7
Lou Whitaker	26.3
Devon White	11.0
Deacon White	11.0
Rondell White	9.0
Roy White	20.8
Pinky Whitney	8.2
Bernie Williams	28.6
Billy Williams	30.1
Cy Williams	9.2
Jimmy Williams	15.9
Ken Williams	18.2
Matt Williams	22.6
Ted Williams	83.0
Ned Williamson	11.1
Bump Wills	8.5
Maury Wills	12.2
Hack Wilson	17.9
Dave Winfield	36.9
Jimmy Wolf	11.8
Gene Woodling	7.9
Jimmy Wynn	35.9
Carl Yastrzemski	46.7
Rudy York	11.0
Ross Youngs	11.5
Robin Yount	46.0
Chief Zimmer	15.6
Heinie Zimmerman	10.6
Richie Zisk	12.9

Total Player Rating (by era)

1876-1892

Rank	Player	Rating
1	Roger Connor	43.3
2	Dan Brouthers	42.1
3	Bid McPhee	41.0
4	Jack Glasscock	36.0
5	Cap Anson	32.6
6	Sam Thompson	30.7
7	Buck Ewing	29.6
8	Pete Browning	28.5
9	Fred Dunlap	27.8
10	Hardy Richardson	27.4
11	King Kelly	26.1
12	Fred Pfeffer	22.8
13	Harry Stovey	22.4
14	Charley Jones	19.9
15	Charlie Bennett	19.8
16	Denny Lyons	19.1
17	Jocko Milligan	16.2
18	Paul Hines	15.7
19	George Gore	15.4
20	Jim O'Rourke	15.3
21	Henry Larkin	14.6
22	Fred Carroll	13.6
	Dave Orr	13.6
24	Orator Shaffer	13.2
25	Jack Clements	12.7

1893-1919

Rank	Player	Rating
1	Nap Lajoie	95.5
2	Ty Cobb	92.0
3	Tris Speaker	88.2
4	Honus Wagner	81.8
5	Eddie Collins	73.3
6	George Davis	51.4
7	Bill Dahlen	51.1
8	Ed Delahanty	42.9
9	Joe Jackson	39.0
10	Bobby Wallace	35.7
11	Frank Baker	34.6
12	Sam Crawford	31.3
13	Elmer Flick	30.4
14	Cupid Childs	30.0
15	Heinie Groh	28.1
16	Billy Hamilton	27.4
17	Jesse Burkett	27.0
18	Fred Clarke	26.7
19	Hughie Jennings	26.3
20	Art Fletcher	26.2
21	Sherry Magee	26.0
22	Zack Wheat	25.7
23	Jimmy Collins	24.0
24	Roy Thomas	23.6
25	Joe Tinker	23.4

1920-1941

Rank	Player	Rating
1	Babe Ruth	108.9
2	Rogers Hornsby	82.7
3	Lou Gehrig	68.9
4	Mel Ott	61.4
5	Jimmie Foxx	55.9
6	Charlie Gehringer	45.0
7	Luke Appling	42.4
8	Gabby Hartnett	40.3
9	Joe Cronin	39.9
10	Arky Vaughan	39.7
11	Frankie Frisch	38.6
12	Dave Bancroft	37.5
13	Joe Sewell	35.5
14	Bill Dickey	35.4
15	Bob Johnson	34.9
16	Paul Waner	33.5
17	Harry Heilmann	32.2
18	Mickey Cochrane	31.8
	Billy Herman	31.8
20	Hank Greenberg	31.5
21	Dick Bartell	28.3
22	Stan Hack	28.2
23	Al Simmons	26.9
24	Bill Terry	26.1
25	2 players tied	25.0

Total Player Rating (by era)

1942-1960

Rank	Player	Rating
1	Ted Williams	83.0
2	Mickey Mantle	77.4
3	Stan Musial	71.5
4	Eddie Mathews	52.2
5	Joe DiMaggio	50.2
6	Lou Boudreau	42.5
7	Bobby Doerr	40.5
8	Yogi Berra	37.4
9	Johnny Mize	36.2
10	Richie Ashburn	32.8
11	Jackie Robinson	32.0
12	Joe Gordon	28.8
13	Minnie Minoso	26.0
14	Ralph Kiner	25.9
15	Duke Snider	24.1
16	Larry Doby	22.7
17	Roy Campanella	22.5
	Charlie Keller	22.5
19	Vern Stephens	20.7
20	Bob Elliott	19.6
21	Bill Nicholson	18.7
22	Eddie Stanky	18.4
23	Roy Cullenbine	18.0
	Gil McDougald	18.0
25	Johnny Logan	17.7

1961-1976

Rank	Player	Rating
1	Willie Mays	95.9
2	Hank Aaron	89.1
3	Frank Robinson	67.6
4	Joe Morgan	54.8
5	Carl Yastrzemski	46.7
6	Al Kaline	45.2
7	Roberto Clemente	42.2
8	Ron Santo	40.9
9	Reggie Smith	37.5
10	Willie McCovey	37.3
11	Bill Mazeroski	36.3
12	Dick Allen	35.9
	Jimmy Wynn	35.9
14	Rod Carew	34.2
15	Willie Stargell	31.6
16	Billy Williams	30.1
17	Bobby Bonds	29.6
18	Norm Cash	28.8
19	Harmon Killebrew	27.3
20	Ernie Banks	26.9
21	Rusty Staub	26.4
22	Johnny Bench	25.6
23	Rocky Colavito	25.5
24	Tony Oliva	24.0
25	Amos Otis	23.1

1977-2000

Rank	Player	Rating
1	Barry Bonds	89.4
2	Mike Schmidt	79.6
3	Rickey Henderson	77.0
4	Ken Griffey Jr.	51.6
5	Tim Raines	47.9
6	Robin Yount	46.0
7	Bobby Grich	45.8
8	Tony Gwynn	45.6
9	Jeff Bagwell	45.2
10	Wade Boggs	44.4
11	Ozzie Smith	42.4
12	Reggie Jackson	42.2
	Cal Ripken	42.2
14	Barry Larkin	41.2
15	Frank Thomas	40.7
16	George Brett	40.0
17	Mark McGwire	38.4
18	Dave Winfield	36.9
19	Ryne Sandberg	36.6
20	Mike Piazza	36.0
21	Edgar Martinez	35.7
22	Craig Biggio	35.6
23	Darrell Evans	35.5
24	Keith Hernandez	34.8
25	Albert Belle	34.3

Wins

1	Cy Young	511
2	Walter Johnson	417
3	Grover Alexander	373
	Christy Mathewson	373
5	Warren Spahn	363
6	Jim Galvin	361
	Kid Nichols	361
8	Tim Keefe	342
9	Steve Carlton	329
10	John Clarkson	328
11	Eddie Plank	326
12	Nolan Ryan	324
	Don Sutton	324
14	Phil Niekro	318
15	Gaylord Perry	314
16	Tom Seaver	311
17	Charley Radbourn	309
18	Mickey Welch	307
19	Lefty Grove	300
	Early Wynn	300
21	Tommy John	288
22	Bert Blyleven	287
23	Robin Roberts	286
24	Fergie Jenkins	284
	Tony Mullane	284
26	Jim Kaat	283
27	Red Ruffing	273
28	Burleigh Grimes	270
29	Jim Palmer	268
30	Bob Feller	266
	Eppa Rixey	266
32	Jim McCormick	265
33	Gus Weyhing	264
34	Roger Clemens	260
	Ted Lyons	260
36	Red Faber	254
	Jack Morris	254
38	Carl Hubbell	253
39	Bob Gibson	251
40	Vic Willis	249
41	Jack Quinn	247
42	Joe McGinnity	246
	Amos Rusie	246
44	Dennis Martinez	245
	Jack Powell	245
46	Juan Marichal	243
47	Herb Pennock	241
48	Greg Maddux	240
	Frank Tanana	240
50	Mordecai Brown	239
51	Clark Griffith	237
	Waite Hoyt	237
53	Whitey Ford	236
54	Charlie Buffinton	233
55	Sam Jones	229
	Luis Tiant	229
	Will White	229
58	George Mullin	228
59	Jim Bunning	224
	Catfish Hunter	224
61	Hooks Dauss	223
	Paul Derringer	223
	Mel Harder	223
64	Jerry Koosman	222
65	Joe Niekro	221
66	Jerry Reuss	220
67	Bob Caruthers	218
	Earl Whitehill	218
69	Freddie Fitzsimmons	217
	Mickey Lolich	217
71	Wilbur Cooper	216
	Charlie Hough	216
73	Stan Coveleski	215
	Jim Perry	215
75	Rick Reuschel	214
76	Chief Bender	212
77	Bobo Newsom	211
	Billy Pierce	211
	Bob Welch	211
80	Jesse Haines	210
81	Vida Blue	209
	Eddie Cicotte	209
	Don Drysdale	209
	Milt Pappas	209
85	Tom Glavine	208
	Carl Mays	208
87	Bob Lemon	207
	Hal Newhouser	207
89	Orel Hershiser	204
	Al Orth	204
91	Lew Burdette	203
	Silver King	203
	Jack Stivetts	203
94	Rube Marquard	201
	Charlie Root	201
96	George Uhle	200
97	Jack Chesbro	198
	Bucky Walters	198
99	6 players tied	197

Losses

1	Cy Young	316
2	Jim Galvin	308
3	Nolan Ryan	292
4	Walter Johnson	279
5	Phil Niekro	274
6	Gaylord Perry	265
7	Don Sutton	256
8	Jack Powell	254
9	Eppa Rixey	251
10	Bert Blyleven	250
11	Robin Roberts	245
	Warren Spahn	245
13	Steve Carlton	244
	Early Wynn	244
15	Jim Kaat	237
16	Frank Tanana	236
17	Gus Weyhing	232
18	Tommy John	231
19	Bob Friend	230
	Ted Lyons	230
21	Fergie Jenkins	226
22	Tim Keefe	225
	Red Ruffing	225
24	Bobo Newsom	222
25	Tony Mullane	220
26	Jack Quinn	218
27	Sam Jones	217
28	Charlie Hough	216
29	Jim McCormick	214
30	Red Faber	213
31	Paul Derringer	212
	Chick Fraser	212
	Burleigh Grimes	212
34	Mickey Welch	210
35	Jerry Koosman	209
36	Grover Alexander	208
	Kid Nichols	208
38	Tom Seaver	205
	Vic Willis	205
40	Joe Niekro	204
	Jim Whitney	204
42	George Mullin	196
	Adonis Terry	196
44	Claude Osteen	195
45	Eddie Plank	194
	Charley Radbourn	194
47	Dennis Martinez	193
48	Mickey Lolich	191
	Rick Reuschel	191
	Jerry Reuss	191
	Tom Zachary	191
52	Al Orth	189
53	Christy Mathewson	188
54	Mel Harder	186
	Jack Morris	186
56	Mike Morgan	185
	Earl Whitehill	185
58	Jim Bunning	184
	Joe Bush	184
60	Larry Jackson	183
	Curt Simmons	183
62	Danny Darwin	182
	Hooks Dauss	182
	Waite Hoyt	182
65	Murry Dickson	181
	Dutch Leonard	181
	Rick Wise	181
68	Lee Meadows	180
69	Pink Hawley	179
	Dolf Luque	179
71	John Clarkson	178
	Wilbur Cooper	178
73	Bill Dinneen	177
	Rube Marquard	177
75	Mike Moore	176
76	Red Donahue	175
77	Doyle Alexander	174
	Bob Gibson	174
	Tom Hughes	174
	Jim Perry	174
	Amos Rusie	174
82	Luis Tiant	172
83	Dennis Eckersley	171
	Larry French	171
85	Ted Breitenstein	170
	Camilo Pascual	170
87	Billy Pierce	169
88	Red Ames	167
	Jim Clancy	167
	Bert Cunningham	167
	Red Ehret	167
92	Don Drysdale	166
	Howard Ehmke	166
	Catfish Hunter	166
	George Uhle	166
	Will White	166
97	Mark Baldwin	165
	Bump Hadley	165
	Si Johnson	165
100	4 players tied	164

Winning Percentage

1	Pedro Martinez	.691
2	Dave Foutz	.690
3	Whitey Ford	.690
4	Bob Caruthers	.688
5	Lefty Grove	.680
6	Vic Raschi	.667
7	Larry Corcoran	.665
8	Christy Mathewson	.665
9	Sam Leever	.660
10	Sal Maglie	.657
11	Sandy Koufax	.655
12	Johnny Allen	.654
13	Randy Johnson	.653
14	Ron Guidry	.651
15	Lefty Gomez	.649
16	John Clarkson	.648
17	Mordecai Brown	.648
18	Roger Clemens	.647
19	Mike Mussina	.645
20	Dizzy Dean	.644
21	Grover Alexander	.642
22	Greg Maddux	.640
23	Jim Palmer	.638
24	Kid Nichols	.634
25	Deacon Phillippe	.634
26	Joe McGinnity	.634
27	Dwight Gooden	.634
28	Ed Reulbach	.632
29	Juan Marichal	.631
30	Mort Cooper	.631
31	Allie Reynolds	.630
32	Jesse Tannehill	.627
33	Ray Kremer	.627
34	Firpo Marberry	.627
35	Eddie Plank	.627
36	Tommy Bond	.627
37	Chief Bender	.625
38	Tom Glavine	.625
39	Don Newcombe	.623
40	Nig Cuppy	.623
41	Carl Mays	.623
42	Addie Joss	.623
43	Fred Goldsmith	.622
44	Doc Crandall	.622
45	Carl Hubbell	.622
46	Bob Feller	.621
47	Mel Parnell	.621
48	John Tudor	.619
49	Clark Griffith	.619
50	Bob Lemon	.618
51	Cy Young	.618
52	Urban Shocker	.615
53	Jeff Tesreau	.615
54	Jim Maloney	.615
55	Charley Radbourn	.614
56	John Ward	.614
57	Jimmy Key	.614
58	Lon Warneke	.613
59	David Cone	.613
60	Gary Nolan	.611
61	Ramon Martinez	.611
62	Schoolboy Rowe	.610
63	Carl Erskine	.610
64	Ed Walsh	.607
65	Charlie Ferguson	.607
66	Dave McNally	.607
67	Hooks Wiltse	.607
68	Jack Stivetts	.606
69	Art Nehf	.605
70	Charlie Buffinton	.605
71	Denny Neagle	.603
72	Orval Overall	.603
73	Tim Keefe	.603
74	Tom Seaver	.603
75	Stan Coveleski	.602
76	Preacher Roe	.602
77	Wes Ferrell	.601
78	J.R. Richard	.601
79	David Wells	.601
80	Jack Chesbro	.600
81	Walter Johnson	.599
82	Kevin Brown	.599
83	Herb Pennock	.598
84	Freddie Fitzsimmons	.598
85	Ed Lopat	.597
86	Warren Spahn	.597
87	Rip Sewell	.596
88	Mike Garcia	.594
89	Mickey Welch	.594
90	Jack McDowell	.593
91	Pat Malone	.593
92	Alvin Crowder	.592
93	John Candelaria	.592
94	Harry Brecheen	.591
95	Bob Welch	.591
96	Bret Saberhagen	.591
97	Bob Gibson	.591
98	Dutch Ruether	.591
99	Denny McLain	.590
100	Eddie Rommel	.590

Games

1	Jesse Orosco	1096
2	Dennis Eckersley	1071
3	Hoyt Wilhelm	1070
4	Kent Tekulve	1050
5	Lee Smith	1022
6	Rich Gossage	1002
7	Lindy McDaniel	987
8	Rollie Fingers	944
9	John Franco	940
10	Gene Garber	931
11	Cy Young	906
12	Sparky Lyle	899
13	Jim Kaat	898
14	Paul Assenmacher	884
	Dan Plesac	884
16	Jeff Reardon	880
17	Don McMahon	874
18	Phil Niekro	864
19	Charlie Hough	858
20	Roy Face	848
21	Doug Jones	846
22	Mike Jackson	835
23	Tug McGraw	824
24	Nolan Ryan	807
25	Walter Johnson	802
26	Rick Honeycutt	797
27	Gaylord Perry	777
28	Don Sutton	774
29	Darold Knowles	765
30	Tommy John	760
31	Jack Quinn	756
32	Ron Reed	751
33	Warren Spahn	750
34	Tom Burgmeier	745
	Gary Lavelle	745
36	Willie Hernandez	744
37	Steve Carlton	741
38	Ron Perranoski	737
39	Ron Kline	736
40	Rick Aguilera	732
	Steve Bedrosian	732
42	Clay Carroll	731
43	Randy Myers	728
44	Mike Marshall	723
	Roger McDowell	723
46	Dave Righetti	718
47	Danny Darwin	716
48	Eric Plunk	714
49	Johnny Klippstein	711
50	Greg Minton	710
51	Stu Miller	704
52	Greg Harris	703
53	Joe Niekro	702
54	Bill Campbell	700
	Jeff Montgomery	700
56	Larry Andersen	699
57	Bob McClure	698
58	Jim Galvin	697
59	Grover Alexander	696
	Craig Lefferts	696
61	Bob Miller	694
62	Bert Blyleven	692
	Grant Jackson	692
	Dennis Martinez	692
	Eppa Rixey	692
66	Early Wynn	691
67	Eddie Fisher	690
68	Ted Abernathy	681
69	Mike Stanton	680
70	Robin Roberts	676
71	Waite Hoyt	674
	Dan Quisenberry	674
73	Red Faber	669
74	Dave Giusti	668
75	Fergie Jenkins	664
76	Bruce Sutter	661
77	Tom Seaver	656
78	Paul Lindblad	655
79	Wilbur Wood	651
80	Sam Jones	647
	Dave LaRoche	647
82	Tom Henke	642
83	Dutch Leonard	640
	Gerry Staley	640
85	Dennis Lamp	639
	Diego Segui	639
87	Frank Tanana	638
88	Bob Stanley	637
89	Christy Mathewson	636
90	Charlie Root	632
91	Jim Perry	630
92	Jerry Reuss	628
93	Lew Burdette	626
94	Murry Dickson	625
	Woodie Fryman	625
96	Mark Davis	624
	Red Ruffing	624
98	Eddie Plank	623
99	Kid Nichols	621
100	Dick Tidrow	620

Games Started

1	Cy Young	815
2	Nolan Ryan	773
3	Don Sutton	756
4	Phil Niekro	716
5	Steve Carlton	709
6	Tommy John	700
7	Gaylord Perry	690
8	Bert Blyleven	685
9	Jim Galvin	681
10	Walter Johnson	666
11	Warren Spahn	665
12	Tom Seaver	647
13	Jim Kaat	625
14	Frank Tanana	616
15	Early Wynn	612
16	Robin Roberts	609
17	Grover Alexander	600
18	Fergie Jenkins	594
	Tim Keefe	594
20	Dennis Martinez	562
	Kid Nichols	562
22	Eppa Rixey	554
23	Christy Mathewson	552
24	Mickey Welch	549
25	Jerry Reuss	547
26	Red Ruffing	538
27	Eddie Plank	529
	Rick Reuschel	529
29	Jerry Koosman	527
	Jack Morris	527
31	Jim Palmer	521
32	Jim Bunning	519
33	John Clarkson	518
34	Jack Powell	516
35	Roger Clemens	511
36	Gus Weyhing	505
37	Tony Mullane	504
38	Charley Radbourn	502
39	Joe Niekro	500
40	Bob Friend	497
	Burleigh Grimes	497
42	Mickey Lolich	496
43	Claude Osteen	488
44	Sam Jones	487
45	Jim McCormick	485
46	Bob Feller	484
	Ted Lyons	484
	Luis Tiant	484
49	Red Faber	483
	Bobo Newsom	483
51	Bob Gibson	482
52	Catfish Hunter	476
53	Vida Blue	473
	Earl Whitehill	473
55	Vic Willis	471
56	Greg Maddux	467
57	Orel Hershiser	466
58	Don Drysdale	465
	Milt Pappas	465
60	Doyle Alexander	464
61	Bob Welch	462
62	Curt Simmons	461
63	Mike Torrez	458
64	Lefty Grove	457
	Juan Marichal	457
66	Rick Wise	455
67	Jim Perry	447
68	Paul Derringer	445
69	Jack Quinn	443
70	Charlie Hough	440
	Mike Moore	440
72	Whitey Ford	438
73	Tom Glavine	434
74	Mel Harder	433
	Carl Hubbell	433
76	Billy Pierce	432
77	Larry Jackson	429
78	Mark Langston	428
	George Mullin	428
80	Amos Rusie	427
81	Freddie Fitzsimmons	425
	Waite Hoyt	425
83	Fernando Valenzuela	424
84	Bob Forsch	422
85	Frank Viola	420
86	Herb Pennock	419
87	Chuck Finley	413
	Bob Knepper	413
89	Dave Stieb	412
90	Tom Candiotti	410
	Dwight Gooden	410
	Ken Holtzman	410
	Mike Morgan	410
94	Tom Zachary	408
95	Rube Marquard	407
	Scott Sanderson	407
97	Wilbur Cooper	406
	Lee Meadows	406
	Adonis Terry	406
100	2 players tied	404

Games Started (by era)

1876-1892

1	Jim Galvin	681
2	Tim Keefe	594
3	Mickey Welch	549
4	John Clarkson	518
5	Gus Weyhing	505
6	Tony Mullane	504
7	Charley Radbourn	502
8	Jim McCormick	485
9	Adonis Terry	406
10	Will White	401
11	Charlie Buffinton	396
	Jim Whitney	396
13	Silver King	370
14	Bill Hutchison	346
15	Jack Stivetts	333

1893-1919

1	Cy Young	815
2	Walter Johnson	666
3	Grover Alexander	600
4	Kid Nichols	562
5	Christy Mathewson	552
6	Eddie Plank	529
7	Jack Powell	516
8	Vic Willis	471
9	George Mullin	428
10	Amos Rusie	427
11	Rube Marquard	407
12	Al Orth	394
13	Hooks Dauss	388
	Chick Fraser	388
15	Joe McGinnity	381

1920-1941

1	Eppa Rixey	554
2	Red Ruffing	538
3	Burleigh Grimes	497
4	Sam Jones	487
5	Ted Lyons	484
6	Red Faber	483
	Bobo Newsom	483
8	Earl Whitehill	473
9	Lefty Grove	457
10	Paul Derringer	445
11	Jack Quinn	443
12	Mel Harder	433
	Carl Hubbell	433
14	Freddie Fitzsimmons	425
	Waite Hoyt	425

1942-1960

1	Warren Spahn	665
2	Early Wynn	612
3	Robin Roberts	609
4	Bob Friend	497
5	Bob Feller	484
6	Curt Simmons	461
7	Whitey Ford	438
8	Billy Pierce	432
9	Dutch Leonard	376
10	Hal Newhouser	374
11	Lew Burdette	373
12	Bob Buhl	369
13	Vern Law	364
14	Bob Lemon	350

1961-1976

1	Don Sutton	756
2	Phil Niekro	716
3	Steve Carlton	709
4	Tommy John	700
5	Gaylord Perry	690
6	Tom Seaver	647
7	Jim Kaat	625
8	Fergie Jenkins	594
9	Jerry Koosman	527
10	Jim Palmer	521
11	Jim Bunning	519
12	Mickey Lolich	496
13	Claude Osteen	488
14	Luis Tiant	484
15	Bob Gibson	482

1977-2000

1	Nolan Ryan	773
2	Bert Blyleven	685
3	Frank Tanana	616
4	Dennis Martinez	562
5	Jerry Reuss	547
6	Rick Reuschel	529
7	Jack Morris	527
8	Roger Clemens	511
9	Joe Niekro	500
10	Vida Blue	473
11	Greg Maddux	467
12	Orel Hershiser	466
13	Doyle Alexander	464
14	Bob Welch	462
15	2 players tied	440

Complete Games

1	Cy Young	749
2	Jim Galvin	639
3	Tim Keefe	554
4	Kid Nichols	532
5	Walter Johnson	531
6	Mickey Welch	525
7	Charley Radbourn	488
8	John Clarkson	485
9	Tony Mullane	468
10	Jim McCormick	466
11	Gus Weyhing	449
12	Grover Alexander	437
13	Christy Mathewson	435
14	Jack Powell	422
15	Eddie Plank	410
16	Will White	394
17	Amos Rusie	393
18	Vic Willis	388
19	Warren Spahn	382
20	Jim Whitney	377
21	Adonis Terry	367
22	Ted Lyons	356
23	George Mullin	353
24	Charlie Buffinton	351
25	Chick Fraser	342
26	Clark Griffith	337
27	Red Ruffing	335
28	Silver King	328
29	Al Orth	324
30	Bill Hutchison	321
31	Burleigh Grimes	314
	Joe McGinnity	314
33	Red Donahue	312
	Guy Hecker	312
35	Bill Dinneen	306
36	Robin Roberts	305
37	Gaylord Perry	303
38	Ted Breitenstein	301
39	Bob Caruthers	298
	Lefty Grove	298
41	Pink Hawley	297
	Ed Morris	297
43	Mark Baldwin	295
44	Tommy Bond	294
	Brickyard Kennedy	294
46	Eppa Rixey	290
	Early Wynn	290
48	Bill Donovan	289
	Bobby Mathews	289
50	Bert Cunningham	287
51	Wilbur Cooper	279
	Bob Feller	279
	Sadie McMahon	279
	Jack Taylor	279
55	Jack Stivetts	278
56	Charlie Getzien	277
57	Red Faber	273
58	Mordecai Brown	271
	Frank Dwyer	271
60	Jouett Meekin	270
61	Fergie Jenkins	267
62	Elton Chamberlain	264
	Matt Kilroy	264
	Jesse Tannehill	264
65	Doc White	262
66	Rube Waddell	261
67	Jack Chesbro	260
	Red Ehret	260
	Carl Hubbell	260
70	Larry Corcoran	256
71	Chief Bender	255
	Bob Gibson	255
73	Steve Carlton	254
74	Frank Killen	253
	Win Mercer	253
76	Paul Derringer	251
77	Sam Jones	250
	Ed Walsh	250
79	Eddie Cicotte	249
	Stump Wiedman	249
81	Herb Pennock	247
82	Bobo Newsom	246
83	George Bradley	245
	Hooks Dauss	245
	Phil Niekro	245
	John Ward	245
87	Harry Howell	244
	Juan Marichal	244
89	Jack Quinn	243
90	Bert Blyleven	242
	Deacon Phillippe	242
	Bucky Walters	242
93	Sam Leever	241
94	Kid Gleason	240
95	Addie Joss	234
96	George Uhle	232
97	Carl Mays	231
	Tom Seaver	231
	Harry Staley	231
100	Earl Moore	230

Complete Games (by era)

1876-1892

1	Jim Galvin	639
2	Tim Keefe	554
3	Mickey Welch	525
4	Charley Radbourn	488
5	John Clarkson	485
6	Tony Mullane	468
7	Jim McCormick	466
8	Gus Weyhing	449
9	Will White	394
10	Jim Whitney	377
11	Adonis Terry	367
12	Charlie Buffinton	351
13	Silver King	328
14	Bill Hutchison	321
15	Guy Hecker	312

1893-1919

1	Cy Young	749
2	Kid Nichols	532
3	Walter Johnson	531
4	Grover Alexander	437
5	Christy Mathewson	435
6	Jack Powell	422
7	Eddie Plank	410
8	Amos Rusie	393
9	Vic Willis	388
10	George Mullin	353
11	Chick Fraser	342
12	Clark Griffith	337
13	Al Orth	324
14	Joe McGinnity	314
15	Red Donahue	312

1920-1941

1	Ted Lyons	356
2	Red Ruffing	335
3	Burleigh Grimes	314
4	Lefty Grove	298
5	Eppa Rixey	290
6	Wilbur Cooper	279
7	Red Faber	273
8	Carl Hubbell	260
9	Paul Derringer	251
10	Sam Jones	250
11	Herb Pennock	247
12	Bobo Newsom	246
13	Jack Quinn	243
14	Bucky Walters	242
15	George Uhle	232

1942-1960

1	Warren Spahn	382
2	Robin Roberts	305
3	Early Wynn	290
4	Bob Feller	279
5	Hal Newhouser	212
6	Billy Pierce	193
7	Dutch Leonard	192
8	Bob Lemon	188
9	Ed Lopat	164
10	Bob Friend	163
	Curt Simmons	163
12	Lew Burdette	158
	Dizzy Trout	158
14	Whitey Ford	156
	Jim Tobin	156

1961-1976

1	Gaylord Perry	303
2	Fergie Jenkins	267
3	Bob Gibson	255
4	Steve Carlton	254
5	Phil Niekro	245
6	Juan Marichal	244
7	Tom Seaver	231
8	Jim Palmer	211
9	Mickey Lolich	195
10	Luis Tiant	187
11	Catfish Hunter	181
12	Jim Kaat	180
13	Don Sutton	178
14	Mike Cuellar	172
15	Don Drysdale	167

1977-2000

1	Bert Blyleven	242
2	Nolan Ryan	222
3	Jack Morris	175
4	Vida Blue	143
	Frank Tanana	143
6	Steve Rogers	129
7	Jerry Reuss	127
8	Dennis Martinez	122
9	Roger Clemens	116
10	Fernando Valenzuela	113
11	Charlie Hough	107
	Joe Niekro	107
13	Dennis Leonard	103
	Dave Stieb	103
15	Rick Reuschel	102

Shutouts

Rank	Player	SHO
1	Walter Johnson	110
2	Grover Alexander	90
3	Christy Mathewson	79
4	Cy Young	76
5	Eddie Plank	69
6	Warren Spahn	63
7	Nolan Ryan	61
	Tom Seaver	61
9	Bert Blyleven	60
10	Don Sutton	58
11	Jim Galvin	57
	Ed Walsh	57
13	Bob Gibson	56
14	Mordecai Brown	55
	Steve Carlton	55
16	Jim Palmer	53
	Gaylord Perry	53
18	Juan Marichal	52
19	Rube Waddell	50
	Vic Willis	50
21	Don Drysdale	49
	Fergie Jenkins	49
	Luis Tiant	49
	Early Wynn	49
25	Kid Nichols	48
26	Tommy John	46
	Jack Powell	46
28	Roger Clemens	45
	Whitey Ford	45
	Addie Joss	45
	Phil Niekro	45
	Robin Roberts	45
	Red Ruffing	45
	Doc White	45
35	Babe Adams	44
	Bob Feller	44
37	Milt Pappas	43
38	Catfish Hunter	42
	Bucky Walters	42
40	Mickey Lolich	41
	Hippo Vaughn	41
	Mickey Welch	41
43	Chief Bender	40
	Jim Bunning	40
	Larry French	40
	Sandy Koufax	40
	Claude Osteen	40
	Ed Reulbach	40
	Mel Stottlemyre	40
50	Tim Keefe	39
	Sam Leever	39
	Jerry Reuss	39
53	Stan Coveleski	38
	Billy Pierce	38
	Nap Rucker	38
56	Vida Blue	37
	John Clarkson	37
	Larry Jackson	37
	Eppa Rixey	37
	Steve Rogers	37
61	Mike Cuellar	36
	Bob Friend	36
	Carl Hubbell	36
	Sam Jones	36
	Camilo Pascual	36
	Allie Reynolds	36
	Curt Simmons	36
	Will White	36
69	Tommy Bond	35
	Joe Bush	35
	Jack Chesbro	35
	Eddie Cicotte	35
	Jack Coombs	35
	Wilbur Cooper	35
	Bill Donovan	35
	Burleigh Grimes	35
	Lefty Grove	35
	George Mullin	35
	Herb Pennock	35
	Charley Radbourn	35
81	Bill Doak	34
	Earl Moore	34
	Frank Tanana	34
	Jesse Tannehill	34
85	Tommy Bridges	33
	Lew Burdette	33
	Dean Chance	33
	Mort Cooper	33
	Jerry Koosman	33
	Dutch Leonard	33
	Jim McCormick	33
	Dave McNally	33
	Hal Newhouser	33
	Bob Shawkey	33
	Virgil Trucks	33
96	Paul Derringer	32
	Lefty Leifield	32
	Joe McGinnity	32
	Jim Perry	32
100	8 players tied	31

Saves

Rank	Player	SV
1	Lee Smith	478
2	John Franco	420
3	Dennis Eckersley	390
4	Jeff Reardon	367
5	Randy Myers	347
6	Rollie Fingers	341
7	John Wetteland	330
8	Rick Aguilera	318
9	Tom Henke	311
10	Rich Gossage	310
11	Jeff Montgomery	304
12	Doug Jones	303
13	Bruce Sutter	300
14	Trevor Hoffman	271
15	Roberto Hernandez	266
16	Rod Beck	260
17	Todd Worrell	256
18	Dave Righetti	252
19	Dan Quisenberry	244
20	Sparky Lyle	238
21	Hoyt Wilhelm	227
22	Robb Nen	226
23	Gene Garber	218
24	Gregg Olson	217
25	Dave Smith	216
26	Bobby Thigpen	201
27	Roy Face	193
	Mike Henneman	193
29	Mitch Williams	192
30	Mike Marshall	188
31	Jeff Russell	186
32	Steve Bedrosian	184
	Kent Tekulve	184
34	Tug McGraw	180
35	Ron Perranoski	179
36	Bryan Harvey	177
37	Jeff Brantley	172
	Lindy McDaniel	172
39	Troy Percival	171
40	Todd Jones	170
41	Mariano Rivera	165
42	Jeff Shaw	160
43	Roger McDowell	159
44	Jay Howell	155
45	Stu Miller	154
	Dan Plesac	154
47	Don McMahon	153
48	Greg Minton	150
49	Ted Abernathy	148
50	Willie Hernandez	147
51	Dave Giusti	145
52	Clay Carroll	143
	Darold Knowles	143
54	Jesse Orosco	141
55	Mike Jackson	138
	Jose Mesa	138
57	Gary Lavelle	136
58	Jim Brewer	132
	Steve Farr	132
	Bob Stanley	132
61	Ron Davis	130
62	Terry Forster	127
63	Bill Campbell	126
	Dave LaRoche	126
	Mel Rojas	126
66	John Hiller	125
67	Jack Aker	123
68	Dick Radatz	122
69	Duane Ward	121
70	Tippy Martinez	115
71	Mark Wohlers	112
72	Ricky Bottalico	111
	Frank Linzy	111
	Mike Timlin	111
75	Ugueth Urbina	110
	Al Worthington	110
77	Fred Gladding	109
78	Wayne Granger	108
	Ron Kline	108
80	Johnny Murphy	107
	Billy Wagner	107
82	Bill Caudill	106
83	Bob Wickman	104
84	Ron Reed	103
	John Wyatt	103
86	Tom Burgmeier	102
	Tim Burke	102
	Ellis Kinder	102
89	Craig Lefferts	101
	Firpo Marberry	101
91	Armando Benitez	100
	Billy Taylor	100
93	Joe Hoerner	99
94	Mike Schooler	98
	Heathcliff Slocumb	98
96	Al Hrabosky	97
	Tom Niedenfuer	97
98	4 players tied	96

Innings Pitched

Rank	Player	IP
1	Cy Young	7356.0
2	Jim Galvin	5941.1
3	Walter Johnson	5914.1
4	Phil Niekro	5404.1
5	Nolan Ryan	5386.0
6	Gaylord Perry	5350.1
7	Don Sutton	5282.1
8	Warren Spahn	5243.2
9	Steve Carlton	5217.1
10	Grover Alexander	5190.0
11	Kid Nichols	5066.1
12	Tim Keefe	5049.2
13	Bert Blyleven	4970.0
14	Mickey Welch	4802.0
15	Christy Mathewson	4788.2
16	Tom Seaver	4782.2
17	Tommy John	4710.1
18	Robin Roberts	4688.2
19	Early Wynn	4564.0
20	John Clarkson	4536.1
21	Tony Mullane	4531.1
22	Jim Kaat	4530.1
23	Charley Radbourn	4527.1
24	Fergie Jenkins	4500.2
25	Eddie Plank	4495.2
26	Eppa Rixey	4494.2
27	Jack Powell	4389.0
28	Red Ruffing	4344.0
29	Gus Weyhing	4337.1
30	Jim McCormick	4275.2
31	Frank Tanana	4188.1
32	Burleigh Grimes	4179.2
33	Ted Lyons	4161.0
34	Red Faber	4086.2
35	Dennis Martinez	3999.2
36	Vic Willis	3996.0
37	Jim Palmer	3948.0
38	Lefty Grove	3940.2
39	Jack Quinn	3920.1
40	Bob Gibson	3884.1
41	Sam Jones	3883.0
42	Jerry Koosman	3839.1
43	Bob Feller	3827.0
44	Jack Morris	3824.0
45	Charlie Hough	3801.1
46	Amos Rusie	3778.2
47	Waite Hoyt	3762.1
48	Jim Bunning	3760.1
49	Bobo Newsom	3759.1
50	George Mullin	3686.2
51	Jerry Reuss	3669.2
52	Roger Clemens	3666.2
53	Paul Derringer	3645.0
54	Mickey Lolich	3638.1
55	Bob Friend	3611.0
56	Carl Hubbell	3590.1
57	Joe Niekro	3584.0
58	Herb Pennock	3571.2
59	Earl Whitehill	3564.2
60	Rick Reuschel	3548.1
61	Will White	3542.2
62	Adonis Terry	3514.1
63	Juan Marichal	3507.1
64	Jim Whitney	3496.1
65	Luis Tiant	3486.1
66	Wilbur Cooper	3480.0
67	Claude Osteen	3460.1
68	Catfish Hunter	3449.1
69	Joe McGinnity	3441.1
70	Don Drysdale	3432.0
71	Mel Harder	3426.1
72	Charlie Buffinton	3404.0
73	Hooks Dauss	3390.2
74	Clark Griffith	3385.2
75	Doyle Alexander	3367.2
76	Chick Fraser	3364.0
77	Al Orth	3354.2
78	Curt Simmons	3348.1
79	Vida Blue	3343.1
80	Greg Maddux	3318.0
81	Rube Marquard	3306.2
	Billy Pierce	3306.2
83	Dennis Eckersley	3285.2
	Jim Perry	3285.2
85	Larry Jackson	3262.2
86	Eddie Cicotte	3226.0
87	Freddie Fitzsimmons	3223.2
88	Dolf Luque	3220.1
89	Dutch Leonard	3218.1
90	Jesse Haines	3208.2
91	Red Ames	3198.0
92	Charlie Root	3197.1
93	Milt Pappas	3186.0
94	Silver King	3180.2
95	Mordecai Brown	3172.1
96	Whitey Ford	3170.1
97	Lee Meadows	3160.2
98	Larry French	3152.0
99	Orel Hershiser	3130.1
100	Rick Wise	3127.0

Innings Pitched (by era)

1876-1892

Rank	Player	IP
1	Jim Galvin	5941.1
2	Tim Keefe	5049.2
3	Mickey Welch	4802.0
4	John Clarkson	4536.1
5	Tony Mullane	4531.1
6	Charley Radbourn	4527.1
7	Gus Weyhing	4337.1
8	Jim McCormick	4275.2
9	Will White	3542.2
10	Adonis Terry	3514.1
11	Jim Whitney	3496.1
12	Charlie Buffinton	3404.0
13	Silver King	3180.2
14	Bill Hutchison	3079.2
15	Guy Hecker	2924.0

1893-1919

Rank	Player	IP
1	Cy Young	7356.0
2	Walter Johnson	5914.1
3	Grover Alexander	5190.0
4	Kid Nichols	5066.1
5	Christy Mathewson	4788.2
6	Eddie Plank	4495.2
7	Jack Powell	4389.0
8	Vic Willis	3996.0
9	Amos Rusie	3778.2
10	George Mullin	3686.2
11	Joe McGinnity	3441.1
12	Hooks Dauss	3390.2
13	Clark Griffith	3385.2
14	Chick Fraser	3364.0
15	Al Orth	3354.2

1920-1941

Rank	Player	IP
1	Eppa Rixey	4494.2
2	Red Ruffing	4344.0
3	Burleigh Grimes	4179.2
4	Ted Lyons	4161.0
5	Red Faber	4086.2
6	Lefty Grove	3940.2
7	Jack Quinn	3920.1
8	Sam Jones	3883.0
9	Waite Hoyt	3762.1
10	Bobo Newsom	3759.1
11	Paul Derringer	3645.0
12	Carl Hubbell	3590.1
13	Herb Pennock	3571.2
14	Earl Whitehill	3564.2
15	Wilbur Cooper	3480.0

1942-1960

Rank	Player	IP
1	Warren Spahn	5243.2
2	Robin Roberts	4688.2
3	Early Wynn	4564.0
4	Bob Feller	3827.0
5	Bob Friend	3611.0
6	Curt Simmons	3348.1
7	Billy Pierce	3306.2
8	Dutch Leonard	3218.1
9	Whitey Ford	3170.1
10	Lew Burdette	3067.1
11	Murry Dickson	3052.1
12	Hal Newhouser	2993.0
13	Bob Lemon	2850.0
14	Dizzy Trout	2725.2
15	Virgil Trucks	2682.1

1961-1976

Rank	Player	IP
1	Phil Niekro	5404.1
2	Gaylord Perry	5350.1
3	Don Sutton	5282.1
4	Steve Carlton	5217.1
5	Tom Seaver	4782.2
6	Tommy John	4710.1
7	Jim Kaat	4530.1
8	Fergie Jenkins	4500.2
9	Jim Palmer	3948.0
10	Bob Gibson	3884.1
11	Jerry Koosman	3839.1
12	Jim Bunning	3760.1
13	Mickey Lolich	3638.1
14	Juan Marichal	3507.1
15	Luis Tiant	3486.1

1977-2000

Rank	Player	IP
1	Nolan Ryan	5386.0
2	Bert Blyleven	4970.0
3	Frank Tanana	4188.1
4	Dennis Martinez	3999.2
5	Jack Morris	3824.0
6	Charlie Hough	3801.1
7	Jerry Reuss	3669.2
8	Roger Clemens	3666.2
9	Joe Niekro	3584.0
10	Rick Reuschel	3548.1
11	Doyle Alexander	3367.2
12	Vida Blue	3343.1
13	Greg Maddux	3318.0
14	Dennis Eckersley	3285.2
15	Orel Hershiser	3130.1

Hits per Game

1	Nolan Ryan	6.56
2	Pedro Martinez	6.73
3	Sandy Koufax	6.79
4	Sid Fernandez	6.85
5	J.R. Richard	6.88
6	Andy Messersmith	6.94
7	Randy Johnson	6.96
8	Hoyt Wilhelm	7.01
9	Sam McDowell	7.03
10	Ed Walsh	7.12
11	Bob Turley	7.18
12	Orval Overall	7.22
13	Jeff Tesreau	7.24
14	Ed Reulbach	7.24
15	Mario Soto	7.26
16	Addie Joss	7.30
17	Jose DeLeon	7.38
18	Jim Maloney	7.39
19	Rich Gossage	7.45
20	Tom Seaver	7.47
21	Walter Johnson	7.48
22	Rube Waddell	7.48
23	Bob Gibson	7.60
24	Roger Clemens	7.61
25	Don Wilson	7.61
26	Jim Palmer	7.63
27	David Cone	7.66
28	Larry Cheney	7.68
29	Mordecai Brown	7.68
30	Sam Jones	7.68
31	Bob Feller	7.69
32	Johnny Vander Meer	7.69
33	Catfish Hunter	7.72
34	Al Downing	7.72
35	Jim Scott	7.73
36	Charlie Hough	7.77
37	Bobby Bolin	7.79
38	Stan Williams	7.79
39	Rollie Fingers	7.80
40	John Smoltz	7.80
41	Dean Chance	7.81
42	Frank Smith	7.82
43	Tug McGraw	7.83
44	Barney Pelty	7.84
45	Whitey Ford	7.85
46	Denny McLain	7.85
47	Al Leiter	7.86
48	Bob Veale	7.87
49	Chief Bender	7.89
50	George McQuillan	7.89
51	Jack Coombs	7.89
52	Moe Drabowsky	7.90
53	Vida Blue	7.91
54	Nap Rucker	7.92
55	Allie Reynolds	7.92
56	Eddie Plank	7.92
57	Christy Mathewson	7.94
58	Luis Tiant	7.94
59	Rudy May	7.94
60	Ray Culp	7.95
61	Curt Schilling	7.98
62	Bill Donovan	7.99
63	Howie Camnitz	7.99
64	Don Sutton	7.99
65	Juan Pizarro	7.99
66	Dave Stieb	7.99
67	Gary Bell	8.01
68	Ramon Martinez	8.02
69	Earl Moore	8.02
70	Sonny Siebert	8.03
71	Lefty Tyler	8.03
72	Hal Newhouser	8.04
73	Claude Hendrix	8.06
74	Steve Carlton	8.06
75	Hooks Wiltse	8.06
76	Amos Rusie	8.07
77	Jose Rijo	8.07
78	Willie Mitchell	8.07
79	Bill Singer	8.08
80	Bob Lemon	8.08
81	Eddie Cicotte	8.08
82	Mike Scott	8.08
83	Stu Miller	8.09
84	Don Drysdale	8.09
85	Gary Nolan	8.09
86	Juan Marichal	8.09
87	Greg Maddux	8.10
88	Tim Keefe	8.10
89	Doc White	8.10
90	Virgil Trucks	8.11
91	Hippo Vaughn	8.11
92	Blue Moon Odom	8.12
93	Kirby Higbe	8.13
94	Jim Shaw	8.13
95	Mike Cuellar	8.13
96	Billy Pierce	8.14
97	Mort Cooper	8.15
98	Larry Corcoran	8.15
99	Red Ames	8.15
100	Vic Willis	8.16

Home Runs Allowed

1	Robin Roberts	505
2	Fergie Jenkins	484
3	Phil Niekro	482
4	Don Sutton	472
5	Frank Tanana	448
6	Warren Spahn	434
7	Bert Blyleven	430
8	Steve Carlton	414
9	Gaylord Perry	399
10	Jim Kaat	395
11	Jack Morris	389
12	Charlie Hough	383
13	Tom Seaver	380
14	Catfish Hunter	374
15	Jim Bunning	372
	Dennis Martinez	372
17	Dennis Eckersley	347
	Mickey Lolich	347
19	Luis Tiant	346
20	Early Wynn	338
21	Doyle Alexander	324
22	Danny Darwin	321
	Nolan Ryan	321
24	Juan Marichal	320
25	Pedro Ramos	316
26	Mark Langston	311
27	Jim Perry	308
28	Jim Palmer	303
29	Murry Dickson	302
	Tommy John	302
31	Milt Pappas	298
32	Scott Sanderson	297
33	Frank Viola	294
34	Mudcat Grant	292
35	Floyd Bannister	291
	Mike Moore	291
37	Jerry Koosman	290
38	Lew Burdette	289
39	Bob Friend	286
40	Billy Pierce	284
41	Bill Gullickson	282
42	Don Drysdale	280
43	Chuck Finley	277
	Jim Slaton	277
45	Joe Niekro	276
46	David Wells	273
47	Vern Law	268
48	Bob Welch	267
49	Tim Belcher	264
	Dave Stewart	264
51	Vida Blue	263
52	Mike Morgan	261
	Rick Wise	261
54	Roger Clemens	260
55	Larry Jackson	259
56	Bruce Hurst	258
57	Bob Gibson	257
58	Mike McCormick	256
	Camilo Pascual	256
60	Curt Simmons	255
61	Jimmy Key	254
	Red Ruffing	254
63	Don Newcombe	252
64	Mike Flanagan	251
65	Tom Candiotti	250
66	Andy Benes	249
	Ken Holtzman	249
	Claude Osteen	249
69	Steve Renko	248
70	Doug Drabek	246
	Bobby Witt	246
72	John Candelaria	245
	Jerry Reuss	245
74	Jim Clancy	244
75	Jamie Moyer	243
76	Denny McLain	242
	Johnny Podres	242
	Todd Stottlemyre	242
79	Greg Swindell	241
80	Harvey Haddix	240
	Ray Sadecki	240
82	Ron Darling	239
83	Bob Buhl	238
84	David Cone	237
85	Tom Browning	236
	Rick Sutcliffe	236
	Kevin Tapani	236
	Earl Wilson	236
89	Orel Hershiser	235
	Scott McGregor	235
91	Joe Coleman	233
	Jim Lonborg	233
93	Kevin Gross	230
	Dave McNally	230
95	Whitey Ford	228
	Bob Knepper	228
97	Carl Hubbell	227
98	Ron Guidry	226
	Fernando Valenzuela	226
100	3 players tied	225

Home Runs Allowed (by era)

1876-1892

1	John Clarkson	161
2	Jack Stivetts	131
3	Jim Galvin	122
4	Gus Weyhing	120
5	Charley Radbourn	117
6	Mickey Welch	106
7	Bill Hutchison	104
8	Tony Mullane	98
9	Charlie Getzien	95
10	Harry Staley	92
11	Charlie Buffinton	87
12	Jim McCormick	84
13	Mark Baldwin	82
14	Jim Whitney	79
15	Adonis Terry	76

1893-1919

1	Grover Alexander	164
2	Kid Nichols	156
3	Cy Young	138
4	Jack Powell	110
5	Frank Dwyer	109
6	Rube Marquard	107
7	Walter Johnson	97
8	Brickyard Kennedy	94
9	Christy Mathewson	89
10	Hooks Dauss	87
11	Ad Gumbert	81
12	Kid Carsey	80
13	Ted Breitenstein	79
14	Bill Dinneen	78
15	Clark Griffith	76

1920-1941

1	Red Ruffing	254
2	Carl Hubbell	227
3	Ted Lyons	223
4	Bobo Newsom	206
5	Earl Whitehill	192
6	Charlie Root	187
7	Freddie Fitzsimmons	186
8	Tommy Bridges	181
9	Lon Warneke	175
10	George Blaeholder	173
11	Syl Johnson	172
12	Bump Hadley	167
13	Jesse Haines	165
14	Larry French	164
15	Rube Walberg	163

1942-1960

1	Robin Roberts	505
2	Warren Spahn	434
3	Early Wynn	338
4	Pedro Ramos	316
5	Murry Dickson	302
6	Lew Burdette	289
7	Bob Friend	286
8	Billy Pierce	284
9	Vern Law	268
10	Curt Simmons	255
11	Don Newcombe	252
12	Johnny Podres	242
13	Harvey Haddix	240
14	Bob Buhl	238
15	Whitey Ford	228

1961-1976

1	Fergie Jenkins	484
2	Phil Niekro	482
3	Don Sutton	472
4	Steve Carlton	414
5	Gaylord Perry	399
6	Jim Kaat	395
7	Tom Seaver	380
8	Catfish Hunter	374
9	Jim Bunning	372
10	Mickey Lolich	347
11	Luis Tiant	346
12	Juan Marichal	320
13	Jim Perry	308
14	Jim Palmer	303
15	Tommy John	302

1977-2000

1	Frank Tanana	448
2	Bert Blyleven	430
3	Jack Morris	389
4	Charlie Hough	383
5	Dennis Martinez	372
6	Dennis Eckersley	347
7	Doyle Alexander	324
8	Danny Darwin	321
	Nolan Ryan	321
10	Mark Langston	311
11	Scott Sanderson	297
12	Frank Viola	294
13	Floyd Bannister	291
	Mike Moore	291
15	Bill Gullickson	282

Walks

1	Nolan Ryan	2795
2	Steve Carlton	1833
3	Phil Niekro	1809
4	Early Wynn	1775
5	Bob Feller	1764
6	Bobo Newsom	1732
7	Amos Rusie	1707
8	Charlie Hough	1665
9	Gus Weyhing	1570
10	Red Ruffing	1541
11	Bump Hadley	1442
12	Warren Spahn	1434
13	Earl Whitehill	1431
14	Tony Mullane	1408
15	Sam Jones	1396
16	Jack Morris	1390
	Tom Seaver	1390
18	Gaylord Perry	1379
19	Mike Torrez	1371
20	Walter Johnson	1363
21	Bobby Witt	1350
22	Don Sutton	1343
23	Chick Fraser	1338
24	Bob Gibson	1336
25	Bert Blyleven	1322
26	Sam McDowell	1312
27	Jim Palmer	1311
28	Mark Baldwin	1307
29	Adonis Terry	1298
30	Mickey Welch	1297
31	Burleigh Grimes	1295
32	Mark Langston	1289
33	Kid Nichols	1272
34	Joe Bush	1263
35	Joe Niekro	1262
36	Allie Reynolds	1261
37	Tommy John	1259
38	Frank Tanana	1255
39	Bob Lemon	1251
40	Hal Newhouser	1249
41	George Mullin	1238
42	Tim Keefe	1233
43	Chuck Finley	1219
44	Cy Young	1217
45	Red Faber	1213
46	Vic Willis	1212
47	Ted Breitenstein	1207
48	Brickyard Kennedy	1203
49	Jerry Koosman	1198
50	Tommy Bridges	1192
51	John Clarkson	1191
52	Lefty Grove	1187
53	Roger Clemens	1186
54	Vida Blue	1185
55	Billy Pierce	1178
56	Dennis Martinez	1165
57	Mike Moore	1156
58	Jack Stivetts	1155
59	Fernando Valenzuela	1151
60	Bill Hutchison	1132
	Johnny Vander Meer	1132
62	Jerry Reuss	1127
63	Ted Lyons	1121
	Bucky Walters	1121
65	Mel Harder	1118
66	Earl Moore	1108
67	Bob Buhl	1105
68	Luis Tiant	1104
69	Mickey Lolich	1099
70	Lefty Gomez	1095
71	Randy Johnson	1089
72	Virgil Trucks	1088
73	Whitey Ford	1086
74	Jim Kaat	1083
75	Eppa Rixey	1082
76	Rick Sutcliffe	1081
77	Eddie Plank	1072
78	Camilo Pascual	1069
79	Bob Turley	1068
80	David Cone	1067
	Hooks Dauss	1067
82	Elton Chamberlain	1065
83	Bert Cunningham	1064
84	Curt Simmons	1063
85	Bill Donovan	1059
86	Murry Dickson	1058
87	Jouett Meekin	1056
88	Vern Kennedy	1049
89	Dizzy Trout	1046
90	Howard Ehmke	1042
91	Wes Ferrell	1040
92	Tommy Byrne	1037
93	Red Ames	1034
	Dave Stewart	1034
	Dave Stieb	1034
	Bob Welch	1034
97	Rube Walberg	1031
98	Jack Powell	1021
99	Bob Shawkey	1018
100	Steve Renko	1010

Fewest Walks per Game

1876-1892

Rank	Player	BB/G
1	Tommy Bond	0.58
2	George Bradley	0.67
3	Terry Larkin	0.71
4	John Ward	0.92
5	Fred Goldsmith	0.96
6	Jim Whitney	1.06
7	Bobby Mathews	1.11
8	Jim Galvin	1.13
9	Will White	1.26
10	Jack Lynch	1.38
11	Guy Hecker	1.51
12	Lee Richmond	1.53
13	Jim McCormick	1.58
14	Jumbo McGinnis	1.65
15	Ed Morris	1.67

1893-1919

Rank	Player	BB/G
1	Deacon Phillippe	1.25
2	Babe Adams	1.29
3	Addie Joss	1.41
4	Cy Young	1.49
5	Jesse Tannehill	1.56
6	Christy Mathewson	1.59
7	Nick Altrock	1.62
8	Grover Alexander	1.65
9	Noodles Hahn	1.69
10	Dick Rudolph	1.77
11	Al Orth	1.77
12	Slim Sallee	1.83
13	Bill Bernhard	1.83
14	Ed Siever	1.86
15	Ed Walsh	1.87

1920-1941

Rank	Player	BB/G
1	Red Lucas	1.61
2	Pete Donohue	1.80
3	Jesse Barnes	1.80
4	Carl Hubbell	1.82
5	Curt Davis	1.85
6	Paul Derringer	1.88
7	Bill Swift	1.93
8	Sherry Smith	1.93
9	Watty Clark	1.97
10	Jack Quinn	1.97
11	Syl Johnson	2.03
12	Dizzy Dean	2.07
13	Art Nehf	2.13
14	Sloppy Thurston	2.15
15	Eppa Rixey	2.17

1942-1960

Rank	Player	BB/G
1	Tiny Bonham	1.67
2	Robin Roberts	1.73
3	Lew Burdette	1.84
4	Ken Raffensberger	1.88
5	Vern Law	2.01
6	Don Newcombe	2.05
7	Dutch Leonard	2.06
8	Hal Brown	2.08
9	Larry Jansen	2.09
10	Bob Purkey	2.17
11	Dick Donovan	2.21
12	Bob Friend	2.23
13	Don Mossi	2.24
14	Preacher Roe	2.37
15	Ed Lopat	2.40

1961-1976

Rank	Player	BB/G
1	Fritz Peterson	1.73
2	Juan Marichal	1.82
3	Fergie Jenkins	1.99
4	Jim Barr	2.04
5	Bill Monbouquette	2.12
6	Ken Johnson	2.14
7	Jim Kaat	2.15
8	Ralph Terry	2.17
9	Gary Nolan	2.22
10	Don Drysdale	2.24
11	Bill Hands	2.27
12	Larry Jackson	2.27
13	Don Sutton	2.29
14	Ron Reed	2.30
15	Rick Wise	2.31

1977-2000

Rank	Player	BB/G
1	Bob Tewksbury	1.45
2	Bret Saberhagen	1.77
3	Greg Maddux	1.99
4	Dennis Eckersley	2.02
5	Greg Swindell	2.05
6	Lary Sorensen	2.08
7	Mike Mussina	2.09
8	David Wells	2.10
9	John Candelaria	2.11
10	Bryn Smith	2.17
11	Scott McGregor	2.18
12	Bill Gullickson	2.19
13	Scott Sanderson	2.20
14	Kevin Tapani	2.21
15	Mike Caldwell	2.23

Strikeouts

Rank	Player	SO
1	Nolan Ryan	5714
2	Steve Carlton	4136
3	Bert Blyleven	3701
4	Tom Seaver	3640
5	Don Sutton	3574
6	Gaylord Perry	3534
7	Walter Johnson	3509
8	Roger Clemens	3504
9	Phil Niekro	3342
10	Fergie Jenkins	3192
11	Bob Gibson	3117
12	Randy Johnson	3040
13	Jim Bunning	2855
14	Mickey Lolich	2832
15	Cy Young	2803
16	Frank Tanana	2773
17	Warren Spahn	2583
18	Bob Feller	2581
19	Tim Keefe	2564
20	Jerry Koosman	2556
21	David Cone	2540
22	Christy Mathewson	2507
23	Don Drysdale	2486
24	Jack Morris	2478
25	Mark Langston	2464
26	Jim Kaat	2461
27	Sam McDowell	2453
28	Luis Tiant	2416
29	Dennis Eckersley	2401
30	Sandy Koufax	2396
31	Charlie Hough	2362
32	Robin Roberts	2357
33	Greg Maddux	2350
34	Chuck Finley	2340
35	Early Wynn	2334
36	Rube Waddell	2316
37	Juan Marichal	2303
38	Dwight Gooden	2293
39	Lefty Grove	2266
40	Eddie Plank	2246
41	Tommy John	2245
42	Jim Palmer	2212
43	Grover Alexander	2198
44	Vida Blue	2175
45	Camilo Pascual	2167
46	Dennis Martinez	2149
47	John Smoltz	2098
48	Bobo Newsom	2082
49	Fernando Valenzuela	2074
50	Dazzy Vance	2045
51	Rick Reuschel	2015
52	Orel Hershiser	2014
53	Catfish Hunter	2012
54	Billy Pierce	1999
55	Red Ruffing	1987
56	John Clarkson	1978
57	Bob Welch	1969
58	Whitey Ford	1956
59	Amos Rusie	1950
60	Danny Darwin	1942
61	Bobby Witt	1924
62	Kevin Brown	1917
63	Jerry Reuss	1907
64	Kid Nichols	1880
65	Andy Benes	1858
66	Mickey Welch	1850
67	Frank Viola	1844
68	Charley Radbourn	1830
69	Pedro Martinez	1818
70	Tom Glavine	1811
71	Tony Mullane	1803
72	Jim Galvin	1799
73	Hal Newhouser	1796
74	Ron Guidry	1778
75	Rudy May	1760
76	Joe Niekro	1747
77	Sid Fernandez	1743
78	Dave Stewart	1741
79	Curt Schilling	1739
80	Ed Walsh	1736
81	Tom Candiotti	1735
82	Bob Friend	1734
83	Joe Coleman	1728
	Milt Pappas	1728
85	Kevin Gross	1727
86	Floyd Bannister	1723
87	Chief Bender	1711
88	Larry Jackson	1709
89	Bret Saberhagen	1705
90	Jim McCormick	1704
91	Bob Veale	1703
92	Red Ames	1702
93	Charlie Buffinton	1700
94	Curt Simmons	1697
95	Bruce Hurst	1689
96	Rick Sutcliffe	1679
97	Carl Hubbell	1677
98	Tommy Bridges	1674
99	John Candelaria	1673
100	Dave Stieb	1669

Strikeouts per Game

Rank	Player	SO/G
1	Randy Johnson	10.95
2	Pedro Martinez	10.38
3	Nolan Ryan	9.55
4	Sandy Koufax	9.28
5	Sam McDowell	8.86
6	Roger Clemens	8.60
7	Sid Fernandez	8.40
8	J.R. Richard	8.37
9	David Cone	8.33
10	Curt Schilling	8.23
11	Bob Veale	7.96
12	Jose Rijo	7.84
13	Tom Gordon	7.83
14	Al Leiter	7.83
15	John Smoltz	7.82
16	Jim Maloney	7.81
17	Jose DeLeon	7.56
18	Mario Soto	7.54
19	Sam Jones	7.54
20	Mark Langston	7.49
21	Jeff Fassero	7.48
22	Rich Gossage	7.47
23	Dwight Gooden	7.37
24	Chuck Finley	7.28
25	Andy Benes	7.27
26	Bob Gibson	7.22
27	Bobby Witt	7.15
28	Steve Carlton	7.13
29	Kevin Appier	7.05
30	Rube Waddell	7.04
31	Mickey Lolich	7.01
32	Pedro Astacio	6.99
33	Darryl Kile	6.99
34	Mike Mussina	6.87
35	Rollie Fingers	6.87
36	Tom Seaver	6.85
37	Jim Bunning	6.83
38	Erik Hanson	6.80
39	Ramon Martinez	6.79
40	Denny Neagle	6.77
41	Juan Pizarro	6.73
42	Bobby Bolin	6.71
43	Bert Blyleven	6.70
44	Ron Guidry	6.69
45	Ray Culp	6.69
46	Stan Williams	6.66
47	Camilo Pascual	6.65
48	Bob Turley	6.65
49	Don Wilson	6.60
50	Tug McGraw	6.59
51	Dennis Eckersley	6.58
52	Denny Lemaster	6.57
53	Andy Messersmith	6.56
54	Todd Stottlemyre	6.53
55	Don Drysdale	6.52
56	Al Downing	6.50
57	Floyd Bannister	6.49
58	Toad Ramsey	6.49
59	Kevin Brown	6.48
60	Mark Gardner	6.47
61	Diego Segui	6.46
62	Dean Chance	6.43
63	Hoyt Wilhelm	6.43
64	Alex Fernandez	6.40
65	Mike Scott	6.39
66	Fergie Jenkins	6.38
67	Greg Maddux	6.37
68	Moe Drabowsky	6.37
69	Fernando Valenzuela	6.37
70	Earl Wilson	6.37
71	Harvey Haddix	6.34
72	Sonny Siebert	6.32
73	Pete Harnisch	6.32
74	Chris Short	6.31
75	Bruce Hurst	6.29
76	Bill Singer	6.27
77	Kevin Gross	6.25
78	Jack McDowell	6.25
79	Luis Tiant	6.24
80	Turk Farrell	6.21
81	Dazzy Vance	6.20
82	Greg Swindell	6.19
83	Stu Miller	6.18
84	Clay Kirby	6.17
85	Gary Bell	6.15
86	David Wells	6.15
87	Gary Peters	6.14
88	Denny McLain	6.12
89	Don Sutton	6.09
90	Mike Krukow	6.07
91	Bob Feller	6.07
92	Ron Darling	6.06
93	John Smiley	6.06
94	Joe Coleman	6.05
95	Fred Norman	6.05
96	Rudy May	6.04
97	Bret Saberhagen	6.02
98	Jerry Koosman	5.99
99	John Candelaria	5.96
100	Frank Tanana	5.96

Ratio

Rank	Player	Ratio
1	Addie Joss	8.9
2	Ed Walsh	9.2
3	John Ward	9.4
4	Pedro Martinez	9.6
	Christy Mathewson	9.6
6	Tommy Bond	9.8
	Mordecai Brown	9.8
8	George Bradley	9.9
	Walter Johnson	9.9
10	Babe Adams	10.0
	Larry Corcoran	10.0
	Sandy Koufax	10.0
	Juan Marichal	10.0
14	Charlie Ferguson	10.1
	Terry Larkin	10.1
	Deacon Phillippe	10.1
17	Grover Alexander	10.2
	Jim McCormick	10.2
	Ed Morris	10.2
	Tom Seaver	10.2
	Will White	10.2
22	Chief Bender	10.3
	Catfish Hunter	10.3
	Tim Keefe	10.3
	Greg Maddux	10.3
	Rube Waddell	10.3
27	Nick Altrock	10.4
	Tiny Bonham	10.4
	Fred Goldsmith	10.4
	Noodles Hahn	10.4
	Fergie Jenkins	10.4
	George McQuillan	10.4
	Gary Nolan	10.4
	Don Sutton	10.4
	Doc White	10.4
	Jim Whitney	10.4
	Hoyt Wilhelm	10.4
	Hooks Wiltse	10.4
	Cy Young	10.4
40	Eddie Cicotte	10.5
	Sid Fernandez	10.5
	Andy Messersmith	10.5
	Eddie Plank	10.5
	Charley Radbourn	10.5
	Dick Rudolph	10.5
	Bret Saberhagen	10.5
	Curt Schilling	10.5
	Jeff Tesreau	10.5
49	Rollie Fingers	10.6
	Carl Hubbell	10.6
	Sam Leever	10.6
	Denny McLain	10.6
	Robin Roberts	10.6
54	Bob Caruthers	10.7
	Jack Chesbro	10.7
	Don Drysdale	10.7
	Dennis Eckersley	10.7
	Ron Guidry	10.7
	Guy Hecker	10.7
	Jumbo McGinnis	10.7
	Mike Mussina	10.7
	Orval Overall	10.7
	Jim Palmer	10.7
	Ed Reulbach	10.7
	Slim Sallee	10.7
	Frank Smith	10.7
	George Winter	10.7
68	John Candelaria	10.8
	Roger Clemens	10.8
	Mike Cuellar	10.8
	Bob Ewing	10.8
	Jim Galvin	10.8
	Barney Pelty	10.8
	Gaylord Perry	10.8
	Nap Rucker	10.8
	Dupee Shaw	10.8
	John Smoltz	10.8
	Mario Soto	10.8
	Warren Spahn	10.8
	Ralph Terry	10.8
81	Harry Brecheen	10.9
	Phil Douglas	10.9
	Eddie Fisher	10.9
	Dave Foutz	10.9
	Bob Gibson	10.9
	Claude Hendrix	10.9
	Fritz Peterson	10.9
	Jim Scott	10.9
	Jack Taylor	10.9
	Luis Tiant	10.9
	Fred Toney	10.9
	John Tudor	10.9
	Carl Weilman	10.9
94	9 players tied	11.0

Earned Run Average

Rank	Player	ERA
1	Ed Walsh	1.82
2	Addie Joss	1.89
3	Mordecai Brown	2.06
4	John Ward	2.10
5	Christy Mathewson	2.13
6	Rube Waddell	2.16
7	Walter Johnson	2.17
8	Orval Overall	2.23
9	Tommy Bond	2.25
10	Ed Reulbach	2.28
	Will White	2.28
12	Jim Scott	2.30
13	Eddie Plank	2.35
14	Larry Corcoran	2.36
15	Eddie Cicotte	2.38
	Ed Killian	2.38
	George McQuillan	2.38
18	Doc White	2.39
19	Nap Rucker	2.42
20	Terry Larkin	2.43
	Jim McCormick	2.43
	Jeff Tesreau	2.43
23	Chief Bender	2.46
24	Sam Leever	2.47
	Lefty Leifield	2.47
	Hooks Wiltse	2.47
27	Bob Ewing	2.49
	Hippo Vaughn	2.49
29	George Bradley	2.50
30	Hoyt Wilhelm	2.52
31	Noodles Hahn	2.55
32	Grover Alexander	2.56
	Slim Sallee	2.56
34	Deacon Phillippe	2.59
	Frank Smith	2.59
36	Ed Siever	2.60
37	Bob Rhoads	2.61
38	Tim Keefe	2.62
39	Red Ames	2.63
	Barney Pelty	2.63
	Vic Willis	2.63
	Cy Young	2.63
43	Claude Hendrix	2.65
	Jack Taylor	2.65
45	Joe McGinnity	2.66
	Dick Rudolph	2.66
47	Nick Altrock	2.67
	Charlie Ferguson	2.67
	Carl Weilman	2.67
50	Jack Chesbro	2.68
	Cy Falkenberg	2.68
	Pedro Martinez	2.68
	Charley Radbourn	2.68
54	Bill Donovan	2.69
	Fred Toney	2.69
56	Larry Cheney	2.70
57	Mickey Welch	2.71
58	Fred Goldsmith	2.73
59	Harry Howell	2.74
60	Howie Camnitz	2.75
	Whitey Ford	2.75
	Dummy Taylor	2.75
63	Babe Adams	2.76
	Sandy Koufax	2.76
	Dutch Leonard	2.76
66	Jeff Pfeffer	2.77
67	Jack Coombs	2.78
	Earl Moore	2.78
69	Phil Douglas	2.80
	Jesse Tannehill	2.80
71	John Clarkson	2.81
72	Ray Fisher	2.82
	Ed Morris	2.82
	George Mullin	2.82
	Tully Sparks	2.82
76	Bob Caruthers	2.83
	Greg Maddux	2.83
78	Dave Foutz	2.84
79	Andy Messersmith	2.86
	Jim Palmer	2.86
	Tom Seaver	2.86
82	Jim Galvin	2.87
	George Winter	2.87
84	Willie Mitchell	2.88
85	Wilbur Cooper	2.89
	Stan Coveleski	2.89
	Juan Marichal	2.89
88	Rollie Fingers	2.90
89	Bob Gibson	2.91
90	Harry Brecheen	2.92
	Dean Chance	2.92
	Doc Crandall	2.92
	Carl Mays	2.92
94	Dave Davenport	2.93
	Guy Hecker	2.93
96	Don Drysdale	2.95
	Jumbo McGinnis	2.95
	Kid Nichols	2.95
	Lefty Tyler	2.95
100	Charlie Buffinton	2.96

Earned Run Average (by era)

1876-1892

Rank	Player	ERA
1	John Ward	2.10
2	Tommy Bond	2.25
3	Will White	2.28
4	Larry Corcoran	2.36
5	Terry Larkin	2.43
	Jim McCormick	2.43
7	George Bradley	2.50
8	Tim Keefe	2.62
9	Charlie Ferguson	2.67
10	Charley Radbourn	2.68
11	Mickey Welch	2.71
12	Fred Goldsmith	2.73
13	John Clarkson	2.81
14	Ed Morris	2.82
15	Bob Caruthers	2.83

1893-1919

Rank	Player	ERA
1	Ed Walsh	1.82
2	Addie Joss	1.89
3	Mordecai Brown	2.06
4	Christy Mathewson	2.13
5	Rube Waddell	2.16
6	Walter Johnson	2.17
7	Orval Overall	2.23
8	Ed Reulbach	2.28
9	Jim Scott	2.30
10	Eddie Plank	2.35
11	Eddie Cicotte	2.38
	Ed Killian	2.38
	George McQuillan	2.38
14	Doc White	2.39
15	Nap Rucker	2.42

1920-1941

Rank	Player	ERA
1	Wilbur Cooper	2.89
	Stan Coveleski	2.89
3	Carl Mays	2.92
4	Carl Hubbell	2.98
5	Dizzy Dean	3.02
6	Lefty Grove	3.06
7	Bob Shawkey	3.09
8	Red Faber	3.15
	Eppa Rixey	3.15
10	Urban Shocker	3.17
11	Lon Warneke	3.18
12	Art Nehf	3.20
13	Jesse Barnes	3.22
14	George Mogridge	3.23
15	2 players tied	3.24

1942-1960

Rank	Player	ERA
1	Hoyt Wilhelm	2.52
2	Whitey Ford	2.75
3	Harry Brecheen	2.92
4	Mort Cooper	2.97
5	Max Lanier	3.01
6	Tiny Bonham	3.06
	Hal Newhouser	3.06
8	Warren Spahn	3.09
9	Sal Maglie	3.15
10	Ed Lopat	3.21
11	Bob Lemon	3.23
	Dizzy Trout	3.23
13	Stu Miller	3.24
14	Bob Feller	3.25
	Dutch Leonard	3.25

1961-1976

Rank	Player	ERA
1	Sandy Koufax	2.76
2	Andy Messersmith	2.86
	Jim Palmer	2.86
	Tom Seaver	2.86
5	Juan Marichal	2.89
6	Rollie Fingers	2.90
7	Bob Gibson	2.91
8	Dean Chance	2.92
9	Don Drysdale	2.95
10	Mel Stottlemyre	2.97
11	Bob Veale	3.07
12	Gary Nolan	3.08
13	Joe Horlen	3.11
	Gaylord Perry	3.11
15	2 players tied	3.14

1977-2000

Rank	Player	ERA
1	Pedro Martinez	2.68
2	Greg Maddux	2.83
3	Rich Gossage	3.01
4	Roger Clemens	3.07
5	John Tudor	3.12
6	J.R. Richard	3.15
7	Jose Rijo	3.16
8	Steve Rogers	3.17
9	Randy Johnson	3.19
	Nolan Ryan	3.19
11	Kevin Brown	3.21
12	Vida Blue	3.27
13	Ron Guidry	3.29
14	Bert Blyleven	3.31
15	2 players tied	3.33

Adjusted Earned Run Average

Rank	Player	Adj. ERA
1	Pedro Martinez	168
2	Lefty Grove	148
3	Walter Johnson	147
4	Roger Clemens	146
	Hoyt Wilhelm	146
6	Greg Maddux	145
	Ed Walsh	145
8	Addie Joss	142
9	Kid Nichols	139
10	Randy Johnson	138
	Cy Young	138
12	Mordecai Brown	137
13	Christy Mathewson	136
14	Grover Alexander	135
	Rube Waddell	135
16	John Clarkson	134
17	Harry Brecheen	133
	Whitey Ford	133
	Noodles Hahn	133
20	Sandy Koufax	131
21	Kevin Brown	130
	Dizzy Dean	130
	Carl Hubbell	130
	Mike Mussina	130
	Hal Newhouser	130
	Amos Rusie	130
27	Stan Coveleski	128
28	Nig Cuppy	127
	Bob Gibson	127
	Sal Maglie	127
	Tom Seaver	127
32	Kevin Appier	126
	Tommy Bridges	126
	Rich Gossage	126
	Tim Keefe	126
	Bret Saberhagen	126
37	Lefty Gomez	125
	Max Lanier	125
	Jim Palmer	125
	Mel Parnell	125
	Dazzy Vance	125
42	Dave Foutz	124
	Urban Shocker	124
	Dizzy Trout	124
	John Tudor	124
46	Bob Caruthers	123
	Eddie Cicotte	123
	Mort Cooper	123
	Larry Corcoran	123
	Sam Leever	123
	Orval Overall	123
	Jose Rijo	123
53	David Cone	122
	Bob Feller	122
	Charlie Ferguson	122
	Tom Glavine	122
	Jimmy Key	122
	Silver King	122
	Juan Marichal	122
	Eddie Plank	122
	Ed Reulbach	122
	Eddie Rommel	122
	Curt Schilling	122
	John Smoltz	122
	Dave Stieb	122
66	Don Drysdale	121
	Clark Griffith	121
	Andy Messersmith	121
	Jack Stivetts	121
70	Tiny Bonham	120
	Joe McGinnity	120
	Deacon Phillippe	120
	Charley Radbourn	120
	Jim Scott	120
	Hippo Vaughn	120
	Will White	120
77	Dean Chance	119
	Red Faber	119
	Rollie Fingers	119
	Ron Guidry	119
	Thornton Lee	119
	Bob Lemon	119
	Dutch Leonard	119
	Carl Mays	119
	Billy Pierce	119
	Nap Rucker	119
	Bobby Shantz	119
	Lon Warneke	119
89	Babe Adams	118
	Bert Blyleven	118
	Chuck Finley	118
	Ted Lyons	118
	Sadie McMahon	118
	Tony Mullane	118
	Warren Spahn	118
	Bob Stanley	118
	John Ward	118
	Vic Willis	118
99	8 players tied	117

Adjusted ERA (by era)

1876-1892

Rank	Player	Adj. ERA
1	John Clarkson	134
2	Tim Keefe	126
3	Dave Foutz	124
4	Bob Caruthers	123
	Larry Corcoran	123
6	Charlie Ferguson	122
	Silver King	122
8	Jack Stivetts	121
9	Charley Radbourn	120
	Will White	120
11	Sadie McMahon	118
	Tony Mullane	118
	John Ward	118
14	Jim McCormick	117
	Toad Ramsey	117

1893-1919

Rank	Player	Adj. ERA
1	Walter Johnson	147
2	Ed Walsh	145
3	Addie Joss	142
4	Kid Nichols	139
5	Cy Young	138
6	Mordecai Brown	137
7	Christy Mathewson	136
8	Grover Alexander	135
	Rube Waddell	135
10	Noodles Hahn	133
11	Amos Rusie	130
12	Nig Cuppy	127
13	Eddie Cicotte	123
	Sam Leever	123
	Orval Overall	123

1920-1941

Rank	Player	Adj. ERA
1	Lefty Grove	148
2	Dizzy Dean	130
	Carl Hubbell	130
4	Stan Coveleski	128
5	Tommy Bridges	126
6	Lefty Gomez	125
	Dazzy Vance	125
8	Urban Shocker	124
9	Eddie Rommel	122
10	Red Faber	119
	Thornton Lee	119
	Carl Mays	119
	Lon Warneke	119
14	Ted Lyons	118
15	2 players tied	117

1942-1960

Rank	Player	Adj. ERA
1	Hoyt Wilhelm	146
2	Harry Brecheen	133
	Whitey Ford	133
4	Hal Newhouser	130
5	Sal Maglie	127
6	Max Lanier	125
	Mel Parnell	125
8	Dizzy Trout	124
9	Mort Cooper	123
10	Bob Feller	122
11	Tiny Bonham	120
12	Bob Lemon	119
	Dutch Leonard	119
	Billy Pierce	119
	Bobby Shantz	119

1961-1976

Rank	Player	Adj. ERA
1	Sandy Koufax	131
2	Bob Gibson	127
	Tom Seaver	127
4	Jim Palmer	125
5	Juan Marichal	122
6	Don Drysdale	121
	Andy Messersmith	121
8	Dean Chance	119
	Rollie Fingers	119
10	Gaylord Perry	117
11	Tug McGraw	116
	Gary Nolan	116
13	4 players tied	115

1977-2000

Rank	Player	Adj. ERA
1	Pedro Martinez	168
2	Roger Clemens	146
3	Greg Maddux	145
4	Randy Johnson	138
5	Kevin Brown	130
	Mike Mussina	130
7	Kevin Appier	126
	Rich Gossage	126
	Bret Saberhagen	126
10	John Tudor	124
11	Jose Rijo	123
12	6 players tied	122

Pitching Runs

Rank	Player	Runs
1	Cy Young	753
2	Walter Johnson	706
3	Lefty Grove	595
4	Kid Nichols	534
5	Roger Clemens	529
6	Grover Alexander	484
7	Warren Spahn	470
8	Greg Maddux	436
9	Tom Seaver	422
10	Christy Mathewson	421
11	Amos Rusie	418
12	Tim Keefe	405
13	Carl Hubbell	394
14	Whitey Ford	386
15	Bob Feller	385
16	Jim Palmer	378
17	John Clarkson	371
18	Randy Johnson	329
19	Lefty Gomez	322
20	Kevin Brown	319
21	Gaylord Perry	315
22	Nolan Ryan	314
23	Ted Lyons	313
24	Ed Walsh	310
	Hoyt Wilhelm	310
26	Pedro Martinez	309
27	Charley Radbourn	300
28	Red Faber	294
29	Bob Gibson	291
30	Dazzy Vance	281
31	Mordecai Brown	279
32	Bert Blyleven	276
33	Red Ruffing	272
34	Dutch Leonard	267
35	Don Drysdale	266
36	Robin Roberts	264
37	Don Sutton	263
38	Juan Marichal	262
39	Stan Coveleski	259
40	Hal Newhouser	257
	Eddie Plank	257
42	Tommy Bridges	256
43	Bob Lemon	251
	Eppa Rixey	251
45	Billy Pierce	250
46	David Cone	248
47	Dolf Luque	245
	Tony Mullane	245
49	Mike Mussina	244
50	Sandy Koufax	243
51	Steve Carlton	240
	Rube Waddell	240
53	Bret Saberhagen	237
54	Clark Griffith	233
55	Jimmy Key	225
56	Chuck Finley	218
57	Tommy John	217
	Carl Mays	217
59	Addie Joss	216
	Mickey Welch	216
61	Bob Caruthers	214
62	Waite Hoyt	210
	Urban Shocker	210
64	Tom Glavine	209
65	Silver King	205
66	Ron Guidry	204
67	Kevin Appier	203
68	Jim McCormick	202
69	Eddie Cicotte	201
	Dave Stieb	201
71	Nig Cuppy	200
72	Will White	198
73	Phil Niekro	196
74	Harry Brecheen	194
75	Mel Harder	190
76	Lon Warneke	188
77	Dizzy Dean	187
78	Ed Lopat	186
	Joe McGinnity	186
80	Orel Hershiser	181
81	Jim Bunning	179
	Ed Morris	179
	Eddie Rommel	179
84	Larry French	178
85	Dizzy Trout	177
86	Spud Chandler	176
87	Sam Leever	175
88	Freddie Fitzsimmons	174
	Mike Garcia	174
	Andy Messersmith	174
91	Sadie McMahon	172
	Vic Willis	172
93	John Smoltz	170
	Early Wynn	170
95	Thornton Lee	169
96	Wilbur Cooper	168
	Dennis Eckersley	168
98	Charlie Buffinton	162
99	3 players tied	161

Adjusted Pitching Runs

Rank	Player	Runs
1	Cy Young	801
2	Walter Johnson	680
3	Lefty Grove	628
4	Kid Nichols	621
5	Roger Clemens	561
6	Grover Alexander	512
7	Greg Maddux	460
8	John Clarkson	450
9	Tom Seaver	416
10	Christy Mathewson	408
11	Amos Rusie	391
12	Tim Keefe	382
13	Carl Hubbell	364
14	Warren Spahn	351
15	Randy Johnson	333
16	Whitey Ford	332
17	Jim Palmer	330
18	Bob Gibson	326
19	Bob Feller	316
20	Bert Blyleven	315
	Pedro Martinez	315
22	Gaylord Perry	310
23	Ted Lyons	304
24	Hoyt Wilhelm	295
25	Hal Newhouser	294
26	Kevin Brown	290
27	Phil Niekro	289
28	Tommy Bridges	284
29	Ed Walsh	282
30	Red Faber	277
31	Steve Carlton	275
	Charley Radbourn	275
33	Stan Coveleski	272
34	Mordecai Brown	270
35	Dazzy Vance	269
36	Tony Mullane	267
37	Clark Griffith	259
38	Eddie Plank	255
39	Juan Marichal	251
40	Eppa Rixey	248
41	Lefty Gomez	247
42	Fergie Jenkins	245
	Rube Waddell	245
44	Bret Saberhagen	244
45	Silver King	243
46	Mike Mussina	239
	Robin Roberts	239
48	Don Drysdale	237
49	Dave Stieb	235
50	Nolan Ryan	233
51	Tom Glavine	232
	Billy Pierce	232
53	Dutch Leonard	231
54	Nig Cuppy	230
55	David Cone	229
	Jack Stivetts	229
57	Sandy Koufax	226
58	Urban Shocker	223
59	Dizzy Trout	221
60	Jimmy Key	220
61	Chuck Finley	219
62	Kevin Appier	216
63	Eddie Rommel	210
64	Addie Joss	209
65	Bob Caruthers	208
66	Dolf Luque	207
67	Joe McGinnity	203
68	Harry Brecheen	202
	Bob Lemon	202
	Vic Willis	202
71	Dennis Eckersley	201
72	Jim McCormick	200
73	Dizzy Dean	198
	Mickey Welch	198
75	Eddie Cicotte	196
76	Carl Mays	194
77	John Smoltz	192
78	Jim Bunning	191
79	Wes Ferrell	188
	Lon Warneke	188
81	Tommy John	186
82	Mel Harder	183
83	Sadie McMahon	182
	Red Ruffing	182
	Will White	182
86	Noodles Hahn	180
87	Wilbur Cooper	178
88	Waite Hoyt	177
	Jack Quinn	177
	Rick Reuschel	177
91	Ron Guidry	175
92	Larry French	172
	Thornton Lee	172
94	Sam Leever	170
95	Frank Dwyer	169
96	Luis Tiant	168
97	Bucky Walters	166
98	Virgil Trucks	164
99	Jim Galvin	162
100	2 players tied	161

Pitching Wins

Rank	Player	Wins
1	Walter Johnson	77.1
2	Cy Young	73.2
3	Lefty Grove	58.2
4	Roger Clemens	54.2
5	Grover Alexander	51.7
6	Warren Spahn	49.2
7	Kid Nichols	49.1
8	Greg Maddux	46.4
9	Christy Mathewson	46.1
10	Tom Seaver	45.9
11	Whitey Ford	41.2
12	Jim Palmer	40.9
13	Carl Hubbell	40.4
14	Bob Feller	38.9
15	Tim Keefe	37.5
16	Amos Rusie	37.3
17	Ed Walsh	35.1
18	John Clarkson	34.1
19	Gaylord Perry	33.8
20	Randy Johnson	33.5
21	Nolan Ryan	33.4
22	Kevin Brown	32.6
23	Hoyt Wilhelm	32.4
24	Bob Gibson	31.7
25	Pedro Martinez	31.5
26	Lefty Gomez	31.2
27	Mordecai Brown	30.8
28	Ted Lyons	30.2
29	Red Faber	29.6
30	Bert Blyleven	29.0
31	Don Drysdale	28.6
32	Juan Marichal	28.6
33	Dazzy Vance	27.9
34	Eddie Plank	27.9
35	Don Sutton	27.9
36	Charley Radbourn	27.3
37	Robin Roberts	27.2
38	Dutch Leonard	27.0
39	Hal Newhouser	26.8
40	Stan Coveleski	26.7
41	Rube Waddell	26.1
42	Red Ruffing	26.1
43	Sandy Koufax	26.1
44	Bob Lemon	25.8
45	Billy Pierce	25.7
46	Eppa Rixey	25.7
47	Steve Carlton	25.7
48	David Cone	25.3
49	Tommy Bridges	24.8
50	Addie Joss	24.6
51	Dolf Luque	24.5
52	Bret Saberhagen	24.2
53	Mike Mussina	24.1
54	Tommy John	22.8
55	Jimmy Key	22.5
56	Carl Mays	22.5
57	Eddie Cicotte	22.0
58	Tony Mullane	21.9
59	Tom Glavine	21.6
60	Chuck Finley	21.5
61	Clark Griffith	21.2
62	Urban Shocker	21.1
63	Ron Guidry	21.0
64	Phil Niekro	20.7
65	Dave Stieb	20.6
66	Waite Hoyt	20.5
67	Harry Brecheen	20.3
68	Kevin Appier	20.1
69	Mickey Welch	20.0
70	Lon Warneke	19.4
71	Ed Lopat	19.4
72	Bob Caruthers	19.3
73	Dizzy Dean	19.2
74	Andy Messersmith	19.0
75	Joe McGinnity	18.9
76	Jim Bunning	18.9
77	Jim McCormick	18.8
78	Will White	18.6
79	Orel Hershiser	18.6
80	Spud Chandler	18.4
81	Mel Harder	18.3
82	Dizzy Trout	18.3
83	Sam Leever	18.2
84	Silver King	18.0
85	Vic Willis	17.9
86	Larry French	17.9
87	Mike Garcia	17.8
88	Wilbur Cooper	17.8
89	John Smoltz	17.6
90	Ed Reulbach	17.5
91	Nig Cuppy	17.5
92	Early Wynn	17.4
93	Freddie Fitzsimmons	17.3
94	Eddie Rommel	17.3
95	Dennis Eckersley	17.1
96	Fergie Jenkins	17.1
97	Babe Adams	17.0
98	Thornton Lee	16.7
99	Rich Gossage	16.6
100	Vida Blue	16.5

Adjusted Pitching Wins

Rank	Player	Wins
1	Cy Young	77.9
2	Walter Johnson	74.3
3	Lefty Grove	61.5
4	Roger Clemens	57.5
5	Kid Nichols	57.0
6	Grover Alexander	54.7
7	Greg Maddux	48.9
8	Tom Seaver	45.3
9	Christy Mathewson	44.7
10	John Clarkson	41.3
11	Carl Hubbell	37.3
12	Warren Spahn	36.7
13	Jim Palmer	35.7
14	Bob Gibson	35.5
15	Whitey Ford	35.4
16	Tim Keefe	35.3
17	Amos Rusie	34.8
18	Randy Johnson	33.9
19	Gaylord Perry	33.3
20	Bert Blyleven	33.1
21	Pedro Martinez	32.1
22	Bob Feller	31.9
23	Ed Walsh	31.9
24	Hoyt Wilhelm	30.9
25	Hal Newhouser	30.7
26	Phil Niekro	30.5
27	Mordecai Brown	29.8
28	Kevin Brown	29.7
29	Steve Carlton	29.4
30	Ted Lyons	29.3
31	Stan Coveleski	28.1
32	Red Faber	27.9
33	Eddie Plank	27.7
34	Tommy Bridges	27.5
35	Juan Marichal	27.4
36	Dazzy Vance	26.8
37	Rube Waddell	26.7
38	Fergie Jenkins	26.0
39	Don Drysdale	25.5
40	Eppa Rixey	25.4
41	Charley Radbourn	25.1
42	Bret Saberhagen	25.0
43	Nolan Ryan	24.8
44	Robin Roberts	24.7
45	Sandy Koufax	24.3
46	Dave Stieb	24.1
47	Lefty Gomez	23.9
48	Tom Glavine	23.9
49	Billy Pierce	23.9
50	Tony Mullane	23.8
51	Addie Joss	23.8
52	Mike Mussina	23.6
53	Clark Griffith	23.6
54	Dutch Leonard	23.3
55	David Cone	23.3
56	Dizzy Trout	22.8
57	Urban Shocker	22.4
58	Jimmy Key	22.0
59	Chuck Finley	21.6
60	Eddie Cicotte	21.5
61	Silver King	21.4
62	Kevin Appier	21.3
63	Harry Brecheen	21.2
64	Vic Willis	21.1
65	Bob Lemon	20.7
66	Dolf Luque	20.7
67	Joe McGinnity	20.7
68	Dennis Eckersley	20.5
69	Dizzy Dean	20.3
70	Eddie Rommel	20.3
71	Jim Bunning	20.2
72	Carl Mays	20.1
73	Nig Cuppy	20.1
74	John Smoltz	19.9
75	Jack Stivetts	19.7
76	Tommy John	19.5
77	Lon Warneke	19.4
78	Wilbur Cooper	18.8
79	Bob Caruthers	18.8
80	Rick Reuschel	18.7
81	Jim McCormick	18.6
82	Mickey Welch	18.3
83	Noodles Hahn	18.2
84	Ron Guidry	18.0
85	Luis Tiant	17.9
86	Jack Quinn	17.8
87	Sam Leever	17.7
88	Wes Ferrell	17.7
89	Mel Harder	17.6
90	Red Ruffing	17.5
91	Waite Hoyt	17.3
92	Larry French	17.2
93	Bucky Walters	17.2
94	Will White	17.1
95	Babe Adams	17.0
96	Thornton Lee	16.9
97	Virgil Trucks	16.9
98	Don Sutton	16.7
99	Steve Rogers	16.7
100	Andy Messersmith	16.6

Opponents' Batting Average

Rank	Player	Avg
1	Nolan Ryan	.204
2	Sandy Koufax	.205
3	Pedro Martinez	.206
4	Sid Fernandez	.209
5	Andy Messersmith	.212
	J.R. Richard	.212
7	Randy Johnson	.213
8	Sam McDowell	.215
9	Hoyt Wilhelm	.216
10	Ed Walsh	.218
11	Mario Soto	.220
	Bob Turley	.220
13	Addie Joss	.223
	Orval Overall	.223
	Jeff Tesreau	.223
16	Jose DeLeon	.224
	Jim Maloney	.224
	Ed Reulbach	.224
19	Tom Seaver	.226
20	Larry Corcoran	.227
	Walter Johnson	.227
22	Roger Clemens	.228
	Bob Gibson	.228
	Rich Gossage	.228
	Rube Waddell	.228
	Don Wilson	.228
27	David Cone	.230
	Sam Jones	.230
	Jim Palmer	.230
30	Bobby Bolin	.231
	Bob Feller	.231
	Catfish Hunter	.231
	Tim Keefe	.231
34	Al Downing	.232
	Johnny Vander Meer	.232
	Stan Williams	.232
37	Mordecai Brown	.233
	Charlie Hough	.233
	John Smoltz	.233
40	Dean Chance	.234
	Larry Cheney	.234
	Denny McLain	.234
	Amos Rusie	.234
	John Ward	.234
45	Ray Culp	.235
	Rollie Fingers	.235
	Whitey Ford	.235
48	Moe Drabowsky	.236
	Christy Mathewson	.236
	Don Sutton	.236
	Luis Tiant	.236
	Bob Veale	.236
53	Vida Blue	.237
	Al Leiter	.237
	Juan Marichal	.237
	Tug McGraw	.237
	Juan Pizarro	.237
	Curt Schilling	.237
	Frank Smith	.237
60	Ramon Martinez	.238
	Rudy May	.238
	Allie Reynolds	.238
	Jim Scott	.238
	Sonny Siebert	.238
65	Gary Bell	.239
	Chief Bender	.239
	Bill Donovan	.239
	Don Drysdale	.239
	Charlie Ferguson	.239
	Hal Newhouser	.239
	Gary Nolan	.239
	Barney Pelty	.239
	Eddie Plank	.239
	Dave Stieb	.239
	Will White	.239
76	Steve Carlton	.240
	Mort Cooper	.240
	Ed Morris	.240
	Billy Pierce	.240
	Jose Rijo	.240
	Mike Scott	.240
	Bill Singer	.240
	Virgil Trucks	.240
84	Jack Coombs	.241
	Kirby Higbe	.241
	Bob Lemon	.241
	Greg Maddux	.241
	George McQuillan	.241
	Earl Moore	.241
	Tony Mullane	.241
	Hooks Wiltse	.241
92	Harry Brecheen	.242
	Jim Bunning	.242
	Howie Camnitz	.242
	Lefty Gomez	.242
	Stu Miller	.242
	Doc White	.242
	Earl Wilson	.242
99	13 players tied	.243

Opponents' On-Base Pctg.

Rank	Player	Pct
1	John Ward	.254
2	Addie Joss	.260
3	George Bradley	.262
4	Terry Larkin	.263
5	Larry Corcoran	.264
	Ed Walsh	.264
7	Tommy Bond	.267
8	Will White	.268
9	Charlie Ferguson	.270
10	Pedro Martinez	.271
11	Christy Mathewson	.273
	Ed Morris	.273
13	Jim McCormick	.274
14	Fred Goldsmith	.275
	Tim Keefe	.275
	Jim Whitney	.275
17	Sandy Koufax	.276
18	Mordecai Brown	.278
	Juan Marichal	.278
	Charley Radbourn	.278
21	Walter Johnson	.279
	Dupee Shaw	.279
23	Guy Hecker	.281
	Jumbo McGinnis	.281
25	Deacon Phillippe	.283
26	Babe Adams	.284
	Jim Galvin	.284
28	Bob Caruthers	.285
	Bobby Mathews	.285
	Tom Seaver	.285
31	Dave Foutz	.286
32	Catfish Hunter	.287
	Gary Nolan	.287
	Don Sutton	.287
	Cy Young	.287
36	Grover Alexander	.288
	Sid Fernandez	.288
	Greg Maddux	.288
	Rube Waddell	.288
40	Tiny Bonham	.289
	Henry Boyle	.289
	Noodles Hahn	.289
	Fergie Jenkins	.289
	Jack Lynch	.289
	Andy Messersmith	.289
46	Bret Saberhagen	.290
	Curt Schilling	.290
	Hoyt Wilhelm	.290
	Hooks Wiltse	.290
50	Nick Altrock	.291
	Chief Bender	.291
	John Clarkson	.291
	Carl Hubbell	.291
54	Charlie Buffinton	.292
	Dennis Eckersley	.292
	Denny McLain	.292
	Mickey Welch	.292
	Doc White	.292
59	Sam Leever	.293
	Eddie Plank	.293
	Robin Roberts	.293
62	Don Drysdale	.294
	Ron Guidry	.294
	George McQuillan	.294
	Mike Mussina	.294
66	Roger Clemens	.295
	Rollie Fingers	.295
	Toad Ramsey	.295
	Jeff Tesreau	.295
70	Jim Palmer	.296
	Mario Soto	.296
	Ralph Terry	.296
73	Jack Chesbro	.297
	Eddie Cicotte	.297
	Gaylord Perry	.297
	Frank Smith	.297
	John Smoltz	.297
	Warren Spahn	.297
	Jack Taylor	.297
	George Winter	.297
81	Harry Brecheen	.298
	John Candelaria	.298
	Dizzy Dean	.298
	Tony Mullane	.298
	Orval Overall	.298
	Lee Richmond	.298
	Dick Rudolph	.298
	Luis Tiant	.298
89	Jim Bunning	.299
	Mike Cuellar	.299
	Eddie Fisher	.299
	Bob Gibson	.299
	Don Mossi	.299
	Don Newcombe	.299
	Ed Reulbach	.299
	Slim Sallee	.299
97	5 players tied	.300

Wins Above Team

Rank	Player	Wins
1	Cy Young	99.7
2	Walter Johnson	90.0
3	Grover Alexander	81.6
4	Christy Mathewson	64.9
5	Lefty Grove	62.9
6	Tom Seaver	58.9
7	Roger Clemens	57.4
8	Jim McCormick	56.3
9	Jim Galvin	54.3
10	Charley Radbourn	52.2
11	Warren Spahn	45.8
12	Clark Griffith	45.6
13	Randy Johnson	45.5
14	Whitey Ford	44.4
15	Will White	43.5
16	Juan Marichal	38.7
17	Greg Maddux	38.0
18	Bob Feller	36.8
	Amos Rusie	36.8
	Mickey Welch	36.8
21	Ted Lyons	36.2
	Phil Niekro	36.2
23	Tony Mullane	35.8
	Eddie Plank	35.8
25	Dwight Gooden	35.3
26	Jesse Tannehill	35.2
27	Charlie Buffinton	35.0
28	Wes Ferrell	34.8
29	Carl Hubbell	34.6
30	Kid Nichols	34.4
31	Mike Mussina	34.0
32	Steve Carlton	33.5
33	Pedro Martinez	33.2
	Dazzy Vance	33.2
35	Jim Devlin	32.5
36	Joe McGinnity	32.4
37	Guy Hecker	31.5
	Ed Walsh	31.5
39	Bob Gibson	31.0
40	Ed Morris	30.8
	Eddie Rommel	30.8
42	Sandy Koufax	30.6
43	Bob Caruthers	30.4
44	Jim Palmer	30.2
	Urban Shocker	30.2
46	Robin Roberts	30.0
47	Sadie McMahon	29.5
48	Fergie Jenkins	29.3
49	Ron Guidry	29.1
50	Mordecai Brown	29.0
51	Tom Glavine	28.9
52	Addie Joss	28.7
53	Kevin Brown	27.8
54	Dizzy Dean	27.6
55	Bobby Mathews	26.7
56	Schoolboy Rowe	26.5
57	Sam Leever	25.7
58	Rip Sewell	25.4
59	Frank Killen	25.1
	Bret Saberhagen	25.1
61	Jack Chesbro	24.8
62	Nap Rucker	24.7
63	Red Lucas	24.5
	Herb Pennock	24.5
65	Russ Ford	24.3
66	John Candelaria	23.9
67	David Cone	23.8
68	Charlie Ferguson	23.6
69	Red Faber	23.5
	Joe Wood	23.5
71	Johnny Allen	23.4
	Chief Bender	23.4
	Ramon Martinez	23.4
74	John Clarkson	23.2
75	Gaylord Perry	23.1
	Rick Reuschel	23.1
77	Noodles Hahn	22.9
	Firpo Marberry	22.9
79	Orel Hershiser	22.7
	Sal Maglie	22.7
81	Gus Weyhing	22.6
82	Tim Keefe	22.5
83	Tommy John	22.2
84	Mark Langston	22.1
85	Carl Mays	21.9
	Bob Welch	21.9
87	Chuck Finley	21.5
88	Burleigh Grimes	21.3
	Claude Passeau	21.3
	Hippo Vaughn	21.3
91	Spud Chandler	21.2
92	Dutch Leonard	21.1
	J.R. Richard	21.1
94	John Tudor	21.0
	George Uhle	21.0
	Bucky Walters	21.0
97	Jim Maloney	20.9
98	Slim Sallee	20.6
99	Vida Blue	20.4
	Hal Newhouser	20.4

Wins Above League

Rank	Player	Wins
1	Cy Young	491.4
2	Walter Johnson	422.3
3	Jim Galvin	349.3
4	Grover Alexander	345.2
5	Kid Nichols	341.5
6	Warren Spahn	340.7
7	Nolan Ryan	332.8
8	Phil Niekro	326.5
9	Christy Mathewson	325.2
10	Gaylord Perry	322.8
11	Tim Keefe	318.8
12	Steve Carlton	315.9
13	Don Sutton	306.7
14	Tom Seaver	303.3
15	Bert Blyleven	301.6
16	John Clarkson	294.3
17	Robin Roberts	290.2
18	Eddie Plank	287.7
19	Early Wynn	283.9
20	Eppa Rixey	283.9
21	Lefty Grove	282.0
22	Fergie Jenkins	281.0
23	Tommy John	279.0
24	Mickey Welch	276.8
25	Charley Radbourn	276.6
26	Tony Mullane	275.8
27	Ted Lyons	274.3
28	Jim Kaat	272.5
29	Red Ruffing	266.5
30	Red Faber	261.4
31	Jack Powell	258.9
32	Roger Clemens	258.5
33	Jim McCormick	258.1
34	Burleigh Grimes	253.1
35	Gus Weyhing	251.3
36	Jack Quinn	250.3
37	Frank Tanana	248.3
38	Vic Willis	248.1
39	Bob Gibson	248.0
40	Bob Feller	245.9
41	Jim Palmer	245.7
42	Amos Rusie	244.8
43	Carl Hubbell	240.8
44	Greg Maddux	236.4
45	Jerry Koosman	230.9
46	Dennis Martinez	229.6
47	Sam Jones	229.0
48	Paul Derringer	228.6
49	Jack Morris	227.9
50	Bobo Newsom	226.9
51	Waite Hoyt	226.8
52	Charlie Hough	226.3
53	Jim Bunning	224.2
54	Bob Friend	223.8
55	Mel Harder	222.1
56	Rick Reuschel	221.2
57	Juan Marichal	219.9
58	Luis Tiant	218.4
59	Wilbur Cooper	215.8
60	Clark Griffith	215.1
61	Joe McGinnity	214.7
62	Will White	214.6
63	Mordecai Brown	214.3
64	Billy Pierce	213.9
65	Don Drysdale	213.0
66	George Mullin	212.7
67	Mickey Lolich	210.2
68	Herb Pennock	209.8
69	Dutch Leonard	209.3
70	Hal Newhouser	209.2
71	Joe Niekro	208.6
72	Dolf Luque	207.2
73	Charlie Buffinton	207.0
74	Stan Coveleski	206.6
75	Whitey Ford	206.4
76	Hooks Dauss	206.0
77	Jerry Reuss	205.1
78	Dennis Eckersley	204.5
79	Larry Jackson	204.0
80	Jim Whitney	202.5
81	Jim Perry	202.4
82	Curt Simmons	202.3
83	Earl Whitehill	202.1
84	Larry French	201.2
85	Claude Osteen	201.2
86	Catfish Hunter	201.0
87	Adonis Terry	200.2
88	Eddie Cicotte	200.0
89	Silver King	198.9
90	Milt Pappas	198.9
91	Al Orth	197.9
92	Tom Zachary	196.7
93	Bucky Walters	196.2
94	Freddie Fitzsimmons	196.2
95	Vida Blue	195.8
96	Dazzy Vance	195.3
97	Rube Waddell	194.7
98	Jesse Haines	194.3
99	Tommy Bridges	193.5
100	Charlie Root	193.5

Relief Games

1	Jesse Orosco	1092
2	Kent Tekulve	1050
3	Hoyt Wilhelm	1018
4	Lee Smith	1016
5	Rich Gossage	965
6	John Franco	940
7	Gene Garber	922
8	Lindy McDaniel	913
9	Rollie Fingers	907
10	Sparky Lyle	899
11	Paul Assenmacher	883
12	Jeff Reardon	880
13	Don McMahon	872
14	Dan Plesac	870
15	Doug Jones	842
16	Mike Jackson	828
17	Roy Face	821
18	Tug McGraw	785
19	Darold Knowles	757
20	Tom Burgmeier	742
	Gary Lavelle	742
22	Ron Perranoski	736
23	Willie Hernandez	733
24	Roger McDowell	721
25	Randy Myers	716
26	Dennis Eckersley	710
27	Clay Carroll	703
	Greg Minton	703
29	Mike Marshall	699
	Jeff Montgomery	699
31	Larry Andersen	698
32	Bill Campbell	691
33	Steve Bedrosian	686
34	Mike Stanton	679
35	Dan Quisenberry	674
36	Eric Plunk	673
37	Bruce Sutter	661
38	Craig Lefferts	651
39	Ted Abernathy	647
40	Rick Aguilera	643
41	Tom Henke	642
42	Dave LaRoche	632
43	Dave Righetti	629
44	Eddie Fisher	627
45	Bob McClure	625
46	Paul Lindblad	623
47	Todd Worrell	617
48	Mitch Williams	616
49	Stu Miller	611
50	Grant Jackson	609

Relief Wins

1	Hoyt Wilhelm	124
2	Lindy McDaniel	119
3	Rich Gossage	115
4	Rollie Fingers	107
5	Sparky Lyle	99
6	Roy Face	96
7	Gene Garber	94
	Kent Tekulve	94
9	Mike Marshall	92
10	Don McMahon	90
11	Tug McGraw	89
12	Clay Carroll	88
13	Bob Stanley	85
14	Jesse Orosco	84
15	John Franco	82
16	Bill Campbell	80
	Gary Lavelle	80
18	Tom Burgmeier	79
	Stu Miller	79
	Ron Perranoski	79
21	Johnny Murphy	73
	Jeff Reardon	73
23	John Hiller	72
24	Mark Clear	71
	Dick Hall	71
	Lee Smith	71
27	Willie Hernandez	70
	Roger McDowell	70
29	Pedro Borbon	69
30	Bruce Sutter	68
31	Doug Jones	66
32	Steve Bedrosian	65
33	Al Hrabosky	64
34	Darold Knowles	63
	Clem Labine	63
	Dave LaRoche	63
	Eric Plunk	63
38	Jim Brewer	62
	Turk Farrell	62
	Eddie Fisher	62
	Grant Jackson	62
	Paul Lindblad	62
	Frank Linzy	62
44	Paul Assenmacher	61
45	Joe Heving	60
46	Johnny Klippstein	59
	Elias Sosa	59
48	Aurelio Lopez	58
	Phil Regan	58
50	4 players tied	57

Relief Losses

1	Gene Garber	108
2	Hoyt Wilhelm	103
3	Rollie Fingers	101
4	Mike Marshall	98
5	Kent Tekulve	90
6	Lindy McDaniel	88
7	Lee Smith	87
8	Rich Gossage	85
9	Roy Face	82
10	Doug Jones	78
11	Jeff Reardon	77
12	Sparky Lyle	76
13	Gary Lavelle	75
14	John Franco	74
	Ron Perranoski	74
16	Jesse Orosco	73
17	Darold Knowles	71
	Bruce Sutter	71
19	Roger McDowell	69
	Tug McGraw	69
21	Stu Miller	67
22	Clay Carroll	66
	Don McMahon	66
24	Bill Campbell	65
25	Greg Minton	62
26	Steve Bedrosian	61
	Bob Stanley	61
28	John Hiller	58
	Dan Plesac	58
30	Mike Jackson	57
	Frank Linzy	57
	Randy Myers	57
33	Mitch Williams	56
34	Willie Hernandez	55
35	Craig Lefferts	54
36	Tom Burgmeier	53
	Ron Davis	53
	Greg Harris	53
	Dave Smith	53
40	Rick Aguilera	52
	Jim Kern	52
	Randy Moffitt	52
	Dave Righetti	52
	Todd Worrell	52
45	Turk Farrell	51
	Eddie Fisher	51
	Dave LaRoche	51
	Jeff Montgomery	51
	Claude Raymond	51
50	3 players tied	50

Relief Innings Pitched

1	Hoyt Wilhelm	1871.0
2	Lindy McDaniel	1694.0
3	Rich Gossage	1556.2
4	Rollie Fingers	1500.1
5	Gene Garber	1452.2
6	Kent Tekulve	1436.2
7	Sparky Lyle	1390.1
8	Tug McGraw	1301.1
9	Don McMahon	1297.0
10	Mike Marshall	1259.1
11	Lee Smith	1252.1
12	Tom Burgmeier	1248.2
13	Roy Face	1212.1
14	Clay Carroll	1204.2
15	Jesse Orosco	1200.0
16	Eddie Fisher	1186.0
17	Bill Campbell	1177.1
18	Ron Perranoski	1170.2
19	Bob Stanley	1157.0
20	Jeff Reardon	1132.1
21	Doug Jones	1097.1
22	John Franco	1097.0
23	Stu Miller	1094.2
24	Greg Minton	1087.1
25	Gary Lavelle	1077.2
26	Darold Knowles	1052.1
27	Paul Lindblad	1043.1
	Dan Quisenberry	1043.1
29	Bruce Sutter	1042.0
30	Johnny Klippstein	1040.2
31	Roger McDowell	1039.2
32	Pedro Borbon	1016.1
33	Willie Hernandez	994.1
34	Bob Miller	992.2
35	Larry Andersen	990.2
36	Mike Jackson	984.0
37	Dave LaRoche	976.0
38	Ted Abernathy	970.0
39	John Hiller	962.2
40	Steve Bedrosian	931.0
41	Greg Harris	923.0
42	Eric Plunk	917.0
43	Elias Sosa	905.0
44	Dale Murray	901.1
45	Doug Bair	889.1
46	Terry Forster	888.0
	Dan Plesac	888.0
48	Craig Lefferts	881.2
49	Bob Locker	879.0
50	Dennis Lamp	876.0

Relief Points

1	Lee Smith	1011
2	John Franco	930
3	Dennis Eckersley	835
4	Jeff Reardon	803
5	Rollie Fingers	795
6	Rich Gossage	765
7	Randy Myers	721
8	John Wetteland	716
9	Rick Aguilera	676
10	Bruce Sutter	665
11	Tom Henke	662
12	Doug Jones	660
13	Jeff Montgomery	649
14	Hoyt Wilhelm	599
15	Sparky Lyle	598
16	Trevor Hoffman	587
17	Roberto Hernandez	572
18	Todd Worrell	560
19	Dan Quisenberry	554
20	Dave Righetti	544
21	Rod Beck	541
22	Gene Garber	516
23	Roy Face	496
24	Lindy McDaniel	494
25	Dave Smith	485
26	Robb Nen	484
27	Gregg Olson	476
28	Tug McGraw	469
29	Kent Tekulve	466
30	Mike Marshall	462
31	Mike Henneman	458
32	Ron Perranoski	442
33	Steve Bedrosian	437
34	Bobby Thigpen	428
35	Don McMahon	420
36	Mitch Williams	418
37	Jeff Russell	406
38	Stu Miller	399
39	Clay Carroll	396
40	Roger McDowell	389
41	Jeff Brantley	380
42	Willie Hernandez	379
43	Jesse Orosco	377
44	Mariano Rivera	376
45	Bob Stanley	373
46	Todd Jones	372
47	Jay Howell	369
48	Dave Giusti	363
	Bryan Harvey	363
50	Ted Abernathy	362

Relief Ranking

1	Hoyt Wilhelm	366
2	Rich Gossage	314
3	John Franco	271
4	John Wetteland	249
5	Lee Smith	219
6	Dan Quisenberry	218
7	Rollie Fingers	215
8	Tom Henke	212
	Roberto Hernandez	212
10	Kent Tekulve	199
11	Doug Jones	190
12	Jesse Orosco	188
13	Sparky Lyle	187
14	Dennis Eckersley	186
15	Mike Marshall	185
16	Mariano Rivera	183
17	John Hiller	179
18	Trevor Hoffman	178
19	Rick Aguilera	175
20	Jeff Montgomery	173
21	Bruce Sutter	172
22	Tug McGraw	162
23	Bob Stanley	156
24	Ron Perranoski	155
25	Ellis Kinder	154
26	Robb Nen	151
27	Gary Lavelle	147
28	Mike Jackson	142
	Lindy McDaniel	142
30	Stu Miller	141
31	Gregg Olson	138
32	Mark Eichhorn	137
	Roy Face	137
34	Gene Garber	132
35	Mike Henneman	130
	Randy Myers	130
	Jeff Reardon	130
38	Clay Carroll	127
39	Dave Righetti	125
40	Bryan Harvey	119
	Jeff Russell	119
42	Willie Hernandez	118
	Dan Plesac	118
44	Dave Smith	117
45	Jeff Shaw	115
46	Lefty Grove	113
47	Johnny Murphy	110
48	Tom Burgmeier	109
	Frank Linzy	109
50	Jim Brewer	108

Relievers' Runs

1	Hoyt Wilhelm	261
2	Rich Gossage	186
3	Rollie Fingers	157
4	John Franco	149
5	Dan Quisenberry	145
6	Jesse Orosco	139
7	Tom Henke	130
	John Wetteland	130
9	Kent Tekulve	129
10	Mark Eichhorn	123
11	Dennis Eckersley	122
	Sparky Lyle	122
13	Doug Jones	120
	Lee Smith	120
15	Roberto Hernandez	118
16	Mariano Rivera	117
17	Mike Jackson	115
18	Tug McGraw	111
19	Jeff Montgomery	104
20	Mike Marshall	102
21	Trevor Hoffman	101
	Ron Perranoski	101
23	Clay Carroll	100
	Gary Lavelle	100
25	John Hiller	99
	Don McMahon	99
27	Stu Miller	96
28	Lindy McDaniel	94
	Bob Stanley	94
30	Bruce Sutter	92
31	Rick Aguilera	91
32	Greg Minton	89
	Dave Smith	89
34	Eric Plunk	88
35	Johnny Murphy	85
36	Jeff Nelson	83
37	Ellis Kinder	82
38	Mike Henneman	81
	Jeff Reardon	81
40	Tom Burgmeier	79
41	Jeff Shaw	78
42	Greg Harris	77
	Robb Nen	77
	Paul Quantrill	77
45	Jeff Russell	76
46	Steve Farr	75
	Willie Hernandez	75
	Jay Howell	75
	Bob Wickman	75
50	Randy Myers	74

Adjusted Relievers' Runs

1	Hoyt Wilhelm	252
2	Rich Gossage	183
3	John Franco	150
4	Dan Quisenberry	147
5	Kent Tekulve	139
6	Lee Smith	136
7	John Wetteland	133
8	Jesse Orosco	132
9	Tom Henke	131
10	Rollie Fingers	129
11	Mark Eichhorn	125
12	Sparky Lyle	121
13	Doug Jones	118
14	Mike Jackson	117
15	Bob Stanley	115
16	Roberto Hernandez	114
	Mariano Rivera	114
18	Tug McGraw	113
19	John Hiller	110
	Jeff Montgomery	110
	Bruce Sutter	110
22	Dennis Eckersley	109
23	Lindy McDaniel	105
24	Mike Marshall	103
25	Clay Carroll	98
26	Gary Lavelle	97
27	Trevor Hoffman	94
28	Rick Aguilera	93
	Ellis Kinder	93
30	Gene Garber	90
31	Greg Harris	88
	Ron Perranoski	88
33	Don McMahon	86
34	Tom Burgmeier	85
	Stu Miller	85
	Eric Plunk	85
37	Willie Hernandez	84
	Jeff Reardon	84
39	Jeff Nelson	81
	Paul Quantrill	81
41	Mike Henneman	80
42	Jeff Russell	79
	Dave Smith	79
44	Greg Minton	78
45	Jeff Shaw	77
46	Steve Farr	76
	Terry Forster	76
48	Ron Reed	73
	Bob Wickman	73
50	3 players tied	72

Clutch Pitching Index

1	Bob Rhoads	117
2	Ed Killian	116
	Ed Siever	116
4	Win Mercer	115
5	Ron Kline	113
	Bill Lee	113
	Will White	113
8	Al Benton	112
	Ed Lopat	112
	Bob Stanley	112
	Tom Zachary	112
12	Whitey Ford	111
	Preacher Roe	111
14	Steve Blass	110
	Frank Dwyer	110
	Max Lanier	110
	Bob Miller	110
	Gerry Staley	110
	Bill Wight	110
20	Bob Buhl	109
	Max Butcher	109
	Dan Casey	109
	Chuck Finley	109
	Lefty Leifield	109
	Sal Maglie	109
	Mel Parnell	109
	Bob Shaw	109
	Geoff Zahn	109
29	Steve Barber	108
	Sheriff Blake	108
	Lefty Grove	108
	Carl Morton	108
	George Mullin	108
	Dizzy Trout	108
	Bob Veale	108
36	Jim Abbott	107
	Mark Baldwin	107
	Nelson Briles	107
	Lloyd Brown	107
	Nixey Callahan	107
	Nig Cuppy	107
	Larry French	107
	Clark Griffith	107
	Claude Osteen	107
	Eddie Rommel	107
	Dutch Ruether	107
	Eddie Smith	107
	Dummy Taylor	107
	Steve Trout	107
	Mickey Welch	107
51	Jim Bagby	106
	Roger Craig	106
	Red Donahue	106
	Red Faber	106
	Dave Foutz	106
	Gene Garber	106
	Mel Harder	106
	Joe Haynes	106
	Guy Hecker	106
	Tommy John	106
	Jim McCormick	106
	Cal McLish	106
	Jeff Pfeffer	106
	Togie Pittinger	106
	Howie Pollet	106
	Nap Rucker	106
	Jim Scott	106
	Sherry Smith	106
	Zane Smith	106
	Bill Swift	106
	Sloppy Thurston	106
	John Tudor	106
	Rube Waddell	106
	Bucky Walters	106
75	30 players tied	105

Pitcher Batting Runs

Rank	Player	Runs
1	Red Ruffing	143
2	Bob Caruthers	111
3	Wes Ferrell	100
4	Walter Johnson	99
5	Red Lucas	98
6	George Uhle	92
7	Guy Hecker	90
	Bob Lemon	90
9	Jim Whitney	89
10	Warren Spahn	88
11	George Mullin	87
12	Don Newcombe	79
13	Babe Ruth	78
14	Schoolboy Rowe	76
15	Early Wynn	72
16	Bob Gibson	65
	Jack Stivetts	65
18	Carl Mays	64
19	Al Orth	63
20	Don Drysdale	60
21	Christy Mathewson	59
22	Gary Peters	57
	Bucky Walters	57
	Earl Wilson	57
25	Doc Crandall	54
	Jesse Tannehill	54
	Jim Tobin	54
28	Ad Gumbert	53
29	Burleigh Grimes	52
30	Claude Hendrix	50
	Tony Mullane	50
32	Joe Bush	49
	Steve Carlton	49
	Charlie Ferguson	49
35	Bob Forsch	48
	Scott Stratton	48
37	Don Larsen	46
38	Dave Foutz	45
	Vern Law	45
	Rick Rhoden	45
	Dutch Ruether	45
	Adonis Terry	45
43	Frank Killen	44
	Jack Scott	44
45	Tommy Byrne	41
	Jim Kaat	41
	Don Robinson	41
48	Johnny Sain	40
49	Wilbur Cooper	39
	Fred Hutchinson	39
	Charley Radbourn	39
52	Claude Osteen	38
	Sloppy Thurston	38
54	Dolf Luque	37
	Doc White	37
56	Jack Coombs	36
	Mickey McDermott	36
58	Clark Griffith	35
	Harvey Haddix	35
	Win Mercer	35
	Frank Smith	35
62	Art Nehf	34
	Robin Roberts	34
	Jack Taylor	34
	Rick Wise	34
66	Chief Bender	33
	Erv Brame	33
	Ken Brett	33
	Orel Hershiser	33
	Catfish Hunter	33
	Ben Sanders	33
72	Hooks Dauss	32
	Ted Lyons	32
	Al Maul	32
	Fernando Valenzuela	32
76	Ray Caldwell	31
	Dizzy Trout	31
	John Ward	31
	Joe Wood	31
80	Ed Brandt	30
	Lew Burdette	30
	Dwight Gooden	30
	Lefty Tyler	30
84	Jack Harshman	29
	Ed Lopat	29
	Jouett Meekin	29
	Camilo Pascual	29
	Juan Pizarro	29
89	Jack Bentley	28
	Tom Glavine	28
	Mike Hampton	28
	Joe Nuxhall	28
	Tom Seaver	28
	Urban Shocker	28
95	Charlie Buffinton	27
	Whitey Ford	27
	Brickyard Kennedy	27
	Frank Kitson	27
	Bill Sherdel	27
	Lon Warneke	27

Pitcher Fielding Runs

Rank	Player	Runs
1	Ed Walsh	83
2	Greg Maddux	82
3	Carl Mays	74
4	Christy Mathewson	68
5	Freddie Fitzsimmons	60
	Bob Lemon	60
7	Burleigh Grimes	58
8	Tommy John	55
9	Harry Howell	51
10	Harry Gumbert	50
11	John Clarkson	45
12	Bill Doak	43
	Dennis Martinez	43
14	Willis Hudlin	42
	Eddie Rommel	42
16	Kevin Brown	41
17	Jack Quinn	40
18	Jim Galvin	39
	Rick Reuschel	39
	Bobby Shantz	39
21	Hooks Dauss	38
	Kenny Rogers	38
	Dizzy Trout	38
24	Orel Hershiser	36
	Jack Russell	36
	Mel Stottlemyre	36
	Fernando Valenzuela	36
28	Charlie Buffinton	35
	Johnny Schmitz	35
	Willie Sudhoff	35
31	Nick Altrock	34
32	Tony Mullane	33
33	Red Ames	32
	Murry Dickson	32
	Howard Ehmke	32
	Randy Jones	32
37	Grover Alexander	31
	Russ Christopher	31
	Curt Davis	31
	John Denny	31
41	Tommy Bond	30
	Chick Fraser	30
	Addie Joss	30
	Hal Schumacher	30
45	Gerry Staley	29
	Dave Stieb	29
47	Mike Boddicker	28
	Ben Cantwell	28
	Sid Hudson	28
	Matt Kilroy	28
	George Mullin	28
	Phil Niekro	28
	Ed Willett	28
54	Ted Abernathy	27
	Tom Burgmeier	27
	Spud Chandler	27
	Tom Glavine	27
	Amos Rusie	27
	Bucky Walters	27
	Vic Willis	27
61	Nixey Callahan	26
	Whitey Ford	26
	Frank Smith	26
	Sherry Smith	26
65	Don Drysdale	25
	Guy Hecker	25
	Larry Jackson	25
	Charlie Leibrandt	25
	Dan Quisenberry	25
	Elmer Stricklett	25
	Doc White	25
72	Mike Caldwell	24
	Frank Corridon	24
	Ned Garvin	24
	Dutch Leonard	24
	Cy Seymour	24
	John Ward	24
78	Jean Dubuc	23
	Jim McCormick	23
	Lindy McDaniel	23
	Roger McDowell	23
	Charles Nagy	23
	Bill Swift	23
84	Tom Brewer	22
	Scott Erickson	22
	Bill Hart	22
	Joe Horlen	22
	Carl Hubbell	22
	Stu Miller	22
	Mike Moore	22
	Hal Newhouser	22
	Frank Owen	22
	Dan Petry	22
	Ed Reulbach	22
	Bob Stanley	22
	Kent Tekulve	22
97	11 players tied	21

Pitcher Batting Average

1	Babe Ruth	.299
2	Guy Hecker	.297
3	Jack Stivetts	.295
4	Jim Devlin	.293
5	Charlie Ferguson	.288
6	George Uhle	.286
7	Wes Ferrell	.284
8	Charlie Sweeney	.284
9	Cy Seymour	.280
10	Doc Crandall	.279
11	Al Orth	.277
12	Bob Caruthers	.276
13	Fred Hutchinson	.276
14	Jack Scott	.276
15	Ben Sanders	.275
16	Scott Stratton	.275
17	Ad Gumbert	.274
18	Sloppy Thurston	.270
19	Red Ruffing	.269
20	Carl Mays	.268
21	Don Newcombe	.266
22	Johnny Marcum	.265
23	Dutch Ruether	.264
24	Dave Foutz	.262
25	George Mullin	.262
26	Win Mercer	.261
27	Brickyard Kennedy	.261
28	Jim Whitney	.261
29	Nixey Callahan	.260
	Joe Shaute	.260
31	Schoolboy Rowe	.257
32	Jesse Tannehill	.256
33	Joe Bush	.253
34	Jack Taylor	.252
35	Elmer Smith	.251
36	Lee Richmond	.250
37	Mickey McDermott	.250
	Carl Scheib	.250
	Phenomenal Smith	.250
40	Amos Rusie	.248
41	Burleigh Grimes	.248
42	John Ward	.247
43	Clarence Mitchell	.247
44	Adonis Terry	.247
45	Tommy Byrne	.246
46	Pete Donohue	.246
47	Al Maul	.246
48	Johnny Sain	.245
49	Jack Dunn	.244
50	Vern Kennedy	.244
51	Jouett Meekin	.243
52	Elam Vangilder	.243
53	Bucky Walters	.242
54	Willard Nixon	.242
55	Frank Killen	.241
56	Pink Hawley	.241
57	Joe Wood	.241
58	Charlie Buffinton	.241
59	Duke Esper	.241
60	Terry Larkin	.241
61	Claude Hendrix	.241
62	Ray Caldwell	.241
63	Frank Kitson	.240
64	Kid Gleason	.240
65	Don Larsen	.240
66	Wiley Piatt	.239
67	Tony Mullane	.239
68	Wilbur Cooper	.239
69	Tommy Bond	.238
70	Rick Rhoden	.238
71	Fred Heimach	.236
72	Charley Radbourn	.236
73	Jim McCormick	.236
74	Ed Brandt	.236
	Bob Smith	.236
76	Walter Johnson	.235
77	Ed Crane	.234
78	Fritz Ostermueller	.234
79	Nig Cuppy	.233
80	Ted Lyons	.233
81	Sherry Smith	.233
82	Clark Griffith	.233
83	Bob Lemon	.233
84	Don Robinson	.231
85	Lady Baldwin	.231
86	Murry Dickson	.231
87	Jean Dubuc	.231
88	Ben Cantwell	.231
89	George Earnshaw	.230
90	Jim Tobin	.230
91	Jack Coombs	.230
92	Frank Dwyer	.229
93	Vic Aldridge	.229
94	Bill Hoffer	.229
95	John Harkins	.228
96	Monte Pearson	.228
97	George Bradley	.228
98	Nels Potter	.228
99	Dolf Luque	.227
100	George Haddock	.227

Total Pitcher Index

1	Walter Johnson	91.4
2	Cy Young	78.0
3	Grover Alexander	64.6
4	Christy Mathewson	62.9
5	Greg Maddux	60.0
6	Lefty Grove	59.7
7	Roger Clemens	57.5
	Kid Nichols	57.5
9	Warren Spahn	50.2
10	Tom Seaver	48.7
11	John Clarkson	46.0
12	Ed Walsh	44.9
13	Bob Gibson	43.7
14	Carl Hubbell	41.1
15	Hoyt Wilhelm	40.8
16	Amos Rusie	39.8
17	Hal Newhouser	39.3
18	Whitey Ford	39.2
19	Bob Lemon	38.4
20	Tim Keefe	38.1
21	Ted Lyons	37.1
22	Carl Mays	36.6
23	Mordecai Brown	35.3
24	Jim Palmer	34.9
	Gaylord Perry	34.9
26	Don Drysdale	34.6
27	Phil Niekro	33.8
28	Steve Carlton	33.7
29	Dizzy Trout	33.3
30	Pedro Martinez	32.9
31	Kevin Brown	32.8
32	Tony Mullane	32.3
33	Randy Johnson	31.8
34	Tom Glavine	30.9
35	Bert Blyleven	30.7
36	Wes Ferrell	30.5
37	Bob Feller	30.2
38	Fergie Jenkins	29.8
39	John Franco	29.5
	Juan Marichal	29.5
	Charley Radbourn	29.5
42	Bob Caruthers	29.3
43	Bucky Walters	29.0
44	Rich Gossage	28.9
45	Clark Griffith	28.3
46	Bret Saberhagen	28.1
47	Tommy Bridges	28.0
	Red Ruffing	28.0
49	Dazzy Vance	27.4
50	Dennis Eckersley	27.3
51	Red Faber	27.2
52	Stan Coveleski	27.0
53	Eddie Plank	26.9
54	Dolf Luque	26.8
	Dave Stieb	26.8
56	Dutch Leonard	26.7
57	Eppa Rixey	26.6
58	Jack Stivetts	26.5
59	Robin Roberts	25.9
60	Addie Joss	25.8
	Urban Shocker	25.8
62	Tommy John	25.6
63	Eddie Cicotte	25.4
64	Eddie Rommel	25.2
65	Dan Quisenberry	25.1
66	Harry Brecheen	25.0
67	Mike Mussina	24.8
68	Rick Reuschel	24.7
69	Rube Waddell	24.4
70	Guy Hecker	24.3
71	Jimmy Key	24.2
72	Joe Wood	24.1
73	Billy Pierce	23.9
74	Burleigh Grimes	23.7
75	Jack Quinn	23.3
76	David Cone	23.1
77	Freddie Fitzsimmons	22.9
	John Smoltz	22.9
	Kent Tekulve	22.9
80	Lon Warneke	22.8
81	Rollie Fingers	22.5
82	Dizzy Dean	21.8
83	Nig Cuppy	21.7
84	Orel Hershiser	21.5
	John Wetteland	21.5
86	Silver King	21.4
87	Tom Henke	21.3
88	Lee Smith	21.2
	Vic Willis	21.2
90	Jesse Tannehill	21.1
91	Spud Chandler	21.0
92	Chuck Finley	20.9
	Bobby Shantz	20.9
94	Jim McCormick	20.7
	Nolan Ryan	20.7
96	Curt Davis	20.5
	Sandy Koufax	20.5
98	Roberto Hernandez	20.3
	John Hiller	20.3
100	Mike Marshall	20.2

Total Pitcher Index

101	Doc White	20.1
102	Charlie Buffinton	20.0
	Wilbur Cooper	20.0
104	Lefty Gomez	19.9
	Jesse Orosco	19.9
106	Doug Jones	19.8
	Sparky Lyle	19.8
108	Murry Dickson	19.5
109	Mel Harder	19.4
110	Dave Foutz	19.1
	Ed Lopat	19.1
112	Jim Kaat	19.0
113	Kevin Appier	18.8
	Red Lucas	18.8
	Joe McGinnity	18.8
116	Bruce Sutter	18.6
117	Ron Guidry	18.5
	Luis Tiant	18.5
119	Don Newcombe	18.4
120	Larry Jackson	18.2
121	Mel Stottlemyre	18.1
122	Bob Stanley	18.0
123	Wilbur Wood	17.9
124	Andy Messersmith	17.8
	Ed Reulbach	17.8
126	Dwight Gooden	17.7
127	Hippo Vaughn	17.6
128	Rick Aguilera	17.5
129	Trevor Hoffman	17.4
130	Larry French	17.3
	Jeff Montgomery	17.3
	Mariano Rivera	17.3
	Schoolboy Rowe	17.3
	Jack Taylor	17.3
135	Babe Ruth	17.2
136	Mel Parnell	17.1
	Early Wynn	17.1
138	John Tudor	17.0
139	Stu Miller	16.9
	Claude Passeau	16.9
141	Ned Garver	16.8
142	Thornton Lee	16.7
	Hal Schumacher	16.7
144	Harry Howell	16.6
145	Gene Garber	16.2
146	Max Lanier	16.1
	Ron Perranoski	16.1
148	Noodles Hahn	16.0
149	Johnny Antonelli	15.9
150	Jose Rijo	15.7
151	Sadie McMahon	15.6
152	Virgil Trucks	15.5
153	Mike Garcia	15.4
	Sam Leever	15.4
155	Steve Rogers	15.3
156	Babe Adams	15.2
	Jim Whitney	15.2
158	Waite Hoyt	15.1
	Deacon Phillippe	15.1
	Mickey Welch	15.1
161	Bob Shawkey	14.9
	John Ward	14.9
163	Mark Eichhorn	14.8
	Claude Hendrix	14.8
	Robb Nen	14.8
166	Frank Viola	14.7
167	John Candelaria	14.6
168	Charlie Hough	14.5
	George Mullin	14.5
170	Chief Bender	14.4
	Frank Linzy	14.4
172	Larry Corcoran	14.3
	Ellis Kinder	14.3
	Gary Lavelle	14.3
	Tug McGraw	14.3
	Gregg Olson	14.3
177	Fred Hutchinson	14.2
	Curt Schilling	14.2
179	Nap Rucker	14.1
180	Tom Burgmeier	14.0
181	Clay Carroll	13.9
	Frank Dwyer	13.9
	Mike Hampton	13.9
	Jerry Koosman	13.9
	George Uhle	13.9
186	Charlie Ferguson	13.7
	Claude Osteen	13.7
	Dave Righetti	13.7
189	Frank Lary	13.6
	Sal Maglie	13.6
	Dennis Martinez	13.6
	Howie Pollet	13.6
193	Jim Bunning	13.4
	Lindy McDaniel	13.4
195	Bill Hutchison	13.3
	Mike Jackson	13.3
	Randy Myers	13.3
198	Firpo Marberry	13.2
	Don Sutton	13.2
200	Mike Henneman	13.1

Total Pitcher Index

201	Jim Galvin	13.0
202	Alex Fernandez	12.9
	Van Mungo	12.9
204	Mort Cooper	12.8
	Jim Maloney	12.8
206	Jim Tobin	12.7
	Will White	12.7
208	Frank Killen	12.6
	Jon Matlack	12.6
210	Roy Face	12.5
211	Steve Farr	12.3
	Kenny Rogers	12.3
213	Gary Peters	12.2
	Sherry Smith	12.2
	Frank Tanana	12.2
216	Dean Chance	12.0
	Willie Hernandez	12.0
	Curt Simmons	12.0
219	Ewell Blackwell	11.9
	Mark Langston	11.9
	Greg Minton	11.9
	Milt Pappas	11.9
223	Jake Weimer	11.8
224	Orval Overall	11.7
225	Ted Breitenstein	11.6
	Bryan Harvey	11.6
	Jeff Reardon	11.6
228	Harvey Haddix	11.5
	Johnny Sain	11.5
230	Jim Devlin	11.4
231	Lefty Leifield	11.3
232	Al Brazle	11.2
233	Dave Smith	11.1
234	Mike Boddicker	11.0
	Nixey Callahan	11.0
	Terry Forster	11.0
	Fernando Valenzuela	11.0
238	Jack Chesbro	10.9
	Bob Rush	10.9
240	Vida Blue	10.7
	Tom Candiotti	10.7
	Roger McDowell	10.7
	Charlie Root	10.7
	Mike Timlin	10.7
245	Hooks Wiltse	10.6
	Todd Worrell	10.6
247	Camilo Pascual	10.5
	David Wells	10.5
	Tom Zachary	10.5
250	Matt Kilroy	10.4
	Charlie Leibrandt	10.4
	Andy Pettitte	10.4
	Sonny Siebert	10.4
254	Bob Locker	10.3
	Don McMahon	10.3
	Win Mercer	10.3
	Johnny Murphy	10.3
	Jeff Russell	10.3
259	Jeff Fassero	10.2
	Tex Hughson	10.2
	Jim Kern	10.2
262	Russ Ford	10.1
263	Jim Brewer	10.0
	Hooks Dauss	10.0
	Dan Plesac	10.0
	Dick Radatz	10.0
267	Tim Burke	9.9
	Steve Howe	9.9
	Art Nehf	9.9
270	Ned Garvin	9.8
	Mark Gubicza	9.8
	Fritz Ostermueller	9.8
	Slim Sallee	9.8
274	Clint Brown	9.7
	Elton Chamberlain	9.7
	Al Leiter	9.7
	Ed Morris	9.7
	Ben Sanders	9.7
	Jeff Shaw	9.7
	Gerry Staley	9.7
281	Sam McDowell	9.6
	Jeff Nelson	9.6
	Jim Perry	9.6
284	Greg Harris	9.5
	Monte Pearson	9.5
	Jeff Pfeffer	9.5
	Jim Scott	9.5
288	Joe Dobson	9.4
	Bob Ewing	9.4
	Pink Hawley	9.4
	Teddy Higuera	9.4
	Darold Knowles	9.4
	Bob Wickman	9.4
	Al Worthington	9.4
295	Al Orth	9.3
296	Larry Jansen	9.2
	Jack McDowell	9.2
	Brad Radke	9.2
	Rip Sewell	9.2
300	3 players tied	9.1

Total Pitcher Index (alpha.)

Babe Adams	15.2
Rick Aguilera	17.5
Grover Alexander	64.6
Johnny Antonelli	15.9
Kevin Appier	18.8
Chief Bender	14.4
Ewell Blackwell	11.9
Vida Blue	10.7
Bert Blyleven	30.7
Mike Boddicker	11.0
Al Brazle	11.2
Harry Brecheen	25.0
Ted Breitenstein	11.6
Jim Brewer	10.0
Tommy Bridges	28.0
Clint Brown	9.7
Kevin Brown	32.8
Mordecai Brown	35.3
Charlie Buffinton	20.0
Jim Bunning	13.4
Tom Burgmeier	14.0
Tim Burke	9.9
Nixey Callahan	11.0
John Candelaria	14.6
Tom Candiotti	10.7
Steve Carlton	33.7
Clay Carroll	13.9
Bob Caruthers	29.3
Elton Chamberlain	9.7
Dean Chance	12.0
Spud Chandler	21.0
Jack Chesbro	10.9
Eddie Cicotte	25.4
John Clarkson	46.0
Roger Clemens	57.5
David Cone	23.1
Wilbur Cooper	20.0
Mort Cooper	12.8
Larry Corcoran	14.3
Stan Coveleski	27.0
Nig Cuppy	21.7
Hooks Dauss	10.0
Curt Davis	20.5
Dizzy Dean	21.8
Jim Devlin	11.4
Murry Dickson	19.5
Joe Dobson	9.4
Don Drysdale	34.6
Frank Dwyer	13.9
Dennis Eckersley	27.3
Mark Eichhorn	14.8
Bob Ewing	9.4
Red Faber	27.2
Roy Face	12.5
Steve Farr	12.3
Jeff Fassero	10.2
Bob Feller	30.2
Charlie Ferguson	13.7
Alex Fernandez	12.9
Wes Ferrell	30.5
Rollie Fingers	22.5
Chuck Finley	20.9
Freddie Fitzsimmons	22.9
Whitey Ford	39.2
Russ Ford	10.1
Terry Forster	11.0
Dave Foutz	19.1
John Franco	29.5
Larry French	17.3
Jim Galvin	13.0
Gene Garber	16.2
Mike Garcia	15.4
Ned Garver	16.8
Ned Garvin	9.8
Bob Gibson	43.7
Tom Glavine	30.9
Lefty Gomez	19.9
Dwight Gooden	17.7
Rich Gossage	28.9
Clark Griffith	28.3
Burleigh Grimes	23.7
Lefty Grove	59.7
Mark Gubicza	9.8
Ron Guidry	18.5
Harvey Haddix	11.5
Noodles Hahn	16.0
Mike Hampton	13.9
Mel Harder	19.4
Greg Harris	9.5
Bryan Harvey	11.6
Pink Hawley	9.4
Guy Hecker	24.3
Claude Hendrix	14.8
Tom Henke	21.3
Mike Henneman	13.1
Willie Hernandez	12.0
Roberto Hernandez	20.3
Orel Hershiser	21.5
Teddy Higuera	9.4
John Hiller	20.3

Total Pitcher Index (alpha.)

Pitcher	TPI
Trevor Hoffman	17.4
Charlie Hough	14.5
Steve Howe	9.9
Harry Howell	16.6
Waite Hoyt	15.1
Carl Hubbell	41.1
Tex Hughson	10.2
Fred Hutchinson	14.2
Bill Hutchison	13.3
Larry Jackson	18.2
Mike Jackson	13.3
Larry Jansen	9.2
Fergie Jenkins	29.8
Tommy John	25.6
Randy Johnson	31.8
Walter Johnson	91.4
Doug Jones	19.8
Addie Joss	25.8
Jim Kaat	19.0
Tim Keefe	38.1
Jim Kern	10.2
Jimmy Key	24.2
Frank Killen	12.6
Matt Kilroy	10.4
Ellis Kinder	14.3
Silver King	21.4
Darold Knowles	9.4
Jerry Koosman	13.9
Sandy Koufax	20.5
Mark Langston	11.9
Max Lanier	16.1
Frank Lary	13.6
Gary Lavelle	14.3
Thornton Lee	16.7
Sam Leever	15.4
Charlie Leibrandt	10.4
Lefty Leifield	11.3
Al Leiter	9.7
Bob Lemon	38.4
Dutch Leonard	26.7
Frank Linzy	14.4
Bob Locker	10.3
Ed Lopat	19.1
Red Lucas	18.8
Dolf Luque	26.8
Sparky Lyle	19.8
Ted Lyons	37.1
Greg Maddux	60.0
Sal Maglie	13.6
Jim Maloney	12.8
Firpo Marberry	13.2
Juan Marichal	29.5
Mike Marshall	20.2
Dennis Martinez	13.6
Pedro Martinez	32.9
Christy Mathewson	62.9
Jon Matlack	12.6
Carl Mays	36.6
Jim McCormick	20.7
Lindy McDaniel	13.4
Jack McDowell	9.2
Roger McDowell	10.7
Sam McDowell	9.6
Joe McGinnity	18.8
Tug McGraw	14.3
Don McMahon	10.3
Sadie McMahon	15.6
Win Mercer	10.3
Andy Messersmith	17.8
Stu Miller	16.9
Greg Minton	11.9
Jeff Montgomery	17.3
Ed Morris	9.7
Tony Mullane	32.3
George Mullin	14.5
Van Mungo	12.9
Johnny Murphy	10.3
Mike Mussina	24.8
Randy Myers	13.3
Art Nehf	9.9
Jeff Nelson	9.6
Robb Nen	14.8
Don Newcombe	18.4
Hal Newhouser	39.3
Kid Nichols	57.5
Phil Niekro	33.8
Gregg Olson	14.3
Jesse Orosco	19.9
Al Orth	9.3
Claude Osteen	13.7
Fritz Ostermueller	9.8
Orval Overall	11.7
Jim Palmer	34.9
Milt Pappas	11.9
Mel Parnell	17.1
Camilo Pascual	10.5
Claude Passeau	16.9
Monte Pearson	9.5
Ron Perranoski	16.1
Gaylord Perry	34.9

Total Pitcher Index (alpha.)

Pitcher	TPI
Jim Perry	9.6
Gary Peters	12.2
Andy Pettitte	10.4
Jeff Pfeffer	9.5
Deacon Phillippe	15.1
Billy Pierce	23.9
Eddie Plank	26.9
Dan Plesac	10.0
Howie Pollet	13.6
Jack Quinn	23.3
Dan Quisenberry	25.1
Dick Radatz	10.0
Charley Radbourn	29.5
Brad Radke	9.2
Jeff Reardon	11.6
Ed Reulbach	17.8
Rick Reuschel	24.7
Dave Righetti	13.7
Jose Rijo	15.7
Mariano Rivera	17.3
Eppa Rixey	26.6
Robin Roberts	25.9
Kenny Rogers	12.3
Steve Rogers	15.3
Eddie Rommel	25.2
Charlie Root	10.7
Schoolboy Rowe	17.3
Nap Rucker	14.1
Red Ruffing	28.0
Bob Rush	10.9
Amos Rusie	39.8
Jeff Russell	10.3
Babe Ruth	17.2
Nolan Ryan	20.7
Bret Saberhagen	28.1
Johnny Sain	11.5
Slim Sallee	9.8
Ben Sanders	9.7
Curt Schilling	14.2
Hal Schumacher	16.7
Jim Scott	9.5
Tom Seaver	48.7
Rip Sewell	9.2
Bobby Shantz	20.9
Jeff Shaw	9.7
Bob Shawkey	14.9
Urban Shocker	25.8
Sonny Siebert	10.4
Curt Simmons	12.0
Dave Smith	11.1
Lee Smith	21.2
Sherry Smith	12.2
John Smoltz	22.9
Warren Spahn	50.2
Gerry Staley	9.7
Bob Stanley	18.0
Dave Stieb	26.8
Jack Stivetts	26.5
Mel Stottlemyre	18.1
Bruce Sutter	18.6
Don Sutton	13.2
Frank Tanana	12.2
Jesse Tannehill	21.1
Jack Taylor	17.3
Kent Tekulve	22.9
Luis Tiant	18.5
Mike Timlin	10.7
Jim Tobin	12.7
Dizzy Trout	33.3
Virgil Trucks	15.5
John Tudor	17.0
George Uhle	13.9
Fernando Valenzuela	11.0
Dazzy Vance	27.4
Hippo Vaughn	17.6
Frank Viola	14.7
Rube Waddell	24.4
Ed Walsh	44.9
Bucky Walters	29.0
John Ward	14.9
Lon Warneke	22.8
Jake Weimer	11.8
Mickey Welch	15.1
David Wells	10.5
John Wetteland	21.5
Doc White	20.1
Will White	12.7
Jim Whitney	15.2
Bob Wickman	9.4
Hoyt Wilhelm	40.8
Vic Willis	21.2
Hooks Wiltse	10.6
Joe Wood	24.1
Wilbur Wood	17.9
Todd Worrell	10.6
Al Worthington	9.4
Early Wynn	17.1
Cy Young	78.0
Tom Zachary	10.5

Total Pitcher Index (by era)

1876-1892

Rank	Pitcher	TPI
1	John Clarkson	46.0
2	Tim Keefe	38.1
3	Tony Mullane	32.3
4	Charley Radbourn	29.5
5	Bob Caruthers	29.3
6	Jack Stivetts	26.5
7	Guy Hecker	24.3
8	Silver King	21.4
9	Jim McCormick	20.7
10	Charlie Buffinton	20.0
11	Dave Foutz	19.1
12	Sadie McMahon	15.6
13	Jim Whitney	15.2
14	Mickey Welch	15.1
15	John Ward	14.9
16	Larry Corcoran	14.3
17	Charlie Ferguson	13.7
18	Bill Hutchison	13.3
19	Jim Galvin	13.0
20	Will White	12.7
21	Jim Devlin	11.4
22	Matt Kilroy	10.4
23	Elton Chamberlain	9.7
	Ed Morris	9.7
	Ben Sanders	9.7

1893-1919

Rank	Pitcher	TPI
1	Walter Johnson	91.4
2	Cy Young	78.0
3	Grover Alexander	64.6
4	Christy Mathewson	62.9
5	Kid Nichols	57.5
6	Ed Walsh	44.9
7	Amos Rusie	39.8
8	Mordecai Brown	35.3
9	Clark Griffith	28.3
10	Eddie Plank	26.9
11	Addie Joss	25.8
12	Eddie Cicotte	25.4
13	Rube Waddell	24.4
14	Joe Wood	24.1
15	Nig Cuppy	21.7
16	Vic Willis	21.2
17	Jesse Tannehill	21.1
18	Doc White	20.1
19	Joe McGinnity	18.8
20	Ed Reulbach	17.8
21	Hippo Vaughn	17.6
22	Jack Taylor	17.3
23	Babe Ruth	17.2
24	Harry Howell	16.6
25	Noodles Hahn	16.0

1920-1941

Rank	Pitcher	TPI
1	Lefty Grove	59.7
2	Carl Hubbell	41.1
3	Ted Lyons	37.1
4	Carl Mays	36.6
5	Wes Ferrell	30.5
6	Bucky Walters	29.0
7	Tommy Bridges	28.0
	Red Ruffing	28.0
9	Dazzy Vance	27.4
10	Red Faber	27.2
11	Stan Coveleski	27.0
12	Dolf Luque	26.8
13	Eppa Rixey	26.6
14	Urban Shocker	25.8
15	Eddie Rommel	25.2
16	Burleigh Grimes	23.7
17	Jack Quinn	23.3
18	Freddie Fitzsimmons	22.9
19	Lon Warneke	22.8
20	Dizzy Dean	21.8
21	Curt Davis	20.5
22	Wilbur Cooper	20.0
23	Lefty Gomez	19.9
24	Mel Harder	19.4
25	Red Lucas	18.8

Total Pitcher Index (by era)

1942-1960

Rank	Pitcher	TPI
1	Warren Spahn	50.2
2	Hoyt Wilhelm	40.8
3	Hal Newhouser	39.3
4	Whitey Ford	39.2
5	Bob Lemon	38.4
6	Dizzy Trout	33.3
7	Bob Feller	30.2
8	Dutch Leonard	26.7
9	Robin Roberts	25.9
10	Harry Brecheen	25.0
11	Billy Pierce	23.9
12	Spud Chandler	21.0
13	Bobby Shantz	20.9
14	Murry Dickson	19.5
15	Ed Lopat	19.1
16	Don Newcombe	18.4
17	Mel Parnell	17.1
	Early Wynn	17.1
19	Stu Miller	16.9
20	Ned Garver	16.8
21	Max Lanier	16.1
22	Johnny Antonelli	15.9
23	Virgil Trucks	15.5
24	Mike Garcia	15.4
25	Ellis Kinder	14.3

1961-1976

Rank	Pitcher	TPI
1	Tom Seaver	48.7
2	Bob Gibson	43.7
3	Jim Palmer	34.9
	Gaylord Perry	34.9
5	Don Drysdale	34.6
6	Phil Niekro	33.8
7	Steve Carlton	33.7
8	Fergie Jenkins	29.8
9	Juan Marichal	29.5
10	Tommy John	25.6
11	Rollie Fingers	22.5
12	Sandy Koufax	20.5
13	John Hiller	20.3
14	Mike Marshall	20.2
15	Sparky Lyle	19.8
16	Jim Kaat	19.0
17	Luis Tiant	18.5
18	Larry Jackson	18.2
19	Mel Stottlemyre	18.1
20	Wilbur Wood	17.9
21	Andy Messersmith	17.8
22	Ron Perranoski	16.1
23	Frank Linzy	14.4
24	Tug McGraw	14.3
25	Tom Burgmeier	14.0

1977-2000

Rank	Pitcher	TPI
1	Greg Maddux	60.0
2	Roger Clemens	57.5
3	Pedro Martinez	32.9
4	Kevin Brown	32.8
5	Randy Johnson	31.8
6	Tom Glavine	30.9
7	Bert Blyleven	30.7
8	John Franco	29.5
9	Rich Gossage	28.9
10	Bret Saberhagen	28.1
11	Dennis Eckersley	27.3
12	Dave Stieb	26.8
13	Dan Quisenberry	25.1
14	Mike Mussina	24.8
15	Rick Reuschel	24.7
16	Jimmy Key	24.2
17	David Cone	23.1
18	John Smoltz	22.9
	Kent Tekulve	22.9
20	Orel Hershiser	21.5
	John Wetteland	21.5
22	Tom Henke	21.3
23	Lee Smith	21.2
24	Chuck Finley	20.9
25	Nolan Ryan	20.7

Total Baseball Ranking

1	Babe Ruth	126.1
2	Willie Mays	95.9
3	Nap Lajoie	95.5
4	Ty Cobb	92.1
5	Walter Johnson	91.0
6	Barry Bonds	89.4
7	Hank Aaron	89.1
8	Tris Speaker	88.2
9	Ted Williams	83.0
10	Rogers Hornsby	82.7
11	Honus Wagner	82.0
12	Mike Schmidt	79.6
13	Cy Young	78.0
14	Mickey Mantle	77.4
15	Rickey Henderson	77.0
16	Eddie Collins	73.3
17	Stan Musial	71.5
18	Lou Gehrig	68.9
19	Frank Robinson	67.6
20	Grover Alexander	64.6
21	Christy Mathewson	62.9
22	Mel Ott	61.4
23	Greg Maddux	60.0
24	Lefty Grove	59.7
25	Roger Clemens	57.5
	Kid Nichols	57.5
27	Jimmie Foxx	56.3
28	Joe Morgan	54.8
29	Eddie Mathews	52.2
30	Ken Griffey Jr.	51.6
31	Bill Dahlen	51.1
32	George Davis	50.6
33	Warren Spahn	50.2
	Joe DiMaggio	50.2
35	Tom Seaver	48.7
36	Tim Raines	47.9
37	Carl Yastrzemski	46.7
38	John Clarkson	46.0
	Robin Yount	46.0
40	Bobby Grich	45.8
41	Tony Gwynn	45.6
42	Jeff Bagwell	45.2
	Al Kaline	45.2
44	Charlie Gehringer	45.0
45	Ed Walsh	44.9
46	Wade Boggs	44.4
47	Bob Gibson	43.7
48	Roger Connor	43.3
49	Ed Delahanty	42.9
50	Lou Boudreau	42.5
51	Luke Appling	42.4
	Ozzie Smith	42.4
53	Roberto Clemente	42.2
	Reggie Jackson	42.2
	Cal Ripken	42.2
56	Dan Brouthers	41.4
57	Barry Larkin	41.2
58	Carl Hubbell	41.1
59	Bid McPhee	41.0
60	Ron Santo	40.9
61	Hoyt Wilhelm	40.8
62	Frank Thomas	40.7
63	Bobby Doerr	40.5
64	Gabby Hartnett	40.3
65	George Brett	40.0
66	Joe Cronin	39.9
67	Amos Rusie	39.8
68	Arky Vaughan	39.7
69	Bobby Wallace	39.4
70	Hal Newhouser	39.3
71	Whitey Ford	39.2
72	Joe Jackson	39.0
73	Frankie Frisch	38.6
74	Mark McGwire	38.4
75	Tim Keefe	38.1
76	Bob Lemon	37.9
77	Dave Bancroft	37.5
	Reggie Smith	37.5
79	Yogi Berra	37.4
80	Willie McCovey	37.3
81	Ted Lyons	37.1
82	Dave Winfield	36.9
83	Carl Mays	36.6
	Ryne Sandberg	36.6
85	Bill Mazeroski	36.3
86	Johnny Mize	36.2
87	Mike Piazza	36.0
88	Dick Allen	35.9
	Jack Glasscock	35.9
	Jimmy Wynn	35.9
91	Edgar Martinez	35.7
92	Craig Biggio	35.6
93	Darrell Evans	35.5
	Joe Sewell	35.5
95	Bill Dickey	35.4
96	Mordecai Brown	35.3
97	Jim Palmer	34.9
	Gaylord Perry	34.9
	Bob Johnson	34.9
100	Keith Hernandez	34.8

Total Baseball Ranking

101	Don Drysdale	34.6
	Frank Baker	34.6
103	Albert Belle	34.3
104	Rod Carew	34.2
105	Eddie Murray	34.1
106	Phil Niekro	33.8
	Roberto Alomar	33.8
108	Steve Carlton	33.7
109	Paul Waner	33.5
110	Dizzy Trout	33.3
111	Pedro Martinez	32.9
112	Kevin Brown	32.8
	Richie Ashburn	32.8
114	Paul Molitor	32.6
115	Cap Anson	32.5
116	Tony Mullane	32.3
	Kirby Puckett	32.3
118	Harry Heilmann	32.2
119	Jackie Robinson	32.0
120	Randy Johnson	31.8
	Mickey Cochrane	31.8
	Billy Herman	31.8
123	Willie Stargell	31.6
124	Bob Caruthers	31.5
	Hank Greenberg	31.5
126	Cesar Cedeno	31.3
	Sam Crawford	31.3
128	Andre Dawson	31.0
129	Tom Glavine	30.9
130	Bert Blyleven	30.7
	Jack Clark	30.7
	Sam Thompson	30.7
133	Wes Ferrell	30.6
134	Elmer Flick	30.4
135	Bob Feller	30.2
136	Gary Carter	30.1
	Billy Williams	30.1
138	Cupid Childs	30.0
139	Fergie Jenkins	29.8
	Buck Ewing	29.8
141	Bobby Bonds	29.6
142	John Franco	29.5
	Juan Marichal	29.5
144	Rich Gossage	28.9
145	Norm Cash	28.8
	Joe Gordon	28.8
147	Brett Butler	28.7
148	Bernie Williams	28.6
149	Jose Cruz	28.5
	Dwight Evans	28.5
151	Dick Bartell	28.3
152	Pete Browning	28.2
	Stan Hack	28.2
154	Bret Saberhagen	28.1
	Heinie Groh	28.1
156	Tommy Bridges	28.0
157	Red Ruffing	27.9
158	Fred Dunlap	27.7
	Lenny Dykstra	27.7
160	Clark Griffith	27.6
161	Gary Sheffield	27.5
162	Dazzy Vance	27.4
	Billy Hamilton	27.4
164	Dennis Eckersley	27.3
	Harmon Killebrew	27.3
	Hardy Richardson	27.3
167	Red Faber	27.2
168	Charley Radbourn	27.1
	Chet Lemon	27.1
170	Stan Coveleski	27.0
171	Eddie Plank	26.9
	Ernie Banks	26.9
	Fred Lynn	26.9
	Al Simmons	26.9
175	Dolf Luque	26.8
	Dave Stieb	26.8
177	Dutch Leonard	26.7
	Fred Clarke	26.7
179	Eppa Rixey	26.6
	Bucky Walters	26.6
	Ray Lankford	26.6
182	Rafael Palmeiro	26.5
	Darryl Strawberry	26.5
184	Jim Rice	26.4
	Rusty Staub	26.4
186	Hughie Jennings	26.3
	George Sisler	26.3
	Lou Whitaker	26.3
189	Art Fletcher	26.2
190	Bill Terry	26.1
191	Sherry Magee	26.0
	Minnie Minoso	26.0
193	Robin Roberts	25.9
	Ralph Kiner	25.9
195	Addie Joss	25.8
	Urban Shocker	25.8
	Rocky Colavito	25.8
	King Kelly	25.8
199	Zack Wheat	25.7
200	Tommy John	25.6

Total Baseball Ranking

	Johnny Bench	25.6
202	Eddie Cicotte	25.4
203	Alex Rodriguez	25.3
204	Eddie Rommel	25.2
	Jose Canseco	25.2
206	Dan Quisenberry	25.1
	Jesse Burkett	25.1
	Larry Walker	25.1
209	Harry Brecheen	25.0
	Goose Goslin	25.0
	Joe Medwick	25.0
212	Carlton Fisk	24.9
213	Mike Mussina	24.8
214	Rick Reuschel	24.7
215	Jack Stivetts	24.6
	Buddy Bell	24.6
217	Jack Fournier	24.5
218	Rube Waddell	24.4
	Harlond Clift	24.4
220	Jimmy Key	24.2
221	Eric Davis	24.1
	Duke Snider	24.1
223	Wally Berger	24.0
	Jimmy Collins	24.0
	Tony Oliva	24.0
226	Billy Pierce	23.9
227	Burleigh Grimes	23.7
	Travis Jackson	23.7
229	Roy Thomas	23.6
230	Willie Randolph	23.5
231	Max Carey	23.4
	Will Clark	23.4
	Tim Salmon	23.4
	Joe Tinker	23.4
235	Jack Quinn	23.3
	John Ward	23.3
	Alan Trammell	23.3
238	David Cone	23.1
	Amos Otis	23.1
	Fred Pfeffer	23.1
241	Freddie Fitzsimmons	22.9
	John Smoltz	22.9
	Kent Tekulve	22.9
244	Lon Warneke	22.8
	Joe Wood	22.8
	Kenny Lofton	22.8
247	Larry Doby	22.7
248	Matt Williams	22.6
249	Rollie Fingers	22.5
	Roy Campanella	22.5
	Ron Cey	22.5
	Charlie Keller	22.5
253	Jake Beckley	22.4
254	Graig Nettles	22.2
	Harry Stovey	22.2
256	Dizzy Dean	21.8
	Guy Hecker	21.8
258	Nig Cuppy	21.7
	Del Pratt	21.7
260	George Foster	21.6
	Andy Van Slyke	21.6
262	Orel Hershiser	21.5
	John Wetteland	21.5
	Glenn Hubbard	21.5
	Dave Parker	21.5
266	Silver King	21.4
	Ed Konetchy	21.4
	Dale Murphy	21.4
	Pete Rose	21.4
270	Tom Henke	21.3
	Jim Fregosi	21.3
272	Lee Smith	21.2
	Vic Willis	21.2
	Fred Tenney	21.2
275	Earl Averill	21.1
276	Spud Chandler	21.0
	Frank Chance	21.0
	Miller Huggins	21.0
279	Chuck Finley	20.9
	Bobby Shantz	20.9
281	Robin Ventura	20.8
	Roy White	20.8
283	Jim McCormick	20.7
	Nolan Ryan	20.7
	Vern Stephens	20.7
286	Frank Howard	20.6
287	Curt Davis	20.5
	Sandy Koufax	20.5
289	Ken Singleton	20.4
290	Roberto Hernandez	20.3
	John Hiller	20.3
	Art Devlin	20.3
	Mike Griffin	20.3
294	Mike Marshall	20.2
	Dwayne Murphy	20.2
296	Ken Boyer	20.1
	Roger Bresnahan	20.1
	Kevin Mitchell	20.1
	Brooks Robinson	20.1
300	Wilbur Cooper	20.0

Total Baseball Ranking

	Jesse Tannehill	20.0
	Chuck Klein	20.0
	Manny Ramirez	20.0
304	Lefty Gomez	19.9
	Jesse Orosco	19.9
	Tony Fernandez	19.9
	Charley Jones	19.9
308	Doug Jones	19.8
	Sparky Lyle	19.8
	Charlie Bennett	19.8
311	Pie Traynor	19.7
312	Bob Elliott	19.6
	Joe Kelley	19.6
	Joe Torre	19.6
315	Murry Dickson	19.5
	Fred McGriff	19.5
317	Mel Harder	19.4
318	Jay Bell	19.2
	David Justice	19.2
320	Ed Lopat	19.1
	Brian Downing	19.1
	Denny Lyons	19.1
323	Jim Kaat	19.0
	Paul O'Neill	19.0
	Sammy Sosa	19.0
326	Ken Caminiti	18.9
	Gavvy Cravath	18.9
328	Kevin Appier	18.8
	Joe McGinnity	18.8
	Chili Davis	18.8
	Wally Schang	18.8
332	Doc White	18.7
	Bill Joyce	18.7
	Bill Nicholson	18.7
335	Bruce Sutter	18.6
336	Ron Guidry	18.5
	Luis Tiant	18.5
	Jimmy Sheckard	18.5
339	Don Newcombe	18.4
	Ted Simmons	18.4
	Eddie Stanky	18.4
342	Orlando Cepeda	18.3
343	Larry Jackson	18.2
	Ken Williams	18.2
345	Red Lucas	18.1
	Mel Stottlemyre	18.1
347	Bob Stanley	18.0
	Roy Cullenbine	18.0
	Gil McDougald	18.0
350	Wilbur Wood	17.9
	Hack Wilson	17.9
352	Andy Messersmith	17.8
	Ed Reulbach	17.8
354	Dwight Gooden	17.7
	Johnny Logan	17.7
	Jim Thome	17.7
357	Hippo Vaughn	17.6
	Gene Alley	17.6
	Rico Carty	17.6
	Jeff Kent	17.6
361	Rick Aguilera	17.5
	Tony Lazzeri	17.5
	Ernie Lombardi	17.5
364	Trevor Hoffman	17.4
	Jim Edmonds	17.4
	Ferris Fain	17.4
367	Larry French	17.3
	Jeff Montgomery	17.3
	Mariano Rivera	17.3
	Schoolboy Rowe	17.3
	Jack Taylor	17.3
	Cy Seymour	17.3
373	Thurman Munson	17.2
374	Mel Parnell	17.1
	Early Wynn	17.1
376	John Tudor	17.0
	Luis Gonzalez	17.0
378	Stu Miller	16.9
	Claude Passeau	16.9
	Harold Baines	16.9
	Pedro Guerrero	16.9
382	Ned Garver	16.8
	Steve Finley	16.8
	Mark Grace	16.8
	John Olerud	16.8
	Bobby Veach	16.8
387	Thornton Lee	16.7
	Hal Schumacher	16.7
	Tommy Leach	16.7
390	Ellis Burks	16.6
391	John McGraw	16.5
	Gene Tenace	16.5
393	Kiki Cuyler	16.4
	Babe Herman	16.4
395	Edd Roush	16.3
396	Gene Garber	16.2
	Ray Chapman	16.2
	Jocko Milligan	16.2
399	Max Lanier	16.1
	Ron Perranoski	16.1

Total Baseball Ranking

Rank	Player	TB
	Willie Davis	16.1
	Davey Johnson	16.1
	Phil Rizzuto	16.1
404	Noodles Hahn	16.0
	Bobby Knoop	16.0
406	Johnny Antonelli	15.9
	Al Oliver	15.9
	Jimmy Williams	15.9
409	Enos Slaughter	15.8
410	Jose Rijo	15.7
	Paul Hines	15.7
412	Sadie McMahon	15.6
	Mike Hargrove	15.6
	Tommy Holmes	15.6
	Chief Zimmer	15.6
416	Virgil Trucks	15.5
	Jeff Heath	15.5
418	Mike Garcia	15.4
	Sam Leever	15.4
	Lave Cross	15.4
	George Gore	15.4
	Boog Powell	15.4
423	Steve Rogers	15.3
	Earle Combs	15.3
	Bobby Murcer	15.3
	Jim O'Rourke	15.3
	John Valentin	15.3
428	Babe Adams	15.2
	Jesse Barfield	15.2
430	Waite Hoyt	15.1
	Deacon Phillippe	15.1
	Mickey Welch	15.1
	Johnny Evers	15.1
	Juan Gonzalez	15.1
	Ron Hansen	15.1
	Kevin McReynolds	15.1
	Ivan Rodriguez	15.1
438	Jason Kendall	15.0
	Roger Peckinpaugh	15.0
440	Bob Shawkey	14.9
	Ben Chapman	14.9
	Dom DiMaggio	14.9
	Kirk Gibson	14.9
444	Charlie Buffinton	14.8
	Mark Eichhorn	14.8
	Claude Hendrix	14.8
	Robb Nen	14.8
	Bobby Bonilla	14.8
449	Frank Viola	14.7
	Mark Belanger	14.7
	Pee Wee Reese	14.7
	Mike Scioscia	14.7
	Danny Tartabull	14.7
454	John Candelaria	14.6
	Tommy Henrich	14.6
	Chipper Jones	14.6
	Henry Larkin	14.6
458	Charlie Hough	14.5
	Johnny Pesky	14.5
	Jimmy Ryan	14.5
461	Chief Bender	14.4
	Frank Linzy	14.4
463	Ellis Kinder	14.3
	Gary Lavelle	14.3
	Tug McGraw	14.3
	Gregg Olson	14.3
467	Curt Schilling	14.2
	Andruw Jones	14.2
	Benny Kauff	14.2
	Roy Smalley	14.2
471	Fred Hutchinson	14.1
	Nap Rucker	14.1
	Duke Farrell	14.1
474	Tom Burgmeier	14.0
	Harry Howell	14.0
	George Mullin	14.0
	Bob Allison	14.0
	Greg Luzinski	14.0
	Rabbit Maranville	14.0
	Stan Spence	14.0
481	Clay Carroll	13.9
	Frank Dwyer	13.9
	Mike Hampton	13.9
	Jerry Koosman	13.9
	George Uhle	13.9
	Doug DeCinces	13.9
487	Augie Galan	13.8
	Nomar Garciaparra	13.8
	Vladimir Guerrero	13.8
	Harry Hooper	13.8
491	Charlie Ferguson	13.7
	Claude Osteen	13.7
	Dave Righetti	13.7
	Elmer Smith	13.7
495	9 players tied	13.6

Total Baseball Rank (alpha.)

Player	TB
Hank Aaron	89.1
Babe Adams	15.2
Rick Aguilera	17.5
Grover Alexander	64.6
Dick Allen	35.9
Gene Alley	17.6
Bob Allison	14.0
Roberto Alomar	33.8
Cap Anson	32.5
Johnny Antonelli	15.9
Kevin Appier	18.8
Luke Appling	42.4
Richie Ashburn	32.8
Earl Averill	21.1
Jeff Bagwell	45.2
Harold Baines	16.9
Frank Baker	34.6
Dave Bancroft	37.5
Ernie Banks	26.9
Jesse Barfield	15.2
Dick Bartell	28.3
Jake Beckley	22.4
Mark Belanger	14.7
Buddy Bell	24.6
Jay Bell	19.2
Albert Belle	34.3
Johnny Bench	25.6
Chief Bender	14.4
Charlie Bennett	19.8
Wally Berger	24.0
Yogi Berra	37.4
Craig Biggio	35.6
Bert Blyleven	30.7
Wade Boggs	44.4
Barry Bonds	89.4
Bobby Bonds	29.6
Bobby Bonilla	14.8
Lou Boudreau	42.5
Ken Boyer	20.1
Harry Brecheen	25.0
Roger Bresnahan	20.1
George Brett	40.0
Tommy Bridges	28.0
Dan Brouthers	41.4
Kevin Brown	32.8
Mordecai Brown	35.3
Pete Browning	28.2
Charlie Buffinton	14.8
Tom Burgmeier	14.0
Jesse Burkett	25.1
Ellis Burks	16.6
Brett Butler	28.7
Ken Caminiti	18.9
Roy Campanella	22.5
John Candelaria	14.6
Jose Canseco	25.2
Rod Carew	34.2
Max Carey	23.4
Steve Carlton	33.7
Clay Carroll	13.9
Gary Carter	30.1
Rico Carty	17.6
Bob Caruthers	31.5
Norm Cash	28.8
Cesar Cedeno	31.3
Orlando Cepeda	18.3
Ron Cey	22.5
Frank Chance	21.0
Spud Chandler	21.0
Ray Chapman	16.2
Ben Chapman	14.9
Cupid Childs	30.0
Eddie Cicotte	25.4
Jack Clark	30.7
Will Clark	23.4
Fred Clarke	26.7
John Clarkson	46.0
Roger Clemens	57.5
Roberto Clemente	42.2
Harlond Clift	24.4
Ty Cobb	92.1
Mickey Cochrane	31.8
Rocky Colavito	25.8
Eddie Collins	73.3
Jimmy Collins	24.0
Earle Combs	15.3
David Cone	23.1
Roger Connor	43.3
Wilbur Cooper	20.0
Stan Coveleski	27.0
Gavvy Cravath	18.9
Sam Crawford	31.3
Joe Cronin	39.9
Lave Cross	15.4
Jose Cruz	28.5
Roy Cullenbine	18.0
Nig Cuppy	21.7
Kiki Cuyler	16.4
Bill Dahlen	51.1
Curt Davis	20.5

Total Baseball Rank (alpha.)

Player	TB
Chili Davis	18.8
Eric Davis	24.1
George Davis	50.6
Willie Davis	16.1
Andre Dawson	31.0
Dizzy Dean	21.8
Doug DeCinces	13.9
Ed Delahanty	42.9
Art Devlin	20.3
Bill Dickey	35.4
Murry Dickson	19.5
Dom DiMaggio	14.9
Joe DiMaggio	50.2
Larry Doby	22.7
Bobby Doerr	40.5
Brian Downing	19.1
Don Drysdale	34.6
Fred Dunlap	27.7
Frank Dwyer	13.9
Lenny Dykstra	27.7
Dennis Eckersley	27.3
Jim Edmonds	17.4
Mark Eichhorn	14.8
Bob Elliott	19.6
Darrell Evans	35.5
Dwight Evans	28.5
Johnny Evers	15.1
Buck Ewing	29.8
Red Faber	27.2
Ferris Fain	17.4
Duke Farrell	14.1
Bob Feller	30.2
Charlie Ferguson	13.7
Tony Fernandez	19.9
Wes Ferrell	30.6
Rollie Fingers	22.5
Chuck Finley	20.9
Steve Finley	16.8
Carlton Fisk	24.9
Freddie Fitzsimmons	22.9
Art Fletcher	26.2
Elmer Flick	30.4
Whitey Ford	39.2
George Foster	21.6
Jack Fournier	24.5
Jimmie Foxx	56.3
John Franco	29.5
Jim Fregosi	21.3
Larry French	17.3
Frankie Frisch	38.6
Augie Galan	13.8
Gene Garber	16.2
Mike Garcia	15.4
Nomar Garciaparra	13.8
Ned Garver	16.8
Lou Gehrig	68.9
Charlie Gehringer	45.0
Bob Gibson	43.7
Kirk Gibson	14.9
Jack Glasscock	35.9
Tom Glavine	30.9
Lefty Gomez	19.9
Juan Gonzalez	15.1
Luis Gonzalez	17.0
Dwight Gooden	17.7
Joe Gordon	28.8
George Gore	15.4
Goose Goslin	25.0
Rich Gossage	28.9
Mark Grace	16.8
Hank Greenberg	31.5
Bobby Grich	45.8
Ken Griffey Jr.	51.6
Mike Griffin	20.3
Clark Griffith	27.6
Burleigh Grimes	23.7
Heinie Groh	28.1
Lefty Grove	59.7
Pedro Guerrero	16.9
Vladimir Guerrero	13.8
Ron Guidry	18.5
Tony Gwynn	45.6
Stan Hack	28.2
Noodles Hahn	16.0
Billy Hamilton	27.4
Mike Hampton	13.9
Ron Hansen	15.1
Mel Harder	19.4
Mike Hargrove	15.6
Gabby Hartnett	40.3
Jeff Heath	15.5
Guy Hecker	21.8
Harry Heilmann	32.2
Rickey Henderson	77.0
Claude Hendrix	14.8
Tom Henke	21.3
Tommy Henrich	14.6
Babe Herman	16.4
Billy Herman	31.8
Roberto Hernandez	20.3

Total Baseball Rank (alpha.)

Player	TB
Keith Hernandez	34.8
Orel Hershiser	21.5
John Hiller	20.3
Paul Hines	15.7
Trevor Hoffman	17.4
Tommy Holmes	15.6
Harry Hooper	13.8
Rogers Hornsby	82.7
Charlie Hough	14.5
Frank Howard	20.6
Harry Howell	14.0
Waite Hoyt	15.1
Glenn Hubbard	21.5
Carl Hubbell	41.1
Miller Huggins	21.0
Fred Hutchinson	14.1
Larry Jackson	18.2
Joe Jackson	39.0
Reggie Jackson	42.2
Travis Jackson	23.7
Fergie Jenkins	29.8
Hughie Jennings	26.3
Tommy John	25.6
Randy Johnson	31.8
Walter Johnson	91.0
Davey Johnson	16.1
Bob Johnson	34.9
Doug Jones	19.8
Andruw Jones	14.2
Charley Jones	19.9
Chipper Jones	14.6
Addie Joss	25.8
Bill Joyce	18.7
David Justice	19.2
Jim Kaat	19.0
Al Kaline	45.2
Benny Kauff	14.2
Tim Keefe	38.1
Charlie Keller	22.5
Joe Kelley	19.6
King Kelly	25.8
Jason Kendall	15.0
Jeff Kent	17.6
Jimmy Key	24.2
Harmon Killebrew	27.3
Ellis Kinder	14.3
Ralph Kiner	25.9
Silver King	21.4
Chuck Klein	20.0
Bobby Knoop	16.0
Ed Konetchy	21.4
Jerry Koosman	13.9
Sandy Koufax	20.5
Nap Lajoie	95.5
Max Lanier	16.1
Ray Lankford	26.6
Barry Larkin	41.2
Henry Larkin	14.6
Gary Lavelle	14.3
Tony Lazzeri	17.5
Tommy Leach	16.7
Thornton Lee	16.7
Sam Leever	15.4
Bob Lemon	37.9
Chet Lemon	27.1
Dutch Leonard	26.7
Frank Linzy	14.4
Kenny Lofton	22.8
Johnny Logan	17.7
Ernie Lombardi	17.5
Ed Lopat	19.1
Red Lucas	18.1
Dolf Luque	26.8
Greg Luzinski	14.0
Sparky Lyle	19.8
Fred Lynn	26.9
Ted Lyons	37.1
Denny Lyons	19.1
Greg Maddux	60.0
Sherry Magee	26.0
Mickey Mantle	77.4
Rabbit Maranville	14.0
Juan Marichal	29.5
Mike Marshall	20.2
Pedro Martinez	32.9
Edgar Martinez	35.7
Eddie Mathews	52.2
Christy Mathewson	62.9
Carl Mays	36.6
Willie Mays	95.9
Bill Mazeroski	36.3
Jim McCormick	20.7
Willie McCovey	37.3
Gil McDougald	18.0
Joe McGinnity	18.8
Tug McGraw	14.3
John McGraw	16.5
Fred McGriff	19.5
Mark McGwire	38.4
Sadie McMahon	15.6

Total Baseball Rank (alpha.)

Bid McPhee	41.0
Kevin McReynolds	15.1
Joe Medwick	25.0
Andy Messersmith	17.8
Stu Miller	16.9
Jocko Milligan	16.2
Minnie Minoso	26.0
Kevin Mitchell	20.1
Johnny Mize	36.2
Paul Molitor	32.6
Jeff Montgomery	17.3
Joe Morgan	54.8
Tony Mullane	32.3
George Mullin	14.0
Thurman Munson	17.2
Bobby Murcer	15.3
Dale Murphy	21.4
Dwayne Murphy	20.2
Eddie Murray	34.1
Stan Musial	71.5
Mike Mussina	24.8
Robb Nen	14.8
Graig Nettles	22.2
Don Newcombe	18.4
Hal Newhouser	39.3
Kid Nichols	57.5
Bill Nicholson	18.7
Phil Niekro	33.8
John Olerud	16.8
Tony Oliva	24.0
Al Oliver	15.9
Gregg Olson	14.3
Paul O'Neill	19.0
Jesse Orosco	19.9
Jim O'Rourke	15.3
Claude Osteen	13.7
Amos Otis	23.1
Mel Ott	61.4
Rafael Palmeiro	26.5
Jim Palmer	34.9
Dave Parker	21.5
Mel Parnell	17.1
Claude Passeau	16.9
Roger Peckinpaugh	15.0
Ron Perranoski	16.1
Gaylord Perry	34.9
Johnny Pesky	14.5
Fred Pfeffer	23.1
Deacon Phillippe	15.1
Mike Piazza	36.0
Billy Pierce	23.9
Eddie Plank	26.9
Boog Powell	15.4
Del Pratt	21.7
Kirby Puckett	32.3
Jack Quinn	23.3
Dan Quisenberry	25.1
Charley Radbourn	27.1
Tim Raines	47.9
Manny Ramirez	20.0
Willie Randolph	23.5
Pee Wee Reese	14.7
Ed Reulbach	17.8
Rick Reuschel	24.7
Jim Rice	26.4
Hardy Richardson	27.3
Dave Righetti	13.7
Jose Rijo	15.7
Cal Ripken	42.2
Mariano Rivera	17.3
Eppa Rixey	26.6
Phil Rizzuto	16.1
Robin Roberts	25.9
Brooks Robinson	20.1
Frank Robinson	67.6
Jackie Robinson	32.0
Alex Rodriguez	25.3
Ivan Rodriguez	15.1
Steve Rogers	15.3
Eddie Rommel	25.2
Pete Rose	21.4
Edd Roush	16.3
Schoolboy Rowe	17.3
Nap Rucker	14.1
Red Ruffing	27.9
Amos Rusie	39.8
Babe Ruth	126.1
Nolan Ryan	20.7
Jimmy Ryan	14.5
Bret Saberhagen	28.1
Tim Salmon	23.4
Ryne Sandberg	36.6
Ron Santo	40.9
Wally Schang	18.8
Curt Schilling	14.2
Mike Schmidt	79.6
Hal Schumacher	16.7
Mike Scioscia	14.7
Tom Seaver	48.7
Joe Sewell	35.5
Cy Seymour	17.3
Bobby Shantz	20.9
Bob Shawkey	14.9
Jimmy Sheckard	18.5
Gary Sheffield	27.5
Urban Shocker	25.8
Al Simmons	26.9
Ted Simmons	18.4
Ken Singleton	20.4
George Sisler	26.3
Enos Slaughter	15.8
Roy Smalley	14.2
Lee Smith	21.2
Reggie Smith	37.5
Elmer Smith	13.7
Ozzie Smith	42.4
John Smoltz	22.9
Duke Snider	24.1
Sammy Sosa	19.0
Warren Spahn	50.2
Tris Speaker	88.2
Stan Spence	14.0
Eddie Stanky	18.4
Bob Stanley	18.0
Willie Stargell	31.6
Rusty Staub	26.4
Vern Stephens	20.7
Dave Stieb	26.8
Jack Stivetts	24.6
Mel Stottlemyre	18.1
Harry Stovey	22.2
Darryl Strawberry	26.5
Bruce Sutter	18.6
Jesse Tannehill	20.0
Danny Tartabull	14.7
Jack Taylor	17.3
Kent Tekulve	22.9
Gene Tenace	16.5
Fred Tenney	21.2
Bill Terry	26.1
Frank Thomas	40.7
Roy Thomas	23.6
Jim Thome	17.7
Sam Thompson	30.7
Luis Tiant	18.5
Joe Tinker	23.4
Joe Torre	19.6
Alan Trammell	23.3
Pie Traynor	19.7
Dizzy Trout	33.3
Virgil Trucks	15.5
John Tudor	17.0
George Uhle	13.9
John Valentin	15.3
Dazzy Vance	27.4
Andy Van Slyke	21.6
Arky Vaughan	39.7
Hippo Vaughn	17.6
Bobby Veach	16.8
Robin Ventura	20.8
Frank Viola	14.7
Rube Waddell	24.4
Honus Wagner	82.0
Larry Walker	25.1
Bobby Wallace	39.4
Ed Walsh	44.9
Bucky Walters	26.6
Paul Waner	33.5
John Ward	23.3
Lon Warneke	22.8
Mickey Welch	15.1
John Wetteland	21.5
Zack Wheat	25.7
Lou Whitaker	26.3
Doc White	18.7
Roy White	20.8
Hoyt Wilhelm	40.8
Bernie Williams	28.6
Billy Williams	30.1
Jimmy Williams	15.9
Ken Williams	18.2
Matt Williams	22.6
Ted Williams	83.0
Vic Willis	21.2
Hack Wilson	17.9
Dave Winfield	36.9
Joe Wood	22.8
Wilbur Wood	17.9
Early Wynn	17.1
Jimmy Wynn	35.9
Carl Yastrzemski	46.7
Cy Young	78.0
Robin Yount	46.0
Chief Zimmer	15.6

Total Baseball Rank (by era)

1876-1892

Rank	Player	Rating
1	John Clarkson	46.0
2	Roger Connor	43.3
3	Dan Brouthers	41.4
4	Bid McPhee	41.0
5	Tim Keefe	38.1
6	Jack Glasscock	35.9
7	Cap Anson	32.5
8	Tony Mullane	32.3
9	Bob Caruthers	31.5
10	Sam Thompson	30.7
11	Buck Ewing	29.8
12	Pete Browning	28.2
13	Fred Dunlap	27.7
14	Hardy Richardson	27.3
15	Charley Radbourn	27.1
16	King Kelly	25.8
17	Jack Stivetts	24.6
18	John Ward	23.3
19	Fred Pfeffer	23.1
20	Harry Stovey	22.2
21	Guy Hecker	21.8
22	Silver King	21.4
23	Jim McCormick	20.7
24	Charley Jones	19.9
25	Charlie Bennett	19.8

1893-1919

Rank	Player	Rating
1	Nap Lajoie	95.5
2	Ty Cobb	92.1
3	Walter Johnson	91.0
4	Tris Speaker	88.2
5	Honus Wagner	82.0
6	Cy Young	78.0
7	Eddie Collins	73.3
8	Grover Alexander	64.6
9	Christy Mathewson	62.9
10	Kid Nichols	57.5
11	Bill Dahlen	51.1
12	George Davis	50.6
13	Ed Walsh	44.9
14	Ed Delahanty	42.9
15	Amos Rusie	39.8
16	Bobby Wallace	39.4
17	Joe Jackson	39.0
18	Mordecai Brown	35.3
19	Frank Baker	34.6
20	Sam Crawford	31.3
21	Elmer Flick	30.4
22	Cupid Childs	30.0
23	Heinie Groh	28.1
24	Clark Griffith	27.6
25	Billy Hamilton	27.4

1920-1941

Rank	Player	Rating
1	Babe Ruth	126.1
2	Rogers Hornsby	82.7
3	Lou Gehrig	68.9
4	Mel Ott	61.4
5	Lefty Grove	59.7
6	Jimmie Foxx	56.3
7	Charlie Gehringer	45.0
8	Luke Appling	42.4
9	Carl Hubbell	41.1
10	Gabby Hartnett	40.3
11	Joe Cronin	39.9
12	Arky Vaughan	39.7
13	Frankie Frisch	38.6
14	Dave Bancroft	37.5
15	Ted Lyons	37.1
16	Carl Mays	36.6
17	Joe Sewell	35.5
18	Bill Dickey	35.4
19	Bob Johnson	34.9
20	Paul Waner	33.5
21	Harry Heilmann	32.2
22	Mickey Cochrane	31.8
	Billy Herman	31.8
24	Hank Greenberg	31.5
25	Wes Ferrell	30.6

1942-1960

Rank	Player	Rating
1	Ted Williams	83.0
2	Mickey Mantle	77.4
3	Stan Musial	71.5
4	Eddie Mathews	52.2
5	Warren Spahn	50.2
	Joe DiMaggio	50.2
7	Lou Boudreau	42.5
8	Hoyt Wilhelm	40.8
9	Bobby Doerr	40.5
10	Hal Newhouser	39.3
11	Whitey Ford	39.2
12	Bob Lemon	37.9
13	Yogi Berra	37.4
14	Johnny Mize	36.2
15	Dizzy Trout	33.3
16	Richie Ashburn	32.8
17	Jackie Robinson	32.0
18	Bob Feller	30.2
19	Joe Gordon	28.8
20	Dutch Leonard	26.7
21	Minnie Minoso	26.0
22	Robin Roberts	25.9
	Ralph Kiner	25.9
24	Harry Brecheen	25.0
25	Duke Snider	24.1

1961-1976

Rank	Player	Rating
1	Willie Mays	95.9
2	Hank Aaron	89.1
3	Frank Robinson	67.6
4	Joe Morgan	54.8
5	Tom Seaver	48.7
6	Carl Yastrzemski	46.7
7	Al Kaline	45.2
8	Bob Gibson	43.7
9	Roberto Clemente	42.2
10	Ron Santo	40.9
11	Reggie Smith	37.5
12	Willie McCovey	37.3
13	Bill Mazeroski	36.3
14	Dick Allen	35.9
	Jimmy Wynn	35.9
16	Jim Palmer	34.9
	Gaylord Perry	34.9
18	Don Drysdale	34.6
19	Rod Carew	34.2
20	Phil Niekro	33.8
21	Steve Carlton	33.7
22	Willie Stargell	31.6
23	Billy Williams	30.1
24	Fergie Jenkins	29.8
25	Bobby Bonds	29.6

1977-2000

Rank	Player	Rating
1	Barry Bonds	89.4
2	Mike Schmidt	79.6
3	Rickey Henderson	77.0
4	Greg Maddux	60.0
5	Roger Clemens	57.5
6	Ken Griffey Jr.	51.6
7	Tim Raines	47.9
8	Robin Yount	46.0
9	Bobby Grich	45.8
10	Tony Gwynn	45.6
11	Jeff Bagwell	45.2
12	Wade Boggs	44.4
13	Ozzie Smith	42.4
14	Reggie Jackson	42.2
	Cal Ripken	42.2
16	Barry Larkin	41.2
17	Frank Thomas	40.7
18	George Brett	40.0
19	Mark McGwire	38.4
20	Dave Winfield	36.9
21	Ryne Sandberg	36.6
22	Mike Piazza	36.0
23	Edgar Martinez	35.7
24	Craig Biggio	35.6
25	Darrell Evans	35.5

At Bats

Rank	Player	AB
1	Willie Wilson, 1980	705
2	Juan Samuel, 1984	701
3	Dave Cash, 1975	699
4	Matty Alou, 1969	698
5	Woody Jensen, 1936	696
6	Maury Wills, 1962	695
	Omar Moreno, 1979	695
8	Bobby Richardson, 1962	692
9	Kirby Puckett, 1985	691
10	Neifi Perez, 1999	690
11	Lou Brock, 1967	689
	Sandy Alomar, 1971	689
13	Dave Cash, 1974	687
	Tony Fernandez, 1986	687
15	Horace Clarke, 1970	686
	Alex Rodriguez, 1998	686
17	Nomar Garciaparra, 1997	684
18	Lance Johnson, 1996	682
19	Lloyd Waner, 1931	681
	Jo-Jo Moore, 1935	681
21	Pete Rose, 1973	680
	Frank Taveras, 1979	680
	Kirby Puckett, 1986	680
24	Harvey Kuenn, 1953	679
	Curt Flood, 1964	679
	Bobby Richardson, 1964	679
27	Dick Groat, 1962	678
	Doug Glanville, 1998	678
29	Matty Alou, 1970	677
	Jim Rice, 1978	677
	Don Mattingly, 1986	677
32	Felix Millan, 1975	676
	Omar Moreno, 1980	676
	Darin Erstad, 2000	676
35	Rennie Stennett, 1974	673
	Bill Buckner, 1985	673
	B.J. Surhoff, 1999	673
38	Arlie Latham, 1887	672
	Rabbit Maranville, 1922	672
	Tony Oliva, 1964	672
	Sandy Alomar, 1970	672
	Garry Templeton, 1979	672
43	Jack Tobin, 1921	671
	Marquis Grissom, 1996	671
45	Al Simmons, 1932	670
	Pete Rose, 1965	670
	Buddy Bell, 1979	670
48	Vada Pinson, 1965	669
	Larry Bowa, 1974	669
50	Buddy Lewis, 1937	668
	Brooks Robinson, 1961	668
	Ralph Garr, 1973	668
53	Carl Furillo, 1951	667
54	Billy Herman, 1935	666
	Zoilo Versalles, 1965	666
	Felipe Alou, 1966	666
	Dave Cash, 1976	666
	Ron LeFlore, 1978	666
	Paul Molitor, 1982	666
60	Tommy Davis, 1962	665
	Pete Rose, 1976	665
	Paul Molitor, 1991	665
63	Taylor Douthit, 1930	664
	Bobby Richardson, 1965	664
	Don Kessinger, 1969	664
	Lou Brock, 1970	664
67	Jake Wood, 1961	663
	Bill Virdon, 1962	663
	Bobby Bonds, 1970	663
	Rick Burleson, 1977	663
	Cal Ripken, 1983	663
	Juan Samuel, 1985	663
	Joe Carter, 1986	663
	Carlos Beltran, 1999	663
75	Lloyd Waner, 1929	662
	Hughie Critz, 1930	662
	Richie Ashburn, 1949	662
	Granny Hamner, 1949	662
	Bobby Richardson, 1961	662
	Curt Flood, 1963	662
	Felipe Alou, 1968	662
	Pete Rose, 1975	662
	Kenny Lofton, 1996	662
	Dante Bichette, 1998	662
85	Doc Cramer, 1933	661
	Doc Cramer, 1940	661
	Ken Hubbs, 1962	661
	Cecil Cooper, 1983	661
	Ruben Sierra, 1991	661
90	Tom Brown, 1892	660
	Doc Cramer, 1941	660
	Lou Brock, 1968	660
	Enos Cabell, 1978	660
	Paul Molitor, 1996	660
95	9 players tied	659

Runs

Rank	Player	R
1	Billy Hamilton, 1894	198
2	Tom Brown, 1891	177
	Babe Ruth, 1921	177
4	Tip O'Neill, 1887	167
	Lou Gehrig, 1936	167
6	Billy Hamilton, 1895	166
7	Willie Keeler, 1894	165
	Joe Kelley, 1894	165
9	Arlie Latham, 1887	163
	Babe Ruth, 1928	163
	Lou Gehrig, 1931	163
12	Willie Keeler, 1895	162
13	Hugh Duffy, 1890	161
14	Fred Dunlap, 1884	160
	Hugh Duffy, 1894	160
	Jesse Burkett, 1896	160
17	Hughie Jennings, 1895	159
18	Bobby Lowe, 1894	158
	Babe Ruth, 1920	158
	Babe Ruth, 1927	158
	Chuck Klein, 1930	158
22	John McGraw, 1894	156
	Rogers Hornsby, 1929	156
24	King Kelly, 1886	155
	Kiki Cuyler, 1930	155
26	Dan Brouthers, 1887	153
	Jesse Burkett, 1895	153
	Billy Hamilton, 1896	153
	Willie Keeler, 1896	153
30	Arlie Latham, 1886	152
	Mike Griffin, 1889	152
	Harry Stovey, 1889	152
	Billy Hamilton, 1897	152
	Lefty O'Doul, 1929	152
	Woody English, 1930	152
	Al Simmons, 1930	152
	Chuck Klein, 1932	152
	Jeff Bagwell, 2000	152
39	Babe Ruth, 1923	151
	Jimmie Foxx, 1932	151
	Joe DiMaggio, 1937	151
42	George Gore, 1886	150
	Bill Dahlen, 1894	150
	Jake Stenzel, 1894	150
	Babe Ruth, 1930	150
	Ted Williams, 1949	150
47	Herman Long, 1893	149
	Ed Delahanty, 1895	149
	Lou Gehrig, 1927	149
	Babe Ruth, 1931	149
51	Hub Collins, 1890	148
	Ed Delahanty, 1894	148
	Joe Kelley, 1895	148
	Joe Kelley, 1896	148
55	Mike Tiernan, 1889	147
	Hugh Duffy, 1893	147
	Patsy Donovan, 1894	147
	Ty Cobb, 1911	147
59	Darby O'Brien, 1889	146
	Tom Brown, 1890	146
	Hack Wilson, 1930	146
	Rickey Henderson, 1985	146
	Craig Biggio, 1997	146
64	Jesse Burkett, 1893	145
	Cupid Childs, 1893	145
	Ed Delahanty, 1893	145
	Willie Keeler, 1897	145
	Nap Lajoie, 1901	145
	Harlond Clift, 1936	145
70	Hugh Duffy, 1889	144
	Billy Hamilton, 1889	144
	Ty Cobb, 1915	144
	Kiki Cuyler, 1925	144
	Charlie Gehringer, 1930	144
	Al Simmons, 1932	144
	Charlie Gehringer, 1936	144
	Hank Greenberg, 1938	144
78	Cupid Childs, 1894	143
	John McGraw, 1898	143
	Babe Ruth, 1924	143
	Babe Herman, 1930	143
	Lou Gehrig, 1930	143
	Earle Combs, 1932	143
	Red Rolfe, 1937	143
	Lenny Dykstra, 1993	143
	Larry Walker, 1997	143
	Jeff Bagwell, 1999	143
88	Mike Griffin, 1887	142
	Harry Stovey, 1890	142
	Jesse Burkett, 1901	142
	Paul Waner, 1928	142
	Ted Williams, 1946	142
	Ellis Burks, 1996	142
94	Billy Hamilton, 1891	141
	Rogers Hornsby, 1922	141
	Ted Williams, 1942	141
	Alex Rodriguez, 1996	141
98	9 players tied	140

Runs per Game (by era)

1876-1892

Rank	Player	R/G
1	Ross Barnes, 1876	1.91
2	Fred Dunlap, 1884	1.58
3	George Gore, 1890	1.42
4	Tip O'Neill, 1887	1.35
5	King Kelly, 1886	1.31
6	Tom Brown, 1891	1.29
7	George Gore, 1886	1.27
8	Dan Brouthers, 1887	1.24
9	Orator Shaffer, 1884	1.23
10	Mike Tiernan, 1889	1.20
11	Harry Stovey, 1890	1.20
12	Arlie Latham, 1887	1.20
13	Harry Stovey, 1884	1.19
14	George Gore, 1882	1.18
15	George Gore, 1881	1.18

1893-1919

Rank	Player	R/G
1	Billy Hamilton, 1894	1.50
2	Billy Hamilton, 1895	1.35
3	Billy Hamilton, 1893	1.34
4	Herman Long, 1894	1.31
5	Ed Delahanty, 1895	1.28
6	Hugh Duffy, 1894	1.28
7	Willie Keeler, 1894	1.28
	Joe Kelley, 1894	1.28
9	Ed Delahanty, 1894	1.28
10	John McGraw, 1894	1.26
11	Willie Keeler, 1895	1.24
12	Bill Dahlen, 1894	1.23
13	Willie Keeler, 1896	1.21
14	Hughie Jennings, 1895	1.21
15	Cupid Childs, 1894	1.21

1920-1941

Rank	Player	R/G
1	Babe Ruth, 1921	1.16
2	Babe Ruth, 1920	1.11
3	Al Simmons, 1930	1.10
4	Lou Gehrig, 1936	1.08
5	Babe Ruth, 1928	1.06
6	Lou Gehrig, 1931	1.05
7	Jimmie Foxx, 1939	1.05
8	Babe Ruth, 1927	1.05
9	Babe Ruth, 1930	1.03
10	Babe Ruth, 1931	1.03
11	Chuck Klein, 1930	1.01
12	Rogers Hornsby, 1929	1.00
	Joe DiMaggio, 1937	1.00
14	Kiki Cuyler, 1930	.99
15	Babe Ruth, 1923	.99

1942-1960

Rank	Player	R/G
1	Ted Williams, 1949	.97
2	Ted Williams, 1946	.95
3	Tommy Henrich, 1948	.95
4	Ted Williams, 1942	.94
5	Dom DiMaggio, 1950	.93
6	Ted Williams, 1948	.91
7	Johnny Mize, 1947	.89
8	Eddie Joost, 1949	.89
9	Mickey Mantle, 1954	.88
10	Johnny Pesky, 1950	.88
11	Mickey Mantle, 1956	.88
12	Stan Musial, 1948	.87
13	Goody Rosen, 1945	.87
	Dom DiMaggio, 1949	.87
15	Johnny Pesky, 1948	.87

1961-1976

Rank	Player	R/G
1	Mickey Mantle, 1961	.86
2	Bobby Bonds, 1970	.85
3	Billy Williams, 1970	.85
4	Willie Mays, 1961	.84
5	Frank Robinson, 1962	.83
6	Roger Maris, 1961	.82
7	Joe Morgan, 1972	.82
8	Bobby Bonds, 1973	.82
9	Hank Aaron, 1962	.81
10	Don Buford, 1971	.81
11	Reggie Jackson, 1969	.81
12	Jimmy Wynn, 1972	.81
13	Lou Brock, 1971	.80
14	Willie Mays, 1962	.80
	Pete Rose, 1976	.80

1977-2000

Rank	Player	R/G
1	Rickey Henderson, 1985	1.02
2	Paul Molitor, 1987	.97
3	Alex Rodriguez, 1996	.97
4	Jeff Bagwell, 2000	.96
5	Jeff Bagwell, 1994	.95
6	Frank Thomas, 1994	.94
7	Kenny Lofton, 1994	.94
8	Larry Walker, 1997	.93
9	Eric Davis, 1987	.93
10	Kenny Lofton, 1999	.92
11	Chuck Knoblauch, 1996	.92
12	Ellis Burks, 1996	.91
13	Alex Rodriguez, 2000	.91
14	Barry Bonds, 2000	.90
15	Craig Biggio, 1997	.90

Hits

Rank	Player	H
1	Pete Browning, 1887	275
	Tip O'Neill, 1887	275
3	George Sisler, 1920	257
4	Denny Lyons, 1887	256
5	Lefty O'Doul, 1929	254
	Bill Terry, 1930	254
7	Al Simmons, 1925	253
8	Oyster Burns, 1887	251
9	Rogers Hornsby, 1922	250
	Chuck Klein, 1930	250
11	Ty Cobb, 1911	248
12	George Sisler, 1922	246
13	Arlie Latham, 1887	243
14	Heinie Manush, 1928	241
	Babe Herman, 1930	241
16	Dan Brouthers, 1887	240
	Jesse Burkett, 1896	240
	Wade Boggs, 1985	240
	Darin Erstad, 2000	240
20	Willie Keeler, 1897	239
	Rod Carew, 1977	239
22	Ed Delahanty, 1899	238
	Don Mattingly, 1986	238
24	Hugh Duffy, 1894	237
	Harry Heilmann, 1921	237
	Paul Waner, 1927	237
	Joe Medwick, 1937	237
28	Jack Tobin, 1921	236
29	Sam Thompson, 1887	235
	Paul Radford, 1887	235
	Rogers Hornsby, 1921	235
32	Lloyd Waner, 1929	234
	Kirby Puckett, 1988	234
34	Joe Jackson, 1911	233
35	Nap Lajoie, 1901	232
	Earl Averill, 1936	232
37	Earle Combs, 1927	231
	Freddie Lindstrom, 1928	231
	Freddie Lindstrom, 1930	231
	Matty Alou, 1969	231
41	Reddy Mack, 1887	230
	Stan Musial, 1948	230
	Tommy Davis, 1962	230
	Joe Torre, 1971	230
	Pete Rose, 1973	230
	Willie Wilson, 1980	230
47	Rogers Hornsby, 1929	229
48	Kiki Cuyler, 1930	228
	Stan Musial, 1946	228
50	Nap Lajoie, 1910	227
	Rogers Hornsby, 1924	227
	Jim Bottomley, 1925	227
	Sam Rice, 1925	227
	Billy Herman, 1935	227
	Charlie Gehringer, 1936	227
	Lance Johnson, 1996	227
57	Jesse Burkett, 1901	226
	Joe Jackson, 1912	226
	Ty Cobb, 1912	226
	Bill Terry, 1929	226
	Chuck Klein, 1932	226
62	Billy Hamilton, 1894	225
	Jesse Burkett, 1895	225
	Ty Cobb, 1917	225
	Harry Heilmann, 1925	225
	Johnny Hodapp, 1930	225
	Bill Terry, 1932	225
	Paul Molitor, 1996	225
69	Cap Anson, 1887	224
	Bill McClellan, 1887	224
	Eddie Collins, 1920	224
	George Sisler, 1925	224
	Joe Medwick, 1935	224
	Tommy Holmes, 1945	224
75	Yank Robinson, 1887	223
	Frankie Frisch, 1923	223
	Lloyd Waner, 1927	223
	Paul Waner, 1928	223
	Chuck Klein, 1933	223
	Joe Medwick, 1936	223
	Hank Aaron, 1959	223
	Kirby Puckett, 1986	223
83	Frank Fennelly, 1887	222
	Sam Thompson, 1893	222
	Tris Speaker, 1912	222
	Charlie Jamieson, 1923	222
87	Jesse Burkett, 1899	221
	Zack Wheat, 1925	221
	Lloyd Waner, 1928	221
	Heinie Manush, 1933	221
	Richie Ashburn, 1951	221
92	Jimmy Williams, 1899	220
	Kiki Cuyler, 1925	220
	Lou Gehrig, 1930	220
	Stan Musial, 1943	220
	Tony Gwynn, 1997	220
97	10 players tied	219

Doubles

Rank	Player	2B
1	Earl Webb, 1931	67
2	George Burns, 1926	64
	Joe Medwick, 1936	64
4	Hank Greenberg, 1934	63
5	Paul Waner, 1932	62
6	Charlie Gehringer, 1936	60
7	Tris Speaker, 1923	59
	Chuck Klein, 1930	59
	Todd Helton, 2000	59
10	Billy Herman, 1935	57
	Billy Herman, 1936	57
	Carlos Delgado, 2000	57
13	Joe Medwick, 1937	56
	George Kell, 1950	56
	Craig Biggio, 1999	56
16	Ed Delahanty, 1899	55
	Gee Walker, 1936	55
18	Hal McRae, 1977	54
	John Olerud, 1993	54
	Alex Rodriguez, 1996	54
	Mark Grudzielanek, 1997	54
22	Tris Speaker, 1912	53
	Al Simmons, 1926	53
	Paul Waner, 1936	53
	Stan Musial, 1953	53
	Don Mattingly, 1986	53
	Jeff Cirillo, 2000	53
28	Tip O'Neill, 1887	52
	Tris Speaker, 1921	52
	Tris Speaker, 1926	52
	Lou Gehrig, 1927	52
	Johnny Frederick, 1929	52
	Enos Slaughter, 1939	52
	Albert Belle, 1995	52
	Edgar Martinez, 1995	52
	Edgar Martinez, 1996	52
37	Hugh Duffy, 1894	51
	Nap Lajoie, 1910	51
	Baby Doll Jacobson, 1926	51
	George Burns, 1927	51
	Johnny Hodapp, 1930	51
	Beau Bell, 1937	51
	Joe Cronin, 1938	51
	Stan Musial, 1944	51
	Mickey Vernon, 1946	51
	Frank Robinson, 1962	51
	Pete Rose, 1978	51
	Wade Boggs, 1989	51
	Mark Grace, 1995	51
	Craig Biggio, 1998	51
	Jose Vidro, 2000	51
	Nomar Garciaparra, 2000	51
53	Tris Speaker, 1920	50
	Harry Heilmann, 1927	50
	Paul Waner, 1928	50
	Kiki Cuyler, 1930	50
	Chuck Klein, 1932	50
	Charlie Gehringer, 1934	50
	Odell Hale, 1936	50
	Ben Chapman, 1936	50
	Hank Greenberg, 1940	50
	Stan Musial, 1946	50
	Stan Spence, 1946	50
	Juan Gonzalez, 1998	50
65	Ned Williamson, 1883	49
	Ed Delahanty, 1895	49
	Nap Lajoie, 1904	49
	George Sisler, 1920	49
	Heinie Manush, 1930	49
	Riggs Stephenson, 1932	49
	Hank Greenberg, 1937	49
	Robin Yount, 1980	49
	Rafael Palmeiro, 1991	49
	Tony Gwynn, 1997	49
75	Joe Kelley, 1894	48
	Nap Lajoie, 1901	48
	Nap Lajoie, 1906	48
	Tris Speaker, 1922	48
	Joe Sewell, 1927	48
	Babe Herman, 1930	48
	Dick Bartell, 1932	48
	Earl Averill, 1934	48
	Wally Moses, 1937	48
	Joe Medwick, 1939	48
	Stan Musial, 1943	48
	Keith Hernandez, 1979	48
	Don Mattingly, 1985	48
	Jeff Bagwell, 1996	48
	Dante Bichette, 1998	48
	Dmitri Young, 1998	48
	Albert Belle, 1998	48
92	27 players tied	47

Triples

Rank	Player	3B
1	Chief Wilson, 1912	36
2	Dave Orr, 1886	31
	Heinie Reitz, 1894	31
4	Perry Werden, 1893	29
5	Sam Thompson, 1894	28
	Harry Davis, 1897	28
7	George Davis, 1893	27
	Jimmy Williams, 1899	27
9	John Reilly, 1890	26
	George Treadway, 1894	26
	Joe Jackson, 1912	26
	Sam Crawford, 1914	26
	Kiki Cuyler, 1925	26
14	Roger Connor, 1894	25
	Buck Freeman, 1899	25
	Sam Crawford, 1903	25
	Larry Doyle, 1911	25
	Tom Long, 1915	25
19	Ed McKean, 1893	24
	Ty Cobb, 1911	24
	Ty Cobb, 1917	24
22	Harry Stovey, 1884	23
	Sam Thompson, 1887	23
	Elmer Smith, 1893	23
	Dan Brouthers, 1894	23
	Nap Lajoie, 1897	23
	Ty Cobb, 1912	23
	Sam Crawford, 1913	23
	Earle Combs, 1927	23
	Adam Comorosky, 1930	23
	Dale Mitchell, 1949	23
32	Roger Connor, 1887	22
	Bid McPhee, 1890	22
	Jake Beckley, 1890	22
	Joe Visner, 1890	22
	Willie Keeler, 1894	22
	Kip Selbach, 1895	22
	John Anderson, 1898	22
	Honus Wagner, 1900	22
	Tommy Leach, 1902	22
	Sam Crawford, 1902	22
	Bill Bradley, 1903	22
	Elmer Flick, 1906	22
	Mike Mitchell, 1911	22
	Birdie Cree, 1911	22
	Tris Speaker, 1913	22
	Hy Myers, 1920	22
	Jake Daubert, 1922	22
	Paul Waner, 1926	22
	Earle Combs, 1930	22
	Snuffy Stirnweiss, 1945	22
52	Dave Orr, 1885	21
	Mike Tiernan, 1890	21
	Billy Shindle, 1890	21
	Tom Brown, 1891	21
	Ed Delahanty, 1892	21
	Sam Thompson, 1895	21
	Mike Tiernan, 1895	21
	Tom McCreery, 1896	21
	George Van Haltren, 1896	21
	Bobby Wallace, 1897	21
	Jimmy Williams, 1901	21
	Bill Keister, 1901	21
	Jimmy Williams, 1902	21
	Cy Seymour, 1905	21
	Frank Schulte, 1911	21
	Frank Baker, 1912	21
	Sam Crawford, 1912	21
	Vic Saier, 1913	21
	Joe Jackson, 1916	21
	Edd Roush, 1924	21
	Earle Combs, 1928	21
	Willie Wilson, 1985	21
	Lance Johnson, 1996	21
75	37 players tied	20

Triples (by era)

1876-1892

Rank	Player	3B
1	Dave Orr, 1886	31
2	John Reilly, 1890	26
3	Harry Stovey, 1884	23
	Sam Thompson, 1887	23
5	Roger Connor, 1887	22
	Bid McPhee, 1890	22
	Jake Beckley, 1890	22
	Joe Visner, 1890	22
9	Dave Orr, 1885	21
	Mike Tiernan, 1890	21
	Billy Shindle, 1890	21
	Tom Brown, 1891	21
	Ed Delahanty, 1892	21
14	10 players tied	20

1893-1919

Rank	Player	3B
1	Chief Wilson, 1912	36
2	Heinie Reitz, 1894	31
3	Perry Werden, 1893	29
4	Sam Thompson, 1894	28
	Harry Davis, 1897	28
6	George Davis, 1893	27
	Jimmy Williams, 1899	27
8	George Treadway, 1894	26
	Joe Jackson, 1912	26
	Sam Crawford, 1914	26
11	Roger Connor, 1894	25
	Buck Freeman, 1899	25
	Sam Crawford, 1903	25
	Larry Doyle, 1911	25
	Tom Long, 1915	25

1920-1941

Rank	Player	3B
1	Kiki Cuyler, 1925	26
2	Earle Combs, 1927	23
	Adam Comorosky, 1930	23
4	Hy Myers, 1920	22
	Jake Daubert, 1922	22
	Paul Waner, 1926	22
	Earle Combs, 1930	22
8	Edd Roush, 1924	21
	Earle Combs, 1928	21
10	12 players tied	20

1942-1960

Rank	Player	3B
1	Dale Mitchell, 1949	23
2	Snuffy Stirnweiss, 1945	22
3	Stan Musial, 1943	20
	Stan Musial, 1946	20
	Willie Mays, 1957	20
6	Johnny Barrett, 1944	19
7	Stan Musial, 1948	18
	Minnie Minoso, 1954	18
9	Enos Slaughter, 1942	17
	Jim Gilliam, 1953	17
11	6 players tied	16

1961-1976

Rank	Player	3B
1	Ralph Garr, 1974	17
2	Johnny Callison, 1965	16
	Willie Davis, 1970	16
4	Gino Cimoli, 1962	15
5	Jake Wood, 1961	14
	Vada Pinson, 1963	14
	Dick Allen, 1965	14
	Roberto Clemente, 1965	14
	Donn Clendenon, 1965	14
	Lou Brock, 1968	14
	Don Kessinger, 1970	14
	Roger Metzger, 1973	14
	George Brett, 1976	14
14	10 players tied	13

1977-2000

Rank	Player	3B
1	Willie Wilson, 1985	21
	Lance Johnson, 1996	21
3	George Brett, 1979	20
	Cristian Guzman, 2000	20
5	Garry Templeton, 1979	19
	Juan Samuel, 1984	19
	Ryne Sandberg, 1984	19
8	Garry Templeton, 1977	18
	Willie McGee, 1985	18
10	Tony Fernandez, 1990	17
11	Rod Carew, 1977	16
	Paul Molitor, 1979	16
13	11 players tied	15

Home Runs

Rank	Player	HR
1	Mark McGwire, 1998	70
2	Sammy Sosa, 1998	66
3	Mark McGwire, 1999	65
4	Sammy Sosa, 1999	63
5	Roger Maris, 1961	61
6	Babe Ruth, 1927	60
7	Babe Ruth, 1921	59
8	Mark McGwire, 1997	58
	Jimmie Foxx, 1932	58
	Hank Greenberg, 1938	58
11	Hack Wilson, 1930	56
	Ken Griffey Jr., 1997	56
	Ken Griffey Jr., 1998	56
14	Babe Ruth, 1920	54
	Babe Ruth, 1928	54
	Ralph Kiner, 1949	54
	Mickey Mantle, 1961	54
18	Mickey Mantle, 1956	52
	Willie Mays, 1965	52
	George Foster, 1977	52
	Mark McGwire, 1996	52
22	Ralph Kiner, 1947	51
	Johnny Mize, 1947	51
	Willie Mays, 1955	51
	Cecil Fielder, 1990	51
26	Jimmie Foxx, 1938	50
	Albert Belle, 1995	50
	Brady Anderson, 1996	50
	Greg Vaughn, 1998	50
	Sammy Sosa, 2000	50
31	Babe Ruth, 1930	49
	Lou Gehrig, 1934	49
	Lou Gehrig, 1936	49
	Ted Kluszewski, 1954	49
	Willie Mays, 1962	49
	Harmon Killebrew, 1964	49
	Frank Robinson, 1966	49
	Harmon Killebrew, 1969	49
	Andre Dawson, 1987	49
	Mark McGwire, 1987	49
	Ken Griffey Jr., 1996	49
	Larry Walker, 1997	49
	Albert Belle, 1998	49
	Barry Bonds, 2000	49
45	Jimmie Foxx, 1933	48
	Harmon Killebrew, 1962	48
	Frank Howard, 1969	48
	Willie Stargell, 1971	48
	Dave Kingman, 1979	48
	Mike Schmidt, 1980	48
	Albert Belle, 1996	48
	Ken Griffey Jr., 1999	48
53	Babe Ruth, 1926	47
	Lou Gehrig, 1927	47
	Ralph Kiner, 1950	47
	Eddie Mathews, 1953	47
	Ted Kluszewski, 1955	47
	Ernie Banks, 1958	47
	Willie Mays, 1964	47
	Reggie Jackson, 1969	47
	Hank Aaron, 1971	47
	George Bell, 1987	47
	Kevin Mitchell, 1989	47
	Andres Galarraga, 1996	47
	Juan Gonzalez, 1996	47
	Rafael Palmeiro, 1999	47
	Jeff Bagwell, 2000	47
	Troy Glaus, 2000	47
69	Babe Ruth, 1924	46
	Babe Ruth, 1929	46
	Babe Ruth, 1931	46
	Lou Gehrig, 1931	46
	Joe DiMaggio, 1937	46
	Eddie Mathews, 1959	46
	Orlando Cepeda, 1961	46
	Jim Gentile, 1961	46
	Harmon Killebrew, 1961	46
	Jim Rice, 1978	46
	Barry Bonds, 1993	46
	Juan Gonzalez, 1993	46
	Vinny Castilla, 1998	46
	Jose Canseco, 1998	46
83	Ernie Banks, 1959	45
	Rocky Colavito, 1961	45
	Hank Aaron, 1962	45
	Harmon Killebrew, 1963	45
	Willie McCovey, 1969	45
	Johnny Bench, 1970	45
	Mike Schmidt, 1979	45
	Gorman Thomas, 1979	45
	Ken Griffey Jr., 1993	45
	Juan Gonzalez, 1998	45
	Manny Ramirez, 1998	45
	Chipper Jones, 1999	45
	Greg Vaughn, 1999	45
96	24 players tied	44

Home Runs (by era)

1876-1892

1	Ned Williamson, 1884	27
2	Fred Pfeffer, 1884	25
3	Abner Dalrymple, 1884	22
4	Cap Anson, 1884	21
5	Sam Thompson, 1889	20
6	Billy O'Brien, 1887	19
	Bug Holliday, 1889	19
	Harry Stovey, 1889	19
9	Jerry Denny, 1889	18
10	Roger Connor, 1887	17
	Jimmy Ryan, 1889	17
12	5 players tied	16

1893-1919

1	Babe Ruth, 1919	29
2	Buck Freeman, 1899	25
3	Gavvy Cravath, 1915	24
4	Frank Schulte, 1911	21
5	Ed Delahanty, 1893	19
	Gavvy Cravath, 1913	19
	Gavvy Cravath, 1914	19
8	Hugh Duffy, 1894	18
	Sam Thompson, 1895	18
	Fred Luderus, 1913	18
	Vic Saier, 1914	18
12	5 players tied	17

1920-1941

1	Babe Ruth, 1927	60
2	Babe Ruth, 1921	59
3	Jimmie Foxx, 1932	58
	Hank Greenberg, 1938	58
5	Hack Wilson, 1930	56
6	Babe Ruth, 1920	54
	Babe Ruth, 1928	54
8	Jimmie Foxx, 1938	50
9	Babe Ruth, 1930	49
	Lou Gehrig, 1934	49
	Lou Gehrig, 1936	49
12	Jimmie Foxx, 1933	48
13	Babe Ruth, 1926	47
	Lou Gehrig, 1927	47
15	5 players tied	46

1942-1960

1	Ralph Kiner, 1949	54
2	Mickey Mantle, 1956	52
3	Ralph Kiner, 1947	51
	Johnny Mize, 1947	51
	Willie Mays, 1955	51
6	Ted Kluszewski, 1954	49
7	Ralph Kiner, 1950	47
	Eddie Mathews, 1953	47
	Ted Kluszewski, 1955	47
	Ernie Banks, 1958	47
11	Eddie Mathews, 1959	46
12	Ernie Banks, 1959	45
13	Hank Greenberg, 1946	44
	Ernie Banks, 1955	44
	Hank Aaron, 1957	44

1961-1976

1	Roger Maris, 1961	61
2	Mickey Mantle, 1961	54
3	Willie Mays, 1965	52
4	Willie Mays, 1962	49
	Harmon Killebrew, 1964	49
	Frank Robinson, 1966	49
	Harmon Killebrew, 1969	49
8	Harmon Killebrew, 1962	48
	Frank Howard, 1969	48
	Willie Stargell, 1971	48
11	Willie Mays, 1964	47
	Reggie Jackson, 1969	47
	Hank Aaron, 1971	47
14	3 players tied	46

1977-2000

1	Mark McGwire, 1998	70
2	Sammy Sosa, 1998	66
3	Mark McGwire, 1999	65
4	Sammy Sosa, 1999	63
5	Mark McGwire, 1997	58
6	Ken Griffey Jr., 1997	56
	Ken Griffey Jr., 1998	56
8	George Foster, 1977	52
	Mark McGwire, 1996	52
10	Cecil Fielder, 1990	51
11	Albert Belle, 1995	50
	Brady Anderson, 1996	50
	Greg Vaughn, 1998	50
	Sammy Sosa, 2000	50
15	6 players tied	49

Home Run Percentage

1	Mark McGwire, 1998	13.75
2	Mark McGwire, 1999	12.48
3	Mark McGwire, 1996	12.29
4	Babe Ruth, 1920	11.79
5	Babe Ruth, 1927	11.11
6	Babe Ruth, 1921	10.93
7	Mark McGwire, 1997	10.74
8	Mickey Mantle, 1961	10.51
9	Hank Greenberg, 1938	10.43
10	Roger Maris, 1961	10.34
11	Sammy Sosa, 1998	10.26
12	Barry Bonds, 2000	10.21
13	Sammy Sosa, 1999	10.08
14	Babe Ruth, 1928	10.07
15	Jimmie Foxx, 1932	9.91
16	Ralph Kiner, 1949	9.84
17	Mickey Mantle, 1956	9.76
18	Jeff Bagwell, 1994	9.75
19	Kevin Mitchell, 1994	9.68
20	Matt Williams, 1994	9.66
21	Hack Wilson, 1930	9.57
22	Frank Thomas, 1994	9.52
23	Babe Ruth, 1926	9.49
	Hank Aaron, 1971	9.49
25	Jim Gentile, 1961	9.47
26	Barry Bonds, 1994	9.46
27	Babe Ruth, 1930	9.46
28	Willie Stargell, 1971	9.39
29	Willie Mays, 1965	9.32
30	Ken Griffey Jr., 1994	9.24
31	Babe Ruth, 1929	9.22
32	Ken Griffey Jr., 1997	9.21
33	Boog Powell, 1964	9.20
34	Willie McCovey, 1969	9.16
35	Albert Belle, 1995	9.16
36	Ted Williams, 1957	9.05
37	Ralph Kiner, 1947	9.03
38	Dave Kingman, 1979	9.02
39	Mark McGwire, 1992	8.99
40	Ken Griffey Jr., 1996	8.99
41	Babe Ruth, 1932	8.97
42	Cecil Fielder, 1990	8.90
43	Jimmie Foxx, 1938	8.85
44	Ken Griffey Jr., 1998	8.85
45	Harmon Killebrew, 1969	8.83
46	Mark McGwire, 1987	8.80
47	Willie Mays, 1955	8.79
48	Mike Schmidt, 1980	8.76
49	Mike Schmidt, 1981	8.76
50	Harmon Killebrew, 1963	8.74
	Albert Belle, 1994	8.74
52	Greg Vaughn, 1998	8.73
53	Johnny Mize, 1947	8.70
54	Babe Ruth, 1924	8.70
	Harmon Killebrew, 1962	8.70
56	Juan Gonzalez, 1996	8.69
57	Manny Ramirez, 2000	8.66
58	Kevin Mitchell, 1989	8.66
59	Brady Anderson, 1996	8.64
60	Larry Walker, 1997	8.63
61	Babe Ruth, 1922	8.62
62	Babe Ruth, 1931	8.61
63	Ralph Kiner, 1950	8.59
64	Gary Sheffield, 2000	8.58
65	Juan Gonzalez, 1993	8.58
66	Reggie Jackson, 1969	8.56
67	Ted Kluszewski, 1954	8.55
68	Barry Bonds, 1993	8.53
69	Jay Buhner, 1995	8.51
70	Frank Robinson, 1966	8.51
71	Harmon Killebrew, 1961	8.50
72	Harmon Killebrew, 1964	8.49
73	Lou Gehrig, 1934	8.46
	Lou Gehrig, 1936	8.46
75	George Foster, 1977	8.46
76	Larry Walker, 1999	8.45
77	Jason Giambi, 2000	8.43
78	Willie Stargell, 1973	8.43
	Manny Ramirez, 1999	8.43
80	Hank Greenberg, 1946	8.41
81	Eddie Mathews, 1954	8.40
82	Gary Sheffield, 1994	8.39
83	Rocky Colavito, 1958	8.38
84	Jimmie Foxx, 1933	8.38
85	Joe Adcock, 1956	8.37
86	Alex Rodriguez, 1999	8.37
87	Jack Clark, 1987	8.35
88	Troy Glaus, 2000	8.35
89	Rafael Palmeiro, 1999	8.32
90	Mike Schmidt, 1979	8.32
91	Sammy Sosa, 2000	8.28
92	Eddie Mathews, 1955	8.22
93	Greg Vaughn, 1999	8.18
94	Jimmie Foxx, 1934	8.16
95	Willie Mays, 1964	8.13
96	Barry Bonds, 1996	8.12
97	Eddie Mathews, 1953	8.12
98	Ted Williams, 1941	8.11
99	Frank Thomas, 1995	8.11
100	Frank Howard, 1969	8.11

Home Run Pctg.(by era)

1876-1892

1	Ned Williamson, 1884	6.47
2	Fred Pfeffer, 1884	5.35
3	Cap Anson, 1884	4.42
4	Abner Dalrymple, 1884	4.22
5	Billy O'Brien, 1887	4.01
6	Sam Thompson, 1889	3.75
7	Dan Brouthers, 1884	3.52
8	Harry Stovey, 1889	3.42
9	Bug Holliday, 1889	3.37
10	Harry Stovey, 1883	3.33
11	Charlie Duffee, 1889	3.14
12	Fred Pfeffer, 1887	3.12
13	Jerry Denny, 1889	3.11
14	Roger Connor, 1887	3.11
15	Dan Brouthers, 1881	2.96

1893-1919

1	Babe Ruth, 1919	6.71
2	Bill Joyce, 1894	4.79
3	Gavvy Cravath, 1915	4.60
4	Jack Clements, 1893	4.52
5	Buck Freeman, 1899	4.25
6	Gavvy Cravath, 1914	3.81
7	Frank Schulte, 1911	3.64
8	Gavvy Cravath, 1913	3.62
9	Jim Canavan, 1894	3.57
10	Bill Joyce, 1895	3.55
11	Sherry Magee, 1911	3.37
12	Vic Saier, 1914	3.35
13	Sam Thompson, 1895	3.35
14	Hugh Duffy, 1894	3.34
15	Ed Delahanty, 1893	3.19

1920-1941

1	Babe Ruth, 1920	11.79
2	Babe Ruth, 1927	11.11
3	Babe Ruth, 1921	10.93
4	Hank Greenberg, 1938	10.43
5	Babe Ruth, 1928	10.07
6	Jimmie Foxx, 1932	9.91
7	Hack Wilson, 1930	9.57
8	Babe Ruth, 1926	9.49
9	Babe Ruth, 1930	9.46
10	Babe Ruth, 1929	9.22
11	Babe Ruth, 1932	8.97
12	Jimmie Foxx, 1938	8.85
13	Babe Ruth, 1924	8.70
14	Babe Ruth, 1922	8.62
15	Babe Ruth, 1931	8.61

1942-1960

1	Ralph Kiner, 1949	9.84
2	Mickey Mantle, 1956	9.76
3	Ted Williams, 1957	9.05
4	Ralph Kiner, 1947	9.03
5	Willie Mays, 1955	8.79
6	Johnny Mize, 1947	8.70
7	Ralph Kiner, 1950	8.59
8	Ted Kluszewski, 1954	8.55
9	Hank Greenberg, 1946	8.41
10	Eddie Mathews, 1954	8.40
11	Rocky Colavito, 1958	8.38
12	Joe Adcock, 1956	8.37
13	Eddie Mathews, 1955	8.22
14	Eddie Mathews, 1953	8.12
15	Mickey Mantle, 1958	8.09

1961-1976

1	Mickey Mantle, 1961	10.51
2	Roger Maris, 1961	10.34
3	Hank Aaron, 1971	9.49
4	Jim Gentile, 1961	9.47
5	Willie Stargell, 1971	9.39
6	Willie Mays, 1965	9.32
7	Boog Powell, 1964	9.20
8	Willie McCovey, 1969	9.16
9	Harmon Killebrew, 1969	8.83
10	Harmon Killebrew, 1963	8.74
11	Harmon Killebrew, 1962	8.70
12	Reggie Jackson, 1969	8.56
13	Frank Robinson, 1966	8.51
14	Harmon Killebrew, 1961	8.50
15	Harmon Killebrew, 1964	8.49

1977-2000

1	Mark McGwire, 1998	13.75
2	Mark McGwire, 1999	12.48
3	Mark McGwire, 1996	12.29
4	Mark McGwire, 1997	10.74
5	Sammy Sosa, 1998	10.26
6	Barry Bonds, 2000	10.21
7	Sammy Sosa, 1999	10.08
8	Jeff Bagwell, 1994	9.75
9	Kevin Mitchell, 1994	9.68
10	Matt Williams, 1994	9.66
11	Frank Thomas, 1994	9.52
12	Barry Bonds, 1994	9.46
13	Ken Griffey Jr., 1994	9.24
14	Ken Griffey Jr., 1997	9.21
15	Albert Belle, 1995	9.16

Total Bases

1	Babe Ruth, 1921	457
2	Rogers Hornsby, 1922	450
3	Lou Gehrig, 1927	447
4	Chuck Klein, 1930	445
5	Jimmie Foxx, 1932	438
6	Stan Musial, 1948	429
7	Hack Wilson, 1930	423
8	Chuck Klein, 1932	420
9	Lou Gehrig, 1930	419
10	Joe DiMaggio, 1937	418
11	Babe Ruth, 1927	417
12	Babe Herman, 1930	416
	Sammy Sosa, 1998	416
14	Lou Gehrig, 1931	410
15	Rogers Hornsby, 1929	409
	Lou Gehrig, 1934	409
	Larry Walker, 1997	409
18	Tip O'Neill, 1887	407
19	Joe Medwick, 1937	406
	Jim Rice, 1978	406
21	Chuck Klein, 1929	405
	Hal Trosky, 1936	405
	Todd Helton, 2000	405
24	Jimmie Foxx, 1933	403
	Lou Gehrig, 1936	403
26	Hank Aaron, 1959	400
27	George Sisler, 1920	399
	Babe Ruth, 1923	399
	Albert Belle, 1998	399
30	Jimmie Foxx, 1938	398
31	Lefty O'Doul, 1929	397
	Hank Greenberg, 1937	397
	Sammy Sosa, 1999	397
34	Ken Griffey Jr., 1997	393
35	Al Simmons, 1925	392
	Bill Terry, 1930	392
	Al Simmons, 1930	392
	Ellis Burks, 1996	392
39	Babe Ruth, 1924	391
40	Hank Greenberg, 1935	389
41	Babe Ruth, 1920	388
	George Foster, 1977	388
	Don Mattingly, 1986	388
44	Ken Griffey Jr., 1998	387
45	Earl Averill, 1936	385
46	Hank Greenberg, 1940	384
	Alex Rodriguez, 1998	384
48	Mark McGwire, 1998	383
	Sammy Sosa, 2000	383
50	Stan Musial, 1949	382
	Willie Mays, 1955	382
	Willie Mays, 1962	382
	Jim Rice, 1977	382
	Juan Gonzalez, 1998	382
55	Rogers Hornsby, 1925	381
56	Babe Ruth, 1928	380
	Hank Greenberg, 1938	380
	Frank Robinson, 1962	380
	Vinny Castilla, 1998	380
60	Babe Ruth, 1930	379
	Ernie Banks, 1958	379
	Alex Rodriguez, 1996	379
	Vladimir Guerrero, 2000	379
64	Rogers Hornsby, 1921	378
	Duke Snider, 1954	378
	Carlos Delgado, 2000	378
67	Willie Mays, 1954	377
	Albert Belle, 1995	377
69	Mickey Mantle, 1956	376
	Andres Galarraga, 1996	376
71	Albert Belle, 1996	375
72	Hugh Duffy, 1894	374
	Babe Ruth, 1931	374
	Hal Trosky, 1934	374
	Tony Oliva, 1964	374
76	Rogers Hornsby, 1924	373
	Al Simmons, 1929	373
	Bill Terry, 1932	373
	Billy Williams, 1970	373
80	Lou Gehrig, 1932	370
	Duke Snider, 1953	370
	Hank Aaron, 1963	370
	Don Mattingly, 1985	370
	Mo Vaughn, 1996	370
85	Kiki Cuyler, 1925	369
	Ripper Collins, 1934	369
	Jimmie Foxx, 1936	369
	Hank Aaron, 1957	369
	Jim Rice, 1979	369
	George Bell, 1987	369
	Brady Anderson, 1996	369
92	Johnny Mize, 1940	368
	Ted Williams, 1949	368
	Ted Kluszewski, 1954	368
	Cal Ripken, 1991	368
96	11 players tied	367

Runs Batted In

Rank	Player, Year	RBI
1	Hack Wilson, 1930	191
2	Lou Gehrig, 1931	184
3	Hank Greenberg, 1937	183
4	Lou Gehrig, 1927	175
	Jimmie Foxx, 1938	175
6	Lou Gehrig, 1930	174
7	Babe Ruth, 1921	171
8	Chuck Klein, 1930	170
	Hank Greenberg, 1935	170
10	Jimmie Foxx, 1932	169
11	Joe DiMaggio, 1937	167
12	Sam Thompson, 1887	166
13	Sam Thompson, 1895	165
	Al Simmons, 1930	165
	Lou Gehrig, 1934	165
	Manny Ramirez, 1999	165
17	Babe Ruth, 1927	164
18	Babe Ruth, 1931	163
	Jimmie Foxx, 1933	163
20	Hal Trosky, 1936	162
21	Hack Wilson, 1929	159
	Lou Gehrig, 1937	159
	Ted Williams, 1949	159
	Vern Stephens, 1949	159
25	Sammy Sosa, 1998	158
26	Al Simmons, 1929	157
	Juan Gonzalez, 1998	157
28	Jimmie Foxx, 1930	156
29	Ken Williams, 1922	155
	Joe DiMaggio, 1948	155
31	Babe Ruth, 1929	154
	Joe Medwick, 1937	154
33	Babe Ruth, 1930	153
	Tommy Davis, 1962	153
35	Rogers Hornsby, 1922	152
	Lou Gehrig, 1936	152
	Albert Belle, 1998	152
38	Mel Ott, 1929	151
	Lou Gehrig, 1932	151
	Al Simmons, 1932	151
41	Hank Greenberg, 1940	150
	Andres Galarraga, 1996	150
43	Rogers Hornsby, 1929	149
	George Foster, 1977	149
45	Johnny Bench, 1970	148
	Albert Belle, 1996	148
	Rafael Palmeiro, 1999	148
48	Cap Anson, 1886	147
	Sam Thompson, 1894	147
	Ken Griffey Jr., 1997	147
	Mark McGwire, 1998	147
	Mark McGwire, 1999	147
	Todd Helton, 2000	147
54	Hardy Richardson, 1890	146
	Ed Delahanty, 1893	146
	Babe Ruth, 1926	146
	Hank Greenberg, 1938	146
	Ken Griffey Jr., 1998	146
59	Hugh Duffy, 1894	145
	Chuck Klein, 1929	145
	Ted Williams, 1939	145
	Al Rosen, 1953	145
	Don Mattingly, 1985	145
	Manny Ramirez, 1998	145
	Edgar Martinez, 2000	145
66	Walt Dropo, 1950	144
	Vern Stephens, 1950	144
	Juan Gonzalez, 1996	144
	Vinny Castilla, 1998	144
	Mike Sweeney, 2000	144
71	Rogers Hornsby, 1925	143
	Earl Averill, 1931	143
	Don Hurst, 1932	143
	Jimmie Foxx, 1936	143
	Ernie Banks, 1959	143
	Mo Vaughn, 1996	143
	Frank Thomas, 2000	143
78	Lou Gehrig, 1928	142
	Babe Ruth, 1928	142
	Hal Trosky, 1934	142
	Roy Campanella, 1953	142
	Orlando Cepeda, 1961	142
	Roger Maris, 1961	142
	Rafael Palmeiro, 1996	142
	Matt Williams, 1999	142
86	Ted Kluszewski, 1954	141
	Jim Gentile, 1961	141
	Willie Mays, 1962	141
	Dante Bichette, 1996	141
	Tino Martinez, 1997	141
	Sammy Sosa, 1999	141
92	Joe DiMaggio, 1938	140
	Rocky Colavito, 1961	140
	Harmon Killebrew, 1969	140
	Ken Griffey Jr., 1996	140
	Andres Galarraga, 1997	140
97	5 players tied	139

Runs Batted In per Game

Rank	Player, Year	RBI/G
1	Sam Thompson, 1894	1.44
2	Sam Thompson, 1895	1.39
3	Sam Thompson, 1887	1.31
4	Hack Wilson, 1930	1.23
5	Al Simmons, 1930	1.20
6	Hank Greenberg, 1937	1.19
7	Lou Gehrig, 1931	1.19
8	Cap Anson, 1886	1.18
9	Jimmie Foxx, 1938	1.17
10	Hugh Duffy, 1894	1.16
11	Dave Orr, 1890	1.16
12	Ed Delahanty, 1894	1.15
13	Babe Ruth, 1929	1.14
14	Lou Gehrig, 1930	1.13
15	Lou Gehrig, 1927	1.13
16	Babe Ruth, 1921	1.13
17	Babe Ruth, 1931	1.12
18	Hardy Richardson, 1890	1.12
19	Manny Ramirez, 1999	1.12
20	Hank Greenberg, 1935	1.12
21	Ed Delahanty, 1893	1.11
22	Joe DiMaggio, 1937	1.11
23	Al Simmons, 1929	1.10
24	Jimmie Foxx, 1932	1.10
25	Jimmie Foxx, 1933	1.09
26	Chuck Klein, 1930	1.09
27	Babe Ruth, 1927	1.09
28	Lave Cross, 1894	1.08
29	Oyster Burns, 1890	1.08
30	Juan Gonzalez, 1996	1.07
31	Hal Trosky, 1936	1.07
32	Lou Gehrig, 1934	1.07
33	Ed McKean, 1893	1.06
34	Hack Wilson, 1929	1.06
35	Dave Foutz, 1887	1.06
	Walt Dropo, 1950	1.06
37	Babe Ruth, 1930	1.06
38	Jeff Bagwell, 1994	1.05
39	Buck Ewing, 1893	1.05
40	Joe DiMaggio, 1939	1.05
41	Dan Brouthers, 1894	1.04
42	George Davis, 1897	1.04
43	Kirby Puckett, 1994	1.04
44	Rogers Hornsby, 1925	1.04
45	Jim O'Rourke, 1890	1.04
46	Manny Ramirez, 2000	1.03
47	Babe Ruth, 1932	1.03
48	Ted Williams, 1949	1.03
	Vern Stephens, 1949	1.03
50	Ed Delahanty, 1896	1.02
51	Steve Brodie, 1895	1.02
	Joe Kelley, 1895	1.02
53	Jimmie Foxx, 1930	1.02
54	Juan Gonzalez, 1998	1.02
55	Dave Orr, 1884	1.02
56	Hank Greenberg, 1940	1.01
57	Ken Williams, 1922	1.01
	Joe DiMaggio, 1948	1.01
59	Lou Gehrig, 1937	1.01
60	Cap Anson, 1882	1.01
61	George Brett, 1980	1.01
62	Joe DiMaggio, 1940	1.01
63	Mel Ott, 1929	1.01
64	George Decker, 1894	1.00
	Bug Holliday, 1894	1.00
	Nap Lajoie, 1897	1.00
	Al Simmons, 1931	1.00
	Ken Griffey Jr., 1996	1.00
69	Sammy Sosa, 1998	.99
70	Roger Connor, 1889	.99
71	Tommy McCarthy, 1894	.99
72	Tip O'Neill, 1887	.99
73	Jake Beckley, 1890	.99
74	Dan Brouthers, 1883	.99
75	Joe Medwick, 1937	.99
76	Rogers Hornsby, 1922	.99
77	Roy Campanella, 1953	.99
78	Jimmy Collins, 1897	.98
79	Juan Gonzalez, 1997	.98
80	Ed McKean, 1894	.98
81	Lou Gehrig, 1936	.98
82	Al Simmons, 1932	.98
83	Cap Anson, 1881	.98
84	Chuck Klein, 1929	.97
	Ted Williams, 1939	.97
86	Heinie Reitz, 1894	.97
87	Lou Gehrig, 1932	.97
88	Manny Ramirez, 1998	.97
89	Vern Stephens, 1950	.97
90	Joe DiMaggio, 1938	.97
91	Babe Ruth, 1920	.96
92	Cap Anson, 1885	.96
93	Walt Wilmot, 1894	.96
94	Hugh Duffy, 1897	.96
95	Sam Thompson, 1893	.96
96	Billy Nash, 1893	.96
97	Mark McGwire, 1999	.96
98	Babe Ruth, 1926	.96
99	Jay Buhner, 1995	.96
100	Harry Heilmann, 1929	.96

Walks

Rank	Player, Year	BB
1	Babe Ruth, 1923	170
2	Ted Williams, 1947	162
	Ted Williams, 1949	162
	Mark McGwire, 1998	162
5	Ted Williams, 1946	156
6	Eddie Yost, 1956	151
	Barry Bonds, 1996	151
8	Babe Ruth, 1920	150
9	Eddie Joost, 1949	149
	Jeff Bagwell, 1999	149
11	Eddie Stanky, 1945	148
	Jimmy Wynn, 1969	148
13	Jimmy Sheckard, 1911	147
14	Mickey Mantle, 1957	146
15	Babe Ruth, 1921	145
	Ted Williams, 1941	145
	Ted Williams, 1942	145
	Harmon Killebrew, 1969	145
	Barry Bonds, 1997	145
20	Babe Ruth, 1926	144
	Eddie Stanky, 1950	144
	Ted Williams, 1951	144
23	Babe Ruth, 1924	142
	Gary Sheffield, 1996	142
25	Eddie Yost, 1950	141
26	Frank Thomas, 1991	138
27	Babe Ruth, 1927	137
	Babe Ruth, 1928	137
	Eddie Stanky, 1946	137
	Roy Cullenbine, 1947	137
	Ralph Kiner, 1951	137
	Willie McCovey, 1970	137
	Jason Giambi, 2000	137
34	Jack Crooks, 1892	136
	Babe Ruth, 1930	136
	Ferris Fain, 1949	136
	Ted Williams, 1954	136
	Jack Clark, 1987	136
	Frank Thomas, 1995	136
40	Eddie Yost, 1959	135
	Jeff Bagwell, 1996	135
42	Ferris Fain, 1950	133
	Mark McGwire, 1999	133
44	Lou Gehrig, 1935	132
	Frank Howard, 1970	132
	Joe Morgan, 1975	132
	Jack Clark, 1989	132
	Tony Phillips, 1993	132
49	Bob Elliott, 1948	131
	Eddie Yost, 1954	131
	Harmon Killebrew, 1967	131
52	Babe Ruth, 1932	130
	Lou Gehrig, 1936	130
	Barry Bonds, 1998	130
55	Eddie Yost, 1952	129
	Mickey Mantle, 1958	129
	Lenny Dykstra, 1993	129
58	Billy Hamilton, 1894	128
	Max Bishop, 1929	128
	Max Bishop, 1930	128
	Babe Ruth, 1931	128
	Harmon Killebrew, 1970	128
	Carl Yastrzemski, 1970	128
	Mike Schmidt, 1983	128
65	Lu Blue, 1931	127
	Lou Gehrig, 1937	127
	Eddie Stanky, 1951	127
	Jimmy Wynn, 1976	127
	Barry Bonds, 1992	127
	Jeff Bagwell, 1997	127
	Jim Thome, 1999	127
72	Lu Blue, 1929	126
	Ted Williams, 1948	126
	Eddie Yost, 1951	126
	Mickey Mantle, 1961	126
	Darrell Evans, 1974	126
	Rickey Henderson, 1989	126
	Barry Bonds, 1993	126
	Chipper Jones, 1999	126
80	Richie Ashburn, 1954	125
	Eddie Yost, 1960	125
	Gene Tenace, 1977	125
	Wade Boggs, 1988	125
	Rickey Henderson, 1996	125
	Tony Phillips, 1996	125
	John Olerud, 1999	125
87	John McGraw, 1899	124
	Norm Cash, 1961	124
	Eddie Mathews, 1963	124
	Darrell Evans, 1973	124
91	Bill Joyce, 1890	123
	Eddie Yost, 1953	123
	Ken Singleton, 1973	123
	Edgar Martinez, 1996	123
	Jim Thome, 1996	123
	Carlos Delgado, 2000	123
97	9 players tied	122

Strikeouts

Rank	Player, Year	SO
1	Bobby Bonds, 1970	189
2	Bobby Bonds, 1969	187
	Preston Wilson, 2000	187
4	Rob Deer, 1987	186
5	Pete Incaviglia, 1986	185
6	Cecil Fielder, 1990	182
7	Mo Vaughn, 2000	181
8	Mike Schmidt, 1975	180
9	Rob Deer, 1986	179
10	Dave Nicholson, 1963	175
	Gorman Thomas, 1979	175
	Jose Canseco, 1986	175
	Rob Deer, 1991	175
	Jay Buhner, 1997	175
15	Sammy Sosa, 1997	174
16	Jim Presley, 1986	172
	Bo Jackson, 1989	172
18	Reggie Jackson, 1968	171
	Sammy Sosa, 1998	171
	Sammy Sosa, 1999	171
	Jim Thome, 1999	171
	Jim Thome, 2000	171
23	Gorman Thomas, 1980	170
24	Andres Galarraga, 1990	169
	Rob Deer, 1993	169
26	Juan Samuel, 1984	168
	Pete Incaviglia, 1987	168
	Sammy Sosa, 2000	168
29	Jim Edmonds, 2000	167
30	Gary Alexander, 1978	166
	Steve Balboni, 1985	166
	Cory Snyder, 1987	166
33	Donn Clendenon, 1968	163
	Troy Glaus, 2000	163
35	Butch Hobson, 1977	162
	Juan Samuel, 1987	162
	Ron Gant, 1997	162
38	Dick Allen, 1968	161
	Reggie Jackson, 1971	161
40	Mickey Tettleton, 1990	160
	Henry Rodriguez, 1996	160
42	Mark McGwire, 1997	159
	Richie Sexson, 2000	159
	Jay Buhner, 1996	159
	Jose Canseco, 1998	159
46	Bo Jackson, 1987	158
	Andres Galarraga, 1989	158
	Rob Deer, 1989	158
	Jose Canseco, 1990	158
	Melvin Nieves, 1996	158
	Jeromy Burnitz, 1998	158
52	Danny Tartabull, 1986	157
	Jose Canseco, 1987	157
	Jim Presley, 1987	157
	Andres Galarraga, 1996	157
	Melvin Nieves, 1997	157
57	Tommie Agee, 1970	156
	Dave Kingman, 1982	156
	Reggie Jackson, 1982	156
	Tony Armas, 1984	156
	Danny Tartabull, 1993	156
	Preston Wilson, 1999	156
63	Frank Howard, 1967	155
	Jeff Burroughs, 1975	155
	Mark McGwire, 1998	155
66	Willie Stargell, 1971	154
	Larry Parrish, 1987	154
	Dean Palmer, 1992	154
	Dean Palmer, 1993	154
	Mo Vaughn, 1996	154
	Mo Vaughn, 1997	154
72	Dave Kingman, 1975	153
	Andres Galarraga, 1988	153
	Rob Deer, 1988	153
	Pete Incaviglia, 1988	153
	Dean Palmer, 1999	153
77	George Scott, 1966	152
	Larry Hisle, 1969	152
	Jose Canseco, 1991	152
80	Don Lock, 1963	151
	Greg Luzinski, 1975	151
	Juan Samuel, 1988	151
	Delino DeShields, 1991	151
	Cecil Fielder, 1991	151
	Cecil Fielder, 1992	151
	Ray Lankford, 1998	151
	Jorge Posada, 2000	151
88	Dick Allen, 1965	150
	Nate Colbert, 1970	150
	Ron Kittle, 1983	150
	Jesse Barfield, 1989	150
	Jesse Barfield, 1990	150
	Sammy Sosa, 1990	150
	Mo Vaughn, 1995	150
95	Billy Grabarkewitz, 1970	149
	Mike Schmidt, 1976	149
	Fred McGriff, 1988	149
	Travis Fryman, 1991	149
	Henry Rodriguez, 1997	149
100	5 players tied	148

At Bats per Strikeout

1876-1892

1	Mike McGeary, 1876	278.0
2	Cap Anson, 1878	261.0
3	John Peters, 1876	159.5
4	John Clapp, 1876	153.0
5	Joe Start, 1877	135.5
6	Joe Start, 1876	132.5
7	Levi Meyerle, 1876	129.5
8	Jim Holdsworth, 1876	121.0
	Lon Knight, 1876	121.0
10	Ezra Sutton, 1876	119.5
11	Bobby Mathews, 1876	110.5
12	Deacon White, 1876	103.3
13	Paul Hines, 1876	102.0
14	Al Spalding, 1876	99.3
15	Davy Force, 1876	97.3

1893-1919

1	Jack Doyle, 1894	142.3
2	John Ward, 1893	117.6
3	Willie Keeler, 1894	98.3
4	John Ward, 1894	91.5
5	Joe Quinn, 1893	78.1
	Joe Quinn, 1895	78.1
7	Lave Cross, 1894	77.4
8	Steve Brodie, 1894	71.6
9	Jack Glasscock, 1893	69.7
10	Lave Cross, 1895	66.9
11	Ed McKean, 1896	63.4
12	Dummy Hoy, 1893	62.7
13	Patsy Donovan, 1893	62.4
14	Farmer Vaughn, 1896	61.9
15	Willie Keeler, 1896	60.4

1920-1941

1	Joe Sewell, 1932	167.7
2	Joe Sewell, 1925	152.0
3	Joe Sewell, 1929	144.5
4	Joe Sewell, 1933	131.0
5	Charlie Hollocher, 1922	118.4
6	Stuffy McInnis, 1922	107.4
7	Stuffy McInnis, 1924	96.8
8	Joe Sewell, 1926	96.3
9	Joe Sewell, 1927	81.3
10	Pie Traynor, 1929	77.1
11	Sam Rice, 1929	68.4
12	Tris Speaker, 1927	65.4
13	Joe Sewell, 1928	65.3
14	Sam Rice, 1925	64.9
15	Stuffy McInnis, 1921	64.9

1942-1960

1	Tommy Holmes, 1945	70.7
2	Emil Verban, 1947	67.5
3	Lou Boudreau, 1948	62.2
4	Dale Mitchell, 1949	58.2
5	Tommy Holmes, 1944	57.4
6	Dale Mitchell, 1952	56.8
7	Nellie Fox, 1958	56.6
8	Tommy Holmes, 1942	55.8
9	Jimmy Brown, 1942	55.1
10	Nellie Fox, 1951	54.9
11	Lou Boudreau, 1947	53.8
12	Nellie Fox, 1954	52.6
13	Harvey Kuenn, 1954	50.5
14	Don Mueller, 1955	50.4
15	Yogi Berra, 1950	49.8

1961-1976

1	Nellie Fox, 1962	51.8
2	Dave Cash, 1976	51.2
3	Nellie Fox, 1961	50.5
4	Matty Alou, 1970	37.6
5	Felix Millan, 1974	37.0
6	Vic Power, 1961	35.2
7	Nellie Fox, 1964	34.0
8	Glenn Beckert, 1968	32.2
9	Nellie Fox, 1963	31.7
10	Felix Millan, 1973	29.0
11	Bobby Richardson, 1962	28.8
12	Bobby Richardson, 1961	28.8
13	Bobby Richardson, 1963	28.6
14	Felix Millan, 1976	27.9
15	Glenn Beckert, 1972	27.9

1977-2000

1	Tim Foli, 1979	38.0
2	Tony Gwynn, 1995	35.7
3	Felix Fermin, 1993	34.3
4	Tony Gwynn, 1992	32.5
5	Bill Buckner, 1980	32.1
6	Tim Foli, 1981	31.6
7	Ozzie Smith, 1993	30.3
8	Bob Bailor, 1978	29.6
9	Rich Dauer, 1980	29.3
10	Tony Gwynn, 1991	27.9
11	Tony Gwynn, 1984	26.3
12	Bill Buckner, 1981	26.3
13	Tony Gwynn, 1993	25.7
14	Tony Gwynn, 1998	25.6
15	Bill Buckner, 1982	25.3

Strikeout Percentage

1876-1892

1	Frank Meinke, 1884	26.10
2	Jim Galvin, 1883	24.53
3	Sam Wise, 1884	24.41
4	Jim Galvin, 1879	21.13
5	Charlie Bastian, 1885	21.08
6	Will White, 1878	20.81
7	Silver Flint, 1883	20.78
8	John Morrill, 1884	19.86
9	John Morrill, 1885	19.80
10	Charlie Bastian, 1886	19.57
11	Jim Lillie, 1886	19.23
12	Will White, 1879	19.05
13	John Morrill, 1886	18.84
14	Sam Wise, 1883	18.23
15	Bill Crowley, 1884	18.18

1893-1919

1	Gus Williams, 1914	24.05
2	Grover Gilmore, 1914	20.38
3	Gavvy Cravath, 1916	19.87
4	Ed McDonald, 1912	19.83
5	Art Wilson, 1914	18.18
6	Gavvy Cravath, 1912	17.66
7	Cozy Dolan, 1914	17.58
8	Max Carey, 1911	17.56
9	Danny Moeller, 1913	17.49
10	Doug Baird, 1915	17.19
11	Al Boucher, 1914	17.05
12	Wally Pipp, 1915	16.91
13	Joe Agler, 1914	16.85
14	Ray Powell, 1919	16.81
15	Cy Williams, 1917	16.67

1920-1941

1	Vince DiMaggio, 1938	24.81
2	Vince DiMaggio, 1937	22.52
3	Chet Ross, 1940	22.32
4	Dolph Camilli, 1941	21.74
5	Joe Orengo, 1940	21.69
6	Jimmie Foxx, 1941	21.15
7	Boze Berger, 1935	21.04
8	Jimmie Foxx, 1936	20.34
9	Dolph Camilli, 1938	19.84
10	Babe Ruth, 1922	19.70
11	Babe Ruth, 1933	19.61
12	Jimmy Dykes, 1922	19.56
13	Hank Greenberg, 1939	19.00
14	Vince DiMaggio, 1941	18.94
15	Dolph Camilli, 1939	18.94

1942-1960

1	Pancho Herrera, 1960	26.56
2	Jim Lemon, 1956	25.65
3	Dick Stuart, 1960	24.43
4	Frank Howard, 1960	24.11
5	Harmon Killebrew, 1960	23.98
6	Jim Lemon, 1958	23.95
7	Mickey Mantle, 1960	23.72
8	Larry Doby, 1953	23.59
9	Pat Seerey, 1945	23.43
10	Mickey Mantle, 1959	23.29
11	Mickey Mantle, 1958	23.12
12	Wally Post, 1956	23.01
13	Woodie Held, 1959	22.48
14	Gil Hodges, 1959	22.28
15	Norm Zauchin, 1955	22.01

1961-1976

1	Dave Nicholson, 1963	38.98
2	Dick Allen, 1969	32.88
3	Mike Schmidt, 1975	32.03
4	Reggie Jackson, 1970	31.69
5	Larry Hisle, 1969	31.54
6	Reggie Jackson, 1968	30.92
7	Dick Allen, 1968	30.90
8	Dave Kingman, 1975	30.48
9	Willie Stargell, 1971	30.14
10	Bobby Bonds, 1969	30.06
11	Frank Howard, 1967	29.87
12	Rick Monday, 1968	29.67
13	Dave Kingman, 1972	29.66
14	Willie Mays, 1971	29.50
15	Jimmy Wynn, 1969	28.69

1977-2000

1	Rob Deer, 1987	39.24
2	Rob Deer, 1991	39.06
3	Rob Deer, 1986	38.41
4	Rob Deer, 1993	36.27
5	Mickey Tettleton, 1990	36.04
6	Benji Gil, 1995	35.42
7	Jim Thome, 1999	34.62
8	Pete Incaviglia, 1986	34.26
9	Rob Deer, 1989	33.91
10	Rob Deer, 1990	33.41
11	Bo Jackson, 1989	33.40
12	Gary Alexander, 1978	33.33
13	Jack Clark, 1987	33.17
14	Pete Incaviglia, 1987	33.01
15	Jose Canseco, 1990	32.85

Batting Average

1	Tip O'Neill, 1887	.485
2	Pete Browning, 1887	.457
3	Bob Caruthers, 1887	.456
4	Hugh Duffy, 1894	.440
5	Yank Robinson, 1887	.427
6	Nap Lajoie, 1901	.426
7	Willie Keeler, 1897	.424
8	Rogers Hornsby, 1924	.424
9	Cap Anson, 1887	.421
10	Dan Brouthers, 1887	.420
11	George Sisler, 1922	.420
12	Ty Cobb, 1911	.420
13	Denny Lyons, 1887	.415
14	Sam Thompson, 1894	.415
15	Fred Dunlap, 1884	.412
16	Reddy Mack, 1887	.410
17	Ed Delahanty, 1899	.410
18	Jesse Burkett, 1896	.410
19	Oyster Burns, 1887	.409
20	Ty Cobb, 1912	.409
21	Joe Jackson, 1911	.408
22	George Sisler, 1920	.407
23	Sam Thompson, 1887	.407
24	Ted Williams, 1941	.406
25	Jesse Burkett, 1895	.405
26	Ed Delahanty, 1895	.404
27	Ed Delahanty, 1894	.404
28	Ross Barnes, 1876	.404
29	Billy Hamilton, 1894	.403
30	Rogers Hornsby, 1925	.403
31	Harry Heilmann, 1923	.403
32	Rogers Hornsby, 1922	.401
33	Bill Terry, 1930	.401
34	Hughie Jennings, 1896	.401
35	Ty Cobb, 1922	.401
36	Cap Anson, 1881	.399
37	Lefty O'Doul, 1929	.398
38	Harry Heilmann, 1927	.398
39	Paul Radford, 1887	.397
	Rogers Hornsby, 1921	.397
41	Ed Delahanty, 1896	.397
42	Jesse Burkett, 1899	.396
43	Joe Jackson, 1912	.395
44	Tony Gwynn, 1994	.394
45	Harry Heilmann, 1921	.394
46	Babe Ruth, 1923	.393
47	Harry Heilmann, 1925	.393
48	Babe Herman, 1930	.393
49	Joe Kelley, 1894	.393
50	Sam Thompson, 1895	.392
51	King Kelly, 1887	.391
52	John McGraw, 1899	.391
53	Ty Cobb, 1913	.390
54	Dave Foutz, 1887	.390
55	Al Simmons, 1931	.390
56	George Brett, 1980	.390
57	Fred Clarke, 1897	.390
58	Otto Schomberg, 1887	.389
59	Tris Speaker, 1925	.389
60	Bill Lange, 1895	.389
61	Billy Hamilton, 1895	.389
62	Ty Cobb, 1921	.389
63	Ted Williams, 1957	.388
64	King Kelly, 1886	.388
65	Rod Carew, 1977	.388
66	Luke Appling, 1936	.388
67	Tris Speaker, 1920	.388
68	Lave Cross, 1894	.387
69	Deacon White, 1877	.387
70	Al Simmons, 1925	.387
71	Rogers Hornsby, 1928	.387
72	Tris Speaker, 1916	.386
73	Willie Keeler, 1896	.386
74	Chuck Klein, 1930	.386
75	Hughie Jennings, 1895	.386
76	Willie Keeler, 1898	.385
77	Arky Vaughan, 1935	.385
78	Rogers Hornsby, 1923	.384
79	Ty Cobb, 1919	.384
80	Nap Lajoie, 1910	.384
81	Ty Cobb, 1910	.383
82	Jesse Burkett, 1897	.383
83	Roger Connor, 1887	.383
84	Tris Speaker, 1912	.383
85	Ty Cobb, 1917	.383
86	Lefty O'Doul, 1930	.383
87	Joe Jackson, 1920	.382
88	Ty Cobb, 1918	.382
89	Sam Wise, 1887	.382
90	Honus Wagner, 1900	.381
91	Babe Herman, 1929	.381
92	Joe DiMaggio, 1939	.381
93	Al Simmons, 1930	.381
94	Fred Carroll, 1887	.381
95	Paul Waner, 1927	.380
96	Rogers Hornsby, 1929	.380
97	Billy Hamilton, 1893	.380
98	Tris Speaker, 1923	.380
99	Goose Goslin, 1928	.379
100	Freddie Lindstrom, 1930	.379

Batting Average (by era)

1876-1892

1	Tip O'Neill, 1887	.485
2	Pete Browning, 1887	.457
3	Bob Caruthers, 1887	.456
4	Yank Robinson, 1887	.427
5	Cap Anson, 1887	.421
6	Dan Brouthers, 1887	.420
7	Denny Lyons, 1887	.415
8	Fred Dunlap, 1884	.412
9	Reddy Mack, 1887	.410
10	Oyster Burns, 1887	.409
11	Sam Thompson, 1887	.407
12	Ross Barnes, 1876	.404
13	Cap Anson, 1881	.399
14	Paul Radford, 1887	.397
15	King Kelly, 1887	.391

1893-1919

1	Hugh Duffy, 1894	.440
2	Nap Lajoie, 1901	.426
3	Willie Keeler, 1897	.424
4	Ty Cobb, 1911	.420
5	Sam Thompson, 1894	.415
6	Ed Delahanty, 1899	.410
7	Jesse Burkett, 1896	.410
8	Ty Cobb, 1912	.409
9	Joe Jackson, 1911	.408
10	Jesse Burkett, 1895	.405
11	Ed Delahanty, 1895	.404
12	Ed Delahanty, 1894	.404
13	Billy Hamilton, 1894	.403
14	Hughie Jennings, 1896	.401
15	Ed Delahanty, 1896	.397

1920-1941

1	Rogers Hornsby, 1924	.424
2	George Sisler, 1922	.420
3	George Sisler, 1920	.407
4	Ted Williams, 1941	.406
5	Rogers Hornsby, 1925	.403
6	Harry Heilmann, 1923	.403
7	Rogers Hornsby, 1922	.401
8	Bill Terry, 1930	.401
9	Ty Cobb, 1922	.401
10	Lefty O'Doul, 1929	.398
11	Harry Heilmann, 1927	.398
12	Rogers Hornsby, 1921	.397
13	Harry Heilmann, 1921	.394
14	Babe Ruth, 1923	.393
15	Harry Heilmann, 1925	.393

1942-1960

1	Ted Williams, 1957	.388
2	Stan Musial, 1948	.376
3	Ted Williams, 1948	.369
4	Stan Musial, 1946	.365
5	Mickey Mantle, 1957	.365
6	Harry Walker, 1947	.363
7	Dixie Walker, 1944	.357
8	Stan Musial, 1943	.357
9	Ted Williams, 1942	.356
10	Phil Cavarretta, 1945	.355
11	Lou Boudreau, 1948	.355
12	Stan Musial, 1951	.355
13	Hank Aaron, 1959	.355
14	Billy Goodman, 1950	.354
15	Harvey Kuenn, 1959	.353

1961-1976

1	Rico Carty, 1970	.366
2	Rod Carew, 1974	.364
3	Joe Torre, 1971	.363
4	Norm Cash, 1961	.361
5	Rod Carew, 1975	.359
6	Roberto Clemente, 1967	.357
7	Bill Madlock, 1975	.354
8	Ralph Garr, 1974	.353
9	Roberto Clemente, 1961	.351
10	Rod Carew, 1973	.350
11	Pete Rose, 1969	.348
12	Tommy Davis, 1962	.346
13	Roberto Clemente, 1969	.345
14	Ralph Garr, 1971	.343
15	Vada Pinson, 1961	.343

1977-2000

1	Tony Gwynn, 1994	.394
2	George Brett, 1980	.390
3	Rod Carew, 1977	.388
4	Larry Walker, 1999	.379
5	Todd Helton, 2000	.372
6	Nomar Garciaparra, 2000	.372
7	Tony Gwynn, 1997	.372
8	Andres Galarraga, 1993	.370
9	Tony Gwynn, 1987	.370
10	Tony Gwynn, 1995	.368
11	Wade Boggs, 1985	.368
12	Jeff Bagwell, 1994	.368
13	Wade Boggs, 1988	.366
14	Larry Walker, 1997	.366
15	Larry Walker, 1998	.363

Batting Average (by position)

First Base

1	Cap Anson, 1887	.421
2	Dan Brouthers, 1887	.420
3	George Sisler, 1922	.420
4	George Sisler, 1920	.407
5	Bill Terry, 1930	.401
6	Cap Anson, 1881	.399
7	Otto Schomberg, 1887	.389
8	Rod Carew, 1977	.388
9	Roger Connor, 1887	.383
10	Lou Gehrig, 1930	.379

Second Base

1	Yank Robinson, 1887	.427
2	Nap Lajoie, 1901	.426
3	Rogers Hornsby, 1924	.424
4	Fred Dunlap, 1884	.412
5	Reddy Mack, 1887	.410
6	Ross Barnes, 1876	.404
7	Rogers Hornsby, 1925	.403
8	Rogers Hornsby, 1922	.401
9	Rogers Hornsby, 1921	.397
10	Rogers Hornsby, 1928	.387

Shortstop

1	Oyster Burns, 1887	.409
2	Hughie Jennings, 1896	.401
3	Luke Appling, 1936	.388
4	Hughie Jennings, 1895	.386
5	Arky Vaughan, 1935	.385
6	Nomar Garciaparra, 2000	.372
7	Ned Williamson, 1887	.371
8	John Ward, 1887	.371
9	Frank Fennelly, 1887	.365
10	Jack Rowe, 1887	.365

Third Base

1	Denny Lyons, 1887	.415
2	John McGraw, 1899	.391
3	George Brett, 1980	.390
4	Lave Cross, 1894	.387
5	Freddy Lindstrom, 1930	.379
6	Billy Nash, 1887	.374
7	Heinie Zimmerman, 1912	.372
8	John McGraw, 1895	.369
9	Wade Boggs, 1985	.368
10	Wade Boggs, 1988	.366

Outfield

1	Tip O'Neill, 1887	.485
2	Pete Browning, 1887	.457
3	Hugh Duffy, 1894	.440
4	Willie Keeler, 1897	.424
5	Ty Cobb, 1911	.420
6	Sam Thompson, 1894	.415
7	Ed Delahanty, 1899	.410
8	Jesse Burkett, 1896	.410
9	Ty Cobb, 1912	.409
10	Joe Jackson, 1911	.408
11	Sam Thompson, 1887	.407
12	Ted Williams, 1941	.406
13	Jesse Burkett, 1895	.405
14	Ed Delahanty, 1895	.404
15	Ed Delahanty, 1894	.404
16	Billy Hamilton, 1894	.403
17	Harry Heilmann, 1923	.403
18	Ty Cobb, 1922	.401
19	Lefty O'Doul, 1929	.398
20	Harry Heilmann, 1927	.398

Catcher

1	Cal McVey, 1877	.368
2	Mike Piazza, 1997	.362
3	Mickey Cochrane, 1930	.357
4	Wilbert Robinson, 1894	.353
5	Spud Davis, 1933	.349
6	Mickey Cochrane, 1931	.349
7	Mike Piazza, 1995	.346
8	Ernie Lombardi, 1938	.342
9	Gabby Hartnett, 1930	.339
10	Mickey Cochrane, 1927	.338

Relative Batting Average

1	Ross Barnes, 1876	1.540
2	Nap Lajoie, 1910	1.537
3	Ty Cobb, 1910	1.534
4	Pete Browning, 1882	1.526
5	Cap Anson, 1881	1.512
6	King Kelly, 1886	1.508
7	Roger Connor, 1885	1.506
8	Tris Speaker, 1916	1.506
9	Ty Cobb, 1917	1.501
10	Ty Cobb, 1912	1.501
11	Nap Lajoie, 1901	1.501
12	Nap Lajoie, 1904	1.499
13	Ty Cobb, 1911	1.493
14	Ty Cobb, 1909	1.492
15	Ted Williams, 1957	1.476
16	Ty Cobb, 1913	1.475
17	Ted Williams, 1941	1.472
18	Ty Cobb, 1918	1.469
19	George Gore, 1880	1.462
20	Rogers Hornsby, 1924	1.461
21	Rod Carew, 1977	1.458
22	Dan Brouthers, 1885	1.455
23	Joe Jackson, 1911	1.452
24	Joe Jackson, 1912	1.451
25	Dan Brouthers, 1882	1.449
26	Dave Orr, 1884	1.448
27	George Brett, 1980	1.448
28	Ty Cobb, 1915	1.448
29	Ty Cobb, 1916	1.445
30	Cap Anson, 1886	1.442
31	Pete Browning, 1885	1.439
32	Dan Brouthers, 1886	1.439
33	Tony Gwynn, 1994	1.436
34	Honus Wagner, 1908	1.434
35	George Sisler, 1922	1.433
36	Cap Anson, 1882	1.428
37	Cy Seymour, 1905	1.425
38	Willie Keeler, 1897	1.423
39	Tip O'Neill, 1887	1.416
40	Ed Delahanty, 1899	1.414
41	Wade Boggs, 1988	1.413
42	King Kelly, 1884	1.411
43	Joe Jackson, 1913	1.411
44	Rod Carew, 1974	1.408
45	Wade Boggs, 1985	1.407
46	Tris Speaker, 1912	1.406
47	Deacon White, 1877	1.405
48	Dan Brouthers, 1883	1.402
49	Jimmy Wolf, 1890	1.401
50	George Stone, 1906	1.400
51	Stan Musial, 1948	1.400
52	Cap Anson, 1888	1.399
53	George Sisler, 1920	1.398
54	Joe Torre, 1971	1.397
55	Hugh Duffy, 1894	1.393
56	Stan Musial, 1946	1.393
57	Ed Swartwood, 1883	1.392
58	Ty Cobb, 1919	1.392
59	Rod Carew, 1975	1.391
60	Tommy Tucker, 1889	1.391
61	Nap Lajoie, 1906	1.390
62	John Reilly, 1884	1.389
63	Harry Heilmann, 1923	1.389
64	Mickey Mantle, 1957	1.388
65	Willie Keeler, 1898	1.387
66	Honus Wagner, 1907	1.387
67	Roberto Clemente, 1967	1.385
68	George Sisler, 1917	1.383
69	Jim O'Rourke, 1884	1.383
70	Pete Browning, 1886	1.382
71	Tris Speaker, 1917	1.380
72	Ezra Sutton, 1884	1.380
73	Ty Cobb, 1907	1.379
74	Hick Carpenter, 1882	1.379
75	Roger Connor, 1886	1.378
76	Jesse Burkett, 1896	1.378
77	Paul Hines, 1879	1.377
78	Tony Gwynn, 1987	1.375
79	Larry Walker, 1999	1.375
80	Pete Browning, 1884	1.374
81	Tris Speaker, 1913	1.374
82	Tony Gwynn, 1997	1.374
83	Kirby Puckett, 1988	1.374
84	John Cassidy, 1877	1.373
85	Eddie Collins, 1909	1.373
86	Honus Wagner, 1905	1.372
87	Dave Orr, 1886	1.372
88	Rico Carty, 1970	1.372
89	Tip O'Neill, 1888	1.370
90	Wade Boggs, 1987	1.370
91	Ty Cobb, 1922	1.370
92	Dan Brouthers, 1889	1.370
93	Cap Anson, 1880	1.368
94	Norm Cash, 1961	1.368
95	Jesse Burkett, 1899	1.367
96	Andres Galarraga, 1993	1.366
97	Jesse Burkett, 1901	1.365
98	Hardy Richardson, 1886	1.365
99	Willie Keeler, 1904	1.365
100	Wade Boggs, 1986	1.365

On-Base Percentage

1	Ted Williams, 1941	.551
2	John McGraw, 1899	.547
3	Babe Ruth, 1923	.545
4	Babe Ruth, 1920	.532
5	Ted Williams, 1957	.528
6	Billy Hamilton, 1894	.522
7	Ted Williams, 1954	.516
8	Babe Ruth, 1926	.516
9	Mickey Mantle, 1957	.515
10	Babe Ruth, 1924	.513
11	Babe Ruth, 1921	.512
12	Rogers Hornsby, 1924	.507
13	John McGraw, 1900	.505
14	Joe Kelley, 1894	.502
15	Hugh Duffy, 1894	.502
16	Ed Delahanty, 1895	.500
17	Ted Williams, 1942	.499
18	Ted Williams, 1947	.499
19	Rogers Hornsby, 1928	.498
20	Ted Williams, 1946	.497
21	Ted Williams, 1948	.497
22	Bill Joyce, 1894	.496
23	Babe Ruth, 1931	.495
24	Frank Thomas, 1994	.494
25	Babe Ruth, 1930	.493
26	Arky Vaughan, 1935	.491
27	Ted Williams, 1949	.490
28	Billy Hamilton, 1895	.490
29	Billy Hamilton, 1893	.490
30	Tip O'Neill, 1887	.490
31	Rogers Hornsby, 1925	.489
	Babe Ruth, 1932	.489
33	Norm Cash, 1961	.488
34	Mickey Mantle, 1962	.488
35	Ty Cobb, 1915	.486
36	Babe Ruth, 1927	.486
37	Tris Speaker, 1920	.483
38	King Kelly, 1886	.483
39	Jesse Burkett, 1895	.482
40	Edgar Martinez, 1995	.482
41	Jason Giambi, 2000	.482
42	Harry Heilmann, 1923	.481
43	Wade Boggs, 1988	.480
44	Billy Hamilton, 1898	.480
45	Tris Speaker, 1925	.479
	Ted Williams, 1956	.479
47	Billy Hamilton, 1896	.478
48	John Olerud, 1993	.478
49	Lou Gehrig, 1936	.478
50	Cupid Childs, 1894	.475
51	John McGraw, 1898	.475
52	Ed Delahanty, 1894	.475
53	Harry Heilmann, 1927	.475
54	Tris Speaker, 1922	.474
55	Lou Gehrig, 1927	.474
56	Luke Appling, 1936	.474
57	Lou Gehrig, 1930	.473
58	Lou Gehrig, 1937	.473
59	Mark McGwire, 1998	.473
60	Carlos Delgado, 2000	.472
61	Hughie Jennings, 1896	.472
62	Ed Delahanty, 1896	.472
63	John McGraw, 1897	.471
64	Joe Morgan, 1975	.471
65	Dan Brouthers, 1891	.471
66	Todd Helton, 2000	.470
67	Tris Speaker, 1916	.470
68	Bill Joyce, 1896	.470
69	Joe Kelley, 1896	.469
70	Tris Speaker, 1923	.469
	Gary Sheffield, 1996	.469
72	Jimmie Foxx, 1932	.469
73	Jesse Burkett, 1897	.468
74	Ty Cobb, 1925	.468
75	Mark McGwire, 1996	.468
76	Joe Jackson, 1911	.468
77	Lou Gehrig, 1928	.467
78	Ty Cobb, 1913	.467
79	George Sisler, 1922	.467
80	Cupid Childs, 1896	.467
81	Mickey Mantle, 1956	.467
82	Edgar Martinez, 1996	.467
83	Wade Boggs, 1987	.467
84	Ty Cobb, 1911	.467
85	Dan Brouthers, 1890	.466
86	Lou Gehrig, 1935	.466
87	Lou Gehrig, 1934	.465
88	Lefty O'Doul, 1929	.465
89	Mike Griffin, 1894	.465
90	Frank Thomas, 1996	.465
91	Barry Bonds, 1996	.465
92	Sam Thompson, 1894	.465
93	Jimmie Foxx, 1939	.464
94	Tris Speaker, 1912	.464
95	Ed Delahanty, 1899	.464
96	Pete Browning, 1887	.464
97	Ted Williams, 1951	.464
98	Willie Keeler, 1897	.464
99	Paul O'Neill, 1994	.464
100	Larry Walker, 1999	.464

Slugging Average

1	Babe Ruth, 1920	.847
2	Babe Ruth, 1921	.846
3	Babe Ruth, 1927	.772
4	Lou Gehrig, 1927	.765
5	Babe Ruth, 1923	.764
6	Rogers Hornsby, 1925	.756
7	Mark McGwire, 1998	.752
8	Jeff Bagwell, 1994	.750
9	Jimmie Foxx, 1932	.749
10	Babe Ruth, 1924	.739
11	Babe Ruth, 1926	.737
12	Ted Williams, 1941	.735
13	Babe Ruth, 1930	.732
14	Ted Williams, 1957	.731
15	Mark McGwire, 1996	.730
16	Frank Thomas, 1994	.729
17	Hack Wilson, 1930	.723
18	Rogers Hornsby, 1922	.722
19	Lou Gehrig, 1930	.721
20	Larry Walker, 1997	.720
21	Albert Belle, 1994	.714
22	Larry Walker, 1999	.710
23	Babe Ruth, 1928	.709
24	Al Simmons, 1930	.708
25	Lou Gehrig, 1934	.706
26	Mickey Mantle, 1956	.705
27	Jimmie Foxx, 1938	.704
28	Jimmie Foxx, 1933	.703
29	Stan Musial, 1948	.702
30	Babe Ruth, 1931	.700
31	Todd Helton, 2000	.698
32	Babe Ruth, 1929	.697
33	Manny Ramirez, 2000	.697
34	Mark McGwire, 1999	.697
35	Sam Thompson, 1894	.696
36	Lou Gehrig, 1936	.696
37	Rogers Hornsby, 1924	.696
38	Hugh Duffy, 1894	.694
39	Jimmie Foxx, 1939	.694
40	Tip O'Neill, 1887	.691
41	Albert Belle, 1995	.690
42	Barry Bonds, 2000	.688
43	Mickey Mantle, 1961	.687
44	Chuck Klein, 1930	.687
45	Hank Greenberg, 1938	.683
46	Kevin Mitchell, 1994	.681
47	Rogers Hornsby, 1929	.679
48	Babe Herman, 1930	.678
49	Barry Bonds, 1993	.677
50	Ken Griffey Jr., 1994	.674
51	Joe DiMaggio, 1937	.673
52	Babe Ruth, 1922	.672
53	Joe DiMaggio, 1939	.671
54	Hank Greenberg, 1940	.670
55	Hank Aaron, 1971	.669
56	Hank Greenberg, 1937	.668
57	Ted Williams, 1946	.667
58	Willie Mays, 1954	.667
59	Mickey Mantle, 1957	.665
60	Carlos Delgado, 2000	.664
61	Vladimir Guerrero, 2000	.664
62	George Brett, 1980	.664
63	Manny Ramirez, 1999	.663
64	Lou Gehrig, 1931	.662
65	Norm Cash, 1961	.662
66	Babe Ruth, 1932	.661
67	Willie Mays, 1955	.659
68	Ralph Kiner, 1949	.658
69	Chuck Klein, 1929	.657
70	Babe Ruth, 1919	.657
71	Willie McCovey, 1969	.656
72	Albert Belle, 1998	.655
73	Sam Thompson, 1895	.654
74	Jimmie Foxx, 1934	.653
75	Chick Hafey, 1930	.652
76	Ted Williams, 1949	.650
77	Bill Joyce, 1894	.648
78	Lou Gehrig, 1928	.648
79	Ted Williams, 1942	.648
80	Duke Snider, 1954	.647
81	Barry Bonds, 1994	.647
	Jason Giambi, 2000	.647
83	Sammy Sosa, 1998	.647
84	Ken Griffey Jr., 1997	.646
85	Mark McGwire, 1997	.646
86	Chuck Klein, 1932	.646
87	Jim Gentile, 1961	.646
88	Willie Stargell, 1973	.646
89	Willie Mays, 1965	.645
90	Mike Schmidt, 1981	.644
91	Hal Trosky, 1936	.644
92	Nap Lajoie, 1901	.643
93	Joe DiMaggio, 1941	.643
	Juan Gonzalez, 1996	.643
95	Lou Gehrig, 1937	.643
96	Gary Sheffield, 2000	.643
97	Ted Kluszewski, 1954	.642
98	Al Simmons, 1929	.642
99	Joe Medwick, 1937	.641
100	Al Simmons, 1931	.641

On-Base Plus Slugging

1	Babe Ruth, 1920	1379
2	Babe Ruth, 1921	1359
3	Babe Ruth, 1923	1309
4	Ted Williams, 1941	1286
5	Ted Williams, 1957	1259
6	Babe Ruth, 1927	1258
7	Babe Ruth, 1926	1253
8	Babe Ruth, 1924	1252
9	Rogers Hornsby, 1925	1245
10	Lou Gehrig, 1927	1240
11	Mark McGwire, 1998	1225
12	Babe Ruth, 1930	1225
13	Frank Thomas, 1994	1223
14	Jimmie Foxx, 1932	1218
15	Jeff Bagwell, 1994	1211
16	Rogers Hornsby, 1924	1203
17	Mark McGwire, 1996	1199
18	Hugh Duffy, 1894	1196
19	Babe Ruth, 1931	1195
20	Lou Gehrig, 1930	1194
21	Rogers Hornsby, 1922	1181
22	Tip O'Neill, 1887	1180
23	Mickey Mantle, 1957	1179
24	Hack Wilson, 1930	1177
25	Larry Walker, 1997	1175
26	Lou Gehrig, 1936	1174
27	Larry Walker, 1999	1174
28	Mickey Mantle, 1956	1172
29	Babe Ruth, 1928	1172
30	Lou Gehrig, 1934	1172
31	Todd Helton, 2000	1168
32	Jimmie Foxx, 1938	1166
33	Ted Williams, 1946	1164
34	Sam Thompson, 1894	1161
35	Jimmie Foxx, 1939	1158
36	Manny Ramirez, 2000	1157
37	Albert Belle, 1994	1156
38	Jimmie Foxx, 1933	1153
39	Stan Musial, 1948	1152
40	Ted Williams, 1954	1151
41	Babe Ruth, 1932	1150
42	Norm Cash, 1961	1150
43	Ted Williams, 1942	1147
44	Bill Joyce, 1894	1143
45	Ted Williams, 1949	1141
46	Barry Bonds, 1993	1140
47	Rogers Hornsby, 1929	1139
48	Mickey Mantle, 1961	1138
49	Carlos Delgado, 2000	1137
50	Ted Williams, 1947	1133
51	Barry Bonds, 2000	1133
52	Babe Herman, 1930	1132
53	Al Simmons, 1930	1130
54	Rogers Hornsby, 1928	1130
55	Jason Giambi, 2000	1129
56	Babe Ruth, 1929	1128
57	George Brett, 1980	1124
58	Mark McGwire, 1999	1124
59	Chuck Klein, 1930	1123
60	Hank Greenberg, 1938	1122
61	Joe DiMaggio, 1939	1119
62	Kevin Mitchell, 1994	1119
63	Ed Delahanty, 1895	1117
64	Lou Gehrig, 1937	1116
65	Lou Gehrig, 1928	1115
66	Babe Ruth, 1919	1114
67	Willie McCovey, 1969	1114
68	Harry Heilmann, 1923	1113
69	Ted Williams, 1948	1112
70	Manny Ramirez, 1999	1111
71	Edgar Martinez, 1995	1110
72	Lou Gehrig, 1931	1108
73	Nap Lajoie, 1901	1106
74	Babe Ruth, 1922	1106
75	Hank Greenberg, 1937	1105
76	Joe Kelley, 1894	1104
77	Hank Greenberg, 1940	1103
78	Ed Delahanty, 1896	1103
79	Jimmie Foxx, 1934	1102
80	Arky Vaughan, 1935	1098
81	Rogers Hornsby, 1921	1097
82	Jimmie Foxx, 1935	1096
83	Gary Sheffield, 1996	1094
84	Albert Belle, 1995	1094
85	Mickey Mantle, 1962	1093
86	Frank Thomas, 1996	1091
87	Harry Heilmann, 1927	1091
88	Ralph Kiner, 1949	1089
89	Jimmie Foxx, 1929	1088
90	Ty Cobb, 1911	1088
91	Lefty O'Doul, 1929	1087
92	Rogers Hornsby, 1923	1086
93	Al Simmons, 1931	1085
94	Gary Sheffield, 2000	1085
95	Barry Bonds, 1992	1085
96	Joe DiMaggio, 1937	1085
97	Sam Thompson, 1895	1085
98	Ted Williams, 1956	1084
99	Mel Ott, 1929	1084
100	Joe DiMaggio, 1941	1083

Adjusted OPS

1	Babe Ruth, 1920	252
2	Babe Ruth, 1923	238
3	Babe Ruth, 1921	236
4	Ted Williams, 1941	232
5	Babe Ruth, 1927	229
6	Pete Browning, 1882	229
7	Babe Ruth, 1926	228
8	Ted Williams, 1957	227
9	Lou Gehrig, 1927	224
10	Babe Ruth, 1919	224
11	Babe Ruth, 1931	223
12	Mickey Mantle, 1957	223
13	Rogers Hornsby, 1924	223
14	Ross Barnes, 1876	222
15	Babe Ruth, 1924	221
16	Jeff Bagwell, 1994	220
17	Mark McGwire, 1998	218
18	Babe Ruth, 1930	216
19	Frank Thomas, 1994	214
20	Ted Williams, 1942	214
21	Lou Gehrig, 1934	213
22	Mickey Mantle, 1956	213
23	Willie McCovey, 1969	212
24	Ted Williams, 1946	211
25	Babe Ruth, 1928	211
26	Mickey Mantle, 1961	210
27	Rogers Hornsby, 1922	210
28	Ty Cobb, 1917	210
29	George Hall, 1876	208
30	Rogers Hornsby, 1925	208
31	Lou Gehrig, 1930	207
32	Barry Bonds, 1993	207
33	Barry Bonds, 1992	207
34	Babe Ruth, 1932	206
35	Tip O'Neill, 1887	205
36	Honus Wagner, 1908	205
37	Rogers Hornsby, 1928	204
38	Dan Brouthers, 1886	204
39	Nap Lajoie, 1904	204
40	Ty Cobb, 1912	203
41	Jimmie Foxx, 1932	203
42	Roger Connor, 1885	203
43	George Brett, 1980	203
44	Ty Cobb, 1910	202
45	Mark McGwire, 1996	201
46	Frank Robinson, 1966	200
47	Jimmie Foxx, 1933	199
48	Ted Williams, 1947	199
49	Lou Gehrig, 1931	199
50	Dan Brouthers, 1885	199
51	Babe Ruth, 1929	199
52	Dick Allen, 1972	199
53	Norm Cash, 1961	198
54	Mickey Mantle, 1962	198
55	Dan Brouthers, 1882	198
56	Nap Lajoie, 1910	198
57	Dave Orr, 1885	197
58	Ed Swartwood, 1882	197
59	Lou Gehrig, 1928	197
60	Stan Musial, 1948	196
61	Ty Cobb, 1918	196
62	Ty Cobb, 1913	196
63	Nap Lajoie, 1901	196
64	Orator Shaffer, 1878	196
65	Mike Schmidt, 1981	195
66	George Stone, 1906	195
67	Harry Heilmann, 1923	195
68	Dave Orr, 1884	195
69	Kevin Mitchell, 1989	194
70	Barry Bonds, 2000	194
71	Lou Gehrig, 1936	193
72	Ed Delahanty, 1899	193
73	Ty Cobb, 1911	193
74	Ted Williams, 1954	193
75	Joe Jackson, 1911	192
76	Gary Sheffield, 1996	192
77	Ed Delahanty, 1896	192
78	Mike Piazza, 1997	191
79	Rogers Hornsby, 1921	191
80	Albert Belle, 1994	191
81	Ty Cobb, 1909	190
82	Joe Jackson, 1913	190
83	Rickey Henderson, 1990	190
84	Pete Browning, 1885	190
85	Hank Aaron, 1971	190
86	Reggie Jackson, 1969	190
87	Deacon White, 1877	190
88	Joe Jackson, 1912	190
89	Rogers Hornsby, 1920	190
90	Cap Anson, 1881	189
91	Jim Gentile, 1961	189
92	Cupid Childs, 1890	189
93	Carl Yastrzemski, 1967	189
94	Mickey Mantle, 1958	189
95	Frank Robinson, 1967	189
96	Barry Bonds, 1996	189
97	Willie Stargell, 1973	189
98	Willie Stargell, 1971	188
99	King Kelly, 1879	188
100	Jimmie Foxx, 1934	188

Batting Runs

1	Babe Ruth, 1921	120
2	Babe Ruth, 1923	119
3	Babe Ruth, 1920	114
4	Tip O'Neill, 1887	110
5	Ted Williams, 1941	102
6	Babe Ruth, 1924	101
7	Lou Gehrig, 1927	101
8	Babe Ruth, 1927	100
9	Babe Ruth, 1926	97
10	Jimmie Foxx, 1932	97
11	Ted Williams, 1946	94
12	Rogers Hornsby, 1924	94
13	Mark McGwire, 1998	93
14	Ted Williams, 1942	93
15	Babe Ruth, 1931	92
16	Ted Williams, 1947	91
17	Stan Musial, 1948	90
18	Rogers Hornsby, 1922	90
19	Ted Williams, 1957	90
20	Babe Ruth, 1930	90
21	Mickey Mantle, 1957	89
22	Ted Williams, 1949	89
23	Lou Gehrig, 1930	88
24	Rogers Hornsby, 1925	87
25	Pete Browning, 1887	87
26	Norm Cash, 1961	86
27	Lou Gehrig, 1934	86
28	Larry Walker, 1997	85
29	Babe Ruth, 1928	85
30	Dan Brouthers, 1887	84
31	Mickey Mantle, 1956	83
32	Todd Helton, 2000	83
33	Jimmie Foxx, 1933	83
34	Lou Gehrig, 1936	82
35	Barry Bonds, 1993	82
36	Lou Gehrig, 1931	80
37	Carlos Delgado, 2000	79
38	Ty Cobb, 1911	78
39	Jimmie Foxx, 1938	78
40	Carl Yastrzemski, 1967	76
41	Mickey Mantle, 1961	76
42	Willie McCovey, 1969	76
43	Lou Gehrig, 1928	76
44	Ted Williams, 1948	76
45	Hugh Duffy, 1894	76
46	Hack Wilson, 1930	75
47	Rogers Hornsby, 1921	74
48	Ty Cobb, 1917	74
49	John Olerud, 1993	74
50	Rogers Hornsby, 1929	74
51	Nap Lajoie, 1901	74
52	Bob Caruthers, 1887	74
53	Frank Robinson, 1966	74
54	Oyster Burns, 1887	73
55	Lou Gehrig, 1937	73
56	George Sisler, 1920	73
57	Yank Robinson, 1887	73
58	Tris Speaker, 1912	73
59	Rogers Hornsby, 1928	72
60	Stan Musial, 1949	72
61	Roger Connor, 1887	72
62	Gary Sheffield, 1996	72
63	Jason Giambi, 2000	72
64	Arky Vaughan, 1935	72
65	Barry Bonds, 1992	72
66	Joe Jackson, 1911	72
67	Carl Yastrzemski, 1970	72
68	Ty Cobb, 1915	72
69	Edgar Martinez, 1995	71
70	Frank Thomas, 1994	71
71	Babe Ruth, 1932	71
72	Ted Williams, 1954	71
73	Tris Speaker, 1923	71
74	Stan Musial, 1946	71
75	Ralph Kiner, 1951	71
76	Harry Heilmann, 1923	71
77	Joe Jackson, 1912	70
78	Stan Musial, 1951	70
79	Ralph Kiner, 1949	70
80	Barry Bonds, 1996	69
81	Chuck Klein, 1933	69
82	Joe Medwick, 1937	69
83	Hank Greenberg, 1940	69
84	Denny Lyons, 1887	69
85	Johnny Mize, 1939	69
86	Babe Herman, 1930	69
87	Lou Gehrig, 1932	69
88	Lefty O'Doul, 1929	69
89	Nap Lajoie, 1910	68
90	Chuck Klein, 1932	68
91	Ty Cobb, 1910	68
92	Ed Delahanty, 1899	68
93	Cap Anson, 1887	68
94	Chuck Klein, 1930	67
95	Mark McGwire, 1996	67
96	Jimmie Foxx, 1935	67
97	Hank Greenberg, 1937	67
98	Ty Cobb, 1912	67
99	Rod Carew, 1977	67
100	Frank Robinson, 1962	67

Adjusted Batting Runs

1	Babe Ruth, 1923	116
2	Babe Ruth, 1921	115
3	Babe Ruth, 1920	107
4	Lou Gehrig, 1927	107
5	Babe Ruth, 1927	106
6	Babe Ruth, 1931	102
7	Babe Ruth, 1924	101
8	Babe Ruth, 1926	100
9	Rogers Hornsby, 1922	99
10	Lou Gehrig, 1934	98
11	Babe Ruth, 1930	98
12	Ted Williams, 1941	98
13	Rogers Hornsby, 1924	97
14	Lou Gehrig, 1930	97
15	Mark McGwire, 1998	95
16	Mickey Mantle, 1957	91
17	Lou Gehrig, 1931	90
18	Jimmie Foxx, 1932	90
19	Babe Ruth, 1928	90
20	Tip O'Neill, 1887	89
21	Lou Gehrig, 1936	89
22	Mickey Mantle, 1956	89
23	Barry Bonds, 1993	87
24	Ted Williams, 1942	87
25	Ted Williams, 1946	85
26	Oyster Burns, 1887	85
27	Mickey Mantle, 1961	85
28	Rogers Hornsby, 1925	83
29	Pete Browning, 1887	83
30	Ted Williams, 1957	82
31	Norm Cash, 1961	82
32	Lou Gehrig, 1928	81
33	Stan Musial, 1948	81
34	Jimmie Foxx, 1933	81
35	Roger Connor, 1887	81
36	Rogers Hornsby, 1928	81
37	Ted Williams, 1947	80
38	Babe Ruth, 1932	79
39	Willie McCovey, 1969	79
40	Dan Brouthers, 1887	78
41	Rogers Hornsby, 1921	78
42	Gary Sheffield, 1996	78
43	Lou Gehrig, 1932	78
44	Ted Williams, 1949	77
45	Carlos Delgado, 2000	77
46	Jason Giambi, 2000	76
47	Jeff Bagwell, 1996	76
48	Frank Robinson, 1966	76
49	Hank Aaron, 1959	76
50	Barry Bonds, 1996	75
51	Ty Cobb, 1917	75
52	Babe Ruth, 1919	74
53	Hack Wilson, 1930	74
54	Frank Thomas, 1994	74
55	Mike Piazza, 1997	74
56	Rogers Hornsby, 1929	74
57	Harry Heilmann, 1923	74
58	John Olerud, 1993	74
59	Ed Delahanty, 1899	74
60	Barry Bonds, 1992	73
61	Barry Bonds, 1998	73
62	Barry Bonds, 2000	73
63	Lou Gehrig, 1937	72
64	Jimmie Foxx, 1934	72
65	Ty Cobb, 1912	72
66	Babe Ruth, 1929	72
67	Jeff Bagwell, 1994	71
68	Tris Speaker, 1923	71
69	Frank Thomas, 1996	71
70	Frank Thomas, 1997	71
71	Ty Cobb, 1911	71
72	Babe Herman, 1930	71
73	Jimmie Foxx, 1938	71
74	Paul Radford, 1887	71
75	Lou Gehrig, 1935	70
76	Mark McGwire, 1996	70
77	Joe Jackson, 1911	70
78	Edgar Martinez, 1995	70
79	Frank Thomas, 1991	69
80	Mickey Mantle, 1958	69
81	Rod Carew, 1977	69
82	Stan Musial, 1951	69
83	Frank Thomas, 1995	69
84	Lou Gehrig, 1933	69
85	Denny Lyons, 1887	69
86	George Sisler, 1920	69
87	Jimmie Foxx, 1935	68
88	Ted Williams, 1948	68
89	Reggie Jackson, 1969	68
90	Rogers Hornsby, 1920	68
91	Nap Lajoie, 1901	68
92	Arky Vaughan, 1935	67
93	Al Rosen, 1953	67
94	Albert Belle, 1998	67
95	Ralph Kiner, 1951	67
96	Ed Delahanty, 1896	67
97	Nap Lajoie, 1910	66
98	Joe DiMaggio, 1941	66
99	Ralph Kiner, 1949	66
100	Jesse Burkett, 1901	66

Batting Wins

1	Babe Ruth, 1923	11.1
2	Babe Ruth, 1921	10.8
3	Babe Ruth, 1920	10.6
4	Ted Williams, 1941	9.5
5	Ted Williams, 1946	9.5
6	Lou Gehrig, 1927	9.3
7	Babe Ruth, 1927	9.2
8	Babe Ruth, 1924	9.2
9	Ted Williams, 1942	9.2
10	Babe Ruth, 1926	9.1
11	Ted Williams, 1947	9.1
12	Rogers Hornsby, 1924	9.0
13	Ted Williams, 1957	8.9
14	Mark McGwire, 1998	8.9
15	Mickey Mantle, 1957	8.9
16	Stan Musial, 1948	8.7
17	Jimmie Foxx, 1932	8.7
18	Tip O'Neill, 1887	8.6
19	Ted Williams, 1949	8.4
20	Norm Cash, 1961	8.3
21	Babe Ruth, 1931	8.3
22	Rogers Hornsby, 1922	8.3
23	Carl Yastrzemski, 1967	8.2
24	Larry Walker, 1997	8.1
25	Ty Cobb, 1917	8.0
26	Barry Bonds, 1993	8.0
27	Babe Ruth, 1928	7.9
28	Mickey Mantle, 1956	7.9
29	Rogers Hornsby, 1925	7.9
30	Babe Ruth, 1930	7.9
31	Lou Gehrig, 1930	7.8
32	Lou Gehrig, 1934	7.8
33	Willie McCovey, 1969	7.7
34	Frank Robinson, 1966	7.7
35	Jimmie Foxx, 1933	7.6
36	Todd Helton, 2000	7.6
37	Barry Bonds, 1992	7.5
38	Ty Cobb, 1911	7.5
39	Ty Cobb, 1915	7.4
40	Mickey Mantle, 1961	7.4
41	Nap Lajoie, 1910	7.4
42	Stan Musial, 1946	7.3
43	Honus Wagner, 1908	7.3
44	Ty Cobb, 1910	7.3
45	Dick Allen, 1972	7.3
46	Lou Gehrig, 1931	7.3
47	Carl Yastrzemski, 1970	7.3
48	Rogers Hornsby, 1921	7.2
49	Lou Gehrig, 1928	7.2
50	Ted Williams, 1948	7.1
51	Chuck Klein, 1933	7.1
52	Lou Gehrig, 1936	7.1
53	Tris Speaker, 1912	7.1
54	Ted Williams, 1954	7.1
55	John Olerud, 1993	7.1
56	Carlos Delgado, 2000	7.1
57	Stan Musial, 1949	7.0
58	Ty Cobb, 1909	7.0
59	Tris Speaker, 1916	7.0
60	George Sisler, 1920	6.9
61	Ralph Kiner, 1951	6.9
62	Gary Sheffield, 1996	6.9
63	Dan Brouthers, 1887	6.9
64	Jimmie Foxx, 1938	6.9
65	Rogers Hornsby, 1928	6.9
66	Joe Jackson, 1911	6.9
67	Joe Jackson, 1912	6.9
68	Pete Browning, 1887	6.9
69	Stan Musial, 1951	6.8
70	Stan Musial, 1943	6.8
71	Arky Vaughan, 1935	6.8
72	Hank Aaron, 1971	6.8
73	Joe Jackson, 1913	6.8
74	Ralph Kiner, 1949	6.8
75	Babe Ruth, 1919	6.7
76	Harmon Killebrew, 1969	6.7
77	Harmon Killebrew, 1967	6.7
78	Johnny Mize, 1939	6.7
79	Tris Speaker, 1923	6.7
80	Nap Lajoie, 1904	6.7
81	Willie Mays, 1965	6.7
82	Joe Medwick, 1937	6.7
83	Hank Aaron, 1963	6.7
84	Harry Heilmann, 1923	6.7
85	Barry Bonds, 1996	6.6
86	Rogers Hornsby, 1929	6.6
87	Lou Gehrig, 1937	6.6
88	Chuck Klein, 1932	6.6
89	Cy Seymour, 1905	6.6
90	Ty Cobb, 1912	6.5
91	Edgar Martinez, 1995	6.5
92	Joe Torre, 1971	6.5
93	Rogers Hornsby, 1920	6.5
94	Hack Wilson, 1930	6.5
95	Nap Lajoie, 1901	6.5
96	Rod Carew, 1977	6.5
97	Frank Robinson, 1962	6.5
98	Wade Boggs, 1988	6.5
99	Kevin Mitchell, 1989	6.5
100	Jason Giambi, 2000	6.5

Adjusted Batting Wins

1	Babe Ruth, 1923	10.8
2	Babe Ruth, 1921	10.4
3	Babe Ruth, 1920	10.0
4	Lou Gehrig, 1927	9.8
5	Babe Ruth, 1927	9.7
6	Babe Ruth, 1926	9.4
7	Rogers Hornsby, 1924	9.3
8	Babe Ruth, 1924	9.3
9	Babe Ruth, 1931	9.2
10	Ted Williams, 1941	9.2
11	Mickey Mantle, 1957	9.1
12	Mark McGwire, 1998	9.1
13	Rogers Hornsby, 1922	9.0
14	Lou Gehrig, 1934	8.9
15	Ted Williams, 1946	8.7
16	Ted Williams, 1942	8.6
17	Babe Ruth, 1930	8.6
18	Lou Gehrig, 1930	8.5
19	Babe Ruth, 1928	8.5
20	Barry Bonds, 1993	8.4
21	Mickey Mantle, 1956	8.4
22	Lou Gehrig, 1931	8.2
23	Mickey Mantle, 1961	8.1
24	Ted Williams, 1957	8.1
25	Jimmie Foxx, 1932	8.1
26	Ty Cobb, 1917	8.1
27	Ted Williams, 1947	8.0
28	Willie McCovey, 1969	8.0
29	Frank Robinson, 1966	7.9
30	Stan Musial, 1948	7.9
31	Norm Cash, 1961	7.9
32	Lou Gehrig, 1936	7.7
33	Barry Bonds, 1992	7.6
34	Lou Gehrig, 1928	7.6
35	Rogers Hornsby, 1928	7.6
36	Rogers Hornsby, 1925	7.6
37	Babe Ruth, 1919	7.5
38	Rogers Hornsby, 1921	7.5
39	Jimmie Foxx, 1933	7.5
40	Hank Aaron, 1959	7.4
41	Gary Sheffield, 1996	7.4
42	Honus Wagner, 1908	7.3
43	Ted Williams, 1949	7.3
44	Jeff Bagwell, 1996	7.3
45	Barry Bonds, 1996	7.2
46	Nap Lajoie, 1910	7.2
47	Babe Ruth, 1932	7.1
48	Mike Piazza, 1997	7.1
49	Carl Yastrzemski, 1967	7.1
50	Rogers Hornsby, 1920	7.0
51	Tip O'Neill, 1887	7.0
52	Dick Allen, 1972	7.0
53	Barry Bonds, 1998	7.0
54	Lou Gehrig, 1932	7.0
55	John Olerud, 1993	7.0
56	Ty Cobb, 1912	7.0
57	Mickey Mantle, 1958	7.0
58	Reggie Jackson, 1969	6.9
59	Harry Heilmann, 1923	6.9
60	Carlos Delgado, 2000	6.9
61	Kevin Mitchell, 1989	6.9
62	Jason Giambi, 2000	6.8
63	Hank Aaron, 1963	6.8
64	Frank Thomas, 1991	6.8
65	Nap Lajoie, 1904	6.8
66	Jeff Bagwell, 1994	6.8
67	Ty Cobb, 1911	6.8
68	George Stone, 1906	6.8
69	Stan Musial, 1951	6.8
70	Oyster Burns, 1887	6.7
71	Stan Musial, 1946	6.7
72	Joe Jackson, 1911	6.7
73	Rod Carew, 1977	6.7
74	Tris Speaker, 1923	6.7
75	Barry Bonds, 2000	6.7
76	Ty Cobb, 1915	6.7
77	Roger Connor, 1887	6.7
78	Frank Thomas, 1994	6.6
79	Frank Thomas, 1997	6.6
80	Al Rosen, 1953	6.6
81	Babe Ruth, 1929	6.6
82	Rogers Hornsby, 1929	6.6
83	Jimmie Foxx, 1934	6.6
84	Pete Browning, 1887	6.6
85	Frank Howard, 1969	6.6
86	Ralph Kiner, 1951	6.5
87	Ed Delahanty, 1899	6.5
88	Lou Gehrig, 1937	6.5
89	George Sisler, 1920	6.5
90	Ted Williams, 1948	6.5
91	Ty Cobb, 1910	6.5
92	Lou Gehrig, 1935	6.4
93	Dan Brouthers, 1887	6.4
94	Joe Jackson, 1912	6.4
95	Bobby Murcer, 1971	6.4
96	Edgar Martinez, 1995	6.4
97	Harmon Killebrew, 1969	6.4
98	Hack Wilson, 1930	6.4
99	Joe Jackson, 1913	6.4
100	Ralph Kiner, 1949	6.4

Runs Created

1	Babe Ruth, 1921	239
2	Pete Browning, 1887	238
3	Tip O'Neill, 1887	238
4	Babe Ruth, 1923	223
5	Hugh Duffy, 1894	217
6	Lou Gehrig, 1927	212
7	Babe Ruth, 1920	212
8	Billy Hamilton, 1894	210
9	Jimmie Foxx, 1932	209
10	Babe Ruth, 1927	208
11	Ty Cobb, 1911	207
12	Babe Ruth, 1924	205
13	Ted Williams, 1941	202
14	Rogers Hornsby, 1922	200
15	Lou Gehrig, 1936	199
16	Denny Lyons, 1887	198
17	Babe Ruth, 1926	196
18	Lou Gehrig, 1930	195
19	Oyster Burns, 1887	195
20	Lou Gehrig, 1934	195
21	Dan Brouthers, 1887	194
22	Babe Ruth, 1931	194
23	Mark McGwire, 1998	193
24	Ted Williams, 1949	193
25	Todd Helton, 2000	192
26	Babe Ruth, 1930	191
27	Stan Musial, 1948	191
28	Hack Wilson, 1930	189
29	Jimmie Foxx, 1938	189
30	Ted Williams, 1946	188
31	Mickey Mantle, 1956	188
32	Rogers Hornsby, 1925	187
33	Larry Walker, 1997	187
34	Ted Williams, 1947	186
35	Rogers Hornsby, 1924	186
36	Carlos Delgado, 2000	186
37	Chuck Klein, 1930	186
38	Ted Williams, 1942	185
39	Jimmie Foxx, 1933	184
40	Yank Robinson, 1887	184
41	Lou Gehrig, 1931	184
42	Rogers Hornsby, 1929	183
43	Babe Ruth, 1928	183
44	Babe Herman, 1930	183
45	Joe Kelley, 1894	182
46	Lou Gehrig, 1937	181
47	Chuck Klein, 1932	180
48	Arlie Latham, 1887	180
49	Lefty O'Doul, 1929	180
50	Jim Fogarty, 1887	180
51	Nap Lajoie, 1901	179
52	Mickey Mantle, 1957	178
53	Billy Hamilton, 1895	178
54	Joe Kelley, 1896	178
55	Norm Cash, 1961	178
56	Hank Greenberg, 1937	178
57	Roger Connor, 1887	177
58	Ed Delahanty, 1895	176
59	George Sisler, 1920	176
60	Willie Keeler, 1897	176
61	Ed Delahanty, 1899	175
62	Benny Kauff, 1914	175
63	Tris Speaker, 1912	175
64	Joe Jackson, 1911	175
65	Paul Radford, 1887	174
66	Mickey Mantle, 1961	174
67	Stan Musial, 1949	173
68	Joe DiMaggio, 1937	173
69	Ty Cobb, 1912	173
70	King Kelly, 1887	172
71	Barry Bonds, 1993	172
72	Bob Caruthers, 1887	172
73	Jason Giambi, 2000	172
74	Hank Greenberg, 1938	172
75	Ted Williams, 1948	172
76	Hank Greenberg, 1940	171
77	Ed Delahanty, 1896	170
78	Joe Medwick, 1937	170
79	Bill Terry, 1930	170
80	Stan Musial, 1951	169
81	Lou Gehrig, 1928	169
82	Lou Gehrig, 1932	169
83	Rogers Hornsby, 1921	169
84	Earl Averill, 1936	168
85	Jimmie Foxx, 1936	168
86	Sam Thompson, 1895	167
87	Ted Williams, 1957	167
88	Frank Fennelly, 1887	167
89	Ed Delahanty, 1893	167
90	Jesse Burkett, 1896	166
91	Stan Musial, 1953	166
92	Joe Jackson, 1912	166
93	Sam Thompson, 1887	166
94	Tris Speaker, 1923	166
95	Jimmie Foxx, 1934	165
96	Ralph Kiner, 1951	165
97	Mike Griffin, 1887	165
98	Chipper Jones, 1999	165
99	Ty Cobb, 1917	164
100	Jake Stenzel, 1894	164

Total Average

1	Babe Ruth, 1920	1.803
2	Babe Ruth, 1921	1.748
3	Ted Williams, 1941	1.688
4	Tip O'Neill, 1887	1.685
5	Babe Ruth, 1923	1.683
6	Bob Caruthers, 1887	1.650
7	Hugh Duffy, 1894	1.619
8	Babe Ruth, 1926	1.606
9	John McGraw, 1899	1.601
10	Ted Williams, 1957	1.599
11	Billy Hamilton, 1894	1.592
12	Pete Browning, 1887	1.590
13	Babe Ruth, 1927	1.568
14	Babe Ruth, 1924	1.558
15	Rogers Hornsby, 1925	1.539
16	Mickey Mantle, 1957	1.534
17	Bill Joyce, 1894	1.528
18	Ed Delahanty, 1895	1.517
19	Mark McGwire, 1998	1.512
20	Babe Ruth, 1930	1.509
21	Yank Robinson, 1887	1.505
22	Joe Kelley, 1894	1.503
23	Lou Gehrig, 1927	1.500
24	Babe Ruth, 1931	1.487
25	Ty Cobb, 1911	1.464
26	Frank Thomas, 1994	1.453
27	Ted Williams, 1954	1.452
28	Jimmie Foxx, 1932	1.451
29	Sam Thompson, 1894	1.451
30	Billy Hamilton, 1895	1.443
31	Babe Ruth, 1932	1.432
32	Ted Williams, 1946	1.431
33	Joe Kelley, 1896	1.430
34	Lou Gehrig, 1936	1.426
35	Mickey Mantle, 1956	1.426
36	Rogers Hornsby, 1924	1.424
37	Mark McGwire, 1996	1.420
38	Jeff Bagwell, 1994	1.413
39	Hack Wilson, 1930	1.411
40	Babe Ruth, 1928	1.410
41	Rogers Hornsby, 1928	1.409
42	Ed Delahanty, 1896	1.405
43	Lou Gehrig, 1934	1.401
44	Dan Brouthers, 1887	1.399
45	Ted Williams, 1942	1.394
46	Jimmie Foxx, 1938	1.392
47	Ted Williams, 1947	1.391
48	Lou Gehrig, 1930	1.389
49	Billy Hamilton, 1893	1.386
50	Mickey Mantle, 1962	1.385
51	Mickey Mantle, 1961	1.384
52	Larry Walker, 1997	1.373
53	Bill Lange, 1895	1.373
54	Jason Giambi, 2000	1.370
55	King Kelly, 1886	1.366
56	Babe Ruth, 1919	1.358
57	Norm Cash, 1961	1.358
58	Todd Helton, 2000	1.356
59	Rogers Hornsby, 1922	1.353
60	Roger Connor, 1887	1.353
61	Babe Herman, 1930	1.351
62	Jimmie Foxx, 1933	1.348
63	Ted Williams, 1948	1.347
64	Ted Williams, 1949	1.347
65	Larry Walker, 1999	1.344
66	Barry Bonds, 2000	1.339
67	Manny Ramirez, 2000	1.339
68	Lou Gehrig, 1937	1.339
69	Barry Bonds, 1993	1.339
70	Rogers Hornsby, 1929	1.338
71	Barry Bonds, 1996	1.338
72	Barry Bonds, 1992	1.335
73	Carlos Delgado, 2000	1.334
74	Nap Lajoie, 1901	1.327
75	Billy Hamilton, 1896	1.325
76	Ty Cobb, 1912	1.321
77	Ty Cobb, 1910	1.321
78	Joe Morgan, 1976	1.319
79	Arky Vaughan, 1935	1.317
80	King Kelly, 1887	1.314
81	Jake Stenzel, 1894	1.312
82	Ty Cobb, 1913	1.310
83	Jimmie Foxx, 1934	1.310
84	Tris Speaker, 1912	1.310
85	Jim Fogarty, 1887	1.309
86	Oyster Burns, 1887	1.309
87	Joe Jackson, 1911	1.308
88	Bill Joyce, 1896	1.306
89	Hank Greenberg, 1938	1.306
90	Denny Lyons, 1887	1.305
91	Albert Belle, 1994	1.304
92	Jimmie Foxx, 1939	1.304
93	Edgar Martinez, 1995	1.300
94	Stan Musial, 1948	1.298
95	Willie McCovey, 1969	1.296
96	Joe Kelley, 1895	1.289
97	Jimmie Foxx, 1935	1.288
98	Babe Ruth, 1929	1.288
99	Harry Heilmann, 1923	1.288
100	Mel Ott, 1929	1.287

Runs Produced

1	Lou Gehrig, 1931	301
2	Babe Ruth, 1921	289
3	Chuck Klein, 1930	288
4	Hugh Duffy, 1894	287
5	Billy Hamilton, 1894	284
6	Hack Wilson, 1930	281
	Al Simmons, 1930	281
8	Hughie Jennings, 1895	280
	Hank Greenberg, 1937	280
10	Sam Thompson, 1895	278
11	Ed Delahanty, 1894	277
	Lou Gehrig, 1927	277
13	Tip O'Neill, 1887	276
	Kiki Cuyler, 1930	276
	Lou Gehrig, 1930	276
16	Sam Thompson, 1887	274
17	Ed Delahanty, 1893	272
	Joe Kelley, 1895	272
	Joe DiMaggio, 1937	272
20	Joe Kelley, 1894	270
	Lou Gehrig, 1936	270
22	Ty Cobb, 1911	266
	Rogers Hornsby, 1929	266
	Babe Ruth, 1931	266
	Ted Williams, 1949	266
26	Jimmie Foxx, 1938	264
27	Ed Delahanty, 1899	263
28	Babe Ruth, 1927	262
	Jimmie Foxx, 1932	262
30	Walt Wilmot, 1894	261
31	Al Simmons, 1932	260
	Lou Gehrig, 1937	260
33	Hardy Richardson, 1890	259
	Hugh Duffy, 1893	259
35	Jake Stenzel, 1894	258
36	Dan Brouthers, 1894	256
	Bobby Lowe, 1894	256
	Nap Lajoie, 1901	256
39	Hack Wilson, 1929	255
	Lou Gehrig, 1932	255
	Hank Greenberg, 1935	255
42	Cap Anson, 1886	254
	Willie Keeler, 1894	254
	Lou Gehrig, 1928	254
	Babe Ruth, 1930	254
46	Lave Cross, 1894	253
47	Harry Stovey, 1889	252
	Manny Ramirez, 1999	252
49	Pete Browning, 1887	251
	Rogers Hornsby, 1922	251
	Babe Ruth, 1928	251
	Earl Averill, 1931	251
	Chuck Klein, 1932	251
54	Charlie Gehringer, 1934	250
55	Sam Thompson, 1894	248
	Hugh Duffy, 1897	248
57	John McGraw, 1894	247
	Mel Ott, 1929	247
59	Hughie Jennings, 1896	246
	Tris Speaker, 1923	246
	Jimmie Foxx, 1930	246
	Zeke Bonura, 1936	246
	Tommy Davis, 1962	246
64	Sam Thompson, 1893	245
	Bill Terry, 1930	245
	Lou Gehrig, 1933	245
	Charlie Gehringer, 1936	245
	Ted Williams, 1939	245
69	Arlie Latham, 1887	244
	Tom Brown, 1891	244
	Steve Brodie, 1894	244
	Ed Delahanty, 1895	244
	Ed Delahanty, 1896	244
	Ken Williams, 1922	244
	Lou Gehrig, 1934	244
	Hal Trosky, 1936	244
77	Bill Dahlen, 1894	243
	Todd Helton, 2000	243
79	Dan Brouthers, 1887	242
	Ed McKean, 1895	242
	Lefty O'Doul, 1929	242
	Ted Williams, 1942	242
83	Babe Ruth, 1920	241
	Babe Ruth, 1923	241
85	Dan Brouthers, 1892	240
	Joe Kelley, 1896	240
	Ty Cobb, 1915	240
	George Sisler, 1920	240
	Joe Cronin, 1930	240
	Jimmie Foxx, 1933	240
91	Hughie Jennings, 1894	239
	Vern Stephens, 1950	239
93	Charlie Comiskey, 1887	238
	Jake Beckley, 1894	238
	George Davis, 1897	238
	Babe Ruth, 1926	238
	Babe Herman, 1930	238
	Hank Greenberg, 1940	238
99	4 players tied	237

Clutch Hitting Index

1	Cap Anson, 1880	178
2	Tom Herr, 1987	172
3	Ed Abbaticchio, 1907	166
4	Bill McClellan, 1878	165
	Ed McKean, 1892	165
6	Lon Knight, 1881	164
7	Jack Barry, 1913	163
8	George Stovall, 1911	163
9	John Sullivan, 1943	162
10	Tom Herr, 1985	161
11	Cookie Lavagetto, 1941	160
12	Fred Hartman, 1902	160
13	Cap Anson, 1886	158
14	Sherry Magee, 1918	158
15	John Gochnauer, 1903	155
16	Tommy Davis, 1969	155
17	Maurice Van Robays, 1940	154
18	George Davis, 1906	154
19	Art Devlin, 1904	154
20	Frank LaPorte, 1910	154
21	Jack Rowe, 1888	153
22	Pete Hotaling, 1888	153
23	John Ward, 1886	153
24	Sam Crawford, 1910	153
25	Johnny Berardino, 1941	152
26	Jackie Hayes, 1937	152
27	Rebel Oakes, 1915	152
28	Sam Thompson, 1887	151
29	Bill Harbidge, 1878	151
	Pop Corkhill, 1886	151
	Frank LaPorte, 1914	151
	Possum Whitted, 1920	151
33	Heinie Reitz, 1896	151
34	Earl Sheely, 1931	151
35	Joe Gerhardt, 1879	150
	Oyster Burns, 1890	150
	Socks Seybold, 1907	150
38	Cy Seymour, 1908	150
39	Tom Burns, 1888	150
40	Joe Battin, 1876	150
41	Norm Larker, 1960	149
42	Chick Galloway, 1925	149
43	Earl Sheely, 1924	149
	Vic Wertz, 1960	149
45	Jack Crooks, 1890	149
46	Hugh Duffy, 1896	148
47	Cap Anson, 1893	148
48	Roger Connor, 1884	148
49	Farmer Vaughn, 1893	148
	Bill Brubaker, 1936	148
51	Pie Traynor, 1928	147
52	Reddy Mack, 1889	147
	Larry Kopf, 1920	147
54	Pete Hotaling, 1880	147
55	Fred Pfeffer, 1882	147
56	Doc Gessler, 1911	147
57	Stuffy McInnis, 1914	147
58	Heinie Zimmerman, 1917	146
59	Bill Dahlen, 1904	146
60	Bill Holbert, 1882	146
61	Deacon White, 1885	146
62	Ned Williamson, 1885	146
	Clyde Barnhart, 1925	146
64	Jimmy Brown, 1942	146
65	Nap Lajoie, 1912	145
66	Cap Anson, 1881	145
	Cap Anson, 1890	145
68	Cap Anson, 1885	145
69	Dave Foutz, 1889	145
70	Mike Mowrey, 1916	145
71	Roy McMillan, 1956	145
72	Joe Kelley, 1898	145
73	Larry Gardner, 1920	144
74	Lave Cross, 1903	144
75	Jose Cardenal, 1971	144
76	Ty Cobb, 1907	144
77	Cap Anson, 1882	143
	Ed Delahanty, 1900	143
79	Hal Chase, 1909	143
80	Cal McVey, 1879	143
	Jim O'Rourke, 1887	143
	Ferris Fain, 1949	143
83	Kirby Puckett, 1994	143
84	John Ward, 1881	143
	Maurice Van Robays, 1941	143
	Joe Medwick, 1942	143
87	Eddie Collins, 1919	143
	Bobby Veach, 1922	143
89	Bill Hague, 1878	142
	Ron Fairly, 1964	142
91	Hick Carpenter, 1886	142
	Ross Youngs, 1921	142
93	Bob Ferguson, 1877	142
94	Monte Cross, 1900	142
	Milt Stock, 1921	142
	Enos Slaughter, 1953	142
97	Deacon White, 1876	142
	Fred Pfeffer, 1892	142
99	Cap Anson, 1896	141
	Tommy Corcoran, 1903	141

Isolated Power

1	Babe Ruth, 1920	.472
2	Babe Ruth, 1921	.469
3	Mark McGwire, 1998	.454
4	Mark McGwire, 1996	.418
5	Mark McGwire, 1999	.418
6	Babe Ruth, 1927	.417
7	Lou Gehrig, 1927	.392
8	Babe Ruth, 1928	.386
9	Jimmie Foxx, 1932	.385
10	Jeff Bagwell, 1994	.382
11	Barry Bonds, 2000	.381
12	Frank Thomas, 1994	.376
13	Albert Belle, 1995	.374
14	Babe Ruth, 1930	.373
15	Mark McGwire, 1997	.372
16	Babe Ruth, 1923	.372
17	Mickey Mantle, 1961	.370
18	Hank Greenberg, 1938	.369
19	Hack Wilson, 1930	.368
20	Babe Ruth, 1926	.366
21	Babe Ruth, 1924	.361
22	Babe Ruth, 1922	.357
23	Albert Belle, 1994	.357
24	Jimmie Foxx, 1938	.356
25	Kevin Mitchell, 1994	.355
26	Larry Walker, 1997	.354
27	Rogers Hornsby, 1925	.353
28	Mickey Mantle, 1956	.353
29	Babe Ruth, 1929	.353
30	Ken Griffey Jr., 1994	.351
31	Roger Maris, 1961	.351
32	Ralph Kiner, 1949	.348
33	Jimmie Foxx, 1933	.347
34	Sammy Sosa, 1999	.347
35	Willie Stargell, 1973	.347
36	Manny Ramirez, 2000	.346
37	Kevin Mitchell, 1989	.344
38	Lou Gehrig, 1934	.344
39	Jim Gentile, 1961	.344
40	Ted Williams, 1957	.343
41	Lou Gehrig, 1930	.343
42	Ken Griffey Jr., 1997	.342
43	Lou Gehrig, 1936	.342
44	Hank Aaron, 1971	.341
45	Barry Bonds, 1993	.341
46	Brady Anderson, 1996	.340
47	Willie Mays, 1955	.340
48	Matt Williams, 1994	.339
49	Sammy Sosa, 1998	.339
50	Mike Schmidt, 1980	.338
51	Willie McCovey, 1969	.336
52	Babe Ruth, 1919	.336
53	Barry Bonds, 1994	.335
54	Jimmie Foxx, 1939	.334
55	Reggie Jackson, 1969	.333
56	Willie Stargell, 1971	.333
57	Hank Greenberg, 1937	.332
58	Larry Walker, 1999	.331
59	Hank Greenberg, 1940	.330
60	Manny Ramirez, 1999	.330
61	Juan Gonzalez, 1996	.329
62	Ted Williams, 1941	.329
63	Mark McGwire, 1987	.329
64	Willie Mays, 1965	.328
65	Babe Ruth, 1931	.328
66	Mike Schmidt, 1981	.328
67	Ken Griffey Jr., 1998	.327
68	Hank Greenberg, 1946	.327
69	Joe DiMaggio, 1937	.327
70	Albert Belle, 1998	.327
71	Al Simmons, 1930	.327
72	Todd Helton, 2000	.326
73	Stan Musial, 1948	.326
74	Ralph Kiner, 1947	.326
75	Dave Kingman, 1979	.325
76	Ted Williams, 1946	.325
77	Ken Griffey Jr., 1996	.325
78	Eddie Mathews, 1953	.325
79	Greg Vaughn, 1998	.325
80	Willie McCovey, 1970	.323
81	Juan Gonzalez, 1993	.323
82	Richard Hidalgo, 2000	.323
83	Willie Mays, 1954	.322
84	Lou Gehrig, 1931	.321
85	Johnny Mize, 1940	.321
86	Frank Robinson, 1966	.321
87	Rogers Hornsby, 1922	.321
88	Carlos Delgado, 2000	.320
89	Troy Glaus, 2000	.320
90	Duke Snider, 1955	.320
91	Babe Ruth, 1932	.319
92	Jimmie Foxx, 1934	.319
93	Vladimir Guerrero, 2000	.319
94	Ralph Kiner, 1951	.318
95	Ralph Kiner, 1950	.318
96	Harmon Killebrew, 1961	.318
97	Gary Sheffield, 2000	.317
98	Bob Hamelin, 1994	.317
99	Rocky Colavito, 1958	.317
100	Mark McGwire, 1992	.317

Extra Base Hits

1	Babe Ruth, 1921	119
2	Lou Gehrig, 1927	117
3	Chuck Klein, 1930	107
4	Chuck Klein, 1932	103
	Hank Greenberg, 1937	103
	Stan Musial, 1948	103
	Albert Belle, 1995	103
	Todd Helton, 2000	103
9	Rogers Hornsby, 1922	102
10	Lou Gehrig, 1930	100
	Jimmie Foxx, 1932	100
12	Babe Ruth, 1920	99
	Babe Ruth, 1923	99
	Hank Greenberg, 1940	99
	Larry Walker, 1997	99
	Albert Belle, 1998	99
	Carlos Delgado, 2000	99
18	Hank Greenberg, 1935	98
19	Babe Ruth, 1927	97
	Hack Wilson, 1930	97
	Joe Medwick, 1937	97
	Juan Gonzalez, 1998	97
23	Hank Greenberg, 1934	96
	Hal Trosky, 1936	96
	Joe DiMaggio, 1937	96
26	Lou Gehrig, 1934	95
	Joe Medwick, 1936	95
28	Rogers Hornsby, 1929	94
	Chuck Klein, 1929	94
	Babe Herman, 1930	94
	Jimmie Foxx, 1933	94
32	Jim Bottomley, 1928	93
	Al Simmons, 1930	93
	Lou Gehrig, 1936	93
	Ellis Burks, 1996	93
	Ken Griffey Jr., 1997	93
37	Babe Ruth, 1924	92
	Lou Gehrig, 1931	92
	Jimmie Foxx, 1938	92
	Stan Musial, 1953	92
	Hank Aaron, 1959	92
	Frank Robinson, 1962	92
	Brady Anderson, 1996	92
	Ken Griffey Jr., 1998	92
45	Babe Ruth, 1928	91
	Alex Rodriguez, 1996	91
	Mark McGwire, 1998	91
48	Rogers Hornsby, 1925	90
	Stan Musial, 1949	90
	Willie Mays, 1962	90
	Willie Stargell, 1973	90
52	Hal Trosky, 1934	89
	Duke Snider, 1954	89
	Andres Galarraga, 1996	89
	Albert Belle, 1996	89
	Sammy Sosa, 1999	89
	Richard Hidalgo, 2000	89
	Sammy Sosa, 2000	89
59	Joe DiMaggio, 1936	88
	Barry Bonds, 1993	88
	Barry Bonds, 1998	88
62	Tris Speaker, 1923	87
	Kiki Cuyler, 1925	87
	Lou Gehrig, 1928	87
	Ripper Collins, 1934	87
	Charlie Gehringer, 1936	87
	Johnny Mize, 1940	87
	Willie Mays, 1954	87
	Robin Yount, 1982	87
	Kevin Mitchell, 1989	87
	Chipper Jones, 1999	87
	Mark McGwire, 1999	87
	Shawn Green, 1999	87
	Frank Thomas, 2000	87
75	George Sisler, 1920	86
	Babe Ruth, 1930	86
	Wally Moses, 1937	86
	Johnny Mize, 1939	86
	Ted Williams, 1939	86
	Stan Musial, 1946	86
	Eddie Mathews, 1953	86
	Reggie Jackson, 1969	86
	Hal McRae, 1977	86
	Jim Rice, 1978	86
	Don Mattingly, 1985	86
	Don Mattingly, 1986	86
	Ken Griffey Jr., 1993	86
	Sammy Sosa, 1998	86
89	20 players tied	85

Pinch Hits

1	John Vander Wal, 1995	28
2	Lenny Harris, 1999	26
3	Jose Morales, 1976	25
4	Dave Philley, 1961	24
	Vic Davalillo, 1970	24
	Rusty Staub, 1983	24
	Gerald Perry, 1993	24
8	Sam Leslie, 1932	22
	Peanuts Lowrey, 1953	22
	Red Schoendienst, 1962	22
	Wallace Johnson, 1988	22
	Mark Sweeney, 1997	22
13	Doc Miller, 1913	21
	Smoky Burgess, 1966	21
	Merv Rettenmund, 1977	21
16	Ed Coleman, 1936	20
	Frenchy Bordagaray, 1938	20
	Joe Frazier, 1954	20
	Smoky Burgess, 1965	20
	Ken Boswell, 1976	20
	Jerry Turner, 1978	20
	Thad Bosley, 1985	20
	Chris Chambliss, 1986	20
	Dave Clark, 1997	20
25	Many players tied	19

Pinch Hit Average (30 at-bats minimum)

1	Ed Kranepool, 1974	.486
2	Smead Jolley, 1931	.467
3	Frenchy Bordagaray, 1938	.465
4	Rick Miller, 1983	.457
5	Bill Spiers, 1997	.455
6	Jose Pagan, 1969	.452
7	Elmer Valo, 1955	.452
	Mark Johnson, 1996	.452
9	Gates Brown, 1968	.450
10	Ted Easterly, 1912	.433
	Milt Thompson, 1985	.433
	Randy Bush, 1986	.433
13	Joe Cronin, 1943	.429
	Don Dillard, 1961	.429
15	Candy Maldonado, 1986	.425
16	Richie Ashburn, 1962	.419
	Dick Williams, 1962	.419
18	Merritt Ranew, 1963	.415
	Carl Taylor, 1969	.415
20	Kurt Bevacqua, 1983	.412
21	Jerry Turner, 1978	.408
22	Bob Bowman, 1958	.406
	Chico Walker, 1991	.406
	Sid Bream, 1994	.406
25	Frankie Baumholtz, 1955	.405

Pinch Hit Home Runs

1	Dave Hansen, 2000	7
2	Johnny Frederick, 1932	6
3	Joe Cronin, 1943	5
	Butch Nieman, 1945	5
	Gene Freese, 1959	5
	Jerry Lynch, 1961	5
	Cliff Johnson, 1974	5
	Lee Lacy, 1978	5
	Jerry Turner, 1978	5
	Billy Ashley, 1996	5
11	Ernie Lombardi, 1946	4
	Del Wilber, 1953	4
	Bill Taylor, 1955	4
	Bob Thurman, 1957	4
	Rip Repulski, 1958	4
	George Crowe, 1959	4
	George Crowe, 1960	4
	Johnny Blanchard, 1961	4
	Carl Sawatski, 1961	4
	Jerry Lynch, 1963	4
	Don Mincher, 1964	4
	Hal Breeden, 1973	4
	Mike Ivie, 1978	4
	Del Unser, 1979	4
	Jeff Burroughs, 1982	4
	Danny Heep, 1983	4
	Candy Maldonado, 1986	4
	Mark Carreon, 1989	4
	Tommy Gregg, 1990	4
	Ernest Riles, 1990	4
	Howard Johnson, 1994	4
	John Vander Wal, 1995	4
	Jack Howell, 1996	4
	Mark Johnson, 1996	4
	Bob Hamelin, 1998	4
	Angelo Echevarria, 1999	4
	Bubba Trammell, 2000	4

Total Player Rating / 150g

1	Babe Ruth, 1923	10.66
2	Fred Dunlap, 1884	10.54
3	Pete Browning, 1882	10.43
4	Jeff Bagwell, 1994	10.36
5	Mike Schmidt, 1981	10.29
6	Nap Lajoie, 1901	9.73
7	Nap Lajoie, 1903	9.72
8	Babe Ruth, 1920	9.61
9	Rogers Hornsby, 1924	9.55
10	Barry Bonds, 1992	9.54
11	Babe Ruth, 1921	9.47
12	Ross Barnes, 1876	9.09
13	Mickey Mantle, 1957	9.06
14	Babe Ruth, 1927	8.94
15	Rickey Henderson, 1990	8.71
16	Mickey Mantle, 1956	8.70
17	Cal Ripken, 1984	8.61
18	Rogers Hornsby, 1922	8.47
19	Fred Pfeffer, 1884	8.44
20	Babe Ruth, 1924	8.43
21	Ted Williams, 1941	8.39
22	George Brett, 1980	8.33
23	Nap Lajoie, 1910	8.30
24	Nap Lajoie, 1906	8.29
	Babe Ruth, 1926	8.29
26	Rogers Hornsby, 1917	8.28
27	Barry Bonds, 1993	8.21
28	Ty Cobb, 1917	8.19
29	Rogers Hornsby, 1920	8.15
30	Eric Davis, 1987	8.14
31	Mickey Mantle, 1961	8.14
32	Ted Williams, 1957	8.07
33	Lou Gehrig, 1927	8.03
34	Ted Williams, 1942	8.00
35	King Kelly, 1879	7.99
36	Hughie Jennings, 1896	7.96
37	Barry Bonds, 1996	7.88
38	Orator Shaffer, 1878	7.86
	Cupid Childs, 1890	7.86
40	Honus Wagner, 1906	7.82
41	Alex Rodriguez, 2000	7.80
42	Lou Boudreau, 1944	7.80
43	Rickey Henderson, 1985	7.76
44	Nap Lajoie, 1908	7.74
45	Cal Ripken, 1991	7.69
46	Nap Lajoie, 1907	7.66
47	Barry Bonds, 2000	7.66
48	Babe Ruth, 1930	7.66
	Babe Ruth, 1931	7.66
50	Honus Wagner, 1905	7.65
51	Ron Santo, 1966	7.65
52	Babe Ruth, 1919	7.62
53	George Sisler, 1920	7.60
54	Nap Lajoie, 1904	7.50
	Lou Gehrig, 1934	7.50
	Ted Williams, 1946	7.50
	Willie Mays, 1955	7.50
	Barry Bonds, 1994	7.50
	Ken Caminiti, 1996	7.50
	Mike Piazza, 1997	7.50
61	Joe DiMaggio, 1941	7.45
62	Andre Dawson, 1981	7.43
63	Craig Biggio, 1997	7.41
64	Lou Gehrig, 1930	7.40
65	Cupid Childs, 1896	7.39
66	Nap Lajoie, 1900	7.35
	Eddie Collins, 1910	7.35
68	Tris Speaker, 1913	7.34
69	Hughie Jennings, 1897	7.31
70	Mike Schmidt, 1980	7.30
71	Ty Cobb, 1910	7.29
72	Buddy Bell, 1981	7.27
73	Dick Bartell, 1937	7.27
74	Tris Speaker, 1912	7.25
75	Joe DiMaggio, 1939	7.25
76	Rickey Henderson, 1981	7.22
77	Tris Speaker, 1914	7.22
78	Barry Bonds, 1998	7.21
79	Honus Wagner, 1903	7.21
80	Rogers Hornsby, 1921	7.21
81	Ed Delahanty, 1896	7.20
82	Joe Morgan, 1975	7.19
83	Robin Yount, 1981	7.19
84	Willie Mays, 1965	7.17
85	Honus Wagner, 1908	7.15
86	Jack Glasscock, 1882	7.14
87	Snuffy Stirnweiss, 1945	7.11
	Willie Mays, 1958	7.11
89	Norm Cash, 1961	7.08
	Albert Belle, 1994	7.08
91	Harlond Clift, 1937	7.06
92	Frankie Frisch, 1927	7.06
93	Barry Bonds, 1990	7.05
94	Rico Petrocelli, 1969	7.01
95	Frank Fennelly, 1884	7.00
96	Eddie Collins, 1913	6.99
97	Ron Santo, 1967	6.99
98	Ty Cobb, 1911	6.99
99	Hughie Jennings, 1895	6.98
100	Barry Bonds, 1995	6.98

Stolen Bases

1	Hugh Nicol, 1887	138
2	Rickey Henderson, 1982	130
3	Arlie Latham, 1887	129
4	Lou Brock, 1974	118
5	Charlie Comiskey, 1887	117
6	John Ward, 1887	111
	Billy Hamilton, 1889	111
	Billy Hamilton, 1891	111
9	Vince Coleman, 1985	110
10	Arlie Latham, 1888	109
	Vince Coleman, 1987	109
12	Rickey Henderson, 1983	108
13	Vince Coleman, 1986	107
14	Tom Brown, 1891	106
15	Maury Wills, 1962	104
16	Pete Browning, 1887	103
	Hugh Nicol, 1888	103
18	Jim Fogarty, 1887	102
	Billy Hamilton, 1890	102
20	Billy Hamilton, 1894	100
	Rickey Henderson, 1980	100
22	Jim Fogarty, 1889	99
23	Harry Stovey, 1890	97
	Billy Hamilton, 1895	97
	Ron LeFlore, 1980	97
26	Ty Cobb, 1915	96
	Omar Moreno, 1980	96
28	Bid McPhee, 1887	95
	Curt Welch, 1888	95
30	Mike Griffin, 1887	94
	Maury Wills, 1965	94
32	Tommy McCarthy, 1888	93
	Rickey Henderson, 1988	93
34	Darby O'Brien, 1889	91
35	Tim Raines, 1983	90
36	Curt Welch, 1887	89
	Herman Long, 1889	89
38	Tom Poorman, 1887	88
	Blondie Purcell, 1887	88
	John Ward, 1892	88
	Clyde Milan, 1912	88
42	Harry Stovey, 1888	87
	Arlie Latham, 1891	87
	Joe Kelley, 1896	87
	Rickey Henderson, 1986	87
46	Cub Stricker, 1887	86
47	Tommy Tucker, 1887	85
	Hub Collins, 1890	85
	Hugh Duffy, 1891	85
50	King Kelly, 1887	84
	Chippy McGarr, 1887	84
	Billy Sunday, 1890	84
	Bill Lange, 1896	84
54	Tommy McCarthy, 1890	83
	Billy Hamilton, 1896	83
	Ty Cobb, 1911	83
	Willie Wilson, 1979	83
58	Dummy Hoy, 1888	82
	John Reilly, 1888	82
60	Eddie Collins, 1910	81
	Bob Bescher, 1911	81
	Vince Coleman, 1988	81
63	Emmett Seery, 1888	80
	Hugh Nicol, 1889	80
	Rickey Henderson, 1985	80
	Eric Davis, 1986	80
67	Tom Brown, 1890	79
	Dave Collins, 1980	79
	Willie Wilson, 1980	79
70	Hugh Duffy, 1890	78
	Tom Brown, 1892	78
	John McGraw, 1894	78
	Ron LeFlore, 1979	78
	Tim Raines, 1982	78
	Marquis Grissom, 1992	78
76	Ted Scheffler, 1890	77
	Jimmy Sheckard, 1899	77
	Davey Lopes, 1975	77
	Omar Moreno, 1979	77
	Rudy Law, 1983	77
	Rickey Henderson, 1989	77
	Vince Coleman, 1990	77
83	Ed McKean, 1887	76
	Walt Wilmot, 1890	76
	Walt Wilmot, 1894	76
	Dusty Miller, 1896	76
	Ty Cobb, 1909	76
	Marquis Grissom, 1991	76
89	Yank Robinson, 1887	75
	George Van Haltren, 1891	75
	Clyde Milan, 1913	75
	Benny Kauff, 1914	75
	Billy North, 1976	75
	Tim Raines, 1984	75
	Kenny Lofton, 1996	75
96	Frank Fennelly, 1887	74
	Harry Stovey, 1887	74
	Fritz Maisel, 1914	74
	Lou Brock, 1966	74
	Brian Hunter, 1997	74

Stolen Base Average

1	Kevin McReynolds, 1988	100.0
	Paul Molitor, 1994	100.0
3	Brady Anderson, 1994	96.9
4	Max Carey, 1922	96.2
5	Ken Griffey Sr., 1980	95.8
6	Stan Javier, 1988	95.2
7	Doug Glanville, 1999	94.4
8	Amos Otis, 1970	94.3
9	Jack Perconte, 1985	93.9
10	Miguel Dilone, 1984	93.1
	Bob Dernier, 1986	93.1
12	Kirk Gibson, 1990	92.9
	Barry Larkin, 1994	92.9
14	Don Baylor, 1972	92.3
	Oddibe McDowell, 1987	92.3
16	Davey Lopes, 1985	92.2
17	Eric Davis, 1988	92.1
18	Henry Cotto, 1992	92.0
	Mike Cameron, 1997	92.0
20	Bobby Bonds, 1969	91.8
	Davey Lopes, 1978	91.8
22	Davey Lopes, 1979	91.7
	Marquis Grissom, 1990	91.7
24	Jimmy Wynn, 1965	91.5
25	Larry Bowa, 1977	91.4
26	Ryne Sandberg, 1987	91.3
	Alan Trammell, 1987	91.3
	Rich Amaral, 1995	91.3
29	Jerry Mumphrey, 1980	91.2
30	Tom Herr, 1985	91.2
31	Barry Larkin, 1995	91.1
32	Jack Smith, 1925	90.9
	Davey Lopes, 1981	90.9
	Tim Raines, 1987	90.9
	Bip Roberts, 1995	90.9
	Roberto Alomar, 1995	90.9
37	Craig Biggio, 1994	90.7
	Roberto Alomar, 2000	90.7
39	Derek Bell, 1996	90.6
	Pokey Reese, 2000	90.6
41	Willie Wilson, 1984	90.4
42	Bake McBride, 1978	90.3
43	Devon White, 1992	90.2
44	Henry Cotto, 1988	90.0
45	Barry Larkin, 1998	89.7
46	Tony Womack, 1997	89.6
47	Devon White, 1993	89.5
48	Mitchell Page, 1977	89.4
49	5 players tied	89.3

Stolen Base Runs

1	Vince Coleman, 1986	19
2	Maury Wills, 1962	18
3	Rickey Henderson, 1983	17
4	Vince Coleman, 1987	16
5	Rickey Henderson, 1988	16
6	Vince Coleman, 1985	15
7	Tim Raines, 1983	15
8	Ron LeFlore, 1980	15
9	Lou Brock, 1974	14
10	Rickey Henderson, 1985	14
11	Willie Wilson, 1979	14
12	Rickey Henderson, 1982	14
13	Willie Wilson, 1980	14
14	Eric Davis, 1986	14
15	Tim Raines, 1984	13
16	Rickey Henderson, 1980	13
17	Rickey Henderson, 1986	13
18	Davey Lopes, 1975	13
	Rudy Law, 1983	13
20	Marquis Grissom, 1992	13
21	Ron LeFlore, 1979	12
22	Tim Raines, 1985	12
	Tim Raines, 1986	12
24	Rickey Henderson, 1989	12
25	Tim Raines, 1981	12
26	Tim Raines, 1982	12
27	Tony Womack, 1999	11
28	Joe Morgan, 1975	11
29	Vince Coleman, 1990	11
30	Bert Campaneris, 1969	11
31	Vince Coleman, 1989	11
	Rickey Henderson, 1990	11
33	Marquis Grissom, 1991	11
34	Tony Womack, 1997	11
35	Juan Samuel, 1984	11
36	Kenny Lofton, 1996	11
37	Max Carey, 1922	11
38	Mickey Rivers, 1975	11
	Kenny Lofton, 1993	11
40	Davey Lopes, 1976	10
41	Fritz Maisel, 1914	10
42	Kenny Lofton, 1992	10
43	Willie Wilson, 1983	10
44	Chuck Knoblauch, 1997	10
45	Joe Morgan, 1976	10
46	Dave Collins, 1980	10
47	Lou Brock, 1966	10
	Brian Hunter, 1997	10
49	Alan Wiggins, 1983	10
	Rickey Henderson, 1998	10

Stolen Base Wins

1	Vince Coleman, 1986	2.0
2	Maury Wills, 1962	1.8
3	Rickey Henderson, 1983	1.7
4	Vince Coleman, 1985	1.6
5	Vince Coleman, 1987	1.6
6	Rickey Henderson, 1988	1.6
7	Ron LeFlore, 1980	1.6
8	Tim Raines, 1983	1.5
9	Lou Brock, 1974	1.5
10	Eric Davis, 1986	1.4
11	Willie Wilson, 1980	1.4
12	Rickey Henderson, 1982	1.4
13	Willie Wilson, 1979	1.4
14	Rickey Henderson, 1985	1.4
15	Marquis Grissom, 1992	1.4
16	Tim Raines, 1984	1.3
17	Davey Lopes, 1975	1.3
18	Rudy Law, 1983	1.3
19	Rickey Henderson, 1980	1.3
20	Tim Raines, 1985	1.3
21	Rickey Henderson, 1986	1.3
22	Tim Raines, 1986	1.3
23	Tim Raines, 1981	1.3
24	Tim Raines, 1982	1.2
25	Rickey Henderson, 1989	1.2
26	Ron LeFlore, 1979	1.2
27	Vince Coleman, 1989	1.2
28	Joe Morgan, 1975	1.1
29	Bert Campaneris, 1969	1.1
30	Fritz Maisel, 1914	1.1
31	Vince Coleman, 1990	1.1
32	Marquis Grissom, 1991	1.1
33	Juan Samuel, 1984	1.1
34	Davey Lopes, 1976	1.1
35	Tony Womack, 1999	1.1
36	Lou Brock, 1968	1.1
37	Mickey Rivers, 1975	1.1
38	Rickey Henderson, 1990	1.1
39	Tony Womack, 1997	1.1
40	Dave Collins, 1980	1.1
41	Kenny Lofton, 1992	1.0
42	Lou Brock, 1966	1.0
43	Alan Wiggins, 1983	1.0
44	Maury Wills, 1965	1.0
45	Joe Morgan, 1976	1.0
46	Tommy Harper, 1969	1.0
47	Willie Wilson, 1983	1.0
48	Jerry Mumphrey, 1980	1.0
49	Omar Moreno, 1980	1.0
50	Kenny Lofton, 1993	1.0

Fielding Average

First Base

1	Steve Garvey, 1984	1.000
2	Stuffy McInnis, 1921	.999
3	Frank McCormick, 1946	.999
4	David Segui, 1998	.999
5	J. T. Snow, 1998	.999
6	Steve Garvey, 1981	.999
7	Jim Spencer, 1973	.999
8	Wes Parker, 1968	.999
9	Eddie Murray, 1981	.999
10	Hal Morris, 1992	.999

Second Base

1	Bret Boone, 1997	.997
2	Bobby Grich, 1985	.997
3	Jose Oquendo, 1990	.996
4	Ryne Sandberg, 1991	.995
5	Jody Reed, 1994	.995
6	Rob Wilfong, 1980	.995
7	Bobby Grich, 1973	.995
8	Frank White, 1988	.994
9	Mark Lemke, 1994	.994
10	Jose Oquendo, 1989	.994

Shortstop

1	Cal Ripken, 1990	.996
2	Omar Vizquel, 2000	.995
3	Rey Sanchez, 2000	.994
4	Rey Ordonez, 1999	.994
5	Omar Vizquel, 1998	.993
6	Tony Fernandez, 1989	.992
7	Larry Bowa, 1979	.991
8	Ed Brinkman, 1972	.990
9	Cal Ripken, 1989	.990
10	Mike Bordick, 1998	.990

Third Base

1	Tony Fernandez, 1994	.991
2	Don Money, 1974	.989
3	Hank Majeski, 1947	.988
4	Aurelio Rodriguez, 1978	.987
5	Willie Kamm, 1933	.984
6	Steve Buechele, 1991	.983
7	Gary Gaetti, 1998	.983
8	George Kell, 1946	.983
9	Heinie Groh, 1924	.983
10	Carney Lansford, 1979	.983

Outfield (250 chances accepted)

1	Danny Litwhiler, 1942	1.000
	Tony Gonzalez, 1962	1.000
	Rocky Colavito, 1965	1.000
	Curt Flood, 1966	1.000
	Mickey Stanley, 1968	1.000
	Mickey Stanley, 1970	1.000
	Roy White, 1971	1.000
	Ken Berry, 1972	1.000
	Carl Yastrzemski, 1977	1.000
	Terry Puhl, 1979	1.000
	Brian Downing, 1982	1.000
	Brian Downing, 1984	1.000
	Brett Butler, 1991	1.000
	Darryl Hamilton, 1992	1.000
	Brett Butler, 1993	1.000
	Darren Lewis, 1993	1.000
	Lance Johnson, 1994	1.000
	Stan Javier, 1995	1.000
	Darryl Hamilton, 1996	1.000
	Paul O'Neill, 1996	1.000
	Darryl Hamilton, 1999	1.000
	B.J. Surhoff, 2000	1.000
	Eric Owens, 2000	1.000
	Bernie Williams, 2000	1.000

Catcher

1	Spud Davis, 1939	1.000
	Buddy Rosar, 1946	1.000
	Lou Berberet, 1957	1.000
	Pete Daley, 1957	1.000
	Yogi Berra, 1958	1.000
	Rick Cerone, 1988	1.000
	Charles Johnson, 1997	1.000
	Chris Hoiles, 1997	1.000
9	Tom Pagnozzi, 1992	.999
10	Joe Azcue, 1967	.999

Pitcher (90 chances accepted)

1	Kid Nichols, 1896	1.000
	Frank Owen, 1904	1.000
	Mordecai Brown, 1908	1.000
	Grover Alexander, 1913	1.000
	Walter Johnson, 1913	1.000
	Eppa Rixey, 1917	1.000
	Walter Johnson, 1917	1.000
	Grover Alexander, 1919	1.000
	Jesse Barnes, 1921	1.000
	Hal Schumacher, 1935	1.000
	Larry Jackson, 1964	1.000
	Randy Jones, 1976	1.000
	Greg Maddux, 1990	1.000

Total Chances per Game

First Base

1	Joe Gerhardt, 1876	13.28
2	Jiggs Donahue, 1907	12.73
3	Oscar Walker, 1879	12.60
4	Joe Start, 1878	12.54
5	Tim Murnane, 1878	12.52
6	Joe Start, 1879	12.49
7	Jake Goodman, 1878	12.45
8	Herman Dehlman, 1876	12.36
9	Phil Todt, 1926	12.36
10	Joe Start, 1877	12.35

Second Base

1	Thorny Hawkes, 1879	8.44
2	Chick Fulmer, 1879	8.34
3	Jack Burdock, 1878	8.30
4	Ed Somerville, 1876	8.28
5	Joe Gerhardt, 1877	8.12
6	Fred Pfeffer, 1884	8.08
7	Jack Burdock, 1879	7.88
8	Joe Quest, 1878	7.81
9	Pop Smith, 1885	7.74
10	Joe Quest, 1879	7.73

Shortstop

1	Herman Long, 1889	7.27
2	Hughie Jennings, 1895	7.16
3	Dave Bancroft, 1918	7.14
4	Phil Tomney, 1889	7.12
5	George Davis, 1899	7.10
6	Hughie Jennings, 1896	7.07
7	Hughie Jennings, 1897	7.03
8	Bobby Wallace, 1901	6.97
9	Monte Cross, 1897	6.97
10	Bill Dahlen, 1895	6.93

Third Base

1	Al Nichols, 1876	5.81
2	Bob Ferguson, 1877	5.61
3	Jumbo Davis, 1888	5.13
4	Billy Alvord, 1891	5.03
5	Cap Anson, 1876	5.03
6	George Bradley, 1880	4.93
7	Billy Shindle, 1892	4.93
8	Jack Gleason, 1882	4.90
9	Bill Bradley, 1900	4.87
10	Will Foley, 1877	4.79

Outfield

1	Fred Treacey, 1876	4.39
2	Redleg Snyder, 1876	3.84
3	Charley Jones, 1877	3.77
4	Taylor Douthit, 1928	3.68
5	Mike Mansell, 1879	3.64
6	Richie Ashburn, 1951	3.64
7	Chet Lemon, 1977	3.60
8	Thurman Tucker, 1944	3.58
9	Kirby Puckett, 1984	3.57
10	Irv Noren, 1951	3.53
11	Richie Ashburn, 1949	3.49
12	Carden Gillenwater, 1945	3.46
13	Taylor Douthit, 1926	3.43
14	Sam West, 1935	3.41
15	Richie Ashburn, 1956	3.40
16	Dom DiMaggio, 1948	3.39
17	Richie Ashburn, 1957	3.38
18	Lloyd Waner, 1932	3.37
19	Lloyd Waner, 1931	3.37
20	Richie Ashburn, 1958	3.36

Catcher

1	Bill Holbert, 1883	10.63
2	Sam Trott, 1884	10.35
3	Bill Holbert, 1884	9.51
4	Jocko Milligan, 1884	9.40
5	Mert Hackett, 1884	9.35
6	Barney Gilligan, 1884	9.30
7	Mike Hines, 1883	9.27
8	George Baker, 1884	8.99
9	Jocko Milligan, 1885	8.82
10	Lew Brown, 1877	8.65

Pitcher

1	Harry Howell, 1905	5.42
2	Harry Howell, 1904	5.12
3	Will White, 1882	4.76
4	Ed Walsh, 1907	4.75
5	George Mullin, 1904	4.53
6	Tony Mullane, 1882	4.38
7	Red Donahue, 1902	4.37
8	Harry Howell, 1906	4.34
9	Jack Katoll, 1902	4.31
10	Nick Altrock, 1904	4.26
	Nick Altrock, 1905	4.26

Chances Accepted per Game

First Base

1	Jiggs Donahue, 1907	12.65
2	Joe Gerhardt, 1876	12.54
3	Phil Todt, 1926	12.21
4	Joe Start, 1879	12.15
5	George Burns, 1914	12.10
6	Stuffy McInnis, 1918	12.10
7	George Stovall, 1908	12.08
8	George Kelly, 1920	12.01
9	Joe Start, 1878	12.00
10	Oscar Walker, 1879	11.92

Second Base

1	Jack Burdock, 1878	7.62
2	Thorny Hawkes, 1879	7.56
3	Chick Fulmer, 1879	7.55
4	Fred Pfeffer, 1884	7.29
5	Joe Gerhardt, 1877	7.21
6	Ed Somerville, 1876	7.20
7	Jack Burdock, 1879	7.18
8	Joe Quest, 1879	7.16
9	Pop Smith, 1885	7.13
10	Bid McPhee, 1886	7.09

Shortstop

1	Hughie Jennings, 1895	6.73
2	George Davis, 1899	6.72
3	Dave Bancroft, 1918	6.62
4	Hughie Jennings, 1896	6.56
5	Hughie Jennings, 1897	6.55
6	Rabbit Maranville, 1919	6.48
7	Bobby Wallace, 1901	6.48
8	Monte Cross, 1897	6.40
9	Dave Bancroft, 1920	6.40
10	George Davis, 1900	6.39

Third Base

1	Bob Ferguson, 1877	4.71
2	Al Nichols, 1876	4.53
3	Billy Shindle, 1892	4.34
4	Jumbo Davis, 1888	4.33
5	Billy Alvord, 1891	4.31
6	Bill Bradley, 1900	4.29
7	Cap Anson, 1876	4.27
8	George Bradley, 1880	4.23
9	Joe Battin, 1883	4.17
10	Bill Hague, 1878	4.16

Outfield

1	Fred Treacey, 1876	3.70
2	Taylor Douthit, 1928	3.62
3	Richie Ashburn, 1951	3.59
4	Thurman Tucker, 1944	3.55
5	Kirby Puckett, 1984	3.55
6	Chet Lemon, 1977	3.52
7	Irv Noren, 1951	3.45
8	Richie Ashburn, 1949	3.42
9	Carden Gillenwater, 1945	3.39
10	Sam West, 1935	3.38
11	Richie Ashburn, 1956	3.34
12	Richie Ashburn, 1957	3.33
13	Dom DiMaggio, 1948	3.33
14	Lloyd Waner, 1932	3.32
15	Jim Busby, 1953	3.31
16	Richie Ashburn, 1958	3.31
17	Jim Busby, 1952	3.31
18	Richie Ashburn, 1953	3.29
19	Lloyd Waner, 1931	3.29
20	Dwayne Murphy, 1980	3.29

Catcher

1	Bill Holbert, 1883	9.78
2	Sam Trott, 1884	9.63
3	Jocko Milligan, 1884	8.83
4	Bill Holbert, 1884	8.75
5	Mert Hackett, 1884	8.68
6	Barney Gilligan, 1884	8.63
7	Duffy Dyer, 1972	8.25
8	Jocko Milligan, 1885	8.25
9	Mike Hines, 1883	8.22
10	Javy Lopez, 1998	8.17

Pitcher

1	Harry Howell, 1905	5.24
2	Harry Howell, 1904	4.97
3	Ed Walsh, 1907	4.68
4	Will White, 1882	4.56
5	George Mullin, 1904	4.24
6	Nick Altrock, 1905	4.21
7	Tony Mullane, 1882	4.20
8	Willie Sudhoff, 1904	4.19
9	Red Donahue, 1902	4.14
10	Nick Altrock, 1904	4.13

Putouts

First Base

1	Jiggs Donahue, 1907	1846
2	George Kelly, 1920	1759
3	Phil Todt, 1926	1755
4	Wally Pipp, 1926	1710
5	Jiggs Donahue, 1906	1697
6	Candy LaChance, 1904	1691
7	Tom Jones, 1907	1687
8	Ernie Banks, 1965	1682
9	Wally Pipp, 1922	1667
10	Lou Gehrig, 1927	1662

Second Base

1	Bid McPhee, 1886	529
2	Bobby Grich, 1974	484
3	Bucky Harris, 1922	483
4	Nellie Fox, 1956	478
5	Lou Bierbauer, 1889	472
6	Billy Herman, 1933	466
7	Bill Wambsganss, 1924	463
8	Cub Stricker, 1887	461
9	Buddy Myer, 1935	460
10	Bill Sweeney, 1912	459

Shortstop

1	Hughie Jennings, 1895	425
	Donie Bush, 1914	425
3	Joe Cassidy, 1905	408
4	Rabbit Maranville, 1914	407
5	Dave Bancroft, 1922	405
	Eddie Miller, 1940	405
7	Monte Cross, 1898	404
8	Dave Bancroft, 1921	396
9	Mickey Doolan, 1906	395
10	Buck Weaver, 1913	392

Third Base

1	Denny Lyons, 1887	255
2	Jimmy Williams, 1899	251
	Jimmy Collins, 1900	251
4	Jimmy Collins, 1898	243
	Willie Kamm, 1928	243
6	Willie Kamm, 1927	236
7	Frank Baker, 1913	233
8	Bill Coughlin, 1901	232
9	Ernie Courtney, 1905	229
10	Jimmy Austin, 1911	228

Outfield

1	Taylor Douthit, 1928	547
2	Richie Ashburn, 1951	538
3	Richie Ashburn, 1949	514
4	Chet Lemon, 1977	512
5	Dwayne Murphy, 1980	507
6	Dom DiMaggio, 1948	503
	Richie Ashburn, 1956	503
8	Richie Ashburn, 1957	502
9	Richie Ashburn, 1953	496
10	Richie Ashburn, 1958	495
11	Andruw Jones, 1999	492
12	Jim Busby, 1954	491
13	Omar Moreno, 1979	490
14	Baby Doll Jacobson, 1924	488
	Bobby Thomson, 1949	488
	Al Bumbry, 1980	488
17	Lloyd Waner, 1931	484
18	Richie Ashburn, 1954	483
19	Jim Busby, 1953	482
	Willie Wilson, 1980	482

Catcher

1	Johnny Edwards, 1969	1135
2	Mike Piazza, 1996	1055
3	Dan Wilson, 1997	1051
4	Mike Piazza, 1997	1045
5	Jason Kendall, 1998	1015
6	Johnny Edwards, 1963	1008
7	Javy Lopez, 1996	993
8	Jason Kendall, 2000	990
9	Mike Piazza, 1998	984
10	Darren Daulton, 1993	981

Pitcher

1	Dave Foutz, 1886	57
2	Tony Mullane, 1882	54
3	George Bradley, 1876	50
	Guy Hecker, 1884	50
5	Mike Boddicker, 1984	49
6	Larry Corcoran, 1884	47
7	Ted Breitenstein, 1895	46
8	Al Spalding, 1876	45
9	Jim Devlin, 1876	44
	Dave Foutz, 1887	44
	Bill Hutchison, 1890	44

Putouts per Game

First Base

1	Joe Gerhardt, 1876	12.30
2	Joe Start, 1879	11.98
3	Joe Start, 1878	11.79
4	Jiggs Donahue, 1907	11.76
5	Joe Start, 1877	11.73
6	Herman Dehlman, 1876	11.72
7	Joe Start, 1880	11.63
8	Jake Goodman, 1878	11.55
9	George Burns, 1914	11.53
10	Oscar Walker, 1879	11.50

Second Base

1	Jack Burdock, 1878	4.08
2	Jack Burdock, 1880	3.81
3	Bid McPhee, 1886	3.78
4	Bid McPhee, 1884	3.71
5	Joe Quest, 1878	3.68
6	Cub Stricker, 1887	3.66
7	Lou Bierbauer, 1889	3.63
8	Jack Burdock, 1879	3.61
9	Chick Fulmer, 1879	3.59
10	Bob Ferguson, 1880	3.59

Shortstop

1	Hughie Jennings, 1895	3.24
2	Dave Bancroft, 1918	2.97
3	George Davis, 1899	2.91
4	Hughie Jennings, 1896	2.90
5	Hughie Jennings, 1897	2.89
6	George Davis, 1898	2.88
7	Rabbit Maranville, 1919	2.76
8	Honus Wagner, 1913	2.75
9	Kid Elberfeld, 1901	2.74
10	Buck Weaver, 1914	2.74

Third Base

1	Al Nichols, 1876	2.16
2	Cap Anson, 1876	2.05
3	Hick Carpenter, 1880	2.03
4	Bob Ferguson, 1877	1.95
5	Denny Lyons, 1887	1.86
6	Patsy Tebeau, 1890	1.85
7	Cap Anson, 1877	1.85
8	Joe Battin, 1876	1.83
9	Jerry Denny, 1883	1.82
10	Frank Hankinson, 1881	1.80

Outfield

1	Taylor Douthit, 1928	3.55
2	Fred Treacey, 1876	3.54
3	Richie Ashburn, 1951	3.49
4	Thurman Tucker, 1944	3.45
5	Chet Lemon, 1977	3.44
6	Kirby Puckett, 1984	3.42
7	Richie Ashburn, 1949	3.34
8	Irv Noren, 1951	3.33
9	Sam West, 1935	3.33
10	Jim Busby, 1952	3.28
11	Richie Ashburn, 1956	3.27
12	Richie Ashburn, 1958	3.26
13	Lloyd Waner, 1932	3.25
14	Dom DiMaggio, 1948	3.25
15	Carden Gillenwater, 1945	3.22
16	Richie Ashburn, 1957	3.22
17	Jim Busby, 1953	3.21
18	Baby Doll Jacobson, 1924	3.21
19	Dwayne Murphy, 1980	3.21
20	Taylor Douthit, 1926	3.19

Catcher

1	Sam Trott, 1884	8.18
2	Bill Holbert, 1883	7.75
3	Javy Lopez, 1998	7.64
4	Duffy Dyer, 1972	7.58
5	Dan Wilson, 1995	7.52
6	Mike Piazza, 1997	7.52
7	Johnny Edwards, 1969	7.52
8	Joe Girardi, 1997	7.48
9	Barney Gilligan, 1884	7.47
10	Javy Lopez, 1994	7.45

Pitcher

1	Kevin Brown, 1995	1.54
2	Mike Boddicker, 1984	1.44
3	Oil Can Boyd, 1985	1.20
4	Kevin Brown, 1999	1.17
5	Nick Altrock, 1904	1.13
6	Greg Maddux, 1990	1.11
7	Dave Foutz, 1887	1.10
8	Dwight Gooden, 1986	1.09
	Kevin Brown, 1997	1.09
10	Dan Petry, 1984	1.09

Assists

First Base

1	Bill Buckner, 1985	184
2	Mark Grace, 1990	180
3	Mark Grace, 1991	167
4	Sid Bream, 1986	166
5	Bill Buckner, 1983	161
6	Bill Buckner, 1982	159
7	Bill Buckner, 1986	157
8	Mickey Vernon, 1949	155
9	Fred Tenney, 1905	152
	Eddie Murray, 1985	152

Second Base

1	Frankie Frisch, 1927	641
2	Hughie Critz, 1926	588
3	Rogers Hornsby, 1927	582
4	Ski Melillo, 1930	572
5	Ryne Sandberg, 1983	571
6	Rabbit Maranville, 1924	568
7	Frank Parkinson, 1922	562
8	Tony Cuccinello, 1936	559
9	Johnny Hodapp, 1930	557
10	Lou Bierbauer, 1892	555

Shortstop

1	Ozzie Smith, 1980	621
2	Glenn Wright, 1924	601
3	Dave Bancroft, 1920	598
4	Tommy Thevenow, 1926	597
5	Ivan DeJesus, 1977	595
6	Cal Ripken, 1984	583
7	Whitey Wietelmann, 1943	581
8	Dave Bancroft, 1922	579
9	Rabbit Maranville, 1914	574
10	Don Kessinger, 1968	573

Third Base

1	Graig Nettles, 1971	412
2	Graig Nettles, 1973	410
	Brooks Robinson, 1974	410
4	Harlond Clift, 1937	405
	Brooks Robinson, 1967	405
6	Mike Schmidt, 1974	404
7	Doug DeCinces, 1982	399
8	Clete Boyer, 1962	396
	Mike Schmidt, 1977	396
	Buddy Bell, 1982	396

Outfield

1	Orator Shaffer, 1879	50
2	Hugh Nicol, 1884	48
3	Hardy Richardson, 1881	45
4	Tommy McCarthy, 1888	44
	Chuck Klein, 1930	44
6	Charlie Duffee, 1889	43
	Jimmy Bannon, 1894	43
8	Jim Fogarty, 1889	42
9	Orator Shaffer, 1883	41
	Jim Lillie, 1884	41
11	Jim Fogarty, 1887	39
	Tom Brown, 1893	39
	Mike Mitchell, 1907	39
14	King Kelly, 1883	38
	Harry Stovey, 1889	38
	Tommy McCarthy, 1889	38
17	Jack Manning, 1883	37
	Tom Brown, 1892	37
19	Lon Knight, 1884	36
	Jimmy Ryan, 1889	36
	Jack McGeachy, 1889	36

Catcher

1	Bill Rariden, 1915	238
2	Bill Rariden, 1914	215
3	Pat Moran, 1903	214
4	Oscar Stanage, 1911	212
	Art Wilson, 1914	212
6	Gabby Street, 1909	210
7	Frank Snyder, 1915	204
8	George Gibson, 1910	203
9	Bill Bergen, 1909	202
	Claude Berry, 1914	202

Pitcher

1	Ed Walsh, 1907	227
2	Will White, 1882	223
3	Ed Walsh, 1908	190
4	Harry Howell, 1905	178
5	Tony Mullane, 1882	177
6	John Clarkson, 1885	174
7	John Clarkson, 1889	172
8	Jack Chesbro, 1904	166
9	George Mullin, 1904	163
10	Ed Walsh, 1911	159

Assists per Game

First Base

1	Mark Grace, 1990	1.18
2	Bill Buckner, 1986	1.14
3	Bill Buckner, 1985	1.14
4	Jeff Bagwell, 1995	1.13
5	Bill Buckner, 1983	1.12
6	Jeff Bagwell, 1994	1.10
7	Sid Bream, 1986	1.08
8	Eric Karros, 1994	1.08
9	Cecil Fielder, 1994	1.06
10	Ferris Fain, 1951	1.05

Second Base

1	Joe Gerhardt, 1877	4.28
2	Frankie Frisch, 1927	4.19
3	Thorny Hawkes, 1879	4.13
4	Hughie Critz, 1933	4.07
5	Frank Parkinson, 1922	4.04
6	Joe Quest, 1879	3.99
7	Chick Fulmer, 1879	3.96
8	Ed Somerville, 1876	3.92
9	Ski Melillo, 1930	3.86
10	Glenn Hubbard, 1985	3.85

Shortstop

1	Germany Smith, 1885	4.21
2	Arthur Irwin, 1880	4.13
3	Art Fletcher, 1919	4.10
4	Bill Dahlen, 1895	4.09
5	Phil Tomney, 1889	4.05
6	Bobby Wallace, 1901	4.04
7	Jack Glasscock, 1887	4.04
8	Germany Smith, 1892	4.04
9	Henry Easterday, 1888	3.99
10	Dave Bancroft, 1920	3.99

Third Base

1	Jumbo Davis, 1888	2.96
2	Buddy Bell, 1981	2.93
3	George Bradley, 1880	2.89
4	Bill Hague, 1878	2.85
5	Billy Shindle, 1892	2.85
6	Bob Ferguson, 1877	2.77
7	Ned Williamson, 1879	2.76
8	Arlie Latham, 1884	2.75
9	Bill Bradley, 1900	2.75
10	Arlie Latham, 1891	2.74

Outfield

1	Orator Shaffer, 1879	0.69
2	Hardy Richardson, 1881	0.57
3	Hugh Nicol, 1884	0.55
4	King Kelly, 1878	0.51
5	John Cassidy, 1878	0.50
	King Kelly, 1880	0.50
7	King Kelly, 1883	0.46
8	Jake Evans, 1882	0.46
9	Orator Shaffer, 1878	0.44
10	Dick Higham, 1878	0.44
11	Orator Shaffer, 1883	0.43
12	King Kelly, 1881	0.43
13	Orator Shaffer, 1880	0.42
14	Jake Evans, 1879	0.42
15	Jack Manning, 1883	0.38
16	Jake Evans, 1881	0.37
17	Jimmy Wolf, 1883	0.37
18	Hugh Nicol, 1883	0.37
19	Jim Lillie, 1884	0.36
20	Buttercup Dickerson, 1883	0.36

Catcher

1	Bill Holbert, 1884	2.41
2	Tom Daly, 1887	2.31
3	Bill Holbert, 1882	2.14
4	Pop Snyder, 1884	2.08
5	Bill Holbert, 1883	2.03
6	Buck Ewing, 1881	2.02
7	Pat Moran, 1903	2.00
8	Charlie Reipschlager, 1885	1.98
9	Connie Mack, 1888	1.92
10	King Kelly, 1888	1.92

Pitcher

1	Harry Howell, 1905	4.68
2	Harry Howell, 1904	4.21
3	Will White, 1882	4.13
4	Ed Walsh, 1907	4.05
5	Willie Sudhoff, 1904	3.85
6	Red Donahue, 1902	3.71
7	George Mullin, 1904	3.62
8	Frank Owen, 1904	3.51
9	Carl Mays, 1918	3.49
10	Jack Katoll, 1902	3.44

Double Plays

First Base

1	Ferris Fain, 1949	194
2	Ferris Fain, 1950	192
3	Donn Clendenon, 1966	182
4	Andres Galarraga, 1997	176
5	Ron Jackson, 1979	175
6	Gil Hodges, 1951	171
7	Mickey Vernon, 1949	168
8	Ted Kluszewski, 1954	166
9	Rudy York, 1944	163
10	Donn Clendenon, 1965	161
	Rod Carew, 1977	161

Second Base

1	Bill Mazeroski, 1966	161
2	Jerry Priddy, 1950	150
3	Bill Mazeroski, 1961	144
4	Nellie Fox, 1957	141
	Dave Cash, 1974	141
6	Buddy Myer, 1935	138
	Bill Mazeroski, 1962	138
	Carlos Baerga, 1992	138
9	Jerry Coleman, 1950	137
	Jackie Robinson, 1951	137
	Red Schoendienst, 1954	137

Shortstop

1	Rick Burleson, 1980	147
2	Roy Smalley, 1979	144
3	Bobby Wine, 1970	137
4	Lou Boudreau, 1944	134
5	Spike Owen, 1986	133
6	Mike Bordick, 1999	132
7	Rafael Ramirez, 1982	130
8	Roy McMillan, 1954	129
9	Hod Ford, 1928	128
	Vern Stephens, 1949	128
	Gene Alley, 1966	128

Third Base

1	Graig Nettles, 1971	54
2	Harlond Clift, 1937	50
3	Johnny Pesky, 1949	48
	Paul Molitor, 1982	48
5	Sammy Hale, 1927	46
	Clete Boyer, 1965	46
	Gary Gaetti, 1983	46
8	Eddie Yost, 1950	45
	Frank Malzone, 1961	45
	Darrell Evans, 1974	45
	Jeff Cirillo, 1998	45

Outfield

1	Happy Felsch, 1919	15
2	Jimmy Sheckard, 1899	14
3	Tom Brown, 1893	13
4	Tom Brown, 1886	12
	Tommy McCarthy, 1888	12
	Jimmy Bannon, 1894	12
	Mike Griffin, 1895	12
	Danny Green, 1899	12
	Cy Seymour, 1905	12
	Ginger Beaumont, 1907	12
	Ty Cobb, 1907	12
	Tris Speaker, 1909	12
	Jimmy Sheckard, 1911	12
	Tris Speaker, 1914	12
	Mel Ott, 1929	12
16	11 players tied	11

Catcher

1	Steve O'Neill, 1916	36
2	Frankie Hayes, 1945	29
3	Ray Schalk, 1916	25
	Yogi Berra, 1951	25
5	Jack Lapp, 1915	23
	Muddy Ruel, 1924	23
	Tom Haller, 1968	23
8	Steve O'Neill, 1914	22
	Bob O'Farrell, 1922	22
10	Gabby Hartnett, 1927	21
	Wes Westrum, 1950	21

Pitcher

1	Bob Lemon, 1953	15
2	Eddie Rommel, 1924	12
	Curt Davis, 1934	12
	Randy Jones, 1976	12
5	Scott Perry, 1919	11
	Tom Rogers, 1919	11
	Art Nehf, 1920	11
	Burleigh Grimes, 1925	11
	Gene Bearden, 1948	11
10	10 players tied	10

Fielding Runs

1	Glenn Hubbard, 1985	61.8
2	Danny Richardson, 1892	57.4
3	Bill Mazeroski, 1963	56.7
4	Rabbit Maranville, 1914	51.8
5	Freddie Maguire, 1928	50.5
6	Nap Lajoie, 1908	49.4
7	Danny Richardson, 1891	49.1
8	George Davis, 1899	48.9
9	Frankie Frisch, 1927	48.6
10	Hughie Critz, 1933	46.5
11	Nap Lajoie, 1907	45.9
12	Fred Pfeffer, 1884	45.5
13	Dick Bartell, 1936	44.8
14	Ozzie Guillen, 1988	42.6
15	Dave Shean, 1910	42.5
	Lee Tannehill, 1911	42.5
17	Cupid Childs, 1896	42.4
18	Graig Nettles, 1971	42.3
19	Joe Gerhardt, 1890	41.5
20	Bid McPhee, 1889	41.1
	Bill Mazeroski, 1962	41.1
	Ryne Sandberg, 1983	41.1
23	Harlond Clift, 1937	41.0
	Glenn Hubbard, 1986	41.0
25	Bill Mazeroski, 1966	40.8
	Ozzie Smith, 1980	40.8
27	Felix Martinez, 2000	40.2
28	Nap Lajoie, 1903	40.1
29	Germany Smith, 1885	39.9
30	Arlie Latham, 1884	39.5
31	Lee Tannehill, 1906	39.3
32	John Kerins, 1886	39.0
	Dave Bancroft, 1920	39.0
34	Neifi Perez, 2000	38.9
35	Bobby Wallace, 1899	38.8
	Cal Ripken, 1984	38.8
37	Bob Allen, 1890	38.6
38	Fred Pfeffer, 1888	38.3
39	Everett Scott, 1921	38.1
40	Bill Dahlen, 1908	37.5
	Dick Bartell, 1937	37.5
	Dal Maxvill, 1970	37.5
43	Bobby Knoop, 1964	37.2
44	Al Weis, 1966	36.9
45	Billy Shindle, 1888	36.8
46	Tim Wallach, 1985	36.7
47	Lou Bierbauer, 1889	36.6
48	Mike Benjamin, 1999	36.3
49	Miller Huggins, 1905	36.2
	Clete Boyer, 1962	36.2
51	Hughie Jennings, 1895	36.0
52	Bill Dahlen, 1895	35.9
53	Tommy Leach, 1904	35.8
	Ivan DeJesus, 1977	35.8
55	Harry Steinfeldt, 1900	35.6
56	Jack Glasscock, 1889	35.5
57	Billy Shindle, 1892	35.4
58	Freddie Patek, 1973	35.3
59	Bobby Knoop, 1970	35.1
60	Jack Glasscock, 1887	35.0
	Andruw Jones, 1999	35.0
62	Bill Dahlen, 1894	34.9
	Chet Lemon, 1977	34.9
64	Jimmy Bloodworth, 1941	34.7
65	George Davis, 1898	34.6
66	Bill Holbert, 1883	34.4
	Buddy Bell, 1982	34.4
68	Shorty Fuller, 1895	34.3
69	Hughie Jennings, 1896	34.2
	Doc Lavan, 1916	34.2
71	Bid McPhee, 1893	33.9
	Joe Cassidy, 1905	33.9
	Buck Weaver, 1913	33.9
	Bill Mazeroski, 1964	33.9
75	Mark Belanger, 1978	33.8
76	Bid McPhee, 1894	33.7
	Eddie Collins, 1910	33.7
	Gene Alley, 1970	33.7
79	Lave Cross, 1895	33.5
	John Farrell, 1902	33.5
	Donie Bush, 1914	33.5
	Leo Cardenas, 1969	33.5
83	Pop Smith, 1885	33.2
84	Ski Melillo, 1931	33.1
	Roy Smalley, 1979	33.1
	Ozzie Smith, 1982	33.1
87	Mickey Doolan, 1915	33.0
88	Tom Daly, 1887	32.9
	Hughie Jennings, 1894	32.9
	Red Schoendienst, 1952	32.9
	Red Schoendienst, 1954	32.9
92	Lave Cross, 1899	32.7
93	Don Zimmer, 1958	32.6
94	Art Fletcher, 1915	32.5
	Dave Parker, 1977	32.5
96	Richie Ashburn, 1957	32.4
97	Richie Ashburn, 1951	32.3
	Marty Barrett, 1987	32.3
99	Herman Long, 1889	32.2
100	5 players tied	32.0

Fielding Runs

First Base

1	Mark Grace, 1990	27
2	Bill Buckner, 1985	25
3	Chick Gandil, 1914	24
4	Sid Bream, 1986	24
5	Fred Tenney, 1905	22
6	Bill Buckner, 1983	22
7	Vic Power, 1960	21
8	Sid Bream, 1988	21
9	Jake Beckley, 1892	21
	Jiggs Donahue, 1907	21

Second Base

1	Glenn Hubbard, 1985	62
2	Bill Mazeroski, 1963	57
3	Freddie Maguire, 1928	50
4	Frankie Frisch, 1927	49
5	Nap Lajoie, 1908	48
6	Hughie Critz, 1933	46
7	Fred Pfeffer, 1884	46
8	Danny Richardson, 1891	44
9	Nap Lajoie, 1907	44
10	Dave Shean, 1910	42

Shortstop

1	Rabbit Maranville, 1914	52
2	George Davis, 1899	49
3	Dick Bartell, 1936	45
4	Ozzie Guillen, 1988	43
5	Ozzie Smith, 1980	41
6	Felix Martinez, 2000	40
7	Germany Smith, 1885	40
8	Dave Bancroft, 1920	39
9	Neifi Perez, 2000	39
10	Cal Ripken, 1984	39

Third Base

1	Graig Nettles, 1971	42
2	Harlond Clift, 1937	41
3	Arlie Latham, 1884	40
4	Billy Shindle, 1892	38
5	Billy Shindle, 1888	37
6	Tim Wallach, 1985	37
7	Clete Boyer, 1962	36
8	Tommy Leach, 1904	36
9	Lee Tannehill, 1906	35
10	Buddy Bell, 1982	35

Outfield

1	Andruw Jones, 1999	35
2	Chet Lemon, 1977	35
3	Dave Parker, 1977	33
4	Richie Ashburn, 1957	32
5	Richie Ashburn, 1951	32
6	Andruw Jones, 1998	32
7	Jim Fogarty, 1887	32
8	Kirby Puckett, 1984	30
9	Tommy McCarthy, 1888	30
10	Max Carey, 1916	30
11	Eric Davis, 1987	28
12	Tris Speaker, 1914	28
13	Omar Moreno, 1980	27
14	Tom Brown, 1893	27
15	Garry Maddox, 1979	27
16	Carl Yastrzemski, 1964	27
17	Gerald Young, 1989	26
18	Ed Delahanty, 1893	26
19	Gary Ward, 1983	26
20	Richie Ashburn, 1953	26

Catcher

1	John Kerins, 1886	37
2	Bill Holbert, 1883	36
3	Tom Daly, 1887	32
4	Duke Farrell, 1894	31
5	John Kerins, 1887	27
6	Pop Snyder, 1884	26
7	Wilbert Robinson, 1888	26
8	Connie Mack, 1892	25
9	Pop Snyder, 1879	25
10	George Mitterwald, 1970	24

Pitcher

1	Ed Walsh, 1907	22
2	Harry Howell, 1905	18
3	Ed Walsh, 1911	15
4	Ed Walsh, 1908	14
5	Will White, 1882	13
6	John Clarkson, 1889	11
7	Sadie McMahon, 1890	11
8	Tony Mullane, 1882	11
9	Carl Mays, 1926	10
10	Frank Smith, 1909	10

Fielding Wins

1	Glenn Hubbard, 1985	6.5
2	Bill Mazeroski, 1963	6.2
3	Rabbit Maranville, 1914	5.6
4	Nap Lajoie, 1908	5.6
5	Danny Richardson, 1892	5.3
6	Nap Lajoie, 1907	5.0
7	Freddie Maguire, 1928	5.0
8	Hughie Critz, 1933	5.0
9	Frankie Frisch, 1927	4.8
10	Graig Nettles, 1971	4.5
11	Dave Shean, 1910	4.5
12	George Davis, 1899	4.4
13	Danny Richardson, 1891	4.4
14	Lee Tannehill, 1906	4.4
15	Dick Bartell, 1936	4.4
16	Ozzie Smith, 1980	4.3
17	Bill Dahlen, 1908	4.3
18	Ozzie Guillen, 1988	4.3
19	Ryne Sandberg, 1983	4.3
20	Bill Mazeroski, 1966	4.3
21	Glenn Hubbard, 1986	4.3
22	Lee Tannehill, 1911	4.2
23	Dave Bancroft, 1920	4.2
24	Bill Mazeroski, 1962	4.1
25	Nap Lajoie, 1903	4.1
26	Fred Pfeffer, 1884	4.0
27	Al Weis, 1966	4.0
28	Bobby Knoop, 1964	3.9
29	Cal Ripken, 1984	3.8
30	Tim Wallach, 1985	3.8
31	Doc Lavan, 1916	3.8
32	Tommy Leach, 1904	3.8
33	Dal Maxvill, 1970	3.8
34	Joe Cassidy, 1905	3.8
35	Fred Pfeffer, 1888	3.8
36	Miller Huggins, 1905	3.7
37	Harlond Clift, 1937	3.7
38	Felix Martinez, 2000	3.7
39	Neifi Perez, 2000	3.7
40	Dick Bartell, 1937	3.7
41	Donie Bush, 1914	3.7
42	Eddie Collins, 1910	3.7
43	Joe Gerhardt, 1890	3.7
44	Bobby Knoop, 1970	3.7
45	Ivan DeJesus, 1977	3.6
46	George McBride, 1908	3.6
47	Freddie Patek, 1973	3.6
48	Clete Boyer, 1962	3.6
49	Heinie Wagner, 1908	3.6
50	Art Fletcher, 1915	3.6
51	Mickey Doolan, 1915	3.6
52	Buck Weaver, 1913	3.6
53	Everett Scott, 1921	3.6
54	Arlie Latham, 1884	3.6
55	Bill Mazeroski, 1964	3.6
56	Germany Smith, 1885	3.6
57	Cupid Childs, 1896	3.6
58	John Farrell, 1902	3.5
59	Mark Belanger, 1978	3.5
60	Leo Cardenas, 1969	3.5
61	Joe Tinker, 1908	3.5
62	Bobby Wallace, 1899	3.5
63	Ozzie Smith, 1982	3.5
64	Bid McPhee, 1889	3.5
65	Mike Benjamin, 1999	3.5
66	Chet Lemon, 1977	3.5
67	Buck Herzog, 1915	3.4
68	Horace Clarke, 1968	3.4
69	Bob Allen, 1890	3.4
70	Billy Shindle, 1888	3.4
71	Buddy Bell, 1982	3.4
72	John Kerins, 1886	3.4
73	Max Carey, 1916	3.4
74	Nap Lajoie, 1916	3.4
75	Freddie Patek, 1972	3.4
76	Red Schoendienst, 1952	3.4
77	Jimmy Bloodworth, 1941	3.4
78	Gene Alley, 1970	3.4
79	Brooks Robinson, 1967	3.4
80	Nap Lajoie, 1906	3.3
81	Johnny Evers, 1904	3.3
82	Don Zimmer, 1958	3.3
83	Andruw Jones, 1999	3.3
84	Buck Herzog, 1914	3.3
85	Billy Shindle, 1892	3.3
86	Richie Ashburn, 1957	3.3
87	Harry Steinfeldt, 1900	3.3
88	Bruno Betzel, 1916	3.3
89	Ron Santo, 1967	3.3
90	Red Schoendienst, 1954	3.2
91	Ed Brinkman, 1970	3.2
92	Dave Parker, 1977	3.2
93	Terry Pendleton, 1989	3.2
94	George Davis, 1898	3.2
95	Roy Smalley, 1979	3.2
96	Richie Ashburn, 1951	3.2
97	Pep Young, 1938	3.2
98	Zoilo Versalles, 1962	3.2
99	Hal Lanier, 1967	3.2
100	Rabbit Maranville, 1919	3.2

Total Player Rating

1	Babe Ruth, 1923	10.8
2	Babe Ruth, 1921	9.6
3	Cal Ripken, 1984	9.3
4	Babe Ruth, 1920	9.1
	Rogers Hornsby, 1924	9.1
6	Babe Ruth, 1927	9.0
7	Barry Bonds, 1992	8.9
8	Nap Lajoie, 1910	8.8
9	Rogers Hornsby, 1922	8.7
	Mickey Mantle, 1956	8.7
	Mickey Mantle, 1957	8.7
	Barry Bonds, 1993	8.7
13	Babe Ruth, 1924	8.6
14	Nap Lajoie, 1901	8.5
15	Nap Lajoie, 1906	8.4
	Babe Ruth, 1926	8.4
17	Ty Cobb, 1917	8.3
	Lou Gehrig, 1927	8.3
	Mickey Mantle, 1961	8.3
	Cal Ripken, 1991	8.3
	Barry Bonds, 1996	8.3
22	Nap Lajoie, 1903	8.1
	Nap Lajoie, 1908	8.1
	Rogers Hornsby, 1920	8.1
25	Rogers Hornsby, 1917	8.0
	Ted Williams, 1941	8.0
	Ted Williams, 1942	8.0
	Craig Biggio, 1997	8.0
29	Ron Santo, 1966	7.9
	Rickey Henderson, 1990	7.9
31	George Sisler, 1920	7.8
	Lou Boudreau, 1944	7.8
33	Lou Gehrig, 1934	7.7
	Alex Rodriguez, 2000	7.7
35	Tris Speaker, 1914	7.6
	Lou Gehrig, 1930	7.6
	Willie Mays, 1955	7.6
	Jeff Bagwell, 1994	7.6
	Mike Piazza, 1997	7.6
40	Honus Wagner, 1905	7.5
	Eddie Collins, 1910	7.5
	Ted Williams, 1946	7.5
	Norm Cash, 1961	7.5
	Willie Mays, 1965	7.5
	Ron Santo, 1967	7.5
	Barry Bonds, 1998	7.5
47	Honus Wagner, 1906	7.4
	Tris Speaker, 1912	7.4
	Rogers Hornsby, 1921	7.4
	Babe Ruth, 1930	7.4
	Babe Ruth, 1931	7.4
	Carl Yastrzemski, 1967	7.4
	Rickey Henderson, 1985	7.4
54	Harlond Clift, 1937	7.3
	Mike Schmidt, 1980	7.3
	Ken Caminiti, 1996	7.3
	Barry Bonds, 2000	7.3
58	Honus Wagner, 1908	7.2
	Frankie Frisch, 1927	7.2
	Snuffy Stirnweiss, 1945	7.2
	Willie Mays, 1958	7.2
	Rico Petrocelli, 1969	7.2
	Robin Yount, 1982	7.2
	Mark McGwire, 1998	7.2
65	Fred Dunlap, 1884	7.1
	Ted Williams, 1957	7.1
	Mike Schmidt, 1974	7.1
	George Brett, 1985	7.1
	Barry Bonds, 1990	7.1
70	Nap Lajoie, 1904	7.0
	Nap Lajoie, 1907	7.0
	Babe Ruth, 1928	7.0
	Rogers Hornsby, 1929	7.0
	Lou Boudreau, 1948	7.0
	Willie Mays, 1963	7.0
	Joe Morgan, 1975	7.0
	Mike Schmidt, 1981	7.0
	Cal Ripken, 1983	7.0
	Eric Davis, 1987	7.0
	Kevin Mitchell, 1989	7.0
	Barry Bonds, 1997	7.0
82	Hughie Jennings, 1896	6.9
	Eddie Collins, 1913	6.9
	Tris Speaker, 1913	6.9
	Tris Speaker, 1923	6.9
	Joe DiMaggio, 1941	6.9
	Lou Boudreau, 1943	6.9
	Snuffy Stirnweiss, 1944	6.9
	Ted Williams, 1947	6.9
	Jackie Robinson, 1951	6.9
	Ken Griffey Jr., 1997	6.9
92	Ty Cobb, 1910	6.8
	Ty Cobb, 1911	6.8
	Joe Jackson, 1912	6.8
	Rogers Hornsby, 1927	6.8
	Joe Cronin, 1930	6.8
	Hank Aaron, 1959	6.8
98	12 players tied	6.7

Total Player Rating (alpha.)

Hank Aaron, 1959	6.8
Jeff Bagwell, 1994	7.6
Craig Biggio, 1997	8.0
Barry Bonds, 1990	7.1
Barry Bonds, 1992	8.9
Barry Bonds, 1993	8.7
Barry Bonds, 1996	8.3
Barry Bonds, 1997	7.0
Barry Bonds, 1998	7.5
Barry Bonds, 2000	7.3
Lou Boudreau, 1943	6.9
Lou Boudreau, 1944	7.8
Lou Boudreau, 1948	7.0
George Brett, 1985	7.1
Ken Caminiti, 1996	7.3
Norm Cash, 1961	7.5
Harlond Clift, 1937	7.3
Ty Cobb, 1910	6.8
Ty Cobb, 1911	6.8
Ty Cobb, 1917	8.3
Eddie Collins, 1910	7.5
Eddie Collins, 1913	6.9
Joe Cronin, 1930	6.8
Eric Davis, 1987	7.0
Joe DiMaggio, 1941	6.9
Fred Dunlap, 1884	7.1
Frankie Frisch, 1927	7.2
Lou Gehrig, 1927	8.3
Lou Gehrig, 1930	7.6
Lou Gehrig, 1934	7.7
Ken Griffey Jr., 1997	6.9
Rickey Henderson, 1985	7.4
Rickey Henderson, 1990	7.9
Rogers Hornsby, 1917	8.0
Rogers Hornsby, 1920	8.1
Rogers Hornsby, 1921	7.4
Rogers Hornsby, 1922	8.7
Rogers Hornsby, 1924	9.1
Rogers Hornsby, 1927	6.8
Rogers Hornsby, 1929	7.0
Joe Jackson, 1912	6.8
Hughie Jennings, 1896	6.9
Nap Lajoie, 1901	8.5
Nap Lajoie, 1903	8.1
Nap Lajoie, 1904	7.0
Nap Lajoie, 1906	8.4
Nap Lajoie, 1907	7.0
Nap Lajoie, 1908	8.1
Nap Lajoie, 1910	8.8
Mickey Mantle, 1956	8.7
Mickey Mantle, 1957	8.7
Mickey Mantle, 1961	8.3
Willie Mays, 1955	7.6
Willie Mays, 1958	7.2
Willie Mays, 1963	7.0
Willie Mays, 1965	7.5
Mark McGwire, 1998	7.2
Kevin Mitchell, 1989	7.0
Joe Morgan, 1975	7.0
Rico Petrocelli, 1969	7.2
Mike Piazza, 1997	7.6
Cal Ripken, 1983	7.0
Cal Ripken, 1984	9.3
Cal Ripken, 1991	8.3
Jackie Robinson, 1951	6.9
Alex Rodriguez, 2000	7.7
Babe Ruth, 1920	9.1
Babe Ruth, 1921	9.6
Babe Ruth, 1923	10.8
Babe Ruth, 1924	8.6
Babe Ruth, 1926	8.4
Babe Ruth, 1927	9.0
Babe Ruth, 1928	7.0
Babe Ruth, 1930	7.4
Babe Ruth, 1931	7.4
Ron Santo, 1966	7.9
Ron Santo, 1967	7.5
Mike Schmidt, 1974	7.1
Mike Schmidt, 1980	7.3
Mike Schmidt, 1981	7.0
George Sisler, 1920	7.8
Tris Speaker, 1912	7.4
Tris Speaker, 1913	6.9
Tris Speaker, 1914	7.6
Tris Speaker, 1923	6.9
Snuffy Stirnweiss, 1944	6.9
Snuffy Stirnweiss, 1945	7.2
Honus Wagner, 1905	7.5
Honus Wagner, 1906	7.4
Honus Wagner, 1908	7.2
Ted Williams, 1941	8.0
Ted Williams, 1942	8.0
Ted Williams, 1946	7.5
Ted Williams, 1947	6.9
Ted Williams, 1957	7.1
Carl Yastrzemski, 1967	7.4
Robin Yount, 1982	7.2

Total Player Rating (by era)

1876-1892

1	Fred Dunlap, 1884	7.1
2	Dan Brouthers, 1892	6.7
3	Cupid Childs, 1890	6.6
4	Fred Pfeffer, 1884	6.3
5	Jack Glasscock, 1889	5.6
6	Harry Stovey, 1889	4.9
	Bid McPhee, 1892	4.9
8	Pete Browning, 1882	4.8
	Ned Williamson, 1884	4.8
	Billy Nash, 1888	4.8
11	King Kelly, 1886	4.7
	Hardy Richardson, 1886	4.7
	Tip O'Neill, 1887	4.7
14	3 players tied	4.6

1893-1919

1	Nap Lajoie, 1910	8.8
2	Nap Lajoie, 1901	8.5
3	Nap Lajoie, 1906	8.4
4	Ty Cobb, 1917	8.3
5	Nap Lajoie, 1903	8.1
	Nap Lajoie, 1908	8.1
7	Rogers Hornsby, 1917	8.0
8	Tris Speaker, 1914	7.6
9	Honus Wagner, 1905	7.5
	Eddie Collins, 1910	7.5
11	Honus Wagner, 1906	7.4
	Tris Speaker, 1912	7.4
13	Honus Wagner, 1908	7.2
14	Nap Lajoie, 1904	7.0
	Nap Lajoie, 1907	7.0

1920-1941

1	Babe Ruth, 1923	10.8
2	Babe Ruth, 1921	9.6
3	Babe Ruth, 1920	9.1
	Rogers Hornsby, 1924	9.1
5	Babe Ruth, 1927	9.0
6	Rogers Hornsby, 1922	8.7
7	Babe Ruth, 1924	8.6
8	Babe Ruth, 1926	8.4
9	Lou Gehrig, 1927	8.3
10	Rogers Hornsby, 1920	8.1
11	Ted Williams, 1941	8.0
12	George Sisler, 1920	7.8
13	Lou Gehrig, 1934	7.7
14	Lou Gehrig, 1930	7.6
15	3 players tied	7.4

1942-1960

1	Mickey Mantle, 1956	8.7
	Mickey Mantle, 1957	8.7
3	Ted Williams, 1942	8.0
4	Lou Boudreau, 1944	7.8
5	Willie Mays, 1955	7.6
6	Ted Williams, 1946	7.5
7	Snuffy Stirnweiss, 1945	7.2
	Willie Mays, 1958	7.2
9	Ted Williams, 1957	7.1
10	Lou Boudreau, 1948	7.0
11	Lou Boudreau, 1943	6.9
	Snuffy Stirnweiss, 1944	6.9
	Ted Williams, 1947	6.9
	Jackie Robinson, 1951	6.9
15	Hank Aaron, 1959	6.8

1961-1976

1	Mickey Mantle, 1961	8.3
2	Ron Santo, 1966	7.9
3	Norm Cash, 1961	7.5
	Willie Mays, 1965	7.5
	Ron Santo, 1967	7.5
6	Carl Yastrzemski, 1967	7.4
7	Rico Petrocelli, 1969	7.2
8	Mike Schmidt, 1974	7.1
9	Willie Mays, 1963	7.0
	Joe Morgan, 1975	7.0
11	Willie Mays, 1962	6.7
	Willie Mays, 1964	6.7
	Ron Santo, 1964	6.7
	Reggie Jackson, 1969	6.7
15	Carl Yastrzemski, 1968	6.6

1977-2000

1	Cal Ripken, 1984	9.3
2	Barry Bonds, 1992	8.9
3	Barry Bonds, 1993	8.7
4	Cal Ripken, 1991	8.3
	Barry Bonds, 1996	8.3
6	Craig Biggio, 1997	8.0
7	Rickey Henderson, 1990	7.9
8	Alex Rodriguez, 2000	7.7
9	Jeff Bagwell, 1994	7.6
	Mike Piazza, 1997	7.6
11	Barry Bonds, 1998	7.5
12	Rickey Henderson, 1985	7.4
13	Mike Schmidt, 1980	7.3
	Ken Caminiti, 1996	7.3
	Barry Bonds, 2000	7.3

Wins

1	Charley Radbourn, 1884	59
2	John Clarkson, 1885	53
3	Guy Hecker, 1884	52
4	John Clarkson, 1889	49
5	Charley Radbourn, 1883	48
	Charlie Buffinton, 1884	48
7	Al Spalding, 1876	47
	John Ward, 1879	47
9	Jim Galvin, 1883	46
	Jim Galvin, 1884	46
	Matt Kilroy, 1887	46
12	George Bradley, 1876	45
	Jim McCormick, 1880	45
	Silver King, 1888	45
15	Mickey Welch, 1885	44
	Bill Hutchison, 1891	44
17	Billy Taylor, 1884	43
	Tommy Bond, 1879	43
	Will White, 1879	43
	Larry Corcoran, 1880	43
	Will White, 1883	43
22	Lady Baldwin, 1886	42
	Tim Keefe, 1886	42
	Bill Hutchison, 1890	42
25	Charlie Sweeney, 1884	41
	Tim Keefe, 1883	41
	Dave Foutz, 1886	41
	Ed Morris, 1886	41
	Jack Chesbro, 1904	41
30	Jim McCormick, 1884	40
	Tommy Bond, 1877	40
	Tommy Bond, 1878	40
	Will White, 1882	40
	Bill Sweeney, 1884	40
	Bob Caruthers, 1885	40
	Bob Caruthers, 1889	40
	Ed Walsh, 1908	40
38	John Ward, 1880	39
	Mickey Welch, 1884	39
	Ed Morris, 1885	39
41	Toad Ramsey, 1886	38
	John Clarkson, 1887	38
	Kid Gleason, 1890	38
44	Jim Galvin, 1879	37
	Jim Whitney, 1883	37
	Tim Keefe, 1884	37
	Jack Lynch, 1884	37
	Toad Ramsey, 1887	37
	Christy Mathewson, 1908	37
50	Jim McCormick, 1882	36
	Tony Mullane, 1884	36
	John Clarkson, 1886	36
	Sadie McMahon, 1890	36
	Bill Hutchison, 1892	36
	Cy Young, 1892	36
	Frank Killen, 1893	36
	Amos Rusie, 1894	36
	Walter Johnson, 1913	36
59	Jim Devlin, 1877	35
	Tony Mullane, 1883	35
	Larry Corcoran, 1884	35
	Tim Keefe, 1887	35
	Tim Keefe, 1888	35
	Ed Seward, 1888	35
	Silver King, 1889	35
	Sadie McMahon, 1891	35
	Kid Nichols, 1892	35
	Jack Stivetts, 1892	35
	Cy Young, 1895	35
	Joe McGinnity, 1904	35
71	Mickey Welch, 1880	34
	Larry Corcoran, 1883	34
	Ed Morris, 1884	34
	Will White, 1884	34
	Elmer Smith, 1887	34
	Scott Stratton, 1890	34
	George Haddock, 1891	34
	Kid Nichols, 1893	34
	Cy Young, 1893	34
	Joe Wood, 1912	34
81	Charley Radbourn, 1882	33
	Dave Foutz, 1885	33
	Henry Porter, 1885	33
	Mickey Welch, 1886	33
	Tony Mullane, 1886	33
	John Clarkson, 1888	33
	Mark Baldwin, 1890	33
	John Clarkson, 1891	33
	Amos Rusie, 1891	33
	Jack Stivetts, 1891	33
	Amos Rusie, 1893	33
	Jouett Meekin, 1894	33
	Cy Young, 1901	33
	Christy Mathewson, 1904	33
	Walter Johnson, 1912	33
	Grover Alexander, 1916	33
97	10 players tied	32

Wins (by era)

1876-1892

1	Charley Radbourn, 1884	59
2	John Clarkson, 1885	53
3	Guy Hecker, 1884	52
4	John Clarkson, 1889	49
5	Charley Radbourn, 1883	48
	Charlie Buffinton, 1884	48
7	Al Spalding, 1876	47
	John Ward, 1879	47
9	Jim Galvin, 1883	46
	Jim Galvin, 1884	46
	Matt Kilroy, 1887	46
12	George Bradley, 1876	45
	Jim McCormick, 1880	45
	Silver King, 1888	45
15	2 players tied	44

1893-1919

1	Jack Chesbro, 1904	41
2	Ed Walsh, 1908	40
3	Christy Mathewson, 1908	37
4	Frank Killen, 1893	36
	Amos Rusie, 1894	36
	Walter Johnson, 1913	36
7	Cy Young, 1895	35
	Joe McGinnity, 1904	35
9	Kid Nichols, 1893	34
	Cy Young, 1893	34
	Joe Wood, 1912	34
12	6 players tied	33

1920-1941

1	Jim Bagby, 1920	31
	Lefty Grove, 1931	31
3	Dizzy Dean, 1934	30
4	Dazzy Vance, 1924	28
	Lefty Grove, 1930	28
	Dizzy Dean, 1935	28
7	Grover Alexander, 1920	27
	Carl Mays, 1921	27
	Urban Shocker, 1921	27
	Eddie Rommel, 1922	27
	Dolf Luque, 1923	27
	George Uhle, 1926	27
	Bucky Walters, 1939	27
	Bob Feller, 1940	27
15	7 players tied	26

1942-1960

1	Hal Newhouser, 1944	29
2	Robin Roberts, 1952	28
3	Dizzy Trout, 1944	27
	Don Newcombe, 1956	27
5	Hal Newhouser, 1946	26
	Bob Feller, 1946	26
7	Hal Newhouser, 1945	25
	Dave Ferriss, 1946	25
	Mel Parnell, 1949	25
10	Johnny Sain, 1948	24
	Bobby Shantz, 1952	24
12	13 players tied	23

1961-1976

1	Denny McLain, 1968	31
2	Sandy Koufax, 1966	27
	Steve Carlton, 1972	27
4	Sandy Koufax, 1965	26
	Juan Marichal, 1968	26
6	Whitey Ford, 1961	25
	Don Drysdale, 1962	25
	Sandy Koufax, 1963	25
	Juan Marichal, 1963	25
	Juan Marichal, 1966	25
	Jim Kaat, 1966	25
	Tom Seaver, 1969	25
	Mickey Lolich, 1971	25
	Catfish Hunter, 1974	25
	Fergie Jenkins, 1974	25

1977-2000

1	Bob Welch, 1990	27
2	Ron Guidry, 1978	25
	Steve Stone, 1980	25
4	Steve Carlton, 1980	24
	La Marr Hoyt, 1983	24
	Dwight Gooden, 1985	24
	Roger Clemens, 1986	24
	Frank Viola, 1988	24
	John Smoltz, 1996	24
10	7 players tied	23

Losses

1	John Coleman, 1883	48
2	Will White, 1880	42
3	Larry McKeon, 1884	41
4	George Bradley, 1879	40
	Jim McCormick, 1879	40
6	Henry Porter, 1888	37
	Kid Carsey, 1891	37
	George Cobb, 1892	37
9	Stump Wiedman, 1886	36
	Bill Hutchison, 1892	36
11	Jim Devlin, 1876	35
	Jim Galvin, 1880	35
	Fleury Sullivan, 1884	35
	Adonis Terry, 1884	35
	Hardie Henderson, 1885	35
	Red Donahue, 1897	35
17	Bobby Mathews, 1876	34
	Bob Barr, 1884	34
	Matt Kilroy, 1886	34
	Al Mays, 1887	34
	Mark Baldwin, 1889	34
	Amos Rusie, 1890	34
23	Hardie Henderson, 1883	33
	Dupee Shaw, 1884	33
	Harry McCormick, 1879	33
	Jim Whitney, 1881	33
	Lee Richmond, 1882	33
	Frank Mountain, 1883	33
	Jersey Bakely, 1888	33
30	Lee Richmond, 1880	32
	John Harkins, 1884	32
	Jim Whitney, 1885	32
	Jim Whitney, 1886	32
34	Sam Weaver, 1878	31
	Will White, 1879	31
	Charley Radbourn, 1886	31
	Dupee Shaw, 1886	31
	Billy Crowell, 1887	31
	Amos Rusie, 1892	31
40	Mickey Welch, 1880	30
	Jim McCormick, 1881	30
	Jim McCormick, 1882	30
	Jersey Bakely, 1884	30
	Jack Lynch, 1886	30
	Phenomenal Smith, 1887	30
	Toad Ramsey, 1888	30
	John Ewing, 1889	30
	Ed Beatin, 1890	30
	Ted Breitenstein, 1895	30
	Jim Hughey, 1899	30
51	Tommy Bond, 1880	29
	Doc Landis, 1882	29
	Jim Galvin, 1883	29
	John Healy, 1887	29
	Hank O'Day, 1888	29
	Bert Cunningham, 1888	29
	Red Ehret, 1889	29
	Silver King, 1891	29
	Bill Hart, 1896	29
	Jack Taylor, 1898	29
	Vic Willis, 1905	29
62	Jim McCormick, 1880	28
	Hank O'Day, 1884	28
	Hugh Daily, 1884	28
	Gus Weyhing, 1887	28
	Mark Baldwin, 1891	28
	Duke Esper, 1893	28
	Bill Hill, 1896	28
69	Jim Galvin, 1879	27
	Tim Keefe, 1881	27
	Tim Keefe, 1883	27
	Charlie Buffinton, 1885	27
	Al Mays, 1886	27
	Tony Mullane, 1886	27
	Toad Ramsey, 1886	27
	Toad Ramsey, 1887	27
	Park Swartzel, 1889	27
	Phil Knell, 1891	27
	Mark Baldwin, 1892	27
	Pink Hawley, 1894	27
	Chick Fraser, 1896	27
	Bill Hart, 1897	27
	Willie Sudhoff, 1898	27
	Bill Carrick, 1899	27
	Dummy Taylor, 1901	27
	George Bell, 1910	27
	Paul Derringer, 1933	27
88	20 players tied	26

Winning Percentage

1	Roy Face, 1959	.947
2	Johnny Allen, 1937	.938
3	Greg Maddux, 1995	.905
4	Randy Johnson, 1995	.900
5	Ron Guidry, 1978	.893
6	Freddie Fitzsimmons, 1940	.889
7	Lefty Grove, 1931	.886
8	Bob Stanley, 1978	.882
9	Preacher Roe, 1951	.880
10	Fred Goldsmith, 1880	.875
11	Joe Wood, 1912	.872
12	David Cone, 1988	.870
13	Orel Hershiser, 1985	.864
14	Bill Donovan, 1907	.862
	Whitey Ford, 1961	.862
16	Dwight Gooden, 1985	.857
	Roger Clemens, 1986	.857
18	Pedro Martinez, 1999	.852
19	Chief Bender, 1914	.850
	John Smoltz, 1998	.850
21	Lefty Grove, 1930	.848
22	Mike Hampton, 1999	.846
23	Tom Hughes, 1916	.842
	Emil Yde, 1924	.842
	Schoolboy Rowe, 1940	.842
	Sandy Consuegra, 1954	.842
	Ralph Terry, 1961	.842
	Ron Perranoski, 1963	.842
29	Lefty Gomez, 1934	.839
30	Bill Hoffer, 1895	.838
	Denny McLain, 1968	.838
32	Walter Johnson, 1913	.837
33	Henry Boyle, 1884	.833
	King Cole, 1910	.833
	Spud Chandler, 1943	.833
	Hoyt Wilhelm, 1952	.833
	Sandy Koufax, 1963	.833
	Randy Johnson, 1997	.833
39	Charley Radbourn, 1884	.831
40	Ed Reulbach, 1906	.826
	Elmer Riddle, 1941	.826
	Greg Maddux, 1997	.826
43	Jay Hughes, 1899	.824
	Jack Chesbro, 1902	.824
	Dazzy Vance, 1924	.824
46	Chief Bender, 1910	.821
	Bob Purkey, 1962	.821
48	Sal Maglie, 1950	.818
	Bob Welch, 1990	.818
	Mark Portugal, 1993	.818
	David Wells, 1998	.818
52	Joe McGinnity, 1904	.814
53	Mordecai Brown, 1906	.813
	Russ Ford, 1910	.813
	Eddie Plank, 1912	.813
	Carl Hubbell, 1936	.813
57	Dizzy Dean, 1934	.811
58	Ed Reulbach, 1907	.810
	Doc Crandall, 1910	.810
	Johnny Allen, 1932	.810
	Ted Wilks, 1944	.810
	Phil Niekro, 1982	.810
	Jimmy Key, 1994	.810
64	Alvin Crowder, 1928	.808
	Bobo Newsom, 1940	.808
	Tiny Bonham, 1942	.808
	Larry Jansen, 1947	.808
	Dave McNally, 1971	.808
	Catfish Hunter, 1973	.808
70	Christy Mathewson, 1909	.806
	Howie Camnitz, 1909	.806
	Dave Ferriss, 1946	.806
	Juan Marichal, 1966	.806
74	Eddie Cicotte, 1919	.806
75	Mickey Welch, 1885	.800
	Ed Doheny, 1902	.800
	Sam Leever, 1905	.800
	Bert Humphries, 1913	.800
	Stan Coveleski, 1925	.800
	Firpo Marberry, 1931	.800
	Robin Roberts, 1952	.800
	Ed Lopat, 1953	.800
	Don Newcombe, 1955	.800
	Jim Palmer, 1969	.800
	John Candelaria, 1977	.800
	Larry Gura, 1978	.800
	Tommy Greene, 1993	.800
	Denny Neagle, 1997	.800
89	Al Spalding, 1876	.797
90	Don Newcombe, 1956	.794
91	Jocko Flynn, 1886	.793
	Ellis Kinder, 1949	.793
	Sal Maglie, 1951	.793
	Bret Saberhagen, 1989	.793
95	Dutch Leonard, 1914	.792
	Sandy Koufax, 1964	.792
	Wally Bunker, 1964	.792
	Shawn Estes, 1997	.792
99	8 players tied	.789

Winning Percentage (by era)

1876-1892

1	Fred Goldsmith, 1880	.875
2	Henry Boyle, 1884	.833
3	Charley Radbourn, 1884	.831
4	Mickey Welch, 1885	.800
5	Al Spalding, 1876	.797
6	Jocko Flynn, 1886	.793
7	Bob Caruthers, 1889	.784
8	Jack Manning, 1876	.783
9	Will White, 1882	.769
	Charlie Ferguson, 1886	.769
11	John Clarkson, 1885	.768
12	Lady Baldwin, 1886	.764
13	Bob Caruthers, 1887	.763
	Charlie Buffinton, 1891	.763
15	George Haddock, 1891	.756

1893-1919

1	Joe Wood, 1912	.872
2	Bill Donovan, 1907	.862
3	Chief Bender, 1914	.850
4	Tom Hughes, 1916	.842
5	Bill Hoffer, 1895	.838
6	Walter Johnson, 1913	.837
7	King Cole, 1910	.833
8	Ed Reulbach, 1906	.826
9	Jay Hughes, 1899	.824
	Jack Chesbro, 1902	.824
11	Chief Bender, 1910	.821
12	Joe McGinnity, 1904	.814
13	Mordecai Brown, 1906	.813
	Russ Ford, 1910	.813
	Eddie Plank, 1912	.813

1920-1941

1	Johnny Allen, 1937	.938
2	Freddie Fitzsimmons, 1940	.889
3	Lefty Grove, 1931	.886
4	Lefty Grove, 1930	.848
5	Emil Yde, 1924	.842
	Schoolboy Rowe, 1940	.842
7	Lefty Gomez, 1934	.839
8	Elmer Riddle, 1941	.826
9	Dazzy Vance, 1924	.824
10	Carl Hubbell, 1936	.813
11	Dizzy Dean, 1934	.811
12	Johnny Allen, 1932	.810
13	Alvin Crowder, 1928	.808
	Bobo Newsom, 1940	.808
15	2 players tied	.800

1942-1960

1	Roy Face, 1959	.947
2	Preacher Roe, 1951	.880
3	Sandy Consuegra, 1954	.842
4	Spud Chandler, 1943	.833
	Hoyt Wilhelm, 1952	.833
6	Sal Maglie, 1950	.818
7	Ted Wilks, 1944	.810
8	Tiny Bonham, 1942	.808
	Larry Jansen, 1947	.808
10	Dave Ferriss, 1946	.806
11	Robin Roberts, 1952	.800
	Ed Lopat, 1953	.800
	Don Newcombe, 1955	.800
14	Don Newcombe, 1956	.794
15	2 players tied	.793

1961-1976

1	Whitey Ford, 1961	.862
2	Ralph Terry, 1961	.842
	Ron Perranoski, 1963	.842
4	Denny McLain, 1968	.838
5	Sandy Koufax, 1963	.833
6	Bob Purkey, 1962	.821
7	Dave McNally, 1971	.808
	Catfish Hunter, 1973	.808
9	Juan Marichal, 1966	.806
10	Jim Palmer, 1969	.800
11	Sandy Koufax, 1964	.792
	Wally Bunker, 1964	.792
13	Don Gullett, 1975	.789
14	Johnny Podres, 1961	.783
15	Tom Seaver, 1969	.781

1977-2000

1	Greg Maddux, 1995	.905
2	Randy Johnson, 1995	.900
3	Ron Guidry, 1978	.893
4	Bob Stanley, 1978	.882
5	David Cone, 1988	.870
6	Orel Hershiser, 1985	.864
7	Dwight Gooden, 1985	.857
	Roger Clemens, 1986	.857
9	Pedro Martinez, 1999	.852
10	John Smoltz, 1998	.850
11	Mike Hampton, 1999	.846
12	Randy Johnson, 1997	.833
13	Greg Maddux, 1997	.826
14	3 players tied	.818

Games

1	Mike Marshall, 1974	106
2	Kent Tekulve, 1979	94
3	Mike Marshall, 1973	92
4	Kent Tekulve, 1978	91
5	Wayne Granger, 1969	90
	Mike Marshall, 1979	90
	Kent Tekulve, 1987	90
8	Mark Eichhorn, 1987	89
	Julian Tavarez, 1997	89
10	Wilbur Wood, 1968	88
	Mike Myers, 1997	88
	Sean Runyan, 1998	88
13	Rob Murphy, 1987	87
14	Kent Tekulve, 1982	85
	Frank Williams, 1987	85
	Mitch Williams, 1987	85
17	Ted Abernathy, 1965	84
	Enrique Romo, 1979	84
	Dick Tidrow, 1980	84
	Dan Quisenberry, 1985	84
	Stan Belinda, 1997	84
22	Ken Sanders, 1971	83
	Craig Lefferts, 1986	83
	Eddie Guardado, 1996	83
	Mike Myers, 1996	83
	Steve Kline, 2000	83
	Kelly Wunsch, 2000	83
28	Eddie Fisher, 1965	82
	Bill Campbell, 1983	82
	Juan Agosto, 1990	82
	Paul Quantrill, 1998	82
	Steve Kline, 1999	82
33	John Wyatt, 1964	81
	Dale Murray, 1976	81
	Jeff Robinson, 1987	81
	Duane Ward, 1991	81
	Joe Boever, 1992	81
	Kenny Rogers, 1992	81
	Mike Jackson, 1993	81
	Brad Clontz, 1996	81
	Mike Stanton, 1996	81
	Rod Beck, 1998	81
	Greg Swindell, 1998	81
44	Mudcat Grant, 1970	80
	Pedro Borbon, 1973	80
	Willie Hernandez, 1984	80
	Mitch Williams, 1986	80
	Doug Jones, 1992	80
	Greg Harris, 1993	80
	Turk Wendell, 1999	80
51	Dick Radatz, 1964	79
	Duane Ward, 1992	79
	Bob Patterson, 1996	79
	Eddie Guardado, 1998	79
	Scott Sullivan, 1999	79
	Anthony Telford, 1999	79
	Scott Sullivan, 2000	79
58	Hal Woodeshick, 1965	78
	Ted Abernathy, 1968	78
	Bill Campbell, 1976	78
	Rollie Fingers, 1977	78
	Tom Hume, 1980	78
	Kent Tekulve, 1980	78
	Greg Minton, 1982	78
	Ed Vande Berg, 1982	78
	Ted Power, 1984	78
	Tim Burke, 1985	78
	Lance McCullers, 1987	78
	Mark Dewey, 1996	78
	Jeff Shaw, 1996	78
	Jeff Shaw, 1997	78
	Buddy Groom, 1997	78
	Steve Kline, 1998	78
	Chuck McElroy, 1998	78
	Robb Nen, 1998	78
	Dan Plesac, 1998	78
	Mike Myers, 2000	78
78	Dick Tidrow, 1979	77
	Bob Locker, 1967	77
	Wilbur Wood, 1970	77
	Charlie Hough, 1976	77
	Butch Metzger, 1976	77
	Rick Camp, 1980	77
	Gary Lavelle, 1984	77
	Mark Davis, 1985	77
	Craig Lefferts, 1987	77
	Bobby Thigpen, 1990	77
	Barry Jones, 1991	77
	Xavier Hernandez, 1992	77
	Mike Perez, 1992	77
	Mark Wohlers, 1996	77
	Mel Rojas, 1997	77
	Jeff Nelson, 1997	77
	Paul Quantrill, 1997	77
	Anthony Telford, 1998	77
	Mike Trombley, 1998	77
	Armando Benitez, 1999	77
	Turk Wendell, 2000	77
	Mike Venafro, 2000	77
100	31 players tied	76

Games (by era)

1876-1892

1	Will White, 1879	76
	Jim Galvin, 1883	76
	Charley Radbourn, 1883	76
4	Charley Radbourn, 1884	75
	Guy Hecker, 1884	75
	Bill Hutchison, 1892	75
7	Jim McCormick, 1880	74
	Lee Richmond, 1880	74
9	John Clarkson, 1889	73
10	Jim Galvin, 1884	72
11	Bill Hutchison, 1890	71
12	John Ward, 1879	70
	John Ward, 1880	70
	John Clarkson, 1885	70
15	Matt Kilroy, 1887	69

1893-1919

1	Ed Walsh, 1908	66
2	Ed Walsh, 1912	62
3	Dave Davenport, 1916	59
4	Amos Rusie, 1893	56
	Ted Breitenstein, 1894	56
	Pink Hawley, 1895	56
	Ed Walsh, 1907	56
	Christy Mathewson, 1908	56
	Ed Walsh, 1911	56
	Reb Russell, 1916	56
11	Frank Killen, 1893	55
	Ted Breitenstein, 1895	55
	Joe McGinnity, 1903	55
	Jack Chesbro, 1904	55
	Dave Davenport, 1915	55

1920-1941

1	Firpo Marberry, 1926	64
2	Clint Brown, 1939	61
3	Garland Braxton, 1927	58
	Russ Van Atta, 1935	58
5	Eddie Rommel, 1923	56
	Firpo Marberry, 1927	56
	Hugh Mulcahy, 1937	56
8	Firpo Marberry, 1925	55
	Bump Hadley, 1931	55
	Jim Walkup, 1935	55
11	George Uhle, 1923	54
	Firpo Marberry, 1932	54
	Jack Russell, 1934	54
	Chubby Dean, 1939	54
	Clyde Shoun, 1940	54

1942-1960

1	Jim Konstanty, 1950	74
2	Hoyt Wilhelm, 1952	71
3	Ace Adams, 1943	70
	Mike Fornieles, 1960	70
5	Ellis Kinder, 1953	69
	Don Elston, 1958	69
7	Hoyt Wilhelm, 1953	68
	Roy Face, 1956	68
	Roy Face, 1960	68
10	Andy Karl, 1945	67
	Turk Lown, 1957	67
	Gerry Staley, 1959	67
13	6 players tied	65

1961-1976

1	Mike Marshall, 1974	106
2	Mike Marshall, 1973	92
3	Wayne Granger, 1969	90
4	Wilbur Wood, 1968	88
5	Ted Abernathy, 1965	84
6	Ken Sanders, 1971	83
7	Eddie Fisher, 1965	82
8	John Wyatt, 1964	81
	Dale Murray, 1976	81
10	Mudcat Grant, 1970	80
	Pedro Borbon, 1973	80
12	Dick Radatz, 1964	79
13	Hal Woodeshick, 1965	78
	Ted Abernathy, 1968	78
	Bill Campbell, 1976	78

1977-2000

1	Kent Tekulve, 1979	94
2	Kent Tekulve, 1978	91
3	Mike Marshall, 1979	90
	Kent Tekulve, 1987	90
5	Mark Eichhorn, 1987	89
	Julian Tavarez, 1997	89
7	Mike Myers, 1997	88
	Sean Runyan, 1998	88
9	Rob Murphy, 1987	87
10	Kent Tekulve, 1982	85
	Frank Williams, 1987	85
	Mitch Williams, 1987	85
13	4 players tied	84

Games Started

1	Will White, 1879	75
	Jim Galvin, 1883	75
3	Jim McCormick, 1880	74
4	Charley Radbourn, 1884	73
	Guy Hecker, 1884	73
6	Jim Galvin, 1884	72
	John Clarkson, 1889	72
8	John Clarkson, 1885	70
	Bill Hutchison, 1892	70
10	Matt Kilroy, 1887	69
11	Jim Devlin, 1876	68
	Charley Radbourn, 1883	68
	Tim Keefe, 1883	68
	Matt Kilroy, 1886	68
15	John Ward, 1880	67
	Jim McCormick, 1882	67
	Charlie Buffinton, 1884	67
	Toad Ramsey, 1886	67
19	Dupee Shaw, 1884	66
	Jim Galvin, 1879	66
	Lee Richmond, 1880	66
	Bill Hutchison, 1890	66
23	Jim McCormick, 1884	65
	Mickey Welch, 1884	65
	Tony Mullane, 1884	65
26	George Bradley, 1876	64
	Tommy Bond, 1879	64
	Mickey Welch, 1880	64
	Will White, 1883	64
	Tim Keefe, 1886	64
	Toad Ramsey, 1887	64
	Silver King, 1888	64
33	Jim Whitney, 1881	63
	Ed Morris, 1885	63
	Ed Morris, 1886	63
36	Will White, 1880	62
	Amos Rusie, 1890	62
	Amos Rusie, 1892	62
39	Jim Devlin, 1877	61
	John Coleman, 1883	61
	Hardie Henderson, 1885	61
	Jersey Bakely, 1888	61
43	Al Spalding, 1876	60
	Jim McCormick, 1879	60
	John Ward, 1879	60
	Larry Corcoran, 1880	60
	Larry McKeon, 1884	60
	Bill Sweeney, 1884	60
49	Billy Taylor, 1884	59
	Tommy Bond, 1878	59
	Frank Mountain, 1883	59
	Larry Corcoran, 1884	59
	Mickey Welch, 1886	59
	John Clarkson, 1887	59
	Mark Baldwin, 1889	59
56	Tommy Bond, 1877	58
	Terry Larkin, 1879	58
	Jim McCormick, 1881	58
	Tim Keefe, 1884	58
	Hugh Daily, 1884	58
	Charley Radbourn, 1886	58
	Bill Hutchison, 1891	58
	Sadie McMahon, 1891	58
64	Tommy Bond, 1880	57
	Dave Foutz, 1886	57
	Ed Seward, 1888	57
	Sadie McMahon, 1890	57
	Amos Rusie, 1891	57
69	Charlie Sweeney, 1884	56
	Bobby Mathews, 1876	56
	Terry Larkin, 1877	56
	Terry Larkin, 1878	56
	Jim Whitney, 1883	56
	Lady Baldwin, 1886	56
	Tony Mullane, 1886	56
	Tim Keefe, 1887	56
	Matt Kilroy, 1889	56
	Mark Baldwin, 1890	56
	Silver King, 1890	56
	Jack Stivetts, 1891	56
81	George Derby, 1881	55
	Tony Mullane, 1882	55
	Adonis Terry, 1884	55
	Mickey Welch, 1885	55
	John Clarkson, 1886	55
	Phenomenal Smith, 1887	55
	Gus Weyhing, 1887	55
	Ed Morris, 1888	55
	Kid Gleason, 1890	55
90	George Bradley, 1879	54
	Harry McCormick, 1879	54
	Jim Galvin, 1880	54
	Will White, 1882	54
	Henry Porter, 1885	54
	John Clarkson, 1888	54
	Henry Porter, 1888	54
	Ed Beatin, 1890	54
	Bob Barr, 1890	54
99	9 players tied	53

Games Started (by era)

1876-1892

1	Will White, 1879	75
	Jim Galvin, 1883	75
3	Jim McCormick, 1880	74
4	Charley Radbourn, 1884	73
	Guy Hecker, 1884	73
6	Jim Galvin, 1884	72
	John Clarkson, 1889	72
8	John Clarkson, 1885	70
	Bill Hutchison, 1892	70
10	Matt Kilroy, 1887	69
11	Jim Devlin, 1876	68
	Charley Radbourn, 1883	68
	Tim Keefe, 1883	68
	Matt Kilroy, 1886	68
15	4 players tied	67

1893-1919

1	Amos Rusie, 1893	52
2	Ted Breitenstein, 1895	51
	Jack Chesbro, 1904	51
4	Ted Breitenstein, 1894	50
	Amos Rusie, 1894	50
	Pink Hawley, 1895	50
	Frank Killen, 1896	50
8	Jouett Meekin, 1894	49
	Ed Walsh, 1908	49
10	Frank Killen, 1893	48
	Joe McGinnity, 1903	48
12	Cy Young, 1894	47
	Amos Rusie, 1895	47
	Jack Taylor, 1898	47
15	8 players tied	46

1920-1941

1	George Uhle, 1923	44
2	Grover Alexander, 1920	40
	Stan Coveleski, 1921	40
	George Uhle, 1922	40
	George Caster, 1938	40
	Bobo Newsom, 1938	40
	Bob Feller, 1941	40
8	Red Faber, 1920	39
	Red Faber, 1921	39
	Hooks Dauss, 1923	39
	Howard Ehmke, 1923	39
	Watty Clark, 1929	39
	George Earnshaw, 1930	39
	Alvin Crowder, 1932	39
	Kirby Higbe, 1941	39

1942-1960

1	Bob Feller, 1946	42
	Bob Friend, 1956	42
3	Bill Voiselle, 1944	41
	Robin Roberts, 1953	41
5	Dizzy Trout, 1944	40
6	Johnny Sain, 1948	39
	Robin Roberts, 1950	39
	Warren Spahn, 1950	39
	Vern Bickford, 1950	39
	Robin Roberts, 1951	39
	Ron Kline, 1956	39
	Lew Burdette, 1959	39
13	10 players tied	38

1961-1976

1	Wilbur Wood, 1972	49
2	Wilbur Wood, 1973	48
3	Mickey Lolich, 1971	45
4	Wilbur Wood, 1975	43
5	Don Drysdale, 1963	42
	Jack Sanford, 1963	42
	Don Drysdale, 1965	42
	Jim Kaat, 1965	42
	Fergie Jenkins, 1969	42
	Wilbur Wood, 1971	42
	Stan Bahnsen, 1973	42
	Mickey Lolich, 1973	42
	Wilbur Wood, 1974	42
14	22 players tied	41

1977-2000

1	Phil Niekro, 1979	44
2	Phil Niekro, 1977	43
3	Phil Niekro, 1978	42
4	Steve Rogers, 1977	40
	Mike Flanagan, 1978	40
	Dennis Leonard, 1978	40
	Jim Clancy, 1982	40
	Charlie Hough, 1987	40
9	9 players tied	39

Complete Games

Rank	Player	CG
1	Will White, 1879	75
2	Charley Radbourn, 1884	73
3	Jim McCormick, 1880	72
	Jim Galvin, 1883	72
	Guy Hecker, 1884	72
6	Jim Galvin, 1884	71
7	Tim Keefe, 1883	68
	John Clarkson, 1885	68
	John Clarkson, 1889	68
10	Bill Hutchison, 1892	67
11	Jim Devlin, 1876	66
	Charley Radbourn, 1883	66
	Matt Kilroy, 1886	66
	Toad Ramsey, 1886	66
	Matt Kilroy, 1887	66
16	Jim Galvin, 1879	65
	Jim McCormick, 1882	65
	Bill Hutchison, 1890	65
19	Mickey Welch, 1880	64
	Will White, 1883	64
	Tony Mullane, 1884	64
	Silver King, 1888	64
23	Jim McCormick, 1884	63
	George Bradley, 1876	63
	Charlie Buffinton, 1884	63
	Ed Morris, 1885	63
	Ed Morris, 1886	63
28	Mickey Welch, 1884	62
	Tim Keefe, 1886	62
30	Jim Devlin, 1877	61
	Toad Ramsey, 1887	61
32	Dupee Shaw, 1884	60
	Jersey Bakely, 1888	60
34	Billy Taylor, 1884	59
	Tommy Bond, 1879	59
	Jim McCormick, 1879	59
	John Ward, 1880	59
	John Coleman, 1883	59
	Larry McKeon, 1884	59
	Hardie Henderson, 1885	59
	Amos Rusie, 1892	59
42	Tommy Bond, 1877	58
	John Ward, 1879	58
	Will White, 1880	58
	Bill Sweeney, 1884	58
46	Tommy Bond, 1878	57
	Terry Larkin, 1879	57
	Larry Corcoran, 1880	57
	Lee Richmond, 1880	57
	Jim McCormick, 1881	57
	Jim Whitney, 1881	57
	Frank Mountain, 1883	57
	Larry Corcoran, 1884	57
	Charley Radbourn, 1886	57
	Ed Seward, 1888	57
56	Terry Larkin, 1878	56
	Tim Keefe, 1884	56
	Hugh Daily, 1884	56
	Mickey Welch, 1886	56
	John Clarkson, 1887	56
	Amos Rusie, 1890	56
	Bill Hutchison, 1891	56
63	Bobby Mathews, 1876	55
	Terry Larkin, 1877	55
	George Derby, 1881	55
	Mickey Welch, 1885	55
	Lady Baldwin, 1886	55
	Dave Foutz, 1886	55
	Tony Mullane, 1886	55
	Matt Kilroy, 1889	55
	Sadie McMahon, 1890	55
72	Jim Whitney, 1883	54
	Adonis Terry, 1884	54
	Tim Keefe, 1887	54
	Phenomenal Smith, 1887	54
	Ed Morris, 1888	54
	Mark Baldwin, 1889	54
	Kid Gleason, 1890	54
79	Charlie Sweeney, 1884	53
	Al Spalding, 1876	53
	George Bradley, 1879	53
	Jack Lynch, 1884	53
	Bob Caruthers, 1885	53
	Henry Porter, 1885	53
	Gus Weyhing, 1887	53
	John Clarkson, 1888	53
	Henry Porter, 1888	53
	Ed Beatin, 1890	53
	Mark Baldwin, 1890	53
	Sadie McMahon, 1891	53
91	Will White, 1878	52
	Will White, 1882	52
	Will White, 1884	52
	Ed Seward, 1887	52
	Bob Barr, 1890	52
	Amos Rusie, 1891	52
97	6 players tied	51

Complete Games (by era)

1876-1892

Rank	Player	CG
1	Will White, 1879	75
2	Charley Radbourn, 1884	73
3	Jim McCormick, 1880	72
	Jim Galvin, 1883	72
	Guy Hecker, 1884	72
6	Jim Galvin, 1884	71
7	Tim Keefe, 1883	68
	John Clarkson, 1885	68
	John Clarkson, 1889	68
10	Bill Hutchison, 1892	67
11	Jim Devlin, 1876	66
	Charley Radbourn, 1883	66
	Matt Kilroy, 1886	66
	Toad Ramsey, 1886	66
	Matt Kilroy, 1887	66

1893-1919

Rank	Player	CG
1	Amos Rusie, 1893	50
2	Jack Chesbro, 1904	48
3	Ted Breitenstein, 1895	47
4	Ted Breitenstein, 1894	46
5	Amos Rusie, 1894	45
	Vic Willis, 1902	45
7	Cy Young, 1894	44
	Pink Hawley, 1895	44
	Frank Killen, 1896	44
	Joe McGinnity, 1903	44
11	Kid Nichols, 1893	43
	Kid Nichols, 1895	43
13	6 players tied	42

1920-1941

Rank	Player	CG
1	Grover Alexander, 1920	33
	Burleigh Grimes, 1923	33
3	Red Faber, 1921	32
	George Uhle, 1926	32
5	Red Faber, 1922	31
	Wes Ferrell, 1935	31
	Bobo Newsom, 1938	31
	Bucky Walters, 1939	31
	Bob Feller, 1940	31
10	8 players tied	30

1942-1960

Rank	Player	CG
1	Bob Feller, 1946	36
2	Dizzy Trout, 1944	33
	Robin Roberts, 1953	33
4	Robin Roberts, 1952	30
5	Hal Newhouser, 1945	29
	Hal Newhouser, 1946	29
	Robin Roberts, 1954	29
8	Jim Tobin, 1942	28
	Jim Tobin, 1944	28
	Johnny Sain, 1948	28
	Bob Lemon, 1952	28
12	Bucky Walters, 1944	27
	Mel Parnell, 1949	27
	Vern Bickford, 1950	27
	Bobby Shantz, 1952	27

1961-1976

Rank	Player	CG
1	Juan Marichal, 1968	30
	Fergie Jenkins, 1971	30
	Steve Carlton, 1972	30
	Catfish Hunter, 1975	30
5	Mickey Lolich, 1971	29
	Gaylord Perry, 1972	29
	Gaylord Perry, 1973	29
	Fergie Jenkins, 1974	29
9	Bob Gibson, 1968	28
	Denny McLain, 1968	28
	Bob Gibson, 1969	28
	Gaylord Perry, 1974	28
13	4 players tied	27

1977-2000

Rank	Player	CG
1	Rick Langford, 1980	28
2	Mike Norris, 1980	24
	Bert Blyleven, 1985	24
4	Mike Caldwell, 1978	23
	Phil Niekro, 1979	23
6	Jim Palmer, 1977	22
	Nolan Ryan, 1977	22
	Phil Niekro, 1978	22
9	Wayne Garland, 1977	21
	Dennis Leonard, 1977	21
	Ron Guidry, 1983	21
12	6 players tied	20

Shutouts

1	George Bradley, 1876	16
	Grover Alexander, 1916	16
3	Jack Coombs, 1910	13
	Bob Gibson, 1968	13
5	Jim Galvin, 1884	12
	Ed Morris, 1886	12
	Grover Alexander, 1915	12
8	Tommy Bond, 1879	11
	Charley Radbourn, 1884	11
	Dave Foutz, 1886	11
	Christy Mathewson, 1908	11
	Ed Walsh, 1908	11
	Walter Johnson, 1913	11
	Sandy Koufax, 1963	11
	Dean Chance, 1964	11
16	Jim McCormick, 1884	10
	John Clarkson, 1885	10
	Cy Young, 1904	10
	Ed Walsh, 1906	10
	Joe Wood, 1912	10
	Dave Davenport, 1915	10
	Carl Hubbell, 1933	10
	Mort Cooper, 1942	10
	Bob Feller, 1946	10
	Bob Lemon, 1948	10
	Juan Marichal, 1965	10
	Jim Palmer, 1975	10
	John Tudor, 1985	10
29	Tommy Bond, 1878	9
	George Derby, 1881	9
	Cy Young, 1892	9
	Joe McGinnity, 1904	9
	Mordecai Brown, 1906	9
	Addie Joss, 1906	9
	Mordecai Brown, 1908	9
	Addie Joss, 1908	9
	Orval Overall, 1909	9
	Grover Alexander, 1913	9
	Walter Johnson, 1914	9
	Cy Falkenberg, 1914	9
	Babe Ruth, 1916	9
	Stan Coveleski, 1917	9
	Grover Alexander, 1919	9
	Bill Lee, 1938	9
	Bob Porterfield, 1953	9
	Luis Tiant, 1968	9
	Denny McLain, 1969	9
	Don Sutton, 1972	9
	Nolan Ryan, 1972	9
	Bert Blyleven, 1973	9
	Ron Guidry, 1978	9
52	50 players tied	8

Saves

1	Bobby Thigpen, 1990	57
2	Randy Myers, 1993	53
	Trevor Hoffman, 1998	53
4	Dennis Eckersley, 1992	51
	Rod Beck, 1998	51
6	Dennis Eckersley, 1990	48
	Rod Beck, 1993	48
	Jeff Shaw, 1998	48
9	Lee Smith, 1991	47
10	Lee Smith, 1993	46
	Dave Righetti, 1986	46
	Bryan Harvey, 1991	46
	Jose Mesa, 1995	46
	Tom Gordon, 1998	46
15	Dan Quisenberry, 1983	45
	Bruce Sutter, 1984	45
	Dennis Eckersley, 1988	45
	Bryan Harvey, 1993	45
	Jeff Montgomery, 1993	45
	Duane Ward, 1993	45
	Randy Myers, 1997	45
	Mariano Rivera, 1999	45
	Antonio Alfonseca, 2000	45
24	Dan Quisenberry, 1984	44
	Mark Davis, 1989	44
	Jeff Brantley, 1996	44
	Todd Worrell, 1996	44
28	Doug Jones, 1990	43
	Dennis Eckersley, 1991	43
	Lee Smith, 1992	43
	John Wetteland, 1993	43
	Mitch Williams, 1993	43
	John Wetteland, 1996	43
	Mariano Rivera, 1997	43
	Roberto Hernandez, 1999	43
	John Wetteland, 1999	43
	Trevor Hoffman, 2000	43
38	Jeff Reardon, 1988	42
	Rick Aguilera, 1991	42
	Trevor Hoffman, 1996	42
	Jeff Shaw, 1997	42
	Troy Percival, 1998	42
	John Wetteland, 1998	42
	Todd Jones, 2000	42
	Derek Lowe, 2000	42
46	Jeff Reardon, 1985	41
	Rick Aguilera, 1992	41
	Ugueth Urbina, 1999	41
	Armando Benitez, 2000	41
	Robb Nen, 2000	41
51	Steve Bedrosian, 1987	40
	Jeff Reardon, 1991	40
	Tom Henke, 1993	40
	Robb Nen, 1998	40
	Mike Jackson, 1998	40
	Trevor Hoffman, 1999	40
57	John Franco, 1988	39
	Jeff Montgomery, 1992	39
	Mark Wohlers, 1996	39
	Jose Mesa, 1996	39
	Billy Wagner, 1999	39
	Mike Jackson, 1999	39
63	John Hiller, 1973	38
	Jeff Russell, 1989	38
	Randy Myers, 1992	38
	Roberto Hernandez, 1993	38
	Randy Myers, 1995	38
	Roberto Hernandez, 1996	38
	John Franco, 1998	38
	Rick Aguilera, 1998	38
	John Rocker, 1999	38
72	Clay Carroll, 1972	37
	Rollie Fingers, 1978	37
	Bruce Sutter, 1979	37
	Dan Quisenberry, 1985	37
	Doug Jones, 1988	37
	Gregg Olson, 1990	37
	John Wetteland, 1992	37
	Lee Smith, 1995	37
	Rod Beck, 1997	37
	Trevor Hoffman, 1997	37
	Robb Nen, 1999	37
	Bob Wickman, 1999	37
	Kazuhiro Sasaki, 2000	37
85	18 players tied	36

Innings Pitched

1	Will White, 1879	680.0
2	Charley Radbourn, 1884	678.2
3	Guy Hecker, 1884	670.2
4	Jim McCormick, 1880	657.2
5	Jim Galvin, 1883	656.1
6	Jim Galvin, 1884	636.1
7	Charley Radbourn, 1883	632.1
8	John Clarkson, 1885	623.0
9	Jim Devlin, 1876	622.0
	Bill Hutchison, 1892	622.0
11	John Clarkson, 1889	620.0
12	Tim Keefe, 1883	619.0
13	Bill Hutchison, 1890	603.0
14	Jim McCormick, 1882	595.2
15	John Ward, 1880	595.0
16	Jim Galvin, 1879	593.0
17	Lee Richmond, 1880	590.2
18	Matt Kilroy, 1887	589.1
19	Toad Ramsey, 1886	588.2
20	John Ward, 1879	587.0
	Charlie Buffinton, 1884	587.0
22	Silver King, 1888	584.2
23	Matt Kilroy, 1886	583.0
24	Ed Morris, 1885	581.0
25	Will White, 1883	577.0
26	Mickey Welch, 1880	574.0
27	George Bradley, 1876	573.0
28	Jim McCormick, 1884	569.0
29	Tony Mullane, 1884	567.0
30	Toad Ramsey, 1887	561.0
	Bill Hutchison, 1891	561.0
32	Jim Devlin, 1877	559.0
33	Mickey Welch, 1884	557.1
34	Tommy Bond, 1879	555.1
	Ed Morris, 1886	555.1
36	Jim Whitney, 1881	552.1
37	Amos Rusie, 1890	548.2
38	Jim McCormick, 1879	546.1
39	Dupee Shaw, 1884	543.1
40	Amos Rusie, 1892	541.0
41	Hardie Henderson, 1885	539.1
42	John Coleman, 1883	538.1
43	Bill Sweeney, 1884	538.0
44	Larry Corcoran, 1880	536.1
45	Tim Keefe, 1886	535.0
46	Tommy Bond, 1878	532.2
	Jersey Bakely, 1888	532.2
48	Tony Mullane, 1886	529.2
49	Al Spalding, 1876	528.2
50	Jim McCormick, 1881	526.0
51	Billy Taylor, 1884	523.0
	John Clarkson, 1887	523.0
53	Tommy Bond, 1877	521.0
54	Ed Seward, 1888	518.2
55	Will White, 1880	517.1
56	Larry Corcoran, 1884	516.2
57	Bobby Mathews, 1876	516.0
58	Jim Whitney, 1883	514.0
59	Mark Baldwin, 1889	513.2
60	Terry Larkin, 1879	513.1
61	Larry McKeon, 1884	512.0
62	Charley Radbourn, 1886	509.1
63	Sadie McMahon, 1890	509.0
64	Terry Larkin, 1878	506.0
	Kid Gleason, 1890	506.0
66	Dave Foutz, 1886	504.0
67	Frank Mountain, 1883	503.0
	Sadie McMahon, 1891	503.0
69	Terry Larkin, 1877	501.0
70	Hugh Daily, 1884	500.2
71	Amos Rusie, 1891	500.1
72	Mickey Welch, 1886	500.0
73	Jack Lynch, 1884	496.0
74	George Derby, 1881	494.2
75	Bob Barr, 1890	493.1
76	Tommy Bond, 1880	493.0
77	Charlie Sweeney, 1884	492.0
	Mickey Welch, 1885	492.0
	Mark Baldwin, 1890	492.0
80	Phenomenal Smith, 1887	491.1
81	George Bradley, 1879	487.0
	Lady Baldwin, 1886	487.0
83	John Clarkson, 1888	483.1
84	Tim Keefe, 1884	483.0
85	Bob Caruthers, 1885	482.1
86	Amos Rusie, 1893	482.0
87	Henry Porter, 1885	481.2
88	Matt Kilroy, 1889	480.2
89	Will White, 1882	480.0
	Guy Hecker, 1885	480.0
	Ed Morris, 1888	480.0
92	Tim Keefe, 1887	476.2
93	Adonis Terry, 1884	476.0
94	Ed Beatin, 1890	474.1
95	Jim Galvin, 1881	474.0
	Henry Porter, 1888	474.0
97	Larry Corcoran, 1883	473.2
98	Ed Seward, 1887	470.2
99	Gus Weyhing, 1892	469.2
100	Guy Hecker, 1883	469.0

Innings Pitched (by era)

1876-1892

1	Will White, 1879	680.0
2	Charley Radbourn, 1884	678.2
3	Guy Hecker, 1884	670.2
4	Jim McCormick, 1880	657.2
5	Jim Galvin, 1883	656.1
6	Jim Galvin, 1884	636.1
7	Charley Radbourn, 1883	632.1
8	John Clarkson, 1885	623.0
9	Jim Devlin, 1876	622.0
	Bill Hutchison, 1892	622.0
11	John Clarkson, 1889	620.0
12	Tim Keefe, 1883	619.0
13	Bill Hutchison, 1890	603.0
14	Jim McCormick, 1882	595.2
15	John Ward, 1880	595.0

1893-1919

1	Amos Rusie, 1893	482.0
2	Ed Walsh, 1908	464.0
3	Jack Chesbro, 1904	454.2
4	Ted Breitenstein, 1894	447.1
5	Pink Hawley, 1895	444.1
6	Amos Rusie, 1894	444.0
7	Ted Breitenstein, 1895	438.2
8	Joe McGinnity, 1903	434.0
9	Frank Killen, 1896	432.1
10	Kid Nichols, 1893	425.0
11	Cy Young, 1893	422.2
12	Ed Walsh, 1907	422.1
13	Jouett Meekin, 1894	418.1
14	Frank Killen, 1893	415.0
15	Cy Young, 1896	414.1

1920-1941

1	Grover Alexander, 1920	363.1
2	George Uhle, 1923	357.2
3	Red Faber, 1922	352.0
4	Urban Shocker, 1922	348.0
5	Bob Feller, 1941	343.0
6	Jim Bagby, 1920	339.2
7	Carl Mays, 1921	336.2
8	Red Faber, 1921	330.2
	Burleigh Grimes, 1928	330.2
10	Bobo Newsom, 1938	329.2
11	Wilbur Cooper, 1920	327.0
	Wilbur Cooper, 1921	327.0
	Burleigh Grimes, 1923	327.0
	Alvin Crowder, 1932	327.0
15	Urban Shocker, 1921	326.2

1942-1960

1	Bob Feller, 1946	371.1
2	Dizzy Trout, 1944	352.1
3	Robin Roberts, 1953	346.2
4	Robin Roberts, 1954	336.2
5	Robin Roberts, 1952	330.0
6	Robin Roberts, 1951	315.0
7	Johnny Sain, 1948	314.2
8	Bob Friend, 1956	314.1
9	Hal Newhouser, 1945	313.1
10	Bill Voiselle, 1944	312.2
11	Hal Newhouser, 1944	312.1
12	Vern Bickford, 1950	311.2
13	Warren Spahn, 1951	310.2
14	Bob Lemon, 1952	309.2
15	Robin Roberts, 1955	305.0

1961-1976

1	Wilbur Wood, 1972	376.2
2	Mickey Lolich, 1971	376.0
3	Wilbur Wood, 1973	359.1
4	Steve Carlton, 1972	346.1
5	Gaylord Perry, 1973	344.0
6	Gaylord Perry, 1972	342.2
7	Denny McLain, 1968	336.0
8	Sandy Koufax, 1965	335.2
9	Wilbur Wood, 1971	334.0
10	Nolan Ryan, 1974	332.2
11	Gaylord Perry, 1970	328.2
12	Fergie Jenkins, 1974	328.1
13	Catfish Hunter, 1975	328.0
14	Mickey Lolich, 1972	327.1
15	2 players tied	326.0

1977-2000

1	Phil Niekro, 1979	342.0
2	Phil Niekro, 1978	334.1
3	Phil Niekro, 1977	330.1
4	Jim Palmer, 1977	319.0
5	Steve Carlton, 1980	304.0
6	Dave Goltz, 1977	303.0
7	Steve Rogers, 1977	301.2
8	Nolan Ryan, 1977	299.0
9	Jim Palmer, 1978	296.0
10	Steve Carlton, 1982	295.2
11	Dennis Leonard, 1978	294.2
12	Jack Morris, 1983	293.2
	Bert Blyleven, 1985	293.2
14	Mike Caldwell, 1978	293.1
15	Dennis Leonard, 1977	292.2

Hits per Game

1	Nolan Ryan, 1972	5.26
2	Luis Tiant, 1968	5.30
3	Nolan Ryan, 1991	5.31
4	Pedro Martinez, 2000	5.31
5	Ed Reulbach, 1906	5.33
6	Dutch Leonard, 1914	5.57
7	Carl Lundgren, 1907	5.65
8	Sid Fernandez, 1985	5.71
9	Tommy Byrne, 1949	5.74
10	Dave McNally, 1968	5.77
11	Sandy Koufax, 1965	5.79
12	Russ Ford, 1910	5.83
13	Tim Keefe, 1880	5.83
14	Hideo Nomo, 1995	5.83
15	Al Downing, 1963	5.84
16	Herb Score, 1956	5.85
17	Bob Gibson, 1968	5.85
18	Sam McDowell, 1965	5.87
19	Ed Walsh, 1910	5.89
20	Pedro Martinez, 1997	5.89
21	Mike Scott, 1986	5.95
22	Mario Soto, 1980	5.96
23	Floyd Youmans, 1986	5.96
24	Nolan Ryan, 1977	5.96
25	Nolan Ryan, 1974	5.98
26	Nolan Ryan, 1981	5.98
27	Nolan Ryan, 1986	6.02
28	Sam McDowell, 1966	6.02
29	Vida Blue, 1971	6.03
30	Walter Johnson, 1913	6.03
31	Nolan Ryan, 1990	6.04
32	Grover Alexander, 1915	6.05
33	Sam McDowell, 1968	6.06
34	Joe Horlen, 1964	6.07
35	Andy Messersmith, 1969	6.08
36	Nolan Ryan, 1989	6.09
37	Stan Coveleski, 1917	6.09
38	Catfish Hunter, 1972	6.09
39	Nolan Ryan, 1976	6.11
40	Sid Fernandez, 1988	6.11
41	Bob Turley, 1957	6.12
42	Bob Turley, 1955	6.13
43	Don Sutton, 1972	6.14
44	Nolan Ryan, 1983	6.14
45	Ron Guidry, 1978	6.15
46	Mordecai Brown, 1908	6.17
47	Sandy Koufax, 1963	6.19
48	Randy Johnson, 1997	6.21
49	Jack Pfiester, 1906	6.21
50	Sandy Koufax, 1964	6.22
51	Roger Nelson, 1972	6.23
52	Herb Score, 1955	6.26
53	Cy Morgan, 1909	6.26
54	Dean Chance, 1964	6.27
55	Christy Mathewson, 1909	6.28
	J.R. Richard, 1978	6.28
57	Art Fromme, 1909	6.28
58	Greg Maddux, 1995	6.31
59	Walter Johnson, 1912	6.32
60	Kerry Wood, 1998	6.32
61	Jack Coombs, 1910	6.32
62	Rube Waddell, 1905	6.33
63	Vean Gregg, 1911	6.33
64	Jeff Robinson, 1988	6.33
65	Larry Cheney, 1916	6.33
66	Sonny Siebert, 1968	6.33
67	Allie Reynolds, 1943	6.34
68	Roger Clemens, 1986	6.34
69	Willie Mitchell, 1913	6.35
70	Jose DeLeon, 1989	6.36
71	Pascual Perez, 1988	6.37
72	Walter Johnson, 1910	6.37
73	Dave Boswell, 1966	6.38
74	Harry Krause, 1909	6.38
75	Dutch Leonard, 1915	6.38
76	Eddie Cicotte, 1917	6.39
77	Wayne Simpson, 1970	6.39
78	Al Leiter, 1996	6.39
79	Babe Ruth, 1916	6.40
80	Spec Shea, 1947	6.40
81	Jim Bibby, 1973	6.42
82	Ed Reulbach, 1905	6.42
83	Gaylord Perry, 1974	6.42
84	Eddie Fisher, 1965	6.42
85	Addie Joss, 1908	6.42
86	Mordecai Brown, 1906	6.43
87	Luis Tiant, 1972	6.44
88	Frank Smith, 1908	6.44
89	Dwight Gooden, 1985	6.44
90	Orval Overall, 1909	6.44
91	Sid Fernandez, 1989	6.44
92	Denny McLain, 1968	6.46
93	Mordecai Brown, 1909	6.46
94	Ray Caldwell, 1914	6.46
95	Fred Toney, 1915	6.47
96	Gary Peters, 1967	6.47
97	Bob Turley, 1954	6.48
98	Roger Clemens, 1998	6.48
99	Ed Walsh, 1909	6.49
100	Eddie Cicotte, 1909	6.49

Hits per Game (by era)

1876-1892

1	Tim Keefe, 1880	5.83
2	Guy Hecker, 1882	6.49
3	Tim Keefe, 1888	6.57
4	Charlie Sweeney, 1884	6.59
5	Adonis Terry, 1888	6.69
6	Silver King, 1888	6.70
7	Frank Knauss, 1890	6.73
8	Ed Seward, 1888	6.73
9	Tim Keefe, 1885	6.75
10	Tony Mullane, 1892	6.77
11	Larry Corcoran, 1880	6.78
12	Mickey Welch, 1885	6.80
13	Cannonball Titcomb, 1888	6.81
14	Amos Rusie, 1892	6.82
15	Toad Ramsey, 1886	6.83

1893-1919

1	Ed Reulbach, 1906	5.33
2	Dutch Leonard, 1914	5.57
3	Carl Lundgren, 1907	5.65
4	Russ Ford, 1910	5.83
5	Ed Walsh, 1910	5.89
6	Walter Johnson, 1913	6.03
7	Grover Alexander, 1915	6.05
8	Stan Coveleski, 1917	6.09
9	Mordecai Brown, 1908	6.17
10	Jack Pfiester, 1906	6.21
11	Cy Morgan, 1909	6.26
12	Christy Mathewson, 1909	6.28
13	Art Fromme, 1909	6.28
14	Walter Johnson, 1912	6.32
15	Jack Coombs, 1910	6.32

1920-1941

1	Johnny Vander Meer, 1941	6.84
2	Bob Feller, 1940	6.88
3	Bob Feller, 1939	6.89
4	Hal Schumacher, 1933	6.92
5	Dazzy Vance, 1924	6.95
6	Whit Wyatt, 1941	6.96
7	Bucky Walters, 1939	7.05
8	Johnny Vander Meer, 1938	7.07
9	Bucky Walters, 1940	7.11
10	Lefty Gomez, 1934	7.13
11	Ernie White, 1941	7.24
12	Dazzy Vance, 1928	7.26
13	Bump Hadley, 1931	7.26
14	Dolf Luque, 1920	7.28
15	Bob Feller, 1938	7.29

1942-1960

1	Tommy Byrne, 1949	5.74
2	Herb Score, 1956	5.85
3	Bob Turley, 1957	6.12
4	Bob Turley, 1955	6.13
5	Herb Score, 1955	6.26
6	Allie Reynolds, 1943	6.34
7	Spec Shea, 1947	6.40
8	Bob Turley, 1954	6.48
9	Sam Jones, 1955	6.52
10	Bob Turley, 1958	6.53
11	Hal Newhouser, 1946	6.61
12	Johnny Niggeling, 1943	6.66
13	Don Larsen, 1956	6.66
14	Whitey Ford, 1955	6.67
15	Mort Cooper, 1942	6.69

1961-1976

1	Nolan Ryan, 1972	5.26
2	Luis Tiant, 1968	5.30
3	Dave McNally, 1968	5.77
4	Sandy Koufax, 1965	5.79
5	Al Downing, 1963	5.84
6	Bob Gibson, 1968	5.85
7	Sam McDowell, 1965	5.87
8	Nolan Ryan, 1974	5.98
9	Sam McDowell, 1966	6.02
10	Vida Blue, 1971	6.03
11	Sam McDowell, 1968	6.06
12	Joe Horlen, 1964	6.07
13	Andy Messersmith, 1969	6.08
14	Catfish Hunter, 1972	6.09
15	Nolan Ryan, 1976	6.11

1977-2000

1	Nolan Ryan, 1991	5.31
2	Pedro Martinez, 2000	5.31
3	Sid Fernandez, 1985	5.71
4	Hideo Nomo, 1995	5.83
5	Pedro Martinez, 1997	5.89
6	Mike Scott, 1986	5.95
7	Mario Soto, 1980	5.96
8	Floyd Youmans, 1986	5.96
9	Nolan Ryan, 1977	5.96
10	Nolan Ryan, 1981	5.98
11	Nolan Ryan, 1986	6.02
12	Nolan Ryan, 1990	6.04
13	Nolan Ryan, 1989	6.09
14	Sid Fernandez, 1988	6.11
15	Nolan Ryan, 1983	6.14

Home Runs Allowed

1	Bert Blyleven, 1986	50
2	Jose Lima, 2000	48
3	Robin Roberts, 1956	46
	Bert Blyleven, 1987	46
5	Pedro Ramos, 1957	43
6	Denny McLain, 1966	42
7	Robin Roberts, 1955	41
	Phil Niekro, 1979	41
	Rick Helling, 1999	41
10	Bill Gullickson, 1987	40
	Robin Roberts, 1957	40
	Ralph Terry, 1962	40
	Orlando Pena, 1964	40
	Phil Niekro, 1970	40
	Fergie Jenkins, 1979	40
	Jack Morris, 1986	40
	Shawn Boskie, 1996	40
	Brad Radke, 1996	40
19	Murry Dickson, 1948	39
	Pedro Ramos, 1961	39
	Jim Perry, 1971	39
	Catfish Hunter, 1973	39
	Jack Morris, 1987	39
	Brian Anderson, 1998	39
	Pedro Astacio, 1998	39
26	Warren Hacker, 1955	38
	Pedro Ramos, 1958	38
	Lew Burdette, 1959	38
	Jim Bunning, 1963	38
	Don Sutton, 1970	38
	Mickey Lolich, 1974	38
	Matt Keough, 1982	38
	Floyd Bannister, 1987	38
	Don Sutton, 1987	38
	Curt Young, 1987	38
	Tim Wakefield, 1996	38
	Pedro Astacio, 1999	38
	Brian Anderson, 2000	38
39	Jim Bunning, 1959	37
	Earl Wilson, 1964	37
	Luis Tiant, 1969	37
	Fergie Jenkins, 1975	37
	Jack Morris, 1982	37
	Dan Petry, 1983	37
	Frank Viola, 1986	37
	Mark Leiter, 1996	37
	Allen Watson, 1997	37
	Livan Hernandez, 1998	37
	Tim Belcher, 1998	37
50	Dennis Rasmussen, 1987	36
	Larry Jansen, 1949	36
	Art Mahaffey, 1962	36
	Pete Richert, 1966	36
	Mickey Lolich, 1971	36
	Ed Whitson, 1987	36
	Charlie Hough, 1987	36
	Tom Browning, 1988	36
	Woody Williams, 1998	36
	Chad Ogea, 1999	36
	Jon Lieber, 2000	36
	Jeff Suppan, 2000	36
62	Larry Corcoran, 1884	35
	Warren Hacker, 1953	35
	Robin Roberts, 1954	35
	Don Newcombe, 1955	35
	Jim Perry, 1960	35
	Roger Craig, 1962	35
	Robin Roberts, 1963	35
	Sammy Ellis, 1966	35
	Denny McLain, 1967	35
	Fergie Jenkins, 1973	35
	Mickey Lolich, 1973	35
	Mike Caldwell, 1983	35
	Mike Smithson, 1984	35
	Scott McGregor, 1986	35
	Scott Bankhead, 1987	35
	Bruce Hurst, 1987	35
	Bill Gullickson, 1992	35
	Mike Moore, 1993	35
	Sidney Ponson, 1999	35
	Jeff Fassero, 1999	35
	Kevin Tapani, 2000	35
	Eric Milton, 2000	35
84	30 players tied	34

Home Runs Allowed (by era)

1876-1892

1	Larry Corcoran, 1884	35
2	Charlie Getzien, 1889	27
3	Bill Hutchison, 1891	26
4	Charlie Getzien, 1887	24
	John Healy, 1887	24
6	Jim Galvin, 1884	23
	Mark Baldwin, 1887	23
	Lev Shreve, 1888	23
9	Billy Serad, 1884	21
	John Clarkson, 1885	21
	Park Swartzel, 1889	21
	George Cobb, 1892	21
13	8 players tied	20

1893-1919

1	Frank Dwyer, 1894	27
	Jack Stivetts, 1894	27
3	Kid Nichols, 1894	23
4	Harry Staley, 1893	22
	Kid Carsey, 1894	22
6	Ted Breitenstein, 1894	21
7	Jack Stivetts, 1896	20
8	Tom Parrott, 1894	19
	Cy Young, 1894	19
10	Kid Gleason, 1893	18
	Al Orth, 1902	18
12	5 players tied	17

1920-1941

1	Lon Warneke, 1937	32
2	Phil Collins, 1934	30
	Bobo Newsom, 1938	30
4	Ray Kremer, 1930	29
	Lynn Nelson, 1938	29
6	George Earnshaw, 1932	28
	George Earnshaw, 1934	28
8	Roy Mahaffey, 1932	27
	Carl Hubbell, 1935	27
	Luke Hamlin, 1939	27
	Lynn Nelson, 1939	27
	Johnny Marcum, 1939	27
13	Freddie Fitzsimmons, 1930	26
	Gordon Rhodes, 1936	26
	Nels Potter, 1939	26

1942-1960

1	Robin Roberts, 1956	46
2	Pedro Ramos, 1957	43
3	Robin Roberts, 1955	41
4	Robin Roberts, 1957	40
5	Murry Dickson, 1948	39
6	Warren Hacker, 1955	38
	Pedro Ramos, 1958	38
	Lew Burdette, 1959	38
9	Jim Bunning, 1959	37
10	Larry Jansen, 1949	36
11	Warren Hacker, 1953	35
	Robin Roberts, 1954	35
	Don Newcombe, 1955	35
	Jim Perry, 1960	35
15	5 players tied	34

1961-1976

1	Denny McLain, 1966	42
2	Ralph Terry, 1962	40
	Orlando Pena, 1964	40
	Phil Niekro, 1970	40
5	Pedro Ramos, 1961	39
	Jim Perry, 1971	39
	Catfish Hunter, 1973	39
8	Jim Bunning, 1963	38
	Don Sutton, 1970	38
	Mickey Lolich, 1974	38
11	Earl Wilson, 1964	37
	Luis Tiant, 1969	37
	Fergie Jenkins, 1975	37
14	3 players tied	36

1977-2000

1	Bert Blyleven, 1986	50
2	Jose Lima, 2000	48
3	Bert Blyleven, 1987	46
4	Phil Niekro, 1979	41
	Rick Helling, 1999	41
6	Bill Gullickson, 1987	40
	Fergie Jenkins, 1979	40
	Jack Morris, 1986	40
	Shawn Boskie, 1996	40
	Brad Radke, 1996	40
11	Jack Morris, 1987	39
	Brian Anderson, 1998	39
	Pedro Astacio, 1998	39
14	7 players tied	38

Walks

1	Amos Rusie, 1890	289
2	Mark Baldwin, 1889	274
3	Amos Rusie, 1892	270
4	Amos Rusie, 1891	262
5	Mark Baldwin, 1890	249
6	Jack Stivetts, 1891	232
7	Mark Baldwin, 1891	227
8	Phil Knell, 1891	226
9	Bob Barr, 1890	219
10	Amos Rusie, 1893	218
11	Cy Seymour, 1898	213
12	Gus Weyhing, 1889	212
13	Ed Crane, 1890	208
	Bob Feller, 1938	208
15	Toad Ramsey, 1886	207
16	Elton Chamberlain, 1891	206
17	Mike Morrison, 1887	205
18	Henry Gruber, 1890	204
	Nolan Ryan, 1977	204
20	Ed Crane, 1891	203
	John Clarkson, 1889	203
22	Nolan Ryan, 1974	202
23	Bert Cunningham, 1890	201
24	Amos Rusie, 1894	200
25	Bill Hutchison, 1890	199
26	Mark Baldwin, 1892	194
	Bob Feller, 1941	194
28	Bobo Newsom, 1938	192
29	Ted Breitenstein, 1894	191
30	Bill Hutchison, 1892	190
31	Ed Crane, 1892	189
	Tony Mullane, 1893	189
33	Tony Mullane, 1891	187
	Kid Gleason, 1893	187
35	Ed Beatin, 1890	186
36	Sam Jones, 1955	185
37	Tom Vickery, 1890	184
38	Nolan Ryan, 1976	183
39	Matt Kilroy, 1886	182
	Frank Killen, 1892	182
	Ted Breitenstein, 1895	182
42	Willie McGill, 1893	181
	Bob Harmon, 1911	181
	Bob Turley, 1954	181
45	Jack Stivetts, 1890	179
	Gus Weyhing, 1890	179
	Tommy Byrne, 1949	179
48	Bill Hutchison, 1891	178
49	Bob Turley, 1955	177
50	Phenomenal Smith, 1887	176
	Jouett Meekin, 1894	176
52	George Hemming, 1893	175
53	Silver King, 1892	171
	Jack Stivetts, 1892	171
	Bump Hadley, 1932	171
56	Elton Chamberlain, 1892	170
	Ed Stein, 1894	170
	Cy Seymour, 1899	170
59	Gus Weyhing, 1892	168
	Brickyard Kennedy, 1893	168
	Cy Seymour, 1897	168
	Elmer Myers, 1916	168
63	Toad Ramsey, 1887	167
	Gus Weyhing, 1887	167
	Darby O'Brien, 1889	167
	Kid Gleason, 1890	167
	Bill Daley, 1890	167
	Bobo Newsom, 1937	167
69	Tony Mullane, 1886	166
	Sadie McMahon, 1890	166
	Phil Knell, 1890	166
	Chick Fraser, 1896	166
73	Elton Chamberlain, 1889	165
	Dan Casey, 1890	165
	Kid Gleason, 1891	165
	Weldon Wyckoff, 1915	165
77	Earl Moore, 1911	164
	Phil Niekro, 1977	164
79	Mickey Welch, 1886	163
	Silver King, 1890	163
	Willie McGill, 1891	163
	George Haddock, 1892	163
83	Johnny Vander Meer, 1943	162
	Nolan Ryan, 1973	162
85	Hank O'Day, 1890	161
	John Sowders, 1890	161
	Kid Carsey, 1891	161
	Gus Weyhing, 1891	161
89	Tommy Byrne, 1950	160
90	George Hemming, 1894	159
	Amos Rusie, 1895	159
	Marty O'Toole, 1912	159
93	Ed Doheny, 1899	158
	Joe Coleman, 1974	158
95	Matt Kilroy, 1887	157
	Bert Cunningham, 1888	157
	Pink Hawley, 1896	157
	Grover Lowdermilk, 1915	157
	Nolan Ryan, 1972	157
100	4 players tied	156

Fewest Walks/Game (by era)

1876-1892

1	George Zettlein, 1876	0.23
2	Cherokee Fisher, 1876	0.24
3	George Bradley, 1880	0.28
4	Tommy Bond, 1876	0.29
5	Tommy Bond, 1879	0.39
6	Bobby Mathews, 1876	0.42
7	Guy Hecker, 1882	0.43
8	Dale Williams, 1876	0.43
9	Al Spalding, 1876	0.44
10	Jim Galvin, 1879	0.47
11	George Bradley, 1879	0.48
12	Sam Weaver, 1878	0.49
13	Terry Larkin, 1879	0.53
14	Jim Devlin, 1876	0.54
15	Denny Driscoll, 1882	0.54

1893-1919

1	Christy Mathewson, 1913	0.62
2	Christy Mathewson, 1914	0.66
3	Cy Young, 1904	0.69
4	Cy Young, 1906	0.78
5	Babe Adams, 1919	0.79
6	Slim Sallee, 1919	0.79
7	Slim Sallee, 1918	0.82
8	Addie Joss, 1908	0.83
9	Cy Young, 1905	0.84
10	Deacon Phillippe, 1902	0.86
11	Cy Young, 1901	0.90
12	Deacon Phillippe, 1903	0.90
13	Christy Mathewson, 1908	0.97
14	Christy Mathewson, 1915	0.97
15	Jesse Tannehill, 1902	0.97

1920-1941

1	Babe Adams, 1920	0.62
2	Red Lucas, 1933	0.74
3	Babe Adams, 1922	0.79
4	Grover Alexander, 1923	0.89
5	Babe Adams, 1921	1.01
6	Paul Derringer, 1939	1.05
7	Carl Hubbell, 1934	1.06
8	Bill Swift, 1932	1.09
9	Grover Alexander, 1925	1.11
10	Herb Pennock, 1930	1.15
11	Red Lucas, 1932	1.17
12	Grover Alexander, 1921	1.18
13	Watty Clark, 1935	1.22
14	Pete Donohue, 1926	1.23
15	Grover Alexander, 1922	1.25

1942-1960

1	Tiny Bonham, 1942	0.96
2	Don Newcombe, 1959	1.09
3	Tiny Bonham, 1945	1.10
4	Lew Burdette, 1960	1.14
5	Lew Burdette, 1959	1.18
6	Robin Roberts, 1956	1.21
7	Robin Roberts, 1959	1.22
8	Robin Roberts, 1952	1.23
9	Hal Brown, 1960	1.25
10	Ray Prim, 1945	1.25
11	Robin Roberts, 1960	1.29
12	Fred Hutchinson, 1951	1.29
13	Ted Lyons, 1942	1.30
14	Schoolboy Rowe, 1943	1.31
15	Vern Law, 1960	1.33

1961-1976

1	Gary Nolan, 1976	1.02
2	Fergie Jenkins, 1971	1.02
3	Juan Marichal, 1966	1.05
4	Lew Burdette, 1961	1.09
5	Jim Merritt, 1967	1.19
6	Vern Law, 1966	1.22
7	Dick Donovan, 1963	1.22
8	Fritz Peterson, 1968	1.23
9	Fergie Jenkins, 1974	1.23
10	Gary Nolan, 1975	1.24
11	Ralph Terry, 1965	1.25
12	Bill Hands, 1968	1.25
13	Jim Kaat, 1976	1.27
14	Juan Marichal, 1968	1.27
15	Catfish Hunter, 1974	1.30

1977-2000

1	Bret Saberhagen, 1994	0.66
2	Bob Tewksbury, 1992	0.77
3	Greg Maddux, 1997	0.77
4	Bob Tewksbury, 1993	0.84
5	La Marr Hoyt, 1985	0.86
6	Greg Maddux, 1995	0.99
7	Dennis Eckersley, 1985	1.01
8	Greg Maddux, 1996	1.03
9	Brian Anderson, 1998	1.04
10	La Marr Hoyt, 1983	1.07
11	Jimmy Key, 1989	1.13
12	Zane Smith, 1991	1.14
13	Greg Swindell, 1991	1.17
14	Scott McGregor, 1979	1.19
15	Rick Honeycutt, 1981	1.20

Strikeouts

1	Matt Kilroy, 1886	513
2	Toad Ramsey, 1886	499
3	Hugh Daily, 1884	483
4	Dupee Shaw, 1884	451
5	Charley Radbourn, 1884	441
6	Charlie Buffinton, 1884	417
7	Guy Hecker, 1884	385
8	Nolan Ryan, 1973	383
9	Sandy Koufax, 1965	382
10	Bill Sweeney, 1884	374
11	Jim Galvin, 1884	369
12	Mark Baldwin, 1889	368
13	Nolan Ryan, 1974	367
14	Randy Johnson, 1999	364
15	Tim Keefe, 1883	359
16	Toad Ramsey, 1887	355
17	Rube Waddell, 1904	349
18	Bob Feller, 1946	348
19	Randy Johnson, 2000	347
20	Hardie Henderson, 1884	346
21	Jim Whitney, 1883	345
	Mickey Welch, 1884	345
23	Jim McCormick, 1884	343
24	Amos Rusie, 1890	341
	Nolan Ryan, 1977	341
26	Charlie Sweeney, 1884	337
	Amos Rusie, 1891	337
28	Tim Keefe, 1888	335
29	Tim Keefe, 1884	334
30	Randy Johnson, 1998	329
	Nolan Ryan, 1972	329
32	Nolan Ryan, 1976	327
33	Ed Morris, 1886	326
34	Tony Mullane, 1884	325
	Sam McDowell, 1965	325
36	Lady Baldwin, 1886	323
37	Curt Schilling, 1997	319
38	Sandy Koufax, 1966	317
39	Charley Radbourn, 1883	315
40	Bill Hutchison, 1892	314
41	John Clarkson, 1886	313
	Walter Johnson, 1910	313
	J.R. Richard, 1979	313
	Pedro Martinez, 1999	313
45	Steve Carlton, 1972	310
46	Larry McKeon, 1884	308
	John Clarkson, 1885	308
	Mickey Lolich, 1971	308
	Randy Johnson, 1993	308
50	Sandy Koufax, 1963	306
	Mike Scott, 1986	306
52	Pedro Martinez, 1997	305
53	Amos Rusie, 1892	304
	Sam McDowell, 1970	304
55	Walter Johnson, 1912	303
	J.R. Richard, 1978	303
57	Ed Morris, 1884	302
	Rube Waddell, 1903	302
59	Vida Blue, 1971	301
	Nolan Ryan, 1989	301
61	Curt Schilling, 1998	300
62	Ed Morris, 1885	298
63	Tim Keefe, 1886	297
64	Randy Johnson, 1995	294
65	Jack Lynch, 1884	292
	Roger Clemens, 1997	292
67	Sadie McMahon, 1890	291
	Roger Clemens, 1988	291
	Randy Johnson, 1997	291
70	Bill Hutchison, 1890	289
	Jack Stivetts, 1890	289
	Tom Seaver, 1971	289
73	Rube Waddell, 1905	287
74	Bobby Mathews, 1884	286
	Bobby Mathews, 1885	286
	Steve Carlton, 1980	286
	Steve Carlton, 1982	286
78	Billy Taylor, 1884	284
	John Clarkson, 1889	284
	Pedro Martinez, 2000	284
81	Dave Foutz, 1886	283
	Sam McDowell, 1968	283
	Tom Seaver, 1970	283
84	Denny McLain, 1968	280
85	Jim Galvin, 1883	279
	Sam McDowell, 1969	279
87	Bob Veale, 1965	276
	Dwight Gooden, 1984	276
	John Smoltz, 1996	276
90	Hal Newhouser, 1946	275
	Steve Carlton, 1983	275
92	Bob Gibson, 1970	274
	Fergie Jenkins, 1970	274
	Mario Soto, 1982	274
95	Fergie Jenkins, 1969	273
96	Larry Corcoran, 1884	272
	Mickey Welch, 1886	272
	Ed Seward, 1888	272
99	Mickey Lolich, 1969	271
	Roger Clemens, 1998	271

Strikeouts (by era)

1876-1892

1	Matt Kilroy, 1886	513
2	Toad Ramsey, 1886	499
3	Hugh Daily, 1884	483
4	Dupee Shaw, 1884	451
5	Charley Radbourn, 1884	441
6	Charlie Buffinton, 1884	417
7	Guy Hecker, 1884	385
8	Bill Sweeney, 1884	374
9	Jim Galvin, 1884	369
10	Mark Baldwin, 1889	368
11	Tim Keefe, 1883	359
12	Toad Ramsey, 1887	355
13	Hardie Henderson, 1884	346
14	Jim Whitney, 1883	345
	Mickey Welch, 1884	345

1893-1919

1	Rube Waddell, 1904	349
2	Walter Johnson, 1910	313
3	Walter Johnson, 1912	303
4	Rube Waddell, 1903	302
5	Rube Waddell, 1905	287
6	Ed Walsh, 1908	269
7	Christy Mathewson, 1903	267
8	Christy Mathewson, 1908	259
9	Ed Walsh, 1910	258
	Joe Wood, 1912	258
11	Ed Walsh, 1911	255
12	Ed Walsh, 1912	254
13	Walter Johnson, 1913	243
14	Grover Alexander, 1915	241

1920-1941

1	Dazzy Vance, 1924	262
2	Bob Feller, 1940	261
3	Bob Feller, 1941	260
4	Bob Feller, 1939	246
5	Bob Feller, 1938	240
6	Van Mungo, 1936	238
7	Bobo Newsom, 1938	226
8	Dazzy Vance, 1925	221
9	Lefty Grove, 1930	209
10	Johnny Vander Meer, 1941	202
11	Dazzy Vance, 1928	200
12	Dizzy Dean, 1933	199
13	Dazzy Vance, 1923	197
14	Dizzy Dean, 1934	195
	Dizzy Dean, 1936	195

1942-1960

1	Bob Feller, 1946	348
2	Hal Newhouser, 1946	275
3	Herb Score, 1956	263
4	Don Drysdale, 1960	246
5	Herb Score, 1955	245
6	Don Drysdale, 1959	242
7	Sam Jones, 1958	225
8	Hal Newhouser, 1945	212
9	Bob Turley, 1955	210
10	Sam Jones, 1959	209
11	Jim Bunning, 1959	201
	Jim Bunning, 1960	201
13	Robin Roberts, 1953	198
	Sam Jones, 1955	198
15	Sandy Koufax, 1960	197

1961-1976

1	Nolan Ryan, 1973	383
2	Sandy Koufax, 1965	382
3	Nolan Ryan, 1974	367
4	Nolan Ryan, 1972	329
5	Nolan Ryan, 1976	327
6	Sam McDowell, 1965	325
7	Sandy Koufax, 1966	317
8	Steve Carlton, 1972	310
9	Mickey Lolich, 1971	308
10	Sandy Koufax, 1963	306
11	Sam McDowell, 1970	304
12	Vida Blue, 1971	301
13	Tom Seaver, 1971	289
14	Sam McDowell, 1968	283
	Tom Seaver, 1970	283

1977-2000

1	Randy Johnson, 1999	364
2	Randy Johnson, 2000	347
3	Nolan Ryan, 1977	341
4	Randy Johnson, 1998	329
5	Curt Schilling, 1997	319
6	J.R. Richard, 1979	313
	Pedro Martinez, 1999	313
8	Randy Johnson, 1993	308
9	Mike Scott, 1986	306
10	Pedro Martinez, 1997	305
11	J.R. Richard, 1978	303
12	Nolan Ryan, 1989	301
13	Curt Schilling, 1998	300
14	Randy Johnson, 1995	294
15	Roger Clemens, 1997	292

Strikeouts per Game

1	Pedro Martinez, 1999	13.20
2	Kerry Wood, 1998	12.58
3	Randy Johnson, 2000	12.56
4	Randy Johnson, 1995	12.35
5	Randy Johnson, 1997	12.30
6	Randy Johnson, 1998	12.12
7	Randy Johnson, 1999	12.06
8	Pedro Martinez, 2000	11.78
9	Nolan Ryan, 1987	11.48
10	Dwight Gooden, 1984	11.39
11	Pedro Martinez, 1997	11.37
12	Nolan Ryan, 1989	11.32
13	Curt Schilling, 1997	11.29
14	Hideo Nomo, 1995	11.10
15	Randy Johnson, 1993	10.86
16	Sam McDowell, 1965	10.71
17	Randy Johnson, 1994	10.67
18	Nolan Ryan, 1973	10.57
19	Nolan Ryan, 1991	10.56
20	Sandy Koufax, 1962	10.55
21	Nolan Ryan, 1972	10.43
22	Sam McDowell, 1966	10.42
23	Roger Clemens, 1998	10.39
24	Nolan Ryan, 1976	10.35
25	Randy Johnson, 1992	10.31
26	Nolan Ryan, 1977	10.26
27	David Cone, 1997	10.25
28	Sandy Koufax, 1965	10.24
29	Nolan Ryan, 1990	10.24
30	Randy Johnson, 1991	10.19
31	Bartolo Colon, 2000	10.15
32	Sandy Koufax, 1960	10.13
33	Hideo Nomo, 1997	10.11
34	Curt Schilling, 1998	10.05
35	Mike Scott, 1986	10.00
36	Rick Ankiel, 2000	9.98
37	Nolan Ryan, 1978	9.97
38	Roger Clemens, 1997	9.95
39	Nolan Ryan, 1974	9.93
40	Roger Clemens, 1988	9.92
41	David Cone, 1990	9.91
42	J.R. Richard, 1978	9.90
43	Andy Benes, 1994	9.87
44	Nolan Ryan, 1986	9.81
45	John Smoltz, 1996	9.79
46	Herb Score, 1955	9.70
47	Pedro Martinez, 1998	9.67
48	Nolan Ryan, 1984	9.65
49	J.R. Richard, 1979	9.64
50	Mario Soto, 1982	9.57
51	Tom Griffin, 1969	9.56
52	Roger Clemens, 1996	9.53
53	Jim Maloney, 1963	9.53
54	Sid Fernandez, 1985	9.51
55	Herb Score, 1956	9.49
56	Sandy Koufax, 1961	9.47
57	Sam McDowell, 1968	9.47
58	David Cone, 1992	9.41
59	Frank Tanana, 1975	9.41
60	Don Wilson, 1969	9.40
61	Bob Veale, 1965	9.34
62	Nolan Ryan, 1988	9.33
63	David Cone, 1991	9.32
64	John Smoltz, 1998	9.29
65	Luis Tiant, 1967	9.22
66	Hideo Nomo, 1996	9.22
67	Pedro Martinez, 1996	9.22
68	Mark Langston, 1986	9.21
69	Luis Tiant, 1968	9.20
70	Dave Boswell, 1966	9.19
71	Sam McDowell, 1964	9.19
72	Sonny Siebert, 1965	9.11
73	Sid Fernandez, 1988	9.10
74	Tom Seaver, 1971	9.08
75	Sid Fernandez, 1990	9.08
76	David Cone, 1998	9.06
77	Dennis Eckersley, 1976	9.03
78	John Smoltz, 1995	9.02
79	Nolan Ryan, 1979	9.01
80	Sandy Koufax, 1964	9.00
	Darryl Kile, 1996	9.00
	Kevin Brown, 1998	9.00
83	Sam McDowell, 1967	8.99
84	Sam McDowell, 1970	8.97
85	Bobby Witt, 1990	8.96
86	Curt Schilling, 1996	8.93
87	Jose Rijo, 1994	8.93
88	Jim Maloney, 1964	8.92
89	Andy Benes, 1997	8.90
90	Jose Rijo, 1988	8.89
91	Roger Clemens, 1994	8.86
92	Sandy Koufax, 1963	8.86
93	Pedro Astacio, 2000	8.85
94	Pedro Martinez, 1994	8.83
95	Sandy Koufax, 1966	8.83
96	Kevin Appier, 1996	8.82
97	Sam McDowell, 1969	8.81
98	Sid Fernandez, 1986	8.81
99	Nolan Ryan, 1982	8.81
100	Todd Stottlemyre, 1995	8.80

Strikeouts per Game (by era)

1876-1892

1	Hugh Daily, 1884	8.68
2	Matt Kilroy, 1886	7.92
3	Charlie Gagus, 1884	7.92
4	John Clarkson, 1884	7.78
5	Toad Ramsey, 1886	7.63
6	Dupee Shaw, 1884	7.47
7	Jim Whitney, 1884	7.23
8	Mike Dorgan, 1884	7.17
9	James Burke, 1884	7.13
10	Hardie Henderson, 1884	7.09
11	Tim Keefe, 1888	6.94
12	Bob Black, 1884	6.80
13	Lady Baldwin, 1885	6.78
14	Jack Stivetts, 1889	6.71
15	Toad Ramsey, 1890	6.63

1893-1919

1	Rube Waddell, 1903	8.39
2	Rube Waddell, 1904	8.20
3	Rube Waddell, 1905	7.86
4	Rube Marquard, 1911	7.68
5	Walter Johnson, 1910	7.61
6	Joe Wood, 1911	7.54
7	Walter Johnson, 1912	7.39
8	Rube Waddell, 1907	7.33
9	Rube Waddell, 1908	7.31
10	Dutch Leonard, 1914	7.05
11	Red Ames, 1906	6.90
12	Rube Waddell, 1902	6.84
13	Red Ames, 1905	6.78
14	Joe Wood, 1912	6.75
15	Orval Overall, 1908	6.68

1920-1941

1	Johnny Vander Meer, 1941	8.03
2	Bob Feller, 1938	7.78
3	Dazzy Vance, 1924	7.65
4	Dazzy Vance, 1925	7.50
5	Bob Feller, 1939	7.46
6	Dazzy Vance, 1926	7.46
7	Bob Feller, 1940	7.33
8	Van Mungo, 1936	6.87
9	Bob Feller, 1941	6.82
10	Van Mungo, 1937	6.82
11	Lefty Grove, 1926	6.77
12	Bill Hallahan, 1930	6.71
13	George Earnshaw, 1928	6.65
14	Red Ruffing, 1932	6.60
15	Lefty Grove, 1930	6.46

1942-1960

1	Sandy Koufax, 1960	10.13
2	Herb Score, 1955	9.70
3	Herb Score, 1956	9.49
4	Hal Newhouser, 1946	8.46
5	Bob Feller, 1946	8.43
6	Sam Jones, 1956	8.40
7	Herb Score, 1959	8.23
8	Don Drysdale, 1960	8.23
9	Sam Jones, 1958	8.10
10	Don Drysdale, 1959	8.05
11	Bob Turley, 1957	7.76
12	Camilo Pascual, 1956	7.73
13	Bob Turley, 1955	7.66
14	Stan Williams, 1960	7.60
15	Sam Jones, 1957	7.59

1961-1976

1	Sam McDowell, 1965	10.71
2	Nolan Ryan, 1973	10.57
3	Sandy Koufax, 1962	10.55
4	Nolan Ryan, 1972	10.43
5	Sam McDowell, 1966	10.42
6	Nolan Ryan, 1976	10.35
7	Sandy Koufax, 1965	10.24
8	Nolan Ryan, 1974	9.93
9	Tom Griffin, 1969	9.56
10	Jim Maloney, 1963	9.53
11	Sandy Koufax, 1961	9.47
12	Sam McDowell, 1968	9.47
13	Frank Tanana, 1975	9.41
14	Don Wilson, 1969	9.40
15	Bob Veale, 1965	9.34

1977-2000

1	Pedro Martinez, 1999	13.20
2	Kerry Wood, 1998	12.58
3	Randy Johnson, 2000	12.56
4	Randy Johnson, 1995	12.35
5	Randy Johnson, 1997	12.30
6	Randy Johnson, 1998	12.12
7	Randy Johnson, 1999	12.06
8	Pedro Martinez, 2000	11.78
9	Nolan Ryan, 1987	11.48
10	Dwight Gooden, 1984	11.39
11	Pedro Martinez, 1997	11.37
12	Nolan Ryan, 1989	11.32
13	Curt Schilling, 1997	11.29
14	Hideo Nomo, 1995	11.10
15	Randy Johnson, 1993	10.86

Ratio

1	Guy Hecker, 1882	6.92
2	Tim Keefe, 1880	7.20
3	Pedro Martinez, 2000	7.22
4	Walter Johnson, 1913	7.26
5	Addie Joss, 1908	7.31
6	Charlie Sweeney, 1884	7.35
7	Christy Mathewson, 1909	7.45
8	Greg Maddux, 1995	7.47
9	Ed Walsh, 1910	7.47
10	George Bradley, 1880	7.53
11	Christy Mathewson, 1908	7.60
12	Henry Boyle, 1884	7.68
13	Mordecai Brown, 1908	7.72
14	Denny Driscoll, 1882	7.79
15	Grover Alexander, 1915	7.82
16	Sandy Koufax, 1965	7.83
17	Juan Marichal, 1966	7.88
18	Bob Gibson, 1968	7.89
19	Roger Nelson, 1972	7.89
20	Dave McNally, 1968	7.91
21	Ed Walsh, 1908	7.91
22	Sandy Koufax, 1963	7.96
23	Luis Tiant, 1968	7.98
24	George Bradley, 1876	7.98
25	Jim Whitney, 1884	8.01
26	Guy Hecker, 1884	8.02
27	Cy Young, 1905	8.03
28	Mordecai Brown, 1909	8.04
29	Cy Young, 1908	8.07
30	Tommy Bond, 1876	8.12
31	Babe Adams, 1919	8.17
32	Russ Ford, 1910	8.17
33	John Ward, 1880	8.26
34	Lady Baldwin, 1885	8.28
35	Eddie Cicotte, 1917	8.28
36	Dutch Leonard, 1914	8.29
37	Charley Radbourn, 1884	8.30
38	Denny McLain, 1968	8.30
39	Catfish Hunter, 1972	8.32
40	Silver King, 1888	8.33
41	Doc White, 1906	8.33
42	Greg Maddux, 1994	8.33
43	Grover Alexander, 1919	8.35
44	Juan Marichal, 1965	8.35
45	Don Sutton, 1972	8.35
46	Sandy Koufax, 1964	8.35
47	Ed Morris, 1884	8.36
48	Mike Scott, 1986	8.37
49	Christy Mathewson, 1905	8.42
50	Larry Corcoran, 1880	8.44
51	Addie Joss, 1906	8.49
52	Reb Russell, 1916	8.51
53	Cy Young, 1904	8.53
54	Mordecai Brown, 1906	8.53
55	Walter Johnson, 1910	8.54
56	Ron Guidry, 1978	8.55
57	Claude Hendrix, 1914	8.55
58	Walter Johnson, 1912	8.56
59	Warren Hacker, 1952	8.56
60	Jack Lynch, 1884	8.56
61	Jack Chesbro, 1904	8.57
62	John Clarkson, 1885	8.58
63	Joe Horlen, 1964	8.59
64	Ed Walsh, 1909	8.60
65	Perry Werden, 1884	8.60
66	Chief Bender, 1910	8.60
67	John Tudor, 1985	8.61
68	Bill Burns, 1908	8.62
69	Addie Joss, 1909	8.64
70	Tom Seaver, 1971	8.64
71	Russ Ford, 1914	8.66
72	Tim Keefe, 1883	8.67
73	Bill Bernhard, 1902	8.68
74	Tim Keefe, 1888	8.68
75	Vida Blue, 1971	8.68
76	Tim Keefe, 1884	8.68
77	Pedro Martinez, 1999	8.69
78	Charlie Buffinton, 1888	8.70
79	Lady Baldwin, 1886	8.70
80	Larry Corcoran, 1882	8.70
81	Frank Smith, 1908	8.71
82	Tony Mullane, 1883	8.71
83	Bret Saberhagen, 1989	8.71
84	Christy Mathewson, 1907	8.71
85	Joe Horlen, 1967	8.72
86	Jim Devlin, 1876	8.73
87	Pedro Martinez, 1997	8.73
88	Frank Smith, 1909	8.73
89	Mordecai Brown, 1907	8.73
90	Charlie Getzien, 1884	8.74
91	Greg Maddux, 1997	8.74
92	Dwight Gooden, 1985	8.75
93	Fred Anderson, 1917	8.78
94	Charlie Ferguson, 1886	8.78
95	Dick Hughes, 1967	8.78
96	Ray Caldwell, 1914	8.79
97	Walter Johnson, 1918	8.81
98	Turk Farrell, 1963	8.81
99	Pascual Perez, 1988	8.81
100	Charley Radbourn, 1883	8.81

Earned Run Average

1	Tim Keefe, 1880	0.86
2	Dutch Leonard, 1914	0.96
3	Mordecai Brown, 1906	1.04
4	Bob Gibson, 1968	1.12
5	Christy Mathewson, 1909	1.14
6	Walter Johnson, 1913	1.14
7	Jack Pfiester, 1907	1.15
8	Addie Joss, 1908	1.16
9	Carl Lundgren, 1907	1.17
10	Denny Driscoll, 1882	1.21
11	Grover Alexander, 1915	1.22
12	George Bradley, 1876	1.23
13	Cy Young, 1908	1.26
14	Ed Walsh, 1910	1.27
15	Walter Johnson, 1918	1.27
16	Christy Mathewson, 1905	1.28
17	Jack Taylor, 1902	1.29
18	Guy Hecker, 1882	1.30
19	Jack Coombs, 1910	1.30
20	Mordecai Brown, 1909	1.31
21	Walter Johnson, 1910	1.36
22	George Bradley, 1880	1.38
23	Charley Radbourn, 1884	1.38
24	Walter Johnson, 1912	1.39
25	Mordecai Brown, 1907	1.39
26	Harry Krause, 1909	1.39
27	Ed Walsh, 1909	1.41
28	Ed Walsh, 1908	1.42
29	Ed Reulbach, 1905	1.42
30	Orval Overall, 1909	1.42
31	Christy Mathewson, 1908	1.43
32	Fred Anderson, 1917	1.44
33	Mordecai Brown, 1908	1.47
34	Rube Waddell, 1905	1.48
35	Joe Wood, 1915	1.49
36	Walter Johnson, 1919	1.49
37	Jack Pfiester, 1906	1.51
38	John Ward, 1878	1.51
39	Harry McCormick, 1882	1.52
40	Doc White, 1906	1.52
41	George McQuillan, 1908	1.53
42	Dwight Gooden, 1985	1.53
43	Eddie Cicotte, 1917	1.53
44	Will White, 1882	1.54
45	Cy Morgan, 1910	1.55
46	Grover Alexander, 1916	1.55
47	Walter Johnson, 1915	1.55
48	Howie Camnitz, 1908	1.56
49	Greg Maddux, 1994	1.56
50	Jim Devlin, 1876	1.56
51	Tim Keefe, 1885	1.58
52	Fred Toney, 1915	1.58
53	Eddie Cicotte, 1913	1.58
54	Rube Marquard, 1916	1.58
55	Chief Bender, 1910	1.58
56	Barney Pelty, 1906	1.59
57	Addie Joss, 1904	1.59
58	Ed Walsh, 1907	1.60
59	Luis Tiant, 1968	1.60
60	Joe McGinnity, 1904	1.61
61	Ray Collins, 1910	1.62
62	Rube Waddell, 1904	1.62
63	Howie Camnitz, 1909	1.62
64	Cy Young, 1901	1.62
65	Greg Maddux, 1995	1.63
66	Silver King, 1888	1.63
67	Spud Chandler, 1943	1.64
68	Ernie Shore, 1915	1.64
69	Ed Summers, 1908	1.64
70	Dean Chance, 1964	1.65
71	Walter Johnson, 1908	1.65
72	Ed Reulbach, 1906	1.65
73	Russ Ford, 1910	1.65
74	Chief Bender, 1909	1.66
75	Sam Leever, 1907	1.66
76	Carl Hubbell, 1933	1.66
77	Mickey Welch, 1885	1.66
78	Candy Cummings, 1876	1.67
79	Tommy Bond, 1876	1.68
80	Orval Overall, 1907	1.68
81	Ed Reulbach, 1907	1.69
82	Claude Hendrix, 1914	1.69
83	Nolan Ryan, 1981	1.69
84	Jim McCormick, 1878	1.69
85	Joe Wood, 1910	1.69
86	Rube Foster, 1914	1.70
87	Charlie Sweeney, 1884	1.70
	Bill Burns, 1908	1.70
89	Addie Joss, 1909	1.71
90	Ed Killian, 1909	1.71
91	Walter Johnson, 1914	1.72
92	Ned Garvin, 1904	1.72
93	Doc White, 1909	1.72
94	Bill Doak, 1914	1.72
95	Addie Joss, 1906	1.72
	Grover Alexander, 1919	1.72
97	Sandy Koufax, 1966	1.73
98	Bob Ewing, 1907	1.73
99	Vic Willis, 1906	1.73
100	Sandy Koufax, 1964	1.74

Earned Run Average (by era)

1876-1892

1	Tim Keefe, 1880	0.86
2	Denny Driscoll, 1882	1.21
3	George Bradley, 1876	1.23
4	Guy Hecker, 1882	1.30
5	George Bradley, 1880	1.38
6	Charley Radbourn, 1884	1.38
7	John Ward, 1878	1.51
8	Harry McCormick, 1882	1.52
9	Will White, 1882	1.54
10	Jim Devlin, 1876	1.56
11	Tim Keefe, 1885	1.58
12	Silver King, 1888	1.63
13	Mickey Welch, 1885	1.66
14	Candy Cummings, 1876	1.67
15	Tommy Bond, 1876	1.68

1893-1919

1	Dutch Leonard, 1914	0.96
2	Mordecai Brown, 1906	1.04
3	Christy Mathewson, 1909	1.14
4	Walter Johnson, 1913	1.14
5	Jack Pfiester, 1907	1.15
6	Addie Joss, 1908	1.16
7	Carl Lundgren, 1907	1.17
8	Grover Alexander, 1915	1.22
9	Cy Young, 1908	1.26
10	Ed Walsh, 1910	1.27
11	Walter Johnson, 1918	1.27
12	Christy Mathewson, 1905	1.28
13	Jack Taylor, 1902	1.29
14	Jack Coombs, 1910	1.30
15	Mordecai Brown, 1909	1.31

1920-1941

1	Carl Hubbell, 1933	1.66
2	Grover Alexander, 1920	1.91
3	Dolf Luque, 1923	1.93
4	Lon Warneke, 1933	2.00
5	Lefty Grove, 1931	2.06
6	Dazzy Vance, 1928	2.09
7	Babe Adams, 1920	2.16
8	Hal Schumacher, 1933	2.16
9	Dazzy Vance, 1924	2.16
10	Burleigh Grimes, 1920	2.22
11	Elmer Riddle, 1941	2.24
12	Bill Walker, 1931	2.26
13	Wilcy Moore, 1927	2.28
14	Bucky Walters, 1939	2.29
15	Carl Hubbell, 1934	2.30

1942-1960

1	Spud Chandler, 1943	1.64
2	Mort Cooper, 1942	1.78
3	Hal Newhouser, 1945	1.81
4	Max Lanier, 1943	1.90
5	Hal Newhouser, 1946	1.94
6	Billy Pierce, 1955	1.97
7	Whitey Ford, 1958	2.01
8	Al Benton, 1945	2.02
9	Allie Reynolds, 1952	2.06
10	Ted Lyons, 1942	2.10
11	Howie Pollet, 1946	2.10
12	Spud Chandler, 1946	2.10
13	Warren Spahn, 1953	2.10
14	Dizzy Trout, 1944	2.12
15	Roger Wolff, 1945	2.12

1961-1976

1	Bob Gibson, 1968	1.12
2	Luis Tiant, 1968	1.60
3	Dean Chance, 1964	1.65
4	Sandy Koufax, 1966	1.73
5	Sandy Koufax, 1964	1.74
6	Tom Seaver, 1971	1.76
7	Sam McDowell, 1968	1.81
8	Vida Blue, 1971	1.82
9	Phil Niekro, 1967	1.87
10	Joe Horlen, 1964	1.88
11	Sandy Koufax, 1963	1.88
12	Luis Tiant, 1972	1.91
13	Wilbur Wood, 1971	1.91
14	Gaylord Perry, 1972	1.92
15	Dave McNally, 1968	1.95

1977-2000

1	Dwight Gooden, 1985	1.53
2	Greg Maddux, 1994	1.56
3	Greg Maddux, 1995	1.63
4	Nolan Ryan, 1981	1.69
5	Pedro Martinez, 2000	1.74
6	Ron Guidry, 1978	1.74
7	Kevin Brown, 1996	1.89
8	Pedro Martinez, 1997	1.90
9	John Tudor, 1985	1.93
10	Roger Clemens, 1990	1.93
11	Orel Hershiser, 1985	2.03
12	Roger Clemens, 1997	2.05
13	Pedro Martinez, 1999	2.07
14	Bill Swift, 1992	2.08
15	Bret Saberhagen, 1989	2.16

Adjusted Earned Run Average

1	Tim Keefe, 1880	294
2	Pedro Martinez, 2000	292
3	Dutch Leonard, 1914	280
4	Greg Maddux, 1994	272
5	Greg Maddux, 1995	262
6	Walter Johnson, 1913	258
7	Bob Gibson, 1968	258
8	Mordecai Brown, 1906	254
9	Pedro Martinez, 1999	241
10	Walter Johnson, 1912	240
11	Christy Mathewson, 1905	230
12	Dwight Gooden, 1985	226
13	Grover Alexander, 1915	225
14	Roger Clemens, 1997	225
15	Christy Mathewson, 1909	223
16	Pedro Martinez, 1997	221
17	Lefty Grove, 1931	218
18	Cy Young, 1901	217
19	Jack Pfiester, 1907	216
20	Denny Driscoll, 1882	216
21	Walter Johnson, 1919	216
22	Kevin Brown, 1996	215
23	Walter Johnson, 1918	215
24	Carl Lundgren, 1907	213
25	Roger Clemens, 1990	212
26	Ed Reulbach, 1905	210
27	Jack Taylor, 1902	209
28	Ron Guidry, 1978	209
29	Charley Radbourn, 1884	206
30	Addie Joss, 1908	206
31	Billy Pierce, 1955	201
32	Dolf Luque, 1923	200
33	Silver King, 1888	200
34	Dean Chance, 1964	199
35	Randy Johnson, 1997	197
36	Spud Chandler, 1943	197
37	Al Maul, 1895	196
38	Nolan Ryan, 1981	195
39	Cy Young, 1908	195
40	Hal Newhouser, 1945	194
41	Tom Seaver, 1971	194
42	Mordecai Brown, 1909	193
43	Carl Hubbell, 1933	193
44	Mort Cooper, 1942	193
45	Randy Johnson, 1995	191
46	Walter Johnson, 1915	191
47	Monty Stratton, 1937	191
48	Guy Hecker, 1882	191
49	Lefty Gomez, 1937	191
50	Sandy Koufax, 1966	191
51	Greg Maddux, 1997	191
52	Ed Siever, 1902	191
53	Clark Griffith, 1898	191
54	Dazzy Vance, 1928	191
55	Lefty Grove, 1936	189
56	Vean Gregg, 1911	189
57	Ed Walsh, 1910	189
58	Amos Rusie, 1894	189
59	Hal Newhouser, 1946	189
60	Dazzy Vance, 1930	188
61	Billy Rhines, 1896	188
62	Wilbur Wood, 1971	188
63	Jack Stivetts, 1889	188
64	Greg Maddux, 1998	187
65	Joe Wood, 1915	187
66	Warren Spahn, 1953	187
67	Sandy Koufax, 1964	187
68	Lefty Grove, 1939	186
69	Eddie Cicotte, 1913	185
70	Luis Tiant, 1968	185
71	Lefty Grove, 1930	184
72	Hank Aguirre, 1962	184
73	Randy Johnson, 1999	184
74	Joe Horlen, 1964	184
75	Vida Blue, 1971	184
76	Henry Boyle, 1886	184
77	John Tudor, 1985	183
78	Walter Johnson, 1910	183
79	Harry Brecheen, 1948	183
80	Jack Coombs, 1910	182
81	Billy Rhines, 1890	182
82	Steve Carlton, 1972	182
83	Fred Toney, 1915	182
84	Johnny Allen, 1937	181
85	Rube Waddell, 1905	180
86	Mordecai Brown, 1907	179
87	Kevin Appier, 1993	179
88	Orval Overall, 1909	179
89	Rube Waddell, 1902	179
90	Bret Saberhagen, 1989	178
91	Joe Wood, 1912	178
92	Phil Niekro, 1967	178
93	Max Lanier, 1943	177
94	Roger Clemens, 1994	177
95	Fred Anderson, 1917	177
96	Roger Clemens, 1998	176
97	Cy Young, 1892	176
98	Johnny Antonelli, 1954	176
99	Whitey Ford, 1958	176
100	Lefty Grove, 1935	176

Adjusted ERA (by era)

1876-1892

1	Tim Keefe, 1880	294
2	Denny Driscoll, 1882	216
3	Charley Radbourn, 1884	206
4	Silver King, 1888	200
5	Guy Hecker, 1882	191
6	Jack Stivetts, 1889	188
7	Henry Boyle, 1886	184
8	Billy Rhines, 1890	182
9	Cy Young, 1892	176
10	Harry McCormick, 1882	174
11	George Bradley, 1876	174
12	Jim Devlin, 1876	174
13	Will White, 1882	172
14	Guy Hecker, 1884	172
15	Jim McCormick, 1883	171

1893-1919

1	Dutch Leonard, 1914	280
2	Walter Johnson, 1913	258
3	Mordecai Brown, 1906	254
4	Walter Johnson, 1912	240
5	Christy Mathewson, 1905	230
6	Grover Alexander, 1915	225
7	Christy Mathewson, 1909	223
8	Cy Young, 1901	217
9	Jack Pfiester, 1907	216
10	Walter Johnson, 1919	216
11	Walter Johnson, 1918	215
12	Carl Lundgren, 1907	213
13	Ed Reulbach, 1905	210
14	Jack Taylor, 1902	209
15	Addie Joss, 1908	206

1920-1941

1	Lefty Grove, 1931	218
2	Dolf Luque, 1923	200
3	Carl Hubbell, 1933	193
4	Monty Stratton, 1937	191
5	Lefty Gomez, 1937	191
6	Dazzy Vance, 1928	191
7	Lefty Grove, 1936	189
8	Dazzy Vance, 1930	188
9	Lefty Grove, 1939	186
10	Lefty Grove, 1930	184
11	Johnny Allen, 1937	181
12	Lefty Grove, 1935	176
13	Mel Harder, 1934	174
14	Lefty Gomez, 1934	174
15	Dazzy Vance, 1924	173

1942-1960

1	Billy Pierce, 1955	201
2	Spud Chandler, 1943	197
3	Hal Newhouser, 1945	194
4	Mort Cooper, 1942	193
5	Hal Newhouser, 1946	189
6	Warren Spahn, 1953	187
7	Harry Brecheen, 1948	183
8	Max Lanier, 1943	177
9	Johnny Antonelli, 1954	176
10	Whitey Ford, 1958	176
11	Al Benton, 1945	174
12	Hoyt Wilhelm, 1959	173
13	Ted Lyons, 1942	172

1961-1976

1	Bob Gibson, 1968	258
2	Dean Chance, 1964	199
3	Tom Seaver, 1971	194
4	Sandy Koufax, 1966	191
5	Wilbur Wood, 1971	188
6	Sandy Koufax, 1964	187
7	Luis Tiant, 1968	185
8	Hank Aguirre, 1962	184
9	Joe Horlen, 1964	184
10	Vida Blue, 1971	184
11	Steve Carlton, 1972	182
12	Phil Niekro, 1967	178
13	Tom Seaver, 1973	174
14	Whitey Ford, 1964	170
15	Luis Tiant, 1972	169

1977-2000

1	Pedro Martinez, 2000	292
2	Greg Maddux, 1994	272
3	Greg Maddux, 1995	262
4	Pedro Martinez, 1999	241
5	Dwight Gooden, 1985	226
6	Roger Clemens, 1997	225
7	Pedro Martinez, 1997	221
8	Kevin Brown, 1996	215
9	Roger Clemens, 1990	212
10	Ron Guidry, 1978	209
11	Randy Johnson, 1997	197
12	Nolan Ryan, 1981	195
13	Randy Johnson, 1995	191
14	Greg Maddux, 1997	191
15	Greg Maddux, 1998	187

Pitching Runs

1	Amos Rusie, 1894	125.8
2	Charley Radbourn, 1884	120.9
3	Guy Hecker, 1884	108.0
4	Silver King, 1888	92.9
5	John Clarkson, 1889	88.7
6	Cy Young, 1901	84.2
7	Matt Kilroy, 1887	80.4
8	Walter Johnson, 1912	79.1
9	Pink Hawley, 1895	79.0
10	Silver King, 1890	78.9
11	Will White, 1883	77.7
12	Jouett Meekin, 1894	77.6
13	Amos Rusie, 1893	76.9
14	Pedro Martinez, 2000	76.7
15	Charley Radbourn, 1883	76.5
16	Dave Foutz, 1886	75.2
17	Lefty Grove, 1931	74.5
18	Dolf Luque, 1923	74.2
19	Roger Clemens, 1997	74.1
20	Scott Stratton, 1890	72.3
21	Billy Rhines, 1890	72.2
22	Lefty Gomez, 1937	70.9
23	Jim Galvin, 1884	69.8
24	Walter Johnson, 1913	68.8
25	George Bradley, 1876	68.8
26	Cy Young, 1892	68.5
27	Lefty Grove, 1930	68.4
28	Kid Nichols, 1897	68.1
29	Dazzy Vance, 1930	67.9
30	Lefty Gomez, 1934	67.7
31	Elmer Smith, 1887	67.6
32	Sandy Koufax, 1966	67.5
33	John Clarkson, 1885	67.3
34	Pedro Martinez, 1999	66.5
35	Red Faber, 1921	66.4
36	Toad Ramsey, 1886	65.7
37	Christy Mathewson, 1905	65.0
38	Warren Spahn, 1953	64.5
39	Grover Alexander, 1915	64.1
40	Dwight Gooden, 1985	63.6
41	Kid Nichols, 1896	63.6
42	Kid Nichols, 1898	63.5
43	Ted Breitenstein, 1893	63.4
44	Amos Rusie, 1897	63.3
45	Mickey Welch, 1885	63.3
46	Kid Nichols, 1890	63.2
47	Bob Gibson, 1968	63.1
48	Bob Caruthers, 1885	63.1
49	Bob Feller, 1940	63.0
50	Cy Young, 1894	62.9
51	Randy Johnson, 1999	62.9
52	Lefty Grove, 1936	62.8
53	Clark Griffith, 1898	62.6
54	Cy Young, 1895	62.3
55	Ron Guidry, 1978	61.9
56	Ed Morris, 1886	61.9
57	Pedro Martinez, 1997	61.8
58	Amos Rusie, 1890	61.6
59	Carl Hubbell, 1934	61.3
60	Will White, 1882	61.3
61	Cy Young, 1893	61.1
62	Dean Chance, 1964	61.1
63	Tim Keefe, 1883	61.1
64	Jim Palmer, 1975	61.0
65	Kid Nichols, 1895	61.0
66	Cy Young, 1902	60.8
67	Ed Seward, 1888	60.5
68	Kevin Brown, 1996	60.3
69	Greg Maddux, 1994	59.7
70	Greg Maddux, 1995	59.5
71	Dazzy Vance, 1928	59.4
72	Thornton Lee, 1941	59.4
73	Robin Roberts, 1953	59.1
74	Charlie Ferguson, 1886	58.6
75	Dazzy Vance, 1924	58.5
76	Bob Feller, 1939	58.3
77	Bill Hutchison, 1890	58.2
78	Lady Baldwin, 1886	58.2
79	Bucky Walters, 1939	57.8
80	Carl Hubbell, 1936	57.8
81	Wilbur Wood, 1971	57.7
82	John Clarkson, 1887	57.7
83	Ed Morris, 1885	57.7
84	Jesse Duryea, 1889	57.5
85	Carl Hubbell, 1933	57.5
86	Guy Hecker, 1885	57.2
87	Vida Blue, 1971	57.2
88	Steve Carlton, 1972	57.0
89	Tony Mullane, 1883	57.0
90	Greg Maddux, 1998	56.2
91	Walter Johnson, 1919	56.1
92	Sandy Koufax, 1965	56.0
93	Win Mercer, 1894	55.8
94	Warren Spahn, 1947	55.7
95	Tim Keefe, 1885	55.4
96	Jack Taylor, 1902	55.2
97	Randy Johnson, 2000	55.1
98	Bill Hoffer, 1895	54.8
99	Walter Johnson, 1918	54.6
100	Bob Feller, 1946	54.5

Adjusted Pitching Runs

1	Amos Rusie, 1894	123.7
2	Charley Radbourn, 1884	116.0
3	Guy Hecker, 1884	101.0
4	Silver King, 1888	99.4
5	John Clarkson, 1889	95.4
6	Silver King, 1890	82.4
7	Cy Young, 1901	81.6
8	Walter Johnson, 1912	79.4
9	Pedro Martinez, 2000	78.1
10	Jim Galvin, 1884	77.4
11	Amos Rusie, 1893	76.5
12	Lefty Grove, 1931	76.2
13	Will White, 1883	75.4
14	John Clarkson, 1885	75.3
15	Jouett Meekin, 1894	75.0
16	Dave Foutz, 1886	74.8
17	Roger Clemens, 1997	74.4
18	John Clarkson, 1887	74.3
19	Toad Ramsey, 1886	74.0
20	Charley Radbourn, 1883	74.0
21	Kid Nichols, 1897	72.0
22	Billy Rhines, 1890	71.9
23	Scott Stratton, 1890	71.8
24	Dolf Luque, 1923	71.8
25	Cy Young, 1892	71.5
26	Matt Kilroy, 1887	70.7
27	Kid Nichols, 1895	70.1
28	Pink Hawley, 1895	69.9
29	Elmer Smith, 1887	69.2
30	Walter Johnson, 1913	68.9
31	Lefty Grove, 1930	68.8
32	Kid Nichols, 1890	68.3
33	Kid Nichols, 1896	68.2
34	Cy Young, 1893	68.2
35	Lefty Gomez, 1937	68.1
36	Cy Young, 1895	67.9
37	Jim Devlin, 1876	67.7
38	Pedro Martinez, 1999	67.5
39	Cy Young, 1894	67.4
40	Dazzy Vance, 1930	67.0
41	Lefty Grove, 1936	66.9
42	Kid Nichols, 1898	65.7
43	Red Faber, 1921	65.3
44	Ted Breitenstein, 1893	65.3
45	Grover Alexander, 1915	63.9
46	Bob Caruthers, 1885	63.8
47	Christy Mathewson, 1905	63.8
48	Kid Nichols, 1893	63.4
49	Tim Keefe, 1883	63.1
50	Randy Johnson, 1999	63.0
51	Tony Mullane, 1883	62.9
52	Bill Hutchison, 1890	62.6
53	George Bradley, 1876	62.5
54	Clark Griffith, 1898	62.1
55	Bob Gibson, 1968	61.9
56	Dwight Gooden, 1985	61.8
57	Pedro Martinez, 1997	61.7
58	Sandy Koufax, 1966	61.6
59	Cy Young, 1902	60.8
60	Wilbur Wood, 1971	60.2
61	Greg Maddux, 1995	60.2
62	Lefty Gomez, 1934	60.0
63	Steve Carlton, 1972	60.0
64	Greg Maddux, 1994	59.9
65	Amos Rusie, 1897	59.9
66	Will White, 1882	59.8
67	Ron Guidry, 1978	59.8
68	Bob Feller, 1940	59.3
69	Jesse Duryea, 1889	59.2
70	Dazzy Vance, 1928	59.1
71	Ed Morris, 1886	59.1
72	Warren Spahn, 1953	58.8
73	Vic Willis, 1899	58.7
74	Amos Rusie, 1890	58.6
75	Kevin Brown, 1996	58.6
76	Toad Ramsey, 1887	58.5
77	Thornton Lee, 1941	58.4
78	Charlie Ferguson, 1886	58.3
79	Lady Baldwin, 1886	58.3
80	Lefty Grove, 1935	58.1
81	Mickey Welch, 1885	58.1
82	Cy Young, 1896	57.7
83	Jack Stivetts, 1891	57.6
84	Ed Seward, 1888	57.6
85	John Clarkson, 1886	57.4
86	Dan Casey, 1887	57.3
87	Matt Kilroy, 1889	57.3
88	Carl Hubbell, 1934	57.3
89	Robin Roberts, 1953	57.1
90	Hal Newhouser, 1945	56.9
91	Guy Hecker, 1885	56.4
92	Ed Morris, 1885	56.3
93	Kid Gleason, 1890	56.2
94	Dazzy Vance, 1924	56.1
95	Bucky Walters, 1939	56.0
96	Walter Johnson, 1919	55.8
97	Dean Chance, 1964	55.8
98	Joe Wood, 1912	55.6
99	Jim Devlin, 1877	55.6
100	Cy Young, 1899	55.5

Pitching Wins

1	Charley Radbourn, 1884	11.0
2	Amos Rusie, 1894	10.4
3	Guy Hecker, 1884	10.2
4	Walter Johnson, 1912	9.7
5	Silver King, 1888	9.2
6	Walter Johnson, 1913	9.2
7	Cy Young, 1901	8.7
8	Lefty Grove, 1931	8.6
9	Christy Mathewson, 1905	8.1
10	Pedro Martinez, 2000	8.1
11	John Clarkson, 1889	8.0
12	Sandy Koufax, 1966	7.9
13	Pedro Martinez, 1999	7.9
14	Dolf Luque, 1923	7.8
15	Grover Alexander, 1915	7.8
16	Bob Gibson, 1968	7.8
17	Roger Clemens, 1997	7.6
18	Lefty Gomez, 1937	7.5
19	Red Faber, 1921	7.4
20	Dazzy Vance, 1930	7.3
21	Will White, 1883	7.3
22	Pink Hawley, 1895	7.3
23	Charley Radbourn, 1883	7.3
24	Lefty Grove, 1930	7.2
25	Warren Spahn, 1953	7.2
26	Dave Foutz, 1886	7.1
27	Kevin Brown, 1996	7.1
28	Bob Feller, 1940	7.0
29	Carl Hubbell, 1933	7.0
30	Billy Rhines, 1890	7.0
31	Dwight Gooden, 1985	6.9
32	Walter Johnson, 1919	6.9
33	Lefty Gomez, 1934	6.9
34	Walter Johnson, 1918	6.9
35	Scott Stratton, 1890	6.8
36	Dean Chance, 1964	6.8
37	Bucky Walters, 1939	6.8
38	Matt Kilroy, 1887	6.8
39	Amos Rusie, 1893	6.7
40	Silver King, 1890	6.7
41	Ed Walsh, 1908	6.7
42	Greg Maddux, 1994	6.7
43	John Clarkson, 1885	6.6
44	Dazzy Vance, 1928	6.6
45	Ron Guidry, 1978	6.6
46	Jim Palmer, 1975	6.6
47	Kid Nichols, 1897	6.5
48	Steve Carlton, 1972	6.5
49	Walter Johnson, 1915	6.5
50	Kid Nichols, 1898	6.5
51	Wilbur Wood, 1971	6.5
52	Cy Young, 1892	6.5
53	Carl Hubbell, 1934	6.4
54	Mordecai Brown, 1906	6.4
55	Pedro Martinez, 1997	6.4
56	George Bradley, 1876	6.4
57	Mickey Welch, 1885	6.4
58	Dazzy Vance, 1924	6.4
59	Hal Newhouser, 1946	6.3
60	Lefty Grove, 1936	6.3
61	Thornton Lee, 1941	6.3
62	Hal Newhouser, 1945	6.3
63	Vida Blue, 1971	6.3
64	Robin Roberts, 1953	6.3
65	Jim Galvin, 1884	6.3
66	Bob Feller, 1946	6.3
67	Cy Young, 1902	6.2
68	Amos Rusie, 1897	6.2
69	Mel Harder, 1934	6.2
70	Tom Seaver, 1971	6.1
71	Kid Nichols, 1896	6.1
72	Roger Clemens, 1990	6.0
73	Dizzy Trout, 1944	6.0
74	Grover Alexander, 1916	6.0
75	Greg Maddux, 1995	6.0
76	Clark Griffith, 1898	6.0
77	Christy Mathewson, 1911	6.0
78	Toad Ramsey, 1886	6.0
79	Sandy Koufax, 1965	6.0
80	Grover Alexander, 1920	6.0
81	Joe Wood, 1912	6.0
82	Jack Taylor, 1902	5.9
83	Ed Walsh, 1910	5.9
84	Bob Caruthers, 1885	5.9
85	Lefty Grove, 1932	5.9
86	Greg Maddux, 1998	5.9
87	Amos Rusie, 1890	5.9
88	Carl Hubbell, 1936	5.9
89	Elmer Smith, 1887	5.9
90	Jack Coombs, 1910	5.9
91	Walter Johnson, 1910	5.9
92	Warren Spahn, 1947	5.9
93	Ed Reulbach, 1905	5.9
94	Walter Johnson, 1911	5.9
95	Jesse Duryea, 1889	5.9
96	Bob Feller, 1939	5.8
97	Kid Nichols, 1890	5.8
98	Cy Young, 1895	5.8
99	Will White, 1882	5.8
100	Randy Johnson, 1997	5.8

Adjusted Pitching Wins

1	Charley Radbourn, 1884	10.5
2	Amos Rusie, 1894	10.2
3	Silver King, 1888	9.9
4	Walter Johnson, 1912	9.7
5	Guy Hecker, 1884	9.5
6	Walter Johnson, 1913	9.2
7	Lefty Grove, 1931	8.9
8	John Clarkson, 1889	8.7
9	Cy Young, 1901	8.4
10	Pedro Martinez, 2000	8.2
11	Pedro Martinez, 1999	8.0
12	Christy Mathewson, 1905	7.9
13	Grover Alexander, 1915	7.8
14	Roger Clemens, 1997	7.7
15	Bob Gibson, 1968	7.6
16	Dolf Luque, 1923	7.6
17	John Clarkson, 1885	7.5
18	Red Faber, 1921	7.2
19	Lefty Grove, 1930	7.2
20	Dazzy Vance, 1930	7.2
21	Lefty Gomez, 1937	7.2
22	Sandy Koufax, 1966	7.2
23	Dave Foutz, 1886	7.1
24	Will White, 1883	7.1
25	Silver King, 1890	7.0
26	Charley Radbourn, 1883	7.0
27	Jim Galvin, 1884	7.0
28	Billy Rhines, 1890	6.9
29	Kid Nichols, 1897	6.9
30	Kevin Brown, 1996	6.9
31	Steve Carlton, 1972	6.9
32	Walter Johnson, 1919	6.9
33	Wilbur Wood, 1971	6.8
34	Toad Ramsey, 1886	6.8
35	Lefty Grove, 1936	6.8
36	Walter Johnson, 1918	6.8
37	Cy Young, 1892	6.8
38	Scott Stratton, 1890	6.8
39	Carl Hubbell, 1933	6.7
40	Kid Nichols, 1898	6.7
41	Greg Maddux, 1994	6.7
42	John Clarkson, 1887	6.7
43	Amos Rusie, 1893	6.7
44	Hal Newhouser, 1946	6.7
45	Dwight Gooden, 1985	6.7
46	Hal Newhouser, 1945	6.7
47	Bob Feller, 1940	6.6
48	Dazzy Vance, 1928	6.6
49	Walter Johnson, 1915	6.6
50	Kid Nichols, 1896	6.6
51	Bucky Walters, 1939	6.6
52	Warren Spahn, 1953	6.5
53	Dizzy Trout, 1944	6.4
54	Mordecai Brown, 1906	6.4
55	Pink Hawley, 1895	6.4
56	Pedro Martinez, 1997	6.4
57	Cy Young, 1895	6.4
58	Ron Guidry, 1978	6.3
59	Kid Nichols, 1890	6.3
60	Ed Walsh, 1908	6.3
61	Lefty Grove, 1935	6.3
62	Roger Clemens, 1990	6.3
63	Cy Young, 1893	6.3
64	Mel Harder, 1934	6.3
65	Gaylord Perry, 1972	6.2
66	Cy Young, 1902	6.2
67	Thornton Lee, 1941	6.2
68	Grover Alexander, 1920	6.2
69	Joe Wood, 1912	6.2
70	Dean Chance, 1964	6.2
71	Grover Alexander, 1916	6.1
72	Greg Maddux, 1995	6.1
73	Dazzy Vance, 1924	6.1
74	Robin Roberts, 1953	6.1
75	Lefty Gomez, 1934	6.0
76	Elmer Smith, 1887	6.0
77	Dizzy Dean, 1934	6.0
78	Jesse Duryea, 1889	6.0
79	Lefty Grove, 1932	6.0
80	Bob Caruthers, 1885	6.0
81	Vida Blue, 1971	6.0
82	Tom Seaver, 1971	6.0
83	Carl Hubbell, 1934	6.0
84	Clark Griffith, 1898	5.9
85	Kid Nichols, 1895	5.9
86	Matt Kilroy, 1887	5.9
87	Jim Palmer, 1975	5.9
88	Christy Mathewson, 1911	5.9
89	Jim Devlin, 1876	5.9
90	Christy Mathewson, 1908	5.8
91	Jack Stivetts, 1891	5.8
92	Bill Hutchison, 1890	5.8
93	Amos Rusie, 1897	5.8
94	Juan Marichal, 1965	5.8
95	Mickey Welch, 1885	5.8
96	Curt Davis, 1934	5.8
97	Ed Reulbach, 1905	5.8
98	Walter Johnson, 1914	5.8
99	Greg Maddux, 1998	5.8
100	Walter Johnson, 1910	5.8

Opponents' Batting Average

1	Pedro Martinez, 2000	.167
2	Luis Tiant, 1968	.168
3	Nolan Ryan, 1972	.171
4	Nolan Ryan, 1991	.172
5	Ed Reulbach, 1906	.175
6	Tim Keefe, 1880	.178
7	Sandy Koufax, 1965	.179
8	Dutch Leonard, 1914	.180
9	Sid Fernandez, 1985	.181
10	Hideo Nomo, 1995	.182
11	Dave McNally, 1968	.182
12	Tommy Byrne, 1949	.183
13	Pedro Martinez, 1997	.184
14	Al Downing, 1963	.184
15	Bob Gibson, 1968	.184
16	Sam McDowell, 1965	.185
17	Carl Lundgren, 1907	.185
18	Herb Score, 1956	.186
19	Mike Scott, 1986	.186
20	Nolan Ryan, 1989	.187
21	Ed Walsh, 1910	.187
22	Mario Soto, 1980	.187
23	Walter Johnson, 1913	.187
24	Nolan Ryan, 1981	.188
25	Russ Ford, 1910	.188
26	Nolan Ryan, 1986	.188
27	Nolan Ryan, 1990	.188
28	Floyd Youmans, 1986	.188
29	Sam McDowell, 1966	.188
30	Guy Hecker, 1882	.188
31	Sandy Koufax, 1963	.189
32	Sam McDowell, 1968	.189
33	Don Sutton, 1972	.189
34	Catfish Hunter, 1972	.189
35	Vida Blue, 1971	.189
36	Nolan Ryan, 1974	.190
37	Andy Messersmith, 1969	.190
38	Joe Horlen, 1964	.190
39	Sid Fernandez, 1988	.191
40	Grover Alexander, 1915	.191
41	Sandy Koufax, 1964	.191
42	Bob Turley, 1955	.193
43	Nolan Ryan, 1977	.193
44	Fred Beebe, 1908	.193
45	Charlie Sweeney, 1884	.193
46	Ron Guidry, 1978	.193
47	Stan Coveleski, 1917	.194
48	Bob Turley, 1957	.194
49	Randy Johnson, 1997	.194
50	Herb Score, 1955	.194
51	Jack Pfiester, 1906	.194
52	Mordecai Brown, 1908	.195
53	Nolan Ryan, 1976	.195
54	Nolan Ryan, 1983	.195
55	Dean Chance, 1964	.195
56	Roger Clemens, 1986	.195
57	Tim Keefe, 1888	.196
58	Kerry Wood, 1998	.196
59	Walter Johnson, 1912	.196
60	Roger Nelson, 1972	.196
61	J.R. Richard, 1978	.196
62	Pascual Perez, 1988	.196
63	Greg Maddux, 1995	.197
64	Jeff Robinson, 1988	.197
65	Lady Baldwin, 1885	.197
66	Jose DeLeon, 1989	.197
67	Dave Boswell, 1966	.197
68	Sandy Koufax, 1962	.197
69	Addie Joss, 1908	.197
70	Roger Clemens, 1998	.197
71	Sonny Siebert, 1968	.198
72	Sid Fernandez, 1989	.198
73	Toad Ramsey, 1886	.198
74	Larry Cheney, 1916	.198
75	Wayne Simpson, 1970	.198
76	Orval Overall, 1909	.198
77	Gary Peters, 1967	.199
78	Larry Corcoran, 1880	.199
79	Willie Mitchell, 1913	.199
80	Adonis Terry, 1888	.199
81	Nolan Ryan, 1987	.199
82	Mordecai Brown, 1904	.199
83	Silver King, 1888	.200
84	Christy Mathewson, 1909	.200
85	Rube Waddell, 1905	.200
86	Denny McLain, 1968	.200
87	Larry Corcoran, 1882	.200
88	Bobby Bolin, 1968	.200
	Jim Palmer, 1969	.200
	Sid Fernandez, 1990	.200
91	Christy Mathewson, 1908	.200
92	Spec Shea, 1947	.200
93	Ed Seward, 1888	.200
94	Tony Mullane, 1892	.201
95	Art Fromme, 1909	.201
96	Babe Ruth, 1916	.201
97	Randy Johnson, 1995	.201
98	Dwight Gooden, 1985	.201
99	Cannonball Titcomb, 1888	.201
100	Curt Schilling, 1992	.201

Opponents' On-Base Pctg.

1	Guy Hecker, 1882	.199
2	Charlie Sweeney, 1884	.211
3	Tim Keefe, 1880	.212
4	Pedro Martinez, 2000	.214
5	Henry Boyle, 1884	.215
6	George Bradley, 1880	.217
7	Walter Johnson, 1913	.217
8	Denny Driscoll, 1882	.218
9	Addie Joss, 1908	.218
10	Jim Whitney, 1884	.223
11	George Bradley, 1876	.224
12	Greg Maddux, 1995	.225
13	Christy Mathewson, 1908	.225
14	Guy Hecker, 1884	.226
15	Ed Walsh, 1910	.226
16	Tommy Bond, 1876	.227
17	Lady Baldwin, 1885	.228
18	Sandy Koufax, 1965	.228
19	Christy Mathewson, 1909	.228
20	Sandy Koufax, 1963	.230
21	Juan Marichal, 1966	.230
22	John Ward, 1880	.232
23	Mordecai Brown, 1908	.232
24	Ed Walsh, 1908	.232
25	Luis Tiant, 1968	.233
26	Bob Gibson, 1968	.233
27	Grover Alexander, 1915	.234
28	Dave McNally, 1968	.234
29	Larry Corcoran, 1882	.234
30	Charley Radbourn, 1884	.234
31	Ed Morris, 1884	.234
32	Perry Werden, 1884	.235
33	Jim Devlin, 1876	.235
34	Jack Lynch, 1884	.236
35	Larry Corcoran, 1880	.236
36	Roger Nelson, 1972	.236
37	Silver King, 1888	.237
38	Charlie Getzien, 1884	.237
39	Tim Keefe, 1883	.237
40	Tony Mullane, 1883	.238
41	John Clarkson, 1885	.239
42	Tim Keefe, 1884	.239
43	Mordecai Brown, 1909	.239
44	Fred Corey, 1880	.239
45	Juan Marichal, 1965	.240
46	Cy Young, 1908	.240
47	Don Sutton, 1972	.240
48	Cy Young, 1905	.241
49	Babe Adams, 1919	.241
50	Sandy Koufax, 1964	.241
51	Catfish Hunter, 1972	.242
52	Pete Conway, 1888	.243
53	Harry McCormick, 1882	.243
54	Denny McLain, 1968	.243
55	Tim Keefe, 1888	.243
56	Lady Baldwin, 1886	.243
57	Mike Scott, 1986	.244
58	Charley Radbourn, 1883	.244
59	Will White, 1883	.244
60	Charlie Ferguson, 1886	.244
61	Charlie Buffinton, 1888	.244
62	Will White, 1882	.244
63	Charlie Buffinton, 1884	.244
64	Russ Ford, 1910	.245
65	Grover Alexander, 1919	.245
66	Christy Mathewson, 1905	.245
67	Greg Maddux, 1994	.245
68	Dutch Leonard, 1914	.246
69	Bobby Mathews, 1882	.246
70	Jim Galvin, 1884	.246
71	Sam Weaver, 1878	.247
72	Charley Radbourn, 1882	.247
73	Charlie Gagus, 1884	.247
74	Christy Mathewson, 1907	.247
75	Warren Hacker, 1952	.247
76	Jim McCormick, 1880	.247
77	Ed Morris, 1885	.247
78	Fred Goldsmith, 1880	.247
79	Dupee Shaw, 1884	.247
80	Eddie Cicotte, 1917	.248
81	Walter Johnson, 1912	.248
82	Doc White, 1906	.249
83	John Clarkson, 1884	.249
84	Jumbo McGinnis, 1883	.249
85	John Tudor, 1985	.249
86	Pedro Martinez, 1999	.249
87	Henry Gruber, 1888	.249
88	Hugh Daily, 1884	.250
89	Ron Guidry, 1978	.250
90	Joe Horlen, 1964	.250
91	Pedro Martinez, 1997	.250
92	Terry Larkin, 1879	.250
93	John Ward, 1879	.250
94	John Ward, 1878	.251
95	Billy Taylor, 1884	.251
96	Candy Cummings, 1876	.251
97	Jim Whitney, 1883	.251
98	Cy Young, 1904	.251
99	Claude Hendrix, 1914	.251
100	Dick Burns, 1884	.252

Wins Above Team

1	George Bradley, 1876	22.5
2	Will White, 1879	21.5
3	Charley Radbourn, 1884	20.1
4	Jim McCormick, 1880	19.4
5	Guy Hecker, 1884	18.0
6	Jim Galvin, 1883	17.6
7	Jim Devlin, 1877	17.5
8	Charley Radbourn, 1883	15.7
9	Matt Kilroy, 1887	15.4
10	Jim Galvin, 1884	15.1
11	Jim Devlin, 1876	15.0
12	Charlie Buffinton, 1884	14.9
13	Walter Johnson, 1913	14.7
14	Jim McCormick, 1884	14.6
15	Jack Chesbro, 1904	14.0
16	Tony Mullane, 1884	13.9
17	Sadie McMahon, 1890	13.4
18	Will White, 1882	13.1
19	Ed Morris, 1885	12.9
20	Joe Wood, 1912	12.8
21	Bill Sweeney, 1884	12.7
	Ed Walsh, 1908	12.7
23	John Clarkson, 1889	12.1
24	Tommy Bond, 1879	12.0
25	Lefty Grove, 1931	11.8
26	Steve Carlton, 1972	11.7
27	Cy Young, 1901	11.6
28	Bill Hutchison, 1891	11.4
	Denny McLain, 1968	11.4
30	Terry Larkin, 1878	11.2
	Mickey Welch, 1884	11.2
	Bob Caruthers, 1889	11.2
33	Henry Porter, 1885	11.0
	Bill Hoffer, 1895	11.0
	Christy Mathewson, 1908	11.0
36	Cy Young, 1902	10.9
37	Cy Young, 1895	10.7
38	Dazzy Vance, 1924	10.6
	Robin Roberts, 1952	10.6
	Ron Guidry, 1978	10.6
41	Bobby Mathews, 1876	10.5
	Dizzy Dean, 1934	10.5
43	Toad Ramsey, 1886	10.2
	Cy Young, 1892	10.2
	Joe McGinnity, 1904	10.2
	Eddie Rommel, 1922	10.2
47	Lefty Grove, 1930	10.1
48	Ed Morris, 1886	10.0
	Bill Donovan, 1907	10.0
50	Frank Mountain, 1883	9.9
	Eddie Cicotte, 1919	9.9
	Lefty Gomez, 1934	9.9
53	Kid Gleason, 1890	9.8
	Grover Alexander, 1915	9.8
	Hal Newhouser, 1944	9.8
56	Bobby Mathews, 1885	9.7
	Russ Ford, 1910	9.7
	Roger Clemens, 1986	9.7
59	Charlie Ferguson, 1886	9.6
	Pete Conway, 1888	9.6
	Eddie Plank, 1912	9.6
62	Grover Alexander, 1916	9.5
	Carl Hubbell, 1936	9.5
	Dwight Gooden, 1985	9.5
65	Jouett Meekin, 1894	9.4
	Walter Johnson, 1912	9.4
	Claude Hendrix, 1914	9.4
68	Joe McGinnity, 1900	9.3
	Sandy Koufax, 1963	9.3
	Pedro Martinez, 1999	9.3
71	Bert Cunningham, 1898	9.2
	Walter Johnson, 1911	9.2
	Bobby Shantz, 1952	9.2
	Don Newcombe, 1956	9.2
	Juan Marichal, 1966	9.2
	Bob Gibson, 1970	9.2
	Bob Welch, 1990	9.2
78	Tim Keefe, 1888	9.1
	Whitey Ford, 1961	9.1
80	Jim McCormick, 1882	9.0
	Cy Young, 1893	9.0
	Preacher Roe, 1951	9.0
83	Frank Killen, 1892	8.9
	Red Faber, 1921	8.9
85	Tim Keefe, 1883	8.8
	Tim Keefe, 1887	8.8
	Christy Mathewson, 1909	8.8
	Dolf Luque, 1923	8.8
89	Lee Richmond, 1881	8.7
	Frank Killen, 1893	8.7
	Jay Hughes, 1899	8.7
	Juan Marichal, 1963	8.7
	Juan Marichal, 1968	8.7
94	Jim McCormick, 1883	8.6
	Lefty Grove, 1933	8.6
	Bob Feller, 1946	8.6
	Roy Face, 1959	8.6
98	8 players tied	8.5

Wins Above League

1	Charley Radbourn, 1884	46.0
2	Guy Hecker, 1884	45.5
3	Charley Radbourn, 1883	43.5
4	John Clarkson, 1889	42.7
5	Silver King, 1888	42.4
6	John Clarkson, 1885	42.0
7	Jim Galvin, 1884	41.0
8	Jim Galvin, 1883	40.5
9	Jim McCormick, 1880	40.2
10	Bill Hutchison, 1892	39.8
11	Tim Keefe, 1883	39.7
12	Will White, 1883	39.6
13	Will White, 1879	39.6
14	Bill Hutchison, 1890	39.3
15	Toad Ramsey, 1886	39.3
16	Matt Kilroy, 1887	38.4
17	Jim Devlin, 1876	38.4
18	George Bradley, 1876	37.8
19	Amos Rusie, 1890	37.1
20	Toad Ramsey, 1887	37.0
21	Ed Morris, 1885	36.7
22	Charlie Buffinton, 1884	36.5
23	John Clarkson, 1887	36.2
24	Tony Mullane, 1884	36.0
25	Ed Morris, 1886	35.9
26	Jim McCormick, 1882	35.7
27	Jim McCormick, 1884	35.6
28	Dave Foutz, 1886	35.6
29	Jim Devlin, 1877	35.0
30	Tim Keefe, 1886	34.9
31	Amos Rusie, 1894	34.7
32	John Ward, 1880	34.7
33	Lee Richmond, 1880	34.6
34	Bill Hutchison, 1891	34.5
35	John Ward, 1879	34.4
36	Sadie McMahon, 1891	34.3
37	Tommy Bond, 1879	34.1
38	Jim Galvin, 1879	33.9
39	Ed Walsh, 1908	33.8
40	Amos Rusie, 1892	33.8
41	Billy Taylor, 1884	33.7
42	Amos Rusie, 1893	33.7
43	Jim Whitney, 1883	33.6
44	Jack Stivetts, 1891	33.3
45	Mickey Welch, 1885	33.3
46	Dupee Shaw, 1884	33.2
47	Jim Whitney, 1881	33.1
48	Lady Baldwin, 1886	33.1
49	Mark Baldwin, 1890	33.1
50	Silver King, 1890	33.0
51	Al Spalding, 1876	33.0
52	Pink Hawley, 1895	32.9
53	Charlie Sweeney, 1884	32.8
54	Larry Corcoran, 1884	32.7
55	Kid Gleason, 1890	32.6
56	Mickey Welch, 1884	32.6
57	Bob Caruthers, 1885	32.5
58	Ed Seward, 1888	32.2
59	Walter Johnson, 1912	32.2
60	Tommy Bond, 1877	32.2
61	Matt Kilroy, 1889	32.1
62	John Clarkson, 1886	32.1
63	Will White, 1880	31.9
64	Mickey Welch, 1880	31.9
65	Jack Chesbro, 1904	31.9
66	Matt Kilroy, 1886	31.8
67	Guy Hecker, 1885	31.8
68	Will White, 1882	31.7
69	Tim Keefe, 1884	31.6
70	Sadie McMahon, 1890	31.6
71	Elmer Smith, 1887	31.5
72	Jesse Duryea, 1889	31.5
73	Cy Young, 1893	31.3
74	Larry Corcoran, 1880	31.2
75	Tommy Bond, 1878	31.1
76	George Derby, 1881	31.1
77	Bill Sweeney, 1884	30.9
78	Cy Young, 1892	30.8
79	Scott Stratton, 1890	30.8
80	Larry Corcoran, 1883	30.7
81	Tony Mullane, 1883	30.7
82	Walter Johnson, 1913	30.7
83	Mark Baldwin, 1889	30.6
84	Jim McCormick, 1879	30.4
85	Hardie Henderson, 1885	30.4
86	Tony Mullane, 1882	30.3
87	Tim Keefe, 1887	30.3
88	Phil Knell, 1891	30.3
89	Joe McGinnity, 1903	30.1
90	Charley Radbourn, 1886	30.0
91	Cy Young, 1901	29.9
92	Silver King, 1889	29.9
93	John Clarkson, 1891	29.9
94	Christy Mathewson, 1908	29.8
95	Amos Rusie, 1891	29.8
96	Jersey Bakely, 1888	29.6
97	Kid Nichols, 1893	29.6
98	Charley Radbourn, 1882	29.6
99	Gus Weyhing, 1892	29.5
100	Henry Porter, 1885	29.5

Relief Games

1	Mike Marshall, 1974	106
2	Kent Tekulve, 1979	94
3	Mike Marshall, 1973	92
4	Kent Tekulve, 1978	91
5	Wayne Granger, 1969	90
	Kent Tekulve, 1987	90
7	Mike Marshall, 1979	89
	Mark Eichhorn, 1987	89
	Julian Tavarez, 1997	89
10	Mike Myers, 1997	88
	Sean Runyan, 1998	88
12	Rob Murphy, 1987	87
13	Wilbur Wood, 1968	86
14	Kent Tekulve, 1982	85
	Frank Williams, 1987	85
16	Ted Abernathy, 1965	84
	Enrique Romo, 1979	84
	Dick Tidrow, 1980	84
	Dan Quisenberry, 1985	84
	Mitch Williams, 1987	84
	Stan Belinda, 1997	84
22	Ken Sanders, 1971	83
	Craig Lefferts, 1986	83
	Eddie Guardado, 1996	83
	Mike Myers, 1996	83
	Steve Kline, 2000	83
	Kelly Wunsch, 2000	83
28	Eddie Fisher, 1965	82
	Bill Campbell, 1983	82
	Juan Agosto, 1990	82
	Paul Quantrill, 1998	82
	Steve Kline, 1999	82
33	John Wyatt, 1964	81
	Dale Murray, 1976	81
	Jeff Robinson, 1987	81
	Duane Ward, 1991	81
	Joe Boever, 1992	81
	Kenny Rogers, 1992	81
	Mike Jackson, 1993	81
	Brad Clontz, 1996	81
	Mike Stanton, 1996	81
	Rod Beck, 1998	81
	Greg Swindell, 1998	81
44	Mudcat Grant, 1970	80
	Pedro Borbon, 1973	80
	Willie Hernandez, 1984	80
	Mitch Williams, 1986	80
	Doug Jones, 1992	80
	Greg Harris, 1993	80
	Turk Wendell, 1999	80

Relief Wins

1	Roy Face, 1959	18
2	John Hiller, 1974	17
	Bill Campbell, 1976	17
4	Jim Konstanty, 1950	16
	Ron Perranoski, 1963	16
	Dick Radatz, 1964	16
	Tom Johnson, 1977	16
8	Mace Brown, 1938	15
	Hoyt Wilhelm, 1952	15
	Luis Arroyo, 1961	15
	Dick Radatz, 1963	15
	Eddie Fisher, 1965	15
	Mike Marshall, 1974	15
	Dale Murray, 1975	15
15	Joe Page, 1947	14
	Joe Black, 1952	14
	Hersh Freeman, 1956	14
	Stu Miller, 1961	14
	Stu Miller, 1965	14
	Phil Regan, 1966	14
	Frank Linzy, 1969	14
	Mike Marshall, 1972	14
	Mike Marshall, 1973	14
	Ron Davis, 1979	14
	Mark Clear, 1982	14
	Jim Slaton, 1983	14
	Roger McDowell, 1986	14
	Mark Eichhorn, 1986	14
29	Dick Tidrow, 1979	13
	Wilcy Moore, 1927	13
	Earl Caldwell, 1946	13
	Clyde Shoun, 1943	13
	Joe Page, 1949	13
	Clyde King, 1951	13
	Lindy McDaniel, 1959	13
	Larry Sherry, 1960	13
	Gerry Staley, 1960	13
	Lindy McDaniel, 1963	13
	Al Hrabosky, 1975	13
	Rollie Fingers, 1976	13
	Bill Campbell, 1977	13
	Sparky Lyle, 1977	13
	Gary Lavelle, 1978	13
	Bob Stanley, 1978	13
	Ron Reed, 1979	13
	Jim Kern, 1979	13
	Aurelio Lopez, 1980	13
	Jesse Orosco, 1983	13
	Rich Gossage, 1983	13
50	32 players tied	12

Relief Losses

1	Gene Garber, 1979	16
2	Darold Knowles, 1970	14
	John Hiller, 1974	14
	Mike Marshall, 1975	14
	Mike Marshall, 1979	14
6	Wilbur Wood, 1970	13
	Rollie Fingers, 1978	13
	Skip Lockwood, 1978	13
9	Roy Face, 1956	12
	Roy Face, 1961	12
	Ken Sanders, 1971	12
	Mike Marshall, 1974	12
	Gene Garber, 1975	12
	Jim Willoughby, 1976	12
	Charlie Hough, 1977	12
	Mike Marshall, 1978	12
	Kent Tekulve, 1980	12
	Ken Howell, 1986	12
	Roger Mason, 1993	12
20	Nels Potter, 1949	11
	Frank Funk, 1961	11
	Dick Radatz, 1965	11
	Frank Linzy, 1966	11
	Wilbur Wood, 1968	11
	Wilbur Wood, 1969	11
	Mike Marshall, 1973	11
	Rollie Fingers, 1976	11
	Rich Gossage, 1978	11
	Dave Heaverlo, 1979	11
	Mark Clear, 1980	11
	Greg Minton, 1983	11
	Ron Davis, 1984	11
	Mark Davis, 1985	11
	Joe Boever, 1989	11
	Jose Paniagua, 1999	11
36	47 players tied	10

Relief Innings Pitched

1	Mike Marshall, 1974	208.1
2	Mike Marshall, 1973	179.0
3	Bob Stanley, 1982	168.1
4	Bill Campbell, 1976	167.2
5	Andy Karl, 1945	166.2
6	Eddie Fisher, 1965	165.1
7	Hoyt Wilhelm, 1952	159.1
8	Dick Radatz, 1964	157.0
	Mark Eichhorn, 1986	157.0
10	Jim Konstanty, 1950	152.0
11	John Hiller, 1974	150.0
12	Tom Johnson, 1977	146.2
13	Garland Braxton, 1927	146.0
14	Bob Stanley, 1983	145.1
15	Hoyt Wilhelm, 1953	145.0
	Wilbur Wood, 1968	145.0
17	Allan Russell, 1923	144.2
	Wayne Granger, 1969	144.2
19	Steve Foucault, 1974	144.1
20	Hoyt Wilhelm, 1965	144.0
21	Jim Kern, 1979	143.0
22	Charlie Hough, 1976	142.2
23	Rich Gossage, 1975	141.2
24	Mike Marshall, 1979	140.2
25	Sammy Stewart, 1983	140.1
	Willie Hernandez, 1984	140.1
27	Bill Campbell, 1977	140.0
28	Jack Lamabe, 1963	139.2
29	Pedro Borbon, 1974	139.0
	Dan Quisenberry, 1983	139.0
31	Lindy McDaniel, 1973	138.1
32	Aurelio Lopez, 1984	137.2
33	Clay Carroll, 1966	137.1
34	Sparky Lyle, 1977	137.0
	Tom Hume, 1980	137.0
36	Dan Quisenberry, 1982	136.2
37	Ted Abernathy, 1965	136.1
	Ken Sanders, 1971	136.1
	Doug Corbett, 1980	136.1
40	Mudcat Grant, 1970	135.1
	Joe Page, 1949	135.1
	Kent Tekulve, 1978	135.1
43	Clay Carroll, 1968	135.0
44	Ted Abernathy, 1968	134.2
	Phil Regan, 1968	134.2
	Rollie Fingers, 1976	134.2
47	Bill Henry, 1959	134.1
	Dick Selma, 1970	134.1
	Rich Gossage, 1978	134.1
	Kent Tekulve, 1979	134.1

Relief Points

1	Bobby Thigpen, 1990	116
2	Dennis Eckersley, 1992	115
3	Trevor Hoffman, 1998	112
4	Randy Myers, 1993	106
5	Rod Beck, 1998	104
6	Lee Smith, 1991	103
7	Dennis Eckersley, 1990	102
	Tom Gordon, 1998	102
9	Rod Beck, 1993	101
	John Wetteland, 1993	101
11	Dave Righetti, 1986	100
12	Jeff Montgomery, 1993	99
13	Jose Mesa, 1995	98
14	Dan Quisenberry, 1983	97
	Dan Quisenberry, 1984	97
	Trevor Hoffman, 1996	97
17	Dennis Eckersley, 1988	96
18	Mariano Rivera, 1999	95
19	Mariano Rivera, 1997	94
	Jeff Shaw, 1998	94
	Antonio Alfonseca, 2000	94
22	Bruce Sutter, 1984	93
	Mark Davis, 1989	93
24	Lee Smith, 1993	92
	Dennis Eckersley, 1991	92
	Bryan Harvey, 1991	92
27	John Hiller, 1973	91
	Doug Jones, 1990	91
	Duane Ward, 1993	91
	Randy Myers, 1997	91
31	Todd Worrell, 1996	90
	Jeff Shaw, 1997	90
	John Wetteland, 1999	90
34	John Wetteland, 1998	89
35	Jeff Brantley, 1996	88
	Ugueth Urbina, 1999	88
	Derek Lowe, 2000	88
38	Steve Bedrosian, 1987	87
	Rick Aguilera, 1991	87
	Bryan Harvey, 1993	87
	John Wetteland, 1996	87
	Robb Nen, 1998	87
	Roberto Hernandez, 1999	87
	Trevor Hoffman, 2000	87
	Robb Nen, 2000	87
46	Doug Jones, 1992	86
	Armando Benitez, 2000	86
48	5 players tied	85

Relief Ranking

Rank	Player	Ranking
1	Jim Kern, 1979	66.5
2	John Hiller, 1973	60.7
3	Rich Gossage, 1977	60.1
4	Roberto Hernandez, 1996	56.2
5	Mark Eichhorn, 1986	55.0
6	Mike Marshall, 1979	53.3
7	Lindy McDaniel, 1960	52.8
8	John Wetteland, 1993	51.5
9	Robb Nen, 1998	51.5
10	Ellis Kinder, 1953	50.9
11	Jesse Orosco, 1983	50.8
12	Donnie Moore, 1985	50.2
13	Sid Monge, 1979	49.4
14	Dennis Eckersley, 1990	47.6
15	Dick Radatz, 1963	47.4
16	Rich Gossage, 1978	46.9
17	Rich Gossage, 1975	46.8
18	Bruce Sutter, 1977	46.3
19	Dick Radatz, 1964	46.2
20	Bob James, 1985	46.2
21	Doug Jones, 1997	46.0
22	Mariano Rivera, 1999	45.9
23	Scott Williamson, 1999	45.8
24	Ugueth Urbina, 1998	45.1
25	Sparky Lyle, 1977	45.1
26	Dan Quisenberry, 1985	44.6
27	Jose Mesa, 1995	44.6
28	Mike Marshall, 1972	44.4
29	Robb Nen, 2000	43.9
30	Luis Arroyo, 1961	43.6
31	Al Hrabosky, 1975	43.6
32	Danny Graves, 2000	43.6
33	Doug Corbett, 1980	43.5
34	Dan Spillner, 1982	43.2
35	Tom Murphy, 1974	43.1
36	Jeff Montgomery, 1993	42.6
37	Trevor Hoffman, 1998	42.6
38	Bruce Sutter, 1984	42.2
39	Mariano Rivera, 1997	42.0
40	Joe Page, 1949	41.8
41	Ken Sanders, 1971	41.7
42	Bill Campbell, 1977	41.6
43	Roy Face, 1962	41.6
44	Hoyt Wilhelm, 1964	41.6
45	Stu Miller, 1965	41.4
46	Lee Smith, 1983	41.0
47	Ron Perranoski, 1969	40.9
48	Derek Lowe, 2000	40.8
49	Billy Koch, 2000	40.6
50	Rollie Fingers, 1981	40.6

Relievers' Runs

1	Mark Eichhorn, 1986	43.0
2	Jim Kern, 1979	42.2
3	Mariano Rivera, 1996	34.8
4	Rich Gossage, 1977	33.8
5	John Hiller, 1973	33.2
6	Dan Quisenberry, 1983	33.0
7	Willie Hernandez, 1984	32.3
8	Doug Corbett, 1980	31.2
9	Keith Foulke, 1999	31.0
10	Bruce Sutter, 1977	30.7
11	Rich Gossage, 1975	30.6
12	Tim Burke, 1987	29.3
13	Wilcy Moore, 1927	29.2
14	Roberto Hernandez, 1996	29.0
15	Sparky Lyle, 1977	29.0
16	Lindy McDaniel, 1960	28.6
17	Bob Lee, 1964	28.4
18	Mudcat Grant, 1970	28.4
19	Garland Braxton, 1927	28.2
20	Mike Marshall, 1974	28.0
21	Bruce Sutter, 1984	28.0
22	Derek Lowe, 1999	27.2
23	Dennis Eckersley, 1990	26.9
24	Robb Nen, 1998	26.7
25	Sid Monge, 1979	26.6
26	Jesse Orosco, 1983	26.5
27	Rich Gossage, 1978	26.4
28	Hoyt Wilhelm, 1965	26.3
29	Jeff Montgomery, 1989	25.8
30	Phil Regan, 1966	25.8
31	Aurelio Lopez, 1979	25.7
32	Paul Quantrill, 1997	25.7
33	Jose Mesa, 1995	25.6
34	Ellis Kinder, 1953	25.5
35	Donnie Moore, 1985	25.5
36	Dan Quisenberry, 1985	25.5
37	John Wetteland, 1993	25.4
38	Ellis Kinder, 1951	25.1
39	Jim Konstanty, 1950	25.0
40	Sparky Lyle, 1974	24.9
41	Billy Wagner, 1999	24.9
42	Ted Abernathy, 1967	24.9
43	Mike Marshall, 1979	24.9
44	Bob James, 1985	24.7
45	Gary Lavelle, 1977	24.5
46	Jeff Zimmerman, 1999	24.5
47	Rollie Fingers, 1973	24.5
48	Dick Radatz, 1963	24.4
49	Hoyt Wilhelm, 1954	24.4
50	Greg Minton, 1982	24.3

Adjusted Relievers' Runs

1	Mark Eichhorn, 1986	43.3
2	Jim Kern, 1979	41.8
3	John Hiller, 1973	34.6
4	Mariano Rivera, 1996	34.5
5	Rich Gossage, 1977	34.3
6	Doug Corbett, 1980	33.5
7	Dan Quisenberry, 1983	33.0
8	Bruce Sutter, 1977	32.4
9	Willie Hernandez, 1984	31.8
10	Rich Gossage, 1975	31.3
11	Keith Foulke, 1999	31.1
12	Lindy McDaniel, 1960	29.8
13	Tim Burke, 1987	29.7
14	Roberto Hernandez, 1996	28.1
15	Sparky Lyle, 1977	28.0
16	Derek Lowe, 1999	27.9
17	Wilcy Moore, 1927	27.3
18	Bruce Sutter, 1984	27.3
19	Ellis Kinder, 1951	27.1
20	Mudcat Grant, 1970	27.0
21	Sid Monge, 1979	26.9
22	Bob Lee, 1964	26.8
23	Dennis Eckersley, 1990	26.7
24	Mike Marshall, 1979	26.7
25	Ellis Kinder, 1953	26.6
26	Aurelio Lopez, 1979	26.6
27	Jesse Orosco, 1983	26.5
28	Ted Abernathy, 1967	26.4
29	Paul Quantrill, 1997	25.8
30	John Wetteland, 1993	25.8
31	Bob James, 1985	25.7
32	Robb Nen, 1998	25.7
33	Jeff Montgomery, 1989	25.7
34	Dick Radatz, 1964	25.6
35	Dan Quisenberry, 1985	25.6
36	Dick Radatz, 1963	25.6
37	Jose Mesa, 1995	25.5
38	Jeff Zimmerman, 1999	25.4
39	Donnie Moore, 1985	25.3
40	Rich Gossage, 1978	25.2
41	Dick Radatz, 1962	25.2
42	Derek Lowe, 2000	24.8
43	Gary Lavelle, 1977	24.5
44	Mike Marshall, 1974	24.5
45	Billy Wagner, 1999	24.4
46	Sparky Lyle, 1974	24.4
47	Greg Minton, 1982	24.3
48	Hoyt Wilhelm, 1954	24.1
49	Jim Konstanty, 1950	23.9
50	Hoyt Wilhelm, 1965	23.9

Percent of Team Wins (by era)

1876-1892

1	Will White, 1879	100.0
	Bobby Mathews, 1876	100.0
	Jim Devlin, 1877	100.0
	Jim Devlin, 1876	100.0
	George Bradley, 1876	100.0
6	Tommy Bond, 1878	97.6
7	Terry Larkin, 1878	96.7
8	Jim McCormick, 1880	95.7
9	Tommy Bond, 1877	95.2
10	Terry Larkin, 1877	93.5
11	Al Spalding, 1876	90.4
	Jim Galvin, 1883	88.5
13	Will White, 1880	85.7
	Jim McCormick, 1882	85.7
15	Mickey Welch, 1880	82.9

1893-1919

1	Ted Breitenstein, 1895	48.7
2	Amos Rusie, 1893	48.5
3	Ted Breitenstein, 1894	48.2
4	Cy Young, 1893	46.6
5	Ed Walsh, 1908	45.5
	Frank Killen, 1896	45.5
7	Ted Breitenstein, 1896	45.0
8	Jack Chesbro, 1904	44.6
9	Frank Killen, 1893	44.4
10	Pink Hawley, 1895	43.7
11	Win Mercer, 1896	43.1
12	Noodles Hahn, 1901	42.3
13	Cy Young, 1901	41.8
14	Cy Young, 1895	41.6
15	Cy Young, 1902	41.6

1920-1941

1	Eddie Rommel, 1922	41.5
2	Red Faber, 1921	40.3
3	Buck Newsom, 1938	36.4
4	Jimmy Ring, 1923	36.0
	Pete Alexander, 1920	36.0
6	Ted Lyons, 1930	35.5
7	Curt Davis, 1934	33.9
8	Urban Shocker, 1921	33.3
	Bob Feller, 1941	33.3
	Ed Morris, 1928	33.3
11	Howard Ehmke, 1923	32.8
12	Dazzy Vance, 1925	32.4
	Paul Derringer, 1935	32.4
14	Wes Ferrell, 1935	32.1
15	George Uhle, 1923	31.7

1942-1960

1	Ned Garver, 1951	38.5
2	Bob Feller, 1946	38.2
3	Murry Dickson, 1952	33.3
4	Robin Roberts, 1952	32.2
5	Bill Voiselle, 1944	31.3
6	Murry Dickson, 1951	31.3
7	Phil Marchildon, 1942	30.9
8	Dizzy Trout, 1944	30.7
9	Robin Roberts, 1954	30.7
10	Bobby Shantz, 1952	30.4
11	Ewell Blackwell, 1947	30.1
12	Robin Roberts, 1955	29.9
13	Johnny Antonelli, 1956	29.9
14	Dave Ferriss, 1945	29.6
15	2 players tied	29.0

1961-1976

1	Steve Carlton, 1972	45.8
2	Gaylord Perry, 1972	33.3
3	Nolan Ryan, 1974	32.4
4	Larry Jackson, 1964	31.6
5	Wilbur Wood, 1973	31.2
6	Bob Gibson, 1970	30.3
7	Randy Jones, 1976	30.1
8	Denny McLain, 1968	30.1
9	Fergie Jenkins, 1974	29.8
10	Juan Marichal, 1968	29.5
11	Sam McDowell, 1969	29.0
12	Fergie Jenkins, 1971	28.9
13	Steve Busby, 1974	28.6
14	Sandy Koufax, 1966	28.4
15	Juan Marichal, 1963	28.4

1977-2000

1	Phil Niekro, 1979	31.8
2	Dave Stieb, 1981	29.7
3	Brad Radke, 1997	29.4
4	Fernando Valenzuela, 1986	28.8
5	Roger Clemens, 1997	27.6
6	Phil Niekro, 1978	27.5
7	Kevin Brown, 1992	27.3
8	Pat Hentgen, 1996	27.0
9	Mike Mussina, 1995	26.8
10	Randy Johnson, 1994	26.5
11	Mike Norris, 1980	26.5
12	Danny Jackson, 1988	26.4
13	Steve Carlton, 1980	26.4
	Frank Viola, 1988	26.4
15	Ross Grimsley, 1978	26.3

Clutch Pitching Index

1	Doc White, 1904	152.8
2	Mordecai Brown, 1903	152.7
3	Ned Garvin, 1904	152.6
4	Jim McCormick, 1878	152.3
5	Max Lanier, 1943	150.8
6	Pete Schneider, 1917	145.4
7	Sammy Stewart, 1981	145.0
8	Ed Killian, 1907	144.4
9	Carl Lundgren, 1902	144.2
10	Bill Burns, 1909	142.4
11	Cy Morgan, 1910	142.2
12	Ed Summers, 1908	142.1
13	Andy Coakley, 1905	141.7
	Fred Olmstead, 1910	141.7
15	Ben Tincup, 1914	141.6
16	Dick Rudolph, 1919	141.2
17	Sherry Smith, 1919	141.1
18	Fred Blanding, 1913	140.8
19	Charlie Hodnett, 1884	140.3
20	Ed Poole, 1902	139.9
21	Ed Willett, 1908	139.6
22	Bert Humphries, 1915	139.5
23	Doug Rau, 1976	139.4
24	Sloppy Thurston, 1923	139.0
25	Vic Willis, 1906	138.7
	Al Benton, 1945	138.7
	Al Brazle, 1947	138.7
28	Dummy Taylor, 1902	138.4
29	Allan Anderson, 1988	138.3
30	Mark Baldwin, 1888	137.4
31	Al Maul, 1895	136.9
32	Bob Rhoads, 1908	136.8
33	Chuck Finley, 1990	136.6
34	Mike Sullivan, 1892	136.2
	Spud Chandler, 1942	136.2
36	Mal Eason, 1902	135.9
	Red Faber, 1917	135.9
38	King Cole, 1910	135.8
39	Clark Griffith, 1898	135.4
40	John Tudor, 1988	135.1
41	Bob Buhl, 1957	134.8
42	Doug Rau, 1978	134.6
43	Stu Miller, 1959	134.4
44	Ken Chase, 1940	134.2
	Dutch Leonard, 1948	134.2
46	Andy Coakley, 1908	134.1
	Mike Marshall, 1973	134.1
48	Ed Siever, 1904	133.9
	Joe McGinnity, 1908	133.9
50	Win Mercer, 1894	133.7
51	Ned Garvin, 1902	133.5
52	Mike Hampton, 1998	133.2
53	Joe Horlen, 1968	133.1
54	Art Nehf, 1928	133.0
55	Eddie Plank, 1911	132.8
56	Charlie Chech, 1905	132.7
57	Andy Coakley, 1907	132.6
58	Gene Bearden, 1948	132.3
	Hoyt Wilhelm, 1959	132.3
60	Stan Baumgartner, 1924	132.1
	Jim Abbott, 1992	132.1
62	Ed Killian, 1909	131.9
	Bump Hadley, 1939	131.9
64	Lew Brockett, 1909	131.8
65	Win Mercer, 1897	131.6
	Jose DeLeon, 1991	131.6
67	Steve Blass, 1972	131.5
68	Chick Fraser, 1900	131.2
69	Rick Honeycutt, 1983	131.1
	Don Schwall, 1961	131.1
71	Mike O'Neill, 1904	131.0
72	Ted Lyons, 1942	130.9
	Bobby Shantz, 1957	130.9
	Bill Lee, 1978	130.9
	Pete Vuckovich, 1982	130.9
	Bill Swift, 1992	130.9
77	Tony Mullane, 1890	130.7
78	Lon Warneke, 1933	130.6
79	John Cerutti, 1989	130.5
	Bill Krueger, 1991	130.5
81	Bill Bernhard, 1904	130.4
82	Hal McKain, 1929	130.3
83	Larry Pape, 1911	130.2
	Hi Bithorn, 1942	130.2
85	Vean Gregg, 1913	130.0
	Wilson Alvarez, 1993	130.0
87	Brickyard Kennedy, 1899	129.9
	Rollie Naylor, 1920	129.9
89	Larry McWilliams, 1984	129.8
90	Earl Moore, 1911	129.6
	Ruben Gomez, 1954	129.6
92	Jim Galvin, 1886	129.5
93	Lefty Weinert, 1922	129.4
94	Harry Moran, 1915	129.3
	Ned Garver, 1948	129.3
	John Denny, 1976	129.3
	Geoff Zahn, 1978	129.3
98	4 players tied	129.2

Pitcher Batting Runs

1	Guy Hecker, 1884	27.5
2	Bob Caruthers, 1886	23.4
3	Jim Whitney, 1882	22.2
4	Don Drysdale, 1965	21.6
5	Wes Ferrell, 1935	20.2
6	Don Newcombe, 1955	19.6
7	Guy Hecker, 1886	18.4
8	Jim Whitney, 1883	17.7
9	Schoolboy Rowe, 1943	17.4
10	Warren Spahn, 1958	17.4
11	Charlie Ferguson, 1885	17.1
12	Wes Ferrell, 1931	16.9
13	Babe Ruth, 1917	16.5
14	Scott Stratton, 1890	16.5
15	George Uhle, 1923	16.4
16	Red Ruffing, 1930	16.4
17	Walter Johnson, 1925	16.2
18	Tony Mullane, 1884	16.2
19	Bob Lemon, 1950	16.1
20	Bob Caruthers, 1887	15.8
21	Bob Caruthers, 1889	15.7
22	Red Lucas, 1930	15.4
23	Bob Lemon, 1949	15.0
24	Jack Bentley, 1923	15.0
25	Babe Ruth, 1915	15.0
26	John Ward, 1879	15.0
27	Claude Hendrix, 1912	14.8
28	Don Newcombe, 1959	14.7
29	Red Ruffing, 1936	14.3
30	Jim Tobin, 1942	14.3
31	Red Lucas, 1932	14.2
32	Frank Killen, 1893	14.1
33	Robin Roberts, 1955	13.9
34	Jack Stivetts, 1892	13.8
35	Pete Conway, 1888	13.8
36	Pink Hawley, 1895	13.6
37	Charlie Ferguson, 1887	13.4
38	Scott Stratton, 1888	13.4
39	Red Ruffing, 1932	13.2
40	Jack Coombs, 1911	13.1
41	Clark Griffith, 1901	13.1
42	Jack Stivetts, 1890	13.1
43	Joe Bush, 1924	13.1
44	Babe Ruth, 1916	13.0
45	Adonis Terry, 1890	13.0
46	Schoolboy Rowe, 1935	12.9
47	Bob Lemon, 1948	12.9
48	Red Ruffing, 1935	12.9
49	Elam Vangilder, 1922	12.9
50	Dave Foutz, 1887	12.9
51	Terry Larkin, 1878	12.8
52	Red Lucas, 1933	12.7
53	Bucky Walters, 1939	12.7
54	Red Ruffing, 1928	12.4
55	Catfish Hunter, 1971	12.3
56	Ad Gumbert, 1891	12.2
57	Johnny Sain, 1947	12.0
58	Joe Bowman, 1939	12.0
59	Bob Gibson, 1970	11.9
60	Jouett Meekin, 1896	11.8
61	Doc Crandall, 1915	11.8
62	Babe Ruth, 1918	11.7
63	Cy Young, 1903	11.7
64	George Mullin, 1904	11.7
65	Curt Davis, 1939	11.6
66	Red Lucas, 1931	11.6
67	Jim Whitney, 1881	11.5
68	Charley Radbourn, 1883	11.5
69	Tim Keefe, 1884	11.4
70	Billy Taylor, 1884	11.4
71	Wes Ferrell, 1936	11.3
72	Red Lucas, 1929	11.3
73	Jim Whitney, 1887	11.3
74	Erv Brame, 1929	11.3
75	Dizzy Trout, 1944	11.3
76	Adonis Terry, 1889	11.2
77	Schoolboy Rowe, 1934	11.2
78	Dutch Ruether, 1921	11.2
79	Frank Foreman, 1891	11.1
80	Charlie Ferguson, 1886	11.1
81	Jack Stivetts, 1896	11.1
82	Ad Gumbert, 1895	11.1
83	Guy Hecker, 1883	11.0
84	Blue Moon Odom, 1969	10.9
85	Red Ruffing, 1941	10.9
86	Bob Caruthers, 1891	10.9
87	Jack Scott, 1921	10.9
88	Charlie Buffinton, 1884	10.8
89	Ben Sanders, 1892	10.8
90	Guy Hecker, 1887	10.8
91	Scott Stratton, 1892	10.8
92	Carl Mays, 1921	10.7
93	Erv Brame, 1930	10.7
94	Ken Brett, 1974	10.7
95	Dave Ferriss, 1945	10.6
96	Mike Hampton, 1999	10.6
97	Tony Mullane, 1882	10.5
98	Claude Hendrix, 1915	10.5
99	Al Maul, 1893	10.5
100	George Van Haltren, 1888	10.4

Pitcher Fielding Runs

1	Ed Walsh, 1907	21.7
2	Harry Howell, 1905	17.8
3	Ed Walsh, 1911	14.6
4	Ed Walsh, 1908	13.6
5	Will White, 1882	12.9
6	John Clarkson, 1889	11.3
7	Tony Mullane, 1882	10.7
	Sadie McMahon, 1890	10.7
9	Carl Mays, 1926	10.1
10	Frank Smith, 1909	10.0
11	Tommy Bond, 1880	9.8
	Greg Maddux, 1996	9.8
13	Mike Morrison, 1887	9.7
	Ed Walsh, 1910	9.7
15	Tony Mullane, 1884	9.6
	Christy Mathewson, 1908	9.6
17	Matt Kilroy, 1887	9.5
	Charlie Buffinton, 1888	9.5
19	Harry Howell, 1904	9.4
20	Ed Scott, 1900	9.1
	Elmer Stricklett, 1906	9.1
	Carl Mays, 1916	9.1
	Carl Mays, 1918	9.1
	Curt Davis, 1934	9.1
25	John Clarkson, 1887	9.0
	Elmer Stricklett, 1905	9.0
27	Hooks Dauss, 1915	8.9
28	Addie Joss, 1907	8.7
29	Gene Packard, 1914	8.6
30	Park Swartzel, 1889	8.5
	Bucky Walters, 1936	8.5
32	Jack Taylor, 1898	8.4
	Hooks Dauss, 1920	8.4
	Wilcy Moore, 1927	8.4
	Bob Lemon, 1948	8.4
	Greg Maddux, 2000	8.4
37	Cy Seymour, 1898	8.3
	Harry Howell, 1907	8.3
	Randy Jones, 1976	8.3
40	Burleigh Grimes, 1925	8.2
41	Matt Kilroy, 1889	8.1
	Cy Seymour, 1897	8.1
	George Mullin, 1904	8.1
	Carl Mays, 1924	8.1
	Eddie Rommel, 1924	8.1
46	Cy Young, 1895	8.0
	Fred Newman, 1965	8.0
48	Cy Young, 1896	7.9
	Nick Altrock, 1905	7.9
	Bob Lemon, 1953	7.9
	Mel Stottlemyre, 1969	7.9
52	Jim Galvin, 1887	7.8
	Carl Mays, 1917	7.8
	Freddie Fitzsimmons, 1931	7.8
	Harry Gumbert, 1938	7.8
	John Denny, 1978	7.8
57	John Clarkson, 1885	7.7
	Amos Rusie, 1894	7.7
	Joe Wood, 1912	7.7
	Mel Harder, 1933	7.7
	Harry Gumbert, 1937	7.7
	Russ Christopher, 1943	7.7
63	Larry McKeon, 1884	7.6
	Ed Walsh, 1906	7.6
65	Willie Sudhoff, 1898	7.5
	Christy Mathewson, 1901	7.5
	Ned Garvin, 1903	7.5
	Harry Howell, 1906	7.5
	Jean Dubuc, 1913	7.5
	Greg Maddux, 1990	7.5
71	Christy Mathewson, 1911	7.4
	Carl Hubbell, 1933	7.4
	Greg Maddux, 1998	7.4
74	Tommy Bond, 1879	7.3
	Charlie Buffinton, 1887	7.3
	Bob Caruthers, 1887	7.3
	Bill Doak, 1915	7.3
78	Jim Galvin, 1881	7.2
	Russ Christopher, 1945	7.2
80	Jim Galvin, 1884	7.1
	George Mullin, 1905	7.1
	Ed Walsh, 1912	7.1
	Eddie Cicotte, 1913	7.1
	Harry Coveleski, 1914	7.1
	Kenny Rogers, 1998	7.1
86	Kenny Rogers, 1999	7.0
	Doc White, 1908	7.0
	Red Ames, 1909	7.0
	Hal Schumacher, 1935	7.0
90	Guy Hecker, 1884	6.9
	Dave Foutz, 1885	6.9
	Red Donahue, 1902	6.9
	Elmer Stricklett, 1907	6.9
	Lefty Tyler, 1913	6.9
	Gene Krapp, 1915	6.9
	Larry Jackson, 1964	6.9
	Greg Maddux, 1999	6.9
98	9 players tied	6.8

Total Pitcher Index

1	Guy Hecker, 1884	13.1
2	Amos Rusie, 1894	11.1
	Walter Johnson, 1912	11.1
4	Walter Johnson, 1913	10.8
5	Silver King, 1888	10.6
6	Charley Radbourn, 1884	10.4
7	Christy Mathewson, 1905	9.9
8	John Clarkson, 1889	9.8
9	Scott Stratton, 1890	9.0
10	Dizzy Trout, 1944	8.8
11	Grover Alexander, 1915	8.7
12	Cy Young, 1901	8.6
	Bucky Walters, 1939	8.6
14	Charley Radbourn, 1883	8.5
	Pedro Martinez, 2000	8.5
16	Ed Walsh, 1908	8.4
	Joe Wood, 1912	8.4
	Lefty Grove, 1931	8.4
19	John Clarkson, 1885	8.2
20	Dave Foutz, 1886	8.1
	Pedro Martinez, 1999	8.1
22	Roger Clemens, 1997	8.0
23	Pink Hawley, 1895	7.8
	Walter Johnson, 1918	7.8
	Carl Hubbell, 1933	7.8
26	Walter Johnson, 1915	7.7
	Dolf Luque, 1923	7.7
28	John Clarkson, 1887	7.6
	Matt Kilroy, 1887	7.6
	Bob Gibson, 1968	7.6
	Dwight Gooden, 1985	7.6
	Kevin Brown, 1996	7.6
33	Hal Newhouser, 1945	7.5
34	Will White, 1882	7.4
	Tony Mullane, 1884	7.4
	Ed Walsh, 1910	7.4
37	Grover Alexander, 1916	7.3
	Warren Spahn, 1953	7.3
	Greg Maddux, 1994	7.3
40	Amos Rusie, 1893	7.2
	Christy Mathewson, 1908	7.2
	Walter Johnson, 1919	7.2
	Lefty Grove, 1930	7.2
44	Christy Mathewson, 1909	7.1
	Walter Johnson, 1914	7.1
	Red Faber, 1921	7.1
	Steve Carlton, 1972	7.1
	Greg Maddux, 1998	7.1
49	Amos Rusie, 1890	7.0
	Kid Nichols, 1897	7.0
	Grover Alexander, 1920	7.0
	Dazzy Vance, 1928	7.0
	Bob Lemon, 1948	7.0
54	Silver King, 1890	6.9
	Jack Stivetts, 1891	6.9
56	Will White, 1883	6.8
	Bob Caruthers, 1886	6.8
	Matt Kilroy, 1889	6.8
	Mordecai Brown, 1906	6.8
	Ed Walsh, 1912	6.8
	Curt Davis, 1934	6.8
	Wes Ferrell, 1935	6.8
	Hal Newhouser, 1946	6.8
	Jim Kern, 1979	6.8
65	Charlie Sweeney, 1884	6.7
	Guy Hecker, 1885	6.7
	Cy Young, 1895	6.7
	Kid Nichols, 1898	6.7
	Jack Taylor, 1902	6.7
	Jack Chesbro, 1904	6.7
	Ed Walsh, 1907	6.7
	Christy Mathewson, 1911	6.7
	Dazzy Vance, 1930	6.7
	Lefty Gomez, 1937	6.7
	Thornton Lee, 1941	6.7
	Gaylord Perry, 1972	6.7
	Greg Maddux, 1995	6.7
78	Jesse Duryea, 1889	6.6
	Joe Wood, 1911	6.6
	Lefty Grove, 1936	6.6
	Tom Seaver, 1971	6.6
	John Hiller, 1973	6.6
83	Tim Keefe, 1883	6.5
	Bob Caruthers, 1885	6.5
	Charlie Ferguson, 1886	6.5
	Billy Rhines, 1890	6.5
	Walter Johnson, 1911	6.5
	Ron Guidry, 1978	6.5
	Roger Clemens, 1990	6.5
90	Jim Galvin, 1884	6.4
	Cy Young, 1892	6.4
	Kid Nichols, 1896	6.4
	Ed Walsh, 1911	6.4
	Mel Harder, 1934	6.4
	Bob Feller, 1940	6.4
	Wilbur Wood, 1971	6.4
97	8 players tied	6.3

Total Pitcher Index (alpha.)

Grover Alexander, 1915	8.7
Grover Alexander, 1916	7.3
Grover Alexander, 1920	7.0
Mordecai Brown, 1906	6.8
Kevin Brown, 1996	7.6
Steve Carlton, 1972	7.1
Bob Caruthers, 1885	6.5
Bob Caruthers, 1886	6.8
Jack Chesbro, 1904	6.7
John Clarkson, 1885	8.2
John Clarkson, 1887	7.6
John Clarkson, 1889	9.8
Roger Clemens, 1990	6.5
Roger Clemens, 1997	8.0
Curt Davis, 1934	6.8
Jesse Duryea, 1889	6.6
Red Faber, 1921	7.1
Bob Feller, 1940	6.4
Charlie Ferguson, 1886	6.5
Wes Ferrell, 1935	6.8
Dave Foutz, 1886	8.1
Jim Galvin, 1884	6.4
Bob Gibson, 1968	7.6
Lefty Gomez, 1937	6.7
Dwight Gooden, 1985	7.6
Lefty Grove, 1930	7.2
Lefty Grove, 1931	8.4
Lefty Grove, 1936	6.6
Ron Guidry, 1978	6.5
Mel Harder, 1934	6.4
Pink Hawley, 1895	7.8
Guy Hecker, 1884	13.1
Guy Hecker, 1885	6.7
John Hiller, 1973	6.6
Carl Hubbell, 1933	7.8
Walter Johnson, 1911	6.5
Walter Johnson, 1912	11.1
Walter Johnson, 1913	10.8
Walter Johnson, 1914	7.1
Walter Johnson, 1915	7.7
Walter Johnson, 1918	7.8
Walter Johnson, 1919	7.2
Tim Keefe, 1883	6.5
Jim Kern, 1979	6.8
Matt Kilroy, 1887	7.6
Matt Kilroy, 1889	6.8
Silver King, 1888	10.6
Silver King, 1890	6.9
Thornton Lee, 1941	6.7
Bob Lemon, 1948	7.0
Dolf Luque, 1923	7.7
Greg Maddux, 1994	7.3
Greg Maddux, 1995	6.7
Greg Maddux, 1998	7.1
Pedro Martinez, 1999	8.1
Pedro Martinez, 2000	8.5
Christy Mathewson, 1905	9.9
Christy Mathewson, 1908	7.2
Christy Mathewson, 1909	7.1
Christy Mathewson, 1911	6.7
Tony Mullane, 1884	7.4
Hal Newhouser, 1945	7.5
Hal Newhouser, 1946	6.8
Kid Nichols, 1896	6.4
Kid Nichols, 1897	7.0
Kid Nichols, 1898	6.7
Gaylord Perry, 1972	6.7
Charley Radbourn, 1883	8.5
Charley Radbourn, 1884	10.4
Billy Rhines, 1890	6.5
Amos Rusie, 1890	7.0
Amos Rusie, 1893	7.2
Amos Rusie, 1894	11.1
Tom Seaver, 1971	6.6
Warren Spahn, 1953	7.3
Jack Stivetts, 1891	6.9
Scott Stratton, 1890	9.0
Charlie Sweeney, 1884	6.7
Jack Taylor, 1902	6.7
Dizzy Trout, 1944	8.8
Dazzy Vance, 1928	7.0
Dazzy Vance, 1930	6.7
Ed Walsh, 1907	6.7
Ed Walsh, 1908	8.4
Ed Walsh, 1910	7.4
Ed Walsh, 1911	6.4
Ed Walsh, 1912	6.8
Bucky Walters, 1939	8.6
Will White, 1882	7.4
Will White, 1883	6.8
Joe Wood, 1911	6.6
Joe Wood, 1912	8.4
Wilbur Wood, 1971	6.4
Cy Young, 1892	6.4
Cy Young, 1895	6.7
Cy Young, 1901	8.6

Total Pitcher Index (by era)

1876-1892

1	Guy Hecker, 1884	13.1
2	Silver King, 1888	10.6
3	Charley Radbourn, 1884	10.4
4	John Clarkson, 1889	9.8
5	Scott Stratton, 1890	9.0
6	Charley Radbourn, 1883	8.5
7	John Clarkson, 1885	8.2
8	Dave Foutz, 1886	8.1
9	John Clarkson, 1887	7.6
	Matt Kilroy, 1887	7.6
11	Will White, 1882	7.4
	Tony Mullane, 1884	7.4
13	Amos Rusie, 1890	7.0
14	Silver King, 1890	6.9
	Jack Stivetts, 1891	6.9

1893-1919

1	Amos Rusie, 1894	11.1
	Walter Johnson, 1912	11.1
3	Walter Johnson, 1913	10.8
4	Christy Mathewson, 1905	9.9
5	Grover Alexander, 1915	8.7
6	Cy Young, 1901	8.6
7	Ed Walsh, 1908	8.4
	Joe Wood, 1912	8.4
9	Pink Hawley, 1895	7.8
	Walter Johnson, 1918	7.8
11	Walter Johnson, 1915	7.7
12	Ed Walsh, 1910	7.4
13	Grover Alexander, 1916	7.3
14	3 players tied	7.2

1920-1941

1	Bucky Walters, 1939	8.6
2	Lefty Grove, 1931	8.4
3	Carl Hubbell, 1933	7.8
4	Dolf Luque, 1923	7.7
5	Lefty Grove, 1930	7.2
6	Red Faber, 1921	7.1
7	Grover Alexander, 1920	7.0
	Dazzy Vance, 1928	7.0
9	Curt Davis, 1934	6.8
	Wes Ferrell, 1935	6.8
11	Dazzy Vance, 1930	6.7
	Lefty Gomez, 1937	6.7
	Thornton Lee, 1941	6.7
14	Lefty Grove, 1936	6.6
15	2 players tied	6.4

1942-1960

1	Dizzy Trout, 1944	8.8
2	Hal Newhouser, 1945	7.5
3	Warren Spahn, 1953	7.3
4	Bob Lemon, 1948	7.0
5	Hal Newhouser, 1946	6.8
6	Hal Newhouser, 1944	6.2
	Robin Roberts, 1953	6.2
8	Johnny Sain, 1946	5.9
9	Spud Chandler, 1943	5.8
	Gene Bearden, 1948	5.8
	Bob Lemon, 1949	5.8
12	Ellis Kinder, 1953	5.6
13	Johnny Antonelli, 1954	5.5
14	Johnny Sain, 1948	5.4
15	6 players tied	5.3

1961-1976

1	Bob Gibson, 1968	7.6
2	Steve Carlton, 1972	7.1
3	Gaylord Perry, 1972	6.7
4	Tom Seaver, 1971	6.6
	John Hiller, 1973	6.6
6	Wilbur Wood, 1971	6.4
7	Bob Gibson, 1969	6.1
	Jim Palmer, 1975	6.1
9	Sandy Koufax, 1966	6.0
10	Juan Marichal, 1965	5.9
11	Fergie Jenkins, 1971	5.8
12	Juan Marichal, 1966	5.7
13	Juan Marichal, 1969	5.6
14	4 players tied	5.5

1977-2000

1	Pedro Martinez, 2000	8.5
2	Pedro Martinez, 1999	8.1
3	Roger Clemens, 1997	8.0
4	Dwight Gooden, 1985	7.6
	Kevin Brown, 1996	7.6
6	Greg Maddux, 1994	7.3
7	Greg Maddux, 1998	7.1
8	Jim Kern, 1979	6.8
9	Greg Maddux, 1995	6.7
10	Ron Guidry, 1978	6.5
	Roger Clemens, 1990	6.5
12	Rich Gossage, 1977	6.3
	Pedro Martinez, 1997	6.3
14	Greg Maddux, 1992	6.1
	Greg Maddux, 1993	6.1

Total Baseball Ranking

1	Guy Hecker, 1884	13.1
2	Amos Rusie, 1894	11.1
	Walter Johnson, 1912	11.1
4	Walter Johnson, 1913	10.8
	Babe Ruth, 1923	10.8
6	Silver King, 1888	10.6
7	Charley Radbourn, 1884	10.4
8	Christy Mathewson, 1905	9.9
9	John Clarkson, 1889	9.8
10	Babe Ruth, 1921	9.6
11	Cal Ripken, 1984	9.3
12	Babe Ruth, 1920	9.1
	Rogers Hornsby, 1924	9.1
14	Scott Stratton, 1890	9.0
	Babe Ruth, 1927	9.0
16	Barry Bonds, 1992	8.9
17	Dizzy Trout, 1944	8.8
	Nap Lajoie, 1910	8.8
19	Grover Alexander, 1915	8.7
	Rogers Hornsby, 1922	8.7
	Mickey Mantle, 1956	8.7
	Mickey Mantle, 1957	8.7
	Barry Bonds, 1993	8.7
24	Cy Young, 1901	8.6
	Bucky Walters, 1939	8.6
	Babe Ruth, 1924	8.6
27	Charley Radbourn, 1883	8.5
	Pedro Martinez, 2000	8.5
	Nap Lajoie, 1901	8.5
30	Ed Walsh, 1908	8.4
	Joe Wood, 1912	8.4
	Lefty Grove, 1931	8.4
	Nap Lajoie, 1906	8.4
	Babe Ruth, 1926	8.4
35	Ty Cobb, 1917	8.3
	Lou Gehrig, 1927	8.3
	Mickey Mantle, 1961	8.3
	Cal Ripken, 1991	8.3
	Barry Bonds, 1996	8.3
40	John Clarkson, 1885	8.2
41	Dave Foutz, 1886	8.1
	Pedro Martinez, 1999	8.1
	Nap Lajoie, 1903	8.1
	Nap Lajoie, 1908	8.1
	Rogers Hornsby, 1920	8.1
46	Roger Clemens, 1997	8.0
	Rogers Hornsby, 1917	8.0
	Ted Williams, 1941	8.0
	Ted Williams, 1942	8.0
	Craig Biggio, 1997	8.0
51	Ron Santo, 1966	7.9
	Rickey Henderson, 1990	7.9
53	Pink Hawley, 1895	7.8
	Walter Johnson, 1918	7.8
	Carl Hubbell, 1933	7.8
	George Sisler, 1920	7.8
	Lou Boudreau, 1944	7.8
58	Walter Johnson, 1915	7.7
	Dolf Luque, 1923	7.7
	Lou Gehrig, 1934	7.7
	Alex Rodriguez, 2000	7.7
62	John Clarkson, 1887	7.6
	Matt Kilroy, 1887	7.6
	Bob Gibson, 1968	7.6
	Dwight Gooden, 1985	7.6
	Kevin Brown, 1996	7.6
	Tris Speaker, 1914	7.6
	Lou Gehrig, 1930	7.6
	Willie Mays, 1955	7.6
	Jeff Bagwell, 1994	7.6
	Mike Piazza, 1997	7.6
72	Hal Newhouser, 1945	7.5
	Honus Wagner, 1905	7.5
	Eddie Collins, 1910	7.5
	Ted Williams, 1946	7.5
	Norm Cash, 1961	7.5
	Willie Mays, 1965	7.5
	Ron Santo, 1967	7.5
	Barry Bonds, 1998	7.5
80	Will White, 1882	7.4
	Tony Mullane, 1884	7.4
	Ed Walsh, 1910	7.4
	Honus Wagner, 1906	7.4
	Tris Speaker, 1912	7.4
	Rogers Hornsby, 1921	7.4
	Babe Ruth, 1930	7.4
	Babe Ruth, 1931	7.4
	Carl Yastrzemski, 1967	7.4
	Rickey Henderson, 1985	7.4
90	Grover Alexander, 1916	7.3
	Warren Spahn, 1953	7.3
	Greg Maddux, 1994	7.3
	Harlond Clift, 1937	7.3
	Mike Schmidt, 1980	7.3
	Ken Caminiti, 1996	7.3
	Barry Bonds, 2000	7.3
97	11 players tied	7.2

Total Baseball Rank (alpha.)

Grover Alexander, 1915	8.7
Grover Alexander, 1916	7.3
Jeff Bagwell, 1994	7.6
Craig Biggio, 1997	8.0
Barry Bonds, 1992	8.9
Barry Bonds, 1993	8.7
Barry Bonds, 1996	8.3
Barry Bonds, 1998	7.5
Barry Bonds, 2000	7.3
Lou Boudreau, 1944	7.8
Kevin Brown, 1996	7.6
Ken Caminiti, 1996	7.3
Norm Cash, 1961	7.5
John Clarkson, 1885	8.2
John Clarkson, 1887	7.6
John Clarkson, 1889	9.8
Roger Clemens, 1997	8.0
Harlond Clift, 1937	7.3
Ty Cobb, 1917	8.3
Eddie Collins, 1910	7.5
Dave Foutz, 1886	8.1
Lou Gehrig, 1927	8.3
Lou Gehrig, 1930	7.6
Lou Gehrig, 1934	7.7
Bob Gibson, 1968	7.6
Dwight Gooden, 1985	7.6
Lefty Grove, 1931	8.4
Pink Hawley, 1895	7.8
Guy Hecker, 1884	13.1
Rickey Henderson, 1985	7.4
Rickey Henderson, 1990	7.9
Rogers Hornsby, 1917	8.0
Rogers Hornsby, 1920	8.1
Rogers Hornsby, 1921	7.4
Rogers Hornsby, 1922	8.7
Rogers Hornsby, 1924	9.1
Carl Hubbell, 1933	7.8
Walter Johnson, 1912	11.1
Walter Johnson, 1913	10.8
Walter Johnson, 1915	7.7
Walter Johnson, 1918	7.8
Matt Kilroy, 1887	7.6
Silver King, 1888	10.6
Nap Lajoie, 1901	8.5
Nap Lajoie, 1903	8.1
Nap Lajoie, 1906	8.4
Nap Lajoie, 1908	8.1
Nap Lajoie, 1910	8.8
Dolf Luque, 1923	7.7
Greg Maddux, 1994	7.3
Mickey Mantle, 1956	8.7
Mickey Mantle, 1957	8.7
Mickey Mantle, 1961	8.3
Pedro Martinez, 1999	8.1
Pedro Martinez, 2000	8.5
Christy Mathewson, 1905	9.9
Willie Mays, 1955	7.6
Willie Mays, 1965	7.5
Tony Mullane, 1884	7.4
Hal Newhouser, 1945	7.5
Mike Piazza, 1997	7.6
Charley Radbourn, 1883	8.5
Charley Radbourn, 1884	10.4
Cal Ripken, 1984	9.3
Cal Ripken, 1991	8.3
Alex Rodriguez, 2000	7.7
Amos Rusie, 1894	11.1
Babe Ruth, 1920	9.1
Babe Ruth, 1921	9.6
Babe Ruth, 1923	10.8
Babe Ruth, 1924	8.6
Babe Ruth, 1926	8.4
Babe Ruth, 1927	9.0
Babe Ruth, 1930	7.4
Babe Ruth, 1931	7.4
Ron Santo, 1966	7.9
Ron Santo, 1967	7.5
Mike Schmidt, 1980	7.3
George Sisler, 1920	7.8
Warren Spahn, 1953	7.3
Tris Speaker, 1912	7.4
Tris Speaker, 1914	7.6
Scott Stratton, 1890	9.0
Dizzy Trout, 1944	8.8
Honus Wagner, 1905	7.5
Honus Wagner, 1906	7.4
Ed Walsh, 1908	8.4
Ed Walsh, 1910	7.4
Bucky Walters, 1939	8.6
Will White, 1882	7.4
Ted Williams, 1941	8.0
Ted Williams, 1942	8.0
Ted Williams, 1946	7.5
Joe Wood, 1912	8.4
Carl Yastrzemski, 1967	7.4
Cy Young, 1901	8.6

Total Baseball Rank (by era)

1876-1892

1	Guy Hecker, 1884	13.1
2	Silver King, 1888	10.6
3	Charley Radbourn, 1884	10.4
4	John Clarkson, 1889	9.8
5	Scott Stratton, 1890	9.0
6	Charley Radbourn, 1883	8.5
7	John Clarkson, 1885	8.2
8	Dave Foutz, 1886	8.1
9	John Clarkson, 1887	7.6
	Matt Kilroy, 1887	7.6
11	Will White, 1882	7.4
	Tony Mullane, 1884	7.4
13	Fred Dunlap, 1884	7.1
14	Amos Rusie, 1890	7.0
15	2 players tied	6.9

1893-1919

1	Amos Rusie, 1894	11.1
	Walter Johnson, 1912	11.1
3	Walter Johnson, 1913	10.8
4	Christy Mathewson, 1905	9.9
5	Nap Lajoie, 1910	8.8
6	Grover Alexander, 1915	8.7
7	Cy Young, 1901	8.6
8	Nap Lajoie, 1901	8.5
9	Ed Walsh, 1908	8.4
	Joe Wood, 1912	8.4
	Nap Lajoie, 1906	8.4
12	Ty Cobb, 1917	8.3
13	Nap Lajoie, 1903	8.1
	Nap Lajoie, 1908	8.1
15	Rogers Hornsby, 1917	8.0

1920-1941

1	Babe Ruth, 1923	10.8
2	Babe Ruth, 1921	9.6
3	Babe Ruth, 1920	9.1
	Rogers Hornsby, 1924	9.1
5	Babe Ruth, 1927	9.0
6	Rogers Hornsby, 1922	8.7
7	Bucky Walters, 1939	8.6
	Babe Ruth, 1924	8.6
9	Lefty Grove, 1931	8.4
	Babe Ruth, 1926	8.4
11	Lou Gehrig, 1927	8.3
12	Rogers Hornsby, 1920	8.1
13	Ted Williams, 1941	8.0
14	Carl Hubbell, 1933	7.8
	George Sisler, 1920	7.8

1942-1960

1	Dizzy Trout, 1944	8.8
2	Mickey Mantle, 1956	8.7
	Mickey Mantle, 1957	8.7
4	Ted Williams, 1942	8.0
5	Lou Boudreau, 1944	7.8
6	Willie Mays, 1955	7.6
7	Hal Newhouser, 1945	7.5
	Ted Williams, 1946	7.5
9	Warren Spahn, 1953	7.3
10	Snuffy Stirnweiss, 1945	7.2
	Willie Mays, 1958	7.2
12	Ted Williams, 1957	7.1
13	Bob Lemon, 1948	7.0
	Lou Boudreau, 1948	7.0
15	4 players tied	6.9

1961-1976

1	Mickey Mantle, 1961	8.3
2	Ron Santo, 1966	7.9
3	Bob Gibson, 1968	7.6
4	Norm Cash, 1961	7.5
	Willie Mays, 1965	7.5
	Ron Santo, 1967	7.5
7	Carl Yastrzemski, 1967	7.4
8	Rico Petrocelli, 1969	7.2
9	Steve Carlton, 1972	7.1
	Mike Schmidt, 1974	7.1
11	Willie Mays, 1963	7.0
	Joe Morgan, 1975	7.0
13	5 players tied	6.7

1977-2000

1	Cal Ripken, 1984	9.3
2	Barry Bonds, 1992	8.9
3	Barry Bonds, 1993	8.7
4	Pedro Martinez, 2000	8.5
5	Cal Ripken, 1991	8.3
	Barry Bonds, 1996	8.3
7	Pedro Martinez, 1999	8.1
8	Roger Clemens, 1997	8.0
	Craig Biggio, 1997	8.0
10	Rickey Henderson, 1990	7.9
11	Alex Rodriguez, 2000	7.7
12	Dwight Gooden, 1985	7.6
	Kevin Brown, 1996	7.6
	Jeff Bagwell, 1994	7.6
	Mike Piazza, 1997	7.6

Team Rosters

The Team Roster, like the five rosters that follow it, is offered as an adjunct to the five principal statistical sections of *Total Baseball:* the Annual Record, the Player Register, and the Pitcher Register. Employed together, these rosters and registers give a thorough accounting of major league baseball records. And as we observe the 130th anniversary of professional baseball, it can be said that these records are the very core of the game, the only imperishable remains of men who strode the fields of play yesterday or a hundred years ago.

The Team Roster lists the regular players, pitchers, key substitutes, and managers for all 2,355 team seasons in the history of professional league play since 1871. It does not contain the name of every man who played for every team in every year, for many teams have employed up to 50 or more players in a single season. The Team Roster allows the reader, by scanning its pages, to find who were the prominent players for a given team in a given year, or to track over time a team's personnel at a particular position (such as the "turnstile" at third base for the New York Mets since their inception). For a complete record of every one of the 15,416 major league players, consult the Player and Pitcher Registers.

Those included in a team roster are

- All managers
- All everyday players at eight positions, plus designated hitters
- Key utility or substitute players
- Starting pitchers (the top five, provided they have pitched at least 60 percent of the innings that together would yield one inning per scheduled game—that is, 98 innings in a 162-game season)
- Relief pitchers (up to three, provided they have pitched at least 30 percent of the innings that would yield a rate of one inning per scheduled game—50 innings in a 162-game season; and provided that they averaged less than three innings pitched per appearance).

The yearly team rosters are grouped alphabetically by city. At the head of each city's entry is a listing of the leagues and years in which that city was represented in the top rank of baseball. The teams representing that city are grouped by league in the order shown at the head of the entry; the organizing principle is to present the teams in the order of the leagues' demise (excepting, of course, the National and American Leagues). Accordingly, for a city like Chicago, represented in all six major leagues, the teams would be presented in this order:

National Association (last year, 1875)
Union Association (last year, 1884)
Players League (last year, 1890)
American Association (last year, 1891)
Federal League (last year, 1915)
National League (first year, 1876)
American League (first year, 1901)

The team and league abbreviations used in this section are found on the final pages of this book. Other abbreviations used in the Team Roster are these:

M	Manager
1B	First Base
2B	Second Base
SS	Shortstop
3B	Third Base
LF	Left Field
CF	Center Field
RF	Right Field
C	Catcher
DH	Designated Hitter
UT	Utility (substitute)
P	Pitcher
RP	Relief Pitcher

Altoona

ALT U 1884

ALT 1884U

M E.Curtis
1B F.Harris
2B C.Dougherty
SS G.Smith
3B H.Koons
LF J.Murphy
CF F.Shaffer
RF J.Brown
C J.Moore
P J.Murphy

Anaheim

ANA A 1997-2000

ANA 1997A

M T.Collins
1B D.Erstad
2B L.Alicea
SS G.DiSarcina
3B D.Hollins
LF G.Anderson
CF J.Edmonds
RF T.Salmon
C C.Kreuter
DH E.Murray
UT T.Phillips
P J.Dickson
P A.Watson
P D.Springer
P C.Finley
RP S.Hasegawa
RP P.Harris
RP M.James

ANA 1998A

M T.Collins
1B C.Fielder
2B J.Baughman
SS G.DiSarcina
3B D.Hollins
LF D.Erstad
CF J.Edmonds
RF G.Anderson
C M.Walbeck
DH T.Salmon
P C.Finley
P O.Olivares
P S.Sparks
P J.Dickson
P K.Hill
RP S.Hasegawa
RP R.DeLucia
RP T.Percival

ANA 1999A

M T.Collins
M J.Maddon
1B D.Erstad
2B R.Velarde
SS G.DiSarcina
3B T.Glaus
LF O.Palmeiro
CF G.Anderson
RF T.Salmon
C M.Walbeck
DH M.Vaughn
UT T.Greene
UT J.Huson
P C.Finley
P S.Sparks
P T.Belcher
P O.Olivares
P K.Hill
RP A.Levine
RP M.Petkovsek
RP S.Hasegawa

ANA 2000A

M M.Scioscia
1B M.Vaughn
2B A.Kennedy
SS B.Gil
3B T.Glaus
LF D.Erstad
CF G.Anderson
RF T.Salmon
C B.Molina
DH S.Spiezio
UT O.Palmeiro
P S.Schoeneweis
P K.Bottenfield
P R.Ortiz
RP S.Hasegawa
RP A.Levine
RP M.Petkovsek

Arizona

ARI N 1998-2000

ARI 1998N

M B.Showalter
1B T.Lee
2B A.Stankiewicz
SS J.Bell
3B M.Williams
LF D.Dellucci
CF D.White
RF K.Garcia
C K.Stinnett
UT T.Batista
UT B.Brede
UT A.Fox
P A.Benes
P B.Anderson
P O.Daal
P W.Blair
P A.Telemaco
RP C.Sodowsky
RP G.Olson

ARI 1999N

M B.Showalter
1B T.Lee
2B J.Bell
SS A.Fox
3B M.Williams
LF L.Gonzalez
CF S.Finley
RF T.Womack
C K.Stinnett
P R.Johnson
P O.Daal
P A.Benes
P A.Reynoso
P B.Anderson
RP G.Swindell
RP G.Olson
RP D.Holmes

ARI 2000N

M B.Showalter
1B G.Colbrunn
2B J.Bell
SS T.Womack
3B M.Williams
LF L.Gonzalez
CF S.Finley
RF D.Bautista
C D.Miller
P R.Johnson
P B.Anderson
P A.Reynoso
P C.Schilling
P O.Daal
RP M.Morgan
RP G.Swindell
RP B.Kim

Atlanta

ATL N 1966-2000

ATL 1966N

M B.Bragan
M B.Hitchcock
1B F.Alou
2B W.Woodward
SS D.Menke
3B E.Mathews
LF R.Carty
CF M.Jones
RF H.Aaron
C J.Torre
P T.Cloninger
P K.Johnson
P D.Lemaster
RP C.Carroll
RP C.Olivo
RP T.Abernathy

ATL 1967N

M B.Hitchcock
M K.Silvestri
1B F.Alou
2B W.Woodward
SS D.Menke
3B C.Boyer
LF R.Carty
CF M.Jones
RF H.Aaron
C J.Torre
P D.Lemaster
P K.Johnson
P P.Niekro
P P.Jarvis
RP D.Kelley
RP C.Carroll
RP J.Ritchie

ATL 1968N

M L.Harris
1B D.Johnson
2B F.Millan
SS S.Jackson
3B C.Boyer
LF M.Lum
CF F.Alou
RF H.Aaron
C J.Torre
UT T.Francona
UT M.Martinez
P P.Niekro
P P.Jarvis
P R.Reed
P K.Johnson
P M.Pappas
RP C.Upshaw
RP J.Britton
RP C.Raymond

ATL 1969N

M L.Harris
1B O.Cepeda
2B F.Millan
SS S.Jackson
3B C.Boyer
LF T.Gonzalez
CF F.Alou
RF H.Aaron
C B.Didier
UT R.Carty
UT M.Lum
P P.Niekro
P R.Reed
P P.Jarvis
P G.Stone
P M.Pappas
RP C.Upshaw
RP G.Neibauer
RP C.Raymond

ATL 1970N

M L.Harris
1B O.Cepeda
2B F.Millan
SS S.Jackson
3B C.Boyer
LF R.Carty
CF T.Gonzalez
RF H.Aaron
C B.Tillman
UT G.Garrido
UT M.Lum
P P.Jarvis
P P.Niekro
P J.Nash
P G.Stone
P R.Reed
RP H.Wilhelm
RP B.Priddy

ATL 1971N

M L.Harris
1B H.Aaron
2B F.Millan
SS M.Perez
3B D.Evans
LF R.Garr
CF S.Jackson
RF M.Lum
C E.Williams
P P.Niekro
P R.Reed
P G.Stone
P P.Jarvis
P T.Kelley
RP C.Upshaw
RP S.Barber
RP B.Priddy

ATL 1972N

M L.Harris
M E.Mathews
1B H.Aaron
2B F.Millan
SS M.Perez
3B D.Evans
LF R.Carty
CF D.Baker
RF R.Garr
C E.Williams
UT M.Lum
P P.Niekro
P R.Reed
P R.Schueler
P T.Kelley
P G.Stone
RP P.Jarvis
RP C.Upshaw

ATL 1973N

M E.Mathews
1B M.Lum
2B D.Johnson
SS M.Perez
3B D.Evans
LF H.Aaron
CF D.Baker
RF R.Garr
C J.Oates
UT S.Jackson
P C.Morton
P P.Niekro
P R.Schueler
P R.Harrison
P R.Reed
RP T.House

ATL 1974N

M E.Mathews
M C.King
1B D.Johnson
2B M.Perez
SS C.Robinson
3B D.Evans
LF H.Aaron
CF D.Baker
RF R.Garr
C J.Oates
UT R.Office
UT M.Lum
P P.Niekro
P C.Morton
P B.Capra
P R.Reed
P R.Harrison
RP T.House
RP M.Leon
RP L.Krausse

ATL 1975N

M C.King
M C.Ryan
1B E.Williams
2B M.Perez
SS L.Blanks
3B D.Evans
LF R.Garr
CF R.Office
RF D.Baker
C V.Correll
UT M.Lum
P C.Morton
P P.Niekro
RP M.Leon
RP T.House
RP M.Beard

ATL 1976N

M D.Bristol
1B W.Montanez
2B R.Gilbreath
SS D.Chaney
3B J.Royster
LF J.Wynn
CF R.Office
RF K.Henderson
C V.Correll
UT D.May
UT T.Paciorek
P P.Niekro
P D.Ruthven
P A.Messersmith
P C.Morton
P F.LaCorte
RP R.Moret
RP A.Devine
RP B.Dal Canton

ATL 1977N

M D.Bristol
M T.Turner
M V.Benson
M D.Bristol
1B W.Montanez
2B R.Gilbreath
SS P.Rockett
3B J.Moore
LF G.Matthews
CF R.Office
RF J.Burroughs
C B.Pocoroba
UT B.Bonnell
UT J.Royster
P P.Niekro
P D.Ruthven
P B.Capra
P A.Messersmith
RP D.Campbell
RP M.Leon
RP R.Camp

ATL 1978N

M B.Cox
1B D.Murphy
2B J.Royster
SS D.Chaney
3B B.Horner
LF J.Burroughs
CF R.Office
RF G.Matthews
C B.Pocoroba
UT B.Beall
UT B.Bonnell
UT R.Gilbreath
P P.Niekro
P P.Hanna
P M.Mahler
P L.McWilliams
RP E.Solomon
RP G.Garber
RP J.Easterly

ATL 1979N

M B.Cox
1B D.Murphy
2B G.Hubbard
SS P.Frias
3B B.Horner
LF J.Burroughs
CF R.Office
RF G.Matthews
C B.Benedict
UT M.Lum
UT B.Bonnell
UT J.Royster
P P.Niekro
P E.Solomon
P R.Matula
P T.Brizzolara
P M.Mahler
RP G.Garber
RP J.McLaughlin
RP A.Devine

ATL 1980N

M B.Cox
1B C.Chambliss
2B G.Hubbard
SS L.Gomez
3B B.Horner
LF J.Burroughs
CF D.Murphy
RF G.Matthews
C B.Benedict
UT J.Royster
P P.Niekro
P D.Alexander
P T.Boggs
P R.Matula
P L.McWilliams
RP R.Camp
RP G.Garber
RP P.Hanna

ATL 1981N

M B.Cox
1B C.Chambliss
2B G.Hubbard
SS R.Ramirez
3B B.Horner
LF R.Linares
CF D.Murphy
RF C.Washington
C B.Benedict
UT J.Royster
P G.Perry
P T.Boggs
P P.Niekro
P R.Mahler
RP J.Montefusco
RP R.Camp
RP G.Garber

ATL 1982N

M J.Torre
1B C.Chambliss
2B G.Hubbard
SS R.Ramirez
3B B.Horner
LF R.Linares
CF D.Murphy
RF C.Washington
C B.Benedict
UT J.Royster
UT B.Butler
P P.Niekro
P R.Mahler
P R.Camp
P B.Walk
RP S.Bedrosian
RP G.Garber

ATL 1983N

M J.Torre
1B C.Chambliss
2B G.Hubbard
SS R.Ramirez
3B B.Horner
LF B.Butler
CF D.Murphy
RF C.Washington
C B.Benedict
P C.McMurtry
P P.Perez
P P.Niekro
P R.Camp
P P.Falcone
RP S.Bedrosian
RP T.Forster
RP D.Moore

ATL 1984N

M J.Torre
1B C.Chambliss
2B G.Hubbard
SS R.Ramirez
3B R.Johnson
LF B.Komminsk
CF D.Murphy
RF C.Washington
C B.Benedict
UT G.Perry
P R.Mahler
P P.Perez
P C.McMurtry
P R.Camp
P L.Barker
RP G.Garber
RP S.Bedrosian
RP J.Dedmon

ATL 1985N

M E.Haas
M B.Wine
1B B.Horner
2B G.Hubbard
SS R.Ramirez
3B K.Oberkfell
LF T.Harper
CF D.Murphy
RF C.Washington
C R.Cerone
UT C.Chambliss
UT B.Komminsk
UT G.Perry
P R.Mahler
P S.Bedrosian
P Z.Smith
RP R.Camp
RP G.Garber
RP B.Sutter

ATL 1986N

M C.Tanner
1B B.Horner
2B G.Hubbard
SS A.Thomas
3B K.Oberkfell
LF T.Harper
CF D.Murphy
RF O.Moreno
C O.Virgil
UT C.Chambliss
UT R.Ramirez
P R.Mahler
P D.Palmer
P Z.Smith
P D.Alexander
RP J.Dedmon
RP C.McMurtry
RP G.Garber

ATL 1987N

M C.Tanner
1B G.Perry
2B G.Hubbard
SS A.Thomas
3B K.Oberkfell
LF K.Griffey
CF D.James
RF D.Murphy
C O.Virgil
UT G.Nettles
P Z.Smith
P R.Mahler
P D.Palmer
P C.Puleo
P D.Alexander
RP J.Acker
RP J.Dedmon
RP G.Garber

ATL 1988N

M C.Tanner
M R.Nixon
1B G.Perry
2B R.Gant
SS A.Thomas
3B K.Oberkfell
LF D.James
CF A.Hall
RF D.Murphy
C O.Virgil
P R.Mahler
P P.Smith
P T.Glavine
P Z.Smith
RP C.Puleo
RP J.Alvarez
RP P.Assenmacher

ATL 1989N

M R.Nixon
1B G.Perry
2B J.Treadway
SS A.Thomas
3B J.Blauser
LF L.Smith
CF O.McDowell
RF D.Murphy
C J.Davis
UT D.Evans
UT T.Gregg
P J.Smoltz
P T.Glavine
P D.Lilliquist
P P.Smith
P M.Clary
RP J.Acker
RP J.Boever
RP M.Eichhorn

ATL 1990N

M R.Nixon
M B.Cox
1B D.Justice
2B J.Treadway
SS J.Blauser
3B J.Presley
LF L.Smith
CF R.Gant
RF D.Murphy
C G.Olson
UT T.Gregg
UT M.Lemke
UT O.McDowell
P J.Smoltz
P T.Glavine
P C.Leibrandt
P M.Clary
P S.Avery
RP T.Castillo
RP R.Luecken
RP M.Grant

ATL 1991N

M B.Cox
1B B.Hunter
2B M.Lemke
SS R.Belliard
3B T.Pendleton
LF O.Nixon
CF R.Gant
RF D.Justice
C G.Olson
UT J.Blauser
UT L.Smith
UT J.Treadway
P T.Glavine
P J.Smoltz
P C.Leibrandt
P S.Avery
RP M.Stanton
RP K.Mercker
RP J.Berenguer

ATL 1992N

M B.Cox
1B S.Bream
2B M.Lemke
SS R.Belliard
3B T.Pendleton
LF R.Gant
CF O.Nixon
RF D.Justice

C G.Olson
UT D.Berryhill
UT J.Blauser
UT B.Hunter
UT D.Sanders
P J.Smoltz
P S.Avery
P T.Glavine
P C.Leibrandt
RP K.Mercker
RP M.Stanton
RP M.Freeman

ATL 1993N

M B.Cox
1B S.Bream
2B M.Lemke
SS J.Blauser
3B T.Pendleton
LF R.Gant
CF O.Nixon
RF D.Justice
C D.Berryhill
P G.Maddux
P J.Smoltz
P T.Glavine
P S.Avery
RP G.McMichael
RP K.Mercker
RP J.Howell

ATL 1994N

M B.Cox
1B F.McGriff
2B M.Lemke
SS J.Blauser
3B T.Pendleton
LF R.Klesko
CF R.Kelly
RF D.Justice
C J.Lopez
UT T.Tarasco
UT D.Gallagher
P G.Maddux
P T.Glavine
P S.Avery
P J.Smoltz
P K.Mercker
RP G.McMichael
RP M.Wohlers
RP M.Stanton

ATL 1995N

M B.Cox
1B F.McGriff
2B M.Lemke
SS J.Blauser
3B C.Jones
LF R.Klesko
CF M.Grissom
RF D.Justice
C J.Lopez
UT M.Kelly
UT D.Smith
P G.Maddux
P T.Glavine
P J.Smoltz
P S.Avery
P K.Mercker
RP G.McMichael
RP B.Clontz
RP M.Wohlers

ATL 1996N

M B.Cox
1B F.McGriff
2B M.Lemke
SS J.Blauser
3B C.Jones
LF R.Klesko
CF M.Grissom
RF J.Dye
C J.Lopez
UT D.Smith
P J.Smoltz
P G.Maddux
P T.Glavine
P S.Avery
RP G.McMichael
RP B.Clontz
RP M.Wohlers

ATL 1997N

M B.Cox
1B F.McGriff
2B M.Lemke
SS J.Blauser
3B C.Jones
LF R.Klesko
CF A.Jones
RF M.Tucker
C J.Lopez
UT T.Graffanino
UT K.Lofton
P J.Smoltz
P T.Glavine
P D.Neagle
P G.Maddux
RP M.Wohlers
RP M.Bielecki
RP P.Byrd

ATL 1998N

M B.Cox
1B A.Galarraga
2B K.Lockhart
SS W.Weiss
3B C.Jones
LF R.Klesko
CF A.Jones
RF G.Williams
C J.Lopez
UT T.Graffanino
UT M.Tucker
P G.Maddux
P T.Glavine
P D.Neagle
P K.Millwood
P J.Smoltz
RP D.Martinez
RP K.Ligtenberg

ATL 1999N

M B.Cox
1B B.Hunter
2B B.Boone
SS W.Weiss
3B C.Jones
LF G.Williams
CF A.Jones
RF B.Jordan
C E.Perez
UT R.Klesko
UT K.Lockhart
P T.Glavine
P K.Millwood
P G.Maddux
P J.Smoltz
RP M.Remlinger
RP J.Rocker
RP K.McGlinchy

ATL 2000N

M B.Cox
1B A.Galarraga
2B Q.Veras
SS R.Furcal
3B C.Jones
LF R.Sanders
CF A.Jones
RF B.Jordan
C J.Lopez
UT B.Bonilla
UT W.Joyner
UT K.Lockhart
P G.Maddux
P T.Glavine
P K.Millwood
P J.Burkett
P A.Ashby
RP T.Mulholland
RP M.Remlinger
RP J.Rocker

Baltimore

MAR n 1873
BAL n 1872-1874
BAL U 1884
BAL a 1882-1889
BAL a 1890-1891
BAL N 1892-1899
BAL A 1901-1902
BAL F 1914-1915
BAL A 1954-2000

MAR 1873n

M B.Smith
1B B.Lennon
2B M.Simpson
SS L.Say
3B H.Kohler
LF M.Hooper
CF J.Smith
RF B.French
C B.Smith
P E.Stratton
P F.Selman
P Mc Doolan

BAL 1872n

M B.Craver
M E.Mills
1B E.Mills
2B T.Carey
SS J.Radcliff
3B D.Force
LF T.York
CF G.Hall
RF L.Pike
C B.Craver
UT D.Higham
P B.Mathews
P C.Fisher

BAL 1873n

M C.McVey
M T.Carey
1B E.Mills
2B T.Carey
SS J.Radcliff
3B D.Force
LF T.York
CF G.Hall
RF L.Pike
C C.McVey
UT B.Craver
P C.Cummings
P A.Brainard

BAL 1874n

M W.White
1B C.Gould
2B J.Manning
SS L.Say
3B W.White
LF J.Ryan
CF H.Deane
RF O.Bielaski
C P.Snyder
P A.Brainard
P J.Manning

BAL 1884U

M B.Henderson
1B C.Levis
2B D.Phelan
SS L.Say
3B Y.Robinson
LF E.Seery
CF N.Cuthbert
RF B.Graham
C E.Fusselback
P B.Sweeney
P T.Lee
P A.Atkinson

BAL 1882a

M H.Myers
1B C.Householder
2B G.Pierce
SS H.Myers
3B J.Shetzline
LF C.Waitt
CF M.Cline
RF T.Brown
C E.Whiting
P D.Landis
P T.Nichols
P E.Geis

BAL 1883a

M B.Barnie
1B E.Stearns
2B T.Manning
SS L.Say
3B J.McCormick
LF J.Clinton
CF D.Eggler
RF D.Rowe
C J.Kelly
P H.Henderson
P B.Emslie
P J.Fox

BAL 1884a

M B.Barnie
1B E.Stearns
2B T.Manning
SS J.Macullar
3B J.Sommer
LF T.York
CF J.Clinton
RF G.Gardner
C S.Trott
P B.Emslie
P H.Henderson

BAL 1885a

M B.Barnie
1B E.Stearns
2B T.Manning
SS J.Macullar
3B M.Muldoon
LF J.Sommer
CF D.Casey
RF O.Burns
C B.Traffley
P H.Henderson
P B.Emslie
P J.Henry

BAL 1886a

M B.Barnie
1B M.Scott
2B M.Muldoon
SS J.Macullar
3B J.Davis
LF J.Sommer
CF P.O'Connell
RF J.Manning
C C.Fulmer
P M.Kilroy
P J.McGinnis
P H.Henderson

BAL 1887a

M B.Barnie
1B T.Tucker
2B B.Greenwood
SS O.Burns
3B J.Davis
LF J.Sommer
CF M.Griffin
RF B.Purcell
C S.Trott
P M.Kilroy
P P.Smith

BAL 1888a

M B.Barnie
1B T.Tucker
2B B.Greenwood
SS J.Farrell
3B B.Shindle
LF O.Burns
CF M.Griffin
RF B.Purcell
C C.Fulmer
P B.Cunningham
P M.Kilroy
P P.Smith

BAL 1889a

M B.Barnie
1B T.Tucker
2B R.Mack
SS J.Farrell
3B B.Shindle
LF J.Hornung
CF M.Griffin
RF J.Sommer
C P.Tate
P M.Kilroy
P F.Foreman
P B.Cunningham

BAL 1890a

M B.Barnie
1B T.Power
2B R.Mack
SS I.Ray
3B P.Gilbert
LF J.Sommer
CF D.Long
RF B.Johnson
C G.Townsend
P L.German
P S.McMahon
P M.O'Rourke
P M.Morrison

BAL 1891a

M B.Barnie
1B P.Werden
2B S.Wise
SS G.Van Haltren
3B P.Gilbert
LF B.Johnson
CF C.Welch
RF I.Ray
C W.Robinson
P S.McMahon
P B.Cunningham
P K.Madden
P J.Healy

BAL 1892N

M G.Van Haltren
M J.Waltz
M N.Hanlon
1B S.Sutcliffe
2B C.Stricker
SS T.O'Rourke
3B B.Shindle
LF H.Stovey
CF C.Welch
RF G.Van Haltren
C W.Robinson
P S.McMahon
P G.Cobb
P T.Vickery
P C.Buffinton

BAL 1893N

M N.Hanlon
1B H.Taylor
2B H.Reitz
SS J.McGraw
3B B.Shindle
LF J.Long
CF J.Kelley
RF G.Treadway
C W.Robinson
P S.McMahon
P T.Mullane
P B.Hawke
P E.McNabb
P K.Baker

BAL 1894N

M N.Hanlon
1B D.Brouthers
2B H.Reitz
SS H.Jennings
3B J.McGraw
LF J.Kelley
CF S.Brodie
RF W.Keeler
C W.Robinson
P S.McMahon
P B.Hawke
P K.Gleason
P B.Inks
P T.Mullane

BAL 1895N

M N.Hanlon
1B S.Carey
2B K.Gleason
SS H.Jennings
3B J.McGraw
LF J.Kelley
CF S.Brodie
RF W.Keeler
C W.Robinson
P B.Hoffer
P G.Hemming
P D.Esper
P D.Clarkson
P S.McMahon

BAL 1896N

M N.Hanlon
1B J.Doyle
2B H.Reitz
SS H.Jennings
3B J.Donnelly
LF J.Kelley
CF S.Brodie
RF W.Keeler
C W.Robinson
UT B.Clarke
P B.Hoffer
P A.Pond
P G.Hemming
P S.McMahon
P D.Esper

BAL 1897N

M N.Hanlon
1B J.Doyle
2B H.Reitz
SS H.Jennings
3B J.McGraw
LF J.Kelley
CF J.Stenzel
RF W.Keeler
C B.Clarke
P J.Corbett
P B.Hoffer
P A.Pond
P J.Nops

BAL 1898N

M N.Hanlon
1B D.McGann
2B De Montreville
SS H.Jennings
3B J.McGraw
LF D.Holmes
CF J.Kelley
RF W.Keeler
C W.Robinson
P D.McJames
P J.Hughes
P A.Maul
P J.Nops
P F.Kitson

BAL 1899N

M J.McGraw
1B C.LaChance
2B De Montreville
SS B.Keister
3B J.McGraw
LF D.Holmes
CF S.Brodie
RF J.Sheckard
C W.Robinson
P J.McGinnity
P F.Kitson
P J.Nops
P H.Howell

BAL 1901A

M J.McGraw
1B B.Hart
2B J.Williams
SS B.Keister
3B J.McGraw
LF J.Jackson
CF S.Brodie
RF C.Seymour
C R.Bresnahan
UT M.Donlin
UT J.Dunn
P J.McGinnity
P H.Howell
P F.Foreman
P J.Nops

BAL 1902A

M J.McGraw
M W.Robinson
1B D.McGann
2B J.Williams
SS B.Gilbert
3B R.Bresnahan
LF K.Selbach
CF H.McFarland
RF C.Seymour
C W.Robinson
P J.McGinnity
P H.Howell
P S.Wiltse
P C.Shields
P J.Katoll

BAL 1914F

M O.Knabe
1B H.Swacina
2B O.Knabe
SS M.Doolan
3B J.Walsh
LF H.Simmons
CF V.Duncan
RF B.Meyer
C F.Jacklitsch
P J.Quinn
P G.Suggs
P K.Wilhelm
P F.Smith
P B.Bailey

BAL 1915F

M O.Knabe
1B H.Swacina
2B O.Knabe
SS M.Doolan
3B J.Walsh
LF V.Duncan
CF J.McCandless
RF S.Evans
C F.Owens
UT G.Zinn
P J.Quinn
P G.Suggs
P B.Bailey
P C.Bender
P R.Johnson

BAL 1954A

M J.Dykes
1B E.Waitkus
2B B.Young
SS B.Hunter
3B V.Stephens
LF J.Fridley
CF C.Diering
RF C.Abrams
C C.Courtney
UT G.Coan
UT B.Kennedy
UT D.Kryhoski
P B.Turley
P J.Coleman
P D.Larsen
P D.Pillette
P L.Kretlow
RP B.Chakales
RP M.Blyzka
RP H.Fox

BAL 1955A

M P.Richards
1B G.Triandos
2B F.Marsh
SS W.Miranda
3B W.Causey
LF D.Philley
CF C.Diering
RF C.Abrams
C H.Smith
P J.Wilson
P E.Palica
P R.Moore
P B.Wight
RP A.Schallock
RP D.Johnson
RP H.Dorish

BAL 1956A

M P.Richards
1B B.Boyd
2B B.Gardner
SS W.Miranda
3B G.Kell
LF B.Nieman
CF D.Williams
RF T.Francona
C G.Triandos
P R.Moore
P C.Johnson
P B.Wight
P H.Brown
P E.Palica
RP D.Ferrarese
RP G.Zuverink
RP B.Loes

BAL 1957A

M P.Richards
1B B.Boyd
2B B.Gardner
SS W.Miranda
3B G.Kell
LF B.Nieman
CF J.Busby
RF A.Pilarcik
C G.Triandos
UT T.Francona
P C.Johnson
P R.Moore
P B.Loes
P H.Brown
P B.O'Dell
RP G.Zuverink
RP K.Lehman
RP A.Ceccarelli

BAL 1958A

M P.Richards
1B B.Boyd
2B B.Gardner
SS W.Miranda
3B B.Robinson
LF G.Woodling
CF J.Busby
RF A.Pilarcik
C G.Triandos
UT F.Castleman
UT B.Nieman
UT D.Williams
P J.Harshman
P B.O'Dell
P A.Portocarrero
P M.Pappas
P C.Johnson
RP G.Zuverink
RP K.Lehman
RP C.Beamon

BAL 1959A

M P.Richards
1B B.Boyd
2B B.Gardner

SS C.Carrasquel
3B B.Robinson
LF G.Woodling
CF W.Tasby
RF A.Pilarcik
C G.Triandos
UT B.Klaus
UT B.Nieman
P H.Wilhelm
P M.Pappas
P B.O'Dell
P J.Walker
P H.Brown
RP B.Loes
RP E.Johnson

BAL 1960A

M P.Richards
1B J.Gentile
2B M.Breeding
SS R.Hansen
3B B.Robinson
LF G.Woodling
CF J.Brandt
RF G.Stephens
C G.Triandos
UT A.Pilarcik
P C.Estrada
P M.Pappas
P J.Fisher
P S.Barber
P H.Brown
RP G.Jones

BAL 1961A

M P.Richards
M L.Harris
1B J.Gentile
2B J.Adair
SS R.Hansen
3B B.Robinson
LF R.Snyder
CF J.Brandt
RF W.Herzog
C G.Triandos
UT D.Williams
P S.Barber
P C.Estrada
P J.Fisher
P M.Pappas
P H.Brown
RP H.Wilhelm
RP W.Stock

BAL 1962A

M B.Hitchcock
1B J.Gentile
2B M.Breeding
SS J.Adair
3B B.Robinson
LF B.Powell
CF J.Brandt
RF R.Snyder
C G.Triandos
UT W.Herzog
UT D.Nicholson
P C.Estrada
P M.Pappas
P R.Roberts
P J.Fisher
P S.Barber
RP D.Hall
RP B.Hoeft
RP H.Wilhelm

BAL 1963A

M B.Hitchcock
1B J.Gentile
2B J.Adair
SS L.Aparicio
3B B.Robinson
LF B.Powell
CF J.Brandt
RF R.Snyder
C J.Orsino
UT B.Saverine
UT A.Smith
P S.Barber
P R.Roberts
P M.Pappas
P M.McCormick
P D.McNally
RP S.Miller
RP D.Hall
RP W.Stock

BAL 1964A

M H.Bauer
1B N.Siebern
2B J.Adair
SS L.Aparicio
3B B.Robinson
LF B.Powell
CF J.Brandt
RF S.Bowens
C D.Brown
P M.Pappas
P W.Bunker
P R.Roberts
P D.McNally
P S.Barber
RP S.Miller
RP H.Haddix
RP D.Hall

BAL 1965A

M H.Bauer
1B B.Powell
2B J.Adair
SS L.Aparicio
3B B.Robinson
LF C.Blefary
CF P.Blair
RF R.Snyder
C D.Brown
UT N.Siebern
P M.Pappas
P S.Barber
P D.McNally
P W.Bunker
P R.Roberts
RP S.Miller
RP D.Hall
RP D.Larsen

BAL 1966A

M H.Bauer
1B B.Powell
2B D.Johnson
SS L.Aparicio
3B B.Robinson
LF C.Blefary
CF P.Blair
RF F.Robinson
C A.Etchebarren
UT R.Snyder
P D.McNally
P J.Palmer
P E.Watt
P W.Bunker
P S.Barber
RP M.Drabowsky
RP S.Miller
RP E.Fisher

BAL 1967A

M H.Bauer
1B B.Powell
2B D.Johnson
SS L.Aparicio
3B B.Robinson
LF C.Blefary
CF P.Blair
RF F.Robinson
C A.Etchebarren
UT R.Snyder
P T.Phoebus
P P.Richert
P B.Dillman
P D.McNally
P J.Hardin
RP E.Watt
RP M.Drabowsky
RP E.Fisher

BAL 1968A

M H.Bauer
M E.Weaver
1B B.Powell
2B D.Johnson
SS M.Belanger
3B B.Robinson
LF C.Blefary
CF P.Blair
RF F.Robinson
C A.Etchebarren
UT D.Buford
P D.McNally
P J.Hardin
P T.Phoebus
P D.Leonhard
P G.Brabender
RP E.Watt
RP P.Richert
RP M.Drabowsky

BAL 1969A

M E.Weaver
1B B.Powell
2B D.Johnson
SS M.Belanger
3B B.Robinson
LF D.Buford
CF P.Blair
RF F.Robinson
C E.Hendricks
P M.Cuellar
P D.McNally
P T.Phoebus
P J.Palmer
P J.Hardin
RP D.Leonhard
RP E.Watt
RP M.Lopez

BAL 1970A

M E.Weaver
1B B.Powell
2B D.Johnson
SS M.Belanger
3B B.Robinson
LF D.Buford
CF P.Blair
RF F.Robinson
C E.Hendricks
UT M.Rettenmund
P J.Palmer
P M.Cuellar
P D.McNally
P J.Hardin
P T.Phoebus
RP M.Lopez
RP D.Hall
RP E.Watt

BAL 1971A

M E.Weaver
1B B.Powell
2B D.Johnson
SS M.Belanger
3B B.Robinson
LF D.Buford
CF P.Blair
RF M.Rettenmund
C E.Hendricks
UT F.Robinson
P M.Cuellar
P J.Palmer
P P.Dobson
P D.McNally
RP G.Jackson

BAL 1972A

M E.Weaver
1B B.Powell
2B D.Johnson
SS M.Belanger
3B B.Robinson
LF D.Buford
CF P.Blair
RF M.Rettenmund
C J.Oates
UT D.Baylor
UT T.Crowley
UT B.Grich
P J.Palmer
P P.Dobson
P M.Cuellar
P D.McNally
P D.Alexander
RP R.Harrison

BAL 1973A

M E.Weaver
1B B.Powell
2B B.Grich
SS M.Belanger
3B B.Robinson
LF D.Baylor
CF P.Blair
RF R.Coggins
C E.Williams
DH T.Davis
UT A.Bumbry
P J.Palmer
P M.Cuellar
P D.McNally
P D.Alexander
P J.Jefferson
RP B.Reynolds
RP G.Jackson
RP E.Watt

BAL 1974A

M E.Weaver
1B B.Powell
2B B.Grich
SS M.Belanger
3B B.Robinson
LF D.Baylor
CF P.Blair
RF R.Coggins
C E.Williams
DH T.Davis
P R.Grimsley
P M.Cuellar
P D.McNally
P J.Palmer
P D.Alexander
RP B.Reynolds
RP G.Jackson
RP J.Jefferson

BAL 1975A

M E.Weaver
1B L.May
2B B.Grich
SS M.Belanger
3B B.Robinson
LF D.Baylor
CF P.Blair
RF K.Singleton
C D.Duncan
DH T.Davis
UT A.Bumbry
P J.Palmer
P M.Torrez
P M.Cuellar
P R.Grimsley
P D.Alexander
RP G.Jackson

BAL 1976A

M E.Weaver
1B T.Muser
2B B.Grich
SS M.Belanger
3B D.DeCinces
LF K.Singleton
CF P.Blair
RF R.Jackson
C D.Duncan
DH L.May
UT A.Bumbry
P J.Palmer
P W.Garland
P R.May
P R.Grimsley
P M.Cuellar
RP D.Miller

BAL 1977A

M E.Weaver
1B L.May
2B B.Smith
SS M.Belanger
3B D.DeCinces
LF P.Kelly
CF A.Bumbry
RF K.Singleton
C R.Dempsey
DH E.Murray
UT T.Muser
P J.Palmer
P R.May
P M.Flanagan
P R.Grimsley
P D.Martinez
RP T.Martinez

BAL 1978A

M E.Weaver
1B E.Murray
2B R.Dauer
SS M.Belanger
3B D.DeCinces
LF P.Kelly
CF L.Harlow
RF K.Singleton
C R.Dempsey
DH L.May
UT C.Lopez
P J.Palmer
P M.Flanagan
P D.Martinez
P S.McGregor
RP D.Stanhouse
RP J.Kerrigan
RP T.Martinez

BAL 1979A

M E.Weaver
1B E.Murray
2B R.Dauer
SS K.Garcia
3B D.DeCinces
LF G.Roenicke
CF A.Bumbry
RF K.Singleton
C R.Dempsey
DH L.May
UT M.Belanger
UT J.Lowenstein
P D.Martinez
P M.Flanagan
P S.Stone
P S.McGregor
P J.Palmer
RP T.Martinez
RP D.Stanhouse
RP T.Stoddard

BAL 1980A

M E.Weaver
1B E.Murray
2B R.Dauer
SS M.Belanger
3B D.DeCinces
LF G.Roenicke
CF A.Bumbry
RF K.Singleton
C R.Dempsey
DH T.Crowley
UT K.Garcia
UT J.Lowenstein
P S.McGregor
P S.Stone
P M.Flanagan
P J.Palmer
P S.Stewart
RP T.Stoddard
RP T.Martinez
RP D.Ford

BAL 1981A

M E.Weaver
1B E.Murray
2B R.Dauer
SS M.Belanger
3B D.DeCinces
LF J.Lowenstein
CF A.Bumbry
RF G.Roenicke
C R.Dempsey
DH T.Crowley
UT J.Dwyer
UT K.Singleton
P D.Martinez
P S.McGregor
P J.Palmer
P M.Flanagan
P S.Stewart
RP T.Martinez
RP D.Ford
RP T.Stoddard

BAL 1982A

M E.Weaver
1B E.Murray
2B R.Dauer
SS L.Sakata
3B C.Ripken
LF G.Roenicke
CF A.Bumbry
RF D.Ford
C R.Dempsey
DH K.Singleton
UT J.Lowenstein
P D.Martinez
P M.Flanagan
P J.Palmer
P S.McGregor
P S.Stewart
RP T.Martinez
RP R.Grimsley
RP T.Stoddard

BAL 1983A

M J.Altobelli
1B E.Murray
2B R.Dauer
SS C.Ripken
3B T.Cruz
LF J.Lowenstein
CF J.Shelby
RF D.Ford
C R.Dempsey
UT J.Dwyer
UT A.Bumbry
UT G.Roenicke
P S.McGregor
P S.Davis
P M.Boddicker
P D.Martinez
P M.Flanagan
RP S.Stewart
RP T.Martinez
RP T.Stoddard

BAL 1984A

M J.Altobelli
1B E.Murray
2B R.Dauer
SS C.Ripken
3B W.Gross
LF G.Roenicke
CF J.Shelby
RF M.Young
C R.Dempsey
DH K.Singleton
UT A.Bumbry
UT J.Lowenstein
P M.Boddicker
P M.Flanagan
P S.Davis
P S.McGregor
P D.Martinez
RP S.Stewart
RP T.Martinez
RP T.Underwood

BAL 1985A

M J.Altobelli
M C.Ripken
M E.Weaver
1B E.Murray
2B A.Wiggins
SS C.Ripken
3B F.Rayford
LF M.Young
CF F.Lynn
RF L.Lacy
C R.Dempsey
DH L.Sheets
UT J.Dwyer
UT W.Gross
UT G.Roenicke
P S.McGregor
P M.Boddicker
P D.Martinez
P S.Davis
P K.Dixon
RP S.Stewart
RP N.Snell
RP D.Aase

BAL 1986A

M E.Weaver
1B E.Murray
2B J.Bonilla
SS C.Ripken
3B F.Rayford
LF J.Shelby
CF F.Lynn
RF L.Lacy
C R.Dempsey
DH L.Sheets
UT J.Beniquez
UT M.Young
P M.Boddicker
P S.McGregor
P K.Dixon
P M.Flanagan
P S.Davis
RP R.Bordi
RP D.Aase
RP N.Snell

BAL 1987A

M C.Ripken
1B E.Murray
2B B.Ripken
SS C.Ripken
3B R.Knight
LF K.Gerhart
CF F.Lynn
RF L.Sheets
C T.Kennedy
DH M.Young
P M.Boddicker
P E.Bell
P D.Schmidt
P J.Habyan
P K.Dixon
RP M.Williamson
RP T.Arnold
RP T.Niedenfuer

BAL 1988A

M C.Ripken
M F.Robinson
1B J.Traber
2B B.Ripken
SS C.Ripken
3B R.Gonzales
LF P.Stanicek
CF F.Lynn
RF J.Orsulak
C M.Tettleton
DH E.Murray
UT L.Sheets
UT K.Gerhart
P J.Bautista
P J.Tibbs
P J.Ballard
P M.Boddicker
P D.Schmidt
RP D.Sisk
RP M.Thurmond
RP T.Niedenfuer

BAL 1989A

M F.Robinson
1B R.Milligan
2B B.Ripken
SS C.Ripken
3B C.Worthington
LF P.Bradley
CF M.Devereaux
RF J.Orsulak
C M.Tettleton
DH L.Sheets
P B.Milacki
P J.Ballard
P D.Schmidt
P P.Harnisch
RP B.Holton
RP M.Williamson
RP M.Thurmond

BAL 1990A

M F.Robinson
1B R.Milligan
2B B.Ripken
SS C.Ripken
3B C.Worthington
LF P.Bradley
CF M.Devereaux
RF S.Finley
C M.Tettleton
DH S.Horn
UT J.Orsulak
P P.Harnisch
P D.Johnson
P B.Milacki
P J.Ballard
P B.McDonald
RP M.Williamson
RP G.Olson
RP J.Price

BAL 1991A

M F.Robinson
M J.Oates
1B R.Milligan
2B B.Ripken
SS C.Ripken
3B L.Gomez
LF B.Anderson
CF M.Devereaux
RF J.Orsulak
C C.Hoiles
DH S.Horn
UT J.Bell
UT D.Evans
P B.Milacki
P B.McDonald
P J.Mesa
P J.Ballard
P J.Robinson
RP M.Flanagan
RP T.Frohwirth
RP M.Williamson

BAL 1992A

M J.Oates
1B R.Milligan
2B B.Ripken
SS C.Ripken
3B L.Gomez
LF B.Anderson
CF M.Devereaux
RF J.Orsulak
C C.Hoiles
DH G.Davis
UT M.McLemore
UT D.Segui
P M.Mussina
P R.Sutcliffe
P B.McDonald
P B.Milacki
RP T.Frohwirth
RP A.Mills
RP S.Davis

BAL 1993A

M J.Oates
1B D.Segui
2B H.Reynolds
SS C.Ripken
3B T.Hulett
LF B.Anderson
CF M.Devereaux
RF M.McLemore
C C.Hoiles
DH H.Baines
P B.McDonald
P F.Valenzuela

P M.Mussina
P R.Sutcliffe
P J.Moyer
RP A.Mills
RP T.Frohwirth
RP M.Williamson

BAL 1994A

M J.Oates
1B R.Palmeiro
2B M.McLemore
SS C.Ripken
3B L.Gomez
LF B.Anderson
CF M.Devereaux
RF J.Hammonds
C C.Hoiles
DH H.Baines
UT C.Sabo
P M.Mussina
P B.McDonald
P J.Moyer
P S.Fernandez
RP M.Eichhorn
RP M.Williamson
RP A.Mills

BAL 1995A

M P.Regan
1B R.Palmeiro
2B M.Alexander
SS C.Ripken
3B J.Manto
LF B.Anderson
CF C.Goodwin
RF K.Bass
C C.Hoiles
DH H.Baines
UT B.Barberie
P M.Mussina
P K.Brown
P J.Moyer
P S.Erickson
RP M.Oquist
RP J.Orosco
RP A.Benitez

BAL 1996A

M D.Johnson
1B R.Palmeiro
2B R.Alomar
SS C.Ripken
3B B.Surhoff
LF M.Devereaux
CF B.Anderson
RF B.Bonilla
C C.Hoiles
DH E.Murray
P M.Mussina
P D.Wells
P S.Erickson
P R.Coppinger
RP R.Myers
RP R.McDowell
RP J.Orosco

BAL 1997A

M D.Johnson
1B R.Palmeiro
2B R.Alomar
SS M.Bordick
3B C.Ripken
LF B.Surhoff
CF B.Anderson
RF J.Hammonds
C L.Webster
DH G.Berroa
UT C.Hoiles
UT J.Reboulet
UT T.Tarasco
P M.Mussina
P S.Erickson
P J.Key
P S.Kamieniecki
RP A.Rhodes
RP S.Boskie
RP A.Benitez

BAL 1998A

M R.Miller
1B R.Palmeiro
2B R.Alomar
SS M.Bordick
3B C.Ripken
LF B.Surhoff
CF B.Anderson
RF E.Davis
C L.Webster
DH H.Baines
UT C.Hoiles
P S.Erickson
P M.Mussina
P S.Ponson
P D.Drabek
RP D.Johns
RP A.Rhodes
RP A.Mills

BAL 1999A

M R.Miller
1B J.Conine
2B D.DeShields
SS M.Bordick
3B C.Ripken
LF B.Surhoff
CF B.Anderson
RF A.Belle
C C.Johnson
DH H.Baines
UT J.Reboulet
P S.Erickson
P S.Ponson
P M.Mussina
P J.Guzman
P J.Johnson
RP D.Johns
RP M.Timlin
RP S.Kamieniecki

BAL 2000A

M M.Hargrove
1B W.Clark
2B D.DeShields
SS M.Bordick
3B C.Ripken
LF B.Surhoff
CF B.Anderson
RF A.Belle
C C.Johnson
DH H.Baines
UT J.Conine
P M.Mussina
P S.Ponson
P P.Rapp
P J.Mercedes
P J.Johnson
RP M.Trombley
RP C.McElroy
RP B.Groom

Boston

BOS n 1871-1875
BOS U 1884
BOS P 1890
BOS a 1891
BOS N 1876-1952
BOS A 1901-2000

BOS 1871n

M H.Wright
1B C.Gould
2B R.Barnes
SS G.Wright
3B H.Schafer
LF F.Cone
CF H.Wright
RF D.Birdsall
C C.McVey
P A.Spalding

BOS 1872n

M H.Wright
1B C.Gould
2B R.Barnes
SS G.Wright
3B H.Schafer
LF A.Leonard
CF H.Wright
RF F.Rogers
C C.McVey
P A.Spalding

BOS 1873n

M H.Wright
1B J.O'Rourke
2B R.Barnes
SS G.Wright
3B H.Schafer
LF A.Leonard
CF H.Wright
RF B.Addy
C D.White
P A.Spalding

BOS 1874n

M H.Wright
1B J.O'Rourke
2B R.Barnes
SS G.Wright
3B H.Schafer
LF A.Leonard
CF G.Hall
RF C.McVey
C D.White
P A.Spalding

BOS 1875n

M H.Wright
1B C.McVey
2B R.Barnes
SS G.Wright
3B H.Schafer
LF A.Leonard
CF J.O'Rourke
RF J.Manning
C D.White
P A.Spalding

BOS 1884U

M T.Murnane
1B T.Murnane
2B T.O'Brien
SS W.Hackett
3B J.Irwin
LF K.Butler
CF M.Slattery
RF E.Crane
C L.Brown
P J.Burke
P D.Shaw
P T.Bond

BOS 1890P

M K.Kelly
1B D.Brouthers
2B J.Quinn
SS A.Irwin
3B B.Nash
LF H.Richardson
CF T.Brown
RF H.Stovey
C M.Murphy
UT K.Kelly
P C.Radbourn
P A.Gumbert
P B.Daley
P M.Kilroy

BOS 1891a

M A.Irwin
1B D.Brouthers
2B C.Stricker
SS P.Radford
3B D.Farrell
LF H.Richardson
CF T.Brown
RF H.Duffy
C M.Murphy
P G.Haddock
P C.Buffinton
P D.O'Brien
P B.Daley

BOS 1876N

M H.Wright
1B T.Murnane
2B J.Morrill
SS G.Wright
3B H.Schafer
LF A.Leonard
CF J.O'Rourke
RF J.Manning
C L.Brown
P J.Borden
P F.Bradley

BOS 1877N

M H.Wright
1B D.White
2B G.Wright
SS E.Sutton
3B J.Morrill
LF A.Leonard
CF J.O'Rourke
RF G.Schafer
C L.Brown
P T.Bond

BOS 1878N

M H.Wright
1B J.Morrill
2B J.Burdock
SS G.Wright
3B E.Sutton
LF A.Leonard
CF J.O'Rourke
RF J.Manning
C P.Snyder
P T.Bond

BOS 1879N

M H.Wright
1B E.Cogswell
2B J.Burdock
SS E.Sutton
3B J.Morrill
LF C.Jones
CF J.O'Rourke
RF S.Houck
C P.Snyder
P T.Bond
P C.Foley

BOS 1880N

M H.Wright
1B C.Foley
2B J.Burdock
SS E.Sutton
3B J.Morrill
LF C.Jones
CF Jn.O'Rourke
RF Js.O'Rourke
C P.Powers
P T.Bond
P C.Foley

BOS 1881N

M H.Wright
1B J.Morrill
2B J.Burdock
SS R.Barnes
3B E.Sutton
LF J.Hornung
CF B.Crowley
RF F.Lewis
C P.Snyder
P J.Whitney
P J.Fox

BOS 1882N

M J.Morrill
1B J.Morrill
2B J.Burdock
SS S.Wise
3B E.Sutton
LF J.Hornung
CF P.Hotaling
RF E.Rowen
C P.Deasley
P J.Whitney
P B.Mathews

BOS 1883N

M J.Burdock
M J.Morrill
1B J.Morrill
2B J.Burdock
SS S.Wise
3B E.Sutton
LF J.Hornung
CF A.Smith
RF P.Radford
C M.Hines
UT C.Buffinton
P J.Whitney

BOS 1884N

M J.Morrill
1B J.Morrill
2B J.Burdock
SS S.Wise
3B E.Sutton
LF J.Hornung
CF J.Manning
RF B.Crowley
C M.Hackett
P C.Buffinton
P J.Whitney

BOS 1885N

M J.Morrill
1B J.Morrill
2B J.Burdock
SS S.Wise
3B E.Sutton
LF T.McCarthy
CF J.Manning
RF T.Poorman
C T.Gunning
P J.Whitney
P C.Buffinton
P D.Davis

BOS 1886N

M J.Morrill
1B S.Wise
2B J.Burdock
SS J.Morrill
3B B.Nash
LF J.Hornung
CF D.Johnston
RF T.Poorman
C C.Daily
UT E.Sutton
P C.Radbourn
P B.Stemmeyer

BOS 1887N

M K.Kelly
M J.Morrill
1B J.Morrill
2B J.Burdock
SS S.Wise
3B B.Nash
LF J.Hornung
CF D.Johnston
RF K.Kelly
C P.Tate
UT E.Sutton
P C.Radbourn
P K.Madden
P D.Conway
P B.Stemmeyer

BOS 1888N

M J.Morrill
1B J.Morrill
2B J.Quinn
SS S.Wise
3B B.Nash
LF J.Hornung
CF D.Johnston
RF T.Brown
C K.Kelly
P J.Clarkson
P B.Sowders
P C.Radbourn
P K.Madden

BOS 1889N

M J.Hart
1B D.Brouthers
2B H.Richardson
SS J.Quinn
3B B.Nash
LF T.Brown
CF D.Johnston
RF K.Kelly
C C.Bennett
P J.Clarkson
P C.Radbourn
P K.Madden

BOS 1890N

M F.Selee
1B T.Tucker
2B P.Smith
SS H.Long
3B C.McGarr
LF M.Sullivan
CF P.Hines
RF S.Brodie
C C.Bennett
P K.Nichols
P J.Clarkson
P C.Getzien

BOS 1891N

M F.Selee
1B T.Tucker
2B J.Quinn
SS H.Long
3B B.Nash
LF B.Lowe
CF S.Brodie
RF H.Stovey
C C.Bennett
P J.Clarkson
P K.Nichols
P H.Staley
P C.Getzien

BOS 1892N

M F.Selee
1B T.Tucker
2B J.Quinn
SS H.Long
3B B.Nash
LF B.Lowe
CF H.Duffy
RF T.McCarthy
C K.Kelly
P K.Nichols
P J.Stivetts
P H.Staley
P J.Clarkson

BOS 1893N

M F.Selee
1B T.Tucker
2B B.Lowe
SS H.Long
3B B.Nash
LF T.McCarthy
CF H.Duffy
RF C.Carroll
C C.Bennett
P K.Nichols
P J.Stivetts
P H.Staley
P H.Gastright

BOS 1894N

M F.Selee
1B T.Tucker
2B B.Lowe
SS H.Long
3B B.Nash
LF T.McCarthy
CF H.Duffy
RF J.Bannon
C C.Ganzel
P K.Nichols
P J.Stivetts
P H.Staley
P T.Lovett

BOS 1895N

M F.Selee
1B T.Tucker
2B B.Lowe
SS H.Long
3B B.Nash
LF T.McCarthy
CF H.Duffy
RF J.Bannon
C C.Ganzel
P K.Nichols
P J.Stivetts
P C.Dolan
P J.Sullivan

BOS 1896N

M F.Selee
1B T.Tucker
2B B.Lowe
SS H.Long
3B J.Collins
LF H.Duffy
CF B.Hamilton
RF J.Bannon
C M.Bergen
UT F.Tenney
P K.Nichols
P J.Stivetts
P J.Sullivan
P F.Klobedanz

BOS 1897N

M F.Selee
1B F.Tenney
2B B.Lowe
SS H.Long
3B J.Collins
LF H.Duffy
CF B.Hamilton
RF C.Stahl
C M.Bergen
P K.Nichols
P F.Klobedanz
P T.Lewis
P J.Sullivan

BOS 1898N

M F.Selee
1B F.Tenney
2B B.Lowe
SS H.Long
3B J.Collins
LF H.Duffy
CF B.Hamilton
RF C.Stahl
C M.Bergen
P K.Nichols
P T.Lewis
P V.Willis
P F.Klobedanz

BOS 1899N

M F.Selee
1B F.Tenney
2B B.Lowe
SS H.Long
3B J.Collins
LF H.Duffy
CF B.Hamilton
RF C.Stahl
C M.Bergen
P V.Willis
P K.Nichols
P T.Lewis
P J.Meekin
P F.Killen

BOS 1900N

M F.Selee
1B F.Tenney
2B B.Lowe
SS H.Long
3B J.Collins
LF C.Stahl
CF B.Hamilton
RF B.Freeman
C B.Clarke
P B.Dinneen
P V.Willis
P K.Nichols
P T.Lewis
P T.Pittinger

BOS 1901N

M F.Selee
1B F.Tenney
2B De Montreville
SS H.Long
3B B.Lowe
LF D.Cooley
CF B.Hamilton
RF J.Slagle
C M.Kittridge
P K.Nichols
P B.Dinneen
P V.Willis
P T.Pittinger

BOS 1902N

M A.Buckenberger
1B F.Tenney
2B De Montreville
SS H.Long
3B E.Gremminger
LF D.Cooley
CF B.Lush
RF P.Carney
C M.Kittridge
P V.Willis
P T.Pittinger
P M.Eason
P J.Malarkey

BOS 1903N

M A.Buckenberger
1B F.Tenney
2B E.Abbaticchio
SS H.Aubrey
3B E.Gremminger
LF D.Cooley
CF C.Dexter
RF P.Carney
C P.Moran
UT J.Stanley
P T.Pittinger
P V.Willis
P J.Malarkey
P W.Piatt

BOS 1904N

M A.Buckenberger
1B F.Tenney
2B F.Raymer
SS E.Abbaticchio
3B J.Delahanty
LF D.Cooley
CF P.Geier
RF R.Cannell
C T.Needham
UT P.Moran
P V.Willis
P T.Pittinger
P K.Wilhelm
P T.Fisher
P E.McNichol

BOS 1905N

M F.Tenney
1B F.Tenney
2B F.Raymer
SS E.Abbaticchio
3B H.Wolverton
LF J.Delahanty
CF R.Cannell
RF C.Dolan
C P.Moran
P I.Young
P V.Willis
P C.Fraser

P K.Wilhelm

BOS 1906N

M F.Tenney
1B F.Tenney
2B A.Strobel
SS A.Bridwell
3B D.Brain
LF D.Howard
CF J.Bates
RF C.Dolan
C T.Needham
P I.Young
P V.Lindaman
P B.Pfeffer
P G.Dorner

BOS 1907N

M F.Tenney
1B F.Tenney
2B C.Ritchey
SS A.Bridwell
3B D.Brain
LF N.Randall
CF G.Beaumont
RF J.Bates
C T.Needham
P G.Dorner
P V.Lindaman
P I.Young
P P.Flaherty
P B.Pfeffer

BOS 1908N

M J.Kelley
1B D.McGann
2B C.Ritchey
SS B.Dahlen
3B B.Sweeney
LF J.Bates
CF G.Beaumont
RF G.Browne
C F.Bowerman
P V.Lindaman
P P.Flaherty
P G.Dorner
P G.Ferguson
P T.McCarthy

BOS 1909N

M F.Bowerman
M H.Smith
1B F.Stem
2B D.Shean
SS J.Coffey
3B B.Sweeney
LF R.Thomas
CF G.Beaumont
RF B.Becker
C P.Graham
UT F.Beck
P A.Mattern
P G.Ferguson
P K.White
P L.Richie
P B.Brown

BOS 1910N

M F.Lake
1B B.Sharpe
2B D.Shean
SS B.Sweeney
3B B.Herzog
LF B.Collins
CF F.Beck
RF D.Miller
C P.Graham
P A.Mattern
P B.Brown
P S.Frock
P C.Curtis
P G.Ferguson

BOS 1911N

M F.Tenney
1B F.Tenney
2B B.Sweeney
SS B.Herzog
3B S.Ingerton
LF A.Kaiser
CF M.Donlin
RF D.Miller
C J.Kling
P B.Brown
P A.Mattern
P L.Tyler
P H.Perdue
P O.Weaver

BOS 1912N

M J.Kling
1B B.Houser
2B B.Sweeney
SS F.O'Rourke
3B E.McDonald
LF G.Jackson
CF V.Campbell
RF J.Titus
C J.Kling
UT A.Devlin
UT J.Kirke
P L.Tyler
P O.Hess
P H.Perdue
P W.Dickson
P E.Donnelly

BOS 1913N

M G.Stallings
1B H.Myers
2B B.Sweeney
SS R.Maranville
3B A.Devlin
LF J.Connolly
CF L.Mann
RF J.Titus
C B.Rariden
P L.Tyler
P D.Rudolph
P O.Hess
P H.Perdue
P B.James

BOS 1914N

M G.Stallings
1B B.Schmidt
2B J.Evers
SS R.Maranville
3B C.Deal
LF J.Connolly
CF L.Mann
RF L.Gilbert
C H.Gowdy
P D.Rudolph
P B.James
P L.Tyler
P D.Crutcher

BOS 1915N

M G.Stallings
1B B.Schmidt
2B J.Evers
SS R.Maranville
3B R.Smith
LF J.Connolly
CF S.Magee
RF H.Moran
C H.Gowdy
UT E.Fitzpatrick
P D.Rudolph
P T.Hughes
P P.Ragan
P L.Tyler

BOS 1916N

M G.Stallings
1B E.Konetchy
2B J.Evers
SS R.Maranville
3B R.Smith
LF S.Magee
CF F.Snodgrass
RF J.Wilhoit
C H.Gowdy
P D.Rudolph
P L.Tyler
P P.Ragan
P J.Barnes
P T.Hughes

BOS 1917N

M G.Stallings
1B E.Konetchy
2B J.Rawlings
SS R.Maranville
3B R.Smith
LF J.Kelly
CF R.Powell
RF W.Rehg
C W.Tragesser
P J.Barnes
P D.Rudolph
P L.Tyler
P A.Nehf
P P.Ragan

BOS 1918N

M G.Stallings
1B E.Konetchy
2B B.Herzog
SS J.Rawlings
3B R.Smith
LF R.Massey
CF R.Powell
RF A.Wickland
C A.Wilson
P A.Nehf
P P.Ragan
P D.Rudolph
P B.Hearn
P D.Fillingim

BOS 1919N

M G.Stallings
1B W.Holke
2B B.Herzog
SS R.Maranville
3B T.Boeckel
LF W.Cruise
CF J.Riggert
RF R.Powell
C H.Gowdy
UT R.Smith
P D.Rudolph
P D.Fillingim
P A.Nehf
P R.Keating
P A.Demaree

BOS 1920N

M G.Stallings
1B W.Holke
2B C.Pick
SS R.Maranville
3B T.Boeckel
LF L.Mann
CF R.Powell
RF W.Cruise
C M.O'Neil
P J.Oeschger
P J.Scott
P D.Fillingim
P H.McQuillan

BOS 1921N

M F.Mitchell
1B W.Holke
2B H.Ford
SS W.Barbare
3B T.Boeckel
LF W.Cruise
CF R.Powell
RF B.Southworth
C M.O'Neil
P J.Oeschger
P M.Watson
P H.McQuillan
P D.Fillingim
P J.Scott

BOS 1922N

M F.Mitchell
1B W.Holke
2B L.Kopf
SS H.Ford
3B T.Boeckel
LF A.Nixon
CF R.Powell
RF W.Cruise
C M.O'Neil
UT W.Barbare
P M.Watson
P F.Miller
P R.Marquard
P J.Oeschger
P H.McQuillan
RP T.McNamara
RP G.Braxton

BOS 1923N

M F.Mitchell
1B S.McInnis
2B H.Ford
SS B.Smith
3B T.Boeckel
LF G.Felix
CF R.Powell
RF B.Southworth
C M.O'Neil
P R.Marquard
P J.Genewich
P J.Barnes
P J.Oeschger
P T.McNamara
RP D.Fillingim

BOS 1924N

M D.Bancroft
M R.Rudolph
M D.Bancroft
1B S.McInnis
2B C.Tierney
SS B.Smith
3B E.Padgett
LF B.Cunningham
CF G.Felix
RF C.Stengel
C M.O'Neil
P J.Barnes
P J.Genewich
P J.Cooney
P T.McNamara
P A.Yeargin

BOS 1925N

M D.Bancroft
1B D.Burrus
2B D.Gautreau
SS D.Bancroft
3B W.Marriott
LF D.Harris
CF G.Felix
RF J.Welsh
C F.Gibson
UT B.Neis
P J.Cooney
P J.Barnes
P L.Benton
P J.Genewich
P S.Graham
RP R.Marquard
RP I.Kamp

BOS 1926N

M D.Bancroft
1B D.Burrus
2B D.Gautreau
SS D.Bancroft
3B A.High
LF E.Brown
CF J.Smith
RF J.Welsh
C Z.Taylor
P L.Benton
P J.Genewich
P B.Smith
P J.Werts
P G.Mogridge

BOS 1927N

M D.Bancroft
1B J.Fournier
2B D.Gautreau
SS D.Bancroft
3B A.High
LF E.Brown
CF J.Welsh
RF L.Richbourg
C S.Hogan
UT D.Farrell
UT E.Moore
P B.Smith
P K.Greenfield
P J.Genewich
P J.Werts
P C.Robertson
RP G.Mogridge

BOS 1928N

M J.Slattery
M R.Hornsby
1B G.Sisler
2B R.Hornsby
SS D.Farrell
3B L.Bell
LF E.Brown
CF J.Smith
RF L.Richbourg
C Z.Taylor
P B.Smith
P E.Brandt
P A.Delaney
P K.Greenfield
RP F.Edwards

BOS 1929N

M J.Fuchs
1B G.Sisler
2B F.Maguire
SS R.Maranville
3B L.Bell
LF G.Harper
CF E.Clark
RF L.Richbourg
C A.Spohrer
P B.Smith
P S.Seibold
P P.Jones
P E.Brandt
P B.Cantwell

BOS 1930N

M B.McKechnie
1B G.Sisler
2B F.Maguire
SS R.Maranville
3B B.Chatham
LF W.Berger
CF J.Welsh
RF L.Richbourg
C A.Spohrer
P S.Seibold
P B.Smith
P B.Cantwell
P T.Zachary
P E.Brandt
RP B.Cunningham

BOS 1931N

M B.McKechnie
1B E.Sheely
2B F.Maguire
SS R.Maranville
3B B.Urbanski
LF R.Worthington
CF W.Berger
RF W.Schulmerich
C A.Spohrer
UT L.Richbourg
P E.Brandt
P T.Zachary
P S.Seibold
P B.Cantwell
P B.Sherdel
RP H.Haid

BOS 1932N

M B.McKechnie
1B A.Shires
2B R.Maranville
SS B.Urbanski
3B F.Knothe
LF R.Worthington
CF W.Berger
RF W.Schulmerich
C A.Spohrer
UT R.Moore
P E.Brandt
P H.Betts
P B.Brown
P T.Zachary
P B.Cantwell
RP F.Frankhouse
RP B.Cunningham

BOS 1933N

M B.McKechnie
1B B.Jordan
2B R.Maranville
SS B.Urbanski
3B P.Whitney
LF H.Lee
CF W.Berger
RF R.Moore
C S.Hogan
P E.Brandt
P B.Cantwell
P F.Frankhouse
P H.Betts
P T.Zachary

BOS 1934N

M B.McKechnie
1B B.Jordan
2B M.McManus
SS B.Urbanski
3B P.Whitney
LF H.Lee
CF W.Berger
RF T.Thompson
C A.Spohrer
UT S.Hogan
UT R.Moore
P E.Brandt
P F.Frankhouse
P H.Betts
P F.Rhem
P B.Cantwell

BOS 1935N

M B.McKechnie
1B B.Jordan
2B L.Mallon
SS B.Urbanski
3B P.Whitney
LF H.Lee
CF W.Berger
RF T.Thompson
C A.Spohrer
UT R.Moore
P F.Frankhouse
P B.Cantwell
P B.Smith
P E.Brandt
P H.Betts
RP L.Benton

BOS 1936N

M B.McKechnie
1B B.Jordan
2B T.Cuccinello
SS B.Urbanski
3B J.Coscarart
LF H.Lee
CF W.Berger
RF G.Moore
C A.Lopez
UT T.Thompson
P D.Mac Fayden
P T.Chaplin
P J.Lanning
P B.Reis
P B.Smith

BOS 1937N

M B.McKechnie
1B E.Fletcher
2B T.Cuccinello
SS R.Warstler
3B G.English
LF D.Garms
CF V.DiMaggio
RF G.Moore
C A.Lopez
P L.Fette
P J.Turner
P D.Mac Fayden
P G.Bush
P J.Lanning
RP I.Hutchinson

BOS 1938N

M C.Stengel
1B E.Fletcher
2B T.Cuccinello
SS R.Warstler
3B J.Stripp
LF M.West
CF V.DiMaggio
RF J.Cooney
C R.Mueller
UT D.Garms
P J.Turner
P L.Fette
P D.Mac Fayden
P I.Hutchinson
P M.Shoffner

BOS 1939N

M C.Stengel
1B B.Hassett
2B T.Cuccinello
SS E.Miller
3B H.Majeski
LF M.West
CF J.Cooney
RF D.Garms
C A.Lopez
UT A.Simmons
UT R.Warstler
P B.Posedel
P D.Mac Fayden
P J.Turner
P L.Fette
P M.Shoffner

BOS 1940N

M C.Stengel
1B B.Hassett
2B B.Rowell
SS E.Miller
3B S.Sisti
LF C.Ross
CF J.Cooney
RF M.West
C R.Berres
UT G.Moore
P D.Errickson
P B.Posedel
P J.Sullivan
P M.Salvo
P N.Strincevich
RP A.Javery
RP A.Piechota
RP D.Coffman

BOS 1941N

M C.Stengel
1B B.Hassett
2B B.Rowell
SS E.Miller
3B S.Sisti
LF M.West
CF J.Cooney
RF G.Moore
C R.Berres
UT P.Waner
P J.Tobin
P M.Salvo
P A.Johnson
P D.Errickson
P A.Javery
RP J.Hutchings
RP F.LaManna

BOS 1942N

M C.Stengel
1B M.West
2B S.Sisti
SS E.Miller
3B N.Fernandez
LF C.Ross
CF T.Holmes
RF P.Waner
C E.Lombardi
P J.Tobin
P A.Javery
P L.Tost
P M.Salvo
P T.Earley
RP J.Sain
RP B.Donovan
RP D.Errickson

BOS 1943N

M B.Coleman
M C.Stengel
1B J.McCarthy
2B C.Ryan
SS W.Wietelmann
3B E.Joost
LF B.Nieman
CF T.Holmes
RF C.Workman
C P.Masi
UT C.Ross
P A.Javery
P N.Andrews
P R.Barrett
P J.Tobin
P M.Salvo
RP D.Odom

BOS 1944N

M B.Coleman
1B B.Etchison
2B C.Ryan
SS W.Wietelmann
3B D.Phillips
LF B.Nieman
CF T.Holmes
RF C.Workman
C P.Masi
UT M.Macon
P J.Tobin
P N.Andrews
P A.Javery
P R.Barrett
P I.Hutchinson

BOS 1945N

M B.Coleman
M D.Bissonette
1B V.Shupe
2B W.Wietelmann
SS D.Culler
3B C.Workman
LF B.Nieman
CF C.Gillenwater
RF T.Holmes
C P.Masi
P J.Tobin
P B.Logan
P J.Hutchings
P N.Andrews
P E.Wright
RP D.Hendrickson

BOS 1946N

M B.Southworth
1B R.Sanders
2B C.Ryan
SS D.Culler
3B N.Fernandez
LF B.Rowell
CF C.Gillenwater
RF T.Holmes
C P.Masi
UT J.Hopp
P J.Sain

P M.Cooper
P E.Wright
P B.Lee
P S.Johnson
RP L.Wallace

BOS 1947N

M B.Southworth
1B E.Torgeson
2B C.Ryan
SS D.Culler
3B B.Elliott
LF B.Rowell
CF J.Hopp
RF T.Holmes
C P.Masi
P W.Spahn
P J.Sain
P R.Barrett
P B.Voiselle
P S.Johnson
RP C.Shoun
RP E.Wright
RP W.Lanfranconi

BOS 1948N

M B.Southworth
1B E.Torgeson
2B E.Stanky
SS A.Dark
3B B.Elliott
LF J.Heath
CF J.Russell
RF T.Holmes
C P.Masi
UT M.McCormick
P J.Sain
P W.Spahn
P B.Voiselle
P V.Bickford
P R.Barrett
RP B.Hogue
RP C.Shoun

BOS 1949N

M B.Southworth
M J.Cooney
1B E.Fletcher
2B E.Stanky
SS A.Dark
3B B.Elliott
LF M.Rickert
CF J.Russell
RF T.Holmes
C B.Salkeld
UT S.Sisti
P W.Spahn
P J.Sain
P V.Bickford
P B.Voiselle
P J.Antonelli
RP N.Potter
RP B.Hall
RP B.Hogue

BOS 1950N

M B.Southworth
1B E.Torgeson
2B R.Hartsfield
SS B.Kerr
3B B.Elliott
LF S.Gordon
CF S.Jethroe
RF T.Holmes
C W.Cooper
UT W.Marshall
P V.Bickford
P W.Spahn
P J.Sain
P B.Chipman
RP B.Hogue
RP J.Antonelli
RP B.Hall

BOS 1951N

M B.Southworth
M T.Holmes
1B E.Torgeson
2B R.Hartsfield
SS B.Kerr
3B B.Elliott
LF S.Gordon
CF S.Jethroe
RF W.Marshall
C W.Cooper
UT S.Sisti
P W.Spahn
P M.Surkont
P V.Bickford
P J.Sain
P C.Nichols
RP D.Cole
RP G.Estock
RP B.Chipman

BOS 1952N

M T.Holmes
M C.Grimm
1B E.Torgeson
2B J.Dittmer
SS J.Logan
3B E.Mathews
LF S.Gordon
CF S.Jethroe
RF J.Daniels
C W.Cooper
P W.Spahn
P J.Wilson
P M.Surkont
P V.Bickford
P L.Burdette
RP S.Jones

BOS 1901A

M J.Collins
1B B.Freeman
2B H.Ferris
SS F.Parent
3B J.Collins
LF T.Dowd
CF C.Stahl
RF C.Hemphill
C O.Schreckengost
P C.Young
P T.Lewis
P G.Winter
P F.Mitchell
P N.Cuppy

BOS 1902A

M J.Collins
1B C.LaChance
2B H.Ferris
SS F.Parent
3B J.Collins
LF P.Dougherty
CF C.Stahl
RF B.Freeman
C L.Criger
P C.Young
P B.Dinneen
P G.Winter
P T.Sparks

BOS 1903A

M J.Collins
1B C.LaChance
2B H.Ferris
SS F.Parent
3B J.Collins
LF P.Dougherty
CF C.Stahl
RF B.Freeman
C L.Criger
UT J.O'Brien
P C.Young
P B.Dinneen
P T.Hughes
P N.Gibson
P G.Winter

BOS 1904A

M J.Collins
1B C.LaChance
2B H.Ferris
SS F.Parent
3B J.Collins
LF K.Selbach
CF C.Stahl
RF B.Freeman
C L.Criger
P C.Young
P B.Dinneen
P J.Tannehill
P N.Gibson
P G.Winter

BOS 1905A

M J.Collins
1B M.Grimshaw
2B H.Ferris
SS F.Parent
3B J.Collins
LF J.Burkett
CF C.Stahl
RF K.Selbach
C L.Criger
UT B.Freeman
P C.Young
P J.Tannehill
P G.Winter
P B.Dinneen
P N.Gibson

BOS 1906A

M J.Collins
M C.Stahl
1B M.Grimshaw
2B H.Ferris
SS F.Parent
3B R.Morgan
LF J.Hoey
CF C.Stahl
RF J.Hayden
C C.Armbruster
UT B.Freeman
P C.Young
P J.Harris
P B.Dinneen
P G.Winter
P J.Tannehill

BOS 1907A

M C.Young
M G.Huff
M B.Unglaub
M D.McGuire
1B B.Unglaub
2B H.Ferris
SS H.Wagner
3B J.Knight
LF J.Barrett
CF D.Sullivan
RF B.Congalton
C L.Criger
UT F.Parent
P C.Young
P G.Winter
P R.Glaze
P T.Pruiett
P J.Tannehill

BOS 1908A

M D.McGuire
M F.Lake
1B J.Stahl
2B A.McConnell
SS H.Wagner
3B H.Lord
LF J.Thoney
CF D.Sullivan
RF D.Gessler
C L.Criger
UT G.Cravath
P C.Young
P E.Cicotte
P C.Morgan
P F.Burchell
P G.Winter

BOS 1909A

M F.Lake
1B J.Stahl
2B A.McConnell
SS H.Wagner
3B H.Lord
LF H.Niles
CF T.Speaker
RF D.Gessler
C B.Carrigan
P F.Arellanes
P E.Cicotte
P J.Wood
P C.Chech

BOS 1910A

M P.Donovan
1B J.Stahl
2B L.Gardner
SS H.Wagner
3B H.Lord
LF D.Lewis
CF T.Speaker
RF H.Hooper
C B.Carrigan
UT C.Engle
P E.Cicotte
P R.Collins
P J.Wood
P C.Hall
P E.Karger

BOS 1911A

M P.Donovan
1B C.Engle
2B H.Wagner
SS S.Yerkes
3B L.Gardner
LF D.Lewis
CF T.Speaker
RF H.Hooper
C B.Carrigan
UT R.Williams
P J.Wood
P E.Cicotte
P R.Collins
P L.Pape
P C.Hall

BOS 1912A

M J.Stahl
1B J.Stahl
2B S.Yerkes
SS H.Wagner
3B L.Gardner
LF D.Lewis
CF T.Speaker
RF H.Hooper
C B.Carrigan
P J.Wood
P B.O'Brien
P H.Bedient
P R.Collins
P C.Hall

BOS 1913A

M J.Stahl
M B.Carrigan
1B C.Engle
2B S.Yerkes
SS H.Wagner
3B L.Gardner
LF D.Lewis
CF T.Speaker
RF H.Hooper
C B.Carrigan
P D.Leonard
P H.Bedient
P R.Collins
P J.Wood
P E.Moseley

BOS 1914A

M B.Carrigan
1B D.Hoblitzel
2B S.Yerkes
SS E.Scott
3B L.Gardner
LF D.Lewis
CF T.Speaker
RF H.Hooper
C B.Carrigan
UT H.Janvrin
P R.Collins
P D.Leonard
P R.Foster
P H.Bedient
P E.Shore

BOS 1915A

M B.Carrigan
1B D.Hoblitzel
2B H.Wagner
SS E.Scott
3B L.Gardner
LF D.Lewis
CF T.Speaker
RF H.Hooper
C P.Thomas
UT H.Janvrin
P R.Foster
P E.Shore
P B.Ruth
P D.Leonard
P J.Wood

BOS 1916A

M B.Carrigan
1B D.Hoblitzel
2B J.Barry
SS E.Scott
3B L.Gardner
LF D.Lewis
CF T.Walker
RF H.Hooper
C P.Thomas
UT H.Janvrin
P B.Ruth
P D.Leonard
P C.Mays
P E.Shore
P R.Foster

BOS 1917A

M J.Barry
1B D.Hoblitzel
2B J.Barry
SS E.Scott
3B L.Gardner
LF D.Lewis
CF T.Walker
RF H.Hooper
C S.Agnew
P B.Ruth
P D.Leonard
P C.Mays
P E.Shore
P R.Foster

BOS 1918A

M E.Barrow
1B S.McInnis
2B D.Shean
SS E.Scott
3B F.Thomas
LF G.Whiteman
CF A.Strunk
RF H.Hooper
C S.Agnew
UT B.Ruth
UT W.Schang
P C.Mays
P J.Bush
P S.Jones
P D.Leonard

BOS 1919A

M E.Barrow
1B S.McInnis
2B R.Shannon
SS E.Scott
3B O.Vitt
LF B.Ruth
CF B.Roth
RF H.Hooper
C W.Schang
P S.Jones
P H.Pennock
P C.Mays
P A.Russell
P W.Hoyt

BOS 1920A

M E.Barrow
1B S.McInnis
2B M.McNally
SS E.Scott
3B E.Foster
LF M.Menosky
CF T.Hendryx
RF H.Hooper
C R.Walters
UT W.Schang
P S.Jones
P J.Bush
P H.Pennock
P H.Harper
P W.Hoyt

BOS 1921A

M H.Duffy
1B S.McInnis
2B D.Pratt
SS E.Scott
3B E.Foster
LF M.Menosky
CF N.Leibold
RF S.Collins
C M.Ruel
P S.Jones
P J.Bush
P H.Pennock
P A.Russell
P E.Myers

BOS 1922A

M H.Duffy
1B G.Burns
2B D.Pratt
SS J.Mitchell
3B J.Dugan
LF M.Menosky
CF N.Leibold
RF S.Collins
C M.Ruel
UT J.Harris
P J.Quinn
P R.Collins
P H.Pennock
P A.Ferguson
P B.Karr
RP C.Fullerton

BOS 1923A

M F.Chance
1B G.Burns
2B C.Fewster
SS J.Mitchell
3B H.Shanks
LF J.Harris
CF D.Reichle
RF I.Flagstead
C V.Picinich
UT S.Collins
UT N.McMillan
P H.Ehmke
P J.Quinn
P A.Ferguson
P B.Piercy
P G.Murray
RP L.O'Doul

BOS 1924A

M L.Fohl
1B J.Harris
2B B.Wambsganss
SS D.Lee
3B D.Clark
LF B.Veach
CF I.Flagstead
RF I.Boone
C S.O'Neill
P H.Ehmke
P A.Ferguson
P J.Quinn
P C.Fullerton
P B.Piercy
RP G.Murray

BOS 1925A

M L.Fohl
1B P.Todt
2B B.Wambsganss
SS D.Lee
3B D.Prothro
LF R.Carlyle
CF I.Flagstead
RF I.Boone
C V.Picinich
UT T.Vache
P H.Ehmke
P T.Wingfield
P R.Ruffing
P P.Zahniser
P J.Quinn
RP B.Ross
RP O.Fuhr

BOS 1926A

M L.Fohl
1B P.Todt
2B B.Regan
SS T.Rigney
3B F.Haney
LF S.Rosenthal
CF I.Flagstead
RF B.Jacobson
C A.Gaston
P H.Wiltse
P T.Wingfield
P P.Zahniser
P R.Ruffing
P T.Welzer
RP J.Russell

BOS 1927A

M B.Carrigan
1B P.Todt
2B B.Regan
SS B.Myer
3B B.Rogell
LF W.Shaner
CF I.Flagstead
RF J.Tobin
C G.Hartley
UT C.Carlyle
UT J.Rothrock
P H.Wiltse
P S.Harriss
P T.Welzer
P D.Mac Fayden
P R.Ruffing

BOS 1928A

M B.Carrigan
1B P.Todt
2B B.Regan
SS W.Gerber
3B B.Myer
LF K.Williams
CF I.Flagstead
RF D.Taitt
C F.Hofmann
UT B.Rogell
UT J.Rothrock
P R.Ruffing
P E.Morris
P J.Russell
P D.Mac Fayden
P S.Harriss
RP M.Settlemire
RP P.Simmons

BOS 1929A

M B.Carrigan
1B P.Todt
2B B.Regan
SS H.Rhyne
3B B.Reeves
LF R.Scarritt
CF J.Rothrock
RF B.Barrett
C C.Berry
UT E.Bigelow
UT B.Narleski
P R.Ruffing
P M.Gaston
P J.Russell
P D.Mac Fayden
P E.Morris
RP E.Carroll

BOS 1930A

M H.Wagner
1B P.Todt
2B B.Regan
SS H.Rhyne
3B O.Miller
LF R.Scarritt
CF T.Oliver
RF E.Webb
C C.Berry
UT C.Durst
P M.Gaston
P D.Mac Fayden
P H.Lisenbee
P J.Russell
P E.Durham
RP G.Smith

BOS 1931A

M S.Collins
1B B.Sweeney
2B R.Warstler
SS H.Rhyne
3B O.Miller
LF J.Rothrock
CF T.Oliver
RF E.Webb
C C.Berry
UT U.Pickering
UT A.Van Camp
P J.Russell
P D.Mac Fayden
P W.Moore
P H.Lisenbee
P E.Durham

BOS 1932A

M S.Collins
M M.McManus
1B D.Alexander
2B M.Olson
SS R.Warstler
3B U.Pickering
LF S.Jolley
CF T.Oliver
RF R.Johnson
C B.Tate
UT J.Watwood
P B.Weiland
P E.Durham
P B.Kline
P I.Andrews
RP W.Moore
RP J.Michaels
RP L.Boerner

BOS 1933A

M M.McManus
1B D.Alexander
2B J.Hodapp
SS R.Warstler
3B M.McManus
LF S.Jolley
CF D.Cooke
RF R.Johnson
C R.Ferrell
UT B.Werber
P G.Rhodes
P B.Weiland
P L.Brown
P H.Johnson
P I.Andrews
RP J.Welch
RP B.Kline

BOS 1934A

M B.Harris
1B E.Morgan
2B B.Cissell
SS L.Lary
3B B.Werber

LF R.Johnson
CF C.Reynolds
RF D.Porter
C R.Ferrell
UT M.Bishop
UT M.Solters
P G.Rhodes
P J.Welch
P F.Ostermueller
P W.Ferrell
P H.Johnson
RP H.Pennock

BOS 1935A

M J.Cronin
1B B.Dahlgren
2B S.Melillo
SS J.Cronin
3B B.Werber
LF R.Johnson
CF M.Almada
RF D.Cooke
C R.Ferrell
P W.Ferrell
P L.Grove
P G.Rhodes
P J.Welch
P R.Walberg
RP J.Wilson
RP G.Hockette

BOS 1936A

M J.Cronin
1B J.Foxx
2B S.Melillo
SS E.McNair
3B B.Werber
LF H.Manush
CF D.Cramer
RF D.Cooke
C R.Ferrell
UT M.Almada
P W.Ferrell
P L.Grove
P F.Ostermueller
P J.Marcum
P J.Wilson

BOS 1937A

M J.Cronin
1B J.Foxx
2B E.McNair
SS J.Cronin
3B P.Higgins
LF B.Mills
CF D.Cramer
RF B.Chapman
C G.Desautels
P L.Grove
P J.Wilson
P B.Newsom
P J.Marcum
P A.McKain

BOS 1938A

M J.Cronin
1B J.Foxx
2B B.Doerr
SS J.Cronin
3B P.Higgins
LF J.Vosmik
CF D.Cramer
RF B.Chapman
C G.Desautels
P J.Bagby
P J.Wilson
P F.Ostermueller
P L.Grove
P E.Dickman
RP A.McKain

BOS 1939A

M J.Cronin
1B J.Foxx
2B B.Doerr
SS J.Cronin
3B J.Tabor
LF J.Vosmik
CF D.Cramer
RF T.Williams
C J.Peacock
UT L.Finney
P L.Grove
P J.Wilson
P F.Ostermueller
P E.Auker
P D.Galehouse
RP E.Dickman
RP J.Heving
RP J.Wade

BOS 1940A

M J.Cronin
1B J.Foxx
2B B.Doerr
SS J.Cronin
3B J.Tabor
LF T.Williams
CF D.DiMaggio
RF D.Cramer
C G.Desautels
UT L.Finney
P J.Bagby
P J.Wilson
P L.Grove
P F.Ostermueller
P H.Hash
RP E.Dickman

BOS 1941A

M J.Cronin
1B J.Foxx
2B B.Doerr
SS J.Cronin
3B J.Tabor
LF T.Williams
CF D.DiMaggio
RF L.Finney
C F.Pytlak
P D.Newsome
P M.Harris
P C.Wagner
P L.Grove
P J.Dobson

BOS 1942A

M J.Cronin
1B T.Lupien
2B B.Doerr
SS J.Pesky
3B J.Tabor
LF T.Williams
CF D.DiMaggio
RF L.Finney
C B.Conroy
P T.Hughson
P C.Wagner
P J.Dobson
P D.Newsome
P O.Judd
RP M.Brown

BOS 1943A

M J.Cronin
1B T.Lupien
2B B.Doerr
SS S.Newsome
3B J.Tabor
LF L.Culberson
CF C.Metkovich
RF P.Fox
C R.Partee
P T.Hughson
P Y.Terry
P J.Dobson
P O.Judd
P D.Newsome
RP M.Brown

BOS 1944A

M J.Cronin
1B L.Finney
2B B.Doerr
SS S.Newsome
3B J.Tabor
LF B.Johnson
CF C.Metkovich
RF P.Fox
C R.Partee
P T.Hughson
P P.Woods
P J.Bowman
P E.O'Neill
P M.Ryba
RP F.Barrett

BOS 1945A

M J.Cronin
1B C.Metkovich
2B S.Newsome
SS E.Lake
3B J.Tobin
LF B.Johnson
CF L.Culberson
RF J.Lazor
C B.Garbark
UT T.McBride
P D.Ferriss
P J.Wilson
P E.O'Neill
P C.Hausmann
P M.Ryba
RP F.Barrett

BOS 1946A

M J.Cronin
1B R.York
2B B.Doerr
SS J.Pesky
3B R.Russell
LF T.Williams
CF D.DiMaggio
RF C.Metkovich
C H.Wagner
P T.Hughson
P D.Ferriss
P M.Harris
P J.Dobson
P J.Bagby
RP E.Johnson
RP B.Klinger
RP C.Dreisewerd

BOS 1947A

M J.Cronin
1B J.Jones
2B B.Doerr
SS J.Pesky
3B S.Dente
LF T.Williams
CF D.DiMaggio
RF S.Mele
C B.Tebbetts
P J.Dobson
P D.Ferriss
P T.Hughson
P D.Galehouse
P E.Johnson
RP J.Murphy
RP B.Zuber

BOS 1948A

M J.McCarthy
1B B.Goodman
2B B.Doerr
SS V.Stephens
3B J.Pesky
LF T.Williams
CF D.DiMaggio
RF S.Spence
C B.Tebbetts
P J.Dobson
P M.Parnell
P J.Kramer
P E.Kinder
P D.Galehouse
RP E.Johnson

BOS 1949A

M J.McCarthy
1B B.Goodman
2B B.Doerr
SS V.Stephens
3B J.Pesky
LF T.Williams
CF D.DiMaggio
RF A.Zarilla
C B.Tebbetts
P M.Parnell
P E.Kinder
P J.Dobson
P C.Stobbs
P J.Kramer
RP T.Hughson
RP E.Johnson

BOS 1950A

M J.McCarthy
M S.O'Neill
1B W.Dropo
2B B.Doerr
SS V.Stephens
3B J.Pesky
LF T.Williams
CF D.DiMaggio
RF A.Zarilla
C B.Tebbetts
UT B.Goodman
P M.Parnell
P E.Kinder
P J.Dobson
P C.Stobbs
P M.McDermott

BOS 1951A

M S.O'Neill
1B W.Dropo
2B B.Doerr
SS J.Pesky
3B V.Stephens
LF T.Williams
CF D.DiMaggio
RF C.Vollmer
C L.Moss
UT B.Goodman
P M.Parnell
P R.Scarborough
P M.McDermott
P C.Stobbs
P W.Nixon
RP E.Kinder
RP H.Taylor
RP W.Masterson

BOS 1952A

M L.Boudreau
1B D.Gernert
2B B.Goodman
SS J.Lipon
3B G.Kell
LF H.Evers
CF D.DiMaggio
RF F.Throneberry
C S.White
P M.Parnell
P M.McDermott
P D.Trout
P S.Hudson
P D.Brodowski
RP I.Delock
RP R.Scarborough

BOS 1953A

M L.Boudreau
1B D.Gernert
2B B.Goodman
SS M.Bolling
3B G.Kell
LF H.Evers
CF T.Umphlett
RF J.Piersall
C S.White
P M.Parnell
P M.McDermott
P H.Brown
P S.Hudson
P W.Nixon
RP E.Kinder
RP B.Flowers
RP I.Delock

BOS 1954A

M L.Boudreau
1B H.Agganis
2B T.Lepcio
SS M.Bolling
3B G.Hatton
LF T.Williams
CF J.Jensen
RF J.Piersall
C S.White
UT B.Goodman
UT K.Olson
P F.Sullivan
P W.Nixon
P T.Brewer
P L.Kiely
P B.Henry
RP H.Brown
RP E.Kinder
RP S.Hudson

BOS 1955A

M P.Higgins
1B N.Zauchin
2B B.Goodman
SS B.Klaus
3B G.Hatton
LF T.Williams
CF J.Piersall
RF J.Jensen
C S.White
UT G.Stephens
P F.Sullivan
P W.Nixon
P T.Brewer
P G.Susce
P I.Delock
RP L.Kiely
RP T.Hurd
RP E.Kinder

BOS 1956A

M P.Higgins
1B M.Vernon
2B B.Goodman
SS D.Buddin
3B B.Klaus
LF T.Williams
CF J.Piersall
RF J.Jensen
C S.White
UT D.Gernert
UT G.Stephens
P T.Brewer
P F.Sullivan
P W.Nixon
P D.Sisler
P M.Parnell
RP I.Delock
RP T.Hurd

BOS 1957A

M P.Higgins
1B D.Gernert
2B T.Lepcio
SS B.Klaus
3B F.Malzone
LF T.Williams
CF J.Piersall
RF J.Jensen
C S.White
UT G.Stephens
UT M.Vernon
P F.Sullivan
P T.Brewer
P W.Nixon
P M.Fornieles
P I.Delock
P D.Sisler
RP I.Delock

BOS 1958A

M P.Higgins
1B D.Gernert
2B P.Runnels
SS D.Buddin
3B F.Malzone
LF T.Williams
CF J.Piersall
RF J.Jensen
C S.White
UT G.Stephens
P T.Brewer
P F.Sullivan
P I.Delock
P D.Sisler
P M.Fornieles
RP M.Wall
RP L.Kiely

BOS 1959A

M P.Higgins
M R.York
M B.Jurges
1B D.Gernert
2B P.Runnels
SS D.Buddin
3B F.Malzone
LF G.Stephens
CF G.Geiger
RF J.Jensen
C S.White
UT M.Keough
UT V.Wertz
UT T.Williams
P T.Brewer
P J.Casale
P F.Sullivan
P B.Monbouquette
P I.Delock
RP M.Fornieles
RP L.Kiely

BOS 1960A

M B.Jurges
M D.Baker
M P.Higgins
1B V.Wertz
2B P.Runnels
SS D.Buddin
3B F.Malzone
LF T.Williams
CF W.Tasby
RF L.Clinton
C R.Nixon
UT P.Green
P B.Monbouquette
P T.Brewer
P F.Sullivan
P I.Delock
P B.Muffett
RP M.Fornieles
RP T.Sturdivant
RP T.Borland

BOS 1961A

M P.Higgins
1B P.Runnels
2B C.Schilling
SS D.Buddin
3B F.Malzone
LF C.Yastrzemski
CF G.Geiger
RF J.Jensen
C J.Pagliaroni
P B.Monbouquette
P G.Conley
P D.Schwall
P I.Delock
P T.Stallard
RP M.Fornieles
RP B.Muffett
RP D.Hillman

BOS 1962A

M P.Higgins
1B P.Runnels
2B C.Schilling
SS E.Bressoud
3B F.Malzone
LF C.Yastrzemski
CF G.Geiger
RF C.Hardy
C J.Pagliaroni
UT L.Clinton
P G.Conley
P B.Monbouquette
P E.Wilson
P D.Schwall
RP D.Radatz
RP M.Fornieles
RP A.Earley

BOS 1963A

M J.Pesky
1B D.Stuart
2B C.Schilling
SS E.Bressoud
3B F.Malzone
LF C.Yastrzemski
CF G.Geiger
RF L.Clinton
C B.Tillman
UT R.Mejias
UT R.Nixon
P B.Monbouquette
P E.Wilson
P D.Morehead
P B.Heffner
RP J.Lamabe
RP D.Radatz
RP A.Earley

BOS 1964A

M J.Pesky
M .Herman
1B D.Stuart
2B D.Jones
SS E.Bressoud
3B F.Malzone
LF T.Conigliaro
CF C.Yastrzemski
RF L.Thomas
C B.Tillman
UT F.Mantilla
P B.Monbouquette
P E.Wilson
P J.Lamabe
P D.Morehead
RP B.Heffner
RP D.Radatz
RP B.Spanswick

BOS 1965A

M .Herman
1B L.Thomas
2B F.Mantilla
SS R.Petrocelli
3B F.Malzone
LF C.Yastrzemski
CF L.Green
RF T.Conigliaro
C B.Tillman
UT E.Bressoud
UT D.Jones
P E.Wilson
P B.Monbouquette
P D.Morehead
P J.Lonborg
P D.Bennett
RP D.Radatz
RP A.Earley
RP J.Ritchie

BOS 1966A

M .Herman
M P.Runnels
1B G.Scott
2B G.Smith
SS R.Petrocelli
3B J.Foy
LF C.Yastrzemski
CF D.Demeter
RF T.Conigliaro
C M.Ryan
UT D.Jones
P J.Lonborg
P J.Santiago
P B.Brandon
P L.Stange
P E.Wilson
RP D.Stigman
RP D.McMahon
RP J.Wyatt

BOS 1967A

M D.Williams
1B G.Scott
2B M.Andrews
SS R.Petrocelli
3B J.Foy
LF C.Yastrzemski
CF R.Smith
RF T.Conigliaro
C M.Ryan
UT J.Tartabull
P J.Lonborg
P L.Stange
P G.Bell
P B.Brandon
RP J.Santiago
RP J.Wyatt
RP D.Osinski

BOS 1968A

M D.Williams
1B G.Scott
2B M.Andrews
SS R.Petrocelli
3B J.Foy
LF C.Yastrzemski
CF R.Smith
RF K.Harrelson
C R.Gibson
UT D.Jones
P R.Culp
P G.Bell
P D.Ellsworth
P J.Santiago
P J.Lonborg
RP L.Stange
RP S.Lyle
RP B.Landis

BOS 1969A

M D.Williams
M E.Popowski
1B D.Jones
2B M.Andrews
SS R.Petrocelli
3B G.Scott
LF C.Yastrzemski
CF R.Smith
RF T.Conigliaro
C R.Gibson
UT J.Lahoud
UT S.O'Brien
P R.Culp
P M.Nagy
P S.Siebert
P J.Lonborg
P L.Stange
RP V.Romo
RP S.Lyle
RP B.Landis

BOS 1970A

M E.Kasko
1B C.Yastrzemski
2B M.Andrews
SS R.Petrocelli
3B G.Scott
LF B.Conigliaro
CF R.Smith
RF T.Conigliaro
C J.Moses
P R.Culp
P S.Siebert
P G.Peters
P K.Brett
P M.Nagy
RP V.Romo
RP S.Lyle

BOS 1971A

M E.Kasko
1B G.Scott
2B D.Griffin
SS L.Aparicio
3B R.Petrocelli
LF C.Yastrzemski
CF B.Conigliaro
RF R.Smith
C D.Josephson
UT J.Lahoud

P R.Culp
P S.Siebert
P G.Peters
P J.Lonborg
RP B.Lee
RP B.Bolin
RP K.Brett

BOS 1972 A

M E.Kasko
1B D.Cater
2B D.Griffin
SS L.Aparicio
3B R.Petrocelli
LF C.Yastrzemski
CF T.Harper
RF R.Smith
C C.Fisk
UT B.Oglivie
P M.Pattin
P S.Siebert
P L.Tiant
P J.Curtis
P L.McGlothen
RP G.Peters
RP B.Lee
RP L.Krausse

BOS 1973 A

M E.Kasko
M E.Popowski
1B C.Yastrzemski
2B D.Griffin
SS L.Aparicio
3B R.Petrocelli
LF T.Harper
CF R.Miller
RF R.Evans
C C.Fisk
DH O.Cepeda
UT R.Smith
P B.Lee
P L.Tiant
P J.Curtis
P M.Pattin
P R.Moret
RP B.Bolin

BOS 1974 A

M D.Johnson
1B C.Yastrzemski
2B D.Griffin
SS M.Guerrero
3B R.Petrocelli
LF B.Carbo
CF J.Beniquez
RF D.Evans
C B.Montgomery
DH T.Harper
UT R.Burleson
UT R.Miller
UT C.Cooper
UT D.McAuliffe
P L.Tiant
P B.Lee
P R.Cleveland
P D.Drago
P R.Moret
RP D.Segui

BOS 1975 A

M D.Johnson
1B C.Yastrzemski
2B D.Griffin
SS R.Burleson
3B R.Petrocelli
LF B.Carbo
CF F.Lynn
RF D.Evans
C C.Fisk
DH J.Rice
UT C.Cooper
P L.Tiant
P B.Lee
P R.Wise
P R.Cleveland
P R.Moret
RP D.Drago
RP D.Segui
RP J.Burton

BOS 1976 A

M D.Johnson
M D.Zimmer
1B C.Yastrzemski
2B D.Doyle
SS R.Burleson
3B B.Hobson
LF J.Rice
CF F.Lynn
RF D.Evans
C C.Fisk
DH C.Cooper
UT R.Miller
P L.Tiant
P R.Wise
P F.Jenkins
P R.Cleveland
P D.Pole
RP J.Willoughby
RP T.Murphy

BOS 1977 A

M D.Zimmer
1B G.Scott
2B D.Doyle
SS R.Burleson
3B B.Hobson
LF C.Yastrzemski
CF F.Lynn
RF R.Miller
C C.Fisk
DH J.Rice
P F.Jenkins
P R.Cleveland
P L.Tiant
P B.Stanley
P R.Wise
RP B.Campbell
RP J.Willoughby

BOS 1978 A

M D.Zimmer
1B G.Scott
2B J.Remy
SS R.Burleson
3B B.Hobson
LF C.Yastrzemski
CF F.Lynn
RF D.Evans
C C.Fisk
DH J.Rice
P D.Eckersley
P M.Torrez
P L.Tiant
P B.Lee
P J.Wright
RP B.Stanley
RP D.Drago
RP T.Burgmeier

BOS 1979 A

M D.Zimmer
1B B.Watson
2B J.Remy
SS R.Burleson
3B B.Hobson
LF J.Rice
CF F.Lynn
RF D.Evans
C C.Fisk
DH C.Yastrzemski
P M.Torrez
P D.Eckersley
P B.Stanley
P S.Renko
P C.Rainey
RP D.Drago
RP T.Burgmeier
RP B.Campbell

BOS 1980 A

M D.Zimmer
M J.Pesky
1B T.Perez
2B D.Stapleton
SS R.Burleson
3B G.Hoffman
LF J.Rice
CF F.Lynn
RF D.Evans
C C.Fisk
DH C.Yastrzemski
P M.Torrez
P D.Eckersley
P B.Stanley
P S.Renko
P D.Drago
RP T.Burgmeier

BOS 1981 A

M R.Houk
1B T.Perez
2B J.Remy
SS G.Hoffman
3B C.Lansford
LF J.Rice
CF R.Miller
RF D.Evans
C R.Gedman
DH C.Yastrzemski
UT D.Stapleton
P D.Eckersley
P F.Tanana
P M.Torrez
P J.Tudor
P B.Ojeda
RP B.Stanley
RP M.Clear
RP T.Burgmeier

BOS 1982A

M R.Houk
1B D.Stapleton
2B J.Remy
SS G.Hoffman
3B C.Lansford
LF J.Rice
CF R.Miller
RF D.Evans
C G.Allenson
DH C.Yastrzemski
UT W.Boggs
P D.Eckersley
P J.Tudor
P M.Torrez
P B.Stanley
P C.Rainey
RP M.Clear
RP T.Burgmeier
RP L.Aponte

BOS 1983A

M R.Houk
1B D.Stapleton
2B J.Remy
SS G.Hoffman
3B W.Boggs
LF J.Rice
CF T.Armas
RF D.Evans
C G.Allenson
DH C.Yastrzemski
UT R.Miller
UT R.Nichols
P J.Tudor
P B.Hurst
P D.Eckersley
P B.Ojeda
P M.Brown
RP B.Stanley
RP M.Clear
RP L.Aponte

BOS 1984A

M R.Houk
1B B.Buckner
2B M.Barrett
SS J.Gutierrez
3B W.Boggs
LF J.Rice
CF T.Armas
RF D.Evans
C R.Gedman
DH M.Easler
P B.Hurst
P B.Ojeda
P O.Boyd
P A.Nipper
P R.Clemens
RP B.Stanley
RP M.Clear
RP J.Johnson

BOS 1985A

M J.McNamara
1B B.Buckner
2B M.Barrett
SS J.Gutierrez
3B W.Boggs
LF J.Rice
CF S.Lyons
RF D.Evans
C R.Gedman
DH M.Easler
UT T.Armas
P O.Boyd
P B.Hurst
P A.Nipper
P B.Ojeda
RP S.Crawford
RP B.Stanley
RP M.Clear

BOS 1986A

M J.McNamara
1B B.Buckner
2B M.Barrett
SS E.Romero
3B W.Boggs
LF J.Rice
CF T.Armas
RF D.Evans
C R.Gedman
DH D.Baylor
P R.Clemens
P O.Boyd
P B.Hurst
P A.Nipper
P T.Seaver
RP B.Stanley
RP S.Stewart
RP S.Crawford

BOS 1987A

M J.McNamara
1B D.Evans
2B M.Barrett
SS S.Owen
3B W.Boggs
LF J.Rice
CF E.Burks
RF M.Greenwell
C M.Sullivan
DH D.Baylor
P R.Clemens
P B.Hurst
P A.Nipper
P B.Stanley
P J.Sellers
RP W.Gardner
RP C.Schiraldi
RP S.Crawford

BOS 1988A

M J.McNamara
M J.Morgan
1B T.Benzinger
2B M.Barrett
SS J.Reed
3B W.Boggs
LF M.Greenwell
CF E.Burks
RF D.Evans
C R.Gedman
DH J.Rice
P R.Clemens
P B.Hurst
P W.Gardner
P O.Boyd
P M.Smithson
RP B.Stanley
RP L.Smith
RP D.Lamp

BOS 1989A

M J.Morgan
1B N.Esasky
2B M.Barrett
SS L.Rivera
3B W.Boggs
LF M.Greenwell
CF E.Burks
RF K.Romine
C R.Cerone
DH D.Evans
UT D.Heep
UT J.Reed
P R.Clemens
P M.Boddicker
P J.Dopson
P M.Smithson
RP D.Lamp
RP R.Murphy
RP B.Stanley

BOS 1990A

M J.Morgan
1B C.Quintana
2B J.Reed
SS L.Rivera
3B W.Boggs
LF M.Greenwell
CF E.Burks
RF T.Brunansky
C T.Pena
DH D.Evans
P R.Clemens
P M.Boddicker
P G.Harris
P D.Kiecker
P T.Bolton
RP D.Lamp
RP W.Gardner
RP R.Murphy

BOS 1991A

M J.Morgan
1B C.Quintana
2B J.Reed
SS L.Rivera
3B W.Boggs
LF M.Greenwell
CF E.Burks
RF T.Brunansky
C T.Pena
DH J.Clark
P R.Clemens
P G.Harris
P J.Hesketh
P M.Gardiner
P T.Bolton
RP D.Lamp
RP J.Gray
RP J.Reardon

BOS 1992A

M B.Hobson
1B M.Vaughn
2B J.Reed
SS L.Rivera
3B W.Boggs
LF B.Hatcher
CF B.Zupcic
RF T.Brunansky
C T.Pena
DH J.Clark
UT S.Cooper
UT H.Winningham
UT P.Plantier
P R.Clemens
P F.Viola
P D.Darwin
P J.Hesketh
P J.Dopson
RP G.Harris
RP M.Young
RP P.Quantrill

BOS 1993A

M B.Hobson
1B M.Vaughn
2B S.Fletcher
SS J.Valentin
3B S.Cooper
LF M.Greenwell
CF B.Hatcher
RF B.Zupcic
C T.Pena
DH A.Dawson
UT C.Quintana
P D.Darwin
P R.Clemens
P F.Viola
P J.Dopson
P A.Sele
RP P.Quantrill
RP G.Harris
RP S.Bankhead

BOS 1994A

M B.Hobson
1B M.Vaughn
2B S.Fletcher
SS J.Valentin
3B S.Cooper
LF M.Greenwell
CF O.Nixon
RF T.Brunansky
C D.Berryhill
DH A.Dawson
UT T.Naehring
P R.Clemens
P A.Sele
P J.Hesketh
P D.Darwin
RP K.Ryan
RP G.Harris
RP C.Howard

BOS 1995A

M K.Kennedy
1B M.Vaughn
2B L.Alicea
SS J.Valentin
3B T.Naehring
LF M.Greenwell
CF L.Tinsley
RF T.O'Leary
C M.Macfarlane
DH J.Canseco
P T.Wakefield
P E.Hanson
P R.Clemens
P Z.Smith
RP R.Cormier
RP M.Maddux
RP S.Belinda

BOS 1996A

M K.Kennedy
1B M.Vaughn
2B J.Frye
SS J.Valentin
3B T.Naehring
LF M.Greenwell
CF L.Tinsley
RF T.O'Leary
C M.Stanley
DH J.Canseco
UT R.Jefferson
P R.Clemens
P T.Gordon
P T.Wakefield
P A.Sele
RP V.Eshelman
RP H.Slocumb
RP M.Maddux

BOS 1997A

M J.Williams
1B M.Vaughn
2B J.Frye
SS N.Garciaparra
3B T.Naehring
LF W.Cordero
CF D.Bragg
RF T.O'Leary
C S.Hatteberg
DH R.Jefferson
UT M.Stanley
UT J.Valentin
P T.Wakefield
P T.Gordon
P A.Sele
P J.Suppan
P S.Avery
RP J.Wasdin
RP B.Henry
RP C.Hammond

BOS 1998A

M J.Williams
1B M.Vaughn
2B M.Benjamin
SS N.Garciaparra
3B J.Valentin
LF T.O'Leary
CF D.Lewis
RF D.Bragg
C S.Hatteberg
DH R.Jefferson
P P.Martinez
P T.Wakefield
P B.Saberhagen
P S.Avery
RP D.Lowe
RP J.Wasdin
RP T.Gordon

BOS 1999A

M J.Williams
1B M.Stanley
2B J.Offerman
SS N.Garciaparra
3B J.Valentin
LF T.O'Leary
CF D.Lewis
RF T.Nixon
C J.Varitek
DH R.Jefferson
UT B.Daubach
P P.Martinez
P M.Portugal
P P.Rapp
P B.Saberhagen
P B.Rose
RP T.Wakefield
RP D.Lowe
RP J.Wasdin

BOS 2000A

M J.Williams
1B M.Stanley
2B J.Offerman
SS N.Garciaparra
3B M.Alexander
LF T.O'Leary
CF C.Everett
RF T.Nixon
C J.Varitek
DH B.Daubach
UT D.Lewis
P P.Martinez
P T.Wakefield
P J.Fassero
P R.Martinez
P P.Schourek
RP D.Lowe
RP R.Garces
RP R.Cormier

Brooklyn

ECK n 1872
ATL n 1872-1875
BRO a 1884-1889
BRO a 1890
BRO P 1890
BRO F 1914-1915
BRO N 1890-1957

ECK 1872n

M A.Allison
M J.Wood
M P.Martin
1B A.Allison
2B C.Nelson
SS J.Snyder
3B F.Fleet
LF C.Gedney
CF D.Patterson
RF J.Clinton
C D.Allison
P P.Martin
P G.Zettlein
P J.McDermott
P M.Malone

ATL 1872n

M B.Ferguson
1B H.Dehlman
2B J.Hall
SS J.Burdock
3B B.Ferguson
LF A.Thake
CF J.Remsen
RF J.McDonald
C T.Barlow
P J.Britt

ATL 1873n

M B.Ferguson
1B H.Dehlman
2B J.Burdock
SS D.Pearce
3B B.Ferguson
LF C.Pabor
CF J.Remsen
RF B.Boyd
C T.Barlow
P J.Britt

ATL 1874n

M B.Ferguson
1B H.Dehlman
2B J.Farrow
SS D.Pearce
3B B.Ferguson
LF E.Booth
CF B.Clack
RF J.Chapman
C J.Knowdell
P T.Bond

ATL 1875n

M C.Pabor
M B.Boyd
1B F.Crane
2B F.Fleet
SS H.Kessler
3B A.Nichols
LF C.Pabor
CF B.Clack
RF B.Boyd
C J.Knowdell
P J.Cassidy
P J.Clinton
P J.O'Neill

BRO 1884a

M G.Taylor
1B C.Householder
2B B.Greenwood
SS B.Geer
3B F.Warner
LF I.Benners
CF J.Remsen
RF J.Cassidy
C J.Corcoran
UT O.Walker
P A.Terry
P S.Kimber
P J.Conway

BRO 1885a

M C.Hackett
M C.Byrne
1B B.Phillips
2B G.Pinkney
SS G.Smith
3B B.McClellan
LF E.Swartwood
CF P.Hotaling
RF J.Cassidy

C J.Hayes
UT A.Terry
P H.Porter
P J.Harkins

BRO 1886a

M C.Byrne
1B B.Phillips
2B B.McClellan
SS G.Smith
3B G.Pinkney
LF E.Burch
CF J.McTamany
RF E.Swartwood
C J.Peoples
P H.Porter
P J.Harkins
P A.Terry
P H.Henderson
P S.Toole

BRO 1887a

M C.Byrne
1B B.Phillips
2B B.McClellan
SS G.Smith
3B G.Pinkney
LF E.Greer
CF J.McTamany
RF E.Swartwood
C J.Peoples
UT A.Terry
P H.Porter
P J.Harkins
P S.Toole
P H.Henderson

BRO 1888a

M B.McGunnigle
1B D.Orr
2B J.Burdock
SS G.Smith
3B G.Pinkney
LF D.O'Brien
CF P.Radford
RF D.Foutz
C D.Bushong
UT B.Caruthers
P M.Hughes
P A.Terry
P A.Mays

BRO 1889a

M B.McGunnigle
1B D.Foutz
2B H.Collins
SS G.Smith
3B G.Pinkney
LF D.O'Brien
CF P.Corkhill
RF O.Burns
C J.Visner
P B.Caruthers
P A.Terry
P T.Lovett
P M.Hughes

BRO 1890a

M J.Kennedy
1B B.O'Brien
2B J.Gerhardt
SS C.Nelson
3B J.Davis
LF H.Simon
CF J.Peltz
RF E.Daily
C J.Toy
UT F.Bowes
UT H.Pitz
P C.McCullough
P M.Mattimore
P B.Murphy

BRO 1890P

M M.Ward
1B D.Orr
2B L.Bierbauer
SS J.Ward
3B B.Joyce
LF E.Seery
CF E.Andrews
RF J.McGeachy
C T.Kinslow
UT G.Van Haltren
P G.Weyhing
P J.Sowders
P C.Murphy
P G.Hemming

BRO 1914F

M B.Bradley
1B H.Myers
2B S.Hofman
SS E.Gagnier
3B T.Wisterzil
LF C.Cooper
CF A.Shaw
RF S.Evans
C G.Land
UT G.Anderson
P T.Seaton
P E.Lafitte
P H.Finneran

BRO 1915F

M L.Magee
M J.Ganzel
1B H.Myers
2B L.Magee
SS F.Smith
3B A.Halt
LF C.Cooper
CF B.Kauff
RF G.Anderson
C G.Land
P H.Finneran
P D.Marion
P T.Seaton
P J.Bluejacket
P B.Upham

BRO 1890N

M B.McGunnigle
1B D.Foutz
2B H.Collins
SS G.Smith
3B G.Pinkney
LF A.Terry
CF D.O'Brien
RF O.Burns
C T.Daly
P T.Lovett

BRO 1891N

M M.Ward
1B D.Foutz
2B H.Collins
SS J.Ward
3B G.Pinkney
LF D.O'Brien
CF M.Griffin
RF O.Burns
C T.Kinslow
P T.Lovett
P B.Caruthers
P G.Hemming
P A.Terry
P B.Inks

BRO 1892N

M M.Ward
1B D.Brouthers
2B J.Ward
SS T.Corcoran
3B B.Joyce
LF D.O'Brien
CF M.Griffin
RF O.Burns
C C.Daily
UT T.Daly
P G.Haddock
P E.Stein
P B.Hart
P B.Kennedy

BRO 1893N

M D.Foutz
1B D.Brouthers
2B D.Richardson
SS T.Corcoran
3B T.Daly
LF D.Foutz
CF M.Griffin
RF O.Burns
C T.Kinslow
UT G.Shoch
P B.Kennedy
P E.Stein
P G.Haddock
P D.Daub
P T.Lovett

BRO 1894N

M D.Foutz
1B D.Foutz
2B T.Daly
SS T.Corcoran
3B B.Shindle
LF G.Treadway
CF M.Griffin
RF O.Burns
C T.Kinslow
P B.Kennedy
P E.Stein
P D.Daub
P H.Gastright

BRO 1895N

M D.Foutz
1B C.LaChance
2B T.Daly
SS T.Corcoran
3B B.Shindle
LF J.Anderson
CF M.Griffin
RF G.Treadway
C J.Grim
P B.Kennedy
P E.Stein
P A.Gumbert
P D.Daub
P C.Lucid

BRO 1896N

M D.Foutz
1B C.LaChance
2B T.Daly
SS T.Corcoran
3B B.Shindle
LF T.McCarthy
CF M.Griffin
RF F.Jones
C J.Grim
UT J.Anderson
P B.Kennedy
P H.Payne
P D.Daub
P B.Abbey
P E.Stein

BRO 1897N

M B.Barnie
1B C.LaChance
2B G.Shoch
SS G.Smith
3B B.Shindle
LF J.Anderson
CF M.Griffin
RF F.Jones
C J.Grim
P B.Kennedy
P H.Payne
P J.Dunn
P C.Fisher
P D.Daub

BRO 1898N

M B.Barnie
M M.Griffin
M C.Ebbets
1B C.LaChance
2B B.Hallman
SS G.Magoon
3B B.Shindle
LF J.Sheckard
CF M.Griffin
RF F.Jones
C J.Ryan
P B.Kennedy
P J.Dunn
P J.Yeager
P R.Miller
P K.McKenna

BRO 1899N

M N.Hanlon
1B D.McGann
2B T.Daly
SS B.Dahlen
3B D.Casey
LF J.Kelley
CF F.Jones
RF W.Keeler
C D.Farrell
UT J.Anderson
P J.Dunn
P J.Hughes
P B.Kennedy
P D.McJames

BRO 1900N

M N.Hanlon
1B H.Jennings
2B T.Daly
SS B.Dahlen
3B L.Cross
LF J.Sheckard
CF F.Jones
RF W.Keeler
C D.Farrell
UT J.Kelley
P J.McGinnity
P B.Kennedy
P F.Kitson
P H.Howell

BRO 1901N

M N.Hanlon
1B J.Kelley
2B T.Daly
SS B.Dahlen
3B C.Irwin
LF J.Sheckard
CF T.McCreery
RF W.Keeler
C D.McGuire
P B.Donovan
P F.Kitson
P J.Hughes
P D.Newton
P D.McJames

BRO 1902N

M N.Hanlon
1B T.McCreery
2B T.Flood
SS B.Dahlen
3B C.Irwin
LF J.Sheckard
CF C.Dolan
RF W.Keeler
C H.Hearne
P B.Donovan
P F.Kitson
P D.Newton
P J.Hughes
P R.Evans

BRO 1903N

M N.Hanlon
1B J.Doyle
2B T.Flood
SS B.Dahlen
3B S.Strang
LF J.Sheckard
CF J.Dobbs
RF W.McCredie
C L.Ritter
P O.Jones
P H.Schmidt
P N.Garvin
P R.Evans
P B.Reidy

BRO 1904N

M N.Hanlon
1B P.Dillon
2B D.Jordan
SS C.Babb
3B M.McCormick
LF J.Sheckard
CF J.Dobbs
RF H.Lumley
C B.Bergen
UT D.Gessler
P O.Jones
P J.Cronin
P N.Garvin
P E.Poole
P D.Scanlan

BRO 1905N

M N.Hanlon
1B D.Gessler
2B C.Malay
SS P.Lewis
3B E.Batch
LF J.Sheckard
CF J.Dobbs
RF H.Lumley
C L.Ritter
P H.McIntire
P D.Scanlan
P E.Stricklett
P M.Eason
P O.Jones

BRO 1906N

M P.Donovan
1B T.Jordan
2B W.Alperman
SS P.Lewis
3B D.Casey
LF J.McCarthy
CF B.Maloney
RF H.Lumley
C B.Bergen
UT J.Hummel
P E.Stricklett
P D.Scanlan
P H.McIntire
P M.Eason
P J.Pastorius

BRO 1907N

M P.Donovan
1B T.Jordan
2B W.Alperman
SS P.Lewis
3B D.Casey
LF E.Batch
CF B.Maloney
RF H.Lumley
C L.Ritter
UT J.Hummel
P N.Rucker
P G.Bell
P E.Stricklett
P J.Pastorius
P H.McIntire

BRO 1908N

M P.Donovan
1B T.Jordan
2B H.Pattee
SS P.Lewis
3B T.Sheehan
LF A.Burch
CF B.Maloney
RF H.Lumley
C B.Bergen
UT J.Hummel
P N.Rucker
P K.Wilhelm
P H.McIntire
P J.Pastorius
P G.Bell

BRO 1909N

M H.Lumley
1B T.Jordan
2B W.Alperman
SS T.McMillan
3B E.Lennox
LF W.Clement
CF A.Burch
RF H.Lumley
C B.Bergen
UT J.Hummel
P N.Rucker
P G.Bell
P H.McIntire
P K.Wilhelm
P D.Scanlan

BRO 1910N

M B.Dahlen
1B J.Daubert
2B J.Hummel
SS T.Smith
3B E.Lennox
LF Z.Wheat
CF B.Davidson
RF J.Dalton
C B.Bergen
UT A.Burch
P N.Rucker
P G.Bell
P C.Barger
P D.Scanlan
P E.Knetzer
RP R.Dessau

BRO 1911N

M B.Dahlen
1B J.Daubert
2B J.Hummel
SS B.Tooley
3B E.Zimmerman
LF Z.Wheat
CF B.Davidson
RF B.Coulson
C B.Bergen
P N.Rucker
P C.Barger
P E.Knetzer
P B.Schardt
P D.Scanlan

BRO 1912N

M B.Dahlen
1B J.Daubert
2B G.Cutshaw
SS B.Tooley
3B R.Smith
LF Z.Wheat
CF H.Moran
RF H.Northen
C O.Miller
UT J.Hummel
P N.Rucker
P P.Ragan
P E.Yingling
P E.Stack
P E.Knetzer

BRO 1913N

M B.Dahlen
1B J.Daubert
2B G.Cutshaw
SS B.Fisher
3B R.Smith
LF Z.Wheat
CF C.Stengel
RF H.Moran
C O.Miller
P P.Ragan
P N.Rucker
P F.Allen
P C.Curtis
P E.Yingling

BRO 1914N

M W.Robinson
1B J.Daubert
2B G.Cutshaw
SS D.Egan
3B R.Smith
LF Z.Wheat
CF J.Dalton
RF C.Stengel
C L.McCarty
P J.Pfeffer
P E.Reulbach
P P.Ragan
P R.Aitchison
P F.Allen

BRO 1915N

M W.Robinson
1B J.Daubert
2B G.Cutshaw
SS O.O'Mara
3B G.Getz
LF Z.Wheat
CF H.Myers
RF C.Stengel
C O.Miller
P J.Pfeffer
P W.Dell
P J.Coombs
P S.Smith
P E.Appleton

BRO 1916N

M W.Robinson
1B J.Daubert
2B G.Cutshaw
SS I.Olson
3B M.Mowrey
LF Z.Wheat
CF H.Myers
RF C.Stengel
C C.Meyers
UT J.Johnston
P J.Pfeffer
P L.Cheney
P S.Smith
P R.Marquard
P J.Coombs

BRO 1917N

M W.Robinson
1B J.Daubert
2B G.Cutshaw
SS I.Olson
3B M.Mowrey
LF Z.Wheat
CF J.Hickman
RF C.Stengel
C O.Miller
UT J.Johnston
UT H.Myers
P J.Pfeffer
P L.Cadore
P R.Marquard
P S.Smith
P L.Cheney

BRO 1918N

M W.Robinson
1B J.Daubert
2B M.Doolan
SS I.Olson
3B O.O'Mara
LF Z.Wheat
CF H.Myers
RF J.Johnston
C O.Miller
P B.Grimes
P R.Marquard
P L.Cheney
P J.Coombs
P D.Robertson

BRO 1919N

M W.Robinson
1B E.Konetchy
2B J.Johnston
SS I.Olson
3B L.Malone
LF Z.Wheat
CF H.Myers
RF T.Griffith
C E.Krueger
P J.Pfeffer
P L.Cadore
P A.Mamaux
P B.Grimes
P S.Smith

BRO 1920N

M W.Robinson
1B E.Konetchy
2B P.Kilduff
SS I.Olson
3B J.Johnston
LF Z.Wheat
CF H.Myers
RF T.Griffith
C O.Miller
UT B.Neis
P B.Grimes
P L.Cadore
P J.Pfeffer
P A.Mamaux
P R.Marquard

BRO 1921N

M W.Robinson
1B R.Schmandt
2B P.Kilduff
SS I.Olson
3B J.Johnston
LF Z.Wheat
CF H.Myers
RF T.Griffith
C O.Miller
UT B.Neis
P B.Grimes
P L.Cadore
P D.Ruether
P C.Mitchell
P S.Smith

BRO 1922N

M W.Robinson
1B R.Schmandt
2B J.Johnston
SS I.Olson
3B A.High
LF Z.Wheat
CF H.Myers
RF T.Griffith
C H.DeBerry
UT B.Griffith
P D.Ruether
P B.Grimes
P D.Vance
P L.Cadore
P S.Smith
RP A.Mamaux

BRO 1923N

M W.Robinson
1B J.Fournier
2B I.Olson
SS J.Johnston
3B A.High
LF Z.Wheat
CF B.Neis
RF T.Griffith
C Z.Taylor
UT G.Bailey
P B.Grimes
P D.Vance
P D.Ruether
P L.Dickerman
P D.Henry
RP A.Decatur

BRO 1924N

M W.Robinson
1B J.Fournier
2B A.High
SS J.Mitchell
3B M.Stock
LF Z.Wheat

CF E.Brown
RF T.Griffith
C Z.Taylor
P B.Grimes
P D.Vance
P D.Ruether
P B.Doak
P A.Decatur

BRO 1925N

M W.Robinson
1B J.Fournier
2B M.Stock
SS J.Mitchell
3B J.Johnston
LF Z.Wheat
CF E.Brown
RF D.Cox
C Z.Taylor
P D.Vance
P B.Grimes
P R.Ehrhardt
P T.Osborne
P J.Petty
RP B.Hubbell

BRO 1926N

M W.Robinson
1B B.Herman
2B C.Fewster
SS J.Butler
3B W.Marriott
LF Z.Wheat
CF G.Felix
RF D.Cox
C M.O'Neil
UT M.Jacobson
P J.Petty
P B.Grimes
P D.McWeeny
P B.McGraw
P D.Vance
RP R.Ehrhardt

BRO 1927N

M W.Robinson
1B B.Herman
2B J.Partridge
SS J.Butler
3B B.Barrett
LF G.Felix
CF J.Statz
RF M.Carey
C H.DeBerry
UT H.Hendrick
P D.Vance
P J.Petty
P J.Elliott
P D.McWeeny
P B.Doak
RP R.Ehrhardt
RP W.Clark

BRO 1928N

M W.Robinson
1B D.Bissonette
2B J.Flowers
SS D.Bancroft
3B H.Hendrick
LF R.Bressler
CF M.Carey
RF B.Herman
C H.DeBerry
P D.Vance
P D.McWeeny
P J.Petty
P W.Clark
P J.Elliott
RP R.Moss
RP R.Ehrhardt

BRO 1929N

M W.Robinson
1B D.Bissonette
2B E.Moore
SS D.Bancroft
3B W.Gilbert
LF R.Bressler
CF J.Frederick
RF B.Herman
C V.Picinich
UT H.Hendrick
P W.Clark
P D.Vance
P R.Moss
P C.Dudley
P D.McWeeny
RP C.Moore
RP W.Ballou

BRO 1930N

M W.Robinson
1B D.Bissonette
2B N.Finn
SS G.Wright
3B W.Gilbert
LF R.Bressler
CF J.Frederick
RF B.Herman
C A.Lopez
P D.Vance
P W.Clark
P D.Luque
P J.Elliott
P R.Phelps

BRO 1931N

M W.Robinson
1B D.Bissonette
2B N.Finn
SS G.Slade
3B W.Gilbert
LF L.O'Doul
CF J.Frederick
RF B.Herman
C A.Lopez
P W.Clark
P D.Vance
P R.Phelps
P S.Thurston
P F.Heimach
RP J.Quinn
RP C.Moore
RP P.Day

BRO 1932N

M M.Carey
1B G.Kelly
2B T.Cuccinello
SS G.Wright
3B J.Stripp
LF L.O'Doul
CF D.Taylor
RF H.Wilson
C A.Lopez
UT J.Frederick
P W.Clark
P V.Mungo
P D.Vance
P F.Heimach
P S.Thurston
RP J.Quinn
RP C.Moore

BRO 1933N

M M.Carey
1B S.Leslie
2B T.Cuccinello
SS G.Wright
3B J.Stripp
LF H.Wilson
CF D.Taylor
RF J.Frederick
C A.Lopez
P B.Beck
P V.Mungo
P R.Benge
P O.Carroll
P S.Thurston
RP J.Shaute
RP R.Ryan

BRO 1934N

M C.Stengel
1B S.Leslie
2B T.Cuccinello
SS L.Frey
3B J.Stripp
LF D.Taylor
CF L.Koenecke
RF B.Boyle
C A.Lopez
UT J.Frederick
UT J.Jordan
P V.Mungo
P R.Benge
P D.Leonard
P J.Babich
P T.Zachary
RP O.Carroll
RP B.Beck

BRO 1935N

M C.Stengel
1B S.Leslie
2B T.Cuccinello
SS L.Frey
3B J.Stripp
LF D.Taylor
CF F.Bordagaray
RF B.Boyle
C A.Lopez
UT J.Bucher
UT J.Jordan
UT L.Koenecke
P V.Mungo
P W.Clark
P G.Earnshaw
P T.Zachary
P J.Babich
RP L.Munns
RP D.Vance

BRO 1936N

M C.Stengel
1B B.Hassett
2B J.Jordan
SS L.Frey
3B J.Stripp
LF G.Watkins
CF J.Cooney
RF F.Bordagaray
C R.Berres
UT J.Bucher
UT B.Phelps
P V.Mungo
P F.Frankhouse
P E.Brandt
P M.Butcher
P W.Clark
RP G.Jeffcoat
RP T.Baker

BRO 1937N

M B.Grimes
1B B.Hassett
2B C.Lavagetto
SS W.English
3B J.Stripp
LF T.Winsett
CF J.Cooney
RF H.Manush
C B.Phelps
UT G.Brack
UT J.Bucher
P M.Butcher
P L.Hamlin
P F.Frankhouse
P W.Hoyt
P V.Mungo
RP G.Jeffcoat

BRO 1938N

M B.Grimes
1B D.Camilli
2B J.Hudson
SS L.Durocher
3B C.Lavagetto
LF B.Hassett
CF E.Koy
RF G.Rosen
C B.Phelps
P L.Hamlin
P F.Fitzsimmons
P T.Pressnell
P V.Tamulis
P B.Posedel

BRO 1939N

M L.Durocher
1B D.Camilli
2B P.Coscarart
SS L.Durocher
3B C.Lavagetto
LF E.Koy
CF D.Walker
RF G.Moore
C B.Phelps
UT J.Hudson
P L.Hamlin
P H.Casey
P V.Tamulis
P T.Pressnell
P F.Fitzsimmons
RP I.Hutchinson
RP R.Evans

BRO 1940N

M L.Durocher
1B D.Camilli
2B P.Coscarart
SS P.Reese
3B C.Lavagetto
LF J.Medwick
CF D.Walker
RF J.Vosmik
C B.Phelps
P W.Wyatt
P L.Hamlin
P V.Tamulis
P H.Casey
P T.Carleton
RP T.Pressnell

BRO 1941N

M L.Durocher
1B D.Camilli
2B B.Herman
SS P.Reese
3B C.Lavagetto
LF J.Medwick
CF P.Reiser
RF D.Walker
C M.Owen
UT J.Wasdell
P K.Higbe
P W.Wyatt
P H.Casey
P C.Davis
P L.Hamlin

BRO 1942N

M L.Durocher
1B D.Camilli
2B B.Herman
SS P.Reese
3B A.Vaughan
LF J.Medwick
CF P.Reiser
RF D.Walker
C M.Owen
P K.Higbe
P W.Wyatt
P C.Davis
P L.French
P E.Head
RP H.Casey
RP L.Webber

BRO 1943N

M L.Durocher
1B D.Camilli
2B B.Herman
SS A.Glossop
3B A.Vaughan
LF D.Walker
CF A.Galan
RF P.Waner
C M.Owen
P K.Higbe
P W.Wyatt
P E.Head
P C.Davis
P B.Newsom
RP L.Webber

BRO 1944N

M L.Durocher
1B H.Schultz
2B E.Stanky
SS B.Bragan
3B F.Bordagaray
LF A.Galan
CF G.Rosen
RF D.Walker
C M.Owen
UT L.Olmo
P H.Gregg
P C.Davis
P R.Melton
RP L.Webber

BRO 1945N

M L.Durocher
1B A.Galan
2B E.Stanky
SS E.Basinski
3B F.Bordagaray
LF L.Olmo
CF G.Rosen
RF D.Walker
C M.Sandlock
P H.Gregg
P V.Lombardi
P C.Davis
P A.Herring
P T.Seats
RP C.King
RP C.Buker

BRO 1946N

M L.Durocher
1B E.Stevens
2B E.Stanky
SS P.Reese
3B C.Lavagetto
LF P.Reiser
CF C.Furillo
RF D.Walker
C B.Edwards
UT A.Galan
UT D.Whitman
P J.Hatten
P K.Higbe
P V.Lombardi
P H.Behrman
P H.Gregg
RP H.Casey
RP A.Herring
RP R.Branca

BRO 1947N

M C.Sukeforth
M B.Shotton
1B J.Robinson
2B E.Stanky
SS P.Reese
3B S.Jorgensen
LF P.Reiser
CF C.Furillo
RF D.Walker
C B.Edwards
P R.Branca
P J.Hatten
P V.Lombardi
P H.Taylor
RP H.Gregg
RP H.Behrman
RP R.Barney

BRO 1948N

M L.Durocher
M R.Blades
M B.Shotton
1B G.Hodges
2B J.Robinson
SS P.Reese
3B B.Cox
LF M.Rackley
CF C.Furillo
RF G.Hermanski
C R.Campanella
UT B.Edwards
P R.Barney
P R.Branca
P J.Hatten
P P.Roe
P E.Palica
RP H.Behrman
RP P.Minner
RP W.Ramsdell

BRO 1949N

M B.Shotton
1B G.Hodges
2B J.Robinson
SS P.Reese
3B B.Cox
LF G.Hermanski
CF D.Snider
RF C.Furillo
C R.Campanella
P D.Newcombe
P P.Roe
P J.Hatten
P R.Branca
P J.Banta
RP E.Palica
RP P.Minner

BRO 1950N

M B.Shotton
1B G.Hodges
2B J.Robinson
SS P.Reese
3B B.Cox
LF G.Hermanski
CF D.Snider
RF C.Furillo
C R.Campanella
P D.Newcombe
P P.Roe
P E.Palica
P R.Branca
P D.Bankhead

BRO 1951N

M C.Dressen
1B G.Hodges
2B J.Robinson
SS P.Reese
3B B.Cox
LF A.Pafko
CF D.Snider
RF C.Furillo
C R.Campanella
P D.Newcombe
P P.Roe
P R.Branca
P C.Erskine
RP C.King
RP B.Podbielan
RP E.Palica

BRO 1952N

M C.Dressen
1B G.Hodges
2B J.Robinson
SS P.Reese
3B B.Cox
LF A.Pafko
CF D.Snider
RF C.Furillo
C R.Campanella
UT G.Shuba
P C.Erskine
P B.Loes
P B.Wade
P P.Roe
P C.Van Cuyk
RP J.Black

BRO 1953N

M C.Dressen
1B G.Hodges
2B J.Gilliam
SS P.Reese
3B B.Cox
LF D.Thompson
CF D.Snider
RF C.Furillo
C R.Campanella
UT J.Robinson
P C.Erskine
P R.Meyer
P B.Loes
P P.Roe
P B.Milliken
RP C.Labine
RP B.Wade
RP J.Hughes

BRO 1954N

M W.Alston
1B G.Hodges
2B J.Gilliam
SS P.Reese
3B D.Hoak
LF J.Robinson
CF D.Snider
RF C.Furillo
C R.Campanella
P C.Erskine
P R.Meyer
P J.Podres
P B.Loes
P D.Newcombe
RP C.Labine
RP J.Hughes
RP E.Palica

BRO 1955N

M W.Alston
1B G.Hodges
2B J.Gilliam
SS P.Reese
3B J.Robinson
LF S.Amoros
CF D.Snider
RF C.Furillo
C R.Campanella
UT D.Hoak
P D.Newcombe
P C.Erskine
P J.Podres
P B.Loes
P K.Spooner
RP C.Labine
RP E.Roebuck
RP D.Bessent

BRO 1956N

M W.Alston
1B G.Hodges
2B J.Gilliam
SS P.Reese
3B R.Jackson
LF S.Amoros
CF D.Snider
RF C.Furillo
C R.Campanella
UT J.Robinson
P D.Newcombe
P R.Craig
P S.Maglie
P C.Erskine
P D.Drysdale
RP C.Labine
RP E.Roebuck
RP D.Bessent

BRO 1957N

M W.Alston
1B G.Hodges
2B J.Gilliam
SS C.Neal
3B P.Reese
LF G.Cimoli
CF D.Snider
RF C.Furillo
C R.Campanella
UT S.Amoros
P D.Drysdale
P D.Newcombe
P J.Podres
P D.McDevitt
P R.Craig
RP C.Labine
RP E.Roebuck

Buffalo

BUF N 1879-1885
BUF P 1890
BUF F 1914-1915

BUF 1879N

M J.Clapp
1B O.Walker
2B C.Fulmer
SS D.Force
3B H.Richardson
LF J.Hornung
CF D.Eggler
RF B.Crowley
C J.Clapp
P J.Galvin

BUF 1880N

M S.Crane
1B D.Esterbrook
2B D.Force
SS M.Moynahan
3B H.Richardson
LF J.Hornung
CF B.Crowley
RF E.Stearns
C J.Rowe
P J.Galvin
P S.Wiedman
P T.Poorman

BUF 1881N

M J.O'Rourke
1B D.Brouthers
2B D.Force
SS J.Peters
3B J.O'Rourke
LF B.Purcell
CF H.Richardson
RF C.Foley
C J.Rowe
UT D.White
P J.Galvin
P J.Lynch

BUF 1882N

M J.O'Rourke
1B D.Brouthers
2B H.Richardson
SS D.Force
3B D.White
LF B.Purcell
CF J.O'Rourke
RF C.Foley
C J.Rowe
P J.Galvin
P H.Daily

BUF 1883N

M J.O'Rourke
1B D.Brouthers
2B H.Richardson
SS D.Force
3B D.White
LF J.O'Rourke
CF J.Lillie
RF O.Shaffer
C J.Rowe
P J.Galvin
P G.Derby

BUF 1884N

M J.O'Rourke
1B D.Brouthers
2B H.Richardson
SS D.Force
3B D.White
LF J.O'Rourke

CF D.Eggler
RF J.Lillie
C J.Rowe
UT G.Myers
P J.Galvin
P B.Serad

BUF 1885N

M J.Galvin
M J.Chapman
1B D.Brouthers
2B D.Force
SS J.Rowe
3B D.White
LF B.Crowley
CF H.Richardson
RF J.Lillie
C G.Myers
P J.Galvin
P B.Serad
P P.Conway
P P.Wood

BUF 1890P

M J.Rowe
M J.Faatz
M J.Rowe
1B D.White
2B S.Wise
SS J.Rowe
3B J.Irwin
LF E.Beecher
CF D.Hoy
RF J.Halligan
C C.Mack
P G.Haddock
P B.Cunningham
P G.Keefe
P G.Stafford

BUF 1914F

M L.Schlafly
1B J.Agler
2B T.Downey
SS B.Louden
3B F.Smith
LF F.Delahanty
CF C.Hanford
RF T.McDonald
C W.Blair
P F.Anderson
P G.Krapp
P R.Ford
P E.Moore
P A.Schulz

BUF 1915F

M L.Schlafly
M W.Blair
M H.Lord
1B H.Chase
2B B.Louden
SS R.Roach
3B H.Lord
LF B.Meyer
CF C.Engle
RF J.Dalton
C W.Blair
UT S.Hofman
P A.Schulz
P H.Bedient
P F.Anderson
P G.Krapp
P R.Ford
RP R.Marshall

California

CAL A 1965-1996

CAL 1965A

M B.Rigney
1B V.Power
2B B.Knoop
SS J.Fregosi
3B P.Schaal
LF W.Smith
CF J.Cardenal
RF A.Pearson
C B.Rodgers
UT J.Adcock
P F.Newman
P D.Chance
P M.Lopez
P G.Brunet
P R.May
RP B.Lee
RP A.Gatewood

CAL 1966A

M B.Rigney
1B N.Siebern
2B B.Knoop
SS J.Fregosi
3B P.Schaal
LF R.Reichardt
CF J.Cardenal
RF E.Kirkpatrick
C B.Rodgers
UT T.Satriano
P D.Chance
P G.Brunet
P M.Lopez
P F.Newman
RP J.Sanford
RP B.Lee
RP M.Rojas

CAL 1967A

M B.Rigney
1B D.Mincher
2B B.Knoop
SS J.Fregosi
3B P.Schaal
LF R.Reichardt
CF J.Cardenal
RF J.Hall
C B.Rodgers
P G.Brunet
P J.McGlothlin
P R.Clark
P J.Hamilton
RP M.Rojas
RP B.Kelso
RP P.Cimino

CAL 1968A

M B.Rigney
1B D.Mincher
2B B.Knoop
SS J.Fregosi
3B A.Rodriguez
LF R.Reichardt
CF V.Davalillo
RF R.Repoz
C B.Rodgers
UT C.Hinton
UT T.Satriano
P G.Brunet
P J.McGlothlin
P S.Ellis
P C.Wright
P T.Murphy
RP M.Pattin
RP A.Messersmith
RP T.Burgmeier

CAL 1969A

M B.Rigney
M L.Phillips
1B J.Spencer
2B S.Alomar
SS J.Fregosi
3B A.Rodriguez
LF R.Reichardt
CF J.Johnstone
RF B.Voss
C J.Azcue
UT R.Repoz
P A.Messersmith
P T.Murphy
P J.McGlothlin
P R.May
P G.Brunet
RP E.Fisher
RP K.Tatum
RP H.Wilhelm

CAL 1970A

M L.Phillips
1B J.Spencer
2B S.Alomar
SS J.Fregosi
3B K.McMullen
LF A.Johnson
CF J.Johnstone
RF R.Repoz
C J.Azcue
P C.Wright
P T.Murphy
P R.May
P A.Messersmith
RP E.Fisher
RP K.Tatum
RP G.Garrett

CAL 1971A

M L.Phillips
1B J.Spencer
2B S.Alomar
SS J.Fregosi
3B K.McMullen
LF T.Gonzalez
CF K.Berry
RF R.Repoz
C J.Stephenson
P C.Wright
P A.Messersmith
P T.Murphy
P R.May
RP E.Fisher
RP L.Allen
RP D.LaRoche

CAL 1972A

M D.Rice
1B B.Oliver
2B S.Alomar
SS L.Cardenas
3B K.McMullen
LF V.Pinson
CF K.Berry
RF L.Stanton
C A.Kusnyer
P N.Ryan
P C.Wright
P R.May
P A.Messersmith
P R.Clark
RP L.Allen
RP E.Fisher
RP S.Barber

CAL 1973A

M B.Winkles
1B M.Epstein
2B S.Alomar
SS R.Meoli
3B A.Gallagher
LF V.Pinson
CF K.Berry
RF L.Stanton
C J.Torborg
DH F.Robinson
UT T.McCraw
UT B.Oliver
P N.Ryan
P B.Singer
P C.Wright
P R.May
RP S.Barber
RP D.Sells

CAL 1974A

M B.Winkles
M W.Herzog
M D.Williams
1B J.Doherty
2B D.Doyle
SS D.Chalk
3B P.Schaal
LF J.Lahoud
CF M.Rivers
RF L.Stanton
C E.Rodriguez
DH F.Robinson
UT B.Oliver
UT B.Valentine
P N.Ryan
P F.Tanana
P A.Hassler
P D.Lange
P B.Singer
RP S.Lockwood

CAL 1975A

M D.Williams
1B B.Bochte
2B J.Remy
SS M.Miley
3B D.Chalk
LF M.Nettles
CF M.Rivers
RF L.Stanton
C E.Rodriguez
DH T.Harper
P F.Tanana
P E.Figueroa
P N.Ryan
P B.Singer
P A.Hassler
RP D.Kirkwood
RP M.Scott

CAL 1976A

M D.Williams
M N.Sherry
1B B.Bochte
2B J.Remy
SS D.Chalk
3B R.Jackson
LF L.Stanton
CF R.Torres
RF B.Bonds
C A.Etchebarren
DH T.Davis
UT D.Collins
UT B.Melton
P F.Tanana
P N.Ryan
P G.Ross
P P.Hartzell
P D.Kirkwood
RP D.Drago

CAL 1977A

M N.Sherry
M D.Garcia
1B T.Solaita
2B J.Remy
SS R.Mulliniks
3B D.Chalk
LF J.Rudi
CF G.Flores
RF B.Bonds
C T.Humphrey
DH D.Baylor
UT R.Jackson
P N.Ryan
P F.Tanana
P P.Hartzell
P K.Brett
P W.Simpson
RP D.Miller
RP D.LaRoche
RP M.Barlow

CAL 1978A

M D.Garcia
M J.Fregosi
1B R.Fairly
2B B.Grich
SS D.Chalk
3B C.Lansford
LF J.Rudi
CF R.Miller
RF L.Bostock
C B.Downing
DH D.Baylor
UT R.Jackson
P F.Tanana
P N.Ryan
P C.Knapp
P D.Aase
P K.Brett
RP P.Hartzell
RP D.LaRoche
RP D.Miller

CAL 1979A

M J.Fregosi
1B R.Carew
2B B.Grich
SS B.Campaneris
3B C.Lansford
LF J.Rudi
CF R.Miller
RF D.Ford
C B.Downing
DH D.Baylor
UT W.Aikens
P D.Frost
P N.Ryan
P J.Barr
P D.Aase
P C.Knapp
RP M.Clear
RP D.LaRoche
RP M.Barlow

CAL 1980A

M J.Fregosi
1B R.Carew
2B B.Grich
SS F.Patek
3B C.Lansford
LF J.Rudi
CF R.Miller
RF L.Harlow
C T.Donohue
DH J.Thompson
P F.Tanana
P D.Aase
P A.Martinez
P C.Knapp
RP D.LaRoche
RP M.Clear
RP A.Hassler

CAL 1981A

M J.Fregosi
M G.Mauch
1B R.Carew
2B B.Grich
SS R.Burleson
3B B.Hobson
LF B.Downing
CF F.Lynn
RF D.Ford
C E.Ott
DH D.Baylor
P G.Zahn
P K.Forsch
P M.Witt
P S.Renko
RP J.Jefferson
RP A.Hassler
RP D.Aase

CAL 1982A

M G.Mauch
1B R.Carew
2B B.Grich
SS T.Foli
3B D.DeCinces
LF B.Downing
CF F.Lynn
RF R.Jackson
C B.Boone
DH D.Baylor
UT J.Beniquez
UT B.Clark
P G.Zahn
P K.Forsch
P M.Witt
P S.Renko
P B.Kison
RP L.Sanchez
RP A.Hassler
RP D.Corbett

CAL 1983A

M J.McNamara
1B R.Carew
2B B.Grich
SS T.Foli
3B D.DeCinces
LF B.Downing
CF F.Lynn
RF E.Valentine
C B.Boone
DH Re.Jackson
UT Ro.Jackson
UT D.Sconiers
P T.John
P K.Forsch
P G.Zahn
P M.Witt
P B.Kison
RP L.Sanchez
RP J.Curtis

CAL 1984A

M J.McNamara
1B R.Carew
2B R.Wilfong
SS D.Schofield
3B D.DeCinces
LF B.Downing
CF G.Pettis
RF F.Lynn
C B.Boone
DH R.Jackson
UT J.Beniquez
UT B.Grich
P M.Witt
P R.Romanick
P G.Zahn
P T.John
P J.Slaton
RP D.Corbett
RP L.Sanchez
RP C.Kaufman

CAL 1985A

M G.Mauch
1B R.Carew
2B B.Grich
SS D.Schofield
3B D.DeCinces
LF B.Downing
CF G.Pettis
RF R.Jones
C B.Boone
DH R.Jackson
UT J.Beniquez
P M.Witt
P R.Romanick
P K.McCaskill
P J.Slaton
RP D.Moore
RP S.Cliburn
RP P.Clements

CAL 1986A

M G.Mauch
1B W.Joyner
2B R.Wilfong
SS D.Schofield
3B D.DeCinces
LF B.Downing
CF G.Pettis
RF R.Jones
C B.Boone
DH R.Jackson
UT B.Grich
UT G.Hendrick
P M.Witt
P K.McCaskill
P D.Sutton
P R.Romanick
RP D.Corbett
RP D.Moore

CAL 1987A

M G.Mauch
1B W.Joyner
2B M.McLemore
SS D.Schofield
3B D.DeCinces
LF J.Howell
CF G.Pettis
RF D.White
C B.Boone
DH B.Downing
P M.Witt
P D.Sutton
P W.Fraser
P J.Lazorko
P J.Candelaria
RP D.Buice
RP C.Finley
RP G.Minton

CAL 1988A

M C.Rojas
M M.Stubing
1B W.Joyner
2B J.Ray
SS D.Schofield
3B J.Howell
LF T.Armas
CF D.White
RF C.Davis
C B.Boone
DH B.Downing
P M.Witt
P W.Fraser
P C.Finley
P K.McCaskill
P D.Petry
RP S.Cliburn
RP G.Minton
RP B.Harvey

CAL 1989A

M D.Rader
1B W.Joyner
2B J.Ray
SS D.Schofield
3B J.Howell
LF C.Davis
CF D.White
RF C.Washington
C L.Parrish
DH B.Downing
P B.Blyleven
P M.Witt
P K.McCaskill
P C.Finley
P J.Abbott
RP W.Fraser
RP G.Minton
RP B.Harvey

CAL 1990A

M D.Rader
1B W.Joyner
2B J.Ray
SS D.Schofield
3B J.Howell
LF D.Bichette
CF D.White
RF D.Winfield
C L.Parrish
DH B.Downing
UT C.Davis
UT D.Hill
UT L.Polonia
P C.Finley
P M.Langston
P J.Abbott
P K.McCaskill
P B.Blyleven
RP M.Eichhorn
RP W.Fraser
RP M.Fetters

CAL 1991A

M D.Rader
M B.Rodgers
1B W.Joyner
2B L.Sojo
SS D.Schofield
3B G.Gaetti
LF L.Polonia
CF D.Gallagher
RF D.Winfield
C L.Parrish
DH D.Parker
P M.Langston
P J.Abbott
P C.Finley
P K.McCaskill
RP M.Eichhorn
RP B.Harvey
RP J.Robinson

CAL 1992A

M B.Rodgers
M J.Wathan
M B.Rodgers
1B L.Stevens
2B L.Sojo
SS G.DiSarcina
3B G.Gaetti
LF L.Polonia
CF J.Felix
RF C.Curtis
C M.Fitzgerald
DH H.Brooks
UT R.Gonzales
P M.Langston
P J.Abbott
P C.Finley
P J.Valera
P B.Blyleven
RP J.Grahe
RP C.Crim
RP M.Eichhorn

CAL 1993A

M B.Rodgers
1B J.Snow
2B T.Lovullo
SS G.DiSarcina
3B R.Gonzales
LF L.Polonia
CF C.Curtis
RF T.Salmon
C G.Myers
DH C.Davis
P M.Langston
P C.Finley
P S.Sanderson
RP K.Patterson
RP J.Grahe
RP J.Valera

CAL 1994A

M B.Rodgers
M B.Knoop
M M.Lachemann
1B J.Snow
2B H.Reynolds
SS G.DiSarcina
3B S.Owen
LF J.Edmonds
CF C.Curtis
RF T.Salmon
C C.Turner
DH C.Davis
UT D.Easley
UT B.Jackson
P C.Finley
P M.Langston
P P.Leftwich
P B.Anderson
P J.Magrane
RP M.Leiter
RP J.Dopson
RP R.Springer

CAL 1995A

M M.Lachemann
1B J.Snow
2B D.Easley
SS G.DiSarcina
3B T.Phillips
LF G.Anderson
CF J.Edmonds
RF T.Salmon

C J.Fabregas
DH C.Davis
P C.Finley
P M.Langston
P S.Boskie
P B.Anderson
RP T.Percival
RP M.James
RP B.Patterson

CAL 1996A

M M.Lachemann
M J.McNamara
1B J.Snow
2B R.Velarde
SS G.DiSarcina
3B G.Arias
LF G.Anderson
CF J.Edmonds
RF T.Salmon
C J.Fabregas
DH C.Davis
P C.Finley
P S.Boskie
P J.Abbott
P J.Grimsley
P M.Langston
RP M.James
RP T.Percival

Chicago

CHI n 1871
CHI n 1874-1875
CPU 1884
CHI P 1890
CHI F 1914-1915
CHI A 1901-2000
CHI N 1876-2000

CHI 1871n

M J.Wood
1B B.McAtee
2B J.Wood
SS E.Duffy
3B E.Pinkham
LF F.Treacey
CF T.Foley
RF J.Simmons
C C.Hodes
UT M.King
P G.Zettlein

CHI 1874n

M F.Malone
M J.Wood
1B J.Glenn
2B L.Meyerle
SS J.Peters
3B D.Force
LF N.Cuthbert
CF P.Hines
RF F.Treacey
C F.Malone
UT J.Devlin
P G.Zettlein

CHI 1875n

M J.Wood
1B J.Devlin
2B J.Miller
SS J.Peters
3B W.White
LF J.Glenn
CF P.Hines
RF O.Bielaski
C S.Hastings
P G.Zettlein

CP1884U

M E.Hengle
M J.Battin
M J.Ellick
1B J.Schoeneck
2B M.Hengle
SS S.Matthias
3B W.Foley
LF C.Householder
CF H.Wheeler
RF J.Ellick
C B.Krieg
P H.Daily
P A.Atkinson
P J.Horan

CHI 1890P

M C.Comiskey
1B C.Comiskey
2B F.Pfeffer
SS C.Bastian
3B N.Williamson
LF T.O'Neill
CF J.Ryan
RF H.Duffy
C D.Farrell
UT J.Boyle
P M.Baldwin
P S.King
P C.Bartson

CHI 1914F

M J.Tinker
1B F.Beck
2B J.Farrell
SS J.Tinker
3B R.Zeider
LF M.Flack
CF D.Zwilling
RF A.Wickland
C A.Wilson
P C.Hendrix
P M.Fiske
P E.Lange
P D.Watson
P M.Prendergast

CHI 1915F

M J.Tinker
1B F.Beck
2B R.Zeider
SS J.Smith
3B H.Fritz
LF L.Mann
CF D.Zwilling
RF M.Flack
C A.Wilson
UT W.Fischer
P G.McConnell
P C.Hendrix
P M.Prendergast
P M.Brown
P D.Black

CHI 1901A

M C.Griffith
1B F.Isbell
2B S.Mertes
SS F.Shugart
3B F.Hartman
LF H.McFarland
CF D.Hoy
RF F.Jones
C B.Sullivan
P R.Patterson
P C.Griffith
P N.Callahan
P J.Katoll
P Z.Harvey

CHI 1902A

M C.Griffith
1B F.Isbell
2B T.Daly
SS G.Davis
3B S.Strang
LF S.Mertes
CF F.Jones
RF D.Green
C B.Sullivan
P N.Callahan
P R.Patterson
P W.Piatt
P C.Griffith
P N.Garvin

CHI 1903A

M J.Callahan
1B F.Isbell
2B G.Magoon
SS L.Tannehill
3B N.Callahan
LF D.Holmes
CF F.Jones
RF D.Green
C J.Slattery
P D.White
P P.Flaherty
P R.Patterson
P F.Owen

CHI 1904A

M J.Callahan
M F.Jones
1B J.Donahue
2B G.Dundon
SS G.Davis
3B L.Tannehill
LF N.Callahan
CF F.Jones
RF D.Green
C B.Sullivan
UT F.Isbell
P F.Owen
P N.Altrock
P D.White
P F.Smith
P R.Patterson

CHI 1905A

M F.Jones
1B J.Donahue
2B G.Dundon
SS G.Davis
3B L.Tannehill
LF N.Callahan
CF F.Jones
RF D.Green
C B.Sullivan
P F.Owen
P N.Altrock
P F.Smith
P D.White
P E.Walsh

CHI 1906A

M F.Jones
1B J.Donahue
2B F.Isbell
SS G.Davis
3B L.Tannehill
LF E.Hahn
CF F.Jones
RF B.O'Neill
C B.Sullivan
P F.Owen
P N.Altrock
P E.Walsh
P D.White
P R.Patterson

CHI 1907A

M F.Jones
1B J.Donahue
2B F.Isbell
SS G.Davis
3B G.Rohe
LF P.Dougherty
CF F.Jones
RF E.Hahn
C B.Sullivan
P E.Walsh
P F.Smith
P D.White
P N.Altrock
P R.Patterson

CHI 1908A

M F.Jones
1B J.Donahue
2B G.Davis
SS F.Parent
3B L.Tannehill
LF P.Dougherty
CF F.Jones
RF E.Hahn
C B.Sullivan
UT J.Anderson
P E.Walsh
P F.Smith
P D.White
P F.Owen
P N.Altrock

CHI 1909A

M B.Sullivan
1B F.Isbell
2B J.Atz
SS F.Parent
3B L.Tannehill
LF P.Dougherty
CF D.Altizer
RF E.Hahn
C B.Sullivan
UT B.Purtell
P F.Smith
P J.Scott
P E.Walsh
P B.Burns

CHI 1910A

M H.Duffy
1B C.Gandil
2B R.Zeider
SS L.Blackburne
3B B.Purtell
LF P.Dougherty
CF F.Parent
RF S.Collins
C F.Payne
P E.Walsh
P D.White
P J.Scott
P F.Olmstead
P I.Young

CHI 1911A

M H.Duffy
1B S.Collins
2B A.McConnell
SS L.Tannehill
3B H.Lord
LF N.Callahan
CF P.Bodie
RF M.McIntyre
C B.Sullivan
P E.Walsh
P J.Scott
P D.White
P F.Lange
P F.Olmstead

CHI 1912A

M J.Callahan
1B R.Zeider
2B M.Rath
SS B.Weaver
3B H.Lord
LF N.Callahan
CF P.Bodie
RF S.Collins
C W.Kuhn
P E.Walsh
P J.Benz
P D.White
P F.Lange
P E.Cicotte

CHI 1913A

M J.Callahan
1B H.Chase
2B M.Rath
SS B.Weaver
3B H.Lord
LF P.Bodie
CF W.Mattick
RF S.Collins
C R.Schalk
P R.Russell
P J.Scott
P E.Cicotte
P J.Benz
P D.White

CHI 1914A

M J.Callahan
1B J.Fournier
2B L.Blackburne
SS B.Weaver
3B J.Breton
LF R.Demmitt
CF P.Bodie
RF S.Collins
C R.Schalk
P J.Benz
P E.Cicotte
P J.Scott
P R.Faber
P R.Russell
RP B.Lathrop

CHI 1915A

M P.Rowland
1B J.Fournier
2B E.Collins
SS B.Weaver
3B L.Blackburne
LF S.Collins
CF H.Felsch
RF E.Murphy
C R.Schalk
P R.Faber
P J.Scott
P J.Benz
P R.Russell
P E.Cicotte

CHI 1916A

M P.Rowland
1B J.Fournier
2B E.Collins
SS Z.Terry
3B B.Weaver
LF J.Jackson
CF H.Felsch
RF S.Collins
C R.Schalk
P R.Russell
P L.Williams
P R.Faber
P E.Cicotte
P J.Scott

CHI 1917A

M P.Rowland
1B C.Gandil
2B E.Collins
SS S.Risberg
3B B.Weaver
LF J.Jackson
CF H.Felsch
RF N.Leibold
C R.Schalk
P E.Cicotte
P R.Faber
P L.Williams
P R.Russell
P D.Danforth

CHI 1918A

M P.Rowland
1B C.Gandil
2B E.Collins
SS B.Weaver
3B F.McMullin
LF N.Leibold
CF S.Collins
RF E.Murphy
C R.Schalk
UT S.Risberg
P E.Cicotte
P F.Shellenback
P J.Benz
P D.Danforth
P R.Russell

CHI 1919A

M K.Gleason
1B C.Gandil
2B E.Collins
SS S.Risberg
3B B.Weaver
LF J.Jackson
CF H.Felsch
RF N.Leibold
C R.Schalk
P E.Cicotte
P L.Williams
P D.Kerr
P R.Faber
P G.Lowdermilk
RP D.Danforth

CHI 1920A

M K.Gleason
1B S.Collins
2B E.Collins
SS S.Risberg
3B B.Weaver
LF J.Jackson
CF H.Felsch
RF N.Leibold
C R.Schalk
P R.Faber
P E.Cicotte
P L.Williams
P D.Kerr
P R.Wilkinson

CHI 1921A

M K.Gleason
1B E.Sheely
2B E.Collins
SS E.Johnson
3B E.Mulligan
LF B.Falk
CF A.Strunk
RF H.Hooper
C R.Schalk
UT J.Mostil
P R.Faber
P D.Kerr
P R.Wilkinson
P S.Hodge
P D.McWeeny

CHI 1922A

M K.Gleason
1B E.Sheely
2B E.Collins
SS E.Johnson
3B E.Mulligan
LF B.Falk
CF J.Mostil
RF H.Hooper
C R.Schalk
P R.Faber
P C.Robertson
P D.Leverett
P S.Hodge
P T.Blankenship

CHI 1923A

M K.Gleason
1B E.Sheely
2B E.Collins
SS H.McClellan
3B W.Kamm
LF B.Falk
CF J.Mostil
RF H.Hooper
C R.Schalk
P C.Robertson
P R.Faber
P M.Cvengros
P T.Blankenship
P D.Leverett

CHI 1924A

M J.Evers
M E.Walsh
M .Collins
M J.Evers
1B E.Sheely
2B E.Collins
SS B.Barrett
3B W.Kamm
LF B.Falk
CF J.Mostil
RF H.Hooper
C B.Crouse
UT M.Archdeacon
P S.Thurston
P T.Lyons
P R.Faber
P S.Connally
P T.Blankenship

CHI 1925A

M .Collins
1B E.Sheely
2B E.Collins
SS I.Davis
3B W.Kamm
LF B.Falk
CF J.Mostil
RF H.Hooper
C R.Schalk
P T.Lyons
P R.Faber
P T.Blankenship
P S.Thurston
P C.Robertson
RP S.Connally

CHI 1926A

M .Collins
1B E.Sheely
2B E.Collins
SS B.Hunnefield
3B W.Kamm
LF B.Falk
CF J.Mostil
RF B.Barrett
C R.Schalk
P T.Lyons
P T.Thomas
P T.Blankenship
P R.Faber
P J.Edwards

CHI 1927A

M R.Schalk
1B B.Clancy
2B A.Ward
SS B.Hunnefield
3B W.Kamm
LF B.Falk
CF A.Metzler
RF B.Barrett
C H.McCurdy
P T.Thomas
P T.Lyons
P T.Blankenship
P S.Connally
P R.Faber
RP E.Jacobs
RP B.Cole

CHI 1928A

M R.Schalk
M L.Blackburne
1B B.Clancy
2B B.Hunnefield
SS B.Cissell
3B W.Kamm
LF B.Falk
CF J.Mostil
RF A.Metzler
C B.Crouse
P T.Thomas
P T.Lyons
P G.Adkins
P R.Faber
P T.Blankenship
RP S.Connally

CHI 1929A

M L.Blackburne
1B A.Shires
2B J.Kerr
SS B.Cissell
3B W.Kamm
LF A.Metzler
CF D.Hoffman
RF C.Reynolds
C M.Berg
UT B.Clancy
P T.Thomas
P T.Lyons
P R.Faber
P H.McKain
P G.Adkins

CHI 1930A

M D.Bush
1B J.Watwood
2B B.Cissell
SS G.Mulleavy
3B W.Kamm
LF S.Jolley
CF R.Barnes
RF C.Reynolds
C B.Tate
P T.Lyons
P P.Caraway
P T.Thomas
P R.Faber
P D.Henry
RP E.Walsh
RP H.McKain

CHI 1931A

M D.Bush
1B L.Blue
2B J.Kerr
SS B.Cissell
3B B.Sullivan
LF L.Fonseca
CF J.Watwood
RF C.Reynolds
C B.Tate
UT L.Appling
UT B.Fothergill
P V.Frasier
P T.Thomas
P P.Caraway
P R.Faber
P H.McKain
RP J.Moore
RP G.Braxton

CHI 1932A

M L.Fonseca
1B L.Blue
2B J.Hayes
SS L.Appling
3B C.Selph
LF B.Fothergill
CF L.Funk
RF B.Seeds
C F.Grube
UT R.Kress
UT B.Sullivan
P T.Lyons
P S.Jones
P M.Gaston
P V.Frasier
P P.Gregory
RP R.Faber

CHI 1933A

M L.Fonseca
1B R.Kress
2B J.Hayes
SS L.Appling
3B J.Dykes
LF A.Simmons
CF M.Haas
RF E.Swanson
C F.Grube
P T.Lyons
P S.Jones
P M.Gaston
P E.Durham
P J.Miller
RP J.Heving
RP R.Faber

CHI 1934A
M L.Fonseca
M J.Dykes
1B Z.Bonura
2B J.Hayes
SS L.Appling
3B J.Dykes
LF A.Simmons
CF M.Haas
RF E.Swanson
C E.Madjeski
P G.Earnshaw
P T.Lyons
P M.Gaston
P S.Jones
P L.Tietje
RP J.Heving
RP W.Wyatt

CHI 1935A
M J.Dykes
1B Z.Bonura
2B J.Hayes
SS L.Appling
3B J.Dykes
LF R.Radcliff
CF A.Simmons
RF M.Haas
C L.Sewell
UT G.Washington
P J.Whitehead
P V.Kennedy
P T.Lyons
P L.Tietje
P S.Jones
RP W.Wyatt

CHI 1936A
M J.Dykes
1B Z.Bonura
2B J.Hayes
SS L.Appling
3B J.Dykes
LF R.Radcliff
CF M.Kreevich
RF M.Haas
C L.Sewell
UT T.Piet
P V.Kennedy
P J.Whitehead
P S.Cain
P T.Lyons
P M.Stratton
RP C.Brown
RP R.Evans

CHI 1937A
M J.Dykes
1B Z.Bonura
2B J.Hayes
SS L.Appling
3B T.Piet
LF R.Radcliff
CF M.Kreevich
RF D.Walker
C L.Sewell
P V.Kennedy
P T.Lee
P T.Lyons
P J.Whitehead
P M.Stratton
RP C.Brown

CHI 1938A
M J.Dykes
1B J.Kuhel
2B J.Hayes
SS L.Appling
3B M.Owen
LF G.Walker
CF M.Kreevich
RF H.Steinbacher
C L.Sewell
UT B.Berger
UT R.Radcliff
P T.Lee
P T.Lyons
P M.Stratton
P J.Whitehead
P J.Rigney

CHI 1939A
M J.Dykes
1B J.Kuhel
2B O.Bejma
SS L.Appling
3B E.McNair
LF G.Walker
CF M.Kreevich
RF L.Rosenthal
C M.Tresh
UT R.Radcliff
P T.Lee
P J.Rigney
P E.Smith
P T.Lyons
P J.Knott
RP C.Brown

CHI 1940A
M J.Dykes
1B J.Kuhel
2B S.Webb
SS L.Appling
3B B.Kennedy
LF M.Solters
CF M.Kreevich
RF T.Wright
C M.Tresh
UT L.Rosenthal
P J.Rigney
P T.Lee
P E.Smith
P T.Lyons
P J.Knott
RP C.Brown
RP P.Appleton

CHI 1941A
M J.Dykes
1B J.Kuhel
2B B.Knickerbocker
SS L.Appling
3B D.Lodigiani
LF M.Hoag
CF M.Kreevich
RF T.Wright
C M.Tresh
P T.Lee
P E.Smith
P J.Rigney
P T.Lyons
P B.Dietrich

CHI 1942A
M J.Dykes
1B J.Kuhel
2B D.Kolloway
SS L.Appling
3B B.Kennedy
LF T.Wright
CF M.Hoag
RF W.Moses
C M.Tresh
P J.Humphries
P E.Smith
P T.Lyons
P B.Dietrich
P B.Ross
RP J.Haynes

CHI 1943A
M J.Dykes
1B J.Kuhel
2B D.Kolloway
SS L.Appling
3B R.Hodgin
LF G.Curtright
CF T.Tucker
RF W.Moses
C M.Tresh
P O.Grove
P E.Smith
P J.Humphries
P B.Dietrich
P B.Ross
RP G.Maltzberger
RP B.Swift

CHI 1944A
M J.Dykes
1B H.Trosky
2B R.Schalk
SS S.Webb
3B R.Hodgin
LF E.Carnett
CF T.Tucker
RF W.Moses
C M.Tresh
P B.Dietrich
P O.Grove
P E.Lopat
P J.Humphries
P J.Haynes
RP G.Maltzberger

CHI 1945A
M J.Dykes
1B K.Farrell
2B R.Schalk
SS C.Michaels
3B T.Cuccinello
LF J.Dickshot
CF O.Hockett
RF W.Moses
C M.Tresh
UT G.Curtright
P T.Lee
P O.Grove
P E.Lopat
P J.Humphries
P B.Dietrich
RP J.Johnson

CHI 1946A
M J.Dykes
M T.Lyons
1B H.Trosky
2B D.Kolloway
SS L.Appling
3B D.Lodigiani
LF B.Kennedy
CF T.Tucker
RF T.Wright
C M.Tresh
P E.Lopat
P O.Grove
P J.Haynes
P E.Smith
P F.Papish
RP E.Caldwell
RP R.Hamner
RP A.Hollingsworth

CHI 1947A
M T.Lyons
1B R.York
2B D.Kolloway
SS L.Appling
3B F.Baker
LF T.Wright
CF D.Philley
RF B.Kennedy
C M.Tresh
UT C.Michaels
P E.Lopat
P F.Papish
P J.Haynes
P O.Grove
P B.Gillespie
RP E.Harrist
RP P.Gebrian
RP G.Maltzberger

CHI 1948A
M T.Lyons
1B T.Lupien
2B D.Kolloway
SS C.Michaels
3B L.Appling
LF P.Seerey
CF D.Philley
RF T.Wright
C A.Robinson
UT F.Baker
UT R.Hodgin
P B.Wight
P J.Haynes
P A.Gettel
P M.Pieretti
P R.Gumpert
RP H.Judson
RP F.Papish
RP O.Grove

CHI 1949A
M J.Onslow
1B C.Kress
2B C.Michaels
SS L.Appling
3B F.Baker
LF G.Zernial
CF C.Metkovich
RF D.Philley
C D.Wheeler
P B.Wight
P R.Gumpert
P B.Pierce
P B.Kuzava
P H.Judson
RP M.Pieretti
RP M.Surkont

CHI 1950A
M J.Onslow
M R.Corriden
1B E.Robinson
2B N.Fox
SS C.Carrasquel
3B H.Majeski
LF G.Zernial
CF D.Philley
RF M.Rickert
C P.Masi
P B.Pierce
P B.Wight
P B.Cain
P R.Gumpert
P R.Scarborough
RP H.Judson
RP L.Aloma
RP M.Haefner

CHI 1951A
M P.Richards
1B E.Robinson
2B N.Fox
SS C.Carrasquel
3B B.Dillinger
LF M.Minoso
CF J.Busby
RF A.Zarilla
C P.Masi
UT B.Stewart
P B.Pierce
P S.Rogovin
P K.Holcombe
P J.Dobson
P R.Gumpert
RP L.Aloma
RP M.Rotblatt

CHI 1952A
M P.Richards
1B E.Robinson
2B N.Fox
SS C.Carrasquel
3B H.Rodriguez
LF M.Minoso
CF R.Coleman
RF S.Mele
C S.Lollar
P B.Pierce
P S.Rogovin
P J.Dobson
P M.Grissom
P C.Stobbs
RP H.Dorish
RP B.Kennedy

CHI 1953A
M P.Richards
1B F.Fain
2B N.Fox
SS C.Carrasquel
3B B.Elliott
LF M.Minoso
CF J.Rivera
RF S.Mele
C S.Lollar
P B.Pierce
P V.Trucks
P M.Fornieles
P S.Rogovin
P S.Consuegra
RP H.Dorish
RP G.Bearden

CHI 1954A
M P.Richards
M M.Marion
1B F.Fain
2B N.Fox
SS C.Carrasquel
3B C.Michaels
LF M.Minoso
CF J.Groth
RF J.Rivera
C S.Lollar
P V.Trucks
P B.Keegan
P B.Pierce
P J.Harshman
P S.Consuegra
RP H.Dorish
RP M.Martin

CHI 1955A
M M.Marion
1B W.Dropo
2B N.Fox
SS C.Carrasquel
3B G.Kell
LF M.Minoso
CF J.Busby
RF J.Rivera
C S.Lollar
UT B.Nieman
P B.Pierce
P D.Donovan
P J.Harshman
P V.Trucks
P C.Johnson
RP S.Consuegra
RP D.Howell
RP M.Martin

CHI 1956A
M M.Marion
1B W.Dropo
2B N.Fox
SS L.Aparicio
3B F.Hatfield
LF M.Minoso
CF L.Doby
RF J.Rivera
C S.Lollar
P B.Pierce
P D.Donovan
P J.Harshman
P J.Wilson
P B.Keegan
RP D.Howell

CHI 1957A
M A.Lopez
1B E.Torgeson
2B N.Fox
SS L.Aparicio
3B B.Phillips
LF M.Minoso
CF L.Doby
RF J.Landis
C S.Lollar
UT S.Esposito
UT J.Rivera
P B.Pierce
P D.Donovan
P J.Wilson
P J.Harshman
P B.Keegan
RP G.Staley
RP D.Howell

CHI 1958A
M A.Lopez
1B E.Torgeson
2B N.Fox
SS L.Aparicio
3B B.Goodman
LF J.Rivera
CF J.Landis
RF A.Smith
C S.Lollar
UT S.Esposito
P D.Donovan
P B.Pierce
P E.Wynn
P J.Wilson
P R.Moore
RP G.Staley
RP B.Shaw

CHI 1959A
M A.Lopez
1B E.Torgeson
2B N.Fox
SS L.Aparicio
3B B.Phillips
LF A.Smith
CF J.Landis
RF J.Rivera
C S.Lollar
UT B.Goodman
P E.Wynn
P B.Shaw
P B.Pierce
P D.Donovan
P B.Latman
RP G.Staley
RP T.Lown

CHI 1960A
M A.Lopez
1B R.Sievers
2B N.Fox
SS L.Aparicio
3B G.Freese
LF M.Minoso
CF J.Landis
RF A.Smith
C S.Lollar
P E.Wynn
P B.Pierce
P B.Shaw
P F.Baumann
P R.Kemmerer
RP G.Staley
RP D.Donovan
RP T.Lown

CHI 1961A
M A.Lopez
1B R.Sievers
2B N.Fox
SS L.Aparicio
3B A.Smith
LF M.Minoso
CF J.Landis
RF F.Robinson
C S.Lollar
UT J.Martin
P J.Pizarro
P F.Baumann
P B.Pierce
P C.McLish
P R.Herbert
RP T.Lown
RP R.Kemmerer
RP D.Larsen

CHI 1962A
M A.Lopez
1B J.Cunningham
2B N.Fox
SS L.Aparicio
3B A.Smith
LF F.Robinson
CF J.Landis
RF M.Hershberger
C C.Carreon
P R.Herbert
P J.Pizarro
P E.Fisher
P E.Wynn
P J.Buzhardt
RP D.Zanni
RP T.Lown

CHI 1963A
M A.Lopez
1B T.McCraw
2B N.Fox
SS R.Hansen
3B P.Ward
LF D.Nicholson
CF J.Landis
RF F.Robinson
C J.Martin
UT C.Carreon
UT M.Hershberger
UT A.Weis
P G.Peters
P R.Herbert
P J.Pizarro
P J.Buzhardt
P J.Horlen
RP H.Wilhelm
RP J.Brosnan
RP F.Baumann

CHI 1964A
M A.Lopez
1B T.McCraw
2B A.Weis
SS R.Hansen
3B P.Ward
LF F.Robinson
CF J.Landis
RF M.Hershberger
C J.Martin
UT D.Buford
UT D.Nicholson
P G.Peters
P J.Pizarro
P J.Horlen
P J.Buzhardt
P R.Herbert
RP H.Wilhelm
RP E.Fisher

CHI 1965A
M A.Lopez
1B B.Skowron
2B D.Buford
SS R.Hansen
3B P.Ward
LF D.Cater
CF K.Berry
RF F.Robinson
C J.Martin
UT T.McCraw
UT J.Romano
UT A.Weis
P J.Horlen
P J.Buzhardt
P T.John
P G.Peters
P B.Howard
RP E.Fisher
RP H.Wilhelm
RP B.Locker

CHI 1966A
M E.Stanky
1B T.McCraw
2B A.Weis
SS L.Elia
3B D.Buford
LF K.Berry
CF T.Agee
RF F.Robinson
C J.Romano
UT J.Adair
UT B.Skowron
P T.John
P J.Horlen
P G.Peters
P J.Buzhardt
P B.Howard
RP B.Locker
RP D.Higgins
RP J.Pizarro

CHI 1967A
M E.Stanky
1B T.McCraw
2B W.Causey
SS R.Hansen
3B D.Buford
LF P.Ward
CF T.Agee
RF K.Berry
C J.Martin
UT W.Williams
P G.Peters
P J.Horlen
P T.John
P B.Howard
RP B.Locker
RP W.Wood
RP D.McMahon

CHI 1968A
M E.Stanky
M L.Moss
M A.Lopez
M L.Moss
M A.Lopez
1B T.McCraw
2B S.Alomar
SS L.Aparicio
3B P.Ward
LF T.Davis
CF K.Berry
RF B.Bradford
C D.Josephson
P J.Horlen
P J.Fisher
P T.John
P G.Peters
P C.Carlos
RP W.Wood
RP H.Wilhelm
RP B.Locker

CHI 1969A
M A.Lopez
M D.Gutteridge
1B G.Hopkins
2B B.Knoop
SS L.Aparicio
3B B.Melton
LF C.May
CF K.Berry
RF W.Williams
C E.Herrmann
UT P.Ward
P J.Horlen
P T.John
P G.Peters
P B.Wynne
RP W.Wood
RP D.Osinski
RP C.Carlos

CHI 1970A
M D.Gutteridge
M B.Adair
M C.Tanner
1B G.Hopkins
2B B.Knoop
SS L.Aparicio
3B B.Melton
LF C.May
CF K.Berry
RF W.Williams
C E.Herrmann
UT T.McCraw
UT S.O'Brien
P T.John
P J.Janeski
P J.Horlen
RP W.Wood

RP J.Crider
RP D.Murphy

CHI 1971A
M C.Tanner
1B C.May
2B M.Andrews
SS L.Alvarado
3B B.Melton
LF R.Reichardt
CF J.Johnstone
RF W.Williams
C E.Herrmann
UT R.McKinney
P W.Wood
P T.Bradley
P T.John
P B.Johnson
P J.Horlen
RP S.Kealey
RP V.Romo
RP T.Forster

CHI 1972A
M C.Tanner
1B D.Allen
2B M.Andrews
SS R.Morales
3B E.Spiezio
LF C.May
CF J.Johnstone
RF P.Kelly
C E.Herrmann
UT L.Alvarado
UT R.Reichardt
P W.Wood
P T.Bradley
P S.Bahnsen
P D.Lemonds
RP T.Forster
RP R.Gossage
RP S.Kealey

CHI 1973A
M C.Tanner
1B T.Muser
2B J.Orta
SS E.Leon
3B B.Melton
LF C.May
CF J.Jeter
RF P.Kelly
C E.Herrmann
DH K.Henderson
P W.Wood
P S.Bahnsen
P S.Stone
P T.Forster
P E.Fisher
RP C.Acosta
RP R.Gossage

CHI 1974A
M C.Tanner
1B D.Allen
2B J.Orta
SS B.Dent
3B B.Melton
LF C.May
CF K.Henderson
RF B.Sharp
C E.Herrmann
DH P.Kelly
UT B.Downing
UT T.Muser
UT R.Santo
P W.Wood
P J.Kaat
P S.Bahnsen
P B.Johnson
RP T.Forster
RP S.Pitlock
RP R.Gossage

CHI 1975A
M C.Tanner
1B C.May
2B J.Orta
SS B.Dent
3B B.Melton
LF N.Nyman
CF K.Henderson
RF P.Kelly
C B.Downing
DH D.Johnson
P J.Kaat
P W.Wood
P C.Osteen
P J.Jefferson
RP R.Gossage
RP D.Hamilton
RP O.Osborn

CHI 1976A
M P.Richards
1B J.Spencer
2B J.Brohamer
SS B.Dent
3B K.Bell
LF J.Orta
CF C.Lemon
RF R.Garr
C B.Downing
DH P.Kelly
UT B.Stein
P R.Gossage
P B.Johnson
P K.Brett
P F.Barrios
P T.Forster
RP D.Hamilton
RP C.Carroll

CHI 1977A
M B.Lemon
1B J.Spencer
2B J.Orta
SS A.Bannister
3B E.Soderholm
LF R.Garr
CF C.Lemon
RF R.Zisk
C J.Essian
DH O.Gamble
UT L.Johnson
P F.Barrios
P S.Stone
P K.Kravec
P C.Knapp
P W.Wood
RP L.LaGrow
RP D.Hamilton

CHI 1978A
M B.Lemon
M L.Doby
1B M.Squires
2B J.Orta
SS D.Kessinger
3B E.Soderholm
LF R.Garr
CF C.Lemon
RF C.Washington
C B.Nahorodny
DH L.Johnson
UT B.Molinaro
P S.Stone
P K.Kravec
P F.Barrios
P W.Wood
RP J.Willoughby
RP L.LaGrow
RP R.Schueler

CHI 1979A
M D.Kessinger
M T.LaRussa
1B M.Squires
2B A.Bannister
SS G.Pryor
3B K.Bell
LF R.Torres
CF C.Lemon
RF C.Washington
C M.May
DH J.Orta
UT R.Garr
UT L.Johnson
P K.Kravec
P R.Wortham
P R.Baumgarten
P S.Trout
RP R.Scarbery
RP M.Proly
RP E.Farmer

CHI 1980A
M T.LaRussa
1B M.Squires
2B J.Morrison
SS T.Cruz
3B K.Bell
LF W.Nordhagen
CF C.Lemon
RF H.Baines
C B.Kimm
DH L.Johnson
UT B.Molinaro
UT G.Pryor
P B.Burns
P S.Trout
P R.Dotson
P R.Baumgarten
P L.Hoyt
RP M.Proly
RP E.Farmer
RP R.Wortham

CHI 1981A
M T.LaRussa
1B M.Squires
2B T.Bernazard
SS B.Almon
3B J.Morrison
LF R.LeFlore
CF C.Lemon
RF H.Baines
C C.Fisk
DH G.Luzinski
UT R.Kuntz
UT W.Nordhagen
P B.Burns
P R.Dotson
P D.Lamp
P S.Trout
P R.Baumgarten
RP L.Hoyt
RP E.Farmer
RP K.Hickey

CHI 1982A
M T.LaRussa
1B M.Squires
2B T.Bernazard
SS B.Almon
3B A.Rodriguez
LF S.Kemp
CF R.Law
RF H.Baines
C C.Fisk
DH G.Luzinski
UT V.Law
UT T.Paciorek
P L.Hoyt
P R.Dotson
P D.Lamp
P J.Koosman
P B.Burns
RP S.Barojas
RP K.Hickey
RP C.Escarrega

CHI 1983A
M T.LaRussa
1B M.Squires
2B J.Cruz
SS J.Dybzinski
3B V.Law
LF R.Kittle
CF R.Law
RF H.Baines
C C.Fisk
DH G.Luzinski
UT S.Fletcher
UT J.Hairston
UT T.Paciorek
UT G.Walker
P L.Hoyt
P R.Dotson
P F.Bannister
P B.Burns
P J.Koosman
RP D.Lamp
RP D.Tidrow
RP S.Barojas

CHI 1984A
M T.LaRussa
1B G.Walker
2B J.Cruz
SS S.Fletcher
3B V.Law
LF R.Kittle
CF R.Law
RF H.Baines
C C.Fisk
DH G.Luzinski
UT J.Hairston
UT T.Paciorek
UT M.Squires
P R.Dotson
P T.Seaver
P L.Hoyt
P F.Bannister
P B.Burns
RP R.Reed
RP J.Agosto
RP D.Spillner

CHI 1985A
M T.LaRussa
1B G.Walker
2B J.Cruz
SS O.Guillen
3B T.Hulett
LF R.Law
CF D.Boston
RF H.Baines
C C.Fisk
DH R.Kittle
UT S.Fletcher
UT L.Salazar
P T.Seaver
P B.Burns
P F.Bannister
P G.Nelson
RP B.James
RP D.Spillner
RP J.Agosto

CHI 1986A
M T.LaRussa
M D.Rader
M J.Fregosi
1B G.Walker
2B J.Cruz
SS O.Guillen
3B T.Hulett
LF R.Nichols
CF J.Cangelosi
RF H.Baines
C C.Fisk
DH R.Kittle
UT J.Hairston
P R.Dotson
P F.Bannister
P J.Cowley
P N.Allen
P J.Davis
RP G.Nelson
RP B.Dawley
RP D.Schmidt

CHI 1987A
M J.Fregosi
1B G.Walker
2B F.Manrique
SS O.Guillen
3B T.Hulett
LF G.Redus
CF K.Williams
RF I.Calderon
C C.Fisk
DH H.Baines
UT D.Boston
UT D.Hill
P F.Bannister
P R.Dotson
P J.DeLeon
P B.Long
RP J.Winn
RP B.Thigpen
RP R.Searage

CHI 1988A
M J.Fregosi
1B G.Walker
2B F.Manrique
SS O.Guillen
3B S.Lyons
LF D.Boston
CF D.Gallagher
RF D.Pasqua
C C.Fisk
DH H.Baines
P M.Perez
P J.Reuss
P B.Long
P D.LaPoint
P J.McDowell
RP R.Horton
RP B.Thigpen
RP J.Davis

CHI 1989A
M J.Torborg
1B G.Walker
2B S.Lyons
SS O.Guillen
3B C.Martinez
LF D.Boston
CF D.Gallagher
RF I.Calderon
C C.Fisk
DH H.Baines
P M.Perez
P E.King
P S.Rosenberg
P G.Hibbard
P J.Reuss
RP S.Hillegas
RP D.Pall
RP B.Thigpen

CHI 1990A
M J.Torborg
1B C.Martinez
2B S.Fletcher
SS O.Guillen
3B R.Ventura
LF I.Calderon
CF L.Johnson
RF S.Sosa
C C.Fisk
DH D.Pasqua
P G.Hibbard
P J.McDowell
P M.Perez
P E.King
RP W.Edwards
RP B.Thigpen
RP D.Pall

CHI 1991A
M J.Torborg
1B D.Pasqua
2B S.Fletcher
SS O.Guillen
3B R.Ventura
LF T.Raines
CF L.Johnson
RF S.Sosa
C C.Fisk
DH F.Thomas
UT J.Cora
UT C.Grebeck
P J.McDowell
P C.Hough
P G.Hibbard
P A.Fernandez
RP M.Perez
RP S.Radinsky
RP D.Pall

CHI 1992A
M G.Lamont
1B F.Thomas
2B S.Sax
SS C.Grebeck
3B R.Ventura
LF T.Raines
CF L.Johnson
RF S.Abner
C R.Karkovice
DH G.Bell
P J.McDowell
P K.McCaskill
P A.Fernandez
P C.Hough
P G.Hibbard
RP W.Alvarez
RP T.Leach
RP D.Pall

CHI 1993A
M G.Lamont
1B F.Thomas
2B J.Cora
SS O.Guillen
3B R.Ventura
LF T.Raines
CF L.Johnson
RF E.Burks
C R.Karkovice
DH G.Bell
P J.McDowell
P A.Fernandez
P W.Alvarez
P J.Bere
P K.McCaskill
RP R.Hernandez
RP D.Pall
RP S.Radinsky

CHI 1994A
M G.Lamont
1B F.Thomas
2B J.Cora
SS O.Guillen
3B R.Ventura
LF T.Raines
CF L.Johnson
RF D.Jackson
C R.Karkovice
DH J.Franco
P J.McDowell
P A.Fernandez
P W.Alvarez
P J.Bere
P S.Sanderson
RP J.DeLeon
RP K.McCaskill
RP R.Hernandez

CHI 1995A
M G.Lamont
M T.Bevington
1B D.Martinez
2B R.Durham
SS O.Guillen
3B R.Ventura
LF T.Raines
CF L.Johnson
RF M.Devereaux
C R.Karkovice
DH F.Thomas
P A.Fernandez
P W.Alvarez
P J.Bere
P J.Abbott
P B.Keyser
RP K.McCaskill
RP J.DeLeon
RP R.Hernandez

CHI 1996A
M T.Bevington
1B F.Thomas
2B R.Durham
SS O.Guillen
3B R.Ventura
LF T.Phillips
CF D.Lewis
RF D.Tartabull
C R.Karkovice
DH H.Baines
UT D.Martinez
P A.Fernandez
P K.Tapani
P W.Alvarez
P J.Baldwin
RP R.Hernandez
RP B.Simas
RP B.Keyser

CHI 1997A
M T.Bevington
1B F.Thomas
2B R.Durham
SS O.Guillen
3B C.Snopek
LF A.Belle
CF M.Cameron
RF D.Martinez
C J.Fabregas
DH H.Baines
P J.Navarro
P J.Baldwin
P D.Drabek
P W.Alvarez
P D.Darwin
RP C.Castillo
RP T.Castillo
RP C.McElroy

CHI 1998A
M J.Manuel
1B W.Cordero
2B R.Durham
SS M.Caruso
3B R.Ventura
LF A.Belle
CF M.Cameron
RF M.Ordonez
C C.Kreuter
DH F.Thomas
UT G.Norton
P M.Sirotka
P J.Navarro
P J.Baldwin
P J.Parque
P S.Eyre
RP C.Castillo
RP B.Simas
RP K.Foulke

CHI 1999A
M J.Manuel
1B P.Konerko
2B R.Durham
SS M.Caruso
3B G.Norton
LF C.Lee
CF C.Singleton
RF M.Ordonez
C B.Fordyce
DH F.Thomas
UT C.Wilson
P M.Sirotka
P J.Baldwin
P J.Parque
P J.Navarro
P J.Snyder
RP K.Foulke
RP S.Lowe
RP B.Simas

CHI 2000A
M J.Manuel
1B P.Konerko
2B R.Durham
SS J.Valentin
3B H.Perry
LF C.Lee
CF C.Singleton
RF M.Ordonez
C M.Johnson
DH F.Thomas
P M.Sirotka
P J.Parque
P J.Baldwin
P C.Eldred
P K.Wells
RP K.Foulke
RP S.Lowe
RP B.Howry

CHI 1876N
M A.Spalding
1B C.McVey
2B R.Barnes
SS J.Peters
3B C.Anson
LF J.Glenn
CF P.Hines
RF O.Bielaski
C D.White
P A.Spalding

CHI 1877N
M A.Spalding
1B A.Spalding
2B R.Barnes
SS J.Peters
3B C.Anson
LF J.Glenn
CF D.Eggler
RF P.Hines
C C.McVey
P G.Bradley
P L.Reis

CHI 1878N
M B.Ferguson
1B J.Start
2B B.McClellan
SS B.Ferguson
3B F.Hankinson
LF C.Anson
CF J.Remsen
RF J.Cassidy
C B.Harbidge
P T.Larkin
P L.Reis

CHI 1879N
M C.Anson
M S.Flint
1B C.Anson
2B J.Quest
SS J.Peters
3B N.Williamson
LF A.Dalrymple
CF G.Gore
RF O.Shaffer
C S.Flint
P T.Larkin
P F.Hankinson

CHI 1880N
M C.Anson
1B C.Anson
2B J.Quest
SS T.Burns
3B N.Williamson
LF A.Dalrymple
CF G.Gore
RF K.Kelly
C S.Flint
P L.Corcoran
P F.Goldsmith

CHI 1881N
M C.Anson
1B C.Anson
2B J.Quest
SS T.Burns
3B N.Williamson
LF A.Dalrymple
CF G.Gore
RF K.Kelly
C S.Flint
P L.Corcoran
P F.Goldsmith

CHI 1882N
M C.Anson
1B C.Anson
2B T.Burns
SS K.Kelly
3B N.Williamson
LF A.Dalrymple
CF G.Gore
RF H.Nicol
C S.Flint
P F.Goldsmith
P L.Corcoran

CHI 1883N
M C.Anson
1B C.Anson
2B F.Pfeffer
SS T.Burns
3B N.Williamson
LF A.Dalrymple
CF G.Gore
RF K.Kelly
C S.Flint
P L.Corcoran
P F.Goldsmith

CHI 1884N
M C.Anson
1B C.Anson
2B F.Pfeffer
SS T.Burns
3B N.Williamson
LF A.Dalrymple
CF G.Gore
RF K.Kelly
C S.Flint
P L.Corcoran
P F.Goldsmith
P J.Clarkson

CHI 1885N
M C.Anson
1B C.Anson
2B F.Pfeffer
SS T.Burns
3B N.Williamson
LF A.Dalrymple
CF G.Gore
RF K.Kelly
C S.Flint
P J.Clarkson
P J.McCormick
P T.Kennedy

CHI 1886N
M C.Anson
1B C.Anson
2B F.Pfeffer
SS N.Williamson
3B T.Burns
LF A.Dalrymple
CF G.Gore
RF K.Kelly
C S.Flint
UT J.Ryan
P J.Clarkson
P J.McCormick
P J.Flynn

CHI 1887N
M C.Anson
1B C.Anson
2B F.Pfeffer
SS N.Williamson
3B T.Burns
LF M.Sullivan
CF J.Ryan
RF B.Sunday
C T.Daly
P J.Clarkson
P M.Baldwin

CHI 1888N
M C.Anson
1B C.Anson
2B F.Pfeffer
SS N.Williamson
3B T.Burns
LF M.Sullivan
CF J.Ryan
RF H.Duffy
C T.Daly
P G.Krock
P M.Baldwin
P J.Tener

CHI 1889N
M C.Anson
1B C.Anson
2B F.Pfeffer
SS N.Williamson
3B T.Burns
LF G.Van Haltren
CF J.Ryan
RF H.Duffy
C D.Farrell
P B.Hutchison
P J.Tener
P F.Dwyer
P A.Gumbert

CHI 1890N
M C.Anson
1B C.Anson
2B B.Glenalvin
SS J.Cooney
3B T.Burns
LF C.Carroll
CF W.Wilmot
RF J.Andrews
C M.Kittridge
UT H.Earl
P B.Hutchison
P P.Luby
P E.Stein
P M.Sullivan
P R.Coughlin

CHI 1891N
M C.Anson
1B C.Anson
2B F.Pfeffer
SS J.Cooney
3B B.Dahlen
LF W.Wilmot
CF J.Ryan
RF C.Carroll
C M.Kittridge
P B.Hutchison
P A.Gumbert
P P.Luby
P E.Stein

CHI 1892N
M C.Anson
1B C.Anson
2B J.Canavan
SS B.Dahlen
3B J.Parrott
LF W.Wilmot
CF J.Ryan
RF S.Dungan
C P.Schriver
P B.Hutchison
P A.Gumbert
P P.Luby

CHI 1893N
M C.Anson
1B C.Anson
2B B.Lange
SS B.Dahlen
3B J.Parrott
LF W.Wilmot
CF J.Ryan
RF S.Dungan
C M.Kittridge
UT G.Decker
P B.Hutchison
P W.McGill
P H.Mauck

CHI 1894N
M C.Anson
1B C.Anson
2B J.Parrott
SS B.Dahlen
3B C.Irwin
LF W.Wilmot
CF B.Lange
RF J.Ryan
C P.Schriver
UT G.Decker
P B.Hutchison
P C.Griffith
P W.McGill
P A.Terry
P S.Stratton

CHI 1895N
M C.Anson
1B C.Anson
2B A.Stewart
SS B.Dahlen
3B B.Everitt
LF W.Wilmot
CF B.Lange
RF J.Ryan
C T.Donahue
P C.Griffith
P A.Terry
P B.Hutchison

CHI 1896N
M C.Anson
1B C.Anson
2B F.Pfeffer
SS B.Dahlen
3B B.Everitt
LF G.Decker
CF B.Lange
RF J.Ryan
C M.Kittridge
P C.Griffith
P D.Friend
P A.Terry
P B.Briggs

CHI 1897N
M C.Anson
1B C.Anson
2B J.Connor
SS B.Dahlen
3B B.Everitt
LF G.Decker
CF B.Lange
RF J.Ryan
C M.Kittridge
UT N.Callahan
UT B.McCormick
P C.Griffith
P D.Friend
P B.Briggs
P R.Denzer

CHI 1898N
M T.Burns
1B B.Everitt
2B J.Connor
SS B.Dahlen
3B B.McCormick
LF J.Ryan
CF B.Lange
RF S.Mertes
C T.Donahue
P C.Griffith
P N.Callahan
P W.Woods
P M.Kilroy

CHI 1899N
M T.Burns
1B B.Everitt
2B B.McCormick
SS De Montreville
3B H.Wolverton
LF J.Ryan
CF S.Mertes
RF D.Green
C T.Donahue
UT B.Lange
P J.Taylor
P C.Griffith
P N.Callahan
P N.Garvin

CHI 1900N
M T.Loftus
1B J.Ganzel
2B C.Childs
SS B.McCormick
3B B.Bradley
LF J.McCarthy
CF D.Green
RF J.Ryan
C T.Donahue
UT S.Mertes
P N.Callahan
P C.Griffith
P N.Garvin
P J.Taylor
P J.Menefee

CHI 1901N
M T.Loftus
1B J.Doyle
2B C.Childs
SS B.McCormick
3B F.Raymer
LF T.Hartsel
CF D.Green
RF F.Chance
C J.Kling
UT C.Dexter
P T.Hughes
P J.Taylor
P R.Waddell
P M.Eason

CHI 1902N
M F.Selee
1B F.Chance
2B B.Lowe
SS J.Tinker
3B G.Schaefer
LF J.Slagle
CF J.Dobbs
RF D.Jones
C J.Kling
P J.Taylor
P P.Williams
P C.Lundgren
P B.Rhoads
P J.St.Vrain

CHI 1903N
M F.Selee
1B F.Chance
2B J.Evers
SS J.Tinker
3B D.Casey
LF J.Slagle
CF D.Jones
RF D.Harley
C J.Kling
P J.Taylor
P J.Weimer
P B.Wicker
P C.Lundgren
P J.Menefee

CHI 1904N
M F.Selee
1B F.Chance
2B J.Evers
SS J.Tinker
3B D.Casey
LF J.Slagle
CF J.McCarthy
RF D.Jones
C J.Kling
P J.Weimer
P B.Briggs
P C.Lundgren
P B.Wicker
P M.Brown

CHI 1905N
M F.Selee
M F.Chance
1B F.Chance
2B J.Evers
SS J.Tinker
3B D.Casey
LF F.Schulte
CF J.Slagle
RF B.Maloney
C J.Kling
P E.Reulbach
P J.Weimer
P M.Brown
P B.Wicker
P C.Lundgren

CHI 1906N
M F.Chance
1B F.Chance
2B J.Evers
SS J.Tinker
3B H.Steinfeldt
LF J.Sheckard
CF J.Slagle
RF F.Schulte
C J.Kling
P M.Brown
P J.Pfiester
P E.Reulbach
P C.Lundgren
P J.Taylor

CHI 1907N
M F.Chance
1B F.Chance
2B J.Evers
SS J.Tinker
3B H.Steinfeldt
LF J.Sheckard
CF J.Slagle
RF F.Schulte
C J.Kling
UT S.Hofman
P O.Overall
P M.Brown
P C.Lundgren
P J.Pfiester
P E.Reulbach

CHI 1908N
M F.Chance
1B F.Chance
2B J.Evers
SS J.Tinker
3B H.Steinfeldt
LF J.Sheckard
CF J.Slagle
RF F.Schulte
C J.Kling
UT S.Hofman
P M.Brown
P E.Reulbach
P J.Pfiester
P O.Overall
P C.Fraser

CHI 1909N
M F.Chance
1B F.Chance
2B J.Evers
SS J.Tinker
3B H.Steinfeldt
LF J.Sheckard
CF S.Hofman
RF F.Schulte
C J.Archer
P M.Brown
P O.Overall
P E.Reulbach
P J.Pfiester
P R.Kroh

CHI 1910N
M F.Chance
1B F.Chance
2B J.Evers
SS J.Tinker
3B H.Steinfeldt
LF J.Sheckard
CF S.Hofman
RF F.Schulte
C J.Kling
UT J.Archer
UT H.Zimmerman
P M.Brown
P K.Cole
P H.McIntire
P E.Reulbach
P O.Overall

CHI 1911N
M F.Chance
1B V.Saier
2B H.Zimmerman
SS J.Tinker
3B J.Doyle
LF J.Sheckard
CF S.Hofman
RF F.Schulte
C J.Archer
P M.Brown
P L.Richie
P E.Reulbach
P K.Cole
P H.McIntire
RP R.Richter

CHI 1912N
M F.Chance
1B V.Saier
2B J.Evers
SS J.Tinker
3B H.Zimmerman
LF J.Sheckard
CF T.Leach
RF F.Schulte
C J.Archer
P L.Cheney
P J.Lavender
P L.Richie
P E.Reulbach
P C.Smith

CHI 1913N
M J.Evers
1B V.Saier
2B J.Evers
SS A.Bridwell
3B H.Zimmerman
LF M.Mitchell
CF T.Leach
RF F.Schulte
C J.Archer
P L.Cheney
P J.Lavender
P B.Humphries
P G.Pearce
P C.Smith

CHI 1914N
M H.O'Day
1B V.Saier
2B B.Sweeney
SS R.Corriden
3B H.Zimmerman
LF F.Schulte
CF T.Leach
RF W.Good
C R.Bresnahan
P L.Cheney
P H.Vaughn
P J.Lavender
P B.Humphries
P G.Pearce
RP C.Hageman

CHI 1915N
M R.Bresnahan
1B V.Saier
2B H.Zimmerman
SS B.Fisher
3B A.Phelan
LF F.Schulte
CF C.Williams
RF W.Good
C J.Archer
P H.Vaughn
P J.Lavender
P G.Pearce
P B.Humphries
P Z.Zabel

CHI 1916N
M J.Tinker
1B V.Saier
2B O.Knabe
SS C.Wortman
3B H.Zimmerman
LF L.Mann
CF C.Williams
RF M.Flack
C J.Archer
UT R.Zeider
P H.Vaughn
P C.Hendrix
P J.Lavender
P G.McConnell
P G.Packard

CHI 1917N
M F.Mitchell
1B F.Merkle
2B L.Doyle
SS C.Wortman
3B C.Deal
LF L.Mann
CF C.Williams
RF M.Flack
C A.Wilson
UT H.Wolter
UT R.Zeider
P H.Vaughn
P P.Douglas
P C.Hendrix
P A.Demaree
P P.Carter
RP M.Prendergast

CHI 1918N
M F.Mitchell
1B F.Merkle
2B R.Zeider
SS C.Hollocher
3B C.Deal
LF L.Mann
CF D.Paskert
RF M.Flack
C B.Killefer
P H.Vaughn
P L.Tyler
P C.Hendrix
P P.Douglas

CHI 1919N
M F.Mitchell
1B F.Merkle
2B C.Pick
SS C.Hollocher
3B C.Deal
LF L.Mann
CF D.Paskert
RF M.Flack
C B.Killefer
P H.Vaughn
P G.Alexander
P C.Hendrix
P S.Martin
P P.Douglas

CHI 1920N
M F.Mitchell
1B F.Merkle
2B Z.Terry
SS C.Hollocher
3B C.Deal
LF D.Robertson
CF D.Paskert
RF M.Flack
C B.O'Farrell
UT T.Barber
P G.Alexander
P H.Vaughn
P C.Hendrix
P L.Tyler
P S.Martin

CHI 1921N
M J.Evers
M B.Killefer
1B R.Grimes
2B Z.Terry
SS C.Hollocher
3B C.Deal
LF T.Barber
CF G.Maisel
RF M.Flack
C B.O'Farrell
UT J.Kelleher
P G.Alexander
P S.Martin
P B.Freeman
P V.Cheeves
P L.York

CHI 1922N
M B.Killefer
1B R.Grimes
2B Z.Terry
SS C.Hollocher
3B M.Krug
LF H.Miller
CF J.Statz
RF B.Friberg
C B.O'Farrell
P V.Aldridge
P G.Alexander
P T.Osborne
P V.Cheeves
P P.Jones

CHI 1923N
M B.Killefer
1B R.Grimes
2B G.Grantham
SS S.Adams
3B B.Friberg
LF H.Miller
CF J.Statz
RF C.Heathcote
C B.O'Farrell
P G.Alexander
P V.Aldridge
P T.Kaufmann
P T.Osborne
P V.Keen
RP F.Fussell

CHI 1924N
M B.Killefer
1B H.Cotter
2B G.Grantham
SS S.Adams
3B B.Friberg
LF D.Grigsby
CF J.Statz
RF C.Heathcote
C G.Hartnett
P V.Aldridge
P V.Keen
P T.Kaufmann
P E.Jacobs
P G.Alexander

CHI 1925N
M B.Killefer
M W.Maranville
M M.Gibson
1B C.Grimm
2B S.Adams
SS R.Maranville
3B H.Freigau
LF A.Jahn
CF M.Brooks
RF C.Heathcote
C G.Hartnett
P G.Alexander
P S.Blake
P W.Cooper
P T.Kaufmann

P G.Bush
RP V.Keen

CHI 1926N

M J.McCarthy
1B C.Grimm
2B S.Adams
SS J.Cooney
3B H.Freigau
LF R.Stephenson
CF H.Wilson
RF C.Heathcote
C G.Hartnett
P C.Root
P S.Blake
P T.Kaufmann
P P.Jones
P G.Bush

CHI 1927N

M J.McCarthy
1B C.Grimm
2B C.Beck
SS W.English
3B S.Adams
LF R.Stephenson
CF H.Wilson
RF E.Webb
C G.Hartnett
P C.Root
P S.Blake
P G.Bush
P H.Carlson
P J.Brillheart

CHI 1928N

M J.McCarthy
1B C.Grimm
2B F.Maguire
SS W.English
3B C.Beck
LF R.Stephenson
CF H.Wilson
RF K.Cuyler
C G.Hartnett
P P.Malone
P S.Blake
P C.Root
P G.Bush
P A.Nehf
RP H.Carlson

CHI 1929N

M J.McCarthy
1B C.Grimm
2B R.Hornsby
SS W.English
3B N.McMillan
LF R.Stephenson
CF H.Wilson
RF K.Cuyler
C Z.Taylor
P C.Root
P G.Bush
P P.Malone
P S.Blake
P A.Nehf
RP M.Cvengros

CHI 1930N

M J.McCarthy
M R.Hornsby
1B C.Grimm
2B F.Blair
SS W.English
3B L.Bell
LF R.Stephenson
CF H.Wilson
RF K.Cuyler
C G.Hartnett
P P.Malone
P G.Bush
P C.Root
P S.Blake
P B.Teachout
RP L.Nelson

CHI 1931N

M R.Hornsby
1B C.Grimm
2B R.Hornsby
SS W.English
3B L.Bell
LF D.Taylor
CF H.Wilson
RF K.Cuyler
C G.Hartnett
P C.Root
P B.Smith
P P.Malone
P G.Bush
P L.Sweetland
RP J.May
RP B.Teachout

CHI 1932N

M R.Hornsby
M C.Grimm
1B C.Grimm
2B B.Herman
SS B.Jurges
3B W.English
LF R.Stephenson
CF J.Moore
RF K.Cuyler
C G.Hartnett
P L.Warneke
P G.Bush
P P.Malone
P C.Root
P B.Grimes
RP J.May

CHI 1933N

M C.Grimm
1B C.Grimm
2B Bi.Herman
SS B.Jurges
3B W.English
LF R.Stephenson
CF F.Demaree
RF Ba.Herman
C G.Hartnett
P L.Warneke
P G.Bush
P C.Root
P P.Malone
P B.Tinning

CHI 1934N

M C.Grimm
1B C.Grimm
2B Bi.Herman
SS B.Jurges
3B S.Hack
LF C.Klein
CF K.Cuyler
RF Ba.Herman
C G.Hartnett
UT W.English
UT T.Stainback
P L.Warneke
P B.Lee
P G.Bush
P P.Malone
P J.Weaver

CHI 1935N

M C.Grimm
1B P.Cavarretta
2B B.Herman
SS B.Jurges
3B S.Hack
LF A.Galan
CF F.Demaree
RF C.Klein
C G.Hartnett
P L.Warneke
P B.Lee
P L.French
P C.Root
P T.Carleton
RP F.Kowalik

CHI 1936N

M C.Grimm
1B P.Cavarretta
2B B.Herman
SS B.Jurges
3B S.Hack
LF E.Allen
CF A.Galan
RF F.Demaree
C G.Hartnett
P B.Lee
P L.French
P L.Warneke
P T.Carleton
P C.Davis
RP C.Root
RP C.Bryant

CHI 1937N

M C.Grimm
1B R.Collins
2B B.Herman
SS B.Jurges
3B S.Hack
LF A.Galan
CF J.Marty
RF F.Demaree
C G.Hartnett
UT P.Cavarretta
P B.Lee
P L.French
P T.Carleton
P C.Root
P R.Parmelee
RP C.Shoun

CHI 1938N

M C.Grimm
M G.Hartnett
1B R.Collins
2B B.Herman
SS B.Jurges
3B S.Hack
LF A.Galan
CF C.Reynolds
RF F.Demaree
C G.Hartnett
P B.Lee
P C.Bryant
P L.French
P T.Carleton
P C.Root
RP J.Russell

CHI 1939N

M G.Hartnett
1B R.Russell
2B B.Herman
SS D.Bartell
3B S.Hack
LF A.Galan
CF H.Leiber
RF J.Gleeson
C G.Hartnett
P B.Lee
P C.Passeau
P L.French
P C.Root
P V.Page
RP J.Russell
RP G.Lillard

CHI 1940N

M G.Hartnett
1B P.Cavarretta
2B B.Herman
SS B.Mattick
3B S.Hack
LF B.Nicholson
CF J.Gleeson
RF H.Leiber
C A.Todd
UT D.Dallessandro
P C.Passeau
P L.French
P B.Lee
P V.Olsen
P J.Mooty
RP K.Raffensberger
RP V.Page

CHI 1941N

M J.Wilson
1B B.Dahlgren
2B L.Stringer
SS B.Sturgeon
3B S.Hack
LF D.Dallessandro
CF P.Cavarretta
RF B.Nicholson
C C.McCullough
P C.Passeau
P V.Olsen
P B.Lee
P J.Mooty
P P.Erickson
RP T.Pressnell
RP V.Page

CHI 1942N

M J.Wilson
1B P.Cavarretta
2B L.Stringer
SS L.Merullo
3B S.Hack
LF L.Novikoff
CF D.Dallessandro
RF B.Nicholson
C C.McCullough
UT R.Russell
P C.Passeau
P B.Lee
P H.Bithorn
P V.Olsen
P B.Fleming

CHI 1943N

M J.Wilson
1B P.Cavarretta
2B E.Stanky
SS L.Merullo
3B S.Hack
LF L.Novikoff
CF P.Lowrey
RF B.Nicholson
C C.McCullough
P C.Passeau
P H.Bithorn
P P.Derringer
P H.Wyse
P E.Hanyzewski
RP R.Prim

CHI 1944N

M J.Wilson
M R.Johnson
M C.Grimm
1B P.Cavarretta
2B D.Johnson
SS L.Merullo
3B S.Hack
LF D.Dallessandro
CF A.Pafko
RF B.Nicholson
C D.Williams
UT R.Hughes
P H.Wyse
P C.Passeau
P P.Derringer
P B.Fleming
P B.Chipman

CHI 1945N

M C.Grimm
1B P.Cavarretta
2B D.Johnson
SS L.Merullo
3B S.Hack
LF P.Lowrey
CF A.Pafko
RF B.Nicholson
C M.Livingston
P H.Wyse
P C.Passeau
P P.Derringer
P R.Prim
P H.Borowy
RP B.Chipman

CHI 1946N

M C.Grimm
1B E.Waitkus
2B D.Johnson
SS B.Jurges
3B S.Hack
LF M.Rickert
CF P.Lowrey
RF P.Cavarretta
C C.McCullough
UT B.Nicholson
UT B.Sturgeon
P J.Schmitz
P H.Wyse
P H.Borowy
P P.Erickson
P E.Kush

CHI 1947N

M C.Grimm
1B E.Waitkus
2B D.Johnson
SS L.Merullo
3B P.Lowrey
LF P.Cavarretta
CF A.Pafko
RF B.Nicholson
C B.Scheffing
P J.Schmitz
P D.Lade
P H.Borowy
P P.Erickson
P H.Wyse
RP E.Kush
RP R.Meers

CHI 1948N

M C.Grimm
1B E.Waitkus
2B H.Schenz
SS R.Smalley
3B A.Pafko
LF P.Lowrey
CF H.Jeffcoat
RF B.Nicholson
C B.Scheffing
UT P.Cavarretta
P J.Schmitz
P R.Meyer
P D.McCall
P B.Rush
P H.Borowy
RP J.Dobernic
RP E.Kush
RP B.Chipman

CHI 1949N

M C.Grimm
M F.Frisch
1B H.Reich
2B E.Verban
SS R.Smalley
3B F.Gustine
LF H.Sauer
CF A.Pafko
RF H.Jeffcoat
C M.Owen
UT P.Cavarretta
P J.Schmitz
P B.Rush
P D.Leonard
P M.Dubiel
P D.Lade
RP B.Chipman
RP D.Adkins
RP B.Muncrief

CHI 1950N

M F.Frisch
1B P.Ward
2B W.Terwilliger
SS R.Smalley
3B B.Serena
LF H.Sauer
CF A.Pafko
RF B.Borkowski
C M.Owen
P B.Rush
P J.Schmitz
P P.Minner
P F.Hiller
P M.Dubiel
RP J.Vander Meer
RP D.Leonard
RP B.Voiselle

CHI 1951N

M F.Frisch
M P.Cavarretta
1B C.Connors
2B E.Miksis
SS R.Smalley
3B R.Jackson
LF H.Sauer
CF H.Jeffcoat
RF F.Baumholtz
C S.Burgess
P B.Rush
P P.Minner
P C.McLish
P F.Hiller
P T.Lown
RP D.Leonard
RP M.Dubiel

CHI 1952N

M P.Cavarretta
1B D.Fondy
2B E.Miksis
SS R.Smalley
3B R.Jackson
LF H.Sauer
CF H.Jeffcoat
RF F.Baumholtz
C T.Atwell
UT G.Hermanski
UT B.Serena
P B.Rush
P J.Klippstein
P W.Hacker
P P.Minner
P T.Lown
RP B.Schultz
RP D.Leonard

CHI 1953N

M P.Cavarretta
1B D.Fondy
2B E.Miksis
SS R.Smalley
3B R.Jackson
LF R.Kiner
CF F.Baumholtz
RF H.Sauer
C C.McCullough
UT H.Jeffcoat
P W.Hacker
P P.Minner
P J.Klippstein
P B.Rush
P T.Lown
RP D.Leonard

CHI 1954N

M S.Hack
1B D.Fondy
2B G.Baker
SS E.Banks
3B R.Jackson
LF R.Kiner
CF B.Talbot
RF H.Sauer
C J.Garagiola
P B.Rush
P P.Minner
P W.Hacker
P J.Klippstein
P H.Pollet
RP J.Davis
RP H.Jeffcoat
RP B.Tremel

CHI 1955N

M S.Hack
1B D.Fondy
2B G.Baker
SS E.Banks
3B R.Jackson
LF H.Sauer
CF E.Miksis
RF J.King
C H.Chiti
UT F.Baumholtz
UT B.Speake
P S.Jones
P B.Rush
P W.Hacker
P P.Minner
P J.Davis
RP H.Jeffcoat
RP H.Pollet
RP D.Hillman

CHI 1956N

M S.Hack
1B D.Fondy
2B G.Baker
SS E.Banks
3B D.Hoak
LF M.Irvin
CF P.Whisenant
RF W.Moryn
C H.Landrith
UT J.King
UT E.Miksis
P B.Rush
P S.Jones
P W.Hacker
P D.Kaiser
P J.Brosnan
RP J.Davis
RP T.Lown
RP V.Valentinetti

CHI 1957N

M B.Scheffing
1B D.Long
2B B.Morgan
SS J.Littrell
3B E.Banks
LF L.Walls
CF B.Speake
RF W.Moryn
C C.Neeman
UT J.Bolger
P M.Drabowsky
P D.Drott
P B.Rush
P D.Elston
P D.Hillman
RP J.Brosnan
RP T.Lown
RP D.Littlefield

CHI 1958N

M B.Scheffing
1B D.Long
2B T.Taylor
SS E.Banks
3B A.Dark
LF W.Moryn
CF B.Thomson
RF L.Walls
C S.Taylor
P T.Phillips
P G.Hobbie
P D.Drott
P D.Hillman
P M.Drabowsky
RP D.Elston
RP B.Henry

CHI 1959N

M B.Scheffing
1B D.Long
2B T.Taylor
SS E.Banks
3B A.Dark
LF B.Thomson
CF G.Altman
RF L.Walls
C S.Taylor
UT J.Marshall
UT W.Moryn
P B.Anderson
P G.Hobbie
P D.Hillman
P M.Drabowsky
P A.Ceccarelli
RP B.Henry
RP D.Elston

CHI 1960N

M C.Grimm
M L.Boudreau
1B E.Bouchee
2B J.Kindall
SS E.Banks
3B R.Santo
LF R.Ashburn
CF G.Altman
RF B.Will
C M.Thacker
UT F.Thomas
UT D.Zimmer
P G.Hobbie
P B.Anderson
P D.Ellsworth
P D.Cardwell
RP D.Elston
RP S.Morehead
RP M.Freeman

CHI 1961N

M V.Himsl
M H.Craft
M V.Himsl
M E.Tappe
M H.Craft
M V.Himsl
M E.Tappe
M L.Klein
M E.Tappe
1B E.Bouchee
2B D.Zimmer
SS E.Banks
3B R.Santo
LF B.Williams
CF A.Heist
RF G.Altman
C D.Bertell
UT R.Ashburn
UT J.Kindall
P D.Cardwell
P G.Hobbie
P D.Ellsworth
P J.Curtis
RP B.Anderson
RP D.Drott
RP D.Elston

CHI 1962N

M E.Tappe
M L.Klein
M C.Metro
1B E.Banks
2B K.Hubbs
SS A.Rodgers
3B R.Santo
LF B.Williams
CF L.Brock
RF G.Altman
C D.Bertell
P B.Buhl
P D.Ellsworth
P D.Cardwell
P C.Koonce
P G.Hobbie
RP B.Anderson
RP B.Schultz
RP D.Elston

CHI 1963N

M B.Kennedy
1B E.Banks
2B K.Hubbs
SS A.Rodgers
3B R.Santo
LF B.Williams
CF E.Burton

RF L.Brock
C D.Bertell
OF D.Ellsworth
P L.Jackson
P B.Buhl
P G.Hobbie
P P.Toth
RP L.McDaniel
RP D.Elston
RP J.Brewer

CHI 1964N

M B.Kennedy
1B E.Banks
2B J.Amalfitano
SS A.Rodgers
3B R.Santo
LF B.Williams
CF B.Cowan
RF L.Gabrielson
C D.Bertell
UT J.Stewart
P L.Jackson
P D.Ellsworth
P B.Buhl
P L.Burdette
P E.Broglio
RP L.McDaniel
RP D.Elston
RP S.Slaughter

CHI 1965N

M B.Kennedy
M L.Klein
1B E.Banks
2B G.Beckert
SS D.Kessinger
3B R.Santo
LF D.Clemens
CF D.Landrum
RF B.Williams
C V.Roznovsky
UT J.Stewart
P L.Jackson
P D.Ellsworth
P B.Buhl
P C.Koonce
RP T.Abernathy
RP L.McDaniel
RP B.Humphreys

CHI 1966N

M L.Durocher
1B E.Banks
2B G.Beckert
SS D.Kessinger
3B R.Santo
LF B.Browne
CF A.Phillips
RF B.Williams
C R.Hundley
P D.Ellsworth
P K.Holtzman
P F.Jenkins
P B.Hands
RP C.Koonce
RP B.Hendley

CHI 1967N

M L.Durocher
1B E.Banks
2B G.Beckert
SS D.Kessinger
3B R.Santo
LF B.Williams
CF A.Phillips
RF T.Savage
C R.Hundley
P F.Jenkins
P R.Nye
P J.Niekro
P R.Culp
P B.Hands
RP C.Hartenstein
RP B.Stoneman
RP C.Koonce

CHI 1968N

M L.Durocher
1B E.Banks
2B G.Beckert
SS D.Kessinger
3B R.Santo
LF B.Williams
CF A.Phillips
RF J.Hickman
C R.Hundley
P F.Jenkins
P B.Hands
P K.Holtzman
P J.Niekro
P R.Nye
RP P.Regan
RP J.Lamabe

CHI 1969N

M L.Durocher
1B E.Banks
2B G.Beckert
SS D.Kessinger
3B R.Santo
LF B.Williams
CF D.Young
RF J.Hickman
C R.Hundley
UT W.Smith
P F.Jenkins
P B.Hands
P K.Holtzman
P D.Selma
RP P.Regan
RP T.Abernathy
RP R.Nye

CHI 1970N

M L.Durocher
1B E.Banks
2B G.Beckert
SS D.Kessinger
3B R.Santo
LF B.Williams
CF J.Hickman
RF J.Callison
C R.Hundley
UT C.James
P F.Jenkins
P K.Holtzman
P B.Hands
P M.Pappas
P J.Decker
RP P.Regan
RP J.Colborn

CHI 1971N

M L.Durocher
1B J.Pepitone
2B G.Beckert
SS D.Kessinger
3B R.Santo
LF B.Williams
CF B.Davis
RF J.Callison
C C.Cannizzaro
UT J.Hickman
P F.Jenkins
P M.Pappas
P B.Hands
P K.Holtzman
P J.Pizarro
RP P.Regan
RP B.Bonham

CHI 1972N

M L.Durocher
M W.Lockman
1B J.Hickman
2B G.Beckert
SS D.Kessinger
3B R.Santo
LF B.Williams
CF R.Monday
RF J.Cardenal
C R.Hundley
P F.Jenkins
P B.Hooton
P M.Pappas
P B.Hands
P R.Reuschel
RP T.Phoebus
RP J.Aker
RP D.McGinn

CHI 1973N

M W.Lockman
1B J.Hickman
2B G.Beckert
SS D.Kessinger
3B R.Santo
LF B.Williams
CF R.Monday
RF J.Cardenal
C R.Hundley
UT G.Hiser
UT P.Popovich
P F.Jenkins
P B.Hooton
P R.Reuschel
P M.Pappas
P B.Bonham
RP B.Locker
RP R.Burris
RP J.Aker

CHI 1974N

M W.Lockman
M J.Marshall
1B A.Thornton
2B V.Harris
SS D.Kessinger
3B B.Madlock
LF J.Morales
CF R.Monday
RF J.Cardenal
C S.Swisher
UT B.Williams
P B.Bonham
P R.Reuschel
P B.Hooton
P S.Stone
RP K.Frailing
RP D.LaRoche
RP J.Todd

CHI 1975N

M J.Marshall
1B A.Thornton
2B M.Trillo
SS D.Kessinger
3B B.Madlock
LF J.Cardenal
CF R.Monday
RF J.Morales
C S.Swisher
UT P.LaCock
P R.Burris
P R.Reuschel
P B.Bonham
P S.Stone
RP D.Knowles
RP T.Dettore
RP O.Zamora

CHI 1976N

M J.Marshall
1B P.LaCock
2B M.Trillo
SS M.Kelleher
3B B.Madlock
LF J.Cardenal
CF R.Monday
RF J.Morales
C S.Swisher
UT G.Mitterwald
UT J.Wallis
P R.Reuschel
P R.Burris
P B.Bonham
P S.Renko
RP P.Reuschel
RP B.Sutter
RP J.Coleman

CHI 1977N

M H.Franks
1B B.Buckner
2B M.Trillo
SS I.DeJesus
3B S.Ontiveros
LF J.Cardenal
CF J.Morales
RF B.Murcer
C G.Mitterwald
UT L.Biittner
UT G.Gross
UT G.Clines
P R.Reuschel
P R.Burris
P B.Bonham
P M.Krukow
RP W.Hernandez
RP B.Sutter
RP P.Reuschel

CHI 1978N

M H.Franks
1B B.Buckner
2B M.Trillo
SS I.DeJesus
3B S.Ontiveros
LF D.Kingman
CF G.Gross
RF B.Murcer
C D.Rader
UT L.Biittner
UT G.Clines
P R.Reuschel
P D.Lamp
P R.Burris
P D.Roberts
P M.Krukow
RP D.Moore
RP B.Sutter
RP L.McGlothen

CHI 1979N

M H.Franks
M J.Amalfitano
1B B.Buckner
2B T.Sizemore
SS I.DeJesus
3B S.Ontiveros
LF D.Kingman
CF J.Martin
RF S.Thompson
C B.Foote
UT L.Biittner
P R.Reuschel
P L.McGlothen
P D.Lamp
P M.Krukow
P K.Holtzman
RP D.Tidrow
RP B.Sutter
RP W.Hernandez

CHI 1980N

M P.Gomez
M J.Amalfitano
1B B.Buckner
2B M.Tyson
SS I.DeJesus
3B L.Randle
LF D.Kingman
CF J.Martin
RF M.Vail
C T.Blackwell
UT L.Biittner
UT S.Dillard
UT J.Figueroa
UT M.Kelleher
UT S.Thompson
P R.Reuschel
P M.Krukow
P D.Lamp
P L.McGlothen
RP B.Caudill
RP D.Tidrow
RP W.Hernandez

CHI 1981N

M J.Amalfitano
1B B.Buckner
2B M.Tyson
SS I.DeJesus
3B K.Reitz
LF S.Henderson
CF J.Morales
RF L.Durham
C J.Davis
P M.Krukow
P R.Martz
P R.Reuschel
P K.Kravec
P D.Bird
RP D.Tidrow
RP B.Caudill
RP L.Smith

CHI 1982N

M L.Elia
1B B.Buckner
2B B.Wills
SS L.Bowa
3B R.Sandberg
LF K.Moreland
CF G.Woods
RF L.Durham
C J.Davis
UT J.Johnstone
UT J.Kennedy
P F.Jenkins
P D.Bird
P D.Noles
P R.Martz
P A.Ripley
RP L.Smith
RP D.Tidrow
RP B.Campbell

CHI 1983N

M L.Elia
M C.Fox
1B B.Buckner
2B R.Sandberg
SS L.Bowa
3B R.Cey
LF L.Durham
CF M.Hall
RF K.Moreland
C J.Davis
P C.Rainey
P S.Trout
P F.Jenkins
P D.Ruthven
P D.Noles
RP B.Campbell
RP L.Smith
RP C.Lefferts

CHI 1984N

M J.Frey
1B L.Durham
2B R.Sandberg
SS L.Bowa
3B R.Cey
LF G.Matthews
CF B.Dernier
RF K.Moreland
C J.Davis
UT H.Cotto
P S.Trout
P D.Eckersley
P R.Sutcliffe
P S.Sanderson
P D.Ruthven
RP L.Smith
RP T.Stoddard
RP R.Bordi

CHI 1985N

M J.Frey
1B L.Durham
2B R.Sandberg
SS S.Dunston
3B R.Cey
LF G.Matthews
CF B.Dernier
RF K.Moreland
C J.Davis
UT T.Bosley
UT D.Lopes
UT C.Speier
P D.Eckersley
P R.Fontenot
P S.Trout
P R.Sutcliffe
P S.Sanderson
RP L.Smith
RP L.Sorensen
RP G.Frazier

CHI 1986N

M J.Frey
M J.Vukovich
M G.Michael
1B L.Durham
2B R.Sandberg
SS S.Dunston
3B R.Cey
LF G.Matthews
CF B.Dernier
RF K.Moreland
C J.Davis
UT J.Mumphrey
P D.Eckersley
P R.Sutcliffe
P S.Sanderson
P S.Trout
P E.Lynch
RP L.Smith
RP G.Hoffman
RP D.Gumpert

CHI 1987N

M G.Michael
M F.Lucchesi
1B L.Durham
2B R.Sandberg
SS S.Dunston
3B K.Moreland
LF J.Mumphrey
CF D.Martinez
RF A.Dawson
C J.Davis
UT B.Dayett
UT M.Trillo
P R.Sutcliffe
P J.Moyer
P G.Maddux
P S.Sanderson
P L.Lancaster
RP E.Lynch
RP L.Smith
RP F.DiPino

CHI 1988N

M D.Zimmer
1B M.Grace
2B R.Sandberg
SS S.Dunston
3B V.Law
LF R.Palmeiro
CF D.Jackson
RF A.Dawson
C D.Berryhill
P G.Maddux
P R.Sutcliffe
P J.Moyer
P C.Schiraldi
P J.Pico
RP F.DiPino
RP L.Lancaster

CHI 1989N

M D.Zimmer
1B M.Grace
2B R.Sandberg
SS S.Dunston
3B V.Law
LF D.Smith
CF J.Walton
RF A.Dawson
C D.Berryhill
UT M.Webster
P G.Maddux
P R.Sutcliffe
P M.Bielecki
P S.Sanderson
P P.Kilgus
RP J.Pico
RP S.Wilson
RP M.Williams

CHI 1990N

M D.Zimmer
1B M.Grace
2B R.Sandberg
SS S.Dunston
3B L.Salazar
LF D.Dascenzo
CF J.Walton
RF A.Dawson
C J.Girardi
UT D.Ramos
UT D.Smith
P G.Maddux
P M.Harkey
P M.Bielecki
P S.Wilson
P S.Boskie
RP L.Lancaster
RP P.Assenmacher
RP J.Pico

CHI 1991N

M D.Zimmer
M J.Altobelli
M J.Essian
1B M.Grace
2B R.Sandberg
SS S.Dunston
3B L.Salazar
LF G.Bell
CF J.Walton
RF A.Dawson
C R.Wilkins
UT D.Dascenzo
UT C.Walker
P G.Maddux
P M.Bielecki
P S.Boskie
P F.Castillo
P R.Sutcliffe
RP L.Lancaster
RP B.Scanlan
RP P.Assenmacher

CHI 1992N

M J.Lefebvre
1B M.Grace
2B R.Sandberg
SS R.Sanchez
3B S.Buechele
LF D.May
CF D.Dascenzo
RF A.Dawson
C J.Girardi
UT L.Salazar
UT D.Smith
P G.Maddux
P M.Morgan
P F.Castillo
P D.Jackson
RP B.Scanlan
RP J.Bullinger
RP C.McElroy

CHI 1993N

M J.Lefebvre
1B M.Grace
2B R.Sandberg
SS R.Sanchez
3B S.Buechele
LF D.May
CF D.Smith
RF S.Sosa
C R.Wilkins
UT J.Vizcaino
UT W.Wilson
P M.Morgan
P G.Hibbard
P J.Guzman
P M.Harkey
P F.Castillo
RP J.Bautista
RP B.Scanlan
RP R.Myers

CHI 1994N

M T.Trebelhorn
1B M.Grace
2B R.Sandberg
SS S.Dunston
3B S.Buechele
LF D.May
CF G.Hill
RF S.Sosa
C R.Wilkins
UT K.Rhodes
UT R.Sanchez
P S.Trachsel
P W.Banks
P A.Young
P J.Bullinger
P M.Morgan
RP J.Bautista
RP C.Crim
RP D.Plesac

CHI 1995N

M J.Riggleman
1B M.Grace
2B R.Sanchez
SS S.Dunston
3B T.Zeile
LF L.Gonzalez
CF B.McRae
RF S.Sosa
C S.Servais
UT S.Bullett
UT J.Hernandez
P J.Navarro
P F.Castillo
P K.Foster
P S.Trachsel
P J.Bullinger
RP M.Perez
RP T.Wendell
RP R.Myers

CHI 1996N

M J.Riggleman
1B M.Grace
2B R.Sandberg
SS R.Sanchez
3B L.Gomez
LF L.Gonzalez
CF B.McRae
RF S.Sosa
C S.Servais
UT S.Bullett
UT J.Hernandez
P J.Navarro
P S.Trachsel
P F.Castillo
P J.Bullinger
P A.Telemaco
RP T.Adams
RP T.Wendell
RP R.Myers

CHI 1997N

M J.Riggleman
1B M.Grace
2B R.Sandberg
SS S.Dunston
3B K.Orie
LF D.Glanville
CF B.McRae
RF S.Sosa
C S.Servais
UT D.Clark
UT J.Hernandez
UT R.Sanchez
P S.Trachsel
P T.Mulholland
P K.Foster
P J.Gonzalez
P F.Castillo
RP K.Bottenfield
RP T.Adams
RP T.Wendell

CHI 1998N

M J.Riggleman
1B M.Grace
2B M.Morandini
SS J.Blauser

3B J.Hernandez
LF H.Rodriguez
CF B.Brown
RF S.Sosa
C S.Servais
UT M.Alexander
P K.Tapani
P M.Clark
P S.Trachsel
P K.Wood
P J.Gonzalez
RP T.Mulholland
RP R.Beck
RP T.Adams

CHI 1999N

M J.Riggleman
1B M.Grace
2B M.Morandini
SS J.Hernandez
3B G.Gaetti
LF H.Rodriguez
CF L.Johnson
RF S.Sosa
C B.Santiago
UT J.Blauser
UT G.Hill
UT T.Houston
P S.Trachsel
P J.Lieber
P K.Tapani
P K.Farnsworth
P T.Mulholland
RP S.Sanders
RP T.Adams
RP R.Myers

CHI 2000N

M D.Baylor
1B M.Grace
2B E.Young
SS R.Gutierrez
3B W.Greene
LF H.Rodriguez
CF D.Buford
RF S.Sosa
C J.Girardi
P J.Lieber
P K.Tapani
P K.Wood
RP T.Van Poppel
RP K.Farnsworth
RP D.Garibay

Cincinnati

CIN N 1876-1880
CIN U 1884
CIN a 1882-1889
CIN a 1891
CIN N 1890-2000

CIN 1876N

M C.Gould
1B C.Gould
2B C.Sweasy
SS H.Kessler
3B W.Foley
LF R.Snyder
CF C.Jones
RF D.Pierson
C A.Booth
P D.Dean
P C.Fisher
P D.Williams

CIN 1877N

M L.Pike
M B.Addy
M J.Manning
1B C.Gould
2B J.Hallinan
SS J.Manning
3B W.Foley
LF C.Jones
CF L.Pike
RF B.Addy
C S.Hastings
UT A.Booth
P C.Cummings
P B.Mathews
P B.Mitchell

CIN 1878N

M C.McVey
1B C.Sullivan
2B J.Gerhardt
SS B.Geer
3B C.McVey
LF C.Jones
CF L.Pike
RF K.Kelly
C D.White
P W.White
P B.Mitchell

CIN 1879N

M D.White
M C.McVey
1B C.McVey
2B J.Gerhardt
SS R.Barnes
3B W.Foley
LF B.Dickerson
CF P.Hotaling
RF K.Kelly
C D.White
P W.White

CIN 1880N

M J.Clapp
1B J.Reilly
2B P.Smith
SS L.Say
3B H.Carpenter
LF M.Mansell
CF B.Purcell
RF J.Manning
C J.Clapp
P W.White

CIN 1884U

M D.O'Leary
M S.Crane
1B M.Powell
2B S.Crane
SS J.Jones
3B C.Barber
LF L.Sylvester
CF B.Harbidge
RF B.Hawes
C J.Kelly
UT D.Burns
P G.Bradley
P J.McCormick

CIN 1882a

M P.Snyder
1B E.Stearns
2B B.McPhee
SS C.Fulmer
3B H.Carpenter
LF J.Sommer
CF J.Macullar
RF H.Wheeler
C P.Snyder
P W.White
P H.McCormick

CIN 1883a

M P.Snyder
1B J.Reilly
2B B.McPhee
SS C.Fulmer
3B H.Carpenter
LF J.Sommer
CF C.Jones
RF P.Corkhill
C P.Snyder
P W.White
P R.Deagle
P H.McCormick

CIN 1884a

M W.White
M P.Snyder
1B J.Reilly
2B B.McPhee
SS J.Peoples
3B H.Carpenter
LF T.Mansell
CF C.Jones
RF P.Corkhill
C P.Snyder
P W.White
P B.Mountjoy
P G.Shallix

CIN 1885a

M O.Caylor
1B J.Reilly
2B B.McPhee
SS F.Fennelly
3B H.Carpenter
LF C.Jones
CF J.Clinton
RF P.Corkhill
C P.Snyder
P W.White
P L.McKeon
P B.Mountjoy
P G.Pechiney
P G.Shallix

CIN 1886a

M O.Caylor
1B J.Reilly
2B B.McPhee
SS F.Fennelly
3B H.Carpenter
LF C.Jones
CF F.Lewis
RF P.Corkhill
C K.Baldwin
P T.Mullane
P G.Pechiney
P L.McKeon

CIN 1887a

M G.Schmelz
1B J.Reilly
2B B.McPhee
SS F.Fennelly
3B H.Carpenter
LF G.Tebeau
CF P.Corkhill
RF H.Nicol
C K.Baldwin
P E.Smith
P T.Mullane
P B.Serad

CIN 1888a

M G.Schmelz
1B J.Reilly
2B B.McPhee
SS F.Fennelly
3B H.Carpenter
LF G.Tebeau
CF P.Corkhill
RF H.Nicol
C J.Keenan
P L.Viau
P T.Mullane
P E.Smith

CIN 1889a

M G.Schmelz
1B J.Reilly
2B B.McPhee
SS O.Beard
3B H.Carpenter
LF G.Tebeau
CF B.Holliday
RF H.Nicol
C J.Keenan
P J.Duryea
P L.Viau
P T.Mullane
P E.Smith

CIN 1891a

M K.Kelly
1B J.Carney
2B Y.Robinson
SS J.Canavan
3B A.Whitney
LF E.Andrews
CF D.Johnston
RF E.Seery
C K.Kelly
P F.Dwyer
P E.Crane
P W.Mains
P W.McGill

CIN 1890N

M T.Loftus
1B J.Reilly
2B B.McPhee
SS O.Beard
3B L.Marr
LF J.Knight
CF B.Holliday
RF H.Nicol
C J.Harrington
P B.Rhines
P J.Duryea
P F.Foreman
P L.Viau

CIN 1891N

M T.Loftus
1B J.Reilly
2B B.McPhee
SS G.Smith
3B A.Latham
LF P.Browning
CF B.Holliday
RF L.Marr
C J.Harrington
P T.Mullane
P B.Rhines
P C.Radbourn
P E.Crane

CIN 1892N

M C.Comiskey
1B C.Comiskey
2B B.McPhee
SS G.Smith
3B A.Latham
LF T.O'Neill
CF P.Browning
RF B.Holliday
C M.Murphy
P E.Chamberlain
P T.Mullane
P F.Dwyer
P M.Sullivan

CIN 1893N

M C.Comiskey
1B C.Comiskey
2B B.McPhee
SS G.Smith
3B A.Latham
LF J.Canavan
CF B.Holliday
RF J.McCarthy
C F.Vaughn
P F.Dwyer
P E.Chamberlain
P M.Sullivan
P T.Parrott
P T.Mullane

CIN 1894N

M C.Comiskey
1B C.Comiskey
2B B.McPhee
SS G.Smith
3B A.Latham
LF B.Holliday
CF D.Hoy
RF J.Canavan
C M.Murphy
P F.Dwyer
P T.Parrott
P E.Chamberlain
P C.Fisher

CIN 1895N

M B.Ewing
1B B.Ewing
2B B.McPhee
SS G.Smith
3B A.Latham
LF D.Hoy
CF G.Hogriever
RF D.Miller
C F.Vaughn
P F.Dwyer
P B.Rhines
P T.Parrott
P F.Foreman
P B.Phillips

CIN 1896N

M B.Ewing
1B B.Ewing
2B B.McPhee
SS G.Smith
3B C.Irwin
LF E.Burke
CF D.Hoy
RF D.Miller
C H.Peitz
UT F.Vaughn
P F.Dwyer
P R.Ehret
P F.Foreman
P C.Fisher
P B.Rhines

CIN 1897N

M B.Ewing
1B J.Beckley
2B B.McPhee
SS C.Ritchey
3B C.Irwin
LF E.Burke
CF D.Hoy
RF D.Miller
C H.Peitz
UT T.Corcoran
P T.Breitenstein
P B.Rhines
P F.Dwyer
P R.Ehret
P B.Dammann

CIN 1898N

M B.Ewing
1B J.Beckley
2B B.McPhee
SS T.Corcoran
3B C.Irwin
LF E.Smith
CF A.McBride
RF D.Miller
C H.Peitz
P P.Hawley
P T.Breitenstein
P B.Hill
P F.Dwyer
P B.Dammann

CIN 1899N

M B.Ewing
1B J.Beckley
2B B.McPhee
SS T.Corcoran
3B C.Irwin
LF E.Smith
CF K.Selbach
RF D.Miller
C H.Peitz
UT H.Steinfeldt
P N.Hahn
P P.Hawley
P B.Phillips
P T.Breitenstein
P J.Taylor

CIN 1900N

M B.Allen
1B J.Beckley
2B J.Quinn
SS T.Corcoran
3B H.Steinfeldt
LF S.Crawford
CF J.Barrett
RF A.McBride
C H.Peitz
P E.Scott
P N.Hahn
P D.Newton
P B.Phillips
P T.Breitenstein

CIN 1901N

M B.McPhee
1B J.Beckley
2B H.Steinfeldt
SS G.Magoon
3B C.Irwin
LF D.Harley
CF J.Dobbs
RF S.Crawford
C B.Bergen
P N.Hahn
P B.Phillips
P D.Newton
P A.Stimmel

CIN 1902N

M B.McPhee
M F.Bancroft
M J.Kelley
1B J.Beckley
2B H.Peitz
SS T.Corcoran
3B H.Steinfeldt
LF J.Dobbs
CF D.Hoy
RF S.Crawford
C B.Bergen
P N.Hahn
P B.Phillips
P H.Thielman
P E.Poole
P B.Ewing

CIN 1903N

M J.Kelley
1B J.Beckley
2B T.Daly
SS T.Corcoran
3B H.Steinfeldt
LF M.Donlin
CF C.Seymour
RF C.Dolan
C H.Peitz
UT J.Kelley
P N.Hahn
P B.Ewing
P J.Sutthoff
P E.Poole
P J.Harper

CIN 1904N

M J.Kelley
1B J.Kelley
2B M.Huggins
SS T.Corcoran
3B H.Steinfeldt
LF F.Odwell
CF C.Seymour
RF C.Dolan
C A.Schlei
P N.Hahn
P J.Harper
P W.Kellum
P T.Walker
P B.Ewing

CIN 1905N

M J.Kelley
1B S.Barry
2B M.Huggins
SS T.Corcoran
3B H.Steinfeldt
LF J.Kelley
CF C.Seymour
RF F.Odwell
C A.Schlei
P O.Overall
P B.Ewing
P C.Chech
P J.Harper
P T.Walker

CIN 1906N

M N.Hanlon
1B S.Deal
2B M.Huggins
SS T.Corcoran
3B J.Delahanty
LF J.Kelley
CF C.Seymour
RF F.Jude
C A.Schlei
P J.Weimer
P B.Ewing
P C.Fraser
P B.Wicker
P C.Hall

CIN 1907N

M N.Hanlon
1B J.Ganzel
2B M.Huggins
SS H.Lobert
3B M.Mowrey
LF F.Odwell
CF A.Kruger
RF M.Mitchell
C L.McLean
P B.Ewing
P A.Coakley
P J.Weimer
P R.Hitt
P D.Mason

CIN 1908N

M J.Ganzel
1B J.Ganzel
2B M.Huggins
SS R.Hulswitt
3B H.Lobert
LF D.Paskert
CF J.Kane
RF M.Mitchell
C A.Schlei
UT L.McLean
P B.Ewing
P B.Spade
P A.Coakley
P B.Campbell
P J.Weimer

CIN 1909N

M C.Griffith
1B D.Hoblitzel
2B D.Egan
SS T.Downey
3B H.Lobert
LF B.Bescher
CF R.Oakes
RF M.Mitchell
C L.McLean
UT D.Paskert
P A.Fromme
P H.Gaspar
P J.Rowan
P B.Ewing
P B.Campbell

CIN 1910N

M C.Griffith
1B D.Hoblitzel
2B D.Egan
SS T.McMillan
3B H.Lobert
LF B.Bescher
CF D.Paskert
RF M.Mitchell
C L.McLean
UT T.Downey
P H.Gaspar
P G.Suggs
P J.Rowan
P F.Beebe
P B.Burns

CIN 1911N

M C.Griffith
1B D.Hoblitzel
2B D.Egan
SS T.Downey
3B E.Grant
LF B.Bescher
CF J.Bates
RF M.Mitchell
C L.McLean
P G.Suggs
P H.Gaspar
P B.Keefe
P A.Fromme
P F.Smith

CIN 1912N

M H.O'Day
1B D.Hoblitzel
2B D.Egan
SS J.Esmond
3B A.Phelan
LF B.Bescher
CF A.Marsans
RF M.Mitchell
C L.McLean
UT E.Grant
P G.Suggs
P R.Benton
P A.Fromme
P B.Humphries

CIN 1913N

M J.Tinker
1B D.Hoblitzel
2B H.Groh
SS J.Tinker
3B J.Dodge
LF B.Bescher
CF A.Marsans
RF J.Bates
C T.Clarke
P C.Johnson
P G.Suggs
P G.Packard
P R.Ames
P M.Brown
RP F.Harter

CIN 1914N

M B.Herzog
1B D.Hoblitzel
2B H.Groh
SS B.Herzog
3B B.Niehoff
LF G.Twombly
CF B.Daniels
RF H.Moran
C T.Clarke
UT M.Gonzalez
P R.Ames
P R.Benton
P P.Douglas
P E.Yingling
P P.Schneider

CIN 1915N

M B.Herzog
1B F.Mollwitz
2B B.Rodgers
SS B.Herzog
3B H.Groh
LF R.Killefer
CF T.Leach
RF T.Griffith
C I.Wingo
P G.Dale
P P.Schneider
P F.Toney
P R.Benton
P K.Lear

CIN 1916N

M B.Herzog
M I.Wingo
M C.Mathewson
1B H.Chase
2B B.Louden
SS B.Herzog
3B H.Groh
LF G.Neale
CF E.Roush
RF T.Griffith
C I.Wingo
P F.Toney
P P.Schneider
P A.Schulz
P C.Mitchell
P E.Knetzer

CIN 1917N

M C.Mathewson
1B H.Chase
2B D.Shean
SS L.Kopf
3B H.Groh
LF G.Neale
CF E.Roush
RF T.Griffith
C I.Wingo
P F.Toney
P P.Schneider
P M.Regan
P C.Mitchell
P H.Eller

CIN 1918N

M C.Mathewson
M H.Groh
1B H.Chase
2B L.Magee
SS L.Blackburne
3B H.Groh
LF G.Neale
CF E.Roush
RF T.Griffith
C I.Wingo
UT S.Magee
P H.Eller
P P.Schneider
P J.Ring
P F.Toney
P R.Bressler

CIN 1919N

M P.Moran
1B J.Daubert
2B M.Rath
SS L.Kopf
3B H.Groh
LF R.Bressler
CF E.Roush
RF G.Neale
C I.Wingo
P H.Eller
P D.Ruether
P S.Sallee
P J.Ring
P R.Fisher

CIN 1920N

M P.Moran
1B J.Daubert
2B M.Rath
SS L.Kopf
3B H.Groh
LF P.Duncan
CF E.Roush
RF G.Neale
C I.Wingo
P J.Ring
P D.Ruether
P H.Eller
P D.Luque
P R.Fisher

CIN 1921N

M P.Moran
1B J.Daubert
2B S.Bohne
SS L.Kopf
3B H.Groh
LF P.Duncan
CF E.Roush
RF R.Bressler
C I.Wingo
P D.Luque
P E.Rixey
P R.Marquard
P P.Donohue
RP B.Napier

CIN 1922N

M P.Moran
1B J.Daubert
2B S.Bohne
SS I.Caveney
3B B.Pinelli
LF P.Duncan
CF G.Burns
RF G.Harper
C B.Hargrave
P E.Rixey
P J.Couch
P D.Luque
P P.Donohue
P C.Keck
RP D.Gillespie

CIN 1923N

M P.Moran
1B J.Daubert
2B S.Bohne
SS I.Caveney
3B B.Pinelli
LF P.Duncan
CF E.Roush
RF G.Burns
C B.Hargrave
P D.Luque
P E.Rixey
P P.Donohue
P R.Benton
RP C.Keck

CIN 1924N

M J.Hendricks
1B J.Daubert
2B H.Critz
SS I.Caveney
3B B.Pinelli
LF P.Duncan
CF E.Roush
RF C.Walker
C B.Hargrave
UT S.Bohne
UT R.Bressler
UT G.Burns
P E.Rixey
P C.Mays
P P.Donohue
P D.Luque
P T.Sheehan
RP J.May

CIN 1925N

M J.Hendricks
1B W.Holke
2B H.Critz
SS I.Caveney
3B B.Pinelli
LF B.Zitzmann
CF E.Roush
RF C.Walker
C B.Hargrave
UT R.Bressler
UT E.Smith
P P.Donohue
P D.Luque
P E.Rixey
P R.Benton
P J.May
RP H.Biemiller

CIN 1926N

M J.Hendricks
1B W.Pipp
2B H.Critz
SS F.Emmer
3B C.Dressen
LF C.Christensen
CF E.Roush
RF C.Walker
C B.Hargrave
P P.Donohue
P C.Mays
P D.Luque
P E.Rixey
P J.May

CIN 1927N

M J.Hendricks
1B W.Pipp
2B H.Critz
SS H.Ford
3B C.Dressen
LF R.Bressler
CF E.Allen
RF C.Walker
C B.Hargrave
P R.Lucas
P J.May
P D.Luque
P E.Rixey
P P.Donohue

CIN 1928N

M J.Hendricks
1B G.Kelly
2B H.Critz
SS H.Ford
3B C.Dressen
LF B.Zitzmann
CF E.Allen
RF C.Walker
C V.Picinich
UT W.Pipp
P E.Rixey
P D.Luque
P R.Kolp
P R.Lucas
P P.Donohue
RP P.Appleton

CIN 1929N

M J.Hendricks
1B G.Kelly
2B H.Critz
SS H.Ford
3B C.Dressen
LF E.Swanson
CF E.Allen
RF C.Walker
C J.Gooch
P R.Lucas
P E.Rixey
P J.May
P P.Donohue
P D.Luque
RP K.Ash
RP R.Ehrhardt

CIN 1930N

M D.Howley
1B J.Stripp
2B H.Ford
SS L.Durocher
3B T.Cuccinello
LF C.Walker
CF B.Meusel
RF H.Heilmann
C C.Sukeforth
UT E.Swanson
P B.Frey
P R.Lucas
P L.Benton
P R.Kolp
P E.Rixey
RP S.Johnson
RP A.Campbell

CIN 1931N

M D.Howley
1B H.Hendrick
2B T.Cuccinello
SS L.Durocher
3B J.Stripp
LF E.Roush
CF T.Douthit
RF E.Crabtree
C C.Sukeforth
UT N.Cullop
P S.Johnson
P R.Lucas
P L.Benton
P B.Frey
P E.Rixey

CIN 1932N

M D.Howley
1B H.Hendrick
2B G.Grantham
SS L.Durocher
3B W.Gilbert
LF W.Roettger
CF E.Crabtree
RF B.Herman
C E.Lombardi
UT T.Douthit
P R.Lucas
P S.Johnson
P O.Carroll
P L.Benton
P R.Kolp
RP J.Ogden

CIN 1933N

M D.Bush
1B J.Bottomley
2B J.Morrissey
SS O.Bluege
3B S.Adams
LF J.Moore
CF C.Hafey
RF H.Rice
C E.Lombardi
P P.Derringer
P R.Lucas
P S.Johnson
P L.Benton
P R.Kolp

CIN 1934N

M B.O'Farrell
M B.Shotton
M C.Dressen
1B J.Bottomley
2B T.Piet
SS G.Slade
3B M.Koenig
LF H.Pool
CF C.Hafey
RF A.Comorosky
C E.Lombardi
P P.Derringer
P B.Frey
P S.Johnson
P T.Freitas
P A.Stout
RP D.Brennan
RP R.Kolp

CIN 1935N

M C.Dressen
1B J.Bottomley
2B A.Kampouris
SS B.Myers
3B L.Riggs
LF B.Herman
CF S.Byrd
RF I.Goodman
C E.Lombardi
P P.Derringer
P A.Hollingsworth
P G.Schott
P T.Freitas
P S.Johnson

CIN 1936N

M C.Dressen
1B L.Scarsella
2B A.Kampouris
SS B.Myers
3B L.Riggs
LF B.Herman
CF K.Cuyler
RF I.Goodman
C E.Lombardi
UT C.Chapman
UT T.Thevenow
P P.Derringer
P A.Hollingsworth
P G.Schott
P B.Hallahan
P B.Frey
RP D.Brennan

CIN 1937N

M C.Dressen
M B.Wallace
1B B.Jordan
2B A.Kampouris
SS B.Myers
3B L.Riggs
LF K.Cuyler
CF C.Hafey
RF I.Goodman
C E.Lombardi
UT L.Scarsella
P L.Grissom
P P.Derringer
P P.Davis
P A.Hollingsworth
P G.Schott

CIN 1938N

M B.McKechnie
1B F.McCormick
2B L.Frey
SS B.Myers
3B L.Riggs
LF W.Berger
CF H.Craft
RF I.Goodman
C E.Lombardi
P P.Derringer
P J.Vander Meer
P B.Walters
P P.Davis
P J.Weaver
RP G.Schott
RP J.Cascarella

CIN 1939N

M B.McKechnie
1B F.McCormick
2B L.Frey
SS B.Myers
3B B.Werber
LF W.Berger
CF H.Craft
RF I.Goodman
C E.Lombardi
P B.Walters
P P.Derringer
P W.Moore
P L.Grissom
P J.Thompson

CIN 1940N

M B.McKechnie
1B F.McCormick
2B L.Frey
SS B.Myers
3B B.Werber
LF M.McCormick
CF H.Craft
RF I.Goodman
C E.Lombardi
P B.Walters
P P.Derringer
P J.Thompson
P J.Turner
P W.Moore
RP J.Beggs
RP M.Shoffner
RP J.Hutchings

CIN 1941N

M B.McKechnie
1B F.McCormick
2B L.Frey
SS E.Joost
3B B.Werber
LF M.McCormick
CF H.Craft
RF J.Gleeson
C E.Lombardi
P B.Walters
P P.Derringer
P J.Vander Meer
P E.Riddle
P J.Turner
RP W.Moore
RP J.Beggs

CIN 1942N

M B.McKechnie
1B F.McCormick
2B L.Frey
SS E.Joost
3B B.Haas
LF E.Tipton
CF G.Walker
RF M.Marshall
C R.Lamanno
P R.Starr
P B.Walters
P J.Vander Meer
P P.Derringer
P E.Riddle
RP J.Beggs
RP C.Shoun

CIN 1943N

M B.McKechnie
1B F.McCormick
2B L.Frey
SS E.Miller
3B S.Mesner
LF E.Tipton
CF G.Walker
RF M.Marshall
C R.Mueller
UT E.Crabtree
UT B.Haas
P J.Vander Meer
P E.Riddle
P B.Walters
P R.Starr
P C.Shoun
RP J.Beggs

CIN 1944N

M B.McKechnie
1B F.McCormick
2B W.Williams
SS E.Miller
3B S.Mesner
LF E.Tipton
CF D.Clay
RF G.Walker
C R.Mueller
P B.Walters
P C.Shoun
P E.Heusser
P T.DeLa Cruz
P H.Gumbert

CIN 1945N

M B.McKechnie
1B F.McCormick
2B W.Williams
SS E.Miller
3B S.Mesner
LF E.Tipton
CF D.Clay
RF A.Libke
C A.Lakeman
UT G.Walker
P E.Heusser
P J.Bowman
P B.Walters
P H.Fox
P V.Kennedy
RP H.Lisenbee

CIN 1946N

M B.McKechnie
M H.Gowdy
1B B.Haas
2B B.Adams
SS E.Miller
3B G.Hatton
LF E.Lukon
CF D.Clay
RF A.Libke
C R.Mueller
UT L.Frey
P J.Vander Meer
P E.Blackwell
P J.Beggs
P E.Heusser
P B.Walters
RP C.Shoun
RP B.Malloy
RP C.Lambert

CIN 1947N

M J.Neun
1B B.Young
2B B.Zientara
SS E.Miller
3B G.Hatton
LF A.Galan
CF B.Haas
RF F.Baumholtz
C R.Lamanno
P E.Blackwell
P J.Vander Meer
P K.Peterson
P B.Lively
P B.Walters
RP J.Hetki
RP H.Gumbert

CIN 1948N

M J.Neun
M B.Walters
1B T.Kluszewski
2B B.Adams
SS V.Stallcup
3B G.Hatton
LF H.Sauer
CF J.Wyrostek
RF F.Baumholtz
C R.Lamanno
UT D.Litwhiler
P J.Vander Meer
P K.Raffensberger
P H.Fox
P H.Wehmeier
P E.Blackwell
RP H.Gumbert
RP W.Cress

CIN 1949N

M B.Walters
M L.Sewell
1B T.Kluszewski
2B J.Bloodworth
SS V.Stallcup
3B G.Hatton
LF P.Lowrey
CF L.Merriman
RF J.Wyrostek
C W.Cooper
UT B.Adams
UT D.Litwhiler
P K.Raffensberger
P H.Fox
P H.Wehmeier
P J.Vander Meer
P B.Lively
RP E.Erautt
RP E.Blackwell
RP K.Peterson

CIN 1950N

M L.Sewell
1B T.Kluszewski
2B C.Ryan
SS V.Stallcup
3B G.Hatton
LF J.Adcock
CF B.Usher
RF J.Wyrostek
C D.Howell
UT B.Adams
UT L.Merriman
P E.Blackwell
P K.Raffensberger
P H.Wehmeier
P H.Fox
P W.Ramsdell
RP F.Smith
RP E.Erautt
RP J.Hetki

CIN 1951N

M L.Sewell
1B T.Kluszewski
2B C.Ryan
SS V.Stallcup
3B G.Hatton
LF J.Adcock
CF L.Merriman
RF J.Wyrostek
C D.Howell
UT B.Adams
UT B.Usher
P K.Raffensberger
P E.Blackwell
P H.Fox
P W.Ramsdell
P H.Wehmeier
RP H.Perkowski
RP F.Smith
RP B.Byerly

CIN 1952N

M L.Sewell
M E.Brucker
M R.Hornsby
1B T.Kluszewski
2B G.Hatton
SS R.McMillan
3B B.Adams
LF J.Adcock
CF B.Borkowski
RF W.Marshall
C A.Seminick
P K.Raffensberger
P H.Perkowski
P H.Wehmeier
P B.Church
P F.Hiller
RP F.Smith
RP J.Nuxhall

CIN 1953N

M R.Hornsby
M B.Mills
1B T.Kluszewski
2B R.Bridges
SS R.McMillan
3B B.Adams
LF J.Greengrass
CF G.Bell
RF W.Marshall
C A.Seminick
UT B.Borkowski
P H.Perkowski
P B.Podbielan
P K.Raffensberger
P J.Nuxhall
P F.Baczewski
RP F.Smith
RP H.Wehmeier
RP C.King

CIN 1954N

M B.Tebbetts
1B T.Kluszewski
2B J.Temple
SS R.McMillan
3B B.Adams
LF J.Greengrass
CF G.Bell
RF W.Post
C A.Seminick
UT C.Harmon
P A.Fowler
P C.Valentine
P J.Nuxhall

P B.Podbielan
P F.Baczewski
RP H.Judson
RP F.Smith
RP J.Collum

CIN 1955N
M B.Tebbetts
1B T.Kluszewski
2B J.Temple
SS R.McMillan
3B R.Bridges
LF S.Palys
CF G.Bell
RF W.Post
C S.Burgess
UT C.Harmon
P J.Nuxhall
P A.Fowler
P J.Klippstein
P J.Collum
P G.Staley
RP R.Minarcin
RP H.Freeman

CIN 1956N
M B.Tebbetts
1B T.Kluszewski
2B J.Temple
SS R.McMillan
3B R.Jablonski
LF F.Robinson
CF G.Bell
RF W.Post
C E.Bailey
P B.Lawrence
P J.Klippstein
P J.Nuxhall
P A.Fowler
P H.Jeffcoat
RP H.Freeman
RP T.Acker
RP J.Black

CIN 1957N
M B.Tebbetts
1B G.Crowe
2B J.Temple
SS R.McMillan
3B D.Hoak
LF F.Robinson
CF G.Bell
RF W.Post
C E.Bailey
P B.Lawrence
P H.Jeffcoat
P J.Nuxhall
P D.Gross
P J.Klippstein
RP T.Acker
RP A.Fowler
RP H.Freeman

CIN 1958N
M B.Tebbetts
M J.Dykes
1B G.Crowe
2B J.Temple
SS R.McMillan
3B D.Hoak
LF F.Robinson
CF G.Bell
RF J.Lynch
C E.Bailey
UT S.Burgess
UT A.Grammas
UT B.Thurman
P B.Purkey
P H.Haddix
P B.Lawrence
P J.Nuxhall
P D.Newcombe
RP H.Jeffcoat
RP W.Schmidt

CIN 1959N
M M.Smith
M F.Hutchinson
1B F.Robinson
2B J.Temple
SS E.Kasko
3B W.Jones
LF J.Lynch
CF V.Pinson
RF G.Bell
C E.Bailey
UT F.Thomas
P D.Newcombe
P B.Purkey
P J.Nuxhall
P J.O'Toole
RP O.Pena
RP B.Lawrence
RP W.Schmidt

CIN 1960N
M F.Hutchinson
1B F.Robinson
2B B.Martin
SS R.McMillan
3B E.Kasko
LF W.Post
CF V.Pinson
RF G.Bell
C E.Bailey
UT J.Lynch
P B.Purkey
P J.Hook
P J.O'Toole
P C.McLish
RP J.Nuxhall
RP J.Brosnan
RP B.Henry

CIN 1961N
M F.Hutchinson
1B G.Coleman
2B D.Blasingame
SS E.Kasko
3B G.Freese
LF W.Post
CF V.Pinson
RF F.Robinson
C J.Zimmerman
UT G.Bell
UT J.Lynch
P J.O'Toole
P J.Jay
P B.Purkey
P K.Hunt
P J.Maloney
RP J.Brosnan
RP J.Hook
RP S.Jones

CIN 1962N
M F.Hutchinson
1B G.Coleman
2B D.Blasingame
SS L.Cardenas
3B E.Kasko
LF W.Post
CF V.Pinson
RF F.Robinson
C J.Edwards
UT M.Keough
UT J.Lynch
P B.Purkey
P J.Jay
P J.O'Toole
P J.Maloney
RP J.Klippstein
RP J.Brosnan
RP T.Wills

CIN 1963N
M F.Hutchinson
1B G.Coleman
2B P.Rose
SS L.Cardenas
3B G.Freese
LF F.Robinson
CF V.Pinson
RF T.Harper
C J.Edwards
P J.Maloney
P J.O'Toole
P J.Nuxhall
P J.Tsitouris
P J.Jay
RP A.Worthington
RP B.Henry

CIN 1964N
M F.Hutchinson
M D.Sisler
M F.Hutchinson
M D.Sisler
1B D.Johnson
2B P.Rose
SS L.Cardenas
3B S.Boros
LF T.Harper
CF V.Pinson
RF F.Robinson
C J.Edwards
UT M.Keough
P J.O'Toole
P J.Maloney
P B.Purkey
P J.Jay
P J.Tsitouris
RP S.Ellis
RP B.McCool
RP B.Henry

CIN 1965N
M D.Sisler
1B T.Perez
2B P.Rose
SS L.Cardenas
3B D.Johnson
LF T.Harper
CF V.Pinson
RF F.Robinson
C J.Edwards
UT G.Coleman
P S.Ellis
P J.Maloney
P J.Jay
P J.Nuxhall
P J.Tsitouris
RP B.McCool
RP T.Davidson
RP R.Craig

CIN 1966N
M D.Heffner
M D.Bristol
1B T.Perez
2B P.Rose
SS L.Cardenas
3B T.Helms
LF D.Johnson
CF V.Pinson
RF T.Harper
C J.Edwards
P J.Maloney
P S.Ellis
P M.Pappas
P J.O'Toole
P J.Nuxhall
RP D.Nottebart
RP B.McCool
RP T.Davidson

CIN 1967N
M D.Bristol
1B L.May
2B T.Helms
SS L.Cardenas
3B T.Perez
LF P.Rose
CF V.Pinson
RF T.Harper
C J.Edwards
UT D.Johnson
UT C.Ruiz
P G.Nolan
P M.Pappas
P M.Queen
P J.Maloney
P S.Ellis
RP T.Abernathy
RP D.Nottebart
RP G.Arrigo

CIN 1968N
M D.Bristol
1B L.May
2B T.Helms
SS L.Cardenas
3B T.Perez
LF A.Johnson
CF V.Pinson
RF P.Rose
C J.Bench
UT M.Jones
P G.Culver
P J.Maloney
P G.Arrigo
P G.Nolan
RP T.Abernathy
RP C.Carroll
RP B.Lee

CIN 1969N
M D.Bristol
1B L.May
2B T.Helms
SS W.Woodward
3B T.Perez
LF A.Johnson
CF B.Tolan
RF P.Rose
C J.Bench
UT J.Stewart
P J.Merritt
P T.Cloninger
P J.Maloney
P J.Fisher
P G.Nolan
RP C.Carroll
RP W.Granger
RP P.Ramos

CIN 1970N
M S.Anderson
1B L.May
2B T.Helms
SS D.Concepcion
3B T.Perez
LF B.Carbo
CF B.Tolan
RF P.Rose
C J.Bench
UT J.Stewart
UT W.Woodward
P G.Nolan
P J.Merritt
P J.McGlothlin
P W.Simpson
P T.Cloninger
RP C.Carroll
RP W.Granger
RP D.Gullett

CIN 1971N
M S.Anderson
1B L.May
2B T.Helms
SS D.Concepcion
3B T.Perez
LF H.McRae
CF G.Foster
RF P.Rose
C J.Bench
UT B.Carbo
UT W.Woodward
P G.Nolan
P D.Gullett
P J.McGlothlin
P R.Grimsley
P W.Simpson
RP W.Granger
RP C.Carroll
RP J.Gibbon

CIN 1972N
M S.Anderson
1B T.Perez
2B J.Morgan
SS D.Concepcion
3B D.Menke
LF P.Rose
CF B.Tolan
RF C.Geronimo
C J.Bench
P J.Billingham
P R.Grimsley
P G.Nolan
P J.McGlothlin
P D.Gullett
RP T.Hall
RP P.Borbon
RP C.Carroll

CIN 1973N
M S.Anderson
1B T.Perez
2B J.Morgan
SS D.Concepcion
3B D.Menke
LF P.Rose
CF C.Geronimo
RF B.Tolan
C J.Bench
UT D.Chaney
UT D.Driessen
P J.Billingham
P R.Grimsley
P D.Gullett
P F.Norman
RP P.Borbon
RP T.Hall
RP C.Carroll

CIN 1974N
M S.Anderson
1B T.Perez
2B J.Morgan
SS D.Concepcion
3B D.Driessen
LF P.Rose
CF C.Geronimo
RF G.Foster
C J.Bench
UT D.Chaney
P D.Gullett
P C.Kirby
P J.Billingham
P F.Norman
RP P.Borbon
RP C.Carroll
RP T.Hall

CIN 1975N
M S.Anderson
1B T.Perez
2B J.Morgan
SS D.Concepcion
3B P.Rose
LF G.Foster
CF C.Geronimo
RF K.Griffey
C J.Bench
P G.Nolan
P J.Billingham
P F.Norman
P D.Gullett
P P.Darcy
RP P.Borbon
RP C.Carroll
RP W.McEnaney

CIN 1976N
M S.Anderson
1B T.Perez
2B J.Morgan
SS D.Concepcion
3B P.Rose
LF G.Foster
CF C.Geronimo
RF K.Griffey
C J.Bench
UT D.Driessen
P G.Nolan
P P.Zachry
P F.Norman
P J.Billingham
P S.Alcala
RP P.Borbon
RP R.Eastwick
RP W.McEnaney

CIN 1977N
M S.Anderson
1B D.Driessen
2B J.Morgan
SS D.Concepcion
3B P.Rose
LF G.Foster
CF C.Geronimo
RF K.Griffey
C J.Bench
P F.Norman
P T.Seaver
P J.Billingham
P P.Moskau
P D.Capilla
RP P.Borbon
RP D.Murray

CIN 1978N
M S.Anderson
1B D.Driessen
2B J.Morgan
SS D.Concepcion
3B P.Rose
LF G.Foster
CF C.Geronimo
RF K.Griffey
C J.Bench
UT D.Collins
P T.Seaver
P F.Norman
P T.Hume
P P.Moskau
P B.Bonham
RP M.Sarmiento
RP D.Bair
RP P.Borbon

CIN 1979N
M J.McNamara
1B D.Driessen
2B J.Morgan
SS D.Concepcion
3B R.Knight
LF G.Foster
CF C.Geronimo
RF K.Griffey
C J.Bench
UT D.Collins
P T.Seaver
P M.LaCoss
P F.Norman
P B.Bonham
P P.Moskau
RP T.Hume
RP D.Bair
RP D.Tomlin

CIN 1980N
M J.McNamara
1B D.Driessen
2B J.Kennedy
SS D.Concepcion
3B R.Knight
LF G.Foster
CF D.Collins
RF K.Griffey
C J.Bench
UT C.Geronimo
UT R.Oester
P M.Soto
P F.Pastore
P C.Leibrandt
P M.LaCoss
P T.Seaver
RP T.Hume
RP D.Bair

CIN 1981N
M J.McNamara
1B D.Driessen
2B R.Oester
SS D.Concepcion
3B R.Knight
LF G.Foster
CF K.Griffey
RF D.Collins
C J.Nolan
P M.Soto
P T.Seaver
P F.Pastore
P B.Berenyi
P M.LaCoss
RP T.Hume
RP P.Moskau
RP J.Price

CIN 1982N
M J.McNamara
M R.Nixon
1B D.Driessen
2B R.Oester
SS D.Concepcion
3B J.Bench
LF E.Milner
CF C.Cedeno
RF P.Householder
C A.Trevino
UT L.Biittner
P M.Soto
P B.Berenyi
P F.Pastore
P B.Shirley
P T.Seaver
RP G.Harris
RP J.Kern
RP J.Price

CIN 1983N
M R.Nixon
1B D.Driessen
2B R.Oester
SS D.Concepcion
3B N.Esasky
LF G.Redus
CF E.Milner
RF P.Householder
C D.Bilardello
UT J.Bench
UT C.Cedeno
UT D.Walker
P M.Soto
P B.Berenyi
P F.Pastore
P C.Puleo
P J.Price
RP T.Power
RP B.Scherrer
RP R.Gale

CIN 1984N
M V.Rapp
M P.Rose
1B D.Driessen
2B R.Oester
SS D.Concepcion
3B N.Esasky
LF G.Redus
CF E.Milner
RF D.Parker
C B.Gulden
UT C.Cedeno
UT T.Foley
UT W.Krenchicki
P M.Soto
P J.Russell
P J.Price
P J.Tibbs
P F.Pastore
RP T.Hume
RP T.Power
RP B.Owchinko

CIN 1985N
M P.Rose
1B P.Rose
2B R.Oester
SS D.Concepcion
3B B.Bell
LF G.Redus
CF E.Milner
RF D.Parker
C D.Van Gorder
UT N.Esasky
P T.Browning
P M.Soto
P J.Tibbs
P R.Robinson
P J.Stuper
RP J.Franco
RP T.Power
RP T.Hume

CIN 1986N
M P.Rose
1B N.Esasky
2B R.Oester
SS K.Stillwell
3B B.Bell
LF E.Davis
CF E.Milner
RF D.Parker
C B.Diaz
UT M.Venable
P B.Gullickson
P T.Browning
P J.Denny
P C.Welsh
P M.Soto
RP T.Power
RP R.Robinson
RP J.Franco

CIN 1987N
M P.Rose
1B N.Esasky
2B R.Oester
SS B.Larkin
3B B.Bell
LF T.Jones
CF E.Davis
RF D.Parker
C B.Diaz
UT D.Concepcion
UT K.Daniels
UT T.Francona
UT K.Stillwell
P T.Power
P T.Browning
P B.Gullickson
P G.Hoffman
P R.Robinson
RP F.Williams
RP R.Murphy
RP J.Franco

CIN 1988N
M P.Rose
M T.Helms
M P.Rose
1B N.Esasky
2B J.Treadway
SS B.Larkin
3B C.Sabo
LF K.Daniels
CF E.Davis
RF P.O'Neill
C B.Diaz
UT D.Collins
P D.Jackson
P T.Browning
P J.Rijo
RP J.Franco
RP R.Murphy
RP T.Birtsas

CIN 1989N
M P.Rose
M T.Helms
1B T.Benzinger
2B R.Oester
SS B.Larkin
3B C.Sabo
LF R.Roomes
CF E.Davis
RF P.O'Neill
C J.Reed
UT K.Griffey
UT L.Quinones
UT H.Winningham

P T.Browning
P R.Mahler
P D.Jackson
P J.Rijo
P S.Scudder
RP R.Dibble
RP N.Charlton
RP J.Franco

CIN 1990N

M L.Piniella
1B T.Benzinger
2B M.Duncan
SS B.Larkin
3B C.Sabo
LF B.Hatcher
CF E.Davis
RF P.O'Neill
C J.Oliver
UT H.Morris
P T.Browning
P J.Rijo
P J.Armstrong
P R.Mahler
P D.Jackson
RP N.Charlton
RP R.Dibble
RP R.Myers

CIN 1991N

M L.Piniella
1B H.Morris
2B B.Doran
SS B.Larkin
3B C.Sabo
LF B.Hatcher
CF E.Davis
RF P.O'Neill
C J.Oliver
UT M.Duncan
UT L.Quinones
UT H.Winningham
P T.Browning
P J.Rijo
P J.Armstrong
P S.Scudder
P C.Hammond
RP R.Myers
RP N.Charlton
RP T.Power

CIN 1992N

M L.Piniella
1B H.Morris
2B B.Doran
SS B.Larkin
3B C.Sabo
LF R.Sanders
CF D.Martinez
RF P.O'Neill
C J.Oliver
UT B.Roberts
P T.Belcher
P G.Swindell
P J.Rijo
P C.Hammond
RP D.Henry
RP N.Charlton
RP S.Bankhead

CIN 1993N

M T.Perez
M D.Johnson
1B H.Morris
2B J.Samuel
SS B.Larkin
3B C.Sabo
LF K.Mitchell
CF J.Brumfield
RF R.Sanders
C J.Oliver
UT J.Branson
P J.Rijo
P T.Pugh
P T.Belcher
P T.Browning
P J.Smiley
RP B.Ayala
RP J.Reardon
RP J.Spradlin

CIN 1994N

M D.Johnson
1B H.Morris
2B B.Boone
SS B.Larkin
3B T.Fernandez
LF K.Mitchell
CF D.Sanders
RF R.Sanders
C B.Dorsett
P J.Rijo
P J.Smiley
P E.Hanson
P J.Roper
P P.Schourek
RP J.Ruffin
RP J.Brantley
RP C.McElroy

CIN 1995N

M D.Johnson
1B H.Morris
2B B.Boone
SS B.Larkin
3B J.Branson
LF R.Gant
CF J.Walton
RF R.Sanders
C B.Santiago
UT L.Harris
UT T.Howard
P P.Schourek
P J.Smiley
P T.Pugh
RP X.Hernandez
RP H.Carrasco
RP J.Brantley

CIN 1996N

M R.Knight
1B H.Morris
2B B.Boone
SS B.Larkin
3B W.Greene
LF T.Howard
CF E.Davis
RF R.Sanders
C J.Oliver
UT J.Branson
UT L.Harris
UT E.Taubensee
P J.Smiley
P D.Burba
P M.Portugal
P K.Jarvis
P R.Salkeld
RP J.Shaw
RP H.Carrasco
RP J.Brantley

CIN 1997N

M R.Knight
M J.McKeon
1B H.Morris
2B B.Boone
SS P.Reese
3B W.Greene
LF C.Goodwin
CF D.Sanders
RF R.Sanders
C J.Oliver
UT L.Harris
UT E.Perez
UT E.Taubensee
P M.Morgan
P D.Burba
P K.Mercker
P B.Tomko
P J.Smiley
RP M.Remlinger
RP S.Belinda
RP S.Sullivan

CIN 1998N

M J.McKeon
1B S.Casey
2B B.Boone
SS B.Larkin
3B W.Greene
LF D.Young
CF R.Sanders
RF J.Nunnally
C E.Taubensee
UT C.Stynes
P B.Tomko
P P.Harnisch
P M.Remlinger
P S.Parris
RP S.Sullivan
RP G.White
RP D.Graves

CIN 1999N

M J.McKeon
1B S.Casey
2B P.Reese
SS B.Larkin
3B A.Boone
LF G.Vaughn
CF M.Cameron
RF M.Tucker
C E.Taubensee
UT J.Hammonds
UT D.Young
P P.Harnisch
P B.Tomko
P R.Villone
P S.Parris
P D.Neagle
RP S.Sullivan
RP D.Graves
RP S.Williamson

CIN 2000N

M J.McKeon
1B S.Casey
2B P.Reese
SS B.Larkin
3B A.Boone
UT D.Young
CF K.Griffey
RF D.Bichette
C B.Santiago
UT A.Ochoa
UT C.Stynes
LF M.Tucker
P S.Parris
P E.Dessens
P R.Villone
P R.Bell
P P.Harnisch
RP S.Williamson
RP S.Sullivan
RP D.Graves

Cleveland

CLE n 1871-1872
CLE N 1879-1884
CLE a 1887-1888
CLE P 1890
CLE N 1889-1899
CLE A 1901-2000

CLE 1871n

M C.Pabor
1B J.Carleton
2B G.Kimball
SS J.Bass
3B E.Sutton
LF C.Pabor
CF A.Allison
RF E.White
C D.White
P A.Pratt

CLE 1872n

M S.Hastings
M D.White
1B J.Simmons
2B C.Sweasy
SS J.Holdsworth
3B E.Sutton
LF C.Pabor
CF A.Allison
RF R.Wolters
C D.White
UT S.Hastings
P A.Pratt
P R.Wolters

CLE 1879N

M J.McCormick
1B B.Phillips
2B J.Glasscock
SS T.Carey
3B F.Warner
LF B.Riley
CF G.Strief
RF C.Eden
C D.Kennedy
UT B.Gilligan
P J.McCormick
P B.Mitchell

CLE 1880N

M J.McCormick
1B B.Phillips
2B F.Dunlap
SS J.Glasscock
3B F.Hankinson
LF N.Hanlon
CF P.Hotaling
RF O.Shaffer
C D.Kennedy
P J.McCormick
P G.Gardner

CLE 1881N

M M.McGeary
M J.Clapp
1B B.Phillips
2B F.Dunlap
SS J.Glasscock
3B G.Bradley
LF M.Moynahan
CF J.Remsen
RF O.Shaffer
C J.Clapp
P J.McCormick
P T.Nolan

CLE 1882N

M J.McCormick
M F.Dunlap
1B B.Phillips
2B F.Dunlap
SS J.Glasscock
3B M.Muldoon
LF D.Esterbrook
CF J.Richmond
RF O.Shaffer
C F.Briody
P J.McCormick
P G.Bradley

CLE 1883N

M F.Bancroft
1B B.Phillips
2B F.Dunlap
SS J.Glasscock
3B M.Muldoon
LF T.York
CF P.Hotaling
RF J.Evans
C D.Bushong
P H.Daily
P J.McCormick
P W.Sawyer

CLE 1884N

M C.Hackett
1B B.Phillips
2B G.Smith
SS J.Glasscock
3B M.Muldoon
LF W.Murphy
CF P.Hotaling
RF J.Evans
C D.Bushong
P J.Harkins
P J.McCormick

CLE 1887a

M J.Williams
1B J.Toy
2B C.Stricker
SS E.McKean
3B P.Reccius
LF F.Mann
CF P.Hotaling
RF M.Allen
C P.Snyder
P B.Crowell
P M.Morrison
P H.Daily
P B.Gilks
P G.Pechiney

CLE 1888a

M J.Williams
M T.Loftus
1B J.Faatz
2B C.Stricker
SS E.McKean
3B G.Alberts
LF B.Gilks
CF P.Hotaling
RF E.Hogan
C C.Zimmer
P J.Bakely
P D.O'Brien
P B.Crowell

CLE 1890P

M T.Larkin
M P.Tebeau
1B H.Larkin
2B C.Stricker
SS E.Delahanty
3B P.Tebeau
LF P.Browning
CF J.McAleer
RF P.Radford
C S.Sutcliffe
P H.Gruber
P J.Bakely
P D.O'Brien
P W.McGill

CLE 1889N

M T.Loftus
1B J.Faatz
2B C.Stricker
SS E.McKean
3B P.Tebeau
LF L.Twitchell
CF J.McAleer
RF P.Radford
C C.Zimmer
P D.O'Brien
P E.Beatin
P J.Bakely
P H.Gruber

CLE 1890N

M G.Schmelz
M B.Leadley
1B P.Veach
2B J.Ardner
SS E.McKean
3B W.Smalley
LF B.Gilks
CF G.Davis
RF V.Dailey
C C.Zimmer
P E.Beatin
P J.Wadsworth
P C.Young
P E.Lincoln
P L.Viau

CLE 1891N

M B.Leadley
M P.Tebeau
1B J.Virtue
2B C.Childs
SS E.McKean
3B P.Tebeau
LF J.McAleer
CF G.Davis
RF S.Johnson
C C.Zimmer
P C.Young
P H.Gruber
P L.Viau

CLE 1892N

M P.Tebeau
1B J.Virtue
2B C.Childs
SS E.McKean
3B G.Davis
LF J.Burkett
CF J.McAleer
RF J.O'Connor
C C.Zimmer
P C.Young
P N.Cuppy
P J.Clarkson
P G.Davies

CLE 1893N

M P.Tebeau
1B J.Virtue
2B C.Childs
SS E.McKean
3B C.McGarr
LF J.Burkett
CF J.McAleer
RF B.Ewing
C C.Zimmer
UT J.O'Connor
UT P.Tebeau
P C.Young
P J.Clarkson
P N.Cuppy
P C.Hastings

CLE 1894N

M P.Tebeau
1B P.Tebeau
2B C.Childs
SS E.McKean
3B C.McGarr
LF J.Burkett
CF J.McAleer
RF H.Blake
C C.Zimmer
UT J.O'Connor
P C.Young
P N.Cuppy
P J.Clarkson
P M.Sullivan

CLE 1895N

M P.Tebeau
1B P.Tebeau
2B C.Childs
SS E.McKean
3B C.McGarr
LF J.Burkett
CF J.McAleer
RF H.Blake
C C.Zimmer
UT J.O'Connor
UT G.Tebeau
P C.Young
P N.Cuppy
P B.Wallace
P P.Knell

CLE 1896N

M P.Tebeau
1B P.Tebeau
2B C.Childs
SS E.McKean
3B C.McGarr
LF J.Burkett
CF J.McAleer
RF H.Blake
C C.Zimmer
P C.Young
P N.Cuppy
P Z.Wilson

CLE 1897N

M P.Tebeau
1B P.Tebeau
2B C.Childs
SS E.McKean
3B B.Wallace
LF J.Burkett
CF J.O'Connor
RF C.Sockalexis
C C.Zimmer
P C.Young
P Z.Wilson
P J.Powell
P N.Cuppy

CLE 1898N

M P.Tebeau
1B P.Tebeau
2B C.Childs
SS E.McKean
3B B.Wallace
LF J.Burkett
CF J.McAleer
RF H.Blake
C L.Criger
UT J.O'Connor
P C.Young
P J.Powell
P Z.Wilson
P N.Cuppy

CLE 1899N

M L.Cross
M J.Quinn
1B T.Tucker
2B J.Quinn
SS H.Lochhead
3B S.Sullivan
LF D.Harley
CF T.Dowd
RF S.McAllister
C J.Sugden
P J.Hughey
P C.Knepper
P F.Bates
P C.Schmit
P H.Colliflower

CLE 1901A

M J.McAleer
1B C.LaChance
2B E.Beck
SS F.Scheibeck
3B B.Bradley
LF J.McCarthy
CF O.Pickering
RF J.O'Brien
C B.Wood
P P.Dowling
P E.Moore
P B.Hart
P E.Scott
P J.Bracken

CLE 1902A

M B.Armour
1B C.Hickman
2B N.Lajoie
SS J.Gochnauer
3B B.Bradley
LF J.McCarthy
CF H.Bay
RF E.Flick
C H.Bemis
P E.Moore
P A.Joss
P B.Bernhard
P G.Wright

CLE 1903A

M B.Armour
1B C.Hickman
2B N.Lajoie
SS J.Gochnauer
3B B.Bradley
LF J.McCarthy
CF H.Bay
RF E.Flick
C H.Bemis
P A.Joss
P E.Moore
P B.Bernhard
P R.Donahue
P G.Wright

CLE 1904A

M B.Armour
1B C.Hickman
2B N.Lajoie
SS T.Turner
3B B.Bradley
LF B.Lush
CF H.Bay
RF E.Flick
C H.Bemis
P B.Bernhard
P R.Donahue
P E.Moore
P A.Joss
P B.Rhoads

CLE 1905A

M N.Lajoie
M B.Bradley
M N.Lajoie
1B C.Carr
2B N.Lajoie
SS T.Turner
3B B.Bradley
LF J.Jackson
CF H.Bay
RF E.Flick
C F.Buelow
UT G.Stovall
P A.Joss
P E.Moore
P B.Rhoads
P B.Bernhard
P R.Donahue

CLE 1906A

M N.Lajoie
1B C.Rossman
2B N.Lajoie
SS T.Turner
3B B.Bradley
LF J.Jackson
CF E.Flick
RF B.Congalton
C H.Bemis
UT G.Stovall
P O.Hess
P B.Rhoads
P A.Joss
P B.Bernhard
P H.Townsend

CLE 1907A

M N.Lajoie
1B G.Stovall
2B N.Lajoie
SS T.Turner
3B B.Bradley
LF B.Hinchman
CF J.Birmingham
RF E.Flick
C N.Clarke
P A.Joss
P G.Liebhardt
P B.Rhoads
P J.Thielman

CLE 1908A

M N.Lajoie
1B G.Stovall
2B N.Lajoie
SS G.Perring
3B B.Bradley
LF J.Clarke
CF J.Birmingham
RF B.Hinchman
C N.Clarke
P A.Joss

P B.Rhoads
P G.Liebhardt
P H.Berger
P C.Chech

CLE 1909A

M N.Lajoie
M D.McGuire
1B G.Stovall
2B N.Lajoie
SS N.Ball
3B B.Bradley
LF B.Hinchman
CF J.Birmingham
RF W.Good
C T.Easterly
P C.Young
P H.Berger
P A.Joss
P C.Falkenberg
P B.Rhoads

CLE 1910A

M D.McGuire
1B G.Stovall
2B N.Lajoie
SS T.Turner
3B B.Bradley
LF J.Graney
CF J.Birmingham
RF B.Lord
C T.Easterly
P C.Falkenberg
P W.Mitchell
P C.Young
P E.Koestner
P S.Harkness

CLE 1911A

M D.McGuire
M G.Stovall
1B G.Stovall
2B N.Ball
SS I.Olson
3B T.Turner
LF J.Graney
CF J.Birmingham
RF J.Jackson
C G.Fisher
UT T.Easterly
P V.Gregg
P G.Krapp
P W.Mitchell
P F.Blanding
P G.Kahler

CLE 1912A

M H.Davis
M J.Birmingham
1B A.Griggs
2B N.Lajoie
SS R.Peckinpaugh
3B T.Turner
LF B.Ryan
CF J.Birmingham
RF J.Jackson
C S.O'Neill
UT I.Olson
P V.Gregg
P F.Blanding
P G.Kahler
P W.Mitchell
P B.Steen

CLE 1913A

M J.Birmingham
1B D.Johnston
2B N.Lajoie
SS R.Chapman
3B I.Olson
LF J.Graney
CF N.Leibold
RF J.Jackson
C S.O'Neill
UT T.Turner
P V.Gregg
P C.Falkenberg
P W.Mitchell
P F.Blanding
P B.Steen

CLE 1914A

M J.Birmingham
1B D.Johnston
2B N.Lajoie
SS R.Chapman
3B T.Turner
LF J.Graney
CF N.Leibold
RF J.Jackson
C S.O'Neill
P W.Mitchell
P B.Steen
P R.Hagerman
P G.Morton
P F.Blanding

CLE 1915A

M J.Birmingham
M L.Fohl
1B J.Kirke
2B B.Wambsganss
SS R.Chapman
3B W.Barbare
LF J.Graney
CF N.Leibold
RF E.Smith
C S.O'Neill
P G.Morton
P W.Mitchell
P R.Hagerman
P S.Jones
P R.Walker
RP O.Harstad

CLE 1916A

M L.Fohl
1B C.Gandil
2B I.Howard
SS B.Wambsganss
3B T.Turner
LF J.Graney
CF T.Speaker
RF B.Roth
C S.O'Neill
UT R.Chapman
P J.Bagby
P S.Coveleski
P G.Morton
P E.Klepfer
P F.Coumbe

CLE 1917A

M L.Fohl
1B J.Harris
2B B.Wambsganss
SS R.Chapman
3B J.Evans
LF J.Graney
CF T.Speaker
RF B.Roth
C S.O'Neill
P J.Bagby
P S.Coveleski
P E.Klepfer
P G.Morton
P F.Coumbe

CLE 1918A

M L.Fohl
1B D.Johnston
2B B.Wambsganss
SS R.Chapman
3B J.Evans
LF J.Wood
CF T.Speaker
RF B.Roth
C S.O'Neill
P S.Coveleski
P J.Bagby
P G.Morton
P F.Coumbe
P J.Enzmann

CLE 1919A

M L.Fohl
M T.Speaker
1B D.Johnston
2B B.Wambsganss
SS R.Chapman
3B L.Gardner
LF J.Graney
CF T.Speaker
RF E.Smith
C S.O'Neill
P S.Coveleski
P J.Bagby
P G.Morton
P E.Myers
P G.Uhle
RP T.Phillips

CLE 1920A

M T.Speaker
1B D.Johnston
2B B.Wambsganss
SS R.Chapman
3B L.Gardner
LF C.Jamieson
CF T.Speaker
RF E.Smith
C S.O'Neill
P J.Bagby
P S.Coveleski
P R.Caldwell
P G.Morton

CLE 1921A

M T.Speaker
1B D.Johnston
2B B.Wambsganss
SS J.Sewell
3B L.Gardner
LF C.Jamieson
CF T.Speaker
RF E.Smith
C S.O'Neill
P S.Coveleski
P G.Uhle
P D.Mails
P J.Bagby
P R.Caldwell

CLE 1922A

M T.Speaker
1B S.McInnis
2B B.Wambsganss
SS J.Sewell
3B L.Gardner
LF C.Jamieson
CF T.Speaker
RF J.Wood
C S.O'Neill
P G.Uhle
P S.Coveleski
P G.Morton
P D.Mails
P J.Bagby
RP J.Lindsey

CLE 1923A

M T.Speaker
1B F.Brower
2B B.Wambsganss
SS J.Sewell
3B R.Lutzke
LF C.Jamieson
CF T.Speaker
RF H.Summa
C S.O'Neill
P G.Uhle
P S.Coveleski
P J.Edwards
P J.Shaute
P G.Morton
RP D.Metivier
RP D.Boone

CLE 1924A

M T.Speaker
1B G.Burns
2B C.Fewster
SS J.Sewell
3B R.Lutzke
LF C.Jamieson
CF T.Speaker
RF H.Summa
C G.Myatt
UT P.McNulty
P J.Shaute
P S.Smith
P S.Coveleski
P G.Uhle
RP D.Metivier

CLE 1925A

M T.Speaker
1B G.Burns
2B C.Fewster
SS J.Sewell
3B R.Lutzke
LF C.Jamieson
CF T.Speaker
RF P.McNulty
C G.Myatt
UT F.Spurgeon
P S.Smith
P G.Uhle
P B.Karr
P J.Miller
P G.Buckeye

CLE 1926A

M T.Speaker
1B G.Burns
2B F.Spurgeon
SS J.Sewell
3B R.Lutzke
LF C.Jamieson
CF T.Speaker
RF H.Summa
C L.Sewell
P G.Uhle
P D.Levsen
P J.Shaute
P S.Smith
P G.Buckeye

CLE 1927A

M J.McCallister
1B G.Burns
2B L.Fonseca
SS J.Sewell
3B R.Lutzke
LF C.Jamieson
CF I.Eichrodt
RF H.Summa
C L.Sewell
P W.Hudlin
P J.Shaute
P G.Buckeye
P J.Miller
P G.Uhle

CLE 1928A

M R.Peckinpaugh
1B L.Fonseca
2B C.Lind
SS J.Sewell
3B J.Hodapp
LF C.Jamieson
CF S.Langford
RF H.Summa
C L.Sewell
P J.Shaute
P W.Hudlin
P G.Uhle
P J.Miller
P G.Grant
RP B.Bayne
RP M.Harder

CLE 1929A

M R.Peckinpaugh
1B L.Fonseca
2B J.Hodapp
SS J.Tavener
3B J.Sewell
LF C.Jamieson
CF E.Averill
RF B.Falk
C L.Sewell
UT E.Morgan
P W.Hudlin
P W.Ferrell
P J.Miller
P J.Shaute
P J.Miljus

CLE 1930A

M R.Peckinpaugh
1B E.Morgan
2B J.Hodapp
SS J.Goldman
3B J.Sewell
LF C.Jamieson
CF E.Averill
RF D.Porter
C L.Sewell
P W.Ferrell
P W.Hudlin
P C.Brown
P M.Harder
P P.Appleton

CLE 1931A

M R.Peckinpaugh
1B E.Morgan
2B J.Hodapp
SS E.Montague
3B W.Kamm
LF J.Vosmik
CF E.Averill
RF D.Porter
C L.Sewell
UT J.Burnett
P W.Ferrell
P W.Hudlin
P C.Brown
P M.Harder
RP P.Appleton

CLE 1932A

M R.Peckinpaugh
1B E.Morgan
2B B.Cissell
SS J.Burnett
3B W.Kamm
LF J.Vosmik
CF E.Averill
RF D.Porter
C L.Sewell
P W.Ferrell
P C.Brown
P M.Harder
P W.Hudlin
P O.Hildebrand

CLE 1933A

M R.Peckinpaugh
M B.Falk
M W.Johnson
1B H.Boss
2B O.Hale
SS B.Knickerbocker
3B W.Kamm
LF J.Vosmik
CF E.Averill
RF D.Porter
C R.Spencer
UT B.Cissell
P M.Harder
P O.Hildebrand
P W.Ferrell
P C.Brown
P W.Hudlin
RP S.Connally
RP B.Bean

CLE 1934A

M W.Johnson
1B H.Trosky
2B O.Hale
SS B.Knickerbocker
3B W.Kamm
LF J.Vosmik
CF E.Averill
RF S.Rice
C F.Pytlak
P M.Pearson
P M.Harder
P O.Hildebrand
P W.Hudlin
P L.Brown
RP B.Bean
RP C.Brown

CLE 1935A

M W.Johnson
M S.O'Neill
1B H.Trosky
2B B.Berger
SS B.Knickerbocker
3B O.Hale
LF J.Vosmik
CF E.Averill
RF M.Galatzer
C E.Phillips
P M.Harder
P W.Hudlin
P M.Pearson
P T.Lee
P O.Hildebrand
RP L.Brown
RP R.Winegarner
RP C.Brown

CLE 1936A

M S.O'Neill
1B H.Trosky
2B R.Hughes
SS B.Knickerbocker
3B O.Hale
LF J.Vosmik
CF E.Averill
RF R.Weatherly
C B.Sullivan
P J.Allen
P M.Harder
P O.Hildebrand
P D.Galehouse
P L.Brown
RP T.Lee
RP W.Hudlin

CLE 1937A

M S.O'Neill
1B H.Trosky
2B J.Kroner
SS L.Lary
3B O.Hale
LF M.Solters
CF E.Averill
RF B.Campbell
C F.Pytlak
UT R.Hughes
P M.Harder
P D.Galehouse
P W.Hudlin
P J.Allen
P B.Feller
RP L.Brown
RP W.Wyatt
RP J.Heving

CLE 1938A

M O.Vitt
1B H.Trosky
2B O.Hale
SS L.Lary
3B K.Keltner
LF J.Heath
CF E.Averill
RF B.Campbell
C F.Pytlak
P B.Feller
P M.Harder
P J.Allen
P E.Whitehill
P W.Hudlin
RP J.Humphries
RP A.Milnar

CLE 1939A

M O.Vitt
1B H.Trosky
2B O.Hale
SS S.Webb
3B K.Keltner
LF J.Heath
CF B.Chapman
RF B.Campbell
C R.Hemsley
UT O.Grimes
UT R.Weatherly
P B.Feller
P A.Milnar
P M.Harder
P J.Allen
P W.Hudlin
RP J.Dobson

CLE 1940A

M O.Vitt
1B H.Trosky
2B R.Mack
SS L.Boudreau
3B K.Keltner
LF B.Chapman
CF R.Weatherly
RF B.Bell
C R.Hemsley
UT J.Heath
P B.Feller
P A.Milnar
P M.Harder
P A.Smith
P J.Allen
RP J.Dobson
RP H.Eisenstat

CLE 1941A

M R.Peckinpaugh
1B H.Trosky
2B R.Mack
SS L.Boudreau
3B K.Keltner
LF G.Walker
CF R.Weatherly
RF J.Heath
C R.Hemsley
UT S.Campbell
P B.Feller
P A.Milnar
P A.Smith
P J.Bagby
RP C.Brown
RP J.Heving

CLE 1942A

M L.Boudreau
1B L.Fleming
2B R.Mack
SS L.Boudreau
3B K.Keltner
LF J.Heath
CF R.Weatherly
RF O.Hockett
C O.Denning
P J.Bagby
P M.Harder
P C.Dean
P A.Smith
P A.Milnar
RP T.Ferrick
RP H.Eisenstat

CLE 1943A

M L.Boudreau
1B M.Rocco
2B R.Mack
SS L.Boudreau
3B K.Keltner
LF J.Heath
CF O.Hockett
RF R.Cullenbine
C B.Rosar
P J.Bagby
P A.Smith
P A.Reynolds
P V.Kennedy
P M.Harder
RP J.Heving
RP M.Naymick

CLE 1944A

M L.Boudreau
1B M.Rocco
2B R.Mack
SS L.Boudreau
3B K.Keltner
LF P.Seerey
CF O.Hockett
RF R.Cullenbine
C B.Rosar
P S.Gromek
P M.Harder
P A.Smith
P E.Klieman
P A.Reynolds
RP J.Heving
RP R.Poat
RP P.Calvert

CLE 1945A

M L.Boudreau
1B M.Rocco
2B D.Meyer
SS L.Boudreau
3B D.Ross
LF J.Heath
CF F.Mackiewicz
RF P.Seerey
C F.Hayes
UT A.Cihocki
P S.Gromek
P A.Reynolds
P J.Bagby
P A.Smith
P E.Klieman
RP P.Center
RP J.Salveson

CLE 1946A

M L.Boudreau
1B L.Fleming
2B D.Meyer
SS L.Boudreau
3B K.Keltner
LF G.Case
CF P.Seerey
RF H.Edwards
C J.Hegan
P B.Feller
P R.Embree
P A.Reynolds
P S.Gromek
RP B.Lemon
RP J.Krakauskas

CLE 1947A

M L.Boudreau
1B E.Robinson
2B J.Gordon
SS L.Boudreau
3B K.Keltner
LF D.Mitchell
CF C.Metkovich
RF H.Edwards
C J.Hegan
UT L.Fleming
UT H.Peck
P B.Feller
P D.Black
P B.Lemon
P R.Embree
P A.Gettel
RP B.Stephens
RP E.Klieman
RP S.Gromek

CLE 1948A

M L.Boudreau
1B E.Robinson
2B J.Gordon
SS L.Boudreau
3B K.Keltner
LF D.Mitchell
CF T.Tucker
RF L.Doby
C J.Hegan
P B.Lemon

P B.Feller
P G.Bearden
P S.Gromek
P S.Zoldak
RP E.Klieman
RP R.Christopher
RP D.Black

CLE 1949A

M L.Boudreau
1B M.Vernon
2B J.Gordon
SS L.Boudreau
3B K.Keltner
LF D.Mitchell
CF L.Doby
RF B.Kennedy
C J.Hegan
P B.Lemon
P B.Feller
P M.Garcia
P E.Wynn
P A.Benton
RP S.Paige
RP F.Papish
RP S.Zoldak

CLE 1950A

M L.Boudreau
1B L.Easter
2B J.Gordon
SS R.Boone
3B A.Rosen
LF D.Mitchell
CF L.Doby
RF B.Kennedy
C J.Hegan
P B.Lemon
P B.Feller
P E.Wynn
P M.Garcia
P S.Gromek
RP S.Zoldak
RP A.Benton
RP J.Flores

CLE 1951A

M A.Lopez
1B L.Easter
2B B.Avila
SS R.Boone
3B A.Rosen
LF D.Mitchell
CF L.Doby
RF B.Kennedy
C J.Hegan
UT S.Chapman
UT H.Simpson
P E.Wynn
P B.Lemon
P M.Garcia
P B.Feller
P S.Gromek
RP L.Brissie

CLE 1952A

M A.Lopez
1B L.Easter
2B B.Avila
SS R.Boone
3B A.Rosen
LF D.Mitchell
CF L.Doby
RF H.Simpson
C J.Hegan
P B.Lemon
P M.Garcia
P E.Wynn
P B.Feller
P S.Gromek
RP L.Brissie
RP M.Harris

CLE 1953A

M A.Lopez
1B B.Glynn
2B B.Avila
SS G.Strickland
3B A.Rosen
LF D.Mitchell
CF L.Doby
RF B.Kennedy
C J.Hegan
P B.Lemon
P M.Garcia
P E.Wynn
P B.Feller
P D.Hoskins
RP B.Hooper

CLE 1954A

M A.Lopez
1B B.Glynn
2B B.Avila
SS G.Strickland
3B A.Rosen
LF A.Smith
CF L.Doby
RF D.Philley
C J.Hegan
UT V.Wertz
P E.Wynn
P M.Garcia
P B.Lemon
P A.Houtteman
P B.Feller
RP D.Mossi
RP R.Narleski
RP H.Newhouser

CLE 1955A

M A.Lopez
1B V.Wertz
2B B.Avila
SS G.Strickland
3B A.Rosen
LF R.Kiner
CF L.Doby
RF A.Smith
C J.Hegan
P E.Wynn
P H.Score
P B.Lemon
P M.Garcia
P A.Houtteman
RP R.Narleski
RP D.Mossi

CLE 1956A

M A.Lopez
1B V.Wertz
2B B.Avila
SS C.Carrasquel
3B A.Rosen
LF A.Smith
CF J.Busby
RF R.Colavito
C J.Hegan
UT G.Woodling
P E.Wynn
P B.Lemon
P H.Score
P M.Garcia
RP D.Mossi
RP C.McLish
RP R.Narleski

CLE 1957A

M K.Farrell
1B V.Wertz
2B B.Avila
SS C.Carrasquel
3B A.Smith
LF G.Woodling
CF R.Maris
RF R.Colavito
C J.Hegan
UT L.Raines
P E.Wynn
P M.Garcia
P D.Mossi
P R.Narleski
P C.McLish
RP B.Daley
RP D.Tomanek
RP S.Pitula

CLE 1958A

M B.Bragan
M J.Gordon
1B M.Vernon
2B B.Avila
SS B.Hunter
3B B.Harrell
LF M.Minoso
CF L.Doby
RF R.Colavito
C R.Nixon
UT B.Moran
P C.McLish
P M.Grant
P R.Narleski
P G.Bell
P D.Ferrarese
RP D.Mossi

CLE 1959A

M J.Gordon
1B V.Power
2B B.Martin
SS W.Held
3B G.Strickland
LF M.Minoso
CF J.Piersall
RF R.Colavito
C R.Nixon
UT T.Francona
P C.McLish
P G.Bell
P M.Grant
P H.Score
P J.Perry
RP M.Garcia

CLE 1960A

M J.Gordon
M J.White
M J.Dykes
1B V.Power
2B K.Aspromonte
SS W.Held
3B B.Phillips
LF T.Francona
CF J.Piersall
RF H.Kuenn
C J.Romano
UT J.Temple
P J.Perry
P M.Grant
P G.Bell
P B.Latman
P D.Stigman
RP J.Klippstein
RP D.Newcombe

CLE 1961A

M J.Dykes
M M.Harder
1B V.Power
2B J.Temple
SS W.Held
3B B.Phillips
LF T.Francona
CF J.Piersall
RF W.Kirkland
C J.Romano
P M.Grant
P G.Bell
P J.Perry
P B.Latman
P W.Hawkins
RP B.Locke
RP F.Funk
RP B.Allen

CLE 1962A

M M.McGaha
M M.Harder
1B T.Francona
2B J.Kindall
SS W.Held
3B B.Phillips
LF C.Essegian
CF T.Cline
RF W.Kirkland
C J.Romano
UT A.Luplow
P D.Donovan
P P.Ramos
P J.Perry
P B.Latman
P M.Grant
RP G.Bell
RP F.Funk

CLE 1963A

M B.Tebbetts
1B F.Whitfield
2B W.Held
SS J.Kindall
3B M.Alvis
LF T.Francona
CF V.Davalillo
RF W.Kirkland
C J.Azcue
UT J.Adcock
UT A.Luplow
P M.Grant
P D.Donovan
P J.Kralick
P P.Ramos
P B.Latman
RP G.Bell
RP J.Walker
RP T.Abernathy

CLE 1964A

M G.Strickland
M B.Tebbetts
1B B.Chance
2B L.Brown
SS D.Howser
3B M.Alvis
LF L.Wagner
CF V.Davalillo
RF T.Francona
C J.Romano
UT W.Held
UT F.Whitfield
P J.Kralick
P S.McDowell
P D.Donovan
P S.Siebert
P P.Ramos
RP G.Bell
RP D.McMahon
RP T.Abernathy

CLE 1965A

M B.Tebbetts
1B F.Whitfield
2B P.Gonzalez
SS L.Brown
3B M.Alvis
LF L.Wagner
CF V.Davalillo
RF R.Colavito
C J.Azcue
UT C.Hinton
UT D.Howser
P S.McDowell
P L.Tiant
P S.Siebert
P R.Terry
P L.Stange
RP G.Bell
RP J.Kralick
RP D.McMahon

CLE 1966A

M B.Tebbetts
M G.Strickland
1B F.Whitfield
2B P.Gonzalez
SS L.Brown
3B M.Alvis
LF L.Wagner
CF V.Davalillo
RF R.Colavito
C J.Azcue
UT C.Hinton
UT C.Salmon
P G.Bell
P S.Siebert
P S.McDowell
P S.Hargan
P L.Tiant
RP J.Kralick
RP D.Radatz
RP B.Allen

CLE 1967A

M J.Adcock
1B T.Horton
2B P.Gonzalez
SS L.Brown
3B M.Alvis
LF L.Wagner
CF V.Davalillo
RF C.Hinton
C J.Azcue
UT L.Maye
UT F.Whitfield
P S.McDowell
P S.Hargan
P L.Tiant
P S.Siebert
P J.O'Donoghue
RP O.Pena
RP G.Culver
RP S.Bailey

CLE 1968A

M A.Dark
1B T.Horton
2B V.Fuller
SS L.Brown
3B M.Alvis
LF L.Maye
CF J.Cardenal
RF T.Harper
C J.Azcue
UT C.Salmon
UT D.Sims
P S.McDowell
P L.Tiant
P S.Siebert
P S.Williams
P S.Hargan
RP E.Fisher
RP M.Paul
RP V.Romo

CLE 1969A

M A.Dark
1B T.Horton
2B V.Fuller
SS L.Brown
3B M.Alvis
LF R.Snyder
CF J.Cardenal
RF K.Harrelson
C D.Sims
UT R.Scheinblum
P S.McDowell
P L.Tiant
P S.Hargan
P D.Ellsworth
RP S.Williams
RP M.Paul
RP J.Pizarro

CLE 1970A

M A.Dark
1B T.Horton
2B E.Leon
SS J.Heidemann
3B G.Nettles
LF R.Foster
CF T.Uhlaender
RF V.Pinson
C R.Fosse
UT C.Hinton
UT D.Sims
P S.McDowell
P R.Hand
P D.Chance
P S.Hargan
RP D.Higgins
RP M.Paul
RP P.Hennigan

CLE 1971A

M A.Dark
M J.Lipon
1B C.Chambliss
2B E.Leon
SS J.Heidemann
3B G.Nettles
LF T.Uhlaender
CF V.Pinson
RF R.Foster
C R.Fosse
P S.McDowell
P S.Dunning
P A.Foster
P R.Lamb
P S.Hargan
RP V.Colbert
RP P.Hennigan
RP E.Farmer

CLE 1972A

M K.Aspromonte
1B C.Chambliss
2B J.Brohamer
SS F.Duffy
3B G.Nettles
LF A.Johnson
CF D.Unser
RF B.Bell
C R.Fosse
UT T.McCraw
P G.Perry
P D.Tidrow
P M.Wilcox
P R.Lamb
P S.Dunning
RP P.Hennigan
RP E.Farmer
RP M.Kilkenny

CLE 1973A

M K.Aspromonte
1B C.Chambliss
2B J.Brohamer
SS F.Duffy
3B B.Bell
LF C.Spikes
CF G.Hendrick
RF R.Torres
C D.Duncan
DH O.Gamble
UT J.Ellis
UT J.Lowenstein
UT W.Williams
P G.Perry
P D.Tidrow
P M.Wilcox
P T.Timmermann
P B.Strom
RP T.Hilgendorf
RP R.Lamb
RP J.Johnson

CLE 1974A

M K.Aspromonte
1B J.Ellis
2B J.Brohamer
SS F.Duffy
3B B.Bell
LF J.Lowenstein
CF G.Hendrick
RF C.Spikes
C D.Duncan
DH O.Gamble
UT R.Torres
P G.Perry
P J.Perry
P F.Peterson
P D.Bosman
RP T.Buskey
RP F.Beene
RP M.Wilcox

CLE 1975A

M F.Robinson
1B B.Powell
2B D.Kuiper
SS F.Duffy
3B B.Bell
LF O.Gamble
CF R.Manning
RF G.Hendrick
C A.Ashby
DH R.Carty
UT C.Spikes
P D.Eckersley
P F.Peterson
P D.Hood
P R.Harrison
P G.Perry
RP D.LaRoche
RP T.Buskey
RP J.Brown

CLE 1976A

M F.Robinson
1B B.Powell
2B D.Kuiper
SS F.Duffy
3B B.Bell
LF G.Hendrick
CF R.Manning
RF C.Spikes
C A.Ashby
DH R.Carty
UT L.Blanks
P P.Dobson
P D.Eckersley
P J.Brown
P J.Bibby
P R.Waits
RP J.Kern
RP S.Thomas
RP D.LaRoche

CLE 1977A

M F.Robinson
M J.Torborg
1B A.Thornton
2B D.Kuiper
SS F.Duffy
3B B.Bell
LF B.Bochte
CF J.Norris
RF P.Dade
C F.Kendall
DH R.Carty
UT L.Blanks
P W.Garland
P D.Eckersley
P J.Bibby
P R.Waits
P A.Fitzmorris
RP D.Hood
RP J.Kern

CLE 1978A

M J.Torborg
1B A.Thornton
2B D.Kuiper
SS T.Veryzer
3B B.Bell
LF J.Grubb
CF R.Manning
RF P.Dade
C G.Alexander
DH B.Carbo
UT J.Norris
P R.Waits
P R.Wise
P M.Paxton
P D.Hood
P D.Clyde
RP J.Kern
RP S.Monge
RP D.Spillner

CLE 1979A

M J.Torborg
M D.Garcia
1B A.Thornton
2B D.Kuiper
SS T.Veryzer
3B T.Harrah
LF J.Norris
CF R.Manning
RF B.Bonds
C G.Alexander
DH C.Johnson
UT M.Hargrove
P R.Wise
P R.Waits
P M.Paxton
P D.Spillner
P L.Barker
RP S.Monge
RP V.Cruz

CLE 1980A

M D.Garcia
1B M.Hargrove
2B J.Brohamer
SS T.Veryzer
3B T.Harrah
LF M.Dilone
CF R.Manning
RF J.Orta
C R.Hassey
DH J.Charboneau
UT J.Dybzinski
P L.Barker
P R.Waits
P D.Spillner
P W.Garland
P B.Owchinko
RP S.Monge
RP M.Stanton
RP V.Cruz

CLE 1981A

M D.Garcia
1B M.Hargrove
2B D.Kuiper
SS T.Veryzer
3B T.Harrah
LF M.Dilone
CF R.Manning
RF J.Orta
C R.Hassey
DH A.Thornton
UT A.Bannister
P B.Blyleven
P L.Barker
P J.Denny
P R.Waits
P D.Spillner
RP S.Monge
RP M.Stanton

CLE 1982A

M D.Garcia
1B M.Hargrove
2B J.Perconte
SS M.Fischlin
3B T.Harrah
LF M.Dilone
CF R.Manning
RF V.Hayes
C R.Hassey
DH A.Thornton
UT A.Bannister
P L.Barker
P R.Sutcliffe
P L.Sorensen
P J.Denny
P R.Waits
RP D.Spillner
RP E.Whitson
RP E.Glynn

CLE 1983A

M M.Ferraro
M P.Corrales
1B M.Hargrove
2B M.Trillo
SS J.Franco
3B T.Harrah
LF A.Bannister
CF G.Thomas
RF G.Vukovich
C R.Hassey
DH A.Thornton
UT P.Tabler
P R.Sutcliffe
P L.Sorensen

P B.Blyleven
P L.Barker
P N.Heaton
RP D.Spillner
RP B.Anderson
RP J.Easterly

CLE 1984A
M P.Corrales
1B M.Hargrove
2B T.Bernazard
SS J.Franco
3B B.Jacoby
LF M.Hall
CF B.Butler
RF G.Vukovich
C J.Willard
DH A.Thornton
UT P.Tabler
P B.Blyleven
P N.Heaton
P S.Comer
P S.Farr
RP E.Camacho
RP T.Waddell
RP M.Jeffcoat

CLE 1985A
M P.Corrales
1B P.Tabler
2B T.Bernazard
SS J.Franco
3B B.Jacoby
LF J.Carter
CF B.Butler
RF G.Vukovich
C J.Willard
DH A.Thornton
UT M.Hargrove
UT O.Nixon
P N.Heaton
P B.Blyleven
RP V.Ruhle
RP T.Waddell
RP J.Easterly

CLE 1986A
M P.Corrales
1B P.Tabler
2B T.Bernazard
SS J.Franco
3B B.Jacoby
LF M.Hall
CF B.Butler
RF J.Carter
C A.Allanson
DH A.Thornton
UT O.Nixon
UT C.Snyder
P T.Candiotti
P P.Niekro
P K.Schrom
RP S.Bailes
RP R.Yett
RP B.Oelkers

CLE 1987A
M P.Corrales
M D.Edwards
1B J.Carter
2B T.Bernazard
SS J.Franco
3B B.Jacoby
LF M.Hall
CF B.Butler
RF C.Snyder
C C.Bando
DH P.Tabler
P T.Candiotti
P K.Schrom
P P.Niekro
P S.Bailes
P S.Carlton
RP R.Yett
RP D.Jones
RP E.Vande Berg

CLE 1988A
M D.Edwards
1B W.Upshaw
2B J.Franco
SS J.Bell
3B B.Jacoby
LF M.Hall
CF J.Carter
RF C.Snyder
C A.Allanson
DH R.Kittle
P G.Swindell
P T.Candiotti
P J.Farrell
P S.Bailes
P R.Yett
RP D.Jones
RP D.Gordon
RP B.Havens

CLE 1989A
M D.Edwards
M J.Hart
1B P.O'Brien
2B J.Browne
SS F.Fermin
3B B.Jacoby
LF J.Carter
CF B.Komminsk
RF C.Snyder
C A.Allanson
DH D.Clark
P B.Black
P J.Farrell
P T.Candiotti
P G.Swindell
P S.Bailes
RP D.Jones
RP J.Orosco

CLE 1990A
M J.McNamara
1B B.Jacoby
2B J.Browne
SS F.Fermin
3B C.Baerga
LF C.Maldonado
CF M.Webster
RF C.Snyder
C S.Alomar
DH C.James
P G.Swindell
P T.Candiotti
P B.Black
P S.Valdez
P J.Farrell
RP S.Olin
RP D.Jones
RP J.Orosco

CLE 1991A
M J.McNamara
M M.Hargrove
1B B.Jacoby
2B M.Lewis
SS F.Fermin
3B C.Baerga
LF A.Belle
CF A.Cole
RF M.Whiten
C J.Skinner
DH C.James
UT J.Browne
P G.Swindell
P C.Nagy
P E.King
P R.Nichols
P T.Candiotti
RP S.Hillegas
RP J.Shaw
RP D.Jones

CLE 1992A
M M.Hargrove
1B P.Sorrento
2B C.Baerga
SS M.Lewis
3B B.Jacoby
LF T.Howard
CF K.Lofton
RF M.Whiten
C S.Alomar
DH A.Belle
UT G.Hill
P C.Nagy
P J.Armstrong
P D.Cook
P S.Scudder
P R.Nichols
RP T.Power
RP S.Olin
RP E.Plunk

CLE 1993A
M M.Hargrove
1B P.Sorrento
2B C.Baerga
SS F.Fermin
3B A.Espinoza
LF A.Belle
CF K.Lofton
RF W.Kirby
C J.Ortiz
DH R.Jefferson
UT J.Treadway
P J.Mesa
P T.Kramer
P M.Clark
RP J.Hernandez
RP E.Plunk
RP D.Lilliquist

CLE 1994A
M M.Hargrove
1B P.Sorrento
2B C.Baerga
SS O.Vizquel
3B J.Thome
LF A.Belle
CF K.Lofton
RF M.Ramirez
C S.Alomar
DH E.Murray
UT A.Espinoza
UT W.Kirby
P D.Martinez
P C.Nagy
P J.Morris
P M.Clark
P J.Grimsley
RP J.Mesa
RP E.Plunk

CLE 1995A
M M.Hargrove
1B P.Sorrento
2B C.Baerga
SS O.Vizquel
3B J.Thome
LF A.Belle
CF K.Lofton
RF M.Ramirez
C T.Pena
DH E.Murray
UT W.Kirby
P D.Martinez
P C.Nagy
P O.Hershiser
P M.Clark
P C.Ogea
RP J.Tavarez
RP E.Plunk
RP J.Mesa

CLE 1996A
M M.Hargrove
1B J.Franco
2B C.Baerga
SS O.Vizquel
3B J.Thome
LF A.Belle
CF K.Lofton
RF M.Ramirez
C S.Alomar
DH E.Murray
P C.Nagy
P O.Hershiser
P J.McDowell
P C.Ogea
P D.Martinez
RP J.Tavarez
RP E.Plunk
RP J.Mesa

CLE 1997A
M M.Hargrove
1B J.Thome
2B T.Fernandez
SS O.Vizquel
3B M.Williams
LF B.Giles
CF M.Grissom
RF M.Ramirez
C S.Alomar
DH D.Justice
P C.Nagy
P O.Hershiser
P C.Ogea
RP J.Mesa
RP A.Lopez
RP M.Jackson

CLE 1998A
M M.Hargrove
1B J.Thome
2B D.Bell
SS O.Vizquel
3B T.Fryman
LF B.Giles
CF K.Lofton
RF M.Ramirez
C S.Alomar
DH D.Justice
P C.Nagy
P B.Colon
P D.Burba
P J.Wright
P D.Gooden
RP M.Jackson
RP J.Mesa
RP P.Shuey

CLE 1999A
M M.Hargrove
1B R.Sexson
2B R.Alomar
SS O.Vizquel
3B T.Fryman
LF D.Justice
CF K.Lofton
RF M.Ramirez
C E.Diaz
DH J.Thome
UT E.Wilson
P D.Burba
P B.Colon
P C.Nagy
P J.Wright
P D.Gooden
RP P.Shuey
RP S.Karsay
RP M.Jackson

CLE 2000A
M C.Manuel
1B D.Segui
2B R.Alomar
SS O.Vizquel
3B T.Fryman
LF R.Sexson
CF K.Lofton
RF M.Ramirez
C S.Alomar
DH J.Thome
UT J.Cabrera
P C.Finley
P D.Burba
P B.Colon
RP S.Karsay
RP J.Speier
RP P.Shuey

Columbus

COL a 1883-1884
COL a 1889-1891

COL 1883a
M H.Phillips
1B J.Field
2B P.Smith
SS J.Richmond
3B B.Kuehne
LF H.Wheeler
CF F.Mann
RF T.Brown
C R.Kemmler
P F.Mountain
P E.Dundon
P J.Valentine

COL 1884a
M G.Schmelz
1B J.Field
2B P.Smith
SS J.Richmond
3B B.Kuehne
LF J.Cahill
CF F.Mann
RF T.Brown
C R.Kemmler
UT F.Carroll
P E.Morris
P F.Mountain

COL 1889a
M A.Buckenberger
1B D.Orr
2B B.Greenwood
SS H.Easterday
3B L.Marr
LF E.Daily
CF J.McTamany
RF S.Johnson
C J.O'Connor
P M.Baldwin
P W.Widner
P H.Gastright
P A.Mays

COL 1890a
M A.Buckenberger
M G.Schmelz
M J.Sullivan
1B M.Lehane
2B J.Crooks
SS H.Easterday
3B C.Reilly
LF S.Johnson
CF J.McTamany
RF J.Sneed
C J.O'Connor
P H.Gastright
P F.Knauss
P J.Easton
P E.Chamberlain
P W.Widner

COL 1891a
M G.Schmelz
1B M.Lehane
2B J.Crooks
SS B.Wheelock
3B B.Kuehne
LF C.Duffee
CF J.McTamany
RF J.Sneed
C J.Donahue
P P.Knell
P H.Gastright
P J.Dolan
P J.Easton

Colorado

COL N 1993-2000

COL 1993N
M D.Baylor
1B A.Galarraga
2B E.Young
SS V.Castilla
3B C.Hayes
LF J.Clark
CF A.Cole
RF D.Bichette
C J.Girardi
UT D.Boston
P A.Reynoso
P W.Blair
RP B.Ruffin
RP S.Reed
RP J.Parrett

COL 1994N
M D.Baylor
1B A.Galarraga
2B N.Liriano
SS W.Weiss
3B C.Hayes
LF H.Johnson
CF M.Kingery
RF D.Bichette
C J.Girardi
UT J.Vander Wal
UT E.Young
P G.Harris
P D.Nied
P M.Freeman
P M.Harkey
P K.Ritz
RP W.Blair
RP S.Reed
RP B.Ruffin

COL 1995N
M D.Baylor
1B A.Galarraga
2B J.Bates
SS W.Weiss
3B V.Castilla
LF D.Bichette
CF M.Kingery
RF L.Walker
C J.Girardi
UT E.Burks
UT J.Vander Wal
UT E.Young
P K.Ritz
P B.Swift
P M.Freeman
P A.Reynoso
RP C.Leskanic
RP S.Reed
RP R.Bailey

COL 1996N
M D.Baylor
1B A.Galarraga
2B E.Young
SS W.Weiss
3B V.Castilla
LF E.Burks
CF Q.McCracken
RF D.Bichette
C J.Reed
UT J.Vander Wal
P K.Ritz
P M.Thompson
P A.Reynoso
P M.Freeman
RP D.Holmes
RP S.Reed
RP C.Leskanic

COL 1997N
M D.Baylor
1B A.Galarraga
2B E.Young
SS W.Weiss
3B V.Castilla
LF D.Bichette
CF Q.McCracken
RF L.Walker
C K.Manwaring
UT E.Burks
P R.Bailey
P J.Thomson
P J.Wright
P K.Ritz
RP J.Dipoto
RP D.Holmes
RP M.DeJean

COL 1998N
M D.Baylor
1B T.Helton
2B M.Lansing
SS N.Perez
3B V.Castilla
LF D.Bichette
CF E.Burks
RF L.Walker
C K.Manwaring
UT C.Goodwin
UT J.Reed
P D.Kile
P P.Astacio
P J.Wright
P J.Thomson
P B.Jones
RP D.Veres
RP C.Leskanic
RP M.DeJean

COL 1999N
M J.Leyland
1B T.Helton
2B K.Abbott
SS N.Perez
3B V.Castilla
LF D.Bichette
CF D.Hamilton
RF L.Walker
C H.Blanco
UT A.Echevarria
P P.Astacio
P B.Bohanon
P D.Kile
P B.Jones
RP J.Dipoto
RP C.Leskanic
RP D.Veres

COL 2000N
M B.Bell
1B T.Helton
2B M.Lansing
SS N.Perez
3B J.Cirillo
RF J.Hammonds
CF T.Goodwin
LF L.Walker
C B.Mayne
UT T.Shumpert
P P.Astacio
P B.Bohanon
P M.Yoshii
P K.Jarvis
P R.Arrojo
RP J.Tavarez
RP G.White
RP J.Jimenez

Detroit

DET N 1881-1888
DET A 1901-2000

DET 1881N
M F.Bancroft
1B M.Powell
2B J.Gerhardt
SS S.Houck
3B A.Whitney
LF G.Wood
CF N.Hanlon
RF L.Knight
C C.Bennett
P G.Derby
P S.Wiedman
P F.Mountain

DET 1882N
M F.Bancroft
1B M.Powell
2B D.Troy
SS M.McGeary
3B J.Farrell
LF G.Wood
CF N.Hanlon
RF L.Knight
C C.Bennett
P S.Wiedman
P G.Derby

DET 1883N
M J.Chapman
1B M.Powell
2B S.Trott
SS S.Houck
3B J.Farrell
LF G.Wood
CF N.Hanlon
RF S.Wiedman
C C.Bennett
P S.Wiedman
P D.Shaw
P J.Jones

DET 1884N
M J.Chapman
1B M.Scott
2B B.Geis
SS F.Meinke
3B J.Farrell
LF G.Wood
CF N.Hanlon
RF S.Wiedman
C C.Bennett
P D.Shaw
P C.Getzien
P F.Brill

DET 1885N
M C.Morton
M B.Watkins
1B M.McQuery
2B S.Crane
SS M.Phillips
3B J.Donnelly
LF G.Wood
CF N.Hanlon
RF S.Thompson
C C.Bennett
P S.Wiedman
P C.Getzien
P L.Baldwin
P D.Casey

DET 1886N
M B.Watkins
1B D.Brouthers
2B F.Dunlap
SS J.Rowe
3B D.White
LF H.Richardson
CF N.Hanlon
RF S.Thompson
C C.Bennett
P L.Baldwin
P C.Getzien
P P.Conway
P B.Smith

DET 1887N
M B.Watkins
1B D.Brouthers
2B F.Dunlap
SS J.Rowe
3B D.White
LF H.Richardson
CF N.Hanlon
RF S.Thompson
C C.Ganzel
P C.Getzien
P L.Baldwin
P S.Wiedman
P P.Conway

DET 1888N
M B.Watkins
M B.Leadley
1B D.Brouthers

2B H.Richardson
SS J.Rowe
3B D.White
LF L.Twitchell
CF N.Hanlon
RF C.Campau
C C.Bennett
UT C.Ganzel
P C.Getzien
P P.Conway
P H.Gruber
P E.Beatin

DET 1901A

M G.Stallings
1B P.Dillon
2B K.Gleason
SS K.Elberfeld
3B D.Casey
LF D.Nance
CF J.Barrett
RF D.Holmes
C F.Buelow
UT S.McAllister
P R.Miller
P E.Siever
P J.Cronin
P J.Yeager

DET 1902A

M F.Dwyer
1B P.Dillon
2B K.Gleason
SS K.Elberfeld
3B D.Casey
LF D.Harley
CF J.Barrett
RF D.Holmes
C D.McGuire
P W.Mercer
P G.Mullin
P E.Siever
P R.Miller
P J.Yeager

DET 1903A

M E.Barrow
1B C.Carr
2B H.Smith
SS S.McAllister
3B J.Yeager
LF B.Lush
CF J.Barrett
RF S.Crawford
C D.McGuire
P G.Mullin
P B.Donovan
P F.Kitson
P R.Kisinger

DET 1904A

M E.Barrow
M B.Lowe
1B C.Carr
2B B.Lowe
SS C.O'Leary
3B E.Gremminger
LF M.McIntyre
CF J.Barrett
RF S.Crawford
C L.Drill
UT R.Robinson
P G.Mullin
P E.Killian
P B.Donovan
P F.Kitson
P J.Stovall

DET 1905A

M B.Armour
1B C.Lindsay
2B G.Schaefer
SS C.O'Leary
3B B.Coughlin
LF M.McIntyre
CF D.Cooley
RF S.Crawford
C L.Drill
P G.Mullin
P E.Killian
P B.Donovan
P F.Kitson

DET 1906A

M B.Armour
1B C.Lindsay
2B G.Schaefer
SS C.O'Leary
3B B.Coughlin
LF M.McIntyre
CF T.Cobb
RF S.Crawford
C B.Schmidt
P G.Mullin
P R.Donahue
P E.Siever
P B.Donovan
P E.Killian

DET 1907A

M H.Jennings
1B C.Rossman
2B R.Downs
SS C.O'Leary
3B B.Coughlin
LF D.Jones
CF S.Crawford
RF T.Cobb
C B.Schmidt
UT G.Schaefer
P G.Mullin
P E.Killian
P E.Siever
P B.Donovan

DET 1908A

M H.Jennings
1B C.Rossman
2B R.Downs
SS G.Schaefer
3B B.Coughlin
LF M.McIntyre
CF S.Crawford
RF T.Cobb
C B.Schmidt
P E.Summers
P G.Mullin
P B.Donovan
P E.Willett
P E.Killian

DET 1909A

M H.Jennings
1B C.Rossman
2B G.Schaefer
SS D.Bush
3B G.Moriarty
LF M.McIntyre
CF S.Crawford
RF T.Cobb
C B.Schmidt
P G.Mullin
P E.Willett
P E.Summers
P E.Killian
P B.Donovan

DET 1910A

M H.Jennings
1B T.Jones
2B J.Delahanty
SS D.Bush
3B G.Moriarty
LF D.Jones
CF T.Cobb
RF S.Crawford
C O.Stanage
P G.Mullin
P E.Willett
P E.Summers
P B.Donovan
P S.Stroud

DET 1911A

M H.Jennings
1B J.Delahanty
2B C.O'Leary
SS D.Bush
3B G.Moriarty
LF D.Jones
CF T.Cobb
RF S.Crawford
C O.Stanage
UT D.Drake
P G.Mullin
P E.Willett
P E.Summers
P E.Lafitte
P B.Donovan

DET 1912A

M H.Jennings
1B G.Moriarty
2B B.Louden
SS D.Bush
3B C.Deal
LF D.Jones
CF T.Cobb
RF S.Crawford
C O.Stanage
P E.Willett
P J.Dubuc
P G.Mullin
P J.Lake
P R.Works

DET 1913A

M H.Jennings
1B D.Gainer
2B O.Vitt
SS D.Bush
3B G.Moriarty
LF B.Veach
CF T.Cobb
RF S.Crawford
C O.Stanage
P J.Dubuc
P E.Willett
P H.Dauss
P M.Hall
P J.Lake
RP F.House

DET 1914A

M H.Jennings
1B G.Burns
2B M.Kavanagh
SS D.Bush
3B G.Moriarty
LF B.Veach
CF T.Cobb
RF S.Crawford
C O.Stanage
P H.Coveleski
P H.Dauss
P J.Dubuc
P P.Cavet
P A.Main

DET 1915A

M H.Jennings
1B G.Burns
2B R.Young
SS D.Bush
3B O.Vitt
LF B.Veach
CF T.Cobb
RF S.Crawford
C O.Stanage
UT M.Kavanagh
P H.Coveleski
P H.Dauss
P J.Dubuc
P B.Boland

DET 1916A

M H.Jennings
1B G.Burns
2B R.Young
SS D.Bush
3B O.Vitt
LF B.Veach
CF T.Cobb
RF S.Crawford
C O.Stanage
UT H.Heilmann
P H.Coveleski
P H.Dauss
P J.Dubuc
P B.James
P G.Cunningham
RP B.Boland

DET 1917A

M H.Jennings
1B G.Burns
2B R.Young
SS D.Bush
3B O.Vitt
LF B.Veach
CF T.Cobb
RF H.Heilmann
C O.Stanage
P H.Dauss
P B.Boland
P H.Ehmke
P B.James
P W.Mitchell

DET 1918A

M H.Jennings
1B H.Heilmann
2B R.Young
SS D.Bush
3B O.Vitt
LF B.Veach
CF T.Cobb
RF G.Harper
C A.Yelle
P H.Dauss
P B.Boland
P R.Kallio
P G.Cunningham
P B.James

DET 1919A

M H.Jennings
1B H.Heilmann
2B R.Young
SS D.Bush
3B B.Jones
LF B.Veach
CF T.Cobb
RF I.Flagstead
C E.Ainsmith
UT C.Shorten
P H.Dauss
P H.Ehmke
P B.Boland
P D.Leonard
P D.Ayers
RP G.Cunningham

DET 1920A

M H.Jennings
1B H.Heilmann
2B R.Young
SS D.Bush
3B B.Pinelli
LF B.Veach
CF T.Cobb
RF C.Shorten
C O.Stanage
UT I.Flagstead
P H.Dauss
P H.Ehmke
P R.Oldham
P D.Ayers
P D.Leonard

DET 1921A

M T.Cobb
1B L.Blue
2B R.Young
SS D.Bush
3B B.Jones
LF B.Veach
CF T.Cobb
RF H.Heilmann
C J.Bassler
P D.Leonard
P H.Dauss
P R.Oldham
P H.Ehmke
P C.Holling

DET 1922A

M T.Cobb
1B L.Blue
2B G.Cutshaw
SS T.Rigney
3B B.Jones
LF B.Veach
CF T.Cobb
RF H.Heilmann
C J.Bassler
P H.Ehmke
P H.Pillette
P H.Dauss
P R.Oldham
P O.Olsen

DET 1923A

M T.Cobb
1B L.Blue
2B F.Haney
SS T.Rigney
3B B.Jones
LF B.Veach
CF T.Cobb
RF H.Heilmann
C J.Bassler
UT B.Fothergill
UT H.Manush
UT D.Pratt
P H.Dauss
P H.Pillette
P K.Holloway
P S.Johnson
P B.Cole
RP R.Francis

DET 1924A

M T.Cobb
1B L.Blue
2B D.Pratt
SS T.Rigney
3B B.Jones
LF H.Manush
CF T.Cobb
RF H.Heilmann
C J.Bassler
P E.Whitehill
P L.Stoner
P R.Collins
P K.Holloway
P H.Dauss

DET 1925A

M T.Cobb
1B L.Blue
2B F.O'Rourke
SS J.Tavener
3B F.Haney
LF A.Wingo
CF T.Cobb
RF H.Heilmann
C J.Bassler
UT H.Manush
P E.Whitehill
P H.Dauss
P K.Holloway
P L.Stoner
P R.Collins
RP J.Doyle

DET 1926A

M T.Cobb
1B L.Blue
2B C.Gehringer
SS J.Tavener
3B J.Warner
LF B.Fothergill
CF H.Manush
RF H.Heilmann
C C.Manion
UT J.Neun
UT F.O'Rourke
UT A.Wingo
P E.Whitehill
P S.Gibson
P E.Wells
P L.Stoner
P K.Holloway

DET 1927A

M G.Moriarty
1B L.Blue
2B C.Gehringer
SS J.Tavener
3B J.Warner
LF B.Fothergill
CF H.Manush
RF H.Heilmann
C L.Woodall
UT M.McManus
P E.Whitehill
P L.Stoner
P S.Gibson
P K.Holloway
P R.Collins
RP G.Smith

DET 1928A

M G.Moriarty
1B B.Sweeney
2B C.Gehringer
SS J.Tavener
3B M.McManus
LF B.Fothergill
CF H.Rice
RF H.Heilmann
C P.Hargrave
P O.Carroll
P E.Whitehill
P V.Sorrell
P E.Vangilder
P L.Stoner
RP G.Smith

DET 1929A

M B.Harris
1B D.Alexander
2B C.Gehringer
SS H.Schuble
3B M.McManus
LF R.Johnson
CF H.Rice
RF H.Heilmann
C E.Phillips
UT B.Fothergill
P G.Uhle
P E.Whitehill
P V.Sorrell
P O.Carroll
RP A.Prudhomme
RP L.Stoner

DET 1930A

M B.Harris
1B D.Alexander
2B C.Gehringer
SS M.Koenig
3B M.McManus
LF J.Stone
CF L.Funk
RF R.Johnson
C R.Hayworth
P G.Uhle
P V.Sorrell
P E.Whitehill
P C.Hogsett
P W.Hoyt
RP C.Sullivan

DET 1931A

M B.Harris
1B D.Alexander
2B C.Gehringer
SS B.Rogell
3B M.McManus
LF J.Stone
CF H.Walker
RF R.Johnson
C R.Hayworth
UT M.Koenig
UT M.Owen
P E.Whitehill
P V.Sorrell
P G.Uhle
P T.Bridges
P A.Herring

DET 1932A

M B.Harris
1B H.Davis
2B C.Gehringer
SS B.Rogell
3B H.Schuble
LF J.Stone
CF G.Walker
RF E.Webb
C R.Hayworth
P E.Whitehill
P V.Sorrell
P W.Wyatt
P T.Bridges
P C.Hogsett

DET 1933A

M B.Harris
M D.Baker
1B H.Greenberg
2B C.Gehringer
SS B.Rogell
3B M.Owen
LF G.Walker
CF P.Fox
RF J.Stone
C R.Hayworth
P F.Marberry
P V.Sorrell
P T.Bridges
P C.Fischer
P S.Rowe
RP C.Hogsett
RP A.Herring

DET 1934A

M M.Cochrane
1B H.Greenberg
2B C.Gehringer
SS B.Rogell
3B M.Owen
LF G.Goslin
CF J.White
RF P.Fox
C M.Cochrane
UT G.Walker
P T.Bridges
P S.Rowe
P E.Auker
P F.Marberry
P V.Sorrell
RP C.Hogsett

DET 1935A

M M.Cochrane
1B H.Greenberg
2B C.Gehringer
SS B.Rogell
3B M.Owen
LF G.Goslin
CF J.White
RF P.Fox
C M.Cochrane
UT G.Walker
P S.Rowe
P T.Bridges
P A.Crowder
P E.Auker
P J.Sullivan
RP C.Hogsett

DET 1936A

M M.Cochrane
M D.Baker
M M.Cochrane
1B J.Burns
2B C.Gehringer
SS B.Rogell
3B M.Owen
LF G.Goslin
CF A.Simmons
RF G.Walker
C R.Hayworth
P T.Bridges
P S.Rowe
P E.Auker
P V.Sorrell
P R.Lawson
RP C.Kimsey

DET 1937A

M M.Cochrane
M D.Baker
M M.Cochrane
M D.Baker
M C.Perkins
1B H.Greenberg
2B C.Gehringer
SS B.Rogell
3B M.Owen
LF G.Walker
CF J.White
RF P.Fox
C R.York
P E.Auker
P T.Bridges
P R.Lawson
P J.Wade
P B.Poffenberger

DET 1938A

M M.Cochrane
M D.Baker
1B H.Greenberg
2B C.Gehringer
SS B.Rogell
3B D.Ross
LF D.Walker
CF C.Morgan
RF P.Fox
C R.York
UT M.Christman
P V.Kennedy
P G.Gill
P E.Auker
P T.Bridges
P R.Lawson
RP S.Coffman
RP J.Wade

DET 1939A

M D.Baker
1B H.Greenberg
2B C.Gehringer
SS F.Croucher
3B P.Higgins
LF E.Averill
CF B.McCosky
RF P.Fox
C B.Tebbetts
UT R.York
P B.Newsom
P T.Bridges
P S.Rowe
P D.Trout
P A.Benton
RP B.Thomas

DET 1940A

M D.Baker
1B R.York
2B C.Gehringer
SS D.Bartell
3B P.Higgins
LF H.Greenberg
CF B.McCosky
RF P.Fox
C B.Tebbetts
UT B.Campbell
P B.Newsom
P T.Bridges
P S.Rowe
P J.Gorsica
P H.Newhouser
RP A.Benton
RP T.Seats
RP A.McKain

DET 1941A
M D.Baker
1B R.York
2B C.Gehringer
SS F.Croucher
3B P.Higgins
LF R.Radcliff
CF B.McCosky
RF B.Campbell
C B.Tebbetts
UT T.Stainback
P B.Newsom
P H.Newhouser
P J.Gorsica
P A.Benton
P D.Trout
RP B.Thomas

DET 1942A
M D.Baker
1B R.York
2B J.Bloodworth
SS B.Hitchcock
3B P.Higgins
LF B.McCosky
CF D.Cramer
RF N.Harris
C B.Tebbetts
P A.Benton
P D.Trout
P H.White
P H.Newhouser
P T.Bridges
RP R.Henshaw
RP J.Gorsica

DET 1943A
M S.O'Neill
1B R.York
2B J.Bloodworth
SS J.Hoover
3B P.Higgins
LF D.Wakefield
CF D.Cramer
RF N.Harris
C P.Richards
P D.Trout
P V.Trucks
P H.Newhouser
P T.Bridges
P H.White
RP J.Gorsica
RP R.Henshaw

DET 1944A
M S.O'Neill
1B R.York
2B E.Mayo
SS J.Hoover
3B P.Higgins
LF D.Wakefield
CF D.Cramer
RF J.Outlaw
C P.Richards
P D.Trout
P H.Newhouser
P R.Gentry
P S.Overmire
P J.Gorsica
RP B.Beck

DET 1945A
M S.O'Neill
1B R.York
2B E.Mayo
SS S.Webb
3B B.Maier
LF J.Outlaw
CF D.Cramer
RF R.Cullenbine
C B.Swift
P H.Newhouser
P D.Trout
P A.Benton
P S.Overmire
P L.Mueller
RP W.Wilson
RP G.Caster

DET 1946A
M S.O'Neill
1B H.Greenberg
2B J.Bloodworth
SS E.Lake
3B G.Kell
LF D.Wakefield
CF H.Evers
RF R.Cullenbine
C B.Tebbetts
P H.Newhouser
P D.Trout
P V.Trucks
P F.Hutchinson
P A.Benton

DET 1947A
M S.O'Neill
1B R.Cullenbine
2B E.Mayo
SS E.Lake
3B G.Kell
LF D.Wakefield
CF H.Evers
RF P.Mullin
C B.Swift
UT V.Wertz
P H.Newhouser
P F.Hutchinson
P D.Trout
P V.Trucks
P S.Overmire
RP H.White
RP J.Gorsica

DET 1948A
M S.O'Neill
1B G.Vico
2B E.Mayo
SS J.Lipon
3B G.Kell
LF V.Wertz
CF H.Evers
RF P.Mullin
C B.Swift
UT D.Wakefield
P H.Newhouser
P F.Hutchinson
P V.Trucks
P D.Trout
P A.Houtteman
RP S.Overmire
RP B.Pierce

DET 1949A
M R.Rolfe
1B P.Campbell
2B N.Berry
SS J.Lipon
3B G.Kell
LF H.Evers
CF J.Groth
RF V.Wertz
C A.Robinson
UT D.Kolloway
UT E.Lake
UT P.Mullin
P H.Newhouser
P V.Trucks
P A.Houtteman
P T.Gray
P F.Hutchinson
RP D.Trout

DET 1950A
M R.Rolfe
1B D.Kolloway
2B J.Priddy
SS J.Lipon
3B G.Kell
LF H.Evers
CF J.Groth
RF V.Wertz
C A.Robinson
P A.Houtteman
P F.Hutchinson
P H.Newhouser
P D.Trout
P T.Gray
RP H.White
RP P.Calvert

DET 1951A
M R.Rolfe
1B D.Kryhoski
2B J.Priddy
SS J.Lipon
3B G.Kell
LF H.Evers
CF J.Groth
RF V.Wertz
C J.Ginsberg
UT P.Mullin
P T.Gray
P D.Trout
P F.Hutchinson
P V.Trucks
P B.Cain
RP G.Bearden
RP H.White

DET 1952A
M R.Rolfe
M F.Hutchinson
1B W.Dropo
2B J.Priddy
SS N.Berry
3B F.Hatfield
LF P.Mullin
CF J.Groth
RF V.Wertz
C J.Ginsberg
P T.Gray
P A.Houtteman
P V.Trucks
P H.Newhouser
P B.Wight
RP H.White
RP D.Littlefield

DET 1953A
M F.Hutchinson
1B W.Dropo
2B J.Pesky
SS H.Kuenn
3B R.Boone
LF B.Nieman
CF J.Delsing
RF D.Lund
C M.Batts
UT F.Hatfield
P B.Hoeft
P N.Garver
P T.Gray
P S.Gromek
P R.Branca
RP D.Marlowe
RP R.Herbert
RP D.Madison

DET 1954A
M F.Hutchinson
1B W.Dropo
2B F.Bolling
SS H.Kuenn
3B R.Boone
LF J.Delsing
CF B.Tuttle
RF A.Kaline
C F.House
P S.Gromek
P N.Garver
P G.Zuverink
P B.Hoeft
P A.Aber
RP D.Marlowe
RP R.Herbert
RP B.Miller

DET 1955A
M B.Harris
1B E.Torgeson
2B F.Hatfield
SS H.Kuenn
3B R.Boone
LF J.Delsing
CF B.Tuttle
RF A.Kaline
C F.House
UT B.Phillips
P F.Lary
P N.Garver
P B.Hoeft
P S.Gromek
RP B.Birrer
RP A.Aber
RP P.Foytack

DET 1956A
M B.Harris
1B E.Torgeson
2B F.Bolling
SS H.Kuenn
3B R.Boone
LF C.Maxwell
CF B.Tuttle
RF A.Kaline
C F.House
P F.Lary
P P.Foytack
P B.Hoeft
P S.Gromek
P V.Trucks
RP D.Maas
RP A.Aber
RP W.Masterson

DET 1957A
M J.Tighe
1B R.Boone
2B F.Bolling
SS H.Kuenn
3B R.Bertoia
LF C.Maxwell
CF B.Tuttle
RF A.Kaline
C F.House
P J.Bunning
P F.Lary
P D.Maas
P P.Foytack
P B.Hoeft
RP L.Sleater
RP H.Byrd

DET 1958A
M J.Tighe
M B.Norman
1B G.Harris
2B F.Bolling
SS B.Martin
3B R.Bertoia
LF C.Maxwell
CF H.Kuenn
RF A.Kaline
C R.Wilson
P F.Lary
P P.Foytack
P J.Bunning
P B.Hoeft
P H.Moford
RP H.Aguirre
RP T.Morgan

DET 1959A
M B.Norman
M J.Dykes
1B G.Harris
2B F.Bolling
SS R.Bridges
3B E.Yost
LF C.Maxwell
CF A.Kaline
RF H.Kuenn
C L.Berberet
P J.Bunning
P P.Foytack
P D.Mossi
P F.Lary
RP R.Narleski
RP T.Morgan
RP P.Burnside

DET 1960A
M J.Dykes
M B.Hitchcock
M J.Gordon
1B N.Cash
2B F.Bolling
SS C.Fernandez
3B E.Yost
LF C.Maxwell
CF A.Kaline
RF R.Colavito
C L.Berberet
UT N.Chrisley
P F.Lary
P J.Bunning
P D.Mossi
P P.Bruce
P P.Burnside
RP H.Aguirre
RP D.Sisler
RP B.Fischer

DET 1961A
M B.Scheffing
1B N.Cash
2B J.Wood
SS C.Fernandez
3B S.Boros
LF R.Colavito
CF B.Bruton
RF A.Kaline
C D.Brown
P F.Lary
P J.Bunning
P D.Mossi
P P.Foytack
P P.Regan
RP T.Fox
RP H.Aguirre

DET 1962A
M B.Scheffing
1B N.Cash
2B J.Wood
SS C.Fernandez
3B S.Boros
LF R.Colavito
CF B.Bruton
RF A.Kaline
C D.Brown
UT D.McAuliffe
P J.Bunning
P H.Aguirre
P D.Mossi
P P.Regan
P P.Foytack
RP S.Jones
RP R.Kline
RP R.Nischwitz

DET 1963A
M B.Scheffing
M C.Dressen
1B N.Cash
2B J.Wood
SS D.McAuliffe
3B B.Phillips
LF R.Colavito
CF B.Bruton
RF A.Kaline
C G.Triandos
UT B.Freehan
P J.Bunning
P H.Aguirre
P P.Regan
P M.Lolich
P D.Mossi
RP T.Fox
RP B.Anderson
RP T.Sturdivant

DET 1964A
M C.Dressen
1B N.Cash
2B J.Lumpe
SS D.McAuliffe
3B D.Wert
LF G.Brown
CF G.Thomas
RF A.Kaline
C B.Freehan
UT B.Bruton
UT D.Demeter
P D.Wickersham
P M.Lolich
P H.Aguirre
P E.Rakow
P P.Regan
RP F.Gladding
RP L.Sherry
RP T.Fox

DET 1965A
M B.Swift
M C.Dressen
1B N.Cash
2B J.Lumpe
SS D.McAuliffe
3B D.Wert
LF W.Horton
CF D.Demeter
RF A.Kaline
C B.Freehan
P M.Lolich
P D.McLain
P H.Aguirre
P D.Wickersham
P J.Sparma
RP L.Sherry
RP T.Fox
RP F.Gladding

DET 1966A
M C.Dressen
M B.Swift
M F.Skaff
1B N.Cash
2B J.Lumpe
SS D.McAuliffe
3B D.Wert
LF W.Horton
CF A.Kaline
RF J.Northrup
C B.Freehan
UT J.Wood
P D.McLain
P M.Lolich
P E.Wilson
P D.Wickersham
P J.Podres
RP O.Pena
RP L.Sherry
RP F.Gladding

DET 1967A
M M.Smith
1B N.Cash
2B D.McAuliffe
SS R.Oyler
3B D.Wert
LF J.Northrup
CF M.Stanley
RF A.Kaline
C B.Freehan
UT W.Horton
P E.Wilson
P D.McLain
P J.Sparma
P M.Lolich
RP D.Wickersham
RP F.Gladding
RP J.Hiller

DET 1968A
M M.Smith
1B N.Cash
2B D.McAuliffe
SS R.Oyler
3B D.Wert
LF W.Horton
CF M.Stanley
RF J.Northrup
C B.Freehan
UT A.Kaline
P D.McLain
P E.Wilson
P M.Lolich
P J.Sparma
P J.Hiller
RP P.Dobson
RP D.Patterson

DET 1969A
M M.Smith
1B N.Cash
2B D.McAuliffe
SS T.Tresh
3B D.Wert
LF W.Horton
CF J.Northrup
RF A.Kaline
C B.Freehan
UT M.Stanley
P D.McLain
P M.Lolich
P E.Wilson
P M.Kilkenny
RP P.Dobson
RP J.Hiller
RP T.Timmermann

DET 1970A
M M.Smith
1B N.Cash
2B D.McAuliffe
SS C.Gutierrez
3B D.Wert
LF W.Horton
CF M.Stanley
RF J.Northrup
C B.Freehan
UT A.Kaline
UT E.Maddox
P M.Lolich
P J.Niekro
P L.Cain
P M.Kilkenny
P E.Wilson
RP J.Hiller
RP T.Timmermann
RP D.Patterson

DET 1971A
M B.Martin
1B N.Cash
2B D.McAuliffe
SS E.Brinkman
3B A.Rodriguez
LF W.Horton
CF M.Stanley
RF A.Kaline
C B.Freehan
UT J.Northrup
P M.Lolich
P J.Coleman
P L.Cain
P J.Niekro
RP F.Scherman
RP D.Chance
RP M.Kilkenny

DET 1972A
M B.Martin
1B N.Cash
2B D.McAuliffe
SS E.Brinkman
3B A.Rodriguez
LF W.Horton
CF M.Stanley
RF J.Northrup
C B.Freehan
UT G.Brown
UT A.Kaline
P M.Lolich
P J.Coleman
P T.Timmermann
P W.Fryman
RP C.Seelbach
RP F.Scherman
RP J.Niekro

DET 1973A
M B.Martin
M J.Schultz
1B N.Cash
2B D.McAuliffe
SS E.Brinkman
3B A.Rodriguez
LF W.Horton
CF M.Stanley
RF J.Northrup
C B.Freehan
DH G.Brown
P M.Lolich
P J.Coleman
P J.Perry
P W.Fryman
RP J.Hiller
RP F.Scherman
RP L.LaGrow

DET 1974A
M R.Houk
1B B.Freehan
2B G.Sutherland
SS E.Brinkman
3B A.Rodriguez
LF W.Horton
CF M.Stanley
RF J.Northrup
C J.Moses
DH A.Kaline
P M.Lolich
P J.Coleman
P L.LaGrow
P W.Fryman
RP J.Hiller
RP J.Ray

DET 1975A
M R.Houk
1B J.Pierce
2B G.Sutherland
SS T.Veryzer
3B A.Rodriguez
LF B.Oglivie
CF R.LeFlore
RF L.Roberts
C B.Freehan
DH W.Horton
UT D.Meyer
P M.Lolich
P J.Coleman
P V.Ruhle
P L.LaGrow
P R.Bare
RP J.Hiller

DET 1976A
M R.Houk
1B J.Thompson
2B P.Garcia
SS T.Veryzer
3B A.Rodriguez
LF A.Johnson
CF R.LeFlore
RF R.Staub
C B.Kimm
DH W.Horton
UT D.Meyer
UT B.Oglivie
P D.Roberts
P M.Fidrych
P V.Ruhle
P R.Bare
P J.Crawford
RP J.Hiller
RP S.Grilli

DET 1977A
M R.Houk
1B J.Thompson
2B T.Fuentes
SS T.Veryzer
3B A.Rodriguez
LF S.Kemp
CF R.LeFlore
RF B.Oglivie
C M.May
DH R.Staub
P D.Rozema
P F.Arroyo

P B.Sykes
P D.Roberts
P J.Crawford
RP J.Hiller
RP S.Foucault
RP S.Grilli

DET 1978A

M R.Houk
1B J.Thompson
2B L.Whitaker
SS A.Trammell
3B A.Rodriguez
LF S.Kemp
CF R.LeFlore
RF T.Corcoran
C M.May
DH R.Staub
P J.Slaton
P M.Wilcox
P D.Rozema
P J.Billingham
P K.Young
RP J.Hiller

DET 1979A

M L.Moss
M D.Tracewski
M S.Anderson
1B J.Thompson
2B L.Whitaker
SS A.Trammell
3B A.Rodriguez
LF S.Kemp
CF R.LeFlore
RF J.Morales
C L.Parrish
DH R.Staub
P J.Morris
P M.Wilcox
P J.Billingham
P P.Underwood
P D.Petry
RP A.Lopez
RP J.Hiller
RP D.Tobik

DET 1980A

M S.Anderson
1B R.Hebner
2B L.Whitaker
SS A.Trammell
3B T.Brookens
LF S.Kemp
CF R.Peters
RF A.Cowens
C L.Parrish
DH C.Summers
UT J.Wockenfuss
P J.Morris
P M.Wilcox
P D.Schatzeder
P D.Petry
P D.Rozema
RP A.Lopez
RP P.Underwood

DET 1981A

M S.Anderson
1B R.Hebner
2B L.Whitaker
SS A.Trammell
3B T.Brookens
LF S.Kemp
CF A.Cowens
RF K.Gibson
C L.Parrish
DH J.Wockenfuss
UT L.Jones
P J.Morris
P M.Wilcox
P D.Petry
P D.Rozema
P D.Schatzeder
RP A.Lopez
RP D.Tobik
RP K.Saucier

DET 1982A

M S.Anderson
1B E.Cabell
2B L.Whitaker
SS A.Trammell
3B T.Brookens
LF L.Herndon
CF G.Wilson
RF C.Lemon
C L.Parrish
DH M.Ivie
P J.Morris
P D.Petry
P M.Wilcox
P J.Ujdur
P P.Underwood
RP D.Tobik
RP D.Rucker
RP E.Sosa

DET 1983A

M S.Anderson
1B E.Cabell
2B L.Whitaker
SS A.Trammell
3B T.Brookens
LF L.Herndon
CF C.Lemon
RF G.Wilson
C L.Parrish
DH K.Gibson
UT R.Leach
P J.Morris
P D.Petry
P M.Wilcox
P J.Berenguer
P D.Rozema
RP A.Lopez
RP H.Bailey
RP D.Bair

DET 1984A

M S.Anderson
1B D.Bergman
2B L.Whitaker
SS A.Trammell
3B H.Johnson
LF L.Herndon
CF C.Lemon
RF K.Gibson
C L.Parrish
DH D.Evans
UT T.Brookens
UT B.Garbey
P J.Morris
P D.Petry
P M.Wilcox
P J.Berenguer
P D.Rozema
RP W.Hernandez
RP A.Lopez
RP D.Bair

DET 1985A

M S.Anderson
1B D.Evans
2B L.Whitaker
SS A.Trammell
3B T.Brookens
LF L.Herndon
CF C.Lemon
RF K.Gibson
C L.Parrish
DH J.Grubb
P J.Morris
P D.Petry
P W.Terrell
P F.Tanana
RP W.Hernandez
RP A.Lopez
RP B.Scherrer

DET 1986A

M S.Anderson
1B D.Evans
2B L.Whitaker
SS A.Trammell
3B D.Coles
LF D.Collins
CF C.Lemon
RF K.Gibson
C L.Parrish
DH J.Grubb
UT T.Brookens
UT L.Herndon
UT P.Sheridan
P J.Morris
P W.Terrell
P F.Tanana
P E.King
P R.O'Neal
RP W.Hernandez
RP B.Campbell
RP M.Thurmond

DET 1987A

M S.Anderson
1B D.Evans
2B L.Whitaker
SS A.Trammell
3B T.Brookens
LF K.Gibson
CF C.Lemon
RF P.Sheridan
C M.Nokes
DH B.Madlock
P J.Morris
P W.Terrell
P F.Tanana
P D.Petry
P J.Robinson
RP E.King
RP M.Henneman
RP M.Thurmond

DET 1988A

M S.Anderson
1B R.Knight
2B L.Whitaker
SS A.Trammell
3B T.Brookens
LF P.Sheridan
CF G.Pettis
RF C.Lemon
C M.Nokes
DH D.Evans
UT D.Bergman
UT L.Salazar
P J.Morris
P D.Alexander
P W.Terrell
P F.Tanana
P J.Robinson
RP P.Gibson
RP M.Henneman
RP W.Hernandez

DET 1989A

M S.Anderson
1B D.Bergman
2B L.Whitaker
SS A.Trammell
3B R.Schu
LF F.Lynn
CF G.Pettis
RF C.Lemon
C M.Heath
DH K.Moreland
UT G.Ward
P F.Tanana
P D.Alexander
P J.Morris
RP P.Gibson
RP M.Henneman
RP F.Williams

DET 1990A

M S.Anderson
1B C.Fielder
2B L.Whitaker
SS A.Trammell
3B T.Phillips
LF G.Ward
CF L.Moseby
RF C.Lemon
C M.Heath
DH D.Bergman
UT L.Sheets
P J.Morris
P F.Tanana
P D.Petry
P J.Robinson
RP P.Gibson
RP M.Henneman
RP J.Gleaton

DET 1991A

M S.Anderson
1B D.Bergman
2B L.Whitaker
SS A.Trammell
3B T.Fryman
LF L.Moseby
CF M.Cuyler
RF R.Deer
C M.Tettleton
DH C.Fielder
UT P.Incaviglia
UT T.Phillips
P B.Gullickson
P W.Terrell
P F.Tanana
P M.Leiter
RP P.Gibson
RP J.Cerutti
RP M.Henneman

DET 1992A

M S.Anderson
1B D.Bergman
2B L.Whitaker
SS T.Fryman
3B S.Livingstone
LF D.Gladden
CF M.Cuyler
RF R.Deer
C M.Tettleton
DH C.Fielder
UT M.Carreon
UT T.Phillips
P B.Gullickson
P F.Tanana
P W.Terrell
P M.Leiter
RP J.Doherty
RP L.Lancaster
RP M.Henneman

DET 1993A

M S.Anderson
1B C.Fielder
2B L.Whitaker
SS A.Trammell
3B T.Fryman
LF T.Phillips
CF M.Cuyler
RF R.Deer
C C.Kreuter
DH K.Gibson
UT S.Livingstone
UT M.Tettleton
P M.Moore
P D.Wells
P J.Doherty
P B.Gullickson
P M.Leiter
RP T.Bolton
RP B.Krueger
RP M.Henneman

DET 1994A

M S.Anderson
1B C.Fielder
2B L.Whitaker
SS A.Trammell
3B T.Fryman
LF T.Phillips
CF M.Cuyler
RF J.Felix
C C.Kreuter
DH K.Gibson
UT C.Gomez
UT M.Tettleton
P T.Belcher
P M.Moore
P B.Gullickson
P D.Wells
P J.Doherty
RP J.Boever
RP M.Gardiner
RP S.Davis

DET 1995A

M S.Anderson
1B C.Fielder
2B L.Whitaker
SS C.Gomez
3B T.Fryman
LF B.Higginson
CF C.Curtis
RF D.Bautista
C J.Flaherty
DH K.Gibson
P F.Lira
P S.Bergman
P M.Moore
P D.Wells
RP J.Doherty
RP B.Bohanon
RP J.Boever

DET 1996A

M B.Bell
1B T.Clark
2B M.Lewis
SS A.Cedeno
3B T.Fryman
LF B.Higginson
CF C.Curtis
RF M.Nieves
C B.Ausmus
DH E.Williams
UT K.Bartee
UT C.Fielder
P F.Lira
P O.Olivares
P B.Williams
RP R.Lewis
RP J.Lima
RP M.Myers

DET 1997A

M B.Bell
1B T.Clark
2B D.Easley
SS D.Cruz
3B T.Fryman
LF B.Higginson
CF B.Hunter
RF M.Nieves
C R.Casanova
DH B.Hamelin
P J.Thompson
P B.Moehler
P W.Blair
P O.Olivares
RP A.Sager
RP D.Miceli
RP D.Brocail

DET 1998A

M B.Bell
M L.Parrish
1B T.Clark
2B D.Easley
SS D.Cruz
3B J.Randa
LF L.Gonzalez
CF B.Hunter
RF B.Higginson
C P.Bako
DH G.Berroa
P J.Thompson
P B.Moehler
P B.Florie
P S.Greisinger
P F.Castillo
RP D.Bochtler
RP T.Jones
RP D.Brocail

DET 1999A

M L.Parrish
1B T.Clark
2B D.Easley
SS D.Cruz
3B D.Palmer
LF J.Encarnacion
CF G.Kapler
RF B.Higginson
C B.Ausmus
DH L.Polonia
UT F.Catalanotto
P B.Moehler
P D.Mlicki
P J.Weaver
P J.Thompson
P W.Blair
RP C.Nitkowski
RP D.Brocail
RP N.Cruz

DET 2000A

M P.Garner
1B T.Clark
2B D.Easley
SS D.Cruz
3B D.Palmer
LF B.Higginson
CF J.Encarnacion
RF R.Becker
C B.Ausmus
DH J.Gonzalez
UT S.Halter
P J.Weaver
P H.Nomo
P B.Moehler
P W.Blair
P D.Mlicki
RP C.Nitkowski
RP M.Anderson
RP T.Jones

Elizabeth

RES n 1873

RES 1873n

M D.Allison
1B M.Campbell
2B B.Laughlin
SS F.Wordsworth
3B A.Nevin
LF E.Booth
CF A.Allison
RF H.Austin
C D.Allison
UT F.Fleet
P H.Campbell

Florida

FLA N 1993-2000

FLA 1993N

M R.Lachemann
1B O.Destrade
2B B.Barberie
SS W.Weiss
3B G.Sheffield
LF J.Conine
CF C.Carr
RF D.Whitmore
C B.Santiago
UT G.Briley
UT R.Renteria
P C.Hough
P J.Armstrong
P C.Hammond
P R.Bowen
RP L.Aquino
RP R.Lewis
RP B.Harvey

FLA 1994N

M R.Lachemann
1B G.Colbrunn
2B B.Barberie
SS K.Abbott
3B J.Browne
LF J.Conine
CF C.Carr
RF G.Sheffield
C B.Santiago
UT M.Carrillo
UT D.Magadan
P J.Weathers
P P.Rapp
P C.Hough
P M.Gardner
P C.Hammond
RP R.Nen
RP R.Lewis
RP L.Aquino

FLA 1995N

M R.Lachemann
1B G.Colbrunn
2B Q.Veras
SS K.Abbott
3B T.Pendleton
LF J.Conine
CF C.Carr
RF Sheffield
C C.Johnson
UT A.Arias
P J.Burkett
P P.Rapp
P C.Hammond
P B.Witt
P J.Weathers
RP M.Gardner
RP T.Mathews
RP R.Nen

FLA 1996N

M R.Lachemann
M C.Rojas
M J.Boles
1B G.Colbrunn
2B Q.Veras
SS E.Renteria
3B T.Pendleton
LF J.Conine
CF D.White
RF G.Sheffield
C C.Johnson
UT K.Abbott
UT A.Arias
UT J.Orsulak
UT J.Tavarez
P K.Brown
P A.Leiter
P P.Rapp
P J.Burkett
RP R.Nen
RP C.Hammond
RP J.Weathers

FLA 1997N

M J.Leyland
1B J.Conine
2B L.Castillo
SS E.Renteria
3B B.Bonilla
LF M.Alou
CF D.White
RF G.Sheffield
C C.Johnson
UT J.Cangelosi
UT J.Eisenreich
P K.Brown
P A.Fernandez
P A.Leiter
P T.Saunders
P P.Rapp
RP J.Powell
RP R.Helling
RP R.Nen

FLA 1998N

M J.Leyland
1B D.Lee
2B C.Counsell
SS E.Renteria
3B T.Zeile
LF C.Floyd
CF T.Dunwoody
RF M.Kotsay
C G.Zaun
UT J.Cangelosi
UT R.Jackson
P L.Hernandez
P B.Meadows
P J.Sanchez
P K.Ojala
RP V.Darensbourg
RP A.Alfonseca
RP B.Edmondson

FLA 1999N

M J.Boles
1B K.Millar
2B L.Castillo
SS A.Gonzalez
3B M.Lowell
LF B.Aven
CF P.Wilson
RF M.Kotsay
C M.Redmond
UT D.Berg
P D.Springer
P B.Meadows
P R.Dempster
P A.Fernandez
P L.Hernandez
RP B.Edmondson
RP B.Looper
RP A.Alfonseca

FLA 2000N

M J.Boles
1B D.Lee
2B L.Castillo
SS A.Gonzalez
3B M.Lowell
LF C.Floyd
CF P.Wilson
RF M.Kotsay
C M.Redmond
UT K.Millar
UT M.Smith
P R.Dempster
P J.Sanchez
P R.Cornelius
P C.Smith
P B.Penny
RP R.Bones
RP A.Alfonseca
RP B.Looper

Fort Wayne

KEK n 1871

KEK 1871n

M B.Lennon
M H.Deane
1B J.Foran
2B T.Carey
SS W.Goldsmith
3B F.Selman
LF E.Mincher
CF B.Armstrong
RF B.Kelly
C B.Lennon
P B.Mathews

Hartford

HAR n 1874-1875
HAR N 1876-1877

HAR 1874n

M L.Pike
1B E.Mills
2B B.Addy
SS T.Barlow
3B B.Boyd
LF J.Tipper
CF L.Pike
RF B.Barnie
C S.Hastings
P C.Fisher

P B.Stearns

HAR 1875n

M B.Ferguson
1B E.Mills
2B J.Burdock
SS T.Carey
3B B.Ferguson
LF T.York
CF J.Remsen
RF A.Allison
C D.Allison
UT B.Harbidge
P C.Cummings
P T.Bond

HAR 1876N

M B.Ferguson
1B E.Mills
2B J.Burdock
SS T.Carey
3B B.Ferguson
LF T.York
CF J.Remsen
RF D.Higham
C D.Allison
P T.Bond
P C.Cummings

HAR 1877N

M B.Ferguson
1B J.Start
2B J.Burdock
SS T.Carey
3B B.Ferguson
LF T.York
CF J.Holdsworth
RF J.Cassidy
C B.Harbidge
P T.Larkin

Houston

HOU N 1962-2000

HOU 1962N

M H.Craft
1B N.Larker
2B J.Amalfitano
SS B.Lillis
3B B.Aspromonte
LF A.Spangler
CF C.Warwick
RF R.Mejias
C H.Smith
UT J.Pendleton
P T.Farrell
P K.Johnson
P B.Bruce
P J.Golden
P H.Woodeshick
RP B.Tiefenauer
RP D.McMahon
RP R.Kemmerer

HOU 1963N

M H.Craft
1B R.Staub
2B E.Fazio
SS B.Lillis
3B B.Aspromonte
LF A.Spangler
CF H.Goss
RF C.Warwick
C J.Bateman
UT P.Runnels
UT J.Temple
P K.Johnson
P T.Farrell
P D.Nottebart
P B.Bruce
P H.Brown
RP H.Woodeshick
RP D.McMahon
RP J.Umbricht

HOU 1964N

M H.Craft
M L.Harris
1B W.Bond
2B N.Fox
SS E.Kasko
3B B.Aspromonte
LF A.Spangler
CF M.White
RF J.Gaines
C J.Grote
UT B.Lillis
P K.Johnson
P B.Bruce
P T.Farrell
P D.Nottebart
P H.Brown
RP J.Owens
RP C.Raymond
RP H.Woodeshick

HOU 1965N

M L.Harris
1B W.Bond
2B J.Morgan
SS B.Lillis
3B B.Aspromonte
LF L.Maye
CF J.Wynn
RF R.Staub
C R.Brand
UT J.Gaines
P B.Bruce
P T.Farrell
P D.Nottebart
P L.Dierker
P D.Giusti
RP C.Raymond
RP J.Owens
RP R.Taylor

HOU 1966N

M G.Hatton
1B C.Harrison
2B J.Morgan
SS S.Jackson
3B B.Aspromonte
LF L.Maye
CF J.Wynn
RF R.Staub
C J.Bateman
UT D.Nicholson
P M.Cuellar
P D.Giusti
P L.Dierker
P T.Farrell
P B.Bruce
RP C.Raymond
RP R.Taylor
RP J.Owens

HOU 1967N

M G.Hatton
1B E.Mathews
2B J.Morgan
SS S.Jackson
3B B.Aspromonte
LF R.Davis
CF J.Wynn
RF R.Staub
C J.Bateman
P M.Cuellar
P D.Giusti
P D.Wilson
P B.Belinsky
P L.Dierker
RP B.Latman
RP C.Sembera
RP D.Eilers

HOU 1968N

M G.Hatton
M H.Walker
1B R.Staub
2B D.Menke
SS H.Torres
3B D.Rader
LF J.Wynn
CF R.Davis
RF N.Miller
C J.Bateman
UT B.Aspromonte
P D.Giusti
P L.Dierker
P D.Lemaster
P D.Wilson
P M.Cuellar
RP J.Buzhardt
RP J.Ray
RP T.Dukes

HOU 1969N

M H.Walker
1B C.Blefary
2B J.Morgan
SS D.Menke
3B D.Rader
LF J.Alou
CF J.Wynn
RF N.Miller
C J.Edwards
P L.Dierker
P D.Lemaster
P D.Wilson
P T.Griffin
P J.Ray
RP J.Billingham
RP F.Gladding

HOU 1970N

M H.Walker
1B B.Watson
2B J.Morgan
SS D.Menke
3B D.Rader
LF J.Wynn
CF C.Cedeno
RF J.Alou
C J.Edwards
P L.Dierker
P J.Billingham
P D.Wilson
P D.Lemaster
P T.Griffin
RP J.Ray
RP R.Cook
RP J.Bouton

HOU 1971N

M H.Walker
1B D.Menke
2B J.Morgan
SS R.Metzger
3B D.Rader
LF J.Alou
CF C.Cedeno
RF J.Wynn
C J.Edwards
UT B.Watson
P D.Wilson
P J.Billingham
P K.Forsch
P L.Dierker
P W.Blasingame
RP J.Ray
RP G.Culver
RP D.Lemaster

HOU 1972N

M H.Walker
M S.Parker
M L.Durocher
1B L.May
2B T.Helms
SS R.Metzger
3B D.Rader
LF B.Watson
CF C.Cedeno
RF J.Wynn
C J.Edwards
P D.Wilson
P L.Dierker
P D.Roberts
P J.Reuss
P K.Forsch
RP G.Culver
RP T.Griffin
RP J.Ray

HOU 1973N

M L.Durocher
1B L.May
2B T.Helms
SS R.Metzger
3B D.Rader
LF B.Watson
CF C.Cedeno
RF J.Wynn
C S.Jutze
P J.Reuss
P D.Roberts
P D.Wilson
P K.Forsch
P T.Griffin
RP J.Crawford
RP J.Ray
RP J.York

HOU 1974N

M P.Gomez
1B L.May
2B T.Helms
SS R.Metzger
3B D.Rader
LF B.Watson
CF C.Cedeno
RF G.Gross
C M.May
UT B.Gallagher
UT L.Milbourne
P L.Dierker
P T.Griffin
P D.Wilson
P D.Roberts
P C.Osteen
RP K.Forsch
RP M.Cosgrove
RP F.Scherman

HOU 1975N

M P.Gomez
M B.Virdon
1B B.Watson
2B R.Andrews
SS R.Metzger
3B D.Rader
LF W.Howard
CF C.Cedeno
RF G.Gross
C M.May
UT E.Cabell
UT J.Cruz
UT C.Johnson
P L.Dierker
P J.Richard
P D.Roberts
P D.Konieczny
P K.Forsch
RP J.Niekro
RP J.Crawford
RP W.Granger

HOU 1976N

M B.Virdon
1B B.Watson
2B R.Andrews
SS R.Metzger
3B E.Cabell
LF J.Cruz
CF C.Cedeno
RF G.Gross
C E.Herrmann
UT C.Johnson
P J.Richard
P L.Dierker
P J.Andujar
P J.Niekro
RP K.Forsch
RP G.Pentz
RP G.Rondon

HOU 1977N

M B.Virdon
1B B.Watson
2B A.Howe
SS R.Metzger
3B E.Cabell
LF T.Puhl
CF C.Cedeno
RF J.Cruz
C J.Ferguson
UT J.Gonzalez
P J.Richard
P M.Lemongello
P J.Niekro
P J.Andujar
P F.Bannister
RP J.Sambito
RP G.Pentz
RP K.Forsch

HOU 1978N

M B.Virdon
1B B.Watson
2B A.Howe
SS J.Sexton
3B E.Cabell
LF D.Walling
CF T.Puhl
RF J.Cruz
C L.Pujols
UT D.Bergman
P J.Richard
P M.Lemongello
P J.Niekro
P T.Dixon
P J.Andujar
RP K.Forsch
RP J.Sambito

HOU 1979N

M B.Virdon
1B C.Cedeno
2B R.Landestoy
SS C.Reynolds
3B E.Cabell
LF J.Cruz
CF T.Puhl
RF J.Leonard
C A.Ashby
UT A.Howe
P J.Richard
P J.Niekro
P J.Andujar
P K.Forsch
P R.Williams
RP J.Sambito
RP R.Niemann

HOU 1980N

M B.Virdon
1B A.Howe
2B J.Morgan
SS C.Reynolds
3B E.Cabell
LF J.Cruz
CF C.Cedeno
RF T.Puhl
C A.Ashby
UT R.Landestoy
UT D.Walling
P J.Niekro
P N.Ryan
P K.Forsch
P V.Ruhle
P J.Andujar
RP D.Smith
RP J.Sambito
RP F.LaCorte

HOU 1981N

M B.Virdon
1B C.Cedeno
2B J.Pittman
SS C.Reynolds
3B A.Howe
LF J.Cruz
CF T.Scott
RF T.Puhl
C A.Ashby
P J.Niekro
P D.Sutton
P B.Knepper
P N.Ryan
P V.Ruhle
RP D.Smith
RP J.Sambito
RP F.LaCorte

HOU 1982N

M B.Virdon
M B.Lillis
1B R.Knight
2B P.Garner
SS D.Thon
3B A.Howe
LF J.Cruz
CF T.Scott
RF T.Puhl
C A.Ashby
P J.Niekro
P N.Ryan
P D.Sutton
P B.Knepper
P V.Ruhle
RP M.LaCoss
RP F.LaCorte
RP D.Smith

HOU 1983N

M B.Lillis
1B R.Knight
2B B.Doran
SS D.Thon
3B P.Garner
LF J.Cruz
CF O.Moreno
RF T.Puhl
C A.Ashby
UT D.Walling
P J.Niekro
P B.Knepper
P N.Ryan
P M.Scott
P M.LaCoss
RP V.Ruhle
RP B.Dawley
RP D.Smith

HOU 1984N

M B.Lillis
1B E.Cabell
2B B.Doran
SS C.Reynolds
3B P.Garner
LF J.Cruz
CF J.Mumphrey
RF T.Puhl
C M.Bailey
UT K.Bass
P J.Niekro
P B.Knepper
P N.Ryan
P M.Scott
P M.LaCoss
RP B.Dawley
RP V.Ruhle
RP D.Smith

HOU 1985N

M B.Lillis
1B G.Davis
2B B.Doran
SS C.Reynolds
3B P.Garner
LF J.Cruz
CF K.Bass
RF J.Mumphrey
C M.Bailey
UT D.Walling
P B.Knepper
P N.Ryan
P M.Scott
P J.Niekro
RP B.Dawley
RP D.Smith
RP F.DiPino

HOU 1986N

M H.Lanier
1B G.Davis
2B B.Doran
SS D.Thon
3B D.Walling
LF J.Cruz
CF B.Hatcher
RF K.Bass
C A.Ashby
UT P.Garner
UT C.Reynolds
P M.Scott
P B.Knepper
P N.Ryan
P J.Deshaies
RP C.Kerfeld
RP A.Lopez
RP L.Andersen

HOU 1987N

M H.Lanier
1B G.Davis
2B B.Doran
SS C.Reynolds
3B D.Walling
LF J.Cruz
CF B.Hatcher
RF K.Bass
C A.Ashby
P M.Scott
P N.Ryan
P D.Darwin
P B.Knepper
P J.Deshaies
RP L.Andersen
RP D.Smith
RP D.Meads

HOU 1988N

M H.Lanier
1B G.Davis
2B B.Doran
SS R.Ramirez
3B B.Bell
LF B.Hatcher
CF G.Young
RF K.Bass
C A.Trevino
UT T.Puhl
P N.Ryan
P M.Scott
P J.Deshaies
P D.Darwin
P B.Knepper
RP J.Agosto
RP L.Andersen
RP D.Smith

HOU 1989N

M A.Howe
1B G.Davis
2B B.Doran
SS R.Ramirez
3B K.Caminiti
LF B.Hatcher
CF G.Young
RF T.Puhl
C C.Biggio
UT C.Reynolds
P M.Scott
P J.Deshaies
P J.Clancy
P B.Knepper
P M.Portugal
RP D.Darwin
RP B.Forsch
RP L.Andersen

HOU 1990N

M A.Howe
1B G.Davis
2B B.Doran
SS R.Ramirez
3B K.Caminiti
LF F.Stubbs
CF E.Yelding
RF G.Wilson
C C.Biggio
UT C.Candaele
P J.Deshaies
P M.Scott
P M.Portugal
P B.Gullickson
P D.Darwin
RP J.Agosto
RP J.Clancy
RP L.Andersen

HOU 1991N

M A.Howe
1B J.Bagwell
2B C.Candaele
SS E.Yelding
3B K.Caminiti
LF L.Gonzalez
CF G.Young
RF S.Finley
C C.Biggio
UT R.Ramirez
P P.Harnisch
P M.Portugal
P J.Deshaies
P D.Kile
P J.Jones
RP A.Osuna
RP J.Corsi
RP C.Schilling

HOU 1992N

M A.Howe
1B J.Bagwell
2B C.Biggio
SS A.Cedeno
3B K.Caminiti
LF L.Gonzalez
CF S.Finley
RF E.Anthony
C E.Taubensee
UT C.Candaele
UT P.Incaviglia
P P.Harnisch
P B.Henry
P J.Jones
P D.Kile
P M.Portugal
RP D.Jones
RP X.Hernandez
RP J.Boever

HOU 1993N

M A.Howe
1B J.Bagwell
2B C.Biggio
SS A.Cedeno
3B K.Caminiti
LF L.Gonzalez
CF S.Finley
RF E.Anthony
C E.Taubensee
UT K.Bass
P D.Drabek
P P.Harnisch
P M.Portugal
P G.Swindell
P D.Kile
RP X.Hernandez
RP D.Jones
RP B.Williams

HOU 1994N

M T.Collins
1B J.Bagwell
2B C.Biggio
SS A.Cedeno
3B K.Caminiti
LF L.Gonzalez
CF S.Finley
RF J.Mouton
C S.Servais
UT K.Bass
P D.Drabek
P G.Swindell
P D.Kile
P S.Reynolds
P P.Harnisch
RP T.Jones
RP T.Edens
RP D.Veres

HOU 1995N

- M T.Collins
- 1B J.Bagwell
- 2B C.Biggio
- SS O.Miller
- 3B D.Magadan
- LF J.Mouton
- CF B.Hunter
- RF D.Bell
- C T.Eusebio
- UT J.Cangelosi
- UT C.Shipley
- UT M.Thompson
- P S.Reynolds
- P D.Drabek
- P G.Swindell
- P M.Hampton
- P D.Kile
- RP D.Veres
- RP T.Jones
- RP D.Brocail

HOU 1996N

- M T.Collins
- 1B J.Bagwell
- 2B C.Biggio
- SS O.Miller
- 3B S.Berry
- LF J.Mouton
- CF B.Hunter
- RF D.Bell
- C R.Wilkins
- UT J.Cangelosi
- UT D.May
- UT B.Spiers
- P S.Reynolds
- P D.Kile
- P D.Drabek
- P M.Hampton
- P D.Wall
- RP X.Hernandez
- RP T.Jones
- RP D.Brocail

HOU 1997N

- M L.Dierker
- 1B J.Bagwell
- 2B C.Biggio
- SS T.Bogar
- 3B S.Berry
- LF L.Gonzalez
- CF T.Howard
- RF D.Bell
- C B.Ausmus
- UT R.Gutierrez
- UT B.Spiers
- P D.Kile
- P M.Hampton
- P C.Holt
- P S.Reynolds
- P R.Garcia
- RP J.Lima
- RP B.Wagner
- RP T.Martin

HOU 1998N

- M L.Dierker
- 1B J.Bagwell
- 2B C.Biggio
- SS R.Gutierrez
- 3B B.Spiers
- LF M.Alou
- CF C.Everett
- RF D.Bell
- C B.Ausmus
- UT S.Berry
- P S.Reynolds
- P J.Lima
- P M.Hampton
- P S.Bergman
- RP D.Henry
- RP B.Wagner
- RP C.Nitkowski

HOU 1999N

- M L.Dierker
- M M.Galante
- M L.Dierker
- 1B J.Bagwell
- 2B C.Biggio
- SS T.Bogar
- 3B K.Caminiti
- LF R.Hidalgo
- CF C.Everett
- RF D.Bell
- C T.Eusebio
- UT B.Spiers
- P J.Lima
- P M.Hampton
- P S.Reynolds
- P C.Holt
- P S.Bergman
- RP S.Elarton
- RP B.Wagner
- RP J.Powell

HOU 2000N

- M L.Dierker
- 1B J.Bagwell
- 2B C.Biggio
- SS T.Bogar
- 3B C.Truby
- LF M.Alou
- CF R.Hidalgo
- RF L.Berkman
- C M.Meluskey
- UT J.Lugo
- UT B.Spiers
- UT D.Ward
- P C.Holt
- P J.Lima
- P S.Elarton
- P S.Reynolds
- P W.Miller
- RP O.Dotel
- RP J.Slusarski
- RP J.Cabrera

Indianapolis

IND N 1878
IND a 1884
IND N 1887-1889
IND F 1914

IND 1878N

- M J.Clapp
- 1B A.Croft
- 2B J.Quest
- SS F.Warner
- 3B N.Williamson
- LF J.Clapp
- CF R.McKelvy
- RF O.Shaffer
- C S.Flint
- P T.Nolan
- P J.McCormick
- P T.Healey

IND 1884a

- M J.Gifford
- M B.Watkins
- 1B J.Kerins
- 2B E.Merrill
- SS M.Phillips
- 3B P.Callahan
- LF J.Peltz
- CF J.Morrison
- RF P.Weihe
- C J.Keenan
- P L.McKeon
- P B.Barr
- P J.Aydelott
- P A.McCauley

IND 1887N

- M W.Burnham
- M F.Thomas
- M H.Fogel
- 1B O.Schomberg
- 2B C.Bassett
- SS J.Glasscock
- 3B J.Denny
- LF E.Seery
- CF J.McGeachy
- RF J.Cahill
- C G.Myers
- P J.Healy
- P H.Boyle
- P L.Shreve

IND 1888N

- M H.Spence
- 1B D.Esterbrook
- 2B C.Bassett
- SS J.Glasscock
- 3B J.Denny
- LF E.Seery
- CF P.Hines
- RF J.McGeachy
- C D.Buckley
- P H.Boyle
- P J.Healy
- P L.Shreve
- P B.Burdick

IND 1889N

- M F.Bancroft
- M J.Glasscock
- 1B P.Hines
- 2B C.Bassett
- SS J.Glasscock
- 3B J.Denny
- LF E.Seery
- CF M.Sullivan
- RF J.McGeachy
- C D.Buckley
- P H.Boyle
- P C.Getzien
- P A.Rusie

IND 1914F

- M B.Phillips
- 1B C.Carr
- 2B F.LaPorte
- SS J.Esmond
- 3B B.McKechnie
- LF A.Scheer
- CF V.Campbell
- RF B.Kauff
- C B.Rariden
- P C.Falkenberg
- P E.Moseley
- P G.Kaiserling
- P G.Mullin
- P H.Billiard

Kansas City

KCU 1884
KCN 1886
KCa 1888-1889
KCF 1914-1915
KCA 1955-1967
KCA 1969-2000

KC 1884U

- M H.Wheeler
- M M.Porter
- M T.Sullivan
- 1B J.Sweeney
- 2B C.Berry
- SS C.Cross
- 3B P.Sullivan
- LF F.Wyman
- CF B.McLaughlin
- RF F.Shaffer
- C K.Baldwin
- P E.Hickman

KC 1886N

- M D.Rowe
- 1B M.McQuery
- 2B A.Myers
- SS C.Bassett
- 3B J.Donnelly
- LF J.Lillie
- CF D.Rowe
- RF P.Radford
- C F.Briody
- P S.Wiedman
- P J.Whitney

KC 1888a

- M D.Rowe
- M S.Barkley
- M B.Watkins
- 1B B.Phillips
- 2B S.Barkley
- SS H.Easterday
- 3B J.Davis
- LF M.Cline
- CF J.McTamany
- RF B.Hamilton
- C J.Donahue
- P H.Porter
- P T.Sullivan
- P B.Fagan
- P F.Hoffman
- P S.Toole

KC 1889a

- M B.Watkins
- 1B E.Stearns
- 2B S.Barkley
- SS H.Long
- 3B J.Davis
- LF J.Manning
- CF J.Burns
- RF B.Hamilton
- C C.Hoover
- P P.Swartzel
- P J.Conway
- P J.Sowders
- P J.McCarty
- P T.Sullivan

KC 1914F

- M G.Stovall
- 1B G.Stovall
- 2B B.Kenworthy
- SS P.Goodwin
- 3B G.Perring
- LF C.Chadbourne
- CF A.Kruger
- RF G.Gilmore
- C T.Easterly
- P G.Packard
- P N.Cullop
- P D.Stone
- P B.Harris
- P P.Henning

KC 1915F

- M G.Stovall
- 1B G.Stovall
- 2B B.Kenworthy
- SS J.Rawlings
- 3B G.Perring
- LF A.Shaw
- CF C.Chadbourne
- RF G.Gilmore
- C T.Easterly
- P N.Cullop
- P G.Packard
- P C.Johnson
- P A.Main
- P P.Henning

KC 1955A

- M L.Boudreau
- 1B V.Power
- 2B J.Finigan
- SS J.DeMaestri
- 3B H.Lopez
- LF G.Zernial
- CF H.Simpson
- RF E.Slaughter
- C J.Astroth
- UT B.Renna
- UT B.Wilson
- UT E.Valo
- P A.Ditmar
- P A.Kellner
- P B.Shantz
- P A.Ceccarelli
- P A.Portocarrero
- RP T.Gorman
- RP B.Harrington

KC 1956A

- M L.Boudreau
- 1B V.Power
- 2B J.Finigan
- SS J.DeMaestri
- 3B H.Lopez
- LF L.Skizas
- CF J.Groth
- RF H.Simpson
- C T.Thompson
- UT G.Zernial
- P A.Ditmar
- P T.Gorman
- P W.Burnette
- P L.Kretlow
- P T.Herriage
- RP J.Crimian
- RP B.Shantz
- RP J.McMahan

KC 1957A

- M L.Boudreau
- M H.Craft
- 1B V.Power
- 2B B.Hunter
- SS J.DeMaestri
- 3B H.Lopez
- LF G.Zernial
- CF W.Held
- RF L.Skizas
- C H.Smith
- UT B.Cerv
- P N.Garver
- P T.Morgan
- P A.Kellner
- P R.Terry
- P J.Urban
- RP V.Trucks
- RP W.Burnette
- RP M.McDermott

KC 1958A

- M H.Craft
- 1B V.Power
- 2B M.Baxes
- SS J.DeMaestri
- 3B H.Lopez
- LF B.Cerv
- CF B.Tuttle
- RF R.Maris
- C H.Chiti
- UT B.Martyn
- UT H.Smith
- P R.Terry
- P N.Garver
- P R.Herbert
- P J.Urban
- P B.Grim
- RP T.Gorman
- RP D.Tomanek
- RP B.Daley

KC 1959A

- M H.Craft
- 1B K.Hadley
- 2B W.Terwilliger
- SS J.DeMaestri
- 3B D.Williams
- LF B.Cerv
- CF B.Tuttle
- RF R.Maris
- C F.House
- UT J.Lumpe
- UT H.Smith
- P B.Daley
- P N.Garver
- P R.Herbert
- P J.Kucks
- P B.Grim
- RP R.Coleman
- RP T.Sturdivant
- RP M.Dickson

KC 1960A

- M B.Elliott
- 1B M.Throneberry
- 2B J.Lumpe
- SS K.Hamlin
- 3B A.Carey
- LF N.Siebern
- CF B.Tuttle
- RF R.Snyder
- C P.Daley
- UT H.Bauer
- UT D.Williams
- P R.Herbert
- P B.Daley
- P D.Hall
- P N.Garver
- P J.Kucks
- RP K.Johnson
- RP M.Kutyna

KC 1961A

- M J.Gordon
- M H.Bauer
- 1B N.Siebern
- 2B J.Lumpe
- SS D.Howser
- 3B W.Causey
- LF L.Posada
- CF B.Del Greco
- RF D.Johnson
- C H.Sullivan
- P J.Archer
- P N.Bass
- P J.Walker
- P B.Shaw
- P J.Nuxhall
- RP E.Rakow
- RP B.Kunkel
- RP A.Ditmar

KC 1962A

- M H.Bauer
- 1B N.Siebern
- 2B J.Lumpe
- SS D.Howser
- 3B E.Charles
- LF M.Jimenez
- CF B.Del Greco
- RF G.Cimoli
- C H.Sullivan
- UT W.Causey
- UT J.Tartabull
- P E.Rakow
- P D.Pfister
- P J.Walker
- P B.Fischer
- P D.Segui
- RP J.Wyatt
- RP D.McDevitt

KC 1963A

- M E.Lopat
- 1B N.Siebern
- 2B J.Lumpe
- SS W.Causey
- 3B E.Charles
- LF B.Del Greco
- CF J.Tartabull
- RF G.Cimoli
- C D.Edwards
- UT C.Essegian
- P D.Wickersham
- P O.Pena
- P E.Rakow
- P M.Drabowsky
- P D.Segui
- RP T.Bowsfield
- RP B.Fischer
- RP J.Wyatt

KC 1964A

- M E.Lopat
- M M.McGaha
- 1B J.Gentile
- 2B D.Green
- SS W.Causey
- 3B E.Charles
- LF J.Tartabull
- CF N.Mathews
- RF R.Colavito
- C D.Edwards
- UT G.Alusik
- P O.Pena
- P D.Segui
- P J.O'Donoghue
- P M.Drabowsky
- RP J.Wyatt
- RP T.Bowsfield
- RP W.Stock

KC 1965A

- M M.McGaha
- M H.Sullivan
- 1B K.Harrelson
- 2B D.Green
- SS B.Campaneris
- 3B E.Charles
- LF T.Reynolds
- CF J.Landis
- RF M.Hershberger
- C B.Bryan
- UT W.Causey
- P F.Talbot
- P R.Sheldon
- P J.O'Donoghue
- P D.Segui
- P C.Hunter
- RP W.Stock
- RP J.Wyatt
- RP J.Dickson

KC 1966A

- M A.Dark
- 1B K.Harrelson
- 2B D.Green
- SS B.Campaneris
- 3B E.Charles
- LF L.Stahl
- CF J.Nossek
- RF M.Hershberger
- C P.Roof
- UT D.Cater
- UT R.Repoz
- P L.Krausse
- P C.Hunter
- P J.Nash
- P P.Lindblad
- RP J.Aker
- RP K.Sanders

KC 1967A

- M A.Dark
- M L.Appling
- 1B R.Webster
- 2B J.Donaldson
- SS B.Campaneris
- 3B D.Green
- LF J.Gosger
- CF R.Monday
- RF M.Hershberger
- C P.Roof
- UT D.Cater
- P C.Hunter
- P J.Nash
- P C.Dobson
- P L.Krausse
- P B.Odom
- RP P.Lindblad
- RP T.Pierce
- RP J.Aker

KC 1969A

- M J.Gordon
- 1B M.Fiore
- 2B J.Adair
- SS J.Hernandez
- 3B J.Foy
- LF L.Piniella
- CF B.Oliver
- RF P.Kelly
- C E.Rodriguez
- UT E.Kirkpatrick
- P W.Bunker
- P D.Drago
- P B.Butler
- P R.Nelson
- P J.Rooker
- RP M.Drabowsky
- RP T.Burgmeier
- RP D.Wickersham

KC 1970A

- M C.Metro
- M B.Lemon
- 1B B.Oliver
- 2B C.Rojas
- SS J.Hernandez
- 3B P.Schaal
- LF L.Piniella
- CF A.Otis
- RF P.Kelly
- C E.Kirkpatrick
- P D.Drago
- P B.Johnson
- P J.Rooker
- P B.Butler
- P D.Morehead
- RP A.Fitzmorris
- RP T.Burgmeier
- RP T.Abernathy

KC 1971A

- M B.Lemon
- 1B G.Hopkins
- 2B C.Rojas
- SS F.Patek
- 3B P.Schaal
- LF L.Piniella
- CF A.Otis
- RF J.Keough
- C J.May
- UT E.Kirkpatrick
- UT B.Oliver
- P D.Drago
- P M.Hedlund
- P P.Splittorff
- P B.Dal Canton
- P A.Fitzmorris
- RP J.York
- RP T.Burgmeier
- RP T.Abernathy

KC 1972A

- M B.Lemon
- 1B J.Mayberry
- 2B C.Rojas
- SS F.Patek
- 3B P.Schaal
- LF L.Piniella
- CF A.Otis
- RF R.Scheinblum
- C E.Kirkpatrick
- UT S.Hovley
- P D.Drago
- P P.Splittorff
- P R.Nelson
- P B.Dal Canton
- P M.Hedlund
- RP A.Fitzmorris
- RP T.Abernathy
- RP T.Burgmeier

KC 1973A

- M J.McKeon
- 1B J.Mayberry
- 2B C.Rojas
- SS F.Patek
- 3B P.Schaal
- LF L.Piniella
- CF A.Otis
- RF E.Kirkpatrick
- C F.Healy
- DH H.McRae
- UT K.Bevacqua
- UT S.Hovley
- P P.Splittorff
- P S.Busby
- P D.Drago
- P G.Garber
- P B.Dal Canton
- RP D.Bird
- RP S.Mingori

KC 1974A

- M J.McKeon
- 1B J.Mayberry
- 2B C.Rojas
- SS F.Patek
- 3B G.Brett
- LF J.Wohlford

CF A.Otis
RF V.Pinson
C F.Healy
DH H.McRae
UT A.Cowens
UT F.White
P S.Busby
P P.Splittorff
P A.Fitzmorris
P B.Dal Canton
P M.Pattin
RP L.McDaniel
RP D.Bird
RP S.Mingori

KC 1975A

M J.McKeon
M W.Herzog
1B J.Mayberry
2B C.Rojas
SS F.Patek
3B G.Brett
LF H.McRae
CF A.Otis
RF A.Cowens
C B.Martinez
DH H.Killebrew
UT V.Pinson
UT F.White
UT J.Wohlford
P S.Busby
P A.Fitzmorris
P D.Leonard
P M.Pattin
P P.Splittorff
RP D.Bird
RP L.McDaniel
RP S.Mingori

KC 1976A

M W.Herzog
1B J.Mayberry
2B F.White
SS F.Patek
3B G.Brett
LF T.Poquette
CF A.Otis
RF A.Cowens
C B.Martinez
DH H.McRae
UT J.Wohlford
P D.Leonard
P A.Fitzmorris
P D.Bird
P P.Splittorff
P M.Pattin
RP M.Littell
RP S.Mingori

KC 1977A

M W.Herzog
1B J.Mayberry
2B F.White
SS F.Patek
3B G.Brett
LF T.Poquette
CF A.Otis
RF A.Cowens
C D.Porter
DH H.McRae
UT J.Zdeb
P D.Leonard
P J.Colborn
P P.Splittorff
P A.Hassler
P M.Pattin
RP D.Bird
RP L.Gura
RP M.Littell

KC 1978A

M W.Herzog
1B P.LaCock
2B F.White
SS F.Patek
3B G.Brett
LF W.Wilson
CF A.Otis
RF A.Cowens
C D.Porter
DH H.McRae
UT C.Hurdle
P D.Leonard
P P.Splittorff
P L.Gura
P R.Gale
RP D.Bird
RP M.Pattin
RP A.Hrabosky

KC 1979A

M W.Herzog
1B P.LaCock
2B F.White
SS F.Patek
3B G.Brett
LF W.Wilson
CF A.Otis
RF A.Cowens
C D.Porter
DH H.McRae
UT U.Washington
P P.Splittorff
P D.Leonard
P L.Gura
P R.Gale
RP E.Rodriguez
RP A.Hrabosky

KC 1980A

M J.Frey
1B W.Aikens
2B F.White
SS U.Washington
3B G.Brett
LF W.Wilson
CF A.Otis
RF C.Hurdle
C D.Porter
DH H.McRae
UT P.LaCock
UT J.Wathan
P L.Gura
P D.Leonard
P P.Splittorff
P R.Gale
P R.Martin
RP D.Quisenberry
RP M.Pattin

KC 1981A

M J.Frey
M D.Howser
1B W.Aikens
2B F.White
SS U.Washington
3B G.Brett
LF W.Wilson
CF A.Otis
RF C.Geronimo
C J.Wathan
DH H.McRae
P D.Leonard
P L.Gura
P R.Gale
P P.Splittorff
P M.Jones
RP D.Quisenberry
RP R.Martin
RP K.Brett

KC 1982A

M D.Howser
1B W.Aikens
2B F.White
SS U.Washington
3B G.Brett
LF W.Wilson
CF A.Otis
RF J.Martin
C J.Wathan
DH H.McRae
P L.Gura
P V.Blue
P P.Splittorff
P D.Leonard
RP D.Quisenberry
RP M.Armstrong
RP D.Hood

KC 1983A

M D.Howser
1B W.Aikens
2B F.White
SS U.Washington
3B G.Brett
LF W.Wilson
CF A.Otis
RF P.Sheridan
C J.Wathan
DH H.McRae
P L.Gura
P B.Black
P P.Splittorff
P S.Renko
RP D.Quisenberry
RP M.Armstrong

KC 1984A

M D.Howser
1B S.Balboni
2B F.White
SS O.Concepcion
3B G.Pryor
LF D.Motley
CF W.Wilson
RF P.Sheridan
C D.Slaught
DH H.McRae
UT G.Brett
UT J.Orta
UT J.Wathan
P B.Black
P M.Gubicza
P L.Gura
P B.Saberhagen
P C.Leibrandt
RP D.Quisenberry
RP J.Beckwith
RP M.Huismann

KC 1985A

M D.Howser
1B S.Balboni
2B F.White
SS O.Concepcion
3B G.Brett
LF L.Smith
CF W.Wilson
RF D.Motley
C J.Sundberg
DH H.McRae
UT L.Jones
UT J.Orta
P C.Leibrandt
P B.Saberhagen
P D.Jackson
P B.Black
P M.Gubicza
RP D.Quisenberry
RP J.Beckwith
RP M.Jones

KC 1986A

M D.Howser
M M.Ferraro
1B S.Balboni
2B F.White
SS A.Salazar
3B G.Brett
LF L.Smith
CF W.Wilson
RF R.Law
C J.Sundberg
DH J.Orta
UT B.Biancalana
UT H.McRae
P C.Leibrandt
P D.Leonard
P D.Jackson
P M.Gubicza
P B.Saberhagen
RP B.Black
RP S.Farr
RP D.Quisenberry

KC 1987A

M B.Gardner
M J.Wathan
1B G.Brett
2B F.White
SS A.Salazar
3B K.Seitzer
LF B.Jackson
CF W.Wilson
RF D.Tartabull
C J.Quirk
DH S.Balboni
P B.Saberhagen
P M.Gubicza
P C.Leibrandt
P D.Jackson
P B.Black
RP S.Farr
RP J.Gleaton
RP D.Quisenberry

KC 1988A

M J.Wathan
1B G.Brett
2B F.White
SS K.Stillwell
3B K.Seitzer
LF B.Jackson
CF W.Wilson
RF D.Tartabull
C J.Quirk
DH B.Buckner
P M.Gubicza
P B.Saberhagen
P C.Leibrandt
P F.Bannister
RP S.Farr
RP J.Montgomery

KC 1989A

M J.Wathan
1B G.Brett
2B F.White
SS K.Stillwell
3B K.Seitzer
LF B.Jackson
CF W.Wilson
RF J.Eisenreich
C B.Boone
DH D.Tartabull
UT P.Tabler
UT B.Wellman
P B.Saberhagen
P M.Gubicza
P T.Gordon
P C.Leibrandt
P L.Aquino
RP J.Montgomery
RP T.Leach
RP S.Farr

KC 1990A

M J.Wathan
1B G.Brett
2B F.White
SS K.Stillwell
3B K.Seitzer
LF W.Wilson
CF B.Jackson
RF J.Eisenreich
C M.Macfarlane
DH G.Perry
P T.Gordon
P K.Appier
P B.Saberhagen
P S.Davis
RP S.Farr
RP J.Montgomery
RP S.Crawford

KC 1991A

M J.Wathan
M B.Schaefer
M H.McRae
1B T.Benzinger
2B T.Shumpert
SS K.Stillwell
3B B.Pecota
LF J.Eisenreich
CF B.McRae
RF D.Tartabull
C B.Mayne
DH G.Brett
UT K.Gibson
P K.Appier
P B.Saberhagen
P M.Boddicker
P T.Gordon
P L.Aquino
RP S.Davis
RP J.Montgomery
RP M.Davis

KC 1992A

M H.McRae
1B W.Joyner
2B K.Miller
SS D.Howard
3B G.Jefferies
LF K.McReynolds
CF B.McRae
RF J.Eisenreich
C M.Macfarlane
DH G.Brett
UT C.Wilkerson
P K.Appier
P H.Pichardo
P M.Gubicza
P R.Reed
RP T.Gordon
RP R.Meacham
RP M.Magnante

KC 1993A

M H.McRae
1B W.Joyner
2B J.Lind
SS G.Gagne
3B G.Gaetti
LF K.McReynolds
CF B.McRae
RF F.Jose
C M.Macfarlane
DH G.Brett
UT C.Gwynn
P D.Cone
P K.Appier
P H.Pichardo
P T.Gordon
P C.Haney
RP M.Gubicza
RP J.Montgomery

KC 1994A

M H.McRae
1B W.Joyner
2B J.Lind
SS G.Gagne
3B G.Gaetti
LF V.Coleman
CF B.McRae
RF F.Jose
C M.Macfarlane
DH B.Hamelin
P D.Cone
P T.Gordon
P K.Appier
P M.Gubicza
RP H.Pichardo
RP R.Meacham
RP S.Belinda

KC 1995A

M B.Boone
1B W.Joyner
2B K.Lockhart
SS G.Gagne
3B G.Gaetti
LF V.Coleman
CF T.Goodwin
RF J.Nunnally
C B.Mayne
DH B.Hamelin
UT D.Howard
P M.Gubicza
P K.Appier
P T.Gordon
RP J.Montgomery
RP H.Pichardo
RP R.Meacham

KC 1996A

M B.Boone
1B J.Offerman
2B K.Lockhart
SS D.Howard
3B J.Randa
LF T.Goodwin
CF J.Damon
RF M.Tucker
C M.Macfarlane
DH J.Vitiello
UT C.Paquette
P T.Belcher
P C.Haney
P K.Appier
P M.Gubicza
P J.Rosado
RP H.Pichardo
RP J.Montgomery
RP J.Valera

KC 1997A

M B.Boone
M T.Muser
1B J.King
2B J.Offerman
SS J.Bell
3B C.Paquette
LF B.Roberts
CF T.Goodwin
RF J.Damon
C M.Macfarlane
DH C.Davis
P K.Appier
P T.Belcher
P J.Rosado
P G.Rusch
P J.Pittsley
RP J.Montgomery
RP H.Pichardo

KC 1998A

M T.Muser
1B J.King
2B J.Offerman
SS M.Lopez
3B D.Palmer
LF J.Conine
CF J.Damon
RF L.Sutton
C M.Sweeney
DH T.Pendleton
UT H.Morris
P T.Belcher
P P.Rapp
P J.Rosado
P G.Rusch
P H.Pichardo
RP C.Haney
RP S.Service
RP J.Pittsley

KC 1999A

M T.Muser
1B M.Sweeney
2B C.Febles
SS R.Sanchez
3B J.Randa
LF J.Damon
CF C.Beltran
RF J.Dye
C C.Kreuter
DH J.Giambi
P J.Suppan
P J.Rosado
P J.Witasick
P K.Appier
RP S.Service
RP A.Morman
RP J.Montgomery

KC 2000A

M T.Muser
1B M.Sweeney
2B C.Febles
SS R.Sanchez
3B J.Randa
LF J.Damon
CF C.Beltran
RF J.Dye
C G.Zaun
DH M.Quinn
UT D.McCarty
P J.Suppan
P M.Suzuki
P D.Reichert
P B.Stein
RP J.Spradlin
RP R.Bottalico
RP J.Santiago

Keokuk

WES n 1875

WES 1875n

M J.Simmons
1B J.Carbine
2B J.Miller
SS J.Hallinan
3B W.Goldsmith
LF C.Jones
CF J.Simmons
RF B.Riley
C P.Quinn
UT B.Barnie
P M.Golden

Los Angeles

LAA 1961-1964
LAN 1958-2000

LA 1961A

M B.Rigney
1B S.Bilko
2B K.Aspromonte
SS J.Koppe
3B E.Yost
LF L.Wagner
CF K.Hunt
RF A.Pearson
C E.Averill
UT T.Kluszewski
UT L.Thomas
P K.McBride
P E.Grba
P T.Bowsfield
P R.Moeller
P R.Kline
RP J.Donohue
RP R.Duren
RP T.Morgan

LA 1962A

M B.Rigney
1B L.Thomas
2B B.Moran
SS J.Koppe
3B F.Torres
LF L.Wagner
CF A.Pearson
RF G.Thomas
C B.Rodgers
P D.Chance
P B.Belinsky
P E.Grba
P D.Lee
P K.McBride
RP A.Fowler
RP R.Duren
RP J.Spring

LA 1963A

M B.Rigney
1B L.Thomas
2B B.Moran
SS J.Fregosi
3B F.Torres
LF L.Wagner
CF A.Pearson
RF B.Perry
C B.Rodgers
P K.McBride
P D.Chance
P D.Osinski
P D.Lee
RP J.Navarro
RP A.Fowler
RP P.Foytack

LA 1964A

M B.Rigney
1B J.Adcock
2B B.Knoop
SS J.Fregosi
3B F.Torres
LF W.Smith
CF J.Piersall
RF L.Clinton
C B.Rodgers
UT A.Pearson
UT T.Satriano
P D.Chance
P F.Newman
P B.Latman
P B.Belinsky
P K.McBride
RP B.Lee
RP D.Osinski
RP D.Lee

LA 1958N

M W.Alston
1B G.Hodges
2B C.Neal
SS D.Zimmer
3B D.Gray
LF J.Gilliam
CF G.Cimoli
RF C.Furillo
C J.Roseboro
UT D.Snider
UT N.Larker
P D.Drysdale
P J.Podres
P S.Koufax
P S.Williams
P C.Erskine
RP C.Labine
RP F.Kipp
RP J.Klippstein

LA 1959N

M W.Alston
1B G.Hodges
2B C.Neal
SS D.Zimmer
3B J.Gilliam
LF W.Moon
CF D.Demeter
RF D.Snider
C J.Roseboro
UT R.Fairly
UT N.Larker
P D.Drysdale
P J.Podres
P S.Koufax
P R.Craig
P D.McDevitt
RP C.Labine
RP A.Fowler

LA 1960N

M W.Alston
1B N.Larker
2B C.Neal
SS M.Wills
3B J.Gilliam
LF W.Moon
CF T.Davis
RF F.Howard
C J.Roseboro
UT G.Hodges
UT D.Snider

P D.Drysdale
P J.Podres
P S.Williams
P S.Koufax
P R.Craig
RP L.Sherry
RP E.Roebuck
RP D.McDevitt

LA 1961N

M W.Alston
1B G.Hodges
2B C.Neal
SS M.Wills
3B J.Gilliam
LF W.Moon
CF W.Davis
RF T.Davis
C J.Roseboro
UT R.Fairly
UT N.Larker
P S.Koufax
P D.Drysdale
P S.Williams
P J.Podres
RP R.Craig
RP L.Sherry
RP R.Perranoski

LA 1962N

M W.Alston
1B R.Fairly
2B L.Burright
SS M.Wills
3B J.Gilliam
LF T.Davis
CF W.Davis
RF F.Howard
C J.Roseboro
P D.Drysdale
P J.Podres
P S.Williams
P S.Koufax
RP E.Roebuck
RP R.Perranoski
RP L.Sherry

LA 1963N

M W.Alston
1B R.Fairly
2B J.Gilliam
SS M.Wills
3B K.McMullen
LF T.Davis
CF W.Davis
RF F.Howard
C J.Roseboro
UT W.Moon
UT D.Tracewski
P D.Drysdale
P S.Koufax
P J.Podres
P B.Miller
RP R.Perranoski
RP L.Sherry

LA 1964N

M W.Alston
1B R.Fairly
2B N.Oliver
SS M.Wills
3B J.Gilliam
LF T.Davis
CF W.Davis
RF F.Howard
C J.Roseboro
UT W.Parker
UT D.Tracewski
P D.Drysdale
P S.Koufax
P P.Ortega
P J.Moeller
RP B.Miller
RP R.Perranoski
RP J.Brewer

LA 1965N

M W.Alston
1B W.Parker
2B J.Lefebvre
SS M.Wills
3B J.Kennedy
LF L.Johnson
CF W.Davis
RF R.Fairly
C J.Roseboro
UT J.Gilliam
P S.Koufax
P D.Drysdale
P C.Osteen
P J.Podres
RP R.Perranoski
RP B.Miller
RP H.Reed

LA 1966N

M W.Alston
1B W.Parker
2B J.Lefebvre
SS M.Wills
3B J.Kennedy
LF L.Johnson
CF W.Davis
RF R.Fairly
C J.Roseboro
UT T.Davis
P S.Koufax
P D.Drysdale
P C.Osteen
P D.Sutton
RP P.Regan
RP B.Miller
RP R.Perranoski

LA 1967N

M W.Alston
1B W.Parker
2B R.Hunt
SS G.Michael
3B J.Lefebvre
LF L.Johnson
CF W.Davis
RF R.Fairly
C J.Roseboro
UT B.Bailey
UT A.Ferrara
P C.Osteen
P D.Drysdale
P D.Sutton
P B.Singer
P J.Brewer
RP R.Perranoski
RP P.Regan
RP B.Miller

LA 1968N

M W.Alston
1B W.Parker
2B P.Popovich
SS Z.Versalles
3B B.Bailey
LF L.Gabrielson
CF W.Davis
RF R.Fairly
C T.Haller
UT J.Fairey
P B.Singer
P C.Osteen
P D.Drysdale
P D.Sutton
P M.Kekich
RP M.Grant
RP J.Brewer
RP J.Billingham

LA 1969N

M W.Alston
1B W.Parker
2B T.Sizemore
SS M.Wills
3B B.Sudakis
LF W.Crawford
CF W.Davis
RF A.Kosco
C T.Haller
UT B.Russell
P C.Osteen
P B.Singer
P D.Sutton
P A.Foster
RP J.Brewer
RP P.Mikkelsen
RP J.Moeller

LA 1970N

M W.Alston
1B W.Parker
2B T.Sizemore
SS M.Wills
3B B.Grabarkewitz
LF M.Mota
CF W.Davis
RF W.Crawford
C T.Haller
UT J.Lefebvre
P D.Sutton
P C.Osteen
P A.Foster
P J.Moeller
P S.Vance
RP J.Brewer
RP F.Norman
RP P.Mikkelsen

LA 1971N

M W.Alston
1B W.Parker
2B J.Lefebvre
SS M.Wills
3B S.Garvey
LF D.Allen
CF W.Davis
RF B.Buckner
C D.Sims
UT W.Crawford
UT B.Valentine
P D.Sutton
P A.Downing
P C.Osteen
P B.Singer
RP J.Brewer
RP P.Mikkelsen
RP J.Moeller

LA 1972N

M W.Alston
1B W.Parker
2B L.Lacy
SS B.Russell
3B S.Garvey
LF M.Mota
CF W.Davis
RF F.Robinson
C C.Cannizzaro
UT B.Buckner
UT W.Crawford
UT B.Valentine
P D.Sutton
P C.Osteen
P A.Downing
P T.John
P B.Singer
RP J.Brewer
RP P.Mikkelsen
RP P.Richert

LA 1973N

M W.Alston
1B B.Buckner
2B D.Lopes
SS B.Russell
3B R.Cey
LF M.Mota
CF W.Davis
RF W.Crawford
C J.Ferguson
UT S.Garvey
P D.Sutton
P A.Messersmith
P C.Osteen
P T.John
P A.Downing
RP C.Hough
RP J.Brewer
RP D.Rau

LA 1974N

M W.Alston
1B S.Garvey
2B D.Lopes
SS B.Russell
3B R.Cey
LF B.Buckner
CF J.Wynn
RF W.Crawford
C S.Yeager
UT J.Ferguson
P A.Messersmith
P D.Sutton
P D.Rau
P T.John
P A.Downing
RP M.Marshall
RP C.Hough

LA 1975N

M W.Alston
1B S.Garvey
2B D.Lopes
SS B.Russell
3B R.Cey
LF B.Buckner
CF J.Wynn
RF W.Crawford
C S.Yeager
UT L.Lacy
P A.Messersmith
P D.Rau
P D.Sutton
P B.Hooton
P R.Rhoden
RP M.Marshall
RP C.Hough

LA 1976N

M W.Alston
M T.Lasorda
1B S.Garvey
2B D.Lopes
SS B.Russell
3B R.Cey
LF B.Buckner
CF D.Baker
RF R.Smith
C S.Yeager
P D.Sutton
P D.Rau
P B.Hooton
P T.John
P R.Rhoden
RP C.Hough
RP M.Marshall
RP S.Wall

LA 1977N

M T.Lasorda
1B S.Garvey
2B D.Lopes
SS B.Russell
3B R.Cey
LF D.Baker
CF R.Monday
RF R.Smith
C S.Yeager
P D.Sutton
P B.Hooton
P T.John
P R.Rhoden
P D.Rau
RP C.Hough
RP E.Sosa
RP M.Garman

LA 1978N

M T.Lasorda
1B S.Garvey
2B D.Lopes
SS B.Russell
3B R.Cey
LF D.Baker
CF B.North
RF R.Smith
C S.Yeager
UT L.Lacy
UT R.Monday
P D.Sutton
P B.Hooton
P T.John
P D.Rau
P R.Rhoden
RP C.Hough
RP T.Forster
RP L.Rautzhan

LA 1979N

M T.Lasorda
1B S.Garvey
2B D.Lopes
SS B.Russell
3B R.Cey
LF D.Baker
CF D.Thomas
RF G.Thomasson
C S.Yeager
UT J.Ferguson
P R.Sutcliffe
P D.Sutton
P B.Hooton
P J.Reuss
P C.Hough
RP D.Patterson

LA 1980N

M T.Lasorda
1B S.Garvey
2B D.Lopes
SS B.Russell
3B R.Cey
LF D.Baker
CF R.Law
RF R.Smith
C S.Yeager
UT J.Johnstone
UT D.Thomas
P J.Reuss
P B.Welch
P D.Sutton
P B.Hooton
P D.Goltz
RP R.Sutcliffe
RP B.Castillo
RP S.Howe

LA 1981N

M T.Lasorda
1B S.Garvey
2B D.Lopes
SS B.Russell
3B R.Cey
LF D.Baker
CF K.Landreaux
RF P.Guerrero
C M.Scioscia
UT D.Thomas
P F.Valenzuela
P J.Reuss
P B.Hooton
P B.Welch
RP D.Goltz
RP S.Howe
RP B.Castillo

LA 1982N

M T.Lasorda
1B S.Garvey
2B S.Sax
SS B.Russell
3B R.Cey
LF D.Baker
CF K.Landreaux
RF P.Guerrero
C M.Scioscia
UT R.Monday
UT R.Roenicke
P F.Valenzuela
P J.Reuss
P B.Welch
P D.Stewart
P B.Hooton
RP S.Howe
RP T.Forster
RP T.Niedenfuer

LA 1983N

M T.Lasorda
1B G.Brock
2B S.Sax
SS B.Russell
3B P.Guerrero
LF D.Baker
CF K.Landreaux
RF M.Marshall
C S.Yeager
UT D.Thomas
P F.Valenzuela
P J.Reuss
P B.Welch
P A.Pena
P B.Hooton
RP T.Niedenfuer
RP D.Stewart
RP J.Beckwith

LA 1984N

M T.Lasorda
1B G.Brock
2B S.Sax
SS D.Anderson
3B G.Rivera
LF M.Marshall
CF K.Landreaux
RF C.Maldonado
C M.Scioscia
UT P.Guerrero
P F.Valenzuela
P A.Pena
P O.Hershiser
P R.Honeycutt
P B.Welch
RP B.Hooton
RP P.Zachry
RP K.Howell

LA 1985N

M T.Lasorda
1B G.Brock
2B S.Sax
SS M.Duncan
3B D.Anderson
LF C.Maldonado
CF K.Landreaux
RF M.Marshall
C M.Scioscia
UT P.Guerrero
P F.Valenzuela
P O.Hershiser
P J.Reuss
P B.Welch
P R.Honeycutt
RP T.Niedenfuer
RP K.Howell
RP C.Diaz

LA 1986N

M T.Lasorda
1B G.Brock
2B S.Sax
SS M.Duncan
3B B.Madlock
LF F.Stubbs
CF R.Williams
RF M.Marshall
C M.Scioscia
UT E.Cabell
UT K.Landreaux
UT B.Russell
P F.Valenzuela
P B.Welch
P O.Hershiser
P R.Honeycutt
RP K.Howell
RP T.Niedenfuer
RP E.Vande Berg

LA 1987N

M T.Lasorda
1B F.Stubbs
2B S.Sax
SS M.Duncan
3B M.Hatcher
LF P.Guerrero
CF J.Shelby
RF M.Marshall
C M.Scioscia
UT D.Anderson
UT K.Landreaux
P O.Hershiser
P B.Welch
P F.Valenzuela
P R.Honeycutt
RP T.Leary
RP A.Pena
RP B.Holton

LA 1988N

M T.Lasorda
1B F.Stubbs
2B S.Sax
SS A.Griffin
3B J.Hamilton
LF K.Gibson
CF J.Shelby
RF M.Marshall
C M.Scioscia
UT D.Anderson
UT M.Davis
P O.Hershiser
P T.Leary
P T.Belcher
P F.Valenzuela
RP A.Pena
RP B.Holton
RP T.Crews

LA 1989N

M T.Lasorda
1B E.Murray
2B W.Randolph
SS A.Griffin
3B J.Hamilton
LF K.Gibson
CF J.Shelby
RF M.Marshall
C M.Scioscia
P O.Hershiser
P T.Belcher
P F.Valenzuela
P M.Morgan
P T.Leary
RP J.Howell
RP A.Pena
RP T.Crews

LA 1990N

M T.Lasorda
1B E.Murray
2B J.Samuel
SS A.Griffin
3B M.Sharperson
LF K.Daniels
CF S.Javier
RF H.Brooks
C M.Scioscia
UT J.Gonzalez
UT C.Gwynn
UT L.Harris
P R.Martinez
P M.Morgan
P F.Valenzuela
P T.Belcher
RP T.Crews
RP M.Hartley
RP J.Howell

LA 1991N

M T.Lasorda
1B E.Murray
2B J.Samuel
SS A.Griffin
3B L.Harris
LF K.Daniels
CF B.Butler
RF D.Strawberry
C M.Scioscia
UT G.Carter
UT S.Javier
UT M.Sharperson
P M.Morgan
P R.Martinez
P T.Belcher
P B.Ojeda
P O.Hershiser
RP K.Gross
RP J.Gott
RP T.Crews

LA 1992N

M T.Lasorda
1B E.Karros
2B L.Harris
SS J.Offerman
3B D.Hansen
LF E.Davis
CF B.Butler
RF M.Webster
C M.Scioscia
UT T.Benzinger
UT M.Sharperson
P O.Hershiser
P K.Gross
P T.Candiotti
P B.Ojeda
P R.Martinez
RP J.Gott
RP R.McDowell
RP T.Crews

LA 1993N

M T.Lasorda
1B E.Karros
2B J.Reed
SS J.Offerman
3B T.Wallach
LF E.Davis
CF B.Butler
RF C.Snyder
C M.Piazza
UT L.Harris
P O.Hershiser
P T.Candiotti
P R.Martinez
P K.Gross
P P.Astacio
RP P.Martinez
RP J.Gott
RP R.McDowell

LA 1994N

M T.Lasorda
1B E.Karros
2B D.DeShields
SS J.Offerman
3B T.Wallach
LF H.Rodriguez
CF B.Butler
RF R.Mondesi
C M.Piazza
UT C.Snyder
UT M.Webster
P R.Martinez
P K.Gross
P T.Candiotti
P P.Astacio
P O.Hershiser
RP T.Worrell
RP R.McDowell
RP J.Gott

LA 1995N

M T.Lasorda
1B E.Karros
2B D.DeShields
SS J.Offerman
3B T.Wallach
LF B.Ashley
CF R.Kelly
RF R.Mondesi
C M.Piazza
UT C.Fonville
UT D.Hansen
P R.Martinez
P I.Valdes
P H.Nomo
P T.Candiotti
RP P.Astacio

RP T.Worrell
RP A.Osuna

LA 1996N
M T.Lasorda
M B.Russell
1B E.Karros
2B D.DeShields
SS G.Gagne
3B M.Blowers
LF T.Hollandsworth
CF R.Cedeno
RF R.Mondesi
C M.Piazza
UT C.Fonville
P H.Nomo
P I.Valdes
P P.Astacio
P R.Martinez
P T.Candiotti
RP C.Park
RP A.Osuna
RP M.Guthrie

LA 1997N
M B.Russell
1B E.Karros
2B W.Guerrero
SS G.Gagne
3B T.Zeile
LF T.Hollandsworth
CF B.Butler
RF R.Mondesi
C M.Piazza
P H.Nomo
P I.Valdes
P C.Park
P P.Astacio
P T.Candiotti
RP M.Guthrie
RP D.Dreifort
RP S.Radinsky

LA 1998N
M B.Russell
M G.Hoffman
1B E.Karros
2B E.Young
SS J.Vizcaino
3B A.Beltre
LF T.Hubbard
CF R.Mondesi
RF G.Sheffield
C C.Johnson
UT R.Cedeno
P C.Park
P D.Dreifort
P I.Valdes
P D.Mlicki
P R.Martinez
RP A.Osuna
RP S.Radinsky
RP M.Guthrie

LA 1999N
M D.Johnson
1B E.Karros
2B E.Young
SS M.Grudzielanek
3B A.Beltre
LF G.Sheffield
CF D.White
RF R.Mondesi
C T.Hundley
UT D.Hansen
P K.Brown
P I.Valdes
P C.Park
P D.Dreifort
RP A.Mills
RP J.Arnold
RP J.Shaw

LA 2000N
M D.Johnson
1B E.Karros
2B M.Grudzielanek
SS A.Cora
3B A.Beltre
LF G.Sheffield
CF T.Hollandsworth
RF S.Green
C T.Hundley
UT D.Hansen
P K.Brown
P C.Park
P D.Dreifort
P C.Perez
P E.Gagne
RP M.Herges
RP T.Adams
RP A.Osuna

Louisville

LOU N 1876-1877
LOU a 1882-1891
LOU N 1892-1899

LOU 1876N
M J.Chapman
1B J.Gerhardt
2B E.Somerville
SS C.Fulmer
3B B.Hague
LF J.Ryan
CF S.Hastings
RF A.Allison
C P.Snyder
P J.Devlin

LOU 1877N
M J.Chapman
1B J.Latham
2B J.Gerhardt
SS B.Craver
3B B.Hague
LF G.Hall
CF B.Crowley
RF O.Shaffer
C P.Snyder
P J.Devlin

LOU 1882a
M D.Mack
1B G.Hecker
2B P.Browning
SS D.Mack
3B B.Schenck
LF L.Maskrey
CF J.Reccius
RF J.Wolf
C D.Sullivan
P T.Mullane

LOU 1883a
M J.Gerhardt
1B J.Latham
2B J.Gerhardt
SS J.Leary
3B J.Gleason
LF P.Browning
CF L.Maskrey
RF J.Wolf
C E.Whiting
P G.Hecker
P S.Weaver

LOU 1884a
M M.Walsh
1B J.Latham
2B J.Gerhardt
SS T.McLaughlin
3B P.Browning
LF L.Maskrey
CF M.Cline
RF J.Wolf
C D.Sullivan
UT P.Reccius
P G.Hecker
P D.Driscoll
P R.Deagle

LOU 1885a
M J.Hart
1B J.Kerins
2B T.McLaughlin
SS J.Miller
3B P.Reccius
LF L.Maskrey
CF P.Browning
RF J.Wolf
C J.Crotty
P G.Hecker
P N.Baker
P A.Mays
P T.Ramsey

LOU 1886a
M J.Hart
1B J.Kerins
2B R.Mack
SS B.White
3B J.Werrick
LF J.Strauss
CF P.Browning
RF J.Wolf
C A.Cross
P T.Ramsey
P G.Hecker

LOU 1887a
M J.Kelly
1B J.Kerins
2B R.Mack
SS B.White
3B J.Werrick
LF H.Collins
CF P.Browning
RF J.Wolf
C P.Cook
UT G.Hecker
P T.Ramsey
P E.Chamberlain

LOU 1888a
M J.Kelly
M M.Davidson
M J.Kerins
M M.Davidson
1B S.Smith
2B R.Mack
SS B.White
3B J.Werrick
LF H.Collins
CF P.Browning
RF J.Wolf
C P.Cook
P T.Ramsey
P E.Chamberlain
P J.Ewing

LOU 1889a
M D.Esterbrook
M C.Wolf
M D.Shannon
M J.Chapman
1B G.Hecker
2B D.Shannon
SS P.Tomney
3B H.Raymond
LF P.Browning
CF F.Weaver
RF J.Wolf
C P.Cook
UT F.Vaughn
P R.Ehret
P J.Ewing
P T.Ramsey
P M.McDermott

LOU 1890a
M J.Chapman
1B H.Taylor
2B T.Shinnick
SS P.Tomney
3B H.Raymond
LF C.Hamburg
CF F.Weaver
RF J.Wolf
C J.Ryan
P S.Stratton
P R.Ehret
P G.Meakim
P H.Goodall
P E.Daily

LOU 1891a
M J.Chapman
1B H.Taylor
2B T.Shinnick
SS H.Jennings
3B O.Beard
LF P.Donovan
CF F.Weaver
RF J.Wolf
C J.Ryan
UT T.Cahill
P W.Fitzgerald
P J.Meekin
P R.Ehret
P S.Stratton
P J.Doran

LOU 1892N
M J.Chapman
M F.Pfeffer
1B L.Whistler
2B F.Pfeffer
SS H.Jennings
3B B.Kuehne
LF F.Weaver
CF T.Brown
RF H.Taylor
C J.Grim
P S.Stratton
P B.Sanders
P F.Clausen
P J.Meekin
P A.Jones

LOU 1893N
M B.Barnie
1B W.Brown
2B F.Pfeffer
SS T.O'Rourke
3B G.Pinkney
LF P.Browning
CF T.Brown
RF F.Weaver
C J.Grim
P G.Hemming
P S.Stratton
P B.Rhodes
P J.Menefee

LOU 1894N
M B.Barnie
1B L.Lutenberg
2B F.Pfeffer
SS D.Richardson
3B J.Denny
LF F.Clarke
CF T.Brown
RF O.Smith
C J.Grim
P G.Hemming
P P.Knell
P J.Menefee
P J.Wadsworth

LOU 1895N
M J.McCloskey
1B H.Spies
2B J.O'Brien
SS F.Shugart
3B J.Collins
LF F.Clarke
CF J.Wright
RF T.Gettinger
C J.Warner
P B.Cunningham
P G.Weyhing
P M.McDermott
P B.Inks

LOU 1896N
M J.McCloskey
M B.McGunnigle
1B J.Rogers
2B J.O'Brien
SS J.Dolan
3B B.Clingman
LF F.Clarke
CF C.Dexter
RF T.McCreery
C D.Miller
P C.Fraser
P B.Hill
P B.Cunningham
P A.Herman

LOU 1897N
M J.Rogers
M F.Clarke
1B P.Werden
2B J.Rogers
SS G.Stafford
3B B.Clingman
LF F.Clarke
CF O.Pickering
RF T.McCreery
C B.Wilson
P C.Fraser
P B.Cunningham
P B.Hill
P B.Magee

LOU 1898N
M F.Clarke
1B H.Wagner
2B H.Smith
SS C.Ritchey
3B B.Clingman
LF F.Clarke
CF D.Hoy
RF C.Dexter
C M.Kittridge
P B.Cunningham
P B.Magee
P P.Dowling
P C.Fraser

LOU 1899N
M F.Clarke
1B M.Kelley
2B C.Ritchey
SS B.Clingman
3B T.Leach
LF F.Clarke
CF D.Hoy
RF C.Dexter
C C.Zimmer
UT H.Wagner
P B.Cunningham
P D.Phillippe
P P.Dowling
P W.Woods

Middletown

MAN n 1872

MAN 1872n
M J.Clapp
1B T.Murnane
2B E.Booth
SS J.O'Rourke
3B G.Fields
LF J.Tipper
CF F.McCarton
RF C.Bentley
C J.Clapp
UT H.Allen
P C.Bentley
P F.Buttery

Milwaukee

MIL N 1878
MIL U 1884
MIL a 1891
MIL A 1901
MIL N 1953-1965
MIL A 1970-1997
MIL N 1998-2000

MIL 1878N
M J.Chapman
1B J.Goodman
2B J.Peters
SS B.Redmon
3B W.Foley
LF A.Dalrymple
CF M.Golden
RF B.Holbert
C C.Bennett
UT G.Creamer
P S.Weaver

MIL 1884U
M T.Loftus
1B T.Griffin
2B A.Myers
SS T.Sexton
3B T.Morrissey
LF S.Behel
CF L.Baldwin
RF E.Hogan
C C.Broughton
P H.Porter
P E.Cushman

MIL 1891a
M C.Cushman
1B J.Carney
2B J.Canavan
SS G.Shoch
3B G.Alberts
LF A.Dalrymple
CF E.Burke
RF H.Earl
C F.Vaughn
UT J.Grim
P G.Davies
P F.Killen
P F.Dwyer

MIL 1901A
M H.Duffy
1B J.Anderson
2B B.Gilbert
SS W.Conroy
3B J.Burke
LF B.Hallman
CF H.Duffy
RF I.Waldron
C B.Maloney
UT B.Friel
P B.Reidy
P N.Garvin
P B.Husting
P T.Sparks
P P.Hawley

MIL 1953N
M C.Grimm
1B J.Adcock
2B J.Dittmer
SS J.Logan
3B E.Mathews
LF S.Gordon
CF B.Bruton
RF A.Pafko
C D.Crandall
UT J.Pendleton
P W.Spahn
P L.Burdette
P J.Antonelli
P M.Surkont
P B.Buhl
RP E.Johnson
RP V.Bickford

MIL 1954N
M C.Grimm
1B J.Adcock
2B D.O'Connell
SS J.Logan
3B E.Mathews
LF H.Aaron
CF B.Bruton
RF A.Pafko
C D.Crandall
P W.Spahn
P L.Burdette
P G.Conley
P J.Wilson
P C.Nichols
RP D.Jolly
RP E.Johnson
RP R.Crone

MIL 1955N
M C.Grimm
1B G.Crowe
2B D.O'Connell
SS J.Logan
3B E.Mathews
LF B.Thomson
CF B.Bruton
RF H.Aaron
C D.Crandall
UT C.Tanner
P W.Spahn
P L.Burdette
P B.Buhl
P G.Conley
P C.Nichols
RP E.Johnson
RP D.Jolly

MIL 1956N
M C.Grimm
M F.Haney
1B J.Adcock
2B D.O'Connell
SS J.Logan
3B E.Mathews
LF B.Thomson
CF B.Bruton
RF H.Aaron
C D.Crandall
UT F.Torre
P W.Spahn
P L.Burdette
P B.Buhl
P R.Crone
P G.Conley
RP B.Trowbridge
RP E.Johnson

MIL 1957N
M F.Haney
1B F.Torre
2B R.Schoendienst
SS J.Logan
3B E.Mathews
LF W.Covington
CF B.Bruton
RF H.Aaron
C D.Crandall
P W.Spahn
P L.Burdette
P B.Buhl
P G.Conley
P B.Trowbridge
RP T.Phillips
RP E.Johnson
RP D.McMahon

MIL 1958N
M F.Haney
1B F.Torre
2B R.Schoendienst
SS J.Logan
3B E.Mathews
LF A.Pafko
CF B.Bruton
RF H.Aaron
C D.Crandall
UT J.Adcock
P W.Spahn
P L.Burdette
P B.Rush
P C.Willey
P J.Pizarro
RP G.Conley
RP D.McMahon
RP B.Trowbridge

MIL 1959N
M F.Haney
1B J.Adcock
2B F.Mantilla
SS J.Logan
3B E.Mathews
LF W.Covington
CF B.Bruton
RF H.Aaron
C D.Crandall
UT F.Torre
P W.Spahn
P L.Burdette
P B.Buhl
P J.Jay
P J.Pizarro
RP D.McMahon

MIL 1960N
M C.Dressen
1B J.Adcock
2B C.Cottier
SS J.Logan
3B E.Mathews
LF A.Spangler
CF B.Bruton
RF H.Aaron
C D.Crandall
UT W.Covington
P L.Burdette
P W.Spahn
P B.Buhl
P C.Willey
P J.Jay
RP D.McMahon
RP G.Brunet
RP R.Piche

MIL 1961N
M C.Dressen
M B.Tebbetts
1B J.Adcock
2B F.Bolling
SS R.McMillan
3B E.Mathews
LF F.Thomas
CF H.Aaron
RF L.Maye
C J.Torre
P L.Burdette
P W.Spahn
P B.Buhl
P C.Willey
P D.Nottebart
RP D.McMahon

MIL 1962N
M B.Tebbetts
1B J.Adcock
2B F.Bolling
SS R.McMillan
3B E.Mathews
LF L.Maye
CF H.Aaron
RF M.Jones
C D.Crandall
UT T.Aaron
P W.Spahn
P B.Shaw
P B.Hendley
P L.Burdette
P T.Cloninger
RP J.Curtis
RP C.Willey
RP D.Nottebart

MIL 1963N
M B.Bragan
1B G.Oliver
2B F.Bolling
SS R.McMillan
3B E.Mathews
LF L.Maye
CF M.Jones
RF H.Aaron

C J.Torre
UT D.Menke
P W.Spahn
P D.Lemaster
P B.Hendley
P B.Shaw
P T.Cloninger
RP H.Fischer
RP C.Raymond
RP R.Piche

MIL 1964N

M B.Bragan
1B G.Oliver
2B F.Bolling
SS D.Menke
3B E.Mathews
LF R.Carty
CF L.Maye
RF H.Aaron
C J.Torre
UT F.Alou
UT T.Cline
P T.Cloninger
P D.Lemaster
P W.Spahn
P H.Fischer
P B.Sadowski
RP B.Tiefenauer
RP B.Hoeft
RP C.Olivo

MIL 1965N

M B.Bragan
1B F.Alou
2B F.Bolling
SS W.Woodward
3B E.Mathews
LF R.Carty
CF M.Jones
RF H.Aaron
C J.Torre
UT G.Oliver
UT T.Cline
P T.Cloninger
P W.Blasingame
P K.Johnson
P D.Lemaster
P B.Sadowski
RP B.O'Dell
RP D.Osinski
RP P.Niekro

MIL 1970A

M D.Bristol
1B M.Hegan
2B T.Kubiak
SS R.Pena
3B T.Harper
LF D.Walton
CF D.May
RF R.Snyder
C P.Roof
UT J.McNertney
UT T.Savage
P M.Pattin
P L.Krausse
P S.Lockwood
P B.Bolin
P G.Brabender
RP K.Sanders
RP J.Gelnar

MIL 1971A

M D.Bristol
1B J.Briggs
2B R.Theobald
SS R.Auerbach
3B T.Matchick
LF T.Harper
CF D.May
RF B.Voss
C E.Rodriguez
UT A.Kosco
UT R.Pena
P M.Pattin
P B.Parsons
P S.Lockwood
P L.Krausse
P J.Slaton
RP K.Sanders
RP J.Morris
RP M.Lopez

MIL 1972A

M D.Bristol
M R.McMillan
M D.Crandall
1B G.Scott
2B R.Theobald
SS R.Auerbach
3B M.Ferraro
LF J.Briggs
CF D.May
RF J.Lahoud
C E.Rodriguez
UT B.Heise
P J.Lonborg
P B.Parsons
P S.Lockwood
P J.Colborn
P K.Brett
RP K.Sanders
RP E.Stephenson
RP F.Linzy

MIL 1973A

M D.Crandall
1B G.Scott
2B P.Garcia
SS T.Johnson
3B D.Money
LF J.Briggs
CF D.May
RF B.Coluccio
C D.Porter
DH O.Brown
P J.Colborn
P J.Slaton
P J.Bell
P S.Lockwood
P B.Champion
RP E.Rodriguez
RP C.Short
RP F.Linzy

MIL 1974A

M D.Crandall
1B G.Scott
2B P.Garcia
SS R.Yount
3B D.Money
LF J.Briggs
CF B.Coluccio
RF D.May
C D.Porter
DH B.Mitchell
UT K.Berry
P J.Slaton
P C.Wright
P J.Colborn
P K.Kobel
P B.Champion
RP T.Murphy
RP E.Rodriguez
RP B.Travers

MIL 1975A

M D.Crandall
M H.Kuenn
1B G.Scott
2B P.Garcia
SS R.Yount
3B D.Money
LF B.Sharp
CF G.Thomas
RF S.Lezcano
C D.Porter
DH H.Aaron
UT K.Bevacqua
P P.Broberg
P J.Slaton
P J.Colborn
P B.Travers
P T.Hausman
RP E.Rodriguez
RP T.Murphy

MIL 1976A

M A.Grammas
1B G.Scott
2B T.Johnson
SS R.Yount
3B D.Money
LF S.Lezcano
CF V.Joshua
RF G.Thomas
C D.Porter
DH H.Aaron
P J.Slaton
P B.Travers
P J.Colborn
P J.Augustine
P E.Rodriguez
RP B.Castro
RP D.Frisella

MIL 1977A

M A.Grammas
1B C.Cooper
2B D.Money
SS R.Yount
3B S.Bando
LF J.Wohlford
CF V.Joshua
RF S.Lezcano
C C.Moore
DH J.Quirk
P J.Slaton
P J.Augustine
P M.Haas
P E.Rodriguez
P L.Sorensen
RP S.Hinds
RP B.McClure
RP B.Castro

MIL 1978A

M G.Bamberger
1B C.Cooper
2B P.Molitor
SS R.Yount
3B S.Bando
LF B.Oglivie
CF G.Thomas
RF S.Lezcano
C C.Moore
DH L.Hisle
UT D.Money
P M.Caldwell
P L.Sorensen
P J.Augustine
P B.Travers
P A.Replogle
RP R.Stein
RP B.McClure
RP B.Castro

MIL 1979A

M G.Bamberger
1B C.Cooper
2B P.Molitor
SS R.Yount
3B S.Bando
LF B.Oglivie
CF G.Thomas
RF S.Lezcano
C C.Moore
DH D.Davis
P L.Sorensen
P M.Caldwell
P J.Slaton
P B.Travers
P M.Haas
RP J.Augustine
RP R.Cleveland
RP B.McClure

MIL 1980A

M B.Rodgers
M G.Bamberger
M B.Rodgers
1B C.Cooper
2B P.Molitor
SS R.Yount
3B J.Gantner
LF B.Oglivie
CF G.Thomas
RF S.Lezcano
C C.Moore
DH D.Davis
P M.Haas
P M.Caldwell
P L.Sorensen
P B.Travers
P R.Cleveland
RP B.McClure
RP B.Castro
RP J.Augustine

MIL 1981A

M B.Rodgers
1B C.Cooper
2B J.Gantner
SS R.Yount
3B D.Money
LF B.Oglivie
CF G.Thomas
RF M.Brouhard
C T.Simmons
DH L.Hisle
UT R.Howell
P P.Vuckovich
P M.Caldwell
P M.Haas
P J.Slaton
P R.Lerch
RP R.Fingers
RP R.Cleveland
RP J.Easterly

MIL 1982A

M B.Rodgers
M H.Kuenn
1B C.Cooper
2B J.Gantner
SS R.Yount
3B P.Molitor
LF B.Oglivie
CF G.Thomas
RF C.Moore
C T.Simmons
DH R.Howell
P M.Caldwell
P P.Vuckovich
P M.Haas
P B.McClure
P J.Slaton
RP R.Fingers
RP D.Bernard

MIL 1983A

M H.Kuenn
1B C.Cooper
2B J.Gantner
SS R.Yount
3B P.Molitor
LF B.Oglivie
CF R.Manning
RF C.Moore
C N.Yost
DH T.Simmons
P M.Caldwell
P D.Sutton
P M.Haas
P B.McClure
P C.Porter
RP J.Slaton
RP T.Tellmann
RP J.Augustine

MIL 1984A

M R.Lachemann
1B C.Cooper
2B J.Gantner
SS R.Yount
3B E.Romero
LF B.Oglivie
CF R.Manning
RF D.James
C J.Sundberg
DH T.Simmons
P D.Sutton
P M.Haas
P J.Cocanower
P B.McClure
P M.Caldwell
RP P.Ladd
RP T.Tellmann
RP R.Waits

MIL 1985A

M G.Bamberger
1B C.Cooper
2B J.Gantner
SS E.Riles
3B P.Molitor
LF B.Oglivie
CF R.Yount
RF P.Householder
C C.Moore
DH T.Simmons
P D.Darwin
P T.Higuera
P R.Burris
P M.Haas
P J.Cocanower
RP B.Gibson
RP B.McClure
RP R.Fingers

MIL 1986A

M G.Bamberger
M T.Trebelhorn
1B B.Robidoux
2B J.Gantner
SS E.Riles
3B P.Molitor
LF R.Manning
CF R.Yount
RF R.Deer
C C.Moore
DH C.Cooper
UT B.Oglivie
P T.Higuera
P B.Wegman
P T.Leary
P J.Nieves
P D.Darwin
RP D.Plesac
RP M.Clear
RP B.Clutterbuck

MIL 1987A

M T.Trebelhorn
1B G.Brock
2B J.Castillo
SS D.Sveum
3B E.Riles
LF R.Deer
CF R.Yount
RF G.Braggs
C B.Surhoff
DH C.Cooper
UT M.Felder
UT R.Manning
UT P.Molitor
P T.Higuera
P B.Wegman
P J.Nieves
P C.Bosio
RP C.Crim
RP D.Plesac
RP M.Clear

MIL 1988A

M T.Trebelhorn
1B G.Brock
2B J.Gantner
SS D.Sveum
3B P.Molitor
LF J.Leonard
CF R.Yount
RF R.Deer
C B.Surhoff
DH J.Meyer
P T.Higuera
P B.Wegman
P C.Bosio
P D.August
P M.Birkbeck
RP C.Crim
RP O.Jones
RP P.Mirabella

MIL 1989A

M T.Trebelhorn
1B G.Brock
2B J.Gantner
SS B.Spiers
3B P.Molitor
LF G.Braggs
CF R.Yount
RF R.Deer
C B.Surhoff
DH J.Meyer
UT M.Felder
P C.Bosio
P D.August
P T.Higuera
P M.Knudson
P J.Navarro
RP C.Crim
RP B.Krueger
RP D.Plesac

MIL 1990A

M T.Trebelhorn
1B G.Brock
2B J.Gantner
SS B.Spiers
3B G.Sheffield
LF M.Felder
CF R.Yount
RF R.Deer
C B.Surhoff
DH D.Parker
UT P.Molitor
UT G.Vaughn
P T.Higuera
P M.Knudson
P J.Navarro
P R.Robinson
P C.Bosio
RP T.Edens
RP C.Crim
RP D.Plesac

MIL 1991A

M T.Trebelhorn
1B F.Stubbs
2B W.Randolph
SS B.Spiers
3B J.Gantner
LF G.Vaughn
CF R.Yount
RF D.Bichette
C B.Surhoff
DH P.Molitor
UT D.Hamilton
P J.Navarro
P C.Bosio
P B.Wegman
P D.August
RP D.Plesac
RP C.Crim
RP J.Machado

MIL 1992A

M P.Garner
1B F.Stubbs
2B S.Fletcher
SS P.Listach
3B K.Seitzer
LF G.Vaughn
CF R.Yount
RF D.Hamilton
C B.Surhoff
DH P.Molitor
UT D.Bichette
UT J.Gantner
P B.Wegman
P J.Navarro
P C.Bosio
P R.Bones
P C.Eldred
RP D.Plesac
RP D.Henry
RP M.Fetters

MIL 1993A

M P.Garner
1B J.Jaha
2B B.Spiers
SS P.Listach
3B B.Surhoff
LF G.Vaughn
CF R.Yount
RF D.Hamilton
C D.Nilsson
DH K.Reimer
P C.Eldred
P J.Navarro
P R.Bones
P B.Wegman
P A.Miranda
RP G.Lloyd
RP M.Fetters
RP J.Orosco

MIL 1994A

M P.Garner
1B J.Jaha
2B J.Reed
SS J.Valentin
3B K.Seitzer
LF G.Vaughn
CF T.Ward
RF M.Mieske
C D.Nilsson
DH B.Harper
UT A.Diaz
UT B.Spiers
P C.Eldred
P R.Bones
P B.Wegman
P B.Scanlan
P J.Navarro
RP M.Ignasiak
RP G.Lloyd
RP M.Fetters

MIL 1995A

M P.Garner
1B J.Jaha
2B F.Vina
SS J.Valentin
3B J.Cirillo
LF D.Hulse
CF D.Hamilton
RF M.Mieske
C J.Oliver
DH G.Vaughn
UT P.Listach
UT K.Seitzer
UT B.Surhoff
P S.Sparks
P R.Bones
P S.Karl
P B.Givens
RP A.Miranda
RP B.Wegman
RP M.Kiefer

MIL 1996A

M P.Garner
1B K.Seitzer
2B F.Vina
SS J.Valentin
3B J.Cirillo
LF G.Vaughn
CF P.Listach
RF M.Mieske
C M.Matheny
DH J.Jaha
UT J.Levis
UT D.Nilsson
P B.McDonald
P S.Karl
P R.Bones
RP A.Miranda
RP R.Garcia
RP M.Fetters

MIL 1997A

M P.Garner
1B D.Nilsson
2B F.Vina
SS J.Valentin
3B J.Cirillo
LF M.Mieske
CF G.Williams
RF J.Burnitz
C M.Matheny
DH J.Franco
UT J.Levis
UT M.Loretta
P C.Eldred
P S.Karl
P J.Mercedes
P J.D'Amico
P B.McDonald
RP B.Wickman
RP D.Jones
RP J.Adamson

MIL 1998N

M P.Garner
1B M.Loretta
2B F.Vina
SS J.Valentin
3B J.Cirillo
LF D.Jackson
CF M.Grissom
RF J.Burnitz
C M.Matheny
UT B.Hamelin
UT D.Nilsson
P S.Karl
P S.Woodard
P B.Woodall
P J.Juden
P C.Eldred
RP B.Wickman
RP B.Patrick
RP A.Reyes

MIL 1999N

M P.Garner
M J.Lefebvre
1B M.Loretta
2B R.Belliard
SS J.Valentin
3B J.Cirillo
LF G.Jenkins
CF M.Grissom
RF J.Burnitz
C D.Nilsson
UT B.Banks
UT S.Berry
UT A.Ochoa
P S.Karl
P S.Woodard
P H.Nomo
RP J.Weathers
RP R.Roque
RP E.Plunk

MIL 2000N

M D.Lopes
1B R.Sexson
2B R.Belliard
SS M.Loretta
3B J.Hernandez
LF G.Jenkins
CF M.Grissom
RF J.Burnitz
C H.Blanco
UT C.Hayes
UT T.Houston
P J.Haynes
P J.Wright
P J.D'Amico
P J.Snyder
P J.Bere
RP J.Acevedo
RP C.Leskanic
RP J.Weathers

Minnesota

MIN A 1961-2000

MIN 1961A

M C.Lavagetto

M S.Mele
M C.Lavagetto
M S.Mele
1B H.Killebrew
2B B.Martin
SS Z.Versalles
3B B.Tuttle
LF J.Lemon
CF L.Green
RF B.Allison
C E.Battey
P P.Ramos
P C.Pascual
P J.Kralick
P J.Kaat
P D.Lee
RP B.Pleis
RP R.Moore

MIN 1962A

M S.Mele
1B V.Power
2B B.Allen
SS Z.Versalles
3B R.Rollins
LF H.Killebrew
CF L.Green
RF B.Allison
C E.Battey
UT B.Tuttle
P J.Kaat
P C.Pascual
P J.Kralick
P D.Stigman
P J.Bonikowski
RP L.Stange
RP G.Maranda
RP R.Moore

MIN 1963A

M S.Mele
1B V.Power
2B B.Allen
SS Z.Versalles
3B R.Rollins
LF H.Killebrew
CF J.Hall
RF B.Allison
C E.Battey
UT L.Green
P C.Pascual
P D.Stigman
P J.Kaat
P J.Perry
P L.Stange
RP B.Dailey
RP B.Pleis
RP G.Roggenburk

MIN 1964A

M S.Mele
1B B.Allison
2B B.Allen
SS Z.Versalles
3B R.Rollins
LF H.Killebrew
CF J.Hall
RF T.Oliva
C E.Battey
UT D.Mincher
P C.Pascual
P J.Kaat
P D.Stigman
P M.Grant
RP G.Arrigo
RP A.Worthington
RP J.Perry

MIN 1965A

M S.Mele
1B D.Mincher
2B J.Kindall
SS Z.Versalles
3B R.Rollins
LF B.Allison
CF J.Hall
RF T.Oliva
C E.Battey
UT H.Killebrew
UT S.Valdespino
P M.Grant
P J.Kaat
P J.Perry
P C.Pascual
P D.Boswell
RP A.Worthington
RP J.Klippstein
RP D.Stigman

MIN 1966A

M S.Mele
1B D.Mincher
2B B.Allen
SS Z.Versalles
3B H.Killebrew
LF J.Hall
CF T.Uhlaender
RF T.Oliva
C E.Battey
UT C.Tovar
P J.Kaat
P M.Grant
P J.Perry
P D.Boswell
P J.Merritt
RP A.Worthington
RP P.Cimino
RP D.Siebler

MIN 1967A

M S.Mele
M C.Ermer
1B H.Killebrew
2B R.Carew
SS Z.Versalles
3B R.Rollins
LF B.Allison
CF T.Uhlaender
RF T.Oliva
C J.Zimmerman
UT C.Tovar
P D.Chance
P J.Kaat
P J.Merritt
P D.Boswell
P J.Perry
RP A.Worthington
RP R.Kline

MIN 1968A

M C.Ermer
1B R.Reese
2B R.Carew
SS J.Hernandez
3B C.Tovar
LF B.Allison
CF T.Uhlaender
RF T.Oliva
C J.Roseboro
UT R.Clark
UT H.Killebrew
UT F.Quilici
P D.Chance
P J.Merritt
P J.Kaat
P D.Boswell
P J.Perry
RP R.Perranoski
RP A.Worthington
RP B.Miller

MIN 1969A

M B.Martin
1B R.Reese
2B R.Carew
SS L.Cardenas
3B H.Killebrew
LF T.Uhlaender
CF C.Tovar
RF T.Oliva
C J.Roseboro
UT F.Quilici
P J.Perry
P D.Boswell
P J.Kaat
P T.Hall
RP R.Perranoski
RP B.Miller
RP D.Woodson

MIN 1970A

M B.Rigney
1B R.Reese
2B D.Thompson
SS L.Cardenas
3B H.Killebrew
LF J.Holt
CF C.Tovar
RF T.Oliva
C G.Mitterwald
UT F.Quilici
P J.Perry
P J.Kaat
P B.Blyleven
P B.Zepp
RP T.Hall
RP S.Williams
RP R.Perranoski

MIN 1971A

M B.Rigney
1B R.Reese
2B R.Carew
SS L.Cardenas
3B S.Braun
LF C.Tovar
CF J.Holt
RF T.Oliva
C G.Mitterwald
UT H.Killebrew
P B.Blyleven
P J.Perry
P J.Kaat
RP R.Corbin
RP T.Hall
RP S.Williams

MIN 1972A

M B.Rigney
M F.Quilici
1B H.Killebrew
2B R.Carew
SS D.Thompson
3B E.Soderholm
LF S.Brye
CF B.Darwin
RF C.Tovar
C P.Roof
UT S.Braun
UT J.Nettles
UT R.Reese
P B.Blyleven
P D.Woodson
P J.Perry
P R.Corbin
P J.Kaat
RP D.LaRoche
RP W.Granger

MIN 1973A

M F.Quilici
1B J.Lis
2B R.Carew
SS D.Thompson
3B S.Braun
LF J.Holt
CF L.Hisle
RF B.Darwin
C G.Mitterwald
DH T.Oliva
UT J.Terrell
P B.Blyleven
P J.Kaat
P J.Decker
P B.Hands
P D.Woodson
RP R.Corbin
RP E.Bane
RP B.Campbell

MIN 1974A

M F.Quilici
1B C.Kusick
2B R.Carew
SS D.Thompson
3B E.Soderholm
LF L.Hisle
CF S.Brye
RF B.Darwin
C G.Borgmann
DH T.Oliva
UT S.Braun
UT H.Killebrew
UT J.Terrell
P B.Blyleven
P J.Decker
P D.Goltz
P V.Albury
P B.Hands
RP B.Campbell
RP T.Burgmeier

MIN 1975A

M F.Quilici
1B C.Kusick
2B R.Carew
SS D.Thompson
3B E.Soderholm
LF S.Braun
CF D.Ford
RF L.Bostock
C G.Borgmann
DH T.Oliva
UT J.Terrell
P B.Blyleven
P J.Hughes
P D.Goltz
P V.Albury
RP B.Campbell
RP T.Burgmeier

MIN 1976A

M G.Mauch
1B R.Carew
2B B.Randall
SS R.Smalley
3B M.Cubbage
LF L.Hisle
CF L.Bostock
RF D.Ford
C B.Wynegar
DH C.Kusick
UT S.Braun
P D.Goltz
P J.Hughes
P B.Singer
P S.Luebber
P P.Redfern
RP B.Campbell
RP T.Burgmeier
RP V.Albury

MIN 1977A

M G.Mauch
1B R.Carew
2B B.Randall
SS R.Smalley
3B M.Cubbage
LF L.Hisle
CF L.Bostock
RF D.Ford
C B.Wynegar
DH C.Kusick
UT R.Chiles
P D.Goltz
P P.Thormodsgard
P G.Zahn
P P.Redfern
RP T.Johnson
RP R.Schueler
RP T.Burgmeier

MIN 1978A

M G.Mauch
1B R.Carew
2B B.Randall
SS R.Smalley
3B M.Cubbage
LF W.Norwood
CF D.Ford
RF H.Powell
C B.Wynegar
DH G.Adams
UT J.Morales
UT B.Rivera
P R.Erickson
P G.Zahn
P D.Goltz
P G.Serum
RP M.Marshall

MIN 1979A

M G.Mauch
1B R.Jackson
2B R.Wilfong
SS R.Smalley
3B J.Castino
LF B.Rivera
CF K.Landreaux
RF H.Powell
C B.Wynegar
DH J.Morales
UT G.Adams
P J.Koosman
P D.Goltz
P G.Zahn
P P.Hartzell
P R.Erickson
RP M.Marshall
RP P.Redfern
RP D.Jackson

MIN 1980A

M G.Mauch
M J.Goryl
1B R.Jackson
2B R.Wilfong
SS R.Smalley
3B J.Castino
LF R.Sofield
CF K.Landreaux
RF H.Powell
C B.Wynegar
DH J.Morales
UT G.Adams
UT M.Cubbage
UT P.Mackanin
P J.Koosman
P G.Zahn
P R.Erickson
P D.Jackson
P P.Redfern
RP D.Corbett
RP J.Verhoeven

MIN 1981A

M J.Goryl
M B.Gardner
1B D.Goodwin
2B R.Wilfong
SS R.Smalley
3B J.Castino
LF G.Ward
CF M.Hatcher
RF D.Engle
C S.Butera
DH G.Adams
UT P.Mackanin
UT H.Powell
P A.Williams
P P.Redfern
P F.Arroyo
P J.Koosman
P R.Erickson
RP D.Corbett
RP D.Cooper
RP J.Verhoeven

MIN 1982A

M B.Gardner
1B K.Hrbek
2B J.Castino
SS R.Washington
3B G.Gaetti
LF G.Ward
CF B.Mitchell
RF T.Brunansky
C T.Laudner
DH R.Johnson
P B.Castillo
P B.Havens
P A.Williams
P F.Viola
P J.O'Connor
RP T.Felton
RP R.Davis
RP J.Pacella

MIN 1983A

M B.Gardner
1B K.Hrbek
2B J.Castino
SS R.Washington
3B G.Gaetti
LF G.Ward
CF D.Brown
RF T.Brunansky
C D.Engle
DH R.Bush
UT M.Hatcher
P F.Viola
P K.Schrom
P A.Williams
P B.Castillo
RP R.Lysander
RP R.Davis
RP L.Whitehouse

MIN 1984A

M B.Gardner
1B K.Hrbek
2B T.Teufel
SS H.Jimenez
3B G.Gaetti
LF M.Hatcher
CF K.Puckett
RF T.Brunansky
C D.Engle
DH R.Bush
P F.Viola
P M.Smithson
P J.Butcher
P K.Schrom
P E.Hodge
RP P.Filson
RP R.Davis
RP R.Lysander

MIN 1985A

M B.Gardner
M R.Miller
1B K.Hrbek
2B T.Teufel
SS G.Gagne
3B G.Gaetti
LF M.Hatcher
CF K.Puckett
RF T.Brunansky
C M.Salas
DH R.Smalley
UT R.Bush
P M.Smithson
P F.Viola
P J.Butcher
P K.Schrom
P B.Blyleven
RP P.Filson
RP R.Davis
RP F.Eufemia

MIN 1986A

M R.Miller
M T.Kelly
1B K.Hrbek
2B S.Lombardozzi
SS G.Gagne
3B G.Gaetti
LF R.Bush
CF K.Puckett
RF T.Brunansky
C M.Salas
DH R.Smalley
UT M.Hatcher
P B.Blyleven
P F.Viola
P M.Smithson
P N.Heaton
P M.Portugal
RP K.Atherton
RP R.Jackson
RP F.Pastore

MIN 1987A

M T.Kelly
1B K.Hrbek
2B S.Lombardozzi
SS G.Gagne
3B G.Gaetti
LF D.Gladden
CF K.Puckett
RF T.Brunansky
C T.Laudner
DH R.Smalley
UT R.Bush
UT M.Davidson
UT A.Newman
P B.Blyleven
P F.Viola
P L.Straker
P M.Smithson
P J.Niekro
RP J.Berenguer
RP G.Frazier
RP J.Reardon

MIN 1988A

M T.Kelly
1B K.Hrbek
2B S.Lombardozzi
SS G.Gagne
3B G.Gaetti
LF D.Gladden
CF K.Puckett
RF R.Bush
C T.Laudner
DH G.Larkin
UT M.Davidson
UT J.Moses
UT A.Newman
P F.Viola
P B.Blyleven
P A.Anderson
P C.Lea
P F.Toliver
RP J.Berenguer
RP K.Atherton
RP J.Reardon

MIN 1989A

M T.Kelly
1B K.Hrbek
2B A.Newman
SS G.Gagne
3B G.Gaetti
LF D.Gladden
CF K.Puckett
RF R.Bush
C B.Harper
DH J.Dwyer
UT G.Larkin
UT T.Laudner
UT J.Moses
P A.Anderson
P F.Viola
P R.Smith
P S.Rawley
RP J.Berenguer
RP J.Reardon
RP G.Wayne

MIN 1990A

M T.Kelly
1B K.Hrbek
2B A.Newman
SS G.Gagne
3B G.Gaetti
LF D.Gladden
CF K.Puckett
RF S.Mack
C B.Harper
DH G.Larkin
UT J.Moses
P A.Anderson
P K.Tapani
P R.Smith
P D.West
P M.Guthrie
RP J.Berenguer
RP T.Drummond
RP T.Leach

MIN 1991A

M T.Kelly
1B K.Hrbek
2B C.Knoblauch
SS G.Gagne
3B M.Pagliarulo
LF D.Gladden
CF K.Puckett
RF S.Mack
C B.Harper
DH C.Davis
UT G.Larkin
UT S.Leius
UT A.Newman
P J.Morris
P K.Tapani
P S.Erickson
P A.Anderson
RP M.Guthrie
RP C.Willis
RP S.Bedrosian

MIN 1992A

M T.Kelly
1B K.Hrbek
2B C.Knoblauch
SS G.Gagne
3B S.Leius
LF S.Mack
CF K.Puckett
RF P.Munoz
C B.Harper
DH C.Davis
UT R.Bush
UT G.Larkin
P J.Smiley
P K.Tapani
P S.Erickson
P B.Krueger
RP C.Willis
RP T.Edens
RP M.Guthrie

MIN 1993A

M T.Kelly
1B K.Hrbek
2B C.Knoblauch
SS P.Meares
3B M.Pagliarulo
LF P.Munoz
CF S.Mack
RF K.Puckett
C B.Harper
DH D.Winfield
UT D.McCarty
UT J.Reboulet
P K.Tapani
P S.Erickson
P W.Banks
P J.Deshaies
RP M.Trombley
RP M.Hartley
RP R.Aguilera

MIN 1994A

M T.Kelly
1B K.Hrbek
2B C.Knoblauch
SS P.Meares
3B S.Leius
LF S.Mack
CF A.Cole
RF K.Puckett
C M.Walbeck
DH D.Winfield
UT P.Munoz
UT J.Reboulet
P K.Tapani
P S.Erickson
P J.Deshaies
P P.Mahomes
P C.Pulido
RP C.Willis
RP M.Guthrie
RP M.Trombley

MIN 1995A
M T.Kelly
1B S.Stahoviak
2B C.Knoblauch
SS P.Meares
3B S.Leius
LF M.Cordova
CF R.Becker
RF K.Puckett
C M.Walbeck
DH P.Munoz
P B.Radke
P K.Tapani
P M.Trombley
P F.Rodriguez
P S.Erickson
RP P.Mahomes
RP E.Guardado
RP D.Stevens

MIN 1996A
M T.Kelly
1B S.Stahoviak
2B C.Knoblauch
SS P.Meares
3B D.Hollins
LF M.Cordova
CF R.Becker
RF R.Kelly
C G.Myers
DH P.Molitor
UT J.Reboulet
P B.Radke
P F.Rodriguez
P R.Robertson
P S.Aldred
P R.Aguilera
RP G.Hansell
RP E.Guardado
RP J.Parra

MIN 1997A
M T.Kelly
1B S.Stahoviak
2B C.Knoblauch
SS P.Meares
3B R.Coomer
LF M.Cordova
CF R.Becker
RF M.Lawton
C T.Steinbach
DH P.Molitor
UT D.Hocking
P B.Radke
P B.Tewksbury
P R.Robertson
P F.Rodriguez
P L.Hawkins
RP G.Swindell
RP M.Trombley
RP T.Ritchie

MIN 1998A
M T.Kelly
1B D.Ortiz
2B T.Walker
SS P.Meares
3B B.Gates
LF M.Cordova
CF O.Nixon
RF M.Lawton
C T.Steinbach
DH P.Molitor
UT R.Coomer
UT D.Hocking
P B.Radke
P L.Hawkins
P E.Milton
P B.Tewksbury
P M.Morgan
RP M.Trombley
RP D.Serafini
RP R.Aguilera

MIN 1999A
M T.Kelly
1B D.Mientkiewicz
2B T.Walker
SS C.Guzman
3B C.Koskie
LF C.Allen
CF T.Hunter
RF M.Lawton
C T.Steinbach
DH M.Cordova
UT R.Coomer
UT B.Gates
UT D.Hocking
P B.Radke
P E.Milton
P L.Hawkins
P J.Mays
RP B.Wells
RP M.Trombley
RP B.Sampson

MIN 2000A
M T.Kelly
1B R.Coomer
2B J.Canizaro
SS C.Guzman
3B C.Koskie
LF J.Jones
CF T.Hunter
RF M.Lawton
C M.LeCroy
DH D.Ortiz
UT D.Hocking
P B.Radke
P E.Milton
P J.Mays
P M.Redman
RP L.Hawkins
RP B.Wells
RP J.Santana

Montreal

MON N 1969-2000

MON 1969N
M G.Mauch
1B B.Bailey
2B G.Sutherland
SS B.Wine
3B C.Laboy
LF M.Jones
CF A.Phillips
RF R.Staub
C R.Brand
UT T.Cline
P B.Stoneman
P J.Robertson
P M.Wegener
P G.Waslewski
P H.Reed
RP D.McGinn
RP D.Shaw
RP R.Face

MON 1970N
M G.Mauch
1B R.Fairly
2B G.Sutherland
SS B.Wine
3B C.Laboy
LF M.Jones
CF A.Phillips
RF R.Staub
C J.Bateman
UT B.Bailey
UT M.Staehle
P C.Morton
P S.Renko
P B.Stoneman
P M.Wegener
RP D.McGinn
RP H.Reed
RP C.Raymond

MON 1971N
M G.Mauch
1B R.Fairly
2B R.Hunt
SS B.Wine
3B B.Bailey
LF J.Fairey
CF B.Day
RF R.Staub
C J.Bateman
UT G.Sutherland
P B.Stoneman
P S.Renko
P C.Morton
P E.McAnally
P J.Strohmayer
RP M.Marshall
RP D.McGinn
RP H.Reed

MON 1972N
M G.Mauch
1B M.Jorgensen
2B R.Hunt
SS T.Foli
3B B.Bailey
LF K.Singleton
CF B.Day
RF C.Mashore
C J.Boccabella
UT R.Fairly
UT R.Woods
P B.Stoneman
P M.Torrez
P C.Morton
P E.McAnally
P B.Moore
RP M.Marshall
RP J.Strohmayer
RP T.Walker

MON 1973N
M G.Mauch
1B M.Jorgensen
2B R.Hunt
SS T.Foli
3B B.Bailey
LF R.Fairly
CF R.Woods
RF K.Singleton
C J.Boccabella
UT H.Breeden
UT B.Day
UT P.Frias
P S.Renko
P M.Torrez
P B.Moore
P E.McAnally
P S.Rogers
RP M.Marshall
RP T.Walker

MON 1974N
M G.Mauch
1B M.Jorgensen
2B J.Cox
SS T.Foli
3B R.Hunt
LF B.Bailey
CF W.Davis
RF K.Singleton
C B.Foote
UT R.Fairly
UT L.Lintz
P S.Rogers
P S.Renko
P M.Torrez
P D.Blair
P E.McAnally
RP C.Taylor
RP T.Walker
RP J.Montague

MON 1975N
M G.Mauch
1B M.Jorgensen
2B P.Mackanin
SS T.Foli
3B L.Parrish
LF L.Biittner
CF P.Mangual
RF G.Carter
C B.Foote
UT B.Bailey
P S.Rogers
P S.Renko
P D.Warthen
P D.Blair
P W.Fryman
RP D.Murray
RP D.DeMola
RP F.Scherman

MON 1976N
M K.Kuehl
M C.Fox
1B M.Jorgensen
2B P.Mackanin
SS T.Foli
3B L.Parrish
LF D.Unser
CF J.White
RF E.Valentine
C B.Foote
UT J.Morales
P S.Rogers
P W.Fryman
P D.Stanhouse
P D.Carrithers
RP D.Murray
RP S.Dunning
RP C.Lang

MON 1977N
M D.Williams
1B T.Perez
2B D.Cash
SS C.Speier
3B L.Parrish
LF W.Cromartie
CF A.Dawson
RF E.Valentine
C G.Carter
UT D.Unser
P S.Rogers
P J.Brown
P D.Stanhouse
P W.Twitchell
P S.Bahnsen
RP J.Kerrigan
RP W.McEnaney
RP B.Atkinson

MON 1978N
M D.Williams
1B T.Perez
2B D.Cash
SS C.Speier
3B L.Parrish
LF W.Cromartie
CF A.Dawson
RF E.Valentine
C G.Carter
UT D.Unser
P R.Grimsley
P S.Rogers
P D.Schatzeder
P R.May
P W.Twitchell
RP S.Bahnsen
RP D.Knowles
RP M.Garman

MON 1979N
M D.Williams
1B T.Perez
2B R.Scott
SS C.Speier
3B L.Parrish
LF W.Cromartie
CF A.Dawson
RF E.Valentine
C G.Carter
P S.Rogers
P B.Lee
P S.Sanderson
P D.Schatzeder
P R.Grimsley
RP E.Sosa
RP R.May
RP S.Bahnsen

MON 1980N
M D.Williams
1B W.Cromartie
2B R.Scott
SS C.Speier
3B L.Parrish
LF R.LeFlore
CF A.Dawson
RF R.Office
C G.Carter
UT J.White
P S.Rogers
P S.Sanderson
P B.Gullickson
P D.Palmer
P B.Lee
RP F.Norman
RP E.Sosa
RP S.Bahnsen

MON 1981N
M D.Williams
M J.Fanning
1B W.Cromartie
2B R.Scott
SS C.Speier
3B L.Parrish
LF T.Raines
CF A.Dawson
RF J.White
C G.Carter
UT T.Wallach
P S.Rogers
P B.Gullickson
P S.Sanderson
P R.Burris
RP B.Lee
RP S.Bahnsen
RP W.Fryman

MON 1982N
M J.Fanning
1B A.Oliver
2B D.Flynn
SS C.Speier
3B T.Wallach
LF T.Raines
CF A.Dawson
RF W.Cromartie
C G.Carter
P S.Rogers
P B.Gullickson
P S.Sanderson
P C.Lea
P R.Burris
RP J.Reardon
RP B.Smith
RP W.Fryman

MON 1983N
M B.Virdon
1B A.Oliver
2B D.Flynn
SS C.Speier
3B T.Wallach
LF T.Raines
CF A.Dawson
RF W.Cromartie
C G.Carter
UT T.Francona
UT B.Little
P S.Rogers
P B.Gullickson
P C.Lea
P B.Smith
P R.Burris
RP J.Reardon
RP D.Schatzeder
RP B.James

MON 1984N
M B.Virdon
M J.Fanning
1B T.Francona
2B D.Flynn
SS A.Salazar
3B T.Wallach
LF J.Wohlford
CF T.Raines
RF A.Dawson
C G.Carter
UT D.Thomas
P B.Gullickson
P C.Lea
P B.Smith
P S.Rogers
P D.Schatzeder
RP B.James
RP J.Reardon
RP G.Lucas

MON 1985N
M B.Rodgers
1B D.Driessen
2B V.Law
SS H.Brooks
3B T.Wallach
LF T.Raines
CF H.Winningham
RF A.Dawson
C M.Fitzgerald
UT T.Francona
P B.Smith
P B.Gullickson
P J.Hesketh
P D.Palmer
P D.Schatzeder
RP T.Burke
RP J.Reardon
RP R.St.Claire

MON 1986N
M B.Rodgers
1B A.Galarraga
2B V.Law
SS H.Brooks
3B T.Wallach
LF T.Raines
CF M.Webster
RF A.Dawson
C D.Bilardello
UT W.Krenchicki
P F.Youmans
P J.Tibbs
P B.Smith
P D.Martinez
RP A.McGaffigan
RP T.Burke
RP J.Reardon

MON 1987N
M B.Rodgers
1B A.Galarraga
2B V.Law
SS H.Brooks
3B T.Wallach
LF T.Raines
CF H.Winningham
RF M.Webster
C M.Fitzgerald
UT C.Candaele
UT T.Foley
P N.Heaton
P B.Sebra
P B.Smith
P D.Martinez
P F.Youmans
RP A.McGaffigan
RP T.Burke
RP R.St.Claire

MON 1988N
M B.Rodgers
1B A.Galarraga
2B T.Foley
SS L.Rivera
3B T.Wallach
LF T.Raines
CF O.Nixon
RF H.Brooks
C N.Santovenia
P D.Martinez
P B.Smith
P P.Perez
P J.Dopson
P B.Holman
RP J.Parrett
RP A.McGaffigan
RP T.Burke

MON 1989N
M B.Rodgers
1B A.Galarraga
2B T.Foley
SS S.Owen
3B T.Wallach
LF T.Raines
CF Da.Martinez
RF H.Brooks
C N.Santovenia
UT M.Fitzgerald
UT O.Nixon
P De.Martinez
P B.Smith
P K.Gross
P P.Perez
P M.Langston
RP T.Burke
RP A.McGaffigan
RP Z.Smith

MON 1990N
M B.Rodgers
1B A.Galarraga
2B D.DeShields
SS S.Owen
3B T.Wallach
LF T.Raines
CF Da.Martinez
RF L.Walker
C M.Fitzgerald
UT M.Grissom
UT O.Nixon
P De.Martinez
P O.Boyd
P K.Gross
P M.Gardner
P Z.Smith
RP B.Sampen
RP T.Burke
RP D.Hall

MON 1991N
M B.Rodgers
M T.Runnells
1B A.Galarraga
2B D.DeShields
SS S.Owen
3B T.Wallach
LF I.Calderon
CF M.Grissom
RF Da.Martinez
C G.Reyes
UT L.Walker
P De.Martinez
P M.Gardner
P B.Barnes
P C.Nabholz
P O.Boyd
RP B.Sampen
RP B.Jones
RP S.Ruskin

MON 1992N
M T.Runnells
M F.Alou
1B T.Wallach
2B D.DeShields
SS S.Owen
3B B.Barberie
LF M.Alou
CF M.Grissom
RF L.Walker
C G.Carter
UT J.Vander Wal
P D.Martinez
P K.Hill
P C.Nabholz
P M.Gardner
P B.Barnes
RP M.Rojas
RP J.Fassero
RP J.Wetteland

MON 1993N
M F.Alou
1B G.Colbrunn
2B D.DeShields
SS W.Cordero
3B S.Berry
LF M.Alou
CF M.Grissom
RF L.Walker
C D.Fletcher
UT L.Frazier
UT M.Lansing
UT J.Vander Wal
P D.Martinez
P K.Hill
P C.Nabholz
RP J.Fassero
RP B.Barnes
RP J.Shaw

MON 1994N
M F.Alou
1B C.Floyd
2B M.Lansing
SS W.Cordero
3B S.Berry
LF M.Alou
CF M.Grissom
RF L.Walker
C D.Fletcher
UT L.Frazier
P K.Hill
P P.Martinez
P J.Fassero
P B.Henry
P K.Rueter
RP M.Rojas
RP G.Heredia
RP J.Shaw

MON 1995N
M F.Alou
1B D.Segui
2B M.Lansing
SS W.Cordero
3B S.Berry
LF M.Alou
CF R.White
RF T.Tarasco
C D.Fletcher
P P.Martinez
P J.Fassero
P C.Perez
P B.Henry
RP G.Heredia
RP M.Rojas
RP T.Scott

MON 1996N
M F.Alou
1B D.Segui
2B M.Lansing
SS M.Grudzielanek
3B S.Andrews
LF H.Rodriguez
CF F.Santangelo
RF M.Alou
C D.Fletcher
UT C.Floyd
P J.Fassero
P P.Martinez
P R.Cormier
P U.Urbina
RP O.Daal
RP B.Manuel
RP M.Rojas

MON 1997N
M F.Alou
1B D.Segui
2B M.Lansing
SS M.Grudzielanek
3B D.Strange
LF H.Rodriguez
CF R.White
RF F.Santangelo
C C.Widger
UT J.Orsulak
P P.Martinez
P C.Perez

P D.Hermanson
P J.Bullinger
P J.Juden
RP M.Valdes
RP A.Telford
RP U.Urbina

MON 1998N

M F.Alou
1B B.Fullmer
2B J.Vidro
SS M.Grudzielanek
3B S.Andrews
LF F.Santangelo
CF R.White
RF V.Guerrero
C C.Widger
UT R.McGuire
P D.Hermanson
P J.Vazquez
P C.Perez
P C.Pavano
RP M.Batista
RP S.Bennett
RP A.Telford

MON 1999N

M F.Alou
1B B.Fullmer
2B J.Vidro
SS O.Cabrera
3B S.Andrews
LF R.White
CF M.Martinez
RF V.Guerrero
C C.Widger
UT M.Barrett
UT W.Guerrero
UT M.Mordecai
P D.Hermanson
P J.Vazquez
P M.Thurman
P M.Batista
P C.Pavano
RP A.Telford
RP U.Urbina
RP S.Kline

MON 2000N

M F.Alou
1B L.Stevens
2B J.Vidro
SS O.Cabrera
3B M.Mordecai
LF T.Jones
CF P.Bergeron
RF V.Guerrero
C C.Widger
UT G.Blum
UT W.Guerrero
P J.Vazquez
P D.Hermanson
P T.Armas
RP F.Lira
RP A.Telford
RP S.Kline

Newark

NEW F 1915

NEW 1915F

M B.Phillips
M B.McKechnie
1B E.Huhn
2B F.LaPorte
SS J.Esmond
3B B.McKechnie
LF A.Scheer
CF E.Roush
RF V.Campbell
C B.Rariden
P E.Reulbach
P E.Moseley
P G.Kaiserling
P H.Moran
P C.Falkenberg

New Haven

NHn 1875

NH1875n

M C.Gould
M J.Latham
M C.Pabor
1B C.Gould
2B E.Somerville
SS S.Wright
3B H.Luff
LF J.Ryan
CF J.Tipper
RF J.McKelvey
C T.McGinley
UT B.Geer
P T.Nichols

New York

MUT n 1871-1875
NYN 1876
NYa 1883-1887
NYP 1890
NYN 1883-1957
NYN 1962-2000
NYA 1903-2000

MUT 1871n

M B.Ferguson
1B J.Start
2B D.Higham
SS D.Pearce
3B B.Ferguson
LF J.Hatfield
CF D.Eggler
RF D.Patterson
C C.Mills
P R.Wolters

MUT 1872n

M D.Pearce
M J.Hatfield
1B J.Start
2B J.Hatfield
SS D.Pearce
3B B.Boyd
LF J.McMullin
CF D.Eggler
RF G.Bechtel
C N.Hicks
UT C.Fulmer
P C.Cummings

MUT 1873n

M J.Hatfield
M J.Start
1B J.Start
2B C.Nelson
SS J.Holdsworth
3B J.Hatfield
LF C.Gedney
CF D.Eggler
RF P.Martin
C N.Hicks
UT D.Higham
P B.Mathews

MUT 1874n

M T.Carey
M D.Higham
1B J.Start
2B C.Nelson
SS T.Carey
3B J.Burdock
LF J.Hatfield
CF J.Remsen
RF D.Allison
C D.Higham
P B.Mathews

MUT 1875n

M N.Hicks
1B J.Start
2B C.Nelson
SS J.Hallinan
3B J.Gerhardt
LF C.Gedney
CF J.Holdsworth
RF E.Booth
C N.Hicks
P B.Mathews

NY 1876N

M B.Craver
1B J.Start
2B B.Craver
SS J.Hallinan
3B A.Nichols
LF F.Treacey
CF J.Holdsworth
RF E.Booth
C N.Hicks
P B.Mathews

NY 1883a

M J.Mutrie
1B S.Brady
2B S.Crane
SS C.Nelson
3B D.Esterbrook
LF E.Kennedy
CF J.O'Rourke
RF C.Roseman
C B.Holbert
P T.Keefe
P J.Lynch

NY 1884a

M J.Mutrie
1B D.Orr
2B D.Troy
SS C.Nelson
3B D.Esterbrook
LF E.Kennedy
CF C.Roseman
RF S.Brady
C B.Holbert
P J.Lynch
P T.Keefe

NY 1885a

M J.Gifford
1B D.Orr
2B T.Forster
SS C.Nelson
3B F.Hankinson
LF E.Kennedy
CF C.Roseman
RF S.Brady
C C.Reipschlager
P J.Lynch
P E.Cushman
P D.Crothers
P E.Begley
P B.Becannon

NY 1886a

M J.Gifford
M B.Ferguson
1B D.Orr
2B T.Forster
SS C.Nelson
3B F.Hankinson
LF C.Roseman
CF S.Behel
RF S.Brady
C C.Reipschlager
P J.Lynch
P A.Mays
P E.Cushman

NY 1887a

M B.Ferguson
M D.Orr
M O.Caylor
1B D.Orr
2B J.Gerhardt
SS P.Radford
3B F.Hankinson
LF D.O'Brien
CF C.Jones
RF C.Roseman
C B.Holbert
P A.Mays
P E.Cushman
P J.Lynch
P J.Shaffer
P S.Wiedman

NY 1890P

M B.Ewing
1B R.Connor
2B D.Shannon
SS D.Richardson
3B A.Whitney
LF G.Gore
CF M.Slattery
RF J.O'Rourke
C B.Ewing
P E.Crane
P H.O'Day
P J.Ewing
P T.Keefe

NY 1883N

M J.Clapp
1B R.Connor
2B D.Troy
SS E.Caskin
3B F.Hankinson
LF P.Gillespie
CF J.Ward
RF M.Dorgan
C B.Ewing
P M.Welch
P T.O'Neill

NY 1884N

M J.Price
M M.Ward
1B A.McKinnon
2B R.Connor
SS E.Caskin
3B F.Hankinson
LF P.Gillespie
CF J.Ward
RF M.Dorgan
C B.Ewing
UT D.Richardson
P M.Welch
P E.Begley

NY 1885N

M J.Mutrie
1B R.Connor
2B J.Gerhardt
SS J.Ward
3B D.Esterbrook
LF P.Gillespie
CF J.O'Rourke
RF M.Dorgan
C B.Ewing
P M.Welch
P T.Keefe

NY 1886N

M J.Mutrie
1B R.Connor
2B J.Gerhardt
SS J.Ward
3B D.Esterbrook
LF P.Gillespie
CF D.Richardson
RF M.Dorgan
C B.Ewing
UT J.O'Rourke
P T.Keefe
P M.Welch

NY 1887N

M J.Mutrie
1B R.Connor
2B D.Richardson
SS J.Ward
3B B.Ewing
LF P.Gillespie
CF G.Gore
RF M.Tiernan
C W.Brown
UT J.O'Rourke
P T.Keefe
P M.Welch
P B.George

NY 1888N

M J.Mutrie
1B R.Connor
2B D.Richardson
SS J.Ward
3B A.Whitney
LF J.O'Rourke
CF M.Slattery
RF M.Tiernan
C B.Ewing
P T.Keefe
P M.Welch
P C.Titcomb
P E.Crane

NY 1889N

M J.Mutrie
1B R.Connor
2B D.Richardson
SS J.Ward
3B A.Whitney
LF J.O'Rourke
CF G.Gore
RF M.Tiernan
C B.Ewing
P M.Welch
P T.Keefe
P E.Crane
P H.O'Day

NY 1890N

M J.Mutrie
1B L.Whistler
2B C.Bassett
SS J.Glasscock
3B J.Denny
LF J.Hornung
CF M.Tiernan
RF J.Burkett
C D.Buckley
UT A.Clarke
P A.Rusie
P M.Welch
P J.Sharrott

NY 1891N

M J.Mutrie
1B R.Connor
2B D.Richardson
SS J.Glasscock
3B C.Bassett
LF J.O'Rourke
CF G.Gore
RF M.Tiernan
C D.Buckley
P A.Rusie
P J.Ewing
P M.Welch

NY 1892N

M P.Powers
1B B.Ewing
2B E.Burke
SS S.Fuller
3B D.Lyons
LF J.O'Rourke
CF H.Lyons
RF M.Tiernan
C J.Boyle
P A.Rusie
P S.King
P E.Crane

NY 1893N

M M.Ward
1B R.Connor
2B J.Ward
SS S.Fuller
3B G.Davis
LF E.Burke
CF G.Stafford
RF M.Tiernan
C J.Doyle
P A.Rusie
P M.Baldwin
P L.German

NY 1894N

M M.Ward
1B J.Doyle
2B J.Ward
SS S.Fuller
3B G.Davis
LF E.Burke
CF G.Van Haltren
RF M.Tiernan
C D.Farrell
P A.Rusie
P J.Meekin
P L.German
P H.Westervelt
P D.Clarke

NY 1895N

M G.Davis
M J.Doyle
M H.Watkins
1B J.Doyle
2B G.Stafford
SS S.Fuller
3B G.Davis
LF E.Burke
CF G.Van Haltren
RF M.Tiernan
C D.Farrell
P A.Rusie
P D.Clarke
P J.Meekin
P L.German

NY 1896N

M A.Irwin
M B.Joyce
1B W.Clark
2B K.Gleason
SS F.Connaughton
3B G.Davis
LF G.Stafford
CF G.Van Haltren
RF M.Tiernan
C P.Wilson
P D.Clarke
P J.Meekin
P M.Sullivan
P E.Doheny

NY 1897N

M B.Joyce
1B W.Clark
2B K.Gleason
SS G.Davis
3B B.Joyce
LF D.Holmes
CF G.Van Haltren
RF M.Tiernan
C J.Warner
P A.Rusie
P J.Meekin
P C.Seymour
P M.Sullivan
P E.Doheny

NY 1898N

M B.Joyce
M C.Anson
M B.Joyce
1B B.Joyce
2B K.Gleason
SS G.Davis
3B F.Hartman
LF M.Tiernan
CF G.Van Haltren
RF J.Doyle
C J.Warner
P C.Seymour
P J.Meekin
P A.Rusie
P E.Doheny

NY 1899N

M J.Day
M F.Hoey
1B J.Doyle
2B K.Gleason
SS G.Davis
3B F.Hartman
LF T.O'Brien
CF G.Van Haltren
RF P.Foster
C J.Warner
UT P.Wilson
P B.Carrick
P E.Doheny
P C.Seymour
P J.Meekin
P C.Gettig

NY 1900N

M B.Ewing
M G.Davis
1B J.Doyle
2B K.Gleason
SS G.Davis
3B C.Hickman
LF K.Selbach
CF G.Van Haltren
RF E.Smith
C F.Bowerman
P B.Carrick
P P.Hawley
P W.Mercer
P E.Doheny

NY 1901N

M G.Davis
1B J.Ganzel
2B R.Nelson
SS G.Davis
3B S.Strang
LF K.Selbach
CF G.Van Haltren
RF A.McBride
C J.Warner
UT C.Hickman
P D.Taylor
P C.Mathewson
P B.Phyle

NY 1902N

M H.Fogel
M H.Smith
M J.McGraw
1B D.McGann
2B H.Smith
SS J.Bean
3B B.Lauder
LF J.Jones
CF S.Brodie
RF J.Dunn
C F.Bowerman
UT G.Browne
P C.Mathewson
P D.Taylor
P R.Evans
P J.McGinnity
P T.Sparks

NY 1903N

M J.McGraw
1B D.McGann
2B B.Gilbert
SS C.Babb
3B B.Lauder
LF S.Mertes
CF R.Bresnahan
RF G.Browne
C J.Warner
P J.McGinnity
P C.Mathewson
P D.Taylor
P J.Cronin
P R.Miller

NY 1904N

M J.McGraw
1B D.McGann
2B B.Gilbert
SS B.Dahlen
3B A.Devlin
LF S.Mertes
CF R.Bresnahan
RF G.Browne
C J.Warner
P J.McGinnity
P C.Mathewson
P D.Taylor
P H.Wiltse
P R.Ames

NY 1905N

M J.McGraw
1B D.McGann
2B B.Gilbert
SS B.Dahlen
3B A.Devlin
LF S.Mertes
CF M.Donlin
RF G.Browne
C R.Bresnahan
UT F.Bowerman
UT S.Strang
P C.Mathewson
P J.McGinnity
P R.Ames
P D.Taylor
P H.Wiltse

NY 1906N

M J.McGraw
1B D.McGann
2B B.Gilbert
SS B.Dahlen
3B A.Devlin
LF S.Shannon
CF C.Seymour
RF G.Browne
C R.Bresnahan
UT F.Bowerman
UT S.Strang
P J.McGinnity
P C.Mathewson
P H.Wiltse
P D.Taylor
P R.Ames
RP G.Ferguson

NY 1907N

M J.McGraw
1B D.McGann
2B L.Doyle
SS B.Dahlen
3B A.Devlin
LF S.Shannon
CF C.Seymour
RF G.Browne
C R.Bresnahan
UT F.Bowerman
UT S.Strang
P C.Mathewson
P J.McGinnity
P R.Ames
P H.Wiltse
P D.Taylor

NY 1908N

M J.McGraw
1B F.Tenney
2B L.Doyle
SS A.Bridwell
3B A.Devlin
LF S.Shannon
CF C.Seymour
RF M.Donlin
C R.Bresnahan
P C.Mathewson
P H.Wiltse
P D.Crandall
P J.McGinnity
P D.Taylor

NY 1909N

M J.McGraw
1B F.Tenney
2B L.Doyle
SS A.Bridwell
3B A.Devlin
LF M.McCormick
CF B.O'Hara
RF R.Murray
C A.Schlei
P C.Mathewson
P B.Raymond
P H.Wiltse
P R.Ames
P R.Marquard

NY 1910N

M J.McGraw
1B F.Merkle
2B L.Doyle
SS A.Bridwell
3B A.Devlin
LF J.Devore
CF F.Snodgrass
RF R.Murray
C C.Meyers
P C.Mathewson
P H.Wiltse
P L.Drucke
P D.Crandall
P R.Ames

NY 1911N

M J.McGraw
1B F.Merkle
2B L.Doyle
SS A.Bridwell
3B A.Devlin
LF J.Devore
CF F.Snodgrass
RF R.Murray
C C.Meyers
UT A.Fletcher
P C.Mathewson
P R.Marquard
P R.Ames
P D.Crandall
P H.Wiltse

NY 1912N

M J.McGraw
1B F.Merkle
2B L.Doyle
SS A.Fletcher
3B B.Herzog
LF F.Snodgrass
CF B.Becker
RF R.Murray
C C.Meyers
UT J.Devore
P C.Mathewson
P R.Marquard
P J.Tesreau
P R.Ames
P D.Crandall

NY 1913N

M J.McGraw
1B F.Merkle
2B L.Doyle
SS A.Fletcher
3B B.Herzog
LF G.Burns
CF F.Snodgrass
RF R.Murray
C C.Meyers
UT T.Shafer
P C.Mathewson
P R.Marquard
P J.Tesreau
P A.Demaree
P A.Fromme
RP D.Crandall

NY 1914N

M J.McGraw
1B F.Merkle
2B L.Doyle
SS A.Fletcher
3B M.Stock
LF G.Burns
CF B.Bescher
RF F.Snodgrass
C C.Meyers
P J.Tesreau
P C.Mathewson
P R.Marquard
P A.Demaree
P A.Fromme

NY 1915N

M J.McGraw
1B F.Merkle
2B L.Doyle
SS A.Fletcher
3B H.Lobert
LF G.Burns
CF F.Snodgrass
RF D.Robertson
C C.Meyers
P J.Tesreau
P P.Perritt
P C.Mathewson
P S.Stroud
P R.Marquard
RP H.Ritter
RP F.Schupp

NY 1916N

M J.McGraw
1B F.Merkle
2B L.Doyle
SS A.Fletcher
3B B.McKechnie
LF G.Burns
CF B.Kauff
RF D.Robertson
C B.Rariden
P J.Tesreau
P P.Perritt
P R.Benton
P F.Anderson
P F.Schupp

NY 1917N

M J.McGraw
1B W.Holke
2B B.Herzog
SS A.Fletcher
3B H.Zimmerman
LF G.Burns
CF B.Kauff
RF D.Robertson
C B.Rariden
P F.Schupp
P S.Sallee
P P.Perritt
P R.Benton
P J.Tesreau

NY 1918N

M J.McGraw
1B W.Holke
2B L.Doyle
SS A.Fletcher
3B H.Zimmerman
LF G.Burns
CF B.Kauff
RF R.Youngs
C L.McCarty
P P.Perritt
P R.Causey
P A.Demaree
P S.Sallee
P F.Toney

NY 1919N

M J.McGraw
1B H.Chase
2B L.Doyle
SS A.Fletcher
3B H.Zimmerman
LF G.Burns
CF B.Kauff
RF R.Youngs
C L.McCarty
P J.Barnes
P R.Benton
P F.Toney
P J.Dubuc
P R.Causey

NY 1920N

M J.McGraw
1B G.Kelly
2B L.Doyle
SS D.Bancroft
3B F.Frisch
LF G.Burns
CF L.King
RF R.Youngs
C F.Snyder
P J.Barnes
P A.Nehf
P F.Toney
P P.Douglas
P R.Benton

NY 1921N

M J.McGraw
1B G.Kelly
2B J.Rawlings
SS D.Bancroft
3B F.Frisch
LF I.Meusel
CF G.Burns
RF R.Youngs
C F.Snyder
P A.Nehf
P J.Barnes
P F.Toney
P P.Douglas
P R.Ryan
RP S.Sallee

NY 1922N

M J.McGraw
1B G.Kelly
2B F.Frisch
SS D.Bancroft
3B H.Groh
LF I.Meusel
CF C.Stengel
RF R.Youngs
C F.Snyder
P A.Nehf
P J.Barnes
P R.Ryan
P P.Douglas
P H.McQuillan
RP C.Jonnard
RP R.Causey
RP V.Barnes

NY 1923N

M J.McGraw
1B G.Kelly
2B F.Frisch
SS D.Bancroft
3B H.Groh
LF I.Meusel
CF B.Cunningham
RF R.Youngs
C F.Snyder
UT T.Jackson
P H.McQuillan
P J.Scott
P A.Nehf
P J.Bentley
P R.Ryan
RP C.Jonnard
RP V.Barnes

NY 1924N

M J.McGraw
M H.Jennings
M J.McGraw
1B G.Kelly
2B F.Frisch
SS T.Jackson
3B H.Groh
LF I.Meusel
CF H.Wilson
RF R.Youngs
C F.Snyder
UT B.Southworth
P V.Barnes
P J.Bentley
P H.McQuillan
P A.Nehf
P W.Dean
RP C.Jonnard

NY 1925N

M J.McGraw
M H.Jennings
M J.McGraw
1B B.Terry
2B G.Kelly
SS T.Jackson
3B F.Lindstrom
LF I.Meusel
CF B.Southworth
RF R.Youngs
C F.Snyder
UT F.Frisch
P J.Scott
P V.Barnes
P K.Greenfield
P J.Bentley
P A.Nehf
RP W.Huntzinger

NY 1926N

M J.McGraw
1B G.Kelly
2B F.Frisch
SS T.Jackson
3B F.Lindstrom
LF I.Meusel
CF T.Tyson
RF R.Youngs
C P.Florence
UT B.Terry
P J.Scott
P K.Greenfield
P F.Fitzsimmons
P V.Barnes
P J.Ring
RP C.Davies

NY 1927N

M J.McGraw
M R.Hornsby
1B B.Terry
2B R.Hornsby
SS T.Jackson
3B F.Lindstrom
LF H.Mueller
CF E.Roush
RF G.Harper
C Z.Taylor
UT R.Reese
P B.Grimes
P F.Fitzsimmons
P V.Barnes
P L.Benton
P D.Henry
RP D.Songer

NY 1928N

M J.McGraw
1B B.Terry
2B A.Cohen
SS T.Jackson
3B F.Lindstrom
LF L.O'Doul
CF J.Welsh
RF M.Ott
C S.Hogan
UT R.Reese
P L.Benton
P F.Fitzsimmons
P J.Genewich
P C.Hubbell
P V.Aldridge

NY 1929N

M J.McGraw
1B B.Terry
2B A.Cohen
SS T.Jackson
3B F.Lindstrom
LF F.Leach
CF E.Roush
RF M.Ott
C S.Hogan
UT B.O'Farrell
P C.Hubbell
P L.Benton
P F.Fitzsimmons
P B.Walker
P C.Mays
RP R.Judd

NY 1930N

M J.McGraw
1B B.Terry
2B H.Critz
SS T.Jackson
3B F.Lindstrom
LF F.Leach
CF W.Roettger
RF M.Ott
C S.Hogan
UT B.O'Farrell
P B.Walker
P C.Hubbell
P F.Fitzsimmons
P H.Pruett
P C.Mitchell
RP J.Heving

NY 1931N

M J.McGraw
1B B.Terry
2B B.Hunnefield
SS T.Jackson
3B J.Vergez
LF F.Leach
CF E.Allen
RF M.Ott
C S.Hogan
P F.Fitzsimmons
P C.Hubbell
P B.Walker
P C.Mitchell
P J.Berly

NY 1932N

M J.McGraw
M B.Terry
1B B.Terry
2B H.Critz
SS D.Marshall
3B J.Vergez
LF J.Moore
CF F.Lindstrom
RF M.Ott
C S.Hogan
UT C.Fullis
P C.Hubbell
P F.Fitzsimmons
P B.Walker
P J.Mooney
P H.Bell
RP D.Luque
RP S.Gibson

NY 1933N

M B.Terry
1B B.Terry
2B H.Critz
SS B.Ryan
3B J.Vergez
LF J.Moore
CF K.Davis
RF M.Ott
C G.Mancuso
P C.Hubbell
P H.Schumacher
P F.Fitzsimmons
P R.Parmelee
RP H.Bell
RP D.Luque
RP G.Spencer

NY 1934N

M B.Terry
1B B.Terry
2B H.Critz
SS T.Jackson
3B J.Vergez
LF J.Moore
CF G.Watkins
RF M.Ott
C G.Mancuso
UT B.Ryan
P C.Hubbell
P H.Schumacher
P F.Fitzsimmons
P R.Parmelee
P J.Bowman
RP A.Smith
RP H.Bell

NY 1935N

M B.Terry
1B B.Terry
2B M.Koenig
SS D.Bartell
3B T.Jackson
LF J.Moore
CF H.Leiber
RF M.Ott
C G.Mancuso
P C.Hubbell
P H.Schumacher
P R.Parmelee
P S.Castleman
P A.Smith
RP A.Stout
RP F.Gabler

NY 1936N

M B.Terry
1B S.Leslie
2B B.Whitehead
SS D.Bartell
3B T.Jackson
LF J.Moore
CF H.Leiber
RF M.Ott
C G.Mancuso
UT J.Ripple
P C.Hubbell
P H.Schumacher
P A.Smith
P F.Gabler
P H.Gumbert
RP D.Coffman

NY 1937N

M B.Terry
1B J.McCarthy
2B B.Whitehead
SS D.Bartell
3B L.Chiozza
LF J.Moore
CF J.Ripple
RF M.Ott
C H.Danning
P C.Hubbell
P C.Melton
P H.Schumacher
P H.Gumbert
P S.Castleman
RP A.Smith
RP D.Coffman

NY 1938N

M B.Terry
1B J.McCarthy
2B A.Kampouris
SS D.Bartell
3B M.Ott
LF J.Moore
CF H.Leiber
RF J.Ripple
C H.Danning
P C.Melton
P H.Gumbert
P H.Schumacher
P C.Hubbell
P B.Lohrman
RP D.Coffman
RP J.Brown

NY 1939N

M B.Terry
1B Z.Bonura
2B B.Whitehead
SS B.Jurges
3B T.Hafey
LF J.Moore
CF F.Demaree
RF M.Ott
C H.Danning
P H.Gumbert
P C.Melton
P B.Lohrman
P H.Schumacher
P C.Hubbell
RP J.Brown
RP R.Lynn

NY 1940N

M B.Terry
1B B.Young
2B T.Cuccinello
SS M.Witek
3B B.Whitehead
LF J.Moore
CF F.Demaree
RF M.Ott
C H.Danning
P H.Gumbert
P H.Schumacher
P C.Hubbell
P B.Lohrman
P C.Melton
RP J.Brown
RP R.Joiner

NY 1941N

M B.Terry
1B B.Young
2B B.Whitehead
SS B.Jurges
3B D.Bartell
LF J.Moore
CF J.Rucker
RF M.Ott
C H.Danning
P H.Schumacher
P C.Melton
P C.Hubbell
P B.Lohrman
P B.Carpenter
RP B.Bowman
RP A.Adams
RP J.Brown

NY 1942N

M M.Ott
1B J.Mize
2B M.Witek
SS B.Jurges
3B B.Werber
LF B.Barna
CF W.Marshall
RF M.Ott
C H.Danning
UT B.Young
P H.Schumacher
P B.Carpenter
P B.Lohrman
P C.Hubbell
P C.Melton
RP A.Adams

NY 1943N

M M.Ott
1B J.Orengo
2B M.Witek
SS B.Jurges
3B D.Bartell
LF J.Medwick
CF J.Rucker
RF M.Ott
C G.Mancuso
UT S.Gordon
UT E.Lombardi
UT B.Maynard
P C.Melton
P J.Wittig
P V.Mungo
P R.Fischer
P K.Chase
RP A.Adams
RP B.Sayles

NY 1944N

M M.Ott
1B P.Weintraub
2B G.Hausmann
SS B.Kerr
3B H.Luby
LF J.Medwick
CF J.Rucker
RF M.Ott
C E.Lombardi
UT N.Reyes
P B.Voiselle
P H.Feldman
P E.Pyle
P R.Fischer
RP A.Adams
RP A.Hansen

NY 1945N

M M.Ott
1B P.Weintraub
2B G.Hausmann
SS B.Kerr
3B N.Reyes
LF D.Gardella
CF J.Rucker
RF M.Ott
C E.Lombardi
P B.Voiselle
P H.Feldman
P V.Mungo
P J.Brewer
P S.Emmerich
RP A.Adams
RP R.Fischer

NY 1946N

M M.Ott
1B J.Mize
2B B.Blattner
SS B.Kerr
3B B.Rigney
LF S.Gordon
CF W.Marshall
RF G.Rosen
C W.Cooper
UT J.Graham
UT J.Rucker
UT B.Young
P D.Koslo
P M.Kennedy
P B.Voiselle
P K.Trinkle
P H.Schumacher
RP M.Budnick
RP J.Thompson

NY 1947N

M M.Ott
1B J.Mize
2B B.Rigney
SS B.Kerr
3B J.Lohrke
LF S.Gordon
CF B.Thomson
RF W.Marshall
C W.Cooper
P L.Jansen
P D.Koslo
P M.Kennedy
P C.Hartung
RP K.Trinkle
RP J.Beggs

NY 1948N

M M.Ott
M L.Durocher
1B J.Mize
2B B.Rigney

SS B.Kerr
3B S.Gordon
LF B.Thomson
CF W.Lockman
RF W.Marshall
C W.Cooper
UT J.Lohrke
P L.Jansen
P S.Jones
P R.Poat
P C.Hartung
P D.Koslo
RP A.Hansen
RP K.Trinkle

NY 1949N
M L.Durocher
1B J.Mize
2B H.Thompson
SS B.Kerr
3B S.Gordon
LF W.Lockman
CF B.Thomson
RF W.Marshall
C W.Westrum
UT B.Rigney
P L.Jansen
P M.Kennedy
P D.Koslo
P S.Jones
P C.Hartung
RP K.Higbe
RP H.Behrman
RP A.Hansen

NY 1950N
M L.Durocher
1B T.Gilbert
2B E.Stanky
SS A.Dark
3B H.Thompson
LF W.Lockman
CF B.Thomson
RF D.Mueller
C W.Westrum
UT M.Irvin
P L.Jansen
P S.Maglie
P S.Jones
P D.Koslo
P J.Hearn
RP J.Kramer
RP A.Hansen

NY 1951N
M L.Durocher
1B W.Lockman
2B E.Stanky
SS A.Dark
3B H.Thompson
LF M.Irvin
CF W.Mays
RF D.Mueller
C W.Westrum
UT B.Thomson
P S.Maglie
P L.Jansen
P J.Hearn
P D.Koslo
RP G.Spencer
RP S.Jones
RP M.Kennedy

NY 1952N
M L.Durocher
1B W.Lockman
2B D.Williams
SS A.Dark
3B B.Thomson
LF B.Elliott
CF H.Thompson
RF D.Mueller
C W.Westrum
P J.Hearn
P S.Maglie
P L.Jansen
P D.Koslo
P M.Lanier
RP H.Wilhelm
RP M.Kennedy
RP G.Spencer

NY 1953N
M L.Durocher
1B W.Lockman
2B D.Williams
SS A.Dark
3B H.Thompson
LF M.Irvin
CF B.Thomson
RF D.Mueller
C W.Westrum
UT D.Spencer
P R.Gomez
P J.Hearn
P L.Jansen
P S.Maglie
P D.Koslo
RP H.Wilhelm
RP A.Corwin

NY 1954N
M L.Durocher
1B W.Lockman
2B D.Williams
SS A.Dark
3B H.Thompson
LF M.Irvin
CF W.Mays
RF D.Mueller
C W.Westrum
P J.Antonelli
P R.Gomez
P S.Maglie
P J.Hearn
P D.Liddle
RP M.Grissom
RP H.Wilhelm
RP W.McCall

NY 1955N
M L.Durocher
1B G.Harris
2B W.Terwilliger
SS A.Dark
3B H.Thompson
LF W.Lockman
CF W.Mays
RF D.Mueller
C R.Katt
UT B.Hofman
UT D.Rhodes
P J.Antonelli
P J.Hearn
P R.Gomez
P S.Maglie
P D.Liddle
RP H.Wilhelm
RP W.McCall
RP M.Grissom

NY 1956N
M B.Rigney
1B B.White
2B R.Schoendienst
SS D.Spencer
3B F.Castleman
LF J.Brandt
CF W.Mays
RF D.Mueller
C B.Sarni
UT D.Rhodes
P J.Antonelli
P R.Gomez
P A.Worthington
P J.Hearn
P D.Littlefield
RP S.Ridzik
RP H.Wilhelm
RP M.Grissom

NY 1957N
M B.Rigney
1B W.Lockman
2B D.O'Connell
SS D.Spencer
3B R.Jablonski
LF H.Sauer
CF W.Mays
RF D.Mueller
C V.Thomas
UT O.Virgil
P R.Gomez
P J.Antonelli
P C.Barclay
P S.Miller
P R.Crone
RP A.Worthington
RP M.Grissom
RP R.Monzant

NY 1962N
M C.Stengel
1B M.Throneberry
2B C.Neal
SS E.Chacon
3B F.Mantilla
LF F.Thomas
CF J.Hickman
RF R.Ashburn
C C.Cannizzaro
UT J.Christopher
UT R.Kanehl
P R.Craig
P A.Jackson
P J.Hook
P B.Miller
RP C.Anderson
RP B.Moorhead
RP R.Daviault

NY 1963N
M C.Stengel
1B T.Harkness
2B R.Hunt
SS A.Moran
3B C.Neal
LF F.Thomas
CF J.Hickman
RF D.Snider
C C.Coleman
UT R.Kanehl
P R.Craig
P A.Jackson
P C.Willey
P G.Cisco
P T.Stallard
RP L.Bearnarth
RP K.Mac Kenzie
RP D.Rowe

NY 1964N
M C.Stengel
1B E.Kranepool
2B R.Hunt
SS R.McMillan
3B C.Smith
LF G.Altman
CF J.Hickman
RF J.Christopher
C J.Gonder
P J.Fisher
P T.Stallard
P A.Jackson
P G.Cisco
RP B.Wakefield
RP L.Bearnarth

NY 1965N
M C.Stengel
M W.Westrum
1B E.Kranepool
2B C.Hiller
SS R.McMillan
3B C.Smith
LF R.Swoboda
CF J.Hickman
RF J.Lewis
C C.Cannizzaro
UT J.Christopher
UT B.Klaus
P J.Fisher
P A.Jackson
P W.Spahn
P G.Cisco
RP T.McGraw
RP T.Parsons
RP G.Kroll

NY 1966N
M W.Westrum
1B E.Kranepool
2B R.Hunt
SS E.Bressoud
3B K.Boyer
LF R.Swoboda
CF C.Jones
RF A.Luplow
C J.Grote
UT C.Hiller
P J.Fisher
P D.Ribant
P B.Shaw
P R.Gardner
RP J.Hamilton
RP D.Selma
RP B.Hepler

NY 1967N
M W.Westrum
M S.Parker
1B E.Kranepool
2B J.Buchek
SS B.Harrelson
3B E.Charles
LF T.Davis
CF C.Jones
RF R.Swoboda
C J.Grote
UT T.Reynolds
P T.Seaver
P J.Fisher
P D.Cardwell
P B.Shaw
RP D.Selma
RP R.Taylor
RP D.Shaw

NY 1968N
M G.Hodges
1B E.Kranepool
2B P.Linz
SS B.Harrelson
3B E.Charles
LF C.Jones
CF T.Agee
RF R.Swoboda
C J.Grote
UT A.Shamsky
P T.Seaver
P J.Koosman
P D.Cardwell
P D.Selma
P N.Ryan
RP C.Koonce
RP R.Taylor
RP D.Frisella

NY 1969N
M G.Hodges
1B E.Kranepool
2B K.Boswell
SS B.Harrelson
3B W.Garrett
LF C.Jones
CF T.Agee
RF R.Swoboda
C J.Grote
UT R.Gaspar
UT A.Shamsky
UT A.Weis
P T.Seaver
P J.Koosman
P G.Gentry
P D.Cardwell
P J.McAndrew
RP T.McGraw
RP C.Koonce
RP R.Taylor

NY 1970N
M G.Hodges
1B D.Clendenon
2B K.Boswell
SS B.Harrelson
3B J.Foy
LF C.Jones
CF T.Agee
RF R.Swoboda
C J.Grote
UT W.Garrett
UT A.Shamsky
P T.Seaver
P J.Koosman
P G.Gentry
P J.McAndrew
P R.Sadecki
RP T.McGraw
RP R.Taylor
RP D.Frisella

NY 1971N
M G.Hodges
1B E.Kranepool
2B K.Boswell
SS B.Harrelson
3B B.Aspromonte
LF C.Jones
CF T.Agee
RF K.Singleton
C J.Grote
UT T.Foli
UT D.Hahn
UT D.Marshall
P T.Seaver
P G.Gentry
P J.Koosman
P R.Sadecki
P N.Ryan
RP T.McGraw
RP D.Frisella
RP C.Williams

NY 1972N
M Y.Berra
1B E.Kranepool
2B K.Boswell
SS B.Harrelson
3B J.Fregosi
LF J.Milner
CF T.Agee
RF R.Staub
C D.Dyer
UT W.Garrett
UT T.Martinez
UT C.Jones
P T.Seaver
P J.Matlack
P G.Gentry
P J.Koosman
P J.McAndrew
RP T.McGraw
RP R.Sadecki
RP D.Frisella

NY 1973N
M Y.Berra
1B J.Milner
2B F.Millan
SS B.Harrelson
3B W.Garrett
LF C.Jones
CF D.Hahn
RF R.Staub
C J.Grote
UT E.Kranepool
P T.Seaver
P J.Koosman
P J.Matlack
P G.Stone
P R.Sadecki
RP T.McGraw
RP H.Parker

NY 1974N
M Y.Berra
1B J.Milner
2B F.Millan
SS B.Harrelson
3B W.Garrett
LF C.Jones
CF D.Hahn
RF R.Staub
C J.Grote
UT T.Martinez
P J.Matlack
P J.Koosman
P T.Seaver
P H.Parker
P R.Sadecki
RP B.Apodaca
RP T.McGraw
RP B.Miller

NY 1975N
M Y.Berra
M R.McMillan
1B E.Kranepool
2B F.Millan
SS M.Phillips
3B W.Garrett
LF D.Kingman
CF D.Unser
RF R.Staub
C J.Grote
UT J.Torre
P T.Seaver
P J.Koosman
P J.Matlack
P R.Tate
P H.Webb
RP R.Baldwin
RP B.Apodaca
RP T.Hall

NY 1976N
M J.Frazier
1B E.Kranepool
2B F.Millan
SS B.Harrelson
3B R.Staiger
LF J.Milner
CF D.Unser
RF D.Kingman
C J.Grote
UT J.Torre
UT B.Boisclair
P T.Seaver
P J.Matlack
P J.Koosman
P M.Lolich
P C.Swan
RP S.Lockwood
RP B.Apodaca

NY 1977N
M J.Frazier
M J.Torre
1B J.Milner
2B F.Millan
SS B.Harrelson
3B L.Randle
LF S.Henderson
CF L.Mazzilli
RF M.Vail
C J.Stearns
UT E.Kranepool
UT B.Boisclair
P J.Koosman
P N.Espinosa
P J.Matlack
P C.Swan
P P.Zachry
RP S.Lockwood
RP B.Myrick
RP B.Apodaca

NY 1978N
M J.Torre
1B W.Montanez
2B D.Flynn
SS T.Foli
3B L.Randle
LF S.Henderson
CF L.Mazzilli
RF E.Maddox
C J.Stearns
UT B.Boisclair
UT J.Youngblood
P J.Koosman
P C.Swan
P N.Espinosa
P P.Zachry
P M.Bruhert
RP S.Lockwood
RP D.Murray
RP D.Bernard

NY 1979N
M J.Torre
1B W.Montanez
2B D.Flynn
SS F.Taveras
3B R.Hebner
LF S.Henderson
CF L.Mazzilli
RF J.Youngblood
C J.Stearns
P C.Swan
P P.Falcone
P K.Kobel
RP N.Allen
RP D.Murray
RP A.Hassler

NY 1980N
M J.Torre
1B L.Mazzilli
2B D.Flynn
SS F.Taveras
3B E.Maddox
LF S.Henderson
CF J.Youngblood
RF C.Washington
C A.Trevino
UT M.Jorgensen
P R.Burris
P P.Zachry
P M.Bomback
P P.Falcone
P C.Swan
RP T.Hausman
RP J.Reardon
RP N.Allen

NY 1981N
M J.Torre
1B D.Kingman
2B D.Flynn
SS F.Taveras
3B H.Brooks
LF L.Mazzilli
CF M.Wilson
RF E.Valentine
C J.Stearns
UT M.Cubbage
UT M.Jorgensen
UT R.Staub
P P.Zachry
P M.Scott
P E.Lynch
P G.Harris
RP P.Falcone
RP N.Allen
RP D.Miller

NY 1982N
M G.Bamberger
1B D.Kingman
2B W.Backman
SS R.Gardenhire
3B H.Brooks
LF G.Foster
CF M.Wilson
RF E.Valentine
C J.Stearns
UT B.Bailor
UT M.Jorgensen
UT R.Staub
P C.Puleo
P P.Falcone
P C.Swan
P M.Scott
P E.Lynch
RP J.Orosco
RP N.Allen

NY 1983N
M G.Bamberger
M F.Howard
1B K.Hernandez
2B B.Giles
SS J.Oquendo
3B H.Brooks
LF G.Foster
CF M.Wilson
RF D.Strawberry
C R.Hodges
UT B.Bailor
UT D.Heep
UT D.Kingman
UT R.Staub
P T.Seaver
P M.Torrez
P E.Lynch
P W.Terrell
P C.Swan
RP J.Orosco
RP D.Sisk
RP S.Holman

NY 1984N
M D.Johnson
1B K.Hernandez
2B W.Backman
SS J.Oquendo
3B H.Brooks
LF G.Foster
CF M.Wilson
RF D.Strawberry
C M.Fitzgerald
UT D.Heep
P D.Gooden
P W.Terrell
P R.Darling
P E.Lynch
P B.Berenyi
RP J.Orosco
RP B.Gaff
RP D.Sisk

NY 1985N
M D.Johnson
1B K.Hernandez
2B W.Backman
SS R.Santana
3B H.Johnson
LF G.Foster
CF M.Wilson
RF D.Strawberry
C G.Carter
P D.Gooden
P R.Darling
P E.Lynch
P S.Fernandez
P R.Aguilera
RP R.McDowell
RP J.Orosco
RP D.Sisk

NY 1986N
M D.Johnson
1B K.Hernandez
2B W.Backman
SS R.Santana
3B R.Knight
LF M.Wilson
CF L.Dykstra
RF D.Strawberry
C G.Carter
UT K.Mitchell
P D.Gooden
P R.Darling
P B.Ojeda
P S.Fernandez
P R.Aguilera
RP R.McDowell
RP J.Orosco
RP D.Sisk

NY 1987N
M D.Johnson
1B K.Hernandez
2B T.Teufel
SS R.Santana
3B H.Johnson
LF K.McReynolds

CF L.Dykstra
RF D.Strawberry
C G.Carter
UT M.Wilson
P R.Darling
P D.Gooden
P S.Fernandez
P R.Aguilera
P J.Mitchell
RP T.Leach
RP R.McDowell
RP D.Sisk

NY 1988N

M D.Johnson
1B K.Hernandez
2B W.Backman
SS K.Elster
3B H.Johnson
LF K.McReynolds
CF L.Dykstra
RF D.Strawberry
C G.Carter
UT D.Magadan
UT M.Wilson
P D.Gooden
P R.Darling
P D.Cone
P B.Ojeda
P S.Fernandez
RP T.Leach
RP R.McDowell
RP R.Myers

NY 1989N

M D.Johnson
1B D.Magadan
2B G.Jefferies
SS K.Elster
3B H.Johnson
LF K.McReynolds
CF J.Samuel
RF D.Strawberry
C B.Lyons
P D.Cone
P S.Fernandez
P R.Darling
P B.Ojeda
P D.Gooden
RP R.Myers
RP R.Aguilera
RP D.Aase

NY 1990N

M D.Johnson
M B.Harrelson
1B D.Magadan
2B G.Jefferies
SS K.Elster
3B H.Johnson
LF K.McReynolds
CF D.Boston
RF D.Strawberry
C M.Sasser
P F.Viola
P D.Gooden
P D.Cone
P S.Fernandez
P R.Darling
RP A.Pena
RP J.Franco
RP W.Whitehurst

NY 1991N

M B.Harrelson
M M.Cubbage
1B D.Magadan
2B G.Jefferies
SS K.Elster
3B H.Johnson
LF K.McReynolds
CF D.Boston
RF H.Brooks
C R.Cerone
UT M.Carreon
UT K.Miller
P D.Cone
P F.Viola
P D.Gooden
P W.Whitehurst
P R.Darling
RP P.Schourek
RP J.Innis
RP A.Pena

NY 1992N

M J.Torborg
1B E.Murray
2B W.Randolph
SS D.Schofield
3B D.Magadan
LF D.Boston
CF H.Johnson
RF B.Bonilla
C T.Hundley
UT D.Gallagher
UT B.Pecota
UT C.Walker
P S.Fernandez
P D.Gooden
P D.Cone
P P.Schourek
P B.Saberhagen
RP A.Young
RP W.Whitehurst
RP J.Innis

NY 1993N

M J.Torborg
M D.Green
1B E.Murray
2B J.Kent
SS T.Bogar
3B H.Johnson
LF V.Coleman
CF J.Orsulak
RF B.Bonilla
C T.Hundley
UT D.Gallagher
UT J.McKnight
UT C.Walker
P D.Gooden
P F.Tanana
P E.Hillman
P B.Saberhagen
P P.Schourek
RP A.Young
RP J.Innis
RP M.Maddux

NY 1994N

M D.Green
1B D.Segui
2B J.Kent
SS J.Vizcaino
3B B.Bonilla
LF J.Cangelosi
CF R.Thompson
RF J.Orsulak
C T.Hundley
UT F.Vina
P B.Saberhagen
P B.Jones
P P.Smith
P M.Gozzo
RP R.Mason
RP D.Linton
RP J.Franco

NY 1995N

M D.Green
1B R.Brogna
2B J.Kent
SS J.Vizcaino
3B E.Alfonzo
LF J.Orsulak
CF B.Butler
RF C.Everett
C T.Hundley
P B.Jones
P D.Mlicki
P B.Pulsipher
P B.Saberhagen
P P.Harnisch
RP J.Dipoto
RP D.Henry
RP J.Franco

NY 1996N

M D.Green
M B.Valentine
1B B.Huskey
2B J.Vizcaino
SS R.Ordonez
3B J.Kent
LF B.Gilkey
CF L.Johnson
RF A.Ochoa
C T.Hundley
UT E.Alfonzo
UT C.Everett
P M.Clark
P B.Jones
P P.Harnisch
P J.Isringhausen
P P.Wilson
RP D.Mlicki
RP J.Dipoto
RP D.Henry

NY 1997N

M B.Valentine
1B J.Olerud
2B C.Baerga
SS R.Ordonez
3B E.Alfonzo
LF B.Gilkey
CF C.Everett
RF B.Huskey
C T.Hundley
UT M.Franco
UT A.Ochoa
P R.Reed
P D.Mlicki
P B.Jones
P M.Clark
RP G.McMichael
RP C.Lidle
RP J.Franco

NY 1998N

M B.Valentine
1B J.Olerud
2B C.Baerga
SS R.Ordonez
3B E.Alfonzo
LF B.Gilkey
CF B.McRae
RF B.Huskey
C M.Piazza
UT M.Franco
UT L.Lopez
P R.Reed
P B.Jones
P A.Leiter
P M.Yoshii
RP T.Wendell
RP D.Cook
RP J.Franco

NY 1999N

M B.Valentine
1B J.Olerud
2B E.Alfonzo
SS R.Ordonez
3B R.Ventura
LF R.Henderson
CF B.McRae
RF R.Cedeno
C M.Piazza
UT B.Agbayani
UT M.Franco
P A.Leiter
P O.Hershiser
P M.Yoshii
P R.Reed
RP T.Wendell
RP A.Benitez
RP P.Mahomes

NY 2000N

M B.Valentine
1B T.Zeile
2B E.Alfonzo
SS M.Bordick
3B R.Ventura
LF B.Agbayani
CF J.Payton
RF D.Bell
C M.Piazza
UT M.Franco
UT M.Hampton
P A.Leiter
P G.Rusch
P R.Reed
P B.Jones
RP P.Mahomes
RP T.Wendell
RP A.Benitez

NY 1903A

M C.Griffith
1B J.Ganzel
2B J.Williams
SS K.Elberfeld
3B W.Conroy
LF L.Davis
CF H.McFarland
RF W.Keeler
C M.Beville
P J.Chesbro
P J.Tannehill
P C.Griffith
P H.Howell
P B.Wolfe

NY 1904A

M C.Griffith
1B J.Ganzel
2B J.Williams
SS K.Elberfeld
3B W.Conroy
LF P.Dougherty
CF J.Anderson
RF W.Keeler
C D.McGuire
UT D.Fultz
P J.Chesbro
P J.Powell
P A.Orth
P T.Hughes
P C.Griffith

NY 1905A

M C.Griffith
1B H.Chase
2B J.Williams
SS K.Elberfeld
3B J.Yeager
LF P.Dougherty
CF D.Fultz
RF W.Keeler
C R.Kleinow
UT W.Conroy
P A.Orth
P J.Chesbro
P B.Hogg
P J.Powell
P C.Griffith

NY 1906A

M C.Griffith
1B H.Chase
2B J.Williams
SS K.Elberfeld
3B F.LaPorte
LF W.Conroy
CF D.Hoffman
RF W.Keeler
C R.Kleinow
P A.Orth
P J.Chesbro
P B.Hogg
P W.Clarkson
P D.Newton

NY 1907A

M C.Griffith
1B H.Chase
2B J.Williams
SS K.Elberfeld
3B G.Moriarty
LF W.Conroy
CF D.Hoffman
RF W.Keeler
C R.Kleinow
UT F.LaPorte
P A.Orth
P J.Chesbro
P S.Doyle
P B.Hogg
P D.Newton

NY 1908A

M C.Griffith
M K.Elberfeld
1B H.Chase
2B H.Niles
SS N.Ball
3B W.Conroy
LF J.Stahl
CF C.Hemphill
RF W.Keeler
C R.Kleinow
UT G.Moriarty
P J.Chesbro
P J.Lake
P R.Manning
P B.Hogg
P A.Orth

NY 1909A

M G.Stallings
1B H.Chase
2B F.LaPorte
SS J.Knight
3B J.Austin
LF C.Engle
CF R.Demmitt
RF W.Keeler
C R.Kleinow
UT B.Cree
UT K.Elberfeld
P J.Warhop
P J.Lake
P R.Manning
P L.Brockett
P S.Doyle

NY 1910A

M G.Stallings
M H.Chase
1B H.Chase
2B F.LaPorte
SS J.Knight
3B J.Austin
LF B.Cree
CF C.Hemphill
RF H.Wolter
C E.Sweeney
UT B.Daniels
P R.Ford
P J.Warhop
P J.Quinn
P H.Vaughn
P T.Hughes

NY 1911A

M H.Chase
1B H.Chase
2B E.Gardner
SS J.Knight
3B R.Hartzell
LF B.Cree
CF B.Daniels
RF H.Wolter
C W.Blair
P R.Ford
P R.Caldwell
P J.Warhop
P J.Quinn
P R.Fisher

NY 1912A

M H.Wolverton
1B H.Chase
2B H.Simmons
SS J.Martin
3B R.Hartzell
LF B.Daniels
CF C.Sterrett
RF G.Zinn
C E.Sweeney
P R.Ford
P J.Warhop
P R.Caldwell
P G.McConnell
P J.Quinn

NY 1913A

M F.Chance
1B J.Knight
2B R.Hartzell
SS R.Peckinpaugh
3B E.Midkiff
LF B.Cree
CF H.Wolter
RF B.Daniels
C E.Sweeney
P R.Fisher
P R.Ford
P A.Schulz
P G.McConnell
P R.Caldwell

NY 1914A

M F.Chance
M R.Peckinpaugh
1B C.Mullen
2B L.Boone
SS R.Peckinpaugh
3B F.Maisel
LF R.Hartzell
CF B.Cree
RF D.Cook
C E.Sweeney
P J.Warhop
P R.Caldwell
P R.Keating
P R.Fisher
P M.McHale

NY 1915A

M B.Donovan
1B W.Pipp
2B L.Boone
SS R.Peckinpaugh
3B F.Maisel
LF R.Hartzell
CF H.High
RF D.Cook
C L.Nunamaker
P R.Caldwell
P R.Fisher
P J.Warhop
P B.Brown
P C.Pieh

NY 1916A

M B.Donovan
1B W.Pipp
2B J.Gedeon
SS R.Peckinpaugh
3B F.Baker
LF H.High
CF L.Magee
RF F.Gilhooley
C L.Nunamaker
P B.Shawkey
P G.Mogridge
P R.Fisher
P A.Russell
P N.Cullop
RP S.Love

NY 1917A

M B.Donovan
1B W.Pipp
2B F.Maisel
SS R.Peckinpaugh
3B F.Baker
LF H.High
CF E.Miller
RF T.Hendryx
C L.Nunamaker
P B.Shawkey
P R.Caldwell
P G.Mogridge
P N.Cullop
P U.Shocker

NY 1918A

M M.Huggins
1B W.Pipp
2B D.Pratt
SS R.Peckinpaugh
3B F.Baker
LF P.Bodie
CF E.Miller
RF F.Gilhooley
C T.Hannah
P G.Mogridge
P S.Love
P R.Caldwell
P A.Russell
P H.Finneran

NY 1919A

M M.Huggins
1B W.Pipp
2B D.Pratt
SS R.Peckinpaugh
3B F.Baker
LF D.Lewis
CF P.Bodie
RF S.Vick
C M.Ruel
P J.Quinn
P B.Shawkey
P H.Thormahlen
P G.Mogridge
P C.Mays

NY 1920A

M M.Huggins
1B W.Pipp
2B D.Pratt
SS R.Peckinpaugh
3B A.Ward
LF D.Lewis
CF P.Bodie
RF B.Ruth
C M.Ruel
UT B.Meusel
P C.Mays
P B.Shawkey
P J.Quinn
P R.Collins
P H.Thormahlen

NY 1921A

M M.Huggins
1B W.Pipp
2B A.Ward
SS R.Peckinpaugh
3B F.Baker
LF B.Ruth
CF E.Miller
RF B.Meusel
C W.Schang
P C.Mays
P W.Hoyt
P B.Shawkey
P R.Collins
P J.Quinn

NY 1922A

M M.Huggins
1B W.Pipp
2B A.Ward
SS E.Scott
3B J.Dugan
LF B.Ruth
CF W.Witt
RF B.Meusel
C W.Schang
P B.Shawkey
P W.Hoyt
P S.Jones
P J.Bush
P C.Mays
RP G.Murray

NY 1923A

M M.Huggins
1B W.Pipp
2B A.Ward
SS E.Scott
3B J.Dugan
LF B.Meusel
CF W.Witt
RF B.Ruth
C W.Schang
P J.Bush
P B.Shawkey
P S.Jones
P W.Hoyt
P H.Pennock

NY 1924A

M M.Huggins
1B W.Pipp
2B A.Ward
SS E.Scott
3B J.Dugan
LF B.Meusel
CF W.Witt
RF B.Ruth
C W.Schang
P H.Pennock
P J.Bush
P W.Hoyt
P B.Shawkey
P S.Jones
RP M.Gaston

NY 1925A

M M.Huggins
1B L.Gehrig
2B A.Ward
SS P.Wanninger
3B J.Dugan
LF B.Meusel
CF E.Combs
RF B.Ruth
C B.Bengough
P H.Pennock
P S.Jones
P U.Shocker
P W.Hoyt
P B.Shawkey
RP H.Johnson
RP A.Ferguson

NY 1926A

M M.Huggins
1B L.Gehrig
2B T.Lazzeri
SS M.Koenig
3B J.Dugan
LF B.Meusel
CF E.Combs
RF B.Ruth
C P.Collins
UT B.Paschal
P H.Pennock
P U.Shocker
P W.Hoyt
P S.Jones
P M.Thomas
RP G.Braxton

NY 1927A

M M.Huggins
1B L.Gehrig
2B T.Lazzeri
SS M.Koenig
3B J.Dugan
LF B.Meusel
CF E.Combs
RF B.Ruth
C P.Collins
P W.Hoyt
P W.Moore
P H.Pennock
P U.Shocker
P D.Ruether

NY 1928A

M M.Huggins
1B L.Gehrig
2B T.Lazzeri
SS M.Koenig

3B J.Dugan
LF B.Meusel
CF E.Combs
RF B.Ruth
C J.Grabowski
UT L.Durocher
P G.Pipgras
P W.Hoyt
P H.Pennock
P H.Johnson
P A.Shealy
RP W.Moore

NY 1929A

M M.Huggins
M A.Fletcher
1B L.Gehrig
2B T.Lazzeri
SS L.Durocher
3B G.Robertson
LF B.Meusel
CF E.Combs
RF B.Ruth
C B.Dickey
UT M.Koenig
P G.Pipgras
P W.Hoyt
P E.Wells
P H.Pennock
P R.Sherid
RP W.Moore

NY 1930A

M B.Shawkey
1B L.Gehrig
2B T.Lazzeri
SS L.Lary
3B B.Chapman
LF E.Combs
CF H.Rice
RF B.Ruth
C B.Dickey
P G.Pipgras
P R.Ruffing
P R.Sherid
P H.Johnson
P H.Pennock
RP L.McEvoy

NY 1931A

M J.McCarthy
1B L.Gehrig
2B T.Lazzeri
SS L.Lary
3B J.Sewell
LF B.Chapman
CF E.Combs
RF B.Ruth
C B.Dickey
UT S.Byrd
P L.Gomez
P R.Ruffing
P H.Johnson
P H.Pennock
P G.Pipgras

NY 1932A

M J.McCarthy
1B L.Gehrig
2B T.Lazzeri
SS F.Crosetti
3B J.Sewell
LF B.Chapman
CF E.Combs
RF B.Ruth
C B.Dickey
UT S.Byrd
P L.Gomez
P R.Ruffing
P G.Pipgras
P J.Allen
P H.Pennock
RP J.Brown

NY 1933A

M J.McCarthy
1B L.Gehrig
2B T.Lazzeri
SS F.Crosetti
3B J.Sewell
LF B.Chapman
CF E.Combs
RF B.Ruth
C B.Dickey
UT D.Walker
P R.Ruffing
P L.Gomez
P J.Allen
P R.Van Atta
P D.Mac Fayden
RP H.Pennock
RP W.Moore

NY 1934A

M J.McCarthy
1B L.Gehrig
2B T.Lazzeri
SS F.Crosetti
3B J.Saltzgaver
LF M.Hoag
CF B.Chapman
RF B.Ruth
C B.Dickey
UT S.Byrd
P L.Gomez
P R.Ruffing
P J.Murphy
P J.Broaca
P J.DeShong

NY 1935A

M J.McCarthy
1B L.Gehrig
2B T.Lazzeri
SS F.Crosetti
3B R.Rolfe
LF J.Hill
CF B.Chapman
RF G.Selkirk
C B.Dickey
P L.Gomez
P R.Ruffing
P J.Broaca
P J.Allen
P V.Tamulis
RP J.Murphy
RP J.DeShong
RP P.Malone

NY 1936A

M J.McCarthy
1B L.Gehrig
2B T.Lazzeri
SS F.Crosetti
3B R.Rolfe
LF J.DiMaggio
CF J.Powell
RF G.Selkirk
C B.Dickey
P R.Ruffing
P M.Pearson
P J.Broaca
P L.Gomez
P B.Hadley

NY 1937A

M J.McCarthy
1B L.Gehrig
2B T.Lazzeri
SS F.Crosetti
3B R.Rolfe
LF J.Powell
CF J.DiMaggio
RF M.Hoag
C B.Dickey
P L.Gomez
P R.Ruffing
P B.Hadley
P M.Pearson
RP J.Murphy
RP F.Makosky

NY 1938A

M J.McCarthy
1B L.Gehrig
2B J.Gordon
SS F.Crosetti
3B R.Rolfe
LF G.Selkirk
CF J.DiMaggio
RF T.Henrich
C B.Dickey
P R.Ruffing
P L.Gomez
P M.Pearson
P S.Chandler
P B.Hadley
RP J.Murphy
RP I.Andrews

NY 1939A

M J.McCarthy
1B B.Dahlgren
2B J.Gordon
SS F.Crosetti
3B R.Rolfe
LF G.Selkirk
CF J.DiMaggio
RF C.Keller
C B.Dickey
UT T.Henrich
P R.Ruffing
P L.Gomez
P B.Hadley
P A.Donald
P M.Pearson
RP J.Murphy

NY 1940A

M J.McCarthy
1B B.Dahlgren
2B J.Gordon
SS F.Crosetti
3B R.Rolfe
LF G.Selkirk
CF J.DiMaggio
RF C.Keller
C B.Dickey
P R.Ruffing
P M.Russo
P S.Chandler
P M.Breuer
P A.Donald
RP J.Murphy

NY 1941A

M J.McCarthy
1B J.Sturm
2B J.Gordon
SS P.Rizzuto
3B R.Rolfe
LF C.Keller
CF J.DiMaggio
RF T.Henrich
C B.Dickey
P M.Russo
P R.Ruffing
P S.Chandler
P A.Donald
P L.Gomez
RP J.Murphy
RP C.Stanceu
RP N.Branch

NY 1942A

M J.McCarthy
1B B.Hassett
2B J.Gordon
SS P.Rizzuto
3B F.Crosetti
LF C.Keller
CF J.DiMaggio
RF T.Henrich
C B.Dickey
P T.Bonham
P S.Chandler
P R.Ruffing
P H.Borowy
P M.Breuer
RP J.Murphy
RP J.Lindell

NY 1943A

M J.McCarthy
1B N.Etten
2B J.Gordon
SS F.Crosetti
3B B.Johnson
LF C.Keller
CF J.Lindell
RF B.Metheny
C B.Dickey
P S.Chandler
P T.Bonham
P B.Wensloff
P H.Borowy
P A.Donald
RP J.Murphy

NY 1944A

M J.McCarthy
1B N.Etten
2B S.Stirnweiss
SS M.Milosevich
3B O.Grimes
LF H.Martin
CF J.Lindell
RF B.Metheny
C M.Garbark
P H.Borowy
P M.Dubiel
P T.Bonham
P A.Donald
P B.Zuber

NY 1945A

M J.McCarthy
1B N.Etten
2B S.Stirnweiss
SS F.Crosetti
3B O.Grimes
LF H.Martin
CF T.Stainback
RF B.Metheny
C M.Garbark
P B.Bevens
P T.Bonham
P A.Gettel
P M.Dubiel
P H.Borowy
RP K.Holcombe
RP J.Turner

NY 1946A

M J.McCarthy
M B.Dickey
M J.Neun
1B N.Etten
2B J.Gordon
SS P.Rizzuto
3B S.Stirnweiss
LF C.Keller
CF J.DiMaggio
RF T.Henrich
C A.Robinson
UT J.Lindell
P S.Chandler
P B.Bevens
P J.Page
P R.Gumpert
P T.Bonham

NY 1947A

M B.Harris
1B G.McQuinn
2B S.Stirnweiss
SS P.Rizzuto
3B B.Johnson
LF J.Lindell
CF J.DiMaggio
RF T.Henrich
C A.Robinson
P A.Reynolds
P S.Shea
P B.Bevens
P S.Chandler
P B.Newsom
RP J.Page
RP R.Gumpert

NY 1948A

M B.Harris
1B G.McQuinn
2B S.Stirnweiss
SS P.Rizzuto
3B B.Johnson
LF J.Lindell
CF J.DiMaggio
RF T.Henrich
C G.Niarhos
UT Y.Berra
UT B.Brown
P A.Reynolds
P E.Lopat
P V.Raschi
P S.Shea
P T.Byrne
RP J.Page
RP F.Hiller

NY 1949A

M C.Stengel
1B T.Henrich
2B J.Coleman
SS P.Rizzuto
3B B.Brown
LF G.Woodling
CF C.Mapes
RF H.Bauer
C Y.Berra
UT B.Johnson
P V.Raschi
P E.Lopat
P A.Reynolds
P T.Byrne
P F.Sanford
RP J.Page
RP S.Shea
RP C.Marshall

NY 1950A

M C.Stengel
1B J.Collins
2B J.Coleman
SS P.Rizzuto
3B B.Johnson
LF G.Woodling
CF J.DiMaggio
RF H.Bauer
C Y.Berra
UT B.Brown
UT C.Mapes
P V.Raschi
P A.Reynolds
P E.Lopat
P T.Byrne
P F.Sanford
RP T.Ferrick
RP J.Page

NY 1951A

M C.Stengel
1B J.Collins
2B J.Coleman
SS P.Rizzuto
3B B.Brown
LF G.Woodling
CF J.DiMaggio
RF H.Bauer
C Y.Berra
UT M.Mantle
UT G.McDougald
UT J.Mize
P V.Raschi
P E.Lopat
P A.Reynolds
P T.Morgan
P S.Shea
RP J.Ostrowski

NY 1952A

M C.Stengel
1B J.Collins
2B B.Martin
SS P.Rizzuto
3B G.McDougald
LF G.Woodling
CF M.Mantle
RF H.Bauer
C Y.Berra
P A.Reynolds
P V.Raschi
P E.Lopat
P J.Sain
P B.Kuzava
RP J.McDonald
RP B.Hogue

NY 1953A

M C.Stengel
1B J.Collins
2B B.Martin
SS P.Rizzuto
3B G.McDougald
LF G.Woodling
CF M.Mantle
RF H.Bauer
C Y.Berra
UT I.Noren
P W.Ford
P J.Sain
P V.Raschi
P E.Lopat
P A.Reynolds
RP B.Kuzava
RP T.Gorman
RP R.Scarborough

NY 1954A

M C.Stengel
1B J.Collins
2B G.McDougald
SS P.Rizzuto
3B A.Carey
LF I.Noren
CF M.Mantle
RF H.Bauer
C Y.Berra
UT J.Coleman
UT G.Woodling
P W.Ford
P B.Grim
P E.Lopat
P A.Reynolds
P T.Morgan
RP J.Sain

NY 1955A

M C.Stengel
1B B.Skowron
2B G.McDougald
SS B.Hunter
3B A.Carey
LF I.Noren
CF M.Mantle
RF H.Bauer
C Y.Berra
UT J.Collins
UT E.Howard
P W.Ford
P B.Turley
P T.Byrne
P J.Kucks
P D.Larsen
RP J.Konstanty
RP T.Morgan
RP T.Sturdivant

NY 1956A

M C.Stengel
1B B.Skowron
2B B.Martin
SS G.McDougald
3B A.Carey
LF E.Howard
CF M.Mantle
RF H.Bauer
C Y.Berra
UT J.Collins
P W.Ford
P J.Kucks
P D.Larsen
P T.Sturdivant
P B.Turley
RP T.Byrne
RP B.Grim
RP T.Morgan

NY 1957A

M C.Stengel
1B B.Skowron
2B B.Richardson
SS G.McDougald
3B A.Carey
LF E.Howard
CF M.Mantle
RF H.Bauer
C Y.Berra
UT T.Kubek
UT E.Slaughter
P T.Sturdivant
P J.Kucks
P B.Turley
P B.Shantz
P D.Larsen
RP A.Ditmar
RP T.Byrne
RP B.Grim

NY 1958A

M C.Stengel
1B B.Skowron
2B G.McDougald
SS T.Kubek
3B A.Carey
LF N.Siebern
CF M.Mantle
RF H.Bauer
C Y.Berra
UT E.Howard
P B.Turley
P W.Ford
P A.Ditmar
P B.Shantz
P J.Kucks
RP R.Duren
RP Z.Monroe

NY 1959A

M C.Stengel
1B B.Skowron
2B B.Richardson
SS T.Kubek
3B H.Lopez
LF N.Siebern
CF M.Mantle
RF H.Bauer
C Y.Berra
UT E.Howard
UT G.McDougald
P W.Ford
P A.Ditmar
P B.Turley
P D.Maas
P R.Terry
RP J.Coates
RP B.Shantz
RP R.Duren

NY 1960A

M C.Stengel
1B B.Skowron
2B B.Richardson
SS T.Kubek
3B C.Boyer
LF H.Lopez
CF M.Mantle
RF R.Maris
C E.Howard
UT Y.Berra
UT G.McDougald
P A.Ditmar
P W.Ford
P B.Turley
P R.Terry
P J.Coates
RP D.Maas
RP B.Shantz
RP G.Gabler

NY 1961A

M R.Houk
1B B.Skowron
2B B.Richardson
SS T.Kubek
3B C.Boyer
LF Y.Berra
CF M.Mantle
RF R.Maris
C E.Howard
P W.Ford
P B.Stafford
P R.Terry
P R.Sheldon
P J.Coates
RP L.Arroyo

NY 1962A

M R.Houk
1B B.Skowron
2B B.Richardson
SS T.Tresh
3B C.Boyer
LF H.Lopez
CF M.Mantle
RF R.Maris
C E.Howard
P R.Terry
P W.Ford
P B.Stafford
P J.Bouton
P R.Sheldon
RP J.Coates
RP B.Daley
RP M.Bridges

NY 1963A

M R.Houk
1B J.Pepitone
2B B.Richardson
SS T.Kubek
3B C.Boyer
LF H.Lopez
CF T.Tresh
RF J.Reed
C E.Howard
P W.Ford
P R.Terry
P J.Bouton
P A.Downing
P S.Williams
RP H.Reniff
RP S.Hamilton

NY 1964A

M Y.Berra
1B J.Pepitone
2B B.Richardson
SS T.Kubek
3B C.Boyer
LF T.Tresh
CF M.Mantle
RF R.Maris
C E.Howard
UT P.Linz
UT H.Lopez
P J.Bouton
P W.Ford
P A.Downing
P R.Terry
P R.Sheldon
RP P.Mikkelsen
RP H.Reniff
RP B.Stafford

NY 1965A

M J.Keane
1B J.Pepitone
2B B.Richardson
SS T.Kubek
3B C.Boyer
LF M.Mantle
CF T.Tresh
RF H.Lopez
C E.Howard
UT R.Barker
UT P.Linz
P M.Stottlemyre
P W.Ford
P A.Downing
P J.Bouton
P B.Stafford
RP P.Ramos
RP H.Reniff
RP P.Mikkelsen

NY 1966A

M J.Keane
M R.Houk
1B J.Pepitone
2B B.Richardson
SS H.Clarke
3B C.Boyer
LF T.Tresh
CF M.Mantle
RF R.Maris
C E.Howard
UT R.White
P M.Stottlemyre
P F.Peterson
P A.Downing
P F.Talbot
P J.Bouton
RP H.Reniff
RP P.Ramos
RP S.Hamilton

NY 1967A

M R.Houk
1B M.Mantle
2B H.Clarke
SS R.Amaro
3B C.Smith
LF T.Tresh
CF J.Pepitone
RF S.Whitaker
C J.Gibbs
UT B.Robinson
P M.Stottlemyre
P A.Downing
P F.Peterson
P F.Talbot
P B.Monbouquette
RP T.Tillotson
RP D.Womack
RP J.Verbanic

NY 1968A

M R.Houk
1B M.Mantle
2B H.Clarke
SS T.Tresh
3B B.Cox
LF R.White
CF B.Robinson
RF A.Kosco
C J.Gibbs
UT J.Pepitone
P M.Stottlemyre
P S.Bahnsen
P F.Peterson
P S.Barber
P F.Talbot
RP J.Verbanic
RP D.Womack
RP L.McDaniel

NY 1969A

M R.Houk
1B J.Pepitone
2B H.Clarke
SS G.Michael
3B J.Kenney
LF R.White
CF R.Woods
RF B.Murcer
C J.Gibbs
P M.Stottlemyre
P F.Peterson
P S.Bahnsen
P B.Burbach
P A.Downing
RP L.McDaniel
RP J.Aker
RP S.Hamilton

NY 1970A

M R.Houk
1B D.Cater
2B H.Clarke
SS G.Michael
3B J.Kenney
LF R.White
CF B.Murcer
RF C.Blefary
C T.Munson
P M.Stottlemyre
P F.Peterson
P S.Bahnsen
P S.Kline
P M.Kekich
RP L.McDaniel
RP R.Klimkowski
RP J.Aker

NY 1971A

M R.Houk
1B D.Cater
2B H.Clarke
SS G.Michael
3B J.Kenney
LF R.White
CF B.Murcer
RF F.Alou
C T.Munson
P F.Peterson
P M.Stottlemyre
P S.Bahnsen
P S.Kline
P M.Kekich
RP L.McDaniel
RP J.Aker

NY 1972A

M R.Houk
1B R.Blomberg
2B H.Clarke
SS G.Michael
3B C.Sanchez
LF R.White
CF B.Murcer
RF J.Callison
C T.Munson
UT F.Alou
P M.Stottlemyre
P F.Peterson
P S.Kline
P M.Kekich
P R.Gardner
RP S.Lyle
RP L.McDaniel
RP F.Beene

NY 1973A

M R.Houk
1B F.Alou
2B H.Clarke
SS G.Michael
3B G.Nettles
LF R.White
CF B.Murcer
RF M.Alou
C T.Munson
DH J.Hart
UT R.Blomberg
P M.Stottlemyre
P D.Medich
P F.Peterson
P L.McDaniel
P P.Dobson
RP S.Lyle

NY 1974A

M B.Virdon
1B C.Chambliss
2B S.Alomar
SS J.Mason
3B G.Nettles
LF L.Piniella
CF E.Maddox
RF B.Murcer
C T.Munson
DH R.Blomberg
UT R.White
P P.Dobson
P D.Medich
P D.Tidrow
P R.May
P M.Stottlemyre
RP S.Lyle
RP C.Upshaw
RP M.Wallace

NY 1975A

M B.Virdon
M B.Martin
1B C.Chambliss
2B S.Alomar
SS J.Mason
3B G.Nettles
LF R.White
CF E.Maddox
RF B.Bonds
C T.Munson
DH E.Herrmann
UT F.Stanley
P C.Hunter
P D.Medich
P R.May
P P.Dobson
P L.Gura
RP S.Lyle
RP D.Tidrow

NY 1976A

M B.Martin
1B C.Chambliss
2B W.Randolph
SS F.Stanley
3B G.Nettles
LF R.White
CF M.Rivers
RF O.Gamble
C T.Munson
DH C.May
UT L.Piniella
P C.Hunter
P E.Figueroa
P D.Ellis
P K.Holtzman
P D.Alexander
RP S.Lyle
RP D.Tidrow
RP G.Jackson

NY 1977A

M B.Martin
1B C.Chambliss
2B W.Randolph
SS B.Dent
3B G.Nettles
LF R.White
CF M.Rivers
RF R.Jackson
C T.Munson
DH C.May
UT L.Piniella
P E.Figueroa
P M.Torrez
P R.Guidry
P D.Gullett
P D.Tidrow
RP S.Lyle
RP K.Clay

NY 1978A

M B.Martin
M D.Howser
M B.Lemon
1B C.Chambliss
2B W.Randolph
SS B.Dent
3B G.Nettles
LF L.Piniella
CF M.Rivers
RF R.Jackson
C T.Munson
DH C.Johnson
UT R.White
P R.Guidry
P E.Figueroa
P D.Tidrow
P J.Beattie
P C.Hunter
RP R.Gossage
RP S.Lyle
RP K.Clay

NY 1979A

M B.Lemon
M B.Martin
1B C.Chambliss
2B W.Randolph
SS B.Dent
3B G.Nettles
LF L.Piniella
CF B.Murcer
RF R.Jackson
C T.Munson
DH J.Spencer
P T.John
P R.Guidry
P L.Tiant
P C.Hunter
P E.Figueroa
RP R.Davis
RP K.Clay
RP D.Hood

NY 1980A

M D.Howser
1B B.Watson
2B W.Randolph
SS B.Dent
3B G.Nettles
LF L.Piniella
CF B.Brown
RF R.Jackson
C R.Cerone
DH E.Soderholm
UT B.Murcer
UT J.Spencer
P T.John
P R.Guidry
P T.Underwood
P R.May
P L.Tiant
RP R.Davis
RP R.Gossage
RP D.Bird

NY 1981A

M G.Michael
M B.Lemon
1B B.Watson
2B W.Randolph
SS B.Dent
3B G.Nettles
LF D.Winfield
CF J.Mumphrey
RF R.Jackson
C R.Cerone
DH B.Murcer
UT O.Gamble
P R.May
P T.John
P R.Guidry
P D.Righetti
P R.Reuschel
RP R.Davis
RP D.LaRoche
RP R.Gossage

NY 1982A

M B.Lemon
M G.Michael
M C.King
1B J.Mayberry
2B W.Randolph
SS R.Smalley
3B G.Nettles
LF D.Winfield
CF J.Mumphrey
RF K.Griffey
C R.Cerone
DH O.Gamble
UT D.Collins
UT L.Piniella
P R.Guidry
P T.John
P D.Righetti
P S.Rawley
P M.Morgan
RP G.Frazier
RP R.May
RP R.Gossage

NY 1983A

M B.Martin
1B K.Griffey
2B W.Randolph
SS R.Smalley
3B G.Nettles
LF D.Winfield
CF J.Mumphrey
RF S.Kemp
C B.Wynegar
DH D.Baylor
UT A.Robertson
P R.Guidry
P S.Rawley
P D.Righetti
P B.Shirley
P R.Fontenot
RP G.Frazier
RP D.Murray
RP R.Gossage

NY 1984A

M Y.Berra
1B D.Mattingly
2B W.Randolph
SS B.Meacham
3B T.Harrah
LF K.Griffey
CF O.Moreno
RF D.Winfield
C B.Wynegar
DH D.Baylor
P P.Niekro
P R.Guidry
P R.Fontenot
P D.Rasmussen
RP B.Shirley
RP J.Howell
RP D.Righetti

NY 1985A

M Y.Berra
M B.Martin
1B D.Mattingly
2B W.Randolph
SS B.Meacham
3B M.Pagliarulo
LF K.Griffey
CF R.Henderson
RF D.Winfield
C B.Wynegar
DH D.Baylor
P R.Guidry
P P.Niekro
P J.Cowley
P E.Whitson
P D.Rasmussen
RP B.Shirley
RP D.Righetti
RP B.Fisher

NY 1986A

M L.Piniella
1B D.Mattingly
2B W.Randolph
SS W.Tolleson
3B M.Pagliarulo
LF D.Pasqua
CF R.Henderson
RF D.Winfield
C B.Wynegar
DH M.Easler
P D.Rasmussen
P R.Guidry
P D.Drabek
P B.Tewksbury
P J.Niekro
RP D.Righetti
RP B.Shirley
RP B.Fisher

NY 1987A

M L.Piniella
1B D.Mattingly
2B W.Randolph
SS W.Tolleson
3B M.Pagliarulo
LF G.Ward
CF C.Washington
RF D.Winfield
C R.Cerone
UT D.Pasqua
P T.John
P R.Rhoden
P C.Hudson
P D.Rasmussen
P R.Guidry
RP D.Righetti
RP T.Stoddard
RP P.Clements

NY 1988A

M B.Martin
M L.Piniella
1B D.Mattingly
2B W.Randolph
SS R.Santana
3B M.Pagliarulo
LF R.Henderson
CF C.Washington
RF D.Winfield
C D.Slaught
DH J.Clark
P R.Rhoden
P T.John
P R.Dotson
P J.Candelaria
P C.Hudson
RP N.Allen
RP D.Righetti
RP S.Shields

NY 1989A

M D.Green
M B.Dent
1B D.Mattingly
2B S.Sax
SS A.Espinoza
3B M.Pagliarulo
LF M.Hall
CF R.Kelly
RF J.Barfield
C D.Slaught
DH S.Balboni
P A.Hawkins
P C.Parker
P D.LaPoint
P C.Cary
RP L.Guetterman
RP L.McCullers
RP E.Plunk

NY 1990A

M B.Dent
M S.Merrill
1B D.Mattingly
2B S.Sax
SS A.Espinoza
3B R.Velarde
LF O.Azocar
CF R.Kelly
RF J.Barfield
C B.Geren
DH S.Balboni
UT M.Hall
P T.Leary
P D.LaPoint
P A.Hawkins
P C.Cary
P M.Witt
RP G.Cadaret
RP L.Guetterman
RP J.Robinson

NY 1991A

M S.Merrill
1B D.Mattingly
2B S.Sax
SS A.Espinoza
3B P.Kelly
LF R.Kelly
CF B.Williams
RF M.Hall
C M.Nokes
DH K.Maas
P S.Sanderson
P J.Johnson
P T.Leary
P W.Taylor
RP G.Cadaret
RP E.Plunk
RP J.Habyan

NY 1992A

M B.Showalter
1B D.Mattingly
2B P.Kelly
SS A.Stankiewicz
3B C.Hayes
LF M.Hall
CF R.Kelly
RF D.Tartabull
C M.Nokes
DH K.Maas
UT R.Velarde
P M.Perez
P S.Sanderson
P S.Kamieniecki
P T.Leary
RP G.Cadaret
RP R.Monteleone
RP J.Habyan

NY 1993A

M B.Showalter
1B D.Mattingly
2B P.Kelly
SS S.Owen
3B W.Boggs
LF D.James
CF B.Williams
RF P.O'Neill
C M.Stanley
DH D.Tartabull
UT M.Gallego
P J.Key
P J.Abbott
P M.Perez
P S.Kamieniecki
P B.Wickman
RP R.Monteleone
RP S.Howe

NY 1994A

M B.Showalter
1B D.Mattingly
2B P.Kelly
SS M.Gallego
3B W.Boggs
LF L.Polonia
CF B.Williams
RF P.O'Neill
C M.Stanley
DH D.Tartabull
UT J.Leyritz
UT R.Velarde
P J.Key
P J.Abbott
P M.Perez
P T.Mulholland
P S.Kamieniecki
RP B.Wickman
RP S.Hitchcock
RP S.Howe

NY 1995A

M B.Showalter
1B D.Mattingly
2B P.Kelly
SS T.Fernandez
3B W.Boggs
LF G.Williams
CF B.Williams
RF P.O'Neill
C M.Stanley
DH R.Sierra
UT R.Velarde
P J.McDowell
P A.Pettitte
P S.Hitchcock
P D.Cone
P S.Kamieniecki
RP B.Wickman
RP J.Wetteland
RP S.Howe

NY 1996A

M J.Torre
1B T.Martinez
2B M.Duncan
SS D.Jeter
3B W.Boggs
LF G.Williams
CF B.Williams
RF P.O'Neill
C J.Girardi
DH R.Sierra
UT A.Fox
P A.Pettitte
P K.Rogers
P D.Gooden
P J.Key
RP M.Rivera
RP B.Wickman
RP J.Nelson

NY 1997A

M J.Torre
1B T.Martinez
2B L.Sojo
SS D.Jeter
3B C.Hayes
LF C.Curtis
CF B.Williams
RF P.O'Neill
C J.Girardi
DH C.Fielder
UT W.Boggs
P A.Pettitte
P D.Wells
P D.Cone
P K.Rogers
P R.Mendoza
RP J.Nelson
RP M.Rivera
RP M.Stanton

NY 1998A

M J.Torre
1B T.Martinez
2B C.Knoblauch
SS D.Jeter
3B S.Brosius
LF C.Curtis
CF B.Williams
RF P.O'Neill
C J.Posada
DH D.Strawberry
UT T.Raines
P A.Pettitte
P D.Wells
P D.Cone
P H.Irabu
P O.Hernandez
RP M.Stanton
RP M.Rivera
RP D.Holmes

NY 1999A

M D.Zimmer
M J.Torre
1B T.Martinez
2B C.Knoblauch
SS D.Jeter
3B S.Brosius
LF C.Curtis
CF B.Williams
RF P.O'Neill
C J.Posada
DH C.Davis
P O.Hernandez
P D.Cone
P A.Pettitte
P R.Clemens
P H.Irabu
RP R.Mendoza
RP J.Grimsley
RP M.Rivera

NY 2000A

M J.Torre
1B T.Martinez

2B C.Knoblauch
SS D.Jeter
3B S.Brosius
LF D.Justice
CF B.Williams
RF P.O'Neill
C J.Posada
DH S.Spencer
UT C.Bellinger
P A.Pettitte
P R.Clemens
P O.Hernandez
P D.Cone
RP J.Grimsley
RP M.Rivera
RP J.Nelson

Oakland

OAK A 1968-2000

OAK 1968A

M B.Kennedy
1B D.Cater
2B J.Donaldson
SS B.Campaneris
3B S.Bando
LF M.Hershberger
CF R.Monday
RF R.Jackson
C D.Duncan
P C.Hunter
P B.Odom
P J.Nash
P C.Dobson
P L.Krausse
RP D.Segui
RP J.Aker
RP E.Sprague

OAK 1969A

M H.Bauer
M J.McNamara
1B D.Cater
2B D.Green
SS B.Campaneris
3B S.Bando
LF T.Reynolds
CF R.Monday
RF R.Jackson
C P.Roof
P C.Hunter
P C.Dobson
P B.Odom
P L.Krausse
P J.Nash
RP R.Fingers
RP J.Roland
RP P.Lindblad

OAK 1970A

M J.McNamara
1B D.Mincher
2B D.Green
SS B.Campaneris
3B S.Bando
LF F.Alou
CF R.Monday
RF R.Jackson
C F.Fernandez
UT J.Rudi
P C.Dobson
P C.Hunter
P D.Segui
P B.Odom
P R.Fingers
RP M.Grant
RP P.Lindblad
RP M.Lachemann

OAK 1971A

M D.Williams
1B M.Epstein
2B D.Green
SS B.Campaneris
3B S.Bando
LF J.Rudi
CF R.Monday
RF R.Jackson
C D.Duncan
P V.Blue
P C.Hunter
P C.Dobson
P D.Segui
P B.Odom
RP R.Fingers
RP B.Locker
RP D.Knowles

OAK 1972A

M D.Williams
1B M.Epstein
2B T.Cullen
SS B.Campaneris
3B S.Bando
LF J.Rudi
CF R.Jackson
RF A.Mangual
C D.Duncan
UT M.Hegan
P C.Hunter
P K.Holtzman
P B.Odom
P V.Blue
P D.Hamilton
RP R.Fingers
RP J.Horlen
RP B.Locker

OAK 1973A

M D.Williams
1B G.Tenace
2B D.Green
SS B.Campaneris
3B S.Bando
LF J.Rudi
CF B.North
RF R.Jackson
C R.Fosse
DH D.Johnson
UT T.Kubiak
P K.Holtzman
P V.Blue
P C.Hunter
P B.Odom
RP R.Fingers
RP D.Knowles
RP H.Pina

OAK 1974A

M A.Dark
1B G.Tenace
2B D.Green
SS B.Campaneris
3B S.Bando
LF J.Rudi
CF B.North
RF R.Jackson
C L.Haney
DH J.Alou
UT T.Kubiak
UT A.Mangual
P C.Hunter
P V.Blue
P K.Holtzman
P D.Hamilton
P G.Abbott
RP R.Fingers
RP P.Lindblad
RP B.Odom

OAK 1975A

M A.Dark
1B J.Rudi
2B P.Garner
SS B.Campaneris
3B S.Bando
LF C.Washington
CF B.North
RF R.Jackson
C G.Tenace
DH B.Williams
UT J.Holt
P V.Blue
P K.Holtzman
P D.Bosman
P G.Abbott
P S.Bahnsen
RP R.Fingers
RP J.Todd
RP P.Lindblad

OAK 1976A

M C.Tanner
1B G.Tenace
2B P.Garner
SS B.Campaneris
3B S.Bando
LF J.Rudi
CF B.North
RF C.Washington
C L.Haney
DH B.Williams
UT D.Baylor
UT K.McMullen
P V.Blue
P M.Torrez
P S.Bahnsen
P P.Mitchell
P D.Bosman

RP R.Fingers
RP P.Lindblad
RP J.Todd

OAK 1977A

M J.McKeon
M B.Winkles
1B D.Allen
2B M.Perez
SS R.Picciolo
3B W.Gross
LF M.Page
CF T.Armas
RF J.Tyrone
C J.Newman
DH M.Sanguillen
UT R.Scott
UT E.Williams
P V.Blue
P R.Langford
P D.Medich
RP J.Coleman
RP B.Lacey
RP P.Torrealba

OAK 1978A

M B.Winkles
M J.McKeon
1B D.Revering
2B M.Edwards
SS M.Guerrero
3B W.Gross
LF M.Page
CF M.Dilone
RF T.Armas
C J.Essian
DH G.Alexander
UT T.Duncan
UT J.Newman
P M.Keough
P J.Johnson
P R.Langford
P P.Broberg
P S.Renko
RP D.Heaverlo
RP B.Lacey
RP E.Sosa

OAK 1979A

M J.Marshall
1B D.Revering
2B M.Edwards
SS R.Picciolo
3B W.Gross
LF R.Henderson
CF D.Murphy
RF L.Murray
C J.Newman
DH M.Page
UT J.Essian
P R.Langford
P S.McCatty
P M.Keough
P M.Norris
P C.Minetto
RP D.Heaverlo
RP D.Hamilton
RP J.Todd

OAK 1980A

M B.Martin
1B D.Revering
2B D.McKay
SS M.Guerrero
3B W.Gross
LF R.Henderson
CF D.Murphy
RF T.Armas
C J.Essian
DH M.Page
UT J.Newman
P R.Langford
P M.Norris
P M.Keough
P S.McCatty
P B.Kingman
RP B.Lacey

OAK 1981A

M B.Martin
1B J.Spencer
2B S.Babitt
SS R.Picciolo
3B W.Gross
LF R.Henderson
CF D.Murphy
RF T.Armas
C M.Heath
DH C.Johnson
UT D.McKay
UT J.Newman

P R.Langford
P S.McCatty
P M.Norris
P M.Keough
P B.Kingman
RP J.Jones
RP B.Owchinko

OAK 1982A

M B.Martin
1B D.Meyer
2B D.Lopes
SS F.Stanley
3B W.Gross
LF R.Henderson
CF D.Murphy
RF T.Armas
C M.Heath
DH C.Johnson
UT J.Burroughs
P R.Langford
P M.Keough
P M.Norris
P S.McCatty
P B.Kingman
RP T.Underwood
RP B.Owchinko
RP D.Beard

OAK 1983A

M S.Boros
1B W.Gross
2B D.Lopes
SS T.Phillips
3B C.Lansford
LF R.Henderson
CF D.Murphy
RF M.Davis
C B.Kearney
DH J.Burroughs
UT B.Almon
UT G.Hancock
P C.Codiroli
P S.McCatty
P T.Conroy
P B.Krueger
RP T.Underwood
RP T.Burgmeier
RP K.Atherton

OAK 1984A

M S.Boros
M J.Moore
1B B.Bochte
2B J.Morgan
SS T.Phillips
3B C.Lansford
LF R.Henderson
CF D.Murphy
RF M.Davis
C M.Heath
DH D.Kingman
UT B.Almon
P R.Burris
P L.Sorensen
P S.McCatty
P B.Krueger
P C.Young
RP K.Atherton
RP B.Caudill
RP T.Conroy

OAK 1985A

M J.Moore
1B B.Bochte
2B D.Hill
SS A.Griffin
3B C.Lansford
LF D.Collins
CF D.Murphy
RF M.Davis
C M.Heath
DH D.Kingman
UT D.Baker
P C.Codiroli
P D.Sutton
P B.Krueger
P T.Birtsas
RP K.Atherton
RP J.Howell
RP S.McCatty

OAK 1986A

M J.Moore
M J.Newman
M T.LaRussa
1B B.Bochte
2B T.Phillips
SS A.Griffin
3B C.Lansford
LF J.Canseco

CF D.Murphy
RF M.Davis
C M.Tettleton
DH D.Kingman
UT D.Hill
P C.Young
P J.Rijo
P J.Andujar
P D.Stewart
P E.Plunk
RP B.Mooneyham
RP S.Ontiveros
RP J.Howell

OAK 1987A

M T.LaRussa
1B M.McGwire
2B T.Phillips
SS A.Griffin
3B C.Lansford
LF J.Canseco
CF L.Polonia
RF M.Davis
C T.Steinbach
DH R.Jackson
P D.Stewart
P C.Young
P S.Ontiveros
RP G.Nelson
RP D.Eckersley
RP E.Plunk

OAK 1988A

M T.LaRussa
1B M.McGwire
2B G.Hubbard
SS W.Weiss
3B C.Lansford
LF S.Javier
CF D.Henderson
RF J.Canseco
C R.Hassey
DH D.Baylor
UT M.Gallego
UT D.Parker
UT T.Steinbach
P D.Stewart
P B.Welch
P S.Davis
P C.Young
P T.Burns
RP G.Nelson
RP R.Honeycutt
RP E.Plunk

OAK 1989A

M T.LaRussa
1B M.McGwire
2B T.Phillips
SS M.Gallego
3B C.Lansford
LF R.Henderson
CF D.Henderson
RF S.Javier
C T.Steinbach
DH D.Parker
UT R.Hassey
P D.Stewart
P M.Moore
P B.Welch
P S.Davis
P C.Young
RP T.Burns
RP G.Nelson
RP R.Honeycutt

OAK 1990A

M T.LaRussa
1B M.McGwire
2B W.Randolph
SS W.Weiss
3B C.Lansford
LF R.Henderson
CF D.Henderson
RF F.Jose
C T.Steinbach
DH J.Canseco
UT M.Gallego
P D.Stewart
P B.Welch
P S.Sanderson
P M.Moore
P C.Young
RP T.Burns
RP G.Nelson
RP D.Eckersley

OAK 1991A

M T.LaRussa
1B M.McGwire
2B M.Gallego

SS M.Bordick
3B E.Riles
LF R.Henderson
CF D.Henderson
RF J.Canseco
C T.Steinbach
DH H.Baines
UT W.Wilson
P D.Stewart
P B.Welch
P M.Moore
P J.Slusarski
RP D.Eckersley
RP C.Young
RP J.Klink

OAK 1992A

M T.LaRussa
1B M.McGwire
2B M.Bordick
SS W.Weiss
3B C.Lansford
LF R.Henderson
CF W.Wilson
RF J.Canseco
C T.Steinbach
DH H.Baines
UT L.Blankenship
UT J.Browne
P M.Moore
P R.Darling
P D.Stewart
P B.Welch
RP J.Parrett
RP D.Eckersley
RP K.Campbell

OAK 1993A

M T.LaRussa
1B M.Aldrete
2B B.Gates
SS M.Bordick
3B C.Paquette
LF R.Henderson
CF D.Henderson
RF R.Sierra
C T.Steinbach
DH T.Neel
P B.Witt
P R.Darling
P B.Welch
RP K.Downs
RP J.Boever
RP E.Nunez

OAK 1994A

M T.LaRussa
1B T.Neel
2B B.Gates
SS M.Bordick
3B S.Brosius
LF R.Henderson
CF S.Javier
RF R.Sierra
C T.Steinbach
DH G.Berroa
UT M.Aldrete
UT S.Hemond
P R.Darling
P B.Witt
P T.Van Poppel
P S.Ontiveros
RP C.Reyes
RP B.Welch
RP J.Briscoe

OAK 1995A

M T.LaRussa
1B M.McGwire
2B B.Gates
SS M.Bordick
3B C.Paquette
LF R.Henderson
CF S.Javier
RF R.Sierra
C T.Steinbach
DH G.Berroa
UT S.Brosius
P T.Stottlemyre
P T.Van Poppel
P S.Ontiveros
P R.Darling
RP C.Reyes
RP M.Acre
RP D.Eckersley

OAK 1996A

M A.Howe
1B M.McGwire
2B R.Bournigal
SS M.Bordick

3B S.Brosius
LF P.Plantier
CF E.Young
RF J.Herrera
C T.Steinbach
DH G.Berroa
UT J.Giambi
P D.Wengert
P D.Johns
P J.Wasdin
P A.Prieto
RP C.Reyes
RP M.Mohler
RP B.Groom

OAK 1997A

M A.Howe
1B M.McGwire
2B S.Spiezio
SS R.Bournigal
3B S.Brosius
LF J.Giambi
CF D.Mashore
RF M.Stairs
C B.Mayne
UT J.McDonald
UT D.Magadan
P S.Karsay
P A.Prieto
P M.Oquist
P D.Telgheder
RP D.Wengert
RP M.Mohler
RP A.Small

OAK 1998A

M A.Howe
1B J.Giambi
2B S.Spiezio
SS M.Tejada
3B M.Blowers
LF R.Henderson
CF R.Christenson
RF B.Grieve
C A.Hinch
DH M.Stairs
P K.Rogers
P T.Candiotti
P J.Haynes
P M.Oquist
P B.Stein
RP B.Taylor
RP T.Mathews
RP M.Mohler

OAK 1999A

M A.Howe
1B J.Giambi
2B T.Phillips
SS M.Tejada
3B E.Chavez
LF B.Grieve
CF R.Christenson
RF M.Stairs
C M.Macfarlane
DH J.Jaha
UT J.McDonald
UT O.Saenz
P G.Heredia
P J.Haynes
P M.Oquist
P T.Hudson
P K.Rogers
RP D.Jones
RP T.Worrell
RP B.Rigby

OAK 2000A

M A.Howe
1B Ja.Giambi
2B R.Velarde
SS M.Tejada
3B E.Chavez
LF B.Grieve
CF T.Long
RF M.Stairs
C R.Hernandez
DH Je.Giambi
UT R.Christenson
P T.Hudson
P G.Heredia
P K.Appier
P M.Mulder
P O.Olivares
RP J.Tam
RP D.Jones
RP J.Isringhausen

Philadelphia

CEN n 1875

PHI n 1873-1875
ATH n 1871-1875
PHI N 1876
PHI U 1884
PHI P 1890
PHI a 1882-1891
PHI A 1901-1954
PHI N 1883-2000

CEN 1875n
M B.Craver
1B J.Abadie
2B E.Somerville
SS B.Craver
3B G.Trenwith
LF F.Treacey
CF F.Warner
RF C.Mason
C T.McGinley
P G.Bechtel

PHI 1873n
M F.Malone
1B D.Mack
2B J.Wood
SS C.Fulmer
3B L.Meyerle
LF N.Cuthbert
CF F.Treacey
RF G.Bechtel
C F.Malone
P G.Zettlein

PHI 1874n
M N.Hicks
1B D.Mack
2B B.Craver
SS C.Fulmer
3B J.Holdsworth
LF T.York
CF D.Eggler
RF G.Bechtel
C N.Hicks
P C.Cummings

PHI 1875n
M M.McGeary
M B.Addy
1B T.Murnane
2B L.Meyerle
SS C.Fulmer
3B M.McGeary
LF F.Treacey
CF J.McMullin
RF B.Addy
C P.Snyder
P C.Fisher
P G.Zettlein
P J.Borden

ATH 1871n
M D.McBride
1B W.Fisler
2B A.Reach
SS J.Radcliff
3B L.Meyerle
LF N.Cuthbert
CF C.Sensenderfer
RF G.Heubel
C F.Malone
UT G.Bechtel
P D.McBride

ATH 1872n
M D.McBride
1B D.Mack
2B W.Fisler
SS M.McGeary
3B C.Anson
LF N.Cuthbert
CF F.Treacey
RF L.Meyerle
C F.Malone
P D.McBride

ATH 1873n
M D.McBride
1B C.Anson
2B W.Fisler
SS M.McGeary
3B E.Sutton
LF J.McMullin
CF T.Murnane
RF C.Fisher
C J.Clapp
P D.McBride

ATH 1874n
M D.McBride
1B W.Fisler
2B J.Battin
SS E.Sutton
3B C.Anson
LF C.Gedney
CF J.McMullin
RF J.Clapp
C M.McGeary
P D.McBride

ATH 1875n
M D.McBride
M C.Anson
1B W.Fisler
2B B.Craver
SS D.Force
3B E.Sutton
LF G.Hall
CF D.Eggler
RF G.Bechtel
C J.Clapp
UT C.Anson
P D.McBride
P L.Knight

PHI 1876N
M A.Wright
1B E.Sutton
2B W.Fisler
SS D.Force
3B L.Meyerle
LF G.Hall
CF D.Eggler
RF W.Coon
C F.Malone
P L.Knight
P G.Zettlein

PHI 1884U
M F.Malone
1B J.McGuinness
2B E.Peak
SS H.Easterday
3B J.McCormick
LF B.Hoover
CF B.Kienzle
RF J.Flynn
C T.Gillen
UT J.Clements
P J.Bakely
P S.Weaver
P Fisher

PHI 1890P
M J.Fogarty
M C.Buffinton
1B S.Farrar
2B J.Pickett
SS B.Shindle
3B J.Mulvey
LF G.Wood
CF M.Griffin
RF J.Fogarty
C J.Milligan
UT B.Hallman
P B.Sanders
P P.Knell
P C.Buffinton
P B.Husted
P B.Cunningham

PHI 1882a
M J.Latham
1B J.Latham
2B C.Stricker
SS L.Say
3B F.Mann
LF J.Birchall
CF J.Mansell
RF B.Blakiston
C J.O'Brien
P S.Weaver
P B.Sweeney
P F.Mountain

PHI 1883a
M L.Knight
1B H.Stovey
2B C.Stricker
SS M.Moynahan
3B G.Bradley
LF J.Birchall
CF B.Blakiston
RF L.Knight
C J.O'Brien
UT F.Corey
P B.Mathews
P J.Jones
P J.Bakely

PHI 1884a
M L.Knight
1B H.Stovey
2B C.Stricker
SS S.Houck
3B F.Corey
LF J.Birchall
CF H.Larkin
RF L.Knight
C J.Milligan
P B.Mathews
P B.Taylor
P A.Atkinson

PHI 1885a
M H.Stovey
1B H.Stovey
2B C.Stricker
SS S.Houck
3B F.Corey
LF B.Purcell
CF H.Larkin
RF J.Coleman
C J.Milligan
P B.Mathews
P T.Lovett
P E.Knouff
P E.Cushman

PHI 1886a
M L.Simmons
M B.Sharsig
1B H.Stovey
2B L.Bierbauer
SS C.McGarr
3B J.Gleason
LF H.Larkin
CF E.Greer
RF J.Coleman
C W.Robinson
UT J.O'Brien
P A.Atkinson
P B.Mathews
P B.Hart
P T.Kennedy
P C.Miller

PHI 1887a
M F.Bancroft
M C.Mason
1B J.Milligan
2B L.Bierbauer
SS C.McGarr
3B D.Lyons
LF H.Larkin
CF H.Stovey
RF T.Poorman
C W.Robinson
P E.Seward
P G.Weyhing
P A.Atkinson

PHI 1888a
M B.Sharsig
1B H.Larkin
2B L.Bierbauer
SS B.Gleason
3B D.Lyons
LF H.Stovey
CF C.Welch
RF T.Poorman
C W.Robinson
P E.Seward
P G.Weyhing
P M.Mattimore

PHI 1889a
M B.Sharsig
1B H.Larkin
2B L.Bierbauer
SS F.Fennelly
3B D.Lyons
LF H.Stovey
CF C.Welch
RF B.Purcell
C W.Robinson
P G.Weyhing
P E.Seward
P S.McMahon

PHI 1890a
M B.Sharsig
1B J.O'Brien
2B T.Shaffer
SS B.Conroy
3B D.Lyons
LF B.Purcell
CF C.Welch
RF O.Shaffer
C W.Robinson
P S.McMahon
P E.Green
P E.Seward
P D.Esper

PHI 1891a
M B.Sharsig
M G.Wood
1B H.Larkin
2B B.Hallman
SS T.Corcoran
3B J.Mulvey
LF G.Wood
CF P.Corkhill
RF L.Cross
C J.Milligan
P G.Weyhing
P E.Chamberlain
P W.Calihan

PHI 1901A
M C.Mack
1B H.Davis
2B N.Lajoie
SS J.Dolan
3B L.Cross
LF M.McIntyre
CF D.Fultz
RF S.Seybold
C D.Powers
P C.Fraser
P E.Plank
P B.Bernhard
P S.Wiltse
P W.Piatt

PHI 1902A
M C.Mack
1B H.Davis
2B D.Murphy
SS M.Cross
3B L.Cross
LF T.Hartsel
CF D.Fultz
RF S.Seybold
C O.Schreckengost
P E.Plank
P R.Waddell
P B.Husting
P S.Wiltse
P F.Mitchell

PHI 1903A
M C.Mack
1B H.Davis
2B D.Murphy
SS M.Cross
3B L.Cross
LF T.Hartsel
CF O.Pickering
RF S.Seybold
C O.Schreckengost
P E.Plank
P R.Waddell
P C.Bender
P W.Henley

PHI 1904A
M C.Mack
1B H.Davis
2B D.Murphy
SS M.Cross
3B L.Cross
LF T.Hartsel
CF O.Pickering
RF S.Seybold
C O.Schreckengost
P R.Waddell
P E.Plank
P W.Henley
P C.Bender

PHI 1905A
M C.Mack
1B H.Davis
2B D.Murphy
SS J.Knight
3B L.Cross
LF T.Hartsel
CF D.Hoffman
RF S.Seybold
C O.Schreckengost
P E.Plank
P R.Waddell
P A.Coakley
P C.Bender
P W.Henley

PHI 1906A
M C.Mack
1B H.Davis
2B D.Murphy
SS M.Cross
3B J.Knight
LF T.Hartsel
CF B.Lord
RF S.Seybold
C O.Schreckengost
UT H.Armbruster
P R.Waddell
P C.Bender
P J.Dygert
P E.Plank
P J.Coombs

PHI 1907A
M C.Mack
1B H.Davis
2B D.Murphy
SS S.Nicholls
3B J.Collins
LF T.Hartsel
CF R.Oldring
RF S.Seybold
C O.Schreckengost
P E.Plank
P R.Waddell
P J.Dygert
P C.Bender
P J.Coombs

PHI 1908A
M C.Mack
1B H.Davis
2B E.Collins
SS S.Nicholls
3B J.Collins
LF T.Hartsel
CF R.Oldring
RF D.Murphy
C O.Schreckengost
P R.Vickers
P E.Plank
P J.Dygert
P C.Bender
P B.Schlitzer

PHI 1909A
M C.Mack
1B H.Davis
2B E.Collins
SS J.Barry
3B F.Baker
LF T.Hartsel
CF R.Oldring
RF D.Murphy
C I.Thomas
P E.Plank
P C.Bender
P C.Morgan
P H.Krause
P J.Coombs

PHI 1910A
M C.Mack
1B H.Davis
2B E.Collins
SS J.Barry
3B F.Baker
LF T.Hartsel
CF R.Oldring
RF D.Murphy
C J.Lapp
P J.Coombs
P C.Morgan
P E.Plank
P C.Bender
P H.Krause

PHI 1911A
M C.Mack
1B S.McInnis
2B E.Collins
SS J.Barry
3B F.Baker
LF B.Lord
CF R.Oldring
RF D.Murphy
C I.Thomas
P J.Coombs
P E.Plank
P C.Morgan
P C.Bender
P H.Krause

PHI 1912A
M C.Mack
1B S.McInnis
2B E.Collins
SS J.Barry
3B F.Baker
LF A.Strunk
CF R.Oldring
RF B.Lord
C J.Lapp
P J.Coombs
P E.Plank
P B.Brown
P B.Houck
P C.Bender
RP H.Pennock

PHI 1913A
M C.Mack
1B S.McInnis
2B E.Collins
SS J.Barry
3B F.Baker
LF R.Oldring
CF J.Walsh
RF E.Murphy
C J.Lapp
UT A.Strunk
P E.Plank
P C.Bender
P B.Brown
P J.Bush
P B.Houck

PHI 1914A
M C.Mack
1B S.McInnis
2B E.Collins
SS J.Barry
3B F.Baker
LF R.Oldring
CF A.Strunk
RF E.Murphy
C W.Schang
P B.Shawkey
P J.Bush
P W.Wyckoff
P E.Plank
P C.Bender

PHI 1915A
M C.Mack
1B S.McInnis
2B N.Lajoie
SS L.Kopf
3B W.Schang
LF R.Oldring
CF J.Walsh
RF A.Strunk
C J.Lapp
P W.Wyckoff
P R.Bressler
P J.Bush
P T.Sheehan
P T.Knowlson

PHI 1916A
M C.Mack
1B S.McInnis
2B N.Lajoie
SS W.Witt
3B C.Pick
LF W.Schang
CF A.Strunk
RF J.Walsh
C B.Meyer
P E.Myers
P J.Bush
P J.Nabors
P T.Sheehan

PHI 1917A
M C.Mack
1B S.McInnis
2B R.Grover
SS W.Witt
3B R.Bates
LF P.Bodie
CF A.Strunk
RF C.Jamieson
C W.Schang
P J.Bush
P R.Schauer
P E.Myers
P J.Johnson
P W.Noyes

PHI 1918A
M C.Mack
1B G.Burns
2B J.Dykes
SS J.Dugan
3B L.Gardner
LF M.Kopp
CF T.Walker
RF C.Jamieson
C W.McAvoy
P S.Perry
P V.Gregg
P W.Adams
P M.Watson
P E.Myers

PHI 1919A
M C.Mack
1B G.Burns
2B W.Witt
SS J.Dugan
3B F.Thomas
LF M.Kopp
CF T.Walker
RF A.Strunk
C C.Perkins
P R.Naylor
P W.Kinney
P J.Johnson
P S.Perry
P T.Rogers

PHI 1920A
M C.Mack
1B I.Griffin
2B J.Dykes
SS C.Galloway
3B F.Thomas
LF T.Walker
CF F.Welch
RF A.Strunk
C C.Perkins
UT J.Dugan
P S.Perry
P R.Naylor
P S.Harriss
P E.Rommel
P R.Moore

PHI 1921A
M C.Mack
1B J.Walker
2B J.Dykes
SS C.Galloway
3B J.Dugan
LF T.Walker
CF F.Welch
RF W.Witt
C C.Perkins
P E.Rommel
P S.Harriss
P R.Moore
P B.Hasty
P D.Keefe
RP H.Freeman

PHI 1922A
M C.Mack
1B J.Hauser
2B R.Young
SS C.Galloway
3B J.Dykes
LF T.Walker
CF B.Miller
RF F.Welch
C C.Perkins
UT B.McGowan
P E.Rommel
P S.Harriss
P B.Hasty
P F.Heimach
P R.Naylor
RP J.Sullivan
RP C.Eckert

PHI 1923A
M C.Mack
1B J.Hauser
2B J.Dykes
SS C.Galloway
3B S.Hale
LF B.Miller
CF W.Matthews
RF F.Welch
C C.Perkins
UT B.McGowan
P E.Rommel
P B.Hasty
P S.Harriss
P F.Heimach
P R.Naylor

PHI 1924A
M C.Mack
1B J.Hauser
2B M.Bishop
SS C.Galloway
3B H.Riconda
LF B.Lamar
CF A.Simmons
RF B.Miller
C C.Perkins
UT J.Dykes
UT F.Welch
P E.Rommel
P F.Heimach
P S.Baumgartner
P D.Burns
P D.Gray
RP B.Hasty

PHI 1925A
M C.Mack
1B J.Poole
2B M.Bishop
SS C.Galloway
3B S.Hale
LF B.Lamar
CF A.Simmons
RF B.Miller
C M.Cochrane
UT J.Dykes
P E.Rommel
P S.Harriss
P D.Gray
P L.Grove
P R.Walberg

PHI 1926A
M C.Mack
1B J.Poole
2B M.Bishop
SS C.Galloway
3B J.Dykes
LF B.Lamar
CF A.Simmons
RF W.French
C M.Cochrane
UT S.Hale
UT J.Hauser
P L.Grove
P E.Rommel
P J.Quinn
P R.Walberg
P D.Gray
RP J.Pate

PHI 1927A
M C.Mack
1B J.Dykes
2B M.Bishop
SS J.Boley
3B S.Hale
LF W.Lamar
CF A.Simmons
RF T.Cobb
C M.Cochrane
UT E.Collins
UT W.French
P L.Grove
P R.Walberg
P J.Quinn
P H.Ehmke
P E.Rommel
RP J.Pate

PHI 1928A
M C.Mack
1B J.Hauser
2B M.Bishop
SS J.Boley
3B S.Hale
LF A.Simmons
CF B.Miller
RF T.Cobb
C M.Cochrane
UT J.Foxx
P L.Grove
P R.Walberg
P J.Quinn
P E.Rommel
P G.Earnshaw

PHI 1929A
M C.Mack
1B J.Foxx
2B M.Bishop
SS J.Boley
3B S.Hale
LF A.Simmons
CF M.Haas
RF B.Miller
C M.Cochrane
UT J.Dykes
P L.Grove
P R.Walberg
P G.Earnshaw
P J.Quinn
P B.Shores

PHI 1930A
M C.Mack
1B J.Foxx
2B M.Bishop
SS J.Boley
3B J.Dykes
LF A.Simmons
CF M.Haas
RF B.Miller
C M.Cochrane
P G.Earnshaw
P L.Grove
P R.Walberg
P B.Shores
P R.Mahaffey
RP J.Quinn

PHI 1931A
M C.Mack
1B J.Foxx
2B M.Bishop
SS D.Williams
3B J.Dykes
LF A.Simmons
CF M.Haas
RF B.Miller
C M.Cochrane
P R.Walberg
P L.Grove
P G.Earnshaw
P R.Mahaffey
P E.Rommel

PHI 1932A
M C.Mack
1B J.Foxx
2B M.Bishop
SS E.McNair
3B J.Dykes
LF A.Simmons
CF M.Haas
RF D.Cramer
C M.Cochrane
UT B.Miller
P L.Grove
P R.Walberg
P G.Earnshaw
P R.Mahaffey
P T.Freitas
RP L.Krausse

PHI 1933A
M C.Mack
1B J.Foxx
2B M.Bishop
SS D.Williams
3B P.Higgins
LF B.Johnson
CF D.Cramer
RF E.Coleman
C M.Cochrane
P L.Grove
P S.Cain
P R.Walberg
P R.Mahaffey
P G.Earnshaw
RP J.Peterson

PHI 1934A
M C.Mack
1B J.Foxx
2B R.Warstler
SS E.McNair
3B P.Higgins
LF B.Johnson
CF D.Cramer
RF E.Coleman
C C.Berry
P J.Marcum
P S.Cain
P B.Dietrich
P J.Cascarella
P A.Benton

PHI 1935A
M C.Mack
1B J.Foxx
2B R.Warstler
SS E.McNair
3B P.Higgins
LF B.Johnson
CF D.Cramer
RF W.Moses
C P.Richards
UT L.Finney
P J.Marcum
P B.Dietrich
P G.Blaeholder
P W.Wilshere
P R.Mahaffey
RP A.Benton
RP G.Caster
RP D.Lieber

PHI 1936A
M C.Mack
1B L.Finney
2B R.Warstler
SS S.Newsome
3B P.Higgins
LF B.Johnson
CF W.Moses
RF G.Puccinelli
C F.Hayes
UT C.Dean
P H.Kelley
P G.Rhodes
P B.Ross
P H.Fink
RP R.Gumpert

PHI 1937A
M C.Mack
M E.Mack
1B C.Dean
2B R.Peters
SS S.Newsome
3B B.Werber
LF B.Johnson
CF J.Hill
RF W.Moses
C E.Brucker
P G.Caster
P H.Kelley
P E.Smith
P B.Thomas
P B.Ross
RP H.Fink
RP G.Turbeville

PHI 1938A
M C.Mack
1B L.Finney
2B D.Lodigiani
SS W.Ambler
3B B.Werber
LF S.Chapman
CF B.Johnson
RF W.Moses
C F.Hayes
P G.Caster
P B.Thomas
P L.Nelson
P B.Ross
P E.Smith

PHI 1939A
M C.Mack
M E.Mack
1B D.Siebert
2B J.Gantenbein
SS S.Newsome
3B D.Lodigiani
LF B.Johnson
CF S.Chapman
RF W.Moses
C F.Hayes
UT W.Ambler
UT D.Miles
UT B.Nagel
P L.Nelson
P N.Potter
P B.Ross
P B.Beckmann
P G.Caster
RP C.Dean

PHI 1940A
M C.Mack
1B D.Siebert
2B B.McCoy
SS A.Brancato
3B A.Rubeling
LF B.Johnson
CF S.Chapman
RF W.Moses
C F.Hayes
P J.Babich
P N.Potter
P G.Caster
P C.Dean
P B.Ross
RP E.Heusser

PHI 1941A
M C.Mack
1B D.Siebert
2B B.McCoy
SS A.Brancato
3B P.Suder
LF B.Johnson
CF S.Chapman
RF W.Moses
C F.Hayes
P P.Marchildon
P J.Knott
P L.McCrabb
P L.Harris
P B.Beckmann

PHI 1942A
M C.Mack
1B D.Siebert
2B B.Knickerbocker
SS P.Suder
3B B.Blair
LF B.Johnson
CF M.Kreevich
RF E.Valo
C H.Wagner
UT D.Miles
P P.Marchildon
P R.Wolff
P L.Harris
P R.Christopher
P D.Fowler

PHI 1943A
M C.Mack
1B D.Siebert
2B P.Suder
SS I.Hall
3B E.Mayo
LF B.Estalella
CF J.White
RF J.Welaj
C H.Wagner
P J.Flores
P R.Wolff
P L.Harris
P D.Black
P O.Arntzen

PHI 1944A
M C.Mack
1B B.McGhee
2B I.Hall
SS E.Busch
3B G.Kell
LF F.Garrison
CF B.Estalella
RF J.White
C F.Hayes
UT D.Siebert
P B.Newsom
P R.Christopher
P L.Hamlin
P J.Flores
P D.Black
RP J.Berry

PHI 1945A
M C.Mack
1B D.Siebert
2B I.Hall
SS E.Busch
3B G.Kell
LF M.Smith
CF B.Estalella
RF H.Peck
C B.Rosar
P B.Newsom
P R.Christopher
P J.Flores
P L.Knerr
P D.Black
RP J.Berry

PHI 1946A
M C.Mack
1B G.McQuinn
2B G.Handley
SS P.Suder
3B H.Majeski
LF S.Chapman
CF B.McCosky
RF E.Valo
C B.Rosar
P P.Marchildon
P D.Fowler
P B.Savage
P J.Flores
P L.Knerr

PHI 1947A
M C.Mack
1B F.Fain
2B P.Suder
SS E.Joost
3B H.Majeski
LF B.McCosky
CF S.Chapman
RF E.Valo
C B.Rosar
UT G.Binks
P P.Marchildon
P D.Fowler
P B.McCahan
P J.Coleman
P J.Flores
RP R.Christopher

PHI 1948A
M C.Mack
1B F.Fain
2B P.Suder
SS E.Joost
3B H.Majeski
LF B.McCosky
CF S.Chapman
RF E.Valo
C B.Rosar
P P.Marchildon
P J.Coleman
P D.Fowler
P C.Scheib
P L.Brissie
RP B.Harris
RP B.Savage

PHI 1949A
M C.Mack
1B F.Fain
2B P.Suder
SS E.Joost
3B H.Majeski
LF E.Valo
CF S.Chapman
RF W.Moses
C M.Guerra
P A.Kellner
P J.Coleman
P L.Brissie
P D.Fowler
P C.Scheib
RP B.Harris

PHI 1950A
M C.Mack
1B F.Fain
2B B.Hitchcock
SS E.Joost
3B B.Dillinger
LF P.Lehner
CF S.Chapman
RF E.Valo
C M.Guerra
P L.Brissie
P A.Kellner
P B.Shantz
P H.Wyse
P B.Hooper
RP C.Scheib

PHI 1951A
M J.Dykes
1B F.Fain
2B P.Suder
SS E.Joost
3B H.Majeski
LF G.Zernial
CF D.Philley
RF E.Valo
C J.Tipton
UT L.Limmer
P A.Kellner
P B.Shantz
P B.Hooper
P C.Scheib
P M.Martin
RP J.Kucab

PHI 1952A
M J.Dykes
1B F.Fain
2B S.Kell
SS E.Joost
3B B.Hitchcock
LF G.Zernial
CF D.Philley
RF E.Valo
C J.Astroth
P B.Shantz
P A.Kellner
P H.Byrd
P C.Scheib
P B.Hooper
RP J.Kucab

PHI 1953A
M J.Dykes
1B E.Robinson
2B C.Michaels
SS J.DeMaestri
3B L.Babe
LF G.Zernial
CF E.McGhee
RF D.Philley
C J.Astroth
UT P.Suder
P H.Byrd
P M.Fricano
P A.Kellner
P C.Bishop
P B.Shantz
RP M.Martin
RP F.Fanovich

PHI 1954A
M E.Joost
1B L.Limmer
2B S.Jacobs
SS J.DeMaestri
3B J.Finigan
LF G.Zernial
CF V.Power
RF B.Renna
C J.Astroth
UT D.Bollweg
UT E.Valo
UT B.Wilson
P A.Portocarrero
P A.Kellner
P M.Fricano
P B.Trice
P J.Gray
RP S.Dixon
RP M.Burtschy
RP A.Sima

PHI 1883N
M B.Ferguson
M B.Purcell
1B S.Farrar
2B B.Ferguson
SS B.McClellan
3B F.Warner
LF B.Purcell
CF B.Harbidge
RF J.Manning
C E.Gross
P J.Coleman
P A.Hagan

PHI 1884N
M H.Wright
1B S.Farrar
2B E.Andrews
SS B.McClellan
3B J.Mulvey
LF B.Purcell
CF J.Fogarty
RF J.Manning
C J.Crowley
P C.Ferguson
P B.Vinton
P J.McElroy

PHI 1885N
M H.Wright
1B S.Farrar
2B A.Myers
SS C.Bastian
3B J.Mulvey
LF E.Andrews
CF J.Fogarty
RF J.Manning
C J.Clements
P E.Daily
P C.Ferguson
P B.Vinton

PHI 1886N
M H.Wright
1B S.Farrar
2B C.Bastian
SS A.Irwin
3B J.Mulvey
LF G.Wood
CF E.Andrews
RF J.Fogarty
C D.McGuire
UT E.Daily
P C.Ferguson
P D.Casey

PHI 1887N
M H.Wright
1B S.Farrar
2B B.McLaughlin
SS A.Irwin
3B J.Mulvey
LF G.Wood
CF E.Andrews
RF J.Fogarty
C J.Clements
P D.Casey
P C.Buffinton
P C.Ferguson

PHI 1888N
M H.Wright
1B S.Farrar
2B C.Bastian
SS A.Irwin
3B J.Mulvey
LF G.Wood
CF E.Andrews
RF J.Fogarty
C J.Clements
P C.Buffinton
P D.Casey
P B.Sanders
P K.Gleason

PHI 1889N
M H.Wright
1B S.Farrar
2B A.Myers
SS B.Hallman
3B J.Mulvey
LF G.Wood
CF J.Fogarty
RF S.Thompson
C J.Clements
P C.Buffinton
P B.Sanders
P K.Gleason
P D.Casey

PHI 1890N
M H.Wright
M J.Clements
M A.Reach
M B.Allen
M H.Wright
1B A.McCauley
2B A.Myers
SS B.Allen
3B E.Mayer
LF B.Hamilton
CF E.Burke
RF S.Thompson
C J.Clements
P K.Gleason
P T.Vickery
P P.Smith

PHI 1891N
M H.Wright
1B W.Brown
2B A.Myers
SS B.Allen
3B B.Shindle
LF B.Hamilton
CF E.Delahanty
RF S.Thompson
C J.Clements
P K.Gleason
P D.Esper
P J.Thornton

PHI 1892N
M H.Wright
1B R.Connor
2B B.Hallman
SS B.Allen
3B C.Reilly
LF B.Hamilton
CF E.Delahanty
RF S.Thompson
C J.Clements
UT L.Cross
P G.Weyhing
P K.Carsey
P T.Keefe
P D.Esper

PHI 1893N
M H.Wright
1B J.Boyle
2B B.Hallman
SS B.Allen

3B C.Reilly
LF E.Delahanty
CF B.Hamilton
RF S.Thompson
C J.Clements
UT L.Cross
P G.Weyhing
P K.Carsey
P T.Keefe
P J.Taylor

PHI 1894N
M A.Irwin
1B J.Boyle
2B B.Hallman
SS J.Sullivan
3B L.Cross
LF E.Delahanty
CF B.Hamilton
RF S.Thompson
C J.Clements
UT T.Turner
P J.Taylor
P K.Carsey
P G.Weyhing
P G.Harper

PHI 1895N
M A.Irwin
1B J.Boyle
2B B.Hallman
SS J.Sullivan
3B L.Cross
LF E.Delahanty
CF B.Hamilton
RF S.Thompson
C J.Clements
P K.Carsey
P J.Taylor
P W.McGill
P A.Orth

PHI 1896N
M B.Nash
1B D.Brouthers
2B B.Hallman
SS B.Hulen
3B B.Nash
LF E.Delahanty
CF D.Cooley
RF S.Thompson
C M.Grady
UT L.Cross
P J.Taylor
P A.Orth
P K.Carsey
P H.Keener
P W.McGill

PHI 1897N
M G.Stallings
1B N.Lajoie
2B L.Cross
SS S.Gillen
3B B.Nash
LF E.Delahanty
CF D.Cooley
RF T.Dowd
C J.Boyle
UT P.Geier
P J.Taylor
P A.Orth
P J.Fifield
P G.Wheeler

PHI 1898N
M G.Stallings
M B.Shettsline
1B K.Douglass
2B N.Lajoie
SS M.Cross
3B B.Lauder
LF E.Delahanty
CF D.Cooley
RF E.Flick
C E.McFarland
P W.Piatt
P R.Donahue
P A.Orth
P J.Fifield
P G.Wheeler

PHI 1899N
M B.Shettsline
1B D.Cooley
2B N.Lajoie
SS M.Cross
3B B.Lauder
LF E.Delahanty
CF R.Thomas
RF E.Flick
C E.McFarland
UT P.Chiles
P W.Piatt
P R.Donahue
P C.Fraser
P A.Orth
P B.Bernhard

PHI 1900N
M B.Shettsline
1B E.Delahanty
2B N.Lajoie
SS M.Cross
3B H.Wolverton
LF J.Slagle
CF R.Thomas
RF E.Flick
C E.McFarland
P A.Orth
P R.Donahue
P C.Fraser
P B.Bernhard
P W.Piatt

PHI 1901N
M B.Shettsline
1B H.Jennings
2B B.Hallman
SS M.Cross
3B H.Wolverton
LF E.Delahanty
CF R.Thomas
RF E.Flick
C E.McFarland
P R.Donahue
P B.Duggleby
P A.Orth
P D.White
P H.Townsend

PHI 1902N
M B.Shettsline
1B H.Jennings
2B P.Childs
SS R.Hulswitt
3B B.Hallman
LF G.Browne
CF R.Thomas
RF S.Barry
C R.Dooin
UT K.Douglass
P D.White
P B.Duggleby
P H.Iburg
P C.Fraser

PHI 1903N
M C.Zimmer
1B K.Douglass
2B K.Gleason
SS R.Hulswitt
3B H.Wolverton
LF S.Barry
CF R.Thomas
RF B.Keister
C F.Roth
P B.Duggleby
P C.Fraser
P T.Sparks
P F.Mitchell
P J.McFetridge

PHI 1904N
M H.Duffy
1B J.Doyle
2B K.Gleason
SS R.Hulswitt
3B H.Wolverton
LF J.Titus
CF R.Thomas
RF S.Magee
C R.Dooin
UT J.Lush
P C.Fraser
P B.Duggleby
P T.Sparks
P J.Sutthoff
P J.McPherson

PHI 1905N
M H.Duffy
1B K.Bransfield
2B K.Gleason
SS M.Doolan
3B E.Courtney
LF S.Magee
CF R.Thomas
RF J.Titus
C R.Dooin
P T.Pittinger
P B.Duggleby
P T.Sparks
P F.Corridon
P K.Nichols

PHI 1906N
M H.Duffy
1B K.Bransfield
2B K.Gleason
SS M.Doolan
3B E.Courtney
LF S.Magee
CF R.Thomas
RF J.Titus
C R.Dooin
P T.Sparks
P J.Lush
P B.Duggleby
P L.Richie
P T.Pittinger

PHI 1907N
M B.Murray
1B K.Bransfield
2B O.Knabe
SS M.Doolan
3B E.Courtney
LF S.Magee
CF R.Thomas
RF J.Titus
C R.Dooin
P F.Corridon
P T.Sparks
P L.Moren
P B.Brown
P L.Richie

PHI 1908N
M B.Murray
1B K.Bransfield
2B O.Knabe
SS M.Doolan
3B E.Grant
LF S.Magee
CF F.Osborn
RF J.Titus
C R.Dooin
P G.McQuillan
P T.Sparks
P F.Corridon
P L.Richie
P L.Moren

PHI 1909N
M B.Murray
1B K.Bransfield
2B O.Knabe
SS M.Doolan
3B E.Grant
LF S.Magee
CF J.Bates
RF J.Titus
C R.Dooin
P E.Moore
P L.Moren
P G.McQuillan
P F.Corridon
P T.Sparks

PHI 1910N
M R.Dooin
1B K.Bransfield
2B O.Knabe
SS M.Doolan
3B E.Grant
LF S.Magee
CF J.Bates
RF J.Titus
C R.Dooin
P E.Moore
P B.Ewing
P L.Moren
P G.McQuillan
P E.Stack

PHI 1911N
M R.Dooin
1B F.Luderus
2B O.Knabe
SS M.Doolan
3B H.Lobert
LF S.Magee
CF D.Paskert
RF F.Beck
C R.Dooin
UT J.Walsh
P G.Alexander
P E.Moore
P G.Chalmers
P B.Burns

PHI 1912N
M R.Dooin
1B F.Luderus
2B O.Knabe
SS M.Doolan
3B H.Lobert
LF S.Magee
CF D.Paskert
RF G.Cravath
C B.Killefer
P G.Alexander
P T.Seaton
P E.Moore
P A.Brennan
P E.Rixey
RP T.Shultz

PHI 1913N
M R.Dooin
1B F.Luderus
2B O.Knabe
SS M.Doolan
3B H.Lobert
LF S.Magee
CF D.Paskert
RF G.Cravath
C B.Killefer
P T.Seaton
P G.Alexander
P A.Brennan
P E.Mayer
P E.Rixey

PHI 1914N
M R.Dooin
1B F.Luderus
2B B.Byrne
SS J.Martin
3B H.Lobert
LF B.Becker
CF D.Paskert
RF G.Cravath
C B.Killefer
UT S.Magee
P G.Alexander
P E.Mayer
P B.Tincup
P R.Marshall
P J.Oeschger

PHI 1915N
M P.Moran
1B F.Luderus
2B B.Niehoff
SS D.Bancroft
3B B.Byrne
LF B.Becker
CF P.Whitted
RF G.Cravath
C B.Killefer
UT D.Paskert
P G.Alexander
P E.Mayer
P A.Demaree
P E.Rixey
P G.Chalmers

PHI 1916N
M P.Moran
1B F.Luderus
2B B.Niehoff
SS D.Bancroft
3B M.Stock
LF P.Whitted
CF D.Paskert
RF G.Cravath
C B.Killefer
P G.Alexander
P E.Rixey
P A.Demaree
P E.Mayer
P C.Bender
RP G.McQuillan

PHI 1917N
M P.Moran
1B F.Luderus
2B B.Niehoff
SS D.Bancroft
3B M.Stock
LF P.Whitted
CF D.Paskert
RF G.Cravath
C B.Killefer
P G.Alexander
P E.Rixey
P J.Oeschger
P E.Mayer
P J.Lavender

PHI 1918N
M P.Moran
1B F.Luderus
2B P.McGaffigan
SS D.Bancroft
3B M.Stock
LF I.Meusel
CF C.Williams
RF G.Cravath
C B.Adams
P M.Prendergast
P B.Hogg
P J.Oeschger
P E.Jacobs
P M.Watson
RP D.Davis

PHI 1919N
M J.Coombs
M G.Cravath
1B F.Luderus
2B G.Paulette
SS D.Bancroft
3B L.Blackburne
LF I.Meusel
CF C.Williams
RF L.Callahan
C B.Adams
P G.Smith
P L.Meadows
P E.Rixey
P B.Hogg
P G.Packard

PHI 1920N
M G.Cravath
1B G.Paulette
2B J.Rawlings
SS A.Fletcher
3B R.Miller
LF I.Meusel
CF C.Williams
RF C.Stengel
C M.Wheat
UT D.Miller
P E.Rixey
P G.Smith
P L.Meadows
P R.Causey
P B.Hubbell

PHI 1921N
M B.Donovan
M K.Wilhelm
1B E.Konetchy
2B J.Smith
SS F.Parkinson
3B R.Wrightstone
LF I.Meusel
CF C.Williams
RF B.LeBourveau
C F.Bruggy
P J.Ring
P G.Smith
P B.Hubbell
P L.Meadows
P J.Winters

PHI 1922N
M K.Wilhelm
1B R.Leslie
2B F.Parkinson
SS A.Fletcher
3B G.Rapp
LF C.Lee
CF C.Williams
RF C.Walker
C B.Henline
UT R.Wrightstone
P J.Ring
P L.Meadows
P G.Smith
P B.Hubbell
P L.Weinert

PHI 1923N
M A.Fletcher
1B W.Holke
2B C.Tierney
SS H.Sand
3B R.Wrightstone
LF J.Mokan
CF C.Williams
RF C.Walker
C B.Henline
UT C.Lee
P J.Ring
P W.Glazner
P L.Weinert
P C.Mitchell
P R.Head
RP B.Hubbell

PHI 1924N
M A.Fletcher
1B W.Holke
2B H.Ford
SS H.Sand
3B R.Wrightstone
LF J.Mokan
CF C.Williams
RF G.Harper
C B.Henline
UT J.Wilson
P J.Ring
P H.Carlson
P B.Hubbell
P C.Mitchell
P W.Glazner

PHI 1925N
M A.Fletcher
1B C.Hawks
2B B.Friberg
SS H.Sand
3B C.Huber
LF G.Burns
CF G.Harper
RF C.Williams
C J.Wilson
UT L.Fonseca
P J.Ring
P H.Carlson
P C.Mitchell
P A.Decatur
P J.Knight
RP H.Betts
RP J.Couch

PHI 1926N
M A.Fletcher
1B J.Bentley
2B B.Friberg
SS H.Sand
3B C.Huber
LF J.Mokan
CF F.Leach
RF C.Williams
C J.Wilson
UT B.Henline
UT A.Nixon
UT R.Wrightstone
P H.Carlson
P W.Dean
P C.Mitchell
P C.Willoughby
P D.Ulrich
RP R.Pierce
RP E.Baecht

PHI 1927N
M S.McInnis
1B R.Wrightstone
2B F.Thompson
SS H.Sand
3B B.Friberg
LF D.Spalding
CF F.Leach
RF C.Williams
C J.Wilson
P J.Scott
P A.Ferguson
P D.Ulrich
P H.Pruett
P L.Sweetland
RP C.Willoughby

PHI 1928N
M B.Shotton
1B D.Hurst
2B F.Thompson
SS H.Sand
3B P.Whitney
LF F.Leach
CF D.Sothern
RF C.Williams
C W.Lerian
P R.Benge
P J.Ring
P L.Sweetland
P A.Ferguson
P C.Willoughby

PHI 1929N
M B.Shotton
1B D.Hurst
2B F.Thompson
SS T.Thevenow
3B P.Whitney
LF L.O'Doul
CF D.Sothern
RF C.Klein
C W.Lerian
UT S.Davis
UT B.Friberg
P C.Willoughby
P L.Sweetland
P R.Benge
P P.Collins
RP H.Elliott
RP B.McGraw
RP S.Dailey

PHI 1930N
M B.Shotton
1B D.Hurst
2B F.Thompson
SS T.Thevenow
3B P.Whitney
LF L.O'Doul
CF D.Sothern
RF C.Klein
C S.Davis
UT B.Friberg
P P.Collins
P R.Benge
P L.Sweetland
P C.Willoughby
P H.Collard
RP H.Elliott
RP H.Smythe

PHI 1931N
M B.Shotton
1B D.Hurst
2B L.Mallon
SS D.Bartell
3B P.Whitney
LF C.Klein
CF F.Brickell
RF B.Arlett
C S.Davis
UT B.Friberg
P J.Elliott
P R.Benge
P P.Collins
P C.Dudley
P F.Watt

PHI 1932N
M B.Shotton
1B D.Hurst
2B L.Mallon
SS D.Bartell
3B P.Whitney
LF H.Lee
CF K.Davis
RF C.Klein
C S.Davis
P E.Holley
P R.Benge
P S.Hansen
P P.Collins
P F.Rhem

PHI 1933N
M B.Shotton
1B D.Hurst
2B J.Warner
SS D.Bartell
3B J.McLeod
LF W.Schulmerich
CF C.Fullis
RF C.Klein
C S.Davis
P E.Holley
P S.Hansen
P J.Elliott
P C.Moore
P P.Collins
RP A.Liska

PHI 1934N
M J.Wilson
1B D.Camilli
2B L.Chiozza
SS D.Bartell
3B B.Walters
LF E.Allen
CF K.Davis
RF J.Moore
C A.Todd
UT J.Wilson
P C.Davis
P P.Collins
P S.Hansen
P S.Johnson
P C.Moore
RP R.Grabowski

RP G.Darrow

PHI 1935N

M J.Wilson
1B D.Camilli
2B L.Chiozza
SS M.Haslin
3B J.Vergez
LF G.Watkins
CF E.Allen
RF J.Moore
C A.Todd
P C.Davis
P O.Jorgens
P S.Johnson
P J.Bivin
P B.Walters
RP P.Pezzullo
RP R.Prim
RP H.Mulcahy

PHI 1936N

M J.Wilson
1B D.Camilli
2B C.Gomez
SS L.Norris
3B P.Whitney
LF J.Moore
CF E.Sulik
RF C.Klein
C E.Grace
UT L.Chiozza
P B.Walters
P C.Passeau
P J.Bowman
P O.Jorgens
RP S.Johnson
RP E.Moore

PHI 1937N

M J.Wilson
1B D.Camilli
2B D.Young
SS G.Scharein
3B P.Whitney
LF M.Arnovich
CF H.Martin
RF C.Klein
C B.Atwood
UT E.Browne
UT J.Moore
UT L.Norris
P C.Passeau
P B.Walters
P W.LaMaster
P H.Mulcahy
P S.Johnson
RP O.Jorgens
RP H.Kelleher

PHI 1938N

M J.Wilson
M H.Lobert
1B P.Weintraub
2B H.Mueller
SS D.Young
3B P.Whitney
LF M.Arnovich
CF H.Martin
RF C.Klein
C B.Atwood
UT G.Scharein
P H.Mulcahy
P C.Passeau
P A.Hollingsworth
P M.Butcher
RP P.Sivess
RP A.Smith

PHI 1939N

M D.Prothro
1B G.Suhr
2B R.Hughes
SS G.Scharein
3B P.May
LF M.Arnovich
CF H.Martin
RF L.Scott
C S.Davis
UT G.Brack
UT H.Mueller
P H.Mulcahy
P K.Higbe
P B.Beck
P I.Pearson
P S.Johnson
RP B.Kerksieck

PHI 1940N

M D.Prothro
1B A.Mahan
2B H.Schulte
SS B.Bragan
3B P.May
LF J.Rizzo
CF J.Marty
RF C.Klein
C B.Warren
UT H.Mueller
P K.Higbe
P H.Mulcahy
P I.Pearson
P S.Johnson
P B.Beck

PHI 1941N

M D.Prothro
1B N.Etten
2B D.Murtaugh
SS B.Bragan
3B P.May
LF D.Litwhiler
CF J.Marty
RF S.Benjamin
C B.Warren
UT M.Livingston
UT J.Rizzo
P J.Podgajny
P T.Hughes
P C.Blanton
P S.Johnson
P L.Grissom
RP I.Pearson
RP L.Hoerst
RP B.Beck

PHI 1942N

M H.Lobert
1B N.Etten
2B A.Glossop
SS B.Bragan
3B P.May
LF D.Litwhiler
CF E.Koy
RF R.Northey
C B.Warren
UT D.Murtaugh
UT L.Waner
P T.Hughes
P R.Melton
P S.Johnson
P J.Podgajny
P L.Hoerst
RP I.Pearson
RP S.Nahem
RP B.Beck

PHI 1943N

M B.Harris
M F.Fitzsimmons
1B J.Wasdell
2B D.Murtaugh
SS G.Stewart
3B P.May
LF C.Triplett
CF B.Adams
RF R.Northey
C M.Livingston
UT B.Dahlgren
P A.Gerheauser
P J.Kraus
P S.Rowe
P D.Barrett
P S.Johnson
RP N.Kimball

PHI 1944N

M F.Fitzsimmons
1B T.Lupien
2B M.Mullen
SS R.Hamrick
3B G.Stewart
LF J.Wasdell
CF B.Adams
RF R.Northey
C B.Finley
UT C.Letchas
P K.Raffensberger
P C.Schanz
P D.Barrett
P B.Lee
P A.Gerheauser
RP A.Karl

PHI 1945N

M F.Fitzsimmons
M B.Chapman
1B J.Wasdell
2B T.Daniels
SS B.Mott
3B J.Antonelli
LF C.Triplett
CF V.DiMaggio
RF V.Dinges
C A.Seminick
UT R.Monteagudo
P D.Barrett
P C.Schanz
P C.Sproull
P D.Mauney
RP A.Karl

PHI 1946N

M B.Chapman
1B F.McCormick
2B E.Verban
SS S.Newsome
3B J.Tabor
LF D.Ennis
CF J.Wyrostek
RF R.Northey
C A.Seminick
P K.Raffensberger
P O.Judd
P S.Rowe
P C.Schanz
P T.Hughes
RP A.Karl
RP D.Mulligan

PHI 1947N

M B.Chapman
1B H.Schultz
2B E.Verban
SS S.Newsome
3B L.Handley
LF D.Ennis
CF H.Walker
RF J.Wyrostek
C A.Seminick
P D.Leonard
P S.Rowe
P O.Judd
P K.Heintzelman
P T.Hughes
RP F.Schmidt

PHI 1948N

M B.Chapman
M D.Cooke
M E.Sawyer
1B D.Sisler
2B G.Hamner
SS E.Miller
3B P.Caballero
LF J.Blatnik
CF R.Ashburn
RF D.Ennis
C A.Seminick
UT B.Haas
UT H.Walker
P D.Leonard
P C.Simmons
P M.Dubiel
P S.Rowe
P R.Roberts
RP E.Heusser
RP S.Nahem

PHI 1949N

M E.Sawyer
1B D.Sisler
2B E.Miller
SS G.Hamner
3B W.Jones
LF D.Ennis
CF R.Ashburn
RF B.Nicholson
C A.Seminick
P K.Heintzelman
P R.Roberts
P R.Meyer
P H.Borowy
P C.Simmons
RP J.Konstanty
RP K.Trinkle
RP S.Rowe

PHI 1950N

M E.Sawyer
1B E.Waitkus
2B M.Goliat
SS G.Hamner
3B W.Jones
LF D.Sisler
CF R.Ashburn
RF D.Ennis
C A.Seminick
P R.Roberts
P C.Simmons
P B.Miller
P R.Meyer
P B.Church
RP J.Konstanty

PHI 1951N

M E.Sawyer
1B E.Waitkus
2B P.Caballero
SS G.Hamner
3B W.Jones
LF D.Sisler
CF R.Ashburn
RF D.Ennis
C A.Seminick
P R.Roberts
P B.Church
P R.Meyer
P J.Thompson
P K.Heintzelman
RP J.Konstanty

PHI 1952N

M E.Sawyer
M S.O'Neill
1B E.Waitkus
2B C.Ryan
SS G.Hamner
3B W.Jones
LF D.Ennis
CF R.Ashburn
RF J.Wyrostek
C S.Burgess
P R.Roberts
P R.Meyer
P K.Drews
P C.Simmons
P S.Ridzik
RP J.Konstanty
RP A.Hansen

PHI 1953N

M S.O'Neill
1B E.Torgeson
2B G.Hamner
SS T.Kazanski
3B W.Jones
LF D.Ennis
CF R.Ashburn
RF J.Wyrostek
C S.Burgess
P R.Roberts
P C.Simmons
P K.Drews
P J.Konstanty
P B.Miller
RP S.Ridzik
RP A.Hansen

PHI 1954N

M S.O'Neill
M T.Moore
1B E.Torgeson
2B G.Hamner
SS B.Morgan
3B W.Jones
LF D.Schell
CF R.Ashburn
RF D.Ennis
C S.Burgess
P R.Roberts
P C.Simmons
P M.Dickson
P B.Miller
P H.Wehmeier
RP S.Ridzik
RP J.Konstanty

PHI 1955N

M M.Smith
1B M.Blaylock
2B B.Morgan
SS R.Smalley
3B W.Jones
LF D.Ennis
CF R.Ashburn
RF J.Greengrass
C A.Seminick
UT G.Hamner
UT S.Lopata
P R.Roberts
P M.Dickson
P H.Wehmeier
P C.Simmons
RP J.Meyer
RP B.Miller

PHI 1956N

M M.Smith
1B M.Blaylock
2B T.Kazanski
SS G.Hamner
3B W.Jones
LF D.Ennis
CF R.Ashburn
RF E.Valo
C S.Lopata
P R.Roberts
P H.Haddix
P C.Simmons
P S.Rogovin
P S.Miller
RP B.Miller
RP J.Meyer
RP R.Negray

PHI 1957N

M M.Smith
1B E.Bouchee
2B G.Hamner
SS C.Fernandez
3B W.Jones
LF H.Anderson
CF R.Ashburn
RF R.Repulski
C S.Lopata
UT B.Bowman
P R.Roberts
P J.Sanford
P C.Simmons
P H.Haddix
P D.Cardwell
RP T.Farrell
RP J.Hearn
RP B.Miller

PHI 1958N

M M.Smith
M E.Sawyer
1B E.Bouchee
2B S.Hemus
SS C.Fernandez
3B W.Jones
LF H.Anderson
CF R.Ashburn
RF W.Post
C S.Lopata
UT T.Kazanski
P R.Roberts
P R.Semproch
P J.Sanford
P C.Simmons
P D.Cardwell
RP T.Farrell
RP J.Meyer
RP J.Hearn

PHI 1959N

M E.Sawyer
1B E.Bouchee
2B S.Anderson
SS J.Koppe
3B G.Freese
LF H.Anderson
CF R.Ashburn
RF W.Post
C C.Sawatski
UT D.Philley
P R.Roberts
P J.Owens
P G.Conley
P D.Cardwell
P R.Semproch
RP J.Meyer
RP H.Robinson
RP T.Phillips

PHI 1960N

M E.Sawyer
M A.Cohen
M G.Mauch
1B P.Herrera
2B T.Taylor
SS R.Amaro
3B A.Dark
LF B.Smith
CF B.Del Greco
RF K.Walters
C J.Coker
UT T.Curry
UT J.Callison
P R.Roberts
P J.Buzhardt
P G.Conley
P J.Owens
P D.Green
RP C.Short
RP T.Farrell
RP R.Gomez

PHI 1961N

M G.Mauch
1B P.Herrera
2B T.Taylor
SS R.Amaro
3B C.Smith
LF J.Callison
CF T.Gonzalez
RF K.Walters
C C.Dalrymple
UT B.Malkmus
UT D.Demeter
P A.Mahaffey
P J.Buzhardt
P F.Sullivan
P D.Ferrarese
P D.Green
RP J.Baldschun
RP K.Lehman

PHI 1962N

M G.Mauch
1B R.Sievers
2B T.Taylor
SS B.Wine
3B D.Demeter
LF T.Savage
CF T.Gonzalez
RF J.Callison
C C.Dalrymple
UT W.Covington
UT B.Klaus
UT F.Torre
P A.Mahaffey
P J.Hamilton
P D.Bennett
P C.McLish
P C.Short
RP J.Baldschun
RP P.Brown
RP B.Smith

PHI 1963N

M G.Mauch
1B R.Sievers
2B T.Taylor
SS B.Wine
3B D.Hoak
LF T.Gonzalez
CF D.Demeter
RF J.Callison
C C.Dalrymple
UT R.Amaro
UT W.Covington
P C.McLish
P R.Culp
P C.Short
P A.Mahaffey
P D.Green
RP J.Baldschun
RP J.Klippstein
RP R.Duren

PHI 1964N

M G.Mauch
1B J.Herrnstein
2B T.Taylor
SS B.Wine
3B D.Allen
LF W.Covington
CF T.Gonzalez
RF J.Callison
C C.Dalrymple
UT R.Amaro
UT C.Rojas
P J.Bunning
P C.Short
P D.Bennett
P A.Mahaffey
P R.Culp
RP J.Baldschun
RP E.Roebuck
RP R.Wise

PHI 1965N

M G.Mauch
1B D.Stuart
2B T.Taylor
SS B.Wine
3B D.Allen
LF A.Johnson
CF T.Gonzalez
RF J.Callison
C C.Dalrymple
UT R.Amaro
UT W.Covington
UT C.Rojas
P C.Short
P J.Bunning
P R.Culp
P R.Herbert
P B.Belinsky
RP G.Wagner
RP J.Baldschun
RP E.Roebuck

PHI 1966N

M G.Mauch
1B B.White
2B C.Rojas
SS D.Groat
3B D.Allen
LF T.Gonzalez
CF J.Briggs
RF J.Callison
C C.Dalrymple
UT T.Taylor
P J.Bunning
P C.Short
P L.Jackson
P B.Buhl
P R.Culp
RP D.Knowles
RP R.Herbert

PHI 1967N

M G.Mauch
1B B.White
2B C.Rojas
SS B.Wine
3B D.Allen
LF T.Gonzalez
CF J.Briggs
RF J.Callison
C C.Dalrymple
UT D.Lock
UT G.Sutherland
UT T.Taylor
P J.Bunning
P L.Jackson
P C.Short
P R.Wise
P D.Ellsworth
RP T.Farrell
RP D.Hall
RP G.Jackson

PHI 1968N

M G.Mauch
M G.Myatt
M B.Skinner
1B B.White
2B C.Rojas
SS R.Pena
3B T.Taylor
LF D.Allen
CF T.Gonzalez
RF J.Callison
C M.Ryan
UT J.Briggs
UT D.Lock
P C.Short
P L.Jackson
P W.Fryman
P R.Wise
P J.James
RP T.Farrell
RP G.Wagner
RP J.Boozer

PHI 1969N

M B.Skinner
M G.Myatt
1B D.Allen
2B C.Rojas
SS D.Money
3B T.Taylor
LF J.Briggs
CF L.Hisle
RF J.Callison
C M.Ryan
UT D.Johnson
UT R.Joseph
UT R.Stone
P G.Jackson
P W.Fryman
P R.Wise
P J.Johnson
P B.Champion
RP J.Boozer
RP T.Farrell
RP A.Raffo

PHI 1970N

M F.Lucchesi
1B D.Johnson
2B D.Doyle
SS L.Bowa
3B D.Money
LF J.Briggs
CF L.Hisle
RF R.Stone
C M.Ryan
UT B.Browne
UT T.Taylor
P R.Wise
P J.Bunning

P C.Short
P G.Jackson
P B.Lersch
RP D.Selma
RP L.Palmer
RP B.Wilson

PHI 1971N

M F.Lucchesi
1B D.Johnson
2B D.Doyle
SS L.Bowa
3B J.Vukovich
LF O.Gamble
CF W.Montanez
RF R.Freed
C T.McCarver
UT D.Money
P R.Wise
P B.Lersch
P C.Short
P K.Reynolds
P W.Fryman
RP B.Champion
RP B.Brandon
RP J.Hoerner

PHI 1972N

M F.Lucchesi
M P.Owens
1B T.Hutton
2B D.Doyle
SS L.Bowa
3B D.Money
LF G.Luzinski
CF W.Montanez
RF B.Robinson
C J.Bateman
UT D.Johnson
P S.Carlton
P K.Reynolds
P B.Champion
P W.Fryman
RP W.Twitchell
RP B.Brandon
RP B.Lersch

PHI 1973N

M D.Ozark
1B W.Montanez
2B D.Doyle
SS L.Bowa
3B M.Schmidt
LF G.Luzinski
CF D.Unser
RF B.Robinson
C B.Boone
UT T.Hutton
UT C.Tovar
P S.Carlton
P W.Twitchell
P K.Brett
P J.Lonborg
P D.Ruthven
RP B.Lersch
RP M.Scarce
RP B.Brandon

PHI 1974N

M D.Ozark
1B W.Montanez
2B D.Cash
SS L.Bowa
3B M.Schmidt
LF G.Luzinski
CF D.Unser
RF M.Anderson
C B.Boone
UT B.Robinson
P S.Carlton
P J.Lonborg
P D.Ruthven
P R.Schueler
P W.Twitchell
RP M.Scarce
RP G.Garber

PHI 1975N

M D.Ozark
1B D.Allen
2B D.Cash
SS L.Bowa
3B M.Schmidt
LF G.Luzinski
CF G.Maddox
RF M.Anderson
C B.Boone
UT T.Hutton
UT J.Johnstone
P S.Carlton
P T.Underwood
P L.Christenson
P J.Lonborg
P W.Twitchell
RP G.Garber
RP T.McGraw
RP T.Hilgendorf

PHI 1976N

M D.Ozark
1B D.Allen
2B D.Cash
SS L.Bowa
3B M.Schmidt
LF G.Luzinski
CF G.Maddox
RF J.Johnstone
C B.Boone
UT J.Martin
UT B.Tolan
P S.Carlton
P J.Kaat
P J.Lonborg
P L.Christenson
P T.Underwood
RP R.Reed
RP T.McGraw
RP G.Garber

PHI 1977N

M D.Ozark
1B R.Hebner
2B T.Sizemore
SS L.Bowa
3B M.Schmidt
LF G.Luzinski
CF G.Maddox
RF J.Johnstone
C B.Boone
UT T.Hutton
UT J.Martin
P S.Carlton
P L.Christenson
P R.Lerch
P J.Kaat
P J.Lonborg
RP R.Reed
RP G.Garber
RP T.McGraw

PHI 1978N

M D.Ozark
1B R.Hebner
2B T.Sizemore
SS L.Bowa
3B M.Schmidt
LF G.Luzinski
CF G.Maddox
RF B.McBride
C B.Boone
UT J.Martin
P S.Carlton
P L.Christenson
P R.Lerch
P D.Ruthven
P J.Kaat
RP R.Reed
RP T.McGraw
RP W.Brusstar

PHI 1979N

M D.Ozark
M D.Green
1B P.Rose
2B M.Trillo
SS L.Bowa
3B M.Schmidt
LF G.Luzinski
CF G.Maddox
RF B.McBride
C B.Boone
UT G.Gross
P S.Carlton
P R.Lerch
P N.Espinosa
P D.Ruthven
P L.Christenson
RP R.Reed
RP T.McGraw
RP R.Eastwick

PHI 1980N

M D.Green
1B P.Rose
2B M.Trillo
SS L.Bowa
3B M.Schmidt
LF G.Luzinski
CF G.Maddox
RF B.McBride
C B.Boone
UT G.Gross
UT L.Smith
P S.Carlton
P D.Ruthven
P B.Walk
P R.Lerch
RP T.McGraw
RP R.Reed
RP D.Noles

PHI 1981N

M D.Green
1B P.Rose
2B M.Trillo
SS L.Bowa
3B M.Schmidt
LF G.Matthews
CF G.Maddox
RF B.McBride
C B.Boone
UT G.Gross
P S.Carlton
P D.Ruthven
P L.Christenson
P N.Espinosa
RP S.Lyle
RP M.Proly
RP R.Reed

PHI 1982N

M P.Corrales
1B P.Rose
2B M.Trillo
SS I.DeJesus
3B M.Schmidt
LF G.Matthews
CF G.Maddox
RF G.Vukovich
C B.Diaz
UT G.Gross
UT B.Dernier
P S.Carlton
P L.Christenson
P M.Krukow
P D.Ruthven
RP R.Reed
RP E.Farmer
RP S.Monge

PHI 1983N

M P.Corrales
M P.Owens
1B P.Rose
2B J.Morgan
SS I.DeJesus
3B M.Schmidt
LF G.Matthews
CF G.Maddox
RF V.Hayes
C B.Diaz
UT G.Gross
UT J.Lefebvre
UT B.Dernier
P S.Carlton
P J.Denny
P C.Hudson
P M.Bystrom
RP R.Reed
RP W.Hernandez
RP A.Holland

PHI 1984N

M P.Owens
1B L.Matuszek
2B J.Samuel
SS I.DeJesus
3B M.Schmidt
LF G.Wilson
CF V.Hayes
RF S.Lezcano
C O.Virgil
UT T.Corcoran
UT G.Gross
P S.Carlton
P J.Koosman
P C.Hudson
P J.Denny
P S.Rawley
RP K.Gross
RP A.Holland
RP L.Andersen

PHI 1985N

M J.Felske
1B M.Schmidt
2B J.Samuel
SS S.Jeltz
3B R.Schu
LF V.Hayes
CF G.Maddox
RF G.Wilson
C O.Virgil
UT T.Corcoran
P J.Denny
P K.Gross
P S.Rawley
P C.Hudson
P J.Koosman
RP D.Carman
RP D.Rucker
RP L.Andersen

PHI 1986N

M J.Felske
1B V.Hayes
2B J.Samuel
SS S.Jeltz
3B M.Schmidt
LF G.Redus
CF M.Thompson
RF G.Wilson
C J.Russell
UT R.Roenicke
P K.Gross
P S.Rawley
P B.Ruffin
P C.Hudson
RP D.Carman
RP K.Tekulve
RP T.Hume

PHI 1987N

M J.Felske
M L.Elia
1B V.Hayes
2B J.Samuel
SS S.Jeltz
3B M.Schmidt
LF C.James
CF M.Thompson
RF G.Wilson
C L.Parrish
UT G.Gross
P S.Rawley
P D.Carman
P B.Ruffin
P K.Gross
RP M.Jackson
RP K.Tekulve
RP S.Bedrosian

PHI 1988N

M L.Elia
M J.Vukovich
1B V.Hayes
2B J.Samuel
SS S.Jeltz
3B M.Schmidt
LF P.Bradley
CF M.Thompson
RF C.James
C L.Parrish
UT G.Gross
P K.Gross
P D.Carman
P S.Rawley
P D.Palmer
RP B.Ruffin
RP G.Harris
RP K.Tekulve

PHI 1989N

M N.Leyva
1B R.Jordan
2B T.Herr
SS D.Thon
3B C.Hayes
LF J.Kruk
CF L.Dykstra
RF V.Hayes
C D.Daulton
UT C.Ford
UT S.Jeltz
UT B.Dernier
P K.Howell
P D.Carman
P B.Ruffin
P L.McWilliams
P D.Cook
RP J.Parrett
RP G.Harris
RP T.Frohwirth

PHI 1990N

M N.Leyva
1B R.Jordan
2B T.Herr
SS D.Thon
3B C.Hayes
LF J.Kruk
CF L.Dykstra
RF V.Hayes
C D.Daulton
UT R.Ready
P P.Combs
P T.Mulholland
P B.Ruffin
P D.Cook
P J.DeJesus
RP D.Akerfelds
RP D.Carman
RP R.McDowell

PHI 1991N

M N.Leyva
M J.Fregosi
1B J.Kruk
2B M.Morandini
SS D.Thon
3B C.Hayes
LF W.Chamberlain
CF V.Hayes
RF D.Murphy
C D.Daulton
UT R.Jordan
P T.Mulholland
P T.Greene
P J.DeJesus
P B.Ruffin
P D.Cox
RP J.Boever
RP M.Williams
RP R.McDowell

PHI 1992N

M J.Fregosi
1B J.Kruk
2B M.Morandini
SS J.Bell
3B D.Hollins
LF M.Duncan
CF L.Dykstra
RF R.Amaro
C D.Daulton
UT S.Javier
P T.Mulholland
P C.Schilling
P K.Abbott
P B.Rivera
RP M.Williams
RP C.Brantley
RP M.Hartley

PHI 1993N

M J.Fregosi
1B J.Kruk
2B M.Morandini
SS K.Stocker
3B D.Hollins
LF M.Thompson
CF L.Dykstra
RF J.Eisenreich
C D.Daulton
UT M.Duncan
UT P.Incaviglia
P C.Schilling
P D.Jackson
P T.Greene
P T.Mulholland
P B.Rivera
RP D.West
RP M.Williams
RP L.Andersen

PHI 1994N

M J.Fregosi
1B J.Kruk
2B M.Morandini
SS K.Stocker
3B D.Hollins
LF M.Thompson
CF L.Dykstra
RF J.Eisenreich
C D.Daulton
UT M.Duncan
UT P.Incaviglia
UT R.Jordan
P D.Jackson
P B.Munoz
P D.West
P S.Boskie
P C.Schilling
RP H.Slocumb
RP D.Jones

PHI 1995N

M J.Fregosi
1B D.Hollins
2B M.Morandini
SS K.Stocker
3B C.Hayes
LF A.Van Slyke
CF L.Dykstra
RF J.Eisenreich
C D.Daulton
P P.Quantrill
P T.Green
P M.Mimbs
P C.Schilling
RP M.Williams
RP R.Bottalico
RP T.Borland

PHI 1996N

M J.Fregosi
1B G.Jefferies
2B M.Morandini
SS K.Stocker
3B T.Zeile
LF P.Incaviglia
CF R.Otero
RF J.Eisenreich
C B.Santiago
P C.Schilling
P M.Williams
P T.Mulholland
P M.Mimbs
RP R.Springer
RP T.Borland
RP K.Ryan

PHI 1997N

M T.Francona
1B R.Brogna
2B M.Morandini
SS K.Stocker
3B S.Rolen
LF G.Jefferies
CF R.Amaro
RF D.Daulton
C M.Lieberthal
P C.Schilling
P M.Leiter
P M.Beech
P G.Stephenson
RP J.Spradlin
RP R.Bottalico
RP R.Harris

PHI 1998N

M T.Francona
1B R.Brogna
2B M.Lewis
SS D.Relaford
3B S.Rolen
LF G.Jefferies
CF D.Glanville
RF B.Abreu
C M.Lieberthal
UT K.Jordan
UT K.Sefcik
P C.Schilling
P M.Portugal
P T.Green
P C.Loewer
P M.Beech
RP W.Gomes
RP M.Leiter
RP J.Spradlin

PHI 1999N

M T.Francona
1B R.Brogna
2B M.Anderson
SS A.Arias
3B S.Rolen
LF R.Gant
CF D.Glanville
RF B.Abreu
C M.Lieberthal
UT D.Doster
UT R.Ducey
UT K.Jordan
UT K.Sefcik
P P.Byrd
P C.Schilling
P C.Ogea
P R.Person
P R.Wolf
RP W.Gomes
RP S.Montgomery
RP M.Grace

PHI 2000N

M T.Francona
1B P.Burrell
2B M.Morandini
SS D.Relaford
3B S.Rolen
LF R.Gant
CF D.Glanville
RF B.Abreu
C M.Lieberthal
UT K.Jordan
UT K.Sefcik
P R.Wolf
P R.Person
P C.Schilling
P A.Ashby
RP C.Brock
RP W.Gomes
RP J.Brantley

Pittsburgh

CPU 1884
PIT a 1882-1886
PIT P 1890
PIT F 1914-1915
PIT N 1887-2000

CP1884U

M E.Hengle
M J.Battin
M J.Ellick
1B J.Schoeneck
2B M.Hengle
SS S.Matthias
3B W.Foley
LF C.Householder
CF H.Wheeler
RF J.Ellick
C B.Krieg
P H.Daily
P A.Atkinson
P J.Horan

PIT 1882a

M A.Pratt
1B C.Lane
2B G.Strief
SS J.Peters
3B J.Battin
LF M.Mansell
CF E.Swartwood
RF J.Leary
C B.Taylor
P H.Salisbury
P D.Driscoll
P H.Arundel

PIT 1883a

M A.Pratt
M O.Butler
M J.Battin
1B E.Swartwood
2B G.Creamer
SS D.Mack
3B J.Battin
LF M.Mansell
CF B.Dickerson
RF B.Taylor
C J.Hayes
P D.Driscoll
P B.Barr
P J.Neagle

PIT 1884a

M D.McKnight
M B.Ferguson
M J.Battin
M G.Creamer
M H.Phillips
1B J.Knowles
2B G.Creamer
SS B.White
3B J.Battin
LF D.Miller
CF L.Taylor
RF E.Swartwood
C E.Colgan
P F.Sullivan
P J.Neagle

PIT 1885a

M H.Phillips
1B J.Field
2B P.Smith
SS A.Whitney
3B B.Kuehne
LF C.Eden
CF F.Mann
RF T.Brown
C F.Carroll
P E.Morris
P P.Meegan
P H.O'Day
P J.Galvin

PIT 1886a

M H.Phillips
1B O.Schomberg
2B S.Barkley
SS P.Smith

3B A.Whitney
LF E.Glenn
CF F.Mann
RF T.Brown
C F.Carroll
UT B.Kuehne
P E.Morris
P J.Galvin
P J.Handiboe

PIT 1890P

M N.Hanlon
1B J.Beckley
2B Y.Robinson
SS T.Corcoran
3B B.Kuehne
LF J.Fields
CF N.Hanlon
RF J.Visner
C F.Carroll
P H.Staley
P A.Maul
P J.Galvin
P E.Morris
P J.Tener

PIT 1914F

M D.Gessler
M R.Oakes
1B H.Bradley
2B J.Lewis
SS E.Holly
3B E.Lennox
LF D.Jones
CF R.Oakes
RF J.Savage
C C.Berry
P E.Knetzer
P H.Camnitz
P W.Dickson
P C.Barger
P M.Walker

PIT 1915F

M R.Oakes
1B E.Konetchy
2B S.Yerkes
SS M.Berghammer
3B M.Mowrey
LF A.Wickland
CF R.Oakes
RF J.Kelly
C C.Berry
P F.Allen
P E.Knetzer
P C.Rogge
P B.Hearn
P C.Barger

PIT 1887N

M H.Phillips
1B S.Barkley
2B P.Smith
SS B.Kuehne
3B A.Whitney
LF A.Dalrymple
CF T.Brown
RF J.Coleman
C D.Miller
UT F.Carroll
P J.Galvin
P J.McCormick
P E.Morris

PIT 1888N

M H.Phillips
1B J.Beckley
2B F.Dunlap
SS P.Smith
3B B.Kuehne
LF A.Dalrymple
CF B.Sunday
RF J.Coleman
C D.Miller
UT F.Carroll
P E.Morris
P J.Galvin
P H.Staley

PIT 1889N

M H.Phillips
M F.Dunlap
M N.Hanlon
1B J.Beckley
2B F.Dunlap
SS J.Rowe
3B B.Kuehne
LF A.Maul
CF N.Hanlon
RF B.Sunday
C D.Miller
UT F.Carroll
P H.Staley
P J.Galvin
P E.Morris

PIT 1890N

M G.Hecker
1B G.Hecker
2B S.LaRoque
SS E.Sales
3B D.Miller
LF J.Kelty
CF B.Sunday
RF T.Berger
C H.Decker
P K.Baker
P D.Anderson
P B.Sowders

PIT 1891N

M N.Hanlon
M B.McGunnigle
1B J.Beckley
2B L.Bierbauer
SS F.Shugart
3B C.Reilly
LF P.Browning
CF N.Hanlon
RF F.Carroll
C C.Mack
UT D.Miller
P M.Baldwin
P S.King
P J.Galvin

PIT 1892N

M A.Buckenberger
M T.Burns
M A.Buckenberger
1B J.Beckley
2B L.Bierbauer
SS F.Shugart
3B D.Farrell
LF E.Smith
CF D.Miller
RF P.Donovan
C C.Mack
P M.Baldwin
P R.Ehret
P A.Terry
P J.Galvin

PIT 1893N

M A.Buckenberger
1B J.Beckley
2B L.Bierbauer
SS J.Glasscock
3B D.Lyons
LF E.Smith
CF G.Van Haltren
RF P.Donovan
C D.Miller
P F.Killen
P R.Ehret
P A.Terry
P A.Gumbert

PIT 1894N

M A.Buckenberger
M C.Mack
1B J.Beckley
2B L.Bierbauer
SS J.Glasscock
3B D.Lyons
LF E.Smith
CF J.Stenzel
RF P.Donovan
C C.Mack
P R.Ehret
P A.Gumbert
P F.Killen
P T.Colcolough
P J.Menefee

PIT 1895N

M C.Mack
1B J.Beckley
2B L.Bierbauer
SS M.Cross
3B B.Clingman
LF E.Smith
CF J.Stenzel
RF P.Donovan
C B.Merritt
P P.Hawley
P B.Hart
P B.Foreman
P F.Killen
P J.Gardner

PIT 1896N

M C.Mack
1B J.Beckley
2B D.Padden
SS B.Ely
3B D.Lyons
LF E.Smith
CF J.Stenzel
RF P.Donovan
C J.Sugden
P F.Killen
P P.Hawley
P J.Hughey
P C.Hastings

PIT 1897N

M P.Donovan
1B H.Davis
2B D.Padden
SS B.Ely
3B J.Hoffmeister
LF E.Smith
CF S.Brodie
RF P.Donovan
C J.Sugden
P F.Killen
P P.Hawley
P J.Hughey
P C.Hastings
P J.Gardner

PIT 1898N

M B.Watkins
1B W.Clark
2B D.Padden
SS B.Ely
3B B.Grey
LF J.McCarthy
CF T.O'Brien
RF P.Donovan
C P.Schriver
P J.Tannehill
P B.Rhines
P J.Gardner
P F.Killen
P C.Hastings

PIT 1899N

M B.Watkins
M P.Donovan
1B W.Clark
2B J.O'Brien
SS B.Ely
3B J.Williams
LF J.McCarthy
CF G.Beaumont
RF P.Donovan
C F.Bowerman
UT T.McCreery
P S.Leever
P J.Tannehill
P T.Sparks
P B.Hoffer
P J.Chesbro

PIT 1900N

M F.Clarke
1B D.Cooley
2B C.Ritchey
SS B.Ely
3B J.Williams
LF F.Clarke
CF G.Beaumont
RF H.Wagner
C C.Zimmer
UT T.O'Brien
P D.Phillippe
P J.Tannehill
P S.Leever
P J.Chesbro
P R.Waddell

PIT 1901N

M F.Clarke
1B K.Bransfield
2B C.Ritchey
SS B.Ely
3B T.Leach
LF F.Clarke
CF G.Beaumont
RF L.Davis
C C.Zimmer
UT H.Wagner
P D.Phillippe
P J.Chesbro
P J.Tannehill
P S.Leever

PIT 1902N

M F.Clarke
1B K.Bransfield
2B C.Ritchey
SS W.Conroy
3B T.Leach
LF F.Clarke
CF G.Beaumont
RF H.Wagner
C H.Smith
P J.Chesbro
P D.Phillippe
P J.Tannehill
P S.Leever
P E.Doheny

PIT 1903N

M F.Clarke
1B K.Bransfield
2B C.Ritchey
SS H.Wagner
3B T.Leach
LF F.Clarke
CF G.Beaumont
RF J.Sebring
C E.Phelps
P D.Phillippe
P S.Leever
P E.Doheny
P B.Kennedy
P K.Wilhelm

PIT 1904N

M F.Clarke
1B K.Bransfield
2B C.Ritchey
SS H.Wagner
3B T.Leach
LF F.Clarke
CF G.Beaumont
RF J.Sebring
C E.Phelps
P S.Leever
P P.Flaherty
P M.Lynch
P D.Phillippe
P C.Case

PIT 1905N

M F.Clarke
1B D.Howard
2B C.Ritchey
SS H.Wagner
3B D.Brain
LF F.Clarke
CF G.Beaumont
RF O.Clymer
C H.Peitz
UT T.Leach
P D.Phillippe
P S.Leever
P C.Case
P M.Lynch
P P.Flaherty

PIT 1906N

M F.Clarke
1B J.Nealon
2B C.Ritchey
SS H.Wagner
3B T.Sheehan
LF F.Clarke
CF G.Beaumont
RF B.Ganley
C G.Gibson
UT T.Leach
P V.Willis
P S.Leever
P L.Leifield
P D.Phillippe
P M.Lynch

PIT 1907N

M F.Clarke
1B J.Nealon
2B E.Abbaticchio
SS H.Wagner
3B A.Storke
LF F.Clarke
CF T.Leach
RF G.Anderson
C G.Gibson
UT B.Hallman
P V.Willis
P L.Leifield
P S.Leever
P D.Phillippe
P H.Camnitz

PIT 1908N

M F.Clarke
1B H.Swacina
2B E.Abbaticchio
SS H.Wagner
3B T.Leach
LF F.Clarke
CF R.Thomas
RF C.Wilson
C G.Gibson
P V.Willis
P N.Maddox
P H.Camnitz
P L.Leifield
P S.Leever

PIT 1909N

M F.Clarke
1B B.Abstein
2B D.Miller
SS H.Wagner
3B J.Barbeau
LF F.Clarke
CF T.Leach
RF C.Wilson
C G.Gibson
P V.Willis
P H.Camnitz
P N.Maddox
P L.Leifield
P D.Phillippe

PIT 1910N

M F.Clarke
1B J.Flynn
2B D.Miller
SS H.Wagner
3B B.Byrne
LF F.Clarke
CF T.Leach
RF C.Wilson
C G.Gibson
UT V.Campbell
P H.Camnitz
P B.Adams
P L.Leifield
P K.White
P D.Phillippe

PIT 1911N

M F.Clarke
1B N.Hunter
2B D.Miller
SS H.Wagner
3B B.Byrne
LF F.Clarke
CF M.Carey
RF C.Wilson
C G.Gibson
UT T.Leach
UT B.McKechnie
P L.Leifield
P B.Adams
P H.Camnitz
P E.Steele
P C.Hendrix

PIT 1912N

M F.Clarke
1B D.Miller
2B A.McCarthy
SS H.Wagner
3B B.Byrne
LF M.Carey
CF C.Wilson
RF M.Donlin
C G.Gibson
P C.Hendrix
P H.Camnitz
P M.O'Toole
P H.Robinson
P B.Adams

PIT 1913N

M F.Clarke
1B D.Miller
2B J.Viox
SS H.Wagner
3B B.Byrne
LF M.Carey
CF M.Mitchell
RF C.Wilson
C M.Simon
P B.Adams
P C.Hendrix
P H.Robinson
P H.Camnitz
P M.O'Toole

PIT 1914N

M F.Clarke
1B E.Konetchy
2B J.Viox
SS H.Wagner
3B M.Mowrey
LF M.Carey
CF J.Kelly
RF M.Mitchell
C G.Gibson
P B.Adams
P W.Cooper
P G.McQuillan
P B.Harmon
P J.Conzelman

PIT 1915N

M F.Clarke
1B D.Johnston
2B J.Viox
SS H.Wagner
3B D.Baird
LF M.Carey
CF Z.Collins
RF B.Hinchman
C G.Gibson
P B.Harmon
P A.Mamaux
P B.Adams
P W.Cooper
P E.Kantlehner
RP J.Conzelman

PIT 1916N

M J.Callahan
1B D.Johnston
2B J.Farmer
SS H.Wagner
3B D.Baird
LF F.Schulte
CF M.Carey
RF B.Hinchman
C W.Schmidt
P A.Mamaux
P W.Cooper
P F.Miller
P B.Harmon
P E.Kantlehner

PIT 1917N

M J.Callahan
M H.Wagner
M H.Bezdek
1B H.Wagner
2B J.Pitler
SS C.Ward
3B T.Boeckel
LF C.Bigbee
CF M.Carey
RF L.King
C W.Fischer
P W.Cooper
P E.Jacobs
P F.Miller
P B.Grimes
P B.Steele

PIT 1918N

M H.Bezdek
1B F.Mollwitz
2B G.Cutshaw
SS H.Caton
3B B.McKechnie
LF C.Bigbee
CF M.Carey
RF B.Southworth
C W.Schmidt
P W.Cooper
P F.Miller
P R.Sanders
P E.Mayer
P B.Harmon

PIT 1919N

M H.Bezdek
1B F.Mollwitz
2B G.Cutshaw
SS Z.Terry
3B W.Barbare
LF B.Southworth
CF C.Bigbee
RF C.Stengel
C W.Schmidt
P W.Cooper
P B.Adams
P F.Miller
P E.Hamilton
P H.Carlson

PIT 1920N

M M.Gibson
1B C.Grimm
2B G.Cutshaw
SS H.Caton
3B P.Whitted
LF C.Bigbee
CF M.Carey
RF B.Southworth
C W.Schmidt
UT F.Nicholson
P W.Cooper
P B.Adams
P H.Carlson
P E.Hamilton
P E.Ponder

PIT 1921N

M M.Gibson
1B C.Grimm
2B G.Cutshaw
SS R.Maranville
3B C.Barnhart
LF C.Bigbee
CF M.Carey
RF P.Whitted
C W.Schmidt
UT C.Tierney
P W.Cooper
P W.Glazner
P E.Hamilton
P B.Adams
P J.Morrison

PIT 1922N

M M.Gibson
M B.McKechnie
1B C.Grimm
2B C.Tierney
SS R.Maranville
3B P.Traynor
LF C.Bigbee
CF M.Carey
RF R.Russell
C J.Gooch
P W.Cooper
P J.Morrison
P W.Glazner
P B.Adams
P E.Hamilton
RP C.Yellowhorse

PIT 1923N

M B.McKechnie
1B C.Grimm
2B J.Rawlings
SS R.Maranville
3B P.Traynor
LF C.Bigbee
CF M.Carey
RF C.Barnhart
C W.Schmidt
UT R.Russell
P J.Morrison
P W.Cooper
P L.Meadows
P B.Adams
P E.Hamilton

PIT 1924N

M B.McKechnie
1B C.Grimm
2B R.Maranville
SS G.Wright
3B P.Traynor
LF K.Cuyler
CF M.Carey
RF C.Barnhart
C J.Gooch
P W.Cooper
P R.Kremer
P J.Morrison
P L.Meadows
P E.Yde
RP A.Stone

PIT 1925N

M B.McKechnie
1B G.Grantham
2B E.Moore
SS G.Wright
3B P.Traynor
LF C.Barnhart
CF M.Carey
RF K.Cuyler
C E.Smith
P L.Meadows
P R.Kremer
P V.Aldridge
P J.Morrison

P E.Yde
RP T.Sheehan

PIT 1926N

M B.McKechnie
1B G.Grantham
2B H.Rhyne
SS G.Wright
3B P.Traynor
LF K.Cuyler
CF M.Carey
RF P.Waner
C E.Smith
P R.Kremer
P L.Meadows
P V.Aldridge
P E.Yde
P D.Songer

PIT 1927N

M D.Bush
1B J.Harris
2B G.Grantham
SS G.Wright
3B P.Traynor
LF C.Barnhart
CF L.Waner
RF P.Waner
C J.Gooch
P L.Meadows
P C.Hill
P V.Aldridge
P R.Kremer
RP J.Morrison
RP M.Cvengros

PIT 1928N

M D.Bush
1B G.Grantham
2B S.Adams
SS G.Wright
3B P.Traynor
LF F.Brickell
CF L.Waner
RF P.Waner
C C.Hargreaves
P B.Grimes
P C.Hill
P R.Kremer
P F.Fussell
P J.Dawson

PIT 1929N

M D.Bush
M J.Ens
1B E.Sheely
2B G.Grantham
SS D.Bartell
3B P.Traynor
LF A.Comorosky
CF L.Waner
RF P.Waner
C C.Hargreaves
P B.Grimes
P E.Brame
P R.Kremer
P J.Petty
P S.Swetonic
RP C.Hill

PIT 1930N

M J.Ens
1B G.Suhr
2B G.Grantham
SS D.Bartell
3B P.Traynor
LF A.Comorosky
CF L.Waner
RF P.Waner
C R.Hemsley
P R.Kremer
P L.French
P E.Brame
P G.Spencer
P H.Meine

PIT 1931N

M J.Ens
1B G.Suhr
2B G.Grantham
SS T.Thevenow
3B P.Traynor
LF A.Comorosky
CF L.Waner
RF P.Waner
C E.Phillips
P H.Meine
P L.French
P R.Kremer
P G.Spencer
P E.Brame
RP B.Osborn

PIT 1932N

M M.Gibson
1B G.Suhr
2B T.Piet
SS A.Vaughan
3B P.Traynor
LF A.Comorosky
CF L.Waner
RF P.Waner
C E.Grace
UT D.Barbee
P L.French
P B.Swift
P H.Meine
P B.Harris
P S.Swetonic
RP E.Brame

PIT 1933N

M M.Gibson
1B G.Suhr
2B T.Piet
SS A.Vaughan
3B P.Traynor
LF L.Waner
CF F.Lindstrom
RF P.Waner
C E.Grace
P L.French
P B.Swift
P H.Meine
P S.Swetonic
P H.Smith
RP L.Chagnon
RP B.Harris

PIT 1934N

M M.Gibson
M P.Traynor
1B G.Suhr
2B C.Lavagetto
SS A.Vaughan
3B P.Traynor
LF F.Lindstrom
CF L.Waner
RF P.Waner
C E.Grace
UT T.Thevenow
P L.French
P B.Swift
P R.Birkofer
P W.Hoyt
P R.Lucas
RP L.Chagnon
RP H.Smith

PIT 1935N

M P.Traynor
1B G.Suhr
2B P.Young
SS A.Vaughan
3B T.Thevenow
LF W.Jensen
CF L.Waner
RF P.Waner
C T.Padden
P C.Blanton
P B.Swift
P G.Bush
P J.Weaver
P W.Hoyt

PIT 1936N

M P.Traynor
1B G.Suhr
2B P.Young
SS A.Vaughan
3B B.Brubaker
LF W.Jensen
CF L.Waner
RF P.Waner
C T.Padden
P B.Swift
P C.Blanton
P J.Weaver
P R.Lucas
P M.Brown

PIT 1937N

M P.Traynor
1B G.Suhr
2B L.Handley
SS A.Vaughan
3B B.Brubaker
LF W.Jensen
CF L.Waner
RF P.Waner
C A.Todd
UT P.Young
P C.Blanton
P R.Bauers
P E.Brandt
P B.Swift
P J.Bowman
RP M.Brown

PIT 1938N

M P.Traynor
1B G.Suhr
2B P.Young
SS A.Vaughan
3B L.Handley
LF J.Rizzo
CF L.Waner
RF P.Waner
C A.Todd
P R.Bauers
P J.Tobin
P C.Blanton
P B.Klinger
P B.Swift
RP M.Brown

PIT 1939N

M P.Traynor
1B E.Fletcher
2B P.Young
SS A.Vaughan
3B L.Handley
LF J.Rizzo
CF L.Waner
RF P.Waner
C R.Mueller
UT B.Brubaker
P B.Klinger
P M.Brown
P J.Bowman
P R.Sewell
P J.Tobin

PIT 1940N

M F.Frisch
1B E.Fletcher
2B F.Gustine
SS A.Vaughan
3B L.Handley
LF M.Van Robays
CF V.DiMaggio
RF B.Elliott
C S.Davis
UT D.Garms
P R.Sewell
P J.Bowman
P M.Brown
P K.Heintzelman
P B.Klinger
RP D.Lanahan
RP D.Mac Fayden

PIT 1941N

M F.Frisch
1B E.Fletcher
2B F.Gustine
SS A.Vaughan
3B L.Handley
LF M.Van Robays
CF V.DiMaggio
RF B.Elliott
C A.Lopez
P R.Sewell
P M.Butcher
P K.Heintzelman
P J.Lanning
P B.Klinger

PIT 1942N

M F.Frisch
1B E.Fletcher
2B F.Gustine
SS P.Coscarart
3B B.Elliott
LF J.Wasdell
CF V.DiMaggio
RF J.Barrett
C A.Lopez
UT B.Phelps
UT M.Van Robays
P R.Sewell
P B.Klinger
P M.Butcher
P D.Dietz
P K.Heintzelman

PIT 1943N

M F.Frisch
1B E.Fletcher
2B P.Coscarart
SS F.Gustine
3B B.Elliott
LF J.Russell
CF V.DiMaggio
RF J.Barrett
C A.Lopez
P R.Sewell
P B.Klinger
P M.Butcher
P W.Hebert
P H.Gornicki
RP B.Brandt

PIT 1944N

M F.Frisch
1B B.Dahlgren
2B P.Coscarart
SS F.Gustine
3B B.Elliott
LF J.Russell
CF V.DiMaggio
RF J.Barrett
C A.Lopez
UT F.Colman
P R.Sewell
P F.Ostermueller
P M.Butcher
P N.Strincevich
P P.Roe
RP X.Rescigno

PIT 1945N

M F.Frisch
1B B.Dahlgren
2B P.Coscarart
SS F.Gustine
3B B.Elliott
LF J.Russell
CF A.Gionfriddo
RF J.Barrett
C A.Lopez
UT L.Handley
UT B.Salkeld
P P.Roe
P N.Strincevich
P R.Sewell
P M.Butcher
P A.Gerheauser
RP X.Rescigno
RP C.Cuccurullo

PIT 1946N

M F.Frisch
M S.Davis
1B E.Fletcher
2B F.Gustine
SS B.Cox
3B L.Handley
LF J.Russell
CF R.Kiner
RF B.Elliott
C A.Lopez
P F.Ostermueller
P N.Strincevich
P K.Heintzelman
P R.Sewell
P E.Bahr
RP A.Gerheauser

PIT 1947N

M .Herman
M B.Burwell
1B H.Greenberg
2B J.Bloodworth
SS B.Cox
3B F.Gustine
LF R.Kiner
CF J.Russell
RF W.Westlake
C D.Howell
UT C.Rikard
P K.Higbe
P F.Ostermueller
P T.Bonham
P P.Roe
P R.Sewell
RP N.Strincevich
RP E.Singleton

PIT 1948N

M B.Meyer
1B E.Stevens
2B D.Murtaugh
SS S.Rojek
3B F.Gustine
LF R.Kiner
CF W.Westlake
RF D.Walker
C E.Fitz Gerald
UT J.Hopp
UT C.Kluttz
P B.Chesnes
P E.Riddle
P V.Lombardi
P T.Bonham
P F.Ostermueller
RP K.Higbe
RP E.Singleton
RP M.Queen

PIT 1949N

M B.Meyer
1B J.Hopp
2B M.Basgall
SS S.Rojek
3B P.Castiglione
LF R.Kiner
CF D.Restelli
RF W.Westlake
C C.McCullough
P M.Dickson
P B.Werle
P C.Chambers
P B.Chesnes
P V.Lombardi
RP R.Sewell

PIT 1950N

M B.Meyer
1B J.Hopp
2B D.Murtaugh
SS S.Rojek
3B N.Fernandez
LF R.Kiner
CF W.Westlake
RF G.Bell
C C.McCullough
UT P.Castiglione
P C.Chambers
P M.Dickson
P B.Werle
P B.Macdonald
P V.Law
RP V.Lombardi
RP J.Walsh

PIT 1951N

M B.Meyer
1B J.Phillips
2B D.Murtaugh
SS G.Strickland
3B P.Castiglione
LF R.Kiner
CF C.Metkovich
RF G.Bell
C C.McCullough
P M.Dickson
P M.Queen
P B.Friend
P H.Pollet
P V.Law
RP B.Werle
RP T.Wilks
RP J.Walsh

PIT 1952N

M B.Meyer
1B T.Bartirome
2B J.Merson
SS D.Groat
3B P.Castiglione
LF R.Kiner
CF B.Del Greco
RF G.Bell
C J.Garagiola
UT C.Koshorek
UT C.Metkovich
P M.Dickson
P H.Pollet
P B.Friend
P W.Main
RP R.Kline
RP T.Wilks
RP P.LaPalme

PIT 1953N

M F.Haney
1B P.Ward
2B J.O'Brien
SS E.O'Brien
3B D.O'Connell
LF H.Rice
CF F.Thomas
RF C.Abrams
C M.Sandlock
UT D.Cole
UT P.Smith
UT C.Bernier
P M.Dickson
P J.Lindell
P P.LaPalme
P B.Friend
P B.Hall
RP R.Face
RP J.Hetki
RP R.Bowman

PIT 1954N

M F.Haney
1B B.Skinner
2B C.Roberts
SS G.Allie
3B D.Cole
LF D.Hall
CF F.Thomas
RF S.Gordon
C T.Atwell
UT J.Lynch
UT P.Ward
P M.Surkont
P B.Friend
P V.Law
P D.Littlefield
P B.Purkey
RP J.Hetki

PIT 1955N

M F.Haney
1B D.Long
2B J.O'Brien
SS D.Groat
3B G.Freese
LF J.Lynch
CF F.Thomas
RF R.Clemente
C J.Shepard
P V.Law
P B.Friend
P M.Surkont
P R.Kline
P D.Littlefield

PIT 1956N

M B.Bragan
1B D.Long
2B B.Mazeroski
SS D.Groat
3B F.Thomas
LF L.Walls
CF B.Virdon
RF R.Clemente
C J.Shepard
UT B.Skinner
P B.Friend
P R.Kline
P V.Law
P R.Munger
RP R.Face
RP N.King
RP F.Waters

PIT 1957N

M B.Bragan
M D.Murtaugh
1B D.Fondy
2B B.Mazeroski
SS D.Groat
3B G.Freese
LF B.Skinner
CF B.Virdon
RF R.Clemente
C H.Foiles
UT G.Baker
UT F.Thomas
P B.Friend
P R.Kline
P B.Purkey
P V.Law
RP L.Arroyo
RP R.Face
RP R.Swanson

PIT 1958N

M D.Murtaugh
1B T.Kluszewski
2B B.Mazeroski
SS D.Groat
3B F.Thomas
LF B.Skinner
CF B.Virdon
RF R.Clemente
C H.Foiles
P B.Friend
P R.Kline
P V.Law
P C.Raydon
P G.Witt
RP B.Porterfield
RP R.Face
RP D.Gross

PIT 1959N

M D.Murtaugh
1B D.Stuart
2B B.Mazeroski
SS D.Groat
3B D.Hoak
LF B.Skinner
CF B.Virdon
RF R.Clemente
C S.Burgess
UT R.Mejias
UT R.Nelson
P V.Law
P B.Friend
P H.Haddix
P R.Kline
RP B.Daniels
RP R.Face

PIT 1960N

M D.Murtaugh
1B D.Stuart
2B B.Mazeroski
SS D.Groat
3B D.Hoak
LF B.Skinner
CF B.Virdon
RF R.Clemente
C S.Burgess
UT G.Cimoli
P B.Friend
P V.Law
P H.Haddix
P V.Mizell
RP R.Face
RP J.Gibbon
RP F.Green

PIT 1961N

M D.Murtaugh
1B D.Stuart
2B B.Mazeroski
SS D.Groat
3B D.Hoak
LF B.Skinner
CF B.Virdon
RF R.Clemente
C S.Burgess
P B.Friend
P J.Gibbon
P H.Haddix
P E.Francis
P V.Mizell
RP C.Labine
RP R.Face
RP B.Shantz

PIT 1962N

M D.Murtaugh
1B D.Stuart
2B B.Mazeroski
SS D.Groat
3B D.Hoak
LF B.Skinner
CF B.Virdon
RF R.Clemente
C S.Burgess
P B.Friend
P A.McBean
P E.Francis
P H.Haddix
P V.Law
RP T.Sturdivant
RP R.Face
RP D.Olivo

PIT 1963N

M D.Murtaugh
1B D.Clendenon
2B B.Mazeroski
SS D.Schofield
3B B.Bailey
LF W.Stargell
CF B.Virdon
RF R.Clemente
C J.Pagliaroni
P B.Friend
P D.Cardwell
P D.Schwall
P J.Gibbon
RP A.McBean
RP T.Sisk
RP E.Francis

PIT 1964N

M D.Murtaugh
1B D.Clendenon
2B B.Mazeroski
SS D.Schofield
3B B.Bailey

LF M.Mota
CF B.Virdon
RF R.Clemente
C J.Pagliaroni
UT G.Freese
UT J.Lynch
UT W.Stargell
P B.Veale
P B.Friend
P V.Law
P J.Gibbon
P S.Blass
RP A.McBean
RP R.Face
RP T.Butters

PIT 1965N

M H.Walker
1B D.Clendenon
2B B.Mazeroski
SS G.Alley
3B B.Bailey
LF W.Stargell
CF B.Virdon
RF R.Clemente
C J.Pagliaroni
UT M.Mota
P B.Veale
P D.Cardwell
P B.Friend
P V.Law
P J.Gibbon
RP A.McBean
RP T.Sisk
RP D.Schwall

PIT 1966N

M H.Walker
1B D.Clendenon
2B B.Mazeroski
SS G.Alley
3B B.Bailey
LF W.Stargell
CF M.Alou
RF R.Clemente
C J.Pagliaroni
UT M.Mota
UT J.Pagan
P B.Veale
P W.Fryman
P V.Law
P S.Blass
P T.Sisk
RP P.Mikkelsen
RP A.McBean
RP B.O'Dell

PIT 1967N

M H.Walker
M D.Murtaugh
1B D.Clendenon
2B B.Mazeroski
SS G.Alley
3B M.Wills
LF W.Stargell
CF M.Alou
RF R.Clemente
C J.May
UT M.Mota
P T.Sisk
P B.Veale
P D.Ribant
P S.Blass
P W.Fryman
RP A.McBean
RP J.Pizarro
RP R.Face

PIT 1968N

M L.Shepard
1B D.Clendenon
2B B.Mazeroski
SS G.Alley
3B M.Wills
LF W.Stargell
CF M.Alou
RF R.Clemente
C J.May
UT M.Mota
P B.Veale
P S.Blass
P A.McBean
P B.Moose
P J.Bunning
RP R.Kline
RP T.Sisk
RP L.Walker

PIT 1969N

M L.Shepard
M A.Grammas
1B A.Oliver
2B B.Mazeroski
SS F.Patek
3B R.Hebner
LF W.Stargell
CF M.Alou
RF R.Clemente
C M.Sanguillen
UT J.Pagan
UT C.Taylor
P B.Veale
P D.Ellis
P S.Blass
P B.Moose
P J.Bunning
RP C.Hartenstein
RP B.Dal Canton
RP J.Gibbon

PIT 1970N

M D.Murtaugh
1B B.Robertson
2B B.Mazeroski
SS G.Alley
3B R.Hebner
LF W.Stargell
CF M.Alou
RF R.Clemente
C M.Sanguillen
UT A.Oliver
P B.Veale
P D.Ellis
P S.Blass
P B.Moose
P L.Walker
RP D.Giusti
RP B.Dal Canton

PIT 1971N

M D.Murtaugh
1B B.Robertson
2B D.Cash
SS G.Alley
3B R.Hebner
LF W.Stargell
CF A.Oliver
RF R.Clemente
C M.Sanguillen
UT G.Clines
UT V.Davalillo
P S.Blass
P D.Ellis
P B.Johnson
P L.Walker
P B.Moose
RP D.Giusti
RP M.Grant

PIT 1972N

M B.Virdon
1B W.Stargell
2B D.Cash
SS G.Alley
3B R.Hebner
LF V.Davalillo
CF A.Oliver
RF R.Clemente
C M.Sanguillen
UT G.Clines
UT B.Robertson
UT R.Stennett
P S.Blass
P B.Moose
P N.Briles
P D.Ellis
P B.Kison
RP D.Giusti
RP R.Hernandez
RP B.Miller

PIT 1973N

M B.Virdon
M D.Murtaugh
1B B.Robertson
2B D.Cash
SS D.Maxvill
3B R.Hebner
LF W.Stargell
CF A.Oliver
RF R.Zisk
C M.Sanguillen
UT G.Clines
UT M.May
UT R.Stennett
P N.Briles
P B.Moose
P D.Ellis
P J.Rooker
P L.Walker
RP D.Giusti
RP B.Johnson
RP R.Hernandez

PIT 1974N

M D.Murtaugh
1B B.Robertson
2B R.Stennett
SS F.Taveras
3B R.Hebner
LF W.Stargell
CF A.Oliver
RF R.Zisk
C M.Sanguillen
UT G.Clines
UT E.Kirkpatrick
P J.Rooker
P J.Reuss
P K.Brett
P D.Ellis
P B.Kison
RP D.Giusti
RP R.Hernandez
RP J.Morlan

PIT 1975N

M D.Murtaugh
1B W.Stargell
2B R.Stennett
SS F.Taveras
3B R.Hebner
LF R.Zisk
CF A.Oliver
RF D.Parker
C M.Sanguillen
P J.Reuss
P J.Rooker
P B.Kison
P D.Ellis
P J.Candelaria
RP L.Demery
RP D.Giusti
RP B.Moose

PIT 1976N

M D.Murtaugh
1B W.Stargell
2B R.Stennett
SS F.Taveras
3B R.Hebner
LF R.Zisk
CF A.Oliver
RF D.Parker
C M.Sanguillen
UT B.Robinson
P J.Candelaria
P J.Reuss
P J.Rooker
P B.Kison
P D.Medich
RP K.Tekulve
RP B.Moose
RP D.Giusti

PIT 1977N

M C.Tanner
1B B.Robinson
2B R.Stennett
SS F.Taveras
3B P.Garner
LF A.Oliver
CF O.Moreno
RF D.Parker
C D.Dyer
UT E.Ott
P J.Candelaria
P J.Reuss
P J.Rooker
P B.Kison
P O.Jones
RP R.Gossage
RP K.Tekulve
RP G.Jackson

PIT 1978N

M C.Tanner
1B W.Stargell
2B R.Stennett
SS F.Taveras
3B P.Garner
LF B.Robinson
CF O.Moreno
RF D.Parker
C E.Ott
UT J.Milner
P B.Blyleven
P D.Robinson
P J.Candelaria
P J.Rooker
P J.Bibby
RP K.Tekulve
RP G.Jackson
RP E.Whitson

PIT 1979N

M C.Tanner
1B W.Stargell
2B R.Stennett
SS T.Foli
3B B.Madlock
LF B.Robinson
CF O.Moreno
RF D.Parker
C E.Ott
UT P.Garner
UT J.Milner
P B.Blyleven
P J.Candelaria
P B.Kison
P D.Robinson
P J.Bibby
RP K.Tekulve
RP E.Romo
RP G.Jackson

PIT 1980N

M C.Tanner
1B J.Milner
2B P.Garner
SS T.Foli
3B B.Madlock
LF M.Easler
CF O.Moreno
RF D.Parker
C E.Ott
UT L.Lacy
UT B.Robinson
P J.Bibby
P J.Candelaria
P B.Blyleven
P D.Robinson
P R.Rhoden
RP E.Romo
RP K.Tekulve
RP G.Jackson

PIT 1981N

M C.Tanner
1B J.Thompson
2B P.Garner
SS T.Foli
3B B.Madlock
LF M.Easler
CF O.Moreno
RF D.Parker
C T.Pena
UT D.Berra
UT L.Lacy
P R.Rhoden
P E.Solomon
P J.Bibby
P P.Perez
RP R.Scurry
RP K.Tekulve
RP E.Romo

PIT 1982N

M C.Tanner
1B J.Thompson
2B J.Ray
SS D.Berra
3B B.Madlock
LF M.Easler
CF O.Moreno
RF L.Lacy
C T.Pena
P R.Rhoden
P D.Robinson
P J.Candelaria
P M.Sarmiento
P L.McWilliams
RP K.Tekulve
RP R.Scurry
RP E.Romo

PIT 1983N

M C.Tanner
1B J.Thompson
2B J.Ray
SS D.Berra
3B B.Madlock
LF M.Easler
CF M.Wynne
RF D.Parker
C T.Pena
UT L.Lacy
UT L.Mazzilli
P R.Rhoden
P L.McWilliams
P J.Candelaria
P L.Tunnell
P J.DeLeon
RP C.Guante
RP K.Tekulve
RP M.Sarmiento

PIT 1984N

M C.Tanner
1B J.Thompson
2B J.Ray
SS D.Berra
3B B.Madlock
LF L.Lacy
CF M.Wynne
RF D.Frobel
C T.Pena
UT L.Mazzilli
UT J.Morrison
P R.Rhoden
P L.McWilliams
P J.Tudor
P J.DeLeon
P J.Candelaria
RP D.Robinson
RP K.Tekulve
RP L.Tunnell

PIT 1985N

M C.Tanner
1B J.Thompson
2B J.Ray
SS S.Khalifa
3B B.Madlock
LF J.Orsulak
CF M.Wynne
RF G.Hendrick
C T.Pena
P R.Rhoden
P R.Reuschel
P J.DeLeon
P L.Tunnell
P L.McWilliams
RP C.Guante
RP D.Robinson
RP J.Winn

PIT 1986N

M J.Leyland
1B S.Bream
2B J.Ray
SS R.Belliard
3B J.Morrison
LF R.Reynolds
CF B.Bonds
RF J.Orsulak
C T.Pena
UT B.Almon
UT M.Diaz
P R.Rhoden
P R.Reuschel
P M.Bielecki
P B.Walk
P B.Kipper
RP L.McWilliams
RP J.Winn
RP C.Guante

PIT 1987N

M J.Leyland
1B S.Bream
2B J.Ray
SS A.Pedrique
3B B.Bonilla
LF B.Bonds
CF A.Van Slyke
RF R.Reynolds
C M.LaValliere
UT J.Cangelosi
UT M.Diaz
P B.Fisher
P R.Reuschel
P D.Drabek
P M.Dunne
P B.Walk
RP J.Smiley
RP D.Robinson

PIT 1988N

M J.Leyland
1B S.Bream
2B J.Lind
SS R.Belliard
3B B.Bonilla
LF B.Bonds
CF A.Van Slyke
RF R.Reynolds
C M.LaValliere
P D.Drabek
P B.Walk
P J.Smiley
P M.Dunne
P B.Fisher
RP J.Robinson
RP J.Gott
RP B.Kipper

PIT 1989N

M J.Leyland
1B G.Redus
2B J.Lind
SS J.Bell
3B B.Bonilla
LF B.Bonds
CF A.Van Slyke
RF R.Reynolds
C J.Ortiz
UT J.Cangelosi
UT G.Wilson
P D.Drabek
P J.Smiley
P B.Walk
P N.Heaton
P R.Kramer
RP J.Robinson
RP B.Kipper
RP B.Landrum

PIT 1990N

M J.Leyland
1B S.Bream
2B J.Lind
SS J.Bell
3B J.King
LF B.Bonds
CF A.Van Slyke
RF B.Bonilla
C M.LaValliere
UT W.Backman
P D.Drabek
P J.Smiley
P N.Heaton
P B.Walk
RP B.Patterson
RP B.Landrum
RP B.Kipper

PIT 1991N

M J.Leyland
1B O.Merced
2B J.Lind
SS J.Bell
3B B.Bonilla
LF B.Bonds
CF A.Van Slyke
RF G.Varsho
C M.LaValliere
UT G.Redus
P D.Drabek
P Z.Smith
P J.Smiley
P R.Tomlin
P B.Walk
RP V.Palacios
RP S.Belinda
RP B.Landrum

PIT 1992N

M J.Leyland
1B O.Merced
2B J.Lind
SS J.Bell
3B S.Buechele
LF B.Bonds
CF A.Van Slyke
RF C.Espy
C M.LaValliere
UT J.King
UT G.Varsho
P D.Drabek
P R.Tomlin
P Z.Smith
P B.Walk
RP R.Mason
RP D.Neagle
RP S.Belinda

PIT 1993N

M J.Leyland
1B K.Young
2B C.Garcia
SS J.Bell
3B J.King
LF A.Martin
CF A.Van Slyke
RF O.Merced
C D.Slaught
UT D.Clark
P S.Cooke
P B.Walk
P P.Wagner
P T.Wakefield
P R.Tomlin
RP B.Minor
RP D.Neagle
RP D.Otto

PIT 1994N

M J.Leyland
1B B.Hunter
2B C.Garcia
SS J.Bell
3B J.King
LF A.Martin
CF A.Van Slyke
RF O.Merced
C D.Slaught
UT D.Clark
P Z.Smith
P D.Neagle
P S.Cooke
P P.Wagner
P J.Lieber
RP R.White
RP M.Dewey
RP R.Manzanillo

PIT 1995N

M J.Leyland
1B M.Johnson
2B C.Garcia
SS J.Bell
3B J.King
LF A.Martin
CF J.Brumfield
RF O.Merced
C M.Parent
UT N.Liriano
P D.Neagle
P E.Loaiza
P P.Wagner
P J.Ericks
RP M.Dyer
RP J.McCurry
RP D.Plesac

PIT 1996N

M J.Leyland
1B M.Johnson
2B C.Garcia
SS J.Bell
3B C.Hayes
LF A.Martin
CF M.Kingery
RF O.Merced
C J.Kendall
UT J.King
UT N.Liriano
P D.Neagle
P D.Darwin
RP J.Lieber
RP F.Cordova
RP D.Miceli

PIT 1997N

M G.Lamont
1B K.Young
2B T.Womack
SS K.Polcovich
3B J.Randa
LF A.Martin
CF J.Allensworth
RF J.Guillen
C J.Kendall
UT D.Sveum
P E.Loaiza
P J.Schmidt
P J.Lieber
P F.Cordova
P S.Cooke
RP M.Wilkins
RP R.Loiselle
RP M.Ruebel

PIT 1998N

M G.Lamont
1B K.Young
2B T.Womack
SS L.Collier
3B A.Ramirez
LF A.Martin
CF T.Ward
RF J.Guillen
C J.Kendall
P F.Cordova
P J.Schmidt
P J.Lieber
P C.Peters
P J.Silva
RP E.Dessens
RP R.Rincon
RP J.Christiansen

PIT 1999N

M G.Lamont
1B K.Young
2B W.Morris

SS M.Benjamin
3B E.Sprague
LF A.Martin
CF B.Giles
RF A.Brown
C J.Kendall
UT B.Brown
P J.Schmidt
P K.Benson
P T.Ritchie
P F.Cordova
P P.Schourek
RP J.Silva
RP S.Sauerbeck
RP M.Williams

PIT 2000N

M G.Lamont
1B K.Young
2B W.Morris
SS P.Meares
3B A.Ramirez
LF W.Cordero
CF A.Brown
RF B.Giles
C J.Kendall
UT J.Vander Wal
P K.Benson
P T.Ritchie
P J.Anderson
RP J.Silva
RP S.Sauerbeck
RP M.Williams

Providence

PRO N 1878-1885

PRO 1878N

M T.York
1B T.Murnane
2B C.Sweasy
SS T.Carey
3B B.Hague
LF T.York
CF P.Hines
RF D.Higham
C L.Brown
P J.Ward
P T.Nichols
P H.Wheeler

PRO 1879N

M G.Wright
1B J.Start
2B M.McGeary
SS G.Wright
3B B.Hague
LF T.York
CF P.Hines
RF J.O'Rourke
C L.Brown
P J.Ward
P B.Mathews

PRO 1880N

M M.McGeary
M M.Ward
M M.Dorgan
1B J.Start
2B J.Farrell
SS J.Peters
3B G.Bradley
LF T.York
CF P.Hines
RF M.Dorgan
C E.Gross
P J.Ward

PRO 1881N

M J.Farrell
M T.York
1B J.Start
2B J.Farrell
SS B.McClellan
3B J.Denny
LF T.York
CF P.Hines
RF J.Ward
C E.Gross
P C.Radbourn
P B.Mathews

PRO 1882N

M H.Wright
1B J.Start
2B J.Farrell
SS G.Wright
3B J.Denny
LF T.York
CF P.Hines
RF J.Ward
C B.Gilligan
P C.Radbourn

PRO 1883N

M H.Wright
1B J.Start
2B J.Farrell
SS A.Irwin
3B J.Denny
LF C.Carroll
CF P.Hines
RF J.Cassidy
C B.Gilligan
P C.Radbourn
P C.Sweeney

PRO 1884N

M F.Bancroft
1B J.Start
2B J.Farrell
SS A.Irwin
3B J.Denny
LF C.Carroll
CF P.Hines
RF P.Radford
C B.Gilligan
P C.Radbourn
P C.Sweeney
P E.Conley

PRO 1885N

M F.Bancroft
1B J.Start
2B J.Farrell
SS A.Irwin
3B J.Denny
LF C.Carroll
CF P.Hines
RF P.Radford
C B.Gilligan
UT C.Bassett
P C.Radbourn
P D.Shaw

Richmond

RIC a 1884

RIC 1884a

M F.Moses
1B J.Powell
2B T.Larkin
SS B.Schenck
3B B.Nash
LF E.Glenn
CF D.Johnston
RF M.Mansell
C J.Hanna
P P.Meegan
P E.Dugan

Rochester

ROC a 1890

ROC 1890a

M P.Powers
1B T.O'Brien
2B B.Greenwood
SS M.Phillips
3B J.Knowles
LF H.Lyons
CF S.Griffin
RF T.Scheffler
C D.McGuire
P B.Barr
P W.Calihan
P C.Titcomb
P B.Miller

Rockford

ROK n 1871

ROK 1871n

M S.Hastings
1B D.Mack
2B B.Addy
SS C.Fulmer
3B C.Anson
LF R.Ham
CF G.Bird
RF G.Stires
C S.Hastings
P C.Fisher

St. Louis

STL n 1875
RSn 1875
STL N 1876-1877
STL U 1884
STL N 1885-1886
STL a 1882-1891
STL F 1914-1915
STL A 1902-1953
STL N 1892-2000

STL 1875n

M D.Pearce
1B H.Dehlman
2B J.Battin
SS D.Pearce
3B B.Hague
LF N.Cuthbert
CF L.Pike
RF J.Chapman
C T.Miller
P G.Bradley
P J.Galvin

RS1875n

M C.Sweasy
1B C.Hautz
2B C.Sweasy
SS B.Redmon
3B T.McSorley
LF A.Croft
CF B.Morgan
RF T.Oran
C S.Flint
P J.Blong

STL 1876N

M M.Graffen
M G.McManus
1B H.Dehlman
2B M.McGeary
SS D.Mack
3B J.Battin
LF N.Cuthbert
CF L.Pike
RF J.Blong
C J.Clapp
P G.Bradley

STL 1877N

M G.McManus
1B H.Dehlman
2B M.McGeary
SS D.Force
3B J.Battin
LF J.Blong
CF J.Remsen
RF M.Dorgan
C J.Clapp
UT A.Croft
P T.Nichols

STL 1884U

M T.Sullivan
M F.Dunlap
1B J.Quinn
2B F.Dunlap
SS M.Whitehead
3B J.Gleason
LF H.Boyle
CF D.Rowe
RF O.Shaffer
C G.Baker
P C.Sweeney
P B.Taylor
P P.Werden
P C.Hodnett

STL 1885N

M F.Dunlap
M A.McKinnon
M F.Dunlap
1B A.McKinnon
2B F.Dunlap
SS J.Glasscock
3B E.Caskin
LF E.Seery
CF F.Lewis
RF O.Shaffer
C F.Briody
UT C.Sweeney
UT J.Quinn
P H.Boyle
P J.Kirby
P H.Daily
P J.Healy

STL 1886N

M G.Schmelz
1B A.McKinnon
2B F.Dunlap
SS J.Glasscock
3B J.Denny
LF E.Seery
CF J.McGeachy
RF J.Cahill
C G.Myers
P J.Healy
P J.Kirby
P H.Boyle
P C.Sweeney

STL 1882a

M N.Cuthbert
1B C.Comiskey
2B B.Smiley
SS B.Gleason
3B J.Gleason
LF N.Cuthbert
CF O.Walker
RF G.Seward
C S.Sullivan
P J.McGinnis
P J.Schappert
P B.Dorr

STL 1883a

M T.Sullivan
M C.Comiskey
1B C.Comiskey
2B G.Strief
SS B.Gleason
3B A.Latham
LF T.Dolan
CF F.Lewis
RF H.Nicol
C P.Deasley
P T.Mullane
P J.McGinnis

STL 1884a

M J.Williams
M C.Comiskey
1B C.Comiskey
2B J.Quest
SS B.Gleason
3B A.Latham
LF T.O'Neill
CF F.Lewis
RF H.Nicol
C P.Deasley
P J.McGinnis
P D.Foutz
P D.Davis

STL 1885a

M C.Comiskey
1B C.Comiskey
2B S.Barkley
SS B.Gleason
3B A.Latham
LF Y.Robinson
CF C.Welch
RF H.Nicol
C D.Bushong
P B.Caruthers
P D.Foutz
P J.McGinnis

STL 1886a

M C.Comiskey
1B C.Comiskey
2B Y.Robinson
SS B.Gleason
3B A.Latham
LF T.O'Neill
CF C.Welch
RF H.Nicol
C D.Bushong
P D.Foutz
P B.Caruthers
P N.Hudson
P J.McGinnis

STL 1887a

M C.Comiskey
1B C.Comiskey
2B Y.Robinson
SS B.Gleason
3B A.Latham
LF T.O'Neill
CF C.Welch
RF B.Caruthers
C J.Boyle
UT D.Foutz
P S.King

STL 1888a

M C.Comiskey
1B C.Comiskey
2B Y.Robinson
SS B.White
3B A.Latham
LF T.O'Neill
CF H.Lyons
RF T.McCarthy
C J.Boyle
P S.King
P N.Hudson
P E.Chamberlain
P J.Devlin
P E.Knouff

STL 1889a

M C.Comiskey
1B C.Comiskey
2B Y.Robinson
SS S.Fuller
3B A.Latham
LF T.O'Neill
CF C.Duffee
RF T.McCarthy
C J.Boyle
P S.King
P E.Chamberlain
P J.Stivetts

STL 1890a

M T.McCarthy
M J.Kerins
M C.Roseman
M C.Campau
M T.McCarthy
M J.Gerhardt
1B E.Cartwright
2B B.Higgins
SS S.Fuller
3B C.Duffee
LF C.Campau
CF C.Roseman
RF T.McCarthy
C J.Munyan
P J.Stivetts
P T.Ramsey
P B.Hart
P B.Whitrock

STL 1891a

M C.Comiskey
1B C.Comiskey
2B B.Eagan
SS S.Fuller
3B D.Lyons
LF T.O'Neill
CF D.Hoy
RF T.McCarthy
C J.Boyle
P J.Stivetts
P W.McGill
P C.Griffith
P J.Neale
P G.Rettger

STL 1914F

M M.Brown
M F.Jones
1B H.Miller
2B D.Crandall
SS A.Bridwell
3B A.Boucher
LF W.Miller
CF D.Drake
RF J.Tobin
C M.Simon
UT J.Misse
P B.Groom
P D.Davenport
P H.Keupper
P E.Willett
P M.Brown
RP E.Herbert

STL 1915F

M F.Jones
1B B.Borton
2B B.Vaughn
SS E.Johnson
3B C.Deal
LF W.Miller
CF D.Drake
RF J.Tobin
C G.Hartley
P D.Davenport
P D.Crandall
P E.Plank
P B.Groom
P D.Watson

STL 1902A

M J.McAleer
1B J.Anderson
2B D.Padden
SS B.Wallace
3B B.McCormick
LF J.Burkett
CF E.Heidrick
RF C.Hemphill
C J.Sugden
P J.Powell
P R.Donahue
P J.Harper
P W.Sudhoff
P B.Reidy

STL 1903A

M J.McAleer
1B J.Anderson
2B B.Friel
SS B.Wallace
3B H.Hill
LF J.Burkett
CF E.Heidrick
RF C.Hemphill
C M.Kahoe
P J.Powell
P W.Sudhoff
P E.Siever
P R.Donahue

STL 1904A

M J.McAleer
1B T.Jones
2B D.Padden
SS B.Wallace
3B C.Moran
LF J.Burkett
CF E.Heidrick
RF C.Hemphill
C J.Sugden
P B.Pelty
P H.Howell
P F.Glade
P W.Sudhoff
P E.Siever

STL 1905A

M J.McAleer
1B T.Jones
2B I.Rockenfield
SS B.Wallace
3B H.Gleason
LF G.Stone
CF B.Koehler
RF E.Frisk
C J.Sugden
UT I.Van Zandt
P H.Howell
P F.Glade
P B.Pelty
P W.Sudhoff
P J.Buchanan

STL 1906A

M J.McAleer
1B T.Jones
2B P.O'Brien
SS B.Wallace
3B R.Hartzell
LF G.Stone
CF C.Hemphill
RF H.Niles
C B.Rickey
P H.Howell
P F.Glade
P B.Pelty
P J.Powell
P E.Smith

STL 1907A

M J.McAleer
1B T.Jones
2B H.Niles
SS B.Wallace
3B J.Yeager
LF G.Stone
CF C.Hemphill
RF O.Pickering
C T.Spencer
P H.Howell
P B.Pelty
P J.Powell
P F.Glade
P B.Dinneen

STL 1908A

M J.McAleer
1B T.Jones
2B J.Williams
SS B.Wallace
3B H.Ferris
LF G.Stone
CF D.Hoffman
RF R.Hartzell
C T.Spencer
P H.Howell
P R.Waddell
P J.Powell
P B.Dinneen
P B.Pelty

STL 1909A

M J.McAleer
1B T.Jones
2B J.Williams
SS B.Wallace
3B H.Ferris
LF G.Stone
CF D.Hoffman
RF R.Hartzell
C L.Criger
UT A.Griggs
P J.Powell
P R.Waddell
P B.Pelty
P B.Bailey
P B.Grahame

STL 1910A

M J.O'Connor
1B P.Newnam
2B F.Truesdale
SS B.Wallace
3B R.Hartzell
LF G.Stone
CF D.Hoffman
RF A.Schweitzer
C J.Stephens
UT A.Griggs
P J.Lake
P B.Bailey
P B.Pelty
P F.Ray
P J.Powell

STL 1911A

M B.Wallace
1B J.Black
2B F.LaPorte
SS B.Wallace
3B J.Austin
LF W.Hogan
CF B.Shotton
RF A.Schweitzer
C N.Clarke
P J.Lake
P J.Powell
P B.Pelty
P E.Hamilton
P R.Mitchell

STL 1912A

M B.Wallace
M G.Stovall
1B G.Stovall
2B D.Pratt
SS B.Wallace
3B J.Austin
LF W.Hogan
CF B.Shotton
RF G.Williams
C J.Stephens
UT P.Compton
P E.Hamilton
P J.Powell
P G.Baumgardner
P M.Allison
P E.Brown

STL 1913A

M G.Stovall
M J.Austin
M B.Rickey
1B G.Stovall
2B D.Pratt
SS M.Balenti
3B J.Austin
LF J.Johnston
CF B.Shotton
RF G.Williams
C S.Agnew
P G.Baumgardner
P C.Weilman
P R.Mitchell
P E.Hamilton
P W.Leverenz

STL 1914A

M B.Rickey
1B J.Leary
2B D.Pratt
SS D.Lavan
3B J.Austin
LF T.Walker
CF B.Shotton
RF G.Williams
C S.Agnew
P E.Hamilton
P C.Weilman
P B.James
P G.Baumgardner
P W.Leverenz

STL 1915A

M B.Rickey
1B J.Leary
2B D.Pratt
SS D.Lavan
3B J.Austin
LF B.Shotton
CF T.Walker
RF D.Walsh
C S.Agnew
UT I.Howard
P C.Weilman
P G.Lowdermilk
P E.Hamilton
P B.James
P E.Koob
RP P.Perryman

STL 1916A

M F.Jones
1B G.Sisler
2B D.Pratt
SS D.Lavan
3B J.Austin
LF B.Shotton
CF A.Marsans
RF W.Miller
C H.Severeid
P D.Davenport
P C.Weilman
P E.Plank
P B.Groom
P E.Koob

STL 1917A

M F.Jones
1B G.Sisler
2B D.Pratt
SS D.Lavan
3B J.Austin
LF B.Shotton
CF B.Jacobson
RF T.Sloan
C H.Severeid
P D.Davenport
P A.Sothoron
P B.Groom
P E.Koob
P E.Plank

STL 1918A

M F.Jones
M J.Austin
M J.Burke
1B G.Sisler
2B J.Gedeon
SS J.Austin
3B F.Maisel
LF E.Smith
CF J.Tobin
RF R.Demmitt
C L.Nunamaker
UT T.Hendryx
P A.Sothoron
P D.Davenport
P T.Rogers
P B.Gallia
P R.Wright
RP B.Houck

STL 1919A

M J.Burke
1B G.Sisler
2B J.Gedeon
SS W.Gerber
3B J.Austin
LF J.Tobin
CF B.Jacobson
RF E.Smith
C H.Severeid
P A.Sothoron
P B.Gallia
P U.Shocker
P C.Weilman
P D.Davenport
RP E.Koob
RP R.Wright

STL 1920A

M J.Burke
1B G.Sisler
2B J.Gedeon
SS W.Gerber
3B J.Austin
LF K.Williams
CF B.Jacobson
RF J.Tobin
C H.Severeid
UT E.Smith
P D.Davis
P U.Shocker
P A.Sothoron
P C.Weilman
P B.Burwell

STL 1921A

M L.Fohl
1B G.Sisler
2B M.McManus
SS W.Gerber
3B F.Ellerbe
LF K.Williams
CF B.Jacobson
RF J.Tobin
C H.Severeid
P U.Shocker
P D.Davis
P E.Vangilder
P R.Kolp
P B.Bayne
RP B.Burwell

STL 1922A

M L.Fohl
1B G.Sisler
2B M.McManus
SS W.Gerber
3B F.Ellerbe
LF K.Williams
CF B.Jacobson
RF J.Tobin
C H.Severeid
P U.Shocker
P E.Vangilder
P D.Davis
P R.Kolp
P R.Wright

STL 1923A

M L.Fohl
M J.Austin
1B D.Schliebner
2B M.McManus
SS W.Gerber
3B G.Robertson
LF K.Williams
CF B.Jacobson
RF J.Tobin
C H.Severeid
P E.Vangilder
P U.Shocker
P D.Danforth
P R.Kolp
P D.Davis
RP C.Root

STL 1924A

M G.Sisler
1B G.Sisler
2B M.McManus
SS W.Gerber
3B G.Robertson
LF K.Williams
CF B.Jacobson
RF J.Tobin
C H.Severeid
P U.Shocker
P D.Danforth
P E.Wingard
P D.Davis
P E.Vangilder
RP H.Pruett
RP G.Grant
RP B.Bayne

STL 1925A

M G.Sisler
1B G.Sisler
2B M.McManus
SS B.LaMotte
3B G.Robertson
LF K.Williams
CF B.Jacobson
RF H.Rice
C L.Dixon
P M.Gaston
P J.Bush
P E.Vangilder
P D.Davis
P J.Giard

STL 1926A

M G.Sisler
1B G.Sisler
2B S.Melillo
SS W.Gerber
3B M.McManus
LF K.Williams
CF H.Rice
RF B.Miller
C W.Schang
P T.Zachary
P M.Gaston
P E.Vangilder
P E.Wingard
P W.Ballou

STL 1927A

M D.Howley
1B G.Sisler
2B S.Melillo
SS W.Gerber
3B F.O'Rourke
LF K.Williams
CF B.Miller
RF H.Rice
C W.Schang
P M.Gaston
P E.Vangilder
P S.Jones
P E.Wingard
P L.Stewart

STL 1928A

M D.Howley
1B L.Blue
2B O.Brannan
SS R.Kress
3B F.O'Rourke
LF H.Manush
CF F.Schulte
RF E.McNeely
C W.Schang
P D.Gray
P A.Crowder
P J.Ogden
P G.Blaeholder
P L.Stewart
RP D.Coffman
RP H.Wiltse
RP E.Strelecki

STL 1929A

M D.Howley
1B L.Blue
2B S.Melillo
SS R.Kress
3B F.O'Rourke
LF H.Manush
CF F.Schulte
RF B.McGowan
C W.Schang
P D.Gray
P A.Crowder
P G.Blaeholder
P R.Collins
P L.Stewart
RP C.Kimsey
RP D.Coffman

STL 1930A

M B.Killefer
1B L.Blue
2B S.Melillo
SS R.Kress
3B F.O'Rourke
LF G.Goslin
CF F.Schulte
RF T.Gullic
C R.Ferrell
P L.Stewart
P D.Coffman
P G.Blaeholder
P R.Collins
P D.Gray
RP C.Kimsey
RP H.Holshouser

STL 1931A

M B.Killefer
1B J.Burns
2B S.Melillo
SS J.Levey
3B R.Kress
LF G.Goslin
CF F.Schulte
RF T.Jenkins
C R.Ferrell
P L.Stewart
P D.Gray
P G.Blaeholder
P D.Coffman
P R.Collins
RP C.Kimsey
RP R.Stiles

STL 1932A

M B.Killefer
1B J.Burns
2B S.Melillo
SS J.Levey
3B A.Scharein
LF G.Goslin
CF F.Schulte
RF B.Campbell
C R.Ferrell
P L.Stewart
P G.Blaeholder
P B.Hadley
P D.Gray
P W.Hebert
RP C.Kimsey

STL 1933A

M B.Killefer
M A.Sothoron
M R.Hornsby
1B J.Burns
2B S.Melillo
SS J.Levey
3B A.Scharein
LF C.Reynolds
CF S.West
RF B.Campbell
C M.Shea
UT T.Gullic
P B.Hadley
P G.Blaeholder
P E.Wells
P R.Stiles
RP D.Gray
RP W.Hebert
RP H.McDonald

STL 1934A

M R.Hornsby
1B J.Burns
2B S.Melillo
SS A.Strange
3B H.Clift
LF R.Pepper
CF S.West
RF B.Campbell
C R.Hemsley
UT O.Bejma
P B.Newsom
P G.Blaeholder
P B.Hadley
P D.Coffman
P I.Andrews
RP E.Wells
RP B.McAfee

STL 1935A

M R.Hornsby
1B J.Burns
2B T.Carey
SS L.Lary
3B H.Clift
LF M.Solters
CF S.West
RF E.Coleman
C R.Hemsley
P I.Andrews
P J.Knott
P J.Walkup
P R.Van Atta
P S.Cain

STL 1936A

M R.Hornsby
1B J.Bottomley
2B T.Carey
SS L.Lary
3B H.Clift
LF M.Solters
CF S.West
RF B.Bell
C R.Hemsley
P C.Hogsett
P J.Knott
P I.Andrews
P E.Caldwell
P T.Thomas
RP R.Van Atta
RP R.Mahaffey
RP G.Liebhardt

STL 1937A

M R.Hornsby
M J.Bottomley
1B H.Davis
2B T.Carey
SS B.Knickerbocker
3B H.Clift
LF J.Vosmik
CF S.West
RF B.Bell
C R.Hemsley
UT E.Allen
P O.Hildebrand
P J.Knott
P C.Hogsett
P J.Walkup
P J.Bonetti

STL 1938A

M G.Street
M S.Melillo
1B G.McQuinn
2B D.Heffner
SS R.Kress
3B H.Clift
LF B.Mills
CF M.Almada
RF B.Bell
C B.Sullivan
P B.Newsom
P L.Mills
P O.Hildebrand
P R.Van Atta
P J.Walkup
RP E.Cole
RP B.Cox

STL 1939A

M F.Haney
1B G.McQuinn
2B J.Berardino
SS D.Heffner
3B H.Clift
LF J.Gallagher
CF C.Laabs
RF M.Hoag
C J.Glenn
UT B.Sullivan
P J.Kramer
P V.Kennedy
P B.Trotter
P R.Lawson
P L.Mills
RP J.Whitehead

STL 1940A

M F.Haney
1B G.McQuinn
2B D.Heffner
SS J.Berardino
3B H.Clift
LF R.Radcliff
CF W.Judnich
RF R.Cullenbine
C B.Swift
UT C.Laabs
P E.Auker
P V.Kennedy
P B.Harris
P J.Niggeling
P E.Bildilli
RP B.Trotter
RP S.Coffman
RP R.Lawson

STL 1941A

M F.Haney
M L.Sewell
1B G.McQuinn
2B D.Heffner
SS J.Berardino
3B H.Clift
LF R.Cullenbine
CF W.Judnich
RF C.Laabs
C R.Ferrell
UT J.Grace
UT J.Lucadello
P E.Auker
P B.Muncrief
P D.Galehouse
P B.Harris
P J.Niggeling
RP J.Kramer
RP B.Trotter

STL 1942A

M L.Sewell
1B G.McQuinn
2B D.Gutteridge
SS V.Stephens
3B H.Clift
LF G.McQuillen
CF W.Judnich
RF C.Laabs
C R.Ferrell
UT T.Criscola
P E.Auker
P J.Niggeling
P D.Galehouse
P A.Hollingsworth
P B.Muncrief
RP G.Caster

STL 1943A

M L.Sewell
1B G.McQuinn
2B D.Gutteridge
SS V.Stephens
3B H.Clift
LF C.Laabs
CF M.Byrnes
RF M.Chartak
C F.Hayes
UT M.Christman
P D.Galehouse
P S.Sundra
P B.Muncrief
P N.Potter
P A.Hollingsworth
RP G.Caster

STL 1944A

M L.Sewell
1B G.McQuinn
2B D.Gutteridge
SS V.Stephens
3B M.Christman
LF M.Byrnes
CF M.Kreevich
RF G.Moore
C F.Mancuso
UT A.Zarilla
P J.Kramer
P N.Potter
P B.Muncrief
P S.Jakucki
P D.Galehouse
RP G.Caster

STL 1945A

M L.Sewell
1B G.McQuinn
2B D.Gutteridge
SS V.Stephens
3B M.Christman
LF M.Byrnes
CF M.Kreevich
RF G.Moore
C F.Mancuso
UT L.Schulte
P N.Potter
P J.Kramer
P S.Jakucki
P T.Shirley
P A.Hollingsworth
RP S.Zoldak

STL 1946A

M L.Sewell
M Z.Taylor
1B C.Stevens
2B J.Berardino
SS V.Stephens
3B M.Christman
LF J.Heath
CF W.Judnich
RF A.Zarilla
C F.Mancuso
P J.Kramer
P D.Galehouse
P S.Zoldak
P N.Potter
P T.Shirley
RP S.Ferens
RP E.Kinder

STL 1947A

M M.Ruel
1B W.Judnich
2B J.Berardino
SS V.Stephens
3B B.Dillinger
LF J.Heath
CF P.Lehner
RF A.Zarilla
C L.Moss
UT R.Coleman
P J.Kramer
P E.Kinder
P F.Sanford
P B.Muncrief
P S.Zoldak
RP G.Moulder

STL 1948A

M Z.Taylor
1B C.Stevens
2B J.Priddy
SS E.Pellagrini
3B B.Dillinger
LF W.Platt
CF P.Lehner
RF A.Zarilla
C L.Moss
UT S.Dente
P F.Sanford
P C.Fannin
P N.Garver
P B.Kennedy
RP B.Stephens
RP F.Biscan
RP A.Widmar

STL 1949A

M Z.Taylor
1B J.Graham
2B J.Priddy
SS E.Pellagrini
3B B.Dillinger
LF R.Sievers
CF S.Spence
RF D.Kokos
C S.Lollar
UT P.Lehner
UT L.Moss
UT W.Platt
UT J.Sullivan
P N.Garver
P B.Kennedy
P C.Fannin
P A.Papai
P J.Ostrowski
RP T.Ferrick
RP D.Starr

STL 1950A

M Z.Taylor
1B D.Lenhardt
2B O.Friend
SS T.Upton
3B B.Sommers
LF D.Kokos
CF R.Coleman
RF K.Wood
C S.Lollar
UT H.Arft
UT R.Sievers
P N.Garver
P A.Widmar
P S.Overmire
P D.Starr
P H.Dorish
RP C.Marshall

STL 1951A

M Z.Taylor
1B H.Arft
2B B.Young
SS B.Jennings
3B F.Marsh
LF R.Coleman
CF J.Delsing
RF K.Wood
C S.Lollar
P N.Garver
P D.Pillette
P T.Byrne
P A.Widmar
RP B.Mahoney
RP S.Paige
RP B.Kennedy

STL 1952A

M R.Hornsby
M M.Marion
1B D.Kryhoski
2B B.Young
SS J.DeMaestri
3B J.Dyck
LF J.Delsing
CF J.Rivera
RF B.Nieman
C C.Courtney
P D.Pillette
P T.Byrne
P B.Cain

P G.Bearden
P N.Garver
RP D.Madison

STL 1953A

M M.Marion
1B D.Kryhoski
2B B.Young
SS B.Hunter
3B J.Dyck
LF D.Kokos
CF J.Groth
RF V.Wertz
C C.Courtney
UT D.Lenhardt
P D.Larsen
P D.Pillette
P D.Littlefield
P H.Brecheen
P B.Cain
RP S.Paige
RP M.Stuart
RP M.Blyzka

STL 1892N

M J.Glasscock
M C.Stricker
M J.Crooks
M G.Gore
M B.Caruthers
1B P.Werden
2B J.Crooks
SS J.Glasscock
3B G.Pinkney
LF C.Carroll
CF S.Brodie
RF B.Caruthers
C D.Buckley
P K.Gleason
P T.Breitenstein
P P.Hawley
P C.Getzien
P B.Hawke

STL 1893N

M B.Watkins
1B P.Werden
2B J.Quinn
SS J.Glasscock
3B J.Crooks
LF C.Frank
CF S.Brodie
RF T.Dowd
C H.Peitz
P T.Breitenstein
P K.Gleason
P P.Hawley
P D.Clarkson

STL 1894N

M G.Miller
1B R.Connor
2B J.Quinn
SS B.Ely
3B H.Peitz
LF C.Frank
CF F.Shugart
RF T.Dowd
C D.Miller
P T.Breitenstein
P P.Hawley
P D.Clarkson

STL 1895N

M A.Buckenberger
M C.Von Der Ahe
M J.Quinn
M L.Phelan
1B R.Connor
2B J.Quinn
SS B.Ely
3B D.Miller
LF D.Cooley
CF T.Brown
RF T.Dowd
C H.Peitz
P T.Breitenstein
P R.Ehret
P H.Staley
P B.Kissinger
P D.McDougal

STL 1896N

M H.Diddlebock
M A.Latham
M C.Von Der Ahe
M R.Connor
M T.Dowd
1B R.Connor
2B T.Dowd
SS M.Cross
3B B.Myers
LF J.Sullivan
CF T.Parrott
RF K.Douglass
C E.McFarland
P T.Breitenstein
P B.Hart
P R.Donahue
P B.Kissinger

STL 1897N

M T.Dowd
M H.Nicol
M B.Hallman
M C.Von Der Ahe
1B M.Grady
2B B.Hallman
SS M.Cross
3B F.Hartman
LF D.Lally
CF D.Harley
RF T.Turner
C K.Douglass
P R.Donahue
P B.Hart
P K.Carsey
P W.Sudhoff

STL 1898N

M T.Hurst
1B G.Decker
2B J.Crooks
SS G.Smith
3B L.Cross
LF D.Harley
CF J.Stenzel
RF T.Dowd
C J.Clements
UT J.Quinn
P J.Taylor
P W.Sudhoff
P J.Hughey
P K.Carsey

STL 1899N

M P.Tebeau
1B P.Tebeau
2B C.Childs
SS B.Wallace
3B L.Cross
LF J.Burkett
CF H.Blake
RF E.Heidrick
C L.Criger
P J.Powell
P C.Young
P W.Sudhoff
P N.Cuppy

STL 1900N

M P.Tebeau
M L.Heilbroner
1B D.McGann
2B B.Keister
SS B.Wallace
3B J.McGraw
LF J.Burkett
CF E.Heidrick
RF P.Donovan
C L.Criger
P C.Young
P C.Jones
P J.Powell
P W.Sudhoff
P J.Hughey

STL 1901N

M P.Donovan
1B D.McGann
2B D.Padden
SS B.Wallace
3B O.Krueger
LF J.Burkett
CF E.Heidrick
RF P.Donovan
C J.Ryan
UT A.Nichols
P J.Powell
P J.Harper
P W.Sudhoff
P E.Murphy

STL 1902N

M P.Donovan
1B R.Brashear
2B J.Farrell
SS O.Krueger
3B F.Hartman
LF G.Barclay
CF H.Smoot
RF P.Donovan
C J.Ryan
P M.O'Neill
P S.Yerkes
P E.Murphy
P B.Wicker
P C.Currie

STL 1903N

M P.Donovan
1B J.Hackett
2B J.Farrell
SS D.Brain
3B J.Burke
LF G.Barclay
CF H.Smoot
RF P.Donovan
C J.O'Neill
P C.McFarland
P M.Brown
P C.Currie
P M.O'Neill
P B.Rhoads

STL 1904N

M K.Nichols
1B J.Beckley
2B J.Farrell
SS D.Shay
3B J.Burke
LF G.Barclay
CF H.Smoot
RF S.Shannon
C M.Grady
UT D.Brain
P J.Taylor
P K.Nichols
P C.McFarland
P M.O'Neill
P J.Corbett

STL 1905N

M K.Nichols
M J.Burke
M S.Robison
1B J.Beckley
2B H.Arndt
SS G.McBride
3B J.Burke
LF S.Shannon
CF H.Smoot
RF J.Dunleavy
C M.Grady
P J.Taylor
P C.McFarland
P J.Thielman
P B.Brown
P W.Egan

STL 1906N

M J.McCloskey
1B J.Beckley
2B P.Bennett
SS G.McBride
3B H.Arndt
LF S.Shannon
CF H.Smoot
RF A.Burch
C M.Grady
UT A.Hoelskoetter
P B.Brown
P E.Karger
P F.Beebe
P J.Taylor
P C.Druhot

STL 1907N

M J.McCloskey
1B E.Konetchy
2B P.Bennett
SS E.Holly
3B B.Byrne
LF R.Murray
CF J.Burnett
RF S.Barry
C D.Marshall
UT A.Hoelskoetter
P S.McGlynn
P E.Karger
P F.Beebe
P A.Fromme
P J.Lush

STL 1908N

M J.McCloskey
1B E.Konetchy
2B B.Gilbert
SS P.O'Rourke
3B B.Byrne
LF J.Delahanty
CF A.Shaw
RF R.Murray
C B.Ludwig
UT C.Charles
P B.Raymond
P J.Lush
P F.Beebe
P E.Karger
P S.Sallee

STL 1909N

M R.Bresnahan
1B E.Konetchy
2B C.Charles
SS R.Hulswitt
3B B.Byrne
LF R.Ellis
CF A.Shaw
RF S.Evans
C E.Phelps
UT J.Delahanty
P F.Beebe
P J.Lush
P S.Sallee
P B.Harmon
P L.Backman
RP S.Melter

STL 1910N

M R.Bresnahan
1B E.Konetchy
2B M.Huggins
SS A.Hauser
3B M.Mowrey
LF R.Ellis
CF R.Oakes
RF S.Evans
C E.Phelps
P B.Harmon
P J.Lush
P V.Willis
P F.Corridon
P L.Backman

STL 1911N

M R.Bresnahan
1B E.Konetchy
2B M.Huggins
SS A.Hauser
3B M.Mowrey
LF R.Ellis
CF R.Oakes
RF S.Evans
C J.Bliss
P B.Harmon
P B.Steele
P S.Sallee
P R.Golden
P R.Geyer

STL 1912N

M R.Bresnahan
1B E.Konetchy
2B M.Huggins
SS A.Hauser
3B M.Mowrey
LF L.Magee
CF R.Oakes
RF S.Evans
C I.Wingo
UT R.Ellis
P S.Sallee
P B.Harmon
P B.Steele
P R.Geyer
P J.Willis
RP G.Woodburn

STL 1913N

M M.Huggins
1B E.Konetchy
2B M.Huggins
SS C.O'Leary
3B M.Mowrey
LF L.Magee
CF R.Oakes
RF S.Evans
C I.Wingo
UT P.Whitted
P S.Sallee
P B.Harmon
P D.Griner
P P.Perritt
P B.Doak
RP R.Geyer

STL 1914N

M M.Huggins
1B D.Miller
2B M.Huggins
SS A.Butler
3B Z.Beck
LF C.Dolan
CF L.Magee
RF C.Wilson
C F.Snyder
UT W.Cruise
P P.Perritt
P S.Sallee
P B.Doak
P D.Griner
P H.Perdue

STL 1915N

M M.Huggins
1B D.Miller
2B M.Huggins
SS A.Butler
3B B.Betzel
LF B.Bescher
CF C.Wilson
RF T.Long
C F.Snyder
UT C.Dolan
UT H.Hyatt
P B.Doak
P S.Sallee
P L.Meadows
P D.Griner
P H.Robinson

STL 1916N

M M.Huggins
1B D.Miller
2B B.Betzel
SS R.Corhan
3B R.Hornsby
LF B.Bescher
CF J.Smith
RF C.Wilson
C M.Gonzalez
UT T.Long
UT F.Snyder
P L.Meadows
P R.Ames
P B.Doak
P B.Steele
P H.Jasper
RP S.Williams

STL 1917N

M M.Huggins
1B G.Paulette
2B D.Miller
SS R.Hornsby
3B D.Baird
LF W.Cruise
CF J.Smith
RF T.Long
C F.Snyder
UT B.Betzel
UT M.Gonzalez
P B.Doak
P L.Meadows
P R.Ames
P M.Watson
P G.Packard

STL 1918N

M J.Hendricks
1B G.Paulette
2B B.Fisher
SS R.Hornsby
3B D.Baird
LF A.McHenry
CF C.Heathcote
RF W.Cruise
C M.Gonzalez
P B.Doak
P R.Ames
P B.Sherdel
P G.Packard
P L.Meadows

STL 1919N

M B.Rickey
1B D.Miller
2B M.Stock
SS D.Lavan
3B R.Hornsby
LF A.McHenry
CF C.Heathcote
RF J.Smith
C V.Clemons
UT J.Schultz
UT B.Shotton
P B.Doak
P M.Goodwin
P O.Tuero
P B.Sherdel
P J.May

STL 1920N

M B.Rickey
1B J.Fournier
2B R.Hornsby
SS D.Lavan
3B M.Stock
LF A.McHenry
CF J.Smith
RF C.Heathcote
C V.Clemons
UT J.Schultz
P J.Haines
P B.Doak
P F.Schupp
P B.Sherdel
P M.Goodwin

STL 1921N

M B.Rickey
1B J.Fournier
2B R.Hornsby
SS D.Lavan
3B M.Stock
LF A.McHenry
CF L.Mann
RF J.Smith
C V.Clemons
P J.Haines
P B.Doak
P B.Pertica
P R.Walker
P B.Sherdel
RP L.North

STL 1922N

M B.Rickey
1B J.Fournier
2B R.Hornsby
SS S.Toporcer
3B M.Stock
LF J.Schultz
CF J.Smith
RF M.Flack
C E.Ainsmith
P J.Pfeffer
P B.Sherdel
P J.Haines
P B.Doak
P B.Pertica
RP L.North
RP C.Barfoot

STL 1923N

M B.Rickey
1B J.Bottomley
2B R.Hornsby
SS H.Freigau
3B M.Stock
LF J.Smith
CF H.Myers
RF M.Flack
C E.Ainsmith
UT R.Blades
UT S.Toporcer
P J.Haines
P B.Sherdel
P F.Toney
P B.Doak
P J.Pfeffer
RP L.North

STL 1924N

M B.Rickey
1B J.Bottomley
2B R.Hornsby
SS J.Cooney
3B H.Freigau
LF R.Blades
CF W.Holm
RF J.Smith
C M.Gonzalez
P J.Haines
P A.Sothoron
P B.Sherdel
P J.Stuart
P E.Dyer

STL 1925N

M B.Rickey
M R.Hornsby
1B J.Bottomley
2B R.Hornsby
SS S.Toporcer
3B L.Bell
LF R.Blades
CF H.Mueller
RF C.Hafey
C B.O'Farrell
P J.Haines
P B.Sherdel
P F.Rhem
P A.Sothoron
P A.Reinhart

STL 1926N

M R.Hornsby
1B J.Bottomley
2B R.Hornsby
SS T.Thevenow
3B L.Bell
LF R.Blades
CF T.Douthit
RF B.Southworth
C B.O'Farrell
P F.Rhem
P B.Sherdel
P J.Haines
P V.Keen
P G.Alexander
RP S.Johnson

STL 1927N

M B.O'Farrell
1B J.Bottomley
2B F.Frisch
SS H.Schuble
3B L.Bell
LF C.Hafey
CF T.Douthit
RF B.Southworth
C F.Snyder
UT W.Holm
P J.Haines
P G.Alexander
P B.Sherdel
P F.Rhem
P B.McGraw
RP H.Bell

STL 1928N

M B.McKechnie
1B J.Bottomley
2B F.Frisch
SS R.Maranville
3B W.Holm
LF C.Hafey
CF T.Douthit
RF G.Harper
C J.Wilson
UT A.High
P B.Sherdel
P G.Alexander
P J.Haines
P F.Rhem
P C.Mitchell
RP H.Haid

STL 1929N

M B.Southworth
M G.Street
M B.McKechnie
1B J.Bottomley
2B F.Frisch
SS C.Gelbert
3B A.High
LF C.Hafey
CF T.Douthit
RF E.Orsatti
C J.Wilson
P B.Sherdel
P S.Johnson
P J.Haines
P C.Mitchell
P H.Haid

STL 1930N

M G.Street
1B J.Bottomley
2B F.Frisch
SS C.Gelbert
3B S.Adams
LF C.Hafey
CF T.Douthit
RF G.Watkins
C J.Wilson
P B.Hallahan
P S.Johnson
P J.Haines
P B.Grimes
P F.Rhem
RP H.Bell
RP J.Lindsey

STL 1931N

M G.Street
1B J.Bottomley
2B F.Frisch
SS C.Gelbert

3B S.Adams
LF C.Hafey
CF P.Martin
RF G.Watkins
C J.Wilson
P B.Hallahan
P B.Grimes
P P.Derringer
P F.Rhem
P S.Johnson
RP J.Lindsey
RP A.Stout

STL 1932N

M G.Street
1B R.Collins
2B J.Reese
SS C.Gelbert
3B J.Flowers
LF E.Orsatti
CF P.Martin
RF G.Watkins
C G.Mancuso
UT F.Frisch
P D.Dean
P P.Derringer
P T.Carleton
P B.Hallahan
P S.Johnson
RP J.Lindsey
RP A.Stout

STL 1933N

M G.Street
M F.Frisch
1B R.Collins
2B F.Frisch
SS L.Durocher
3B P.Martin
LF J.Medwick
CF E.Orsatti
RF G.Watkins
C J.Wilson
P D.Dean
P T.Carleton
P B.Hallahan
P B.Walker
P J.Haines
RP S.Johnson

STL 1934N

M F.Frisch
1B R.Collins
2B F.Frisch
SS L.Durocher
3B P.Martin
LF J.Medwick
CF E.Orsatti
RF J.Rothrock
C S.Davis
UT B.Whitehead
P D.Dean
P T.Carleton
P P.Dean
P B.Hallahan
P B.Walker
RP J.Haines
RP J.Mooney

STL 1935N

M F.Frisch
1B R.Collins
2B F.Frisch
SS L.Durocher
3B P.Martin
LF J.Medwick
CF T.Moore
RF J.Rothrock
C B.DeLancey
UT S.Davis
UT B.Whitehead
P D.Dean
P P.Dean
P B.Walker
P B.Hallahan
P E.Heusser

STL 1936N

M F.Frisch
1B J.Mize
2B S.Martin
SS L.Durocher
3B C.Gelbert
LF J.Medwick
CF T.Moore
RF P.Martin
C S.Davis
UT R.Collins
UT B.Ogrodowski
P D.Dean
P R.Parmelee
P J.Winford
P J.Haines
RP E.Heusser
RP G.Earnshaw

STL 1937N

M F.Frisch
1B J.Mize
2B J.Brown
SS L.Durocher
3B D.Gutteridge
LF J.Medwick
CF T.Moore
RF D.Padgett
C B.Ogrodowski
UT F.Bordagaray
UT P.Martin
P B.Weiland
P L.Warneke
P D.Dean
P S.Johnson
P M.Ryba
RP R.Harrell

STL 1938N

M F.Frisch
M M.Gonzalez
1B J.Mize
2B S.Martin
SS L.Myers
3B D.Gutteridge
LF J.Medwick
CF T.Moore
RF E.Slaughter
C M.Owen
UT J.Brown
UT D.Padgett
P B.Weiland
P B.McGee
P L.Warneke
P C.Davis
P R.Henshaw
RP C.Shoun
RP R.Harrell

STL 1939N

M R.Blades
1B J.Mize
2B S.Martin
SS J.Brown
3B D.Gutteridge
LF J.Medwick
CF T.Moore
RF E.Slaughter
C M.Owen
P C.Davis
P M.Cooper
P B.Bowman
P L.Warneke
P B.McGee
RP C.Shoun

STL 1940N

M R.Blades
M M.Gonzalez
M B.Southworth
1B J.Mize
2B J.Orengo
SS M.Marion
3B S.Martin
LF E.Koy
CF T.Moore
RF E.Slaughter
C M.Owen
UT J.Brown
P L.Warneke
P M.Cooper
P B.McGee
P C.Shoun
P B.Bowman
RP J.Russell

STL 1941N

M B.Southworth
1B J.Mize
2B C.Crespi
SS M.Marion
3B J.Brown
LF J.Hopp
CF T.Moore
RF E.Slaughter
C G.Mancuso
UT D.Padgett
P L.Warneke
P E.White
P M.Cooper
P M.Lanier
P H.Gumbert
RP C.Shoun
RP I.Hutchinson

STL 1942N

M B.Southworth
1B J.Hopp
2B C.Crespi
SS M.Marion
3B W.Kurowski
LF S.Musial
CF T.Moore
RF E.Slaughter
C W.Cooper
UT J.Brown
UT R.Sanders
P M.Cooper
P J.Beazley
P H.Gumbert
P M.Lanier
P E.White

STL 1943N

M B.Southworth
1B R.Sanders
2B L.Klein
SS M.Marion
3B W.Kurowski
LF D.Litwhiler
CF H.Walker
RF S.Musial
C W.Cooper
P M.Cooper
P M.Lanier
P H.Krist
P H.Brecheen
P H.Gumbert
RP R.Munger

STL 1944N

M B.Southworth
1B R.Sanders
2B E.Verban
SS M.Marion
3B W.Kurowski
LF D.Litwhiler
CF J.Hopp
RF S.Musial
C W.Cooper
P M.Cooper
P M.Lanier
P T.Wilks
P H.Brecheen
P A.Jurisich
RP B.Donnelly

STL 1945N

M B.Southworth
1B R.Sanders
2B E.Verban
SS M.Marion
3B W.Kurowski
LF R.Schoendienst
CF B.Adams
RF J.Hopp
C K.O'Dea
UT A.Bergamo
P R.Barrett
P K.Burkhart
P B.Donnelly
P H.Brecheen
P G.Dockins
RP B.Byerly
RP A.Jurisich

STL 1946N

M E.Dyer
1B S.Musial
2B R.Schoendienst
SS M.Marion
3B W.Kurowski
LF E.Dusak
CF H.Walker
RF E.Slaughter
C J.Garagiola
P H.Pollet
P H.Brecheen
P M.Dickson
P A.Brazle
P J.Beazley
RP T.Wilks
RP R.Barrett

STL 1947N

M E.Dyer
1B S.Musial
2B R.Schoendienst
SS M.Marion
3B W.Kurowski
LF E.Slaughter
CF T.Moore
RF R.Northey
C D.Rice
UT C.Diering
UT E.Dusak
P M.Dickson
P R.Munger
P H.Brecheen
P H.Pollet
P A.Brazle
RP K.Burkhart
RP T.Wilks

STL 1948N

M E.Dyer
1B N.Jones
2B R.Schoendienst
SS M.Marion
3B D.Lang
LF E.Slaughter
CF T.Moore
RF S.Musial
C D.Rice
UT E.Dusak
UT R.Northey
P M.Dickson
P H.Brecheen
P H.Pollet
P R.Munger
P A.Brazle
RP T.Wilks
RP J.Hearn
RP G.Staley

STL 1949N

M E.Dyer
1B N.Jones
2B R.Schoendienst
SS M.Marion
3B E.Kazak
LF E.Slaughter
CF C.Diering
RF S.Musial
C D.Rice
P H.Pollet
P H.Brecheen
P A.Brazle
P R.Munger
P G.Staley
RP T.Wilks

STL 1950N

M E.Dyer
1B R.Nelson
2B R.Schoendienst
SS M.Marion
3B T.Glaviano
LF S.Musial
CF B.Howerton
RF E.Slaughter
C D.Rice
UT C.Diering
P H.Pollet
P M.Lanier
P G.Staley
P A.Brazle
P H.Brecheen
RP F.Martin

STL 1951N

M M.Marion
1B N.Jones
2B R.Schoendienst
SS S.Hemus
3B B.Johnson
LF S.Musial
CF P.Lowrey
RF E.Slaughter
C D.Rice
P G.Staley
P T.Poholsky
P M.Lanier
P H.Brecheen
P C.Chambers
RP A.Brazle
RP D.Bokelmann

STL 1952N

M E.Stanky
1B D.Sisler
2B R.Schoendienst
SS S.Hemus
3B B.Johnson
LF P.Lowrey
CF S.Musial
RF E.Slaughter
C D.Rice
UT H.Rice
P G.Staley
P V.Mizell
P J.Presko
P C.Boyer
P H.Brecheen
RP A.Brazle
RP E.Yuhas

STL 1953N

M E.Stanky
1B S.Bilko
2B R.Schoendienst
SS S.Hemus
3B R.Jablonski
LF S.Musial
CF R.Repulski
RF E.Slaughter
C D.Rice
UT P.Lowrey
P H.Haddix
P G.Staley
P V.Mizell
P J.Presko
P S.Miller
RP A.Brazle
RP H.White
RP C.Chambers

STL 1954N

M E.Stanky
1B J.Cunningham
2B R.Schoendienst
SS A.Grammas
3B R.Jablonski
LF R.Repulski
CF W.Moon
RF S.Musial
C B.Sarni
UT S.Hemus
P H.Haddix
P V.Raschi
P B.Lawrence
P G.Staley
P T.Poholsky
RP A.Brazle
RP J.Presko
RP C.Deal

STL 1955N

M E.Stanky
M H.Walker
1B S.Musial
2B R.Schoendienst
SS A.Grammas
3B K.Boyer
LF R.Repulski
CF B.Virdon
RF W.Moon
C B.Sarni
UT S.Hemus
P H.Haddix
P L.Jackson
P L.Arroyo
P T.Poholsky
P W.Schmidt
RP B.Lawrence
RP P.LaPalme

STL 1956N

M F.Hutchinson
1B S.Musial
2B D.Blasingame
SS A.Dark
3B K.Boyer
LF R.Repulski
CF B.Del Greco
RF W.Moon
C H.Smith
P V.Mizell
P T.Poholsky
P M.Dickson
P H.Wehmeier
P W.Schmidt
RP L.McDaniel
RP L.Jackson
RP J.Collum

STL 1957N

M F.Hutchinson
1B S.Musial
2B D.Blasingame
SS A.Dark
3B E.Kasko
LF W.Moon
CF K.Boyer
RF D.Ennis
C H.Smith
UT J.Cunningham
P L.Jackson
P L.McDaniel
P S.Jones
P H.Wehmeier
P V.Mizell
RP W.Schmidt
RP L.Merritt
RP H.Wilhelm

STL 1958N

M F.Hutchinson
M S.Hack
1B S.Musial
2B D.Blasingame
SS E.Kasko
3B K.Boyer
LF D.Ennis
CF C.Flood
RF W.Moon
C H.Smith
UT J.Cunningham
UT G.Green
UT I.Noren
P S.Jones
P L.Jackson
P V.Mizell
P J.Brosnan
P B.Mabe
RP B.Muffett
RP P.Paine
RP B.Wight

STL 1959N

M S.Hemus
1B S.Musial
2B D.Blasingame
SS A.Grammas
3B K.Boyer
LF G.Cimoli
CF C.Flood
RF J.Cunningham
C H.Smith
UT B.White
P L.Jackson
P V.Mizell
P E.Broglio
P G.Blaylock
RP L.McDaniel
RP M.Bridges

STL 1960N

M S.Hemus
1B B.White
2B J.Javier
SS D.Spencer
3B K.Boyer
LF S.Musial
CF C.Flood
RF J.Cunningham
C H.Smith
UT A.Grammas
UT W.Moryn
P L.Jackson
P E.Broglio
P R.Sadecki
P C.Simmons
P R.Kline
RP L.McDaniel

STL 1961N

M S.Hemus
M J.Keane
1B B.White
2B J.Javier
SS A.Grammas
3B K.Boyer
LF S.Musial
CF C.Flood
RF C.James
C J.Schaffer
UT J.Cunningham
UT D.Taussig
P R.Sadecki
P L.Jackson
P B.Gibson
P C.Simmons
P E.Broglio
RP L.McDaniel
RP A.Cicotte
RP B.Miller

STL 1962N

M J.Keane
1B B.White
2B J.Javier
SS J.Gotay
3B K.Boyer
LF S.Musial
CF C.Flood
RF C.James
C G.Oliver
P L.Jackson
P B.Gibson
P E.Broglio
P R.Washburn
P C.Simmons
RP L.McDaniel
RP B.Shantz
RP D.Ferrarese

STL 1963N

M J.Keane
1B B.White
2B J.Javier
SS D.Groat
3B K.Boyer
LF C.James
CF C.Flood
RF G.Altman
C T.McCarver
UT S.Musial
P B.Gibson
P E.Broglio
P C.Simmons
P R.Sadecki
P L.Burdette
RP R.Taylor
RP B.Shantz
RP E.Bauta

STL 1964N

M J.Keane
1B B.White
2B J.Javier
SS D.Groat
3B K.Boyer
LF L.Brock
CF C.Flood
RF M.Shannon
C T.McCarver
P B.Gibson
P C.Simmons
P R.Sadecki
P R.Craig
RP R.Taylor
RP M.Cuellar
RP B.Schultz

STL 1965N

M R.Schoendienst
1B B.White
2B J.Javier
SS D.Groat
3B K.Boyer
LF L.Brock
CF C.Flood
RF M.Shannon
C T.McCarver
UT P.Gagliano
P B.Gibson
P C.Simmons
P T.Stallard
P R.Sadecki
P B.Purkey
RP N.Briles
RP H.Woodeshick
RP D.Dennis

STL 1966N

M R.Schoendienst
1B O.Cepeda
2B J.Javier
SS D.Maxvill
3B C.Smith
LF L.Brock
CF C.Flood
RF M.Shannon
C T.McCarver
UT J.Buchek
P B.Gibson
P A.Jackson
P R.Washburn
P N.Briles
P L.Jaster
RP J.Hoerner
RP H.Woodeshick
RP D.Dennis

STL 1967N

M R.Schoendienst
1B O.Cepeda
2B J.Javier
SS D.Maxvill
3B M.Shannon
LF L.Brock
CF C.Flood
RF R.Maris
C T.McCarver
UT B.Tolan
P D.Hughes
P S.Carlton
P R.Washburn
P B.Gibson
P N.Briles
RP A.Jackson
RP R.Willis
RP J.Hoerner

STL 1968N

M R.Schoendienst

1B O.Cepeda
2B J.Javier
SS D.Maxvill
3B M.Shannon
LF L.Brock
CF C.Flood
RF R.Maris
C T.McCarver
P B.Gibson
P N.Briles
P S.Carlton
P R.Washburn
P L.Jaster
RP R.Willis
RP D.Hughes
RP M.Nelson

STL 1969N

M R.Schoendienst
1B J.Torre
2B J.Javier
SS D.Maxvill
3B M.Shannon
LF L.Brock
CF C.Flood
RF V.Pinson
C T.McCarver
P B.Gibson
P S.Carlton
P N.Briles
P R.Washburn
P C.Taylor
RP M.Grant
RP J.Hoerner

STL 1970N

M R.Schoendienst
1B J.Hague
2B J.Javier
SS D.Maxvill
3B J.Torre
LF L.Brock
CF J.Cardenal
RF L.Lee
C T.Simmons
UT D.Allen
UT V.Davalillo
UT Ca.Taylor
P B.Gibson
P S.Carlton
P M.Torrez
P J.Reuss
P N.Briles
RP Ch.Taylor
RP F.Linzy
RP S.Campisi

STL 1971N

M R.Schoendienst
1B J.Hague
2B T.Sizemore
SS D.Maxvill
3B J.Torre
LF L.Brock
CF M.Alou
RF J.Cardenal
C T.Simmons
UT J.Cruz
P S.Carlton
P B.Gibson
P R.Cleveland
P J.Reuss
RP C.Taylor
RP M.Drabowsky
RP F.Linzy

STL 1972N

M R.Schoendienst
1B M.Alou
2B T.Sizemore
SS D.Maxvill
3B J.Torre
LF L.Brock
CF J.Cruz
RF L.Melendez
C T.Simmons
UT B.Carbo
UT E.Crosby
P B.Gibson
P R.Wise
P R.Cleveland
P A.Santorini
P S.Spinks
RP D.Segui

STL 1973N

M R.Schoendienst
1B J.Torre
2B T.Sizemore
SS M.Tyson
3B K.Reitz
LF L.Brock
CF L.Melendez
RF J.Cruz
C T.Simmons
UT B.Carbo
UT T.McCarver
P R.Wise
P R.Cleveland
P A.Foster
P B.Gibson
RP D.Segui
RP R.Folkers
RP O.Pena

STL 1974N

M R.Schoendienst
1B J.Torre
2B T.Sizemore
SS M.Tyson
3B K.Reitz
LF L.Brock
CF B.McBride
RF R.Smith
C T.Simmons
UT J.Cruz
P B.Gibson
P L.McGlothen
P J.Curtis
P A.Foster
P S.Siebert
RP R.Folkers
RP A.Hrabosky
RP M.Garman

STL 1975N

M R.Schoendienst
1B R.Smith
2B T.Sizemore
SS M.Tyson
3B K.Reitz
LF L.Brock
CF B.McBride
RF W.Davis
C T.Simmons
UT R.Fairly
UT L.Melendez
P L.McGlothen
P B.Forsch
P R.Reed
P J.Curtis
P J.Denny
RP A.Hrabosky
RP M.Garman

STL 1976N

M R.Schoendienst
1B K.Hernandez
2B M.Tyson
SS D.Kessinger
3B H.Cruz
LF L.Brock
CF J.Mumphrey
RF W.Crawford
C T.Simmons
UT V.Harris
P P.Falcone
P J.Denny
P L.McGlothen
P B.Forsch
P E.Rasmussen
RP A.Hrabosky
RP M.Wallace
RP B.Greif

STL 1977N

M V.Rapp
1B K.Hernandez
2B M.Tyson
SS G.Templeton
3B K.Reitz
LF L.Brock
CF J.Mumphrey
RF H.Cruz
C T.Simmons
P E.Rasmussen
P B.Forsch
P J.Denny
P J.Urrea
P P.Falcone
RP B.Metzger
RP C.Carroll
RP A.Hrabosky

STL 1978N

M V.Rapp
M J.Krol
M K.Boyer
1B K.Hernandez
2B M.Tyson
SS G.Templeton
3B K.Reitz
LF L.Brock
CF G.Hendrick
RF J.Morales
C T.Simmons
UT J.Mumphrey
P B.Forsch
P J.Denny
P P.Vuckovich
P S.Martinez
P J.Urrea
RP M.Littell
RP B.Schultz
RP A.Lopez

STL 1979N

M K.Boyer
1B K.Hernandez
2B K.Oberkfell
SS G.Templeton
3B K.Reitz
LF L.Brock
CF T.Scott
RF G.Hendrick
C T.Simmons
UT J.Mumphrey
P P.Vuckovich
P B.Forsch
P S.Martinez
P J.Denny
P J.Fulgham
RP M.Littell
RP R.Thomas
RP W.McEnaney

STL 1980N

M K.Boyer
M J.Krol
M W.Herzog
M R.Schoendienst
1B K.Hernandez
2B K.Oberkfell
SS G.Templeton
3B K.Reitz
LF B.Bonds
CF T.Scott
RF G.Hendrick
C T.Simmons
UT D.Iorg
P P.Vuckovich
P B.Forsch
P B.Sykes
P S.Martinez
RP J.Kaat
RP D.Hood
RP J.Littlefield

STL 1981N

M W.Herzog
1B K.Hernandez
2B T.Herr
SS G.Templeton
3B K.Oberkfell
LF D.Iorg
CF G.Hendrick
RF S.Lezcano
C D.Porter
P L.Sorensen
P B.Forsch
P J.Martin
P S.Martinez
RP B.Sutter
RP B.Shirley
RP J.Kaat

STL 1982N

M W.Herzog
1B K.Hernandez
2B T.Herr
SS O.Smith
3B K.Oberkfell
LF L.Smith
CF W.McGee
RF G.Hendrick
C D.Porter
UT D.Iorg
UT M.Ramsey
P J.Andujar
P B.Forsch
P S.Mura
P D.LaPoint
P J.Stuper
RP B.Sutter
RP D.Bair
RP J.Kaat

STL 1983N

M W.Herzog
1B G.Hendrick
2B T.Herr
SS O.Smith
3B K.Oberkfell
LF L.Smith
CF W.McGee
RF D.Green
C D.Porter
UT M.Ramsey
UT A.Van Slyke
P J.Andujar
P J.Stuper
P D.LaPoint
P B.Forsch
P N.Allen
RP B.Sutter
RP J.Lahti
RP D.Von Ohlen

STL 1984N

M W.Herzog
1B D.Green
2B T.Herr
SS O.Smith
3B T.Pendleton
LF L.Smith
CF W.McGee
RF G.Hendrick
C D.Porter
UT T.Landrum
UT A.Van Slyke
P J.Andujar
P D.LaPoint
P D.Cox
P R.Horton
P K.Kepshire
RP B.Sutter
RP N.Allen
RP J.Lahti

STL 1985N

M W.Herzog
1B J.Clark
2B T.Herr
SS O.Smith
3B T.Pendleton
LF V.Coleman
CF W.McGee
RF A.Van Slyke
C T.Nieto
P J.Tudor
P J.Andujar
P D.Cox
P K.Kepshire
P B.Forsch
RP R.Horton
RP J.Lahti
RP K.Dayley

STL 1986N

M W.Herzog
1B J.Clark
2B T.Herr
SS O.Smith
3B T.Pendleton
LF V.Coleman
CF W.McGee
RF A.Van Slyke
C M.LaValliere
P B.Forsch
P D.Cox
P J.Tudor
P G.Mathews
P T.Conroy
RP T.Worrell
RP R.Horton
RP P.Perry

STL 1987N

M W.Herzog
1B J.Clark
2B T.Herr
SS O.Smith
3B T.Pendleton
LF V.Coleman
CF W.McGee
RF C.Ford
C T.Pena
UT J.Morris
UT J.Oquendo
P D.Cox
P G.Mathews
P B.Forsch
P J.Magrane
P J.Tudor
RP R.Horton
RP B.Dawley
RP T.Worrell

STL 1988N

M W.Herzog
1B B.Horner
2B L.Alicea
SS O.Smith
3B T.Pendleton
LF V.Coleman
CF W.McGee
RF T.Brunansky
C T.Pena
UT J.Oquendo
UT J.DeLeon
P J.Magrane
P J.Tudor
P L.McWilliams
P B.Forsch
RP S.Terry
RP T.Worrell
RP K.Dayley

STL 1989N

M W.Herzog
1B P.Guerrero
2B J.Oquendo
SS O.Smith
3B T.Pendleton
LF V.Coleman
CF M.Thompson
RF T.Brunansky
C T.Pena
P J.DeLeon
P J.Magrane
P K.Hill
P S.Terry
RP F.DiPino
RP D.Quisenberry
RP K.Dayley

STL 1990N

M W.Herzog
M R.Schoendienst
M J.Torre
1B P.Guerrero
2B J.Oquendo
SS O.Smith
3B T.Pendleton
LF V.Coleman
CF W.McGee
RF M.Thompson
C T.Zeile
UT D.Collins
P J.Magrane
P J.DeLeon
P J.Tudor
P B.Tewksbury
P B.Smith
RP F.DiPino
RP K.Dayley
RP S.Terry

STL 1991N

M J.Torre
1B P.Guerrero
2B J.Oquendo
SS O.Smith
3B T.Zeile
LF M.Thompson
CF R.Lankford
RF F.Jose
C T.Pagnozzi
UT R.Hudler
UT G.Pena
UT G.Perry
P B.Smith
P B.Tewksbury
P K.Hill
P O.Olivares
P J.DeLeon
RP J.Agosto
RP S.Terry
RP L.Smith

STL 1992N

M J.Torre
1B A.Galarraga
2B L.Alicea
SS O.Smith
3B T.Zeile
LF B.Gilkey
CF R.Lankford
RF F.Jose
C T.Pagnozzi
UT M.Thompson
P B.Tewksbury
P O.Olivares
P R.Cormier
P D.Osborne
P M.Clark
RP M.Perez
RP C.Carpenter
RP L.Smith

STL 1993N

M J.Torre
1B G.Jefferies
2B L.Alicea
SS O.Smith
3B T.Zeile
LF B.Gilkey
CF R.Lankford
RF M.Whiten
C T.Pagnozzi
UT R.Brewer
P B.Tewksbury
P R.Arocha
P D.Osborne
P R.Cormier
P J.Magrane
RP O.Olivares
RP M.Perez
RP R.Murphy

STL 1994N

M J.Torre
1B G.Jefferies
2B G.Pena
SS O.Smith
3B T.Zeile
LF B.Gilkey
CF R.Lankford
RF M.Whiten
C T.Pagnozzi
UT L.Alicea
P B.Tewksbury
P V.Palacios
P A.Watson
P T.Urbani
P O.Olivares
RP R.Arocha
RP B.Eversgerd
RP R.Rodriguez

STL 1995N

M J.Torre
M M.Jorgensen
1B J.Mabry
2B J.Oquendo
SS T.Cromer
3B S.Cooper
LF B.Gilkey
CF R.Lankford
RF B.Jordan
C D.Sheaffer
P M.Petkovsek
P A.Watson
P D.Osborne
P K.Hill
P M.Morgan
RP R.DeLucia
RP J.Parrett
RP T.Henke

STL 1996N

M T.LaRussa
1B J.Mabry
2B L.Alicea
SS R.Clayton
3B G.Gaetti
LF R.Gant
CF R.Lankford
RF B.Jordan
C T.Pagnozzi
UT W.McGee
UT M.Sweeney
P An.Benes
P T.Stottlemyre
P D.Osborne
P Al.Benes
P M.Morgan
RP M.Petkovsek
RP T.Mathews
RP D.Eckersley

STL 1997N

M T.LaRussa
1B D.Young
2B D.DeShields
SS R.Clayton
3B G.Gaetti
LF R.Gant
CF R.Lankford
RF W.McGee
C M.Difelice
UT T.Lampkin
UT J.Mabry
P M.Morris
P T.Stottlemyre
P An.Benes
P Al.Benes
RP M.Petkovsek
RP J.Frascatore
RP R.Beltran

STL 1998N

M T.LaRussa
1B M.McGwire
2B D.DeShields
SS R.Clayton
3B G.Gaetti
LF R.Gant
CF R.Lankford
RF B.Jordan
C E.Marrero
UT J.Mabry
UT W.McGee
P K.Mercker
P T.Stottlemyre
P K.Bottenfield
P M.Morris
RP M.Petkovsek
RP J.Acevedo
RP J.Frascatore

STL 1999N

M T.LaRussa
1B M.McGwire
2B J.McEwing
SS E.Renteria
3B F.Tatis
LF R.Lankford
CF J.Drew
RF W.McGee
C E.Marrero
UT T.Howard
P D.Oliver
P K.Bottenfield
P J.Jimenez
P K.Mercker
RP J.Acevedo
RP M.Aybar
RP R.Bottalico

STL 2000N

M T.LaRussa
1B M.McGwire
2B F.Vina
SS E.Renteria
3B F.Tatis
LF R.Lankford
CF J.Edmonds
RF J.Drew
C M.Matheny
UT S.Dunston
UT C.Paquette
UT P.Polanco
P D.Kile
P G.Stephenson
P P.Hentgen
P R.Ankiel
P A.Benes
RP D.Veres
RP M.Morris
RP M.James

St. Paul

STP U 1884

STP 1884U

M A.Thompson
1B S.Dunn
2B M.Hengle
SS J.Werrick
3B B.O'Brien
LF J.Tilley
CF B.Barnes
RF S.Carroll
C C.Ganzel
P J.Brown
P L.Galvin

San Diego

SDN 1969-2000

SD 1969N

M P.Gomez
1B N.Colbert
2B J.Arcia
SS T.Dean
3B E.Spiezio
LF A.Ferrara
CF C.Gaston
RF O.Brown
C C.Cannizzaro
UT I.Murrell
UT R.Pena
P C.Kirby
P J.Niekro
P A.Santorini
P D.Kelley
RP T.Sisk
RP G.Ross
RP F.Reberger

SD 1970N

M P.Gomez

1B N.Colbert
2B D.Campbell
SS J.Arcia
3B E.Spiezio
LF A.Ferrara
CF C.Gaston
RF O.Brown
C C.Cannizzaro
UT I.Murrell
UT S.Huntz
P P.Dobson
P C.Kirby
P D.Coombs
P D.Roberts
P M.Corkins
RP R.Herbel
RP T.Dukes
RP G.Ross

SD 1971N

M P.Gomez
1B N.Colbert
2B D.Mason
SS E.Hernandez
3B E.Spiezio
LF L.Stahl
CF C.Gaston
RF O.Brown
C B.Barton
UT D.Campbell
UT I.Murrell
P D.Roberts
P C.Kirby
P S.Arlin
P T.Phoebus
P F.Norman
RP A.Severinsen
RP B.Miller
RP D.Kelley

SD 1972N

M P.Gomez
M D.Zimmer
1B N.Colbert
2B D.Thomas
SS E.Hernandez
3B D.Roberts
LF L.Lee
CF J.Jeter
RF C.Gaston
C F.Kendall
UT J.Morales
UT L.Stahl
P S.Arlin
P C.Kirby
P F.Norman
P M.Caldwell
P B.Greif
RP M.Corkins
RP G.Ross
RP E.Acosta

SD 1973N

M D.Zimmer
1B N.Colbert
2B R.Morales
SS D.Thomas
3B D.Roberts
LF L.Lee
CF J.Grubb
RF C.Gaston
C F.Kendall
UT J.Morales
P B.Greif
P C.Kirby
P S.Arlin
P R.Troedson
P R.Jones
RP M.Caldwell
RP M.Corkins
RP V.Romo

SD 1974N

M J.McNamara
1B W.McCovey
2B D.Thomas
SS E.Hernandez
3B D.Roberts
LF D.Winfield
CF J.Grubb
RF B.Tolan
C F.Kendall
UT N.Colbert
UT C.Gaston
P B.Greif
P D.Freisleben
P R.Jones
P D.Spillner
RP L.Hardy
RP V.Romo
RP D.Tomlin

SD 1975N

M J.McNamara
1B W.McCovey
2B T.Fuentes
SS E.Hernandez
3B T.Kubiak
LF B.Tolan
CF J.Grubb
RF D.Winfield
C F.Kendall
UT M.Ivie
UT G.Locklear
UT H.Torres
P R.Jones
P J.McIntosh
P D.Freisleben
P D.Spillner
P R.Folkers
RP D.Frisella
RP D.Tomlin
RP B.Greif

SD 1976N

M J.McNamara
1B M.Ivie
2B T.Fuentes
SS E.Hernandez
3B D.Rader
LF J.Grubb
CF W.Davis
RF D.Winfield
C F.Kendall
UT J.Turner
P R.Jones
P B.Strom
P D.Freisleben
P D.Spillner
RP B.Metzger
RP D.Tomlin
RP R.Folkers

SD 1977N

M J.McNamara
M B.Skinner
M A.Dark
1B M.Ivie
2B M.Champion
SS B.Almon
3B T.Ashford
LF G.Richards
CF G.Hendrick
RF D.Winfield
C G.Tenace
UT M.Rettenmund
UT J.Turner
P B.Shirley
P B.Owchinko
P T.Griffin
P R.Jones
P D.Freisleben
RP R.Fingers
RP D.Spillner
RP R.Sawyer

SD 1978N

M R.Craig
1B G.Tenace
2B F.Gonzalez
SS O.Smith
3B B.Almon
LF G.Richards
CF D.Winfield
RF O.Gamble
C R.Sweet
UT D.Thomas
UT J.Turner
P G.Perry
P R.Jones
P B.Owchinko
P B.Shirley
P E.Rasmussen
RP R.Fingers
RP J.D'Acquisto
RP M.Lee

SD 1979N

M R.Craig
1B G.Tenace
2B F.Gonzalez
SS O.Smith
3B P.Dade
LF J.Turner
CF G.Richards
RF D.Winfield
C B.Fahey
UT B.Almon
UT K.Bevacqua
UT D.Briggs
P R.Jones
P G.Perry
P B.Shirley
P E.Rasmussen
P B.Owchinko
RP J.D'Acquisto
RP R.Fingers
RP S.Mura

SD 1980N

M J.Coleman
1B W.Montanez
2B D.Cash
SS O.Smith
3B A.Rodriguez
LF G.Richards
CF J.Mumphrey
RF D.Winfield
C G.Tenace
P J.Curtis
P S.Mura
P R.Wise
P R.Jones
P G.Lucas
RP B.Shirley
RP E.Rasmussen
RP R.Fingers

SD 1981N

M F.Howard
1B B.Perkins
2B J.Bonilla
SS O.Smith
3B L.Salazar
LF G.Richards
CF R.Jones
RF J.Lefebvre
C T.Kennedy
UT R.Bass
P J.Eichelberger
P S.Mura
P C.Welsh
P R.Wise
P T.Lollar
RP G.Lucas
RP J.Curtis
RP J.Littlefield

SD 1982N

M D.Williams
1B B.Perkins
2B T.Flannery
SS G.Templeton
3B L.Salazar
LF G.Richards
CF R.Jones
RF S.Lezcano
C T.Kennedy
UT J.Lefebvre
P T.Lollar
P J.Montefusco
P J.Eichelberger
P E.Show
P C.Welsh
RP L.DeLeon
RP G.Lucas
RP F.Chiffer

SD 1983N

M D.Williams
1B S.Garvey
2B J.Bonilla
SS G.Templeton
3B L.Salazar
LF A.Wiggins
CF R.Jones
RF S.Lezcano
C T.Kennedy
P E.Show
P D.Dravecky
P T.Lollar
P E.Whitson
P A.Hawkins
RP L.DeLeon
RP G.Lucas
RP E.Sosa

SD 1984N

M D.Williams
1B S.Garvey
2B A.Wiggins
SS G.Templeton
3B G.Nettles
LF C.Martinez
CF K.McReynolds
RF T.Gwynn
C T.Kennedy
P E.Show
P T.Lollar
P E.Whitson
P M.Thurmond
P D.Dravecky
RP C.Lefferts
RP R.Gossage
RP G.Booker

SD 1985N

M D.Williams
1B S.Garvey
2B T.Flannery
SS G.Templeton
3B G.Nettles
LF C.Martinez
CF K.McReynolds
RF T.Gwynn
C T.Kennedy
P E.Show
P A.Hawkins
P D.Dravecky
P L.Hoyt
P M.Thurmond
RP C.Lefferts
RP R.Gossage
RP T.Stoddard

SD 1986N

M S.Boros
1B S.Garvey
2B T.Flannery
SS G.Templeton
3B G.Nettles
LF K.McReynolds
CF M.Wynne
RF T.Gwynn
C T.Kennedy
UT J.Kruk
UT C.Martinez
UT B.Roberts
UT J.Royster
P A.Hawkins
P D.Dravecky
P L.Hoyt
P E.Show
RP L.McCullers
RP C.Lefferts
RP G.Walter

SD 1987N

M L.Bowa
1B J.Kruk
2B T.Flannery
SS G.Templeton
3B R.Ready
LF S.Jefferson
CF S.Mack
RF T.Gwynn
C B.Santiago
UT C.Martinez
UT M.Wynne
P E.Whitson
P E.Show
P J.Jones
P A.Hawkins
P M.Grant
RP L.McCullers
RP D.Dravecky
RP G.Booker

SD 1988N

M L.Bowa
M J.McKeon
1B K.Moreland
2B R.Alomar
SS G.Templeton
3B C.Brown
LF C.Martinez
CF M.Wynne
RF T.Gwynn
C B.Santiago
UT J.Kruk
UT R.Ready
P E.Show
P A.Hawkins
P E.Whitson
P J.Jones
P D.Rasmussen
RP L.McCullers
RP M.Grant
RP M.Davis

SD 1989N

M J.McKeon
1B J.Clark
2B R.Alomar
SS G.Templeton
3B L.Salazar
LF C.James
CF M.Wynne
RF T.Gwynn
C B.Santiago
UT C.Martinez
UT B.Roberts
P B.Hurst
P E.Whitson
P D.Rasmussen
P W.Terrell
P E.Show
RP G.Harris
RP M.Grant
RP M.Davis

SD 1990N

M J.McKeon
M G.Riddoch
1B J.Clark
2B R.Alomar
SS G.Templeton
3B M.Pagliarulo
LF B.Roberts
CF J.Carter
RF T.Gwynn
C B.Santiago
UT P.Stephenson
P E.Whitson
P B.Hurst
P A.Benes
P D.Rasmussen
RP G.Harris
RP E.Show
RP C.Schiraldi

SD 1991N

M G.Riddoch
1B F.McGriff
2B B.Roberts
SS T.Fernandez
3B J.Howell
LF J.Clark
CF D.Jackson
RF T.Gwynn
C B.Santiago
UT T.Howard
UT T.Teufel
P A.Benes
P B.Hurst
P D.Rasmussen
P G.Harris
RP M.Maddux
RP R.Rodriguez
RP C.Lefferts

SD 1992N

M G.Riddoch
M J.Riggleman
1B F.McGriff
2B K.Stillwell
SS T.Fernandez
3B G.Sheffield
LF J.Clark
CF D.Jackson
RF T.Gwynn
C B.Santiago
UT O.Azocar
UT T.Teufel
P A.Benes
P B.Hurst
P C.Lefferts
P G.Harris
P F.Seminara
RP R.Rodriguez
RP J.Melendez
RP R.Myers

SD 1993N

M J.Riggleman
1B F.McGriff
2B J.Gardner
SS R.Gutierrez
3B G.Sheffield
LF P.Plantier
CF D.Bell
RF T.Gwynn
C K.Higgins
UT P.Clark
UT C.Shipley
P A.Benes
P Gr.Harris
P D.Brocail
P W.Whitehurst
P T.Worrell
RP K.Taylor
RP Ge.Harris
RP T.Hoffman

SD 1994N

M J.Riggleman
1B E.Williams
2B B.Roberts
SS R.Gutierrez
3B C.Shipley
LF P.Plantier
CF D.Bell
RF T.Gwynn
C B.Ausmus
UT B.Bean
UT L.Lopez
P A.Benes
P A.Ashby
P S.Sanders
P J.Hamilton
RP P.Martinez
RP T.Hoffman
RP T.Mauser

SD 1995N

M B.Bochy
1B E.Williams
2B J.Reed
SS A.Cedeno
3B K.Caminiti
LF M.Nieves
CF S.Finley
RF T.Gwynn
C B.Ausmus
UT S.Livingstone
UT R.Petagine
P J.Hamilton
P A.Ashby
P A.Benes
P G.Dishman
P F.Valenzuela
RP W.Blair
RP B.Williams
RP B.Florie

SD 1996N

M B.Bochy
1B W.Joyner
2B J.Reed
SS C.Gomez
3B K.Caminiti
LF R.Henderson
CF S.Finley
RF T.Gwynn
C J.Flaherty
UT S.Livingstone
P J.Hamilton
P B.Tewksbury
P F.Valenzuela
P A.Ashby
P S.Sanders
RP T.Worrell
RP S.Bergman
RP T.Hoffman

SD 1997N

M B.Bochy
1B W.Joyner
2B Q.Veras
SS C.Gomez
3B K.Caminiti
LF G.Vaughn
CF S.Finley
RF T.Gwynn
C J.Flaherty
P A.Ashby
P J.Hamilton
P S.Hitchcock
P P.Smith
RP T.Worrell
RP S.Bergman
RP W.Cunnane

SD 1998N

M B.Bochy
1B W.Joyner
2B Q.Veras
SS C.Gomez
3B K.Caminiti
LF G.Vaughn
CF S.Finley
RF T.Gwynn
C C.Hernandez
UT M.Sweeney
P K.Brown
P A.Ashby
P J.Hamilton
P S.Hitchcock
RP B.Boehringer
RP D.Miceli
RP T.Hoffman

SD 1999N

M B.Bochy
1B W.Joyner
2B Q.Veras
SS D.Jackson
3B P.Nevin
LF E.Owens
CF R.Rivera
RF R.Sanders
C B.Davis
UT T.Gwynn
UT D.Magadan
UT J.Vander Wal
P W.Williams
P S.Hitchcock
P A.Ashby
P M.Clement
RP B.Boehringer
RP C.Reyes
RP D.Wall

SD 2000N

M B.Bochy
1B R.Klesko
2B B.Boone
SS D.Jackson
3B P.Nevin
LF A.Martin
CF R.Rivera
RF E.Owens
C W.Gonzalez
P M.Clement
P W.Williams
P A.Eaton
P B.Meadows
P B.Tollberg
RP T.Hoffman
RP C.Almanzar
RP K.Walker

San Francisco

SFN 1958-2000

SF 1958N

M B.Rigney
1B O.Cepeda
2B D.O'Connell
SS D.Spencer
3B J.Davenport
LF H.Sauer
CF W.Mays
RF W.Kirkland
C B.Schmidt
P J.Antonelli
P R.Gomez
P S.Miller
P M.McCormick
P R.Monzant
RP A.Worthington
RP M.Grissom

SF 1959N

M B.Rigney
1B O.Cepeda
2B D.Spencer
SS E.Bressoud
3B J.Davenport
LF J.Brandt
CF W.Mays
RF W.Kirkland
C H.Landrith
UT F.Alou
P J.Antonelli
P S.Jones
P M.McCormick
P J.Sanford
RP S.Miller
RP A.Worthington

SF 1960N

M B.Rigney
M T.Sheehan
1B W.McCovey
2B D.Blasingame
SS E.Bressoud
3B J.Davenport
LF F.Alou
CF W.Mays
RF W.Kirkland
C B.Schmidt
UT J.Amalfitano
UT O.Cepeda
P M.McCormick
P S.Jones
P J.Sanford
P B.O'Dell
RP J.Antonelli
RP S.Miller

SF 1961N

M A.Dark
1B W.McCovey
2B J.Amalfitano
SS J.Pagan
3B J.Davenport
LF H.Kuenn
CF W.Mays
RF F.Alou
C E.Bailey
UT O.Cepeda
P M.McCormick
P J.Sanford

P J.Marichal
P S.Jones
P B.Loes
RP B.O'Dell
RP S.Miller
RP J.Duffalo

SF 1962N

M A.Dark
1B O.Cepeda
2B C.Hiller
SS J.Pagan
3B J.Davenport
LF H.Kuenn
CF W.Mays
RF F.Alou
C T.Haller
P B.O'Dell
P J.Sanford
P J.Marichal
P B.Pierce
P M.McCormick
RP S.Miller
RP B.Bolin
RP D.Larsen

SF 1963N

M A.Dark
1B O.Cepeda
2B C.Hiller
SS J.Pagan
3B J.Davenport
LF W.McCovey
CF W.Mays
RF F.Alou
C E.Bailey
UT T.Haller
UT H.Kuenn
P J.Marichal
P J.Sanford
P B.O'Dell
P J.Fisher
RP B.Bolin
RP B.Pierce
RP G.Perry

SF 1964N

M A.Dark
1B O.Cepeda
2B H.Lanier
SS J.Pagan
3B J.Hart
LF H.Kuenn
CF W.Mays
RF J.Alou
C T.Haller
UT M.Alou
UT J.Davenport
UT W.McCovey
P J.Marichal
P G.Perry
P B.Bolin
P B.Hendley
P R.Herbel
RP B.Shaw
RP B.O'Dell
RP J.Duffalo

SF 1965N

M H.Franks
1B W.McCovey
2B H.Lanier
SS D.Schofield
3B J.Hart
LF M.Alou
CF W.Mays
RF J.Alou
C T.Haller
UT J.Davenport
P J.Marichal
P B.Shaw
P G.Perry
P R.Herbel
P B.Bolin
RP F.Linzy
RP M.Murakami

SF 1966N

M H.Franks
1B W.McCovey
2B H.Lanier
SS T.Fuentes
3B J.Hart
LF J.Alou
CF W.Mays
RF O.Brown
C T.Haller
UT J.Davenport
P J.Marichal
P G.Perry
P B.Bolin
P R.Herbel
P R.Sadecki
RP L.McDaniel
RP F.Linzy
RP B.Priddy

SF 1967N

M H.Franks
1B W.McCovey
2B T.Fuentes
SS H.Lanier
3B J.Hart
LF J.Alou
CF W.Mays
RF O.Brown
C T.Haller
UT J.Davenport
P G.Perry
P M.McCormick
P J.Marichal
P R.Sadecki
P R.Herbel
RP F.Linzy
RP J.Gibbon
RP L.McDaniel

SF 1968N

M H.Franks
1B W.McCovey
2B R.Hunt
SS H.Lanier
3B J.Davenport
LF J.Alou
CF W.Mays
RF B.Bonds
C D.Dietz
UT T.Cline
UT J.Hart
P J.Marichal
P G.Perry
P R.Sadecki
P M.McCormick
P B.Bolin
RP F.Linzy

SF 1969N

M C.King
1B W.McCovey
2B R.Hunt
SS H.Lanier
3B J.Davenport
LF K.Henderson
CF W.Mays
RF B.Bonds
C D.Dietz
UT B.Burda
UT D.Marshall
UT D.Mason
P G.Perry
P J.Marichal
P M.McCormick
P B.Bolin
P R.Sadecki
RP F.Linzy
RP R.Herbel

SF 1970N

M C.King
M C.Fox
1B W.McCovey
2B R.Hunt
SS H.Lanier
3B A.Gallagher
LF K.Henderson
CF W.Mays
RF B.Bonds
C D.Dietz
UT T.Fuentes
P G.Perry
P J.Marichal
P R.Robertson
P F.Reberger
RP R.Bryant
RP D.McMahon
RP J.Johnson

SF 1971N

M C.Fox
1B W.McCovey
2B T.Fuentes
SS C.Speier
3B A.Gallagher
LF K.Henderson
CF W.Mays
RF B.Bonds
C D.Dietz
UT H.Lanier
P G.Perry
P J.Marichal
P J.Cumberland
P R.Bryant
P S.Stone
RP J.Johnson
RP D.McMahon
RP R.Robertson

SF 1972N

M C.Fox
1B W.McCovey
2B T.Fuentes
SS C.Speier
3B A.Gallagher
LF K.Henderson
CF G.Maddox
RF B.Bonds
C D.Rader
UT D.Kingman
P R.Bryant
P J.Barr
P J.Marichal
P S.McDowell
P S.Stone
RP J.Johnson
RP R.Moffitt
RP D.McMahon

SF 1973N

M C.Fox
1B W.McCovey
2B T.Fuentes
SS C.Speier
3B E.Goodson
LF G.Matthews
CF G.Maddox
RF B.Bonds
C D.Rader
UT D.Kingman
UT G.Thomasson
P R.Bryant
P J.Barr
P T.Bradley
P J.Marichal
P J.Willoughby
RP E.Sosa
RP R.Moffitt
RP D.Carrithers

SF 1974N

M C.Fox
M W.Westrum
1B D.Kingman
2B T.Fuentes
SS C.Speier
3B S.Ontiveros
LF G.Matthews
CF G.Maddox
RF B.Bonds
C D.Rader
UT E.Goodson
UT M.Phillips
UT G.Thomasson
P J.Barr
P J.D'Acquisto
P M.Caldwell
P T.Bradley
P R.Bryant
RP R.Moffitt
RP E.Sosa
RP C.Williams

SF 1975N

M W.Westrum
1B W.Montanez
2B D.Thomas
SS C.Speier
3B S.Ontiveros
LF G.Matthews
CF V.Joshua
RF B.Murcer
C D.Rader
UT B.Miller
UT G.Thomasson
P J.Montefusco
P J.Barr
P P.Falcone
P M.Caldwell
P E.Halicki
RP C.Williams
RP G.Lavelle
RP R.Moffitt

SF 1976N

M B.Rigney
1B D.Evans
2B M.Perez
SS C.Speier
3B K.Reitz
LF G.Matthews
CF L.Herndon
RF B.Murcer
C D.Rader
UT G.Thomasson
P J.Montefusco
P J.Barr
P E.Halicki
P R.Dressler
P J.D'Acquisto
RP G.Lavelle
RP M.Caldwell
RP R.Moffitt

SF 1977N

M J.Altobelli
1B W.McCovey
2B R.Andrews
SS T.Foli
3B B.Madlock
LF G.Thomasson
CF D.Thomas
RF J.Clark
C M.Hill
UT D.Evans
UT T.Whitfield
P E.Halicki
P J.Barr
P B.Knepper
P J.Montefusco
RP C.Williams
RP G.Lavelle
RP D.Heaverlo

SF 1978N

M J.Altobelli
1B W.McCovey
2B B.Madlock
SS J.LeMaster
3B D.Evans
LF T.Whitfield
CF L.Herndon
RF J.Clark
C M.Hill
UT M.Ivie
P B.Knepper
P V.Blue
P J.Montefusco
P E.Halicki
P J.Barr
RP G.Lavelle
RP R.Moffitt
RP J.Curtis

SF 1979N

M J.Altobelli
M D.Bristol
1B M.Ivie
2B J.Strain
SS J.LeMaster
3B D.Evans
LF L.Herndon
CF B.North
RF J.Clark
C D.Littlejohn
UT W.McCovey
UT T.Whitfield
P V.Blue
P B.Knepper
P J.Montefusco
P E.Halicki
P J.Curtis
RP G.Lavelle
RP T.Griffin
RP G.Minton

SF 1980N

M D.Bristol
1B M.Ivie
2B R.Stennett
SS J.LeMaster
3B D.Evans
LF L.Herndon
CF B.North
RF J.Clark
C M.May
UT T.Whitfield
P V.Blue
P B.Knepper
P E.Whitson
P A.Ripley
P J.Montefusco
RP T.Griffin
RP G.Lavelle
RP G.Minton

SF 1981N

M F.Robinson
1B E.Cabell
2B J.Morgan
SS J.LeMaster
3B D.Evans
LF L.Herndon
CF J.Martin
RF J.Clark
C M.May
P D.Alexander
P T.Griffin
P V.Blue
P E.Whitson
P A.Ripley
RP A.Holland
RP G.Minton
RP F.Breining

SF 1982N

M F.Robinson
1B R.Smith
2B J.Morgan
SS J.LeMaster
3B D.Evans
LF J.Leonard
CF C.Davis
RF J.Clark
C M.May
UT D.Bergman
UT D.Kuiper
UT J.Wohlford
P B.Laskey
P A.Hammaker
P R.Gale
P R.Martin
RP F.Breining
RP A.Holland
RP J.Barr

SF 1983N

M F.Robinson
1B D.Evans
2B B.Wellman
SS J.LeMaster
3B T.O'Malley
LF J.Leonard
CF C.Davis
RF J.Clark
C B.Brenly
UT J.Youngblood
P F.Breining
P M.Krukow
P A.Hammaker
P B.Laskey
P A.McGaffigan
RP G.Minton
RP R.Martin
RP J.Barr

SF 1984N

M F.Robinson
M D.Ozark
1B S.Thompson
2B M.Trillo
SS J.LeMaster
3B J.Youngblood
LF J.Leonard
CF D.Gladden
RF C.Davis
C B.Brenly
UT D.Baker
P B.Laskey
P M.Krukow
P M.Davis
P J.Robinson
RP G.Minton
RP F.Williams
RP G.Lavelle

SF 1985N

M J.Davenport
M R.Craig
1B D.Green
2B M.Trillo
SS J.Uribe
3B C.Brown
LF J.Leonard
CF D.Gladden
RF C.Davis
C B.Brenly
P D.LaPoint
P M.Krukow
P A.Hammaker
P J.Gott
P V.Blue
RP M.Davis
RP S.Garrelts
RP G.Minton

SF 1986N

M R.Craig
1B W.Clark
2B R.Thompson
SS J.Uribe
3B C.Brown
LF C.Maldonado
CF D.Gladden
RF C.Davis
C B.Brenly
UT J.Youngblood
P M.Krukow
P M.LaCoss
P S.Garrelts
P V.Blue
RP J.Robinson
RP M.Davis
RP J.Berenguer

SF 1987N

M R.Craig
1B W.Clark
2B R.Thompson
SS J.Uribe
3B K.Mitchell
LF J.Leonard
CF C.Davis
RF C.Maldonado
C B.Brenly
UT M.Aldrete
UT E.Milner
UT C.Speier
P K.Downs
P M.LaCoss
P A.Hammaker
P M.Krukow
P D.Dravecky
RP S.Garrelts
RP J.Robinson
RP J.Gott

SF 1988N

M R.Craig
1B W.Clark
2B R.Thompson
SS J.Uribe
3B K.Mitchell
LF M.Aldrete
CF B.Butler
RF C.Maldonado
C B.Melvin
P R.Reuschel
P D.Robinson
P K.Downs
P A.Hammaker
P M.Krukow
RP S.Garrelts
RP C.Lefferts
RP J.Price

SF 1989N

M R.Craig
1B W.Clark
2B R.Thompson
SS J.Uribe
3B E.Riles
LF K.Mitchell
CF B.Butler
RF C.Maldonado
C T.Kennedy
P R.Reuschel
P D.Robinson
P S.Garrelts
P M.LaCoss
RP C.Lefferts
RP J.Brantley
RP A.Hammaker

SF 1990N

M R.Craig
1B W.Clark
2B R.Thompson
SS J.Uribe
3B M.Williams
LF K.Mitchell
CF B.Butler
RF M.Kingery
C T.Kennedy
P J.Burkett
P S.Garrelts
P D.Robinson
P T.Wilson
RP J.Brantley
RP S.Bedrosian
RP A.Hammaker

SF 1991N

M R.Craig
1B W.Clark
2B R.Thompson
SS J.Uribe
3B M.Williams
LF M.Felder
CF W.McGee
RF K.Bass
C S.Decker
UT D.Anderson
UT K.Mitchell
P B.Black
P J.Burkett
P T.Wilson
P D.Robinson
RP K.Downs
RP J.Brantley
RP F.Oliveras

SF 1992N

M R.Craig
1B W.Clark
2B R.Thompson
SS R.Clayton
3B M.Williams
LF M.Felder
CF D.Lewis
RF W.McGee
C K.Manwaring
UT C.James
UT C.Snyder
P J.Burkett
P B.Black
P B.Swift
P T.Wilson
RP J.Brantley
RP R.Beck
RP B.Hickerson

SF 1993N

M D.Baker
1B W.Clark
2B R.Thompson
SS R.Clayton
3B M.Williams
LF B.Bonds
CF D.Lewis
RF W.McGee
C K.Manwaring
P B.Swift
P J.Burkett
P T.Wilson
RP B.Hickerson
RP J.Brantley
RP D.Burba

SF 1994N

M D.Baker
1B T.Benzinger
2B J.Patterson
SS R.Clayton
3B M.Williams
LF B.Bonds
CF D.Lewis
RF D.Martinez
C K.Manwaring
P J.Burkett
P M.Portugal
P B.Swift
P B.Hickerson
P Van Landingham
RP D.Burba
RP R.Beck
RP R.Monteleone

SF 1995N

M D.Baker
1B M.Carreon
2B R.Thompson
SS R.Clayton
3B M.Williams
LF B.Bonds
CF D.Lewis
RF G.Hill
C K.Manwaring
UT J.Patterson
UT J.Phillips
P M.Leiter
P T.Mulholland
P Van Landingham
P M.Portugal
RP J.Bautista
RP R.Beck
RP C.Hook

SF 1996N

M D.Baker
1B M.Carreon
2B S.Scarsone
SS R.Aurilia
3B M.Williams
LF B.Bonds
CF M.Benard
RF G.Hill
C T.Lampkin
P A.Watson
P Van Landingham
P M.Gardner
P O.Fernandez
P M.Leiter
RP M.Dewey
RP J.Bautista
RP R.DeLucia

SF 1997N
M D.Baker
1B J.Snow
2B J.Kent
SS J.Vizcaino
3B B.Mueller
LF B.Bonds
CF D.Hamilton
RF S.Javier
C R.Wilkins
UT G.Hill
UT M.Lewis
P S.Estes
P K.Rueter
P M.Gardner
RP J.Tavarez
RP D.Henry
RP R.Beck

SF 1998N
M D.Baker
1B J.Snow
2B J.Kent
SS R.Aurilia
3B B.Mueller
LF B.Bonds
CF D.Hamilton
RF S.Javier
C B.Johnson
UT M.Benard
UT C.Hayes
UT R.Sanchez
P M.Gardner
P O.Hershiser
P K.Rueter
P S.Estes
P D.Darwin
RP R.Nen
RP J.Johnstone
RP J.Tavarez

SF 1999N
M D.Baker
1B J.Snow
2B J.Kent
SS R.Aurilia
3B B.Mueller
LF B.Bonds
CF M.Benard
RF E.Burks
C B.Mayne
UT S.Javier
UT F.Santangelo
P R.Ortiz
P S.Estes
P K.Rueter
P M.Gardner
P C.Brock
RP R.Nen
RP F.Rodriguez
RP J.Johnstone

SF 2000N
M D.Baker
1B J.Snow
2B J.Kent
SS R.Aurilia
3B B.Mueller
LF B.Bonds
CF M.Benard
RF E.Burks
C B.Estalella
UT C.Murray
UT A.Rios
P L.Hernandez
P R.Ortiz
P S.Estes
P K.Rueter
P M.Gardner
RP F.Rodriguez
RP A.Fultz
RP R.Nen

Seattle

SEA A 1969
SEA A 1977-2000

SEA 1969A
M J.Schultz
1B D.Mincher
2B J.Donaldson
SS R.Oyler
3B T.Harper
LF T.Davis
CF W.Comer
RF S.Hovley
C J.McNertney
P G.Brabender
P M.Pattin
P F.Talbot
RP D.Segui
RP J.Gelnar
RP J.Bouton

SEA 1977A
M D.Johnson
1B D.Meyer
2B J.Baez
SS C.Reynolds
3B B.Stein
LF S.Braun
CF R.Jones
RF L.Stanton
C B.Stinson
DH J.Bernhardt
UT D.Collins
UT C.Lopez
P G.Abbott
P J.Montague
P D.Pole
RP E.Romo
RP D.Segui
RP M.Kekich

SEA 1978A
M D.Johnson
1B D.Meyer
2B J.Cruz
SS C.Reynolds
3B B.Stein
LF B.Bochte
CF R.Jones
RF L.Roberts
C B.Stinson
UT J.Hale
P P.Mitchell
P G.Abbott
P R.Honeycutt
P T.House
P J.Colborn
RP S.Rawley
RP J.Todd
RP E.Romo

SEA 1979A
M D.Johnson
1B B.Bochte
2B J.Cruz
SS M.Mendoza
3B D.Meyer
LF L.Roberts
CF R.Jones
RF J.Simpson
C L.Cox
DH W.Horton
UT L.Milbourne
UT T.Paciorek
P M.Parrott
P R.Honeycutt
P F.Bannister
P O.Jones
P G.Abbott
RP B.McLaughlin
RP J.Montague
RP S.Rawley

SEA 1980A
M D.Johnson
M M.Wills
1B B.Bochte
2B J.Cruz
SS M.Mendoza
3B T.Cox
LF D.Meyer
CF J.Simpson
RF L.Roberts
C L.Cox
DH W.Horton
UT J.Anderson
UT L.Milbourne
UT T.Paciorek
P F.Bannister
P G.Abbott
P R.Honeycutt
P J.Beattie
P R.Dressler
RP S.Rawley
RP B.McLaughlin
RP D.Roberts

SEA 1981A
M M.Wills
M R.Lachemann
1B B.Bochte
2B J.Cruz
SS J.Anderson
3B L.Randle
LF T.Paciorek
CF J.Simpson
RF J.Burroughs
C J.Narron
DH R.Zisk
UT G.Gray
UT D.Meyer
P G.Abbott
P F.Bannister
P K.Clay
P B.Clark
P M.Parrott
RP S.Rawley
RP L.Andersen
RP D.Drago

SEA 1982A
M R.Lachemann
1B G.Gray
2B J.Cruz
SS T.Cruz
3B M.Castillo
LF B.Bochte
CF D.Henderson
RF A.Cowens
C R.Sweet
DH R.Zisk
UT J.Simpson
P F.Bannister
P G.Perry
P J.Beattie
P M.Moore
P G.Nelson
RP B.Caudill
RP L.Andersen
RP E.Vande Berg

SEA 1983A
M R.Lachemann
M D.Crandall
1B P.Putnam
2B T.Bernazard
SS S.Owen
3B J.Allen
LF S.Henderson
CF D.Henderson
RF A.Cowens
C R.Sweet
DH R.Zisk
P M.Young
P J.Beattie
P B.Stoddard
P B.Clark
P M.Moore
RP R.Thomas
RP B.Caudill
RP M.Stanton

SEA 1984A
M D.Crandall
M C.Cottier
1B A.Davis
2B J.Perconte
SS S.Owen
3B J.Presley
LF P.Bradley
CF D.Henderson
RF A.Cowens
C B.Kearney
DH K.Phelps
UT B.Bonnell
UT S.Henderson
P M.Langston
P M.Moore
P J.Beattie
P M.Young
RP E.Vande Berg
RP B.Stoddard
RP D.Beard

SEA 1985A
M C.Cottier
1B A.Davis
2B J.Perconte
SS S.Owen
3B J.Presley
LF P.Bradley
CF D.Henderson
RF A.Cowens
C B.Kearney
DH G.Thomas
P M.Moore
P M.Young
P M.Langston
P F.Wills
P B.Swift
RP R.Thomas
RP E.Nunez
RP E.Vande Berg

SEA 1986A
M C.Cottier
M M.Martinez
M D.Williams
1B A.Davis
2B H.Reynolds
SS S.Owen
3B J.Presley
LF P.Bradley
CF J.Moses
RF D.Tartabull
C B.Kearney
DH G.Thomas
UT D.Henderson
UT K.Phelps
P M.Moore
P M.Langston
P M.Morgan
P B.Swift
RP M.Young
RP M.Huismann
RP L.Guetterman

SEA 1987A
M D.Williams
1B A.Davis
2B H.Reynolds
SS R.Quinones
3B J.Presley
LF P.Bradley
CF J.Moses
RF M.Kingery
C S.Bradley
DH K.Phelps
P M.Langston
P M.Moore
P M.Morgan
P S.Bankhead
P L.Guetterman
RP J.Reed
RP B.Wilkinson
RP M.Trujillo

SEA 1988A
M D.Williams
M J.Snyder
1B A.Davis
2B H.Reynolds
SS R.Quinones
3B J.Presley
LF M.Brantley
CF H.Cotto
RF G.Wilson
C S.Bradley
DH K.Phelps
UT S.Balboni
P M.Langston
P M.Moore
P B.Swift
P S.Bankhead
P M.Campbell
RP M.Jackson
RP J.Reed
RP M.Schooler

SEA 1989A
M J.Lefebvre
1B A.Davis
2B H.Reynolds
SS O.Vizquel
3B J.Presley
LF G.Briley
CF K.Griffey
RF D.Coles
C D.Valle
UT S.Bradley
UT H.Cotto
P S.Bankhead
P B.Holman
P R.Johnson
P B.Swift
P E.Hanson
RP J.Reed
RP M.Jackson
RP M.Schooler

SEA 1990A
M J.Lefebvre
1B P.O'Brien
2B H.Reynolds
SS O.Vizquel
3B E.Martinez
LF G.Briley
CF K.Griffey
RF H.Cotto
C D.Valle
DH A.Davis
UT S.Bradley
UT J.Leonard
P E.Hanson
P M.Young
P R.Johnson
P B.Holman
RP B.Swift
RP M.Jackson
RP M.Schooler

SEA 1991A
M J.Lefebvre
1B P.O'Brien
2B H.Reynolds
SS O.Vizquel
3B E.Martinez
LF G.Briley
CF K.Griffey
RF J.Buhner
C D.Valle
DH A.Davis
P R.Johnson
P B.Holman
P R.DeLucia
P B.Krueger
P E.Hanson
RP B.Swift
RP M.Jackson
RP R.Swan

SEA 1992A
M B.Plummer
1B P.O'Brien
2B H.Reynolds
SS O.Vizquel
3B E.Martinez
LF H.Cotto
CF K.Griffey
RF J.Buhner
C D.Valle
DH T.Martinez
UT K.Mitchell
P D.Fleming
P R.Johnson
P E.Hanson
RP R.Swan
RP R.DeLucia
RP J.Nelson

SEA 1993A
M L.Piniella
1B T.Martinez
2B R.Amaral
SS O.Vizquel
3B M.Blowers
LF M.Felder
CF K.Griffey
RF J.Buhner
C D.Valle
DH P.O'Brien
P R.Johnson
P E.Hanson
P T.Leary
P D.Fleming
P C.Bosio
RP J.Nelson
RP D.Henry
RP D.Powell

SEA 1994A
M L.Piniella
1B T.Martinez
2B R.Amaral
SS F.Fermin
3B E.Martinez
LF E.Anthony
CF K.Griffey
RF J.Buhner
C D.Wilson
DH R.Jefferson
UT M.Blowers
P R.Johnson
P C.Bosio
P D.Fleming
P G.Hibbard
RP B.Ayala
RP B.Risley
RP T.Davis

SEA 1995A
M L.Piniella
1B T.Martinez
2B J.Cora
SS L.Sojo
3B M.Blowers
LF R.Amaral
CF A.Diaz
RF J.Buhner
C D.Wilson
DH E.Martinez
P R.Johnson
P T.Belcher
P C.Bosio
RP J.Nelson
RP B.Wells
RP B.Ayala

SEA 1996A
M L.Piniella
1B P.Sorrento
2B J.Cora
SS A.Rodriguez
3B R.Davis
LF R.Amaral
CF K.Griffey
RF J.Buhner
C D.Wilson
DH E.Martinez
P S.Hitchcock
P B.Wolcott
P B.Wells
RP R.Carmona
RP N.Charlton
RP M.Jackson

SEA 1997A
M L.Piniella
1B P.Sorrento
2B J.Cora
SS A.Rodriguez
3B R.Davis
LF R.Ducey
CF K.Griffey
RF J.Buhner
C D.Wilson
DH E.Martinez
P J.Fassero
P R.Johnson
P J.Moyer
P B.Wolcott
RP B.Ayala
RP N.Charlton
RP B.Wells

SEA 1998A
M L.Piniella
1B D.Segui
2B J.Cora
SS A.Rodriguez
3B R.Davis
LF G.Hill
CF K.Griffey
RF R.Ducey
C D.Wilson
DH E.Martinez
P J.Moyer
P J.Fassero
P R.Johnson
P K.Cloude
P B.Swift
RP P.Spoljaric
RP M.Timlin
RP B.Ayala

SEA 1999A
M L.Piniella
1B D.Segui
2B D.Bell
SS A.Rodriguez
3B R.Davis
LF B.Hunter
CF K.Griffey
RF J.Buhner
C D.Wilson
DH E.Martinez
P J.Moyer
P F.Garcia
P J.Halama
P J.Fassero
RP J.Paniagua
RP F.Rodriguez
RP P.Abbott

SEA 2000A
M L.Piniella
1B J.Olerud
2B M.McLemore
SS A.Rodriguez
3B D.Bell
LF S.Javier
CF M.Cameron
RF J.Buhner
C D.Wilson
DH E.Martinez
P A.Sele
P P.Abbott
P J.Halama
P J.Moyer
P F.Garcia
RP B.Tomko
RP J.Mesa
RP J.Paniagua

Syracuse

SYR N 1879
SYR a 1890

SYR 1879N
M M.Dorgan
M B.Holbert
M J.Macullar
1B H.Carpenter
2B J.Farrell
SS J.Macullar
3B R.Woodhead
LF M.Mansell
CF J.Richmond
RF B.Purcell
C B.Holbert
UT M.Dorgan
P H.McCormick

SYR 1890a
M G.Frazer
M W.Fessenden
M G.Frazer
1B M.McQuery
2B C.Childs
SS B.McLaughlin
3B T.O'Rourke
LF B.Ely
CF R.Wright
RF P.Friel
C G.Briggs
P D.Casey
P J.Keefe
P M.Morrison
P E.Mars

Tampa Bay

TBA 1998-2000

TB 1998A
M L.Rothschild
1B F.McGriff
2B M.Cairo
SS K.Stocker
3B B.Smith
LF Q.McCracken
CF R.Winn
RF M.Kelly
C J.Flaherty
DH P.Sorrento
UT W.Boggs
P R.Arrojo
P T.Saunders
P W.Alvarez
P J.Santana
P D.Springer
RP E.Yan
RP J.Mecir
RP A.Lopez

TB 1999A
M L.Rothschild
1B F.McGriff
2B M.Cairo
SS K.Stocker
3B W.Boggs
LF B.Trammell
CF R.Winn
RF D.Martinez
C J.Flaherty
DH J.Canseco
UT P.Sorrento
P B.Witt
P W.Alvarez
P R.Rupe
P R.Arrojo
RP R.White
RP R.Hernandez
RP A.Lopez

TB 2000A
M L.Rothschild
1B F.McGriff
2B M.Cairo
SS F.Martinez
3B V.Castilla
LF G.Vaughn
CF G.Williams
RF J.Guillen
C J.Flaherty
DH J.Canseco
UT S.Cox
P A.Lopez
P B.Rekar
P E.Yan
P S.Trachsel
P C.Lidle
RP R.Hernandez
RP R.White
RP D.Creek

Texas

TEX A 1972-2000

TEX 1972A

M T.Williams
1B F.Howard
2B L.Randle
SS T.Harrah
3B D.Nelson
LF L.Biittner
CF J.Lovitto
RF T.Ford
C D.Billings
UT E.Maddox
P P.Broberg
P D.Bosman
P R.Hand
P M.Paul
P B.Gogolewski
RP P.Lindblad
RP J.Panther
RP H.Pina

TEX 1973A

M W.Herzog
M D.Wilber
M B.Martin
1B J.Spencer
2B D.Nelson
SS J.Mason
3B T.Harrah
LF R.Carty
CF V.Harris
RF J.Burroughs
C K.Suarez
DH A.Johnson
UT E.Maddox
P J.Bibby
P J.Merritt
P S.Siebert
P P.Broberg
RP B.Gogolewski
RP M.Paul
RP J.Brown

TEX 1974A

M B.Martin
1B M.Hargrove
2B D.Nelson
SS T.Harrah
3B L.Randle
LF C.Tovar
CF J.Lovitto
RF J.Burroughs
C J.Sundberg
DH J.Spencer
UT A.Johnson
P F.Jenkins
P J.Bibby
P J.Brown
P S.Hargan
P D.Clyde
RP S.Foucault

TEX 1975A

M B.Martin
M F.Lucchesi
1B J.Spencer
2B L.Randle
SS T.Harrah
3B R.Howell
LF M.Hargrove
CF D.Moates
RF J.Burroughs
C J.Sundberg
DH C.Tovar
UT T.Grieve
P F.Jenkins
P S.Hargan
P G.Perry
P B.Hands
RP J.Umbarger
RP S.Foucault
RP S.Thomas

TEX 1976A

M F.Lucchesi
1B M.Hargrove
2B L.Randle
SS T.Harrah
3B R.Howell
LF G.Clines
CF J.Beniquez
RF J.Burroughs
C J.Sundberg
DH T.Grieve
P G.Perry
P N.Briles
P B.Blyleven
P J.Umbarger
P S.Hargan
RP S.Foucault
RP M.Bacsik
RP J.Terpko

TEX 1977A

M F.Lucchesi
M E.Stanky
M C.Ryan
M B.Hunter
1B M.Hargrove
2B B.Wills
SS B.Campaneris
3B T.Harrah
LF C.Washington
CF J.Beniquez
RF D.May
C J.Sundberg
DH W.Horton
P G.Perry
P D.Alexander
P B.Blyleven
P D.Ellis
P N.Briles
RP A.Devine
RP P.Lindblad
RP D.Knowles

TEX 1978A

M B.Hunter
M P.Corrales
1B M.Hargrove
2B B.Wills
SS B.Campaneris
3B T.Harrah
LF A.Oliver
CF J.Beniquez
RF B.Bonds
C J.Sundberg
DH R.Zisk
P J.Matlack
P F.Jenkins
P D.Alexander
P D.Medich
P D.Ellis
RP R.Cleveland
RP L.Barker

TEX 1979A

M P.Corrales
1B P.Putnam
2B B.Wills
SS N.Norman
3B B.Bell
LF B.Sample
CF A.Oliver
RF R.Zisk
C J.Sundberg
DH J.Ellis
UT J.Grubb
P F.Jenkins
P S.Comer
P D.Medich
P D.Alexander
RP J.Kern
RP S.Lyle
RP D.Rajsich

TEX 1980A

M P.Corrales
1B P.Putnam
2B B.Wills
SS P.Frias
3B B.Bell
LF A.Oliver
CF M.Rivers
RF J.Norris
C J.Sundberg
DH R.Zisk
UT J.Grubb
UT D.Roberts
UT R.Staub
P J.Matlack
P D.Medich
P F.Jenkins
P G.Perry
RP D.Darwin
RP S.Lyle
RP J.Kern

TEX 1981A

M D.Zimmer
1B P.Putnam
2B B.Wills
SS M.Mendoza
3B B.Bell
LF B.Sample
CF M.Rivers
RF L.Roberts
C J.Sundberg
DH A.Oliver
UT J.Grubb
P D.Darwin
P D.Medich
P R.Honeycutt
P F.Jenkins
P J.Matlack
RP S.Comer
RP D.Schmidt

TEX 1982A

M D.Zimmer
M D.Johnson
1B D.Hostetler
2B M.Richardt
SS M.Wagner
3B B.Bell
LF B.Sample
CF G.Wright
RF L.Parrish
C J.Sundberg
DH L.Johnson
UT J.Grubb
P C.Hough
P F.Tanana
P R.Honeycutt
P J.Matlack
P D.Medich
RP S.Comer
RP D.Darwin
RP P.Mirabella

TEX 1983A

M D.Rader
1B P.O'Brien
2B W.Tolleson
SS B.Dent
3B B.Bell
LF B.Sample
CF G.Wright
RF L.Parrish
C J.Sundberg
DH D.Hostetler
P C.Hough
P M.Smithson
P D.Darwin
P R.Honeycutt
P F.Tanana
RP J.Matlack
RP O.Jones

TEX 1984A

M D.Rader
1B P.O'Brien
2B W.Tolleson
SS C.Wilkerson
3B B.Bell
LF B.Sample
CF G.Wright
RF G.Ward
C D.Scott
DH L.Parrish
UT M.Rivers
P C.Hough
P F.Tanana
P D.Darwin
P D.Stewart
P M.Mason
RP D.Schmidt
RP O.Jones

TEX 1985A

M D.Rader
M B.Valentine
1B P.O'Brien
2B T.Harrah
SS C.Wilkerson
3B B.Bell
LF G.Ward
CF O.McDowell
RF G.Wright
C D.Slaught
DH C.Johnson
UT W.Tolleson
P C.Hough
P M.Mason
P B.Hooton
P D.Noles
RP G.Harris
RP D.Rozema
RP D.Schmidt

TEX 1986A

M B.Valentine
1B P.O'Brien
2B T.Harrah
SS S.Fletcher
3B S.Buechele
LF R.Sierra
CF O.McDowell
RF P.Incaviglia
C D.Slaught
DH L.Parrish
UT G.Ward
UT C.Wilkerson
P C.Hough
P E.Correa
P J.Guzman
P B.Witt
P M.Mason
RP G.Harris
RP M.Williams
RP J.Russell

TEX 1987A

M B.Valentine
1B P.O'Brien
2B J.Browne
SS S.Fletcher
3B S.Buechele
LF P.Incaviglia
CF O.McDowell
RF R.Sierra
C D.Slaught
DH L.Parrish
UT B.Brower
UT G.Petralli
P C.Hough
P J.Guzman
P B.Witt
P G.Harris
RP M.Williams
RP D.Mohorcic
RP J.Russell

TEX 1988A

M B.Valentine
1B P.O'Brien
2B C.Wilkerson
SS S.Fletcher
3B S.Buechele
LF C.Espy
CF O.McDowell
RF R.Sierra
C G.Petralli
DH L.Parrish
UT P.Incaviglia
P C.Hough
P J.Guzman
P P.Kilgus
P J.Russell
P B.Witt
RP M.Williams
RP C.McMurtry
RP D.Mohorcic

TEX 1989A

M B.Valentine
1B R.Palmeiro
2B J.Franco
SS S.Fletcher
3B S.Buechele
LF P.Incaviglia
CF C.Espy
RF R.Sierra
C C.Kreuter
DH H.Baines
UT J.Kunkel
UT R.Leach
P N.Ryan
P B.Witt
P K.Brown
P C.Hough
P M.Jeffcoat
RP K.Rogers
RP J.Russell
RP C.Guante

TEX 1990A

M B.Valentine
1B R.Palmeiro
2B J.Franco
SS J.Huson
3B S.Buechele
LF P.Incaviglia
CF G.Pettis
RF R.Sierra
C G.Petralli
DH H.Baines
UT J.Daugherty
UT J.Kunkel
UT M.Stanley
P B.Witt
P C.Hough
P N.Ryan
P K.Brown
P J.Moyer
RP M.Jeffcoat
RP K.Rogers
RP B.Arnsberg

TEX 1991A

M B.Valentine
1B R.Palmeiro
2B J.Franco
SS J.Huson
3B S.Buechele
LF J.Gonzalez
CF G.Pettis
RF R.Sierra
C I.Rodriguez
DH B.Downing
UT K.Reimer
P K.Brown
P N.Ryan
P J.Guzman
RP K.Rogers
RP G.Alexander
RP J.Barfield

TEX 1992A

M B.Valentine
M T.Harrah
1B R.Palmeiro
2B A.Newman
SS D.Thon
3B D.Palmer
LF K.Reimer
CF J.Gonzalez
RF R.Sierra
C I.Rodriguez
DH B.Downing
UT J.Huson
P K.Brown
P J.Guzman
P B.Witt
P N.Ryan
RP T.Burns
RP K.Rogers
RP J.Russell

TEX 1993A

M K.Kennedy
1B R.Palmeiro
2B D.Strange
SS M.Lee
3B D.Palmer
LF J.Gonzalez
CF D.Hulse
RF J.Canseco
C I.Rodriguez
DH J.Franco
P K.Brown
P K.Rogers
P R.Pavlik
P C.Leibrandt
RP B.Bohanon
RP C.Lefferts
RP T.Henke

TEX 1994A

M K.Kennedy
1B W.Clark
2B J.Frye
SS M.Lee
3B D.Palmer
LF J.Gonzalez
CF D.Hulse
RF R.Greer
C I.Rodriguez
DH J.Canseco
UT D.Strange
P K.Brown
P K.Rogers
P H.Fajardo
RP M.Whiteside
RP C.Carpenter
RP D.Oliver

TEX 1995A

M J.Oates
1B W.Clark
2B J.Frye
SS B.Gil
3B M.Pagliarulo
LF M.McLemore
CF O.Nixon
RF R.Greer
C I.Rodriguez
DH J.Gonzalez
UT M.Tettleton
P K.Rogers
P R.Pavlik
P K.Gross
P B.Tewksbury
RP R.McDowell
RP M.Whiteside
RP D.Oliver

TEX 1996A

M J.Oates
1B W.Clark
2B M.McLemore
SS K.Elster
3B D.Palmer
LF R.Greer
CF D.Hamilton
RF J.Gonzalez
C I.Rodriguez
DH M.Tettleton
P K.Hill
P R.Pavlik
P B.Witt
P D.Oliver
P K.Gross
RP G.Heredia
RP D.Cook
RP J.Russell

TEX 1997A

M J.Oates
1B W.Clark
2B M.McLemore
SS B.Gil
3B D.Palmer
LF R.Greer
CF D.Buford
RF W.Newson
C I.Rodriguez
DH J.Gonzalez
UT D.Cedeno
UT L.Stevens
P B.Witt
P D.Oliver
P J.Burkett
P K.Hill
P J.Santana
RP M.Whiteside
RP D.Patterson
RP J.Wetteland

TEX 1998A

M J.Oates
1B W.Clark
2B M.McLemore
SS K.Elster
3B F.Tatis
LF R.Greer
CF T.Goodwin
RF J.Gonzalez
C I.Rodriguez
DH L.Stevens
UT L.Alicea
P R.Helling
P A.Sele
P J.Burkett
P D.Oliver
RP T.Crabtree
RP E.Gunderson
RP J.Wetteland

TEX 1999A

M J.Oates
1B L.Stevens
2B M.McLemore
SS R.Clayton
3B T.Zeile
LF R.Greer
CF T.Goodwin
RF J.Gonzalez
C I.Rodriguez
DH R.Palmeiro
P R.Helling
P A.Sele
P J.Burkett
P M.Morgan
P E.Loaiza
RP J.Zimmerman
RP M.Venafro
RP J.Wetteland

TEX 2000A

M J.Oates
1B R.Palmeiro
2B L.Alicea
SS R.Clayton
3B M.Lamb
LF R.Greer
CF G.Kapler
RF C.Curtis
C I.Rodriguez
DH D.Segui
UT F.Catalanotto
P K.Rogers
P R.Helling
P D.Oliver
P E.Loaiza
P M.Perisho
RP T.Crabtree
RP F.Cordero
RP J.Zimmerman

Toledo

TOL a 1884
TOL a 1890-1890

TOL 1884a

M C.Morton
1B C.Lane
2B S.Barkley
SS J.Miller
3B E.Brown
LF F.Olin
CF C.Welch
RF T.Poorman
C F.Walker
P T.Mullane
P H.O'Day

TOL 1890a

M C.Morton
1B P.Werden
2B P.Nicholson
SS F.Scheibeck
3B B.Alvord
LF B.Van Dyke
CF G.Tebeau
RF E.Swartwood
C H.Sage
P J.Healy
P E.Cushman
P F.Smith

Toronto

TOR A 1977-2000

TOR 1977A

M R.Hartsfield
1B D.Ault
2B S.Staggs
SS H.Torres
3B R.Howell
LF A.Woods
CF B.Bailor
RF O.Velez
C A.Ashby
DH R.Fairly
UT S.Ewing
P D.Lemanczyk
P J.Garvin
P J.Jefferson
RP P.Vuckovich
RP M.Willis
RP J.Johnson

TOR 1978A

M R.Hartsfield
1B J.Mayberry
2B D.McKay
SS L.Gomez
3B R.Howell
LF O.Velez
CF R.Bosetti
RF B.Bailor
C R.Cerone
DH R.Carty
P J.Jefferson
P T.Underwood
P J.Clancy
P J.Garvin
P B.Moore
RP M.Willis
RP T.Murphy
RP J.Coleman

TOR 1979A

M R.Hartsfield
1B J.Mayberry
2B D.Ainge
SS A.Griffin
3B R.Howell
LF A.Woods
CF R.Bosetti
RF B.Bailor
C R.Cerone
DH R.Carty
UT O.Velez
P T.Underwood
P P.Huffman
P D.Lemanczyk
P B.Moore
P D.Stieb
RP D.Freisleben
RP T.Buskey

TOR 1980A

M B.Mattick
1B J.Mayberry
2B D.Garcia
SS A.Griffin
3B R.Howell
LF B.Bailor
CF B.Bonnell
RF L.Moseby
C E.Whitt
DH O.Velez
UT A.Woods

P J.Clancy
P D.Stieb
P P.Mirabella
P J.Jefferson
RP J.McLaughlin
RP J.Garvin
RP J.Kucek

TOR 1981A

M B.Mattick
1B J.Mayberry
2B D.Garcia
SS A.Griffin
3B D.Ainge
LF A.Woods
CF L.Moseby
RF B.Bonnell
C E.Whitt
DH O.Velez
UT G.Iorg
P D.Stieb
P L.Leal
P J.Clancy
P J.Todd
P M.Bomback
RP R.Jackson
RP J.McLaughlin
RP J.Garvin

TOR 1982A

M B.Cox
1B W.Upshaw
2B D.Garcia
SS A.Griffin
3B R.Mulliniks
LF B.Bonnell
CF L.Moseby
RF J.Barfield
C E.Whitt
DH D.Revering
UT G.Iorg
UT H.Powell
P D.Stieb
P J.Clancy
P L.Leal
P J.Gott
RP D.Murray
RP R.Jackson
RP J.McLaughlin

TOR 1983A

M B.Cox
1B W.Upshaw
2B D.Garcia
SS A.Griffin
3B R.Mulliniks
LF B.Bonnell
CF L.Moseby
RF J.Barfield
C E.Whitt
DH C.Johnson
UT D.Collins
UT G.Iorg
UT J.Orta
P D.Stieb
P J.Clancy
P L.Leal
P J.Gott
P D.Alexander
RP J.Acker
RP R.Jackson
RP J.McLaughlin

TOR 1984A

M B.Cox
1B W.Upshaw
2B D.Garcia
SS A.Griffin
3B R.Mulliniks
LF D.Collins
CF L.Moseby
RF G.Bell
C E.Whitt
DH C.Johnson
UT J.Barfield
UT G.Iorg
UT B.Martinez
P D.Stieb
P D.Alexander
P L.Leal
P J.Clancy
P J.Gott
RP R.Jackson
RP D.Lamp
RP J.Acker

TOR 1985A

M B.Cox
1B W.Upshaw
2B D.Garcia
SS T.Fernandez
3B R.Mulliniks
LF G.Bell
CF L.Moseby
RF J.Barfield
C E.Whitt
DH J.Burroughs
UT G.Iorg
P D.Stieb
P D.Alexander
P J.Key
P J.Clancy
RP D.Lamp
RP J.Acker
RP G.Lavelle

TOR 1986A

M J.Williams
1B W.Upshaw
2B D.Garcia
SS T.Fernandez
3B R.Mulliniks
LF G.Bell
CF L.Moseby
RF J.Barfield
C E.Whitt
DH C.Johnson
UT G.Iorg
UT R.Leach
P J.Key
P J.Clancy
P D.Stieb
P J.Cerutti
P D.Alexander
RP M.Eichhorn
RP T.Henke
RP D.Lamp

TOR 1987A

M J.Williams
1B W.Upshaw
2B G.Iorg
SS T.Fernandez
3B K.Gruber
LF G.Bell
CF L.Moseby
RF J.Barfield
C E.Whitt
DH F.McGriff
UT R.Leach
UT R.Mulliniks
P J.Key
P J.Clancy
P D.Stieb
P J.Cerutti
RP M.Eichhorn
RP J.Nunez
RP T.Henke

TOR 1988A

M J.Williams
1B F.McGriff
2B M.Lee
SS T.Fernandez
3B K.Gruber
LF G.Bell
CF L.Moseby
RF J.Barfield
C E.Whitt
DH R.Mulliniks
UT N.Liriano
P M.Flanagan
P D.Stieb
P J.Clancy
P J.Key
P T.Stottlemyre
RP J.Cerutti
RP D.Ward
RP T.Henke

TOR 1989A

M J.Williams
M C.Gaston
1B F.McGriff
2B N.Liriano
SS T.Fernandez
3B K.Gruber
LF G.Bell
CF L.Moseby
RF J.Felix
C E.Whitt
DH R.Mulliniks
UT M.Lee
P J.Key
P D.Stieb
P J.Cerutti
P M.Flanagan
P T.Stottlemyre
RP D.Ward
RP T.Henke
RP D.Wells

TOR 1990A

M C.Gaston
1B F.McGriff
2B M.Lee
SS T.Fernandez
3B K.Gruber
LF G.Bell
CF M.Wilson
RF J.Felix
C P.Borders
DH J.Olerud
P D.Stieb
P T.Stottlemyre
P D.Wells
P J.Key
P J.Cerutti
RP D.Ward
RP F.Wills
RP J.Acker

TOR 1991A

M C.Gaston
M G.Tenace
M C.Gaston
1B J.Olerud
2B R.Alomar
SS M.Lee
3B K.Gruber
LF C.Maldonado
CF D.White
RF J.Carter
C G.Myers
DH R.Mulliniks
UT P.Borders
P T.Stottlemyre
P J.Key
P D.Wells
P J.Guzman
P T.Candiotti
RP M.Timlin
RP D.Ward
RP J.Acker

TOR 1992A

M C.Gaston
1B J.Olerud
2B R.Alomar
SS M.Lee
3B K.Gruber
LF C.Maldonado
CF D.White
RF J.Carter
C P.Borders
DH D.Winfield
P J.Morris
P J.Key
P J.Guzman
P T.Stottlemyre
P D.Stieb
RP D.Wells
RP D.Ward
RP T.Henke

TOR 1993A

M C.Gaston
1B J.Olerud
2B R.Alomar
SS T.Fernandez
3B E.Sprague
LF T.Ward
CF D.White
RF J.Carter
C P.Borders
DH P.Molitor
P J.Guzman
P P.Hentgen
P T.Stottlemyre
P D.Stewart
P J.Morris
RP D.Cox
RP M.Eichhorn
RP D.Ward

TOR 1994A

M C.Gaston
1B J.Olerud
2B R.Alomar
SS D.Schofield
3B E.Sprague
LF M.Huff
CF D.White
RF J.Carter
C P.Borders
DH P.Molitor
P P.Hentgen
P J.Guzman
P T.Stottlemyre
P D.Stewart
P A.Leiter
RP T.Castillo
RP W.Williams
RP M.Timlin

TOR 1995A

M C.Gaston
1B J.Olerud
2B R.Alomar
SS A.Gonzalez
3B E.Sprague
LF J.Carter
CF D.White
RF S.Green
C L.Parrish
DH P.Molitor
P P.Hentgen
P A.Leiter
P J.Guzman
P D.Cone
RP T.Castillo
RP W.Williams
RP D.Cox

TOR 1996A

M C.Gaston
1B J.Olerud
2B T.Perez
SS A.Gonzalez
3B E.Sprague
LF J.Carter
CF O.Nixon
RF S.Green
C C.O'Brien
DH C.Delgado
P P.Hentgen
P E.Hanson
P J.Guzman
P P.Quantrill
RP T.Castillo
RP T.Crabtree
RP M.Timlin

TOR 1997A

M C.Gaston
M M.Queen
1B C.Delgado
2B C.Garcia
SS A.Gonzalez
3B E.Sprague
LF S.Green
CF O.Nixon
RF O.Merced
C B.Santiago
DH J.Carter
P P.Hentgen
P R.Clemens
P W.Williams
P R.Person
RP P.Quantrill
RP D.Plesac
RP L.Andujar

TOR 1998A

M T.Johnson
1B C.Delgado
2B C.Grebeck
SS A.Gonzalez
3B E.Sprague
LF S.Stewart
CF J.Cruz
RF S.Green
C D.Fletcher
DH J.Canseco
UT T.Fernandez
P R.Clemens
P W.Williams
P P.Hentgen
P C.Carpenter
P J.Guzman
RP P.Quantrill
RP B.Risley
RP D.Stieb

TOR 1999A

M J.Fregosi
1B C.Delgado
2B H.Bush
SS T.Batista
3B T.Fernandez
LF S.Stewart
CF J.Cruz
RF S.Green
C D.Fletcher
DH W.Greene
P D.Wells
P P.Hentgen
P K.Escobar
P C.Carpenter
P R.Halladay
RP G.Lloyd
RP B.Koch
RP P.Spoljaric

TOR 2000A

M J.Fregosi
1B C.Delgado
2B H.Bush
SS A.Gonzalez
3B T.Batista
LF S.Stewart
CF J.Cruz
RF R.Mondesi
C D.Fletcher
DH B.Fullmer
P D.Wells
P K.Escobar
P C.Carpenter
P F.Castillo
RP P.Quantrill
RP B.Koch
RP J.Frascatore

Troy

TRO n 1871-1872
TRO N 1879-1882

TRO 1871n

M L.Pike
M B.Craver
1B C.Flynn
2B B.Craver
SS D.Flowers
3B S.Bellan
LF S.King
CF T.York
RF L.Pike
C M.McGeary
P J.McMullin

TRO 1872n

M J.Wood
1B B.McAtee
2B J.Wood
SS S.Bellan
3B D.Force
LF S.King
CF C.Gedney
RF P.Martin
C D.Allison
P G.Zettlein

TRO 1879N

M H.Phillips
M B.Ferguson
1B D.Brouthers
2B T.Hawkes
SS E.Caskin
3B H.Doscher
LF T.Mansell
CF A.Hall
RF J.Evans
C C.Reilley
P G.Bradley
P H.Salisbury
P F.Goldsmith

TRO 1880N

M B.Ferguson
1B E.Cogswell
2B B.Ferguson
SS E.Caskin
3B R.Connor
LF P.Gillespie
CF J.Cassidy
RF J.Evans
C B.Holbert
P M.Welch
P T.Keefe

TRO 1881N

M B.Ferguson
1B R.Connor
2B B.Ferguson
SS E.Caskin
3B F.Hankinson
LF P.Gillespie
CF J.Cassidy
RF J.Evans
C B.Ewing
P T.Keefe
P M.Welch

TRO 1882N

M B.Ferguson
1B J.Smith
2B B.Ferguson
SS F.Pfeffer
3B B.Ewing
LF P.Gillespie
CF R.Connor
RF C.Roseman
C B.Holbert
P T.Keefe
P M.Welch

Washington

OLY n 1871-1872
NAT n 1872
WAS n 1873
WAS n 1875
WAS a 1884
WAS U 1884
WAS N 1886-1889
WAS a 1891
WAS N 1892-1899
WAS A 1901-1960
WAS A 1961-1971

OLY 1871n

M N.Young
1B E.Mills
2B A.Leonard
SS D.Force
3B F.Waterman
LF H.Berthrong
CF G.Hall
RF J.Glenn
C D.Allison
P A.Brainard
P B.Stearns

OLY 1872n

M F.Waterman
1B C.Flynn
2B T.Beals
SS W.Goldsmith
3B F.Waterman
LF J.Glenn
CF G.Heubel
RF V.Robinson
C F.Selman
P A.Brainard

NAT 1872n

M W.White
1B P.Hines
2B H.Hollingshead
SS J.Doyle
3B W.White
LF E.Mincher
CF S.Studley
RF O.Bielaski
C B.Lennon
UT D.Coughlin
P B.Stearns

WAS 1873n

M N.Young
1B J.Glenn
2B T.Beals
SS J.Gerhardt
3B W.White
LF P.Hines
CF H.Hollingshead
RF O.Bielaski
C P.Snyder
UT J.Donnelly
P B.Stearns
P Greason

WAS 1875n

M H.Hollingshead
M B.Parks
1B A.Allison
2B S.Brady
SS J.Dailey
3B H.Doscher
LF B.Parks
CF H.Hollingshead
RF L.Ressler
C A.Thompson
P B.Stearns

WAS 1884a

M H.Hollingshead
M Bickerson
1B W.Prince
2B T.Hawkes
SS F.Fennelly
3B B.Gladman
LF B.Morgan
CF H.Mullin
RF E.Trumbull
C J.Humphries
P B.Barr
P J.Hamill

WAS 1884U

M M.Scanlon
1B P.Joy
2B T.Evers
SS J.Halpin
3B J.McCormick
LF H.Moore
CF P.Baker
RF B.Wise
C C.Fulmer
P B.Wise
P A.Voss
P C.Gagus

WAS 1886N

M M.Scanlon
M J.Gaffney
1B P.Baker
2B J.Farrell
SS D.Force
3B J.Knowles
LF C.Carroll
CF P.Hines
RF E.Crane
C B.Gilligan
P D.Shaw
P B.Barr
P T.Madigan
P F.Gilmore

WAS 1887N

M J.Gaffney
1B B.O'Brien
2B A.Myers
SS J.Farrell
3B J.Donnelly
LF C.Carroll
CF P.Hines
RF E.Daily
C C.Mack
P J.Whitney
P H.O'Day
P F.Gilmore
P D.Shaw

WAS 1888N

M W.Hewett
M T.Sullivan
1B B.O'Brien
2B A.Myers
SS G.Shoch
3B J.Donnelly
LF W.Wilmot
CF D.Hoy
RF E.Daily
C C.Mack
P H.O'Day
P J.Whitney
P W.Widner
P G.Keefe
P F.Gilmore

WAS 1889N

M J.Morrill
M A.Irwin
1B J.Carney
2B S.Wise
SS A.Irwin
3B J.Irwin
LF W.Wilmot
CF D.Hoy
RF E.Beecher
C T.Daly
UT C.Mack
P A.Ferson
P G.Haddock
P G.Keefe
P H.O'Day
P J.Healy

WAS 1891a

M S.Trott
M P.Snyder
M D.Shannon
M S.Griffin
1B M.McQuery
2B T.Dowd
SS G.Hatfield
3B B.Alvord
LF E.Beecher
CF P.Hines
RF L.Murphy
C D.McGuire
P K.Carsey
P F.Foreman
P J.Bakely

WAS 1892N

M B.Barnie

M A.Irwin
M D.Richardson
1B H.Larkin
2B T.Dowd
SS D.Richardson
3B Y.Robinson
LF C.Duffee
CF D.Hoy
RF P.Radford
C D.McGuire
P F.Killen
P B.Abbey
P P.Knell
P J.Duryea
P J.Meekin

WAS 1893N

M J.O'Rourke
1B H.Larkin
2B S.Wise
SS J.Sullivan
3B J.Mulvey
LF J.O'Rourke
CF D.Hoy
RF P.Radford
C D.Farrell
P D.Esper
P A.Maul
P J.Meekin
P J.Duryea

WAS 1894N

M G.Schmelz
1B E.Cartwright
2B P.Ward
SS F.Scheibeck
3B B.Joyce
LF K.Selbach
CF C.Abbey
RF B.Hassamaer
C D.McGuire
UT P.Radford
P W.Mercer
P A.Maul
P M.Sullivan
P O.Stocksdale
P D.Esper

WAS 1895N

M G.Schmelz
1B E.Cartwright
2B J.Crooks
SS F.Scheibeck
3B B.Joyce
LF K.Selbach
CF C.Abbey
RF B.Hassamaer
C D.McGuire
P W.Mercer
P V.Anderson
P O.Stocksdale
P A.Maul
P J.Malarkey

WAS 1896N

M G.Schmelz
1B E.Cartwright
2B J.O'Brien
SS De Montreville
3B B.Joyce
LF K.Selbach
CF T.Brown
RF B.Lush
C D.McGuire
P W.Mercer
P D.McJames
P L.German
P S.King

WAS 1897N

M G.Schmelz
M T.Brown
1B T.Tucker
2B J.O'Brien
SS De Montreville
3B C.Reilly
LF K.Selbach
CF T.Brown
RF C.Abbey
C D.McGuire
UT Z.Wrigley
P W.Mercer
P D.McJames
P C.Swaim
P S.King
P L.German

WAS 1898N

M T.Brown
M J.Doyle

M D.McGuire
M A.Irwin
1B J.Doyle
2B H.Reitz
SS Z.Wrigley
3B J.Smith
LF K.Selbach
CF J.Anderson
RF J.Gettman
C D.McGuire
UT D.Farrell
P G.Weyhing
P W.Mercer
P B.Dinneen
P F.Killen
P C.Swaim

WAS 1899N

M A.Irwin
1B D.McGann
2B F.Bonner
SS D.Padden
3B C.Atherton
LF J.O'Brien
CF J.Slagle
RF B.Freeman
C D.McGuire
UT W.Mercer
P G.Weyhing
P B.Dinneen
P D.McFarlan

WAS 1901A

M J.Manning
1B M.Grady
2B J.Farrell
SS B.Clingman
3B B.Coughlin
LF P.Foster
CF I.Waldron
RF S.Dungan
C B.Clarke
P B.Carrick
P W.Lee
P C.Patten
P W.Mercer

WAS 1902A

M T.Loftus
1B S.Carey
2B J.Doyle
SS B.Ely
3B B.Coughlin
LF E.Delahanty
CF J.Ryan
RF W.Lee
C B.Clarke
UT B.Keister
P A.Orth
P C.Patten
P B.Carrick
P H.Townsend

WAS 1903A

M T.Loftus
1B B.Clarke
2B B.McCormick
SS C.Moran
3B B.Coughlin
LF K.Selbach
CF J.Ryan
RF W.Lee
C M.Kittridge
UT R.Robinson
P C.Patten
P A.Orth
P H.Wilson
P H.Townsend
P D.Dunkle

WAS 1904A

M M.Kittridge
M P.Donovan
1B J.Stahl
2B B.McCormick
SS J.Cassidy
3B H.Hill
LF F.Huelsman
CF B.O'Neill
RF P.Donovan
C M.Kittridge
P C.Patten
P H.Townsend
P B.Jacobson
P B.Wolfe
P T.Hughes

WAS 1905A

M J.Stahl
1B J.Stahl

2B C.Hickman
SS J.Cassidy
3B H.Hill
LF F.Huelsman
CF C.Jones
RF J.Anderson
C M.Heydon
UT R.Nill
P C.Patten
P T.Hughes
P H.Townsend
P B.Wolfe
P B.Jacobson

WAS 1906A

M J.Stahl
1B J.Stahl
2B L.Schlafly
SS D.Altizer
3B L.Cross
LF J.Anderson
CF C.Jones
RF C.Hickman
C H.Wakefield
P C.Falkenberg
P C.Patten
P C.Smith
P T.Hughes
P F.Kitson

WAS 1907A

M J.Cantillon
1B J.Anderson
2B J.Delahanty
SS D.Altizer
3B B.Shipke
LF O.Clymer
CF C.Jones
RF B.Ganley
C J.Warner
P C.Smith
P C.Patten
P C.Falkenberg
P T.Hughes
P W.Johnson

WAS 1908A

M J.Cantillon
1B J.Freeman
2B J.Delahanty
SS G.McBride
3B B.Shipke
LF B.Ganley
CF C.Milan
RF O.Pickering
C G.Street
UT O.Clymer
P T.Hughes
P W.Johnson
P C.Smith
P B.Keeley
P B.Burns

WAS 1909A

M J.Cantillon
1B J.Donahue
2B J.Delahanty
SS G.McBride
3B W.Conroy
LF J.Lelivelt
CF C.Milan
RF G.Browne
C G.Street
UT B.Unglaub
P W.Johnson
P B.Groom
P D.Gray
P C.Smith
P T.Hughes

WAS 1910A

M J.McAleer
1B B.Unglaub
2B R.Killefer
SS G.McBride
3B K.Elberfeld
LF J.Lelivelt
CF C.Milan
RF D.Gessler
C G.Street
UT W.Conroy
P W.Johnson
P B.Groom
P D.Gray
P D.Walker
P D.Reisling

WAS 1911A

M J.McAleer
1B G.Schaefer

2B B.Cunningham
SS G.McBride
3B W.Conroy
LF T.Walker
CF C.Milan
RF D.Gessler
C G.Street
UT K.Elberfeld
P W.Johnson
P B.Groom
P T.Hughes
P D.Walker
P D.Gray

WAS 1912A

M C.Griffith
1B C.Gandil
2B R.Morgan
SS G.McBride
3B E.Foster
LF H.Shanks
CF C.Milan
RF D.Moeller
C J.Henry
P W.Johnson
P B.Groom
P T.Hughes
P C.Cashion

WAS 1913A

M C.Griffith
1B C.Gandil
2B R.Morgan
SS G.McBride
3B E.Foster
LF H.Shanks
CF C.Milan
RF D.Moeller
C J.Henry
P W.Johnson
P B.Groom
P J.Boehling
P J.Engel
P T.Hughes

WAS 1914A

M C.Griffith
1B C.Gandil
2B R.Morgan
SS G.McBride
3B E.Foster
LF H.Shanks
CF C.Milan
RF D.Moeller
C J.Henry
P W.Johnson
P D.Ayers
P J.Shaw
P J.Boehling
P J.Bentley
RP H.Harper

WAS 1915A

M C.Griffith
1B C.Gandil
2B R.Morgan
SS G.McBride
3B E.Foster
LF H.Shanks
CF C.Milan
RF D.Moeller
C J.Henry
P W.Johnson
P B.Gallia
P J.Boehling
P D.Ayers
P J.Shaw

WAS 1916A

M C.Griffith
1B J.Judge
2B R.Morgan
SS G.McBride
3B E.Foster
LF H.Shanks
CF C.Milan
RF D.Moeller
C J.Henry
P W.Johnson
P B.Gallia
P H.Harper
P D.Ayers
P J.Boehling

WAS 1917A

M C.Griffith
1B J.Judge
2B R.Morgan
SS H.Shanks
3B E.Foster

LF M.Menosky
CF C.Milan
RF S.Rice
C E.Ainsmith
UT J.Leonard
P W.Johnson
P J.Shaw
P B.Gallia
P D.Ayers
P G.Dumont

WAS 1918A

M C.Griffith
1B J.Judge
2B R.Morgan
SS D.Lavan
3B E.Foster
LF B.Shotton
CF C.Milan
RF F.Schulte
C E.Ainsmith
UT H.Shanks
P W.Johnson
P H.Harper
P J.Shaw
P D.Ayers

WAS 1919A

M C.Griffith
1B J.Judge
2B H.Janvrin
SS H.Shanks
3B E.Foster
LF M.Menosky
CF C.Milan
RF S.Rice
C V.Picinich
UT P.Gharrity
P J.Shaw
P W.Johnson
P H.Harper
P E.Erickson

WAS 1920A

M C.Griffith
1B J.Judge
2B B.Harris
SS J.O'Neill
3B F.Ellerbe
LF C.Milan
CF S.Rice
RF B.Roth
C P.Gharrity
UT H.Shanks
P T.Zachary
P E.Erickson
P J.Shaw
P H.Courtney
P W.Johnson

WAS 1921A

M G.McBride
1B J.Judge
2B B.Harris
SS F.O'Rourke
3B H.Shanks
LF B.Miller
CF S.Rice
RF C.Milan
C P.Gharrity
P G.Mogridge
P W.Johnson
P T.Zachary
P E.Erickson
P H.Courtney
RP A.Schacht

WAS 1922A

M C.Milan
1B J.Judge
2B B.Harris
SS R.Peckinpaugh
3B B.LaMotte
LF G.Goslin
CF S.Rice
RF F.Brower
C P.Gharrity
P W.Johnson
P G.Mogridge
P R.Francis
P T.Zachary
P E.Erickson

WAS 1923A

M D.Bush
1B J.Judge
2B B.Harris
SS R.Peckinpaugh
3B O.Bluege
LF G.Goslin

CF N.Leibold
RF S.Rice
C M.Ruel
UT J.Evans
P W.Johnson
P G.Mogridge
P T.Zachary
P A.Russell
P P.Zahniser

WAS 1924A

M B.Harris
1B J.Judge
2B B.Harris
SS R.Peckinpaugh
3B O.Bluege
LF G.Goslin
CF N.Leibold
RF S.Rice
C M.Ruel
P W.Johnson
P G.Mogridge
P T.Zachary
P F.Marberry
P J.Martina
RP A.Russell
RP B.Speece

WAS 1925A

M B.Harris
1B J.Judge
2B B.Harris
SS R.Peckinpaugh
3B O.Bluege
LF G.Goslin
CF E.McNeely
RF S.Rice
C M.Ruel
UT J.Harris
P S.Coveleski
P W.Johnson
P D.Ruether
P T.Zachary
RP F.Marberry
RP V.Gregg
RP A.Russell

WAS 1926A

M B.Harris
1B J.Judge
2B B.Harris
SS B.Myer
3B O.Bluege
LF E.McNeely
CF G.Goslin
RF S.Rice
C M.Ruel
UT J.Harris
P W.Johnson
P S.Coveleski
P D.Ruether
P A.Crowder
P C.Ogden
RP F.Marberry
RP B.Morrell
RP A.Ferguson

WAS 1927A

M B.Harris
1B J.Judge
2B B.Harris
SS B.Reeves
3B O.Bluege
LF G.Goslin
CF T.Speaker
RF S.Rice
C M.Ruel
P H.Lisenbee
P S.Thurston
P B.Hadley
P W.Johnson
P T.Zachary
RP F.Marberry
RP G.Braxton
RP B.Burke

WAS 1928A

M B.Harris
1B J.Judge
2B B.Harris
SS B.Reeves
3B O.Bluege
LF G.Goslin
CF S.West
RF S.Rice
C M.Ruel
UT R.Barnes
P B.Hadley
P S.Jones
P G.Braxton
P F.Marberry

P M.Gaston

WAS 1929A

M W.Johnson
1B J.Judge
2B B.Myer
SS J.Cronin
3B J.Hayes
LF G.Goslin
CF S.West
RF S.Rice
C B.Tate
P F.Marberry
P B.Hadley
P G.Braxton
P L.Brown
P S.Jones

WAS 1930A

M W.Johnson
1B J.Judge
2B B.Myer
SS J.Cronin
3B O.Bluege
LF H.Manush
CF S.West
RF S.Rice
C R.Spencer
P B.Hadley
P A.Crowder
P L.Brown
P F.Marberry
P S.Jones

WAS 1931A

M W.Johnson
1B J.Kuhel
2B B.Myer
SS J.Cronin
3B O.Bluege
LF H.Manush
CF S.West
RF S.Rice
C R.Spencer
P L.Brown
P A.Crowder
P F.Marberry
P C.Fischer
P B.Hadley

WAS 1932A

M W.Johnson
1B J.Kuhel
2B B.Myer
SS J.Cronin
3B O.Bluege
LF H.Manush
CF S.West
RF C.Reynolds
C R.Spencer
UT S.Rice
P A.Crowder
P M.Weaver
P L.Brown
P F.Marberry
P T.Thomas

WAS 1933A

M J.Cronin
1B J.Kuhel
2B B.Myer
SS J.Cronin
3B O.Bluege
LF H.Manush
CF F.Schulte
RF G.Goslin
C L.Sewell
P A.Crowder
P E.Whitehill
P L.Stewart
P M.Weaver
P T.Thomas
RP J.Russell
RP B.Burke
RP B.McAfee

WAS 1934A

M J.Cronin
1B J.Kuhel
2B B.Myer
SS J.Cronin
3B C.Travis
LF H.Manush
CF F.Schulte
RF J.Stone
C E.Phillips
UT O.Bluege
UT D.Harris
P E.Whitehill
P M.Weaver

P B.Burke
P L.Stewart
P T.Thomas
RP J.Russell
RP A.McColl

WAS 1935A

M B.Harris
1B J.Kuhel
2B B.Myer
SS O.Bluege
3B C.Travis
LF H.Manush
CF J.Powell
RF J.Stone
C C.Bolton
P E.Whitehill
P B.Hadley
P B.Newsom
P E.Linke
RP J.Russell
RP L.Pettit

WAS 1936A

M B.Harris
1B J.Kuhel
2B O.Bluege
SS C.Travis
3B B.Lewis
LF J.Stone
CF B.Chapman
RF C.Reynolds
C C.Bolton
UT R.Kress
P B.Newsom
P J.DeShong
P E.Whitehill
P P.Appleton
P J.Cascarella
RP J.Russell

WAS 1937A

M B.Harris
1B J.Kuhel
2B B.Myer
SS C.Travis
3B B.Lewis
LF A.Simmons
CF M.Almada
RF J.Stone
C R.Ferrell
P J.DeShong
P W.Ferrell
P M.Weaver
P P.Appleton
P E.Linke
RP S.Cohen

WAS 1938A

M B.Harris
1B Z.Bonura
2B B.Myer
SS C.Travis
3B B.Lewis
LF A.Simmons
CF S.West
RF G.Case
C R.Ferrell
UT T.Wright
P D.Leonard
P P.Appleton
P K.Chase
P W.Ferrell
P H.Kelley
RP C.Hogsett

WAS 1939A

M B.Harris
1B M.Vernon
2B J.Bloodworth
SS C.Travis
3B B.Lewis
LF T.Wright
CF S.West
RF G.Case
C R.Ferrell
P D.Leonard
P K.Chase
P J.Krakauskas
P J.Haynes
P A.Carrasquel
RP P.Appleton
RP W.Masterson

WAS 1940A

M B.Harris
1B Z.Bonura
2B J.Bloodworth
SS J.Pofahl
3B C.Travis
LF G.Walker
CF G.Case
RF B.Lewis
C R.Ferrell
P D.Leonard
P K.Chase
P S.Hudson
P W.Masterson
P J.Krakauskas
RP J.Haynes
RP A.Carrasquel

WAS 1941A

M B.Harris
1B M.Vernon
2B J.Bloodworth
SS C.Travis
3B G.Archie
LF G.Case
CF D.Cramer
RF B.Lewis
C J.Early
P D.Leonard
P S.Hudson
P K.Chase
P S.Sundra
P R.Anderson
RP A.Carrasquel
RP B.Zuber
RP W.Masterson

WAS 1942A

M B.Harris
1B M.Vernon
2B E.Clary
SS J.Sullivan
3B B.Estalella
LF G.Case
CF S.Spence
RF B.Campbell
C J.Early
P S.Hudson
P B.Newsom
P E.Wynn
P A.Carrasquel
P W.Masterson

WAS 1943A

M O.Bluege
1B M.Vernon
2B J.Priddy
SS J.Sullivan
3B E.Clary
LF B.Johnson
CF S.Spence
RF G.Case
C J.Early
P E.Wynn
P D.Leonard
P M.Candini
P M.Haefner
P A.Carrasquel

WAS 1944A

M O.Bluege
1B J.Kuhel
2B G.Myatt
SS J.Sullivan
3B G.Torres
LF G.Case
CF S.Spence
RF R.Ortiz
C R.Ferrell
UT J.Powell
P D.Leonard
P M.Haefner
P E.Wynn
P J.Niggeling
P R.Wolff
RP B.Lefebvre

WAS 1945A

M O.Bluege
1B J.Kuhel
2B G.Myatt
SS G.Torres
3B H.Clift
LF G.Case
CF G.Binks
RF B.Lewis
C R.Ferrell
P R.Wolff
P M.Haefner
P M.Pieretti
P D.Leonard
P J.Niggeling
RP S.Ullrich

WAS 1946A

M O.Bluege
1B M.Vernon
2B J.Priddy
SS B.Hitchcock
3B C.Travis
LF J.Grace
CF S.Spence
RF B.Lewis
C A.Evans
P M.Haefner
P B.Newsom
P D.Leonard
P R.Scarborough
P S.Hudson
RP M.Pieretti

WAS 1947A

M O.Bluege
1B M.Vernon
2B J.Priddy
SS M.Christman
3B E.Yost
LF J.Grace
CF S.Spence
RF B.Lewis
C A.Evans
UT S.Robertson
P W.Masterson
P E.Wynn
P M.Haefner
P R.Scarborough
P S.Hudson
RP M.Candini
RP T.Ferrick
RP S.Cary

WAS 1948A

M J.Kuhel
1B M.Vernon
2B A.Kozar
SS M.Christman
3B E.Yost
LF G.Coan
CF J.Wooten
RF B.Stewart
C J.Early
P E.Wynn
P W.Masterson
P R.Scarborough
P S.Hudson
P M.Haefner
RP F.Thompson
RP M.Candini
RP T.Ferrick

WAS 1949A

M J.Kuhel
1B E.Robinson
2B A.Kozar
SS S.Dente
3B E.Yost
LF B.Stewart
CF C.Vollmer
RF B.Lewis
C A.Evans
UT G.Coan
UT S.Robertson
P S.Hudson
P R.Scarborough
P P.Calvert
P M.Harris
P L.Hittle
RP J.Haynes
RP D.Welteroth

WAS 1950A

M B.Harris
1B M.Vernon
2B C.Michaels
SS S.Dente
3B E.Yost
LF B.Stewart
CF I.Noren
RF S.Mele
C A.Evans
UT G.Coan
P S.Hudson
P B.Kuzava
P C.Marrero
P S.Consuegra
P J.Haynes
RP M.Harris
RP J.Pearce

WAS 1951A

M B.Harris
1B M.Vernon
2B C.Michaels
SS P.Runnels
3B E.Yost
LF G.Coan
CF I.Noren
RF S.Mele
C M.Guerra
P C.Marrero
P S.Consuegra
P D.Johnson
P S.Hudson
P B.Porterfield
RP M.Harris
RP J.Haynes

WAS 1952A

M B.Harris
1B M.Vernon
2B F.Baker
SS P.Runnels
3B E.Yost
LF G.Coan
CF J.Busby
RF J.Jensen
C M.Grasso
P B.Porterfield
P C.Marrero
P S.Shea
P W.Masterson
P J.Moreno
RP S.Consuegra
RP D.Johnson
RP T.Ferrick

WAS 1953A

M B.Harris
1B M.Vernon
2B W.Terwilliger
SS P.Runnels
3B E.Yost
LF C.Vollmer
CF J.Busby
RF J.Jensen
C E.Fitz Gerald
P B.Porterfield
P W.Masterson
P S.Shea
P C.Stobbs
P C.Marrero
RP S.Dixon
RP A.Sima
RP J.Lane

WAS 1954A

M B.Harris
1B M.Vernon
2B W.Terwilliger
SS P.Runnels
3B E.Yost
LF R.Sievers
CF J.Busby
RF T.Umphlett
C E.Fitz Gerald
P B.Porterfield
P M.McDermott
P J.Schmitz
P C.Stobbs
P D.Stone
RP C.Pascual
RP G.Keriazakos
RP B.Stewart

WAS 1955A

M C.Dressen
1B M.Vernon
2B P.Runnels
SS J.Valdivielso
3B E.Yost
LF R.Sievers
CF T.Umphlett
RF C.Paula
C E.Fitz Gerald
UT E.Oravetz
P D.Stone
P B.Porterfield
P J.Schmitz
P M.McDermott
P C.Stobbs
RP P.Ramos
RP T.Abernathy
RP S.Shea

WAS 1956A

M C.Dressen
1B P.Runnels
2B H.Plews
SS J.Valdivielso
3B E.Yost
LF R.Sievers
CF W.Herzog
RF J.Lemon
C C.Courtney
UT L.Berberet
UT K.Olson
P C.Stobbs
P C.Pascual
P P.Ramos
P D.Stone
P B.Wiesler
RP H.Griggs
RP B.Chakales
RP C.Grob

WAS 1957A

M C.Dressen
M C.Lavagetto
1B P.Runnels
2B H.Plews
SS R.Bridges
3B E.Yost
LF R.Sievers
CF B.Usher
RF J.Lemon
C L.Berberet
UT J.Becquer
P P.Ramos
P C.Stobbs
P C.Pascual
P R.Kemmerer
RP T.Clevenger
RP D.Hyde
RP B.Byerly

WAS 1958A

M C.Lavagetto
1B N.Zauchin
2B K.Aspromonte
SS R.Bridges
3B E.Yost
LF R.Sievers
CF A.Pearson
RF J.Lemon
C C.Courtney
UT N.Chrisley
UT H.Plews
P P.Ramos
P R.Kemmerer
P C.Pascual
P H.Griggs
P V.Valentinetti
RP T.Clevenger
RP D.Hyde

WAS 1959A

M C.Lavagetto
1B R.Sievers
2B R.Bertoia
SS B.Consolo
3B H.Killebrew
LF J.Lemon
CF B.Allison
RF F.Throneberry
C H.Naragon
UT J.Becquer
P C.Pascual
P P.Ramos
P R.Kemmerer
P B.Fischer
RP T.Clevenger
RP H.Griggs
RP C.Stobbs

WAS 1960A

M C.Lavagetto
1B J.Becquer
2B B.Gardner
SS J.Valdivielso
3B R.Bertoia
LF J.Lemon
CF L.Green
RF B.Allison
C E.Battey
UT B.Consolo
UT D.Dobbek
UT H.Killebrew
P P.Ramos
P D.Lee
P C.Pascual
P J.Kralick
RP T.Clevenger
RP C.Stobbs
RP H.Woodeshick

WAS 1961A

M M.Vernon
1B D.Long
2B C.Cottier
SS C.Veal
3B D.O'Connell
LF M.Keough
CF W.Tasby
RF G.Woodling
C G.Green
UT J.King
UT C.Hinton
P J.McClain
P B.Daniels
P D.Donovan
P E.Hobaugh
P P.Burnside
RP M.Kutyna
RP J.Klippstein
RP D.Sisler

WAS 1962A

M M.Vernon
1B H.Bright
2B C.Cottier
SS K.Hamlin
3B B.Johnson
LF C.Hinton
CF J.Piersall
RF J.King
C K.Retzer
UT J.Hicks
P D.Stenhouse
P D.Rudolph
P T.Cheney
P B.Daniels
P C.Osteen
RP S.Hamilton
RP M.Kutyna
RP E.Hobaugh

WAS 1963A

M M.Vernon
M E.Yost
M G.Hodges
1B B.Osborne
2B C.Cottier
SS E.Brinkman
3B D.Zimmer
LF C.Hinton
CF D.Lock
RF J.King
C K.Retzer
UT M.Minoso
UT D.Phillips
P C.Osteen
P D.Rudolph
P B.Daniels
P T.Cheney
P J.Duckworth
RP R.Kline
RP P.Burnside
RP E.Roebuck

WAS 1964A

M G.Hodges
1B B.Skowron
2B D.Blasingame
SS E.Brinkman
3B J.Kennedy
LF C.Hinton
CF D.Lock
RF J.King
C M.Brumley
UT D.Phillips
UT F.Valentine
UT D.Zimmer
P C.Osteen
P B.Narum
P B.Daniels
P A.Koch
RP S.Ridzik
RP J.Hannan
RP R.Kline

WAS 1965A

M G.Hodges
1B D.Nen
2B D.Blasingame
SS E.Brinkman
3B K.McMullen
LF F.Howard
CF D.Lock
RF W.Held
C M.Brumley
UT K.Hamlin
UT J.King
UT W.Kirkland
P P.Richert
P P.Ortega
P B.Narum
P M.McCormick
P B.Daniels
RP S.Ridzik
RP R.Kline
RP F.Kreutzer

WAS 1966A

M G.Hodges
1B D.Nen
2B B.Saverine
SS E.Brinkman
3B K.McMullen
LF F.Howard
CF D.Lock
RF F.Valentine
C P.Casanova
UT J.King
UT W.Kirkland
P P.Richert
P M.McCormick
P P.Ortega
P J.Hannan
RP C.Cox
RP B.Humphreys
RP R.Kline

WAS 1967A

M G.Hodges
1B M.Epstein
2B B.Allen
SS E.Brinkman
3B K.McMullen
LF F.Howard
CF F.Valentine
RF C.Peterson
C P.Casanova
UT H.Allen
UT T.Cullen
UT D.Nen
P P.Ortega
P C.Pascual
P B.Moore
P J.Coleman
P F.Bertaina
RP D.Knowles
RP B.Priddy
RP B.Humphreys

WAS 1968A

M J.Lemon
1B M.Epstein
2B B.Allen
SS R.Hansen
3B K.McMullen
LF F.Howard
CF D.Unser
RF E.Stroud
C P.Casanova
P J.Coleman
P C.Pascual
P J.Hannan
P D.Bosman
P F.Bertaina
RP D.Higgins
RP B.Humphreys

WAS 1969A

M T.Williams
1B M.Epstein
2B B.Allen
SS E.Brinkman
3B K.McMullen
LF F.Howard
CF D.Unser
RF H.Allen
C P.Casanova
UT B.Alyea
UT T.Cullen
UT E.Stroud
P J.Coleman
P D.Bosman
P C.Cox
P J.Hannan
P B.Moore
RP J.Shellenback
RP D.Higgins
RP D.Knowles

WAS 1970A

M T.Williams
1B M.Epstein
2B T.Cullen
SS E.Brinkman
3B A.Rodriguez
LF F.Howard
CF E.Stroud
RF D.Unser
C P.Casanova
UT B.Allen
UT R.Reichardt
P D.Bosman
P J.Coleman
P C.Cox
P J.Hannan
P G.Brunet
RP D.Knowles
RP J.Grzenda
RP H.Pina

WAS 1971A

M	T.Williams
1B	D.Mincher
2B	T.Cullen
SS	T.Harrah
3B	D.Nelson
LF	F.Howard
CF	E.Maddox
RF	D.Unser
C	P.Casanova
UT	B.Allen
UT	D.Billings
UT	T.McCraw
P	D.Bosman
P	D.McLain
P	P.Broberg
P	B.Gogolewski
P	J.Shellenback
RP	C.Cox
RP	P.Lindblad
RP	D.Riddleberger

Wilmington

WIL U 1884

WIL 1884U

M	J.Simmons
1B	R.Snyder
2B	C.Bastian
SS	H.Myers
3B	J.Say
LF	T.Lynch
CF	G.Fisher
RF	J.Munce
C	T.Cusick
P	J.Murphy
P	T.Nolan
P	D.Casey
P	J.Bakely

Worcester

WOR N 1880-1882

WOR 1880N

M	F.Bancroft
1B	C.Sullivan
2B	G.Creamer
SS	A.Irwin
3B	A.Whitney
LF	G.Wood
CF	H.Stovey
RF	L.Knight
C	C.Bennett
P	L.Richmond

WOR 1881N

M	M.Dorgan
M	H.Stovey
1B	H.Stovey
2B	G.Creamer
SS	A.Irwin
3B	H.Carpenter
LF	B.Dickerson
CF	P.Hotaling
RF	F.Corey
C	D.Bushong
P	L.Richmond
P	H.McCormick

WOR 1882N

M	F.Brown
M	T.Bond
M	J.Chapman
1B	H.Stovey
2B	G.Creamer
SS	A.Irwin
3B	F.Mann
LF	J.Clinton
CF	J.Hayes
RF	J.Evans
C	D.Bushong
UT	F.Corey
P	L.Richmond
P	F.Mountain

Manager Roster

This section details the managerial record of every man who ever held the reins of a major league club from 1871 through 2000. For many years, the assignment of wins and losses was thought a relatively simple task—almost as simple as identifying the managers themselves. In recent years, however, Richard Topp and Robert Tiemann wondered how it was that "managers" who never set foot on the field to lead their charges or even accompanied their clubs on road trips could be regarded as managers at all, at least in the commonly understood sense of field manager rather than business manager. Topp and Tiemann wondered how John McGraw, for example, could be credited as manager of the New York Giants for all of 1924 when a knee injury kept him from the bench for seven weeks: Somebody else must have run the team, they figured, so why not credit that man as interim manager?

That there were record-keeping errors in the 1870s or even the early 1900s may strike the average fan as unsurprising, but the incorrect assignment of decisions to helmsmen has been characteristic of every decade, up to and including the 1990s. Tiemann and Topp undertook a complete review of managerial records dating back to the National Association and found that the records published in previous baseball encyclopedias were wrong—so wrong that they had to be refigured from scratch. Here are the criteria they established for their groundbreaking study:

1. *Definition* A manager is the person designated by the club ownership to run the club on the field.

2. *Absences* When the regular manager is unable to be with the team for 30 or more days, the assistant in charge during his absence should be credited with the team's record from the time the absence begins until the regular manager returns to active duty.

3. *Interim manager* When a manager is removed, either by resignation or by being fired, and his designated replacement is not present to replace him, the assistant temporarily in charge of the team shall be credited with the team's record during the interim.

4. *Head coaches* From 1961 through 1964, the Chicago Cubs had a "panel of coaches" rather than a single manager. One of these coaches was designated *head coach* for a period of time; and that coach is credited with the team's record during his term as head coach.

5. *Captains* During the early years of professional baseball, the man who had the title of "manager" often served merely as the club's business manager, while the captain (a player) was responsible for the team on the field. Some captains were also managers. Each ambiguous situation is judged according to its particular circumstances, but in general the captain, rather than the manager, is credited with the team's record if the manager did not travel with the team or did not have previous baseball experience.

6. *Suspended games* If a game was suspended when one man was managing the team and was completed on a later date when another man was managing, the second manager is credited if the game was suspended before five innings were completed. If the game was suspended after five or more innings were played, then:

(a) credit the first manager with a win if the team was leading at the point of suspension and maintained the lead to win the game; or

(b) credit the first manager with a loss if the team was losing at the point of suspension and remained behind to lose the game; or

(c) credit the second manager with a win (or tie) if the team was losing at the point of suspension but came back to tie the score or win the game; or

(d) credit the second manager with a loss if the team was winning at the point of suspension but then lost the lead and/or game; or

(e) credit the second manager with the win or loss if the score was tied at the point of suspension.

7. *Protested games* If a protest was granted and the game was ordered resumed from the point of protest, then the same rules used for suspended games apply. If a protested game of at least five innings' duration was ordered replayed in its entirety, then no win or loss is credited, but both managers are credited with a no-decision game.

8. *Forfeited games* All forfeited games are counted as games managed, even if the game did not start or if it did not go five innings.

9. *Split seasons* In 1892 the National League played a split season, the winners meeting for the championship. In 1981, because of a players' strike, the National and American Leagues played split seasons. The managers' totals will have entries for each half-season.

10. *Replacement clubs* In the American Association (1882–1891), there were three instances in which one club dropped out during the season and was replaced by another club. In 1884 Richmond replaced Washington; in 1890 Baltimore replaced Brooklyn; and in 1891 Milwaukee replaced Cincinnati. In each case, the new club inherited the old club's won-lost record. Therefore, the manager of the new club is credited with starting in the

position (standing) in which the old club finished.

In the Union Association (1884), when a new club replaced an old one, the new club started with a 0–0 record rather than inheriting the old club's record, except in the case of the Chicago franchise, which moved to Pittsburgh. Therefore, all such Union Association managers are credited with a finish as if their teams had begun their season at the beginning of the league season. The finish for each manager is his club's standing in the eight-team league when (a) he left the job, (b) his club dropped out of the league, or (c) his club finished the season. The clubs that dropped out were Altoona (replaced by Kansas City); Philadelphia (replaced by Wilmington); Wilmington (replaced by St. Paul); and Pittsburgh (replaced by Milwaukee).

In a typical entry in the Manager Roster (a hypothetical entry has been created below), the column marked STANDING will, in cases where a team has had only one manager throughout the year, show the team's final standing (in the example below, see the entry for 1972). In the case of a manager who began the season but was replaced midway, however, the figure on the left of the column shows the team's standing when he departed and the figure on the right shows the team's final standing (in the example below, see the entry for 1976). In the case of a manager who finished the season but did not begin it, the team's standing when he took over is shown on the left and the final standing on the right (see the entry for 1978). In the case of a manager who began when the season was already under way but who failed to finish, the figure on the left of the column shows the team's standing when he took over; the middle figure shows the team's standing when he departed; and a third figure shows the team's final standing (see the entry for 1977). The figure in the next column represents the number of wins predicted by the team's runs scored and runs allowed, with about 10 extra runs being required for each win beyond .500. Last, the number of wins in the A-E column, which may be a positive figure or a negative figure, reflects the extent to which a manager may have stretched (or hindered) his available talent. The bottom line of a manager's entry provides his career totals, beginning at the left with the number of years, full or partial, in which he managed a major league club. The symbols shown in the sample entry are explained after the example.

YEAR	TM/L	G	W	L	PCT	STANDING			M/Y	W-EXP	A-E
Blow, Josiah H. "Joe"											
1969	Det-A*	134	71	63	.530	3 E	3 E		1/2	66.8	4.2
1971	Tex-A*	23	9	14	.391	6 W	6 W		3/3	12.0	-3.0
1972	Tex-A	161	84	76	.525	2 W				79.1	4.9
1973	Tex-A	95	44	51	.463	4 W	3 W		1/2	44.2	-0.2
1973	NY-A	56	30	26	.535	3 E	3 E		2/2	28.7	1.3
1974	NY-A	159	97	62	.610	★◆1 E				82.8	14.2
1975	NY-A	162	100	62	.617	◆1 E				90.0	10.0
1976	NY-A	94	52	42	.553	▲◆3 E	1 E		1/3	53.8	-1.8
1977	Bos-A	95	55	40	.579	4 E	4 E	2 E	2/3	50.4	4.6
1978	Oak-A	152	83	69	.546	●5 W	2 W		2/2	75.2	7.8
1979	Oak-A	60	37	23	.617	1 W	2 W		1/2	33.0	4.0
1980	Oak-A	49	27	22	.551	2 W	3 W		2/2	27.4	-0.4
1981(1)	Oak-A	62	24	38	.387	6 W				32.4	-7.6
1981(2)	Oak-A	100	44	56	.440	5 W				57.0	-13.0
1982	NY-A	162	91	71	.562	3 E				81.5	10.5
1983	NY-A	145	91	54	.628	6 E	2 E		2/2	84.0	7.0
1996	Atl-N	10	3	7	.300	■○◆6 E	2 E		1/2	6.0	-3.0
	15	1719	942	776	.548					904.3	39.5

Whenever a manager served two or more teams in the same year, the totals for each club are shown separately (see the sample entry for 1973). The split seasons of 1892 and 1981 are indicated with separate records for each half. A figure to the right of the year indicates first half or second half (see sample entry for 1981).

TM/L	Team and League
G	Games managed (including ties)
W	Wins
L	Losses
PCT	Percentage of games won
M/Y	Manager/Year (The latter figure indicates how many managers the team employed that year, while the former indicates the chronological position of the manager whose entry it is; "2/5," for example, would mean that this manager was the second of the team's five managers during that year.)
W-EXP	Expected Wins Calculated for the team based on its actual runs scored and allowed, not its predicted runs scored and runs allowed. A team that allows exactly as many runs as it scores is predicted to play .500 ball. The equation for expected wins is: $\frac{\text{(Runs Scored – Runs Allowed)}}{\text{Runs Per Win}} + \frac{\text{(Wins + Losses)}}{2}$
A-E	Actual Wins Minus Expected Wins (A measure of the extent to which a team outperformed or underperformed its talent; for a single season or two a high figure may be attributable to chance, but over time one must credit good managing.)
E	Eastern Division
W	Western Division
*	Indicates playing manager; for vital statistics, consult the player or pitcher register
▲	Tied for first place, involved in league or division playoff
●	Tied for position in standings
◆	League Championship Series win
★	World Series win
■	Wild Card
○	Lost Divisional Playoffs

The team and league abbreviations used in this section can be found on the last page of the book.

YEAR	TM/L	G	W	L	PCT	STANDING			M/Y	W-EXP	A-E
Adair, Marion Danne "Bill"											
1970	Chi-A	10	4	6	.400	6 W	6 W	6 W	2/3	3.8	0.2
Adcock, Joseph Wilbur "Joe"											
1967	Cle-A	162	75	87	.463	8				75.0	0.0
Addy, Robert Edward "Bob"											
1875	Phi-n*	7	3	4	.429	4	5		2/2	4.3	-1.3
1877	Cin-N*	24	5	19	.208	6	6	6	2/3	5.3	-0.3
	2	31	8	23	.258						-1.6
Allen, Robert Gilman "Bob"											
1890	Phi-N*	35	25	10	.714	3	2	3	4/5	20.2	4.8
1900	Cin-N*	144	62	77	.446	7				65.5	-3.5
	2	179	87	87	.500						1.3
Allison, Andrew K. "Andy"											
1872	Eck-n*	11	0	11	.000	10	9		1/3	-1.2	1.2
Allison, Douglas L. "Doug"											
1873	Res-n*	23	2	21	.087	8				-3.0	5.0
Alou, Felipe Rojas											
1992	Mon-N	125	70	55	.560	4 E	2 E		2/2	68.1	1.9
1993	Mon-N	163	94	68	.580	2 E				86.1	7.9
1994	Mon-N	114	74	40	.649	1 E				70.0	4.0
1995	Mon-N	144	66	78	.458	5 E				70.3	-4.3
1996	Mon-N	162	88	74	.543	2 E				88.4	-0.4
1997	Mon-N	162	78	84	.481	4 E				76.1	1.9
1998	Mon-N	162	65	97	.401	4 E				66.9	-1.9
1999	Mon-N	162	68	94	.420	4 E				68.0	0.0
2000	Mon-N	162	67	95	.414	4 E				65.5	1.5
	9	1356	670	685	.494						10.5
Alston, Walter Emmons											
1954	Bro-N	154	92	62	.597	2				80.6	11.4
1955	Bro-N	154	98	55	.641	★1				96.4	1.6
1956	Bro-N	154	93	61	.604	1				89.2	3.8
1957	Bro-N	154	84	70	.545	3				87.3	-3.3
1958	LA-N	154	71	83	.461	7				67.8	3.2
1959	LA-N	156	88	68	.564	▲★1				81.5	6.5
1960	LA-N	154	82	72	.532	4				84.3	-2.3
1961	LA-N	154	89	65	.578	2				80.7	8.3
1962	LA-N	165	102	63	.618	▲2				96.7	5.3
1963	LA-N	163	99	63	.611	★1				91.0	8.0
1964	LA-N	164	80	82	.494	●6				85.7	-5.7
1965	LA-N	162	97	65	.599	★1				90.9	6.1
1966	LA-N	162	95	67	.586	1				94.4	0.6
1967	LA-N	162	73	89	.451	8				72.3	0.7
1968	LA-N	162	76	86	.469	●7				76.2	-0.2
1969	LA-N	162	85	77	.525	4 W				90.2	-5.2
1970	LA-N	161	87	74	.540	2 W				87.0	-0.0
1971	LA-N	162	89	73	.549	2 W				89.2	-0.2
1972	LA-N	155	85	70	.548	3 W				83.9	1.1
1973	LA-N	162	95	66	.590	2 W				92.4	2.6
1974	LA-N	162	102	60	.630	♦1 W				105.6	-3.6
1975	LA-N	162	88	74	.543	2 W				93.7	-5.7
1976	LA-N	158	90	68	.570	2 W	2 W		1/2	86.1	3.9
	23	3658	2040	1613	.558						36.8
Altobelli, Joseph "Joe"											
1977	SF-N	162	75	87	.463	4 W				77.1	-2.1
1978	SF-N	162	89	73	.549	3 W				83.1	5.9
1979	SF-N	140	61	79	.436	4 W	4 W		1/2	63.1	-2.1
1983	Bal-A	162	98	64	.605	★1 E				95.7	2.3
1984	Bal-A	162	85	77	.525	5 E				82.5	2.5
1985	Bal-A	55	29	26	.527	4 E	4 E		1/3	29.3	-0.3
1991	Chi-N	1	0	1	.000	4 E	5 E	4 E	2/3	0.5	-0.5
	7	844	437	407	.518						5.8
Amalfitano, John Joseph "Joey"											
1979	Chi-N	7	2	5	.286	5 E	5 E		2/2	3.5	-1.5
1980	Chi-N	72	26	46	.361	6 E	6 E		2/2	30.7	-4.7
1981(1)	Chi-N	54	15	37	.288	6 E					
(2)	Chi-N	52	23	28	.451	5 E				39.5	-1.5
	3	185	66	116	.363						-7.8
Anderson, George Lee "Sparky"											
1970	Cin-N	162	102	60	.630	♦1 W				90.4	11.6
1971	Cin-N	162	79	83	.488	●4 W				81.6	-2.6
1972	Cin-N	154	95	59	.617	♦1 W				92.7	2.3
1973	Cin-N	162	99	63	.611	1 W				93.4	5.6
1974	Cin-N	163	98	64	.605	2 W				95.8	2.2
1975	Cin-N	162	108	54	.667	★1 W				106.7	1.3
1976	Cin-N	162	102	60	.630	★1 W				103.2	-1.2
1977	Cin-N	162	88	74	.543	2 W				88.5	-0.5
1978	Cin-N	161	92	69	.571	2 W				82.7	9.3
1979	Det-A	106	56	50	.528	5 E	5 E		3/3	55.1	0.9
1980	Det-A	163	84	78	.519	5 E				88.0	-4.0
1981(1)	Det-A	57	31	26	.544	4 E					
(2)	Det-A	52	29	23	.558	●2 E				57.0	3.0
1982	Det-A	162	83	79	.512	4 E				85.5	-2.5
1983	Det-A	162	92	70	.568	2 E				92.0	0.0
1984	Det-A	162	104	58	.642	★1 E				99.5	4.5
1985	Det-A	161	84	77	.522	3 E				84.6	-0.6
1986	Det-A	162	87	75	.537	3 E				89.2	-2.2
1987	Det-A	162	98	64	.605	1 E				96.2	1.8
1988	Det-A	162	88	74	.543	2 E				85.7	2.3
1989	Det-A	162	59	103	.364	7 E				60.9	-1.9
1990	Det-A	162	79	83	.488	3 E				80.6	-1.6
1991	Det-A	162	84	78	.519	●2 E				83.2	0.8
1992	Det-A	162	75	87	.463	6 E				80.7	-5.7
1993	Det-A	162	85	77	.525	●3 E				86.7	-1.7
1994	Det-A	115	53	62	.461	5 E				55.8	-2.8
1995	Det-A	144	60	84	.417	4 E				54.3	5.7
	26	4030	2194	1834	.545						23.9
Anson, Adrian Constantine "Cap"											
1875	Ath-n*	8	4	2	.667	2	2		2/2	4.9	-0.9
1879	Chi-N*	64	41	21	.661	2	4		1/2	32.9	8.1
1880	Chi-N*	86	67	17	.798	1				63.0	4.0
1881	Chi-N*	84	56	28	.667	1				57.4	-1.4
1882	Chi-N*	84	55	29	.655	1				64.3	-9.3
1883	Chi-N*	98	59	39	.602	2				60.8	-1.8
1884	Chi-N*	113	62	50	.554	●4				71.5	-9.5
1885	Chi-N*	113	87	25	.777	1				88.1	-1.1
1886	Chi-N*	126	90	34	.726	1				92.5	-2.5
1887	Chi-N*	127	71	50	.587	3				68.9	2.1
1888	Chi-N*	136	77	58	.570	2				74.5	2.5
1889	Chi-N*	136	67	65	.508	3				70.5	-3.5
1890	Chi-N*	139	84	53	.613	2				82.5	1.5
1891	Chi-N*	137	82	53	.607	2				76.6	5.4
1892(1)	Chi-N*	71	31	39	.443	8					
(2)	Chi-N*	76	39	37	.513	7				63.2	6.8
1893	Chi-N*	128	56	71	.441	9				59.8	-3.8
1894	Chi-N*	132	57	75	.432	8				64.2	-7.2
1895	Chi-N*	133	72	58	.554	4				66.0	6.0
1896	Chi-N*	132	71	57	.555	5				64.9	6.1
1897	Chi-N*	138	59	73	.447	9				60.7	-1.7
1898	NY-N	22	9	13	.409	6	7	7	2/3	11.5	-2.5
	21	2288	1296	947	.578						-2.9
Appling, Lucius Benjamin "Luke"											
1967	KC-A	40	10	30	.250	10	10		2/2	16.5	-6.5
Armour, William Clark "Bill"											
1902	Cle-A	137	69	67	.507	5				69.8	-0.8
1903	Cle-A	140	77	63	.550	3				76.1	0.9
1904	Cle-A	154	86	65	.570	4				93.8	-7.8
1905	Det-A	154	79	74	.516	3				66.2	12.8
1906	Det-A	151	71	78	.477	6				65.7	5.3
	5	736	382	347	.524						10.4
Aspromonte, Kenneth Joseph "Ken"											
1972	Cle-A	156	72	84	.462	5 E				72.4	-0.4
1973	Cle-A	162	71	91	.438	6 E				66.6	4.4
1974	Cle-A	162	77	85	.475	4 E				77.7	-0.7
	3	480	220	260	.458						3.3
Austin, James Philip "Jimmy"											
1913	StL-A*	8	2	6	.250	7	7	8	2/3	3.3	-1.3
1918	StL-A*	16	7	9	.438	6	6	5	2/3	7.7	-0.7
1923	StL-A*	51	22	29	.431	3	5		2/2	24.4	-2.4
	3	75	31	44	.413						-4.5
Baker, Delmer David "Del"											
1933	Det-A	2	2	0	1.000	5	5		2/2	1.0	1.0
1936	Det-A	34	18	16	.529	3	4	2	2/3	18.0	0.0
1937	Det-A	54	34	20	.630	3	3	2	2/5	29.9	4.1
	Det-A	10	7	3	.700	2	2	2	4/5	5.5	1.5
1938	Det-A	57	37	19	.661	5	4		2/2	30.2	6.8
1939	Det-A	155	81	73	.526	5				85.1	-4.1
1940	Det-A	155	90	64	.584	1				92.9	-2.9
1941	Det-A	155	75	79	.487	●4				71.4	3.6
1942	Det-A	156	73	81	.474	5				77.2	-4.2
1960	Bos-A	7	2	5	.286	8	8	7	2/3	3.0	-1.0
	9	785	419	360	.538						4.7
Baker, Johnnie B "Dusty"											
1993	SF-N	162	103	59	.636	2 W				98.3	4.7
1994	SF-N	115	55	60	.478	2 W				57.9	-2.9
1995	SF-N	144	67	77	.465	4 W				60.2	6.8
1996	SF-N	162	68	94	.420	4 W				70.5	-2.5
1997	SF-N	162	90	72	.556	○1 W				80.1	9.9
1998	SF-N	163	89	74	.546	▲2 W				91.7	-2.7
1999	SF-N	162	86	76	.531	2 W				84.8	1.2
2000	SF-N	162	97	65	.599	○1 W				97.6	-0.6
	8	1232	655	577	.532						13.8
Bamberger, George Irvin											
1978	Mil-A	162	93	69	.574	3 E				96.4	-3.4
1979	Mil-A	161	95	66	.590	2 E				88.8	6.2
1980	Mil-A	92	47	45	.511	2 E	4 E	3 E	2/3	53.2	-6.2
1982	NY-N	162	65	97	.401	6 E				69.1	-4.1
1983	NY-N	46	16	30	.348	6 E	6 E		1/2	19.8	-3.8
1985	Mil-A	161	71	90	.441	6 E				69.5	1.5
1986	Mil-A	152	71	81	.467	6 E	6 E		1/2	69.6	1.4
	7	936	458	478	.489						-8.3
Bancroft, David James "Dave"											
1924	Bos-N*	66	27	38	.415	6	8		1/3	20.4	6.6
	Bos-N*	50	15	35	.300	8	8		3/3	15.7	-0.7
1925	Bos-N*	153	70	83	.458	5				67.5	2.5

YEAR	TM/L	G	W	L	PCT	STANDING			M/YW-EXP		A-E
1926	Bos-N*	153	66	86	.434	7				66.4	-0.4
1927	Bos-N*	155	60	94	.390	7				65.1	-5.1
	4	577	238	336	.415						2.9
Bancroft, Frank Carter											
1880	Wor-N	85	40	43	.482	5				45.7	-5.7
1881	Det-N	84	41	43	.488	4				42.9	-1.9
1882	Det-N	86	42	41	.506	6				34.0	8.0
1883	Cle-N	100	55	42	.567	4				51.8	3.2
1884	Pro-N	114	84	28	.750	1				83.3	0.7
1885	Pro-N	110	53	57	.482	4				46.0	7.0
1887	Phi-a	55	26	29	.473	6	5		1/2	27.6	-1.6
1889	Ind-N	68	25	43	.368	7	7		1/2	30.8	-5.8
1902	Cin-N	16	9	7	.563	6	6	4	2/3	8.8	0.2
	9	718	375	333	.530						4.1
Barkley, Samuel E. "Sam"											
1888	KC-a*	58	21	36	.368	8	8	8	2/3	16.2	4.8
Barnie, William Harrison "Billy"											
1883	Bal-a*	96	28	68	.292	8				25.1	2.9
1884	Bal-a	109	63	43	.594	6				64.1	-1.1
1885	Bal-a	110	41	68	.376	8				41.7	-0.7
1886	Bal-a	139	48	83	.366	8				42.4	5.6
1887	Bal-a	141	77	58	.570	3				77.0	0.0
1888	Bal-a	139	57	80	.416	5				56.8	0.2
1889	Bal-a	139	70	65	.519	5				67.1	2.9
1890	Bal-a	38	15	19	.441	8				16.0	-1.0
1891	Bal-a	139	71	64	.526	3				72.0	-1.0
1892(1)	Was-N	2	0	2	.000	●11	7		1/2	0.8	-0.8
1893	Lou-N	126	50	75	.400	11				47.6	2.4
1894	Lou-N	131	36	94	.277	12				38.4	-2.4
1897	Bro-N	136	61	71	.462	●6				62.3	-1.3
1898	Bro-N	35	15	20	.429	9	10		1/3	13.5	1.5
	14	1480	632	810	.438						7.0
Barrow, Edward Grant "Ed"											
1903	Det-A	137	65	71	.478	5				71.0	-6.0
1904	Det-A	84	32	46	.410	7	7		1/2	31.9	0.1
1918	Bos-A	126	75	51	.595	★1				73.8	1.2
1919	Bos-A	138	66	71	.482	6				69.8	-3.8
1920	Bos-A	154	72	81	.471	5				71.6	0.4
	5	639	310	320	.492						-8.1
Barry, John Joseph "Jack"											
1917	Bos-A*	157	90	62	.592	2				87.8	2.2
Battin, Joseph V. "Joe"											
1883	Pit-a*	13	2	11	.154	7	7		3/3	4.2	-2.2
1884	Pit-a*	13	6	7	.462	11	10	10	3/5	2.9	3.1
	CP-U*	6	1	5	.167	5	5		2/3	2.7	-1.7
	2	32	9	23	.281						-0.9
Bauer, Henry Albert "Hank"											
1961	KC-A*	102	35	67	.343	8	●9		2/2	39.9	-4.9
1962	KC-A	162	72	90	.444	9				72.2	-0.2
1964	Bal-A	163	97	65	.599	3				93.2	3.8
1965	Bal-A	162	94	68	.580	3				87.9	6.1
1966	Bal-A	160	97	63	.606	★1				95.9	1.1
1967	Bal-A	161	76	85	.472	●6				87.2	-11.2
1968	Bal-A	80	43	37	.538	3	2		1/2	44.7	-1.7
1969	Oak-A	149	80	69	.537	2 W	2 W		1/2	80.3	-0.3
	8	1139	594	544	.522						-7.2
Baylor, Donald Edward "Don"											
1993	Col-N	162	67	95	.414	6 W				61.8	5.2
1994	Col-N	117	53	64	.453	3 W				52.4	0.6
1995	Col-N	144	77	67	.535	■2 W				72.2	4.8
1996	Col-N	162	82	79	.509	3 W				80.7	2.3
1997	Col-N	162	83	79	.512	3 W				82.3	0.7
1998	Col-N	162	77	85	.475	4 W				78.3	-1.3
2000	Chi-N	162	65	97	.401	6 C				67.9	-2.9
	7	1071	504	566	.471						9.3
Bell, David Gus "Buddy"											
1996	Det-A	162	53	109	.327	5 E				52.9	0.1
1997	Det-A	162	79	83	.488	3 E				80.4	-1.4
1998	Det-A	137	52	85	.380	5 C	5 C		1/2	57.1	-5.1
2000	Col-N	162	82	80	.506	4 W				87.3	-5.3
	4	623	266	357	.427						-11.6
Benson, Vernon Adair "Vern"											
1977	Atl-N	1	1	0	1.000	6 W	6 W	6 W	3/4	0.4	0.6
Berra, Lawrence Peter "Yogi"											
1964	NY-A	164	99	63	.611	1				97.3	1.7
1972	NY-N	156	83	73	.532	3 E				72.4	10.6
1973	NY-N	161	82	79	.509	♦1 E				82.7	-0.7
1974	NY-N	162	71	91	.438	5 E				72.9	-1.9
1975	NY-N	109	56	53	.514	3 E	●3 E		1/2	56.0	-0.0
1984	NY-A	162	87	75	.537	3 E				89.0	-2.0
1985	NY-A	16	6	10	.375	7 E	2 E		1/2	9.7	-3.7
	7	930	484	444	.522						4.0
Bevington, Terry Paul											
1995	Chi-A	113	57	56	.504	4 C	3 C		2/2	56.3	0.7
1996	Chi-A	162	85	77	.525	2 C				90.7	-5.7
1997	Chi-A	161	80	81	.497	2 C				75.4	4.6
	3	436	222	214	.509						-0.3
Bezdek, Hugo Frank											
1917	Pit-N	91	30	59	.337	8	8		3/3	35.8	-5.8
1918	Pit-N	126	65	60	.520	4				68.6	-3.6
1919	Pit-N	139	71	68	.511	4				70.2	0.8
	3	356	166	187	.470						-8.6
Bickerson											
1884	Was-a	1	0	1	.000	12	12		2/2	0.2	-0.2
Birmingham, Joseph Leo "Joe"											
1912	Cle-A*	28	21	7	.750	6	5		2/2	13.9	7.1
1913	Cle-A*	155	86	66	.566	3				86.6	-0.6
1914	Cle-A*	157	51	102	.333	8				58.3	-7.3
1915	Cle-A	28	12	16	.429	6	7		1/2	11.4	0.6
	4	368	170	191	.471						-0.2
Bissonette, Adelphia Louis "Del"											
1945	Bos-N	60	25	34	.424	7	6		2/2	29.2	-4.2
Blackburne, Russell Aubrey "Lena"											
1928	Chi-A	80	40	40	.500	6	5		2/2	36.4	3.6
1929	Chi-A*	152	59	93	.388	7				59.8	-0.8
	2	232	99	133	.427						2.8
Blades, Francis Raymond "Ray"											
1939	StL-N	155	92	61	.601	2				91.0	1.0
1940	StL-N	39	14	24	.368	6	3		1/3	20.2	-6.2
1948	Bro-N	1	1	0	1.000	5	5	3	2/3	0.5	0.5
	3	195	107	85	.557						-4.7
Blair, Walter Allen "Walter"											
1915	Buf-F*	2	1	1	.500	8	8	6	2/3	0.9	0.1
Bluege, Oswald Louis "Ossie"											
1943	Was-A	153	84	69	.549	2				83.9	0.1
1944	Was-A	154	64	90	.416	8				69.4	-5.4
1945	Was-A	156	87	67	.565	2				83.5	3.5
1946	Was-A	155	76	78	.494	4				66.9	9.1
1947	Was-A	154	64	90	.416	7				57.5	6.5
	5	772	375	394	.488						13.7
Bochy, Bruce Douglas											
1995	SD-N	144	70	74	.486	3 W				71.6	-1.6
1996	SD-N	162	91	71	.562	○1 W				89.9	1.1
1997	SD-N	162	76	86	.469	4 W				72.1	3.9
1998	SD-N	162	98	64	.605	♦1 W				92.7	5.3
1999	SD-N	162	74	88	.457	4 W				74.0	0.0
2000	SD-N	162	76	86	.469	5 W				74.9	1.1
	6	954	485	469	.508						9.8
Boles, John											
1996	Fla-N	75	40	35	.533	4 E	3 E		3/3	36.8	3.2
1999	Fla-N	162	64	98	.395	5 E				65.3	-1.3
2000	Fla-N	161	79	82	.491	3 E				74.1	4.9
	3	398	183	215	.460						6.8
Bond, Thomas Henry "Tommy"											
1882	Wor-N*	6	2	4	.333	8	8	8	2/3	1.3	0.7
Boone, Robert Raymond "Bob"											
1995	KC-A	144	70	74	.486	2 C				65.9	4.1
1996	KC-A	161	75	86	.466	5 C				76.6	-1.6
1997	KC-A	82	36	46	.439	4 C	5 C		1/2	37.4	-1.4
	3	387	181	206	.468						1.1
Boros, Stephen "Steve"											
1983	Oak-A	162	74	88	.457	4 W				73.7	0.3
1984	Oak-A	44	20	24	.455	5 W	4 W		1/2	20.5	-0.5
1986	SD-N	162	74	88	.457	4 W				74.1	-0.1
	3	368	168	200	.457						-0.3
Bottomley, James Leroy "Jim"											
1937	StL-A*	78	21	56	.273	7	8		2/2	24.7	-3.7
Boudreau, Louis "Lou"											
1942	Cle-A*	156	75	79	.487	4				69.7	5.3
1943	Cle-A*	153	82	71	.536	3				79.0	3.0
1944	Cle-A*	155	72	82	.468	●5				73.5	-1.5
1945	Cle-A*	147	73	72	.503	5				73.5	-0.5
1946	Cle-A*	156	68	86	.442	6				66.0	2.0
1947	Cle-A*	157	80	74	.519	4				87.4	-7.4
1948	Cle-A*	156	97	58	.626	▲★1				104.7	-7.7
1949	Cle-A*	154	89	65	.578	3				87.6	1.4
1950	Cle-A*	155	92	62	.597	4				91.9	0.1
1952	Bos-A*	154	76	78	.494	6				78.0	-2.0
1953	Bos-A	153	84	69	.549	4				79.0	5.0
1954	Bos-A	156	69	85	.448	4				74.2	-5.2
1955	KC-A	155	63	91	.409	6				51.1	11.9
1956	KC-A	154	52	102	.338	8				56.3	-4.3
1957	KC-A	104	36	67	.350	8	7		1/2	41.2	-5.2
1960	Chi-N	139	54	83	.394	7	7		2/2	55.9	-1.9
	16	2404	1162	1224	.487						-6.9
Bowa, Lawrence Robert "Larry"											
1987	SD-N	162	65	97	.401	6 W				71.4	-6.4
1988	SD-N	46	16	30	.348	5 W	3 W		1/2	23.3	-7.3
	2	208	81	127	.389						-13.8

YEAR	TM/L	G	W	L	PCT	STANDING			M/Y	W-EXP	A-E
Bowerman, Frank Eugene "Frank"											
1909	Bos-N*	76	22	54	.289	8	8		1/2	24.2	-2.2
Boyd, William J. "Bill"											
1875	Atl-n*	2	0	2	.000	12	12		2/2	-0.2	0.2
Boyer, Kenton Lloyd "Ken"											
1978	StL-N	143	62	81	.434	6 E	5 E		3/3	66.1	-4.1
1979	StL-N	163	86	76	.531	3 E				84.9	1.1
1980	StL-N	51	18	33	.353	6 E	4 E		1/4	26.4	-8.4
	3	357	166	190	.466						-11.3
Bradley, William Joseph "Bill"											
1905	Cle-A*	41	20	21	.488	●1	2	5	2/3	19.8	0.2
1914	Bro-F*	157	77	77	.500	5				75.5	1.5
	2	198	97	98	.497						1.7
Bragan, Robert Randall "Bobby"											
1956	Pit-N	157	66	88	.429	7				70.1	-4.1
1957	Pit-N	104	36	67	.350	7	●7		1/2	43.8	-7.8
1958	Cle-A	67	31	36	.463	6	4		1/2	36.1	-5.1
1963	Mil-N	163	84	78	.519	6				88.9	-4.9
1964	Mil-N	162	88	74	.543	5				86.7	1.3
1965	Mil-N	162	86	76	.531	5				88.8	-2.8
1966	Atl-N	112	52	59	.468	7	5		1/2	62.3	-10.3
	7	927	443	478	.481						-33.8
Bresnahan, Roger Philip											
1909	StL-N*	154	54	98	.355	7				60.8	-6.8
1910	StL-N*	153	63	90	.412	7				68.5	-5.5
1911	StL-N*	158	75	74	.503	5				67.1	7.9
1912	StL-N*	153	63	90	.412	6				60.1	2.9
1915	Chi-N*	157	73	80	.477	4				71.1	1.9
	5	775	328	432	.432						0.5
Bristol, James David "Dave"											
1966	Cin-N	77	39	38	.506	8	7		2/2	38.0	1.0
1967	Cin-N	162	87	75	.537	4				85.6	1.4
1968	Cin-N	163	83	79	.512	4				82.8	0.2
1969	Cin-N	163	89	73	.549	3 W				83.9	5.1
1970	Mil-A	163	65	97	.401	●4 W				66.7	-1.7
1971	Mil-A	161	69	92	.429	6 W				72.1	-3.1
1972	Mil-A	30	10	20	.333	6 E	6 E		1/3	12.8	-2.8
1976	Atl-N	162	70	92	.432	6 W				72.6	-2.6
1977	Atl-N	29	8	21	.276	6 W	6 W		1/4	10.8	-2.8
	Atl-N	131	52	79	.397	6 W	6 W		4/4	48.6	3.4
1979	SF-N	22	10	12	.455	4 W	4 W		2/2	9.9	0.1
1980	SF-N	161	75	86	.466	5 W				73.8	1.2
	11	1424	657	764	.462						-0.5
Brown, Freeman											
1882	Wor-N	41	9	32	.220	8	8		1/3	9.1	-0.1
Brown, Mordecai Peter Centennial "Three Finger"											
1914	StL-F*	114	50	63	.442	7	8		1/2	46.1	3.9
Brown, Thomas T. "Tom"											
1897	Was-N*	99	52	46	.531	11	●6		2/2	48.2	3.8
1898	Was-N*	38	12	26	.316	11	11		1/4	13.6	-1.6
	2	137	64	72	.471						2.2
Brucker, Earle Francis Sr											
1952	Cin-N	5	3	2	.600	7	7	6	2/3	2.4	0.6
Buckenberger, Albert C. "Al"											
1889	Col-a	140	60	78	.435	6				56.5	3.5
1890	Col-a	80	39	41	.488	5	2		1/3	51.9	-12.9
1892(1)	Pit-N	29	15	14	.517	7	6		1/2		
(2)	Pit-N	66	38	27	.585	10	4		2/2	47.3	5.7
1893	Pit-N	131	81	48	.628	2				81.3	-0.3
1894	Pit-N	110	53	55	.491	7	7		1/2	51.7	1.3
1895	StL-N	50	16	34	.320	11	11		1/4	16.0	-0.0
1902	Bos-N	142	73	64	.533	3				74.6	-1.6
1903	Bos-N	140	58	80	.420	6				57.0	1.0
1904	Bos-N	155	55	98	.359	7				49.1	5.9
	9	1043	488	539	.475						2.5
Buffinton, Charles G. "Charlie"											
1890	Phi-P*	116	61	54	.530	5	5		2/2	63.6	-2.6
Burdock, John Joseph "Jack"											
1883	Bos-N*	54	30	24	.556	4	1		1/2	37.4	-7.4
Burke, James Timothy "Jimmy"											
1905	StL-N*	90	34	56	.378	7	6	6	2/3	32.8	1.2
1918	StL-A	61	29	31	.483	6	5		3/3	28.8	0.2
1919	StL-A	140	67	72	.482	5				65.9	1.1
1920	StL-A	154	76	77	.497	4				79.4	-3.4
	4	445	206	236	.466						-0.9
Burnham, George Walter "Watch"											
1887	Ind-N	28	6	22	.214	8	8		1/3	7.7	-1.7
Burns, Thomas Everett "Tom"											
1892(1)	Pit-N*	47	22	25	.468	7	6		2/2		
(2)	Pit-N*	13	5	7	.417	10	4		1/2	29.7	-2.7
1898	Chi-N	152	85	65	.567	4				89.2	-4.2
1899	Chi-N	152	75	73	.507	8				78.6	-3.6
	3	364	187	170	.524						-10.5
Burwell, William Edwin "Bill"											
1947	Pit-N	1	1	0	1.000	8	●7		2/2	0.5	0.5
Bush, Owen Joseph "Donie"											
1923	Was-A*	155	75	78	.490	4				73.9	1.1
1927	Pit-N	156	94	60	.610	1				92.4	1.6
1928	Pit-N	152	85	67	.559	4				88.5	-3.5
1929	Pit-N	119	67	51	.568	2	2		1/2	67.7	-0.7
1930	Chi-A	154	62	92	.403	7				62.6	-0.6
1931	Chi-A	156	56	97	.366	8				54.8	1.2
1933	Cin-N	153	58	94	.382	8				59.8	-1.8
	7	1045	497	539	.480						-2.7
Butler, Ormond Hook											
1883	Pit-a	53	17	36	.321	6	6	7	2/3	17.3	-0.3
Byrne, Charles H. "Charlie"											
1885	Bro-a	75	38	37	.507	7	●5		2/2	36.0	2.0
1886	Bro-a	141	76	61	.555	3				68.5	7.5
1887	Bro-a	138	60	74	.448	6				65.8	-5.8
	3	354	174	172	.503						3.7
Callahan, James Joseph "Jim"											
1903	Chi-A*	138	60	77	.438	7				58.3	1.7
1904	Chi-A*	42	23	18	.561	4	3		1/2	24.1	-1.1
1912	Chi-A*	158	78	76	.506	4				76.1	1.9
1913	Chi-A*	153	78	74	.513	5				74.8	3.2
1914	Chi-A	157	70	84	.455	●6				68.5	1.5
1916	Pit-N	157	65	89	.422	6				65.3	-0.3
1917	Pit-N	61	20	40	.333	8	8		1/3	24.1	-4.1
	7	866	394	458	.462						2.8
Campau, Charles Columbus "Count"											
1890	StL-a*	42	27	14	.659	5	2	3	4/6	24.1	2.9
Cantillon, Joseph D. "Joe"											
1907	Was-A	154	49	102	.325	8				55.4	-6.4
1908	Was-A	155	67	85	.441	7				69.0	-2.0
1909	Was-A	156	42	110	.276	8				43.9	-1.9
	3	465	158	297	.347						-10.2
Carey, Max George											
1932	Bro-N	154	81	73	.526	3				77.5	3.5
1933	Bro-N	157	65	88	.425	6				68.4	-3.4
	2	311	146	161	.476						0.1
Carey, Thomas John "Tom"											
1873	Bal-n*	24	14	9	.609	3	3		2/2	16.9	-2.9
1874	Mut-n*	25	13	12	.520	3	2		1/2	16.4	-3.4
	2	49	27	21	.563						-6.3
Carrigan, William Francis "Bill"											
1913	Bos-A*	70	40	30	.571	5	4		2/2	36.0	4.0
1914	Bos-A*	159	91	62	.595	2				85.5	5.5
1915	Bos-A*	155	101	50	.669	★1				94.1	6.9
1916	Bos-A*	156	91	63	.591	★1				85.2	5.8
1927	Bos-A	154	51	103	.331	8				51.7	-0.7
1928	Bos-A	154	57	96	.373	8				58.2	-1.2
1929	Bos-A	155	58	96	.377	8				57.3	0.7
	7	1003	489	500	.494						21.0
Caruthers, Robert Lee "Bob"											
1892(2)	StL-N*	50	16	32	.333	12	11		3/3	17.5	-1.5
Cavarretta, Philip Joseph "Phil"											
1951	Chi-N*	74	27	47	.365	7	8		2/2	30.4	-3.4
1952	Chi-N*	155	77	77	.500	5				76.7	0.3
1953	Chi-N*	155	65	89	.422	7				57.3	7.7
	3	384	169	213	.442						4.6
Caylor, Oliver Perry "O.P."											
1885	Cin-a	112	63	49	.563	2				62.1	0.9
1886	Cin-a	141	65	73	.471	5				70.5	-5.5
1887	NY-a	100	35	60	.368	7	7		3/3	27.6	7.4
	3	353	163	182	.472						2.7
Chance, Frank Leroy											
1905	Chi-N*	90	55	33	.625	4	3		2/2	58.5	-3.5
1906	Chi-N*	155	116	36	.763	1				112.6	3.4
1907	Chi-N*	155	107	45	.704	★1				98.1	8.9
1908	Chi-N*	158	99	55	.643	★1				95.7	3.3
1909	Chi-N*	155	104	49	.680	2				105.1	-1.1
1910	Chi-N*	154	104	50	.675	1				99.8	4.2
1911	Chi-N*	158	92	62	.597	2				92.3	-0.3
1912	Chi-N*	153	91	59	.607	3				83.6	7.4
1913	NY-A*	153	57	94	.377	7				60.6	-3.6
1914	NY-A*	137	60	74	.448	7	●6		1/2	65.7	-5.7
1923	Bos-A	154	61	91	.401	8				53.6	7.4
	11	1622	946	648	.593						20.4
Chapman, John Curtis "Jack"											
1876	Lou-N*	69	30	36	.455	5				26.6	3.4
1877	Lou-N	61	35	25	.583	2				34.8	0.2
1878	Mil-N	61	15	45	.250	6				18.0	-3.0
1882	Wor-N	37	7	30	.189	8	8		3/3	8.2	-1.2
1883	Det-N	101	40	58	.408	7				37.9	2.1
1884	Det-N	114	28	84	.250	8				28.9	-0.9
1885	Buf-N	88	31	57	.352	7	7		2/4	25.3	5.7
1889	Lou-a	7	1	6	.143	8	8		4/4	1.5	-0.5

YEAR	TM/L	G	W	L	PCT	STANDING			M/YW-EXP		A-E
1890	Lou-a	136	88	44	.667	1				87.5	0.5
1891	Lou-a	139	54	83	.394	7				52.9	1.1
1892(1)	Lou-N	54	21	33	.389	10	11		1/2	21.5	-0.5
	11	867	350	501	.411						7.0
Chapman, William Benjamin "Ben"											
1945	Phi-N*	85	28	57	.329	8	8		2/2	25.2	2.8
1946	Phi-N*	155	69	85	.448	5				61.8	7.2
1947	Phi-N	155	62	92	.403	●7				66.8	-4.8
1948	Phi-N	79	37	42	.468	7	6		1/3	32.3	4.7
	4	474	196	276	.415						10.0
Chase, Harold Homer "Hal"											
1910	NY-A*	14	10	4	.714	3	2		2/2	7.7	2.3
1911	NY-A*	153	76	76	.500	6				72.1	3.9
	2	167	86	80	.518						6.2
Clapp, John Edgar											
1872	Man-n*	24	5	19	.208	8				4.1	0.9
1878	Ind-N*	63	24	36	.400	5				26.7	-2.7
1879	Buf-N*	79	46	32	.590	3				41.8	4.2
1880	Cin-N*	82	21	59	.262	8				22.6	-1.6
1881	Cle-N*	74	32	41	.438	6	7		2/2	34.6	-2.6
1883	NY-N*	98	46	50	.479	6				43.8	2.2
	6	420	174	237	.423						0.3
Clarke, Fred Clifford											
1897	Lou-N*	92	35	54	.393	9	11		2/2	32.7	2.3
1898	Lou-N*	154	70	81	.464	9				65.6	4.4
1899	Lou-N*	156	75	76	.497	9				80.3	-5.3
1900	Pit-N*	140	79	60	.568	2				81.2	-2.2
1901	Pit-N*	140	90	49	.647	1				93.2	-3.2
1902	Pit-N*	142	103	36	.741	1				103.9	-0.9
1903	Pit-N*	141	91	49	.650	1				87.1	3.9
1904	Pit-N*	156	87	66	.569	4				85.2	1.8
1905	Pit-N*	155	96	57	.627	2				89.3	6.7
1906	Pit-N*	154	93	60	.608	3				93.7	-0.7
1907	Pit-N*	157	91	63	.591	2				90.8	0.2
1908	Pit-N*	155	98	56	.636	●2				90.5	7.5
1909	Pit-N*	154	110	42	.724	★1				103.7	6.3
1910	Pit-N*	154	86	67	.562	3				84.9	1.1
1911	Pit-N*	156	85	69	.552	3				96.4	-11.4
1912	Pit-N	153	93	58	.616	2				94.5	-1.5
1913	Pit-N*	155	78	71	.523	4				83.8	-5.8
1914	Pit-N*	158	69	85	.448	7				72.7	-3.7
1915	Pit-N*	157	73	81	.474	5				81.2	-8.2
	19	2829	1602	1180	.576						-8.6
Clements, John J. "Jack"											
1890	Phi-N*	19	13	6	.684	1	2	3	2/5	11.0	2.0
Cobb, Tyrus Raymond "Ty"											
1921	Det-A*	154	71	82	.464	6				79.3	-8.3
1922	Det-A*	155	79	75	.513	3				80.4	-1.4
1923	Det-A*	155	83	71	.539	2				85.5	-2.5
1924	Det-A*	156	86	68	.558	3				81.9	4.1
1925	Det-A*	156	81	73	.526	4				83.7	-2.7
1926	Det-A*	157	79	75	.513	6				73.5	5.5
	6	933	479	444	.519						-5.3
Cochrane, Gordon Stanley "Mickey"											
1934	Det-A*	154	101	53	.656	1				99.8	1.2
1935	Det-A*	152	93	58	.616	★1				99.1	-6.1
1936	Det-A*	53	29	24	.547	3	2		1/3	28.0	1.0
	Det-A*	67	36	31	.537	4	2		3/3	35.4	0.6
1937	Det-A*	29	16	13	.552	3	2		1/5	16.1	-0.1
	Det-A*	47	26	20	.565	3	2	2	3/5	25.5	0.5
1938	Det-A	98	47	51	.480	5	4		1/2	52.9	-5.9
	5	600	348	250	.582						-8.8
Cohen, Andrew Howard "Andy"											
1960	Phi-N	1	1	0	1.000	●6	●4	8	2/3	0.4	0.6
Coleman, Gerald Francis "Jerry"											
1980	SD-N	163	73	89	.451	6 W				74.2	-1.2
Coleman, Robert Hunter "Bob"											
1943	Bos-N	46	21	25	.457	6	6		1/2	18.0	3.0
1944	Bos-N	155	65	89	.422	6				68.5	-3.5
1945	Bos-N	94	42	51	.452	7	6		1/2	46.1	-4.1
	3	295	128	165	.437						-4.6
Collins, Edward Trowbridge Sr. "Eddie"											
1924	Chi-A*	27	14	13	.519	6			3/4	12.4	1.6
1925	Chi-A*	154	79	75	.513	5				80.8	-1.8
1926	Chi-A*	155	81	72	.529	5				83.0	-2.0
	3	336	174	160	.521						-2.3
Collins, James Joseph "Jimmy"											
1901	Bos-A*	138	79	57	.581	2				82.4	-3.4
1902	Bos-A*	138	77	60	.562	3				74.8	2.2
1903	Bos-A*	141	91	47	.659	★1				89.9	1.1
1904	Bos-A*	157	95	59	.617	1				93.3	1.7
1905	Bos-A*	153	78	74	.513	4				77.5	0.5
1906	Bos-A*	115	35	79	.307	8	8		1/2	37.3	-2.3
	6	842	455	376	.548						-0.3

YEAR	TM/L	G	W	L	PCT	STANDING			M/YW-EXP		A-E
Collins, John Francis "Shano"											
1931	Bos-A	153	62	90	.408	6				58.8	3.2
1932	Bos-A	55	11	44	.200	8	8		1/2	15.4	-4.4
	2	208	73	134	.353						-1.2
Collins, Terry Lee											
1994	Hou-N	115	66	49	.574	2 C				67.1	-1.1
1995	Hou-N	144	76	68	.528	2 C				79.0	-3.0
1996	Hou-N	162	82	80	.506	2 C				77.2	4.8
1997	Ana-A	162	84	78	.519	2 W				84.3	-0.3
1998	Ana-A	162	85	77	.525	2 W				81.4	3.6
1999	Ana-A	133	51	82	.383	4 W	4 W		1/2	57.3	-6.3
	6	878	444	434	.506						-2.3
Comiskey, Charles Albert "Charlie"											
1883	StL-a*	19	12	7	.632	2	2		2/2	12.1	-0.1
1884	StL-a*	25	16	7	.696	5	4		2/2	13.8	2.2
1885	StL-a*	112	79	33	.705	1				76.3	2.7
1886	StL-a*	139	93	46	.669	1				101.3	-8.3
1887	StL-a*	138	95	40	.704	1				97.5	-2.5
1888	StL-a*	137	92	43	.681	1				95.7	-3.7
1889	StL-a*	141	89	46	.659	2				91.9	-1.9
1890	Chi-P*	138	75	62	.547	4				78.5	-3.5
1891	StL-a*	139	85	51	.625	2				87.0	-2.0
1892(1)	Cin-N*	77	44	31	.587	4					
(2)	Cin-N*	78	38	37	.507	8				78.4	3.6
1893	Cin-N*	131	65	63	.508	●6				59.2	5.8
1894	Cin-N*	134	55	75	.423	10				51.8	3.2
	12	1408	838	541	.608						-4.5
Connor, Roger											
1896	StL-N*	46	8	37	.178	11	11	11	4/5	12.3	-4.3
Cooke, Allen Lindsey "Dusty"											
1948	Phi-N	13	6	6	.500	7	6	6	2/3	4.9	1.1
Coombs, John Wesley "Jack"											
1919	Phi-N	63	18	44	.290	8	8		1/2	22.3	-4.3
Cooney, John Walter "Johnny"											
1949	Bos-N	46	20	25	.444	4	4		2/2	22.1	-2.1
Corrales, Patrick "Pat"											
1978	Tex-A	1	1	0	1.000	●2 W	●2 W		2/2	0.5	0.5
1979	Tex-A	162	83	79	.512	3 W				86.2	-3.2
1980	Tex-A	163	76	85	.472	4 W				80.9	-4.9
1982	Phi-N	162	89	73	.549	2 E				82.1	6.9
1983	Phi-N	86	43	42	.506	1 E	♦1 E		1/2	45.9	-2.9
	Cle-A	62	30	32	.484	7 E	7 E		2/2	27.9	2.1
1984	Cle-A	163	75	87	.463	6 E				80.5	-5.5
1985	Cle-A	162	60	102	.370	7 E				68.4	-8.4
1986	Cle-A	163	84	78	.519	5 E				80.1	3.9
1987	Cle-A	87	31	56	.356	7 E	7 E		1/2	32.8	-1.8
	9	1211	572	634	.474						-13.2
Corriden, John Michael Sr. "Red"											
1950	Chi-A	125	52	72	.419	8	6		2/2	51.9	0.1
Cottier, Charles Keith "Chuck"											
1984	Sea-A	27	15	12	.556	7 W	●5 W		2/2	12.0	3.0
1985	Sea-A	162	74	88	.457	6 W				71.4	2.6
1986	Sea-A	28	9	19	.321	6 W	7 W		1/3	12.0	-3.0
	3	217	98	119	.452						2.6
Cox, Robert Joseph "Bobby"											
1978	Atl-N	162	69	93	.426	6 W				65.4	3.6
1979	Atl-N	160	66	94	.412	6 W				70.6	-4.6
1980	Atl-N	161	81	80	.503	4 W				77.3	3.7
1981(1)	Atl-N	55	25	29	.463	4 W					
(2)	Atl-N	52	25	27	.481	5 W				50.7	-0.7
1982	Tor-A	162	78	84	.481	●6 E				75.8	2.2
1983	Tor-A	162	89	73	.549	4 E				87.8	1.2
1984	Tor-A	163	89	73	.549	2 E				86.4	2.6
1985	Tor-A	161	99	62	.615	1 E				98.2	0.8
1990	Atl-N	97	40	57	.412	6 W	6 W		2/2	40.3	-0.3
1991	Atl-N	162	94	68	.580	♦1 W				91.7	2.3
1992	Atl-N	162	98	64	.605	♦1 W				93.2	4.8
1993	Atl-N	162	104	58	.642	1 W				102.8	1.2
1994	Atl-N	114	68	46	.596	2 E				66.6	1.4
1995	Atl-N	144	90	54	.625	★1 E				83.0	7.0
1996	Atl-N	162	96	66	.593	♦1 E				93.7	2.3
1997	Atl-N	162	101	61	.623	1 E				102.7	-1.7
1998	Atl-N	162	106	56	.654	1 E				105.9	0.1
1999	Atl-N	162	103	59	.636	♦1 E				98.6	4.4
2000	Atl-N	162	95	67	.586	○1 E				90.4	4.6
	19	2889	1616	1271	.560						34.8
Craft, Harry Francis											
1957	KC-A	50	23	27	.460	8	7		2/2	20.0	3.0
1958	KC-A	156	73	81	.474	7				69.8	3.2
1959	KC-A	154	66	88	.429	7				69.3	-3.3
1961	Chi-N	12	4	8	.333	●6	7	7	2/9	5.2	-1.2
	Chi-N	4	3	1	.750	7	7	7	5/9	1.7	1.3
1962	Hou-N	162	64	96	.400	8				66.8	-2.8
1963	Hou-N	162	66	96	.407	9				60.8	5.2
1964	Hou-N	149	61	88	.409	9	9		1/2	60.6	0.4
	7	849	360	485	.426						6.0

YEAR	TM/L	G	W	L	PCT	STANDING			M/YW-EXP		A-E
Craig, Roger Lee											
1978	SD-N	162	84	78	.519	4 W				80.2	3.8
1979	SD-N	161	68	93	.422	5 W				72.2	-4.2
1985	SF-N	18	6	12	.333	6 W	6 W		2/2	7.6	-1.6
1986	SF-N	162	83	79	.512	3 W				89.4	-6.4
1987	SF-N	162	90	72	.556	1 W				92.4	-2.4
1988	SF-N	162	83	79	.512	4 W				85.7	-2.7
1989	SF-N	162	92	70	.568	♦1 W				91.5	0.5
1990	SF-N	162	85	77	.525	3 W				81.9	3.1
1991	SF-N	162	75	87	.463	4 W				76.0	-1.0
1992	SF-N	162	72	90	.444	5 W				73.0	-1.0
	10	1475	738	737	.500						-11.9
Crandall, Delmar Wesley "Del"											
1972	Mil-A	124	54	70	.435	6 E	6 E		3/3	52.8	1.2
1973	Mil-A	162	74	88	.457	5 E				78.7	-4.7
1974	Mil-A	162	76	86	.469	5 E				79.6	-3.6
1975	Mil-A	161	67	94	.416	5 E	5 E		1/2	68.9	-1.9
1983	Sea-A	89	34	55	.382	7 W	7 W		2/2	33.9	0.1
1984	Sea-A	135	59	76	.437	7 W	●5 W		1/2	59.8	-0.8
	6	833	364	469	.437						-9.7
Crane, Samuel Newhall "Sam"											
1880	Buf-N*	84	24	58	.293	7				24.6	-0.6
1884	Cin-U*	70	49	21	.700	5	3		2/2	49.2	-0.2
	2	154	73	79	.480						-0.8
Cravath, Clifford Carlton "Gavvy"											
1919	Phi-N*	75	29	46	.387	8	8		2/2	27.0	2.0
1920	Phi-N*	153	62	91	.405	8				61.0	1.0
	2	228	91	137	.399						2.9
Craver, William H. "Bill"											
1871	Tro-n*	25	12	12	.500	7	6		2/2	11.4	0.6
1872	Bal-n*	41	27	13	.675	2	2		1/2	29.6	-2.6
1875	Cen-n*	14	2	12	.143	11				1.7	0.3
1876	NY-N*	57	21	35	.375	6				14.7	6.3
	4	137	62	72	.463						4.6
Creamer, George W.											
1884	Pit-a*	8	0	8	.000	10	10	10	4/5	1.8	-1.8
Cronin, Joseph Edward "Joe"											
1933	Was-A*	153	99	53	.651	1				93.6	5.4
1934	Was-A*	155	66	86	.434	7				68.7	-2.7
1935	Bos-A*	154	78	75	.510	4				75.1	2.9
1936	Bos-A*	155	74	80	.481	6				78.0	-4.0
1937	Bos-A*	154	80	72	.526	5				80.3	-0.3
1938	Bos-A*	150	88	61	.591	2				88.1	-0.1
1939	Bos-A*	152	89	62	.589	2				84.1	4.9
1940	Bos-A*	154	82	72	.532	●4				81.2	0.8
1941	Bos-A*	155	84	70	.545	2				87.7	-3.7
1942	Bos-A*	152	93	59	.612	2				92.8	0.2
1943	Bos-A*	155	68	84	.447	7				71.2	-3.2
1944	Bos-A*	156	77	77	.500	4				83.3	-6.3
1945	Bos-A*	157	71	83	.461	7				69.1	1.9
1946	Bos-A	156	104	50	.675	1				96.9	7.1
1947	Bos-A	157	83	71	.539	3				82.1	0.9
	15	2315	1236	1055	.540						3.7
Crooks, John Charles											
1892(1)	StL-N*	47	24	22	.522	11	9		3/3		
(2)	StL-N*	15	3	11	.214	12	11		1/3	21.9	5.1
Cross, Lafayette Napoleon "Lave"											
1899	Cle-N*	38	8	30	.211	12	12		1/2	3.3	4.7
Cubbage, Michael Lee "Mike"											
1991	NY-N	7	3	4	.429	3 E	5 E		2/2	3.5	-0.5
Curtis, Edwin R. "Ed"											
1884	Alt-U	25	6	19	.240	6				1.7	4.3
Cushman, Charles H. "Charlie"											
1891	Mil-a	36	21	15	.583	5				24.5	-3.5
Cuthbert, Edgar Edward "Ned"											
1882	StL-a*	80	37	43	.463	5				31.3	5.7
Dahlen, William Frederick "Bill"											
1910	Bro-N*	156	64	90	.416	6				62.9	1.1
1911	Bro-N*	154	64	86	.427	7				62.1	1.9
1912	Bro-N	153	58	95	.379	7				67.3	-9.3
1913	Bro-N	152	65	84	.436	6				72.6	-7.6
	4	615	251	355	.414						-13.8
Dark, Alvin Ralph											
1961	SF-N	155	85	69	.552	3				88.7	-3.7
1962	SF-N	165	103	62	.624	▲1				100.8	2.2
1963	SF-N	162	88	74	.543	3				89.7	-1.7
1964	SF-N	162	90	72	.556	4				88.5	1.5
1966	KC-A	160	74	86	.463	7				70.8	3.2
1967	KC-A	121	52	69	.430	10	10		1/2	50.0	2.0
1968	Cle-A	162	86	75	.534	3				81.9	4.1
1969	Cle-A	161	62	99	.385	6 E				65.2	-3.2
1970	Cle-A	162	76	86	.469	5 E				78.3	-2.3
1971	Cle-A	103	42	61	.408	6 E	6 E		1/2	37.7	4.3
1974	Oak-A	162	90	72	.556	★1 W				96.0	-6.0
1975	Oak-A	162	98	64	.605	1 W				96.7	1.3

YEAR	TM/L	G	W	L	PCT	STANDING			M/YW-EXP		A-E
1977	SD-N	113	48	65	.425	4 W	5 W		3/3	46.8	1.2
	13	1950	994	954	.510						2.9
Davenport, James Houston "Jim"											
1985	SF-N	144	56	88	.389	6 W	6 W		1/2	60.6	-4.6
Davidson, Mordecai H.											
1888	Lou-a	3	1	2	.333	8	8	7	2/4	1.1	-0.1
	Lou-a	90	34	52	.395	8	7		4/4	32.7	1.3
Davis, George Stacey											
1895	NY-N*	33	16	17	.485	8	9		1/3	16.9	-0.9
1900	NY-N*	78	39	37	.513	8	8		2/2	32.5	6.5
1901	NY-N*	141	52	85	.380	7				47.6	4.4
	3	252	107	139	.435						10.0
Davis, Harry H											
1912	Cle-A*	127	54	71	.432	6	5		1/2	62.2	-8.2
Davis, Virgil Lawrence "Spud"											
1946	Pit-N	3	1	2	.333	7	7		2/2	1.3	-0.3
Day, John B.											
1899	NY-N	66	29	35	.453	9	10		1/2	27.0	2.0
Deane, John Henry "Harry"											
1871	Kek-n*	5	2	3	.400	7	8		2/2	0.6	1.4
Dent, Russell Earl "Bucky"											
1989	NY-A	40	18	22	.450	6 E	5 E		2/2	17.7	0.3
1990	NY-A	49	18	31	.367	7 E	7 E		1/2	19.9	-1.9
	2	89	36	53	.404						-1.6
Dickey, William Malcolm "Bill"											
1946	NY-A*	105	57	48	.543	2	3	3	2/3	62.4	-5.4
Diddlebock, Henry H. "Harry"											
1896	StL-N	17	7	10	.412	10	11		1/5	4.6	2.4
Dierker, Lawrence Edward "Larry"											
1997	Hou-N	162	84	78	.519	○1 C				92.8	-8.8
1998	Hou-N	162	102	60	.630	○1 C				106.1	-4.1
1999	Hou-N	60	37	23	.617	1 C	○1 C		1/3	35.4	1.6
	Hou-N	75	47	28	.627	●1 C	○1 C		3/3	44.3	2.7
2000	Hou-N	162	72	90	.444	4 C				80.5	-8.5
	4	621	342	279	.551						-17.0
Doby, Lawrence Eugene "Larry"											
1978	Chi-A	87	37	50	.425	5 W	5 W		2/2	38.1	-1.1
Donovan, Patrick Joseph "Patsy"											
1897	Pit-N*	135	60	71	.458	8				51.2	8.8
1899	Pit-N*	131	69	58	.543	10	7		2/2	69.1	-0.1
1901	StL-N*	142	76	64	.543	4				79.6	-3.6
1902	StL-N*	140	56	78	.418	6				48.8	7.2
1903	StL-N*	139	43	94	.314	8				40.0	3.0
1904	Was-A*	139	37	97	.276	8	8		2/2	37.3	-0.3
1906	Bro-N*	153	66	86	.434	5				61.7	4.3
1907	Bro-N*	153	65	83	.439	5				64.9	0.1
1908	Bro-N	154	53	101	.344	7				59.4	-6.4
1910	Bos-A	158	81	72	.529	4				84.9	-3.9
1911	Bos-A	153	78	75	.510	5				80.3	-2.3
	11	1597	684	879	.438						6.8
Donovan, William Edward "Bill"											
1915	NY-A*	154	69	83	.454	5				75.6	-6.6
1916	NY-A*	156	80	74	.519	4				78.8	1.2
1917	NY-A	155	71	82	.464	6				72.6	-1.6
1921	Phi-N	87	25	62	.287	8	8		1/2	27.3	-2.3
	4	552	245	301	.449						-9.3
Dooin, Charles Sebastian "Red"											
1910	Phi-N*	157	78	75	.510	4				80.1	-2.1
1911	Phi-N*	153	79	73	.520	4				74.9	4.1
1912	Phi-N*	152	73	79	.480	5				74.2	-1.2
1913	Phi-N*	159	88	63	.583	2				81.4	6.6
1914	Phi-N*	154	74	80	.481	6				73.3	0.7
	5	775	392	370	.514						8.0
Dorgan, Michael Cornelius "Mike"											
1879	Syr-N*	43	17	26	.395	6	7		1/3	10.9	6.1
1880	Pro-N*	39	26	12	.684	3	2		3/3	24.7	1.3
1881	Wor-N*	56	24	32	.429	7	8		1/2	22.9	1.1
	3	138	67	70	.489						8.6
Dowd, Thomas Jefferson "Tom"											
1896	StL-N*	63	25	38	.397	11	11		5/5	17.2	7.8
1897	StL-N*	29	6	22	.214	12	12		1/4	5.1	0.9
	2	92	31	60	.341						8.8
Doyle, John Joseph "Jack"											
1895	NY-N*	64	32	31	.508	8	9	9	2/3	32.2	-0.2
1898	Was-N*	17	8	9	.471	11	10	11	2/4	6.1	1.9
	2	81	40	40	.500						1.7
Dressen, Charles Walter "Chuck"											
1934	Cin-N	60	21	39	.350	8	8		3/3	21.7	-0.7
1935	Cin-N	154	68	85	.444	6				64.0	4.0
1936	Cin-N	154	74	80	.481	5				73.3	0.7
1937	Cin-N	130	51	78	.395	8	8		1/2	56.4	-5.4
1951	Bro-N	158	97	60	.618	▲2				96.2	0.8
1952	Bro-N	155	96	57	.627	1				93.8	2.2

YEAR	TM/L	G	W	L	PCT	STANDING			M/YW-EXP		A-E
1953	Bro-N	155	105	49	.682	1				101.5	3.5
1955	Was-A	154	53	101	.344	8				57.9	-4.9
1956	Was-A	155	59	95	.383	7				51.4	7.6
1957	Was-A	20	4	16	.200	8	8		1/2	7.4	-3.4
1960	Mil-N	154	88	66	.571	2				83.6	4.4
1961	Mil-N	130	71	58	.550	3	4		1/2	69.2	1.8
1963	Det-A	102	55	47	.539	9	●5		2/2	50.8	4.2
1964	Det-A	163	85	77	.525	4				83.2	1.8
1965	Det-A	120	65	55	.542	3	4		2/2	66.2	-1.2
1966	Det-A	26	16	10	.615	3	3		1/3	13.3	2.7
	16	1990	1008	973	.509						18.1
Duffy, Hugh											
1901	Mil-A*	139	48	89	.350	8				51.2	-3.2
1904	Phi-N*	155	52	100	.342	8				54.4	-2.4
1905	Phi-N*	155	83	69	.546	4				86.8	-3.8
1906	Phi-N*	154	71	82	.464	4				72.4	-1.4
1910	Chi-A	156	68	85	.444	6				73.8	-5.8
1911	Chi-A	154	77	74	.510	4				85.1	-8.1
1921	Bos-A	154	75	79	.487	5				74.2	0.8
1922	Bos-A	154	61	93	.396	8				59.8	1.2
	8	1221	535	671	.444						-22.7
Dunlap, Frederick C. "Fred"											
1882	Cle-N*	80	42	36	.538	8	5		2/2	38.2	3.8
1884	StL-U*	83	66	16	.805	1	1		2/2	70.3	-4.3
1885	StL-N*	50	21	29	.420	5	8		1/3	15.5	5.5
	StL-N*	22	9	11	.450	8	8		3/3	6.2	2.8
1889	Pit-N*	17	7	10	.412	6	7	5	2/3	7.6	-0.6
	4	252	145	102	.587						7.1
Durocher, Leo Ernest											
1939	Bro-N*	157	84	69	.549	3				82.9	1.1
1940	Bro-N*	156	88	65	.575	2				84.3	3.7
1941	Bro-N*	157	100	54	.649	1				99.2	0.8
1942	Bro-N	155	104	50	.675	2				101.3	2.7
1943	Bro-N*	153	81	72	.529	3				80.6	0.4
1944	Bro-N	155	63	91	.409	7				63.4	-0.4
1945	Bro-N*	155	87	67	.565	3				83.8	3.2
1946	Bro-N	157	96	60	.615	▲2				91.8	4.2
1948	Bro-N	73	35	37	.486	5	3		1/3	39.5	-4.5
	NY-N	79	41	38	.519	4	5		2/2	43.3	-2.3
1949	NY-N	156	73	81	.474	5				81.3	-8.3
1950	NY-N	154	86	68	.558	3				86.2	-0.2
1951	NY-N	157	98	59	.624	▲1				92.5	5.5
1952	NY-N	154	92	62	.597	2				85.4	6.6
1953	NY-N	155	70	84	.455	5				79.0	-9.0
1954	NY-N	154	97	57	.630	★1				95.9	1.1
1955	NY-N	154	80	74	.519	3				79.9	0.1
1966	Chi-N	162	59	103	.364	10				64.5	-5.5
1967	Chi-N	162	87	74	.540	3				88.7	-1.7
1968	Chi-N	163	84	78	.519	3				81.1	2.9
1969	Chi-N	163	92	70	.568	2 E				92.4	-0.4
1970	Chi-N	162	84	78	.519	2 E				93.6	-9.6
1971	Chi-N	162	83	79	.512	●3 E				79.8	3.2
1972	Chi-N	91	46	44	.511	4 E	2 E		1/2	52.3	-6.3
	Hou-N	31	16	15	.516	2 W	2 W		3/3	17.0	-1.0
1973	Hou-N	162	82	80	.506	4 W				81.9	0.1
	24	3739	2008	1709	.540						-13.6
Dwyer, John Francis "Frank"											
1902	Det-A	137	52	83	.385	7				58.4	-6.4
Dyer, Edwin Hawley "Eddie"											
1946	StL-N	156	98	58	.628	▲★1				95.7	2.3
1947	StL-N	156	89	65	.578	2				91.5	-2.5
1948	StL-N	155	85	69	.552	2				86.6	-1.6
1949	StL-N	157	96	58	.623	2				92.2	3.8
1950	StL-N	153	78	75	.510	5				78.8	-0.8
	5	777	446	325	.578						1.2
Dykes, James Joseph "Jimmy"											
1934	Chi-A*	138	49	88	.358	8	8		2/2	48.6	0.4
1935	Chi-A*	153	74	78	.487	5				74.8	-0.8
1936	Chi-A*	153	81	70	.536	3				79.6	1.4
1937	Chi-A*	154	86	68	.558	3				81.8	4.2
1938	Chi-A*	149	65	83	.439	6				69.9	-4.9
1939	Chi-A*	155	85	69	.552	4				78.7	6.3
1940	Chi-A	155	82	72	.532	●4				83.3	-1.3
1941	Chi-A	156	77	77	.500	3				75.9	1.1
1942	Chi-A	148	66	82	.446	6				66.3	-0.3
1943	Chi-A	155	82	72	.532	4				74.7	7.3
1944	Chi-A	154	71	83	.461	7				64.2	6.8
1945	Chi-A	150	71	78	.477	6				70.6	0.4
1946	Chi-A	30	10	20	.333	7	5		1/2	14.3	-4.3
1951	Phi-A	154	70	84	.455	6				76.1	-6.1
1952	Phi-A	155	79	75	.513	4				71.1	7.9
1953	Phi-A	157	59	95	.383	7				60.4	-1.4
1954	Bal-A	154	54	100	.351	7				56.7	-2.7
1958	Cin-N	41	24	17	.585	8	4		2/2	22.5	1.5
1959	Det-A	137	74	63	.540	8	4		2/2	66.8	7.2
1960	Det-A	96	44	52	.458	6	6		1/3	47.3	-3.3
	Cle-A	58	26	32	.448	4	4		3/3	28.0	-2.0
1961	Cle-A	160	77	83	.481	5	5		1/2	78.5	-1.5

YEAR	TM/L	G	W	L	PCT	STANDING			M/YW-EXP		A-E
	21	2962	1406	1541	.477						15.7
Ebbets, Charles Hercules "Charlie"											
1898	Bro-N	110	38	68	.358	9	10		3/3	40.8	-2.8
Edwards, Howard Rodney "Doc"											
1987	Cle-A	75	30	45	.400	7 E	7 E		2/2	28.3	1.7
1988	Cle-A	162	78	84	.481	6 E				74.4	3.6
1989	Cle-A	143	65	78	.455	6 E	6 E		1/2	66.7	-1.7
	3	380	173	207	.455						3.6
Elberfeld, Norman Arthur "Kid"											
1908	NY-A*	98	27	71	.276	6	8		2/2	31.4	-4.4
Elia, Lee Constantine											
1982	Chi-N	162	73	89	.451	5 E				77.6	-4.6
1983	Chi-N	123	54	69	.439	5 E	5 E		1/2	60.1	-6.1
1987	Phi-N	101	51	50	.505	5 E	●4 E		2/2	47.6	3.4
1988	Phi-N	153	60	92	.395	6 E	6 E		1/2	62.5	-2.5
	4	539	238	300	.442						-9.8
Ellick, Joseph J. "Joe"											
1884	CP-U*	13	6	6	.500	5	5		3/3	5.4	0.6
Elliott, Robert Irving "Bob"											
1960	KC-A	155	58	96	.377	8				62.8	-4.8
Ens, Jewel Winklemeyer											
1929	Pit-N	35	21	14	.600	2	2		2/2	20.1	0.9
1930	Pit-N	154	80	74	.519	5				73.8	6.2
1931	Pit-N	155	75	79	.487	5				71.4	3.6
	3	344	176	167	.513						10.8
Ermer, Calvin Coolidge "Cal"											
1967	Min-A	114	66	46	.589	6	●2		2/2	62.1	3.9
1968	Min-A	162	79	83	.488	7				82.8	-3.8
	2	276	145	129	.529						0.1
Essian, James Sarkis "Jim"											
1991	Chi-N	122	59	63	.484	5 E	4 E		3/3	58.0	1.0
Esterbrook, Thomas Jefferson "Dude"											
1889	Lou-a*	10	2	8	.200	7	8		1/4	2.2	-0.2
Evers, John Joseph "Johnny"											
1913	Chi-N*	155	88	65	.575	3				85.6	2.4
1921	Chi-N	96	41	55	.427	6	7		1/2	41.6	-0.6
1924	Chi-A	21	10	11	.476	6			1/4	9.7	0.3
	Chi-A	103	41	61	.402	8			4/4	47.0	-6.0
	3	375	180	192	.484						-3.9
Ewing, William "Buck"											
1890	NY-P*	132	74	57	.565	3				76.8	-2.8
1895	Cin-N*	132	66	64	.508	8				69.0	-3.0
1896	Cin-N*	128	77	50	.606	3				78.3	-1.3
1897	Cin-N*	134	76	56	.576	4				71.3	4.7
1898	Cin-N	157	92	60	.605	3				84.6	7.4
1899	Cin-N	157	83	67	.553	6				82.8	0.2
1900	NY-N	63	21	41	.339	8	8		1/2	26.5	-5.5
	7	903	489	395	.553						-0.3
Faatz, Jayson S. "Jay"											
1890	Buf-P*	34	9	24	.273	8	8	8	2/3	8.6	0.4
Falk, Bibb August											
1933	Cle-A	1	1	0	1.000	5	5	4	2/3	0.5	0.5
Fanning, William James "Jim"											
1981(2)	Mon-N	27	16	11	.593	2 E	○1 E		2/2	14.8	1.2
1982	Mon-N	162	86	76	.531	3 E				89.5	-3.5
1984	Mon-N	30	14	16	.467	5 E	5 E		2/2	15.2	-1.2
	3	219	116	103	.530						-3.5
Farrell, John A. "Jack"											
1881	Pro-N*	51	24	27	.471	4	2		1/2	26.7	-2.7
Farrell, Major Kerby "Kerby"											
1957	Cle-A	153	76	77	.497	6				72.5	3.5
Felske, John Frederick											
1985	Phi-N	162	75	87	.463	5 E				80.4	-5.4
1986	Phi-N	161	86	75	.534	2 E				83.1	2.9
1987	Phi-N	61	29	32	.475	5 E	●4 E		1/2	28.7	0.3
	3	384	190	194	.495						-2.2
Ferguson, Robert V. "Bob"											
1871	Mut-n*	33	16	17	.485	4				15.7	0.3
1872	Atl-n*	37	9	28	.243	6				2.3	6.7
1873	Atl-n*	55	17	37	.315	6				13.5	3.5
1874	Atl-n*	56	22	33	.400	6				15.3	6.7
1875	Har-n*	86	54	28	.659	3				60.8	-6.8
1876	Har-N*	69	47	21	.691	3				49.9	-2.9
1877	Har-N*	60	31	27	.534	3				31.7	-0.7
1878	Chi-N*	61	30	30	.500	4				33.5	-3.5
1879	Tro-N*	30	7	22	.241	8	8		2/2	6.8	0.2
1880	Tro-N*	83	41	42	.494	4				37.1	3.9
1881	Tro-N*	85	39	45	.464	5				39.1	-0.1
1882	Tro-N*	85	35	48	.422	7				33.3	1.7
1883	Phi-N*	17	4	13	.235	8	8		1/2	2.1	1.9
1884	Pit-a*	42	11	31	.262	9	11	10	2/5	9.4	1.6
1886	NY-a	120	48	70	.407	8	7		2/2	47.7	0.3
1887	NY-a	30	6	24	.200	8	7		1/3	8.7	-2.7

YEAR	TM/L	G	W	L	PCT	STANDING			M/YW-EXP		A-E
	16	949	417	516	.447						9.9
Ferraro, Michael Dennis "Mike"											
1983	Cle-A	100	40	60	.400	7 E	7 E		1/2	45.1	-5.1
1986	KC-A	74	36	38	.486	4 W	●3 W		2/2	36.1	-0.1
	2	174	76	98	.437						-5.1
Fessenden, Wallace Clifton											
1890	Syr-a	11	4	7	.364	7	7	6	2/3	4.5	-0.5
Fitzsimmons, Frederick Landis "Freddie"											
1943	Phi-N	65	26	38	.406	7	7		2/2	27.4	-1.4
1944	Phi-N	154	61	92	.399	8				63.7	-2.7
1945	Phi-N	69	18	51	.261	8	8		1/2	20.4	-2.4
	3	288	105	181	.367						-6.5
Fletcher, Arthur "Art"											
1923	Phi-N	155	50	104	.325	8				53.8	-3.8
1924	Phi-N	152	55	96	.364	7				59.1	-4.1
1925	Phi-N	153	68	85	.444	●6				66.0	2.0
1926	Phi-N	152	58	93	.384	8				55.7	2.3
1929	NY-A	11	6	5	.545	2	2		2/2	6.3	-0.3
	5	623	237	383	.382						-4.0
Flint, Frank Sylvester "Silver"											
1879	Chi-N*	19	5	12	.294	2	4		2/2	9.0	-4.0
Fogarty, James G. "Jim"											
1890	Phi-P*	16	7	9	.438	5	5		1/2	8.9	-1.9
Fogel, Horace S.											
1887	Ind-N	70	20	49	.290	8	8		3/3	18.9	1.1
1902	NY-N	44	18	23	.439	4	8		1/3	13.8	4.2
	2	114	38	72	.345						5.4
Fohl, Leo Alexander "Lee"											
1915	Cle-A	127	45	79	.363	6	7		2/2	50.6	-5.6
1916	Cle-A	157	77	77	.500	6				80.0	-3.0
1917	Cle-A	156	88	66	.571	3				81.6	6.4
1918	Cle-A	129	73	54	.575	2				69.8	3.2
1919	Cle-A	78	44	34	.564	3	2		1/2	44.7	-0.7
1921	StL-A	154	81	73	.526	3				76.1	4.9
1922	StL-A	154	93	61	.604	2				98.5	-5.5
1923	StL-A	103	52	49	.515	3	5		1/2	48.4	3.6
1924	Bos-A	157	67	87	.435	7				70.2	-3.2
1925	Bos-A	152	47	105	.309	8				49.5	-2.5
1926	Bos-A	154	46	107	.301	8				49.3	-3.3
	11	1521	713	792	.474						-5.6
Fonseca, Lewis Albert "Lew"											
1932	Chi-A*	152	49	102	.325	7				54.0	-5.0
1933	Chi-A*	151	67	83	.447	6				62.5	4.5
1934	Chi-A	15	4	11	.267	8	8		1/2	5.3	-1.3
	3	318	120	196	.380						-1.8
Foutz, David Luther "Dave"											
1893	Bro-N*	130	65	63	.508	●6				58.1	6.9
1894	Bro-N*	135	70	61	.534	5				65.8	4.2
1895	Bro-N*	134	71	60	.542	●5				68.9	2.1
1896	Bro-N*	133	58	73	.443	●9				59.0	-1.0
	4	532	264	257	.507						12.2
Fox, Charles Francis "Charlie"											
1970	SF-N	120	67	53	.558	4 W	3 W		2/2	60.3	6.7
1971	SF-N	162	90	72	.556	1 W				87.4	2.6
1972	SF-N	155	69	86	.445	5 W				78.8	-9.8
1973	SF-N	162	88	74	.543	3 W				84.7	3.3
1974	SF-N	76	34	42	.447	5 W	5 W		1/2	33.7	0.3
1976	Mon-N	34	12	22	.353	6 E	6 E		2/2	12.4	-0.4
1983	Chi-N	39	17	22	.436	5 E	5 E		2/2	19.1	-2.1
	7	748	377	371	.504						0.5
Francona, Terry Jon											
1997	Phi-N	162	68	94	.420	5 E				64.1	3.9
1998	Phi-N	162	75	87	.463	3 E				71.7	3.3
1999	Phi-N	162	77	85	.475	3 E				80.5	-3.5
2000	Phi-N	162	65	97	.401	5 E				69.1	-4.1
	4	648	285	363	.440						-0.4
Franks, Herman Louis											
1965	SF-N	163	95	67	.586	2				90.5	4.5
1966	SF-N	161	93	68	.578	2				85.7	7.3
1967	SF-N	162	91	71	.562	2				92.1	-1.1
1968	SF-N	163	88	74	.543	2				89.0	-1.0
1977	Chi-N	162	81	81	.500	4 E				76.3	4.7
1978	Chi-N	162	79	83	.488	3 E				74.8	4.2
1979	Chi-N	155	78	77	.503	5 E	5 E		1/2	77.4	0.6
	7	1128	605	521	.537						19.2
Frazer, George Kasson											
1890	Syr-a	71	31	40	.437	7	6		1/3	29.0	2.0
	Syr-a	46	20	25	.444	7	6		3/3	18.4	1.6
Frazier, Joseph Filmore "Joe"											
1976	NY-N	162	86	76	.531	3 E				89.7	-3.7
1977	NY-N	45	15	30	.333	6 E	6 E		1/2	20.2	-5.2
	2	207	101	106	.488						-8.9
Fregosi, James Louis "Jim"											
1978	Cal-A	116	62	54	.534	3 W	●2 W		2/2	59.9	2.1

YEAR	TM/L	G	W	L	PCT	STANDING			M/YW-EXP		A-E
1979	Cal-A	162	88	74	.543	1 W				90.3	-2.3
1980	Cal-A	160	65	95	.406	6 W				70.3	-5.3
1981(1)	Cal-A	47	22	25	.468	4 W	4 W		1/2	24.5	-2.5
1986	Chi-A	96	45	51	.469	5 W	5 W		3/3	44.6	0.4
1987	Chi-A	162	77	85	.475	5 W				81.2	-4.2
1988	Chi-A	161	71	90	.441	5 W				67.6	3.4
1991	Phi-N	149	74	75	.497	6 E	3 E		2/2	69.5	4.5
1992	Phi-N	162	70	92	.432	6 E				77.8	-7.8
1993	Phi-N	162	97	65	.599	♦1 E				94.0	3.0
1994	Phi-N	115	54	61	.470	4 E				59.9	-5.9
1995	Phi-N	144	69	75	.479	●2 E				67.7	1.3
1996	Phi-N	162	67	95	.414	5 E				66.9	0.1
1999	Tor-A	162	84	78	.519	3 E				82.9	1.1
2000	Tor-A	162	83	79	.512	3 E				76.7	6.3
	15	2122	1028	1094	.484						-5.9
Frey, James Gottfried "Jim"											
1980	KC-A	162	97	65	.599	♦1 W				92.3	4.7
1981(1)	KC-A	50	20	30	.400	5 W					
(2)	KC-A	20	10	10	.500	●2 W	1 W		1/2	34.4	-4.4
1984	Chi-N	161	96	65	.596	1 E				91.0	5.0
1985	Chi-N	162	77	84	.478	4 E				76.1	0.9
1986	Chi-N	56	23	33	.411	5 E	5 E		1/3	24.5	-1.5
	5	611	323	287	.530						4.6
Frisch, Frank Francis "Frankie"											
1933	StL-N*	63	36	26	.581	5	5		2/2	34.3	1.7
1934	StL-N*	154	95	58	.621	★1				90.5	4.5
1935	StL-N*	154	96	58	.623	2				96.9	-0.9
1936	StL-N*	155	87	67	.565	●2				77.1	9.9
1937	StL-N*	157	81	73	.526	4				82.4	-1.4
1938	StL-N	139	63	72	.467	6	6		1/2	67.8	-4.8
1940	Pit-N	156	78	76	.506	4				79.4	-1.4
1941	Pit-N	156	81	73	.526	4				81.8	-0.8
1942	Pit-N	151	66	81	.449	5				68.6	-2.6
1943	Pit-N	157	80	74	.519	4				83.7	-3.7
1944	Pit-N	158	90	63	.588	2				84.7	5.3
1945	Pit-N	155	82	72	.532	4				83.6	-1.6
1946	Pit-N	152	62	89	.411	7	7		1/2	63.3	-1.3
1949	Chi-N	104	42	62	.404	7	8		2/2	39.8	2.2
1950	Chi-N	154	64	89	.418	7				63.7	0.3
1951	Chi-N	81	35	45	.438	7	8		1/2	32.9	2.1
	16	2246	1138	1078	.514						7.4
Fuchs, Emil Edmund "Judge"											
1929	Bos-N	154	56	98	.364	8				56.2	-0.2
Gaffney, John H.											
1886	Was-N	43	15	25	.375	8			2/2	9.0	6.0
1887	Was-N	126	46	76	.377	7				41.6	4.4
	2	169	61	101	.377						10.4
Galante, Matthew Joseph "Matt"											
1999	Hou-N	27	13	14	.481	●1 C	○1 C		2/3	15.9	-2.9
Galvin, James Francis "Jim"											
1885	Buf-N*	24	7	17	.292	7	7		1/2	6.9	0.1
Ganzel, John Henry											
1908	Cin-N*	155	73	81	.474	5				70.6	2.4
1915	Bro-F	35	17	18	.486	7	7		2/2	16.9	0.1
	2	190	90	99	.476						2.5
Garcia, David "Dave"											
1977	Cal-A	81	35	46	.432	5 W	5 W		2/2	39.5	-4.5
1978	Cal-A	46	25	21	.543	3 W	●2 W		1/2	23.7	1.3
1979	Cle-A	66	38	28	.576	6 E	6 E		2/2	31.2	6.8
1980	Cle-A	160	79	81	.494	6 E				73.3	5.7
1981(1)	Cle-A	50	26	24	.520	6 E					
(2)	Cle-A	53	26	27	.491	5 E				50.4	1.6
1982	Cle-A	162	78	84	.481	●6 E				74.4	3.6
	6	618	307	311	.497						14.4
Gardner, William Frederick "Billy"											
1981(1)	Min-A	20	6	14	.300	6 W	7 W		2/2		
(2)	Min-A	53	24	29	.453	4 W				28.8	1.2
1982	Min-A	162	60	102	.370	7 W				64.9	-4.9
1983	Min-A	162	70	92	.432	5 W				70.0	0.0
1984	Min-A	162	81	81	.500	2 W				80.8	0.2
1985	Min-A	62	27	35	.435	6 W	4 W		1/2	28.1	-1.1
1987	KC-A	126	62	64	.492	4 W	2 W		1/2	64.9	-2.9
	6	747	330	417	.442						-7.4
Garner, Philip Mason "Phil"											
1992	Mil-A	162	92	70	.568	2 E				95.2	-3.2
1993	Mil-A	162	69	93	.426	7 E				75.2	-6.2
1994	Mil-A	115	53	62	.461	5 C				53.8	-0.8
1995	Mil-A	144	65	79	.451	4 C				71.3	-6.3
1996	Mil-A	162	80	82	.494	3 C				80.5	-0.5
1997	Mil-A	161	78	83	.484	3 C				74.3	3.7
1998	Mil-N	162	74	88	.457	5 C				70.7	3.3
1999	Mil-N	112	52	60	.464	5 C	5 C		1/2	51.4	0.6
2000	Det-A	162	79	83	.488	3 C				80.6	-1.6
	9	1342	642	700	.478						-11.2
Gaston, Clarence Edwin "Cito"											
1989	Tor-A	126	77	49	.611	6 E	1 E		2/2	69.4	7.6

YEAR	TM/L	G	W	L	PCT	STANDING			M/Y	W-EXP	A-E
1990	Tor-A	162	86	76	.531	2 E				91.7	-5.7
1991	Tor-A	120	66	54	.550	1 E	1 E		1/3	64.9	1.1
	Tor-A	9	6	3	.667	1 E	1 E		3/3	4.9	1.1
1992	Tor-A	162	96	66	.593	★1 E				90.8	5.2
1993	Tor-A	162	95	67	.586	★1 E				91.1	3.9
1994	Tor-A	115	55	60	.478	3 E				56.3	-1.3
1995	Tor-A	144	56	68	.452	5 E				59.1	-3.1
1996	Tor-A	162	74	88	.457	4 E				76.9	-2.9
1997	Tor-A	157	72	85	.459	5 E	5 E		1/2	74.5	-2.5
	9	1319	683	616	.526						3.6
Gerhardt, John Joseph "Joe"											
1883	Lou-a*	98	52	45	.536	5				48.7	3.3
1890	StL-a*	38	20	16	.556	2	3		6/6	21.1	-1.1
	2	136	72	61	.541						2.2
Gessler, Harry Homer "Doc"											
1914	Pit-F	11	3	8	.273	8	7		1/2	4.8	-1.8
Gibson, George C. "Moon"											
1920	Pit-N	155	79	75	.513	4				74.5	4.5
1921	Pit-N	154	90	63	.588	2				86.6	3.4
1922	Pit-N	65	32	33	.492	5	●3		1/2	37.6	-5.6
1925	Chi-N	26	12	14	.462	7	8		3/3	12.2	-0.2
1932	Pit-N	154	86	68	.558	2				76.0	10.0
1933	Pit-N	154	87	67	.565	2				82.0	5.0
1934	Pit-N	51	27	24	.529	4	5		1/2	26.2	0.8
	7	759	413	344	.546						17.9
Gifford, James H. "Jim"											
1884	Ind-a	87	25	60	.294	10	11		1/2	21.5	3.5
1885	NY-a	108	44	64	.407	7				39.5	4.5
1886	NY-a	17	5	12	.294	8	7		1/2	6.9	-1.9
	3	212	74	136	.352						6.1
Glasscock, John Wesley "Jack"											
1889	Ind-N*	67	34	32	.515	7	7		2/2	29.9	4.1
1892(1)	StL-N*	4	1	3	.250	10	9		1/3	1.5	-0.5
	2	71	35	35	.500						3.6
Gleason, William J. "Kid"											
1919	Chi-A	140	88	52	.629	1				83.6	4.4
1920	Chi-A	154	96	58	.623	2				89.6	6.4
1921	Chi-A	154	62	92	.403	7				60.4	1.6
1922	Chi-A	155	77	77	.500	5				77.0	0.0
1923	Chi-A	156	69	85	.448	7				72.1	-3.1
	5	759	392	364	.519						9.3
Gomez, Pedro W. [Martinez] "Preston"											
1969	SD-N	162	52	110	.321	6 W				50.5	1.5
1970	SD-N	162	63	99	.389	6 W				70.3	-7.3
1971	SD-N	161	61	100	.379	6 W				66.2	-5.2
1972	SD-N	11	4	7	.364	4 W	6 W		1/2	4.1	-0.1
1974	Hou-N	162	81	81	.500	4 W				83.2	-2.2
1975	Hou-N	127	47	80	.370	6 W	6 W		1/2	59.7	-12.7
1980	Chi-N	90	38	52	.422	6 E	6 E		1/2	38.4	-0.4
	7	875	346	529	.395						-26.5
Gonzalez, Miguel Angel "Mike"											
1938	StL-N	17	8	8	.500	6	6		2/2	8.0	-0.0
1940	StL-N	6	1	5	.167	6	7	3	2/3	3.2	-2.2
	2	23	9	13	.409						-2.2
Gordon, Joseph Lowell "Joe"											
1958	Cle-A	86	46	40	.535	6	4		2/2	46.4	-0.4
1959	Cle-A	154	89	65	.578	2				86.9	2.1
1960	Cle-A	95	49	46	.516	4	4		1/3	45.9	3.1
	Det-A	57	26	31	.456	6	6		3/3	28.1	-2.1
1961	KC-A	60	26	33	.441	8	●9		1/2	23.1	2.9
1969	KC-A	163	69	93	.426	4 W				70.1	-1.1
	5	615	305	308	.498						4.6
Gore, George F.											
1892(2)	StL-N*	16	6	9	.400	12	12	11	2/3	5.5	0.5
Goryl, John Albert "Johnny"											
1980	Min-A	36	23	13	.639	4 W	3 W		2/2	16.8	6.2
1981(1)	Min-A	37	11	25	.306	6 W	7 W		1/2	14.2	-3.2
	2	73	34	38	.472						3.0
Gould, Charles Harvey "Charlie"											
1875	NH-n*	23	2	21	.087	11	8		1/3	1.9	0.1
1876	Cin-N*	65	9	56	.138	8				3.6	5.4
	2	88	11	77	.125						5.5
Gowdy, Henry Morgan "Hank"											
1946	Cin-N	4	3	1	.750	6	6		2/2	1.9	1.1
Graffen, Samuel Mason "Mase"											
1876	StL-N	56	39	17	.696	2	2		1/2	41.3	-2.3
Grammas, Alexander Peter "Alex"											
1969	Pit-N	5	4	1	.800	3 E	3 E		2/2	2.7	1.3
1976	Mil-A	161	66	95	.410	6 E				71.3	-5.3
1977	Mil-A	162	67	95	.414	6 E				68.2	-1.2
	3	328	137	191	.418						-5.1
Green, George Dallas "Dallas"											
1979	Phi-N	30	19	11	.633	5 E	4 E		2/2	14.3	4.7
1980	Phi-N	162	91	71	.562	★1 E				90.2	0.8

YEAR	TM/L	G	W	L	PCT	STANDING			M/Y	W-EXP	A-E
1981(1)	Phi-N	55	34	21	.618	1 E					
(2)	Phi-N	52	25	27	.481	3 E				55.4	3.6
1989	NY-A	121	56	65	.463	6 E	5 E		1/2	53.5	2.5
1993	NY-N	124	46	78	.371	7 E	7 E		2/2	56.4	-10.4
1994	NY-N	113	55	58	.487	3 E				54.5	0.5
1995	NY-N	144	69	75	.479	●2 E				75.9	-6.9
1996	NY-N	131	59	72	.450	4 E	4 E		1/2	62.9	-3.9
	8	932	454	478	.487						-9.2
Griffin, Michael Joseph "Mike"											
1898	Bro-N*	4	1	3	.250	9	9	10	2/3	1.5	-0.5
Griffin, Tobias Charles "Sandy"											
1891	Was-a*	6	2	4	.333	8	8		4/4	1.6	0.4
Griffith, Clark Calvin											
1901	Chi-A*	137	83	53	.610	1				85.3	-2.3
1902	Chi-A*	138	74	60	.552	4				74.2	-0.2
1903	NY-A*	136	72	62	.537	4				67.6	4.4
1904	NY-A*	155	92	59	.609	2				83.5	8.5
1905	NY-A*	152	71	78	.477	6				70.8	0.2
1906	NY-A*	155	90	61	.596	2				86.0	4.0
1907	NY-A*	152	70	78	.473	5				67.6	2.4
1908	NY-A	57	24	32	.429	6	8		1/2	18.0	6.0
1909	Cin-N*	157	77	76	.503	4				77.3	-0.3
1910	Cin-N*	156	75	79	.487	5				70.4	4.6
1911	Cin-N	159	70	83	.458	6				74.1	-4.1
1912	Was-A*	154	91	61	.599	2				88.3	2.7
1913	Was-A*	155	90	64	.584	2				80.7	9.3
1914	Was-A*	158	81	73	.526	3				83.1	-2.1
1915	Was-A	155	85	68	.556	4				85.4	-0.4
1916	Was-A	159	76	77	.497	7				75.7	0.3
1917	Was-A	158	74	79	.484	5				74.0	-0.0
1918	Was-A	130	72	56	.563	3				69.7	2.3
1919	Was-A	142	56	84	.400	7				66.0	-10.0
1920	Was-A	153	68	84	.447	6				68.5	-0.5
	20	2918	1491	1367	.522						24.9
Grimes, Burleigh Arland											
1937	Bro-N	155	62	91	.405	6				60.9	1.1
1938	Bro-N	151	69	80	.463	7				73.9	-4.9
	2	306	131	171	.434						-3.8
Grimm, Charles John "Charlie"											
1932	Chi-N*	55	37	18	.673	2	1		2/2	30.6	6.4
1933	Chi-N*	154	86	68	.558	3				88.9	-2.9
1934	Chi-N*	152	86	65	.570	3				82.2	3.8
1935	Chi-N*	154	100	54	.649	1				101.5	-1.5
1936	Chi-N*	154	87	67	.565	●2				92.4	-5.4
1937	Chi-N	154	93	61	.604	2				89.4	3.6
1938	Chi-N	81	45	36	.556	3	1		1/2	46.9	-1.9
1944	Chi-N	146	74	69	.517	8	4		3/3	74.6	-0.6
1945	Chi-N	155	98	56	.636	1				98.3	-0.3
1946	Chi-N	155	82	71	.536	3				81.3	0.7
1947	Chi-N	155	69	85	.448	6				61.1	7.9
1948	Chi-N	155	64	90	.416	8				65.8	-1.8
1949	Chi-N	50	19	31	.380	7	8		1/2	19.1	-0.1
1952	Bos-N	120	51	67	.432	7	7		2/2	52.2	-1.2
1953	Mil-N	157	92	62	.597	2				92.4	-0.4
1954	Mil-N	154	89	65	.578	3				89.1	-0.1
1955	Mil-N	154	85	69	.552	2				84.4	0.6
1956	Mil-N	46	24	22	.522	5	2		1/2	27.4	-3.4
1960	Chi-N	17	6	11	.353	7	7		1/2	6.9	-0.9
	19	2368	1287	1067	.547						2.4
Groh, Henry Knight "Heinie"											
1918	Cin-N*	10	7	3	.700	4	3		2/2	5.3	1.7
Gutteridge, Donald Joseph "Don"											
1969	Chi-A	145	60	85	.414	4 W	5 W		2/2	63.4	-3.4
1970	Chi-A	136	49	87	.360	6 W	6 W		1/3	52.1	-3.1
	2	281	109	172	.388						-6.5
Haas, George Edwin "Eddie"											
1985	Atl-N	121	50	71	.413	5 W	5 W		1/2	49.2	0.8
Hack, Stanley Camfield "Stan"											
1954	Chi-N	154	64	90	.416	7				70.6	-6.6
1955	Chi-N	154	72	81	.471	6				67.6	4.4
1956	Chi-N	157	60	94	.390	8				65.4	-5.4
1958	StL-N	10	3	7	.300	5	●5		2/2	4.4	-1.4
	4	475	199	272	.423						-9.1
Hackett, Charles M. "Charlie"											
1884	Cle-N	113	35	77	.313	7				32.0	3.0
1885	Bro-a	37	15	22	.405	7	●5		1/2	17.7	-2.7
	2	150	50	99	.336						0.3
Hallman, William Wilson "Bill"											
1897	StL-N*	50	13	36	.265	12	12	12	3/4	8.8	4.2
Haney, Fred Girard											
1939	StL-A	156	43	111	.279	8				50.1	-7.1
1940	StL-A	156	67	87	.435	6				65.4	1.6
1941	StL-A	44	15	29	.341	7	●6		1/2	20.4	-5.4
1953	Pit-N	154	50	104	.325	8				51.6	-1.6
1954	Pit-N	154	53	101	.344	8				48.4	4.6
1955	Pit-N	154	60	94	.390	8				55.8	4.2

YEAR	TM/L	G	W	L	PCT	STANDING			M/YW-EXP		A-E
1956	Mil-N	109	68	40	.630	5	2		2/2	64.3	3.7
1957	Mil-N	155	95	59	.617	★1				93.0	2.0
1958	Mil-N	154	92	62	.597	1				91.3	0.7
1959	Mil-N	157	86	70	.551	▲2				88.3	-2.3
	10	1393	629	757	.454						0.4
Hanlon, Edward Hugh "Ned"											
1889	Pit-N*	46	26	18	.591	7	5		3/3	19.8	6.2
1890	Pit-P*	131	60	68	.469	6				59.3	0.7
1891	Pit-N*	78	31	47	.397	8	8		1/2	35.5	-4.5
1892(1)	Bal-N*	56	17	39	.304	12	12		3/3		
(2)	Bal-N*	77	26	46	.361	10				45.7	-2.7
1893	Bal-N	130	60	70	.462	8				59.0	1.0
1894	Bal-N	129	89	39	.695	1				90.9	-1.9
1895	Bal-N	132	87	43	.669	1				95.8	-8.8
1896	Bal-N	132	90	39	.698	1				92.7	-2.7
1897	Bal-N	136	90	40	.692	2				90.1	-0.1
1898	Bal-N	154	96	53	.644	2				103.8	-7.8
1899	Bro-N	150	100	47	.680	1				95.3	4.7
1900	Bro-N	142	82	54	.603	1				76.6	5.4
1901	Bro-N	137	79	57	.581	3				81.8	-2.8
1902	Bro-N	141	75	63	.543	2				73.9	1.1
1903	Bro-N	139	70	66	.515	5				66.6	3.4
1904	Bro-N	154	56	97	.366	6				63.4	-7.4
1905	Bro-N	155	48	104	.316	8				45.0	3.0
1906	Cin-N	155	64	87	.424	6				70.0	-6.0
1907	Cin-N	156	66	87	.431	6				77.3	-11.3
	19	2530	1312	1164	.530						-30.3
Harder, Melvin Leroy "Mel"											
1961	Cle-A	1	1	0	1.000	5	5		2/2	0.5	0.5
1962	Cle-A	2	2	0	1.000	6	6		2/2	0.9	1.1
	2	3	3	0	1.000						1.6
Hargrove, Dudley Michael "Mike"											
1991	Cle-A	85	32	53	.376	7 E	7 E		2/2	32.5	-0.5
1992	Cle-A	162	76	86	.469	●4 E				73.7	2.3
1993	Cle-A	162	76	86	.469	6 E				78.8	-2.8
1994	Cle-A	113	66	47	.584	2 C				67.1	-1.1
1995	Cle-A	144	100	44	.694	♦1 C				94.1	5.9
1996	Cle-A	161	99	62	.615	○1 C				97.3	1.7
1997	Cle-A	161	86	75	.534	♦1 C				85.4	0.6
1998	Cle-A	162	89	73	.549	1 C				87.7	1.3
1999	Cle-A	162	97	65	.599	○1 C				94.2	2.8
2000	Bal-A	162	74	88	.457	4 E				70.0	4.0
	10	1474	795	679	.539						14.3
Harrah, Colbert Dale "Toby"											
1992	Tex-A	76	32	44	.421	3 W	4 W		2/2	34.6	-2.6
Harrelson, Derrel Mc Kinley "Bud"											
1990	NY-N	120	71	49	.592	4 E	2 E		2/2	72.3	-1.3
1991	NY-N	154	74	80	.481	3 E	5 E		1/2	76.4	-2.4
	2	274	145	129	.529						-3.7
Harris, Chalmer Luman "Lum"											
1961	Bal-A	27	17	10	.630	3	3		2/2	15.3	1.7
1964	Hou-N	13	5	8	.385	9	9		2/2	5.3	-0.3
1965	Hou-N	162	65	97	.401	9				65.8	-0.8
1968	Atl-N	163	81	81	.500	5				76.9	4.1
1969	Atl-N	162	93	69	.574	1 W				87.3	5.7
1970	Atl-N	162	76	86	.469	5 W				77.5	-1.5
1971	Atl-N	162	82	80	.506	3 W				75.2	6.8
1972	Atl-N	105	47	57	.452	4 W	4 W		1/2	45.0	2.0
	8	956	466	488	.488						17.7
Harris, Stanley Raymond "Bucky"											
1924	Was-A*	156	92	62	.597	★1				91.4	0.6
1925	Was-A*	152	96	55	.636	1				90.7	5.3
1926	Was-A*	152	81	69	.540	4				78.8	2.2
1927	Was-A*	157	85	69	.552	3				82.0	3.0
1928	Was-A*	155	75	79	.487	4				78.3	-3.3
1929	Det-A*	155	70	84	.455	6				76.8	-6.8
1930	Det-A	154	75	79	.487	5				72.4	2.6
1931	Det-A*	154	61	93	.396	7				59.1	1.9
1932	Det-A	153	76	75	.503	5				76.6	-0.6
1933	Det-A	153	73	79	.480	5	5		1/2	74.9	-1.9
1934	Bos-A	153	76	76	.500	4				80.2	-4.2
1935	Was-A	154	67	86	.438	6				69.3	-2.3
1936	Was-A	153	82	71	.536	4				84.6	-2.6
1937	Was-A	158	73	80	.477	6				68.6	4.4
1938	Was-A	152	75	76	.497	5				70.2	4.8
1939	Was-A	153	65	87	.428	6				66.9	-1.9
1940	Was-A	154	64	90	.416	7				62.9	1.1
1941	Was-A	156	70	84	.455	●6				70.3	-0.3
1942	Was-A	151	62	89	.411	7				59.7	2.3
1943	Phi-N	92	38	52	.422	7	7		1/2	38.5	-0.5
1947	NY-A	155	97	57	.630	★1				99.9	-2.9
1948	NY-A	154	94	60	.610	3				98.6	-4.6
1950	Was-A	155	67	87	.435	5				65.1	1.9
1951	Was-A	154	62	92	.403	7				68.0	-6.0
1952	Was-A	157	78	76	.506	5				75.9	2.1
1953	Was-A	152	76	76	.500	5				83.5	-7.5
1954	Was-A	155	66	88	.429	6				72.1	-6.1
1955	Det-A	154	79	75	.513	5				88.5	-9.5

YEAR	TM/L	G	W	L	PCT	STANDING			M/YW-EXP		A-E
1956	Det-A	155	82	72	.532	5				85.7	-3.7
	29	4408	2157	2218	.493						-32.5
Hart, James Aristotle "Jim"											
1885	Lou-a	112	53	59	.473	●5				52.8	0.2
1886	Lou-a	138	66	70	.485	4				70.4	-4.4
1889	Bos-N	133	83	45	.648	2				82.2	0.8
	3	383	202	174	.537						-3.4
Hart, John Henry											
1989	Cle-A	19	8	11	.421	6 E	6 E		2/2	8.9	-0.9
Hartnett, Charles Leo "Gabby"											
1938	Chi-N*	73	44	27	.620	3	1		2/2	41.1	2.9
1939	Chi-N*	156	84	70	.545	4				81.6	2.4
1940	Chi-N*	154	75	79	.487	5				81.6	-6.6
	3	383	203	176	.536						-1.3
Hartsfield, Roy Thomas											
1977	Tor-A	161	54	107	.335	7 E				58.6	-4.6
1978	Tor-A	161	59	102	.366	7 E				61.4	-2.4
1979	Tor-A	162	53	109	.327	7 E				56.2	-3.2
	3	484	166	318	.343						-10.3
Hastings, Winfield Scott "Scott"											
1871	Rok-n*	25	4	21	.160	9				8.8	-4.8
1872	Cle-n*	20	6	14	.300	6	7		1/2	5.1	0.9
	2	45	10	35	.222						-3.9
Hatfield, John Van Buren											
1872	Mut-n*	40	24	14	.632	4	3		2/2	27.6	-3.6
1873	Mut-n*	28	11	17	.393	5	4		1/2	15.6	-4.6
	2	68	35	31	.530						-8.1
Hatton, Grady Edgebert											
1966	Hou-N	163	72	90	.444	8				72.2	-0.2
1967	Hou-N	162	69	93	.426	9				69.0	-0.0
1968	Hou-N	61	23	38	.377	10	10		1/2	27.1	-4.1
	3	386	164	221	.426						-4.3
Hecker, Guy Jackson											
1890	Pit-N*	138	23	113	.169	8				15.5	7.5
Heffner, Donald Henry "Don"											
1966	Cin-N	83	37	46	.446	8	7		1/2	41.0	-4.0
Heilbroner, Louis Wilbur "Louie"											
1900	StL-N	50	23	25	.479	7	●5		2/2	23.9	-0.9
Helms, Tommy Vann											
1988	Cin-N	27	12	15	.444	4 W	4 W	2 W	2/3	14.3	-2.3
1989	Cin-N	37	16	21	.432	●4 W	5 W		2/2	17.1	-1.1
	2	64	28	36	.438						-3.4
Hemus, Solomon Joseph "Solly"											
1959	StL-N*	154	71	83	.461	7				68.5	2.5
1960	StL-N	155	86	68	.558	3				79.4	6.6
1961	StL-N	75	33	41	.446	6	5		1/2	38.7	-5.7
	3	384	190	192	.497						3.3
Henderson, William C. "Bill"											
1884	Bal-U	106	58	47	.552	4				55.5	2.5
Hendricks, John Charles "Jack"											
1918	StL-N	133	51	78	.395	8				56.5	-5.5
1924	Cin-N	153	83	70	.542	4				83.9	-0.9
1925	Cin-N	153	80	73	.523	3				81.3	-1.3
1926	Cin-N	157	87	67	.565	2				86.7	0.3
1927	Cin-N	153	75	78	.490	5				75.5	-0.5
1928	Cin-N	153	78	74	.513	5				72.1	5.9
1929	Cin-N	155	66	88	.429	7				69.7	-3.7
	7	1057	520	528	.496						-5.7
Hengle, Edward S. "Ed"											
1884	CP-U	74	34	39	.466	5			1/3	33.1	0.9
Herman, William Jennings Bryan "Billy"											
1947	Pit-N*	155	61	92	.399	8	●7		1/2	69.7	-8.7
1964	Bos-A	2	2	0	1.000	8	8		2/2	0.9	1.1
1965	Bos-A	162	62	100	.383	9				68.8	-6.8
1966	Bos-A	146	64	82	.438	9	9		1/2	66.0	-2.0
	4	465	189	274	.408						-16.4
Herzog, Charles Lincoln "Buck"											
1914	Cin-N*	157	60	94	.390	8				63.8	-3.8
1915	Cin-N*	160	71	83	.461	7				69.1	1.9
1916	Cin-N*	84	34	49	.410	8	●7		1/3	34.7	-0.7
	3	401	165	226	.422						-2.6
Herzog, Dorrel Norman Elvert "Whitey"											
1973	Tex-A	138	47	91	.341	6 W	6 W		1/3	49.9	-2.9
1974	Cal-A	4	2	2	.500	6 W	6 W	6 W	2/3	1.9	0.1
1975	KC-A	66	41	25	.621	2 W	2 W		2/2	35.6	5.4
1976	KC-A	162	90	72	.556	1 W				91.7	-1.7
1977	KC-A	162	102	60	.630	1 W				98.0	4.0
1978	KC-A	162	92	70	.568	1 W				92.2	-0.2
1979	KC-A	162	85	77	.525	2 W				84.3	0.7
1980	StL-N	73	38	35	.521	6 E	5 E	4 E	3/4	37.8	0.2
1981(1)	StL-N	51	30	20	.600	2 E					
(2)	StL-N	52	29	23	.558	2 E				55.8	3.2
1982	StL-N	162	92	70	.568	★1 E				89.1	2.9

YEAR	TM/L	G	W	L	PCT	STANDING			M/YW-EXP		A-E
1983	StL-N	162	79	83	.488	4 E				77.8	1.2
1984	StL-N	162	84	78	.519	4 E				81.7	2.3
1985	StL-N	162	101	61	.623	♦1 E				99.4	1.0
1986	StL-N	161	79	82	.491	3 E				79.4	-0.4
1987	StL-N	162	95	67	.586	♦1 E				91.4	3.6
1988	StL-N	162	76	86	.469	5 E				75.0	1.0
1989	StL-N	164	86	76	.531	3 E				83.6	2.4
1990	StL-N	80	33	47	.412	6 E	6 E		1/3	34.8	-1.8
	18	2409	1281	1125	.532						21.6
Hewett, Walter F.											
1888	Was-N	40	10	29	.256	8	8		1/2	12.2	-2.2
Hicks, Nathaniel Woodhull "Nat"											
1874	Phi-n*	58	29	29	.500	4				32.6	-3.6
1875	Mut-n*	71	30	38	.441	7				25.1	4.9
	2	129	59	67	.468						1.3
Higgins, Michael Franklin "Pinky"											
1955	Bos-A	154	84	70	.545	4				87.2	-3.2
1956	Bos-A	155	84	70	.545	4				79.8	4.2
1957	Bos-A	154	82	72	.532	3				82.3	-0.3
1958	Bos-A	155	79	75	.513	3				77.6	1.4
1959	Bos-A	73	31	42	.425	8	8		1/3	37.9	-6.9
1960	Bos-A	105	48	57	.457	8	7		3/3	44.7	3.3
1961	Bos-A	163	76	86	.469	6				74.8	1.2
1962	Bos-A	160	76	84	.475	8				75.1	0.9
	8	1119	560	556	.502						0.6
Higham, Richard "Dick"											
1874	Mut-n*	40	29	11	.725	3	2		2/2	26.2	2.8
Himsl, Avitus Bernard "Vedie"											
1961	Chi-N	11	5	6	.455	6	●6		1/9	4.7	0.3
	Chi-N	17	5	12	.294	7	7	7	3/9	7.3	-2.3
	Chi-N	4	0	3	.000	7	7	7	6/9	1.3	-1.3
Hitchcock, William Clyde "Billy"											
1960	Det-A	1	1	0	1.000	6	6	6	2/3	0.5	0.5
1962	Bal-A	162	77	85	.475	7				78.1	-1.1
1963	Bal-A	162	86	76	.531	4				83.5	2.5
1966	Atl-N	51	33	18	.647	7	5		2/2	28.6	4.4
1967	Atl-N	159	77	82	.484	7	7		1/2	78.6	-1.6
	5	535	274	261	.512						4.8
Hobson, Clell Lavern "Butch"											
1992	Bos-A	162	73	89	.451	7 E				73.5	-0.5
1993	Bos-A	162	80	82	.494	5 E				79.8	0.2
1994	Bos-A	115	54	61	.470	4 E				51.0	3.0
	3	439	207	232	.472						2.7
Hodges, Gilbert Raymond "Gil"											
1963	Was-A	121	42	79	.347	10	10		3/3	42.6	-0.6
1964	Was-A	162	62	100	.383	9				64.7	-2.7
1965	Was-A	162	70	92	.432	8				67.3	2.7
1966	Was-A	159	71	88	.447	8				68.4	2.6
1967	Was-A	161	76	85	.472	●6				70.9	5.1
1968	NY-N	163	73	89	.451	9				77.8	-4.8
1969	NY-N	162	100	62	.617	★1 E				91.1	8.9
1970	NY-N	162	83	79	.512	3 E				87.8	-4.8
1971	NY-N	162	83	79	.512	●3 E				85.3	-2.3
	9	1414	660	753	.467						4.1
Hoey, Frederick C. "Fred"											
1899	NY-N	87	31	55	.360	9	10		2/2	36.3	-5.3
Hoffman, Glenn Edward											
1998	LA-N	88	47	41	.534	3 W	3 W		2/2	43.5	3.5
Holbert, William H. "Bill"											
1879	Syr-N*	1	0	1	.000	6	6	7	2/3	0.3	-0.3
Hollingshead, John Samuel "Holly"											
1875	Was-n*	20	4	16	.200	8	10		1/2	-2.4	6.4
1884	Was-a	62	12	50	.194	12	12		1/2	10.8	1.2
	2	82	16	66	.195						7.6
Holmes, Thomas Francis "Tommy"											
1951	Bos-N*	95	48	47	.505	5	4		2/2	51.3	-3.3
1952	Bos-N	35	13	22	.371	7	7		1/2	15.5	-2.5
	2	130	61	69	.469						-5.8
Hornsby, Rogers											
1925	StL-N*	115	64	51	.557	8	4		2/2	62.0	2.0
1926	StL-N*	156	89	65	.578	★1				90.5	-1.5
1927	NY-N*	33	22	10	.688	4	3		2/2	17.9	4.1
1928	Bos-N*	122	39	83	.320	7	7		2/2	42.2	-3.2
1930	Chi-N*	4	4	0	1.000	2	2		2/2	2.3	1.7
1931	Chi-N*	156	84	70	.545	3				88.3	-4.3
1932	Chi-N*	99	53	46	.535	2	1		1/2	55.2	-2.2
1933	StL-A*	54	19	33	.365	8	8		3/3	21.0	-2.0
1934	StL-A*	154	67	85	.441	6				63.8	3.2
1935	StL-A*	155	65	87	.428	7				56.5	8.5
1936	StL-A*	155	57	95	.375	7				53.5	3.5
1937	StL-A*	78	25	52	.325	7	8		1/2	24.7	0.3
1952	StL-A	51	22	29	.431	8	7		1/2	21.1	0.9
	Cin-N	51	27	24	.529	7	6		3/3	24.0	3.0
1953	Cin-N	147	64	82	.438	6	6		1/2	66.2	-2.2
	14	1530	701	812	.463						11.9
Houk, Ralph George "Ralph"											
1961	NY-A	163	109	53	.673	★1				102.7	6.3
1962	NY-A	162	96	66	.593	★1				94.5	1.5
1963	NY-A	161	104	57	.646	1				98.4	5.6
1966	NY-A	140	66	73	.475	10	10		2/2	69.4	-3.4
1967	NY-A	163	72	90	.444	9				69.8	2.2
1968	NY-A	164	83	79	.512	5				81.6	1.4
1969	NY-A	162	80	81	.497	5 E				77.7	2.3
1970	NY-A	163	93	69	.574	2 E				88.2	4.8
1971	NY-A	162	82	80	.506	4 E				81.7	0.3
1972	NY-A	155	79	76	.510	4 E				80.9	-1.9
1973	NY-A	162	80	82	.494	4 E				84.3	-4.3
1974	Det-A	162	72	90	.444	6 E				65.8	6.2
1975	Det-A	159	57	102	.358	6 E				57.3	-0.3
1976	Det-A	161	74	87	.460	5 E				70.0	4.0
1977	Det-A	162	74	88	.457	4 E				77.3	-3.3
1978	Det-A	162	86	76	.531	5 E				87.3	-1.3
1981(1)	Bos-A	56	30	26	.536	5 E					
(2)	Bos-A	52	29	23	.558	●2 E				57.7	1.3
1982	Bos-A	162	89	73	.549	3 E				85.0	4.0
1983	Bos-A	162	78	84	.481	6 E				76.0	2.0
1984	Bos-A	162	86	76	.531	4 E				85.4	0.6
	20	3157	1619	1531	.514						27.8
Howard, Frank Oliver											
1981(1)	SD-N	56	23	33	.411	6 W					
(2)	SD-N	54	18	36	.333	6 W				47.1	-6.1
1983	NY-N	116	52	64	.448	6 E	6 E		2/2	49.9	2.1
	2	226	93	133	.412						-4.0
Howe, Arthur Henry "Art"											
1989	Hou-N	162	86	76	.531	3 W				78.7	7.3
1990	Hou-N	162	75	87	.463	●4 W				72.0	3.0
1991	Hou-N	162	65	97	.401	6 W				69.2	-4.2
1992	Hou-N	162	81	81	.500	4 W				74.6	6.4
1993	Hou-N	162	85	77	.525	3 W				90.0	-5.0
1996	Oak-A	162	78	84	.481	3 W				77.5	0.5
1997	Oak-A	162	65	97	.401	4 W				64.2	0.8
1998	Oak-A	162	74	88	.457	4 W				75.2	-1.2
1999	Oak-A	162	87	75	.537	2 W				85.3	1.7
2000	Oak-A	161	91	70	.565	○1 W				92.7	-1.7
	10	1619	787	832	.486						7.8
Howley, Daniel Philip "Dan"											
1927	StL-A	155	59	94	.386	7				59.8	-0.8
1928	StL-A	154	82	72	.532	3				79.9	2.1
1929	StL-A	154	79	73	.520	4				78.0	1.0
1930	Cin-N	154	59	95	.383	7				58.7	0.3
1931	Cin-N	154	58	96	.377	8				61.7	-3.7
1932	Cin-N	155	60	94	.390	8				62.4	-2.4
	6	926	397	524	.431						-3.5
Howser, Richard Dalton "Dick"											
1978	NY-A	1	0	1	.000	3 E	4 E	▲★1 E	2/3	0.6	-0.6
1980	NY-A	162	103	59	.636	1 E				96.7	6.3
1981(2)	KC-A	33	20	13	.606	●2 W	1 W		2/2	16.2	3.8
1982	KC-A	162	90	72	.556	2 W				87.6	2.4
1983	KC-A	163	79	83	.488	2 W				73.9	5.1
1984	KC-A	162	84	78	.519	1 W				79.7	4.3
1985	KC-A	162	91	71	.562	★1 W				86.0	5.0
1986	KC-A	88	40	48	.455	4 W	●3 W		1/2	42.9	-2.9
	8	933	507	425	.544						23.4
Huff, George A.											
1907	Bos-A	8	2	6	.250	●4	6	7	2/4	3.4	-1.4
Huggins, Miller James											
1913	StL-N*	153	51	99	.340	8				51.5	-0.5
1914	StL-N*	157	81	72	.529	3				78.5	2.5
1915	StL-N*	157	72	81	.471	6				75.3	-3.3
1916	StL-N*	153	60	93	.392	●7				59.4	0.6
1917	StL-N	154	82	70	.539	3				72.0	10.0
1918	NY-A	126	60	63	.488	4				63.4	-3.4
1919	NY-A	141	80	59	.576	3				77.3	2.7
1920	NY-A	154	95	59	.617	3				97.3	-2.3
1921	NY-A	153	98	55	.641	1				98.4	-0.4
1922	NY-A	154	94	60	.610	1				91.1	2.9
1923	NY-A	152	98	54	.645	★1				95.6	2.4
1924	NY-A	153	89	63	.586	2				88.7	0.3
1925	NY-A	156	69	85	.448	7				70.4	-1.4
1926	NY-A	155	91	63	.591	1				89.7	1.3
1927	NY-A	155	110	44	.714	★1				112.4	-2.4
1928	NY-A	154	101	53	.656	★1				96.6	4.4
1929	NY-A	143	82	61	.573	2	2		1/2	82.0	0.0
	17	2570	1413	1134	.555						13.5
Hunter, Gordon William "Billy"											
1977	Tex-A	93	60	33	.645	5 W	2 W		4/4	52.9	7.1
1978	Tex-A	161	86	75	.534	●2 W	●2 W		1/2	86.8	-0.8
	2	254	146	108	.575						6.4
Hurst, Timothy Carroll "Tim"											
1898	StL-N	154	39	111	.260	12				40.6	-1.6
Hutchinson, Frederick Charles "Fred"											
1952	Det-A*	83	27	55	.329	8	8		2/2	31.0	-4.0

YEAR	TM/L	G	W	L	PCT	STANDING			M/Y	W-EXP	A-E
1953	Det-A*	158	60	94	.390	6				55.6	4.4
1954	Det-A	155	68	86	.442	5				68.5	-0.5
1956	StL-N	156	76	78	.494	4				75.0	1.0
1957	StL-N	154	87	67	.565	2				84.1	2.9
1958	StL-N	144	69	75	.479	5	●5		1/2	63.9	5.1
1959	Cin-N	74	39	35	.527	7	●5		2/2	38.2	0.8
1960	Cin-N	154	67	87	.435	6				71.7	-4.7
1961	Cin-N	154	93	61	.604	1				82.7	10.3
1962	Cin-N	162	98	64	.605	3				92.6	5.4
1963	Cin-N	162	86	76	.531	5				86.9	-0.9
1964	Cin-N	100	54	45	.545	3	●2		1/4	55.8	-1.8
	Cin-N	10	6	4	.600	4	3	●2	3/4	5.6	0.4
	12	1666	830	827	.501						18.5
Irwin, Arthur Albert											
1889	Was-N*	76	28	45	.384	8	8		2/2	23.2	4.8
1891	Bos-a*	139	93	42	.689	1				97.8	-4.8
1892(1)	Was-N	74	35	39	.473	●11	7		2/2		
(2)	Was-N	34	11	21	.344	11	12		1/2	44.0	2.0
1894	Phi-N*	132	71	57	.555	4				77.6	-6.6
1895	Phi-N	133	78	53	.595	3				74.0	4.0
1896	NY-N	90	36	53	.404	10	7		1/2	45.0	-9.0
1898	Was-N	30	10	19	.345	11	11		4/4	10.4	-0.4
1899	Was-N	155	54	98	.355	11				54.4	-0.4
	8	863	416	427	.493						-10.4
Jennings, Hugh Ambrose "Hughie"											
1907	Det-A*	153	92	58	.613	1				92.2	-0.2
1908	Det-A	154	90	63	.588	1				87.3	2.7
1909	Det-A*	158	98	54	.645	1				95.2	2.8
1910	Det-A	155	86	68	.558	3				87.0	-1.0
1911	Det-A	154	89	65	.578	2				82.0	7.0
1912	Det-A*	154	69	84	.451	6				71.0	-2.0
1913	Det-A	153	66	87	.431	6				67.3	-1.3
1914	Det-A	157	80	73	.523	4				76.2	3.8
1915	Det-A	156	100	54	.649	2				95.3	4.7
1916	Det-A	155	87	67	.565	3				84.9	2.1
1917	Det-A	155	78	75	.510	4				83.1	-5.1
1918	Det-A*	128	55	71	.437	7				54.4	0.6
1919	Det-A	140	80	60	.571	4				74.1	5.9
1920	Det-A	155	61	93	.396	7				59.5	1.5
1924	NY-N	44	32	12	.727	3	1	1	2/3	28.0	4.0
1925	NY-N	32	21	11	.656	1	1	2	2/3	16.7	4.3
	16	2203	1184	995	.543						29.9
Johnson, Darrell Dean											
1974	Bos-A	162	84	78	.519	3 E				84.6	-0.6
1975	Bos-A	160	95	65	.594	♦1 E				88.5	6.5
1976	Bos-A	86	41	45	.477	5 E	3 E		1/2	46.1	-5.1
1977	Sea-A	162	64	98	.395	6 W				58.1	5.9
1978	Sea-A	160	56	104	.350	7 W				58.1	-2.1
1979	Sea-A	162	67	95	.414	6 W				70.4	-3.4
1980	Sea-A	105	39	65	.375	6 W	7 W		1/2	40.0	-1.0
1982	Tex-A	66	26	40	.394	6 W	6 W		2/2	26.2	-0.2
	8	1063	472	590	.444						0.1
Johnson, David Allen "Davey"											
1984	NY-N	162	90	72	.556	2 E				78.5	11.5
1985	NY-N	162	98	64	.605	2 E				94.6	3.4
1986	NY-N	162	108	54	.667	★1 E				102.2	5.8
1987	NY-N	162	92	70	.568	2 E				93.2	-1.2
1988	NY-N	160	100	60	.625	1 E				98.5	1.5
1989	NY-N	162	87	75	.537	2 E				90.4	-3.4
1990	NY-N	42	20	22	.476	4 E	2 E		1/2	25.3	-5.3
1993	Cin-N	118	53	65	.449	5 W	5 W		2/2	54.5	-1.5
1994	Cin-N	115	66	48	.579	1 C				68.5	-2.5
1995	Cin-N	144	85	59	.590	○1 C				84.1	0.9
1996	Bal-A	163	88	74	.543	■2 E				85.1	2.9
1997	Bal-A	162	98	64	.605	1 E				93.9	4.1
1999	LA-N	162	77	85	.475	3 W				81.6	-4.6
2000	LA-N	162	86	76	.531	2 W				87.7	-1.7
	14	2038	1148	888	.564						9.8
Johnson, Roy J											
1944	Chi-N	1	0	1	.000	8	8	4	2/3	0.5	-0.5
Johnson, Timothy Evald "Tim"											
1998	Tor-A	163	88	74	.543	3 E				85.6	2.4
Johnson, Walter Perry											
1929	Was-A	153	71	81	.467	5				71.6	-0.6
1930	Was-A	154	94	60	.610	2				96.0	-2.0
1931	Was-A	156	92	62	.597	3				91.6	0.4
1932	Was-A	154	93	61	.604	3				88.7	4.3
1933	Cle-A	99	48	51	.485	5	4		3/3	48.5	-0.5
1934	Cle-A	154	85	69	.552	3				81.8	3.2
1935	Cle-A	96	46	48	.489	5	3		1/2	49.2	-3.2
	7	966	529	432	.550						1.6
Jones, Fielder Allison											
1904	Chi-A*	114	66	47	.584	4	3		2/2	66.4	-0.4
1905	Chi-A*	158	92	60	.605	2				94.6	-2.6
1906	Chi-A*	154	93	58	.616	★1				88.3	4.7
1907	Chi-A*	157	87	64	.576	3				88.7	-1.7
1908	Chi-A*	156	88	64	.579	3				83.9	4.1

YEAR	TM/L	G	W	L	PCT	STANDING			M/Y	W-EXP	A-E
1914	StL-F*	40	12	26	.316	7	8		2/2	15.5	-3.5
1915	StL-F*	159	87	67	.565	2				88.9	-1.9
1916	StL-A	158	79	75	.513	5				81.8	-2.8
1917	StL-A	155	57	97	.370	7				57.9	-0.9
1918	StL-A	46	22	24	.478	6	5		1/3	22.1	-0.1
	10	1297	683	582	.540						-5.0
Joost, Edwin David "Eddie"											
1954	Phi-A*	156	51	103	.331	8				43.8	7.2
Jorgensen, Michael "Mike"											
1995	StL-N	96	42	54	.438	4 C	4 C		2/2	41.5	0.5
Joyce, William Michael "Bill"											
1896	NY-N*	43	28	14	.667	10	7		2/2	21.2	6.8
1897	NY-N*	138	83	48	.634	3				83.6	-0.6
1898	NY-N*	43	22	21	.512	6	7		1/3	22.5	-0.5
	NY-N*	92	46	39	.541	7	7		3/3	44.4	1.6
	3	316	179	122	.595						7.3
Jurges, William Frederick "Billy"											
1959	Bos-A	80	44	36	.550	8	5		3/3	41.5	2.5
1960	Bos-A	42	15	27	.357	8	7		1/3	17.9	-2.9
	2	122	59	63	.484						-0.4
Kasko, Edward Michael "Eddie"											
1970	Bos-A	162	87	75	.537	3 E				87.3	-0.3
1971	Bos-A	162	85	77	.525	3 E				83.5	1.5
1972	Bos-A	155	85	70	.548	2 E				79.6	5.4
1973	Bos-A	161	88	73	.547	2 E	2 E		1/2	89.8	-1.8
	4	640	345	295	.539						4.8
Keane, John Joseph "Johnny"											
1961	StL-N	80	47	33	.587	6	5		2/2	41.8	5.2
1962	StL-N	163	84	78	.519	6				92.1	-8.1
1963	StL-N	162	93	69	.574	2				93.3	-0.3
1964	StL-N	162	93	69	.574	★1				87.5	5.5
1965	NY-A	162	77	85	.475	6				81.8	-4.8
1966	NY-A	20	4	16	.200	10	10		1/2	10.0	-6.0
	6	749	398	350	.532						-8.5
Kelley, Joseph James "Joe"											
1902	Cin-N*	60	34	26	.567	6	4		3/3	33.0	1.0
1903	Cin-N*	141	74	65	.532	4				79.8	-5.8
1904	Cin-N*	157	88	65	.575	3				92.3	-4.3
1905	Cin-N*	155	79	74	.516	5				80.2	-1.2
1908	Bos-N*	156	63	91	.409	6				67.6	-4.6
	5	669	338	321	.513						-14.9
Kelly, Jay Thomas "Tom"											
1986	Min-A	23	12	11	.522	7 W	6 W		2/2	10.2	1.8
1987	Min-A	162	85	77	.525	★1 W				79.1	5.9
1988	Min-A	162	91	71	.562	2 W				89.8	1.2
1989	Min-A	162	80	82	.494	5 W				81.2	-1.2
1990	Min-A	162	74	88	.457	7 W				74.6	-0.6
1991	Min-A	162	95	67	.586	★1 W				93.5	1.5
1992	Min-A	162	90	72	.556	2 W				90.6	-0.6
1993	Min-A	162	71	91	.438	●5 W				67.6	3.4
1994	Min-A	113	53	60	.469	4 C				48.1	4.9
1995	Min-A	144	56	88	.389	5 C				55.2	0.8
1996	Min-A	162	78	84	.481	4 C				78.9	-0.9
1997	Min-A	162	68	94	.420	4 C				72.6	-4.6
1998	Min-A	162	70	92	.432	4 C				72.9	-2.9
1999	Min-A	161	63	97	.394	5 C				64.5	-1.5
2000	Min-A	162	69	93	.426	5 C				68.5	0.5
	15	2223	1055	1167	.475						7.7
Kelly, John O.											
1887	Lou-a	139	76	60	.559	4				76.5	-0.5
1888	Lou-a	39	10	29	.256	8	7		1/4	14.8	-4.8
	2	178	86	89	.491						-5.3
Kelly, Michael Joseph "King"											
1887	Bos-N*	95	49	43	.533	5	5		1/2	48.5	0.5
1890	Bos-P*	133	81	48	.628	1				82.9	-1.9
1891	Cin-a*	102	43	57	.430	6				41.7	1.3
	3	330	173	148	.539						-0.1
Kennedy, James C. "Jim"											
1890	Bro-a	100	26	73	.263	8				28.8	-2.8
Kennedy, Kevin Curtis											
1993	Tex-A	162	86	76	.531	2 W				89.1	-3.1
1994	Tex-A	114	52	62	.456	1 W				49.6	2.4
1995	Bos-A	144	86	58	.597	1 E				80.7	5.3
1996	Bos-A	162	85	77	.525	3 E				81.6	3.4
	4	582	309	273	.531						8.1
Kennedy, Robert Daniel "Bob"											
1963	Chi-N	162	82	80	.506	7				80.1	1.9
1964	Chi-N	162	76	86	.469	8				73.3	2.7
1965	Chi-N	58	24	32	.429	9	8		1/2	24.8	-0.8
1968	Oak-A	163	82	80	.506	6				83.9	-1.9
	4	545	264	278	.487						1.9
Kerins, John Nelson											
1888	Lou-a*	7	3	4	.429	8	8	7	3/4	2.7	0.3
1890	StL-a*	17	9	8	.529	4	4	3	2/6	10.0	-1.0
	2	24	12	12	.500						-0.6

YEAR	TM/L	G	W	L	PCT	STANDING			M/Y	W-EXP	A-E
Kessinger, Donald Eulon "Don"											
1979	Chi-A*	106	46	60	.434	5 W	5 W		1/2	51.8	-5.8
Killefer, William Lavier "Bill"											
1921	Chi-N*	57	23	34	.404	6	7		2/2	24.7	-1.7
1922	Chi-N	156	80	74	.519	5				73.5	6.5
1923	Chi-N	154	83	71	.539	4				82.1	0.9
1924	Chi-N	154	81	72	.529	5				76.4	4.6
1925	Chi-N	75	33	42	.440	7	8		1/3	35.2	-2.2
1930	StL-A	154	64	90	.416	6				64.6	-0.6
1931	StL-A	154	63	91	.409	5				63.1	-0.1
1932	StL-A	154	63	91	.409	6				62.1	0.9
1933	StL-A	91	34	57	.374	8	8		1/3	36.7	-2.7
	9	1149	524	622	.457						5.7
King, Clyde Edward											
1969	SF-N	162	90	72	.556	2 W				89.0	1.0
1970	SF-N	42	19	23	.452	4 W	3 W		1/2	21.1	-2.1
1974	Atl-N	64	38	25	.603	4 W	3 W		2/2	35.7	2.3
1975	Atl-N	134	58	76	.433	5 W	5 W		1/2	53.4	4.6
1982	NY-A	62	29	33	.468	●5 E	5 E		3/3	30.7	-1.7
	5	464	234	229	.505						4.1
Kittridge, Malachi J.											
1904	Was-A*	18	1	16	.059	8	8		1/2	4.7	-3.7
Klein, Louis Frank "Lou"											
1961	Chi-N	11	5	6	.455	7	7	7	8/9	4.7	0.3
1962	Chi-N	30	12	18	.400	9	9	9	2/3	11.4	0.6
1965	Chi-N	106	48	58	.453	9	8		2/2	47.0	1.0
	3	147	65	82	.442						1.9
Kling, John "Johnny"											
1912	Bos-N*	155	52	101	.340	8				59.7	-7.7
Knabe, Franz Otto "Otto"											
1914	Bal-F*	160	84	70	.545	3				78.8	5.2
1915	Bal-F*	155	47	107	.305	8				55.4	-8.4
	2	315	131	177	.425						-3.2
Knight, Alonzo P. "Lon"											
1883	Phi-a*	98	66	32	.673	1				63.4	2.6
1884	Phi-a*	109	61	46	.570	7				67.1	-6.1
	2	207	127	78	.620						-3.5
Knight, Charles Ray "Ray"											
1996	Cin-N	162	81	81	.500	3 C				81.5	-0.5
1997	Cin-N	99	43	56	.434	4 C	3 C		1/2	42.5	0.5
	2	261	124	137	.475						0.0
Knoop, Robert Frank "Bobby"											
1994	Cal-A	2	1	1	.500	3 W	2 W	4 W	2/3	0.8	0.2
Krol, John Thomas "Jack"											
1978	StL-N	2	1	1	.500	6 E	6 E	5 E	2/3	0.9	0.1
1980	StL-N	1	0	1	.000	6 E	6 E	4 E	2/4	0.5	-0.5
	2	3	1	2	.333						-0.4
Kuehl, Karl Otto											
1976	Mon-N	128	43	85	.336	6 E	6 E		1/2	46.8	-3.8
Kuenn, Harvey Edward											
1975	Mil-A	1	1	0	1.000	5 E	5 E		2/2	0.4	0.6
1982	Mil-A	116	72	43	.626	5 E	♦1 E		2/2	69.3	2.7
1983	Mil-A	162	87	75	.537	5 E				86.6	0.4
	3	279	160	118	.576						3.7
Kuhel, Joseph Anthony "Joe"											
1948	Was-A	154	56	97	.366	7				54.6	1.4
1949	Was-A	154	50	104	.325	8				49.3	0.7
	2	308	106	201	.345						2.1
Lachemann, Marcel Ernest											
1994	Cal-A	74	30	44	.405	2 W	4 W		3/3	30.0	-0.0
1995	Cal-A	145	78	67	.538	▲2 W				82.2	-4.2
1996	Cal-A	111	52	59	.468	4 W			1/2	44.0	8.0
	3	330	160	170	.485						3.8
Lachemann, Rene George											
1981(1)	Sea-A	33	15	18	.455	7 W	6 W		2/2		
(2)	Sea-A	52	23	29	.442	5 W				34.9	3.1
1982	Sea-A	162	76	86	.469	4 W				74.7	1.3
1983	Sea-A	73	26	47	.356	7 W	7 W		1/2	27.8	-1.8
1984	Mil-A	161	67	94	.416	7 E				71.0	-4.0
1993	Fla-N	162	64	98	.395	6 E				65.9	-1.9
1994	Fla-N	115	51	54	.486	5 E				46.7	4.3
1995	Fla-N	143	67	76	.469	4 E				71.5	-4.5
1996	Fla-N	86	39	47	.453	4 E	3 E		1/3	42.2	-3.2
	8	987	428	549	.438						-6.7
Lajoie, Napoleon "Nap"											
1905	Cle-A*	58	37	21	.638	●1	5		1/3	28.0	9.0
	Cle-A*	56	19	36	.345	2	5		3/3	26.6	-7.6
1906	Cle-A*	157	89	64	.582	3				96.7	-7.7
1907	Cle-A*	158	85	67	.559	4				76.7	8.3
1908	Cle-A*	157	90	64	.584	2				89.9	0.1
1909	Cle-A*	114	57	57	.500	4	6		1/2	53.6	3.4
	5	700	377	309	.550						5.4
Lake, Frederick Lovett "Fred"											
1908	Bos-A	40	22	17	.564	6	5		2/2	21.0	1.0
1909	Bos-A	152	88	63	.583	3				81.2	6.8
1910	Bos-N*	157	53	100	.346	8				54.1	-1.1
	3	349	163	180	.475						6.8
Lamont, Gene William											
1992	Chi-A	162	86	76	.531	3 W				85.9	0.1
1993	Chi-A	162	94	68	.580	1 W				92.3	1.7
1994	Chi-A	113	67	46	.593	1 C				69.3	-2.3
1995	Chi-A	31	11	20	.355	4 C	3 C		1/2	15.4	-4.4
1997	Pit-N	162	79	83	.488	2 C				77.5	1.5
1998	Pit-N	163	69	93	.426	6 C				74.0	-5.0
1999	Pit-N	161	78	83	.484	3 C				79.8	-1.8
2000	Pit-N	162	69	93	.426	5 C				72.2	-3.2
	8	1116	553	562	.496						-13.3
Lanier, Harold Clifton "Hal"											
1986	Hou-N	162	96	66	.593	1 W				90.3	5.7
1987	Hou-N	162	76	86	.469	3 W				77.9	-1.9
1988	Hou-N	162	82	80	.506	5 W				79.5	2.5
	3	486	254	232	.523						6.4
Larkin, Henry E. "Ted"											
1890	Cle-P*	79	34	45	.430	7	7		1/2	30.9	3.1
LaRussa, Anthony "Tony"											
1979	Chi-A	54	27	27	.500	5 W	5 W		2/2	26.4	0.6
1980	Chi-A	162	70	90	.438	5 W				65.8	4.2
1981(1)	Chi-A	53	31	22	.585	3 W					
(2)	Chi-A	53	23	30	.434	6 W				58.5	-4.5
1982	Chi-A	162	87	75	.537	3 W				88.5	-1.5
1983	Chi-A	162	99	63	.611	1 W				96.0	3.0
1984	Chi-A	162	74	88	.457	●5 W				75.2	-1.2
1985	Chi-A	163	85	77	.525	3 W				82.6	2.4
1986	Chi-A	64	26	38	.406	6 W	5 W		1/3	29.7	-3.7
	Oak-A	79	45	34	.570	7 W	●3 W		3/3	38.1	6.9
1987	Oak-A	162	81	81	.500	3 W				82.6	-1.6
1988	Oak-A	162	104	58	.642	♦1 W				99.2	4.8
1989	Oak-A	162	99	63	.611	★1 W				95.5	3.5
1990	Oak-A	162	103	59	.636	♦1 W				98.2	4.8
1991	Oak-A	162	84	78	.519	4 W				79.4	4.6
1992	Oak-A	162	96	66	.593	1 W				88.4	7.6
1993	Oak-A	162	68	94	.420	7 W				68.3	-0.3
1994	Oak-A	114	51	63	.447	2 W				53.2	-2.2
1995	Oak-A	144	67	77	.465	4 W				69.1	-2.1
1996	StL-N	162	88	74	.543	1 C				86.3	1.7
1997	StL-N	162	73	89	.451	4 C				79.1	-6.1
1998	StL-N	163	83	79	.512	3 C				83.7	-0.7
1999	StL-N	161	75	86	.466	4 C				77.8	-2.8
2000	StL-N	162	95	67	.586	1 C				91.9	3.1
	22	3316	1734	1578	.524						20.4
Lasorda, Thomas Charles "Tom"											
1976	LA-N	4	2	2	.500	2 W	2 W		2/2	2.2	-0.2
1977	LA-N	162	98	64	.605	♦1 W				100.4	-2.4
1978	LA-N	162	95	67	.586	♦1 W				97.3	-2.3
1979	LA-N	162	79	83	.488	3 W				83.2	-4.2
1980	LA-N	163	92	71	.564	▲2 W				89.3	2.7
1981(1)	LA-N	57	36	21	.632	★1 W					
(2)	LA-N	53	27	26	.509	4 W				65.4	-2.4
1982	LA-N	162	88	74	.543	2 W				89.4	-1.4
1983	LA-N	163	91	71	.562	1 W				85.9	5.1
1984	LA-N	162	79	83	.488	4 W				78.8	0.2
1985	LA-N	162	95	67	.586	1 W				92.1	2.9
1986	LA-N	162	73	89	.451	5 W				76.7	-3.7
1987	LA-N	162	73	89	.451	4 W				76.8	-3.8
1988	LA-N	162	94	67	.584	★1 W				89.9	4.1
1989	LA-N	160	77	83	.481	4 W				82.1	-5.1
1990	LA-N	162	86	76	.531	2 W				85.4	0.6
1991	LA-N	162	93	69	.574	2 W				91.9	1.1
1992	LA-N	162	63	99	.389	6 W				71.2	-8.2
1993	LA-N	162	81	81	.500	4 W				82.4	-1.4
1994	LA-N	114	58	56	.509	1 W				59.3	-1.3
1995	LA-N	144	78	66	.542	1 W				74.6	3.4
1996	LA-N	76	41	35	.539	1 W	2 W		1/2	40.5	0.5
	21	3040	1599	1439	.526						-15.5
Latham, George Warren "Juice"											
1875	NH-n*	18	4	14	.222	11	8	8	2/3	1.5	2.5
1882	Phi-a*	75	41	34	.547	2				39.1	1.9
	2	93	45	48	.484						4.4
Latham, Walter Arlington "Arlie"											
1896	StL-N*	3	0	3	.000	10	10	11	2/5	0.8	-0.8
Lavagetto, Harry Arthur "Cookie"											
1957	Was-A	134	51	83	.381	8	8		2/2	49.3	1.7
1958	Was-A	156	61	93	.396	8				56.8	4.2
1959	Was-A	154	63	91	.409	8				68.6	-5.6
1960	Was-A	154	73	81	.474	5				74.6	-1.6
1961	Min-A	49	19	30	.388	8	7		1/4	22.4	-3.4
	Min-A	10	4	6	.400	9	9	7	3/4	4.6	-0.6
	5	657	271	384	.414						-5.3
Leadley, Robert H. "Bob"											
1888	Det-N	40	19	19	.500	3	5		2/2	21.5	-2.5
1890	Cle-N	58	23	33	.411	7	7		2/2	20.2	2.8

YEAR	TM/L	G	W	L	PCT	STANDING			M/YW-EXP		A-E
1891	Cle-N	68	34	34	.500	4	5		1/2	31.8	2.2
	3	166	76	86	.469						2.5
Lefebvre, James Kenneth "Jim"											
1989	Sea-A	162	73	89	.451	6 W				77.6	-4.6
1990	Sea-A	162	77	85	.475	5 W				76.8	0.2
1991	Sea-A	162	83	79	.512	5 W				83.9	-0.9
1992	Chi-N	162	78	84	.481	4 E				77.6	0.4
1993	Chi-N	163	84	78	.519	4 E				80.9	3.1
1999	Mil-N	49	22	27	.449	5 C	5 C		2/2	22.5	-0.5
	6	860	417	442	.485						-2.2
Lemon, James Robert "Jim"											
1968	Was-A	161	65	96	.404	10				64.9	0.1
Lemon, Robert Granville "Bob"											
1970	KC-A	110	46	64	.418	5 W	●4 W		2/2	48.3	-2.3
1971	KC-A	161	85	76	.528	2 W				84.6	0.4
1972	KC-A	154	76	78	.494	4 W				80.9	-4.9
1977	Chi-A	162	90	72	.556	3 W				87.9	2.1
1978	Chi-A	74	34	40	.459	5 W	5 W		1/2	32.4	1.6
	NY-A	68	48	20	.706	4 E	▲★1 E		3/3	40.7	7.3
1979	NY-A	65	34	31	.523	4 E	4 E		1/2	35.0	-1.0
1981(2)	NY-A	25	11	14	.440	4 E	6 E		2/2	14.5	-3.5
1982	NY-A	14	6	8	.429	●4 E	5 E		1/3	6.9	-0.9
	8	833	430	403	.516						-1.4
Lennon, William F. "Bill"											
1871	Kek-n*	14	5	9	.357	7	8		1/2	1.8	3.2
Leyland, James Richard "Jim"											
1986	Pit-N	162	64	98	.395	6 E				77.2	-13.2
1987	Pit-N	162	80	82	.494	●4 E				78.9	1.1
1988	Pit-N	160	85	75	.531	2 E				83.7	1.3
1989	Pit-N	164	74	88	.457	5 E				76.4	-2.4
1990	Pit-N	162	95	67	.586	1 E				92.8	2.2
1991	Pit-N	162	98	64	.605	1 E				94.9	3.1
1992	Pit-N	162	96	66	.593	1 E				91.4	4.6
1993	Pit-N	162	75	87	.463	5 E				71.3	3.7
1994	Pit-N	114	53	61	.465	●3 C				45.7	7.3
1995	Pit-N	144	58	86	.403	5 C				61.6	-3.6
1996	Pit-N	162	73	89	.451	5 C				75.6	-2.6
1997	Fla-N	162	92	70	.568	■★2 E				88.2	3.8
1998	Fla-N	162	54	108	.333	5 E				56.5	-2.5
1999	Col-N	162	72	90	.444	5 W				70.4	1.6
	14	2202	1069	1131	.486						4.3
Leyva, Nicolas Tomas "Nick"											
1989	Phi-N	163	67	95	.414	6 E				70.0	-3.0
1990	Phi-N	162	77	85	.475	●4 E				72.5	4.5
1991	Phi-N	13	4	9	.308	6 E	3 E		1/2	6.1	-2.1
	3	338	148	189	.439						-0.5
Lillis, Robert Perry "Bob"											
1982	Hou-N	51	28	23	.549	5 W	5 W		2/2	23.7	4.3
1983	Hou-N	162	85	77	.525	3 W				80.7	4.3
1984	Hou-N	162	80	82	.494	●2 W				87.6	-7.6
1985	Hou-N	162	83	79	.512	●3 W				82.5	0.5
	4	537	276	261	.514						1.5
Lipon, John Joseph "Johnny"											
1971	Cle-A	59	18	41	.305	6 E	6 E		2/2	21.6	-3.6
Lobert, John Bernard "Hans"											
1938	Phi-N	2	0	2	.000	8	8		2/2	0.6	-0.6
1942	Phi-N	151	42	109	.278	8				40.8	1.2
	2	153	42	111	.275						0.6
Lockman, Carroll Walter "Whitey"											
1972	Chi-N	65	39	26	.600	4 E	2 E		2/2	37.7	1.3
1973	Chi-N	161	77	84	.478	5 E				76.1	0.9
1974	Chi-N	93	41	52	.441	5 E	6 E		1/2	37.6	3.4
	3	319	157	162	.492						5.5
Loftus, Thomas Joseph "Tom"											
1884	Mil-U	12	8	4	.667	2				8.1	-0.1
1888	Cle-a	71	30	38	.441	8	6		2/2	25.3	4.7
1889	Cle-N	136	61	72	.459	6				60.5	0.5
1890	Cin-N	134	77	55	.583	4				77.2	-0.2
1891	Cin-N	138	56	81	.409	7				55.1	0.9
1900	Chi-N	146	65	75	.464	●5				58.7	6.3
1901	Chi-N	140	53	86	.381	6				57.5	-4.5
1902	Was-A	138	61	75	.449	6				60.4	0.6
1903	Was-A	140	43	94	.314	8				41.7	1.3
	9	1055	454	580	.439						9.6
Lopat, Edmund Walter "Ed"											
1963	KC-A	162	73	89	.451	8				71.6	1.4
1964	KC-A	52	17	35	.327	10	10		1/2	19.1	-2.1
	2	214	90	124	.421						-0.7
Lopes, David Earl "Davey"											
2000	Mil-N	163	73	89	.451	3 C				72.7	0.3
Lopez, Alfonso Ramon "Al"											
1951	Cle-A	155	93	61	.604	2				87.6	5.4
1952	Cle-A	155	93	61	.604	2				92.8	0.2
1953	Cle-A	155	92	62	.597	2				91.3	0.7
1954	Cle-A	156	111	43	.721	1				102.7	8.3

YEAR	TM/L	G	W	L	PCT	STANDING			M/YW-EXP		A-E
1955	Cle-A	154	93	61	.604	2				87.0	6.0
1956	Cle-A	155	88	66	.571	2				90.6	-2.6
1957	Chi-A	155	90	64	.584	2				91.8	-1.8
1958	Chi-A	155	82	72	.532	2				79.0	3.0
1959	Chi-A	156	94	60	.610	1				85.6	8.4
1960	Chi-A	154	87	67	.565	3				89.5	-2.5
1961	Chi-A	163	86	76	.531	4				84.9	1.1
1962	Chi-A	162	85	77	.525	5				86.1	-1.1
1963	Chi-A	162	94	68	.580	2				96.2	-2.2
1964	Chi-A	162	98	64	.605	2				96.9	1.1
1965	Chi-A	162	95	67	.586	2				91.1	3.9
1968	Chi-A	11	6	5	.545	9	9	●8	3/5	5.0	1.0
	Chi-A	36	15	21	.417	9	●8		5/5	16.3	-1.3
1969	Chi-A	17	8	9	.471	4 W	5 W		1/2	7.4	0.6
	17	2425	1410	1004	.584						28.3
Lord, Harry Donald											
1915	Buf-F*	110	60	49	.550	8	6		3/3	49.9	10.1
Lowe, Robert Lincoln "Bobby"											
1904	Det-A*	78	30	44	.405	7	7		2/2	30.3	-0.3
Lucchesi, Frank Joseph											
1970	Phi-N	161	73	88	.453	5 E				66.3	6.7
1971	Phi-N	162	67	95	.414	6 E				66.9	0.1
1972	Phi-N	76	26	50	.342	6 E	6 E		1/2	30.9	-4.9
1975	Tex-A	67	35	32	.522	4 W	3 W		2/2	32.7	2.3
1976	Tex-A	162	76	86	.469	●4 W				77.1	-1.1
1977	Tex-A	62	31	31	.500	●3 W	2 W		1/4	35.3	-4.3
1987	Chi-N	25	8	17	.320	5 E	6 E		2/2	11.3	-3.3
	7	715	316	399	.442						-4.4
Lumley, Harry G											
1909	Bro-N*	155	55	98	.359	6				55.6	-0.6
Lyons, Theodore Amar "Ted"											
1946	Chi-A	125	64	60	.516	7	5		2/2	59.1	4.9
1947	Chi-A	155	70	84	.455	6				65.4	4.6
1948	Chi-A	154	51	101	.336	8				50.4	0.6
	3	434	185	245	.430						10.1
Mack, Cornelius Alexander "Connie"											
1894	Pit-N*	23	12	10	.545	7	7		2/2	10.5	1.5
1895	Pit-N*	135	71	61	.538	7				67.4	3.6
1896	Pit-N*	131	66	63	.512	6				68.5	-2.5
1901	Phi-A	137	74	62	.544	4				72.0	2.0
1902	Phi-A	137	83	53	.610	1				81.0	2.0
1903	Phi-A	137	75	60	.556	2				75.7	-0.7
1904	Phi-A	155	81	70	.536	5				81.7	-0.7
1905	Phi-A	152	92	56	.622	1				89.0	3.0
1906	Phi-A	149	78	67	.538	4				74.9	3.1
1907	Phi-A	150	88	57	.607	2				80.6	7.4
1908	Phi-A	157	68	85	.444	6				67.7	0.3
1909	Phi-A	153	95	58	.621	2				99.1	-4.1
1910	Phi-A	155	102	48	.680	★1				100.9	1.1
1911	Phi-A	152	101	50	.669	★1				100.5	0.5
1912	Phi-A	153	90	62	.592	3				87.8	2.2
1913	Phi-A	153	96	57	.627	★1				96.6	-0.6
1914	Phi-A	158	99	53	.651	1				99.2	-0.2
1915	Phi-A	154	43	109	.283	8				42.2	0.8
1916	Phi-A	154	36	117	.235	8				41.5	-5.5
1917	Phi-A	154	55	98	.359	8				59.2	-4.2
1918	Phi-A	130	52	76	.406	8				50.0	2.0
1919	Phi-A	140	36	104	.257	8				40.8	-4.8
1920	Phi-A	156	48	106	.312	8				49.3	-1.3
1921	Phi-A	155	53	100	.346	8				54.0	-1.0
1922	Phi-A	155	65	89	.422	7				65.1	-0.1
1923	Phi-A	153	69	83	.454	6				66.2	2.8
1924	Phi-A	152	71	81	.467	5				67.0	4.0
1925	Phi-A	153	88	64	.579	2				87.1	0.9
1926	Phi-A	150	83	67	.553	3				86.1	-3.1
1927	Phi-A	155	91	63	.591	2				87.9	3.1
1928	Phi-A	153	98	55	.641	2				97.4	0.6
1929	Phi-A	151	104	46	.693	★1				102.1	1.9
1930	Phi-A	154	102	52	.662	★1				95.0	7.0
1931	Phi-A	153	107	45	.704	1				98.4	8.6
1932	Phi-A	154	94	60	.610	2				97.5	-3.5
1933	Phi-A	152	79	72	.523	3				77.5	1.5
1934	Phi-A	153	68	82	.453	5				68.1	-0.1
1935	Phi-A	149	58	91	.389	8				59.8	-1.8
1936	Phi-A	154	53	100	.346	8				47.1	5.9
1937	Phi-A	120	39	80	.328	7	7		1/2	48.0	-9.0
1938	Phi-A	154	53	99	.349	8				55.1	-2.1
1939	Phi-A	62	25	37	.403	6	7		1/2	19.7	5.3
1940	Phi-A	154	54	100	.351	8				55.9	-1.9
1941	Phi-A	154	64	90	.416	8				65.0	-1.0
1942	Phi-A	154	55	99	.357	8				51.5	3.5
1943	Phi-A	155	49	105	.318	8				53.4	-4.4
1944	Phi-A	155	72	82	.468	●5				69.3	2.7
1945	Phi-A	153	52	98	.347	8				59.1	-7.1
1946	Phi-A	155	49	105	.318	8				60.8	-11.8
1947	Phi-A	156	78	76	.506	5				79.0	-1.0
1948	Phi-A	154	84	70	.545	4				76.4	7.6
1949	Phi-A	154	81	73	.526	5				77.1	3.9

YEAR	TM/L	G	W	L	PCT	STANDING			M/Y	W-EXP	A-E
1950	Phi-A	154	52	102	.338	8				54.3	-2.3
	53	7755	3731	3948	.486						13.9
Mack, Dennis Joseph "Denny"											
1882	Lou-a*	80	42	38	.525	3				48.7	-6.7
Mack, Earle Thaddeus											
1937	Phi-A	34	15	17	.469	7	7		2/2	12.9	2.1
1939	Phi-A	91	30	60	.333	6	7		2/2	28.6	1.4
	2	125	45	77	.369						3.5
Macullar, James F. "Jimmy"											
1879	Syr-N*	27	5	21	.192	6	7		3/3	6.6	-1.6
Maddon, Joseph John "Joe"											
1999	Ana-A	29	19	10	.655	4 W	4 W		2/2	12.5	6.5
Magee, Leo Christopher "Lee"											
1915	Bro-F*	118	53	64	.453	7	7		1/2	56.5	-3.5
Malone, Ferguson G. "Fergy"											
1873	Phi-n*	53	36	27	.571	2				35.9	0.1
1874	Chi-n*	36	18	18	.500	4	5		1/2	15.1	2.9
1884	Phi-U*	67	21	46	.313	7				23.1	-2.1
	3	156	75	91	.452						0.9
Manning, James H. "Jimmy"											
1901	Was-A	138	61	72	.459	6				58.3	2.7
Manning, John E. "Jack"											
1877	Cin-N*	20	7	12	.368	6	6		3/3	4.2	2.8
Manuel, Charles Fuqua "Charlie"											
2000	Cle-A	162	90	72	.556	2 C				93.2	-3.2
Manuel, Jerry											
1998	Chi-A	163	80	82	.494	2 C				74.7	5.3
1999	Chi-A	162	75	86	.466	2 C				71.7	3.3
2000	Chi-A	162	95	67	.586	○1 C				93.5	1.5
	3	487	250	235	.515						10.1
Maranville, Walter James Vincent "Rabbit"											
1925	Chi-N*	53	23	30	.434	7	7	8	2/3	24.8	-1.8
Marion, Martin Whitford "Marty"											
1951	StL-N	155	81	73	.526	3				78.2	2.8
1952	StL-A*	104	42	61	.408	8	7		2/2	42.7	-0.7
1953	StL-A*	154	54	100	.351	8				54.3	-0.3
1954	Chi-A	9	3	6	.333	3	3		2/2	5.7	-2.7
1955	Chi-A	155	91	63	.591	3				94.5	-3.5
1956	Chi-A	154	85	69	.552	3				91.1	-6.1
	6	731	356	372	.489						-10.5
Marshall, Rufus James "Jim"											
1974	Chi-N	69	25	44	.362	5 E	6 E		2/2	27.9	-2.9
1975	Chi-N	162	75	87	.463	●5 E				69.8	5.2
1976	Chi-N	162	75	87	.463	4 E				68.8	6.2
1979	Oak-A	162	54	108	.333	7 W				52.0	2.0
	4	555	229	326	.413						10.5
Martin, Alfred Manuel "Billy"											
1969	Min-A	162	97	65	.599	1 W				98.5	-1.5
1971	Det-A	162	91	71	.562	2 E				86.8	4.2
1972	Det-A	156	86	70	.551	1 E				83.0	3.0
1973	Det-A	134	71	63	.530	3 E	3 E		1/2	64.2	6.8
	Tex-A	23	9	14	.391	6 W	6 W		3/3	8.3	0.7
1974	Tex-A	161	84	76	.525	2 W				79.2	4.8
1975	Tex-A	95	44	51	.463	4 W	3 W		1/2	46.4	-2.4
	NY-A	56	30	26	.536	3 E	3 E		2/2	31.5	-1.5
1976	NY-A	159	97	62	.610	♦1 E				95.7	1.3
1977	NY-A	162	100	62	.617	★1 E				98.9	1.1
1978	NY-A	94	52	42	.553	3 E	▲★1 E		1/3	56.3	-4.3
1979	NY-A	95	55	40	.579	4 E	4 E		2/2	51.2	3.8
1980	Oak-A	162	83	79	.512	2 W				85.6	-2.6
1981(1)	Oak-A	60	37	23	.617	○1 W					
(2)	Oak-A	49	27	22	.551	2 W				60.4	3.6
1982	Oak-A	162	68	94	.420	5 W				68.4	-0.4
1983	NY-A	162	91	71	.562	3 E				87.7	3.3
1985	NY-A	145	91	54	.628	7 E	2 E		2/2	88.4	2.6
1988	NY-A	68	40	28	.588	2 E	5 E		1/2	35.0	5.0
	16	2267	1253	1013	.553						27.5
Martin, Alphonse Case "Phonney"											
1872	Eck-n*	9	1	8	.111	10	9		3/3	-1.0	2.0
Martinez, Orlando iva] "Marty"											
1986	Sea-A	1	0	1	.000	6 W	6 W	7 W	2/3	0.4	-0.4
Mason, Charles E. "Charlie"											
1887	Phi-a	82	38	40	.487	6	5		2/2	39.1	-1.1
Mathews, Edwin Lee "Eddie"											
1972	Atl-N	50	23	27	.460	4 W	4 W		2/2	21.6	1.4
1973	Atl-N	162	76	85	.472	5 W				82.9	-6.9
1974	Atl-N	99	50	49	.505	4 W	3 W		1/2	56.1	-6.1
	3	311	149	161	.481						-11.6
Mathewson, Christopher "Christy"											
1916	Cin-N*	69	25	43	.368	8	●7		3/3	28.4	-3.4
1917	Cin-N	157	78	76	.506	4				75.9	2.1
1918	Cin-N	120	61	57	.517	4	3		1/2	62.3	-1.3
	3	346	164	176	.482						-2.7

YEAR	TM/L	G	W	L	PCT	STANDING			M/Y	W-EXP	A-E
Mattick, Robert James "Bobby"											
1980	Tor-A	162	67	95	.414	7 E				66.8	0.2
1981(1)	Tor-A	58	16	42	.276	7 E					
(2)	Tor-A	48	21	27	.438	7 E				38.0	-1.0
	2	268	104	164	.388						-0.8
Mauch, Gene William											
1960	Phi-N	152	58	94	.382	●4	8		3/3	60.8	-2.8
1961	Phi-N	155	47	107	.305	8				55.7	-8.7
1962	Phi-N	161	81	80	.503	7				75.1	5.9
1963	Phi-N	162	87	75	.537	4				88.0	-1.0
1964	Phi-N	162	92	70	.568	●2				87.4	4.6
1965	Phi-N	162	85	76	.528	6				79.1	5.9
1966	Phi-N	162	87	75	.537	4				86.9	0.1
1967	Phi-N	162	82	80	.506	5				84.4	-2.4
1968	Phi-N	54	27	27	.500	●6	●7		1/3	24.3	2.7
1969	Mon-N	162	52	110	.321	6 E				59.5	-7.5
1970	Mon-N	162	73	89	.451	6 E				69.1	3.9
1971	Mon-N	162	71	90	.441	5 E				69.4	1.6
1972	Mon-N	156	70	86	.449	5 E				67.3	2.7
1973	Mon-N	162	79	83	.488	4 E				77.5	1.5
1974	Mon-N	161	79	82	.491	4 E				81.0	-2.0
1975	Mon-N	162	75	87	.463	●5 E				71.5	3.5
1976	Min-A	162	85	77	.525	3 W				84.9	0.1
1977	Min-A	161	84	77	.522	4 W				89.0	-5.0
1978	Min-A	162	73	89	.451	4 W				79.8	-6.8
1979	Min-A	162	82	80	.506	4 W				84.9	-2.9
1980	Min-A	125	54	71	.432	4 W	3 W		1/2	58.2	-4.2
1981(1)	Cal-A	13	9	4	.692	4 W	4 W		2/2		
(2)	Cal-A	50	20	30	.400	7 W				32.9	-3.9
1982	Cal-A	162	93	69	.574	1 W				95.3	-2.3
1985	Cal-A	162	90	72	.556	2 W				83.9	6.1
1986	Cal-A	162	92	70	.568	1 W				91.2	0.8
1987	Cal-A	162	75	87	.463	●6 W				77.8	-2.8
	26	3942	1902	2037	.483						-12.9
McAleer, James Robert "Jimmy"											
1901	Cle-A*	138	54	82	.397	7				53.0	1.0
1902	StL-A*	140	78	58	.574	2				69.2	8.8
1903	StL-A	139	65	74	.468	6				66.7	-1.7
1904	StL-A	156	65	87	.428	6				62.0	3.0
1905	StL-A	156	54	99	.353	8				65.8	-11.8
1906	StL-A	154	76	73	.510	5				81.5	-5.5
1907	StL-A*	155	69	83	.454	6				74.4	-5.4
1908	StL-A	155	83	69	.546	4				83.1	-0.1
1909	StL-A	154	61	89	.407	7				59.3	1.7
1910	Was-A	157	66	85	.437	7				69.7	-3.7
1911	Was-A	154	64	90	.416	7				62.9	1.1
	11	1658	735	889	.453						-12.7
McBride, George Florian											
1921	Was-A	154	80	73	.523	4				73.2	6.8
McBride, James Dickson "Dick"											
1871	Ath-n*	28	21	7	.750	1				20.9	0.1
1872	Ath-n*	47	30	14	.682	4				35.1	-5.1
1873	Ath-n*	52	28	23	.549	5				30.7	-2.7
1874	Ath-n*	56	33	23	.589	3				35.2	-2.2
1875	Ath-n*	69	49	18	.731	2	2		1/2	55.1	-6.1
	5	252	161	85	.654						-16.0
McCallister, John "Jack"											
1927	Cle-A	153	66	87	.431	6				66.9	-0.9
McCarthy, Joseph Vincent "Joe"											
1926	Chi-N	155	82	72	.532	4				85.3	-3.3
1927	Chi-N	153	85	68	.556	4				85.3	-0.3
1928	Chi-N	154	91	63	.591	3				87.1	3.9
1929	Chi-N	156	98	54	.645	1				96.1	1.9
1930	Chi-N	152	86	64	.573	2	2		1/2	85.8	0.2
1931	NY-A	155	94	59	.614	2				103.3	-9.3
1932	NY-A	156	107	47	.695	★1				102.1	4.9
1933	NY-A	152	91	59	.607	2				89.3	1.7
1934	NY-A	154	94	60	.610	2				93.6	0.4
1935	NY-A	149	89	60	.597	2				92.4	-3.4
1936	NY-A	155	102	51	.667	★1				105.9	-3.9
1937	NY-A	157	102	52	.662	★1				105.5	-3.5
1938	NY-A	157	99	53	.651	★1				99.5	-0.5
1939	NY-A	152	106	45	.702	★1				114.5	-8.5
1940	NY-A	155	88	66	.571	3				91.1	-3.1
1941	NY-A	156	101	53	.656	★1				96.5	4.5
1942	NY-A	154	103	51	.669	1				107.3	-4.3
1943	NY-A	155	98	56	.636	★1				90.6	7.4
1944	NY-A	154	83	71	.539	3				82.9	0.1
1945	NY-A	152	81	71	.533	4				83.2	-2.2
1946	NY-A	35	22	13	.629	2	3		1/3	20.8	1.2
1948	Bos-A	155	96	59	.619	▲2				94.8	1.2
1949	Bos-A	155	96	58	.623	2				98.6	-2.6
1950	Bos-A	59	31	28	.525	4	3		1/2	36.9	-5.9
	24	3487	2125	1333	.615						-23.6
McCarthy, Thomas Francis "Tommy"											
1890	StL-a*	22	11	11	.500	4	3		1/6	12.9	-1.9
	StL-a*	5	4	1	.800	2	2	3	5/6	2.9	1.1

YEAR	TM/L	G	W	L	PCT	STANDING			M/Y	W-EXP	A-E
McCloskey, John Joseph											
1895	Lou-N	133	35	96	.267	12				33.4	1.6
1896	Lou-N	19	2	17	.105	12	12		1/2	5.2	-3.2
1906	StL-N	154	52	98	.347	7				59.5	-7.5
1907	StL-N	155	52	101	.340	8				54.3	-2.3
1908	StL-N	154	49	105	.318	8				47.1	1.9
	5	615	190	417	.313						-9.4
McCormick, James "Jim"											
1879	Cle-N*	82	27	55	.329	6				27.5	-0.5
1880	Cle-N*	85	47	37	.560	3				47.1	-0.1
1882	Cle-N*	4	0	4	.000	8	5		1/2	2.0	-2.0
	3	171	74	96	.435						-2.6
McGaha, Fred Melvin "Mel"											
1962	Cle-A	160	78	82	.488	6	6		1/2	73.7	4.3
1964	KC-A	111	40	70	.364	10	10		2/2	40.3	-0.3
1965	KC-A	26	5	21	.192	10	10		1/2	10.2	-5.2
	3	297	123	173	.416						-1.2
McGeary, Michael Henry "Mike"											
1875	Phi-n*	63	34	27	.557	4	5		1/2	37.8	-3.8
1880	Pro-N*	16	8	7	.533	4	2		1/3	9.7	-1.7
1881	Cle-N*	11	4	7	.364	6	7		1/2	5.2	-1.2
	3	90	46	41	.529						-6.7
McGraw, John Joseph											
1899	Bal-N*	152	86	62	.581	4				86.9	-0.9
1901	Bal-A*	135	68	65	.511	5				67.4	0.6
1902	Bal-A*	58	26	31	.456	7	8		1/2	23.5	2.5
	NY-N*	65	25	38	.397	8	8		3/3	21.2	3.8
1903	NY-N*	142	84	55	.604	2				85.6	-1.6
1904	NY-N*	158	106	47	.693	1				105.7	0.3
1905	NY-N*	155	105	48	.686	★1				105.2	-0.2
1906	NY-N*	153	96	56	.632	2				88.8	7.2
1907	NY-N	155	82	71	.536	4				83.8	-1.8
1908	NY-N	157	98	56	.636	●2				99.2	-1.2
1909	NY-N	158	92	61	.601	3				85.0	7.0
1910	NY-N	155	91	63	.591	2				92.4	-1.4
1911	NY-N	154	99	54	.647	1				98.6	0.4
1912	NY-N	154	103	48	.682	1				100.6	2.4
1913	NY-N	156	101	51	.664	1				94.3	6.7
1914	NY-N	156	84	70	.545	2				87.2	-3.2
1915	NY-N	155	69	83	.454	8				71.1	-2.1
1916	NY-N	155	86	66	.566	4				86.5	-0.5
1917	NY-N	158	98	56	.636	1				97.3	0.7
1918	NY-N	124	71	53	.573	2				69.3	1.7
1919	NY-N	140	87	53	.621	2				84.6	2.4
1920	NY-N	155	86	68	.558	2				91.8	-5.8
1921	NY-N	153	94	59	.614	★1				96.1	-2.1
1922	NY-N	156	93	61	.604	★1				95.7	-2.7
1923	NY-N	153	95	58	.621	1				93.1	1.9
1924	NY-N	29	16	13	.552	3	1		1/3	18.4	-2.4
	NY-N	81	45	35	.563	1	1		3/3	50.9	-5.9
1925	NY-N	14	10	4	.714	1	2		1/3	7.3	2.7
	NY-N	106	55	51	.519	1	2		3/3	55.3	-0.3
1926	NY-N	151	74	77	.490	5				75.0	-1.0
1927	NY-N	122	70	52	.574	4	3		1/2	68.3	1.7
1928	NY-N	155	93	61	.604	2				92.1	0.9
1929	NY-N	152	84	67	.556	3				92.9	-8.9
1930	NY-N	154	87	67	.565	3				89.8	-2.8
1931	NY-N	153	87	65	.572	2				93.0	-6.0
1932	NY-N	40	17	23	.425	8	●6		1/2	21.2	-4.2
	33	4769	2763	1948	.586						-11.9
McGuire, James Thomas "Deacon"											
1898	Was-N*	70	21	47	.309	10	11	11	3/4	24.3	-3.3
1907	Bos-A*	112	45	61	.425	8	7		4/4	45.4	-0.4
1908	Bos-A*	115	53	62	.461	6	5		1/2	61.8	-8.8
1909	Cle-A	41	14	25	.359	4	6		2/2	18.3	-4.3
1910	Cle-A*	161	71	81	.467	5				64.0	7.0
1911	Cle-A	17	6	11	.353	7	3		1/2	8.3	-2.3
	6	516	210	287	.423						-12.2
McGunnigle, William Henry "Bill"											
1888	Bro-a	143	88	52	.629	2				87.0	1.0
1889	Bro-a	140	93	44	.679	1				93.4	-0.4
1890	Bro-N	129	86	43	.667	1				87.7	-1.7
1891	Pit-N	59	24	33	.421	8	8		2/2	25.9	-1.9
1896	Lou-N	115	36	76	.321	12	12		2/2	30.9	5.1
	5	586	327	248	.569						2.1
McInnis, John Phalen "Stuffy"											
1927	Phi-N*	155	51	103	.331	8				55.9	-4.9
McKechnie, William Boyd "Bill"											
1915	New-F*	102	54	45	.545	6	5		2/2	51.2	2.8
1922	Pit-N	90	53	36	.596	5	●3		2/2	51.5	1.5
1923	Pit-N	154	87	67	.565	3				85.7	1.3
1924	Pit-N	153	90	63	.588	3				90.6	-0.6
1925	Pit-N	153	95	58	.621	★1				94.6	0.4
1926	Pit-N	157	84	69	.549	3				84.4	-0.4
1928	StL-N	154	95	59	.617	1				93.8	1.2
1929	StL-N	63	34	29	.540	4	4		3/3	32.5	1.5
1930	Bos-N	154	70	84	.455	6				63.5	6.5
1931	Bos-N	156	64	90	.416	7				61.2	2.8
1932	Bos-N	155	77	77	.500	5				76.4	0.6
1933	Bos-N	156	83	71	.539	4				79.4	3.6
1934	Bos-N	152	78	73	.517	4				72.4	5.6
1935	Bos-N	153	38	115	.248	8				49.3	-11.3
1936	Bos-N	157	71	83	.461	6				68.4	2.6
1937	Bos-N	152	79	73	.520	5				78.5	0.5
1938	Cin-N	151	82	68	.547	4				83.9	-1.9
1939	Cin-N	156	97	57	.630	1				94.5	2.5
1940	Cin-N	155	100	53	.654	★1				95.5	4.5
1941	Cin-N	154	88	66	.571	3				82.6	5.4
1942	Cin-N	154	76	76	.500	4				74.0	2.0
1943	Cin-N	155	87	67	.565	2				84.2	2.8
1944	Cin-N	155	89	65	.578	3				81.0	8.0
1945	Cin-N	154	61	93	.396	7				60.2	0.8
1946	Cin-N	152	64	86	.427	6	6		1/2	69.8	-5.8
	25	3647	1896	1723	.524						37.0
McKeon, John Aloysius "Jack"											
1973	KC-A	162	88	74	.543	2 W				81.3	6.7
1974	KC-A	162	77	85	.475	5 W				81.5	-4.5
1975	KC-A	96	50	46	.521	2 W	2 W		1/2	51.7	-1.7
1977	Oak-A	53	26	27	.491	●5 W	7 W		1/2	21.6	4.4
1978	Oak-A	123	45	78	.366	1 W	6 W		2/2	48.4	-3.4
1988	SD-N	115	67	48	.583	5 W	3 W		2/2	58.4	8.6
1989	SD-N	162	89	73	.549	2 W				82.7	6.3
1990	SD-N	80	37	43	.463	4 W	5 W		1/2	40.0	-3.0
1997	Cin-N	63	33	30	.524	4 C	3 C		2/2	27.0	6.0
1998	Cin-N	162	77	85	.475	4 C				80.0	-3.0
1999	Cin-N	163	96	67	.589	▲2 C				96.4	-0.4
2000	Cin-N	163	85	77	.525	2 C				86.8	-1.8
	12	1504	770	733	.512						14.2
McKinnon, Alexander J. "Alex"											
1885	StL-N*	39	6	32	.158	5	8	8	2/3	11.8	-5.8
McKnight, Dennis Hamar "Denny"											
1884	Pit-a	12	4	8	.333	9	10		1/5	2.7	1.3
McManus, George											
1876	StL-N	8	6	2	.750	2	2		2/2	5.9	0.1
1877	StL-N	60	28	32	.467	4				26.8	1.2
	2	68	34	34	.500						1.3
McManus, Martin Joseph "Marty"											
1932	Bos-A*	99	32	67	.323	8	8		2/2	27.8	4.2
1933	Bos-A*	149	63	86	.423	7				68.9	-5.9
	2	248	95	153	.383						-1.7
McMillan, Roy David											
1972	Mil-A	2	1	1	.500	6 E	6 E	6 E	2/3	0.9	0.1
1975	NY-N	53	26	27	.491	3 E	●3 E		2/2	27.2	-1.2
	2	55	27	28	.491						-1.1
McNamara, John Francis											
1969	Oak-A	13	8	5	.615	2 W	2 W		2/2	7.0	1.0
1970	Oak-A	162	89	73	.549	2 W				90.1	-1.1
1974	SD-N	162	60	102	.370	6 W				51.2	8.8
1975	SD-N	162	71	91	.438	4 W				66.8	4.2
1976	SD-N	162	73	89	.451	5 W				71.0	2.0
1977	SD-N	48	20	28	.417	4 W	5 W		1/3	19.9	0.1
1979	Cin-N	161	90	71	.559	1 W				89.4	0.6
1980	Cin-N	163	89	73	.549	3 W				84.8	4.2
1981(1)	Cin-N	56	35	21	.625	2 W					
(2)	Cin-N	52	31	21	.596	2 W				56.5	9.5
1982	Cin-N	92	34	58	.370	6 W	6 W		1/2	38.8	-4.8
1983	Cal-A	162	70	92	.432	●5 W				75.4	-5.4
1984	Cal-A	162	81	81	.500	●2 W				80.9	0.1
1985	Bos-A	163	81	81	.500	5 E				88.9	-7.9
1986	Bos-A	161	95	66	.590	♦1 E				90.2	4.8
1987	Bos-A	162	78	84	.481	5 E				82.6	-4.6
1988	Bos-A	85	43	42	.506	4 E	1 E		1/2	48.9	-5.9
1990	Cle-A	162	77	85	.475	4 E				80.5	-3.5
1991	Cle-A	77	25	52	.325	7 E	7 E		1/2	29.4	-4.4
1996	Cal-A	50	18	32	.360	4 W			2/2	19.8	-1.8
	19	2417	1168	1247	.484						-4.0
McPhee, John Alexander "Bid"											
1901	Cin-N	142	52	87	.374	8				44.8	7.2
1902	Cin-N	65	27	37	.422	6	4		1/3	35.2	-8.2
	2	207	79	124	.389						-0.9
McRae, Harold Abraham "Hal"											
1991	KC-A	124	66	58	.532	7 W	6 W		3/3	62.4	3.6
1992	KC-A	162	72	90	.444	●5 W				74.9	-2.9
1993	KC-A	162	84	78	.519	3 W				79.0	5.0
1994	KC-A	115	64	51	.557	3 C				61.6	2.4
	4	563	286	277	.508						8.1
McVey, Calvin Alexander "Cal"											
1873	Bal-n*	33	20	13	.606	3	3		1/2	24.3	-4.3
1878	Cin-N*	61	37	23	.617	2				34.9	2.1
1879	Cin-N*	63	34	28	.548	4	5		2/2	32.4	1.6
	3	157	91	64	.587						-0.6
Mele, Sabath Anthony "Sam"											
1961	Min-A	7	2	5	.286	8	9	7	2/4	3.2	-1.2

YEAR	TM/L	G	W	L	PCT	STANDING			M/YW-EXP		A-E
	Min-A	95	45	49	.479	9	7		4/4	42.9	2.1
1962	Min-A	163	91	71	.562	2				89.4	1.6
1963	Min-A	161	91	70	.565	3				97.5	-6.5
1964	Min-A	163	79	83	.488	●6				87.0	-8.0
1965	Min-A	162	102	60	.630	1				98.9	3.1
1966	Min-A	162	89	73	.549	2				89.9	-0.9
1967	Min-A	50	25	25	.500	6	●2		1/2	27.7	-2.7
	7	963	524	436	.546						-12.4
Melillo, Oscar Donald "Ski"											
1938	StL-A	10	2	7	.222	7	7		2/2	3.4	-1.4
Merrill, Carl Harrison "Stump"											
1990	NY-A	113	49	64	.434	7 E	7 E		2/2	45.9	3.1
1991	NY-A	162	71	91	.438	5 E				70.7	0.3
	2	275	120	155	.436						3.4
Metro, Charles "Charlie"											
1962	Chi-N	112	43	69	.384	9	9		3/3	42.5	0.5
1970	KC-A	52	19	33	.365	5 W	●4 W		1/2	22.8	-3.8
	2	164	62	102	.378						-3.3
Meyer, William Adam "Billy"											
1948	Pit-N	156	83	71	.539	4				77.5	5.5
1949	Pit-N	154	71	83	.461	6				69.3	1.7
1950	Pit-N	154	57	96	.373	8				59.8	-2.8
1951	Pit-N	155	64	90	.416	7				62.1	1.9
1952	Pit-N	155	42	112	.273	8				48.3	-6.3
	5	774	317	452	.412						0.0
Michael, Eugene Richard "Gene"											
1981(1)	NY-A	56	34	22	.607	♦1 E					
(2)	NY-A	26	14	12	.538	4 E	6 E		1/2	47.7	0.3
1982	NY-A	86	44	42	.512	●4 E	●5 E	5 E	2/3	42.6	1.4
1986	Chi-N	102	46	56	.451	5 E	5 E		3/3	44.6	1.4
1987	Chi-N	136	68	68	.500	5 E	6 E		1/2	61.3	6.7
	4	406	206	200	.507						9.7
Milan, Jesse Clyde "Clyde"											
1922	Was-A*	154	69	85	.448	6				71.3	-2.3
Miller, George Frederick											
1894	StL-N*	133	56	76	.424	9				50.8	5.2
Miller, Raymond Roger "Ray"											
1985	Min-A	100	50	50	.500	6 W	4 W		2/2	45.3	4.7
1986	Min-A	139	59	80	.424	7 W	6 W		1/2	61.4	-2.4
1998	Bal-A	162	79	83	.488	4 E				84.1	-5.1
1999	Bal-A	162	78	84	.481	4 E				84.4	-6.4
	4	563	266	297	.472						-9.1
Mills, Colonel Buster "Buster"											
1953	Cin-N	8	4	4	.500	6	6		2/2	3.6	0.4
Mills, Everett											
1872	Bal-n*	17	8	6	.571	2	2		2/2	10.3	-2.3
Mitchell, Frederick Francis "Fred"											
1917	Chi-N	157	74	80	.481	5				75.3	-1.3
1918	Chi-N	131	84	45	.651	1				80.8	3.2
1919	Chi-N	140	75	65	.536	3				75.7	-0.7
1920	Chi-N	154	75	79	.487	●5				75.3	-0.3
1921	Bos-N	153	79	74	.516	4				78.9	0.1
1922	Bos-N	154	53	100	.346	8				54.2	-1.2
1923	Bos-N	155	54	100	.351	7				61.0	-7.0
	7	1044	494	543	.476						-7.2
Moore, Jackie Spencer											
1984	Oak-A	118	57	61	.483	5 W	4 W		2/2	54.9	2.1
1985	Oak-A	162	77	85	.475	●4 W				78.1	-1.1
1986	Oak-A	73	29	44	.397	●6 W	●3 W		1/3	35.2	-6.2
	3	353	163	190	.462						-5.2
Moore, Terry Bluford											
1954	Phi-N	77	35	42	.455	3	4		2/2	40.8	-5.8
Moran, Patrick Joseph "Pat"											
1915	Phi-N	153	90	62	.592	1				90.4	-0.4
1916	Phi-N	154	91	62	.595	2				87.0	4.0
1917	Phi-N	155	87	65	.572	2				84.8	2.2
1918	Phi-N	125	55	68	.447	6				53.1	1.9
1919	Cin-N	140	96	44	.686	★1				90.0	6.0
1920	Cin-N	154	82	71	.536	3				84.0	-2.0
1921	Cin-N	153	70	83	.458	6				73.3	-3.3
1922	Cin-N	156	86	68	.558	2				85.8	0.2
1923	Cin-N	154	91	63	.591	2				85.0	6.0
	9	1344	748	586	.561						14.6
Morgan, Joseph Michael "Joe"											
1988	Bos-A	77	46	31	.597	4 E	1 E		2/2	44.3	1.7
1989	Bos-A	162	83	79	.512	3 E				84.8	-1.8
1990	Bos-A	162	88	74	.543	1 E				84.6	3.4
1991	Bos-A	162	84	78	.519	●2 E				82.9	1.1
	4	563	301	262	.535						4.3
Moriarty, George Joseph											
1927	Det-A	156	82	71	.536	4				80.2	1.8
1928	Det-A	154	68	86	.442	6				71.3	-3.3
	2	310	150	157	.489						-1.5

YEAR	TM/L	G	W	L	PCT	STANDING			M/YW-EXP		A-E
Morrill, John Francis											
1882	Bos-N*	85	45	39	.536	●3				47.4	-2.4
1883	Bos-N*	44	33	11	.750	4	1		2/2	30.5	2.5
1884	Bos-N*	116	73	38	.658	2				76.1	-3.1
1885	Bos-N*	113	46	66	.411	5				50.2	-4.2
1886	Bos-N*	118	56	61	.479	5				58.1	-2.1
1887	Bos-N*	32	12	17	.414	5	5		2/2	15.3	-3.3
1888	Bos-N*	137	70	64	.522	4				71.9	-1.9
1889	Was-N*	51	13	38	.255	8	8		1/2	16.2	-3.2
	8	696	348	334	.510						-17.7
Morton, Charles Hazen "Charlie"											
1884	Tol-a*	110	46	58	.442	8				41.4	4.6
1885	Det-N*	38	7	31	.184	8	6		1/2	16.7	-9.7
1890	Tol-a	134	68	64	.515	4				70.6	-2.6
	3	282	121	153	.442						-7.8
Moses, Felix I.											
1884	Ric-a	46	12	30	.286	12				11.8	0.2
Moss, John Lester "Les"											
1968	Chi-A	2	0	2	.000	9	9	●8	2/5	0.9	-0.9
	Chi-A	34	12	22	.353	9	9	●8	4/5	15.4	-3.4
1979	Det-A	53	27	26	.509	5 E	5 E		1/3	27.5	-0.5
	2	89	39	50	.438						-4.8
Murnane, Timothy Hayes "Tim"											
1884	Bos-U*	111	58	51	.532	5				61.6	-3.6
Murray, William Jeremiah "Billy"											
1907	Phi-N	149	83	64	.565	3				77.9	5.1
1908	Phi-N	155	83	71	.539	4				84.2	-1.2
1909	Phi-N	154	74	79	.484	5				76.3	-2.3
	3	458	240	214	.529						1.7
Murtaugh, Daniel Edward "Danny"											
1957	Pit-N	51	26	25	.510	7	●7		2/2	21.7	4.3
1958	Pit-N	154	84	70	.545	2				82.7	1.3
1959	Pit-N	155	78	76	.506	4				74.0	4.0
1960	Pit-N	155	95	59	.617	★1				91.5	3.5
1961	Pit-N	154	75	79	.487	6				78.9	-3.9
1962	Pit-N	161	93	68	.578	4				88.8	4.2
1963	Pit-N	162	74	88	.457	8				77.9	-3.9
1964	Pit-N	162	80	82	.494	●6				83.9	-3.9
1967	Pit-N	79	39	39	.500	6	6		2/2	38.3	0.7
1970	Pit-N	162	89	73	.549	1 E				87.7	1.3
1971	Pit-N	162	97	65	.599	★1 E				100.4	-3.4
1973	Pit-N	26	13	13	.500	2 E	3 E		2/2	13.2	-0.2
1974	Pit-N	162	88	74	.543	1 E				90.6	-2.6
1975	Pit-N	161	92	69	.571	1 E				96.2	-4.2
1976	Pit-N	162	92	70	.568	2 E				89.1	2.9
	15	2068	1115	950	.540						0.2
Muser, Anthony Joseph "Tony"											
1997	KC-A	79	31	48	.392	4 C	5 C		2/2	36.1	-5.1
1998	KC-A	161	72	89	.447	3 C				63.0	9.0
1999	KC-A	161	64	97	.398	4 C				74.6	-10.6
2000	KC-A	162	77	85	.475	4 C				76.4	0.6
	4	563	244	319	.433						-6.1
Mutrie, James J. "Jim"											
1883	NY-a	97	54	42	.563	4				57.1	-3.1
1884	NY-a	112	75	32	.701	1				82.5	-7.5
1885	NY-N	112	85	27	.759	2				87.3	-2.3
1886	NY-N	124	75	44	.630	3				72.2	2.8
1887	NY-N	129	68	55	.553	4				69.6	-1.6
1888	NY-N	138	84	47	.641	1				84.3	-0.3
1889	NY-N	131	83	43	.659	1				82.2	0.8
1890	NY-N	135	63	68	.481	6				66.9	-3.9
1891	NY-N	136	71	61	.538	3				69.9	1.1
	9	1114	658	419	.611						-14.1
Myatt, George Edward "George"											
1968	Phi-N	1	1	0	1.000	●6	5	●7	2/3	0.5	0.5
1969	Phi-N	54	19	35	.352	5 E	5 E		2/2	23.6	-4.6
	2	55	20	35	.364						-4.0
Myers, Henry C.											
1882	Bal-a*	74	19	54	.260	6				14.2	4.8
Nash, William Mitchell "Billy"											
1896	Phi-N*	130	62	68	.477	8				64.9	-2.9
Neun, John Henry "Johnny"											
1946	NY-A	14	8	6	.571	3	3		3/3	8.3	-0.3
1947	Cin-N	154	73	81	.474	5				69.7	3.3
1948	Cin-N	100	44	56	.440	7	7		1/2	39.2	4.8
	3	268	125	143	.466						7.8
Newman, Jeffrey Lynn "Jeff"											
1986	Oak-A	10	2	8	.200	●6 W	7 W	●3 W	2/3	4.8	-2.8
Nichols, Charles Augustus "Kid"											
1904	StL-N*	155	75	79	.487	5				77.8	-2.8
1905	StL-N*	14	5	9	.357	7	6		1/3	5.1	-0.1
	2	169	80	88	.476						-2.9
Nicol, Hugh											
1897	StL-N	40	8	32	.200	12	12	12	2/4	7.2	0.8

YEAR	TM/L	G	W	L	PCT	STANDING			M/Y	W-EXP	A-E
Nixon, Russell Eugene "Russ"											
1982	Cin-N	70	27	43	.386	6 W	6 W		2/2	29.5	-2.5
1983	Cin-N	162	74	88	.457	6 W				71.9	2.1
1988	Atl-N	121	42	79	.347	6 W	6 W		2/2	45.7	-3.7
1989	Atl-N	161	63	97	.394	6 W				69.7	-6.7
1990	Atl-N	65	25	40	.385	6 W	6 W		1/2	27.0	-2.0
	5	579	231	347	.400						-12.8
Norman, Henry Willis Patrick "Bill"											
1958	Det-A	105	56	49	.533	8	5		2/2	56.3	-0.3
1959	Det-A	17	2	15	.118	8	4		1/2	8.3	-6.3
	2	122	58	64	.475						-6.6
Oakes, Ennis Telfair "Rebel"											
1914	Pit-F*	143	61	78	.439	8	7		2/2	60.6	0.4
1915	Pit-F*	156	86	67	.562	3				84.1	1.9
	2	299	147	145	.503						2.3
Oates, Johnny Lane											
1991	Bal-A	125	54	71	.432	7 E	6 E		2/2	54.1	-0.1
1992	Bal-A	162	89	73	.549	3 E				86.1	2.9
1993	Bal-A	162	85	77	.525	●3 E				85.0	-0.0
1994	Bal-A	112	63	49	.563	2 E				64.9	-1.9
1995	Tex-A	144	74	70	.514	3 W				69.2	4.8
1996	Tex-A	163	90	72	.556	○1 W				92.9	-2.9
1997	Tex-A	162	77	85	.475	3 W				79.5	-2.5
1998	Tex-A	162	88	74	.543	○1 W				87.2	0.8
1999	Tex-A	162	95	67	.586	○1 W				88.7	6.3
2000	Tex-A	162	71	91	.438	4 W				69.7	1.3
	10	1516	786	729	.519						8.7
O'Connor, John Joseph "Jack"											
1910	StL-A*	158	47	107	.305	8				45.1	1.9
O'Day, Henry Francis "Hank"											
1912	Cin-N	155	75	78	.490	4				69.9	5.1
1914	Chi-N	156	78	76	.506	4				73.5	4.5
	2	311	153	154	.498						9.6
O'Farrell, Robert Arthur "Bob"											
1927	StL-N*	153	92	61	.601	2				85.3	6.7
1934	Cin-N*	91	30	60	.333	8	8		1/3	32.5	-2.5
	2	244	122	121	.502						4.2
O'Leary, Daniel "Dan"											
1884	Cin-U*	35	20	15	.571	5	3		1/2	24.6	-4.6
O'Neill, Stephen Francis "Steve"											
1935	Cle-A	60	36	23	.610	5	3		2/2	30.9	5.1
1936	Cle-A	157	80	74	.519	5				82.3	-2.3
1937	Cle-A	156	83	71	.539	4				81.6	1.4
1943	Det-A	155	78	76	.506	5				84.8	-6.8
1944	Det-A	156	88	66	.571	2				85.2	2.8
1945	Det-A	155	88	65	.575	★1				83.8	4.2
1946	Det-A	155	92	62	.597	2				91.4	0.6
1947	Det-A	158	85	69	.552	2				84.4	0.6
1948	Det-A	154	78	76	.506	5				74.4	3.6
1950	Bos-A	95	63	32	.663	4	3		2/2	59.5	3.5
1951	Bos-A	154	87	67	.565	3				84.5	2.5
1952	Phi-N	91	59	32	.648	6	4		2/2	52.1	6.9
1953	Phi-N	156	83	71	.539	●3				82.0	1.0
1954	Phi-N	77	40	37	.519	3	4		1/2	40.8	-0.8
	14	1879	1040	821	.559						22.2
Onslow, John James "Jack"											
1949	Chi-A	154	63	91	.409	6				68.1	-5.1
1950	Chi-A	31	8	22	.267	8	6		1/2	12.6	-4.6
	2	185	71	113	.386						-9.7
O'Rourke, James Henry "Jim"											
1881	Buf-N*	83	45	38	.542	3				40.9	4.1
1882	Buf-N*	84	45	39	.536	●3				45.5	-0.5
1883	Buf-N*	98	52	45	.536	5				51.8	0.2
1884	Buf-N*	115	64	47	.577	3				62.0	2.0
1893	Was-N*	130	40	89	.310	12				39.2	0.8
	5	510	246	258	.488						6.7
Orr, David L. "Dave"											
1887	NY-a*	8	3	5	.375	8	7	7	2/3	2.3	0.7
Ott, Melvin Thomas "Mel"											
1942	NY-N*	154	85	67	.559	3				83.8	1.2
1943	NY-N*	156	55	98	.359	8				60.2	-5.2
1944	NY-N*	155	67	87	.435	5				68.1	-1.1
1945	NY-N*	154	78	74	.513	5				72.7	5.3
1946	NY-N*	154	61	93	.396	8				69.5	-8.5
1947	NY-N*	155	81	73	.526	4				83.5	-2.5
1948	NY-N	76	37	38	.493	4	5		1/2	41.1	-4.1
	7	1004	464	530	.467						-14.8
Owens, Paul Francis											
1972	Phi-N	80	33	47	.412	6 E	6 E		2/2	32.5	0.5
1983	Phi-N	77	47	30	.610	1 E	◆1 E		2/2	41.5	5.5
1984	Phi-N	162	81	81	.500	4 E				84.1	-3.1
	3	319	161	158	.505						2.9
Ozark, Daniel Leonard "Danny"											
1973	Phi-N	162	71	91	.438	6 E				73.2	-2.2
1974	Phi-N	162	80	82	.494	3 E				78.4	1.6
1975	Phi-N	162	86	76	.531	2 E				85.1	0.9
1976	Phi-N	162	101	61	.623	1 E				103.3	-2.3
1977	Phi-N	162	101	61	.623	1 E				98.6	2.4
1978	Phi-N	162	90	72	.556	1 E				94.0	-4.0
1979	Phi-N	133	65	67	.492	5 E	4 E		1/2	63.1	1.9
1984	SF-N	56	24	32	.429	6 W	6 W		2/2	23.7	0.3
	8	1161	618	542	.533						-1.4
Pabor, Charles Henry "Charlie"											
1871	Cle-n*	29	10	19	.345	7				8.4	1.6
1875	Atl-n*	42	2	40	.048	12	12		1/2	-3.3	5.3
	NH-n*	6	1	5	.167	8	8		3/3	0.5	0.5
	2	77	13	64	.169						7.5
Parker, Francis James "Salty"											
1967	NY-N	11	4	7	.364	10	10		2/2	4.2	-0.2
1972	Hou-N	1	1	0	1.000	2 W	2 W		2/3	0.5	0.5
	2	12	5	7	.417						0.3
Parks, William Robert "Bill"											
1875	Was-n*	8	1	7	.125	8	10		2/2	-1.0	2.0
Parrish, Larry Alton											
1998	Det-A	25	13	12	.520	5 C	5 C		2/2	10.4	2.6
1999	Det-A	161	69	92	.429	3 C				67.8	1.2
	2	186	82	104	.441						3.8
Pearce, Richard J. "Dickey"											
1872	Mut-n*	16	10	6	.625	4	3		1/2	11.6	-1.6
1875	StL-n*	70	39	29	.574	4				35.6	3.4
	2	86	49	35	.583						1.8
Peckinpaugh, Roger Thorpe											
1914	NY-A*	20	10	10	.500	7	●6		2/2	9.8	0.2
1928	Cle-A	155	62	92	.403	7				62.0	0.0
1929	Cle-A	152	81	71	.533	3				74.2	6.8
1930	Cle-A	154	81	73	.526	4				74.8	6.2
1931	Cle-A	155	78	76	.506	4				81.7	-3.7
1932	Cle-A	153	87	65	.572	4				85.1	1.9
1933	Cle-A	51	26	25	.510	5	4		1/3	25.0	1.0
1941	Cle-A	155	75	79	.487	●4				77.9	-2.9
	8	995	500	491	.505						9.5
Perez, Atanasio "Tony"											
1993	Cin-N	44	20	24	.455	5 W	5 W		1/2	20.3	-0.3
Perkins, Ralph Foster "Cy"											
1937	Det-A	15	6	9	.400	2	2		5/5	8.3	-2.3
Pesky, John Michael "Johnny"											
1963	Bos-A	161	76	85	.472	7				76.6	-0.6
1964	Bos-A	160	70	90	.438	8	8		1/2	69.7	0.3
1980	Bos-A	5	1	4	.200	3 E	4 E		2/2	2.5	-1.5
	3	326	147	179	.451						-1.8
Pfeffer, Nathaniel Frederick "Fred"											
1892(1)	Lou-N*	23	9	14	.391	10	11		2/2		
(2)	Lou-N*	77	33	42	.440	9				39.2	2.8
Phelan, Lewis G. "Lew"											
1895	StL-N	45	11	30	.268	11	11		4/4	13.1	-2.1
Phillips, Harold Ross "Lefty"											
1969	Cal-A	124	60	63	.488	6 W	3 W		2/2	51.0	9.0
1970	Cal-A	162	86	76	.531	3 W				81.1	4.9
1971	Cal-A	162	76	86	.469	4 W				73.5	2.5
	3	448	222	225	.497						16.4
Phillips, Horace B.											
1879	Tro-N	47	12	34	.261	8	8		1/2	10.8	1.2
1883	Col-a	97	32	65	.330	6				32.4	-0.4
1884	Pit-a	35	9	24	.273	10	10		5/5	7.4	1.6
1885	Pit-a	111	56	55	.505	3				56.3	-0.3
1886	Pit-a	140	80	57	.584	2				83.7	-3.7
1887	Pit-N	125	55	69	.444	6				50.3	4.7
1888	Pit-N	139	66	68	.493	6				62.1	3.9
1889	Pit-N	71	28	43	.394	6	5		1/3	31.9	-3.9
	8	765	338	415	.449						3.1
Phillips, William Corcoran "Bill"											
1914	Ind-F	157	88	65	.575	1				90.6	-2.6
1915	New-F	53	26	27	.491	6	5		1/2	27.4	-1.4
	2	210	114	92	.553						-4.0
Pike, Lipman Emanuel "Lip"											
1871	Tro-n*	4	1	3	.250	7	6		1/2	1.9	-0.9
1874	Har-n*	53	16	37	.302	7				19.0	-3.0
1877	Cin-N*	14	3	11	.214	6	6		1/3	3.1	-0.1
	3	71	20	51	.282						-4.0
Piniella, Louis Victor "Lou"											
1986	NY-A	162	90	72	.556	2 E				86.8	3.2
1987	NY-A	162	89	73	.549	4 E				83.9	5.1
1988	NY-A	93	45	48	.484	2 E	5 E		2/2	47.9	-2.9
1990	Cin-N	162	91	71	.562	★1 W				91.2	-0.2
1991	Cin-N	162	74	88	.457	5 W				80.8	-6.8
1992	Cin-N	162	90	72	.556	2 W				86.5	3.5
1993	Sea-A	162	82	80	.506	4 W				81.3	0.7
1994	Sea-A	112	49	63	.438	3 W				51.7	-2.7
1995	Sea-A	145	79	66	.545	▲1 W	○			80.7	-1.7

YEAR	TM/L	G	W	L	PCT	STANDING			M/YW	EXP	A-E
1996	Sea-A	161	85	76	.528	2 W				89.1	-4.1
1997	Sea-A	162	90	72	.556	○1 W				89.4	0.6
1998	Sea-A	161	76	85	.472	3 W				80.9	-4.9
1999	Sea-A	162	79	83	.488	3 W				76.8	2.2
2000	Sea-A	162	91	71	.562	▲2 W				92.8	-1.8
	14	2130	1110	1020	.521						-9.6
Plummer, William Francis "Bill"											
1992	Sea-A	162	64	98	.395	7 W				69.1	-5.1
Popowski, Edward Joseph "Eddie"											
1969	Bos-A	9	5	4	.556	3 E	3 E		2/2	4.5	0.5
1973	Bos-A	1	1	0	1.000	2 E	2 E		2/2	0.6	0.4
	2	10	6	4	.600						0.9
Porter, Matthew S. "Matt"											
1884	KC-U*	16	3	13	.188	8	8	8	2/3	2.5	0.5
Powers, Patrick Thomas "Pat"											
1890	Roc-a	133	63	63	.500	5				62.8	0.2
1892(1)	NY-N	74	31	43	.419	10					
(2)	NY-N	79	40	37	.519	6				74.1	-3.1
	2	286	134	143	.484						-2.9
Pratt, Albert George "Al"											
1882	Pit-a	79	39	39	.500	4				39.9	-0.9
1883	Pit-a	32	12	20	.375	6	7		1/3	10.4	1.6
	2	111	51	59	.464						0.6
Price, James L. "Jim"											
1884	NY-N	100	56	42	.571	4	●4		1/2	54.5	1.5
Prothro, James Thompson "Doc"											
1939	Phi-N	152	45	106	.298	8				45.6	-0.6
1940	Phi-N	153	50	103	.327	8				49.6	0.4
1941	Phi-N	155	43	111	.279	8				46.7	-3.7
	3	460	138	320	.301						-3.9
Purcell, William Aloysius "Blondie"											
1883	Phi-N*	82	13	68	.160	8	8		2/2	10.0	3.0
Queen, Melvin Douglas "Mel"											
1997	Tor-A	5	4	1	.800	5 E	5 E		2/2	2.4	1.6
Quilici, Francis Ralph "Frank"											
1972	Min-A	84	41	43	.488	3 W	3 W		2/2	42.1	-1.1
1973	Min-A	162	81	81	.500	3 W				85.6	-4.6
1974	Min-A	163	82	80	.506	3 W				81.4	0.6
1975	Min-A	159	76	83	.478	4 W				78.3	-2.3
	4	568	280	287	.494						-7.5
Quinn, Joseph J. "Joe"											
1895	StL-N*	40	11	28	.282	11	11	11	3/4	12.5	-1.5
1899	Cle-N*	116	12	104	.103	12	12		2/2	10.0	2.0
	2	156	23	132	.148						0.5
Rader, Douglas Lee "Doug"											
1983	Tex-A	163	77	85	.475	3 W				84.3	-7.3
1984	Tex-A	161	69	92	.429	7 W				74.5	-5.5
1985	Tex-A	32	9	23	.281	7 W	7 W		1/2	12.6	-3.6
1986	Chi-A	2	1	1	.500	6 W	5 W	5 W	2/3	0.9	0.1
1989	Cal-A	162	91	71	.562	3 W				90.8	0.2
1990	Cal-A	162	80	82	.494	4 W				79.4	0.6
1991	Cal-A	124	61	63	.492	7 W	7 W		1/2	62.3	-1.3
	7	806	388	417	.482						-16.9
Rapp, Vernon Fred "Vern"											
1977	StL-N	162	83	79	.512	3 E				86.0	-3.0
1978	StL-N	17	6	11	.353	6 E	5 E		1/3	7.9	-1.9
1984	Cin-N	121	51	70	.421	5 W	5 W		1/2	51.3	-0.3
	3	300	140	160	.467						-5.1
Reach, Alfred James "Al"											
1890	Phi-N	11	4	7	.364	2	3	3	3/5	6.4	-2.4
Regan, Philip Raymond "Phil"											
1995	Bal-A	144	71	73	.493	3 E				78.3	-7.3
Rice, Delbert "Del"											
1972	Cal-A	155	75	80	.484	5 W				68.1	6.9
Richards, Paul Rapier											
1951	Chi-A	155	81	73	.526	4				84.1	-3.1
1952	Chi-A	156	81	73	.526	3				81.6	-0.6
1953	Chi-A	156	89	65	.578	3				89.8	-0.8
1954	Chi-A	146	91	54	.628	3	3		1/2	91.5	-0.5
1955	Bal-A	156	57	97	.370	7				54.7	2.3
1956	Bal-A	154	69	85	.448	6				63.0	6.0
1957	Bal-A	154	76	76	.500	5				77.0	-1.0
1958	Bal-A	154	74	79	.484	6				70.4	3.6
1959	Bal-A	155	74	80	.481	6				69.4	4.6
1960	Bal-A	154	89	65	.578	2				84.9	4.1
1961	Bal-A	136	78	57	.578	3	3		1/2	76.7	1.3
1976	Chi-A	161	64	97	.398	6 W				63.9	0.1
	12	1837	923	901	.506						15.9
Richardson, Daniel "Danny"											
1892(2)	Was-N*	43	12	31	.279	11	12		2/2	17.9	-5.9
Rickey, Wesley Branch "Branch"											
1913	StL-A	12	5	6	.455	7	8		3/3	4.6	0.4
1914	StL-A*	159	71	82	.464	5				66.2	4.8

YEAR	TM/L	G	W	L	PCT	STANDING			M/YW	EXP	A-E
1915	StL-A	159	63	91	.409	6				59.8	3.2
1919	StL-N	138	54	83	.394	7				58.7	-4.7
1920	StL-N	155	75	79	.487	●5				76.3	-1.3
1921	StL-N	154	87	66	.569	3				88.8	-1.8
1922	StL-N	154	85	69	.552	●3				81.0	4.0
1923	StL-N	154	79	74	.516	5				77.9	1.1
1924	StL-N	154	65	89	.422	6				76.0	-11.0
1925	StL-N	38	13	25	.342	8	4		1/2	20.5	-7.5
	10	1277	597	664	.473						-12.7
Riddoch, Gregory Lee "Greg"											
1990	SD-N	82	38	44	.463	4 W	5 W		2/2	41.0	-3.0
1991	SD-N	162	84	78	.519	3 W				79.9	4.1
1992	SD-N	150	78	72	.520	3 W	3 W		1/2	73.1	4.9
	3	394	200	194	.508						6.0
Riggleman, James David "Jim"											
1992	SD-N	12	4	8	.333	3 W	3 W		2/2	5.8	-1.8
1993	SD-N	162	61	101	.377	7 W				71.7	-10.7
1994	SD-N	117	47	70	.402	4 W				53.2	-6.2
1995	Chi-N	144	73	71	.507	3 C				74.1	-1.1
1996	Chi-N	162	76	86	.469	4 C				81.1	-5.1
1997	Chi-N	162	68	94	.420	5 C				73.8	-5.8
1998	Chi-N	163	90	73	.552	▲○■2 C				85.2	4.8
1999	Chi-N	162	67	95	.414	6 C				64.8	2.2
	8	1084	486	598	.448						-23.8
Rigney, William Joseph "Bill"											
1956	NY-N	154	67	87	.435	6				65.1	1.9
1957	NY-N	154	69	85	.448	6				71.1	-2.1
1958	SF-N	154	80	74	.519	3				79.9	0.1
1959	SF-N	154	83	71	.539	3				86.4	-3.4
1960	SF-N	58	33	25	.569	2	5		1/2	30.6	2.4
1961	LA-A	162	70	91	.435	8				76.6	-6.6
1962	LA-A	162	86	76	.531	3				82.2	3.8
1963	LA-A	161	70	91	.435	9				73.7	-3.7
1964	LA-A	162	82	80	.506	5				80.2	1.8
1965	Cal-A	162	75	87	.463	7				76.2	-1.2
1966	Cal-A	162	80	82	.494	6				76.8	3.2
1967	Cal-A	161	84	77	.522	5				78.3	5.7
1968	Cal-A	162	67	95	.414	8				67.6	-0.6
1969	Cal-A	39	11	28	.282	6 W	3 W		1/2	16.2	-5.2
1970	Min-A	162	98	64	.605	1 W				95.5	2.5
1971	Min-A	160	74	86	.463	5 W				78.3	-4.3
1972	Min-A	70	36	34	.514	3 W	3 W		1/2	35.1	0.9
1976	SF-N	162	74	88	.457	4 W				71.3	2.7
	18	2561	1239	1321	.484						-2.0
Ripken, Calvin Edwin Sr. "Cal"											
1985	Bal-A	1	1	0	1.000	4 E	4 E	4 E	2/3	0.5	0.5
1987	Bal-A	162	67	95	.414	6 E				66.6	0.4
1988	Bal-A	6	0	6	.000	7 E	7 E		1/2	2.1	-2.1
	3	169	68	101	.402						-1.2
Robinson, Frank											
1975	Cle-A*	159	79	80	.497	4 E				78.0	1.0
1976	Cle-A*	159	81	78	.509	4 E				79.5	1.5
1977	Cle-A	57	26	31	.456	5 E	5 E		1/2	26.2	-0.2
1981(1)	SF-N	59	27	32	.458	5 W					
(2)	SF-N	52	29	23	.558	3 W				56.9	-0.9
1982	SF-N	162	87	75	.537	3 W				79.6	7.4
1983	SF-N	162	79	83	.488	5 W				80.0	-1.0
1984	SF-N	106	42	64	.396	6 W	6 W		1/2	44.9	-2.9
1988	Bal-A	155	54	101	.348	7 E	7 E		2/2	53.6	0.4
1989	Bal-A	162	87	75	.537	2 E				83.3	3.7
1990	Bal-A	161	76	85	.472	5 E				77.5	-1.5
1991	Bal-A	37	13	24	.351	7 E	6 E		1/2	16.0	-3.0
	11	1432	680	751	.475						4.6
Robinson, Wilbert											
1902	Bal-A*	83	24	57	.296	7	8		2/2	33.5	-9.5
1914	Bro-N	154	75	79	.487	5				77.4	-2.4
1915	Bro-N	154	80	72	.526	3				73.3	6.7
1916	Bro-N	156	94	60	.610	1				90.1	3.9
1917	Bro-N	156	70	81	.464	7				70.0	-0.0
1918	Bro-N	127	57	69	.452	5				50.9	6.1
1919	Bro-N	141	69	71	.493	5				71.3	-2.3
1920	Bro-N	155	93	61	.604	1				91.3	1.7
1921	Bro-N	152	77	75	.507	5				74.6	2.4
1922	Bro-N	155	76	78	.494	6				75.9	0.1
1923	Bro-N	155	76	78	.494	6				78.2	-2.2
1924	Bro-N	154	92	62	.597	2				80.8	11.2
1925	Bro-N	153	68	85	.444	●6				69.2	-1.2
1926	Bro-N	155	71	82	.464	6				68.1	2.9
1927	Bro-N	154	65	88	.425	6				68.0	-3.0
1928	Bro-N	155	77	76	.503	6				79.1	-2.1
1929	Bro-N	153	70	83	.458	6				64.3	5.7
1930	Bro-N	154	86	68	.558	4				89.3	-3.3
1931	Bro-N	153	79	73	.520	4				76.8	2.2
	19	2819	1399	1398	.500						16.8
Robison, Matthew Stanley "Stanley"											
1905	StL-N	50	19	31	.380	6	6		3/3	18.2	0.8

YEAR	TM/L	G	W	L	PCT	STANDING			M/YW-EXP		A-E
Rodgers, Robert Leroy "Buck"											
1980	Mil-A	47	26	21	.553	2 E	3 E		1/3	27.2	-1.2
	Mil-A	23	13	10	.565	4 E	3 E		3/3	13.3	-0.3
1981(1)	Mil-A	56	31	25	.554	3 E					
(2)	Mil-A	53	31	22	.585	1 E				58.0	4.0
1982	Mil-A	47	23	24	.489	5 E	◆1 E		1/2	28.3	-5.3
1985	Mon-N	161	84	77	.522	3 E				80.2	3.8
1986	Mon-N	161	78	83	.484	4 E				75.2	2.8
1987	Mon-N	162	91	71	.562	3 E				83.1	7.9
1988	Mon-N	163	81	81	.500	3 E				84.9	-3.9
1989	Mon-N	162	81	81	.500	4 E				81.2	-0.2
1990	Mon-N	162	85	77	.525	3 E				87.9	-2.9
1991	Mon-N	49	20	29	.408	6 E	6 E		1/2	22.0	-2.0
	Cal-A	38	20	18	.526	7 W	7 W		2/2	19.1	0.9
1992	Cal-A	39	19	20	.487	5 W	●5 W		1/3	17.1	1.9
	Cal-A	34	14	20	.412	5 W	●5 W		3/3	14.9	-0.9
1993	Cal-A	162	71	91	.438	●5 W				72.4	-1.4
1994	Cal-A	39	16	23	.410	3 W	4 W		1/3	15.8	0.2
	13	1558	784	773	.504						3.4
Rogers, James F. "Jim"											
1897	Lou-N*	44	17	24	.415	9	11		1/2	15.1	1.9
Rojas, Octavio Victor "Cookie"											
1988	Cal-A	154	75	79	.487	4 W	4 W		1/2	71.6	3.4
1996	Fla-N	1	1	0	1.000	4 E	4 E	3 E	2/3	0.5	0.5
	2	155	76	79	.490						3.9
Rolfe, Robert Abial "Red"											
1949	Det-A	155	87	67	.565	4				86.6	0.4
1950	Det-A	157	95	59	.617	2				88.8	6.2
1951	Det-A	154	73	81	.474	5				71.5	1.5
1952	Det-A	73	23	49	.319	8	8		1/2	27.2	-4.2
	4	539	278	256	.521						3.9
Rose, Peter Edward "Pete"											
1984	Cin-N*	41	19	22	.463	5 W	5 W		2/2	17.4	1.6
1985	Cin-N*	162	89	72	.553	2 W				81.6	7.4
1986	Cin-N*	162	86	76	.531	2 W				82.5	3.5
1987	Cin-N	162	84	78	.519	2 W				84.0	-0.0
1988	Cin-N	23	11	12	.478	4 W	2 W		1/3	12.2	-1.2
	Cin-N	111	64	47	.577	4 W	2 W		3/3	58.9	5.1
1989	Cin-N	125	59	66	.472	●4 W	5 W		1/2	57.7	1.3
	6	786	412	373	.525						17.7
Roseman, James John "Chief"											
1890	StL-a*	15	7	8	.467	4	5	3	3/6	8.8	-1.8
Rothschild, Lawrence Lee "Larry"											
1998	TB-A	162	63	99	.389	5 E				67.5	-4.5
1999	TB-A	162	69	93	.426	5 E				67.9	1.1
2000	TB-A	161	69	92	.429	5 E				70.0	-1.0
	3	485	201	284	.414						-4.4
Rowe, David E. "Dave"											
1886	KC-N*	126	30	91	.248	7				26.1	3.9
1888	KC-a*	50	14	36	.280	8	8		1/3	14.2	-0.2
	2	176	44	127	.257						3.7
Rowe, John Charles "Jack"											
1890	Buf-P*	81	22	58	.275	8	8		1/3	20.9	1.1
	Buf-P*	19	5	14	.263	8	8		3/3	5.0	0.0
Rowland, Clarence Henry "Pants"											
1915	Chi-A	156	93	61	.604	3				99.2	-6.2
1916	Chi-A	155	89	65	.578	2				88.7	0.3
1917	Chi-A	156	100	54	.649	★1				98.5	1.5
1918	Chi-A	124	57	67	.460	6				63.2	-6.2
	4	591	339	247	.578						-10.7
Rudolph, Richard											
1924	Bos-N	38	11	27	.289	6	8		2/3	11.9	-0.9
Ruel, Herold Dominic "Muddy"											
1947	StL-A	154	59	95	.383	8				58.5	0.5
Runnells, Thomas William "Tom"											
1991	Mon-N	112	51	61	.455	6 E	6 E		2/2	50.3	0.7
1992	Mon-N	37	17	20	.459	4 E	2 E		1/2	20.2	-3.2
	2	149	68	81	.456						-2.4
Runnels, James Edward "Pete"											
1966	Bos-A	16	8	8	.500	9	9		2/2	7.2	0.8
Russell, William Ellis "Bill"											
1996	LA-N	86	49	37	.570	1 W	■2 W	○	2/2	45.8	3.2
1997	LA-N	162	88	74	.543	2 W				90.9	-2.9
1998	LA-N	74	36	38	.486	3 W	3 W		1/2	36.6	-0.6
	3	322	173	149	.537						-0.3
Ryan, Cornelius Joseph "Connie"											
1975	Atl-N	27	9	18	.333	5 W	5 W		2/2	10.8	-1.8
1977	Tex-A	6	2	4	.333	3 W	5 W	2 W	3/4	3.4	-1.4
	2	33	11	22	.333						-3.2
Sawyer, Edwin Milby "Eddie"											
1948	Phi-N	63	23	40	.365	6	6		3/3	25.7	-2.7
1949	Phi-N	154	81	73	.526	3				76.4	4.6
1950	Phi-N	157	91	63	.591	1				87.0	4.0
1951	Phi-N	154	73	81	.474	5				77.4	-4.4
1952	Phi-N	63	28	35	.444	6	4		1/2	36.1	-8.1
1958	Phi-N	70	30	40	.429	8	8		2/2	30.6	-0.6
1959	Phi-N	155	64	90	.416	8				64.1	-0.1
1960	Phi-N	1	0	1	.000	●6	8		1/3	0.4	-0.4
	8	817	390	423	.480						-7.8
Scanlon, Michael B. "Mike"											
1884	Was-U	114	47	65	.420	6				46.3	0.7
1886	Was-N	82	13	67	.162	8	8		1/2	18.0	-5.0
	2	196	60	132	.313						-4.3
Schaefer, Robert Wald "Bob"											
1991	KC-A	1	1	0	1.000	7 W	7 W	6 W	2/3	0.5	0.5
Schalk, Raymond William "Ray"											
1927	Chi-A*	153	70	83	.458	5				71.9	-1.9
1928	Chi-A*	75	32	42	.432	6	5		1/2	33.7	-1.7
	2	228	102	125	.449						-3.6
Scheffing, Robert Boden "Bob"											
1957	Chi-N	156	62	92	.403	●7				67.4	-5.4
1958	Chi-N	154	72	82	.468	●5				75.4	-3.4
1959	Chi-N	155	74	80	.481	●5				75.5	-1.5
1961	Det-A	163	101	61	.623	2				97.7	3.3
1962	Det-A	161	85	76	.528	4				87.1	-2.1
1963	Det-A	60	24	36	.400	9	●5		1/2	29.9	-5.9
	6	849	418	427	.495						-15.1
Schlafly, Harry Linton "Larry"											
1914	Buf-F*	156	80	71	.530	4				77.4	2.6
1915	Buf-F	41	13	28	.317	8	6		1/3	18.8	-5.8
	2	197	93	99	.484						-3.2
Schmelz, Gustavius Heinrich "Gus"											
1884	Col-a	110	69	39	.639	2				66.3	2.7
1886	StL-N	126	43	79	.352	6				45.3	-2.3
1887	Cin-a	136	81	54	.600	2				80.2	0.8
1888	Cin-a	137	80	54	.597	4				78.1	1.9
1889	Cin-a	141	76	63	.547	4				80.7	-4.7
1890	Cle-N	78	21	55	.276	7	7		1/2	27.4	-6.4
	Col-a	57	38	13	.745	5	2		2/3	33.1	4.9
1891	Col-a	138	61	76	.445	6				61.6	-0.6
1894	Was-N	132	45	87	.341	11				47.5	-2.5
1895	Was-N	133	43	85	.336	10				47.1	-4.1
1896	Was-N	133	58	73	.443	●9				57.0	1.0
1897	Was-N	36	9	25	.265	11	●6		1/2	16.7	-7.7
	11	1357	624	703	.470						-17.1
Schoendienst, Albert Fred "Red"											
1965	StL-N	162	80	81	.497	7				83.9	-3.9
1966	StL-N	162	83	79	.512	6				80.3	2.7
1967	StL-N	161	101	60	.627	★1				95.3	5.7
1968	StL-N	162	97	65	.599	1				94.1	2.9
1969	StL-N	162	87	75	.537	4 E				87.2	-0.2
1970	StL-N	162	76	86	.469	4 E				80.7	-4.7
1971	StL-N	163	90	72	.556	2 E				85.0	5.0
1972	StL-N	156	75	81	.481	4 E				74.5	0.5
1973	StL-N	162	81	81	.500	2 E				85.3	-4.3
1974	StL-N	161	86	75	.534	2 E				84.1	1.9
1975	StL-N	163	82	80	.506	●3 E				78.2	3.8
1976	StL-N	162	72	90	.444	5 E				76.6	-4.6
1980	StL-N	37	18	19	.486	5 E	4 E		4/4	19.1	-1.1
1990	StL-N	24	13	11	.542	6 E	6 E	6 E	2/3	10.4	2.6
	14	1999	1041	955	.522						6.2
Schultz, Joseph Charles Jr. "Joe"											
1969	Sea-A	163	64	98	.395	6 W				64.8	-0.8
1973	Det-A	28	14	14	.500	3 E	3 E		2/2	13.4	0.6
	2	191	78	112	.411						-0.3
Scioscia, Michael Lorri "Mike"											
2000	Ana-A	162	82	80	.506	3 W				80.5	1.5
Selee, Frank Gibson											
1890	Bos-N	134	76	57	.571	5				82.5	-6.5
1891	Bos-N	140	87	51	.630	1				86.3	0.7
1892(1)	Bos-N	75	52	22	.703	1					
(2)	Bos-N	77	50	26	.658	2				95.3	6.7
1893	Bos-N	131	86	43	.667	1				81.7	4.3
1894	Bos-N	133	83	49	.629	3				82.0	1.0
1895	Bos-N	133	71	60	.542	●5				72.3	-1.3
1896	Bos-N	132	74	57	.565	4				74.4	-0.4
1897	Bos-N	135	93	39	.705	1				96.5	-3.5
1898	Bos-N	152	102	47	.685	1				99.3	2.7
1899	Bos-N	153	95	57	.625	2				96.4	-1.4
1900	Bos-N	142	66	72	.478	4				72.6	-6.6
1901	Bos-N	140	69	69	.500	5				66.3	2.7
1902	Chi-N	143	68	69	.496	5				72.8	-4.8
1903	Chi-N	139	82	56	.594	3				78.4	3.6
1904	Chi-N	156	93	60	.608	2				85.5	7.5
1905	Chi-N	65	37	28	.569	4	3		1/2	43.2	-6.2
	16	2180	1284	862	.598						-1.5
Sewell, James Luther "Luke"											
1941	StL-A	113	55	55	.500	7	●6		2/2	51.1	3.9
1942	StL-A*	151	82	69	.543	3				84.8	-2.8
1943	StL-A	153	72	80	.474	6				75.1	-3.1

YEAR	TM/L	G	W	L	PCT	STANDING			M/YW	EXP	A-E
1944	StL-A	154	89	65	.578	1				87.1	1.9
1945	StL-A	154	81	70	.536	3				80.9	0.1
1946	StL-A	125	53	71	.427	7	7		1/2	54.6	-1.6
1949	Cin-N	3	1	2	.333	7	7		2/2	1.2	-0.2
1950	Cin-N	153	66	87	.431	6				68.5	-2.5
1951	Cin-N	155	68	86	.442	6				65.5	2.5
1952	Cin-N	98	39	59	.398	7	6		1/3	46.1	-7.1
	10	1259	606	644	.485						-9.0
Shannon, Daniel W. "Dan"											
1889	Lou-a*	58	10	46	.179	8	8	8	3/4	12.1	-2.1
1891	Was-a*	51	15	34	.306	7	8	8	3/4	13.0	2.0
	2	109	25	80	.238						-0.1
Sharsig, William A. "Bill"											
1886	Phi-a	41	22	17	.564	6	6		2/2	15.3	6.7
1888	Phi-a	137	81	52	.609	3				88.1	-7.1
1889	Phi-a	138	75	58	.564	3				74.5	0.5
1890	Phi-a	132	54	78	.409	7				45.4	8.6
1891	Phi-a	18	6	11	.353	7	4		1/2	8.8	-2.8
	5	466	238	216	.524						5.9
Shawkey, James Robert "Bob"											
1930	NY-A	154	86	68	.558	3				90.8	-4.8
Sheehan, Thomas Clancy "Tom"											
1960	SF-N	98	46	50	.479	2	5		2/2	50.6	-4.6
Shepard, Lawrence William "Larry"											
1968	Pit-N	163	80	82	.494	6				86.9	-6.9
1969	Pit-N	157	84	73	.535	3 E	3 E		1/2	85.8	-1.8
	2	320	164	155	.514						-8.6
Sherry, Norman Burt "Norm"											
1976	Cal-A	66	37	29	.561	6 W	●4 W		2/2	29.3	7.7
1977	Cal-A	81	39	42	.481	5 W	5 W		1/2	39.5	-0.5
	2	147	76	71	.517						7.2
Shettsline, William Joseph "Bill"											
1898	Phi-N	104	59	44	.573	●8	6		2/2	54.0	5.0
1899	Phi-N	154	94	58	.618	3				91.8	2.2
1900	Phi-N	141	75	63	.543	3				70.6	4.4
1901	Phi-N	140	83	57	.593	2				82.8	0.2
1902	Phi-N	138	56	81	.409	7				51.2	4.8
	5	677	367	303	.548						16.6
Shotton, Burton Edwin "Burt"											
1928	Phi-N	152	43	109	.283	8				48.7	-5.7
1929	Phi-N	154	71	82	.464	5				65.1	5.9
1930	Phi-N	156	52	102	.338	8				56.4	-4.4
1931	Phi-N	155	66	88	.429	6				63.2	2.8
1932	Phi-N	154	78	76	.506	4				81.4	-3.4
1933	Phi-N	152	60	92	.395	7				60.7	-0.7
1934	Cin-N	1	1	0	1.000	8	8	8	2/3	0.4	0.6
1947	Bro-N	153	92	60	.605	●1	1		2/2	86.4	5.6
1948	Bro-N	81	48	33	.593	5	3		3/3	44.4	3.6
1949	Bro-N	156	97	57	.630	1				98.8	-1.8
1950	Bro-N	155	89	65	.578	2				88.6	0.4
	11	1469	697	764	.477						3.0
Showalter, William Nathaniel "Buck"											
1992	NY-A	162	76	86	.469	●4 E				79.7	-3.7
1993	NY-A	162	88	74	.543	2 E				86.8	1.2
1994	NY-A	113	70	43	.619	1 E				69.0	1.0
1995	NY-A	144	79	65	.549	■2 E				77.8	1.2
1998	Ari-N	162	65	97	.401	5 W				66.4	-1.4
1999	Ari-N	162	100	62	.617	○1 W				103.3	-3.3
2000	Ari-N	162	85	77	.525	3 W				84.7	0.3
	7	1067	563	504	.528						-4.6
Silvestri, Kenneth Joseph "Ken"											
1967	Atl-N	3	0	3	.000	7	7		2/2	1.5	-1.5
Simmons, Joseph S. "Joe"											
1875	Wes-n*	13	1	12	.077	13				2.5	-1.5
1884	Wil-U	18	2	16	.111	8				0.8	1.2
	2	31	3	28	.097						-0.2
Simmons, Lewis "Lew"											
1886	Phi-a	98	41	55	.427	6	6		1/2	37.7	3.3
Sisler, George Harold											
1924	StL-A*	153	74	78	.487	4				72.4	1.6
1925	StL-A*	154	82	71	.536	3				76.0	6.0
1926	StL-A*	155	62	92	.403	7				61.4	0.6
	3	462	218	241	.475						8.2
Sisler, Richard Allan "Dick"											
1964	Cin-N	6	3	3	.500	3	4	●2	2/4	3.4	-0.4
	Cin-N	47	29	18	.617	3	●2		4/4	26.5	2.5
1965	Cin-N	162	89	73	.549	4				92.8	-3.8
	2	215	121	94	.563						-1.7
Skaff, Francis Michael "Frank"											
1966	Det-A	79	40	39	.506	2	3		3/3	40.5	-0.5
Skinner, Robert Ralph "Bob"											
1968	Phi-N	107	48	59	.449	5	●7		3/3	48.2	-0.2
1969	Phi-N	108	44	64	.407	5 E	5 E		1/2	47.2	-3.2
1977	SD-N	1	1	0	1.000	4 W	4 W	5 W	2/3	0.4	0.6

YEAR	TM/L	G	W	L	PCT	STANDING			M/YW	EXP	A-E
	3	216	93	123	.431						-2.7
Slattery, John Terrence "Jack"											
1928	Bos-N	31	11	20	.355	7	7		1/2	10.7	0.3
Smith, Edward Mayo "Mayo"											
1955	Phi-N	154	77	77	.500	4				77.9	-0.9
1956	Phi-N	154	71	83	.461	5				70.0	1.0
1957	Phi-N	156	77	77	.500	5				73.5	3.5
1958	Phi-N	84	39	45	.464	8	8		1/2	36.7	2.3
1959	Cin-N	80	35	45	.438	7	●5		1/2	41.3	-6.3
1967	Det-A	163	91	71	.562	●2				91.3	-0.3
1968	Det-A	164	103	59	.636	★1				101.2	1.8
1969	Det-A	162	90	72	.556	2 E				91.6	-1.6
1970	Det-A	162	79	83	.488	4 E				74.4	4.6
	9	1279	662	612	.520						4.0
Smith, George Henry "Heinie"											
1902	NY-N*	32	5	27	.156	4	8	8	2/3	10.7	-5.7
Smith, Harry Thomas											
1909	Bos-N*	79	23	54	.299	8	8		2/2	24.6	-1.6
Smith, William J. "Bill"											
1873	Mar-n*	6	0	6	.000	9				-3.9	3.9
Snyder, Charles N. "Pop"											
1882	Cin-a*	80	55	25	.688	1				61.6	-6.6
1883	Cin-a*	98	61	37	.622	3				71.6	-10.6
1884	Cin-a*	40	24	14	.632	5	5		2/2	26.5	-2.5
1891	Was-a*	70	23	46	.333	6	7	8	2/4	18.3	4.7
	4	288	163	122	.572						-14.9
Snyder, James Robert "Jim"											
1988	Sea-A	105	45	60	.429	6 W	7 W		2/2	47.2	-2.2
Sothoron, Allen Sutton											
1933	StL-A	8	2	6	.250	8	8	8	2/3	3.2	-1.2
Southworth, William Harrison "Billy"											
1929	StL-N*	90	43	45	.489	4	4		1/3	45.3	-2.3
1940	StL-N	111	69	40	.633	7	3		3/3	57.9	11.1
1941	StL-N	155	97	56	.634	2				91.4	5.6
1942	StL-N	156	106	48	.688	★1				106.3	-0.3
1943	StL-N	157	105	49	.682	1				99.6	5.4
1944	StL-N	157	105	49	.682	★1				106.8	-1.8
1945	StL-N	155	95	59	.617	2				94.8	0.2
1946	Bos-N	154	81	72	.529	4				80.5	0.5
1947	Bos-N	154	86	68	.558	3				84.7	1.3
1948	Bos-N	154	91	62	.595	1				92.4	-1.4
1949	Bos-N	111	55	54	.505	4	4		1/2	53.6	1.4
1950	Bos-N	156	83	71	.539	4				81.7	1.3
1951	Bos-N	60	28	31	.475	5	4		1/2	31.8	-3.8
	13	1770	1044	704	.597						17.2
Spalding, Albert Goodwill "Al"											
1876	Chi-N*	66	52	14	.788	1				63.1	-11.1
1877	Chi-N*	60	26	33	.441	5				28.7	-2.7
	2	126	78	47	.624						-13.9
Speaker, Tristram E "Tris"											
1919	Cle-A*	61	40	21	.656	3	2		2/2	35.0	5.0
1920	Cle-A*	154	98	56	.636	★1				97.7	0.3
1921	Cle-A*	154	94	60	.610	2				96.6	-2.6
1922	Cle-A*	155	78	76	.506	4				72.4	5.6
1923	Cle-A*	153	82	71	.536	3				89.5	-7.5
1924	Cle-A*	153	67	86	.438	6				71.0	-4.0
1925	Cle-A*	155	70	84	.455	6				73.7	-3.7
1926	Cle-A*	154	88	66	.571	2				89.8	-1.8
	8	1139	617	520	.543						-8.7
Spence, Harrison L. "Harry"											
1888	Ind-N	136	50	85	.370	7				55.2	-5.2
Stahl, Charles Sylvester "Chick"											
1906	Bos-A*	40	14	26	.350	8	8		2/2	13.1	0.9
Stahl, Garland "Jake"											
1905	Was-A*	154	64	87	.424	7				68.6	-4.6
1906	Was-A*	151	55	95	.367	7				59.4	-4.4
1912	Bos-A*	154	105	47	.691	★1				101.9	3.1
1913	Bos-A*	81	39	41	.488	5	4		1/2	41.2	-2.2
	4	540	263	270	.493						-8.0
Stallings, George Tweedy											
1897	Phi-N*	134	55	77	.417	10				62.5	-7.5
1898	Phi-N*	46	19	27	.413	●8	6		1/2	24.1	-5.1
1901	Det-A	136	74	61	.548	3				71.8	2.2
1909	NY-A	153	74	77	.490	5				75.7	-1.7
1910	NY-A	142	78	59	.569	3	2		1/2	75.3	2.7
1913	Bos-N	154	69	82	.457	5				70.5	-1.5
1914	Bos-N	158	94	59	.614	★1				88.3	5.7
1915	Bos-N	157	83	69	.546	2				80.1	2.9
1916	Bos-N	158	89	63	.586	3				86.6	2.4
1917	Bos-N	158	72	81	.471	6				74.7	-2.7
1918	Bos-N	124	53	71	.427	7				57.0	-4.0
1919	Bos-N	140	57	82	.410	6				58.6	-1.6
1920	Bos-N	153	62	90	.408	7				60.2	1.8
	13	1813	879	898	.495						-6.6

YEAR	TM/L	G	W	L	PCT	STANDING			M/Y	W-EXP	A-E
Stanky, Edward Raymond "Eddie"											
1952	StL-N*	154	88	66	.571	3				81.8	6.2
1953	StL-N*	157	83	71	.539	●3				82.4	0.6
1954	StL-N	154	72	82	.468	6				77.8	-5.8
1955	StL-N	36	17	19	.472	5	7		1/2	15.6	1.4
1966	Chi-A	163	83	79	.512	4				87.6	-4.6
1967	Chi-A	162	89	73	.549	4				85.8	3.2
1968	Chi-A	79	34	45	.430	9	8		1/5	35.7	-1.7
1977	Tex-A	1	1	0	1.000	●3 W	3 W	2 W	2/4	0.6	0.4
	8	906	467	435	.518						-0.3
Start, Joseph "Joe"											
1873	Mut-n*	25	18	7	.720	5	4		2/2	13.9	4.1
Stengel, Charles Dillon "Casey"											
1934	Bro-N	153	71	81	.467	6				71.6	-0.6
1935	Bro-N	154	70	83	.458	5				71.1	-1.1
1936	Bro-N	156	67	87	.435	7				68.0	-1.0
1938	Bos-N	153	77	75	.507	5				69.8	7.2
1939	Bos-N	152	63	88	.417	7				66.3	-3.3
1940	Bos-N	152	65	87	.428	7				63.8	1.2
1941	Bos-N	156	62	92	.403	7				63.8	-1.8
1942	Bos-N	150	59	89	.399	7				60.0	-1.0
1943	Bos-N	107	47	60	.439	6	6		2/2	41.9	5.1
1949	NY-A	155	97	57	.630	★1				95.7	1.3
1950	NY-A	155	98	56	.636	★1				97.8	0.2
1951	NY-A	154	98	56	.636	★1				94.5	3.5
1952	NY-A	154	95	59	.617	★1				94.7	0.3
1953	NY-A	151	99	52	.656	★1				101.0	-2.0
1954	NY-A	155	103	51	.669	2				101.4	1.6
1955	NY-A	154	96	58	.623	1				96.7	-0.7
1956	NY-A	154	97	57	.630	★1				98.8	-1.8
1957	NY-A	154	98	56	.636	1				96.8	1.2
1958	NY-A	155	92	62	.597	★1				95.6	-3.6
1959	NY-A	155	79	75	.513	3				81.1	-2.1
1960	NY-A	155	97	57	.630	1				89.0	8.0
1962	NY-N	161	40	120	.250	10				48.1	-8.1
1963	NY-N	162	51	111	.315	10				51.8	-0.8
1964	NY-N	163	53	109	.327	10				59.4	-6.4
1965	NY-N	96	31	64	.326	10	10		1/2	31.1	-0.1
	25	3766	1905	1842	.508						-4.8
Stovall, George Thomas											
1911	Cle-A*	139	74	62	.544	7	3		2/2	66.3	7.7
1912	StL-A*	117	41	74	.357	8	7		2/2	41.1	-0.1
1913	StL-A*	135	50	84	.373	7	8		1/3	56.1	-6.1
1914	KC-F*	154	67	84	.444	6				71.5	-4.5
1915	KC-F*	153	81	72	.529	4				76.1	4.9
	5	698	313	376	.454						1.9
Stovey, Harry Duffield											
1881	Wor-N*	27	8	18	.308	7	8		2/2	10.6	-2.6
1885	Phi-a*	113	55	57	.491	4				62.1	-7.1
	2	140	63	75	.457						-9.7
Street, Charles Evard "Gabby"											
1929	StL-N	1	1	0	1.000	4	4	4	2/3	0.5	0.5
1930	StL-N	154	92	62	.597	1				96.4	-4.4
1931	StL-N*	154	101	53	.656	★1				96.8	4.2
1932	StL-N	156	72	82	.468	●6				73.7	-1.7
1933	StL-N	91	46	45	.505	5	5		1/2	50.3	-4.3
1938	StL-A	146	53	90	.371	7	7		1/2	53.9	-0.9
	6	702	365	332	.524						-6.6
Stricker, John A. "Cub"											
1892(1)	StL-N*	23	6	17	.261	10	11	9	2/3	8.4	-2.4
Strickland, George Bevan											
1964	Cle-A	73	33	39	.458	8	●6		1/2	35.8	-2.8
1966	Cle-A	39	15	24	.385	3	5		2/2	19.2	-4.2
	2	112	48	63	.432						-7.0
Stubing, Lawrence George "Moose"											
1988	Cal-A	8	0	8	.000	4 W	4 W		2/2	3.7	-3.7
Sukeforth, Clyde Leroy											
1947	Bro-N	2	2	0	1.000	●1	1		1/2	1.1	0.9
Sullivan, Haywood Cooper											
1965	KC-A	136	54	82	.397	10	10		2/2	53.1	0.9
Sullivan, James Patrick "Pat"											
1890	Col-a	3	2	1	.667	5	5	2	3/3	1.9	0.1
Sullivan, Timothy Paul "Ted"											
1883	StL-a	79	53	26	.671	2	2		1/2	50.3	2.7
1884	StL-U	31	28	3	.903	1	1		1/2	26.6	1.4
	KC-U*	62	13	46	.220	8	8		3/3	9.1	3.9
1888	Was-N	96	38	57	.400	8	8		2/2	29.8	8.2
	3	268	132	132	.500						16.2
Sullivan, William Joseph Sr. "Billy"											
1909	Chi-A*	159	78	74	.513	4				79.4	-1.4
Sweasy, Charles James "Charlie"											
1875	RS-n*	19	4	15	.211	9				0.6	3.4
Swift, Robert Virgil "Bob"											
1965	Det-A	42	24	18	.571	3	4		1/2	23.2	0.8
1966	Det-A	57	32	25	.561	3	2	3	2/3	29.2	2.8

YEAR	TM/L	G	W	L	PCT	STANDING			M/Y	W-EXP	A-E
	2	99	56	43	.566						3.6
Tanner, Charles William "Chuck"											
1970	Chi-A	16	3	13	.188	6 W	6 W		3/3	6.1	-3.1
1971	Chi-A	162	79	83	.488	3 W				83.2	-4.2
1972	Chi-A	154	87	67	.565	2 W				80.1	6.9
1973	Chi-A	162	77	85	.475	5 W				75.5	1.5
1974	Chi-A	163	80	80	.500	4 W				76.2	3.8
1975	Chi-A	161	75	86	.466	5 W				75.5	-0.5
1976	Oak-A	161	87	74	.540	2 W				89.8	-2.8
1977	Pit-N	162	96	66	.593	2 E				88.0	8.0
1978	Pit-N	161	88	73	.547	2 E				85.4	2.6
1979	Pit-N	163	98	64	.605	★1 E				94.4	3.6
1980	Pit-N	162	83	79	.512	3 E				83.1	-0.1
1981(1)	Pit-N	49	25	23	.521	4 E					
(2)	Pit-N	54	21	33	.389	6 E				49.1	-3.1
1982	Pit-N	162	84	78	.519	4 E				83.8	0.2
1983	Pit-N	162	84	78	.519	2 E				82.2	1.8
1984	Pit-N	162	75	87	.463	6 E				86.3	-11.3
1985	Pit-N	161	57	104	.354	6 E				65.6	-8.6
1986	Atl-N	161	72	89	.447	6 W				69.7	2.3
1987	Atl-N	161	69	92	.429	5 W				72.6	-3.6
1988	Atl-N	39	12	27	.308	6 W	6 W		1/2	14.7	-2.7
	19	2738	1352	1381	.495						-9.6
Tappe, Elvin Walter "El"											
1961	Chi-N	2	2	0	1.000	7	7	7	4/9	0.9	1.1
	Chi-N	79	35	43	.449	7	7	7	7/9	33.5	1.5
	Chi-N	16	5	11	.313	7	7		9/9	6.9	-1.9
1962	Chi-N	20	4	16	.200	9	9		1/3	7.6	-3.6
	2	117	46	70	.397						-2.9
Taylor, George J.											
1884	Bro-a	109	40	64	.385	9				36.3	3.7
Taylor, James Wren "Zack"											
1946	StL-A	31	13	17	.433	7	7		2/2	13.2	-0.2
1948	StL-A	155	59	94	.386	6				59.4	-0.4
1949	StL-A	155	53	101	.344	7				53.9	-0.9
1950	StL-A	154	58	96	.377	7				55.4	2.6
1951	StL-A	154	52	102	.338	8				50.9	1.1
	5	649	235	410	.364						2.2
Tebbetts, George Robert "Birdie"											
1954	Cin-N	154	74	80	.481	5				73.7	0.3
1955	Cin-N	154	75	79	.487	5				84.5	-9.5
1956	Cin-N	155	91	63	.591	3				88.5	2.5
1957	Cin-N	154	80	74	.519	4				73.8	6.2
1958	Cin-N	113	52	61	.460	8	4		1/2	62.1	-10.1
1961	Mil-N	25	12	13	.480	3	4		2/2	13.4	-1.4
1962	Mil-N	162	86	76	.531	5				87.6	-1.6
1963	Cle-A	162	79	83	.488	●5				74.0	5.0
1964	Cle-A	91	46	44	.511	8	●6		2/2	44.8	1.2
1965	Cle-A	162	87	75	.537	5				86.3	0.7
1966	Cle-A	123	66	57	.537	3	5		1/2	60.5	5.5
	11	1455	748	705	.515						-1.3
Tebeau, Oliver Wendell "Patsy"											
1890	Cle-P*	52	21	30	.412	7	7		2/2	20.0	1.0
1891	Cle-N*	73	31	40	.437	4	5		2/2	33.2	-2.2
1892(1)	Cle-N*	74	40	33	.548	5					
(2)	Cle-N*	79	53	23	.697	1				97.9	-4.9
1893	Cle-N*	129	73	55	.570	3				75.0	-2.0
1894	Cle-N*	130	68	61	.527	6				67.4	0.6
1895	Cle-N*	132	84	46	.646	2				81.7	2.3
1896	Cle-N*	135	80	48	.625	2				81.2	-1.2
1897	Cle-N*	132	69	62	.527	5				73.9	-4.9
1898	Cle-N*	156	81	68	.544	5				79.2	1.8
1899	StL-N*	155	84	67	.556	5				83.1	0.9
1900	StL-N*	92	42	50	.457	7	●5		1/2	45.8	-3.8
	11	1339	726	583	.555						-12.2
Tenace, Fury Gene "Gene"											
1991	Tor-A	33	19	14	.576	1 E	1 E	1 E	2/3	17.8	1.2
Tenney, Frederick "Fred"											
1905	Bos-N*	156	51	103	.331	7				48.3	2.7
1906	Bos-N*	152	49	102	.325	8				48.1	0.9
1907	Bos-N*	152	58	90	.392	7				57.7	0.3
1911	Bos-N*	156	44	107	.291	8				46.4	-2.4
	4	616	202	402	.334						1.5
Terry, William Harold "Bill"											
1932	NY-N*	114	55	59	.482	8	●6		2/2	60.5	-5.5
1933	NY-N*	156	91	61	.599	★1				89.4	1.6
1934	NY-N*	153	93	60	.608	2				94.4	-1.4
1935	NY-N*	156	91	62	.595	3				85.9	5.1
1936	NY-N*	154	92	62	.597	1				89.2	2.8
1937	NY-N	152	95	57	.625	1				89.2	5.8
1938	NY-N	152	83	67	.553	3				81.9	1.1
1939	NY-N	151	77	74	.510	5				77.3	-0.3
1940	NY-N	152	72	80	.474	6				76.4	-4.4
1941	NY-N	156	74	79	.484	5				72.6	1.4
	10	1496	823	661	.555						6.3
Thomas, Frederick L. "Fred"											
1887	Ind-N	29	11	18	.379	8	8	8	2/3	7.9	3.1

YEAR	TM/L	G	W	L	PCT	STANDING			M/Y	W-EXP	A-E
Thompson, Andrew M. “A. M.”											
1884	Stp-U	9	2	6	.250	7				0.7	1.3
Tighe, John Thomas “Jack”											
1957	Det-A	154	78	76	.506	4				77.0	1.0
1958	Det-A	49	21	28	.429	8	5		1/2	26.3	-5.3
	2	203	99	104	.488						-4.3
Tinker, Joseph Bert “Joe”											
1913	Cin-N*	156	64	89	.418	7				65.2	-1.2
1914	Chi-F*	158	87	67	.565	2				88.6	-1.6
1915	Chi-F*	156	86	66	.566	1				87.1	-1.1
1916	Chi-N*	156	67	86	.438	5				74.1	-7.1
	4	626	304	308	.497						-10.9
Torborg, Jeffrey Allen “Jeff”											
1977	Cle-A	104	45	59	.433	5 E	5 E		2/2	47.9	-2.9
1978	Cle-A	159	69	90	.434	6 E				73.8	-4.8
1979	Cle-A	95	43	52	.453	6 E	6 E		1/2	44.9	-1.9
1989	Chi-A	161	69	92	.429	7 W				74.8	-5.8
1990	Chi-A	162	94	68	.580	2 W				86.2	7.8
1991	Chi-A	162	87	75	.537	2 W				88.8	-1.8
1992	NY-N	162	72	90	.444	5 E				75.2	-3.2
1993	NY-N	38	13	25	.342	7 E	7 E		1/2	17.3	-4.3
	8	1043	492	551	.472						-16.8
Torre, Joseph Paul “Joe”											
1977	NY-N*	117	49	68	.419	6 E	6 E		2/2	52.6	-3.6
1978	NY-N	162	66	96	.407	6 E				72.2	-6.2
1979	NY-N	163	63	99	.389	6 E				69.0	-6.0
1980	NY-N	162	67	95	.414	5 E				71.4	-4.4
1981(1)	NY-N	52	17	34	.333	5 E					
(2)	NY-N	53	24	28	.462	4 E				42.3	-1.3
1982	Atl-N	162	89	73	.549	1 W				84.7	4.3
1983	Atl-N	162	88	74	.543	2 W				91.9	-3.9
1984	Atl-N	162	80	82	.494	●2 W				78.6	1.4
1990	StL-N	58	24	34	.414	6 E	6 E		3/3	25.2	-1.2
1991	StL-N	162	84	78	.519	2 E				81.3	2.7
1992	StL-N	162	83	79	.512	3 E				83.9	-0.9
1993	StL-N	162	87	75	.537	3 E				82.4	4.6
1994	StL-N	115	53	61	.465	●3 C				48.9	4.1
1995	StL-N	47	20	27	.426	4 C	4 C		1/2	20.3	-0.3
1996	NY-A	162	92	70	.568	★1 E				88.9	3.1
1997	NY-A	162	96	66	.593	■○2 E				100.5	-4.5
1998	NY-A	162	114	48	.704	★1 E				110.3	3.7
1999	NY-A	126	77	49	.611	1 E	★1 E		2/2	75.4	1.6
2000	NY-A	161	87	74	.540	1 E	★1 E			85.8	1.2
	19	2674	1360	1310	.509						-5.5
Tracewski, Richard Joseph “Dick”											
1979	Det-A	2	2	0	1.000	5 E	5 E	5 E	2/3	1.0	1.0
Traynor, Harold Joseph “Pie”											
1934	Pit-N*	100	47	52	.475	4	5		2/2	50.9	-3.9
1935	Pit-N*	153	86	67	.562	4				86.1	-0.1
1936	Pit-N	156	84	70	.545	4				85.3	-1.3
1937	Pit-N*	154	86	68	.558	3				82.8	3.2
1938	Pit-N	152	86	64	.573	2				82.8	3.2
1939	Pit-N	153	68	85	.444	6				71.0	-3.0
	6	868	457	406	.530						-1.8
Trebelhorn, Thomas Lynn “Tom”											
1986	Mil-A	9	6	3	.667	6 E	6 E		2/2	4.1	1.9
1987	Mil-A	162	91	71	.562	3 E				85.2	5.8
1988	Mil-A	162	87	75	.537	●3 E				88.0	-1.0
1989	Mil-A	162	81	81	.500	4 E				83.9	-2.9
1990	Mil-A	162	74	88	.457	6 E				78.2	-4.2
1991	Mil-A	162	83	79	.512	3 E				86.3	-3.3
1994	Chi-N	113	49	64	.434	5 C				51.7	-2.7
	7	932	471	461	.505						-6.4
Trott, Samuel W. “Sam”											
1891	Was-a	12	4	7	.364	6	9		1/4	2.9	1.1
Turner, Robert Edward “Ted”											
1977	Atl-N	1	0	1	.000	6 W	6 W	6 W	2/4	0.4	-0.4
Unglaub, Robert Alexander “Bob”											
1907	Bos-A*	29	9	20	.310	6	8	7	3/4	12.4	-3.4
Valentine, Robert John “Bobby”											
1985	Tex-A	129	53	76	.411	7 W	7 W		2/2	50.8	2.2
1986	Tex-A	162	87	75	.537	2 W				83.7	3.3
1987	Tex-A	162	75	87	.463	●6 W				78.6	-3.6
1988	Tex-A	161	70	91	.435	6 W				70.4	-0.4
1989	Tex-A	162	83	79	.512	4 W				79.1	3.9
1990	Tex-A	162	83	79	.512	3 W				78.9	4.1
1991	Tex-A	162	85	77	.525	3 W				82.4	2.6
1992	Tex-A	86	45	41	.523	3 W	4 W		1/2	39.2	5.8
1996	NY-N	31	12	19	.387	4 E	4 E		2/2	14.9	-2.9
1997	NY-N	162	88	74	.543	3 E				87.7	0.3
1998	NY-N	162	88	74	.543	2 E				87.3	0.7
1999	NY-N	163	97	66	.595	▲2 E	■			95.3	1.7
2000	NY-N	162	94	68	.580	▲2 E	◆			87.7	6.3
	13	1866	960	906	.514						23.9
Van Haltren, George Edward											
1892(1)	Bal-N*	11	1	10	.091	12	12		1/3	3.9	-2.9

YEAR	TM/L	G	W	L	PCT	STANDING			M/Y	W-EXP	A-E
Vernon, James Barton “Mickey”											
1961	Was-A	161	61	100	.379	●9				64.4	-3.4
1962	Was-A	162	60	101	.373	10				68.2	-8.2
1963	Was-A	40	14	26	.350	10	10		1/3	14.1	-0.1
	3	363	135	227	.373						-11.7
Virdon, William Charles “Bill”											
1972	Pit-N	155	96	59	.619	1 E				96.8	-0.8
1973	Pit-N	136	67	69	.493	2 E	3 E		1/2	68.9	-1.9
1974	NY-A	162	89	73	.549	2 E				86.1	2.9
1975	NY-A	104	53	51	.510	3 E	3 E		1/2	58.4	-5.4
	Hou-N	35	17	17	.500	6 W	6 W		2/2	16.0	1.0
1976	Hou-N	162	80	82	.494	3 W				77.6	2.4
1977	Hou-N	162	81	81	.500	3 W				84.1	-3.1
1978	Hou-N	162	74	88	.457	5 W				77.9	-3.9
1979	Hou-N	162	89	73	.549	2 W				81.1	7.9
1980	Hou-N	163	93	70	.571	▲1 W				86.8	6.2
1981(1)	Hou-N	57	28	29	.491	3 W					
(2)	Hou-N	53	33	20	.623	1 W				62.4	-1.4
1982	Hou-N	111	49	62	.441	5 W	5 W		1/2	51.6	-2.6
1983	Mon-N	163	82	80	.506	3 E				84.3	-2.3
1984	Mon-N	131	64	67	.489	5 E	5 E		1/2	66.2	-2.2
	13	1918	995	921	.519						-3.2
Vitt, Oscar Joseph “Ossie”											
1938	Cle-A	153	86	66	.566	3				82.0	4.0
1939	Cle-A	154	87	67	.565	3				86.3	0.7
1940	Cle-A	155	89	65	.578	2				84.4	4.6
	3	462	262	198	.570						9.3
Von Der Ahe, Christian Frederick Wilhelm “Chris”											
1895	StL-N	1	1	0	1.000	11	11	11	2/4	0.3	0.7
1896	StL-N	2	0	2	.000	10	11	11	3/5	0.5	-0.5
1897	StL-N	14	2	12	.143	12	12		4/4	2.5	-0.5
	3	17	3	14	.176						-0.4
Vukovich, John Christopher											
1986	Chi-N	2	1	1	.500	5 E	5 E	5 E	2/3	0.9	0.1
1988	Phi-N	9	5	4	.556	6 E	6 E		2/2	3.7	1.3
	2	11	6	5	.545						1.4
Wagner, Charles F. “Heinie”											
1930	Bos-A	154	52	102	.338	8				57.1	-5.1
Wagner, John Peter “Honus”											
1917	Pit-N*	5	1	4	.200	8	8	8	2/3	2.0	-1.0
Walker, Harry William											
1955	StL-N*	118	51	67	.432	5	7		2/2	51.2	-0.2
1965	Pit-N	163	90	72	.556	3				91.3	-1.3
1966	Pit-N	162	92	70	.568	3				93.0	-1.0
1967	Pit-N	84	42	42	.500	6	6		1/2	41.2	0.8
1968	Hou-N	101	49	52	.485	10	10		2/2	44.9	4.1
1969	Hou-N	162	81	81	.500	5 W				81.8	-0.8
1970	Hou-N	162	79	83	.488	4 W				79.1	-0.1
1971	Hou-N	162	79	83	.488	●4 W				83.0	-4.0
1972	Hou-N	121	67	54	.554	2 W	2 W		1/3	66.3	0.7
	9	1235	630	604	.511						-1.9
Wallace, Roderick John “Bobby”											
1911	StL-A*	152	45	107	.296	8				51.6	-6.6
1912	StL-A*	40	12	27	.308	8	7		1/2	13.9	-1.9
1937	Cin-N	25	5	20	.200	8	8		2/2	10.9	-5.9
	3	217	62	154	.287						-14.5
Walsh, Edward Augustine “Ed”											
1924	Chi-A	3	1	2	.333	6			2/4	1.4	-0.4
Walsh, Michael John “Mike”											
1884	Lou-a	110	68	40	.630	3				68.7	-0.7
Walters, William Henry “Bucky”											
1948	Cin-N*	53	20	33	.377	7	7		2/2	20.8	-0.8
1949	Cin-N	153	61	90	.404	7	7		1/2	61.4	-0.4
	2	206	81	123	.397						-1.2
Waltz, John J.											
1892(1)	Bal-N	8	2	6	.250	12	12	12	2/3	2.9	-0.9
Ward, John Montgomery “Monte”											
1880	Pro-N*	32	18	13	.581	4	3	2	2/3	20.1	-2.1
1884	NY-N*	16	6	8	.429	4	●4		2/2	7.8	-1.8
1890	Bro-P*	133	76	56	.576	2				71.7	4.3
1891	Bro-N*	137	61	76	.445	6				63.6	-2.6
1892(1)	Bro-N*	78	51	26	.662	2					
(2)	Bro-N*	80	44	33	.571	3				95.7	-0.7
1893	NY-N*	136	68	64	.515	5				73.9	-5.9
1894	NY-N*	139	88	44	.667	2				79.6	8.4
	7	751	412	320	.563						-0.4
Waterman, Frederick A. “Fred”											
1872	Oly-n*	9	2	7	.222	10				-1.1	3.1
Wathan, John David											
1987	KC-A	36	21	15	.583	4 W	2 W		2/2	18.5	2.5
1988	KC-A	161	84	77	.522	3 W				86.3	-2.3
1989	KC-A	162	92	70	.568	2 W				86.8	5.2
1990	KC-A	161	75	86	.466	6 W				80.3	-5.3
1991	KC-A	37	15	22	.405	7 W	6 W		1/3	18.6	-3.6

YEAR	TM/L	G	W	L	PCT	STANDING			M/Y	W-EXP	A-E
1992	Cal-A	89	39	50	.438	5 W	5 W	●5 W	2/3	39.0	-0.0
	6	646	326	320	.505						-3.6
Watkins, Harvey L.											
1895	NY-N	35	18	17	.514	9	9		3/3	17.9	0.1
Watkins, William Henry "Bill"											
1884	Ind-a*	23	4	18	.182	10	11		2/2	5.6	-1.6
1885	Det-N	70	34	36	.486	8	6		2/2	30.8	3.2
1886	Det-N	126	87	36	.707	2				88.0	-1.0
1887	Det-N	127	79	45	.637	1				83.0	-4.0
1888	Det-N	94	49	44	.527	3	5		1/2	52.7	-3.7
	KC-a	25	8	17	.320	8	8		3/3	7.1	0.9
1889	KC-a	139	55	82	.401	7				53.9	1.1
1893	StL-N	135	57	75	.432	10				58.6	-1.6
1898	Pit-N	151	72	76	.486	8				67.9	4.1
1899	Pit-N	24	7	15	.318	10	7		1/2	12.0	-5.0
	9	914	452	444	.504						-7.6
Weaver, Earl Sidney											
1968	Bal-A	82	48	34	.585	3	2		2/2	45.8	2.2
1969	Bal-A	162	109	53	.673	♦1 E				108.8	0.2
1970	Bal-A	162	108	54	.667	★1 E				103.5	4.5
1971	Bal-A	158	101	57	.639	♦1 E				101.4	-0.4
1972	Bal-A	154	80	74	.519	3 E				87.8	-7.8
1973	Bal-A	162	97	65	.599	1 E				101.3	-4.3
1974	Bal-A	162	91	71	.562	1 E				86.0	5.0
1975	Bal-A	159	90	69	.566	2 E				93.4	-3.4
1976	Bal-A	162	88	74	.543	2 E				83.3	4.7
1977	Bal-A	161	97	64	.602	●2 E				87.3	9.7
1978	Bal-A	161	90	71	.559	4 E				83.3	6.7
1979	Bal-A	159	102	57	.642	♦1 E				97.6	4.4
1980	Bal-A	162	100	62	.617	2 E				97.6	2.4
1981(1)	Bal-A	54	31	23	.574	2 E					
(2)	Bal-A	51	28	23	.549	4 E				51.7	7.3
1982	Bal-A	163	94	68	.580	2 E				89.7	4.3
1985	Bal-A	105	53	52	.505	4 E	4 E		3/3	55.9	-2.9
1986	Bal-A	162	73	89	.451	7 E				75.8	-2.8
	17	2541	1480	1060	.583						29.9
Westrum, Wesley Noreen "Wes"											
1965	NY-N	68	19	48	.284	10	10		2/2	21.9	-2.9
1966	NY-N	161	66	95	.410	9				62.5	3.5
1967	NY-N	151	57	94	.377	10	10		1/2	57.4	-0.4
1974	SF-N	86	38	48	.442	5 W	5 W		2/2	38.1	-0.1
1975	SF-N	161	80	81	.497	3 W				79.2	0.8
	5	627	260	366	.415						0.9
Wheeler, Harry Eugene											
1884	KC-U*	4	0	4	.000	8	8		1/3	0.6	-0.6
White, James Laurie "Deacon"											
1872	Cle-n*	2	0	2	.000	6	7		2/2	0.5	-0.5
1879	Cin-N*	18	9	9	.500	4	5		1/2	9.4	-0.4
	2	20	9	11	.450						-0.9
White, Joyner Clifford "Jo-Jo"											
1960	Cle-A	1	1	0	1.000	4	4	4	2/3	0.5	0.5
White, William Henry "Will"											
1884	Cin-a*	72	44	27	.620	5			1/2	49.6	-5.6
White, William Warren "Warren"											
1872	Nat-n*	11	0	11	.000	11				-1.2	1.2
1874	Bal-n*	47	9	38	.191	8				2.4	6.6
	2	58	9	49	.155						7.8
Wilber, Delbert Quentin "Del"											
1973	Tex-A	1	1	0	1.000	6 W	6 W	6 W	2/3	0.4	0.6
Wilhelm, Irvin Key "Kaiser"											
1921	Phi-N*	67	26	41	.388	8	8		2/2	21.0	5.0
1922	Phi-N	154	57	96	.373	7				59.9	-2.9
	2	221	83	137	.377						2.1
Williams, James A. "Jimmy"											
1884	StL-a	85	51	33	.607	5	4		1/2	50.5	0.5
1887	Cle-a	133	39	92	.298	8				34.6	4.4
1888	Cle-a	64	20	44	.313	8	6		1/2	23.8	-3.8
	3	282	110	169	.394						1.1
Williams, James Francis "Jimy"											
1986	Tor-A	163	86	76	.531	4 E				88.4	-2.4
1987	Tor-A	162	96	66	.593	2 E				99.7	-3.7
1988	Tor-A	162	87	75	.537	●3 E				89.3	-2.3
1989	Tor-A	36	12	24	.333	6 E	1 E		1/2	19.8	-7.8
1997	Bos-A	162	78	84	.481	4 E				80.4	-2.4
1998	Bos-A	162	92	70	.568	■○2 E				95.0	-3.0
1999	Bos-A	162	94	68	.580	■2 E				92.4	1.6
2000	Bos-A	162	85	77	.525	2 E				85.6	-0.6
	8	1171	630	540	.538						-20.8
Williams, Richard Hirschfeld "Dick"											
1967	Bos-A	162	92	70	.568	1				92.3	-0.3
1968	Bos-A	162	86	76	.531	4				81.3	4.7
1969	Bos-A	153	82	71	.536	3 E	3 E		1/2	77.2	4.8
1971	Oak-A	161	101	60	.627	1 W				94.1	6.9
1972	Oak-A	155	93	62	.600	★1 W				94.4	-1.4
1973	Oak-A	162	94	68	.580	★1 W				95.7	-1.7

YEAR	TM/L	G	W	L	PCT	STANDING			M/Y	W-EXP	A-E
1974	Cal-A	84	36	48	.429	6 W	6 W		3/3	39.8	-3.8
1975	Cal-A	161	72	89	.447	6 W				70.7	1.3
1976	Cal-A	96	39	57	.406	6 W	●4 W		1/2	42.7	-3.7
1977	Mon-N	162	75	87	.463	5 E				73.8	1.2
1978	Mon-N	162	76	86	.469	4 E				83.4	-7.4
1979	Mon-N	160	95	65	.594	2 E				92.7	2.3
1980	Mon-N	162	90	72	.556	2 E				87.8	2.2
1981(1)	Mon-N	55	30	25	.545	3 E					
(2)	Mon-N	26	14	12	.538	2 E	○1 E		1/2	44.5	-0.5
1982	SD-N	162	81	81	.500	4 W				82.8	-1.8
1983	SD-N	163	81	81	.500	4 W				81.0	0.0
1984	SD-N	162	92	70	.568	♦1 W				86.5	5.5
1985	SD-N	162	83	79	.512	●3 W				84.0	-1.0
1986	Sea-A	133	58	75	.436	6 W	7 W		3/3	57.2	0.8
1987	Sea-A	162	78	84	.481	4 W				77.0	1.0
1988	Sea-A	56	23	33	.411	6 W	7 W		1/2	25.2	-2.2
	21	3023	1571	1451	.520						7.0
Williams, Theodore Samuel "Ted"											
1969	Was-A	162	86	76	.531	4 E				86.2	-0.2
1970	Was-A	162	70	92	.432	6 E				74.4	-4.4
1971	Was-A	159	63	96	.396	5 E				66.1	-3.1
1972	Tex-A	154	54	100	.351	6 W				58.2	-4.2
	4	637	273	364	.429						-11.8
Wills, Maurice Morning "Maury"											
1980	Sea-A	58	20	38	.345	6 W	7 W		2/2	22.3	-2.3
1981(1)	Sea-A	25	6	18	.250	7 W	6 W		1/2	9.9	-3.9
	2	83	26	56	.317						-6.2
Wilson, James "Jimmie"											
1934	Phi-N*	149	56	93	.376	7				63.1	-7.1
1935	Phi-N*	156	64	89	.418	7				58.8	5.2
1936	Phi-N*	154	54	100	.351	8				63.2	-9.2
1937	Phi-N*	155	61	92	.399	7				62.9	-1.9
1938	Phi-N*	149	45	103	.304	8	8		1/2	45.7	-0.7
1941	Chi-N	155	70	84	.455	6				76.6	-6.6
1942	Chi-N	155	68	86	.442	6				69.2	-1.2
1943	Chi-N	154	74	79	.484	5				80.0	-6.0
1944	Chi-N	10	1	9	.100	8	4		1/3	5.2	-4.2
	9	1237	493	735	.401						-31.8
Wine, Robert Paul Sr. "Bobby"											
1985	Atl-N	41	16	25	.390	5 W	5 W		2/2	16.7	-0.7
Wingo, Ivey Brown											
1916	Cin-N*	2	1	1	.500	8	8	●7	2/3	0.8	0.2
Winkles, Bobby Brooks											
1973	Cal-A	162	79	83	.488	4 W				78.0	1.0
1974	Cal-A	75	30	44	.405	6 W	6 W		1/3	35.1	-5.1
1977	Oak-A	108	37	71	.343	●5 W	7 W		2/2	44.0	-7.0
1978	Oak-A	39	24	15	.615	1 W	6 W		1/2	15.3	8.7
	4	384	170	213	.444						-2.5
Wolf, William Van Winkle "Chicken"											
1889	Lou-a*	65	14	51	.215	8	8	8	2/4	14.0	-0.0
Wolverton, Harry Sterling											
1912	NY-A*	153	50	102	.329	8				55.5	-5.5
Wood, George A.											
1891	Phi-a*	125	67	55	.549	7	4		2/2	62.8	4.2
Wood, James Leon "Jimmy"											
1871	Chi-n*	28	19	9	.679	2				18.2	0.8
1872	Tro-n*	25	15	10	.600	5				18.2	-3.2
	Eck-n*	9	2	7	.222	10	10	9	2/3	-1.0	3.0
1874	Chi-n	23	10	13	.435	4	5		2/2	9.6	0.4
1875	Chi-n	69	30	37	.448	6				30.2	-0.2
	4	154	76	76	.500						0.8
Wright, Alfred Hector "Al"											
1876	Phi-N	60	14	45	.237	7				17.5	-3.5
Wright, George											
1879	Pro-N*	85	59	25	.702	1				64.9	-5.9
Wright, William Henry "Harry"											
1871	Bos-n*	31	20	10	.667	3				21.2	-1.2
1872	Bos-n*	48	39	8	.830	1				45.0	-6.0
1873	Bos-n*	60	43	16	.729	1				48.2	-5.2
1874	Bos-n*	71	52	18	.743	1				58.9	-6.9
1875	Bos-n*	82	71	8	.899	1				78.2	-7.2
1876	Bos-N*	70	39	31	.557	4				36.7	2.3
1877	Bos-N*	61	42	18	.700	1				44.0	-2.0
1878	Bos-N	60	41	19	.683	1				35.7	5.3
1879	Bos-N	84	54	30	.643	2				61.5	-7.5
1880	Bos-N	86	40	44	.476	6				38.2	1.8
1881	Bos-N	83	38	45	.458	6				35.4	2.6
1882	Pro-N	84	52	32	.619	2				52.3	-0.3
1883	Pro-N	98	58	40	.592	3				67.1	-9.1
1884	Phi-N	113	39	73	.348	6				32.3	6.7
1885	Phi-N	111	56	54	.509	3				55.2	0.8
1886	Phi-N	119	71	43	.623	4				69.0	2.0
1887	Phi-N	128	75	48	.610	2				78.4	-3.4
1888	Phi-N	132	69	61	.531	3				67.8	1.2
1889	Phi-N	130	63	64	.496	3				63.0	0.0

YEAR	TM/L	G	W	L	PCT	STANDING			M/YW	EXP	A-E
1890	Phi-N	22	14	8	.636	1	3		1/5	12.7	1.3
	Phi-N	46	22	23	.489	2	3		5/5	26.0	-4.0
1891	Phi-N	138	68	69	.496	4				67.0	1.0
1892(1)	Phi-N	77	46	30	.605	3					
(2)	Phi-N	78	41	36	.532	5				92.6	-5.6
1893	Phi-N	133	72	57	.558	4				78.2	-6.2
	23	2145	1225	885	.581						-39.7
York, Preston Rudolph "Rudy"											
1959	Bos-A	1	0	1	.000	8	8	5	2/3	0.5	-0.5
York, Thomas J. "Tom"											
1878	Pro-N*	62	33	27	.550	3				31.4	1.6
1881	Pro-N*	34	23	10	.697	4	2		2/2	17.3	5.7
	2	96	56	37	.602						7.3
Yost, Edward Frederick "Eddie"											
1963	Was-A	1	0	1	.000	10	10	10	2/3	0.4	-0.4
Young, Denton True "Cy"											
1907	Bos-A*	6	3	3	.500	●4	7		1/4	2.6	0.4
Young, Nicholas Ephraim "Nick"											
1871	Oly-n	32	15	15	.500	5				15.5	-0.5
1873	Was-n	39	8	31	.205	7				5.8	2.2

YEAR	TM/L	G	W	L	PCT	STANDING			M/YW	EXP	A-E
	2	71	23	46	.333						1.7
Zimmer, Charles Louis "Chief"											
1903	Phi-N*	139	49	86	.363	7				55.9	-6.9
Zimmer, Donald William "Don"											
1972	SD-N	142	54	88	.380	4 W	6 W		2/2	53.0	1.0
1973	SD-N	162	60	102	.370	6 W				57.6	2.4
1976	Bos-A	76	42	34	.553	5 E	3 E		2/2	40.7	1.3
1977	Bos-A	161	97	64	.602	●2 E				94.6	2.4
1978	Bos-A	163	99	64	.607	▲2 E				95.5	3.5
1979	Bos-A	160	91	69	.569	3 E				92.5	-1.5
1980	Bos-A	155	82	73	.529	3 E	4 E		1/2	76.6	5.4
1981(1)	Tex-A	55	33	22	.600	2 W					
(2)	Tex-A	50	24	26	.480	3 W				59.2	-2.2
1982	Tex-A	96	38	58	.396	6 W	6 W		1/2	38.2	-0.2
1988	Chi-N	163	77	85	.475	4 E				77.5	-0.5
1989	Chi-N	162	93	69	.574	1 E				89.3	3.7
1990	Chi-N	162	77	85	.475	●4 E				72.6	4.4
1991	Chi-N	37	18	19	.486	4 E	4 E		1/3	17.6	0.4
1999	NY-A	36	21	15	.583	1 E	1 E		1/2	21.6	-0.6
	14	1780	906	873	.509						19.6

Biographical Data for Managers Not Appearing in the Player/Pitcher Registers

BILL ADAIR Adair, Marion Danne b: 2/10/13, Mobile, Ala.
BILL ARMOUR Armour, William Clark b: 9/3/1869, Homestead, Pa. d: 12/2/22, Minneapolis, Minn.
FRANK BANCROFT Bancroft, Frank Carter b: 5/9/1846, Lancaster, Mass. d: 3/30/21, Cincinnati, Ohio
ED BARROW Barrow, Edward Grant "Cousin Ed" b: 5/10/1868, Springfield, Ill. d: 12/15/53, Port Chester, N.Y.
TERRY BEVINGTON Bevington, Terry Paul b: 7/7/56, Akron, Ohio
HUGO BEZDEK Bezdek, Hugo Frank b: 4/1/1884, Prague, Czechoslovakia d: 9/19/52, Atlantic City, N.J.
BICKERSON Bickerson
JOHN BOLES Boles, John b: 8/19/48, Chicago, Ill.
DAVE BRISTOL Bristol, James David b: 6/23/33, Macon, Ga.
FREEMAN BROWN Brown, Freeman b: 1/31/1845, Hubbardston, Mass d: 12/27/16, Worcester, Mass.
AL BUCKENBERGER Buckenberger, Albert C. b: 1/31/1861, Detroit, Mich. d: 7/1/17, Syracuse, N.Y.
GEORGE BURNHAM Burnham, George Walter "Watch" b: 5/20/1860, Albion, Mich. d: 11/18/02, Detroit, Mich.
ORMOND BUTLER Butler, Ormond Hook b: 11/1854, West Virginia d: 9/12/15, Mt.Hope, Md.
CHARLIE BYRNE Byrne, Charles H. b: 9/1843, New York, N.Y. d: 1/4/1898, New York, N.Y.
JOE CANTILLON Cantillon, Joseph D. "Pongo Joe" b: 8/19/1861, Janesville, Wis. d: 1/31/30, Hickman, Ky.
O. P. CAYLOR Caylor, Oliver Perry b: 12/17/1849, Near Dayton, Ohio d: 10/19/1897, Winona, Minn:
TERRY COLLINS Collins, Terry Lee b: 5/27/49, Midland, Mich.
ED CURTIS Curtis, Edwin R.
CHARLIE CUSHMAN Cushman, Charles H. b: 5/25/1850, New York, N.Y. d: 6/29/09, Milwaukee, Wis.
MORDECAI DAVIDSON Davidson, Mordecai H. b: 11/30/1846, Port Washington, Ohio d: 9/6/40, Louisville, Ky.
JOHN DAY Day, John B. b: 9/23/47, Colchester, Conn. d: 1/25/25, Cliffside, N.J.
HARRY DIDDLEBOCK Diddlebock, Henry H. b: 6/27/1854, Philadelphia, Pa. d: 2/5/1900, Philadelphia, Pa.
CHARLIE EBBETS Ebbets, Charles Hercules b: 10/29/1859, New York, N.Y. d: 4/18/25, New York, N.Y.
WALLACE FESSENDEN Fessenden, Wallace Clifton b: 10/5/1860, Windham, N.H.
HORACE FOGEL Fogel, Horace S. b: 3/2/1861, Macungie, Pa. d: 11/15/28, Philadelphia, Pa.
GEORGE FRAZER Frazer, George Kasson b: 1/7/1861, Syracuse, N.Y. d: 2/5/13, Philadelphia, Pa.
JIM FREY Frey, James Gottfried b: 5/26/31, Cleveland, Ohio
JUDGE FUCHS Fuchs, Emil Edwin b: 4/17/1878, Hamburg, Germany d: 12/5/61, Boston, Mass.
JOHN GAFFNEY Gaffney, John H. b: 6/29/1855, Roxbury, Mass. d: 8/8/13, New York, N.Y.
DAVE GARCIA Garcia, David b: 9/15/20, E.St.Louis, Ill.
JIM GIFFORD Gifford, James H. b: 10/18/1845, Warren, N.Y. d: 12/19/01, Columbus, Ohio
MASE GRAFFEN Graffen, Samuel Mason b: 1845, Philadelphia, Pa. d: 11/18/1883, Silver City, N.Mex
CHARLIE HACKETT Hackett, Charles M. b: 1855, Lee, Mass. d: 8/1/1898, Holyoke, Mass.
JIM HART Hart, James Aristotle b: 7/10/1855, Fairview, Pa. d: 7/18/19, Chicago, Ill.
JOHN HART Hart, John Henry (born John Henry Reen) b: 7/21/48, Tampa, Fla.
LOUIE HEILBRONER Heilbroner, Louis Wilbur b: 7/4/1861, Ft.Wayne, Ind. d: 12/21/33, Ft.Wayne, Ind.
BILL HENDERSON Henderson, William C.
ED HENGLE Hengle, Edward Siegfried b: Chicago, Ill. d: 11/4/27, Norwich, England
WALTER HEWETT Hewett, Walter F. b: 1861, Washington, D.C. d: 10/7/44, Washington, D.C.
VEDIE HIMSL Himsl, Avitus Bernard b: 4/2/17, Plevna, Mont.
FRED HOEY Hoey, Frederick Chamberlain b: 1866, New York, N.Y. d: 12/7/33, Paris, France
GEORGE HUFF Huff, George A. "Gee" b: 6/11/1872, Champaign, Ill. d: 10/1/36, Champaign, Ill.
TIM HURST Hurst, Timothy Carroll b: 6/30/1865, Ashland, Pa. d: 6/4/15, Pottsville, Pa.
JOHNNY KEANE Keane, John Joseph b: 11/3/11, St.Louis, Mo. d: 1/6/67, Houston, Tex.
JIM KENNEDY Kennedy, James C. b: 1867, New York, N.Y. d: 4/20/04, Brighton Beach, N.Y.
KEVIN KENNEDY Kennedy, Kevin Curtis b: 9/26/54, Los Angeles, Cal.
JACK KROL Krol, John Thomas b: 7/5/36, Chicago, Ill. d: 5/30/94, Winston-Salem, N.C.
KARL KUEHL Kuehl, Karl Otto b: 9/5/37, Monterey Park, Cal.
BOB LEADLEY Leadley, Robert H. b: 1858, Brooklyn, N.Y.
JIM LEYLAND Leyland, James Richard b: 12/15/44, Toledo, Ohio
NICK LEYVA Leyva, Nicholas Tomas b: 8/16/53, Ontario, Cal.
FRANK LUCCHESI Lucchesi, Frank Joseph b: 4/24/27, San Francisco, Cal.
JACK McCALLISTER McCallister, John b: 1/19/1879, Marietta, Ohio d: 10/18/46, Columbus, Ohio
JOE McCARTHY McCarthy, Joseph Vincent "Marse Joe" b: 4/21/1887, Philadelphia, Pa. d: 1/13/78, Buffalo, N.Y.
JOHN McCLOSKEY McCloskey, John Joseph "Honest John" b: 4/4/1862, Louisville, Ky. d: 11/17/40, Louisville, Ky.
MEL McGAHA McGaha, Fred Melvin b: 9/26/26, Bastrop, La.
JACK McKEON McKeon, John Aloysius b: 11/23/30, South Amboy, N.J.
DENNY McKNIGHT McKnight, Dennis Hamar b: 1847, Pittsburgh, Pa. d: 5/5/1900, Pittsburgh, Pa.
GEORGE McMANUS McManus, George b: 6/28/1846, Ireland d: 10/2/18, New York, N.Y.
JOHN McNAMARA McNamara, John Francis b: 6/4/32, Sacramento, Cal.
STUMP MERRILL Merrill, Carl Harrison b: 2/25/44, Brunswick, Me.
RAY MILLER Miller, Raymond Roger b: 4/30/45, Takoma Park, Md.
FELIX MOSES Moses, Felix I. b: Richmond, Va.

BILLY MURRAY Murray, William Jeremiah b: 4/13/1864, Peabody, Mass. d: 3/25/37, Youngstown, Ohio
JIM MUTRIE Mutrie, James J. "Truthful Jim" b: 6/13/1851, Chelsea, Mass. d: 1/24/38, New York, N.Y.
PAUL OWENS Owens, Paul Francis b: 2/7/24, Salamanca, N.Y.
DANNY OZARK Ozark, Daniel Leonard (born Daniel Leonard Orzechowski) b: 11/26/23, Buffalo, N.Y.
LEW PHELAN Phelan, Lewis G.
LEFTY PHILLIPS Phillips, Harold Ross b: 6/16/19, Los Angeles, Cal. d: 6/12/72, Fullerton, Cal.
HORACE PHILLIPS Phillips, Horace B. b: 5/14/1853, Salem, Ohio
EDDIE POPOWSKI Popowski, Edward Joseph b: 8/20/13, Sayreville, N.J.
PAT POWERS Powers, Patrick Thomas b: 6/27/1860, Trenton, N.J. d: 8/29/25, Belmar, N.J.
JIM PRICE Price, James L. b: 1847, New York, N.Y. d: 10/6/31, Chicago, Ill.
VERN RAPP Rapp, Vernon Fred b: 5/11/28, St.Louis, Mo.
GREG RIDDOCH Riddoch, Gregory Lee b: 7/17/45, Greeley, Colo.
JIM RIGGLEMAN Riggleman, James David b: 11/9/52, Fort Dix, N.J.
CAL RIPKEN Ripken, Calvin Edwin Sr. b: 12/17/35, Aberdeen, Md.
STAN ROBISON Robison, Matthew Stanley b: 3/30/1859, Pittsburgh, Pa. d: 3/24/11, Cleveland, Ohio
PANTS ROWLAND Rowland, Clarence Henry b: 2/12/1879, Platteville, Wis. d: 5/17/69, Chicago, Ill.
EDDIE SAWYER Sawyer, Edwin Milby b: 9/10/10, Westerly, R.I. d: 9/22/97, Phoenixville, Pa.
MIKE SCANLON Scanlon, Michael B. b: 11/1843, Cork, Ireland d: 1/18/29, Washington, D.C.
BOB SCHAEFER Schaefer, Robert Walden b: 5/22/44, Putnam, Conn. 5'11", 180 lbs. Deb: 5/22/91
M **GUS SCHMELZ** Schmelz, Gustavius Heinrich b: 9/26/1850, Columbus, Ohio d: 10/13/25, Columbus, Ohio
FRANK SELEE Selee, Frank Gibson b: 10/26/1859, Amherst, N.Y. d: 7/5/09, Denver, Colo.
BILL SHARSIG Sharsig, William A. b: 1855, Philadelphia, Pa. d: 2/1/02, Philadelphia, Pa.
LARRY SHEPARD Shepard, Lawrence William b: 4/3/19, Lakewood, Ohio
BILL SHETTSLINE Shettsline, William Joseph b: 10/25/1863, Philadelphia, Pa. d: 2/22/33, Philadelphia, Pa.
BUCK SHOWALTER Showalter, William Nathaniel b: 5/23/56, DeFuniak Springs, Fla.
LEW SIMMONS Simmons, Lewis b: 8/27/1838, New Castle, Pa. d: 9/2/11, Jamestown, Pa.
HARRY SPENCE Spence, Harrison L. b: 2/2/1856, New York, N.Y. d: 5/17/08, Chicago, Ill.
PAT SULLIVAN Sullivan, James Patrick d: 5/22/1898,
GEORGE TAYLOR Taylor, George J. b: 11/22/1853, New York
FRED THOMAS Thomas, Frederick L. b: Indiana
JACK TIGHE Tighe, John Thomas b: 8/9/13, Kearny, N.J.
TOM TREBELHORN Trebelhorn, Thomas Lynn b: 1/27/48, Portland, Ore.
TED TURNER Turner, Robert Edward b: 11/19/38, Cincinnati, Ohio
CHRIS VonDER AHE Von Der Ahe, Christian Frederick Wilhelm b: 10/7/1851, Hille, Prussia d: 6/5/13, St.Louis, Mo.
MIKE WALSH Walsh, Michael John b: 4/29/1850, Ireland d: 2/2/29, Louisville, Ky.
JOHN WALTZ Waltz, John J.
HARVEY WATKINS Watkins, Harvey L.
EARL WEAVER Weaver, Earl Sidney b: 8/14/30, St.Louis, Mo.
JIMMY WILLIAMS Williams, James Andrews b: 1/3/1848, Columbus, Ohio d: 10/24/18, N.Hempstead Twsp., N.Y.
BOBBY WINKLES Winkles, Bobby Brooks b: 3/11/30, Tuckerman, Ark.
AL WRIGHT Wright, Alfred Hector b: 3/30/1842, Cedar Grove, N.J. d: 4/20/05, New York, N.Y.
NICK YOUNG Young, Nicholas Ephraim b: 9/12/1840, Fort Johnson, N.Y. d: 10/31/16, Washington, D.C.

The Coach Roster

In an age of ever greater specialization in baseball, coaches have become increasingly important to the successful management of a team. The need for such assistance did not occur to any manager until John McGraw took on Arlie Latham as baseball's first full-time coach in 1909; today, teams employ separate coaches for first base, third base, pitching, the bullpen, hitting, baserunning, strength, conditioning, and more. Some coaches, like Charlie Lau and Roger Craig, have achieved fame exceeding that of the managers under whom they served. But coaches leave no statistical trail by which to track them. Players and pitchers have official records, and so do managers, but the accomplishments of coaches (and umpires) have until now resided largely in memory.

In the first edition of *Total Baseball,* the Coach Roster that follows represented a first attempt in a baseball encyclopedia to recognize these foot soldiers, who too often serve as scapegoats when a team fails but are invisible when it succeeds. We offered the roster in full knowledge that there were gaps and probably gaffes in our research; we hoped that our readers would advise us of omissions so that we could improve this roster in future editions of *Total Baseball*—and they have. We owe particular thanks to Bob Hoie and Walt Wilson. An additional feature, besides the inclusion of many new names, is full biographical data for all coaches who did not play at the major league level and so are absent from the Registers.

The principal sources of the data herein are, for 1921–1939, the *Baseball Blue Book*; for 1940–1981, *The Sporting News Dope Book of 1961,* the *Baseball Register*, and for years since 1982, the *American League Red Book* and the *National League Green Book.* We have done our best to reconcile the many differences among the lists. The team and league abbreviations used in the Coach Roster are found on the final page of this book.

Aaron, Tommie Lee Atl-N 1979-83
Abbott, Spencer Was-A 1935
Acosta, Oscar C. Chi-N 2000
Adair, James A. "Jimmy" Chi-A 1951-52, Bal-A 1957-61, Hou-N 1962-65
Adair, K. Jerry Oak-A 1972-74, Cal-A 1975
Adair, Marion D. "Bill" Mil-N 1962, Atl-N 1967, Chi-A 1970, Mon-N 1976
Adair, M. Richard "Rick" Cle-A 1992-93, Det-A 1996-99
Adams, Charles D. "Red" LA-N 1969-80
Adams, Robert H. "Bobby" Chi-N 1961-65, 1973
Aguirre, Henry J. "Hank" Chi-N 1972-74
Aker, Jackie D. "Jack" Cle-A 1985-87
Alejo, Robert K. "Bob" Oak-A 1997
Alfonso, Carlos SF-N 1992, 1997-99
Allenson, Gary M. Bos-A 1992-94, Mil-N 2000
Alomar, Santos C. "Sandy" SD-N 1986-90, Chi-N 2000
Alou, Felipe R. Mon-N 1979-80, 1984, 1992
Alou, Jesus M. R. Hou-N 1979
Altobelli, Joseph S. "Joe" NY-A 1981-82, 1986, Chi-N 1988-91
Altrock, Nicholas "Nick" Was-A 1912-53
Amalfitano, J. Joseph "Joey" Chi-N 1967-71, SF-N 1972-75, SD-N 1976-77, Chi-N 1978-80, Cin-N 1982, LA-N 1983-98
Amaro, Ruben Phi-N 1980-81, Chi-N 1983-86
Anderson, George L. "Sparky" SD-N 1969
Apodaca, Robert J. "Bob" NY-N 1996-99, Mil-N 2000
Appling, Lucius B. "Luke" Det-A 1960, Cle-A 1960-61, Bal-A 1963, KC-A 1964-67, Chi-A 1970-71
Arnsberg, Bradley J. "Brad" Mon-N 2000
Arsenault, Pierre J. Mon-N 1992-00
Ashby, Alan D. Hou-N 1997
Auferio, Anthony P. "Tony" StL-N 1973
Austin, James P. "Jimmy" StL-A 1923-32, Chi-A 1933-40
Babe, Loren R. NY-A 1967, Chi-A 1980-81, 1983
Bader, Lore V. Bos-N 1926
Bailey, Welby S. "Buddy" Bos-A 2000
Bailor, Robert M. "Bob" Tor-A 1992-95
Baker, Delmer D. "Del" Det-A 1933-38, Cle-A 1943-44, Bos-A 1945-48, 1953-60
Baker, Eugene W. "Gene" Pit-N 1963
Baker, Floyd W. Min-A 1961-64
Baker, Johnnie B "Dusty" SF-N 1988-92
Baker, William P. "Bill" Chi-N 1950
Bamberger, George I. Bal-A 1968-77
Bancroft, David J. "Dave" NY-N 1930-32
Bando, Christopher M. "Chris" Mil-A 1996-97, Mil-N 1998
Bando, Salvatore L. "Sal" Mil-A 1980-81
Banks, Ernest "Ernie" Chi-N 1967-73
Barfield, Jesse L. Hou-N 1995, Sea-A 1998-99
Bartell, Richard W. "Dick" NY-N 1946, Det-A 1949-52, Cin-N 1954-55
Bartirome, Anthony J. "Tony" Atl-N 1986-88
Basgall, Romanus "Monty" LA-N 1973-86
Bassler, John L. "Johnny" Cle-A 1938-40, StL-A 1941
Baylor, Don E. Mil-A 1990-91, StL-N 1992, Atl-N 1999
Bauer, Henry A. "Hank" Bal-A 1963
Beauchamp, James E. "Jim" Atl-N 1991-98
Bearnarth, Lawrence D. "Larry" Mon-N 1976, 1985-91, Col-N 1993-95
Beck, Walter W. "Boom-Boom" Was-A 1957-59
Becker, Joseph E. "Joe" Bro-N 1955-57, LA-N 1958-64, StL-N 1965-66, Chi-N 1967-70
Bedell, Howard W. "Howie" KC-A 1984, SE-A 1988
Bell, David G. "Buddy" Cle-A 1994-95
Bender, Charles A. "Chief" Chi-A 1925-26, NY-N 1931, Phi-A 1951-53
Bengough, Bernard O. "Benny" Was-A 1940-43, Bos-N 1944-45, Phi-N 1946-58
Benedict, Bruce E. NY-N 1997-99
Benson, Vernon A. "Vern" StL-N 1961-64, NY-A 1965-66, Cin-N 1966-69, StL-N 1970-75, Atl-N 1976-77, SF-N 1980
Berardino, John "Johnny" StL-A 1951
Berardino, Richard J. "Dick" Bos-A 1989-91
Berg, Morris "Moe" Bos-A 1940-41
Beringer, Carroll J. "C. B." LA-N 1967-72, Phi-N 1973-78
Bernhardt, Carlos Bal-A 1998
Berra, Lawrence P. "Yogi" NY-A 1963, NY-N 1965-71, NY-A 1976-83, Hou-N 1986-89
Berres, Raymond F. "Ray" Chi-A 1949-66, 1968-69
Berry, Charles F. "Charlie" Phi-A 1936-40
Bevington, Terry Paul Chi-A 1989-95, TO-R 1999-00
Biagini, Gregory P. "Greg" Bal-A 1992-94
Bialas, David B. "Dave" SD-N 1993-94, Chi-N 1995-99
Bissonette, Adelphia L. "Del" Bos-N 1945, Pit-N 1946
Black, William C. "Bud" Ana-A 2000
Blackburn, Wayne C. Det-A 1963-64
Blackburne, Russell A. "Lena" Chi-A 1927-28, StL-A 1930, Phi-A 1933-40, 1942-43
Blades, F. Raymond "Ray" StL-N 1930-32, Cin-N 1942, Bro-N 1947-48, StL-N 1951, Chi-N 1953-56
Blaylock, Gary N. KC-A 1984-87
Bloomfield, Gordon L. "Jack" SD-N 1974, Chi-N 1975-76, 1977
Bluege, Oswald L. "Ossie" Was-A 1940-42
Bochy, Bruce D. SD-N 1993-94
Bombard, Marc Cin-N 1996
Bonds, Bobby L. Cle-A 1984-87, SF-N 1993-96
Booker, Gregory S. "Greg" SD-N 1997-00
Boone, Robert R. "Bob" Cin-N 1994
Boros, Stephen "Steve" KC-A 1975-79, Mon-N 1981-82, KC-A 1993-94, Bal-A 1995
Bosley, Thaddis "Thad" Oak-A 1999-00
Bosman, Richard A. "Dick" Chi-A 1986-87, Bal-A 1992-94, Tex-A 1995-00
Bottomley, James L. "Jim" StL-A 1937
Bowa, Lawrence R. "Larry" Phi-N 1988-96, Ana-A 1997-99, Sea-A 2000
Boyer, Cletis L. "Clete" Oak-A 1980-85, NY-A 1988, 1992-94
Boyer, Cloyd V. NY-A 1975, 1977, Atl-N 1978-81, KC-A 1982-83
Boyer, Kenton L. "Ken" StL-N 1971-72
Bragan, James A. "Jimmy" Cin-N 1967-69, Mon-N 1970-72, Mil-A 1976-77
Bragan, Robert R. "Bobby" LA-N 1960, Hou-N 1962
Brantley, Michael C. "Mickey" NY-N 1999
Braun, Stephen R. "Steve" StL-N 1990
Brecheen, Harry D. Bal-A 1954-67
Breeden, H. Scott Cin-N 1986-89
Breeden, Joseph T. "Joe" Fla-N 1995-96, 1999-00
Brenly, Robert E. "Bob" SF-N 1992-96
Bresnahan, Roger P. NY-N 1925-28, Det-A 1930-31
Brewer, James T. "Jim" Mon-N 1977-79
Bridges, Everett L. "Rocky" LA-A 1962-63, Cal-A 1968-71, SF-N 1985
Bridges, Thomas J. "Tommy" Det-A 1946, Cin-N 1951
Brinkman, Edwin A. "Ed" Det-A 1979, SD-N 1981, Chi-A 1983-88
Bristol, J. David "Dave" Cin-N 1966, Mon-N 1973-75, SF-N 1978-79, Phi-N 1982-85, 1988, Cin-N 1989, 1993
Brown, H. Harold "Hal" Bal-A 1964
Brown, Jackie G. Tex-A 1979-82, Chi-A 1992-95
Brown, James R. "Jimmy" Bos-N 1949-51
Brown, Mace S. Bos-A 1965
Brown, William J. "Gates" Det-A 1978-84
Brucker, Earle F., Sr. Phi-A 1941-49, StL-A 1950, Cin-N 1952
Bryant, Claiborne H. "Clay" LA-N 1961, Cle-A 1967, 1974
Bryant, Donald R. "Don" Bos-A 1974-76, Sea-A 1977-80
Buckner, William J. "Bill" Chi-A 1996-97
Buford, Donald A. "Don" SF-N 1981-84, Bal-A 1994
Bumbry, Alonza B. "Al" Bos-A 1988-93, Bal-A 1995, Cle-A 1998
Bundy, C. Lorenzo Fla-N 1998, Col-N 1999
Burdette, S. Lewis "Lew" Atl-N 1972-73
Burgess, Thomas R. "Tom" NY-N 1977, Atl-N 1978
Burgmeier, Thomas H. "Tom" KC-A 1991, 1998-00
Burke, James T. "Jimmy" Det-A 1914-17, Bos-A 1921-23, Chi-N 1926-30, NY-A 1931-33
Burkett, Jesse C. NY-N 1921
Burleson, Richard P. "Rick" Oak-A 1991, Bos-A 1992-93, Cal-A 1995-96
Burns, George J. NY-N 1931
Burns, John I. "Jack" Bos-A 1955-59
Burris, B. Ray Mil-A 1990-91, Tex-A 1992
Burwell, William E. "Bill" Bos-A 1944, Pit-N 1947-48, 1958-62
Busby, James F. "Jim" Bal-A 1961, Hou-N 1962, 1963-67, Atl-N 1968-75, Chi-A 1976, Sea-A 1977-78
Butera, Salvatore P. "Sal" Tor-A 1998-99
Butler, John S. "Johnny" Chi-A 1932
Butterfield, Brian J. NY-A 1994-95, Ari-N 1998-00
Camacho, Joseph G. "Joe" Was-A 1969-71, Tex-A 1972
Camilli, Douglas J. "Doug" Was-A 1968-69, Bos-A 1970-73
Campbell, William R. "Bill" Mil-N 1999
Cannizzaro, Christopher J. "Chris" Atl-N 1976-78
Cardenal, Jose R. D. Cin-N 1993, StL-N 1994-95, NY-A 1996-99, TB-A 2000
Carew, Rodney C. "Rod" Cal-A 1992-96, Ana-A 1997-99, Mil-N 2000
Carey, Max G. Pit-N 1930
Carey, Paul J. "P. J." Col-N 1997
Carey, Thomas F. "Tom" Bos-A 1946-47
Carisch, Frederick B. "Fred" Det-A 1923-24
Carlucci, David M. "Dave" Bos-A 1996
Carnevale, Daniel J. "Danny" KC-A 1970
Carrion, Leonel S. Mon-N 1988
Carter, Richard J. "Dick" Phi-N 1959-60
Case, George W. Was-A 1961-63, Min-A 1968
Cash, David "Dave" Phi-N 1996
Castro, William R. "Bill" Mil-A 1992-95, NY-A 1996, Mil-A 1997, Mil-N 1998-00
Cavarretta, Philip J. "Phil" Det-A 1961-63, NY-N 1978
Cepeda, Orlando M. Chi-A 1980
Chambliss, C. Christopher "Chris" NY-A 1988, StL-N 1993-95, NY-A 1997-00
Chandler, Spurgeon F. "Spud" KC-A 1957-58
Chapman, W. Benjamin "Ben" Cin-N 1952
Chesbro, John D. "Jack" Was-A 1924
Chiti, H. Dominic "Dom" Cle-A 1991-93
Cisco, Galen B. KC-A 1971-79, Mon-N 1980-84, SD-N 1985-87, Tor-A 1988, 1990-95, Phi-N 1997-00
Clark, Ronald B. "Ron" Chi-A 1988-90, Sea-A 1991, Cle-A 1992-93
Clarke, Fred C. Pit-N 1925
Clarke, Thomas A. "Tommy" NY-N 1932-35, 1938
Clary, Ellis Was-A 1955-60, Tor-A 1989
Clear, E. Robert "Bob" Cal-A 1976-87
Clines, Eugene A. "Gene" Chi-N 1979-81, Hou-N 1988, Sea-A 1989-92, Mil-A 1993-94, SF-N 1997-00
Cloninger, Tony L. NY-A 1992-00
Cluck, Robert A. "Bob" Hou-N 1979, 1990-93, Oak-A 1996-98
Clymer, William J. "Bill" Cin-N 1925
Cochrane, Gordon S. "Mickey" Phi-A 1950
Cohen, Andrew H. "Andy" Phi-N 1960
Colavito, Rocco D. "Rocky" Cle-A 1973, 1976-78, KC-A 1982-83
Cole, Richard R. "Dick" Chi-N 1961
Coleman, Joseph H. "Joe" Cal-A 1988-90, StL-N 1991-94, Cal-A 1996, Ana-A 1997-99
Coleman, Robert H. "Bob" Bos-A 1926, Det-A 1932, Bos-N 1943
Collins, David S "Dave" StL-N 1991-92, Cin-N 1999-00
Collins, Edward T. "Eddie" Phi-A 1931-32
Collins, James A. "Ripper" Chi-N 1961-63
Collins, Terry L. Pit-N 1992-93
Combs, Earle B. NY-A 1936-44, StL-A 1947, Bos-A 1948-52, Phi-N 1954
Combs, Merrill R. "Merl" Tex-A 1974-75
Comer, Stephen M. "Steve" Cle-A 1987
Connor, Mark P. NY-A 1984-85, 1986-87, 1990-93, Ari-N 1998-00
Connors, William J. "Billy" KC-A 1980-81, Chi-N 1982-86, Sea-A 1987-88, NY-A 1989-90, Chi-N 1991-93, NY-A 1994-95, 2000
Conroy, William E. "Wid" Phi-N 1922
Consolo, William A. "Billy" Det-A 1979-92, 1995
Contreras, Arnaldo J. "Nardi" NY-A 1995, Sea-A 1997-98, Chi-A 1998-00
Cooke, Allen L. "Dusty" Phi-N 1948-52
Coombs, John W. "Jack" Det-A 1920
Cooney, John W. "Johnny" Bos-N 1940-42, 1946-49, 1950-52, Mil-N 1953-55, Chi-A 1957-64
Cooper, Donald J. "Don" Chi-A 1995
Cooper, W. Walker StL-N 1957, KC-A 1960
Corrales, Patrick "Pat" Tex-A 1975-78, NY-A 1989, Atl-N 1990-00
Corriden, John M., Sr "Red" Chi-N 1932-40, Bro-N 1941-46, NY-A 1947-48, Chi-A 1950
Cottier, Charles K. "Chuck" NY-N 1979-81, Sea-A 1982-84, Chi-N 1988-94, Bal-A 1995,

Phi-N 1997-00
Couchee, Michael "Mike" Cal-A 1996
Courtney, Clinton D. "Clint" Hou-N 1965
Cox, Jeffrey L. "Jeff" KC-A 1995
Cox, Larry E. Chi-N 1988-89
Cox, Robert J. "Bobby" NY-A 1977
Crabtree, Estel C. Cin-N 1943-44
Craft, Harry F. KC-A 1955-57, Chi-N 1960-61
Craig, Roger L. SD-N 1969-72, Hou-N 1974-75, SD-N 1976-77, Det-A 1980-84
Cramer, Roger M. "Doc" Det-A 1948, Chi-A 1951-53
Crandall, Delmar W. "Del" Cal-A 1977
Crandall, J. Otis "Doc" Pit-N 1931-34
Crandall, James M. "Jim" StL-A 1953
Cravath, Clifford C. "Gavvy" Phi-N 1923
Cresse, Mark E. LA-N 1977-98
Crosetti, Frank P. J. "Frankie" NY-A 1947-68, Sea-A 1969, Min-A 1970-71
Crowley, Terrence M. "Terry" Bal-A 1985-88, Min-A 1991-98, Bal-A 1999-00
Cruz, Jose Hou-N 1997-00
Cubbage, Michael L. "Mike" NY-N 1990-91, 1992-96, Hou-N 1997-00
Cuccinello, Anthony F. "Tony" Cin-N 1949-51, Cle-A 1952-56, Chi-A 1957-66, Det-A 1967-68, Chi-A 1969
Cuellar, Robert "Bobby" Sea-A 1995-96, Mon-N 1997-00
Culp, Benjamin B. "Benny" Phi-N 1946-47
Cumberland, John S. Bos-A 1995, 1999-00
Cunningham, Joseph R. "Joe" StL-N 1982
Cunningham, William A. "Bill" Chi-A 1932
Cuyler, Hazen S. "Kiki" Chi-N 1941-43, Bos-A 1949
Dahlgren, Ellsworth T. "Babe" KC-A 1964
Dal Canton, J. Bruce Chi-A 1978, Atl-N 1987-90
Daly, Thomas D. "Tom" Bos-A 1933-46
Dark, Alvin R. Chi-N 1965, 1977
Dauer, Richard F. "Rich" Cle-A 1990-91, KC-A 1997-00
Davenport, James H. "Jim" SF-N 1970, SD-N 1974-75, SF-N 1976-82, 1984, Phi-N 1986-87, Cle-A 1989, SF-N 1995
Davis, Harry H. Phi-A 1913-17, 1919
Davis, H. Thomas "Tommy" Sea-A 1981
Davis, R. Brandon "Brandy" Phi-N 1972
Davis, Virgil L. "Spud" Pit-N 1942-46, Chi-N 1950-53
Deal, Ellis F. "Cot" Cin-N 1959-60, Hou-N 1962-64, NY-A 1965, KC-A 1966-67, Cle-A 1970-71, Det-A 1973-74, Hou-N 1983-85
Dean, Jay H. "Dizzy" Chi-N 1941
DeArmas, Rolando J. "Roly" Chi-A 1995-96, Tor-A 2000
DeJohn, Mark S. StL-N 1996-00
DeMars, William L. "Billy" Phi-N 1969-81, Mon-N 1982-84, Cin-N 1985-87
DeMerritt, Martin G. "Marty" SF-N 1989, Chi-N 1999
Demeter, Stephen "Steve" Pit-N 1985
Dempsey, J. Rikard "Rick" LA-N 1999-00
Dent, Russell E. "Bucky" StL-N 1991-94, Tex-A 1995-00
Detore, George F. Pit-N 1959
Devlin, Arthur M. "Art" Bos-N 1926, 1928
Dews, Robert W. "Bobby" Atl-N 1979-81, 1985, 1997-00
Dickey, William M. "Bill" NY-A 1949-57, 1960
Didier, Robert D. "Bob" Oak-A 1984-86, Sea-A 1989-90
DiMaggio, Joseph P. "Joe" Oak-A 1968-69
Dixon, Walter "Walt" Chi-N 1964-65
Dobson, Patrick E. "Pat" Mil-A 1982-84, SD-N 1988-90, KC-A 1991, Bal-A 1996
Doby, Lawrence E. "Larry" Mon-N 1971-73, Cle-A 1974, Mon-N 1976, Chi-A 1977-78
Doerr, Robert P. "Bobby" Bos-A 1967-69, Tor-A 1977-81
Dolan, Albert J. "Cozy" NY-N 1922-24
Donnelly, Richard F. "Rich" Tex-A 1980, 1983-85, Pit-N 1986-95, Fla-N 1997-98, Col-N 1999-00
Donovan, William E. "Bill" Det-A 1918
Doolan, Michael J. "Mickey" Chi-N 1926-29, Cin-N 1930-32
Dorish, Harry "Fritz" Bos-A 1963, Atl-N 1968-71
Douglas, Otis W. Cin-N 1961-62
Down, Richard J. "Rick" Cal-A 1987-88, NY-A 1993-95, Bal-A 1996-98, LA-N 1999-00
Drabowsky, Myron W. "Moe" Chi-A 1986, Chi-N 1994
Dressen, Charles W. "Chuck" Bro-N 1939-42, 1943-46, NY-A 1947-48, LA-N 1958-59
Dubee, Richard P. "Rich" Fla-N 1998-00
Dubuc, Jean J. Det-A 1930-31
Duffy, Hugh Bos-A 1932
Dugey, Oscar J. Bos-N 1920, Chi-N 1921-24
Duncan, David E. "Dave" Cle-A 1978-81, Sea-A 1982, Chi-A 1983-86, Oak-A 1986-95, StL-N 1996-00
Dunlop, Harry A. KC-A 1969-75, Chi-N 1976, Cin-N 1979-82, SD-N 1983-86, Cin-N 1998
Durocher, Leo E. LA-N 1961-64
Dusan, Eugene P. "Gene" NY-N 1983
Dyer, Don R. "Duffy" Chi-N 1983, Mil-A 1989-95, Oak-A 1996-98
Dykes, James J. "Jimmy" Phi-A 1949-50, Cin-N 1955-58, Pit-N 1959, Mil-N 1962, KC-A 1963-64
Earnshaw, George L. Phi-N 1949-50
Easler, Michael A. "Mike" Mil-A 1992, Bos-A 1993-94, StL-N 1999-00
Easter, L. Luke Cle-A 1969
Edwards, Howard R. "Doc" Phi-N 1970-72, Cle-A 1985-87, NY-N 1990-91
Egan, Arthur A. "Ben" Bro-N 1925, Chi-A 1926
Egan, Richard W. "Dick" Tex-A 1988-89
Elia, Lee C. Phi-N 1980-81, 1985-87, NY-A 1989, Sea-A 1993-97, Tor-A 2000
Elliott, Robert I. "Bob" LA-A 1961
Ellis, Samuel J. "Sammy" NY-A 1982, 1983-84, 1986, Chi-A 1989-91, Chi-N 1992, Sea-A 1993-94, Bos-A 1996, Bal-A 2000
Emery, Calvin W. "Cal" Chi-A 1988
Engle, R. David "Dave" Hou-N 1998
Ens, Jewel W. Pit-N 1926-29, Det-A 1932, Cin-N 1933, Bos-N 1934, Pit-N 1935-39, Cin-N 1941
Ermer, Calvin C. "Cal" Bal-A 1962, Mil-A 1970-71, Oak-A 1977
Estrada, Charles L. "Chuck" Tex-A 1973, SD-N 1978-81, Cle-A 1983
Etchebarren, Andrew A. "Andy" Cal-A 1977, Mil-A 1985-91, Bal-A 1996-97
Evans, Darrell W. NY-A 1990
Evans, Dwight M. Col-N 1994
Evers, John J. "Johnny" NY-N 1920, Chi-A 1922-23, Bos-N 1929-32
Evers, Walter A. "Hoot" Cle-A 1970
Ezell, Glenn W. Tex-A 1983-85, KC-A 1989-94, Det-A 1996
Faber, Urban C. "Red" Chi-A 1946-48
Fahey, William R. "Bill" SF-N 1986-91
Falk, Bibb A. Cle-A 1933, Bos-A 1934
Fanning, W. James "Jim" Atl-N 1967
Farrell, M. Kerby Chi-A 1966-69, Cle-A 1970-71
Felske, John F. Tor-A 1980-81, Phi-N 1984
Ferguson, Joseph V. "Joe" Tex-A 1986-87, LA-N 1988-89, 1992-93
Ferraro, Michael D. "Mike" NY-A 1979-82, KC-A 1984-86, NY-A 1987-88, 1989-91, Bal-A 1993
Ferrell, Richard B. "Rick" Was-A 1946-49, Det-A 1950-53
Ferrick, Thomas J. "Tom" Cin-N 1954-58, Phi-N 1959, Det-A 1960-63, KC-A 1964-65
Ferriss, David M. "Dave" Bos-A 1955-59
Fischer, Bradley J. "Brad" Oak-A 1996-00
Fischer, William C. "Bill" Cin-N 1979-83, Bos-A 1985-91, TB-A 2000
Fitzgerald, Edward R. "Ed" Cle-A 1960, KC-A 1961, Min-A 1962-64
Fitzgerald, Joseph P. "Joe" Was-A 1947-56
Fitzpatrick, John A. Pit-N 1953-56, Mil-N 1958-59
Fitzsimmons, Frederick "Freddie" Bro-N 1942, Bos-N 1948, NY-N 1949-53, 1954-55, Chi-N 1957-59, KC-A 1960, Chi-N 1966
Flanagan, Michael K. "Mike" Bal-A 1995, 1998
Flannery, Timothy E. "Tim" SD-N 1996-00
Fletcher, Arthur "Art" NY-A 1927-45
Flowers, D'Arcy R. "Jake" Pit-N 1940-45, Bos-N 1946, Cle-A 1951-52
Fohl, Leo A. "Lee" StL-A 1920
Foley, Marvis E. "Marv" Chi-N 1994, Bal-A 1999
Foli, Timothy J. "Tim" Tex-A 1986-87, Mil-A 1992-95, KC-A 1996
Foote, Barry C. Chi-A 1991, NY-N 1992-93
Ford, Edward C. "Whitey" NY-A 1964, 1968, 1974-75
Fowler, J. Arthur "Art" LA-A 1964, Min-A 1969, Det-A 1971-73, Tex-A 1973-75, NY-A 1977-79, Oak-A 1980-82, NY-A 1983, 1988
Fox, Charles F. "Charlie" SF-N 1965-68, NY-A 1989
Fox, J. Nelson "Nellie" Hou-N 1965, 1966-67, Was-A 1968-71, Tex-A 1972
Foxx, James E. "Jimmie" Chi-N 1944
Francona, Terry J. Det-A 1996
Franks, Herman L. NY-N 1949-55, SF-N 1958, 1964, Chi-N 1970
Fraser, Charles C. "Chick" Pit-N 1923
Freese, George W. Chi-N 1964-65
Frey, James G. "Jim" Bal-A 1970-79, NY-N 1982-83
Friel, William E. "Bill" StL-A 1920
Friend, Owen L. KC-A 1969
Frisch, Frank F. "Frankie" NY-N 1949
Funk, Franklin R. "Frank" SF-N 1976, Sea-A 1980-81, 1983-84, KC-A 1988-90, Col-N 1996-98
Galan, August J. "Augie" Phi-A 1954
Galante, Matthew "Matt" Hou-N 1985-96, 1998-00
Gale, Richard B. "Rich" Bos-A 1992-93
Gamboa, Thomas Harold "Tom" Chi-N 1998-99
Gantner, James E. "Jim" Mil-A 1996-97
Garcia, David "Dave" SD-N 1970-73, Cle-A 1975-76, Cal-A 1977, Cle-A 1979, Mil-A 1983-84
Gardenhire, Ronald C. "Ron" Min-A 1991-00
Gardner, William F. "Billy" Bos-A 1965-66, Mon-N 1977-78, Min-A 1981
Garner, Philip M. "Phil" Hou-N 1989-91
Garrett, H. Adrian KC-A 1988-92
Garrison, R. Ford Cin-N 1953
Gaston, Clarence E. "Cito" Tor-A 1982-89, 2000
Gebhard, Robert H. "Bob" Mon-N 1982
Gehringer, Charles L. "Charlie" Det-A 1942
Gernert, Richard E. "Dick" Tex-A 1975-76
Gharrity, E. Patrick "Patsy" Was-A 1929-32, Cle-A 1933-35
Gibson, George C. Was-A 1923, Chi-N 1925, 1926
Gibson, Robert "Bob" NY-N 1981, Atl-N 1982-84, StL-N 1995
Gilbert, Andrew "Andy" SF-N 1972-75
Gilliam, James W. "Jim" LA-N 1965-78
Gladding, Fred E. Det-A 1976-78
Gleason, William J. "Kid" Phi-N 1908-11, Chi-A 1912-14, 1916-17, Phi-A 1926-32
Gleeson, James J. "Jim" KC-A 1957, NY-A 1964
Glynn, Eugene P. "Gene" Col-N 1994, 1995-98, Mon-N 1999, Chi-N 2000
Gomez, Juan A. "Orlando" Tex-A 1991-92, TB-A 1998-00
Gomez, Pedro "Preston" LA-N 1965-68, Hou-N 1973, StL-N 1976, LA-N 1977-79, Cal-A 1981-84
Gonzalez, Fredi J. Fla-N 1999-00
Gonzalez, Miguel A. "Mike" StL-N 1934-46
Gooch, John B. "Johnny" Pit-N 1937-39
Goodman, William D. "Billy" Atl-N 1968-70
Gordon, Joseph L. "Joe" Det-A 1956
Goryl, John A. "Johnny" Min-A 1968-69, 1979-80, Cle-A 1982-88, 1997-98
Gowdy, Henry M. "Hank" Bos-N 1929-37, Cin-N 1938-42, 1945-46, NY-N 1947-48
Graff, Milton E. "Milt" Pit-N 1985
Graham, J. Brian Cle-A 1999, Bal-A 2000
Grammas, Alexander P. "Alex" Chi-N 1964, Pit-N 1965-69, Cin-N 1970-75, 1978, Atl-N 1979, Det-A 1980-91
Gregson, Glenn LA-N 1998
Griffey, G. Kenneth Sr. "Ken" Sea-A 1993-94, Col-N 1996, Cin-N 1997-00
Griffin, Alfredo C. Tor-A 1996-97, Ana-A 2000
Grimes, Burleigh A. KC-A 1955
Grimm, Charles J. "Charlie" Chi-N 1941, 1961-63
Grissom, Marvin E. "Marv" LA-A 1961-65, Cal-A 1966, Chi-A 1967-68, Cal-A 1969, Min-A 1970-71, Chi-N 1975-76, Cal-A 1977-78
Grodzicki, John "Johnny" Det-A 1979
Guerrero, Epifanio O. "Epy" Tor-A 1981
Gullett, Donald E. "Don" Cin-N 1993-00
Gustine, Frank W. "Frankie" Pit-N 1950
Gutteridge, Donald J. "Don" Chi-A 1955-66, 1968-69
Haas, G. Edward "Eddie" Atl-N 1974-77, 1984
Haas, George W. "Mule" Chi-A 1940-46
Hack, Stanley C. "Stan" StL-N 1957-58, Chi-N 1965
Hacker, Richard W. "Rich" StL-N 1986-90, Tor-A 1991-94
Haddix, Harvey NY-N 1966-67, Cin-N 1969, Bos-A 1971, Cle-A 1975-78, Pit-N 1979-84
Haines, Jesse J. Bro-N 1938
Hairston, Samuel "Sammy" Chi-A 1978
Haller, Thomas F. "Tom" SF-N 1977-79
Hamilton, Steve A. Det-A 1975
Hancken, Morris M. "Buddy" Hou-N 1968-72
Haney, Fred G. Mil-N 1956
Haney, W. Larry Mil-A 1978-91

Hansen, Guy C. KC-A 1991-93, 1996-97
Hansen, Roger C. Sea-A 1992
Hansen, Ronald L. "Ron" Mil-A 1980-83, Mon-N 1985-89
Harder, Melvin L. "Mel" Cle-A 1947, 1948-63, NY-N 1964, Chi-N 1965, Cin-N 1966-68, KC-A 1969
Hardy, H. Lawrence "Larry" Tex-A 1995-00
Hargrove, D. Michael "Mike" Cle-A 1990-91
Harmon, Thomas "Tom" Chi-N 1982
Harper, Tommy Bos-A 1980-84, Mon-N 1990-99, Bos-A 2000
Harrah, Colbert D. "Toby" Tex-A 1989-92, Cle-A 1996, Col-N 2000
Harrelson, Derrel M. "Bud" NY-N 1982, 1985-90
Harris, C. Luman "Lum" Chi-A 1951-54, Bal-A 1955-61, Hou-N 1962-64
Hart, John H. Bal-A 1988
Hartenstein, Charles O. "Chuck" Cle-A 1979, Mil-A 1987-89
Hartley, Grover A. Cle-A 1928-30, Pit-N 1931-33, StL-A 1934-36, NY-N 1946
Hartnett, Charles L. "Gabby" Chi-N 1938, NY-N 1941, KC-A 1965
Hartsfield, Roy T. LA-N 1969-72, Atl-N 1973
Hassey, Ronald W. "Ron" Col-N 1993-95, StL-N 1996
Hatcher, Michael V. "Mickey" Tex-A 1993-94, LA-N 1998, Ana-A 2000
Hatcher, William A. "Billy" TB-A 1998-00
Hatfield, Fred J. Det-A 1977-78
Hatton, Grady E. Chi-N 1960, Hou-N 1973-74
Hayes, William E. "Bill" Col-N 1998
Haynes, Joseph W. "Joe" Was-A 1953-55
Hayworth, Raymond H. "Ray" Bro-N 1945, Chi-N 1955
Hebner, Richard J. "Richie" Bos-A 1989-91
Heffner, Donald H. "Don" KC-A 1958-60, Det-A 1961, NY-N 1964-65, Cal-A 1967-68
Hegan, James E. "Jim" NY-A 1960-73, Det-A 1974-78, NY-A 1979-80
Heilmann, Harry E. Cin-N 1932
Heist, Alfred M. "Al" Hou-N 1966-67, SD-N 1980
Helms, Tommy V. Tex-A 1981-82, Cin-N 1983-89
Hemsley, Ralston B. "Rollie" Phi-A 1954, Was-A 1961-62
Hemus, Solomon J. "Solly" NY-N 1962-63, Cle-A 1964-65
Henderson, Ramon G. Phi-N 1998-00
Henderson, Stephen C. "Steve" Hou-N 1994-96, TB-A 1998
Hendrick, George A. StL-N 1996-97, Ana-A 1998-99
Hendricks, Elrod J. Bal-A 1978-00
Henrich, Thomas D. "Tommy" NY-A 1951, NY-N 1957, Det-A 1958-59
Herman, Floyd C. "Babe" Pit-N 1951
Herman, William J. "Billy" Bro-N 1952-57, Mil-N 1958-59, Bos-A 1960-64, Cal-A 1967, SD-N 1978-79
Hernandez, Carlo A "Chuck" Cal-A 1992-96
Herndon, Larry D. Det-A 1992-98
Herzog, Dorrel N. "Whitey" KC-A 1965, NY-N 1966, Cal-A 1974-75
Hiatt, Jack E Chi-N 1981
High, Andrew A. "Andy" Bro-N 1937-38
Hill, Marc K. Hou-N 1988, NY-A 1991
Hill, Perry W. Tex-A 1992-94, 1995, Det-A 1997-99, Mon-N 2000
Hiller, Charles J. "Chuck" Tex-A 1973, KC-A 1976-79, StL-N 1981-83, SF-N 1985, NY-N 1990
Hilton, J. David "Dave" Mil-A 1987-88
Himsl, Avitus B. "Vedie" Chi-N 1960-64
Hinchman, William W. "Bill" Pit-N 1923
Hines, Benjamin T. "Ben" Sea-A 1984, LA-N 1986, 1988-93, Hou-N 1994
Hines, Bruce E. Cal-A 1991
Hisle, Larry E. Tor-A 1992-95
Hitchcock, William C. "Billy" Det-A 1955-60, Atl-N 1966
Hoak, Donald A. "Don" Phi-N 1967
Hoffman, Glenn E. LA-N 1999-00
Hofman, Robert G. "Bobby" KC-A 1966-67, Was-A 1968, Oak-A 1969-70, Cle-A 1971-72, Oak-A 1974-75, 1978
Hofmann, Fred StL-A 1938-49, 1951
Holke, Walter H. StL-A 1940
Hollingsworth, Albert W. "Al" StL-N 1957-58
Holmberg, Dennis Tor-A 1994-95
Holmquist, Douglas L. "Doug" NY-A 1984, 1985
Holt, Golden D. "Goldie" Pit-N 1948-50, Chi-N 1961-65
Hooten, Burt C. Hou-N 2000
Hopp, John L. "Johnny" Det-A 1954, StL-N 1956
Hornsby, Rogers Chi-N 1958-59, NY-N 1962
Horton, Willie W. NY-A 1985, Chi-A 1986
Hoscheit, Vernard A. "Vern" Bal-A 1968, Oak-A 1969-74, Cal-A 1976, NY-N 1984-87
Hough, Charles O. "Charlie" LA-N 1998-99
Houk, Ralph G. NY-A 1954, 1958-60
House, Thomas R. "Tom" Tex-A 1985-92
Howard, Elston G. NY-A 1969-79
Howard, Frank O. Mil-A 1977-80, NY-N 1982-83, 1984, Mil-A 1985-86, Sea-A 1987-88, NY-A 1989, 1991-92, NY-N 1994-96, TB-A 1998-99
Howe, Arthur H. "Art" Tex-A 1985-88, Col-N 1995
Howley, Daniel P. "Dan" Det-A 1919, 1921-22
Howser, Richard D. "Dick" NY-A 1969-78
Hriniak, Walter J. "Walt" Mon-N 1974-75, Bos-A 1977-88, Chi-A 1989-95
Hudlin, G. Willis Det-A 1957-59
Hubbard, Glenn D. Atl-N 1999-00
Hubbard, John H. "Jack" StL-N 1993, Tor-A 1998
Hudgens, David M. "Dave" Oak-A 1999
Hudson, Sidney C. "Sid" Was-A 1961-65, 1968-71, Tex-A 1972, 1975-78
Hulswitt, Rudolph E. "Rudy" Bos-A 1931-33
Hume, Thomas H. "Tom" Cin-N 1996-00
Hundley, C. Randolph "Randy" Chi-N 1977
Hunter, Frederick C. "Newt" Phi-N 1928-31, 1933
Hunter, G. William "Billy" Bal-A 1964-77
Hurdle, Clinton M. "Clint" Col-N 1997-00
Isaac, Luis Cle-A 1987-91, 1994-00
Jackson, Alvin N. "Al" Bos-A 1977-79, Bal-A 1989-91, NY-N 1999-00
Jackson, Grant D. Pit-N 1984-85, Cin-N 1994-95
Jackson, Roland T. "Sonny" Atl-N 1982-83, SF-N 1997-00
Jackson, Ronnie D. "Ron" Chi-A 1995-98, Mil-N 1999
Jackson, Travis C. NY-N 1939-40, 1947-48
Jansen, Lawrence J. "Larry" NY-N 1954, SF-N 1961-71, Chi-N 1972-73
Jaramillo, Rudolph "Rudy" Hou-N 1990-93, Tex-A 1995-00
Jauss, David P. "Dave" Bos-A 1997-99
Jenkins, Ferguson A. "Fergie" Chi-N 1995-96
Jennings, Hugh A. "Hughie" NY-N 1921-25
Johnson, Darrell D. StL-N 1960-61, Bal-A 1962, Bos-A 1968-69, Tex-A 1981-82, NY-N 1993
Johnson, Deron R. Cal-A 1979-80, NY-N 1981, Phi-N 1982-84, Sea-A 1985-86, Chi-A 1987, Cal-A 1989-91
Johnson, Lamar Mil-A 1995-97, Mil-N 1998, KC-A 1999-00
Johnson, Roy J Chi-N 1935-39, 1944-53
Johnson, Sylvester W. "Syl" Phi-N 1937-40
Johnson, Timothy E. "Tim" Mon-N 1993-94, Bos-A 1995-96
Johnson, Wallace D. Chi-A 1998-00
Johnston, James H. "Jimmy" Bro-N 1931
Jones, Clarence W. Atl-N 1985, 1988-98, Cle-A 1999-00
Jones, Gary W. Oak-A 1998
Jones, Gordon B. Hou-N 1966-67
Jones, Grover W. "Deacon" Hou-N 1976-82, SD-N 1984-87
Jones, Jeffrey A. "Jeff" Det-A 1995, 1999
Jones, Joseph C. "Joe" KC-A 1987, 1992, Pit-N 1997-00
Jones, Lynn M. KC-A 1991-92
Jonnard, Clarence J. "Bubber" Phi-N 1935, NY-N 1942-46
Joshua, Von E. Chi-A 1998-00
Judge, Joseph I. "Joe" Was-A 1945-46
Jurges, William F. "Billy" Chi-N 1947-48, Was-A 1956-59
Kaat, James L. "Jim" Cin-N 1984-85
Kahn, Louis "Lou" StL-N 1955
Katt, Raymond F. "Ray" StL-N 1959-60, Cle-A 1962
Kaufmann, Anthony C. "Tony" StL-N 1947-50
Keane, John J. "Johnny" StL-N 1959-61
Keefe, David E. "Dave" Phi-A 1940-49
Keely, Robert W. "Bob" Bos-N 1946-52, Mil-N 1953-57
Kelleher, Michael D. "Mick" Pit-N 1986
Keller, Charles E. "Charlie" NY-A 1957, 1959
Kelley, Joseph J. "Joe" Bro-N 1926
Kelly, Bernard F. "Mike" Chi-A 1930-31, Chi-N 1934, Bos-N 1937-39, Pit-N 1940-41
Kelly, George L. Cin-N 1935-37, Bos-N 1938-43, Cin-N 1947-48
Kelly, J. Thomas "Tom" Min-A 1983-86
Kendall, Fred L. Det-A 1996-98, Col-N 2000
Kennedy, Kevin Mon-N 1992
Kennedy, Robert D. "Bob" Chi-N 1962-65, Atl-N 1967
Kerr, John F. Was-A 1935
Kerrigan, Joseph T. "Joe" Mon-N 1983-86, 1992-96, Bos-A 1997-00
Killefer, William L. "Bill" StL-N 1926, StL-A 1927-29, Bro-N 1939, Phi-N 1942
Kim, Wendell K. SF-N 1989-96, Bos-A 1997-00
Kimm, Bruce E. Cin-N 1984-88, Pit-N 1989, SD-N 1991-92, Fla-N 1997-98, Col-N 1999
King, Clyde E. Cin-N 1959, Pit-N 1965-67, NY-A 1978, 1981, 1988
Kison, Bruce E. KC-A 1992-98, Bal-A 1999
Kissell, George M. StL-N 1969-75
Kittle, Hubert M. "Hub" Hou-N 1971-75, StL-N 1981-83
Klein, Charles H. "Chuck" Phi-N 1942-45
Klein, Louis F. "Lou" Chi-N 1960-65
Kluszewski, Theodore B. "Ted" Cin-N 1970-78
Knight, C. Ray Cin-N 1993-95
Knoop, Robert F. "Bobby" Chi-A 1977-78, Cal-A 1979-96, Tor-A 2000
Knowles, Darold D. StL-N 1983, Phi-N 1989-90
Koenig, Fred Carl Cal-A 1970-71, StL-N 1976, Tex-A 1977-82, Chi-N 1983, Cle-A 1985-86
Kress, Ralph "Red" Det-A 1940, NY-N 1946-49, Cle-A 1953-60, LA-A 1961, NY-N 1962
Krol, John T. "Jack" StL-N 1977-80, SD-N 1981-86
Krug, Everett B. "Chris" SD-N 1969
Kuehl, Karl O. Min-A 1977-82
Kuenn, Harvey E. Mil-A 1971-82
Kuntz, Russell J. "Rusty" Sea-A 1989-92, Fla-N 1995-96, 1999-00
Kusnyer, Arthur W. "Art" Chi-A 1980-87, Oak-A 1989-95, Chi-A 1997-00
Lachemann, Marcel E. Cal-A 1984-92, Fla-N 1993-94, Ana-A 1997-98, Col-N 2000
Lachemann, Rene G. Bos-A 1985-86, Oak-A 1987-92, StL-N 1997-99, Chi-N 2000
Lachemann, William C. "Bill" Cal-A 1995-96
Lakeman, Albert W. "Al" Bos-A 1963-64, 1967-69
Lamont, Gene W. Pit-N 1986-91, 1996
Land, Grover C. Pit-N 1914, Cin-N 1925-28, Chi-N 1929-30
Landestoy, Rafael S. Mon-N 1989, NY-N 1996
Landrith, Hobert N. "Hobie" Was-A 1964
Langford, J. Rick Tor-A 2000
Lanier, Harold C. "Hal" StL-N 1981-85, Phi-N 1990-91
Lansford, Carney R. Oak-A 1995, StL-N 1997
LaRoche, David E. "Dave" Chi-A 1989-91, NY-N 1992-93
LaRussa, Anthony "Tony" Chi-A 1978
Lasorda, Thomas C. "Tommy" LA-N 1973-76
Latham, W. Arlington "Arlie" Cin-N 1900, NY-N 1909
Lau, Charles R. "Charley" Bal-A 1969, Oak-A 1970, KC-A 1971-74, 1975-78, NY-A 1979-81, Chi-A 1982-83
Lauder, William "Billy" Chi-A 1925
Lavagetto, Harry A. "Cookie" Bro-N 1951-53, Was-A 1955-57, NY-N 1962-63, SF-N 1964-67
Law, Vernon S. "Vern" Pit-N 1968-69
Lazzeri, Anthony M. "Tony" Chi-N 1938
Lefebvre, James K. "Jim" LA-N 1978-79, SF-N 1980-82, Oak-A 1987-88, 1994-95, Mil-N 1999
Leifield, Albert P. "Lefty" StL-N 1920-23, Bos-A 1924-26, Det-A 1927-28
Lemon, James R. "Jim" Min-A 1965-67, 1981-84
Lemon, Robert G. "Bob" Cle-A 1960, Phi-N 1961, Cal-A 1967-68, KC-A 1970, NY-A 1976
Lenhardt, Donald E. "Don" Bos-A 1970-73
Leonard, Emil J. "Dutch" Chi-N 1954-56
Leppert, Donald G. "Don" Pit-N 1968-76, Tor-A 1977-79, Hou-N 1980-85
Lett, James C. "Jim" Cin-N 1988-89, 1996, Tor-A 1997-99
Levy, Leonard "Len" Pit-N 1957-63
Lewis, George E. "Duffy" Bos-N 1931-35
Lewis, Johnny J. StL-N 1973-76, 1985-89
Leyland, James R. "Jim" Chi-A 1982-85
Leyva, Nicolas T. "Nick" StL-N 1984-88, Tor-A 1993-97
Lillis, Robert P. "Bob" Hou-N 1967, 1973-82, SF-N 1986-96
Linares, Julio Hou-N 1994-96
Lind, Jackson H. "Jack" Pit-N 1997-00
Lipon, John J. "Johnny" Cle-A 1968-71

Little, R. Bryan Chi-A 1998-00
Little, W. Grady SD-N 1996, Bos-A 1997-99, Cle-A 2000
Litwhiler, Daniel W. "Danny" Cin-N 1951
Livingston, Patrick J. "Paddy" Phi-A 1919
Llenas, Winston E. Tor-A 1988
Lobe, William C. "Bill" Cle-A 1951-56
Lobert, John B. "Hans" NY-N 1928, Phi-N 1934-41, Cin-N 1943-44
Lockman, Carroll W. "Whitey" Cin-N 1960, SF-N 1961-64, Chi-N 1965-66
Lodigiani, Dario A. KC-A 1961-62
Lollar, J. Sherman "Sherm" Bal-A 1964-67, Oak-A 1968
Long, R. Dale NY-A 1963
Lonnett, Joseph P. "Joe" Chi-A 1971-75, Oak-A 1976, Pit-N 1977-84
Lopat, Edmund W. "Ed" NY-A 1960, Min-A 1961, KC-A 1962
Lopes, David E. "Davey" Tex-A 1988-91, Bal-A 1992-94, SD-N 1995-99
Lopez, Juan E. SF-N 1999-00
Lowe, Q. V. "Q. V." Chi-N 1972
Lowrey, Harry L. "Peanuts" Phi-N 1960-66, SF-N 1967-68, Mon-N 1969, Chi-N 1970-71, Cal-A 1972, Chi-N 1977-79, 1981
Lucchesi, Frank J. Tex-A 1974-75, 1979-80
Lum, Michael K. "Mike" Chi-A 1985, KC-A 1988-89
Lumpe, Jerry D. Oak-A 1971
Lund, Donald A. "Don" Det-A 1957-58
Luque, Adolfo "Dolf" NY-N 1935-38, 1941-45
Lutz, R. Joseph "Joe" Cle-A 1971-73
Luzinski, Gregory M. "Greg" Oak-A 1993, KC-A 1995-97
Lyons, Edward H. "Eddie" Min-A 1976
Lyons, Theodore A. "Ted" Det-A 1949-53, Bro-N 1954
Macha, Kenneth E. "Ken" Mon-N 1986-91, Cal-A 1992-94, Oak-A 1999-00
Mack, Earle T. Phi-A 1924-50
Mackanin, Peter Mon-N 1997-00
MacKenzie, H. Gordon "Gordy" KC-A 1980-81, Chi-N 1982, SF-N 1986-88, Cle-A 1991
Macko, Joseph "Joe" Chi-N 1964
Maddon, Joseph J. "Joe" Cal-A 1995-96, Ana-A 1997-00
Madlock, Bill Det-A 2000
Maglie, Salvatore A. "Sal" Bos-A 1960-62, 1966-67, Sea-A 1969
Mahoney, James T. "Jim" Chi-A 1972-76, Sea-A 1985-86
Majtyka, LeRoy W. "Roy" Atl-N 1988-90
Malmberg, Harry W. Bos-A 1963-64
Maloof, Jack G. SD-N 1990, Fla-N 1999-00
Maltzberger, Gordon R. Min-A 1962-64
Mancuso, August R. "Gus" Cin-N 1950
Mansolino, Douglas "Doug" Chi-A 1992-96, Mil-N 1998-99, Det-A 2000
Mantle, Mickey C. NY-A 1970
Manuel, Charles F. "Charlie" Cle-A 1988-89, 1994-99
Manuel, Jerry Mon-N 1991-96, Fla-N 1997
Manush, Henry E. "Heinie" Was-A 1953-54
Marion, Martin W. "Marty" StL-A 1952, Chi-A 1954
Marshall, R. James "Jim" Chi-N 1974
Martin, Alfred M. "Billy" Min-A 1965-68, Tex-A 1974
Martin, Fred T. Chi-N 1961-65, Chi-A 1979
Martin, John L. "Pepper" Chi-N 1956
Martin, Joseph C. "J. C." Chi-N 1974
Martinez, Jose KC-A 1980-87, Chi-N 1988-94
Martinez, Orlando "Marty" Sea-A 1984-86, 1992
Mason, Martin L. "Marty" StL-N 2000
Mathews, Edwin L. "Eddie" Atl-N 1971-72
Mathews, Henry "Harry" Cle-A 1926-27, NY-A 1929
Mathews, Rick R. Col-N 1993, 1995
Mathewson, Christopher "Christy" NY-N 1919-20
Matlack, Jonathan T. "Jon" Det-A 1996
Matthews, Gary N. Tor-A 1998-99
Mauch, Gene W. KC-A 1995
Maxvill, C. Dallan "Dal" Oak-A 1975, NY-N 1978, StL-N 1979-80, Atl-N 1982-84
May, Lee A. KC-A 1984-86, Cin-N 1988-89, KC-A 1992-93, Bal-A 1995
May, Milton S. "Milt" Pit-N 1987-96, Fla-N 1997-98, Col-N 1999
Mayberry, John C. KC-A 1989-90
Mayo, Edward J. "Eddie" Bos-A 1951, Phi-N 1952-54
Mays, Willie H. NY-N 1974-79
Mazeroski, William S. "Bill" Pit-N 1973, Sea-A 1979-80
Mazzilli, Lee L. NY-A 2000
Mazzone, Leo D. Atl-N 1985, 1990-00
McBride, George F. Det-A 1925-26, 1929
McBride, Kenneth F. "Ken" Mil-A 1975
McCallister, John "Jack" Cle-A 1920-26, Bos-A 1930
McClendon, Lloyd G. Pit-N 1997-00
McClure, Robert C. "Bob" Fla-N 1994
McCormick, Frank A. Cin-N 1956-57
McCrabb, Lester W. "Les" Phi-A 1950-54
McCraw, Tommy L. "Tom" Cle-A 1975, 1979-82, SF-N 1983-85, Bal-A 1989-91, NY-N 1992-96, Hou-N 1997-00
McCullough, Clyde E. Was-A 1960, Min-A 1961, NY-N 1963, SD-N 1982
McDermott, Maurice J. "Mickey" Cal-A 1968
McDonnell, Robert A. "Maje" Phi-N 1951-57
McGaha, F. Melvin "Mel" Cle-A 1961, KC-A 1963-64, Hou-N 1968-70
McGinnity, Joseph J. "Joe" Bro-N 1926
McGuire, James T. "Deacon" Det-A 1911-16
McKay, David L. "Dave" Oak-A 1984-95, StL-N 1996-00
McKechnie, William B. "Bill" Pit-N 1922, StL-N 1927, Cle-A 1947-49, Bos-A 1952-53
McKee, J. R. Pit-N 1947
McKeon, John A. "Jack" Oak-A 1978
McLaren, John L. Tor-A 1986-90, Bos-A 1991, Cin-N 1992, Sea-A 1993-00
McLish, Calvin C. "Cal" Phi-N 1965-66, Mon-N 1969-75, Mil-A 1976-82
McMahon, Donald J. "Don" SF-N 1973-75, Min-A 1976-77, SF-N 1980-82, Cle-A 1983-85
McMillan, Roy D. Mil-A 1970-72, NY-N 1973-76
McNamara, John F. Oak-A 1968-69, SF-N 1971-73, Cal-A 1978
McNeely, G. Earl StL-A 1931, Was-A 1936-37
McNertney, Gerald E. "Jerry" Bos-A 1988
McRae, Harold A. "Hal" KC-A 1987, Mon-N 1990-91, Cin-N 1995-96, Phi-N 1997-00
Mejias, Samuel E. "Sammy" Sea-A 1993-99
Mele, Sabath A. "Sam" Was-A 1959-60, Min-A 1961
Melillo, Oscar D. "Ski" StL-A 1938, Cle-A 1939-40, 1942, 1945-48, 1950, Bos-A 1952-53, KC-A 1955-56
Melvin, Robert P. "Bob" Mil-N 1999, Det-A 2000
Mendoza, C. Rigoberto "Minnie" Bal-A 1988
Menke, Denis J. Tor-A 1980-81, Hou-N 1983-88, Phi-N 1989-96, Cin-N 1997-00
Merkle, Frederick C. "Fred" NY-A 1925-26
Merrill, Carl H. "Stump" NY-A 1985, 1986-87
Metro, Charles "Charlie" Chi-N 1962, Chi-A 1965, Oak-A 1982
Meusel, Emil F. "Irish" NY-N 1930
Meyer, Bernhard "Benny" Phi-N 1924-26, Det-A 1928-30
Meyer, Russell C. "Russ"Or "Monk" NY-A 1992
Michael, Eugene R. "Gene" NY-A 1976-77, 1978, 1984-86, 1988, 1989
Milan, J. Clyde Was-A 1928-29, 1938-52
Miley, David A. "Dave" Cin-N 1993
Miller, Dyar K Chi-A 1987-88
Miller, Edmund J. "Bing" Bos-A 1937, Det-A 1938-41, Chi-A 1942-49, Phi-A 1950-53
Miller, L. Otto Bro-N 1926-36
Miller, Raymond R. "Ray" Bal-A 1978-85, Pit-N 1987-96, Bal-A 1997
Miller, Robert L. "Bob" Tor-A 1977-79, SF-N 1985
Milliken, Robert F. "Bob" StL-N 1965-70, 1976
Mills, Arthur G. "Art" Det-A 1944-48
Mills, C. Buster Cle-A 1946, Chi-A 1947-50, Cin-N 1953, Bos-A 1954
Mills, J. Bradley "Brad" Phi-N 1997-00
Minoso, S. Orestes "Minnie" Chi-A 1976-78, 1980-81
Mitchell, Clarence E. NY-N 1932-33
Mitchell, Frederick F. "Fred" Bos-N 1914-16
Mitterwald, George E. Oak-A 1979-82, NY-A 1988
Mize, John R. "Johnny" KC-A 1961
Molitor, Paul L. Min-A 2000
Monbouquette, William C. "Bill" NY-N 1982-83, NY-A 1985
Monchak, Alex "Al" Chi-A 1971-75, Oak-A 1976, Pit-N 1977-84, Atl-N 1986-88
Moon, Wallace W. "Wally" SD-N 1969
Moore, Jackie S. Mil-A 1970-72, Tex-A 1973-74, 1975-76, Tor-A 1977-79, Tex-A 1980, Oak-A 1981-84, Mon-N 1987-89, Cin-N 1990-92, Tex-A 1993-94, Col-N 1996-98
Moore, Terry B. StL-N 1949-52, 1956-58
Morales, Jose M. SF-N 1986-88, Cle-A 1990-93, Fla-N 1995-96
Morales, Richard A. "Rich" Atl-N 1986-87
Morgan, Joseph M. "Joe" Pit-N 1972, Bos-A 1985-88
Morgan, Tom S. Cal-A 1972-74, SD-N 1975, NY-A 1979, Cal-A 1981-83
Morgan, Vernon T. "Vern" Min-A 1969-75
Moseby, Lloyd A. Tor-A 1999
Moses, John W. Sea-A 2000
Moses, Wallace "Wally" Phi-A 1952-54, Phi-N 1955-58, Cin-N 1959-60, NY-A 1961-62, 1966, Det-A 1967-70
Moss, J. Lester "Les" Chi-A 1967-68, 1969-70, Chi-N 1981, Hou-N 1982-84, 1985-89
Mota, Manuel R. "Manny" LA-N 1980-89
Motton, Curtell H. "Curt" Bal-A 1991
Mozzali, Maurice J. "Mo" StL-N 1977-78
Mueller, Ray C. NY-N 1956, Chi-N 1957
Muffett, Billy A. StL-N 1967-70, Cal-A 1974-77, Det-A 1985-94
Mulcahy, Hugh N. Chi-A 1970
Mull, Jack L. SF-N 1985
Mulleavy, Gregory T. "Greg" Bro-N 1957, LA-N 1958-60, 1962-64
Mullin, Patrick J. "Pat" Det-A 1963-66, Cle-A 1967, Mon-N 1979-81
Mungo, Van Lingle Bro-N 1940
Murphy, Daniel F. "Danny" Phi-A 1920-24, Phi-N 1927
Murphy, Dwayne K. Ari-N 1998-00
Murray, Eddie C. Bal-A 1998-00
Murtaugh, Daniel E. "Danny" Pit-N 1956-57
Muser, Anthony J. "Tony" Mil-A 1985-89, Chi-N 1993-97
Myatt, George E. Was-A 1950-54, Chi-A 1955-56, Chi-N 1957-59, Mil-N 1960-61, Det-A 1962-63, Phi-N 1964-72
Napoleon, Edward G. "Ed" Cle-A 1983-85, KC-A 1987-88, Hou-N 1989, NY-A 1992-93, Tex-A 1995-00
Naragon, Harold R. "Hal" Min-A 1963-66, Det-A 1967-69
Narron, Jerry A. Bal-A 1993-94, Tex-A 1995-00
Narron, Samuel "Sam" Pit-N 1952-64
Neale, A. Earle "Greasy" StL-N 1929
Nelson, David E. "Dave" Chi-A 1981-84, Cle-A 1992-97
Nettles, Graig NY-A 1991, SD-N 1995
Neun, John H. "Johnny" NY-A 1944-46
Newman, Jeffrey L. "Jeff" Oak-A 1986, Cle-A 1992-99, Bal-A 2000
Niarhos, C. Gus KC-A 1962-64
Niehoff, J. Albert "Bert" NY-N 1929
Niemann, Randal H. "Randy" NY-N 1997-99
Nipper, Albert S, "Al" Bos-A 1995-96
Nixon, Russell E. "Russ" Cin-N 1976-82, Mon-N 1984-85, Atl-N 1986-87, Sea-A 1992
Noren, Irving A. "Irv" Oak-A 1971-74, Chi-N 1975
Norman, H. Willis P. "Bill" StL-A 1952-53
Northey, Ronald J. "Ron" Pit-N 1961-63
Nossek, Joseph R. "Joe" Mil-A 1973-75, Min-A 1976, Cle-A 1977-81, KC-A 1982-83, Chi-A 1984-85, 1986, 1991-00
Nottle, Edward W. "Ed" Oak-A 1983
Oates, Johnny L. Chi-N 1984-87, Bal-A 1989-91
O'Brien, Edward J. "Eddie" Sea-A 1969
Oceak, Frank J. Pit-N 1958-64, Cin-N 1965, Pit-N 1970-72
O'Connell, Daniel F. "Danny" Was-A 1963-64
O'Connor, Patrick F. "Paddy" NY-A 1918-21
Oester, Ronald J. "Ron" Cin-N 1993, Cal-A 1996, Cin-N 1997-00
Oglivie, Benjamin A. "Ben" SD-N 2000
Okrie, Leonard J. "Len" Bos-A 1961-62, 1965-66, Det-A 1970
Oldis, Robert C. "Bob" Phi-N 1964-66, Min-A 1968, Mon-N 1969
O'Leary, Charles T. "Charley" StL-N 1913, NY-A 1920-30, Chi-N 1931-33, StL-A 1934-37
Oliva, Pedro "Tony" Min-A 1976-78, 1985-91
Oliveras, Max "Mako" Cal-A 1994, Chi-N 1995-97
Oliver, David J. "Dave" Tex-A 1987-94, Bos-A 1995-96
Oliver, Thomas N. "Tom" Phi-A 1951-53, Bal-A 1954
Olson, Ivan M. "Ivy" Bro-N 1924, 1930-31, NY-N 1932
O'Neil, G. Michael "Mickey" Cle-A 1930

O'Neil, John S. "Buck" Chi-N 1962-65
O'Neill, Stephen F. "Steve" Cle-A 1935, Det-A 1941, Cle-A 1949, Bos-A 1950
Onslow, John J. "Jack" Pit-N 1925-26, Was-A 1927, StL-N 1928, Phi-N 1931-32, Bos-A 1934
Oquendo, Jose M. StL-N 1999-00
Osborn, Donald E. "Don" Pit-N 1963-64, 1970-72, 1974-76
Osteen, Claude W. StL-N 1977-80, Phi-N 1982-88, Tex-A 1993-94, NY-N 1999, LA-N 2000
Otero, Regino J. "Regie" Cin-N 1959-65, Cle-A 1966
Otis, Amos J. SD-N 1988-90, Col-N 1993
Ott, N. Edward "Ed" Hou-N 1989-93
Overmire, Frank "Stubby" Det-A 1963-66
Owen, Arnold M. "Mickey" Bos-A 1955-56
Owens, James P. "Jim" Hou-N 1967-72
Ozark, Daniel L. "Danny" LA-N 1965-72, 1980-82, SF-N 1983-84
Pacheco, Antonio A. "Tony" Cle-A 1974, Hou-N 1976-79, 1982
Paepke, Jack LA-A 1961-64, Cal-A 1965-66
Pafko, Andrew "Andy" Mil-N 1960-62
Pagan, Jose A. Pit-N 1974-78
Page, Mitchell O. KC-A 1995-97
Page, Philippe R. "Phil" Cin-N 1947-52
Paige, Leroy R. "Satchell" Atl-N 1968-69
Parker, David G. "Dave" Ana-A 1997, StL-N 1998
Parker, Francis J. "Salty" SF-N 1958-61, Cle-A 1962, LA-A 1964, Cal-A 1965-66, NY-N 1967, Hou-N 1968-72, Cal-A 1973-74
Parrish, Lance M. Det-A 1999-00
Parrish, Larry A. Det-A 1997-98
Pascual, Camilo A. Min-A 1978-80
Patkin, Max Cle-A 1946-47, StL-A 1951, Chi-A 1976, 1978
Patterson, Henry J. C. "Hank" Bos-A 1932
Pattin, Martin W. "Marty" Tor-A 1989
Paul, Michael G. "Mike" Oak-A 1987-88, Sea-A 1989-91, Oak-A 1993
Pavlick, Gregory M. "Greg" NY-N 1985-86, 1988-91, 1994-96
Pazik, Michael J. "Mike" Chi-A 1995-98
Peden, Leslie E. "Les" Chi-N 1965
Peitz, Henry C. "Heinie" StL-N 1913
Pennock, Herbert J. "Herb" Bos-A 1936-39
Pentland, Jeffrey W. "Jeff" Fla-N 1996, Chi-N 1997-00
Pepitone, Joseph A. "Joe" NY-A 1982
Perez, Atanacio R. "Tony" Cin-N 1987-92
Perkins, Ralph F. "Cy" NY-A 1932-33, Det-A 1934-39, Phi-N 1946-54
Perlozzo, Samuel B. "Sam" NY-N 1987-89, Cin-N 1990-92, Sea-A 1993-95, Bal-A 1996-00
Perranoski, Ronald P. "Ron" LA-N 1981-94, SF-N 1997-99
Perry, Gerald J. Sea-A 2000
Pesky, John M. "Johnny" Pit-N 1965-67, Bos-A 1975-84
Peterson, Eric H. "Rick" Pit-N 1984-85, Chi-A 1995, Oak-A 1999-00
Pevey, Marty A. Tor-A 1999
Pfister, George E. Bro-N 1952
Phillips, Harold R. "Lefty" LA-N 1965-68, Cal-A 1969
Phillips, Richard E. "Dick" SD-N 1980
Picciolo, Robert M. "Rob" SD-N 1990-00
Piche, Ronald J. "Ron" Mon-N 1976
Picinich, Valentine J. "Val" Cin-N 1934
Piersall, James A. "Jimmy" Tex-A 1975
Pignatano, Joseph B. "Joe" Was-A 1965-67, NY-N 1968-81, Atl-N 1982-85
Piniella, Louis V. "Lou" NY-A 1984-85
Pinson, Vada E. Sea-A 1977-80, Chi-A 1981, Sea-A 1982-83, Det-A 1985-91, Fla-N 1993-94
Pitler, Jacob A. "Jake" Bro-N 1947-57
Pitts, Gaylen R. StL-N 1991-95
Plaza, Ronald C. "Ron" Sea-A 1969, Cin-N 1978-83, Oak-A 1986
Plummer, William F. "Bill" Sea-A 1982-83, 1988-91, Col-N 1993
Podres, John J. "Johnny" SD-N 1973, Bos-A 1980, Min-A 1981-85, Phi-N 1991-96
Pole, Richard H. "Dick" Chi-N 1988-91, SF-N 1993-97, Bos-A 1998, Ana-A 1999, Cle-A 2000
Pollet, Howard J. "Howie" StL-N 1959-64, Hou-N 1965
Popowski, Edward J. "Eddie" Bos-A 1967-76
Poquette, Thomas A. "Tom" KC-A 1997-98
Posedel, William J. "Bill" Pit-N 1949-53, StL-N 1954-57, Phi-N 1958, SF-N 1959-60, Oak-A 1968-72, SD-N 1974
Presley, James A. "Jim" Ari-N 1998-00
Price, Bryan R. Sea-A 2000
Pujols, Luis B. Mon-N 1993-00
Quade, G. Mike Oak-A 2000
Queen, Melvin D. "Mel" Cle-A 1982, Tor-A 1996-99
Quilici, Francis R. "Frank" Min-A 1971-72
Quirk, James P. "Jamie" StL-N 1984, KC-A 1994-00
Rader, Douglas L. "Doug" SD-N 1978-79, Chi-A 1986-87, Oak-A 1992, Fla-N 1993-94, Chi-A 1997
Radison, Daniel J. "Dan" SD-N 1993-94, Chi-N 1995-99
Ragan, D. C. Patrick "Pat" Phi-N 1924
Ramos, Roberto "Bobby" Ana-A 2000
Randall, Robert L. "Bobby" Min-A 1980
Randolph, Willie L. NY-A 1994-00
Rapp, Vernon F. "Vern" Mon-N 1979-83
Reberger, Frank B. Cal-A 1991, Fla-N 1993-94
Redys, Edward "Ed" StL-A 1950-51
Reese, Harold H. "Pee Wee" LA-N 1959
Reese, James H. "Jimmie" Cal-A 1973-94
Regan, Philip R. "Phil" Sea-A 1984-86, Cle-A 1994, Chi-N 1997-98, Cle-A 1999
Reiser, Harold P. "Pete" LA-N 1960-64, Chi-N 1966-69, Cal-A 1970-71, Chi-N 1972-74
Renick, W. Richard "Rick" KC-A 1981, Mon-N 1985-86, Min-A 1987-90, Pit-N 1997-00
Resinger, Grover S. Atl-N 1966, Chi-A 1967-68, Det-A 1969-70, Cal-A 1975-76
Rettenmund, Mervin W. "Merv" Cal-A 1980-82, Tex-A 1983-85, Oak-A 1989-90, SD-N 1991-99, Atl-N 2000
Reyes, Benjamin "Cananea" Sea-A 1981
Reynolds, Tommie D Oak-A 1989-95, StL-N 1996
Rice, Delbert "Del" StL-N 1959, LA-A 1962-64, Cal-A 1965-66, Cle-A 1967
Rice, James E. "Jim" Bos-A 1994-00
Ricketts, David W. "Dave" Pit-N 1971-73, StL-N 1974-75, 1978-91
Riddle, John L. "Johnny" Pit-N 1948-50, StL-N 1952-55, Mil-N 1956-57, Cin-N 1958, Phi-N 1959
Riddoch, Gregory L. "Greg" SD-N 1987-90, TB-A 1998-99
Riggins, Mark A. StL-N 1995
Riggleman, James D. "Jim" StL-N 1989-90, Cle-A 2000
Righetti, David A. "Dave" SF-N 2000
Rigney, William J. "Bill" SD-N 1975
Rigoli, Joseph M. "Joe" Phi-N 1996-97
Ripken, Calvin E., Sr. "Cal" Bal-A 1976-86, 1989-92
Rippelmeyer, Raymond R. "Ray" Phi-N 1970-78
Roarke, Michael T. "Mike" Det-A 1965-66, Cal-A 1967-69, Det-A 1970, Chi-N 1978-80, StL-N 1984-90, SD-N 1991-93, Bos-A 1994
Roberts, David W. "Dave" Cle-A 1987
Roberts, Leon K. TB-A 1999-00
Roberts, Melvin H. "Mel" Phi-N 1992-95
Robertson, Sherrard A. "Sherry" Min-A 1970
Robinson, Brooks C. Bal-A 1977
Robinson, Dewey E. Chi-A 1993-94
Robinson, Frank Cal-A 1977, Bal-A 1978-80, 1985-87
Robinson, Warren G. "Sheriff" NY-N 1964, 1965-67, 1972
Robinson, Wilbert NY-N 1911-13
Robinson, William H. "Bill" NY-N 1984-89
Robinson, W. Edward "Eddie" Bal-A 1957-59
Robson, Thomas J. "Tom" Tex-A 1986-92, NY-N 1997-99, 2000
Rodgers, Robert L. "Bob" Min-A 1970-74, SF-N 1976, Mil-A 1978-80
Rodriguez, Eduardo "Eddie" Cal-A 1996, Tor-A 1998
Roenicke, Ronald J. "Ron" Ana-A 2000
Roessler, Patrick A. "Pat" Mon-N 2000
Rojas, Octavio V. "Cookie" Chi-N 1978-81, Fla-N 1993-96, NY-N 1997-00
Rolfe, Robert A. "Red" NY-A 1946
Rommel, Edwin A. "Eddie" Phi-A 1933-34
Roof, Eugene L.'Gene" Det-A 1992-95
Roof, Phillip A. "Phil" SD-N 1978, Sea-A 1983-88, Chi-N 1990-91
Root, Charles H. "Charlie" Chi-N 1951-53, Mil-N 1956-57, Chi-N 1960
Roseboro, John J. Was-A 1970-71, Cal-A 1972-74
Rosenbaum, Glen O. Chi-A 1973-75, 1986-88
Roth, Francis C. "Frank" Pit-N 1917, NY-A 1921-22, Cle-A 1923-25, Chi-A 1927
Rothschild, Lawrence L. "Larry" Cin-N 1990-93, Fla-N 1995-97
Roush, Edd J Cin-N 1938
Rowe, Donald H. "Don" Chi-A 1988, Mil-A 1992-97, Mil-N 1998
Rowe, Kenneth D. "Ken" Bal-A 1985-86
Rowe, Lynwood T. "Schoolboy" Det-A 1954-55
Rowe, Ralph E. Min-A 1972-75, Bal-A 1981-84
Royster, Jeron K. "Jerry" Col-N 1993, Mil-N 2000
Ruberto, John E. "Sonny" StL-N 1977-78
Rudi, Joseph O. "Joe" Oak-A 1986-87
Rudolph, Richard "Dick" Bos-N 1921-27
Ruel, Herold D. "Muddy" Chi-A 1935-45, Cle-A 1948-50
Ruffing, Charles H. "Red" NY-N 1962
Ruhle, Vernon G. "Vern" Hou-N 1997-00
Runnels, James E. "Pete" Bos-A 1965-66
Runnells, Thomas W. "Tom" Mon-N 1990-91
Russell, William E. "Bill" LA-N 1987-91, 1994-96, TB-A 2000
Ruth, George H. "Babe" Bro-N 1938
Ryan, Cornelius J. "Connie" Mil-N 1957, Atl-N 1971, 1973-75, Tex-A 1977-79
Ryan, John B. "Jack" Was-A 1912-13, Bos-A 1923-27
Ryan, Michael J. "Mike" Phi-N 1980-95
Ryba, Dominic J. "Mike" StL-N 1951-54
Sain, John F. "Johnny" KC-A 1959, NY-A 1961-63, Min-A 1965-66, Det-A 1967-69, Chi-A 1971-75, Atl-N 1977, 1985-86
Samuel, Juan M. Det-A 1999-00
Sanford, John A. "Jack" Cle-A 1968-69
Sandt, Thomas J. "Tommy" Pit-N 1987-96, Fla-N 1997-98, Col-N 1999
Sarni, William F. "Bill" NY-N 1957
Sauer, Henry J. "Hank" SF-N 1959
Saul, James A. "Jim" Chi-N 1975-76, Oak-A 1979
Scarborough, Ray W. Bal-A 1968
Schacht, Alexander "Al" Was-A 1925-34, Bos-A 1935-36
Schaefer, Robert W. "Bob" KC-A 1988-91
Schaffer, Jimmie R. "Jim" Tex-A 1978, KC-A 1980-88
Schalk, Raymond W. "Ray" Chi-N 1930-31
Schang, Walter H. "Wally" Cle-A 1936-38
Scheffing, Robert B. "Bob" StL-A 1952-53, Chi-N 1954-55, Mil-N 1960
Scherger, George R. Cin-N 1970-78, 1982-86
Schoendienst, Albert F. "Red" StL-N 1961-64, Oak-A 1977-78, StL-N 1979-89
Schreiber, Paul F. NY-A 1942, Bos-A 1947-58
Schueler, Ronald R. "Ron" Chi-A 1979-82, Oak-A 1983-84, Pit-N 1986
Schulte, John C. "Johnny" Chi-N 1933, NY-A 1934-48, Bos-A 1949-50
Schultz, George W. "Barney" StL-N 1971-75, Chi-N 1977
Schultz, Joseph C., Jr. "Joe" StL-A 1949, StL-N 1963-68, KC-A 1970, Det-A 1971-76
Scioscia, Michael L. "Mike" LA-N 1997-98
Seminick, Andrew W. "Andy" Phi-N 1957-58, 1967-69
Sewell, J. Luther "Luke" Cle-A 1939-41, Cin-N 1949
Sewell, Joseph W. "Joe" NY-A 1934-35
Sewell, Truett B. "Rip" Pit-N 1948
Shanks, Howard S. "Howie" Cle-A 1928-32
Shaughnessy, Francis J. "Shag" Det-A 1928
Shaw, Robert J. "Bob" Mil-A 1973
Shawkey, J. Robert "Bob" NY-A 1929
Shea, Mervyn D. "Merv" Det-A 1939-42, Phi-N 1944-45, Chi-N 1948-49
Sheehan, Thomas C. "Tom" Cin-N 1935-37, Bro-N 1938, Bos-N 1944
Shelby, John T. LA-N 1998-00
Shellenback, Frank V. StL-A 1939, Bos-A 1940-44, Det-A 1946-47, NY-N 1949-55
Shellenback, James P. "Jim" Min-A 1983
Shepard, Robert E. "Bert" Was-A 1946
Shepard, Lawrence W. "Larry" Phi-N 1967, Cin-N 1970-78, SF-N 1979
Sherlock, Glenn P. Ari-N 1998-00
Sherry, Lawrence "Larry" Pit-N 1977-78, Cal-A 1979-80
Sherry, Norman B. "Norm" Cal-A 1970-71, 1976, Mon-N 1978-81, SD-N 1982-84, SF-N 1986-91
Shore, Raymond E. "Ray" Cin-N 1963-67
Shotton, Burton E. "Burt" StL-N 1923-25, Cin-N 1934, Cle-A 1942-45
Showalter, William N. "Buck" NY-A 1990-91
Siebert, Wilfred C. "Sonny" SD-N 1994-95
Sievers, Roy E. Cin-N 1966
Silvera, Charles A. "Charlie" Min-A 1969, Det-A 1971-73, Tex-A 1973-75

Silvestri, Kenneth J. "Ken" Phi-N 1959-60, Mil-N 1963-65, Atl-N 1966-75, Chi-A 1976, 1982
Simmons, Aloysius H. "Al" Phi-A 1940-42, 1944-49, Cle-A 1950-51
Sinatro, Matthew Stephen "Matt" Sea-A 1995-00
Sisler, George H. Bos-N 1930
Sisler, Richard A. "Dick" Cin-N 1961-64, StL-N 1966-70, SD-N 1975-76, NY-N 1979-80
Sisti, Sebastian D. "Sibby" Mil-N 1954, Sea-A 1969
Skaff, Francis M. "Frank" Bal-A 1954, Det-A 1965-66, 1971
Skinner, Robert R. "Bob" SD-N 1970-73, Pit-N 1974-76, SD-N 1977, Cal-A 1978, Pit-N 1979-85, Atl-N 1986-88
Slattery, John T. "Jack" Bos-N 1918-19
Slider, Rachel W. "Rac" Bos-A 1987-90
Smith, Alfred J. "Al" NY-N 1933
Smith, Billy F. Tor-A 1984-88
Smith, C. Reginald "Reggie" LA-N 1994-98
Smith, David S. "Dave" SD-N 1999-00
Smith, Harold R. "Hal" StL-N 1962, Pit-N 1965-67, Cin-N 1968-69, Mil-A 1976-77
Smith, Richard P. "Red" Chi-N 1945-48
Smith, Steven J. "Steve" Sea-A 1996-99
Snider, Edwin D. "Duke" Mon-N 1974-75
Snitker, Brian G. Atl-N 1985, 1988-90
Snyder, Francis E. "Frank" NY-N 1933-41
Snyder, James R. "Jim" Chi-N 1987, Sea-A 1988, SD-N 1991-92
Sommers, Dennis J. "Denny" NY-N 1977-78, Cle-A 1980-85, SD-N 1988-90
Sothoron, Allen S. StL-N 1927-28, StL-A 1932-33
Southworth, William H. "Billy" NY-N 1933
Spahn, Warren E. NY-N 1965, Cle-A 1972-73
Spalding, Charles H. "Dick" Phi-N 1934-36, Chi-N 1941-43
Spangler, Albert D. "Al" Chi-N 1970-71, 1974
Sparks, Joseph E. "Joe" Chi-A 1979, Cin-N 1984, Mon-N 1989, NY-A 1990
Speier, Chris E. Mil-N 2000
Spencer, H. Thomas "Tom" Cle-A 1988-89, NY-N 1991, Hou-N 1992-93
Spilman, W. Harry Hou-N 2000
Squires, Michael L. "Mike" Tor-A 1989-91, Chi-A 1992
Staller, George W. Bal-A 1962, 1969-75
Stanage, Oscar H. Pit-N 1927-31
Stange, A. Lee Bos-A 1969, 1972-74, Min-A 1975, Oak-A 1977-79, Bos-A 1981-84
Stanky, Edward R. "Eddie" Cle-A 1957-58
Stanley, Frederick B. "Fred" Mil-A 1991
Stargell, Wilver D. "Willie" Pit-N 1985, Atl-N 1986-88
Starrette, Herman P. "Herm" Atl-N 1974-76, SF-N 1977-78, Phi-N 1979-81, SF-N 1983-84, Mil-A 1985-86, Chi-N 1987, Bal-A 1988, Bos-A 1995, 1996-97
Staub, Daniel J. "Rusty" NY-N 1982
Stearns, John H. NY-A 1989, Bal-A 1996-97, NY-N 2000
Stelmaszek, Richard F. "Rick" Min-A 1981-00
Stengel, Charles D. "Casey" Bro-N 1932-33
Stevens, Edward L. "Ed" SD-N 1981
Stewart, David K. "Dave" SD-N 1998, Tor-A 2000
Stock, Milton J. "Milt" Chi-N 1944-48, Bro-N 1949-50, Pit-N 1951-52
Stock, Wesley G. "Wes" KC-A 1967, Mil-A 1970-72, Oak-A 1972-76, Sea-A 1977-81, Oak-A 1984-86
Stottlemyre, Melvin L. "Mel" NY-N 1984-93, Hou-N 1994-95, NY-A 1996-00
Stratton, Monty F. Chi-A 1939-41
Street, Charles E. "Gabby" StL-N 1929, StL-A 1937
Strickland, George B. Min-A 1962, Cle-A 1963-69, KC-A 1970-72
Strom, Brent T. Hou-N 1996, KC-A 2000
Stubing, Lawrence G. "Moose" Cal-A 1985-88, 1989-90
Such, Richard S. "Dick" Tex-A 1983-85, Min-A 1985-00
Sugden, Joseph "Joe" StL-N 1921-25, Phi-N 1926-27
Sukeforth, Clyde L. Bro-N 1943-51, Pit-N 1952-57
Sullivan, John P. KC-A 1979, Atl-N 1980-81, Tor-A 1982-93
Summers, John J. "Champ" NY-A 1989-90
Susce, George C. M. Cle-A 1941-47, 1948-49, Bos-A 1950-54, KC-A 1955-56, Mil-N 1958-59, Was-A 1961-67, 1969-71, Tex-A 1972
Sweeney, William J. "Bill" Det-A 1947-48
Sweet, Ricky J. "Rick" Sea-A 1984, Hou-N 1996
Swift, Robert V. "Bob" Det-A 1953-54, KC-A 1957-59, Was-A 1960, Det-A 1963-66
Swisher, Steven E. "Steve" NY-N 1993-96
Tamargo, John F. Hou-N 1999-00
Tannehill, Jesse N. Phi-N 1920
Tappe, Elvin W. "El" Chi-N 1958-65
Taylor, Antonio N. "Tony" Phi-N 1977-79, 1988-89, Fla-N 1999-00
Taylor, James W. "Zack" Bro-N 1936, StL-A 1941-46, Pit-N 1947
Temple, John E. "Johnny" Cin-N 1964
Tenace, F. Gene Hou-N 1986-87, Tor-A 1990-97
Terwilliger, W. Wayne Was-A 1969-71, Tex-A 1972, 1981-85, Min-A 1986-94
Testa, Nicholas "Nick" SF-N 1958
Thomas, George E. Bos-A 1970
Thomas, Ira F. Phi-A 1914-17, 1925-26
Thomas, J. Leroy "Lee" StL-N 1972, 1983
Thomas, Roy A. StL-N 1922
Thompson, Charles L. "Tim" StL-N 1981
Thompson, Robert R. "Robby" SF-N 2000
Tiefenauer, Bobby G. Phi-N 1979
Tighe, John T. "Jack" Det-A 1942, 1955-56
Tincup, A. Ben Bro-N 1940
Tobin, John T. "Jack" StL-A 1949-51
Tolan, Robert "Bobby" SD-N 1980-83, Sea-A 1987
Torborg, Jeffrey A. "Jeff" Cle-A 1975-77, NY-A 1979-88
Torchia, Anthony L. "Tony" Bos-A 1985
Torgeson, C. Earl NY-A 1961
Torres, Hector E. Tor-A 1991
Tosca, Carlos Ari-N 1998-00
Tracewski, Richard J. "Dick" Det-A 1972-95
Tracy, James E. "Jim" Mon-N 1995-98, LA-N 1999-00
Trammell, Alan S. Det-A 1999, SD-N 2000
Trebelhorn, Thomas L. "Tom" Mil-A 1984, 1986, Chi-N 1992-93
Treuel, Ralph M. Det-A 1995
Trucks, Virgil O. Pit-N 1963
Tesreau, Charles M. "Jeff" Chi-A 1928
Turley, Robert L. "Bob" Bos-A 1964
Turner, James R. "Jim" NY-A 1949-59, Cin-N 1961-65, NY-A 1966-73
Turner, Terrence L. "Terry" StL-N 1924
Uhlaender, Theodore O. "Ted" Cle-A 2000
Uhle, George E. Cle-A 1936-37, Chi-N 1940, Was-A 1944
Ullger, Scott M. Min-A 1995-00
Unser, Delbert B. "Del" Phi-N 1985-88
Upshaw, Willie C. Tex-A 1993-94, Tor-A 1996-97
Valentine, Robert J. "Bobby" NY-N 1983-85, Cin-N 1993
Valo, Elmer W. Cle-A 1963-64
Van Ornum, John C. SF-N 1980-84
Vernon, James B. "Mickey" Pit-N 1960, 1964, StL-N 1965, Mon-N 1977-78, NY-A 1982
Vincent, Albert L. "Al" Det-A 1943-44, Bal-A 1955-59, Phi-N 1961-63, KC-A 1966-67
Virdon, William C. "Bill" Pit-N 1968-71, 1986, Hou-N 1997
Virgil, Osvaldo Jose Sr. "Ozzie" SF-N 1969-72, 1974-75, Mon-N 1976-81, SD-N 1982-85, Sea-A 1986-88
Vuckovich, Peter D. "Pete" Pit-N 1997-00
Vukovich, John C. Chi-N 1982-87, Phi-N 1988, 1989-00
Wagner, Charles F. "Heinie" Bos-A 1916-19, 1927-29
Wagner, Charles T. "Charley" Bos-A 1970
Wagner, John P. "Honus" Pit-N 1933-51
Walker, Albert B. "Rube" LA-N 1958, Was-A 1965-67, NY-N 1968-81, Atl-N 1982-84
Walker, Fred "Dixie" StL-N 1953, 1955, Mil-N 1963-65
Walker, Gerald H. "Gee" Cin-N 1946
Walker, Harry W. StL-N 1959-62
Walker, Jerry A. NY-A 1981-82, Hou-N 1983-85
Walker, Verlon L. Chi-N 1961-70
Wallace, David W. "Dave" LA-N 1995-97, NY-N 1999-00
Wallace, Roderick J. "Bobby" Cin-N 1926
Waller, Tyrone E. "Tye" SD-N 1995
Walling, Dennis M. "Denny" Oak-A 1996-98
Walls, R. Lee Oak-A 1979-82, NY-A 1983
Walsh, Edward A. "Ed" Chi-A 1923-25, 1928-30
Walters, William H. "Bucky" Bos-N 1950-52, Mil-N 1953-55, NY-N 1956-57
Walton, James R. "Jim" Mil-A 1973-75
Waner, Paul G. Phi-N 1965
Ward, John F. "Jay" NY-A 1987, Mon-N 1991-92
Ward, Peter T. "Pete" Atl-N 1978
Wares, Clyde E. "Buzzy" StL-N 1930-35, 1937-52
Warner, Harry C. Tor-A 1977-79, 1980, Mil-A 1981-82
Warthen, Daniel D. "Dan" Sea-A 1991-92, SD-N 1996-97, Det-A 1999-00
Washington, Ronald "Ron" Oak-A 1996-00
Wathan, John D. KC-A 1986, Cal-A 1992-93, Bos-A 1994
Watson, Robert J. "Bob" Oak-A 1986-88
Weaver, Earl S. Bal-A 1968
Webb, William J. "Billy" Chi-A 1935-39
Werle, William G. "Bill" SF-N 1966
West, Samuel F. "Sam" Was-A 1947-49
Westrum, Wesley N. "Wes" SF-N 1958-63, NY-N 1964-65, SF-N 1968-71
Whisenant, T. Peter "Pete" Cin-N 1961-62
White, Ernest D. "Ernie" Bos-N 1947-48, NY-N 1963
White, Frank Bos-A 1994-96, KC-A 1997-00
White, Jerome C. "Jerry" Det-A 1997-98, Min-A 1999-00
White, Joyner C. "Jo-Jo" Cle-A 1958-60, Det-A 1960, KC-A 1961-62, Mil-N 1963-65, Atl-N 1966, KC-A 1969
White, Roy H. NY-A 1983-84, 1986
Whitehill, Earl O. Cle-A 1941, Phi-N 1943
Whitmer, Daniel C. "Dan" Det-A 1992-94
Widmar, Albert J. "Al" Phi-N 1962-64, 1968-69, Mil-A 1973-74, Tor-A 1980-88, 1989
Wietelmann, William F. "Whitey" Cin-N 1966-67, SD-N 1969-79
Wilber, Delbert Q. "Del" Chi-A 1955-56, Was-A 1970, Tex-A 1973
Wiley, Mark E. Bal-A 1987, Cle-A 1988-91, 1995-98, KC-A 1999
Wilhelm, Irvin K. "Kaiser" Phi-N 1921
Wilks, Theodore "Ted" Cle-A 1960, KC-A 1961
Williams, Billy L. Chi-N 1980-82, Oak-A 1983-85, Chi-N 1986-87, 1992-00
Williams, Dallas M. Col-N 2000
Williams, Dana Cle-A 1993
Williams, Daniel L. "Dan" Cle-A 1995-00
Williams, David C. "Davey" NY-N 1956-57
Williams, Donald E. "Don" SD-N 1977-80
Williams, Donald R. "Spin" Pit-N 1994-00
Williams, James B. "Jimmy" Hou-N 1975, Bal-A 1981-87
Williams, James F. "Jimy" Tor-A 1980-85, Atl-N 1990-96
Williams, Otto G. Det-A 1925, StL-N 1926, StL-A 1927, Cin-N 1930
Williams, Richard A. "Rick" Fla-N 1995-96, TB-A 1998-00
Williams, Richard H. "Dick" Mon-N 1970
Williams, Stanley W. "Stan" Bos-A 1975-76, Chi-A 1977-78, NY-A 1980-81, 1982, Cin-N 1984, NY-A 1987, 1988, Cin-N 1990-91, Sea-A 1998-99
Williams, Walter A. "Walt" Chi-A 1988
Wilson, James "Jimmy" Cin-N 1939-40, 1944-46
Wilson, William H. "Mookie" NY-N 1997-00
Wiltse, George L. "Hooks" NY-A 1925
Wine, Robert P. Sr. "Bobby" Phi-N 1972-83, Atl-N 1985, 1988-90, NY-N 1993-96
Winegarner, Ralph L. StL-A 1948-51
Wingo, Ivey B. Cin-N 1928-29, 1936
Winkles, Bobby B. Cal-A 1972, Oak-A 1974-75, SF-N 1976-77, Chi-A 1979-81, Mon-N 1986-88
Wolgamot, C. Earl Cle-A 1931-33
Woodall, C. Lawrence "Larry" Bos-A 1942-48
Woodling, Eugene R. "Gene" Bal-A 1964-67
Worthington, Allan F. "Al" Min-A 1972-73
Wotus, Ronald A. "Ron" SF-N 1998-00
Wright, James I. "Jim" Phi-N 1996
Wright, Melvin J. "Mel" Chi-N 1963-64, 1971, Pit-N 1973, NY-A 1974-75, Hou-N 1976-82
Wyatt, J. Whitlow "Whit" Phi-N 1955-57, Mil-N 1958-65, Atl-N 1966-67
Wynn, Early Cle-A 1964-66, Min-A 1967-69
York, P. Rudolph "Rudy" Bos-A 1959-62
Yost, Edgar F. "Ned" Atl-N 1991-00
Yost, Edward F. "Eddie" LA-A 1962, Was-A 1963-67, NY-N 1968-76, Bos-A 1977-84
Youngblood, Joel R. Cin-N 1994-97, Mil-N 1998
Zarilla, Allen L. "Al" Was-A 1971
Zeller, Barton W. "Bart" StL-N 1970
Zimmer, Donald W. "Don" Mon-N 1971, SD-N 1972, Bos-A 1974-76, NY-A 1983, Chi-N 1984-86, NY-A 1986, SF-N 1987, Bos-A 1992, Col-N 1993-95, NY-A 1996-00
Zimmer, Thomas J. "Tom" StL-N 1976
Zimmerman, Gerald R. "Gerry" Min-A 1967, Mon-N 1969-75, Min-A 1976-80
Zuvella, Paul Col-N 1996
Zwilling, Edward H. "Dutch" Cle-A 1941

Biographical Data for Coaches Not Appearing in the Player/Pitcher Register

SPENCER ABBOTT Abbott, Spencer Arthur b: 8/27/1877, Chicago, Ill. d: 12/18/51, Washington, D.C. BL/TL, (1B)
OSCAR ACOSTA Acosta, Oscar Carlos b: 3/21/57, Portales, N.Mex. BR/TR, 6'1", 175 lbs. (P)
RICK ADAIR Adair, Michael Richard b: 1/19/58, Spartanburg, S.C. BL/TL, 6', 185 lbs. (P)
BOB ALEJO Alejo, Robert Kevin b: 11/19/57, Sacramento, Cal. BR/TR, 5'10", 185 lbs. (DNP)
CARLOS ALFONSO Alfonso, Carlos b: 12/18/50, Havana, Cuba BR/TR, 6'2", 205 lbs. (P)
PIERRE ARSENAULT Arsenault, Pierre Jean b: 10/12/63, Roberval, Que., Can. BR/TR, 5'11", 180 lbs. (C)
TONY AUFERIO Auferio, Anthony Patrick b: 6/13/47, Orange, N.J. BR/TR, 5'10", 185 lbs. (3B)
BUDDY BAILEY Bailey, Welby Sheldon b: 3/28/57, Norristown, Pa. BR/TR, 6', 193 lbs. (C)
DICK BERARDINO Berardino, Richard J. b: 7/2/37, Cambridge, Mass. BR/TR, 6'1", 190 lbs. (OF)
C. B. BERINGER Beringer, Carroll James b: 8/14/28, Bellwood, Neb. BR/TR, 6', 195 lbs. (P)
CARLOS BERNHARDT Bernhardt, Carlos b: 9/9/50, San Pedro De Macoris, D.R. BR/TR, 5'11", 195 lbs. (P)
GREG BIAGINI Biagini, Gregory Peter b: 5/12/52, Chicago, Ill. BB/TR, 6'2", 205 lbs. (1B-OF)
DAVE BIALAS Bialas, David Bruce b: 3/6/54, Houston, Tex. BR/TR, 6'1", 210 lbs. (OF)
WAYNE BLACKBURN Blackburn, Wayne Clark b: 7/10/16, Mount Joy, Ohio BL/TR, 5'10", 165 lbs. (OF-3B-2B)
JACK BLOOMFIELD Bloomfield, Gordon Leigh b: 8/7/32, Monte Alto, Tex. BL/TR, 6'2", 185 lbs. (2B)
MARC BOMBARD Bombard, Marc b: 11/15/49, Tampa, Fla. BR/TL, 5'8", 180 lbs. (P)
JIMMY BRAGAN Bragan, James Alton b: 3/12/29, Birmingham, Ala. BR/TR, 6', 198 lbs. (2B) (Brother of Bobby Bragan)
SCOTT BREEDEN Breeden, Harold Scott b: 9/17/37, Charlottesville, Va. BR/TR, 6'2", 210 lbs. (P)
JOE BREEDEN Breeden, Joseph Thomas b: 10/11/56, Newport News, Va. BR/TR, 5'11", 195 lbs. (C)
LORENZO BUNDY Bundy, Charles Lorenzo b: 11/6/59, Philadelphia, Pa. BL/TR, 6'2", 205 lbs. (1B)
BRIAN BUTTERFIELD Butterfield, Brian James b: 3/9/58, Bangor, Maine BB/TR, 6', 200 lbs. (2B)
JOE CAMACHO Camacho, Joseph Gomes b: 5/29/28, New Bedford, Mass. BR/TR, 6', 185 lbs. (SS-2B)
P. J. CAREY Carey, Paul Jerome b: 11/4/53, Scranton, Pa. BR/TR, 6'1", 190 lbs. (C)
DAVE CARLUCCI Carlucci, David Mario b: 5/1/63, Milford, Mass. BR/TR, 6'1", 195 lbs. (C)
DANNY CARNEVALE Carnevale, Daniel Joseph b: 2/8/18, Buffalo, N.Y. BR/TR, 6', 195 lbs. (SS)
LEONEL CARRION Carrion, Leonel Santiago (Matheus) b: 2/15/52, Maracaibo, Venez. BR/TR, 5'11", 185 lbs. (OF)
DICK CARTER Carter, Richard Joseph b: 8/31/16, Philadelphia, Pa. d: 9/11/69, Philadelphia, Pa. BR/TR, 5'10", 190 lbs. (P-OF)
DOM CHITI Chiti, Harry Dominic b: 12/10/58, Independence, Mo. BL/TL, 6'2", 200 lbs. (P)
BOB CLEAR Clear, Elwood Robert b: 12/14/27, Denver, Colo. BR/TR, 5'10", 170 lbs. (P)
BOB CLUCK Cluck, Robert Alton b: 1/10/46, San Diego, Cal. BL/TL, 6'2", 195 lbs. (P)
MARK CONNOR Connor, Mark Peter b: 5/27/49, Brooklyn, N.Y. BR/TR, 6'3", 195 lbs. (P)
JIMMIE CRANDALL Crandall, James Mark b: 12/7/12, Wadena, Ind. d: 2/83, Bullhead City, Ariz. BB/TR, 5'11", 190 lbs. (P-C) (Son of Doc Crandall)
MARK CRESSE Cresse, Mark Emery b: 9/21/51, St.Albans, N.Y. BR/TR, 6'3", 220 lbs. (C)
ROLY DeARMAS DeArmas, Rolando Jesus b: 12/29/51, New York, N.Y. BR/TR, 6'1", 190 lbs. (C)
MARTY DeMERRITT DeMerritt, Martin Gordon b: 3/4/53, San Francisco, Cal. BR/TR, 6'2.5", 205 lbs. (P)
BOBBY DEWS Dews, Robert Walter b: 3/23/38, Clinton, Iowa BR/TR, 6'1", 175 lbs. (SS)
WALT DIXON Dixon, Walter Edward b: 11/25/20, Mount Vernon Springs, N.C. BR/TR, 6'2", 220 lbs. (P)
RICH DONNELLY Donnelly, Richard Francis b: 8/3/46, Steubenville, Ohio BL/TR, 6', 185 lbs. (C)
OTIS DOUGLAS Douglas, Otis Whitfield b: 7/25/11, Reedville, Va. d: 3/21/89, Kilmarnock, Va. BR/TR, 6'1", 230 lbs. (DNP)
RICK DOWN Down, Richard John b: 12/14/50, Wyandotte, Mich. BR/TR, 5'11", 220 lbs. (OF)
RICH DUBEE Dubee, Richard Peter b: 10/19/57, Brockton, Mass. BB/TR, 6'2", 200 lbs. (P)
HARRY DUNLOP Dunlop, Harry Alexander b: 9/6/33, Sacramento, Cal. BL/TR, 6'3", 200 lbs. (C)
GENE DUSAN Dusan, Eugene Paul b: 11/9/49, Los Angeles, Cal. BB/TR, 6', 200 lbs. (C)
GLENN EZZELL Ezzell, Glenn Wayne b: 10/29/44, Kentwood, La. BR/TR, 6', 190 lbs. (C)
BRAD FISCHER Fischer, Bradley James b: 6/28/56, Toledo, Ohio BR/TR, 6'3", 198 lbs. (C)
JOE FITZGERALD Fitzgerald, Joseph Patrick b: 3/17/1897, Washington, D.C. d: 8/29/67, Orlando, Fla. BR/TR, 5'11", 200 lbs. (C)
JOHN FITZPATRICK Fitzpatrick, John Arthur b: 3/19/04, LaSalle, Ill. d: 11/19/90, BR/TR, 6'1.5", 185 lbs. (C)
TOM GAMBOA Gamboa, Thomas Harold b: 2/28/48, Los Angeles, Cal. BL/TL, 5'10", 175 lbs. (OF)
GENE GLYNN Glynn, Eugene Patrick b: 9/22/56, Waseca, Minn. BR/TR, 5'9", 165 lbs. (SS)
ORLANDO GOMEZ Gomez, Juan Alejandro b: 6/24/46, Juana Diaz, P.R. BR/TR, 6', 190 lbs. (C)
FREDI GONZALEZ Gonzalez, Fredi Jesus b: 1/28/64, Havana, Cuba BR/TR, 5'11", 200 lbs. (C)
BRIAN GRAHAM Graham, John Brian b: 4/9/60, San Diego, Cal. BR/TR, 6'1", 195 lbs. (2)
GLENN GREGSON Gregson, Glenn b: 2/10/50, Hamlet, N.C. BB/TR, 6'3", 185 lbs. (P)
EPY GUERRERO Guerrero, Epifanio Obdulio (Abud) b: 1/3/42, Santo Domingo, D.R. BR/TR, 5'11", 168 lbs. (OF) (Brother of Mario Guerrero)
GUY HANSEN Hansen, Guy Christopher b: 11/12/47, Los Angeles, Cal. BR/TR, 6', 170 lbs. (P)
ROGER HANSEN Hansen, Roger Christian b: 8/28/61, Johnstown, Pa. BR/TR, 6', 200 lbs. (C)
TOM HARMON Harmon, Thomas Harold b: 12/16/48, Lubbock, Tex. BL/TR, 5'11", 185 lbs. (C)
RAMON HENDERSON Henderson, Ramon Gaspar b: 8/18/63, Moncion, D.R. BR/TR, 5'11", 175 lbs. (3B)
CHUCK HERNANDEZ Hernandez, Carlo Amado b: 11/11/60, Tampa, Fla. BL/TL, 6'3", 200 lbs. (P)
PERRY HILL Hill, Perry Wendell b: 3/19/52, Salina, Kan. BR/TR, 5'10", 170 lbs. (2B)
BEN HINES Hines, Benjamin Thortan b: 11/7/35, Yeager, Okla. BR/TR, 5'11", 205 lbs. (3B-C) (Father of Bruce Hines)
BRUCE HINES Hines, Bruce Edwin b: 11/7/57, Pomona, Cal. BB/TR, 5'10", 180 lbs. (2B) (Son of Ben Hines)
DENNIS HOLMBERG Holmberg, Dennis Nels b: 8/2/51, Fremont, Neb. BL/TR, 6', 190 lbs. (3B)
DOUG HOLMQUIST Holmquist, Douglas Leonard b: 10/4/41, Bridgeport, Conn. d: 2/27/88, Altamonte Springs, Fla. BR/TR, 6'2", 195 lbs. (C)
GOLDIE HOLT Holt, Golden Desmond b: 3/22/02, Enloe, Tex. d: 6/11/91, Sherman Oaks, Cal. BR/TR, 5'7.5", 165 lbs. (3B-OF-2B)
VERN HOSCHEIT Hoscheit, Vernard Arthur b: 4/1/22, Brunswick, Neb. BR/TR, 5'9", 185 lbs. (C)
JACK HUBBARD Hubbard, John H. b: 10/4/50, Rock Hall, Md. BR/TR, 5'11", 175 lbs. (DNP)
LUIS ISAAC Isaac, Luis (Aponte) b: 6/19/46, Rio Piedras, P.R. BR/TR, 5'11.5", 195 lbs. (C)
RUDY JARAMILLO Jaramillo, Rudolph b: 9/20/50, Beeville, Tex. BL/TR, 5'11", 180 lbs. (OF)
DAVE JAUSS Jauss, David Patrick b: 1/16/57, Chicago, Ill. BR/TR, 5'11", 170 lbs. (DNP)
GARY JONES Jones, Gary Wayne b: 11/11/60, Henderson, Tex. BL/TR, 5'9", 163 lbs. (2B)
JOE JONES Jones, Joseph Carmack b: 12/13/41, Lebanon, Tenn. BR/TR, 5'9", 155 lbs. (2B)
LOU KAHN Kahn, Louis b: 12/4/16, St.Louis, Mo. BR/TR, 5'11", 195 lbs. (C)
MIKE KELLY Kelly, Bernard Francis b: 5/1/1896, Indianapolis, Ind. d: 10/23/68, Indianapolis, Ind. BR/TR, 6', 198 lbs. (1B)
WENDELL KIM Kim, Wendell Kealohapauloe b: 3/9/51, Honolulu, Hawaii BR/TR, 5'5", 160 lbs. (2B)
GEORGE KISSELL Kissell, George Marshall b: 9/9/21, Watertown, N.Y. BR/TR, 5'8", 175 lbs. (3B)
HUB KITTLE Kittle, Hubert Milton b: 2/19/17, Los Angeles, Cal. BR/TR, 6'1", 195 lbs. (P)
FRED KOENIG Koenig, Fred Carl b: 4/27/31, St.Louis, Mo. d: 1/12/93, Wagoner, Okla. BR/TR, 6'3", 200 lbs. (1B-3B)
BILL LACHEMANN Lachemann, William Charles b: 4/5/34, Los Angeles, Cal. BL/TR, 5'9", 195 lbs. (C)
JIM LETT Lett, James Curtis b: 1/3/51, Charleston, W.Va. BR/TR, 6'2", 185 lbs. (3B)
LENNY LEVY Levy, Leonard Howard b: 6/11/13, Pittsburgh, Pa. d: 2/2/93, Palm Desert, Cal. BR/TR, 5'10.5", 190 lbs. (C)
JULIO LINARES Linares, Julio Mairenu (Rijo) b: 12/26/40, San Pedro De Macoris, D.R. BR/TR, 5'9", 165 lbs. (3B)
GRADY LITTLE Little, William Grady b: 3/30/50, Abilene, Tex. BR/TR, 5'11", 190 lbs. (C)
BILL LOBE Lobe, William Charles b: 3/24/12, Cleveland, Ohio d: 1/7/69, Cleveland, Ohio BR/TR, 5'9.5", 178 lbs. (C)
JUAN LOPEZ Lopez, Juan Enrique b: 5/16/62, Bayamon, P.R. BR/TR, 5'10", 187 lbs. (C)
Q. V. LOWE Lowe, Q. V. b: 1/15/45, Red Level, Ala. BR/TR, 6'1", 185 lbs. (P)
JOE MACKO Macko, Joseph John b: 2/19/28, Port Clinton, Ohio BR/TR, 6'2", 195 lbs. (1B) (Father of Steve Macko)
ROY MAJTYKA Majtyka, Le Roy Walter b: 6/1/39, Buffalo, N.Y. BR/TR, 5'10", 170 lbs. (2B)
JACK MALOOF Maloof, Jack Garth b: 10/12/49, Redlands, Cal. BL/TL, 6', 175 lbs. (1B-OF)
DOUG MANSOLINO Mansolino, Douglas b: 9/20/56, Plainfield, N.J. BR/TR, 5'7", 155 lbs. (IF)

MARTY MASON Mason, Martin Lee b: 4/4/58, Central City, Ky. BR/TR, 6'1", 175 lbs. (P)
HARRY MATHEWS Mathews, Henry b: 7/23/1876, Newport, Ky. BR/TR, (C)
RICK MATHEWS Mathews, Rick Ray b: 10/9/47, Centerville, Iowa BR/TR, 5'11", 180 lbs. (P)
LEO MAZZONE Mazzone, Leo David b: 10/16/48, Keyser, W.Va. BL/TL, 5'10", 185 lbs. (P)
MAJE McDONNELL McDonnell, Robert A. b: 7/20/20, Philadelphia, Pa. BR/TR, 5'6", 135 lbs. (P)
J. R. McKEE McKee, John R.
JOHN McLAREN McLaren, John Lowell b: 9/29/51, Galveston, Tex. BR/TR, 6', 200 lbs. (C)
DAVE MILEY Miley, David Allen b: 4/3/62, Tampa, Fla. BL/TR, 6'3", 220 lbs. (C)
MO MOZZALI Mozzali, Maurice Joseph b: 12/12/22, Louisville, Ky. d: 3/2/87, Lakeland, Fla. BL/TL, 5'10", 160 lbs. (1B)
JACK MULL Mull, Jack Leroy b: 9/29/43, Chambersburg, Pa. BR/TR, 5'10", 188 lbs. (C)
ED NAPOLEON Napoleon, Edward George b: 9/17/37, Baltimore, Md. BR/TR, 5'8", 165 lbs. (OF-3B-1B)
ED NOTTLE Nottle, Edward William b: 10/22/39, Philadelphia, Pa. BR/TR, 5'10", 180 lbs. (P)
FRANK OCEAK Oceak, Frank John "Fez" b: 9/8/12, Pocahontas, Va. d: 3/19/83, Johnstown, Pa. BR/TR, 5'9", 172 lbs. (2B)
MAKO OLIVERAS Oliveras, Max b: 9/10/46, Santurce, P.R. BR/TR, 6', 195 lbs. (2B)
BUCK O'NEIL O'Neil, John Jordan b: 11/13/11, Carrabelle, Fla. BR/TR, 6'2", 190 lbs. (1B)
DON OSBORN Osborn, Donald Edwin b: 6/3/08, Sandpoint, Idaho d: 3/23/79, Torrance, Cal. BR/TR, 6', 185 lbs. (P)
TONY PACHECO Pacheco, Antonio Aristides b: 8/9/27, Havana, Cuba d: 3/23/87, Miami Beach, Fla. BR/TR, 6', 190 lbs. (2B)
JACK PAEPKE Paepke, Jack b: 8/28/22, Provo, Utah BR/TR, 6'2.5", 220 lbs. (C-P) (Father of Dennis Paepke)
MAX PATKIN Patkin, Max b: 1/10/20, Philadelphia, Pa. d: 10/30/99, Paoli, Pa. BR/TR, 6'2", 170 lbs. (P)
GREG PAVLICK Pavlick, Gregory Michael b: 3/10/50, Washington, D.C. BR/TR, 6'3", 205 lbs. (P)
JEFF PENTLAND Pentland, Jeffrey William b: 9/18/46, Hollywood, Cal. BL/TL, 5'10", 185 lbs. (1B)
RICK PETERSON Peterson, Eric Harding b: 10/30/54, Brunswick, N.J. BL/TL, 6', 175 lbs. (P) (Son of Harding Peterson)
RON PLAZA Plaza, Ronald Charles b: 8/24/34, Passaic, N.J. BL/TR, 6', 180 lbs. (3B)
BRYAN PRICE Price, Bryan Roberts b: 6/22/62, San Francisco, Cal. BL/TL, 6'2", 200 lbs. (P)
MIKE QUADE Quade, Gregory Mike b: 3/12/57, Evanston, Ill. BR/TR, 6', 182 lbs. (OF)
DAN RADISON Radison, Daniel John b: 8/24/50, St.Louis, Mo. BR/TR, 6'2", 190 lbs. (C)
ED REDYS Redys, Edward b: 6/23/21, Detroit, Mich. BR/TR, 6', 185 lbs. (P)
GROVER RESINGER Resinger, Grover S b: 10/20/15, St.Louis, Mo. d: 1/11/86, St.Louis, Mo. BR/TR, 5'9", 180 lbs. (3B)
CANANEA REYES Reyes, Benjamin (Chavez) b: 2/18/37, Nacozari, Mexico d: 11/11/91, Hermosillo, Mexico BR/TR, (OF)
MARK RIGGINS Riggins, Mark Alan b: 1/3/57, Jasper, Ind. BR/TL, 5'10", 180 lbs. (P)
JOE RIGOLI Rigoli, Joseph M. b: 12/14/56, New York, N.Y. BR/TR, 6'2", 190 lbs. (C)
MEL ROBERTS Roberts, Melvin Henry b: 1/18/43, Abington, Pa. BR/TR, 6', 180 lbs. (OF)
SHERIFF ROBINSON Robinson, Warren Grant b: 9/8/21, Cambridge, Md. BR/TR, 6'1", 195 lbs. (C)
EDDIE RODRIGUEZ Rodriguez, Eduardo b: 3/11/59, Havana, Cuba BR/TR, 5'8", 165 lbs. (SS)
PAT ROESSLER Roessler, Patrick Alan b: 12/27/59, Phoenix, Ariz. BR/TR, 6', 200 lbs. (IF)
GLEN ROSENBAUM Rosenbaum, Glen Otis b: 6/14/36, Union Mills, Ind. BR/TR, 5'11", 180 lbs. (P)
RALPH ROWE Rowe, Ralph Emanuel b: 7/14/24, Newberry, S.C. d: 2/29/96, Newberry, S.C. BL/TR, 5'6", 160 lbs. (OF)
JIM SAUL Saul, James Allen b: 11/24/39, Bristol, Va. BL/TR, 6'3", 210 lbs. (C)
GEORGE SCHERGER Scherger, George Richard b: 11/20/20, Dickinson, N.Dak. BR/TR, 5'8", 170 lbs. (2B)
GLENN SHERLOCK Sherlock, Glenn Patrick b: 9/26/60, Nahant, Mass. BL/TR, 6'1", 200 lbs. (C)
RAC SLIDER Slider, Rachel W. b: 12/23/33, Simms, Tex. BL/TR, 5'8", 160 lbs. (SS)
BILLY SMITH Smith, Billy Franklin b: 1/14/30, High Point, N.C. BL/TL, 5'9", 160 lbs. (1B-OF)
STEVE SMITH Smith, Steven J. b: 7/21/53, Canton, Ohio BR/TR, 5'11", 180 lbs. (2B-SS)
BRIAN SNITKER Snitker, Brian Gerald b: 10/17/55, Decatur, Ill. BR/TR, 6'1", 192 lbs. (C)
DENNY SOMMERS Sommers, Dennis James b: 7/12/40, New London, Wis. BL/TR, 6'2", 205 lbs. (C)
JOE SPARKS Sparks, Joseph Everett b: 3/15/38, McComas, W.Va. BL/TR, 6', 195 lbs. (3B-2B)
TONY TORCHIA Torchia, Anthony Lewis b: 12/13/43, Chicago, Ill. BR/TL, 5'10", 180 lbs. (1B-OF)
CARLOS TOSCA Tosca, Carlos b: 9/29/53, Pinar Del Rio, Cuba BR/TR, 5'7", 155 lbs. (P)
RALPH TREUEL Treuel, Ralph Martin b: 6/7/55, Elyria, Ohio BR/TR, 6'4", 220 lbs. (P)
JOHN VanORNUM Van Ornum, John Clayton b: 10/20/39, Pasadena, Cal. BR/TR, 5'11", 175 lbs. (C)
AL VINCENT Vincent, Albert Linder b: 12/23/06, Birmingham, Ala. BR/TR, 5'9.5", 170 lbs. (2B)
VERLON WALKER Walker, Verlon Lee "Rube" b: 3/7/29, Lenoir, N.C. d: 3/24/71, Chicago, Ill. BL/TR, 6', 210 lbs. (C) (Brother of Rube Walker)
JIM WALTON Walton, James Robert b: 9/5/35, Shattuck, Okla. BR/TR, 6'2", 190 lbs. (P)
HARRY WARNER Warner, Harry Clinton b: 12/11/28, Reeders, Pa. BL/TR, 6'2", 215 lbs. (1B)
DAN WILLIAMS Williams, Daniel Lawrence b: 9/3/66, San Gabriel, Cal. BR/TR, 6'3", 245 lbs. (C)
DON WILLIAMS Williams, Donald Ellis b: 12/24/37, Paragould, Ark. BR/TR, 5'10", 185 lbs. (SS)
SPIN WILLIAMS Williams, Donald Ray b: 1/5/56, Davenport, Iowa BL/TL, 6'3", 230 lbs. (P)
JIMMY WILLIAMS Williams, James Bernard b: 5/15/26, Toronto, Ont., Can. BR/TR, 5'10", 180 lbs. (OF)
RICK WILLIAMS Williams, Richard Anthony b: 11/21/56, Ft.Worth, Tex. BL/TL, 6'1", 205 lbs. (P) (Son of Dick Williams)
EARL WOLGAMOT Wolgamot, Clinton Earl b: 12/21/1895, Fairbank, Iowa d: 4/25/70, Independence, Iowa BR/TR, 5'8", 155 lbs. (C)
TOM ZIMMER Zimmer, Thomas Jeffrey b: 6/30/52, Mobile, Ala. BR/TR, 5'8", 165 lbs. (C) (Son of Don Zimmer)

The Umpire Roster

The men in blue have been rebuked and scorned since the Knickerbockers cavorted on the Elysian Fields of Hoboken. The first to incur an umpire's wrath in return was Knickerbocker player Davis, fined 6 cents for swearing, perhaps understandably since his team was being trounced by the New York Club, 23–1. The name of the umpire in that historic game of June 19, 1846—the first match game under Alexander Cartwright's new rules—was not recorded. Ever since, a handful of researchers have scrambled to find out who umpired the league games of baseball's early history.

Larry Gerlach, who knows more about umpires and umpiring than anybody, has created the Umpire Roster that follows. The basis of his roster is the list compiled by S. C. Thompson in the 1930s and 1940s, but his research has corrected several errors and omissions in that list and has scrupulously brought the umpire roster up to date. In the first edition of *Total Baseball,* he hoped that "by the next edition we will have finished a complete re-study of the umpire roster. . . . I am going to try to fashion a biographical encyclopedia of major league umpires—vital statistics; minor and major league service; All-Star, World Series, Playoff games; special achievements; and so on. One of the more frustrating things about the Turkin/Thompson roster (and even ours) is how years of service are noted in terms of seasons; it really is misleading to identify someone as working from 1980–1987 when he may have broken into the majors on September 24, 1980."

The data presented here does not meet those lofty goals, but it is vastly increased and improved, as well as reorganized. Separate rosters exist for each league, showing the few instances where an umpire worked in more than one league. The American League and National League maintained separate umpiring crews until the 2000 season, when they were consolidated into a single pool. All umpires added in 2000 are listed under the heading Major League Baseball; all other current umpires are listed under the league in which they debuted.

Umpires are divided into four categories: regular, league-employed umpires; substitutes; player-umpires, pressed into emergency service; and those subs used during the recent strikes. New leads continue to flow in, especially about the early days, when umpires were not assigned by the leagues but were supplied by the teams, recruited from among the fans in attendance (this explains why so many given names are lacking for pre-1900 arbiters), or, not infrequently, plucked from the team's reserve players.

A feature unique to *Total Baseball* is the identification of substitute umpires in the National Association years 1871–75. An instance of this last practice occurred as late as 1935, when Chicago White Sox outfielder Jocko Conlan was recruited to fill in for umpire Red Ormsby in a game between the Sox and the St. Louis Browns. Conlan, of course, went on to a Hall of Fame career as a man in blue.

Let's call the roll.

REGULAR UMPIRES

National Association (1871-75)

Avery, C. Hamilton 1875
Beardslee, John J. 1871
Blodgett, C. W. 1875
Boardman, Frederick "Fred" 1875
Bomeisler, Theodore 1871-73
Boyd, William J. "Bill" 1875
Burdock, John J. "Jack" 1872-74
Carey, Thomas J. "Tom" 1874
Clapp, John E. 1874-75
Cone, J. Frederick "Fred" 1875
Daniels, Charles F. 1874-75
Dehlman, Herman J. 1874
Dole, Lester C. 1875
Ferguson, Robert V. "Bob" 1872-73, 1875
Fulmer, Charles J. "Chick" 1873
Heubel, George A. 1875
Hodges, Amory G. 1874-75
Holly, Samuel J. "Sam" 1871
Lennon, William F. "Bill" 1871-72, 1873-74
Mack, Dennis J. "Denny" 1875
Martin, Alphonse C. "Phonney" 1875
Mathews, Robert T. "Bobby" 1873-75
McLean, William H. "Billy" 1874-75
Mills, Charles "Charlie" 1872-73
Patterson, Daniel T. "Dan" 1874
Rogers, M. Mortimer "Mort" 1871
Sensenderfer, John P. J. "Count" 1874
Swandell, J. Martin "Marty" 1872-73
Tate, William 1874
Walsh, Michael F. "Mike" 1875
Young, Nicholas E. "Nick" 1871-75

National League (1876-)

Andrews, G. Edward "Ed" 1895, 1898-99
Baker, William P. "Bill" 1957
Ballanfant, E. Lee 1936-57
Barlick, Albert J. "Al" 1940-43, 1946-55, 1958-71
Barnes, Ronald E. "Ron" 1990-94, 1996-97
Barnie, William S. "Billy" 1892
Barr, George M. 1931-49
Barron, Mark E. 1992-97
Battin, Joseph V. "Joe" 1891
Bausewine, George 1905
Behle, Frank 1901
Bell, Wally 1992-2000
Betts, William G. 1894-96, 1898-99
Betz, Edwin J. 1961
Boggess, Lynton R. "Dusty" 1944-48, 1950-62
Boles, Charles 1877
Bond, Thomas H. "Tommy" 1883, 1885
Bonin, Gregory "Greg" 1984-2000
Bradley, George H. "Foghorn" 1879-83
Brady, Jackson 1887
Bransfield, William E. "Kitty" 1917
Bredburg, George W. 1877
Brennan, John E. "Jack" 1899
Brennan, William T. "Bill" 1909-13, 1921
Brocklander, Fred W. 1979-90
Brown, Thomas T. "Tom" 1898-99, 1901-02
Bucknor, C. B. 1996-2000
Bunce, Joshua 1877
Burkhart, W. Kenneth "Ken" 1957-73
Burnham, George W. 1883, 1889, 1895
Burns, John S. 1884
Burns, Thomas E. "Tom" 1892
Burns, Thomas P. "Oyster" 1899
Burtis, L. W. 1876-77
Bush, Garnet C. 1911-12
Byron, William J. "Bill"or "Lord" 1913-19
Callahan, Edward J. "Ed" 1881
Campbell, Daniel "Dan" 1894-96
Campbell, William M. "Bick" 1939-40
Cantillon, Joseph D. "Joe" 1902
Carlson, Mark C. 1999-2000
Carpenter, William B. "Bill" 1897, 1904, 1906-07
Chapman, John C. "Jack" 1880
Chipman, Harry F. 1883
Clarke, Robert M. "Bob" 1930-31
Cockill, George W. 1915
Colgan, Harry W. 1901
Colosi, Nicholas "Nick" 1968-82
Conahan, Edward J. "Ed" 1896
Cone, J. F. "Fred" 1877
Conlan, John B. "Jocko" 1941-64
Connolly, John M. "Red" 1886
Connolly, Thomas H. "Tommy" 1898-1900
Connors, Patrick "Pat" 1998
Conway, John H. 1906
Cook, Robert "Robb" 1999-2000
Crandall, Robert 1877
Crawford, Gerald J. "Jerry" 1975-2000
Crawford, Henry C. "Shag" 1956-75
Cross, John A. 1878
Cunningham, Elmer E. "Bert" 1901
Curry, Wesley "Wes" 1885-86, 1889, 1898
Cusack, Stephen P. 1909
Cushman, Charles H. "Charlie" 1885, 1898
Cuzzi, Phil 1991-93, 1999-2000
Dailey, John J. 1882
Dale, Jerry P. 1970-85
Daniels, Charles F. 1876, 1878-80, 1887-88
Danley, Kerwin J. 1991-2000
Darling, Gary R. 1986-99
Dascoli, Frank 1948-62
Davidson, David L. "Satch" 1969-84
Davidson, Robert A. "Bob" 1982-99
Davis, Gerald S. "Gerry" 1982-2000
Decker, Stewart M. 1883-85, 1888
Delmore, Victor "Vic" 1956-59
DeMuth, Dana A. 1983-2000
Derr, Doll 1923
Devinney, P. H. "Dan" 1877
Dezelan, Frank J. 1966-68, 1969-71
Dixon, Hal H. 1953-59
Donatelli, August J. "Augie" 1950-73
Donnelly, Charles H. 1931-32
Donohue, Michael R. 1930
Doscher, John H. Sr. "Herm" 1880-81, 1887
Doyle, John J. "Jack" 1911
Drake, Robert "Rob" 1999-2000
Dreckman, Bruce M. 1996-99
Ducharme, — 1876-77
Dunn, Thomas P. "Tom" 1939-46
Dunnigan, Joseph 1881-82
Dwyer, J. Francis "Frank" 1899, 1901
Eagan, John J. 1878, 1886
Eason, Malcolm W. "Mal" 1902, 1910-16
Ellick, Joseph J. "Joe" 1886
Emmel, Paul L. 1999-2000
Emslie, Robert D. "Bob" 1891-1924
Engel, Robert A. "Bob" 1965-90
Engeln, William R. "Bill" 1952-56
Ferguson, Robert V. "Bob" 1879, 1884-85
Fessenden, Wallace C. "Wally" 1889-90
Fields, Stephen H. "Steve" 1979-82
Finneran, William F. 1911-12
Fletcher, Andrew J. 1999-2000
Forman, Allen S. "Al" 1961-65
Fountain, Edward G. 1879
Frary, Ralph 1911
Froemming, Bruce N. 1971-2000
Fulmer, Charles J. "Chick" 1886
Furlong, William E. "Bill" 1878-79, 1883-84
Fyfe, Lee C. 1920
Gaffney, John H. 1884-86, 1891-94, 1899-1900
Galvin, James F. "Jim" 1895
Gibbons, Brian 1994-99
Gibson, Gregory A. "Greg" 1997-2000
Gillean, Thomas 1879-80
Goetz, Lawrence J. "Larry" 1936-57
Gore, Arthur J. "Artie" 1947-56
Gorman, Brian 1991-2000
Gorman, Thomas D. "Tom" 1951-76
Gregg, Eric E. 1975-91, 1993-99
Guglielmo, A. Augie 1952
Gunning, Thomas F. "Tom" 1887
Guthrie, William J. "Bill" 1913, 1915
Hallion, Thomas F. "Tom" 1985-99
Harris, Lanny D. 1979-85
Harrison, Peter A. "Pete" 1916-20
Hart, Eugene F. "Bob" 1920-29
Hart, William F. "Bill" 1914-15
Harvey, H. Douglas "Doug" 1962-92
Hautz, Charles A. "Charlie" 1876, 1879
Henderson, J. Harding "Hardie" 1895-96
Hengle, Edward S. "Ed" 1887
Henline, Walter J. "Butch" 1945-48
Hernandez, Angel 1991-2000
Heuble, George A. 1876
Heydler, John A. 1898
Higham, Richard "Dick" 1881-82
Hirschbeck, Mark 1987-2000
Hoagland, Willard A. 1894
Hodges, A. D. 1876
Hodges, Morris 1999-2000
Hohn, William J. "Bill"1987-99
Holland, John A. 1887
Holbrook, Samuel "Sam" 1997-99
Holliday, James W. "Bug" 1903
Holmes, Howard E. "Ducky" 1921
Hornung, M. Joseph "Joe" 1893, 1896
Hudson, Marvin L. 1998-2000
Hunt, John T. 1895, 1898-99
Hurst, Timothy C. "Tim" 1891-97, 1900, 1903
Iassogna, Dan 1999-2000
Irwin, Arthur A. 1902
Jackowski, William A. "Bill" 1952-68
Jeffers, W. W. 1881
Jevne, Frederick "Fred" 1895
Johnson, Harry S. "Steamboat" 1914
Johnstone, James E. "Jim" 1903-12
Jorda, Louis D. "Lou" 1927-31, 1940-52
Julian, Joseph O. 1878
Kane, Stephen J. 1909-10
Keefe, Timothy J. "Tim" 1894-96
Kellogg, Jeffery "Jeff" 1991-2000
Kelly, John O. "Kick" 1882, 1888, 1897
Kennedy, Charles 1904
Kenney, John 1877
Kibler, John W. 1963-89
Klem, William J. "Bill" 1905-41
Knight, Alonzo P. "Lon" 1889
Kulpa, Ronald "Ron" 1998-2000
Lally, Bud 1896
Lamplugh, Ian 1999-2000
Landes, Stanley A. "Stan" 1955-72
Lane, Frank H. 1883
Latham, W. Arlington "Arlie" 1899, 1902
Layne, Jerry B. 1989-2000
Libby, Stephen A. 1880
Lincoln, Frederick H. 1914
Long, Robert "Bob" 1992
Long, William H. "Billy" 1895
Lynch, Thomas J. "Tom" 1888-99
Macullar, James F. "Jimmy" 1892
Magee, Sherwood R. "Sherry" 1928
Magerkurth, George L. 1929-47
Mahoney, Michael J. 1892
Malone, Ferguson G. "Fergy" 1884
Manassau, Alfred S. "Al" 1899
Marquez, Alfonso 1999-2000
Marsh, Randall G. "Randy" 1981-2000
Mathews, Robert T. "Bobby" 1880
McCafferty, Charles 1921, 1923
McCormick, William J. "Barry" 1919-29
McDermott, Michael J. "Sandy" 1890, 1897
McDonald, James F.1895, 1897-99
McElwee, Harvey 1877
McFarland, Horace 1896-97
McGarr, James B. "Chippy" 1899
McGrew, Harry T. "Ted" 1930-31, 1933-34
McLaughlin, Edward J. 1929
McLaughlin, Michael 1893
McLaughlin, Peter J. 1924-28
McLean, William H. "Billy" 1876, 1878-80, 1882-84
McQuaid, John H. "Jack" 1889-94
McSherry, John P. 1971-96
Meals, Gerald W. "Jerry" 1992-94, 1996-2000
Miller, George E. 1879
Mitchell, Charles 1892
Montague, Edward M. "Ed" 1974-2000
Moran, August "Augie" 1903-04, 1910, 1918
Moran, Charles B. "Charlie" 1918-39
Mullin, John 1909
Nash, William M. "Billy" 1901
Nauert, Paul 1995-99
Nelson, Jeff 1997-2000
O'Connor, Arthur 1914
O'Day, Henry F. "Hank" 1895, 1897-1911, 1913, 1915-27
Odlin, Albert F. 1883
Olsen, Andrew H. "Andy" 1968-8l
O'Rourke, James H. "Jim" 1894
Orth, Albert L. "Al" 1912-17
O'Sullivan, John J. 1922
Owens, Clarence B. "Brick" 1908, 1912-13
Pallone, David M. "Dave" 1979-88
Parker, George L. 1936-38
Pearce, Richard J. "Dicky" 1878, 1882
Pears, Frank H. 1897, 1905
Pelekoudas, Christos G. "Chris" 1960-75
Pfirman, Charles H. "Cy" 1922-36
Pierce, Grayson S. "Gracie" 1886-87
Pinelli, Ralph A. "Babe" 1935-56
Poncino, Larry L. 1985-88, 1991-99
Potter, Scott A. 1991-95, 1997
Powell, Cornelius J. "Jack" 1923-24, 1933
Power, Charles B. 1902
Powers, Philip B. "Phil" 1879, 1881, 1886-91
Pratt, Albert G. "Al" 1879
Pratt, Thomas J. "Tom" 1886
Pryor, J. Paul 1961-8l
Pulli, Frank V. 1972-99
Quest, Joseph L. "Joe" 1886-87
Quick, James E. "Jim" 1974-98
Quigley, Ernest C. "Ernie" 1913-37
Quinn, Joseph C. "Joe" 1882
Randazzo, Anthony J. "Tony" 1999-2000
Rapuano, Edward "Ed" 1990-2000
Reardon, John E. "Beans" 1926-49
Reliford, Charles H. "Charlie" 1989-2000
Rennert, Laurence H. "Dutch" 1973-92
Rieker, Richard G. "Rich" 1992-2000
Rigler, Charles "Cy" 1906-22, 1924-35
Riley, William J. "Billy" 1880
Rippley, T. Steven "Steve" 1983-2000
Robb, Douglas W. "Scotty" 1948-52
Roberts, Leonard W. "Lenny" 1953-55
Rudderham, John E. 1908
Runge, Brian 1999-2000
Runge, Paul E. 1973-97
Ryan, Walter 1946
Schrieber, Paul W.1997-2000
Scott, James "Jim" 1930-31
Sears, John W. "Ziggy" 1934-45

Secory, Frank E. 1952-70
Sentelle, Leopold T. "Paul" 1922-23
Seward, Edward W. "Ed" 1893
Seward, George E. 1876, 1878
Sheridan, John F. "Jack" 1892, 1896-97
Smith, Charles M. "Pop" 1881
Smith, Vincent A. "Vinnie" 1957-65
Smith, William W. "Billy" 1898-99
Snyder, Charles N. "Pop" 1892-93, 1898-1901
Stage, Charles W. "Billy" 1894
Stambaugh, Calvin G. 1877-78
Stark, Albert D. "Dolly" 1928-35, 1937-40, 1942
Steiner, Melvin J. "Mel" 1961-72
Steinfeldt, Harry M. 1905
Stello, Richard J. "Dick" 1969-87
Sternburg, Paul 1909
Stewart, William J. "Bill" 1933-54
Stockdale, M. J. 1915
Strief, George A. -1889, 1890
Sudol, Edward L. "Ed" 1957-77
Sullivan, David F. "Dave" 1882, 1885
Sullivan, Jeremiah "Jerry" 1887
Sullivan, T. P. 1880
Summer, James G. 1877
Swartwood, C. Edward "Ed" 1894, 1898-1900
Sweeney, James M. "Jim" 1924-26
Tata, Terry A. 1973-99
Terry, William H. "Adonis" 1900
Tilden, Otis 1880
Tremblay, Richard H. "Dick" 1971
Truby, Harry G. 1909
Valentine, John G. 1887-88
Van Court, Eugene 1884
Vanover, Larry W. 1991, 1993-99
Vargo, Edward P. "Ed" 1960-83
Venzon, Anthony "Tony" 1957-71
Walker, William E. 1876-77
Walsh, Francis D. "Frank" 1961-63
Walsh, Michael F. "Mike" 1876, 1878, 1880
Warneke, Lonnie "Lon" 1949-55
Warner, Albert "Al" 1898-1900
Wegner, Mark P. 1998-2000
Wendelstedt, Harry H. Sr. 1966-98
Wendelstedt, H. Hunter Jr. 1998-2000
West, Joseph H. "Joe" 1976, 1978-99
Westervelt, Frederick E. 1922-23
Weyer, Lee H. 1961, 1963-88
White, Gideon F. 1878
Wickham, Daniel "Dan" 1990-92
Wiedman, George E. "Stump" 1896
Wilbur, Charles E. 1879
Williams, Arthur "Art" 1972-77
Williams, Charles H. "Charlie" 1978, 1983-2000
Williams, William G. "Bill" 1963-87
Wilson, Frank 1922-28
Wilson, John A. 1887
Winters, Michael J. "Mike" 1988-2000
Wise, Samuel W. "Sam" 1889
Wood, George A. 1898
York, Thomas J. "Tom" 1886
Young, Joseph 1879
Zacharias, Thomas 1890
Zimmer, Charles L. "Chief" 1904

American Association (1882-91)

Barnum, George W. 1890
Bauers, Albert J. "Al" 1887
Becannon, William H. 1883
Bradley, George H. "Foghorn" 1886
Brennan, John E. "Jack" 1884
Butler, Ormond H. 1883
Carey, Thomas J. "Tom" 1882
Clinton, James L. "Jim" 1886
Connell, Terence G. 1884, 1890
Connelly, John M. 1885, 1887
Connelly, William 1884
Curry, Wesley "Wes" 1887, 1890
Cuthbert, Edgar E. "Ned" 1887
Dailey, John J. 1884
Daniels, Charles F. 1883-85, 1889
Davis, James J. "Jumbo" 1891
Devinney, P. H. "Dan" 1884
Doscher, John H. Sr. "Herm" 1888, 1890
Dyler, John F. 1884
Emslie, Robert D. "Bob" 1890
Ferguson, Robert V. "Bob" 1886-89, 1891
Gaffney, John H. 1888-89
Gleason, William G. "Bill" 1891
Goldsmith, Frederick E. "Fred" 1888-89
Griffith, E. A. 1884
Hautz, Charles A. "Charlie" 1882
Hecker, Guy J. 1889
Holland, John A. 1884
Holland, Willard A. 1889
Hurley, Daniel "Dan" 1887
Jennings, Alfred J. "Al" 1887
Jones, Charles W. "Charley" 1891
Kelly, John O. "Kick" 1883-86
Kerins, John A. "Jack" 1889-91
Knight, Alonzo P. "Lon" 1887
Lawler, John F. 1884
Mack, Dennis J. "Denny" 1886
Macullar, James F. "Jimmy" 1891
Magner, John T. 1883
Mahoney, Michael J. 1891
Mathews, Robert T. "Bobby" 1891
McLaughlin, Thomas 1891
McLean, William H. "Billy" 1885
McNichol, Robert T. 1883
McQuaid, John H. "Jack" 1886-88
Morton, Charles H. "Charlie" 1886
O'Brien, Frank 1890
Peoples, James E. "Jimmy" 1890
Pike, Lipman E. "Lip" 1889
Pratt, Albert G. "Al" 1883
Quinn, A. J. 1886
Riley, William J. "Billy" 1882
Ross, Robert T. 1882
Seward, George E. 1884
Simmons, Joseph S. "Joe" 1882
Smith, Charles M. "Pop"1882
Snyder, Charles N. "Pop" 1891
Sommer, Benjamin F. 1883
Sullivan, Jeremiah "Jerry" 1887
Sullivan, Timothy P. "Ted" 1887
Taylor, Walter 1890
Toole, Stephen J. "Steve" 1890
Tunison, William 1885-86
Valentine, John G. 1884-87
Walsh, Michael F. "Mike" 1882-83, 1885-86
York, Thomas J. "Tom" 1886
Young, Benjamin F. "Ben" 1886

Union Association (1884)

Crawford, Alexander 1884
Devinney, P. H. "Dan" 1884
Dutton, Patrick J. 1884
Hengle, Emery J. "Moxie" 1884
Holland, John A. 1884
Hooper, Michael H. 1884
Jennings, Alfred "Al" 1884
Jordan, William H. "Bill" 1884
Mapledoram, Blake A. 1884
McCaffrey, Harry C. 1884
Seward, George E. 1884
Stearns, D. Eckford "Ecky" 1884
Sullivan, David F. "Dave" 1884

Players League (1890)

Barnes, Roscoe C. "Ross" 1890
Ferguson, Robert V. "Bob" 1890
Gaffney, John H. 1890
Gunning, Thomas F. "Tom" 1890
Holbert, William H. "Bill" 1890
Jones, Charles W. "Charley" 1890
Knight, Alonzo P. "Lon" 1890
Leach, Henry 1890
Mathews, Robert T. "Bobby" 1890
Pierce, Grayson S. "Gracie" 1890
Sheridan, John F. "Jack" 1890
Snyder, Charles N. "Pop" 1890

American League (1901-)

Adams, John H. 1903
Anthony, G. Merlyn 1969-75
Ashford, Emmett L. 1966-70
Avants, Nick R. 1969-71
Barnett, Lawrence R. "Larry" 1968-99
Barrett, Ted 1994-2000
Barry, Daniel "Dan" 1928
Basil, Stephen J. "Steve" 1936-42
Bean, Ed 1994
Berry, Charles F. "Charlie" 1942-62
Betts, William G. 1901
Boyer, James M. "Jim" 1944-50
Bremigan, Nicholas G. "Nick" 1974-88
Brinkman, Joseph N. "Joe" 1973-2000
Campbell, William M. "Bick" 1928-31
Cantillon, Joseph D. "Joe" 1901
Carrigan, H. Sam 1961-65
Carpenter, William B. "Bill" 1904
Caruthers, Robert L. "Bob" 1902-03
Cederstrom, Gary L. 1989-2000
Chill, Oliver P. "Ollie" 1914-16, 1919-22
Chylak, Nestor L. 1954-78
Clark, Alan M. "Al" 1976-2000
Coble, G. Drew 1983-99
Colliflower, J. Harry 1910
Connolly, Thomas H. "Tommy" 1901-31
Connor, Thomas "Tom" 1905-06
Cooney, Terrance J. "Terry" 1975-92
Cooper, Erik R. 1996-2000
Cousins, Derryl 1979-2000
Craft, Terry 1989-2000
Culbreth, Fieldin "Field" 1993-2000
Deegan, William E. J. "Bill" 1970-80
Denkinger, Donald A. "Don" 1968-98
Diaz, Lazaro "Laz" 1995, 1997-2000
DiMuro, Louis J. "Lou" 1963-80
DiMuro, Michael "Mike" 1997, 1999-2000
DiMuro, Raymond "Ray" 1996-99
Dinneen, William H. "Bill" 1909-37
Donnelly, Charles H. 1934-35
Doyle, Walter J. 1963
Drummond, Calvin T. "Cal" 1960-69
Duffy, James F. "Jim" 1951-55
Dwyer, J. Francis "Frank" 1904
Eddings, Douglas "Doug" 1998-2000
Egan, John J. "Rip" 1903, 1907-14
Eldridge, Clarence E. 1914-15
Evans, James B. "Jim" 1971-99
Evans, William G. "Billy" 1906-27
Everitt, Michael "Mike" 1996-2000
Ferguson, Charles A. 1913
Fichter, Michael 1999-2000
Flaherty, John F. "Red" 1953-73
Ford, R. Dale 1975-99
Foster, Martin "Marty" 1996-2000
Frantz, Arthur F. "Art" 1969-77
Friel, William E. "Bill" 1920
Froese, Grover A. 1952-53
Garcia, Richard P. "Rich" 1975-99
Geisel, Harry C. 1925-42
Goetz, Russell L. "Russ" 1968-83
Grieve, William T. "Bill" 1938-55
Guthrie, William J. "Bill" 1922, 1928-32
Haller, William E. "Bill" 1961, 1963-82
Hart, Robert F. "Bertie" 1912-13
Hart, William F. "Bill" 1901
Haskell, John E. 1901
Hassett, James E. 1903
Hayes, Gerald 1925-26
Hendry, Eugene "Ted" 1978-99
Henrichs, Jeff 1993
Hickox, Edwin W. "Ed" 1990-99
Hildebrand, George A. 1913-34
Hirschbeck, John F. 1984-2000
Holbrook, Samuel "Sam" 1996
Holmes, Howard E. "Ducky" 1923-24
Honochick, G. James "Jim" 1949-73
Hubbard, R. Cal 1936-51
Hurley, Edwin H. "Eddie" 1947-65
Hurst, Timothy C. "Tim" 1905-09
Iassogna, Dan 1999
Johnson, Mark S. 1980-99
Johnston, Charles E. 1936-37
Johnstone, James E. "Jim" 1902
Jones, Nicholas I. "Red" 1944-49
Joyce, James A. "Jim" 1989-2000
Kaiser, Kenneth J. "Ken" 1977-99
Katzenmeier, Travis 1999-2000
Kelly, Thomas B. 1905
Kerin, John 1909-10
King, Charles F. 1904
Kinnamon, William E. "Bill" 1960-69
Kolls, Louis C. "Lou" 1933-40
Kosc, Gregory J. "Greg" 1976-99
Kunkel, William G. "Bill" 1968-84
Leppart, Thomas E. "Tom" 1984-86
Linsalata, Joseph N. "Joe" 1961-62
Luciano, Ronald M. "Ron" 1968-80
Maloney, George P. 1969-83
Manassau, Alfred S. "Al" 1901
Marberry, Frederick "Firpo" 1935
McCarthy, John "Jack" 1905
McClelland, Timothy R. "Tim" 1984-2000
McCormick, William J. "Barry" 1917
McCoy, Larry S. 1970-99
McGowan, William A. "Bill" 1925-54
McGreevy, Edward 1912-13
McKean, James G. "Jim" 1974-2000
McKinley, William F. "Bill" 1946-65
Meriwether, Julius E. "Chuck" 1988-2000
Merrill, E. Durwood 1977-99
Miller, William "Bill" 1997-2000
Morgenweck, Henry C. "Hank" 1972-75
Moriarty, George J. 1917-26, 1929-40
Morrison, Daniel G. "Dan" 1979-2000
Mullaney, Dominic J. 1915
Mullin, John 1911
Nallin, Richard F. "Dick" 1915-32
Napp, Larry A. 1951-74
Nelson, Jeff 1998
Neudecker, Jerome A. "Jerry" 1965-85
O'Brien, Joseph "Joe" 1912, 1914
Odom, James C. "Jim" 1965-74
O'Donnell, James M. "Jake" 1968-71
O'Loughlin, Francis H. "Silk" 1902-18
O'Nora, Brian 1992-2000
Ormsby, Emmett T. "Red" 1923-41
Owens, Clarence B. "Brick" 1916-37
Palermo, Stephen M. "Steve" 1977-91
Paparella, Joseph J. "Joe" 1946-65
Parker, Harley P. "Doc" 1911
Parks, Dallas F. 1979-83
Passarella, Arthur M. "Art" 1941-42, 1945-53
Perrine, Fred "Bull" 1909-12
Phillips, David R. "Dave"

1971-99
Pipgras, George W. 1938-46
Quinn, John A. 1935-42
Reed, Rick A. 1984-2000
Reilly, Michael E. "Mike" 1978-2000
Reynolds, James "Jim" 1999-2000
Rice, John L. 1955-73
Robb, Douglas W. "Scotty" 1952-53
Rodriguez, Armando H. 1974-75
Roe, John A. "Rocky" 1979-2000
Rommel, Edwin A. "Eddie" 1938-59
Rowland, Clarence H. "Pants" 1923-27
Rue, Joseph W. "Joe" 1938-47
Runge, Edward P. "Ed" 1954-70
Salerno, Alexander J. "Al" 1961-68
Schwarts, Harry C. 1960-62
Scott, Dale A. 1986-2000
Sheridan, John F. "Jack" 1901-14
Shulock, John R. 1979-2000
Smith, W. Alaric "Al" 1960-65
Soar, A. Henry "Hank" 1950-73
Spenn, Frederick C. "Fred" 1979-80
Springstead, Martin J. "Marty" 1965-86
Stafford, John H. 1907
Stevens, John W. "Johnny" 1948-71
Stewart, Ernest D. 1941-45
Stewart, Robert W. "Bob" 1959-70
Summers, William R. "Bill" 1933-59
Tabacchi, Frank T. 1956-59
Tschida, Timothy J. "Tim" 1986-2000
Umont, Frank W. 1954-73
Valentine, William T. "Bill" 1963-68
Van Graflan, Roy R. 1927-33
Voltaggio, Vito H. "Vic" 1977-96
Wallace, Roderick J. "Bobby" 1915
Walsh, Edward A. "Ed" 1922
Walton, Bennie 1996
Weafer, Harold L. "Hal" 1943-47
Welke, Timothy J. "Tim" 1985-2000
Welke, William "Bill" 1999-2000
Westervelt, Frederick E. 1911-12
Wilson, Frank 1921-22
Winans, Mathew "Matt" 1994
Young, Larry E. 1985-2000

Federal League (1914-15)

Anderson, Oliver O. "Ollie" 1914
Brennan, William T. "Bill" 1914-15
Bush, Garnet C. 1914
Corcoran, Thomas W. "Tommy" 1915
Cross, Montford M. "Monte" 1914
Cusack, Stephen P. 1914
Finneran, William F. 1915
Fyfe, Louis 1915
Goeckel, E. 1914
Howell, H. Harry 1915
Johnstone, James E. "Jim" 1915
Kane, Stephen J. 1914
Langden, Joseph 1915
Manassau, Alfred S. "Al" 1914
McCormick, William J. "Barry"1914-15
Mullin, John 1915
O'Brien, Joseph "Joe" 1915
Shannon, William P. "Spike" 1914-15
Stocksdale, Otis H. 1915
Van Sickle, Charles F. 1914
Westervelt, Frederick E. 1915
Wilhelm, Irving K. "Kaiser" 1915

Major League Baseball (2000-)

Barksdale, Lance 2000
Guccione, Chris 2000
Higgins, Scott 2000
Hollowell, Matthew "Matt" 2000
Klemm, Justin 2000
Packard, Scott 2000
Spieler, Patrick "Pat" 2000
Timmoms, Tim 2000
Van Vleet, Mike 2000
Wolf, James "Jim" 2000

SUBSTITUTE UMPIRES

National Association (1871-75)

Addy, Robert E. "Bob" 1875
Allison, Andrew K. "Andy" 1872, 1874
Allison, Arthur A. "Art" 1872
Allison, Douglas L. "Doug" 1872-73, 1875
Alston, David 1871-72, 1875
Annan, William H. 1873
Arnold, Willis S. "Billy" 1875
Avery, C. Hamilton 1874
Barlow, Thomas H. "Tom" 1875
Barnes, Roscoe C. "Ross" 1874
Barrett, William "Bill" 1872, 1874
Barron, James "Jim" 1875
Barrows, Franklin L. "Frank" 1872
Battin, Joseph V. "Joe" 1874
Beals, Thomas L. "Tommy" 1872, 1874-75
Beardslee, John J. 1872-73
Bechtel, George A. 1874
Beck, W. S. 1872
Berthrong, Henry W. "Harry" 1872
Bielaski, Oscar 1874-75
Bigelow, W. J. 1875
Birdsall, David S. "Dave" 1873-74
Blair, William J. 1873
Boake, John L. 1871
Bomeisler, Theodore 1874-75
Bond, Thomas H. "Tommy" 1875
Bonse, Nicholas 1871
Boyd, William J. "Bill"1873
Bradley, George H. "Foghorn" 1875
Brainard, Asa 1872, 1875
Briggs, Warren R. 1874
Brown, William 1872, 1875
Bruce, D. W. 1875
Buck, William F. 1871
Bunce, Frederick L. "Fred" 1874
Bunce, H. C. 1872
Bush, Archibald M. "Archie" 1871
Carey, Thomas J. "Tom" 1873, 1875
Carpenter, John R. 1874
Cassidy, John P. 1875
Cavanaugh, J. H. "Harry" 1875
Chandler, Moses E. 1872-1875
Chapman, John C. "Jack"1871, 1873-74
Clifton, — 1872
Clinton, James L. "Jim" 1873, 1875
Colby, — 1873
Collins, Daniel T. "Dan" 1875
Cone, J. Frederick "Fred" 1873-74
Cope, Elias 1871
Craver, William H. "Bill" 1873
Cuthbert, Edgar E. "Ned" 1875
Daubney, Thomas 1871
David, L. N. 1874
Dawson, Mort 1871
Deane, J. Henry "Harry" 1871, 1874
Dehlman, Herman J. 1873, 1875
Demorest, D. P. 1872-73
Dobson, H. A. 1871
Dornlach, D. E. 1872
Draper, John H. 1871
Ellis, William R. 1871-72, 1875
English, John W. 1874-75
Erby, Frederick 1872
Evans, George 1872
Fellows, T. E. 1871
Ferguson, Robert V. "Bob" 1871, 1874
Fisher, William C. "Cherokee" 1871, 1875
Foley, Thomas J. "Tom" 1874-75
Force, David W. "Davy" 1873
Fulmer, Charles J. "Chick" 1872, 1874-75
Garrigan, Charles 1873
Geer, William H. "Billy" 1874-75
Gerhardt, Joseph J. "Joe" 1875
Glenn, John W. 1874
Glover, Frank 1873
Goodwin, J. Cheever 1871-72
Gould, Charles H. "Charlie" 1874-75
Graham, J. S. 1871-72
Halback, A. C. N.1871, 1873-75
Hall, George W. 1873-75
Hall, James "Jim" 1872-73
Hall, N. Samuel 1873
Hanna, Dr. 1872
Hartenstein, Isaac 1875
Hastings, W. Scott 1871-74
Hatfield, John V. B. 1872-73
Hayhurst, E. Hicks 1875
Haynie, James L. 1871
Hegeman, William H. 1871
Helm, J. 1871-72
Higham, Richard "Dick" 1872-75
Hodes, Charles "Charlie" 1874
Hooper, Michael H. "Mike" 1872-74
Hosworth, — 1872-74
Hough, Pliny 1875
Howard, Charles 1872
Jennings, Alfred J. "Al" 1873
Johns, William R. 1873
Kahn, S. L. 1875
Keerl, George W. 1872
Kenney, John 1872
Kent, John 1875
Knight, George H. 1875
Kohler, Henry C. 1873
Lamb, Henry W. "Harry" 1875
Laughlin, Benjamin "Ben" 1873
Leonard, Andrew J. "Andy" 1872-73, 1875
Leonard, J. 1872
Leroy, Isaac 1871
Locke, Marshall 1873-74
Lovett, James D. 1871
Lowell, John A. 1872-73
Lush, M. R. 1873
MacDiarmed, Thomas 1872
Mack, Dennis J. "Denny" 1873-74
Malone, — 1875
Malone, Ferguson G. "Fergy" 1875
Martin, Alphonse C. "Phonney" 1871, 1873
Martin, Lewis G. 1871, 1873-74
Mathews, Robert T. "Bobby" 1871
Mawny, J. H. 1871
Maxwell, Cortez "Corty"1875
Mays, — 1871
McCrea, — 1872
McDonald, James F. 1872
McGeary, Michael H. 1872, 1875
McLean, Harry C. 1871, 1873
McLean, William H. "Billy" 1872-73
McMahon, William 1871
McMullin, John F. 1874
McVey, Calvin A. "Cal" 1871, 1873, 1875
Meacham, — 1875
Miller, Joseph W. "Joe" 1872-73
Mills, Charles "Charlie" 1871
Mincher, Edward J. "Ed" 1872, 1875
Mincher, William E. 1875
Mitchell, Franklin B. 1874-75
Murnane, Timothy H. "Tim" 1873-75
Nelson, John W. "Candy" 1872
Nichols, A. N. 1871
Norton, Frank P. 1872
O'Brien, P. 1875
Pabor, Charles H. "Charlie" 1875
Parks, William R. "Bill" 1875
Patterson, Daniel T. "Dan" 1872
Peak, Frank 1871
Pearson, S. W. 1872
Phelps, Cornelius C. "Neal" 1874
Pike, Jacob Emanuel "Jay" 1875
Porter, — 1874
Powers, W. 1872-73, 1875
Pratt, Thomas J. "Tom" 1871-73
Quinn, — 1875
Radcliff, John Y. 1873
Ramsay, R. 1875
Rastall, Joseph H. 1872
Reach, Albert J. 1872-75
Reed, Hugh 1871, 1873-74
Remsen, John J. "Jack" 1873-74
Robinson, A. Valentine "Val" 1872
Robinson, Miley 1873
Rockwell, Horace T. 1874
Rogers, George R. 1871-72
Ryan, John J. 1872, 1875
Sawyer, Dent 1871
Schafer, Harry C. 1875
Schrader, Louis 1875
Schuester, John A.1874-75
Scofield, John W. 1871
Sears, John K. 1873
Selman, Frank C. 1873
Sensenderfer, John P. J. "Count" 1872-73, 1875
Simmons, Joseph S. "Joe" 1871, 1873-74
Smith, Eb 1872
Smith, George 1872
Smith, Gustavus 1872
Snyder, Charles N. "Pop" 1875
Stahl, George 1875
Stanwood, — 1872-73
Stires, Garrett "Gat" 1875
Stophlet, J. 1871
Sutton, Ezra B. 1875
Swandell, J. Martin "Marty" 1871, 1874
Sweasy, Charles J. "Charlie" 1871, 1873-74
Tighe, Edward 1871
Treacey, Frederick S. "Fred" 1871, 1873, 1875
Tyler, Columbus T. 1871-73
Urell, M. E. 1873
Van Delft, Benjamin 1875
Voltz, Edward "Ed" 1871-72
Walk, Frank 1871
Wardell, — 1874
Waterman, Frederick A. "Fred" 1873
Weaver, Charles 1873
Weigel, William H.1873-74
White, Horatio S. 1873
White, W. Warren 1874
White, William H. "Will" 1875
Wiggins, — 1875
Wildey, John 1871
Willard, Gardner 1871
Wirth, Adam 1875
Wood, James L. "Jimmy" 1871
Worth, Herb 1872
Wright, W. Harrison "Harry" 1875
York, Thomas J. "Tom" 1874

National League (1876-)

Adams, James 1897
Allen, Hezekiah "Ham" 1876
Ayers, — 1876
Baker, Charles 1884
Barker, Alfred L. 1881
Barnie, William S. "Billy" 1882
Barnum, George W. 1896
Barton, — 1876
Battin, Joseph V. "Joe" 1895-96
Beard, Oliver P. "Ollie" 1894
Becannon, James M. "Buck" 1885
Behle, Frank 1895-96
Berger, Frederick 1886
Bigelow, — 1877
Bittman, Henry P. "Red" 1892, 1894-95, 1897
Blakiston, Robert J. "Bob" 1884
Blodgett, C. W. 1876
Bradley, George H. "Foghorn" 1877
Brady, — 1877
Bredburg, George W. 1878-79
Brennan, John E. "Jack" 1887
Brockway, John 1877, 1879
Bullymore, Charles L. 1882
Burke, — 1892
Burlingame, Frank A. 1878
Burnham, George W. 1886-87
Campbell, Al 1886
Campbell, Daniel "Dan" 1897
Carsey, Wilfred "Kid" 1901
Caruthers, Robert L. "Bob" 1886, 1893
Chandler, Moses E. 1877
Chapman, John C. "Jack" 1876, 1882
Cheppy, John T. 1876
Chipman, Harry F. 1886
Clack, Robert H. "Bobby" 1897
Cohen, George 1893
Colgan, Harry W. 1899
Collins, Daniel T. "Dan" 1876
Cone, J. F. "Fred" 1876
Connell, Terence G. 1885, 1887
Connolly, John M. 1885, 1887, 1892-93
Cook, W. H. 1879
Crandall, Robert 1876, 1878
Crane, Edward N. "Ed" 1893
Crane, Samuel N. "Sam" 1879, 1887
Cray, P. C. 1893
Cross, John A. 1876
Cudworth, Al 1880

Curren, Peter 1876
Cushman, Charles H. "Charley" 1894
Daniels, — 1885
Deane, J. Henry "Harry" 1876, 1878
Devinney, P. H. "Dan" 1876
Doscher, John H. Sr. "Herm" 1879
Draper, John H. 1877
Dunlap, Frederick C. "Fred" 1879
Dyler, John F. 1892, 1897
Eagan, John J. 1879
Earle, William M. "Billy" 1892
Eason, Malcolm W. "Mal" 1901
English, John W. 1876
Evans, Jacob "Jake" 1886
Fenno, Norman 1876
Finneran, William F. 1923
Fisher, William C. "Cherokee" 1876
Flaherty, — 1882
Flaherty, Patrick J. "Patsy" 07
Flynn, John A. "Jocko" 1893
Fouser, William C. 1876
Fulmer, Charles J. "Chick" 1881
Furlong, William E. "Bill" 1877, 1880, 1888
Gaffney, John H. 1887, 1898
Galvin, James F. "Jim" 1886
Ganzel, Charles W. "Charlie" 1901
Gifford, James H. 1881
Gillean, Thomas 1881
Gleason, John D. 1877
Gleason, William G. "Bill" 1877
Glenn, John W. 1880
Goldsmith, Frederick E. "Fred" 1886
Graves, Frank M. 1895
Griffiths, — 1884
Gross, Edward M. 1881
Guinney, Daniel 1882
Hardie, Louis W. "Lou" 1887
Hartley, John "Jack" 1894
Hastings, W. Scott 1877
Hatfield, John V. B. 1876
Hawes, William A. 1880-82
Hegeman, William H. 1881
Herrin, W. E. 1894
Heydler, John A. 1895-97
Hickey, James L. 1882
Hodges, A. D. 1877
Hogan, — 1897
Hogriever, George C. 1893
Hornung, M. Joseph "Joe" 1892
Howard, C. F. 1884
Hurll, George 1876
Hurst, Timothy C. "Tim" 1904
Jevne, Frederick "Fred" 1892, 1894
Jose, — 1889
Joyce, C. E. 1879
Kane, Stephen J. 1906
Keefe, Timothy J. "Tim" 1893
Keenan, James W. "Jim" 1893
Kelley, J. P. 1879
Kelley, W. W. 1877
Kelly, John O. 1884-85
Kennedy, — 1893
Kennedy, Michael J. "Doc" 1884
Kenney, John 1876
Kerins, John A. "Jack" 1888
Kipp, Eden 1881
Kling, William "Bill" 1892
Klusman, William F. "Billy" 1893
Knight, Alonzo P. "Lon" 1876, 1888
Lanigan, Charles 1908
Latham, W. Arlington "Arlie" 1900
Laughlin, —, 1876
Lawler, Michael H. 1882
Leary, — 1879
Libby, Stephen A. 1879
Long, William H. "Billy" 1893, 1897
Lynch, F. G. 1892
Lynch, Thomas J. "Tom" 1902
Maddox, Charles 1882
Maginnis, Jim 1910
Malone, Ferguson G. "Fergy" 1892
Maloney, James "Jim" 1893
Manning, James H. "Jim" 1893
Manning, John E. "Jack" 1881
Mapledoram, Blake A. 1886
Martin, Alphonse C. "Phonney" 1876
Mason, Charles E. "Charlie" 1876
Mathews, Robert T. "Bobby" 1876
Mayer, Ed 1893
McCaffrey, Harry 1885-86
McCrum, — 1892
McGee, — 1876
McGinty, — 1897
McGunnigle, Edward 1888
McKinney, — 1883
McLeod, — 1895
McMullen, John F. 1876
Meagher, John 1877
Mears, Charles W. 1894
Medart, William 1876-77
Megrue, Cliff 1876
Mills, Abraham G. 1877
Montague, — 1877
Morrill, John F. 1891, 1896
Morris, Edward 1895, 1897
Morris, John S. 1876
Muir, Thomas 1876
Mullane, Anthony J. "Tony" 1897
Mullen, Peter C. 1893
Murnane, Timothy H. "Tim" 1886
Murphy, Henry 1880
Murphy, Martin W. 1886
Murray, Jeremiah J. "Miah" 1894, 1900, 1905, 1910
Myers, Henry C. 1890
Nicol, Hugh N. 1894
O'Brien, William 1876
O'Day, Henry F. "Hank" 1896
Orr, David L. "Dave" 1891
Osborne, William 1876
Pfeffer, Nathaniel F. "Nate" 1897
Phelan, — 1896
Pierce, — 1893
Pierce, Grayson S. "Gracie" 1892
Pike, Lipman E. "Lip" 1890
Power, Charles B. 1893-95
Pratt, Albert G. "Al" 1880, 1887
Quincy, W. 1893
Quinn, Joseph C. "Joe" 1881
Quinn, P. J. 1876
Quinn, William H. "Billy" 1887, 1889
Redheffer, — 1895
Reid, William A. 1882
Reilly, Charles 1880
Remsen, John J. "Jack" 1880
Rhodes, Eugene A. 1887
Richards, J. E. 1880
Ritchie, F. 1876
Rocap, Adam 1876
Roll, — 1876
Rowe, John C. "Jack" 1881
Rudderham, Francis F. "Frank" 1907
Say, Louis I. "Lou" 1879
Schofield, J. W. 1879
Seward, Edward W. "Ed" 1892
Seward, George E. 1877
Shepard, W. L. 1879
Sheridan, John F. "Jack" 1893
Sick, — 1884
Simmons, Joseph S. "Joe" 1876
Skelly, — 1880
Skinner, S. A. 1886
Smith, — 1876
Sneeden, George W. 1895
Snodd, Carey 1877
Snyder, Charles N. "Pop" 1895
Sommers, Joseph A. "Joe" 1893
Stack, W. Edward "Eddie" 1934
Stafford, John H. "Jack" 1906
Stage, Charles W. "Billy" 1895
Stambaugh, Calvin G. 1879
Strief, George A. 1880
Sullivan, — 1889
Sullivan, David F. "Dave" 1883, 1887-88
Summer, James G. 1876, 1878
Supple, William N. 1906
Sutton, Ezra B. 1876
Sweasy, Charles J. "Charlie" 1879
Tilden, Otis 1876
Tindall, — 1890, 1896
Toole, Stephen J. "Steve" 1888
Tuthill, Benjamin "Ben" 1895
Twitchell, Lawrence G. "Larry" 1894
Wade, Ben F. 1879-80
Walker, William E. 1878
Walsh, Michael F. "Mike" 1879
Walters, —, 1892-93
Walton, G. W. 1876
Warren, L. B. 1876
Wash, Frank 1877
Weeden, —, 1889-90
West, — 1885
West, George 1878
West, Milton D. "Buck" 1890
White, Gideon F. 1876-77
White, W. Warren 1876
Williams, Elisha A. "Dale" 1876
Wilson, William G. "Bill" 1892-93
Witham, C. B. 1879
Wolf, William V. "Jimmy" 1893, 1895-97
Wood, George A. 1899
Wood, James B. "Jimmy" 1876
Wright, W. Harrison "Harry" 1885
Wycoff, — 1892

American Association (1882-91)

Arnold, Frank W. 1889
Austin, Ed 1890
Barnie, William S. "Billy" 1882, 1884, 1887, 1889
Battin, Joseph V. "Joe" 1882, 1886
Bauers, Albert J. "Al" 1890
Bell, Frank G. 1889
Bittman, Henry P. "Red" 1889
Blogg, Wesley C. "Wes" 1886
Bloom, Ed 1887
Bond, Thomas H. "Tommy"1891
Bowes, Frank M. 1890
Brown, J. 1887
Burdock, John J. "Jack"1887
Burkalow, Isaac 1888
Burns, — 1882
Butler, Charles 1889
Butler, Ormond H. 1886
Campbell, Daniel "Dan" 1890
Carlin, William J. "Billy" 1885-86, 1888-89
Connell, Terence G. 1885-86, 1889, 1891
Cornell, — 1884
Crandall, Robert 1882
Creighton, — 1889-90
Critchley, Morris A. "Morrie" 1884-85
Curry, Frank 1884, 1886
Cuthbert, Edgar E. "Ned" 1888
Dailey, John J. 1889
Daniels, Lawrence L. 1887
Devine, W. James "Jim" 1890
Devinney, P. H. "Dan" 1887
Devlin, Charles "Charlie" 1888
Dolan, Thomas J. "Tom" 1890-91
Dow, Clarence 1891
Dugan, — 1887
Duke, Martin F. 1890
Dunlevy, Hugh 1887
Dyler, John F. 1883, 1885-86
Ellick, Joseph J. "Joe" 1888-89
Ewing, William "Buck" 1882
Fell, — 1885
Fountain, Henry V. 1888
Galvin, James F. "Jim" 1885
Geer, William H. "Billy" 1887
Gill, Thomas H. "Tommy" 1886
Helburn, Hugo 1887
Henderson, J. Harding "Hardie" 1889
Hengle, Edward S. "Ed" 1889
Hicks, Nathaniel W. "Nat" 1885
Holliday, James W. "Bug" 1888
Irwin, — 1882
Irwin, Arthur A. 1885
Jennings, Alfred J. "Al" 1882, 1884-85, 1889, 1891
Julian, Joseph O. 1888
Kelly, John O. "Kick" 1887
Kelly, William 1884
Kleinbacker, — 1886
Levis, Charles H. "Charlie" 1882
Lilly, J. 1884
Little, — 1884
Loughlin, — 1885
Loughlin, William H. 1882
Lyons, Thomas A. "Toby" 1891
Lyston, William E. 1890
Magner, John T. 1882, 1884, 1887
Malone, J. R. 1888
Marshall, — 1887
Mathews, Robert T. "Bobby" 1888
McCartney, Joseph 1882
McCormick, — 1888
McGee, Patrick 1882, 1884
McGinnis, George W. "Jumbo" 1888-89
McIntosh, — 1882
McLaughlin, William 1882
McLean, William H. "Billy" 1882, 1889-90
McSorley, John B. "Trick" 1888
Medart, William 1887
Miller, Charles A. 1884
Mitchell, — 1887
Morgan, H. William "Bill" 1884
Morton, Charles H. "Charlie" 1884
Mullen, Peter C. 1891
Norton, Lee 1890
O'Dea, Lawrence 1890
Paasch, William 1887-89
Parker, H. 1887
Phillips, Horace B. 1882
Pierce, Grayson S. "Gracie" 1884
Pike, Lipman E. "Lip" 1887
Pratt, Albert G. "Al" 1886
Quinn, William H. "Billy" 1884-85
Ramsey, Dick 1887
Reeder, James E. "Icicle" 1884
Reising, Charles 1882
Rice, — 1885
Riley, William J. "Billy" 1885
Robb, John 1886
Ross, Robert T. 1884
Ruhl, Gus 1882
Ryan, John 1882
Selman, Frank C. 1882
Sherman, Sharon L. "Shang" 1890
Shraeder, Louis 1890
Simpson, Lew 1882
Skerritt, Jim 1890
Skinner, — 1884, 1886
Smith, George 1887
Sneed, Jonathon L.1885
Sullivan, David F. "Dave" 1884
Talbot, John 1887
Tinney, — 1882
Walsh, Michael F. "Mike" 1887-88
West, Edward 1885, 1887
Wood, George A. 1886
Wright, — 1884
Young, Benjamin F. "Ben" 1887
Young, Joseph 1890

Union Association (1884)

Adler, — 1884
Burlingame, Frank A. 1884
Donovan, Timothy H. 1884
Furlong, William E. "Bill" 1884
Hudson, Vincent D. 1884
Lee, Thomas F. 1884
McGunningle, William H. "Bill" 1884
McManaway, D. 1884
McMinimum, Dennis 1884
Montgomery, — 1884
Power, Charles B. 1884
Timblin, — 1884
Torry, — 1884

Players' League (1890)

Caskin, Edward J. "Ed" 1890

American League (1901-)

Betts, William G. 1903
Bierhalter, "Bits" 1918, 1922, 1924
Brown, Thomas T. "Tom" 1907
Carney, "Red" 1924
Connolly, Thomas H. "Tommy" 1932
Donlin, Michael J. "Mike" 1918
Howley, Daniel P. "Dan" 1922
Kennedy, Michael J. "Doc" 1910
Kerin, John 1908
Kerins, John A. "Jack" 1903
Mace, Harry L. 1903
Monahan, Pat 1931
Nallin, Richard F. "Dick" 1933
Pears, Frank H. 1903
Quigley, Ernest C. "Ernie" 1906
Soar, A. Henry "Hank" 1975
Stevens, John W. "Johnny" 1975
Terry, William H. "Adonis" 1901

Federal League (1914-15)

Murphy, J. A. 1914
Quisser, Arthur 1914

UMPIRES DURING STRIKES

National League (1876-)

Anderson, Lewis E. "Andy" 1978-79
Andress, William J. "Bill" 1979
Baird, John 1979
Ballina, Frank 1991, 1995

Barston, Michael "Mike" 1979
Baswell, Jack S. 1979
Beck, Robert "Bob" 1979
Bendekovits, Joseph "Joe" 1979
Betcher, Ralph A. 1976
Blandford, Fred 1970
Bovey, Terry R. 1979, 1984, 1995
Bruns, Randy 1991
Campagna, Frank J.1979, 1984
Cavenaugh, Richard P. "Dick" 1979, 1984
Cohen, Alfred A. "Al" 1976
Costello, Perry 1995
Cote, Emilien 1979
Cuneo, James "Jim" 1978-79
Davidson, — 1995
Davis, Bill 1995
Deniston, Shannon W. "Shan" 1978
Dierking, Roger A. 1978
Edwards, Larry 1978
Fick, Jerry D. 1978-79
Fisher, Frank 1979, 1984
Fleming, Thomas E. "Tom" 1979
Floras, John 1991
Ford, Wade 1995
Fowler, A. Wheeler 1978
Freels, Robert L. "Bob" 1979
Garman, Jim 1995
Gisondi, Tony 1991
Graham, Scott 1991, 1995
Grimsley, John 1970
Grinder, Scott 1976
Grooms, Roger C. 1979
Grygiel, George R. 1970
Guckert, Elmer 1976
Hadry, Merrill A. 1979
Hamil, Ray 1979
Hansen, Howard 1978-79
Hantak, H. Robert "Bob" 1979
Harris, Vance 1995
Henry, William E. "Bill" 1979
Hernandez, Bob 1995
Holoka, Mike 1991, 1995
Homolka, Bob 1995
Humphrey, Rich 1995
Hutson, Ronald "Ron" 1979
Jackson, Dick 1995
January, Don1991, 1995
Jeffers, Ronald L. "Ron" 1979
Jenkins, Jeff 1995
Jones, Bob 1995
Jones, James "Jim" 1979
Jumper, Howard 1979
Lambeth, Jim 1995
Lauzon, Jacques 1979
Lawson, William R. "Bill" 1979
Loeber, Gerald G. "Jerry" 1979
Lospitalier, Philip A. "Phil" 1979
Lupo, Charles "Charlie" 1978-79
Maher, Robert J. "Bob" 1979, 1984
Martine, Bruce 1991
Mauer, Boyd 1978-79
Melton, David "Dave" 1978
Miller, Marvin G. "Bud" 1979
Mills, Greg 1979
Morgenweck, Henry C. "Hank" 1970
Mrvos, Joseph S. "Joe" 1979
Myers, Joseph "Joe" 1979
Negri, Peter "Pete" 1979
Nelson, Robert "Bob" 1979, 1991, 1995
Norris, Edward E. "Ed" 1978-79
Oliger, Edward C. "Ed" 1979
Pacheco, Jim 1995
Padilla, Joe 1995
Patch, Tony D. 1978-79
Perez, J. Ray 1979
Pomponi, Joseph L. "Joe" 1979, 1984
Rains, James "Jim" 1978-79
Randall, Larry 1995
Riccio, Dennis R. 1979
Riccio, L. Leonard "Len" 1979
Riggers, Mike 1995
Rodriguez, Gus 1995
Rosenberry, Bill 1995
Roth, Roy 1978-79
Rountree, Henry J. "Hank" 1978-79
Ryberg, Sy 1995
Schaff, Fred 1995
Schaller, Cliff 1978-79
Schleyer, John 1979
Schratz, Joseph "Joe" 1979
Schroeder, Robert L. "Bobby" 1978-79
Scott, James "Jim" 1978-79
Sharkey, Michael E. "Mick" 1978-79
Sharp, Robert C. "Bob" 1979
Siroka, Harold L. 1979
Slattery, Donald L. "Don" 1979
Slickenmeyer, David W. "Dave" 1979, 1984
Smail, Harry F. 1979
Spange, John 1991
Spinelli, Michel 1979
Stansell, B. Jack 1979
Stewart, John 1979, 1984
Strey, Murray W. 1978-79
Sylvester, Frank 1995
Telford, Thomas "Tom" 1979
Tillman, Henry T. "Hank" 1978-79
Treitel, Leslie J. "Les" 1978-79
Tremblay, Richard H. "Dick" 1979
Urlage, Richard C. "Dick" 1979, 1991
Waller, James "Jim" 1979
Whaley, Bart 1995
Widlowski, Mark 1995
Williams, Dale 1978-79
Willman, Bob 1991, 1995
Yeast, Dave 1995

American League (1901-)

Arata, Mark 1991
Berry, Charles F. "Charlie" 1970
Bialorucko, Larry 1995
Bible, Jonathan D. "Jon" 1984
Bishop, Homer L. 1979
Bohn, Matt 1995
Borga, Steven A. "Steve" 1979
Briscese, Michael L. "Mike" 1979
Brown, Buddy Lee "Bud" 1979
Brown, Douglas D. "Doug" 1979
Brown, Jeff 1978-79
Camp, John W. 1979
Campbell, Robert "Bob" 1979
Caraco, Joe 1995
Clegg, Richard "Dick" 1979
Clement, Robert F. "Bob" 1978-79
Compton, Craig 1995
Contant, Alan 1978-79
Cossey, Douglas C. "Doug" 1978-79, 1984
Cuneo, James "Jim" 1979
Cristal, W. Randle "Randy" 1984
Davidson, Dale F. 1979
Deegan, William E. J. "Bill" 1970, 1984, 1991, 1995
DeFlesco, Pete 1991
Denny, Richard 1984
Dreke, Roy 1979
Dresser, Al 1995
Driscoll, Joseph M. "Joe" 1978
Duncan, Robert 1995
Dunne, James "Jim" 1978-79
Easley, Harold L. 1979
Eshelman, George R. 1979
Evans, Jeff 1991
Farmer, Michael "Mike" 1979
Farnsworth, Harry 1979
Feaser, Richard L. "Dick" 1979
Fitzpatrick, Michael N. "Mike" 1979
Follmer, William A. "Bill" 1979
Forman, Allen S. "Al" 1978-79
Freese, Todd 1995
Fuchs, Lester 1978-79
Gallagher, Lawrence E. "Larry" 1979
George, Edward "Ed" 1979
Giard, Robert "Bob" 1978
Gustafson, G. David "Dave" 1978
Hafner, William F. "Bill" 1979
Hadry, Merrill A. 1979
Harris, Vance 1995
Harvey, Randy 1991, 1995
Heitzer, Richard "Dick" 1979
Henrichs, Jeff 1995
Henry, William E. "Bill" 1979
Higgins, John 1991, 1995
Huber, Mike 1995
Ivory, William J. "Bill" 1979
Jackson, Charles L. 1979
James, John F. "Johnny" 1978-79
Jones, Robert G. "Bob" 1979, 1984
Jordan, Harold E. 1984
Kaplan, Al 1995
Kavulich, Joseph "Joe" 1978-79
Keister, R. Wayne 1978-79
Kelly, Eugene C. "Gene" 1979
Kimball, Shawn 1991
Kirby, Kenneth "Ken" 1979
Klein, Gus 1991, 1995
Knauss, Jim 1991
LaPierre, Richard 1979
Laude, William F. "Bill" 1978-79
Lazar, Richard R. "Richie" 1978-79
Levet, Jay 1979
Loeber, Gerald G. "Jerry" 1979
Lospitalier, Philip A. "Phil" 1979
Luker, Dale 1995
Lupo, Charles "Charlie" 1979
Mabbot, Frederick J. "Fred" 1979
Mackin, John F. 1979
Mann, Terry 1995
Marino, James H. "Jimmy" 1979
Mason, Danny 1995
Mauer, Boyd 1979
McDougall, Scott 1991
McNally, James "Jim" 1979
Merritt, Clarence 1979
Miller, Gale 1979
Miller, John A. "Jack" 1979
Moyer, Robert "Bob" 1979
Mulcahy, James "Jim" 1979
Murray, Ed 1991
Nelson, Richard "Dick" 1979
Nothhnagel, Carl L. 1984
Novack, Lester A. "Les" 1979
O'Brien, James D. "Jim" 1979
O'Connor, James "Jim" 1978-79
O'Connor, Thomas M. "Tom" 1979
O'Dell, Mikel R. "Mike" 1984
Panas, Richard J. "Rich" 1978-79
Parks, Dallas F. 1991, 1995
Patch, Tony D. 1979
Paylor, Jim 1995
Perez, David A. "Dave" 1979
Phipps, George H. "Jerry" 1978-79
Pilato, Mike 1995
Pratt, Lester 1979
Purduski, Al J. 1979
Ravan, Bruce 1995
Ravashiere, Thomas "Tom" 1979
Riccio, L. Leonard "Len" 1979
Rice, Robert W. "Bob" 1979
Robinson, William N. "Bill" 1978-79
Roesner, Robert A. "Bob" 1978-79
Roth, Roy 1979
Rountree, Henry J. "Hank" 1991
Runchey, Richard D. "Dick" 1979, 1984
Satchell, Darold L. 1970
Sawchuk, Joseph W. "Joe" 1978-79
Schaly, Jim 1995
Scheel, Alfred M. "Al" 1979
Schirmer, Donald A. "Don" 1979
Schulte, Donald E. "Don" 1979
Schwarz, Henry "Hank" 1995
Shaw, A. Duane 1979
Shewmake, James B. "Jim" 1978
Siroka, Harold L. 1979
Slattery, Donald L. "Don" 1979
Slickenmeyer, David W. "Dave" 1979, 1991, 1995
Spenn, Frederick C. "Fred" 1991
Sprincz, William "Bill" 1978-79
Stevens, John W. "Johnny" 1970
Sweeney, George P. 1979
Swenson, Charles H. 1979
Taylor, Joe Bob 1979
Terlop, Russell F. "Russ" 1979
Theilander, Theodore "Ted" 1979
Thompson, Michael G. "Mike" 1978-79
Tillman, Henry T. "Hank" 1979
Travis, Vic 1995
Trimmer, Harry 1979
Turner, Leo I. 1978
Ulrich, George 1995
Urchak, Woody J. 1978-79
Uremovich, Jim 1991, 1995
Walding, Larry 1995
Williams, Dale 1979
Wright, Marvin 1995
Zirbel, Lawrence A. "Larry" 1979, 1984
Zivic, Richard J. "Dick" 1984
Zuccaro, Amerigo J. "Rico" 1978-79

ACTIVE PLAYERS WHO UMPIRED

National League (1876-)

Abbey, Charles S. "Charlie" 1897
Abbott, Frederick H. "Fred" 1905
Andrews, G. Edward "Ed" 1889
Arundel, John T. "Tug" 1888
Baker, Philip "Phil" 1889
Baldwin, Marcus E. "Mark" 1892
Bannon, James H. "Jimmy" 1894
Beatin, Ebenezer "Ed" 1889
Beck, Erwin T. "Erve" 1902
Beckley, Jacob P. "Jake" 1906
Beebe, Fred L. 1907
Berger, John H. "Tun" 1891
Bonner, Frank J. 1894
Boyle, Henry J. 1886
Boyle, John A. "Jack" 1892, 1897
Breitenstein, Theodore P. "Ted" 1900
Briody, Charles F. "Fatty" 1881
Brown, Samuel W. "Sam" 1907
Brown, Thomas T. "Tom" 1896
Buelow, Charles J. "Charlie" 1901
Buffinton, Charles G. "Charlie" 1883, 1888-89, 1892
Burdock, John J. "Jack" 1881
Burns, Thomas P. "Oyster" 1895
Bushong, Albert J. "Doc" 1880, 1890
Butler, Richard H. "Dick" 1897
Carrick, William M. "Bill" 1900
Carroll, Frederick H. "Fred" 1887
Carsey, Wilfred "Kid" 1894, 1896
Caruthers, Robert L. "Bob" 1891
Casey, Daniel M. "Dan" 1888
Caskin, Edward J. "Ed" 1884
Cassidy, John P. 1882
Chamberlain, Elton P. 1894
Chance, Frank L. 1902
Clack, Robert H. "Bobby" 1876
Clarke, Arthur F. "Artie" 1890
Clarke, William J. "Boileryard" 1893-94, 1896
Clarkson, Arthur H. "Dad" 1893-96
Clarkson, John G. 1888, 1892-93
Clements, John J. "Jack" 1892
Coleman, John F. 1884
Coogan, Daniel G. "Dan" 1895
Cooney, John W. "Johnny" 1941
Crane, Edward N. "Ed" 1892
Crane, Samuel N. "Sam" 1886, 1890
Crolius, Frederick J. "Fred" 1901
Cronin, John J. "Jack" 1902-03
Cross, Lafayette N. "Lave" 1892
Culler, Richard B. "Dick" 1947
Cunningham, Elmer E. "Bert" 1896-97, 1900
Cuppy, George M. 1894
Cusick, Andrew D. "Tony" 1886-87
Daily, Cornelius F. "Con" 1891, 1894, 1896
Daly, Thomas P. "Tom" 1901
Darling, Conrad "Dell" 1887
Dealy, Patrick E. "Pat" 1886
Dexter, Charles D. "Charlie" 1896-97
Donahue, Francis R. "Red" 1897
Donahue, Timothy C. "Tim" 1895-96
Donlin, Michael J. "Mike" 1900
Donnelly, James B. "Jim" 1896
Donovan, William E. "Bill" 1902
Dooin, Charles S. "Red" 1904
Douglass, William B.

"Klondike" 1903
Dowse, Thomas J. "Tom" 1890
Duggleby, William J. "Bill" 1905
Dwyer, J. Francis "Frank" 1889, 1893-94, 1896-97
Earle, William M. "Billy" 1894
Ehret, Philip S. "Phil" 1892, 1895-97
Farrell, Charles A. "Duke" 1901-02
Ferguson, Charles J. "Charlie" 1886
Fitzsimmons, Frederick "Freddie" 1941
Flaherty, Patrick J. "Patsy" 1904
Force, David W. "Davy" 1881
Foreman, Francis I. "Frank" 1895
Foreman, John D. "Brownie" 1896
Foster, Clarence F. "Pop" 1900
Fouser, William C. 1876
Freeman, John F. "Buck" 1900
Galvin, James F. "Jim" 1881, 1887, 1889
Gardner, James A. "Jim" 1899
George, William M. "Bill" 1889
German, Lester S. "Les" 1895
Getzien, Charles H. "Charlie" 1890
Gleason, William J. "Kid" 1890, 1892
Grady, Michael W. "Mike" 1895
Graves, Frank M. 1886
Griffith, Clark C. 1894-95
Grim, John H. 1892, 1895-96
Gruber, Henry J. 1889
Gumbert, Addison C. "Ad" 1892, 1895-96
Gunning, Thomas F. "Tom" 1884-85
Gunson, Joseph B. "Joe" 1892
Hackett, Mortimer M. "Mert" 1886
Haddock, George S. 1889
Hallman, William W. "Bill" 1903
Hanlon, Edward H. "Ned" 1892
Hart, William F. "Bill" 1896-97
Hatfield, Gilbert "Gil" 1889
Healy, John J. 1887
Hemming, George E. 1895-96
Hines, Michael P. "Mike" 1884
Hoffer, William L. "Bill" 1896
Holliday, James W. "Bug" 1897
Howe, John "Shorty" 1890
Hurst, Timothy C. "Tim" 1898
Hyatt, R. Hamilton "Ham" 1912
Irwin, Arthur A. 1881
Jacklitsch, Fred L. 1901
Jennings, Hugh A. "Hughie" 1893, 1900
Johnson, Sylvester "Syl" 1934
Jones, Henry M. 1890
Kahoe, Michael J. "Mike" 1905
Karger, Edwin "Ed" 1906
Keefe, Timothy J. "Tim" 1880-82, 1884-85, 1887, 1892
Keeler, William H. "Willie" 1910
Keenan, James W. "Jim" 1890
Kellum, Winford A. "Win" 1905
Kelly, Michael J. "King" 1892-93
Killen, Frank B. 1896-97
Kinslow, Thomas F. "Tom" 1892
Kitson, Frank R. 1902
Kittridge, Malachi J. 1890, 1899
Klein, Charles H. "Chuck" 1942
Kling, John G. "Johnny" 1901
Knell, Philip H. "Phil" 1895
Knowles, James "Jimmy" 1892
Krieg, William F. "Bill" 1887
Leever, Samuel W. "Sam" 1900, 1904
Lindaman, Vivian A. "Vive" 1907
Lundgren, Carl L. 1905-06
Maloney, William A. "Billy" 1902
Manning, James H. "Jim" 1886
Mathews, Robert T. "Bobby" 1882
Mathewson, Christopher "Christy" 1901, 1907
McAleer, James R. "Jim" 1893
McAllister, Lewis W. "Sport" 1899
McCarthy, Thomas F. M. "Tommy" 1896
McCauley, Allen A. "Al" 1890
McCauley, Patrick M. "Pat" 1896
McCormick, James "Jim" 1885
McFarland, Edward W. "Ed" 1896
McGarr, James B. "Chippy" 1895
McGinnity, Joseph J. "Joe" 1900
McGuire, James T. "Deacon" 1886-87, 1894, 1896-97, 1901
McKinnon, Alexander J. "Alex" 1886
Meekin, Jouette 1895-96
Menefee, John "Jock" 1903
Mercer, George B. "Win" 1896
Mertes, Samuel B. "Sam" 1905
Miller, George F. "Doggie" 1893, 1896
Miller, Joseph H. 1884
Miller, L. Otto 1934
Moran, Patrick J. "Pat" 1901
Mullane, Anthony J. "Tony" 1893
Mulvey, Joseph H. "Joe" 1895
Murphy, Morgan E. 1893, 1896, 1898
Murphy, William H. "Yale" 1895, 1897
Murray, Jeremiah J. "Miah" 1895
Myers, George D. 1886
Needham, Thomas J. "Tom" 1904, 1907
Newton, Eustace J. "Doc" 1902
Nichols, Charles A. "Kid" 1900-01
Nolan, Edward S. "The Only" 1881
Noonan, Peter J. "Pete" 1906-07
O'Brien, John F. "Darby" 1889
O'Connor, John J. "Jack" 1893, 1901
O'Day, Henry F. "Hank" 1888-89
O'Neill, Michael J. "Mike" 1904
Orth, Albert L. "Al" 1901
Overall, Orval 1905, 1910
Peitz, Henry C. "Heinie" 1901, 1906
Phelps, Edward J. "Ed" 1912
Phillippe, Charles L. "Deacon" 1903
Quinn, Joseph J. "Joe" 1889, 1894, 1896
Reilly, Charles T. "Charlie" 1892, 1894-95
Reitz, Henry P. "Heinie" 1895
Rhines, William P. "Billy" 1891, 1896
Richardson, A. Harding "Hardie" 1892
Richmond, J. Lee 1883
Robinson, Wilbert 1898
Ryan, James E. "Jimmy" 1892
Sanders, A. Bennett "Ben" 1889
Schmidt, Henry M. 1903
Schriver, William F. "Pop" 1901
Serad, William I. "Billy" 1884
Smith, A. Edgar 1883
Smith, Edgar E. 1890
Smith, George H. "Heinie" 1901
Smith, Harry T. 1903
Smith, William E. "Bill" 1886
Sommers, Joseph A. "Joe" 1889
Staley, Harry E. 1892, 1895
Stearns, D. Eckford "Ecky" 1881
Stein, Edward F. "Ed" 1890, 1894, 1896
Stivetts, John C. "Jack" 1894
Stocksdale, Otis H. 1895
Stricker, John A. "Cub" 1892
Stricklett, Elmer E. 1907
Sugden, Joseph "Joe" 1897
Sullivan, James E. "Jim" 1896
Sullivan, Martin C. "Marty" 1889
Sullivan, Michael J. "Mike" 1897
Sullivan, Thomas J. "Sleeper" 1881
Sutcliffe, Elmer E. "Sy" 1889, 1892
Tannehill, Jesse N. 1897, 1901-02
Tate, Edward C. "Pop" 1888
Taylor, John B. "Jack" 1899
Taylor, John W. "Jack" 1901, 1905
Tener, John K. 1889
Terry, William H. "Adonis" 1892, 1895-96
Tiernan, Michael J. "Mike" 1895
Vaughn, Harry F. "Farmer" 1892, 1899
Viau, Leon "Lee" 1891
Vickery, Thomas G. "Tom" 1890
Walker, Thomas W. "Tom" 1905
Wall, Joseph F. "Joe" 1901
Wallace, Roderick J. "Bobby" 1895
Walters, William H. "Bucky" 1942, 1947
Ward, John M. 1888
Warneke, Lonnie "Lon" 1940
Warner, John J. "Jack" 1896-97, 1901, 1903
Weaver, William B. "Farmer" 1893
Weimer, Jacob W. "Jake" 1905, 1907
Welch, Michael F. "Mickey" 1881-82, 1885-86, 1888
Weyhing, August "Gus" 1894, 1899-1900
Whistler, Lewis "Lew" 1891
White, Guy H. "Doc" 1901-02
White, James L. "Deacon" 1880
Whitney, James E. "Jim" 1884, 1886
Wilhelm, Irving K. "Kaiser" 1904-05
Williamson, Edward N. "Ned" 1878, 1880
Willis, Victor G. "Vic" 1903
Wilmot, Walter R. "Walt" 1897
Wilson, Frank A. "Zeke" 1896, 1899
Wilson, James "Jimmie" 1940
Wilson, Parke A. 1894-96, 1899
Wilson, William G. "Bill" 1890
Wood, George A. 1889
Wright, W. Harrison "Harry" 1876-77
Yeager, George J. 1901
Young, Denton T. "Cy" 1896
Young, Irving M. "Irv" 1905, 1907
Zimmer, Charles L. "Chief" 1889, 1901

American Association (1882-91)

Bakely, Edward E. "Jersey" 1888
Baldwin, Clarence G. "Kid" 1887
Becannon, James M. "Buck" 1884
Bond, Thomas H. "Tommy" 1884
Booth, Amos S. 1882
Boyle, John A. "Jack" 1888
Brennan, John G. "Jack" 1888
Briody, Charles F. "Fatty" 1888
Burns, Thomas P. "Oyster" 1888
Bushong, Albert J. "Doc" 1888-89
Carsey, Wilfred "Kid" 1891
Cassidy, John P. 1884
Chamberlain, Elton P. 1887, 1891
Cross, Lafayette N. "Lave" 1889
Crowell, William T. "Billy" 1888
Darling, Conrad "Dell" 1891
Donahue, James A. "Jim" 1888
Easton, John S. "Jack" 1891
Ehret, Philip S. "Phil" 1890
Ewing, John 1889
Fulmer, Charles J. "Chick" 1888
Fulmer, Christopher "Chris" 1887
Galvin, James F. "Jim" 1886
Ganzel, Charles W. "Charlie" 1886
Goldsby, Walton H. "Walt" 1888
Greenwood, William F. "Bill" 1884
Griffith, Clark C. 1891
Gunning, Thomas F. "Tom" 1888-89
Healy, John J. 1890
Hecker, Guy J. 1888
Herr, Edward J. "Ed" 1888
Higgins, William E. "Bill" 1890
Holbert, William H. "Bill" 1888
Johnston, Richard F. "Dick" 1884
Keefe, Timothy J. "Tim" 1884
Keenan, James W. "Jim" 1887-88
Kilroy, Matthew A. "Matt" 1887
Kirby, John F. 1888
Knell, Philip H. "Phil" 1891
Latham, George W. "Juice" 1884
Lynch, John H. "Jack" 1884
Macullar, James F. "Jimmy" 1886
Mattimore, Michael J. "Mike" 1888
Mays, Albert C. "Al" 1887
McCarthy, John A. 1889
McKelvy, Russell E. "Russ" 1882
McMahon, John J. "Sadie" 1890
McSorley, John B. "Trick" 1884
Merrill, Edward M. "Ed" 1884
Mountain, Frank H. 1884
Mullane, Anthony J. "Tony" 1888
Murphy, Joseph A. "Joe" 1887
O'Brien, William D. "Darby" 1887-88
O'Connor, John J. "Jack" 1889
O'Day, Henry F. "Hank" 1884
Peoples, James E. "Jimmy" 1888-89
Pierce, Grayson S. "Gracie" 1882
Sage, Harry 1890
Serad, William I. "Billy" 1888
Smith, Charles M. "Pop" 1886
Smith, Frederick C. "Fred" 1890
Smith, John F. "Phenomenal" 1887-88
Snyder, Charles N. "Pop" 1886
Sommer, Joseph J. "Joe" 1888
Sprague, Charles W. "Charlie" 1890
Stivetts, John C. "Jack" 1891
Sweeney, Charles J. "Charley" 1887
Sylvester, Louis J. "Lou" 1888
Terry, William H. "Adonis" 1884, 1888
Townsend, George H. 1890
Traffley, William F. "Bill" 1884
Vaughn, Harry F. "Farmer" 1891
Viau, Leon "Lee" 1888
Weyhing, August "Gus" 1891
Wheeler, Harry E. 1882
Wood, George A. 1891
Zimmer, Charles L. "Chief" 1888

Union Association (1884)

Bradley, George W. 1884
Callahan, Edward J. "Ed" 1884
Carroll, Patrick "Pat" 1884
Cuthbert, Edgar E. "Ned" 1884
Kelly, John F. 1884
McLaughlin, James "Jim" 1884
Oberbeck, Henry A. 1884
Wheeler, Harry E. 1884
Williams, Washington J. "Wash" 1884

Players League (1890)

Bakely, Edward E. "Ed" 1890
Carney, John J. 1890
Comiskey, Charles A. "Charlie" 1890
Daily, Cornelius F. "Con" 1890
Gumbert, Addison C. "Ad" 1890
Haddock, George S. 1890
Hallman, William W. "Bill" 1890
Keefe, Timothy J. "Tim" 1890
Kelly, Michael J. "King" 1890
Madden, Michael J. "Kid" 1890
Milligan, John "Jocko"

1890
O'Day, Henry F. "Hank" 1890
Tener, John K. 1890

American League (1901-)

Altrock, Nicholas "Nick" 1907
Bejma, Alojzy F. "Ollie" 1935
Bender, Charles A. "Chief" 1907
Bernhard, William H. "Bill" 1903, 1907
Beville, H. Monte 1903-04
Blankenship, Clifford D. "Cliff" 1907
Bluege, Oswald L. "Ossie" 1938
Buelow, Frederick W. "Fritz" 1906
Callahan, James J. "Nixey" 1901
Conlan, John B. "Jocko" 1935
Coughlin, William P. "Bill" 1904
Cronin, John J. "Jack" 1901
Davis, Harry H. 1903
Dinneen, William H. "Bill" 1907
Donahue, Francis R. "Red" 1903, 1906
Donovan, William E. "Bill" 1903, 1906
Drill, Lewis L. "Lew" 1903-04
Flaherty, Patrick J. "Patsy" 1903
Foreman, Francis I. "Frank" 1901
Grady, Michael W. "Mike" 1901
Griffith, Clark C. 1903
Harris, Joseph W. "Joe" 1906
Hartley, Grover A. 1935
Hickman, Charles T. "Charlie" 1907
Howell, H. Harry 1904, 1906-07
Kittridge, Malachi J. 1905-06
Leahy, Thomas J. "Tom" 1901
Leppert, Donald G. "Don" 1978
Lowe, Robert L. "Bobby" 1905
McAllister, Lewis W. "Sport" 1901-02
McGuire, James T. "Deacon" 1905
Moore, Earl A. 1903
Newsom, Louis N. "Bobo" 1938
O'Brien, Peter J. "Pete" 1907
Patten, Case L. 1903
Pelty, Barney 1906
Powers, Michael R. "Mike" 1902
Roth, Francis C. "Frank" 1923
Schmidt, Charles "Boss" 1907
Schreckengost, Ossee F. 1903
Siever, Edward T. "Ed" 1901
Warner, John J. "Jack" 1908
White, Guy H. "Doc" 1903
Winter, George L. 1903, 1905
Young, Denton T. "Cy" 1903
Zimmerman, Gerald R. "Jerry" 1978

Federal League (1914-15)

Groom, Robert "Bob" 1914
Maxwell, J. Albert "Bert" 1914

Owner and Executive Roster

Although Major League Baseball began in 1871 with the National Association, it is undeniable that with the founding of the National League in 1876 something dramatic occurred that altered forevermore the character of professional baseball: the division of the game into two classes, labor and management. The National Association of Professional Base Ball Players was an outgrowth of the amateur association of the same name, in which baseball clubs were formed as organizations devoted to social intercourse and fraternal competition. Amateur clubs were organized along the same lines as today's Elks or Odd Fellows, with elected officials and dues-paying members. As players of special skill were invited into these clubs, their dues might be forgiven or "emoluments" offered—no-show jobs or under-the-table payments.

The abuses of the amateur system of the mid-1860s led to the declaration by several clubs of their openly professional status; players would sometimes draw salaries and as often would share in gate receipts. By the end of the decade gambling and game-fixing were rife.

Despite the formation of the National Association, these evils continued largely unabated into the 1870s. A monopolization of talent, largely in Boston, rendered Western clubs uncompetitive, and spectator rowdyism spawned by gambling interest, and the open sale of hard liquor burdened the new league. Clubs were admitted into the NA for paltry fees and fulfilled their schedules halfheartedly. Some of the member clubs had active presidents who functioned much as owners later would; other clubs were "cooperative nines," managed by the players themselves; still others were hybrids, born of civic boosterism. By 1876 the odd amalgam of the NA, presided over by Brooklyn Atlantics star Bob Ferguson, was failing.

Thus in 1876 William Hulbert, president of the Chicago club, combined with seven other team representatives to form the National League, a circuit run entirely by owners. Since then, fan interest has focused on the players, of course, and to a lesser extent on the managers, coaches, and umpires. But it can be said with some justice that while the on-field personnel and personalities "are" the game, it is the club owners, presidents, and league officials who make the game possible and ensure its continuity.

The Owner and Executive Roster that follows represents a first attempt in a baseball encyclopedia to recognize these individuals. As we did with the Coach Roster in the first edition of *Total Baseball*, we offered this section in *Total Baseball*'s second through sixth editions with the full knowledge that there were gaps and probably gaffes in our research; we hope that our readers will advise us of omissions so that we can continue to improve the roster in future editions. (The names of National Association club presidents and officials are listed in this section despite our understanding that these individuals were, by and large, not owners in the sense used after 1876.)

A significant change was made in the role played by league officials after the 1999 season. All duties previously held by the American League and National League presidents were consolidated by the commissioner's office.

Commissioners, Major League Baseball

1920–1944 Kenesaw M. Landis
1945–1951 Albert B. Chandler
1951–1965 Ford C. Frick
1965–1968 William D. Eckert
1969–1984 Bowie K. Kuhn
1984–1989 Peter Ueberroth
1989 A. Bartlett Giamatti
1989–1992 Francis T. Vincent, Jr.
1993–1998 Alan H. "Bud" Selig (Interim)
1998– Alan H. "Bud" Selig

National Association

Association President

1871 James W. Kerns
1872–1875 Robert W. Ferguson

Club Presidents and/or NA Convention Delegates

Baltimore Lord Baltimores
1872 —
1873 R. C. Hall
1874 C. A. Hadel

Baltimore Marylands
1873 W. J. Smith

Boston Red Stockings
1871 Ivers Whitney Adams
1872 Col. Charles H. Porter
1873–1875 Nathan Taylor Appolonio

Brooklyn Atlantics
1872–1873 Robert W. Ferguson
1874 —
1875 B. Van Delft

Brooklyn Eckfords
1872 William H. Ray

Chicago White Stockings
1871 J. M. Thatcher
1874 Mr. Gassette
George W. Gage
1875 William A. Hulbert

Cleveland Forest City
1871 J. S. Evans
1872 H. C. Doolittle

Elizabeth Resolutes
1873 Charles N. Garrighan

Fort Wayne Kekiongas
1871 George J. E. Mayers

Hartford Dark Blues
1874 G. B. Hubbell
1875 Morgan G. Bulkeley

Keokuk Westerns
1875 W. Trimble

Middletown Mansfields
1872 B. Douglass, Jr.
T. W. Ratcliff

New Haven Elm City
1875 W. S. Arnold

New York Mutuals
1871–1872 Alexander V. Davidson
1873 Robert Mathews
1874 Alexander V. Davidson
1875 William H. Cammeyer

Philadelphia Athletics
1871 James W. Kerns
1872–1873 E. Hicks Hayhurst
1874 D. F. Houston
1875 George W. Thompson
C. Spering

Philadelphia White Stockings
1873 Frank McBride
1874 D. L. Reid
1875 George Concannon

Philadelphia Centennials
1875 E. Hicks Hayhurst

Rockford Forest City
1871 Hiram Waldo

St. Louis Brown Stockings
1875 C. O. Bishop

St. Louis Red Stockings
1875 A. Blong

Troy Haymakers
1871 J. W. Scofield
1872 C. C. Clark

Washington Nationals
1872 Mr. Millar
R. Hough

Washington Olympics
1871 Nicholas E. Young
1872 Mr. Pike

Washington
1873 Nicholas E. Young
1875 D. W. Bruce
A. F. Childs

National League

Presidents

1876 Morgan G. Bulkeley
1877–1882 William A. Hulbert
1882 Arthur H. Soden
1883–1884 Abraham G. Mills
1885–1902 Nicholas E. Young
1903–1909 Harry C. Pulliam
1909 John A. Heydler
1910–1913 Thomas J. Lynch
1913–1918 John K. Tener
1918–1934 John A. Heydler
1934–1951 Ford C. Frick
1951–1969 Warren C. Giles
1970–1986 Charles S. Feeney
1986–1989 A. Bartlett Giamatti
1989–1994 William White
1994–1999 Leonard S. Coleman Jr.

Vice Presidents

1929–1932 Barney Dreyfuss
1933–1936 Charles A. Stoneham
1936–1947 Samuel Breadon
1947–1966 Philip K. Wrigley
1966–1969 Horace C. Stoneham
1970–1986 John J. McHale
1987–1994 Phyllis Collins
1994– Katy Feeney

Club Presidents

Arizona
1998– Jerry Colangelo (Chairman)

Atlanta
1966 John J. McHale
1967–1972 William C. Bartholomay
1973–1975 Daniel J. Donahue
1976–1986 R. E. (Ted) Turner
1987– William C. Bartholomay (Ch. of Bd.)

Baltimore
1892 Harry B. Von der Horst
1893–1899 Edward H. Hanlon

Boston (to Milwaukee)
1876 Nathan Taylor Appolonio
1907–1909 George B. Dovey
1909–1910 John S. Dovey
1911 W. Hepburn Russell
1912 John M. Ward
1913–1915 James E. Gaffney
1916–1918 Percy D. Haughton
1919–1922 George W. Grant
1923 Christopher Mathewson
1924 J. A. Robert Quinn
1925 Christopher Mathewson
1926 J. A. Robert Quinn
1927–1935 Emil E. Fuchs (Pres.)
1936–1944 J. A. Robert Quinn (Pres.)
1945–1952 Louis R. Perini (Pres.)

Brooklyn (to Los Angeles)
1890–1897 Charles H. Byrne
1898–1925 Charles H. Ebbets
1925 Edward J. McKeever
1925–1929 Wilbert Robinson (Pres.)
1930–1932 Frank B. York (Pres.)
1933–1938 Stephen W. McKeever
1939–1942 Leland S. MacPhail, Sr. (Exec. VP)
1943–1950 W. Branch Rickey (Pres./GM)
1950–1957 Walter F. O'Malley (Pres.)

Buffalo
1879–1880 E. B. Smith
1880 John B. Sage
1881–1885 Josiah Jewett

Chicago
1876–1881 William A. Hulbert
1882–1891 Albert G. Spalding
1892–1905 James A. Hart
1906–1913 Charles W. Murphy
1914–1915 Charles H. Thomas
1916–1918 Charles H. Weeghman
1919 Fred F. Mitchell
1919–1933 William L. Veeck, Sr. (Pres.)
1934 William M. Walker
1934–1977 Philip K. Wrigley (Pres.)
1977–1981 William J. Hagenah, Jr. (Pres./CEO/Treas.)
1982–1983 Andrew J. McKenna (Ch. of Bd.)
1984 James E. Finks (Pres./CEO)
1985–1987 Dallas Green (Pres./GM)
1988 John W. Madigan (Ch. of Bd.)
1989–1994 Stanton Cook (Ch. of Bd.)
1994– Andy MacPhail (Pres./CEO)

Cincinnati
1876–1877 Josiah L. Keck
1878–1879 J. Wayne Neff
1880 Justus Thorner

Cincinnati
1890 Aaron A. Stern
1891–1902 John T. Brush
1902–1927 August Hermann (Pres.)
1928–1929 C. J. McDiarmid (Pres.)
1930–1933 Sidney Weil (Pres.)
1934–1946 Powel Crosley, Jr. (Pres.)
1946–1951 Warren C. Giles (Pres.)
1951–1961 Powel Crosley, Jr. (Pres.)
1961–1966 William O. DeWitt (Pres./GM/Treas.)
1967–1973 Francis L. Dale (Pres.)
1973–1978 Robert L. Howsam (Pres./CEO)
1979–1983 Richard Wagner (Pres./CEO)
1984–1985 Robert L. Howsam (Pres./CEO)
1986–1995 Marge Schott (Gen. Partner/Pres.)
1996–1999 John Allen (Managing Executive)
2000– Carl Lindner (CEO)

Cleveland
1879–1881 J. Ford Evans
1882–1884 C. H. Bulkley

Cleveland
1889–1898 Frank D. Robison
1899 M. Stanley Robison

Colorado
1992 John Antonucci (Ch./CEO)
1993– Jerry McMorris (Ch./CEO/Pres.)

Detroit
1881–1884 William G. Thompson
1885–1886 Joseph H. Marsh
1887–1888 Fred K. Stearns
1888 Charles W. Smith

Florida
1992–1999 Wayne Huizenga (Chairman)
2000– John Henry (Chairman)

Hartford
1876–1877 Morgan G. Bulkeley

Houston
1962 Craig F. Cullinan, Jr. (Pres.)
1963–1971 Roy Hofheinz (Pres.)
1972–1973 Reuben W. Askanase (Pres./Ch. of Bd.)
1974–1975 T. H. Neyland (Pres.)
1976 Sidney L. Shlenker (Pres.)
1976–1980 Talbot M. Smith (Pres./GM)
1981–1985 Albert L. Rosen (Pres./GM)
1986–1987 Dick Wagner
1988 Fred Stanley
1980–1992 Dr. John J. McMullen (Ch. of Bd.)
1992– Drayton McLane Jr. (Ch. of Bd./CEO)

Indianapolis
1878 William D. Perritt

Indianapolis
1887–1889 John T. Brush

Kansas City
1886 Joseph J. Heim

Los Angeles
1958–1969 Walter F. O'Malley (Pres.)
1970–1997 Peter O'Malley (Pres.)
1998– Rupert Murdoch (Principal Owner)

Louisville
1876–1877 Walter N. Haldeman

Louisville
1892 T. Hunt Stucky

1893–1896 Fred Drexler
1897–1899 Harry C. Pulliam
1899 Barney Dreyfuss

Milwaukee
1878 J. R. Kaine

Milwaukee Braves (to Atlanta Braves)
1953–1956 Louis R. Perini (Pres.)
1957–1961 Joseph F. Cairnes (Pres.)
1962–1966 John J. McHale (Pres.)

Milwaukee Brewers (from American League)
1998 Allan H. "Bud" Selig (Pres./CEO)
1998– Wendy Selig-Prieb (Pres./CEO)

Montreal Expos
1969–1986 John J. McHale (Pres./CEO)
1987–1998 Claude R. Brochu (Pres./CEO)
1998–1999 Jacques Menard (Pres./CEO)
2000– Jeffrey H. Loria (Chair/CEO)

Mutual Club (N.Y.)
1876 William H. Cammeyer

New York Giants (to San Francisco)
1883–1892 John B. Day
1893–1894 C. C. Van Cott
1895–1902 Andrew Freedman
1903–1912 John T. Brush
1912–1918 Harry N. Hempstead
1919–1935 Charles A. Stoneham (Pres.)
1936–1957 Horace C. Stoneham (Pres.)

New York Mets
1962–1966 George M. Weiss (Pres.)
1966–1967 Vaughan P. Devine (Pres.)
1968–1975 Mrs. Joan W. Payson (Pres.)
1976–1979 Mrs. Lorinda de Roulet (Pres.)
1980– Fred Wilpon (Pres./CEO)

Philadelphia Athletics
1876 Thomas J. Smith

Philadelphia Phillies
1883–1902 Alfred J. Reach
1903–1904 James Potter
1905–1908 William J. Shettsline
1909 Israel W. Durham
1909–1912 Horace S. Fogel
1912 Alfred D. Wiler
1913 William H. Locke
1913–1930 William F. Baker (Pres.)
1931–1932 L. Charles Ruch
1933–1942 Gerald P. Nugent (Pres.)
1943 William D. Cox
1943–1972 Robert M. Carpenter, Jr. (Pres.)
1973–1981 Robert M. Carpenter III (Pres.)
1982–1987 Bill Giles (Pres./CEO)
1998– David Montgomery (Pres./CEO)

Pittsburgh
1887–1890 William A. Nimick
1891 J. Palmer O'Neill
1892 William C. Temple
1893 Albert C. Buckenberger
1894–1897 William W. Kerr
1898 William H. Watkins
1899 William W. Kerr
1900–1932 Barney Dreyfuss (Pres.)
1932–1946 William E. Benswanger (Pres./Treas.)
1946–1950 Frank E. McKinney (Pres.)
1951–1969 John W. Galbreath (Pres.)
1970–1985 Daniel M. Galbreath (Pres.)
1986–1987 Malcolm Prine
1988–1990 Carl Barger (Pres.)
1988–1991 Douglas D. Danforth (Chairman/CEO)
1992 Vincent Sarni (Pres./CEO)
1992–1996 Mark Sauer (Pres./CEO)
1996– Kevin S. McClatchy (CEO/Man. Gen. Partner)

Providence
1878 John D. Thurston
1879–1881 Henry T. Root
1882–1883 Henry B. Winship
1884–1885 Henry J. Root

St. Louis Brown Stockings
1876–1877 John R. Lucas

St. Louis Maroons
1885–1886 Henry V. Lucas

St. Louis Cardinals
1892–1897 Chris Von der Ahe
1898 Benjamin S. Muckenfuss
1899–1906 Frank D. Robison
1907–1910 M. Stanley Robison
1911–1912 E. A. Steininger
1912 James C. Jones
1913–1916 Schuyler P. Britton
1916 Mrs. Schuyler P. Britton
1917–1919 W. Branch Rickey
1920–1947 Samuel Breadon (Pres.)
1947–1949 Robert E. Hannegan
1949–1952 Fred M. Saigh, Jr. (Pres.)
1953–1989 August A. Busch, Jr. (Pres.)
1990–1991 Fred L. Kuhlmann (Pres./CEO)
1992–1994 Stuart Meyer (Pres./CEO)
1994– Mark C. Lamping (Pres.)

San Diego
1969–1977 Emil J. Bavasi (Pres.)
1977–1980 Ray A. Kroc
1981–1983 Ray A. Kroc (owner)
1980–1987 Ballard F. Smith, Jr.
1988 Chub Feeney
1990 Dick Freeman
1984–1990 Joan Kroc (owner)
1991–1994 Tom Werner (Prin. Owner/Ch.)
1994– John Moores (Ch. of the Bd.)

San Francisco
1958–1975 Horace C. Stoneham (Pres.)
1976–1979 Robert A. Lurie/Bud Herseth (Co-Chairmen)
1980–1985 Robert A. Lurie (Pres.)
1986–1990 Robert A. Lurie (owner)
1986–1992 Albert L. Rosen (Pres./GM)
1993– Peter A. Magowan (Pres.)

Syracuse
1879 Hamilton S. White

Troy
1879–1880 Gardner Earl
1881–1882 A. L. Hotchkin
1882 Francis N. Mann

Washington
1886–1888 Robert C. Hewitt
1889 Walter F. Hewitt

Washington
1892–1899 George W. Wagner

Worcester
1880–1882 Elbert B. Pratt

American Association

League Presidents

1882–1885 H. D. McKnight
1886–1889 Wheeler C. Wyckoff
1890 Zach Phelps
1891 Louis Kramer
Ed Renau
Zach Phelps

Club Presidents

Baltimore
1882 H. C. Myers (?)
1883 William Barnie (?)
1884 H. T. Houck
1885–1887 William Barnie
1888 Harry Von der Horst
1889 William Barnie
1891 Harry Von der Horst

Boston
1891 Charles A. Prince

Brooklyn
1884–1889 Charles H. Byrne

Brooklyn–Baltimore
1890 James M. Kennedy
Wm. Barnie (?)

Cincinnati
1882 Justus Thorner
1883–1884 Aaron S. Stern
1885 George L. Herancourt
1886 John Hauck
1887–1889 Aaron S. Stern

Cincinnati-Milwaukee
1891 Albert Johnson

Cleveland
1887–1888 Frank Robison

Columbus
1883–1884 H. T. Crittendon (?)
1889–1891 Conrad Born, Jr.

Indianapolis
1884 Joseph Schwabacher

Kansas City
1888 Joseph J. Heim
1889 John W. Speas

Louisville
1882–1883 J. H. Pank
1884 William L. Jackson Jr.
1885–1887 Zach Phelps
1888 W. L. Lyons
1889 M. H. Davidson
1890 Lawrence S. Parsons
1891 Julian B. Hart

New York
1883–1884 John B. Day
1885 Frank Rhouer
1886–1887 Erastus Wiman

Philadelphia
1882 Lew Simmons (?)
1883–1886 William Sharsig
1887 Lew Simmons
1888–1890 H. C. Pennypacker
1891 J. Earle Wagner

Pittsburgh
1882–1883 H. D. McKnight
1884 E. E. Converse
1885–1886 William A. Nimick

Richmond
1884 W. C. Seddon

Rochester
1890 Henry Brinker

St. Louis
1882–1891 Chris Von der Ahe

Syracuse
1890 George K. Frazier

Toledo
1884 W. J. Colburn
1890 V. H. Ketcham

Washington
1884 L. Moxley
1891 H. B. Bennett

Union Association

League Presidents

1883 H. B. Bennett
1883–1885 Henry V. Lucas

Club Presidents

Altoona
1884 W. W. Rich

Baltimore
1884 J. W. Lowe

Boston
1884 Frank E. Winslow

Chicago-Pittsburgh
1884 A. H. Henderson

Cincinnati
1884 Justus Thorner

Kansas City
1884 Americus V. McKim

Milwaukee
1884 Charles Kippen (?)

Philadelphia
1884 Thomas J. Pratt

St. Louis
1884 H. V. Lucas

St. Paul
1884 A. M. Thompson (?)

Washington
1884 H. B. Bennett

Wilmington
1884 John T. West

Players League

League President

1890 Col. Edward A. McAlpin

Club Presidents

Boston
1890 Col. Charles H. Porter

Brooklyn
1890 Wendell Goodwin

Buffalo
1890 Moses Shire

Chicago
1890 John Addison

Cleveland
- 1890 Albert L. Johnson

New York
- 1890 Cornelius Van Cott

Philadelphia
- 1890 H. M. Love

Pittsburgh
- 1890 William McCallin

American League

Presidents

- 1901–1927 B. Bancroft Johnson
- 1927–1931 Ernest S. Barnard
- 1931–1959 William Harridge
- 1959–1973 Joseph E. Cronin
- 1974–1984 Leland S. MacPhail, Jr.
- 1984–1994 Robert W. Brown, M.D.
- 1994–1999 Dr. Gene A. Budig

Vice Presidents

- 1901–1916 Charles W. Somers
- 1917–1919 Charles A. Comiskey
- 1921–1935 Frank J. Navin
- 1935–1938 Jacob Ruppert
- 1939–1955 Clark C. Griffith
- 1955–1976 Thomas A. Yawkey
- 1976–1982 Calvin R. Griffith
- 1983–1984 Calvin R. Griffith / John Fetzer / Gene Autry
- 1985 John Fetzer and Gene Autry
- 1986–1989 Calvin R. Griffith / John Fetzer / Gene Autry
- 1990 John Fetzer and Gene Autry
- 1991 Jean Yawkey and Gene Autry
- 1992–1998 Gene Autry
- 1999– Carl R. Pohlad

Club Presidents

Anaheim (Los Angeles, 1961–1964, California, 1965–1996)
- 1961–1974 Robert Reynolds (Pres.)
- 1975–1977 Arthur E. Patterson (Pres.)
- 1977–1990 Gene Autry (owner/president)
- 1990–1996 Richard M. Brown (Pres./CEO)
- 1996– Michael Eisner (Ch. & CEO)

Baltimore (to New York)
- 1901 Sidney W. Frank
- 1902 John J. Mahon

Baltimore
- 1954–1955 Clarence W. Miles (Pres.)
- 1956–1959 James Keelty, Jr. (Pres.)
- 1960–1965 Leland S. MacPhail, Jr. (Pres./GM)
- 1966–1979 Jerold C. Hoffberger (Ch. of Bd.)
- 1980–1982 Jerold C. Hoffberger (as Pres.)
- 1983–1988 Edward B. Williams (Ch. of Bd./Pres.)
- 1989–1992 Lawrence Lucchino (Pres./CEO)
- 1994– Peter Angelos (Managing Gen. Partner)

Boston
- 1901–1902 Charles W. Somers
- 1903–1904 Henry J. Killilea
- 1904–1911 John I. Taylor
- 1912–1913 James R. McAleer
- 1913–1916 Joseph J. Lannin
- 1917–1923 Harry H. Frazee
- 1923–1932 Robert Quinn (Pres.)
- 1933–1976 Thomas A. Yawkey (Pres.)
- 1977–1988 Jean R. Yawkey (majority owner)
- 1989– John L. Harrington (General Partner)

Chicago
- 1901–1931 Charles A. Comiskey (Pres.)
- 1932–1939 J. Louis Comiskey (Pres./Treas.)
- 1940 Harry Grabiner (VP)
- 1941–1956 Mrs. Grace Comiskey (Pres.)
- 1957–1959 Charles A. Comiskey II/John Rigney (VPs)
- 1959–1961 William L. Veeck, Jr. (Pres.)
- 1961–1969 Arthur C. Allyn, Jr. (Pres.)
- 1970–1975 John W. Allyn (Pres.)
- 1976–1980 William L. Veeck, Jr. (Pres.)
- 1981– Jerry M. Reinsdorf (Chairman)

Cleveland
- 1901–1909 John F. Kilfoyl
- 1910–1915 Charles W. Somers
- 1916–1922 James C. Dunn
- 1922–1927 Ernest S. Barnard (Pres.)
- 1928–1946 Alva Bradley (Pres./Treas.)
- 1946–1949 William L. Veeck, Jr. (Pres.)
- 1950–1952 Ellis W. Ryan (Pres.)
- 1953–1962 Myron H. Wilson, Jr. (Pres.)
- 1963–1971 Gabriel H. Paul (Pres./Treas./GM)
- 1972–1975 Nick Mileti (Pres.)
- 1975–1977 Alva T. Bonda (Pres.)
- 1978–1985 Gabriel H. Paul (Pres./CEO)
- 1986–1987 Patrick J. O'Neill (Chairman)
- 1987– Richard E. Jacobs (Ch. of Bd./CEO)

Detroit
- 1901 James D. Burns (Pres.)
- 1902–1903 Samuel F. Angus (Pres.)
- 1904–1907 William H. Yawkey (Pres.)
- 1908–1935 Frank J. Navin (Pres.)
- 1936–1952 Walter O. Briggs, Sr. (Pres.)
- 1952–1956 Walter O. Briggs, Jr. (Pres.)
- 1957 Frederick A. Knorr (Pres.)
- 1957–1959 Harvey R. Hansen (Pres.)
- 1960 William O. DeWitt (Pres.)
- 1961–1989 John E. Fetzer (Pres.)
- 1978–1989 James Campbell (Pres.)
- 1984–1990 Thomas S. Monaghan (Pres.)
- 1990–1992 Glenn E. (Bo) Schembechler (Pres.)
- 1992– Michael Ilitch (Owner and Chairman)

Kansas City A's (to Oakland)
- 1955–1959 Arnold Johnson (Pres.)
- 1960 Parke Carroll (VP)
- 1961–1967 Charles O. Finley (Pres.)

Kansas City Royals
- 1969–1993 Ewing Kauffman (Ch. of Bd.)
- 1993– David D. Glass (Ch./CEO)

Milwaukee (to St. Louis)
- 1901 Matthew Killilea

Milwaukee Brewers (to National League)
- 1970–1997 Allan H. "Bud" Selig (Pres./CEO)

Minnesota
- 1961–1984 Calvin R. Griffith (Chairman/Pres.)
- 1985–1986 Howard T. Fox, Jr.
- 1987–1989 Jerry Bell
- 1985– Carl R. Pohlad (Owner)

New York
- 1903–1906 Joseph W. Gordon
- 1903–1915 Frank J. Farrell and William S. Devery (owners)
- 1907–1914 Frank J. Farrell
- 1915–1938 Jacob Ruppert (Pres.)
- 1939–1944 Edward G. Barrow (Pres./GM)
- 1945–1947 Leland S. MacPhail, Sr. (Pres./GM/Treas.)
- 1948–1953 Daniel R. Topping (Pres.)
- 1954–1966 Daniel R. Topping/Del E. Webb (co-owners)
- 1966–1973 Michael Burke (Ch. of the Bd./Pres.)
- 1973–1977 Gabriel H. Paul (Pres.)
- 1978–1980 Albert L. Rosen (Pres./CEO)
- 1980–1990 George M. Steinbrenner (Ch. of Bd.)
- 1990–1991 Robert Nederlander (Man. Gen. Part.)
- 1992 Daniel McCarthy (Man. Gen. Part.)
- 1993– George M. Steinbrenner (Prin. Owner)

Oakland
- 1968–1980 Charles O. Finley (Pres.)
- 1981–1990 Roy Eisenhardt (Pres.)
- 1990–1995 Walter J. Haas (Chairman/CEO)
- 1995– Steven C. Schott (Co-Owner/Man. Part.)

Philadelphia (to Kansas City)
- 1901–1921 Benjamin F. Shibe
- 1922–1935 Thomas S. Shibe (Pres.)
- 1936 John D. Shibe
- 1937–1954 Connie Mack (Pres.)

Seattle Pilots (to Milwaukee)
- 1969 Dewey Soriano (Pres.)

Seattle Mariners
- 1977–1979 Danny Kaye and Lester Smith (Man. Gen. Partners)
- 1980–1983 Daniel F. O'Brien (Pres./CEO)
- 1981–1989 George L. Argyros (Ch. of Bd./CEO)
- 1984–1989 Charles G. Armstrong
- 1990–1991 Jeff Smulyan (Ch. of Bd.)
- 1992–1999 John W. Ellis (Ch. of Bd./CEO)
- 1999– Howard Lincoln (Chairman/CEO)

St. Louis (to Baltimore)
- 1902 Ralph T. Orthwein
- 1903–1915 Robert L. Hedges
- 1916–1933 Philip D. Ball (Pres.)
- 1934–1936 Louis B. Von Weise
- 1937–1945 Donald L. Barnes (Pres.)
- 1946–1948 Richard C. Muckerman (Pres.)
- 1949–1951 William O. DeWitt (Pres.)
- 1951–1953 William L. Veeck, Jr. (Pres.)

Tampa Bay
- 1998– Vincent Naimoli (Managing Gen. Partner/CEO)

Texas
- 1972–1974 Robert E. Short (Pres.)
- 1974 Robert W. Brown, M.D.
- 1975–1980 Bradford G. Corbett (Pres.)
- 1980–1987 Eddie Chiles (Owner/Ch. of Bd./CEO)
- 1984–1990 Michael H. Stone (Pres./COO)
- 1991–1998 J. Thomas Schieffer (Pres.)
- 1998– Thomas O. Hicks (Ch./Owner)

Toronto
- 1977–1981 Peter Bavasi (Exec. VP/GM)
- 1977–1988 R. Howard Webster (Ch. of Bd.)
- 1989–1995 Paul Beeston (Pres./CEO)
- 1995– Sam Pollock (Ch. & CEO)

Washington (to Minnesota)
- 1901–1903 Frederick Postal
- 1904 Thomas J. Loftus
- 1904 Harry B. Lambert
- 1905–1912 Thomas C. Noyes
- 1920–1955 Clark C. Griffith (Pres.)
- 1956–1960 Calvin R. Griffith (Pres.)

Washington (to Texas)
- 1961–1962 Elwood R. Quesada (Pres.)
- 1963–1967 James M. Johnston (Ch. of Bd.)
- 1968 James H. Lemon (Ch. of Bd.)
- 1969–1971 Robert E. Short (Pres.)

Federal League

League President

- 1914–1915 James A. Gilmore

Club Presidents

Baltimore
- 1914–1915 Carrol W. Rasin

Brooklyn
- 1914–1915 Robert B. Ward

Buffalo
- 1914 Walter F. Mullen
- William E. Robertson
- 1915 William E. Robertson

Chicago
- 1914–1915 Charles A. Weeghman

Indianapolis
- 1914 J. E. Krause

Kansas City
- 1914 C. C. Madison
- 1915 Charles Baird
- Conrad H. Mann

Newark
- 1915 P. T. Powers
- Harry Sinclair

Pittsburgh
- 1914 John R. Barbour
- 1915 Edward W. Gwinner

St. Louis
- 1914 E. A. Steininger
- 1915 Lloyd H. Rickart

Announcer Roster

Curt Smith

Baseball on the air debuted August 5, 1921, over KDKA—America's first radio station. Soon after that initial broadcast from Forbes Field in Pittsburgh, radio baseball swept the country. The radio voice was a mixture of announcer, writer, director, producer, cameraman, and salesman, linking plots and stories and comedy that rounded out scenes.

Although the television first found its way into American homes in the 1940s, most baseball fans relied on the voices of their hometown radio announcers during the '40s and '50s. Even after TV became prevalent enough to make radio a second option, fans still heard descriptions, explanations, and analysis of their teams' games from two trusted voices. You might disagree with the play-by-play man's interpretation of the action, or the commentator's breakdown of the events; but the voices of your team's announcers often make them seem like an old friend who stops by your home for a few hours 150-plus times per year. Baseball announcers can be entertaining, informative, or irksome. But they have always—in their own unique ways—made the experience of catching a game away from the stadium more comfortable, more complete, and more enjoyable.

No one has ever catalogued all the major league play-by-play men and analysts who enhanced the national pastime's live action for millions of fans. My 1987 book, *Voices of the Game*, relied on a rare recording here, a play-by-play transcript there, photos, magazine stories, and yellowed cartoons: mostly, interviews with the principals to recreate those who broadcast baseball. Until the 1940s radio/TV rosters were as rare, say, as a Red Sox pennant. Even later statistics lag: Many do not exist; others conflict.

To correct that flaw, the Baseball Hall of Fame and Museum has led me through yearbooks, guides, newspapers, and other archives. After *Voices'* release, readers amended dates and names from radio/TV's distant past. Similarly, that invitation is extended to readers of this piece. We have done our best, and hope that you enjoy.

Below is the most exhaustive roster of baseball radio and/or TV announcers yet compiled. Its aim is to list each major league broadcaster—name, date, and for whom. They are listed by club or network: for example, Allen, Mel 1939–42 and 1946–64 NY-A (New York, American League). Many team voices did radio and television: Thus, I do not distinguish. Network abbreviations, on the other hand, distinguish between radio and TV.

TV series include: 1953–54 ABC *Game of the Week* (abbreviation, ABC); 1955–64 CBS *Game* (CBS); 1957–64 NBC *Major League Baseball* (NBC); 1960 ABC *Game of the Week* (ABC); 1965 CBS *Yankee Baseball* (YANKEE); 1965 ABC *Game* (ABC); 1966–89 NBC *Game* (NBC); 1976–89 ABC *Monday Night Baseball* (ABC); 1977–83 USA *Game of the Week* (USA); 1990–93 CBS *Game* (CBS); 1990–2000 ESPN *Sunday Night Baseball* (ESPN); 1994–95 The Baseball Network (BASE); and 1996–2000 Fox *Game* (FOX). *This Week In Baseball* (1977–2000) is also listed (TWIB); to many, it defines the game.

Radio series include: 1949–52 Liberty *Game of the Day* (LIB); 1950–60 Mutual *Game of the Day* (MUT); 1959 Dodgers and Giants games broadcast to New York (DG); 1985–97 CBS *Game of the Week* (CBS); and 1998–2000 ESPN *Game of the Week* (ESPN). Asterisks at entries' end indicate non–regular-season coverage (World Series, League Championship, Division Series, and All-Star Game. For instance: 1969 * ROBERT WOLD, a company which aired the 1959–75 playoffs). Teams and series are listed by abbreviation.

Dizzy Dean often "commertated" how a batter "swang" and a runner "slud" and a slugger stood "confidentially at the plate." We are confident that this roster fills a big league void.

Aaron, Hank 1980 Atl-N
Adderley, Larry 1981–83 Det-A
Aguirre, Hank 1981–83 Det-A
Albert, Kenny 1999–2000 FOX
Albert, Steve 1979–81 NY-N
Alicea, Juan 1982–2000 NY-N
Allbright, Nat 1950–57 Bro-N; 1958–62 LA-N
Allen, Larry 1951 Cle-A
Allen, Lee 1943–45 Cin-N
Allen, Mel 1939–42 and 1946–64 NY-A; 1942 NY-N; 1965 Mil-N; 1968 Cle-A; 1977–96 TWIB; 1984–85 NY-A; 1938* CBS; 1940–42* and 1947–50* MUT; 1951–63* NBC.
Allen, Rod 1998–2000 Ari-N
Allison, Bob 1971 Min-A
Alonzo, Miguel 1958–61 LA-N
Alvarez, Manolo 1993–96 and 1999 Fla-N
Andersen, Larry 1998–2000 Phi-N
Anderson, Sparky 1997–98 Ana-A; 1976*, 1980–81*, and 1984–86* CBS.
Andrews, Mike 1984 Bos-A
Angel, Joe 1977–78 SF-N; 1984–86 Min-A; 1988–90 and 1992 Bal-A; 1991 NY-A; 1993–2000 FLA-N; 1994–95 BASE
Areas, Evelio 1981 SF-N
Arlin, Harold 1921 Pit-N
Armstrong, Dave 1993–95 KC-A; 1996–2000 Col-N
Arthur, Doug 1944 Phi-A; 1944–45 Phi-N
Ashburn, Richie 1963–96 Phi-N
Ashby, Alan 1998–2000 Hou-N
Avila, Juan 1998-2000 SD-N
Baer, Larry 1978 Oak-A
Bailey, Steve 1961–64 LA-A; 1966–69 and 1980 Cal-A
Baker, Roger 1939–1944 Cin-N
Balter, Sam 1943 Cin-N
Barber, Red 1934–38 Cin-N; 1939–53 Bro-N; 1954–66 NY-A; 1935* and 1937–43*, 1947*, and 1949–50* MUT; 1936*, 1948*, and 1952* NBC
Barnett, Dave 1990 Tex-A; 1997–2000 ESPN
Barney, Rex 1956–57 MUT; 1983–92 Bal-A
Barnhart, Brian 1999–2000 Ana-A
Barniak, Jim 1991 Phi-N
Barry, Mike 1979 Det-A
Baruch, Andre 1954–55 Bro-N
Becerra, Rolando 1987–92 Hou-N
Beck, Bill 1984 SD-N
Beckmann, Frank 1995–2000 Det-A
Bench, Johnny 1985–86 (1985–86*) ABC; 1985–91 (1986–93*) CBS; 1987–90 Cin-N
Bender, Gary 1975 Mil-A; 1987–88 (1987–88*) ABC.
Berman, Chris 1990–2000 (1998–2000*) ESPN.
Berroa, Billy 1987–93 and 1997–2000 NY-N.
Bingham, Bob 1948 Sty-A; 1948 Sty-N
Bingham, Dick 1952 Chi-A; 1955–57 Pit-N
Black, Rod 2000 Tor-A
Blass, Steve 1983–84 and 1986–2000 Pit-N
Blattner, Robert (Buddy) 1949–51 LIB; 1950–53 StL-A; 1952 and 1954 MUT; 1953–54 ABC; 1955–59 CBS; 1960–61 StL-N; 1962–65 LA-A; 1966–68 Cal-A; 1969–75 KC-A; 1964* and 1967* NBC
Blyleven, Bert 1995–2000 Min-A; 1999 ESPN
Boeta, Rene 1998–2000 Ari-N
Bond, Ford 1934* NBC
Boudreau, Lou 1958–90 Chi-N
Boyle, Joe 1975–77 Min-A
Bradley, Truman 1935* CBS.
Brando, Tim 1996–97 Atl-N
Bray, Dick 1937–44 Cin-N
Bremer, Dick 1983–85 and 1987–2000 Min-A
Brenly, Bob 1990–91 Chi-N; 1996–2000 (1996–2000*) FOX; 1998–2000 Ari-N
Brennaman, Marty 1974–2000 Cin-N; 1994–95 BASE; 1975* NBC; 1976* CBS
Brennaman, Thom 1989 Cin-N; 1990–95 Chi-N; 1994–95 BASE; 1996–2000 (1996–2000*) FOX; 1998–2000 Ari-N
Brett, George 1999–2000 FOX
Brett, Ken 1986 Sea-A; 1987–96 Cal-A
Brickhouse, Jack 1940–44, 1948, and 1950–81 Chi-N; 1945 and 1948–67 Chi-A; 1946 NY-N; 1950–54* and 1959* NBC; 1952* MUT
Briles, Nelson 1980 Pit-N; 1984–85 Sea-A
Britt, Jim 1940–42 and 1946–50 Bos-A; 1940–42 and 1946–52 Bos-N; 1954–57 Cle-A; 1949–51* NBC; 1951* MUT
Brock, Lou 1981 Chi-A
Brown, Bill 1976–82 Cin-N; 1983–84 Pit-N; 1987–2000 Hou-N
Brown, Bob 1975–76 Cle-A
Brown, Greg 1994–2000 Pit-N
Brown, Lorn 1976–79 and 1983–88 Chi-A; 1980–81 Mil-A; 1982 NY-N
Brown, "Oatmeal" 1933 Cin-N
Brown, Warren 1936* NBC
Brundige, Bill 1950–51 Phi-N
Brulotte, Rodger 1984–2000 Mon-N
Bryson, George 1956–60 Cin-N; 1963–64 KC-A
Buck, Jack, 1954–59 and 1961–2000 StL-N; 1959 DG; 1960 ABC; 1990–91 (1990–91*) CBS; 1994–95 BASE; 1965* and 1967–68* NBC; 1976* and 1979–89* CBS
Buck, Joe 1991–2000 StL-N; 1993–95 CBS; 1996–2000 (1996–2000*) FOX
Buetel, Frank 1967 and 1970–72 Min-A
Burdette, Bob 1929 Cin-N
Busby, Steve 1982–1995 Tex-A; 1996 KC-A; CBS RADIO 1987-95
Buttitta, Joe 1982–84 Cal-A
Cabell, Enos 1991-93 Hou-N
Calton, Larry 1974–75 Min-A
Campbell, Bill 1950 and 1963–70 Phi-N
Campbell, Bud 1950–53 Chi-N
Campbell, Dave 1978 SF-N; 1979–89 SD-N; 1990–2000 (1998–2000*) ESPN; 1993–97 Col-N
Campbell, Don 1946 CLE-A
Cannon, Joe 1997–2000 MON-N
Caray, Chip 1991–92 Atl-N; 1993–95 Sea-A; 1996–2000 (1997*) FOX: 1998–2000 Chi-N
Caray, Harry 1945–69 StL-N; 1946 StL-A; 1970 Oak-A; 1971–81 Chi-A; 1982–1997 ChiN; 1964* and 1967–68* NBC
Caray, Skip 1965 Mil-N; 1976–2000 Atl-N; 1994–95 BASE; 2000* NBC
Cardenas, Rene 1958–61 and 1982–98 LA-N
Carey, Paul 1973–91 Det-A
Carlson, Dick 1976 KC-A
Carmichael, John 1938 Chi-N; 1938* NBC; 1974 Chi-A
Carneal, Herb 1957–61 Bal-A; 1962–2000 Min-A; 1994–95 BASE
Carpenter, Bob 1984 and 1995–2000 StL-N; 1985–89 Tex-A; 1992–93 NY-N; 1994 Min-A; 1991–2000 (1999–2000*) ESPN
Carrasquel, Chico 1990-96 Chi-A
Carter, Boake 1935* NBC
Carter, Gary 1993–96 Fla-N; 1997–99 Mon-N.
Carter, Joe 2000 Tor-A
Casavant, Denis 1990–99 Mon-N
Case, George 1959 CBS
Cash, Norm 1976 ABC; 1981–83 Det-A
Castiglione, Joe 1979 and 1982 Cle-A; 1981 Mil-A; 1983–2000 Bos-A
Cerone, Rick 1995–97 (1997*) CBS
Cerrutti, John 1997–2000 Tor-A
Cesmat, Brad 2000 Ari-N
Chandler, Bob 1972–2000 SD-N
Chandler, Nev 1980–84 Cle-A
Chaney, Darrel 1981–83 Atl-N
Chantelois, Alain 1992–2000 Mon-N
Cheek, Tom 1977–2000 Tor-A; 1994–95 BASE
Cherkin, Carl 1982 Tex-A
Chevrier, Don 1977–1996 Tor-A
Christensen, Ray 1971–73 Min-A
Clemente, Roberto Jr. 1998–2000 NY-A
Cohen, David 1995–96 NY-A
Cohen, Gary 1986 and 1994–97 (1988–91* and 1995–97*) CBS; 1989–2000 NY-N; 1994-n-95 BASE; 1998–2000 (1998–2000*) ESPN
Colavito, Rocky 1972 and 1975–76 Cle-A
Coleman, Ed 1996–2000 NY-N
Coleman, Gordy 1992–94 Cin-N
Coleman, Jerry 1960 CBS; 1963–69 NY-A; 1972–79 and 1981–2000 SD-N; 1985–97 CBS; 1994–95 BASE; 1976–85*, 1988–91*, and 1995–97* CBS
Coleman, Ken 1954–63 Cle-A; 1966–74 Bos-A; 1975–78 Cin-N; 1979–89 Bos-A; 1967* NBC
Collins, Tom 1963–64 Mil-N; 1970–74 Mil-A
Conin, Al 1983–1993 Cal-A
Convey, Thomas Patrick 1931–33 StL-N
Corrigan, Jack 1983 and 1985–2000 Cle-A
Corum, Red 1942* MUT
Cosell, Howard 1965 and 1976–85 (1976–84*) ABC
Cosgrove, Bob 1978 Oak-A
Costas, Bob 1982–89 (1983–89*) and 1996–2000 (1996–2000*) NBC; 1994–95 (1994-n-95*) BASE
Cotroneo, Vince 1991–97 Hou-N; 1998–2000 Tex-A
Coughlin, Dan 1990 Cle-A
Cowan, Tommy 1921* WEST
Craddock, Jack 1942–47 Pit-N
Crandall, Del 1985–88 Chi-A; 1992–94 Mil-A
Creighton, Harry 1948–55 Chi-A; 1951–56 Chi-N
Croghan, Joe 1960–63 Bal-A
Crowley, Bill 1951–52 NY-A; 1958–60 Bos-A
Cutler, Alan 1986 Pit-N
Dailey, Tom 1949 StL-A
D'Ambrosio, Joe 2000 ESPN
Daniels, Dan 1960–68 Was-A
David, Howard 1985–87 CBS
Davis, Bob 1997–2000 KC-A
Davis, Goeff 1955–58 NY-A
Davis, Tom 1985–92 BAL-A
Dean, Jay Hanna (Dizzy) Dean 1941–46 StL-N; 1944–49 and 1952–53 StL-A; 1950–51 NY-A; 1952–54 MUT; 1953–54 ABC; 1955–64 CBS; 1965 YANKEE; 1967–68 Atl-N
DeLaney, Bob 1951–53 Bos-A; 1954–57 NY-N; 1959–65 NY-A
De Gonzalez, Luis 1987 Chi-N
De la Rosa, Rene 1993–98 SF-N
Derdivanis, Kent 1981 Mil-A; 1984 Bos-A; 1990–93 Pit-N
Deshaies, Jim 1997–2000 Hou-N
Desmond, Connie 1943–56 Bro-N
Diaz, Frank 1986 Chi-A
Dibble, Rob 1998–2000 (2000*) ESPN.
Dickerson, Dan 1999–2000 Det-A
Dierker, Larry 1979–97 Hou-N
DiMaggio, Joe 1952 NY-A
Dito, Ken 1985 Oak-A
Doggett, Jerry 1949–51 LIB; 1957 Bro-N; 1958–88 LA-N
Dominguez, Octavio 1991-92 Chi-N
Doucet, Jacques 1972–2000 Mon-N
Doucette, Eddie 1974 Mil-A; 1978 Cle-A; 1980–81 SD-N; 1987 LA-N
Douglas, Paul 1937* CBS
Downing, Al 1978-88, 1991-92 LA-N; 1994–96 (1995–97*) CBS
Drees, Jack 1968–72 CHI-A
Drennan, Bruce 1980–82 Cle-A
Drysdale, Don 1970–71 Mon-N; 1972 Tex-A; 1973–81 Cal-A; 1982–86 (1983–86*) ABC; 1982–87 ChiA; 1988–93 LA-N
Dube, Camille 1994–96 Mon-N
Dudley, Jimmy 1941–42 and 1947 Chi-N; 1948–67 Cle-A; 1969 Sea-A; 1954* MUT.
Dunn, Jack 1962 Bal-A
Dunphy, Don 1944 NY-A; 1944 NY-N; 1959 MUT
Durham, Jim 1984–85 Hou-N; 1990 Chi-A; 1998–2000 (1998–2000*) ESPN
Durney, Bill 1953 StL-A
Durocher, Leo 1957–59 NBC; 1965 ABC
Dyer, Bill 1936–37 Phi-A; 1936–37 Phi-N; 1936–38* CBS
Eckman, Art 1974–75 SF-N
Edge, Bob 1948 Cin-N; 1947* NBC
Edwards, Ed 1954–55 Cle-A; 1957–58 KC-A
Egan, Leo 1934–38 and 1949–50 Bos-A; 1934–38 and 1949–50 Bos-N
Elliot, Win 1976–86* CBS
Elliott, Mike 1984 Hou-N
Ellis, Steve 1946–48 NY-N
Elson, Bob 1931–42 Chi-N; 1931–42 and 1946–70 Chi-A; 1971 Oak-A; 1929–31* and 1933–34* NBC; 1931–32* CBS; 1935–36*, 1938–41*, and 1943* MUT
Elston, Gene 1958–60 MUT; 1954–57 Chi-N; 1962–86 Hou-N; 1987–95 (1995–97*) CBS; 1967* NBC.
Enberg, Dick 1969–78, 1980, and 1985 Cal-A; 1982 (1982*) NBC
Erskine, Carl 1960 ABC
Fairly, Ron 1979–86 Cal-A; 1987–92 SF-N; 1993–2000 Sea-A
Faris, Lynn 1966–67 KC-A; 1972 Min-A
Farmer, Ed 1992–2000 Chi-A
Farrell, Maury 1948 NY-N
Faucher, Ralph 1971–72 CHI-A
Feller, Bob 1958 MUT; 1982–83 CLE-A
Ferron, Guy 1969–81 MON-N
Finnegan, Bob 1958–1961 CBS; 1966 CHI-A
Fitzgerald, John 1959–1961 CBS
Flanagan, Mike 1999–2000 Bal-A
Flanagan, Pat 1929–43

Chi-A; 1929–43 Chi-N; 1929*, 1932*, and 1934* CBS
Flood, Curt 1978 Oak-A
Ford, Whitey 1969–71 NY-A
Fosse, Ray 1986–2000 Oak-A
Foster, Bud 1978 Oak-A
Frattare, Lanny 1976–2000 Pit-N; 1994–95 BASE
Frazier, George 1994–95 BASE; 1998–2000 Col-N
Freehan, Bill 1979-80 Sea-A; 1984–85 Det-A
Frey, Jim 1987 Chi-N
Frisch, Frank 1939 Bos-A; 1939 Bos-N; 1947–48 and 1953 NY-N; 1959–1961 CBS
Fritz, Ralph 1973–74 Min-A
Fuentes, Tito 1981–91 SF-N
Fulton, Bob 1954 MUT
Gamere, Bob 1970 NY-A
Gammons, Peter 1991–2000 ESPN
Garagiola, Joe 1955–62 StL-N; 1961–64 NBC; 1965–67 NY-A; 1975–88 NBC; 1990 Cal-A; 1998–2000 Ari-N; 1961–65* and 1974–88* NBC.
Garceau, Scott 1992–93 Bal-A
Garcia, Jose 1962–72 LA-N
Garvey, Steve 1988–89 CBS
Geitzen, Bruce 1989–90 Hou-N
Gibson, Bob 1976 ABC; 1988–89 CBS; 1973* ROBERT WOLD.
Gibson, Kirk 1998–2000 DET-A
Gillespie, Earl 1953–63 Mil-N; 1957–58* NBC.
Gilmore, Bob 1952–54 Cin-N.
Gladden, Dan 2000 Min-A
Glass, David 1981–85 SF-N
Gleeson, Art 1951–52 NY A; 1950–52 and 1954–57 MUT; 1960–64 Bos-A
Glieber, Frank 1978–80 Tex-A
Goldsholl, Bob 1980 NY-N
Gonzales, Julio 1981 Oak-A; 1989–90 and 1993–1997 SF-N
Gonzalez, Antonio 1983–86 Cal-A
Gonzalez, Danny 1996 Hou-N
Gordon, John 1970–72 Bal-A; 1982–86 NY-A; 1987–2000 Min-A
Goss, Bailey 1953 and 1958–59 Was-A; 1954–56 Bal-A
Gould, Rich 1998–99 StL-N
Gowdy, Curt 1949–50 NY-A; 1951–65 Bos-A; 1966–75 NBC; 1985–86 CBS; 1958–62*, 1964*, 1966–75*, and 1978* NBC; 1980–81*, 1983*, and 1985–86* CBS
Graham, Scott 1999–2000 Phi-N
Grande, George 1988–89 CBS; 1989–90 NY A; 1992 StL-N; 1993–2000 Cin-N; 1994–95 BASE
Graney, Jack 1932–44 and 1946–53 Cle-A; 1932* and 1934–35* CBS
Grant, Mark 1997–2000 SD-N
Grant, Mudcat 1973–74 and 1977 Cle-A
Grant, Taylor 1937 and 1941–42 Phi-N
Greenwald, Hank 1979–86 and 1989–96 SF-N; 1987–88 NY-A; 1994–95 BASE; 1997 (1997*) CBS
Grieve, Tom 1995–2000 Tex-A.
Griffin, Marc 1996–98 Mon-N
Grigsby, Bill 1959–61 KC-A
Grimm, Charlie 1939–42 and 1960 CHI-N
Gross, Jerry 1961 and 1963–67 StL-N; 1969–71 and 1978 SD-N
Guinan, Jack 1959 Was-A
Gumbel, Greg 1990–93 (1990–93*) CBS; 1996 (1996*) NBC
Guy, Raymond 1922* WEST
Hadley, Bump 1949–50 Bos-A; 1949–51 Bos-N
Hagin, Wayne 1981–84 Oak-A; 1987–88 SF-N; 1989–91 Chi-A; 1993–2000 Col-N; 2000 (2000*) ESPN
Hale, Allen 1942 Bro-N
Hall, Halsey 1961–73 Min-A
Hamilton, Milo 1953 StL-A; 1954 StL-N; 1956–57 and 1980–84 Chi-N; 1962–65 Chi-A; 1966–75 Atl-N; 1976–79 Pit-N; 1985–2000 Hou-N; 1994–95 BASE
Hamilton, Tom 1990–2000 Cle-A
Haney, Fred 1960 NBC
Haring, Claude 1944–46 and 1948–54 Phi-A; 1944–46, 1948–49, 1952, and 1955–62 Phi-N; 1963–64 Pit-N
Harmon, Merle, 1955–61 KC-A; 1964–65 Mil-N; 1965 ABC; 1967–69 Min-A; 1970–79 Mil-A; 1980–81 (1980*) NBC; 1982–89 Tex-A.
Harrelson, Bud 1983 NY-N.
Harrelson, Ken 1975–81 Bos-A; 1982–85 and 1990–2000 Chi-A; 1987–88 NY-A; 1994–95 BASE
Harrington, John 1935* NBC.
Harper, Earl 1946 Cle-A
Hartman, Chad 1994–95 Min-A
Hartman, Harry 1930–33 and 1942 Cin-N
Hartman, Sid 1978–79 Min-A
Hartnett, Gabby 1959 CBS
Harwell, Ernie 1948–49 Bro-N; 1950–53 NY-N; 1954–59 Bal-A; 1960–91 and 1993–2000 Det-A; 1992–97 CBS; 1994–95 BASE; 1951* CBS; 1958*, 1961*, 1963*, and 1968* NBC; 1969* ROBERT WOLD; 1976–83*, 1985–86*, and 1988–89* CBS
Hatrick, George 1943 and 1945 Bos-N
Hawk, Bob 1929–33 Chi-A; 1929–33 Chi-N
Hawkins, Burt 1974 Tex-A
Healy, Fran 1978–83 NY-A; 1984–2000 NY-N.
Hearn, Jim 1969 Mon-N
Heatter, Gabriel 1936* and 1939* MUT
Hedrick, Tom 1971-72 Cin-N; 1973 Tex-A
Hegan, Mike 1978–80 and 1982–88 Mil-A; 1990–2000 Cle-A
Heilmann, Harry 1934–50 Det-A
Helfer, Al 1939–41 and 1956–57 Bro-N; 1945 NY-A; 1945 and 1949 NY-N; 1950–54 MUT; 1962, Hou-N; 1968–69 Oak-A; 1955–58* (1957) NBC
Henderson, Dave 1998–2000 Sea-A
Henrich, Tommy 1965 ABC
Herskowitz, Mickey 1963 Hou-N
Higueros, Erwin 1998–2000 SF-N
Hill, Edwin C. 1939* MUT
Hirsch, Larry 1984 Hou-N
Hitzges, Norm 1981, 1986–89, and 1991–95 Tex-A; 1990–91 ESPN
Hoak, Don 1965–66 Pit-N
Hodges, Russ 1932 Cin-N; 1935–38 Chi-N; 1939–45 Was-A; 1946–48 NY-A; 1949–57 NY-N; 1958–70 SF-N; 1951*, 1954*, 1959*, and 1961–62* NBC
Hoegler, Al 1950–52 CLE-A
Hoey, Fred 1925–38 Bos-A; 1925–38 Bos-N; 1933* CBS
Hogan, Marty 1951 Chi-N
Holtz, Mark 1982–97 Tex-A
Howarth, Jerry 1981–2000 Tor-A
Hoyos, Rudy 1973–81 LA-N
Hoyt, Waite 1942–65 and 1972 Cin-N; 1961* NBC
Hrabosky, Al 1985–2000 StL-N
Hrbek, Kent 1995 Min-A
Hudler, Rex 1999–2000 Ana-A
Hughes, Pat 1983 Min-A; 1984–95 Mil-A; 1996–2000 Chi-N
Hughson, Jim 1988–90 Mon-N; 1991–96 Tor-A
Hunter, Jim 1986–97 (1990–91* and 1995–97*) CBS; 1997–2000 Bal-A
Hunter, Pinky 1938–42 Cle-A
Husing, Ted 1924* NBC and 1927–34* CBS
Hussey, Tom 1944–54 Bos-A; 1944–50 Bos-N
Hutton, Tommy 1982–86 Mon-N; 1987–88 NY-A; 1990–93 ESPN; 1993 Tor-A; 1997–2000 Fla-N
Impemba, Mario 1995–1996 Cal-A; 1997–2000 Ana-A
Ingham, Bob 1948 StL-N
Irwin, Jim 1975 JIM Mil-A
Jackson, Darrin 2000 CHI-A
Jackson, Keith 1965 and 1976–82 (1976–82* and 1986*) ABC
Jackson, Reggie 1990 Cal-A; 1991–92 Oak-A; 1976*, 1979*, 1983*, and 1987* ABC
Jamison, Bob 1992 CAL A
Jarrin, Jaime 1959–2000 LA N
John, Tommy 1994–96 Min-A
Johnson, Ernie 1962–65 Mil-N; 1966–91 and 1995–99 Atl-N
Johnson, Len 1966–67 Chi-A
Johnson, Walter 1939 Was-A
Johnstone, Jay 1989–90 and 1993 NY-A
Jones, Bill 1997–2000 Tex-A
Jones, Charlie 1973–74 Cin-N; 1993–95 Col-N
Jones, Harry 1961–76 Cle-A
Jones, Red 1952–53 Cle-A
Kaat, Jim 1986 and 1995–2000 NY-A; 1987 Atl-N; 1988–93 Min-A; 1990–93 (1990–93*) CBS; 1994 ESPN; 1994–95 BASE
Kalas, Harry 1965–70 Hou-N; 1971–2000 Phi-N; 1984* CBS; 1994–95 BASE
Kalas, Todd 1992–93 NY-N; 1994–96 Phi-N; 1998–2000 TB-A
Kaline, Al 1976–2000 Det-A
Karvellas, Jim 1969 Bal-A
Kasey, Sen 1924 Chi-N
Kasper, Len 1999–2000 Mil-N
Kay, Michael 1992–2000 NY-A
Kell, George 1959 CBS; 1959–63 and 1965–97 Det-A; 1962* and 1968* NBC
Kelley, Bob 1953 Mil-N; 1961 LA-A
Kelly, Bud 1971–72 Chi-A
Kelly, Dan 1980–84 StL-N
Kelly, Gene 1950–59 Phi-N; 1962–63 Cin-N
Kelly, Hal 1969–70 Mon-N
Kennedy, Ed 1961–70 Cin-N
Kennedy, Kevin 1998–2000 (1998–2000*) ESPN.
Killebrew, Harmon 1976–78 and 1984–88 Min-A; 1982 Oak-A
Kiner, Ralph 1961 Chi-A; 1962–2000 NY-N; 1976–78* CBS
King, Bill 1981–2000 Oak-A; 1994–95 BASE
King, Larry 1984–85 BAL-A
King, Nellie 1967–75 Pit-N
King, Rich 1980–81 Chi-A
Kingery, Jeff 1993–2000 Col-N
Kirby, Gene 1950–52 MUT; 1953–54 ABC; 1955–64 CBS; 1965 YANKEE
Knight, Ray 1990–93 and 2000 ESPN
Korach, Ken 1993–95 Chi-A; 1996–2000 Oak-A
Koufax, Sandy 1967–72 (1967–68*) NBC
Kremer, Don 1975–76 Det-A
Krukow, Mike 1993–2000 SF-N
Kubek, Tony 1966–89 (1969–89*) NBC; 1977–89 Tor-A; 1990–94 NY-A
Kuiper, Duane 1988–2000 SF-N
Kurtz, Bob 1979–86 Min-A; 1993–2000 Bos-A
LaMar, Steve 1982–84 NY-N; 1985–88 Cle-A; 1991–92 Cin-N
Lane, Ray 1965–72 Det-A; 1979–84 Cin-N
LaPanta, Anthony 1999 Min-A
Lara, Ivan 1998 Ari-N; 1998–2000 Ana-A
Larrivee, Wayne 1996–2000 Chi-N
Laux, France 1929–43 and 1948 StL-A; 1929–43 and 1945 StL-N; 1933–38* CBS; 1939–41* and 1944* MUT
Lebrun, Raymond 1982–93 Mon-N
Lefebvre, Ryan 1995–98 Min-A; 1999–2000 KC-A
Leitner, Ted 1981–2000 SD-N
Levine, Ken 1991 Bal-A; 1992–94 Sea-A.; 1995 SD-N
Lewin, Josh 1997 Chi-N; 1998–2000 Det-A; 1998–2000 (1998–2000*) FOX
Lloyd, Vince 1950 and 1954–86 Chi-N; 1957–64 Chi-A
Lochman, Walt 1944 Chi-A
Logan, Johnny 1973 Mil-A
Lomax, Stan 1939* and 1955 MUT
Long, Paul 1957–62 Pit-N
Lopez, Gustavo Moreno 1983–91 SD-N
Loughlin, Matt 1996–2000 NY-N
Lowenstein, John 1986–95 Bal-A
Lucas, Greg 1989–94 TEX-A
Luciano, Ron 1980* NBC
Lynn, Fred 1993–1997 ESPN
Lyons, Steve 1996–2000 FOX
MacLean, John 1956–60 MUT; 1961–68 Was-A; 1972 Bos-A
MacWilliams, Andy 1987 Cin-N
Maddox, Garry 1987–96 Phi-N
Magrane, Joe 1998 ESPN; 1998–2000 TB-A
Mancuso, Gus 1952–53 StL-N
Manfra, Fred 1993–2000 Bal-A
Manning, Rick 1989–2000 Cle-A
Manning, Tom 1926–31 and 1956–57 Cle-A; 1929–38* NBC
Mantle, Mickey 1969–70 (1969–70*) NBC; 1988 NY-A
Markas, Rory 1992–94 Mil-A
Marks, Garnett 1927–28 StL-A; 1927–28 StL-N
Marr, Tom 1981–86 Bal-A
Martin, Billy 1986-87 NY-A
Martin, Dave 1968 Chi-A; 1969–71 Cle-A; 1972–73 Bos-A; 1980 Pit-N
Martin, J.C. 1975 Chi-A
Martin, Ned 1961–92 Bos-A; 1975* NBC; 1976–78* CBS
Martinez, Buck 1987–2000 Tor-A; 1992–2000 (1996–2000*) ESPN
Martinez, Edgard 1981, 1986–88, and 1993 SF-N
Martinez, Hector 1990–2000 Bos-A
Martinez, Leon 1981–88, 1990-92 Chi-N
Martinez, Ramon 1983 SF-N
Martini, Anita 1976 HOU-N
Matthews, Denny 1969–2000 KC-A; 1994–95 BASE; 1982* CBS
Matthews, Gary 2000 TOR-A
Mayoral, Luis 1998–99 TEX-A
Mazer, Bill 1964 MIL-N
McCarver, Tim 1980–82

Phi-N; 1983–98 NY-N; 1984–89 (1985–89*) ABC; 1990–93 (1990–93*) CBS; 1994–95 (1995*) BASE; 1996–2000 FOX (1996–2000*); 1999–2000 NY-A
McColgan, Bill 1958–60 Cle-A
McConnell, Joe 1978–79 Min-A; 1980–84 Chi-A
McCormick, Frank 1958–68 Cin-N
McDonald, Arch 1934–38 and 1940–56 Was-A; 1939 NY-A
McDonough, Sean 1988–2000 Bos-A; 1990 and 1994 ESPN; 1992–93 (1992–93*) CBS; 1994–95 BASE
McGheehan, W.B. 1922* WEST.
McIntyre, Jim 1966–70 Cin-N; 1970* NBC
McKee, Tom 1977–80 Tor-A
McLaughlin, Dan 1999–2000 StL-N
McLendon, Gordon 1949–52 LIB
McLeod, Fred 1979 Cle-A; 1995-97 Det-A
McLinn, Stoney 1938 Phi-N
McNamee, Graham 1923–25* WEST; 1926–35* NBC
Mee, Tom 1992–93 Min-A
Menchine, Ron 1969–70 Was-A
Mercer, Bill 1972–73 Tex-A; 1974–75 Chi-A
Merrill, Bill 1974–81 Tex-A
Messer, Frank 1964–67 Bal-A; 1968–85 NY-A; 1986–87 Chi-A
Meyer, Russ 1961 CBS
Meyers, Joel 1987–89 Cal-A; 1990–92 LA-N; 1993–97 ESPN
Michaels, Al 1971–73 Cin-N; 1974–76 SF-N; 1976–89 (1976–89*) ABC; 1994–95 (1995*) BASE; 1972* NBC
Miller, Gary 1991–1996 ESPN
Miller, Jon 1974 Oak-A; 1978–79 Tex-A; 1980–82 Bos-A; 1983–96 Bal-A; 1986–89 NBC; 1990–2000 (1996–2000*) ESPN; 1994–95 BASE; 1997–2000 SF-N
Mittendorf, Gene 1924 Cin-N
Molina, Hector 1987-88 Chi-N.; 1992-99 Chi-A
Molitor, Paul 1999 Min-A
Monday, Rick 1985–87 and 1993–2000 LA-N; 1989–92 SD-N
Montgomery, Bob 1982–93 BOS-A
Moore, Monte 1962–67 KC-A; 1968–77 and 1989–92 Oak-A; 1978–82 USA; 1972–74* NBC
Mora, Rene 1999–2000 SD-N
Morgan, Hank 1965 Mil-N
Moran, Jack, 1955–61 Cin-N
Moreland, Tim 1983 Min-A
Morgan, Joe 1985 Cin-N; 1986–87 NBC; 1988–89 (1988*) ABC; 1988–93 SF-N; 1990–2000 (1996–2000*) ESPN; 1994–95 (1995*) BASE; 1996–2000 (1996–2000*) NBC
Morgan, Ray 1947–48 Was-A
Mosley, Dwayne 1982 Mil-A; 1983–84 KC-A
Mueller, Jim 1978 Cle-A
Munday, Bill 1929–34* NBC
Munson, Larry 1966–67 Atl-N
Murcer, Bobby 1983–85 and 1987–2000 NY-A
Murphy, Bob 1954–59 Bos-A; 1960–61 Bal-A; 1962–2000 NY-N; 1985–86 and 1988 CBS; 1994–95 BASE
Musburger, Brent 1985–90 CBS; 1995 BASE; 2000 ESPN; 1976*, 1978–79*, and 1981–89* CBS
Musser, Andy 1976–2000 PHI N; 1976* and 1984* CBS
Nadel, Eric 1979–2000 Tex-A
Nahan, Stu 1981* CBS
Nava, Milt 1958 LA-N
Neal, Bob 1946, 1949, 1952–53, and 1957–67 Cle-A; 1955–56 (1955–56*) MUT; 1957–58* NBC
Neall, Roy 1943–46 Phi-N
Nelson, Dave 1979 KC-A; 1988–89 Chi-N; 1998–99 Cle-A
Nelson, Lindsey 1951–52 LIB; 1957–61 NBC; 1962–78 NY-N; 1979–81 SF-N; 1985–86 CBS; 1964*, 1969*, and 1973* NBC
Nesbitt, Dick 1942–45 Cin-N
Newell, Hal 1951 Cle-A
Newman, Al 1994 Min-A
Newton, Walk 1938–39 Phi-N
Niehaus, Dave 1969–76 Cal-A; 1977–2000 Sea-A; 1994–95 BASE
Northrup, Jim 1985–94 Det-A
Noto, Mike 1988–91 Cal-A
Nuxhall, Joe 1967–2000 Cin-N
O'Brien, Dave 1993–2000 Fla-N; 2000 ESPN
O'Donnell, Bill 1966–82 Bal-A; 1969–76 (1969* and 1971*) NBC
O'Hara, Johnny 1927–33 Chi-A; 1944–47 and 1949 StL-A; 1943–46 StL-N; 1929* NBC; 1936–38* CBS
Olden, Paul 1988–89 Cle-A; 1991 Cal-A; 1991–92 ESPN; 1994–96 NY-A; 1998–2000 TB-A.
Oliu, Enrique 1998–2000 TB-A
Ortega, Eduardo 1987–90 and 1992–2000 SD-N; 1991 SF-N; 1993–2000* CBS
Olver, Fergie 1981–96 Tor-A
Osborn, Gene 1965–66 Det-A; 1970 Pit-N; 1973 Chi-A; 1975 KC-A
Osborn, Wayne 1945 Chi-N
Osterman, Larry 1967–77 and 1984–92 Det-A; 1979–83 Min-A
Ott, Mel 1955 MUT; 1956–58 Det-A
Paciorek, Tom 1988–1999 Chi-A.; 2000 Det-A
Palmer, Jim 1983–89 (1980* and 1983–89*) ABC; 1989–2000 Bal-A; 1995 (1995*) BASE
Papa, Greg 1993–2000 Oak-A
Park, Daryl 1959–61 CBS
Park, Gary 1973–87 SF-N
Parker, Wes 1973 Cin-N
Parnell, Mel 1965–68 Bos-A; 1969 Chi-A
Paschke, Jim 1988–91 and 1995-96 Mil-A
Passe, Loel, 1962–76 Hou-N
Patek, Fred 1985 Tex-A
Patrick, Van 1947–48 Cle-A; 1949 and 1952–59 Det-A; 1960 MUT; 1948* MUT
Patterson, Ted 1983 Bal-A
Pegler, Westbrook 1931* NBC
Pellegrino, Joe 1977–78 Det-A
Perez, Josue 1998–99 Tex-A
Perez, Santos 1992 SD-N
Perez y Martinez, Armando 1986 Chi-A.; 1993 Chi-N
Pesky, Johnny 1969–74 Bos-A
Peterson, Jim 1978 Oak-A
Petrocelli, Rico 1979 Bos-A
Pettit, Lloyd 1963, 1965–66, and 1969–70 Chi-N; 1965–67 Chi-A
Physioc, Steve 1986 Cin-N; 1990–94 ESPN; 1997–2000 Ana-A; 1994-95 BASE
Pierce, Billy 1970 Chi-A
Piersall, Jim 1974 Tex-A; 1977–81 Chi-A
Pi–Gonzalez, Amaury 1981-90 Oak-A; 1985–87 (1985–87*) CBS; 1995–2000 SF-N; 1998–2000 (1998–2000*) ESPN
Poier, Don 1981 Sea-A
Porter, Ross 1977–2000 LA-N; 1977–78* CBS
Pothier, Rene 1997–99 Mon-N
Powell, Jim 1993–94 Min-A; 1996–97 Mil-A; 1998–2000 Mil-N
Price, Elliott 1992–99 Mon-N
Price, Jim 1993–2000 Det-A
Prince, Bob 1948–75 and 1982–85 Pit-N; 1976 Hou-N; 1976 ABC; 1959–60*, 1965–66*, and 1970–71* NBC
Proctor, Mel 1980–81 Tex-A; 1984–96 Bal-A; 1994–95 BASE; 1997–2000 SD-N
Prough, Al 1947 Det-A
Provedor, Armando 1984–85 SF-N
Quilici, Frank 1976–77 and 1980–82 Min-A
Quinlan, Jack 1955–64 Chi-N; 1960* NBC
Quintana, Miguel 1998–2000 Ari-N
Ramey, Hal 1979 Oak-A
Ramirez, Felo 1993–2000 Fla-N
Ramirez, Rafael 1987 Cal-A
Ramos, Christian 1993 Chi-N
Ramsey, Bob 1998–99 StL-N
Randolph, Jay 1975–86 StL-N; 1976–79 NBC; 1988 Cin-N; 1993–96 Fla-N
Rathbun, Bob 1992–94 Det-A; 1997–2000 Atl-N
Rawson, Ron 1943 StL-N
Ray, Larry 1955–56 KC-A; 1957 Bal-A
Raymond, Claude 1973–99 Mon-N
Reagan, Ronald 1933–37 Chi-N; 1989* NBC
Reese, Harold (Pee Wee) 1960–64 CBS; 1965 YANKEE; 1966–68 NBC; 1969–70 Cin-N
Reghi, Michael 1997–2000 Bal-A
Remy, Jerry 1988–2000 Bos-A
Reusch, Ron 1982–90 Mon-N
Reuss, Jerry 1991–93 ESPN; 1997–98 Ana-A
Reynolds, Harold 1996–2000 ESPN
Rice, Bruce 1962 KC-A
Rice, Grantland 1921–23* WEST
Rigney, Bill 1973, 1983–84, and 1991–92 Oak-A
Risenhoover, Dick 1972–77 Tex-A
Rivera, Carlos 1982 and 1992 SF-N
Rizzs, Rick 1983–91 and 1995–2000 Sea-A; 1992–94 Det-A
Rizzuto, Phil 1957–1996 NY-A; 1964* and 1976* NBC
Roberts, Robin 1976 Phi-N
Roberts, Tony 1970 Was-A
Robinson, Brooks 1978–93 Bal-A; 1983* CBS
Robinson, Frank 1999–2000 FOX
Robinson, Jackie 1965 ABC
Robinson, Ted 1980 and 1985–87 Oak-A; 1984 and 1988–92 Min-A; 1985–97 (1985–97*) CBS; 1986–89 NBC; 1993–2000 SF-N
Rojas, Cookie 1984–86 Cal-A
Rooker, Jim 1981–93 Pit-N; 1994–97 ESPN
Rooney, John 1985–97 (1987–92* and 1995–97*) CBS; 1987 Min-A; 1988–2000 Chi-A; 1994–95 BASE; 1997–98 (1997–98*) FOX
Rose, Howie 1995–2000 NY-N
Ross, Spencer 1985–86 NY-A
Rowswell, Rosey 1936–54 Pit-N
Roy, Jean–Pierre 1969–83 Mon-N; 1978 Tor-A
Rucker, Reggie 1983–84 Cle-A
Ruiz, Francisco 1993–2000 Hou-N
Rush, Red 1965 KC-A; 1967–70 Chi-A; 1972 and 1979–80 Oak-A
Ryan, Dave 1997–99 ESPN
Ryan, Quin 1924–31 Chi-A; 1924–31 Chi-N; 1925* NBC; 1935* MUT
Saam, Byrum 1938–54 Phi-A; 1939–49 and 1951–75 Phi-N; 1959* and 1965* NBC
Sample, Billy 1988–89 Atl-N; 1992 Sea-A; 1993–94 Cal-A; 1990–91 ESPN
Sanchez-Diago, Orlando 1962-76, 1987-92 Hou-N
Sanders, John 1981–89 Pit-N; 1991–2000 Cle-A.; 1990 ESPN
Sands, Les 1956 Was-A
Santo, Ron 1990–2000 Chi-N
Santos, Matias 1992–95 SD-N
Sarault, Jean–Paul 1969–71 Mon-N
Saunders, John 1990–93 ESPN
Savage, Guy 1962-64 Hou-N
Schacht, Al 1944 NY-A; 1944 NY-N
Scheffing, Bob 1964 Det-A
Schenkel, Chris 1954 Mil-N; 1958 CBS; 1965 ABC
Schmidt, Mike 1990 Phi- N
Schonely, Bill 1969 Sea-A
Schreiner, Denny 1983 Cle-A
Schroeder, Bill 1995–1997 Mil-A; 1998–2000 Mil-N
Schulte, Greg 1998–2000 Ari-N
Schweizer, Bob 1997 CBS
Sciambi, Jon 1999–2000 Fla-N
Score, Herb 1964–97 Cle-A
Scott, Mark 1956-60 Cin-N
Scott, Ray 1961–66 and 1973–75 Min-A; 1971 Was-A; 1976–77 Mil-A; 1982–93 Pit-N; 1965* NBC
Scully, Vin 1950–57 Bro-N; 1958–2000 LA-N; 1983–89 (1983–89*) NBC; 1953*, 1955–56*, 1959*, 1961–63*, 1965–66*, 1974*, and 1983–89* NBC; 1973* ROBERT WOLD; 1977–83*, 1990–93*, and 1995–97* CBS
Seaver, Tom 1988 CBS; 1989 NBC; 1989–93 NY-A; 1999–2000 NY-N; 1976*, 1979*, 1981*, and 1983* ABC; 1978*, 1980*, and 1982* NBC
Sell, Carl 1968 Atl-N
Serrano, Bobby 1990–2000 Bos-A
Sham, Brad 1990 and 1995–97 Tex-A
Shamsky, Art 1980–81 NY-N
Shane, Mary 1977 Chi-A
Shannon, Mike 1972–2000 StL-N
Shannon, Steve 1978–79 KC-A; 1980 Cal-A; 1981–85 Mil-A
Shaver, Al 1970 Min-A
Shrader, John 1988 Oak-A
Shulman, Dan 1995–2000 Tor-A; 1995–2000 (1996–2000*) ESPN
Simmons, Lon 1958–73, 1976–78, and 1996–2000 SF-N; 1981–95 Oak-A; 1962* NBC
Simpson, Jim 1966–75 (1968–73*) NBC
Simpson, Joe 1987–91 Sea-A; 1992–2000 Atl-N
Sims, Dave 1993–94 ESPN
Sims, Frank 1960–62 Phi-N; 1969–70 SD-N
Singleton, Ken 1985-86 Tor-A; 1985–96 Mon-N; 1996 FOX; 1997–2000 NY-A
Slater, Bill 1944–45 and 1948 NY-A; 1944–45 and 1947 NY-N; 1947* NBC
Slowes, Charlie 1989 NBC; 1995 CBS; 1998–2000 TB-A
Smalley, Roy 1995 ESPN
Smith, Les 1951–52 Bos-N
Smith, Ozzie 1997–99 TWIB; 2000 StL-N
Snider, Duke 1969–71

SD-N; 1973–86 Mon-N; 1990, 92-LA; 1983* CBS
Sorensen, Lary 1992–93 ESPN; 1995–98 Det-A; 1994-95 BASE
Soria, Oscar 1999-2000 Ari-N
Sorrell, Bill 1976* CBS
Speaker, Tris 1949 Cle-A
Splittorff, Paul 1988–2000 KC-A
Staats, Dewayne 1977–84 Hou-N; 1985–89 Chi-N; 1990–94 NY-A; 1994–95 BASE; 1995–1997 (1997*) ESPN; 1998–2000 TB-A
Stanton, Andrew 1932–33 Phi-A; 1932–33 Phi-N
Stanton, Bob 1947* NBC
Stargell, Willie 1983–84 Pit-N
Stark, Dolly 1936 Phi-N
Starr, Bob 1972–79 StL-N; 1980–89 and 1993–97 Cal-A; 1990–92 Bos-A
Staub, Rusty 1986–95 NY-N
Steiner, Charley 1998–2000 (1998–2000*) ESPN
Stembridge, Terry 1973 Tex-A
Stenhouse, Mike 1996 Mon-N
Sterling, John 1982–87 Atl-N; 1989–2000 NY-A
Stern, Bill 1935–36* NBC; 1939 NBC
Stock, Wes 1982–83 Sea-A
Stockton, Dick 1975–78 Bos-A; 1985–90 (1988*) CBS; 1993–95 Oak-A; 1975* NBC
Stoller, Stan 1946 Was-A
Stone, Phil 1984 KC-A; 1985 Tex-A; 1986 SF-N
Stone, Steve 1980–82 (1981–82*) ABC; 1983–2000 Chi-N; 1994–95 BASE
Street, Charles (Gabby) 1945–50 StL-N; 1946 StL-A
Sullivan, Claude 1964–67 Cin-N
Sundberg, Jim 1990–95 Tex-A
Sutcliffe, Rick 1998–2000 SD-N; 1998–2000 (1999–2000*) ESPN
Sutton, Darin 2000 Ana-A
Sutton, Don 1990–2000 Atl-N
Tait, Joe 1973–87 Cle-A
Talavera, Armando 1998–2000 NY-A
Taveres, Ricardo 1998–2000 TB-A
Taylor, Russ 1970–76 Mon-N
Tekulve, Kent 1992–97 Phi-N
Ten-Eyck, Sidney 1930–33 Cin-N
Thomas, Lowell 1939* MUT
Thomas Zapiain, Mario 1983–97 SD-N
Thompson, Bill 1965–73 SF-N
Thompson, Chuck 1946–48 Phi-A; 1947–48 Phi-N; 1955–56, 1962–87, and 1991–2000 Bal-A; 1957–60 Was-A; 1959–60 NBC; 1960*, 1966*, and 1969–70* NBC
Thorne, Gary 1985–88 and 1994–2000 NY-N; 1989 Chi-A; 1990–93, 1996, and 2000 (1996* and 2000*) ESPN
Tolentino, Jose 1998–2000 Ana-A
Tompkins, Barry 1993 SF-N
Torborg, Jeff 1994–97 (1995–97*) CBS; 1994–95 BASE; 1996 Cal-A; 1996–2000 FOX
Torre, Joe 1985–90 Cal-A
Totten, Hal 1924–44 Chi-N; 1926–44 Chi-A; 1945–50 MUT; 1926–27* and 1931–32* CBS; 1933–38* NBC
Trautwig, Al 1991–2000 NY-A
Trease, Denny 1980–92 KC-A
Trevino, Alex 1996–2000 Hou-N
Trout, Dizzy 1953–55 Det-A
Trout, Robert 1938* CBS
Trupiano, Jerry 1985–86 Hou-N; 1989–90 Mon-A; 1991 CBS; 1993–2000 Bos-A
Tucker, Joe 1956 Pit-N
Tyson, Ty 1927–42, 1947–48, and 1951–52 Det-A; 1935–36* NBC
Uecker, Bob 1969 Atl-N; 1971–1997 Mil-A; 1998–2000 Mil-N; 1976–81 (1976–81*) ABC; 1994–95 (1995*) BASE; 1996–1998* NBC
Underwood, Matt 2000 Cle-A
Valentin, Ruben 1981 SF-N; 1986–93 Cal-A
Valentino, Dom 1975 NY-A; 1980 Oak-A
Valle, Dave 1998–2000 Sea-A
Vandergriff, Tom 1975–77 Tex-A
Vander Pyle, Ellis 1932–33 Cle-A
Van Horne, Dave 1969–2000 Mon-N
Van Wieren, Pete 1976–2000 Atl-N
Vasgersian, Matt 1997 Mil-A; 1998–2000 Mil-N
Veeck, Bill 1958–59 NBC
Villa, Beto 1998–2000 NY-A
Villa, Ulpiano Cos 1982–92 Cal-A
Villata, Fernando 1985 SF-N
Villeneuve, Michel 1996–98 Mon-N
Vines, Les 1940 Phi-N
Vukovich, Pete 1989–91 Mil-A
Wakeman, Tony 1936* MUT
Walden, Mike 1970 LA-N; 1972 StL-N
Waldman, Suzyn 1996–2000 NY-A
Walk, Bob 1994–2000 Pit-N
Walker, Harry 1973 StL-N
Walker, Wayne 1976–81 and 1985 Oak-A
Waller, Bob 1971 Cin-N; 1973–74 Chi-A; 1975–78 Oak-A
Walsh, Blaine 1954–65 Mil-N; 1961* NBC
Walsh, George 1949 and 1952 Phi-A; 1949 and 1953–54 Phi-N
Walton, Ray 1951 Phi-A
Wathan, John 1996–97 KC-A
Weaver, Earl 1983–84 (1983–84*) ABC
Weber, Ron 1983 Min-A
Wells, Don 1949–51 LIB; 1953–60 Chi-A; 1961–65 LA-A; 1966–72 Cal-A
Welsh, Chris 1994–2000 Cin-N
West, Jim 1971–76 Chi-N
Wester, Al 1952–60 MUT
Wheeler, Chris 1977–2000 Phi-N
Whitaker, Jack 1959–61 CBS
White, Andrew 1931–32* CBS
White, Bill 1971–88 NY-A; 1985–89 CBS; 1976–79*, 1984–85*, and 1987–88* CBS
White, Fred 1975–98 KC-A
Whitfield, Shelby 1969 Was-A
Wiers, Jack 1987 Bal-A
Wiig, Gunnar 1933* CBS
Williams, Brian 1993–2000 Tor-A
Williams, Howard 1948 Was-A; 1951 StL-A; 1954 Bal-A
Williams, Paul 1948 and 1950–52 Det-A
Wills, Maury 1973 (1973*) NBC
Wilson, Bert 1944–55 Chi-N
Wilson, Jim 1947–51 Chi-N; 1952–53 MUT
Wilson, Joe 1946–51 Chi-N; 1959 MUT
Wilson, Ken 1977–82 Sea-A; 1983–85 Cin-N; 1986–90 StL-N; 1991–95 Cal-A; 1996–98 Oak-A
Winfield, Dave 1996 FOX
Winkles, Bobby 1989–93 Mon-N; 1994 Cal-A
Wisk, Al 1977–79 Cal-A; 1980–82 KC-A
Wismer, Harry 1948 Det-A
Witcher, Geoff 1984 Cal-A
Wolf, Warner, 1969–71 Was-A; 1976 (1976*) ABC
Wolff, Bob 1947–60 Was-A; 1950 MUT; 1961 Min-A; 1962–64 NBC; 1965 ABC; 1956* MUT; 1958* and 1961–62* NBC
Woods, Jim 1953–56 NY-A; 1957 NY-N; 1957 NBC; 1958–69 Pit-N; 1970–71 StL-N; 1972–73 Oak-A; 1974–78 Bos-A; 1978–82 USA
Woodward, Woody 1974–75 Cin-N
Worrell, Bill 1985–2000 Hou-N
Wynn, Early 1977–81 Tor-A; 1982–83 Chi-A
Yniguez, Pepe 1998–2000 LA-N
Young, Kevin 1982 Mil-A
Zabriskie, Steve 1980 ABC; 1983–89 NY-N; 1990–93 ESPN

APPENDIX 1

Baseball Quotations

Sean Lahman

The game of baseball has been a fountain of commentary and wit since it was played in its earliest forms. Everyone from presidents to paupers has played it or watched it, and everyone in between has had something to say about it. Before and after each game, baseball players, managers, and executives alike are asked to dispense their thoughts on everything from that day's opponent to the future of the game—and someone is there to record it. Most of these responses are digested by readers in the next day's newspaper like a quick meal—essential at the time but quickly forgotten. Some statements, like baseball itself, live long after the next afternoon's game or the next evening's deadline.

This section includes some of the most poignant—and humorous—statements made about baseball since people first took the time to record their thoughts about the game. Not only are some of the greatest players in the game's history represented here, but also included are writers, poets, and royalty (or at least Babe Ruth, the "Sultan of Swat"). After his playing days had ended, Ruth reflected, "What I am, what I have, what I am going to leave behind me—all this I owe to the game of baseball, without which I would have come out of St. Mary's Industrial School in Baltimore as a tailor, and a pretty bad one, at that."

Leading Off

"Whoever would understand the heart and mind of America had better learn baseball, the rules and realities of the game—and do it by watching first some high school or small-town teams."

— Jacques Barzun

"It breaks your heart. It is designed to break your heart. The game begins in the spring, when everything else begins again, and it blossoms in the summer, filling the afternoons and evenings, and then as soon as the chill rains come, it stops and leaves you to face the fall alone."

— A. Bartlett Giamatti

"I see great things in baseball. It's our game—the American game. It will take our people out of doors, fill them with oxygen, give them a larger physical stoicism. Tend to relieve us from being a nervous, dyspeptic set. Repair these losses, and be a blessing to us."

— Walt Whitman

"Baseball is the very symbol, the outward and visible expression of the drive and push and rush and struggle of the raging, tearing, booming 19th century."

— Mark Twain

"I enjoy the game because it's a beautifully designed game. It's a beautiful game to watch but principally because it makes me feel American. It makes me feel connected with this culture. And I think there are only three things that America will be known for 2,000 years from now when they study this civilization: the Constitution, jazz music and baseball. They're the three most beautifully designed things this culture's ever produced."

— Gerald Early

"The game itself is like Michelangelo's masterwork in the Sistine Chapel. You can cover it in filth, neglect it to death, attack what it represents and those who supervise it. But the game itself is ever resilient and ever resplendent, and just when you believe you have seen the last of its beauty, some new angle becomes visible to your eye and it is as if you have seen its splendor for the first time."

— Keith Olbermann

Winning

"If you are content with yourself, you'll stop taking those little steps forward and begin taking big steps backward."

— Greg Maddux

"This is not an easy game. To be a champion, you have to invest a little extra."

— Pete Rose

"There are only two places in the league. First and no place."

— Tom Seaver

"The worst thing is the day you realize you want to win more than your players do."

— Gene Mauch

"I'd rather be a swing man on a championship team than a regular on another team."

— Lou Piniella

"What are we out at the park for, except to win? I'd trip my mother. I'd help her up, brush her off, tell her I'm sorry. But mother don't make it to third base."

— Leo Durocher

"Show me a guy who's afraid to look bad, and I'll show you a guy you can beat every time."

— Lou Brock

"The greatest thrill in the world is to end the game with a home run and watch everybody walk off the field while you're running the bases on air."

— Al Rosen

"You may go a long time without winning, but you never forget that scent."

— Steve Busby

"The way a team plays as a whole determines its success. You may have the greatest bunch of individual stars in the world, but if they don't play together, the club won't be worth a dime."

— Babe Ruth

"In the end it all comes down to talent. You can talk all you want about intangibles, I just don't know what that means. Talent makes winners, not intangibles. Can nice guys win? Sure, nice guys can win—if they're nice guys with a lot of talent. Nice guys with a little talent finish fourth, and nice guys with no talent finish last."

— Sandy Koufax

Losing

"If a tie is like kissing your sister, losing is like kissing your grandmother with her teeth out."

— George Brett

On the expansion Mets: "They've shown me ways to lose that I never knew existed."

— Casey Stengel

"The only way to prove that you're a good sport is to lose."

— Ernie Banks

"The losing streak is bad for the fans, no doubt, but look at it this way. We're making a lot of people happy in other cities."

— Ted Turner

Managing the 1973 Texas Rangers: "We need just two players to be a contender. Just Babe Ruth and Sandy Koufax."

— Whitey Herzog

"The fans like to see home runs, and we've assembled a pitching staff for their enjoyment."

— Clark Griffith

"The worst curse in life is unlimited potential."

— Ken Brett

Following a tough loss: "The only reason I'm coming out here tomorrow is the schedule says I have to."

— Sparky Anderson

"When you're a winner you're always happy, but if you're happy as a loser you'll always be a loser."

— Mark Fidrych

"If you don't catch the ball, you catch the bus."

— Rocky Bridges

"Grantland Rice, the great sportswriter once said. 'It's not whether you win or lose, it's how you play the game.' Well Grantland Rice can go to hell as far as I'm concerned."

— Angels owner Gene Autry

"Losing clubs bicker, and you think maybe if they pulled together they would win. No. That's not it. If they won, they would pull together."

— Jim Bouton

"Losing streaks are funny. If you lose at the beginning, you got off to a bad start. If you lose in the middle off the season, you're in a slump. If you lose at the end, you're choking."

— Gene Mauch

Hitters

"I've found that you don't need to wear a necktie if you can hit."

— Ted Williams

"Guessing what the pitcher is going to throw is 80 percent of being a successful hitter. The other 20 percent is just execution."

— Henry Aaron

"You don't always make an out. Sometimes the pitcher gets you out."

— Carl Yastrzemski

When it was suggested he could raise his batting average by choking up on the bat: "Cadillacs are down at the end of the bat."

— Ralph Kiner

"You hit a four-ounce baseball with a 35-ounce bat and there's going to be some damage."

— George Foster

"There is only one legitimate trick to pinch hitting, and that's knowing the pitcher's best pitch when the count is 3-and-2. All the rest is a crapshoot."

— Earl Weaver

"Carrots might be good for my eyes, but they won't straighten out the curveball."

— Carl Furillo

"I have only one superstition. I make sure to touch all the bases when I hit a home run."

— Babe Ruth

"I have observed that baseball is not unlike a war, and when you come right down to it, we batters are the heavy artillery."

— Ty Cobb

"I wanted to be the greatest hitter who ever lived. A man has to have goals and that was mine, to have people say, 'There goes Ted Williams. The greatest hitter who ever lived.' "

— Ted Williams

Pitchers

"Closing games in the big leagues is a lot like landing

airplanes. A successful effort rarely warrants notice and a failure is considered a full-scale disaster."

— John Franco

"The pitcher has to find out if the hitter is timid. And if the hitter is timid, he has to remind the hitter he's timid."

— Don Drysdale

"I throw the ball right down the middle. The high-ball hitters swing over it and the low-ball hitters swing under it."

— Saul Rogovin

Explaining why he pitched so quickly: "What do you want me to do? Let them sons of bitches stand up there and think on my time?"

— Grover Cleveland Alexander

"I've always felt a lot of pitching coaches made a living out of running pitchers so they wouldn't have to spend that same time teaching them how to pitch."

— Johnny Sain

Responding to suggestions that he doctored pitches with a foreign substance: "I'm not going to agree with them and I'm not going to deny it. I do have a tendency to go to my hat a lot. I guess they figure that's where it is. That's not where it is, though."

— Mike Proly

"The way to catch a knuckleball is to wait until the ball stops rolling and then pick it up."

— Bob Uecker

On being a relief pitcher: "Why pitch nine innings when you can get just as famous pitching two?"

— Sparky Lyle

"All pitchers are liars and crybabies."

— Yogi Berra

"If I'd known I was gonna pitch a no-hitter today, I would have gotten a haircut."

— Bo Belinsky, 1962

"To a pitcher, a base hit is the perfect example of negative feedback."

— Steve Holvey

To rookie pitcher Ernie Johnson after he surrendered a mammoth home run to Ted Williams: "Don't worry, he's hit them off better pitchers than you."

— Billy Southworth

"Nothing makes a pitcher feel more secure than the sight of his teammates circling the bases during a ball game."

— Jim Brosnan

"I exploit the greed of all hitters."

— Lew Burdette

Fielders

"Two-thirds of the Earth is covered by water. The other one-third is covered by Garry Maddox."

— Ralph Kiner

"A great catch is like watching girls go by. The last one you see is always the prettiest."

— Bob Gibson

"Pop singer Mariah Carey is now dating Yankee shortstop Derek Jeter —proving that he can catch damn near anything."

— Jim Mullen

On teammate Luis Polonia: "If you hit Polonia 100 flyballs, you could make a movie out of it—*Catch 22.*"

— Dennis Lamp

"Guys who can field you can shake out of any old tree. Find me guys who can hit."

— Rogers Hornsby

"I could field as long as I can remember, but hitting has been a struggle all my life."

— Brooks Robinson

Managers

"The secret of managing is to keep the guys who hate you away from the guys who are undecided."

— Casey Stengel

"When I first became a manager, I asked Chuck Tanner for advice. He told me, 'Always rent.'"

— Tony LaRussa

On his managerial debut: "I had no trouble communicating. The players just didn't like what I had to say."

— Frank Robinson

"You don't save a pitcher for tomorrow. Tomorrow it may rain."

— Leo Durocher

"Bad baseball players make good managers."

— Earl Weaver

During his tenure as a minor league manager: "I like my players to be married and in debt. That's the way you motivate them."

— Ernie Banks

"The best qualification a coach can have is being the manager's drinking buddy."

— Jim Bouton

"If a manager of mine ever said someone was indispensable, I'd fire him."

— Charles Finley

"If you don't win, you're going to be fired. If you do win, you've only put off the day you're going to be fired."

— Leo Durocher

"It's what you learn after you know it all that counts."

— Earl Weaver

"There are three secrets to managing. The first secret is 'have patience.' The second is 'be patient.' And the third most important secret is 'patience.'"

— Chuck Tanner

"Concentration is the ability to think about absolutely

nothing when it is absolutely necessary."

— Ray Knight

"Most ballgames are lost, not won." — Casey Stengel

Words of Praise

"Mark McGwire hit a popup that went so high, all nine guys called for it."

— Randy Bonferraro

"Trying to hit Phil Niekro is like trying to eat Jell-O with chopsticks."

— Bobby Murcer

"I'm not sure I know what the hell charisma is, but I get the feeling it's Willie Mays."

— Ted Kluszewski

"Every time I look at my pocketbook, I see Jackie Robinson."

— Willie Mays

On Cool Papa Bell: "One time he hit a line drive right past my ear. I turned around and saw the ball hit his ass sliding into second."

— Satchel Paige

On Lefty Grove: "He could throw a lamb chop past a wolf."

— Bugs Baer

On the strength of Jimmie Foxx: "He has muscles in his hair."

— Lefty Gomez

On Tom Seaver: "Blind people come to the park just to listen to him pitch."

— Reggie Jackson

After being swept by Sandy Koufax and the Dodgers in the 1963 World Series: "I can see how he won 25 games. What I don't understand is how he lost five."

— Yogi Berra

On Pete Rose: "Does Pete hustle? Before the All-Star Game he came into the clubhouse and took off his shoes—and they ran another mile without him."

— Henry Aaron

"There have been only two authentic geniuses in the world, Willie Mays and Willie Shakespeare."

— Tallulah Bankhead

On Walter Johnson: "He's got a gun concealed on his person. They can't tell me he throws them balls with his arm."

— Ring Lardner

On Steve Carlton: "Sometimes I hit him like I used to hit Koufax, and that's like drinking coffee with a fork."

— Willie Stargell

On Mickey Mantle: "I wish I was half the ballplayer that he is."

— Al Kaline

On Willie Stargell: "He's got power enough to hit home runs in any park, including Yellowstone."

— Sparky Anderson

"Jackie Robinson was the greatest competitor I ever saw. He didn't win. He triumphed."

— Ralph Branca

Insults

On Hack Wilson: "The boy's got talent and desire, but he ain't got no neck."

— John McGraw

To teammate Joe Pepitone: "I wish I could buy you for what you're really worth and sell you for what you think you're worth."

— Mickey Mantle

On Ty Cobb: "He would climb a mountain to take a punch at an echo."

— Bugs Baer

On teammate Reggie Jackson: "Reggie's really a good guy. He'd give you the shirt off his back. Of course, he'd call a press conference to announce it."

— Catfish Hunter

On Lou Boudreau: "He is easily the slowest ballplayer since Ernie Lombardi was thrown out at first base trying to stretch a double into a single."

— Stanley Frank

"Every day in every way, baseball gets fancier and fancier. A few more years and they'll be playing on oriental rugs."

— Russell Baker

On the Chicago Black Sox: "Benedict Arnold—Betrayers of American boyhood. Not to mention American Girlhood and American Womanhood and American Hoodhood."

— Nelson Algren

"My own opinion is that the people who want to put Joe Jackson in the Hall of Fame are baseball's answer to those women who show up at murder trials wanting to marry the cute murderer."

— Bill James

On Hack Wilson: "He was built along the lines of a beer keg and not unfamiliar with its contents."

— Shirley Povich

"If Boog Powell held out his right arm he'd be a railroad crossing."

— Joe Garagiola

On teammate Thurman Munson: "Munson's not moody, he's just mean. When you're moody, you're nice sometimes."

— Sparky Lyle

Self-reflection

On reading that a poll of managers had said he possessed

the best slider in the American League: "I'm flattered, but I don't throw a slider."

— Pedro Martinez

On his pursuit of Ty Cobb's all-time hit record: "When I get the record, all it will make me is the player with the most hits. I'm also the player with the most at bats and the most outs. I never said I was a greater player than Cobb."

— Pete Rose

Nicknamed "The Human Rain Delay" for his behavior in the batter's box: "I feel my ability as a ballplayer is overshadowed by people saying, 'Hey, look at that idiot at the plate.' "

— Mike Hargrove

"I'm the straw that stirs the drink."

— Reggie Jackson

During his Hall of Fame induction: "The Good Lord was good to me. He gave me a strong body, a good right arm, and a weak mind."

— Dizzy Dean

"You can't get rich sitting on the bench, but I'm giving it a try."

— Phil Linz

"I'm in the twilight of a mediocre career."

— Frank Sullivan

"The highlight of my career? Oh, I'd say that was in 1967 in St. Louis. I walked with the bases loaded to drive in the winning run in an intra-squad game in spring training."

— Bob Uecker

"I'm working on a new pitch. It's called a strike."

— Jim Kern

After winning his third consecutive home run title in 1976: "A guy who strikes out as much as I do had better lead in something."

— Mike Schmidt

"If I knew I was going to live this long, I'd have taken better care of myself."

— Mickey Mantle, at age 46

"I ain't what I used to be, but who the hell is?"

— Dizzy Dean

"Trying to think with me is a mismatch. Hell, most of the time I don't know where it's going."

— Sam McDowell

"They shouldn't throw at me, I'm the father of five or six kids."

— Tito Fuentes

"I've heard of guys going 0-for-15, or 0-for-25, but I was 0-for-July."

— Bob Aspromonte

"I loved the game. I loved the competition. But I never had any fun. I never enjoyed it. All hard work, all the time."

— Carl Yastrzemski

"Now they talk on the radio about the records set by Ruth, and DiMaggio and Henry Aaron. But they rarely mention mine. Do you know what I have to show for the 61 home runs? Nothing, exactly nothing."

— Roger Maris

"I didn't come to New York to be a star. I brought my star with me."

— Reggie Jackson

"If I'd done everything I was supposed to, I'd be leading the league in homers, have the highest batting average, have given $100,000 to the Cancer Fund, and be married to Marie Osmond."

— Clint Hurdle

"I owe my success to expansion pitching, a short right field fence, and my hollow bats."

— Norm Cash

"If I did anything funny on the ball field, it was strictly accidental. Like the way I played third. Some people thought it was hilarious, but I was on the level all of the time."

— Rocky Bridges

"There is always some kid who may be seeing me for the first or last time. I owe him my best."

— Joe DiMaggio

The Business of Baseball

"The great trouble with baseball today is that most of the players are in the game for the money and that's it—not for the love of it, the excitement of it, the thrill of it."

— Ty Cobb, 1925

After negotiating his 1945 contract with Dodger's executive Branch Rickey: "I got a million dollars worth of free advice and a very small raise."

— Eddie Stanky

Describing what he would do with his 1975 salary: "Ninety percent I'll spend on good times, women, and Irish whiskey. The other 10 percent I'll probably waste."

— Tug McGraw

On Fernando Valenzuela's 1982 contract holdout: "All last year we tried to teach him English, and the only word he learned was 'million.'"

— Tommy Lasorda

"I don't need an agent. Why should I give somebody 10 percent when I do all the work?"

— Mark Fidrych

Challenging baseball's reserve clause in 1970: "A well-paid slave is nonetheless a slave."

— Curt Flood

"It isn't really the stars that are expensive. It's the high cost of mediocrity."

— Bill Veeck

"I signed Oscar Gamble on the advice of my attorney. I no longer have Gamble and I no longer have my attorney."

— Ray Kroc

"You measure the value of a ballplayer by how many

fannies he puts in the seats."
— George Steinbrenner

"Sometimes the best deals are the ones you don't make."
— Bill Veeck

Speaking of Teams

"Rooting for the New York Yankees is like rooting for U.S. Steel."
— Red Smith

"Cut me and I'll bleed Dodger blue."
— Tommy Lasorda

"All literary men are Red Sox fans. To be a Yankee fan in literary society is to endanger your life."
— John Cheever

After his trade to the Phillies in 1955: "That's too bad. They're the only team I can beat."
— Dave Cole

"When I was a kid, I wanted to play baseball and join the circus. With the Yankees, I've been able to do both."
— Graig Nettles

As manager of the Cardinals "Gashouse Gang": "We could finish first or in an asylum."
— Frankie Frisch

"Baseball isn't a life and death matter, but the Red Sox are."
— Mike Barnicle

The Arts

Fictional manager of the Washington Senators, to the Devil, in the musical *Damn Yankees:* "One longball hitter, that's what we need. I'd sell my soul for one longball hitter . . . hey, where did you come from?"
— Robert Shafer

"Poets are like baseball pitchers. Both have their moments. The intervals are the tough things."
— Robert Frost

"I never thought about being a writer as I grew up; a writer wasn't something to be. An outfielder was something to be. Most of what I know about style I learned from Roberto Clemente."
— John Sayles

Fictional fan in the movie *Bull Durham:* "I believe in the Church of Baseball. I've tried all the major religions and most of the minor ones. And the only church that truly feeds the soul, day-in day-out, is the Church of Baseball."
— Annie Savoy

In *Shoeless Joe:* "If you build it, he will come."
— W.P. Kinsella

The Media

"There's a fly to deep center field. Winfield is going back, back. He hits his head against the wall. It's rolling toward second base."
— Jerry Coleman

On fans who bring their radios to the ballpark: "I always thought it was strange knowing that thousands of people are listening to you describe a play they are watching."
— Vin Scully

"I heard the doctors revived a man after being dead for four-and-a-half minutes. When they asked what it was like being dead, he said it was like listening to New York Yankees announcer Phil Rizzuto during a rain delay."
— David Letterman

"It is interesting about people that leave early from ballgames. It's almost as if they came out to the ballgame to see if they can beat the traffic home."
— Lon Simmons

"The groan is audible. It can also be heard."
— Harry Caray

Umpires

"Many fans look upon an umpire as a sort of necessary evil to the luxury of baseball, like the odor that follows an automobile."
— Christy Mathewson

"Umpiring is the only profession in the world where you have to be perfect when you start and continue to improve."
— Todd Greanier, sportswriter

"If you don't think you're out, read the morning paper."
— Bill McGowan, umpire

"Boys, I'm one of those umpires that misses 'em every once in awhile. So if it's close, you'd better hit it."
— Cal Hubbard

"Whenever you have a tight situation and there's a close pitch, the umpire gets a squawk no matter how he calls it."
— Red Barber

Yogi-isms

"Baseball is 90 percent mental. The other half is physical."
— Yogi Berra

"If the people don't want to come out to the park, nobody's going to stop them."
— Yogi Berra

"If you can't imitate him, don't copy him."
— Yogi Berra

On why he was wearing gloves: "I'm wearing these gloves for my hands."
— Yogi Berra

"You can see a lot just by observing."
— Yogi Berra

APPENDIX 2

Major League Stadiums

Every baseball team, regardless of level, needs three things: a bat, a ball, and a place to play. While sandlots, streets, backyards, and fields have sufficed for amateur clubs, professionals have long preferred enclosed areas in order to charge a fee to spectators.

William Cammeyer is credited as the first to enclose a field and charge money for admittance in 1862. He opened a skating rink at his leased property at the corner of Lee and Rutledge Streets in Brooklyn during the winter, but come the spring he enclosed it for baseball. He allowed teams to play there for free but charged patrons 10 cents apiece to enter what was called Union Grounds. Cammeyer kept all the proceeds for himself. Others soon followed suit.

In the years since, ballparks have gone from modest to modern to high tech. At the start of the 21st century it was common for new stadiums to have retractable roofs to protect patrons and players alike from the elements. Technology also allowed these stadiums to have grass surfaces, whereas a decade earlier it was necessary for all enclosed parks to use artificial turf.

What follows is a list of the venues where each current major league team has played the majority of its games, excluding exhibition sites. Cities in parentheses refer to franchises that have relocated. In the case of Cleveland's League Park, the Indians continued to use that stadium for many weekday games until 1946. PNC Park in Pittsburgh and Miller Park in Milwaukee were scheduled to open in 2001.

Current American League Teams

Anaheim Angels
1961 Wrigley Field (Los Angeles)
1962–1965 Dodger Stadium (Los Angeles)
1966– Edison International Field (Anaheim Stadium until 1997)

Baltimore Orioles
1901 Lloyd Street Grounds (Milwaukee)
1902–1953 Sportsman's Park (St. Louis)
1954–1991 Memorial Stadium
1992– Oriole Park at Camden Yards

Boston Red Sox
1901–1911 Huntington Avenue Grounds
1912– Fenway Park

Chicago White Sox
1901–1910 South Side Park
1910–1990 Comiskey Park
1991– Comiskey Park (new structure)

Cleveland Indians
1901–1946 League Park
1932–1993 Cleveland Stadium
1994– Jacobs Field

Detroit Tigers
1901–1911 Bennett Park
1912–1999 Tiger Stadium (Navin Field 1912–1937, Briggs Stadium 1938–1960)
2000– Comerica Park

Kansas City Royals
1969–1972 Municipal Stadium
1973– Kauffman Stadium (Royals Stadium until 1993)

Minnesota Twins
1901–1910 American League Park (Washington, DC)
1911–1960 Griffith Stadium (Washington, DC)
1961–1981 Metropolitan Stadium
1982– Hubert H. Humphery Metrodome

New York Yankees
1901–1902 American League Park (Baltimore)
1903–1912 Hilltop Park
1913–1922 Polo Grounds
1923–1973 Yankee Stadium
1974–1975 Shea Stadium
1976– Yankee Stadium

Oakland Athletics
1901–1908 Columbia Park (Philadelphia)
1909–1954 Shibe Park (Philadelphia)
1955–1967 Municipal Stadium (Kansas City)
1968– Network Associates Coliseum (Oakland–Alameda County Stadium until 1998)

Seattle Mariners
1977–1999 Kingdome
1999– Safeco Field

Tampa Bay Devil Rays
1998– Tropicana Field

Texas Rangers
1961 Griffith Stadium (Washington, DC)
1962–1971 Robert F. Kennedy Stadium (Washington, DC) (DC Stadium until 1968)
1972–1993 Arlington Stadium
1994– The Ballpark in Arlington

Toronto Blue Jays
1977–1989 Exhibition Stadium
1989– SkyDome

Current National League Teams

Arizona Diamondbacks
1998– Bank One Ballpark

Atlanta Braves
1876–1915 South End Grounds (Boston)
1915–1952 Braves Field (Boston)
1953–1965 County Stadium (Milwaukee)
1966–1996 Atlanta–Fulton County Stadium
1997– Turner Field

Chicago Cubs
1876–1877 23rd Street Grounds
1878–1884 Lakefront Park
1885–1891 West Side Park
1891–1893 South Side Park
1893–1915 West Side Grounds
1916– Wrigley Field (Cubs Park until 1926)

Cincinnati Reds
1876 Lincoln Park Grounds
1877–1879 Avenue Grounds
1880 Bank Street Grounds
1890–1901 League Park
1902–1911 Palace of the Fans
1912–1970 Crosley Field (Redland Field until 1933)
1971– Cinergy Field (Riverfront Stadium until 1996)

Colorado Rockies
1993–1994 Mile High Stadium
1995– Coors Field

Florida Marlins
1993– Pro Player Park (Joe Robbie Stadium until 1997)

Houston Astros
1962–1964 Colt Stadium
1965–1999 Astrodome
2000– Enron Field

Los Angeles Dodgers
1890 Washington Park (Brooklyn)
1891–1897 Eastern Park (Brooklyn)
1898–1912 Washington Park (Brooklyn)
1913–1957 Ebbets Field (Brooklyn)
1958–1961 Memorial Coliseum
1962– Dodger Stadium

Milwaukee Brewers
1969 Sicks Stadium (Seattle)
1970–2000 County Stadium

Montreal Expos
1969–1976 Parc Jarry
1977– Stade Olympique

New York Mets
1962–1963 Polo Grounds
1964– Shea Stadium

Philadelphia Phillies
1883–1886 Recreation Park
1887–1894 Philadelphia Base Ball Grounds
1895–1938 Baker Bowl
1938–1970 Shibe Park (Connie Mack Stadium 1953–1970)
1971– Veterans Stadium

Pittsburgh Pirates
1887–1890 Recreation Park
1891–1909 Exposition Park
1909–1970 Forbes Field
1970–2000 Three Rivers Stadium

St. Louis Cardinals
1892 Sportsman's Park
1893–1920 Robison Field
1920–1966 Sportsman's Park (new structure) (Busch Stadium 1953–1966)
1967– Busch Stadium (new structure)

San Diego Padres
1969– Qualcomm Stadium (San Diego Stadium 1969–1980, Jack Murphy Stadium 1980–1996)

San Francisco Giants
1883–1888 Polo Grounds (New York)
1889 St. George Cricket Grounds (New York)
1889–1957 Polo Grounds (New York)
1958–1959 Seals Stadium
1960–1999 3Com Park (Candlestick Park until 1995)
2000– Pacific Bell Park

APPENDIX 3

The Top Amateur Draft Selections

The 35 years of the Amateur Draft has resulted in literally thousands of picks by major league baseball teams. This section highlights the top 10 picks, and adds perspective by including memorable players who were bypassed by the teams with the first 10 selections in a given year. Hindsight makes experts of us all.

The top 10 selections in baseball's Amateur Draft are listed in the order in which they were drafted in the first round of each year's primary June draft (thanks to Allan Simpson, who provided virtually all of the Top 10 draft picks through 1998). Those who did not make the major leagues are listed with the highest minor league classification they attained as of October 2000. DNP signifies that the draft pick did not play in Organized Baseball, or has not as of this edition of *Total Baseball*. DNS indicates that the player has not signed a contract with the team that drafted him as of this writing.

The notable draft picks at the end of each year are proof as to the inexact science of the draft. These five picks are listed by the draft and round in which they were selected. To keep these selections relevant, the notable picks are only included through 1995. The round the player was picked in is listed as "Rd."

Before 1987 there were regular and secondary phases of the draft in both January and June. "Jan" indicates that the player listed was selected in the January part of the draft; "Sec" shows that the player was selected in a secondary phase of the draft.

For a large variety of reasons—most often the desire of a high school player to go on to college—a large number of players do not sign when they are first drafted. Often these players are drafted again and do sign. Ron Cey is included below as an example of a player who was originally drafted by the Mets in 1966, did not sign, and then went on to be drafted again two years later and signed with the Dodgers (there are similar examples among each year's top 10 draft selections as well).

Tom Seaver is included because of his unique case. He was drafted and signed by the Braves in 1966, but Commissioner William Eckert declared the contract void as a result of the violation of college baseball rules. Meanwhile, Seaver was declared ineligible for further college play because of the contract he had signed with the Braves. So Seaver's professional fate ended up being determined by a lottery of teams willing to match Atlanta's original offer, and the Mets were the lucky winners.

1965

Selection Number	Player	Team	Position—Level Reached
1	Rick Monday	A's	OF
2	Les Rohr	Mets	P
3	Joe Coleman	Senators	P
4	Alex Barrett	Astros	SS-AAA
5	Billy Conigliaro	Red Sox	OF
6	Rick James	Cubs	P
7	Ray Fosse	Indians	C
8	John Wyatt	Dodgers	SS-A
9	Eddie Leon	Twins	SS
10	Doug Dickerson	Pirates	OF-A

Other Picks

Selection Number	Player	Team	Position—Level Reached
Rd. 2	Johnny Bench	Reds	C
Rd. 4	Graig Nettles	Twins	3B
Rd. 5	Amos Otis	Red Sox	OF
Rd. 10	Nolan Ryan	Mets	P
Rd. 11	Gene Tenace	A's	C

1966

Selection Number	Player	Team	Position—Level Reached
1	Steve Chilcott	Mets	C-AAA
2	Reggie Jackson	A's	OF
3	Wayne Twitchell	Astros	P
4	Ken Brett	Red Sox	P-OF
5	Dean Burk	Cubs	P-AAA
6	Tom Grieve	Senators	OF
7	Leron Lee	Cardinals	OF
8	Jim De Neff	Angels	SS-AAA
9	Mike Biko	Phillies	P-A
10	Jim Lyttle	Yankees	OF

Other Picks

Selection Number	Player	Team	Position—Level Reached
Rd. 8	Charlie Hough	Dodgers	P
Rd. 9	Bill Russell	Dodgers	SS
Rd. 19	Ron Cey	Mets	3B-DNS
Rd. 1 (Jan Sec)	Tom Seaver (void)	Braves	P
Rd. 1 (Sec)	Andy Messersmith	Angels	P

1967

Selection Number	Player	Team	Position—Level Reached
1	Ron Blomberg	Yankees	1B
2	Terry Hughes	Cubs	SS
3	Mike Garman	Red Sox	P
4	Jon Matlack	Mets	P
5	John Jones	Senators	C-A
6	John Mayberry	Astros	1B
7	Brian Bickerton	A's	P-AAA
8	Wayne Simpson	Reds	P
9	Mike Nunn	Angel	C-AAA
10	Ted Simmons	Cardinals	C

Other Picks

Selection Number	Player	Team	Position—Level Reached
Rd. 1	Bobby Grich	Orioles	SS
Rd. 2	Vida Blue	A's	P
Rd. 2	Don Baylor	Orioles	OF
Rd. 26	Dusty Baker	Braves	OF
Rd. 1 (Jan)	Carlton Fisk	Red Sox	C

1968

Selection Number	Player	Team	Position—Level Reached
1	Tim Foli	Mets	SS
2	Pete Broberg	A's	P
3	Marty Cott	Astros	C-AAA
4	Thurman Munson	Yankees	C
5	Bobby Valentine	Dodgers	OF
6	Robert Weaver	Indians	SS-AA
7	Curtis Moore	Braves	OF-AAA
8	Donnie Castle	Senators	P-OF
9	Dick Sharon	Pirates	OF
10	Junior Kennedy	Orioles	SS

Other Picks

Selection Number	Player	Team	Position—Level Reached
Rd. 1	Greg Luzinski	Phillies	OF
Rd. 8	Cecil Cooper	Red Sox	1B
Rd. 22	Bill Lee	Red Sox	P
Rd. 1 (Sec)	Steve Garvey	Dodgers	3B
Rd. 3 (Sec)	Ron Cey	Dodgers	3B

1969

Selection Number	Player	Team	Position—Level Reached
1	Jeff Burroughs	Senators	OF
2	J.R. Richard	Astros	P
3	Ted Nicholson	White Sox	3B-A
4	Randy Sterling	Mets	P
5	Alan Bannister	Angels	SS
6	Mike Anderson	Phillies	1B
7	Paul Ray Powell	Twins	OF
8	Terry McDermott	Dodgers	C

Selection Number	Player	Team	Position—Level Reached
9	Don Stanhouse	A's	SS
10	Bob May	Pirates	P-A

Other Picks

Selection Number	Player	Team	Position—Level Reached
Rd. 1	Don Gullet	Reds	P
Rd. 3	Bert Blyleven	Twins	P
Rd. 5	Dwight Evans	Red Sox	OF
Rd. 6	Bob Boone	Phillies	C
Rd. 16	Buddy Bell	Indians	3B

1970

Selection Number	Player	Team	Position—Level Reached
1	Mike Ivie	Padres	C
2	Steve Dunning	Indians	P
3	Barry Foote	Expos	C
4	Darrell Porter	Brewers	C
5	Mike Martin	Phillies	P-AAA
6	Lee Richard	White Sox	SS
7	Randy Scarbery	Astros	P
8	Rex Goodson	Royals	C-AA
9	Jim Haller	Dodgers	P-AAA
10	Paul Dade	Angels	3B-OF

Other Picks

Selection Number	Player	Team	Position—Level Reached
Rd. 3	Rick Reuschel	Cubs	P
Rd. 9	Goose Gossage	White Sox	P
Rd. 14	Dave Parker	Pirates	OF
Rd. 1 (Jan)	Chris Chambliss	Indians	1B
Rd. 1 (Sec)	Dave Kingman	Giants	1B

1971

Selection Number	Player	Team	Position—Level Reached
1	Danny Goodwin	White Sox	C
2	Jay Franklin	Padres	P
3	Tom Bianco	Brewers	SS
4	Condredge Holloway	Expos	SS-DNP
5	Roy Branch	Royals	P
6	Roy Thomas	Phillies	P
7	Roger Quiroga	Senators	P-A
8	Ed Kurpiel	Cardinals	1B-P-AAA
9	David Sloan	Indians	P-AA
10	Taylor Duncan	Braves	SS

Other Picks

Selection Number	Player	Team	Position—Level Reached
Rd. 1	Jim Rice	Red Sox	OF
Rd. 2	George Brett	Royals	3B
Rd. 2	Mike Schmidt	Phillies	P
Rd. 3	Ron Guidry	Yankees	P
Rd. 42	Keith Hernandez	Cardinals	1B

1972

Selection Number	Player	Team	Position—Level Reached
1	Dave Roberts	Padres	3B
2	Rick Manning	Indians	SS
3	Larry Christenson	Phillies	P
4	Roy Howell	Rangers	3B
5	Bobby Goodman	Expos	C-AAA
6	Danny Thomas	Brewers	1B
7	Larry Payne	Reds	P-AAA
8	Dick Ruthven	Twins	P
9	Steve Englishbey	Astros	OF-AA
10	Dave Chalk	Angels	3B

Other Picks

Selection Number	Player	Team	Position—Level Reached
Rd. 1	Chet Lemon	A's	OF
Rd. 2	John Candelaria	Pirates	P
Rd. 3	Dennis Eckersley	Indians	P
Rd. 3	Gary Carter	Expos	C
Rd. 7	Willie Randolph	Pirates	2B

1973

Selection Number	Player	Team	Position—Level Reached
1	David Clyde	Rangers	P
2	John Stearns	Phillies	C
3	Robin Yount	Brewers	SS
4	Dave Winfield	Padres	P-OF
5	Glenn Tufts	Indians	1B-P-AA
6	Johnnie LeMaster	Giants	SS
7	Billy Taylor	Angels	OF-A
8	Gary Roenicke	Expos	SS
9	Lew Olsen	Royals	P-AAA
10	Pat Rockett	Braves	SS

Other Picks

Selection Number	Player	Team	Position—Level Reached
Rd. 2	Fred Lynn	Red Sox	OF
Rd. 3	Eddie Murray	Orioles	1B
Rd. 7	Mike Flanagan	Orioles	P
Rd. 13	Jack Clark	Giants	OF
Rd. 1 (Jan Sec)	Jim Sundberg	Rangers	C

1974

Selection Number	Player	Team	Position—Level Reached
1	Bill Almon	Padres	SS
2	Tommy Boggs	Rangers	P
3	Lonnie Smith	Phillies	OF
4	Tom Brennan	Indians	P
5	Dale Murphy	Braves	C
6	Butch Edge	Brewers	P
7	Scot Thompson	Cubs	OF
8	Larry Monroe	White Sox	P
9	Ron Sorey	Expos	3B-A
10	Mike Miley	Angels	SS

Other Picks

Selection Number	Player	Team	Position—Level Reached
Rd. 1	Garry Templeton	Cardinals	SS
Rd. 1	Lance Parrish	Tigers	C
Rd. 1	Willie Wilson	Royals	OF
Rd. 1	Rick Sutcliffe	Dodgers	P
Rd. 3	Pete Vuckovich	White Sox	P

1975

Selection Number	Player	Team	Position—Level Reached
1	Danny Goodwin	Angels	C
2	Mike Lentz	Padres	P
3	Les Filkins	Tigers	OF-AAA
4	Brian Rosinski	Cubs	OF-AAA
5	Rich O'Keefe	Brewers	OF- AAA
6	Butch Benton	Mets	C
7	Rick Cerone	Indians	C
8	Ted Barnicle	Giants	P-AAA
9	Clint Hurdle	Royals	OF
10	Art Miles	Expos	SS-A

Other Picks

Selection Number	Player	Team	Position—Level Reached
Rd. 2	Lee Smith	Cubs	P
Rd. 3	Carney Lansford	Angels	3B
Rd. 5	Lou Whitaker	Tigers	2B
Rd. 11	Andre Dawson	Expos	OF
Rd. 16	Dave Stewart	Dodgers	P

1976

Selection Number	Player	Team	Position—Level Reached
1	Floyd Bannister	Astros	P
2	Pat Underwood	Tigers	P
3	Ken Smith	Braves	3B
4	Bill Bordley	Brewers	P
5	Bob Owchinko	Padres	P
6	Ken Landreaux	Angels	OF
7	Herm Segelke	Cubs	P
8	Steve Trout	White Sox	P
9	Bob James	Expos	P
10	Jamie Allen	Twins	P

Other Picks

Selection Number	Player	Team	Position—Level Reached
Rd. 1	Mike Scioscia	Dodgers	C
Rd. 2	Alan Trammell	Tigers	SS
Rd. 4	Rickey Henderson	A's	OF
Rd. 5	Jack Morris	Tigers	P
Rd. 3 (Jan Sec)	John Tudor	Red Sox	P

1977

Selection Number	Player	Team	Position—Level Reached
1	Harold Baines	White Sox	1B-OF
2	Bill Gullickson	Expos	P
3	Paul Molitor	Brewers	SS
4	Tim Cole	Braves	P-AAA
5	Kevin Richards	Tigers	P-AA
6	Terry Kennedy	Cardinals	C
7	Richard Dotson	Angels	P
8	Brian Greer	Padres	OF
9	David Hibner	Rangers	SS-A
10	Craig Landis	Giants	SS-AAA

Other Picks

Selection Number	Player	Team	Position—Level Reached
Rd. 4	Ozzie Smith	Padres	SS
Rd. 5	Tim Raines	Expos	2B
Rd. 9	Jesse Barfield	Blue Jays	OF
Rd. 11	Chili Davis	Giants	OF
Rd. 1 (Jan)	Dave Righetti	Rangers	P

1978

Selection Number	Player	Team	Position—Level Reached
1	Bob Horner	Braves	3B
2	Lloyd Moseby	Blue Jays	1B
3	Hubie Brooks	Mets	SS
4	Mike Morgan	A's	P
5	Andy Hawkins	Padres	P
6	Tito Nanni	Mariners	OF-1B-AAA
7	Bob Cummings	Giants	C-AA
8	Nick Hernandez	Brewers	C-A
9	Glenn Franklin	Expos	SS-AAA
10	Phil Lansford	Indians	SS-A

Other Picks

Selection Number	Player	Team	Position—Level Reached
Rd. 1	Kirk Gibson	Tigers	OF
Rd. 2	Cal Ripken Jr.	Orioles	3B
Rd. 5	Dave Stieb	Blue Jays	OF
Rd. 20	Ryne Sandberg	Phillies	SS
Rd. 2 (Jan)	Jesse Orosco	Twins	P

1979

Selection Number	Player	Team	Position—Level Reached
1	Al Chambers	Mariners	OF
2	Tim Leary	Mets	P
3	Jay Schroeder	Blue Jays	C-A
4	Brad Komminsk	Braves	OF
5	Juan Bustabad	A's	SS-AAA
6	Andy Van Slyke	Cardinals	OF
7	Jon Bohnet	Indians	P
8	John Mizerock	Astros	C
9	Steve Buechele	White Sox	SS
10	Tim Wallach	Expos	1B

Other Picks

Selection Number	Player	Team	Position—Level Reached
Rd. 5	Jeff Russell	Reds	P
Rd. 17	Orel Hershiser	Dodgers	P
Rd. 19	Don Mattingly	Yankees	1B
Rd. 23	Brett Butler	Braves	OF
Rd. 1 (Jan Sec)	Howard Johnson	Tigers	3B

1980

Selection Number	Player	Team	Position—Level Reached
1	Darryl Strawberry	Mets	OF
2	Garry Harris	Blue Jays	SS-AA
3	Ken Dayley	Braves	P
4	Mike King	A's	P-AAA
5	Jeff Pyburn	Padres	OF-AAA
6	Darnell Coles	Mariners	SS
7	Jay Reid	Giants	1B
8	Cecil Espy	White Sox	OF
9	Ross Jones	Dodgers	SS
10	Kelly Gruber	Indians	SS

Other Picks

Selection Number	Player	Team	Position—Level Reached
Rd. 2	Tim Burke	Pirates	P
Rd. 3	Danny Tartabull	Reds	3B
Rd. 9	Craig Lefferts	Cubs	P
Rd. 1 (Sec)	Harold Reynolds	Mariners	2B
Rd. 4 (Sec)	Tom Henke	Cubs	P

1981

Selection Number	Player	Team	Position—Level Reached
1	Mike Moore	Mariners	P
2	Joe Carter	Cubs	OF
3	Dick Schofield	Angels	SS

Selection Number	Player	Team	Position—Level Reached
4	Terry Blocker	Mets	OF
5	Matt Williams	Blue Jays	P
6	Kevin McReynolds	Padres	OF
7	Daryl Boston	White Sox	OF
8	Bobby Meacham	Cardinals	SS
9	Ron Darling	Rangers	P
10	Mark Grant	Giants	P

Other Picks

Selection Number	Player	Team	Position—Level Reached
Rd. 2	Mark Langston	Mariners	P
Rd. 2	Frank Viola	Twins	P
Rd. 2	Mark Gubicza	Royals	P
Rd. 3	Tony Gwynn	Padres	OF
Rd. 5	John Franco	Dodgers	P

1982

Selection Number	Player	Team	Position—Level Reached
1	Shawon Dunston	Cubs	SS
2	Augie Schmidt	Blue Jays	SS-AAA
3	Jimmy Jones	Padres	P
4	Bryan Oelkers	Twins	P
5	Dwight Gooden	Mets	P
6	Spike Owen	Mariners	SS
7	Sam Khalifa	Pirates	SS
8	Bob Kipper	Angels	P
9	Duane Ward	Braves	P
10	John Morris	Royals	OF

Other Picks

Selection Number	Player	Team	Position—Level Reached
Rd. 3	Jimmy Key	Blue Jays	P
Rd. 7	Terry Pendleton	Cardinals	3B
Rd. 15	Jose Canseco	A's	OF
Rd. 19	Bret Saberhagen	Royals	P
Rd. 1 (Jan)	Kirby Puckett	Twins	OF

1983

Selection Number	Player	Team	Position—Level Reached
1	Tim Belcher	Twins	P
2	Kurt Stillwell	Reds	SS
3	Jeff Kunkel	Rangers	SS
4	Eddie Williams	Mets	3B
5	Stan Hilton	A's	P-AAA
6	Jackie Davidson	Cubs	P-AAA
7	Darrel Akerfelds	Mariners	P
8	Robbie Wine	Astros	C
9	Matt Stark	Blue Jays	C
10	Ray Hayward	Padres	P

Other Picks

Selection Number	Player	Team	Position—Level Reached
Rd. 1	Roger Clemens	Red Sox	P
Rd. 3	Wally Joyner	Angels	1B
Rd. 1 (Sec)	Robby Thompson	Giants	2B
Rd. 1 (Sec)	Rob Dibble	Reds	P
Rd. 2 (Sec)	Mike Henneman	Phillies	P

1984

Selection Number	Player	Team	Position—Level Reached
1	Shawn Abner	Mets	OF
2	Billy Swift	Mariners	P
3	Drew Hall	Cubs	P
4	Cory Snyder	Indians	3B
5	Pat Pacillo	Reds	P
6	Erik Pappas	Angels	C
7	Mike Dunne	Cardinals	P
8	Jay Bell	Twins	SS
9	Alan Cockrell	Giants	OF
10	Mark McGwire	A's	1B

Other Picks

Selection Number	Player	Team	Position—Level Reached
Rd. 2	Greg Maddux	Cubs	P
Rd. 2	Tom Glavine	Braves	P
Rd. 3	Ken Caminiti	Astros	3B
Rd. 2 (Jan Sec)	Mike Jackson	Phillies	P
Rd. 2 (Jan Sec)	Jay Buhner	Pirates	OF

1985

Selection Number	Player	Team	Position—Level Reached
1	B.J. Surhoff	Brewers	SS
2	Will Clark	Giants	1B
3	Bobby Witt	Rangers	P
4	Barry Larkin	Reds	SS
5	Kurt Brown	White Sox	C-AA
6	Barry Bonds	Pirates	OF
7	Mike Campbell	Mariners	P
8	Pete Incaviglia	Expos	OF
9	Mike Poehl	Indians	P-AA
10	Chris Gwynn	Dodgers	OF

Other Picks

Selection Number	Player	Team	Position—Level Reached
Rd. 1	Rafael Palmeiro	Cubs	OF
Rd. 4	Bobby Thigpen	White Sox	P
Rd. 22	John Smoltz	Tigers	P
Rd. 24	Mark Grace	Cubs	OF
Rd. 1 (Jan Sec)	Chuck Finley	Angels	P

1986

Selection Number	Player	Team	Position—Level Reached
1	Jeff King	Pirates	3B
2	Greg Swindell	Indians	P
3	Matt Williams	Giants	SS
4	Kevin Brown	Rangers	P
5	Kent Mercker	Braves	P
6	Gary Sheffield	Brewers	SS
7	Brad Brink	Phillies	P
8	Patrick Lennon	Mariners	SS
9	Derrick May	Cubs	OF
10	Derek Parks	Twins	C

Other Picks

Selection Number	Player	Team	Position—Level Reached
Rd. 1	Roberto Hernandez	White Sox	P
Rd. 4	Bo Jackson	Royals	OF
Rd. 6	Tom Gordon	Royals	P
Rd. 1 (Jan)	Moises Alou	Pirates	OF
Rd. 2 (Jan)	Curt Schilling	Red Sox	P

1987

Selection Number	Player	Team	Position—Level Reached
1	Ken Griffey Jr.	Mariners	OF
2	Mark Merchant	Pirates	OF-AAA
3	Willie Banks	Twins	P
4	Mike Harkey	Cubs	P
5	Jack McDowell	White Sox	P
6	Derek Lilliquist	Braves	P
7	Chris Myers	Orioles	P-AA
8	Dan Opperman	Dodgers	P-AAA
9	Kevin Appier	Royals	P
10	Kevin Garner	Padres	P-OF-AAA

Other Picks

Selection Number	Player	Team	Position—Level Reached
Rd. 1	Delino DeShields	Expos	SS
Rd. 1	Craig Biggio	Astros	C
Rd. 2	Albert Belle	Indians	OF
Rd. 7	Reggie Sanders	Reds	OF
Rd. 13	Steve Finley	Orioles	OF

1988

Selection Number	Player	Team	Position—Level Reached
1	Andy Benes	Padres	P
2	Mark Lewis	Indians	SS
3	Steve Avery	Braves	P
4	Gregg Olson	Orioles	P
5	Bill Bene	Dodgers	P-AAA
6	Monty Fariss	Rangers	SS
7	Willie Ansley	Astros	OF-AAA
8	Jim Abbott	Angels	P
9	Ty Griffin	Cubs	2B-AA
10	Robin Ventura	White Sox	3B

Other Picks

Selection Number	Player	Team	Position—Level Reached
Rd. 1	Charles Nagy	Indians	P
Rd. 1	Brian Jordan	Cardinals	OF
Rd. 17	Kenny Lofton	Astros	OF
Rd. 30	Deion Sanders	Yankees	OF
Rd. 62	Mike Piazza	Dodgers	OF

1989

Selection Number	Player	Team	Position—Level Reached
1	Ben McDonald	Orioles	P
2	Tyler Houston	Braves	C
3	Roger Salkeld	Mariners	P
4	Jeff Jackson	Phillies	OF-AA
5	Donald Harris	Rangers	OF
6	Paul Coleman	Cardinals	OF-AA
7	Frank Thomas	White Sox	1B
8	Earl Cunningham	Cubs	OF-A
9	Kyle Abbott	Angels	P
10	Charles Johnson	Expos	C

Other Picks

Selection Number	Player	Team	Position—Level Reached
Rd. 1	Chuck Knoblauch	Twins	2B
Rd. 1	Mo Vaughn	Red Sox	1B
Rd. 3	Tim Salmon	Angels	OF
Rd. 3	John Olerud	Blue Jays	1B
Rd. 4	Jeff Bagwell	Red Sox	3B

1990

Selection Number	Player	Team	Position—Level Reached
1	Chipper Jones	Braves	SS
2	Tony Clark	Tigers	1B
3	Mike Lieberthal	Phillies	C
4	Alex Fernandez	White Sox	P
5	Kurt Miller	Pirates	P
6	Marc Newfield	Mariners	1B-OF
7	Dan Wilson	Reds	C
8	Tim Costo	Indians	SS
9	Ron Walden	Dodgers	P-A
10	Carl Everett	Yankees	OF

Other Picks

Selection Number	Player	Team	Position—Level Reached
Rd. 1	Mike Mussina	Orioles	P
Rd. 1	Rondell White	Expos	OF
Rd. 1	Jeromy Burnitz	Mets	OF
Rd. 1	Todd Van Poppel	A's	P
Rd. 6	Troy Percival	Angels	C

1991

Selection Number	Player	Team	Position—Level Reached
1	Brien Taylor	Yankees	P-AA
2	Mike Kelly	Braves	OF
3	David McCarty	Twins	1B
4	Dmitri Young	Cardinals	3B
5	Kenny Henderson	Brewers	P-A
6	John Burke	Astros	P
7	Joe Vitiello	Royals	1B
8	Joey Hamilton	Padres	P
9	Mark Smith	Orioles	OF
10	Tyler Green	Phillies	P

Other Picks

Selection Number	Player	Team	Position—Level Reached
Rd. 1	Manny Ramirez	Indians	OF
Rd. 1	Shawn Green	Blue Jays	OF
Rd. 1	Justin Thompson	Tigers	P
Rd. 11	Jeff Cirillo	Brewers	3B
Rd. 18	Kirk Rueter	Expos	P

1992

Selection Number	Player	Team	Position—Level Reached
1	Phil Nevin	Astros	3B
2	Paul Shuey	Indians	P
3	B.J. Wallace	Expos	P-AA
4	Jeffrey Hammonds	Orioles	OF
5	Chad Mottola	Reds	OF
6	Derek Jeter	Yankees	SS
7	Calvin Murray	Giants	OF
8	Pete Janicki	Angels	P-AAA
9	Preston Wilson	Mets	3B
10	Michael Tucker	Royals	SS

Selection Number	Player	Team	Position—Level Reached
Other Picks			
Rd. 1	Jason Kendall	Pirates	C
Rd. 1	Charles Johnson	Marlins	C
Rd. 1	Johnny Damon	Royals	OF
Rd. 2	Jason Giambi	A's	3B
Rd. 12	Bob Higginson	Tigers	OF
1993			
1	Alex Rodriguez	Mariners	SS
2	Darren Dreifort	Dodgers	P
3	Brian Anderson	Angels	P
4	Wayne Gomes	Phillies	P
5	Jeff Granger	Royals	P
6	Steve Soderstrom	Giants	P
7	Trot Nixon	Red Sox	OF
8	Kirk Presley	Mets	P-A
9	Matt Brunson	Tigers	SS-A
10	Brooks Kieschnick	Cubs	1B-OF
Other Picks			
Rd. 1	Billy Wagner	Astros	P
Rd. 1	Jeff D'Amico	Brewers	P
Rd. 2	Scott Rolen	Phillies	3B
Rd. 2	Brad Fullmer	Expos	3B
Rd. 7	Mark Loretta	Brewers	SS
1994			
1	Paul Wilson	Mets	P
2	Ben Grieve	A's	OF
3	Dustin Hermanson	Padres	P
4	Antone Williamson	Brewers	3B
5	Josh Booty	Marlins	SS
6	McKay Christensen	Angels	OF
7	Doug Million	Rockies	P-AA
8	Todd Walker	Twins	2B
9	C.J. Nitkowski	Reds	P
10	Jaret Wright	Indians	P
Other Picks			
Rd. 1	Nomar Garciaparra	Red Sox	SS
Rd. 1	Paul Konerko	Dodgers	C
Rd. 1	Scott Elarton	Astros	P
Rd. 1	Terrence Long	Mets	1B
Rd. 13	Carl Pavano	Red Sox	P
1995			
1	Darin Erstad	Angels	OF
2	Ben Davis	Padres	C
3	Jose Cruz Jr.	Mariners	OF
4	Kerry Wood	Cubs	P
5	Ariel Prieto	Athletics	P
6	Jaime Jones	Marlins	OF-AAA
7	Jonathan Johnson	Rangers	P
8	Todd Helton	Rockies	1B
9	Geoff Jenkins	Brewers	OF
10	Chad Hermansen	Pirates	SS
Other Picks			
Rd. 1	Matt Morris	Cardinals	P
Rd. 2	Carlos Beltran	Royals	OF
Rd. 2	Sean Casey	Indians	1B
Rd. 2	Brett Tomko	Reds	P
Rd. 4	Russ Ortiz	Giants	P
1996			
1	Kris Benson	Pirates	P
2	Travis Lee	Twins	1B
3	Braden Looper	Cardinals	P
4	Bill Koch	Blue Jays	P
5	John Patterson	Expos	P-AAA
6	Seth Greisinger	Tigers	P
7	Matt White	Giants	P-A
8	Chad Green	Brewers	OF-AAA
9	Mark Kotsay	Marlins	OF
10	Eric Chavez	Athletics	3B
1997			
1	Matt Anderson	Tigers	P
2	J.D. Drew	Phillies	OF
3	Troy Glaus	Angels	3B
4	Jason Grilli	Giants	P
5	Vernon Wells	Blue Jays	OF
6	Geoff Goetz	Mets	P-AA
7	Dan Reichert	Royals	P
8	J.J. Davis	Pirates	OF-AA
9	Michael Cuddyer	Twins	SS-AA
10	Jon Garland	Cubs	P
1998			
1	Pat Burrell	Phillies	3B
2	Mark Mulder	Athletics	P
3	Corey Patterson	Cubs	OF
4	Jeff Austin	Royals	P-AAA
5	J.D. Drew	Cardinals	OF
6	Ryan Mills	Twins	P-AA
7	Austin Kearns	Reds	OF-A
8	Felipe Lopez	Blue Jays	SS-AA
9	Sean Burroughs	Padres	3B-AA
10	Carlos Pena	Rangers	1B-AA
1999			
1	Josh Hamilton	Devil Rays	OF-A
2	Josh Beckett	Marlins	P-A
3	Eric Munson	Tigers	C
4	Corey Myers	Diamondbacks	SS-A
5	B.J. Garbe	Twins	OF-A
6	Josh Girdley	Expos	P-A
7	Kyle Snyder	Royals	P-A
8	Bobby Bradley	Pirates	P-A
9	Barry Zito	A's	P
10	Ben Sheets	Brewers	P-AAA
2000			
1	Adrian Gonzalez	Marlins	1B-A
2	Adam Johnson	Twins	P-A
3	Luis Montanez	Cubs	SS-A
4	Mike Stodolka	Royals	P-A
5	Justin M. Wayne	Expos	P-A
6	Rocco Baldelli	Devil Rays	CF-Rookie
7	Matt Harrington	Rockies	P-DNS
8	Matt Wheatland	Tigers	P-A
9	Mark Phillips	Padres	P-Rookie
10	Joe Torres	Angels	P-A

APPENDIX 4

Spring Training Sites

Baseball teams have been heading South each spring since the 1860s. The emphasis of spring training has changed over the years, as players have evolved from seasonal athletes to year-round weight trainers. Whereas players in years past often showed up at spring training looking to shed some pounds or "regain their wind," today's spring season is more a tryout camp for prospects and other hopefuls. Still, almost no team breaks camp without making a roster decision about a player who either surprised or disappointed the organization during spring training. Sometimes the cut player just stays put, since many organizations use their minor league facilities as a spring training complex.

All 30 franchises now hold spring training in either Florida or Arizona, but it was not always so. Early spring training stops included Arkansas, Louisiana, Georgia, Missouri, and Texas, among other locales. By the 1930s most teams trained in or near Florida, with a few teams training in California. World War II travel restrictions required teams to train close to home, and some, like the Brooklyn Dodgers, even went north for spring training. Most teams returned to Florida after the war, and the Giants and Indians became the first clubs to train in Arizona in 1947.

The fans that traveled to see their favorite teams train proved to be an added benefit to both the team and the town. Municipalities started competing to lure ballclubs—and the accompanying tourist dollars—even though the big leaguers were usually only in town for six weeks or less.

Myles E. Friedman has put together a list of training sites for all current teams. It does not include teams prior to 1900, due to the difficulty of distinguishing teams that were barnstorming from those that were actually training.

Spring Training Sites by Team Nickname

NATIONAL LEAGUE

Astros

1962–63 Apache Junction, Ariz.
1964–84 Cocoa Beach, Fla.
1985– Kissimmee, Fla.

Braves

1901 Norfolk, Va.
1902–04 Thomasville, Ga.
1905 Charleston, S.C.
1906 Jacksonville, Fla.
1907 Thomasville, Ga.
1908–12 Augusta, Ga.
1913 Athens, Ga.
1914–15 Macon, Ga.
1916–18 Miami, Fla.
1919–20 Columbus, Ga.
1921 Galveston, Tex.
1922–37 St. Petersburg, Fla.
1938–40 Bradenton, Fla.
1941 San Antonio, Tex.
1942 Sanford, Fla.
1943–44 Wallingford, Conn.
1945 Washington, D.C.
1946–47 Fort Lauderdale, Fla.
1948–62 Bradenton, Fla.
1963–97 West Palm Beach, Fla.
1998– Walt Disney World, Fla.

Brewers (Pilots)

1969–72 Tempe, Ariz.
1973–85 Sun City, Ariz.
1986–1997 Chandler, Ariz.
1998– Maryvale, Ariz.

Cardinals

1901–02 St. Louis, Mo.
1903 Dallas, Tex.
1904 Houston, Tex.
1905 Marlin Springs, Tex.
1906–08 Houston, Tex.
1909–10 Little Rock, Ark.
1911 West Baden, Ind.
1912 Jackson, Miss.
1913 Columbus, Ga.
1914 St. Augustine, Fla.
1915–17 Hot Wells, Tex.
1918 San Antonio, Tex.
1919 St. Louis, Mo.
1920 Brownsville, Tex.
1921–22 Orange, Tex.
1923–24 Bradenton, Fla.
1925 Stockton, Cal.
1926 San Antonio, Tex.
1927–29 Avon Park, Fla.
1930–36 Bradenton, Fla.
1937 Daytona Beach, Fla.
1938–42 St. Petersburg, Fla.
1943–45 Cairo, Ill.
1946–97 St. Petersburg, Fla.
1998– Jupiter, Fla.

Cubs

1901–02 Champaign, Ill.
1903–04 Los Angeles, Cal.
1905 Santa Monica, Cal.
1906 Champaign, Ill.
1907 New Orleans, La.
1908 Vicksburg, Miss.
1909–10 Hot Springs, Ark.
1911–12 New Orleans, La.
1913–16 Tampa, Fla.
1917–21 Pasadena, Cal.
1922–42 Catalina Island, Cal.
1943–45 French Lick, Ind.
1946–47 Catalina Island, Cal.
1948–49 Los Angeles, Cal.
1950–51 Catalina Island, Cal.
1952–65 Mesa, Ariz.
1966 Long Beach, Cal.
1967–78 Scottsdale, Ariz.
1979– Mesa, Ariz.

Diamondbacks

1998– Tucson, Ariz.

Dodgers

1901 Charlotte, N.C.
1902–06 Columbia, S.C.
1907–09 Jacksonville, Fla.
1910–12 Hot Springs, Ark.
1913–14 Augusta, Ga.
1915–16 Daytona Beach, Fla.
1917–18 Hot Springs, Ark.
1919–20 Jacksonville, Fla.
1921 New Orleans, La.
1922 Jacksonville, Fla.
1923–32 Clearwater, Fla.
1933 Miami, Fla.
1934–35 Orlando, Fla.
1936–40 Clearwater, Fla.
1941–42 Havana, Cuba
1943–45 Bear Mountain, N.Y.
1946 Daytona Beach, Fla.
1947 Havana, Cuba
1948 Ciudad Trujillo, D.R.
1949– Vero Beach, Fla.

Expos

1969–72 West Palm Beach, Fla.
1973–80 Daytona Beach, Fla.
1981–97 West Palm Beach, Fla.
1998– Jupiter, Fla.

Giants

1901–02 N.Y., N.Y.
1903–05 Savannah, Ga.
1906 Memphis, Tenn.
1907 Los Angeles, Cal.
1908–18 Marlin Springs, Tex.
1919 Gainesville, Fla.
1920–23 San Antonio, Tex.
1924–27 Sarasota, Fla.
1928 Augusta, Ga.
1929–31 San Antonio, Tex.
1932–33 Los Angeles, Cal.
1934–35 Miami Beach, Fla.
1936 Pensacola, Fla.
1937 Havana, Cuba
1938–39 Baton Rouge, La.
1940 Winter Haven, Fla.
1941–42 Miami, Fla.
1943–45 Lakewood, N.J.
1946 Miami, Fla.
1947–50 Phoenix, Ariz.
1951 St. Petersburg, Fla.
1952–83 Phoenix, Ariz.
1984– Scottsdale, Ariz.

Marlins

1993 Cocoa, Fla.
1994– Viera, Fla.

Mets

1962–87 St. Petersburg, Fla.
1988– Port St. Lucie, Fla.

Padres

1969–93 Yuma, Ariz.
1994– Peoria, Ariz.

Phillies

1901 Philadelphia, Pa.
1902 Washington, N.C.
1903 Richmond, Va.
1904 Savannah, Ga.
1905 Augusta, Ga.
1906–08 Savannah, Ga.
1909–10 Southern Pines, N.C.
1911 Birmingham, Al.
1912 Hot Springs, Ark.
1913 Southern Pines, N.C.
1914 Wilmington, N.C.
1915–18 St. Petersburg, Fla.
1919 Charlotte, N.C.
1920 Birmingham, Al.
1921 Gainesville, Fla.
1922–24 Leesburg, Fla.
1925–27 Bradenton, Fla.
1928–37 Winter Haven, Fla.
1938 Biloxi, Miss.
1939 New Braunfels, Tex.
1940–42 Miami Beach, Fla.
1943 Hershey, Pa.
1944–45 Wilmington, Del.
1946 Miami Beach, Fla.
1947– Clearwater, Fla.

Pirates

1901–16 Hot Springs, Ark.
1917 Columbus, Ga.
1918 Jacksonville, Fla.

1919 Birmingham, Al.
1920–23 Hot Springs, Ark.
1924–34 Paso Robles, Cal.
1935 San Bernardino, Cal.
1936 San Antonio, Tex.
1937–42 San Bernardino, Cal.
1943–45 Muncie, Ind.
1946 San Bernardino, Cal.
1947 Miami Beach, Fla.
1948 Hollywood, Cal.
1949–52 San Bernardino, Cal.
1953 Havana, Cuba
1954 Fort Pierce, Fla.
1955–68 Fort Myers, Fla.
1969– Bradenton, Fla.

Reds
1901–02 Cincinnati, Oh.
1903 Augusta, Ga.
1904 Dallas, Tex.
1905 Jacksonville, Fla.
1906 San Antonio, Tex.
1907 Marlin Springs, Tex.
1908 St. Augustine, Tex.
1909 Atlanta, Ga.
1910–11 Hot Springs, Ark.
1912 Columbus, Ga.
1913 Mobile, Al.
1914–15 Alexandria, La.
1916–17 Shreveport, La.
1918 Montgomery, Al.
1919 Waxahachie, Tex.
1920 Miami, Fla.
1921 Cisco, Tex.
1922 Mineral Wells, Tex.
1923–30 Orlando, Fla.
1931–42 Tampa, Fla.
1943–45 Bloomington, Ind.
1946–87 Tampa, Fla.
1988–97 Plant City, Fla.
1998– Sarasota, Fla.

Rockies
1993– Tucson, Ariz.

AMERICAN LEAGUE

Angels
1961–92 Mesa/Palm Springs, Ariz./Cal.
1993– Mesa/Tempe, Ariz.

Athletics
1901 Philadelphia, Pa.
1902 Charlotte, N.C.
1903 Jacksonville, Fla.
1904 Spartanburg, S.C.
1905 Shreveport, La.
1906 Montgomery, Al.
1907 Dallas, Tex.
1908–09 New Orleans, La.
1910 Atlanta, Ga.
1911 Savannah, Ga.
1912–13 San Antonio, Tex.
1914–18 Jacksonville, Fla.
1919 Philadelphia, Pa.
1920–21 Lake Charles, La.
1922 Eagle Pass, Tex.
1923–24 Montgomery, Al.
1925–36 Fort Myers, Fla.
1937 Mexico City, Mex.
1938–39 Lake Charles, La.
1940–42 Anaheim, Cal.
1943 Wilmington, Del.
1944–45 Frederick, Md.
1946–62 West Palm Beach, Fla.
1963–68 Bradenton, Fla.
1969–78 Mesa, Ariz.
1979–83 Scottsdale, Ariz.
1984– Phoenix, Ariz.

Blue Jays
1977– Dunedin, Fla.

Devil Rays
1998– St. Petersburg, Fla.

Indians
1901 Cleveland, Oh.
1902–03 New Orleans, La.
1904 San Antonio, Tex.
1905–06 Atlanta, Ga.
1907–08 Macon, Ga.
1909 Mobile, Al.
1910–11 Alexandria, La.
1912 Mobile, Al.
1913 Pensacola, Fla.
1914 Athens, Ga.
1915 San Antonio, Tex.
1916–20 New Orleans, La.
1921–22 Dallas, Tex.
1923–27 Lakeland, Fla.
1928–39 New Orleans, La.
1940–41 Fort Myers, Fla.
1942 Clearwater, Fla.
1943–45 Lafayette, Ind.
1946 Clearwater, Fla.
1947–92 Tucson, Ariz.
1993– Winter Haven, Fla.

Mariners
1977–92 Tempe, Ariz.
1993– Peoria, Ariz.

Orioles (Browns)
1901 St. Louis, Mo.
1902 French Lick, Ind.
1903 Baton Rouge, La.
1904 Corsicana, Tex.
1905–06 Dallas, Tex.
1907 San Antonio, Tex.
1908 Shreveport, La.
1909–10 Houston, Tex.
1911 Hot Springs, Ark.
1912 Montgomery, Al.
1913 Waco, Tex.
1914 St. Petersburg, Fla.
1915 Houston, Tex.
1916–17 Palestine, Tex.
1918 Shreveport, La.
1919 San Antonio, Tex.
1920 Taylor, Al.
1921 Bogalusa, Al.
1922–24 Mobile, Al.
1925–27 Tarpon Springs, Fla.
1928–36 West Palm Beach, Fla.
1937–41 San Antonio, Tex.
1942 Deland, Fla.
1943–45 Cape Girardeau, Mo.
1946 Anaheim, Cal.
1947 Miami, Fla.
1948 San Bernardino, Cal.
1949–52 Burbank, Cal.
1953 San Bernardino, Cal.
1954 Yuma, Ariz.
1955 Daytona Beach, Fla.
1956–58 Scottsdale, Ariz.
1959–88 Miami, Fla.
1989–90 Miami/Sarasota, Fla.
1991 Sarasota, Fla.
1992–95 St. Petersburg/Sarasota, Fla.
1996– Ft. Lauderdale, Fla.

Rangers (Senators)
1961–86 Pompano Beach, Fla.
1987– Port Charlotte, Fla.

Red Sox
1901 Charlottesville, Va.
1902 Augusta, Ga.
1903–06 Macon, Ga.
1907–08 Little Rock, Ark.
1909–10 Hot Springs, Ark.
1911 Redondo Beach, Cal.
1912–18 Hot Springs, Ark.
1919 Tampa, Fla.
1920–23 Hot Springs, Ark.
1924 San Antonio, Tex.
1925–27 New Orleans, La.
1928–29 Bradenton, Fla.
1930–31 Pensacola, Fla.
1932 Savannah, Ga.
1933–42 Sarasota, Fla.
1943–44 Medford, Mass.
1945 Atlantic City, N.J.
1946–58 Sarasota, Fla.
1959–65 Scottsdale, Ariz.
1966–92 Winter Haven, Fla.
1993– Fort Myers, Fla.

Royals
1969–87 Fort Myers, Fla.
1988– Baseball City, Fla.

Tigers
1901 Detroit, Mich.
1902 Ypsilanti, Mich.
1903–04 Shreveport, La.
1905–07 Augusta, Ga.
1908 Hot Springs, Ark.
1909–10 San Antonio, Tex.
1911–12 Monroe, La.
1913–15 Gulfport, Miss.
1916–18 Waxahachie, Tex.
1919–20 Macon, Ga.
1921 San Antonio, Tex.
1922–26 Augusta, Ga.
1927–28 San Antonio, Tex.
1929 Phoenix, Ariz.
1930 Tampa, Fla.
1931 Sacramento, Cal.
1932 Palo Alto, Cal.
1933 San Antonio, Tex.
1934–42 Lakeland, Fla.
1943–45 Evansville, Ind.
1946– Lakeland, Fla.

Twins (Senators)
1901 Phoebus, Va.
1902–04 Washington, D.C.
1905 Hampton, Va.
1906 Charlottesville, Va.
1907–09 Galveston, Tex.
1910 Norfolk, Va.
1911 Atlanta, Ga.
1912–16 Charlottesville, Va.
1917 Atlanta, Ga.
1918–19 Augusta, Ga.
1920–29 Tampa, Fla.
1930–35 Biloxi, Miss.
1936–42 Orlando, Fla.
1943–45 College Park, Md.
1946–90 Orlando, Fla.
1991– Fort Myers, Fla.

White Sox
1901–02 Excelsior Springs, Mo.
1903 Mobile, Al.
1904 Marlin Springs, Tex.
1905–06 New Orleans, La.
1907 Mexico City, Mex.
1908 Los Angeles, Cal.
1909–10 San Francisco, Cal.
1911 Mineral Wells, Tex.
1912 Waco, Tex.
1913–15 Paso Robles, Cal.
1916–19 Mineral Wells, Tex.
1920 Waco, Tex.
1921 Waxahachie, Tex.
1922–23 Seguin, Tex.
1924 Winter Haven, Fla.
1925–28 Shreveport, La.
1929 Dallas, Tex.
1930–32 San Antonio, Tex.
1933–42 Pasadena, Cal.
1943–44 French Lick, Ind.
1945 Terre Haute, Ind.
1946–50 Pasadena, Cal.
1951 Pasadena/Palm Springs, Cal.
1952 Pasadena/El Centro, Cal.
1953 El Centro, Cal.
1954–59 Tampa, Fla.
1960–97 Sarasota, Fla.
1998– Tucson, Ariz.

Yankees
1901 Baltimore, Md.
1902 Savannah, Ga.
1903–04 Atlanta, Ga.
1905 Montgomery, Al.
1906 Birmingham, Al.
1907–08 Atlanta, Ga.
1909 Macon, Ga.
1910–11 Athens, Ga.
1912 Atlanta, Ga.
1913 Hamilton, Berm.
1914 Houston, Tex.
1915 Savannah, Ga.
1916–18 Macon, Ga.
1919–20 Jacksonville, Fla.
1921 Shreveport, La.
1922–24 New Orleans, La.
1925–42 St. Petersburg, Fla.
1943 Asbury Park, N.J.
1944–45 Atlantic City, N.J.
1946–50 St Petersburg, Fla.
1951 Phoenix, Ariz.
1952–61 St. Petersburg, Fla.
1962– Fort Lauderdale, Fla.
1996– Tampa, Fla.

APPENDIX 5

International Baseball Results

Baseball today is truly an international sport that is played all over the world. In the 2000 Olympics in Sydney, teams from five different continents participated in the baseball competition. In some countries, primarily in Asia and the Caribbean, baseball is as much a part of the fabric of life as it is in the United States. Elsewhere, baseball continues to grow in significant pockets.

Below we present many of the professional baseball league results of regional and national championships from around the world. We have divided the list into four sections. The first is Latin America, which includes champions from the Caribbean, the Dominican League, the Mexican League, and Cuba (Cuban League, Cuban Baseball Federation National Series, and Select Series). The second is Asia, which includes champions from Japan (pre-1950 pennant winners and Japan Series results), Korea, and Taiwan (Chinese Professional Baseball League and the Taiwan Major League). The third is Australia, which has had three different methods of selecting champions: the Claxton Shield, the Australian Baseball League Finals, and now the International Baseball League of Australia Claxton Shield Championship Series. The final section covers Olympic competition. It includes the medal winners for the three Olympics at which baseball has been a full medal sport: 1992, 1996 and 2000.

Caribbean Championships
Serie Del Caribe Results

Series	Year	Site	Winning Team/Country
I	1949	Cuba	Almendares/Cuba
II	1950	Puerto Rico	Carta Vieja/Panama
III	1951	Venezuela	Santurce/Puerto Rico
IV	1952	Panama	La Habana/Cuba
V	1953	Cuba	Santurce/Puerto Rico
VI	1954	Puerto Rico	Caguas/Puerto Rico
VII	1955	Venezuela	Santurce/Puerto Rico
VIII	1956	Panama	Cienfuegos/Cuba
IX	1957	Cuba	Marianao/Cuba
X	1958	Puerto Rico	Marianao/Cuba
XI	1959	Venezuela	Almendares/Cuba
XII	1960	Panama	Cienfuegos/Cuba
	1961–69	Not Held	
XIII	1970	Venezuela	Magallanes/Venezuela
XIV	1971	Puerto Rico	Licey/Dominican Republic
XV	1972	Dominican Republic	Ponce/Puerto Rico
XVI	1973	Venezuela	Licey/Dominican Republic
XVII	1974	Mexico	Caguas/Puerto Rico
XVIII	1975	Puerto Rico	Bayamon/Puerto Rico
XIX	1976	Dominican Republic	Hermosillo/Mexico
XX	1977	Venezuela	Licey/Dominican Republic
XXI	1978	Mexico	Mayaguez/Puerto Rico
XXII	1979	Puerto Rico	Magallanes/Venezuela
XXIII	1980	Dominican Republic	Licey/Dominican Republic
	1981	Not Held	
XXIV	1982	Mexico	Caracas/Venezuela
XXV	1983	Venezuela	Arecibo/Puerto Rico
XXVI	1984	Puerto Rico	Zulia/Venezuela
XXVII	1985	Mexico	Licey/Dominican Republic
XXVIII	1986	Venezuela	Mexicali/Mexico
XXIX	1987	Mexico	Caguas/Venezuela
XXX	1988	Dominican Republic	Escogido/Dominican Republic
XXXI	1989	Mazatlan	Zulia/Venezuela
XXXII	1990	Miami	Escogido/Dominican Republic
XXXIII	1991	Miami	Licey/Dominican Republic
XXXIV	1992	Mexico	Mayaguez/Puerto Rico
XXXV	1993	Mexico	Mayaguez/Puerto Rico
XXXVI	1994	Mexico	Licey/Dominican Republic
XXXVII	1995	Puerto Rico	San Juan/Puerto Rico
XXXVIII	1996	Dominican Republic	Culiacan/Mexico
XXXIX	1997	Mexico	Aguilas/Dominican Republic
XL	1998	Venezuela	Aguilas/Dominican Republic
XLI	1999	Puerto Rico	Licey/Dominican Republic
XLII	2000	Dominican Republic	Santurce/Puerto Rico

Dominican League Champions

Year	Winner
1951	Licey
1952	Aguilas
1953	Licey
1954	Estrellas Orientales
1955–56	Escogido*
1956–57	Escogido
1957–58	Escogido
1958–59	Licey
1959–60	Escogido
1960–61	Escogido
1961–62	Incomplete Season
1962–63	Not Held
1963–64	Licey
1964–65	Aguilas
1965–66	Season not organized by league
1966–67	Aguilas
1967–68	Estrellas Orientales
1968–69	Escogido
1969–70	Licey
1970–71	Licey
1971–72	Aguilas
1972–73	Licey
1973–74	Licey
1974–75	Aguilas
1975–76	Aguilas
1976–77	Licey
1977–78	Aguilas
1978–79	Aguilas
1979–80	Licey
1980–81	Escogido
1981–82	Escogido
1982–83	Licey
1983–84	Licey
1984–85	Licey
1985–86	Aguilas
1986–87	Aguilas
1987–88	Escogido
1988–89	Licey
1989–90	Escogido
1990–91	Licey
1991–92	Escogido
1992–93	Aguilas
1993–94	Licey
1994–95	Azucueros
1995–96	Aguilas
1996–97	Aguilas
1997–98	Aguilas
1998–99	Licey
1999–2000	Aguilas

** First year held in winter*

Mexico
Mexican League Champions

Year	Winner
1940	Veracruz Blues
1941	Veracruz Blues
1942	Torreon Cotton Dealers
1943	Monterrey Industrials
1944	Veracruz Blues
1945	Tampico Lightermen
1946	Tampico Lightermen
1947	Monterrey Industrials
1948	Monterrey Industrials
1949	Monterrey Industrials
1950	Torreon Cotton Dealers
1951	Veracruz Blues
1952	Veracruz Eagle
1953	New Laredo Owls
1954	New Laredo Owls
1955	Mexico City Tigers
1956	Mexico City Red Devils
1957	Yucatan Lions
1958	New Laredo Owls
1959	Poza Rica Oilers
1960	Mexico Tigers
1961	Veracruz Eagle
1962	Monterrey Sultans
1963	Puebla Parrots
1964	Mexico Red Devils
1965	Mexico City Tigers
1966	Mexico City Tigers
1967	Jalisco Charros
1968	Mexico City Red Devils
1969	Reynosa Broncos
1970	Veracruz Eagle
1971	Jalisco Charros
1972	Cordoba Coffee Dealers
1973	Mexico City Red Devils
1974	Mexico City Red Devils
1975	Tampico Lightermen
1976	Mexico City Red Devils
1977	New Laredo Owls
1978	Aguascalientes Railers
1979	Puebla Angels
1980	Puebla Angels (Best record in strike-shortened season)
1981	Mexico City Red Devils
1982	Ciudad Juarez Indians
1983	Campeche Pirates
1984	Yucatan Lions
1985	Mexico City Red Devils
1986	Puebla Angels
1987	Mexico City Red Devils
1988	Mexico City Red Devils
1989	Laredo Owls
1990	Leon Braves
1991	Monterrey Sultans
1992	Mexico City Tigers
1993	Tabasco Olmecas
1994	Mexico City Red Devils
1995	Monterrey Sultans
1996	Monterrey Sultans
1997	Mexico City Tigers
1998	Oxaca Warriors
1999	Mexico City Red Devils
2000	Mexico City Tigers

Cuba
Cuban League Champions

Year	Winner
1878–79	Habana
1879–80	Habana
1880–81	Not held
1882	Disputed: Fe and Habana
1882–83	Habana
1885	Habana
1885–86	Habana
1887	Habana
1888	Fe
1889	Habana
1889–90	Habana
1890–91	Fe
1892	Habana
1892–93	Matanzas
1893–94	Almendares
1894–95	Suspended due to War of Independence
1897–98	Not finished
1898	Habanista
1900	San Francisco
1901	Habana
1902	Habana
1903	Habana
1904	Habana
1905	Almendares
1905–06	Fe
1907	Almendares
1908	Almendares
1908–9	Habana
1910	Almendares
1910–11	Almendares
1912	Habana
1913	Fe
1913–14	Almendares
1914–15	Habana
1915–16	Almendares
1917	Orientales
1918–19	Habana
1919–20	Almendares
1920–21	Habana
1921*	Habana
1922–23	Marianao
1923–24	Santa Clara
1924–25	Almendares
1925–26	Almendares
1926–27	Habana
1927–28	Habana
1928–29	Habana
1929–30	Cienfuegos
1930–31*	Not finished
1931–32	Almendares
1932–33	Tie: Habana Almendares
1933–34	No championship held
1934–35	Almendares
1935–36	Santa Clara
1936–37	Marianao
1937–38	Santa Clara
1938–39	Santa Clara
1939–40	Almendares
1940–41	Habana
1941–42	Almendares
1942–43	Almendares
1943–44	Habana
1944–45	Almendares
1945–46	Cienfuegos
1946–47	Almendares
1947–48	Habana
1948–49	Almendares
1949–50	Almendares
1950–51	Habana
1951–52	Habana
1952–53	Habana
1953–54	Almendares
1954–55	Almendares
1955–56	Cienfuegos
1956–57	Marianao
1957–58	Marianao
1958–59	Almendares
1959–60	Cienfuegos
1960-61	Cienfuegos

** Short season*

Cuban Baseball Federation
National Series Champions

Year	Winner
1967	Orientales
1968	Habana
1969	Azucareros
1970	Henequeneros
1971	Azucareros
1972	Azucareros
1973	Industriales
1974	Habana
1975	Agricultores
1976	Ganaderos
1977	Citricultores
1978	Vegueros
1979	Sancti Spiritus
1980	Santiago de Cuba
1981	Vegueros
1982	Vegueros
1983	Villa Clara
1984	Citricultores

Cuban Baseball Federation National Series Champions (continued)

Year	Winner
1985	Vegueros
1986	Industriales
1987	Vegueros
1988	Vegueros
1989	Santiago de Cuba
1990	Henequeneros
1991	Henequeneros
1992	Industriales
1993	Villa Clara
1994	Villa Clara
1995	Villa Clara
1996	Villa Clara
1997	Pinar del Rio
1998	Pinar del Rio
1999	Santiago de Cuba
2000	Santiago de Cuba

Select Series Team Champions (Super–Provincial)

Year	Winner
1975	Orientales
1976	Habana
1977	Camagueyanos
1978	Las Villas
1979	Pinar del Rio
1980	Pinar del Rio
1981	Orientales
1982	Pinar del Rio
1983	Las Villas
1984	Pinar del Rio
1985	Las Villas
1986	Serranos
1987	Serranos
1988	Pinar del Rio
1989	Las Villas
1990	Ciudad Habana
1991	Pinar del Rio
1992	Serranos
1993	Orientales
1994	Occidentales

Japan

Japan Professional–Baseball League Pennant Winners

Year	Team
1936	Fall: Tokyo Giants
1937	Spring: Tokyo Giants Fall: Osaka Tigers
1938	Spring: Osaka Tigers Fall: Tokyo Giants
1939	Tokyo Giants
1940	Tokyo Giants
1941	Tokyo Giants
1942	Tokyo Giants
1943	Tokyo Giants
1944	Hanshin
1945	Play Suspended
1946	Kinki Greatring
1947	Osaka Tigers
1948	Nankai Hawks
1949	Yomiuri Giants

Japan Series Results

Year	Team/League	Won	Team/League	Won
1950	Mainichi Orions, PL	4	Shochiku Robins, CL	2
1951	Yomiuri Giants, CL	4	Nankai Hawks, PL	1
1952	Yomiuri Giants, CL	4	Nankai Hawks, PL	2
1953	Yomiuri Giants, CL	4	Nankai Hawks, PL	2 (1 tie)
1954	Chunichi Dragons, CL	4	Nishitetsu Lions, PL	3
1955	Yomiuri Giants, CL	4	Nankai Hawks, PL	3
1956	Nishitetsu Lions, PL	4	Yomiuri Giants, CL	2
1957	Nishitetsu Lions, PL	4	Yomiuri Giants, CL	0 (1 tie)
1958	Nishitetsu Lions, PL	4	Yomiuri Giants, CL	3
1959	Nankai Hawks, PL	4	Yomiuri Giants, CL	0
1960	Taiyo Whales, CL	4	Daimai Orions, PL	0
1961	Yomiuri Giants, CL	4	Nankai Hawks, PL	2
1962	Toei Flyers, PL	4	Hanshin Tigers, CL	2 (1 tie)
1963	Yomiuri Giants, CL	4	Nishitetsu Lions, PL	3
1964	Nankai Hawks, PL	4	Hanshin Tigers, CL	3
1965	Yomiuri Giants, CL	4	Nankai Hawks, PL	1
1966	Yomiuri Giants, CL	4	Nankai Hawks, PL	2
1967	Yomiuri Giants, CL	4	Hankyu Braves, PL	2
1968	Yomiuri Giants, CL	4	Hankyu Braves, PL	2
1969	Yomiuri Giants, CL	4	Hankyu Braves, PL	2
1970	Yomiuri Giants, CL	4	Lotte Orions, PL	1
1971	Yomiuri Giants, CL	4	Hankyu Braves, PL	1
1972	Yomiuri Giants, CL	4	Hankyu Braves, PL	1
1973	Yomiuri Giants, CL	4	Nankai Hawks, PL	1
1974	Lotte Orions, PL	4	Chunichi Dragons, CL	2
1975	Hankyu Braves, PL	4	Hiroshima Carp, CL	0 (2 ties)
1976	Hankyu Braves, PL	4	Yomiuri Giants, CL	3
1977	Hankyu Braves, PL	4	Yomiuri Giants, CL	1
1978	Yakult Swallows, CL	4	Hankyu Braves, PL	3
1979	Hiroshima Carp, CL	4	Kintetsu Buffaloes, PL	3
1980	Hiroshima Carp, CL	4	Kintetsu Buffaloes, PL	3
1981	Yomiuri Giants, CL	4	Nippon Ham Fighters, PL	2
1982	Seibu Lions, PL	4	Chunichi Dragons, CL	2
1983	Seibu Lions, PL	4	Yomiuri Giants, CL	3
1984	Hiroshima Carp, CL	4	Hankyu Braves, PL	3
1985	Hanshin Tigers, CL	4	Seibu Lions, PL	2
1986	Seibu Lions, PL	4	Hiroshima Carp, CL	3 (1 tie)
1987	Seibu Lions, PL	4	Yomiuri Giants, CL	2
1988	Seibu Lions, PL	4	Chunichi Dragons, CL	1
1989	Yomiuri Giants, CL	4	Kintetsu Buffaloes, PL	3
1990	Seibu Lions, PL	4	Yomiuri Giants, CL	0
1991	Seibu Lions, PL	4	Hiroshima Carp, CL	3
1992	Seibu Lions, PL	4	Yakult Swallows, CL	3
1993	Yakult Swallows, CL	4	Seibu Lions, PL	3
1994	Yomiuri Giants, CL	4	Seibu Lions, PL	2
1995	Yakult Sallows, CL	4	Orix Blue Wave, PL	1
1996	Orix Blue Wave, PL	4	Yomiuri Giants, CL	1
1997	Yakult Swallows, CL	4	Seibu Lions, PL	1
1998	Yokohama Bay Stars, CL	4	Seibu Lions, PL	2
1999	Fukuoka Daiei Hawks, PL	4	Chunichi Dragons, CL	1
2000	Yomiuri Giants, CL	4	Fukuoka Daiei Hawks, PL	2

PL: Pacific League
CL: Central League

Korea

Korean Series Champions

Year	Winner	Record
1982	OB Bears	56–24–0
1983	Haitai Tigers	55–44–1
1984	Lotte Giants	50–48–2
1985	Samsung Lions	77–32–1
1986	Haitai Tigers	67–37–4
1987	Haitai Tigers	55–48–5
1988	Haitai Tigers	68–38–2
1989	Haitai Tigers	65–51–4
1990	LG Twins	71–49–0
1991	Haitai Tigers	79–42–5
1992	Lotte Giants	71–55–0
1993	Haitai Tigers	81–42–3
1994	LG Twins	81–45–0
1995	OB Bears	74–47–5
1996	Haitai Tigers	73–51–2
1997	Haitai Tigers	75–50–1
1998	Hyundai Unicorns	81–45–0
1999	Hanwha Unicorns	72–58
2000	Hyundai Unicorns	91–40–2

Australia
Claxton Shield Winners

Year	State
1934	SA
1935	SA
1936	SA
1937	NSW
1938	NSW
1939	NSW
1940–1945	not held
1946	NSW
1947	Vic
1948	Vic
1949	Vic
1950	NSW
1951	NSW
1952	WA
1953	NSW
1954	Vic
1955	NSW
1956	Vic
1957	SA
1958	Vic
1959	SA
1960	SA
1961	SA
1962	Vic
1963	NSW
1964	SA
1965	Vic
1966	SA
1967	SA
1968	Vic
1969	SA
1970	SA
1971	SA
1972	Vic
1973	Vic
1974	Vic
1975	WA
1976	SA
1977	WA
1978	WA
1979	WA
1980	SA
1981	Vic
1982	Qld
1983	Qld
1984	Vic
1985	WA
1986	Vic
1987	Qld
1988	Qld
1989	NSW

SA: South Australia
NSW: New South Wales
Vic: Victoria
Qld: Queensland
WA: Western Australia

Australian Baseball League Finals Results

Year	Result
1989–90	Best of five: Waverley 3, Melbourne 1
1990–91	Best of five: Perth 3, Gold Coast 2
1991–92	Best of five: Gold Coast 3, Perth 1
1992–93	Best of three: Melbourne 2, Perth 0
1993–94	Best of three: Brisbane 2, Sydney 0
1994–95	Best of three: Waverley 2, Perth 0
1995–96	Best of three: Sydney Blues 2, Melbourne 0
1996–97	Best of three: Perth 2, Brisbane 1
1997–98	Best of three: Melbourne Reds 2, Gold Coast 0
1998–99	Best of three: Gold Coast 2, Sydney 0

International Baseball League of Australia Claxton Shield Championship Series

Year	Result
1999–2000	Best of three: Western Heelers 2, Queensland Rams 1

Taiwan
Chinese Professional Baseball League Champions

Year	Winner
1989	Weichuan Dragons
1990	President Lions
1991	Brother Elephants
1992	Brother Elephants
1993	Brother Elephants
1994	President Lions
1995	President Lions
1996	Weichuan Dragons
1997	Weichuan Dragons
1998	Weichuan Dragons
1999	President Lions

Taiwan Major League Champions

Year	Winner
1997	Chia–nan Luka
1998	Taipei Gida
1999	Taichung Robomen
2000	Taipei Gida

Olympic Medal Winners

1992 Barcelona
Gold: Cuba
Silver: Chinese Taipei
Bronze: Japan

1996 Atlanta
Gold: Cuba
Silver: Japan
Bronze: United States

2000 Sydney
Gold: United States
Silver: Cuba
Bronze: South Korea

APPENDIX 6

Famous Firsts

1845 Alexander Cartwright and the Knickerbocker Base Ball Club codify playing rules; also, first box score of baseball game, eight men to the side, is printed in *New York Morning News*.

1846 At Elysian Fields on June 19 in Hoboken, New Jersey, the New York Knickerbockers lose to the New York Club in first match game under Cartwright's rules.

1849 Knickerbockers develop first uniforms (colors: blue & white).

1853 First box score of Knickerbocker-style game is printed in *New York Clipper*.

1856 Henry Chadwick becomes the first regular baseball reporter.

1858 First admission (50 cents) charged, for game between All-Star teams representing New York and Brooklyn played at Long Island's Fashion Race Course on July 20.

1859 At Pittsfield, Massachusetts, on July 1, Amherst defeats Williams College in first college game, 73-32.

1860 The Excelsiors of Brooklyn make the first "road trip." Their first stop: Albany's Washington Parade Grounds on July 2.

1862 William Cammeyer's Union Grounds in Brooklyn is the first enclosed ballpark; it opens on May 15.

1863 First calling of balls and strikes.

1865 Ed Cuthbert of the Keystones steals the first base.

1866 Bob Addy of Rockford employs the first slide to steal a base; the Brooklyn Atlantics' Tom Barlow lays down the first bunt.

1867 First use of curveball, by W. A. "Candy" Cummings.

1869 The Cincinnati Red Stockings are the first fully professional team; they are also the first team to wear knickers.

1870 First listing of at bats in box scores, in the *New York Clipper*.

1871 First professional league is formed—the National Association; first game: Cleveland Forest Citys lose, 2-0, at Fort Wayne on May 4; first batting averages printed in *The Dime Base Ball Player*.

1873 First doubleheader is played between the Resolutes and Boston, on July 4.

1874 Boston Red Stockings and Philadelphia Athletics conduct first foreign tour.

1875 Philadelphia's Joe Borden hurls first no-hitter in pro ranks on July 28.

1876 National League's first game: Boston at Philadelphia on April 22.

1877 International League becomes the first minor league; Tecumsehs and Maple Leafs are the first foreign professional teams; first professional gambling scandal—four Louisville players expelled from game; Will White is the first player to wear glasses.

1878 Turnstiles introduced (at Providence); Bud Fowler is first black in pro ball, for Lynn Live Oaks of International Association.

1879 Reserve clause first used.

1880 First night game—between two department store teams, at Nantasket Beach in Massachusetts; Worcester's Lee Richmond hurls first perfect game, against Cleveland on June 12.

1882 American Association introduces first salaried umpiring staff; first postseason playoff; first professional doubleheader, Providence vs. Worcester, September 25; Paul Hines is first player to wear sunglasses in field.

1884 First "third major league," the Union Association; first blacks in Major League Baseball—Moses and Weldy Walker of Toledo (AA); hit by pitch allows batter to take first base in AA.

1885 Umpires and catchers use first chest protectors.

1886 Players organize first union, "The Brotherhood of Ball Players"; first spring training camp, Chicago White Stockings at Hot Springs, Ark.

1887 Charles Zimmer is first catcher to play consistently behind the batter; Baltimore's Mike Griffin of Baltimore and Cincinnati's George "White Wings" Tebeau are the first to homer in their first major league at bat; both do it on the same day, April 16.

1887 The Cleveland Blues' James Toy becomes the first American Indian to play in the major leagues.

1888 First round-the-world baseball tour by Chicago White Stockings and all-star squad; "Casey at the Bat" makes its first debut in print and on the stage; Washington Nationals are the first major league club to train in Florida.

1892 National League allows Sunday baseball; first pinch homer, by Brooklyn's Tom Daly on May 24.

1894 Boston's Bobby Lowe is first major league player to smash four homers in one game.

1896 Prof. Charles Hinton demonstrates the first pitching machine.

1900 First pinch-hit grand slam, by St. Louis pitcher Mike O'Neill on September 4.

1901 First American League game, Cleveland loses, 8-7, at Chicago on April 24.

1903 First modern World Series—Boston defeats Pittsburgh, five games to three.

1905 The first "sanitary hose" are introduced.

1907 Giants catcher Roger Bresnahan introduces shin guards.

1909 First concrete-and-steel ballpark opens—Philadelphia's Shibe Park; Cleveland's Neal Ball turns first modern unassisted triple play in majors, on July 19; William Howard Taft is first president to throw out "first ball"; Arlie Latham of the New York Giants is baseball's first full-time coach.

1910 First cork-centered ball.

1911 First MVP Awards to the Cubs' Frank Schulte and the Tigers' Ty Cobb.

1916 Fred Clarke patents the first flip-up sunglasses.

1917 First "knothole gang" organized in St. Louis.

1920 First Japanese pro team, the Nihon Undo Kyokai; first team to draw 1 million fans, Yankees with 1,289,422.

1921 First baseball commissioner, Kenesaw Mountain Landis; first radio broadcast of a game, by Harold Arlin of KDKA from Forbes Field on August 5; first World Series broadcast (Yankees vs. Giants).

1923 Babe Ruth becomes first player to earn $50,000 in a season.

1926 First amplifiers used (at Polo Grounds).

1929 Tigers are the first major league club to train in Arizona.

1930 First successful night ball in minors.

1933 First All-Star Game, at Chicago's Comiskey Park on July 6.

1935 First major league night game: Phils at Reds, May 24.

1936 First pro league in Japan; first players elected to Hall of Fame (Ty Cobb, Babe Ruth, Christy Mathewson, Honus Wagner, and Walter Johnson); the Reds are the first team to fly—from St. Louis to Chicago on July 30.

1939 First AL night game, at Philadelphia Shibe Park on May 16; first televised game, from Ebbets Field on August 26.

1941 Dodgers are first club to wear batting helmets.

1946 Montreal's Jackie Robinson is the century's first black professional player; first team to draw 2 million fans, Yankees with 2,265,512.

1947 Jackie Robinson becomes first modern major league black player; Cleveland's Larry Doby is first black player in AL; first BBWAA Rookie of the Year Awards; Hank Greenberg becomes the first $100,000 player.

1951 Emmett Ashford is first black pro umpire (Southwestern International League); first game televised coast-to-coast (last game of NL playoff); first nationally televised World Series (Yankees vs. Giants); first true baseball encyclopedia, Turkin & Thompson's *The Official Encyclopedia of Baseball;* Paul Pettit is the first $100,000 bonus baby.

1952 Clint Courtney is the first catcher to wear glasses.

1956 Don Larsen hurls first World Series perfect game, on October 8. Frank Umont and Ed Rommel are first major league umps to wear eyeglasses on field.

1957 First Gold Glove Awards.

1959 Joe Cronin becomes first former player to become league president when he assumes leadership of American League.

1962 Jackie Robinson becomes the first black elected to the Hall of Fame.

1965 First enclosed stadium, the Astrodome, opens on April 9; in the first amateur draft Rick Monday is first player selected.

1966 First major league black umpire, Emmett Ashford of AL.

1969 First major league game outside U.S., St. Louis against the Expos at Montreal's Jarry Park on April 14.

1970 First strike by major league umpires occurs during playoffs; first World Series game on artificial turf—Baltimore at Cincinnati on October 10.

1971 First night World Series game—Baltimore at Pittsburgh on October 13; aluminum bats first approved for use in Little League.

1972 First major league player strike; Bernice Gera is first female professional umpire.

1973 The Yankees' Ron Blomberg becomes the first designated hitter, on April 6.

1974 First major league Hispanic umpire: Armando Rodriguez in AL; aluminum bats first approved for use by NCAA.

1975 Indians hire Frank Robinson as first black manager; first players declared free agents (on December 23), Andy Messersmith and Dave McNally; Danny Litwhiler introduces the first radar gun.

1977 Mike Schmidt earns the first $500,000 salary.

1978 First team to draw 3 million fans, Los Angeles Dodgers with 3,347,945.

1980 Nolan Ryan earns the first $1 million annual salary (a four-year contract).

1982 Joel Youngblood becomes first major league player to get hits for two different teams (Mets and Expos) in two different cities (Chicago and Philadelphia) on same day, August 4; George Foster earns the first $2 million salary, $2.04 million a year for five seasons.

1989 Bill White becomes first black league president (NL); the Griffeys become first father-son duo to perform simultaneously.

1990 Kirby Puckett earns the first $3 million salary.

1991 First modern teams to go from last to first (Twins and Braves) meet in World Series; first team to draw 4 million fans, the Toronto Blue Jays with 4,001,527; Roger Clemens becomes first player to top $5 million mark, with $5.38 million salary for five seasons; Brien Taylor becomes first $1 million bonus baby.

1992 First non-U.S. world champion, Toronto Blue Jays.

1993 Carey Schueler, 18-year-old daughter of White Sox general manager Ron Schueler, becomes the first woman chosen in the amateur free agent draft, when the Sox select her in the 43rd round.

1994 First year of three divisions in each league; the Grieves becomes the first father-son duo to be drafted in the first round of the free agent draft (Tom was taken by Washington in 1966, and Ben by Oakland in 1994).

1995 First use of Wild Cards in postseason play; Yankees are first team to have average salary of over $2 million.

1996 First major league game in Mexico, Mets vs. Padres.

1997 Albert Belle earns the first $10 million salary, $11 million a year for five seasons; first regular-season interleague play; Florida Marlins are the first Wild Card team to become world champions.

1998 Mark McGwire is the first player to hit 50 or more home runs in three straight seasons and the first to hit 70 homers; Barry Bonds is first player to hit 400 homers and steal 400 bases; first season two players, 60 or more homers, Mark McGwire and Sammy Sosa; after the season Kevin Brown becomes first player with $15 million contract (seven-year contract).

2000 The Chicago Cubs and New York Mets open the season in Japan on March 29, making it the first regular season game ever played outside of North America.

Notes on Contributors

Larry Amman was born and raised in the suburbs of Detroit. He graduated from Wayne State University with a B.A. in history and political science in 1967, then served in the U.S. Army Intelligence in Vietnam and Germany. Germany remains a very special place to him. In the last few years he has made several trips to that country to help with baseball programs. Larry has lived in the Washington area for 20 years. He is employed as a travel agent.

Marty Appel, a former public relations director and television producer for the New York Yankees, is the author of 15 books, including the Casey Award-winning *Slide, Kelly, Slide,* and collaborations with Bowie Kuhn, Tom Seaver, Thurman Munson, and umpire Eric Gregg. His autobiography, *Now Pitching for the Yankees: Spinning the News for Mickey, Billy, and George,* is a 2001 publication from Total Sports Publishing.

Bill Deane is a freelance baseball researcher and writer stationed near Cooperstown, New York, where he spent eight years as senior research Associate for the National Baseball Library & Archive. He has published seven books and nearly 200 articles for such publications as *Baseball America* and *USA Today Baseball Weekly,* and was a recipient of the 1989 SABR-Macmillan Baseball Research Award. Deane resides in Fly Creek, New York, with his wife, Pam, and daughter, Sarah.

Michael Gershman was best known among baseball fans for *Diamonds: The Evolution of the Ballpark,* which won the 1993 CASEY Award and also received that year's SABR-Macmillan Award. He was also familiar to collectors for his series of *Baseball Card Engagement Books and Baseball Stadium Postcard Albums.* He was co-editor of *Total Baseball* and *Total Football* and co-founder of Total Sports. He was editor-in-chief of the biographical component of Microsoft's *Complete Baseball* CD-ROM and served as a co-editor for *Baseball: The Biographical Encyclopedia.* He passed away on January 4, 2000.

Gary Gillette is a nationally known baseball author, analyst, and editor. He is currently working on an updated and revised edition of the renowned baseball classic, *The Hidden Game of Baseball,* scheduled for publication by Total Sports Publishing in January 2002. Gillette was a vice president of Total Sports, Inc., an Internet and print sports information publisher, from 1997 to 1999, serving as the executive editor of *Total Baseball Daily* from 1996 to 1999. He has written or edited many baseball books, including the *Baseball Weekly Insider 1999 and 2000; The Spy: Baseball '98; The Scouting Report: 1995* and *1996;* and *The Great American Baseball Stat Book 1992, 1993,* and *1994.* Gillette also works as a legal expert witness on baseball-related litigation and has been a consultant for prominent player agents and for insurance companies. From 1992 to 1997, Gillette was the president and owner of The Baseball Workshop, which he sold to Total Sports in 1997. Gillette was a baseball commentator for the Sports Fans Radio Network in 1999 and has also served as a baseball commentator for several National Public Radio stations.

Bob Hoie has long been an active member of the Society for American Baseball Research, receiving the Society's Bob Davids Award for meritorious service in 1987. He has served as chairman of SABR's Minor League Committee, was a principal contributor to *Minor League Baseball Stars,* volumes 1, 2, and 3, and contributed to *The Encyclopedia of Minor League Baseball.* A native of Los Angeles and a fan of the Pacific Coast League Angels until their demise in 1957, Hoie is retired after 30 years of service as an urban planner for Los Angeles County.

Mikhail Horowitz is a senior editor at Total Sports. He is the author of *Big League Poets* (City Lights, 1978), a wry collection of collages and captions illuminating the baseball careers of immortal bards. His poem, "Pearly Babe," was featured in 1999 on the Los Angeles Dodgers' website, where you could click to hear it read by Vin Scully.

Frederick Ivor-Campbell is vice president of the Society for American Baseball Research, and a contributor of baseball history and biography to numerous reference works and journals, including *American National Biography, Biographical Dictionary of American Sports,* and *The National Pastime.* His work as general editor of *Baseball's First Stars (1996)* earned him The Sporting News-SABR Baseball Research Award. He and his wife Alma live in Bristol, Rhode Island.

Sean Lahman is director of digital publishing for Total Sports Publishing. His Baseball Archive web site was one of the early sources for baseball information on the Internet, and he headed the first significant effort to make a database of baseball statistics freely available to the general public. He has written for or edited a number of books, including *Total Baseball* and *Baseball: The Biographical Encyclopedia.* He is the project editor for *Total Stock Car Racing,* and co-editor of *Total Basketball.* He attended the University of Cincinnati and lives in Woodstock, New York, with his wife Heather and their three children.

Bruce Markusen is manager of program presentations at the National Baseball Hall of Fame and Museum, where he has worked since 1995. After graduating from Hamilton College in 1987, Markusen began a seven-year stint at WIBX Radio in Utica, New York. Markusen hosted a nightly sports talk show, anchored daily afternoon sports updates, and performed play-by-play of Utica Blue Sox baseball. In March of 1995 Markusen joined the staff of the National Baseball Hall of Fame as a senior researcher. As part of his duties in Cooperstown, he has conducted numerous audio-visual interviews for the Hall's archives, narrated several Hall of Fame video productions, and delivered a variety of presentations on baseball history to the general public. Markusen has also written three books. His first book, *Baseball's Last Dynasty: Charlie Finley's Oakland A's*, won the Seymour Award from the Society for American Baseball Research as the best baseball book of 1998. His second release, *Roberto Clemente: The Great One*, was also published in 1998. A third book, *The Orlando Cepeda Story*, is scheduled for release in the spring of 2001. Markusen has also written numerous articles for *Baseball Digest, Elysian Fields Quarterly,* and *Oldtyme Baseball News.* Markusen lives in Cooperstown, New York, with his wife, the former Sue Ellen Bartow.

Patricia Millen has spent most of her career in history museums in New York and New Jersey. She is author of *Bare Trees; Zadock Pratt Master Tanner and the Story of What Happened to the Catskill Mountain Forests,* and numerous published articles on 19th century American history. A Civil War enthusiast, she became interested in the connection between baseball and the war while living in Cooperstown, New York. Her second book, *From Pastime to Passion: Baseball and the Civil War,* is due out from Heritage Books in 2001. Millen now works in the education field and lives in Titusville, New Jersey, with her husband and two children. She holds a B.S. in American Studies from the State University of New York.

Pete Palmer is the former editor of the Barnes *Official Encyclopedia of Baseball.* He began compiling his historical and analytical data in the mid-1960s, and from 1978 to 1987 he was chairman of SABR's statistical analysis committee. In that time he also served as a consultant for the Sports Information Center, the official statisticians of the American League. He was on the board of directors of Project Scoresheet. Palmer has contributed articles to *Sport, USA Today, Sports Heritage, The National Pastime,* and *Baseball Research Journal.* He is co-author, with John Thorn, of *The Hidden Game of Baseball* and *The Official Major League Baseball Record Book;* with Thorn and Bob Carroll of *The Hidden Game of Football* and *The Football Abstract;* and with Thorn and Eliot Cohen of *The Baseball Annual 1990.* He won SABR's Bob Davids Award in 1989.

David Pietrusza, former president of the Society for American Baseball Research (SABR) and editor-in-chief of Total Sports, is the author of *Judge and Jury: The Life and Times of Judge Kenesaw Mountain Landis,* winner of the 1998 CASEY Award. He is also the author of *Lights On!: The Wild Century-Long Saga of Night Baseball* (a finalist for the 1997 CASEY Award), *Minor Miracles: The Legend and Lure of Minor League Baseball, Major Leagues,* and *Baseball's Canadian-American League.* He co-edited *Total Baseball, The Total Baseball Catalog, Baseball: The Biographical Encyclopedia, Total Mets, Total Braves, Total Indians. Ted Williams: My Life in Pictures,* written by Pietrusza and Williams, will be published by Total Sports Publishing in 2001. Pietrusza served as managing editor of the first edition of *Total Football: The Official Encyclopedia of the NFL,* and edited seven books on football. Pietrusza served as producer for the documentary *Local Heroes* for PBS station WMHT and as a consultant for the Baseball Online segment of the PBS LearningLink system. He has appeared on ABC-TV, ESPN, and National Public Radio and written for numerous publications including *USA Today Baseball Weekly* and *Baseball America.* A former member of the Amsterdam (New York) City Council, Pietrusza serves as public information officer for the New York State Governor's Office of Regulatory Reform.

Beau Riffenburgh was formerly editor-in-chief for Total Sports. He was on the public relations staff of the Los Angeles Lakers before serving eight years as an associate editor and senior writer for NFL Properties, where he was the author of *The Official NFL Encyclopedia, Running Wild, and Great Ones.* He has written 15 books and contributed to many more. He has spent 12 years in Cambridge, England, where he is a lecturer in the History Faculty at the University of Cambridge and is editor of *Polar Record,* the world's oldest journal of polar research. In Britain he also coached "American football" for eight years at the university level, posting an overall record of 68–12–2 and winning three national titles.

Tom Ruane is a member of the Society for American Baseball Research and past contributor to *The Big Bad Baseball Annual, NINE,* and *The Baseball Research Journal.* He is a researcher and writer for Diamond Mind Baseball as well as a computer programmer for IBM. His fiction has appeared in several magazines, including *The Yale Review, ACM, Carolina Quarterly,* and *Witness.* He lives and works in Poughkeepsie, New York, where he is a liability to his recreational softball team.

Debra A. Shattuck was born in Lorain, Ohio in 1959. She received her B.A. in history from Cedarville College in 1981 and her M.A. in history from Brown University in 1988. Her master's thesis was on female baseball players in the United States, 1866–1954. She later was a captain in the U.S. Air Force.

Matthew Silverman is associate publisher in charge of reference at Total Sports Publishing. He co-edited *Baseball: The Biographical Encyclopedia* with David Pietrusza and Michael Gershman. He served as managing editor for the sixth edition of *Total Baseball* and the second edition of *Total Football.* He has edited seven offshoots of *Total Football,* including *Total Packers, Total Steelers, Total Cowboys,* and *Total Super Bowl.* He also co-edited *Total Mets* in 1997. Formerly a junior editor for *Variety* in New York, he worked for three New England newspapers before joining Total Sports Publishing. He resides in High Falls, New York, with his wife, Debbie, and daughter, Jan.

Curt Smith is the author of eight books, including *The Storytellers, Our House: A Tribute to Fenway Park,* and his seminal work on broadcasting, *Voices of the Game.* He has also written and produced the ESPN Television documentary, *Voices of the Game,* and contributed to the network's *SportsCentury* series. A former speechwriter to President Bush, Smith has hosted sports symposia at the Smithsonian Institution. Today, he is senior lecturer in

English at the University of Rochester and hosts several political series for CBS television affiliate WROC.

David W. Smith is the founder and president of Retrosheet, a non-profit, all-volunteer organization dedicated to the collection, computerization and distribution at no charge of play by play accounts of major league games (www.retrosheet.org). He is a long-time member of the Society for American Baseball Research who makes frequent research presentations at annual meetings and also served as co-chair of SABR's statistical analysis committee with Pete Palmer from 1980 to 1982. Smith has contributed to the media guides and public relations departments of many teams, as well as to *USA Today's Baseball Weekly* and several daily newspapers, including the *NewYork Times.* He is a co- author, along with David Vincent and Lyle Spatz, of *The Midsummer Classic,* a comprehensive history of baseball's All-Star Game. He is a biology professor at the University of Delaware and lives with his wife, Amy Tetlow Smith, and son, Graham, in Newark, Delaware.

Lyle Spatz is the chairman of the Society for American Baseball Research's Baseball Records Committee, a post he has held since 1991. He is the author of *New York Yankee Openers—1903–1996; Yankees Coming, Yankees Going—New York Yankee Player Transactions, 1903–1999;* and a co-author of *The Midsummer Classic—The Complete History of Baseball's All-Star Game.* Spatz has also contributed chapters to *The Dictionary of Literary Biography—Sportswriters; The Biographical Dictionary of American Sports—Baseball; Jackie Robinson: Race, Sports, and the American Dream;* and *The Perfect Game.* His articles have appeared in *The Washington Post, Baseball Weekly, Baseball Digest, The National Pastime,* and *The Baseball Research Journal.* He has also presented papers at the Babe Ruth Conference at Hofstra University and at the Jackie Robinson Conference at Long Island University.

Greg Spira has been a member of the Society for Baseball Researcher and a writer of baseball articles on the Internet for over a decade. He has contributed to such books as *The Baseball Prospectus* and *Baseball: The Biographical Encyclopedia.* He continues to write regularly on baseball for various sites on the net and maintains on-line guides to finding baseball information and buying baseball books on the net. He is a graduate of Harvard College and currently lives in Kingston, New York.

John Thorn is the author/editor of many baseball books, including *Treasures of the Hall of Fame, The Game for All America, The Armchair Books of Baseball, Ted Williams: Seasons of the Kid* (with Richard Ben Cramer and Mark Rucker), *The National Pastime,* and *The Relief Pitcher.* He co-authored *The Pitcher* with John Holway, and *The Hidden Game of Baseball* and *The Baseball Record Book* with Pete Palmer. With Palmer and Bob Carroll he also co-authored *The Hidden Game of Football* and *The Football Abstract.* He has written for several periodicals, among them *The Sporting News, Sport,* and *American Heritage.* Thorn was Senior Creative Consultant to Baseball, Ken Burns's nine-part film for the Public Broadcasting System, and serves as a consultant to the National Baseball Hall of Fame Committee on Baseball Veterans. The publisher of Total Sports Publishing, Thorn is also a co-editor of *Total Football.*

Robert L. Tiemann served as chairman of the 19th-century research committee of the Society for American Baseball Research and is the author of *Cardinal Classics* and *Dodger Classics.* He headed the SABR research project that reconstructed from newspaper play-by-play accounts much of the missing data for the National Association of 1871 to 1875. With Rich Topp, Tiemann shared a SABR award for his redevelopment of the Manager Roster as it appears in *Total Baseball,* and in 1992 won SABR's Bob Davids Award.

Jules Tygiel is a professor of history at San Francisco State University. He is the author of *Baseball's Great Experiment: Jackie Robinson and his Legacy* (Oxford University Press, 1983; Expanded Paperback edition, 1997), and has contributed articles to many periodicals.

Joseph M. Wayman, publisher and editor of *Grandstand Baseball Annual,* which he founded in 1985, has been the subject of a "SABR Salute," which commended him for his steadfast "investigative reporting of questionable baseball records." Several of his discoveries have been accepted as fact by *Total Baseball* and the Elias Sports Bureau and have resulted in a rewriting of the baseball record books. His writings have also appeared in the *Baseball Research Journal* and *Baseball Bulletin.*

With appreciation to these readers of the first edition of *Total Baseball* who sent in corrections or made suggestions on how to improve the second edition:

Larry Amman, Ray Andreotti, Mel Bailey, Craig Barbarino, Edgar K. Beatty, James M. Beck, Joseph R. Bender, Robert Beukelher, John Booth, Jim Bostain, Therese R. Brown, J. Paul Browne, Bob Cambris, Kevin A. Carleton, Bob Carroll, Anthony M. Chieco, Ken Coleman, Steve Cooper, Owen Curtis, Clay Davenport, L. Robert Davids, Bill Deane, Harold Dellinger, Ted D. DeVries, Don Dewey, Raymond A. DiSanto, Sam Elfand, Don Elliott, John Emerson, Eddie Epstein, Kenneth Fink, Robert L. Franz, Andrew Fussner, Cam Gibson, Steven Goldberg, Ray Gonzalez, Dan Greenia, Bill Haber, Rod Hay, Bob Hoie, Frederick Ivor-Campbell, Tom Jennings, Bill Jensen, Warren Johnson, Cliff Kachline, James Kaufman, Dave Kemp, Larry Kempster, Randall Kleinman, Jack Lang, Ron Liebman, Jerry Malloy, James F. Maxfield, Bob McConnell, Joe M. McGowan, David Molnar, George S. Moskal, Frank J. Mueller, Neil Munro, Thomas L. Nester, Dave Nichols, Tom O'Brien, Yoshio Ohno, S. Mark Parker, Paul E. Pennebaker, Peretz Perl, David Pietrusza, Mike Post, Jorgen Rasmussen, Allan Rausch, Andrew Richardson, John Rickert, John M. Roca, Winslow Rogers, Tom Ruane, Bill Rubenstein, David Schermer, Leon Schmerhold, John Schwartz, Alfred Secondi, Sy Siegel, Richard Siegelman, Al Smith, David M. Snyder, David Stephan, Mike Sparks, Lyle Spatz, Dean Sullivan, Isaac Thorn, Richard Topp, Stephen Toth, T. Brook Treakle III, Jim Troisi, Jim Tuttle, Jim Vail, Cullen P. Vane, David Vincent, Joseph M. Wayman, Jim Weigand, Bernard Weisberger, Christopher Williams, Frank Williams, Joseph C. Williams, Ralph Winnie, Jim Wright, and Ed Yerha.

And to those whose suggestions have improved the third edition:

David Aceto, Tim Anderson, Andrew J. Balog, Robert Browning, Chuck Carey, Keith Carlson, Garrett M. Casey, Jim Conroy, Bob Davids, Bill Deane, Dennis DeValeria, Ted DiTullio, Robert Downer, Tom Dunken, Jules Egyrd, Eddie Epstein, Ken Fetterman, Bob Franzosa, Gary Gillette, Jay Gregory, Charlie Harville, Jeffrey Hatt, Ralph Horton, Jeff James, Darlene Kadlecik, Jerry Kahn, John Kenyon, Patrick Kinas, D.C. Larkin, II, Matthew Lesniewski, Morris Levin, Don Luce, Michael Lucich, Ed Luteran, Jeff Magalif, E.H. Marshall, Richard A. Marston, Ronald A. Mayer, John P. McBride, John McClaran, Randy Messel, Scott Messinger, Steve Moore, Neil Munro, John O'Malley, Ed Oswalt, Douglas R. Pappas, Richard Pardoe, Danny Radakovich, Matt Rapacz, Louis Rauco, Matt Reese, Eric Reinholdt, Dennis Repp, John Richards, Bob Richardson, John M. Roca, Seth D. Rodgers, Robert Schulz, John Schwartz, John Scott, Jamie Selko, Jim Smith, Dave Smith, Lewis J. Snyder, Lyle Spatz, Alan Steinberg, David Stephan, A.D. Suehsdorf, James Swetnam, Blair D. Tarr, Robert Tiemann, Harry L. Turtledove, Bill Wallace, Patrick K. Walsh, Joe Wayman, Jim Weigand, Frank Williams, Walt Wilson, and Edgar M. Wyatt.

The fourth edition has benefited from the comments of:

Tim Anderson, Arnie Braunstein, Chuck Carey, Bill Carle, Tim Cashion, Tom Chase, Ed Coen, Bob Davids, Bill Deane, Dan Dischley, Ted DiTullio, Jules Egyrd, Eddie Epstein, Bill French, Campbell Gibson, Gary Gillette, Herb Goldman, Albert A. Gunnell, Robert Kern, Joe Kinsman, Joe Klein, Joe Marchetto, Jeff Marcus, Bob McConnell, Randy Messell, Scott Messinger, Neil Munro, John O'Malley, Ed Oswalt, Doug Pappas, Jeffrey Platt, Frank Phelps, Bob Richardson, Win Rogers, Bob Rosiek, Jim Sargent, Robert Schulz, John Schwartz, Jamie Selko, Dave Smith, Jim Smith, David Stephan, Chuck Stevens, David Stone, Adie Suehsdorf, Bob Tiemann, David Vincent, Bill Way, Joe Wayman, Jim Weigand, Roy White, Alan Whitney, Frank Williams, Walt Wilson, and Ed Yerha.

The fifth edition has benefited from the comments of:

Arnie Braunstein, Chuck Carey, Keith Carlson, Bill Carle, Bill Carr, Tim Cashion, Tom Chase, Bob Davids, Bill Deane, Dan Dischley, Bill Doig, Jeff Fox, Tate Giersdorf, Gary Gillette, Herb Goldberg, Ed Hartig, Bob Hoie, Frederick Ivor-Campbell, Herm Krabbenhoft, Dan Levitt, Fred Lenger, David Marasco, John Matthew IV, Neil Munro, John O'Malley, David Neft, Doug Pappas, Bob Richardson, Patrick Rock, Jim Sargent, John Schultz, John Schwartz, Jamie Selko, Joe Simenic, Allan Simpson, Lyle Spatz, Dick Thompson, Bob Tiemann, Dixie Torangeau, Jim Troisi, Frank Vaccaro, Paul Walker, Bill Way, Joe Wayman, Jim Weigand, Frank Williams, Walt Wilson, and Dave Zeman.

The sixth edition has benefited from the comments of:

Carlos Bauer, Randy Bonferraro, Bill Carle, Tim Cashion, Bill Carr, Ryall Carroll, Bill Deane, Dan Dischley, Harvey Frankel, Gary Gillette, Todd Greanier, Rich Hancock, Ed Hartig, Herm Krabbenhoft, Fred Lenger, Jamie Lotze, Chuck Lumb, Bob McConnell, Neil Munro, Rob Neyer, John O'Malley, Jeff Ouriel, Frank Peters, Frank Phelps, Bob Richardson, Tom Ruane, John Schwartz, Stuart Shea, Dave Smith, Lyle Spatz, John Steele, Dick Thompson, Bob Tiemann, Dixie Torangeau, Wayne Townsend, Frank Vaccaro, David Vincent, Bill Way, Joe Wayman, Frank Williams, Vic Wilson, Walt Wilson and Ken Zweibel.

The seventh edition has benefited from the comments of:

Carlos Bauer, Greg Beston, G. Betor, Peter Bjarkman, Al Bokar, Randy Bonferraro, Timm Boyle, Adrian Burgos Jr., Jeffrey Burk, Bill Carle, Keith Carlson, Bob Carroll, Kevin Clark, Clem Comly, Thomas Crimmins, Clay Davenport, Aaron Davis, Darl Edward Devault, Brandon L. Dillard, Terry Dinan, Dan Dischley, Bruce Fleming, Sean Forman, Bill Fort, Myles E. Friedman, Jim Furtado, Jim Gates, Larry R. Gerlach, Steve Gietschier, Todd Greanier, Marc Guarino, G. Michael Hall, Ed Hartig, Bruce Hobbs, John B. Holway, Jonathan Jacobs, Gary A. Kizer, Nathan Kunkel, Robert Laidlaw, Robert Langenderfer, Gary Lee, Fred Lenger, Michael Levett, Jamie Lotze, Philip J. Lowry, Bill Lussenheide, Lillian Madden, Kenneth Matinale, Bob McConnell, Wayne McElreavy, Todd McGee, William J. Melzer, Mike Meserole, Richard Minteer, Peter Morris, Yoichi Nagata, Rob Neyer, Mat Olkin, John O'Malley, Edwin Orenberg, Jeff Ouriel, Robert Panara, Mark Pankin, Pat Parker, Doug Pappas, Dave Pease, Fred Percival, Juan Fernando Rivera Pernia, Hayford Pierce, Bob Richardson, Rob Ruck, Thomas St. John, Mike Sandler, John Schwartz, Stuart Shea, Joseph Sheehan, Tom Shieber, Scott Silveri, Allan Simpson, Herb Soltman, Nicolas Tavuchis, Neal Traven, Rob Tucker, Frank Vacarro, John Vaughan, David Vincent, Patrick W. Walsh, Bill Way, Tim Wiles, Jeffrey Wilson, Frank Williams, Walt Wilson, and Keith Woolner.

Glossary of Statistical Terms

This Glossary contains definitions of the statistical terms and measures that may be unfamiliar to the average baseball fan or that represent what today might seem odd scoring practices. The Glossary will also be of value to the advanced fan who wishes to know more about the mathematical and theoretical foundations of certain statistics.

+ indicates an adjusted statistic, meaning that the statistic to the immediate left of this mark has been normalized to league average and adjusted for home park factor. Stats that are normalized in this book are Batting Runs, Production (On-Base Plus Slugging), Batting Average, On-Base Percentage, Slugging Average, Earned Run Average, and Pitcher Runs.

Assist Although credited to pitchers on strikeouts in some of baseball's early years, not counted as such in this volume.

Assist Average Assists divided by games played. Stat created by Philadelphia baseball writer Al Wright in 1875.

At Bats Charged to batters on sacrifice hits, 1889–1893; on sacrifice-fly situations, 1931–1938 and 1940–1953; bases on balls, 1876, 1887. However, we did not count at bats for bases on balls.

Average and Over Early form of expressing averages for base hits, runs, and outs. The average of a batter with 23 hits in six games would be not 3.83 but 3–5 (an average of 3 with an overage, or remainder, of 5); borrowed from cricket.

Average Bases Allowed A pitcher's total bases allowed, divided by his innings pitched—what might be termed Opponents' Slugging Average. Created by Alfred P. Berry in 1951.

Average Batting (Pitching, Fielding) Skill The great philosophical as well as statistical puzzler: after one has normalized a player's performance to that of his league, how does one compare one season's league average with that of another far removed in time? Does a .266 batting average in the NL of 1902 mean the same thing as a .266 batting average in the AL of 1977?

Bases on Balls Counted as outs for batters in 1876 and as hits for batters in 1887, but as neither throughout this book. Awarded for a varying number of errant pitches since 1876, from nine in that year to the current four, standardized in 1889. (After 1887, the batter was no longer allowed to specify strike zone as waist to shoulders or waist to shins.)

Bases on Balls Percentage Batters' stat: most walks per 100 at bats plus bases on balls.

Bases on Balls Per Game Game defined as nine innings; league-leading pitchers calculated on basis of lowest mark; computed as bases on balls times nine, divided by innings.

Base-Out Percentage Barry Codell's stat for measuring complete offensive performance, in which the elements of the numerator represent bases gained while the events in the denominator represent outs produced (sacrifices and sacrifice flies appear in both because they achieve both—gaining a base for the team while costing it an out). The formula:

$$\frac{\text{Total Bases} + \text{Walks} + \text{HBP} + \text{Steals} + \text{Sacrifices} + \text{Sacrifice Flies}}{\text{At bats} - \text{Hits} + \text{Caught Stealing} + \text{GIDP} + \text{Sac.} + \text{Sac. Flies}}$$

(GIDP, in the equation above, stands for Grounded Into Double Play; HBP for Hit By Pitch.)

Batters Facing Pitcher Unavailable before 1903 in the National League. The 1903 and 1908 data was not published and has been reconstructed. BFP was unavailable for the American League of 1901-1907. Excepting the NL of 1876-1888 and the AA of 1882 and 1884-1887, for which John Tattersall calculated BFP from box scores, earlier years in both leagues have had their BFP constructed from available data in this manner: subtract league base hits from league at bats, divide by league innings pitched, multiply by the pitcher's innings, and add his hits allowed, walks, hit by pitch, and sacrifice hits, if available. Abbreviated as BFP.

Batter's Park Factor The Park Factor shown in the batters' section of the team statistics in the Annual Record, Player Register, and Home-Road Statistics. Above 100 means batters benefited from playing half their games in a good hitting park. Abbreviated as BPF or, in what are clearly batters' stats (as in the Player Register) simply as PF. See entry for *Park Factor* for the computation.

Battery Errors In baseball's early years, wild pitches, passed balls, and hit batsmen were lumped together in the statistical summary of a game as *battery errors* and were charged against the fielding percentage of the pitcher or catcher. Such battery errors have been removed from individual and team stats for this book.

Batting Average Calculated as base hits divided by at bats ever since its first appearance in print in 1874. In 1876 walks were counted as at bats, and in 1887 they were counted as at bats and as hits. Abbreviated in Part 2 of this volume as AVG, although it is also commonly abbreviated BA.

Batting Runs The Linear Weights measure of runs contributed *beyond* those of a league-average batter or team, such league average defined as zero. The formula depends upon the run values for each offensive event that resulted from Pete Palmer's 1978 computer simulation of all major league games played since 1901. Run values change marginally with changing conditions of play (an out costs a team more in a hitters' year, such as 1930, than in a pitchers' year, such as 1908), and they differ slightly up and down the batting order (a homer is not worth as much to the leadoff hitter as it is to the fifth-place batter; a walk is worth more for the man batting second than for the man batting eighth); however, these differences have been averaged out historically in the figures that follow.

$$\text{Runs} = (.47)1B + (.78)2B + (1.09)3B + (1.40)HR + (.33)(BB + HB) - (.25)(AB - H) - (.50)OOB$$

(An out is considered to be a hitless at bat and its value is set so that the sum of all events times their frequency is zero, thus establishing zero as the baseline, or norm, for performance.)

Some events one might expect to see included in this formula but that do not appear are sacrifices, sacrifice hits, grounded into double plays, and reached on error. The last is not known for most years and in the official statistics is indistinguishable from outs on base (OOB). The sacrifice has values that essentially cancel one another, trading an out for an advanced base which, often as not, leaves the team in a situation with poorer run potential than it had before the sacrifice. The sacrifice fly has dubious run value because it is entirely dependent on a situation not under the batter's control: while a single or a walk or a hit by pitch always has potential run value, a long fly does not unless a man happens to be poised at third base. Last, the grounded into double play is to a far greater extent a function of one's place in the batting order than it is of poor speed or failure in the clutch, and thus it does not find a home in a formula applicable to all batters. It is no accident that Hank Aaron, who ran well for most of his long career and wasn't too shabby in the clutch, hit into more DPs than anyone else, nor that Roberto Clemente, Al Kaline, and Frank Robinson, who fit the same description, are also among the ten "worst" in this department.

The Batting Runs formula can be condensed by eliminating the components for steals, caught stealing, and outs on base. Outs on base (calculated as *Hits + Walks + Hit Batsman – Left on Base – Runs – Caught Stealing*) is meaningful only for teams, not individuals. We eliminate steals from the formula in those years in which caught-stealing figures are not available, but the surviving data for the early years indicate that few of the men with high base-stealing totals exceeded the break-even point of 66.7 percent by a margin large enough to produce even one additional Batting Win. A further condensation that we have used for our historical data, as indicated in the formula above, involves setting the value of a single at .47 runs and each extra base at .31, making a double .78, a triple 1.09, and a homer 1.40. (This tends to even out the fluctuations in run values for base hits and extra bases over time: a double, for example, was in fact worth .82 runs from 1901–1920, .80 runs from 1941–1960, and .77 runs from 1961–1977.) Subtract the hits from the total bases and multiply the resulting extra bases by .31 and the hits by .47. This may introduce small variations from a more rigorous formula that includes differing run values for the differing periods or even for single years (generally amounting to a fraction of a run), but the calculation is much snappier for those without a computer.

The Batting Runs formula may be long, even in its condensed form, but it calls for only addition, subtraction, and multiplication and thus is as simple as Slugging Average, whose incorrect weights (1, 2, 3, and 4) it revises and expands upon. Each event has a value and frequency, just as in Slugging Average, yet in Batting Runs outs are treated as offensive events with a run value of their own (albeit a negative one). Just as the run potential for a team in a given half-inning is boosted by a man reaching base, it is diminished by a man being retired; not only has he failed to brighten the situation on the bases but he has deprived his team of the services of a man further down the order who might have come up in this half-inning, either with men on base and/or with scores already in.

The Batting Runs stat treats every offensive event in terms of its impact upon the team—an *average* team, so that a man does not benefit in his individual record for having the good fortune to bat cleanup with the Rockies or suffer for batting cleanup with the White Sox. The relationship of individual performance to team play is stated poorly or not at all in conventional baseball statistics. In Batting Runs it is crystal clear.

Recognizing that some readers will wish to keep track of batting performance by compiling Batting Runs themselves over the course of a season and that they may be frustrated by the difficulty of separating out pitcher batting or of calculating the (At Bats – Hits) factor for the league, we advise that using the fixed value of –.25 for outs will tend to work quite well if you wish to include pitcher batting performance, and a fixed value of –.27 will serve if you wish to exclude it. Actually, any fixed value will suffice in midseason; it's only when all the numbers are in and you care to compare this year's results with last year's (or, e.g., with those of the 1927 Yankees) that more precision is desirable. At that point the value of the out may be calculated by the more ambitious among you, but, ideally, the sporting press will provide accurate Batting Runs figures. (Who calculates ERA for himself?) Batting Runs are abbreviated as BR.

Batting Wins Adjusted Batting Runs divided by the number of runs required to create an additional win beyond average (see *Runs Per Win*). That average is defined as a team record of .500 because a league won-lost average must be .500, or as an individual record of zero because the value of the out for a given year is calculated to establish a baseline of zero. Abbreviated as BW.

Calculated Stat One or more counting stats (see below) subjected to a mathematical process such as averaging.

Chances Accepted Putouts and assists, minus errors.

Clutch Hitting Index Calculated for individuals, actual RBIs over expected RBIs, adjusted for league average and slot in batting order; 100 is a league-average performance. The spot in the batting order is figured as

$$5 - (9 \times \text{BFPGP} - \text{BFPGT})$$

where BFPGP is the batters facing pitcher per game for the player, or plate appearances divided by games, and BFPGT is the batters facing pitcher per game of the entire team.

Expected RBIs are calculated as

$$(.25 \text{ singles} + .50 \text{ doubles} + .75 \text{ triples} + 1.75 \text{ homers}) \times \text{LGAV} \times \text{EXPSL}$$

where LGAV (league average) = league RBIs divided by (.25 singles + .50 doubles + .75 triples + 1.75 homers), and EXPSL (expected RBI by slot number) = .88 for the leadoff batter, and for the remaining slots, descending to ninth, .90, .98, 1.08, 1.08, 1.04, 1.04, 1.04, and 1.02.

Calculated for teams, Clutch Hitting Index is actual runs scored over Batting Runs. Abbreviated as CHI.

Clutch Pitching Index Expected runs allowed over actual runs allowed, with 100 being a league-average performance. Expected runs are figured on the basis of the pitcher's opposing at bats, hits, walks, and hit batsmen (doubles and triples estimated at league average). Abbreviated as CPI.

Counting Stat A raw figure that tells how many of an item have been accumulated, as opposed to a calculated or derived figure such as an average.

Differential The difference between a team's actual won-lost record and that predicted by the total of its Pitching Wins, Batting Wins, Fielding Wins, and Stolen Base Wins; this measure indicates the extent to which a team outperformed or underperformed its talent. Abbreviated as DIF.

Earned Run Average Calculated as earned runs times nine, divided by innings pitched. For a few years after being introduced as an official stat in the National League in 1912 and the American League in 1913, runs aided by stolen bases were not counted as earned (see Chronology of Scoring Rules in Appendix 1, Rules and Scoring). For years before 1912, ERA has been constructed from raw data, but for some teams in some seasons, earned runs cannot be identified with perfect certainty. For those teams, we use the estimating procedure created by Information Concepts, Inc., of assigning to those runs whose earned/unearned status is unknown the percentage of earned runs to runs that characterize the team's known runs. In *Total Baseball*, we have created an Adjusted ERA by normalizing to the league average—which is done by dividing the league average ERA by the individual ERA—and then factoring in home park.

Expected Wins Calculated for the team based on its actual runs scored and allowed, not its predicted runs scored and allowed. A team that allows exactly as many runs as it scores is predicted to play .500 ball. The equation for expected wins is:

$$\frac{(\text{Runs Scored} - \text{Runs Allowed})}{\text{Runs Per Win}} + \frac{(\text{Wins} + \text{Losses})}{2}$$

Abbreviated as W– EXP.

Fielding Average Defined as putouts and assists divided by the total of putouts, assists, and errors. The weakness of this stat is that it values a player with minimal range but good hands over another player who may accept many more chances but mishandle a few of these. Abbreviated as FA. See *Range Factor, Total Chances*.

Fielding Runs The Linear Weights measure of runs saved *beyond* what a league-average player at that position might have saved, defined as zero; this stat is calculated to take account of the particular demands of the different positions.

For second basemen, shortstops, and third basemen, the formula begins by calculating the league average for the position:

$$\text{AVG}_{\text{pos. lg.}} = \left(\frac{.20\ (\text{PO} + 2\text{A} - \text{E} + \text{DP})\ \text{league at position}}{\text{PO league total} - \text{K league total}} \right)$$

where A = assists, PO = putouts, E = errors, DP = double plays, and K = strikeouts. Then we estimate the number of innings for each player at each position based upon each player's entire fielding record and his number of plate appearances. So, if the team played 1,500 innings and one player was calculated to have played 1,000 of those innings at a given position, his Fielding Runs (FR) would be calculated as:

$$\text{FR} = .20\ (\text{PO} + 2\text{A} - \text{E} + \text{DP})\ \text{player} - \text{avg. pos. lg.} \times \left(\text{PO}_{\text{team}} - \text{K}_{\text{team}} \right) \frac{\text{innings, player}}{\text{innings, team}}$$

Assists are doubly weighted because more fielding skill is generally required to get one than to record a putout.

For catchers, the above formula is modified by removing strikeouts from their formulas and subtracting not only errors but also passed balls divided by two. Also incorporated in the catcher's Fielding Runs is one tenth of the adjusted Pitching Runs for the team, times the percentage of games behind the plate by that catcher.

For pitchers, the above formula is modified to subtract individual pitcher strikeouts from the total number of potential outs (otherwise, exceptional strikeout pitchers like Nolan Ryan or Bob Feller would see their Fielding Runs artificially depressed). Also, pitchers' chances are weighted less than infielders' assists because a pitcher's style may produce fewer ground balls. Thus the formula for pitchers is .10(PO + 2A – E + DP), whereas for second basemen, shortstops, and third basemen it is .20(PO + 2A – E + DP).

For first basemen, because putouts and double plays require so little skill in all but the odd case, these plays are eliminated, leaving only .20(2A – E) in the numerator.

For outfielders, the formula becomes .20(PO + 4A – E + 2DP). The weighting for assists is boosted here because a good outfielder can prevent runs through the threat of assists that are never made; for them, unlike infielders, the assist is essentially an elective play, like the stolen base. Outfielders' Fielding Runs were subject to some degree of error because outfielders sometimes switch fields within a game or season (Babe Ruth, for example, was positioned in the field that required the lesser range—right field in Yankee Stadium, left field in most road parks). Also, short distances to left or right field walls in some parks tend to depress putout totals.

Since the third edition of *Total Baseball,* however, we have researched and obtained breakouts of all outfielders' games in left, center, and right fields. Center fielders now have higher ratings than they did in the first and second editions. Abbreviated as FR.

Fielding Wins Fielding Runs divided by the number of runs required to create an additional win beyond average. That average is defined as a team record of .500 because a league won-lost average must be .500. Abbreviated as FW. See *Runs Per Win*.

Games Behind Figured by adding the difference in wins between a trailing team and the leader to the difference in losses, and dividing by two. Thus a team that is three games behind may trail by three in the win column and three in the loss column, or four and two, or any other combination of wins and losses totaling six. Abbreviated as GB.

Game-Winning Run Batted In Credited to the batter who drives in a run that gives his club a lead that it never relinquishes, no matter when that run is driven in nor what the final score is. Introduced in 1980 as an official stat and later disowned, the GWRBI is not recorded in this volume.

Grounded into Double Play Kept officially since 1933 in the NL and 1939 in the AL (though the NL data of

1933-1938 made no distinction between lined-into double plays and grounded-into double plays, and the AL data of 1939 was not published). This stat tends to be overvalued by the general public as an indicator of rally-killing ineptitude. Instead, it is largely a function of high totals of at bats, which tend to be accumulated by the game's best players, not its worst. Abbreviated as GIDP.

Hands Out The original 1840s scoring term for batters producing outs either at the plate or on the bases. On a force out, the runner retired on the bases would be charged with a hand out, not the batter. Also called Hands Lost, and abbreviated as HO or HL.

Hit by Pitch A batter struck by a pitched ball was not awarded first base until 1884 in the American Association and 1887 in the National League. Reconstruction of stats for batters and pitchers in the years 1897-1908 has been accomplished. Abbreviated as HBP.

Home Run Factor A measure of the home runs hit in a given ballpark, with 100 representing the average home park and the highest figure above that representing the best home-run park. Computed in the same manner as Home Run Batter Rating (see above). Abbreviated as HRF.

Home Run Percentage Home runs per 100 at bats.

Home Run Pitcher Rating A measure of a team's ability to prevent home runs, taking into account the Home Run Factor (see above) of the park and the team's not having to face its own batters. The average mark is represented as 100, and the lowest figure beneath that indicates the best.

Home Runs When is a home run not a home run? Before 1920, not if it came with men on base in the ultimate inning and created a margin of victory greater than one run. A ruling of the Special Baseball Records Committee in 1969 reversed its earlier decision that had made home runs of 37 disputed final-inning, game-winning base hits. In accordance with the practice of the day, such a hit, even if it sailed out of the park, would be credited with only as many bases as necessary to plate the winning run. Thus Babe Ruth's "715th home run," hit on July 8, 1918, to win a game against Cleveland, remained a triple, and Jimmy Collins and Sherry Magee were each deprived of two home runs.

Innings Pitched Official baseball practice was, until 1982, to round off fractional innings for individuals to the next highest inning. Since then fractional innings have been kept for individuals and teams. In this volume fractional innings are supplied for all individuals and all teams in all years. Those men who took a turn on the mound but failed to retire a batter are credited with no innings pitched and, if they allowed a runner or runners to score, an ERA of infinity.

Intentional Bases on Balls Recorded only since 1955.

Isolated Power Total bases minus hits, divided by at bats; in other words, Slugging Average minus Batting Average. Appears to have been created by Allan Roth and Branch Rickey in the 1950s.

League-Average Replacement Player That model player who performs at precisely the league average, creating a baseline against which to measure others.

League Performance: Because the caliber of play in the Union Association of 1884 and the Federal League of 1914-1915 was substantially below that of its rivals in those years, we have made an upward adjustment to overall league performance, thus lowering individual ratings or computed stats, while leaving unaffected the raw statistics of Organized Baseball. League at bats were reduced to 80 percent for the UA and 90 percent for the FL.

We tested all players who appeared in at least 30 games for the UA in 1884 and 30 or more games in the NL or AA in the 1883-1885 period. There were 31 players who played 2,182 games in the UA and had a Total Player Rating 2.6 wins higher per 112 games in the UA. There were 17 pitchers who pitched 3,678 innings in the UA with at least 30 innings in the UA and 30 innings in other leagues in the 1883-1985 period). These pitchers had a Total Pitcher Index 0.8 wins higher in the UA per 112 innings.

For the Federal League, there were 54 players with 30 games in the FL and at least 30 games in other leagues in the 1913-1916 period. These players had 10,401 games in the FL and had a Total Player Rating 1.26 wins higher per 154 games. For pitchers, there were 39 with 30 or more innings in the FL and 30 innings in other leagues in the 1913-1916 period). These pitchers had 13,872 innings and a Total Pitcher Index .49 wins higher in the FL per 154 innings.

Actually, the calculations for the UA produced a .76 multiplier for on base percentage and slugging, which we have rounded to .80. The calculations for the FL produced a .90 multiplier for on base percentage and slugging, which we have incorporated. UA pitchers had an .875 multiplier for earned run average, which we have expressed as .80 for consistency with the batting figure. Federal League pitchers had a multiplier of .924, which we have rounded to .90.

Linear Weights A system created by Pete Palmer to measure all the events on a ballfield in terms of runs. At the root of this system, as with other sabermetric figures such as Runs Created, is the knowledge that wins and losses are what the game of baseball is about, that wins and losses are proportional in some way to runs scored and runs allowed, and that runs in turn are proportional to the events that go into their making.

Normalizing Restating a figure as a ratio by comparing it to the league average, or norm.

On-Base Percentage Created by Roth and Rickey in its current form—hits plus walks plus hit by pitch, divided by at bats plus walks plus hit by pitch—in the early 1950s, although there were nineteenth-century forebears such as "Reached First Base." When OBP, as it is abbreviated, was adopted as an official stat in 1984, the denominator was expanded to include sacrifice flies. The effect is to penalize a batter in his on base percentage by giving him a plate appearance while at the same time crediting him in his batting average by deleting the plate appearance. In this book we calculate OBP without considering sacrifice flies, which in any event are calculable on a continuing basis only since 1954.

On-Base plus Slugging See *Production*.

Opponents' Batting Average Hits allowed divided by at bats allowed (or, if at bats allowed is unknown, then at bats equals hits plus inning times "K," where "K" is the league average of at bats minus hits, all over innings). Abbreviated as OAV.

Opponents' On-Base Percentage For years before 1908 in the American League and 1903 in the National League, the number of batters facing a pitcher has been constructed from the available raw data. We have subtracted league base hits from league at bats, divided by league innings pitched, multiplied by the pitcher's innings, and added his hits and walks allowed and hit by pitch and sacrifices, if available. Abbreviated as OOB.

Outs Until 1883, included catching a ball on one bounce in foul ground. Not credited after three strikes in 1887, when the rule was "four strikes and yer out"—as it was, in fact, from 1871–1881, when batters commonly received "warning pitches" rather than called strikes.

Outs Per Game The 1860s successor to Hands Out (see above), it joined with Runs Per Game to form the batting record before the rise of professional league play.

Park Factor Calculated separately for batters and pitchers. Above 100 signifies a park favorable to hitters; below 100 signifies a park favorable to pitchers. The computation of PF is admittedly daunting, and what follows is probably of interest to the merest handful of readers, but we feel obliged to state the mathematical underpinnings for those few who may care. We use a three-year average Park Factor for players and teams unless they change home parks. Then a two-year average is used, unless the park existed for only one year. Then a one-year mark is used. If a team started up in Year 1, played two years in the first park, one in the next, and three in the park after that and then stopped play, the average would be as follows (where F*n* is the one-year park factor for year *n*):

Year 1 and 2 = (F1 + F2)/2	Year 4 = (F4 + F5)/2
Year 3 = F3	Year 5 = (F4 + F5 + F6)/3
	Year 6 = (F5 + F6)/2

Step 1. Find games, losses, and runs scored and allowed for each team at home and on the road. Take runs per game scored and allowed at home over runs per game scored and allowed on the road. This is the initial figure, but we must make two corrections to it.

Step 2. The first correction is for innings pitched at home and on the road. This is a bit complicated, so the mathematically faint of heart may want to head back at this point. First, find the team's home winning percentage (wins at home over games at home). Do the same for road games. Calculate the Innings Pitched Corrector (IPC) shown below. If it is greater than 1, this means the innings pitched on the road are higher because the other team is batting more often in the last of the ninth. This rating is divided by the Innings Pitched Corrector, like so:

$$\text{IPC} = \frac{(18.5 - \text{Wins at home / Games at home})}{(18.5 - \text{Losses on road / Games on road})}$$

Note: 18.5 is the average number of half-innings per game if the home team always bats in the ninth.

Step 3. Make corrections for the fact that the other road parks' total difference from the league average is offset by the park rating of the club that is being rated. Multiply rating by this Other Parks Corrector (OPC):

$$\text{OPC} = \frac{\text{No. of teams}}{\text{No. of teams} - 1 + \text{Run Factor, team}}$$

(Note that this OPC differs from that presented earlier in *The Hidden Game of Baseball*, for in preparing the pre-1900 data for *Total Baseball*, we discovered that for some parks with extreme characteristics, like Chicago's Lake Front Park of 1884, which had a Home Run Factor of nearly 5, the earlier formula produced wrong results. For parks with factors of 1.5 or less, either formula works well.)

Example. In 1982, Atlanta scored 388 runs and allowed 387 runs at home in 81 games, and scored 351 and allowed 315 on the road in 81 games. The initial factor is (775/81) ÷ (666/81) = 1.164. The Braves' home record was 42–39, or .519, and their road record was 47–34, or .580. Thus the IPC = (18.5 – .519) ÷ (18.5 – .420) = .995. The team rating is now 1.164/.995 = 1.170. The OPC = (12) ÷ (12 – 1 + 1.170) = .986. The final runs-allowed rating is 1.170 × .986, or 1.154.

We warned you it wouldn't be easy!

The batter adjustment factor is composed of two parts, one the park factor and the other the fact that a batter does not have to face his own team's pitchers. The initial correction takes care of only the second factor. Start with the following (SF = Scoring Factor, previously determined [for Atlanta, 1.154], and SF1 = Scoring Factor of the other clubs [NT = number of teams]):

$$\frac{\text{NT}}{\text{NT} - 1 + \text{SF}}$$

Next is an iterative process in which the initial team pitching rating is assumed to be 1, and the following factors are employed:

RHT, RAT = Runs per game scored at home (H) and away (A), by team

OHT, OAT = Runs per game allowed at home, away, by team

RAL = Runs per game by both teams

Now, with the Team Pitching Rating (TPR) = 1, we proceed to calculate Team Batting Rating (TBR):

$$\text{TBR} = \left(\frac{\text{RAT}}{\text{SF1}} + \frac{\text{RHT}}{\text{SF}}\right)\left(1 + \frac{\text{TPR} - 1}{\text{NT} - 1}\right)\Big/\text{RAL}$$

$$\text{TPR} = \left(\frac{\text{OAT}}{\text{SF1}} + \frac{\text{OHT}}{\text{SF}}\right)\left(1 + \frac{\text{TBR} - 1}{\text{NT} - 1}\right)\Big/\text{RAL}$$

The last two steps are repeated three more times. The final Batting Corrector, or Batters' Park Factor (BPF) is

$$\text{BPF} = \frac{(\text{SF} + \text{SF1})}{\left(2 \times \left[1 + \frac{\text{TPR} - 1}{\text{NT} - 1}\right]\right)}$$

Similarly, the final Pitching Corrector, or Pitchers' Park Factor (PPF) is

$$\text{PPF} = \frac{(\text{SF} + \text{SF1})}{\left(2 \times \left[1 + \frac{\text{TBR} - 1}{\text{NT} - 1}\right]\right)}$$

Now an example, using the 1982 Atlanta Braves once again.

$$\text{RHT} — \frac{388}{81} — 4.79 \qquad \text{RAT} — \frac{351}{81} — 4.33$$

$$\text{OHT} = \frac{387}{81} = 4.78 \qquad \text{OAT} = \frac{315}{81} = 3.89$$

$$\text{RAL} = \frac{7947}{972} = 8.18 \qquad \text{NT} = 12$$

$$\text{SF} = 1.154 \qquad \text{SF1} = 1 - \left(\frac{1.154 - 1}{11}\right) = .986$$

$$\text{TBR} = \left(\frac{4.33}{.986} + \frac{4.79}{1.154}\right)\left(1 + \frac{1-1}{11}\right) \Big/ 8.18 = 1.044$$

$$\text{TPR} = \left(\frac{3.89}{.986} + \frac{4.78}{1.154}\right)\left(1 + \frac{1.044-1}{11}\right) \Big/ 8.18 = .993$$

Repeating these steps gives a TBR of 1.04 and a TPR of .97. The Batters' Park Factor is

$$\text{BPF} = \frac{(1.154 + .970)}{\left(2 \times \left[1 + \frac{.97-1}{11}\right]\right)} = 1.07$$

This is not a great deal removed from taking the original ratio,

$$\frac{1.170 + 1}{2}, \text{ which is } 1.08.$$

The Pitchers' Park Factor may be calculated in analogous fashion.

To apply the Batters' Park Factor to Batting Runs, one must use this formula:

$$\underset{\text{corr.}}{\text{BR}} = \frac{\underset{\text{uncorr.}}{\text{BR}} - \frac{\text{Runs (league)}}{\text{AB+BB+HBP (league)}} \times \text{AB + BB + HBP (player)} \times (\text{BPF} - 1)}{\text{BPF}}$$

For example, if a player produces 20 runs above average in 700 plate appearances with a Batters' Park Factor of 1.10, and the league average of runs produced per plate appearance is .11, his uncorrected Batting Runs is 20. Therefore, 77 runs is the average run contribution expected of this batter were he playing in an average home park. But because his home park was 10 percent kinder to hitters than average, you would really expect an average run production of 1.1 × 77, or 85 runs from a player in that ballpark. Thus the player whose uncorrected Batting Runs is 97 with a BF of 1.1 is only +12 runs before adjustment (rather than +20), and Park Adjusted Batting Runs is only 11 (in the Player Register, BR/A):

$$11 = \frac{20 - .11 \times 700 \times 0.10}{1.10}$$

Percentage of Team Wins A simple but deceiving measure of a good pitcher's contribution to a bad club; in this, it shares the virtues and flaws of Ted Oliver's Weighted Rating System and, to a lesser degree, our own Wins Above Team (both of which see). Steve Carlton had the highest single-season rating in this century when, in 1972, he went 27–10 for a Phillie club that won only 59 games. Yet his mark of 45.8 percent of his team's wins would not make the top 100 list of seasons since 1876, making this stat nearly useless for historical analysis.

Pitcher Defense Abbreviated as PD. See *Fielding Runs*.

Pitchers' Park Factor The same as the Park Factor shown in the pitchers' section of the team statistics portion of the Annual Record and in the Pitcher Register; above 100 means a pitcher was hurt by playing half his games in a good hitting park. See *Park Factor*.

Pitcher Strikeouts Made tougher or easier by cyclically varying rules and conditions. For instance, foul tips did not count as strikes for many years, even when deliberate, as with bunts; fouls caught on a bounce were outs until 1883; the ball-strike count underwent much experimentation until settling at four balls and three strikes in 1889; not to mention the high-low strike zone, warning pitches, varying pitching distances, and restricted deliveries. It helps to know some history before rattling off stats to prove this or that, but normalizing a stat to its league helps, even with counting stats such as strikeouts.

Pitching Runs The Linear Weights measure of runs saved *beyond* what a league-average pitcher or team might have saved, defined as zero. The math is simple: *Pitching Runs = Innings Pitched × (League ERA/9) − Earned Runs Allowed*. An alternate version is: *Innings Pitched/9 × (League ERA − Individual ERA)*. Abbreviated as PR.

Pitching Wins Park Adjusted Pitching Runs divided by the number of runs required to create an additional win beyond average. That average is defined as a team record of .500 because a league won-lost average must be .500. Abbreviated as PW. See *Pitching Runs*, above, and *Runs Per Win*.

Player Win Averages The title of a 1970 book issued by the Mills brothers, Harlan and Eldon, as well as the name of their overall method of determining not only the *what* of baseball statistics but also the *when*, or clutch element. Computerizing complete play-by-play data for a full season for their book, they assigned "Win Points"—reflective of that event's potential impact on the team's prospects of victory—to *every* event on a baseball field.

Positional Adjustment A key factor in the Total Player Rating that addresses the relative worth to a ball club of the defensive positions. A man who bats .270, hits 25 homers, and drives in 80 runs may be an average performer in left field, no matter how good his glove; but credit those batting stats to a shortstop or second baseman and you have a star, because the defensive demands of the position are so much greater. To balance the abundance of good-hitting outfielders or first basemen against the scarcity of such players at catcher or shortstop, we created a positional adjustment expressed in terms of the average batting skill needed to hold down a major league spot at that position.

To determine the average defensive skill required of a position, simply subtract the average batting skill at that position from his Total Player Rating. This may seem strange at first glance, but it does put, for example, shortstops, first basemen, and left fielders on the same footing. In this edition, we have increased the periods used to determine the positional adjustments to an era, and we have used the same rating for the entire era, rather than a moving average. We have also, for the first time, broken down the outfield into left, center and right. Normally center fielders need more fielding skill and therefore do not hit as well as left and right fielders. The result is that center field Total Player Ratings will increase slightly and left and right field ratings will decrease slightly.

Here are the eras and their positional adjustments:

YEARS	P	C	1B	2B	3B	SS	LF	CF	RF	DH
1871–75	-21.217	-0.631	-3.315	9.537	4.798	3.685	-4.502	0.207	-9.801	
1876–81	-17.824	-4.044	6.569	-6.927	-4.731	-6.436	9.489	6.372	-0.171	
1882–91	-29.589	-13.166	13.753	-5.651	-2.564	-4.613	3.786	5.152	1.246	
1892–00	-37.794	-14.223	0.611	-7.015	-2.506	-7.809	13.556	9.928	7.611	
1901–10	-37.160	-15.350	2.879	-1.306	-4.023	-5.043	8.775	7.319	6.783	
1911–20	-38.455	-13.589	3.874	-2.543	-4.194	-10.513	6.716	10.610	8.130	
1921–30	-47.793	-10.597	10.037	-4.255	-9.528	-16.624	12.018	6.536	12.395	
1931–42	-51.226	-9.754	14.359	-9.747	-5.428	-11.244	8.639	3.839	9.372	
1943–45	-42.246	-9.572	7.943	-8.325	-1.707	-12.151	9.302	4.382	10.160	
1946–52	-48.296	-8.481	5.166	-8.428	0.429	-9.538	11.703	4.150	5.015	
1953–60	-48.555	-7.766	9.018	-11.286	0.525	-12.872	9.496	7.273	5.633	
1969–76	-45.696	-7.214	12.400	-10.181	0.820	-18.347	9.197	3.997	8.123	4.948
1977–87	-45.170	-6.804	9.671	-8.484	2.464	-16.139	6.861	1.324	8.251	5.733
1988–92	-43.487	-9.283	11.195	-4.159	-0.252	-11.627	4.817	1.294	4.957	6.125
1993–00	-41.423	-8.578	12.620	-6.582	-0.511	-11.505	4.056	-1.363	7.149	9.513

Production On-Base Percentage plus Slugging Average: a simple but elegant measure of batting prowess, in that the weaknesses of one-half of the formulation, On-Base Percentage, are countered by the strengths of the other, Slugging Average, and vice versa. When OPS, as it is abbreviated, is adjusted for home park and normalized to league average to become OPS$^+$, the calculation is modified slightly to create a baseline of 100 for a league-average performance. For OPS$^+$, the calculation is

$$\frac{\text{Player On Base Pct.}}{\text{League On Base Pct.}} + \frac{\text{Player Slugging Avg.}}{\text{League Slugging Avg.}} - 1$$

This produces a figure with a decimal point—an above-average figure, like 1.46, or a below-average figure, like 0.82. For ease of display, in this book we drop the decimal and express these as 146 and 82.

Putout Average Putouts divided by games played; a stat created by Philadelphia baseball writer Al Wright in 1875.

Quality Start A game started in which a pitcher lasts for six innings or more and allows three runs or less.

Ratio Hits plus walks plus hit batsmen allowed per nine innings. Abbreviated as RAT.

RBI Opportunities An official American League stat for the first three weeks of 1918, until the league saw how much work it involved and scrapped it. Still a good idea, sort of, and the folks at the Elias Sports Bureau have tracked this type of "situational stat" since 1975.

Reached First Base A precursor of the On Base Percentage, this stat was introduced as an official National League measure in 1879, its one and only year of existence. It included times reached via hits, walks, and errors, but not hit by pitch because putting their bodies on the line did not yet, in 1879, send batters to first base. Trivia: the league leader in this stat's lone year of life was Providence outfielder Paul Hines, with 193.

Relative Batting Average Pioneered by David Shoebotham in a *Baseball Research Journal* article in 1976, this was the first traditional stat normalized to league average so as to permit cross-era comparison. Most folks who have employed this measure simply divide individual batting average by league batting average. Shoebotham's original computation was more precise:

$$\text{RBA} = \frac{\text{player's hits}}{\text{player's AB}} \Big/ \frac{\text{league hits} - \text{player's hits}}{\text{league AB} - \text{player's AB}}$$

In this manner a player's own performance would not be compared with itself.

Relief Points Relief wins plus saves minus losses was the original formula used as the basis for the Rolaids Company's annual award to the top reliever in each league. Recently the formula has been changed to include a debit for blown saves.

Relief Ranking Takes *Relief Runs* (which see), adjusts them for home park, then weights them by a factor (F in the formula below) reflecting the greater value of the innings pitched by a bullpen "closer." Relief Runs, which weights all innings identically, will tend to benefit long and middle relievers who are effective over many innings, while Relief Ranking—which was initially designed for those men who pitch less than three innings per game over a season or career—will tend to benefit relievers who may have fewer innings but who have more saves and decisions. The formula is

$$\text{(Relief Runs)} \times \text{F where the Factor} = \frac{9 \times \text{(Wins + Losses + K* [Saves])}}{\text{IP}}$$

*K = either .25 or 1 over 10 times fraction of league wins that are saved, whichever is smaller.

The multiplier, or Factor, is usually around 1, but can get up to 1.5 or even 2 for some relievers, and can get down as low as 0.8 for some starters who have a lot of no-decision games. The value of Factor is set to no higher than 2 or no lower than 0.5.

Relief Runs Identical to Pitching Runs but confined to relief pitchers, defined as those who average less than three innings per appearance. Abbreviated as RR. See *Relief Ranking*.

Run Batted In Though widely regarded as a good measure of a batter's overall productivity and value to his team, the RBI is extremely situation-dependent, denying equal access to opportunity on the basis of a player's team, slot in the batting order, and particularly the men surrounding him in the batting order.

Run Factor A measure of the run scoring in a given ballpark compared to other ballparks, with 100 representing the average home park and the highest figure above that representing the best hitters' park. Abbreviated as RF, it is computed on the basis of comparing runs scored and allowed per inning at home and on the road. Innings are estimated from the number of games and games won, allowing for the home team not batting in the final inning of a game in which it leads. The resulting Run Factor is then compared to the league average.

Run Rating for Batters A measure of a team's run-scoring ability, taking into account the park's *Run Factor* (see above) and the team's batters not having to face its own pitchers, with 100 representing the average and the highest figure above that representing the best. Run Batting for Batters is abbreviated as RB.

Run Rating for Pitchers A measure of a team's run-prevention ability, taking into account the *Run Factor* (see above) and the team's pitchers not having to face its own batters, with 100 representing the average and the lowest figure beneath that representing the best. Abbreviated as RP.

Runs Created Bill James's formulation for run contribution from a variety of batting and baserunning events.

Many different formulas are used, depending upon data available. In its basic expression, the formula is:

$$\frac{\text{(Hits + Walks) (Total Bases)}}{\text{At Bats + Walks}}$$

The essence of this formulation is that the ability to get on base and the ability to push baserunners around fairly describes offensive ability. James later refined the formula with a "stolen base version":

$$\frac{\text{(Hits + Walks − Caught Stealing) (Total Bases + .55} \times \text{Stolen Bases)}}{\text{At Bats + Walks}}$$

Next came the "technical version": a longer formulation, presented below using the standard abbreviations for the various offensive events (the two elements multiplied in the numerator are referred to below as "A" and "B," and the denominator is referred to as "C"):

$$\frac{\text{(H + BB + HBP − CS − GIDP) (TB + .26[BB − IBB + HBP] + .52[SH + SF + SB])}}{\text{AB + BB + HBP + SH + SF}}$$

From this technical version (Tech-1), James spun off 13 additional technical versions. "The reason that we have to do this," he wrote in *The Bill James Historical Baseball Abstract*, "is that the data set changes and evolves rapidly throughout the century, or at least up until about 1955, when the progress of evolution in statistical information came to a temporary halt (it stopped moving forward until Bill James and Pete Palmer came around, about twenty years later). In 1900 we have no data for how many times a player grounded into a double play, how many times he was hit by a pitch, how many of his walks might have been intentional, how many times he was caught stealing, or how many sacrifice flies he hit." Accordingly, James adjusted his Runs Created formula to fit the available data; some versions, such as Tech-3, cover as much as a decade in a given league, while others, such as Tech-4, are in force for only a single league season. In *Total Baseball*, we have computed Runs Created values for all players since 1876 using the version most applicable to the period, with the single exception of Tech-9, which James applied only to the American League of 1916 but which we use for 1914–1916 in the AL and 1915–1916 in the NL because we have discovered additional caught-stealing data. (For those players whose careers began before 1900, James used the Tech-11 formula "to estimate how many runs they had created," but appended a note saying that "these estimates were of indeterminate accuracy.")

Here are the formulas for Runs Created (RC) technical versions 2–14 (Tech-1 was used for both the American and National leagues in 1955–1988):

Tech-2 (1954)
Factors A and C of Tech-1 remain the same, while Part B simply drops Intentional Bases on Balls.

Tech-3 (AL 1940–1953; NL 1951–1953)
Factor A remains the same, while SF is dropped from Factor C; Factor B changes to: 1.025 TB + .26(BB + HBP) + .52(SH + SB).

Tech-4 (AL 1939)
Factors A and C remain the same, while B becomes: TB + .26(BB + HBP) + .52(SH + SB).

Tech-5 (AL 1931–1938)
Factors B and C remain the same, while A becomes: .96(H + BB + HBP − CS).

Tech-6 (AL 1920–1930; NL 1920–1925)
Factors A and C remain the same, while B changes only in the value placed on the sacrifice hit and stolen base, which declines from .52 to .51.

Tech-7 (NL 1926–1930)
C remains the same, while A changes to: .93(H + BB + HBP), and B becomes: TB + .26(BB + HBP) + .46(SH).

Tech-8 (AL 1913, 1917–1919; NL 1913–1914, 1917–1919)
C remains the same, while A becomes: H + W + HBP − .02(AB), and B becomes: TB + .85(SH + SB).

Tech-9 (AL 1914–1916; NL 1915–1916)
B and C are the same, while A becomes: H + BB + HBP − CS.

Tech-10 (AL, NL 1908–1912)
A and C remain the same, while B becomes: 1.025(TB + SB) + .75(SH).

Tech-11 (AL, NL 1900–1907)
B and C remain the same, while A becomes: H + BB + HBP.

Tech-12 (NL 1939–1950)
A Factor: H + BB + HBP − GIDP
B Factor: TB + .26(BB +HBP) + .52(SH)

Tech-13 (NL 1933–1938)
A and C remain the same as above, while B becomes: 1.025(TB) + .26(BB + HBP) + .52(SH)

Tech-14 (NL 1931–1932)
B and C remain the same, but A becomes: .95(H + BB + HBP).

Runs Per Game With its mate *Outs Per Game* (which see), this was the precursor, in the 1860s, of the batting average; by the end of that decade it gave way to Hits Per Game.

Runs Per Win Branch Rickey and Allan Roth first stated the proportional nature of runs and wins in their 1954 article in *Life*. Since then the point has been expanded upon by George Lindsey, Pete Palmer, Bill James, and every sabermetrician worth his salt: the point being that just as runs scored and allowed are the key to victory in a given game, so are they the key to success over the course of a season and the predictors of won-lost record with a surprising degree of precision. In 1982, Palmer wrote in *The National Pastime*, "My work showed that as a rough rule of thumb, each additional ten runs scored (or ten less runs allowed) produced one extra win. . . . However, breaking the teams into groups showed that high-scoring teams needed more runs to produce a win. This runs-per-win factor I determined to be ten times the square root of the average number of runs scored per inning by both teams. Thus in normal play, when 4.5 runs per game are scored by each club, each team scores .5 runs per inning—totaling one run, the square root of which is one, times ten."

For *Total Baseball*, we have improved the Runs Per

Win figure used in calculating the overall win figures in the Total Player Rating and the Total Pitcher Index. Rather than using 10 times the square root of the average number of runs scored per inning by both teams, we use adjusted runs per inning based on what the player or pitcher rating is. A hitter will increase the figure by adding in his rating over the number of games played, while a pitcher will have his rating subtracted. Say the average number of runs scored per inning is 1, as in the model above; then Runs Per Win = 10. Take a pitcher who allows 45 runs less than average in 25 games. This lowers the runs per game by 1.8, or runs per inning by .2, so the new Runs Per Win figure is 10 times the square root of the average number of runs scored per inning by both teams, *minus the pitcher's rating*. So we take from the one run per inning the .2 run saved by the pitcher, giving a result of 0.8. Ten times the square root of 0.8 is 8.9, so the pitcher gets 45/8.9, or 5.1, wins instead of 4.5. A hitter with plus 45 runs in 150 games, or .3 runs per game, contributes .03 runs per inning. His Runs Per Win is now 10 times the square root of the average number of runs scored per inning *plus the batter's rating*. So we add to the 1 run per inning the .03 runs added by the batter, giving a result of 10.1. Ten times the square root of 10.1 gives the batter 4.4 wins. (This method makes makes more of a difference in pitching because the runs are contributed over fewer games. With the same run contribution—45 beyond average—the pitcher gains 0.7 wins over the batter. This is because when the total number of runs scored is lowered, the value of each run is greater).

Runs Produced Runs batted in plus runs scored minus home runs.

Sabermetrics Defined by Bill James, who coined the term in honor of the Society for American Baseball Research, as "the search for objective knowledge about baseball" and, earlier, as "the mathematical and statistical analysis of baseball records."

SABR Pronounced "saber," this is the acronym for the Society for American Baseball Research, the organization that has, since its founding by Bob Davids in 1971, steadily advanced the state of baseball knowledge.

Sacrifice Fly First recognized as an event in 1908 but indistinguishable in the official records from sacrifice hits until 1954. There has been much flip-flopping since 1930 on whether to credit the sacrifice flier with an at bat or an RBI or whether a fly ball that advances a runner to a base other than home plate also should exempt a man from an at bat.

Sacrifice Hits Invented in the 1860s, recorded since 1889; sacrificer charged with an at bat until 1894. Sabermetricians frown on the strategy because all the studies show that the trading of an out for a base advanced is a losing strategy—lowering the run expectations of the team that attempts it—in all but the most unusual of cases . . . even if the sacrifice "succeeds."

Sacrifice Hits Allowed Computed officially in the National League since 1913 but not published until 1916, and kept in the American League since 1921 but not published until 1922; what it signified about anything is unclear.

Save Created by Jerome Holtzman of the *Chicago Sun-Times*, the save began to be reported by *The Sporting News* on a regular basis in 1960. The major leagues adopted the save in 1969, at which time it was credited to a reliever who finished a game that his team won. In 1973 the save was redefined so that a reliever had not only to finish the game but also to find the potential tying or winning run on base or at the plate, or, alternately, to pitch the final three innings of a victorious contest. In 1975 the rule was liberalized to include a reliever's appearance of one inning or more in which he protects a lead of three runs or less; or he enters the game with the tying or winning run on base, at bat, or on deck; or he pitches three innings to the game's conclusion. In this book, the 1969 definition is applied to all games before 1969; otherwise the rule in force at the time prevails. Abbreviated as SV.

Shutouts On an individual basis, credited only to pitchers of complete-game scoreless victories or ties; former practice was to credit combined shutouts to the starting pitcher if he had pitched most of the way. Abbreviated as SH.

Situational Statistics How does a batter perform with the bases loaded? At night? On artificial turf? With no one on base? After the seventh inning when his team is tied or trails? The specialty of Baseball Workshop, Stats, Inc., and the Elias Sports Bureau.

Slugging Average Total bases divided by at bats; combines nicely with On Base Percentage to create *Production* (which see). Abbreviated as SLG.

Starter Runs Identical to *Pitching Runs* (which see) but confined to starting pitchers, defined as those who average more than three innings per appearance. Abbreviated as SR.

Stolen Base Average Stolen bases divided by attempts; its computation is dependent upon the availability of caught-stealing numbers. Abbreviated as SBA.

Stolen Base Runs For teams, the Linear Weights measure of runs contributed *beyond* what a league-average basestealing team might have gained, defined as zero; for individuals, Stolen Base Runs are calculated on the basis of the 62.8 percent success rate that sabermetric studies have shown to be the break-even point for producing runs beyond the average. Availability dependent upon caught stealing data as with Stolen Base Average. The formula is simple: .22(Stolen Bases) – .35(Caught Stealing). A man who steals two bases in three attempts is more or less spinning his wheels in terms of value to his team, and even a man who succeeds at an 80 percent clip will have to steal a lot of bases—about 75—to create just one win beyond average. Abbreviated as SBR.

Stolen Base Wins Stolen Base Runs divided by the number of runs required to create an additional win beyond average. Those runs are generally around around 10—historically in the range of 9–11. Abbreviated as SBW. See *Runs Per Win*.

Stolen Bases Recorded since 1886, but until 1898 steals are thought to have included a variety of daring baserunning exploits, such as going from first to third on a single or advancing an extra base on an out. Abbreviated as SB.

Strikeouts Varying rules concerning the strike zone, the foul strike, and the warning pitch—not to mention the fourth strike of 1887—all contribute to making the cross-era comparison of strikeout accomplishments a very sticky business. Abbreviated as SO.

Strikeout Percentage A batters' stat: fewest strikeouts

per 100 at bats.

Total Average Tom Boswell's formulation for offensive contribution from a variety of batting and baserunning events; as with Runs Created, we have calculated Total Average to make use of the maximum available data in a given year. The concept of the numerator is bases gained, that of the denominator is outs made:

$$\frac{\text{(Total Bases + Steals + Walks + HBP − Caught Stealing)}}{\text{(At Bats − Hits + Caught Stealing + GIDP)}}$$

Abbreviated as TA. See *Base-Out Percentage*.

Total Baseball Ranking The "MVP" of statistics, this ranks pitchers and position players by their total wins contributed in all their endeavors, revealing the most valuable performers in a given year. Abbreviated as TBR, it is not a computed stat but a sorting of players and pitchers by, respectively, the sum of their Total Batter Rating and Total Pitcher Index.

Total Bases Average Henry Chadwick's measure that divided total bases by games played; a forerunner of the Slugging Average.

Total Bases Run A silly stat of one year's duration, 1880, this was sort of an RBI in reverse, from the runner's perspective. Also called "Bases Touched," it was nothing more than that and signified nothing about individual talent. Trivia: the National League's leader in 1880 was Abner Dalrymple, with 501 bases touched.

Total Chances Putouts plus assists plus errors; in other words, total chances offered, not total chances accepted.

Total Pitcher Index The sum of a pitcher's Pitching Runs—expressed as Ranking Runs, employing the same formula used to compute Relief Ranking Runs—Batting Runs (in the AL since 1973, zero), and Fielding Runs, all divided by the Runs Per Win factor for that year (generally around 10, historically in the 9–11 range); abbreviated as TPI. See *Runs Per Win, Relief Ranking*.

Total Player Rating The sum of a player's Adjusted Batting Runs, Fielding Runs, and Base Stealing Runs, minus his positional adjustment, all divided by the Runs Per Win factor for that year (generally around 10, historically in the 9–11 range). See *Runs Per Win*.

Triple Crown Long regarded as consisting of batting average, home runs, and RBIs, but was not always so. In the early years of this century, newspapers spoke of Ty Cobb shooting for the "triple crown" of batting average, runs, and hits.

Weighted Average The next step in statistical sophistication after first, counting and, next, averaging. Chadwick's Total Bases Average was probably the first weighted average, in that it assigned values of 1 to a single, 2 to a double, 3 to a triple, and 4 to a home run.

Weighted Rating System Ted Oliver's invention, promoted in a 1944 self-published booklet called *Kings of the Mound*. We have modified Oliver's pioneering effort to create *Wins Above Team* (see below), which entry presents a discussion of Oliver's effort.

Win Points See *Player Win Averages*.

Wins Above League A pitcher's won-lost record restated by adding his Pitching Wins above the league average to the record that a league-average pitcher would have had with his number of decisions. Example: Tom Seaver has a hard-luck season, going only 16–14 despite a 1.76 ERA and five Pitching Wins; applying the five wins to a league-average 15–15 mark in the same 30 decisions results in a WAL of 20-10.

Wins Above Team How many wins a pitcher garnered beyond those expected of an average pitcher for that team. As the editors of this volume, in their earlier *Hidden Game of Baseball*, modified Ted Oliver's *Weighted Rating System* (see above), they now improve this statistic thanks to Bill Deane's corrective for its tendency to overvalue the contributions of good pitchers on awful teams.

Oliver's Weighted Rating System for pitchers was motivated by the inadequacies of both the won-lost percentage and the ERA when it came to evaluating pitchers laboring for poor teams. The Oliver formula, ingenious if flawed, was: pitcher's won-lost percentage minus the team's won-lost percentage—after removing the pitcher's decisions from the team's record—then multiplying the difference by the pitcher's number of decisions. Here is an example of the Oliver method as applied to Bobby Castillo, who in 1982 pitched very well in going 13–11 for a very bad Minnesota club (60–102; without him, 47–91):

$$\left(\frac{13}{24} - \frac{47}{138}\right) \times 24$$

or

$$(.542 - .341) \times 24$$

or

$$.201 \times 24 = 4.824$$

The figure of 4.824 would have been represented by Ted Oliver as "4,824 points"; he did not seem to recognize that had he retained the decimal point, his rating would have been expressed directly in *wins*. Thus the number of wins Castillo accounted for in his 24 decisions that an average Minnesota pitcher would *not* have gained was 4.8.

Thanks to a key modification of our earlier formula for Wins Above Team, abbreviated as WAT, we now propose the following: calculate the pitcher's won-lost percentage and the team's winning percentage after his decisions have been set aside. If the pitcher's percentage is higher, then WAT is

$$\text{Pitcher decisions} \times \left(\frac{\text{Pitcher pct.} - \text{Team pct.}}{2 - 2 \times \text{Team pct.}}\right)$$

If the pitcher's percentage is lower, then WAT is

$$\text{Pitcher decisions} \times \left(\frac{\text{Pitcher pct.} - \text{Team pct.}}{2 \times \text{Team pct.}}\right)$$

Won-lost percentage Computed as wins over decisions.

Team and League Abbreviations

These are the franchises, seven principal leagues and their abbreviations as used throughout this book.

NATIONAL ASSOCIATION, 1871–1875 (Shown as n or NA)

Abbrev.	First	Last	Team
ATH n	1871	1875	Philadelphia Athletics
ATL n	1872	1875	Brooklyn Atlantics
BAL n	1872	1874	Baltimore Lord Baltimores
BOS n	1871	1875	Boston Red Stockings
CEN n	1875	1875	Philadelphia Centennials
CHI n	1871	1871	Chicago White Stockings
CHI n	1874	1875	Chicago White Stockings
CLE n	1871	1872	Cleveland Forest City
ECK n	1872	1872	Brooklyn Eckfords
HAR n	1874	1875	Hartford Dark Blues
KEK n	1871	1871	Fort Wayne Kekiongas
MAN n	1872	1872	Middletown (Conn.) Mansfields
MUT n	1871	1875	New York Mutuals
NAT n	1872	1872	Washington, D.C., Nationals
NH n	1875	1875	New Haven Elm City
OLY n	1871	1872	Washington, D.C., Olympics
PHI n	1873	1875	Philadelphia White Stockings
RES n	1873	1873	Elizabeth (N.J.) Resolutes
ROK n	1871	1871	Rockford (Ill.) Forest City
RS n	1875	1875	St. Louis Red Stockings
STL n	1875	1875	St. Louis Brown Stockings
TRO n	1871	1872	Troy Haymakers
WAS n	1873	1873	Washington Washingtons
WAS n	1875	1875	Washington Washingtons
WES n	1875	1875	Keokuk (Iowa) Westerns

NATIONAL LEAGUE, 1876– (Shown as N or NL)

Abbrev.	First	Last	Team
ARI N	1998		Arizona
ATL N	1966		Atlanta
BAL N	1892	1899	Baltimore
BOS N	1876	1952	Boston (transferred to Milwaukee)
BRO N	1890	1957	Brooklyn (transferred to Los Angeles)
BUF N	1879	1885	Buffalo
CHI N	1876		Chicago
CIN N	1876	1880	Cincinnati
CIN N	1890		Cincinnati
CLE N	1879	1884	Cleveland
CLE N	1889	1899	Cleveland
COL N	1993		Colorado
DET N	1881	1888	Detroit
FLA N	1993		Florida
HAR N	1876	1877	Hartford (played in Brooklyn in 1877)
HOU N	1962		Houston
IND N	1878	1878	Indianapolis
IND N	1887	1889	Indianapolis
KC N	1886	1886	Kansas City
LA N	1958		Los Angeles
LOU N	1876	1877	Louisville
LOU N	1892	1899	Louisville
MIL N	1878	1878	Milwaukee
MIL N	1953	1965	Milwaukee (transferred to Atlanta)
MON N	1969		Montreal
NY N	1876	1876	New York (played in Brooklyn)
NY N	1883	1957	New York (transferred to San Francisco)
NY N	1962		New York
PHI N	1876	1876	Philadelphia
PHI N	1883		Philadelphia
PIT N	1887		Pittsburgh
PRO N	1878	1885	Providence
STL N	1876	1877	St. Louis
STL N	1885	1886	St. Louis
STL N	1892		St. Louis
SD N	1969		San Diego
SF N	1958		San Francisco
SYR N	1879	1879	Syracuse
TRO N	1879	1882	Troy (N.Y.)
WAS N	1886	1889	Washington, D.C.
WAS N	1892	1899	Washington, D.C.
WOR N	1880	1882	Worcester (Mass.)

AMERICAN ASSOCIATION, 1882-1891 (Shown as a or AA)

Abbrev.	First	Last	Team
BAL a	1882	1889	Baltimore
BAL a	1890	1891	Baltimore (transferred to National League)
BOS a	1891	1891	Boston
BRO a	1884	1889	Brooklyn (transferred to National League)
BRO a	1890	1890	Brooklyn
CIN a	1882	1889	Cincinnati (transferred to National League)
CIN a	1891	1891	Cincinnati
CLE a	1887	1888	Cleveland (transferred to National League)
COL a	1883	1884	Columbus (Ohio)
COL a	1889	1891	Columbus (Ohio)
IND a	1884	1884	Indianapolis
KC a	1888	1889	Kansas City
LOU a	1882	1891	Louisville (transferred to National League)
MIL a	1891	1891	Milwaukee
NY a	1883	1887	New York
PHI a	1882	1891	Philadelphia
PIT a	1882	1886	Pittsburgh (transferred to National League)
RIC a	1884	1884	Richmond
ROC a	1890	1890	Rochester
STL a	1882	1891	St. Louis (transferred to National League)
SYR a	1890	1890	Syracuse
TOL a	1884	1884	Toledo
TOL a	1890	1890	Toledo
WAS a	1884	1884	Washington, D.C.
WAS a	1891	1891	Washington, D.C. (transferred to National League)

UNION ASSOCIATION, 1884 (Shown as U or UA)

Abbrev.	First	Last	Team
ALT U	1884	1884	Altoona (Pa.)
BAL U	1884	1884	Baltimore
BOS U	1884	1884	Boston
CHI U	1884	1884	Chicago (combined with Pittsburgh, shown as CP)
CIN U	1884	1884	Cincinnati
KC U	1884	1884	Kansas City
MIL U	1884	1884	Milwaukee
PHI U	1884	1884	Philadelphia
PIT U	1884	1884	Pittsburgh (combined with Chicago, shown as CP)
STL U	1884	1884	St. Louis
STP U	1884	1884	St. Paul (Minn.)
WAS U	1884	1884	Washington, D.C.
WIL U	1884	1884	Wilmington (Del.)

PLAYERS LEAGUE, 1890 (Shown as P or PL)

Abbrev.	First	Last	Team
BOS P	1890	1890	Boston
BRO P	1890	1890	Brooklyn
BUF P	1890	1890	Buffalo
CHI P	1890	1890	Chicago
CLE P	1890	1890	Cleveland
NY P	1890	1890	New York
PHI P	1890	1890	Philadelphia
PIT P	1890	1890	Pittsburgh

AMERICAN LEAGUE, 1901– (Shown as A or AL)

Abbrev.	First	Last	Team
BAL A	1901	1902	Baltimore (replaced by New York)
BAL A	1954		Baltimore
BOS A	1901		Boston
CAL A	1965		California
CHI A	1901		Chicago
CLE A	1901		Cleveland
DET A	1901		Detroit
KC A	1955	1967	Kansas City (transferred to Oakland)
KC A	1969		Kansas City
LA A	1961	1964	Los Angeles (transferred to California)
MIL A	1901	1901	Milwaukee (replaced by St. Louis)
MIL A	1970		Milwaukee
MIN A	1961		Minnesota
NY A	1903		New York
OAK A	1968		Oakland
PHI A	1901	1954	Philadelphia (transferred to Kansas City)
STL A	1902	1953	St. Louis (transferred to Baltimore)
SEA A	1969	1969	Seattle (transferred to Milwaukee)
SEA A	1977		Seattle
TB A	1998		Tampa Bay
TEX A	1972		Texas
TOR A	1977		Toronto
WAS A	1901	1960	Washington, D.C. (transferred to Minnesota)
WAS A	1961	1971	Washington, D.C. (transferred to Texas)

FEDERAL LEAGUE, 1914-1915 (Shown as F or FL)

Abbrev.	First	Last	Team
BAL F	1914	1915	Baltimore
BRO F	1914	1915	Brooklyn
BUF F	1914	1915	Buffalo
CHI F	1914	1915	Chicago
IND F	1914	1914	Indianapolis (transferred to Newark)
KC F	1914	1915	Kansas City
NEW F	1915	1915	Newark
PIT F	1914	1915	Pittsburgh
STL F	1914	1915	St. Louis